Income
Tax
Regulations

Including
Proposed
Regulations

As of January 13, 2003

Volume 1
§1.0-1–§1.197-2

CCH Editorial Staff Publication

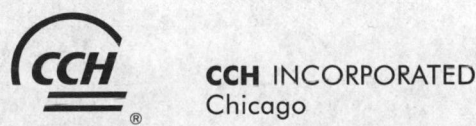

CCH INCORPORATED
Chicago

This publication is designed to provide accurate and authoritative information in regard to the subject matter covered. It is sold with the understanding that the publisher is not engaged in rendering legal, accounting, or other professional service. If legal advice or other expert assistance is required, the services of a competent professional person should be sought.

ISBN 0-8080-0930-3

©2003, **CCH** INCORPORATED

4025 W. Peterson Ave.
Chicago, IL 60646-6085
1 800 248 3248
http://tax.cchgroup.com

FOREWORD

The federal income tax regulations are the official Treasury Department interpretation of the Internal Revenue Code and follow the number sequence of the Internal Revenue Code sections. Title 26 of the Code of Federal Regulations pertains to the Internal Revenue Code of 1986. Part 1 of Title 26 relates to federal income tax, Part 31 to employment tax and withholding of income tax, and Part 301 to procedure and administration.

All regulations are written either by the Legislation and Regulations Division or the Employee Plans, Exempt Organizations Division of the Office of the Chief Counsel, IRS, and are approved by the Chief Counsel and the IRS Commissioner. The Treasury Department's Assistant Secretary for Tax Policy, or his deputy, has final approval over regulations.

● Classes of Regulations

The three classifications of regulations are described below:

Proposed Regulations. Proposed regulations are issued to solicit public written comments, and public hearings are held if written requests are made.

Temporary Regulations. Temporary regulations are issued to provide guidance for the public and for IRS employees until final regulations are released. Public hearings are not held on temporary regulations.

Final Regulations. Final regulations are issued after public comments on proposed regulations are evaluated. Final regulations supersede any existing temporary regulations.

● Finding Aids

A complete topical index to the final and temporary regulations begins on page 19,003; for proposed regulations, a complete topical index begins on page 73,001. A list indicating the subject of each part of the regulations for Title 26 of the Code, which is represented in the regulations reproduced in Volumes 1 through 6, appears at page 20,101. A list of irregularly numbered regulations giving the page on which the text of the regulation begins and the subject of the regulation is at page 20,201. A table of public laws by number and title appears at page 20,301, and a table of regulations that do not reflect changes made by recently enacted public laws appears at page 20,601.

January 2003

CONTENTS

TABLE OF CONTENTS

[The next page is 19,003.]

INDEX
FINAL AND TEMPORARY REGULATIONS UNDER
THE 1986 CODE

[References are to Reg. § numbers.]

[Index for Proposed Regulations Begins on Page 73,001.]

A

ACC

BAR

DEF

DEF

DEP

DES

DOM

EXE

EXE

INC

Injuries or sickness
. compensation received for, exclusion...
1.104-1(a)

Insolvency reorganizations...1.371-1—1.373-3
. exchanges by security holders...1.371-2

Inspection of applications for tax exemption
...301.6104(a)-1—301.6104(d)-3

Inspection of returns
. authorization...601.702

Installment method of accounting...1.453A-0—
1.453A-3
. adoption of...1.453A-3
. change to...1.453A-3
. dealers in personal property...1.453A-3
. interest paid, deductibility where charge not
separately stated...1.163-2
. real estate sales...1.453-5
. revolving credit plan sales...1.453A-0—
1.453A-3

Installment obligations
. carryover by acquiring corporation...
1.381(c)(8)-1
. gain on disposition...1.453-9
. liquidating corporation...1.453-11
. transmission at death...1.691(e)-1

Installment payments of tax...1.6152-1

Installment reporting
. personal property...15a.453-1
. real property...15a.453-1

Installment sales
. depreciable real property
.. capital gains...1.453-12

Insurance
. health insurance
.. group health plans, nondiscrimination...
54.9802-1, 54.9802-1T
. life insurance
.. mortality tables...1.101-7
.. premiums paid, deductibility...1.264-1—
1.264-3
.. proceeds received...1.101-1—1.101-5
. living expense reimbursement...1.123-1
. policies
.. exchanges...1.1035-1

Insurance companies
. controlled foreign corporations...1.953-2
. foreign insurers
.. premium excise tax...46.4374-1
. mutual life insurance companies
.. differential dividends earnings rate...
1.809-9
.. equity base computation on differential
earnings...1.809-10
. other than life or mutual...1.831-2—1.832-6
.. computation of "losses incurred"
deduction...1.832-7T
.. deductions...1.832-5
.. gross income...1.832-4
.. investment income...1.822-8
.. multiple line companies, election to be
taxed on total income...1.831-4
.. policyholders, taxable income
determination...1.832-6
. policy acquisition expenses
.. capitalization...1.848-1—1.848-4
. reserves
.. unpaid losses...1.846-3
.. returns...1.6012-2(c)
. salvage and reinsurance
.. gross income...1.832-4
. underwriting income, determination of...
1.832-4

Insurance companies—continued
. unpaid losses
.. discount factors...1.846-1
.. election of pattern...1.846-2
.. reserves...1.846-3

Intangible drilling costs...1.612-4
. geothermal wells...1.162-5
. transfers...1.367(a)-4T

Intangible property
. allocation of income from transfers of...
1.482-4
. amortization...1.197-2
. depreciation...1.167(a)-3
. election...1.167(a)-13T, 1.197-1T
. property excluded from Code Sec. 197
.. amortization...1.167(a)-14

Intangibles
. election for straight-line recovery...7.57(d)-1

Interest on tax
. abatement of
.. unreasonable IRS errors or delays...
301.6404-2
. computed daily...301.6622-1
. overpayments
.. period in which interest allowed...
301.6611-1
. rate...301.6621-1

Interest on underpayments of tax...1.9006-1
. large corporate underpayments, higher rate
...301.6621-3T

Interest paid
. allocation of...1.163-8T
. annuities purchased...1.72-14
. backup withholding...35a.3406-1, 35a.9999-1—
35a.9999-5
. banks...1.163-1(c)
. capitalization...1.263A-8—1.263A-15
.. property production...1.263A(f)-0—
1.263A(f)-9, 1.266-1
. cooperative housing tenant-stockholders...
1.216-1
. corporate acquisition indebtedness...
1.279-1—1.279-7
. exempt-interest dividends...1.265-3
. foreign corporations...1.882-5
. governmental obligations...1.103-8
. home mortgages
.. credit against tax...1.25-1T—1.25-8T
. imputed interest...1.1274-1—1.1274-5
. industrial development bonds...1.103-7
. information returns...1.6049-1—1.6049-6
. installment purchases...1.163-2
. life insurance companies...1.803-3
. loans to purchase tax-free obligations...
1.265-2
. Maryland ground rent...1.163-1(b)
. mortgage interest...1.163-1(b)
.. reduction where credit taken...1.163-6T
. nonbusiness interest limitations...1.163-8T
. original issue discount as...1.6049-5
. price level adjusted mortgage...1.6050H-2
. partially exempt interest...1.216-1
. personal interest...1.163-9T
. real estate mortgage investment conduits
.. variable rate...1.860A-0, 1.860A-1, 1.860G-1
. registration-required obligations...1.163-5,
1.1287-1
. residence interest...1.163-10T
. reimbursements
.. reporting requirements...1.6050H-2
. trusts, substantial owners
.. pass-through certificates...1.163-5T
. underpayment of tax...301.6601-1

19,040

Index—Final and Temporary Regulations Under 1986 Code
[References are to Reg. § numbers.]

S

UNE

[The next page is 20,101.]

HOW TO LOCATE REGULATIONS

The INCOME TAX REGULATIONS volumes contain the final and temporary income tax regulations, as well as the procedural and administrative regulations, under the Internal Revenue Code, i.e., Title 26 of the United States Code. They are arranged in strict Code sequence. To locate a particular regulation, always keep the Code section number in mind. This Code section number, in most instances, follows the decimal point in the regulation § number.

Example 1: § 1.641(a)-1 is an income tax regulation that explains or interprets Code section 641(a). It can be located in Volume 3.

Example 2: § 31.3402(b)-1 is a withholding regulation that explains or interprets Code section 3402(b). It is among the regulations included in Volume 5.

Example 3: §§ 1.6655-1 and 301.6655-1 were both issued under Code section 6655. While § 301.6655-1 is merely a cross reference to § 1.6655-1, it has been retained in the interest of completeness. Both of these regulation sections appear in Code order in Volume 5.

For a list of irregularly numbered regulations and their locations, see page 20,201.

Part Designation

The number preceding the decimal point in the regulation section number indicates the subject of the regulation. The following table indicates the subject of each part of the regulations for Title 26 of the United States Code that is represented in the regulations, which are reproduced in Volumes 1 through 6.

Part	Title
1	Final income tax regulations
4	Temporary regs. relating to foreign base company income
5	Temporary regs. under the Revenue Act of 1978
5c	Temporary regs. under the Economic Recovery Tax Act of 1981
5e	Temporary regs. on travel expenses of members of Congress
5f	Temporary regs. under the Tax Equity and Fiscal Responsibility Act of 1982
6a	Temporary regs. under the Omnibus Budget Reconciliation Act of 1981
7	Temporary regs. under the Tax Reform Act of 1976
8	Temporary regulation relating to charitable remainder trusts
11	Temporary regs. under the Employee Retirement Income Security Act of 1974
12	Temporary regs. under the Revenue Act of 1971
14a	Temporary regs. relating to incentive stock options
15A	Temporary regs. under the Installment Sales Revision Act of 1980
16	Temporary regs. under the Revenue Act of 1962
16A	Temporary regs. on the partial exclusion for certain conservation cost-sharing payments
17	Temporary regs. under 26 U.S.C. § 103(c)
18	Temporary regs. under the Subchapter S Revision Act of 1982
20	Estate taxes
25	Gift taxes
26	Tax on certain generation-skipping transfers

Regulations relating to estate and gift taxes, generation-skipping transfer taxes, and 31 C.F.R. Part 10, relating to practice before the IRS, are not included in the INCOME TAX REGULATIONS. For a list of regulations that have been proposed but not adopted, see the "List of Proposed Regulations" in Volume 6.

Subsequent Legislation

Not all regulations have been amended to reflect changes made in the related Code section by legislation. Check the Law Changes Not Yet in the Regulations Table (beginning on page 20,601) for regulations that do not reflect laws passed after the regulations were issued or amended.

[The next page is 20,201.]

IRREGULARLY NUMBERED REGULATIONS

There are a few exceptions to the standard method of numbering regulations. The following table indicates the page on which the text of the irregularly numbered regulation begins and the subject of the regulation. Unless otherwise indicated, regulations are part of Title 26 of the Code of Federal Regulations.

[The next page is 20,301.]

[The next page is 20,301.]

TABLE OF PUBLIC LAWS BY NUMBER AND TITLE

Following is a list of the Public Laws referred to in "Law Changes Not Yet in the Regulations" (beginning on page 20,601) that have designated titles:

[The next page is 20,601.]

LAW CHANGES NOT YET IN THE REGULATIONS

There is a lapse of time between amendments to the Code and a corresponding change in the Regulations. This table shows those Regulations that do not yet reflect changes made in the Code. For a list of the designated or popular titles of Public Laws noted below, see the table beginning on page 20,301.

When a Regulation is adopted, it is reflected as a final Regulation. The reader, however, should always check this table to determine whether a particular Regulation has been amended for the latest change in the law.

Regulations Section	Public Law Making Changes Not Reflected	Regulations Section	Public Law Making Changes Not Reflected
1.0-1	99-514	1.38-1	95-600, 98-369
1.1-1	95-600, 97-34, 97-488, 99-514, 100-647, 103-66, 107-16	1.41-3A	101-239, 103-66
1.1(i)-1T	100-647, 101-508, 105-34, 105-206, 107-16	1.41-5A, 1.41-6, 1.41-7	101-239
		1.42-1T	100-647, 101-239, 103-66
1.2-1	99-514	1.42-2	101-239, 103-66
1.2-2	93-597, 94-569, 97-448, 98-369, 99-514	1.44A-1	98-369 (redesignated Code Sec. 44A as 21), 99-514, 100-485, 104-188
1.3-1	94-12, 94-164, 94-455, 95-30, 95-600, 96-222, 97-34, 99-514	1.44A-2	98-369 (redesignated Code Sec. 44A as 21), 100-485, 104-188, 107-16, 107-147
1.11-1	94-164, 94-455, 95-30, 95-600, 97-34, 98-369, 99-514, 100-203, 100-647	1.44A-3	98-369 (redesignated Code Sec 44A as 21), 99-514, 104-188
1.21-1	95-30, 95-600, 97-34, 98-369 (redesignated Code Sec. 21 as 15), 99-514, 100-647, 107-16	1.44A-4	98-369 (redesignated Code Sec. 44A as 21), 99-514, 104-188
		5c.44F-1	98-369 (redesignated Code Sec. 44F as 30), 99-514 (redesignated Code Sec. 30 as 41)
1.25-1T	99-514, 100-647, 101-239	1.46-1	100-647, 101-239, 101-508
1.25-2T	99-514, 100-647, 101-239, 104-188, 105-206, 107-16	1.46-2	96-222, 96-223, 97-34, 97-248, 97-354, 98-369, 101-508
1.25-3T	99-514, 100-647, 101-239, 103-66, 105-34	1.46-3	97-34, 98-369, 99-514, 100-647, 101-508
1.25-4T	99-514, 100-647, 101-239	1.46-4	97-34, 98-369, 99-514, 100-647, 101-508
1.25-5T	99-514, 100-647, 101-239		
1.25-6T	99-514, 100-647, 101-239	1.46-5	97-34, 98-369, 100-647, 101-508
1.25-7T	99-514, 100-647, 101-239	1.46-6	98-369, 99-514, 101-508
1.25-8T	99-514, 100-647, 101-239	1.47-1	97-34, 97-248, 98-369, 98-443, 99-121, 99-514, 100-647, 101-508, 104-188, 105-206
1.28-0	104-188, 106-170		
1.28-1	100-647, 101-239, 102-227, 103-66, 104-188, 105-34, 106-170	1.47-2	91-676, 97-34, 97-248, 98-369, 98-443, 99-121, 99-514, 100-647, 101-508, 104-88
1.30-1	104-188	1.47-3	97-34, 97-248, 98-369, 101-508, 104-188
1.31-1	97-248, 97-354, 98-67, 98-369		
1.31-2	(does not reflect current taxable wage base for FICA tax purposes)	1.47-4	97-34, 97-248, 97-354, 98-369, 101-508
		1.47-5	97-34, 97-248, 98-369
1.32-2	96-222, 98-21, 98-369 (redesignated Code Sec. 43 as 32), 99-514, 100-647, 101-508, 103-66, 103-465, 104-7, 104-193, 105-34, 105-206, 107-16	1.47-6	97-34, 97-248, 98-369
		1.48-1	101-508
		1.48-2	97-34, 97-248, 98-369, 99-514, 101-508
1.37-1	98-21, 98-369, 99-514		
1.37-2	98-21, 98-369		
1.37-3	98-21, 98-369, 99-514		

Regulations Section	Public Law Making Changes Not Reflected
1.167(g)-1	97-32, 99-514
1.167(l)-1	101-508
1.167(l)-l(d)	97-34
1.167(l)-2	101-508
1.167(l)-3	101-508
1.167(l)-4	101-508
1.167(m)-1	101-508
1.168(d)-1	96-223, 101-508
5c.168(f)(8)-1—5c.168(f)(8)-8	97-248, 98-369, 99-514, 100-647
5f.168(f)(8)-1	98-369, 99-514, 100-647
1.169-1	92-178, 94-455
1.169-2	92-178, 94-455
1.169-3	92-178
1.170A-1	97-34, 97-248, 98-369, 99-514, 100-647
1.170A-4	95-600, 97-34, 97-248, 97-354, 98-369, 99-514
1.170A-4A	98-369, 99-514, 100-203
1.170A-5	98-369, 99-514, 100-203
1.170A-6	98-369, 99-514, 100-203
1.170A-8	94-455, 97-34, 98-369, 99-514, 100-203, 100-647
1.170A-10	97-34, 98-369, 99-514, 100-203
1.170A-11	97-34, 98-369, 99-514, 100-203, 100-647
1.170A-13(c)	100-647
1.170A-14	105-34
1.171-1	94-455, 103-66
1.171-2	85-866, 94-455, 99-514
1.171-3	94-455
1.171-4	94-455
1.172-2	100-203, 101-239
1.172-3	99-514, 103-66
1.172-4	99-514, 101-508, 105-34, 107-147
1.172-5	99-514, 103-66
1.172-9	101-508
1.172-10	105-34
1.172-13	101-508, 105-277
1.173-1(c)	97-248
1.174-4	97-248
1.175-1—1.175-2	90-630, 99-514
1.178-1—1.178-3	99-514
1.179-1—1.179-2	103-66, 104-188
1.183-1(c)	92-178, 99-514
1.190-1	96-167, 98-369, 99-514, 101-508
1.190-3	98-369, 101-508
1.213-1	97-248, 98-369, 99-514, 100-647, 101-508, 103-66, 104-191
1.217-2	103-66
1.219-1	94-455, 95-600, 97-34, 97-248, 98-369, 99-514, 100-203, 100-647, 101-239, 102-318, 104-188

Regulations Section	Public Law Making Changes Not Reflected
1.219-2	97-34, 98-369, 99-514, 100-203, 100-647, 101-239
1.243-1	99-514, 100-203
1.243-3	100-203
1.243-4	101-508, 104-188
1.243-5	94-455, 98-369, 99-514
1.244-2	88-272, 95-600, 99-514, 100-203
1.245-1	89-809, 99-514, 100-647
1.246-1	94-455, 98-369, 99-514
1.246-2	98-369, 99-514
1.246-3	98-369, 99-514, 105-34
1.247-1	94-455, 95-600
1.263(a)-1(c)	99-514, 105-34
1.263(a)-3(b)	99-514
1.263(b)-1	101-508
1.263(e)-1	94-455
1.263(f)-1	97-34
1.263A-1	106-170
1.263A-3	106-170
1.263A-8	106-170
1.264-1	104-191, 105-34
1.264-2	99-514, 104-191, 105-34
1.264-4	99-514, 104-191, 105-34
1.265-2	94-455, 96-223, 97-34, 98-369, 99-514, 105-34
1.267(a)-1	95-628, 97-354, 98-369, 99-514, 100-647
1.267(a)-2T	99-514, 100-647, 105-34
1.267(b)-1	95-628, 97-354, 98-369, 105-34
1.269-4	98-369
1.274-4	96-222, 96-605, 96-608, 97-34, 97-424, 98-67, 99-44, 99-514, 100-647, 103-66
1.276-1(b)(1)	90-364, 93-443
1.280C-1	97-414, 98-369, 99-514, 100-647, 103-66
1.280C-3	104-188
1.280F-2T	98-369, 99-44, 99-514, 101-508, 105-34, 107-147
1.280F-3T, 1.280F-4T	99-44, 99-514, 101-508
1.280F-6T	101-508
1.281-3	104-88
1.301-1	95-628, 98-369, 100-203, 100-647
1.302-1	96-589, 97-248
1.302-2	96-589, 97-248
1.302-4	97-248
1.303-2	94-455, 97-34
1.304-2	97-248, 98-369, 105-34
1.304-3	98-369
1.305-1	101-508
1.306-2	95-600, 97-248, 98-369
1.306-3	97-248, 98-369
1.312-1	98-369

Regulations Section	Public Law Making Changes Not Reflected
1.312-2	99-514, 100-647
1.312-3	94-455, 95-628, 99-514
1.312-4	87-834, 88-272, 88-484, 89-570, 91-172, 94-455, 95-628, 99-514
1.312-5	97-248, 98-369
1.312-6	89-570, 91-172, 96-589, 97-34, 97-248, 98-369, 99-121, 99-514, 100-647
1.312-10	94-455, 98-369
1.312-15	94-455, 97-34, 97-248, 98-369, 99-121, 99-514, 100-647, 105-34
1.318-2	98-369
1.331-1	97-248
1.332-1	96-471
1.332-2	99-514
1.332-7	99-514
1.341-1—1.341-7	97-248, 98-369, 99-514
1.346-1—1.346-3	97-248, 99-514
1.351-1	96-589, 100-647, 101-239
1.354-1	96-589, 105-34
1.355-1—1.355-2	100-203, 100-647, 105-34
1.355-3—1.355-4	100-203, 100-647
1.356-1	97-248, 105-34
1.357-1	101-508
1.357-2	95-600, 96-222, 96-589
1.358-1—1.358-2	100-647
1.358-3	95-600, 107-147
1.361-1	100-647
1.367(d)-1T	99-514, 100-647, 105-34
1.368-1	96-589, 97-248, 98-369, 99-514, 100-647, 101-73
1.368-2	94-455, 96-589, 97-248, 98-369, 99-514, 100-647
1.381(a)-1	96-589, 98-369
1.381(b)-1	105-34
1.381(c)(1)-1	105-34
1.381(c)(1)-2	105-34
1.381(c)(10)-1	94-455
1.381(c)(12)-1	99-514
1.381(c)(15)-1	94-455, 101-508
1.381(c)(22)-1	90-240
1.381(c)(23)-1—1.381(c)(25)-1	98-369
1.381(d)-1	98-369
1.401-1	93-406
1.401-2	87-863
1.401-4	97-248, 98-397
1.401-7	105-34
1.401-10—1.401-12	93-406
1.401-14	99-514, 101-239, 101-508
1.401(a)(4)-1	104-188, 105-34
1.401(a)(4)-3	104-188
1.401(a)(4)-4	104-188, 105-34
1.401(a)(4)-12	104-188
1.401(a)(4)-13	105-34
1.401(a)-1	98-397
1.401(a)-11	104-188
1.401(a)-12	96-364
1.401(a)-13	105-34
1.401(a)-20	105-34
1.401(a)(17)-1	107-16
1.401(a)(26)-1	104-188, 105-34
1.401(a)(26)-2	104-188
1.401(a)(26)-3	104-188
1.401(a)(26)-6(c)(4), (d)	105-34
1.401(a)(26)-9(b)(1)	105-34
1.401(a)(31)-1	107-16
1.401(e)-1—1.401(e) 6	97-248
1.401(f)-1	98-369
1.401(k)-1	104-188, 105-34, 107-16
1.401(m)-1	104-188
1.401(m)-2	104-188, 107-16
1.402(a)-1	94-267, 94-455, 95-30, 96-222, 96-608, 98-369, 98-397, 99-514, 100-647, 102-318, 104-188
1.402(a)(5)-1T	99-514, 100-647, 102-318, 104-188, 107-16
1.402(b)-1	99-514, 100-647, 102-318
1.402(c)-1	104-188
1.402(c)-2	104-188, 105-206, 107-16
11.402(e)(4)(A)-1	102-318
11.402(e)(4)(B)-1	99-514, 102-318
1.402(f)-1	107-16
1.402(g)-1	107-16
1.403(a)-1	99-514
1.403(a)-2	94-267, 94-455, 95-30, 96-222, 96-608, 98-397, 99-514, 100-647, 104-188
1.403(b)-1	99-514, 100-647, 104-188, 107-16
1.043(b)-2	107-16
1.404(a)-1	93-406, 97-34, 97-248, 98-369, 99-514, 100-203, 100-647
1.404(a)-3	93-406, 97-34, 97-248, 98-369, 99-514, 100-203, 100-647
1.404(a)-4	93-406, 97-34, 97-248, 98-369, 99-514, 100-203, 100-647, 107-16
1.404(a)-5—1.404(a)-6	93-406, 97-34, 97-248, 98-369, 99-514, 100-203, 100-647
1.404(a)-7	93-406, 97-34, 97-248, 98-369, 99-514, 100-203, 100-647, 107-16
1.404(a)-8	93-406, 97-34, 97-248, 98-369, 99-514, 100-203, 100-647, 104-188
1.404(a)-9—1.404(a)-10	93-406, 97-34, 97-248, 98-369, 99-514, 100-203, 100-647, 107-16

Regulations Section	Public Law Making Changes Not Reflected
1.593-4—1.593-5 . .	91-172, 97-34, 99-514, 100-647, 104-188
1.593-6A . .	91-172, 96-222, 97-34, 99-514, 100-647, 104-188
1.593-7 . .	91-172, 97-34, 99-514, 100-647, 104-188
1.593-10 .	91-172, 97-34, 99-514, 100-647, 104-188
1.593-11	104-188
1.594-1	98-369
1.595-1	104-188
1.596-1	99-514, 104-188
1.612-4	99-514
1.612-5	99-514
1.613-2 . . . . 89-809, 91-172, 94-12, 95-618
1.613-4	95-618
1.613A-5—1.613A-6	101-508
1.614-0	95-618
1.614-1	95-618
1.614-2	101-508
1.614-3	95-618
1.614-8	95-618
1.616-1	99-514
1.617-1—1.617-4	99-514
1.631-1(a)(4), (b)(1), (d)(4)	98-369
1.631-2	98-369
1.631-3	98-369, 99-514
1.641(a)-0	95-600, 98-369, 99-514, 100-647
1.641(a)-1	95-30, 104-188
1.641(a)-2	94-455, 99-514, 104-188
1.641(b)-3	104-188
1.642(a)(3)-1—1.642(a)(3)-2	99-514
1.642(b)-1	107-134
1.642(c)-3	99-514
1.642(c)-5	98-369, 99-514, 100-647
1.642(c)-7	100-647
1.642(e)-1	97-34
1.642(f)-1	97-34
1.642(g)-1	94-455, 101-239
1.642(h)-1	91-172, 99-514
1.643(a)-1	97-248
1.643(a)-3	99-514, 105-34
1.643(a)-6	94-455, 99-514, 101-239, 104-188
1.643(a)-7	99-514
1.643(d)-1	94-455, 98-369, 99-514, 100-647, 104-188
1.643(d)-2	99-514, 105-34
1.652(b)-2	99-514
1.652(b)-3	99-514
1.652(c)-1	99-514, 105-34
1.652(c)-2	99-514, 105-34
1.652(c)-4	99-514, 105-34
1.661(a)-2(f)	98-369

Regulations Section	Public Law Making Changes Not Reflected
1.661(c)-1	99-514
1.661(c)-2	99-514
1.662(b)-2	99-514
1.662(c)-1	99-514
1.662(c)-4	99-514
1.663(b)-1	105-34
1.663(b)-2	105-34
1.664-1	99-514, 105-34
1.664-1(f)	93-483, 94-455, 98-369, 100-647
8.1	95-600, 96-222, 96-605, 98-369, 100-647
1.664-2	105-34
1.664-2(a)(5)	98-369
1.664-3	105-34
1.664-3(a)(5)	98-369
1.665(a)-0A—1.665(b)-1A	94-455, 95-600, 105-34
1.665(b)-2A	94-455, 95-600
1.665(c)-1A—1.665(d)-1A	94-455, 95-600, 104-188, 105-34
1.665(e)-1A—1.665(g)-2A	94-455, 95-600, 105-34
1.666(a)-1A	94-455, 95-600, 105-34
1.666(b)-1A	94-455, 95-600, 105-34
1.666(c)-1A	94-455, 95-600, 105-34
1.666(c)-2A	94-455, 95-600, 105-34
1.666(d)-1A	94-455, 95-600, 105-34
1.667(a)-1A	94-455, 95-600, 99-514, 105-34
1.667(b)-1A	94-455, 95-600, 99-514, 105-34
1.671-2	99-514, 100-647
1.672(a)-1	99-514, 100-647, 101-508
1.672(c)-1	99-514, 100-647, 104-188
1.672(d)-1	99-514, 100-647
1.673(a)-1	99-514, 100-647
1.673(d)-1	99-514, 100-647
1.674(a)-1	99-514, 100-647, 105-34
1.674(b)-1	99-514, 100-647, 105-34
1.674(c)-1—1.674(d)-2 . .	99-514, 100-647
1.675-1	99-514, 100-647
1.676(a)-1	99-514, 100-647
1.676(b)-1	99-514, 100-647
1.677(a)-1	99-514, 100-647
1.677(b)-1	94-455, 99-514, 100-647
1.678(a)-1	99-514, 100-647
1.683-1—1.683-3	94-455
1.691(a)-1—1.691(a)-3 . .	94-455, 95-600, 96-222, 96-471, 99-514, 100-203, 100-647
1.691(a)-5	94-455, 95-600, 96-222, 96-471, 99-514, 100-203, 100-647
1.691(c)-1	94-455, 95-600, 96-222, 96-471, 99-514, 100-203, 100-647

Regulations Section	Public Law Making Changes Not Reflected
1.691(c)-2	94-455, 95-600, 96-222, 96-471, 99-514, 100-203, 100-647, 105-34
1.691(e)-1	94-455
1.692-1	98-259, 98-369, 99-514, 107-134
1.701-2	105-34
1.702-1	105-34
1.702-1(a)(5)	99-514
1.702-3T(g)	99-514, 100-647
1.703-1	94-12, 94-455, 95-30, 96-589
7.704-1	98-369
1.704-4	105-34
1.706-1	94-455, 98-369, 105-34
1.707-1	98-369
1.721-1	94-455, 105-34
1.722-1	94-455, 105-34
1.723-1	94-455
1.731-1	103-465, 105-34
1.732-2	106-170
1.734-1	98-369
1.735-1	98-369, 105-34
1.736-1	103-66
1.737-1	105-34
1.743-1	98-369
1.751-1	94-455, 95-600, 95-618, 97-448, 98-369, 103-66, 105-34, 106-170
1.761-2	96-222
1.801-2—1.801-8	98-369 (repealed and partially incorporated Code Sec. 801 as 816 and/or 817)
1.802-2—1.802-4	98-369 (repealed and partially incorporated Code Sec. 802 as 801)
1.804-3	98-369 (repealed and partially incorporated Code Sec. 804 as 812)
1.804-4	98-369 (repealed and partially incorporated Code Sec. 804 as 805)
1.806-2—1.806-4	98-369 (repealed and partially incorporated Code Sec. 806 as 807)
1.809-1—1.809-8	98-369 (repealed and partially incorporated Code Sec. 809 as 803 and/or 805)
1.810-1—1.810-4	98-369 (repealed and partially incorporated Code Sec. 810 as 807)
1.811-1—1.811-2	98-369 (repealed and partially incorporated Code Sec. 811 as 808)
1.812-1—1.812-8	98-369 (repealed and substantially incorporated Code Sec. 812 as 810)

Regulations Section	Public Law Making Changes Not Reflected
1.815-1—1.815-6	98-369 (repealed and substantially incorporated Code Sec. 815 as 815)
1.817-1—1.817-4	98-369 (repealed and partially incorporated Code Sec. 817 as 818)
1.818-1—1.818-8	98-369 (repealed and partially incorporated Code Sec. 818 as 811)
1.822-4	99-514 (redesignated Code Sec. 822 as 834)
1.822-8—1.822-12	99-514 (redesignated Code Sec. 822 as 834)
1.826-1—1.826-7	99-514 (redesignated Code Sec. 826 as 835)
1.831-3	99-514
1.831-4	99-514
1.832-5	99-514
1.851-1	91-172, 94-12, 95-345, 99-514
1.851-2	91-172, 94-12, 95-600, 99-514, 105-34
1.851-3—1.851-4	91-172, 94-12, 105-34
1.851-5—1.851-6	105-34
1.852-1	99-514
1.852-2	95-600, 99-514
1.852-3	105-34
1.852-4	94-455, 95-600, 98-369, 99-514, 105-34
1.852-5	99-514, 105-34
1.852-9	99-514
1.852-11	105-34
1.853-1	105-206
1.853-3	99-514
1.854-1	97-34, 98-369, 99-514
1.854-2	99-514
1.854-3	99-514
1.856-1	99-514
1.856-2	99-514, 105-34
1.856-2(d)(2)	106-170
1.856-3	99-514, 105-34
1.856-4	99-514, 105-34
1.856-4(b)	106-170
1.856-5	99-514
1.856-6	105-34, 106-170
5.856-1	105-34, 106-170
1.857-1	105-34
1.857-2	106-170
1.857-3	99-514
1.857-5	99-514, 105-34
1.857-6	98-369, 99-514, 105-34, 106-170
1.857-7	99-514, 105-34, 105-206
1.857-8	105-34
1.857-11	105-206
1.860E-1	104-188

Regulations Section	Public Law Making Changes Not Reflected
1.860G-2	104-188
1.861-1	94-455, 95-30, 95-600, 96-605, 99-514, 100-647
1.861-2	93-625, 95-600, 99-514, 101-508
1.861-3	87-834, 89-809, 99-514, 100-203, 100-647
1.861-4	105-34, 107-16
1.861-7	99-514
1.861-8	95-30, 98-369, 99-514
1.861-15	95-600, 99-514
1.861-16	99-514
1.862-1	94-445, 95-30, 97-34, 99-514
1.863-4	105-34
1.864-2	105-34
1.864-3	99-514, 100-647
1.864-4	98-369, 99-514, 100-647
1.864-6	98-369, 99-514, 100-647
1.864-7	98-369, 99-514, 100-647
1.871-7	94-455, 98-369, 99-514, 100-647, 103-465
1.871-8	94-455, 98-369, 99-514, 100-647, 103-66, 103-465
1.872-2	99-514, 100-647, 101-239
1.873-1	89-809, 92-580, 95-30, 98-369, 105-277
1.875-1	89-809
1.876-1	99-514
1.879-1	98-369, 99-514
1.881-1	98-369, 99-514, 103-66
1.881-2	98-369, 99-514, 103-66
1.882-1	99-514, 100-647
1.882-2	100-647
1.883-1	94-164, 99-514, 100-647
1.884-4(a)(2)	104-188
1.892-2T	100-647
1.893-1	100-647
1.894-1	99-514, 100-647
1.897-3	104-188
1.897-5T(c)(6)	100-647
1.901-1(a)	104-188, 105-34
1.901-1(f)	97-248, 98-369
1.902-1	105-34
1.902-2	105-34
1.902-3	94-455
1.902-4	94-455
1.904-1	94-455, 99-514, 100-647, 105-34
1.904-2	94-455, 99-514, 100-647
1.904-3	99-514, 100-647
1.904-4(b)	103-66
1.904-4(e), (g)	105-34
1.904-5	103-66
1.904-5(c)	104-188
1.904(b)-1—1.904(b)-3	99-514, 100-647
1.904(f)-1—1.904(f)-6	99-514, 100-647
1.905-3T—1.905-4T	105-34
1.907(a)-1—1.907(c)-3	103-66
1.911-2	99-514
1.911-3—1.911-6	99-514, 105-34
1.912-1	86-707, 87-293, 100-647
1.931-1	89-809, 99-514
1.934-1	99-514
1.936-1	104-188
1.936-4—1.936-7	99-514, 100-647, 104-188
1.936-10	104-188
1.951-1	94-12, 94-455, 98-369, 99-514, 100-647, 103-66, 105-34
1.951-3	98-369, 103-66
1.952-1(a)-(d)	99-509, 99-514, 100-647
1.952-1(b)	105-34
1.953-1—1.953-2	98-369, 99-514, 100-647, 105-277, 106-170, 107-147
1.953-3—1.953-4	98-369, 99-514, 100-647, 105-277, 106-170
1.953-5—1.953-6	98-369, 99-514, 100-647, 105-277, 106-170, 107-147
1.954-2	105-34, 105-277, 106-170, 107-147
1.954-3	99-514, 100-647, 103-66
1.954-4	98-369, 99-514, 106-170, 107-147
1.954-6	99-514, 103-66
1.954-7	99-514, 103-66
1.954-8	99-514, 103-66
1.955-5	94-12
1.955-6	94-12
1.956-1	103-66, 105-34
1.956-1T	103-66, 105-34
1.956-2	103-66, 105-34
1.956-3T	103-66, 105-34
1.957-2—1.957-4	99-514
1.958-2	103-66
1.959-1—1.959-3	103-66
1.960-1	99-514, 105-34
1.960-2	99-514, 105-34
1.961-1	105-34
1.961-2	105-34
1.962-1	95-600, 100-647
1.970-1—1.970-3	94-455
1.971-1	94-455
1.988-1(a)(9)	105-34
1.988-3	103-66
1.988-5	103-66
1.989(b)-1	105-34
1.991-1	105-34, 105-206
1.992-1	98-369
1.992-1(f)	104-188
1.993-3(f)	103-66

Regulations Section	Public Law Making Changes Not Reflected
31.3402(f)(1)-1	99-514, 100-203
31.3402(f)(3)-1	100-203
31.3402(f)(4)-2	99-514, 100-203
31.3402(g)-1	103-66, 107-16
31.3402(i)-2	99-514
31.3402(m)-1	98-369, 99-514, 100-647 (and the latest tables for determining the number of withholding allowances as set forth in Form W-4)
31.3402(n)-1	100-203
31.3402(o)-2	97-248
31.3402(p)-1	103-465
31.3402(p)-1(b)(2)	100-203
31.3402(q)-1	102-486, 107-16
35.3405(c)-1	107-16
35.3405-1T	98-369, 99-514, 100-647, 102 318
31.3406(a)-1	107-16
31.3406(c)-1	107-16
31.3406(d)-3	107-16
31.3406(d)-4	107-16
31.3406(d)-5	102-486
31.3406(e)-1	107-16
31.3406(g)-3	107-16
31.3406(h)-2	107-16
31.3501(a)-1T	103-66, 107-16
31.3507-1	98-369, 99-514, 101-508, 103-465
31.3507-2	98-369, 99-514, 100-203, 100-647
48.4041-3—48.4041-7	101-508, 103-66, 104-188, 105-34
48.4041-8	104-188, 105-34
48.4041-9	101-508, 102-240, 103-66
48.4041-11	101-508, 103-66, 104-188, 105-2, 105-34
48.4041-13(c)	104-188
48.4041-18	101-508, 103-66, 104-188, 105-34, 105-178
48.4041-19, 48.4041-20	101-508, 103-66, 105-34, 105-178
145.4051-1	98-369, 105-34
145.4052-1(d)(8)(iii)	105-34
48.4061(a)-1—48.4061(a)-5	98-369 (Code Sec. 4061 stricken but regulations still in effect)
48.4061(b)-1, 48.4061(b)-2	98-369 (Code Sec. 4061 stricken but regulations still in effect)
48.4062(a)-1, 48.4062(b)-1	98-369 (Code Sec. 4062 stricken but regulations still in effect)
48.4063-1—48.4063-3	98-369 (Code Sec. 4063 stricken but regulations still in effect)
48.4064-1	101-508
48.4072-1(b)	98-369
48.4073-1, 48.4073-3	98-369
48.4121-1(b)	97-119, 99-272
48.4161(a)-1, 48.4161(a)-3	98-369
48.4161(b)-1	105-34
48.4161(b)-1(a)(3)	98-369
48.4161(b)-2	105-34
48.4161(b)-5	98-369
48.4216(b)-1(b)(5)	98-369
48.4216(b)-3(a)(4)	98-369
48.4216(b)-4(e)	98-369
48.4216(f)-1	98-369
48.4218-1	89-44, 95-227, 98-369 (repealed Code Secs. 4061 and 4141)
48 4218-5	89-44, 95-227
48.4221-7	95-618
48.4222(b)-1	105-34
48.4222(c)-1	101-508
48.4222(d)-1	105-34
49.4251-1—49.4251-2	89 44, 89-368, 90-285, 90-364, 91-172, 91-614, 96-499, 97-34, 97-248, 98-369, 101-508, 105-34, 105-206
49.4251-3	89-44, 89-368, 90-285, 90-364, 91-172, 91-614, 96-499, 97-34, 97-248, 101-508, 105-206
49.4252-1—49.4252-7	89-44
49.4253-1, 49.4253-2	89-44
49.4253-3	89-44, 101-508
49.4253-4—49.4253-10	89-44
49.4253-11, 49.4253-12	89-44, 101-508
49.4254-1	89-44, 95-172
49.4254-2	89-44
49.4261-1	89-44, 91-258, 97-248, 101-508, 104-188, 105-2, 105-34
49.4261-3—49.4261-7	89-44, 91-258, 97-248, 101-508, 105-34
49.4261-8	89-44, 91-258, 97-248, 101-508, 104-188, 105-34
49.4261-9	89-44, 91-258, 97-248, 101-508, 105-34
49.4261-10	89-44, 91-258, 97-248, 101-508
49.4262(a)-1	89-44, 91-258, 97-248
49.4262(b)-1, 49.4262(c)-1	89-44, 97-248
49.4264(a)-1—49.4264(f)-1	91-258 (redesignated former Code Sec. 4264 as Code Sec. 4263)
49.4264(c)-1	105-34

[The next page is 21,011.]

INCOME TAX

Normal Tax and Surtax

EXPLANATION OF REGULATIONS

[Reg. § 1.0-1]

§ 1.0-1. **Internal Revenue Code of 1954 and regulations.**—(a) *Enactment of law.* The Internal Revenue Code of 1954 which became law upon enactment of Public Law 591, 83d Congress, approved August 16, 1954, provides in part as follows:

Be it enacted by the Senate and House of Representatives of the United States of America in Congress assembled, That (a) *Citation.* (1) The provisions of this Act set forth under the heading "Internal Revenue Title" may be cited as the "Internal Revenue Code of 1954".

(2) The Internal Revenue Code enacted on February 10, 1939, as amended, may be cited as the "Internal Revenue Code of 1939".

(b) *Publication.* This Act shall be published as volume 68A of the United States Statutes at Large, with a comprehensive table of contents and an appendix; but without an index or marginal references. The date of enactment, bill number, public law number, and chapter number, shall be printed as a headnote.

(c) *Cross reference.* For saving provisions, effective date provisions, and other related provisions, see chapter 80 (sec. 7801 and following) of the Internal Revenue Code of 1954.

(d) *Enactment of Internal Revenue Title into law.* The Internal Revenue Title referred to in subsection (a)(1) is as follows:

* * * * *

In general, the provisions of the Internal Revenue Code of 1954 are applicable with respect to taxable years beginning after December 31, 1953, and ending after August 16, 1954. Certain provisions of that Code are deemed to be included in the Internal Revenue Code of 1939. See section 7851.

(b) *Scope of regulations.* The regulations in this part deal with (1) the income taxes imposed under subtitle A of the Internal Revenue Code of 1954, and (2) certain administrative provisions contained in subtitle F of such Code relating to such taxes. In general, the applicability of such regulations is commensurate with the applicability of the respective provisions of the Internal Revenue Code of 1954 except that with respect to the provisions of the Internal Revenue Code of 1954 which are deemed to be included in the Internal Revenue Code of 1939, the regulations relating to such provisions are applicable to certain fiscal years and short taxable years which are subject to the Internal Revenue Code of 1939. Those provisions of the regulations which are applicable to taxable years subject to the Internal Revenue Code of 1939 and the specific taxable years to which such provisions are so applicable are identified in each instance. The regulations in 26 CFR (1939) Part 39 (Regulations 118) are continued in effect until superseded by the regulations in this part. See Treasury Decision 6091, approved August 16, 1954 (19 F.R. 5167, C.B. 1954-2, 47). [Reg. § 1.0-1.]

☐ [*T.D.* 6161, 2-3-56.]

DETERMINATION OF TAX LIABILITY

Tax on Individuals

[Reg. § 1.1-1]

§ 1.1-1. **Income tax on individuals.**—(a) *General rule.* (1) Section 1 of the Code imposes an income tax on the income of every individual who is a citizen or resident of the United States and, to the extent provided by section 871(b) or 877(b), on the income of a nonresident alien individual. For optional tax in the case of taxpayers with adjusted gross income of less than $10,000 (less than $5,000 for taxable years beginning before January 1, 1970) see section 3. The tax imposed is upon taxable income (determined by subtracting the allowable deductions from gross income). The tax is determined in accordance with the table

contained in section 1. See subparagraph (2) of this paragraph for reference guides to the appropriate table for taxable years beginning on or after January 1, 1964, and before January 1, 1965, taxable years beginning after December 31, 1964, and before January 1, 1971, and taxable years beginning after December 31, 1970. In certain cases credits are allowed against the amount of the tax. See part IV (section 31 and following), subchapter A, chapter 1 of the Code. In general, the tax is payable upon the basis of returns rendered by persons liable therefor (subchapter A (sections 6001 and following), chapter 61 of the Code) or at the source of the income by withholding. For the computation of tax in the case of a joint return of a husband and wife, or a return of a surviving spouse, for taxable years beginning before January 1, 1971, see section 2. The computation of tax in such a case for taxable years beginning after December 31, 1970, is determined in accordance with the table contained in section 1(a) as amended by the Tax Reform Act of 1969. For other rates of tax on individuals, see section 5(a). For the imposition of an additional tax for the calendar years 1968, 1969, and 1970, see section 51(a).

(2)(i) For taxable years beginning on or after January 1, 1964, the tax imposed upon a single individual, a head of a household, a married individual filing a separate return, and estates and trusts is the tax imposed by section 1 determined in accordance with the appropriate table contained in the following subsection of section 1:

	Taxable years beginning in 1964	Taxable years beginning after 1964 but before 1971	Taxable years beginning after December 31, 1970. (References in this column are to the Code as amended by the Tax Reform Act of 1969)
Single individual	Sec. 1(a)(1)	Sec. 1(a)(2)	Sec. 1(c)
Head of a household	Sec. 1(b)(1)	Sec. 1(b)(2)	Sec. 1(b)
Married individual			
Filing a separate return	Sec. 1(a)(1)	Sec. 1(a)(2)	Sec. 1(d)
Estates and trusts	Sec. 1(a)(1)	Sec. 1(a)(2)	Sec. 1(d)

(ii) For taxable years beginning after December 31, 1970, the tax imposed by section 1(d), as amended by the Tax Reform Act of 1969, shall apply to the income effectively connected with the conduct of a trade or business in the United States by a married alien individual who is a nonresident of the United States for all or part of the taxable year or by a foreign estate or trust. For such years the tax imposed by section 1(c), as amended by such Act, shall apply to the income effectively connected with the conduct of a trade or business in the United States by an unmarried alien individual (other than a surviving spouse) who is a nonresident of the United States for all or part of the taxable year. See paragraph (b)(2) of § 1.871-8.

(3) The income tax imposed by section 1 upon any amount of taxable income is computed by adding to the income tax for the bracket in which that amount falls in the appropriate table in section 1 the income tax upon the excess of the amount over the bottom of the bracket at the rate indicated in such table.

(4) The provisions of section 1 of the Code, as amended by the Tax Reform Act of 1969, and of this paragraph may be illustrated by the following examples:

Example (1). A, an unmarried individual, had taxable income for the calendar year 1964 of $15,750. Accordingly, the tax upon such taxable income would be $4,507.50, computed as follows from the table in section 1(a)(1):

Tax on $14,000 (from table)	$3,790.00
Tax on $1,750 (at 41% as determined from the table)	717.50
Total tax on $15,750	$4,507.50

Example (2). Assume the same facts as in example (1), except the figures are for the calendar year 1965. The tax upon such taxable income would be $4,232.50, computed as follows from the table in section 1(a)(2):

Tax on $14,000 (from table)	$3,550.00
Tax on $1,750 (at 39% as determined from the table)	682.50
Total tax on $15,750	$4,232.50

Example (3). Assume the same facts as in example (1), except the figures are for the calendar year 1971. The tax upon such taxable income would be $3,752.50, computed as follows from the table in section 1(c), as amended:

Tax on $14,000 (from table)	$3,210.00
Tax on $1,750 (at 31% as determined from the table)	542.50
Total tax on $15,750	$3,752.50

(b) *Citizens or residents of the United States liable to tax.* In general, all citizens of the United States, wherever resident, and all resident alien individuals are liable to the income taxes imposed by the Code whether the income is received from sources within or without the United States. Pursuant to section 876, a nonresident alien individual who is a bona fide resident of Puerto Rico during the entire taxable year is, except as provided in section 933 with respect to Puerto Rican source income, subject to taxation in the same manner as a resident alien individual. As to tax on nonresident alien individuals, see sections 871 and 877.

(c) *Who is a citizen.* Every person born or naturalized in the United States and subject to its jurisdiction is a citizen. For other rules governing the acquisition of citizenship, see chapters 1 and 2 of title III of the Immigration and Nationality Act (8 U.S.C. 1401-1459). For rules governing loss of citizenship, see sections 349 to 357, inclusive, of such Act (8 U.S.C. 1481-1489), *Schneider v. Rusk,* (1964) 377 U.S. 163, and Rev. Rul. 70-506, C.B. 1970-2, 1. For rules pertaining to persons who are nationals but not citizens at birth, e.g., a person born in American Samoa, see section 308 of such Act (8 U.S.C. 1408). For special rules applicable to certain expatriates who have lost citizenship with a principal purpose of avoiding certain taxes, see section 877. A foreigner who has filed his declaration of intention of becoming a citizen but who has not yet been admitted to citizenship by a final order of a naturalization court is an alien. [Reg. § 1.1-1.]

□ [*T.D.* 6161, 2-3-56. *Amended by T.D.* 7117, 5-24-71, *and T.D.* 7332, 12-20-74.]

[Reg. § 1.1(h)-1]

§ 1.1(h)-1. Capital gains look-through rule for sales or exchanges of interests in a partnership, S corporation, or trust.—(a) *In general.* When an interest in a partnership held for more than one year is sold or exchanged, the transferor may recognize ordinary income (e.g., under section 751(a)), collectibles gain, section 1250 capital gain, and residual long-term capital gain or loss. When stock in an S corporation held for more than one year is sold or exchanged, the transferor may recognize ordinary income (e.g., under sections 304, 306, 341, 1254), collectibles gain, and residual long-term capital gain or loss. When an interest in a trust held for more than one year is sold or exchanged, a transferor who is not treated as the owner of the portion of the trust attributable to the interest sold or exchanged (sections 673 through 679) (a non-grantor transferor) may recognize collectibles gain and residual long-term capital gain or loss.

(b) *Look-through capital gain*—(1) *In general.* Look-through capital gain is the share of collectibles gain allocable to an interest in a partnership, S corporation, or trust, plus the share of section 1250 capital gain allocable to an interest in a partnership, determined under paragraphs (b)(2) and (3) of this section.

(2) *Collectibles gain*—(i) *Definition.* For purposes of this section, *collectibles gain* shall be treated as gain from the sale or exchange of a collectible (as defined in section 408(m) without regard to section 408(m)(3)) that is a capital asset held for more than 1 year.

(ii) *Share of collectibles gain allocable to an interest in a partnership, S corporation, or a trust.* When an interest in a partnership, S corporation, or trust held for more than one year is sold or exchanged in a transaction in which all realized gain is recognized, the transferor shall recognize as collectibles gain the amount of net gain (but not net loss) that would be allocated to that partner (taking into account any remedial allocation under § 1.704-3(d)), shareholder, or beneficiary (to the extent attributable to the portion of the partnership interest, S corporation stock, or trust interest transferred that was held for more than one year) if the partnership, S corporation, or trust transferred all of its collectibles for cash equal to the fair market value of the assets in a fully taxable transaction immediately before the transfer of the interest in the partnership, S corporation, or trust. If less than all of the realized gain is recognized upon the sale or exchange of an interest in a partnership, S corporation, or trust, the same methodology shall apply to determine the collectibles gain recognized by the transferor, except that the partnership, S corporation, or trust shall be treated as transferring only a proportionate amount of each of its collectibles determined as a fraction that is the amount of gain recognized in the sale or exchange over the amount of gain realized in the sale or exchange. With respect to the transfer of an interest in a trust, this paragraph (b)(2) applies only to transfers by non-grantor transferors (as defined in paragraph (a) of this section). This paragraph (b)(2) does not apply to a transaction that is treated, for Federal income tax purposes, as a redemption of an interest in a partnership, S corporation, or trust.

(3) *Section 1250 capital gain*—(i) *Definition.* For purposes of this section, *section 1250 capital gain* means the capital gain (not otherwise treated as ordinary income) that would be treated as ordinary income if section 1250(b)(1) included all depreciation and the applicable percentage under section 1250(a) were 100 percent.

(ii) *Share of section 1250 capital gain allocable to interest in partnership.* When an interest in a partnership held for more than one year is sold or exchanged in a transaction in which all realized gain is recognized, there shall be taken into account under section 1(h)(7)(A)(i) in determining the partner's unrecaptured section 1250 gain the amount of section 1250 capital gain that would be allocated (taking into account any remedial allocation under § 1.704-3(d)) to that partner (to the extent attributable to the portion of the partnership interest transferred that was held for more than one year) if the partnership transferred all of its section 1250 property in a fully taxable transaction for cash equal to the fair market value of the assets immediately before the transfer of the interest in the partnership. If less than all of the realized gain is recognized upon the sale or exchange of an interest in a partnership, the same methodology shall apply to determine the section 1250 capital gain recognized by the transferor, except that the partnership shall be treated as transferring only a proportionate amount of each section 1250 property determined as a fraction that is the amount of gain recognized in the sale or exchange over the amount of gain realized in the sale or exchange. This paragraph (b)(3) does not apply to a transaction that is treated, for Federal income tax purposes, as a redemption of a partnership interest.

(iii) *Limitation with respect to net section 1231 gain.* In determining a transferor partner's net section 1231 gain (as defined in section 1231(c)(3)) for purposes of section 1(h)(7)(B), the transferor partner's allocable share of section 1250 capital gain in partnership property shall not be treated as section 1231 gain, regardless of whether the partnership property is used in the trade or business (as defined in section 1231(b)).

(c) *Residual long-term capital gain or loss.* The amount of residual long-term capital gain or loss recognized by a partner, shareholder of an S corporation, or beneficiary of a trust on account of the sale or exchange of an interest in a partnership, S corporation, or trust shall equal the amount of long-term capital gain or loss that the partner would recognize under section 741, that

the shareholder would recognize upon the sale or exchange of stock of an S corporation, or that the beneficiary would recognize upon the sale or exchange of an interest in a trust (pre-look-through long-term capital gain or loss) minus the amount of look-through capital gain determined under paragraph (b) of this section.

(d) *Special rule for tiered entities.* In determining whether a partnership, S corporation, or trust has gain from collectibles, such partnership, S corporation, or trust shall be treated as owning its proportionate share of the collectibles of any partnership, S corporation, or trust in which it owns an interest either directly or indirectly through a chain of such entities. In determining whether a partnership has section 1250 capital gain, such partnership shall be treated as owning its proportionate share of the section 1250 property of any partnership in which it owns an interest, either directly or indirectly through a chain of partnerships.

(e) *Notification requirements.* Reporting rules similar to those that apply to the partners and the partnership under section 751(a) shall apply in the case of sales or exchanges of interests in a partnership, S corporation, or trust that cause holders of such interests to recognize collectibles gain and in the case of sales or exchanges of interests in a partnership that cause holders of such interests to recognize section 1250 capital gain. See § 1.751-1(a)(3).

(f) *Examples.* The following examples illustrate the requirements of this section:

Example 1. Collectibles gain. (i) *A* and *B* are equal partners in a personal service partnership (*PRS*). *B* transfers *B*'s interest in *PRS* to *T* for $15,000 when *PRS*'s balance sheet (reflecting a cash receipts and disbursements method of accounting) is as follows:

	ASSETS	
	Adjusted Basis	*Market Value*
Cash	$ 3,000	$ 3,000
Loans Owed to Partnership	10,000	10,000
Collectibles	1,000	3,000
Other Capital Assets	6,000	2,000
Capital Assets	7,000	5,000
Unrealized Receivables	0	14,000
Total	$20,000	$32,000

	LIABILITIES AND CAPITAL	
Liabilities	$ 2,000	$ 2,000
Capital:		
A	9,000	15,000
B	9,000	15,000
Total	$20,000	$32,000

Reg. § 1.1(h)-1(c)

(ii) At the time of the transfer, B has held the interest in PRS for more than one year, and B's basis for the partnership interest is $10,000 ($9,000 plus $1,000, B's share of partnership liabilities). None of the property owned by PRS is section 704(c) property. The total amount realized by B is $16,000, consisting of the cash received, $15,000, plus $1,000, B's share of the partnership liabilities assumed by T. See section 752. B's undivided one-half interest in PRS includes a one-half interest in the partnership's unrealized receivables and a one-half interest in the partnership's collectibles.

(iii) If PRS were to sell all of its section 751 property in a fully taxable transaction for cash equal to the fair market value of the assets immediately prior to the transfer of B's partnership interest to T, B would be allocated $7,000 of ordinary income from the sale of PRS's unrealized receivables. Therefore, B will recognize $7,000 of ordinary income with respect to the unrealized receivables. The difference between the amount of capital gain or loss that the partner would realize in the absence of section 751 ($6,000) and the amount of ordinary income or loss determined under § 1.751-1(a)(2) ($7,000) is the partner's capital gain or loss on the sale of the partnership interest under section 741. In this case, the transferor has a $1,000 pre-look-through long-term capital loss.

(iv) If PRS were to sell all of its collectibles in a fully taxable transaction for cash equal to the fair market value of the assets immediately prior to the transfer of B's partnership interest to T, B would be allocated $1,000 of gain from the sale of the collectibles. Therefore, B will recognize $1,000 of collectibles gain on account of the collectibles held by PRS.

(v) The difference between the transferor's pre-look-through long-term capital gain or loss (−$1,000) and the look-through capital gain determined under this section ($1,000) is the transferor's residual long-term capital gain or loss on the sale of the partnership interest. Under these facts, B will recognize a $2,000 residual long-term capital loss on account of the sale or exchange of the interest in PRS.

Example 2. Special allocations. Assume the same facts as in *Example 1*, except that under the partnership agreement, all gain from the sale of the collectibles is specially allocated to B, and B transfers B's interest to T for $16,000. All items of income, gain, loss, or deduction of PRS, other than the gain from the collectibles, are divided equally between A and B. Under these facts, B's amount realized is $17,000, consisting of the cash received, $16,000, plus $1,000, B's share of the partnership liabilities assumed by T. See section 752. B will recognize $7,000 of ordinary income with respect to the unrealized receivables (determined under § 1.751-1(a)(2)). Accordingly, B's pre-look-through long-term capital gain would be $0. If PRS were to sell all of its collectibles in a fully taxable transaction for cash equal to the fair market value of the assets immediately prior to the transfer of B's partnership interest to T, B would be allocated $2,000 of gain from the sale of the collectibles. Therefore, B will recognize $2,000 of collectibles gain on account of the collectibles held by PRS. B will recognize a $2,000 residual long-term capital loss on account of the sale of B's interest in PRS.

Example 3. Net collectibles loss ignored. Assume the same facts as in *Example 1*, except that the collectibles held by PRS have an adjusted basis of $3,000 and a fair market value of $1,000, and the other capital assets have an adjusted basis of $4,000 and a fair market value of $4,000. (The total adjusted basis and fair market value of the partnership's capital assets are the same as in *Example 1*.) If PRS were to sell all of its collectibles in a fully taxable transaction for cash equal to the fair market value of the assets immediately prior to the transfer of B's partnership interest to T, B would be allocated $1,000 of loss from the sale of the collectibles. Because none of the gain from the sale of the interest in PRS is attributable to unrealized appreciation in the value of collectibles held by PRS, the net loss in collectibles held by PRS is not recognized at the time B transfers the interest in PRS. B will recognize $7,000 of ordinary income (determined under § 1.751-1(a)(2)) and a $1,000 long-term capital loss on account of the sale of B's interest in PRS.

Example 4. Collectibles gain in an S corporation. (i) A corporation (X) has always been an S corporation and is owned by individuals A, B, and C. In 1996, X invested in antiques. Subsequent to their purchase, the antiques appreciated in value by $300. A owns one-third of the shares of X stock and has held that stock for more than one year. A's adjusted basis in the X stock is $100. If A were to sell all of A's X stock to T for $150, A would realize $50 of pre-look-through long-term capital gain.

(ii) If X were to sell its antiques in a fully taxable transaction for cash equal to the fair market value of the assets immediately before the transfer to T, A would be allocated $100 of gain on account of the sale. Therefore, A will recognize $100 of collectibles gain (look-through capital gain) on account of the collectibles held by X.

Reg. § 1.1(h)-1(f)

(iii) The difference between the transferor's pre-look-through long-term capital gain or loss ($50) and the look-through capital gain determined under this section ($100) is the transferor's residual long-term capital gain or loss on the sale of the S corporation stock. Under these facts, A will recognize $100 of collectibles gain and a $50 residual long-term capital loss on account of the sale of A's interest in X.

Example 5. Sale or exchange of partnership interest where part of the interest has a short-term holding period. (i) A, B, and C form an equal partnership (PRS). In connection with the forma-tion, A contributes $5,000 in cash and a capital asset with a fair market value of $5,000 and a basis of $2,000; B contributes $7,000 in cash and a collectible with a fair market value of $3,000 and a basis of $3,000; and C contributes $10,000 in cash. At the time of the contribution, A had held the contributed property for two years. Six months later, when A's basis in PRS is $7,000, A transfers A's interest in PRS to T for $14,000 at a time when PRS's balance sheet (reflecting a cash receipts and disbursements method of accounting) is as follows:

	ASSETS	
	Adjusted Basis	*Market Value*
Cash	$22,000	$22,000
Unrealized Receivables	0	6,000
Capital Asset	2,000	5,000
Collectible	3,000	9,000
Capital Assets	5,000	14,000
Total	$27,000	$42,000

(ii) Although at the time of the transfer A has not held A's interest in PRS for more than one year, 50 percent of the fair market value of A's interest in PRS was received in exchange for a capital asset with a long-term holding period. Therefore, 50 percent of A's interest in PRS has a long-term holding period. See § 1.1223-3(b)(1).

(iii) If PRS were to sell all of its section 751 property in a fully taxable transaction immediately before A's transfer of the partnership interest, A would be allocated $2,000 of ordinary income. Accordingly, A will recognize $2,000 ordinary income and $5,000 ($7,000 − $2,000) of capital gain on account of the transfer to T of A's interest in PRS. Fifty percent ($2,500) of that gain is long-term capital gain and 50 percent ($2,500) is short-term capital gain. See § 1.1223-3(c)(1).

(iv) If the collectible were sold or exchanged in a fully taxable transaction immediately before A's transfer of the partnership interest, A would be allocated $2,000 of gain attributable to the col-lectible. The gain attributable to the collectible that is allocable to the portion of the transferred interest in PRS with a long-term holding period is $1,000 (50 percent of $2,000). Accordingly, A will recognize $1,000 of collectibles gain on account of the transfer of A's interest in PRS.

(v) The difference between the amount of pre-look-through long-term capital gain or loss ($2,500) and the look-through capital gain ($1,000) is the amount of residual long-term capi-tal gain or loss that A will recognize on account of the transfer of A's interest in PRS. Under these facts, A will recognize a residual long-term capital gain of $1,500 and a short-term capital gain of $2,500.

(g) *Effective date.* This section applies to trans-fers of interests in partnerships, S corporations, and trusts that occur on or after September 21, 2000. [Reg. § 1.1(h)-1.]

☐ [*T.D.* 8902, 9-20-2000.]

[Reg. § 1.1(i)-1T]

§ 1.1(i)-1T. Questions and answers relating to the tax on unearned income of certain mi-nor children (Temporary).

In general.

Q-1. To whom does section 1(i) apply?

A-1. Section 1(i) applies to any child who is under 14 years of age at the close of the taxable year, who has at least one living parent at the close of the taxable year, and who recognizes over $1,000 of unearned income during the taxable year.

Q-2. What is the effective date of section 1(i)?

A-2. Section 1(i) applies to taxable years of the child beginning after December 31, 1986.

Computation of tax.

Q-3. What is the amount of tax imposed by section 1 on a child to whom section 1(i) applies?

A-3. In the case of a child to whom section 1(i) applies, the amount of tax imposed by section 1 equals the greater of (A) the tax imposed by section 1 without regard to section 1(i) or (B) the sum of the tax that would be imposed by section 1 if the child's taxable income was reduced by the

Reg. § 1.1(i)-1T

child's net unearned income, plus the child's share of the allocable parental tax.

Q-4. What is the allocable parental tax?

A-4. The allocable parental tax is the excess of (A) the tax that would be imposed by section 1 on the sum of the parent's taxable income plus the net unearned income of all children of such parent to whom section 1(i) applies, over (B) the tax imposed by section 1 on the parent's taxable income. Thus, the allocable parental tax is not computed with reference to unearned income of a child over 14 or a child under 14 with less than $1,000 of unearned income. See A-10 through A-13 for rules regarding the determination of the parent(s) whose taxable income is taken into account under section 1(i). See A-14 for rules regarding the determination of children of the parent whose net unearned income is taken into account under section 1(i).

Q-5. What is the child's share of the allocable parental tax?

A-5. The child's share of the allocable parental tax is an amount that bears the same ratio to the total allocable parental tax as the child's net unearned income bears to the total net unearned income of all children of such parent to whom section 1(i) applies. See A-14.

Example (1). During 1988, D, a 12 year old, receives $5,000 of unearned income and no earned income. D has no itemized deductions and is not eligible for a personal exemption. D's parents have two other children, E, a 15 year old, and F, a 10 year old. E has $10,000 of unearned income and F has $100 of unearned income. D's parents file a joint return for 1988 and report taxable income of $70,000. Neither D's nor his parent's taxable income is attributable to net capital gain. D's tax liability for 1988, determined without regard to section 1(i), is $675 on $4,500 of taxable income ($5,000 less $500 allowable standard deduction). In applying section 1(i), D's tax would be equal to the sum of (A) the tax that would be imposed on D's taxable income if it were reduced by any net unearned income, plus (B) D's share of the allocable parental tax. Only D's unearned income is taken into account in determining the allocable parental tax because E is over 14 and F has less than $1,000 of unearned income. See A-4. D's net unearned income is $4,000 ($4,500 taxable unearned income less $500). The tax imposed on D's taxable income as reduced by D's net unearned income is $75 ($500 × 15%). The allocable parental tax is $1,225, the excess of $16,957.50 (the tax on $74,000, the parent's taxable income plus D's net unearned income) over $15,732.50 (the tax on $70,000, the parent's taxable income). See A-4. Thus, D's tax under section

1(i)(1)(B) is $1,300 ($1,225 + $75). Since this amount is greater than the amount of D's tax liability as determined without regard to section 1(i), the amount of tax imposed on D for 1988 is $1,300. See A-3.

Example (2). H and W have 3 children, A, B, and C, who are all under 14 years of age. For the taxable year 1988, H and W file a joint return and report taxable income of $129,750. The tax imposed by section 1 on H and W is $35,355. A has $5,000 of net unearned income and B and C each have $2,500 of net unearned income during 1988. The allocable parental tax imposed on A, B, and C's combined net unearned income of $10,000 is $3,300. This tax is the excess of $38,655, which is the tax imposed by section 1 on $139,750 ($129,750 + 10,000), over $35,355 (the tax imposed by section 1 on H and W's taxable income of $129,750). See A-4. Each child's share of the allocable parental tax is an amount that bears the same ratio to the total allocable parental tax as the child's net unearned income bears to the total net unearned income of A, B, and C. Thus, A's share of the allocable parental tax is $1,650

$$(\frac{5,000}{10,000} \times 3,300)$$

and B and C's share of the tax is $825

$$(\frac{2,500}{10,000} \times 3,300) \text{ each. See A-5.}$$

Definition of net unearned income.

Q-6. What is net unearned income?

A-6. Net unearned income is the excess of the portion of adjusted gross income for the taxable year that is not "earned income" as defined in section 911(d)(2) (income that is not attributable to wages, salaries, or other amounts received as compensation for personal services), over the sum of the standard deduction amount provided for under section 63(c)(5)(A) ($500 for 1987 and 1988; adjusted for inflation thereafter), plus the greater of (A) $500 (adjusted for inflation after 1988) or (B) the amount of allowable itemized deductions that are directly connected with the production of unearned income. A child's net unearned income for any taxable year shall not exceed the child's taxable income for such year.

Example (3). A is a child who is under 14 years of age at the end of the taxable year 1987. Both of A's parents are alive at this time. During 1987, A receives $3,000 of interest from a bank savings account and earns $1,000 from a paper route and performing odd jobs. A has no itemized deductions for 1987. A's standard deduction is $1,000, which is an amount equal to A's earned income for 1987. Of this amount, $500 is applied against A's unearned income and the remaining $500 is ap-

Reg. § 1.1(i)-1T

plied against A's earned income. Thus, A's $500 of taxable earned income ($1,000 less the remaining $500 of the standard deduction) is taxed without regard to section 1(i); A has $2,500 of taxable unearned income ($3,000 gross unearned income less $500 of the standard deduction) of which $500 is taxed without regard to section 1(i). The remaining $2,000 of taxable unearned income is A's net unearned income and is taxed under section 1(i).

Example (4). B is a child who is subject to tax under section 1(i). B has $400 of earned income and $2,000 of unearned income. B has itemized deductions of $800 (net of the 2 percent of adjusted gross income (AGI) floor on miscellaneous itemized deductions under section 67) of which $200 are directly connected with the production of unearned income. The amount of itemized deductions that B may apply against unearned income is equal to the greater of $500 or the deductions directly connected with the production of unearned income. *See* A-6. Thus, $500 of B's itemized deductions are applied against the $2,000 of unearned income and the remaining $300 of deductions are applied against earned income. As a result, B has taxable earned income of $100 and taxable unearned income of $1,500. Of these amounts, all of the earned income and $500 of the unearned income are taxed without regard to section 1(i). The remaining $1,000 of unearned income is net unearned income and is taxed under section 1(i).

Unearned income subject to tax under section 1(i).

Q-7. Will a child be subject to tax under section 1(i) on net unearned income (as defined in section 1(i)(4) and A-6 of this section) that is attributable to property transferred to the child prior to 1987?

A-7. Yes. the tax imposed by section 1(i) on a child's net unearned income applies to any net unearned income of the child for taxable years beginning after December 31, 1986, regardless of when the underlying assets were transferred to the child.

Q-8. Will a child be subject to tax under section 1(i) on net unearned income that is attributable to gifts from persons other than the child's parents or attributable to assets resulting from child's earned income?

A-8. Yes. The tax imposed by section 1(i) applies to all net unearned income of the child, regardless of the source of the assets that produced such income. Thus, the rules of section 1(i) apply to income attributable to gifts not only from the parents but also from any other source, such as the child's grandparents. Section 1(i) also applies to unearned income derived with respect

to assets resulting from earned income of the child, such as interest earned on bank deposits.

Example (5). A is a child who is under 14 years of age at the end of the taxable year beginning on January 1, 1987. Both of A's parents are alive at the end of the taxable year. During 1987, A receives $2,000 in interest from his bank account and $1,500 from a paper route. Some of the interest earned by A from the bank account is attributable to A's paper route earnings that were deposited in the account. The balance of the account is attributable to cash gifts from A's parents and grandparents and interest earned prior to 1987. Some cash gifts were received by A prior to 1987. A has no itemized deductions and is eligible to be claimed as a dependent on his parent's return. Therefore, for the taxable year 1987, A's standard deduction is $1,500, the amount of A's earned income. Of this standard deduction amount, $500 is allocated against unearned income and $1,000 is allocated against earned income. A's taxable unearned income is $1,500 of which $500 is taxed without regard to section 1(i). The remaining taxable unearned income of $1,000 is net unearned income and is taxed under section 1(i). The fact that some of A's unearned income is attributable to interest on principal created by earned income and gifts from persons other than A's parents or that some of the unearned income is attributable to property transferred to A prior to 1987, will not affect the tax treatment of this income under section 1(i). *See* A-8.

Q-9. For purposes of section 1(i), does income which is not earned income (as defined in section 911(d)(2)) include social security benefits or pension benefits that are paid to the child?

A-9. Yes. For purposes of section 1(i), earned income (as defined in section 911(d)(2)) does not include any social security or pension benefits paid to the child. Thus, such amounts are included in unearned income to the extent they are includible in the child's gross income.

Determination of the parent's taxable income.

Q-10. If a child's parents file a joint return, what is the taxable income that must be taken into account by the child in determining tax liability under section 1(i)?

A-10. In the case of parents who file a joint return, the parental taxable income to be taken into account in determining the tax liability of a child is the total taxable income shown on the joint return.

Q-11. If a child's parents are married and file separate tax returns, which parent's taxable income must be taken into account by the child in determining tax liability under section 1(i)?

Reg. § 1.1(i)-1T

A-11. For purposes of determining the tax liability of a child under section 1(i), where such child's parents are married and file separate tax returns, the parent whose taxable income is the greater of the two for the taxable year shall be taken into account.

Q-12. If the parents of a child are divorced, legally separated, or treated as not married under section 7703(b), which parent's taxable income is taken into account in computing the child's tax liability?

A-12. If the child's parents are divorced, legally separated, or treated as not married under section 7703(b), the taxable income of the custodial parent (within the meaning of section 152(e)) of the child is taken into account under section 1(i) in determining the child's tax liability.

Q-13. If a parent whose taxable income must be taken into account in determining a child's tax liability under section 1(i) files a joint return with a spouse who is not a parent of the child, what taxable income must the child take into account?

A-13. The amount of a parent's taxable income that a child must take into account for purposes of section 1(i) where the parent files a joint return with a spouse who is not a parent of the child is the total taxable income shown on such joint return.

Children of the parent.

Q-14. In determining a child's share of the allocable parental tax, is the net unearned income of legally adopted children, children related to such child by half-blood, or children from a prior marriage of the spouse of such child's parent taken into account in addition to the natural children of such child's parent?

A-14. Yes. In determining a child's share of the allocable parental tax, the net unearned income of all children subject to tax under section 1(i) and who use the same parent's taxable income as such child to determine their tax liability under section 1(i) must be taken into account. Such children are taken into account regardless of whether they are adopted by the parent, related to such child by half-blood, or are children from a prior marriage of the spouse of such child's parent.

Rules regarding income from a trust or similar instrument.

Q-15. Will the unearned income of a child who is subject to section 1(i) that is attributable to gifts given to the child under the Uniform Gift to Minors Act (UGMA) be subject to tax under section 1(i)?

A-15. Yes. A gift under the UGMA vests legal title to the property in the child although an adult custodian is given certain rights to deal with the property until the child attains majority. Any unearned income attributable to such a gift is the child's unearned income and is subject to tax under section 1(i), whether distributed to the child or not.

Q-16. Will a child who is a beneficiary of a trust be required to take into account the income of a trust in determining the child's tax liability under section 1(i)?

A-16. The income of a trust must be taken into account for purposes of determining the tax liability of a beneficiary who is subject to section 1(i) only to the extent it is included in the child's gross income for the taxable year under sections 652(a) or 662(a). Thus, income from a trust for the fiscal taxable year of a trust ending during 1987, that is included in the gross income of a child who is subject to section 1(i) and who has a calendar taxable year, will be subject to tax under section 1(i) for the child's 1987 taxable year.

Subsequent adjustments.

Q-17. What effect will a subsequent adjustment to a parent's taxable income have on the child's tax liability if such parent's taxable income was used to determine the child's tax liability under section 1(i) for the same taxable year?

A-17. If the parent's taxable income is adjusted and if, for the same taxable year as the adjustment, the child paid tax determined under section 1(i) with reference to that parent's taxable income, then the child's tax liability under section 1(i) must be recomputed using the parent's taxable income as adjusted.

Q-18. In the case where more than one child who is subject to section 1(i) uses the same parent's taxable income to determine their allocable parental tax, what effect will a subsequent adjustment to the net unearned income of one child have on the other child's share of the allocable parental tax?

A-18. If, for the same taxable year, more than one child uses the same parent's taxable income to determine their share of the allocable parental tax and a subsequent adjustment is made to one or more of such children's net unearned income, each child's share of the allocable parental tax must be recomputed using the combined net unearned income of all such children as adjusted.

Q-19. If a recomputation of a child's tax under section 1(i), as a result of an adjustment to the taxable income of the child's parents or another child's net unearned income, results in additional tax being imposed by section 1(i) on the child, is the child subject to interest and penalties on such additional tax?

Reg. § 1.1(i)-1T

A-19. Any additional tax resulting from an adjustment to the taxable income of the child's parents or the net unearned income of another child shall be treated as an underpayment of tax and interest shall be imposed on such underpayment as provided in section 6601. However, the child shall not be liable for any penalties on the underpayment resulting from additional tax's being imposed under section 1(i) due to such an adjustment.

Example (6). D and M are the parents of C, a child under the age of 14. D and M file a joint return for 1988 and report taxable income of $69,900. C has unearned income of $3,000 and no itemized deductions for 1988. C properly reports a total tax liability of $635 for 1988. This amount is the sum of the allocable parental tax of $560 on C's net unearned income of $2,000 (the excess of $3,000 over the sum of $500 standard deduction and the first $500 of taxable unearned income) plus $75 (the tax imposed on C's first $500 of taxable unearned income). *See* A-3. One year later, D and M's 1988 tax return is adjusted on audit by adding an additional $1,000 of taxable income. No adjustment is made to the amount reported as C's net unearned income for 1988. However, the adjustment to D and M's taxable income causes C's tax liability under section 1(i) for 1988 to be increased by $50 as a result of the phase-out of the 15 percent rate bracket. *See* A-20. In addition to this further tax liability, C will be liable for interest on the $50. However, C will not have to pay any penalty on the delinquent amount.

Miscellaneous rules.

Q-20. Does the phase-out of the parent's 15 percent rate bracket and personal exemptions under section 1(g), if applicable, have any effect on the calculation of the allocable parental tax imposed on a child's net unearned income under section 1(i)?

A-20. Yes. Any phase-out of the parent's 15 percent rate bracket or personal exemptions under section 1(g) is given full effect in determining the tax that would be imposed on the sum of the parent's taxable income and the total net unearned income of all children of the parent. Thus, any additional tax on a child's net unearned income resulting from the phase-out of the 15 percent rate bracket and the personal exemptions is reflected in the tax liability of the child.

Q-21. For purposes of calculating a parent's tax liability or the allocable parental tax imposed on a child, are other phase-outs, limitations, or floors on deductions or credits, such as the phase-out of the $25,000 passive loss allowance for rental real estate activities under section 469(i)(3) or the 2

percent of AGI floor on miscellaneous itemized deductions under section 67, affected by the addition of a child's net unearned income to the parent's taxable income?

A-21. No. A child's net unearned income is not taken into account in computing any deduction or credit for purposes of determining the parent's tax liability or the child's allocable parental tax. Thus, for example, although the amounts allowable to the parent as a charitable contribution deduction, medical expense deduction, section 212 deduction, or a miscellaneous itemized deduction are affected by the amount of the parent's adjusted gross income, the amount of these deductions that is allowed does not change as a result of the application of section 1(i) because the amount of the parent's adjusted gross income does not include the child's net unearned income. Similarly, the amount of itemized deductions that is allowed to a child does not change as a result of section 1(i) because section 1(i) only affects the amount of tax liability and not the child's adjusted gross income.

Q-22. If a child is unable to obtain information concerning the tax return of the child's parents directly from such parents, how may the child obtain information from the parent's tax return which is necessary to determine the child's tax liability under section 1(i)?

A-22. Under section 6103(e)(1)(A)(iv), a return of a parent shall, upon written request, be open to inspection or disclosure to a child of that individual (or the child's legal representative) to the extent necessary to comply with section 1(i). Thus, a child may request the Internal Revenue Service to disclose sufficient tax information about the parent to the child so that the child can properly file his or her return. [Temporary Reg. § 1.1(i)-1T.]

☐ [*T.D.* 8158, 9-3-87.]

[Reg. § 1.1-3]

§ 1.1-3. **Change in rates applicable to taxable year.**—For computation of the tax for a taxable year during which a change in the tax rates occurs, see section [15]21 and the regulations thereunder. [Reg. § 1.1-3.]

☐ [*T.D.* 6161, 2-3-56. *Amended by T.D.* 7117, 5-24-71.]

[Reg. § 1.2-1]

§ 1.2-1. **Tax in case of joint return of husband and wife or the return of a surviving spouse.**—(a) *Taxable year ending before January 1, 1971.* * * *

(b) *Taxable years beginning after December 31, 1970.* (1) For taxable years beginning after December 31, 1970, in the case of a joint return of husband and wife, or the return of a surviving spouse as defined in section 2(a) of the Code as amended by the Tax Reform Act of 1969, the tax shall be determined in accordance with the table contained in section 1(a) of the Code as so amended. For rules relating to the filing of joint returns of husband and wife see section 6013 as amended and the regulations thereunder.

(2) The following computation illustrates the method of computing the tax of a husband and wife filing a joint return for calendar year 1971. If the combined gross income is $8,200, and the only deductions are the two exemptions of the taxpayers under section 151(b), as amended, and the standard deduction under section 141, as amended, the tax on the joint return for 1971, without regard to any credits against the tax, is $968.46, determined as follows:

1. Gross income			$8,200.00
2. Less: Standard deduction, section 141		$1,066.00	
	Deduction for personal exemption, section 151	1,300.00	2,366.00
3. Taxable income			$5,834.00
4. Tax computed by the tax table provided under section 1(a) ($620 plus 19% of excess over $4,000)			968.46

(3) The limitation under section 1348 with respect to the maximum rate of tax on earned income shall apply to a married individual only if such individual and his spouse file a joint return for the taxable year.

(c) *Death of a spouse.* If a joint return of a husband and wife is filed under the provisions of section 6013 and if the husband and wife have different taxable years solely because of the death of either spouse, the taxable year of the deceased spouse covered by the joint return shall, for the purpose of the computation of the tax in respect of such joint return, be deemed to have ended on the date of the closing of the surviving spouse's taxable year.

(d) *Computation of optional tax.* For computation of optional tax in the case of a joint return or the return of a surviving spouse, see section 3 and the regulations thereunder.

(e) *Change in rates.* For treatment of taxable years during which a change in the tax rates occurs see section 21 and the regulations thereunder. [Reg. § 1.2-1.]

☐ [*T.D.* 6161, 2-3-56. *Amended by T.D.* 7117, 5-24-71.]

[Reg. § 1.2-2]

§ 1.2-2. **Definitions and special rules.**—(a) *Surviving spouse.* (1) If a taxpayer is eligible to file a joint return under the Internal Revenue Code of 1954 without regard to section 6013(a)(3) thereof for the taxable year in which his spouse dies, his return for each of the next two taxable years following the year of the death of the spouse shall be treated as a joint return for all purposes if all three of the following requirements are satisfied:

(i) He has not remarried before the close of the taxable year the return for which is sought to be treated as a joint return, and

(ii) He maintains as his home a household which constitutes for the taxable year the principal place of abode as a member of such household of a person who is (whether by blood or adoption) a son, stepson, daughter, or stepdaughter of the taxpayer, and

(iii) He is entitled for the taxable year to a deduction under section 151 (relating to deductions for dependents) with respect to such son, stepson, daughter, or stepdaughter.

(2) See paragraphs (c)(1) and (d) of this section for rules for the determination of when the taxpayer maintains as his home a household which constitutes for the taxable year the principal place of abode, as a member of such household, of another person.

(3) If the taxpayer does not qualify as a surviving spouse he may nevertheless qualify as a head of a household if he meets the requirements of § 1.2-2(b).

(4) The following example illustrates the provisions relating to a surviving spouse:

Example: Assume that the taxpayer meets the requirements of this paragraph for the years 1967 through 1971, and that the taxpayer, whose wife died during 1966 while married to him, remarried in 1968. In 1969, the taxpayer's second wife died while married to him, and he remained single thereafter. For 1967 the taxpayer will qualify as a surviving spouse, provided that neither the taxpayer nor the first wife was a nonresident alien at any time during 1966 and that she (immediately prior to her death) did not have a taxable year different from that of the taxpayer. For 1968 the taxpayer does not qualify as a surviving spouse because he remarried before the close of the taxable year. The taxpayer will qualify as a surviving spouse for 1970 and 1971, provided that neither the taxpayer nor the second wife was a nonresident alien at any time during

Reg. § 1.2-2(a)(4)

1969 and that she (immediately prior to her death) did not have a taxable year different from that of the taxpayer. On the other hand, if the taxpayer, in 1969, was divorced or legally separated from his second wife, the taxpayer will not qualify as a surviving spouse for 1970 or 1971, since he could not have filed a joint return for 1969 (the year in which his second wife died).

(b) *Head of household.* (1) A taxpayer shall be considered the head of a household if, and only if, he is not married at the close of his taxable year, is not a surviving spouse, (as defined in paragraph (a) of this section), and (i) maintains as his home a household which constitutes for such taxable year the principal place of abode, as a member of such household, of at least one of the individuals described in subparagraph (3), or (ii) maintains (whether or not as his home) a household which constitutes for such taxable year the principal place of abode of one of the individuals described in subparagraph (4).

(2) Under no circumstances shall the same person be used to qualify more than one taxpayer as the head of a household for the same taxable year.

(3) Any of the following persons may qualify the taxpayer as a head of a household:

(i) A son, stepson, daughter, or stepdaughter of the taxpayer, or a descendant of a son or daughter of the taxpayer. For the purpose of determining whether any of the stated relationships exist, a legally adopted child of a person is considered a child of such person by blood. If any such person is not married at the close of the taxable year of the taxpayer, the taxpayer may qualify as the head of a household by reason of such person even though the taxpayer may not claim a deduction for such person under section 151, for example, because the taxpayer does not furnish more than half of the support of such person. However, if any such person is married at the close of the taxable year of the taxpayer, the taxpayer may qualify as the head of a household by reason of such person only if the taxpayer is entitled to a deduction for such person under section 151 and the regulations thereunder. In applying the preceding sentence there shall be disregarded any such person for whom a deduction is allowed under section 151 only by reason of section 152(c) (relating to persons covered by a multiple support agreement).

(ii) Any other person who is a dependent of the taxpayer, if the taxpayer is entitled to a deduction for the taxable year for such person under section 151 and paragraphs (3) through (8) of section 152(a) and the regulations thereunder.

Under section 151 the taxpayer may be entitled to a deduction for any of the following persons:

(a) His brother, sister, stepbrother, or stepsister;

(b) His father or mother, or an ancestor of either;

(c) His stepfather or stepmother;

(d) A son or a daughter of his brother or sister;

(e) A brother or sister of his father or mother; or

(f) His son-in-law, daughter-in-law, father-in-law, mother-in-law, brother-in-law or sister-in-law;

if such person has a gross income of less than the amount determined pursuant to § 1.151-2 applicable to the calendar year in which the taxable year of the taxpayer begins, if the taxpayer supplies more than one-half of the support of such person for such calendar year and if such person does not make a joint return with his spouse for the taxable year beginning in such calendar year. The taxpayer may not be considered to be a head of a household by reason of any person for whom a deduction is allowed under section 151 only by reason of sections 152(a)(9), 152(a)(10) or 152(c) (relating to persons not related to the taxpayer, persons receiving institutional care, and persons covered by multiple support agreements).

(4) The father or mother of the taxpayer may qualify the taxpayer as a head of a household, but only if the taxpayer is entitled to a deduction for the taxable year for such father or mother under section 151 (determined without regard to section 152(c)). For example, an unmarried taxpayer who maintains a home for his widowed mother may not qualify as the head of a household by reason of his maintenance of a home for his mother if his mother has gross income equal to or in excess of the amount determined pursuant to § 1.151-2 applicable to the calendar year in which the taxable year of the taxpayer begins, or if he does not furnish more than one-half of the support of his mother for such calendar year. For this purpose, a person who legally adopted the taxpayer is considered the father or mother of the taxpayer.

(5) For the purpose of this paragraph, the status of the taxpayer shall be determined as of the close of the taxpayer's taxable year. A taxpayer shall be considered as not married if at the close of his taxable year he is legally separated from his spouse under a decree of divorce or separate maintenance, or if at any time during the taxable year the spouse to whom the taxpayer is married at the close of his taxable year was a nonresident alien.

Reg. § 1.2-2(b)(2)

A taxpayer shall be considered married at the close of his taxable year if his spouse (other than a spouse who is a nonresident alien) dies during such year.

(6) If the taxpayer is a nonresident alien during any part of the taxable year he may not qualify as a head of a household even though he may comply with the other provisions of this paragraph. See the regulations prescribed under section 871 for a definition of nonresident alien.

(c) *Household.* (1) In order for a taxpayer to be considered as maintaining a household by reason of any individual described in paragraph (a)(1) or (b)(3) of this section, the household must actually constitute the home of the taxpayer for his taxable year. A physical change in the location of such home will not prevent a taxpayer from qualifying as a head of a household. Such home must also constitute the principal place of abode of at least one of the persons specified in such paragraph (a)(1) or (b)(3) of this section. It is not sufficient that the taxpayer maintain the household without being its occupant. The taxpayer and such other person must occupy the household for the entire taxable year of the taxpayer. However, the fact that such other person is born or dies within the taxable year will not prevent the taxpayer from qualifying as a head of household if the household constitutes the principal place of abode of such other person for the remaining or preceding part of such taxable year. The taxpayer and such other person will be considered as occupying the household for such entire taxable year notwithstanding temporary absences from the household due to special circumstances. A nonpermanent failure to occupy the common abode by reason of illness, education, business, vacation, military service, or a custody agreement under which a child or stepchild is absent for less than six months in the taxable year of the taxpayer, shall be considered temporary absence due to special circumstances. Such absence will not prevent the taxpayer from being considered as maintaining a household if (i) it is reasonable to assume that the taxpayer or such other person will return to the household, and (ii) the taxpayer continues to maintain such household or a substantially equivalent household in anticipation of such return.

(2) In order for a taxpayer to be considered as maintaining a household by reason of any individual described in paragraph (b)(4) of this section, the household must actually constitute the principal place of abode of the taxpayer's dependent father or mother, or both of them. It is not, however, necessary for the purposes of such subparagraph for the taxpayer also to reside in such place of abode. A physical change in the location of such home will not prevent a taxpayer from qualifying as a head of a household. The father or mother of the taxpayer, however, must occupy the household for the entire taxable year of the taxpayer. They will be considered as occupying the household for such entire year notwithstanding temporary absences from the household due to special circumstances. For example, a nonpermanent failure to occupy the household by reason of illness or vacation shall be considered temporary absence due to special circumstances. Such absence will not prevent the taxpayer from qualifying as the head of a household if (i) it is reasonable to assume that such person will return to the household, and (ii) the taxpayer continues to maintain such household or a substantially equivalent household in anticipation of such return. However, the fact that the father or mother of the taxpayer dies within the year will not prevent the taxpayer from qualifying as a head of a household if the household constitutes the principal place of abode of the father or mother for the preceding part of such taxable year.

(d) *Cost of maintaining a household.* A taxpayer shall be considered as maintaining a household only if he pays more than one-half the cost thereof for his taxable year. The cost of maintaining a household shall be the expenses incurred for the mutual benefit of the occupants thereof by reason of its operation as the principal place of abode of such occupants for such taxable year. The cost of maintaining a household shall not include expenses otherwise incurred. The expenses of maintaining a household include property taxes, mortgage interest, rent, utility charges, upkeep and repairs, property insurance, and food consumed on the premises. Such expenses do not include the cost of clothing, education, medical treatment, vacations, life insurance, and transportation. In addition, the cost of maintaining a household shall not include any amount which represents the value of services rendered in the household by the taxpayer or by a person qualifying the taxpayer as a head of a household or as a surviving spouse.

(e) *Certain married individuals living apart.* For taxable years beginning after December 31, 1969, an individual who is considered as not married under section 143(b) shall be considered as not married for purposes of determining whether he or she qualifies as a single individual, a married individual, a head of household or a surviving spouse under sections 1 and 2 of the Code. [Reg. § 1.2-2.]

☐ [*T.D.* 6161, 2-3-56. *Amended by T.D.* 6792, 1-14-65, *and T.D.* 7117, 5-24-71.]

Reg. § 1.2-2(e)

[Reg. § 1.3-1]

§ 1.3-1. Application of optional tax.—(a) *General rules.* (1) For taxable years ending before January 1, 1970, an individual whose adjusted gross income is less than $5,000 (or a husband and wife filing a joint return whose combined adjusted gross income is less than $5,000) may elect to pay the tax imposed by section 3 in place of the tax imposed by section 1(a) or (b). For taxable years beginning after December 31, 1969 and before January 1, 1971 an individual whose adjusted gross income is less than $10,000 (or a husband and wife filing a joint return whose combined adjusted gross income is less than $10,000) may elect to pay the tax imposed by section 3 as amended by the Tax Reform Act of 1969 in place of the tax imposed by section 1(a) or (b). For taxable years beginning after December 31, 1970 an individual whose adjusted gross income is less than $10,000 (or a husband and wife filing a joint return whose combined adjusted gross income is less than $10,000) may elect to pay the tax imposed by section 3 as amended in place of the tax imposed by section 1 as amended. See § 1.4-2 for the manner of making such election. A taxpayer may make such election regardless of the sources from which his income is derived and regardless of whether his income is computed by the cash method or the accrual method. See section 62 and the regulations thereunder for the determination of adjusted gross income. For the purpose of determining whether a taxpayer may elect to pay the tax under section 3, the amount of the adjusted gross income is controlling, without reference to the number of exemptions to which the taxpayer may be entitled. See section 4 and the regulations thereunder for additional rules applicable to section 3.

(2) The following examples illustrate the rule that section 3 applies only if the adjusted gross income is less than $10,000 ($5,000 for taxable years ending before January 1, 1970).

Example (1). A is employed at a salary of $9,200 for the calendar year 1970. In the course of such employment, he incurred travel expenses of $1,500 for which he was reimbursed during the year. Such items constitute his sole income for 1970. In such case the gross income is $10,700 but the amount of $1,500 is deducted from gross income in the determination of adjusted gross income and thus A's adjusted gross income for 1970 is $9,200. Hence, the adjusted gross income being less than $10,000, he may elect to pay his tax for 1970 under section 3. Similarly, in the case of an individual engaged in trade or business (excluding from the term "engaged in trade or business" the performance of personal services as an employee),

there may be deducted from gross income in ascertaining adjusted gross income those expenses directly relating to the carrying on of such trade or business.

Example (2). If B has, as his only income for 1970, a salary of $11,600 and his spouse has no gross income, then B's adjusted gross income is $11,600 (not $11,600 reduced by exemptions of $1,250) and he is not, for such year, entitled to pay his tax under section 3. If, however, B has for 1970 a salary of $13,000 and incident to his employment he incurs expenses in the amount of $3,400 for travel, meals, and lodging while away from home, for which he is not reimbursed, the adjusted gross income is $13,000 minus $3,400 or $9,600. In such case his adjusted gross income being less than $10,000, B may elect to pay the tax under section 3. However, if B's wife has adjusted gross income of $400, the total adjusted gross income is $10,000. In such case, if B and his wife file a joint return, they may not elect to pay the optional tax since the combined adjusted gross income is not less than $10,000. B may nevertheless elect to pay the optional tax, but if he makes this election he must file a separate return and, since his wife has gross income, he may not claim an exemption for her in computing the optional tax.

(b) *Surviving spouse.* The return of a surviving spouse is treated as a joint return for purposes of section 3. See section 2, and the regulations thereunder, with respect to the qualifications of a taxpayer as a surviving spouse. Accordingly, if the taxpayer qualifies as a surviving spouse and elects to pay the optional tax, he shall use the column in the tax table, appropriate to his number of exemptions, provided for cases in which a joint return is filed.

(c) *Use of tax table.* (1) To determine the amount of the tax, the individual ascertains the amount of his adjusted gross income, refers to the appropriate table set forth in section 3 or the regulations thereunder, ascertains the income bracket into which such income falls, and, using the number of exemptions applicable to his case, finds the tax in the vertical column having at the top thereof a number corresponding to the number of exemptions to which the taxpayer is entitled.

(2) Section 3(b) (relating to taxable years beginning after December 31, 1964 and ending before January 1, 1970) contains 5 tables for use in computing the tax. Table I is to be used by a single person who is not a head of household. Table II is to be used by a head of household. Table III is to be used by married persons filing joint returns and by a surviving spouse. Table IV

is to be used by married persons filing separate returns using the 10% standard deduction. Table V is to be used by married persons filing separate returns using the minimum standard deduction. For an explanation of the standard deduction see section 141 and the regulations thereunder.

(3) 30 tables are provided for use in computing the tax under the Tax Reform Act of 1969. Tables I through XV apply for taxable years beginning after December 31, 1969 and ending before January 1, 1971. Tables XVI through XXX apply for taxable years beginning after December 31, 1970. The standard deduction for Tables I through XV, applicable to taxable years beginning in 1970 is 10%. The standard deduction for Tables XVI through XXX, applicable to taxable years beginning in 1971 is 13%. For an explanation of the standard deduction and the low income allowance see section 141 as amended by the Tax Reform Act of 1969.

(4) In the case of married persons filing separate returns who qualify to use the optional tax imposed by section 3, such persons shall use the tax imposed by the table for the applicable year in accordance with the rules prescribed by sections 4(c) and 141 and the regulations thereunder governing the use and application of the standard deduction and the low income allowance.

(5) The tax shown in the tax tables set forth in section 3 or the regulations thereunder reflects full income splitting in the case of a joint return (including the return of a surviving spouse) and lesser income splitting in the case of a head of household. Therefore, it is possible for the tax shown in the tables relating to joint returns, or relating to a return of a head of a household, to be lower than that shown in the table for separate returns even though the amounts of adjusted gross income and the number of exemptions are the same. [Reg. § 1.3-1.]

☐ [*T.D. 6161, 2-3-56. Amended by T.D. 7117, 5-24-71.*]

Tax on Corporations

[Reg. § 1.11-1]

§ 1.11-1. Tax on corporations.—(a) Every corporation, foreign or domestic, is liable to the tax imposed under section 11 except (1) corporations specifically excepted under such section from such tax: (2) corporations expressly exempt from all taxation under subtitle A of the Code (see section 501); and (3) corporations subject to tax under section 511(a). For taxable years beginning after December 31, 1966, foreign corporations engaged in trade or business in the United States shall be taxable under section 11 only on their taxable income which is effectively connected with the conduct of a trade or business in the United States (see section 882(a)(1)). For definition of the terms "corporations," "domestic," and "foreign," see section 7701(a)(3), (4), and (5), respectively. It is immaterial that a domestic corporation, and for taxable years beginning after December 31, 1966, a foreign corporation engaged in trade or business in the United States, which is subject to the tax imposed by section 11 may derive no income from sources within the United States. The tax imposed by section 11 is payable upon the basis of the returns rendered by the corporations liable thereto, except that in some cases a tax is to be paid at the source of the income. See subchapter A (sections 6001 and following), chapter 61 of the Code, and section 1442.

(b) The tax imposed by section 11 consists of a normal tax and a surtax. The normal tax and the surtax are both computed upon the taxable income of the corporation for the taxable year, that is, upon the gross income of the corporation minus the deductions allowed by chapter 1 of the Code. However, the deduction provided in section 242 for partially tax-exempt interest is not allowed in computing the taxable income subject to the surtax.

(c) The normal tax is at the rate of 22 percent and is applied to the taxable income for the taxable year. However, in the case of a taxable year ending after December 31, 1974, and before January 1, 1976, the normal tax is at the rate of 20 percent of so much of the taxable income as does not exceed $25,000 and at the rate of 22 percent of so much of the taxable income as does exceed $25,000 and is applied to the taxable income for the taxable year.

(d) The surtax is at the rate of 26 percent and is upon the taxable income (computed without regard to the deduction, if any, provided in section 242 for partially tax-exempt interest) in excess of $25,000. However, in the case of a taxable year ending after December 31, 1974, and before January 1, 1976, the surtax is upon the taxable income (computed as provided in the preceding sentence) in excess of $50,000. In certain circumstances the exemption from surtax may be disallowed in whole or in part. See sections 269, 1551, 1561, and 1564 and the regulations thereunder. For purposes of sections 244, 247, 804, 907, 922, and § § 1.51-1 and 1.815-4, when the phrase "the sum of the normal tax rate and the surtax rate for the taxable year" is used in any such section, the normal tax rate for all taxable years beginning after December 31, 1963, and ending before January 1, 1976, shall be considered to be 22 percent.

(e) The computation of the tax on corporations imposed under section 11 may be illustrated by the following example:

Example. The X Corporation, a domestic corporation, has gross income of $86,000 for the calendar year 1964. The gross income includes interest

of $5,000 on United States obligations for which a deduction under section 242 is allowable in determining taxable income subject to the normal tax. It has other deductions of $11,000. The tax of the X Corporation under section 11 for the calendar year is $28,400 ($15,400 normal tax and $13,000 surtax) computed as follows:

Computation of Normal Tax

Gross income		$86,000
Deductions:		
Partially tax-exempt interest	$ 5,000	
Other	11,000	16,000
Taxable income		70,000
Normal tax (22% of $70,000)		15,400

Computation of Surtax

Taxable income	$70,000
Add: Amount of partially tax-exempt interest deducted in computed taxable income ..	5,000
Taxable income subject to surtax	75,000
Less: Exemption from surtax	25,000
Excess of taxable income subject to surtax over exemption	50,000
Surtax (26% of $50,000)	$13,000

(f) For special rules applicable to foreign corporations engaged in trade or business within the United States, see section 882 and the regulations thereunder. For additional tax on personal holding companies, see part II of (section 541 and following), subchapter G, chapter 1 of the Code, and the regulations thereunder. For additional tax on corporations improperly accumulating surplus, see part I (section 531 and following), subchapter G, chapter 1 of the Code, and the regulations thereunder. For treatment of China Trade Act corporations, see sections 941 and 942 and the regulations thereunder. For treatment of Western Hemisphere trade corporations, see sections 921 and

922 and the regulations thereunder. For treatment of capital gains and losses, see subchapter P (sections 1201 and following), chapter 1 of the Code. For computation of the tax for a taxable year during which a change in the tax rates occurs, see section 21 and the regulations thereunder. [Reg. § 1.11-1.]

☐ [*T.D.* 6161, 2-3-56. *Amended by T.D.* 6237, 6-10-57; *T.D.* 6350, 1-6-59; *T.D.* 6407, 8-14-59; *T.D.* 6610, 8-30-62; *T.D.* 6681, 10-16-63, *T.D.* 7100, 3-19-71, *T.D.* 7181, 4-24-72, *T.D.* 7293, 11-27-73 *and T.D.* 7413, 3-25-76.]

Changes in Rates During a Taxable Year

→ *Caution: Code Sec. 15 was formerly Code Sec. 21. See Reg. § 1.21-1 for rules issued under former Code Sec. 21.*←

Credits Against Tax

→ *Caution: Former Code Sec. 21 has been redesignated as Code Sec. 15. Reg. § 1.21-1, below, covers rules issued under former Code Sec. 21.*

[Reg. § 1.21-1]

§ 1.21-1. Changes in rate during a taxable year.—(a) Section 21 applies to all taxpayers, including individuals and corporations. It provides a general rule applicable in any case where (1) any rate of tax imposed by chapter 1 of the Code upon the taxpayer is increased or decreased,

or any such tax is repealed, and (2) the taxable year includes the effective date of the change, except where that date is the first day of the taxable year. For example, the normal tax on corporations under section 11(b) was decreased from 30 percent to 22 percent in the case of a taxable year beginning after December 31, 1963.

→ *Caution: Former Code Sec. 21 has been redesignated as Code Sec. 15. Reg.*
§ 1.21-1, below, covers rules issued under former Code Sec. 21.

Accordingly, the tax for a taxable year of a corporation beginning on January 1, 1964, would be computed under section 11(b) at the new rate without regard to section 21. However, for any taxable year beginning before January 1, 1964, and ending on or after that date, the tax would be computed under section 21. For additional circumstances under which section 21 is not applicable, see paragraph (k) of this section.

(b) In any case in which section 21 is applicable, a tentative tax shall be computed by applying to the taxable income for the entire taxable year the rate for the period within the taxable year before the effective date of change, and another tentative tax shall be computed by applying to the taxable income for the entire taxable year the rate for the period within the taxable year on or after such effective date. The tax imposed on the taxpayer is the sum of—

(1) An amount which bears the same ratio to the tentative tax computed at the rate applicable to the period within the taxable year before the effective date of the change that the number of days in such period bears to the number of days in the taxable year, and

(2) An amount which bears the same ratio to the tentative tax computed at the rate applicable to the period within the taxable year on and after the effective date of the change that the number of days in such period bears to the number of days in the taxable year.

(c) If the rate of tax is changed for taxable years "beginning after" or "ending after" a certain date, the following day is considered the effective date of the change for purposes of section 21. If the rate is changed for taxable years "beginning on or after" a certain date, that date is considered the effective date of the change for purposes of section 21. This rule may be illustrated by the following examples:

Example (1). Assume that the law provides that a change in a certain rate of tax shall be effective only with respect to taxable years beginning after December 31, 1969. The effective date of change for purposes of section 21 is January 1, 1970, and section 21 must be applied to any taxable year which begins before and ends on or after January 1, 1970.

Example (2). Assume that the law provides that a change in a certain rate of tax shall be applicable only with respect to taxable years ending after December 31, 1970. For purposes of section 21, the effective date of change is January 1, 1971, and section 21 must be applied to any

taxable year which begins before and ends on or after January 1, 1971.

Example (3). Assume that the law provides that a change in a certain rate of tax shall be effective only with respect to taxable years beginning on or after January 1, 1971. The effective date of change for purposes of section 21 is January 1, 1971, and section 21 must be applied to any taxable year which begins before and ends on or after January 1, 1971.

(d) If a tax is repealed, the repeal will be treated as a change of rate for purposes of section 21, and the rate for the period after the repeal (for purposes of computing the tentative tax with respect to that period) will be considered zero. For example, the Tax Reform Act of 1969 repealed section 1562, which imposed a 6 percent additional tax on controlled corporations electing multiple surtax exemptions, effective for taxable years beginning after December 31, 1974. For such controlled corporations having taxable years beginning in 1974 and ending in 1975, the rate for the period ending before January 1, 1975, would be 6 percent; the rate for the period beginning after December 31, 1974, would be zero. However, subject to the rules stated in this section, section 21 does not apply to the imposition of a new tax. For example, if a new tax is imposed for taxable years beginning on or after July 1, 1972, a computation under section 21 would not be required with respect to such new tax in the case of taxable years beginning before July 1, 1972, and ending on or after that date. If the effective date of the imposition of a new tax and the effective date of a change in rate of such tax fall in the same taxable year, section 21 is not applicable in computing the taxpayer's liability for such tax for such year unless the new tax is expressly imposed upon the taxpayer for a portion of his taxable year prior to the change in rate.

(e) If a husband and wife have different taxable years because of the death of either spouse, and if a joint return is filed with respect to the taxable years of each, then, for purposes of section 21, the joint return shall be treated as if the taxable years of both spouses ended on the date of the closing of the surviving spouse's taxable year. See section 6013(c), relating to treatment of joint return after death of either spouse. Accordingly, if a change in the rate of tax is effective during the taxable year of the surviving spouse, the tentative taxes with respect to the joint return shall be computed on the basis of the number of days during which each rate of tax was in effect for the taxable year of the surviving spouse.

Reg. § 1.21-1(e)

→ *Caution: Former Code Sec. 21 has been redesignated as Code Sec. 15. Reg.*
§ 1.21-1, below, covers rules issued under former Code Sec. 21.

(f) Section 21 applies whether or not the taxpayer has a taxable year of less than 12 months. Moreover, section 21 applies whether or not the taxable income for a taxable year of less than 12 months is required to be placed on an annual basis under section 443. If the taxable income is required to be computed under section 443(b) then the tentative taxes under section 21 are computed as provided in paragraph (1) or (2) of section 443(b) and are reduced as provided in those paragraphs. The tentative taxes so computed and reduced are then apportioned as provided in section 21(a)(2) to determine the tax for such taxable years as computed under section 21.

(g) If a taxpayer has made the election under section 441(f) (relating to computation of taxable income on the basis of an annual accounting period varying from 52 to 53 weeks), the rules provided in section 441(f)(2) shall be applicable for purposes of determining whether section 21 applies to the taxable year of the taxpayer. Where a taxpayer has made the election under section 441(f) and where section 21 applies to the taxable year of the taxpayer the computation under section 21(a)(2) shall be made upon the basis of the actual number of days in the taxable year and in each period thereof.

(h)(1) Section 21 is applicable only if the rate of tax imposed by chapter 1 changes. Sections in which rates of tax are specified or incorporated by reference include the following: 1, 2, 3, 11, 511, 531, 541, 821, 831, 871, 881, 1201 and 1348 (for taxable years beginning after December 31, 1970). Except as provided in subparagraph (3) of this paragraph, section 21 is not applicable with respect to changes in the law relating to deductions from gross income, exclusions from or inclusions in gross income, or other items taken into account in determining the amount or character of income subject to tax. Moreover, section 21 is not applicable with respect to changes in the law relating to credits against the tax or with respect to changes in the law relating to limitations on the amount of tax. Section 21 is applicable, however, to all those computations specified in the section providing the rate of tax which are implicit in determining the rate. For example, if one of the tax brackets in the tax tables under section 3 were to be changed, section 21 would be applicable to that change. Thus, if the bracket relating to "at least $4,200 but not less than $4,250" for heads of households should be changed to increase or decrease the last sum specified, with corresponding changes being made in subsequent brackets, section 21 would be applicable. The enactment of

sections 1561 and 1562 is considered a change in section 11(d) which constitutes a change in rate for the period ending after December 31, 1963. The amendment of section 1561 and the repeal of section 1562 by the Tax Reform Act of 1969 is considered a change in section 11(d) which constitutes a change in rate for the period ending after December 31, 1974. The repeal of the 2 percent additional tax imposed under section 1503 on corporations filing consolidated returns constitutes a change in rate for the period ending after December 31, 1963. The addition to the Code of section 1348 (relating to 50 percent maximum rate on earned income) is a change in rate to which section 21(a) is applicable. The amendment of section 11(d) by the Tax Reduction Act of 1975 which increases to $50,000 the surtax exemption for a taxable year ending during 1975 constitutes a change in rate for such portion of the taxable year (if less than the entire taxable year) as follows December 31, 1974. Similarly, the return of the surtax exemption to $25,000 for a taxable year ending during 1976 constitutes a change in rate for such portion of the taxable year (if less than the entire taxable year) as follows December 31, 1975.

(2) Ordinarily, both the old and the new rates are applied to the same amount of taxable income. However, where the rate of tax is itself taken into account in determining taxable income (for example, the special deduction for Western Hemisphere trade corporations under section 922), the taxable income used in determining the tentative tax employing the rate before the effective date of change shall be determined by reference to that rate of tax, and the taxable income for the purpose of determining the tentative tax employing the rate for the period on and after the effective date of the change shall be determined by reference to the new tax rate.

(3) Section 21 is applicable with respect to changes in the law relating to the standard deduction for individuals provided in part IV of subchapter B and to the deduction for personal exemptions for individuals provided in part V of subchapter B.

(i) If the rate of tax changes more than once during the taxable year, section 21 is applicable to each change in rate. For example, if the rate of normal tax changed for taxable years beginning on or after March 1, 1954, and changed again for taxable years beginning on or after June 1, 1954, section 21 requires computation of 3 tentative taxes for any taxable year which began before March 1, 1954, and ended on or after June 1,

Reg. § 1.21-1(f)

→ *Caution: Former Code Sec. 21 has been redesignated as Code Sec. 15. Reg. § 1.21-1, below, covers rules issued under former Code Sec. 21.*

1954: One tentative tax at the rate in effect before the March 1 change; another tentative tax at the rate in effect from March 1 to May 31; and a third tentative tax at the rate in effect from June 1 to the end of the taxable year. The proportion of each such tentative tax taken into account in determining the tax imposed on the taxpayer is computed by reference to the portion of the taxable year before March 1, 1954, by reference to the portion of the taxable year from March 1, 1954, through May 31, 1954, and by reference to the portion of the taxable year from June 1, 1954, to the end of the taxable year, respectively.

(j)(1) If a change in the rate of one tax imposed by chapter 1 of the Code does not affect the amount of other taxes imposed by chapter 1 of the Code the other taxes may be determined without regard to section 21 and section 21 will be applied only to the tax for which a change in rate is made. However, if the change of rate of one tax does affect the amount of other taxes imposed under chapter 1 of the Code, then the computation of the taxes under chapter 1 of the Code, so affected shall be made by applying section 21. For example, if section 1201 applies to an individual taxpayer for a taxable year containing the effective date of a change in a rate of tax provided in section 1, then under section 21 the taxpayer must compute a tentative tax for each period for which a different rate of tax is effective under section 1. The tentative tax for each such period as computed under section 1201 will reflect the rate of tax provided by section 1 for such period.

(2) In certain cases chapter 1 of the Code provides that the particular tax to be imposed upon the taxpayer shall be one of several taxes, the basis of selection being the tax that is greater or lesser. See, for example, sections 821 and 1201. If in any such case the rate of any one of these taxes changes, then the tentative taxes computed as provided by section 21 for each period shall be computed employing the tax selected in accordance with the general rule of selection for such a case, at the rate of tax in effect for such period. Thus, if a change in the rate of the alternative tax under section 1201 is such that the alternative tax under section 1201 is applicable if the old rate is used and is not applicable if the new rate is used, one tentative tax will consist of the alternative tax under section 1201 and the other tentative tax will consist of the tax imposed by the other appli-

cable sections of chapter 1 of the Code. The two tentative taxes so computed are then prorated in accordance with section 21(a)(2) and the sum of the proportionate amounts is the tax imposed for the taxable year under chapter 1 of the Code. See the examples in paragraph (n) of this section.

(k) Section 21 does not apply in the following situations:

(1) The provisions of section 21 do not apply to the imposition of the tax surcharge by section 51. The proration rules of section 51(a) apply in the case of a taxable year ending on or after the effective date of the surcharge and beginning before July 1, 1970.

(2) The provisions of section 21 do not apply to the imposition of the minimum tax for tax preferences by section 56. The proration rules of section 301(c) of the Tax Reform Act of 1969 (83 Stat. 586) apply in the case of a taxable year beginning in 1969 and ending in 1970.

(l) In computing the number of days each rate of tax is in effect during the taxable year for purposes of section 21(a)(2) the effective date of the change in rate shall be counted in the period for which the new rate is in effect.

(m) Any credits against tax, and any limitation in any credit against tax, shall be based upon the tax computed under section 21. For credits against tax, see Part IV (sections 31 and following), subchapter A, chapter 1 of the Code.

(n) The application of section 21 may be illustrated by the following examples: (See also the examples in § 1.1561-2A(a)(3).)

Example (1). A, a married taxpayer filing a joint return, reports his income on the basis of a fiscal year ending June 30. For his fiscal year ending June 30, 1970, A reports taxable income (exclusive of capital gains and losses) of $50,000 and net long-term capital gain (section 1201 gain (net capital gain for taxable years beginning after December 31, 1976)) of $75,000. The rate of tax on capital gains under section 1201(b) relating to the alternative tax has been increased from 25 percent to a maximum rate of 29½ percent with respect to gain in excess of $50,000 and the effective date of the change in rate is January 1, 1970. The income tax for the taxable year ended June 30, 1970, would be computed under section 21 as follows:

Reg. § 1.21-1(n)

→ *Caution: Former Code Sec. 21 has been redesignated as Code Sec. 15. Reg.*
§ 1.21-1, below, covers rules issued under former Code Sec. 21.

Tentative Tax

Taxable income exclusive of capital gains and losses	$ 50,000
Long-term capital gain	75,000
	$125,000
Deduct 50% of long-term capital gain	37,500
Taxable income	$ 87,500
Tax under section 1 (1969 and 1970 rates)	$ 37,690

Alternative tax under section 1201(b) (1969 rates)

Taxable income ($50,000 + 50% of $75,000)	$ 87,500
Less 50% of long-term capital gain	37,500
Taxable income exclusive of capital gains	$ 50,000
Partial tax (tax on $50,000)	$ 17,060
Plus 25% of $75,000	18,750
Alternative tax under section 1201(b) at 1969 rates	$ 35,810

Alternative tax under section 1201(b) (1970 rates)

Step I

Taxable income ($50,000 + 50% of $75,000)	$ 87,500
Deduct 50% of net section 1201 gain	37,500
	$ 50,000
Tax on $50,000 (taxable income exclusive of capital gains)	$ 17,060

Step II

(a) Net section 1201 gain (net capital gain for taxable years beginning after December 31, 1976)	$ 75,000	
(b) Subsection (d) gain	$ 50,000	
25% of $50,000 (lesser of (a) or (b))		$ 12,500

Step III

(c) 29½% of $25,000 (excess of (a) over (b))		$ 7,375
(d) Ordinary income	$50,000	
50% of net section 1201 gain	37,500	
	$87,500	
Tax on $87,500		$ 37,690
Ordinary income	$50,000	
50% of subsection (d) gain	25,000	
	$75,000	
Tax on $75,000		30,470
Difference		$ 7,220
Lesser of (c) or (d)		$ 7,220
Alternative tax (total of 3 Steps) at rates effective on and after January 1, 1970		$ 36,780

Reg. § 1.21-1(n)

→ *Caution: Former Code Sec. 21 has been redesignated as Code Sec. 15. Reg. § 1.21-1, below, covers rules issued under former Code Sec. 21.*

Since the alternative tax is less than the tax imposed under section 1 for both the period in 1969 and the period in 1970, the alternative tax applies for both periods. Thus, since the effective date of the change in the rate of tax on capital gains is January 1, 1970, the old rate of alternative tax is effective for 184 days of the taxable year and the new rate of alternative tax is effective for 181 days of the taxable year. The alternative taxes are apportioned as follows:

1969—184/365 of $35,810	$18,052.16
1970—181/365 of $36,780	18,238.85
	$36,291.01
Tax surcharge (See § 1.51-1(d)(1)(i))	2,729.28
Total tax for the taxable year	$39,020.29

Example (2). B, a single individual not a head of a household, has a taxable year ending March 31. For the taxable year ending March 31, 1971, B has adjusted gross income of $18,500. His computation of the tax is as follows:

1970 Tentative Tax

Adjusted gross income		$ 18,500
Less: Standard deduction	$ 1,000	
Personal exemption	625	1,625
Taxable income under 1970 deduction provisions		$ 16,875
Tax on $16,875 (1970 rates)		
Tax on first $16,000	$ 4,330	
42% of $875	367.50	
Tentative tax at rates and deduction provisions effective on or after January 1, 1970		$ 4,697.50

1971 Tentative Tax

Adjusted gross income		$ 18,500
Less: Standard deduction	1,500	
Personal exemption	650	2,150
Taxable income under 1971 deduction provisions		$ 16,350
Tax on $16,350 (1971 rates)		
Tax on first $16,000	$ 3,830	
34% of $350	119	
Tentative tax at rates and deduction provisions effective on or after January 1, 1971		$ 3,949

The 1970 and 1971 tentative taxes are apportioned as follows:		
1970—275/365 of $4,697.50		$ 3,539.21
1971—90/365 of $3,949.00		973.73
		$ 4,512.94
Tax surcharge (See § 1.51-1(d)(1)(i))		56.26
Total tax for the taxable year		$ 4,569.20

Example (3). H and W, husband and wife, have a foster child, C, who qualifies as a dependent under section 152(b)(2) for the period beginning after December 31, 1969. H and W file a joint return on the basis of a taxable year ending August 31. For the taxable year ending August 31, 1970, H and W have adjusted gross income of $12,500. Their computation of the tax imposed is as follows:

→ *Caution: Former Code Sec. 21 has been redesignated as Code Sec. 15. Reg. § 1.21-1, below, covers rules issued under former Code Sec. 21.*

1969 Tentative Tax

Adjusted gross income		$ 12,500
Less: Standard deduction	$ 1,000	
Personal exemption (2)	1,200	2,200
Taxable income under 1969 deduction provision		$ 10,300
Taxable income reduced by one-half		$ 5,150
Tax on $5,150 (1969 rates)		
Tax on first $4,000	$ 690	
22% of $1,150	253	$ 943
Twice the tax on $5,150	$ 1,886	
Tentative tax at rates and deduction provisions effective on or after January 1, 1969		$ 1,886

1970 Tentative Tax

Adjusted gross income		$ 12,500
Less: Standard deduction	$ 1,000	
Personal exemption (3)	1,875	2,875
Taxable income under 1970 deduction provisions		$ 9,625
Tax on $9,625 (1970 rates)		
Tax on first $8,000	$ 1,380	
22% on $1,625	357.50	
Tentative tax at rates and deduction provision effective on or after January 1, 1970		$ 1,737.50

The 1969 and 1970 tentative taxes are apportioned as follows:	
1969—122/365 of $1,886	$ 630.39
1970—243/365 of $1,737.50	1,156.75
	$ 1,787.14
Tax surcharge (See § 1.51-1(d)(1)(i))	104.05
Total tax for the taxable year	$ 1,891.19

Example (4). B, a single individual with one exemption, reports his income on the basis of a fiscal year ending June 30. For fiscal year ending June 30, 1971, B reports adjusted gross income of $250,000, consisting of earned net income of $240,000 and investment income of $10,000. In addition, on April 24, 1971, stock was transferred to B pursuant to his exercise of a qualified stock option, and the fair market value of such stock at that time exceeded the option price by $175,000.

This $175,000 constitutes an item of tax preference described in section 57(a)(6). B claims itemized deductions in the amount of $34,000. By reason of section 1348, the maximum rate of tax on earned taxable income for a taxable year beginning after 1970 but before 1972 is 60 percent. The income tax for the taxable year ending June 30, 1971, would be computed under section 21 as follows:

1970 Tentative Tax

Adjusted gross income		$250,000
Less: Itemized deductions	$ 34,000	
Personal exemption	625	34,625
Taxable income under 1970 deduction provisions		$215,375
Tax on $215,375 (1970 rates)		
Tax on first $100,000	$ 55,490	
70% of $115,375	80,762.50	
Tentative tax at rates and deduction provisions effective on or after January 1, 1970		$136,252.50

Reg. § 1.21-1(n)

→ *Caution: Former Code Sec. 21 has been redesignated as Code Sec. 15. Reg.*
§ 1.21-1, below, covers rules issued under former Code Sec. 21.

Minimum tax:

Total tax preference items		$175,000.00
Less: Exemption	$ 30,000.00	
Income tax	136,252.50	166,252.50
Subject to 10% tax..		$ 8,747.50
10% tax		$ 874.75
Total tentative tax ($136,252.50 + $874.75)		$137,127.25

1971 Tentative Tax

Adjusted gross income		$250,000
Less: Itemized deductions	$ 34,000	
Personal exemption	650	34,650
Taxable income under 1971 deduction provisions		$215,350

(a) Tax on highest amount of taxable income on which rate does not exceed 60% ($50,000)		
(1971 rates)		$ 20,190
(b) Earned taxable income:		
($215,350 × $240,000/$250,000)	$206,736	
Less: Tax preference offset:		
($175,000 − $30,000)	145,000	
	$ 61,736	
(c) 60% of the amount by which $61,736 exceeds $50,000		$ 7,041.60
(d) Tax on $215,350 (1971 rates)		
Tax on first $100,000	$ 53,090	
70% of $115,350	80,745	
Total	$133,835	
(e) Tax on $61,736 (1971 rates)		
Tax on first $60,000	$ 26,390	
64% of $1,736	1,111.04	
Total	$ 27,501.04	
(f) Excess of $133,835 over $27,501.04		$106,333.96

Tentative tax (total of Steps (a), (c), and (f)) at rates and deduction provisions effective on or
after January 1, 1971 .... $133,565.56

Minimum tax:

Total tax preference items...		$175,000
Less: Exemption	$ 30,000	
Income tax	133,565.56	163,565.56
Subject to 10% tax		$ 11,434.44
10% tax		$ 1,143.44
Total tentative tax ($133,565.56 + $1,143.44)		$134,709

The 1970 and 1971 tentative taxes are apportioned as follows:

1970—184/365 of $137,127.25.....................................		$ 69,127.16
1971—181/365 of $134,709		66,800.90
Total tax for the taxable year		$135,928.06

Example (5). The surtax exemption of corporation M (one of 4 subsidiary corporations of W corporation), which files its income tax returns on the basis of a fiscal year ending March 31, 1964, is less than $25,000, by reason of section 1561 of the Code applicable to taxable years ending after December 31, 1963, and beginning before January 1, 1975. The taxable income of corporation M is $100,000, and the amount of the surtax exemption determined under the new rule for the 1964 taxable year is $5,000 ($25,000 ÷ 5). M's income tax liability for the taxable year ending March 31, 1964, is computed as follows:

→ *Caution: Former Code Sec. 21 has been redesignated as Code Sec. 15. Reg.*
§ 1.21-1, below, covers rules issued under former Code Sec. 21.

1963 Tentative Tax

Taxable income		$100,000

Normal tax on $100,000 (1963 rates)		
30% of $100,000	$30,000	
Surtax on $75,000 (1963 rates and $25,000 surtax exemption)		
22% of $75,000	16,500	
Total tentative tax at rates and surtax exemption effective before January 1, 1964		$ 46,500

1964 Tentative Tax

Taxable income		$100,000

Normal tax on $100,000 (1964 rates)		
22% of $100,000	$22,000	
Surtax on $95,000 (1964 rates and a $5,000 surtax exemption)		
28% of $95,000	26,600	
Total tentative tax at rates and surtax exemption effective after January 1, 1964		$ 48,600

The 1963 and 1964 tentative taxes are apportioned as follows:

1963—275/366 of $46,500		$ 34,938.52
1964— 91/366 of $48,600		12,083.61
Total tax for the taxable year		$ 47,022.13

M has the same amount of taxable income in 1965. Its income tax liability for the fiscal year ending March 31, 1965, is computed as follows:

Taxable income		$100,000

Normal tax on $100,000 (1964 rates)		
22% of $100,000	$22,000	
Surtax on $95,000 (1964 rates and a $5,000 surtax exemption)		
28% of $95,000	26,600	
Total tentative tax at the 1964 rates		$ 48,600

1965 Tentative Tax

Taxable income		$100,000

Normal tax on $100,000 (1965 rates)		
22% of $100,000	$22,000	
Surtax on $95,000 (1965 rates and a $5,000 surtax exemption)		
26% of $95,000	24,700	
Total tentative tax at the 1965 rates		$ 46,700

The 1964 and 1965 tentative taxes are apportioned as follows:

1964—275/365 of $48,600		$36,616.44
1965— 90/365 of $46,700		11,515.07
Total tax for the taxable year		$48,131.51

Reg. § 1.21-1(n)

→ *Caution: Former Code Sec. 21 has been redesignated as Code Sec. 15. Reg.*
§ 1.21-1, below, covers rules issued under former Code Sec. 21.

Example (6). Assume the same facts as in example (5), except that M elected the additional tax under section 1562 for its fiscal year ending March 31, 1964. M's tax liability is computed as follows:

1963 Tentative Tax

Taxable income		$100,000
Normal tax on $100,000 (1963 rates)		
30% of $100,000	$30,000	
Surtax on $75,000 (1963 rates and $25,000 surtax exemption)		
22% of $75,000	16,500	
Total tentative tax at rates and surtax exemption effective before January 1, 1964		$ 46,500

1964 Tentative Tax

Taxable income		$100,000
Normal tax on $100,000 (1964 rates)		
22% of $100,000	$22,000	
Surtax on $75,000 (1964 rates and $25,000 surtax exemption)		
28% of $75,000	21,000	
Additional tax on $25,000		
6% of $25,000	1,500	
Total tentative tax at rates and surtax exemption effective on and after January 1, 1964		$ 44,500

The 1963 and 1964 tentative taxes are apportioned as follows:

1963—275/366 of $46,500		$ 34,938.52
1964— 91/366 of $44,500		11,064.21
Total tax for the taxable year		$ 46,002.73

Example (7). Corporation N files its income tax returns on the basis of a fiscal year ending June 30. For its taxable year ending in 1976, the taxable income of N is $100,000. N's income tax liability is determined for the period July 1, 1975, through December 31, 1975, by taking into account two rates of normal tax under section 11(b)(2)(A) and (B) and the increase to $50,000 in the surtax exemption under section 11(d). For the period January 1, 1976, through June 30, 1976, N's income tax liability is determined by taking into account the single normal tax rate under section 11(b)(1) and the $25,000 surtax exemption under section 11(d). N's tax liability for the taxable year ending June 30, 1976, is computed as follows:

1975 Tentative Tax

Taxable income		$100,000
Normal tax on $100,000 (1975 rates)		
20% of $25,000	$ 5,000	
22% of $75,000	16,500	
Surtax on $50,000 (1975 rates and $50,000 surtax exemption)		
26% of $50,000	$13,000	
Total tentative tax at rates and surtax exemption effective on and after January 1, 1975		$ 34,500

→ *Caution: Former Code Sec. 21 has been redesignated as Code Sec. 15. Reg. § 1.21-1, below, covers rules issued under former Code Sec. 21.*

1976 Tentative Tax

Taxable income...		$100,000
Normal tax on $100,000 (1976 rates)		
22% of $100,000	$22,000	
Surtax on $75,000 (1976 rates and $25,000 surtax exemption)		
26% of $75,000	19,500	
Total tentative tax at rates and surtax exemption effective on and after January 1, 1976		$ 41,500

The 1975 and 1976 tentative taxes are apportioned as follows:

1975—184/366 of $34,500		$ 17,344
1976—182/366 of $41,500		20,637
Total tax for the taxable year		$ 37,981

[Reg. § 1.21-1.]

□ [T.D. 6161, 2-3-56. *Amended by* T.D. 6237, 6-10-57; T.D. 6350, 1-6-59; T.D. 6407, 8-14-59; T.D. 7164, 2-28-72; T.D. 7413, 3-25-76; T.D. 7528, 12-27-77; *and* T.D. 7728, 10-31-80.]

→ *Caution: Code Sec. 21 was formerly Code Sec. 44A. See Reg. §§ 1.44A-1—1.44A-4 for rules issued under former Code Sec. 44A.←*

→ *Caution: Code Sec. 22 was formerly Code Sec. 37. See Reg. §§ 1.37-1—1.37-3 for rules issued under former Code Sec. 37.←*

[Reg. § 1.23-1]

§ 1.23-1. Residential energy credit.—(a) *General rule.* Section 23 or former section 44C provides a residential energy credit against the tax imposed by chapter 1 of the Internal Revenue Code. The credit is an amount equal to the individual's qualified energy conservation expenditures (set out in paragraph (b)) plus the individual's qualified renewable energy source expenditures (set out in paragraph (c)) for the taxable year. However, the credit is subject to the limitations described in paragraph (d) and the special rules contained in § 1.23-3. The credit is nonrefundable (that is, the credit may not exceed an individual's tax liability for the taxable year). However, any unused credit may be carried over to succeeding years to the extent permitted under paragraph (e). Renters as well as owners of a dwelling unit may qualify for the credit. See § 1.23-3(h) for the rules relating to the allocation of the credit in the case of joint occupants of a dwelling unit.

(b) *Qualified energy conservation expenditures.* In the case of any dwelling unit, the qualified energy conservation expenditures are 15 percent of the energy conservation expenditures made by the taxpayer with respect to the dwelling unit during the taxable year, but not in excess of $2,000 of such expenditures. See § 1.23-2(a) for the definition of energy conservation expenditures.

(c) *Qualified renewable energy source expenditures.* In the case of taxable years beginning after December 31, 1979, the qualified renewable energy source expenditures are 40 percent of the renewable energy source expenditures made by the taxpayer during the taxable year (and before January 1, 1986) with respect to the dwelling unit that do not exceed $10,000. In the case of taxable years beginning before January 1, 1980, the qualified renewable energy source expenditures are the renewable energy source expenditures made by the taxpayer with respect to the dwelling unit during the taxable year, but not in excess of—

(1) 30 percent of the expenditures up to $2,000, plus

(2) 20 percent of the expenditures over $2,000, but not more than $10,000.

See § 1.23-2(b) for the definition of renewable energy source expenditures.

(d) *Limitations*—(1) *Minimum dollar amount.* No residential energy credit shall be allowed with respect to any return (whether joint or separate) for any taxable year if the amount of the credit otherwise allowable (determined without regard to the tax liability limitation imposed by paragraph (d)(3) of this section) is less than $10.

Reg. § 1.23-1(a)

(2) *Prior expenditures taken into account* — (i) *In general.* For purposes of determining the credit for expenditures made during a taxable year, the taxpayer must reduce the maximum amount of allowable expenditures with respect to the dwelling unit in computing qualified energy conservation expenditures (under paragraph (b)) or qualified renewable energy conservation expenditures (under paragraph (c)) by prior expenditures which were made by the taxpayer or by joint occupants (see § 1.23-3(h)) with respect to the same dwelling unit, and which were taken into account in computing the credit for prior taxable years. In the case of expenditures made during taxable years beginning before January 1, 1980, the reduction of the maximum amount under paragraph (c) must first be made with respect to the first $2,000 of expenditures (to which a 30 percent rate applies) and then with respect to the next $8,000 of expenditures (to which a 20 percent rate applies). This reduction must be made if all or any part of the credit was allowed in or was carried over from a prior taxable year.

(ii) *Change of principal residence.* A taxpayer is eligible for the maximum credit for qualifying expenditures made with respect to a new principal residence notwithstanding the allowance of a credit for qualifying expenditures made with respect to the taxpayer's previous principal residence. Furthermore, except in certain cases involving joint occupancy (see § 1.23-3(h)), a taxpayer is eligible for the maximum credit notwithstanding the allowance of a credit to a prior owner of the taxpayer's new principal residence.

(iii) *Example.* The rules with respect to the reduction for prior expenditures are illustrated by the following example:

Example. In 1978, A has $1,000 of energy conservation expenditures and $5,000 of renewable energy source expenditures in connection with A's principal residence. A's residential energy credit for 1978 is $1,350, made up of $150 of qualified energy conservation expenditures (15 percent of $1,000) plus $1,200 of qualified renewable energy source expenditures (30 percent of the first $2,000 plus 20 percent of the next $3,000). In 1979 A has an additional $2,000 of energy conservation expenditures and $3,000 of renewable energy source expenditures in connection with the same principal residence. A's residential energy credit for 1979 is $750, made up of $150 of qualified energy conservation expenditures (15 percent of the new maximum $1,000, which was reduced from $2,000 by $1,000 of energy conservation expenditures taken into account in 1978) plus $600 of qualified renewable energy source expenditures (20 percent of $3,000, which reflects the reduction of the maximum allowable expenditures

by the $5,000 of renewable energy source expenditures taken into account in 1978). The maximum residential energy credit allowable to A with respect to the same principal residence in subsequent years in which the credit is allowable is $400 (20 percent of the new maximum of $2,000 for renewable energy source expenditures and none for energy conservation expenditures).

(3) *Effects of grants and subsidized energy financing*—(i) *In general.* Qualified expenditures financed with Federal, State, or local grants shall be taken into account for purposes of computing the residential energy credit only if the amount of such grants is taxable as gross income to the taxpayer under section 61 (relating to the definition of gross income) and the regulations thereunder. In the case of taxable years beginning after December 31, 1980, qualified expenditures made from subsidized energy financing (as defined in § 1.23-2(i)) shall not be taken into account (except as provided in the following sentence) for purposes of computing the residential energy credit. In addition, the taxpayer must reduce the maximum amount of allowable expenditures (reduced as provided in paragraph (d)(2) of this section) with respect to the dwelling unit in computing qualified energy conservation expenditures (under paragraph (b) of this section) or qualified renewable energy source expenditures (under paragraph (c) of this section), whichever is appropriate, by an amount equal to the sum of—

(A) The amount of expenditures from subsidized energy financing (as defined in § 1.23-2(i)) that were made by the taxpayer during the taxable year or any prior taxable year beginning after December 31, 1980, with respect to the same dwelling unit, and

(B) The amount of any funds received by the taxpayer during the taxable year or any prior taxable year beginning after December 31, 1980, as a Federal, State, or local government grant made in taxable years beginning after December 31, 1980, that were used to make qualified expenditures with respect to the same dwelling unit and that were not included in the gross income of the taxpayer.

(ii) *Example.* The provisions of this paragraph (d)(3) may be illustrated by the following example:

Example. A had in 1979 made a renewable energy source expenditure of $2,000 in connection with A's residence for which he took the then allowed credit of $600. In 1981 A made additional renewable energy source expenditures of $9,000 with respect to which he received a loan of $5,000 from the Federal Solar-Energy and Energy Conservation Bank. Assume that the loan is subsidized energy financing. A computes the credit as

Reg. § 1.23-1(d)(3)

follows: The initial maximum allowable dollar limit is $10,000 which is reduced by the sum of the prior year expenditures of $2,000 and the subsidized energy financing loan of $5,000 leaving a dollar limit of $3,000 ($10,000 − ($2,000 + 5,000)). The $5,000 portion of the $9,000 funded by the subsidized energy financing loan is not allowed as a renewable energy source expenditure. The remaining expenditures in 1981 are $4,000 ($9,000 − $5,000). However, this amount exceeds the allowed maximum dollar limit of $3,000. Therefore, A's creditable expenses for 1981 are only $3,000 on which the credit is $1,200 (40 percent of $3,000).

(4) *Tax liability limitation*—(i) *For taxable years beginning after December 31, 1983.* For taxable years beginning after December 31, 1983, the credit allowed by this section shall not exceed the amount of tax imposed by chapter 1 of the Internal Revenue Code of 1954 for the taxable year, reduced by the sum of credits allowable under—

(A) Section 21 (relating to expenses for household and dependent care services necessary for gainful employment),

(B) Section 22 (relating to credit for the elderly and the permanently and totally disabled), and

(C) Section 24 (relating to contributions to candidates for public office).

See section 26(b) and (c) for certain taxes that are not treated as imposed by chapter 1.

(ii) *For taxable years beginning before January 1, 1984.* For taxable years beginning before January 1, 1984, the credit allowed by this section shall not exceed the amount of the tax imposed by chapter 1 of the Internal Revenue Code of 1954 for the taxable year, reduced by the sum of the credits allowable under—

(A) Section 32 (relating to tax withheld at source on nonresident aliens and foreign corporations and on tax-free covenant bonds),

(B) Section 33 (relating to the taxes of foreign countries and possessions of the United States),

(C) Section 37 (relating to retirement income),

(D) Section 38 (relating to investment in certain depreciable property),

(E) Section 40 (relating to expenses of work incentive programs),

(F) Section 41 (relating to contributions to candidates for public office),

(G) Section 42 (relating to the general tax credit),

(H) Section 44 (relating to purchase of new personal residence),

(I) Section 44A (relating to expenses for household and dependent care services), and

(J) Section 44B (relating to employment of certain new employees).

(e) *Carryforward of unused credit.* If the credit allowable by this section exceeds the tax liability limitation imposed by section 23(b)(5) (or former section 44C(b)(5)) and paragraph (d)(4) of this section, the excess credit shall be carried forward to the succeeding taxable year and added to the credit allowable under this section for the succeeding taxable year. A carryforward that is not used in the succeeding year because it exceeds the tax liability limitation shall be carried forward to later taxable years until used, except that no excess credit may be carried forward to any taxable year beginning after December 31, 1987. [Reg. § 1.23-1.]

☐ [*T.D. 7717, 8-26-80. Amended by T.D. 8146, 7-15-87.*]

[Reg. § 1.23-2]

§ 1.23-2. **Definitions.**—For purposes of section 23 or former section 44C and the regulations thereunder—(a) *Energy conservation expenditures*—(1) *In general.* The term "energy conservation expenditure" means an expenditure made on or after April 20, 1977, and before January 1, 1986, by a taxpayer for insulation or any other energy-conserving component, or for labor costs allocable to the original installation of such insulation or other component, if all of the following conditions are satisfied:

(i) The insulation (as defined in paragraph (c)) or other energy-conserving component (as defined in paragraph (d)) is installed in or on a dwelling unit that is used as the taxpayer's principal residence when the installation is completed. See § 1.23-3(e) for the definition of principal residence.

(ii) The dwelling unit is located in the United States (as defined in section 7701(a)(9)).

(iii) The construction of the dwelling unit was substantially completed before April 20, 1977. See § 1.23-3(f) for the definition of the terms "construction" and "substantially completed". In the case of expenditures made with respect to the enlargement of a dwelling unit, the construction of the enlargement must have been substantially completed before April 20, 1977.

(2) *Examples.* The application of this paragraph may be illustrated by the following examples:

Example (1). In 1978, A spent $500 for the purchase and installation of new storm windows

Reg. § 1.23-2(a)(1)

to replace old storm windows, $100 to reinstall old storm windows, and $150 to transfer to A's house insulation which had been installed in A's garage. Only the $500 spent for new storm windows qualifies as an energy conservation expenditure. The $100 spent to reinstall storm windows and the $150 spent to transfer insulation to A's house do not qualify since the only installation costs that qualify are those for the original installation of energy conservation property the original use of which commences with the taxpayer.

Example (2). In June 1977, B purchased for B's principal residence a new house that was substantially completed before April 20, 1977. Pursuant to B's request the builder installed storm windows on May 1, 1977, the cost of this option being included in the purchase price of the house. The portion of the purchase price of the residence allocable to the storm windows constitutes an energy conservation expenditure. However, no other part of the purchase price may be allocated to energy conservation property (insulation and other energy conserving components) installed before April 20, 1977. To qualify as an energy conservation expenditure, an expenditure must be made (*i.e.,* installation of the energy conservation property must be completed) on or after April 20, 1977.

(b) *Renewable energy source expenditures.* The term "renewable energy source expenditures" means an expenditure made on or after April 20, 1977, and before January 1, 1986, by a taxpayer for renewable energy source property (as defined in paragraph (e)), or for labor costs properly allocable to the on-site preparation, assembly, or original installation of such property, if both of the following conditions are satisfied:

(1) The renewable energy source property is installed in connection with a dwelling unit that is used as the taxpayer's principal residence when the installation is completed. See § 1.23-3(e).

(2) The dwelling unit is located in the United States (as defined in section 7701(a)(9)).

Additionally, the term "renewable energy source expenditures" includes expenditures made after December 31, 1979, and before January 1, 1986, for an onsite well drilled for any geothermal deposit (as defined in paragraph (h)), or for labor costs properly allocable to onsite preparation, assembly, or original installation of such well, but only if the requirements of paragraph (b)(1) and (2) of this section are met and the taxpayer has not elected under section 263(c) to deduct any portion of such expenditures or allocable labor costs. Eligibility as a renewable energy source expenditure does not depend on the date of construction of the dwelling unit. Thus, such an expenditure may be made in connection with either a new or an existing dwelling unit. Renewable energy source expenditures need only be made in connection with a dwelling, rather than in or on a dwelling unit. For example, a solar collector that otherwise constitutes renewable energy source property is not ineligible merely because it is installed separately from the dwelling unit. The term "renewable energy source expenditure" does not include any expenditure allocable to a swimming pool even when used as an energy storage medium or to any other energy storage medium whose primary function is other than the storage of energy. It also does not include the cost of maintenance of an installed system or the cost of leasing renewable energy source property.

(c) *Insulation.* The term "insulation" means any item that satisfies all of the following conditions:

(1) The item is specifically and primarily designed to reduce, when installed in or on a dwelling or on a water heater, the heat loss or gain or such dwelling or water heater. To qualify as insulation the item must be installed between a conditioned area and a nonconditioned area (except when installed on a water heater, water pipe, or heating/cooling duct). Thus for example, awnings do not qualify as insulation. For purposes of this section the term "conditioned area" means an area that has been heated or cooled by conventional or renewable energy source means. Insulation includes materials made of fiberglass, rock wool, cellulose, urea based foam, urethane, vermiculite, perlite, polystyrene, and extruded polystyrene foam.

(2) The original use of the item begins with the taxpayer.

(3) The item can reasonably be expected to remain in operation at least 3 years.

(4) The item meets the applicable performance and quality standards prescribed in § 1.23-4 (if any) that are in effect at the time the taxpayer acquires the item.

The term "insulation" shall not include items whose primary purpose is not insulation (*e.g.,* whose function is primarily structural, decorative, or safety-related). For example, carpeting, drapes (including linings), shades, wood paneling, fireplace screens (including those made of glass), new or replacement walls (except for qualifying insulation therein) and exterior siding do not qualify although they may have been designed in part to have an insulating effect.

(d) *Other energy-conserving components.* The term "other energy-conserving component" means any item (other than insulation) that satisfies all of the following conditions:

(1) The original use of the item begins with the taxpayer.

Reg. § 1.23-2(d)(1)

(2) The item can reasonably be expected to remain in operation for at least 3 years.

(3) The item meets the applicable performance and quality standards prescribed in § 1.23-4 (if any) that are in effect at the time of the taxpayer's acquisition of the item.

(4) The item is one of the following items:

(i) *A furnace replacement burner.* The term "furnace replacement burner" means a device (for oil and gas-fired furnaces or boilers) that is designed to achieve a reduction in the amount of fuel consumed as a result of increased combustion efficiency. The burner must replace an existing burner. It does not qualify if it is acquired as a component of, or for use in, a new furnace or boiler.

(ii) *A device for modifying flue openings.* The term "device for modifying flue openings" means an automatically operated damper that—

(A) Is designed for installation in the flue, between the barometric damper or draft hood and the chimney, of a furnace; and

(B) Conserves energy by substantially reducing the flow of conditioned air through the chimney when the furnace is not in operation. Conditioned air is air that has been heated or cooled by conventional or renewable energy source means.

(iii) *A furnace ignition system.* The term "furnace ignition system" means an electrical or mechanical device, designed for installation in a gas-fired furnace or boiler that automatically ignites the gas burner. In order to qualify, the device must replace a gas pilot light. Furthermore, it does not qualify if it is acquired as a component of, or for use in, a new furnace or boiler.

(iv) *A storm or thermal window or door.* The terms "storm or thermal window" and "storm or thermal door" mean the following:

(A)(*1*) A window placed outside or inside an ordinary or prime window, creating an insulating air space.

(*2*) A window with enhanced resistance to heat flow through the glazed area by multi-glazing.

(*3*) A window that consists of glass or other glazing materials that have exceptional heat-absorbing or heat-reflecting properties. For purposes of this subdivision (iv), the term "glazing material" does not include films and coatings applied on the surface of a window.

(B)(*1*) A second door, installed outside or inside a prime exterior door, creating an insulating air space.

(*2*) A door with enhanced resistance to heat flow through the glazed area by multi-glazing.

(*3*) A prime exterior door that has an R-value (a measurement of the ability of insulation to resist the flow of heat) of at least 2 throughout.

For purposes of this subdivision, "multi-glazing" is an arrangement in which two or more sheets of glazing material are affixed in a window or door frame to create one or more insulating air spaces. Multi-glazing can be achieved by installing a preassembled, sealed insulating glass unit or by affixing one or more additional sheets of glazing onto an existing window (or sash) or door. For purposes of this subdivision, a storm or thermal window or door does not include any film applied on or over the surface of a window or door.

(v) *Automatic energy-saving setback thermostat.* The term "automatic energy-saving setback thermostat" means a device that is designed to reduce energy consumption by regulating the demand on the heating or cooling system in which it is installed, and uses—

(A) A temperature control device for interior spaces incorporating more than one temperature control level, and

(B) A clock or other automatic mechanism for switching from one control level to another.

(vi) *Caulking and weatherstripping.* The term "caulking" means pliable materials used to fill small gaps at fixed joints on buildings to reduce the passage of air and moisture. Caulking includes, but is not limited to, materials commonly known as "sealants", "putty", and "glazing compounds". The term "weather-stripping" means narrow strips of material placed over or in movable joints of windows and doors to reduce passage of air and moisture.

(vii) *Energy usage display meter.* The term "energy usage display meter" means a device the sole purpose of which is to display the cost (in money) of energy usage in the dwelling. It may show cost information for electricity usage, gas usage, oil usage, or any combination thereof. The device may measure energy usage of the whole dwelling, or individual appliances or systems on an instantaneous or cumulative basis.

(viii) *Components specified by the Secretary.* The Secretary (or his delegate) may, in his discretion, after consultation with the Secretary of Energy and the Secretary of Housing and Urban Development (or their delegates), and any other appropriate Federal officers, specify by regulation other energy-conserving components for addition

Reg. § 1.23-2(d)(2)

to the list of qualified items. See § 1.44C-6 for the procedures and criteria to be used in determining whether an item will be considered for addition to the list of qualified items by the Secretary.

(e) *Renewable energy source property*—(1) *In general.* The term "renewable energy source property" includes any solar energy property, wind energy property, geothermal energy property, or property referred to in subparagraph (2), which meets the following conditions:

(i) The original use of the property begins with the taxpayer.

(ii) The property can reasonably be expected to remain in operation for at least 5 years.

(iii) The property meets the applicable performance and quality standards prescribed in § 1.23-4 (if any) that are in effect at the time of the taxpayer's acquisition of the property.

Renewable energy source property does not include heating or cooling systems, nor systems to provide hot water or electricity, which serve to supplement renewable energy source equipment in heating, cooling, or providing hot water or electricity to a dwelling unit, and which employ a form of energy (such as oil or gas) other than solar, wind, or geothermal energy (or other forms of renewable energy provided in paragraph (e)(2) of this section). Thus, heat pumps or oil or gas furnaces, used in connection with renewable energy source property, are not eligible for the credit. In order to be eligible for the credit for renewable energy source property, the property (as well as labor costs properly allocable to onsite preparation, assembly or installation of equipment) must be clearly identifiable. See § 1.23-3(1) for recordkeeping rules.

(2) *Renewable energy source specified by the Secretary.* In addition to solar, wind, and geothermal energy property, renewable energy source property includes property that transmits or uses another renewable energy source that the Secretary (or his delegate) specifies by regulations, after consultation with the Secretary of Energy and the Secretary of Housing and Urban Development (or their delegates), and any other appropriate Federal officers, to be of a kind that is appropriate for the purpose of heating or cooling the dwelling or providing hot water or (in the case of expenditures made after December 31, 1979) electricity for use within the dwelling. For purposes of this section, references to the transmission or use of energy include its collection and storage. See § 1.23-6 for the procedures and criteria to be used in determining when another energy source will be considered for addition to the list of qualified renewable energy sources.

(f) *Solar energy property*—(1) *In general.* The term "solar energy property" means equipment and materials of a solar energy system as defined in this paragraph (and parts solely related to the functioning of such equipment) which, when installed in connection with a dwelling, transmits or uses solar energy to heat or cool the dwelling or to provide hot water or (in the case of expenditures made after December 31, 1979) electricity for use within the dwelling. For this purpose, solar energy is energy derived directly from sunlight (solar radiation). Property which uses, as an energy source, fuel or energy which is indirectly derived from sunlight (solar radiation), such as fossil fuel or wood or heat in underground water, is not considered solar energy property. Materials and components of "passive solar systems" as well as "active solar systems," or a combination of both types of systems may qualify as solar energy property.

(2) *Active solar system.* An active solar system is based on the use of mechanically forced energy transfer, such as the use of fans or pumps to circulate solar generated energy, or thermal energy transfer, such as systems utilizing thermal siphon principles. Generally, this is accomplished through the use of equipment such as collectors (to absorb sunlight and create hot liquids or air), storage tanks (to store hot liquids), rockbeds (to store hot air), thermostats (to activate pumps or fans which circulate the hot liquids or air), and heat exchangers (to utilize hot liquids or air to heat air or water).

(3) *Passive solar system.* A passive solar system is based on the use of conductive, convective, or radiant energy transfer. In order to qualify as a passive solar system, a solar system used for heating purposes must contain all of the following: a solar collection area, an absorber, a storage mass, a heat distribution method, and heat regulation devices. The term "solar collection area" means an expanse of transparent or translucent material, such as glass which is positioned in such a manner that the rays of the sun directly strike an absorber. The term "absorber" means a surface, such as a floor, that is exposed to the rays of the sun admitted through the solar collection area, which converts solar radiation into heat, and then transfers the heat to a storage mass. The term "storage mass" means material, such as masonry, that receives and holds heat from the absorber and later releases the heat to the interior of the dwelling. The storage mass must be of sufficient volume, depth, and thermal energy capacity to store and deliver adequate amounts of solar heat for the relative size of the dwelling. In addition, the storage mass must be located so that it is capable of distributing the stored heat directly to

Reg. § 1.23-2(f)(3)

the habitable areas of the dwelling through a heat distribution method. The term "heat distribution method" means the release of radiant heating from the storage mass within the habitable areas of the dwelling, or convective heating from the storage mass through airflow paths provided by openings or by ducts in the storage mass, to habitable areas of the dwelling. The term "heat regulation devices" means shading or venting mechanisms (such as awnings or insulated drapes) to control the amount of solar heat admitted through the solar collection areas and nighttime insulation or its equivalent to control the amount of heat permitted to escape from the interior of the dwelling.

(4) *Components with dual function.* To the extent that a passive or active solar system utilizes portions of the structure of a residence, only the materials and components whose sole purpose is to transmit or use solar radiation (and labor costs associated with installing such materials and components) are included within the term "solar energy property". Accordingly, materials and components that serve a dual purpose, *e.g.,* they have a significant structural function or are structural components of the dwelling (and labor costs associated with installing such materials and components) are not included within the term "solar energy property". For example, roof ponds that form part of a roof (including additional structural components to support the roof), windows (including clerestories and skylights), and greenhouses do not qualify as solar energy property. However, with respect to expenditures made after December 31, 1979, a solar collector panel installed as a roof or portion thereof (including additional structural components to support the roof attributable to the collector) does not fail to qualify as solar energy property solely because it constitutes a structural component of the dwelling on which it is installed. For this purpose, the term "solar collector panel" does not include a skylight or other type of window. In the case of a trombe wall (a south facing wall composed of a mass wall and exterior glazing), the mass wall (and labor costs associated with installing the mass wall) will not qualify. However, the exterior (non-window) glazing will qualify. Any shading, venting and heat distribution mechanisms or storage systems that do not have a dual function will also qualify.

(g) *Wind energy property.* The term "wind energy property" means equipment (and parts solely related to the functioning of such equipment) which, when installed in connection with a dwelling, transmits or uses wind energy to produce energy in a useful form for personal residential purposes. Examples of equipment using wind energy to produce energy in a useful form are

windmills, wind-driven generators, power conditioning and storage devices that use wind to generate electricity or mechanical forms of energy. Devices that use wind merely to ventilate do not qualify as wind energy property.

(h) *Geothermal energy property.* The term "geothermal energy property" means equipment (and parts solely related to the functioning of such equipment) necessary to transmit or use energy from a geothermal deposit to heat or cool a dwelling or provide hot water for use within the dwelling. With respect to expenditures made after December 31, 1979, the term "geothermal energy property" also means equipment (and parts solely related to the functioning of such equipment) necessary to transmit or use energy from a geothermal deposit to produce electricity for use within the dwelling. Equipment such as a pipe that serves both a geothermal function (by transmitting hot geothermal water within a dwelling) and a non-geothermal function (by transmitting hot water from a water heater within a dwelling) does not qualify as geothermal property. A geothermal deposit is a geothermal reservoir consisting of natural heat which is from an underground source and is stored in rocks or in an aqueous liquid or vapor (whether or not under pressure), having a temperature exceeding 50 degrees Celsius as measured at the wellhead or, in the case of a natural hot spring (where no well is drilled), at the intake to the distribution system.

(i) *Subsidized energy financing—(1) In general.* The term "subsidized energy financing" means financing (*e.g.,* a loan) made directly or indirectly (such as in association with, or through the facilities of, a bank or other lender) during a taxable year beginning after December 31, 1980, under a Federal, State, or local program, a principal purpose of which is to provide subsidized financing for projects designed to conserve or produce energy. For purposes of this paragraph (i), financing is made when funds that constitute subsidized energy financing are disbursed. Subsidized energy financing includes financing under a Federal, State, or local program having two or more principal purposes (provided that at least one of the principal purposes is to provide subsidized financing for projects designed to conserve or produce energy), but only to the extent that the financing—

(i) Is to be used for energy production or conservation purposes, or

(ii) Is provided out of funds designated specifically for energy production or conservation.

Loan proceeds meet the use test of paragraph (i)(l)(i) of this section only to the extent that the loan application, the loan instrument, or any other loan-related documents indicate that the funds are intended for such use. However, loan proceeds designated for the purchase either of property that contains "insulation" or any "other energy-conserving component" or of "renewable energy source property" as defined in paragraphs (c), (d), and (e), respectively, of this section meet the test of paragraph (i)(l)(i) of this section. Financing is subsidized if the interest rate or other terms of the financing (including any special tax treatment) provided to the taxpayer in connection with the program or used to raise funds for the program are more favorable than the terms generally available commercially. In addition, financing is subsidized if the principal obligation of the financing provided to the taxpayer is reduced by funds provided under the program. The source from which the funds for the program are derived is not a factor to be taken into account in determining whether the financing is subsidized. If a public utility disburses funds for the financing of energy conservation or renewable energy source property under a program that obtains the funds through sales to the utility's ratepayers, the program is not considered to be a Federal, State or local program even though the utility is a governmental agency, and, thus, the funds are not subsidized energy financing. Subsidized energy financing does not include a grant includible in gross income under section 61, nontaxable grants, a credit against State or local taxes made directly to the taxpayer claiming the credit provided for in section 23, or a loan guarantee made directly to the taxpayer claiming the credit provided for in section 23.

(2) *Examples.* The provisions of this paragraph (i) may be illustrated by the following examples:

Example (1). State A has a farm and home loan program. The program is used to provide low interest mortgage loans. In 1984 State A's legislature enacted statutory amendments to its farm and home loan program in an effort to encourage energy conservation-type measures. Low interest loans for such improvements were made available to qualified purchasers and owners under the farm and home loan program. The energy conservation measures subsidized by the program include energy conserving components and renewable energy source devices. State A's tax exempt bonds are the source of funds for loans under the program. Although the 1984 legislation authorizing loans for energy conserving components and renewable energy source improvements did not diminish the original purpose of the farm and home loan program, the 1984 legislation added another principal purpose to the program. Therefore, State A's program which has two prin-

cipal purposes, one of which is the conservation or production of energy, is considered as providing subsidized energy financing for purposes of section 23 (c)(10) of the Code, to the extent that financing is provided by State A out of funds designated specifically for energy production or conservation. State A's program will also be considered as providing subsidized energy financing to the extent that the loan proceeds are to be used for energy production or conservation purposes. Loan proceeds meet the use test of the preceding sentence only to the extent that the loan application, the loan instruments, or any other loan-related documents indicate that the funds are intended for such use.

Example (2). The United States Department of Energy disburses funds to State B that the Department received from settlements from alleged petroleum pricing and allocation violations. State B establishes a program under which B will use the funds to make loans at below market interest rates directly to qualified applicants for the purchase of renewable energy source property. B's loans are subsidized energy financing.

Example (3). State C establishes a program under which C will make loans at below market interest rates directly to qualified applicants for the purchase of renewable energy source property. The program is funded with money that State C was able to borrow after it obtained a loan guarantee from a Federal agency. C's loans provided under the program are subsidized energy financing.

Example (4). Company D is an electric utility that is a federal agency. D purchases its electricity from another federal agency, transmits the electricity over its own distribution system, and sells the electricity to numerous local public utilities that in turn sell the electricity to their customers. D wishes to start a program under which D will make loans at below market interest rates directly to customers of the local utilities for the purchase of renewable energy source property from D. The local public utility will act as the collection agent for repayment of the loans. The loans will be repayable over a period of time not in excess of 15 years. Under law, D must cover its full costs through its own revenues derived from the sale of power and other services. While D may borrow by sale of bonds to the United States Treasury, D must borrow at rates comparable to the rates prevailing in the market for similar bonds. Thus, the subsidized loans made under D's program will be financed by the profits from the sale of electricity to consumers and not by the federal government. D's program, which is substantially the same as that carried out by private

Reg. § 1.23-2(i)(2)

(investor-owned) utilities, is not considered to be a Federal, state or local governmental program. Therefore, D's loans are not subsidized energy financing.

Example (5). The Solar Energy and Energy Conservation Bank (Bank) disburses funds to State E. E disburses a portion of the funds to Financial Institution F. Both the Bank and State E make these disbursements under a program the principal purpose of which is to provide subsidized financing for projects designed to conserve or produce energy. F uses the funds to reduce a portion of the principal obligation on loans it issues to finance energy conservation or solar energy expenditures. Taxpayer G borrows $3,000 from F in order to purchase a solar water heating system. F uses $500 of the funds it received from the Bank to reduce the principal obligation of the loan to G to $2,500. The amount of subsidized energy financing to G is $3,000.

Example (6). State H allows a tax credit to Financial Institution J under a program the principal purpose of which is to provide loans at below market interest rates directly to qualified applicants for the purchase of renewable energy source property. J receives a credit each year in the amount of the excess of the interest that would have been paid at private market rates over the actual interest paid on such loans. The State H tax credit arrangement is an interest subsidy. Thus, any low-interest loans made pursuant to this credit arrangement are subsidized energy financing. [Reg. § 1.23-2.]

☐ [*T.D. 7717, 8-26-80. Amended by T.D. 8146, 7-15-87.*]

[Reg. § 1.23-3]

§ 1.23-3. **Special rules.**—(a) *When expenditures are treated as made*—(1) *Timeliness of an expenditure for the energy credit.* In general, for the purpose of determining whether an expenditure qualifies as being timely for the residential energy credit under section 23 or former section 44C (*i.e.,* is made after April 19, 1977, and before January 1, 1986), the expenditure is treated as made when original installation of the item is completed. Thus, solely for that purpose, the time of payment or accrual is irrelevant.

(2) *Special rule for renewable energy source expenditures in the case of construction or reconstruction of a dwelling.* In the case of renewable energy source expenditures in connection with the construction or reconstruction of a dwelling that becomes the taxpayer's new principal residence, the expenditures are to be treated as made (for the purpose of determining the timeliness of an expenditure for the residential energy credit)

when the taxpayer commences use of the dwelling as his or her principal residence following its construction or reconstruction. The term "reconstruction" means the replacement of most of a dwelling's major structural components such as floors, walls, and ceiling. When a taxpayer reoccupies a reconstructed dwelling that was the taxpayer's principal residence prior to reconstruction, a renewable energy source expenditure is considered made when the original installation of the renewable energy source property is completed.

(3) *Taxable year in which credit is allowable.* For the purpose of determining the taxable year in which the credit for an expenditure is allowable (once it has qualified as timely under subparagraph (1) or (2)), an expenditure is treated as made on the later of (i) the date on which it qualifies as timely, or (ii) the date on which it is paid or incurred by the taxpayer.

(b) *Expenditures in 1977.* No credit under section 23 or former section 44C shall be allowed for any taxable year beginning before 1978. However, the amount of any credit under section 23 or former section 44C for the taxpayer's first taxable year beginning after December 31, 1977, shall take into account qualified energy conservation expenditures and qualified renewable energy source expenditures made during the period beginning April 20, 1977, and ending on the last day of such first taxable year.

(c) *Cross reference.* For rules relating to expenditures financed with Federal, State, or local government grants or subsidized financing see paragraph (d)(3) of § 1.23-1 and paragraph (i) of § 1.23-2.

(d) *Expenditures qualifying both as energy conservation expenditures and renewable source expenditures.* In the case of an expenditure which meets both the definition of an energy conservation expenditure (as defined in § 1.23-2(a)) and a renewable energy source expenditure (as defined in § 1.23-2(b)), the taxpayer may claim either a credit under § 1.23-1(b) (relating to qualified energy conservation expenditures) or § 1.23-1(c) (relating to qualified renewable energy source expenditures) but may not claim both credits with respect to the same expenditure.

(e) *Principal residence.* For purposes of section 23 or former section 44C, the determination of whether a dwelling unit is the taxpayer's principal residence shall be made under principles similar to those applicable to section 1034 and the regulations thereunder (relating to sale or exchange of a principal residence) except that ownership of the dwelling unit is not required. In making this determination, the period for which a dwelling is treated as a taxpayer's principal residence includes the 30-day period ending on the first day on which the dwelling unit would (but for this sentence) be treated as being used as the taxpayer's principal residence under principles similar to those applicable to section 1034. Thus, installations that are completed within that 30-day period may be eligible for the credit although, in the absence of the 30-day rule, the date of habitation of the dwelling unit by the taxpayer would mark the beginning of the taxpayer's use of the unit as a principal residence.

(f) *Construction substantially completed.* Construction of a dwelling unit is substantially completed when construction has progressed to the point where the unit could be put to use as a personal residence, even though comparatively minor items remain to be finished or performed in order to conform to the plans or specifications of the completed building. For this purpose, construction includes reconstruction as defined in paragraph (a)(2). This rule may be illustrated by the following example:

Example. On January 1, 1979, A purchases a dwelling that is to become A's principal residence. The dwelling unit was originally constructed in 1950. A spends $50,000 to reconstruct the dwelling by replacing most of the dwelling's major structural components such as floors, walls and ceilings. Included in the cost is $3,000 attributable to energy-conserving components. Reconstruction is substantially completed on April 1, 1979, and A moves into the reconstructed residence on May 1, 1979. Since construction includes reconstruction, A's reconstructed residence is not considered substantially completed before April 20, 1977. Thus, amounts spent with respect to A's reconstructed residence for energy-conserving components do not qualify as energy conservation expenditures.

(g) *Residential use of property.* To be eligible for the residential energy credit, expenditures must be made for personal residential purposes. If at least 80 percent of the use of a component or item of property is for personal residential purposes, the entire amount of the energy conservation expenditure or the renewable energy source expenditure is taken into account in computing the credit under this section. If less than 80 percent of the use of a component or item of property is for personal residential purposes, the amount of an expenditure taken into account is the amount that bears the same ratio to the amount of the expenditure as the amount of personal residential use of the component or item bears to its total use. For purposes of this paragraph, use of a component or an item of property with respect to a swimming pool is not a use for a personal residential purpose. The rules with respect to residential use of property are illustrated by the following examples:

Example (1). In 1978 A makes an expenditure of $3,000 for the installation of storm windows of which 50 percent is on the portion of A's dwelling used as the principal family residence and 50 percent is on the portion of the dwelling used as an office. A has made no other energy conservation expenditures for the residence. The allowable energy conservation expenditure is $1,500 (50 percent of $3,000), the portion attributable to residential use. Therefore, the residential energy credit is $225 (the qualified conservation expenditure of 15 percent of $1,500).

Example (2). During 1979, B makes $10,000 of renewable energy source expenditures on solar energy property for B's principal residence. Approximately 60 percent of the use of the solar energy property will be for heating B's swimming pool; the other 40 percent will be for heating the dwelling unit. B had not previously made renewable energy source expenditures with respect to the residence. Since use for a swimming pool is not considered a residential use, less than 80 percent of the use of B's solar energy property is considered used for personal residential purposes. Therefore, only $4,000 (40 percent of $10,000), the proportionate part of B's expenditures representing personal residential use, is treated as a renewable energy source expenditure. B is allowed a $1,000 residential energy credit (30 percent of $2,000 plus 20 percent of $2,000) for 1979.

(h) *Joint occupancy*—(1) *In general.* If two or more individuals jointly occupied and used a dwelling unit as their principal residence during any portion of a calendar year—

(i) The amount of the credit allowable under section 23 or former section 44C by reason of energy conservation expenditures or by reason of renewable energy source expenditures shall be determined by treating all of the joint occupants as one taxpayer whose taxable year is such calendar year; and

(ii) The credit under section 23 or former section 44C allowable to each joint occupant for the taxable year with which or in which such calendar year ends shall be an amount which bears the same ratio to the amount determined under paragraph (h)(1)(i) of this section as the amount of energy conservation expenditures or renewable energy source expenditures made by that occupant bears to the total amount of each type of such expenditures made by all joint occupants during such calendar year.

Reg. § 1.23-3(h)(1)

The provisions of this subparagraph may be illustrated by the following example:

Example. A, a calendar year taxpayer, and B, a June 1 fiscal year taxpayer, make energy conservation expenditures of $2,000 (A making expenditures of $500 and B making expenditures of $1,500) on their principal and jointly occupied residence in 1978. A and B have not previously made energy conservation expenditures with respect to this residence. Of the $300 credit (15 percent of $2,000), $75 will be allocated to A ($500/$2,000 × $300) and $225 to B ($1,500/$2,000 × $300). A will claim the allocable share of the credit on A's 1978 tax return and B will claim the allocable share of the credit on B's tax return for the fiscal year ending May 31, 1979.

(2) *Minimum credit.* The fact that one joint occupant may be unable to claim all or part of the credit under section 23 or former section 44C because of insufficient tax liability or because that occupant's allowable credit does not exceed the $10 minimum credit (as set forth in paragraph (d)(1) of § 1.23-1) shall have no effect upon the computation of the amount of the allowable credits for the other joint occupants.

(3) *Prior expenditures.* Because joint occupants are treated as one taxpayer for purposes of determining the residential energy credit, the maximum amount of energy conservation expenditures or renewable energy source expenditures must be reduced by the total amount of such expenditures made in connection with the dwelling unit during prior calendar years in which any one of the residents of the unit during the current calendar year was a resident (whether made by the current resident or by an individual previously occupying the dwelling with the current resident). However, the preceding sentence shall not apply to prior expenditures no part of which was taken into account in computing the credits under section 23 or former section 44C for such years. Prior years' expenditures are not to be allocated among joint occupants to take into account the specific expenditures of each of the occupants in prior years.

(4) The rules of this paragraph may be illustrated by the following examples:

Example (1). Assume A and B have together made prior years' energy conservation expenditures of $1,600 (A having made $1,200 of expenditures and B having made $400) on their principal and jointly occupied residence. In the current year, each makes energy conservation expenditures of $300 with respect to the same residence. The maximum qualified expenditure with respect to the residence is reduced by the $1,600 of prior

expenditures made by A and B. Therefore, only $400 of the $600 current expenditures are eligible as energy conservation expenditures. The resulting residential energy credit is $60 (15 percent of $400) of which $30 apiece will be allocated to A and B ($300/$600 × $60). The fact that A had previously computed the credit in prior years with respect to $1,200 of the total $1,600 of expenditures is irrelevant to the apportionment of the credit in the current year.

Example (2). In 1978, spouses C and D make $10,000 of renewable energy source expenditures with respect to their principal residence, half of which is paid by each spouse. No prior renewable energy source expenditures have been taken into account with respect to that residence by either C or D. C and D file separate returns for the calendar year. Under the joint occupancy rule, the maximum allowable renewable energy source credit with respect to C and D's principal residence is $2,200 (30 percent of the first $2,000, and 20 percent of the next $8,000 of expenditures). Half of this amount, or $1,100, will be allowed to each spouse. If either spouse makes renewable energy source expenditures with respect to the same principal residence in future years, none of those expenditures would be qualified renewable energy source expenditures for which a credit can be claimed. That is, not more than $2,200 may be taken in the aggregate by C and D as a renewable energy source credit with respect to their principal residence.

Example (3). In 1978, E and F make energy conservation expenditures of $1,500 on their principal and jointly occupied residence. In 1979, E moves away and G becomes the other joint occupant of the residence. F and G make energy conservation expenditures of $1,000 in 1979. In 1980 F moves away and H moves in with G. G and H make energy conservation expenditures of $500. The maximum qualified expenditure made by F and G with respect to the residence is reduced by the $1,500 of prior expenditures made in 1978 by E and F. The maximum qualified expenditures made by G and H with respect to the residence is reduced only by the expenditures in prior years in connection with the residence during which either G or H was a joint occupant. Accordingly, the maximum qualified expenditures made by G and H with respect to the residence is reduced only by the $1,000 of prior expenditures made in 1979 by F and G.

(i) *Condominiums and cooperative housing corporations.* An individual who is a tenant-stockholder in a cooperative housing corporation (as defined in section 216) or who is a member of a condominium management association with re-

Reg. § 1.23-3(h)(2)

spect to a condominium which he or she owns shall be treated as having made a proportionate share of the energy conservation expenditures or renewable energy source expenditures of such corporation or association. The cooperative stockholder's allocable share of the expenditures is to be the same as his or her proportionate share of the cooperative's total outstanding stock (including any stock held by the corporation). However, in the case where only certain cooperative stockholders are assessed for the expenditures made by the cooperative housing corporation, only those cooperative stockholders that are assessed shall be treated as having made a share of the expenditures of such corporation. In such case, the cooperative stockholder's share of the expenditures is the amount that the stockholder is assessed. The allocable share of a condominium management association member's energy conservation or renewable energy source expenditures is the amount that the member is assessed (or would be assessed in the case where expenditures are from general funds) by the association as a result of such expenditures. The residential energy credit for a qualified expenditure is allowable for the year in which the association or corporation has completed original installation of the item (or has paid or incurred the expenditure, if later). For purposes of this paragraph, the term "condominium management association" means an organization meeting the requirements of section 528(c)(1) of the Code (other than subparagraph (E) of that section),

$$(\$4,000 \times \frac{\$9,000}{\$9,000 + \$6,000}) \text{ and B is allowed a } \$1,600 \text{ credit}$$

$$(\$4,000 \times \frac{\$6,000}{\$9,000 + \$6,000}) \text{ with respect to the}$$

expenditures attributable to the jointly owned house. C is entitled to a credit of $4,000 with respect to the expenditures attributable to the other house.

(2) *Example.* The application of this subparagraph may be illustrated by the following example:

Example. A, B, and C each has a separate principal residence. They agree to finance jointly the construction of a solar collector, each providing one-third of the costs and taking one-third of the output of the collector. Each will separately pay for the costs of connecting the solar collector with his or her principal residence. Provided the solar collector and connection equipment otherwise qualify as renewable energy source property, A, B, and C will each be considered to have made renewable energy source expenditures equal to one-third of the cost of the collector plus his or her separate connection costs. Such expenditures will

with respect to a condominium project substantially all the units of which are used as residences.

(j) *Joint ownership of energy conservation property or renewable energy source property*—(1) *In general.* Energy conservation property and renewable energy source property include property which is jointly owned by the taxpayer and another person (or persons) and installed in connection with two or more dwelling units. For example, the fact that a windmill, solar collector, or geothermal well and distribution system is owned by two or more individuals does not preclude its qualification as renewable energy source property. The amount of the credit allowable under section 23 shall be computed separately with respect to the amount of the expenditures made by each individual, subject to the limitations of $2,000 imposed by section 23(b)(1) and $10,000 imposed by section 23(b)(2), per dwelling unit of jointly owned property. For example, in 1982, A, B, and C purchased as joint owners renewable energy source property that serviced two houses. One of the houses is jointly owned and occupied by A and B and the other is owned and occupied by C alone. The renewable energy source property cost $30,000 of which A paid $9,000, B paid $6,000, and C paid $15,000. A and B must share the $4,000 credit (40% of $10,000 maximum) with respect to the expenditures for the jointly owned house. Therefore, A is allowed a $2,400 credit

be subject to the limitations and other rules separately applicable to A, B, and C with respect to each principal residence, such as those with respect to the $10 minimum (§ 1.23-1(d)(1)), prior expenditures (§ 1.23-1(d)(2)), residential use (paragraph (g) of this section), and joint occupancy (paragraph (h) of this section).

(k) *Basic adjustments.* If a credit is allowed under section 23 or former section 44C for any expenditure with respect to any property, the increase in the basis of that property which would (but for this paragraph) result from such expenditure shall be reduced by the amount of the credit allowed.

(l) *Recordkeeping*—(1) *In general.* No residential energy credit is allowable unless the taxpayer maintains the records described in paragraph (l)(2) of this section. The records shall be retained so long as the contents thereof may become mate-

Reg. § 1.23-3(l)(1)

rial in the administration of any internal revenue law.

(2) *Records.* The taxpayer must maintain records that clearly identify the energy-conserving components and renewable energy source property with respect to which a residential energy credit is claimed, and substantiate their cost to the taxpayer, any labor costs properly allocable to them paid for by the taxpayer, and the method used for allocating such labor costs. [Reg. § 1.23-3.]

☐ [*T.D. 7717*, 8-26-80. *Amended by T.D.* 8146, 7-15-87.]

[Reg. § 1.23-4]

§ 1.23-4. Performance and quality standards.—[Reserved.]

[Reg. § 1.23-5]

§ 1.23-5. Certification procedures.—(a) *Certification that an item meets the definition of an energy-conserving component or renewable energy source property.* Upon the request of a manufacturer of an item pursuant to paragraph (b) of this section which is supported by proof that the item is entitled to be certified, the Assistant Commissioner (Technical) shall certify (or shall notify the manufacturer that the request is denied) that:

(1) The item meets the definition of insulation (see § 1.23-2(c)(1)).

(2) The item meets the definition of another energy-conserving component specified in section 23(c)(4) (See § 1.23-2(d)(4)).

(3) The item meets the definition of solar energy property (see § 1.23-2(f)), wind energy property (see § 1.23-2(g)), or geothermal energy property (see § 1.23-2(h)).

(4) The item meets the definition of a category of energy-conserving component that has been added to the list of approved items pursuant to paragraph (d)(4)(viii) of § 1.23-2.

(5) The item meets the definition of renewable energy source property that transmits or uses a renewable energy source that has been added to the list of approved renewable energy sources pursuant to paragraph (e)(2) of § 1.23-2.

(b) *Procedure*—(1) *In general.* A manufacturer of an item desiring to apply under paragraph (a) shall submit the application to the Commissioner of Internal Revenue, Attention: Associate Chief Counsel (Technical), CC:C:E, 111 Constitution Avenue, N.W., Washington, D.C. 20224. Upon being advised by the National Office, orally or in writing, that an adverse decision is contemplated a manufacturer may request a conference. The conference must be held within 21 calendar days from the date of that advice. Procedures for re-

questing an extension of the 21-day period and notifying the manufacturer of the Service's decision on that request are the same as those applicable to conferences on ruling requests by taxpayers (see section 9.05 of Rev. Proc. 80-20).

(2) *Contents of application.* The application shall include a description of the item (including appropriate design drawings and specifications) and an explanation of the purpose and function of the item. There shall accompany the application a declaration in the following form: "Under penalties of perjury, I declare that I have examined this application, including accompanying documents and, to the best of my knowledge and belief, the facts presented in support of the application are true, correct, and complete." The statement must be signed by the person or persons making the application.

(c) *Effect of certification under paragraph (a).* Certifications granted under paragraph (a)(1), (2), or (3) will be applied retroactively to April 20, 1977. However, certifications granted under paragraph (a)(4) or (5) will be applied retroactively only to the date the applicable energy-conserving component or renewable energy source was added by Treasury decision to the list of qualifying components or sources. Certification of an item under this section means that the applicable definitional requirement of § 1.23-2 is considered satisfied in the case of any person claiming a residential energy credit with respect to such item. However, it does not relieve manufacturers of the need to establish that their items conform to performance and quality standards (if any) provided under § 1.23-4 and that their items can reasonably be expected to remain in operation at least 3 years, in the case of insulation and other energy-conserving components, or at least 5 years, in the case of renewable energy source property. [Reg. § 1.23-5.]

☐ [*T.D. 7717*, 8-26-80. *Amended by T.D.* 8146, 7-15-87.]

[Reg. § 1.23-6]

§ 1.23-6. Procedure and criteria for additions to the approved list of energy-conserving components or renewable energy sources.—(a) *Procedures for additions to the list of energy-conserving components or renewable energy sources*—(1) *In general.* A manufacturer of an item (or a group of manufacturers) desiring to apply for addition to the approved list of energy-conserving components or renewable energy sources pursuant to paragraph (d)(4)(viii) or (e)(2) of § 1.23-2 shall submit an application to the Internal Revenue Service, Attention: Associate Chief Counsel (Technical), CC:C:E, 1111 Constitution Avenue, N.W., Washington, D.C. 20224. The term "manufacturer" includes a person who assembles an item or a system from components manufactured by other persons. The application shall provide the information required under paragraph (b) of this section. An application may request that more than one item be added to the approved list. It will be the responsibility of the Office of the Associate Chief Counsel (Technical) upon receipt of the application to determine whether all the information required under paragraph (b) of this section has been furnished with the application. If an application lacks essential information, the applicant will be advised of the additional information required. If the information (or a reasonable explanation of the reason why the information cannot be made available) is not forthcoming within 30 days of the date of that advice, the application will be closed and the applicant will be so informed. Any resubmission of information beyond the 30-day period will be treated as a new application. If the Office of the Associate Chief Counsel (Technical) already is considering an application with respect to the same or a similar item, it may consolidate applications. The Office of the Associate Chief Counsel will make a report and recommendation to the ad hoc advisory board as to whether each item that is the subject of an application should be added in accordance with the manufacturer's request to the approved list of energy-conserving components or renewable energy sources in light of the applicable criteria provided in paragraph (c) and the standards for Secretarial determination provided in paragraph (d) of this section. In making this recommendation, the Office of the Associate Chief Counsel shall consult with the Secretary of Energy and the Secretary of Housing and Urban Development (or their delegates) and any other appropriate Federal officers to obtain their views concerning the item in question. In addition, the Office of the Associate Chief Counsel may request from the manufacturer clarification of information submitted with the application. The Office of the Associate Chief Counsel shall report its recommendation and forward the application to the ad hoc advisory board for further consideration.

(2) *Ad hoc advisory board.* The Commissioner of Internal Revenue and the Assistant Secretary (Tax Policy) shall establish an ad hoc advisory board to consider applications and recommendations forwarded by the Office of the Associate Chief Counsel (Technical). If a finding in favor of addition of any item is made, the board shall report its recommendation and forward the application to the Commissioner for further consideration. If the item is approved by the Commissioner, the application will be forwarded to the Secretary (or his delegate) for further consideration. The application will be closed with respect to

an item if the board, the Commissioner, or the Secretary (or his delegate) determines that, under the applicable criteria or the standards for Secretarial determination, the item should not be added to the list of energy-conserving components or renewable energy sources.

(3) *Action on application.* (i) A final decision to grant or deny any application filed under paragraph (a)(1) shall be made within 1 year after the application and all information required to be filed with such request under paragraph (b) have been received by the Office of the Associate Chief Counsel (Technical). The applicant manufacturer shall be notified in writing of the final decision. In the event of a favorable determination, a regulation will be issued in accordance with the procedures contained in § 601.601 to include the item as an energy-conserving component or as a renewable energy source. A final decision to grant approval of an application is made when a Treasury decision adding the item (that is subject of the application) as an energy-conserving component or as a renewable energy source is published in the Federal Register.

(ii) The applicant manufacturer shall be entitled to a conference and be so notified anytime an adverse action is contemplated by the Office of the Associate Chief Counsel, the ad hoc advisory board, the Commissioner of Internal Revenue, or the Secretary (or his delegate) and no conference was previously conducted. Upon being advised in writing that an adverse recommendation or decision as to any item that is the subject of an application is contemplated, a manufacturer may request a conference. The conference must be held within 21 calendar days from the mailing of that advice. Procedures for requesting an extension of the 21-day period and notifying the manufacturer of the recommendation or decision with respect to that request are the same as those applicable to conferences on ruling requests by taxpayers. The applicant is entitled to only one conference. There is no right to another conference when a favorable recommendation or decision is reversed at a higher level.

(iii) A report of any application which has been denied during the preceding month and the reasons for the denial shall be published each month.

(b) *Contents of application.* The application by the manufacturer shall include the following information:

(1) A description of the item and the generic class to which it belongs, including any features relating to safe installation and use of the item. This description shall include appropriate design drawings and technical specifications (or repre-

sentative drawings and specifications when application by a group of manufacturers).

(2) An explanation of the purpose, function, and each recommended use of the item.

(3) An estimate (and explanation of the estimation methods employed and the assumptions made) of the total number of units that would be sold for each recommended use during the first 4 years following the addition of the item to the approved list and of the total number that would be sold for each recommended use during that period in the absence of addition. If the item is sold in more than one size, the estimate shall indicate the projected sales for each size. This estimate shall reflect total industry sales of the item. Past industry sales information for each recommended use for the previous two years shall also be provided.

(4) Whether sufficient capacity is available to increase production to meet any increase in demand for the item, or for associated fuels and materials, caused by such addition. This determination shall be based on industry-wide data and not just the manufacturing capability of the applicant. If the applicant has the exclusive right to manufacture the item, this information shall also be provided in the application.

(5) An estimate (including estimation methods and assumptions) of the energy in Btu's of oil and natural gas used directly or indirectly per unit by the applicant in the manufacture of the item and other items necessary for its use, the type of energy source (e.g., oil, natural gas, coal, electricity), and the extent of its use in the manufacturing process of the item. The applicant must also provide a list of the major components of the item and their composition and weight.

(6) Test data and experience data (where experience data is available) to substantiate for each recommended use the energy savings in Btu's that are claimed will be achieved by one unit during a period of one year. The data shall be obtained by controlled tests in which, if possible, the addition of the item is the only variable. If the item may be sold in various configurations, data shall be provided with respect to energy savings from each configuration with significantly different energy use characteristics. Test methods are to conform to recognized industry or government standards. This determination shall take into account the seasonal use of the item. If the energy savings of the item varies with climatic conditions, data shall be provided with respect to each climate zone. The applicant may use the Department of Energy's climate zones for heating and cooling (see § 450.35 of 10 CFR Part 450 (1980)).

(7) The impact of increased demand on the price of the item and the energy source used by the item.

(8) The energy source which will be replaced or conserved by the item, and, in the case of a request for addition to the approved list of renewable energy sources, data establishing that the energy source is inexhaustible.

(9) Data to show the total estimated savings of energy in Btu's attributable to reduced consumption of oil or natural gas whether directly or indirectly from use of the item, including assumptions underlying this estimate. If the consumption of both oil and natural gas will be reduced, data to show the energy savings in Btu's attributable to each shall be provided. The estimate is to be based on energy savings in Btu's per unit determined under paragraph (b)(6) of this section for the first four years of the useful life of the item and is to take into account only the additional units of the item estimated to be placed in service as a result of the addition using data obtained under paragraph (b)(3) of this section. If the item will result in reduction of oil or natural gas consumption by replacing an item which uses such an energy source, the application shall indicate the item replaced and the extent to which this reduction will occur.

(10) Geographical information if required under paragraph (b)(6) to show the climatic zones of the country where the item is expected to be used, including an estimate of the total number of additional units to be placed in service during the first 4 years following the addition of the item in the area as a result of the addition of the item to the list of qualifying items.

(11) The retail cost of the item (or items if the item is sold in more than one size) including all installation costs necessary for safe and effective use.

(12) Whether the item is designed for residential use.

(13) The estimated useful life of the item and associated equipment necessary for its use.

(14) The type and amount of waste and emissions in weight per unit of energy saved resulting from use of the item.

(15) If the item might reasonably be suspected of presenting any health or safety hazard, test data to show that the item does not present such hazard.

With respect to applications for addition to the approved list of renewable energy sources, the term "item" as used in this paragraph refers to the property which uses the energy source and not the energy source itself. The application should

Reg. § 1.23-6(b)(2)

clearly indicate whether the request is for addition to the approved list of energy-conserving components or renewable energy sources, identify the provisions for which data is being submitted, and present the data in the order requested. The tests required under this paragraph may be conducted by independent laboratories but the underlying data must be submitted along with the test results. There shall accompany the request a declaration in the following form: "Under penalties of perjury, I declare that I have examined this application, including accompanying documents, and, to the best of my knowledge and belief, the facts presented in support of the application are true, correct and complete." The statement must be signed by the person or persons making the application. The declaration shall not be made by the taxpayer's representative.

(c) *Criteria for additions*—(1) *Additions to the approved list of energy-conserving components.* For an item to be considered for addition to the approved list of energy-conserving components, the manufacturer must show that the item increases the energy efficiency of a dwelling. For an item to be considered as increasing the energy efficiency of a dwelling, all of the following criteria must be met:

(i) The use of the item must improve the energy efficiency of the dwelling structure, structural components of the dwelling, hot water heating, or heating or cooling systems.

(ii) The use of the item must result, directly or indirectly, in a significant reduction in the consumption of oil or natural gas.

(iii) The increase in energy efficiency must be established by test data and in accordance with accepted testing standards.

(iv) The item must not present a safety, fire, environmental, or health hazard when properly installed.

(2) *Additions to the approved list of renewable energy sources.* For an energy source to be considered for addition to the approved list of renewable energy sources, the manufacturer must show that the following criteria are met:

(i) As in the case of solar, wind, and geothermal energy, the energy source must be an inexhaustible energy supply. Accordingly, wood and agricultural products and by-products are not considered renewable energy sources. Similarly, no exhaustible or depletable energy source (such as sources that are depletable under 611) will be considered.

(ii) The energy source must be capable of being used for heating or cooling a residential dwelling or providing hot water or electricity for use in such a dwelling.

(iii) A practical working device, machine, or mechanism, etc., must exist and be commercially available to use such renewable energy source.

(iv) The use of the renewable energy source must not present a significant safety, fire, environmental, or health hazard.

(d) *Standards for Secretarial determination*—(1) *In general.* The Secretary will not make any addition to the approved list of energy-conserving components or renewable energy sources unless the Secretary determines that—

(i) There will be a reduction in the total consumption of oil or natural gas as a result of the addition, and that reduction is sufficient to justify any resulting decrease in Federal revenues,

(ii) The addition will not result in an increased use of any item which is known to be, or reasonably suspected to be, environmentally hazardous or a threat to public health or safety, and

(iii) Available Federal subsidies do not make the addition unnecessary or inappropriate (in the light of the most advantageous allocation of economic resources).

(2) *Factors taken into account.* In making any determination under paragraph (d)(1)(i), the Secretary will—

(i) Make an estimate of the amount by which the addition will reduce oil and natural gas consumption, and

(ii) Determine whether the addition compares favorably, on the basis of the reduction in oil and natural gas consumption per dollar of cost to the Federal Government (including revenue loss), with other Federal programs in existence or being proposed.

(3) *Factors taken into account in making estimates.* In making any estimate under subparagraph (2)(i), the Secretary will take into account (among other factors)—

(i) The extent to which the use of any item will be increased as a result of the addition,

(ii) Whether sufficient capacity is available to increase production to meet any increase in demand for the item or associated fuels and materials caused by the addition,

(iii) The amount of oil and natural gas used directly or indirectly in the manufacture of the item and other items necessary for its use,

(iv) The estimated useful life of the item, and

(v) The extent additional use of the item leads, directly or indirectly, to the reduced use of

Reg. § 1.23-6(d)(3)

oil or natural gas. Indirect uses of oil or natural gas include use of electricity derived from oil or natural gas.

(e) *Effective date of addition to approved lists.* In the case of additions to the approved list of energy-conserving components or renewable energy sources, the credit allowable by § 1.23-1 shall apply with respect to expenditures which are made on or after the date a Treasury decision amending the regulations pursuant to the application is published in the Federal Register. However, the Secretary may prescribe by regulations that expenditures for additions made on or after the date referred to in the preceding sentence and before the close of the taxable year in which such date occurs shall be taken into account in the following taxable year. Additions to the list will be subject to the performance and quality standards

(if any) provided under § 1.23-4 which are in effect at the time of the addition. Furthermore, any addition made to the approved list will be subject to revaluation by the Secretary for the purpose of determining whether the item still meets the requisite criteria and standards for addition to the list. If it is determined by the Secretary that an item no longer meets the requisite criteria, the Secretary will amend the regulations to delete the item from the approved list. Removal of an item from the list will be prospective from the date a Treasury decision amending the regulations is published in the Federal Register. [Reg. § 1.23-6.]

☐ [*T.D. 7861, 12-15-86. Amended by T.D. 8146, 7-15-87.*]

→ *Caution: Code Sec. 24 was formerly Code Sec. 41. See Reg. § § 1.41-0—1.41-8 for rules issued under former Code Sec. 41.*←

[Reg. § 1.25-1T]

§ 1.25-1T. Credit for interest paid on certain home mortgages (Temporary).—(a) *In general.* Section 25 permits States and political subdivisions to elect to issue mortgage credit certificates in lieu of qualified mortgage bonds. An individual who holds a qualified mortgage credit certificate (as defined in § 1.25-3T) is entitled to a credit against his Federal income taxes. The amount of the credit depends upon (1) the amount of mortgage interest paid or accrued during the year and (2) the applicable certificate credit rate. See § 1.25-2T. The amount of the deduction under section 163 for interest paid or accrued during any taxable year is reduced by the amount of the credit allowable under section 25 for such year. See § 1.163-6T. The holder of a qualified mortgage credit certificate may be entitled to additional withholding allowances. See section 3402(m) and the regulations thereunder.

(b) *Definitions.* For purposes of § § 1.25-2T through 1.25-8T and this section, the following definitions apply:

(1) *Mortgage.* The term "mortgage" includes deeds of trust, conditional sales contracts, pledges, agreements to hold title in escrow, and any other form of owner financing.

(2) *State.* (i) The term "State" includes a possession of the United States and the District of Columbia.

(ii) Mortgage credit certificates issued by or on behalf of any State or political subdivision ("governmental unit") by constituted authorities empowered to issue such certificates are the certificates of such governmental unit.

(3) *Qualified home improvement loan.* The term "qualified home improvement loan" has the meaning given that term under section 103A(1)(6) and the regulations thereunder.

(4) *Qualified rehabilitation loan.* The term "qualified rehabilitation loan" has the meaning given that term under section 103A(1)(7)(A) and the regulations thereunder.

(5) *Single-family and owner-occupied residences.* The terms "single-family" and "owner-occupied" have the meaning given those terms under section 103A(1)(9) and the regulations thereunder.

(6) *Constitutional home rule city.* The term "constitutional home rule city" means, with respect to any calendar year, any political subdivision of a State which, under a State constitution which was adopted in 1970 and effective on July 1, 1971, had home rule powers on the 1st day of the calendar year.

(7) *Targeted area residence.* The term "targeted area residence" has the meaning given that term under section 103A(k) and the regulations thereunder.

(8) *Acquisition cost.* The term "acquisition cost" has the meaning given that term under section 103A(1)(5) and the regulations thereunder.

(9) *Average area purchase price.* The term "average area purchase price" has the meaning given that term under subparagraphs (2), (3), and (4) of section 103A(f) and the regulations thereunder. For purposes of this paragraph (b)(9), all determinations of average area purchase price shall be made with respect to residences as that

Reg. § 1.25-1T(a)

term is defined in section 103A and the regulations thereunder.

(10) *Total proceeds.* The "total proceeds" of an issue is the sum of the products determined by multiplying—

(i) The certified indebtedness amount of each mortgage credit certificate issued pursuant to such issue, by

(ii) The certificate credit rate specified in such certificate.

Each qualified mortgage credit certificate program shall be treated as a separate issue of mortgage credit certificates.

(11) *Residence.* The term "residence" includes stock held by a tenant-stockholder in a cooperative housing corporation (as those terms are defined in section 216(b)(1) and (2)). It does not include property such as an appliance, a piece of furniture, a radio, etc., which, under applicable local law, is not a fixture. The term also includes any manufactured home which has a minimum of 400 square feet of living space and a minimum width in excess of 102 inches and which is of a kind customarily used at a fixed location. The preceding sentence shall not apply for purposes of determining the average area purchase price for single-family residences, nor shall it apply for purposes of determining the State ceiling amount. The term "residence" does not, however, include recreational vehicles, campers, and other similar vehicles.

(12) *Related person.* The term "related person" has the meaning given that term under section 103(b)(6)(C)(i) and § 1.103-10(e)(1).

(13) *Date of issue.* A mortgage credit certificate is considered issued on the date on which a closing agreement is signed with respect to the certified indebtedness amount.

(c) *Affidavits.* For purposes of § § 1.25-1T through 1.25-8T, an affidavit filed in connection with the requirements of § § 1.25-1T through 1.25-8T shall be made under penalties of perjury. Applicants for mortgage credit certificates who are required by a lender or the issuer to sign affidavits must be informed that any fraudulent statement will result in (i) the revocation of the individual's mortgage credit certificate, and (ii) a $10,000 penalty under section 6709. Other persons required by a lender or an issuer to provide affidavits must receive similar notice. A person may not rely on an affidavit where that person knows or has reason to know that the information contained in the affidavit is false. [Temporary Reg. § 1.25-1T.]

☐ [*T.D.* 8023, 5-3-85.]

[Reg. § 1.25-2T]

§ 1.25-2T. Amount of credit (Temporary).— (a) *In general.* Except as otherwise provided, the amount of the credit allowable for any taxable year to an individual who holds a qualified mortgage credit certificate is equal to the product of the certificate credit rate (as defined in paragraph (b)) and the amount of the interest paid or accrued by the taxpayer during the taxable year on the certified indebtedness amount (as defined in paragraph (c)).

(b) *Certificate credit rate—*(1) *In general.* For purposes of § § 1.25-1T through 1.25-8T, the term "certificate credit rate" means the rate specified by the issuer on the mortgage credit certificate. The certificate credit rate shall not be less than 10 percent nor more than 50 percent.

(2) *Limitation in certain States.* (i) In the case of a State which—

(A) Has a State ceiling for the calendar year in which an election is made that exceeds 20 percent of the average annual aggregate principal amount of mortgages executed during the immediately preceding 3 calendar years for single-family owner-occupied residences located within the jurisdiction of such State, or

(B) Issued qualified mortgage bonds in an aggregate amount less than $150 million for calendar year 1983,

the certificate credit rate for any mortgage credit certificate issued under such program shall not exceed 20 percent unless the issuing authority submits a plan to the Commissioner to ensure that the weighted average of the certificate credit rates in such mortgage credit certificate program does not exceed 20 percent and the Commissioner approves such plan. For purposes of determining the average annual aggregate principal amount of mortgages executed during the immediately preceding 3 calendar years for single-family owner-occupied residences located within the jurisdiction of such State, an issuer may rely upon the amount published by the Treasury Department for such calendar years. An issuer may rely on a different amount from that safe-harbor limitation where the issuer has made a more accurate and comprehensive determination of that amount. The weighted average of the certificate credit rates in a mortgage credit certificate program is determined by dividing the sum of the products obtained by multiplying the certificate credit rate of each certificate by the certified indebtedness amount with respect to that certificate by the sum of the certified indebtedness amounts of the certificates issued. See section 103A(g) and the regulations thereunder for the definition of the term "State ceiling".

Reg. § 1.25-2T(b)(

(ii) The following example illustrates the application of this paragraph (b)(2):

Example. City Z issues four qualified mortgage credit certificates pursuant to its qualified mortgage credit certificate program. H receives a certificate with a certificate credit rate of 30 percent and a certified indebtedness amount of $50,000. I receives a certificate with a certificate credit rate of 25 percent and a certified indebtedness amount of $100,000. J and K each receive certificates with certificate credit rates of 10 percent; their certified indebtedness amounts are $50,000 and $100,000, respectively. The weighted average of the certificate credit rates is determined by dividing the sum of the products obtained by multiplying the certificate credit rate of each certificate by the certified indebtedness amount with respect to that certificate ((.3 × $50,000) + (.25 × $100,000) + (.1 × $50,000) + (.1 × $100,000)) by the sum of the certified indebtedness amounts of the certificates issued ($50,000 + $100,000 + $50,000 + $100,000). Thus, the weighted average of the certificate credit rates is 18.33 percent ($55,000/$300,000).

(c) *Certified indebtedness amount*—(1) *In general.* The term "certified indebtedness amount" means the amount of indebtedness which is—

(i) Incurred by the taxpayer—

(A) To acquire his principal residence,

(B) As a qualified home improvement loan, or

(C) As a qualified rehabilitation loan, and

(ii) Specified in the mortgage credit certificate.

(2) *Example.* The following example illustrates the application of this paragraph:

Example. On March 1, 1986, State X, pursuant to its qualified mortgage credit certificate program, provides a mortgage credit certificate to B. State X specifies that the maximum amount of the mortgage loan for which B may claim a credit is $65,000. On March 15, B purchases for $67,000 a single-family dwelling for use as his principal residence. B obtains from Bank M a mortgage loan for $60,000. State X, or Bank M acting on behalf of State X, indicates on B's mortgage credit certificate that the certified indebtedness amount of B's loan is $60,000. B may claim a credit under section 25(e) based on this amount.

(d) *Limitation on credit*—(1) *Limitation where certificate credit rate exceeds 20 percent.* (i) If the certificate credit rate of any mortgage credit certificate exceeds 20 percent, the amount of the credit allowed to the taxpayer by section 25(a)(1) any year shall not exceed $2,000. Any amount

denied under this paragraph (d)(1) may not be carried forward under section 25(e)(1) and paragraph (d)(2) of this section.

(ii) If two or more persons hold interests in any residence, the limitation of paragraph (d)(1)(i) shall be allocated among such persons in proportion to their respective interests in the residence.

(2) *Carryforward of unused credit.* (i) If the credit allowable under section 25(a) and § 1.25-2T for any taxable year exceeds the applicable tax limit for that year, the excess (the "unused credit") will be a carryover to each of the 3 succeeding taxable years and, subject to the limitations of paragraph (d)(2)(ii), will be added to the credit allowable by section 25(a) and § 1.25-2T for that succeeding year.

(ii) The amount of the unused credit for any taxable year (the "unused credit year") which may be taken into account under this paragraph (d)(2) for any subsequent taxable year may not exceed the amount by which the applicable tax limit for that subsequent taxable year exceeds the sum of (i) the amount of the credit allowable under section 25(a) and § 1.25-1T for the current taxable year, and (ii) the sum of the unused credits which, by reason of this paragraph (d)(2), are carried to that subsequent taxable year and are attributable to taxable years before the unused credit year. Thus, if by reason of this paragraph (d)(2), unused credits from 2 prior taxable years are carried forward to a subsequent taxable year, the unused credit from the earlier of those 2 prior years must be taken into account before the unused credit from the later of those 2 years is taken into account.

(iii) For purposes of this paragraph (d)(2) the term "applicable tax limit" means the limitation imposed by section 26(a) for the taxable year reduced by the sum of the credits allowable for that year under section 21, relating to expenses for household and dependent care services necessary for gainful employment, section 22, relating to the credit for the elderly and the permanently disabled, section 23, relating to the residential energy credit, and section 24, relating to contributions to candidates for public office. The limitation imposed by section 26(a) for any taxable year is equal to the taxpayer's tax liability (as defined in section 26(b)) for that year.

(iv) The following examples illustrate the application of this paragraph (d)(2):

Example (1). (i) B, a calendar year taxpayer, holds a qualified mortgage credit certificate. For 1986 B's applicable tax limit (*i.e.,* tax liability) is $1,100. The amount of the credit under section 25(a) and § 1.25-2T for 1986 is

$1,700. For 1986 B is not entitled to any of the credits described in sections 21 through 24. Under § 1.25-2T(d)(2), B's unused credit for 1986 is $600, and B is entitled to carry forward that amount to the 3 succeeding years.

(ii) For 1987 B's applicable tax limit is $1,500, the amount of the credit under section 25(a) and § 1.25-2T is $1,700, and the unused credit is $200. For 1988 B's applicable tax limit is $2,000, the amount of the credit under section 25(a) and § 1.25-2T is $1,300, and there is no unused credit. For 1987 and 1988 B is not entitled to any of the credits described in sections 21 through 24. No portion of the unused credit for 1986 may be used in 1987. For 1988 B is entitled to claim a credit of $2,000 under section 25(a) and § 1.25-2T, consisting of a $1,300 credit for 1988, the $600 unused credit for 1986, and $100 of the $200 unused credit for 1987. In addition, B may carry forward the remaining unused credit for 1987 ($100) to 1989 and 1990.

Example (2). The facts are the same as in Example (1) except that for 1988 B is entitled to a credit of $400 under section 23. B's applicable tax limit for 1988 is $1,600 ($2,000 less $400). For 1988 B is entitled to claim a credit of $1,600 under section 25(a) and § 1.25-2T, consisting of a $1,300 credit for 1988 and $300 of the unused credit for 1986. In addition, B may carry forward the remaining unused credits of $300 for 1986 to 1989 and of $200 for 1987 to 1989 and 1990. [Temporary Reg. § 1.25-2T.]

☐ [*T.D. 8023,* 5-3-85.]

[Reg. § 1.25-3]

§ 1.25-3. Qualified mortgage credit certificate.—(a) through (g)(1)(ii) [Reserved] For further guidance, see § 1.25-3T(a) through (g)(1)(ii).

(g)(1)(iii) *Reissued certificate exception.* See paragraph (p) of this section for rules regarding the exception in the case of refinancing existing mortgages.

(g)(2) through (o) [Reserved] For further guidance, see § 1.25-3T(g)(2) through (o).

(p) *Reissued certificates for certain refinancings*—(1) *In general.* If the issuer of a qualified mortgage credit certificate reissues a certificate in place of an existing mortgage credit certificate to the holder of that existing certificate, the reissued certificate is treated as satisfying the requirements of this section. The period for which the reissued certificate is in effect begins with the date of the refinancing (that is, the date on which interest begins accruing on the refinancing loan).

(2) *Meaning of existing certificate.* For purposes of this paragraph (p), a mortgage credit certificate is an existing certificate only if it satis-

fies the requirements of this section. An existing certificate may be the original certificate, a certificate issued to a transferee under § 1.25-3T(h)(2)(ii), or a certificate previously reissued under this paragraph (p).

(3) *Limitations on reissued certificate.* An issuer may reissue a mortgage credit certificate only if all of the following requirements are satisfied:

(i) The reissued certificate is issued to the holder of an existing certificate with respect to same property to which the existing certificate relates.

(ii) The reissued certificate entirely replaces the existing certificate (that is, the holder cannot retain the existing certificate with respect to any portion of the outstanding balance of the certified mortgage indebtedness specified on the existing certificate).

(iii) The certified mortgage indebtedness specified on the reissued certificate does not exceed the remaining outstanding balance of the certified mortgage indebtedness specified on the existing certificate.

(iv) The reissued certificate does not increase the certificate credit rate specified in the existing certificate.

(v) The reissued certificate does not result in an increase in the tax credit that would otherwise have been allowable to the holder under the existing certificate for any taxable year. The holder of a reissued certificate determines the amount of tax credit that would otherwise have been allowable by multiplying the interest that was scheduled to have been paid on the refinanced loan by the certificate rate of the existing certificate. In the case of a series of refinancings, the tax credit that would otherwise have been allowable is determined from the amount of interest that was scheduled to have been paid on the original loan and the certificate rate of the original certificate.

(A) In the case of a refinanced loan that is a fixed interest rate loan, the interest that was scheduled to be paid on the refinanced loan is determined using the scheduled interest method described in paragraph (p)(3)(v)(C) of this section.

(B) In the case of a refinanced loan th~~ is not a fixed interest rate loan, the interest t~ was scheduled to be paid on the refinanced lo~ determined using either the scheduled int~ method described in paragraph (p)(3)(v)(this section or the hypothetical interest ~ described in paragraph (p)(3)(v)(C) section.

(C) The scheduled interest method determines the amount of interest for each taxable year that was scheduled to have been paid in the taxable year based on the terms of the refinanced loan including any changes in the interest rate that would have been required by the terms of the refinanced loan and any payments of principal that would have been required by the terms of the refinanced loan (other than repayments required as a result of any refinancing of the loan).

(D) The hypothetical interest method (which is available only for refinanced loans that are not fixed interest rate loans) determines the amount of interest treated as having been scheduled to be paid for a taxable year by constructing an amortization schedule for a hypothetical self-amortizing loan with level payments. The hypothetical loan must have a principal amount equal to the remaining outstanding balance of the certified mortgage indebtedness specified on the existing certificate, a maturity equal to that of the refinanced loan, and interest equal to the annual percentage rate (APR) of the refinancing loan that is required to be calculated for the Federal Truth in Lending Act.

(E) A holder must consistently apply the scheduled interest method or the hypothetical interest method for all taxable years beginning with the first taxable year the tax credit is claimed by the holder based upon the reissued certificate.

(4) *Examples.* The following examples illustrate the application of paragraph (p)(3)(v) of this section:

Example 1. A holder of an existing certificate that meets the requirements of this section seeks to refinance the mortgage on the property to which the existing certificate relates. The final payment on the holder's existing mortgage is due on December 31, 2000; the final payment on the new mortgage would not be due until January 31, 2004. The holder requests that the issuer provide to the holder a reissued mortgage credit certificate in place of the existing certificate. The requested certificate would have the same certificate credit rate as the existing certificate. For each calendar year through the year 2000, the credit that would be allowable to the holder with respect to the new mortgage under the requested certificate would not exceed the credit allowable that year under the existing certificate. The requested certificate, however, would allow the holder credits for the years 2001 through 2004, for which, due to the earlier scheduled repayment of the existing mortgage, no credit would be allowable under the existing certificate. Under paragraph (p)(3)(v) of this section, the issuer may

not reissue the certificate as requested because, under the existing certificate, no credit would be allowable for the years 2001 through 2004. The issuer may, however, provide a reissued certificate that limits the amount of the credit allowable in each year to the amount allowable under the existing certificate. Because the existing certificate would allow no credit after December 31, 2000, the reissued certificate could expire on December 31, 2000.

Example 2. (a) The facts are the same as *Example 1* except that the existing mortgage loan has a variable rate of interest and the refinancing loan will have a fixed rate of interest. To determine whether the limit under paragraph (p)(3)(v) of this section is met for any taxable year, the holder must calculate the amount of credit that otherwise would have been allowable absent the refinancing. This requires a determination of the amount of interest that would have been payable on the refinanced loan for the taxable year. The holder may determine this amount by—

(1) Applying the terms of the refinanced loan, including the variable interest rate or rates, for the taxable year as though the refinanced loan continued to exist; or

(2) Obtaining the amount of interest, and calculating the amount of credit that would have been available, from the schedule of equal payments that fully amortize a hypothetical loan with the principal amount equal to the remaining outstanding balance of the certified mortgage indebtedness specified on the existing certificate, the interest equal to the annual percentage rate (APR) of the refinacing loan, and the maturity equal to that of the refinanced loan.

(b) The holder must apply the same method for each taxable year the tax credit is claimed based upon the reissued mortgage credit certificate.

(5) *Coordination with Section 143(m)(3).* A refinancing loan underlying a reissued mortgage credit certificate that replaces a mortgage credit certificate issued on or before December 31, 1990, is not a federally subsidized indebtedness for the purposes of section 143(m)(3) of the Internal Revenue Code. [Reg. § 1.25-3.]

☐ [*T.D.* 8692, 12-16-96.]

[Reg. § 1.25-3T]

§ 1.25-3T. Qualified mortgage credit certificate (Temporary).—(a) *Definition of qualified mortgage credit certificate.* For purposes of §§ 1.25-1T through 1.25-8T, the term "qualified mortgage credit certificate" means a certificate that meets all of the requirements of this section.

(b) *Qualified mortgage credit certificate program.* A certificate meets the requirements of this paragraph if it is issued under a qualified mortgage credit certificate program (as defined in § 1.25-4T).

(c) *Required form and information.* A certificate meets the requirements of this paragraph if it is in the form specified in § 1.25-6T and if all the information required by the form is specified on the form.

(d) *Residence requirement* —(1) *In general.* A certificate meets the requirements of this paragraph only if it is provided in connection with the acquisition, qualified rehabilitation, or qualified home improvement of a residence that is—

(i) A single-family residence (as defined in § 1.25-1T(b)(5)) which, at the time the financing on the residence is executed or assumed, can reasonably be expected by the issuer to become (or, in the case of a qualified home improvement loan, to continue to be) the principal residence (as defined in section 1034 and the regulations thereunder) of the holder of the certificate within a reasonable time after the financing is executed or assumed, and

(ii) Located within the jurisdiction of the governmental unit issuing the certificate.

See section 103A(d) and the regulations thereunder for further definitions and requirements.

(2) *Certification procedure.* The requirements of this paragraph will be met if the issuer or its agent obtains from the holder of the certificate and affidavit stating his intent to use (or, in the case of a qualified home improvement loan, that he is currently using and intends to continue to use) the residence as his principal residence within a reasonable time (*e.g.*, 60 days) after the mortgage credit certificate is issued and stating that the holder will notify the issuer of the mortgage credit certificate if the residence ceases to be his principal residence. The affidavit must also state facts that are sufficient for the issuer or his agent to determine whether the residence is located within the jurisdiction of the issuer that issued the mortgage credit certificate.

(e) *3-year requirement* —(1) *In general.* A certificate meets the requirements of this paragraph only if the holder of the certificate had no present ownership interest in a principal residence at any time during the 3-year period prior to the date on which the mortgage on the residence in connection with which the certificate is provided is executed. For purposes of the preceding sentence, the holder's interest in the residence with respect to which the certificate is being provided shall not be taken into account. See section 103A(e) and the

regulations thereunder for further definitions and requirements.

(2) *Exceptions.* Paragraph (e)(1) shall not apply with respect to—

(i) Any certificate provided with respect to a targeted area residence (as defined in § 1.25-1T(b)(7)),

(ii) Any qualified home improvement loan (as defined in § 1.25-1T(b)(3)), and

(iii) Any qualified rehabilitation loan (as defined in § 1.25-1T(b)(4)).

(3) *Certification procedure.* The requirements of paragraph (e)(1) will be met if the issuer or its agent obtains from the holder of the certificate an affidavit stating that he had no present ownership interest in a principal residence at any time during the 3-year period prior to the date on which the certificate is issued and the issuer or its agent obtains from the applicant copies of the applicant's Federal tax returns for the preceding 3 years and examines each statement to determine whether the applicant has claimed a deduction for taxes on property which was the applicant's principal residence pursuant to section 164(a)(1) or a deduction pursuant to section 163 for interest paid on a mortgage secured by property which was the applicant's principal residence. Where the mortgage is executed during the period between January 1 and February 15 and the applicant has not yet filed his Federal income tax return with the Internal Revenue Service, the issuer may, with respect to such year, rely on an affidavit of the applicant that the applicant is not entitled to claim deductions for taxes or interest on indebtedness with respect to property constituting his principal residence for the preceding calendar year. In the alternative, when applicable, the holder may provide an affidavit stating that one of the exceptions provided in paragraph (e)(2) applies.

(4) *Special rule.* An issuer may submit a plan to the Commissioner for distributing certificates, in an amount not to exceed 10 percent of the proceeds of the issue, to individuals who do not meet the requirements of this paragraph. Such plan must describe a procedure for ensuring that no more than 10 percent of the proceeds of such issue will be used to provide certificates to su individuals. If the Commissioner approves the suer's plan, certificates issued in accordance the terms of that plan to holders who do not the 3-year requirement do not fail to satis requirements of this paragraph.

(f) *Purchase price requirement* —(1) eral. A certificate meets the requireme paragraph only if the acquisition cost (in § 1.25-1T(b)(8)) of the residence, o

Reg. § 1.25

targeted area residence, in connection with which the certificate is provided does not exceed 110 percent of the average area purchase price (as defined in § 1.25-1T(b)(9)) applicable to that residence. In the case of a targeted area residence (as defined in § 1.25-1T(b)(7)) the acquisition cost may not exceed 120 percent of the average area purchase price applicable to such residence. See section 103A(f) and the regulations thereunder for further definitions and requirements.

(2) *Certification procedure.* The requirements of paragraph (f)(1) will be met if the issuer or its agent obtains affidavits executed by the seller and the buyer that state that these requirements have been met. Such affidavits must include an itemized list of—

    (i) Any payments made by the buyer (or a related person) or for the benefit of the buyer,

    (ii) If the residence is incomplete, an estimate of the reasonable cost of completing the residence, and

    (iii) If the residence is purchased subject to a ground rent, the capitalized value of the ground rent.

The issuer or his agent must examine such affidavits and determine whether, on the basis of information contained therein, the purchase price requirement is met.

(g) *New mortgage requirement* —(1) *In general.* (i) A certificate meets the requirements of this paragraph only if the certificate is not issued in connection with the acquisition or replacement of an existing mortgage. Except in the case of a qualified home improvement loan, the certificate must be issued to an individual who did not have a mortgage (whether or not paid off) on the residence with respect to which the certificate is issued at any time prior to the execution of the mortgage.

    (ii) *Exceptions.* For purposes of this paragraph, a certificate used in connection with the replacement of—

    (A) Construction period loans,

    (B) Bridge loans or similar temporary initial financing, and

    (C) In the case of a qualified rehabilitaon loan, an existing mortgage,

·ll not be treated as being used to acquire or ~ace an existing mortgage. Generally, tempo- ~initial financing is any financing which has a ~f 24 months or less. See section 103A(j)(1) ~ regulations thereunder for examples illus- ~he application of these requirements.

    Certification procedure. The require- ~aragraph (g)(1) will be met if the issuer ~obtains from the holder of the certifi-

cate an affidavit stating that the mortgage being acquired in connection with the certificate will not be used to acquire or replace an existing mortgage (other than one that falls within the exceptions described in paragraph (g)(1)(ii)).

(h) *Transfer of mortgage credit certificates*— (1) *In general.* A certificate meets the requirements of this paragraph only if it is (i) not transferable or (ii) transferable only with the approval of the issuer.

(2) *Transfer procedure.* A certificate that is transferred with the approval of the issuer is a qualified mortgage credit certificate in the hands of the transferee only if each of the following requirements is met:

    (i) The transferee assumed liability for the remaining balance of the certified indebtedness amount in connection with the acquisition of the residence from the transferor,

    (ii) The issuer issues a new certificate to the transferee, and

    (iii) The new certificate meets each of the requirements of paragraphs (d), (e), (f), and (i) of this section based on the facts as they exist at the time of the transfer as if the mortgage credit certificate were being issued for the first time. For example, the purchase price requirement is to be determined by reference to the average area purchase price at the time of the assumption and not when the mortgage credit certificate was originally issued.

(3) *Statement on certificate.* The requirements of paragraph (h)(1) will be met if the mortgage credit certificate states that the certificate may not be transferred or states that the certificate may not be transferred unless the issuer issues a new certificate in place of the original certificate.

(i) *Prohibited mortgages*—(1) *In general.* A certificate meets the requirements of this paragraph only if it is issued in connection with the acquisition of a residence none of the financing of which is provided from the proceeds of—

    (i) A qualified mortgage bond (as defined under section 103A(c)(1) and the regulations thereunder), or

    (ii) A qualified veterans' mortgage bond (as defined under section 103A(c)(3) and the regulations thereunder).

Thus, for example, if a mortgagor has a mortgage on his principal residence that was obtained from the proceeds of a qualified mortgage bond, a mortgage credit certificate issued to such mortgagor in connection with a qualified home improvement loan with respect to such residence is not a qualified mortgage credit certificate. If, however, the financing provided from the proceeds of the qualified mortgage bond had been paid off in full, the certificate would be a qualified mortgage credit certificate (assuming all the requirements of this paragraph are met).

(2) *Certification procedure.* The requirements of paragraph (i)(1) will be met if the issuer or its agent obtains from the holder of the certificate an affidavit stating that no portion of the financing of the residence in connection with which the certificate is issued is provided from the proceeds of a qualified mortgage bond or a qualified veterans' mortgage bond.

(j) *Particular lenders*—(1) *In general.* Except as otherwise provided in paragraph (j)(2), a certificate meets the requirements of this paragraph only if the certificate is not limited to indebtedness incurred from particular lenders. A certificate is limited to indebtedness from particular lenders if the issuer, directly or indirectly, prohibits the holder of a certificate from obtaining financing from one or more lenders or requires the holder of a certificate to obtain financing from one or more lenders. For purposes of this paragraph, a lender is any person, including an issuer of mortgage credit certificates, that provides financing for the acquisition, qualified rehabilitation, or qualified home improvement of a residence.

(2) *Exception.* A mortgage credit certificate that is limited to indebtedness incurred from particular lenders will not cease to meet the requirements of this paragraph if the Commissioner approves the basis for such limitation. The Commissioner may approve the basis for such limitation if the issuer establishes to the satisfaction of the Commissioner that it will result in a significant economic benefit to the holders of mortgage credit certificates (*e.g.*, substantially lower financing costs) compared to the result without such limitation.

(3) *Taxable bonds.* The requirements of this paragraph do not prevent an issuer of mortgage credit certificates from issuing mortgage subsidy bonds (other than obligations described in section 103(a)) the proceeds of which are to be used to provide mortgages to holders of mortgage credit certificates provided that the holders of such certificates are not required to obtain financing from the proceeds of the bond issue. See § 1.25-4T(h) with respect to permissible fees.

(4) *Lists of participating lenders.* The requirements of this paragraph do not prohibit an issuer from maintaining a list of lenders that have stated that they will make loans to qualified holders of mortgage credit certificates, provided that (i) the issuer solicits such statements in a public notice similar to the notice described in § 1.25-7T,

(ii) lenders are provided a reasonable period of time in which to express their interest in being included in such a list, and (iii) holders of mortgage credit certificates are not required to obtain financing from the lenders on the list. If an issuer maintains such a list, it must update the list at least annually.

(5) *Certification procedure.* The requirements of this paragraph will be met if (i) the issuer or its agent obtains from the holder of the certificate an affidavit stating that the certificate was not limited to indebtedness incurred from particular lenders or (ii) the issuer obtains a ruling from the Commissioner under paragraph (j)(2).

(6) *Examples.* The following examples illustrate the application of this paragraph:

Example (1). Under its mortgage credit certificate program, County Z distributes all the certificates to be issued to a group of 60 participating lenders. Residents of County Z may obtain mortgage credit certificates only from the participating lenders and only in connection with the acquisition of mortgage financing from that lender or one of the other participating lenders. Certificates issued under this program do not meet the requirements of this paragraph since the certificates are limited to indebtedness incurred from particular lenders. The certificates, therefore, are not qualified mortgage credit certificates.

Example (2). In connection with its mortgage credit certificate program, County Y arranges with Bank P for a line of credit to be used to provide mortgage financing to holders of mortgage credit certificates. County Y, pursuant to paragraph (j)(4), maintains a list of lenders participating in the mortgage credit certificate program. County Y distributes the certificates directly to applicants. Holders of the certificates are not required to obtain mortgage financing through the line of credit or through a lender on the list of participating lenders. Certificates issued pursuant to County Y's program satisfy the requirements of this paragraph.

(k) *Developer certification*—(1) *In general.* A mortgage credit certificate that is allocated by the issuer to any particular development meets the requirements of this paragraph only if the developer provides a certification to the purchaser of the residence and the issuer stating that the purchase price of that residence is not higher than the price would be if the issuer had not allocated mortgage credit certificates to the development. The certification must be made by the developer if a natural person or, if not, by a duly authorized official of the developer.

Reg. § 1.25-3T(k)(1)

(2) *Certification procedure.* The requirements of this paragraph will be met if the issuer or its agent obtains from the holder of the certificate an affidavit stating that he has received from the developer the certification described in this paragraph.

(l) *Expiration*—(1) *In general.* A certificate meets the requirements of this paragraph if the certified indebtedness amount is incurred prior to the close of the second calendar year following the calendar year for which the issuer elected not to issue qualified mortgage bonds under § 1.25-4T with respect to that issue of mortgage credit certificates. Thus, for example, if on October 1, 1984, an issuing authority elects under § 1.25-4T not to issue qualified mortgage bonds, a mortgage credit certificate provided under that program does not meet the requirements of this paragraph unless the indebtedness is incurred on or before December 31, 1986.

(2) *Issuer-imposed expiration dates.* An issuer of mortgage credit certificates may provide that a certificate shall expire if the holder of the certificate does not incur certified indebtedness by a date that is prior to the expiration date provided in paragraph (l)(1). A certificate that expires prior to the date provided in paragraph (l)(1) may be reissued provided that the requirements of this paragraph are met.

(m) *Revocation.* A certificate meets the requirements of this paragraph only if it has not been revoked. Thus, the credit provided by section 25 and § 1.25-1T does not apply to interest paid or accrued following the revocation of a certificate. A certificate is treated as revoked when the residence to which the certificate relates ceases to be the holder's principal residence. An issuer may revoke a mortgage credit certificate if the certificate does not meet all the requirements of § 1.25-3T(d), (e), (f), (g), (h), (i), (j), (k), and (n). The certificate is revoked by the issuer's notifying the holder of the certificate and the Internal Revenue Service that the certificate is revoked. The notice to the Internal Revenue Service shall be made as part of the report required by § 1.25-8T(b)(2).

(n) *Interest paid to related person*—(1) *In general.* A certificate does not meet the requirements of this paragraph if interest on the certified indebtedness amount is paid to a person who is a related person to the holder of the certificate.

(2) *Certification procedure.* The requirements of this paragraph will be met if the issuer or its agent obtains from the holder of the certificate an affidavit stating that a related person does not have, and is not expected to have, an interest as a creditor in the certified indebtedness amount.

(o) *Fraud.* Notwithstanding any other provision of this section, a mortgage credit certificate does not meet the requirements of this section and, therefore, the certificate is not a qualified mortgage credit certificate for any calendar year, if the holder of the certificate provides a certification or any other information to the lender providing the mortgage or to the issuer of the certificate containing a material misstatement and such misstatement is due to fraud. In determining whether any misstatement is due to fraud, the rules generally applicable to underpayments of tax due to fraud (including rules relating to the statute of limitations) shall apply. See § 1.6709-1T with respect to the penalty for filing negligent or fraudulent statements. [Temporary Reg. § 1.25-3T.]

☐ [*T.D.* 8023, 5-3-85. *Amended by T.D.* 8502, 12-21-93 *and T.D.* 8692, 12-16-96.]

[Reg. § 1.25-4T]

§ 1.25-4T. Qualified mortgage credit certificate program (Temporary).—(a) *In general* — (1) *Definition of qualified mortgage credit certificate program.* For purposes of § § 1.25-1T through 1.25-8T, the term "qualified mortgage credit certificate program" means a program to issue qualified mortgage credit certificates which meets all of the requirements of paragraphs (b) through (i) of this section.

(2) *Requirements are a minimum.* Except as otherwise provided in this section, the requirements of this section are minimum requirements. Issuers may establish more stringent criteria for participation in a qualified mortgage credit certificate program. Thus, for example, an issuer may target 30 percent of the proceeds of an issue of mortgage credit certificates to targeted areas. Further, issuers may establish additional eligibility criteria for participation in a qualified mortgage credit certificate program. Thus, for example, issuers may impose an income limitation designed to ensure that only those individuals who could not otherwise purchase a residence will benefit from the credit.

(3) Except as otherwise provided in this section and § 1.25-3T, issuers may use mortgage credit certificates in connection with other Federal, State, and local programs provided that such use complies with the requirements of § 1.25-3T(j). Thus, for example, a mortgage credit certificate may be issued in connection with the qualified rehabilitation of a residence part of the cost of which will be paid from the proceeds of a State grant.

Reg. § 1.25-4T(a)(1)

(b) *Establishment of program.* A program meets the requirements of this paragraph only if it is established by a State or political subdivision thereof for any calendar year for which it has the authority to issue qualified mortgage bonds.

(c) *Election not to issue qualified mortgage bonds*—(1) *In general.* A program meets the requirements of this paragraph only if the issuer elects, in the time and manner specified in this paragraph, not to issue an amount of qualified mortgage bonds that it may otherwise issue during the calendar year under section 103A and the regulations thereunder.

(2) *Manner of making election.* On or before the earlier of the date of distribution of mortgage credit certificates under a program or December 31, 1987, the issuer must file an election not to issue an amount of qualified mortgage bonds. The election (and the certification (or affidavit) described in paragraph (d)) shall be filed with the Internal Revenue Service Center, Philadelphia, Pennsylvania 19255. The election should be titled "Mortgage Credit Certificate Election" and must include—

(i) The name, address, and TIN of the issuer,

(ii) The issuer's applicable limit, as defined in section 103A(g) and the regulations thereunder,

(iii) The aggregate amount of qualified mortgage bonds issued by the issuing authority during the calendar year,

(iv) The amount of the issuer's applicable limit that it has surrendered to other issuers during the calendar year,

(v) The date and amount of any previous elections under this paragraph for the calendar year, and

(vi) The amount of qualified mortgage bonds that the issuer elects not to issue.

(3) *Revocation of election.* Any election made under this paragraph may be revoked, in whole or in part, at any time during the calendar year in which the election was made. The revocation, however, may not be made with respect to any part of the nonissued bond amount that has been used to issue mortgage credit certificates pursuant to the election. The revocation shall be filed with the Internal Revenue Service Center, Philadelphia, Pennsylvania 19255. The revocation should be titled "Revocation of Mortgage Credit Certificate Election" and must include—

(i) The name, address, and TIN of the issuer,

(ii) The nonissued bond amount as originally elected, and

(iii) The portion of the nonissued bond amount with respect to which the election is being revoked.

(4) *Special rule.* If at the time that an issuer makes an election under this paragraph it does not know its applicable limit, the issuer may elect not to use all of its remaining authority to issue qualified mortgage bonds; this form of election will be treated as meeting the requirements of paragraph (c)(2) if, prior to the later of the end of the calendar year and December 31, 1985, the issuer amends its election so as to indicate the exact amount of qualified mortgage bond authority that it elected not to issue.

(5) *Limitation on nonissued bond amount.* The amount of qualified mortgage bonds which an issuer elects not to issue may not exceed the issuer's applicable limit (as determined under section 103A(g) and the regulations thereunder. For example, a governmental unit that, pursuant to section 103A(g)(3), may issue $10 million of qualified mortgage bonds that elects to trade in $11 million in qualified mortgage bond authority has not met the requirements of this paragraph, and mortgage credit certificates issued pursuant to such election are not qualified mortgage credit certificates.

(d) *State certification requirement*—(1) *In general.* A program meets the requirements of this paragraph only if the State official designated by law (or, where there is no State official, the Governor) certifies, based on facts and circumstances as of the date on which the certification is requested, following a request for such certification, that the issue meets the requirements of section 103A(g) (relating to volume limitation) and the regulations thereunder. A copy of the State certification must be attached to the issuer's election not to issue qualified mortgage bonds, except that, in the case of elections made during calendar year 1984, the certification may be filed with the Service prior to July 8, 1985, provided that mortgage credit certificates may not be distributed until the certification is filed. In the case of any constitutional home rule city, the certification shall be made by the chief executive officer of the city.

(2) *Certification procedure.* The official making the certification described in this paragraph (d) need not perform an independent investigation to determine whether the issuer has met the requirements of section 103A(g). In determining the aggregate amount of qualified mortgage bonds previously issued by that issuer during the calendar year the official may rely on copies of prior elections under paragraph (c) of this section made by the issuer for that year, together with an affidavit executed by an official of the issuer who

Reg. § 1.25-4T(d)(2)

is responsible for issuing bonds stating that the issuer has not, to date, issued any other issues of qualified mortgage bonds during the calendar year and stating the amount, if any, of the issuer's applicable limit that it has surrendered to other issuers during the calendar year; for any calendar year prior to 1985, the official may rely on an affidavit executed by a duly authorized official of the issuer who states the aggregate amount of qualified mortgage bonds issued by the issuer during the year. In determining the aggregate amount of qualified mortgage bonds that the issuer has previously elected not to issue during that calendar year, the official may rely on copies of any elections not to issue qualified mortgage bonds filed by the issuer for that calendar year, together with an affidavit executed by an official of the issuer responsible for issuing mortgage credit certificates stating that the issuer has not, to date, made any other elections not to issue qualified mortgage bonds. If, based on such information, the certifying official determines that the issuer has not, as of the date on which the certification is provided, exceeded its applicable limit for the year, the official may certify that the issue meets the requirements of section 103A(g). The fact that the certification described in this paragraph (d) is provided does not ensure that the issuer has met the requirements of section 103A(g) and the regulations thereunder, nor does it preclude the application of the penalty for over-issuance of mortgage credit certificates if such over-issuance actually occurs. See § 1.25-5T.

(3) *Special rule.* If within 30 days after the issuer files a proper request for the certification described in this paragraph (d) the issuer has not received from the State official designated by law (or, if there is no State official, the Governor) certification that the issue meets the requirements of section 103A(g) or, in the alternative, a statement that the issue does not meet such requirements, the issuer may submit, in lieu of the certification required by this paragraph (d), an affidavit executed by an officer of the issuer responsible for issuing mortgage credit certificates stating that—

(i) The issue meets the requirements of section 103A(g) and the regulations thereunder,

(ii) At least 30 days before the execution of the affidavit the issuer filed a proper request for the certification described in this paragraph (d), and

(iii) The State official designated by law (or, if there is no State official, the Governor) has not provided the certification described in this paragraph (d) or a statement that the issue does not meet such requirements.

For purposes of this paragraph, a request for certification is proper if the request includes the reports and affidavits described in paragraph (d)(2).

(e) *Information reporting requirement*—(1) *Reports.* With respect to mortgage credit certificates issued after September 30, 1985, a program meets the requirements of this paragraph only if the issuer submits a report containing the information concerning the holders of certificates issued during the preceding reporting period required by this paragraph. The report must be filed for each reporting period in which certificates (other than transferred certificates) are issued under the program. The issuer is not responsible for false information provided by a holder if the issuer did not know or have reason to know that the information was false. The report must be filed on the form prescribed by the Internal Revenue Service. If no form is prescribed, or if the form prescribed is not readily available, the issuer may use its own form provided that such form is in the format set forth in this paragraph and contains the information required by this paragraph. The report must be titled "Mortgage Credit Certificate Information Report" and must include the name, address, and TIN of the issuer, the reporting period for which the information is provided, and the following tables containing information concerning the holders of certificates issued during the reporting period for which the report is filed:

(i) A table titled "Number of Mortgage Credit Certificates by Income and Acquisition Cost" showing the number of mortgage credit certificates issued (other than those issued in connection with qualified home improvement and rehabilitation loans) according to the annualized gross income of the holders (categorized in the following intervals of income: $0-$9,999; $10,000-$19,999; $20,000-$29,999; $30,000-$39,999; $40,000-$49,999; $50,000-$74,999; and $75,000 or more) and according to the acquisition cost of the residences acquired in connection with the mortgage credit certificates (categorized in the following intervals of acquisition cost: $0-$19,999; $20,000-$39,999; $40,000-$59,999; $60,000-$79,999; $80,000-$99,999; $100,000-$119,999; $120,000-$149,999; $150,000-$199,999; and $200,000 or more). For each interval of income and acquisition cost the table must also be categorized according to—

(A) The aggregate amount of fees charged to holders to cover any administrative costs incurred by the issuer in issuing mortgage credit certificates, and

(B) The number of holders that—

Reg. § 1.25-4T(d)(3)

(1) Did not have a present ownership interest in a principal residence at any time during the 3-year period ending on the date the mortgage credit certificate is executed (i.e., satisfied the 3-year requirement) and purchased residences in targeted areas,

(2) Satisfied the 3-year requirement and purchased residences not located in targeted areas,

(3) Did have a present ownership interest in a principal residence at any time during the 3-year period ending on the date the mortgage credit certificate is executed (i.e., did not satisfy the 3-year requirement) and purchased residences in targeted areas, and

(4) Did not satisfy the 3-year requirement and purchased residences not located in targeted areas.

(ii) A table titled "Volume of Mortgage Credit Certificates by Income and Acquisition Cost" containing data on—

(A) The total of the certified indebtedness amounts of the certificates issued (other than those issued in connection with qualified home improvement and rehabilitation loans);

(B) The sum of the products of the certified indebtedness amount and the certificate credit rate for each certificate (other than those issued in connection with qualified home improvement and rehabilitation loans) according to annualized gross income (categorized in the same intervals of income as the preceding table) and according to the acquisition cost of the residences acquired in connection with mortgage credit certificates (categorized in the same intervals of acquisition cost as the preceding table); and

(C) For each interval of income and acquisition cost, the information described in paragraph (e)(1)((ii)(A) and (B) categorized according to the holders that—

(1) Satisfied the 3-year requirement and purchased residences in targeted areas,

(2) Satisfied the 3-year requirement and purchased residences not located in targeted areas,

(3) Did not satisfy the 3-year requirement and purchased residences in targeted areas, and

(4) Did not satisfy the 3-year requirement and purchased residences not located in targeted areas.

(iii) A table titled "Mortgage Credit Certificates for Qualified Home Improvement and Rehabilitation Loans" showing the number of mortgage credit certificates issued in connection with qualified home improvement loans and qualified rehabilitation loans, the total of the certified indebtedness amount with respect to such certificates, and the sum of the products of the certified indebtedness amount and the certificate credit rate for each certificate; the information contained in the table must also be categorized according to whether the residences with respect to which the certificates were provided are located in targeted areas.

(2) *Format.* If no form is prescribed by the Internal Revenue Service, or if the prescribed form is not readily available, the issuer must submit the report in the format specified in this paragraph (e)(2). The specified format of the report is the following:

MORTGAGE CREDIT CERTIFICATE INFORMATION REPORT

Name of issuer:

Address of issuer:

TIN of issuer:

Reporting period:

NUMBER OF MORTGAGE CREDIT CERTIFICATES
BY INCOME AND ACQUISITION COST

3-year Requirement:	Satisfied		Not Satisfied		Totals	Fees
Annualized Gross Monthly Income of Borrowers	Nontargeted Area	Targeted Area	Nontargeted Area	Targeted Area		
$ 0 — 9,999						
$ 10,000— 19,999						
$ 20,000— 29,999						
$ 30,000— 39,999						
$ 40,000— 49,999						
$ 50,000— 74,999						
$ 75,000 or more						
Total						
Acquisition Cost						
$ 0 — 19,999						
$ 20,000— 39,999						
$ 40,000— 59,999						
$ 60,000— 79,999						
$ 80,000— 99,999						
$100,000—119,999						
$120,000—149,999						
$150,000—199,999						
$200,000 or more						
Total						

Reg. § 1.25-4T(e)(2)

VOLUME OF MORTGAGE CREDIT CERTIFICATES BY INCOME AND ACQUISITION COST

	Holders Satisfying the 3-year Requirement			
	Nontargeted Area		*Targeted Area*	
Annualized Gross Monthly Income of Holders	*Total of the Certified Indebtedness Amounts*	*Sum of Products of Certified Indebtedness Amounts and Credit Rates*	*Total of the Certified Indebtedness Amounts*	*Sum of Products of Certified Indebtedness Amounts and Credit Rates*
$ 0 — 9,999				
$ 10,000— 19,999				
$ 20,000— 29,999				
$ 30,000— 39,999				
$ 40,000— 49,999				
$ 50,000— 74,999				
$ 75,000 or more				
Total				
Acquisition Cost				
$ 0 — 19,999				
$ 20,000— 39,999				
$ 40,000— 59,999				
$ 60,000— 79,999				
$ 80,000— 99,999				
$100,000—119,999				
$120,000—149,999				
$150,000—199,999				
$200,000 or more				
Total				

Reg. § 1.25-4T(e)(2)

VOLUME OF MORTGAGE CREDIT CERTIFICATES BY INCOME AND ACQUISITION COST

Annualized Gross Monthly Income of Holders	3-year Requirement Not Satisfied				Totals	
	Nontargeted Area				Targeted Area	
	Total of the Certified Indebtedness Amounts	Sum of Products of Certified Indebtedness Amounts and Credit Rates	Total of the Certified Indebtedness Amounts	Sum of Products of Certified Indebtedness Amounts and Credit Rates	Total Certified Indebtedness Amounts	Total Sum of Products of Certified Indebtedness Amounts and Credit Rates
$ 0 — 9,999						
$ 10,000— 19,999						
$ 20,000— 29,999						
$ 30,000— 39,999						
$ 40,000— 49,999						
$ 50,000— 74,999						
$ 75,000 or more						
Total						

Acquisition Cost

$ 0 — 19,999						
$ 20,000— 39,999						
$ 40,000— 59,999						
$ 60,000— 79,999						
$ 80,000— 99,999						
$100,000—119,999						
$120,000—149,999						
$150,000—199,999						
$200,000 or more						
Total						

Reg. § 1.25-4T(e)(2)

MORTGAGE CREDIT CERTIFICATES FOR QUALIFIED
HOME IMPROVEMENT AND REHABILITATION LOANS

	Nontargeted Area		Targeted Area		Totals
Home Improvement Loans					
Number of mortgage credit certificates					
Total of the certified indebtedness amounts					
Product of certified indebtedness amounts and credit rates					
Rehabilitation Loans					
Number of mortgage credit certificates					
Total of the certified indebtedness amounts					
Product of certified indebtedness amounts and credit rates					

Reg. § 1.25-4T(e)(2)

(3) *Definitions and special rules.* (i) For purposes of this paragraph the term "annualized gross income" means the borrower's gross monthly income multiplied by 12. Gross monthly income is the sum of monthly gross pay, any additional income from investments, pensions, Veterans Administration (VA) compensation, part-time employment, bonuses, dividends, interest, current overtime pay, net rental income, etc., and other income (such as alimony and child support, if the borrower chooses to disclose such income). Information with respect to gross monthly income may be obtained from available loan documents, *e.g.*, the sum of lines 23D and 23E on the Application for VA or FmHA Home Loan Guaranty or for HUD/FHA Insured Mortgage (VA Form 26-1802a, HUD 92900, Jan. 1982), or the total line from the Gross Monthly Income section of FHLMC Residential Loan Application form (FHLMC 65 Rev. 8/78).

(ii) For purposes of this paragraph, the term "reporting period" means each one year period beginning July 1 and ending June 30, except that issuers need not provide data with respect to the period prior to October 1, 1985.

(iii) For purposes of this paragraph, verification of information concerning a holder's gross monthly income by utilizing other available information concerning the holder's income (*e.g.*, Federal income tax returns) is not required. In determining whether the holder of a mortgage credit certificate acquiring a residence in a targeted area satisfies the 3-year requirement, the issuer may rely on a statement signed by the holder.

(4) *Time for filing.* The report required by this paragraph shall be filed not later than the 15th day of the second calendar month after the close of the reporting period. The Commissioner may grant an extension of time for the filing of a report required by this paragraph if there is reasonable cause for the failure to file such report in a timely fashion. The report may be filed at any time before such date but must be complete based on facts and reasonable expectations as of the date the report is filed. The report need not be amended to reflect information learned subsequent to the date of filing, or to reflect changed circumstances with respect to any holder.

(5) *Place for filing.* The report required by this paragraph is to be filed at the Internal Revenue Service Center, Philadelphia, Pennsylvania 19255.

(f) *Policy statement.* A program established pursuant to an election under paragraph (c) made after 1984 meets the requirements of this paragraph only if the applicable elected representative of the governmental unit—

(1) Which is the issuer, or

(2) On whose behalf the certificates were issued,

has published (after a public hearing following reasonable public notice) a policy statement described in § 1.103A-2(l) by the last day of the year preceding the year in which the election under paragraph (c) is made, and a copy of such report has been submitted to the Commissioner on or before such last day. See § 1.103A-2(l) for further definitions and requirements.

(g) *Targeted areas requirement—*(1) *In general.* A program meets the requirements of this paragraph only if—

(i) The portion of the total proceeds of the issue specified in paragraph (g)(2) is made available to provide mortgage credit certificates in connection with owner financing of targeted area residences for at least 1 year after the date on which mortgage credit certificates are first made available with respect to targeted area residences, and

(ii) The issuer attempts with reasonable diligence to place such proceeds with qualified persons.

Mortgage credit certificates are considered first made available with respect to targeted area residences on the date on which the issuer first begins to accept applications for mortgage credit certificates provided under that issue.

(2) *Specified portion.* (i) The specified portion of the total proceeds of an issue is the lesser of—

(A) 20 percent of the total proceeds, or

(B) 8 percent of the average annual aggregate principal amount of mortgages executed during the immediately preceding 3 calendar years for single-family, owner-occupied residences in targeted areas within the jurisdiction of the issuing authority.

For purposes of computing the required portion of the total proceeds specified in paragraph (g)(2)(i)(B) where such provision is applicable, an issuer may rely upon the safe-harbor formula provided in the regulations under section 103A(h).

(ii) See § 1.25-1T(b)(10)(ii) for the definition of "total proceeds".

(h) *Fees—*(1) *In general.* A program meets the requirements of this paragraph only if each applicant is required to pay, directly or indirectly, no fee other than those fees permitted under this paragraph.

Reg. § 1.25-4T(e)(3)

(2) *Permissible fees.* Applicants may be required to pay the following fees provided that they are reasonable:

(i) Points, origination fees, servicing fees, and other fees in amounts that are customarily charged with respect to mortgages not provided in connection with mortgage credit certificates.

(ii) Application fees, survey fees, credit report fees, insurance fees, or similar settlement or financing costs to the extent such amounts do not exceed the amounts charged in the area in cases where mortgages are not provided in connection with mortgage credit certificates. For example, amounts charged for FHA, VA, or similar private mortgage insurance on an individual's mortgage are permissible so long as such amounts do not exceed the amounts charged in the area with respect to a similar mortgage that is not provided in connection with a mortgage credit certificate, and

(iii) Other fees that, taking into account all the facts and circumstances, are reasonably necessary to cover any administrative costs incurred by the issuer or its agent in issuing mortgage credit certificates.

(i) *Qualified mortgage credit certificate.* A program meets the requirement of this paragraph only if each mortgage credit certificate issued under the program meets each of the requirements of paragraphs (c) through (o) of § 1.25-3T.

(j) *Good faith compliance efforts*—(1) *Eligibility requirements.* (i) A program under which each of the mortgage credit certificates issued does not meet each of the requirements of paragraphs (c) through (o) of § 1.25-3T shall be treated as meeting the requirements of paragraph (i) of this section if each of the requirements of this paragraph (j)(1) is satisfied. A mortgage credit certificate program meets the requirements of this paragraph (j)(1) only if each of the following provisions is met:

(A) The issuer in good faith attempted to issue mortgage credit certificates only to individuals meeting each of the requirements of paragraphs (c) through (o) of § 1.25-3T. Good faith requires that agreements with lenders and agents and other relevant instruments contain restrictions that permit the approval of mortgage credit certificates only in accordance with the requirements of paragraphs (c) through (o) of § 1.25-3T. In addition, the issuer must establish reasonable procedures to ensure compliance with those requirements. Reasonable procedures include reasonable investigations by the issuer to determine whether individuals satisfy the requirements of paragraphs (c) through (o) of § 1.25-3T.

(B) 95 percent or more of the total proceeds of the issue were devoted to individuals with respect to whom, at the time that the certificate was issued, all the requirements of paragraphs (c) through (o) of § 1.25-3T were met. If a holder of a mortgage credit certificate fails to meet more than one of these requirements, the amount of the certificate (*i.e.,* the certificate credit rate multiplied by the certified indebtedness amount) issued to that individual will be taken into account only once in determining whether the 95-percent requirement is met. However, all of the defects in that individual's certificate must be corrected pursuant to paragraph (j)(1)(i)(C).

(C) Any failure to meet the requirements of paragraphs (c) through (o) of § 1.25-3T is corrected within a reasonable period after that failure is discovered. For example, if an individual fails to meet one or more of such requirements those failures can be corrected by revoking that individual's certificate.

(ii) *Examples.* The following examples illustrate the application of this paragraph (j)(1):

Example (1). County X only distributes mortgage credit certificates to individuals who have contracted to purchase a principal residence. County X requires that applicants for mortgage credit certificates present the following information:

(i) An affidavit stating that the applicant intends to use the residence in connection with which the mortgage credit certificate is issued as his principal residence within a reasonable time after the certificate is issued by County X, that the applicant will notify the County if the residence ceases to be his principal residence, and facts that are sufficient for County X to determine whether the residence is located within the jurisdiction of County X,

(ii) An affidavit stating that the applicant had no present ownership interest in a principal residence at any time during the 3-year period prior to the date on which the certificate is issued,

(iii) Copies of the applicant's Federal tax returns for the preceding 3 years,

(iv) Affidavits from the seller of the residence with respect to which the certificate is issued and the applicant stating the purchase price of the residence, including an itemized list of (A) payments made by or for the benefit of the applicant, (B) if the residence is incomplete, an estimate of the reasonable cost of completing the residence, and (C) if the residence is subject to a ground rent, the capitalized value of the ground rent,

Reg. § 1.25-4T(j)(1)

(v) An affidavit executed by the applicant stating that the mortgage being acquired in connection with the certificate will not be used to acquire or replace an existing mortgage,

(vi) An affidavit executed by the applicant stating that no portion of the financing for the residence in connection with which the certificate is issued is provided from the proceeds of a qualified mortgage bond or qualified veterans' mortgage bond and that no portion of the mortgage for the residence is provided by a person related to the applicant (as defined in § 1.25-3T(n)),

(vii) An affidavit executed by the applicant stating that the certificate was not limited to indebtedness incurred from particular lenders, and

(viii) In the case of a mortgage credit certificate allocated for use in connection with a particular development, an affidavit executed by the applicant stating that the applicant received from the developer a certification stating that the price of the residence with respect to which the certificate was issued is no higher than it would be without the use of a mortgage credit certificate.

County X examines the information submitted by the applicant to determine whether the requirements of paragraph (c), (d), (e), (f), (g), (i), (j), (k), and (n) of § 1.25-3T are met. County X determines that the certificate has not expired. The mortgage credit certificates issued by County X are in the form prescribed by § 1.25-6T and County X provides all the required information and statements. After determining that the applicant meets all these requirements County X issues a mortgage credit certificate to the applicant. This procedure for issuing mortgage credit certificates is sufficient evidence of the good faith of County X to meet the requirements of § 1.25-4T(j)(1)(i)(A).

    Example (2). County W distributes preliminary mortgage credit certificates to individuals who have not entered into contracts to purchase a principal residence. County W issues preliminary certificates in the form prescribed by § 1.25-6T to those applicants that have submitted statements that they (i) intend to purchase a single-family residence located within the jurisdiction of County W which they will occupy as a principal residence, (ii) have had no present ownership interest in a principal residence within the preceding 3-year period, and (iii) will not use the certificate in connection with the acquisition or replacement of an existing mortgage. The certificates contain a maximum purchase price, the certificate credit rate, and a statement that the certificate will expire if the applicant does not

enter into a closing agreement with respect to a loan within 6 months from the date of preliminary issuance. Holders of these certificates may apply for a mortgage loan from any lender. When the holder of the certificate applies for a loan the lender requires that he submit the following:

(i) An affidavit stating that the applicant intends to use the residence in connection with which the mortgage credit certificate is issued as his principal residence within a reasonable time after the certificate is issued by County W, that the applicant will notify the County if the residence ceases to be his principal residence, and facts that are sufficient for County W to determine whether the residence is located within the jurisdiction of County W,

(ii) An affidavit stating that the applicant had no present ownership interest in a principal residence at any time during the 3-year period prior to the date on which the certificate is issued,

(iii) Copies of the applicant's Federal tax returns for the preceding 3 years,

(iv) Affidavits from the seller of the residence with respect to which the certificate is issued and the applicant stating the purchase price of the residence, including an itemized list of (A) payments made by or for the benefit of the applicant, (B) if the residence is incomplete, an estimate of the reasonable cost of completing the residence, and (C) if the residence is subject to a ground rent, the capitalized value of the ground rent,

(v) An affidavit executed by the applicant stating that the mortgage being acquired in connection with the certificate will not be used to acquire or replace an existing mortgage,

(vi) An affidavit executed by the applicant stating that no portion of the financing for the residence in connection with which the certificate is issued is provided from the proceeds of a qualified mortgage bond or qualified veterans' mortgage bond and that no portion of the mortgage for the residence is provided by a person related to the applicant (as defined in § 1.25-3T(n)),

(vii) An affidavit executed by the applicant stating that the certificate was not limited to indebtedness incurred from particular lenders, and

(viii) In the case of a mortgage credit certificate allocated for use in connection with a particular development, an affidavit executed by the applicant stating that the applicant received from the developer a certification stating that the price of the residence with respect to which the

Reg. § 1.25-4T(j)(1)

certificate was issued is no higher than it would be without the use of a mortgage credit certificate.

The lender then submits those affidavits, together with its statement as to the amount of the indebtedness incurred, to County W. After determining that the requirements of paragraphs (c), (d), (e), (f), (g), (i), (j), (k) and (n) of § 1.25-3T are met and determining that the certificate has not expired, County W completes the mortgage credit certificate. This procedure for issuing mortgage credit certificates is sufficient evidence of the good faith of County W to meet the requirements of § 1.25-4T(j)(1)(i)(A).

(2) *Program requirements.* (i) A mortgage credit certificate program which fails to meet one or more of the requirements of paragraphs (b) through (h) of this section shall be treated as meeting such requirements if the requirements of this paragraph (j)(2) are satisfied. A mortgage credit certificate program meets the requirements of this paragraph (j)(2) only if each of the following provisions is met:

(A) The issuer in good faith attempted to meet all of the requirements of paragraphs (b) through (h) of this section. This good faith requirement will be met if all reasonable steps are taken by the issuer to ensure that the program complies with these requirements.

(B) Any failure to meet such requirements is due to inadvertent error, *e.g.,* mathematical error, after taking reasonable steps to comply with such requirements.

(ii) The following example illustrates the application of this paragraph (j)(2):

Example. City X issues an issue of mortgage credit certificates. However, despite taking all reasonable steps to determine accurately the size of the applicable limit, as provided in section 103A(g)(3) and the regulations thereunder, the limit is exceeded because the amount of the mortgages originated in the area during the past 3 years is incorrectly computed as a result of mathematical error. Such facts are sufficient evidence of the good faith of the issuer to meet the requirements of paragraph (j)(2). [Temporary Reg. § 1.25-4T.]

☐ [*T.D.* 8023, 5-3-85. *Amended by T.D.* 8048, 8-29-85.]

[Reg. § 1.25-5T]

§ 1.25-5T. Limitation on aggregate amount of mortgage credit certificates (Temporary).— (a) *In general.* If the aggregate amount of qualified mortgage credit certificates (as defined in paragraph (b)) issued by an issuer under a qualified mortgage credit certificate program exceeds 20 percent of the nonissued bond amount (as

defined in paragraph (c)), the provisions of paragraph (d) shall apply.

(b) *Aggregate amount of mortgage credit certificates*—(1) *In general.* The aggregate amount of qualified mortgage credit certificates issued under a qualified mortgage credit certificate program is the sum of the products determined by multiplying—

(i) The certified indebtedness amount of each qualified mortgage credit certificate issued under that program, by

(ii) The certificate credit rate with respect to such certificate.

(2) *Examples.* The following examples illustrate the application of this paragraph (b):

Example (1). For 1986 City Q has a nonissued bond amount of $100 million. After making a proper election, Q issues 2,000 qualified mortgage credit certificates each with a certificate credit rate of 20 percent and a certified indebtedness amount of $50,000. The aggregate amount of qualified mortgage credit certificates is $20 million (2,000 × (.2 × $50,000)). Since this amount does not exceed 20 percent of the nonissued bond amount (.2 × $100 million = $20 million), Q has complied with the limitation on the aggregate amount of mortgage credit certificates, provided that it does not issue any additional certificates.

Example (2). The facts are the same as in example (1) except that instead of issuing all its certificates at the 20 percent rate, Q issues (i) qualified mortgage credit certificates with a certificate credit rate of 10 percent and an aggregate principal amount of $25 million, (ii) qualified mortgage credit certificates with a certificate credit rate of 40 percent and an aggregate principal amount of $25 million, and (iii) qualified mortgage credit certificates with a certificate credit rate of 30 percent and an aggregate principal amount of $25 million. The aggregate amount of qualified mortgage credit certificates is $20 million (10 percent of $25 million) plus (40 percent of $25 million) plus (30 percent of $25 million)). Q has complied with the limitation on the aggregate amount of qualified mortgage credit certificates, provided that it does not issue any additional certificates pursuant to the same program.

(c) *Nonissued bond amount.* The term "nonissued bond amount" means, with respect to any qualified mortgage credit certificate program, the amount of qualified mortgage bonds (as defined in section 103A(c)(1) and the regulations thereunder) which the issuer is otherwise authorized to issue and elects not to issue under section 25(c)(2) and § 1.25-4T(b). The amount of qualified mortgage bonds which an issuing authority is author-

Reg. § 1.25-5T(c)

ized to issue is determined under section 103A(g) and the regulations thereunder; such determination shall take into account any prior elections by the issuer not to issue qualified mortgage bonds, the amount of any reduction in the State ceiling under paragraph (d) of this section, and the aggregate amount of qualified mortgage bonds issued by the issuer prior to its election not to issue qualified mortgage bonds.

(d) *Noncompliance with limitation on aggregate amount of mortgage credit certificates*—(1) *In general.* If the provisions of this paragraph apply, the State ceiling under section 103A(g)(4) and the regulations thereunder for the calendar year following the calendar year in which the Commissioner determines the correction amount for the State in which the issuer which exceeded the limitation on the aggregate amount of mortgage credit certificates is located shall be reduced by 1.25 times the correction amount with respect to such failure.

(2) *Correction amount.* (i) The term "correction amount" means an amount equal to the excess credit amount divided by .20.

(ii) The term "excess credit amount" means the excess of—

(A) The credit amount for any mortgage credit certificate program, over

(B) The amount which would have been the credit amount for such program had such program met the requirements of section 25(d)(2) and paragraph (a) of this section.

(iii) The term "credit amount" means the sum of the products determined by multiplying—

(A) The certified indebtedness amount of each qualified mortgage credit certificate issued under the program, by

(B) The certificate credit rate with respect to such certificate.

(3) *Example.* The following example illustrates the application of this paragraph:

Example. For 1987 City R has a nonissued bond amount of $100 million. City R issues all of its mortgage credit certificates with a certificate credit rate of 20 percent. City R issues certificates with an aggregate certified indebtedness amount of $120 million. The aggregate amount of mortgage credit certificates issued by City R is $24 million, which exceeds 20 percent of the nonissued bond amount. The State ceiling for the calendar year following the calendar year in which the Commissioner determines the correction amount is reduced by $25 million (the correction amount multiplied by 1.25). The correction amount is determined as follows: The credit amount is $24

million (.2 × $120 million); the amount which would have been the credit amount for the program had it met the requirements of section 25(d)(2) is $20 million (.2 × $100 million); the excess credit amount is $4 million ($24 million − $20 million); therefore, the correction amount is $20 million ($4 million/.2).

(4) *Cross references.* See section 103A(g)(4) and the regulations thereunder with respect to the reduction of the applicable State ceiling. [Temporary Reg. § 1.25-5T.]

☐ [*T.D.* 8023, 5-3-85.]

[Reg. § 1.25-6T]

§ 1.25-6T. Form of qualified mortgage credit certificate (Temporary).—(a) *In general.* Qualified mortgage credit certificates are to be issued on the form prescribed by the Internal Revenue Service. If no form is prescribed by the Internal Revenue Service, or if the form prescribed by the Internal Revenue Service is not readily available, the issuer may use its own form provided that such form contains the information required by this section. Each mortgage credit certificate must be issued in a form such that there are at least three copies of the form. One copy of the certificate shall be retained by the issuer; one copy shall be retained by the lender; and one copy shall be forwarded to the State official who issued the certification required by § 1.25-4T(d), unless that State official has stated in writing that he does not want to receive such copies.

(b) *Required information.* Each qualified mortgage credit certificate must include the following information:

(1) The name, address, and TIN of the issuer,

(2) The date of the issuer's election not to issue qualified mortgage bonds pursuant to which the certificate is being issued,

(3) The number assigned to the certificate,

(4) The name, address, and TIN of the holder of the certificate,

(5) The certificate credit rate,

(6) The certified indebtedness amount,

(7) The acquisition cost of the residence being acquired in connection with the certificate,

(8) The average area purchase price applicable to the residence,

(9) Whether the certificate meets the requirements of § 1.25-3T(d), relating to residence requirement,

(10) Whether the certificate meets the requirements of § 1.25-3T(e), relating to 3-year requirement,

(11) Whether the certificate meets the requirements of § 1.25-3T(g), relating to new mortgage requirement,

(12) Whether the certificate meets the requirements of § 1.25-3T(i), relating to prohibited mortgages,

(13) Whether the certificate meets the requirements of § 1.25-3T(j), relating to particular lenders,

(14) Whether the certificate meets the requirements of § 1.25-3T(k), relating to allocations to particular developments,

(15) Whether the certificate meets the requirements of § 1.25-3T(n), relating to interest paid to related persons,

(16) Whether the residence in connection with which the certificate is issued is a targeted area residence,

(17) The date on which a closing agreement is signed with respect to the certified indebtedness amount,

(18) The expiration date of the certificate,

(19) A statement that the certificate is not transferable or a statement that the certificate may be transferred only if the issuer issues a new certificate, and

(20) A statement, signed under penalties of perjury by an authorized official of the issuer or its agent, that such person has made the determinations specified in paragraph (b)(9) through (16). [Temporary Reg. § 1.25-6T.]

☐ [*T.D.* 8023, 5-3-85.]

[Reg. § 1.25-7T]

§ 1.25-7T. Public notice (Temporary).—(a) *In general.* At least 90 days prior to the issuance of any mortgage credit certificate under a qualified mortgage credit certificate program, the issuer shall provide reasonable public notice of—

(1) The eligibility requirements for such certificate,

(2) The methods by which such certificates are to be issued, and

(3) The other information required by this section.

(b) *Reasonable public notice*—(1) *In general.* Reasonable public notice means published notice which is reasonably designed to inform individuals who would be eligible to receive mortgage credit certificates of the proposed issuance. Reasonable public notice may be provided through newspapers of general circulation.

(2) *Contents of notice.* The public notice required by paragraph (a) must include a brief description of the principal residence require-

ment, 3-year requirement, purchase price requirement, and new mortgage requirement. The notice must also provide a brief description of the methods by which the certificates are to be issued and the address and telephone number for obtaining further information. [Temporary Reg. § 1.25-7T.]

☐ [*T.D.* 8023, 5-3-85.]

[Reg. § 1.25-8T]

§ 1.25-8T. Reporting requirements (Temporary).—(a) *Lender*—(1) *In general.* Each person who makes a loan that is a certified indebtedness amount with respect to any mortgage credit certificate must file the report described in paragraph (a)(2) and must retain on its books and records the information described in paragraph (a)(3). The report described in paragraph (a)(2) is an annual report and must be filed on or before January 31 of the year following the calendar year to which the report relates. See section 6709(c) and the regulations thereunder for the applicable penalties with respect to failure to file reports.

(2) *Information required.* The report shall be submitted on Form 8329 and shall contain the information required therein. A separate Form 8329 shall be filed for each issue of mortgage credit certificates with respect to which the lender made mortgage loans during the preceding calendar year. Thus, for example, if during 1986 Bank M makes three mortgage loans which are certified indebtedness amounts with respect to State Z's January 15, 1986, issue of mortgage credit certificates, and two mortgage loans which are certified indebtedness amounts with respect to State Z's April 15, 1986, issue of mortgage credit certificates, and fifty mortgage loans which are certified indebtedness amounts with respect to County X's December 31, 1985, issue of mortgage credit certificates, Bank M must file three separate reports for calendar year 1986. The lender must submit the Form 8329 with the information required therein, including—

(i) The name, address, and TIN of the issuer of the mortgage credit certificates,

(ii) The date on which the election not to issue qualified mortgage bonds with respect to that mortgage credit certificate was made,

(iii) The name, address, and TIN of the lender, and

(iv) The sum of the products determined by multiplying—

(A) The certified indebtedness amount of each mortgage credit certificate issued under such program, by

(B) The certificate credit rate with respect to such certificate.

(3) *Recordkeeping requirements.* Each person who makes a loan that is a certified indebtedness amount with respect to any mortgage credit certificate must retain the information specified in this paragraph (a)(3) on its books and records for 6 years following the year in which the loan was made. With respect to each loan the lender must retain the following information:

(i) The name, address, and TIN of each holder of a qualified mortgage credit certificate with respect to which a loan is made,

(ii) The name, address, and TIN of the issuer of such certificate, and

(iii) The date the loan for the certified indebtedness amount is closed, the certified indebtedness amount, and the certificate credit rate of such certificate.

(b) *Issuers*—(1) *In general.* Each issuer of mortgage credit certificates shall file the report described in paragraph (b)(2).

(2) *Quarterly reports.* (i) Each issuer which elects to issue mortgage credit certificates shall file reports on Form 8330. These reports shall be filed on a quarterly basis, beginning with the quarter in which the election is made, and are due on the following dates: April 30 (for the quarter ending March 31), July 31 (for the quarter ending June 30), October 31 (for the quarter ending September 30), and January 31 (for the quarter ending December 31). For elections made prior to May 8, 1985, the first report need not be filed until July 31, 1985. An issuer shall file a separate report for each issue of mortgage credit certificates. In the quarter in which the last qualified mortgage credit certificate that may be issued under a program is issued, the issuer must state that fact on the report to be filed for that quarter; the issuer is not required to file any subsequent reports with respect to that program. See section 6709(c) for the penalties with respect to failure to file a report.

(ii) The report shall be submitted on Form 8330 and shall contain the information required therein, including—

(A) The name, address, and TIN of the issuer of the mortgage credit certificates,

(B) The date of the issuer's election not to issue qualified mortgage bonds with respect to the mortgage credit certificate program and the nonissued bond amount of the program,

(C) The sum of the products determined by multiplying—

(*1*) The certified indebtedness amount of each qualified mortgage credit certificate issued under that program during the calendar quarter, by

(2) The certificate credit rate with respect to such certificate, and

(D) A listing of the name, address, and TIN of each holder of a qualified mortgage credit certificate which has been revoked during the calendar quarter.

(c) *Extensions of time for filing reports.* The Commissioner may grant an extension of time for the filing of a report required by this section if there is reasonable cause for the failure to file such report in a timely fashion.

(d) *Place for filing.* The reports required by this section are to be filed at the Internal Revenue Service Center, Philadelphia, Pennsylvania 19255.

(e) *Cross reference.* See section 6709 and the regulations thereunder with respect to the penalty for failure to file a report required by this section. [Temporary Reg. § 1.25-8T.]

□ [*T.D.* 8023, 5-3-85.]

[Reg. § 1.25A-0]

§ 1.25A-0. Table of contents.—This section lists captions contained in §§ 1.25A-1, 1.25A-2, 1.25A-3, 1.25A-4, and 1.25A-5.

(2) Rules on federal financial aid programs.

(c) Academic period.

(d) Qualified tuition and related expenses.

(1) In general.

(2) Required fees.

(i) In general.

(ii) Books, supplies, and equipment.

(iii) Nonacademic fees.

(3) Personal expenses.

(4) Treatment of a comprehensive or bundled fee.

(5) Hobby courses.

(6) Examples.

§ 1.25A-3 Hope Scholarship Credit.

(a) Amount of the credit.

(1) In general.

(2) Maximum credit.

(b) Per student credit.

(1) In general.

(2) Example.

(c) Credit allowed for only two taxable years.

(d) Eligible student.

(1) Eligible student defined.

(i) Degree requirement.

(ii) Work load requirement.

(iii) Year of study requirement.

(iv) No felony drug conviction.

(2) Examples.

(e) Academic period for prepayments.

(1) In general.

(2) Example.

(f) Effective date.

§ 1.25A-4 Lifetime Learning Credit.

(a) Amount of the credit.

(1) Taxable years beginning before January 1, 2003.

(2) Taxable years beginning after December 31, 2002.

(3) Coordination with the Hope Scholarship Credit.

(4) Examples.

(b) Credit allowed for unlimited number of taxable years.

(c) Both degree and nondegree courses are eligible for the credit.

(1) In general.

(2) Examples.

(d) Effective date.

§ 1.25A-5 Special rules relating to characterization and timing of payments.

(a) Educational expenses paid by claimed dependent.

(b) Educational expenses paid by a third party.

(1) In general.

(2) Special rule for tuition reduction included in gross income of employee.

(3) Examples.

(c) Adjustment to qualified tuition and related expenses for certain excludable educational assistance.

(1) In general.

(2) No adjustment for excludable educational assistance attributable to expenses paid in a prior year.

(3) Scholarships and fellowship grants.

(4) Examples.

(d) No double benefit.

(e) Timing rules.

(1) In general.

(2) Prepayment rule.

(i) In general.

(ii) Example.

(3) Expenses paid with loan proceeds.

(4) Expenses paid through third party installment payment plans.

(i) In general.

(ii) Example.

(f) Refund of qualified tuition and related expenses.

(1) Payment and refund of qualified tuition and related expenses in the same taxable year.

(2) Payment of qualified tuition and related expenses in one taxable year and refund in subsequent taxable year before return filed for prior taxable year.

(3) Payment of qualified tuition and related expenses in one taxable year and refund in subsequent taxable year.

(i) In general.

(ii) Recapture amount.

(4) Refund of loan proceeds treated as refund of qualified tuition and related expenses.

(5) Excludable educational assistance received in a subsequent taxable year treated as a refund.

(6) Examples.

[Reg. § 1.25A-0.]

☐ [*T.D.* 9034, 12-24-2002.]

Reg. § 1.25A-0

[Reg. § 1.25A-1]

§ 1.25A-1. Calculation of education tax credit and general eligibility requirements.— (a) *Amount of education tax credit.* An individual taxpayer is allowed a nonrefundable education tax credit against income tax imposed by chapter 1 of the Internal Revenue Code for the taxable year. The amount of the education tax credit is the total of the Hope Scholarship Credit (as described in § 1.25A-3) plus the Lifetime Learning Credit (as described in § 1.25A-4). For limitations on the credits allowed by subpart A of part IV of subchapter A of chapter 1 of the Internal Revenue Code, see section 26.

(b) *Coordination of Hope Scholarship Credit and Lifetime Learning Credit*—(1) *In general.* In the same taxable year, a taxpayer may claim a Hope Scholarship Credit for each eligible student's qualified tuition and related expenses (as defined in § 1.25A-2(d)) and a Lifetime Learning Credit for one or more other students' qualified tuition and related expenses. However, a taxpayer may not claim both a Hope Scholarship Credit and a Lifetime Learning Credit with respect to the same student in the same taxable year.

(2) *Hope Scholarship Credit.* Subject to certain limitations, a Hope Scholarship Credit may be claimed for the qualified tuition and related expenses paid during a taxable year with respect to each eligible student (as defined in § 1.25A-3(d)). Qualified tuition and related expenses paid during a taxable year with respect to one student may not be taken into account in computing the amount of the Hope Scholarship Credit with respect to any other student. In addition, qualified tuition and related expenses paid during a taxable year with respect to any student for whom a Hope Scholarship Credit is claimed may not be taken into account in computing the amount of the Lifetime Learning Credit.

(3) *Lifetime Learning Credit.* Subject to certain limitations, a Lifetime Learning Credit may be claimed for the aggregate amount of qualified tuition and related expenses paid during a taxable year with respect to students for whom no Hope Scholarship Credit is claimed.

(4) *Examples.* The following examples illustrate the rules of this paragraph (b):

Example 1. In 1999, Taxpayer A pays qualified tuition and related expenses for his dependent, B, to attend College Y during 1999. Assuming all other relevant requirements are met, Taxpayer A may claim either a Hope Scholarship Credit or a Lifetime Learning Credit with respect to dependent B, but not both. See § 1.25A-3(a) and § 1.25A-4(a).

Example 2. In 1999, Taxpayer C pays $2,000 in qualified tuition and related expenses for her dependent, D, to attend College Z during 1999. In 1999, Taxpayer C also pays $500 in qualified tuition and related expenses to attend a computer course during 1999 to improve Taxpayer C's job skills. Assuming all other relevant requirements are met, Taxpayer C may claim a Hope Scholarship Credit for the $2,000 of qualified tuition and related expenses attributable to dependent D (see § 1.25A-3(a)) and a Lifetime Learning Credit (see § 1.25A-4(a))for the $500 of qualified tuition and related expenses incurred to improve her job skills.

Example 3. The facts are the same as in *Example 2*, except that Taxpayer C pays $3,000 in qualified tuition and related expenses for her dependent, D, to attend College Z during 1999. Although a Hope Scholarship Credit is available only with respect to the first $2,000 of qualified tuition and related expenses paid with respect to D (see § 1.25A-3(a)), Taxpayer C may not add the $1,000 of excess expenses to her $500 of qualified tuition and related expenses in computing the amount of the Lifetime Learning Credit.

(c) *Limitation based on modified adjusted gross income*—(1) *In general.* The education tax credit that a taxpayer may otherwise claim is phased out ratably for taxpayers with modified adjusted gross income between $40,000 and $50,000 ($80,000 and $100,000 for married individuals who file a joint return). Thus, taxpayers with modified adjusted gross income above $50,000 (or $100,000 for joint filers) may not claim an education tax credit.

(2) *Modified adjusted gross income defined.* The term *modified adjusted gross income* means the adjusted gross income (as defined in section 62) of the taxpayer for the taxable year increased by any amount excluded from gross income under section 911, 931, or 933 (relating to income earned abroad or from certain U.S. possessions or Puerto Rico).

(3) *Inflation adjustment.* For taxable years beginning after 2001, the amounts in paragraph (c)(1) of this section will be increased for inflation occurring after 2000 in accordance with section 1(f)(3). If any amount adjusted under this paragraph (c)(3) is not a multiple of $1,000, the amount will be rounded to the next lowest multiple of $1,000.

(d) *Election.* No education tax credit is allowed unless a taxpayer elects to claim the credit on the taxpayer's federal income tax return for the taxable year in which the credit is claimed. The election is made by attaching Form 8863, "Education

Reg. § 1.25A-1(a)

Credits (Hope and Lifetime Learning Credits),'' to the Federal income tax return.

(e) *Identification requirement.* No education tax credit is allowed unless a taxpayer includes on the federal income tax return claiming the credit the name and the taxpayer identification number of the student for whom the credit is claimed. For rules relating to assessment for an omission of a correct taxpayer identification number, see section 6213(b) and (g)(2)(J).

(f) *Claiming the credit in the case of a dependent*—(1) *In general.* If a student is a claimed dependent of another taxpayer, only that taxpayer may claim the education tax credit for the student's qualified tuition and related expenses. However, if another taxpayer is eligible to, but does not, claim the student as a dependent, only the student may claim the education tax credit for the student's qualified tuition and related expenses.

(2) *Examples.* The following examples illustrate the rules of this paragraph (f):

Example 1. In 1999, Taxpayer A pays qualified tuition and related expenses for his dependent, B, to attend University Y during 1999. Taxpayer A claims B as a dependent on his federal income tax return. Therefore, assuming all other relevant requirements are met, Taxpayer A is allowed an education tax credit on his federal income tax return, and B is not allowed an education tax credit on B's federal income tax return. The result would be the same if B paid the qualified tuition and related expenses. See § 1.25A-5(a).

Example 2. In 1999, Taxpayer C has one dependent, D. In 1999, D pays qualified tuition and related expenses to attend University Z during 1999. Although Taxpayer C is eligible to claim D as a dependent on her federal income tax return, she does not do so. Therefore, assuming all other relevant requirements are met, D is allowed an education tax credit on D's federal income tax return, and Taxpayer C is not allowed an education tax credit on her federal income tax return, with respect to D's education expenses. The result would be the same if C paid the qualified tuition and related expenses on behalf of D. See § 1.25A-5(b).

(g) *Married taxpayers.* If a taxpayer is married (within the meaning of section 7703), no education tax credit is allowed to the taxpayer unless the taxpayer and the taxpayer's spouse file a joint Federal income tax return for the taxable year.

(h) *Nonresident alien taxpayers and dependents.* If a taxpayer or the taxpayer's spouse is a nonresident alien for any portion of the taxable year, no education tax credit is allowed unless the nonresident alien is treated as a resident alien by reason of an election under section 6013(g) or (h). In addition, if a student is a nonresident alien, a taxpayer may not claim an education tax credit with respect to the qualified tuition and related expenses of the student unless the student is a claimed dependent (as defined in § 1.25A-2(a)). [Reg. § 1.25A-1.]

☐ [*T.D.* 9034, 12-24-2002.]

[Reg. § 1.25A-2]

§ 1.25A-2. **Definitions.**—(a) *Claimed dependent.* A *claimed dependent* means a dependent (as defined in section 152) for whom a deduction under section 151 is allowed on a taxpayer's federal income tax return for the taxable year. Among other requirements under section 152, a nonresident alien student must be a resident of a country contiguous to the United States in order to be treated as a dependent.

(b) *Eligible educational institution*—(1) *In general.* In general, an *eligible educational institution* means a college, university, vocational school, or other postsecondary educational institution that is—

(i) Described in section 481 of the Higher Education Act of 1965 (20 U.S.C. 1088) as in effect on August 5, 1997, (generally all accredited public, nonprofit, and proprietary postsecondary institutions); and

(ii) Participating in a federal financial aid program under title IV of the Higher Education Act of 1965 or is certified by the Department of Education as eligible to participate in such a program but chooses not to participate.

(2) *Rules on federal financial aid programs.* For rules governing an educational institution's eligibility to participate in federal financial aid programs, see 20 U.S.C. 1070; 20 U.S.C. 1094; and 34 CFR 600 and 668.

(c) *Academic period. Academic period* means a quarter, semester, trimester, or other period of study as reasonably determined by an eligible educational institution. In the case of an eligible educational institution that uses credit hours or clock hours, and does not have academic terms, each payment period (as defined in 34 CFR 668.4, revised as of July 1, 2002) may be treated as an academic period.

(d) *Qualified tuition and related expenses*—(1) *In general. Qualified tuition and related expenses* means tuition and fees required for the enrollment or attendance of a student for courses of instruction at an eligible educational institution.

(2) *Required fees*—(i) *In general.* Except as provided in paragraph (d)(3) of this section, the test for determining whether any fee is a qualified

Reg. § 1.25A-2(d)(2)

tuition and related expense is whether the fee is required to be paid to the eligible educational institution as a condition of the student's enrollment or attendance at the institution.

(ii) *Books, supplies, and equipment.* Qualified tuition and related expenses include fees for books, supplies, and equipment used in a course of study only if the fees must be paid to the eligible educational institution for the enrollment or attendance of the student at the institution.

(iii) *Nonacademic fees.* Except as provided in paragraph (d)(3) of this section, qualified tuition and related expenses include fees charged by an eligible educational institution that are not used directly for, or allocated to, an academic course of instruction only if the fee must be paid to the eligible educational institution for the enrollment or attendance of the student at the institution.

(3) *Personal expenses.* Qualified tuition and related expenses do not include the costs of room and board, insurance, medical expenses (including student health fees), transportation, and similar personal, living, or family expenses, regardless of whether the fee must be paid to the eligible educational institution for the enrollment or attendance of the student at the institution.

(4) *Treatment of a comprehensive or bundled fee.* If a student is required to pay a fee (such as a comprehensive fee or a bundled fee) to an eligible educational institution that combines charges for qualified tuition and related expenses with charges for personal expenses described in paragraph (d)(3) of this section, the portion of the fee that is allocable to personal expenses is not included in qualified tuition and related expenses. The determination of what portion of the fee relates to qualified tuition and related expenses and what portion relates to personal expenses must be made by the institution using a reasonable method of allocation.

(5) *Hobby courses.* Qualified tuition and related expenses do not include expenses that relate to any course of instruction or other education that involves sports, games, or hobbies, or any noncredit course, unless the course or other education is part of the student's degree program, or in the case of the Lifetime Learning Credit, the student takes the course to acquire or improve job skills.

(6) *Examples.* The following examples illustrate the rules of this paragraph (d). In each example, assume that the institution is an eligible educational institution and that all other relevant requirements to claim an education tax credit are met. The examples are as follows:

Example 1. University V offers a degree program in dentistry. In addition to tuition, all students enrolled in the program are required to pay a fee to University V for the rental of dental equipment. Because the equipment rental fee must be paid to University V for enrollment and attendance, the tuition and the equipment rental fee are qualified tuition and related expenses.

Example 2. First-year students at College W are required to obtain books and other reading materials used in its mandatory first-year curriculum. The books and other reading materials are not required to be purchased from College W and may be borrowed from other students or purchased from off-campus bookstores, as well as from College W's bookstore. College W bills students for any books and materials purchased from College W's bookstore. The fee that College W charges for the first-year books and materials purchased at its bookstore is not a qualified tuition and related expense because the books and materials are not required to be purchased from College W for enrollment or attendance at the institution.

Example 3. All students who attend College X are required to pay a separate student activity fee in addition to their tuition. The student activity fee is used solely to fund on-campus organizations and activities run by students, such as the student newspaper and the student government (no portion of the fee covers personal expenses). Although labeled as a student activity fee, the fee is required for enrollment or attendance at College X. Therefore, the fee is a qualified tuition and related expense.

Example 4. The facts are the same as in *Example 3*, except that College X offers an optional athletic fee that students may pay to receive discounted tickets to sports events. The athletic fee is not required for enrollment or attendance at College X. Therefore, the fee is not a qualified tuition and related expense.

Example 5. College Y requires all students to live on campus. It charges a single comprehensive fee to cover tuition, required fees, and room and board. Based on College Y's reasonable allocation, sixty percent of the comprehensive fee is allocable to tuition and other required fees not allocable to personal expenses, and the remaining forty percent of the comprehensive fee is allocable to charges for room and board and other personal expenses. Therefore, only sixty percent of College Y's comprehensive fee is a qualified tuition and related expense.

Example 6. As a degree student at College Z, Student A is required to take a certain number of courses outside of her chosen major in Economics. To fulfill this requirement, Student A enrolls in a square dancing class offered by the Physical Education Department. Because Student A receives credit toward her degree program for the square dancing class, the tuition for the square dancing class is included in qualified tuition and related expenses.

[Reg. § 1.25A-2.]

□ [*T.D.* 9034, 12-24-2002.]

[Reg. § 1.25A-3]

§ 1.25A-3. Hope Scholarship Credit.—(a) *Amount of the credit*—(1) *In general.* Subject to the phaseout of the education tax credit described in § 1.25A-1(c), the Hope Scholarship Credit amount is the total of—

(i) 100 percent of the first $1,000 of qualified tuition and related expenses paid during the taxable year for education furnished to an eligible student (as defined in paragraph (d) of this section) who is the taxpayer, the taxpayer's spouse, or any claimed dependent during any academic period beginning in the taxable year (or treated as beginning in the taxable year, see § 1.25A-5(e)(2)); plus

(ii) 50 percent of the next $1,000 of such expenses paid with respect to that student.

(2) *Maximum credit.* For taxable years beginning before 2002, the maximum Hope Scholarship Credit allowed for each eligible student is $1,500. For taxable years beginning after 2001, the amounts used in paragraph (a)(1) of this section to determine the maximum credit will be increased for inflation occurring after 2000 in accordance with section 1(f)(3). If any amount adjusted under this paragraph (a)(2) is not a multiple of $100, the amount will be rounded to the next lowest multiple of $100.

(b) *Per student credit*—(1) *In general.* A Hope Scholarship Credit may be claimed for the qualified tuition and related expenses of each eligible student (as defined in paragraph (d) of this section).

(2) *Example.* The following example illustrates the rule of this paragraph (b). In the example, assume that all the requirements to claim an education tax credit are met. The example is as follows:

Example. In 1999, Taxpayer A has two dependents, B and C, both of whom are eligible students. Taxpayer A pays $1,600 in qualified tuition and related expenses for dependent B to attend a community college. Taxpayer A pays $5,000 in qualified tuition and related expenses for dependent C to attend University X. Taxpayer A may claim a Hope Scholarship Credit of $1,300 ($1,000 + (.50 × $600)) for dependent B, and the maximum $1,500 Hope Scholarship

Credit for dependent C, for a total Hope Scholarship Credit of $2,800.

(c) *Credit allowed for only two taxable years.* For each eligible student, the Hope Scholarship Credit may be claimed for no more than two taxable years.

(d) *Eligible student*—(1) *Eligible student defined.* For purposes of the Hope Scholarship Credit, the term *eligible student* means a student who satisfies all of the following requirements—

(i) *Degree requirement.* For at least one academic period that begins during the taxable year, the student enrolls at an eligible educational institution in a program leading toward a postsecondary degree, certificate, or other recognized postsecondary educational credential;

(ii) *Work load requirement.* For at least one academic period that begins during the taxable year, the student enrolls for at least one-half of the normal full-time work load for the course of study the student is pursuing. The standard for what is half of the normal full-time work load is determined by each eligible educational institution. However, the standard for half-time may not be lower than the applicable standard for half-time established by the Department of Education under the Higher Education Act of 1965 and set forth in 34 CFR 674.2(b) (revised as of July 1, 2002) for a half-time undergraduate student;

(iii) *Year of study requirement.* As of the beginning of the taxable year, the student has not completed the first two years of postsecondary education at an eligible educational institution. Whether a student has completed the first two years of postsecondary education at an eligible educational institution as of the beginning of a taxable year is determined based on whether the institution in which the student is enrolled in a degree program (as described in paragraph (d)(1)(i) of this section) awards the student two years of academic credit at that institution for postsecondary course work completed by the student prior to the beginning of the taxable year. Any academic credit awarded by the eligible educational institution solely on the basis of the student's performance on proficiency examinations is disregarded in determining whether the student has completed two years of postsecondary education; and

(iv) *No felony drug conviction.* The student has not been convicted of a federal or state felony offense for possession or distribution of a controlled substance as of the end of the taxable year for which the credit is claimed.

(2) *Examples.* The following examples illustrate the rules of this paragraph (d). In each example, assume that the student has not been

Reg. § 1.25A-3(d)(2)

convicted of a felony drug offense, that the institution is an eligible educational institution unless otherwise stated, that the qualified tuition and related expenses are paid during the same taxable year that the academic period begins, and that a Hope Scholarship Credit has not previously been claimed for the student (see paragraph (c) of this section). The examples are as follows:

Example 1. Student A graduates from high school in June 1998 and is enrolled in an undergraduate degree program at College U for the 1998 Fall semester on a full-time basis. For the 1999 Spring semester, Student A again is enrolled at College U on a full-time basis. For the 1999 Fall semester, Student A is enrolled in less than half the normal full-time course work for her degree program. Because Student A is enrolled in an undergraduate degree program on at least a half-time basis for at least one academic period that begins during 1998 and at least one academic period that begins during 1999, Student A is an eligible student for taxable years 1998 and 1999 (including the 1999 Fall semester when Student A enrolls at College U on less than a half-time basis).

Example 2. Prior to 1998, Student B attended college for several years on a full-time basis. Student B transfers to College V for the 1998 Spring semester. College V awards Student B credit for some (but not all) of the courses he previously completed, and College V classifies Student B as a first-semester sophomore. During both the Spring and Fall semesters of 1998, Student B is enrolled in at least one-half the normal full-time work load for his degree program at College V. Because College V does not classify Student B as having completed the first two years of postsecondary education as of the beginning of 1998, Student B is an eligible student for taxable year 1998.

Example 3. The facts are the same as in *Example 2.* After taking classes on a half-time basis for the 1998 Spring and Fall semesters, Student B is enrolled at College V for the 1999 Spring semester on a full-time basis. College V classifies Student B as a second-semester sophomore for the 1999 Spring semester and as a first-semester junior for the 1999 Fall semester. Because College V does not classify Student B as having completed the first two years of postsecondary education as of the beginning of 1999, Student B is an eligible student for taxable year 1999. Therefore, the qualified expenses and required fees paid for the 1999 Spring semester and the 1999 Fall semester are taken into account in calculating any Hope Scholarship Credit.

Example 4. Prior to 1998, Student was not enrolled at another eligible educational institu-

tion. At the time that Student C enrolls in a degree program at College W for the 1998 Fall semester, Student C takes examinations to demonstrate her proficiency in several subjects. On the basis of Student C's performance on these examinations, College W classifies Student C as a second-semester sophomore as of the beginning of the 1998 Fall semester. Student C is enrolled at College W during the 1998 Fall semester and during the 1999 Spring and Fall semesters on a full-time basis and is classified as a first-semester junior as of the beginning of the 1999 Spring semester. Because Student C was not enrolled in a college or other eligible educational institution prior to 1998 (but rather was awarded three semesters of academic credit solely because of proficiency examinations), Student C is not treated as having completed the first two years of postsecondary education at an eligible educational institution as of the beginning of 1998 or as of the beginning of 1999. Therefore, Student C is an eligible student for both taxable years 1998 and 1999.

Example 5. During the 1998 Fall semester, Student D is a high school student who takes classes on a half-time basis at College X. Student D is not enrolled as part of a degree program at College X because College X does not admit students to a degree program unless the student has a high school diploma or equivalent. Because Student D is not enrolled in a degree program at College X during 1998, Student D is not an eligible student for taxable year 1998.

Example 6. The facts are the same as in *Example 5.* In addition, during the 1999 Spring semester, Student D again attends College X but not as part of a degree program. Student D graduates from high school in June 1999. For the 1999 Fall semester, Student D enrolls in College X as part of a degree program, and College X awards Student D credit for her prior course work at College X. During the 1999 Fall semester, Student D is enrolled in more than one-half the normal full-time work load of courses for her degree program at College X. Because Student D is enrolled in a degree program at College X for the 1999 Fall term on at least a half-time basis, Student D is an eligible student for all of taxable year 1999. Therefore, the qualified tuition and required fees paid for classes taken at College X during both the 1999 Spring semester (during which Student D was not enrolled in a degree program) and the 1999 Fall semester are taken into account in computing any Hope Scholarship Credit.

Example 7. Student E completed two years of undergraduate study at College S. College S is not an eligible educational institution for purposes of the education tax credit. At the end of 1998,

Reg. § 1.25A-3(d)(2)

Student E enrolls in an undergraduate degree program at College Z, an eligible educational institution, for the 1999 Spring semester on a full-time basis. College Z awards Student E two years of academic credit for his previous course work at College S and classifies Student E as a first-semester junior for the 1999 Spring semester. Student E is treated as having completed the first two years of postsecondary education at an eligible educational institution as of the beginning of 1999. Therefore, Student E is not an eligible student for taxable year 1999.

Example 8. Student F received a degree in 1998 from College R. College R is not an eligible educational institution for purposes of the education tax credit. During 1999, Student F is enrolled in a graduate-degree program at College Y, an eligible educational institution, for the 1999 Fall semester on a full-time basis. By admitting Student F to its graduate degree program, College Y treats Student F as having completed the first two years of postsecondary education as of the beginning of 1999. Therefore, Student F is not an eligible student for taxable year 1999.

Example 9. Student G graduates from high school in June 2001. In January 2002, Student G is enrolled in a one-year postsecondary certificate program on a full-time basis to obtain a certificate as a travel agent. Student G completes the program in December 2002 and is awarded a certificate. In January 2003, Student G enrolls in a one-year postsecondary certificate program on a full-time basis to obtain a certificate as a computer programer. Student G meets the degree requirement, the work load requirement, and the year of study requirement for the taxable years 2002 and 2003. Therefore, Student G is an eligible student for both taxable years 2002 and 2003.

(e) *Academic period for prepayments*—(1) *In general.* For purposes of determining whether a student meets the requirements in paragraph (d) of this section for a taxable year, if qualified tuition and related expenses are paid during one taxable year for an academic period that begins during January, February or March of the next taxable year (for taxpayers on a fiscal taxable year, use the first three months of the next taxable year), the academic period is treated as beginning during the taxable year in which the payment is made.

(2) *Example.* The following example illustrates the rule of this paragraph (e). In the example, assume that all the requirements to claim a Hope Scholarship Credit are met. The example is as follows:

Example. Student G graduates from high school in June 1998. After graduation, Student G works full-time for several months to earn money for college. Student G is enrolled on a full-time basis in an undergraduate degree program at University W, an eligible educational institution, for the 1999 Spring semester, which begins in January 1999. Student G pays tuition to University W for the 1999 Spring semester in December 1998. Because the tuition paid by Student G in 1998 relates to an academic period that begins during the first three months of 1999, Student G's eligibility to claim a Hope Scholarship Credit in 1998 is determined as if the 1999 Spring semester began in 1998. Thus, assuming Student G has not been convicted of a felony drug offense as of December 31, 1998, Student G is an eligible student for 1998.

(f) *Effective date.* The Hope Scholarship Credit is applicable for qualified tuition and related expenses paid after December 31, 1997, for education furnished in academic periods beginning after December 31, 1997. [Reg. § 1.25A-3.]

☐ [*T.D.* 9034, 12-24-2002.]

[Reg. § 1.25A-4]

§ 1.25A-4. Lifetime Learning Credit.—(a) *Amount of the credit*—(1) *Taxable years beginning before January 1, 2003.* Subject to the phaseout of the education tax credit described in § 1.25A-1(c), for taxable years beginning before 2003, the Lifetime Learning Credit amount is 20 percent of up to $5,000 of qualified tuition and related expenses paid during the taxable year for education furnished to the taxpayer, the taxpayer's spouse, and any claimed dependent during any academic period beginning in the taxable year (or treated as beginning in the taxable year, see § 1.25A-5(e)(2)).

(2) *Taxable years beginning after December 31, 2002.* Subject to the phaseout of the education tax credit described in § 1.25A-1(c), for taxable years beginning after 2002, the Lifetime Learning Credit amount is 20 percent of up to $10,000 of qualified tuition and related expenses paid during the taxable year for education furnished to the taxpayer, the taxpayer's spouse, and any claimed dependent during any academic period beginning in the taxable year (or treated as beginning in the taxable year, see § 1.25A-5(e)(2)).

(3) *Coordination with the Hope Scholarship Credit.* Expenses paid with respect to a student for whom the Hope Scholarship Credit is claimed are not eligible for the Lifetime Learning Credit.

(4) *Examples.* The following examples illustrate the rules of this paragraph (a). In each example, assume that all the requirements to claim a Lifetime Learning Credit or a Hope Schol-

arship Credit, as applicable, are met. The examples are as follows:

Example 1. In 1999, Taxpayer A pays qualified tuition and related expenses of $3,000 for dependent B to attend an eligible educational institution, and Taxpayer A pays qualified tuition and related expenses of $4,000 for dependent C to attend an eligible educational institution. Taxpayer A does not claim a Hope Scholarship Credit with respect to either B or C. Although Taxpayer A paid $7,000 of qualified tuition and related expenses during the taxable year, Taxpayer A may claim the Lifetime Learning Credit with respect to only $5,000 of such expenses. Therefore, the maximum Lifetime Learning Credit Taxpayer A may claim for 1999 is $1,000 (.20 × $5,000).

Example 2. In 1999, Taxpayer D pays $6,000 of qualified tuition and related expenses for dependent E, and $2,000 of qualified tuition and related expenses for dependent F, to attend eligible educational institutions. Dependent F has already completed the first two years of postsecondary education. For 1999, Taxpayer D claims the maximum $1,500 Hope Scholarship Credit with respect to dependent E. In computing the amount of the Lifetime Learning Credit, Taxpayer D may not include any of the $6,000 of qualified tuition and related expenses paid on behalf of dependent E but may include the $2,000 of qualified tuition and related expenses of dependent F.

(b) *Credit allowed for unlimited number of taxable years.* There is no limit to the number of taxable years that a taxpayer may claim a Lifetime Learning Credit with respect to any student.

(c) *Both degree and nondegree courses are eligible for the credit*—(1) *In general.* For purposes of the Lifetime Learning Credit, amounts paid for a course at an eligible educational institution are qualified tuition and related expenses if the course is either part of a postsecondary degree program or is not part of a postsecondary degree program but is taken by the student to acquire or improve job skills.

(2) *Examples.* The following examples illustrate the rule of this paragraph (c). In each example, assume that all the requirements to claim a Lifetime Learning Credit are met. The examples are as follows:

Example 1. Taxpayer A, a professional photographer, enrolls in an advanced photography course at a local community college. Although the course is not part of a degree program, Taxpayer A enrolls in the course to improve her job skills. The course fee paid by Taxpayer A is a qualified tuition and related expense for purposes of the Lifetime Learning Credit.

Example 2. Taxpayer B, a stockbroker, plans to travel abroad on a "photo-safari" for his next vacation. In preparation for the trip, Taxpayer B enrolls in a noncredit photography class at a local community college. Because Taxpayer B is not taking the photography course as part of a degree program or to acquire or improve his job skills, amounts paid by Taxpayer B for the course are not qualified tuition and related expenses for purposes of the Lifetime Learning Credit.

(d) *Effective date.* The Lifetime Learning Credit is applicable for qualified tuition and related expenses paid after June 30, 1998, for education furnished in academic periods beginning after June 30, 1998. [Reg. § 1.25A-4.]

☐ [*T.D.* 9034, 12-24-2002.]

[Reg. § 1.25A-5]

§ 1.25A-5. Special rules relating to characterization and timing of payments.—(a) *Educational expenses paid by claimed dependent.* For any taxable year for which the student is a claimed dependent of another taxpayer, qualified tuition and related expenses paid by the student are treated as paid by the taxpayer to whom the deduction under section 151 is allowed.

(b) *Educational expenses paid by a third party*—(1) *In general.* Solely for purposes of section 25A, if a third party (someone other than the taxpayer, the taxpayer's spouse if the taxpayer is treated as married within the meaning of section 7703, or a claimed dependent) makes a payment directly to an eligible educational institution to pay for a student's qualified tuition and related expenses, the student is treated as receiving the payment from the third party and, in turn, paying the qualified tuition and related expenses to the institution.

(2) *Special rule for tuition reduction included in gross income of employee.* Solely for purposes of section 25A, if an eligible educational institution provides a reduction in tuition to an employee of the institution (or to the spouse or dependent child of an employee, as described in section 132(h)(2)) and the amount of the tuition reduction is included in the employee's gross income, the employee is treated as receiving payment of an amount equal to the tuition reduction and, in turn, paying such amount to the institution.

(3) *Examples.* The following examples illustrate the rules of this paragraph (b). In each example, assume that all the requirements to claim an education tax credit are met. The examples are as follows:

Example 1. Grandparent D makes a direct payment to an eligible educational institution for Student E's qualified tuition and related expenses. Student E is not a claimed dependent in 1999. For purposes of claiming an education tax credit, Student E is treated as receiving the money from her grandparent and, in turn, paying her qualified tuition and related expenses.

Example 2. Under a court-approved divorce decree, Parent A is required to pay Student C's college tuition. Parent A makes a direct payment to an eligible educational institution for Student C's 1999 tuition. Under paragraph (b)(1) of this section, Student C is treated as receiving the money from Parent A and, in turn, paying the qualified tuition and related expenses. Under the divorce decree, Parent B has custody of Student C for 1999. Parent B properly claims Student C as a dependent on Parent B's 1999 federal income tax return. Under paragraph (a) of this section, expenses paid by Student C are treated as paid by Parent B. Thus, Parent B may claim an education tax credit for the qualified tuition and related expenses paid directly to the institution by Parent A.

Example 3. University A, an eligible educational institution, offers reduced tuition charges to its employees and their dependent children. F is an employee of University A. F's dependent child, G, enrolls in a graduate-level course at University A. Section 117(d) does not apply, because it is limited to tuition reductions provided for education below the graduate level. Therefore, the amount of the tuition reduction received by G is treated as additional compensation from University A to F and is included in F's gross income. For purposes of claiming a Lifetime Learning Credit, F is treated as receiving payment of an amount equal to the tuition reduction from University A and, in turn, paying such amount to University A on behalf of F's child, G.

(c) *Adjustment to qualified tuition and related expenses for certain excludable educational assistance*—(1) *In general.* In determining the amount of an education tax credit, qualified tuition and related expenses for any academic period must be reduced by the amount of any tax-free educational assistance allocable to such period. For this purpose, *tax-free educational assistance* means—

(i) A qualified scholarship that is excludable from income under section 117;

(ii) A veterans' or member of the armed forces' educational assistance allowance under chapter 30, 31, 32, 34 or 35 of title 38, United States Code, or under chapter 1606 of title 10, United States Code;

(iii) Employer-provided educational assistance that is excludable from income under section 127; or

(iv) Any other educational assistance that is excludable from gross income (other than as a gift, bequest, devise, or inheritance within the meaning of section 102(a)).

(2) *No adjustment for excludable educational assistance attributable to expenses paid in a prior year.* A reduction is not required under paragraph (c)(1) of this section if the amount of excludable educational assistance received during the taxable year is treated as a refund of qualified tuition and related expenses paid in a prior taxable year. See paragraph (f)(5) of this section.

(3) *Scholarships and fellowship grants.* For purposes of paragraph (c)(1)(i) of this section, a scholarship or fellowship grant is treated as a qualified scholarship excludable under section 117 except to the extent—

(i) The scholarship or fellowship grant (or any portion thereof) may be applied, by its terms, to expenses other than qualified tuition and related expenses within the meaning of section 117(b)(2) (such as room and board) and the student reports the grant (or the appropriate portion thereof) as income on the student's federal income tax return if the student is required to file a return; or

(ii) The scholarship or fellowship grant (or any portion thereof) must be applied, by its terms, to expenses other than qualified tuition and related expenses within the meaning of section 117(b)(2) (such as room and board) and the student reports the grant (or the appropriate portion thereof) as income on the student's federal income tax return if the student is required to file a return.

(4) *Examples.* The following examples illustrate the rules of this paragraph (c). In each example, assume that all the requirements to claim an education tax credit are met. The examples are as follows:

Example 1. University X charges Student A, who lives on X's campus, $3,000 for tuition and $5,000 for room and board. University X awards Student A a $2,000 scholarship. The terms of the scholarship permit it to be used to pay any of a student's costs of attendance at University X, including tuition, room and board, and other incidental expenses. University X applies the $2,000 scholarship against Student A's $8,000 total bill, and Student A pays the $6,000 balance of her bill from University X with a combination of savings and amounts she earns from a summer job. University X does not require A to pay any additional fees beyond the $3,000 in tuition in order to enroll in or attend classes. Student A does not report any portion of the scholarship as income on her federal income tax return. Since Student A does not report the scholarship as income, the scholarship is treated under paragraph (c)(3) of this section as a qualified scholarship that is excludable under section 117. Therefore, for purposes of calculating an education tax credit, Student A is treated as having paid only $1,000 ($3,000 tuition − $2,000 scholarship) in qualified tuition and related expenses to University X.

Example 2. The facts are the same as in *Example 1,* except that Student A reports the entire scholarship as income on the student's federal income tax return. Since the full amount of the scholarship may be applied to expenses other than qualified expenses (room and board) and Student A reports the scholarship as income, the exception in paragraph (c)(3) of this section applies and the scholarship is not treated as a qualified scholarship excludable under section 117. Therefore, for purposes of calculating an education tax credit, Student A is treated as having paid $3,000 of qualified tuition and related expenses to University X.

Example 3. The facts are the same as in *Example 1,* except that the terms of the scholarship require it to be used to pay tuition. Under paragraph (c)(3) of this section, the scholarship is treated as a qualified scholarship excludable under section 117. Therefore, for purposes of calculating an education tax credit, Student A is treated as having paid only $1,000 ($3,000 tuition − $2,000 scholarship) in qualified tuition and related expenses to University X.

Example 4. The facts are the same as in *Example 1,* except that the terms of the scholarship require it to be used to pay tuition or room and board charged by University X, and the scholarship amount is $6,000. Under the terms of the scholarship, Student A may allocate the scholarship between tuition and room and board in any manner. However, because room and board totals $5,000, that is the maximum amount that can be applied under the terms of the scholarship to expenses other than qualified expenses and at least $1,000 of the scholarship must be applied to tuition. Therefore, the maximum amount of the exception under paragraph (c)(3) of this section is $5,000 and at least $1,000 is treated as a qualified scholarship excludable under section 117 ($6,000 scholarship − $5,000 room and board). If Student A reports $5,000 of the scholarship as income on the student's federal income tax return, then Student A will be treated as having paid $2,000 ($3,000 tuition − $1,000 qualified scholarship excludable under section 117) in qualified tuition and related expenses to University X.

Example 5. The facts are the same as in *Example 1,* except that in addition to the scholarship that University X awards to Student A, University X also provides Student A with an education loan and pays Student A for working in a work/study job in the campus dining hall. The loan is not excludable educational assistance within the meaning of paragraph (c) of this section. In addition, wages paid to a student who is performing services for the payor are neither a qualified scholarship nor otherwise excludable from gross income. Therefore, Student A is not required to reduce her qualified tuition and related expenses by the amounts she receives from the student loan or as wages from her work/study job.

Example 6. In 1999, Student B pays University Y $1,000 in tuition for the 1999 Spring semester. University Y does not require Student B to pay any additional fees beyond the $1,000 in tuition in order to enroll in classes. Student B is an employee of Company Z. At the end of the academic period and during the same taxable year that Student B paid tuition to University Y, Student B provides Company Z with proof that he has satisfactorily completed his courses at University Y. Pursuant to an educational assistance program described in section 127(b), Company Z reimburses Student B for all of the tuition paid to University Y. Because the reimbursement from Company Z is employer-provided educational assistance that is excludable from Student B's gross income under section 127, the reimbursement reduces Student B's qualified tuition and related expenses. Therefore, for purposes of calculating an education tax credit, Student B is treated as having paid no qualified tuition and related expenses to University Y during 1999.

Example 7. The facts are the same as in *Example 6* except that the reimbursement from Company Z is not pursuant to an educational assistance program described in section 127(b), is not otherwise excludable from Student B's gross income, and is taxed as additional compensation to Student B. Because the reimbursement is not excludable educational assistance within the meaning of paragraph (c)(1) of this section, Student B is not required to reduce his qualified tuition and related expenses by the $1,000 reimbursement he received from his employer. Therefore, for purposes of calculating an education tax credit, Student B is treated as paying $1,000 in qualified tuition and related expenses to University Y during 1999.

(d) *No double benefit.* Qualified tuition and related expenses do not include any expense for which a deduction is allowed under section 162, section 222, or any other provision of chapter 1 of the Internal Revenue Code.

(e) *Timing rules*—(1) *In general.* Except as provided in paragraph (e)(2) of this section, an education tax credit is allowed only for payments of qualified tuition and related expenses for an academic period beginning in the same taxable year as the year the payment is made. Except for certain individuals who do not use the cash receipts and disbursements method of accounting, qualified tuition and related expenses are treated as paid in the year in which the expenses are actually paid. See § 1.461-1(a)(1).

(2) *Prepayment rule*—(i) *In general.* If qualified tuition and related expenses are paid during one taxable year for an academic period that begins during the first three months of the taxpayer's next taxable year (i.e., in January, February, or March of the next taxable year for calendar year taxpayers), an education tax credit is allowed with respect to the qualified tuition and related expenses only in the taxable year in which the expenses are paid.

(ii) *Example.* The following example illustrates the rule of this paragraph (e)(2). In the example, assume that all the requirements to claim an education tax credit are met. The example is as follows:

Example. In December 1998, Taxpayer A, a calendar year taxpayer, pays College Z $1,000 in qualified tuition and related expenses to attend classes during the 1999 Spring semester, which begins in January 1999. Taxpayer A may claim an education tax credit only in 1998 for payments made in 1998 for the 1999 Spring semester.

(3) *Expenses paid with loan proceeds.* An education tax credit may be claimed for qualified tuition and related expenses paid with the proceeds of a loan only in the taxable year in which the expenses are paid, and may not be claimed in the taxable year in which the loan is repaid. Loan proceeds disbursed directly to an eligible educational institution will be treated as paid on the date the institution credits the proceeds to the student's account. For example, in the case of any loan issued or guaranteed as part of a federal student loan program under Title IV of the Higher Education Act of 1965, loan proceeds will be treated as paid on the date of disbursement (as defined in 34 CFR 668.164(a), revised as of July 1, 2002) by the eligible educational institution. If a taxpayer does not know the date the institution credits the student's account, the taxpayer must treat the qualified tuition and related expenses as paid on the last date for payment prescribed by the institution.

(4) *Expenses paid through third party installment payment plans*—(i) *In general.* A taxpayer, an eligible educational institution, and a third party installment payment company may enter into an agreement in which the company agrees to collect installment payments of qualified tuition and related expenses from the taxpayer and to remit the installment payments to the institution. If the third party installment payment company is the taxpayer's agent for purposes of paying qualified tuition and related expenses to the eligible educational institution, the taxpayer is treated as paying the qualified expenses on the date the company pays the institution. However, if the third party installment payment company is the eligible educational institution's agent for purposes of collecting payments of qualified tuition and related expenses from the taxpayer, the taxpayer is treated as paying the qualified expenses on the date the taxpayer pays the company.

(ii) *Example.* The following example illustrates the rule of this paragraph (e)(4). The example is as follows:

Example. Student A, Company B, and College C enter into a written agreement in which Student A agrees to pay the tuition required to attend College C in 10 equal monthly installments to Company B. Under the written agreement, Student A is not relieved of her obligation to pay College C until Company B remits the payments to College C. Under the written agreement, Company B agrees to disburse the monthly installment payments to College C within 30 days of receipt. Because Company B acts as Student A's agent for purposes of paying qualified expenses to College C, Student A is treated as paying qualified expenses on the date Company B disburses payments to College C.

(f) *Refund of qualified tuition and related expenses*—(1) *Payment and refund of qualified tuition and related expenses in the same taxable year.* With respect to any student, the amount of qualified tuition and related expenses for a taxable year is calculated by adding all qualified tuition and related expenses paid for the taxable year, and subtracting any refund of such expenses received from the eligible educational institution during the same taxable year (including refunds of loan proceeds described in paragraph (f)(4) of this section).

(2) *Payment of qualified tuition and related expenses in one taxable year and refund in subsequent taxable year before return filed for prior taxable year.* If, in a taxable year, a taxpayer or someone other than the taxpayer receives a refund (including refunds of loan proceeds described in paragraph (f)(4) of this section) of qualified tuition and related expenses paid on behalf of a student in a prior taxable year and the refund is

Reg. § 1.25A-5(f)(2)

received before the taxpayer files a federal income tax return for the prior taxable year, the amount of the qualified tuition and related expenses for the prior taxable year is reduced by the amount of the refund.

(3) *Payment of qualified tuition and related expenses in one taxable year and refund in subsequent taxable year*—(i) *In general.* If, in a taxable year (refund year), a taxpayer or someone other than the taxpayer receives a refund (including refunds of loan proceeds described in paragraph (f)(4) of this section) of qualified tuition and related expenses paid on behalf of a student for which the taxpayer claimed an education tax credit in a prior taxable year, the tax imposed by chapter 1 of the Internal Revenue Code for the refund year is increased by the recapture amount.

(ii) *Recapture amount.* The recapture amount is the difference in tax liability for the prior taxable year (taking into account any redetermination of such tax liability by audit or amended return) that results when the tax liability for the prior year is calculated using the taxpayer's redetermined credit. The redetermined credit is computed by reducing the amount of the qualified tuition and related expenses taken into account in determining any credit claimed in the prior taxable year by the amount of the refund of the qualified tuition and related expenses (redetermined qualified expenses), and computing the allowable credit using the redetermined qualified expenses and the relevant facts and circumstances of the prior taxable year, such as modified adjusted gross income (redetermined credit).

(4) *Refund of loan proceeds treated as refund of qualified tuition and related expenses.* If loan proceeds used to pay qualified tuition and related expenses (as described in paragraph (e)(3) of this section) during a taxable year are refunded by an eligible educational institution to a lender on behalf of the borrower, the refund is treated as a refund of qualified tuition and related expenses for purposes of paragraphs (f)(1), (2), and (3) of this section.

(5) *Excludable educational assistance received in a subsequent taxable year treated as a refund.* If, in a taxable year, a taxpayer or someone other than the taxpayer receives any excludable educational assistance (described in paragraph (c)(1) of this section) for the qualified tuition and related expenses paid on behalf of a student during a prior taxable year (or attributable to enrollment at an eligible educational institution during a prior taxable year), the educational assistance is treated as a refund of qualified tuition and related expenses for purposes of paragraphs (f)(2) and (3) of this section. If the excludable educa-

tional assistance is received before the taxpayer files a Federal income tax return for the prior taxable year, the amount of the qualified tuition and related expenses for the prior taxable year is reduced by the amount of the excludable educational assistance as provided in paragraph (f)(2) of this section. If the excludable educational assistance is received after the taxpayer has filed a federal income tax return for the prior taxable year, any education tax credit claimed for the prior taxable year is subject to recapture as provided in paragraph (f)(3) of this section.

(6) *Examples.* The following examples illustrate the rules of this paragraph (f). In each example, assume that all the requirements to claim an education tax credit are met. The examples are as follows:

Example 1. In January 1998, Student A, a full-time freshman at University X, pays $2,000 for qualified tuition and related expenses for a 16-hour work load for the 1998 Spring semester. Prior to beginning classes, Student A withdraws from 6 course hours. On February 15, 1998, Student A receives a $750 refund from University X. In September 1998, Student A pays University X $1,000 to enroll half-time for the 1998 Fall semester. Prior to beginning classes, Student A withdraws from a 2-hour course, and she receives a $250 refund in October 1998. Student A computes the amount of qualified tuition and related expenses she may claim for 1998 by:

(i) Adding all qualified expenses paid during the taxable year ($2,000 + 1,000 = $3,000);

(ii) Adding all refunds of qualified tuition and related expenses received during the taxable year ($750 + $250 = $1,000); and, then

(iii) Subtracting paragraph (ii) of this *Example* 1 from paragraph (i) of this *Example* 1 ($3,000 − $1,000 = $2,000). Therefore, Student A's qualified tuition and related expenses for 1998 are $2,000.

Example 2. (i) In December 1998, Student B, a senior at College Y, pays $2,000 for qualified tuition and related expenses for a 16-hour work load for the 1999 Spring semester. Prior to beginning classes, Student B withdraws from a 4-hour course. On January 15, 1999, Student B files her 1998 income tax return and claims a $400 Lifetime Learning Credit for the $2,000 qualified expenses paid in 1998, which reduces her tax liability for 1998 by $400. On February 15, 1999, Student B receives a $500 refund from College Y.

(ii) Student B calculates the increase in tax for 1999 by—

(A) Calculating the redetermined qualified expenses for 1998 ($2,000 − $500 = $1,500);

Reg. § 1.25A-5(f)(3)

(B) Calculating the redetermined credit for the redetermined qualified expenses ($1,500 × .20 = $300); and

(C) Calculating the difference in tax liability for 1998 resulting from the redetermined credit. Because Student B's tax liability for 1998 was reduced by the full amount of the $400 education tax credit claimed on her 1998 income tax return, the difference in tax liability can be determined by subtracting the redetermined credit from the credit claimed in 1998 ($400 − $300 = $100).

(iii) Therefore, Student B must increase the tax on her 1999 Federal income tax return by $100.

Example 3. In September 1998, Student C pays College Z $1,200 in qualified tuition and related expenses to attend evening classes during the 1998 Fall semester. Student C is an employee of Company R. On January 15, 1999, Student C files a federal income tax return for 1998 claiming a Lifetime Learning Credit of $240 (.20 × $1,200), which reduces Student C's tax liability for 1998 by $240. Pursuant to an educational assistance program described in section 127(b), Company R reimburses Student C in February 1999 for the $1,200 of qualified tuition and related expenses paid by Student C in 1998. The $240 education tax credit claimed by Student C for 1998 is subject to recapture. Because Student C paid no net qualified tuition and related expenses for 1998, the redetermined credit for 1998 is zero. Student C must increase the amount of Student C's 1999 tax by the recapture amount, which is $240 (the difference in tax liability for 1998 resulting from the redetermined credit for 1998 ($0)). Because the $1,200 reimbursement relates to expenses for which the taxpayer claimed an education tax credit in a prior year, the reimbursement does not reduce the amount of any qualified tuition and related expenses that Student C paid in 1999.

[Reg. § 1.25A-5.]

☐ [*T.D.* 9034, 12-24-2002.]

[Reg. § 1.28-0]

§ 1.28-0. Credit for clinical testing expenses for certain drugs for rare diseases or conditions; table of contents.—In order to facilitate use of § 1.28-1, this section lists the paragraphs, subparagraphs, and subdivisions contained in § 1.28-1.

(a) General rule.

(b) Qualified clinical testing expenses.

(1) In general.

(2) Modification of section 41(b).

(3) Exclusion for amounts funded by another person.

(i) In general.

(ii) Clinical testing in which taxpayer retains no rights.

(iii) Clinical testing in which taxpayer retains substantial rights.

(A) In general.

(B) Drug by drug determination.

(iv) Funding for qualified clinical testing expenses determinable only in subsequent taxable years.

(4) Special rule governing the application of section 41(b) beyond its expiration date.

(c) Clinical testing.

(1) In general.

(2) Definition of "human clinical testing".

(3) Definition of "carried out under" section 505(i).

(d) Definition and special rules.

(1) Definition of "rare disease or condition".

(i) In general.

(ii) Cost of developing and making available the designated drug.

(A) In general.

(B) Exclusion of costs funded by another person.

(C) Computation of cost.

(D) Allocation of common costs. Costs for developing and making available the designated drug for both the disease or condition for which it is designated and one or more other diseases or conditions.

(iii) Recovery from sales.

(iv) Recordkeeping requirements.

(2) Tax liability limitation.

(i) Taxable years beginning after December 31, 1986.

(ii) Taxable years beginning before January 1, 1987 and after December 31, 1983.

(iii) Taxable years beginning before January 1, 1984.

(3) Special limitations on foreign testing.

(i) Clinical testing conducted outside the United States—In general.

(ii) Insufficient testing population in the United States.

(A) In general.

(B) "Insufficient testing population".

(C) "Unrelated to the taxpayer".

Reg. § 1.28-0

(4) Special limitation for certain corporations.

    (i) Corporations to which section 936 applies.

    (ii) Corporations to which section 934(b) applies.

(5) Aggregation of expenditures.

    (i) Controlled group of corporations: organizations under common control.

        (A) In general.

        (B) Definition of controlled group of corporations.

        (C) Definition of organization.

        (D) Determination of common control.

    (ii) Tax accounting periods used.

        (A) In general.

        (B) Special rule where the timing of clinical testing is manipulated.

    (iii) Membership during taxable year in more than one group.

    (iv) Intra-group transactions.

        (A) In general.

        (B) In-house research expenses.

        (C) Contract research expenses.

        (D) Lease payments.

        (E) Payments for supplies.

(6) Allocations.

    (i) Pass-through in the case of an S corporation.

    (ii) Pass-through in the case of an estate or trust.

    (iii) Pass-through in the case of a partnership.

        (A) In general.

        (B) Certain partnership non-business expenditures.

        (C) Apportionment.

    (iv) Year in which taken into account.

    (v) Credit allowed subject to limitation.

(7) Manner of making an election.

[Reg. § 1.28-0.]

□ [*T.D. 8232, 9-30-88.*]

[Reg. § 1.28-1]

§ 1.28-1. Credit for clinical testing expenses for certain drugs for rare diseases or conditions.—(a) *General rule.* Section 28 provides a credit against the tax imposed by chapter 1 of the Internal Revenue Code. The amount of the credit is equal to 50 percent of the qualified clinical testing expenses (as defined in paragraph (b) of this section) for the taxable year. The credit ap-plies to qualified clinical testing expenses paid or incurred by the taxpayer after December 31, 1982, and before January 1, 1991. The credit may not exceed the taxpayer's tax liability for the taxable year (as determined under paragraph (d)(2) of this section).

(b) *Qualified clinical testing expenses*—(1) *In general.* Except as otherwise provided in para-graph (b)(3) of this section, the term "qualified clinical testing expenses" means the amounts which are paid or incurred during the taxable year which would constitute "qualified research expenses" within the meaning of section 41(b) (relating to the credit for increasing research ac-tivities) as modified by section 28(b)(1)(B) and paragraph (b)(2) of this section. For example, amounts paid or incurred for the acquisition of depreciable property used in the conduct of clinical testing (as defined in paragraph (c) of this section) are not qualified clinical testing expenses.

(2) *Modification of section 41(b).* For pur-poses of paragraph (b)(1) of this section, section 41(b) is modified by substituting "clinical test-ing" for "qualified research" each place it appears in paragraph (2) of section 41(b) (relating to in-house research expenses) and paragraph (3) of section 41(b) (relating to contract research ex-penses). In addition, "100 percent" is substituted for "65 percent" in paragraph (3)(A) of section 41(b).

(3) *Exclusion for amounts funded by another person*—(i) *In general.* The term "qualified clinical testing expenses" shall not include any amount which would otherwise constitute quali-fied clinical testing expenses, to the extent such amount is funded by a grant, contract, or other-wise by another person (or any governmental en-tity). The determination of the extent to which an amount is funded shall be made in light of all the facts and circumstances. For a special rule regard-ing funding between commonly controlled busi-nesses, see paragraph (d)(5)(iv) of § 1.28-1.

(ii) *Clinical testing in which taxpayer re-tains no rights.* If a taxpayer conducting clinical testing with respect to the designated drug for another person retains no substantial rights in the clinical testing under the agreement providing for the clinical testing, the taxpayer's clinical testing expenses are treated as fully funded for purposes of section 28(b)(1)(C). Thus, for example, if the taxpayer incurs clinical testing expenses under an agreement that confers on another person the exclusive right to exploit the results of the clinical testing, those expenses do not constitute qualified clinical testing expenses because they are fully funded under this paragraph (b)(3)(ii). Incidental benefits to the taxpayer from the conduct of the clinical testing (for example, increased experience in the field of human clinical testing) do not constitute substantial rights in the clinical testing.

(iii) *Clinical testing in which taxpayer retains substantial rights—(A) In general.* If a taxpayer conducting clinical testing with respect to the designated drug for another person retains substantial rights in the clinical testing under the agreement providing for the clinical testing, the clinical testing expenses are funded to the extent of the payments (and fair market value of any property at the time of transfer) to which the taxpayer becomes entitled by conducting the clinical testing. The taxpayers shall reduce the amount paid or incurred by the taxpayer for the clinical testing expenses that would, but for section 28(b)(1)(C), constitute qualified clinical testing expenses of the taxpayer by the amount of the funding determined under the preceding sentence. Rights retained in the clinical testing are not treated as property for purposes of this paragraph (b)(3)(iii)(A). If the property that is transferred to the taxpayer is to be consumed in the clinical testing (for example, supplies), the taxpayer should exclude the value of that property from both the payments received and the expenses paid or incurred for the clinical testing.

(B) *Drug by drug determination.* The provisions of this paragraph (b)(3) shall be applied separately to each designated drug tested by the taxpayer.

(iv) *Funding for qualified clinical testing expenses determinable only in subsequent taxable years.* If, at the time the taxpayer files its return for a taxable year, it is impossible to determine to what extent some or all of the qualified clinical testing expenses may be funded, the taxpayer shall treat the clinical testing expenses as fully funded for purposes of that return. When the amount of funding for qualified clinical testing expenses is finally determined, the taxpayers should amend the return and any interim returns to reflect the amount of funding for qualified clinical testing expenses.

(4) *Special rule governing the application of section 41(b) beyond its expiration date.* For purposes of section 28 and this section, section 41(b), as amended, and the regulations thereunder shall be deemed to remain in effect after December 31, 1988.

(c) *Clinical testing—(1) In general.* The term "clinical testing" means any human clinical testing which—

(i) Is carried out under an exemption under section 505(i) of the Federal Food, Drug, and Cosmetic Act (21 U.S.C. 355(i)) and the regulations relating thereto (21 CFR Part 312) for the purpose of testing a drug for a rare disease or condition as defined in paragraph (d)(1) of this section,

(ii) Occurs after the date the drug is designated as a drug for a rare disease or condition under section 526 of the Federal Food, Drug, and Cosmetic Act (21 U.S.C. 360bb),

(iii) Occurs before the date on which an application for the designated drug is approved under section 505(b) of the Federal Food, Drug, and Cosmetic Act (21 U.S.C. 355(b)) or, if the drug is a biological product (other than a radioactive biological product intended for human use), before the date on which a license for such drug is issued under section 351 of the Public Health Services Act (42 U.S.C. 262), and

(iv) Is conducted by or on behalf of the taxpayer to whom the designation under section 526 of the Federal Food, Drug, and Cosmetic Act applies.

Human clinical testing shall be taken into account under this paragraph (c)(1) only to the extent that the testing relates to the use of a drug for the rare disease or condition for which the drug was designated under section 526 of the Federal Food, Drug, and Cosmetic Act. For purposes of paragraph (c)(1)(i) of this section the testing under section 505(i) exemption procedures (21 CFR Part 312) of a biological product (other than a radioactive biological product intended for human use) pursuant to 21 CFR 601.21 is deemed to be carried out under an exemption under section 505(i) of the Federal Food, Drug, and Cosmetic Act.

(2) *Definition of "human clinical testing."* Testing is considered to be human clinical testing only to the extent that it uses human subjects to determine the effect of the designated drug on humans and is necessary for the designated drug either to be approved under section 505(b) of the Federal Food, Drug, and Cosmetic Act and the regulations thereunder (21 CFR Part 314), or if the designated drug is a biological product (other than a radioactive biological product intended for human use), to be licensed under section 351 of the Public Health Services Act and the regulations thereunder (21 CFR Part 601). For purposes of this paragraph (c)(2), a human subject is an individual who is a participant in research, either as a recipient of the drug or as a control. A subject may be either a healthy individual or a patient.

(3) *Definition of "carried out under" section 505(i).* Human clinical testing is not carried out under section 505(i) of the Federal Food, Drug, and Cosmetic Act and the regulations thereunder (21 CFR Part 312) unless the primary purpose of the human clinical testing is to ascertain the data

Reg. § 1.28-1(c)(3)

necessary to qualify the designated drug for sale in the United States, and not to ascertain data unrelated or only incidentally related to that needed to qualify the designated drug. Whether or not this primary purpose test is met shall be determined in light of all of the facts and circumstances.

(d) *Definition and special rules*—(1) *Definition of "rare disease or condition"*—*(i) In general.* The term "rare disease or condition" means any disease or condition which—

(A) Afflicts 200,000 or fewer persons in the United States, or

(B) Afflicts more than 200,000 persons in the United States but for which there is no reasonable expectation that the cost of developing and making available in the United States (as defined in section 7701(a)(9)) a drug for such disease or condition will be recovered from sales in the United States (as so defined) of such drug.

Determinations under paragraph (d)(1)(i)(B) of this section with respect to any drug shall be made on the basis of the facts and circumstances as of the date such drug is designated under section 526 of the Federal Food, Drug, and Cosmetic Act. Examples of diseases or conditions which in 1987 afflicted 200,000 or fewer persons in the United States are Duchenne dystrophy, one of the muscular dystrophies; Huntington's disease, and hereditary chorea; myoclonus; Tourette's syndrome; and amyotrophic lateral sclerosis (ALS or Lou Gehrig's disease).

(ii) *Cost of developing and making available the designated drug*—(A) *In general.* Except as otherwise provided in this paragraph (d)(1)(ii), the taxpayer's computation of the cost of developing and making available in the United States the designated drug shall include only the costs that the taxpayer (or any person whose right to make sales of the drug is directly or indirectly derived from the taxpayer, *e.g.,* a licensee or transferee) has incurred or reasonably expects to incur in developing and making available in the United States the designated drug for the disease or condition for which it is designated. For example, if, prior to designation under section 526, the taxpayer incurred costs of $125,000 to test the drug for the rare disease or condition for which it is subsequently designated and incurred $500,000 to test the same drug for other diseases, and if, on the date of designation, the taxpayer expects to incur costs of $1.2 million to test the drug for the rare disease or condition for which it is designated, the taxpayer shall include in its cost computation both the $125,000 incurred prior to designation and the $1.2 million expected to be incurred after designation to test the drug for the

rare disease or condition for which it is designated. The taxpayer shall not include the $500,000 incurred to test the drug for other diseases.

(B) *Exclusion of costs funded by another person.* In computing the cost of developing and making available in the United States the designated drug, the taxpayer shall not include any cost incurred or expected to be incurred by the taxpayer to the extent that the cost is funded or is reasonably expected to be funded (determined under the principles of paragraph (b)(3)) by a grant, contract, or otherwise by another person (or any governmental entity).

(C) *Computation of cost.* The cost computation shall use only reasonable costs incurred after the first indication of an orphan application for the designated drug. Such costs shall include the costs of obtaining data needed, and of meetings to be held, in connection with a request for FDA assistance under section 525 of the Federal Food, Drug, and Cosmetic Act (21 U.S.C. 360aa) or a request for orphan designation under section 526 of that Act; costs of determining patentability of the drug; costs of screening animal and clinical studies; costs associated with preparation of a Notice of Claimed Investigational Exemption for a New Drug (IND) and a New Drug Application (NDA); costs of possible distribution of drug under a "treatment" protocol; costs of development of a dosage form; manufacturing costs; distribution costs; promotion costs; costs to maintain required records and reports; and costs of the taxpayer in acquiring the right to market a drug from the owner of that right prior to designation. The taxpayer shall also include general overhead, depreciation costs and premiums for insurance against liability losses to the extent that the taxpayer can demonstrate that these costs are properly allocable to the designated drug under the established standards of financial accounting and reporting of research and development costs.

(D) *Allocation of common costs. Costs for developing and making available the designated drug for both the disease or condition for which it is designated and one or more other diseases or conditions.* In the case where the costs incurred or expected to be incurred in developing and making available the designated drug for the disease or condition for which it is designated are also incurred or expected to be incurred in developing and making available in the United States the same drug for one or more other diseases or conditions (whether or not they are also designated or expected to be designated), the costs shall be allocated between the cost of developing and making available the designated drug for the

Reg. § 1.28-1(d)(1)

disease or condition for which the drug is designated and the cost of developing and making available the designated drug for the other diseases or conditions. The amount of the common costs to be allocated to the cost of developing and making available the designated drug for the disease or condition for which it is designated is determined by multiplying the common costs by a fraction the numerator of which is the sum of the expected amount of sales in the United States of the designated drug for the disease or condition for which the drug is designated and the denominator of which is the total expected amount of sales in the United States of the designated drug. For example, if prior to designation, the taxpayer incurs (among other costs) costs of $100,000 in testing the designated drug for its toxic effect on animals (without reference to any disease or condition), and if the taxpayer expects to recover $500,000 from sales in the United States of the designated drug for disease X, the disease for which the drug is designated, and further expects to recover another $1.5 million from the sales in the United States of the designated drug for disease Y, the taxpayer must allocate a proportionate amount of the common costs of $100,000 to the cost of developing and making available the designated drug for both disease X and disease Y. Since the ratio of the expected amount of sales in the United States of the designated drug for disease X to the total of both the expected amount of sales in the United States of the designated drug for disease X and the expected amount of sales in the United States of the designated drug for disease Y is $500,000/$2,000,000, 25% of the common costs of $100,000 (*i.e.*, $25,000) is allocated to the cost of developing and making available the designated drug for disease X.

(iii) *Recovery from sales.* In determining whether the taxpayer's cost described in paragraph (d)(1)(ii) of this section will be recovered from sales in the United States of the designated drug for the disease or condition for which the drug is designated, the taxpayer shall include anticipated sales by the taxpayer or any person whose right to make such sales is directly or indirectly derived from the taxpayer (such as a licensee or transferee). The anticipated sales shall be based upon the size of the anticipated patient population for which the designated drug would be useful, including the following factors: the degree of effectiveness and safety of the designated drug, if known; the projected fraction of the anticipated patient population expected to be given the designated drug and to continue to take it; other available agents and other types of therapy; the likelihood that superior agents will become available within a few years; and the number of

years during which the designated drug would be exclusively available, *e.g.*, under a patent.

(iv) *Recordkeeping requirements.* The taxpayer shall keep records sufficient to substantiate the cost and sales estimates made pursuant to this paragraph (d)(1). The records required by this paragraph (d)(1)(iv) shall be retained so long as the contents thereof may become material in the administration of section 28.

(2) *Tax liability limitation*—(i) *Taxable years beginning after December 31, 1986.* The credit allowed by section 28 shall not exceed the excess (if any) of—

(A) the taxpayer's regular tax liability for the taxable year (as defined in section 26(b)), reduced by the sum of the credits allowable under—

(*1*) Section 21 (relating to expenses for household and dependent care services necessary for gainful employment),

(*2*) Section 22 (relating to the elderly and permanently and totally disabled),

(*3*) Section 23 (relating to residential energy),

(*4*) Section 25 (relating to interest on certain home mortgages), and

(*5*) Section 27 (relating to taxes on foreign countries and possessions of the United States), over

(B) The tentative minimum tax for the taxable year (as determined under section 55(b)(1)).

(ii) *Taxable years beginning before January 1, 1987, and after December 31, 1983.* The credit allowed by section 28 shall not exceed the taxpayer's tax liability for the taxable year (as defined in section 26(b) prior to its amendment by the Tax Reform Act of 1986 (Pub. Law 99-514)), reduced by the sum of the credits allowable under—

(A) Section 21 (relating to expenses for household and dependent care services necessary for gainful employment),

(B) Section 22 (relating to the elderly and permanently and totally disabled),

(C) Section 23 (relating to residential energy),

(D) Section 24 (relating to contributions to candidates for public office),

(E) Section 25 (relating to interest on certain home mortgages), and

(F) Section 27 (relating to the taxes on foreign countries and possessions of the United States).

Reg. § 1.28-1(d)(2)

(iii) *Taxable years beginning before January 1, 1984.* The credit allowed by section 28 shall not exceed the amount of the tax imposed by chapter 1 of the Internal Revenue Code for the taxable year, reduced by the sum of the credits allowable under the following sections as designated prior to the enactment of the Tax Reform Act of 1984 (Pub. Law 98-369):

(A) Section 32 (relating to tax withheld at source on nonresident aliens and foreign corporations and on tax-free covenant bonds),

(B) Section 33 (relating to taxes of foreign countries and possessions of the United States),

(C) Section 37 (relating to the retirement income),

(D) Section 38 (relating to investment in certain depreciable property),

(E) Section 40 (relating to expenses of work incentive programs),

(F) Section 41 (relating to contributions to candidates for public office),

(G) Section 44 (relating to purchase of new principal residence),

(H) Section 44A (relating to expenses for household and dependent care services necessary for gainful employment),

(I) Section 44B (relating to employment of certain new employees),

(J) Section 44C (relating to residential energy),

(K) Section 44D (relating to producing fuel from a nonconventional source),

(L) Section 44E (relating to alcohol used as fuel),

(M) Section 44F (relating to increasing research activities), and

(N) Section 44G (relating to employee stock ownership).

The term "tax imposed by chapter 1," as used in this paragraph (d)(2)(iii) does not include any tax treated as not imposed by chapter 1 of the Internal Revenue Code under the last sentence of section 53(a).

(3) *Special limitations on foreign testing*—(i) *Clinical testing conducted outside of the United States*—*In general.* Except as otherwise provided in this paragraph (d)(3), expenses paid or incurred with respect to clinical testing conducted outside the United States (as defined in section 7701(a)(9)) are not eligible for credit under this section. Thus, for example, wages paid an employee clinical investigator for clinical testing conducted in medical facilities in the United States and Mexico generally must be apportioned between the clinical testing conducted within the United States and the clinical testing conducted outside the United States, and only the wages apportioned to the clinical testing conducted within the United States are qualified clinical testing expenses.

(ii) *Insufficient testing population in the United States*—(A) *In general.* If clinical testing is conducted outside of the United States because there is an insufficient testing population in the United States, and if the clinical testing is conducted by a United States person (as defined in section 7701(a)(30)) or is conducted by any other person unrelated to the taxpayer to whom the designation under section 526 of the Federal Food, Drug, and Cosmetic Act applies, then the expenses paid or incurred for clinical testing conducted outside of the United States are eligible for the credit provided by section 28.

(B) *"Insufficient testing population."* The testing population in the United States is insufficient if there are not within the United States the number of available and appropriate human subjects needed to produce reliable data from the clinical investigation.

(C) *"Unrelated to the taxpayer."* For the purpose of determining whether a person is unrelated to the taxpayer to whom the designation under section 526 of the Federal Food, Drug, and Cosmetic Act and the regulations thereunder applies, the rules of section 613A(d)(3) shall apply except that the number "5" in section 613A(d)(3)(A), (B), and (C) shall be deleted and the number "10" inserted in lieu thereof.

(4) *Special limitations for certain corporations*—(i) *Corporations to which section 936 applies.* Expenses paid or incurred for clinical testing conducted either inside or outside the United States by a corporation to which section 936 (relating to Puerto Rico and possessions tax credit) applies are not eligible for the credit under section 28.

(ii) *Corporations to which section 934(b) applies.* For taxable years beginning before January 1, 1987, expenses paid or incurred for clinical testing conducted either inside or outside the United States by a corporation to which section 934(b) (relating to the limitation on reduction in income tax liability incurred to the Virgin Islands), as in effect prior to its amendment by the Tax Reform Act of 1986, applies are not eligible for the credit under section 28. For taxable years beginning after December 31, 1986, see section 1277(c)(1) of the Tax Reform Act of 1986 (100 Stat. 2600) which makes the rule set forth in the preceding sentence inapplicable with respect to corporations created or organized in the Virgin

Reg. § 1.28-1(d)(3)

Islands only if (and so long as) an implementing agreement described in that section is in effect between the United States and the Virgin Islands.

(5) *Aggregation of expenditures*—(i) *Controlled group of corporations; organizations under common control*—(A) *In general.* In determining the amount of the credit allowable with respect to an organization that at the end of its taxable year is a member of a controlled group of corporations or a member of a group of organizations under common control, all members of the group are treated as a single taxpayer and the credit (if any) allowable to the member is determined on the basis of its proportionate share of the qualified clinical testing expenses of the aggregated group.

(B) *Definition of controlled group of corporations.* For purposes of this section, the term "controlled group of corporations" shall have the meaning given to the term by section 41(f)(5).

(C) *Definition of organization.* For purposes of this section, an organization is a sole proprietorship, a partnership, a trust, an estate, or a corporation, that is carrying on a trade or business (within the meaning of section 162). For purposes of this section, any corporation that is a member of a commonly controlled group shall be deemed to be carrying on a trade or business if any other member of that group is carrying on any trade or business.

(D) *Determination of common control.* Whether organizations are under common control shall be determined under the principles set forth in paragraphs (b)—(g) of 26 CFR § 1.52-1.

(ii) *Tax accounting periods used*—(A) *In general.* The credit allowable to a member of a controlled group of corporations or a group of organizations under common control is that member's share of the aggregate credit computed as of the end of such member's taxable year.

(B) *Special rule where the timing of clinical testing is manipulated.* If the timing of clinical testing by members using different tax accounting periods is manipulated to generate a credit in excess of the amount that would be allowable if all members of the group used the same tax accounting period, the district director may require all members of the group to calculate the credit in the current taxable year and all future years by using the "conformed years" method. Each member computing a credit under the "conformed years" method shall compute the credit as if all members of the group had the same taxable year as the computing member.

(iii) *Membership during taxable year in more than one group.* An organization may be a member of only one group for a taxable year. If, without application of this paragraph (d)(5)(iii),

an organization would be a member of more than one group at the end of its taxable year, the organization shall be treated as a member of the group in which it was included for its preceding taxable year. If the organization was not included for its preceding taxable year in any group in which it could be included as of the end of its taxable year, the organization shall designate in its timely filed return the group in which it is being included. If the return for a taxable year is due before May 1, 1985, the organization may designate its group membership through an amended return for that year filed on or before April 30, 1985. If the organization does not so designate, then the district director with audit jurisdiction of the return will determine the group in which the business is to be included.

(iv) *Intro-group transactions.* (A) *In general.* Because all members of a group under common control are treated as a single taxpayer for purposes of determining the credit, transactions between members of the group are generally disregarded.

(B) *In-house research expenses.* If one member of a group conducts clinical testing on behalf of another member, the member conducting the clinical testing shall include in its qualified clinical testing expenses any in-house research expenses for that work and shall not treat any amount received or accrued from the other member as funding the clinical testing. Conversely, the member for whom the clinical testing is conducted shall not treat any part of any amount paid or incurred as a contract research expense. For purposes of determining whether the in-house research for that work is clinical testing, the member performing the clinical testing shall be treated as carrying on any trade or business carried on by the member on whose behalf the clinical testing is performed.

(C) *Contract research expenses.* If a member of a group pays or incurs contract research expenses to a person outside the group in carrying on the member's trade or business, that member shall include those expenses as qualified clinical testing expenses. However, if the expenses are not paid or incurred in carrying on any trade or business of that member, those expenses may be taken into account as contract research expenses by another member of the group provided that the other member—

(1) Reimburses the member paying or incurring the expenses, and

(2) Carries on a trade or business to which the clinical testing relates.

(D) *Lease payments.* Amounts paid or incurred to another member of the group for the

Reg. § 1.28-1(d)(5)

lease of personal property owned by a person outside the group shall be taken into account as in-house research expenses for purposes of section 28 only to the extent of the lesser of—

    (*1*) The amount paid or incurred to the other member, or

    (*2*) The amount of the lease expense paid to a person outside the group.

    The amount paid or incurred to another member of the group for the lease of personal property owned by a member of the group is not taken into account for purposes of section 28.

    (E) *Payment for supplies.* Amounts paid or incurred to another member of the group for supplies shall be taken into account as in-house research expenses for purposes of section 28 only to the extent of the lesser of—

    (*1*) The amount paid or incurred to the other member, or

    (*2*) The amount of the other member's basis in the supplies.

    (6) *Allocations*—(i) *Pass-through in the case of an S corporation.* In the case of an S corporation (as defined in section 1361), the amount of the credit for qualified clinical testing expenses computed for the corporation for any taxable year shall be allocated among the persons who are shareholders of the corporation during the taxable year according to the provisions of section 1366 and section 1377.

    (ii) *Pass-through in the case of an estate or a trust.* In the case of an estate or a trust, the amount of the credit for qualified clinical testing expenses computed for the estate or trust for any taxable year shall be apportioned between the estate or trust and the beneficiaries on the basis of the income of the estate or trust allocable to each.

    (iii) *Pass-through in the case of a partnership*—(A) *In general.* In the case of a partnership, the credit for qualified clinical testing expenses computed for the partnership for any taxable year shall be apportioned among the persons who are partners during the taxable year in accordance with section 704 and the regulations thereunder.

    (B) *Certain partnership non-business expenditures.* A partner's share of an in-house research expense or contract research expense paid or incurred by a partnership other than in carrying on a trade or business of the partnership constitutes a qualified clinical testing expense of the partner if—

    (*1*) The partner is entitled to make independent use of the result of the clinical testing, and

    (*2*) The clinical testing expense paid or incurred in carrying on the clinical testing would have been paid or incurred by the partner in carrying on a trade or business of the partner if the partner had carried on the clinical testing that was in fact carried on by the partnership.

    (C) *Apportionment.* Qualified clinical testing expenses to which paragraph (d)(6)(iii)(B) of this section applies shall be apportioned among the persons who are partners during the taxable year in accordance with section 704 and the regulations thereunder. For purposes of section 28, these expenses shall be treated as paid or incurred directly by the partners rather than by the partnership. Thus, the partnership shall disregard these expenses in computing the credit to be apportioned under paragraph (d)(6)(iii)(A) of this section, and each partner shall aggregate the portion of these expenses allocated to the partner with other qualified clinical testing expenses of the partner in making the computations under section 28.

    (iv) *Year in which taken into account.* An amount apportioned to a person under paragraph (d)(6) of this section shall be taken into account by the person in the taxable year of such person in which or with which the taxable year of the corporation, estate, trust, or partnership (as the case may be) ends.

    (v) *Credit allowed subject to limitation.* Any person to whom any amount has been apportioned under paragraph (d)(6)(i), (ii), or (iii) of this section is allowed, subject to the limitation provided in section 28(d)(2), a credit for that amount.

    (7) *Manner of making an election.* To make an election to have section 28 apply for its taxable year, the taxpayer shall file Form 6765 (Credit for Increasing Research Activities (or for claiming the orphan drugs credit)) containing all the information required by that form. [Reg. § 1.28-1.]

    ☐ [*T.D.* 8232, 9-30-88.]

[Reg. § 1.30-1]

§ 1.30-1. Definition of qualified electric vehicle and recapture of credit for qualified electric vehicle.—(a) *Definition of qualified electric vehicle.* A qualified electric vehicle is a motor vehicle that meets the requirements of section 30(c). Accordingly, a qualified electric vehicle does not include any motor vehicle that has ever been used (for either personal or business use) as a nonelectric vehicle.

    (b) *Recapture of credit for qualified electric vehicle*—(1) *In general*—(i) *Addition to tax.* If a recapture event occurs with respect to a taxpayer's qualified electric vehicle, the taxpayer must add the recapture amount to the amount of tax due in the taxable year in which the recapture event occurs. The recapture amount is not treated as income tax imposed on the taxpayer by chapter 1 of the Internal Revenue Code for purposes of computing the alternative minimum tax or determining the amount of any other allowable credits for the taxable year in which the recapture event occurs.

(ii) *Reduction of carryover.* If a recapture event occurs with respect to a taxpayer's qualified electric vehicle, and if a portion of the section 30 credit for the cost of that vehicle was disallowed under section 30(b)(3)(B) and consequently added to the taxpayer's minimum tax credit pursuant to section 53(d)(1)(B)(iii), the taxpayer must reduce its minimum tax credit carryover by an amount equal to the portion of any minimum tax credit carryover attributable to the disallowed section 30 credit, multiplied by the recapture percentage for the taxable year of recapture. Similarly, the taxpayer must reduce any other credit carryover amounts (such as under section 469) by the portion of the carryover attributable to section 30, multiplied by the recapture percentage.

(2) *Recapture event*—(i) *In general.* A recapture event occurs if, within 3 full years from the date a qualified electric vehicle is placed in service, the vehicle ceases to be a qualified electric vehicle. A vehicle ceases to be a qualified electric vehicle if—

(A) The vehicle is modified so that it is no longer primarily powered by electricity;

(B) The vehicle is used in a manner described in section 50(b); or

(C) The taxpayer receiving the credit under section 30 sells or disposes of the vehicle and knows or has reason to know that the vehicle will be used in a manner described in paragraph (b)(2)(i)(A) or (B) of this section.

(ii) *Exception for disposition.* Except as provided in paragraph (b)(2)(i)(C) of this section, a sale or other disposition (including a disposition by reason of an accident or other casualty) of a qualified electric vehicle is not a recapture event.

(3) *Recapture amount.* The recapture amount is equal to the recapture percentage times the decrease in the credits allowed under section 30 for all prior taxable years that would have resulted solely from reducing to zero the cost taken into account under section 30 with respect to such vehicle, including any credits allowed attributable to section 30 (such as under sections 53 and 469).

(4) *Recapture date.* The recapture date is the actual date of the recapture event unless a recapture event described in paragraph (b)(2)(i)(B) of this section occurs, in which case the recapture date is the first day of the recapture year.

(5) *Recapture percentage.* For purposes of this section, the recapture percentage is—

(i) 100, if the recapture date is within the first full year after the date the vehicle is placed in service;

(ii) 66⅔, if the recapture date is within the second full year after the date the vehicle is placed in service; or

(iii) 33⅓, if the recapture date is within the third full year after the date the vehicle is placed in service.

(6) *Basis adjustment.* As of the first day of the taxable year in which the recapture event occurs, the basis of the qualified electric vehicle is increased by the recapture amount and the carryover reductions taken into account under paragraphs (b)(1)(i) and (ii) of this section, respectively. For a vehicle that is of a character that is subject to an allowance for depreciation, this increase in basis is recoverable over the remaining recovery period for the vehicle beginning as of the first day of the taxable year of recapture.

(7) *Application of section 1245 for sales and other dispositions.* For purposes of section 1245, the amount of the credit allowable under section 30(a) with respect to any qualified electric vehicle that is (or has been) of a character subject to an allowance for depreciation is treated as a deduction allowed for depreciation under section 167. Therefore, upon a sale or other disposition of a depreciable qualified electric vehicle, section 1245 will apply to any gain recognized to the extent the basis of the depreciable vehicle was reduced under section 30(d)(1) net of any basis increase described in paragraph (b)(6) of this section.

(8) *Examples.* The following examples illustrate the provisions of this section:

Example 1. A, a calendar-year taxpayer, purchases and places in service for personal use on January 1, 1995, a qualified electric vehicle costing $25,000. On A's 1995 federal income tax return, A claims a credit of $2,500. On January 2, 1996, A sells the vehicle to an unrelated third party who subsequently converts the vehicle into a non-electric vehicle on October 15, 1996. There is no recapture upon the sale of the vehicle by A provided A did not know or have reason to know that the purchaser intended to convert the vehicle to non-electric use.

Example 2. B, a calendar-year taxpayer, purchases and places in service for personal use on October 11, 1994, a qualified electric vehicle costing $20,000. On B's 1994 federal income tax return, B claims a credit of $2,000, which reduces

Reg. § 1.30-1(b)(8)

B's tax by $2,000. The basis of the vehicle is reduced to $18,000 ($20,000 − $2,000). On March 8, 1996, B sells the vehicle to a tax-exempt entity. Because B knowingly sold the vehicle to a tax-exempt entity described in section 50(b) in the second full year from the date the vehicle was placed in service, B must recapture $1,333 ($2,000 × 66⅔ percent). This recapture amount increases B's tax by $1,333 on B's 1996 federal income tax return and is added to the basis of the vehicle as of January 1, 1996, the beginning of the taxable year in which the recapture event occurred.

Example 3. X, a calendar-year taxpayer, purchases and places in service for business use on January 1, 1994, a qualified electric vehicle costing $30,000. On X's 1994 federal income tax return, X claims a credit of $3,000, which reduces X's tax by $3,000. The basis of the vehicle is reduced to $27,000 ($30,000 − $3,000) prior to any adjustments for depreciation. On March 8, 1995, X converts the qualified electric vehicle into a gasoline-propelled vehicle. Because X modified the vehicle so that it is no longer primarily powered by electricity in the second full year from the date the vehicle was placed in service, X must recapture $2,000 ($3,000 × 66⅔ percent). This recapture amount increases X's tax by $2,000 on X's 1995 federal income tax return. The recapture amount of $2,000 is added to the basis of the vehicle as of January 1, 1995, the beginning of the taxable year of recapture, and to the extent the property remains depreciable, the adjusted basis is recoverable over the remaining recovery period.

Example 4. The facts are the same as in *Example 3.* In 1996, X sells the vehicle for $31,000, recognizing a gain from this sale. Under paragraph (b)(7) of this section, section 1245 will apply to any gain recognized on the sale of a depreciable vehicle to the extent the basis of the vehicle was reduced by the section 30 credit net of any basis increase from recapture of the section 30 credit. Accordingly, the gain from the sale of the vehicle is subject to section 1245 to the extent of the depreciation allowance for the vehicle plus the credit allowed under section 30 ($3,000), less the previous recapture amount ($2,000). Any remaining amount of gain may be subject to other applicable provisions of the Internal Revenue Code.

(c) *Effective date.* This section is effective on October 14, 1994. If the recapture date is before the effective date of this section, a taxpayer may use any reasonable method to recapture the benefit of any credit allowable under section 30(a) consistent with section 30 and its legislative history. For this purpose, the recapture date is defined in paragraph (b)(4) of this section. [Reg. § 1.30-1.]

☐ [*T.D.* 8606, 8-2-95.]

[Reg. § 1.31-1]

§ 1.31-1. Credit for tax withheld on wages.— (a) The tax deducted and withheld at the source upon wages under chapter 24 of the Internal Revenue Code of 1954 (or in the case of amounts withheld in 1954, under subchapter D, chapter 9 of the Internal Revenue Code of 1939) is allowable as a credit against the tax imposed by subtitle A of the Internal Revenue Code of 1954, upon the recipient of the income. If the tax has actually been withheld at the source, credit or refund shall be made to the recipient of the income even though such tax has not been paid over to the Government by the employer. For the purpose of the credit, the recipient of the income is the person subject to tax imposed under subtitle A upon the wages from which the tax was withheld. For instance, if a husband and wife domiciled in a State recognized as a community property State for Federal tax purposes make separate returns, each reporting for income tax purposes one-half of the wages received by the husband, each spouse is entitled to one-half of the credit allowable for the tax withheld at source with respect to such wages.

(b) The tax withheld during any calendar year shall be allowed as a credit against the tax imposed by subtitle A for the taxable year of the recipient of the income which begins in that calendar year. If such recipient has more than one taxable year beginning in that calendar year, the credit shall be allowed against the tax for the last taxable year so beginning. [Reg. § 1.31-1.]

☐ [*T.D.* 6161, 2-3-56.]

[Reg. § 1.31-2]

§ 1.31-2. Credit for "special refunds" of employee social security tax.—(a) *In general.*—(1) In the case of an employee receiving wages from more than one employer during the calendar year, amounts may be deducted and withheld as employee social security tax with respect to more than $3,600 of wages received during the calendar year 1954, and with respect to more than $4,200 of wages received during a calendar year after 1954. For example, employee social security tax may be deducted and withheld on $5,000 of wages received by an employee during a particular calendar year if the employee is paid wages in such year in the amount of $3,000 by one employer and in the amount of $2,000 by another employer. Section 6413(c) (as amended by section 202 of the Social Security Amendments of 1954 (68 Stat. 1089)), permits, under certain conditions, a so-called "special refund" of the amount of employee social security tax deducted and withheld with respect to wages paid to an employee in a calendar year after 1954 in excess of $4,200 ($3,600 for the calendar year 1954) by reason of the employee receiving wages from more than one employer during the calendar year. For provisions relating to the imposition of the employee tax and the limitation on wages, see with respect to the calendar year 1954, sections 1400 and 1426(a)(1) of the Internal Revenue Code of 1939 and, with respect to calendar years after 1954, sections 3101 and 3121(a)(1) of the Internal Revenue Code of 1954, as amended by sections 208(b) and 204(a), respectively, of the Social Security Amendments of 1954 (68 Stat. 1094, 1091).

(2) An employee who is entitled to a special refund of employee tax with respect to wages received during a calendar year and who is also required to file an income tax return for such calendar year (or for his last taxable year beginning in such calendar year) may obtain the bene fits of such special refund only by claiming credit for such special refund in the same manner as if such special refund were an amount deducted and withheld as income tax at the source. For provisions for claiming special refunds for 1955 and subsequent years in the case of employees not required to file income tax returns, see section 6413(c) and the regulations thereunder. For provisions relating to such refunds for 1954, see 26 CFR (1939) § 408.802 (Regulations 128).

(3) The amount of the special refund allowed as a credit shall be considered as an amount deducted and withheld as income tax at the source under chapter 24 of the Internal Revenue Code of 1954, (or, in the case of a special refund for 1954, subchapter D, chapter 9 of the Internal Revenue Code of 1939). If the amount of such special refund when added to amounts deducted and withheld as income tax exceeds the taxes imposed by subtitle A of the Internal Revenue Code of 1954, the amount of the excess constitutes an overpayment of income tax under subtitle A, and interest on such overpayment is allowed to the extent provided under section 6611 upon an overpayment of income tax resulting from a credit for income tax withheld at source. See section 6401(b).

(b) *Federal and State employees and employees of certain foreign corporations.* The provisions of this section shall apply to the amount of a special refund allowable to an employee of a Federal agency or a wholly owned instrumentality of the United States, to the amount of a special refund allowable to an employee of any State or political subdivision thereof (or any instrumentality of any one or more of the foregoing), and to the amount

of a special refund allowable to employees of certain foreign corporations. See, with respect to such special refunds for 1954, section 1401(d)(4) of the Internal Revenue Code of 1939, and with respect to such special refunds for 1955 and subsequent years, section 6413(c)(2) of the Internal Revenue Code of 1954, as amended by section 202 of the Social Security Amendments of 1954. [Reg. § 1.31-2.]

☐ [*T.D.* 6161, 2-3-56.]

[Reg. § 1.32-2]

§ 1.32-2. Earned income credit for taxable years beginning after December 31, 1978.—(a) *Allowance of credit.* For taxable years beginning after December 31, 1978, subject to the limitations of paragraph (b) of this section, an eligible individual (as defined in paragraph (c)(1) of this section) is allowed as a credit against the tax imposed by subtitle A of the Code for the taxable year, an amount equal to 10 percent of the first $5,000 of earned income (as defined in paragraph (c)(2) of this section) for the taxable year. For earlier taxable years beginning before January 1, 1979, see § 1.43-1.

(b) *Limitations*—(1) *Amount of credit.* The amount of the credit allowed by section 43 and paragraph (a) of this section for the taxable year must not exceed the excess, if any, of $500 over 12.5 percent of that amount of the adjusted gross income (or, if greater, the earned income) of the taxpayer for the taxable year which exceeds $6,000. For the meaning of the term "earned income," see paragraph (c)(2) of this section. Adjusted gross income is determined under section 62 and the regulations thereunder. If an individual has adjusted gross income or earned income of $10,000 or more, the individual is not entitled to the credit.

(2) *Married individuals.* No credit is allowed by section 43 and paragraph (a) of this section in the case of an eligible individual who is married (within the meaning of section 143 and the regulations thereunder) unless the individual and spouse file a single return jointly (a joint return) for the taxable year (see section 6013 and the regulations thereunder relating to joint returns of income tax by husband and wife). The requirements of the preceding sentence do not apply to an eligible individual who is not considered as married under section 143(b) and the regulations thereunder (relating to certain married individuals living apart).

(3) *Length of taxable year.* No credit is allowed by section 143 and paragraph (a) of this section in the case of a taxable year covering a period of less than 12 months. However, the rule

of the preceding sentence does not apply to a taxable year closed by reason of the death of the eligible individual.

(c) *Definitions*—(1) *Eligible individual.* For purposes of this section, an eligible individual is an individual who meets the following requirements of this paragraph (c)(1).

(i) For the taxable year the individual must meet any one of the following three requirements set forth, respectively, in (A), (B), and (C) of this subdivision (i).

(A) The individual must be married (within the meaning of section 143 and the regulations thereunder) and be entitled to a deduction under section 151 for a child (within the meaning of section 151(e)(3) and the regulations thereunder). The child must have the same principal place of abode (as defined in § 1.2-2(c)) as the individual and that principal place of abode must be in the United States for the entire taxable year.

(B) The individual must qualify as a surviving spouse (as determined under section 2(a) and the regulations thereunder). Thus, the spouse of the individual must have died within the period of the 2 taxable years immediately preceding the individual's taxable year. Also, the individual must have furnished over half the cost of maintaining as the individual's home a household in the United States for the entire taxable year which is the principal place of abode of a child of the individual who qualifies as a dependent for whom the individual is entitled to a deduction under section 151.

(C) The individual must qualify as a head of household (as determined under section 2(b) and the regulations thereunder but without regard to section 2(b)(1)(A)(ii) and (B) and the regulations thereunder). Thus, the individual cannot be married as of the close of the taxable year and also cannot qualify as a surviving spouse under section 2(a). Also, the individual must have furnished over half the cost of maintaining as the individual's home a household in the United States for the entire taxable year which is the principal place of abode of a child or descendant of the individual who is unmarried or who qualifies as a dependent for whom the individual is entitled to a deduction under section 151.

(ii) For the entire taxable year, the individual must not be entitled to exclude any amount from gross income under section 911 (relating to earned income by individuals in certain camps outside the United States) or section 931 and the regulations thereunder (relating to income from sources within the possessions of the United States).

(iii) The rules of this paragraph (c)(1) are illustrated by the following examples:

Example (1). A, who is married and a member of the United States Armed Forces, maintains his household outside the United States for part of the taxable year. A is not an eligible individual. However, if A maintains his household inside the United States for the entire taxable year and is only temporarily absent therefrom by reason of military service and if the household is his principal place of abode and the principal place of abode of his child who receives over half of his support from the taxpayer for the calendar year in which the taxable year of the taxpayer begins and who either has less than $1,000 of gross income for the calendar year in which the individual's taxable year begins or who has not attained the age of 19 at the close of the calendar year in which the individual's taxable year begins or is a student, then the individual is an eligible individual if he meets the requirements of subdivision (ii) of this paragraph.

Example (2). B's wife died in 1975 and B has not remarried. For his entire taxable year beginning January 1, 1979, B maintains his household inside the United States. The household is, for the entire year, B's principal place of abode and the principal place of abode of B's unmarried grandchild whose natural parents are deceased. Thus B qualifies as a head of household (as determined under section 2(b) without regard to subparagraphs (A)(ii) and (B) of section 2(b)(1)). In these circumstances, regardless of whether B provides sufficient support to claim the grandchild as a dependent, B is an eligible individual if he meets the requirements of subdivision (ii) of this paragraph.

Example (3). C is married and maintains his household inside the United States for the entire taxable year. The household is his principal place of abode and, for the entire year, is also the principal place of abode of a 12 year old child whose natural parents are deceased and who is placed with C by a State agency to provide the child with foster care. C receives compensation from the State agency to cover all of the cost of maintaining the child in his home. The child is in C's care and is cared for as C's own child. In these circumstances, the child is C's foster child, but C is not able to claim the child as a dependent since C did not provide half the child's support for the year. C is not eligible for the earned income credit.

Example (4). Assume the same facts as in example (3) except that C receives no compensation from the State agency, and C provides over half the child's support and is able to claim the child as a dependent. C is an eligible individual if he meets the requirements of subdivision (ii) of this paragraph.

Example (5). D's husband died in 1974 and D has not remarried. For the entire taxable year beginning January 1, 1979, D maintains her household inside the United States. The household is D's principal place of abode and, for the entire taxable year, is also the principal place of abode of D's unmarried son. D cares for her son in all respects except that her parents provide over half the son's support. D qualifies as a head of household (as determined under section 2(b) without regard to subparagraph (A)(ii) and (B) of section 2(b)(1)). D is an eligible individual if D meets the requirements of subdivision (ii) of this paragraph.

Example (6). Assume the same facts as in example (5) except that D is married. Since D cannot qualify as a head of household, and D's son cannot be claimed as D's dependent, D is not an eligible individual.

(2) *Earned income*. For purposes of this section, earned income means—

(i) Wages, salaries, tips, other employee compensation, and

(ii) Net earnings from self-employment (within the meaning of section 1402(a) and the regulations thereunder).

Earned income includes compensation excluded from gross income, such as disability income excluded under section 105(d), the rental value of a parsonage excluded under section 107, and the value of meals and lodging furnished for the convenience of the employer excluded under section 119. Earned income is computed without regard to any community property laws which may otherwise be applicable. Earned income is reduced by any net loss in earnings from self-employment. Earned income does not include amounts received as a pension, an annuity, unemployment compensation, or workmen's compensation, or an amount to which section 871(a) and the regulations thereunder apply (relating to income of nonresident alien individuals not connected with United States business).

(d) *Examples*. The application of this section is illustrated by the following examples. For purposes of these examples, assume that the eligible individual does not receive a pension, an annuity, or an amount to which section 871(a), 911, or 931 applies.

Example (1). A and B (married individuals) maintain a household inside the United States which is their principal place of abode and the principal place of abode of their two children who are 12 and 14 years old. A and B are calendar year taxpayers and, for 1979, they file a joint return. A and B have a total earned income of $7,600 (computed without regard to any community property laws) and have adjusted gross income of less than $7,600. The earned income credit of $300 is determined as follows:

Basic credit (10 percent of $5,000 under paragraph (a) of this Section)		$500
Initial limitation amount	$500	
Less: Reduction under paragraph (b)(1) of this section:		
Earned income for taxable year	$7,600	
Less	$6,000	
Excess over $6,000	$1,600	
12½ percent of excess ($1,600)		$200
Maximum credit (if less than basic credit)		$300

Example (2). Assume the same facts as in example (1) except that A and B have earned income of $4,000 and adjusted gross income of $7,000. The earned income credit of $375 is determined as follows:

Basic credit (10 percent of $4,000 under paragraph (a) of this section)		$400
Initial limitation amount	$500	
Less: Reduction under paragraph (b)(1) of this section:		
Adjusted gross income for taxable year	$7,000	
Less	$6,000	
Excess over $6,000	$1,000	
12½ percent of excess ($1,000)		$125
Maximum credit (if less than basic credit)		$375

(e) *Coordination of credit with advance payments*—(1) *Recapture of excess advance payments*. If any advance payment of earned income credit under section 3507 is made to an individual by an employer during any calendar year, then the total amount of these advance payments to

Reg. § 1.32-2(e)(1)

the individual in that calendar year is treated as an additional amount of tax imposed (by Chapter 1 of the Code) upon the individual on the tax return for the individual's last taxable year beginning in that calendar year.

(2) *Reconciliation of payments advanced and credit allowed.* Any additional amount of tax under paragraph (e)(1) of this section is not treated as a tax imposed by chapter 1 of the Code for purposes of determining the amount of any credit (other than the earned income credit) allowable under subpart A, part IV, subchapter A, chapter 1 of the Code. [Reg. § 1.32-2.]

☐ [*T.D. 7683, 3-12-80. Redesignated by T.D. 8448, 11-20-92.*]

[Reg. § 1.32-3]

§ 1.32-3. Eligibility requirements after denial of the earned income credit.—(a) *In general.* A taxpayer who has been denied the earned income credit (EIC), in whole or in part, as a result of the deficiency procedures under subchapter B of chapter 63 (deficiency procedures) is ineligible to file a return claiming the EIC subsequent to the denial until the taxpayer demonstrates eligibility for the EIC in accordance with paragraph (c) of this section. If a taxpayer demonstrates eligibility for a taxable year in accordance with paragraph (c) of this section, the taxpayer need not comply with those requirements for any subsequent taxable year unless the Service again denies the EIC as a result of the deficiency procedures.

(b) *Denial of the EIC as a result of the deficiency procedures.* For purposes of this section, denial of the EIC as a result of the deficiency procedures occurs when a tax on account of the EIC is assessed as a deficiency (other than as a mathematical or clerical error under section 6213(b)(1)).

(c) *Demonstration of eligibility.* In the case of a taxpayer to whom paragraph (a) of this section applies, and except as otherwise provided by the Commissioner in the instructions for Form 8862, "Information To Claim Earned Income Credit After Disallowance," no claim for the EIC filed subsequent to the denial is allowed unless the taxpayer properly completes Form 8862, demonstrating eligibility for the EIC, and otherwise is eligible for the EIC. If any item of information on Form 8862 is incorrect or inconsistent with any item on the return, the taxpayer will be treated as not demonstrating eligibility for the EIC. The taxpayer must follow the instructions for Form 8862 to determine the income tax return to which Form 8862 must be attached. If the taxpayer attaches Form 8862 to an incorrect tax return, the taxpayer will not be relieved of the requirement that the taxpayer attach Form 8862 to the correct tax return and will, therefore, not be treated as meeting the taxpayer's obligation under paragraph (a) of this section.

(d) *Failure to demonstrate eligibility.* If a taxpayer to whom paragraph (a) of this section applies fails to satisfy the requirements of paragraph (c) of this section with respect to a particular taxable year, the IRS can deny the EIC as a mathematical or clerical error under section 6213(g)(2)(K).

(e) *Special rule where one spouse denied EIC.* The eligibility requirements set forth in this section apply to taxpayers filing a joint return where one spouse was denied the EIC for a taxable year prior to marriage and has not established eligibility as either an unmarried or married taxpayer for a subsequent taxable year.

(f) *Effective date.* This section applies to returns claiming the EIC for taxable years beginning after December 31, 1997, where the EIC was denied for a taxable year beginning after December 31, 1996. [Reg. § 1.32-3.]

☐ [*T.D. 8953, 6-22-2001.*]

→ *Caution: Reg. § 1.37-1, below, was issued under former Code Sec. 37, which has been redesignated as Code Sec. 22.*←

[Reg. § 1.37-1]

§ 1.37-1. General rules for the credit for the elderly.—(a) *In general.* In the case of an individual, section 37 provides a credit against the tax imposed by chapter 1 of the Internal Revenue Code of 1954. This section and § § 1.37-2 and 1.37-3 provide guidance in the computation of the credit for the elderly provided under section 37 for taxable years beginning after 1975. For rules relating to the computation of the retirement income credit provided under section 37 for taxable years beginning before 1976, see 26 CFR 1.37-1 through 1.37-5 (Rev. as of April 1, 1980). Note that section 403 of the Tax Reduction and Simplification Act of 1977 provides that a taxpayer may elect to compute the credit under section 37 for the taxpayer's first taxable year beginning in 1976 in accordance with the rules applicable to taxable years beginning before 1976.

(b) *Limitation on the amount of the credit.* The credit allowed by section 37 for a taxable year shall not exceed the tax imposed by chapter 1 of the Code for the taxable year (reduced, in the case

→ *Caution: Reg. § 1.37-1, below, was issued under former Code Sec. 37, which has been redesignated as Code Sec. 22.*←

of a taxable year beginning before 1979, by the general tax credit allowed by section 42).

(c) *Married couples must file joint returns.* If the taxpayer is married at the close of the taxable year, the credit provided by section 37 shall be allowed only if the taxpayer and the taxpayer's spouse file a joint return for the taxable year. The preceding sentence shall not apply in the case of a husband and wife who are not members of the same household at any time during the taxable year. For the determination of marital status, see section 143 and § 1.143-1.

(d) *Nonresident aliens ineligible.* No credit is allowed under section 37 to any individual for any taxable year during which that individual is at any time a nonresident alien unless the individual is treated, by reason of an election under section 6013(g) or (h), as a resident of the United States for that taxable year. [Reg. § 1.37-1.]

☐ [*T.D.* 6161, 2-3-56. *Amended by T.D.* 6633, 1-14-63; *T.D.* 6791, 1-5-65 *and T.D.* 7743, 12-19-80.]

→ *Caution: Reg. § 1.37-2, below, was issued under former Code Sec. 37, which has been redesignated as Code Sec. 22.*←

[Reg. § 1.37-2]

§ 1.37-2. Credit for individuals age 65 or over.—(a) *In general.* This section illustrates the computation of the credit for the elderly in the case of an individual who has attained the age of 65 before the close of the taxable year. This section shall not apply to an individual for any taxable year for which the individual makes the election described in section 37(e)(2) and paragraph (b) of § 1.37-3.

(b) *Computation of credit.* The credit for the elderly for an individual to whom this section applies equals 15 percent of the individual's "section 37 amount" for the taxable year. An individual's "section 37 amount" for a taxable year is the initial amount determined under section 37(b)(2), reduced as provided in section 37(b)(3) and (c)(1).

(c) *Examples.* The computation of the credit for the elderly for individuals to whom this section applies may be illustrated by the following examples:

Example (1). A, a single individual who is 67 years old, has adjusted gross income of $8,000 for the calendar year 1977. A also receives social security payments of $1,450 during 1977. A does not itemize deductions. A's credit for the elderly is $120, computed as follows:

Initial amount under section 37(b)(2) . . .		$2,500
Reductions required by Section 37(b)(3) and (c)(1):		
Social security payments . . .	$1,450	
One-half the excess of adjusted gross income over $7,500	250	$1,700

Section 37 amount	800
15% of $800	$ 120

A's tax from the tax tables, which reflect the allowance of the general tax credit, is $662. Accordingly, the limitation of section 37(c)(2) and paragraph (b) of § 1.37-1 does not reduce A's credit for the elderly.

Example (2). H and W, who have both attained the age of 65, file a joint return for calendar year 1977. For that year H and W have adjusted gross income of $8,120; H also receives a railroad retirement pension of $1,550, and W receives social security payments of $1,200. H and W do not itemize deductions. The credit for the elderly allowed to H and W for 1977 is $139, computed as follows:

Initial amount under section 37(b)(2) . . .		$3,750
Railroad retirement pension	$1,550	
Social security payments . . .	1,200	2,750
Section 37 amount		1,000
15% of $1,000		150
Limitation based upon amount of tax (derived from tables reflecting allowance of general tax credit)		$ 139

Since the adjusted gross income of H and W is not greater than $10,000, no reduction of the initial amount is required under section 47(c)(1). [Reg. § 1.37-2.]

☐ [*T.D.* 6161, 2-3-56. *Amended by T.D.* 6791, 1-5-65 *and T.D.* 7743, 12-19-80.]

→ *Caution: Reg. § 1.37-3, below, was issued under former Code Sec. 37, which has been redesignated as Code Sec. 22.*←

[Reg. § 1.37-3]

§ 1.37-3. Credit for individuals under age 65 who have public retirement system income.— (a) *In general*. This section provides rules for the computation of the credit for the elderly under section 37(e) in the case of an individual who has not attained the age of 65 before the close of the taxable year and whose gross income for the taxable year includes retirement income within the meaning of paragraph (d)(1)(ii) of this section (*i.e.*, under a public retirement system). If such an individual is married within the meaning of section 143 at the close of the taxable year and the spouse of the individual has attained the age of 65 before the close of the taxable year, this section shall apply to the individual for the taxable year only if both spouses make the election described in paragraph (b) of this section. If both spouses make the election described in paragraph (b) of this section for the taxable year, the credit of each spouse shall be determined under the rules of this section. See paragraph (f)(2) of this section for a limitation on the effects of community property laws in making determinations and computations under section 37(e) and this section.

(b) *Election by certain married taxpayers*. If a married individual under age 65 at the close of the taxable year has retirement income and the spouse of that individual has attained the age of 65 before the close of the taxable year, both spouses may elect to compute the credit provided by section 37 under the rules of section 37(e) and this section. The spouses shall signify the election on the return (or amended return) for the taxable year in the manner prescribed in the instructions accompanying the return. The election may be made at any time before the expiration of the period of limitation for filing claim for credit or refund for the taxable year. The election may be revoked without the consent of the Commissioner at any time before the expiration of that period by filing an amended return.

(c) *Computation of credit*. The credit of an individual under section 37(e) and this section equals 15 percent of the individual's credit base for the taxable year. The credit base of an individual for a taxable year is the lesser of—

(1) The retirement income of the individual for the taxable year, or

(2) The amount determined under section 37(e)(5), as modified by section 37(e)(6) and (7).

(d) *Retirement income*—(1) *General rule*—(i) *For individuals 65 or over*. Section 37(e)(4)(A) enumerates the kinds of income which may be treated as the retirement income of an individual who has attained the age of 65 before the close of the taxable year. They include income from pensions and annuities, interests, rents, dividends, certain bonds received under a qualified bond purchase plan, and certain individual retirement accounts or annuities.

(ii) *For individuals under 65*. In the case of an individual who has not attained the age of 65 before the close of the taxable year, retirement income consists only of income from pensions and annuities (including disability annuity payments) under a public retirement system which arises from services performed by that individual or by a present or former spouse of that individual. The term "public retirement system" means a pension, annuity, or retirement, or similar fund or system established by the United States, a State, a possession of the United States, any political subdivision of any of the foregoing, or the District of Columbia.

(2) *Rents*. For purposes of section 37(e)(4)(A)(iii), income from rents shall be the gross amount received, not reduced by depreciation or other expenses, except that beneficiaries of a trust or estate shall treat as retirement income only their proportionate shares of the taxable rents of the trust or estate. In the case of an amount received for board and lodging, only the portion of the amount received for lodging is income from rents.

(3) *Disability annuity payments received by individual under age 65*. Disability annuity payments received under a public retirement system by an individual under age 65 at the close of the taxable year shall not be treated as retirement income unless the payments are for periods after the date on which the individual reached minimum retirement age, that is, the age at which the individual would be eligible to receive a pension or annuity without regard to disability, and any of the following conditions is satisfied—

(i) The individual is precluded from seeking the benefits of section 105(d) (relating to certain disability payments) for that taxable year by reason of an irrevocable election;

(ii) The individual was not permanently and totally disabled at the time of retirement (and was not permanently and totally disabled either on January 1, 1976, or on January 1, 1977, if the individual retired before the later date on disability or under circumstances which entitled the individual to retire on disability); or

(iii) The payments are for periods after the individual reached mandatory retirement age.

For purposes of this paragraph, disability annuity payments include payments to an individual who retired on partial or temporary disability.

(4) *Compensation for personal services rendered during taxable year.* Retirement income does not include any amount representing compensation for personal services rendered during the taxable year. For this purpose, amounts received as a pension shall not be treated as representing compensation for personal services rendered during the taxable year if the period of service during the taxable year is not substantial when compared with the total years of service. For example, an individual on the calendar year basis retires on November 30 after 5 years of service and receives a pension during the remainder of his taxable year. The pension is not treated as representing compensation for personal services rendered during such taxable year merely because it is paid by reason of the services of the individual for a period of 5 years which includes a portion of the taxable year.

(5) *Amounts not includible in gross income.* Retirement income does not include any amount not includible in the gross income of the individual for the taxable year. For example, if a portion of an annuity is excluded from gross income under section 72, relating to annuities, that portion of the annuity is not retirement income; similarly, the portion of dividend income excluded from gross income under section 116, relating to the partial exclusion of dividends received by individuals is not retirement income.

(e) *Earned income*—(1) *In general.* The term "earned income" in section 37(e)(5)(B) generally has the same meaning as in section 911(b), except that earned income does not include any amount received as a pension or annuity. See section 911(b) and the regulations thereunder. Section 911(b) provides, in general, that earned income includes wages, salaries, professional fees, and other amounts received as compensation for personal services rendered.

(2) *Earned income from self-employment.* For purposes of section 37(e)(5)(B), the earned income of a taxpayer from self-employment in a trade or business shall not exceed—

(i) The taxpayer's share of the net profits from the trade or business if capital is not a material income-producing factor in that trade or business; or

(ii) Thirty percent of the taxpayer's share of the net profits from the trade or business if capital is a material income-producing factor in that trade or business.

For other rules relating to the determination of earned income from self-employment in a trade or business, see section 911(b) and the regulations thereunder.

(3) *Disability annuity payments received by individuals under age 65.* Disability annuity payments received under a public retirement system by an individual under age 65 at the close of the taxable year shall be treated as earned income for purposes of section 37(e)(5)(B) unless the payments are treated as retirement income under paragraph (d)(3) of this section.

(f) *Computation of credit under section 37(e) in the case of joint returns*—(1) *In general.* In the case of a joint return of husband and wife, the credit base of each spouse under section 37(e) is computed separately. The spouses then combine their credit bases and compute a single credit. The limitation in section 37(c)(2) and paragraph (b) of §1.37-1 on the amount of the credit is determined by reference to the joint tax liability of the spouses. Thus, regardless of whether a spouse would be liable for the tax imposed by chapter 1 of the Code if the joint return had not been filed, the credit base of that spouse is taken into account in computing the credit.

(2) *Community property laws.* For taxable years beginning after 1977, married individuals filing joint returns shall disregard community property laws in making any determination or computation required under section 37(e) or this section. Each item of income is attributed in full to the spouse whose income it would have been in the absence of community property laws. Thus, if a 67-year old individual files a joint return with a 62-year old spouse for 1979 and the only income of the couple is from a public pension of the older spouse, that public pension is attributed in full to the older spouse for purposes of section 37(e) even though the applicable community property law may treat one-half of the pension as the income of the 62-year old spouse. Since the younger spouse consequently has no retirement income within the meaning of paragraph (d) of this section, the couple may not make the election described in paragraph (b) of this section.

(g) *Examples.* The computation of the credit for the elderly under section 37(e) and this section is illustrated by the following examples:

Example (1). B, who is 62 years old and single, receives a fully taxable pension of $2,400 from a public retirement system during 1977. B performed the services giving rise to the pension. During that year, B also earns $2,650 from a part-time job. B receives no tax-exempt pension or annuity in 1977. Subject to the limitation of section 37(c)(2) and paragraph (b) of §1.37-1, B's credit for the elderly for 1977 under section 37(e) is $195, computed as follows:

Reg. § 1.37-3(g)

Maximum retirement income level under section 37(e)(5)		$2,500
Earned income offset under section 37(e)(5)(B)(ii):		
Earned income in excess of $1,700	$ 950	
One-half of earned income in excess of $1,200, but not in excess of $1,700 .	250	
		1,200
Amount determined under section 37(e)(5)		1,300
Retirement income		2,400
Credit for the elderly (15 percent of $1,300)		$ 195

Example (2). During 1978 H, who is 67 years old, has earnings of $1,300 and retirement income (rents, interest, etc.) of $6,000. H also receives social security payments totalling $1,400. During 1978 W, who is 63 years old, earns $1,600 and receives a fully taxable pension of $1,400 from a public retirement system that constitutes retirement income. W performed the services giving rise to the pension. H and W file a joint return for 1978 and elect to compute the credit for the elderly under section 37(e). Under the applicable law these items of income are community income, and both spouses share equally in each item. Because H and W are filing a joint return, they disregard community property laws in computing their credit under section 37(e). The couple allocates $1,600 of the $3,750 referred to in section 37(e)(6) to W and $2,150 to H. Subject to the limitation of section 37(c)(2) and paragraph (b) of § 1.37-1, their credit for the elderly is $315, computed as follows:

Credit base of H:		
Amount allocated to H under section 37(e)(6)		$2,150
Reductions required by section 37(e)(5):		
Social security payments	$1,400	
One-half of excess of earnings over $1,200	50	1,450
Amount determined under section 37(e)(5)		$ 700
Retirement income		6,000
Credit base of H		$ 700
Credit base of W:		
Amount allocated to W under section 37(e)(6)		$1,600
Reduction required by section 37(e)(5)(B):		
One-half of excess of earnings over $1,200	$ 200	
Amount determined under section 37(e)(5)		1,400
Retirement income		1,400
Credit base of W		$1,400
Computation of credit		
Credit base of H		$ 700
Credit base of W		1,400
Combined credit base		2,100
Credit for elderly (15 percent of $2,100)		$ 315

Example (3). (a) Assume the same facts as in example (2) of this paragraph, except that H and W live apart at all times during 1978 and file separate returns. Under these circumstances, H and W must give effect to the applicable community property law in determining their credits under section 37(e). Thus, each spouse must take into account one-half of each item of income.

(b) Subject to the limitation of section 37(c)(2) and paragraph (b) of § 1.37-1, H's credit for the elderly is $157.50, computed as follows:

Maximum retirement income level under section 37(e)(7)		$1,875
Reductions required by section 37(e)(5):		
Social security payments	$ 700	
One-half of excess of earnings over $1,200 (taking into account one-half of		
combined earnings of $2,900)	125	825
Amount determined under section 37(e)(5)		$1,050
Retirement income		3,700
Credit of H (15 percent of $1,050)		$ 157.50

Reg. § 1.37-3(g)

(c) Subject to the limitation of section 37(c)(2) and paragraph (b) of § 1.37-1, W's credit for the elderly is computed as follows:

Maximum retirement income level under section 37(e)(7)		$1,875
Reductions required by section 37(e)(5):		
Social security payments	$ 700	
One-half of excess of earnings over $1,200	125	825
Amount determined under section 37(e)(5)		1,050
Retirement income (limited to W's share of public pension)		700
Credit of W (15 percent of $700)		$ 105

[Reg. § 1.37-3.]

☐ [*T.D.* 6161, 2-3-56. *Amended by T.D.* 6722, 4-13-64; *T.D.* 6791, 1-5-65 *and T.D.* 7743, 12-19-80.]

[Reg. § 1.40-1]

§ 1.40-1. Questions and answers relating to the meaning of the term "qualified mixture" in section 40(b)(1).

Q-1. What is a "qualified mixture" within the meaning of section 40(b)(1)?

A-1. A "qualified mixture" is a mixture of alcohol and gasoline or of alcohol and a special fuel which (1) is sold by the taxpayer producing such mixture to any person for use as a fuel, or (2) is used as a fuel by the taxpayer producing such mixture.

Q-2. Must alcohol be present in a product in order for that product to be considered a mixture of alcohol and either gasoline or a special fuel?

A-2. No. A product is considered to be a mixture of alcohol and gasoline or of alcohol and a special fuel if the product is derived from alcohol and either gasoline or a special fuel even if the alcohol is chemically transformed in producing the product so that the alcohol is no longer present as a separate chemical in the final product, provided that there is no significant loss in the energy content of the alcohol. Thus, a product may be considered to be a "mixture of alcohol and gasoline or of alcohol and a special fuel" within the meaning of section 40(b)(1)(B) if such product is produced in a chemical reaction between alcohol and either gasoline or a special fuel. Similarly a product may be considered to be a "mixture of alcohol and gasoline or of alcohol and a special fuel" if such product is produced by blending a chemical compound derived from alcohol with either gasoline or a special fuel.

Thus, for example, a blend of gasoline and ethyl tertiary butyl ether (ETBE), a compound derived from ethanol (a qualified alcohol), in a chemical reaction in which there is no significant loss in the energy content of the ethanol, is considered for purposes of section 40(b)(1)(B) to be a mixture of gasoline and the ethanol used to produce the ETBE, even though the ethanol is chemically transformed in the production of ETBE and is not present in the final product. [Reg. § 1.40-1.]

☐ [*T.D.* 8291, 3-6-90.]

→ *Caution: Code Sec. 41 was originally enacted as Code Sec. 44F and was redesignated first as Code Sec. 30 and later as Code Sec. 41.*←

[Reg. § 1.41-0]

§ 1.41-0. Table of contents.—This section lists the paragraphs contained in §§ 1.41-1 through 1.41-8 as follows:

§ 1.41-1. Credit for increasing research activities.

(a) Amount of credit.

(b) Introduction to regulations under section 41.

§ 1.41-2. Qualified research expenses.

(a) Trade or business requirement.

  (1) In general.

  (2) New business.

  (3) Research performed for others.

    (i) Taxpayer not entitled to results.

    (ii) Taxpayer entitled to results.

  (4) Partnerships.

    (i) In general.

    (ii) Special rule for certain partnerships and joint ventures.

(b) Supplies and personal property used in the conduct of qualified research.

  (1) In general.

  (2) Certain utility charges.

    (i) In general.

    (ii) Extraordinary expenditures.

  (3) Right to use personal property.

  (4) Use of personal property in taxable years beginning after December 31, 1985.

(c) Qualified services.

  (1) Engaging in qualified research.

Reg. § 1.41-0

(2) Direct supervision.

(3) Direct support.

(d) Wages paid for qualified services.

(1) In general.

(2) "Substantially all."

(e) Contract research expenses.

(1) In general.

(2) Performance of qualified research.

(3) "On behalf of."

(4) Prepaid amounts.

(5) Examples.

§ 1.41-3. Base amount for taxable years beginning on or after January 3, 2001.

(a) New taxpayers.

(b) Special rules for short taxable years.

(1) Short credit year.

(2) Short taxable year preceding credit year.

(3) Short taxable year in determining fixed-base percentage.

(c) Definition of gross receipts.

(1) In general.

(2) Amounts excluded.

(3) Foreign corporations.

(d) Consistency requirement.

(1) In general.

(2) Illustrations.

(e) Effective date.

§ 1.41-4. Qualified research for expenditures paid or incurred on or after January 3, 2001.

(a) Qualified research.

(1) General rule.

(2) Requirements of section 41(d)(1).

(3) Undertaken for the purpose of discovering information.

(i) In general.

(ii) Common knowledge.

(iii) Means of discovery.

(iv) Patent safe harbor.

(v) Rebuttable presumption.

(4) Technological in nature.

(5) Process of experimentation.

(6) Substantially all requirement.

(7) Use of computers and information technology.

(8) Illustrations.

(b) Application of requirements for qualified research.

(1) In general.

(2) Shrinking-back rule.

(3) Illustration.

(c) Excluded activities.

(1) In general.

(2) Research after commercial production.

(i) In general.

(ii) Certain additional activities related to the business component.

(iii) Activities related to production process or technique.

(iv) Clinical testing.

(3) Adaptation of existing business components.

(4) Duplication of existing business component.

(5) Surveys, studies, research relating to management functions, etc.

(6) Internal-use computer software.

(i) General rule.

(ii) Requirements.

(iii) Primarily for internal use.

(iv) Software used in the provision of services.

(A) Computer services.

(B) Noncomputer services.

(v) Exception for certain software used in providing noncomputer services.

(vi) High threshold of innovation test.

(vii) Application of high threshold of innovation test.

(viii) Illustrations.

(ix) Effective dates.

(7) Activities outside the United States, Puerto Rico, and other possessions.

(i) In general.

(ii) Apportionment of in-house research expenses.

(iii) Apportionment of contract research expenses.

(8) Research in the social sciences, etc.

(9) Research funded by any grant, contract, or otherwise.

(10) Illustrations.

(d) Documentation.

(e) Effective dates.

§ 1.41-5. Basic research for taxable years beginning after December 31, 1986. [Reserved]

§ 1.41-6. Aggregation of expenditures.

(a) Controlled group of corporations; trades or businesses under common control.

(1) In general.

(2) Definition of trade or business.

(3) Determination of common control.

(4) Examples.

(b) Minimum base period research expenses.

Reg. § 1.41-0

(c) Tax accounting periods used.

(1) In general.

(2) Special rule where timing of research is manipulated.

(d) Membership during taxable year in more than one group.

(e) Intra-group transactions.

(1) In general.

(2) In-house research expenses.

(3) Contract research expenses.

(4) Lease payments.

(5) Payment for supplies.

§ 1.41-7. Special rules.

(a) Allocations.

(1) Corporation making an election under subchapter S.

(i) Pass-through, for taxable years beginning after December 31, 1982, in the case of an S corporation.

(ii) Pass-through, for taxable years beginning before January 1, 1983, in the case of a subchapter S corporation.

(2) Pass-through in the case of an estate or trust.

(3) Pass-through in the case of a partnership.

(i) In general.

(ii) Certain expenditures by joint ventures.

(4) Year in which taken into account.

(5) Credit allowed subject to limitation.

(b) Adjustments for certain acquisitions and dispositions—Meaning of terms.

(c) Special rule for pass-through of credit.

(d) Carryback and carryover of unused credits.

§ 1.41-8. Special rules for taxable years ending on or after January 3, 2001.

(a) Alternative incremental credit.

(b) Election.

(1) In general.

(2) Time and manner of election.

(3) Revocation.

(4) Effective date.

[Reg. § 1.41-0.]

☐ [T.D. 8251, 5-16-89. Amended by T.D. 8930, 12-27-2000.]

[Reg. § 1.41-1]

§ 1.41-1. Credit for increasing research activities.—(a) Amount of credit. The amount of a taxpayer's credit is determined under section 41(a). For taxable years beginning after June 30, 1996, and at the election of the taxpayer, the portion of the credit determined under section 41(a)(1) may be calculated using the alternative incremental credit set forth in section 41(c)(4).

(b) Introduction to regulations under section 41—(1) Sections 1.41-2 through 1.41-8 and 1.41-3A through 1.41-5A address only certain provisions of section 41. The following table identifies the provisions of section 41 that are addressed, and lists each provision with the section of the regulations in which it is covered.

Section of the regulation	Section of the Internal Revenue Code
§ 1.41-2	41(b)
§ 1.41-3	41(c)
§ 1.41-4	41(d)
§ 1.41-5	41(e)
§ 1.41-6	41(f)
§ 1.41-7	41(f) 41(g)
§ 1.41-8	41(c)
§ 1.41-3A	41(c) (taxable years beginning before January 1, 1990)
§ 1.41-4A	41(d) (taxable years beginning before January 1, 1986)
§ 1.41-5A	41(e) (taxable years beginning before January 1, 1987)

(2) Section 1.41-3A also addresses the special rule in section 221(d)(2) of the Economic Recovery Tax Act of 1981 relating to taxable years overlapping the effective dates of section 41. Section 41 was formerly designated as sections 30 and 44F. Sections 1.41-0 through 1.41-8 and 1.41-0A through 1.41-5A refer to these sections as section 41 for conformity purposes. Whether section 41, former section 30, or former section 44F applies to a particular expenditure depends upon when the expenditure was paid or incurred. [Reg. § 1.41-1.]

☐ [*T.D.* 8251, 5-16-89. *Amended by T.D.* 8930, 12-27-2000.]

[Reg. § 1.41-2]

§ 1.41-2. Qualified research expenses.—(a) *Trade or business requirement*—(1) *In general.* An in-house research expense of the taxpayer or a contract research expense of the taxpayer is a qualified research expense only if the expense is paid or incurred by the taxpayer in carrying on a trade or business of the taxpayer. The phrase "in carrying on a trade or business" has the same meaning for purposes of section 41(b)(1) as it has for purposes of section 162; thus, expenses paid or incurred in connection with a trade or business within the meaning of section 174(a) (relating to the deduction for research and experimental expenses) are not necessarily paid or incurred in carrying on a trade or business for purposes of section 41. A research expense must relate to a particular trade or business being carried on by the taxpayer at the time the expense is paid or incurred in order to be a qualified research expense. For purposes of section 41, a contract research expense of the taxpayer is not a qualified research expense if the product or result of the research is intended to be transferred to another in return for license or royalty payments and the taxpayer does not use the product of the research in the taxpayer's trade or business.

(2) *New business.* Expenses paid or incurred prior to commencing a new business (as distinguished from expanding an existing business) may be paid or incurred in connection with a trade or business but are not paid or incurred in carrying on a trade or business. Thus, research expenses paid or incurred by a taxpayer in developing a product the sale of which would constitute a new trade or business for the taxpayer are not paid or incurred in carrying on a trade or business.

(3) *Research performed for others*—(i) *Taxpayer not entitled to results.* If the taxpayer performs research on behalf of another person and retains no substantial rights in the research, that research shall not be taken into account by the taxpayer for purposes of section 41. See § 1.41-4A(d)(2).

(ii) *Taxpayer entitled to results.* If the taxpayer in carrying on a trade or business performs research on behalf of other persons but retains substantial rights in the research, the taxpayer shall take otherwise qualified expenses for that research into account for purposes of section 41 to the extent provided in § 1.41-4A(d)(3).

(4) *Partnerships*—(i) *In general.* An in-house research expense or a contract research expense paid or incurred by a partnership is a qualified research expense of the partnership if the expense is paid or incurred by the partnership in carrying on a trade or business of the partnership, determined at the partnership level without regard to the trade or business of any partner.

(ii) *Special rule for certain partnerships and joint ventures.*—(A) If a partnership or a joint venture (taxable as a partnership) is not carrying on the trade or business to which the research relates, then the general rule in paragraph (a)(4)(i) of this section would not allow any of such expenditures to qualify as qualified research expenses.

(B) Notwithstanding paragraph (a)(4)(ii)(A) of this section, if all the partners or venturers are entitled to make independent use of the results of the research, this paragraph (a)(4)(ii) may allow a portion of such expenditures to be treated as qualified research expenditures by certain partners or venturers.

(C) First, in order to determine the amount of credit that may be claimed by certain partners or venturers, the amount of qualified research expenditures of the partnership or joint venture is determined (assuming for this purpose that the partnership or joint venture is carrying on the trade or business to which the research relates).

(D) Second, this amount is reduced by the proportionate share of such expenses allocable to those partners or venturers who would not be able to claim such expenses as qualified research expenditures if they had paid or incurred such expenses directly. For this purpose such partners' or venturers' proportionate share of such expenses shall be determined on the basis of such partners' or venturers' share of partnership items of income or gain (excluding gain allocated under section 704(c) which results in the largest proportionate share. Where a partner's or venturer's share of partnership items of income or gain (excluding gain allocated under section 704(c)) may vary during the period such partner or venturer is a partner or venturer in such partnership or joint venture, such share shall be the highest share such partner or venturer may receive.

(E) Third, the remaining amount of qualified research expenses is allocated among those partners or venturers who would have been entitled to claim a credit for such expenses if they had paid or incurred the research expenses in their own trade or business, in the relative proportions that such partners or venturers share deductions for expenses under section 174 for the taxable year that such expenses are paid or incurred.

(F) For purposes of section 41, research expenditures to which this paragraph (a)(4)(ii) applies shall be treated as paid or incurred directly by such partners or venturers. See § 1.41-7(a)(3)(ii) for special rules regarding these expenses.

(iii) The following examples illustrate the application of the principles contained in paragraph (a)(4)(ii) of this section.

Example (1). A joint venture (taxable as a partnership) is formed by corporations A, B, and C to develop and market a supercomputer. A and B are in the business of developing computers, and each has a 30 percent distributive share of each item of income, gain, loss, deduction, credit and basis of the joint venture. C, which is an investment banking firm, has a 40 percent distributive share of each item of income, gain, loss, deduction, credit and basis of the joint venture. The joint venture agreement provides that A's, B's and C's distributive shares will not vary during the life of the joint venture, liquidation proceeds are to be distributed in accordance with the partners' capital account balances, and any partner with a deficit in its capital account following the distribution of liquidation proceeds is required to restore the amount of such deficit to the joint venture. Assume in Year 1 that the joint venture incurs $100x of "qualified research expenses." Assume further that the joint venture cannot claim the research credit for such expenses because it is not carrying on the trade or business to which the research relates. In addition A, B, and C are all entitled to make independent use of the results of the research. First, the amount of qualified research expenses of the joint venture is $100x. Second, this amount is reduced by the proportionate share of such expenses allocable to C, the venturer which would not have been able to claim such expenses as qualified research expenditures if it had paid or incurred them directly, C's proportionate share of such expenses is $40x (40% of $100x). The reduced amount is $60x. Third, the remaining $60x of qualified research expenses is allocated between A and B in the relative proportions that A and B share deductions for expenses under section 174. A is entitled to treat $30x ((30% / (30% + 30%)) $60x) as a qualified research expense. B is also entitled to treat $30x ((30% / (30% + 30%)) $60x) as a qualified research expense.

Example (2). Assume the same facts as in example (1) except that the joint venture agreement provides that during the first 2 years of the joint venture, A and B are each allocated 10 percent of each item of income, gain, loss, deduction, credit and basis, and C is allocated 80 percent of each item of income, gain, loss, deduction, credit and basis. Thereafter the allocations are the same as in example (1). Assume for purposes of this example that such allocations have substantial economic effect for purposes of section 704(b). C's highest share of such items during the life of the joint venture is 80 percent. Therefore C's proportionate share of the joint venture's qualified research expenses is $80x (80% of $100x). The reduced amount of qualified research expenses is $20x ($100x − $80x). A is entitled to treat $10x ((10% / (10% + 10%)) $20x) as a qualified research expense in Year 1. B is also entitled to treat $10x ((10% / (10% + 10%)) $20x) as a qualified research expense in Year 1.

(b) *Supplies and personal property used in the conduct of qualified research*—(1) *In general.* Supplies and personal property (except to the extent provided in paragraph (b)(4) of this section) are used in the conduct of qualified research if they are used in the performance of qualified services (as defined in section 41(b)(2)(B), but without regard to the last sentence thereof) by an employee of the taxpayer (or by a person acting in a capacity similar to that of an employee of the taxpayer; see example (6) of § 1.41-2(e)(5)). Expenditures for supplies or for the use of personal property that are indirect research expenditures or general and administrative expenses do not qualify as in-house research expenses.

(2) *Certain utility charges*—(i) *In general.* In general, amounts paid or incurred for utilities such as water, electricity, and natural gas used in the building in which qualified research is performed are treated as expenditures for general and administrative expenses.

(ii) *Extraordinary expenditures.* To the extent the taxpayer can establish that the special character of the qualified research required additional extraordinary expenditures for utilities, the additional expenditures shall be treated as amounts paid or incurred for supplies used in the conduct of qualified research. For example, amounts paid for electricity used for general laboratory lighting are treated as general and admin-

Reg. § 1.41-2(b)(2)

istrative expenses, but amounts paid for electricity used in operating high energy equipment for qualified research (such as laser or nuclear research) may be treated as expenditures for supplies used in the conduct of qualified research to the extent the taxpayer can establish that the special character of the research required an extraordinary additional expenditure for electricity.

(3) *Right to use personal property.* The determination of whether an amount is paid to or incurred for another person for the right to use personal property in the conduct of qualified research shall be made without regard to the characterization of the transaction as a lease under section 168(f)(8) (as that section read before it was repealed by the Tax Reform Act of 1986). See § 5c.168(f)(8)-1(b).

(4) *Use of personal property in taxable years beginning after December 31, 1985.* For taxable years beginning after December 31, 1985, amounts paid or incurred for the use of personal property are not qualified research expenses, except for any amount paid or incurred to another person for the right to use (time-sharing) computers in the conduct of qualified research. The computer must be owned and operated by someone other than the taxpayer, located off the taxpayer's premises, and the taxpayer must not be the primary user of the computer.

(c) *Qualified services*—(1) *Engaging in qualified research.* The term "engaging in qualified research" as used in section 41(b)(2)(B) means the actual conduct of qualified research (as in the case of a scientist conducting laboratory experiments).

(2) *Direct supervision.* The term "direct supervision" as used in section 41(b)(2)(B) means the immediate supervision (first-line management) of qualified research (as in the case of a research scientist who directly supervises laboratory experiments, but who may not actually perform experiments). "Direct supervision" does not include supervision by a higher-level manager to whom first-line managers report, even if that manager is a qualified research scientist.

(3) *Direct support.* The term "direct support" as used in section 41(b)(2)(B) means services in the direct support of either—

(i) Persons engaging in actual conduct of qualified research, or

(ii) Persons who are directly supervising persons engaging in the actual conduct of qualified research. For example, direct support of research includes the services of a secretary for typing reports describing laboratory results derived from qualified research, of a laboratory worker for cleaning equipment used in qualified research, of a clerk for compiling research data, and of a machinist for machining a part of an experimental model used in qualified research. Direct support of research activities does not include general administrative services, or other services only indirectly of benefit to research activities. For example, services of payroll personnel in preparing salary checks of laboratory scientists, of an accountant for accounting for research expenses, of a janitor for general cleaning of a research laboratory, or of officers engaged in supervising financial or personnel matters do not qualify as direct support of research. This is true whether general administrative personnel are part of the research department or in a separate department. Direct support does not include supervision. Supervisory services constitute "qualified services" only to the extent provided in paragraph (c)(2) of this section.

(d) *Wages paid for qualified services*—(1) *In general.* Wages paid to or incurred for an employee constitute in-house research expenses only to the extent the wages were paid or incurred for qualified services performed by the employee. If an employee has performed both qualified services and nonqualified services, only the amount of wages allocated to the performance of qualified services constitutes an in-house research expense. In the absence of another method of allocation that the taxpayer can demonstrate to be more appropriate, the amount of in-house research expense shall be determined by multiplying the total amount of wages paid to or incurred for the employee during the taxable year by the ratio of the total time actually spent by the employee in the performance of qualified services for the taxpayer to the total time spent by the employee in the performance of all services for the taxpayer during the taxable year.

(2) *"Substantially all."* Notwithstanding paragraph (d)(1) of this section, if substantially all of the services performed by an employee for the taxpayer during the taxable year consist of services meeting the requirements of section 41(b)(2)(B)(i) or (ii), then the term "qualified services" means all of the services performed by the employee for the taxpayer during the taxable year. Services meeting the requirements of section 41(b)(2)(B)(i) or (ii) constitute substantially all of the services performed by the employee during a taxable year only if the wages allocated (on the basis used for purposes of paragraph (d)(1) of this section) to services meeting the requirements of section 41(b)(2)(B)(i) or (ii) constitute at least 80 percent of the wages paid to or incurred by the

Reg. § 1.41-2(b)(3)

taxpayer for the employee during the taxable year.

(e) *Contract research expenses*—(1) *In general.* A contract research expense is 65 percent of any expense paid or incurred in carrying on a trade or business to any person other than an employee of the taxpayer for the performance on behalf of the taxpayer of—

　　(i) Qualified research as defined in § 1.41-4 or 1.41-4A, whichever is applicable, or

　　(ii) Services which, if performed by employees of the taxpayer, would constitute qualified services within the meaning of section 41(b)(2)(B).

Where the contract calls for services other than services described in this paragraph (e)(1), only 65 percent of the portion of the amount paid or incurred that is attributable to the services described in this paragraph (e)(1) is a contract research expense.

(2) *Performance of qualified research.* An expense is paid or incurred for the performance of qualified research only to the extent that it is paid or incurred pursuant to an agreement that—

　　(i) Is entered into prior to the performance of the qualified research,

　　(ii) Provides that research be performed on behalf of the taxpayer, and

　　(iii) Requires the taxpayer to bear the expense even if the research is not successful.

If an expense is paid or incurred pursuant to an agreement under which payment is contingent on the success of the research, then the expense is considered paid for the product or result rather than the performance of the research, and the payment is not a contract research expense. The previous sentence applies only to that portion of a payment which is contingent on the success of the research.

(3) *"On behalf of."* Qualified research is performed on behalf of the taxpayer if the taxpayer has a right to the research results. Qualified research can be performed on behalf of the taxpayer notwithstanding the fact that the taxpayer does not have exclusive rights to the results.

(4) *Prepaid amounts.* Notwithstanding paragraph (e)(1) of this section, if any contract research expense paid or incurred during any taxable year is attributable to qualified research

to be conducted after the close of such taxable year, the expense so attributable shall be treated for purposes of section 41(b)(1)(B) as paid or incurred during the period during which the qualified research is conducted.

(5) *Examples.* The following examples illustrate provisions contained in paragraphs (e)(1) through (4) of this section.

Example (1). A, a cash-method taxpayer using the calendar year as the taxable year, enters into a contract with B Corporation under which B is to perform qualified research on behalf of A. The contract requires A to pay B $300x, regardless of the success of the research. In 1982, B performs all of the research, and A makes full payment of $300x under the contract. Accordingly, during the taxable year 1982, $195x (65 percent of the payment of $300x) constitutes a contract research expense of A.

Example (2). The facts are the same as in example (1), except that B performs 50 percent of the research in 1983. Of the $195x of contract research expense paid in 1982, paragraph (e)(4) of this section provides that $97.5x (50 percent of $195x) is a contract research expense for 1982 and the remaining $97.5x is contract research expense for 1983.

Example (3). The facts are the same as in example (1), except that instead of calling for a flat payment of $300x, the contract requires A to reimburse B for all expenses plus pay B $100x. B incurs expenses attributable to the research as follows:

Labor	$ 90x
Supplies	20x
Depreciation on equipment	50x
Overhead	40x
Total	$200x

Under this agreement A pays B $300x during 1982. Accordingly, during taxable year 1982, $195x (65 percent of $300x) of the payment constitutes a contract research expense of A.

Example (4). The facts are the same as in example (3), except that A agrees to reimburse B for all expenses and agrees to pay B an additional amount of $100x, but the additional $100x is payable only if the research is successful. The research is successful and A pays B $300x during 1982. Paragraph (e)(2) of this section provides that the contingent portion of the payment is not

Reg. § 1.41-2(e)(5)

..n expense incurred for the performance of qualified research. Thus, for taxable year 1982, $130x (65 percent of the payment of $200x) constitutes a contract research expense of A.

Example (5). C conducts in-house qualified research in carrying on a trade or business. In addition, C pays D Corporation, a provider of computer services, $100x to develop software to be used in analyzing the results C derives from its research. Because the software services, if performed by an employee of C, would constitute qualified services, $65x of the $100x constitutes a contract research expense of C.

Example (6). C conducts in-house qualified research in carrying on C's trade or business. In addition, C contracts with E Corporation, a provider of temporary secretarial services, for the services of a secretary for a week. The secretary spends the entire week typing reports describing laboratory results derived from C's qualified research. C pays E $400 for the secretarial service, none of which constitutes wages within the meaning of section 41(b)(2)(D). These services, if performed by employees of C, would constitute qualified services within the meaning of section 41(b)(2)(B). Thus, pursuant to paragraph (e)(1) of this section, $260 (65 percent of $400) constitutes a contract research expense of C.

Example (7). C conducts in-house qualified research in carrying on C's trade or business. In addition, C pays F, an outside accountant, $100x to keep C's books and records pertaining to the research project. The activity carried on by the accountant does not constitute qualified research as defined in section 41(d). The services performed by the accountant, if performed by an employee of C, would not constitute qualified services (as defined in section 41(b)(2)(B)). Thus, under paragraph (e)(1) of this section, no portion of the $100x constitutes a contract research expense. [Reg. § 1.41-2.]

☐ [*T.D. 8251, 5-16-89. Amended by T.D. 8930, 12-27-2000.*]

[Reg. § 1.41-3]

§ 1.41-3. Base amount for taxable years beginning on or after January 3, 2001.—(a) *New taxpayers.* If, with respect to any credit year, the taxpayer has not been in existence for any previous taxable year, the average annual gross receipts of the taxpayer for the four taxable years preceding the credit year shall be zero. If, with respect to any credit year, the taxpayer has been in existence for at least one previous taxable year, but has not been in existence for four taxable years preceding the taxable year, then the average annual gross receipts of the taxpayer for the

four taxable years preceding the credit year shall be the average annual gross receipts for the number of taxable years preceding the credit year for which the taxpayer has been in existence.

(b) *Special rules for short taxable years*—(1) *Short credit year.* If a credit year is a short taxable year, then the base amount determined under section 41(c)(1) (but not section 41(c)(2)) shall be modified by multiplying that amount by the number of months in the short taxable year and dividing the result by 12.

(2) *Short taxable year preceding credit year.* If one or more of the four taxable years preceding the credit year is a short taxable year, then the gross receipts for such year are deemed to be equal to the gross receipts actually derived in that year multiplied by 12 and divided by the number of months in that year.

(3) *Short taxable year in determining fixed-base percentage.* No adjustment shall be made on account of a short taxable year to the computation of a taxpayer's fixed-base percentage.

(c) *Definition of gross receipts*—(1) *In general.* For purposes of section 41, gross receipts means the total amount, as determined under the taxpayer's method of accounting, derived by the taxpayer from all its activities and from all sources (*e.g.*, revenues derived from the sale of inventory before reduction for cost of goods sold).

(2) *Amounts excluded.* For purposes of this paragraph (c), gross receipts do not include amounts representing—

(i) Returns or allowances;

(ii) Receipts from the sale or exchange of capital assets, as defined in section 1221;

(iii) Repayments of loans or similar instruments (e.g., a repayment of the principal amount of a loan held by a commercial lender);

(iv) Receipts from a sale or exchange not in the ordinary course of business, such as the sale of an entire trade or business or the sale of property used in a trade or business as defined under section 1221(2);

(v) Amounts received with respect to sales tax or other similar state and local taxes if, under the applicable state or local law, the tax is legally imposed on the purchaser of the good or service, and the taxpayer merely collects and remits the tax to the taxing authority; and

(vi) Amounts received by a taxpayer in a taxable year that precedes the first taxable year in which the taxpayer derives more than $25,000 in gross receipts other than investment income. For purposes of this paragraph (c)(2)(vi), investment income is interest or distributions with respect to stock (other than the stock of a

20-percent owned corporation as defined in section 243(c)(2).

(3) *Foreign corporations.* For purposes of section 41, in the case of a foreign corporation, gross receipts include only gross receipts that are effectively connected with the conduct of a trade or business within the United States, the Commonwealth of Puerto Rico, or other possessions of the United States. See section 864(c) and applicable regulations thereunder for the definition of effectively connected income.

(d) *Consistency requirement*—(1) *In general.* In computing the credit for increasing research activities for taxable years beginning after December 31, 1989, qualified research expenses and gross receipts taken into account in computing a taxpayer's fixed-base percentage and a taxpayer's base amount must be determined on a basis consistent with the definition of qualified research expenses and gross receipts for the credit year, without regard to the law in effect for the taxable years taken into account in computing the fixed-base percentage or the base amount. This consistency requirement applies even if the period for filing a claim for credit or refund has expired for any taxable year taken into account in computing the fixed-base percentage or the base amount.

(2) *Illustrations.* The following examples illustrate the application of the consistency rule of paragraph (d)(1) of this section:

Example 1. (i) X, an accrual method taxpayer using the calendar year as its taxable year, incurs qualified research expenses in 2001. X wants to compute its research credit under section 41 for the tax year ending December 31, 2001. As part of the computation, X must determine its fixed-base percentage, which depends in part on X's qualified research expenses incurred during the fixed-base period, the taxable years beginning after December 31, 1983, and before January 1, 1989.

(ii) During the fixed-base period, X reported the following amounts as qualified research expenses on its Form 6765:

1984	$100x
1985	120x
1986	150x
1987	180x
1988	170x
Total	$720x

(iii) For the taxable years ending December 31, 1984, and December 31, 1985, X based the amounts reported as qualified research expenses on the definition of qualified research in effect for those taxable years. The definition of qualified research changed for taxable years beginning after December 31, 1985. If X used the definition of

qualified research applicable to its taxable y ending December 31, 2001, the credit year, qualified research expenses for the taxable year ending December 31, 1984, and December 31, 1985, would be reduced to $80x and $100x, respectively. Under the consistency rule in section 41(c)(5) and paragraph (d)(1) of this section, to compute the research credit for the tax year ending December 31, 2001, X must reduce its qualified research expenses for 1984 and 1985 to reflect the change in the definition of qualified research for taxable years beginning after December 31, 1985. Thus, X's total qualified research expenses for the fixed-base period (1984-1988) to be used in computing the fixed-base percentage is $80 + 100 + 150 + 180 + 170 = $680x.

Example 2. The facts are the same as in *Example 1,* except that, in computing its qualified research expenses for the taxable year ending December 31, 2001, X claimed that a certain type of expenditure incurred in 2001 was a qualified research expense. X's claim reflected a change in X's position, because X had not previously claimed that similar expenditures were qualified research expenses. The consistency rule requires X to adjust its qualified research expenses in computing the fixed-base percentage to include any similar expenditures not treated as qualified research expenses during the fixed-base period, regardless of whether the period for filing a claim for credit or refund has expired for any year taken into account in computing the fixed-base percentage.

(e) *Effective date.* The rules in paragraphs (c) and (d) of this section are applicable for taxable years beginning on or after the date final regulations are published in the Federal Register. [Reg. § 1.41-3.]

☐ [*T.D.* 8930, 12-27-2000.]

[Reg. § 1.41-4]

§ 1.41-4. Qualified research for expenditures paid or incurred on or after January 3, 2001.— (a) *Qualified research*—(1) *General rule.* Research activities related to the development or improvement of a business component constitute qualified research only if the research activities meet all of the requirements of section 41(d)(1) and this section, and are not otherwise excluded under section 41(d)(3)(B) or (d)(4), or this section.

(2) *Requirements of section 41(d)(1).* Research constitutes qualified research only if it is research—

(i) With respect to which expenditures may be treated as expenses under section 174, see § 1.174-2;

Reg. § 1.41-4(a)(2)

(ii) That is undertaken for the purpose of discovering information that is technological in nature, and the application of which is intended to be useful in the development of a new or improved business component of the taxpayer; and

(iii) Substantially all of the activities of which constitute elements of a process of experimentation that relates to a new or improved function, performance, reliability or quality.

For certain recordkeeping requirements, see paragraph (d) of this section.

(3) *Undertaken for the purpose of discovering information*—(i) *In general.* For purposes of section 41(d) and this section, research is undertaken for the purpose of discovering information only if it is undertaken to obtain knowledge that exceeds, expands, or refines the common knowledge of skilled professionals in a particular field of science or engineering. A determination that research is undertaken for the purpose of discovering information does not require that the taxpayer succeed in obtaining the knowledge that exceeds, expands, or refines the common knowledge of skilled professionals in a particular field of science or engineering, nor does it require that the advance sought be more than evolutionary. However, research is not undertaken for the purpose of discovering information merely because an expenditure may be treated as an expense under section 174.

(ii) *Common knowledge.* Common knowledge of skilled professionals in a particular field of science or engineering means information that should be known to skilled professionals had they performed, before the research in question is undertaken, a reasonable investigation of the existing level of information in the particular field of science or engineering. Thus, knowledge may, in certain circumstances, exceed, expand, or refine the common knowledge of skilled professionals in a particular field of science or engineering even though such knowledge has previously been obtained by other persons. For example, trade secrets generally are not within the common knowledge of skilled professionals in a particular field of science or engineering because they are not reasonably available to skilled professionals not employed, hired, or licensed by the owner of such trade secrets.

(iii) *Means of discovery.* In seeking to obtain knowledge that exceeds, expands, or refines the common knowledge of skilled professionals in a particular field of science or engineering, a taxpayer may employ existing technologies in a particular field and may rely on existing principles of science or engineering.

(iv) *Patent safe harbor.* For purposes of section 41(d) and paragraph (a)(3)(i) of this section, the issuance of a patent by the Patent and Trademark Office under the provisions of section 151 of title 35, United States Code (other than a patent for design issued under the provisions of section 171 of title 35, United States Code) is conclusive evidence that a taxpayer has obtained knowledge that exceeds, expands, or refines the common knowledge of skilled professionals. However, the issuance of such a patent is not a precondition for credit availability.

(v) *Rebuttable presumption.* If a taxpayer demonstrates with credible evidence that research activities were undertaken to obtain the information described in the taxpayer's contemporaneous documentation required under paragraph (d)(1) of this section, and if that documentation also sets forth the basis for the taxpayer's belief that obtaining this information would exceed, expand, or refine the common knowledge of skilled professionals in the particular field of science or engineering, the research activities are presumed to satisfy the requirements of this paragraph (a)(3). However, the presumption applies only if the taxpayer cooperates with reasonable requests by the Commissioner for witnesses, information, documents, meetings, and interviews. Furthermore, the Commissioner may overcome the presumption in this paragraph if the Commissioner demonstrates that the information described in the taxpayer's documentation was within the common knowledge of skilled professionals (as described in paragraph (a)(3)(ii) of this section), or that the research activities were not undertaken to obtain the information described in the taxpayer's documentation.

(4) *Technological in nature.* For purposes of section 41(d) and this section, information is technological in nature if the process of experimentation used to discover such information fundamentally relies on principles of the physical or biological sciences, engineering, or computer science.

(5) *Process of experimentation.* For purposes of section 41(d) and this section, a process of experimentation is a process to evaluate more than one alternative designed to achieve a result where the capability or method of achieving that result is uncertain at the outset. A process of experimentation does not include the evaluation of alternatives to establish the appropriate design of a business component, if the capability and method for developing or improving the business component are not uncertain. A process of experimentation in the physical or biological sciences, engineering, or computer science may involve—

Reg. § 1.41-4(a)(3)

(i) Developing one or more hypotheses designed to achieve the intended result;

(ii) Designing an experiment (that, where appropriate to the particular field of research, is intended to be replicable with an established experimental control) to test and analyze those hypotheses (through, for example, modeling, simulation, or a systematic trial and error methodology);

(iii) Conducting the experiment; and

(iv) Refining or discarding the hypotheses as part of a sequential design process to develop or improve the business component.

(6) *Substantially all requirement.* The substantially all requirement of section 41(d)(1)(C) and paragraph (a)(2)(iii) of this section is satisfied only if 80 percent or more of the research activities, measured on a cost or other consistently applied reasonable basis (and without regard to § 1.41-2(d)(2)), constitute elements of a process of experimentation for a purpose described in section 41(d)(3). The substantially all requirement is applied separately to each business component.

(7) *Use of computers and information technology.* The employment of computers or information technology, or the reliance on principles of computer science or information technology to store, collect, manipulate, translate, disseminate, produce, distribute, or process data or information, and similar uses of computers and information technology does not itself establish that qualified research has been undertaken.

(8) *Illustrations.* The following examples illustrate the application of this paragraph (a):

Example 1. (i) *Facts.* X and other manufacturing companies have previously designed and manufactured a particular kind of machine using Material S. Material T is less expensive than Material S. X wishes to design a new machine that appears and functions exactly the same as its existing machines, but that is made of Material T instead of Material S. The capability and method necessary to achieve this objective should not have been known to skilled professionals had they conducted a reasonable investigation of the existing information in the relevant field of science or engineering at the time the research was undertaken.

(ii) *Conclusion.* X's activities to design the new machine using Material T may be qualified research within the meaning of section 41(d)(1) and this paragraph (a). In seeking to design the machine, X undertook to obtain knowledge that exceeds, expands, or refines the common knowledge of skilled professionals in the relevant field of science or engineering.

Example 2. (i) *Facts.* X is engaged business of developing and manufacturing gets. X wants to manufacture an improved made out of a material that X has not previ used. Although X is uncertain how to use material to manufacture an improved widget, t capability and method of using the material t manufacture such widgets should have been known to skilled professionals had they conducted a reasonable investigation of the existing level of information in the particular field of science or engineering at the time the research was undertaken.

(ii) *Conclusion.* Even though X's expenditures for the activities to resolve the uncertainty in manufacturing the improved widget may be treated as expenses for research activities under section 174 and § 1.174-2, X's activities to resolve the uncertainty in manufacturing the improved widget are not qualified research within the meaning of section 41(d) and this paragraph (a). Although X's activities were intended to eliminate uncertainty, the activities were not undertaken to obtain knowledge that exceeds, expands, or refines the common knowledge of skilled professionals in the relevant field of science or engineering.

Example 3. (i) *Facts.* X desires to build a bridge that can sustain greater traffic flow without deterioration than can existing bridges. The capability and method used to build such a bridge should not have been known to skilled professionals had they conducted a reasonable investigation of the existing level of information in the particular field of science or engineering at the time the research was undertaken. X eventually abandons the project after attempts to develop the technology prove unsuccessful.

(ii) *Conclusion.* X's activities to develop the technology to build the bridge may be qualified research within the meaning of section 41(d)(1) and this paragraph (a), regardless of the fact that X did not actually succeed in developing that technology. In seeking to develop the technology, X undertook to obtain knowledge that exceeds, expands, or refines the common knowledge of skilled professionals in the relevant field of science or engineering.

Example 4. (i) *Facts.* The facts are the same as in *Example 3*, except that Y successfully builds a bridge that can sustain the greater traffic flow. Thereafter, Z seeks to build a bridge that can also sustain such greater traffic flow. The method Y used to build its bridge is a closely guarded trade secret that is not known to Z and should not have been known to skilled professionals had they conducted a reasonable investigation of the existing level of information in the particular field of sci-

Reg. § 1.41-4(a)(8)

engineering at the time the research was taken.

(ii) *Conclusion.* Z's activities to develop the nology to build the bridge may be qualified search within the meaning of section 41(d)(1) nd this paragraph (a), even if it so happens that the technology Z used to build its bridge is similar or identical to the technology Y used. In developing the technology, Z undertook to obtain knowledge that exceeds, expands, or refines the common knowledge of skilled professionals in the relevant field of science or engineering.

Example 5. (i) *Facts.* X, a widget manufacturer, seeks to develop a new widget and initiates Project A. Before or during the early stages of Project A, X's employees prepare contemporaneous documentation that describes the principal questions to be answered by Project A and the information that X seeks to obtain to exceed, expand, or refine the common knowledge of skilled professionals in the relevant field of science or engineering. The documentation includes a statement from one of X's skilled professionals setting forth the basis for that professional's belief that the information is beyond the common knowledge of skilled professionals in the relevant field. Upon examination by the Commissioner, X presents credible evidence that the research activities were undertaken to obtain the information described in the contemporaneous documentation. X cooperates with all requests by the IRS for witnesses, information, documents, meetings, and interviews.

(ii) *Conclusion.* X's research activities with respect to Project A are presumed to be undertaken for the purpose of obtaining knowledge that exceeds, expands, or refines the common knowledge of skilled professionals in the relevant field of science or engineering. The Commissioner may overcome this presumption by demonstrating that the information X sought to obtain was within the common knowledge of skilled professionals in the relevant field of science or engineering (*i.e.*, by demonstrating that, at the time Project A began, the information should have been known to skilled professionals had they performed a reasonable investigation of the existing level of knowledge in the relevant field).

(b) *Application of requirements for qualified research*—(1) *In general.* The requirements for qualified research in section 41(d)(1) and paragraph (a) of this section, must be applied separately to each business component, as defined in section 41(d)(2)(B). In cases involving development of both a product and a manufacturing or other commercial production process for the product, research activities relating to development of

the process are not qualified research unless the requirements of section 41(d) and this section are met for the research activities relating to the process without taking into account the research activities relating to development of the product. Similarly, research activities relating to development of the product are not qualified research unless the requirements of section 41(d) and this section are met for the research activities relating to the product without taking into account the research activities relating to development of the manufacturing or other commercial production process.

(2) *Shrinking-back rule.* The requirements of section 41(d) and paragraph (a) of this section are to be applied first at the level of the discrete business component, that is, the product, process, computer software, technique, formula, or invention to be held for sale, lease, or license, or used by the taxpayer in a trade or business of the taxpayer. If the requirements for credit eligibility are met at that first level, then some or all of the taxpayer's research expenses are eligible for the credit. A special shrinking-back rule applies in the case where a taxpayer incurs some research expenses with respect to that discrete business component that would constitute qualified research expenses with respect to that business component but for the fact that less than substantially all of the research activities with respect to that component constitute elements of a process of experimentation that relates to a new or improved function, performance, reliability or quality. In such a case, the requirements for the credit are to be applied at the next most significant subset of elements of the business component. The shrinking-back of the applicable business component continues until a subset or series of subsets of elements of the business component satisfies the substantially all requirement of section 41(d)(1)(C) and paragraph (a)(2)(iii) of this section (treating that subset of elements as a business component) or the most basic element fails to satisfy the requirements. This shrinking-back rule is applied only if a taxpayer does not satisfy the requirements of section 41(d)(1)(C) and paragraph (a)(2)(iii) of this section with respect to the overall business component. The shrinking-back rule is not itself applied as a reason to exclude research activities from credit eligibility.

(3) *Illustration.* The following example illustrates the application of this paragraph (b):

(i) *Facts.* X, a widget manufacturer, develops a widget that is improved in several respects. Among the various improvements to the widget is an improvement to the widget's cooling mechanism. Although the capability and method of making the other improvements to the widget would have been known to skilled professionals had they conducted a reasonable investigation of the existing level of information in the particular field of science or engineering, the method of developing the improved cooling mechanism and of incorporating the improved mechanism into the widget would not have been known to skilled professionals had they conducted a reasonable investigation of the existing level of information in the particular field of science or engineering. Substantially all of X's research activities in improving the widget constitute elements of a process of experimentation for purposes of improving the performance of the widget. None of X's research activities in improving the widget are described in section 41(d)(4) or paragraph (c) of this section.

(ii) *Conclusion.* Some, but not all, of X's research activities in developing the improved widget are qualified research within the meaning of section 41(d)(1) and paragraph (a) of this section. In seeking to improve the widget, some of X's activities (related to improving the cooling mechanism and incorporating the improved cooling mechanism into the widget) were undertaken to obtain knowledge that exceeds, expands, or refines the common knowledge of skilled professionals in the relevant field of science or engineering. However, other activities (related to the other improvements) were not undertaken to obtain knowledge that exceeds, expands, or refines the common knowledge of skilled professionals in the relevant field of science or engineering, and thus are not qualified research and are not eligible for the credit. Not all of X's research activities relating to the widget are eligible for the credit because some of the activities are not qualified research as defined in section 41(d) and paragraph (a) of this section, even though the widget qualifies as a business component with respect to which qualified research that satisfies the requirements of section 41(d) and paragraph (a) of this section is undertaken.

(c) *Excluded activities*—(1) *In general.* Qualified research does not include any activity described in section 41(d)(4) and paragraph (c) of this section.

(2) *Research after commercial production*—(i) *In general.* Activities conducted after the beginning of commercial production of a business component are not qualified research. Activities are conducted after the beginning of commercial production of a business component if such activities are conducted after the component is developed to the point where it is ready for commercial sale or use, or meets the basic functional and economic requirements of the taxpayer component's sale or use.

(ii) *Certain additional activities re... the business component.* The following act... are deemed to occur after the beginning of commercial production of a business component—

(A) Preproduction planning for a fin... ished business component;

(B) Tooling-up for production;

(C) Trial production runs;

(D) Trouble shooting involving detecting faults in production equipment or processes;

(E) Accumulating data relating to production processes; and

(F) Debugging flaws in a business component.

(iii) *Activities related to production process or technique.* In cases involving development of both a product and a manufacturing or other commercial production process for the product, the exclusion described in section 41(d)(4)(A) and paragraphs (c)(2)(i) and (ii) of this section applies separately for the activities relating to the development of the product and the activities relating to the development of the process. For example, even after a product meets the taxpayer's basic functional and economic requirements, activities relating to the development of the manufacturing process still may constitute qualified research, provided that the development of the process itself separately satisfies the requirements of section 41(d) and this section, and the activities are conducted before the process meets the taxpayer's basic functional and economic requirements or is ready for commercial use.

(iv) *Clinical testi...* Clinical testing of a pharmaceutical product rior to its commercial production in the United States is not treated as occurring after the beginning of commercial production even if the product is commercially available in other c...tries. Additional clinical testing of a pharma...ical product after a product has been appro... for a specific therapeutic use by the Food... Drug Administration and is ready for com...cial production and sale are not treate... occurring after the beginning of commercial production if such clinical tests are undertaken... merc... establish new functional uses, tal...ristics, indications, combinations, dos... ch... delivery forms for the product. A func...use, characteristic, indication, combination, ... ge or delivery form shall be considered new ... if such functional use, characteristic, indica- ...n, combination, dosage or delivery form must

Reg. § 1.41-4(c)(2)

oved by the Food and Drug
ration.

) *Adaptation of existing business compo-*
. Activities relating to adapting an existing
ness component to a particular customer's
quirement or need are not qualified research.
his exclusion does not apply merely because a
business component is intended for a specific
customer.

(4) *Duplication of existing business component.* Activities relating to reproducing an existing business component (in whole or in part)
from a physical examination of the business component itself or from plans, blueprints, detailed
specifications, or publicly available information
about the business component are not qualified
research. This exclusion does not apply merely
because the taxpayer inspects an existing business
component in the course of developing its own
business component.

(5) *Surveys, studies, research relating to
management functions, etc.* Qualified research
does not include activities relating to—

(i) Efficiency surveys;

(ii) Management functions or techniques,
including such items as preparation of financial
data and analysis, development of employee
training programs and management organization
plans, and management-based changes in production processes (such as rearranging work stations
on an assembly line);

(iii) Market research, testing, or development (including advertising or promotions);

(iv) Routine data collections; or

(v) Routine or ordinary testing or inspections for quality control.

(6) *Internal-use computer software*—(i) *General rule.* Research with respect to computer
software that is developed by (or for the benefit
of) the taxpayer primarily for the taxpayer's internal use is eligible for the research credit only if
the software satisfies the requirements of paragraph (c)(6)(ii) of this section.

(ii) *Requirements.* The requirements of
this paragraph (c)(6)(ii) are—

(A) The research satisfies the requirements of section 41(d)(1);

(B) The research is not otherwise excluded under section 41(d)(4) (other than section
41(d)(4)(E)); and

(C) One of the following conditions is
met—

(1) The taxpayer develops
software for use in an activity that cons

qualified research (other than the development of
the internal-use software itself);

(2) The taxpayer develops the
software for use in a production process that
meets the requirements of section 41(d)(1);

(3) The taxpayer develops a new or
improved package of computer software and hardware together as a single product, of which the
software is an integral part, that is used directly
by the taxpayer in providing technological services in its trade or business to customers. In
these cases, eligibility for the research credit is to
be determined by examining the combined hard-
ware-software product as a single product;

(4) The taxpayer develops the
software for use in providing computer services to
customers; or

(5) The software satisfies the high
threshold of innovation test of paragraph
(c)(6)(vi) of this section.

(iii) *Primarily for internal use.* Software is
developed primarily for the taxpayer's internal
use if the software is to be used internally, for
example, in general administrative functions of
the taxpayer (such as payroll, bookkeeping, or
personnel management) or in providing noncomputer services (such as accounting, consulting or
banking services). If computer software is developed primarily for the taxpayer's internal use, the
requirements of paragraph (c)(6) apply even
though the taxpayer intends to, or subsequently
does, sell, lease, or license the computer software.

(iv) *Software used in the provision of services*—(A) *Computer services.* For purposes of
this section, a computer service is a service offered by a taxpayer to customers who conduct
business with the taxpayer primarily for the use
of the taxpayer's computer or software technology. A taxpayer does not provide a computer
service merely because customers interact with
the taxpayer's software.

(B) *Noncomputer services.* For purposes
of this section, a noncomputer service is a service
offered by a taxpayer to customers who conduct
business with the taxpayer primarily to obtain a
service other than a computer service, even if
such other service is enabled, supported, or facili-
tated by computer or software technology.

(v) *Exception for certain software used in
providing noncomputer services.* The requirements of paragraph (c)(6)(ii)(C) of this section are
deemed satisfied for research with respect to computer software if, at the time the research was
undertaken—

Reg. § 1.41-4(c)(3)

(A) The software is designed to provide customers a new feature with respect to a noncomputer service;

(B) The taxpayer reasonably anticipated that customers would choose to obtain the noncomputer service from the taxpayer (rather than from the taxpayer's competitors) because of those new features provided by the software; and

(C) Those new features were not available from any of the taxpayer's competitors.

(vi) *High threshold of innovation test.* Computer software satisfies the high threshold of innovation test of this paragraph (c)(6)(vi) only if the taxpayer can establish that—

(A) The software is innovative in that the software is intended to result in a reduction in cost, improvement in speed, or other improvement, that is substantial and economically significant;

(B) The software development involves significant economic risk in that the taxpayer commits substantial resources to the development and there is a substantial uncertainty, because of technical risk, that such resources would be recovered within a reasonable period; and

(C) The software is not commercially available for use by the taxpayer in that the software cannot be purchased, leased, or licensed and used for the intended purpose without modifications that would satisfy the requirements of paragraphs (c)(6)(vi)(A) and (B) of this section.

(vii) *Application of high threshold of innovation test.* In determining if the high threshold of innovation test of paragraph (c)(6)(vi) of this section is satisfied, all of the facts and circumstances are considered. The determination of whether the software is intended to result in an improvement or cost reduction that is substantial and economically significant is based on a comparison of the intended result with software that is within the common knowledge of skilled professionals in the relevant field of science or engineering, see § 1.41-4(a)(3)(ii). Similarly, the extent of uncertainty and technical risk is determined with respect to the common knowledge of skilled professionals in the relevant field of science or engineering. Further, in determining if the high threshold of innovation test of paragraph (c)(6)(vi) of this section is satisfied, the activities to develop the new or improved software are considered independent of the effect of any modifications to related hardware or other software.

(viii) *Illustrations.* The following examples illustrate the application of this paragraph (c)(6):

Example 1. (i) *Facts.* X is engaged in the business of manufacturing and selling widgets to wholesalers. X has experienced strong gr‌ at the same time has expanded its produc‌ ings. X also has increased significantly the‌ its business by expanding into new territories‌ increase in the size and scope of its business‌ strained X's existing financial management s‌ tems such that management can no longer obtai‌ timely comprehensive financial data. Accordingly‌ X undertakes the development of a financial man‌ agement computer software system that is more appropriate to its newly expanded operations.

(ii) *Conclusion.* X's new computer software system is developed by X primarily for X's internal use. X's activities to develop the new computer software system may be eligible for the research credit only if the computer software development activities satisfy the requirements of paragraph (c)(6)(ii) of this section.

Example 2. (i) *Facts.* X is engaged in the business of designing, manufacturing, and selling widgets. X delivers its widgets in the same manner and time as its competitors. In keeping with X's corporate commitment to provide customers with top quality service, X undertakes a project to develop for X's internal use a computer software system to facilitate the tracking of the manufacturing and delivery of widgets which will enable X's customers to monitor the progress of their orders and know precisely when their widgets will be delivered. X's computer software activities include research activities that satisfy the discovery requirement in section 41(d)(1) and paragraph (a)(3) of this section. At the time the research is undertaken, X reasonably anticipates that if it is successful, X will increase its market share as compared to X's competitors, none of which has such a tracking feature for its delivery system.

(ii) *Conclusion.* Although X's computer software system is developed primarily for X's internal use, X's activities are excepted from the high threshold of innovation test of paragraph (c)(6)(vi) of this section because, at the time the research is undertaken, X's software is designed to provide improved tracking features, X reasonably anticipates that customers will purchase widgets from X because these improved tracking features, and because comparable tracking features are not available from any of X's competitors.

(ix) *Effective dates.* This paragraph (c)(6) is applicable for taxable years beginning after December 31, 1985, except paragraphs (c)(6)(ii)(C)(4), (c)(6)(iv)(A) and (B), (c)(6)(v), the second and third sentences of paragraph (c)(6)(vii), and paragraph (c)(6)(viii) *Example 2* of this section apply to expenditures paid or incurred on or after January 3, 2001.

*Activities outside the United States, Pu-
~~ico~~, and other possessions—(i) In general.
~~.rch~~ conducted outside the United States, as
~~ned~~ in section 7701(a)(9), the Commonwealth
~~Puerto~~ Rico and other possessions of the United
~~.ates~~ does not constitute qualified research.

(ii) *Apportionment of in-house research expenses.* In-house research expenses paid or incurred for qualified services performed both (A) in
the United States, the Commonwealth of Puerto
Rico and other possessions of the United States
and (B) outside the United States, the Commonwealth of Puerto Rico and other possessions of the
United States must be apportioned between the
services performed in the United States, the Commonwealth of Puerto Rico and other possessions of
the United States and the services performed
outside the United States, the Commonwealth of
Puerto Rico and other possessions of the United
States. Only those in-house research expenses apportioned to the services performed within the
United States, the Commonwealth of Puerto Rico
and other possessions of the United States are
eligible to be treated as qualified research expenses, unless the in-house research expenses are
wages and the 80 percent rule of § 1.41-2(d)(2)
applies.

(iii) *Apportionment of contract research
expenses.* If contract research is performed partly
in the United States, the Commonwealth of Puerto Rico and other possessions of the United
States and partly outside the United States, the
Commonwealth of Puerto Rico and other possessions of the United States, only 65 percent (or 75
percent in the case of amounts paid to qualified
research consortia) of the portion of the contract
amount that is attributable to the research activity performed in the United States, the Commonwealth of Puerto Rico and other possessions of the
United States may qualify as a contract research
expense (even if 80 percent or more of the contract amount is for research performed in the
United States, the Commonwealth of Puerto Rico
and other possessions of the United States).

(8) *Research in the social sciences, etc.* Qualified research does not include research in the
social sciences (including economics, business
management, and behavioral sciences), arts, or
humanities.

(9) *Research funded by any grant, contract,
or otherwise.* Qualified research does not include
any research to the extent funded by any grant,
contract, or otherwise by another person (or governmental entity). To determine the extent to
which research is so funded, § 1.41-4A(d) applies.

(10) *Illustrations.* The following examples illustrate provisions contained in paragraphs (c)(1)

through (9) of this section. No inference should be
drawn from these examples concerning the application of section 41(d)(1) and paragraph (a) of
this section to these facts. The examples are as
follows:

Example 1. (i) *Facts.* X, a tire manufacturer,
seeks to build a tire that will not deteriorate as
rapidly under certain conditions of high speed and
temperature as do existing tires. X commences
laboratory research on January 1. On April 1, X
determines in the laboratory that a certain combination of materials and additives can withstand
higher rotational speeds and temperatures than
the combination of materials and additives used
in existing tires. On the basis of this determination, X undertakes further research activities to
determine how to design a tire using those materials and additives, and to determine whether such
a tire functions outside the laboratory as intended
under various actual road conditions. By September 1, X's research has progressed to the point
where the new tire meets X's basic functional and
economic requirements.

(ii) *Conclusion.* Any research activities conducted by X after September 1 with respect to the
design of the tire are not qualified research within
the meaning of section 41(d)(1) and paragraph (a)
of this section because they are undertaken after
the beginning of commercial production of the
tire. Whether any activities X engaged in to develop a process for manufacturing the new tire
constitute qualified research depends on if the
development of the process itself separately satisfies the requirements of section 41(d) and paragraph (c)(2) of this section, and also depends on if
the activities occur before the point in time when
the process meets the taxpayer's basic functional
and economic requirements or is ready for commercial use.

Example 2. (i) *Facts.* For several years, X
has manufactured and sold a particular kind of
widget. X initiates a new research project to develop an improved widget.

(ii) *Conclusion.* X's activities to develop an
improved widget are not excluded from the definition of qualified research under section
41(d)(4)(A) and paragraph (c)(2) of this section
until the beginning of commercial production of
the improved widget. The fact that X's activities
relating to the improved widget are undertaken
after the beginning of commercial production of
the unimproved widget does not bar the activities
from credit eligibility because those activities constitute a new research project to develop a new
business component, an improved widget.

Example 3. (i) *Facts.* X, a computer software
development firm, owns all substantial rights in a

Reg. § 1.41-4(c)(7)

general ledger accounting software core program that X markets and licenses to customers. X incurs expenditures in adapting the core software program to the requirements of C, one of X's customers.

(ii) *Conclusion.* Because X's activities represent activities to adapt an existing software program to a particular customer's requirement, X's activities are excluded from the definition of qualified research under section 41(d)(4)(B) and paragraph (c)(3) of this section.

Example 4. (i) *Facts.* The facts are the same as in *Example 3,* except that C pays X to adapt the core software program to C's requirements.

(ii) *Conclusion.* Because X's activities are excluded from the definition of qualified research under section 41(d)(4)(B) and paragraph (c)(3) of this section, C's payments to X do not constitute contract research expenses under section 41(b)(3)(A).

Example 5. (i) *Facts.* The facts are the same as in *Example 3,* except that C's own employees adapt the core software program to C's requirements.

(ii) *Conclusion.* Because C's employees' activities are excluded from the definition of qualified research under section 41(d)(4)(B) and paragraph (c)(3) of this section, the wages C paid to its employees do not constitute in-house research expenses under section 41(b)(2)(A).

Example 6. (i) *Facts.* An existing gasoline additive is manufactured by Y using three ingredients, A, B, and C. X seeks to develop and manufacture its own gasoline additive that appears and functions in a manner similar to Y's additive. To develop its own additive, X first inspects the composition of Y's additive, and uses knowledge gained from the inspection to reproduce A and B in the laboratory. Any differences between ingredients A and B that are used in Y's additive and those reproduced by X are insignificant and are not material to the viability, effectiveness, or cost of A and B. X desires to use with A and B an ingredient that has a materially lower cost than ingredient C. Accordingly, X engages in a process of experimentation to discover potential alternative formulations of the additive (i.e., the development and use of various ingredients other than C to use with A and B).

(ii) *Conclusion.* X's activities in analyzing and reproducing ingredients A and B involve duplication of existing business components and are excluded from qualified research under section 41(d)(4)(C) and paragraph (c)(4) of this section. X's experimentation activities to discover potential alternative formulations of the additive do not involve duplication of an existing business

component and are not excluded from qualified research under section 41(d)(4)(C) and paragraph (c)(4) of this section.

Example 7. (i) *Facts.* X, an insurance company, develops a new life insurance product. In the course of developing the product, X engages in research with respect to the effect of pricing and tax consequences on demand for the product, the expected volatility of interest rates, and the expected mortality rates (based on published data and prior insurance claims).

(ii) *Conclusion.* X's activities related to the new product represent research in the social sciences, and are thus excluded from qualified research under section 41(d)(4)(G) and paragraph (c)(8) of this section.

(d) *Documentation.* No credit shall be allowed under section 41 with regard to an expenditure relating to a research project unless the taxpayer—

(1) Prepares documentation before or during the early stages of the research project, that describes the principal questions to be answered and the information the taxpayer seeks to obtain to satisfy the requirements of paragraph (a)(3) of this section, and retains that documentation on paper or electronically in the manner prescribed in applicable regulations, revenue rulings, revenue procedures, or other appropriate guidance until such time as taxes may no longer be assessed (except under section 6501(c)(1), (2), or (3)) for any year in which the taxpayer claims to have qualified research expenditures in connection with the research project; and

(2) Satisfies section 6001 and the regulations thereunder.

(e) *Effective dates.* In general, the rules of this section are applicable for expenditures paid or incurred on or after January 3, 2001. The rules of paragraph (d), however, apply to research projects that begin on or after March 5, 2001. [Reg. § 1.41-4.]

☐ [*T.D.* 8251, 5-16-89. *Amended by T.D.* 8930, 12-27-2000.]

[Reg. § 1.41-5]

§ 1.41-5. **Basic research for taxable years beginning after December 31, 1986.**—[Reserved]

☐ [*T.D.* 8251, 5-16-89. *Redesignated and amended by T.D.* 8930, 12-27-2000.]

[Reg. § 1.41-6]

§ 1.41-6. **Aggregation of expenditures.**—(a) *Controlled group of corporations; trades or businesses under common control*—(1) *In general.* In determining the amount of research credit allowed with respect to a trade or business that at

Reg. § 1.41-6(a)(1)

the end of its taxable year is a member of a controlled group of corporations or a member of a group of trades or businesses under common control, all members of the group are treated as a single taxpayer and the credit (if any) allowed to the member is determined on the basis of its proportionate share (if any) of the increase in qualified research expenses of the aggregated group.

(2) *Definition of trade or business.* For purposes of this section, a trade or business is a sole proprietorship, a partnership, a trust, an estate, or a corporation that is carrying on a trade or business (within the meaning of section 162). For purposes of this section, any corporation that is a member of a commonly controlled group shall be deemed to be carrying on a trade or business if any other member of that group is carrying on any trade or business.

(3) *Determination of common control.* For rules for determining whether trades or businesses are under common control, see paragraphs (b)— (g) of § 1.52-1 except that the words "singly or" in § 1.52-1(d)(1)(i) shall be treated as deleted.

(4) *Examples.* The following examples illustrate provisions of this paragraph.

Example (1). (i) *Facts.* A controlled group of four corporations (all of which are calendar-year taxpayers) had qualified research expenses ("research expenses") during the base period and taxable year as follows:

Corporation	Base Period (average)	Taxable year	Change
A	$60	$40	($20)
B	10	15	5
C	30	70	40
D	15	25	10

(ii) *Total credit.* Because the research expenses of the four corporations are treated as if made by one taxpayer, the total amount of incremental expenses eligible for the credit is $35 ($55 increase attributable to B, C, and D less $20 decrease attributable to A). The total amount of credit allowable to members of the group is 20% of the incremental amount or $7.00.

(iii) *Allocation of credit.* No amount of credit is allocated to A since A's research expenses did not increase in the taxable year. The $7.00 credit is allocated to B, C, and D, the members of the group that increased their research expenses. This allocation is made on the basis of the ratio of each corporation's increase in its research expenses to the sum of increases in those expenses. Inasmuch as the total increase made by those members of the group whose research expenses rose (B, C, and D) was $55, B's share of the $7.00 credit is 5/55; C's share is 40/55; and D's share is 10/55.

Example (2). The facts are the same as in example (1) except that A had zero research expenses in the taxable year. Thus, the controlled group had a decrease rather than an increase in aggregate research expenses. Accordingly, no amount of credit is allowable to any member of the group even though B, C, and D actually increased their research expenses in comparison with their own base period expenses.

(b) *Minimum base period research expenses.* For purposes of this section, the rule in section 41(c)(3) (pertaining to minimum base period research expenses) shall be applied only to the aggregate amount of base period research expenses. See the treatment of corporation C in example (1) of paragraph (a)(4) of this section.

(c) *Tax accounting periods used—(1) In general.* The credit allowable to a member of a controlled group of corporations or of a group of trades or businesses under common control is that member's share of the aggregate credit computed as of the end of such member's taxable year. In computing the aggregate credit in the case of a group whose members have different taxable years, a member shall generally treat the taxable year of another member that ends with or within the determination year of the computing member as the determination year of that other member. The base period research expenses taken into account with respect to a determination year of another member shall be the base period research expenses determined for that year under § 1.41-3A, except that § 1.41-3A(c)(2) shall be applied only at the aggregate level.

(2) *Special rule where timing of research is manipulated.* If the timing of research by members using different tax accounting periods is manipulated to generate a credit in excess of the amount that would be allowable if all members of the group used the same tax accounting period, the district director may require each member of the group to calculate the credit in the current taxable year and all future years as if all members of the group had the same taxable year and base period as the computing member.

(d) *Membership during taxable year in more than one group.* A trade or business may be a member of only one group for a taxable year. If, without application of this paragraph, a business would be a member of more than one group at the end of its taxable year, the business shall be treated as a member of the group in which it was included for its preceding taxable year. If the business was not included for its preceding taxable year in any group in which it could be included as of the end of its taxable year, the business shall designate in its timely filed (includ-

Reg. § 1.41-6(a)(2)

ing extensions) return the group in which it is being included. If the return for a taxable year is due before July 1, 1983, the business may designate its group membership through an amended return for that year filed on or before June 30, 1983. If the business does not so designate, then the district director with audit jurisdiction of the return will determine the group in which the business is to be included.

(e) *Intra-group transactions*—(1) *In general.* Because all members of a group under common control are treated as a single taxpayer for purposes of determining the research credit, transfers between members of the group are generally disregarded.

(2) *In-house research expenses.* If one member of a group performs qualified research on behalf of another member, the member performing the research shall include in its qualified research expenses any in-house research expenses for that work and shall not treat any amount received or accrued as funding the research. Conversely, the member for whom the research is performed shall not treat any part of any amount paid or incurred as a contract research expense. For purposes of determining whether the in-house research for that work is qualified research, the member performing the research shall be treated as carrying on any trade or business carried on by the member on whose behalf the research is performed.

(3) *Contract research expenses.* If a member of a group pays or incurs contract research expenses to a person outside the group in carrying on the member's trade or business, that member shall include those expenses as qualified research expenses. However, if the expenses are not paid or incurred in carrying on any trade or business of that member, those expenses may be taken into account as contract research expenses by another member of the group provided that the other member—

(i) Reimburses the member paying or incurring the expenses, and

(ii) Carries on a trade or business to which the research relates.

(4) *Lease Payments.* The amount paid or incurred to another member of the group for the lease of personal property owned by a member of the group is not taken into account for purposes of section 41. Amounts paid or incurred to another member of the group for the lease of personal property owned by a person outside the group shall be taken into account as in-house research expenses for purposes of section 41 only to the extent of the lesser of—

(i) The amount paid or incurred to the other member, or

(ii) The amount of the lease expenses paid to the person outside the group.

(5) *Payment for supplies.* Amounts paid or incurred to another member of the group for supplies shall be taken into account as in-house research expenses for purposes of section 41 only to the extent of the lesser of—

(i) The amount paid or incurred to the other member, or

(ii) The amount of the other member's basis in the supplies. [Reg. § 1.41-6.]

☐ [*T.D. 8251, 5-16-89. Redesignated and amended by T.D. 8930, 12-27-2000.*]

[Reg. § 1.41-7]

§ 1.41-7. **Special rules.**—(a) *Allocations*—(1) *Corporation making an election under subchapter S*—(i) *Pass-through, for taxable years beginning after December 31, 1982, in the case of an S corporation.* In the case of an S corporation (as defined in section 1361) the amount of research credit computed for the corporation shall be allocated to the shareholders according to the provisions of section 1366 and section 1377.

(ii) *Pass-through, for taxable years beginning before January 1, 1983, in the case of a subchapter S corporation.* In the case of an electing small business corporation (as defined in section 1371 as that section read before the amendments made by the Subchapter S Revision Act of 1982), the amount of the research credit computed for the corporation for any taxable year shall be apportioned pro rata among the persons who are shareholders of the corporation on the last day of the corporation's taxable year.

(2) *Pass-through in the case of an estate or trust.* In the case of an estate or trust, the amount of the research credit computed for the estate or trust for any taxable year shall be apportioned among the estate or trust and the beneficiaries on the basis of the income of the estate or trust allocable to each.

(3) *Pass-through in the case of a partnership*—(i) *In general.* In the case of a partnership, the research credit computed for the partnership for any taxable year shall be apportioned among the persons who are partners during the taxable year in accordance with section 704 and the regulations thereunder. See, for example, § 1.704-1(b)(4)(ii). Because the research credit is an expenditure-based credit, the credit is to be allocated among the partners in the same proportion as section 174 expenditures are allocated for the year.

(ii) *Certain expenditures by joint ventures.* Research expenses to which § 1.41-2(a)(4)(ii) applies shall be apportioned among the persons who are partners during the taxable year in accordance with the provisions of that section. For purposes of section 41, these expenses shall be treated as paid or incurred directly by the partners rather than by the partnership. Thus, the partnership shall disregard these expenses in computing the credit to be apportioned under paragraph (a)(3)(i) of this section, and in making the computations under section 41 each partner shall aggregate its distributive share of these expenses with other research expenses of the partner. The limitation on the amount of the credit set out in section 41(g) and in paragraph (c) of this section shall not apply because the credit is computed by the partner, not the partnership.

(4) *Year in which taken into account.* An amount apportioned to a person under this paragraph shall be taken into account by the person in the taxable year of such person which or within which the taxable year of the corporation, estate, trust, or partnership (as the case may be) ends.

(5) *Credit allowed subject to limitation.* The credit allowable to any person to whom any amount has been apportioned under paragraph (a)(1), (2) or (3)(i) of this section is subject to section 41(g) and sections 38 and 39 of the Code, if applicable.

(b) *Adjustments for certain acquisitions and dispositions—Meaning of terms.* For the meaning of "acquisition," "separate unit," and "major portion," see paragraph (b) of § 1.52-2. An "acquisition" includes an incorporation or a liquidation.

(c) *Special rule for pass-through of credit.* The special rule contained in section 41(g) for the pass-through of the credit in the case of an individual who owns an interest in an unincorporated trade or business, is a partner in a partnership, is a beneficiary of an estate or trust, or is a shareholder in an S corporation shall be applied in accordance with the principles set forth in § 1.53-3.

(d) *Carryback and carryover of unused credits.* The taxpayer to whom the credit is passed through under paragraph (c) of this section shall not be prevented from applying the unused portion in a carryback or carryover year merely because the entity that earned the credit changes its form of conducting business. [Reg. § 1.41-7.]

☐ [*T.D. 8251*, 5-16-89. *Redesignated by T.D. 8930*, 12-27-2000.]

[Reg. § 1.41-8]

§ 1.41-8. Special rules for taxable years ending on or after January 3, 2001.—(a) *Alterna-*

tive incremental credit.* At the election of the taxpayer, the credit determined under section 41(a)(1) equals the amount determined under section 41(c)(4).

(b) *Election*—(1) *In general.* A taxpayer may elect to apply the provisions of the alternative incremental credit in section 41(c)(4) for any taxable year of the taxpayer beginning after June 30, 1996. If a taxpayer makes an election under section 41(c)(4), the election applies to the taxable year for which made and all subsequent taxable years.

(2) *Time and manner of election.* An election under section 41(c)(4) is made by completing the portion of Form 6765, "Credit for Increasing Research Activities," relating to the election of the alternative incremental credit, and attaching the completed form to the taxpayer's timely filed original return (including extensions) for the taxable year to which the election applies.

(3) *Revocation.* An election under this section may not be revoked except with the consent of the Commissioner. A taxpayer must attach the Commissioner's consent to revoke an election under section 41(c)(4) to the taxpayer's timely filed original return (including extensions) for the taxable year of the revocation.

(4) *Effective date.* Paragraphs (b)(2) and (3) of this section are applicable for taxable years ending on or after January 3, 2001. [Reg. § 1.41-8.]

☐ [*T.D. 8930*, 12-27-2000.]

[Reg. § 1.41-0A]

§ 1.41-0A. Table of contents.—This section lists the paragraphs contained in §§ 1.41-0A, 1.41-3A, 1.41-4A and 1.41-5A.

(a) General rule.

(b) Activities outside the United States.

(1) In-house research.

(2) Contract research.

(c) Social sciences or humanities.

(d) Research funded by any grant, contract, or otherwise.

(1) In general.

(2) Research in which taxpayer retains no rights.

(3) Research in which the taxpayer retains substantial rights.

(i) In general.

(ii) Pro rata allocation.

(iii) Project-by-project determination.

(4) Independent research and development under the Federal Acquisition Regulations System and similar provisions.

(5) Funding determinable only in subsequent taxable year.

(6) Examples.

§ 1.41-5A. *Basic research for taxable years beginning before January 1, 1987.*

(a) In general.

(b) Trade or business requirement.

(c) Prepaid amounts.

(1) In general.

(2) Transfers of property.

(d) Written research agreement.

(1) In general.

(2) Agreement between a corporation and a qualified organization after June 30, 1983.

(i) In general.

(ii) Transfers of property.

(3) Agreement between a qualified fund and a qualified educational organization after June 30, 1983.

(e) Exclusions.

(1) Research conducted outside the United States.

(2) Research in the social sciences or humanities.

(f) Procedure for making an election to be treated as a qualified fund.

[Reg. § 1.41-0A.]

□ [*T.D. 8930, 12-27-2000.*]

[Reg. § 1.41-3A]

§ 1.41-3A. **Base period research expense.**—
(a) *Number of years in base period.* The term "base period" generally means the 3 taxable years immediately preceding the year for which a credit is being determined ("determination year"). However, if the first taxable year of the taxpayer ending after June 30, 1981, ends in 1981 or 1982, then with respect to that taxable year the term "base period" means the immediately preceding taxable year. If the second taxable year of the taxpayer ending after June 30, 1981, ends in 1982 or 1983, then with respect to that taxable year the term "base period" means the 2 immediately preceding taxable years.

(b) *New taxpayers.* If, with respect to any determination year, the taxpayer has not been in existence for the number of preceding taxable years that are included under paragraph (a) of this section in the base period for that year, then for purposes of paragraph (c)(1) of this section (relating to the determination of average qualified research expenses during the base period), the taxpayer shall be treated as—

(1) Having been in existence for that number of additional 12-month taxable years that is necessary to complete the base period specified in paragraph (a) of this section, and

(2) Having had qualified research expenses of zero in each of those additional years.

(c) *Definition of base period research expenses.* For any determination year, the term "base period research expenses" means the greater of—

(1) The average qualified research expenses for taxable years during the base period, or

(2) Fifty percent of the qualified research expenses for the determination year.

(d) *Special rules for short taxable years*—(1) *Short determination year.* If the determination year for which a research credit is being taken is a short taxable year, the amount taken into account under paragraph (c)(1) of this section shall be modified by multiplying that amount by the number of months in the short taxable year and dividing the result by 12.

(2) *Short base period year.* For purposes of paragraph (c)(1) of this section, if a year in the base period is a short taxable year, the qualified research expenses paid or incurred in the short taxable year are deemed to be equal to the qualified research expenses actually paid or incurred in that year multiplied by 12 and divided by the number of months in that year.

(3) *Years overlapping the effective dates of section 41 (section 44F)*—(i) *Determination years.* If a determination year includes months before July 1981, the determination year is deemed to be a short taxable year including only the months after June 1981. Accordingly, paragraph (d)(1) of this section is applied for purposes

Reg. § 1.41-3A(d)(3)

of determining the base period expenses for such year. See section 221(d)(2) of the Economic Recovery Tax Act of 1981.

(ii) *Base period years.* No adjustment is required in the case of a base period year merely because it overlaps June 30, 1981.

(4) *Number of months in a short taxable year.* The number of months in a short taxable year is equal to the number of whole calendar months contained in the year plus fractions for any partially included months. The fraction for a partially included month is equal to the number of days in the month that are included in the short taxable year divided by the total number of days in that month. Thus, if a short taxable year begins on January 1, 1982, and ends on June 9, 1982, it consists of 5 and 9/30 months.

(e) *Examples.* The following examples illustrate the application of this section.

Example (1). X Corp., an accrual-method taxpayer using the calendar year as its taxable year, is organized and begins carrying on a trade or business during 1979 and subsequently incurs qualified research expenses as follows:

1979	$ 10x
1980	150x
1/1/81—6/30/81	90x
7/1/81—12/31/81	110x
1982	250x
1983	450x

(i) *Determination year 1981.* For determination year 1981, the base period consists of the immediately preceding taxable year, calendar year 1980. Because the determination year includes months before July 1981, paragraph (d)(3)(i) requires that the determination year be treated as a short taxable year. Thus, for purposes of paragraph (c)(1), as modified by paragraph (d)(1), the average qualified research expenses for taxable years during the base period are $75x ($150x, the average qualified research expenses for the base period, multiplied by 6, the number of months in the determination year after June 30, 1981, and divided by 12). Because this amount is greater than the amount determined under paragraph (c)(2) (50 percent of the determination year's qualified research expense of $110x, or $55x), the amount of base period research expenses is $75x. The credit for determination year 1981 is equal to 25 percent of the excess of $110x (the qualified research expenditures incurred during the determination year including only expenditures accrued on or after July 1, 1981, through the end of the determination year) over $75x (the base period research expenses).

(ii) *Determination year 1982.* For determination year 1982, the base period consists of the 2 immediately preceding taxable years, 1980 and 1981. The amount determined under paragraph (c)(1) of this section (the average qualified research expenses for taxable years during the base period) is $175x (($150x + $90x + $110x) / 2). This amount is greater than the amount determined under paragraph (c)(2) (50 percent of $250x, or $125x). Accordingly, the amount of base period research expenses is $175x. The credit for determination year 1982 is equal to 25 percent of the excess of $250x (the qualified research expenses incurred during the determination year) over $175x (the base period research expenses).

(iii) *Determination year 1983.* For determination year 1983, the base period consists of the 3 immediately preceding taxable years 1980, 1981 and 1982. The amount determined under paragraph (c)(1) of this section (the average qualified research expenses for taxable years during the base period) is $200x (($150x + $200x + $250x) / 3). The amount determined under paragraph (c)(2) is $225x (50 percent of the $450x of qualified research expenses in 1983). Accordingly, the amount of base period research expenses is $225x. The credit for determination year 1983 is equal to 25 percent of the excess of $450x (the qualified research expenses incurred during the determination year) over $225x (the base period research expenses).

Example (2). Y, an accrual-basis corporation using the calendar year as its taxable year comes into existence and begins carrying on a trade or business on July 1, 1983. Y incurs qualified research expenses as follows:

7/1/83—12/31/83	$ 80x
1984	200x
1985	200x

(i) *Determination year 1983.* For determination year 1983, the base period consists of the 3 immediately preceding taxable years: 1980, 1981 and 1982. Although Y was not in existence during 1980, 1981 and 1982, Y is treated under paragraph (b) of this section as having been in existence during those years with qualified research expenses of zero. Thus, the amount determined under paragraph (c)(1) of this section (the average qualified research expenses for taxable years during the base period) is $0x (($0x + $0x + $0x) / 3). The amount determined under paragraph (c)(2) of this section is $40x (50 percent of $80x). Accordingly, the amount of base period research expenses is $40x. The credit for determination year 1983 is equal to 25 percent of the excess of $80x (the qualified research expenses incurred during the determination year) over $40x (the base period research expenses).

Reg. § 1.41-3A(d)(4)

(ii) *Determination year 1984.* For determination year 1984, the base period consists of the 3 immediately preceding taxable years: 1981, 1982, and 1983. Under paragraph (b) of this section, Y is treated as having been in existence during years 1981 and 1982 with qualified research expenses of zero. Because July 1 through December 31, 1983 is a short taxable year, paragraph (d)(2) of this section requires that the qualified research expenses for that year be adjusted to $160x for purposes of determining the average qualified research expenses during the base period. The $160x results from the actual qualified research expenses for that year ($80x) multiplied by 12 and divided by 6 (the number of months in the short taxable year). Accordingly, the amount determined under paragraph (c)(1) of this section (the average qualified research expenses for taxable years during the base period) is $53-1/3x (($0x + $0x + $160x) / 3). The amount determined under paragraph (c)(2) of this section is $100x (50 percent of $200x). The amount of base period research expenses is $100x. The credit for determination year 1984 is equal to 25 percent of the excess of $200x (the qualified research expenses incurred during the determination year) over $100x (the base period research expenses).

(iii) *Determination year 1985.* For determination year 1985, the base period consists of the 3 immediately preceding taxable years: 1982, 1983, and 1984. Pursuant to paragraph (b) of this section, Y is treated as having been in existence during 1982 with qualified research expenses of zero. Because July 1 through December 31, 1982, is a short taxable year, paragraph (d)(2) of this section requires that the qualified research expense for that year be adjusted to $160x for purposes of determining the average qualified research expenses for taxable years during the base period. This $160x is the actual qualified research expense for that year ($80x) multiplied by 12 and divided by 6 (the number of months in the short taxable year). Accordingly, the amount determined under paragraph (c)(1) of this section (the average qualified research expenses for taxable years during the base period) is $120x (($0x + $160x + $200x) / 3). The amount determined under paragraph (c)(2) of this section is $100x (50 percent of $200x). The amount of base period research expenses is $120x. The credit for determination year 1985 is equal to 25 percent of the excess of $200x (the qualified research expenses incurred during the determination year) over $120x (the base period research expenses). [Reg. § 1.41-3A.]

☐ [*T.D.* 8251, 5-16-89. *Redesignated by T.D.* 8930, 12-27-2000.]

[Reg. § 1.41-4A]

§ 1.41-4A. Qualified research for taxable years beginning before January 1, 1986.—(a) *General rule.* Except as otherwise provided in section 30(d) (as that section read before amendment by the Tax Reform Act of 1986) and in this section, the term "qualified research" means research, expenditures for which would be research and experimental expenditures within the meaning of section 174. Expenditures that are ineligible for the section 174 deduction elections are not expenditures for qualified research. For example, expenditures for the acquisition of land or depreciable property used in research, and mineral exploration costs described in section 174(d), are not expenditures for qualified research.

(b) *Activities outside the United States*—(1) *In-house research.* In-house research conducted outside the United States (as defined in section 7701(a)(9)) cannot constitute qualified research. Thus, wages paid to an employee scientist for services performed in a laboratory in the United States and in a test station in Antarctica must be apportioned between the services performed within the United States and the services performed outside the United States, and only the wages apportioned to the services conducted within the United States are qualified research expenses unless the 80 percent rule of § 1.41-2(d)(2) applies.

(2) *Contract research.* If contract research is performed partly within the United States and partly without, only 65 percent of the portion of the contract amount that is attributable to the research performed within the United States can qualify as contract research expense (even if 80 percent or more of the contract amount was for research performed in the United States).

(c) *Social sciences or humanities.* Qualified research does not include research in the social sciences or humanities. For purposes of section 30(d)(2) (as that section read before amendment by the Tax Reform Act of 1986) and of this section, the phrase "research in the social sciences or humanities" encompasses all areas of research other than research in a field of laboratory science (such as physics or biochemistry), engineering or technology. Examples of research in the social sciences or humanities include the development of a new life insurance contract, a new economic model or theory, a new accounting procedure or a new cookbook.

(d) *Research funded by any grant, contract, or otherwise*—(1) *In general.* Research does not constitute qualified research to the extent it is funded by any grant, contract, or otherwise by another person (including any governmental entity). All agreements (not only research contracts) entered into between the taxpayer performing the research and other persons shall be considered in determining the extent to which the research is funded. Amounts payable under any agreement that are contingent on the success of the research and thus considered to be paid for the product or result of the research (see § 1.41-2(e)(2)) are not treated as funding. For special rules regarding funding between commonly controlled businesses, see § 1.41-6(e).

(2) *Research in which taxpayer retains no rights.* If a taxpayer performing research for another person retains no substantial rights in research under the agreement providing for the research, the research is treated as fully funded for purposes of section 41(d)(4)(H), and no expenses paid or incurred by the taxpayer in performing the research are qualified research expenses. For example, if the taxpayer performs research under an agreement that confers on another person the exclusive right to exploit the results of the research, the taxpayer is not performing qualified research because the research is treated as fully funded under this paragraph (d)(2). Incidental benefits to the taxpayer from performance of the research (for example, increased experience in a field of research) do not constitute substantial rights in the research. If a taxpayer performing research for another person retains no substantial rights in the research and if the payments to the researcher are contingent upon the success of the research, neither the performer nor the person paying for the research is entitled to treat any portion of the expenditures as qualified research expenditures.

(3) *Research in which the taxpayer retains substantial rights*—(i) *In general.* If a taxpayer performing research for another person retains substantial rights in the research under the agreement providing for the research, the research is funded to the extent of the payments (and fair market value of any property) to which the taxpayer becomes entitled by performing the research. A taxpayer does not retain substantial rights in the research if the taxpayer must pay for the right to use the results of the research. Except as otherwise provided in paragraph (d)(3)(ii) of this section, the taxpayer shall reduce the amount paid or incurred by the taxpayer for the research that would, but for section 41(d)(4)(H), constitute qualified research expenses of the taxpayer by the amount of funding determined under the preceding sentence.

(ii) *Pro rata allocation.* If the taxpayer can establish to the satisfaction of the district director—

(A) The total amount of research expenses,

(B) That the total amount of research expenses exceed the funding, and

(C) That the otherwise qualified research expenses (that is, the expenses which would be qualified research expenses if there were no funding) exceed 65 percent of the funding, then the taxpayer may allocate the funding pro rata to nonqualified and otherwise qualified research expenses, rather than allocating it 100 percent to otherwise qualified research expenses (as provided in paragraph (d)(3)(i) of this section). In no event, however, shall less than 65 percent of the funding be applied against the otherwise qualified research expenses.

(iii) *Project-by-project determination.* The provisions of this paragraph (d)(3) shall be applied separately to each research project undertaken by the taxpayer.

(4) *Independent research and development under the Federal Acquisition Regulations System and similar provisions.* The Federal Acquisition Regulations System and similar rules and regulations relating to contracts (fixed price, cost plus, etc.) with government entities provide for allocation of certain "independent research and development costs" and "bid and proposal costs" of a contractor to contracts entered into with that contractor. In general, any "independent research and development costs" and "bid and proposal costs" paid to a taxpayer by reason of such a contract shall not be treated as funding the underlying research activities except to the extent the "independent research and development costs" and "bid and proposal costs" are properly severable from the contract. See § 1.451-3(e); see also section 804(d)(2) of the Tax Reform Act of 1986.

(5) *Funding determinable only in subsequent taxable year.* If at the time the taxpayer files its return for a taxable year, it is impossible to determine to what extent particular research performed by the taxpayer during that year may be funded, then the taxpayer shall treat the research as completely funded for purposes of completing that return. When the amount of funding is finally determined, the taxpayer should amend the return and any interim returns to reflect the proper amount of funding.

(6) *Examples.* The following examples illustrate the application of the principles contained in this paragraph.

Example (1). A enters into a contract with B Corporation, a cash-method taxpayer using the calendar year as its taxable year, under which B is to perform research that would, but for section 41(d)(3)(H), be qualified research of B. The agree-

Reg. § 1.41-4A(d)(2)

ment calls for A to pay B $120x, regardless of the outcome of the research. In 1982, A makes full payment of $120x under the contract, B performs all the research, and B pays all the expenses connected with the research, as follows:

In-house research expenses	$ 100x
Outside research	
(amount B paid to third parties for	
research, 65 percent of which	
($26x) is treated as a contract	
research expense of B)	40x
Overhead and other expenses	10x
Total	$150x

If B has no rights to the research, B is fully funded. Alternatively, assume that B retains the right to use the results of the research in carrying on B's business. Of B's otherwise qualified research expenses of $126x ($100x + $26x), $120x is treated as funded by A. Thus $6x ($126x − $120x) is treated as a qualified research expense of B. However, if B establishes the facts required under paragraph (d)(3) of this section, B can allocate the funding pro rata to nonqualified and otherwise qualified research expenses. Thus $100.8x ($120x ($126x/$150x)) would be allocated to otherwise qualified research expenses. B's qualified research expenses would be $25.2x ($126x − $100.8x). For purposes of the following examples (2), (3) and (4) assume that B retains substantial rights to use the results of the research in carrying on B's business.

Example (2). The facts are the same as in example (1) (assuming that B retains the right to use the results of the research in carrying on B's business) except that, although A makes full payment of $120x during 1982, B does not perform the research or pay the associated expenses until 1983. The computations are unchanged. However, B's qualified research expenses determined in example (1) are qualified research expenses during 1983.

Example (3). The facts are the same as in example (1) (assuming that B retains the right to use the results of the research in carrying on B's business) except that, although B performs the research and pays the associated expenses during 1982, A does not pay the $120x until 1983. The computations are unchanged and the amount determined in example (1) is a qualified research expense of B during 1982.

Example (4). The facts are the same as in example (1) (assuming that B retains the right to use the results of the research in carrying on B's business) except that, instead of agreeing to pay B $120x, A agrees to pay $100x regardless of the outcome and an additional $20x only if B's research produces a useful product. B's research produces a useful product and A pays B $120x

during 1982. The $20x payment that is conditional on the success of the research is not treated as funding. Assuming that B establishes to the satisfaction of the district director the actual research expenses, B can allocate the funding to nonqualified and otherwise qualified research expenses. Thus $84x ($100x ($126x/$150x)) would be allocated to otherwise qualified research expenses. B's qualified research expenses would be $42x ($126x − $84x).

Example (5). C enters into a contract with D, a cash-method taxpayer using the calendar year as its taxable year, under which D is to perform research in which both C and D will have substantial rights. C agrees to reimburse D for 80 percent of D's expenses for the research. D performs part of the research in 1982 and the rest in 1983. At the time that D files its return for 1982, D is unable to determine the extent to which the research is funded under the provisions of this paragraph. Under these circumstances, D may not treat any of the expenses paid by D for this research during 1982 as qualified research expenses on its 1982 return. When the project is complete and D can determine the extent of funding, D should file an amended return for 1982 to take into account any qualified research expense for 1982. [Reg. § 1.41-4A.]

☐ [*T.D. 8251*, 5-16-89. *Redesignated and amended by T.D. 8930*, 12-27-2000.]

[Reg. § 1.41-5A]

§ 1.41-5A. Basic research for taxable years beginning before January 1, 1987.—(a) *In general.* The amount expended for basic research within the meaning of section 30(e) (before amendment by the Tax Reform Act of 1986) equals the sum of money plus the taxpayer's basis in tangible property (other than land) transferred for use in the performance of basic research.

(b) *Trade or business requirement.* Any amount treated as a contract research expense under section 30(e) (before amendment by the Tax Reform Act of 1986) shall be deemed to have been paid or incurred in carrying on a trade or business, if the corporation that paid or incurred the expense is actually engaged in carrying on some trade or business.

(c) *Prepaid amounts*—(1) *In general.* If any basic research expense paid or incurred during any taxable year is attributable to research to be conducted after the close of such taxable year, the expense so attributable shall be treated for purposes of section 30(b)(1)(B) (before amendment by the Tax Reform Act of 1986) as paid or incurred during the period in which the basic research is conducted.

Reg. § 1.41-5A(c)(1)

(2) *Transfers of property.* In the case of transfers of property to be used in the performance of basic research, the research in which that property is to be used shall be considered to be conducted ratably over a period beginning on the day the property is first so used and continuing for the number of years provided with respect to property of that class under section 168(c)(2) (before amendment by the Tax Reform Act of 1986). For example, if an item of property which is 3-year property under section 168(c) is transferred to a university for basic research on January 12, 1983, and is first so used by the university on March 1, 1983, then the research in which that property is used is considered to be conducted ratably from March 1, 1983, through February 28, 1986.

(d) *Written research agreement*—(1) *In general.* A written research agreement must be entered into prior to the performance of the basic research.

(2) *Agreement between a corporation and a qualified organization after June 30, 1983*—(i) *In general.* A written research agreement between a corporation and a qualified organization (including a qualified fund) entered into after June 30, 1983, shall provide that the organization shall inform the corporation within 60 days after the close of each taxable year of the corporation what amount of funds provided by the corporation pursuant to the agreement was expended on basic research during the taxable year of the corporation. In determining amounts expended on basic research, the qualified organization shall take into account the exclusions specified in section 30(e)(3) (before amendment by the Tax Reform Act of 1986) and in paragraph (e) of this section.

(ii) *Transfers of property.* In the case of transfers of property to be used in basic research, the agreement shall provide that substantially all use of the property is to be for basic research, as defined in section 30(e)(3) (before amendment by the Tax Reform Act of 1986).

(3) *Agreement between a qualified fund and a qualified educational organization after June 30, 1983.* A written research agreement between a qualified fund and a qualified educational organization (see section 30(e)(4)(B)(iii) (before amendment by the Tax Reform Act of 1986)) entered into after June 30, 1983, shall provide that the qualified educational organization shall furnish sufficient information to the qualified fund to enable the qualified fund to comply with the written research agreements it has entered into with grantor corporations, including the requirement set forth in paragraph (d)(2) of this section.

(e) *Exclusions*—(1) *Research conducted outside the United States.* If a taxpayer pays or incurs an amount for basic research to be performed partly within the United States and partly without, only 65 percent of the portion of the amount attributable to research performed within the United States can be treated as a contract research expense (even if 80 percent or more of the contract amount was for basic research performed in the United States).

(2) *Research in the social sciences or humanities.* Basic research does not include research in the social sciences or humanities, within the meaning of § 1.41-4A(c).

(f) *Procedure for making an election to be treated as a qualified fund.* In order to make an election to be treated as a qualified fund within the meaning of section 30(e)(4)(B)(iii) (before amendment by the Tax Reform Act of 1986) or as an organization described in section 41(e)(6)(D), the organization shall file with the Internal Revenue service center with which it files its annual return a statement that—

(1) Sets out the name, address, and taxpayer identification number of the electing organization (the "taxpayer") and of the organization that established and maintains the electing organization (the "controlling organization"),

(2) Identifies the election as an election under section 41(e)(6)(D) of the Code,

(3) Affirms that the controlling organization and the taxpayer are section 501(c)(3) organizations,

(4) Provides that the taxpayer elects to be treated as a private foundation for all Code purposes other than section 4940,

(5) Affirms that the taxpayer satisfies the requirement of section 41(e)(6)(D)(iii), and

(6) Specifies the date on which the election is to become effective.

If an election to be treated as a qualified fund is filed before February 1, 1982, the election may be made effective as of any date after June 30, 1981, and before January 1, 1986. If an election is filed on or after February 1, 1982, the election may be made effective as of any date on or after the date on which the election is filed. [Reg. § 1.41-5A.]

☐ [*T.D.* 8251, 5-16-89. *Redesignated and amended by T.D. 8930, 12-27-2000.*]

[Reg. § 1.42-0]

§ 1.42-0. **Table of contents.**—This section lists the paragraphs contained in § § 1.42-1 and 1.42-2.

§ 1.42-1. [Reserved]

§ 1.42-2. Waiver of requirement that an existing building eligible for the low-income housing credit

Reg. § 1.42-0

was last placed in service more than 10 years prior to acquisition by the taxpayer.

(a) Low-income housing credit for existing building

(b) Waiver of 10-year holding period requirement

(c) Waiver requirements

    (1) Federally-assisted building

    (2) Federal mortgage funds at risk

    (3) Statement by the Department of Housing and Urban Development or the Farmers' Home Administration

    (4) No prior credit allowed

(d) Application for waiver

    (1) Time and manner

    (2) Information required

    (3) Other rules

    (4) Effective date of waiver

    (5) Attachment to return

(e) Effective date of regulations

[Reg. § 1.42-0.]

☐ [*T.D.* 8302, 5-22-90.]

[Reg. § 1.42-1]

§ 1.42-1. [Reserved]

[Reg. § 1.42-1T]

§ 1.42-1T. Limitation on low-income housing credit allowed with respect to qualified low-income buildings receiving housing credit allocations from a State or local housing credit agency (temporary).—(a) *In general*—(1) *Determination of amount of low-income housing credit.* Section 42 provides that, for purposes of section 38, a low-income housing credit is determined for a building in an amount equal to the applicable percentage of the qualified basis of the qualified low-income building. In general, the credit may be claimed annually for a 10-year credit period, beginning with the taxable year in which the building is placed in service or, at the election of the taxpayer, the succeeding taxable year. If, after the first year of the credit period, the qualified basis of a building is increased in excess of the qualified basis upon which the credit was initially determined, the allowable credit with respect to such additional qualified basis is determined using a credit percentage equal to two-thirds of the applicable percentage for the initial qualified basis. The credit for additions to qualified basis is generally allowable for the remaining years in the 15-year compliance period which begins with the first taxable year of the credit period for the building. In general, the low-income housing credit is available with respect to build-

ings placed in service after December [...] taxable years ending after that date [...] 42 for the definitions of "qualified [...] building", "applicable percentage", "q[...] sis", "credit period", "compliance period [...] other rules relating to determinatio[...] amount of the low-income housing credit. [...]

(2) *Limitation on low-income housing allowed.* Generally, the low-income housing determined under section 42 is allowed and [...] be claimed for any taxable year if, and to [...] extent that, the owner of a qualified low-inc[...] building receives a housing credit allocation fr[...] a State or local housing credit agency. The agg[...] gate amount of housing credit allocations th[...] may be made in any calendar year by all housin[...] credit agencies within a State is limited by a State housing credit ceiling, or volume cap, described in paragraph (b). The authority to make housing credit allocations within the State housing credit ceiling may be apportioned among the State and local housing credit agencies, under the rules prescribed in paragraph (c). Upon apportionment of the State housing credit volume cap, each State or local housing credit agency receives an aggregate housing credit dollar amount that may be used to make housing credit allocations among qualified low-income buildings located within an agency's geographic jurisdiction. The rules governing the making of housing credit allocations by any State or local housing credit agency are provided in paragraph (d). Housing credit allocations are required to be taken into account by owners of qualified low-income buildings under the rules prescribed in paragraph (e). Exceptions to the requirement that a qualified low-income building receive a housing credit allocation from a State or local housing credit agency are provided in paragraph (f). Rules regarding termination of the authority of State and local housing credit agencies to make housing credit allocations after December 31, 1989, are specified in paragraph (g). Rules concerning information reporting by State and local housing credit agencies and owners of qualified low-income buildings are provided in paragraph (h). Special statutory transitional rules are incorporated into this section of the regulations as described in paragraph (i) of this section.

(b) *The State housing credit ceiling.* The aggregate amount of housing credit allocations that may be made in any calendar year by all State and local housing credit agencies within a State may not exceed the State's housing credit ceiling for such calendar year. The State housing credit ceiling for each State for any calendar year is equal to $1.25 multiplied by the State's population. A State's population for any calendar year is determined by reference to the most recent census

Reg. § 1.42-1T(b)

imate (whether final or provisional) of the resi-
nt population of the State released by the Bu-
au of the Census before the beginning of the
lendar year for which the State's housing credit
iling is set. Unless otherwise prescribed by ap-
licable revenue procedure, determinations of
opulation are based on the most recent estimates
f population contained in the Bureau of the Census publication, "Current Population Reports, Series P-25: Population Estimates and Projections,
Estimates of the Population of States". For purposes of this section, the District of Columbia and
United States possessions are treated as States.

(c) *Apportionment of State housing credit ceiling among State and local housing credit agencies*—(1) *In general.* A State's housing credit
ceiling for any calendar year is apportioned
among the State and local housing credit agencies
within such State under the rules prescribed in
this paragraph. A "State housing credit agency"
is any State agency specifically authorized by
gubernatorial act or State statute to make housing
credit allocations on behalf of the State and to
carry out the provisions of section 42(h). A "local
housing credit agency" is any agency of a political
subdivision of the State that is specifically authorized by a State enabling act to make housing
credit allocations on behalf of the State or political subdivision and to carry out the provisions of
section 42(h). A "State enabling act" is any gubernatorial act, State statute, or State housing
credit agency regulation (if authorized by gubernatorial act or State statute). A State enabling act
enacted on or before October 22, 1986, the date of
enactment of the Tax Reform Act of 1986, shall
be given effect for purposes of this paragraph if
such State enabling act expressly carries out the
provisions of section 42(h).

(2) *Primary apportionment.* Except as otherwise provided in paragraph (c)(3) and (4), a
State's housing credit ceiling is apportioned in its
entirety to the State housing credit agency. Such
an apportionment is the "primary apportionment" of a State's housing credit ceiling. There
shall be no primary apportionment of the State
housing credit ceiling and no grants of housing
credit allocations in such State until a State housing credit agency is authorized by gubernatorial
act or State statute. If a State has more than one
State housing credit agency, such agencies shall
be treated as a single agency for purposes of the
primary apportionment. In such a case, the State
housing credit ceiling may be divided among the
multiple State housing credit agencies pursuant to
gubernatorial act or State statute.

(3) *States with 1 or more constitutional home
rule cities*—(i) *In general.* Notwithstanding para-

graph (c)(2), in any State with 1 or more constitutional home rule cities, a portion of the State
housing credit ceiling is apportioned to each constitutional home rule city. In such a State, except
as provided in paragraph (c)(4), the remainder of
the State housing credit ceiling is apportioned to
the State housing credit agency under paragraph
(c)(2). *See* paragraph (c)(3)(iii). The term "constitutional home rule city" means, with respect to
any calendar year, any political subdivision of a
State that, under a State constitution that was
adopted in 1970 and effective on July 1, 1971, had
home rule powers on the first day of the calendar
year.

(ii) *Amount of apportionment to a constitutional home rule city.* The amount of the State
housing credit ceiling apportioned to a constitutional home rule city for any calendar year is an
amount that bears the same ratio to the State
housing credit ceiling for that year as the population of the constitutional home rule city bears to
the population of the entire State. The population
of any constitutional home rule city for any calendar year is determined by reference to the most
recent census estimate (whether final or provisional) of the resident population of the constitutional home rule city released by the Bureau of
the Census before the beginning of the calendar
year for which the State housing credit ceiling is
apportioned. However, determinations of the population of a constitutional home rule city may not
be based on Bureau of the Census estimates that
do not contain estimates for all of the constitutional home rule cities within the State. If no
Bureau of the Census estimate is available for all
such constitutional home rule cities, the most recent decennial census of population shall be relied
on. Unless otherwise prescribed by applicable revenue procedure, determinations of population for
constitutional home rule cities are based on estimates of population contained in the Bureau of
the Census publication, "Current Population Reports, Series P-26: Local Population Estimates".

(iii) *Effect of apportionments to constitutional home rule cities on apportionments to other
housing credit agencies.* The aggregate amounts of
the State housing credit ceiling apportioned to
constitutional home rule cities under this paragraph (c)(3) reduce the State housing credit ceiling available for apportionment under paragraph
(c)(2) or (4). Unless otherwise provided in a State
constitutional amendment or by law changing the
home rule provisions adopted in a manner provided by the State constitution, the power of the
governor or State legislature to apportion the
State housing credit ceiling among local housing
credit agencies under paragraph (c)(4) shall not
be construed as allowing any reduction of the

portion of the State housing credit ceiling apportioned to a constitutional home rule city under this paragraph (c)(3). However, any constitutional home rule city may agree to a reduction in its apportionment of the State housing credit ceiling under this paragraph (c)(3), in which case the amount of the State housing credit ceiling not apportioned to the constitutional home rule city shall be available for apportionment under paragraph (c)(2) or (4).

(iv) *Treatment of governmental authority within constitutional home rule city.* For purposes of determining which agency within a constitutional home rule city receives the apportionment of the State housing credit ceiling under this paragraph (c)(3), the rules of this paragraph (c) shall be applied by treating the constitutional home rule city as a "State", the chief executive officer of a constitutional home rule city as a "governor", and a city council as a "State legislature". A constitutional home rule city is also treated as a "State" for purposes of the set-aside requirement for housing credit allocations to projects involving a qualified nonprofit organization. *See* paragraph (c)(5) for rules governing set-aside requirements. In this connection, a constitutional home rule city may agree with the State housing credit agency to exchange an apportionment set aside for projects involving a qualified nonprofit organization for an apportionment that is not so restricted. In such a case, the authorizing gubernatorial act, State statute, or State housing credit agency regulation (if authorized by gubernatorial act or State statute) must ensure that the set-aside apportionment transferred to the State housing credit agency be used for the purposes described in paragraph (c)(5).

(4) *Apportionment to local housing credit agencies*—(i) *In general.* In lieu of the primary apportionment under paragraph (c)(2), all or a portion of the State housing credit ceiling may be apportioned among housing credit agencies of governmental subdivisions. Apportionments of the State housing credit ceiling to local housing credit agencies must be made pursuant to a State enabling act as defined in paragraph (c)(1). Apportionments of the State housing credit ceiling may be made to housing credit agencies of constitutional home rule cities under this paragraph (c)(4), in addition to apportionments made under paragraph (c)(3). Apportionments of the State housing credit ceiling under this paragraph (c)(4) need not be based on the population of political subdivisions and may, but are not required to, give balanced consideration to the low-income housing needs of the entire State.

(ii) *Change in apportionments during a calendar year.* The apportionment of the State housing credit ceiling among State and local housing credit agencies under this paragraph (c)(4) may be changed after the beginning of a calendar year, pursuant to a State enabling act. No change in apportionments shall retroactively reduce the housing credit allocations made by any agency during such year. Any change in the apportionment of the State housing credit ceiling under this paragraph (c)(4) that occurs during a calendar year is effective only to the extent housing credit agencies have not previously made housing credit allocations during such year from their original apportionments of the State housing credit ceiling for such year. To the extent apportionments of the State housing credit ceiling to local housing credit agencies made pursuant to this paragraph (c)(4) for any calendar year are not used by such local agencies before a certain date (*e.g.,* November 1) to make housing credit allocations in such year, the amount of unused apportionments may revert back to the State housing credit agency for reapportionment. Such reversion must be specifically authorized by the State enabling act.

(iii) *Exchanges of apportionments.* Any State or local housing credit agency that receives an apportionment of the State housing credit ceiling for any calendar year under this paragraph (c)(4) may exchange part or all of such apportionment with another State or local housing credit agency to the extent no housing credit allocations have been made in such year from the exchanged portions. Such exchanges must be made with another housing credit agency in the same State and must be consistent with the State enabling act. If an apportionment set aside for projects involving a qualified nonprofit organization is transferred or exchanged, the transferee housing credit agency shall be required to use the set-aside apportionment for the purposes described in paragraph (c)(5).

(iv) *Written records of apportionments.* All apportionments, exchanges of apportionments, and reapportionments of the State housing credit ceiling which are authorized by this paragraph (c)(4) must be evidenced in the written records maintained by each State and local housing credit agency.

(5) *Set-aside apportionments for projects involving a qualified nonprofit organization*—(i) *In general.* Ten percent of the State housing credit ceiling for a calendar year must be set aside exclusively for projects involving a qualified nonprofit organization (as defined in paragraph (c)(5)(ii)). Thus, at least 10 percent of apportionments of the State housing credit ceiling under

Reg. § 1.42-1T(c)(5)

paragraph (c)(2) and (3) must be used only to make housing credit allocations to buildings that are part of projects involving a qualified nonprofit organization. In the case of apportionments of the State housing credit ceiling under paragraph (c)(4), the State enabling act must ensure that the apportionment of at least 10 percent of the State housing credit ceiling be used exclusively to make housing credit allocations to buildings that are part of projects involving a qualified nonprofit organization. The State enabling act shall prescribe which housing credit agencies in the State receive apportionments that must be set aside for making housing credit allocations to buildings that are part of projects involving a qualified nonprofit organization. These set-aside apportionments may be distributed disproportionately among the State or local housing credit agencies receiving apportionments under paragraph (c)(4). The 10-percent set-aside requirement of this paragraph (c)(4) is a minimum requirement, and the State enabling act may set aside more than 10 percent of the State housing credit ceiling for apportionment to housing credit agencies for exclusive use in making housing credit allocations to buildings that are part of projects involving a qualified nonprofit organization.

(ii) *Projects involving a qualified nonprofit organization.* The term "projects involving a qualified nonprofit organization" means projects with respect to which a qualified nonprofit organization is to materially participate (within the meaning of section 469(h)) in the development and continuing operation of the project throughout the 15-year compliance period. The term "qualified nonprofit organization" means any organization that is described in section 501(c)(3) or (4), is exempt from tax under section 501(a), and includes as one of its exempt purposes the fostering of low-income housing.

(6) *Expiration of unused apportionments.* Apportionments of the State housing credit ceiling under this paragraph (c) for any calendar year may be used by housing credit agencies to make housing credit allocations only in such calendar year. Any part of an apportionment of the State housing credit ceiling for any calendar year that is not used for housing credit allocations in such year expires as of the end of such year and does not carry over to any other year. However, any part of an apportionment for 1989 that is not used to make a housing credit allocation in 1989 may be carried over to 1990 and used to make a housing credit allocation to a qualified low-income building described in section 42(n)(2)(B). *See* paragraph (g)(2).

(d) *Housing credit allocations made by State and local housing credit agencies*—(1) *In general.* This paragraph governs State and local housing credit agencies in making housing credit allocations to qualified low-income buildings. The amount of the apportionment of the State housing credit ceiling for any calendar year received by any State or local housing credit agency under paragraph (c) constitutes the agency's aggregate housing credit dollar amount for such year. The aggregate amount of housing credit allocations made in any calendar year by a State or local housing credit agency may not exceed such agency's aggregate housing credit dollar amount for such year. A State or local housing credit agency may make housing credit allocations only to qualified low-income buildings located within the agency's geographic jurisdiction.

(2) *Amount of a housing credit allocation.* In making a housing credit allocation, a State or local housing credit agency must specify a credit percentage, not to exceed the building's applicable percentage determined under section 42(b), and a qualified basis amount. The amount of the housing credit allocation for any building is the product of the specified credit percentage and the specified qualified basis amount. In specifying the credit percentage and qualified basis amount, the State or local housing credit agency shall not take account of the first-year conventions described in section 42(f)(2)(A) and (3)(B). A State or local housing credit agency may adopt rules or regulations governing conditions for specification of less than the maximum credit percentage and qualified basis amount allowable under section 42(b) and (c), respectively. For example, an agency may specify a credit percentage and a qualified basis amount of less than the maximum credit percentage and qualified basis amount allowable under section 42(b) and (c), respectively, when the financing and rental assistance from all sources for the project of which the building is a part is sufficient to provide the continuing operation of the building without the maximum credit amount allowable under section 42.

(3) *Counting housing credit allocations against an agency's aggregate housing credit dollar amount.* The aggregate amount of housing credit allocations made in any calendar year by a State or local housing credit agency may not exceed such agency's aggregate housing credit dollar amount (*i.e.,* the agency's apportionment of the State housing credit ceiling for such year). This limitation on the aggregate dollar amount of housing credit allocations shall be computed separately for set-aside apportionments received pursuant to paragraph (c)(5) of this section. Housing credit allocations count against an agency's

Reg. § 1.42-1T(c)(6)

aggregate housing credit dollar amount without regard to the amount or credit allowable to or claimed by an owner of a building in the taxable year in which the allocation is made or in any subsequent year. Thus, housing credit allocations (which are computed without regard to the first-year conventions as provided in paragraph (d)(2)) count in full against an agency's aggregate housing credit dollar amount, even though the first-year conventions described in section 42(f)(2)(A) and (3)(B) may reduce the amount of credit claimed by a taxpayer in the first year in which a credit is allowable. *See also* paragraph (e)(2). Housing credit allocations count against an agency's aggregate housing credit dollar amount only in the calendar year in which made and not in subsequent taxable years in the credit period or compliance period during which a taxpayer may claim a credit based on the original housing credit allocation. Since the aggregate amount of housing credit allocations made in any calendar year by a State or local housing credit agency may not exceed such agency's aggregate housing credit dollar amount, an agency shall at all times during a calendar year maintain a record of its cumulative allocations made during such year and its remaining unused aggregate housing credit dollar amount.

(4) *Rules for when applications for housing credit allocations exceed an agency's aggregate housing credit dollar amount.* A State or local housing credit agency may adopt rules or regulations governing the awarding of housing credit allocations when an agency expects that applicants during a calendar year will seek aggregate allocations in excess of the agency's aggregate housing credit dollar amount. The State enabling act may provide uniform standards for the awarding of housing credit allocations when there is actual or anticipated excess demand from applicants in any calendar year.

(5) *Reduced or additional housing credit allocations*—(i) *In general.* A State or local housing credit agency may not reduce or rescind a housing credit allocation made to a qualified low-income building in the manner prescribed in paragraph (d)(8). Thus, a housing credit agency may not reduce or rescind a housing credit allocation made to a qualified low-income building which is acquired by a new owner who is entitled to a carry-over of the allowable credit for such building under section 42(d)(7). A housing credit agency may make additional housing credit allocations to a building in any year in the building's compliance period, whether or not there are additions to qualified basis for which an increased credit is allowable under section 42(f)(3). Each additional housing credit allocation made to a building is

treated as a separate allocation and is subject to the rules and requirements of this section. However, in the case of an additional housing credit allocation made with respect to additions to qualified basis for which an increased credit is allowable under section 42(f)(3), the amount of the allocation that counts against the agency's aggregate housing credit dollar amount shall be computed as if the specified credit percentage were unreduced in the manner prescribed in section 42(f)(3)(A) and the specified qualified basis amount were unreduced by the first-year convention prescribed in section 42(f)(3)(B).

(ii) *Examples.* The rules of paragraph (d)(5)(i) may be illustrated by the following examples:

Example (1). For 1987, the County L Housing Credit Agency has an aggregate housing credit dollar amount of $2 million. D, an individual, places in service on July 1, 1987, a new qualified low-income building. As of the close of each month in 1987 in which the building is in service, the building consists of 100 residential rental units, of which 20 units are both rent-restricted and occupied by individuals whose income is 50 percent or less of area median gross income. The total floor space of the residential rental units is 120,000 square feet, and the total floor space of the low-income units is 20,000 square feet. The building is not Federally subsidized within the meaning of section 42(i)(2). As of the end of 1987, the building has eligible basis under section 42(d) of $1 million. Thus, the qualified basis of the building determined without regard to the first-year convention provided in section 42(f) is $166,666.67 (*i.e.,* $1 million eligible basis times 1/6, the floor space fraction which is required to be used instead of the larger unit fraction). However, the amount of the low-income housing credit determined for 1987 under section 42 reflects the first-year convention provided in section 42(f)(2). Since the building has the same floor space and unit fractions as of the close of each of the six months in 1987 during which it is in service, upon applying the first-year convention in section 42(f)(2), the qualified basis of the building in 1987 is $83,333.33 (*i.e.,* $1 million eligible basis times 1/12, the fraction determined under section 42(f)(2)(A)). Under paragraph (d)(2) of this section, the County L Housing Credit Agency may make a housing credit allocation by specifying a credit percentage, not to exceed 9 percent, and a qualified basis amount, which may be greater or less than the qualified basis of the building in 1987 as determined under section 42(c), without regard to the first-year convention provided in section 42(f)(2). If the County L Housing Credit Agency specifies a credit percentage of 8 percent and a qualified basis amount of $100,000, the amount of the housing credit allocation is $8,000. Under paragraph (d)(3) of this section, the County L Housing Credit Agency's aggregate housing credit dollar amount for 1987 is reduced by $8,000, notwithstanding that D is entitled to claim less than $8,000 of the credit in 1987 under the rules in paragraph (e) of this section. Under paragraph (e)(2), in 1987 D is entitled to claim only $4,000 of the credit, determined by applying the first-year convention of 6/12 to the specified qualified basis amount contained in the housing credit allocation (i.e., .08 × $100,000 × (6/12)).

Example (2). The facts are the same as in *Example (1)* except that on July 1, 1988, the number of occupied low-income units increases to 50 units and the floor space of the occupied low-income units increases to 48,000 square feet. These occupancy fractions remain unchanged as of the close of each month remaining in 1988. Under section 42(c), the qualified basis of the building in 1988, without regard to the first-year convention in section 42(f)(3)(B), is $400,000 (i.e., $1 million eligible basis times .4, the floor space fraction which is required to be used instead of the larger unit fraction). D's 1987 housing credit allocation from the County L Housing Credit Agency remains effective in 1988 and entitles D to a credit of $8,000 (i.e., .08, the specified credit percentage, times $100,000, the specified qualified basis amount). With respect to the additional $300,000 of qualified basis which the 1987 housing credit allocation does not cover, D must apply to the County L Housing Credit Agency for an additional housing credit allocation. Assume that the County L Housing Credit Agency has a sufficient aggregate housing credit dollar amount for 1988 to make a housing credit allocation to D in 1988 by specifying a credit percentage of 9 percent and a qualified basis amount of $300,000. The amount of the housing credit allocation that counts against the County L Housing Credit Agency's aggregate housing credit dollar amount is $27,000 (i.e., the amount counted (.09 times $300,000) is unreduced in the manner prescribed in section 42(f)(3)(A) and (B)). Since D's qualified basis in 1987 was $166,666.67, D is entitled to claim a credit in 1988 with respect to such basis of $14,000 (i.e., .08 × $100,000, the 1987 credit allocation, + .09 × $66,666.67, the 1988 credit allocation). In addition, D is entitled to claim a credit in 1988 and subsequent years in the 15-year compliance period with respect to the additional $233,333.33 of qualified basis covered by the 1988 housing credit allocation. However, the allowable credit for 1988 with respect to this amount of additional qualified basis is subject to

reductions prescribed in section 42(f)(3)(A) and (B). Thus, D is entitled in 1988 to a credit at a 6-percent rate applied to $116,666.67 of additional qualified basis, which is reduced to reflect the first-year convention. D's total allowable low-income housing credit in 1988 is $21,000 (i.e., $14,000 with respect to original qualified basis + $7,000 with respect to 1988 additions to qualified basis). If the County L Housing Credit Agency had specified an 8-percent credit percentage in 1988 with respect to the qualified basis not covered by the 1987 housing credit allocation to D, D's allowable credit with respect to the $233,333.33 of additions to qualified basis would not exceed, in 1988 and subsequent years, an amount determined by applying a specified credit percentage of 5.33 percent (i.e., two-thirds of 8 percent). In 1988, D's specified qualified basis amount would be adjusted for the first-year convention.

(6) *No carryover of unused aggregate housing credit dollar amount*. Any portion of a State or local housing credit agency's aggregate housing credit dollar amount for any calendar year that is not used to make a housing credit allocation in such year may not be carried over to any other year, except as provided in paragraph (g). An agency may not permit owners of qualified low-income buildings to transfer housing credit allocations to other buildings. However, an agency may provide a procedure whereby owners may return to the agency, prior to the end of the calendar year in which housing credit allocations are made, unusable portions of such allocations. In such a case, an owner's housing credit allocation is deemed reduced by the amount of the allocation returned to the agency, and the agency may reallocate such amount to other qualified low-income buildings prior to the end of the year.

(7) *Effect of housing credit allocations in excess of an agency's aggregate housing credit dollar amount*. In the event that a State or local housing credit agency makes housing credit allocations in excess of its aggregate housing credit dollar amount for any calendar year, the allocations shall be deemed reduced (to the extent of such excess) for buildings in the reverse order in which such allocations were made during such year.

(8) *Time and manner for making housing credit allocations*—(i) *Time*. Housing credit allocations are effective for the calendar year in which made in the manner prescribed in paragraph (d)(8)(ii). A State or local housing credit agency may not make a housing credit allocation to a qualified low-income building prior to the calendar year in which such building is placed in

Reg. § 1.42-1T(d)(6)

service. An agency may adopt its own procedures for receiving applications for housing credit allocations from owners of qualified low-income buildings. An agency may provide a procedure for making, in advance of a building's being placed in service, a binding commitment (*e.g.*, by contract, inducement resolution, or other means) to make a housing credit allocation in the calendar year in which a qualified low-income building is placed in service or in a subsequent calendar year. Any advance commitment shall not constitute a housing credit allocation for purposes of this section.

(ii) *Manner.* Housing credit allocations are deemed made when Part I of IRS Form 8609, Low-Income Housing Credit Allocation Certification, is completed and signed by an authorized official of the housing credit agency and mailed to the owner of the qualified low-income building. A copy of all completed (as to Part I) Form 8609 allocations along with a single completed Form 8610, Annual Low-Income Housing Credit Agencies Report, must also be mailed to the Internal Revenue Service not later than the 28th day of the second calendar month after the close of the calendar year in which the housing credit was allocated to the qualified low-income building. Housing credit allocations to a qualified low-income building must be made on Form 8609 and must include—

(A) The address of the building;

(B) The name, address, and taxpayer identification number of the housing credit agency making the housing credit allocation;

(C) The name, address, and taxpayer identification number of the owner of the qualified low-income building;

(D) The date of the allocation of housing credit;

(E) The housing credit dollar amount allocated to the building on such date;

(F) The specified maximum applicable credit percentage allocated to the building on such date;

(G) The specified maximum qualified basis amount;

(H) The percentage of the aggregate basis financed by tax-exempt bonds taken into account for purposes of the volume cap under section 146;

(I) A certification under penalties of perjury by an authorized State or local housing credit agency official that the allocation is made in compliance with the requirements of section 42(h); and

(J) Any additional information that may be required by Form 8609 or by an applicable revenue procedure.

See paragraph (h) for additional rules concerning filing of forms.

(iii) *Certification.* The certifying official for the State or local housing credit agency need not perform an independent investigation of the qualified low-income building in order to certify on Part I of Form 8609 that the housing credit allocation meets the requirements of section 42(h). For example, the certifying official may rely on information contained in an application for a low-income housing credit allocation submitted by the building owner which sets forth facts necessary to determine that the building is eligible for the low-income housing credit under section 42.

(iv) *Fee.* A State or local housing credit agency may charge building owners applying for housing credit allocations a reasonable fee to cover the agency's administrative expenses for processing applications.

(v) *No continuing agency responsibility.* The State or local housing credit agency need not monitor or investigate the continued compliance of a qualified low-income building with the requirements of section 42 throughout the applicable compliance period.

(e) *Housing credit allocation taken into account by owner of a qualified low-income building*—(1) *Time and manner for taking housing credit allocation into account.* An owner of a qualified low-income building may not claim a low-income housing credit determined under section 42 in any year in excess of an effective housing credit allocation received from a State or local housing credit agency. A housing credit allocation made to a qualified low-income building is effective with respect to any owner of the building beginning with the owner's taxable year in which the housing credit allocation is received. A housing credit allocation is deemed received in a taxable year, except as modified in the succeeding sentence, if that allocation is made (in the manner described in paragraph (d)(8)) not later than the earlier of (i) the 60th day after the close of the taxable year, or (ii) the close of the calendar year in which such taxable year ends. A housing credit allocation is deemed received in a taxable year ending in 1987, if such allocation is made (in the manner described in paragraph (d)(8)) on or before December 31, 1987. A housing credit allocation is not effective for any taxable year if received in a calendar year which ends prior to when the qualified low-income building is placed in service. A housing credit allocation made to a qualified low-

Reg. § 1.42-1T(e)(1)

income building remains effective for all taxable years in the compliance period. A taxpayer is required to complete the Form 8609 on which a housing credit agency made the applicable housing credit allocation and submit a copy of such Form 8609 with its Federal income tax return for each year in the compliance period. Failure to comply with the requirement of the preceding sentence with respect to any taxable year after the first taxable year in the credit period shall be treated as a mathematical or clerical error for purposes of the provisions of section 6213(b)(1) and (g)(2).

(2) *First-year convention limitation on housing credit allocation taken into account.* For purposes of the limitation that the allowable low-income housing credit may not exceed the effective housing credit allocation received from a State or local housing credit agency, as provided in paragraph (e)(1), the amount of the effective housing credit allocation shall be adjusted by applying the first-year convention provided in section 42(f)(2)(A) and (3)(B) and the percentage credit reduction provided in section 42(f)(3)(A). Under paragraph (d)(2) and (5), the State or local housing credit agency must specify the credit percentage and qualified basis amount, the product of which is the amount of the housing credit allocation, without taking account of the first-year convention described in section 42(f)(2)(A) and (3)(B) or the percentage credit reduction prescribed in section 42(f)(3)(A). However, for purposes of the limitation on the amount of the allowable low-income housing credit, as provided in paragraph (e)(1), in a taxable year in which the first-year convention applies to the amount of credit determined under section 42(a), the specified qualified basis amount shall be adjusted by the first-year convention fraction which is equal to the number of full months (during the first taxable year) in which the building was in service divided by 12. In addition, for purposes of the limitation on the amount of the allowable low-income housing credit, as provided in paragraph (e)(1), in a taxable year in which the reduction in credit percentage applies to additions to qualified basis, as prescribed in section 42(f)(3), the specified credit percentage shall be reduced by one-third. *See* examples in paragraph (d)(5)(ii) and (e)(3)(ii) of this section.

(3) *Use of excess housing credit allocation for increases in qualified basis*—(i) *In general.* If the housing credit allocation made to a qualified low-income building exceeds the amount of credit allowable with respect to such building in any taxable year (without regard to the first-year conventions under section 42(f)), such excess is not transferable to another qualified low-income

building. However, if in a subsequent year there are increases in the qualified basis for which an increased credit is allowable under section 42(f)(3) at a reduced credit percentage, the original housing credit allocation (including the specified credit percentage and qualified basis amount) would be effective with respect to such increased credit.

(ii) *Example.* The provisions of this paragraph (e)(3) may be illustrated by the following example:

Example. In 1987, a newly-constructed qualified low-income building receives a housing credit allocation of $90,000 based on a specified credit percentage of 9 percent and a specified qualified basis amount of $1,000,000. The building is placed in service in 1987, but the qualified basis in such year is only $800,000, resulting in an allowable credit in 1987 (determined without regard to the first-year conventions) of $72,000. In 1988, the qualified basis is increased to $1,100,000, resulting in an additional credit allowable under section 42(f)(3) (without regard to the first-year conventions) of $18,000 (*i.e.,* $300,000 × .06, or 2/3 of .09). The unused portion of the 1987 housing credit allocation ($18,000) is effective in 1988 and in each subsequent year in the compliance period only with respect to the specified qualified basis for the 1987 housing credit allocation ($1,000,000). Thus, the owner is allowed to claim a credit in 1988 and in each subsequent year (without regard to the first-year conventions), based on the effective housing credit allocation from 1987, of $84,000 (*i.e.,* $72,000 + ($200,000 × .06)). The owner of the qualified low-income building must obtain a new housing credit allocation in 1988 with respect to the additional $100,000 of qualified basis in order to claim a credit on such basis in 1988 and in each subsequent year. If the applicable first-year convention under section 42(f)(3)(B) entitled the owner in 1988 to only 1/2 of the otherwise applicable credit for the additions to qualified basis, under paragraph (e)(2) of this section the owner is allowed to claim a credit in 1988, based on the effective housing credit allocation from 1987, of $78,000 (*i.e.,* $72,000 + ($200,000 × .06 × .5)).

(4) *Separate housing credit allocations for new buildings and increases in qualified basis.* Separate housing credit allocations must be received for each building with respect to which a housing credit may be claimed. Rehabilitation expenditures with respect to a qualified low-income building are treated as a separate new building under section 42(e) and must receive a separate housing credit allocation. Increases in qualified basis in a qualified low-income building

Reg. § 1.42-1T(e)(2)

are not generally treated as a new building for purposes of section 42. To the extent that a prior housing credit allocation received with respect to a qualified low-income building does not allow an increased credit with respect to an increase in the qualified basis of such building, an additional housing credit allocation must be received in order to claim a credit with respect to that portion of increase in qualified basis. *See* paragraph (e)(3) of this section. The amount of credit allowable with respect to an increase in qualified basis is subject to the credit percentage limitation of section 42(f)(3)(A) and the first-year convention of section 42(f)(3)(B). *See* paragraph (d)(5) of this section for a rule requiring that the State or local housing credit agency count a housing credit allocation made with respect to an increase in qualified basis as if the specified credit percentage were unreduced in the manner prescribed in section 42(f)(3) and the specified basis amount were unreduced by the first-year convention prescribed in section 42(f)(3)(B).

(5) *Acquisition of building for which a prior housing credit allocation has been made.* If a carryover credit would be allowable to an acquirer of a qualified low-income building under section 42(d)(1), such acquirer need not obtain a new housing credit allocation with respect to such building. Under section 42(d)(7), the acquirer would be entitled to claim only such credits as would have been allowable to the prior owner of the building.

(6) *Multiple housing credit allocations.* A qualified low-income building may receive multiple housing credit allocations from different housing credit agencies having overlapping jurisdictions. A qualified low-income building that receives a housing credit allocation set aside exclusively for projects involving a qualified nonprofit organization may also receive a housing credit allocation from a housing credit agency's aggregate housing credit dollar amount that is not so set aside.

(f) *Exception to housing credit allocation requirement*—(1) *Tax-exempt bond financing*—(i) *In general.* No housing credit allocation is required in order to claim a credit under section 42 with respect to that portion of the eligible basis (as defined in section 42(d)) of a qualified low-income building that is financed with the proceeds of an obligation described in section 103(a) ("tax-exempt bond") which is taken into account for purposes of the volume cap under section 146. In addition, no housing credit allocation is required in order to claim a credit under section 42 with respect to the entire qualified basis (as defined in section 42(c)) of a qualified low-income building if

70 percent or more of the aggregate basis of the building and the land on which the building is located is financed with the proceeds of tax-exempt bonds which are taken into account for purposes of the volume cap under section 146. For purposes of this paragraph, "land on which the building is located" includes only land that is functionally related and subordinate to the qualified low-income building. *See* § 1.103-8(b)(4)(iii) for the meaning of the term "functionally related and subordinate". For purposes of this paragraph, the basis of the land shall be determined using principles that are consistent with the rules contained in section 42(d).

(ii) *Determining use of bond proceeds.* For purposes of determining the portion of proceeds of an issue of tax-exempt bonds used to finance (A) the eligible basis of a qualfied low-income building, and (B) the aggregate basis of the building and the land on which the building is located, the proceeds of the issue must be allocated in the bond indenture or a related document (as defined in § 1.103-13(b)(8)) in a manner consistent with the method used to allocate the net proceeds of the issue for purposes of determining whether 95 percent or more of the net proceeds of the issue are to be used for the exempt purpose of the issue. If the issuer is not consistent in making this allocation throughout the bond indenture and related documents, or if neither the bond indenture nor a related document provides an allocation, the proceeds of the issue will be allocated on a pro rata basis to all of the property financed by the issue, based on the relative cost of the property.

(iii) *Example.* The provisions of this paragraph may be illustrated by the following example:

Example. In 1987, County K assigns $500,000 of its volume cap for private activity bonds under section 146 to a $500,000 issue of exempt facility bonds to provide a qualified residential rental project to be owned by A, an individual. The aggregate basis of the building and the land on which the building is located is $700,000. Under the terms of the bond indenture, the net proceeds of the issue are to be used to finance $490,000 of the eligible basis of the building. More than 70 percent of the aggregate basis of the qualified low-income building and the land on which the building is located is financed with the proceeds of tax-exempt bonds to which a portion of the volume cap under section 146 was allocated. Accordingly, A may claim a credit under section 42 without regard to whether any housing credit dollar amount was allocated to that building. If, instead, the aggregate basis of the building and land were $800,000, A would be able to claim the credit under section 42 without receiving a housing credit allocation for the building only to the extent that the credit was attributable to eligible basis of the building financed with tax-exempt bonds.

(g) *Termination of authority to make housing credit allocation*—(1) *In general.* No State or local housing credit agency shall receive an apportionment of a State housing credit ceiling for calendar years after 1989. Consequently, no housing credit allocations may be made after 1989, except as provided in paragraph (g)(2). Housing credit allocations made prior to January 1, 1990, remain effective after such date.

(2) *Carryover of unused 1989 apportionment.* Any State or local housing credit agency that has an unused portion of its apportionment of the State housing credit ceiling for 1989 from which housing credit allocations have not been made in 1989 may carry over such unused portion into 1990. Such carryover portion of the 1989 apportionment shall be treated as the agency's apportionment for 1990. From this 1990 apportionment, the State or local housing credit agency may make housing credit allocations only to a qualified low-income building meeting the following requirements:

(i) The building must be constructed, reconstructed, or rehabilitated by the taxpayer seeking the allocation;

(ii) More than 10 percent of the reasonably anticipated cost of such construction, reconstruction, or rehabilitation must have been incurred as of January 1, 1989; and

(iii) The building must be placed in service before January 1, 1991.

(3) *Expiration of exception for tax-exempt bond financed projects.* The exception to the requirement that a housing credit allocation be received with respect to any portion of the eligible basis of a qualified low-income building, as provided in paragraph (f), shall not apply to any building placed in service after 1989, unless such building is described in paragraph (g)(2)(i), (ii), and (iii).

(h) *Filing of forms and special rules*—(1) *Completed form.* For purposes of this section, a form shall be treated as completed if the State or local housing credit agency or the building owner has made a good faith effort to complete the form in accordance with the form and the instructions for the form.

(2) *Manner of filing.* A completed Form 8586, Low-Income Housing Credit, shall be filed with the owner's Federal income tax return for each taxable year the owner of a qualified low-income building is claiming the low-income housing credit during the 10-year credit period. A completed Form 8609 (or copy thereof) shall be filed with the owner's Federal income tax return for each of the 15 taxable years in the compliance period. If a housing credit allocation is not required to be received by an owner under paragraph (f) of this section, the owner shall obtain a blank copy of Form 8609 and fill in the address of the building and the name and address of the owner in Part I. Part II of Form 8609 shall be completed by the owner of the qualified low-income building only for the first year the low-income housing credit is claimed by the building owner. Part III of Form 8609 (Statement of Qualification) shall be completed by the owner of the qualified low-income building for each year of the 15-year compliance period.

(3) *Revised or renumbered forms.* If any form is revised or renumbered, any reference in this section to the form shall be treated as a reference to the revised or renumbered form.

(i) *Transitional rules.* The transitional rules contained in section 252(f)(1) of the Tax Reform Act of 1986 are incorporated into this section of the regulations for purposes of determining whether a qualified low-income building is entitled to receive a housing credit allocation or is excepted from the requirement that a housing credit allocation be received. Housing credit allocations made to qualified low-income buildings described in section 252(f)(1) shall not count against the State or local housing credit agency's aggregate housing credit dollar amount. The transitional rules contained in section 252(f)(2) of the Tax Reform Act of 1986 are incorporated into this section of the regulations for purposes of determining amounts available to certain State or local housing credit agencies for the making of housing credit allocations to certain qualified low-income housing projects. Amounts available to housing credit agencies under section 252(f)(2) shall be treated as special apportionments unavailable for housing credit allocations to qualified low-income buildings not described in section 252(f)(2). Housing credit allocations made from the special apportionments shall not count against the State or local credit agency's aggregate housing credit dollar amount. The set-aside requirements shall not apply to these special apportionments. The transitional rules contained in section 252(f)(3) of the Tax Reform Act of 1986 are incorporated in this section of the regulations for purposes of determining the amount of housing credit allocations received by certain qualified low-income buildings. Housing credit allocations deemed received under section 252(f)(3) shall not count against the State or local housing credit agency's aggregate

Reg. § 1.42-1T(g)(1)

housing credit dollar amount. [Temporary Reg. § 1.42-1T.]

☐ [*T.D.* 8144, 6-17-87.]

[Reg. § 1.42-2]

§ 1.42-2. Waiver of requirement that an existing building eligible for the low-income housing credit was last placed in service more than 10 years prior to acquisition by the taxpayer.

(a) *Low-income housing credit for existing building.* Section 42 provides that, for purposes of section 38, new and existing qualified low-income buildings are eligible for a low-income housing credit. The eligibility rules for new and existing buildings differ. Under section 42(d)(2), an existing building may be eligible for the low-income housing credit based upon the acquisition cost and amounts chargeable to capital account (to the extent properly included in eligible basis) if—

(1) The taxpayer acquires the building by purchase (as defined in section 179(d)(2), as applicable under section 42(d)(2)(D)(iii)(I)),

(2) There is a period of at least 10 years between the date of the building's acquisition by the taxpayer and the later of—(i) The date the building was last placed in service, or

(ii) The date of the most recent nonqualified substantial improvement of the building, and

(3) The building was not previously placed in service by the taxpayer, or by a person who was a related person (as defined in section 42(d)(2)(D)(iii)(II)) with respect to the taxpayer as of the time the building was last previously placed in service.

(b) *Waiver of 10-year holding period requirement.* Section 42(d)(6) provides that a taxpayer may apply for a waiver of the 10-year holding period requirement specified in paragraph (a)(2) of this section. The Internal Revenue Service will grant a waiver only if—

(1) The existing building satisfies all of the requirements in paragraph (c) of this section, and

(2) The taxpayer makes an application in conformity with the requirements in paragraph (d) of this section.

(c) *Waiver requirements*—(1) *Federally-assisted building.* To satisfy the requirement of this paragraph, a building must be a Federally-assisted building. The term "Federally-assisted building" means any building which is substantially assisted, financed, or operated under section 8 of the United States Housing Act of 1937, section 221(d)(3) or 236 of the National Housing Act, or section 515 of the Housing Act of 1949, as such acts were in effect on October 22, 1986.

(2) *Federal mortgage funds at risk.* To satisfy the requirement of this paragraph, Federal mortgage funds must be at risk with respect to a mortgage that is secured by the building or a project of which the building is a part. For purposes of this paragraph, Federal mortgage funds are at risk if, in the event of a default by the mortgagor on the mortgage secured by the building or the project of which the building is a part—

(i) The mortgage could be assigned to the Department of Housing and Urban Development or the Farmers' Home Administration, or

(ii) There could arise a claim against a Federal mortgage insurance fund (or such Department or Administration).

(3) *Statement by the Department of Housing and Urban Development or the Farmers' Home Administration.* (i) To satisfy the requirement of this paragraph, a letter or other written statement must be made or received and approved by the national office of the Department of Housing and Urban Development or the Farmers' Home Administration ("the Federal agency"). This letter or statement shall include the following:

(A) A statement that, as of the earlier of the time of the taxpayer's acquisition of the building or the taxpayer's application for a waiver, the building is a Federally-assisted building within the meaning of paragraph (c)(1) of this section and identifies the source of Federal assistance;

(B) A statement that a waiver of the 10-year holding period requirement is necessary to avert Federal mortgage funds being at risk within the meaning of paragraph (c)(2) of this section; and

(C) A statement that the Federal agency has taken a Federal agency action as described in paragraph (c)(3)(ii) of this section.

(ii) The following specified Federal agency actions shall be the only means of satisfying the requirement of this paragraph:

(A) The Federal agency intends to accept an assignment of a mortgage secured by the building or the project of which the building is a part, and such assignment requires payments by the agency or a mortgage insurance fund maintained by the agency to the prior mortgagee;

(B) The Federal agency or a mortgage insurance fund maintained by the agency intends to accept, as a consequence of foreclosure proceedings or otherwise, conveyance of the building or the project of which the building is a part;

(C) The Federal agency or a mortgage insurance fund maintained by the agency intends, as a consequence of default, to take possession of, hold title to, or otherwise assume ownership of the building or the project of which the building is a part; or

(D) The Federal agency has designated the building or the project of which the building is a part as a troubled building or project. A designation of a troubled building or project must satisfy the following requirements:

(*1*) Designation of troubled status must be based on a review by the Federal agency of the financial condition of the building or project and on a determination by the Federal agency of a history of financial distress or mortgage defaults;

(*2*) Designation of troubled status must be made or received and approved by the national office of the Federal agency; and

(*3*) Federal agency regulations or procedures must provide that, in the event of transfer of the ownership of a designated troubled building or project, the building or project may be subject to continued review by the Federal agency. Each Federal agency may prescribe its own standards and procedures for designating a troubled building or project so long as such standards are consistent with the requirements of this paragraph (c)(3)(ii)(D).

(4) *No prior credit allowed.* The requirement of this paragraph is satisfied only if no prior owner was allowed a low-income housing credit under section 42 for the building.

(d) *Application for waiver*—(1) *Time and manner.* In order to receive a waiver of the 10-year holding period requirement specified in paragraph (a)(2) of this section, a taxpayer must file an application (including the applicable user fee) that complies with the requirements of this paragraph (d) and Rev. Proc. 90-1, 1990-1 I.R.B. 8 (or any subsequent applicable revenue procedure). The application must be filed by a taxpayer who has acquired the building by purchase or who has a binding contract to purchase the building. Such binding contract may be conditioned upon the granting of a waiver under this section. The application may be filed at any time after a binding contract has been entered into, but no later than 12 months after the taxpayer's acquisition of the building. An application for a waiver of the 10-year holding period requirement must not contain a request for a ruling on any other issue arising under section 42 or other sections of the Internal Revenue Code. An application for a waiver of the 10-year holding period requirement must be mailed or delivered to the address listed in section 3.01 of Rev. Proc. 90-1 (or any subsequent applicable revenue procedure).

(2) *Information required.* An application for a waiver of the 10-year holding period requirement must contain the following information:

(i) The taxpayer's name, address and taxpayer identification number;

(ii) The name (if any) and address of the acquired building and the project (if any) of which it is a part;

(iii) The date of acquisition or the date of the binding contract for acquisition of the building by the taxpayer and the expected date of acquisition, the amount of consideration paid or to be paid for the acquisition (including the value of any liabilities assumed by the taxpayer), and the taxpayer's certification that such acquisition is by purchase (as defined in section 179(d)(2), as applicable under section 42(d)(2)(D)(iii)(I));

(iv) The identity of the person from whom the building is acquired, and whether such person is a Federal agency, a mortgagee holding title to the building, or the mortgagor or prior owner;

(v) The date the building was last placed in service and the date of the most recent (if any) nonqualified substantial improvement of the building (as defined in section 42(d)(2)(D)(i));

(vi) The taxpayer's certification that the building was not previously placed in service by the taxpayer, or by a person who was a related person (as defined in section 42(d)(2)(D)(iii)(II)) with respect to the taxpayer as of the time the building was last placed in service;

(vii) The amount and disposition (*e.g.,* discharge, assignment, assumption, or refinance) of the outstanding mortgage at the time of acquisition and the identities of the mortgagee and mortgagor;

(viii) The taxpayer's certification that no prior owner was allowed a low-income housing credit under section 42 for the building (made to the best of the taxpayer's knowledge, with no documentation from other persons needed to be submitted); and

(ix) The statement from the Federal agency required by paragraph (c)(3)(i) of this section.

(3) *Other rules.* (i) In the event that an acquired building will be owned by more than one taxpayer, a single application for waiver may be filed by one taxpayer on behalf of the co-owners if the application contains the names, addresses and taxpayer identification numbers of the other owners. A general partner or a designated limited partner may file an application for waiver on behalf of a partnership.

(ii) In the event that multiple Federally-assisted buildings in a project are being acquired

Reg. § 1.42-2(c)(4)

by the taxpayer, a single application for waiver with respect to such buildings may be filed if the application contains the required information set out for the address of each Federally-assisted building involved.

(iii) In the event that specific Federally-assisted buildings are being acquired by the taxpayer in a project consisting of multiple buildings that may or may not be Federally-assisted, a single application for waiver with respect to the Federally-assisted buildings being acquired may be filed if the application contains the required information set out for the address of each Federally-assisted building being acquired.

(4) *Effective date of waiver.* A waiver will be effective when granted in writing by the Internal Revenue Service after submission of a completed application for waiver filed under this paragraph (d).

(5) *Attachment to return.* A waiver letter granted by the Internal Revenue Service shall be filed with the taxpayer's Federal income tax return for the first taxable year the low-income housing credit is claimed by the taxpayer.

(e) *Effective date of regulations.* The provisions of § 1.42-2 are effective for buildings placed in service by the taxpayer after December 31, 1986. [Reg. § 1.42-2.]

□ [*T.D.* 8302, 5-22-90.]

[Reg. § 1.42-3]

§ 1.42-3. **Treatment of buildings financed with proceeds from a loan under an Affordable Housing Program established pursuant to section 721 of the Financial Institutions Reform, Recovery, and Enforcement Act of 1989 (FIRREA).**—(a) *Treatment under sections 42(i) and 42(b).* A below market loan funded in whole or in part with funds from an Affordable Housing Program established under section 721 of FIRREA is not, solely by reason of the Affordable Housing Program funds, a below market Federal loan as defined in section 42(i)(2)(D). Thus, any building with respect to which the proceeds of the loan are used during the tax year is not, solely by reason of the Affordable Housing Program funds, treated as a federally subsidized building for that tax year and subsequent tax years for purposes of determining the applicable percentage for the building under section 42(b).

(b) *Effective date.* The rules set forth in paragraph (a) of this section are effective for loans made after August 8, 1989. [Reg. § 1.42-3.]

□ [*T.D.* 8368, 9-25-91.]

[Reg. § 1.42-4]

§ 1.42-4. **Application of not-for-profit rules of section 183 to low-income housing credit activities.**—(a) *Inapplicability to section 42.* In the case of a qualified low-income building with respect to which the low-income housing credit under section 42 is allowable, section 183 does not apply to disallow losses, deductions, or credits attributable to the ownership and operation of the building.

(b) *Limitation.* Notwithstanding paragraph (a) of this section, losses, deductions, or credits attributable to the ownership and operation of a qualified low-income building with respect to which the low-income housing credit under section 42 is allowable may be limited or disallowed under other provisions of the Code or principles of tax law. *See, e.g.,* Sections 38(c), 163(d), 465, 469; *Knetsch v. United States,* 364 U.S. 361 (1960), 1961-1 C.B. 34 ("sham" or "economic substance" analysis); and *Frank Lyon Co. v. Commissioner,* 435 U.S. 561 (1978), 1978-1 C.B. 46 ("ownership" analysis).

(c) *Effective date.* The rules set forth in paragraphs (a) and (b) of this section are effective with respect to buildings placed in service after December 31, 1986. [Reg. § 1.42-4.]

□ [*T.D.* 8420, 6-10-92.]

→ *Caution: Reg. § 1.42-5, below, is effective before January 1, 2001.*←

[Reg. § 1.42-5]

§ 1.42-5. **Monitoring compliance with low-income housing credit requirements.**—(a) *Compliance monitoring requirement*—(1) *In general.* Under section 42(m)(1)(B)(iii), an allocation plan is not qualified unless it contains a procedure that the State or local housing credit agency ("Agency") (or an agent of, or other private contractor hired by, the Agency) will follow in monitoring for noncompliance with the provisions of section 42 and in notifying the Internal Revenue Service of any noncompliance of which the Agency becomes aware. These regulations only address compliance monitoring procedures required of Agencies. The regulations do not address forms and other records that may be required by the Service on examination or audit. For example, if a building is sold or otherwise transferred by the owner, the transferee should obtain from the transferor information related to the first year of the credit period so that the transferee can substantiate credits claimed.

(2) *Requirements for a monitoring procedure*—(i) *In general.* A procedure for monitoring for noncompliance under section 42(m)(1)(B)(iii) must include—

Reg. § 1.42-5(a)(2)

→ *Caution: Reg. § 1.42-5, below, is effective before January 1, 2001.*←

(A) The recordkeeping and record retention provisions of paragraph (b) of this section;

(B) The certification and review provisions of paragraph (c) of this section;

(C) The inspection provision of paragraph (d) of this section; and

(D) The notification-of-noncompliance provisions of paragraph (e) of this section.

(ii) *Order and form.* A monitoring procedure will meet the requirements of section 42(m)(1)(B)(iii) if it contains the substance of these provisions. The particular order and form of the provisions in the allocation plan is not material. A monitoring procedure may contain additional provisions or requirements.

(b) *Recordkeeping and record retention provisions*—(1) *Recordkeeping provision.* Under the recordkeeping provision, the owner of a low-income housing project must be required to keep records for each qualified low-income building in the project that show for each year in the compliance period—

(i) The total number of residential rental units in the building (including the number of bedrooms and the size in square feet of each residential rental unit);

(ii) The percentage of residential rental units in the building that are low-income units;

(iii) The rent charged on each residential rental unit in the building (including any utility allowances);

(iv) The number of occupants in each low-income unit, but only if rent is determined by the number of occupants in each unit under section 42(g)(2) (as in effect before the amendments made by the Revenue Reconciliation Act of 1989);

(v) The low-income unit vacancies in the building and information that shows when, and to whom, the next available units were rented;

(vi) The annual income certification of each low-income tenant per unit. For an exception to this requirement, see section 42(g)(8)(B) (which provides a special rule for a 100 percent low-income building);

(vii) Documentation to support each low-income tenant's income certification (for example, a copy of the tenant's federal income tax return, Forms W-2, or verifications of income from third parties such as employers or state agencies paying unemployment compensation). For an exception to this requirement, see section 42(g)(8)(B) (which provides a special rule for a 100 percent low-income building). Tenant income is calculated in a manner consistent with the determination of

annual income under section 8 of the United States Housing Act of 1937 ("Section 8"), not in accordance with the determination of gross income for federal income tax liability. In the case of a tenant receiving housing assistance payments under Section 8, the documentation requirement of this paragraph (b)(1)(vii) is satisfied if the public housing authority provides a statement to the building owner declaring that the tenant's income does not exceed the applicable income limit under section 42(g);

(viii) The eligible basis and qualified basis of the building at the end of the first year of the credit period; and

(ix) The character and use of the nonresidential portion of the building included in the building's eligible basis under section 42(d) (*e.g.,* tenant facilities that are available on a comparable basis to all tenants and for which no separate fee is charged for use of the facilities, or facilities reasonably required by the project).

(2) *Record retention provision.* Under the record retention provision, the owner of a low-income housing project must be required to retain the records described in paragraph (b)(1) of this section for at least 6 years after the due date (with extensions) for filing the federal income tax return for that year. The records for the first year of the credit period, however, must be retained for at least 6 years beyond the due date (with extensions) for filing the federal income tax return for the last year of the compliance period of the building.

(c) *Certification and review provisions*—(1) *Certification.* Under the certification provision, the owner of a low-income housing project must be required to certify at least annually to the Agency that, for the preceding 12-month period—

(i) The project met the requirements of:

(A) The 20-50 test under section 42(g)(1)(A), the 40-60 test under section 42(g)(1)(B), or the 25-60 test under sections 42(g)(4) and 142(d)(6) for New York City, whichever minimum set-aside test was applicable to the project; and

(B) If applicable to the project, the 15-40 test under sections 42(g)(4) and 142(d)(4)(B) for "deep rent skewed" projects;

(ii) There was no change in the applicable fraction (as defined in section 42(c)(1)(B)) of any building in the project, or that there was a change, and a description of the change;

(iii) The owner has received an annual income certification from each low-income tenant, and documentation to support that certification;

Reg. § 1.42-5(b)(1)

→ *Caution: Reg. § 1.42-5, below, is effective before January 1, 2001.*←

or, in the case of a tenant receiving Section 8 housing assistance payments, the statement from a public housing authority described in paragraph (b)(1)(vii) of this section. For an exception to this requirement, see section 42(g)(8)(B) (which provides a special rule for a 100 percent low-income building);

(iv) Each low-income unit in the project was rent-restricted under section 42(g)(2);

(v) All units in the project were for use by the general public and used on a nontransient basis (except for transitional housing for the homeless provided under section 42(i)(3)(B)(iii));

(vi) Each building in the project was suitable for occupancy, taking into account local health, safety, and building codes;

(vii) There was no change in the eligible basis (as defined in section 42(d)) of any building in the project, or if there was a change, the nature of the change (*e.g.*, a common area has become commercial space, or a fee is now charged for a tenant facility formerly provided without charge);

(viii) All tenant facilities included in the eligible basis under section 42(d) of any building in the project, such as swimming pools, other recreational facilities, and parking areas, were provided on a comparable basis without charge to all tenants in the building;

(ix) If a low-income unit in the project became vacant during the year, that reasonable attempts were or are being made to rent that unit or the next available unit of comparable or smaller size to tenants having a qualifying income before any units in the project were or will be rented to tenants not having a qualifying income;

(x) If the income of tenants of a low-income unit in the project increased above the limit allowed in section 42(g)(2)(D)(ii), the next available unit of comparable or smaller size in the project was or will be rented to tenants having a qualifying income; and

(xi) An extended low-income housing commitment as described in section 42(h)(6) was in effect (for buildings subject to section 7108(c)(1) of the Revenue Reconciliation Act of 1989).

(2) *Review.* The review provision must—

(i) Require that the Agency review the certifications submitted under paragraph (c)(1) of this section for compliance with the requirements of section 42;

(ii) Contain at least one of the following requirements:

(A) The owners of at least 50 percent of all low-income housing projects in the Agency's jurisdiction must submit to the Agency for pliance review a copy of the annual income ce fication, the documentation the owner h received to support that certification, and th rent record for each low-income tenant in at least 20 percent of the low-income units in their projects;

(B) The Agency must inspect at least 20 percent of low-income housing projects each year and must inspect the low-income certification, the documentation the owner has received to support that certification, and the rent record for each low-income tenant in at least 20 percent of the low-income units in those projects; or

(C) The owners of all low-income housing projects must submit to the Agency each year information on tenant income and rent for each low-income unit, in the form and manner designated by the Agency, and the owners of at least 20 percent of the projects must submit to the Agency for compliance review a copy of the annual income certification, the documentation the owner has received to support that certification, and the rent record for each low-income tenant in at least 20 percent of the low-income units in their projects; and

(iii) require that the Agency determine which tenants' records are to be inspected or submitted by the owners for review. If a monitoring procedure includes the review provision described in paragraph (c)(2)(ii)(B) of this section, the records to be inspected must be chosen in a manner that will not give owners of low-income housing projects advance notice that their records for a particular year will or will not be inspected. However, an Agency may give an owner reasonable notice that an inspection will occur so that the owner may assemble records (for example, 30 days notice of inspection). See paragraph (d) of this section for the inspection provision that is required to be included in all monitoring procedures.

(3) *Frequency and form of certification.* A monitoring procedure require that the certifications and reviews paragraph (c)(1) and (2) of this section be ma least annually covering each year of the 15-compliance period under section 42(i)(1). Th tifications must be made under penalty of p y. A monitoring procedure may require cert ons and reviews more frequently than on month basis, provided that all months with h 12-month period are subject to certifica.

(4) *Exce* for certain buildings—(i) *In general.* The w requirements under paragraph (c)(2 (B), and (C) of this section

Reg. § 1.42-5(c)(4)

→ *Caution: Reg. § 1.42-5, below, is effective before January 1, 2001.*←

provide that owners are not required to submit, and the Agency is not required to review, the tenant income certifications, supporting documentation, and rent records for buildings financed by the Farmers Home Administration (FmHA) under the section 515 program, or buildings of which 50 percent or more of the aggregate basis (taking into account the building and the land) is financed with the proceeds of obligations the interest on which is exempt from tax under section 103 (tax-exempt bonds). In order for a monitoring procedure to except these buildings, the Agency must meet the requirements of paragraph (c)(4)(ii) of this section.

(ii) *Agreement and review.* The Agency must enter into an agreement with the FmHA or tax-exempt bond issuer. Under the agreement, the FmHA or tax-exempt bond issuer must agree to provide information concerning the income and rent of the tenants in the building to the Agency. The Agency may assume the accuracy of the information provided by FmHA or the tax-exempt bond issuer without verification. The Agency must review the information and determine that the income limitation and rent restriction of section 42(g)(1) and (2) are met. However, if the information provided by the FmHA or tax-exempt bond issuer is not sufficient for the Agency to make this determination, the Agency must request the necessary additional income or rent information from the owner of the buildings. For example, because FmHA determines tenant eligibility based on its definition of "adjusted annual income," rather than "annual income" as defined under Section 8, the Agency may have to calculate the tenant's income for section 42 purposes and may need to request additional income information from the owner.

(iii) *Example.* The exception permitted under paragraph (c)(4) and (ii) of this section is illustrated by the following example.

Example. An Agency chooses the review requirement of paragraph (2)(ii)(A) of this section and some of the buildings selected for review are buildings financed by FmHA. The Agency has entered into an agreement described in paragraph (c)(4)(ii) of this section with the FmHA with respect to those buildings. In reviewing the FmHA-financed buildings, the Agency obtains the tenant income and rent information from the FmHA for 20 percent of the low-income units in each of those buildings. The Agency calculates the tenant income and rent to determine whether the tenants meet the income and rent limitation of section 42(g)(1) and (2). In order to make this determination, the Agency may also request

additional income or rent information from the owners of the FmHA buildings if the information provided by the FmHA is not sufficient.

(5) *Agency reports of compliance monitoring activities.* The Agency must report its compliance monitoring activities annually on Form 8610, "Annual Low-Income Housing Credit Agencies Report."

(d) *Inspection provision.* Under the inspection provision, the Agency must have the right to perform an on-site inspection of any low-income housing project at least through the end of the compliance period of the buildings in the project. The inspection provision of this paragraph (d) is separate from any review of low-income certifications, supporting documents, and rent records under paragraph (c)(2)(ii) of this section.

(e) *Notification-of-noncompliance provisions*— (1) *In general.* Under the notification-of-noncompliance provisions, the Agency must be required to give the notice described in paragraph (e)(2) of this section to the owner of a low-income housing project and the notice described in paragraph (e)(3) of this section to the Service.

(2) *Notice to owner.* The Agency must be required to provide prompt written notice to the owner of a low-income housing project if the Agency does not receive the certification described in paragraph (c)(1) of this section, or does not receive or is not permitted to inspect the tenant income certifications, supporting documentation, and rent records described in paragraph (c)(2)(ii)(A), (B), or (C) of this section (whichever is applicable), or discovers by inspection, review, or in some other manner, that the project is not in compliance with the provisions of section 42.

(3) *Notice to Internal Revenue Service*—(i) *In general.* The Agency must be required to file Form 8823, "Low-Income Housing Credit Agencies Report of Noncompliance," with the Service no later than 45 days after the end of the correction period (as described in paragraph (e)(4) of this section, including extensions permitted under that paragraph) and no earlier than the end of the correction period, whether or not the noncompliance or failure to certify is corrected. The Agency must explain on Form 8823 the nature of the noncompliance or failure to certify and indicate whether the owner has corrected the noncompliance or failure to certify. Any change in either the applicable fraction or eligible basis under paragraph (c)(1)(ii) and (vii) of this section, respectively, that results in a decrease in the qualified basis of the project under section 42(c)(1)(A) is noncompliance that must be reported to the Service under this paragraph (e)(3). If an Agency

→ *Caution: Reg. § 1.42-5, below, is effective before January 1, 2001.*←

reports on Form 8823 that a building is entirely out of compliance and will not be in compliance at any time in the future, the Agency need not file Form 8823 in subsequent years to report that building's noncompliance. If the noncompliance or failure to certify is corrected within 3 years after the end of the correction period, the Agency is required to file Form 8823 with the Service reporting the correction of the noncompliance or failure to certify.

(ii) *Agency retention of records.* An Agency must retain records of noncompliance or failure to certify for 6 years beyond the Agency's filing of the respective Form 8823. In all other cases, the Agency must retain the certifications and records described in paragraph (c) of this section for 3 years from the end of the calendar year the Agency receives the certifications and records.

(4) *Correction period.* The correction period shall be that period specified in the monitoring procedure during which an owner must supply any missing certifications and bring the project into compliance with the provisions of section 42. The correction period is not to exceed 90 days from the date of the notice to the owner described in paragraph (e)(2) of this section. An Agency may extend the correction period for up to 6 months, but only if the Agency determines there is good cause for granting the extension.

(f) *Delegation of authority*—(1) *Agencies permitted to delegate compliance monitoring functions*—(i) *In general.* An Agency may retain an agent or other private contractor ("Authorized Delegate") to perform compliance monitoring. The Authorized Delegate must be unrelated to the owner of any building that the Authorized Delegate monitors. The Authorized Delegate may be delegated all of the functions of the Agency, except for the responsibility of notifying the Service under paragraph (e)(3) of this section. For example, the Authorized Delegate may be delegated the responsibility of reviewing tenant certifications and documentation under paragraph (c)(1) and (2) of this section, the right to inspect buildings and records as described in paragraph (d) of this section, and the responsibility of notifying building owners of lack of certification or noncompliance under paragraph (e)(2) of this section. The Authorized Delegate must notify the Agency of any noncompliance or failure to certify.

(ii) *Limitations.* An Agency that deleg: compliance monitoring to an Authorized Deleg under paragraph (f)(1)(i) of this section must u. reasonable diligence to ensure that the Authorizec Delegate properly performs the delegated monitoring functions. Delegation by an Agency of compliance monitoring functions to an Authorized Delegate does not relieve the Agency of its obligation to notify the Service of any noncompliance of which the Agency becomes aware.

(2) *Agencies permitted to delegate compliance monitoring functions to another Agency.* An Agency may delegate all or some of its compliance monitoring responsibilities for a building to another Agency within the State. This delegation may include the responsibility of notifying the Service under paragraph (e)(3) of this section.

(g) *Liability.* Compliance with the requirements of section 42 is the responsibility of the owner of the building for which the credit is allowable. The Agency's obligation to monitor for compliance with the requirements of section 42 does not make the Agency liable for an owner's noncompliance.

(h) *Effective date.* Allocation plans must comply with these regulations by June 30, 1993. The requirement of section 42(m)(1)(B)(iii) that allocation plans contain a procedure for monitoring for noncompliance becomes effective on January 1, 1992, and applies to buildings for which a low-income housing credit is, or has been, allowable at any time. Thus, allocation plans must comply with section 42(m)(1)(B)(iii) prior to June 30, 1993, the effective date of these regulations. An allocation plan that complies with these regulations, with the notice of proposed rulemaking published in the Federal Register on December 27, 1991, or with a reasonable interpretation of section 42(m)(1)(B)(iii) will satisfy the requirements of section 42(m)(1)(B)(iii) for periods before June 30, 1993. Section 42(m)(1)(B)(iii) and these regulations do not require monitoring for whether a building or project is in compliance with the requirements of section 42 prior to January 1, 1992. However, if an Agency becomes aware of noncompliance that occurred prior to January 1, 1992, the Agency is required to notify the Service of that noncompliance. [Reg. § 1.42-5.]

□ [*T.D.* 8430, 9-1-92. *Amended by T.D.* 8563, 9-30-94 *and T.D.* 8859, 1-13-2000.]

→ *Caution: Reg. § 1.42-5, below, is generally effective on January 1, 2001.*←

§ 1.42-5. **Monitoring compliance with low-income housing credit requirements.**—(a) *Compliance monitoring requirement*—(1) *In gen-*

eral. Under section 42(m)(1)(B)(iii), an allocation plan is not qualified unless it contains a procedure that the State or local housing credit agency

Caution: Reg. § 1.42-5, below, is generally effective on January 1, 2001.

...ency") (or an agent of, or other private con-...ctor hired by, the Agency) will follow in moni-...oring for noncompliance with the provisions of section 42 and in notifying the Internal Revenue Service of any noncompliance of which the Agency becomes aware. These regulations only address compliance monitoring procedures required of Agencies. The regulations do not address forms and other records that may be required by the Service on examination or audit. For example, if a building is sold or otherwise transferred by the owner, the transferee should obtain from the transferor information related to the first year of the credit period so that the transferee can substantiate credits claimed.

(2) *Requirements for a monitoring procedure*—(i) *In general.* A procedure for monitoring for noncompliance under section 42(m)(1)(B)(iii) must include—

(A) The recordkeeping and record retention provisions of paragraph (b) of this section;

(B) The certification and review provisions of paragraph (c) of this section;

(C) The inspection provision of paragraph (d) of this section; and

(D) The notification-of-noncompliance provisions of paragraph (e) of this section.

(ii) *Order and form.* A monitoring procedure will meet the requirements of section 42(m)(1)(B)(iii) if it contains the substance of these provisions. The particular order and form of the provisions in the allocation plan is not material. A monitoring procedure may contain additional provisions or requirements.

(b) *Recordkeeping and record retention provisions*—(1) *Recordkeeping provision.* Under the recordkeeping provision, the owner of a low-income housing project must be required to keep records for each qualified low-income building in the project that show for each year in the compliance period—

(i) The total number of residential rental units in the building (including the number of bedrooms and the size in square feet of each residential rental unit);

(ii) The percentage of residential rental units in the building that are low-income units;

(iii) The rent charged on each residential rental unit in the building (including any utility allowances);

(iv) The number of occupants in each low-income unit, but only if rent is determined by the number of occupants in each unit under section 42(g)(2) (as in effect before the amendments

made by the Omnibus Budget Reconciliation Act of 1989);

(v) The low-income unit vacancies in the building and information that shows when, and to whom, the next available units were rented;

(vi) The annual income certification of each low-income tenant per unit. For an exception to this requirement, see section 42(g)(8)(B) (which provides a special rule for a 100 percent low-income building);

(vii) Documentation to support each low-income tenant's income certification (for example, a copy of the tenant's federal income tax return, Forms W-2, or verifications of income from third parties such as employers or state agencies paying unemployment compensation). For an exception to this requirement, see section 42(g)(8)(B) (which provides a special rule for a 100 percent low-income building). Tenant income is calculated in a manner consistent with the determination of annual income under section 8 of the United States Housing Act of 1937 ("Section 8"), not in accordance with the determination of gross income for federal income tax liability. In the case of a tenant receiving housing assistance payments under Section 8, the documentation requirement of this paragraph (b)(1)(vii) is satisfied if the public housing authority provides a statement to the building owner declaring that the tenant's income does not exceed the applicable income limit under section 42(g);

(viii) The eligible basis and qualified basis of the building at the end of the first year of the credit period; and

(ix) The character and use of the nonresidential portion of the building included in the building's eligible basis under section 42(d) (*e.g.*, tenant facilities that are available on a comparable basis to all tenants and for which no separate fee is charged for use of the facilities, or facilities reasonably required by the project).

(2) *Record retention provision.* Under the record retention provision, the owner of a low-income housing project must be required to retain the records described in paragraph (b)(1) of this section for at least 6 years after the due date (with extensions) for filing the federal income tax return for that year. The records for the first year of the credit period, however, must be retained for at least 6 years beyond the due date (with extensions) for filing the federal income tax return for the last year of the compliance period of the building.

(3) *Inspection record retention provision.* Under the inspection record retention provision,

Reg. § 1.42-5(a)(2)

→ *Caution: Reg. § 1.42-5, below, is generally effective on January 1, 2001.* ◄

the owner of a low-income housing project must be required to retain the original local health, safety, or building code violation reports or notices that were issued by the State or local government unit (as described in paragraph (c)(1)(vi) of this section) for the Agency's inspection under paragraph (d) of this section. Retention of the original violation reports or notices is not required once the Agency reviews the violation reports or notices and completes its inspection, unless the violation remains uncorrected.

(c) *Certification and review provisions*—(1) *Certification.* Under the certification provision, the owner of a low-income housing project must be required to certify at least annually to the Agency that, for the preceding 12-month period—

(i) The project met the requirements of:

(A) The 20-50 test under section 42(g)(1)(A), the 40-60 test under section 42(g)(1)(B), or the 25-60 test under sections 42(g)(4) and 142(d)(6) for New York City, whichever minimum set-aside test was applicable to the project; and

(B) If applicable to the project, the 15-40 test under sections 42(g)(4) and 142(d)(4)(B) for "deep rent skewed" projects;

(ii) There was no change in the applicable fraction (as defined in section 42(c)(1)(B)) of any building in the project, or that there was a change, and a description of the change;

(iii) The owner has received an annual income certification from each low-income tenant, and documentation to support that certification; or, in the case of a tenant receiving Section 8 housing assistance payments, the statement from a public housing authority described in paragraph (b)(1)(vii) of this section. For an exception to this requirement, see section 42(g)(8)(B) (which provides a special rule for a 100 percent low-income building);

(iv) Each low-income unit in the project was rent-restricted under section 42(g)(2);

(v) All units in the project were for use by the general public (as defined in § 1.42-9), including the requirement that no finding of discrimination under the Fair Housing Act, 42 U.S.C. 3601-3619, occurred for the project. A finding of discrimination includes an adverse final decision by the Secretary of the Department of Housing and Urban Development (HUD), 24 CFR 180.680, an adverse final decision by a substantially equivalent state or local fair housing agency, 42 U.S.C. 3616a(a)(1), or an adverse judgment from a federal court;

(vi) The buildings and low-income units the project were suitable for occupancy, taking into account local health, safety, and building codes (or other habitability standards), and the State or local government unit responsible for making local health, safety, or building code inspections did not issue a violation report for any building or low-income unit in the project. If a violation report or notice was issued by the governmental unit, the owner must attach a statement summarizing the violation report or notice or a copy of the violation report or notice to the annual certification submitted to the Agency under paragraph (c)(1) of this section. In addition, the owner must state whether the violation has been corrected;

(vii) There was no change in the eligible basis (as defined in section 42(d)) of any building in the project, or if there was a change, the nature of the change (*e.g.*, a common area has become commercial space, or a fee is now charged for a tenant facility formerly provided without charge);

(viii) All tenant facilities included in the eligible basis under section 42(d) of any building in the project, such as swimming pools, other recreational facilities, and parking areas, were provided on a comparable basis without charge to all tenants in the building;

(ix) If a low-income unit in the project became vacant during the year, that reasonable attempts were or are being made to rent that unit or the next available unit of comparable or smaller size to tenants having a qualifying income before any units in the project were or will be rented to tenants not having a qualifying income;

(x) If the income of tenants of a low-income unit in the building increased above the limit allowed in section 42(g)(2)(D)(ii), the next available unit of comparable or smaller size in the building was or will be rented to tenants having a qualifying income;

(xi) An extended low-income housing commitment as described in section 42(h)(6) was in effect (for buildings subject to section 7108(c)(1) of the Omnibus Budget Reconciliation Act of 1989, 103 Stat. 2106, 2308-2311), including the requirement under section 42(h)(6)(B)(iv) that an owner cannot refuse to lease a unit in the project to an applicant because the applicant holds a voucher or certificate of eligibility under section 8 of the United States Housing Act of 1937, 42 U.S.C. 1437f (for buildings subject to section 13142(b)(4) of the Omnibus Budget Reconciliation Act of 1993, 107 Stat. 312, 438-439); and

Reg. § 1.42-5(c)(1)

▶ *Caution: Reg. § 1.42-5, below, is generally effective on January 1, 2001.*◀

(xii) All low-income units in the project were used on a nontransient basis (except for transitional housing for the homeless provided under section 42(i)(3)(B)(iii) or single-room-occupancy units rented on a month-by-month basis under section 42(i)(3)(B)(iv)).

(2) *Review.* The review provision must—

(i) Require that the Agency review the certifications submitted under paragraph (c)(1) of this section for compliance with the requirements of section 42;

(ii) Require that with respect to each low-income housing project—

(A) The Agency must conduct on-site inspections of all buildings in the project by the end of the second calendar year following the year the last building in the project is placed in service and, for at least 20 percent of the project's low-income units, inspect the units and review the low-income certifications, the documentation supporting the certifications, and the rent records for the tenants in those units; and

(B) At least once every 3 years, the Agency must conduct on-site inspections of all buildings in the project and, for at least 20 percent of the project's low-income units, inspect the units and review the low-income certifications, the documentation supporting the certifications, and the rent records for the tenants in those units; and

(iii) Require that the Agency randomly select which low-income units and tenant records are to be inspected and reviewed by the Agency. The review of tenant records may be undertaken wherever the owner maintains or stores the records (either on-site or off-site). The units and tenant records to be inspected and reviewed must be chosen in a manner that will not give owners of low-income housing projects advance notice that a unit and tenant records for a particular year will or will not be inspected and reviewed. However, an Agency may give an owner reasonable notice that an inspection of the building and low-income units or tenant record review will occur so that the owner may notify tenants of the inspection or assemble tenant records for review (for example, 30 days notice of inspection or review).

(3) *Frequency and form of certification.* A monitoring procedure must require that the certifications and reviews of paragraph (c)(1) and (2) of this section be made at least annually covering each year of the 15-year compliance period under section 42(i)(1). The certifications must be made under penalty of perjury. A monitoring procedure may require certifications and reviews more fre-

quently than on a 12-month basis, provided that all months within each 12-month period are subject to certification.

(4) *Exception for certain buildings*—(i) *In general.* The review requirements under paragraph (c)(2)(ii) of this section may provide that owners are not required to submit, and the Agency is not required to review, the tenant income certifications, supporting documentation, and rent records for buildings financed by the Rural Housing Service (RHS), formerly known as Farmers Home Administration under the section 515 program, or buildings of which 50 percent or more of the aggregate basis (taking into account the building and the land) is financed with the proceeds of obligations the interest on which is exempt from tax under section 103 (tax-exempt bonds). In order for a monitoring procedure to except these buildings, the Agency must meet the requirements of paragraph (c)(4)(ii) of this section.

(ii) *Agreement and review.* The Agency must enter into an agreement with the RHS or tax-exempt bond issuer. Under the agreement, the RHS or tax-exempt bond issuer must agree to provide information concerning the income and rent of the tenants in the building to the Agency. The Agency may assume the accuracy of the information provided by RHS or the tax-exempt bond issuer without verification. The Agency must review the information and determine that the income limitation and rent restriction of section 42(g)(1) and (2) are met. However, if the information provided by the RHS or tax-exempt bond issuer is not sufficient for the Agency to make this determination, the Agency must request the necessary additional income or rent information from the owner of the buildings. For example, because RHS determines tenant eligibility based on its definition of "adjusted annual income," rather than "annual income" as defined under Section 8, the Agency may have to calculate the tenant's income for section 42 purposes and may need to request additional income information from the owner.

(iii) *Example.* The exception permitted under paragraph (c)(4)(i) and (ii) of this section is illustrated by the following example.

Example. An Agency selects for review buildings financed by the RHS. The Agency has entered into an agreement described in paragraph (c)(4)(ii) of this section with the RHS with respect to those buildings. In reviewing the RHS-financed buildings, the Agency obtains the tenant income and rent information from the RHS for 20 percent of the low-income units in each of those buildings.

Reg. § 1.42-5(c)(2)

→ *Caution: Reg. § 1.42-5, below, is generally effective on January 1, 2001.*←

The Agency calculates the tenant income and rent to determine whether the tenants meet the income and rent limitation of section 42(g)(1) and (2). In order to make this determination, the Agency may need to request additional income or rent information from the owners of the RHS buildings if the information provided by the RHS is not sufficient.

(5) *Agency reports of compliance monitoring activities.* The Agency must report its compliance monitoring activities annually on Form 8610, "Annual Low-Income Housing Credit Agencies Report."

(d) *Inspection provision*—(1) *In general.* Under the inspection provision, the Agency must have the right to perform an on-site inspection of any low-income housing project at least through the end of the compliance period of the buildings in the project. The inspection provision of this paragraph (d) is a separate requirement from any tenant file review under paragraph (c)(2)(ii) of this section.

(2) *Inspection standard.* For the on-site inspections of buildings and low-income units required by paragraph (c)(2)(ii) of this section, the Agency must review any local health, safety, or building code violations reports or notices retained by the owner under paragraph (b)(3) of this section and must determine—

(i) Whether the buildings and units are suitable for occupancy, taking into account local health, safety, and building codes (or other habitability standards), or

(ii) Whether the buildings and units satisfy, as determined by the Agency, the uniform physical condition standards for public housing established by HUD (24 CFR 5.703). The HUD physical condition standards do not supersede or preempt local health, safety, and building codes. A low-income housing project under section 42 must continue to satisfy these codes and, if the Agency becomes aware of any violation of these codes, the Agency must report the violation to the Service. However, provided the Agency determines by inspection that the HUD standards are met, the Agency is not required under this paragraph (d)(2)(ii) to determine by inspection whether the project meets local health, safety, and building codes.

(3) *Exception from inspection provision.* An Agency is not required to inspect a building under this paragraph (d) if the building is financed by the RHS under the section 515 program, the RHS inspects the building (under 7 CFR part 1930), and the RHS and Agency enter into a memorandum of understanding, or other similar arrange-

ment, under which, the RHS agrees to notify the Agency of the inspection results.

(4) *Delegation.* An Agency may delegate inspection under this paragraph (d) to an Authorized Delegate retained under paragraph (f) of this section. Such Authorized Delegate, which may include HUD or a HUD-approved inspector, must notify the Agency of the inspection results.

(e) *Notification-of-noncompliance provisions*— (1) *In general.* Under the notification-of-noncompliance provisions, the Agency must be required to give the notice described in paragraph (e)(2) of this section to the owner of a low-income housing project and the notice described in paragraph (e)(3) of this section to the Service.

(2) *Notice to owner.* The Agency must be required to provide prompt written notice to the owner of a low-income housing project if the Agency does not receive the certification described in paragraph (c)(1) of this section, or does not receive or is not permitted to inspect the tenant income certifications, supporting documentation, and rent records described in paragraph (c)(2)(ii) of this section, or discovers by inspection, review, or in some other manner, that the project is not in compliance with the provisions of section 42.

(3) *Notice to Internal Revenue Service*—(i) *In general.* The Agency must be required to file Form 8823, "Low-Income Housing Credit Agencies Report of Noncompliance," with the Service no later than 45 days after the end of the correction period (as described in paragraph (e)(4) of this section, including extensions permitted under that paragraph) and no earlier than the end of the correction period, whether or not the noncompliance or failure to certify is corrected. The Agency must explain on Form 8823 the nature of the noncompliance or failure to certify and indicate whether the owner has corrected the noncompliance or failure to certify. Any change in either the applicable fraction or eligible basis under paragraph (c)(1)(ii) and (vii) of this section, respectively, that results in a decrease in the qualified basis of the project under section 42(c)(1)(A) is noncompliance that must be reported to the Service under this paragraph (e)(3). If an Agency reports on Form 8823 that a building is entirely out of compliance and will not be in compliance at any time in the future, the Agency need not file Form 8823 in subsequent years to report that building's noncompliance. If the noncompliance or failure to certify is corrected within 3 years after the end of the correction period, the Agency is required to file Form 8823 with the Service reporting the correction of the noncompliance or failure to certify.

Reg. § 1.42-5(e)(3)

→ *Caution: Reg. § 1.42-5, below, is generally effective on January 1, 2001.*←

(ii) *Agency retention of records.* An Agency must retain records of noncompliance or failure to certify for 6 years beyond the Agency's filing of the respective Form 8823. In all other cases, the Agency must retain the certifications and records described in paragraph (c) of this section for 3 years from the end of the calendar year the Agency receives the certifications and records.

(4) *Correction period.* The correction period shall be that period specified in the monitoring procedure during which an owner must supply any missing certifications and bring the project into compliance with the provisions of section 42. The correction period is not to exceed 90 days from the date of the notice to the owner described in paragraph (e)(2) of this section. An Agency may extend the correction period for up to 6 months, but only if the Agency determines there is good cause for granting the extension.

(f) *Delegation of authority*—(1) *Agencies permitted to delegate compliance monitoring functions*—(i) *In general.* An Agency may retain an agent or other private contractor ("Authorized Delegate") to perform compliance monitoring. The Authorized Delegate must be unrelated to the owner of any building that the Authorized Delegate monitors. The Authorized Delegate may be delegated all of the functions of the Agency, except for the responsibility of notifying the Service under paragraphs (c)(5) and (e)(3) of this section. For example, the Authorized Delegate may be delegated the responsibility of reviewing tenant certifications and documentation under paragraph (c)(1) and (2) of this section, the right to inspect buildings and records as described in paragraph (d) of this section, and the responsibility of notifying building owners of lack of certification or noncompliance under paragraph (e)(2) of this section. The Authorized Delegate must notify the Agency of any noncompliance or failure to certify.

(ii) *Limitations.* An Agency that delegates compliance monitoring to an Authorized Delegate under paragraph (f)(1)(i) of this section must use reasonable diligence to ensure that the Authorized Delegate properly performs the delegated monitoring functions. Delegation by an Agency of compliance monitoring functions to an Authorized Delegate does not relieve the Agency of its obligation to notify the Service of any noncompliance of which the Agency becomes aware.

(2) *Agencies permitted to delegate compliance monitoring functions to another Agency.* An Agency may delegate all or some of its compliance monitoring responsibilities for a building to another Agency within the State. This delegation may include the responsibility of notifying the Service under paragraph (e)(3) of this section.

(g) *Liability.* Compliance with the requirements of section 42 is the responsibility of the owner of the building for which the credit is allowable. The Agency's obligation to monitor for compliance with the requirements of section 42 does not make the Agency liable for an owner's noncompliance.

(h) *Effective date.* Allocation plans must comply with these regulations by June 30, 1993. The requirement of section 42(m)(1)(B)(iii) that allocation plans contain a procedure for monitoring for noncompliance becomes effective on January 1, 1992, and applies to buildings for which a low-income housing credit is, or has been, allowable at any time. Thus, allocation plans must comply with section 42(m)(1)(B)(iii) prior to June 30, 1993, the effective date of these regulations. An allocation plan that complies with these regulations, with the notice of proposed rulemaking published in the Federal Register on December 27, 1991, or with a reasonable interpretation of section 42(m)(1)(B)(iii) will satisfy the requirements of section 42(m)(1)(B)(iii) for periods before June 30, 1993. Section 42(m)(1)(B)(iii) and these regulations do not require monitoring for whether a building or project is in compliance with the requirements of section 42 prior to January 1, 1992. However, if an Agency becomes aware of noncompliance that occurred prior to January 1, 1992, the Agency is required to notify the Service of that noncompliance. In addition, the requirements in paragraphs (b)(3) and (c)(1)(v), (vi), and (xi) of this section (involving recordkeeping and annual owner certifications) and paragraphs (c)(2)(ii)(B), (c)(2)(iii), and (d) of this section (involving tenant file reviews and physical inspections of existing projects, and the physical inspection standard) are applicable January 1, 2001. The requirement in paragraph (c)(2)(ii)(A) of this section (involving tenant file reviews and physical inspections of new projects) is applicable for buildings placed in service on or after January 1, 2001. The requirements in paragraph (c)(5) of this section (involving Agency reporting of compliance monitoring activities to the Service) and paragraph (e)(3)(i) of this section (involving Agency reporting of corrected noncompliance or failure to certify within 3 years after the end of the correction period) are applicable January 14, 2000. [Reg. § 1.42-5.]

☐ [*T.D.* 8430, 9-1-92. *Amended by T.D.* 8563, 9-30-94 *and T.D.* 8859, 1-13-2000 (*corrected* 3-27-2000).]

Reg. § 1.42-5(e)(4)

[Reg. § 1.42-6]

§ 1.42-6. Buildings qualifying for carryover allocations.—(a) *Carryover allocations.* A carryover allocation is an allocation that meets the requirements of section 42(h)(1)(E) or (F). If the requirements of section 42(h)(1)(E) or (F) that are required to be satisfied by the close of the calendar year are not satisfied, the allocation is treated as if it had not been made. For example, if the taxpayer's basis in the project as of the close of the calendar year of allocation is not more than 10 percent of the taxpayer's reasonably expected basis in the project as of the close of the second calendar year following the year of allocation, the carryover allocation is not valid and is treated as if it had not been made.

(b) *Carryover-allocation basis*—(1) *In general.* Subject to the limitations of paragraph (b)(2) of this section, a taxpayer's basis in a project for purposes of section 42(h)(1)(E)(ii) or (F) (carryover-allocation basis) is the taxpayer's adjusted basis in land or depreciable property that is reasonably expected to be part of the project, whether or not these amounts are includible in eligible basis under section 42(d). Thus, for example, if the project is to include property that is not residential rental property, such as commercial space, the basis attributable to the commercial space, although not includible in eligible basis, is includible in carryover-allocation basis. The adjusted basis of land and depreciable property is determined under sections 1012 and 1016, and generally includes the direct and indirect costs of acquiring, constructing, and rehabilitating the property. Costs otherwise includible in carryover-allocation basis are not excluded by reason of having been incurred prior to the calendar year in which the carryover allocation is made.

(2) *Limitations*—For purposes of determining carryover-allocation basis under paragraph (b)(1) of this section, the following limitations apply.

(i) *Taxpayer must have basis in land or depreciable property related to the project.* A taxpayer has carryover-allocation basis to the extent that it has basis in land or depreciable property and the land or depreciable property is reasonably expected to be part of the project for which the carryover allocation is made. This basis includes all items that are properly capitalizable with respect to the land or depreciable property. For example, a nonrefundable downpayment for, or an amount paid to acquire an option to purchase, land or depreciable property may be included in carryover-allocation basis if properly capitalizable into the basis of land or depreciable property that is reasonably expected to be part of a project.

(ii) *High cost areas.* Any increase in eligible basis that may result under section 42(d)(5)(C) from a building's location in a qualified census tract or difficult development area is not taken into account in determining carryover-allocation basis or reasonably expected basis.

(iii) *Amounts not treated as paid or incurred.* An amount is not includible in carryover-allocation basis unless it is treated as paid or incurred under the method of accounting used by the taxpayer. For example, a cash method taxpayer cannot include construction costs in carryover-allocation basis unless the costs have been paid, and an accrual method taxpayer cannot include construction costs in carryover-allocation basis unless they have been properly accrued. See paragraph (b)(2)(iv) of this section for a special rule for fees.

(iv) *Fees.* A fee is includible in carryover-allocation basis only to the extent the requirements of paragraph (b)(2)(iii) of this section are met and—

(A) The fee is reasonable;

(B) The taxpayer is legally obligated to pay the fee;

(C) The fee is capitalizable as part of the taxpayer's basis in land or depreciable property that is reasonably expected to be part of the project;

(D) The fee is not paid (or to be paid) by the taxpayer to itself; and

(E) If the fee is paid (or to be paid) by the taxpayer to a related person, and the taxpayer uses the cash method of accounting, the taxpayer could properly accrue the fee under the accrual method of accounting (considering, for example, the rules of section 461(h)). A person is a related person if the person bears a relationship to the taxpayer specified in sections 267(b) or 707(b)(1), or if the person and the taxpayer are engaged in trades or businesses under common control (within the meaning of subsections (a) and (b) of section 52).

(3) *Reasonably expected basis.* Rules similar to the rules of paragraphs (a) and (b) of this section apply in determining the taxpayer's reasonably expected basis in a project (land and depreciable basis) as of the close of the second calendar year following the calendar year of the allocation.

(4) *Examples.* The following examples illustrate the rules of paragraphs (a) and (b) of this section.

Example 1. (i) *Facts.* C, an accrual-method taxpayer, receives a carryover allocation from Agency, the state housing credit agency, in September of 1993. As of that date, C has not begun construction of the low-income housing building C plans to build. However, C has owned the land on which C plans to build the building since 1985. C's basis in the land is $100,000. C reasonably expects that by the end of 1995, C's basis in the project of which the building is to be a part will be $2,000,000. C also expects that because the project is located in a qualified census tract, C will be able to increase its basis in the project to $2,600,000. Before the close of 1993, C incurs $150,000 of costs for architects' fees and site preparation. C properly accrues these costs under its method of accounting and capitalizes the costs.

(ii) *Determination of carryover-allocation basis.* C's $100,000 basis in the land is includible in carryover-allocation basis even though C has owned the land since 1985. The $150,000 of costs C has incurred for architects' fees and site preparation are also includible in carryover-allocation basis. The expected increase in basis due to the project's location in a qualified census tract is not taken into account in determining C's carryover-allocation basis. Accordingly, C's carryover-allocation basis in the project of which the building is a part is $250,000.

(iii) *Determination of whether building is qualified.* C's reasonably expected basis in the project at the close of the second calendar year following the calendar year of allocation is $2,000,000. The expected increase in eligible basis due to the project's location in a qualified census tract is not taken into account in determining this amount. Because C's carryover-allocation basis is more than 10 percent of C's reasonably expected basis in the project of which the building is a part, the building for which C received the carryover allocation is a qualified building for purposes of section 42(h)(1)(E)(ii) and paragraph (a) of this section.

Example 2. (i) *Facts.* D, an accrual-method taxpayer, receives a carryover allocation from Agency, the state housing credit agency, on September 11, 1993. As of that date, D has not begun construction of the low-income housing building D plans to build and D does not have basis in the land on which D plans to build the building. In 1993, D incurs some costs related to the planned building, including architects' fees. However, at the close of 1993, these costs do not exceed 10 percent of D's reasonably expected basis in the project.

(ii) *Determination of whether building is qualified.* Because D's carryover-allocation basis is not more than 10 percent of D's reasonably expected basis in the project of which the building is a part, the building for which D received a carryover allocation is not a qualified building for purposes of section 42(h)(1)(E)(ii) and paragraph (a) of this section. The carryover allocation to D is not valid, and is treated as if it had not been made.

(c) *Verification of basis by Agency—*(1) *Verification requirement.* An Agency that makes a carryover allocation to a taxpayer must verify that, as of the close of the calendar year of allocation, the taxpayer has incurred more than 10 percent of the reasonably expected basis in the project (land and depreciable basis).

(2) *Manner of verification.* An Agency may verify that a taxpayer has incurred more than 10 percent of its reasonably expected basis in a project by obtaining a certification from the taxpayer, in writing and under penalty of perjury, that the taxpayer has incurred by the close of the calendar year of the allocation more than 10 percent of the reasonably expected basis in the project. The certification must be accompanied by supporting documentation that the Agency must review. Supporting documentation may include, for example, copies of checks or other records of payments. Alternatively, an Agency may verify that the taxpayer has incurred adequate basis by requiring that the taxpayer obtain from an attorney or certified public accountant a written certification to the Agency, that the attorney or accountant has examined all eligible costs incurred with respect to the project and that, based upon this examination, it is the attorney's or accountant's belief that the taxpayer has incurred more than 10 percent of its reasonably expected basis in the project by the close of the calendar year of the allocation.

(3) *Time of verification.* An Agency may require that the basis certification be submitted to or received by the Agency prior to the close of the calendar year of allocation or within a reasonable time after the close of the calendar year of allocation. The Agency will need to verify basis in order to accurately complete the Form 8610, "Annual Low-Income Housing Credit Agencies Report," for the calendar year. If certification is not timely made, or supporting documentation is lacking, inadequate, or does not actually support the certification, the Agency should notify the taxpayer and try to get adequate documentation. If the Agency cannot verify before the Form 8610

is filed that the taxpayer has satisfied the basis requirement for a carryover allocation, the allocation is treated as if it had not been made and the carryover allocation document should not be filed with the Form 8610.

(d) *Requirements for making carryover allocations*—(1) *In general.* Generally, an allocation is made when an Agency issues the Form 8609, "Low-Income Housing Credit Allocation Certification," for a building. See § 1.42-1T(d)(8)(ii). An Agency does not issue the Form 8609 for a building until the building is placed in service. However, in cases where allocations of credit are made pursuant to section 42(h)(1)(E) (relating to carryover allocations for buildings) or section 42(h)(1)(F) (relating to carryover allocations for multiple-building projects), Form 8609 is not used as the allocating document because the buildings are not yet in service. When an allocation is made pursuant to section 42(h)(1)(E) or (F), the allocating document is the document meeting the requirements of paragraph (d)(2) of this section. In addition, when an allocation is made pursuant to section 42(h)(1)(F), the requirements of paragraph (d)(3) of this section must be met for the allocation to be valid. An allocation pursuant to section 42(h)(1)(E) or (F) reduces the state housing credit ceiling for the year in which the allocation is made, whether or not the Form 8609 is also issued in that year.

(2) *Requirements for allocation.* An allocation pursuant to section 42(h)(1)(E) or (F) is made when an allocation document containing the following information is completed, signed, and dated by an authorized official of the Agency—

(i) The address of each building in the project, or if none exists, a specific description of the location of each building;

(ii) The name, address, and taxpayer identification number of the taxpayer receiving the allocation;

(iii) The name and address of the Agency;

(iv) The taxpayer identification number of the Agency;

(v) The date of the allocation;

(vi) The housing credit dollar amount allocated to the building or project, as applicable;

(vii) The taxpayer's reasonably expected basis in the project (land and depreciable basis) as of the close of the second calendar year following the calendar year in which the allocation is made;

(viii) The taxpayer's basis in the project (land and depreciable basis) as of the close of the calendar year in which the allocation is made and the percentage that basis bears to the reasonably expected basis in the project (land and depreciable basis) as of the close of the second following calendar year;

(ix) The date that each building in the project is expected to be placed in service; and

(x) The Building Identification Number (B.I.N.) to be assigned to each building in the project. The B.I.N. must reflect the year an allocation is first made to the building, regardless of the year that the building is placed in service. This B.I.N. must be used for all allocations of credit for the building. For example, rehabilitation expenditures treated as a separate new building under section 42(e) should not have a separate B.I.N. if the building to which the rehabilitation expenditures are made has a B.I.N. In this case, the B.I.N. used for the rehabilitation expenditures shall be the B.I.N. previously assigned to the building, although the rehabilitation expenditures must have a separate Form 8609 for the allocation. Similarly, a newly constructed building that receives an allocation of credit in different calendar years must have a separate Form 8609 for each allocation. The B.I.N. assigned to the building for the first allocation must be used for the subsequent allocation.

(3) *Special rules for project-based allocations*—(i) *In general.* An allocation pursuant to section 42(h)(1)(F) (a project-based allocation) must meet the requirements of this section as well as the requirements of section 42(h)(1)(F), including the minimum basis requirement of section 42(h)(1)(E)(ii).

(ii) *Requirement of section 42(h)(1)(F)(i)(III).* An allocation satisfies the requirement of section 42(h)(1)(F)(i)(III) if the Form 8609 that is issued for each building that is placed in service in the project states the portion of the project-based allocation that is applied to that building.

(4) *Recordkeeping requirements*—(i) *Taxpayer.* When an allocation is made pursuant to section 42(h)(1)(E) or (F), the taxpayer must retain a copy of the allocation document and file an additional copy with the Form 8609 that is issued to the taxpayer for a building after the building is placed in service. The taxpayer need only file a copy of the allocation document with the Form 8609 for the building for the first year the credit is claimed. However, the Form 8609 must be filed for the first taxable year in which the credit is claimed and for each taxable year thereafter throughout the compliance period, whether or not a credit is claimed for the taxable year.

(ii) *Agency.* The Agency must retain the original carryover allocation document made under paragraph (d)(2) of this section and file Schedule A (Form 8610), "Carryover Allocation of

Reg. § 1.42-6(d)(4)

the Low-Income Housing Credit," with the Agency's Form 8610 for the year the allocation is made. The Agency must also retain a copy of the Form 8609 that is issued to the taxpayer and file the original with the Agency's Form 8610 that reflects the year the form is issued.

(5) *Separate procedure for election of appropriate percentage month.* If a taxpayer receives an allocation under section 42(h)(1)(E) or (F) and wishes to elect under section 42(b)(2)(A)(ii) to use the appropriate percentage for a month other than the month in which a building is placed in service, the requirements specified in § 1.42-8 must be met for the election to be effective.

(e) *Special rules.* The following rules apply for purposes of this section.

(1) *Treatment of partnerships and other flow-through entities.* With respect to taxpayers that own projects through partnerships or other flow-through entities (e.g., S corporations, estates, or trusts), carryover-allocation basis is determined at the entity level using the rules provided by this section. In addition, the entity is responsible for providing to the Agency the certification and documentation required under the basis verification requirement in paragraph (c) of this section.

(2) *Transferees.* If land or depreciable property that is expected to be part of a project is transferred after a carryover allocation has been made for a building that is reasonably expected to be part of the project, but before the close of the calendar year of the allocation, the transferee's carryover-allocation basis is determined under the principles of this section and section 42(d)(7). See also Rev. Rul. 91-38, 1991-2 C.B. 3 (see § 601.601(d)(2)(ii)(*b*) of this chapter). In addition, the transferee is treated as the taxpayer for purposes of the basis verification requirement of this section, and therefore, is responsible for providing to the Agency the required certifications and documentation. [Reg. § 1.42-6.]

☐ [*T.D.* 8520, 3-2-94. *Amended by T.D.* 8859, 1-13-2000.]

[Reg. § 1.42-7]

§ 1.42-7. Substantially bond-financed buildings. [Reserved]

☐ [*T.D.* 8520, 3-2-94.]

[Reg. § 1.42-8]

§ 1.42-8. Election of appropriate percentage month.—(a) *Election under section 42(b)(2)(A)(ii)(I) to use the appropriate percentage for the month of a binding agreement*—(1) *In general.* For purposes of section 42(b)(2)(A)(ii)(I), an agreement between a taxpayer and an Agency

as to the housing credit dollar amount to be allocated to a building is considered binding if it—

(i) Is in writing;

(ii) Is binding under state law on the Agency, the taxpayer, and all successors in interest;

(iii) Specifies the type(s) of building(s) to which the housing credit dollar amount applies (i.e., a newly constructed or existing building, or substantial rehabilitation treated as a separate new building under section 42(e));

(iv) Specifies the housing credit dollar amount to be allocated to the building(s); and

(v) Is dated and signed by the taxpayer and the Agency during the month in which the requirements of paragraphs (a)(1)(i) through (iv) of this section are met.

(2) *Effect on state housing credit ceiling.* Generally, a binding agreement described in paragraph (a)(1) of this section is an agreement by the Agency to allocate credit to the taxpayer at a future date. The binding agreement may include a reservation of credit or a binding commitment (under section 42(h)(1)(C)) to allocate credit in a future taxable year. A reservation or a binding commitment to allocate credit in a future year has no effect on the state housing credit ceiling until the year the Agency actually makes an allocation. However, if the binding agreement is also a carryover allocation under section 42(h)(1)(E) or (F), the state housing credit ceiling is reduced by the amount allocated by the Agency to the taxpayer in the year the carryover allocation is made. For a binding agreement to be a valid carryover allocation, the requirements of paragraph (a)(1) of this section and § 1.42-6 must be met.

(3) *Time and manner of making election.* An election under section 42(b)(2)(A)(ii)(I) may be made either as part of the binding agreement under paragraph (a)(1) of this section to allocate a specific housing credit dollar amount or in a separate document that references the binding agreement. In either case, the election must—

(i) Be in writing;

(ii) Reference section 42(b)(2)(A)(ii)(I);

(iii) Be signed by the taxpayer;

(iv) If it is in a separate document, reference the binding agreement that meets the requirements of paragraph (a)(1) of this section; and

(v) Be notarized by the 5th day following the end of the month in which the binding agreement was made.

(4) *Multiple agreements*— (i) *Rescinded agreements.* A taxpayer may not make an election under section 42(b)(2)(A)(ii)(I) for a building if an election has previously been made for the building for a different month. For example, assume a taxpayer entered into a binding agreement for allocation of a specific housing credit dollar amount to a building and made the election under section 42(b)(2)(A)(ii)(I) to apply the appropriate percentage for the month of the binding agreement. If the binding agreement subsequently is rescinded under state law, and the taxpayer enters into a new binding agreement for allocation of a specific housing credit dollar amount to the building, the taxpayer must apply to the building the appropriate percentage for the elected month of the rescinded binding agreement. However, if no prior election was made with respect to the rescinded binding agreement, the taxpayer may elect the appropriate percentage for the month of the new binding agreement.

(ii) *Increases in credit.* The election under section 42(b)(2)(A)(ii)(I), once made, applies to any increase in the credit amount allocated for a building, whether the increase occurs in the same or in a subsequent year. However, in the case of a binding agreement (or carryover allocation that is treated as a binding agreement) to allocate a credit amount under section 42(e)(1) for substantial rehabilitation treated as a separate new building, a taxpayer may make the election under section 42(b)(2)(A)(ii)(I) notwithstanding that a prior election under section 42(b)(2)(A)(ii)(I) is in effect for a prior allocation of credit for a substantial rehabilitation that was previously placed in service under section 42(e).

(5) *Amount allocated.* The housing credit dollar amount eventually allocated to a building may be more or less than the amount specified in the binding agreement. Depending on the Agency's determination pursuant to section 42(m)(2) as to the financial feasibility of the building (or project), the Agency may allocate a greater housing credit dollar amount to the building (provided that the Agency has additional housing credit dollar amounts available to allocate for the calendar year of the allocation) or the Agency may allocate a lesser housing credit dollar amount. Under section 42(h)(7)(D), in allocating a housing credit dollar amount, the Agency must specify the applicable percentage and maximum qualified basis of the building. The applicable percentage may be less, but not greater than, the appropriate percentage for the month the building is placed in service, or the month elected by the taxpayer under section 42(b)(2)(A)(ii)(I). Whether the appropriate percentage is the appropriate percentage for the 70-percent present value credit or the

30-percent present value credit is determined under section 42(i)(2) when the building is placed in service.

(6) *Procedures*—(i) *Taxpayer.* The taxpayer must give the original notarized election statement to the Agency before the close of the 5th calendar day following the end of the month in which the binding agreement is made. The taxpayer must retain a copy of the binding agreement and the election statement and must file an additional copy of each with the taxpayer's Form 8609, Low-Income Housing Credit Allocation Certification, for the first taxable year in which credit is claimed for the building.

(ii) *Agency.* The Agency must file with the Internal Revenue Service the original of the binding agreement and the election statement with the Agency's Form 8610, Annual Low-Income Housing Credit Agencies Report, that accounts for the year the allocation is actually made. The Agency must also retain a copy of the binding agreement and the election statement.

(7) *Examples.* The following examples illustrate the provisions of this section. In each example, X is the taxpayer, Agency is the state housing credit agency, and the carryover allocations meet the requirements of § 1.42-6 and are otherwise valid.

Example 1. (i) In August 1993, X and Agency enter into an agreement that Agency will allocate $100,000 of housing credit dollar amount for the low-income housing building X is constructing. The agreement is binding and meets all the requirements of paragraph (a)(1) of this section. The agreement is a reservation of credit, not an allocation, and therefore, has no effect on the state housing credit ceiling. On or before September 5, 1993, X signs and has notarized a written election statement that meets the requirements of paragraph (a)(3) of this section. The applicable percentage for the building is the appropriate percentage for the month of August 1993.

(ii) Agency makes a carryover allocation of $100,000 of housing credit dollar amount for the building on October 2, 1993. The carryover allocation reduces Agency's state housing credit ceiling for 1993. Due to unexpectedly high construction costs, when X places the building in service in July 1994, the product of the building's qualified basis and the applicable percentage for the building (the appropriate percentage for the month of August 1993) is $150,000, rather than $100,000. Notwithstanding that only $100,000 of credit was allocated for the building in 1993, Agency may allocate an additional $50,000 of housing credit dollar amount for the building from its state housing credit ceiling for 1994. The appropriate per-

Reg. § 1.42-8(a)(7)

centage for the month of August 1993 is the applicable percentage for the building for the entire $150,000 of credit allocated for the building, even though separate allocations were made in 1993 and 1994. Because allocations were made for the building in two separate calendar years, Agency must issue two Forms 8609 to X. One Form 8609 must reflect the $100,000 allocation made in 1993, and the other Form 8609 must reflect the $50,000 allocation made in 1994.

(iii) X gives the original notarized statement to Agency on or before September 5, 1993, and retains a copy of the binding agreement, election statement, and carryover allocation document. X files a copy of the binding agreement, election statement, and carryover allocation document with X's Form 8609 for the first taxable year in which X claims credit for the building.

(iv) Agency files the original of the binding agreement, election statement, and 1993 carryover allocation document with its 1993 Form 8610. Agency retains a copy of the binding agreement, election statement, and carryover allocation document. After the building is placed in service in 1994, Agency issues to X a copy of the Form 8609 reflecting the 1993 carryover allocation of $100,000 and files the original of that form with its 1994 Form 8610. Agency also files the original of the 1994 Form 8609 reflecting the $50,000 allocation with its 1994 Form 8610 and issues to X a copy of the 1994 Form 8609. Agency retains copies of the Forms 8609 that are issued to X.

Example 2. (i) In September 1993, X and Agency enter into an agreement that Agency will allocate $70,000 of housing credit dollar amount for rehabilitation expenditures that X is incurring and that X will treat as a new low-income housing building under section 42(e)(1). The agreement is binding and meets all the requirements of paragraph (a)(1) of this section. The agreement is a reservation of credit, not an allocation, and therefore, has no effect on Agency's state housing credit ceiling. On or before October 5, 1993, X signs and has notarized a written election statement that meets the requirements of paragraph (a)(3) of this section. The applicable percentage for the building is the appropriate percentage for the month of September 1993. Agency makes a carryover allocation of $70,000 of housing credit dollar amount for the building on November 15, 1993. The carryover allocation reduces by $70,000 Agency's state housing credit ceiling for 1993.

(ii) In October 1994, X and Agency enter into another binding agreement meeting the requirements of paragraph (a)(1) of this section. Under the agreement, Agency will allocate

$50,000 of housing credit dollar amount for additional rehabilitation expenditures by X that qualify as a second separate new building under section 42(e)(1). On or before November 5, 1994, X signs and has notarized a written election statement meeting the requirements of paragraph (a)(3) of this section. On December 1, 1994, X receives a carryover allocation under section 42(h)(1)(E) for $50,000. The carryover allocation reduces by $50,000 Agency's state housing credit ceiling for 1994. The applicable percentage for the rehabilitation expenditures treated as the second separate new building is the appropriate percentage for the month of October 1994, not September 1993. The appropriate percentage for the month of September 1993 still applies to the allocation of $70,000 for the rehabilitation expenditures treated as the first separate new building. Because allocations were made for the building in two separate calendar years, Agency must issue two Forms 8609 to X. One Form 8609 must reflect the $70,000 allocation made in 1993, and the other Form 8609 must reflect the $50,000 allocation made in 1994.

(iii) X gives the first original notarized statement to Agency on or before October 5, 1993, and retains a copy of the first binding agreement, election statement, and carryover allocation document issued in 1993. X gives the second original notarized statement to Agency on or before November 5, 1994, and retains a copy of the second binding agreement, election statement, and carryover allocation document issued in 1994. X files a copy of the binding agreements, election statements, and carryover allocation documents with X's Forms 8609 for the first taxable year in which X claims credit for the buildings.

(iv) Agency retains a copy of the binding agreements, election statements, and carryover allocation documents. Agency files the original of the first binding agreement, election statement, and 1993 carryover allocation document with its 1993 Form 8610. Agency files the original of the second binding agreement, election statement, and 1994 carryover allocation document with its 1994 Form 8610. After X notifies Agency of the date each building is placed in service, the Agency will issue copies of the respective Forms 8609 to X, and file the originals of those forms with the Agency's Form 8610 that reflects the year each form is issued. The Agency also retains copies of the Forms 8609.

(b) *Election under section 42(b)(2)(A)(ii)(II) to use the appropriate percentage for the month tax-exempt bonds are issued*—(1) *Time and manner of making election.* In the case of any building to which section 42(h)(4)(B) applies, an election under section 42(b)(2)(A)(ii)(II) to use the appropriate percentage for the month tax-exempt bonds are issued must—

(i) Be in writing;

(ii) Reference section 42(b)(2)(A)(ii)(II);

(iii) Specify the percentage of the aggregate basis of the building and the land on which the building is located that is financed with the proceeds of obligations described in section 42(h)(4)(A) (tax-exempt bonds);

(iv) State the month in which the tax-exempt bonds are issued;

(v) State that the month in which the tax-exempt bonds are issued is the month elected for the appropriate percentage to be used for the building;

(vi) Be signed by the taxpayer; and

(vii) Be notarized by the 5th day following the end of the month in which the bonds are issued.

(2) *Bonds issued in more than one month.* If a building described in section 42(h)(4)(B) (substantially bond-financed building) is financed with tax-exempt bonds issued in more than one month, the taxpayer may elect the appropriate percentage for any month in which the bonds are issued. Once the election is made, the appropriate percentage elected applies for the building even if all bonds are not issued in that month. The requirements of this paragraph (b), including the time limitation contained in paragraph (b)(1)(vii) of this section, must also be met.

(3) *Limitations on appropriate percentage.* Under section 42(m)(2)(D), the credit allowable for a substantially bond-financed building is limited to the amount necessary to assure the project's feasibility. Accordingly, in making the determination under section 42(m)(2), an Agency may use an applicable percentage that is less, but not greater than, the appropriate percentage for the month the building is placed in service, or the month elected by the taxpayer under section 42(b)(2)(A)(ii)(II).

(4) *Procedures*—(i) *Taxpayer.* The taxpayer must provide the original notarized election statement to the Agency before the close of the 5th calendar day following the end of the month in which the bonds are issued. If an authority other than the Agency issues the tax-exempt bonds, the taxpayer must also give the Agency a signed statement from the issuing authority that certifies the information described in paragraphs (b)(1)(iii) and (iv) of this section. The taxpayer must file a copy of the election statement with the taxpayer's Form 8609 for the first taxable year in which credit is claimed for the building. The tax-

payer must also retain a copy of the election statement.

(ii) *Agency.* The Agency must file with the Internal Revenue Service the original of the election statement and the corresponding Form 8609 for the building with the Agency's Form 8610 that reflects the year the Form 8609 is issued. The Agency must also retain a copy of the election statement and the Form 8609. [Reg. § 1.42-8.]

☐ [*T.D.* 8520, 3-2-94.]

[Reg. § 1.42-9]

§ 1.42-9. **For use by the general public.**—(a) *General rule.* If a residential rental unit in a building is not for use by the general public, the unit is not eligible for a section 42 credit. A residential rental unit is for use by the general public if the unit is rented in a manner consistent with housing policy governing nondiscrimination, as evidenced by rules or regulations of the Department of Housing and Urban Development (HUD) (24 CFR subtitle A and Chapters I through XX). See HUD Handbook 4350.3 (or its successor). A copy of HUD Handbook 4350.3 may be requested by writing to: HUD, Directives Distribution Section, room B-100, 451 7th Street, SW, Washington, DC 20410.

(b) *Limitations.* Notwithstanding paragraph (a) of this section, if a residential rental unit is provided only for a member of a social organization or provided by an employer for its employees, the unit is not for use by the general public and is not eligible for credit under section 42. In addition, any residential rental unit that is part of a hospital, nursing home, sanitarium, lifecare facility, trailer park, or intermediate care facility for the mentally and physically handicapped is not for use by the general public and is not eligible for credit under section 42.

(c) *Treatment of units not for use by the general public.* The costs attributable to a residential rental unit that is not for use by the general public are not excludable from eligible basis by reason of the unit's ineligibility for the credit under this section. However, in calculating the applicable fraction, the unit is treated as a residential rental unit that is not a low-income unit. [Reg. § 1.42-9.]

☐ [*T.D.* 8520, 3-2-94.]

[Reg. § 1.42-10]

§ 1.42-10. **Utility allowances.**—(a) *Inclusion of utility allowances in gross rent.* If the cost of any utilities (other than telephone) for a residential rental unit are paid directly by the tenant(s), the gross rent for that unit includes the applicable utility allowance determined under this section.

Reg. § 1.42-10(a)

This section only applies for purposes of determining gross rent under section 42(g)(2)(B)(ii) as to rent-restricted units.

(b) *Applicable utility allowances*—(1) *FmHA-assisted buildings.* If a building receives assistance from the Farmers Home Administration (FmHA-assisted building), the applicable utility allowance for all rent-restricted units in the building is the utility allowance determined under the method prescribed by the Farmers Home Administration (FmHA) for the building. For example, if a building receives assistance under FmHA's section 515 program (whether or not the building or its tenants also receive other state or federal assistance), the applicable utility allowance for all rent-restricted units in the building is determined using Exhibit A-6 of 7 CFR part 1944, subpart E (or a successor method of determining utility allowances).

(2) *Buildings with FmHA assisted tenants.* If any tenant in a building receives FmHA rental assistance payments (FmHA tenant assistance), the applicable utility allowance for all rent-restricted units in the building (including any units occupied by tenants receiving HUD rental assistance payments) is the applicable FmHA utility allowance.

(3) *HUD-regulated buildings.* If neither a building nor any tenant in the building receives FmHA housing assistance, and the rents and utility allowances of the building are reviewed by HUD on an annual basis (HUD-regulated building), the applicable utility allowance for all rent-restricted units in the building is the applicable HUD utility allowance.

(4) *Other buildings.* If a building is neither an FmHA-assisted nor a HUD-regulated building, and no tenant in the building receives FmHA tenant assistance, the applicable utility allowance for rent-restricted units in the building is determined under the following methods.

(i) *Tenants receiving HUD rental assistance.* The applicable utility allowance for any rent-restricted units occupied by tenants receiving HUD rental assistance payments (HUD tenant assistance) is the applicable Public Housing Authority (PHA) utility allowance established for the Section 8 Existing Housing Program.

(ii) *Other tenants*—(A) *General rule.* If none of the rules of paragraphs (b)(1), (2), (3), and (4)(i) of this section apply to any rent-restricted units in a building, the appropriate utility allowance for the units is the applicable PHA utility allowance. However, if a local utility company estimate is obtained for any unit in the building in accordance with paragraph (b)(4)(ii)(B) of this section, that estimate becomes

the appropriate utility allowance for all rent-restricted units of similar size and construction in the building. This local utility company estimate procedure is not available for and does not apply to units to which the rules of paragraph (b)(1), (2), (3), or (4)(i) of this section apply.

(B) *Utility company estimate.* Any interested party (including a low-income tenant, a building owner, or an Agency) may obtain a local utility company estimate for a unit. The estimate is obtained when the interested party receives, in writing, information from a local utility company providing the estimated cost of that utility for a unit of similar size and construction for the geographic area in which the building containing the unit is located. The local utility company estimate may be obtained by an interested party at any time during the building's extended use period (see section 42(h)(6)(D)) or, if the building does not have an extended use period, during the building's compliance period (see section 42(i)(1)). Unless the parties agree otherwise, costs incurred in obtaining the estimate are borne by the initiating party. The interested party that obtains the local utility company estimate (the initiating party) must retain the original of the utility company estimate and must furnish a copy of the local utility company estimate to the owner of the building (where the initiating party is not the owner), and the Agency that allocated credit to the building (where the initiating party is not the Agency). The owner of the building must make available copies of the utility company estimate to the tenants in the building.

(c) *Changes in applicable utility allowance.* If at any time during the building's extended use period (or, if the building does not have an extended use period, the building's compliance period), the applicable utility allowance for a unit changes, the new utility allowance must be used to compute gross rents of rent-restricted units due 90 days after the change. For example, if rent must be lowered because a local utility company estimate is obtained that shows a higher utility cost than the otherwise applicable PHA utility allowance, the lower rent must be in effect for rent due more than 90 days after the date of the local utility company estimate. [Reg. § 1.42-10.]

☐ [*T.D.* 8520, 3-2-94.]

[Reg. § 1.42-11]

§ 1.42-11. Provision of services.—(a) *General rule.* The furnishing to tenants of services other than housing (whether or not the services are significant) does not prevent the units occupied by the tenants from qualifying as residential rental property eligible for credit under section 42. However, any charges to low-income tenants for services that are not optional generally must be included in gross rent for purposes of section 42(g).

(b) *Services that are optional*—(1) *General rule.* A service is optional if payment for the service is not required as a condition of occupancy. For example, for a qualified low-income building with a common dining facility, the cost of meals is not included in gross rent for purposes of section 42(g)(2)(A) if payment for the meals in the facility is not required as a condition of occupancy and a practical alternative exists for tenants to obtain meals other than from the dining facility.

(2) *Continual or frequent services.* If continual or frequent nursing, medical, or psychiatric services are provided, it is presumed that the services are not optional and the building is ineligible for the credit, as is the case with a hospital, nursing home, sanitarium, lifecare facility, or intermediate care facility for the mentally and physically handicapped. See also § 1.42-9(b).

(3) *Required services*—(i) *General rule.* The cost of services that are required as a condition of occupancy must be included in gross rent even if federal or state law requires that the services be offered to tenants by building owners.

→ *Caution: Reg. § 1.42-11(b)(3)(ii)(A), below, is effective before January 1, 2001.*←

(ii) *Exceptions*—(A) *Supportive services.* Section 42(g)(2)(B)(iii) provides an exception for certain fees paid for supportive services. For purposes of section 42(g)(2)(B)(iii), a supportive service is any service provided under a planned program of services designed to enable residents of a residential rental property to remain independent and avoid placement in a hospital, nursing

home, or intermediate care facility for the mentally or physically handicapped. For a building described in section 42(i)(3)(B)(iii) (relating to transitional housing for the homeless), a supportive service includes any service provided to assist tenants in locating and retaining permanent housing.

→ *Caution: Reg. § 1.42-11(b)(3)(ii)(A), below, is effective on January 1, 2001.*←

(ii) *Exceptions*—(A) *Supportive services.* Section 42(g)(2)(B)(iii) provides an exception for certain fees paid for supportive services. For purposes of section 42(g)(2)(B)(iii), a supportive service is any service provided under a planned program of services designed to enable residents of a residential rental property to remain independent and avoid placement in a hospital, nursing home, or intermediate care facility for the mentally or physically handicapped. For a building described in section 42(i)(3)(B)(iii) (relating to transitional housing for the homeless) or section 42(i)(3)(B)(iv) (relating to single-room occupancy), a supportive service includes any service provided to assist tenants in locating and retaining permanent housing.

(B) *Specific project exception.* Gross rent does not include the cost of mandatory meals in any federally-assisted project for the elderly and handicapped (in existence on or before January 9, 1989) that is authorized by 24 CFR part 278 to provide a mandatory meals program. [Reg. § 1.42-11.]

☐ [*T.D. 8520, 3-2-94. Amended by T.D. 8859, 1-13-2000.*]

[Reg. § 1.42-12]

§ 1.42-12. Effective dates and transitional rules.—(a) *Effective date.* The rules set forth in §§ 1.42-6 and 1.42-8 through 1.42-12 are effective

May 2, 1994. However, binding agreements, election statements, and carryover allocation documents entered into before May 2, 1994, that follow the guidance set forth in Notice 89-1, 1989-1 C.B. 620 (see § 601.601(d)(2)(ii)(*b*) of this chapter) need not be changed to conform to the rules set forth in §§ 1.42-6 and 1.42-8 through 1.42-12.

(b) *Prior periods.* Notice 89-1, 1989-1 C.B. 620 and Notice 89-6, 1989-1 C.B. 625 (see § 601.601(d)(2)(ii)(*b*) of this chapter) may be applied for periods prior to May 2, 1994.

(c) *Carryover allocations.* The rule set forth in § 1.42-6(d)(4)(ii) relating to the requirement that state and local housing agencies file Schedule A (Form 8610), "Carryover Allocation of the Low-Income Housing Credit," is applicable for carryover allocations made after December 31, 1999. [Reg. § 1.42-12.]

☐ [*T.D. 8520, 3-2-94. Amended by T.D. 8859, 1-13-2000.*]

[Reg. § 1.42-13]

§ 1.42-13. Rules necessary and appropriate; housing credit agencies' correction of administrative errors and omissions.—(a) *Publication of guidance.* Under section 42(n), the Secretary has authority to prescribe regulations as may be necessary or appropriate to carry out the purposes of section 42. The Secretary may also provide

Reg. § 1.42-13(a)

guidance through various publications in the Internal Revenue Bulletin. (See § 601.601(d)(2)(ii)(b) of this chapter.)

(b) *Correcting administrative errors and omissions*—(1) *In general.* An Agency may correct an administrative error or omission with respect to allocations and recordkeeping, as described in paragraph (b)(2) of this section, within a reasonable period after the Agency discovers the administrative error or omission. Whether a correction is made within a reasonable period depends on the facts and circumstances of each situation. Except as provided in paragraph (b)(3)(iii) of this section, an Agency need not obtain the prior approval of the Secretary to correct an administrative error or omission, if the correction is made in accordance with paragraph (b)(3)(i) of this section. The administrative errors and omissions to which this paragraph (b) applies are strictly limited to those described in paragraph (b)(2) of this section, and, thus, do not include, for example, any misinterpretation of the applicable rules and regulations under section 42. Accordingly, an Agency's allocation of a particular calendar year's low-income housing credit dollar amount made after the close of that calendar year, or the use of an incorrect population amount in calculating a State's housing credit ceiling for a calendar year are not administrative errors that can be corrected under this paragraph (b).

(2) *Administrative errors and omissions described.* An administrative error or omission is a mistake that results in a document that inaccurately reflects the intent of the Agency at the time the document is originally completed or, if the mistake affects a taxpayer, a document that inaccurately reflects the intent of the Agency and the affected taxpayer at the time the document is originally completed. Administrative errors and omissions described in this paragraph (b)(2) include the following—

(i) A mathematical error;

(ii) An entry on a document that is inconsistent with another entry on the same or another document regarding the same property, or taxpayer;

(iii) A failure in tracking the housing credit dollar amount an Agency has allocated (or that remains to be allocated) in the current calendar year (e.g., a failure to include in its State housing credit ceiling a previously allocated credit dollar amount that has been returned by a taxpayer);

(iv) An omission of information that is required on a document; and

(v) Any other type of error or omission identified by guidance published in the Internal Revenue Bulletin (see § 601.601(d)(2)(ii)(b) of this chapter) as an administrative error or omission covered by this paragraph (b).

(3) *Procedures for correcting administrative errors or omissions*—(i) *In general.* An Agency's correction of an administrative error or omission, as described in paragraph (b)(2) of this section, must amend the document so that the corrected document reflects the original intent of the Agency, or the Agency and the affected taxpayer, and complies with applicable rules and regulations under section 42.

(ii) *Specific procedures.* If a document corrects a document containing an administrative error or omission that has not yet been filed with the Internal Revenue Service, the Agency, or the Agency and the affected taxpayer, should complete and file the corrected document as the original. When a document containing an administrative error or omission has already been filed with the Service, the Agency, or the Agency and the affected taxpayer, should refile a copy of the document containing the administrative error or omission, and prominently and clearly note the correction thereon or on an attached new document. The Agency should indicate at the top of the document(s) that the correction is being made under § 1.42-13 of the Income Tax Regulations.

(iii) *Secretary's prior approval required.* Except as provided in paragraph (b)(3)(vi) of this section, an Agency must obtain the Secretary's prior approval to correct an administrative error or omission, as described in paragraph (b)(2) of this section, if the correction is not made before the close of the calendar year of the error or omission and the correction—

(A) Is a numerical change to the housing credit dollar amount allocated for the building or project;

(B) Affects the determination of any component of the State's housing credit ceiling under section 42(h)(3)(C); or

(C) Affects the State's unused housing credit carryover that is assigned to the Secretary under section 42(h)(3)(D).

(iv) *Requesting the Secretary's approval.* To obtain the Secretary's approval under paragraph (b)(3)(iii) of this section, an Agency must submit a request for the Secretary's approval within a reasonable period after discovering the administrative error or omission, and must agree to any conditions that may be required by the Secretary under paragraph (b)(3)(v) of this section. When requesting the Secretary's approval, the Agency, or the Agency and the affected taxpayer, must file an application that complies with the requirements of this paragraph (b)(3)(iv). For

Reg. § 1.42-13(b)(1)

further information on the application procedure see Rev. Proc. 93-1, 1993-1 I.R.B. 10 (or any subsequent applicable revenue procedure). (See § 601.601(d)(2)(ii)(b) of this chapter.) The application requesting the Secretary's approval must contain the following information—

(A) The name, address, and identification number of each affected taxpayer;

(B) The Building Identification Number (B.I.N.) and address of each building or project affected by the administrative error or omission;

(C) A statement explaining the administrative error or omission and the intent of the Agency, or of the Agency and the affected taxpayer, when the document was originally completed;

(D) Copies of any supporting documentation;

(E) A statement explaining the effect, if any, that a correction of the administrative error or omission would have on the housing credit dollar amount allocated for any building or project; and

(F) A statement explaining the effect, if any, that a correction of the administrative error or omission would have on the determination of the components of the State's housing credit ceiling under section 42(h)(3)(C) or on the State's unused housing credit carryover that is assigned to the Secretary under section 42(h)(3)(D).

(v) *Agreement to conditions.* To obtain the Secretary's approval under paragraph (b)(3)(iii) of this section, an Agency, or the Agency and the affected taxpayer, must agree to the conditions the Secretary considers appropriate.

(vi) *Secretary's automatic approval.* The Secretary grants automatic approval to correct an administrative error or omission described in paragraph (b)(2) of this section if—

(A) The correction is not made before the close of the calendar year of the error or omission and the correction is a numerical change to the housing credit dollar amount allocated for the building or multiple-building project;

(B) The administrative error or omission resulted in an allocation document (the Form 8609, "Low-Income Housing Credit Allocation Certification," or the allocation document under the requirements of section 42(h)(1)(E) or (F), and § 1.42-6(d)(2)) that either did not accurately reflect the number of buildings in a project (for example, an allocation document for a 10-building project only references 8 buildings instead of 10 buildings), or the correct information (other than the amount of credit allocated on the allocation document);

(C) The administrative error or omission does not affect the Agency's ranking of the building(s) or project and the total amount of credit the Agency allocated to the building(s) or project; and

(D) The Agency corrects the administrative error or omission by following the procedures described in paragraph (b)(3)(vii) of this section.

(vii) *How Agency corrects errors or omissions subject to automatic approval.* An Agency corrects an administrative error or omission described in paragraph (b)(3)(vi) of this section by—

(A) Amending the allocation document described in paragraph (b)(3)(vi)(B) of this section to correct the administrative error or omission. The Agency will indicate on the amended allocation document that it is making the "correction under § 1.42-13(b)(3)(vii)." If correcting the allocation document requires including any additional B.I.N.(s) in the document, the document must include any B.I.N.(s) already existing for buildings in the project. If possible, the additional B.I.N.(s) should be sequentially numbered from the existing B.I.N.(s);

(B) Amending, if applicable, the Schedule A (Form 8610), "Carryover Allocation of the Low-Income Housing Credit," and attaching a copy of this schedule to Form 8610, "Annual Low-income Housing Credit Agencies Report," for the year the correction is made. The Agency will indicate on the schedule that it is making the "correction under § 1.42-13(b)(3)(vii)." For a carryover allocation made before January 1, 2000, the Agency must complete Schedule A (Form 8610), and indicate on the schedule that it is making the "correction under § 1.42-13(b)(3)(vii)";

(C) Amending, if applicable, the Form 8609 and attaching the original of this amended form to Form 8610 for the year the correction is made. The Agency will indicate on the Form 8609 that it is making the "correction under § 1.42-13(b)(3)(vii)"; and

(D) Mailing or otherwise delivering a copy of any amended allocation document and any amended Form 8609 to the affected taxpayer.

(viii) *Other approval procedures.* The Secretary may grant automatic approval to correct other administrative errors or omissions as designated in one or more documents published either in the Federal Register or in the Internal Revenue Bulletin (see § 601.601(d)(2) of this chapter).

(c) *Examples.* The following examples illustrate the scope of this section:

Reg. § 1.42-13(c)

Example 1. Individual B applied to Agency X for a reservation of a low-income housing credit dollar amount for a building that is part of a low-income housing project. When applying for the low-income housing credit dollar amount, B informed Agency X that B intended to form Partnership Y to finance the project. After receiving the reservation letter and prior to receiving an allocation, B formed Partnership Y and sold partnership interests to a number of limited partners. B contributed the low-income housing project to Partnership Y in exchange for a partnership interest. B and Partnership Y informed Agency X of the ownership change. When actually allocating the housing credit dollar amount, Agency X sent Partnership Y a document listing B, rather than Partnership Y, as the building's owner. Partnership Y promptly notified Agency X of the error. After reviewing related documents, Agency X determined that it had incorrectly listed B as the building's owner on the allocation document. Since the parties originally intended that Partnership Y would receive the allocation as the owner of the building, Agency X may correct the error without obtaining the Secretary's approval, and insert Partnership Y as the building's owner on the allocation document.

Example 2. Agency Y allocated a lower low-income housing credit dollar amount for a low-income housing building than Agency Y originally intended. After the close of the calendar year of the allocation, B, the building's owner, discovered the error and promptly notified Agency Y. Agency Y reviewed relevant documents and agreed that an error had occurred. Agency Y and B must apply, as provided in paragraph (b)(3)(iv) of this section, for the Secretary's approval before Agency Y may correct the error.

(d) *Effective date.* This section is effective February 24, 1994. However, an Agency may elect to apply these regulations to administrative errors or omissions that occurred before the publication of these regulations. Any reasonable method used by a State or local housing credit agency to correct an administrative error or omission prior to February 24, 1994 will be considered proper, provided that the method is consistent with the rules of section 42. Paragraphs (b)(3)(vi), (vii), and (viii) of this section are effective January 14, 2000. [Reg. § 1.42-13.]

☐ [*T.D.* 8521, 2-23-94. *Amended by T.D.* 8859, 1-13-2000.]

[Reg. § 1.42-14]

§ 1.42-14. Allocation rules for post-1989 State housing credit ceiling amounts.—(a) *In general.* The State housing credit ceiling for a State for any calendar year after 1989 is com-

prised of four components. The four components are—

(1) $1.25 multiplied by the State population (the population component);

(2) The unused State housing credit ceiling, if any, of the State for the preceding calendar year (the unused carryforward component);

(3) The amount of State housing credit ceiling returned in the calendar year (the returned credit component); plus

(4) The amount, if any, allocated to the State by the Secretary under section 42(h)(3)(D) from a national pool of unused credit (the national pool component).

(b) *The population component.* The population component of the State housing credit ceiling of a State for any calendar year is determined pursuant to section 146(j). Thus, a State's population for any calendar year is determined by reference to the most recent census estimate, whether final or provisional, of the resident population of the State released by the Bureau of the Census before the beginning of the calendar year for which the State's housing credit ceiling is set. Unless otherwise prescribed by applicable revenue procedure, determinations of population are based on the most recent estimates of population contained in the Bureau of the Census publication, *Current Population Report, Series P-25; Population Estimates and Projections, Estimates of the Population of States.* For convenience, the Internal Revenue Service publishes the population estimates annually in the Internal Revenue Bulletin. (See § 601.601(d)(2)(ii)(*b*)).

(c) *The unused carryforward component.* The unused carryforward component of the State housing credit ceiling of a State for any calendar year is the excess, if any, of the sum of the population and returned credit components, over the aggregate housing credit dollar amount allocated for the year. Any credit amounts attributable to the national pool component of the State housing credit ceiling that remain unallocated at the close of a calendar year are not carried forward to the succeeding calendar year; instead, the credit expires and cannot be reallocated by any Agency.

(d) *The returned credit component*—(1) *In general.* The returned credit component of the State housing credit ceiling of a State for any calendar year equals the housing credit dollar amount returned during the calendar year that was validly allocated within the State in a prior calendar year to any project that does not become a qualified low-income housing project within the period required by section 42, or as required by the terms of the allocation. The returned credit component also includes credit allocated in a prior calendar year that is returned as a result of the cancellation of an allocation by mutual consent or by an Agency's determination that the amount allocated is not necessary for the financial feasibility of the project. For purposes of this section, credit is allocated within a State if it is allocated from the State's housing credit ceiling by an Agency of the State or of a constitutional home rule city in the State.

(2) *Limitations and special rules.* The following limitations and special rules apply for purposes of this paragraph (d).

(i) *General limitations.* Notwithstanding any other provision of this paragraph (d), returned credit does not include any credit that was—

(A) Allocated prior to calendar year 1990;

(B) Allowable under section 42(h)(4) (relating to the portion of credit attributable to eligible basis financed by certain tax-exempt bonds under section 103); or

(C) Allocated during the same calendar year that it is received back by the Agency.

(ii) *Credit period limitation.* Notwithstanding any other provision of this paragraph (d), an allocation of credit may not be returned any later than 180 days following the close of the first taxable year of the credit period for the building that received the allocation. After this date, credit that might otherwise be returned expires, and cannot be returned to or reallocated by any Agency.

(iii) *Three-month rule for returned credit.* An Agency may, in its discretion, treat any portion of credit that is returned from a project after September 30 of a calendar year and that is not reallocated by the close of the calendar year as returned on January 1 of the succeeding calendar year. In this case, the returned credit becomes part of the returned credit component of the State housing credit ceiling for the succeeding calendar year. Any portion of credit that is returned from a project after September 30 of a calendar year that is reallocated by the close of the calendar year is treated as part of the returned credit component of the State housing credit ceiling for the calendar year that the credit was returned.

(iv) *Returns of credit.* Subject to the limitations of paragraphs (d)(2)(i) and (ii) of this section, credit is returned to the Agency in the following instances in the manner described in paragraph (d)(3) of this section.

(A) *Building not qualified within required time period.* If a building is not a qualified

building within the time period required by section 42, it loses its credit allocation and the credit is returned. For example, a building is not qualified within the required time period if it is not placed in service within the period required by section 42 or if the project of which the building is a part fails to meet the minimum set-aside requirements of section 42(g)(1) by the close of the first year of the credit period.

(B) *Noncompliance with terms of the allocation.* If a building does not comply with the terms of its allocation, it loses the credit allocation and the credit is returned. The terms of an allocation are the written conditions agreed to by the Agency and the allocation recipient in the allocation document.

(C) *Mutual consent.* If the Agency and the allocation recipient cancel an allocation of an amount of credit by mutual consent, that amount of credit is returned.

(D) *Amount not necessary for financial feasibility.* If an Agency determines under section 42(m)(2) that an amount of credit allocated to a project is not necessary for the financial feasibility of the project and its viability as a qualified low-income housing project throughout the credit period, that amount of credit is returned.

(3) *Manner of returning credit*—(i) *Taxpayer notification.* After an Agency determines that a building or project no longer qualifies under paragraph (d)(2)(iv)(A), (B), or (D) of this section for all or part of the allocation it received, the Agency must provide written notification to the allocation recipient, or its successor in interest, that all or part of the allocation is no longer valid. The notification must also state the amount of the allocation that is no longer valid. The date of the notification is the date the credit is returned to the Agency. If an allocation is cancelled by mutual consent under paragraph (d)(2)(iv)(C) of this section, there must be a written agreement signed by the Agency, and the allocation recipient, or its successor in interest, indicating the amount of the allocation that is returned to the Agency. The effective date of the agreement is the date the credit is returned to the Agency.

(ii) *Internal Revenue Service notification.* If a credit is returned within 180 days following the close of the first taxable year of a building's credit period as provided in paragraph (d)(2)(ii) of this section, and a Form 8609, *Low-Income Housing Credit Allocation Certification,* has been issued for the building, the Agency must notify the Internal Revenue Service that the credit has been returned. If only part of the credit has been returned, this notification requirement is satisfied when the Agency attaches to an amended Form

Reg. § 1.42-14(d)(3)

8610, *Annual Low-Income Housing Credit Agencies Report*, the original of an amended Form 8609 reflecting the correct amount of credit attributed to the building together with an explanation for the filing of the amended Forms. The Agency must send a copy of the amended Form 8609 to the taxpayer that owns the building. If the building is not issued an amended Form 8609 because all of the credit allocated to the building is returned, notification to the Internal Revenue Service is satisfied by following the requirements prescribed in § 1.42-5(e)(3) for filing a Form 8823, *Low-Income Housing Credit Agencies Report of Noncompliance.*

(e) *The national pool component.* The national pool component of the State housing credit ceiling of a State for any calendar year is the portion of the National Pool allocated to the State by the Secretary for the calendar year. The national pool component for any calendar year is zero unless a State is a *qualified State.* (See paragraph (i) of this section for rules regarding the National Pool and the description of a qualified State.) Credit from the national pool component of a State housing credit ceiling must be allocated prior to the close of the calendar year or the credit expires and cannot be reallocated by any Agency. A national pool component credit that is allocated during a calendar year and returned after the close of the calendar year may qualify as part of the returned credit component of the State housing credit ceiling for the calendar year that the credit is returned.

(f) *When the State housing credit ceiling is determined.* For purposes of accounting for the State housing credit ceiling on Form 8610 and for purposes of determining the set-aside apportionment for projects involving qualified nonprofit organizations described in section 42(h)(5) and § 1.42-1T(c)(5), the State housing credit ceiling for any calendar year is determined at the close of the calendar year.

(g) *Stacking order.* Under section 42(h)(3)(C), credit is treated as allocated from the various components of the State housing credit ceiling in the following order. The first credit allocated for any calendar year is treated as credit from the sum of the population and returned credit components of the State housing credit ceiling. Once all of the credit in these components has been allocated, the next credit allocated is treated as credit from the unused carryforward component of the State housing credit ceiling. Finally, after all of the credit from the population component, returned credit component, and unused carryforward component has been allocated, any further

credit allocated is treated as credit from the national pool component.

(h) *Nonprofit set-aside*—(1) *Determination of set-aside.* Under section 42(h)(5) and § 1.42-1T(c)(5), at least 10 percent of a State housing credit ceiling in any calendar year must be set aside exclusively for projects involving qualified nonprofit organizations (the nonprofit set-aside). However, credit allocated from the nonprofit set-aside in a calendar year and returned in a subsequent calendar year does not retain its nonprofit set-aside character. The credit becomes part of the returned credit component of the State housing credit ceiling for the calendar year that the credit is returned and must be included in determining the nonprofit set-aside of the State housing credit ceiling for that calendar year. Similarly, credit amounts that are not allocated from the nonprofit set-aside in a calendar year and are returned in a subsequent calendar year become part of the returned credit component of the State housing credit ceiling for that year and are also included in determining the set-aside for that year.

(2) *Allocation rules.* An Agency may allocate credit from any component of the State housing credit ceiling as part of the nonprofit set-aside and need not reserve 10 percent of each component for the nonprofit set-aside. Thus, an Agency may satisfy the nonprofit set-aside requirement of section 42(h)(5) and § 1.42-1T(c)(5) in any calendar year by setting aside for allocation an amount equal to at least 10 percent of the total State housing credit ceiling for the calendar year.

(i) *National Pool*—(1) *In general.* The unused housing credit carryover of a State for any calendar year is assigned to the Secretary for inclusion in a national pool of unused housing credit carryovers (National Pool) that is reallocated among qualified States the succeeding calendar year. The assignment to the Secretary is made on Form 8610.

(2) *Unused housing credit carryover.* The unused housing credit carryover of a State for any calendar year is the excess, if any, of the unused carryforward component of the State housing credit ceiling for the calendar year over the excess, if any, of—

(i) The total housing credit dollar amount allocated for the year; over

(ii) The sum of the population and returned credit components of the State housing credit ceiling for the year.

(3) *Qualified State*—(i) *In general.* The term *qualified State* means, with respect to any calendar year, any State that has allocated its entire State housing credit ceiling for the preceding cal-

Reg. § 1.42-14(e)

endar year and for which a request is made by the State, not later than May 1 of the calendar year, to receive an allocation of credit from the National Pool for that calendar year. Except as provided in paragraph (i)(3)(ii) of this section, a State is not a qualified State in a calendar year if there remains any unallocated credit in its State housing credit ceiling at the close of the preceding calendar year that was apportioned to any Agency within the State for the calendar year.

(ii) *Exceptions*—(A) *De minimis amount.* If the amount remaining unallocated at the close of a calendar year is only a de minimis amount of credit, the State is a qualified State eligible to participate in the National Pool. For that purpose, a credit amount is de minimis if it does not exceed 1 percent of the aggregate State housing credit ceiling of the State for the calendar year.

(B) *Other circumstances.* Pursuant to the authority under section 42(n), the Internal Revenue Service may determine that a State is a qualified State eligible to participate in the National Pool even though the State's unallocated credit is in excess of the 1 percent safe harbor set forth in paragraph (A) of this section. The Internal Revenue Service will make this determination based on all the facts and circumstances, weighing heavily the interests of the States who would otherwise qualify for the National Pool. The Internal Revenue Service will generally grant relief under this paragraph only where a State's unallocated credit is not substantial.

(iii) *Time and manner for making request.* For further guidance as to the time and manner for making a request of housing credit dollar amounts from the National Pool by a qualified State, see Rev. Proc. 92-31, 1992-1 C.B. 775. (See 601.601(d)(2)(ii)(*b*)).

(4) *Formula for determining the National Pool.* The amount allocated to a qualified State in any calendar year is an amount that bears the same ratio to the aggregate unused housing credit carryovers of all States for the preceding calendar year as that State's population for the calendar year bears to the population of all qualified States for the calendar year.

(j) *Coordination between Agencies.* The Agency responsible for filing Form 8610 on behalf of all Agencies within a State and making any request on behalf of the State for credit from the National Pool (the Filing Agency) must coordinate with each Agency within the State to ensure that the various requirements of this section are complied with. For example, the Filing Agency of a State must ensure that all Agencies within the State that were apportioned a credit amount for the calendar year have allocated all of their respec-

tive credit amounts for the calendar year before the Filing Agency can make a request on behalf of the State for a distribution of credit from the National Pool.

(k) *Examples.*—(1) The operation of the rules of this section may be illustrated by the following examples. Unless otherwise stated in an example, Agency A is the sole Agency authorized to make allocations of housing credit dollar amounts in State M, all of Agency A's allocations are valid, and for calendar year 1994 Agency A has available for allocation a State housing credit ceiling consisting of the following housing credit dollar amounts:

A.	population component	$100
B.	unused carryforward component	$ 50
C.	returned credit component	$ 10
D.	national pool component	$ 0
Total		$160

(2) In addition, the $10 of returned credit component was returned before October 1, 1994.

Example 1—(i) *Additional facts.* By the close of 1994, Agency A had allocated $80 of the State M housing credit ceiling. Of the $80 allocated, $16 was allocated to projects involving qualified nonprofit organizations.

(ii) *Application of stacking rules.* The first credit allocated is treated as allocated from the population and returned credit components of the State housing credit ceiling, to the extent of those components. In this case, the $80 of credit allocated is less than the sum of the population and returned credit components. The excess of the sum of the population and returned credit components over the total amount allocated for the calendar year ($110 − 80 = $30) becomes the unused carryforward component of State M's 1995 State housing credit ceiling. Because Agency A did not allocate credit in excess of the sum of the population and returned credit components, no credit is treated as allocated from State M's $50 unused carryforward component in 1994. Because none of this component may be carried forward, all $50 is assigned to the Secretary for inclusion in the National Pool. Under paragraph (i)(3) of this section, State M does not qualify for credit from the National Pool for the 1995 calendar year.

(iii) *Nonprofit set-aside.* Agency A allocated exactly the amount of credit to projects involving qualified nonprofit organizations as necessary to meet the nonprofit set-aside requirement ($16, 10% of the $160 ceiling).

Example 2—(i) *Additional facts.* By the close of 1994, Agency A had allocated $130 of the State M housing credit ceiling. Of the $130 allocated,

Reg. § 1.42-14(k)(2)

$20 was allocated to projects involving qualified nonprofit organizations.

(ii) *Application of stacking rules.* The first $110 of credit allocated is treated as allocated from the population and returned credit components. In this case, because all of the population and returned credit components are allocated, no amount is included in State M's 1995 State housing credit ceiling as an unused carryforward component. The next $20 of credit allocated is treated as allocated from the $50 unused carryforward component. The $30 remaining in the unused carryforward component is assigned to the Secretary for inclusion in the National Pool for the 1995 calendar year. Under paragraph (i)(3) of this section, State M does not qualify for credit from the National Pool for the 1995 calendar year.

(iii) *Nonprofit set-aside.* Agency A allocated $4 more credit to projects involving qualified nonprofit organizations than necessary to meet the nonprofit set-aside requirement. This does not reduce the application of the 10% nonprofit set-aside requirement to the State M housing credit ceiling for the succeeding year.

Example 3—(i) *Additional fact.* None of the applications for credit that Agency A received for 1994 are for projects involving qualified nonprofit organizations.

(ii) *Nonprofit set-aside.* Because at least 10% of the State housing credit ceiling must be set aside for projects involving a qualified nonprofit organization, Agency A can allocate only $144 of the $160 State housing credit ceiling for calendar year 1994 ($160 − 16 = $144). If Agency A allocates $144 of credit, the credit is treated as allocated $110 from the population and returned credit components and $34 from the unused carryforward component. The $16 of unallocated credit that is set aside for projects involving qualified nonprofit organizations is treated as the balance of the unused carryforward component, and is assigned to the Secretary for inclusion in the National Pool. Under paragraph (i)(3) of this section, State M does not qualify for credit from the National Pool for the 1995 calendar year.

Example 4—(i) *Additional facts.* The $10 of returned credit component was returned prior to October 1, 1994. However, a $40 credit that had been allocated in calendar year 1993 to a project involving a qualified nonprofit organization was returned to the Agency by a mutual consent agreement dated November 15, 1994. By the close of 1994, Agency A had allocated $160 of the State M housing credit ceiling, including $16 of credit to projects involving qualified nonprofit organizations.

(ii) *Effect of three-month rule.* Under the three-month rule of paragraph (d)(2)(iii) of this section, Agency A may treat all or part of the $40 of previously allocated credit as returned on January 1, 1995. If Agency A treats all of the $40 amount as having been returned in calendar year 1995, the State M housing credit ceiling for 1994 is $160. This entire amount, including the $16 nonprofit set-aside, has been allocated in 1994. Under paragraph (i)(3) of this section, State M qualifies for the National Pool for the 1995 calendar year.

(iii) *If three-month rule not used.* If Agency A treats all of the $40 of previously allocated credit as returned in calendar year 1994, the State housing credit ceiling for the 1994 calendar year will be $200 of which $50 will be attributable to the returned credit component ($10 + $40 = $50). Because credit amounts allocated in a prior calendar year that are returned in a subsequent calendar year do not retain their nonprofit character, the nonprofit set-aside for calendar year 1994 is $20 (10% of $200). The $160 that Agency A allocated during 1994 is first treated as allocated from the population and returned credit components, which total $150. The next $10 of credit allocated is treated as allocated from the unused carryforward component. The $40 of unallocated credit from the unused carryforward component includes the $4 of unallocated nonprofit set-aside. The entire $40 of credit from the carryforward component is assigned to the Secretary for inclusion in the National Pool for the 1995 calendar year. State M does not qualify for credit from the National Pool for the 1995 calendar year.

Example 5—(i)[(A)] *Additional facts.* For calendar year 1994, Agency A has a State housing credit ceiling that consists of the following housing credit dollar amounts:

A.	population component	$100
B.	unused carryforward component	$ 0
C.	returned credit component	$ 20
D.	national pool component	$ 10
Total		$130
	Minimum nonprofit set-aside	$ 13
	Ceiling amount not set-aside	$117

In addition, the $20 of returned credit component was returned before October 1, 1994. By the close of 1994, Agency A had allocated $100 of the State housing credit ceiling.

(ii) *Application of stacking rules.* The $20 excess of the sum of the population component and the returned credit component over the total amount allocated for the calendar year ($120 − 100 = $20) becomes the unused carryforward component of the State housing credit ceiling for the 1995 calendar year. The $10 of unallocated credit from the national pool component expires and cannot be reallocated. This amount is neither carried over to 1995 by State M nor assigned to the Secretary for inclusion in the National Pool. Under paragraph (i)(3) of this section, State M does not qualify for credit from the National Pool for the 1995 calendar year.

(l) *Effective date.* The rules set forth in § 1.42-14 are effective January 1, 1994. [Reg. § 1.42-14.]

☐ [*T.D.* 8563, 9-30-94.]

[Reg. § 1.42-15]

§ 1.42-15. **Available unit rule.**—(a) *Definitions.* The following definitions apply to this section:

Applicable income limitation means the limitation applicable under section 42(g)(1) or, for deep rent skewed projects described in section 142(d)(4)(B), 40 percent of area median gross income.

Available unit rule means the rule in section 42(g)(2)(D)(ii).

Comparable unit means a residential unit in a low-income building that is comparably sized or smaller than an over-income unit or, for deep rent skewed projects described in section 142(d)(4)(B), any low-income unit. For purposes of determining whether a residential unit is comparably sized, a comparable unit must be measured by the same method used to determine qualified basis for the credit year in which the comparable unit became available.

Current resident means a person who is living in the low-income building.

Low-income unit is defined by section 42(i)(3)(A).

Nonqualified resident means a new occupant or occupants whose aggregate income exceeds the applicable income limitation.

Over-income unit means a low-income unit in which the aggregate income of the occupants of the unit increases above 140 percent of the applicable income limitation under section 42(g)(1), or above 170 percent of the applicable income limitation for deep rent skewed projects described in section 142(d)(4)(B).

Qualified resident means an occupant either whose aggregate income (combined with the income of all other occupants of the unit) does not exceed the applicable income limitation and who is otherwise a low-income resident under section 42, or who is a current resident.

(b) *General section 42(g)(2)(D)(i) rule.* Except as provided in paragraph (c) of this section, notwithstanding an increase in the income of the occupants of a low-income unit above the applicable income limitation, if the income of the occupants initially met the applicable income limitation, and the unit continues to be rent-restricted—

(1) The unit continues to be treated as a low-income unit; and

(2) The unit continues to be included in the numerator and the denominator of the ratio used to determine whether a project satisfies the applicable minimum set-aside requirement of section 42(g)(1).

(c) *Exception.* A unit ceases to be treated as a low-income unit if it becomes an over-income unit and a nonqualified resident occupies any comparable unit that is available or that subsequently becomes available in the same low-income building. In other words, the owner of a low-income building must rent to qualified residents all comparable units that are available or that subsequently become available in the same building to continue treating the over-income unit as a low-income unit. Once the percentage of low-income units in a building (excluding the over-income units) equals the percentage of low-income units on which the credit is based, failure to maintain the over-income units as low-income units has no immediate significance. The failure to maintain the over-income units as low-income units, however, may affect the decision of whether or not to rent a particular available unit at market rate at a later time. A unit is not available for purposes of the available unit rule when the unit is no longer available for rent due to contractual arrangements that are binding under local law (for example, a unit is not available if it is subject to a preliminary reservation that is binding on the owner under local law prior to the date a lease is signed or the unit is occupied).

(d) *Effect of current resident moving within building.* When a current resident moves to a different unit within the building, the newly occupied unit adopts the status of the vacated unit. Thus, if a current resident, whose income exceeds the applicable income limitation, moves from an over-income unit to a vacant unit in the same building, the newly occupied unit is treated as an over-income unit. The vacated unit assumes the status the newly occupied unit had immediately before it was occupied by the current resident.

(e) *Available unit rule applies separately to each building in a project.* In a project containing more than one low-income building, the available unit rule applies separately to each building.

(f) *Result of noncompliance with available unit rule.* If any comparable unit that is available or that subsequently becomes available is rented to a nonqualified resident, all over-income units for which the available unit was a comparable unit within the same building lose their status as low-income units; thus, comparably sized or larger over-income units would lose their status as low-income units.

(g) *Relationship to tax-exempt bond provisions*. Financing arrangements that purport to be exempt-facility bonds under section 142 must meet the requirements of sections 103 and 141 through 150 for interest on the obligations to be excluded from gross income under section 103(a). This section is not intended as an interpretation under section 142.

(h) *Examples*. The following examples illustrate this section:

Example 1. This example illustrates noncompliance with the available unit rule in a low-income building containing three over-income units. On January 1, 1998, a qualified low-income housing project, consisting of one building containing ten identically sized residential units, received a housing credit dollar amount allocation from a state housing credit agency for five low-income units. By the close of 1998, the first year of the credit period, the project satisfied the minimum set-aside requirement of section 42(g)(1)(B). Units 1, 2, 3, 4, and 5 were occupied by individuals whose incomes did not exceed the income limitation applicable under section 42(g)(1) and were otherwise low-income residents under section 42. Units 6, 7, 8, and 9 were occupied by market-rate tenants. Unit 10 was vacant. To avoid recapture of credit, the project owner must maintain five of the units as low-income units. On November 1, 1999, the certificates of annual income state that annual incomes of the individuals in Units 1, 2, and 3 increased above 140 percent of the income limitation applicable under section 42(g)(1), causing those units to become over-income units. On November 30, 1999, Units 8 and 9 became vacant. On December 1, 1999, the project owner rented Units 8 and 9 to qualified residents who were not current residents at rates meeting the rent restriction requirements of section 42(g)(2). On December 31, 1999, the project owner rented Unit 10 to a market-rate tenant. Because Unit 10, an available comparable unit, was leased to a market-rate tenant, Units 1, 2, and 3 ceased to be treated as low-income units. On that date, Units 4, 5, 8, and 9 were the only remaining low-income units. Because the project owner did not maintain five of the residential units as low-income units, the qualified basis in the building is reduced, and credit must be recaptured. If the project owner had rented Unit 10 to a qualified resident who was not

a current resident, eight of the units would be low-income units. At that time, Units 1, 2, and 3, the over-income units, could be rented to market-rate tenants because the building would still contain five low-income units.

Example 2. This example illustrates the provisions of paragraph (d) of this section. A low-income project consists of one six-floor building. The residential units in the building are identically sized. The building contains two over-income units on the sixth floor and two vacant units on the first floor. The project owner, desiring to maintain the over-income units as low-income units, wants to rent the available units to qualified residents. J, a resident of one of the over-income units, wishes to occupy a unit on the first floor. J's income has recently increased above the applicable income limitation. The project owner permits J to move into one of the units on the first floor. Despite J's income exceeding the applicable income limitation, J is a qualified resident under the available unit rule because J is a current resident of the building. The unit newly occupied by J becomes an over-income unit under the available unit rule. The unit vacated by J assumes the status the newly occupied unit had immediately before J occupied the unit. The over-income units in the building continue to be treated as low-income units.

(i) *Effective date*. This section applies to leases entered into or renewed on and after September 26, 1997. [Reg. § 1.42-15.]

☐ [*T.D. 8732, 9-25-97.*]

[Reg. § 1.42-16]

§ 1.42-16. **Eligible basis reduced by federal grants.**—(a) *In general*. If, during any taxable year of the compliance period (described in section 42(i)(1)), a grant is made with respect to any building or the operation thereof and any portion of the grant is funded with federal funds (whether or not includible in gross income), the eligible basis of the building for the taxable year and all succeeding taxable years is reduced by the portion of the grant that is so funded.

(b) *Grants do not include certain rental assistance payments*. A federal rental assistance payment made to a building owner on behalf or in respect of a tenant is not a grant made with respect to a building or its operation if the payment is made pursuant to—

(1) Section 8 of the United States Housing Act of 1937 (42 U.S.C. 1437f);

(2) A qualifying program of rental assistance administered under section 9 of the United States Housing Act of 1937 (42 U.S.C. 1437g); or

(3) A program or method of rental assistance as the Secretary may designate by publication in the Federal Register or in the Internal Revenue Bulletin (see § 601.601(d)(2) of this chapter).

(c) *Qualifying rental assistance program.* For purposes of paragraph (b)(2) of this section, payments are made pursuant to a qualifying rental assistance program administered under section 9 of the United States Housing Act of 1937 to the extent that the payments—

(1) Are made to a building owner pursuant to a contract with a public housing authority with respect to units the owner has agreed to maintain as public housing units (PH-units) in the building;

(2) Are made with respect to units occupied by public housing tenants, provided that, for this purpose, units may be considered occupied during periods of short term vacancy (not to exceed 60 days); and

(3) Do not exceed the difference between the rents received from a building's PH-unit tenants and a pro rata portion of the building's actual operating costs that are reasonably allocable to the PH-units (based on square footage, number of bedrooms, or similar objective criteria), and provided that, for this purpose, operating costs do not include any development costs of a building (including developer's fees) or the principal or interest of any debt incurred with respect to any part of the building.

(d) *Effective date.* This section is effective September 26, 1997. [Reg. § 1.42-16.]

☐ [*T.D.* 8731, 9-25-97.]

→ *Caution: Reg. § 1.42-17, below, is effective on January 1, 2001.*←

[Reg. § 1.42-17]

§ 1.42-17. Qualified allocation plan.—(a) *Requirements*—(1) *In general.* [Reserved]

(2) *Selection criteria.* [Reserved]

(3) *Agency evaluation.* Section 42(m)(2)(A) requires that the housing credit dollar amount allocated to a project is not to exceed the amount the Agency determines is necessary for the financial feasibility of the project and its viability as a qualified low-income housing project throughout the credit period. In making this determination, the Agency must consider—

(i) The sources and uses of funds and the total financing planned for the project. The taxpayer must certify to the Agency the full extent of all federal, state, and local subsidies that apply (or which the taxpayer expects to apply) to the project. The taxpayer must also certify to the Agency all other sources of funds and all development costs for the project. The taxpayer's certification should be sufficiently detailed to enable the Agency to ascertain the nature of the costs that will make up the total financing package, including subsidies and the anticipated syndication or placement proceeds to be raised. Development cost information, whether or not includible in eligible basis under section 42(d), that should be provided to the Agency includes, but is not limited to, site acquisition costs, construction contingency, general contractor's overhead and profit, architect's and engineer's fees, permit and survey fees, insurance premiums, real estate taxes during construction, title and recording fees, construction period interest, financing fees, organizational costs, rent-up and marketing costs, accounting and auditing costs, working capital and operating deficit reserves, syndication and legal fees, and developer fees;

(ii) Any proceeds or receipts expected to be generated by reason of tax benefits;

(iii) The percentage of the housing credit dollar amount used for project costs other than the costs of intermediaries. This requirement should not be applied so as to impede the development of projects in hard-to-develop areas under section 42(d)(5)(C); and

(iv) The reasonableness of the developmental and operational costs of the project.

(4) *Timing of Agency evaluation*—(i) *In general.* The financial determinations and certifications required under paragraph (a)(3) of this section must be made as of the following times—

(A) The time of the application for the housing credit dollar amount;

(B) The time of the allocation of the housing credit dollar amount; and

(C) The date the building is placed in service.

(ii) *Time limit for placed-in-service evaluation.* For purposes of paragraph (a)(4)(i)(C) of this section, the evaluation for when a building is placed in service must be made not later than the date the Agency issues the Form 8609, "Low-Income Housing Credit Allocation Certification." The Agency must evaluate all sources and uses of funds under paragraph (a)(3)(i) of this section paid, incurred, or committed by the taxpayer for the project up until date the Agency issues the Form 8609.

(5) *Special rule for final determinations and certifications.* For the Agency's evaluation under paragraph (a)(4)(i)(C) of this section, the taxpayer must submit a schedule of project costs. Such schedule is to be prepared on the method of accounting used by the taxpayer for federal in-

→ *Caution: Reg. § 1.42-17, below, is effective on January 1, 2001.*←

come tax purposes, and must detail the project's total costs as well as those costs that may qualify for inclusion in eligible basis under section 42(d). For projects with more than 10 units, the schedule of project costs must be accompanied by a Certified Public Accountant's audit report on the schedule (an Agency may require an audited schedule of project costs for projects with fewer than 11 units). The CPA's audit must be conducted in accordance with generally accepted auditing standards. The auditor's report must be unqualified.

(6) *Bond-financed projects.* A project qualifying under section 42(h)(4) is not entitled to any credit unless the governmental unit that issued the bonds (or on behalf of which the bonds were issued), or the Agency responsible for issuing the Form(s) 8609 to the project, makes determinations under rules similar to the rules in paragraphs (a)(3), (4), and (5) of this section.

(b) *Effective date.* This section is effective on January 1, 2001. [Reg. § 1.42-17.]

☐ [*T.D.* 8859, 1-13-2000.]

[Reg. § 1.43-0]

§ 1.43-0. **Table of contents.**—This section lists the captions contained in § § 1.43-0 through 1.43-7.

§ 1.43-1. *The enhanced oil recovery credit—general rules.*

(a) Claiming the credit.

(1) In general.

(2) Examples.

(b) Amount of the credit.

(c) Phase-out of the credit as crude oil prices increase.

(1) In general.

(2) Inflation adjustment.

(3) Examples.

(d) Reduction of associated deductions.

(1) In general.

(2) Certain deductions by an integrated oil company.

(e) Basis adjustment.

(f) Passthrough entity basis adjustment.

(1) Partners' interests in a partnership.

(2) Shareholders' stock in an S corporation.

(g) Examples.

§ 1.43-2. *Qualified enhanced oil recovery project.*

(a) Qualified enhanced oil recovery project.

(b) More than insignificant increase.

(c) First injection of liquids, gases, or other matter.

(1) In general.

(2) Example.

(d) Significant expansion exception.

(1) In general.

(2) Substantially unaffected reservoir volume.

(3) Terminated projects.

(4) Change in tertiary recovery method.

(5) Examples.

(e) Qualified tertiary recovery methods.

(1) In general.

(2) Tertiary recovery methods that qualify.

(3) Recovery methods that do not qualify.

(4) Examples.

§ 1.43-3. *Certification.*

(a) Petroleum engineer's certification of a project.

(1) In general.

(2) Timing of certification.

(3) Content of certification.

(b) Operator's continued certification of a project.

(1) In general.

(2) Timing of certification.

(3) Content of certification.

(c) Notice of project termination.

(1) In general.

(2) Timing of notice.

(3) Content of notice.

(d) Failure to submit certification.

(e) Effective date.

§ 1.43-4. *Qualified enhanced oil recovery costs.*

(a) Qualifying costs.

(1) In general.

(2) Costs paid or incurred for an asset which is used to implement more than one qualified enhanced oil recovery project or for other activities.

(b) Costs defined.

(1) Qualified tertiary injectant expenses.

(2) Intangible drilling and development costs.

(3) Tangible property costs.

(4) Examples.

(c) Primary purpose.

(1) In general.

Reg. § 1.43-0

(2) Tertiary injectant costs.

(3) Intangible drilling and development costs.

(4) Tangible property costs.

(5) Offshore drilling platforms.

(6) Examples.

(d) Costs paid or incurred prior to first injection.

(1) In general.

(2) First injection after filing of return for taxable year costs are allowable.

(3) First injection more than 36 months after close of taxable year costs are paid or incurred.

(4) Injections in volumes less than the volumes specified in the project plan.

(5) Examples.

(e) Other rules.

(1) Anti-abuse rule.

(2) Costs paid or incurred to acquire a project.

(3) Examples.

§ 1.43-5. At-risk limitation. [Reserved]

§ 1.43-6. Election out of section 43.

(a) Election to have the credit not apply.

(1) In general.

(2) Time for making the election.

(3) Manner of making the election.

(b) Election by partnerships and S corporations.

§ 1.43-7. Effective date of regulations.

[Reg. § 1.43-0.]

☐ [*T.D. 8448,* 11-20-92.]

[Reg. § 1.43-1]

§ 1.43-1. The enhanced oil recovery credit— general rules.—(a) *Claiming the credit*—(1) *In general.* The enhanced oil recovery credit (the "credit") is a component of the section 38 general business credit. A taxpayer that owns an operating mineral interest (as defined in § 1.614-2(b)) in a property may claim the credit for qualified enhanced oil recovery costs (as described in § 1.43-4) paid or incurred by the taxpayer in connection with a qualified enhanced oil recovery project (as described in § 1.43-2) undertaken with respect to the property. A taxpayer that does not own an operating mineral interest in a property may not claim the credit. To the extent a credit included in the current year business credit under section 38(b) is unused under section 38, the credit is carried back or forward under the section 39 business credit carryback and carryforward rules.

(2) *Examples.* The following examples illustrate the principles of this paragraph (a).

Example 1. Credit for operating mineral interest owner. In 1992, A, the owner of an operating mineral interest in a property, begins a qualified enhanced oil recovery project using cyclic steam. B, who owns no interest in the property, purchases and places in service a steam generator. B sells A steam, which A uses as a tertiary injectant described in section 193. Because A owns an operating mineral interest in the property with respect to which the project is undertaken, A may claim a credit for the cost of the steam. Although B owns the steam generator used to produce steam for the project, B may not claim a credit for B's costs because B does not own an operating mineral interest in the property.

Example 2. Credit for operating mineral interest owner. C and D are partners in CD, a partnership that owns an operating mineral interest in a property. In 1992, CD begins a qualified enhanced oil recovery project using cyclic steam. D purchases a steam generator and sells steam to CD. Because CD owns an operating mineral interest in the property with respect to which the project is undertaken, CD may claim a credit for the cost of the steam. Although D owns the steam generator used to produce steam for the project, D may not claim a credit for the costs of the steam generator because D paid these costs in a capacity other than that of an operating mineral interest owner.

(b) *Amount of the credit.* A taxpayer's credit is an amount equal to 15 percent of the taxpayer's qualified enhanced oil recovery costs for the taxable year, reduced by the phase-out amount, if any, determined under paragraph (c) of this section.

(c) *Phase-out of the credit as crude oil prices increase*—(1) *In general.* The amount of the credit (determined without regard to this paragraph (c)) for any taxable year is reduced by an amount which bears the same ratio to the amount of the credit (determined without regard to this paragraph (c)) as—

(i) The amount by which the reference price determined under section 29(d)(2)(C) for the calendar year immediately preceding the calendar year in which the taxable year begins exceeds $28 (as adjusted under paragraph (c)(2) of this section); bears to

(ii) $6.

(2) *Inflation adjustment*—(i) *In general.* For any taxable year beginning in a calendar year after 1991, an amount equal to $28 multiplied by the inflation adjustment factor is substituted for the $28 amount under paragraph (c)(1)(i) of this section.

Reg. § 1.43-1(c)(2)

(ii) *Inflation adjustment factor.* For purposes of this paragraph (c), the inflation adjustment factor for any calendar year is a fraction, the numerator of which is the GNP implicit price deflator for the preceding calendar year and the denominator of which is the GNP implicit price deflator for 1990. The "GNP implicit price deflator" is the first revision of the implicit price deflator for the gross national product as computed and published by the Secretary of Commerce. As early as practicable, the inflation adjustment factor for each calendar year will be published by the Internal Revenue Service in the Internal Revenue Bulletin.

(3) *Examples.* The following examples illustrate the principles of this paragraph (c).

Example 1. Reference price exceeds $28. In 1992, E, the owner of an operating mineral interest in a property, incurs $100 of qualified enhanced oil recovery costs. The reference price for 1991 determined under section 29(d)(2)(C) is $30 and the inflation adjustment factor for 1992 is 1. E's credit for 1992 determined without regard to the phase-out for crude oil price increases is $15 ($100 × 15%). In determining E's credit, the credit is reduced by $5 ($15 × ($30 − ($28 × 1))/6). Accordingly, E's credit for 1992 is $10 ($15 − $5).

Example 2. Inflation adjustment. In 1993, F, the owner of an operating mineral interest in a property, incurs $100 of qualified enhanced oil recovery costs. The 1992 reference price is $34, and the 1993 inflation adjustment factor is 1.10. F's credit for 1993 determined without regard to the phase-out for crude oil price increases is $15 ($100 × 15%). In determining F's credit, $30.80 (1.10 × $28) is substituted for $28, and the credit is reduced by $8 ($15 × ($34 − $30.80)/6). Accordingly, F's credit for 1993 is $7 ($15 − $8).

(d) *Reduction of associated deductions*—(1) *In general.* Any deduction allowable under chapter 1 for an expenditure taken into account in computing the amount of the credit determined under paragraph (b) of this section is reduced by the amount of the credit attributable to the expenditure.

(2) *Certain deductions by an integrated oil company.* For purposes of determining the intangible drilling and development costs that an integrated oil company must capitalize under section 291(b), the amount allowable as a deduction under section 263(c) is the deduction allowable after paragraph (d)(1) of this section is applied. *See* § 1.43-4(b)(2) (extent to which integrated oil company intangible drilling and development costs are qualified enhanced oil recovery costs).

(e) *Basis adjustment.* For purposes of subtitle A, the increase in the basis of property which would (but for this paragraph (e)) result from an expenditure with respect to the property is reduced by the amount of the credit determined under paragraph (b) of this section attributable to the expenditure.

(f) *Passthrough entity basis adjustment*—(1) *Partners' interests in a partnership.* To the extent a partnership expenditure is not deductible under paragraph (d)(1) of this section or does not increase the basis of property under paragraph (e) of this section, the expenditure is treated as an expenditure described in section 705(a)(2)(B) (concerning decreases to basis of partnership interests). Thus, the adjusted bases of the partners' interests in the partnership are decreased (but not below zero).

(2) *Shareholders' stock in an S corporation.* To the extent an S corporation expenditure is not deductible under paragraph (d)(1) of this section or does not increase the basis of property under paragraph (e) of this section, the expenditure is treated as an expenditure described in section 1367(a)(2)(D) (concerning decreases to basis of S corporation stock). Thus, the bases of the shareholders' S corporation stock are decreased (but not below zero).

(g) *Examples.* The following examples illustrate the principles of paragraphs (d) through (f) of this section.

Example 1. Deductions reduced for credit amount. In 1992, G, the owner of an operating mineral interest in a property, incurs $100 of intangible drilling and development costs in connection with a qualified enhanced oil recovery project undertaken with respect to the property. G elects under section 263(c) to deduct these intangible drilling and development costs. The amount of the credit determined under paragraph (b) of this section attributable to the $100 of intangible drilling and development costs is $15 ($100 × 15%). Therefore, G's otherwise allowable deduction of $100 for the intangible drilling and development costs is reduced by $15. Accordingly, in 1992, G may deduct under section 263(c) only $85 ($100 − $15) for these costs.

Example 2. Integrated oil company deduction reduced. The facts are the same as in *Example 1*, except that G is an integrated oil company. As in *Example 1*, the amount of the credit determined under paragraph (b) of this section attributable to the $100 of intangible drilling and development costs under section 263(c) is $85. Because G is an integrated oil company, G must capitalize $25.50 ($85 × 30%) under section 291(b). Therefore, in 1992, G may deduct under section 263(c) only $59.50 ($85 − $25.50) for these intangible drilling and development costs.

Example 3. Basis of property reduced. In 1992, H, the owner of an operating mineral interest in a property, pays $100 to purchase tangible property that is an integral part of a qualified enhanced oil recovery project undertaken with respect to the property. The amount of the credit determined under paragraph (b) of this section attributable to the $100 is $15 ($100 × 15%). Therefore, for purposes of subtitle A, H's basis in the tangible property is $85 ($100 − $15).

Example 4. Basis of interest in passthrough entity reduced. In 1992, I is a 50% partner in IJ, a partnership that owns an operating mineral interest in a property. IJ pays $200 to purchase tangible property that is an integral part of a qualified enhanced oil recovery project undertaken with respect to the property. The amount of the credit determined under paragraph (b) of this section attributable to the $200 is $30 ($200 × 15%). Therefore, for purposes of subtitle A, IJ's basis in the tangible property is $170 ($200 − $30). Under paragraph (f) of this section, the amount of the purchase price that does not increase the basis of the property ($30) is treated as an expenditure described in section 705(a)(2)(B). Therefore, I's basis in the partnership interest is reduced by $15 (I's allocable share of the section 705(a)(2)(B) expenditure ($30 × 50%)). [Reg. § 1.43-1.]

☐ [*T.D.* 8448, 11-20-92.]

[Reg. § 1.43-2]

§ 1.43-2. Qualified enhanced oil recovery project.—(a) *Qualified enhanced oil recovery project.* A "qualified enhanced oil recovery project" is any project that meets all of the following requirements—

(1) The project involves the application (in accordance with sound engineering principles) of one or more qualified tertiary recovery methods (as described in paragraph (e) of this section) that is reasonably expected to result in more than an insignificant increase in the amount of crude oil that ultimately will be recovered;

(2) The project is located within the United States (within the meaning of section 638(1));

(3) The first injection of liquids, gases, or other matter for the project (as described in paragraph (c) of this section) occurs after December 31, 1990; and

(4) The project is certified under § 1.43-3.

(b) *More than insignificant increase.* For purposes of paragraph (a)(1) of this section, all the facts and circumstances determine whether the application of a tertiary recovery method can reasonably be expected to result in more than an insignificant increase in the amount of crude oil that ultimately will be recovered. Certain information submitted as part of a project certification is relevant to this determination. *See* § 1.43-3(a)(3)(i)(D). In no event is the application of a recovery method that merely accelerates the recovery of crude oil considered an application of one or more qualified tertiary recovery methods that can reasonably be expected to result in more than an insignificant increase in the amount of crude oil that ultimately will be recovered.

(c) *First injection of liquids, gases, or other matter*—(1) *In general.* The "first injection of liquids, gases, or other matter" generally occurs on the date a tertiary injectant is first injected into the reservoir. The "first injection of liquids, gases, or other matter" does not include—

(i) The injection into the reservoir of any liquids, gases, or other matter for the purpose of pretreating or preflushing the reservoir to enhance the efficiency of the tertiary recovery method; or

(ii) Test or experimental injections.

(2) *Example.* The following example illustrates the principles of this paragraph (c).

Example. Injections to pretreat the reservoir. In 1989, A, the owner of an operating mineral interest in a property, began injecting water into the reservoir for the purpose of elevating reservoir pressure to obtain miscibility pressure to prepare for the injection of miscible gas in connection with an enhanced oil recovery project. In 1992, A obtains miscibility pressure in the reservoir and begins injecting miscible gas into the reservoir. The injection of miscible gas, rather than the injection of water, is the first injection of liquids, gases, or other matter into the reservoir for purposes of determining whether the first injection of liquids, gases, or other matter occurs after December 31, 1990.

(d) *Significant expansion exception*—(1) *In general.* If a project for which the first injection of liquids, gases, or other matter (within the meaning of paragraph (c)(1) of this section) occurred before January 1, 1991, is significantly expanded after December 31, 1990, the expansion is treated as a separate project for which the first injection of liquids, gases, or other matter occurs after December 31, 1990.

(2) *Substantially unaffected reservoir volume.* A project is considered significantly expanded if the injection of liquids, gases, or other matter after December 31, 1990, is reasonably expected to result in more than an insignificant increase in the amount of crude oil that ulti-

mately will be recovered from reservoir volume that was substantially unaffected by the injection of liquids, gases, or other matter before January 1, 1991.

(3) *Terminated projects.* Except as otherwise provided in this paragraph (d)(3), a project is considered significantly expanded if each qualified tertiary recovery method implemented in the project prior to January 1, 1991, terminated more than 36 months before implementing an enhanced oil recovery project that commences after December 31, 1990. Notwithstanding the provisions of the preceding sentence, if a project implemented prior to January 1, 1991, is terminated for less than 36 months before implementing an enhanced oil recovery project that commences after December 31, 1990, a taxpayer may request permission to treat the project that commences after December 31, 1990, as a significant expansion. Permission will not be granted if the Internal Revenue Service determines that a project was terminated to make an otherwise nonqualifying project eligible for the credit. For purposes of section 43, a qualified tertiary recovery method terminates at the point in time when the method no longer results in more than an insignificant increase in the amount of crude oil that ultimately will be recovered. All the facts and circumstances determine whether a tertiary recovery method has terminated. Among the factors considered is the project plan, the unit plan of development, or other similar plan. A tertiary recovery method is not necessarily terminated merely because the injection of the tertiary injectant has ceased. For purposes of this paragraph (d)(1), a project is implemented when costs that will be taken into account in determining the credit with respect to the project are paid or incurred.

(4) *Change in tertiary recovery method.* If the application of a tertiary recovery method or methods with respect to an enhanced oil recovery project for which the first injection of liquids, gases, or other matter occurred before January 1, 1991, has not been terminated for more than 36 months, a taxpayer may request a private letter ruling from the Internal Revenue Service whether the application of a different tertiary recovery method or methods after December 31, 1990, that does not affect reservoir volume substantially unaffected by the previous tertiary recovery method or methods, is treated as a significant expansion. All the facts and circumstances determine whether a change in tertiary recovery method is treated as a significant expansion. Among the factors considered are whether the change in tertiary recovery method is in accordance with sound engineering principles and whether the change in method will result in more than an insignificant

increase in the amount of crude oil that would be recovered using the previous method. A more intensive application of a tertiary recovery method after December 31, 1990, is not treated as a significant expansion.

(5) *Examples.* The following examples illustrate the principles of this paragraph (d).

Example 1. Substantially unaffected reservoir volume. In January 1988, B, the owner of an operating mineral interest in a property, began injecting steam into the reservoir in connection with a cyclic steam enhanced oil recovery project. The project affected only a portion of the reservoir volume. In 1992, B begins cyclic steam injections with respect to reservoir volume that was substantially unaffected by the previous cyclic steam project. Because the injection of steam into the reservoir in 1992 affects reservoir volume that was substantially unaffected by the previous cyclic steam injection, the cyclic steam injection in 1992 is treated as a separate project for which the first injection of liquids, gases, or other matter occurs after December 31, 1990.

Example 2. Tertiary recovery method terminated more than 36 months. In 1982, C, the owner of an operating mineral interest cyclic steam injection as a method for the recovery of crude oil. The project was certified as a tertiary recovery project for purposes of the windfall profit tax. In May 1988, the application of the cyclic steam tertiary recovery method terminated. In July 1992, C begins drilling injection wells as part of a project to apply the steam drive tertiary recovery method with respect to the same project area affected by the cyclic steam method. C begins steam injections in September 1992. Because C commences an enhanced oil recovery project more than 36 months after the previous tertiary recovery method was terminated, the project is treated as a separate project for which the first injection of liquids, gases, or other matter occurs after December 31, 1990.

Example 3. Change in tertiary recovery method affecting substantially unaffected reservoir volume. In 1984, D, the owner of an operating mineral interest in a property implemented a tertiary recovery project using cyclic steam as a method for the recovery of crude oil. The project was certified as a tertiary recovery project for purposes of the windfall profit tax. D continued the cyclic steam injection until 1992, when the tertiary recovery method was changed from cyclic steam injection to steam drive. The steam drive affects reservoir volume that was substantially unaffected by the cyclic steam injection. Because the steam drive affects reservoir volume that was substantially unaffected by the cyclic steam injection, the steam drive is treated as a separate project for which the first injection of liquids, gases, or other matter occurs after December 31, 1990.

Example 4. Change in tertiary recovery method not affecting substantially unaffected reservoir volume. In 1988, E, the owner of an operating mineral interest in a property, undertook an immiscible nitrogen enhanced oil recovery project that resulted in more than an insignificant increase in the ultimate recovery of crude oil from the property. E continued the immiscible nitrogen project until 1992, when the project was converted from immiscible nitrogen displacement to miscible nitrogen displacement by increasing the injection of nitrogen to increase reservoir pressure. The miscible nitrogen displacement affects the same reservoir volume that was affected by the immiscible nitrogen displacement. Because the miscible nitrogen displacement does not affect reservoir volume that was substantially unaffected by the immiscible nitrogen displacement nor was the immiscible nitrogen displacement project terminated for more than 36 months before the miscible nitrogen displacement project was implemented, E must obtain a ruling whether the change from immiscible nitrogen displacement to miscible nitrogen displacement is treated as a separate project for which the first injection of liquids, gases, or other matter occurs after December 31, 1990. If E does not receive a ruling, the miscible nitrogen displacement project is not a qualified project.

Example 5. More intensive application of a tertiary recovery method. In 1989, F, the owner of an operating mineral interest in a property, undertook an immiscible carbon dioxide displacement enhanced oil recovery project. F began injecting carbon dioxide into the reservoir under immiscible conditions. The injection of carbon dioxide under immiscible conditions resulted in more than an insignificant increase in the ultimate recovery of crude oil from the property. F continues to inject the same amount of carbon dioxide into the reservoir until 1992, when new engineering studies indicate that an increase in the amount of carbon dioxide injected is reasonably expected to result in a more than insignificant increase in the amount of crude oil that would be recovered from the property as a result of the previous injection of carbon dioxide. The increase in the amount of carbon dioxide injected affects the same reservoir volume that was affected by the previous injection of carbon dioxide. Because the additional carbon dioxide injected in 1992 does not affect reservoir volume that was substantially unaffected by the previous injection of carbon dioxide and the previous immiscible carbon

dioxide displacement method was not terminated for more than 36 months before additional carbon dioxide was injected, the increase in the amount of carbon dioxide injected into the reservoir is not a significant expansion. Therefore, it is not a separate project for which the first injection of liquids, gases, or other matter occurs after December 31, 1990.

(e) *Qualified tertiary recovery methods*—(1) *In general.* For purposes of paragraph (a)(1) of this section, a "qualified tertiary recovery method" is any one or any combination of the tertiary recovery methods described in paragraph (e)(2) of this section. To account for advances in enhanced oil recovery technology, the Internal Revenue Service may by revenue ruling prescribe that a method not described in paragraph (e)(2) of this section is a "qualified tertiary recovery method." In addition, a taxpayer may request a private letter ruling that a method not described in paragraph (e)(2) of this section or in a revenue ruling is a qualified tertiary recovery method. Generally, the methods identified in revenue rulings or private letter rulings will be limited to those methods that involve the displacement of oil from the reservoir rock by means of modifying the properties of the fluids in the reservoir or providing the energy and drive mechanism to force the oil to flow to a production well. The recovery methods described in paragraph (e)(3) of this section are not "qualified tertiary recovery methods."

(2) *Tertiary recovery methods that qualify*— (i) *Thermal recovery methods*—(A) *Steam drive injection.* The continuous injection of steam into one set of wells (injection wells) or other injection source to effect oil displacement toward and production from a second set of wells (production wells);

(B) *Cyclic steam injection*—The alternating injection of steam and production of oil with condensed steam from the same well or wells; and

(C) *In situ combustion.* The combustion of oil or fuel in the reservoir sustained by injection of air, oxygen-enriched air, oxygen, or supplemental fuel supplied from the surface to displace unburned oil toward producing wells. This process may include the concurrent, alternating, or subsequent injection of water.

(ii) *Gas Flood recovery methods*—(A) *Miscible fluid displacement.* The injection of gas (e.g., natural gas, enriched natural gas, a liquified petroleum slug driven by natural gas; carbon dioxide, nitrogen, or flue gas) or alcohol into the reservoir at pressure levels such that the gas or alcohol and reservoir oil are miscible;

Reg. § 1.43-2(e)(2)

(B) *Carbon dioxide augmented water-flooding.* The injection of carbonated water, or water and carbon dioxide, to increase waterflood efficiency;

(C) *Immiscible carbon dioxide displacement.* The injection of carbon dioxide into an oil reservoir to effect oil displacement under conditions in which miscibility with reservoir oil is not obtained. This process may include the concurrent, alternating, or subsequent injection of water; and

(D) *Immiscible nonhydrocarbon gas displacement.* The injection of nonhydrocarbon gas (*e.g.*, nitrogen) into an oil reservoir, under conditions in which miscibility with reservoir oil is not obtained, to obtain a chemical or physical reaction (other than pressure) between the oil and the injected gas or between the oil and other reservoir fluids. This process may include the concurrent, alternating, or subsequent injection of water.

(iii) *Chemical flood recovery methods*—(A) *Microemulsion flooding.* The injection of a surfactant system (*e.g.*, a surfactant, hydrocarbon, cosurfactant, electrolyte, and water) to enhance the displacement of oil toward producing wells; and

(B) *Caustic flooding*—The injection of water that has been made chemically basic by the addition of alkali metal hydroxides, silicates, or other chemicals.

(iv) *Mobility control recovery method*—*Polymer augmented waterflooding.* The injection of polymeric additives with water to improve the areal and vertical sweep efficiency of the reservoir by increasing the viscosity and decreasing the mobility of the water injected. Polymer augmented waterflooding does not include the injection of polymers for the purpose of modifying the injection profile of the wellbore or the relative permeability of various layers of the reservoir, rather than modifying the water-oil mobility ratio.

(3) *Recovery methods that do not qualify.* The term "qualified tertiary recovery method" does not include—

(i) *Waterflooding*—The injection of water into an oil reservoir to displace oil from the reservoir rock and into the bore of the producing well;

(ii) *Cyclic gas injection*—The increase or maintenance of pressure by injection of hydrocarbon gas into the reservoir from which it was originally produced;

(iii) *Horizontal drilling*—The drilling of horizontal, rather than vertical, wells to penetrate hydrocarbon bearing formations;

(iv) *Gravity drainage*—The production of oil by gravity flow from drainholes that are drilled from a shaft or tunnel dug within or below the oil bearing zones; and

(v) *Other methods*—Any recovery method not specifically designated as a qualified tertiary recovery method in either paragraph (e)(2) of this section or in a revenue ruling or private letter ruling described in paragraph (e)(1) of this section.

(4) *Examples.* The following examples illustrate the principles of this paragraph (e).

Example 1. Polymer augmented waterflooding. In 1992 G, the owner of an operating mineral interest in a property, begins a waterflood project with respect to the property. To reduce the relative permeability in certain areas of the reservoir and minimize water coning, G injects polymers to plug thief zones and improve the areal and vertical sweep efficiency of the reservoir. The injection of polymers into the reservoir does not modify the water-oil mobility ratio. Accordingly, the injection of polymers into the reservoir in connection with the waterflood project does not constitute polymer augmented waterflooding and the project is not a qualified enhanced oil recovery project.

Example 2. Polymer augmented waterflooding. In 1993 H, the owner of an operating mineral interest in a property, begins a caustic flooding project with respect to the property. Engineering studies indicate that the relative permeability of various layers of the reservoir may result in the loss of the injectant to thief zones, thereby reducing the areal and vertical sweep efficiency of the reservoir. As part of the caustic flooding project, H injects polymers to plug the thief zones and improve the areal and vertical sweep efficiency of the reservoir. Because the polymers are injected into the reservoir to improve the effectiveness of the caustic flooding project, the project is a qualified enhanced oil recovery project. [Reg. § 1.43-2.]

☐ [*T.D.* 8448, 11-20-92.]

[Reg. § 1.43-3]

§ 1.43-3. Certification.—(a) *Petroleum engineer's certification of a project*—(1) *In general.* A petroleum engineer must certify, under penalties of perjury, that an enhanced oil recovery project meets the requirements of section 43(c)(2)(A). A petroleum engineer's certification must be submitted for each project. The petroleum engineer certifying a project must be duly registered or certified in any state.

(2) *Timing of certification.* The operator of an enhanced oil recovery project or any other operating mineral interest owner designated by the operated ("designated owner") must submit a

petroleum engineer's certification to the Internal Revenue Service Center, Austin, Texas, or such other place as may be designated by revenue procedure or other published guidance, not later than the last date prescribed by law (including extensions) for filing the operator's or designated owner's federal income tax return for the first taxable year for which the enhanced oil recovery credit (the "credit") is allowable. The operator may designate any other operating mineral interest owner (the "designated owner") to file the petroleum engineer's certification.

(3) *Content of certification*—(i) *In general.* A petroleum engineer's certification must contain the following information—

(A) The name and taxpayer identification number of the operator or the designated owner submitting the certification;

(B) A statement identifying the project, including its geographic location;

(C) A statement that the project involves a tertiary recovery method (as defined in section 43(c)(2)(A)(i)) and a description of the process used, including—

(1) A description of the implementation and operation of the project sufficient to establish that it is implemented and operated in accordance with sound engineering practices;

(2) If the project involves the application of a tertiary recovery method approved in a private letter ruling described in paragraph (e)(1) of section 1.43-2, a copy of the private letter ruling, and

(3) The date on which the first injection of liquids, gases, or other matter occurred or is expected to occur.

(D) A statement that the application of a qualified tertiary recovery method or methods is expected to result in more than an insignificant increase in the amount of crude oil that ultimately will be recovered, including—

(1) Data on crude oil reserve estimates covering the project area with and without the enhanced oil recovery process,

(2) Production history prior to implementation of the project and estimates of production after implementation of the project, and

(3) An adequate delineation of the reservoir, or portion of the reservoir, from which the ultimate recovery of crude oil is expected to be increased as a result of the implementation and operation of the project; and

(E) A statement that the petroleum engineer believes that the project is a qualified enhanced oil recovery project within the meaning of section 43(c)(2)(A).

(ii) *Additional information for significantly expanded projects.* The petroleum engineer's certification for a project that is significantly expanded must in addition contain—

(A) If the expansion affects reservoir volume that was substantially unaffected by a previously implemented project, an adequate delineation of the reservoir volume affected by the previously implemented project;

(B) If the expansion involves the implementation of an enhanced oil recovery project more than 36 months after the termination of a qualified tertiary recovery method that was applied before January 1, 1991, the date on which the previous tertiary recovery method terminated and an explanation of the data or assumptions relied upon to determine the termination date;

(C) If the expansion involves the implementation of an enhanced oil recovery project less than 36 months after the termination of a qualified tertiary recovery method that was applied before January 1, 1991, a copy of a private letter ruling from the Internal Revenue Service that the project implemented after December 31, 1990 is treated as a significant expansion; or

(D) If the expansion involves the application after December 31, 1990, of a tertiary recovery method or methods that do not affect reservoir volume that was substantially unaffected by the application of a different tertiary recovery method or methods before January 1, 1991, a copy of a private letter ruling from the Internal Revenue Service that the change in tertiary recovery method is treated as a significant expansion.

(b) *Operator's continued certification of a project*—(1) *In general.* For each taxable year following the taxable year for which the petroleum engineer's certification is submitted, the operator or designated owner must certify, under penalties of perjury, that an enhanced oil recovery project continues to be implemented substantially in accordance with the petroleum engineer's certification submitted for the project. An operator's certification must be submitted for each project.

(2) *Timing of certification.* The operator or designated owner of an enhanced oil recovery project must submit an operator's certification to the Internal Revenue Service Center, Austin, Texas, or such other place as may be designated by revenue procedure or other published guidance, not later than the last date prescribed by law (including extensions) for filing the operator's or designated owner's federal income tax return for any taxable year after the taxable year for which the petroleum engineer's certification is filed.

Reg. § 1.43-3(b)(2)

(3) *Content of certification.* An operator's certification must contain the following information—

(i) The name and taxpayer identification number of the operator or the designated owner submitting the certification;

(ii) A statement identifying the project, including its geographic location and the date on which the petroleum engineer's certification was filed;

(iii) A statement that the project continues to be implemented substantially in accordance with the petroleum engineer's certification (as described in paragraph (a) of this section) submitted for the project; and

(iv) A description of any significant change or anticipated change in the information submitted under paragraph (a)(3) of this section, including a change in the date on which the first injection of liquids, gases, or other matter occurred or is expected to occur.

(c) *Notice of project termination*—(1) *In general.* If the application of a tertiary recovery method is terminated, the operator or designated owner must submit a notice of project termination to the Internal Revenue Service.

(2) *Timing of notice.* The operator or designated owner of an enhanced oil recovery project must submit the notice of project termination to the Internal Revenue Service Center, Austin, Texas, or such other place as may be designated by revenue procedure or other published guidance, not later than the last date prescribed by law (including extensions) for filing the operator's or designated owner's federal income tax return for the taxable year in which the project terminates.

(3) *Content of notice.* A notice of project termination must contain the following information—

(i) The name and taxpayer identification number of the operator or the designated owner submitting the notice;

(ii) A statement identifying the project, including its geographic location and the date on which the petroleum engineer's certification was filed; and

(iii) The date on which the application of the tertiary recovery method was terminated.

(d) *Failure to submit certification.* If a petroleum engineer's certification (as described in paragraph (a) of this section) or an operator's certification (as described in paragraph (b) of this section) is not submitted in the time or manner prescribed by this section, the credit will be al-lowed only after the appropriate certifications are submitted. [Reg. § 1.43-3.]

☐ [*T.D.* 8448, 11-20-92.]

[Reg. § 1.43-4]

§ 1.43-4. Qualified enhanced oil recovery costs.—(a) *Qualifying costs*—(1) *In general.* Except as provided in paragraph (e) of this section, amounts paid or incurred in any taxable year beginning after December 31, 1990, that are qualified tertiary injectant expenses (as described in paragraph (b)(1) of this section), intangible drilling and development costs (as described in paragraph (b)(2) of this section), and tangible property costs (as described in paragraph (b)(3) of this section) are "qualified enhanced oil recovery costs" if the amounts are paid or incurred with respect to an asset which is used for the primary purpose (as described in paragraph (c) of this section) of implementing an enhanced oil recovery project. Any amount paid or incurred in any taxable year beginning before January 1, 1991, in connection with an enhanced oil recovery project is not a qualified enhanced oil recovery cost.

(2) *Costs paid or incurred for an asset which is used to implement more than one qualified enhanced oil recovery project or for other activities.* Any cost paid or incurred during the taxable year for an asset which is used to implement more than one qualified enhanced oil recovery project is allocated among the projects in determining the qualified enhanced oil recovery costs for each qualified project for the taxable year. Similarly, any cost paid or incurred during the taxable year for an asset which is used to implement a qualified enhanced oil recovery project and which is also used for other activities (for example, an enhanced oil recovery project that is not a qualified enhanced oil recovery project) is allocated among the qualified enhanced oil recovery project and the other activities to determine the qualified enhanced oil recovery costs for the taxable year. See § 1.613-5(a). Any cost paid or incurred for an asset which is used to implement a qualified enhanced oil recovery project and which is also used for other activities is not required to be allocated under this paragraph (a)(2) if the use of the property for nonqualifying activities is *de minimis* (*e.g.,* not greater than 10%). Costs are allocated under this paragraph (a)(2) only if the asset with respect to which the costs are paid or incurred is used for the primary purpose of implementing an enhanced oil recovery project. *See* paragraph (c) of this section. Any reasonable allocation method may be used. A method that allocates costs based on the anticipated use in a project or activity is a reasonable method.

Reg. § 1.43-4(a)(1)

(b) *Costs defined*—(1) *Qualified tertiary injectant expenses.* For purposes of this section, "qualified tertiary injectant expenses" means any costs that are paid or incurred in connection with a qualified enhanced oil recovery project and that are deductible under section 193 for the taxable year. *See* section 193 and § 1.193-1. Qualified tertiary injectant expenses are taken into account in determining the credit with respect to the taxable year in which the tertiary injectant expenses are deductible under section 193.

(2) *Intangible drilling and development costs.* For purposes of this section, "intangible drilling and development costs" means any intangible drilling and development costs that are paid or incurred in connection with a qualified enhanced oil recovery project and for which the taxpayer may make an election under section 263(c) for the taxable year. Intangible drilling and development costs are taken into account in determining the credit with respect to the taxable year in which the taxpayer may deduct the intangible drilling and development costs under section 263(c). For purposes of this paragraph (b)(2), the amount of the intangible drilling and development costs for which an integrated oil company may make an election under section 263(c) is determined without regard to section 291(b).

(3) *Tangible property costs* – (i) *In general.* For purposes of this section, "tangible property costs" means an amount paid or incurred during a taxable year for tangible property that is an integral part of a qualified enhanced oil recovery project and that is depreciable or amortizable under chapter 1. An amount paid or incurred for tangible property is taken into account in determining the credit with respect to the taxable year in which the cost is paid or incurred.

(ii) *Integral part.* For purposes of this paragraph (b), tangible property is an integral part of a qualified enhanced oil recovery project if the property is used directly in the project and is essential to the completeness of the project. All the facts and circumstances determine whether tangible property is used directly in a qualified enhanced oil recovery project and is essential to the completeness of the project. Generally, property used to acquire or produce the tertiary injectant or property used to transport the tertiary injectant to a project site is property that is an integral part of the project.

(4) *Examples.* The following examples illustrate the principles of this paragraph (b). Assume for each of these examples that the qualified enhanced oil recovery costs are paid or incurred with respect to an asset which is used for the primary purpose of implementing an enhanced oil recovery project.

Example 1. Qualified costs—in general. (i) In 1992, X, a corporation, acquires an operating mineral interest in a property and undertakes a cyclic steam enhanced oil recovery project with respect to the property. X pays a fee to acquire a permit to drill and hires a contractor to drill six wells. As part of the project implementation, X constructs a building to serve as an office on the property and purchases equipment, including downhole equipment (*e.g.*, casing, tubing, packers, and sucker rods), pumping units, a steam generator, and equipment to remove gas and water from the oil after it is produced. X constructs roads to transport the equipment to the wellsites and incurs costs for clearing and draining the ground in preparation for the drilling of the wells. X purchases cars and trucks to provide transportation for monitoring the wellsites. In addition, X contracts with Y for the delivery of water to produce steam to be injected in connection with the cyclic steam project, and purchases storage tanks to store the water.

(ii) The leasehold acquisition costs are not qualified enhanced oil recovery costs. However, the costs of the permit to drill are intangible drilling and development costs that are qualified costs. The costs associated with hiring the contractor to drill, constructing roads, and clearing and draining the ground are intangible drilling and development costs that are qualified enhanced oil recovery costs. The downhole equipment, the pumping units, the steam generator, and the equipment to remove the gas and water from the oil after it is produced are used directly in the project and are essential to the completeness of the project. Therefore, this equipment is an integral part of the project and the costs of the equipment are qualified enhanced oil recovery costs. Although the building that X constructs as an office and the cars and trucks X purchases to provide transportation for monitoring the wellsites are used directly in the project, they are not essential to the completeness of the project. Therefore, the building and the cars and trucks are not an integral part of the project and their costs are not qualified enhanced oil recovery costs. The cost of the water X purchases from Y is a tertiary injectant expense that is a qualified enhanced oil recovery cost. The storage tanks X acquires to store the water are required to provide a proximate source of water for the production of steam. Therefore, the water storage tanks are an integral part of the project and the costs of the water storage tanks are qualified enhanced oil recovery costs.

Reg. § 1.43-4(b)(4)

Example 2. Diluent storage tanks. In 1992, A, the owner of an operating mineral interest, undertakes a qualified enhanced oil recovery project with respect to the property. A acquires diluent to be used in connection with the project. A stores the diluent in a storage tank that A acquires for that purpose. The storage tank provides a proximate source of diluent to be used in the tertiary recovery method. Therefore, the storage tank is used directly in the project and is essential to the completeness of the project. Accordingly, the storage tank is an integral part of the project and the cost of the storage tank is a qualified enhanced oil recovery cost.

Example 3. Oil storage tanks. In 1992, Z, a corporation and the owner of an operating mineral interest in a property, undertakes a qualified enhanced oil recovery project with respect to the property. Z acquires storage tanks that Z will use solely to store the crude oil that is produced from the enhanced oil recovery project. The storage tanks are not used directly in the project and are not essential to the completeness of the project. Therefore, the storage tanks are not an integral part of the enhanced oil recovery project and the costs of the storage tanks are not qualified enhanced oil recovery costs.

Example 4. Oil refinery. B, the owner of an operating mineral interest in a property, undertakes a qualified enhanced oil recovery project with respect to the property. Located on B's property is an oil refinery where B will refine the crude oil produced from the project. The refinery is not used directly in the project and is not essential to the completeness of the project. Therefore, the refinery is not an integral part of the enhanced oil recovery project.

Example 5. Gas processing plant. C, the owner of an operating mineral interest in a property, undertakes a qualified enhanced oil recovery project with respect to the property. A gas processing plant where C will process gas produced in the project is located on C's property. The gas processing plant is not used directly in the project and is not essential to the completeness of the project. Therefore, the gas processing plant is not an integral part of the enhanced oil recovery project.

Example 6. Gas processing equipment. The facts are the same as in *Example 5* except that C uses a portion of the gas processing plant to separate and recycle the tertiary injectant. The gas processing equipment used to separate and recycle the tertiary injectant is used directly in the project and is essential to the completeness of the project. Therefore, the gas processing equipment used to separate and recycle the tertiary injectant is an integral part of the enhanced oil recovery project and the costs of this equipment are qualified enhanced oil recovery costs.

Example 7. Steam generator costs allocated. In 1988, D, the owner of an operating mineral interest in a property, undertook a steam drive project with respect to the property. In 1992, D decides to undertake a steam drive project with respect to reservoir volume that was substantially unaffected by the 1988 project. The 1992 project is a significant expansion that is a qualified enhanced oil recovery project. D purchases a new steam generator with sufficient capacity to provide steam for both the 1988 project and the 1992 project. The steam generator is used directly in the 1992 project and is essential to the completeness of the 1992 project. Accordingly, the steam generator is an integral part of the 1992 project. Because the steam generator is also used to provide steam for the 1988 project, D must allocate the cost of the steam generator to the 1988 project and the 1992 project. Only the portion of the cost of the steam generator that is allocable to the 1992 project is a qualified enhanced oil recovery cost.

Example 8. Carbon dioxide pipeline. In 1992, E, the owner of an operating mineral interest in a property, undertakes an immiscible carbon dioxide displacement project with respect to the property. E constructs a pipeline to convey carbon dioxide to the project site. E contracts with F, a producer of carbon dioxide, to purchase carbon dioxide to be injected into injection wells in E's enhanced oil recovery project. The cost of the carbon dioxide is a tertiary injectant expense that is a qualified enhanced oil recovery cost. The pipeline is used by E to transport the tertiary injectant, that is, the carbon dioxide to the project site. Therefore, the pipeline is an integral part of the project. Accordingly, the cost of the pipeline is a qualified enhanced oil recovery cost.

Example 9. Water source wells. In 1992, G the owner of an operating mineral interest in a property, undertakes a polymer augmented waterflood project with respect to the property. G drills water wells to provide water for injection in connection with the project. The costs of drilling the water wells are intangible drilling and development costs that are paid or incurred in connection with the project. Therefore, the costs of drilling the water wells are qualified enhanced oil recovery costs.

Example 10. Leased equipment. In 1992, H, the owner of an operating mineral interest in a property undertakes a steam drive project with respect to the property. H contracts with I, a driller, to drill injection wells in connection with the project. H also leases a steam generator to provide steam for injection in connection with the project. The drilling costs are intangible drilling and development costs that are paid in connection with the project and are qualified enhanced oil recovery costs. The steam generator is used to produce the tertiary injectant. The steam generator is used directly in the project and is essential to the completeness of the project; therefore, it is an integral part of the project. The costs of leasing the steam generator are tangible property costs that are qualified enhanced oil recovery costs.

(c) *Primary purpose*—(1) *In general.* For purposes of this section, a cost is a qualified enhanced oil recovery cost only if the cost is paid or incurred with respect to an asset which is used for the primary purpose of implementing one or more enhanced oil recovery projects, at least one of which is a qualified enhanced oil recovery project. All the facts and circumstances determine whether an asset is used for the primary purpose of implementing an enhanced oil recovery project. For purposes of this paragraph (c), an enhanced oil recovery project is a project that satisfies the requirements of paragraphs (a)(1) and (2) of section 1.43-2.

(2) *Tertiary injectant costs.* Tertiary injectant costs generally satisfy the primary purpose test of this paragraph (c).

(3) *Intangible drilling and development costs.* Intangible drilling and development costs paid or incurred with respect to a well that is used in connection with the recovery of oil by primary or secondary methods are not qualified enhanced oil recovery costs. Except as provided in this paragraph (c)(3), a well used for primary or secondary recovery is not used for the primary purpose of implementing an enhanced oil recovery project. A well drilled for the primary purpose of implementing an enhanced oil recovery project is not considered to be used for primary or secondary recovery, notwithstanding that some primary or secondary production may result when the well is drilled, provided that such primary or secondary production is consistent with the unit plan of development or other similar plan. All the facts and circumstances determine whether primary or secondary recovery is consistent with the unit plan of development or other similar plan.

(4) *Tangible property costs.* Tangible property costs must be paid or incurred with respect to property which is used for the primary purpose of implementing an enhanced oil recovery project. If tangible property is used partly in a qualified enhanced oil recovery project and partly in another activity, the property must be primarily

used to implement the qualified enhanced oil recovery project.

(5) *Offshore drilling platforms.* Amounts paid or incurred in connection with the acquisition, construction, transportation, erection, or installation of an offshore drilling platform (regardless of whether the amounts are intangible drilling and development costs) that is used in connection with the recovery of oil by primary or secondary methods are not qualified enhanced oil recovery costs. An offshore drilling platform used for primary or secondary recovery is not used for the primary purpose of implementing an enhanced oil recovery project.

(6) *Examples.* The following examples illustrate the principles of this paragraph (c).

Example 1. Intangible drilling and development costs. In 1992, J incurs intangible drilling and development costs in drilling a well. J intends to use the well as an injection well in connection with an enhanced oil recovery project in 1994, but in the meantime will use the well in connection with a secondary recovery project. J may not take the intangible drilling and development costs into account in determining the credit because the primary purpose of a well used for secondary recovery is not to implement a qualified enhanced oil recovery project.

Example 2. Offshore drilling platform. K, the owner of an operating mineral interest in an offshore oil field located within the United States, constructs an offshore drilling platform that is designed to accommodate the primary, secondary, and tertiary development of the field. Subsequent to primary and secondary development of the field, K commences an enhanced oil recovery project that involves the application of a qualified tertiary recovery method. As part of the enhanced oil recovery project, K drills injection wells from the offshore drilling platform K used in the primary and secondary development of the field and installs an additional separator on the platform. Because the offshore drilling platform was used in the primary and secondary development of the field and was not used for the primary purpose of implementing tertiary development of the field, costs incurred by K in connection with the acquisition, construction, transportation, erection, or installation of the offshore drilling platform are not qualified enhanced oil recovery costs. However, the costs K incurs for the additional separator are qualified enhanced oil recovery costs because the separator is used for the primary purpose of implementing tertiary development of the field. In addition, the intangible drilling and development costs K incurs in connection with drilling the injection wells are quali-

Reg. § 1.43-4(c)(6)

fied enhanced oil recovery costs with respect to which K may claim the enhanced oil recovery credit.

(d) *Costs paid or incurred prior to first injection*—(1) *In general.* Qualified enhanced oil recovery costs may be paid or incurred prior to the date of the first injection of liquids, gases, or other matter (within the meaning of § 1.43-2(c)). If the first injection of liquids, gases, or other matter occurs on or before the date the taxpayer files the taxpayer's federal income tax return for the taxable year with respect to which the costs are allowable, the costs may be taken into account on that return. If the first injection of liquids, gases, or other matter is expected to occur after the date the taxpayer files that return, costs may be taken into account on that return if the Internal Revenue Service issues a private letter ruling to the taxpayer that so permits.

(2) *First injection after filing of return for taxable year costs are allowable.* Except as provided in paragraph (d)(3) of this section, if the first injection of liquids, gases, or other matter occurs or is expected to occur after the date the taxpayer files the taxpayer's federal income tax return for the taxable year with respect to which the costs are allowable, the costs may be taken into account on an amended return (or in the case of a Coordinated Examination Program taxpayer, on a written statement treated as a qualified return) after the earlier of—

(i) The date the first injection of liquids, gases, or other matter occurs; or

(ii) The date the Internal Revenue Service issues a private letter ruling that provides that the taxpayer may take costs into account prior to the first injection of liquids, gases, or other matter.

(3) *First injection more than 36 months after close of taxable year costs are paid or incurred.* If the first injection of liquids, gases, or other matter occurs more than 36 months after the close of the taxable year in which costs are paid or incurred, the taxpayer may take the costs into account in determining the credit only if the Internal Revenue Service issues a private letter ruling to the taxpayer that so provides.

(4) *Injections in volumes less than the volumes specified in the project plan.* For purposes of this paragraph (d), injections in volumes significantly less than the volumes specified in the project plan, the unit plan of development, or another similar plan do not constitute the first injection of liquids, gases, or other matter.

(5) *Examples.* The following examples illustrate the provisions of paragraph (d) of this section.

Example 1. First injection before return filed. In 1992, L, a calendar year taxpayer, undertakes a qualified enhanced oil recovery project on a property in which L owns an operating mineral interest. L incurs $1,000 of intangible drilling and development costs, which L may elect to deduct under section 263(c) for 1992. The first injection of liquids, gases, or other matter (within the meaning of § 1.43-2(c)) occurs in March 1993. L files a 1992 federal income tax return in April 1993. Because the first injection occurs before the filing of L's 1992 federal income tax return, L may take the $1,000 of intangible drilling and development costs into account in determining the credit for 1992 on that return.

Example 2. First injection after return filed. In 1993, M, a calendar year taxpayer, undertakes a qualified enhanced oil recovery project on a property in which M owns an operating mineral interest. M incurs $2,000 of intangible drilling and development costs, which M elects to deduct under section 263(c) for 1993. The first injection of liquids, gases, or other matter is expected to occur in 1995. M files a 1993 federal income tax return in April 1994. Because the first injection of liquids, gases, or other matter occurs after the date on which M's 1993 federal income tax return is filed in April 1994, M may take the $2,000 of intangible drilling and development costs into account on an amended return for 1993 after the earlier of the date the first injection of liquids, gases, or other matter occurs, or the date the Internal Revenue Service issues a private letter ruling that provides that M may take the $2,000 into account prior to first injection.

Example 3. First injection more than 36 months after taxable year. N, a calendar year taxpayer, owns an operating mineral interest in a property on which N undertakes an immiscible carbon dioxide displacement project. In 1994, N incurs $5,000 in connection with the construction of a pipeline to transport carbon dioxide to the project site. The first injection of liquids, gases, or other matter is expected to occur after the pipeline is completed in 1998. Because the first injection of liquids, gases, or other matter occurs more than 36 months after the close of the taxable year in which the $5,000 is incurred, N may take the $5,000 into account in determining the credit only if N receives a private letter ruling from the Internal Revenue Service that provides that N may take the $5,000 into account prior to first injection.

(e) *Other rules*—(1) *Anti-abuse rule.* Costs paid or incurred with respect to an asset that is acquired, used, or transferred in a manner designed to duplicate or otherwise unreasonably increase

Reg. § 1.43-4(d)(1)

the amount of the credit are not qualified enhanced oil recovery costs, regardless of whether the costs would otherwise be creditable for a single taxpayer or more than one taxpayer.

(2) *Costs paid or incurred to acquire a project.* A purchaser of an existing qualified enhanced oil recovery project may claim the credit for any section 43 costs in excess of the acquisition cost. However, costs paid or incurred to acquire an existing qualified enhanced oil recovery project (or an interest in an existing qualified enhanced oil recovery project) are not eligible for the credit.

(3) *Examples.* The following examples illustrate the principles of paragraph (e) of this section.

Example 1. Duplicating or unreasonably increasing the credit. O owns an operating mineral interest in a property with respect to which a qualified enhanced oil recovery project is implemented. O acquires pumping units, rods, casing, and separators for use in connection with the project from an unrelated equipment dealer in an arm's length transaction. The equipment is used for the primary purpose of implementing the project. Some of the equipment acquired by O is used equipment. The costs paid by O for the used equipment are qualified enhanced oil recovery costs. O does not need to determine whether the equipment has been previously used in an enhanced oil recovery project.

Example 2. Duplicating or unreasonably increasing the credit. P and Q are co-owners of an oil property with respect to which a qualified enhanced oil recovery project is implemented. In 1992, P and Q jointly purchase a nitrogen plant to supply the tertiary injectant used in the project. P and Q claim the credit for their respective costs for the plant. In 1994, X, a corporation unrelated to P or Q, purchases the nitrogen plant and enters into an agreement to sell nitrogen to P and Q. Because this transaction duplicates or otherwise unreasonably increases the credit, the credit is not allowable for the amounts incurred by P and Q for the nitrogen purchased from X.

Example 3. Duplicating or unreasonably increasing the credit. The facts are the same as in *Example 2*. In addition, in 1995, P and Q reacquire the nitrogen plant from X. This constitutes the acquisition of property in a manner designed to duplicate or otherwise unreasonably increase the amount of the credit. Therefore, the credit is not allowable for amounts incurred by P and Q for the nitrogen plant purchased from X.

Example 4. Duplicating or unreasonably increasing the credit. R owns an operating mineral interest in a property with respect to which a qualified enhanced oil recovery project is implemented. R acquires a pump that is installed at the site of the project. After the pump has been placed in service for 6 months, R transfers the pump to a secondary recovery project and acquires a replacement pump for the tertiary project. The original pump is suited to the needs of the secondary recovery project and could have been installed there initially. The pumps have been acquired in a manner designed to duplicate or otherwise unreasonably increase the amount of the credit. Depending on the facts, the cost of one pump or the other may be a qualified enhanced oil recovery cost; however, R may not claim the credit with respect to the cost of both pumps.

Example 5. Acquiring a project. In 1993, S purchases all of T's interest in a qualified enhanced oil recovery project, including all of T's interest in tangible property that is an integral part of the project and all of T's operating mineral interest. In 1994, S incurs costs for additional tangible property that is an integral part of the project and which is used for the primary purpose of implementing the project. S also incurs costs for tertiary injectants that are injected in connection with the project. In determining the credit for 1994, S may take into account costs S incurred for tangible property and tertiary injectants. However, S may not take into account any amount that S paid for T's interest in the project in determining S's credit for any taxable year. [Reg. § 1.43-4.]

☐ [*T.D.* 8448, 11-20-92.]

[Reg. § 1.43-5]

§ 1.43-5. At-risk limitation. [Reserved.]

☐ [*T.D.* 8448, 11-20-92.]

[Reg. § 1.43-6]

§ 1.43-6. Election out of section 43.—(a) *Election to have the credit not apply*—(1) *In general.* A taxpayer may elect to have section 43 not apply for any taxable year. The taxpayer may revoke an election to have section 43 not apply for any taxable year. An election to have section 43 not apply (or a revocation of an election to have section 43 not apply) for any taxable year is effective only for the taxable year to which the election relates.

(2) *Time for making the election.* A taxpayer may make an election under paragraph (a) of this section to have section 43 not apply (or revoke an election to have section 43 not apply) for any taxable year at any time before the expiration of the 3-year period beginning on the last date prescribed by law (determined without regard to extensions) for filing the return for the taxable year. The time for making the election (or revoking the

election) is prescribed by section 43(e)(2) and may not be extended under § 1.9100-1.

(3) *Manner of making the election.* An election (or revocation) under paragraph (a)(1) of this section is made by attaching a statement to the taxpayer's federal income tax return or an amended return (or, in the case of a Coordinated Examination Program taxpayer, on a written statement treated as a qualified amended return) for the taxable year for which the election (or revocation) applies. The taxpayer must indicate whether the taxpayer is electing to not have section 43 apply or is revoking such an election and designate the project or projects to which the election (or revocation) applies. For any taxable year, the last election (or revocation) made by a taxpayer within the period prescribed in paragraph (a)(2) of this section determines whether section 43 applies for that taxable year.

(b) *Election by partnerships and S corporations.* For partnerships and S corporations, an election to have section 43 not apply (or a revocation of an election to have section 43 not apply) for any taxable year is made, in accordance with the requirements of paragraph (a) of this section, by the partnership or S corporation with respect to the qualified enhanced oil recovery costs paid or incurred by the partnership or S corporation for the taxable year to which the election relates. [Reg. § 1.43-6.]

☐ [*T.D.* 8448, 11-20-92.]

[Reg. § 1.43-7]

§ 1.43-7. Effective date of regulations.—The provisions of § § 1.43-1, 1.43-2 and 1.43-4 through 1.43-7 apply with respect to costs paid or incurred after December 31, 1991, in connection with a qualified enhanced oil recovery project. The provisions of § 1.43-3 apply with respect to taxable years beginning after December 31, 1990. For costs paid or incurred after December 31, 1990, and before January 1, 1992, in connection with a qualified enhanced oil recovery project, taxpayers must take reasonable return positions taking into consideration the statute and its legislative history. [Reg. § 1.43-7.]

☐ [*T.D.* 8448, 11-20-92.]

→ *Caution: Former Code Sec. 44A was redesignated as Code Sec. 21.*←

[Reg. § 1.44A-1]

§ 1.44A-1. Expenses for household and dependent care services necessary for gainful employment.—(a) *In general.* (1) This section applies only for expenses incurred in taxable years beginning after December 31, 1975. For deductibility of expenses incurred in taxable years beginning before January 1, 1972, see § 1.214-1. For deductibility of expenses incurred in taxable years beginning after December 31, 1971, and before January 1, 1976, see § § 1.214A-1 through 1.214A-5.

(2) Section 44A allows a credit against the tax imposed by chapter 1 of the Code to an individual who maintains a household (within the meaning of paragraph (d) of this section) which includes as a member one or more qualifying individuals (as defined in paragraph (b) of this section). The amount of the credit is equal to the applicable percentage of the employment-related expenses (as defined in paragraph (c) of this section) paid by the individual during the taxable year (but subject to the limits prescribed in § 1.44A-2(a)). However, the credit cannot exceed the tax imposed by chapter 1, reduced by the sum of the allowable credits enumerated in section 44A(b). The term "applicable percentage" means 30 percent reduced by 1 percentage point for each $2,000 (or fraction thereof) by which the taxpayer's adjusted gross income for the taxable year exceeds $10,000, but in no event shall the percent be less than 20 percent. Thus, for example, if a taxpayer's adjusted gross income is over $10,000, but less than $12,000.01, the applicable percentage is 29 percent. (For expenses incurred in taxable years beginning before January 1, 1982, the applicable percentage is a flat 20 percent.)

(3) Generally, the credit for employment-related expenses is allowable, regardless of the taxpayer's method of accounting, only for expenses which are actually paid during the taxable year and which are incurred during the taxable year or were incurred during a prior taxable year beginning after December 31, 1975. If the expenses are incurred but not paid during the taxable year, no credit may be taken for that year on account of those expenses. Thus, if an expense is incurred in the last month of a taxable year but not paid until the following taxable year, a credit for the expense is not allowed for the earlier taxable year but is allowed for the following taxable year. However, if an expense is incurred in a taxable year beginning before January 1, 1976, and paid in a later taxable year, no credit is allowed with respect to the expense under section 44A. Section 214 and the regulations thereunder are applicable in determining whether a deduction for the expense is allowed in the year of payment.

(4) Since an expense cannot be an employment-related expense until the services for which the expense was incurred are performed (see para-

→ *Caution: Former Code Sec. 44A was redesignated as Code Sec. 21.*←

graph (c) of this section), prepaid expenses may be claimed only in the taxable year in which the services are performed.

(5) The requirements of section 44A, this section, and §§ 1.44A-2 through 1.44A-4 are applied to expenses as of the time they are incurred regardless of when they are paid.

(6) For special rules relating to employment-related expenses which also qualify as medical expenses deductible under section 213, see § 1.44A-4(b).

(7) For substantiation of the credit, see paragraph (e) of this section.

(b) *Qualifying individual.*—(1) *In general.* A person is considered to be a qualifying individual if he or she is—

(i) The taxpayer's dependent who is under the age of 15 and is an individual for whom the taxpayer is entitled to a deduction for a personal exemption under section 151(e);

(ii) The taxpayer's dependent (not described in subdivision (I)) who is physically or mentally incapable of self-care; or

(iii) The taxpayer's spouse who is physically or mentally incapable of self-care.

The term "dependent," as used in this paragraph (b)(1), includes any individual who is a dependent within the meaning of section 152. However, see paragraph (b)(2) of this section for special rules for determining which parent may treat a child as a qualifying individual where the parents are divorced, legally separated, or separated under a written separation agreement.

(2) *Special dependency test in case of divorced or separated parents.* A child (as defined in section 151(e)(3)) who—

(i) Is under age 15 or is physically or mentally incapable of self-care,

(ii) Receives over half of his or her support during the calendar year from his or her parents who are divorced or legally separated under a decree of divorce or separate maintenance or who are separated under a written separation agreement, and

(iii) Is in the custody of one or both of his or her parents for more than one-half of the calendar year,

is treated for any taxable year beginning in the calendar year as a qualifying individual (described in subdivision (i) or (ii), as the case may be, of paragraph (b)(1) of this section) of that parent who has custody for a longer period during the calendar year than the other parent. Accordingly, a child may be treated as a qualifying

individual of a parent even though the parent is not entitled to a dependency exemption for the child. The child cannot be treated as a qualifying individual with respect to more than one parent.

(3) *Qualification on a daily basis.* The status of a person as a qualifying individual is determined on a daily basis. Thus, if a dependent or spouse of a taxpayer ceases to be a qualifying individual on September 16, the dependent or spouse is treated as a qualifying individual through September 15 only.

(4) *Physical or mental incapacity.* An individual is considered to be physically or mentally incapable of self-care if as a result of a physical or mental defect the individual is incapable of caring for his or her hygienical or nutritional needs, or requires full-time attention of another person for his or her own safety or the safety of others. The fact that an individual, by reason of a physical or mental defect, is unable to engage in any substantial gainful activity, or is unable to perform the normal household functions of a homemaker or to care for minor children, does not of itself establish that the individual is physically or mentally incapable of self-care. An individual who is physically handicapped or is mentally defective, and for such reason requires constant attention of another person, is considered to be physically or mentally incapable of self-care.

(c) *Employment-related expenses*—(1) *Gainful employment*—(i) *In general.* Expenses are considered to be employment-related expenses only if they are incurred to enable the taxpayer to be gainfully employed and are paid for household services or for the care of one or more qualifying individuals. The expenses must be incurred while the taxpayer is gainfully employed or is in active search of gainful employment. The employment may consist of service either within or without the home of the taxpayer and may include self-employment. An expense is not considered to be employment-related merely because it is incurred while the taxpayer is gainfully employed. The purpose of the expense must be to enable the taxpayer to be gainfully employed. Volunteer work for a nominal salary does not constitute gainful employment. Whether the purpose of an expense is to enable the taxpayer to be gainfully employed depends upon the facts and circumstances of the particular case. Any tax required to be paid by the taxpayer under sections 3111 (relating to the Federal Insurance Contributions Act) and 3301 (relating to the Federal Unemployment Tax Act), or under similar State payroll taxes, in respect of any wages which otherwise

Reg. § 1.44A-1(c)(1)

→ *Caution: Former Code Sec. 44A was redesignated as Code Sec. 21.*←

constitute employment-related expenses is considered to be an employment-related expense.

(ii) *Determination of period of employment on a daily basis.* An allocation of expenses is required on a daily basis when the expenses cover any period during part of which the taxpayer is gainfully employed or is in active search of gainful employment and during the other part of which there is no employment or active search for gainful employment. Thus, for example, if a taxpayer incurs during each month of the taxable year $60 of expenses which would be employment-related if he or she were gainfully employed all year, and the taxpayer is gainfully employed, or in active search of gainful employment, for only 2 months and 10 days during such year, the amount of employment-related expenses is limited to $140.

(2) *Household services.* Expenses are considered to be paid for household services is they are paid for the performance in and about the taxpayer's home of ordinary and usual services necessary to the maintenance of the household. However, expenses are not considered as paid for household services unless the expenses are attributable in part to the care of the qualifying individual. Thus, amounts paid for the services of a domestic maid or cook are considered to be expenses paid for household services if a part of those services is provided to the qualifying individual. Amounts paid for the services of an individual who is employed as a chauffeur, bartender, or gardener, however, are not considered to be expenses paid for household services.

(3) *Care of qualifying individual.*—(i) *In general.* The primary purpose of expenses for the care of a qualifying individual must be to assure that individual's well-being and protection. Not all benefits bestowed upon a qualifying individual are considered as provided for the individual's care. Accordingly, amounts paid to provide food, clothing, or education are not expenses paid for the care of a qualifying individual. However, where the manner of providing care is such that the expense which is incurred includes expenses for other benefits which are incident to and inseparably a part of the care, the full amount of the expense is considered to be incurred for care. Thus, for example, the full amount paid to a nursery school in which a qualifying child is enrolled is considered as being for the care of the child, even though the school also furnishes lunch and educational services. Educational expenses incurred for a child in the first or higher grade level are not expenses incurred for the care of a qualifying individual. Expenses incurred for

transportation of a qualifying individual described in paragraph (b)(1)(i) of this section between the taxpayer's household and a place outside the taxpayer's household where services for the care of the qualifying individual are provided are not incurred for the care of a qualifying individual.

(ii) *Manner of providing care.* The manner of providing the care need not be the least expensive alternative available to the taxpayer. For example, the taxpayer's mother may reside at the taxpayer's home and be available to provide adequate care at no cost for the taxpayer's wife who is physically or mentally incapable of caring for herself. Nevertheless, the expenses incurred in providing a nurse for the wife may be an expense for the care of the wife. See paragraph (c)(1)(i) of this section with respect to the requirement that the expense must be for the purpose of permitting the taxpayer to be gainfully employed.

(4) *Services outside the taxpayer's household.* The credit is allowed under section 44A with respect to employment-related expenses incurred for services performed outside the taxpayer's household only if those expenses are incurred for the care of—

(i) One or more qualifying individuals who are described in paragraph (b)(1)(i) of this section; or

(ii) One or more qualifying individuals (as to expenses incurred for taxable years beginning after December 31, 1981) who are described in paragraph (b)(1)(ii) or (iii) of this section and who regularly spend at least 8 hours each day in the taxpayer's household.

(5) *Dependent care centers.* The credit is allowed under section 44A with respect to employment-related expenses incurred in taxable years beginning after December 31, 1981, for services provided outside the taxpayer's household by a dependent care center only if—

(i) The center complies with all applicable laws and regulations of a State or unit of local government (*e.g.,* State or local requirements for licensing, if applicable, and building and fire Code regulations); and

(ii) The requirement provided in paragraph (c)(4)(i) or (ii) of this section is met.

The term "dependent care center" means any facility that provides full-time or part-time care for more than six individuals (other than residents of the facility) on a regular basis during the taxpayer's taxable year, and receives a fee, payment, or grant for providing services for any such individuals (regardless of whether such facility is op-

Reg. § 1.44A-1(c)(2)

→ *Caution: Former Code Sec. 44A was redesignated as Code Sec. 21.*←

erated for profit). For purposes of the preceding sentence, a facility will be presumed to provide full-time or part-time care for six or less individuals on a regular basis during the taxpayer's taxable year if the facility has six or less individuals (including the qualifying individual) enrolled for full-time or part-time care on the day the qualifying individual is enrolled in the facility (or on the first day of the taxable year the qualifying individual attends the facility in the case where the individual was enrolled in the facility in the preceding taxable year) unless the Internal Revenue Service demonstrates that the facility provides full-time or part-time care for more than six individuals on a regular basis during the taxpayer's taxable year.

(6) *Allocation of expenses.* Where a portion of an expense is for household services or for the care of a qualifying individual and a portion of such expense is for other purposes, a reasonable allocation must be made and only the portion of the expense paid which is attributable to such household services or care is considered to be an employment-related expense. No allocation is required to be made, however, if the portion of expense for the other purpose is minimal or insignificant. An allocation must be made, for example, if a servant performs household duties, cares for the qualifying children of the taxpayer, and also performs social services for the taxpayer (for which a deduction is not allowable) or clerical services in the office of the taxpayer outside the home (for which a deduction may be allowable under section 162). Employment related expenses include household service expenses which are provided in conjunction with the care of a qualifying individual. Thus, if an expense is in part attributable to the care of a qualifying individual and in part to household services, no allocation is required.

(7) *Illustrations.* The application of this paragraph (c) may be illustrated by the following examples:

Example (1). The taxpayer lives with her mother who is physically incapable of caring for herself. In order to be gainfully employed the taxpayer hires a practical nurse whose sole duty consists of providing for the care of the mother in the home while the taxpayer is at work. All amounts spent for the services of the nurse are employment-related expenses.

Example (2). The taxpayer has a dependent child 10 years of age who has been attending public school. The taxpayer, who has been working part time, is offered a position involving full-time employment which she can accept only if the child is placed in a boarding school. The taxpayer accepts the position and the child is sent to a boarding school. The expenses paid to the school must be allocated between that part of the expenses which represents care for the child and that part which represents tuition for education. The part of the expense representing care of the child is incurred for the purpose of permitting the taxpayer to be gainfully employed.

Example (3). The taxpayer, in order to be gainfully employed, employs a full-time housekeeper who cares for the taxpayer's two children, aged 9 and 15 years, respectively, performs regular household services of cleaning and cooking, and chauffeurs the taxpayer to and from his place of employment. The chauffeuring service never requires more than 30 minutes out of the total period of employment each day. No allocation is required for purposes of determining the portion of the expense attributable to the chauffeuring (not a household service expense) since it is *de minimis.* Further, no allocation is required for the purpose of determining the portion of the expense attributable to the care of the 15 year old child (not a qualifying individual) since the household expense is in part attributable to the care of the 9 year old child, who is a qualifying individual. Accordingly, the entire expense of employing the housekeeper is an employment-related expense. However, the total amount of employment-related expenses taken into account would be limited to the amount allowable for one qualifying individual.

(d) *Maintenance of a household* —(1) *In general.* An individual is considered to have maintained a household for the taxable year (or lesser period) only if the individual (and his or her spouse if the individual is married) have furnished over one-half of the cost incurred for such taxable year (or lesser period) in maintaining the household. The household must actually constitute for the taxable year the principal place of abode of the taxpayer and the qualifying individual or individuals described in paragraph (b) of this section. It is not sufficient that the taxpayer maintain the household without being its occupant. A physical change in the location of the home does not, however, prevent the home from constituting the principal place of abode of the taxpayer and a qualifying individual. The fact that an individual is born or dies during the taxable year does not prevent a home from constituting his or her principal place of abode for such year. An individual is not considered to have terminated a household as his or her principal place of abode merely by reason of temporary absences therefrom by reason

Reg. § 1.44A-1(d)(1)

→ *Caution: Former Code Sec. 44A was redesignated as Code Sec. 21.*←

of illness, education, business, vacation, military service, or a custody agreement.

(2) *Two or more families.* Solely for purposes of section 44A and this section, if two or more families occupy living quarters in common, each of the families is treated as constituting a separate household, and the taxpayer who provides more than one-half of the costs of maintaining such a separate household is treated as maintaining that household. Thus, for example, if two unrelated taxpayers each with children occupy living quarters in common and each taxpayer pays more than one-half of the household costs incurred by each respective family, each taxpayer will be treated as maintaining a separate household.

(3) *Costs of maintaining a household.* The costs of maintaining a household are the expenses incurred for the mutual benefit of the occupants thereof by reason of its operation as the principal place of abode of the occupants. The expenses of maintaining a household include property taxes, mortgage interest, rent, utility charges, upkeep and repairs, property insurance, and food consumed on the premises. These expenses do not include the cost of clothing, education, medical treatment, vacations, life insurance, or transportation or payments on mortgage principal or for the purchase, permanent improvement, betterment, or replacement of property. Further, the costs of maintaining a household do not include the value of services performed in the household by a qualifying individual described in paragraph (b) of this section. An expense incurred by a taxpayer which is paid or reimbursed by another is not considered as a cost of maintaining a household.

(4) *Monthly proration of annual costs.* In determining the cost incurred for a period of less than a taxable year in maintaining a household, the cost incurred during the entire taxable year must be prorated on the basis of the number of calendar months within such lesser period. For this purpose a period of less than a calendar month will be treated as a calendar month. Thus, for example, if the cost of maintaining a household for a taxable year is $6,600, and the period in respect of which a determination is being made under section 44A is from June 20 to December 31, the taxpayer must furnish more than $1,925 [$6,000 × 7/12] × 50%] in maintaining the household from June 1 to December 31.

(e) *Substantiation.* A taxpayer claiming a credit under paragraph (a) of this section for employment-related expenses must substantiate by adequate records or other sufficient evidence any

credit taken under this section. For example, if requested, the taxpayer must furnish information as to the nature and period of the physical or mental incapacity of any dependent or spouse in respect of whom a credit is claimed, including necessary information from the attending physician as to the nature of the physical or mental incapacity. [Reg. § 1.44A-1.]

☐ [*T.D. 7643, 8-27-79. Amended by T.D. 7951, 4-26-84.*]

[Reg. § 1.44A-2]

§ 1.44A-2. Limitations on amount creditable.—(a) *Annual dollar limit on amount creditable.* The amount of the employment-related expenses incurred during any taxable year which may be taken into account under § 1.44A-1(a) cannot exceed—

(1) $2,400 ($2,000 in the case of expenses incurred in taxable years beginning before January 1, 1982) if there is one qualifying individual with respect to the taxpayer at any time during the taxable year, or

(2) $4,800 ($4,000 in the case of expenses incurred in taxable years beginning before January 1, 1982) if there are two or more qualifying individuals with respect to the taxpayer at any one time during the taxable year.

For example, a calendar year taxpayer whose only qualifying individual reaches age 15 on April 1, 1982, is subject for 1982 to the entire annual dollar limit of $2,400, without proration of the $2,400 limit. However, only expenses incurred prior to the child's 15th birthday may be employment-related expenses.

(b) *Earned income limitation*—(1) *In general.* The amount of employment-related expenses incurred during any taxable year which may be taken into account under § 1.44A-1(a) cannot exceed—

(i) For an individual not married at the close of the year, the individual's earned income for the year, or

(ii) For an individual married at the close of the year, the lesser of the individual's earned income or the earned income of his or her spouse for the year.

For purposes of this paragraph (b)(1), the earned income of only the spouse to whom the taxpayer is married at the close of the year is taken into account (and not the earned income of another spouse who died or was divorced from the taxpayer during the year). Further, the spouse's earned income for the entire year is taken into account, even though the taxpayer and his or her spouse were married for only a part of the year. For purposes of this paragraph (b), certain married individuals legally separated or living apart are treated as not married (see § 1.44A-3(b) and (c), respectively).

(2) *Earned income.* For purposes of this section, earned income means—

(i) Wages, salaries, tips, other employee compensation, and

(ii) net earnings from self-employment (within the meaning of section 1402(a) and the regulations thereunder),

For taxable years beginning before January 1, 1979, earned income includes only amounts described in subdivision (i) or (ii) of this paragraph (b)(2) which are includible in the eligible individual's gross income for the taxable year of the individual in which the credit is claimed. For all taxable years, however, earned income is computed without regard to any community property laws which may otherwise be applicable. Earned income is reduced by any net loss in earnings from self-employment. Earned income does not include amounts received as a pension or an annuity, or an amount to which section 871(a) and the regulations thereunder apply (relating to income of nonresident alien individuals not connected with United States business).

(3) *Special rule for spouse who is a student or incapable of self-care.* (i) For purposes of this section, a spouse is deemed, for each month during which the spouse is a full-time student or is a qualifying individual described in § 1.44A-1(b)(1)(iii), to be gainfully employed and to have earned income of not less than—

(A) $200 ($166 for taxable years beginning before January 1, 1982) if there is one quali-

fying individual with respect to the taxpayer at any one time during the taxable year, or

(B) $400 ($333 for taxable years beginning before January 1, 1982), if there are two or more qualifying individuals with respect to the taxpayer at any one time during the taxable year.

However, in the case of any husband and wife, this subparagraph shall apply with respect to only one spouse for any one month.

(ii) A "full-time student" is an individual who is enrolled at and attends an educational institution during each of five calendar months of the taxable year of the taxpayer for the number of course hours which is considered to be a full-time course of study. The enrollment for five calendar months need not be consecutive. School attendance exclusively at night does not constitute a full-time course of study. However, a full-time course of study may include some attendance at night.

(iii) For the definition of "educational institution," see § 1.151-3(c).

(4) *Illustrations.* The application of this paragraph may be illustrated by the following examples:

Example (1). During the 1982 taxable year, A, a married taxpayer, incurs and pays employment-related expenses of $4,000 for the care of a qualifying individual. A's earned income for the taxable year is $20,000 and his wife's earned income is $1,500. Under these circumstances, the amount of employment-related expenses for the year which may be taken into account under § 1.44A-(1)(a) is $1,500, determined as follows:

Employment-related expenses incurred during taxable year ($4,000, but limited to $2,400 by paragraph (a)(1) of this section)	$2,400
Application of paragraph (b)(1)(ii) of this section (employment-related expenses may not exceed wife's earned income of $1,500)	$1,500
Employment-related expenses taken into account	$1,500

Example (2). Assume the same facts as in example (1) except that A's wife is a full-time student for nine months of the taxable year and earns no income for the year. Under these circumstances, the amount of employment-related expenses for the year which may be taken into account under § 1.44A-1(a) is $1,800, determined as follows:

Employment-related expenses incurred during taxable year ($4,000, but limited to $2,400 by paragraph (a)(1) of this section)	$2,400
Application of paragraph (b)(3) of this section [employment-related expenses may not exceed wife's earned income of $1,800 (200 × 9)]	$1,800
Employment-related expenses taken into account	$1,800

[Reg. § 1.44A-2.]

☐ [*T.D. 7643, 8-27-79. Amended by T.D. 7951, 4-26-84.*]

[Reg. § 1.44A-3]

§ 1.44A-3. Special rules applicable to married individuals.—(a) *Joint return requirement.* This section applies only if the taxpayer is married at the close of a taxable year in which employment-related expenses are paid. In such a case the credit provided by section 44A with respect to employment-related expenses is allowed only if for the taxable year the taxpayer and his or her spouse file a joint return. If either spouse dies during the taxable year and a joint return may be made for the year under section 6013(a)(2) for the survivor and the deceased spouse, the credit is allowed for the year only if a joint return is made. If, however, the surviving spouse remarries before the end of the taxable year in which his or her first spouse dies, a credit is allowed on the separate return which is made for the decedent spouse. For purposes of this section, certain married individuals legally separated or living apart are treated as not married, as provided in paragraphs (b) and (c), respectively, of this section.

(b) *Marital status.* For purposes of section 44A, an individual legally separated from his or her spouse under a decree of divorce or of separate maintenance is not considered as married.

(c) *Certain married individuals living apart.* For purposes of section 44A, an individual who is married within the meaning of section 143(a) is treated as not married for the entire taxable year, if the individual—

(1) Files a separate return for the year,

(2) Maintains as his or her home a household which constitutes for more than one-half of the taxable year the principal place of abode of a qualifying individual, and

(3) Furnishes over one-half of the cost of maintaining the household for the year,

and if the individual's spouse is not a member of the household at any time during the last 6 months of the year. Thus, for example, an individual who is married during the taxable year, but is treated as not married by reason of this paragraph, may determine the earned income limitation upon the amount of employment-related expenses without taking into account the earned income of his or her spouse under § 1.44A-2(b). [Reg. § 1.44A-3.]

☐ [*T.D.* 7643, 8-27-79.]

[Reg. § 1.44A-4]

§ 1.44A-4. Other special rules relating to employment-related expenses.—(a) *Payments to related individuals*—(1) *Taxable years beginning after December 31, 1978.* For taxable years beginning after December 31, 1978, a credit is not allowed under section 44A with respect to the amount of any employment-related expenses paid by the taxpayer to an individual—

(i) With respect to whom for the taxable year a deduction under section 151(e) (relating to deduction for personal exemptions for dependents)

is allowable either to the taxpayer or his or her spouse, or

(ii) Who is a child of the taxpayer (within the meaning of section 151(e)(3)) who is under age 19 at the close of the taxable year.

For purposes of this paragraph (a)(1), the term "taxable year" means the taxable year of the taxpayer in which the service is performed.

(2) *Taxable years beginning before January 1, 1979.* For taxable years beginning before January 1, 1979, except as otherwise provided in paragraph (a)(3) of this section, a credit is not allowed under section 44A with respect to the amount of any employment-related expenses paid by the taxpayer to an individual who bears to the taxpayer any relationship described in section 152(a)(1) through (8). These relationships are those of a son or daughter or descendant thereof; a stepson or stepdaughter; a brother, a sister, stepbrother, or stepsister; a father or mother or an ancestor of either; a stepfather or stepmother; a nephew or niece; an uncle or aunt; or a son-in-law, daughter-in-law, father-in-law, mother-in-law, brother-in-law, or sister-in-law. In addition, no credit is allowed with respect to the amount of any employment-related expenses paid by the taxpayer to an individual who qualifies as a dependent of the taxpayer for the taxable year within the meaning of section 152(a)(9), which relates to an individual (other than the taxpayer's spouse) whose principal place of abode for the taxable year is the home of the taxpayer and who is a member of the taxpayer's household.

(3) *Exception for payments to certain related individuals.* For taxable years beginning before January 1, 1979, a credit is allowed for the amount of any employment-related expenses paid by the taxpayer to an individual provided that neither the taxpayer nor his or her spouse is entitled to a deduction under section 151(e) (relating to deduction for personal exemptions for dependents) with respect to such individual for the taxable year in which the service is performed; and the service with respect to which the amount is paid constitutes employment within the meaning of section 3121(b). The following services performed for a taxpayer by a relative who is an employee of the taxpayer may qualify as employment within the meaning of section 3121(b):

(i) Services performed by the taxpayer's child age 21 or over.

(ii) Domestic services in the taxpayer's home performed by the taxpayer's parent if—

(A) The taxpayer has living in his or her home a child (as defined in section 151(e)(3)) who is under age 18 or who has a physical or mental condition requiring the personal care of an adult during at least four continuous weeks in the calendar quarter, and

    (B) The taxpayer is a widow or widower or is divorced, or has a spouse living in the home who, because of a physical or mental condition, is incapable of caring for his or her child during at least four continuous weeks in the calendar quarter in which services are rendered.

    (iii) Services of all relatives other than a child, spouse, or parent of the taxpayer.

For taxable years beginning before January 1, 1979, a credit is not allowed under section 44A with respect to employment-related expenses paid by the taxpayer to a relative for services which do not constitute employment under section 3121(b). Services performed by a relative do not constitute employment if they relate to the relative's trade or business the income from which is includible in computing the relative's net earnings for purposes of the self-employment tax under section 1401.

    (4) *Payments to entities or partnerships.* If the services are performed by an entity or partnership, paragraph (a)(1) and (2) of this section is normally not applicable. If, however, the entity or partnership is established or maintained primarily to avoid the application of paragraph (a)(1) or (2) in order to permit the taxpayer to obtain the credit with respect to employment-related expenses, for purposes of this paragraph (a), the payments of employment-related expenses shall be treated as made directly to each owner of the entity or partner in proportion to his or her share of the entity or partnership. A factor to consider for purposes of determining whether an entity or partnership is so established or maintained is whether the entity or partnership is set up solely to care for the taxpayer's qualifying individual and to provide household services to the taxpayer.

    (5) *Illustrations.* The application of this paragraph may be illustrated by the following examples:

    Example (1). For A's taxable year ending December 31, 1978, A, a divorced taxpayer, pays $5,000 of employment-related expenses to his mother for the care of his child age 5. A's mother cares for the child in her home. The services performed by A's mother do not constitute employment under section 3121(b). Accordingly, A is not allowed a credit with respect to the amounts paid to the mother for the care of his child.

    Example (2). Assume the same facts as in example (1) except that A's taxable year under consideration begins after December 31, 1978. A is not entitled to a deduction under section 151(e) for his mother. Accordingly, A is allowed a credit with respect to the amounts paid to the mother for the care of his child, even though the services

performed by A's mother do not constitute employment under section 3121(b).

    Example (3). For B's taxable year ending December 31, 1978, B, a divorced taxpayer, pays $6,000 of employment-related expenses to his sister (who is not a dependent of the taxpayer) for the care of his child. The services performed by B's sister in the care of his child constitute a trade or business the income from which is includible in computing net earnings for purposes of the self-employment tax under section 1401. Accordingly, B is not allowed a credit with respect to the amounts paid to the sister for the care of his child.

    Example (4). Assume the same facts as in example (3) except that B's taxable year under consideration begins after December 31, 1978. B is allowed a credit with respect to the amounts paid to the sister for the care of his child, even though the services performed by B's sister do not constitute employment under section 3121(b).

    (b) *Expenses qualifying as medical expenses.* An expense which may constitute an amount otherwise deductible under section 213, relating to medical, etc., expenses, may also constitute an expense with respect to which a credit is allowable under section 44A. In such a case, that part of the amount with respect to which a credit is allowed under section 44A will not be considered as an expense for purposes of determining the amount deductible under section 213. On the other hand, where an amount is treated as a medical expense under section 213 for purposes of determining the amount deductible under that section, it may not be treated as an employment-related expense for purposes of section 44A. The application of this paragraph may be illustrated by the following examples:

    Example (1). In 1982, a calendar year taxpayer incurs and pays $5,000 of employment-related expenses during the taxable year for the care of his child when the child is physically incapable of self-care. These expenses are incurred for services performed in the taxpayer's household and are of a nature which qualify as medical expenses under section 213. The taxpayer's adjusted gross income for the taxable year is $100,000. Of the total expenses, the taxpayer may take $2,400 into account under section 44A; the balance of the expenses, or $2,600, may be treated as medical expenses to which section 213 applies. However, this amount does not exceed 3 percent of the taxpayer's adjusted gross income for the taxable year and is thus not allowable as a deduction under section 213.

    Example (2). Assume the same facts as in example (1). It is not proper for the taxpayer first to determine his deductible medical expenses of

$2,000 ($5,000 − [$100,000 × 3%]) under section 213 and then claim the $3,000 balance as employment-related expenses for purposes of section 44A. This is because the $3,000 balance has been treated as a medical expense in computing the amount deductible under section 213.

Example (3). In 1982, a calendar year taxpayer incurs and pays $12,000 of employment-related expenses during the taxable year for the care of his child. These expenses are incurred for services performed in the taxpayer's household, and they also qualify as medical expenses under section 213. The taxpayer's adjusted gross income for the taxable year is $18,000. The taxpayer takes $2,400 of such expenses into account under section 44A. The balance, or $9,600, he treats as medical expenses for purposes of section 213. The allowable deduction under section 213 for the expenses is limited to the excess of the balance of $9,600 over $540 (3 percent of the taxpayer's adjusted gross income of $18,000), or $9,060. [Reg. § 1.44A-4.]

☐ [*T.D. 7643, 8-27-79. Amended by T.D. 7951, 4-26-84.*]

→ *Caution: Former Code Sec. 44F was redesignated as Code Sec. 30 and was redesignated again as Code Sec. 41.*←

[Reg. § 5c.44F-1]

§ 5c.44F-1. Leases and qualified research expenses.—For purposes of section 44F(b)(2)(A)(iii), the determination of whether any amount is paid or incurred to another person for the right to use personal property in the conduct of qualified research shall be made without regard to the characterization of the transaction as a lease under section 168(f)(8). See § 5c.168(f)(8)-1(b). [Temporary Reg. § 5c.44F-1.]

☐ [*T.D. 7791, 10-20-81.*]

[Reg. § 1.45D-1T]

§ 1.45D-1T. New markets tax credit.—(a) *Table of contents.* This paragraph lists the headings that appear in § 1.45D-1T.

(a) Table of contents.

(b) Allowance of credit

(1) In general.

(2) Credit allowance date.

(3) Applicable percentage.

(4) Amount paid at original issue.

(c) Qualified equity investment.

(1) In general.

(2) Equity investment.

(3) Equity investments made prior to allocation.

(i) In general.

(ii) Exception.

(iii) Initial investment date.

(4) Limitations.

(i) In general.

(ii) Allocation limitation.

(5) Substantially all.

(i) In general.

(ii) Direct-tracing calculation.

(iii) Safe harbor calculation.

(iv) Time limit for making investments.

(v) Reduced substantially-all percentage.

(6) Aggregation of equity investments.

(7) Subsequent purchasers.

(d) Qualified low-income community investments.

(1) In general.

(i) Investment in a qualified active low-income community business.

(ii) Purchase of certain loans from CDEs.

(iii) Financial counseling and other services.

(iv) Investments in other CDEs.

(2) Payments of, or for, capital, equity or principal.

(i) In general.

(ii) Subsequent reinvestments.

(iii) Special rule for loans.

(iv) Example.

(3) Special rule for reserves.

(4) Qualified active low-income community business.

(i) In general.

(A) Gross-income requirement.

(B) Use of tangible property.

(C) Services performed.

(D) Collectibles.

(E) Nonqualified financial property.

(ii) Proprietorships.

(iii) Portions of business.

(5) Qualified business.

(i) In general.

(ii) Rental of real property.

(iii) Exclusions.

(A) Trades or businesses involving intangibles.

Reg. § 5c.44F-1

(B) Certain other trades or businesses.

(C) Farming.

(6) Qualifications.

(i) In general.

(ii) Control.

(A) In general.

(B) Definition of control.

(7) Financial counseling and other services.

(e) Recapture.

(1) In general.

(2) Recapture event.

(3) Bankruptcy.

(4) Waiver of requirement or extension of time.

(i) In general.

(ii) Manner for requesting a waiver or extension.

(iii) Terms and conditions.

(5) Example.

(f) Basis reduction.

(1) In general.

(2) Adjustment in basis of interest in partnership or S corporation.

(g) Other rules.

(1) Anti-abuse.

(2) Reporting requirements.

(i) Notification by CDE to taxpayer.

(A) Allowance of new markets tax credit.

(B) Recapture event.

(ii) CDE reporting requirements to Secretary.

(iii) Manner of claiming new markets tax credit.

(iv) Reporting recapture tax.

(h) Effective date.

(b) *Allowance of credit*—(1) *In general.* For purposes of the general business credit under section 38, a taxpayer holding a qualified equity investment on a credit allowance date which occurs during the taxable year may claim the new markets tax credit determined under section 45D and this section for such taxable year in an amount equal to the applicable percentage of the amount paid to a qualified community development entity (CDE) for such investment at its original issue. *Qualified equity investment* is defined in paragraph (c) of this section. *Credit allowance date* is defined in paragraph (b)(2) of this section. *Applicable percentage* is defined in paragraph (b)(3) of this section. A *CDE* is a qualified community development entity as defined in sec-

tion 45D(c). The amount paid at original issue is determined under paragraph (b)(4) of this section.

(2) *Credit allowance date.* The term *credit allowance date* means, with respect to any qualified equity investment—

(i) The date on which the investment is initially made; and

(ii) Each of the 6 anniversary dates of such date thereafter.

(3) *Applicable percentage.* The *applicable percentage* is 5 percent for the first 3 credit allowance dates and 6 percent for the other 4 credit allowance dates.

(4) *Amount paid at original issue.* The amount paid to the CDE for a qualified equity investment at its original issue consists of all amounts paid by the taxpayer to, or on behalf of, the CDE (including any underwriter's fees) to purchase the investment at its original issue.

(c) *Qualified equity investment*—(1) *In general.* The term *qualified equity investment* means any equity investment (as defined in paragraph (c)(2) of this section) in a CDE if—

(i) The investment is acquired by the taxpayer at its original issue (directly or through an underwriter) solely in exchange for cash;

(ii) Substantially all (as defined in paragraph (c)(5) of this section) of such cash is used by the CDE to make qualified low-income community investments (as defined in paragraph (d)(1) of this section); and

(iii) The investment is designated for purposes of section 45D and this section by the CDE on its books and records using any reasonable method.

(2) *Equity investment.* The term *equity investment* means any stock (other than nonqualified preferred stock as defined in section 351(g)(2)) in an entity that is a corporation for Federal tax purposes and any capital interest in an entity that is a partnership for Federal tax purposes. See §§ 301.7701-1 through 301.7701-3 of this chapter for rules governing when a business entity, such as a business trust or limited liability company, is classified as a corporation or a partnership for Federal tax purposes.

(3) *Equity investments made prior to allocation*—(i) *In general.* Except as provided in paragraph (c)(3)(ii) of this section, an equity investment in an entity is not eligible to be designated as a qualified equity investment if it is made before the entity enters into an allocation agreement with the Secretary. An *allocation agreement* is an agreement between the Secretary and a CDE relating to a new markets tax credit allocation under section 45D(f)(2).

Reg. § 1.45D-1T(c)(3)

(ii) *Exception.* Notwithstanding paragraph (c)(3)(i) of this section, an equity investment in an entity is eligible to be designated as a qualified equity investment under paragraph (c)(1)(iii) of this section if—

(A) The equity investment is made on or after April 20, 2001;

(B) The entity in which the equity investment is made is certified by the Secretary as a CDE under section 45D(c) before January 1, 2003;

(C) The entity in which the equity investment is made receives notification of the credit allocation (with the actual receipt of such credit allocation contingent upon subsequently entering into an allocation agreement) from the Secretary before January 1, 2003; and

(D) The equity investment otherwise satisfies the requirements of section 45D and this section.

(iii) *Initial investment date.* If an equity investment is designated as a qualified equity investment in accordance with paragraph (c)(3)(ii) of this section, the investment is treated as initially made on the effective date of the allocation agreement between the CDE and the Secretary.

(4) *Limitations*—(i) *In general.* The term *qualified equity investment* does not include—

(A) Any equity investment issued by a CDE more than 5 years after the date the CDE enters into an allocation agreement (as defined in paragraph (c)(3)(i) of this section) with the Secretary; and

(B) Any equity investment by a CDE in another CDE, if the CDE making the investment has received an allocation under section 45D(f)(2).

(ii) *Allocation limitation.* The maximum amount of equity investments issued by a CDE that may be designated under paragraph (c)(1)(iii) of this section by the CDE may not exceed the portion of the limitation amount allocated to the CDE by the Secretary under section 45D(f)(2).

(5) *Substantially all*—(i) *In general.* Except as provided in paragraph (c)(5)(v) of this section, the term *substantially all* means at least 85 percent. The substantially-all requirement must be satisfied for each annual period in the 7-year credit period using either the direct-tracing calculation under paragraph (c)(5)(ii) of this section, or the safe harbor calculation under paragraph (c)(5)(iii) of this section. The substantially-all requirement is treated as satisfied for an annual period if either the direct-tracing calculation

under paragraph (c)(5)(ii) of this section, or the safe harbor calculation under paragraph (c)(5)(iii) of this section, is performed every six months and the average of the two calculations for the annual period is at least 85 percent. For purposes of this paragraph (c)(5)(i), the *7-year credit period* means the period of 7 years beginning on the date the qualified equity investment is initially made. See paragraph (c)(6) of this section for circumstances in which a CDE may treat more than one equity investment as a single qualified equity investment.

(ii) *Direct-tracing calculation.* The substantially-all requirement is satisfied if at least 85 percent of the taxpayer's investment is directly traceable to qualified low-income community investments as defined in paragraph (d)(1) of this section. The direct-tracing calculation is a fraction the numerator of which is the CDE's aggregate cost basis determined under section 1012 in all of the qualified low-income community investments that are directly traceable to the taxpayer's cash investment, and the denominator of which is the amount of the taxpayer's cash investment under paragraph (b)(4) of this section. For purposes of this paragraph (c)(5)(ii), cost basis includes the cost basis of any qualified low-income community investment that becomes worthless. See paragraph (d)(2) of this section for the treatment of amounts received by a CDE in payment of, or for, capital, equity or principal with respect to a qualified low-income community investment.

(iii) *Safe harbor calculation.* The substantially-all requirement is satisfied if at least 85 percent of the aggregate gross assets of the CDE are invested in qualified low-income community investments as defined in paragraph (d)(1) of this section. The safe harbor calculation is a fraction the numerator of which is the CDE's aggregate cost basis determined under section 1012 in all of its qualified low-income community investments, and the denominator of which is the CDE's aggregate cost basis determined under section 1012 in all of its assets. For purposes of this paragraph (c)(5)(iii), cost basis includes the cost basis of any qualified low-income community investment that becomes worthless. See paragraph (d)(2) of this section for the treatment of amounts received by a CDE in payment of, or for, capital, equity or principal with respect to a qualified low-income community investment.

(iv) *Time limit for making investments.* The taxpayer's cash investment received by a CDE is treated as invested in a qualified low-income community investment as defined in paragraph (d)(1) of this section only to the extent that the cash is so invested no later than 12 months

Reg. § 1.45D-1T(c)(4)

after the date the cash is paid by the taxpayer (directly or through an underwriter) to the CDE.

(v) *Reduced substantially-all percentage.* For purposes of the substantially-all requirement (including the direct-tracing calculation under paragraph (c)(5)(ii) of this section and the safe harbor calculation under paragraph (c)(5)(iii) of this section), 85 percent is reduced to 75 percent for the seventh year of the 7-year credit period (as defined in paragraph (c)(5)(i) of this section).

(6) *Aggregation of equity investments.* A CDE may treat any qualified equity investments issued on the same day as one qualified equity investment. If a CDE aggregates equity investments under this paragraph (c)(6), the rules in this section shall be construed in a manner consistent with that treatment.

(7) *Subsequent purchasers.* A qualified equity investment includes any equity investment that would (but for paragraph (c)(1)(i) of this section) be a qualified equity investment in the hands of the taxpayer if the investment was a qualified equity investment in the hands of a prior holder.

(d) *Qualified low-income community investments*—(1) *In general.* The term *qualified low-income community investment* means any of the following—

(i) *Investment in a qualified active low-income community business.* Any capital or equity investment in, or loan to, any qualified active low-income community business (as defined in paragraph (d)(4) of this section).

(ii) *Purchase of certain loans from CDEs.* The purchase from another CDE (whether or not that CDE has received an allocation from the Secretary under section 45D(f)(2)) of any loan made by such entity that is a qualified low-income community investment. A loan purchased from another CDE is a qualified low-income community investment if it qualifies as such either—

(A) At the time the selling CDE made the loan; or

(B) At the time the loan is purchased from the selling CDE.

(iii) *Financial counseling and other services.* Financial counseling and other services (as defined in paragraph (d)(7) of this section) provided to any qualified active low-income community business, or to any residents of a low-income community (as defined in section 45D(e)).

(iv) *Investments in other CDEs.* Any equity investment in, or loan to, any CDE, but only to the extent that the CDE in which the equity investment or loan is made uses the proceeds of the investment or loan in a manner—

(A) That is described in paragraphs (d)(1)(i) or (iii) of this section; and

(B) That would constitute a qualified low-income community investment if it were made directly by the CDE making such equity investment or loan.

(2) *Payments of, or for, capital, equity or principal*—(i) *In general.* Except as otherwise provided in this paragraph (d)(2), amounts received by a CDE in payment of, or for, capital, equity or principal with respect to a qualified low-income community investment must be reinvested by the CDE in a qualified low-income community investment no later than 12 months from the date of receipt to be treated as continuously invested in a qualified low-income community investment. If the amounts received by the CDE are equal to or greater than the cost basis of the original qualified low-income community investment (or applicable portion thereof), and the CDE reinvests, in accordance with this paragraph (d)(2)(i), an amount at least equal to such original cost basis, then an amount equal to such original cost basis will be treated as continuously invested in a qualified low-income community investment. In addition, if the amounts received by the CDE are equal to or greater than the cost basis of the original qualified low-income community investment (or applicable portion thereof), and the CDE reinvests, in accordance with this paragraph (d)(2)(i), an amount less than such original cost basis, then only the amount so reinvested will be treated as continuously invested in a qualified low-income community investment. If the amounts received by the CDE are less than the cost basis of the original qualified low-income community investment (or applicable portion thereof), and the CDE reinvests an amount in accordance with this paragraph (d)(2)(i), then the amount treated as continuously invested in a qualified low-income community investment will equal the excess (if any) of such original cost basis over the amounts received by the CDE that are not so reinvested. Amounts received by a CDE in payment of, or for, capital, equity or principal with respect to a qualified low-income community investment during the seventh year of the 7-year credit period (as defined in paragraph (c)(5)(i) of this section) do not have to be reinvested by the CDE in a qualified low-income community investment in order to be treated as continuously invested in a qualified low-income community investment.

(ii) *Subsequent reinvestments.* In applying paragraph (d)(2)(i) of this section to subsequent reinvestments, the original cost basis is reduced by the amount (if any) by which the original cost

Reg. § 1.45D-1T(d)(2)

basis exceeds the amount determined to be continuously invested in a qualified low-income community investment.

(iii) *Special rule for loans.* Periodic amounts received during a calendar year as repayment of principal on a loan that is a qualified low-income community investment are treated as continuously invested in a qualified low-income community investment if the amounts are reinvested in another qualified low-income community investment by the end of the following calendar year.

(iv) *Example.* The application of paragraphs (d)(2)(i) and (ii) of this section is illustrated by the following example:

Example. On April 1, 2003, A, B, and C each pay $100,000 to acquire a capital interest in X, a partnership. X is a CDE that has received a new markets tax credit allocation from the Secretary. X treats the 3 partnership interests as one qualified equity investment under paragraph (c)(6) of this section. In August 2003, X uses the $300,000 to make a qualified low-income community investment under paragraph (d)(1) of this section. In August 2005, the qualified low-income community investment is redeemed for $250,000. In February 2006, X reinvests $230,000 of the $250,000 in a second qualified low-income community investment and uses the remaining $20,000 for operating expenses. Under paragraph (d)(2)(i) of this section, $280,000 of the proceeds of the qualified equity investment is treated as continuously invested in a qualified low-income community investment. In December 2008, X sells the second qualified low-income community investment and receives $400,000. In March 2009, X reinvests $320,000 of the $400,000 in a third qualified low-income community investment. Under paragraphs (d)(2)(i) and (ii) of this section, $280,000 of the proceeds of the qualified equity investment is treated as continuously invested in a qualified low-income community investment ($40,000 is treated as invested in another qualified low-income community investment in March 2009).

(3) *Special rule for reserves.* Reserves (not in excess of 5 percent of the taxpayer's cash investment under paragraph (b)(4) of this section) maintained by the CDE for loan losses or for additional investments in existing qualified low-income community investments are treated as invested in a qualified low-income community investment under paragraph (d)(1) of this section.

(4) *Qualified active low-income community business—(i) In general.* The term *qualified active low-income community business* means, with respect to any taxable year, a corporation (including a nonprofit corporation) or a partnership, if the requirements in paragraphs (d)(4)(i)(A), (B), (C), (D), and (E) of this section are met.

(A) *Gross-income requirement.* At least 50 percent of the total gross income of such entity is derived from the active conduct of a qualified business (as defined in paragraph (d)(5) of this section) within any low-income community (as defined in section 45D(e)). An entity is deemed to satisfy this paragraph (d)(4)(i)(A) if the entity meets the requirements of either paragraph (d)(4)(i)(B) or (C) of this section, if "50 percent" is applied instead of *40 percent.* In addition, an entity may satisfy this paragraph (d)(4)(i)(A) based on all the facts and circumstances.

(B) *Use of tangible property.* At least 40 percent of the use of the tangible property of such entity (whether owned or leased) is within any low-income community. This percentage is determined based on a fraction the numerator of which is the average value of the tangible property owned or leased by the entity and used by the entity during the taxable year in a low-income community and the denominator of which is the average value of the tangible property owned or leased by the entity and used by the entity during the taxable year. Property owned by the entity is valued at its cost basis as determined under section 1012. Property leased by the entity is valued at a reasonable amount established by the entity.

(C) *Services performed.* At least 40 percent of the services performed for such entity by its employees are performed in a low-income community. This percentage is determined based on a fraction the numerator of which is the total amount paid by the entity for employee services performed in a low-income community during the taxable year and the denominator of which is the total amount paid by the entity for employee services during the taxable year.

(D) *Collectibles.* Less than 5 percent of the average of the aggregate unadjusted bases of the property of such entity is attributable to collectibles (as defined in section 408(m)(2)) other than collectibles that are held primarily for sale to customers in the ordinary course of business.

(E) *Nonqualified financial property.* Less than 5 percent of the average of the aggregate unadjusted bases of the property of such entity is attributable to nonqualified financial property (as defined in section 1397C(e)). Because the definition of *nonqualified financial property* in section 1397C(e) includes debt instruments with a term in excess of 18 months, banks, credit unions, and other financial institutions are generally excluded from the definition of a *qualified active low-income community business.*

Reg. § 1.45D-1T(d)(3)

(ii) *Proprietorships.* Any business carried on by an individual as a proprietor is a qualified active low-income community business if the business would meet the requirements of paragraph (d)(4)(i) of this section if the business were incorporated.

(iii) *Portions of business.* A CDE may treat any trade or business as a qualified active low-income community business if the trade or business would meet the requirements of paragraph (d)(4)(i) of this section if the trade or business were separately incorporated.

(5) *Qualified business*—(i) *In general.* Except as otherwise provided in this paragraph (d)(5), the term *qualified business* means any trade or business. There is no requirement that employees of a qualified business be residents of a low-income community.

(ii) *Rental of real property.* The rental to others of real property located in any low-income community (as defined in section 45D(e)) is a *qualified business* if and only if the property is not residential rental property (as defined in section 168(e)(2)(A)) and there are substantial improvements located on the real property.

(iii) *Exclusions*—(A) *Trades or businesses involving intangibles.* The term *qualified business* does not include any trade or business consisting predominantly of the development or holding of intangibles for sale or license.

(B) *Certain other trades or businesses.* The term *qualified business* does not include any trade or business consisting of the operation of any private or commercial golf course, country club, massage parlor, hot tub facility, suntan facility, racetrack or other facility used for gambling, or any store the principal business of which is the sale of alcoholic beverages for consumption off premises.

(C) *Farming.* The term *qualified business* does not include any trade or business the principal activity of which is farming (within the meaning of section 2032A(e)(5)(A) or (B)) if, as of the close of the taxable year of the taxpayer conducting such trade or business, the sum of the aggregate unadjusted bases (or, if greater, the fair market value) of the assets owned by the taxpayer that are used in such a trade or business, and the aggregate value of the assets leased by the taxpayer that are used in such a trade or business, exceeds $500,000. For purposes of this paragraph (d)(5)(iii)(C), two or more trades or businesses will be treated as a single trade or business under rules similar to the rules of section 52(a) and (b).

(6) *Qualifications*—(i) *In general.* Except as provided in paragraph (d)(6)(ii) of this section, an entity is treated as a qualified active low-income community business for the duration of the CDE's investment in the entity if the CDE reasonably expects, at the time the CDE makes the capital or equity investment in, or loan to, the entity, that the entity will satisfy the requirements to be a qualified active low-income community business under paragraph (d)(4)(i) of this section throughout the entire period of the investment or loan.

(ii) *Control*—(A) *In general.* If a CDE controls or obtains control of an entity at any time during the 7-year credit period (as defined in paragraph (c)(5)(i) of this section), the entity will be treated as a qualified active low-income community business only if the entity satisfies the requirements of paragraph (d)(4)(i) of this section throughout the entire period the CDE controls the entity.

(B) *Definition of control.* Generally, control means, with respect to an entity, direct or indirect ownership (based on value) or control (based on voting or management rights) of 33 percent or more of the entity. However, a CDE does not control an entity if an unrelated person possesses greater control over the entity than the CDE.

(7) *Financial counseling and other services.* The term *financial counseling and other services* means advice provided by the CDE relating to the organization or operation of a trade or business.

(e) *Recapture*—(1) *In general.* If, at any time during the 7-year period beginning on the date of the original issue of a qualified equity investment in a CDE, there is a recapture event under paragraph (e)(2) of this section with respect to such investment, then the tax imposed by Chapter 1 of the Internal Revenue Code for the taxable year in which the recapture event occurs is increased by the credit recapture amount under section 45D(g)(2). A recapture event under paragraph (e)(2) of this section requires recapture of credits allowed to the taxpayer who purchased the equity investment from the CDE at its original issue and to all subsequent holders of that investment.

(2) *Recapture event.* There is a recapture event with respect to an equity investment in a CDE if—

(i) The entity ceases to be a CDE;

(ii) The proceeds of the investment cease to be used in a manner that satisfies the substantially-all requirement of paragraph (c)(1)(ii) of this section; or

(iii) The investment is redeemed by the CDE.

(3) *Bankruptcy.* Bankruptcy of a CDE is not a recapture event.

Reg. § 1.45D-1T(e)(3)

(4) *Waiver of requirement or extension of time*—(i) *In general*. The Commissioner may waive a requirement or extend a deadline if such waiver or extension does not materially frustrate the purposes of section 45D and this section.

(ii) *Manner for requesting a waiver or extension*. A CDE that believes it has good cause for a waiver or an extension may request relief from the Commissioner in a ruling request. The request should set forth all the relevant facts and include a detailed explanation describing the event or events relating to the request for a waiver or an extension. For further information on the application procedure for a ruling, see Rev. Proc. 2001-1 (2001-1 I.R.B. 1) (see § 601.601(d)(2) of this chapter).

(iii) *Terms and conditions*. The granting of a waiver or an extension to a CDE under this section may require adjustments of the CDE's requirements under section 45D and this section as may be appropriate.

(5) *Example*. The application of this paragraph (e) is illustrated by the following example:

Example. In 2003, A and B acquire separate qualified equity investments in X, a partnership. X is a CDE that has received a new markets tax credit allocation from the Secretary. X uses the proceeds of A's qualified equity investment to make a qualified low-income community investment in Y, and X uses the proceeds of B's qualified equity investment to make a qualified low-income community investment in Z. Y and Z are not CDEs. X controls both Y and Z within the meaning of paragraph (d)(6)(ii)(B) of this section. In 2003, Y and Z are qualified active low-income community businesses. In 2007, Y, but not Z, is a qualified active low-income community business and X does not satisfy the substantially-all requirement using the safe harbor calculation under paragraph (c)(5)(iii) of this section. A's equity investment satisfies the substantially-all requirement of paragraph (c)(1)(ii) of this section using the direct-tracing calculation of paragraph (c)(5)(ii) of this section because A's equity investment is traceable to Y. However, B's equity investment fails the substantially-all requirement using the direct-tracing calculation because B's equity investment is traceable to Z. Therefore, under paragraph (e)(2)(ii) of this section, there is a recapture event for B's equity investment (but not A's equity investment).

(f) *Basis reduction*—(1) *In general*. A taxpayer's basis in a qualified equity investment is reduced by the amount of any new markets tax credit determined under paragraph (b)(1) of this section with respect to the investment. A basis reduction occurs on each credit allowance date

under paragraph (b)(2) of this section. This paragraph (f) does not apply for purposes of sections 1202, 1400B, and 1400F.

(2) *Adjustment in basis of interest in partnership or S corporation*. The adjusted basis of either a partner's interest in a partnership, or stock in an S corporation, must be appropriately adjusted to take into account adjustments made under paragraph (f)(1) of this section in the basis of a qualified equity investment held by the partnership or S corporation (as the case may be).

(g) *Other rules*—(1) *Anti-abuse*. If a principal purpose of a transaction or a series of transactions is to achieve a result that is inconsistent with the purposes of section 45D and this section, the Commissioner may treat the transaction or series of transactions as causing a recapture event under paragraph (e)(2) of this section.

(2) *Reporting requirements*—(i) *Notification by CDE to taxpayer*—(A) *Allowance of new markets tax credit*. A CDE must provide notice to any taxpayer who acquires a qualified equity investment in the CDE at its original issue that the equity investment is a qualified equity investment entitling the taxpayer to claim the new markets tax credit. The notice must be provided by the CDE to the taxpayer no later than 60 days after the date the taxpayer makes the investment in the CDE. The notice must contain the amount paid to the CDE for the qualified equity investment at its original issue and the taxpayer identification number of the CDE.

(B) *Recapture event*. If, at any time during the 7-year period beginning on the date of the original issue of a qualified equity investment in a CDE, there is a recapture event under paragraph (e)(2) of this section with respect to such investment, the CDE must provide notice to each holder, including all prior holders, of the investment that a recapture event has occurred. The notice must be provided by the CDE no later than 60 days after the date the CDE becomes aware of the recapture event.

(ii) *CDE reporting requirements to Secretary*. Each CDE must comply with such reporting requirements to the Secretary as the Secretary may prescribe.

(iii) *Manner of claiming new markets tax credit*. A taxpayer may claim the new markets tax credit for each applicable taxable year by completing Form 8874, "New Markets Credit," and by filing Form 8874 with the taxpayer's Federal income tax return.

(iv) *Reporting recapture tax*. If there is a recapture event with respect to a taxpayer's equity investment in a CDE, the taxpayer must include the credit recapture amount under section

Reg. § 1.45D-1T(e)(4)

45D(g)(2) on the line for recapture taxes on the taxpayer's Federal income tax return for the taxable year in which the recapture event under paragraph (e)(2) of this section occurs (or on the line for total tax, if there is no such line for recapture taxes) and write *NMCR* (new markets credit recapture) next to the entry space.

(h) *Effective date.* This section applies on or after December 26, 2001. [Temporary Reg. § 1.45D-1T.]

☐ [*T.D.* 8971, 12-21-2001.]

[Reg. § 1.46-1]

§ 1.46-1. Determination of amount.—(a) *Effective dates*—(1) *In general.* This section is effective for taxable years beginning after December 31, 1975. However, transitional rules under paragraph (g) of this section are effective for certain earlier taxable years.

(2) *Acts covered.* This section reflects changes made by the following Acts of Congress:

Act and Section

Tax Reduction Act of 1975, section 301.

Tax Reform Act of 1976, section 802, 1701, 1703.

Revenue Act of 1978, section 311, 312, 315.

Energy Tax Act of 1978, section 301.

Economic Recovery Tax Act of 1981, section 212.

Technical Corrections Act of 1982, section 102(f).

Tax Reform Act of 1986, section 251.

(3) *Prior regulations.* For taxable years beginning before January 1, 1976, see 26 CFR § 1.46-1 (Rev. as of April 1, 1979). Those regulations do not reflect changes made by Pub. L. 89-384, Pub. L. 89-389, and Pub. L. 91-172.

(b) *General rule.* The amount of investment credit (credit) allowed by section 38 for the taxable year is the portion of credit available under section 46(a)(1) that does not exceed the limitation based on tax under section 46(a)(3).

(c) *Credit available.* The credit available for the taxable year is the sum of—

(1) Unused credit carried over from prior taxable years under section 46(b) (carryovers),

(2) Amount of credit determined under section 46(a)(2) for the taxable year (credit earned), and

(3) Unused credit carried back from succeeding taxable years under section 46(b) (carrybacks).

(d) *Credit earned.* The credit earned for the taxable year is the sum of the following percentages of qualified investment (as determined under section 46(c) and (d))—

(1) The regular percentage (as determined under section 46),

(2) For energy property, the energy percentage (as determined under section 46), and

(3) For the portion of the basis of a qualified rehabilitated building (as defined in § 1.48-12(b)) that is attributable to qualified rehabilitation expenditures (as defined in § 1.48-12(c)), the rehabilitation percentage (as determined under section 46(b)(4)).

(e) *Designation of credits.* The credit available for the taxable year is designated as follows:

(1) The credit attributable to the regular percentage is the "regular credit".

(2) The credit attributable to the ESOP percentage is the "ESOP credit".

(3) The credit attributable to the energy percentage for energy property other than solar or wind is the "nonrefundable energy credit".

(4) The credit attributable to the energy percentage for solar or wind energy property is the "refundable energy credit".

(5) The credit attributable to the rehabilitation percentage for qualified rehabilitation expenditures is the rehabilitation investment credit.

(f) *Special rules for certain energy property.* Energy property is defined in section 48(l). Under section 46(a)(2)(D), energy property that is section 38 property solely by reason of section 48(l)(1) qualifies only for the energy credit. Other energy property qualifies for both the regular credit (and, if applicable, the ESOP credit) and the energy credit. For limitation on the energy percentage for property financed by industrial development bonds, see section 48(l)(11).

(g) *Transitional rule for regular and ESOP credit* —(1) *In general.* Although section 46(a)(2) was amended by section 301(a)(1) of the Energy Tax Act of 1977 to eliminate the transitional rules under section 46(a)(2)(D), those rules still apply in certain instances. Section 46(a)(2)(D) was added by section 301(a) of the Tax Reduction Act of 1975 and amended by section 802(a) of the Tax Reform Act of 1976.

(2) *Regular credit.* Under section 46(a)(2)(D), the regular credit is 10 percent and applies for the following property: (i) Property to which section 46(d) does not apply, the construction, reconstruction, or erection of which is completed by the taxpayer after January 21, 1975, but only to the extent of basis attributable to construction, reconstruction, or erection after that date.

Reg. § 1.46-1(g)(2)

(ii) Property to which section 46(d) does not apply, acquired by the taxpayer after January 21, 1975.

(iii) Qualified progress expenditures (as defined in section 46(d)) made after January 21, 1975.

(3) *ESOP credit.* See section 48(m) for transitional rules limiting the period for which the ESOP percentage under section 46(a)(2)(E) applies. For prior statutes, see section 46(a)(2)(B) and (D), as added by section 301 of the Tax Reduction Act of 1975 and amended by section 802 of the Tax Reform Act of 1976.

(4) *Cross reference.* (i) The principles of § 1.48-2(b) and (c) apply in determining the portion of basis attributable to construction, reconstruction, or erection after January 21, 1975, and in determining the time when property is acquired.

(ii) Section 311 of the Revenue Act of 1978 made the 10 percent regular credit permanent.

(5) *Seven percent credit.* To the extent that, under paragraph (g)(1) of this section, the 10 percent does not apply, the regular credit, in general, is 7 percent. For a special limitation on qualified investment for public utility property (other than energy property), see section 46(c)(3)(A).

(6) *Qualified progress expenditures.* For progress expenditure property that is constructed, reconstructed, or erected by the taxpayer within the meaning of § 1.48-2(b), the ten-percent credit applies in the year the property is placed in service to the portion of the qualified investment that remains after reduction for qualified progress expenditures under section 46(c)(4), but only to the extent that the remaining qualified investment is attributable to construction, reconstruction, or erection after January 21, 1975. For progress expenditure property that is acquired by the taxpayer (within the meaning of § 1.48-2(b)) after January 21, 1975, and placed in service after that date, the ten-percent credit applies in the year the property is placed in service to the entire portion of qualified investment that remains after reduction for qualified progress expenditures.

(h) *Tax liability limitation*—(1) *In general.* Section 46(a)(3) provides a tax liability limitation on the amount of credit allowed by section 38 (other than the refundable energy credit) for any taxable

year. See section 46(a)(10)(C)(i). Tax liability is defined in paragraph (j) of this section.

The excess of available credit over the applicable tax liability limitation for the year is an unused credit which may be carried forward or carried back under section 46(b).

(2) *Regular and ESOP tax liability limitation.* In general, the tax liability limitation for the regular and ESOP credits is the portion of tax liability that does not exceed $25,000 plus a percentage of the excess, as determined under section 46(a)(3)(B).

(3) *Nonrefundable energy credit tax liability limitation.* (i) For nonrefundable energy credit carrybacks to a taxable year ending before October 1, 1978, the tax liability limitation is the portion of tax liability that does not exceed $25,000 plus a percentage of the excess, as determined under section 46(a)(3)(B).

(ii) For a taxable year ending after September 30, 1978, the tax liability limitation for available nonrefundable energy credit is 100 percent of the year's tax liability.

(4) *Alternative limitations.* Alternative limitations apply for certain utilities, railroads, and airlines in determining the regular tax liability limitation and, for nonrefundable energy credit carrybacks to taxable years ending before October 1, 1978, the nonrefundable energy credit tax liability limitation. These alternative limitations do not apply in determining the energy tax liability limitation for a taxable year ending after October 1, 1978. The provisions listed below set forth the alternative limitations:

Code section, type, and years applicable

46(a)(6),[1] Utilities, Taxable years ending in 1975-1978.

46(a)(7),[2] Utilities, Taxable year ending in 1979.

46(a)(8), Railroads and Airlines, Taxable year ending in 1979 or 1980.

46(a)(8),[3] Railroads, Taxable years ending in 1977 or 1978.

46(a)(9),[3] Airlines, Taxable years ending in 1977 or 1978.

(i) [Reserved]

(j) *Tax liability*—(1) *In general.* "Tax liability" for purposes of the regular and ESOP credit and carrybacks of nonrefundable energy credit to a taxable year ending before October 1, 1978,

---

[1] Section 46(a)(6) was added by section 301(b)(2) of the Tax Reduction Act of 1975 and redesignated as section 46(a)(7) by section 302(a)(1) of the Tax Reform Act of 1976.

[2] Section 46(a)(7) was amended by section 312(b)(1) of the Revenue Act of 1978.

[3] These provisions were repealed by section 312(b)(2) of the Revenue Act of 1978.

Reg. § 1.46-1(g)(3)

means the liability for tax as defined in section 46(a)(4). For ordering of regular, ESOP, and nonrefundable energy credits, see paragraph (m) of this section. In addition to taxes excluded under section 46(a)(4), tax liability does not include tax resulting from recapture of credit under section 47 and the alternative minimum tax imposed by section 55. See sections 47(c) and 55(c)(1).

(2) *Certain nonrefundable energy credit.* For a taxable year ending after September 30, 1978, "tax liability" for purposes of the nonrefundable energy credit is liability for tax, as defined in section 46(a)(4) and paragraph (j)(1) of this section, reduced by the regular and ESOP credit allowed for the taxable year. Thus, carrybacks of regular or ESOP credit to a taxable year may displace nonrefundable energy carryovers or credit earned taken into account in that year. However, carrybacks of regular, ESOP, or nonrefundable energy credit do not affect refundable energy credit which is treated as an overpayment of tax under section 6401(b). See paragraph (k) of this section.

(k) *Special rule for refundable energy credit.* The amount of the refundable energy credit is determined under the rules of section 46 (other than section 46(a)(3)). However, to permit the refund, the refundable energy credit for purposes of the Internal Revenue Code (other than section 38, part IVB, and chapter 63 of the Code) is treated as allowed by section 39 and not by section 38. The refundable credit is not applied against tax liability for purposes of determining the tax liability limitation for other investment credits. Rather, it is treated as an overpayment of tax under section 6401(b).

Regular carryovers	$ 5,000
Regular credit earned	10,000
Regular carrybacks	15,000
Credit available	$30,000

(b) M's "tax liability" for 1979 is $30,000. M's tax liability limitation for 1979 for the regular credit is $28,000, consisting of $25,000 plus 60 percent of the $5,000 of the "tax liability" in excess of $25,000.

(c) The regular carryovers and credit earned are allowed in full. However, only $13,000 of the regular carryback is allowed for 1979. The remaining $2,000 must be carried to the next year to which it may be carried under section 46(b).

Example (2). (a) For its taxable year ending December 31, 1980, corporation N has $30,000 regular credit earned and $9,000 nonrefundable energy credit earned. N has no carryovers to 1980 and no "tax liability" for pre-1980 years.

(l) *FIFO rule.* If the credit available for a taxable year is not allowed in full because of the tax liability limitation, special rules determine the order in which credits are applied. Under the first-in-first-out rule of section 46(a)(1) (FIFO), carryovers are applied against the tax liability limitation first. To the extent the tax liability limitation exceeds carryovers, credit earned, and carrybacks are then applied.

(m) *Special ordering rule—*(1) *In general.* Under section 46(a)(10)(A), the FIFO rule applies separately—

(i) First, with respect to regular and ESOP credits, and

(ii) Second, with respect to nonrefundable energy credit.

(2) *Regular and ESOP credit.* Under § 1.46-8(c)(9)(ii), regular and ESOP credits available are applied in the following order:

(i) Regular carryovers;

(ii) ESOP carryovers;

(iii) Regular credit earned;

(iv) ESOP credit earned;

(v) Regular carrybacks; and

(vi) ESOP carrybacks.

(3) *Example.* For an example of the order of application of regular and ESOP credits, see § 1.46-8(c)(9)(iii).

(n) *Examples.* The following examples illustrate paragraphs (a) through (m) of this section.

Example (1). (a) Corporation M's regular credit available for its taxable year ending December 31, 1979 is as follows:

(b) N's "tax liability" for 1980 for the regular credit is $35,000. N's tax liability limitation for 1980 for the regular credit is $32,000, consisting of $25,000 plus 70 percent of the $10,000 of "tax liability" in excess of $25,000.

(c) The entire regular credit is allowed in 1980.

(d) N's "tax liability" for 1980 for the nonrefundable energy credit is $5,000, consisting of $35,000 less $30,000 regular credit allowed for 1980. N's tax liability limitation for 1980 for the nonrefundable energy credit is 100 percent of $5,000.

(e) $5,000 of the nonrefundable energy credit is allowed for 1980. The remaining $4,000 energy

Reg. § 1.46-1(n)

credit is an unused nonrefundable energy credit which must be carried to the next year to which it may be carried under section 46(b).

Example (3). (a) Assume the same facts as in example (2) except that in its taxable year ended December 31, 1981, N earns a regular credit of which it may carry back $2,000 to 1980.

(b) The $30,000 regular credit earned and $2,000 of the regular carryback is allowed for 1980. N's "tax liability" for 1980 for the nonrefundable energy credit is reduced to $3,000, consisting of $35,000 less $32,000 regular credit allowed for 1980. The nonrefundable energy credit allowed for 1980 is reduced to $3,000. The remaining $6,000 is an unused nonrefundable energy credit which must be carried to the next year to which it may be carried under section 46(b).

Example (4). (a) For its taxable year ending December 31, 1980, corporation P's regular credit earned is $20,000. P also has a $9,000 refundable energy credit for 1980. There are no carryovers or carrybacks to 1980.

(b) P's "tax liability" for 1980 for the regular credit is $25,000 which is also the tax liability limitation for the regular credit.

(c) The entire $20,000 regular credit is allowed for 1980. The entire $9,000 refundable energy credit is treated as an overpayment of tax under section 6401(b), even though "tax liability" remains.

Example (5). Assume the same facts as in example (4), except that in the following year P earns a regular credit, $5,000 of which it may carry back to 1980. The $5,000 carryback is allowed in full in 1980.

Example (6). (i) Corporation X, a calendar year taxpayer, constructs a ship on which it begins construction on January 1, 1973, and which, when placed in service on December 31, 1980, has a basis of $450,000. Of that amount $100,000 is attributable to construction before January 22, 1975. X makes an election under section 46(d) (qualified progress expenditures) for taxable years after 1975.

(ii) For 1976, 1977, 1978, and 1979, qualified progress expenditures total $200,000. The ten-percent credit applies to those expenditures.

(iii) For 1980, qualified investment for the ship is $450,000. Under section 46(c)(4), X must reduce this amount by $200,000, the amount of qualified progress expenditures taken into account. The ten-percent credit applies to the portion of the remaining qualified investment attributable to construction after January 21, 1975 ($150,000). The seven-percent credit applies to the portion of qualified investment attributable

to construction before January 22, 1975 ($100,000).

Example (7). (i) Corporation Y agrees to build a ship for Corporation X, which uses the calendar year. In 1973, Y begins construction of the ship which X acquires and places in service on December 31, 1980. X makes an election under section 46(d) for taxable years after 1974. The contract price is $400,000.

(ii) For 1975, 1976, 1977, 1978, and 1979, qualified progress expenditures total $250,000. The ten-percent credit applies to those expenditures.

(iii) For 1980, qualified investment for the ship is $400,000, which is the contract price. X must reduce qualified investment by $250,000, the amount of qualified progress expenditures. The ten-percent credit applies to the $150,000 of qualified investment that remains after reduction for qualified progress expenditures.

(o) *Married individuals.* If a separate return is filed by a husband or wife, the tax liability limitation is computed by substituting a $12,500 amount for the $25,000 amount that applies under section 46(a)(3). However, this reduction of the $25,000 amount to $12,500 applies only if the taxpayer's spouse is entitled to a credit under section 38 for the taxable year of such spouse which ends with, or within, the taxpayer's taxable year. The taxpayer's spouse is entitled to a credit under section 38 either because of investment made in qualified property for such taxable year of the spouse (whether directly made by such spouse or whether apportioned to such spouse, for example, from an electing small business corporation, as defined in section 1371(b)), or because of an investment credit carryback or carryover to such taxable year. The determination of whether an individual is married shall be made under the principles of section 143 and the regulations thereunder.

(p) *Apportionment of $25,000 amount among component members of a controlled group*—(1) *In general.* In determining the tax liability limitation under section 46(a)(3) for corporations that are component members of a controlled group on a December 31, only one $25,000 amount is available to those component members for their taxable years that include that December 31. See subparagraph (2) of this paragraph for apportionment of such amount among such component members. See subparagraph (3) of this paragraph for definition of "component member".

(2) *Manner of apportionment.* (i) In the case of corporations which are component members of a controlled group on a particular December 31, the $25,000 amount may be apportioned among such members for their taxable years that include

Reg. § 1.46-1(o)

such December 31 in any manner the component members may select, provided that each such member less than 100 percent of whose stock is owned, in the aggregate, by the other component members of the group on such December 31 consents to an apportionment plan. The consent of a component member to an apportionment plan with respect to a particular December 31 shall be made by means of a statement signed by a person duly authorized to act on behalf of the consenting member, stating that such member consents to the apportionment plan with respect to such December 31. The statement shall set forth the name, address, employer identification number, and taxable year of each component member of the group on such December 31, the amount apportioned to each such member under the plan, and the location of the Service Center where the statement is to be filed. The consent of more than one component member may be incorporated in a single statement. The statement shall be timely filed with the Service Center where the component member having the taxable year first ending on or after such December 31 files its return for such taxable year and shall be irrevocable after such filing. If two or more component members have the same such taxable year, a statement of consent may be filed by any one of such members. Such statement shall be considered as timely filed if filed on or before the due date (including any extensions of time) of such member's income tax return which includes such December 31. Each component member of the group on such December 31 shall keep as a part of its records a copy of the statement containing all the required consents.

(ii) An apportionment plan adopted by a controlled group with respect to a particular December 31 shall be valid only for the taxable year of each member of the group which includes such December 31. Thus, a controlled group must file a separate consent to an apportionment plan with respect to each taxable year which includes a December 31 as to which an apportionment plan is desired.

(iii) If the apportionment plan is not timely filed, the $25,000 amount specified in section 46(a)(3) shall be reduced for each component member of the controlled group, for its taxable year which includes a December 31, to an amount equal to $25,000 divided by the number of component members of such group on such December 31.

(iv) If a component member of the controlled group makes its income tax return on the basis of a 52-53 week taxable year, the principles of section 441(f)(2)(A)(ii) and § 1.441-2 apply in determining the last day of such taxable year.

(3) *Definitions of controlled group of corporations and component member of controlled group.* For the purpose of this paragraph, the terms "controlled group of corporations" and "component member" of a controlled group of corporations shall have the same meaning assigned to those terms in section 1563(a) and (b). For purposes of applying § 1.1563-1(b)(2)(ii)(c), an electing small business corporation shall be treated as an excluded member whether or not it is subject to the tax imposed by section 1378.

(4) *Members of a controlled group filing a consolidated return.* If some component members of a controlled group join in filing a consolidated return pursuant to § 1.1502-3(a)(3), and other component members do not join, then, unless a consent is timely filed apportioning the $25,000 amount among the group filing the consolidated return and the other component members of the controlled group, each component member of the controlled group (including each component member which joins in filing the consolidated return) shall be treated as a separate corporation for purposes of equally apportioning the $25,000 amount under subparagraph (2)(iii) of this paragraph. In that case, the tax liability limitation for the group filing the consolidated return is computed by substituting for the $25,000 amount under section 46(a)(3) the total amount apportioned to each component member that joins in filing the consolidated return. If the affiliated group filing the consolidated return and the other component members of the controlled group adopt an apportionment plan, the affiliated group shall be treated as a single member for the purpose of applying subparagraph (2)(i) of this paragraph. Thus, for example, only one consent executed by the common parent to the apportionment plan is required for the group filing the consolidated return. If any component member of the controlled group which joins in the filing of the consolidated return is an organization to which section 593 applies or a cooperative organization described in section 1381(a), see paragraph (a)(3)(ii) of § 1.1502-3.

(5) *Examples.* The provisions of this paragraph may be illustrated by the following examples:

Example (1). At all times during 1976 Smith, an individual, owns all the stock of corporations X, Y, and Z. Corporation X files an income tax return on a calendar year basis. Corporation Y files an income tax return on the basis of a fiscal year ending June 30. Corporation Z files an income tax return on the basis of a fiscal year

Reg. § 1.46-1(p)(5)

ending September 30. On December 31, 1976, X, Y and Z are component members of the same controlled group. X, Y, and Z all consent to an apportionment plan in which the $25,000 amount is apportioned entirely to Y for its taxable year ending June 30, 1977 (Y's taxable year which includes December 31, 1976). Such consent is timely filed. For purposes of computing the credit under section 38, Y's tax liability limitation for its taxable year ending June 30, 1977, is so much of Y's tax liability as does not exceed $25,000, plus 50 percent of Y's tax liability in excess of $25,000. X's and Z's limitations for their taxable years ending December 31, 1976, and September 30, 1977, respectively, are equal to 50 percent of X's tax liability and 50 percent of Z's tax liability. On the other hand, if an apportionment plan is not timely filed, X's limitation would be so much of X's tax liability as does not exceed $8,333.33, plus 50 percent of X's liability in excess of $8,333.33, and Y's and Z's limitations would be computed similarly.

Example (2). At all times during 1976, Jones, an individual, owns all the outstanding stock of corporations P, Q, and R. Corporations Q and R both file returns for taxable years ending December 31, 1970. P files a consolidated return as a common parent for its fiscal year ending June 30, 1977, with its two wholly-owned subsidiaries N and O. On December 31, 1976, N, O, P, Q, and R are component members of the same controlled group. No consent to an apportionment plan is filed. Therefore, each member is apportioned $5,000 of the $25,000 amount ($25,000 divided equally among the five members). The tax liability limitation for the group filing the consolidated return (P, N, and O) for the year ending June 30, 1977 (the consolidated taxable year within which December 31, 1976, falls) is computed by using $15,000 instead of the $25,000 amount. The $15,000 is arrived at by adding together the $5,000 amounts apportioned to P, N, and O.

(q) *Rehabilitation percentage*—(1) *General rule*—(i) *In general.* Due to amendments made by the Tax Reform Act of 1986, different rules apply depending on when the property attributable to the qualified rehabilitated expenditures (as defined in § 1.48-12(c)) is placed in service. Paragraph (q)(1)(ii) of this section contains the general rule relating to property placed in service after December 31, 1986. Paragraph (q)(1)(iii) of this section contains rules relating to property placed in service before January 1, 1987. Paragraph (q)(1)(iv) of this section contains rules relating to property placed in service after December 31, 1986, that qualifies for a transition rule.

(ii) *Property placed in service after December 31, 1986.* Except as otherwise provided in paragraph (q)(1)(iv) of this section, in the case of section 38 property described in section 48(a)(1)(E) placed in service after December 31, 1986, the term "rehabilitation percentage" means—

(A) 10 percent in the case of qualified rehabilitation expenditures with respect to a qualified rehabilitated building other than a certified historic structure, and

(B) 20 percent in the case of qualified rehabilitation expenditures with respect to a certified historic structure.

(iii) *Property placed in service before January 1, 1987.* For qualified rehabilitation expenditures (as defined in § 1.48-12(c)) with respect to property placed in service before January 1, 1987, section 46(b)(4)(A) as in effect prior to the enactment of the Tax Reform Act of 1986 provided for a three-tier rehabilitation percentage. The applicable rehabilitation percentage for such expenditures depends on whether the qualified rehabilitated building is a "30-year building," a "40-year building," or a certified historic structure (as defined in section 48(g)(3) and § 1.48-12(d)(1)). The rehabilitation percentage for such qualified rehabilitation expenditures incurred with respect to a qualified rehabilitated building is 15 percent to the extent that the building is a 30-year building (*i.e.*, at least 30 years, but less than 40 years, has elapsed between the date the physical work on the rehabilitation began and the date the building was first placed in service), 20 percent to the extent that the building is a 40-year building (*i.e.*, at least 40 years has so elapsed), and 25 percent for certified historic structures, regardless of age. See paragraph (q)(2)(ii) of this section for rules concerning buildings to which additions have been added.

(iv) *Property placed in service after December 31, 1986, that qualifies under the transition rules.* In the case of section 38 property described in section 48(a)(1)(E) placed in service after December 31, 1986, and to which the amendments made by section 251 of the Tax Reform Act of 1986 do not apply because the transition rules in section 251(d) of that Act and § 1.48-12(a)(2)(iv)(B) or (C) apply, the rehabilitation percentage for a "30-year building" (within the meaning of paragraph (q)(1)(iii) of this section) shall be 10 percent, the rehabilitation percentage for a "40-year building" (within the meaning of paragraph (q)(1)(iii) of this section) shall be 13 percent, and the rehabilitation percentage for a certified historic structure shall be 25 percent.

Reg. § 1.46-1(q)(1)

(2) *Special rules*—(i) *Moved buildings.* With respect to paragraph (q)(1)(ii) of this section, § 1.48-12(b)(5) provides that a building (other than a certified historic structure) is not a qualified rehabilitated building unless it has been at the location where it is being rehabilitated since January 1, 1936. In addition, for purposes of paragraph (q)(1)(iii) and (iv) of this section, a building is not a "30-year building" unless it has been at the location where it is being rehabilitated for the thirty-year period immediately preceding the beginning of the rehabilitation process, and is not a "40-year building" unless it has been at the location where it is being rehabilitated for the forty-year period immediately preceding the beginning of the rehabilitation process.

(ii) *Building to which additions have been added*—(A) *Property placed in service after December 31, 1986.* For purposes of paragraph (q)(1)(ii) of this section, if part of a building meets the definition of a qualified rehabilitated building, and part of the building does not meet the definition of a qualified rehabilitated building because such part is an addition that was placed in service after December 31, 1935, the qualified rehabilitation expenditures made to the building must be allocated to the pre-1936 portion of the building and the post-1935 portion of the building using the principles in § 1.48-12(c)(10)(ii). Qualified rehabilitation expenditures attributable to the post-1935 addition shall not qualify for the 10 percent rehabilitation percentage.

(B) *Property placed in service before January 1, 1987, and property qualifying for a transitional rule.* For purposes of paragraph (q)(1)(iii) and (iv) of this section, if part of a building meets the definition of a "40-year building" and part of the building is an addition that was placed in service less than forty years before physical work on the rehabilitation began but more than thirty years before such date, then the qualified rehabilitation expenditures made to the building shall be allocated between the forty year old portion of the building and the thirty year old portion of the building, and a 20 percent rehabilitation percentage shall be applied to the forty year old portion of the building and a 15 percent rehabilitation percentage shall be applied to the thirty year old portion. This allocation shall be made using the principles in § 1.48-12(c)(10)(ii). If an allocation cannot be made between the expenditures to the forty year old portion of the building and the thirty year old portion of the building, then the building will be considered to be a 30-year building. Furthermore, for purposes of this paragraph (q), a building (other than a certified historic structure) is not a qualified rehabilitated building to the extent of that portion of the building that is less than 30 years old. If

rehabilitation expenditures are incurred with respect to an addition to a qualified rehabilitated building, but the addition is not considered to be part of the qualified rehabilitated building because the addition does not meet the age requirement in section 48(g)(1)(B) (as in effect prior to its amendment by the Tax Reform Act of 1986) and § 1.48-12(b)(4)(i)(B), then no rehabilitation percentage will be applied to the expenditures attributable to the rehabilitation of the addition. Thus, for purposes of paragraph (q)(1)(iii) and (iv) of this section, it may be necessary to allocate rehabilitation expenditures incurred with respect to a building between the original portion of the building and the addition.

(iii) *Mixed-use buildings.* If qualified rehabilitation expenditures are incurred for property that is excluded from section 38 property described in section 48(a)(1)(E) (because, for example, they are made with respect to a portion of the building used for lodging within the meaning of section 48(a)(3) and § 1.48-1(h)), an allocation of the expenditures must be made between the expenditures that result in an addition to basis that is section 38 property and the expenditures that result in an addition to basis that is excluded from the definition of section 38 property since the rehabilitation percentage is applicable only to section 38 property. These allocations should be made using the principles contained in § 1.48-12(c)(10)(ii).

(3) *Regular and energy percentages not to apply.* The regular percentage and the energy percentage shall not apply to that portion of the basis of any building that is attributable to qualified rehabilitation expenditures (as defined in § 1.48-12(c)).

(4) *Effective date.* The rehabilitation percentage is applicable only to qualified rehabilitation expenditures (as defined in § 1.48-12(c)). For rules relating to applicability of the regular percentage to qualified rehabilitation expenditures (as defined in § 1.48-11(c)), see § 1.48-11. [Reg. § 1.46-1.]

☐ [*T.D.* 6731, 5-7-64. *Amended by T.D.* 6931, 10-9-67; *T.D.* 6958, 6-20-68; *T.D.* 7181, 4-24-72; *T.D.* 7203, 8-24-72; *T.D.* 7564, 9-11-78; *T.D.* 7636, 8-9-79; *T.D.* 7751, 12-30-80; *T.D.* 8183, 3-1-88; *T.D.* 8233, 10-7-88 *and T.D.* 8996, 5-16-2002.]

[Reg. § 1.46-2]

§ 1.46-2. Carryback and carryover of unused credit.—(a) *Effective date.* This section is effective for taxable years beginning after December 31, 1975. For taxable years beginning before January 1, 1976, see 26 CFR 1.46-2 (Rev. as of April 1, 1979).

(b) *In general.* Under section 46(b)(1), unused credit may be carried back and carried over. Carrybacks and carryovers of unused credit are taken into account in determining the amount of credit available and the credit allowed for the taxable years to which they may be carried. In general, the application of the rules of this section to regular and ESOP credits are separate from their application to nonrefundable energy credits. For example, the limitations on carrybacks and carryovers of unused nonrefundable energy credit under section 46(b)(2) and (3), respectively, differ in amount from the limitations on the regular and ESOP credits because the tax liability limitations for those credits differ. See § 1.46-1(h). For a further example, see the special ordering rule in § 1.46-1(m). Section 46(b) does not apply to the refundable energy credit.

(c) *Unused credit.* If carryovers and credit earned (as defined in § 1.46-1(c)(1)) exceed the applicable tax liability limitation, the excess attributable to credit earned is an unused credit. The taxable year in which an unused credit arises is referred to as the "unused credit year".

(d) *Taxable years to which unused credit may be carried.* An unused credit is a carryback to each of the 3 taxable years preceding the unused credit year and a carryover to each of the 7 taxable years succeeding the unused credit year. An unused credit must be carried first to the earliest of those 10 taxable years. An unused credit then must be carried to each of the other 9 taxable years (in order of time) to the extent that the unused credit was not absorbed during a prior taxable year because of the limitations under section 46(b)(2) and (3).

(e) *Special rule for pre-1971 years—(1) In general.* For unused credit years ending before January 1, 1971, unused credit is allowed a 10-year carryover rather than the 7-year carryover. The principles of paragraph (d) of this section apply to this 10-year carryover.

(2) *Cross reference.* For limitations on the taxable years to which unused credit from pre-1971 credit years may be carried, see paragraph (g) of this section.

(f) *Limitations on carrybacks.* Under the FIFO rule to section 46(a)(1), carryovers and credit earned are applied against the tax liability limitation before carrybacks. Thus, carrybacks to a taxable year may not exceed the amount by which the applicable tax liability limitation for that year exceeds the sum of carryovers to and credit earned for that year. Carrybacks from an unused credit year are applied against tax liability before carrybacks from a later unused credit year. To the extent an unused credit cannot be carried back to a particular preceding taxable year, the unused credit must be carried to the next succeeding taxable year to which it may be carried.

(g) *Limitations on carryovers—(1) General rule.* Carryovers to a taxable year may not exceed the applicable tax liability limitation for that year. Carryovers from an unused credit year are applied before carryovers from a later unused credit year.

(2) *Exception.* A 10-year carryover from a pre-1971 unused credit year may, under certain circumstances, be postponed to prevent a later-earned 7-year carryover from expiring. This exception does not extend the 10-year carryover period for pre-1971 unused credit. See section 46(b)(1)(D).

(h) *Examples.* The following examples illustrate paragraphs (a) through (g) of this section.

Example (1). (a) Corporation M is organized on January 1, 1977 and files its income tax return on a calendar year basis. Assume the facts set forth in columns (1) and (2) of the following table. The determination of the regular credit allowed for each of the taxable years indicated is set forth in the remaining portions of the table.

	(1)	(2)	(3)	(4) Tax liability limitation* (remaining from col. (6) on preceding line)	(5) Credit allowed (lower of (1) or (4))	(6) Remaining tax liability limitation ((4)-(5))	(7) Unused credit ((1)-(5)) or (amount absorbed)
	Credit available	Tax liability	Per-cent				
1977:							
A. Credit earned	$20,000	$45,000	50	$35,000	$20,000	$15,000	0
B. Carryback from 1978	*15,000	....	.	[15,000]	15,000	....	....
1978:							
A. Credit earned	80,000	55,000	50	40,000	40,000	0	$20,000
Carryback to 1977	....	....	.	....	....	....	(*15,000)
Carryover to 1979	....	....	.	....	....	....	(* 5,000)

Reg. § 1.46-2(b)

1979:
A. Carryover from 1978 . . . . * 5,000   50,000   60   40,000   6,000   35,000
B. Credit earned 50,000   . . . .   . .   [35,000]   35,000   0   15,000
    Carryover to 1980 . . . .   (*15,000)

1980:
A. Carryover from 1979 . . * 15,000   55,000   70   46,000   15,000   31,000   . . . .
B. Credit earned 25,000   [31,000]   25,000   6,000   0

* For line "A" each year: Lesser of (1) tax liability or (2) $25,000 + (percentage in col. (3) × [col. (2) − $25,000]). See, § 1.46-1(h). For other lines: Amount in col. (6) on preceding line.

Example (2). (a) Assume the same facts as in example (1) except for 1979 M earns a $35,000 nonrefundable energy credit. The following table shows the determinations for each year.

	(1)	(2)		(3)	(4)	(5)	(6)	(7)
		Tax liability			Tax liability limitation* (remaining from col. (6) on preceding line)			Unused credit ((1)-(5)) or (amount absorbed)
	Credit available	(a) Regular	(b) Energy ((2)(a)-(5)(R))	Percent		Credit allowed (lower of (1) or (4))	Remaining tax liability limitation ((4)-(5))	
1977:								
Regular:								
A. Credit earned	$20,000	$45,000	. . . .	50	$35,000	$20,000R	$15,000	0
B. Carryback from 1978	*15,000			. . . .	[15,000]	15,000R	0	. . . .
1978:								
Regular:								
Carryback to 1977	. . . .	. . . .	. . . .	. . . .	. . . .	. . . .	. . . .	(*15,000)
Carryover to 1979	. . . .	. . . .	. . . .	. . . .	. . . .	. . . .	. . . .	(*5,000)
Energy:								
A. Carryback from 1979	*15,000	. . . .	$15,000	100	15,000	15,000E	0	. . . .
1979:								
Regular:								
A. Carryover from 1978	*5,000	50,000	. . . .	60	40,000	5,000R	35,000	. . . .
B. Credit earned	50,000	. . . .	. . . .	. . . .	[35,000]	35,000R	0	15,000
Carryover to 1980	. . . .	. . . .	. . . .	. . . .	. . . .	. . . .	. . . .	(*15,000)
Energy:								
A. Credit earned	35,000	. . . .	10,000	100	10,000	10,000E	0	25,000
Carryback to 1978	. . . .	. . . .	. . . .	. . . .	. . . .	. . . .	. . . .	(*15,000)
Carryover to 1980	. . . .	. . . .	. . . .	. . . .	. . . .	. . . .	. . . .	(*10,000)
1980:								
Regular:								
A. Carryover from 1979	*15,000	55,000	. . . .	70	46,000	15,000R	31,000	. . . .
B. Credit earned	25,000	. . . .	. . . .	. . . .	[31,000]	25,000R	6,000	0
Energy:								
A. Carryover from 1979	*10,000	. . . .	15,000	100	15,000	10,000E	5,000	0

* See footnote to the chart in example (1).

(b) Although, in general, a nonrefundable energy credit may be carried back to taxable years ending before October 1, 1978, in this example the unused nonrefundable energy credit from 1979 may not be absorbed in 1977. The 1977 tax liability limitation for the nonrefundable energy credit is the same as it is for the regular credit, reduced by regular credit previously allowed for 1977. See §§ 1.46-1(h)(3) and 1.46-1(m).

Example (3). (a) Assume the same facts as in example (2) except M has regular credit of $37,000 for 1981 and M's tax liability for 1981 is

Reg. § 1.46-2(h)

$32,500. The determinations for 1980 and 1981 are set forth in the following table:

	(1) Credit available	(2) Tax liability (a) Regular	(2) Tax liability (b) Energy ((2)(a)-(5)(R))	(3) Percent	(4) Tax liability limitation* (remaining from col. (6) on preceding line)	(5) Credit allowed (lower of (1) or (4))	(6) Remaining tax liability limitation ((4)-(5))	(7) Unused credit ((1)-(5)) or (amount absorbed)
1979 (restated):								
Energy:								
To be carried over								$10,000
Carryover to 1980								(*9,000)
Carryover to 1981								(*1,000)
1980 (restated):								
Regular								
A. Carryover from 1979	$15,000	$55,000		70	$46,000	$15,000R	$31,000	
C. Carryback from 1981	*6,000				[6,000]	6,000R	0	
Energy:								
A. Carryover from 1979	*9,000		$9,000	100	9,000	9,000E		
1981:								
Regular:								
A. Credit earned	37,000	32,500		80	31,000	31,000R	0	6,000
Carryback to 1980								(*6,000)
Energy:								
A. Carryover from 1979	*1,000		1,500	100	1,500	1,000E	500	0

* See footnote to chart under example (1).

(b) Allowance of the regular carryback in 1980 from 1981 requires that the computations for 1980 be restated. The energy tax liability limitation for 1980 is reduced from $15,000 (as determined in example (2)) to $9,000. Thus, $1,000 of the $10,000 energy credit allowed for 1980 is displaced by the regular carryback. That amount may not be carried back because there is no remaining energy tax liability limitation for the prior 3 years (see table in example (2)). It may be carried over to 1981 and allowed in full in that year.

(i) [Reserved]

(j) *Electing small business corporation.* A shareholder of an electing small business corporation (as defined in section 1371(b)) may not take into account unused credit of the corporation attributable to unused credit years for which the corporation was not an electing small business corporation. However, a taxable year for which the corporation is an electing small business corporation is counted as a taxable year for determining the taxable years to which that unused credit may be carried.

(k) *Periods of less than 12 months.* A fractional part of a year that is considered a taxable year under sections 441(b) and 7701(a)(23) is treated as a preceding or succeeding taxable year for determining under section 46(b) the taxable years to which an unused credit may be carried.

(l) *Corporate acquisitions.* For carryover of unused credits in the case of certain corporate acquisitions, see section 381(c)(23). [Reg. § 1.46-2.]

☐ [*T.D. 6731, 5-7-64. Amended by T.D. 6931,* 10-9-67, *T.D. 6958, 6-20-68, T.D. 7126, 6-9-71, T.D. 7203, 8-24-72, T.D. 7289, 11-5-73 and T.D.* 7751, 12-30-80.]

[Reg. § 1.46-3]

§ 1.46-3. Qualified investment.—(a) *In general.* (1) With respect to any taxable year, the qualified investment of the taxpayer is the aggregate (expressed in dollars) of (i) the applicable percentage of the basis of each new section 38 property placed in service by the taxpayer during such taxable year, plus (ii) the applicable percentage of the cost of each used section 38 property placed in service by the taxpayer during such taxable year. With respect to any section 38 property, qualified investment means the applicable percentage of the basis (or cost) of such property. Section 38 property placed in service by the taxpayer during the taxable year includes the taxpayer's share of the basis (or cost) of section 38 property placed in service by a partnership in the taxable year of such partnership ending with or within the taxpayer's taxable year. In the case of a shareholder of an electing small business corporation (as defined in section 1371(b)), or a beneficiary of an estate or trust, see §§ 1.48-5 and 1.48-6, respectively, for apportionment of the basis (or cost) of section 38 property placed in service by such corporation, estate, or trust. For the definitions of new section 38 property and used section 38 property, see §§ 1.48-2 and 1.48-3, respectively. See § 1.46-5 for special rules for progress expenditures property.

(2) The basis (or cost) of section 38 property placed in service during a taxable year shall not be taken into account in determining qualified investment for such year if such property is disposed of or otherwise ceases to be section 38 property during such year, except where § 1.47-3 applies. Thus, if individual A places in service during a taxable year section 38 property and later in the same year sells such property, the basis (or cost) of such property shall not be taken into account in determining A's qualified investment. On the other hand, if A places in service section 38 property during a taxable year and dies later in the same year, the basis (or cost) of such property would be taken into account in computing qualified investment. Similarly, if section 38 property is destroyed by fire in the same year in which it is placed in service and paragraph (h) of this section applies to reduce the basis (or cost) of replacement property, the basis (or cost) of the destroyed property would be taken into account in computing qualified investment. In order to determine whether section 38 property is disposed of or otherwise ceases to be section 38 property see § 1.47-2.

(3) Qualified investment is reduced in the case of property which is "public utility property" (see paragraph (h) of this section), and in the case of property of organizations to which section 593 applies, regulated investment companies or real estate investment trusts subject to taxation under subchapter M, chapter 1 of the Code, and cooperative organizations described in section 1381(a) (see § 1.46-4).

(b) *Applicable percentage.* The applicable percentage to be applied to the basis (or cost) of property is 33⅓ percent if the estimated useful life of the property is 3 years or more but less than 5 years; 66⅔ percent if the estimated useful life is 5 years or more but less than 7 years; or 100 percent if the estimated useful life is 7 years or more. In the case of property which is not described in section 50, the preceding sentence shall be applied by substituting "4 years" for "3 years", "6 years" for "5 years", and "8 years" for "7 years". The provisions of this paragraph may be illustrated by the following example:

Example. Corporation Y acquires and places in service during 1972 the following new and used section 38 properties:

Property	Estimated useful life	Basis (or cost)
A (new)	4 years	$ 60,000
B (new)	10 years	90,000
C (new)	6 years	150,000
D (used)	3 years	30,000

Corporation Y's qualified investment for 1972 is $220,000 determined in the following manner:

Property	Basis (or cost)	Applicable percentage	Qualified investment
A	$ 60,000	33⅓	$ 20,000
B	90,000	100	90,000
C	150,000	66⅔	100,000
D	30,000	33⅓	10,000
Total			$220,000

(c) *Basis or cost.* (1) The basis of any new section 38 property shall be determined in accordance with the general rules for determining the basis of property. Thus, the basis of property would generally be its cost (see section 1012), unreduced by the adjustment to basis provided by

Reg. § 1.46-3(c)

section 48 (g) (1) with respect to property placed in service before January 1, 1964, and any other adjustment to basis, such as that for depreciation, and would include all items properly included by the taxpayer in the depreciable basis of the property, such as installation and freight costs. However, for purposes of determining qualified investment, the basis of new section 38 property constructed, reconstructed, or erected by the taxpayer shall not include any depreciation sustained with respect to any other property used in the construction, reconstruction, or erection of such new section 38 property. (See paragraph (b) (4) of § 1.48-1.) If new section 38 property is acquired in exchange for cash and other property in a transaction described in section 1031 in which no gain or loss is recognized, the basis of the newly acquired property for purposes of determining qualified investment would be equal to the adjusted basis of the other property plus the cash paid. See § 1.48-4 for the basis of property to a lessee where the lessor has elected to treat such lessee as a purchaser.

(2) The cost of any used section 38 property shall be determined in accordance with paragraph (b) of § 1.48-3. However, the aggregate cost of used section 38 property which may be taken into account in any taxable year in computing qualified investment cannot exceed $50,000 (see paragraph (c) of § 1.48-3).

(3) For reduction in the basis (or cost) of certain property which replaces other property which was destroyed or damaged by fire, storm, shipwreck, or other casualty, or which was stolen, see paragraph (h) of this section.

(d) *Placed in service.* (1) For purposes of the credit allowed by section 38, property shall be considered placed in service in the earlier of the following taxable years:

(i) The taxable year in which, under the taxpayer's depreciation practice, the period for depreciation with respect to such property begins; or

(ii) The taxable year in which the property is placed in a condition or state of readiness and availability for a specifically assigned function, whether in a trade or business, in the production of income, in a tax-exempt activity, or in a personal activity.

Thus, if property meets the conditions of subdivision (ii) of this subparagraph in a taxable year, it shall be considered placed in service in such year notwithstanding that the period for depreciation with respect to such property begins in a succeeding taxable year because, for example, under the taxpayer's depreciation practice such property is accounted for in a multiple asset account

and depreciation is computed under an "averaging convention" (see § 1.167(a)-10), or depreciation with respect to such property is computed under the completed contract method, the unit of production method, or the retirement method.

(2) In the case of property acquired by a taxpayer for use in his trade or business (or in the production of income), the following are examples of cases where property shall be considered in a condition or state of readiness and availability for a specifically assigned function:

(i) Parts are acquired and set aside during the taxable year for use as replacements for a particular machine (or machines) in order to avoid operational time loss.

(ii) Operational farm equipment is acquired during the taxable year and it is not practicable to use such equipment for its specifically assigned function in the taxpayer's business of farming until the following year.

(iii) Equipment is acquired for a specifically assigned function and is operational but is undergoing testing to eliminate any defects.

(iv) Reforestation expenditures (as defined in § 1.194-3(c)) are incurred during the taxable year in connection with qualified timber property (as defined in § 1.194-3(a)).

However, fruit-bearing trees and vines shall not be considered in a condition or state of readiness and availability for a specifically assigned function until they have reached an income-producing stage. Moreover, materials and parts acquired to be used in the construction of an item of equipment shall not be considered in a condition or state of readiness and availability for a specifically assigned function.

(3) Notwithstanding subparagraph (1) of this paragraph, property with respect to which an election is made under § 1.48-4 to treat the lessee as having purchased such property shall be considered placed in service by the lessor in the taxable year in which possession is transferred to such lessee.

(4)(i) The credit allowed by section 38 with respect to any property shall be allowed only for the first taxable year in which such property is placed in service by the taxpayer. The determination of whether property is section 38 property in the hands of the taxpayer shall be made with respect to such first taxable year. Thus, if a taxpayer places property in service in a taxable year and such property does not qualify as section 38 property (or only a portion of such property qualifies as section 38 property) in such year, no credit (or a credit only as to the portion which qualifies in such year) shall be allowed to the taxpayer with

Reg. § 1.46-3(c)(2)

respect to such property notwithstanding that such property (or a greater portion of such property) qualifies as section 38 property in a subsequent taxable year. For example, if a taxpayer places property in service in 1963 and uses the property entirely for personal purposes in such year, but in 1964 begins using the property in a trade or business, no credit is allowable to the taxpayer under section 38 with respect to such property. See § 1.48-1 for the definition of section 38 property.

(ii) Notwithstanding subdivision (i) of this subparagraph, if, for the first taxable year in which property is placed in service by the taxpayer, the property qualifies as section 38 property but the basis of the property does not reflect its full cost for the reason that the total amount to be paid or incurred by the taxpayer for the property is indeterminate, a credit shall be allowed to the taxpayer for such first taxable year with respect to so much of the cost as is reflected in the basis of the property as of the close of such year, and an additional credit shall be allowed to the taxpayer for any subsequent taxable year with respect to the additional cost paid or incurred during such year and reflected in the basis of the property as of the close of such year. The estimated useful life used in computing each additional credit with respect to the property shall be the same as the estimated useful life used in computing the credit for the first taxable year in which the property was placed in service by the taxpayer. Assume, for example, that in 1964 X Corporation, a utility company which makes its return on the basis of a calendar year, enters into an agreement with Y Corporation, a builder, to construct certain utility facilities for a housing development built by Y. Assume further that part of the funds for the construction of the utility facilities is advanced by Y under a contract providing that X will repay the advances over a 10-year period in accordance with an agreed formula, after which no further amounts will be repayable by X even though the full amount advanced by Y has not been repaid. Assuming that the utility facilities are placed in service in 1964 and qualify as section 38 property, X is allowed a credit for 1964 with respect to its basis in the utility facilities at the close of 1964. For each succeeding taxable year X is allowed an additional credit with respect to the increase in basis of the utility facilities resulting from the repayments to Y during such year.

(e) *Estimated useful life*—(1) *In general.* (i) With respect to assets placed in service by the taxpayer during any taxable year, for the purpose of computing qualified investment the estimated useful lives assigned to all assets which fall within

a particular guideline class (within the mean Revenue Procedure 62-21) may be determine the taxpayer's option, under either subparagr (2) or (3) of this paragraph. Thus, the taxpay may assign estimated useful lives to all the asset falling in one guideline class in accordance with subparagraph (2) of this paragraph, and may assign estimated useful lives to all the assets falling within another guideline class in accordance with subparagraph (3) of this paragraph. See subparagraphs (4) and (5) of this paragraph for determination of estimated useful lives of assets not subject to subparagraph (2) or (3) of this paragraph.

(ii) Except as provided in subparagraph (7), this paragraph shall not apply to property described in section 50.

(2) *Class life system.* The taxpayer may assign to each asset falling within a guideline class, which is placed in service during the taxable year, the class life of the taxpayer for the guideline class for such year as determined under section 4, Part II of Revenue Procedure 62-21. The preceding sentence may be applied to the assets falling within a guideline class irrespective of whether the taxpayer uses single asset accounts or multiple asset accounts in computing depreciation with respect to such assets and irrespective of whether the taxpayer chooses to have his depreciation allowance with respect to such assets examined under the rules provided in Revenue Procedure 62-21.

(3) *Individual useful life system.* (i) The taxpayer may assign an individual estimated useful life to each asset falling within a guideline class which is placed in service during the taxable year. With respect to the assets falling within the guideline class which are placed in single asset accounts for purposes of computing depreciation, the estimated useful life used for each asset for that purpose shall be used in determining qualified investment. With respect to the assets falling within the guideline class which are placed in multiple asset accounts (including a guideline class account described in Revenue Procedure 62-21) for which a group, classified, or composite rate is used in computing depreciation (or in single asset accounts for which an average life rate is used), the determination of estimated useful life for each asset in the account shall be made individually on the best estimate obtainable on the basis of all the facts and circumstances. The individual estimated useful lives used for all the assets placed in a multiple asset account, when viewed together, must be consistent with the group, classified, or composite life used for the account for purposes of computing depreciation.

Reg. § 1.46-3(e)(3)

(ii) In determining the individual estimated useful lives of assets similar in kind contained in a multiple asset account (or in single asset accounts for which an average life rate is used), the taxpayer may (a) assign to each of such assets the average useful life of such assets used for purposes of computing depreciation, or (b) assign separate lives to such assets based on the estimated range of years taken into consideration in establishing the average useful life. Thus, for example, if a taxpayer places 9 similar trucks with an average estimated useful life of 7 years, based on an estimated range of 6 to 8 years (2 trucks with a useful life of 6 years, 5 trucks with a useful life of 7 years, and 2 trucks with a useful life of 8 years), in a multiple asset account for which a group rate is used in computing depreciation, he may either assign a useful life of 6 years to 2 of the trucks, 7 years to 5 of the trucks, and 8 years to 2 of the trucks, or he may assign the average useful life of the trucks (7 years) to each of the 9 trucks. Likewise, if a taxpayer places 100 telephone poles with an average useful life of 28 years, based on an estimated range of 3 to 40 years (2 with a useful life of less than 4 years, 3 with a useful life of 4 to 6 years, 4 with a useful life of 6 to 8 years, and 91 with a useful life of more than 8 years), in a multiple asset account for which a group rate is used in computing depreciation, he may either assign useful lives corresponding to the estimated range of years of the poles (i.e., a useful life of less than 4 years to 2 of the poles, etc.), or he may assign the average useful life of the poles (28 years) to each of the poles.

(iii) [Reserved]

(iv) For purposes of subdivision (ii) of this subparagraph, assets (other than "mass assets") shall not be considered as "similar in kind" in respect of other assets unless all such assets are substantially of the same value, nor shall used section 38 property be considered as "similar in kind" to new section 38 property.

(4) *Useful life of property subject to amortization*—(i) *In general.* In the case of property with respect to which amortization in lieu of depreciation is allowable, the term over which amortization deductions are taken shall be considered as the estimated useful life of such property.

(ii) *Qualified timber property.* In the case of qualified timber property (within the meaning of section 194(c)(1)), the normal growing period of such property shall be considered its estimated useful life.

(5) *Useful life of property subject to certain methods of depreciation.* If a taxpayer is using a method of depreciation, such as the unit of production or retirement method, which does not

measure the useful life of the property in terms of years, he must estimate such useful life in years in order to compute his qualified investment.

(6) *Record requirements.* The taxpayer shall maintain sufficient records to determine whether section 47 (relating to certain dispositions, etc., of section 38 property) applies with respect to any asset.

(7) *Section 50 property.* (i) The provisions of this subparagraph and subparagraphs (4) and (6) of this paragraph shall apply to property which is described in section 50.

(ii) The estimated useful life of property for purposes of computing qualified investment shall be the useful life used or to be used by the taxpayer in computing the allowance for depreciation with respect to such property under section 167 for the taxable year in which the property is placed in service. Thus, if property is placed in service by a taxpayer in a taxable year but the period for depreciation with respect to such property does not begin until a succeeding taxable year (see paragraph (d)(1) of this section), the estimated useful life for purposes of computing qualified investment must be the estimated useful life that the taxpayer uses in computing the allowance for depreciation. See subdivision (iv) of this subparagraph for rules for determining the estimated useful life of property with respect to which the allowance for depreciation under section 167 is computed under the unit of production method, the income-forecast method, or any other method which does not measure the useful life of the property in terms of years.

(iii)(a) The estimated useful life of any section 38 property to which an election under section 167(m) applies shall be the asset depreciation period selected for such property under § 1.167(a)-11(b)(4), whether or not such property constitutes mass assets (as defined in § 1.47-1(e)(4)).

(b) The estimated useful life of any section 38 property to which an election under section 167(m) does not apply and which is placed in a multiple asset account for which a group, classified, or composite rate is used in computing depreciation (or in single asset accounts for which an average life rate is used) shall be determined individually for each asset on the best estimate obtainable on the basis of all the facts and circumstances. The individual estimated useful life for each asset placed in a multiple asset account (including a mass asset account) must be the same as the useful life of such asset used in determining the group, classified, or composite life for the account for purposes of computing depreciation. The individual estimated useful

Reg. § 1.46-3(e)(4)

lives of assets similar in kind may be determined in accordance with subdivisions (ii) and (iv) of subparagraph (3) of this paragraph. In the case of mass assets, subdivision (iii) of subparagraph (3) of this paragraph shall apply.

(iv) [Reserved]

(f) *Partnerships*—(1) *In general.* In the case of a partnership, each partner shall take into account separately, for his taxable year with or within which the partnership taxable year ends, his share of the basis of partnership new section 38 property and his share of the cost of partnership used section 38 property placed in service by the partnership during such partnership taxable year. Each partner shall be treated as the taxpayer with respect to his share of the basis of partnership new section 38 property and his share of the cost of partnership used section 38 property. The estimated useful life to each partner of such property shall be deemed to be the estimated useful life of the property in the hands of the partnership. Partnership section 38 property shall not, by reason of each partner taking his share of the basis or cost into account, lose its character as either new section 38 property or used section 38 property, as the case may be. For computation of each partner's qualified investment for the energy credit for a qualified intercity bus, see § 1.48-9(q) (9)(iv).

(2) *Determination of partner's share.* (i) Each partner's share of the basis (or cost) of any section 38 property shall be determined in accordance with the ratio in which the partners divide the general profits of the partnership (that is, the taxable income of the partnership as described in section 702(a)(9)) regardless of whether the partnership has a profit or a loss for its taxable year during which the section 38 property is placed in service. However, if the ratio in which the partners divide the general profits of the partnership changes during the taxable year of the partnership, the ratio effective for the date on which the property is placed in service shall apply.

(ii) Notwithstanding subdivision (i) of this subparagraph, if all related items of income, gain, loss, and deduction with respect to any item of partnership section 38 property are specially allocated in the same manner and if such special allocation is recognized under section 704(a) (b) and paragraph (b) of § 1.704-1, then a partner's share of the basis of such item of section 38 property or the cost of such used section 38 property shall be determined by reference to such special allocation effective the date on which the property is placed in service.

(iii) Notwithstanding subdivisions (i) and (ii) of this subparagraph, if with respect to a partnership's taxable year the conditions set forth in (a) through (c) of this subdivision are satisfied with respect to a partner, then such partner shall not take into account the basis (or cost) of any section 38 property placed in service by the partnership during such taxable year. The conditions referred to in the preceding sentence are:

(a) Such partner's interest in the general profits of the partnership during the taxable year is 5 percent or less;

(b) Under the partnership agreement, such partner will retire from the partnership during the taxable year or within 7 years after the end of such year; and

(c) The partnership agreement provides that the basis (or cost) of section 38 property placed in service by the partnership during the taxable year shall not be taken into account by a partner described in (*l*) and (*b*) of this subdivision.

Any basis (or cost) of section 38 property which is not taken into account by a partner because of the provisions of this subdivision shall be taken into account by the other partners in accordance with subdivision (i) of this subparagraph.

(3) *Examples.* This paragraph may be illustrated by the following examples:

Example (1). Partnership ABCD acquires and places in service on January 1, 1962, an item of new section 38 property, and acquires and places in service on September 1, 1962, another item of new section 38 property. The ABCD partnership and its partners reports income on a calendar year. Partners A, B, C, and D shall share the basis of each new partnership profits equally. Each partner's property is 25 percent.

Example (2). Assume the same facts as in Example 1 and the following additional facts: A dies June 30, 1962, and B purchases A's interest on such date. Each partner's share of the profits from January 1 to June 30 is 25 percent. From July 1 to December 31, B's share of the profits is 50 percent, and C and D's share of the profits is 25 percent each. For A's last taxable year (January 1 to June 30, 1962), A shall take into account 25 percent of the basis of the section 38 property placed in service on January 1, B shall take into account 25 percent of the basis of the section 38 property placed in service on January 1 and 50 percent of the basis of the section 38 property placed in service on September 1, C and D shall each take into account 25 percent of the basis of each new section 38 property placed in service by the partnership in 1962.

Reg. § 1.46-3(f)(3)

Example (3). Partnership MR is engaged in the business of renting soda fountain equipment and icemakers to restaurants. The partnership makes no elections under § 1.48-4 to treat its lessees as having purchased such property. Under the terms of the partnership agreements, the income, gain or loss on disposition, depreciation, and other deductions attributable to the icemakers are specially allocated 70 percent to partner M and 30 percent to partner R. In all other respects M and R share profits and losses equally. If the special allocation with respect to the icemakers is recognized under section 704(a) and (b) and paragraph (b) of § 1.704-1, the basis (or cost) of the icemakers which qualify as partnership section 38 property shall be taken into account 70 percent by M and 30 percent by R. The basis (or cost) of partnership section 38 property not subject to the special allocation shall be taken into account equally by M and R.

Example (4). Assume the same facts as in example (3) and the following additional facts:

During November 1962, the partnership, which reports its income on the basis of a fiscal year ending May 31, acquires and places in service two items which qualify as new section 38 property, an icemaker and a soda fountain. The icemaker has an estimated useful life of 8 years to the partnership and a basis of $1,000. The soda fountain has an estimated useful life of 6 years to the partnership and a basis of $600. Partner M also owns and operates a business as a sole proprietorship and reports income on the calendar year basis. During 1963, M acquires and places in service in his sole proprietorship a machine which qualifies as new section 38 property. This machine has an estimated useful life of 4 years and a basis of $300. M owns no interest in any other partnerships, electing small business corporations, estates, or trusts. M's total qualified investment for 1963 is $1,000, computed as follows:

Property	Estimated useful life	Basis	M's share of basis	Applicable percentage	Qualified investment
Partnership MR					
Icemaker	8	$1,000	$700	100	$ 700
Soda Fountain	6	600	300	66⅔	200
Sole Proprietorship					
Machine	4	300		33⅓	100
Total					$1,000

(g) *Public utility prope* —(1) *In general* —(i) *Scope of paragraph.* This paragraph only applies to property described in section 50. For rules relating to public utility property not described in section 50, see 26 CFR Part (as revised April 1, 1977). This § 1.46-3(g) (as reflect amendments to section paragraph does not enactment of the Revenue Act) made after

(ii) *Amount of qualified i* payer's qualified investment in ent. A taxerty that is public utility property 38 property amount otherwise determined under of the

(2) *Meaning and use of certai* tion. purposes of this paragraph— For

(i) *Public utility property.* "P property" is property used by a ty predominantly in a trade or business r public utility activity and property tha regulated communication property.

(ii) *Public utility activity.* A "publi ity activity" is any activity in which the go services described in section 46(c)(3)(B)(i), (i (iii) are furnished or sold at regulated rates property is used by a taxpayer both in a pul utility activity and in another activity, the cha

acterization of such property is based on the predominant use of such property during the taxable year in which it is placed in service.

(iii) *Regulated rates.* A taxpayer's rates are "regulated" if they are established or approved on a rate-of-return basis. Rates regulated on a rate-of-return basis are an authorization to collect revenues that cover the taxpayer's cost of providing goods or services, including a fair return on the taxpayer's investment in providing such goods or services, where the taxpayer's costs and investment are determined by use of a uniform system of accounts prescribed by the regulatory body. A taxpayer's rates are not "regulated" if they are established or approved on the basis of maintaining competition within an industry, insuring adequate service to customers of an industry, or charging "reasonable" rates within an industry since the taxpayer is not authorized to collect revenues based on the taxpayer's cost of providing goods or services. Rates are considered have been "established or approved" if a schedule of rates is filed with a regulatory body that the power to approve such rates, even though regulatory body takes no action on the filed

Reg. § 1.46-3(g)(1)

schedule or generally leaves undisturbed rates filed by the taxpayer.

(iv) *Nonregulated communication property.* "Nonregulated communication property" is property that is clearly the same type of property (and is used by the taxpayer predominantly for the same type of communication purposes) as communication property, but it is used by the taxpayer predominantly in a trade or business that is not a public utility activity. For purposes of this subdivision (iv), communication property is property ordinarily used for communication purposes by persons who provide regulated telephone or microwave communication services described in section 46(c)(3)(B)(iii). The determination of whether property is clearly of this same type and is used predominantly for these same communication purposes as communication property is made on the basis of the facts and circumstances of each particular case, including the current state of technology in the communications industry and the range and type of services permitted or required to be provided by the regulated telephone and microwave communication industry. As of 1978, wires or cables used predominantly to distribute to subscribers the signals of one or more television broadcast stations or cablecast stations (such as in a CATV system) are not used for the same type of communication purposes as communication property. Communication property includes microwave transmission equipment, private communication equipment (other than land mobile radio equipment for which the operator must obtain a license from the Federal Communications Commission), private switchboard (PBX) equipment, communications terminal equipment connected to telephone networks, data transmission equipment, and communications satellites. Communication property does not include (as of 1978) computer terminals or facsimile reproduction equipment that is connected to telephone lines to transmit data. It also does not include office furniture stands for communication property, tools, repair vehicles, and similar property, even if such property is exclusively used in providing regulated telephone or microwave communication services.

(3) *Leased property.* Public utility property includes property which is leased to others by a taxpayer where the leasing of such property is part of the lessor's public utility activity. Thus, such leased property is public utility property even though the lessee uses such property in an activity which is not a public utility activity, and whether or not the lessor of such property makes a valid election under § 1.48-4 to treat the lessee as having purchased such property for purposes of the credit allowed by section 38. Property leased

by a lessor, where the leasing is not part public utility activity, to a lessee who uses s property predominantly in a public utility act ity is public utility property for purposes of con puting the lessor's or lessee's qualified investment with respect to such property.

(4) *Property used in both the production or transmission of gas and local distribution of gas.* (i) With respect to properties of a taxpayer engaged in both the production or transmission of gas and the local distribution of gas, section 38 property shall be considered as used predominantly in the trade or business of the furnishing or sale of gas though a local distribution system if expenditures for such property are chargeable to any of the following accounts under either the uniform system of accounts prescribed for natural gas companies (class A and class B) by the Federal Power Commission, effective January 1, 1961, or the uniform system of accounts for class A and B gas utilities adopted in 1958 by the National Association of Railroad and Utility Commissioners (or would be chargeable to any of the following accounts if the taxpayer used either of such systems):

(a) Accounts 360 through 363, inclusive (Local Storage Plant), or

(b) Accounts 374 through 387, inclusive (Distribution Plant).

(ii) If expenditures for section 38 property are chargeable (or would be chargeable) to any of the following accounts under either of the systems named in subdivision (i) of this subparagraph, the determination of whether or not such property is used predominantly in the trade or business of the furnishing or sale of gas through a local distribution system shall be made under all the facts and circumstances relating to the actual use of such property in the year such property is placed in service:

(a) Accounts 304 through 320, inclusive (Manufactured Gas Production Plant), or

(b) Accounts 389 through 399, inclusive (General Plant). For example, if an office machine is used 55 percent of the time for billing customers of the taxpayer's local distribution system in the year in which it is placed in service, such office machine shall be considered as used predominantly in the trade or business of the furnishing or sale of gas through a local distribution system.

(5) *Certain submarine cable property.* In the case of any interest in a submarine cable circuit which is property described in section 50 used to furnish telegraph service between the United States and a point outside the United States of a taxpayer engaged in furnishing international tele-

Reg. § 1.46-3(g)(5)

h service (if the rates for such furnishing
ve been established or approved by a govern-
ental unit, agency, instrumentality, commission, or similar body described in subparagraph
(2) of this paragraph), the qualified investment
shall not exceed the qualified investment attributable to so much of the interest of the taxpayer in
the circuit as does not exceed 50 percent of all
interests in the circuit.

(h) *Certain replacement property.* (1)(i) If section 38 property is placed in service by the taxpayer to replace property (whether or not section
38 property) similar or related in service or use,
which was destroyed or damaged before August
16, 1971, by fire, storm, shipwreck, or other casualty, or was stolen before such date, then for
purposes of paragraph (a) of this section the basis
(or cost) of the replacement section 38 property
otherwise determined under paragraph (c) of this
section shall be reduced by an amount equal to
the lesser of—

(a) The amount of money, or the fair
market value of other property, received as compensation, by insurance or otherwise, for the property which was destroyed, damaged, or stolen, or

(b) The adjusted basis of such destroyed, damaged, or stolen property (immediately before such destruction, damage, or theft).

(ii) For purposes of subdivision (i) of this
subparagraph—

(a) Section 38 property placed in service
after the due date (including extensions of time
thereof) for filing the taxpayer's income tax return for the taxable year in which the other property was destroyed, damaged, or stolen shall not
be considered as replacement section 38 property,
and

(b) If the property which is destroyed,
damaged, or stolen, is leased property, no other
leased property shall be considered as replacement property with respect to the property destroyed, damaged, or stolen, in any case in which
the lessor makes or made an election under section
48(d) (relating to election with respect to certain
leased property) with respect to either the property destroyed, damaged, or stolen, the other
leased property, or both.

(2) Subparagraph (1) of this paragraph shall
not apply to replacement property if the reduction, under such subparagraph (1), in the basis (or
cost) of such replacement property is less than the
excess of—

(i) The qualified investment with respect
to the destroyed, damaged, or stolen property,
over

(ii) The recomputed qualified investment
with respect to such property (determined under
the principles of paragraph (a) of § 1.47-1).

(3) This paragraph may be illustrated by the
following examples:

Example (1). (i) A acquired and placed in
service on January 1, 1962, machine No. 1, which
qualified as section 38 property, with a basis of
$30,000 and an estimated useful life of 6 years.
The amount of qualified investment with respect
to such machine was $20,000. On January 2,
1963, machine No. 1 is completely destroyed by
fire. On January 1, 1963, the adjusted basis of
such machine in A's hands is $24,500. On Nov-
ember 1, 1963, A receives $23,000 in insurance
proceeds as compensation for the destroyed machine, and on December 15, 1963, A acquires and
places in service machine No. 2, which qualifies as
section 38 property, with a basis of $41,000 and
an estimated useful life of 6 years to replace
machine No. 1.

(ii) Under subparagraph (1) of this paragraph, the $41,000 basis of machine No. 2 is
reduced, for purposes of paragraph (a) of this
section, by $23,000 (that is, the $23,000 insurance
proceeds since such amount is less than the
$24,500 adjusted basis of machine No. 1 immedi-
ately before it was destroyed) to $18,000 since
such reduction (that is, $23,000) is greater than
the $20,000 reduction in qualified investment
which would be made if paragraph (a) of § 1.47-1
were to apply to machine No. 1 ($20,000 qualified
investment less zero recomputed qualified
investment).

Example (2). (i) The facts are the same as in
example (1) except that on November 1, 1963, A
receives only $19,000 in insurance proceeds as
compensation for the destroyed machine.

(ii) The $41,000 basis of machine No. 2 is not
reduced, for purposes of paragraph (a) of this
section, under this paragraph since the $19,000
reduction which would have been made under this
paragraph had it applied (that is, the $19,000
insurance proceeds since such amount is less than
the $24,500 adjusted basis of machine No. 1 im-
mediately before it was destroyed) is less than the
$20,000 reduction in qualified investment which
is made since paragraph (a) of § 1.47-1 applies to
machine No. 1 ($20,000 qualified investment less
zero recomputed qualified investment). [Reg.
§ 1.46-3.]

□ [*T.D.* 6731, 5-7-64. *Amended by T.D.* 6931,
10-9-67; *T.D.* 7203, 8-24-72; *T.D.* 7602, 3-20-79;
T.D. 7927, 12-15-83; *T.D.* 7982, 10-5-84; *T.D.*
8183, 3-1-88 *and T.D.* 8474, 4-26-93.]

Reg. § 1.46-3(h)(2)

[Reg. § 1.46-4]

§ 1.46-4. Limitations with respect to certain persons.—(a) *Mutual savings institutions.* In case of an organization to which section 593 applies (that is, a mutual savings bank, a cooperative bank, or a domestic building and loan association)—

(1) The qualified investment with respect to each section 38 property shall be 50 percent of the amount otherwise determined under § 1.46-3, and

(2) The $25,000 amount specified in section 46(a)(2), relating to limitation based on amount of tax, shall be reduced by 50 percent of such amount.

For example, if a domestic building and loan association places in service on January 1, 1963, new section 38 property with a basis of $30,000 and an estimated useful life of 6 years, its qualified investment for 1963 with respect to such property computed under § 1.46-3 is $20,000 (66⅔ percent of $30,000). However, under this paragraph such amount is reduced to $10,000 (50 percent of $20,000). If an organization to which section 593 applies is a member of an affiliated group (as defined in section 46(a)(5)), the $25,000 amount specified in section 46(a)(2) shall be reduced in accordance with the provisions of paragraph (f) of § 1.46-1 before such amount is further reduced under this paragraph.

(b) *Regulated investment companies and real estate investment trusts.* (1) In the case of a regulated investment company or a real estate investment trust subject to taxation under subchapter M, chapter 1 of the Code—

(i) The qualified investment with respect to each section 38 property otherwise determined under § 1.46-3, and

(ii) The $25,000 amount specified in section 46(a)(2), relating to limitation based on amount of tax,

shall be reduced to such person's ratable share of each such amount. If a regulated investment company or a real estate investment trust is a member of an affiliated group (as defined in section 46(a)(5)), the $25,000 amount specified in section 46(a)(2) shall be reduced in accordance with the provisions of paragraph (f) of § 1.46-1 before such amount is further reduced under this paragraph.

(2) A person's ratable share of the amount described in subparagraph (1)(i) and the amount described in subparagraph (1)(ii) of this paragraph shall be the ratio which—

(i) Taxable income for the taxable year, bears to

(ii) Taxable income for the taxable year plus the amount of the deduction for dividends paid taken into account under section 852(b)(2)(D) in computing investment company taxable income, or under section 857(b)(2) (section 857(b)(2)(C), as then in effect, for taxable years ending before October 5, 1976) in computing real estate investment trust taxable income, as the case may be.

For purposes of the preceding sentence, taxable income means, in the case of a regulated investment company its investment company taxable income (within the meaning of section 852(b)(2)), and in the case of a real estate investment trust its real estate investment trust taxable income (within the meaning of section 857(b)(2)). In the case of a taxable year ending after October 4, 1976, real estate investment trust taxable income, for purposes of section 46(e) and this paragraph, is determined by excluding any net capital gain, and by computing the deduction for dividends paid without regard to capital gains dividends (as defined in section 857(b)(3)(C)). The amount of the deduction for dividends paid includes the amount of deficiency dividends (other than capital gains deficiency dividends) taken into account in computing investment company taxable income or real estate investment trust taxable income for the taxable year. See section 860(f) for the definition of deficiency dividends. For purposes of this paragraph only, in computing taxable income for a taxable year beginning before January 1, 1964, a regulated investment company or a real estate investment trust may compute depreciation deductions with respect to section 38 property placed in service before January 1, 1964, without regard to the reduction in basis of such property required under § 1.48-7.

(3) This paragraph may be illustrated by the following example:

Example. (i) Corporation X, a regulated investment company subject to taxation under section 852 of the Code which makes its return on the basis of the calendar year, places in service on January 1, 1964, section 38 property with a basis of $30,000 and an estimated useful life of 6 years. Corporation X's investment company taxable income under section 852(b)(2) is $10,000 after taking into account a deduction for dividends paid of $90,000.

(ii) Under this paragraph, corporation X's qualified investment for the taxable year 1964 with respect to such property is $2,000, computed as follows: (*a*) $20,000 (qualified investment under § 1.46-3), multiplied by (*b*) $10,000 (taxable income), divided by (*c*) $100,000 (taxable income plus the deduction for dividends paid). For 1964, the $25,000 amount specified in section 46(a)(2) is reduced to $2,500.

Cooperatives. (1) In the case of a coopera- organization described in section 1381(a)—

(i) The qualified investment with respect o each section 38 property otherwise determined under § 1.46-3, and

(ii) The $25,000 amount specified in section 46(a)(2), relating to limitation based on amount of tax,

shall be reduced to such cooperative's ratable share of each such amount. If a cooperative organization described in section 1381(a) is a member of an affiliated group (as defined in section 46(a)(5)), the $25,000 amount specified in section 46(a)(2) shall be reduced in accordance with the provisions of paragraph (f) of § 1.46-1 before such amount is further reduced under this paragraph.

(2) A cooperative's ratable share of the amount described in subparagraph (1)(i) and the amount described in subparagraph (1)(ii) of this paragraph shall be the ratio which—

(i) Taxable income for the taxable year, bears to

(ii) Taxable income for the taxable year plus the sum of (a) the amount of the deductions allowed under section 1382(b), (b) the amount of the deductions allowed under section 1382(c), and (c) amounts similar to the amounts described in (a) and (b) of this subdivision the tax treatment of which is determined without regard to subchapter T, chapter 1 of the Code and the regulations thereunder.

Amounts similar to deductions allowed under section 1382(b) or (c) are, for example, in the case of a taxable year of a cooperative organization beginning before January 1, 1963, the amount of patronage dividends which are excluded or deducted and any nonpatronage distributions which are deducted under section 522(b)(1). In the case of a taxable year of a cooperative organization beginning after December 31, 1962, such amounts are the amount of patronage dividends and nonpatronage distributions which are excluded or deducted without regard to section 1382(b) or (c) because they are paid with respect to patronage occurring before 1963. For purposes of this paragraph only, in computing taxable income for a taxable year beginning before January 1, 1964, a cooperative may compute depreciation deductions with respect to section 38 property placed in service before January 1, 1964, without regard to the reduction in basis of such property required under § 1.48-7.

(3) This paragraph may be illustrated by the following example:

Example. (i) Cooperative X, an organization described in section 1381(a) which makes its re- turn on the basis of the calendar year, places in service on January 1, 1964, section 38 property with a basis of $30,000 and an estimated useful life of 6 years. Cooperative X's taxable income is $10,000 after taking into account deductions of $20,000 allowed under section 1382(b), deductions of $60,000 allowed under section 1382(c), and deductions of $10,000 allowed under section 522(b)(1)(B).

(ii) Under this paragraph, cooperative X's qualified investment for the taxable year 1964 with respect to such property is $2,000, computed as follows: (a) $20,000 (qualified investment under § 1.46-3), multiplied by (b) $10,000 (taxable income), divided by (c) $100,000 (taxable income plus the sum of the deductions allowed under sections 1382(b), 1382(c), and 522(b)(1)(B)). For 1964, the $25,000 amount specified in section 46(a)(2) is reduced to $2,500.

(d) *Noncorporate lessors.* (1) In the case of a lease entered into after September 22, 1971, a credit is allowed under section 38 to a noncorporate lessor of property with respect to the leased property only if—

(i) Such property has been manufactured or produced by the lessor in the ordinary course of his business, or

(ii) The term of the lease (taking into account any options to renew) is less than 50 percent of the estimated useful life of the property (determined under § 1.46-3(e)), and for the period consisting of the first 12 months after the date on which the property is transferred to the lessee the sum of the deductions with respect to such property which are allowable to the lessor solely by reason of section 162 (other than rents and reimbursed amounts with respect to such property) exceeds 15 percent of the rental income produced by such property.

In the case of property of which a partnership is the lessor, the credit otherwise allowable under section 38 with respect to such property to any partner which is a corporation shall be allowed notwithstanding the first sentence of this subparagraph. For purposes of this subparagraph, an electing small business corporation (as defined in section 1371) shall be treated as a person which is not a corporation. This paragraph shall not apply to property used by the taxpayer in his trade or business (other than the leasing of property) for a period of at least 24 months preceding the day on which any lease of such property is entered into.

(2) For purposes of subparagraph (1)(ii) of this paragraph, if at the time the lessor files his income tax return for the taxable year in which the property is placed in service, the lessor is unable to show that the more-than-15-percent test

Reg. § 1.46-4(c)(2)

has been satisfied, then no credit may be claimed by the lessor on such return with respect to such property unless (i) taking into account the lessor's obligations under the lease it is reasonable to believe that the more-than-15-percent test will be satisfied, and (ii) the lessor files a statement with his return from which it may be determined that he expects to satisfy the more-than-15-percent test. If the more-than-15-percent test is not satisfied with respect to the property, the taxpayer must file an amended return for the year in which the property is placed in service.

(3)(i) The more-than-15-percent test described in subparagraph (1)(ii) of this paragraph is based on the relationship of the expenses of the lessor relating to or attributable to the property to the gross income from rents of the taxpayer produced by the property. The test is applied with respect to such expenses and gross income as are properly attributable to the period consisting of the first 12 months after the date on which the property is transferred to the lessee. When more than one property is subject to a single lease and, pursuant to subparagraph (4) of this paragraph, the arrangement is considered to be a separate lease of each property, the test is applied separately to each such lease by making an apportionment of the payments received and expenses incurred with respect to each such property, considering all relevant factors. Such apportionment is made in accordance with any reasonable method selected and consistently applied by the taxpayer. For example, under subparagraph (4) of this paragraph, where a taxpayer leases an airplane which he owns to an airline along with a baggage truck, he is treated as having made two separate leases, one covering the airplane and one covering the baggage truck. Thus, the test will be applied by apportioning the related income and expenses between the two leases. Similarly, where a taxpayer leases a factory building erected by him containing section 38 property (machinery and equipment), the test will be applied to the taxpayer as though he had leased (to the lessee) the building and the section 38 property separately. Thus, the rental income and expenses are apportioned between the building and the section 38 property.

(ii) Only those deductions allowable solely by reason of section 162 are taken into account in applying the more-than-15-percent test. Hence, depreciation allowable by reason of section 167 (including amortization allowable in lieu of depreciation); interest allowable by reason of section 163; taxes allowable by reason of section 164; and depletion allowable by reason of section 611 a examples of deductions which are not taken i account in applying the test. Moreover, rents

reimbursed amounts paid or payable by the are not taken into account notwithstanding th deduction in respect of such rents or reimburs amounts is allowable solely by reason of sectio 162. For purposes of this paragraph, a reimbursed amount is any expense for which the lessee or some other party is obligated to reimburse the lessor. Section 162 expenses paid or payable by any person other than the lessor are not taken into account unless the lessor is obligated to reimburse the person paying the expense. Further, if the lessee is obligated to pay to the lessor a charge for services which is separately stated or determinable, the expenses incurred by the lessor with respect to those services are not taken into account.

(iii) For purposes of the more-than-15-percent test, the gross income from rents of the lessor produced by the property is the total amount which is payable to the lessor by reason of the lease agreement other than reimbursements of section 162 expenses and charges for services which are separately stated or determinable. The fact that such amount depends, in whole or in part, on the sales or profits of the lessee or the performance of significant services by the lessor shall not affect the characterization of such amounts as gross income from rents for purposes of this paragraph. Gross income from rents also includes any taxes imposed on the lessor by local law but which are paid directly by the lessee on behalf of the lessor.

(4) For purposes of determining under this paragraph whether property is subject to a lease, the provisions of § 1.46-3(d)(1) (relating to definition of a lease) shall apply. If a noncorporate lessor enters into one or more successive leases with respect to the same or substantially similar items of section 38 property, the terms of such leases shall be aggregated and such leases shall be considered one lease for the purpose of determining whether the form of such leases is less than 50 percent of the estimated useful life of the property subject to such leases. Thus, for example, if erty subject an airplane with an estimated an individual years and enters into 3 successive useful if such airplane, such leases will be 3-year be one lease for a term of 9 years for consof determining whether the term of the less than 3½ years (50 percent of the th nated useful life).

The requirements of this paragraph shall y with respect to any property which is as section 38 property by reason of section)(E). [Reg. § 1.46-4.]

T.D. 6731, 5-7-64. Amended by T.D. 6958, 58; T.D. 7203, 8-24-72; T.D. 7767, 2-3-81; 7936, 1-17-84; and T.D. 8031, 6-27-85.]

[Reg. § 1.46-5]

§ 1.46-5. Qualified progress expenditures.—
a) *Effective date.* This section applies to taxable years ending after December 31, 1974. This section reflects amendments to the Internal Revenue Code made only by the Tax Reduction Act of 1975, the Tax Reform Act of 1976, and the Revenue Act of 1978.

(b) *General rule.* Under section 46(d), a taxpayer may elect to take the investment credit for qualified progress expenditures (as defined in paragraph (g) of this section). In general, qualified progress expenditures are amounts paid (paid or incurred in the case of self-constructed property) for construction of progress expenditure property. The taxpayer must reasonably estimate that the property will take at least 2 years to construct and that the useful life of the property will be 7 years or more. Qualified progress expenditures may not be taken into account if made before the later of January 22, 1975, or the first taxable year to which an election under section 46(d) applies. In general, qualified progress expenditures are not allowed for the year property is placed in service, nor for the first year or any subsequent year recapture is required under section 47(a)(3). There is a percentage limitation on qualified progress expenditure for taxable years beginning before January 1, 1980. For a special rule relating to transfers of progress expenditure property, see paragraph (r) of this section.

(c) *Reduction of qualified investment.* Under section 46(c)(4), a taxpayer must reduce qualified investment for the year property is placed in service by qualified progress expenditures taken into account by that person or a predecessor. A "predecessor" of a taxpayer is a person whose election under section 46 carries over to the taxpayer under paragraph of this section.

(d) *Progress expenditure property.* Progress expenditure property is property constructed by or for the taxpayer, with a normal construction period of 2 years or more. The taxpayer must reasonably believe that the property will be new section 38 property with a useful life of 7 years or more when placed in service. Whether property is progress expenditure property is determined on the basis of facts known at the close of the taxable year of the taxpayer in which construction begins (or, if later, at the close of the first taxable year to which an election under section 46(d) applies). For purposes of this paragraph (d), property is constructed by or for the taxpayer if built or manufactured from materials or component parts. Accordingly, progress expenditure property does not include property

orchards, vineyards, livestock, or motion picture films or videotapes.

(e) *Normal construction period*—(1) *In general.* (i) The normal construction period is the period the taxpayer reasonably expects will be required to construct the property. The period begins on the date physical work on construction of the property commences and ends on the date the property is available to be placed in service. The normal construction period does not include, however, construction before January 22, 1975, nor construction before the first day of the first taxable year for which an election under section 46(d) is in effect. Physical work on construction of property does not include preliminary activities such as planning, designing, preparing blueprints, exploring, or securing financing.

(ii) The determination of the time when physical work on construction commences is based on the facts and circumstances of each case. Physical work on construction of property may include the physical work done by a subcontractor on a component specifically designated as part of the property. Also, the commencement of physical work on construction may occur at a site different from the main site of construction of the property. For example, if a shipyard orders a turbine before it begins work on building a ship, the normal construction period of the ship is measured from the time the subcontractor commences physical work on construction of the turbine (if it is normal for such work to precede the work of the main contractor).

(iii) Generally, physical work on construction does not include physical activity that is not necessary to complete physical construction of the property, nor does it include physical work on construction of a building or other property that will not be new section 38 property when placed in service. Physical work on construction also does not include research and development activities in a laboratory or experimental setting.

(iv) The normal construction period of property ends on the date it is expected the property will be available to be placed in service. Property is considered available to be placed in service when construction is completed and the property is available for delivery to the site of its assigned function. It is not necessary that property be in a state of readiness for a specifically assigned function. Nor is it necessary that it actually be delivered to the site of its assigned function.

(2) *Estimates.* Taxpayers should refer to normal industry practice in estimating the normal construction period of particular items. A different period may be used if special circumstances

Reg. § 1.46-5(a)

exist making it impractical to make the estimate on the basis of normal industry practice. The estimate must be based on information available at the close of the taxable year in which physical work on construction of the property begins, or, if later, at the close of the first taxable year for which an election under section 46(d) is in effect for the taxpayer. If the estimate is reasonable when made, the actual time it takes to complete the work is, in general, irrelevant in determining whether property is progress expenditure property. However, if there is a significant error in estimating the normal construction period, it may be evidence that the estimate was unreasonable when made. For taxable years ending after April 1, 1988, a taxpayer not relying on normal industry practice to estimate the normal construction period of particular property must attach to the tax return for the taxable year in which physical work on construction of the property begins (or, if later, the first taxable year for which an election under section 46(d) is in effect) a statement of the basis relied upon in estimating the normal construction period of the property.

(3) *Integrated unit.* (i) In determining whether property has a normal construction period of 2 years or more, property that will be placed in service separately is to be considered separately. For example, if two ships are contracted for at the same time, each ship is considered separately under this paragraph. However, for property that will be placed in service as an integrated unit, the taxpayer must determine the normal construction period of the integrated unit. If the normal construction period of the integrated unit is 2 years or more, the normal construction period of each item of new section 38 property that is a part of the integrated unit is considered to be 2 years or more. Thus, the normal construction period of an integrated unit may be 2 years or more even if no part of the unit has a normal construction period of 2 years or more.

(ii) Property is part of an integrated unit only if the operation of that item is essential to the performance of the function to which the unit is assigned. Property essential to the performance of the function to which the unit is assigned includes property the use of which is significantly connected to that function and which effects the safe, proper, or efficient performance of the unit. Generally, property must be placed in service at the same time to be considered part of the same integrated unit. Properties are not an integrated unit, however, solely because they are to be placed in service at the same time.

(iii) The normal construction period for an integrated unit begins on the date the normal construction period of the first item of new section 38 property that is part of the unit begins. It is not necessary that physical work commence at the main construction site of the integrated unit.

The period ends on the date the last item of new section 38 property that is part of that unit is available to be placed in service. Property that is not new section 38 property, such as a building, is not considered part of an integrated unit for purposes of determining the normal construction period of that unit. For example, if a manufacturing plant has a normal construction period of two years or more but the equipment (*i.e.,* new section 38 property) to be installed in the plant has a normal construction period of less than two years, the plant and the equipment do not constitute an integrated unit with a construction period of two years or more and the equipment is not progress expenditure property.

(4) *Examples.* The following examples illustrate this paragraph (e).

Example (1). On July 1, 1974, corporation X begins physical work on construction of a machine with an estimated useful life when placed in service of more than 7 years. For its taxable year ending June 30, 1975, X makes an election under section 46(d). For purposes of determining on June 30, 1975, whether the machine is "progress expenditure property", the normal construction period is treated as having begun on January 22, 1975. Thus, the machine will be considered to be progress expenditure property on June 30, 1975, only if the estimated time required to complete construction after June 30 is at least 18 months and 22 days (*i.e.,* 2 years less the period January 22, 1975, through June 30, 1975).

Example (2). (i) Corporation X constructs a pipeline in two sections and simultaneously begins physical work on construction of each section on January 1, 1976. One section extends from city M to city N. The other extends from city N to city O. Oil will be transferred to storage tanks at both city N and city O. Corporation X also begins construction on January 1, 1976, of a pumping station necessary to the operation of the pipeline from city M to city N. Construction of a pumping station necessary to the operation of the pipeline from city N to city O begins on June 30, 1977. For 1976, corporation X makes an election under section 46(d).

(ii) The section of pipeline from city M to city N and the associated pumping station will be available to be placed in service on January 1, 1977. Construction of the section of the pipeline from city N to city O will be completed on June 30, 1977. However, that section of the pipeline will not be available to be placed in service until completion of the associated pumping station on January 1, 1978.

(iii) The section of pipeline from city M to city N and the section from city N to city O must be considered separately in determining the normal construction period of the property. Each section will be placed in service separately. However, each section of the pipeline and the associated pumping station may be considered an integrated unit. The pumping stations are essential to the operation of each section of pipeline. Each section of pipeline and the associated pumping station are placed in service at the same time.

(iv) The section of pipeline from city M to city N and the associated pumping station are not progress expenditure property, because the normal construction period of that unit is only 1 year (January 1, 1976 to January 1, 1977).

(v) The section of pipeline from city N to city O and the associated pumping station are progress expenditure property, because the normal construction of that integrated unit is 2 years (January 1, 1976 to January 1, 1978). It is immaterial that neither the construction period of that section of pipeline (January 1, 1976 to June 30, 1977) nor the construction period of the associated pumping station (June 30, 1977 to January 1, 1978) is 2 years.

(vi) Assume the pumping station associated with the pipeline from city N to city O includes backup pumping equipment that will be used only if the primary pumping equipment fails. The backup equipment is part of the integrated unit because it serves to effect the safe or efficient performance of the unit.

(f) *New section 38 property with a 7-year useful life*—(1) *In general.* The taxpayer must determine if property will be new section 38 property with a useful life of 7 years or more when placed in service. The determination must be made at the close of the taxable year in which construction begins or, if later, at the close of the first taxable year to which an election under section 46(d) applies for the taxpayer.

(2) *Determination based on reasonably expected use.* The determination of whether property will be "new section 38 property" (within the meaning of §§ 1.48-1 and 1.48-2) when placed in service must be based on the reasonably expected use of the property by the taxpayer. There is a presumption that property will be new section 38 property if it would be new section 38 property if placed in service by the taxpayer when the determination is made. For example, in determining if property is an integral part of manufacturing under section 48(a)(1)(B)(i), it will be presumed that property will be new section 38 property if

the taxpayer is engaged in manufacturing when the determination is made. Also, significant steps taken to establish a trade or business will be evidence the taxpayer will be engaged in that trade or business when the property is placed in service.

(3) *Estimated useful life.* The determination of whether property will have an estimated useful life of 7 years or more when placed in service must be made by applying the principles of § 1.46-3(e). If the estimated useful life is less than 7 years when the property is actually placed in service, the credit previously allowed under section 46(d) must be recomputed under section 47(a)(3)(B).

(g) *Definition of qualified progress expenditures*—(1) *In general.* A taxpayer's qualified progress expenditures are the sum of qualified progress expenditures for self-constructed property (determined under paragraph (h) of this section), plus qualified progress expenditures for non-self-constructed property (determined under paragraph (j) of this section). Only amounts includible under § 1.46-3(c) in the basis of new section 38 property may be considered as qualified progress expenditures.

(2) *Excluded amounts.* Qualified progress expenditures do not include:

(i) In the case of non-self-constructed property, amounts incurred (whether or not paid)—

(A) Before the normal construction period begins, or

(B) Before the later of January 22, 1975, or the first day of the first taxable year for which an election under section 46(d) applies for the taxpayer;

(ii) In the case of self-constructed property, amounts chargeable to capital account—

(A) Before the normal construction period begins, or

(B) Before the later of January 22, 1975, or the first day of the first taxable year for which an election under section 46(d) applies for the taxpayer,

(See, however, section 46(d)(4)(A) and paragraph (h)(3)(i) of this section, relating to the time when amounts for component parts and materials are properly chargeable to capital account);

(iii) Expenditures with respect to particular property in the earlier of—

(A) The taxable year in which the property is placed in service, or

(B) The taxable year in which the taxpayer must recapture investment credit under section 47(a)(3) for the property or any subsequent year;

Reg. § 1.46-5(f)(1)

(iv) Expenditures for construction, reconstruction, or erection of property that is not section 38 property; or

(v) Amounts treated as an expense and deducted in the year paid or accrued.

(h) *Qualified progress expenditures for self-constructed property*—(1) *In general.* Qualified progress expenditures for self-constructed property (as defined in paragraph (k) of this section) are amounts properly chargeable to capital account in connection with that property. In general, amounts paid or incurred are chargeable to capital account if under the taxpayer's method of accounting they are properly includible in computing basis under § 1.46-3. Qualified progress expenditures for self-constructed property include both direct costs (*e.g.*, labor, material, parts) and indirect costs (*e.g.*, overhead, insurance) associated with construction of property to the extent those costs are properly chargeable to capital account.

(2) *Property partially non-self-constructed.* If an item of property is self-constructed because more than half of the construction expenditures are made directly by the taxpayer, then any expenditures (whether or not made directly by the taxpayer) for construction of that item of property are not subject to the limitations of section 46(d)(3)(B) and paragraph (j) of this section (relating to actual payment and progress in construction).

(3) *Time when amounts paid or incurred are properly chargeable to capital account.* (i) In general, expenditures for component parts and materials to be used in construction of self-constructed property are not properly chargeable to capital account until consumed or physically attached in the construction process. Component parts and materials that have been neither consumed nor physically attached in the construction process, but which have been irrevocably allocated to construction of that property are properly chargeable to capital account. Component parts and materials designed specifically for the self-constructed property may be considered irrevocably allocated to construction of that property at the time of manufacture of the component parts and materials. Component parts and materials not designed specifically for the property may be considered irrevocably allocated to construction at the time of delivery to the construction site if they would be economically impractical to remove. For example, pumps delivered to sites of construction of a tundra pipeline may be treated as irrevocably allocated to that pipeline on the date of delivery, even if they would be usable, but for their location on the tundra, in connection with other property.

Component parts and materials are not t considered irrevocably allocated to use in s constructed property until physical work on co struction of that property has begun (as deter mined under paragraph (e)(1)(ii) of this section). Mere bookkeeping notations are not sufficient evidence that the necessary allocation has been made.

(ii) A taxpayer's procedure for determining the time when an expenditure is properly chargeable to capital account for self-constructed property is a method of accounting. Under section 446(e), the method of accounting, once adopted, may not be changed without consent of the Secretary.

(4) *Records requirement.* The taxpayer shall maintain detailed records which permit specific identification of the amounts properly chargeable by the taxpayer during each taxable year to capital account for each item of self-constructed property.

(i) [Reserved].

(j) *Qualified progress expenditures for non-self-constructed property*—(1) *In general.* Qualified progress expenditures for non-self-constructed property (as defined in paragraph (l) of this section) are amounts actually paid by the taxpayer to another person for construction of the property, but only to the extent progress is made in construction. For example, such expenditures may include payments to the manufacturer of an item of progress expenditure property, payments to a contractor building progress expenditure property, or payments for engineering designs or blueprints that are drawn up during the normal construction period.

(2) *Property partially self-constructed.* If an item of property is non-self-constructed, but a taxpayer uses its own employees to construct a portion of the property, expenditures for construction of that portion are made directly by the taxpayer (see § 1.46-5(h)(1)). Subject to the limitations of paragraph (g) of this section, those expenditures are qualified progress expenditures for non-self-constructed property if they satisfy the requirements of paragraph (j)(4), (5), and (6) of this section. Wages actually paid to the taxpayer's employees are presumed to correspond to progress in construction. Other amounts, including expenditures for materials, parts, and overhead, must be actually paid, not borrowed from the payee, and attributable to progress made in construction by the taxpayer.

(3) *Property constructed by more than one person.* The percentage of completion limitation (as prescribed in paragraph (j)(6) of this section), including the presumption of ratable progress in

Reg. § 1.46-5(j)(3)

ruction, applies to an item of progress expenditure property as a whole. However, if several manufacturers or contractors do work in connection with the same property, the progress that each person makes toward completion of construction of the property must be determined separately. Section 46(d)(3)(B) is then applied separately to amounts paid to each manufacturer or contractor based on each person's progress in construction. For example, assume the taxpayer contracts with three persons to build an item of equipment. The taxpayer contracts with A to build the frame, B to build the motor, and C to assemble the frame and motor. Assume each contract represents 33⅓ percent of the construction costs of the property. If, within the taxable year in which construction begins, A and B each complete 50 percent of the construction of the frame and motor, respectively, amounts paid to A during that taxable year not in excess of 16⅔ percent of the overall cost of the property, and amounts paid to B during that taxable year not in excess of 16⅔ percent of the overall cost of the property, are qualified progress expenditures. Section 46(d)(3)(B) does not apply, however, to persons, such as lower-tier subcontractors, that do not have a direct contractual relationship with the taxpayer. If, in the above example, A engages a subcontractor to construct part of the frame, section 46(d)(3)(B) is applied only to amounts paid by the taxpayer to A, B, and C, but the portion of construction completed by A during a taxable year includes the portion completed by A's subcontractor.

(4) *Requirement of actual payment.* Qualified progress expenditures for non-self-constructed property must be actually paid and not merely incurred. Amounts paid during the taxable year to another person for construction of non-self-constructed property may be in the form of money or property (*e.g.,* materials). However, property given as payment may be considered only to the extent it will be includible under § 1.46-3(c) in the basis of the non-self-constructed property when it is placed in service.

(5) *Certain borrowing disregarded.* Qualified progress expenditures for non-self-constructed property do not include any amount paid to another person (the "payee") for construction if the amount is paid out of funds borrowed directly or indirectly from the payee. Amounts borrowed directly or indirectly from the payee by any person that is related to the taxpayer (within the meaning of section 267) or that is a member of the same controlled group of corporations (as defined in section 1563(a)) will be considered borrowed indirectly from the payee. Similarly, amounts borrowed under any financing arrangement that has the effect of making the payee a surety will be considered amounts borrowed indirectly by the taxpayer from the payee.

(6) *Percentage of completion limitation.* (i) Under section 46(d)(3)(B)(ii), payments made in any taxable year may be considered qualified progress expenditures for non-self-constructed property only to the extent they are attributable to progress made in construction (percentage of completion limitation). Progress will generally be measured in terms of the manufacturer's incurred cost, as a fraction of the anticipated cost (as adjusted from year to year). Architectural or engineering estimates will be evidence of progress made in construction. Cost accounting records also will be evidence of progress. Progress will be presumed to occur not more rapidly than ratably over the normal construction period. However, the taxpayer may rebut the presumption by clear and convincing evidence of a greater percentage of completion.

(ii) If, after the first year of construction, there is a change in either the total cost to the taxpayer or the total cost of construction by another person, the taxpayer must recompute the percentage of completion limitation on the basis of revised cost. However, the recomputation will affect only amounts allowed as qualified progress expenditures in the taxable year in which change occurs and in subsequent taxable years. The recomputation remains subject to the presumption of pro rata completion.

(iii) If, for any taxable year, the amount paid to another person for construction of an item of property under section 46(d)(3)(B)(i) exceeds the percentage of completion limitation in section 46(d)(3)(B)(ii), the excess is treated as an amount paid to the other person for construction for the succeeding taxable year. If for any taxable year the percentage of completion limitation for an item of property exceeds the amount paid to another during the taxable year for construction, the excess is added to the percentage of completion limitation for that property for the succeeding taxable year.

(iv) The taxpayer must maintain detailed records which permit specific identification of the amounts paid to each person for construction of each item of property and the percentage of construction completed by each person for each taxable year.

(7) *Example.* The following example illustrates paragraph (j)(6) of this section.

Example. (i) Corporation X agrees to build an airplane for corporation Y, a calendar year taxpayer. The airplane is non-self-constructed progress expenditure property. Physical work on

Reg. § 1.46-5(j)(4)

construction begins on January 1, 1980. The normal construction period for the airplane is five years and the airplane is delivered and placed in service on December 31, 1984.

(ii) The cost of construction to corporation X is $500,000. The contract price is $550,000. Corporation Y makes a $110,000 payment in each of the years 1980 and 1981, an $85,000 payment in 1982, a $135,000 payment in 1983, and a $110,000 payment in 1984.

(iii) For 1980, corporation Y makes an election under section 46(d). Progress is presumed to occur ratably over the 5-year construction period, which is 20 percent in each year. Twenty percent of the contract price is $110,000. The percentage of completion limitation for each year, thus, is $110,000.

(iv) For each of the years 1980 and 1981, the $110,000 payments may be treated as qualified progress expenditures. The payments equal the percentage of completion limitation.

(v) For 1982, the $85,000 payment may be treated as a qualified progress expenditure, because it is less than the percentage of completion limitation. The excess of the percentage of completion limitation ($110,000) over the 1982 payment ($85,000) is added to the percentage of completion limitation for 1983. One hundred and ten thousand dollars minus $85,000 equals $25,000. Twenty-five thousand dollars plus $110,000 equals $135,000, which is the percentage of completion limitation for 1983.

(vi) For 1983, the entire $135,000 payment may be treated as a qualifed progress expenditure. The payment equals the percentage of completion limitation for 1983.

(vii) For 1984, no qualified progress expenditures may be taken into account, because the airplane is placed in service in that year.

(viii) See example (2) of paragraph (r)(4) of this section for the result if Y sells its contract rights to the property on December 31, 1982.

(k) *Definition of self-constructed property*—(1) *In general.* Property is self-constructed property if it is reasonable to believe that more than half of the construction expenditures for the property will be made directly by the taxpayer. Construction expenditures made directly by the taxpayer include direct costs such as wages and materials and indirect costs such as overhead attributable to construction of the property. Expenditures for direct and indirect costs of construction will be treated as construction expenditures made directly by the taxpayer only to the extent that the expenditures directly benefit the construction of the property by employees of the taxpayer. Thus, wages paid to taxpayer's employees and expenditures for basic construction materials, such as sheet metal, lumber, glass, and nails, which are used by employees of the taxpayer to construct progress expenditure property, will be considered made directly by the taxpayer. Construction expenditures made by the taxpayer to a contractor or manufacturer, in general, will not be considered made directly by the taxpayer. Thus, the cost of component parts, such as boilers and turbines, which are purchased and merely installed or assembled by the taxpayer, will not be considered expenditures made directly by the taxpayer for construction. (*See* paragraph (h)(3) of this section to determine when such cost is properly chargeable to capital account.)

(2) *Time when determination made.* The determination of whether property is self-constructed is to be made at the close of the taxable year in which physical work on construction of the property begins, or, if later, the close of the first taxable year to which an election under this section applies. Once it is reasonably estimated that more than half of construction expenditures will be made directly by the taxpayer, the fact that the taxpayer actually makes half, or less than half, of the expenditures directly will not affect classification of the property as self-constructed property. Similarly, once a determination has been made, classification of property as self-constructed property is not affected by a change in circumstances in a later taxable year. However, a significant error unrelated to a change in circumstances may be evidence that the estimate was unreasonable when made.

(3) *Determination based on certain expenditures.* For purposes of determining whether more than half of the expenditures for construction of an item of property will be made directly by the taxpayer, the taxpayer may take into account only expenditures properly includable by the taxpayer in the basis of the property under the provisions of § 1.46-3(c). Thus, property is self-constructed property only if more than half of the estimated basis of the property to be used for purposes of determining the credit allowed by section 38 is attributable to expenditures made directly by the taxpayer.

(l) *Definition of non-self-constructed property.* Non-self-constructed property is property that is not self-constructed property. Thus, property is non-self-constructed property if it is reasonable to believe that only half, or less than half, of the expenditures for construction will be made directly by the taxpayer.

(m) *Alternative limitations for public utility, railroad, or airline property.* The alternative limi-

Reg. § 1.46-5(m)

on qualified investment under section
(7) and (8) for public utility, railroad, or
ne property (whichever applies) apply in de-
mining the credit for qualified progress expen-
atures. The determination of whether progress
expenditure property will be public utility, railroad, or airline property (whichever applies) when
placed in service must be made at the close of the
taxable year in which physical work on construction begins or, if later, at the close of the first
taxable year for which an election under section
46(d) is in effect. If, at that time, the taxpayer is
in a trade or business as a public utility, railroad,
or airline (as described in section 46(c)(3)(B) and
46(a)(8)(D) and (E), respectively), it is evidence
the property will be public utility, railroad, or
airline property when placed in service.

(n) *Leased property.* A lessor of progress expenditure property may not elect under section 48(d)
to treat a lessee (or a person who will be a lessee)
as having made qualified progress expenditures.

(o) *Election*—(1) *In general.* The election under
section 46(d)(6) to increase qualified investment
by qualified progress expenditures may be made
for any taxable year ending after December 31,
1974. Except as provided in paragraph (o)(2) of
this section, the election is effective for the first
taxable year for which it is made and for all
taxable years thereafter unless it is revoked with
the consent of the Commissioner. Except as provided in paragraphs (o)(2) and (3) of this section,
the election applies to all qualified progress expenditures made by the taxpayer during the taxable year for construction of any progress
expenditure property. Thus, the taxpayer may
not make the election for one item of progress
expenditure property and not for other items. If
progress expenditure property is being constructed by or for a partnership, S corporation (as
defined in section 1361(a)), trust, or estate, an
election under section 46(d)(6) must be made separately by each partner or shareholder, or each
beneficiary if the beneficiary, in determining his
tax liability, would be allowed investment credit
under section 38 for property subject to the election. The election may not be made by a partnership or S corporation, and may be made by a trust
or estate only if the trust or estate, in determining
its tax liability, would be allowed investment
credit under section 38 for property subject to the
election. The election of any partner, shareholder,
beneficiary, trust, or estate will be effective for
that person, even if a related partner, shareholder,
beneficiary, trust, or estate does not make the
election. An election made by a partner, shareholder, beneficiary, trust, or estate applies to all
progress expenditure property of that person. For
example, an election made by corporation X,

which is a partner in the XYZ partnership, applies to progress expenditure property the corporation holds in its own capacity and also to its
interest in progress expenditure property of the
partnership.

(2) *Time and manner of making election.* An
election under section 46(d)(6) must be made on
Form 3468 and filed with the original income tax
return for the first taxable year ending after December 31, 1974 to which the election will apply.
An election made before March 2, 1988, by filing
a written statement (whether or not attached to
the income tax return) will be considered valid.
The election may not be made on an amended
return filed after the time prescribed for filing the
original return (including extensions) for that taxable year. However, an election under this section
may be made or revoked by filing a statement
with an amended return filed on or before May
31, 1988, if the due date for filing a return for the
first taxable year to which the election applies is
before May 31, 1988.

(3) *Carryover of election in certain transactions.* In general, an election under section
48(d)(6) does not carry over to the transferee of
progress expenditure property (or an interest
therein). However, if under section 47(b) the
property does not cease to be progress expenditure
property because of the transfer, the election will
carry over to the transferee. If so, the election will
apply only to the property transferred. For rules
relating to the determination of qualified progress
expenditures of the transferee, see paragraph (r)
of this section.

(p) *Partnerships, S corporations, trusts, or estates*—(1) *In general.* Each partner, shareholder,
trust, estate, or beneficiary of a trust or estate
that makes an election under section 46(d) shall
take into account its share of qualified progress
expenditures (determined under paragraph (p)(2)
of this section) made by the partnership, S corporation, trust, or estate. In determining qualified
investment for the year in which the property is
placed in service, the basis of the property is
apportioned as provided in § § 1.46-3(f), 1.48-6, or
1.48-5 (whichever applies). Each partner, shareholder, trust, estate, or beneficiary that made the
election must reduce qualified investment under
section 46(c)(4) for the year the property is placed
in service by qualified progress expenditures
taken into account by that person.

(2) *Determination of share of qualified progress expenditures.* The share of qualified progress
expenditures of each partner, shareholder, trust,
estate, or beneficiary that makes an election
under section 46(d) must be determined in accordance with the same ratio used under

Reg. § 1.46-5(n)

§§ 1.46-3(f)(2), 1.48-5(a)(1), or 1.48-6(a)(1) (whichever applies) to determine its share of basis (or cost). The last sentence of § 1.46-3(f)(2)(i) must be applied by referring to the date on which qualified progress expenditures are paid or chargeable to capital amount (whichever is applicable).

(3) *Examples.* The following examples illustrate this paragraph (p).

Example (1). (i) Corporation X contracts to build a ship for partnership AB that qualifies as progress expenditure property. The contract price is $100,000. Physical work on construction of the ship begins on January 1, 1980. The ship is placed in service on December 31, 1983.

(ii) The AB partnership reports income on the calendar year basis. Partners A and B share profits equally. For A's taxable year ending December 31, 1980, A makes an election under section 46(d). B does not make the election.

(iii) For each of the years 1980, 1981, 1982, and 1983, the AB partnership makes $25,000 payments to corporation X. The payments made in 1980, 1981, and 1982 are qualified progress expenditures. The 1983 payment is not a qualified progress expenditure, because the ship is placed in service in that year.

(iv) For each of the years 1980, 1981, and 1982, A may take into account qualified progress expenditures of $12,500 because A had a 50 percent partnership interest in each of those years.

(v) For 1983, qualified investment for the ship is $100,000. A and B's share are $50,000 each, because each had a 50 percent partnership interest in 1983. However, A must reduce its $50,000 share for 1983 by $37,500, the amount of qualified progress expenditures taken into account by A. B's share is not reduced, because B did not take into account qualified progress expenditures.

Example (2). (i) The facts are the same as in example (1) except that on June 30, 1983, the partnership agreement is amended to admit a new partner, C. The partners agree to share profits equally. There is no special allocation in effect under section 704 with respect to the ship.

(ii) For each of the years 1980, 1981, and 1982, A may take into account qualified progress expenditures of $12,500 because A has a 50 percent partnership interest in those years.

(iii) For 1983, A, B, and C's share of qualified investment is $33,333 each, because each had a 33⅓ percent partnership interest in that year. A must reduce its share to zero, because it took $37,500 into account as qualified progress expenditures. In addition, the excess of the $37,500 over

the $33,333 applied as a reduction is subject to recapture under section 47(a)(3)(B). B and C's shares are not reduced, because neither taxpayer took into account qualified progress expenditures.

(q) *Limitation on qualified progress expenditures for taxable years beginning before 1980*—(1) *In general.* (i) Under section 46(d)(7), qualified progress expenditures for any taxable year beginning before January 1, 1980, are limited. The taxpayer must apply the limitation under section 46(d)(7) on an item by item basis. In general, the taxpayer may take into account the applicable percentage (as determined under the table in section 46(d)(7)(A)) of qualified progress expenditures for each of those years. In addition, the taxpayer may take into account for each of those years 20 percent of qualified investment for each of the preceding taxable years determined without applying the limitations of section 46(d)(7).

(ii) The applicable percentage under section 46(d)(7)(A) may be applied only for one taxable year that ends within a calendar year in determining qualified investment for an item of progress expenditure property. For example, calendar year partners of a calendar year partnership may increase qualified investment for 1976 by 20 percent of qualified progress expenditures made in 1975 for an item of property. If the partnership incorporates in 1976 and the taxable year of the corporation begins on July 1, 1976, and ends on June 30, 1977, qualified investment of the corporation for its taxable year beginning on July 1, 1976, cannot be increased by 20 percent of the 1975 expenditure.

(2) *Example.* The following example illustrates this paragraph (q).

Example. (i) Corporation X contracts with A on January 1, 1976, to build an electric generator that qualifies as non-self-constructed progress expenditure property. A will build the generator at a cost of $125,000. Corporation X agrees to pay A $150,000. Corporation X reports income on the calendar year basis. Corporation X makes an election under section 46(d) for 1976. Physical work on construction begins on January 1, 1976. Corporation X makes payments of $30,000 to A for construction of the generator in each of the years 1976, 1977, 1978, 1979, and 1980. A incurs a cost of $25,000 in each of those years for construction of the property. The property is placed in service in 1980.

(ii) For 1976, X may increase qualified investment by $12,000, 40 percent of the payment made in 1976.

(iii) For 1977, corporation X may increase qualified investment by $24,000. Eighteen thousand dollars of that amount is 60 percent of the

✓ payment. The remaining $6,000 is 20 per-
it of the $30,000 payment made in 1976.

(iv) For 1978, corporation X may increase
qualified investment by $36,000. Twenty-four
thousand dollars of that amount is 80 percent of
the 1978 payment. The remaining $12,000 is 20
percent of the $30,000 payment made in 1976,
plus 20 percent of the $30,000 payment made in
1977.

(v) For 1979, corporation X may increase
qualified investment by $48,000. Thirty thousand
dollars of that amount is 100 percent of the 1979
payment. The remaining $18,000 of that amount
is 20 percent of the $30,000 payment made in
each of the years 1976, 1977, and 1978.

(vi) Qualified investment for corporation X
for 1980 is $30,000. The $30,000 is the basis (or
cost) of the generator ($150,000), reduced by
qualified progress expenditures allowed with respect to that property ($120,000).

(r) *Special rules for transferred property*—(1)
In general. A transferee of progress expenditure
property (or an interest therein) may take into
account qualified progress expenditures for the
property only if—

(i) The property is progress expenditure
property in the hands of the transferee, and

(ii) The transferee makes an election under
section 46(d) or the election made by the transferor (or its predecessor) carries over to the transferee under paragraph (o)(3) of this section.

(2) *Status as progress expenditure property.*
(i) If the transfer requires recapture under section
47(a)(3) and § 1.47-1(g) (or would require recapture if the transferor had made an election under
section 46(d)), then—

(A) For purposes of determining if the
property is progress expenditure property in the
hands of the transferee, the normal construction
period for the property begins on the date of the
transfer, or, if later, on the first day of the first
taxable year for which the transferee makes an
election under section 46(d), and

(B) For purposes of determining whether
the property is self-constructed or non-self-constructed in the hands of the transferee, the
amount paid or incurred for the transfer of the
property will not be considered a construction
expenditure made directly by the transferee.

(ii) If the transfer does not require recapture under section 47(a)(3) and § 1.47-1(g), and
the election carries over to the taxpayer under
paragraph (o)(3) of this section, the property does
not lose its status as progress expenditure property because of the transfer.

(3) *Amount of qualified progress expenditures for transferee.* (i) If the transfer does not
require recapture under section 47(a)(3) and
§ 1.47-1(g), and the election carries over to the
taxpayer under paragraph (o)(3) of this section,
the transferee must determine its qualified progress expenditures—

(A) By using the same normal construction period used by the transferor,

(B) By treating the property as having
the same status as self-constructed or non-self-
constructed as the property had in the hands of
the transferor, and

(C) In the case of non-self-constructed
property, by taking into account any excess described in section 46(d)(4)(C)(i) (relating to the
excess of payments over the percentage-of-completion limitation) or section 46(d)(4)(C)(ii) (relating
to the excess of the percentage-of-completion limitation over the amount of payments) that the
transferor would have taken into account with
respect to that property.

(ii) If the transfer requires recapture
under section 47(a)(3) and § 1.47-1(g) (or would
require recapture if the transferor had made an
election under section 46(d)), the amount paid or
incurred for the transfer will be considered a payment for construction of that property to the
extent that—

(A) It is properly includible in the basis
of the property under § 1.46-3(c),

(B) The taxpayer can show the amount
is attributable to construction costs paid or
chargeable to capital account by the transferor or
other person after physical work on construction
of the property began, and

(C) It does not exceed the amount by
which the transferor has increased qualified investment for qualified progress expenditures incurred with respect to the property (or would
have increased qualified investment but for the
"lesser of" limitation of section 46(d)(3)(B) or the
absence of an election under section 46(d)), plus
any amount that would have been treated as a
qualified progress expenditure by the transferor
had the property not been transferred.

Once the status of the property as self-constructed
or non-self-constructed property in the hands of
the transferee has been determined, all rules
under this section for determining the amount of
qualified progress expenditures for that type of
property apply. For example, if the property is
non-self-constructed in the hands of the transferee, amounts merely incurred (but not paid) for
the transfer are not taken into account as qualified progress expenditures. Actual payment is

Reg. § 1.46-5(r)(1)

necessary (see paragraph (j)(3) of this section). In applying section 46(d)(3)(B)(ii), the amount paid or incurred for the transfer (to the extent that it qualifies as a payment for construction under the first sentence of this paragraph (r)(3)(ii)) is considered to be part of the overall cost to the transferee of construction by another person, and the portion of construction which is completed during the taxable year is determined by taking into account construction that was completed before the constructed property was acquired by the transferee. If the transferee makes an election under section 46(d) and this section for the taxable year in which the transfer occurs, then for purposes of applying the presumption in section 46(d)(4)(D) that construction is deemed to occur not more rapidly than ratably over the normal construction period, the transferee's normal construction period is considered to have begun on the date on which physical work on construction of the acquired property began.

(4) *Examples.* The following examples illustrate this paragraph (r).

Example (1). Corporation X begins physical work on construction of progress expenditure property for corporation Y on January 1, 1976. Y accurately estimates a 3-year normal construction period and elects under section 48(d) on its return for its taxable year ending December 31, 1976. On January 1, 1978, Y sells the contract rights for construction of the property to corporation Z, which uses a fiscal year ending June 30. Qualified progress expenditures allowed to Y in 1976 and 1977 are subject to recapture under section 47(a)(3). Because Z's normal construction period for the property is less than 2 years (January 1, 1978 to January 1, 1979), the property is not progress expenditure property in Z's hands. Z may not elect progress expenditure treatment for the property.

Example (2). (i) Assume the same facts as in the example in paragraph (j)(7) of this section, except on December 31, 1982, Y sells its contract rights to the property for $340,000 to corporation Z, which also uses the calendar year. Z pays Y the full $340,000 on that date. The property is still to be placed in service on December 31, 1984, and will not be available for placing in service at an earlier date. Z makes payments to X of $135,000 on December 31, 1983, and $110,000 on December 31, 1984.

(ii) The investment credit allowed Y in 1980 and 1981 for qualified progress expenditures is subject to recapture under section 47(a)(3) and Y may not treat its $85,000 payment in 1982 as a qualified progress expenditure.

(iii) For purposes of determining if the plane is qualified progress expenditure property with respect to Z, the normal construction period for the property for Z begins on December 31, 1982, the date of transfer. Since the remaining construction period is two years, the property is progress expenditure property if it otherwise qualifies in Z's hands.

(iv) Only $305,000 of the $340,000 payment to Y can qualify as a qualified progress expenditure, because only that amount is attributable to construction costs paid by Y and does not exceed the sum of the amount by which Y increased qualified investment in 1980 and 1981 for qualified progress expenditures ($220,000) and the amount that Y would have treated as a qualified progress expenditure in 1982 ($85,000).

(v) Assume that Z cannot establish that progress in construction has been completed more rapidly than ratably. If Z makes an election under section 46(d) for 1982, then for purposes of applying the percentage of completion limitation, Z's normal construction period is considered to begin on January 1, 1980. Progress is presumed to occur ratably over the 5-year construction period, which is 20 percent in each year.

(vi) For 1982, Z may treat the full $305,000 as a qualified progress expenditure because it is less than the percentage of completion limitation, $330,000 ($110,000 a year for 1980, 1981, and 1982).

(vii) For 1983, Z may treat the entire $135,000 payment as a qualified progress expenditure, since it does not exceed the percentage of completion limitation for that year, $135,000 ($110,000 plus the $25,000 excess from 1982).

(viii) For Z's taxable year ending December 31, 1984, no qualified progress expenditures may be taken into account because the property is placed in service during that year. [Reg. § 1.46-5.]

□ [*T.D.* 8183, 3-1-88.]

[Reg. § 1.46-6]

§ 1.46-6. **Limitation in case of certain regulated companies.**—(a) *In general*—(1) *Scope of section.* This section does not reflect amendments made to section 46 after enactment of the Revenue Act of 1971, other than the redesignation of section 46(e) as section 46(f) by the Tax Reduction Act of 1975.

(2) *Disallowance of credit.* Under section 46(f), a credit otherwise allowable under section 38 ("credit") will be disallowed in certain cases with respect to "section 46(f) property" as defined in paragraph (b)(1) of this section. Paragraph (f) of this section describes circumstances

Reg. § 1.46-6(a)(2)

:r which a determination put into effect by a .ulatory body will result in the disallowance of ·e credit. Such a determination will result in a .isallowance only if section 46(f)(1) or (2) applies to such property and such determination affects the taxpayer's cost of service or rate base in a manner inconsistent with section 46(f)(1) or (2) (whichever is applicable).

(3) *General rules.* The provisions of section 46(f)(1) and (2) are limitations on the treatment of the credit for ratemaking purposes and for purposes of the taxpayer's regulated books of account only. Under the provisions of section 46(f)(1), the credit may not be flowed through to income (*i.e.*, used to reduce taxpayer's cost of service) but in certain circumstances may be used to reduce rate base (provided that such reduction is restored not less rapidly than ratably). If an election is made under section 46(f)(2), the credit may be flowed through to income (but not more rapidly than ratably) and there may not be any reduction in rate base. If an election is made under section 46(f)(3), none of the limitations of section 46(f)(1) or (2) apply to certain section 46(f) property of the taxpayer. Thus, under the provisions of section 46(f)(3), no credit is disallowed if the credit is treated in any manner for ratemaking purposes, including any manner of treatment permitted under the limitations of section 46(f)(1) or (2).

(4) *Elections.* For rules relating to the manner of making, on or before March 9, 1972, the three elections listed in section 46(f)(1), (2), and (3), see 26 CFR 12.3. For rules relating to the application of such elections, see paragraph (h) of this section.

(5) *Cross references.* For rules with respect to the treatment of corporate reorganizations, asset acquisitions, and taxpayers subject to the jurisdiction of more than one regulatory body, etc., see paragraph (j) of this section.

(6) *Nonapplication of prior law.* Under section 105(e) of the Revenue Act of 1971, section 203(e) of the Revenue Act of 1964, 78 Stat. 35, does not apply to section 46(f) property.

(b) *Definitions.* For purposes of this section, the following definitions apply:

(1) *Section 46(f) property.* "Section 46(f) property" is property described in section 50 that is—

(i) Public utility property within the meaning of section 46(c)(3)(B) (other than nonregulated communication property described in § 1.46-3(g)(2)(iv)) or

(ii) Property used predominantly in the trade or business of the furnishing or sale of steam through a local distribution system or of the transportation of gas or steam by pipeline, if the rates for the trade or business are regulated within the meaning of § 1.46-3(g)(2)(iii).

For purposes of determining whether property is used predominantly in the trade or business of transportation of gas by pipeline (or of transportation of gas by pipeline and of furnishing or sale of gas through a local distribution system), the rules prescribed in § 1.46-3(g)(4) apply except that accounts 365 through 371 inclusive (Transmission Plant) are added to the accounts listed in § 1.46-3(g)(4)(i).

(2) *Cost of service.* (i) (A) For purposes of this section, "cost of service" is the amount required by a taxpayer to provide regulated goods or services. Cost of service includes operating expenses (including salaries, cost of materials, etc.), maintenance expenses, depreciation expenses, tax expenses, and interest expenses. For purposes of this section, any effect on a taxpayer's permitted return on investment that results from a reduction in the taxpayer's rate base does not constitute a reduction in cost of service, even though, as a technical ratemaking term, "cost of service" ordinarily includes a permitted return on investment. In addition, taking into account a deduction for the additional interest that the taxpayer would pay or accrue if the credit were unavailable in determining Federal income tax expense ("synchronization of interest") does not constitute a reduction in cost of service for purposes of section 46(f)(2). This adjustment to Federal income tax expense may be taken into account in determining cost of service for the regulated accounting period or periods that include the taxable year to which the adjustment relates or for any subsequent regulated accounting period.

(B) See paragraph (b)(3)(ii)(B) of this section for rules relating to the amount of additional interest that the taxpayer would pay or accrue if the credit were unavailable.

(ii) In determining whether, or to what extent, a credit has been used to reduce cost of service, reference shall be made to any accounting treatment that affects cost of service. Examples of such treatment include reducing by all or a portion of the credit the amount of Federal income tax expense taken into account for ratemaking purposes and reducing the depreciable bases of property by all or a portion of the credit for ratemaking purposes.

(3) *Rate base.* (i) For purposes of this section, "rate base" is the monetary amount that is multiplied by a rate of return to determine the permitted return on investment.

Reg. § 1.46-6(a)(3)

(ii)(A) In determining whether, or to what extent, a credit has been used to reduce rate base, reference shall be made to any accounting treatment that affects rate base. In addition, in those cases in which the rate of return is based on the taxpayer's cost of capital, reference shall be made to any accounting treatment that reduces the permitted return on investment by treating the credit less favorably than the capital that would have been provided if the credit were unavailable. Thus, the credit may not be assigned a "cost of capital" rate that is less than the overall cost of capital rate, determined on the basis of a weighted average, for the capital that would have been provided if the credit were unavailable.

(B) For purposes of determining the cost of capital rate assigned to the credit and the amount of additional interest that the taxpayer would pay or accrue, the composition of the capital that would have been provided if the credit were unavailable may be determined—

(1) On the basis of all the relevant facts and circumstances; or

(2) By assuming for both such purposes that such capital would be provided solely by common shareholders, preferred shareholders, and long-term creditors in the same proportions and at the same rates of return as the capital actually provided to the taxpayer by such shareholders and creditors.

For purposes of this section, capital provided by long-term creditors does not include deferred taxes as described in section 167(l)(3)(G) or 168(e)(3)(B)(ii).

(C) If a taxpayer's overall rate of return is based on a deemed or hypothetical capital structure, paragraph (b)(3)(ii)(B) of this section shall be applied by treating the deemed or hypothetical capital as if it were the capital actually provided to the taxpayer and determining the composition of the capital that would have been provided if the credit were unavailable in a manner consistent with such treatment.

(iii) Whether, or to what extent, a credit has been used to reduce rate base for any period to which pre-June 23, 1986, rates apply will be determined under 26 CFR 1.46-6(b)(3) and (4) (revised as of April 1, 1985) if such a determination avoids disallowance of a credit that would be disallowed under paragraph (b)(3)(ii) or (4)(ii) of this section. For this purpose, a period to which pre-June 23, 1986, rates apply is any period for which the effect of the credit on rate base for ratemaking purposes is established under a determination put into effect (within the meaning of paragraph (f) of this section) before June 23, 1986.

(4) *Indirect reductions to cost of service or rate base.* (i) Cost of service or rate base is considered to have been reduced by reason of all or a portion of a credit if such reduction is made in an indirect manner.

(ii) One type of such indirect reduction is any ratemaking decision in which the credit is treated as operating income (subject to ratemaking regulation) or is treated less favorably than the capital that would have been provided if the credit were unavailable. For example, if the credit is accounted for as nonoperating income on a company's regulated books of account but a ratemaking decision has the effect of treating the credit as operating income in determining rate of return to common shareholders, then cost of service has been indirectly reduced by reason of the credit.

(iii) A second type of indirect reduction is any ratemaking decision intended to achieve an effect similar to a direct reduction to cost of service or rate base. In determining whether a ratemaking decision is intended to achieve this effect, consideration is given to all the relevant facts and circumstances of each case, including, but not limited to—

(A) The record of the proceeding,

(B) The regulatory body's orders or opinions (including any dissenting views), and

(C) The anticipated effect of the ratemaking decision on the company's revenues in comparison to a direct reduction to cost of service or rate base by reason of the investment tax credits available to the regulated company.

(iv) This subdivision (iv) describes a situation that is not an indirect reduction to cost of service or rate base by reason of all or a portion of a credit. The ratemaking treatment of credits may affect the financial condition of a company, including the company's ability to attract new capital, the cost of that capital, the company's future financial requirements, the market price of the company's securities, and the degree of risk attributable to investment in those securities. The financial condition may be reflected in certain customary financial indicators such as the comparative capital structure of the company, coverage ratios, price/earnings ratios, and price/book ratios. Under the facts and circumstances test of paragraph (b)(4)(iii) of this section, the consideration of a company's financial condition by a regulatory body is not an indirect reduction to cost of service or rate base, even though such condition, as affected by the ratemaking treatment of the company's investment tax credits, is considered in the development of a reasonable rate of return on common shareholders' investment.

Reg. § 1.46-6(b)(4)

General rule—(1) *In general.* Section)(1) applies to all of the taxpayer's section .f) property except property to which an election under section 46(f)(2) or (3) applies. Under section 46(f)(1), the credit for the taxpayer's section 46(f) property will be disallowed if—

(i) The taxpayer's cost of service for ratemaking purposes is reduced by reason of any portion of such credit, or

(ii) The taxpayer's rate base is reduced by reason of any portion of the credit and such reduction in rate base is not restored or is restored less rapidly than ratably within the meaning of paragraph (g) of this section.

(2) *Insufficient natural domestic supply.* The provisions of paragraph (c)(1)(ii) of this section shall not apply to permit any reduction in taxpayer's rate base with respect to its "short supply property" if it made an election under the last sentence of section 46(f)(1) on or before March 9, 1972.

(3) *Short supply property.* For purposes of this section, section 46(f) property is "short supply property" if—

(i) The property is described in paragraph (b)(1)(ii) of this section,

(ii) The regulatory body described in section 46(c)(3)(B) that has jurisdiction for ratemaking purposes with respect to such trade or business is an agency or instrumentality of the United States, and

(iii) This regulatory body makes a short supply determination and the determination is in effect on the date such property is placed in service.

(4) *Short supply determination.* A short supply determination is made or revoked on the date of its publication in the FEDERAL REGISTER. It is a determination that the natural domestic supply of gas or steam is insufficient to meet the present and future requirements of the domestic economy.

(5) *Dates short supply determination in effect.* (i) A short supply determination is considered to be in effect with respect to section 46(f) property placed in service at any time before the determination is revoked. However, a short supply determination made after June 18, 1979, is not considered to be in effect with respect to section 46(f) property placed in service before such determination was made.

(d) *Special rule for ratable flow-through.* If an election was made under section 46(f)(2) on or before March 9, 1972, section 46(f)(2) applies to all of the taxpayer's section 46(f) property except property to which an election under section 46(f)(3) applies. Under section 46(f)(2), the credit

for the taxpayer's section 46(f) property will be disallowed if—

(1) The taxpayer's cost of service, for ratemaking purposes or in its regulated books of account, is reduced by more than a ratable portion of such credit within the meaning of paragraph (g) of this section or

(2) The taxpayer's rate base is reduced by reason of any portion of such credit.

(e) *Flow-through property.* If a taxpayer made an election under section 46(f)(3) on or before March 9, 1972, section 46(f)(1) and (2) do not apply to the taxpayer's section 46(f) property to which section 167(l)(2)(C) applies. In the case of an election under section 46(f)(3), a credit will not be disallowed, notwithstanding a determination by a regulatory body having jurisdiction over such taxpayer that reduces the taxpayer's cost of service or rate base by reason of such credit. In general, section 167(l)(2)(C) applies to property with respect to which a taxpayer may use a flow-through method of accounting (within the meaning of section 167(l)(3)(H)) to take into account the allowance for depreciation under section 167(a). Section 167(l)(2)(C) applies to property even though the taxpayer does not use a flow-through method of accounting with respect to the property. Section 167(l)(2)(C) does not apply to property if the taxpayer can not use a flow-through method of accounting with respect to the property. For example, section 167(l)(2)(C) does not apply to property with respect to which an election under section 167(l)(4)(A) applies. Thus, such property does not qualify for an election under section 46(f)(3).

(f) *Limitations*—(1) *In general.* This paragraph provides rules relating to limitations on the disallowance of credits under section 46(f)(4). Key terms are defined in paragraphs (f)(7), (8), and (9) of this section.

(2) *Disallowance postponed.* There is no disallowance of a credit before the first final inconsistent determination is put into effect for the taxpayer's section 46(f) property.

(3) *Time of disallowance.* A credit is disallowed—

(i) When the first final inconsistent determination is put into effect and

(ii) When any inconsistent determination (whether or not final) is put into effect after the first final inconsistent determination is put into effect.

(4) *Credits disallowed.* A credit is disallowed for section 46(f) property placed in service (within the meaning of § 1.46-3(d)) by the taxpayer—

Reg. § 1.46-6(c)(1)

(i) Before the date any inconsistent determination described in paragraph (f)(2) of this section is put into effect and

(ii) On or after such date and before the date a subsequent consistent determination (whether or not final) is put into effect.

(5) *Barred years.* No amount of credit for a taxable year is disallowed under paragraph (f)(3) of this section if, for such year, assessment of a deficiency is barred by any law or rule of law.

(6) *Notification and other requirements.* The taxpayer shall notify the district director of a disallowance of a credit under paragraph (f)(3) of this section within 30 days of the date that the applicable determination is put into effect. In the case of such a disallowance, the taxpayer shall recompute its tax liability for any affected taxable year, and such recomputation shall be made in the form of an amended return where necessary.

(7) *Determinations.* For purposes of this paragraph, the term "determination" refers to a determination made with respect to section 46(f) property (other than property to which an election under section 46(f)(3) applies) by a regulatory body described in section 46(c)(3)(B) that determines the effect of the credit—

(i) For purposes of section 46(f)(1), on the taxpayer's cost of service or rate base for ratemaking purposes or

(ii) In the case of a taxpayer that made an election under section 46(f)(2), on the taxpayer's cost of service, for ratemaking purposes or in its regulated books of account, or on the taxpayer's rate base for ratemaking purposes. A regulatory body does not have to take affirmative action to make a determination. Thus, a regulatory body's failure to take action on a rate schedule filed by a taxpayer is a determination if the rates can be put into effect without further action by the regulatory body.

(8) *Types of determinations.* For purposes of this paragraph—

(i) The term "inconsistent" refers to a determination that is inconsistent with section 46(f)(1) or (2) (as the case may be). Thus, for example, a determination to reduce the taxpayer's cost of service by more than a ratable portion of the credit would be a determination that is inconsistent with section 46(f)(2). As a further example, such a determination would also be inconsistent if section 46(f)(1) applied because no reduction in cost of service is permitted under section 46(f)(1).

(ii) The term "consistent" refers to a determination that is consistent with section 46(f)(1) or (2) (as the case may be).

(iii) The term "final determinat[ion]" means a determination with respect to which rights to appeal or to request a review, a rehe[ar]ing, or a redetermination have been exhausted [or] have lapsed.

(iv) The term "first final inconsistent determination" means the first final determination put into effect after December 10, 1971, that is inconsistent with section 46(f)(1) or (2) (as the case may be).

(9) *Put into effect.* A determination is put into effect on the later of—

(i) The date it is issued (or, if a first final inconsistent determination, the date it becomes final) or

(ii) The date it becomes operative.

(10) *Examples.* The provisions of. this paragraph may be illustrated by the following examples:

Example (1). Corporation X, a calendar-year taxpayer engaged in a public utility activity is subject to the jurisdiction of regulatory body A. On September 15, 1971, X purchases section 46(f) property and places it in service on that date. For 1971, X takes the credit allowable by section 38 with respect to such property. X does not make any election permitted by section 46(f). On October 9, 1972, A makes a determination that X must account for the credit allowable under section 38 in a manner inconsistent with section 46(f)(1). The determination, which was the first determination by A after December 10, 1971, becomes final on January 1, 1973, and holds that X must retroactively adjust the manner in which it accounted for the credit allowable under section 38 starting with the taxable year that began on January 1, 1972. Since, under the provisions of paragraph (f)(8) of this section, the determination by A is put into effect on January 1, 1973 (the date it becomes final), the credit is retroactively disallowed with respect to any of X's section 46(f) property placed in service before January 1, 1973, on any date which occurs during a taxable year with respect to which an assessment of a deficiency has not been barred by any law or rule of law. In addition, the credit is disallowed with respect to X's section 46(f) property placed in service on or after January 1, 1973, and before the date that a subsequent determination by A, which as to X is consistent with section 46(f)(1), is put into effect. Thus, X must amend its income tax return for 1971 to reflect the retroactive disallowance of the credit otherwise allowable under section 38 with respect to the section 46(f) property placed in service on September 15, 1971.

Example (2). The facts are the same as in example (1), except that the first inconsistent

Reg. § 1.46-6(f)(10)

rmination by A becomes final on April 5, 72, and requires X to account for the credit for l taxable years beginning on or after January 1, 1973, in a manner inconsistent with section 46(f)(1). Under the provisions of paragraph (f)(8) of this section, the determination was put into effect on January 1, 1973 (the date it became operative). The result is the same as in example (1).

Example (3). The facts are the same as in example (1), except that on June 1, 1975, A issues a determination that X shall retroactively account for the credit allowable by section 38 in a manner consistent with the provisions of section 46(f)(1) for taxable years beginning on or after January 1, 1971. The determination becomes final on January 5, 1976, in the same form as originally issued. The result is the same as in example (1) with respect to property X places in service before June 1, 1975. The credit is allowed with respect to property X places in service on or after June 1, 1975 (the date that the consistent determination is put into effect).

(g) Ratable methods—(1) In general. Under this paragraph (g), rules are prescribed for purposes of determining whether or not, under section 46(f)(1), a reduction in the taxpayer's rate base with respect to the credit is restored less rapidly than ratably and whether or not under section 46(f)(2) the taxpayer's cost of service for ratemaking purposes is reduced by more than a ratable portion of such credit.

(2) Regulated depreciation expense. What is "ratable" is determined by considering the period of time actually used in computing the taxpayer's regulated depreciation expense for the property for which a credit is allowed. "Regulated depreciation expense" is the depreciation expense for the property used by a regulatory body for purposes of establishing the taxpayer's cost of service for ratemaking purposes. Such period of time shall be expressed in units of years (or shorter periods), units of production, or machine hours and shall be determined in accordance with the individual useful life system or composite (or other group asset) account system actually used in computing the taxpayer's regulated depreciation expense. A method of restoring, or reducing, is ratable if the amount to be restored to rate base, or to reduce cost of service (as the case may be), is allocated ratably in proportion to the number of such units. Thus, for example, assume that the regulated depreciation expense is computed under the straight line method by applying a composite annual percentage rate to "original cost" (as defined for purposes of computing regulated depreciation expense). If, with respect to an item of section 46(f)

property, the amount to be restored annually to rate base is computed by applying a composite annual percentage rate to the amount by which the rate base was reduced, then the restoration is ratable. Similarly, if cost of service is reduced annually by an amount computed by applying a composite annual percentage rate to the amount of the credit, cost of service is reduced by a ratable portion. If such composite annual percentage rate were revised for purposes of computing regulated depreciation expense beginning with a particular accounting period, the computation of ratable restoration or ratable portion (as the case may be) must also be revised beginning with such period. A composite annual percentage rate is determined solely by reference to the period of time actually used by the taxpayer in computing its regulated depreciation expense without reduction for salvage or other items such as over and under accruals. A composite annual percentage rate determined by taking into account salvage value or other items shall be considered to be ratable in the case of a determination (whether or not final) issued before March 22, 1979, and any rate order (whether or not final) that is entered into before June 20, 1979, in response to a rate case filed before April 23, 1979. For this purpose, the term "rate order" does not include an order by a regulatory body that perfunctorily adopts rates as filed if such rates are suspended or subject to rebate.

(h) Elections—(1) Applicability of elections. (i) Any election under section 46(f) applies to all of the taxpayer's property eligible for the election, whether or not the taxpayer is regulated by more than one regulatory body.

(ii) Section 46(f)(1) applies to all of the taxpayer's section 46(f) property in the absence of an election under either section 46(f)(2) or (3). If an election is made under section 46(f)(2), section 46(f)(1) does not apply to any of the taxpayer's section 46(f) property.

(iii) An election made under the last sentence of section 46(f)(1) applies to that portion of the taxpayer's section 46(f) property to which section 46(f)(1) applies and which is short supply property within the meaning of paragraph (c)(2) of this section.

(iv) If a taxpayer makes an election under section 46(f)(2) and makes no election under section 46(f)(3), the election under section 46(f)(2) applies to all of the taxpayer's section 46(f) property.

(v) If a taxpayer makes an election under section 46(f)(3), such election applies to all of the taxpayer's section 46(f) property to which section 167(l)(2)(C) applies. Section 46(f)(1) or (2) (as the

Reg. § 1.46-6(g)(1)

case may be) applies to that portion of the taxpayer's section 46(f) property that is not property to which section 167(l)(2)(C) applies. Thus, for example, if a taxpayer makes an election under section 46(f)(2) and also makes an election under section 46(f)(3), section 46(f)(3) applies to all of the taxpayer's section 46(f) property to which section 167(l)(2)(C) applies, and section 46(f)(2) applies to the remainder of the taxpayer's section 46(f) property.

(2) *Method of making elections.* See 26 CFR 12.3 for rules relating to the method of making the elections described in section 46(f)(1), (2), or (3).

(i) [Reserved]

(j) *Reorganizations, asset acquisitions, multiple regulation, etc.*—(1) *Taxpayers not entirely subject to jurisdiction of one regulatory body.* (i) If a taxpayer is required by a regulatory body having jurisdiction over less than all of its property to account for the credit under a determination that is inconsistent with section 46(f)(1) or (2) (as the case may be), such credit shall be disallowed only with respect to property subject to the jurisdiction of such regulatory body.

(ii) For purposes of this paragraph (j), a regulatory body is considered to have jurisdiction over property of a taxpayer if the property is included in the rate base for which the regulatory body determines an allowable rate of return for ratemaking purposes or if expenses with respect to the property are included in cost of service as determined by the regulatory body for ratemaking purposes. For example, if regulatory body A, having jurisdiction over 60 percent of an item of corporation X's section 46(f) property, makes a determination which is inconsistent with section 46(f), and if regulatory body B, having jurisdiction over the remaining 40 percent of such item of property, makes a consistent determination (or if the remaining 40 percent is not subject to the jurisdiction of any regulatory body), then 60 percent of the credit for such item will be disallowed. For a further example, if regulatory body A, having jurisdiction over 60 percent of X's section 46(f) property, has jurisdiction over 100 percent of a particular generator, 100 percent of the credit for such generator will be disallowed.

(iii) For rules which provide that the 3 elections under section 46(f) may not be made with respect to less than all of the taxpayer's property eligible for the election, see paragraph (h)(1)(i) of this section.

(2) [Reserved]

[Reg. § 1.46-6.]

□ [*T.D. 7602, 3-20-79. Amended by T.D.* ⟨ 5-21-86.]

[Reg. § 1.46-11]

§ 1.46-11. Commuter highway vehicles.—(a) *In general.* Section 46(c)(6) provides that the applicable percentage to determine qualified investment under section 46(c)(1) for a qualifying commuter highway vehicle is 100 percent. A qualifying commuter highway vehicle is a vehicle (defined in paragraph (b) of this section)—

(1) Which is acquired by the taxpayer on or after November 9, 1978,

(2) Which is placed in service by the taxpayer before January 1, 1986, and

(3) With respect to which the taxpayer makes an election under paragraph (g) of this section.

(b) *Definition of commuter highway vehicle.* A commuter highway vehicle is a highway vehicle that meets the following requirements:

(1) The vehicle is section 38 property in the hands of the taxpayer. The rule of section 48(d), allowing a lessor to elect to treat the lessee of new section 38 property as having acquired the property, applies to commuter highway vehicles. If the vehicle is leased and that election is made, the lessee is treated as the taxpayer under this section. However, if that election is not made, the lessor, and not the lessee, is treated as the taxpayer under this section;

(2) The vehicle must meet the seating capacity of paragraph (c) of this section; and

(3) The taxpayer reasonably expects to meet the commuter use requirement of paragraph (d) of this section for at least the first 36 months after the vehicle is placed in service.

(c) *Seating capacity.* A commuter highway vehicle must have a seating capacity of at least 8 adults in addition to the driver's seat.

(d) *Commuter use requirement.* A vehicle meets the commuter use requirement only if at least 80 percent of the miles the vehicle is driven are for trips to transport the taxpayer's employees between their residences and their places of employment. A trip for this purpose includes driving the vehicle before or after employees are in the vehicle, so long as the mileage driven is necessary either to pick up or drop off passengers or to park the vehicle in its regular parking space. A trip does not include miles driven solely for maintenance or to refuel the vehicle. A trip is not considered to transport the taxpayer's employees between their residences and their places of employment unless at least one-half the seating capacity (defined in paragraph (c) of this section) is

Reg. § 1.46-11(d)

to seat employees of the taxpayer. In no at is the driver counted as an employee of the payer.

(e) *Definition of employee.* An employee in this section is the same as in section 3121(d) (definition of employee for withholding purposes).

(f) *Transportation between employee's residence and place of employment.* An employee is transported between that employee's residence and place of employment even if that place of employment is not the same as any of the other employees transported, and even if picked up or dropped off at some central point between that residence and place of employment. An employee is not transported between that employee's residence and place of employment if the transportation is of the type for which a deduction would be allowed under § 1.162-2 were the employee providing it, such as the transportation from one work site to another after beginning work for the day.

(g) *Election.* A taxpayer must elect to have the vehicle treated as a qualifying commuter highway vehicle on the return for the taxable year in which the vehicle is placed in service. The election may be made only if the vehicle actually meets the commuter use requirement under paragraph (d) of this section for that taxable year. It must be made on or before the due date (including extensions) of that return. The election is effective as of that due date. [Reg. § 1.46-11.]

□ [*T.D.* 8035, 7-18-85.]

[Reg. § 1.47-1]

§ 1.47-1. Recomputation of credit allowed by section 38.—(a) *General rule*—(1) *In general* — (i) If during the taxable year any section 38 property the basis (or cost) of which was taken into account, under paragraph (a) of § 1.46-3, in computing the taxpayer's qualified investment is disposed of, or otherwise ceases to be section 38 property or becomes public utility property (as defined in paragraph (g) of § 1.46-3) or is a qualifying commuter highway vehicle (as defined in paragraph (a) of § 1.46-11) which undergoes a change in use (as defined in paragraph (m)(2) of this section) with respect to the taxpayer, before the close of the estimated useful life (as determined under subparagraph (2)(i) of this paragraph) which was taken into account in computing such qualified investment, then the credit earned for the credit year (as defined in subdivision (ii)(*a*) of this subparagraph) shall be recomputed under the principles of paragraph (a) of § 1.46-1 and paragraph (a) of § 1.46-3 substituting, in lieu of the estimated useful life of the property that was taken into account originally in

computing qualified investment, the actual useful life of the property as determined under subparagraph (2)(ii) of this paragraph. There shall also be recomputed under the principles of § § 1.46-1 and 1.46-2 the credit allowed for the credit year and for any other taxable year affected by reason of the reduction in credit earned for the credit year, giving effect to such reduction in the computation of carryovers or carrybacks of unused credit. If the recomputation described in the preceding sentence results in the aggregate in a decrease (taking into account any recomputations under this paragraph in respect of prior recapture years, as defined in subdivision (ii)(*b*) of this subparagraph) in the credits allowed for the credit year and for any other taxable year affected by the reduction in credit earned for the credit year, then the income tax for the recapture year shall be increased by the amount of such decrease in credits allowed. For treatment of such increase in tax, see paragraph (b) of this section. For rules relating to "disposition" and "cessation", see § 1.47-2. For rules relating to certain exceptions to the application of this section, see § 1.47-3. For special rules in the case of an electing small business corporation (as defined in section 1371(b)), an estate or trust, or a partnership, see respectively, § 1.47-4, 1.47-5, or 1.47-6. For rules applicable to energy property, see paragraph (h) of this section. For special rules relating to recomputation of credit allowed by section 38 if progress expenditure property (as defined in § 1.46-5(d)) ceases to be progress expenditure property with respect to the taxpayer, see paragraph (g) of this section.

(ii) For purposes of this section and § § 1.47-2 through 1.47-6—

(*a*) The term "credit year" means the taxable year in which section 38 property was taken into account in computing a taxpayer's qualified investment.

(*b*) The term "recapture year" means the taxable year in which section 38 property the basis (or cost) of which was taken into account in computing a taxpayer's qualified investment is disposed of, or otherwise ceases to be section 38 property or becomes public utility property with respect to the taxpayer, before the close of the estimated useful life which was taken into account in computing such qualified investment.

(*c*) The term "recapture determination" means a recomputation made under this paragraph.

(2) *Rules for applying subparagraph (1).* For purposes of subparagraph (1) of this paragraph—

(i) In determining whether section 38 property is disposed of, or otherwise ceases to be section 38 property with respect to the taxpayer,

Reg. § 1.47-1(a)(1)

before the close of the estimated useful life which was taken into account in computing the taxpayer's qualified investment, the term "estimated useful life" means the shortest life of the useful life category within which falls the estimated useful life which was assigned to such property under paragraph (e) of § 1.46-3. Thus, section 38 property which is assigned, under paragraph (e) of § 1.46-3, an estimated useful life of 6 years shall not be treated, for purposes of subparagraph (1) of this paragraph, as having been disposed of before the close of its estimated useful life if such property is sold 5 years (that is, the shortest life of the 5 years or more but less than 7 years useful life category) after the date on which it was placed in service. Likewise, section 38 property with an estimated useful life of 15 years which is placed in service on January 1, 1972, shall not be treated as having been disposed of before the close of its estimated useful life if such property is sold at any time after January 1, 1979 (that is, 7 years or more after the date on which it was placed in service).

(ii) In determining the recomputed qualified investment with respect to property which is disposed of or otherwise ceases to be section 38 property the term "actual useful life" means, except as otherwise provided in this section and §§ 1.47-2 through 1.47-6, the period beginning with the date on which the property was placed in service by the taxpayer and ending with the date of such disposition or cessation. See paragraph (c) of this section.

(iii) In determining the recomputed qualified investment with respect to property which ceases to be section 38 property with respect to the taxpayer after August 15, 1971, or which becomes public utility property after such date, such property shall be treated as if it were property described in section 50 at the time it was placed in service (whether or not it was property described in section 50 at such time). Thus, if property was placed in service on October 15, 1968, and was assigned an estimated useful life of 4 years, there would be no increase in tax under section 47 if the property were disposed of at any time after October 14, 1971, that is, 3 years or more after the property was placed in service.

(b) *Increase in income tax and the investment credit carryover—at re-income*. Except as provided in subparagraph, any increase in income for such section shall be treated the taxpayer by recapture year gard to such tax liability,

taxable year, or no income tax return was otherwise required for such taxable year.

(2) *Special rule*. Any increase in income tax under this section shall not be treated as income tax imposed on the taxpayer by chapter 1 of the Code for purposes of determining the amount of the credits allowable to such taxpayer under—

(i) Section 33 (relating to taxes of foreign countries and possessions of United States),

(ii) Section 34 (relating to dividends received by individuals before January 1, 1965),

(iii) Section 35 (relating to partially tax-exempt interest received by individuals),

(iv) Section 37 (relating to retirement income), and

(v) Section 38 (relating to investment in certain depreciable property).

(3) *Reduction in credit allowed as a result of a net operating loss carryback.* (i) If a net operating loss carryback from the recapture year or from any taxable year subsequent to the recapture year reduces the amount allowed as a credit under section 38 for any taxable year up to and including the recapture year, then there shall be a new recapture determination under paragraph (a) of this section for each recapture year affected, taking into account the reduced amount of credit allowed after application of the net operating loss carryback.

(ii) Subdivision (i) of this subparagraph may be illustrated by the following example:

Example (1). (a) X Corporation, which makes its returns on the basis of a calendar year, acquired and placed in service on January 1, 1962, an item of section 38 property with a basis of $10,000 and an estimated useful life of 8 years. The amount of its qualified investment with respect to such asset was $10,000. In the taxable year 1962, X Corporation earned a credit of $700 (7 percent of its liability) for tax of $700. In as X Corporation had no liability for 1963, such item of section 38 property was sold to Y Corporation. Since the useful life of such item was only one year, was a recapture determination under paragraph (a) of this section. The income tax imposed by chapter 1 of the Code on X Corporation for the taxable year 1963 was increased by the $700 decrease in its credit earned for the taxable year 1962 (that is, $700 the original credit earned minus zero recomputed credit earned).

(b) For the taxable year 1965, X Corporation has a net operating loss which is carried back to the taxable year 1962 and reduces its

Reg. § 1.47-1(b)(3)

bility for tax, as defined in paragraph (c) of 1.46-1, for such taxable year to $200. As a result of such net operating loss carryback, X Corporation's credit allowed under section 38 for the taxable year 1962 is limited to $200 and the excess of $500 ($700 credit earned minus $200 limitation based on amount of tax) is an investment credit carryover to the taxable year 1963.

(c) For 1965, there is a recapture determination under subdivision (i) of this subparagraph for the 1963 recapture year. The $700 increase in the income tax imposed on X Corporation for the taxable year 1963 is redetermined to be $200 (that is, the $200 credit allowed after taking into account the 1965 net operating loss minus zero credit which would have been allowed taking into account the 1963 recapture determination). In addition, X Corporation's $500 investment credit carryover to the taxable year 1963 is reduced by $500 ($700 minus $200) to zero and X Corporation is entitled to a $500 refund of the tax paid as a result of the 1963 determination.

Example (2). (a) X Corporation, which makes its returns on the basis of a calendar year, acquired and placed in service on January 1, 1962, an item of section 38 property with a basis of $10,000 and an estimated useful life of 8 years. The amount of qualified investment with respect to such asset is $10,000. For the taxable year 1962, X Corporation's credit earned of $700 (7 percent of $10) was allowed under section 38 as a credit against its liability for tax of $700. In 1963 and in 19 Corporation had no liability for tax and place service no section 38 property. On January 65, such item of section 38 property is sold porporation. For the taxable year 1965, X Corporation has a net operating loss which is carried back taxable year 1962 and reduces its liability for axable year 1962 and graph (c) of § 1.4 fts defined in paragraph taxable year to $100.

(b) As a result of s carryback, X Corporation's c section 38 for the taxable year rating loss $100 and the excess of $600 ($ d under minus $100 limitation based on a ed to an investment credit carryover ned year 1963.

(c) Since the actual useful item of section 38 property sold to Y C was only 3 years, there is a recapture de tion under paragraph (a) of this section. X ration's $600 investment credit carryover to is reduced by $600 to zero. The income tax posed by chapter 1 of the Code on X Corporat example for the taxable year 1965 is increased by the $10 reduction in credit allowed by section 38 for 1962.

Reg. § 1.47-1(b)(4)

(4) *Statement of recomputation.* The taxpayer shall attach to his income tax return for the recapture year a separate statement showing in detail the computation of the increase in income tax imposed on such taxpayer by chapter 1 of the Code and the reduction in any investment credit carryovers.

(c) *Date placed in service and date of disposition or cessation*—(1) *General rule.* For purposes of this section and §§ 1.47-2 through 1.47-6, in determining the actual useful life of section 38 property—

(i) Such property shall be treated as placed in service on the first day of the month in which such property is placed in service. The month in which property is placed in service shall be determined under the principles of paragraph (d) of § 1.46-3.

(ii) If during the taxable year such property ceases to be section 38 property with respect to the taxpayer—

(a) As a result of the occurrence of an event on a specific date (for example, a sale, transfer, retirement or other disposition), such cessation shall be treated as having occurred on the actual date of such event.

(b) For any reason other than the occurrence of an event on a specific date (for example, because such property is used predominantly in connection with the furnishing of lodging during such taxable year), such cessation shall be treated as having occurred on the first day of such taxable year.

(2) *Special rule.* Notwithstanding subparagraph (1) of this paragraph, if a taxpayer uses an averaging convention (see § 1.167(a)-10) in computing depreciation with respect to section 38 property, then, for purposes of this section and §§ 1.47-2 through 1.47-6, he may use the assumed dates of additions and retirements in determining the actual useful life of such property provided such assumed dates are used consistently for purposes of subpart B of part IV of subchapter A of chapter 1 of the Code with respect to all section 38 property for which such convention is used for purposes of depreciation. This subparagraph shall not apply in any case where from all the facts and circumstances it appears that the use of such med dates results in a substantial distortion investment credit allowed by section 38. example, if the taxpayer computes de under a convention under which the beginning and ending balances of t for the taxable year are taken ay use July 1 as the assumed and retirements to such ac axpayer computes depre-

ciation under a convention under which the average of the beginning and ending balances of the asset account for each month is taken into account, he may use the date determined by reference to the weighted average of the monthly averages as the assumed date of all additions and retirements to such account.

(3) *Example.* This paragraph may be illustrated by the following example:

Example. Assume that section 38 property is placed in service (within the meaning of paragraph (d) of § 1.46-3) on December 1, 1965 (thus the credit is treated as being earned in 1965) but under the taxpayer's depreciation practice the period for depreciation with respect to such property begins on January 1, 1966, and that the property is actually retired on December 2, 1970. Under the general rule of subparagraph (1) of this paragraph, the property is treated as placed in service on December 1, 1965, and as ceasing to be section 38 property with respect to the taxpayer on December 2, 1970, even though under the taxpayer's depreciation practice the period for depreciation with respect to such property begins on January 1, 1966, and terminates on January 1, 1971. However, under the special rule of subparagraph (2) of this paragraph the taxpayer may determine the actual useful life of the property by reference to the assumed dates of January 1, 1966, and January 1, 1971.

(d) *Examples.* Paragraphs (a) through (c) of this section may be illustrated by the following examples:

Example (1). (i) X Corporation, which makes its returns on the basis of the calendar year, acquired and placed in service on January 1, 1962, three items of section 38 property each with a basis of $12,000 and an estimated useful life of 15 years. The amount of qualified investment with respect to each such asset was $12,000. For the taxable year 1962, X Corporation's credit earned of $2,520 was allowed under section 38 as a credit against its liability for tax of $4,000. On December 2, 1965, one of the items of section 38 property is sold to Y Corporation.

(ii) The actual useful life of the item of property which is sold on December 2, 1965, is three years and eleven months. The recomputed qualified investment with respect to such item of property is zero ($12,000 basis multiplied by zero applicable percentage) and X Corporation's recomputed credit earned for the taxable year 1962 is $1,680 (7 percent of $24,000). The income tax imposed by chapter 1 of the Code on X Corporation for the taxable year 1965 is increased by the $840 decrease in its credit earned for the taxable

year 1962 (that is, $2,520 original credit earned minus $1,680 recomputed credit earned).

Example (2). (i) The facts are the same as in example (1) and in addition on December 1, 1966, a second item of section 38 property placed in service in the taxable year 1962 is sold to Y Corporation.

(ii) The actual useful life of the item of property which is sold on December 2, 1966, is four years and eleven months. The recomputed qualified investment with respect to such item of property is $4,000 ($12,000 basis multiplied by 33⅓ percent applicable percentage) and X Corporation's recomputed credit earned for the taxable year 1962 is $1,120 (7 percent of $16,000). The income tax imposed by chapter 1 of the Code on X Corporation for the taxable year 1966 is increased by $560 (that is, $1,400 ($2,520 original credit earned minus $1,120 recomputed credit earned) reduced by the $840 increase in tax for 1965).

Example (3). (i) The facts are the same as in example (1) except that for the taxable year 1962 X Corporation's liability for tax under section 46(a)(3) is only $1,520. Therefore, for such taxable year X Corporation's credit allowed under section 38 is limited to $1,520 and the excess of $1,000 ($2,520 credit earned minus $1,520 limitation based on amount of tax) is an unused credit. Of such $1,000 unused credit, $100 is allowed as a credit under section 38 for the taxable year 1963, $100 is allowed for 1964, and $800 is carried to the taxable year 1965.

(ii) The actual useful life of the item of property which is sold on December 2, 1965, is three years and eleven months. The recomputed qualified investment with respect to such item of property is zero ($12,000 basis multiplied by zero applicable percentage) and X Corporation's recomputed credit earned for the taxable year 1962 is $1,680 (7 percent of $24,000). If such $1,680 recomputed credit earned had been taken into account in place of the $2,520 original credit earned, X's credit allowed for 1962 would have been $1,520, and of the $160 unused credit from 1962 $100 would have been allowed as a credit under section 38 for 1963, and $60 would have been allowed for 1964. X Corporation's $800 investment credit carryover to the taxable year 1965 is reduced by $800 to zero. The income tax imposed by chapter 1 of the Code on X Corporation for the taxable year 1965 is increased by $40 (that is, the aggregate reduction in the credits allowed by section 38 for 1962, 1963, and 1964).

Example (4). (i) X Corporation, which makes its returns on the basis of the calendar year, acquired and placed in service on November 1,

1962, an item of section 38 property with a basis of $12,000 and an estimated useful life of 10 years. The amount of qualified investment with respect to such property was $12,000. For the taxable year 1962, X Corporation's credit earned of $840 was allowed under section 38 as a credit against its liability for tax of $840. For each of the taxable years 1963 and 1964 X Corporation's liability for tax was zero and its credit earned was $400; therefore, for each of such years its unused credit was $400. For the taxable year 1965 its liability for tax was $200 and its credit earned was zero; therefore, $200 of the $400 unused credit from 1963 was allowed as credit for 1965 and $600 ($200 from 1963 and $400 from 1964) is an investment credit carryover to 1966. On February 2, 1966, such item of section 38 property is sold to Y Corporation.

(ii) The actual useful life of such item of property is three years and three months. The recomputed qualified investment with respect to such property is zero ($12,000 basis multiplied by zero) and X Corporation's recomputed credit earned for the taxable year 1962 is zero. If such zero recomputed credit earned had been taken into account in place of the $840 original credit earned, the entire $400 unused credit from 1963 (including the $200 portion which was originally allowed as a credit for 1965) and the $400 unused credit from 1964 would have been allowed as investment credit carrybacks against X Corporation's liability for tax of $840 for 1962. (See § 1.46-2 for rules relating to the carryback of unused credits.)

(iii) Therefore, the $600 carryover from 1963 and 1964 to 1966 is eliminated and the income tax imposed by chapter 1 of the Code on X Corporation for the taxable year 1966 is increased by the $240 aggregate reduction in the credits allowed by section 38 for the taxable years 1962 and 1965 (that is, $1,040 credit allowed minus $800 which would have been allowed).

Example (5). (i) X Corporation, which makes its returns on the basis of the calendar year, acquired and placed in service on November 1, 1962, an item of section 38 property with a basis of $10,000 and an estimated useful life of 8 years. The amount of qualified investment with respect to such asset was $10,000. For the taxable year 1962, X Corporation's credit earned of $700 was allowed as a credit against its liability for tax. For each of the taxable years 1963, 1964, and 1965 X had no taxable income. On July 3, 1966, the item of section 38 property is sold to Y Corporation. For the taxable year 1966 X Corporation has a net operating loss of $3,000.

(ii) The actual useful life of the item of property is three years and eight months. The recomputed qualified investment with respect to such item of property is zero and X Corporation's recomputed credit earned for the taxable year 1962 is zero. Notwithstanding the $3,000 net operating loss for the taxable year 1966, the income tax imposed by chapter 1 of the Code on X Corporation for such year is $700 (that is, the decrease in its credit earned for the taxable year 1962).

(e) *Identification of property*—(1) *General rule*—(i) *Record requirements.* In general, the taxpayer must maintain records from which he can establish, with respect to each item of section 38 property, the following facts:

(*a*) The date the property is disposed of or otherwise ceases to be section 38 property,

(*b*) The estimated useful life which was assigned to the property under paragraph (e) of § 1.46-3,

(*c*) The month and the taxable year in which the property was placed in service, and

(*d*) The basis (or cost), actually or reasonably determined, of the property.

(ii) *Recapture determination.* For purposes of determining whether section 38 property is disposed of, or otherwise ceases to be section 38 property with respect to the taxpayer, before the close of its estimated useful life, and for purposes of determining recomputed qualified investment, the taxpayer must establish from his records the facts required by subdivision (i) of this subparagraph.

(iii) *Examples.* If the taxpayer fails to maintain records from which he can establish the facts required by subdivision (i) of this subparagraph, then this section shall be applied to the taxpayer in the manner indicated in the following examples:

Example (1). Corporation X, organized on January 1, 1964, files its income tax return on the basis of a calendar year. During the years 1964 and 1965, X places in service several items of machinery to which it assigns estimated useful lives of 8 years. X places the items of machinery in a composite account for purposes of computing depreciation. When X's 1966 return is being audited, X is unable to establish whether the items placed in service in 1964 and 1965 were still on hand at the end of 1966. Therefore, for purposes of paragraph (a) of this section, X is treated as having disposed of, in 1966, all of the items of machinery placed in service in 1964 and 1965.

Example (2). Corporation Y, organized on January 1, 1960, files its income tax return on the basis of a calendar year. During each of the years

Reg. § 1.47-1(e)(1)

1960 through 1965, Y places in service 4 items of machinery to each of which it assigns an estimated useful life of 8 years for depreciation purposes (and for purposes of computing qualified investment for relevant years). Y places the items of machinery in a composite account for purposes of computing depreciation (and for purposes of computing qualified investment for relevant years). When Y's 1965 return is being audited, Y can establish that it retired during 1965 only 6 items of this machinery. However, Y cannot establish the date on which these 6 items were placed in service, nor can Y establish that the items placed in service in 1963 or 1964 are still on hand as of the end of 1965. No previous recapture has taken place with respect to any of the items placed in service in 1963 or 1964. Assuming that paragraph (e)(2) and (3) of this section is not applicable, Y is treated, for purposes of paragraph (a) of this section, as having disposed of, in 1965, the 4 items placed in service in 1964, the most recent year before 1965 in which such property was placed in service, and 2 items from 1963, the next most recent year.

Example (3). The facts are the same as in example (2) except that when Y's 1966 return is being audited, Y can establish from its records that all 4 items placed in service in 1965 are still on hand and that only 3 items were retired in 1966. For purposes of paragraph (a) of this section, Y is treated as having disposed of, in 1966, the 2 remaining items of machinery placed in service in 1963, and one of the items placed in service in 1962.

(2) *Treatment of "mass assets."* (i) If, in the case of mass assets (as defined in subparagraph (4) of this paragraph), it is impracticable for the taxpayer to maintain records from which he can establish with respect to each item of section 38 property the facts required by subparagraph (1) of this paragraph, and if he adopts other reasonable recordkeeping practices, consonant with good accounting and engineering practices, and consistent with his prior recordkeeping practices, then he may substitute data from an appropriate mortality dispersion table. An appropriate mortality dispersion table must be based on an acceptable sampling of the taxpayer's actual experience or other acceptable statistical or engineering techniques. In lieu of such mortality dispersion table, the taxpayer may use a standard mortality dispersion table prescribed by the Commissioner. If the taxpayer uses such standard mortality dispersion table for any taxable year, it must be used for all subsequent taxable years unless the taxpayer obtains the consent of the Commissioner to change. If mass assets are placed in a multiple asset account and if the depreciation rate for such account is based on the maximum expected life of the longest lived asset in such account, in applying a mortality dispersion table (including a standard mortality dispersion table) the average expected useful life of the mass assets in such account must be used.

(ii) Subdivision (i) of this subparagraph shall not apply with respect to assets placed in service in a taxable year ending on or after June 30, 1967, and beginning before January 1, 1971, or with respect to assets placed in service for a taxable year beginning after December 31, 1970, for which the taxpayer has not made the election provided by section 167(m), unless the estimated useful lives which were assigned to such assets for purposes of determining qualified investment—

(a) Were separate lives based on the estimated range of years taken into account in establishing the average useful life of assets similar in kind under paragraph (e)(3)(ii)(b) of § 1.46-3, and

(b) Were determined by use of a mortality dispersion table (including a standard mortality dispersion table) [see ¶ 552.70].

(iii) Any standard mortality dispersion table prescribed by the Commissioner shall be based on average useful life categories and with respect to each category shall contain 5 columns, the first 4 of which shall state the percentage of property assumed to have a useful life of—

Column (1): Less than 4 years,

Column (2): 4 years or more but less than 6 years,

Column (3): 6 years or more but less than 8 years, and

Column (4): 8 years or more.

The 5th column shall show the total qualified investment as a percentage and shall be used in connection with the determination to be made under § 1.46-3(e)(3)(iii). In the case of a table which is to apply to property which is described in section 50 or to property which is treated as property described in section 50 under paragraph (a)(2)(iii), of this section shall be applied by substituting "3 years" for "4 years," "5 years" for "6 years," and "7 years" for "8 years."

(iv) Whenever the standard mortality dispersion table is used for a taxable year under subdivision (i) of this subparagraph (whether or not such table was used in determining qualified investment), the percentage of property shown in column (1) of the table shall (for purposes of section 47, this section, and § § 1.47-2 through 1.47-6) be deemed to have been disposed of on the day before the expiration of the 4-year period beginning on the date on which it was considered

Reg. § 1.47-1(e)(2)

as placed in service under § 1.47-1(c); the percentage of property shown in column (2) of the table shall be deemed to have been disposed of on the day before the expiration of the 6-year period beginning on the date on which it was so considered as placed in service; and the percentage of property shown in column (3) shall be deemed to have been disposed of on the day before the expiration of the 8-year period beginning on the date on which it was so considered as placed in service. In applying this subdivision for purposes of recomputing qualified investment, the proper average useful life category shall be used whether or not such category was used in determining qualified investment. In the case of property which is described in section 50 or property which is treated as property described in section 50 under paragraph (a)(2)(iii) of this section (other than property the qualified investment with respect to which was determined by use of the standard or an appropriate mortality dispersion table), this subdivision shall be applied by substituting "3-year period" for "4-year period," "5-year period" for "6-year period," and "7-year period" for "8-year period."

(v) In lieu of using subdivision (iv) of this subparagraph for purposes of recomputing qualified investment, a taxpayer may, for the first recapture year (as defined in paragraph (a)(1)(ii)(b) of this section) to which such subdivision (iv) would otherwise apply with respect to any mass asset account, recompute qualified investment on the basis of the difference between (a) the proper total qualified investment based on the percentage shown in column (5) of the table, and (b) the total qualified investment actually claimed by the taxpayer for the year in which the property was placed in service.

Example. Assume that the taxpayer places in service during 1963 mass assets costing him $100,000, that he places these assets in a multiple asset account for which he properly claims a useful life of 6 years and a qualified investment of $66,667 (⅔ × $100,000), and that he is allowed an investment credit of $4,667.67. When the taxpayer's 1967 return is being audited he is unable to establish that any of the mass assets placed in service in 1963 were still on hand at the end of 1967. The taxpayer elects to use the standard mortality dispersion table prescribed by the Commissioner to determine the amount of recapture with respect to these mass assets. Assume that the table prescribed by the Commissioner shows with respect to mass assets with an average useful life of 6 years the following:

Percent of property assumed to have a useful life of—				
Less than 4 years	4 years or more, but less than 6 years	6 years or more, but less than 8 years	8 years or more	Total qualified investment (Percent)
(1)	(2)	(3)	(4)	(5)
15.87	34.13	34.13	15.87	50.00

(a) Under these circumstances 15.87 percent of the mass assets placed in service in 1963 are deemed to have been disposed of during 1967. With respect to these assets, the amount of qualified investment for 1963 was $10,580 ($15,870 × ⅔) and the amount of credit earned was $740.60 (7% of $10,580), whereas the recomputed qualified investment is zero and the recomputed credit earned is zero. Thus, the tax imposed by chapter 1 of the Code for 1967 is increased by $740.60.

(b) No recapture determination is required for 1968 since no assets are deemed to have been disposed of in that year. During 1969, 34.13 percent of the mass assets placed in service in 1963 are deemed to have been disposed of. With respect to these assets, the amount of qualified investment for 1963 was $22,753.34 ($34,130 × ⅔) and the amount of credit earned was $1,592.73 (7% of $22,753.34), whereas the recomputed qualified investment is $11,376.67 ($34,130 × ⅓ and the recomputed credit earned is $796.37

(7% of $11,376.67). Thus, the tax imposed by chapter 1 of the Code for 1969 is increased by $796.36 ($1,592.73 minus $796.37).

(c) If the taxpayer chooses to recompute qualified investment by using the method provided in subdivision (v) of this subparagraph, the increase in tax for 1967 (the first recapture year) would be $1,167.67, *i.e.,* the original credit earned, $4,667.67, minus the recomputed credit earned, $3,500 (50%, the percentage shown in column (5), of $100,000 multiplied by 7%). As long as the same average useful life category reflects the taxpayer's experience for subsequent years, no recapture determination will be required for any future year, except as provided by subparagraph (3)(iv) of this paragraph.

(vi) Subdivision (i) of this subparagraph shall not apply with respect to section 38 property to which an election under section 167(m) applies unless the taxpayer assigns actual retirements of such section 38 property for all taxable years to

Reg. § 1.47-1(e)(2)

the same vintage account for purposes of section 47 and for purposes of computing the allowance for depreciation under section 167. The assignment of actual retirements of section 38 property for a taxable year to particular vintage accounts may be made on the basis of an appropriate mortality dispersion table (based on an acceptable sampling of the taxpayer's actual experience or other statistical or engineering techniques) or on the basis of a standard mortality dispersion table prescribed by the Commissioner. If the taxpayer assigns actual retirements for any taxable year to particular vintage accounts on the basis of such standard mortality dispersion table, actual retirements for all subsequent taxable years must be assigned to particular vintage accounts on the basis of such table. Actual retirements of section 38 property for a taxable year shall be assigned to particular vintage accounts by—

(a) Determining the expected retirements for such taxable year from each vintage account containing such section 38 property, and

(b) Ratably allocating such actual retirements to each vintage account containing such section 38 property.

However, the unadjusted basis of retired assets assigned to any particular vintage account shall not exceed the unadjusted basis of the property contained in such account.

(3) *Special rules.* (i) Taxpayers who properly determine estimated useful lives under § 1.46-3(e)(3)(ii)(b) or (iii) may treat such assets as having been disposed of or having ceased to be section 38 assets in the order of the estimated useful lives that were assigned to such assets. Thus, the asset that is first disposed of or first ceases to be section 38 property may be treated as the asset to which there was assigned the shortest estimated useful life; the next asset disposed of or ceasing to be section 38 property may be treated as the asset to which there was assigned the second shortest life, etc.

(ii) In the case of taxpayers who use the rule of subdivision (i) of this subparagraph with respect to mass assets for which the estimated useful life was determined under § 1.46-3(e)(3)(iii), if the dispersion shown by the mortality dispersion table effective for a taxable year subsequent to the credit year is the same as the dispersion shown by the mortality table that was effective for the credit year (for example, if the same average useful life on the standard mortality dispersion table reflects the taxpayer's experience for both such years), no recapture determination is required for such subsequent taxable year.

(iii) Notwithstanding subdivision (i) of this subparagraph, taxpayers who, for purposes of determining qualified investment, do not use a mortality dispersion table with respect to certain section 38 assets similar in kind but who consistently assign under paragraph (e)(3)(ii)(b) of § 1.46-3 to such assets separate lives based on the estimated range of years taken into consideration in establishing the average useful life of such assets, may select the order in which such assets shall be considered as having been disposed of, regardless of the taxable years in which such assets were placed in service. If a taxpayer uses the method provided in this subdivision to determine that any asset is considered as having been disposed of, then, in addition to complying with the record requirements of subparagraph (1)(i) of this paragraph, such taxpayer must maintain records from which he can establish to the satisfaction of the district director that such asset has not previously been considered as having been disposed of. In addition, if, for any taxable year, a taxpayer uses the method provided in this subdivision for any asset, he must use for such year and for each subsequent taxable year (unless he obtains the district director's consent to change) with respect to all assets similar in kind to such asset—

(a) The method of determining estimated useful lives described in paragraph (e)(3)(ii)(b) of § 1.46-3, and

(b) The method he has selected under this subdivision for determining the order in which such assets are considered as having been disposed of.

A request by a taxpayer to obtain the district director's consent to change a system or method described in this subdivision with respect to assets similar in kind must be submitted to the district director on or before the last day of the taxable year with respect to which the change is sought.

(iv) Notwithstanding subdivisions (i), (ii), and (iii) of this subparagraph, there shall be taken into account separately any abnormal retirement of section 38 property of substantial value for which the estimated useful life was determined under § 1.46-3(e)(3)(ii)(b) or (iii). For definition of abnormal retirement, see paragraph (b) of § 1.167(a)-8.

(4) [Reserved]

(5) *Example.* This paragraph may be illustrated by the following example:

Example. (i) Taxpayer A uses numerous small returnable containers in his business. It is impracticable for A to keep individual detailed records with respect to such containers which are mass assets. In 1965, A places in service 10 million containers purchased for $1 million, and reasonably determines that each of such containers has a basis of 10 cents. A places such containers in a multiple asset account to which is assigned a 5-year average useful life for purposes of computing depreciation. A has conducted an appropriate mortality study which shows that the containers have the following estimated useful lives:

Percent of assets	Useful life
10%	3 years
20	4
40	5
20	6
10	7

A assigns separate lives to such assets based on the estimated range of years taken into account in establishing the average useful life of such containers. The qualified investment with respect to such containers is $400,000 computed as follows:

Useful life	Basis	Applicable percentage	Qualified investment
4	$200,000	33⅓	$ 66,666
5	400,000	33⅓	133,334
6	200,000	66⅔	133,334
7	100,000	66⅔	66,666
			$400,000

A's credit earned for 1965 of $28,000 (7 percent times $400,000) is allowed as a credit under section 38 against A's liability for tax of $2 million. (For purposes of this example the computations of investment credit and recapture with respect to containers placed in service in years other than 1965 are omitted.) The mortality studies effective for 1966 and 1967 show that none of the containers placed in service in 1965 was retired.

(ii) A's mortality study effective with respect to 1968 shows that the containers are being retired as follows:

Percent of assets	Useful life
30%	3 years
20	4
30	5
10	6
10	7

Thus, the 1968 study shows that 30 percent of the 10 million containers placed in service in 1965 were retired in 1968. Under the rule of subparagraph (3)(i) of this paragraph, the 3 million containers are treated as consisting of the 1 million containers to which was assigned a 3-year useful life and the 2 million containers to which was assigned a 4-year useful life. Taking into account only the fact that 30 percent of the containers placed in service in 1965 had an actual life of less than 4 years, A's recomputed qualified investment for 1965 is $333,333 and his recomputed credit earned is $23,333. A's income tax for 1968

is increased by $4,667 ($28,000 original credit earned minus $23,333 recomputed credit earned).

(iii) The mortality study effective for 1969 shows the same results as the mortality study effective for 1968. Thus, it shows that 2 million containers were retired in 1969 (an actual life of 4 years). Under the rule of subparagraph (3)(i) of this paragraph such 2 million containers are treated as having been among 4,000,000 containers to which were assigned a 5-year useful life. Therefore, no recapture determination is required for 1969.

(iv) The mortality study effective for 1970 shows the same results as the mortality study effective for 1968. Thus, it shows that 3 million containers were retired in 1970 (an actual life of 5 years). Under the rule of subparagraph (3)(i) of this paragraph, the 3 million are treated as having been assigned useful lives as follows: 2 million as having been assigned a useful life of 5 years, and 1 million as having been assigned a useful life of 6 years. Taking into account only the fact that 10 percent of the containers placed in service in 1965 had an actual life of 5 years rather than the 6 years estimated useful life assigned to them, A's recomputed qualified investment is $300,000 and A's credit earned for 1965 is $21,000. Thus, taking into account the 1968 recapture determination, A's income tax for 1970 is increased by $2,333.

(f) *Public utility property*—(1) *Recomputed qualified investment.* In recomputing qualified investment with respect to section 38 property which becomes public utility property (as defined in paragraph (g) of § 1.46-3)—

(i) If such property becomes public utility property less than 3 years from the date on which it was placed in service, then such property shall be treated as public utility property for its entire useful life.

(ii) If such property becomes public utility property 3 years or more but less than 5 years from the date on which it was placed in service, then such property shall be treated as section 38 property which is not public utility property for the first 3 years of its estimated useful life and as public utility property for the remaining period of its estimated useful life.

(iii) If such property becomes public utility property 5 years or more but less than 7 years from the date on which it was placed in service, then such property shall be treated as section 38 property which is not public utility property for the first 5 years of its estimated useful life and as public utility property for the remaining period of its estimated useful life.

Reg. § 1.47-1(f)(1)

If property becomes public utility property before August 16, 1971, this subparagraph shall be applied by substituting "4 years" for "3 years," "6 years" for "5 years," and "8 years" for "7 years."

(2) *Examples.* Subparagraph (1) of this paragraph may be illustrated by the following examples:

Example (1). (i) X Corporation, which makes its returns on the basis of the calendar year, acquired and placed in service on January 1, 1969, an item of section 38 property with a basis of $12,000 and an estimated useful life of 8 years. The amount of qualified investment with respect to such property was $12,000. For the taxable year 1969, X Corporation's credit earned was $840 (7 percent of $12,000) and for such taxable year X Corporation was allowed under section 38 a credit of $840 against its liability for tax. During the taxable year 1972 such property becomes public utility property (as defined in paragraph (g) of § 1.46-3) with respect to X Corporation.

(ii) Such item of section 38 property is treated as section 38 property which is not public utility property for the first 3 years of its 8-year estimated useful life and is treated as public utility property for the remaining 5 years. The recomputed qualified investment with respect to such item of section 38 property is $7,428, computed as follows:

$12,000 basis × 33⅓ percent applicable
  percentage $4,000
$12,000 basis × 3/7 × 66⅔ percent
  applicable percentage 3,428

    Total recomputed qualified investment $7,428

X Corporation's recomputed credit earned for the taxable year 1969 is $520 (7 percent of $7,428). The income tax imposed by chapter 1 of the Code on X Corporation for the taxable year 1972 is increased by the $320 decrease in its credit earned for the taxable year 1969 (that is, $840 original credit earned minus $520 recomputed credit earned).

Example (2). (i) The facts are the same as in example (1) and in addition the item of section 38 property which became public utility property in 1972 is sold to Y Corporation on January 2, 1975.

(ii) The actual useful life of such item of property is 6 years. For the first 3 years of its 8-year estimated useful life such item is treated as section 38 property which is not public utility property and for the remaining 3 years is treated as public utility property. The recomputed qualified investment with respect to such item of property is $5,714, computed as follows:

$12,000 basis × 33⅓ percent applicable
  percentage $4,000
$12,000 basis × 3/7 × 33 1,714

    Total recomputed qualified investment $5,714

X Corporation's recomputed credit earned for the taxable year 1969 is $400 (7 percent of $5,714). The income tax imposed by chapter 1 of the Code on X Corporation for the taxable year 1975 is increased by $120 (that is, $440 ($840 original credit earned minus $400 recomputed credit earned) minus $320 increase in tax for 1969).

(g) *Special rules for progress expenditure property.* Under section 47(a)(3), a recapture determination is required if property ceases to be progress expenditure property (as defined in § 1.46-5(d)). Property ceases to be progress expenditure property if it is sold or otherwise disposed of before it is placed in service. For example, cancellation of the contract for progress expenditure property or abandonment of the project by the taxpayer will be considered a "disposition" within the meaning of § 1.47-2. A cessation occurs if progress expenditure property ceases to be property that will be section 38 property with a useful life of 7 years or more when placed in service. In general, a sale and leaseback is treated as a cessation. However, see paragraph (g)(2) of § 1.47-3 for special rules for certain sale and leaseback transactions. Recapture determinations for progress expenditure property are to be made in a way similar to that provided under §§ 1.47-1 through 1.47-6. Reduction of qualified investment must begin with the most recent credit year (*i.e.*, the most recent taxable year the property is taken into account in computing qualified investment under § 1.46-3 or 1.46-5).

(h) *Special rules for energy property*—(1) *In general.* A recapture determination is required for the investment credit attributable to the energy percentage (energy credit) if property is (i) disposed of or (ii) otherwise ceases to be energy property (as defined in section 48(l)) with regard to the taxpayer before the close of the estimated useful life (as determined under paragraph (a)(2)(i) of this section) which was taken into account in computing qualified investment.

(2) *Dispositions.* The term "disposition" is described in § 1.47-2(a)(1). A transfer of energy property that is a "disposition" requiring a recapture determination for the investment credit attributable to the regular percentage (regular credit) and the ESOP percentage (ESOP credit) will also be a "disposition" requiring a recapture determination for the energy credit.

(3)(i) *Cessation.* The term "cessation" is described in § 1.47-2(a)(2). For energy property, a cessation occurs during a taxable year if, by rea-

Reg. § 1.47-1(h)(3)

son of a change in use or otherwise, the property would not have qualified for an energy credit if placed in service during that year. A change in use will not require a recapture determination for the regular or ESOP credit unless, by reason of the change, the property would not have qualified for the regular or ESOP credit if placed in service during that year.

(ii) A qualified intercity bus described in § 1.48-9(q) must meet the predominant use test (of § 1.48-9(q)(7)) for the remainder of the taxable year from the date it is placed in service and for each taxable year thereafter. A cessation occurs in any taxable year in which the bus is no longer a qualifying bus under § 1.48-9(q)(6). A qualified intercity bus does not cease to be energy property for a taxable year subsequent to the one in which it was placed in service by reason of a decrease in operating capacity (see § 1.48-9(q)(9)) for that year compared to any prior taxable year.

(4) *Recordkeeping requirement.* For recordkeeping requirements with respect to dispositions or cessations, the rules of paragraph (e)(1) of this section apply. For example, the taxpayer must maintain records for each recycling facility indicating the percentage of virgin materials used each year. See, § 1.48-9(g)(5)(ii).

(5) *Examples.* The following examples illustrate this paragraph (h).

Example (1). (a) In 1980, corporation X, a calendar year taxpayer, acquires and places in service a computer that will perform solely energy conserving functions in connection with an existing industrial process. Assume the computer has a 10 year useful life and qualifies for both the regular and energy credits. In 1981, a change is made in the industrial process (within the meaning of § 1.48-9(1)(2)). However, for 1981 the computer continues to perform solely energy conserving functions. In 1982, the computer ceases to perform energy conserving functions and begins to perform a production related function.

(b) For 1981, a recapture determination is not required. For 1982, the entire energy credit must be recaptured, although none of the regular credit is recaptured. If in 1989 the computer first ceased to perform an energy conserving function, no part of the energy credit would be recaptured.

Example (2). Assume the same facts and conclusion as in example (1). Assume further that X sells the computer in 1985. A recapture determination is required for the regular credit.

Example (3). In 1981, corporation Y, a calendar year taxpayer, acquires and places in service recycling equipment. Assume the equipment has a 7-year useful life and qualifies for both the regular credit and energy credit. During the

course of 1982, more than 10 percent of the material recycled is virgin material. The energy credit is recaptured in its entirety, although none of the regular credit is recaptured. See § 1.48-9(g)(5)(B)(ii).

Example (4). In 1980, corporation Z, a calendar year taxpayer, acquires and places in service a boiler the primary fuel for which is an alternate substance. The boiler has a 7-year useful life. Assume the boiler is a structural component of a building within the meaning of § 1.48-1(e)(2). Assume further that the boiler is not a part of a qualified rehabilitated building (as defined in section 48(g)(1)) or a single purpose agricultural or horticultural structure (as defined in section 48(p)). Z is allowed only an energy credit since the boiler is a structural component of a building. In 1984, Z modifies the boiler to use oil as the primary fuel. A recapture determination is required for the energy credit. See § 1.48-9(c)(3).

(i) [Reserved].

(j) [Reserved].

(k) [Reserved].

(l) [Reserved].

(m) *Commuter highway vehicles—(1) Recomputed qualified investment.* (i) If a qualifying commuter highway vehicle (as defined in § 1.46-11(a)) undergoes a change in use but does not cease to be section 38 property, qualified investment for that vehicle is recomputed as if the vehicle was section 38 property which is not a qualifying commuter highway vehicle for its entire useful life.

(ii) The following example illustrates this paragraph (m)(1).

Example. X Corporation, a calendar year taxpayer, acquired and placed in service on January 1, 1982, a qualifying commuter highway vehicle with a basis of $10,000 and which qualified as three year recovery property under section 168(c)(2)(A)(i). The amount of qualified investment for the vehicle under section 46(c)(1) and (6) is $10,000. For the taxable year 1982, X Corporation's credit earned was $1,000 (10 percent of $10,000) and X Corporation was allowed under section 38 a $1,000 credit against its 1982 tax liability. During the taxable year 1984, the vehicle undergoes a change in use but does not cease to be section 38 property. The vehicle is treated as section 38 property which is not a qualifying commuter highway vehicle for its entire useful life. The recomputed qualified investment for the vehicle is $6,000 (60 percent of $10,000) and X Corporation's recomputed credit earned is $600 (10 percent of $6,000). The income tax imposed by chapter 1 of the Code on X Corporation for

1984 is increased by the $400 decrease in its credit earned for 1982 ($1,000 − $600).

(2) *Change in use*—(i) A qualifying commuter highway vehicle undergoes a change in use if the vehicle does not meet the commuter use requirement (as defined in § 1.46-11(d)) for each computation period.

(ii) Each of the following is a computation period:

(A) The period beginning on the date the vehicle was placed in service and ending on the last day of the taxpayer's taxable year in which the vehicle was placed in service;

(B) Each of the taxpayer's taxable years beginning after the date the vehicle was placed in service and ending before the end of the first 36 months after the vehicle was placed in service; and

(C) The period ending at the end of the first 36 months after the vehicle was placed in service and beginning on the first day of the taxpayer's taxable year in which the end of those first 36 months falls.

(iii) The following example illustrates this paragraph (m)(2).

Example. (a) Z Corporation, a calendar year taxpayer, acquired and placed in service a qualifying commuter highway vehicle on January 15, 1979. Z Corporation used the vehicle as set forth in the following table:

Taxable year ending	Total miles	Commuter miles	Ratio
1979	10,000	9,000	.90
1980	10,000	8,000	.80
1981	10,000	8,000	.80
1982 (1-14) .	1,000	100	.10

(b) The first computation period begins on the date the vehicle is placed in service, in this example 1-15-79, and ends 12-31-79. In that computation period, the ratio of commuter miles to total miles is .90 (9,000 miles ÷ 10,000 miles). Therefore, the vehicle meets the commuter use requirement for that period and has not undergone a change in use. Similar calculations for the computation periods 1-1-80 to 12-31-80 and 1-1-81 to 12-31-81 produce the same result.

(c) As of the computation period beginning 1-1-82 and ending 1-14-82, the ratio of commuter use to total mileage is .10 (100 miles ÷ 1,000 miles). Since that ratio is less than .80, the vehicle does not meet the commuter use requirement for the period and the vehicle has undergone a change in use. [Reg. § 1.47-1.]

☐ [*T.D.* 6931, 10-9-67. *Amended by T.D.* 7203, 8-24-72; *T.D.* 7765, 1-19-81; *T.D.* 7982, 10-5-84; *T.D.* 8035, 7-18-85; *T.D.* 8183, 3-1-88 *and T.D.* 8474, 4-26-93.]

[Reg. § 1.47-2]

§ 1.47-2. "Disposition" and "cessation".-
General rule—(1) *"Disposition".* For purposes this section and § 1.47-1 and §§ 1.47-3 throug 1.47-6, the term "disposition" includes a sale in a sale-and-leaseback transaction, a transfer upon the foreclosure of a security interest and a gift, but such term does not include a mere transfer of title to a creditor upon creation of a security interest. See paragraph (g) of § 1.47-3 for treatment of certain sale-and-leaseback transactions.

(2) *"Cessation".* (i) A determination of whether section 38 property ceases to be section 38 property with respect to the taxpayer must be made for each taxable year subsequent to the credit year. Thus, in each such taxable year the taxpayer must determine, as if such property were placed in service in such taxable year, whether such property would qualify as section 38 property (within the meaning of § 1.48-1) in the hands of the taxpayer for such taxable year.

(ii) Section 38 property does not cease to be section 38 property with respect to the taxpayer in any taxable year subsequent to the credit year merely because under the taxpayer's depreciation practice no deduction for depreciation with respect to such property is allowable to the taxpayer for the taxable year, provided that the property continues to be used in the taxpayer's trade or business (or in the production of income) and otherwise qualifies as section 38 property with respect to the taxpayer.

(iii) This subparagraph may be illustrated by the following examples:

Example (1). A, an individual who makes his returns on the basis of the calendar year, on January 1, 1962, acquired and placed in service in his trade or business an item of section 38 property with an estimated useful life of eight years. On January 1, 1965, A removes the item of section 38 property from use in his trade or business by converting such item to personal use. Therefore, no deduction for depreciation with respect to such item of property is allowable to A for the taxable year 1965. On January 1, 1965, such item of property ceases to be section 38 property with respect to A.

Example (2). On January 1, 1965, A placed in service an item of section 38 property with a basis of $10,000 and an estimated useful life of 4 years. A depreciates such item, which has a salvage value of $2,000 (after taking into account section 167(f)), on the declining balance method at a rate of 50 percent (that is, twice the straight line rate of 25 percent). With respect to such item, A is allowed deductions for depreciation of $5,000 for 1965, $2,500 for 1966, and $500

Reg. § 1.47-2(a)(2)

57. A is not allowed a deduction for depreciation for 1968 although he continues to use such item in his trade or business. Such item does not cease to be section 38 property with respect to A in 1968.

(b) *Leased property*—(1) *In general.* For purposes of paragraph (a) of § 1.47-1, generally the mere leasing of section 38 property by a lessor who took the basis of such property into account in computing his qualified investment for the credit year shall not be considered to be a disposition. However, in a case where a lease is treated as a sale for income tax purposes such transaction is considered to be a disposition. Leased section 38 property ceases to be section 38 property with respect to the lessor if, in any taxable year subsequent to the credit year, such property would not qualify as section 38 property (as defined in § 1.48-1) in the hands of the lessor, the lessee, or any sublessee. Thus, if, in a taxable year subsequent to the credit year, a lessee uses the property predominantly outside the United States, such property shall be considered to have ceased to be section 38 property with respect to the lessor.

(2) *Where lessor elects to treat lessee as purchaser.* For purposes of paragraph (a) of § 1.47-1, if, under § 1.48-4, the lessor of new section 38 property made a valid election to treat the lessee as having purchased such property for purposes of the credit allowed by section 38, the following rules apply in determining whether such property is disposed of, or otherwise ceases to be section 38 property with respect to the lessee:

(i) Generally, a mere disposition by the lessor of property subject to a lease shall not be considered to be a disposition by the lessee.

(ii) If the lessor makes a disposition of property subject to a lease to a person who may not, under § 1.48-4, make a valid election to treat the lessee as having purchased such property for purposes of the credit allowed by section 38 (such as a person described in paragraph (a)(5) of § 1.48-4), such property shall be considered to have ceased to be section 38 property with respect to the lessee on the date of such disposition.

(iii) If a lease is terminated and the property is transferred by the lessee to the lessor or to any other person, such transfer shall be considered to be a disposition by the lessee.

(iv) If the lessee actually purchases such property in the credit year or in a taxable year subsequent to the credit year, such purchase shall not be considered to be a disposition.

(v) The property ceases to be section 38 property with respect to the lessee if in any taxable year subsequent to the credit year such property would not qualify as section 38 property (as defined in § 1.48-1) in the hands of the lessor, the lessee, or any sublessee. Thus, for example, if, in a taxable year subsequent to the credit year, a sublessee uses the property predominantly outside the United States, the property ceases to be section 38 property with respect to the lessee.

(c) *Reduction in basis of section 38 property*—(1) *General rule.* If, in the credit year or in any taxable year subsequent to the credit year, the basis (or cost) of section 38 property is reduced, for example, as a result of a refund of part of the cost of the property, then such section 38 property shall be treated as having ceased to be section 38 property with respect to the taxpayer to the extent of the amount of such reduction in basis (or cost) on the date the refund which results in such reduction in basis (or cost) is received or accrued, except that for purposes of § 1.47-1(a) the actual useful life of the property treated as having ceased to be section 38 property shall be considered to be less than 3 years.

(2) *Example.* Subparagraph (1) of this paragraph may be illustrated by the following example:

Example. (i) On January 1, 1962, A, a cash basis taxpayer, acquired from X Cooperative an item of section 38 property with a basis of $100 and an estimated useful life of 10 years which he placed in service on such date. The amount of qualified investment with respect to such asset was $100. For the taxable year 1962 A was allowed under section 38 a credit of $7 against his liability for tax. On June 1, 1963, A receives a $10 patronage dividend from X Cooperative with respect to such asset. Under paragraph (c)(2)(i) of § 1.1385-1, the basis of the asset in A's hands is reduced by $10.

(ii) Under subparagraph (1) of this paragraph, on June 1, 1963, the item of section 38 property ceases to be section 38 property with respect to A to the extent of $10 of the original $100 basis.

(d) *Retirements.* A retirement of section 38 property, including a normal retirement (as defined in paragraph (b) of § 1.167(a)-8, relating to definition of normal and abnormal retirements), whether from a single asset account or a multiple asset account, and an abandonment, are dispositions for purposes of paragraph (a) of § 1.47-1.

(e) *Conversion of section 38 property to personal use.* (1) If, for any taxable year subsequent to the credit year—

(i) A deduction for depreciation is allowable to the taxpayer with respect to only a part of section 38 property because such property is partially devoted to personal use, and

Reg. § 1.47-2(b)(1)

(ii) The part of the property (expressed as a percentage of its total basis (or cost)) with respect to which a deduction for depreciation is allowable for such taxable year is less than the part of the property with respect to which a deduction for depreciation was allowable in the credit year, then such property shall be considered as having ceased to be section 38 property with respect to the taxpayer to such extent. Further, property ceases to be section 38 property with respect to the taxpayer to the extent that a deduction for depreciation thereon is disallowed under section 274 (relating to disallowance of certain entertainment, etc., expenses).

(2) *Examples.* Subparagraph (1) of this paragraph may be illustrated by the following examples:

Example (1). (i) A, a calendar-year taxpayer, acquired and placed in service on January 1, 1962, an automobile with a basis of $2,400 and an estimated useful life of four years. In the taxable year 1962 the automobile was used by A 80 percent of the time in his trade or business and was used 20 percent of the time for personal purposes. Thus, for the taxable year 1962 only 80 percent of the basis of the automobile qualified as section 38 property since a deduction for depreciation was allowable to A only with respect to 80 percent of the basis of the automobile. In the taxable year 1963 the automobile is used by A only 60 percent of the time in his trade or business. Thus, for the taxable year 1963 a deduction for depreciation is allowable to A only with respect to 60 percent of the basis of the automobile.

(ii) Under subparagraph (1) of this paragraph, on January 1, 1963, the automobile ceases to be section 38 property with respect to A to the extent of 20 percent (80 percent minus 60 percent) of the $2,400 basis of the automobile.

Example (2). (i) The facts are the same as in example (1) and in addition for the taxable year 1964 a deduction for depreciation is allowable to A only with respect to 40 percent of the basis of the property.

(ii) Under subparagraph (1) of this paragraph, on January 1, 1964, the automobile ceases to be section 38 property with respect to A to the extent of 20 percent (60 percent minus 40 percent) of the $2,400 basis of the automobile. [Reg. § 1.47-2.]

□ [*T.D. 6931, 10-9-67. Amended by T.D. 7203,* 8-24-72.]

[Reg. § 1.47-3]

§ 1.47-3. **Exceptions to the application of** § 1.47-1.—(a) *In general.* Notwithstanding the provisions of § 1.47-2, relating to "disposition"

and "cessation," paragraph (a) of § 1.47-1 not apply if paragraph (b) of this section (rela~~ to transfers by reason of death), paragraph (c) this section (relating to property destroyed b. casualty), paragraph (d) of this section (relating to reselection of used section 38 property), paragraph (e) of this section (relating to transactions to which section 381(a) applies), paragraph (f) of this section (relating to mere change in form of conducting a trade or business), paragraph (g) of this section (relating to sale-and-leaseback transactions), or paragraph (h) of this section (relating to certain property replaced after Apr. 18, 1969) applies with respect to such disposition or cessation.

(b) *Transfers by reason of death —* (1) *General rule.* Notwithstanding the provisions of § 1.47-2, relating to "disposition" and "cessation", paragraph (a) of § 1.47-1 shall not apply to a transfer of section 38 property by reason of the death of the taxpayer. Thus, for example, with respect to section 38 property held in joint tenancy, paragraph (a) of § 1.47-1 shall not apply to the transfer of the deceased taxpayer's interest to the surviving joint tenant. If, under § 1.48-4, the lessor of new section 38 property made a valid election to treat the lessee as having purchased such property for purposes of the credit allowed by section 38, paragraph (a) of § 1.47-1 does not apply if, by reason of the death of the lessee, there is a termination of the lease and transfer of the leased property to the lessor, or there is an assignment of the lease and transfer of the leased property to another person. Moreover, paragraph (a) of § 1.47-1 does not apply to the transfer of a partner's interest in a partnership, a beneficiary's interest in an estate or trust, or shares of stock of a shareholder of an electing small business corporation (as defined in section 1371(b)) by reason of the death of such partner, beneficiary, or shareholder. Paragraph (a) of § 1.47-1 applies to a gift by a taxpayer prior to his death even if the value of such gift is included in his gross estate for estate tax purposes (such as, a gift in contemplation of death under section 2035). The effect of this subparagraph is that any section 38 property held by a taxpayer at the time of his death is deemed to have been held by him for its entire estimated useful life.

(2) *Examples.* Subparagraph (1) of this paragraph may be illustrated by the following examples:

Example (1). (i) A, an individual, acquired and placed in service on January 1, 1962, an item of section 38 property with a basis of $10,000 and an estimated useful life of eight years. On April 28, 1963, A dies and, as a result of A's death, his est in such item of section 38 property is ansferred to a testamentary trust pursuant to s will, and on February 1, 1967, the trust is erminated and the item of section 38 property is transferred to the beneficiaries of the trust.

(ii) Under subparagraph (1) of this paragraph, paragraph (a) of § 1.47-1 does not apply to the transfer, as a result of A's death, of his interest in such item of section 38 property to the testamentary trust. Moreover, paragraph (a) of § 1.47-1 does not apply to the February 1, 1967, transfer of such item of section 38 property by the trust to its beneficiaries.

Example (2). (i) X Corporation, an electing small business corporation (as defined in section 1371(b)) which makes its returns on the basis of a calendar year, acquired and placed in service during 1962 an item of section 38 property. On December 31, 1962, X Corporation had 10 shares of stock outstanding which were owned as follows: A owned eight shares and B owned two shares. On December 31, 1962, 80 percent of the basis of the item of section 38 property was apportioned to A and 20 percent to B. On June 1, 1964, A dies and, as a result of A's death, his eight shares of stock in X Corporation are transferred to his wife. On July 10, 1965, X Corporation sells the item of section 38 property to Y Corporation.

(ii) Under subparagraph (1) of this paragraph, paragraph (a) of § 1.47-1 does not apply to the transfer, as a result of A's death, of his eight shares of stock in X Corporation to his wife. Moreover, with respect to the July 10, 1965, sale paragraph (a) of § 1.47-1 applies only to the 20 percent of the basis of the item of section 38 property which was apportioned to B.

(c) *Property destroyed by casualty*—(1) *Dispositions after April 18, 1969.* Notwithstanding the provisions of § 1.47-2, relating to "disposition" and "cessation", paragraph (a) of § 1.47-1 shall not apply to property which, after April 18, 1969, and before August 16, 1971, is disposed of or otherwise ceases to be section 38 property with respect to the taxpayer on account of its destruction or damage by fire, storm, shipwreck, or other casualty, or by reason of its theft.

(2) *Dispositions before April 19, 1969.* (i) In the case of property which, before April 19, 1969, is disposed of or otherwise ceases to be section 38 property with respect to the taxpayer on account of its destruction or damage by fire, storm, shipwreck or other casualty, or by reason of its theft, paragraph (a) of § 1.47-1 shall apply except to the extent provided in subdivisions (ii) and (iii) of this subparagraph.

(ii) Paragraph (a) of § 1.47-1 shall not apply if—

(a) Section 38 property is placed in service by the taxpayer to replace (within the meaning of paragraph (h) of § 1.46-3) the destroyed, damaged, or stolen property, and

(b) The basis (or cost) of the section 38 property which is placed in service by the taxpayer to replace the destroyed, damaged, or stolen property is reduced under paragraph (h) of § 1.46-3.

(iii) If property which would be section 38 property but for section 49 is placed in service by the taxpayer to replace the destroyed, damaged, or stolen property, then the provisions of paragraph (h) of this section (other than the requirement that the replacement take place within 6 months after the disposition) shall apply.

(3) *Examples.* The provisions of subparagraph (2)(ii) of this paragraph may be illustrated by the following examples:

Example (1). (i) A acquired and placed in service on January 1, 1962, machine No. 1 which qualified as section 38 property with a basis of $30,000 and an estimated useful life of 6 years. The amount of qualified investment with respect to such machine was $20,000. For the taxable year 1962 A's credit earned of $1,400 was allowed under section 38 as a credit against its liability for tax. On January 1, 1963, machine No. 1 is completely destroyed by fire. On January 1, 1963, the adjusted basis of machine No. 1 in A's hands is $24,500. A receives $23,000 in insurance proceeds as compensation for the destroyed machine, and on February 15, 1964, A acquires and places in service machine No. 2, which qualifies as section 38 property, with a basis of $41,000 and an estimated useful life of six years to replace machine No. 1.

(ii) Under subparagraph (1) of this paragraph, paragraph (a) of § 1.47-1 does not apply with respect to machine No. 1 since machine No. 2 is placed in service to replace machine No. 1 and the $41,000 basis of machine No. 2 is reduced, under paragraph (h) of § 1.46-3, by $23,000. (See example (1) of paragraph (h)(3) of § 1.46-3.)

Example (2). (i) The facts are the same as in example (1) except that A receives only $19,000 in insurance proceeds as compensation for the destroyed machine.

(ii) Although machine No. 2 is placed in service to replace machine No. 1, subparagraph (1) of this paragraph does not apply with respect to machine No. 1 since the basis of machine No. 2 is not reduced under paragraph (h) of § 1.46-3. Paragraph (a) of § 1.47-1 applies with respect to the January 1, 1963, destruction of machine No. 1. The actual useful life of machine No. 1 is one

Reg. § 1.47-3(c)(1)

year. The recomputed qualified investment with respect to such machine is zero ($30,000 basis multiplied by zero applicable percentage) and A's recomputed credit earned for the taxable year 1962 is zero. The income tax imposed by chapter 1 of the Code on A for the taxable year 1963 is increased by $1,400.

(d) *Reselection of used section 38 property*—(1) *Reselection.* If—

(i) Used section 38 property (as defined in § 1.48-3) the cost of which was taken into account in computing the taxpayer's qualified investment is disposed of, or otherwise ceases to be section 38 property with respect to the taxpayer, before the close of the estimated useful life which was taken into account in computing such qualified investment, and

(ii) For the taxable year in which the property described in subdivision (i) of this subparagraph was placed in service, the sum of (a) the cost of used section 38 property placed in service by the taxpayer, and (b) the cost of used section 38 property apportioned to such taxpayer exceeded $50,000,

then such taxpayer may treat the cost of any used section 38 property (regardless of its estimated useful life) which was not originally selected, under paragraph (c)(4) of § 1.48-3, to be taken into account in computing qualified investment for such taxable year (or previously reselected under this subparagraph) as having been selected (in accordance with the principles of paragraph (c)(4)(ii) of § 1.48-3) in place of the cost of the used section 38 property described in subdivision (i) of this subparagraph. Hereinafter such reselected property is referred to as "newly selected used section 38 property". For purposes of this subparagraph, the cost of used section 38 property apportioned to a taxpayer means the sum of the cost of used section 38 property apportioned to him by a trust, estate, or electing small business corporation (as defined in section 1371(b)), and his share of the cost of partnership used section 38 property, with respect to the taxable year of such trust, estate, corporation or partnership ending with or within such taxpayer's taxable year. In the case of a taxpayer to whom paragraph (c)(2) of § 1.48-3 applied for the taxable year in which the property described in subdivision (i) of this subparagraph was placed in service, a $25,000 amount shall be substituted for the $50,0000 amount referred to in subdivision (ii)(b) of this subparagraph, and in the case of a member of an affiliated group (as defined in subparagraph (6) of § 1.48-3(e)) the amount apportioned to such member under paragraph (e) of

§ 1.48-3 shall be substituted for such $50,00(amount.

(2) *Application of paragraph (a) of § 1.47-1.* (i) If a taxpayer treats, under subparagraph (1) of this paragraph, the cost of any used section 38 property which was not originally selected as having been selected in place of the cost of used section 38 property described in subparagraph (1)(i) of this paragraph, then, notwithstanding the provisions of § 1.47-2 (relating to "disposition" and "cessation"), paragraph (a) of § 1.47-1 shall not apply to the property described in subparagraph (1)(i) of this paragraph to the extent of the cost of the newly selected used section 38 property.

(ii) If the cost of the used section 38 property described in subparagraph (1)(i) of this paragraph exceeds the cost of the newly selected used section 38 property, then the property described in subparagraph (1)(i) of this paragraph shall cease to be section 38 property with respect to the taxpayer to the extent of such excess.

(iii) If the newly selected used section 38 property is disposed of, or otherwise ceases to be section 38 property with respect to the taxpayer, before the close of the estimated useful life of the property described in subparagraph (1)(i) of this paragraph, then, unless he reselects other used section 38 property, paragraph (a) of § 1.47-1 shall apply with respect to such newly selected used section 38 property. For purposes of recomputing qualified investment with respect to such newly selected used section 38 property the actual useful life shall be deemed to be the period beginning with the date on which the property described in subparagraph (1)(i) of this paragraph was placed in service by the taxpayer and ending with the date of the disposition or cessation with respect to such newly selected used section 38 property. See paragraph (c) of § 1.47-1, relating to date placed in service and date of disposition or cessation.

(3) *Information requirement.* (i) If in any taxable year this paragraph applies to a taxpayer, such taxpayer, shall attach to his income tax return for such taxable year a statement containing the information required by subdivision (ii) of this subparagraph.

(ii) The statement referred to in subdivision (i) of this subparagraph shall contain the following information:

(a) The taxpayer's name, address and taxpayer account number; and

(b) With respect to the originally selected used section 38 property and the newly selected used section 38 property, the month and

Reg. § 1.47-3(d)(3)

year placed in service, cost, and estimated useful life.

(4) *Examples.* This paragraph may be illustrated by the following examples:

Example (1). (i) X Corporation purchased and placed in service on January 1, 1962, machines No. 1 and No. 2, which qualified as used section 38 property, each with a cost of $50,000 and an estimated useful life of eight years. The aggregate cost of used section 38 property taken into account by X Corporation in computing its qualified investment for the taxable year 1962 could not exceed $50,000; therefore, under paragraph (c)(4) of § 1.48-3, X selected the $50,000 cost of machine No. 1 to be taken into account in computing its qualified investment for the taxable year 1962. The qualified investment with respect to machine No. 1 was $50,000. For the taxable year 1962 X's credit earned of $3,500 was allowed under section 38 as a credit against its liability for tax. On January 2, 1965, X Corporation sells machine No. 1 to Y Corporation.

(ii) Under subparagraph (1) of this paragraph, X Corporation treats the $50,000 cost of machine No. 2 as having been selected to be taken into account in computing its qualified investment for the taxable year 1962 in place of the $50,000 cost of machine No. 1. Therefore, under subparagraph (2)(i) of this paragraph, paragraph (a) of § 1.47-1 does not apply to the January 2, 1965, disposition of machine No. 1.

Example (2). (i) The facts are the same as in example (1) and in addition X Corporation, on December 2, 1966, sells machine No. 2 to Z Corporation.

(ii) Under subparagraph (2)(iii) of this paragraph, paragraph (a) of § 1.47-1 applies with respect to the December 2, 1966, disposition of machine No. 2. The actual useful life of machine No. 2 is four years and eleven months (that is, the period beginning on January 1, 1962, and ending on December 2, 1966). The recomputed qualified investment with respect to machine No. 2 is $16,667 ($50,000 cost multiplied by 33⅓ percent applicable percentage) and X Corporation's recomputed credit earned for the taxable year 1962 is $1,167. The income tax imposed by chapter 1 of the Code on X Corporation for the taxable year 1966 is increased by the $2,333 decrease in its credit earned for the taxable year 1962 (that is, $3,500 original credit earned minus $1,167 recomputed credit earned).

Example (3). (i) The facts are the same as in example (1) except that machine No. 2 had a cost of $30,000.

(ii) Under subparagraph (1) of this paragraph, X Corporation treats the $30,000 cost of machine No. 2 as having been selected to be taken into account in computing its qualified investment for the taxable year 1962 in place of the $50,000 cost of machine No. 1. Therefore, under subparagraph (2)(i) of this paragraph, paragraph (a) of § 1.47-1 does not apply to the January 2, 1965, disposition of machine No. 1 to the extent of $30,000 of the $50,000 cost of machine No. 1. However, under subparagraph (2)(ii) of this paragraph, paragraph (a) of § 1.47-1 applies to the January 2, 1965, disposition of machine No. 1 to the extent of $20,000 (that is, $50,000 cost of machine No. 1 minus $30,000 cost of machine No. 2). The actual useful life of such $20,000 portion of machine No. 1 is three years (that is, the period beginning on January 1, 1962, and ending on January 2, 1965). The recomputed qualified investment with respect to the $20,000 portion of the cost of machine No. 1 is zero ($20,000 portion of the cost multiplied by zero applicable percentage) and X Corporation's recomputed credit earned for the taxable year 1962 is $2,100 (7 percent of $30,000). The income tax imposed by chapter 1 of the Code on X Corporation for the taxable year 1965 is increased by the $1,400 decrease in its credit earned for the taxable year 1962 (that is, $3,500 original credit earned minus $2,100 recomputed credit earned).

(e) *Transactions to which section 381(a) applies*—(1) *General rule.* Notwithstanding the provisions of § 1.47-2, relating to "disposition" and "cessation", paragraph (a) of § 1.47-1 shall not apply to a disposition of section 38 property in a transaction to which section 381(a) (relating to carryovers in certain corporate acquisitions) applies. If the section 38 property described in the preceding sentence is disposed of, or otherwise ceases to be section 38 property with respect to the acquiring corporation, before the close of the estimated useful life which was taken into account in computing the transferor corporation's qualified investment, then paragraph (a) of § 1.47-1 shall apply to the acquiring corporation with respect to such section 38 property. For purposes of recomputing qualified investment with respect to such property its actual useful life shall be the period beginning with the date on which it was placed in service by the transferor corporation and ending with the date of the disposition by, or cessation with respect to, the acquiring corporation.

(2) *Examples.* This paragraph may be illustrated by the following examples:

Example (1). (i) X Corporation, a wholly owned subsidiary of Y Corporation, acquired and placed in service on January 1, 1962, an item of section 38 property with a basis of $12,000 and an estimated useful life of eight years. Both X and Y make their returns on the basis of a calendar year. The qualified investment with respect to such item was $12,000. For the taxable year 1962 X Corporation's credit earned of $840 was allowed under section 38 as a credit against its liability for tax. On January 15, 1967, X Corporation is liquidated under section 332 and all of its properties, including the item of section 38 property, are transferred to Y Corporation. The bases of the properties in the hands of Y Corporation are determined under section 334(b)(1).

(ii) Under subparagraph (1) of this paragraph, paragraph (a) of § 1.47-1 does not apply to the January 15, 1967, transfer to Y Corporation.

Example (2). (i) The facts are the same as in example (1) and in addition on February 2, 1968, Y Corporation sells the item of section 38 property to Z Corporation.

(ii) Under subparagraph (1) of this paragraph, paragraph (a) of § 1.47-1 does not apply to the January 15, 1967, transfer to Y Corporation. However, paragraph (a) of § 1.47 applies to the February 2, 1968, sale of the property by Y Corporation. The actual useful life of the property is six years and one month (that is, the period beginning on January 1, 1962, and ending on February 2, 1968).

(f) *Mere change in form of conducting a trade or business*—(1) *General rule.* (i) Notwithstanding the provisions of § 1.47-2, relating to "disposition" and "cessation", paragraph (a) of § 1.47-1 shall not apply to section 38 property which is disposed of, or otherwise ceases to be section 38 property with respect to the taxpayer, before the close of the estimated useful life which was taken into account in computing the taxpayer's qualified investment by reason of a mere change in the form of conducting the trade or business in which such section 38 property is used provided that conditions set forth in subdivision (ii) of this subparagraph are satisfied.

(ii) The conditions referred to in subdivision (i) of this subparagraph are as follows:

(a) The section 38 property described in subdivision (i) of this subparagraph is retained as section 38 property in the same trade or business,

(b) The transferor (or in a case where the transferor is a partnership, estate, trust, or electing small business corporation, the partner, beneficiary, or shareholder) of such section 38 property retains a substantial interest in such trade or business,

(c) Substantially all the assets (whether or not section 38 property) necessary to operate such trade of business are transferred to the trans-

feree to whom such section 38 property is transferred, and

(d) The basis of such section 38 property in the hands of the transferee is determined in whole or in part by reference to the basis of such section 38 property in the hands of the transferor.

This subparagraph shall not apply to the transfer of section 38 property if paragraph (e) of this section, relating to transactions to which section 381 applies, applies with respect to such transfer.

(2) *Substantial interest.* For purposes of this paragraph, a transferor (or in a case where the transferor is a partnership, estate, trust, or electing small business corporation, the partner, beneficiary, or shareholder) shall be considered as having retained a substantial interest in the trade or business only if, after the change in form, his interest in such trade or business—

(i) Is substantial in relation to the total interest of all persons, or

(ii) Is equal to or greater than his interest prior to the change in form.

Thus, where a taxpayer owns a 5-percent interest in a partnership, and, after the incorporation of that partnership, the taxpayer retains at least a 5-percent interest in the corporation, the taxpayer will be considered as having retained a substantial interest in the trade or business as of the date of the change in form.

(3) *Property held for the production of income.* Subparagraph (1)(i) of this paragraph applies to section 38 property held for the production of income (within the meaning of section 167(a)(2)) as well as to section 38 property used in a trade or business.

(4) *Leased property.* In a case where a lessor of new section 38 property made a valid election, under § 1.48-4, to treat the lessee as having purchased such property for purposes of the credit allowed by section 38, in determining whether subparagraph (1)(i) of this paragraph applies to an assignment of the lease and transfer of possession of such property, the condition contained in subparagraph (1)(ii)(d) of this paragraph is not applicable.

(5) *Disposition or cessation.* (i) If section 38 property described in subparagraph (1)(i) of this paragraph is disposed of by the transferee, or otherwise ceases to be section 38 property with respect to the transferee, before the close of the estimated useful life which was taken into account in computing the qualified investment of the transferor (or in a case where the transferor is a partnership, estate, trust, or electing small business corporation, the qualified investment of the

Reg. § 1.47-3(f)(5)

partners, beneficiaries, or shareholders) then under paragraph (a) of § 1.47-1 such property ceases to be section 38 property with respect to the transferor (or such partners, beneficiaries, or shareholders), and a recapture determination shall be made with respect to such property. For purposes of recomputing qualified investment with respect to such property, the actual useful life shall be the period beginning with the date on which it was placed in service by the transferor and ending with the date of the disposition by, or cessation with respect to, the transferee.

(ii) If in any taxable year the transferor (or in a case where the transferor is a partnership, estate, trust, or electing small business corporation, the partner, beneficiary, or shareholder) of the section 38 property described in subparagraph (1)(i) of this paragraph does not retain a substantial interest in the trade or business directly or indirectly (through ownership in other entities provided that such other entities' bases in such interest are determined in whole or in part by reference to the basis of such interest in the hands of the transferor) then, under paragraph (a) of § 1.47-1, such property ceases to be section 38 property with respect to the transferor and he (or the partner, beneficiary, or shareholder) shall make a recapture determination. For purposes of recomputing qualified investment with respect to property described in this subdivision, its actual useful life shall be the period beginning with the date on which it was placed in service by the transferor and ending with the first date on which the transferor (or the partner, beneficiary, or shareholder) does not retain a substantial interest in the trade or business. Any taxpayer who seeks to establish his interest in a trade or business under the rule of this subdivision shall maintain adequate records to demonstrate his indirect interest in such trade or business after any such transfer or transfers.

(iii) In making a recapture determination under this subparagraph there shall be taken into account any prior recapture determinations with respect to the transferor in connection with the same property.

(iv) Notwithstanding subparagraph (1) of this paragraph and subdivision (ii) of this subparagraph in the case of a mere change in the form of a trade or business, if the interest of a taxpayer in the trade or business is reduced but such taxpayer has retained a substantial interest in such trade or business, paragraph (a)(2) of § 1.47-4 (relating to electing small business corporations), paragraph (a)(2) of § 1.47-5 (relating to estate or trusts) or paragraph (a)(2) of § 1.47-6 (relating to partnerships) shall apply, as the case may be.

(6) *Examples.* This paragraph may be illustrated by the following examples in each of which it is assumed that the transfer satisfies the conditions of subparagraph (1)(ii)(a), (c) and (d) of this paragraph.

Example (1). (i) On January 1, 1962, A, an individual, acquired and placed in service in his sole proprietorship an item of section 38 property with a basis of $12,000 and an estimated useful life of eight years. The qualified investment with respect to such item was $12,000. For the taxable year 1962 A's credit earned of $840 was allowed under section 38 as a credit against his liability for tax. On March 15, 1963, A transfers all of the assets used in his sole proprietorship to X Corporation, a newly formed corporation, in exchange for 45 percent of the stock of X Corporation.

(ii) Under subparagraph (1)(i) of this paragraph, paragraph (a) of § 1.47-1 does not apply to the March 15, 1963, transfer to X Corporation.

Example 2. (i) The facts are the same as in example (1) and in addition on February 2, 1964, X Corporation sells the item of section 38 property to Y Corporation.

(ii) Under subparagraph (1)(i) of this paragraph, paragraph (a) of § 1.47-1 does not apply to the March 15, 1963, transfer to X Corporation. However, under subparagraph (5)(i) of this paragraph, paragraph (a) of § 1.47-1 applies to the February 2, 1964, sale of the item of section 38 property by X Corporation to Y Corporation. The actual useful life of the property is two years and one month (that is, the period beginning on January 1, 1962, and ending on February 2, 1964). The recomputed qualified investment with respect to such property is zero ($12,000 basis multiplied by zero applicable percentage) and A's recomputed credit earned for the taxable year 1962 is zero. The income tax imposed by chapter 1 of the Code on A for 1964 is increased by the $840 decrease in his credit earned for the taxable year 1962 (that is, $840 credit earned minus zero recomputed credit earned).

Example (3). (i) On January 1, 1962, partnership ABC, which makes its returns on the basis of a calendar year, acquired and placed in service an item of section 38 property with a basis of $20,000 and an estimated useful life of eight years. Partnership ABC has 10 partners who make their returns on the basis of a calendar year and share partnership profits equally. Each partner's share of the basis of such item of section 38 property is 10 percent, that is, $2,000. On March 15, 1963, partnership ABC transfers all of the assets used in its trade or business to the X Corporation, a newly formed corporation, in exchange for all of the stock of X Corporation and

Reg. § 1.47-3(f)(6)

immediately thereafter transfers 10 percent of such stock to each of the 10 partners.

(ii) Under subparagraph (1)(i) of this paragraph, paragraph (a) of § 1.47-1 does not apply to the March 15, 1963 transfer by the ABC Partnership to X Corporation.

Example (4). (i) The facts are the same as in example (3) except that partnership ABC transfers 10 percent of the stock in X Corporation to each of 8 partners, 20 percent to partner A, and cash to partner B.

(ii) Under subparagraph (1)(i) of this paragraph, with respect to all of the partners (including partner A) except partner B, paragraph (a) of § 1.47-1 does not apply to the March 15, 1963, transfer by the ABC Partnership to X Corporation. Paragraph (a) of § 1.47-1 applies with respect to partner B's $2,000 share of the item of section 38 property. See paragraph (a)(1) of § 1.47-6.

Example (5). (i) X Corporation operates a manufacturing business and a separate personal service business. On January 1, 1962, X acquired and placed in service a truck, which qualified as section 38 property, in its manufacturing business. The truck had a basis of $10,000 and an estimated useful life of 8 years. On February 10, 1965, X transfers all the assets used in its manufacturing business to Partnership XY in exchange for 50 percent interest in such partnership.

(ii) Under subparagraph (1)(i) of this paragraph, paragraph (a) of § 1.47-1 does not apply to the February 10, 1965, transfer to Partnership XY.

(g) *Sale-and-leaseback transactions*—(1) *In general.* Notwithstanding the provisions of § 1.47-2, relating to "disposition" and "cessation", paragraph (a) of § 1.47-1 shall not apply where section 38 property is disposed of and as part of the same transaction is leased back to the vendor even though gain or loss is recognized to the vendor-lessee and the property ceases to be subject to depreciation in his hands. If paragraph (a) of § 1.47-1 applies with respect to such property subsequent to the transaction, the actual useful life shall begin with the date on which such property was first placed in service by the vendor-lessee as owner.

(2) *Special rule for progress expenditure property.* The sale and leaseback (or agreement or contract to leaseback) of progress expenditure property (including any contract rights to the property), in general, will be treated as a cessation described in section 47(a)(3)(A) with respect to the seller-lessee. However, a sale and leaseback (or agreement or contract to leaseback) will not be treated as a cessation to the extent qualified investment passed through to the lessee under section 48(d) in the year the property is placed in service equals or exceeds qualified progress expenditures for the property taken into account by the lessee. If a sale-leaseback transaction is treated as a cessation, qualified investment must be reduced and the credit recomputed, beginning with the most recent credit year (*i.e.*, the most recent year property is taken into account in computing qualified investment under § 1.46-3 or 1.46-5). The amount of the reduction is the amount, if any, by which qualified progress expenditures taken into account by the lessee in all prior years exceeds qualified investment passed through to the lessee under section 48(d). This paragraph (g)(2) does not apply to any progress expenditure property that has been placed in service by a vendor-lessee (as described in paragraph (g)(1) of this section) prior to a sale-leaseback of that property in a transaction described in paragraph (g)(1) of this section.

(h) *Certain property replaced after April 18, 1969*—(1) *In general.* (i) If section 38 property is disposed of and property which is, for purposes of section 1033 and regulations thereunder, similar or related in service or use to the property disposed of and which would be section 38 property but for the application of section 49 is placed in service to replace the property disposed of, the increase in income tax and adjustment of investment credit carryovers and carrybacks resulting from the recomputation under paragraph (a) of § 1.47-1 shall be reduced (but not below zero) by the credit that would be allowed for the qualified investment of the replacement property (determined as if such property were section 38 property). The preceding sentence shall not apply unless the replacement takes place within 6 months after the disposition. If property otherwise qualifies as replacement property, it is immaterial that it is placed in service (for example, to undergo testing) before the replaced property is disposed of. The assignment by the taxpayer in his return of an estimated useful life to the replacement property in computing its qualified investment will be considered a representation by the taxpayer that he expects to retain the replacement property for its entire estimated useful life. If such property is disposed of before the end of such life, then the circumstances surrounding the replacement will be examined to determine whether the taxpayer's representation was in good faith and, if appropriate, the qualified investment of the replacement property will be recomputed for the year of replacement using the actual useful life of such property.

Reg. § 1.47-3(h)(1)

(ii) The provisions of subdivision (i) of this subparagraph may be illustrated by the following example:

Example: On January 1, 1967, A, a calendar year taxpayer, acquired and placed in service a new machine with a basis of $100 and an estimated useful life of 8 years. A's qualified investment was $100 and his credit earned was $7, which was allowed as a credit against tax for 1967. On January 15, 1971, A disposed of the machine and replaced it with a similar new machine costing $75 and having an estimated useful life of 8 years. The new machine would be section 38 property but for section 49. Since the actual useful life of the original machine was at least 4 but less than 6 years, the recomputed qualified investment of the machine is $33.33 (33⅓ percent of $100) and under paragraph (a) of § 1.47-1 the amount of recapture tax would be $4.67 ($7, the original credit earned, minus $2.33, the recomputed credit earned). However, under the provisions of this paragraph, the recapture tax is reduced (but not below zero) by the credit that would be allowed for the replacement property (determined as if such property were section 38 property). Under these facts the recapture tax is zero ($4.67, the recapture tax with respect to the original machine, minus $5.25, the credit that would be allowed on the new machine).

(2) *Leased property.* Property disposed of may be replaced with property leased from another, provided (i) an election with respect to the newly leased property could be made under section 48(d) but for section 49, and (ii) the lessee obtains the lessor's written statement that he will not claim such property as replacement property under this paragraph. The statement of the lessor shall contain the information specified in subdivisions (i) through (vii) of § 1.48-4(f)(1) and the statement (or a copy thereof) shall be retained in the records of the lessor and the lessee for a period of at least 3 years after the property is transferred to the lessee. [Reg. § 1.47-3.]

☐ [*T.D. 6931, 10-9-67. Amended by T.D. 7126, 6-9-71; T.D. 7203, 8-24-72 and T.D. 8183, 3-1-88.*]

[Reg. § 1.47-4]

§ 1.47-4. **Electing small business corporations.—(a)** *In general*—(1) *Disposition or cessation in hands of corporation.* If an electing small business corporation (as defined in section 1371(b)) or a former electing small business corporation disposes of any section 38 property (or if any section 38 property otherwise ceases to be section 38 property in the hands of the corporation) before the close of the estimated useful life which was taken into account in computing qualified investment with respect to such property, a

recapture determination shall be made with respect to each shareholder who is treated, under § 1.48-5, as a taxpayer with respect to such property. Each such recapture determination shall be made with respect to the pro rata share of the basis (or cost) of such property taken into account by such shareholder in computing his qualified investment. For purposes of each such recapture determination the actual useful life of such property shall be the period beginning with the date on which it was placed in service by the electing small business corporation and ending with the date of the disposition or cessation. In making a recapture determination under this subparagraph there shall be taken into account any prior recapture determinations made with respect to the shareholder in connection with the same property. For definition of "recapture determination" see paragraph (a)(1) of § 1.47-1.

(2) *Disposition of shareholder's interest*—(i) If—

(a) The basis (or cost) of section 38 property is apportioned, under § 1.48-5, to a shareholder of an electing small business corporation who takes such basis (or cost) into account in computing his qualified investment, and

(b) After the end of shareholder's taxable year in which such apportionment was taken into account and before the close of the estimated useful life of the property, such shareholder's proportionate stock interest in such corporation is reduced (for example, by a sale or redemption, or by the issuance of additional shares) below the percentage specified in subdivision (ii) of this subparagraph,

then, on the date of such reduction such section 38 property ceases to be section 38 property with respect to such shareholder to the extent of the actual reduction in such shareholder's proportionate stock interest. (For example, if $100 of the basis of section 38 property was apportioned to a shareholder and if his proportionate stock interest is reduced from 60 percent to 30 percent (that is, 50 percent of his original interest), then such property shall be treated as having ceased to be section 38 property to the extent of $50.) Accordingly, a recapture determination shall be made with respect to such shareholder. For purposes of such recapture determination the actual useful life of such property shall be the period beginning with the date on which it was placed in service by the electing small business corporation and ending with the date on which it is treated as having ceased to be section 38 property with respect to the shareholder. In making a recapture determination under this subparagraph there shall be taken into account any prior recapture determination made with respect to the shareholder in connection with the same property.

(ii) The percentage referred to in subdivision (i)(*b*) of this subparagraph is 66⅔ percent of the shareholder's proportionate stock interest in the corporation on the date of the apportionment under § 1.48-5. However, once property has been treated under this subparagraph as having ceased to be section 38 property to any extent the percentage referred to shall be 33⅓ percent of the shareholder's proportionate stock interest in the corporation on the date of the apportionment under § 1.48-5.

(iii) In determining a shareholder's proportionate stock interest in a former electing small business corporation for purposes of this subparagraph, the shareholder shall be considered to own stock in such corporation which he owns directly or indirectly (through ownership in other entities provided such other entities' bases in such stock are determined in whole or in part by reference to the basis of such stock in the hands of the transferor). For example, if A, who owns all of the 100 shares of the outstanding stock of corporation X, a corporation which was formerly an electing small business corporation, transfers on November 1, 1966, 70 shares of X stock to corporation Y in exchange for 90 percent of the stock of Y in a transaction to which section 351 applies, then, for purposes of subdivision (i) of this subparagraph, A shall be considered to own 93 percent of the stock of X, 30 percent directly and 63 percent indirectly (i.e., 90 percent of 70). Any taxpayer who seeks to establish his interest in the stock of a former electing small business corporation under the rule of this subdivision shall maintain adequate records to demonstrate his indirect interest in the corporation after any such transfer or transfers.

(b) *Election of a small business corporation under section 1372*—(1) *General rule.* If a corporation makes a valid election under section 1372 to be an electing small business corporation (as defined in section 1371(b)), then on the last day of the taxable year immediately preceding the first taxable year for which such election is effective, any section 38 property the basis (or cost) of which was taken into account in computing the corporation's qualified investment in taxable years prior to the first taxable year for which the election is effective (and which has not been disposed of or otherwise ceased to be section 38 property with respect to the corporation prior to such last day) shall be considered as having ceased to be section 38 property with respect to such corporation and § 1.47-1 shall apply. However, if the corporation and each of the persons

who are shareholders of the corporation on the first day of the first taxable year for which the election under section 1372 is to be effective, or on the date of such election, whichever is later, execute the agreement specified in subparagraph (2) of this paragraph, § 1.47-1 shall not apply to any such section 38 property by reason of the election by the corporation under section 1372.

(2) *Agreement of shareholders and corporation.* (i) The agreement referred to in subparagraph (1) of this paragraph shall be signed by the shareholders and the corporation, and shall recite that, in the event the section 38 property described in subparagraph (1) of this paragraph is later disposed of by, or ceases to be section 38 property with respect to, the corporation during a taxable year of the corporation for which the election under section 1372 is effective, each such signer agrees (*a*) to notify the district director of such disposition or cessation, and (*b*) to be jointly and severally liable to pay to the district director an amount equal to the increase in tax provided by section 47. The amount of such increase shall be determined as if such property had ceased to be section 38 property as of the last day of the taxable year immediately preceding the first taxable year for which the election under section 1372 is effective, except that the actual useful life (within the meaning of paragraph (a) of § 1.47-1) of the property shall be considered to have ended on the date of the actual disposition by, or cessation in the hands of, the electing small business corporation.

(ii) The agreement shall set forth the name, address, and taxpayer account number of each party and the internal revenue district in which each such party files his or its income tax return for the taxable year which includes the last day of the corporation's taxable year immediately preceding the first taxable year for which the election under section 1372 is effective. The agreement may be signed on behalf of the corporation by any person who is duly authorized. The agreement shall be filed with the district director with whom the corporation files its income tax return for its taxable year immediately preceding the first taxable year for which the election under section 1372 is effective and shall be filed on or before the due date (including extensions of time) of such return. However, if the due date (including extensions of time) of such income tax return is on or before September 1, 1967, the agreement may be filed on or before December 31, 1967. For purposes of the two preceding sentences, the district director may, if good cause is shown, permit the agreement to be filed on a later date.

Reg. § 1.47-4(b)(2)

(c) *Examples.* This section may be illustrated by the following examples in each of which it is assumed that X Corporation, an electing small business corporation which makes its returns on the basis of the calendar year, acquired and placed in service on June 1, 1962, three items of section 38 property. The basis and estimated useful life of each item of section 38 property are as follows:

Asset number	Basis	Estimated useful life
1	$30,000	4 years
2	30,000	6 years
3	30,000	8 years

On December 31, 1962, X Corporation had 20 shares of stock outstanding which were owned equally by A and B who make their returns on the basis of a calendar year. Under § 1.48-5, the total bases of section 38 properties was apportioned to the shareholders of X Corporation as follows:

	Useful life category		
	4 to 6 years	6 to 8 years	8 years or more
Total bases	$30,000	$30,000	$30,000
Shareholder A (10/20)	$15,000	$15,000	$15,000
Shareholder B (10/20)	15,000	15,000	15,000

Assuming that during 1962 shareholders A and B did not place in service any section 38 property and that they did not own any interests in other electing small business corporations, partnerships, estates, or trusts, the qualified investment of each shareholder is $30,000, computed as follows:

Basis	Applicable percentage	Qualified investment
$5,000	33⅓	$ 5,000
15,000	66⅔	10,000
15,000	100	15,000
		$30,000

For the taxable year 1962, each shareholder's credit earned of $2,100 (7 percent of $30,000) was allowed under section 38 as a credit against his liability for tax.

Example (1). (i) On December 2, 1965, X Corporation sells asset No. 3 to Y Corporation.

(ii) The actual useful life of asset No. 3 is three years and six months. The recomputed qualified investment with respect to each shareholder's share of the basis of asset No. 3 is zero ($15,000 share of basis multiplied by zero applicable percentage) and for the taxable year 1962 each shareholder's recomputed credit earned is $1,050 (7 percent of $15,000). The income tax imposed by chapter 1 of the Code on each of the shareholders for the taxable year 1965 is increased by the $1,050 decrease in his credit earned for the taxable year 1962 (that is, $2,100 original credit earned minus $1,050 recomputed credit earned).

Example (2). (i) On December 3, 1964, shareholder A sells 5 of his 10 shares of stock in X Corporation to C, and on December 3, 1965, A sells his remaining 5 shares of stock to D. In addition, on January 2, 1966, X Corporation sells asset No. 3 to Y Corporation.

(ii) Under paragraph (a)(2) of this section, on December 3, 1964, 50 percent of the share of the basis of each of the three items of section 38 property ceases to be section 38 property with respect to shareholder A since immediately after the December 3, 1964, sale A's proportionate stock interest in X Corporation is reduced to 50 percent of the proportionate stock interest in X Corporation which he held on December 31, 1962. The actual useful life of the share of the basis of the section 38 properties which cease to be section 38 property with respect to A is two years and six months (that is, the period beginning with June 1, 1962, and ending with December 3, 1964). A's recomputed qualified investment with respect to such properties is $15,000, computed as follows:

Basis	Applicable percentage	Recomputed qualified investment
$7,500	33⅓	$ 2,500
7,500	66⅔	5,000
7,500	100	7,500
		$15,000

For the taxable year 1962 shareholder A's recomputed credit earned is $1,050 (7 percent of $15,000). The income tax imposed by chapter 1 of the Code on shareholder A for the taxable year 1964 is increased by the $1,050 decrease in his credit earned for the taxable year 1962 (that is, $2,100 original credit earned minus $1,050 recomputed credit earned).

(iii) Under paragraph (a)(2) of this section, on December 3, 1965, the remaining 50 percent of the share of the basis of each of the three items of section 38 property cease to be section 38 property with respect to shareholder A since immediately after the December 3, 1965, sale A's proportionate stock interest in X Corporation is reduced to zero. The actual useful life of the share of the bases of the section 38 properties which ceases to be section 38 property with respect to A is three years and six months (that is, the period

Reg. § 1.47-4(c)

beginning with June 1, 1962, and ending with December 3, 1965). A's recomputed qualified investment with respect to such properties is zero. For the taxable year 1962 shareholder A's recomputed credit earned is zero. The income tax imposed by chapter 1 of the Code on shareholder A for the taxable year 1965 is increased by $1,050 (that is, $2,100 ($2,100 original credit earned minus zero recomputed credit earned) reduced by the $1,050 increase in tax for 1964).

(iv) The actual useful life of asset No. 3 which was sold on January 2, 1966, is three years and seven months. The recomputed qualified investment with respect to B's share of the basis of asset No. 3 is zero ($15,000 share of basis multiplied by zero applicable percentage) and for the taxable year 1962, B's recomputed credit earned is $1,050 (7 percent of $15,000). The income tax imposed by chapter 1 of the Code on shareholder B for the taxable year 1966 is increased by the $1,050 decrease in his credit earned for the taxable year 1962 ($2,100 original credit earned minus $1,050 recomputed credit earned). The sale of asset No. 3 on January 2, 1966, by X Corporation has no effect on A.

(d) *Termination or revocation of an election under section 1372.* Section 38 property shall not be considered to be disposed of or to have ceased to be section 38 property solely by reason of a termination or revocation of a corporation's election under section 1372. [Reg. § 1.47-4.]

□ [*T.D.* 6931, 10-9-67.]

[Reg. § 1.47-5]

§ 1.47-5. Estates and trusts.—(a) *In general*—(1) *Disposition or cessation in hands of estate or trust.* If an estate or trust disposes of any section 38 property (or if any section 38 property otherwise ceases to be section 38 property in the hands of the estate or trust) before the close of the estimated useful life which was taken into account in computing qualified investment with respect to such property, a recapture determination shall be made with respect to the estate or trust, and each beneficiary who is treated, under § 1.48-6, as a taxpayer with respect to such property. Each such recapture determination shall be made with respect to the share of the basis (or cost) of such property taken into account by such estate or trust and such beneficiary in computing its or his qualified investment. For purposes of each such recapture determination the actual useful life of such property shall be the period beginning with the date on which it was placed in service by the estate or trust and ending with the date of the disposition or cessation. In making a recapture determination under this subparagraph with respect to a taxpayer there shall be taken

into account any prior recapture determinations made with respect to such taxpayer in connection with the same property. For definition of "recapture determination" see paragraph (a)(1) of § 1.47-1.

(2) *Disposition of interest*—(i) If—

(a) The basis (or cost) of section 38 property is apportioned, under § 1.48-6, to an estate or trust which, or to a beneficiary of an estate or trust who, takes such basis (or cost) into account in computing his qualified investment, and

(b) After the date on which such section 38 property was placed in service by the estate or trust and before the close of the estimated useful life of the property, such estate's, trust's, or such beneficiary's proportionate interest in the income of the estate or trust is reduced (for example, by a sale, or by the terms of the estate or trust instrument) below the percentage specified in subdivision (ii) of this subparagraph,

then, on the date of such reduction, such section 38 property ceases to be section 38 property with respect to such estate, trust, or beneficiary to the extent of the actual reduction in such estate's, trust's, or beneficiary's proportionate interest in the income of the estate or trust. (For example, if $100 of the basis of section 38 property was apportioned to a beneficiary and if his proportionate interest in the income of the estate or trust is reduced from 60 percent to 30 percent (that is, 50 percent of his original interest), then such property shall be treated as having ceased to be section 38 property to the extent of $50.) Accordingly, a recapture determination shall be made with respect to such estate, trust, or beneficiary. For purposes of such recapture determination the actual useful life of such property shall be the period beginning with the date on which it was placed in service by the estate or trust and ending with the date on which it is treated as having ceased to be section 38 property with respect to the estate, trust, or beneficiary. In making a recapture determination under this subparagraph there shall be taken into account any prior recapture determination made with respect to the estate, trust, or beneficiary in connection with the same property.

(ii) The percentage referred to in subdivision (i) (b) of this subparagraph is 66⅔ percent of the estate's, trust's, or beneficiary's proportionate interest in the income of the estate or trust for the taxable year of the apportionment under § 1.48-6. However, once property has been treated under this subparagraph as having ceased to be section 38 property to any extent the percentage referred to shall be 33⅓ percent of the estate's, trust's, or beneficiary's proportionate interest in the income of the estate or trust for the taxable year of the apportionment under § 1.48-6.

(iii) In determining a beneficiary's proportionate interest in the income of an estate or trust for purposes of this subparagraph, the beneficiary shall be considered to own any interest in such an estate or trust which he owns directly or indirectly (through ownership in other entities provided such other entities' bases in such interest are determined in whole or in part by reference to the basis of such interest in the hands of the beneficiary). For example, if A, whose proportionate interest in the income of trust X is 30 percent, transfers all of such interest to corporation Y in exchange for all of the stock of Y in a transaction to which section 351 applies, then, for purposes of subdivision (i) of this subparagraph, A shall be considered to own a 30-percent interest in trust X. Any taxpayer who seeks to establish his interest in an estate or trust under the rule of this subdivision shall maintain adequate records to demonstrate his indirect interest in the estate or trust after any such transfer or transfers.

(b) *Examples.* Paragraph (a) of this section may be illustrated by the following examples in each of which it is assumed that XYZ Trust, which makes its returns on the basis of the calendar year, acquired and placed in service on June 1, 1962, three items of section 38 property. The basis and estimated useful life of each item of section 38 property are as follows:

Asset Number	Basis	Estimated useful life
1	$30,000	4 years
2	30,000	6 years
3	30,000	8 years

For the taxable year 1962 the income of XYZ Trust is $20,000, which is allocable equally to XYZ Trust and beneficiary A. Beneficiary A makes his returns on the basis of a calendar year. Under § 1.48-6, the total bases of the section 38 properties was apportioned to XYZ Trust and beneficiary A as follows:

		Useful life category		
		4 to 6 years	6 to 8 years	8 years or more
Total bases		$30,000	$30,000	$30,000
XYZ Trust	($10,000)	15,000	15,000	15,000
	($20,000)			
Beneficiary A	($10,000)	15,000	15,000	15,000
	($20,000)			

Assuming that during 1962 beneficiary A did not place in service any section 38 property and that he did not own any interests in other estates, trusts, electing small business corporations, or

Basis	
$15,000	....
15,000	....
15,000	....

For the taxable year 1962, XYZ Trust and beneficiary A each had a credit earned of $2,100 (7 percent of $30,000). Each such credit earned was allowed under section 38 as a credit against the liability for tax.

Example (1). (i) On December 2, 1965, XYZ Trust sells asset No. 3 to X Corporation.

(ii) The actual useful life of asset No. 3 is three years and six months. The recomputed qualified investment with respect to XYZ Trust's and beneficiary A's share of the basis of asset No. 3 is zero ($15,000 share of basis multiplied by zero applicable percentage) and for the taxable year 1962, XYZ Trust's and beneficiary A's recom-

partnerships, the qualified investment of XYZ Trust and of beneficiary A is $30,000 each, computed as follows:

	Applicable percentage	Qualified investment
....	33⅓	$ 5,000
....	66⅔	10,000
....	100	15,000
		$30,000

puted credit earned is $1,050 (7 percent of $15,000). The income tax imposed by chapter 1 of the Code on XYZ Trust and on beneficiary A for the taxable year 1965 is increased by the $1,050 decrease in his credit earned for the taxable year 1962 (that is, $2,100 original credit earned minus $1,050 recomputed credit earned).

Example (2). (i) On December 3, 1964, beneficiary A sells 50 percent of his interest in the income of XYZ Trust to B, and on December 3, 1965, A sells his remaining 50 percent interest to C. In addition, on January 2, 1966, XYZ Trust sells asset No. 3 to Y Corporation.

Reg. § 1.47-5(b)

(ii) Under paragraph (a)(2) of this section, on December 3, 1964, 50 percent of the basis of each of the three items of section 38 property ceases to be section 38 property with respect to beneficiary A since immediately after the December 3, 1964, sale A's proportionate interest in the income of XYZ Trust is reduced to 50 percent of his proportionate interest in the income of XYZ Trust for the taxable year 1962. The actual useful life of t[...] share of the bases of the section 38 propertie[...] which cease to be section 38 property with respec[...] to A is two years and six months (that is, the period beginning with June 1, 1962, and ending with December 3, 1964). Beneficiary A's recomputed qualified investment with respect to such properties is $15,000, computed as follows:

Basis		Applicable percentage	Qualified investment
$7,500	....	33⅓	$ 2,500
7,500	....	66⅔	5,000
7,500	....	100	7,500
			$15,000

For the taxable year 1962 beneficiary A's recomputed credit earned is $1,050 (7 percent of $15,000). The income tax imposed by chapter 1 of the Code on beneficiary A for the taxable year 1964 is increased by the $1,050 decrease in his credit earned for the taxable year 1962 (that is, $2,100 original credit earned minus $1,050 recomputed credit earned).

(iii) Under paragraph (a)(2) of this section, on December 3, 1965, the remaining 50 percent of the share of the basis of each of the three items of section 38 property ceases to be section 38 property with respect to beneficiary A since immediately after the December 3, 1965, sale A's proportionate interest in the income of XYZ Trust is reduced to zero. The actual useful life of the share of the basis of the section 38 properties which cease to be section 38 property with respect to A is three years and six months (that is, the period beginning with June 1, 1962, and ending with December 3, 1965). A's recomputed qualified investment with respect to such properties is zero. For the taxable year 1962 beneficiary A's recomputed credit earned is zero. The income tax imposed by chapter 1 of the Code on beneficiary A for the taxable year 1965 is increased by $1,050 (that is, $2,100 ($2,100 original credit earned minus zero recomputed credit earned) reduced by the $1,050 increase in tax for 1964).

(iv) The actual useful life of asset No. 3 which was sold on January 2, 1966, is three years and seven months. The recomputed qualified investment with respect to XYZ Trust's share of the basis of asset No. 3 is zero ($15,000 share of basis multiplied by zero applicable percentage) and for the taxable year 1962, XYZ Trust's recomputed credit earned is $1,050 (7 percent of $15,000). The income tax imposed by chapter 1 of the Code on XYZ Trust for the taxable year 1966 is increased by the $1,050 decrease in its credit earned for the taxable year 1962 ($2,100 original credit earned minus $1,050 recomputed credit earned). The sale of asset No. 3 on January 2, 1966, has no effect on A. [Reg. § 1.47-5.]

☐ [T.D. 6931, 10-9-67.]

[Reg. § 1.47-6]

§ 1.47-6. **Partnerships.**—(a) *In general* —(1) *Disposition or cessation in hands of partnership.* If a partnership disposes of any partnership section 38 property (or if any partnership section 38 property otherwise ceases to be section 38 property in the hands of the partnership) before the close of the estimated useful life which was taken into account in computing qualified investment with respect to such property, a recapture determination shall be made with respect to each partner who is treated, under paragraph (f) of § 1.46-3, as a taxpayer with respect to such property. Each such recapture determination shall be made with respect to the share of the basis (or cost) of such property taken into account by such partner in computing his qualified investment. For purposes of each such recapture determination the actual useful life of such property shall be the period beginning with the date on which it was placed in service by the partnership and ending with the date of the disposition or cessation. In making a recapture determination under this subparagraph there shall be taken into account any prior recapture determinations made with respect to the partner in connection with the same property. For definition of "recapture determination" see paragraph (a)(1) of § 1.47-1.

(2) *Disposition of partner's interest.* (i) If—

(a) The basis (or cost) of partnership section 38 property is taken into account by a partner in computing his qualified investment, and

(b) After the date on which such partnership section 38 property was placed in service by the partnership and before the close of the estimated useful life of the property, such partner's proportionate interest in the general profits of the partnership (or in the particular item of property) is reduced (for example, by a sale, by a change in the partnership agreement, or by the

Reg. § 1.47-6(a)(2)

mission of a new partner) below the percentage specified in subdivision (ii) of this subparagraph, then, on the date of such reduction such partnership section 38 property ceases to be section 38 property with respect to such partner to the extent of the actual reduction in such partner's proportionate interest in the general profits of the partnership (or in the particular item of property). (For example, if $100 of the basis of section 38 property was taken into account by a partner and if his proportionate interest in the general profits of the partnership is reduced from 60 percent to 30 percent (that is, 50 percent of his original interest), then such property shall be treated as having ceased to be section 38 property to the extent of $50.) Accordingly, a recapture determination shall be made with respect to such partner. For purposes of such recapture determination the actual useful life of such property shall be the period beginning with the date on which it was placed in service by the partnership and ending with the date on which it is treated as having ceased to be section 38 property with respect to the partner. In making a recapture determination under this subparagraph there shall be taken into account any prior recapture determination made with respect to the partner in connection with the same property.

(ii) The percentage referred to in subdivision (i)(b) of this subparagraph is 66⅔ percent of the partner's proportionate interest in the general profits of the partnership (or in the particular item of property) for the year in which such property was placed in service. However, once property has been treated under this subpara-graph as having ceased to be section 38 property to any extent the percentage referred to shall be 33⅓ percent of the partner's proportionate interest in the general profits of the partnership (or in the particular item of property) for the year in which such property was placed in service.

(iii) In determining a partner's proportionate interest in the general profits of a partnership for purposes of this subparagraph, the partner shall be considered to own any interest in such a partnership which he owns directly or indirectly (through ownership in other entities provided the other entities' bases in such interest are determined in whole or in part by reference to the basis of such interest in the hands of the partner). For example, if A, whose proportionate interest in the general profits of partnership X is 20 percent, transfers all of such interest to corporation Y in exchange for all of the stock of Y in a transaction to which section 351 applies, then, for purposes of subdivision (i) of this subparagraph, A shall be considered to own a 20-percent interest in partnership X. Any taxpayer who seeks to establish his interest in a partnership under the rule of this subdivision shall maintain adequate records to demonstrate his indirect interest in the partnership after any such transfer or transfers.

(b) *Examples.* Paragraph (a) of this section may be illustrated by the following examples in each of which it is assumed that ABC Partnership, which makes its returns on the basis of the calendar year, acquired and placed in service on June 1, 1962, three items of section 38 property. The basis and estimated useful life of each item of section 38 property are as follows:

Asset number	Basis	Estimated useful life
1	$30,000	4 years
2	30,000	6 years
3	30,000	8 years

Partners A and B, who make their returns on the basis of a calendar year, share the profits and losses of ABC Partnership equally. Under paragraph (f)(2) of § 1.46-3, each partner's share of the basis of the partnership section 38 property is as follows:

			Partner's share of basis	
	Estimated		A	B
Asset No.	useful life	Basis	50%	50%
1	4 years	$30,000	$15,000	$15,000
2	6 years	30,000	15,000	15,000
3	8 years	30,000	15,000	15,000

Assuming that during 1962 partners A and B did not place in service any section 38 property and that they did not own any interests in other partnerships, electing small business corporations, estates, or trusts, the qualified investment of each partner is $30,000, computed as follows:

Partnership asset No.	Share of basis	Applicable percentage	Qualified investment
1	$15,000	33⅓	$ 5,000
2	15,000	66⅔	10,000
3	15,000	100	15,000
			$30,000

Reg. § 1.47-6(b)

For the taxable year 1962, each partner's credit earned of $2,100 (7 percent of $30,000) was allowed under section 38 as a credit against his liability for tax.

Example (1). (i) On December 2, 1965, ABC Partnership sells asset No. 3 to X Corporation.

(ii) The actual useful life of asset No. 3 is three years and six months. The recomputed qualified investment with respect to each partner's share of the basis of asset No. 3 is zero ($15,000 share of basis multiplied by zero applicable percentage) and for the taxable year 1962, each partner's recomputed credit earned is $1,050 (7 percent of $15,000). The income tax imposed by chapter 1 of the Code on each of the partners for the taxable year 1965 is increased by the $1,050 decrease in his credit earned for the taxable year 1962 (that is, $2,100 original credit earned minus $1,050 recomputed credit earned).

Example (2). (i) On December 3, 1964, partner A sells one-half of his 50 percent interest in ABC

Partnership asset No.	Share of basis	Applicable percentage	Qualified investment
1	$7,500	33⅓	$ 2,500
2	7,500	66⅔	5,000
3	7,500	100	7,500
			$15,000

For the taxable year 1962 partner A's recomputed credit earned is $1,050 (7 percent of $15,000). The income tax imposed by chapter 1 of the Code on partner A for the taxable year 1964 is increased by the $1,050 decrease in his credit earned for the taxable year 1962 (that is, $2,100 original credit earned minus $1,050 recomputed credit earned).

(iii) Under paragraph (a)(2) of this section, on December 3, 1965, the remaining 50 percent of the share of the basis of each of the three items of section 38 property ceases to be section 38 property with respect to partner A since immediately after the December 3, 1965, sale A's proportionate interest in the general profits of ABC Partnership is reduced to zero. The actual useful life of the share of the bases of the section 38 properties which cease to be section 38 property with respect to A is three years and six months (that is, the period beginning with June 1, 1962, and ending with December 3, 1965). A's recomputed qualified investment with respect to such properties is zero. For the taxable year 1962 partner A's recomputed credit earned is zero. The income tax imposed by chapter 1 of the Code on partner A for the taxable year 1965 is increased by $1,050 (that is, $2,520 ($2,520 original credit earned minus zero recomputed credit earned) reduced by the $1,050 increase in tax for 1964).

Partnership to C, and on December 3, 1965, A sells the remaining one-half of his interest to D. In addition, on January 2, 1966, ABC Partnership sells asset No. 3 to X Corporation.

(ii) Under paragraph (a)(2) of this section, on December 3, 1964, 50 percent of the basis of each of the three items of section 38 property ceases to be section 38 property with respect to partner A since immediately after the December 3, 1964, sale A's proportionate interest in the general profits of ABC Partnership is reduced to 50 percent of his proportionate interest in the general profits of ABC Partnership for 1962. The actual useful life of the share of the basis of each of the section 38 properties which cease to be section 38 property with respect to A is two years and six months (that is, the period beginning with June 1, 1962, and ending with December 3, 1964). Partner A's recomputed qualified investment with respect to such properties is $15,000, computed as follows:

(iv) The actual useful life of asset No. 3 which was sold on January 2, 1966, is three years and seven months. The recomputed qualified investment with respect to partner B's share of basis of asset No. 3 is zero ($15,000 share of basis multiplied by zero applicable percentage) and for the taxable year 1962, partner B's recomputed credit earned is $1,050 (7 percent of $15,000). The income tax imposed by chapter 1 of the Code on partner B for the taxable year 1966 is increased by the $1,050 decrease in his credit earned for the taxable year 1962 ($2,100 original credit earned minus $1,050 recomputed credit earned). The sale of asset No. 3 on January 2, 1966, has no effect on A. [Reg. § 1.47-6.]

☐ [*T.D.* 6931, 10-9-67.]

[Reg. § 1.48-1]

§ 1.48-1. Definition of section 38 property.— (a) *In general.* Property which qualifies for the credit allowed by section 38 is known as "section 38 property". Except as otherwise provided in this section, the term "section 38 property" means property (1) with respect to which depreciation (or amortization in lieu of depreciation) is allowable to the taxpayer, (2) which has an estimated useful life of 3 years or more (determined as of the time such property is placed in service), and (3) which is (i) tangible personal property, (ii)

Reg. § 1.48-1(a)

other tangible property (not including a building and its structural components) but only if such other property is used as an integral part of manufacturing, production, or extraction, or as an integral part of furnishing transportation, communications, electrical energy, gas, water, or sewage disposal services by a person engaged in a trade or business of furnishing any such service, or is a research or storage facility used in connection with any of the foregoing activities, (iii) an elevator or escalator which satisfies the conditions of section 48(a)(1)(C), or (iv) in the case of a qualified rehabilitated building, that portion of the basis which is attributable to qualified rehabilitation expenditures. The determination of whether property qualifies as section 38 property in the hands of the taxpayer for purposes of the credit allowed by section 38 must be made with respect to the first taxable year in which such property is placed in service by the taxpayer. See paragraph (d) of § 1.46-3. For the meaning of "estimated useful life", see paragraph (e) of § 1.46-3. In the case of property which is not described in section 50, this paragraph shall be applied by substituting "4 years" for "3 years".

(b) *Depreciation allowable.* (1) Property (with the exception of property described in section 48 (a)(1)(F) and paragraph (p) of this section) is not section 38 property unless a deduction for depreciation (or amortization in lieu of depreciation) with respect to such property is allowable to the taxpayer for the taxable year. A deduction for depreciation is allowable if the property is of a character subject to the allowance for depreciation under section 167 and the basis (or cost) of the property is recovered through a method of depreciation, including, for example, the unit of production method and the retirement method as well as methods of depreciation which measure the life of the property in terms of years. If property is placed in service (within the meaning of paragraph (d) of § 1.46-3) in a trade or business (or in the production of income), but under the taxpayer's depreciation practice the period for depreciation with respect to such property begins in a taxable year subsequent to the taxable year in which such property is placed in service, then a deduction for depreciation shall be treated as allowable with respect to such property in the earlier taxable year (or years). Thus, for example, if a machine is placed in service in a trade or business in 1963, but the period for depreciation with respect to such machine begins in 1964, because the taxpayer uses an averaging convention (see § 1.167(a)-10) in computing depreciation, then, for purposes of determining whether the machine

qualifies as section 38 property, a deduction for depreciation shall be treated as allowable in 1963.

(2) If, for the taxable year in which property is placed in service, a deduction for depreciation is allowable to the taxpayer only with respect to a part of such property, then only the proportionate part of the property with respect to which such deduction is allowable qualifies as section 38 property for the purpose of determining the amount of credit allowable under section 38. Thus, for example, if property is used 80 percent of the time in a trade or business and is used 20 percent of the time for personal purposes, only 80 percent of the basis (or cost) of such property qualifies as section 38 property. Further, property does not qualify to the extent that a deduction for depreciation thereon is disallowed under section 274 (relating to disallowance of certain entertainment, etc., expenses).

(3) If the cost of property is not recovered through a method of depreciation but through a deduction of the full cost in one taxable year, for purposes of subparagraph (1) of this paragraph a deduction for depreciation with respect to such property is not allowable to the taxpayer. However, if an adjustment with respect to the income tax return for such taxable year requires the cost of such property to be recovered through a method of depreciation, a deduction for depreciation will be considered as allowable to the taxpayer.

(4) If depreciation sustained on property is not an allowable deduction for the taxable year but is added to the basis of property being constructed, reconstructed, or erected by the taxpayer, for purposes of subparagraph (1) of this paragraph a deduction for depreciation shall be treated as allowable for the taxable year with respect to the property on which depreciation is sustained. Thus, if $1,000 of depreciation sustained with respect to property no. 1, which is placed in service in 1964 by taxpayer A, is not allowable to A as a deduction for 1964 but is added to the basis of property being constructed by A (property no. 2), for purposes of subparagraph (1) of this paragraph a deduction for depreciation shall be treated as allowable to A for 1964 with respect to property no. 1. However, the $1,000 amount is not included in the basis of property no. 2 for purposes of determining A's qualified investment with respect to property no. 2. See paragraph (c)(1) of § 1.46-3.

(c) *Definition of tangible personal property.* If property is tangible personal property it may qualify as section 38 property irrespective of whether it is used as an integral part of an activity (or constitutes a research or storage facility

Reg. § 1.48-1(b)(2)

used in connection with such activity) specified in paragraph (a) of this section. Local law shall not be controlling for purposes of determining whether property is or is not "tangible" or "personal". Thus, the fact that under local law property is held to be personal property or tangible property shall not be controlling. Conversely, property may be personal property for purposes of the investment credit even though under local law the property is considered to be a fixture and therefore real property. For purposes of this section, the term "tangible personal property" means any tangible property except land and improvements thereto, such as buildings or other inherently permanent structures (including items which are structural components of such buildings or structures). Thus, buildings, swimming pools, paved parking areas, wharves and docks, bridges, and fences are not tangible personal property. Tangible personal property includes all property (other than structural components) which is contained in or attached to a building. Thus, such property as production machinery, printing presses, transportation and office equipment, refrigerators, grocery counters, testing equipment, display racks and shelves, and neon and other signs, which is contained in or attached to a building constitutes tangible personal property for purposes of the credit allowed by section 38. Further, all property which is in the nature of machinery (other than structural components of a building or other inherently permanent structure) shall be considered tangible personal property even though located outside a building. Thus, for example, a gasoline pump, hydraulic car lift, or automatic vending machine, although annexed to the ground, shall be considered tangible personal property.

(d) *Other tangible property*—(1) *In general.* In addition to tangible personal property, any other tangible property (but not including a building and its structural components) used as an integral part of manufacturing, production, or extraction, or as an integral part of furnishing transportation, communications, electrical energy, gas, water, or sewage disposal services by a person engaged in a trade or business of furnishing any such service, or which constitutes a research or storage facility used in connection with any of the foregoing activities, may qualify as section 38 property.

(2) *Manufacturing, production, and extraction.* For purposes of the credit allowed by section 38, the terms "manufacturing", "production", and "extraction" include the construction, reconstruction, or making of property out of scrap, salvage, or junk material, as well as from new or raw material, by processing, manipulating, refin-

ing, or changing the form of an article, or by combining or assembling two or more articles, and include the cultivation of the soil, the raising of livestock, and the mining of minerals. Thus, section 38 property would include, for example, property used as an integral part of the extracting, processing, or refining of metallic and nonmetallic minerals, including oil, gas, rock, marble, or slate; the construction of roads, bridges, or housing; the processing of meat, fish or other foodstuffs; the cultivation of orchards, gardens, or nurseries; the operation of sawmills, the production of lumber, lumber products or other building materials; the fabrication or treatment of textiles, paper, leather goods, or glass; and the rebuilding, as distinguished from the mere repairing, of machinery.

(3) *Transportation and communications businesses.* Examples of transportation businesses include railroads, airlines, bus companies, shipping or trucking companies, and oil pipeline companies. Examples of communications businesses include telephone or telegraph companies and radio or television broadcasting companies.

(4) *Integral part.* In order to qualify for the credit, property (other than tangible personal property and research or storage facilities used in connection with any of the activities specified in subparagraph (1) of this paragraph) must be used as an integral part of one or more of the activities specified in subparagraph (1) of this paragraph. Property such as pavements, parking areas, inherently permanent advertising displays or inherently permanent outdoor lighting facilities, or swimming pools, although used in the operation of a business, ordinarily is not used as an integral part of any of such specified activities. Property is used as an integral part of one of the specified activities if it is used directly in the activity and is essential to the completeness of the activity. Thus, for example, in determining whether property is used as an integral part of manufacturing, all properties used by the taxpayer in acquiring or transporting raw materials or supplies to the point where the actual processing commences (such as docks, railroad tracks, and bridges), or in processing raw materials into the taxpayer's final product, would be considered as property used as an integral part of manufacturing. Specific examples of property which normally would be used as an integral part of one of the specified activities are blast furnaces, oil and gas pipelines, railroad tracks and signals, telephone poles, broadcasting towers, oil derricks, and fences used to confine livestock. Property shall be considered used as an integral part of one of the specified activities if so used either by the owner of the property or by the lessee of the property.

Reg. § 1.48-1(d)(4)

(5) *Research or storage facilities.* (i) If property (other than a building and its structural components) constitutes a research or storage facility and if it is used in connection with an activity specified in subparagraph (1) of this paragraph, such property may qualify as section 38 property even though it is not used as an integral part of such activity. Examples of research facilities include wind tunnels and test stands. Examples of storage facilities include oil and gas storage tanks and grain storage bins. Although a research or storage facility must be used in connection with, for example, a manufacturing process, the taxpayer-owner of such facility need not be engaged in the manufacturing process.

(ii) In the case of property described in section 50, property will constitute a storage facility only if the facility is used principally for the bulk storage of fungible commodities. Bulk storage means the storage of a commodity in a large mass prior to its consumption or utilization. Thus, if a facility is used to store oranges that have been sorted and boxed, it is not used for bulk storage.

(e) *Definition of building and structural components.* (1) Generally, buildings and structural components thereof do not qualify as section 38 property. See, however, section 48(a)(1)(E) and (g), and § 1.48-11 (relating to investment credit for qualified rehabilitated building). The term "building" generally means any structure or edifice enclosing a space within its walls, and usually covered by a roof, the purpose of which is, for example, to provide shelter or housing, or to provide working, office, parking, display, or sales space. The term includes, for example, structures such as apartment houses, factory and office buildings, warehouses, barns, garages, railway or bus stations, and stores. Such term includes any such structure constructed by, or for, a lessee even if such structure must be removed, or ownership of such structure reverts to the lessor, at the termination of the lease. Such term does not include (i) a structure which is essentially an item of machinery or equipment, or (ii) a structure which houses property used as an integral part of an activity specified in section 48(a)(1)(B)(i) if the use of the structure is so closely related to the use of such property that the structure clearly can be expected to be replaced when the property it initially houses is replaced. Factors which indicate that a structure is closely related to the use of the property it houses include the fact that the structure is specifically designed to provide for the stress and other demands of such property and the fact that the structure could not be economically used for other purposes. Thus, the term "building" does not include such structures as oil and

gas storage tanks, grain storage bins, silos, fractionating towers, blast furnaces, basic oxygen furnaces, coke-ovens, brick kilns, and coal tipples.

(2) The term "structural components" includes such parts of a building as walls, partitions, floors, and ceilings, as well as any permanent coverings therefor such as paneling or tiling; windows and doors; all components (whether in, on, or adjacent to the building) of a central air conditioning or heating system, including motors, compressors, pipes and ducts; plumbing and plumbing fixtures, such as sinks and bathtubs; electric wiring and lighting fixtures; chimneys; stairs, escalators, and elevators, including all components thereof; sprinkler systems; fire escapes; and other components relating to the operation or maintenance of a building. However, the term "structural components" does not include machinery the sole justification for the installation of which is the fact that such machinery is required to meet temperature or humidity requirements which are essential for the operation of other machinery or the processing of materials or foodstuffs. Machinery may meet the "sole justification" test provided by the preceding sentence even though it incidentally provides for the comfort of the employees, or serves, to an insubstantial degree, areas where such temperature or humidity requirements are not essential. For example, an air conditioning and humidification system installed in a textile plant in order to maintain the temperature or humidity within a narrow optimum range which is critical in processing particular types of yarn or cloth is not included within the term "structural components". For special rules with respect to an elevator or escalator, the construction, reconstruction, or erection of which is completed by the taxpayer after June 30, 1963, or which is acquired after June 30, 1963, and the original use of which commences with the taxpayer and commences after such date, see section 48(a)(1)(C) and paragraph (m) of this section.

(f) *Intangible property.* Intangible property, such as patents, copyrights, and subscription lists, does not qualify as section 38 property. The cost of intangible property, in the case of a patent or copyright, includes all costs of purchasing or producing the item patented or copyrighted. Thus, in the case of a motion picture or television film or tape, the cost of the intangible property includes manuscript and screenplay costs, the cost of wardrobe and set design, the salaries of cameramen, actors, directors, etc., and all other costs properly includible in the basis of such film or tape. In the case of a book, the cost of the intangible property includes all costs of producing the original copyrighted manuscript, including the cost of illustra-

Reg. § 1.48-1(d)(5)

tion, research, and clerical and stenographic help. However, if tangible depreciable property is used in the production of such intangible property, see paragraph (b)(4) of this section.

(g) *Property used outside the United States*— (1) *General rule.* (i) Except as provided in subparagraph (2) of this paragraph, the term "section 38 property" does not include property which is used predominantly outside the United States (as defined in section 7701(a)(9)) during the taxable year. The determination of whether property is used prdominantly outside the United States during the taxable year shall be made by comparing the period of time in such year during which the property is physically located outside the United States with the period of time in such year during which the property is physically located within the United States. If the property is physically located outside the United States during more than 50 percent of the taxable year, such property shall be considered used predominantly outside the United States during that year. If property is placed in service after the first day of the taxable year, the determination of whether such property is physically located outside the United States during more than 50 percent of the taxable year shall be made with respect to the period beginning on the date on which the property is placed in service and ending on the last day of such taxable year.

(ii) Since the determination of whether a credit is allowable to the taxpayer with respect to any property may be made only with respect to the taxable year in which the property is placed in service by the taxpayer, property used predominantly outside the United States during the taxable year in which it is placed in service cannot qualify as section 38 property with respect to such taxpayer, regardless of the fact that the property is permanently returned to the United States in a later year. Furthermore, if property is used predominantly in the United States in the year in which it is placed in service by the taxpayer, and a credit under section 38 is allowed with respect to such property, but such property is thereafter in any one year used predominantly outside the United States, such property ceases to be section 38 property with respect to the taxpayer and is subject to the application of section 47.

(iii) This subparagraph applies whether property is used predominantly outside the United States by the owner of the property, or by the lessee of the property. If property is leased and if the lessor makes a valid election under § 1.48-4 to treat the lessee as having purchased such property for purposes of the credit allowed by section 38, the determination of whether such property is physically located outside the United States during more than 50 percent of the taxable year shall be made with respect to the taxable year of the lessee; however, if the lessor does not make such an election, such determination shall be made with respect to the taxable year of the lessor.

(2) *Exceptions.* The provisions of subparagraph (1) of this paragraph do not apply to—

(i) Any aircraft which is registered by the Administrator of the Federal Aviation Agency, and which (*a*) is operated, whether on a scheduled or nonscheduled basis, to and from the United States, or (*b*) is placed in service by the taxpayer during a taxable year ending after March 9, 1967, and is operated under contract with the United States: Provided, That use of the aircraft under the contract constitutes its principal use outside the United States during the taxable year. The term "to and from the United States" is not intended to exclude an aircraft which makes flights from one point in a foreign country to another such point, as long as such aircraft returns to the United States with some degree of frequency;

(ii) Rolling stock, of a domestic railroad corporation subject to part I of the Interstate Commerce Act, which is used within and without the United States. For purposes of this subparagraph, the term "rolling stock" means locomotives, freight and passenger train cars, floating equipment, and miscellaneous transportation equipment on wheels, the expenditures for which are chargeable (or, in the case of leased property, would be chargeable) to the equipment investment accounts in the uniform system of accounts for railroad companies prescribed by the Interstate Commerce Commission;

(iii) Any vessel documented under the laws of the United States which is operated in the foreign or domestic commerce of the United States. A vessel is documented under the laws of the United States if it is registered, enrolled, or licensed under the laws of the United States by the Commandant, United States Coast Guard. Vessels operated in the foreign or domestic commerce of the United States include those documented for use in foreign trade, coast-wise trade, or fisheries;

(iv) Any motor vehicle of a United States person (as defined in section 7701(a)(30)) which is operated to and from the United States with some degree of frequency;

Reg. § 1.48-1(g)(2)

(v) Any container of a United States person which is used in the transportation of property to and from the United States;

(vi) Any property (other than a vessel or an aircraft) of a U.S. person which is used for the purpose of exploring for, developing, removing, or transporting resources from the outer Continental Shelf (within the meaning of section 2 of the Outer Continental Shelf Lands Act, as amended and supplemented; 43 U.S.C., sec. 1331). Thus for example, offshore drilling equipment may be section 38 property;

(vii) Any property placed in service after December 31, 1965 which (a) is owned by a domestic corporation (other than a corporation entitled to the benefits of section 931 or 934(b)) or by a United States citizen (other than a citizen entitled to the benefits of section 931, 932, 933, or 934(c)), and (b) is used predominantly in a possession of the United States during the taxable year by such a corporation or such a citizen, or by a corporation created or organized in, or under the law of, a possession of the United States. Thus, property placed in service after December 31, 1965, which is owned by a domestic corporation not entitled to the benefits of section 931 or 934(b), which is leased to a corporation organized under the laws of a U.S. possession, and which is used by such lessee predominantly in a possession of the United States may qualify as section 38 property. However, property which is owned by a corporation not entitled to the benefits of section 931 or 934(b) but which is leased to a domestic corporation entitled to such benefits would not qualify as section 38 property. The determination of whether property is used predominantly in a possession of the United States during the taxable year shall be made under principles similar to those described in subparagraph (1) of this paragraph. For example, if a machine is placed in service in a possession of the United States on July 1, 1966, by a calendar year taxpayer and if it is physically located in such a possession during more than 50 percent of the period beginning on July 1, 1966 and ending on December 31, 1966, then such machine shall be considered used predominantly in a possession of the United States during the taxable year 1966;

(viii) Any communications satellite (as defined in section 103(3) of the Communications Satellite Act of 1962, 47 U.S.C., sec. 702(3)), or any interest therein, of a U.S. person;

(ix) Any cable which is property described in section 50, or any interest therein, of a domestic corporation engaged in furnishing telephone service to which section 46(c)(3)(B)(iii) applies (or of a wholly owned domestic subsidiary of such corporation), if such cable is part of a submarine cable system which constitutes part of a communications link exclusively between the United States and one or more foreign countries; and

(x) Any property described in section 50 (other than a vessel or an aircraft) of a United States person which is used in international or territorial waters for the purpose of exploring for, developing, removing, or transporting resources from ocean waters or deposits under such waters.

(h) *Property used for lodging*—(1) *In general.* (i) Except as provided in subparagraph (2) of this paragraph, the term "section 38 property" does not include property which is used predominantly to furnish lodging or is used predominantly in connection with the furnishing of lodging during the taxable year. Property used in the living quarters of a lodging facility, including beds and other furniture, refrigerators, ranges, and other equipment, shall be considered as used predominantly to furnish lodging. The term "lodging facility" includes an apartment house, hotel, motel, dormitory, or any other facility (or part of a facility) where sleeping accommodations are provided and let, except that such term does not include a facility used primarily as a means of transportation (such as an aircraft, vessel, or a railroad car) or used primarily to provide medical or convalescent services, even though sleeping accommodations are provided.

(ii) Property which is used predominantly in the operation of a lodging facility or in serving tenants shall be considered used in connection with the furnishing of lodging, whether furnished by the owner of the lodging facility or another person. Thus, for example, lobby furniture, office equipment, and laundry and swimming pool facilities used in the operation of an apartment house or in serving tenants would be considered used predominantly in connection with the furnishing of lodging. However, property which is used in furnishing, to the management of a lodging facility or its tenants, electrical energy, water, sewage disposal services, gas, telephone service, or other similar services shall not be treated as property used in connection with the furnishing of lodging. Thus, such items as gas and electric meters, telephone poles and lines, telephone station and switchboard equipment, and water and gas mains, furnished by a public utility would not be considered as property used in connection with the furnishing of lodging.

(iii) Notwithstanding any other provision of this paragraph (h), in the case of a qualified rehabilitated building (within the meaning of section 48(g)(1) and § 1.48-12(b)), expenditures for property resulting in basis described in section

Reg. § 1.48-1(h)(1)

48(a)(1)(E) shall not be treated as section 38 property to the extent that such property is attributable to a portion of the building that is used for lodging or in connection with lodging. For example, if expenditures are incurred to rehabilitate a five story qualified rehabilitated building, three floors of which are used for apartments and two floors of which are used as commercial office space, the portion of the basis of the building attributable to qualified rehabilitated expenditures attributable to the commercial part of the building shall not be considered to be expenditures for property, or in connection with property, used predominantly for lodging. Allocation of expenditures between the two portions of the building are to be made using the principles contained in § 1.48-12(c)(10)(ii).

(2) *Exceptions*—(i) *Nonlodging commercial facility.* A nonlodging commercial facility which is available to persons not using the lodging facility on the same basis as it is available to the tenants of the lodging facility shall not be treated as property which is used predominantly to furnish lodging or predominantly in connection with the furnishing of lodging. Examples of nonlodging commercial facilities include restaurants, drug stores, grocery stores, and vending machines located in a lodging facility.

(ii) *Property used by a hotel or motel.* Property used by a hotel, motel, inn, or other similar establishment, in connection with the trade or business of furnishing lodging shall not be considered as property which is used predominantly to furnish lodging or predominantly in connection with the furnishing of lodging, provided that the predominant portion of the living accommodations in the hotel, motel, etc., is used by transients during the taxable year. For purposes of the preceding sentence, the term "predominant portion" means "more than one-half". Thus, if more than one-half of the living quarters of a hotel, motel, inn, or other similar establishment is used during the taxable year to accommodate tenants on a transient basis, none of the property used by such hotel, motel, etc., in the trade or business of furnishing lodging shall be considered as property which is used predominantly to furnish lodging or predominantly in connection with the furnishing of lodging. Accommodations shall be considered used on a transient basis if the rental period is normally less than 30 days.

(iii) *Coin-operated machines.* In the case of property which is described in section 50, coin-operated vending machines and coin-operated washing machines and dryers shall not be considered as property which is used predominantly to furnish lodging or predominantly in connection with the furnishing of lodging.

(iv) *Certified historic structures.* For purposes of this paragraph (h), regardless of the actual use of a certified historic structure, that portion of the basis of such certified historic structure which is attributable to qualified rehabilitation expenditures (as defined in § 1.48-12(c)) shall not be considered as property which is either used predominantly to furnish lodging or predominantly in connection with the furnishing of lodging. Accordingly, such portion of the basis may qualify as section 38 property. (For the definition of "certified historic structure," see section 48(g)(3) and § 1.48-12(d).)

(i) [Reserved]

(j) *Property used by certain tax-exempt organizations.* The term "section 38 property" does not include property used by an organization (other than a cooperative described in section 521) which is exempt from the tax imposed by chapter 1 of the Code unless such property is used predominantly in an unrelated trade or business the income of which is subject to tax under section 511. If such property is debt-financed property as defined in section 514(b), the basis or cost of such property for purposes of computing qualified investment under section 46(c) shall include only that percentage of the basis or cost which is the same percentage as is used under section 514(a), for the year the property is placed in service, in computing the amount of gross income to be taken into account during such taxable year with respect to such property. The term "property used by an organization" means (1) property owned by the organization (whether or not leased to another person), and (2) property leased to the organization. Thus, for example, a data processing or copying machine which is leased to an organization exempt from tax would be considered as property used by such organization. Property (unless used predominantly in an unrelated trade or business) leased by another person to an organization exempt from tax or leased by such an organization to another person is not section 38 property to either the lessor or the lessee, and in either case the lessor may not elect under § 1.48-4 to treat the lessee of such property as having purchased such property for purposes of the credit allowed by section 38. This paragraph shall not apply to property leased on a casual or short-term basis to an organization exempt from tax.

(k) *Property used by governmental units.* The term "section 38 property" does not include property used by the United States, any State (including the District of Columbia) or political subdivision thereof, any international organiza-

Reg. § 1.48-1(k)

tion (as defined in section 7701(a)(18)) other than the International Telecommunications Satellite Consortium or any successor organization, or any agency or instrumentality of the United States, of any State or political subdivision thereof, or of any such international organization. The term "property used by the United States, etc." means (1) property owned by any such governmental unit (whether or not leased to another person), and (2) property leased to any such governmental unit. Thus, for example, a data processing or copying machine which is leased to any such governmental unit would be considered as property used by such governmental unit. Property leased by another person to any such governmental unit or leased by such governmental unit to another person is not section 38 property to either the lessor or the lessee, and in either case the lessor may not elect under § 1.48-4 to treat the lessee of such property as having purchased such property for purposes of the credit allowed by section 38. This paragraph shall not apply to property leased on a casual or short-term basis to any such governmental unit.

(l) [Reserved]

(m) *Elevators and escalators*—(1) *In general.* Under section 48(a)(1)(C), an elevator or escalator qualifies as section 38 property if—

(i) The construction, reconstruction, or erection of the elevator or escalator is completed by the taxpayer after June 30, 1963, or

(ii) The elevator or escalator is acquired after June 30, 1963, and the original use of such elevator or escalator commences with the taxpayer and commences after such date.

In the case of construction, reconstruction, or erection of an elevator or escalator commenced before January 1, 1962, and completed after June 30, 1963, there shall be taken into account in determining the qualified investment under section 46(c) only that portion of the basis which is properly attributable to construction, reconstruction, or erection after December 31, 1961. Further, if the construction, reconstruction, or erection of such property is commenced after December 31, 1961, and is completed after June 30, 1963, the entire basis of the elevator or escalator shall be taken into account in determining qualified investment under section 46(c). Also, if an elevator or escalator is reconstructed by the taxpayer after June 30, 1963, the basis attributable to such reconstruction may be taken into account in determining the qualified investment under section 46(c), irrespective of the fact that the original construction or erection of such elevator or escalator may have occurred before January 1, 1962. Paragraph (b) of § 1.48-2 shall be applied in determining the date of acquisition, original use, and basis attributable to construction, reconstruction, or erection.

(2) *Definition of elevators and escalators.* For purposes of this section the term "elevator" means a cage or platform and its hoisting machinery for conveying persons or freight to or from different levels and functionally related equipment which is essential to its operation. The term includes, for example, guide rails and cables, motors and controllers, control panels and landing buttons, and elevator gates and doors, which are essential to the operation of the elevator. The term "elevator" does not, however, include a structure which is considered a building for purposes of the investment credit. The term "escalator" means a moving staircase and functionally related equipment which is essential to its operation. For purposes of determining qualified investment under section 46(c) and § 1.46-3, the basis of an elevator or escalator does not include the cost of any structural alterations to the building, such as the cost of constructing a shaft or of making alterations to the floor, walls, or ceiling, even though such alterations may be necessary in order to install or modernize the elevator or escalator.

(3) *Examples.* The provisions of this paragraph may be illustrated by the following examples:

Example (1). If an elevator with a total basis of $100,000 is completed after June 30, 1963, and the portion attributable to construction by the taxpayer after December 31, 1961, is determined by engineering estimates or by cost accounting records to be $30,000, only the $30,000 portion may be taken into account as an investment in new section 38 property in computing qualified investment.

Example (2). If construction of an elevator with a total basis of $90,000 is commenced by the taxpayer after December 31, 1961, and is completed after June 30, 1963, the entire basis of $90,000 may be taken into account as an investment in new section 38 property.

Example (3). The facts are the same as in example (2) except that construction of the elevator was completed before June 30, 1963. The elevator is not considered to be section 38 property.

Example (4). In 1964, a taxpayer reconditions an elevator, which had been constructed and placed in service in 1962 and which had an adjusted basis in 1964 of $75,000. The cost of reconditioning amounts to an additional $50,000. The basis of the elevator which may be taken into account in computing qualified investment in section 38 property is $50,000, irrespective of whether the taxpayer contracts to have it recondi-

Reg. § 1.48-1(l)

tioned or reconditions it himself, and irrespective of whether the materials used in the process are new in use.

(n) *Amortized property.* Any property with respect to which an election under section 167(k), 169, 184, 187, or 188 applies shall not be treated as section 38 property. In the case of any property to which section 169 applies, the preceding sentence shall apply only to so much of the adjusted basis of the property as (after the application of section 169(f)) constitutes the amortizable basis for purposes of section 169. This paragraph shall not apply to property with respect to which an election under section 167(k), 184, 187, or 188 applies unless such property is described in section 50.

(o) [Reserved]

(p) *Qualified timber property.* (1) Qualified timber property (within the meaning of section 194(c)(1)) shall be treated as section 38 property to the extent of the portion of the basis of such property which is the amortizable basis (as defined in § 1.194-3(b)) acquired during the taxable year and taken into account under section 194 (after applying the limitation of section 194(b)(1)). Such amortizable basis shall qualify as section 38 property whether or not an election is made under section 194. However, any portion of such amortizable basis which is attributable to property which otherwise qualifies as section 38 property shall not be treated as section 38 property under section 48(a)(1)(F) and this paragraph. For example, amortizable basis attributable to depreciation on equipment would not qualify as section 38 property under this paragraph if such equipment qualifies as section 38 property under sections 48(a)(1)(A) or (B). In determining the portion of amortizable basis which qualifies as section 38 property under this paragraph, the reduction in amortizable basis to account for depreciation sustained with respect to property used in the reforestation process (which otherwise qualifies as section 38 property) shall be applied before the $10,000 limitation on eligible costs under section 194(b)(1). For example, if in a taxable year a taxpayer incurs qualifying reforestation costs resulting in $12,000 of amortizable basis with respect to property for which an election is in effect, and $2,000 of these costs are attributable to depreciation of the taxpayer's equipment, such $12,000 would first be reduced by the $2,000 of depreciation, and the $10,000 limitation under section 194(b)(1) would be applied following such reduction.

(2) If a taxpayer makes an election to amortize reforestation expenditures under section 194, and allocates the $10,000 limitation among more than one property under § 1.194-2(b)(2), then such allocation shall apply for purposes of determining the amortizable basis that qualifies as section 38 property under paragraph (p)(1) of this section. If no election is made under section 194, the taxpayer may select the manner in which the $10,000 limitation is to be allocated among the qualified timber properties. [Reg. § 1.48-1.]

[*T.D.* 6731, 5-7-64. *Amended by T.D.* 6838, 7-19-65; *T.D.* 6958, 6-20-68; *T.D.* 6971, 9-11-68; *T.D.* 7203, 8-24-72; *T.D.* 7229, 12-20-72; *T.D.* 7927, 12-15-83; *T.D.* 8031, 6-27-85; *T.D.* 8233, 10-7-88 *and T.D.* 8474, 4-26-93 (*corrected* 1-10-94).]

[Reg. § 1.48-2]

§ 1.48-2. New section 38 property.—(a) *In general.* Section 48 (b) defines "new section 38 property" as section 38 property—

(1) The construction, reconstruction, or erection of which is completed by the taxpayer after December 31, 1961, or

(2) Which is acquired by the taxpayer after December 31, 1961, provided that the original use of such property commences with the taxpayer and commences after such date.

In the case of construction, reconstruction, or erection of such property commenced before January 1, 1962, and completed after December 31, 1961, there shall be taken into account as the basis of new section 38 property in determining qualified investment only that portion of the basis which is properly attributable to construction, reconstruction, or erection after December 31, 1961. See § 1.148-1 for the definition of section 38 property.

(b) *Special rules for determining date of acquisition, original use, and basis attributable to construction, reconstruction, or erection.* For purposes of paragraph (a) of this section, the principles set forth in paragraph (a)(1) and (2) of § 1.167 (c)-1 shall be applied. Thus, for example, the following rules are applicable:

(1) Property is considered as constructed, reconstructed, or erected by the taxpayer if the work is done for him in accordance with his specifications.

(2) The portion of the basis of property attributable to construction, reconstruction, or erection after December 31, 1961, consists of all costs of construction, reconstruction, or erection allocable to the period after December 31, 1961, including the cost or other basis of materials entering into such work (but not including, in the case of reconstruction of property, the adjusted basis of the reconstructed property as of the time such reconstruction is commenced).

Reg. § 1.48-2(b)(2)

(3) It is not necessary that materials entering into construction, reconstruction, or erection be acquired after December 31, 1961, or that they be new in use.

(4) If construction or erection by the taxpayer began after December 31, 1961, the entire cost or other basis of such construction or erection may be taken into account as the basis of new section 38 property.

(5) Construction, reconstruction, or erection by the taxpayer begins when physical work is started on such construction, reconstruction, or erection.

(6) Property shall be deemed to be acquired when reduced to physical possession, or control.

(7) The term "original use" means the first use to which the property is put, whether or not such use corresponds to the use of such property by the taxpayer. For example, a reconditioned or rebuilt machine acquired by the taxpayer will not be treated as being put to original use by the taxpayer. The question of whether property is reconditioned or rebuilt property is a question of fact. Property will not be treated as reconditioned or rebuilt merely because it contains some used parts.

If the cost of reconstruction may properly either be capitalized and recovered through depreciation or charged against the depreciation reserve, such cost may be taken into account as the basis of new section 38 property even though it is charged against the depreciation reserve.

(c) *Examples.* This section may be illustrated by the following examples:

Example (1). If a machine with a total cost of $100,000 is completed after December 31, 1961, and the portion attributable to construction by the taxpayer after December 31, 1961, is determined by engineering estimates or by cost accounting records to be $30,000, the $30,000 amount shall be taken into account by the taxpayer in computing qualified investment in new section 38 property.

Example (2). In 1965, a taxpayer reconditions a machine, which he constructed and placed in service in 1962 and which has an adjusted basis in 1965 of $10,000. The cost of reconditioning amounts to an additional $20,000. The basis of the machine which shall be taken into account in computing qualified investment in new section 38 property for 1965 is $20,000, whether he contracts to have it reconditioned or reconditions it himself, and irrespective of whether the materials used for reconditioning are new in use.

Example (3). In 1961, a taxpayer pays the entire purchase price of $10,000 for section 38 property to be delivered in 1962. In 1962 he takes possession of the property and commences the original use of the asset in that year. The $10,000 amount shall be taken into account in computing qualified investment in new section 38 property for 1962.

Example (4). A taxpayer, instead of reconditioning his old machine, buys a "factory reconditioned" or "rebuilt" machine in 1962 to replace it. The reconditioned or rebuilt machine is not new section 38 property since such taxpayer is not the first user of the machine. See, however, § 1.48-3 (relating to used section 38 property).

Example (5). In 1962, a taxpayer buys from X for $20,000 an item of section 38 property which has been previously used by X. The taxpayer in 1962 makes an expenditure on the property of $5,000 of the type that must be capitalized. Regardless of whether the $5,000 is added to the basis of such property or is capitalized in a separate account, such amount shall be taken into account by the taxpayer in computing qualified investment in new section 38 property for 1962. No part of the $20,000 purchase price may be taken into account for such purpose. See, however, § 1.48-3 (relating to used section 38 property).

(d) *Special rule for qualified rehabilitated buildings.* Notwithstanding the rules in paragraphs (a) through (c) of this section, that portion of the basis of a qualified rehabilitated building attributable to qualified rehabilitation expenditures is treated as new section 38 property. See section 48(a)(1)(E) and (g), and § 1.48-11. [Reg. § 1.48-2.]

☐ [*T.D.* 6731, 5-7-64. *Amended by T.D.* 8031, 6-27-85.]

[Reg. § 1.48-3]

§ 1.48-3. Used section 38 property.—(a) *In general.* (1) Section 48(c) provides that "used section 38 property" means section 38 property acquired by purchase after December 31, 1961, which is not "new section 38 property." See §§ 1.48-1 and 1.48-2, respectively, for definitions of section 38 property and new section 38 property. In determining whether property is acquired by purchase, the provisions of paragraph (c)(1) of § 1.179-3 shall apply, except that (i) "1961" shall be substituted for "1957", and (ii) the definition of "component member" of a controlled group of corporations in paragraph (d)(4) of this section shall be substituted for the definition of such term in paragraph (e) of § 1.179-3.

(2) (i) Property shall not qualify as used section 38 property if, after its acquisition by the taxpayer, it is used by (*a*) a person who used such property before such acquisition, or (*b*) a person

who bears a relationship described in section 179 (d) (2) (A) or (B) to a person who used such property before such acquisition. Thus, for example, if property is used by a person and is later sold by him under a sale and leaseback arrangement, such property in the hands of the purchaser-lessor is not used section 38 property because the property, after its acquisition, is being used by the same person who used it before its acquisition. Similarly, where a lessee has been leasing property and subsequently purchases it (whether or not the lease contains an option to purchase), such property is not used section 38 property with respect to the purchaser because the property is being used by the same person who used it before its acquisition. In addition, if property owned by a lessor is sold subject to the lease, or is sold upon the termination of the lease, the property will not qualify as used section 38 property with respect to the purchaser if, after the purchase, the property is used by a person who used the property as a lessee before the purchase.

(ii) For purposes of applying subdivision (i) of this subparagraph, property shall not be considered as used by a person before its acquisition if such property was used only on a casual basis by such person.

(iii) In determining whether a person bears a relationship described in section 179(d)(2)(A) or (B) to a person who used property before its acquisition by the taxpayer, the provisions of paragraph (c)(1)(i) and (ii) of § 1.179-3 shall apply, except that the definition of "component member" of a controlled group of corporations in paragraph (d)(4) of this section shall be substituted for the definition of such term in paragraph (e) of § 1.179-3.

(3) The provisions of this paragraph may be illustrated by the following examples:

Example (1). Corporation P acquires properties 1 and 2 in 1960 and uses them in its trade or business until 1962. In 1962, corporation P sells such properties to corporation Y, which leases back property 1 to corporation P and leases property 2 to corporation S, a wholly-owned subsidiary of corporation P. Property 1 is not used section 38 property in the hands of corporation Y because, after its acquisition by corporation Y, it is used by a person (corporation P) who used it prior to such acquisition. Property 2 is not used section 38 property because, after its acquisition by corporation Y, it is used by a person (corporation S) who is related, within the meaning of section 179(d)(2)(B), to a person (corporation P) who used it before such acquisition.

Example (2). In 1962, corporation L leases property from corporation M. In 1964, corpora-

tion L acquires the property that it previously had been leasing. The property acquired by corporation L is not used section 38 property because such property is used after such acquisition by the same person (corporation L) who used the property before its acquisition (corporation L).

Example (3). Corporation X buys property in 1962 and leases such property to corporation Y. Corporation X in 1965 sells the property to A subject to the lease. The property acquired by A is not used section 38 property if such property continues to be used by corporation Y, because corporation Y used the property before its acquisition by A.

Example (4). A owns a bulldozer which he rents out to a number of different users, including B. In 1962, B used the bulldozer from February 16 to March 12 and again on October 15 and 16. B purchases the bulldozer from A on December 1, 1962. The prior use of the property by B does not disqualify such property as used section 38 property to B, because he used such property only on a casual basis prior to its purchase.

(b) *Cost.* (1) The cost of used section 38 property is equal to the basis of such property, but does not include so much of such basis as is determined by reference to the adjusted basis of other property (whether or not section 38 property) held at any time by the taxpayer acquiring such used section 38 property.

(2) If property (whether or not section 38 property) is disposed of by the taxpayer (other than by reason of its destruction or damage by fire, storm, shipwreck, or other casualty, or its theft) and used section 38 property similar or related in service or use is acquired as a replacement therefor in a transaction in which the basis of the replacement property is not determined by reference to the adjusted basis of the property replaced, then the cost of the used section 38 property so acquired shall be its basis reduced by the adjusted basis of the property replaced. The preceding sentence shall apply only if the taxpayer acquires (or enters into a contract to acquire) the replacement property within a period of 60 days before or after the date of the disposition.

(3) Notwithstanding subparagraphs (1) and (2) of this paragraph, the cost of used section 38 property shall not be reduced with respect to the adjusted basis of any property disposed of if, by reason of section 47, such disposition resulted in an increase of tax or a reduction of investment credit carrybacks or carryovers described in section 46(b).

(4) The provisions of this paragraph may be illustrated by the following examples:

Reg. § 1.48-3(b)(4)

Example (1). In 1972, A acquires machine 2 (an item of used section 38 property which has a sales price of $5,600) by trading in machine 1 (an item of section 38 property acquired in 1962), and by paying an additional $4,000 cash. The adjusted basis of machine 1 is $1,600. Under the provisions of sections 1012 and 1031(d), the basis of machine 2 is $5,600 ($1,600 adjusted basis of machine 1 plus cash expended of $4,000). The cost of machine 2 which may be taken into account in computing qualified investment for 1972 is $4,000 (basis of $5,600 less $1,600 adjusted basis of machine 1).

Example (2). The facts are the same as in example (1) except that machine 2 has a sales price of $6,000. The trade-in allowance on machine 1 is $2,000. The result is the same as in example (1), that is, the basis of machine 2 is $5,600 ($1,600 plus $4,000); therefore, the cost of machine 2 which may be taken into account in computing qualified investment for 1972 is $4,000 (basis of $5,600 less $1,600 adjusted basis of machine 1).

Example (3). On September 18, 1962, B sells truck 1, which he acquired in 1961 and which has an adjusted basis in his hands of $1,200. On October 15, 1962, he purchases for $2,000 truck 2 (an item of used section 38 property) as a replacement therefor. The cost of truck 2 which may be taken into account in computing qualified investment is $800 ($2,000 less $1,200).

Example (4). In 1962, C acquires property 1, an item of new section 38 property with a basis of $12,000 and a useful life of eight years or more. He is allowed a credit under section 38 of $840 (7 percent of $12,000) with respect to such property. In 1968, C acquires property 2 (an item of used section 38 property) by trading in property 1 and by paying an additional amount in cash. Section 47(a) applies to the disposition of property 1 and C's tax liability for 1968 is increased by $280. Since the application of section 47(a) results in an increase in tax, for purposes of computing qualified investment the cost of property 2 is not reduced by any part of the adjusted basis of the property traded in.

(c) *Dollar limitation*—(1) *In general.* Section 48(c)(2) provides that the aggregate cost of used section 38 property which may be taken into account for any taxable year in computing qualified investment under section 46(c)(1)(B) shall not exceed $50,000. If the total cost of used section 38 property exceeds $50,000, there must be selected, in the manner provided in subparagraph (4) of this paragraph, the particular items of used section 38 property the cost of which is to be taken into account in computing qualified invest-

ment. The cost of used section 38 property that may be taken into account by a person in applying the $50,000 limitation for any taxable year includes not only the cost of used section 38 property placed in service by such person during such taxable year, but also the cost of used section 38 property apportioned to such person. For purposes of this section, the cost of used section 38 property apportioned to any person means the cost of such property apportioned to him by a trust, estate, or electing small business corporation (as defined in section 1371(b)), and his share of the cost of partnership used section 38 property, with respect to the taxable year of such trust, estate, corporation or partnership ending with or within such person's taxable year. Thus, if an individual places in service during his taxable year used section 38 property with a cost of $25,000, if the cost of used section 38 property apportioned to him by an electing small business corporation for such year is $30,000, and if his share for such year of the cost of used section 38 property placed in service by a partnership is $20,000, he may select from the used section 38 property with a total cost of $75,000 the particular used section 38 property the cost of which he wishes to take into account. No part of the excess of $25,000 ($75,000 cost minus $50,000 annual limitation) may be taken into account in any other taxable year. For determining the amount of the cost to be apportioned by an electing small business corporation, see paragraph (a)(2) of § 1.48-5; in the case of estates and trusts, see paragraph (a)(2) of § 1.48-6. See paragraph (e) of this section for application of $50,000 limitation in the case of affiliated groups.

(2) *Married individuals filing separate returns.* In the case of a husband or wife who files a separate return, the aggregate cost of used section 38 property which may be taken into account for the taxable year to which such return relates cannot exceed $25,000. The preceding sentence shall not apply, however, unless the taxpayer's spouse places in service (or is apportioned the cost of) used section 38 property for the taxable year of such spouse which ends with or within the taxpayer's taxable year. Thus, if a husband and wife who file separate returns on a calendar year basis both place in service used section 38 property during the taxable year, the maximum cost of used section 38 property which may be taken into account by each is $25,000. However, in such case, if only one spouse places in service (or is apportioned the cost of) used section 38 property during the taxable year, such spouse may take into account a maximum of $50,000 for such year. The determination of whether an individual is married shall be made under the principles of section 143 and the regulations thereunder.

Reg. § 1.48-3(c)(1)

(3) *Partnerships.* In the case of a partnership, the aggregate cost of used section 38 property placed in service by the partnership (or apportioned to the partnership) which may be taken into account by the partners with respect to any taxable year of the partnership may not exceed $50,000. If such aggregate cost exceeds $50,000, the partnership must make a selection in the manner provided in subparagraph (4) of this paragraph. The $50,000 limitation applies to each partner, as well as to the partnership.

(4) *Selection of $50,000 cost.* (i) If the sum of (a) the cost of used section 38 property placed in service during the taxable year by any person, (b) such person's share of the cost of partnership used section 38 property placed in service during the taxable year of a partnership ending with or within such person's taxable year, and (c) the cost of used section 38 property apportioned to such person for such taxable year by an electing small business corporation, estate, or trust, exceeds $50,000, such person must make a selection for such taxable year in the manner provided in subdivision (ii) of this subparagraph.

(ii) For purposes of computing qualified investment (or, in the case of a partnership, electing small business corporation, estate, or trust, for purposes of selecting used section 38 property the cost of which may be taken into account by the partners, shareholders, or estate or trust and its beneficiaries) any person to whom subdivision (i) of this subparagraph applies must select a total cost of $50,000 from (a) the cost of specific used section 38 property placed in service by such person, (b) such person's share of the cost of specific used section 38 property placed in service by a partnership, and (c) the cost of used section 38 property apportioned to such person by an electing small business corporation, estate, or trust. When a particular property is selected, the entire cost (or entire share of cost of a particular property in the case of partnership property) of such property must be taken into account unless, as a result of the selection of such particular property, the $50,000 limitation is exceeded. Likewise, in the case of an apportionment from an electing small business corporation, estate, or trust, when the cost in a particular useful life category is selected, the entire cost in such category must be taken into account unless, as a result of the selection of such cost, the $50,000 limitation is exceeded. Thus, if a person places in service during the taxable year three items of used section 38 property, each with a cost of $20,000, he must select the entire cost of two of the items and only $10,000 of the cost of the third item; he may not select a portion of the cost of each of the three items. The selection by any person shall be made

by taking the cost of used section 38 property into account in computing qualified investment (or in selecting the used section 38 property the cost of which may be taken into account by the partners, etc.), and if such property was placed in service by such person, he must maintain records which permit specific identification of any item of used section 38 property selected.

(5) *Examples.* The provisions of this paragraph may be illustrated by the following examples:

Example (1). H, who operates a sole proprietorship, purchases and places in service in 1963 used section 38 property with a cost of $60,000. His spouse, W, is a shareholder in an electing small business corporation which purchases and places in service during its fiscal year ending June 30, 1963, used section 38 property with a cost of $50,000. Both spouses file separate returns on a calendar year basis. W, as a 60 percent shareholder on the last day of the taxable year of the corporation, is apportioned $30,000 (60 percent of $50,000) of the cost of the used section 38 property placed in service by the corporation. The cost of used section 38 property that may be taken into account by H on his separate return is $25,000. The cost of used section 38 property that may be taken into account by W on her separate return is $25,000. On the other hand, if the corporation had made no investment in used section 38 property, H could take $50,000 of the $60,000 cost into account.

Example (2). Partners X, Y, and Z share the profits and losses of partnership XYZ in the ratio of 50 percent, 30 percent, and 20 percent, respectively. The partnership and each partner make returns on the basis of the calendar year. Each partner also operates a sole proprietorship. In 1963, the partnership and the partners purchase and place in service the following used section 38 property:

Property	Estimated useful life	Cost
Partnership XYZ		
Property No. 1 ...	9 years	$10,000
Property No. 2 ...	7 years	50,000
Property No. 3 ...	7 years	50,000
Property No. 4 ...	5 years	30,000
Partner X		
Property No. 5 ...	6 years	$30,000
Partner Y		
Property No. 6 ...	10 years	60,000
Partner Z		
Property No. 7 ...	4 years	36,000

(i) *Selection by partnership.* In accordance with subparagraph (4)(ii) of this paragraph, the partnership selects property no. 1 and $40,000 of the cost of property no. 2 to be taken into account.

Reg. § 1.48-3(c)(5)

Therefore, each partner's share of cost of the property selected by the partnership is as follows:

Property	Estimated useful life	Selected cost	X (50%)	Y (30%)	Z (20%)
			Partner's share of cost		
No. 1	9 years	$10,000	$ 5,000	$ 3,000	$ 2,000
No. 2	7 years	40,000	20,000	12,000	8,000
Total		$50,000	$25,000	$15,000	$10,000

(ii) *Selection by partners.* In accordance with subparagraph (4)(ii) of this paragraph, the partners make the following selections: Partner X selects property No. 5 ($30,000), his share of the cost of property No. 1 ($5,000), and $15,000 of his share of the cost of property No. 2. Partner Y selects $50,000 of the cost of property No. 6, and no part of his share of the cost of partnership property. Partner Z, having an aggregate cost of used section 38 property of only $46,000 (partnership property of $10,000 and individually owned property of $36,000), takes into account the entire $46,000.

(iii) *Qualified investment of partner X.* X's total qualified investment in used section 38 property for 1963 is $35,000, computed as follows:

Property	Estimated useful life	Selected cost	Applicable percentage	Qualified investment
No. 1	9 years	$ 5,000	100	$ 5,000
No. 2	7 years	15,000	66⅔	10,000
No. 5	6 years	30,000	66⅔	20,000
Total		$50,000		$35,000

(iv) *Qualified investment of partner Y.* Y's total qualified investment in used section 38 property for 1963 is $50,000 (100 percent of $50,000) since he selected $50,000 of the cost of property No. 6 which has a useful life of 8 years or more.

(v) *Qualified investment of partner Z.* Z's total qualified investment in used section 38 property for 1963 is $19,333, computed as follows:

Property	Estimated useful life	Selected cost	Applicable percentage	Qualified investment
No. 1	9 years	$ 2,000	100	$ 2,000
No. 2	7 years	8,000	66⅔	5,333
No. 7	4 years	36,000	33⅓	12,000
Total		$46,000		$19,333

(d) *Dollar limitation for component members of a controlled group—*(1) *In general.* (i) Section 48(c)(2)(C) provides that the $50,000 limitation on the cost of used section 38 property which may be taken into account for any taxable year shall, in the case of component members of a controlled group (as defined in subparagraph (4) of this paragraph) on a particular December 31, be reduced for each such member by apportioning the $50,000 amount among such component members for their taxable years that include such Decem-

ber 31 in accordance with their respective amounts of used section 38 property which may be taken into account, that is, in accordance with the total cost of used section 38 property placed in service by each such member during its taxable year (without regard to the $50,000 limitation or the applicable percentages to be applied in computing qualified investment).

(ii) Except as otherwise provided in this paragraph, the $50,000 amount shall be apportioned among those corporations which are component members of the controlled group on a December 31. For the taxable year of each such member which includes such December 31, the cost of used section 38 property taken into account in computing qualified investment under section 46(c)(1)(B) shall not exceed the amount which bears the same ratio to $50,000 as the cost of used section 38 property placed in service by such member for such taxable year bears to the total cost of used section 38 property placed in service by all component members of the controlled group for their taxable years which include such December 31.

(iii) If a component member of the group makes its income tax return on the basis of a 52-53 week taxable year, the principles of section 441(f)(2)(A)(ii) and § 1.441-2 apply in determining the last day of such a taxable year.

(2) *Statement by the "filing member".* For purposes of this paragraph, the term "filing member" with respect to a particular December 31 means the member (or members) of a controlled group which has, among those members of the group which are apportioned part of the $50,000 amount for their taxable years which include such December 31, the taxable year including such December 31 which ends on the earliest date. The filing member of the group shall attach to its income tax return a statement containing the name, address, and employer identification number of each component member of the controlled group on such December 31 and a schedule showing the computation of the apportionment of the $50,000 amount among the component members of the group. Each such other member shall retain as part of its records a copy of the statement containing the apportionment schedule. Except as otherwise provided in subparagraph (3)(ii) of this

Reg. § 1.48-3(d)(1)

paragraph, each member which is apportioned part of the $50,000 amount shall take such apportioned amount into account in filing its return for its taxable year which includes such December 31.

(3) *Estimate of used section 38 property to be placed in service.* (i) For purposes of subparagraphs (1) and (2) of this paragraph, if on the date (including extensions of time) for filing the income tax return of the filing member of the group with respect to a particular December 31, the total cost of used section 38 property actually placed in service by a component member of the group during such member's taxable year that includes such December 31 is not known, then such member shall estimate such cost. The estimate shall be made on the basis of the facts and circumstances known as of the time of the estimate. Any such estimate shall also be used in determining the total cost of used section 38 property placed in service by all component members for their taxable years including such December 31.

(ii) If an estimate is used by any component member of a controlled group pursuant to subdivision (i) of this subparagraph, each member may later file an original or amended return in which the apportionment of the $50,000 amount is based upon the cost of used section 38 property actually placed in service by all component members of the group during their taxable year which include such December 31. Such amended apportionment shall be made only if each component member of the group whose limitation would be changed files an original or amended return which reflects the amended apportionment based upon the cost of the used section 38 property actually placed in service by component members of the group. In such case, the new statement reflecting the amended apportionment shall be attached to the amended return of the filing member of the group, and a copy of such statement shall be retained by each such member pursuant to the requirements of subparagraph (2) of this paragraph.

(4) *Definitions of controlled group of corporations and component member of controlled group.* For purposes of this section, the terms "controlled group of corporations" and "component member" of a controlled group of corporations shall have the same meaning assigned to those terms in section 1563(a) and (b), except that the phrase "more than 50 percent" shall be substituted for the phrase "at least 80 percent" each place it appears in section 1563(a)(1). For purposes of applying § 1.1563-1(b)(2)(ii)(c), an electing small business corporation shall be treated as an ex-

cluded member whether or not it is subject to the tax imposed by section 1378.

(5) *Members of controlled group filing a consolidated return.* For the purpose of apportioning the $50,000 amount in the case of component members of a controlled group which join in filing a consolidated return, all such members shall be treated as though they were a single component member of the controlled group. Thus, in determining the limitation on the cost of used section 38 property which may be taken into account by the group filing the consolidated return, the apportionment provided in subparagraph (1)(ii) of this paragraph shall be made by using the aggregate cost of such property placed in service by all members of the group filing the consolidated return. If all component members of the controlled group join in filing a consolidated return, the group may select the items to be taken into account to the extent of an aggregate cost of $50,000; if some component members of the controlled group do not join in filing the consolidated return, then the members of the group which join in filing the consolidated return may select the items to be taken into account to the extent of the amount apportioned to such members under subparagraph (1)(ii) of this paragraph.

(6) *Examples.* This paragraph may be illustrated by the following examples:

Example (1). (i) On December 31, 1970, corporations M, N, and O are component members of the same controlled group. The taxable years of M, N, and O end, respectively, on January 31, March 31, and April 30. During the respective taxable years of each corporation which include December 31, 1970, M places in service no used section 38 property, and N and O place in service used section 38 property with respective costs of $100,000 and $150,000. N is the "filing member" of the group since N, among the members (N and O) which are apportioned part of the $50,000 amount for their taxable years which include such December 31, has the taxable year ending on the earliest date.

(ii) The cost of used section 38 property taken into account by N for its taxable year ending March 31, 1971, may not exceed $20,000, that is, an amount which bears the same ratio to $50,000 as the cost of used section 38 property placed in service by N for its taxable year ($100,000) bears to the total cost of used section 38 property placed in service by all component members of the controlled group (M, N, and O) for their taxable years which include December 31, 1970 ($250,000). Similarly, the cost of used section 38 property taken into account by O for

Reg. § 1.48-3(d)(6)

its taxable year ending April 30, 1971, may not exceed $30,000.

Example (2). (i) On December 31, 1971, corporations S and T are component members of the same controlled group. The taxable year of corporations S and T end, respectively, on January 31 and June 30. On April 15, 1972, S files an income tax return for its taxable year ending January 31, 1972, during which year it places in service used section 38 property costing $100,000. T estimates that it will place in service used section 38 property costing $150,000 during its taxable year ending June 30, 1972.

(ii) S, the "filing member" of the group, must file an apportionment schedule under which it may take into account as the cost of used section 38 property an amount not in excess of $20,000 ($100,000/$250,000 × $50,000). If T actually places in service during its taxable year used section 38 property costing more or less than $150,000, its income tax return for it taxable year ending June 30, 1972, may reflect the amended apportionment of the $50,000 limitation based upon the cost of used section 38 property actually placed in service by the group, provided that S attaches a new apportionment schedule to an amended return to reflect the amended apportionment. For example, if T places in service used section 38 property costing $200,000, the cost of used section 38 property taken into account by S and T for their respective taxable years could not exceed $16,667 ($100,000/$300,000 × $50,000) and $33,333 ($200,000/$300,000 × $50,000), respectively, under an amended apportionment. [Reg. § 1.48-3.]

☐ [*T.D.* 6731, 5-7-64. *Amended by T.D.* 7181, 4-24-72; *T.D.* 7820, 6-9-82 *and T.D.* 8996, 5-16-2002.]

[Reg. § 1.48-4]

§ 1.48-4. Election of lessor of new section 38 property to treat lessee as purchaser.—(a) *In general*—(1) *Lessee treated as purchaser.* Under section 48(d), a lessor of property may elect to treat the lessee of such property as having purchased such property (or, in the case of short-term lease property described in subparagraph (2) of this paragraph, a portion of such property) for purposes of the credit allowed by section 38 if the following conditions are satisfied:

(i) The property must be "section 38 property" in the hands of the lessor; that is, it must be property with respect to which depreciation (or amortization in lieu of depreciation) is allowable to the lessor, it must have a useful life of 3 years (4 years in the case of property which is not described in section 50) or more in his hands, and

in every other respect it must meet the requirements of § 1.48-1. Thus, for example, property leased by a municipality to a taxpayer for use in what is commonly known as an "industrial park" is not eligible for the election since, under paragraph (k) of § 1.48-1, property used by a governmental unit is not section 38 property. In addition, property used by the lessee predominantly outside the United States is not eligible for the election since, under paragraph (g) of § 1.48-1, such property is not section 38 property. For purposes of this subdivision, if the lessor is an estate or trust, depreciation (or amortization in lieu of depreciation) will be considered allowable to the estate or trust even if it is apportioned to the beneficiaries or other persons.

(ii) The property must be "new section 38 property" (within the meaning of § 1.48-2) in the hands of the lessor, and the original use of such property must commence with the lessor. See paragraph (b) of this section for the application of the rules relating to "original use" in the case of leased property.

(iii) The property would constitute "new section 38 property" to the lessee if such lessee had actually purchased the property. Thus, the election is not available if the lessee is not the original user of the property. See paragraph (b) of this section for the application of the rules relating to "original use" in the case of leased property. See paragraph (d) of this section for the determination of the estimated useful life of leased property in the hands of the lessee.

(iv) A statement of election to treat the lessee as a purchaser has been filed in the manner and within the time provided in paragraph (f) or (g) of this section.

(v) The lessor is not a person referred to in section 46(d)(1), that is, a mutual savings bank, cooperative bank, or domestic building and loan association to which section 593 applies; a regulated investment company or real estate investment trust subject to taxation under subchapter M, chapter 1 of the Code; or a cooperative organization described in section 1381(a).

The election may be made on a property-by-property basis or a general election may be made with respect to each taxable year of a particular lessee. If the conditions of this subparagraph have been met, the lessee shall be treated as though he were the actual owner of all or a portion of the property for purposes of the credit allowed by section 38. Thus, the lessee shall be entitled to a credit allowed by section 38 with respect to such property for the taxable year in which he places such property in service, and the lessor shall not be entitled to a credit allowed by section 38 with respect to such property unless the property is short-term lease property (as defined in subparagraph (2) of this paragraph). Moreover, if the leased property is disposed of, or if it otherwise ceases to be section 38 property, the property will be subject to the provisions of section 47 (relating to early dispositions, etc.).

(2) *Short-term lease property.* For purposes of this section, the term "short-term lease property" means property which—

(i) Is new section 38 property;

(ii) Has a class life (determined under section 167(m)) in excess of 14 years;

(iii) Is leased under a lease entered into after November 8, 1971, for a period which is less than 80 percent of the class life of such property; and

(iv) Is not leased subject to a net lease within the meaning of section 57(c)(1)(B) and the regulations thereunder.

The class life of property shall be determined under section 167(m) and the regulations prescribed in connection with that section, except that such class life shall be determined without regard to any variance from the class life permitted under such section. If a class life has not been prescribed for property under section 167(m) on the date such property is leased, the class life of the property shall be the estimated useful life used to compute the allowance for depreciation with respect to such property under section 167. For purposes of subdivision (iii) of this subparagraph, the period for which a lease is entered into shall be determined without regard to any option on the part of the lessee to extend or renew such lease, and without regard to any option on the part of the lessee to cancel the lease after a specified period if under the terms of such lease, such a cancellation would result in the imposition of a substantial penalty upon the lessee. Generally, a penalty equal to 25 percent of the total remaining rental payments due under the lease will be regarded as substantial.

(b) *Original use.* For purposes of this section only, the lessor and the lessee may both be considered as the original users of an item of leased property. The determination of whether the lessor qualifies as the original user of leased property shall be made under paragraph (b)(7) of § 1.48-2. The determination of whether the lessee qualifies as the original user of leased property shall be made, under paragraph (b)(7) of § 1.48-2, as if the lessee actually purchased the property. Thus, the lessee would not be considered the original user of the property if it has been previously used by the lessor or another person, or if it is reconstructed, rebuilt, or reconditioned property. However the

lessee would be considered the original user if he is the first person to use the property for its intended function. Thus, the fact that the lessor may have, for example, tested, stored, or attempted to lease the property to other persons will not preclude the lessee from being considered the original user.

(c) *Qualified investment* —(1) *In general.* If a valid election is made under this section, the amount of qualified investment under section 46(c) with respect to the leased property shall be determined under this paragraph and paragraphs (d) and (e) of this section.

(2) *Nonshort-term lease property.* In the case of property which is not short-term lease property, the lessee is treated as having acquired the entire property for an amount equal to—

(i) The fair market value of such property on the date possession is transferred to the lessee, or

(ii) If the property is leased by a component member of a controlled group to another component member of the same controlled group (within the meaning of paragraph (f)(4) of § 1.46-1) on the date possession of the property is transferred to the lessee, the basis of the property in the hands of the lessor.

(3) *Short-term lease property.* (i) In the case of short-term lease property, the lessee is treated as having acquired a portion of such property. The amount for which the lessee is treated as having acquired such portion is an amount equal to a fraction, the numerator of which is the term of the lease and the denominator of which is the class life of the property leased, of the amount for which the lessee would be treated as having acquired the property under subparagraph (2) of this paragraph if the property were not short-term lease property.

(ii) In the case of short-term lease property, the qualified investment of the lessor is an amount equal to his qualified investment in such property determined under section 46(c) multiplied by a fraction, the numerator of which is the class life of the property leased minus the term of the lease and the denominator of which is the class life of such property.

(4) *Example.* The provisions of this paragraph may be illustrated by the following example:

Example. (a) On December 1, 1971, X corporation completed construction of an item of new section 38 property with a basis of $10,000. Under section 167(m), the property has a class life of 16 years. On December 1, 1971, X leases the property to individual A for 4 years and A immedi-

Reg. § 1.48-4(c)(4)

ately places the property in service. The lease is not a net lease within the meaning of section 57(c)(1)(B). On the date of the lease, the fair market value of the property is $12,000. The property would qualify as new section 38 property in A's hands if it had been purchased by A. Under this section, the property is short-terrm lease property. X makes the election under this section to treat A as having acquired a portion of the property.

(b) A is treated as having acquired from X a portion of the property for $3,000 (the fair market value of the property, $12,000, multiplied by a fraction, 4/16, the numerator of which is the term of the lease and the denominator of which is the class life of the leased property). Since under paragraph (d) of this section the useful life of such property in the hands of A is the same as the useful life of such property in the hands of X, and such useful life is at least 7 years, A's qualified investment with respect to the property is $3,000.

(c) The qualified investment of X is $7,500 (the qualified investment of X under section 46(c), $10,000, multiplied by a fraction, 12/16, the numerator of which is the class life of the leased property, 16 minus the term of the lease, 4, and the denominator of which is the class life of the property).

(d) *Estimated useful life of leased property.* The estimated useful life to the lessee of property subject to the election shall be deemed to be the estimated useful life in the hands of the lessor for purposes of computing depreciation, regardless of the term of the lease. The lessor shall determine the estimated useful life of each leased property on an individual basis even though multiple asset accounts are used. However, in the case of assets similar in kind contained in a multiple asset account, the lessor shall assign to each of such assets the average useful life of such assets used in computing depreciation. Thus, for example, if during a taxable year a lessor leases 10 similar trucks with an average estimated useful life for depreciation purposes of 6 years, based on an estimated range of 5 to 7 years, he must assign a useful life of 6 years to each of the 10 trucks.

(e) *Lessor itself a lessee*—(1) *In general.* If the lessee of property is treated, under this section, as having purchased all or a portion of such property and if such lessee leases such property to a sublessee, the qualified investment with respect to such property in the hands of the sublessee shall be determined under paragraphs (c) and (d) of this section as if the original lessor had leased the property directly to the sublessee for the term of the sublessee's lease on the date possession of the property is transferred to the sublessee. For this

purpose, property which is short-term lease property in the hands of the lessee shall be treated as short-term lease property in the hands of the sublessee regardless of whether such property is leased to the sublessee subject to a net lease (within the meaning of section 57(c)(1)(B)). In the case of property which is short-term lease property in the hands of the sublessee, the amount for which the lessee is treated as having acquired such property under paragraph (c) of this section shall be reduced by an amount equal to such amount multiplied by a fraction, the numerator of which is the term of the lease of the sublessee and the denominator of which is the term of the lease of the lessee.

(2) *Example.* The provisions of this paragraph may be illustrated by the following example:

Example. (a) On December 1, 1971, corporation X completes construction of a machine at a cost of $10,000. The machine has a class life under section 167(m) of 20 years. On December 1, 1971, X leases the machine to corporation Y for 12 years, and Y immediately subleases the machine to individual a for 8 years. X and Y are component members of the same controlled group. The lease between X and Y is not a net lease within the meaning of section 57(c)(1)(B). The fair market value of the property on December 1, 1971, is $16,000. Both X and Y make valid elections under this section.

(b) The property is short-term lease property and this paragraph applies.

(c) The qualified investment of A is $6,400. Such amount is determined by multiplying $16,000, the amount for which A would be treated under paragraph (c)(2) of this section as havng acquired the property if it were not short-term lease property, by 8/20.

(d) The qualified investment of Y is $2,000. Such amount is determined by multiplying $10,000, the amount for which Y would be treated under paragraph (c)(2) of this section as having acquired the property if it were not short-term lease property, by 12/20, and by reducing the amount so determined ($6,000) by 8/12 of such amount ($4,000) to $2,000.

(e) The qualified investment of X is $4,000. Such amount is determined by multiplying the amount of X's qualified investment determined under section 46(c) without regard to this section ($10,000) by 8/20.

(f) *Property-by-property election*—(1) *Manner of making election.* The election of a lessor with respect to a particular property (or properties) shall be made by filing a statement with the lessee, signed by the lessor and including the writ-

Reg. § 1.48-4(d)

ten consent of the lessee, containing the following information:

(i) The name, address, and taxpayer account number of the lessor and the lessee;

(ii) The district director's office with which the income tax returns of the lessor and the lessee are filed;

(iii) A description of each property with respect to which the election is being made;

(iv) The date on which possession of the property (or properties) is transferred to the lessee;

(v) The estimated useful life category of the property (or properties) in the hands of the lessor, that is, 3 years or more but less than 5 years, 5 years or more but less than 7 years, or 7 years or more;

(vi) The amount for which the lessee (or sublessee) is treated as having acquired the leased property under paragraph (c)(2) or (3) of this section; and

(vii) If the lessor is itself a lessee, the name, address, and taxpayer account number of the original lessor, and the district director's office with which the income tax return of such original lessor is filed.

(2) *Time for making election.* The statement referred to in subparagraph (1) of this paragraph shall be filed with the lessee on or before the due date (including any extensions of time) of the lessee's return for the lessee's taxable year during which possession of the property is transferred to the lessee, except that if such taxable year ends after March 31, 1971, and before December 11, 1971, the statement shall be filed with the lessee on or before the due date (including any extensions of time) of the lessee's return for such taxable year, or on or before October 24, 1972, whichever is later.

(3) *Election is irrevocable.* An election under this paragraph shall be irrevocable as of the time the statement referred to in subparagraph (1) of this paragraph is filed with the lessee.

(g) *General election*—(1) *In general.* In lieu of making elections on a property-by-property basis in the manner and time prescribed in paragraph (f) of this section, a lessor may, with respect to a particular taxable year of a particular lessee, make a general election to treat such lessee as having purchased all properties possession of which is transferred under lease by the lessor to the lessee during such taxable year of the lessee.

(2) *Manner and time for making general election.* The general election of a lessor with respect to a taxable year of a lessee shall be made by filing a statement with the lessee, signed by the lessor and including the written consent of the lessee, on or before the due date (including any extensions of time) of the lessee's return for such taxable year, except that if such taxable year ends after March 31, 1971, and before December 11, 1971, the statement shall be filed with the lessee on or before the due date (including any extensions of time) of the lessee's return for such taxable year, or on or before October 24, 1972, whichever is later. Such statement of general election shall contain:

(i) The name, address, and taxpayer account number of the lessor and the lessee;

(ii) The taxable year of the lessee with respect to which such general election is made;

(iii) The district director's office with which the income tax returns of the lessor and the lessee are filed;

(iv) If the lessor is itself a lessee, the name, address, and taxpayer account number of the original lessor, and the district director's office with which the income tax return of such original lessor is filed.

(3) *Election is irrevocable.* A general election under this paragraph shall be irrevocable as of the time the statement referred to in subparagraph (2) of this paragraph is filed with the lessee and shall be binding on the lessor and the lessee for the entire taxable year of the lessee with respect to which such general election is made.

(4) *Information requirement.* If a lessor, with respect to a taxable year of the lessee, makes a general election under this paragraph, such lessor shall provide such lessee, on or before the date required for filing the statement under subparagraph (2) of this paragraph, with a statement (or statements) containing the information required by paragraph (f)(1)(iii), (iv), (v), and (vi) of this section with respect to all properties possession of which is transferred under lease by the lessor to the lessee during such taxable year.

(h) *Signature.* The statement referred to in paragraph (f)(1) of (g)(2) of this section shall not be valid unless signed by both the lessor and the lessee. The signature of the lessee shall constitute the consent of the lessee to the election. The statement shall be signed by the taxpayer or a duly authorized agent of the taxpayer. For purposes of this section, a facsimile signature may be used in lieu of a signature manually executed and, if used, shall be as binding as a signature manually executed.

(i) [Reserved]

(j) *Record requirements.* The lessor and the lessee shall keep as a part of their records the statement referred to in paragraph (f)(1), or the statements referred to in paragraphs (g)(2) and (g)(4), of this section. The lessor shall attach to his income tax return a summary statement of all property leased during his taxable year with respect to which an election is made. In the case of a taxable year ending after March 31, 1971, and before December 11, 1971, a summary statement may be filed on or before the due date (including any extensions of time) of the return or on or before October 24, 1972, whichever is later, with the Internal Revenue Service Center with which the return has been filed. Such summary statement shall contain the following information: (1) The name, address, and taxpayer account number of the lessor; and (2) in numerical account number order, each lessee's account number, name, and address, the estimated useful life category of the property (or, if applicable, the estimated useful life expressed in years), and the basis or fair market value of the property, whichever is applicable.

(k) *Adjustment of rental deductions*—(1) *In general.* The rules of this paragraph apply only to section 38 property placed in service before January 1, 1964, and with respect to any such property only for taxable years of a lessee beginning before January 1, 1964. If a lessor makes a valid election under this section with respect to property placed in service by the lessee before January 1, 1964, section 48(g) and § 1.48-7 (relating to adjustments to basis of property) shall not apply to the lessor with respect to such property. Thus, the lessor is not required to reduce under section 48(g)(1) the basis of such property. However, if such an election is made, the deductions otherwise allowable under section 162 to the lessee for amounts paid or accrued to the lessor under the lease shall be adjusted in the manner provided in this paragraph. For special adjustments for taxable years beginning after December 31, 1963, see paragraph (m) of this section.

(2) *Decrease in rental deduction.* (i) The deductions otherwise allowable under section 162 to the lessee for amounts paid or accrued to the lessor under the lease with respect to leased property placed in service before January 1, 1964, shall be decreased under subdivision (ii) or (iii) of this subparagraph, whichever is applicable, by an amount determined by reference to the credit earned on the leased property. The "credit earned" on the leased property is determined by multiplying the qualified investment (as defined in section 46(c)) with respect to such property by 7 percent. Thus, the credit earned (and the decrease in deductions) is determined without regard to the limitation based on tax which, under section 46(a)(2), may limit the amount of the

credit the lessee may take into account in any one year.

(ii) If, in the case of property placed in service before January 1, 1964, the lessor, under paragraph (f)(1)(v) of this section, supplies the lessee with the useful life of such property expressed in years, then for each taxable year beginning before January 1, 1964, any part of which falls within a period beginning with the month in which the leased property is placed in service by the lessee and ending with the close of the estimated useful life of such property (as determined under paragraph (d) of this section), the lessee shall decrease the deduction otherwise allowable under section 162 for each such taxable year with respect to such property. The decrease for each such taxable year shall be equal to (a) the credit earned, divided by (b) the estimated useful life of the property (expressed in months), multiplied by (c) the number of calendar months in which the leased property was held by the lessee during such taxable year. Thus, if leased property with a basis of $27,000 in the hands of a calendar-year lessee, and with an estimated useful life of 10 years, is placed in service by the lessee on July 15, 1963, the lessee must decrease his section 162 deduction with respect to the leased property for the taxable year 1963 by $94.50 ($1,890 credit earned, divided by 120, multiplied by 6).

(iii) If, in the case of property placed in service before January 1, 1964, the lessor, under paragraph (f)(1)(v) of this section, supplies the lessee with the useful life category of such property, then for each taxable year beginning before January 1, 1964, during a period equal to the shortest life of the useful life category used by the lessee in computing qualified investment under section 46(c) with respect to the leased property, the lessee shall decrease the deduction otherwise allowable under section 162 for such taxable year with respect to such property. The decrease for each such taxable year shall be equal to the credit earned divided by such shortest life, that is, 4, 6, or 8. Such decreases shall begin with the taxable year during which the lessee places the property in service. Thus, if leased property with a basis of $30,000 to the lessee, and an estimated useful life falling within the 4 years or more but less than 6 years useful life category, is placed in service by the lessee within the lessee's taxable year ending December 31, 1962, the lessee must decrease his section 162 deduction with respect to the leased property for each of the taxable years 1962 and 1963 by $175 ($700 credit earned divided by 4).

(iv) To the extent that a required decrease, under subdivision (ii) or (iii) of this subparagraph, is not taken into account for any taxable year

Reg. § 1.48-4(k)(1)

beginning before January 1, 1964, because the deduction otherwise allowable under section 162 for such taxable year with respect to the leased property is less than the required decrease for such taxable year, then the balance of the required decrease not taken into account for such taxable year shall decrease the amount otherwise allowable as a deduction under section 162 with respect to such property for the next succeeding taxable year (or years) beginning before January 1, 1964, if any, for which a deduction is allowable with respect to such property. Thus, if the required decrease with respect to leased property is $200 for 1962 but the lessee's deduction otherwise allowable under section 162 for such taxable year with respect to such property is only $50, the balance of $150 must be applied in 1963 to decrease the deduction otherwise allowable to the lessee with respect to the leased property for such taxable year.

(v) See paragraph (b) of § 1.48-7 for reduction of basis in the case of an actual purchase of leased property by a lessee (in a taxable year of such lessee beginning before January 1, 1964) who has been treated as a purchaser of such property under this section.

(3) *Increase in rental deductions on account of early dispositions, etc.* (i) If, as a result of an early disposition, etc., in a taxable year beginning before January 1, 1964, with respect to leased property placed in service before such date, the lessee's tax is increased under section 47(a)(1) or (?), or an adjustment in a carryback or carryover is made under section 47(a)(3) by reduction of an unused credit, the rental deductions (if any) otherwise allowable under section 162 to such lessee for amounts paid or accrued to the lessor under the lease with respect to such property shall be increased in an amount equal to the total decreases previously made in the lessee's rental deductions under subparagraph (2) of this paragraph.

(ii) Except as provided in subdivision (iii) of this subparagraph, the increase in rental deductions described in subdivision (i) of this subparagraph shall be taken into account as an increase in rental deductions otherwise allowable under section 162 for the taxable year in which the early disposition, etc., occurred.

(iii) If, after the event which caused section 47(a)(1), (2), or (3) to apply, the lessee continues the use of the property in a trade or business or in the production of income, the increase in rental deduction described in subdivision (i) of this subparagraph shall be taken into account ratably over the remaining portion of the useful life of the property which was used in making the decreases in rental deductions with respect to the property under subparagraph (2) of this paragraph.

(iv) If subdivision (iii) of this subparagraph applies, and if, prior to the expiration of the useful life of the property used in making the decreases in rental deductions, the lease is terminated other than by actual purchase of the property by the lessee, any increase in rental deductions not previously taken into account shall be taken into account as an increase in rental deductions for the taxable year in which the lease is terminated. In the case of an actual purchase of the property by the lessee, see paragraph (e) of § 1.48-7.

(l) *Examples.* The provisions of this section may be illustrated by the following examples:

Example (1). X Corporation is engaged in the business of manufacturing and leasing new and reconstructed equipment which in its hands has an estimated useful life of 12 years. After December 31, 1961, X Corporation constructs machine no. 1 at a cost of $20,000 and reconstructs machine no. 2 at a cost of $5,000. On February 15, 1962, Y Corporation, a calendar-year taxpayer, leases both machines from X Corporation and places them in service. The fair market value of machine no. 1 on the date on which possession is transferred to Y is $25,200. Machine no. 1 would qualify as new section 38 property in Y's hands if it had been purchased by Y. If X elects to treat Y as the purchaser of machine no. 1, under paragraph (c)(2)(ii) of this section such machine will have a basis of $25,200 in Y's hands. Under paragraph (f)(1)(v) of this section, X supplies Y with an estimated useful life of 12 years (expressed in years rather than useful life category) with respect to machine no. 1 for purposes of determining Y's qualified investment. Y's credit earned with respect to the property is $1,764 (7 percent of $25,200). Under paragraph (k)(2)(ii) of this section, Y's deduction attributable to the leased property for 1962 will be decreased by $134.75 (credit earned of $1,764, divided by 144, multiplied by 11), and for 1963 such deduction will be decreased by $147 ($1,764, divided by 144, multiplied by 12). The election is not available with respect to machine no. 2 since a reconstructed machine would not constitute new section 38 property if Y had purchased it. In such case, while X cannot make the election to treat Y as a purchaser, X would be entitled to a credit under section 38 based on its expenditure of $5,000 as an investment in new section 38 property, since such amount represents cost of reconstruction after December 31, 1961.

Reg. § 1.48-4(l)

Example (2). Assume the same facts as in example (1) except that under paragraph (f)(1)(v) of this section, X supplies Y with an estimated useful life category of 8 years or more (rather than an estimated useful life expressed in years) with respect to machine no. 1 for purposes of determining Y's qualified investment. Under paragraph (k)(2)(iii) of this section, Y's deduction attributable to the leased property will be decreased by $220.50 (credit earned of $1,764, divided by 8) for each of its taxable years of 1962 and 1963.

Example (3). Assume the same facts as in example (1) except that the lessee disposes of his interest in the lease on January 1, 1963, and that there is an increase in Y's tax for 1963 under section 47(a)(1) in the amount of $1,764. Under paragraph (k)(2) of this section, Y's deductions attributable to the leased property are decreased only in 1962, and the amount of such decrease is $134.75. In 1963 there shall be an increase of $134.75 in the deductions otherwise allowable under section 162 for such taxable year with respect to the leased property.

Example (4). Assume the same facts as in example (1) except that during the year 1963 the property was used by Y predominantly outside the United States within the meaning of paragraph (g) of § 1.48-1, and thereafter was used in Y's trade or business. Under paragraph (k)(3) of this section, the increase of $134.75 described in example (3) is taken into account ratably as an increase in rental deductions otherwise allowable under section 162 in the amount of $12.25 ($134.75 divided by 11 years) for 1963 and each of the 10 succeeding years.

(m) *Increase in rental deductions on account of section 203(a)(2)(B) of the Revenue Act of 1964*— (1) *In general*. (i) Under section 203(a)(2)(B) of the Revenue Act of 1964, if, for any taxable year of a lessee beginning before January 1, 1964, the rental deductions otherwise allowable under section 162 to such lessee for amounts paid or accrued to the lessor under the lease with respect to leased property placed in service before January 1, 1964, were decreased under paragraph (k)(2) of this section, such rental deductions shall be increased.

(ii) The increase in rental deductions described in subdivision (i) of this subparagraph shall be in an amount equal to the total decreases in the lessee's rental deductions previously made under paragraph (k)(2) of this section less any increases in rental deductions made under paragraph (k)(3) of this section.

(iii) Except as provided in subdivision (iv) of this subparagraph, the increase in rental deductions described in subdivision (i) of this subpara-

graph shall be taken into account ratably over the remaining portion of the useful life of the property commencing with the first day of the first taxable year beginning after December 31, 1963. For this purpose, the useful life of the property shall be the useful life used in making the decreases in rental deductions with respect to the property under paragraph (k)(2) of this section.

(iv) If the lease is terminated other than by the lessee's actual purchase of the property during a taxable year beginning after December 31, 1963, and before the end of the remaining useful life of the property used in making the decreases in rental deductions, the amount of the increase in rental deductions described in subdivision (i) of this subparagraph and not previously taken into account shall be allowed as a deduction for the taxable year in which such termination occurs.

(v) The rental deductions with respect to any section 38 property are not to be increased under this paragraph if the lessee dies in a taxable year beginning before January 1, 1964.

(vi) The increase in rental deductions described in subdivision (i) of this subparagraph shall ordinarily be taken into account by the lessee treated as the purchaser, that is, the lessee entitled to the credit. However, if the property under the lease is transferred by the lessee to a successor lessee in a transaction described in section 47(b) (other than a transfer by reason of death) under which the successor lessee assumes the lessee's obligations under the lease, such increase in rental deductions shall be taken into account by the successor lessee in the manner prescribed in this paragraph.

(2) *Examples*. The operation of this paragraph may be illustrated by the following examples:

Example (1). (a) X Corporation acquired on January 1, 1962, an item of new section 38 property with a basis of $24,000 and with a useful life to the lessor of 10 years. Y Corporation, which makes its returns on the basis of a calendar year, leased such property from X Corporation and placed it in service on January 2, 1962. Under this section, X Corporation made a valid election to treat Y Corporation as having purchased such property for purposes of the credit allowed by section 38 and supplied the lessee with information that the property had a useful life of 10 years. The amount of the credit earned with respect to such property was $1,680 (7 percent of $24,000). For each of the taxable years 1962 and 1963, Y Corporation decreased, under paragraph (k)(2) of this section, its deductions otherwise

Reg. § 1.48-4(m)(2)

allowable under section 162 with respect to such property by $168 ($1,680 multiplied by 12/120).

(b) For each of the taxable years 1964 through 1971, Y Corporation increases its deductions otherwise allowable under section 162 for amounts paid to X Corporation under the lease by $42 ($336 (that is, $168 multiplied by 2) divided by the remaining useful life of 8 years).

Example (2). (a) The facts are the same as in example (1) except that the lease is terminated on January 3, 1965.

(b) For the taxable year 1964, Y Corporation increases its deductions otherwise allowable under section 162 by $42.

(c) For the taxable year 1965, Y Corporation increases its deductions otherwise allowable under section 162 for the portion of the increase which had not been taken into account as of the time of the termination of the lease. Thus, the amount of such increase for the taxable year 1965 is $294 ($336 minus $42). [Reg. § 1.48-4.]

☐ [*T.D. 6731, 5-7-64. Amended by T.D. 6838, 7-19-65, T.D. 6953, 4-22-68, T.D. 7181, 1-24-72, and T.D. 7203, 8-24-72.*]

[Reg. § 1.48-5]

§ 1.48-5. Electing small business corporations.—(a) *In general.*—(1) In the case of an electing small business corporation (as defined in section 1371(b)), the basis of "new section 38 property" and the cost of "used section 38 property" placed in service during the taxable year shall be apportioned pro rata among the persons who are shareholders of such corporation on the last day of such corporation's taxable year. Section 38 property shall not (by reason of such apportionment) lose its character as new section 38 property or used section 38 property, as the case may be. The estimated useful life of such property in the hands of a shareholder shall be deemed to be the estimated useful life of such property in the hands of the electing small business corporation. The bases of all new section 38 properties which have a useful life falling within a particular useful life category shall be aggregated; likewise, the cost of all used section 38 properties which have a useful life falling within a particular useful life category shall be aggregated. The total bases of new section 38 properties within each useful life category and the total cost of used section 38 properties within each useful life category shall be apportioned separately. The useful life categories are: (i) 3 years or more but less than 5 years; (ii) 5 years or more but less than 7 years; and (iii) 7 years or more. There shall be apportioned to each person who is a shareholder of the electing small business corporation on the last day of the taxable year of such corporation, for his

taxable year in which or with which the taxable year of such corporation ends, his pro rata share of the total bases of new section 38 properties within each useful life category, and his pro rata share of the total cost of used section 38 properties within each useful life category. In determining who are shareholders of an electing small business corporation on the last day of its taxable year, the rules of paragraph (d)(1) of § 1.1371-1 and of paragraph (a)(2) of § 1.1373-1 shall apply.

(2) The total cost of used section 38 property that may be apportioned by an electing small business corporation to its shareholders for any taxable year of such corporation shall not exceed $50,000. If the total cost of used section 38 property placed in service during the taxable year by the electing small business corporation exceeds $50,000, such corporation must select, under paragraph (c)(4) of § 1.48-3, the used section 38 property the cost of which is to be apportioned to its shareholders.

(3) A shareholder to whom the basis (or cost) of section 38 property is apportioned shall, for purposes of the credit allowed by section 38, be treated as the taxpayer with respect to such property. Thus, the total cost of used section 38 property apportioned to him by the electing small business corporation must be taken into account as cost of used section 38 property in determining whether the $50,000 limitation on the cost of used section 38 property which may be taken into account by the shareholder in computing qualified investment for any taxable year is exceeded. If a shareholder takes into account in determining his qualified investment any portion of the basis (or cost) of section 38 property placed in service by an electing small business corporation and if such property subsequently is disposed of or otherwise ceases to be section 38 property in the hands of the corporation, such shareholder shall be subject to the provisions of section 47. See § 1.47-4.

(b) *Summary statement.* An electing small business corporation shall attach to its return a statement showing the apportionment to each shareholder of the total bases of new, and the total cost of used, section 38 properties within each useful life category.

(c) *Example.* This section may be illustrated by the following example:

Example. (1) X Corporation, an electing small business corporation which makes its return on the basis of the calendar year, acquires and places in service on June 1, 1962, three new assets which qualify as new section 38 property and three used assets which qualify as used section 38 property. The basis of each new, and the cost of each used, section 38 property and the estimated useful life of each property are as follows:

Reg. § 1.48-5(c)

	Basis (or cost)	Estimated useful life
Asset No. 1 (new)	$30,000	4 years
Asset No. 2 (new)	30,000	4 years
Asset No. 3 (new)	30,000	8 years
Asset No. 4 (used)	12,000	6 years
Asset No. 5 (used)	12,000	6 years
Asset No. 6 (used)	12,000	8 years

On December 31, 1962, X Corporation has 10 shares of stock outstanding which are owned as follows: A owns 3 shares, B owns 2 shares, and C owns 5 shares.

(2) Under this section, the total bases of the new, and the total cost of the used, section 38 properties are apportioned to the shareholders of X Corporation as follows:

Useful life category	New— 4 to 6 years	New— 8 years or more	Used— 6 to 8 years	Used—8 years or more
Total bases or total cost	$60,000	$30,000	$24,000	$12,000
Shareholder A (3/10)	$18,000	$ 9,000	$ 7,200	$ 3,600
Shareholder B (2/10)	12,000	6,000	4,800	2,400
Shareholder C (5/10)	30,000	15,000	12,000	6,000

Assume that shareholders A, B, and C did not place in service during their taxable years in which falls December 31, 1962 (the last day of X Corporation's taxable year) any section 38 property and that such shareholders did not own any interests in other electing small business corporations, partnerships, estates, or trusts. Under section 46(c), the qualified investment of shareholder A is $23,400, of shareholder B is $15,600, and of shareholder C is $39,000, computed as follows:

Basis (or cost)	New or used	Applicable percentage	Qualified investment
		Shareholder A	
$18,000 (new)	×33⅓ percent	......	$ 6,000
9,000 (new)	×100 percent	......	9,000
7,200 (used)	×66⅔ percent	......	4,800
3,600 (used)	×100 percent	......	3,600
Total			$23,400

Basis (or cost)	New or used	Applicable percentage	Qualified investment
		Shareholder B	
$12,000 (new)	×33⅓ percent	......	$ 4,000
6,000 (new)	×100 percent	......	6,000
4,800 (used)	×66⅔ percent	......	3,200
2,400 (used)	×100 percent	......	2,400
Total			$15,600

Basis (or cost)	New or used	Applicable percentage	Qualified investment
		Shareholder C	
$30,000 (new)	×33⅓ percent	......	$10,000
15,000 (new)	×100 percent	......	15,000
12,000 (used)	×66⅔ percent	......	8,000
6,000 (used)	×100 percent	......	6,000
Total			$39,000

[Reg. § 1.48-5.]

☐ [T.D. 6731, 5-7-64. *Amended by T.D. 6931, 10-9-67, and T.D. 7203, 8-24-72.*]

[Reg. § 1.48-6]

§ 1.48-6. Estates and trusts.—(a) *In general.* (1) In the case of an estate or trust, the basis of "new section 38 property" and the cost of "used section 38 property" placed in service during the taxable year shall be apportioned among the estate or trust and its beneficiaries on the basis of the income of such estate or trust allocable to each. Section 38 property shall not (by reason of such apportionment) lose its character as new section 38 property or used section 38 property, as the case may be. The estimated useful life of such property in the hands of a beneficiary shall be deemed to be the estimated useful life of such property in the hands of the estate or trust. The bases of all new section 38 properties which have a useful life falling within a particular useful life category shall be aggregated; likewise, the cost of all used section 38 properties which have a useful life falling within a particular useful life category shall be aggregated. The total bases of new section 38 properties within each useful life category and the total cost of used section 38 properties within each useful life category shall be apportioned separately. The useful life categories are: (i) 3 years or more but less than 5 years; (ii) 5 years or more but less than 7 years; and (iii) 7 years or more. There shall be apportioned to the estate or trust for its taxable year, and to each beneficiary of such estate or trust for his taxable year in which or with which the taxable year of such estate or trust ends, his share (as determined under paragraph (b) of this section) of the total bases of new section 38 properties within each useful life category, and his share of the total cost of used section 38 properties within each useful life category.

(2) The total cost of used section 38 property that may be apportioned among an estate or trust and its beneficiaries for any taxable year of such estate or trust shall not exceed $50,000. If the total cost of used section 38 property placed in service during the taxable year by the estate or trust exceeds $50,000, such estate or trust must select, under paragraph (c)(4) of § 1.48-3, the used section 38 property the cost of which is to be apportioned among such estate or trust and its beneficiaries.

(3) A beneficiary to whom the basis (or cost) of section 38 property is apportioned shall, for purposes of the credit allowed by section 38, be treated as the taxpayer with respect to such property. Thus, the total cost of used section 38 property apportioned to him by the estate or trust must be taken into account as cost of used section 38 property in determining whether the $50,000 limitation on the cost of used property which may be taken into account by the beneficiary in computing qualified investment for any taxable year is exceeded. If a beneficiary takes into account in determining his qualified investment any portion of the basis (or cost) of section 38 property placed in service by an estate or trust and if such property subsequently is disposed of or otherwise ceases to be section 38 property in the hands of the estate or trust, such beneficiary shall be subject to the provisions of section 47. See § 1.47-5.

(4) For purposes of this section, the term "beneficiary" includes heir, legatee, and devisee.

(5) If during the taxable year of an estate or trust a beneficiary's interest in the income of such estate or trust terminates, the basis (or cost) of section 38 property placed in service by such estate or trust after such termination shall not be apportioned to such beneficiary.

(b) *Share.* A trust's, estate's, or beneficiary's share of the total bases of new section 38 properties, and the total cost of used section 38 properties, within a useful life category shall be—

(1) The total bases of new (or the total cost of used) section 38 properties which have a useful life falling within such useful life category placed in service in the taxable year of the estate or trust, multiplied by

(2) The amount of income allocable to such estate or trust or to such beneficiary for such taxable year, divided by

(3) The sum of the amounts of income allocable to such estate or trust and all its beneficiaries taken into account under subparagraph (2) of this paragraph.

(c) *Limitation based on amount of tax.* In the case of an estate or trust, the $25,000 amount specified in section 46(a)(2), relating to limitation based on amount of tax, shall be reduced for the taxable year to—

(1) $25,000, multiplied by

(2) The qualified investment with respect to the total bases of new section 38 properties plus the qualified investment with respect to the total cost of used section 38 properties, apportioned to such estate or trust under paragraph (a) of this section, divided by

(3) The qualified investment with respect to the total bases of all new section 38 properties plus the qualified investment with respect to the total cost of all used section 38 properties, apportioned among such estate or trust and its beneficiaries.

For purposes of subparagraph (3) of this paragraph, cost of used section 38 property shall not be considered as apportioned to any beneficiary to the extent that such cost is not taken into account by such beneficiary in computing qualified investment in used section 38 property.

(d) *Summary statement.* An estate or trust shall attach to its return a statement showing the apportionment to such estate or trust and to each beneficiary of the total bases of new, and the total cost of used, section 38 properties within each useful life category.

(e) *Example.* This section may be illustrated by the following example:

Example. (1) XYZ Trust, which makes its return on the basis of the calendar year, acquires and places in service on June 1, 1962, three new assets which qualify as new section 38 property and three used assets which qualify as used section 38 property. The basis of the new, and the cost of the used, section 38 property and the estimated useful life of each property are as follows:

	Basis (or cost)	Estimated useful life
Asset No. 1 (new)	$30,000	4 years
Asset No. 2 (new)	30,000	4 years
Asset No. 3 (new)	30,000	8 years
Asset No. 4 (used)	12,000	6 years
Asset No. 5 (used)	12,000	6 years
Asset No. 6 (used)	12,000	8 years

For the taxable year 1962 the income of XYZ Trust is $20,000 which is allocable as follows: $10,000 to XYZ Trust, $6,000 to beneficiary A, and $4,000 to beneficiary B. Beneficiaries A and B make their returns on the basis of a calendar year.

(2) Under this section, the total bases of the new, and the total cost of the used, section 38 properties are apportioned to XYZ Trust and its beneficiaries as follows:

Useful life category	New— 4 to 6 years	New— 8 years or more	Used— 6 to 8 years	Used— 8 years or more
Total bases or total cost	$60,000	$30,000	$24,000	$12,000
XYZ Trust $\left(\dfrac{\$10,000}{20,000}\right)$	$30,000	$15,000	$12,000	$ 6,000
Beneficiary A $\left(\dfrac{\$ 6,000}{20,000}\right)$	18,000	9,000	7,200	3,600
Beneficiary B $\left(\dfrac{\$ 4,000}{20,000}\right)$	12,000	6,000	4,800	2,400

Assume that beneficiary A placed in service during his taxable year 1962 new section 38 property with a basis of $10,000 and an estimated useful life of 8 years. Also, assume that beneficiary B did not place in service during his taxable year 1962 any section 38 property and that beneficiaries A and B did not own any interests in other trusts, estates, partnerships, or electing small business corporations. Under section 46(c), the qualified investment of XYZ Trust is $39,000, of beneficiary A is $33,400, and of beneficiary B is $15,600, computed as follows:

Basis (or cost)	New or used	XYZ Trust Applicable percentage	Qualified investment
$30,000	(new)	×33⅓ percent	$10,000
15,000	(new)	×100 percent	15,000
12,000	(used)	×66⅔ percent	8,000
6,000	(used)	×100 percent	6,000
Total		....	$39,000

	Beneficiary A		
$18,000	(new)	×33⅓ percent	$ 6,000
9,000	(new)	×100 percent	9,000
7,200	(used)	×66⅔ percent	4,800
3,600	(used)	×100 percent	3,600
			$23,400
$10,000	(new)	×100 percent	$10,000
Total		....	$33,400

	Beneficiary B		
$12,000	(new)	×33⅓ percent	$ 4,000
6,000	(new)	×100 percent	6,000
4,800	(used)	×66⅔ percent	3,200
2,400	(used)	×100 percent	2,400
Total		....	$15,600

(3) In the case of XYZ Trust, the $25,000 amount specified in section 46(a)(2) is reduced to $12,500, computed as follows: (i) $25,000, multiplied by (ii) $39,000 (qualified investment apportioned to the trust), divided by (iii) $78,000 (total qualified investment apportioned among such trust ($39,000), beneficiary A ($23,400), and beneficiary B ($15,600)). [Reg. § 1.48-6.]

☐ [*T.D.* 6731, 5-7-64. *Amended by T.D.* 6931, 10-9-67; *T.D.* 6958, 6-20-68 *and T.D.* 7203, 8-24-72.]

[Reg. § 1.48-9]

§ 1.48-9. Definition of energy property.—(a) *General rule—(1) In general.* Under section 48(l)(2), energy property means property that is described in at least one of 6 categories of energy property and that meets the other requirements of this section. If property is described in more than one of these categories, or is described more than once in a single category, only a single energy investment credit is allowed. In that case, the energy investment credit will be allowed under the category the taxpayer chooses by indicating the chosen category on Form 3468, Schedule B. The 6 categories of energy property are:

    (i) alternative energy property,

    (ii) solar or wind energy property,

    (iii) specially defined energy property,

    (iv) recycling equipment,

    (v) shale oil equipment, and

    (vi) equipment for producing natural gas from geopressured brine.

(2) *Depreciable property with 3-year useful life.* Property is not energy property unless depreciation (or amortization in lieu of depreciation) is

allowable and the property has an estimated useful life (determined at the time when the property is placed in service) of 3 years or more.

(3) *Effective date rules*. To be energy property—

(i) If property is constructed, reconstructed or erected by the taxpayer, the construction, reconstruction, or erection must be completed after September 30, 1978, or

(ii) If the property is acquired, the original use of the property must (A) commence with the taxpayer and (B) commence after September 30, 1978, and before January 1, 1983.

For transitional rules, see section 48(m).

(4) *Cross references*. (i) To determine if depreciation (or amortization in lieu of depreciation) is allowable for property, see § 1.48-1(b).

(ii) For the meaning of "estimated useful life", see § 1.46-3(e)(7).

(iii) The meaning of "acquired", "original use", "construction", "reconstruction", and "erection" is determined under the principles of § 1.48-2(b).

(iv) For the definition of energy investment credit (energy credit), see section 48(o)(2).

(v) For special rules relating to public utility property, see paragraph (n) of this section.

(b) *Relationship to section 38 property*— (1) *In general*. (i) Energy property is treated under section 48(l)(1) as meeting the general requirements for section 38 property set forth in section 48(a)(1). For example, structural components of a building may qualify for the energy credit. In addition, the exclusion from section 38 property under section 48(a)(3) (lodging limitation) does not apply to energy property. For purposes of the energy credit, energy property is treated as section 38 property solely by reason of section 48(l)(1). For example, if property ceases to be energy property, it ceases to be section 38 property for all purposes relating to the energy credit and, thus, is subject to recapture under section 47. See § 1.47-1(h).

(ii) See the effective date rules under paragraph (a)(3) of this section for limitations on the eligibility of property as energy property.

(iii) Section 48(l)(1) does not affect the character of property under sections of the Code outside the investment credit provisions. For example, structural components of a building that are treated as section 38 property under section 48(l)(1) remain section 1250 property and are not section 1245 property.

(2) *Other section 48 rules apply*. (i) In general, section 48(a) otherwise applies in determining if energy property is section 38 property.

Thus, energy property excluded from the definition of section 38 property under section 48(a) (except by reason of section 48(a)(1) or (a)(3)) is not eligible for the energy credit. For example, energy property used predominantly outside the United States (section 48(a)(2)) or used by tax exempt organizations (section 48(a)(4)), in general, is not treated as section 38 property for any purpose and thus, is not eligible for the energy credit.

(ii) Other rules of section 48, such as those for leased property under section 48(d), also apply to energy property.

(3) *Regular credit denied for certain energy property*. In computing the amount of credit under section 46(a)(2), the regular percentage does not apply to any energy property which, but for section 48(l)(1), would not be section 38 property. See section 46(a)(2)(D). For example, energy property used for lodging (section 48(a)(3)) and, in general, structural components of a building (section 48(a)(1)(B)) are not eligible for the regular credit even though they may be eligible for the energy credit. However, a structural component of a qualified rehabilitated building (as defined in section 48(g)(1)) or a single purpose agricultural or horticultural structure (as defined in section 48(p)) may qualify for the regular credit without regard to section 48(l)(1).

(c) *Alternative energy property*—(1) *In general*. Alternative energy property means property described in paragraph (c)(3) through (10) of this section. In general alternative energy property includes certain property that uses an alternate substance as a fuel or feedstock or converts an alternate substance to a synthetic fuel and certain associated equipment.

(2) *Alternate substance*. (i) An alternate substance is any substance or combination of substances other than an oil or gas substance. Alternate substances include coal, wood, and agricultural, industrial, and municipal wastes or by-products. Alternate substances do not include synthetic fuels or other products that are produced from an alternate substance and that have undergone a chemical change as described in paragraph (c)(5)(ii) of this section. For example, methane produced from landfills is not an alternate substance; rather it is a synthetic fuel produced from an alternate substance. However, preparing an alternate substance for use as a fuel or feedstock or for conversion into a fuel does not create a new product if no chemical change occurs. For example, pelletizing, drying, compacting, and liquefying do not result in a new product if no chemical change occurs.

(ii) The term "oil or gas substance" means—

Reg. § 1.48-9(c)(2)

(A) oil or gas and

(B) any primary product of oil or gas.

(iii) For the definition of primary product of oil or gas, see § 1.993-3(g)(3)(i), (ii), and (vi). Thus, petrochemicals are not primary products of oil or gas.

(3) *Boiler*. (i) A boiler that uses an alternate substance as its primary fuel is alternative energy property.

(ii) A boiler is a device for producing vapor from a liquid. Boilers, in general, have a burner in which fuel is burned. A boiler includes a fire box, boiler tubes, the containment shell, pumps, pressure and operating controls, and safety equipment, but not pollution control equipment (as defined in paragraph (c)(8) of this section).

(iii) A "primary fuel" is a fuel comprising more than 50 percent of the fuel requirement of an item of equipment, measured in terms of Btu's for the remainder of the taxable year from the date the equipment is placed in service and for each taxable year thereafter. Electricity and waste heat are not fuels. For example, electric boilers do not qualify as alternative energy property even if the electricity is derived from an alternate substance.

(4) *Burners*. (i) A burner for a combustor other than a burner described in paragraph (c)(3)(ii) of this section is alternative energy property if the burner uses an alternate substance as its primary fuel (as defined in paragraph (c)(3)(iii) of this section).

(ii) A burner is the part of a combustor that produces a flame. A combustor is a process heater which includes ovens, kilns, and furnaces.

(iii) A burner includes equipment (such as conveyors, flame control devices, and safety monitoring devices) located at the site of the burner and necessary to bring the alternate substance to the burner.

(5) *Synthetic fuel production equipment*. (i) Equipment (synthetic fuel equipment) that converts an alternate substance into a synthetic solid, liquid, or gaseous fuel (other than coke or coke gas) is alternative energy property. Synthetic fuel production equipment does not include equipment, such as an oxygen plant, that is not directly involved in the treatment of an alternate substance, but produces a substance that is, like the alternate substance, a basic feedstock or catalyst used in the conversion process. Equipment is not eligible if it is used beyond the point at which a substance usable as a fuel has been produced. Equipment is eligible only to the extent of the equipment's cost or basis allocable to the annual production of substances used as a fuel or used in the production of a fuel. For example, assume for

the taxable year that 50 percent of the output of equipment is used to produce alcohol for production of whiskey and 50 percent is used to produce alcohol for use in a fuel mixture, such as gasohol. The alcohol production equipment qualifies as synthetic fuel equipment but only to the extent of one-half of its cost or basis. If, in a later taxable year, the equipment is used exclusively to produce whiskey, all of the equipment ceases to be synthetic fuel equipment.

(ii) A fuel is a material that produces usable heat upon combustion. To be "synthetic", the fuel either must differ significantly in chemical composition, as opposed to physical composition, from the alternate substance used to produce it or, in the case of solid fuel produced from biomass, the chemical change must consist of defiberization. Examples of synthetic fuels include alcohol derived from coal, peat, and vegetative matter, such as wood and corn, and methane from landfills.

(iii) Synthetic fuel equipment includes coal gasification equipment, coal liquefaction equipment, equipment for recovering methane from landfill, and equipment that converts biomass to a synthetic fuel.

(iv) Synthetic fuel equipment does not include equipment that merely mixes an alternate substance with another substance. For example, synthetic fuel equipment includes neither equipment that mixes coal and water to produce a slurry nor equipment that mixes alcohol and gasoline to produce gasohol. Equipment used to produce coke or coke gas, such as coke ovens, is also ineligible.

(6) *Modification equipment*. (i) Alternative energy property includes equipment (modification equipment) designed to modify existing equipment. For the definition of "existing," see paragraph (l)(1)(i) of this section. To be eligible , the modification must result in a substitution for the remainder of the taxable year from the date the equipment is placed in service and for each taxable year thereafter of the items in paragraph (c)(6)(ii)(A) or (B) of this section for all or a portion of the oil or gas substance used as a fuel or feedstock. As a result of the modification, the substituted alternate substance must comprise at least 25 percent of the fuel or feedstock (determined on the basis of Btu equivalency). If the modification also increases the capacity of the equipment, only the incremental cost (as defined in paragraph (k) of this section) of the equipment qualifies.

(ii) The substitutes for an oil or gas substance are—

(A) An alternate substance or

Reg. § 1.48-9(c)(3)

(B) A mixture of oil and an alternate substance.

(iii) Modification equipment does not include replacements or a boiler or burner. If the boiler or burner is replaced, the items must be described in paragraph (c)(3) or (4) of this section to qualify as alternative energy property. Modification may include, however, replacements of components of a boiler or burner, such as a heat exchanger.

(iv) The following examples illustrate this paragraph (c)(6).

Example (1). On January 1, 1980, corporation X is using oil to fuel its boiler. On June 1, 1980, X modifies the boiler to permit substitution of a coal and oil mixture for 40 percent of X's oil fuel needs. The mixture consists 75 percent of oil and 25 percent of coal. The equipment modifying the boiler does not qualify as modification equipment because the alternate substance comprises only 10 percent of the fuel.

Example (2). Assume the same facts as in example (1) except 75 percent of the mixture is coal. The equipment modifying the boiler qualifies.

Example (3). Assume the same facts as in example (2) except, instead of substituting an oil and coal mixture for 40 percent of X's oil fuel needs, X uses the modification to expand the boiler's fuel capacity by 40 percent using the mixture as additional fuel. The additional fuel mixture comprises only 28 percent of X's total fuel needs. Thus, even though 75 percent of the additional fuel mixture is an alternate substance, the boiler does not qualify as modification equipment because the alternate substance comprises only 21 percent of the total fuel.

(7) *Equipment using coal as feedstock*. Equipment that uses coal (including lignite) to produce a feedstock for the manufacture of chemicals, such as petrochemicals, or other products is alternative energy property. Equipment is not eligible if it is not directly involved in the treatment of coal or a coal product, but produces a substance that is, like coal, a basic feedstock or catalyst used in the coal conversion process. Equipment is not eligible if it is used beyond the point at which the first product marketable as a feedstock has been produced. Equipment used to produce coke or coke gas, such as coke ovens, is ineligible.

(8) *Pollution control equipment*. (i) Pollution control equipment is alternative energy property. Eligible equipment is limited to property or equipment to the extent it qualifies as a pollution control facility under section 103(b)(4)(F) and the regulations thereunder except that, if control of pollution is not the only significant purpose (within the meaning of those regulations), only the incremental cost (as defined in paragraph (k) of this section) of the equipment qualifies. However, if a Treasury decision changes the regulations under section 103(b)(4)(F) and, thus, the rules reflected in this subdivision (i), the rules as changed will apply as of the effective date of the Treasury decision.

(ii) To be eligible, the equipment must be required by a Federal, State, or local government regulation to be installed on, or used in connection with, eligible alternative energy property (as defined in paragraph (c)(8)(v) of this section).

(iii) Under section 48(l)(3)(D) equipment is not eligible if required by a Federal, State, or local government regulation in effect on October 1, 1978, to be installed on, or in connection with, property using coal (including lignite) as of October 1, 1978.

(iv) Under this subparagraph (8), pollution control equipment is required by regulation if it would be necessary to install the equipment to satisfy the requirements of any applicable law, including nuisance law. The pollution control equipment need not be specifically identified in the applicable law. If several different types of equipment may be used to comply with the applicable law, each type of equipment is considered necessary to satisfy the requirements of the law. An order permitting a taxpayer to delay compliance with any applicable law is disregarded.

(v) Under this subparagraph (8) "eligible alternative energy property" is energy property (as defined in section 48(l)(2)) described in paragraph (c)(3) through (7) of this section. If equipment otherwise qualifying as pollution control equipment is installed on, or used in connection with, both eligible alternative energy property and property other than eligible alternative energy property, only the incremental cost (as defined in paragraph (k) of this section) of the equipment qualifies.

(vi) *Examples*. The following examples illustrate this subparagraph (8). Assume that the property or equipment in the examples are described in § 1.103-8(g)(2)(ii) and that their only purpose is control of pollution.

Example (1). On October 1, 1978, corporation X acquires and places in service in State A a paper mill. The facility includes a boiler the primary fuel for which is wood chips. The facility includes equipment necessary to comply with pollution control standards in effect on October 1, 1978 in State A. This equipment qualifies as pollution control equipment.

Reg. § 1.48-9(c)(8)

Example (2). On October 1, 1978, corporation Y was burning coal at its facility in State B. The emissions from the facility exceeded State air pollution control requirements in effect on October 1, 1978. On January 1, 1979, X installed cyclone separators to comply with the State pollution control requirements. The cyclone separators do not qualify as pollution control equipment.

Example (3). Assume the same facts as in example (2) except that Y installs a baghouse instead of cyclone separators to meet more stringent standards that take effect on December 31, 1978. The baghouse qualifies as pollution control equipment because the baghouse was not necessary to meet the standards in effect on October 1, 1978.

Example (4). On October 1, 1978, corporation Z is burning coal at its facility in State C. The emissions from that facility exceed State air pollution control standards in effect on October 1, 1978. C orders Z to install cyclone separators before January 1, 1979. However, C allows Z to operate its facility until January 1, 1979, under less stringent interim standards applicable only to Z. The separators do not qualify as pollution control equipment. The delayed compliance order is disregarded.

(9) *Handling and preparation equipment.* (i) Alternative energy property includes equipment (handling and preparation equipment) used for unloading, transfer, storage, reclaiming from storage, or preparation of an alternate substance for use in eligible alternative energy property (as defined in paragraph (c)(9)(ii) of this section). Handling and preparation equipment must be located at the site the alternate substance is used as a fuel or feedstock. For example, equipment used to screen and prepare coal for use at a power plant qualifies if located at the plant. However, similar equipment located at the coal mine would not qualify.

(ii) Under this subparagraph (9), "eligible alternative energy property" is energy property (as defined in section 48(l)(2)) described in paragraph (c)(3) through (8) of this section. If equipment otherwise qualifying as handling and preparation equipment is installed on, or used in connection with, property other than eligible alternative energy property, only the incremental cost (as defined in paragraph (k) of this section) of the equipment qualifies.

(iii) The term "preparation" includes washing, crushing, drying, compacting, and weighing of an alternate substance. Handling and preparation equipment also includes equipment for shredding, chopping, pulverizing, or screening agricultural or forestry byproducts at the site of use.

(iv) Handling and preparation equipment does not include equipment, such as coal slurry pipelines and railroad cars, that transports a fuel or a feedstock to the site of its use.

(10) *Geothermal equipment*—(i) Alternative energy property includes equipment (geothermal equipment) that produces, distributes, or uses energy derived from a geothermal deposit (as defined in § 1.44C-2(h)).

(ii) In general, production equipment includes equipment necessary to bring geothermal energy from the subterranean deposit to the surface, including well-head and downhole equipment (such as screening or slotting liners, tubing, downhole pumps, and associated equipment). Reinjection wells required for production also may qualify. Production does not include exploration and development.

(iii) Distribution equipment includes equipment that transports geothermal steam or hot water from a geothermal deposit to the site of ultimate use. If geothermal energy is used to generate electricity, distribution equipment includes equipment that transports hot water from the geothermal deposit to a power plant. Distribution equipment also includes components of a heating system, such as pipes and ductwork that distribute within a building the energy derived from the geothermal deposit.

(iv) Geothermal equipment includes equipment that uses energy derived both from a geothermal deposit and from sources other than a geothermal deposit (dual use equipment). Such equipment, however, is geothermal equipment (A) only if its use of energy from sources other than a geothermal deposit does not exceed 25 percent of its total energy input in an annual measuring period and (B) only to the extent of its basis or cost allocable to its use of energy from a geothermal deposit during an annual measuring period. An "annual measuring period" for an item of dual use equipment is the 365 day period beginning with the day it is placed in service or a 365 day period beginning the day after the last day of the immediately preceding annual measuring period. The allocation of energy use required for purposes of paragraph (c)(10)(iv)(A) and (B) of this section may be made by comparing, on a Btu basis, energy input to dual use equipment from the geothermal deposit with energy input from other sources. However, the Commissioner may accept any other method that, in his opinion, accurately establishes the relative annual use by dual use equipment of energy derived from a geothermal deposit and energy derived from other sources.

(v) The existence of a backup system designed for use only in the event of a failure in the system providing energy derived from a geother-

Reg. § 1.48-9(c)(9)

mal deposit will not disqualify any other equipment. If geothermal energy is used to generate electricity, equipment using geothermal energy includes the electrical generating equipment, such as turbines and generators. However, geothermal equipment does not include any electrical transmission equipment, such as transmission lines and towers, or any equipment beyond the electrical transmission stage, such as transformers and distribution lines.

(vi) *Examples.* The following examples illustrate this subparagraph (10):

Example (1). On October 1, 1979, corporation X, a calendar year taxpayer, places in service a system which heats its office building by circulating hot water heated by energy derived from a geothermal deposit through the building. Geothermal equipment includes the circulation system, including the pumps and pipes which circulate the hot water through the building.

Example (2). The facts are the same as in Example (1), except that corporation X also places in service a boiler to produce hot water for heating the building exclusively in the event of a failure of the geothermal equipment. Such a boiler is not geothermal equipment, but the existence of such a backup system does not serve to disqualify property eligible in Example (1).

Example (3). The facts are the same as in Example (1), except that the water heated by energy derived from a geothermal deposit is not hot enough to provide sufficient heat for the building. Therefore, the system includes an electric boiler in which the water is heated before being circulated in the heating system. Assume that, on a Btu basis, eighty percent of the total energy input to the circulating system during the 365 day period beginning on October 1, 1979, is energy derived from a geothermal deposit. The boiler is not geothermal equipment. For the 1979 taxable year, eighty percent of the circulating system is geothermal equipment because eighty percent of its basis or cost is allocable to use of energy from a geothermal deposit. If, in a subsequent taxable year, the basis or cost allocable to use of energy from a geothermal deposit falls below eighty percent, recapture may be required under section 47 and § 1.47-1(h). Thus, if, on a Btu basis, only 70 percent of the total energy input to the circulating system for the 365 day period beginning October 1, 1980, is energy derived from a geothermal deposit, then there will be complete recapture of the credit during the

1980 taxable year. If, however, for that 365 day period, the portion of the total energy input that is derived from a geothermal deposit is less than 80 percent but greater than or equal to 75 percent, then only a proportional amount of credit will be recaptured during the 1980 taxable year. No additional credit is allowable in a subsequent taxable year, however, if the portion of the basis or cost allocable to use of energy from a geothermal deposit increases above what it was for a previous taxable year (see § 1.46-3(d)(4)(i)).

Example (4). Corporation Y acquires a commercial vegetable dehydration system in 1981. The system operates by placing fresh vegetables on a conveyor belt and moving them through a dryer. The conveyor belt is powered by electricity. The dryer uses solely energy derived from a geothermal deposit. The dryer is geothermal equipment while the equipment powered by electricity does not qualify.

(d) *Solar energy property*—(1) *In general.* Energy property includes solar energy property. The term "solar energy property" includes equipment and materials (and parts related to the functioning of such equipment) that use solar energy directly to (i) generate electricity, (ii) heat or cool a building or structure, or (iii) provide hot water for use within a building or structure. Generally, those functions are accomplished through the use of equipment such as collectors (to absorb sunlight and create hot liquids or air), storage tanks (to store hot liquids), rockbeds (to store hot air), thermostats (to activate pumps or fans which circulate the hot liquids or air), and heat exchangers (to utilize hot liquids or air to create hot air or water). Property that uses, as an energy source, fuel or energy derived indirectly from solar energy, such as ocean thermal energy, fossil fuel, or wood, is not considered solar energy property.

(2) *Passive solar excluded*—(i) Solar energy property excludes the materials and components of "passive solar systems," even if combined with "active solar systems."

(ii) An active solar system is based on the use of mechanically forced energy transfer, such as the use of fans or pumps to circulate solar generated energy.

(iii) A passive system is based on the use of conductive, convective, or radiant energy transfer. Passive solar property includes greenhouses, solariums, roof ponds, glazing, and mass or water trombe walls.

Reg. § 1.48-9(d)(2)

(3) *Electric generation equipment.* Solar energy property includes equipment that uses solar energy to generate electricity, and includes storage devices, power conditioning equipment, transfer equipment, and parts related to the functioning of those items. In general, this process involves the transformation of sunlight into electricity through the use of such devices as solar cells or other collectors. However, solar energy property used to generate electricity includes only equipment up to (but not including) the stage that transmits or uses electricity.

(4) *Pipes and ducts.* Pipes and ducts that are used exclusively to carry energy derived from solar energy are solar energy property. Pipes and ducts that are used to carry both energy derived from solar energy and energy derived from other sources are solar energy property (i) only if their use of energy other than solar energy does not exceed 25 percent of their total energy input in an annual measuring period and (ii) only to the extent of their basis or cost allocable to their use of solar energy during an annual measuring period. (See paragraph (d)(6) of this section for the definition of "annual measuring period" and for rules relating to the method of allocation.)

(5) *Specially adapted equipment.* Equipment that uses solar energy beyond the distribution stage is eligible only if specially adapted to use solar energy.

(6) *Auxiliary equipment.* Solar energy property does not include equipment (auxiliary equipment), such as furnaces and hot water heaters, that use a source of power other than solar or wind energy to provide usable energy. Solar energy property does include equipment, such as ducts and hot water tanks, which is utilized by both auxiliary equipment and solar energy equipment (dual use equipment). Such equipment is solar energy property (i) only if its use of energy from sources other than solar energy does not exceed 25 percent of its total energy input in an annual measuring period and (ii) only to the extent of its basis or cost allocable to its use of solar or wind energy during an annual measuring period. An "annual measuring period" for an item of dual use equipment is the 365 day period beginning with the day it is placed in service or a 365 day period beginning the day after the last day of the immediately preceding annual measuring period. The allocation of energy use required for purposes of paragraph (d)(6)(i) and (ii) of this section may be made by comparing, on a Btu basis, energy input to dual use equipment from solar energy with energy input from other sources. However, the Commissioner may accept any other method that, in his opinion, accurately establishes the relative annual use by dual use equipment of solar energy and energy derived from other sources.

(7) *Solar process heat equipment.* Solar energy property does not include equipment that uses solar energy to generate steam at high temperatures for use in industrial or commercial processes (solar process heat).

(8) *Example.* The following example illustrates this paragraph (d).

Example. (a) In 1979, corporation X, a calendar year taxpayer, constructs an apartment building and purchases equipment to convert solar energy into heat for the building. Corporation X also installs an oil-fired water heater and other equipment to provide a backup source of heat when the solar energy equipment cannot meet the energy needs of the building. For purposes of this example, all equipment is placed in service on October 1, 1979. On a Btu basis, eighty percent of the total energy input to the dual use equipment during the 365 day period beginning October 1, 1979, is from solar energy.

(b) The items purchased, in addition to the water heater, include a roof solar collector, a heat exchanger, a hot water tank, a control component, pumps, pipes, fan-coil units, and valves. Assume the fan-coil units could be used with energy derived from an oil or gas substance without significant modification. All items are depreciable and have a useful life of three years or more. The use of the equipment to heat the building is the first use to which the equipment has been put.

(c) Water is pumped from the basement through pipes to the roof solar collector. Heated water returns through pipes to a heat exchanger which transfers heat to the water in the hot water tank.

(d) The hot water tank and the oil-fired water heater utilize the same distribution pipe. Pumps and valves at the points of connection between the hot water tank, the oil-fired water heater, and the distribution pipe regulate the auxiliary energy supply use. They also prevent the oil-fired water heater from heating water in the hot water tank.

(e) An integrated control component determines whether hot water from the hot water tank or from the oil-fired water heater is distributed to fan-coil units located throughout the building.

(f) The roof solar collector is solar energy property. The pump that moves the water to the roof collector and the pipes between the roof collector and the hot water tank qualify because they are solely related to transporting solar heated water. The hot water tank qualifies because it stores water heated solely by solar radiation. The heat exchanger also qualifies.

(g) The oil-fired water heater does not qualify as solar energy property because it is auxiliary equipment.

(h) (i) Because the distribution pipe, the control component, and the pumps and valves serve the oil-fired water heater as well as the solar energy equipment, they qualify only to the extent of eighty percent of their cost or basis, the portion allocable to use of solar energy. If, in a subsequent taxable year, the basis or cost allocable to their use of solar energy falls below eighty percent, recapture may be required under section 47 and § 1.47-1(h). Thus, if, on a Btu basis, only 70 percent of the total energy input to that equipment for the 365 day period beginning October 1, 1980, is from solar energy, then there will be complete recapture of the credit during the 1980 taxable year. If, however, for that 365 day period, the portion of that equipment's total energy input that is from solar energy is less than 80 percent but greater than or equal to 75 percent, then only a proportional amount of credit will be recaptured during the 1980 taxable year. No additional credit is allowable for that equipment in a subsequent taxable year, however, if the portion of its basis or cost allocable to use of solar energy increases above what it was for a previous taxable year (see § 1.46-3(d)(4)(i)).

(ii) The fan-coil units do not qualify as solar energy property because they are not specially adapted to use energy derived from solar energy.

(e) *Wind energy property*—(1) *In general.* Energy property includes wind energy property. Wind energy property is equipment (and parts related to the functioning of that equipment) that performs a function described in paragraph (e)(2) of this section. In general, wind energy property consists of a windmill, wind-driven generator, storage devices, power conditioning equipment, transfer equipment, and parts related to the functioning of those items. Wind energy property does not include equipment that transmits or uses electricity derived from wind energy. In addition, limitations apply similar to those set forth in paragraph (d)(5), (6), and (8) of this section. For example, if equipment is used by both auxiliary equipment and wind energy equipment, such equipment is wind energy property only if its use of energy other than wind energy does not exceed 25 percent of its total energy input in an annual measuring period and only to the extent of its basis or cost allocable to its use of wind energy during an annual measuring period.

(2) *Eligible functions.* Wind energy property is limited to equipment (and parts related to the functioning of that equipment) that—

(i) Uses wind energy to heat or cool, or provide hot water for use in, a building or structure, or

(ii) Uses wind energy to generate electricity (but not mechanical forms of energy).

(f) *Specially defined energy property*—(1) *In general.* Specially defined energy property means only those items described in paragraph (f)(4) through (14) of this section that meet the requirements of paragraph (f)(2) of this section. The items described in paragraph (f)(4) through (14) of this section also consist of related equipment, such as fans, pumps, ductwork, piping, and controls, the installation of which is necessary for the specified item to reduce the energy consumed or heat wasted by the process.

(2) *General requirements* To be eligible, each item described in paragraph (f)(4) through (14) of this section must be installed in connection with an existing industrial or commercial facility. In addition, the principal purpose of each of those items must be reduction of energy consumed or heat wasted in any existing industrial or commercial process. See section 48(l)(10) and paragraph (l) of this section. If an item performs more than one function, only the incremental cost (as defined in paragraph (k) of this section) of this equipment qualifies.

(3) *Industrial or commercial process.* (i) A process is a means or method of producing a desired result by chemical, physical, or mechanical action. For example, equipment installed in connection with retail sales, general office use, and residential use are not used in a process within the meaning of this paragraph (f)(3).

(ii) An industrial process includes agricultural processes and thermal processes relating to production or manufacture, such as those involving boilers and furnaces.

(iii) A commercial process includes laundering and food preparation.

(iv) More than one process may be conducted in a single facility. The fact that several processes involved in the production of a product are integrated does not cause such integrated processes to be treated as one process. For example, in a food canning facility, producing prepared food from fresh vegetables is not one process but rather an integration of several processes including washing, cooking and canning.

(v) The following example illustrates this paragraph (f)(3).

Reg. § 1.48-9(f)(3)

Example. Corporation X, an advertising agency, acquires an automatic energy control system designed to reduce energy consumed by heating and cooling its office building. Although the use of an office for X's business is a commercial activity, heating or cooling an office is not an industrial or commercial process. The automatic energy control system does not qualify because it does not reduce energy consumed in an industrial or commercial process.

(4) *Recuperators.* Recuperators recover energy, usually in the form of waste heat from combustion exhaust gases, hot exiting product, or product cooling air, that is used to heat incoming combustion air, raw materials, or fuel. Recuperators are configurations of equipment consisting in part of fixed heat transfer surfaces between two gas flows, and include related baffles, dividers, entrance flanges, transition sections, and shells or cases enclosing the other components of the recuperator. In general, a fixed heat transfer surface absorbs heat from a gas or liquid flow or dissipates heat to the gas or liquid flow.

(5) *Heat wheels.* Heat wheels recover energy, usually in the form of waste heat, from exhaust gases to preheat incoming gases. Heat wheels are items of equipment consisting in part of regenerators (which rotate between two gas flows) and related drive components, wiper seals, entrance flanges, and transition sections.

(6) *Regenerators.* Regenerators are devices, such as clinker columns or chains, that recover energy by efficiently storing heat while exposed to high temperature gases and releasing heat while exposed to low temperature gases, fluids, or solids.

(7) *Heat exchangers.* Heat exchangers recover energy, usually in the form of waste heat, from high temperature gases, liquids, or solids for transfer to low temperature gases, liquids, or solids. Heat exchangers consist in part of fixed heat transfer surfaces (described in paragraph (f)(4) of this section) separating two media. Heat exchange equipment does not include fluidized bed combustion equipment.

(8) *Waste heat boilers.* Waste heat boilers use waste heat, usually in the form of combustion exhaust gases, as a substantial source of energy. A substantial source of energy is one that comprises more than 20 percent of the energy requirement on the basis of Btu's during the course of each taxable year (including the start-up year).

(9) *Heat pipes.* Heat pipes recover energy, usually in the form of waste heat, from high temperature fluids to heat low temperature fluids. A heat pipe consists in part of sealed heat transfer chambers and a capillary structure. In general, the heat transfer chambers alternatively vaporize and condense a working fluid as it passes from one end of the chamber to the other.

(10) *Automatic energy control systems.* Automatic energy control systems automatically reduce energy consumed in an industrial or commercial process for such purposes as environmental space conditioning (*i.e.,* lighting, heating, cooling or ventilating, etc.). Automatic energy control systems include, for example, automatic equipment settings controls, load shedding devices, and relay devices used as part of such system. Property such as computer hardware installed as a part of the energy control system also qualifies, but only to the extent of its incremental cost (as defined in paragraph (k) of this section).

(11) *Turbulators.* Turbulators increase the rate of transfer of heat from combustion gases to heat exchange surfaces by increasing the turbulence in the gases. A turbulator is a baffle placed in a boiler firetube or in a heat exchange tube in industrial process equipment to deflect gases to the heat transfer surface.

(12) *Preheaters.* Preheaters recover energy, usually in the form of waste heat, from either combustion exhaust gases or steam, to preheat incoming combustion air or boiler feedwater. A preheater consists in part of fixed heat transfer surfaces (described in paragraph (f)(4) of this section) separating two fluids.

(13) *Combustible gas recovery systems.* Combustible gas recovery systems are items of equipment used to recover unburned fuel from combustion exhaust gases.

(14) *Economizers.* Economizers are configurations of equipment used to reduce energy demand or recover energy from combustion exhaust gases and other high temperature sources to preheat boiler feedwater.

(15) *Other property added by the Secretary.* [Reserved]

(g) *Recycling equipment* —(1) *In general.* Recycling equipment is equipment used exclusively to sort and prepare, or recycle, solid waste (other than animal waste) to recover usable raw materials ("recovery equipment") or to convert solid waste (including animal waste) into fuel or other useful forms of energy ("conversion equipment"). Recycling equipment may include certain other onsite related equipment.

(2) *Recovery equipment.* Recovery equipment includes equipment that—

(i) Separates solid waste from a mixture of waste,

(ii) Applies a thermal, mechanical, or chemical treatment to solid waste to ensure the waste will properly respond to recycling, or

(iii) Recycles solid waste to recover usable raw materials, but not beyond occurrence of the first of the following:

(A) The point at which a material has been created that can be used in beginning the fabrication of an end-product in the same way as materials from a virgin substance. Examples are the fiber stage in textile recycling, the newsprint or paperboard stage in paper recycling, and the ingot stage for other metals (other than iron and steel). In the case of recycling iron or steel, recycling equipment does not include any equipment used to reduce solid waste to a molten state or any process thereafter.

(B) The point at which the material is a marketable product (*i.e.*, has a value other than for recycling) even if the material is not marketed by the taxpayer at that point.

(3) *Conversion equipment.* Conversion equipment includes equipment that converts solid waste into a fuel or other usable energy, but not beyond the point at which a fuel, steam, electricity, hot water, or other useful form of energy has been created. Thus, combustors, boilers, and similar equipment may be eligible if used for a conversion process, but steam and heat distribution systems between the combustor or boiler and the point of use are not eligible.

(4) *On-site related equipment.* Recycling equipment also includes onsite loading and transportation equipment, such as conveyors, integrally related to other recycling equipment. This equipment may include equipment to load solid waste into a sorting or preparation machine and also a conveyor belt system that transports solid waste from preparation equipment to other equipment in the recycling process.

(5) *Solid waste.* (i) The term "solid waste" has the same meaning as in § 1.103-8(f)(2)(ii)(*b*), subject to the following exceptions and the other rules of this subparagraph (5):

(A) The date the equipment is placed in service is substituted in the first sentence of § 1.103-8(f)(2)(ii)(*b*) for the date of issue of the obligations, and

(B) Material that has a market value at the place it is located only by reason of its value for recycling is not considered to have a market value.

(ii) Solid waste may include a nominal amount of virgin materials, liquids, or gases, not to exceed 10 percent. If more than 10 percent of the material recycled during the course of any taxable year (including the "start up" year) consists of virgin material, liquids, or gases, the equipment ceases to be energy property and is subject to recapture under section 47. The determination of the portion of virgin material, liquids, or gases used is based on volume, weight, or Btu's, whichever is appropriate.

(6) *Ineligible equipment.* Transportation equipment, such as trucks, that transfer solid waste between geographically separated sites (*e.g.*, the collection point and the recycling point) is not eligible. Steam and heat distribution systems are also ineligible.

(7) *Increased recycling capacity.* If the equipment both replaces recycling capacity and increases that capacity at a particular site, only the incremental cost (as defined in paragraph (k) of this section) of increasing the capacity qualifies. Recycling capacity is determined by the ability to produce a product not previously produced by the taxpayer, or more of an existing product, in a way that does not lower overall production.

(8) *Examples.* The following examples illustrate this paragraph (g).

Example (1). Corporation W recycles aluminum scrap metal. W owns a junk yard where it collects and crushes the metal into compact units. W's trucks bring the scrap metal from the junk yard to its main plant located 3 miles away. W's furnace equipment at the main plant reduces the scrap to the molten state and W's rolling equipment rolls the aluminum into sheets. The furnace qualifies, but for two separate reasons the rolling equipment does not qualify. First, the molten aluminum would be a marketable product if reduced to ingots prior to rolling. It is not necessary that W actually reduce the molten aluminum to ingots. Second, the molten aluminum could be used in the same way as virgin material.

Example (2). Corporation X manufactures newsprint using wood chips discarded during X's lumber operations. Assume X could sell the wood chips to other companies located a short distance from X's mill for use as a fuel. None of the equipment used to manufacture the newsprint qualifies.

Example (3). Assume the same facts as in example (2) except X uses old newspapers which have no value except for recycling in the area where X's mill is located. The equipment qualifies.

Example (4). Corporation Y recycles municipal waste. Assume the municipal waste is "solid waste" under paragraph (g)(5) of this section. During the first taxable year Y operates the equipment, Y uses 8,500 pounds of municipal waste and 1,500 pounds of virgin material and liquids. No energy credit is allowed for the equipment.

Reg. § 1.48-9(g)(8)

Example (5). Corporation Z owns a waste recovery facility. The corrugated paper portion of the waste stream is picked off a conveyor as it enters the facility. The corrugated paper is baled and sold as a secondary paper product. Z acquires shredding and air-classification equipment. Corrugated paper that is not removed from the conveyor belt enters the new equipment for production as a fuel. Z increases the input of corrugated paper so that the same amount of corrugated paper is removed from the conveyor to be baled. The excess paper that is not removed for baling enters the shredding and air-classification equipment. The new equipment qualifies.

(h) *Shale oil equipment* —(1) *In general.* Shale oil equipment used in mining or either surface or *in situ* processing qualifies as energy property. Shale oil equipment means equipment used exclusively to mine, or produce or extract oil from, shale rock.

(2) *Eligible processes.* In general, processing equipment qualifies if used in or after the mining stage and up through the retorting process. Thus, eligible processes include crushing, loading into the retort, and retorting, but not hydrogenation, refining, or any process subsequent to retorting. However, with respect to *in situ* processing, eligible processes include creating the underground cavity.

(3) *Eligible equipment.* Shale oil equipment includes—

(i) Heading jumbos, bulldozers, and scaling and bolting rigs used to create an underground cavity for *in situ* processing.

(ii) On-site water supply and treatment equipment and handling equipment for spent shale.

(iii) Crushing and screening plant equipment, such as hoppers, feeders, vibrating screens, and conveyors.

(iv) Briqueting plant equipment, such as hammer mills and vibratory pan feeders, and

(v) Retort equipment, including direct cooling and condensing equipment.

(i) [Reserved]

(j) *Natural gas from geopressured brine.* Equipment used exclusively to extract natural gas from geopressured brine described in section 613A(b)(3)(C)(i) is energy property. Eligible equipment includes equipment used to separate the gas from saline water and remove other impurities from the gas. Equipment is eligible only up to the point the gas may be introduced into a pipeline.

(k) *Incremental cost.* The term "incremental cost" means the excess of the total cost of equipment over the amount that would have been expended for the equipment if the equipment were not used for a qualifying purpose. For example, assume equipment costing $100 performs a pollution control function and another function. Assuming it would cost $60 solely to perform the nonqualifying function, the incremental cost would be $40.

(l) *Existing*—(1) *In general.* For purposes of section 48(l), the term "existing" means—

(i) When used in connection with a facility or equipment, 50 percent or more of the basis of that facility or equipment is attributable to construction, reconstruction, or erection before October 1, 1978, or

(ii) When used in connection with an industrial or commercial process, that process was carried on in the facility as of October 1, 1978.

(2) *Industrial or commercial process.* (i) A process will be considered the same as the process carried on in the facility as of October 1, 1978, unless and until capitalizable expenditures are paid or incurred for modification of the process. The expenditures need not be capitalized in fact; it is sufficient if the taxpayer has an option or may elect to capitalize. In general, the date of change will be the date the expenditures are properly chargeable to capital account. If the taxpayer properly elects to expense a capitalizable expenditure, the date of change will be the date the expenditure could have been properly chargeable to capital account if the expenditure had been capitalized. Recapture will not occur by reason of a change in a process unless the process change also changes the use of the equipment. See example (1) of § 1.47-1(h)(5).

(m) *Quality and performance standards*—(1) *In general.* Energy property must meet quality and performance standards, if any, that have been prescribed by the Secretary (after consultation with the Secretary of Energy) and are in effect at the time of acquisition.

(2) *Time of acquisition.* Under this paragraph (m) the time of acquisition is—

(i) The date the taxpayer enters into a binding contract to acquire the property or

(ii) For property constructed, reconstructed, or erected by the taxpayer, (A) the earlier of the date it begins construction, reconstruction, or erection of the property, or (B) the date the taxpayer and another person enter into a binding contract requiring each to construct, reconstruct, or erect property and place the property in service for an agreed upon use. See example under paragraph (m)(4) of this section.

Reg. § 1.48-9(h)(1)

(3) *Binding contract.* Under this paragraph (m), a binding contract to construct, reconstruct, or erect property, or to acquire property, is a contract that is binding at all times on the taxpayer under applicable State or local law. A binding contract to construct, reconstruct, or erect property or to acquire property, does not include a contract for preparation of architect's sketches, blueprints, or performance of any other activity not involving the beginning of physical work.

(4) *Example.* The following example illustrates this paragraph (m).

Example. Corporation X owns a junk yard. Corporation Y manufactures recycling equipment and operates several recycling facilities. On January 1, 1979, X and Y enter into a written contract that is binding on both parties on that date and at all times thereafter. Under the contract's terms X will supply scrap metals to Y and Y agrees in return to build a recycling facility on land adjacent to the junk yard. Y will own and operate the facility using the scrap metal supplied by X, Y may treat the agreement as a binding contract under paragraph (m)(2) and (3) of this section.

(n) *Public utility property*—(1) *Inclusions.* Public utility property is included in both of the following categories of energy property:

(i) Shale oil equipment and

(ii) Equipment for producing natural gas from geopressured brine.

(2) *Exclusions.* Public utility property is excluded from each of the following categories of energy property:

(i) Alternative energy property,

(ii) Specially defined energy property,

(iii) Solar or wind energy property, and

(iv) Recycling equipment.

(3) *Public utility property.* The term "public utility property " has the meaning given in section 46(f)(5).

(o) [Reserved].

(p) [Reserved].

(q) *Qualified intercity buses*—(1) *In general.* This paragraph (q) prescribes rules and definitions for purposes of section 48(l)(2)(A)(ix) and (16). Energy property includes qualified intercity buses of an eligible taxpayer, but only to the extent of the increase in the taxpayer's total operating seating capacity (operating capacity) under paragraphs (q)(9), (10), and (11) of this section. For application of recapture rules see § 1.47-1(h)(3)(ii).

(2) *Eligible taxpayer.* A taxpayer is an eligible taxpayer only if it is determined to be both—

(i) A common carrier regulated by the Interstate Commerce Commission or an appropriate State agency and

(ii) Engaged in the trade or business of furnishing intercity transportation by bus.

(3) *Common carrier.* The taxpayer is a common carrier only if the taxpayer holds itself out to the general public as providing passenger bus transportation for compensation over regular or irregular routes, or both.

(4) *Appropriate State agency.* A State agency is appropriate only if it has both—

(i) Power to regulate intrastate transportation provided by a motor carrier, within the meaning of section 10521(b)(1) of the Revised Interstate Commerce Act (49 U.S.C. 10521(b)(1)), and

(ii) Power to initiate an exemption proceeding under section 1025(b) of that Act (49 U.S.C. 10525(b)).

(5) *Intercity transportation.* Intercity transportation means intercity passenger transportation or intercity passenger charter service. Intercity transportation does not include transportation provided entirely within a municipality, contiguous municipalities, or within a zone that is adjacent to, and commercially a part of, the municipality or municipalities (within the meaning of section 10526(b)(1)) of the Revised Interstate Commerce Act (49 U.S.C. 10526(b)(1)). See 49 CFR Part 1048 regulations defining commercial zones under that statute).

(6) *Definition of qualified intercity bus.* A qualified intercity bus (qualifying bus) is an automobile bus—

(i) The chassis and body of which are exempt (under section 4063(a)(6)) from the 10-percent excise tax generally imposed under section 4061(a) on trucks and buses.

(ii) With a seating capacity of at least 36 passengers (in addition to the driver).

(iii) With one or more baggage compartments, in an area separated from the passenger area, with an aggregate capacity of at least 200 cubic feet, and

(iv) Which meets the predominant use test.

(7) *Predominant use test.* (i) A bus meets the predominant use test for a taxable year only if it meets the following conditions:

(A) It is used on a full-time basis during the taxable year, and

(B) At least 70 percent of the total miles driven are driven while furnishing intercity transportation.

Reg. § 1.48-9(q)(7)

(ii) A bus driven from the end point of one trip to the beginning point of another trip ("deadheading"), both of which furnish intercity transportation of passengers, will be considered to have been driven while furnishing intercity transportation of passengers, even if no passengers are carried.

(iii) A bus is considered used on a full-time basis in a taxable year if it was driven 10,000 miles in that year. If available, the best evidence of annual mileage is the difference between odometer readings at the beginning and end of each taxable year. If the bus was placed in service during the taxable year, or for a short taxable year described in section 441(b)(3), that 10,000 mile figure is prorated on a daily basis.

(iv) If a qualifying bus fails to meet the predominant use test in a taxable year, a cessation occurs in that taxable year. See § 1.47-1(h)(3)(ii).

(v) The following examples illustrate this paragraph (q)(7):

Example (1). X, a bus company, used a bus for trips between city M and city N, a distance of 100 miles. These trips qualify as furnishing intercity transportation. During the taxable year, 300 round trips were run carrying passengers both ways and 75 trips were run carrying passengers from city M to city N immediately after each of which the bus was returned to city M for the next trip. The bus was also driven 20,000 miles to furnish passenger service which was local transportation. During the taxable year, the bus was driven a total of 100,000 miles. X makes the following calculations to determine if it met the predominant use test for the taxable year.

1. Total miles driven 100,000
2. Intercity miles driven:
    a. Passenger round trips (100 × 2 × 300) 60,000
    b. Passenger one-way (75 × 100) ... 7,500
    c. Non-passenger return trips (75 × 100) 7,500
3. Total intercity passenger miles (sum of lines 2a, b, and c) 75,000
4. 70% of line 1 70,000

Since line 1 is not less than 10,000 miles, the full-time use requirement is met. Since line 3 is greater than line 4, the 70 percent intercity mileage test is met. Thus, for the taxable year, the bus meets the predominant use test in paragraph (q)(7)(i) of this section.

Example (2). The facts are the same as in example (1), except that the bus was placed in service on the last day of the taxable year. The bus was used only to run one round trip, carrying passengers, between cities M and N. 10,000 miles

× one day ÷ 365 days = 27.4 miles. Because, for the one day of the taxable year that the bus was in service, the bus was driven more than 27.4 miles, and all these miles were driven to furnish intercity transportation, it met the predominant use test for the taxable year.

(8) *Leased buses.* (i) A bus which is leased is energy property only if it meets the requirements of paragraph (q)(6)(i), (ii), and (iii) of this section, the lessee is an eligible taxpayer, and the bus meets the predominant use test in the hands of the lessee. If a leased bus is energy property, the energy credit is available only to the lessee unless paragraph (q)(8)(ii) of this section applies. The lessor must elect under section 48(d) for the lessee to claim the energy credit.

(ii) If a leased bus is energy property and, on or before October 9, 1984, either (A) the lessor and lessee enter into a lease and the lessee places the bus in service, or (B) the bus is not placed in service but the lessor and lessee enter into a binding contract under which the amount of the lease payments cannot be modified, then the energy credit is available to the lessor even if the lessor is not an eligible taxpayer.

(iii) Notwithstanding § 1.47-2(b)(1) (relating to the effect of a disposition by the lessee on the credit claimed by the lessor), if, by reason of a lease or the termination of a lease, a bus is used in a taxable year subsequent to the credit year by a person other than the one whose increase in operating capacity determined the amount of qualified investment for the energy credit, a disposition of the bus under § 1.47-1(h)(2) results. However, if the energy credit for a bus was earned in a taxable year and a lease of the bus which qualifies under section 168(f)(8) (safe-harbor lease) is entered into in a subsequent taxable year, the safe-harbor lease is not a disposition of the bus and the lessee under that lease is treated as the lessee for purposes of this paragraph (q)(8). For the requirement to file an amended return if the energy credit was allowed in a prior taxable year, see § 5c.168(f)(8)-6(b)(2)(ii), (Temporary Income Tax Regulations under the Economic Recovery Tax Act of 1981). For the rule for determining whose operating capacity determines qualified investment for the energy credit, see paragraph (q)(9)(ii) of this section. For the rule for leases to related taxpayers, see paragraph (q)(10)(ii) of this section.

(9) *Operating capacity.* (i) Qualified investment for a qualifying bus is taken into account for the energy credit only to the extent the bus increases the taxpayer's operating capacity. To increase operating capacity, a bus must be counted in operating capacity. The increase in a tax-

Reg. § 1.48-9(q)(8)

payer's operating capacity is the excess of the taxpayer's operating capacity for the current taxable year over its operating capacity for the immediately preceding taxable year. Related taxpayers determine operating capacity on a group basis under paragraph (q)(10) of this section.

(ii) Operating capacity for a particular taxable year is determined by adding together the seating capacities of all intercity buses used by the taxpayer in that year and still owned by the taxpayer at the end of that year. An intercity bus is a bus which meets the chassis and body test and the predominant use test in paragraph (q)(6) of this section whether or not the bus is still in use at the end of the taxable year. In the case of a leased bus to which paragraph (q)(8) of this section applies, the lessee's operating capacity determines qualified investment for the energy credit.

(iii) The qualified investment for the energy credit for a qualifying bus is the bus's qualified investment for the regular credit multiplied by a fraction. The numerator of the fraction is the increase in the taxpayer's operating capacity for the taxable year. The denominator is the added operating capacity for the taxable year. Added operating capacity for the taxable year is determined for a taxpayer by adding together the seating capacities of the taxpayer's intercity buses included in operating capacity for the taxable year which were not included in operating capacity for the immediately preceding taxable year.

(iv) In the case of a partnership, each partner's qualified investment for the energy credit for a qualifying bus is the partner's qualified investment for the regular credit (determined under § 1.46-3(f) multiplied by the fraction referred to in paragraph (q)(9)(iii) of this section for the partnership, as determined for the partnership taxable year in which the bus is placed in service.

(v) The following example illustrates this paragraph (q)(9):

Example. Corporation Y is a calendar year bus company that is an eligible taxpayer under paragraph (q)(2) of this section. Based upon the facts as set forth in the following table, Y makes the following calculations to determine the energy credit earned in 1981:

1. 1980 operating capacity determined as of 12/31/80:
   a. 5 intercity buses × 50 seats each 250
   b. Total 1980 operating capacity 250
2. 1981 operating capacity determined as of 12/31/81:
   a. 2 1980 buses used on a full-time basis in 1981 100
   b. 1981 added capacity:
      i. Qualifying buses:
         Bus 1 45
         Bus 2 55
         Bus 3 50
      ii. Intercity bus not a qualifying bus ... 50
      iii. Total 1981 added capacity 200
   c. Total 1981 operating capacity 300
3. 1981 increase in operating capacity (line 2c − line 1b) 50
4. Fraction for determining qualified investment attributable to increase in capacity (line 3 + line 2(b)(iii)) 1/4

Accordingly, the energy credit earned in 1981 for each of the qualifying buses is determined as follows:

Qualified investment for the regular credit	×	Line 4	×	Energy percentage	=	Energy credit earned
Bus 1: $15,000		1/4		10		$375
Bus 2: $20,000		1/4		10		500
Bus 3: $25,000		1/4		10		625

Total energy credit earned in 1981 .... $1,500

(10) *Related taxpayers.* (i) Related taxpayers are treated as one taxpayer in determining the increase in operating capacity under paragraph (q)(9)(ii) of this section and in determining the qualified investment in qualified intercity buses for the energy credit under paragraph (q)(9)(iii) of this section. Related taxpayers are members of a group of trades or businesses that are under common control (as defined in § 1.52-1(b)).

(ii) Related taxpayers make all computations relating to operating capacity on a group basis. Also, the determination of whether a bus meets the predominant use test is made on a group basis by aggregating bus usage by each member of the group. For example, if a bus is acquired by one member and used by that member for part of a taxable year and used by other members for the remainder, the combined usage is aggregated in determining whether the predominant use test is met. In addition, all related taxpayers are treated as one person in applying paragraph (q)(8) of this section (relating to leasing).

(iii) The energy credit earned for a qualifying bus is allocated to the member which acquired (or is a lessee treated under section 48(d) as having acquired) the bus whether or not that member had a separate increase in operating capacity for the taxable year.

(iv) Each member must make its own computation of the group's increase in operating capacity for the period comprising its taxable year. A member will make this computation as of the end of its taxable year ignoring different taxable years of other members. For the period comprising its taxable year, the member makes all calculations relating to group operating capacity, including the determination of full-time use by other members.

(v) Each member determines the composition of the group as of the end of that member's taxable year. For example, if X uses the calendar year and makes its computation as of December 31, 1981, and Y is a member of X's group at that time, Y's operating capacity determined as of the end of X's immediately preceding taxable year (December 31, 1980) is taken into account by X for 1980 even if Y was not a member of the group for any day prior to December 31, 1981.

(vi) The following example illustrates this paragraph (q)(10):

Example (a). Corporations X and Y are related taxpayers. In this example, each bus is a qualifying bus with a seating capacity of 50. Each bus owned at the close of either X's or Y's taxable year was used on a full-time basis for the relevant period corresponding to X's or Y's taxable year. Other facts are set forth in the following table:

	X	Y
Taxable year ends	Dec. 31.	June 30.
Operating capacity for 1979.	5 buses	10 buses.
Buses added	3 buses Mar. 1, 1980..	3 buses May 15, 1981.
Buses sold	2 buses Mar. 31, 1981..	2 buses Sept. 30, 1980.
Cost of each added bus	$40,000	$60,000

(b) X makes the following calculations to determine the energy credit earned for calendar year 1980.

1. 1979 operating capacity determined as of 12/31/79:
   a. Attributable to X (5 buses × 50 seats) .. 250
   b. Attributable to Y (10 buses × 50 seats) . 500

   c. Total 1979 operating capacity 750
2. 1980 operating capacity determined as of 12/31/80:
   a. X's 5 and Y's 8 1979 buses used on a full-time basis in 1980 and still owned on 12/31/80 650
   b. 1980 added capacity (X's 3 buses × 50 seats) 150

   c. Total 1980 operating capacity 800
3. 1980 increase in operating capacity (line 2c − line 1c) 50
4. Fraction in paragraph (q)(9)(iii) of this section (line 3 ÷ line 2b) 1/3

Accordingly, X earned an energy credit of $4,000 in 1980 ($40,000 × 1/3 × 10% × 3 buses).

(c) Since in calendar year 1981 X placed no qualifying buses in service, X earned no energy credit in 1981.

(d) Since in the taxable year 7/1/79-6/30/80 Y placed no qualifying buses in service, Y earned no energy credit in that taxable year.

(e) Y makes the following calculations to determine the energy credit earned in the taxable year 7/1/80-6/30/81.

1. Operating capacity for the taxable year ending 6/30/80 determined as of the close of that year:
   a. Attributable to X (8 buses × 50 seats) .. 400
   b. Attributable to Y (10 buses × 50 seats) . 500

   c. Total operating capacity for that year .. 900
2. Operating capacity for the taxable year ending 6/30/81 determined as of the close of that year:
   a. X's 6 and Y's 8 buses from prior taxable year used on a full-time basis during current taxable year and still owned on 6/30/81 700
   b. Capacity added during current taxable year (Y's 3 buses × 50 seats) 150

   c. Total operating capacity for that year .. 850
3. Increase in operating capacity for taxable year ending 6/30/81 (line 2c − line 1c) ... (50)

As determined for Y's taxable year ending 6/30/81 the group experienced a decrease in operating capacity. Thus, no energy credit is available for the buses Y placed in service in its taxable year ending 6/30/81.

(11) *Section 381 (a) transactions.* (i) in the case of a transaction described in section 381(a), the operating capacity of each transferor or distributor corporation, determined as of the date of distribution or transfer (within the meaning of § 1.381(b)-1(b)), shall reduce the operating capacity of the acquiring corporation (determined with-

Reg. § 1.48-9(q)(11)

out this paragraph (q)(11)) for its first taxable year ending on or after that date for purposes of determining the acquiring corporation's energy credit for that year. This paragraph (q)(11) shall not apply to any case to which paragraph (q)(10) of this section (dealing with related taxpayers) applies.

(ii) The following example illustrates this paragraph (q)(11):

Example. X and Y are unrelated corporations which use the calendar year. For 1981, each has an operating capacity of 250 seats (5 buses × 50 seats). X merges into Y on January 1, 1982. On May 1, 1982, Y retires and sells two buses and acquires four 50-seat qualifying buses at a cost of $40,000 each. All buses owned by Y on December 31, 1982, are included in operating capacity. Y makes the following calculations to determine the energy credit earned in taxable year 1982.

1. Y's 1981 operating capacity determined as of 12/31/81	250
2. 1982 operating capacity determined as of 12/31/82 without this paragraph (q)(11):	
a. X's 5 buses plus Y's 5 1981 buses less 2 retired buses (8 buses × 50 seats)	400
b. 1982 added capacity (4 buses × 50 seats)	200
c. Total	600
3. Operating capacity of transferor (X) on 1/1/82	250
4. Y's 1982 operating capacity (line 2c − line 3)	350
5. 1982 increase in operating capacity (line 4 − line 1)	100
6. Fraction in paragraph (q)(9)(iii) of this section (line 5 ÷ line 2b)	1/2
7. Energy credit earned in 1982 ($40,000 × 1/2 × 10% × 4 buses)	$8,000

[Reg. § 1.48-9.]

□ [T.D. 7765, 1-19-81. Amended by T.D. 7982, 10-5-84, T.D. 8014, 3-25-85 and T.D. 8147, 7-20-87.]

[Reg. § 1.48-10]

§ 1.48-10. Single purpose agricultural or horticultural structures.—(a) In general —(1) Scope. Under section 48(a)(1)(D), "section 38 property" includes single purpose agricultural and horticultural structures, as defined in section 48(p) and paragraphs (b) and (c) of this section. These structures are subject to a special rule for recapture of the credit. See paragraph (g) of this section. For the relation of this section to section 48(a)(1)(B) (other tangible property) and to sections 1245 and 1250 (depreciation recapture), see paragraph (h) of this section.

(2) Effective date. The provisions of section 48(a)(1)(D) and this section apply to open taxable years ending after August 15, 1971.

(b) Definition of single purpose agricultural structure—(1) In general. Under section 48(p)(2), a single purpose agricultural structure is any structure or enclosure that meets all of the following requirements:

(i) It is specifically designed and constructed exclusively for permissible purposes (as defined in paragraph (b)(2) of this section). See paragraph (d) of this section for the rule regarding "specifically designed and constructed".

(ii) It is specifically used exclusively for those permissible purposes. See paragraph (e) of this section for the rules regarding "specifically used".

(iii) It houses equipment necessary to house, raise, and feed livestock and their produce. See paragraph (b)(3) and (4) of this section.

(2) Permissible purposes. The following are the only permissible purposes for a single purpose agricultural structure:

(i) Housing, raising, and feeding a particular type of livestock and, at the taxpayer's option, its produce. The term "housing, raising, and feeding" includes the full range of livestock breeding and raising activities, including ancillary post-production activities (as defined in paragraph (f) of this section). Thus, for example, use of a structure for breeding livestock, or for producing eggs or livestock, is permitted. The structure may also be used for storing feed or machinery, but more than strictly incidental use for these purposes will disqualify the structure. See paragraph (e)(1) of this section. For the special rule concerning the permissible purposes for a milking parlor, see paragraph (b)(2)(iii) of this section.

(ii) Housing required equipment (including any replacements) as defined in paragraph (b)(4) of this section.

(iii) If the structure is a dairy facility, it will qualify if it is used for: (A) activities consisting of the production of milk or of the production of milk and the housing, raising, or feeding dairy cattle, and (B) housing equipment (including any replacements) necessary for these activities. The term "housing, raising, or feeding" includes the full range of dairy cattle breeding and raising activities including ancillary post-production activities (as defined in paragraph (f) of this section). The structure may also be used for storing feed or machinery, but more than incidental use for these purposes will disqualify the structure. See paragraph (e)(1) of this section.

Reg. § 1.48-10(b)(2)

(3) *Livestock; particular type of livestock* — (i) *Livestock.* Livestock qualifying as "section 38 property" under § 1.48-1(l) constitutes livestock for purposes of this section. Thus, for example, horses are not livestock for purposes of this section since they do not qualify as "section 38 property" under § 1.48-1(l). Under section 48(p)(6), poultry constitutes livestock for purposes of section 48(a)(1)(D). The term "livestock" includes the offspring of livestock. "Livestock" is distinguished from the produce of livestock, such as milk and eggs held for sale. For purposes of this section, eggs held for hatching and newborn livestock are considered livestock. A structure used solely to house produce of livestock or equipment necessary to house produce of livestock will not qualify as a single purpose agricultural structure. Thus, for example, a dairy facility used solely for storing milk will not qualify.

(ii) *Particular type of livestock.* A structure qualifies as a single purpose agricultural structure only if it is specifically designed, constructed, and used exclusively for permissible purposes with respect to one particular type of livestock. For purposes of this section, each species is a different type except that all species of poultry are considered to be of a single type. Thus, for example, a structure specifically designed and constructed as a single purpose hog-raising facility will not qualify if it is used to raise dairy cows, but a structure specifically designed, constructed, and used to raise poultry may house, raise, and feed both chickens and turkeys.

(4) *Required equipment rule.* (i) A single purpose agricultural structure must also house equipment necessary to house, raise, and feed the livestock ("required equipment"). Required equipment must be an integral part of the structure, and includes, but is not limited to, equipment necessary to contain the livestock, to provide them with water or feed, and to control the temperature, lighting, and humidity of the interior of the structure. For purposes of this section, equipment is an integral part of the structure if it is physically attached to or a part of the structure. The useful life of the structure, however, need not be contemporaneous with the life of the equipment it houses. A structure without required equipment is not a single purpose agricultural structure.

(ii) A single purpose agricultural structure may, but is not required to, house equipment (for example, loading chutes) necessary to the conduct of ancillary post-production activities as defined in paragraph (e) of this section.

(5) *Livestock structure.* In section 48(p)(2), the terms "single purpose livestock structure" and "single purpose agricultural structure" are interchangeable.

(c) *Definition of single purpose horticultural structure*—(1) *In general.* Under section 48(p)(3), a single purpose horticultural structure is any structure that meets both of the following requirements:

(i) It is a greenhouse or other structure specifically designed and constructed for permissible purposes (as defined in paragraph (c)(2) of this section). See paragraph (d) of this section for the rule regarding "specifically designed and constructed."

(ii) It is specifically used exclusively for those permissible purposes. See paragraph (e) of this section for the rules regarding "specifically used."

(2) *Permissible purposes.* The following are the only permissible purposes for a single purpose horticultural structure:

(i) The commercial production of plants (including plant products such as flowers, vegetables, or fruit) in a greenhouse.

(ii) The commercial production of mushrooms.

(iii) A single purpose horticultural structure also may, but is not required to, house equipment necessary to carry out these permissible purposes listed in paragraph (c)(2)(i) and (ii) of this section.

(3) *Ancillary post-production activities.* The terms "commercial production of plants" and "commercial production of mushrooms" include ancillary post-production activities (as defined in paragraph (f) of this section).

(d) *Specifically designed and constructed.* A structure is specifically designed and constructed if it is not economic to design and construct the structure for the intended qualifying purpose and then use the structure for a different purpose. For example, if a hog raising structure is designed and constructed in accordance with a standard set of plans for such a structure provided by the Department of Agriculture, it would not be economic to use the structure for purposes other than hog raising.

(e) *Specifically used.* There are two aspects of the specific use requirement—exclusive use and actual use.

(1) *Exclusive use.* (i) A structure qualifies as a single purpose agricultural or horticultural structure only if it is used exclusively for the permitted purposes by reason of which it qualified for the credit. Thus—

(A) The structure may not be used for any nonpermissible purposes (for example,

Reg. § 1.48-10(b)(3)

processing, marketing, or more than incidental use for storing feed or equipment) and

(B) It may not be put to any use other than the specific use by reason of which it qualifies for the credit.

(ii) For purposes of this section, the term "incidental use" means a use which is both related and subordinate to the qualifying purpose. Thus, for example, if feed is stored in an agricultural structure which will be used for raising hogs, the feed must be used only for the hogs in order to be related to the qualifying purpose. In determining whether use of the structure for feed storage is subordinate to the qualifying purpose, all of the facts and circumstances must be considered, including, with respect to feed storage, the following:

(A) Type of animal involved;

(B) Number of, and consumption rate for, each animal;

(C) Climate of area;

(D) Total volume of storage area; or

(E) Percentage of structure's total volume devoted to storage.

(iii) It will be presumed that the storage function is not subordinate to the qualifying purpose of the structure if more than one-third of the structure's total usable volume is devoted to storage. This presumption may be rebutted with clear and convincing evidence.

(iv) A structure may fail the exclusive use test if either of the requirements of paragraph (e)(1)(i) of this section is not met. Thus, for example, a horticultural structure that contains an area for processing plants or plant products will fail the exclusive use test because there is a nonpermissible use. An agricultural structure that is used to house more than one particular type of livestock fails the exclusive use test for the same reason. A change in the use of an agricultural structure from one species of livestock to another will cause the structure to fail the exclusive use test when the change occurs. Thus, for example, a hog-raising facility which qualified for the credit when it was placed in service cannot later be modified and used for producing broiler chickens even if the structure would have qualified for the credit if it had been originally designed, constructed, and used exclusively for producing broiler chickens.

(2) *Actual use.* (i) A single purpose agricultural or horticultural structure also must actually be used for the permissible purpose by reason of which it qualifies for the credit. "Actual use" means "placed in service" (as defined in § 1.46-3(d)). Mere vacancy, on a temporary basis,

will not disqualify the structure. Thus, for example, a structure that is designed and constructed as a hog-raising structure will not qualify if it is never placed in service for raising hogs. However, a turkey-raising facility will not be disqualified if the turkeys are all sent to a packing plant in November and the structure remains vacant until the next spring when newly hatched turkeys are placed in the structure to be raised.

(ii) For purposes of this section, "vacancy on a temporary basis" includes temporary vacancy caused by market fluctuations or other economic considerations and vacancy on a seasonal basis.

(f) *Work space; ancillary post-production activities*—(1) *Permissible work space.* Under section 48(p)(4), a single purpose agricultural or horticultural structure may contain work space only if it is used for—

(i) Stocking, caring for, or collecting livestock, plants, or mushrooms,

(ii) Maintenance of the structure, or

(iii) Maintenance or replacement of the equipment or stock enclosed by or contained in the structure.

Thus, for example, an eligible structure may not contain space devoted to processing or marketing or other nonpermissible purposes.

(2) *Ancillary post-production activities.* The term "stocking, caring for, or collecting" the livestock, plants, or mushrooms includes ancillary post-production activities. These activities, therefore, constitute permissible purposes when carried on in conjunction with other permissible purposes, and a qualifying structure may contain work space devoted to such activities. Ancillary post-production activities include gathering, sorting, and loading livestock, plants, and mushrooms and packing unprocessed plants, mushrooms, and the live offspring and unprocessed produce of the livestock. Ancillary post-production activities do not include processing activities, such as slaughtering or packing meat, nor do they include marketing activities.

(g) *Special rule for recapture under section 47.* Under section 48(p)(5), if a structure which qualifies for the credit under this section becomes ineligible because it ceases to be held for the specific use by reason of which it qualified (or it is used for other than that qualifying use) before the end of the applicable estimated useful life or period specified in section 47(a), then the investment credit previously allowed with respect to the structure may be partially or entirely recaptured under section 47. Unlike other property to which section 47 applies, single purpose structures may

Reg. § 1.48-10(g)

not be converted from one permissible use to another without recapture. See subparagraph (e)(2) of this section.

(h) *Relationship to other sections*—(1) *Relation to section 48(a)(1)(B)*. All structures satisfying the requirements of section 48(a)(1)(B) and (a)(1)(D) will be considered to qualify under either provision.

(2) *Relationship to sections 1245 and 1250*. For purposes of depreciation recapture, property to which section 48(a)(1)(D) applies is section 1245 property, except that property placed in service prior to January 1, 1981, may, at the option of the taxpayer, be treated as section 1250 property if depreciation deductions allowed were not under one of the methods authorized only for section 1245 property.

(i) [Reserved]

(j) *Examples*. The provisions of this section may be illustrated by the following examples:

Example (1). A constructs a rectangular structure for use in an egg-producing facility. The structure has no windows. The walls and roof are made of corrugated steel and there is a door which is 4 feet wide and 8 feet tall at each end of the structure. At the end of each wall are louvered openings approximately 4 feet high and 8 feet long. These openings house thermostatically controlled fans. In the center of the walls are manually operated fresh-air openings. Corrugated steel "curtains" hang from the top of the openings so that the openings can be completely closed in cold weather, but the curtains can be propped open to admit fresh air. The building is well insulated. A has reinforced the roof with extra trusses and rafters and reinforced the building with extra wall studs. Two rows of cages are suspended from the rafters by thin steel girders and wires. The floor of the structure is a sloping concrete slab pierced with long troughs which run the length of the structure beneath the cages. The troughs are used for collection and disposal of chicken wastes. When this structure is placed in service it will qualify for an investment credit under this section.

Example (2). B constructs a greenhouse for the commercial production of plants. The greenhouse is a rectangular structure with translucent fiberglass walls and roof. The structure is equipped with an automatic temperature and humidity control system. Pipes were installed to carry water and liquid fertilizer to the plants and to release minute amounts of carbon dioxide into the air. When the structure was originally placed in service B used the entire structure for growing flowers commercially. In September 1978, B began to use the structure for growing tomatoes.

Because of the success of the venture, in January 1979, B began to use the entire structure for growing tomatoes. In February 1980, B set up a small counter with a cash register at one end of the structure so that workers could sell tomatoes to customers at the greenhouse. Until February 1980, the structure would qualify for the credit under this section. The change in use from growing flowers to growing tomatoes will not affect the eligibility of the structure. Once the cash register is installed, however, the structure fails to meet both the exclusive use test of paragraph (e)(1) of this section and the work space rule of paragraph (f) of this section since a single purpose structure may not be used for marketing activities.

Example (3). C purchases a prefabricated structure and makes modifications so that the structure will meet C's requirements. C adds gates and constructs a partition which divides the structure into two parts. One part of the structure constitutes less than one-third of the total usable volume of the structure and is used to house feeder cattle while they are fed with hay. This part of the structure has a sloping concrete floor. The other part of the structure constitutes more than two-thirds of the total usable volume of the structure and is used to store the hay used to feed the cattle. This structure will not qualify for the credit since it fails the required equipment test. The structure does not contain equipment which is an integral part of the structure. This structure also fails the "specifically designed and constructed" test of paragraph (d) of this section since it would be economical to use the structure for purposes other than housing, raising, and feeding cattle (such as a general purpose barn, for example). Finally, the structure fails the incidental use test of paragraph (e) of this section because the storage function is presumptively not subordinate to the qualifying purpose since more than two-thirds of the structure's total usable volume is devoted to storage and none of the facts will serve to rebut the presumption. [Reg. § 1.48-10.]

☐ [*T.D. 7900, 7-18-83.*]

[Reg. § 1.48-11]

§ 1.48-11. Qualified rehabilitated building; expenditures incurred before January 1, 1982.—(a) *In general*. Under section 48(a)(1)(E), that portion of the basis of a qualified rehabilitated building which is attributable to qualified rehabilitation expenditures qualifies as section 38 property. In general, property which is treated as section 38 property by reason of section 48(a)(1)(E) is treated as new section 38 property and therefore is not subject to the used property limitation. See § 1.48-2(d). Section 48(g)(1) and paragraph (b) of this section define the term "qualified rehabilitated building". Section 48(g)(2) and paragraph (c) of this section define the term "qualified rehabilitation expenditure". Paragraph (d) of this section provides guidance for coordination of these provisions with other sections of the Code.

(b) *Definition of qualified rehabilitated building*—(1) *In general.* The term "qualified rehabilitated building" means any building and its structural components—

(i) Which has been rehabilitated (within the meaning of paragraph (b)(3) of this section),

(ii) Which was placed in service (within the meaning of § 1.46-3(d)) by any person at any time before the beginning of the rehabilitation,

(iii) 75 percent or more of the existing external walls of which are retained in place as external walls (within the meaning of paragraph (b)(4) of this section) in the rehabilitation process, and

(iv) Which meets the twenty-year requirement in paragraph (b)(2) of this section.

In addition, a major portion of a building may be treated as a separate building for purposes of this paragraph if the requirements of paragraph (b)(5) of this section are met.

(2) *Twenty-year requirement*—(i) *In general.* A building is considered a qualified rehabilitated building only if a period of at least 20 years has elapsed between the date physical work on the rehabilitation of the building began, and the later of—

(A) The date the building was first placed in service (see § 1.46-3(d)) by any person as a building, or

(B) The date the building was placed in service by any taxpayer in connection with a prior rehabilitation with respect to which a credit was allowed by reason of section 48(a)(1)(E).

(ii) *Vacant periods.* The 20-year period includes periods during which a building was vacant or devoted to a personal use and is computed without regard to the number of owners or the identity of owners during the period.

(iii) *Physical work on a rehabilitation.* For purposes of this section, "physical work on a rehabilitation" begins when actual construction begins. The term "physical work on a rehabilitation" does not include preliminary activities such as planning, designing, securing financing, exploring, researching, developing plans and specifications, or stabilizing a building to prevent deterioration (*e.g.,* placing boards over broken windows).

(iv) *Special rule.* If a part of a building meets the twenty-years requirement in subdivision (i) of this subparagraph and a part (for example, an addition) does not, a rehabilitation of that part that meets the requirement may qualify for a credit only if that part constitutes a major portion (as defined in paragraph (b)(5) of this section) of the building.

(3) *Rehabilitation*—(i) *In general.* For purposes of this paragraph, rehabilitation includes renovation, restoration, or reconstruction. However, the term "rehabilitation" does not include enlargement (within the meaning of paragraph (c)(7)(ii) of this section), new construction, or the completion of new construction after a building has been placed in service. For purposes of this paragraph (b)(3), whether expenditures are attributable to the rehabilitation of an existing building, or to new construction, is determined upon all the facts and circumstances.

(ii) *Substantial rehabilitation.* For a building to be considered rehabilitated, the rehabilitation must be substantial. Whether a rehabilitation is substantial is determined upon the basis of all the facts and circumstances. In general, to be substantial, the rehabilitation must do one of the following:

(A) materially extend the useful life of the building;

(B) significantly upgrade its usefulness (for either the same or a new use); or

(C) preserve it in a way that significantly improves its condition or enhances its historic value.

A substantial rehabilitation may vary in degree from gutting and extensive reconstruction of a building's major structural components to the cure of a substantial accumulation of major disrepairs. It may also include renovation, alteration, or remodelling for the conversion of a structurally sound building to a design and condition required for a new use. Cosmetic improvements alone, however, do not qualify as a substantial rehabilitation.

(iii) *Aggregation of rehabilitation.* In the case where qualified rehabilitation expenditures are incurred with respect to a rehabilitation of a building by more than one person (*e.g.,* a lessor and a lessee, several lessees, or several condominium owners), the substantial rehabilitation requirement in this paragraph (b)(3) shall be applied by aggregating all the rehabilitation work done by such persons.

(iv) *Special rule for qualified rehabilitation expenditures treated as incurred by the taxpayer.* In the case where qualified rehabilitation

Reg. § 1.48-11(b)(3)

expenditures are treated as having been incurred by a taxpayer because of the application of paragraph (c)(3)(ii) of this section, the substantial rehabilitation test in paragraph (b)(3)(ii) of this section will be applied by aggregating the rehabilitation work done by the transferor and the transferee.

(v) *Examples.* The provisions of this subparagraph (3) may be illustrated by the following examples:

Example (1). Taxpayer A is the owner of a 30-year-old building. The building is air conditioned by means of window air conditioning units. A replaces the window units with a central air conditioning system and no other rehabilitation is performed by A. The expenditures incurred by A did not materially extend the building's useful life, significantly upgrade its usefulness, or preserve it in a manner that significantly improves its condition or enhances its historic value. Although expenditures for replacement of window units with a central air conditioning system may constitute qualified expenditures as part of an overall rehabilitation, alone they do not qualify as a substantial rehabilitation and the building is not considered rehabilitated within the meaning of this subparagraph.

Example (2). Taxpayer B is the owner of a 10 story office building that is 35 years old. The building is in substantial disrepair and in order to modernize it as an office building B installs new plumbing, electrical wiring, and heating and air conditioning systems. In addition, the layout of each floor is changed by means of tearing down many existing interior walls and partitions and building new walls, partitions, and doors. Old plaster is removed from many walls and replaced by new wall covering. New windows and new flooring are installed throughout the building. The improvements made by B materially extend the useful life of the building and significantly upgrade its usefulness. The building is considered rehabilitated within the meaning of the facts and circumstances test in this subparagraph.

Example (3). Taxpayer C is the owner of a 100-year-old building that has substantial historic character, although the building is not a certified historic structure (as defined in section 191(d)(1) and the regulations thereunder). C uncovers and restores the original woodwork, wall coverings and molding throughout the building. The windows and doors are replaced with replicas of the original. The improvements made by C significantly preserve the building and significantly enhance its historic value. Thus, the building is considered rehabilitated within the meaning of this subparagraph.

(4) *Retention of 75 percent of external walls*—(i) *In general.* A building meets the requirements set forth in paragraph (b)(1)(iii) only if 75 percent or more of the existing external walls (as measured by the total area of the existing external walls) are retained in place as external walls in the rehabilitation process. For this purpose, the area of existing external walls includes the area of windows and doors.

(ii) *External wall.* For purposes of this paragraph (b)(4), a wall includes both the supporting elements of the wall and the nonsupporting elements (*e.g.*, a curtain) of the wall. Except as otherwise provided in this paragraph (b)(4), the term "external wall" includes any wall that has one face exposed to the weather, earth, or an abutting wall erected on an adjacent property. An external wall also includes a shared wall (*i.e.*, a single wall shared with an adjacent building), generally referred to as a "party wall".

(iii) *Alternative rule.* Notwithstanding the definition of external wall contained in paragraph (b)(4)(ii) of this section, in any case in which the building being rehabilitated would fail to meet the requirements of a qualified rehabilitation building if the definition of external wall in paragraph (b)(4)(ii) of this section were used, then the term "external wall" shall be defined as a wall, including its supporting elements, with one face exposed to the weather or earth, and a common wall shall not be treated as an external wall.

(iv) *Retained in place.* An existing external wall is retained in place if the supporting elements of the wall are retained in place. An existing external wall is not retained in place if the supporting elements of the wall are replaced by new supporting elements. An external wall is retained in place, however, if the supporting elements are reinforced in the rehabilitation, provided that such supporting elements of the external wall are retained in place. An external wall is retained in place even though it is covered (e.g., with new siding). Moreover, the existing curtain may be replaced with a new curtain provided that the structural framework that provides for the support of the existing curtain is retained in place. An external wall is retained in place notwithstanding that the existing doors and windows in the wall are modified, eliminated, or replaced. A wall may be disassembled and reassembled so long as the same supporting elements are used when the wall is reassembled. Thus, for example, in the case of the brick wall, the wall is considered retained in place even though the original bricks are removed (for cleaning, *etc.*) and put back to form the wall.

Reg. § 1.48-11(b)(4)

(v) *Retention as an external wall*. For purposes of meeting the 75 percent requirement of this subparagraph (4), an existing external wall must be retained in place as an external wall. If an addition is made that results in an existing external wall being converted into an internal wall, the wall is not retained in place as an external wall.

(vi) *Special rule*. Solely for the purpose of meeting the 75 percent requirement of this subparagraph (4), the walls of an uncovered internal shaft designed solely to bring light or air into the center of a building which are completely surrounded by external walls of the building and which enclose space not designated for occupancy or other use by people (other than for maintenance or emergency) are not considered external walls. Thus, a wall of a light well in the center of an office building is not an external wall. However, walls surrounding an uncovered courtyard which is usable by the building's occupants, (*e.g.*, at lunch time) are external walls.

(vii) *Examples*. The provisions of this subparagraph (4) may be illustrated by the following examples:

Example (1). Taxpayer A rehabilitated a building all of the walls of which consisted of wood siding attached to gypsum board sheets (which covered the studs). A covered the existing wood siding with aluminum siding in a part of a rehabilitation that otherwise qualified under this subparagraph. A satisfied the requirement that 75 percent of the existing external walls must be retained in place as external walls.

Example (2). Taxpayer B rehabilitated a building the external walls of which had a masonry curtain. The masonry on the wall face was replaced with a glass curtain. The steel beam and girders supporting the existing curtain were retained in place. B satisfied the requirement that 75 percent of the existing external walls must be retained in place as external walls.

Example (3). Taxpayer C rehabilitated a building which has two external walls measuring 75' × 20' and two other external walls measuring 100' × 20'. C tore down one of the larger walls, including its supporting elements, which accounted for more than 25% of the building's external walls and constructed a new wall. C has not satisfied the requirement that 75 percent of the existing external walls must be retained in place as external walls.

Example (4). The facts are the same as in example 3, except C does not tear down any walls, but makes an addition that results in one of the smaller walls becoming an internal wall. In addition, C enlarged 8 of the existing windows on the larger walls, increasing them from a size of 3' × 4' to 6' × 8'. Since the smaller wall accounts for less than 25 percent of the total wall area, C has satisfied the requirement that 75 percent of the existing external walls must be retained in place as external walls in the rehabilitation process. The enlargement of the existing windows on the larger wall does not change the result.

(5) *Major portion treated as separate building*—(i) *In general*. Where there is a separate rehabilitation of a major portion of a building, such major portion shall be treated as a separate building. Thus, such major portion may qualify as a qualified rehabilitated building if the requirements of this paragraph are met with respect to such major portion. Expenditures for property that services both a major portion of a building and another portion must be specifically allocated to each portion to the extent possible. If it is not possible to make such an allocation, the expenditures must be allocated to each portion on some reasonable basis. What constitutes a reasonable basis for an allocation depends on factors such as the type of improvement and how the improvement relates functionally to the building. For example, in the case of expenditures for an air conditioning system or a roof, a reasonable basis for allocating the expenditures would be the volume of the major portion served by the improvement relative to the volume of the other portion of the building served by the improvement.

(ii) *Major portion defined*. Whether a part of a building constitutes a major portion of the building is determined upon the basis of all the facts and circumstances. A major portion must generally consist of clearly identifiable parts of a building (*e.g.*, a wing of a building or the first 5 stories of a 7 story building). The following factors shall be taken into account:

(A) Whether the portion comprises an entire leasehold interest or an entire ownership (*e.g.*, condominium) interest;

(B) Whether the portion (as measured by volume) is sufficiently large that it would be reasonable to treat it as a separate building; and

(C) Whether the portion is functionally different from other parts of the building.

(6) *Special rule for rehabilitation done in phases*. If rehabilitation which is not continuous is determined under this subparagraph to be a single rehabilitation done in phases, the requirements of this paragraph (b) are to be applied with respect to the overall rehabilitation and not merely to a phase of the rehabilitation. In such case, a phase of a single overall rehabilitation will not be considered as "prior rehabilitation" for purposes of subparagraph (2)(i)(B) of this paragraph (b).

Reg. § 1.48-11(b)(6)

Whether rehabilitation which is not continuous is a single rehabilitation that is done in phases is determined on the basis of all the facts and circumstances. Generally, however, to constitute a single rehabilitation that is done in phases, there must exist, prior to the time any rehabilitation work is commenced, a set of written plans describing generally all phases of the rehabilitation of the building and a reasonable expectation that all phases of the rehabilitation will be completed. Such written plans are not required to contain detailed working drawings or detailed specifications of the material to be used. In addition, the period between the time that physical work on the first phase of the overall rehabilitation begins and physical work on the last phase of the overall rehabilitation begins must be reasonable. In determining whether the rehabilitation is completed within a reasonable time, the fact that a building is occupied during the rehabilitation, the necessity of acquiring a lease (of additional portions of the building), and unforeseen delays shall be taken into account. Other factors that are relevant in determining whether rehabilitation is a single rehabilitation include the length of time between each phase of rehabilitation activities and the extent of rehabilitation activity in each phase.

(7) *Special rule for adjoining buildings that are combined.* For purposes of this paragraph (b), if as part of a rehabilitation process two or more adjoining buildings are combined and placed in service as a single building after the rehabilitation process, then all of the requirements of a qualified rehabilitated building in section 48(g)(1) and this section may be applied to the constituent adjoining buildings in the aggregate. Any party walls or abutting walls between the constituent buildings that would otherwise be treated as external walls (within the meaning of paragraph (b)(4)(ii) of this section) would not be treated as external walls of the building; the substantial rehabilitation test in paragraph (b)(3)(ii) of this section would be applied to the aggregate rehabilitation work with respect to all of the constituent buildings.

(c) *Definition of qualified rehabilitation expenditures*—(1) *In general.* Except as provided in subparagraph (2) of this paragraph, the term "qualified rehabilitation expenditure" means any amount—

(i) Properly chargeable to capital account (as described in subparagraph (2) of this paragraph),

(ii) Incurred after October 31, 1978, for depreciable or amortizable property (or additions or improvements to property) with a useful life of five years or more, and

(iii) Made in connection with the rehabilitation of a qualified rehabilitated building.

(2) *Chargeable to capital account.* For purposes of paragraph (c)(1)(i) of this section, amounts paid or incurred are chargeable to capital account if under the taxpayer's method of accounting they are properly includible in computing basis under § 1.46-3. Amounts treated as an expense and deducted in the year they are paid or incurred are not chargeable to capital account.

(3) *Incurred by the taxpayer*—(i) *In general.* Generally, to qualify for a credit under section 48(a)(1)(E), qualified rehabilitation expenditures must be incurred by the taxpayer after October 31, 1978. An expenditure is incurred for purposes of this paragraph on the date such expenditure would be considered incurred under the accrual method of accounting, regardless of the method of accounting used by the taxpayer with respect to other items of income and expense. If qualified rehabilitation expenditures are treated as having been incurred by a taxpayer under paragraph (c)(3)(ii) of this section, the taxpayer shall be treated as having incurred the expenditures on the date such expenditures were incurred by the transferor.

(ii) *Qualified rehabilitation expenditures treated as incurred by the taxpayer.* (A) Where rehabilitation expenditures are incurred with respect to a building by a person (or persons) other than the taxpayer and the taxpayer acquires the building, or a portion of the building to which the expenditures are allocable, the taxpayer acquiring such property will be treated as having incurred the rehabilitation expenditures actually incurred by the transferor (or treated as incurred by the transferor under this paragraph (c)(3)(ii)) with respect to the acquired property, provided that—

(1) The building, or the portion of the building, acquired by the taxpayer was not used after the rehabilitation expenditures were incurred and prior to the date of acquisition by the taxpayer, and

(2) No credit with respect to such qualified rehabilitation expenditures is claimed by anyone other than the taxpayer acquiring the property.

For purposes of this paragraph (c)(3)(ii), use shall mean actual use, whether personal or business.

(B) The amount of qualified rehabilitation expenditures treated as incurred by the taxpayer under this paragraph is the lesser of—

(1) The qualified rehabilitation expenditures incurred before the date on which the taxpayer acquired the building (or portion

Reg. § 1.48-11(b)(7)

thereof), to which the expenditures are attributable, or

(2) That portion of the taxpayer's cost or other basis for the property which is attributable to the qualified rehabilitation expenditures described in paragraph (c)(3)(B)(1) of this section incurred before such date.

For purposes of paragraph (c)(6)(ii) of this section, the amount of rehabilitation expenditures treated as incurred by the taxpayer under this paragraph (c)(3)(ii) shall not be considered to be part of the cost of acquiring a building or any interest in the building. The portion of the cost of acquiring a building (or an interest therein) which is not treated under this paragraph as qualified rehabilitation expenditures incurred by the taxpayer is not eligible for a rehabilitation investment credit. See paragraph (c)(6)(ii) of this section.

(C) See paragraph (b)(2)(iv) of this section for rules concerning the application of the substantial rehabilitation test to expenditures treated as incurred by the taxpayer.

(iii) *Examples.* The provisions of this subparagraph may be illustrated by the following examples:

Example (1). In 1978, taxpayer A, a cash basis taxpayer, commenced the rehabilitation of a 30-year-old building. In June 1978, A signed a contract with a plumbing contractor for replacement of the plumbing in the building. A agreed to pay the contractor as soon as the work was completed. The work was completed in September 1978, but A did not pay the amount due until November 1, 1978. The expenditures for the plumbing are not qualified rehabilitation expenditures because they were not incurred after October 31, 1978.

Example (2). B incurred qualified rehabilitation expenditures of $300,000 with respect to an existing building between January 1, 1980, and May 15, 1980, and then sold the building to C on June 1, 1980. If the property attributable to the expenditures was not placed in service by A during the period from January 1, 1980, to June 1, 1980, C will be treated as having incurred the expenditures.

(4) *Incurred for 5-year property.* An expenditure is incurred for depreciable or amortizable property if the amount of the expenditure is added to the basis of property which is depreciable or amortizable under section 167. The determination of whether property has a useful life of five years or more is made by applying the principles of § 1.46-3(e). In the case of expenditures for property made by a lessee, see sections 167 and 178 and the regulations thereunder for rules relating to whether improvements made to leased property are depreciable or amortizable.

(5) *Made in connection with the rehabilitation of a qualified rehabilitated building.* Expenditures attributable to work done to facilities related to a building (*e.g.,* sidewalk, parking lot, landscaping) are not considered made in connection with a rehabilitation of a qualified rehabilitated building.

(6) *Certain expenditures excluded from qualified rehabilitation expenditures.* The term "qualified rehabilitation expenditures" does not include the following expenditures:

(i) An expenditure for property which is "section 38 property" (determined without regard to section 48(a)(1)(E) and (1)).

(ii) The cost of acquiring a building or any interest in a building (including a leasehold interest) except as provided in paragraph (c)(3)(ii) of this section.

(iii) An expenditure attributable to enlargement of a building (as defined in paragraph (c)(7) of this section).

(iv) An expenditure attributable to rehabilitation of a certified historic structure (as defined in section 191(d)(1) and the regulations thereunder), unless the rehabilitation is a certified rehabilitation (as defined in paragraph (c)(8) of this section).

(7) *Expenditures for enlargement distinguished* —(i) *In general.* Expenditures attributable to an enlargement of an existing building do not qualify as qualified rehabilitated expenditures. A building is enlarged to the extent that the total volume of the building is increased. An increase in floor space resulting from interior remodelling is not considered an enlargement. Generally, the total volume of a building is equal to the product of the floor area of the base of the building and the height from the underside of the lowest floor (including the basement) to the average height of the finished roof (as it exists or existed). For this purpose, floor area is measured from the exterior faces of external walls (other than shared walls that are external walls) and from the centerline of shared walls that are external walls. In addition, a building is enlarged to the extent of any construction outside the exterior faces of the existing external wall of the building.

(ii) *Rehabilitation which includes enlargement.* If expenditures for property only partially qualify as qualified rehabilitation expenditures because some of the expenditures are also attributable to the enlargement of the building, the expenditures must be apportioned between the original portion of the building and the enlarge-

Reg. § 1.48-11(c)(7)

ment. This allocation should be made using the principles contained in paragraph (b)(5)(i) of this section.

(8) *Certified rehabilitation*—(i) *In general.* For the purpose of this paragraph (c) of this section, the term "certified rehabilitation" means any rehabilitation of a certified historic building in a registered historic district which the Secretary of the Interior has certified to the Secretary as being consistent with the historic character of such building or the district in which such building is located.

(ii) *Revoked or invalidated certifications.* If the Department of Interior revokes or otherwise invalidates a certification after it has been provided to a taxpayer, the decertified property will cease to be section 38 property described in section 48(a)(1)(E). Such cessation shall be effective as of the date the activity giving rise to the revocation or invalidation occurred. See section 47 for the rules applicable to property that ceases to be section 38 property.

(d) *Coordination with other provisions of the Code*—(1) *Credit by lessees*—(i) *Rehabilitation performed by lessor.* A lessee may take the credit for rehabilitation performed by the lessor if the requirements of this section and section 48(d) are satisfied. For purposes of applying section 48(d), the fair market value of section 38 property described in section 48(a)(1)(E) shall be equal to that portion of the lessor's basis in a qualified rehabilitated building that is attributable to qualified rehabilitation expenditures.

(ii) *Rehabilitation performed by lessee.* A lessee may take the credit for rehabilitation performed by the lessee, provided that the property (or improvements or additions to property) for which the rehabilitation expenditures are made is depreciable (or amortizable) by the lessee (see sections 167 and 178, and the regulations thereunder) and the requirements of this section are satisfied.

(2) *When credit may be claimed.* The investment credit for qualified rehabilitation expenditures is allowed generally in the taxable year in which the property to which the rehabilitation expenditures is attributable is placed in service, provided the building is a qualified rehabilitated building for the taxable year. See § 1.46-3(d). Under certain circumstances, however, the credit may be available prior to the date the property is placed in service. See section 46(d) and § 1.46-5 (relating to qualified progress expenditures).

(3) *Recapture.* If property described in section 48(a)(1)(E) is disposed of by the taxpayer, or otherwise ceases to be "section 38 property," recapture may result under section 47. Property

will cease to be section 38 property, and therefore recapture may occur under section 47, in any case where the Department of Interior revokes or otherwise invalidates a certification of rehabilitation (see section 48(g)(2)(C)) after the property is placed in service because, for example, the taxpayer made modifications to the building inconsistent with Department of Interior standards.

(e) *Effective date*—(1) *General rule.* Except as provided in paragraph (e)(2) of this section, this § 1.48-11 shall not apply to expenditures incurred after December 31, 1981.

(2) *Transitional rule.* This § 1.48-11 shall continue to apply to expenditures incurred after December 31, 1981, for the rehabilitation of a building if—

(i) The physical work on the rehabilitation began before January 1, 1982, and

(ii) The building does not meet the requirements of section 48(g)(1) of the Code as amended by the Economic Recovery Tax Act of 1981. [Reg. § 1.48-11.]

□ [*T.D.* 8031, 6-27-85.]

[Reg. § 1.48-12]

§ 1.48-12. **Qualified rehabilitated building; expenditures incurred after December 31, 1981.**—(a) *General rule*—(1) *In general.* Under section 48(a)(1)(E), the portion of the basis of a qualified rehabilitated building that is attributable to qualified rehabilitation expenditures (within the meaning of section 48(g) and this section) is section 38 property. Property that is section 38 property by reason of section 48(a)(1)(E) is treated as new section 38 property and, therefore, is not subject to the used property limitation in section 48(c). Section 48(g)(1) and paragraph (b) of this section define the term "qualified rehabilitated building." Section 48(g)(2) and paragraph (c) of this section define the term "qualified rehabilitation expenditure." Section 48(g)(2)(B)(iv) and (3) and paragraph (d) of this section describe the rules applicable to "certified historic structures." Section 48(q) and paragraph (e) of this section provide rules concerning an adjustment to the basis of the rehabilitated building. Paragraph (f) of this section provides guidance for coordination of these provisions with other sections of the Code, including rules for determining when the rehabilitation credit may be claimed.

(2) *Effective dates and transition rules*—(i) *In general.* Except as otherwise provided in this paragraph (a)(2)(i), this section applies to expenditures incurred after December 31, 1981, in connection with the rehabilitation of a qualified rehabilitated building. (See paragraph (c)(3)(i) of

this section for rules concerning the determination of when an expenditure is incurred.) If, however, physical work on the rehabilitation began before January 1, 1982, and the building does not meet the requirements of paragraph (b) of this section, the rules in § 1.48-11 shall apply to the expenditures incurred after December 31, 1981, in connection with such rehabilitation. (See paragraph (b)(6)(i) of this section for rules determining when physical work on a rehabilitation begins.)

(ii) *Transition rules concerning ACRS lives.* (A) For property placed in service before March 16, 1984, and any property subject to the exception set forth in section 111(g)(2) of Public Law 98-369 (Deficit Reduction Act of 1984), the references to "19 years" in paragraph (c)(4)(ii) and (7)(v) shall be replaced with "15 years" and the reference to "19-year real property" in paragraph (c)(4)(ii) shall be replaced with "15-year real property."

(B) Except as otherwise provided in paragraph (a)(2)(ii)(A) of this section, for property placed in service before May 9, 1985, and any property subject to the exception set forth in section 105(b)(2) and (5) of Public Law 99-121 (99 Stat. 501, 511), the references to "19 years" in paragraph (c)(4)(ii) and (7)(v) shall be replaced with "18 years" and the references to "19-year real property" in paragraph (c)(4)(ii) shall be replaced with "18-year real property."

(iii) *Transition rule concerning external wall definition.* Notwithstanding the definition of external wall contained in paragraph (b)(3)(ii) of this section, in any case in which the written plans and specifications for a rehabilitation were substantially completed on or before June 28, 1985, and the building being rehabilitated would fail to meet the requirement of paragraph (b)(1)(iii) of this section if the definition of external wall in paragraph (b)(3)(ii) of this section were used, the term "external wall" shall be defined as a wall, including its supporting elements, with one face exposed to the weather or earth, and a common wall shall not be treated as an external wall. See paragraph (b)(2)(v) of this section for the definition of written plans and specifications.

(iv) *Transition rules concerning amendments made by the Tax Reform Act of 1986*—(A) *In general.* Except as otherwise provided in section 251(d) of the Tax Reform Act of 1986 and this paragraph (a)(2)(iv), the amendments made by section 251 of the Tax Reform Act of 1986 shall apply to property placed in service after December 31, 1986, in taxable years ending after that date, regardless of when the rehabilitation expenditures attributable to such property were incurred. If property attributable to qualified re-

habilitation expenditures is incurred with respect to a rehabilitation to a building placed in service in segments or phases and some segments are placed in service before January 1, 1987, and the remaining segments are placed in service after December 31, 1986, the amendments under the Tax Reform Act would not apply to the property placed in service before January 1, 1987, but would apply to the segments placed in service after December 31, 1986, unless one of the transition rules in paragraph (a)(2)(iv)(B) or (C) of this section applies.

(B) *General transition rule.* The amendments made by sections 251 and 201 of the Tax Reform Act of 1986 shall not apply to property that qualifies under section 251(d)(2), (3), or (4) of the Tax Reform Act of 1986. Property qualifies for the general transition rule in section 251(d)(2) of the Act if such property is placed in service before January 1, 1994, and if such property is placed in service as part of—

(*1*) A rehabilitation that was completed pursuant to a written contract that was binding on March 1, 1986, or (*2*) A rehabilitation incurred in connection with property (including any leasehold interest) acquired before March 2, 1986, or acquired on or after such date pursuant to a written contract that was binding on March 1, 1986, if—

(*i*) Parts 1 and 2 of the Historic Preservation Certificate Application were filed with the Department of Interior (or its designee) before March 2, 1986, or

(*ii*) The lesser of $1,000,000 or 5 percent of the cost of the rehabilitation is incurred before March 2, 1986, or is required to be incurred pursuant to a written contract which was binding on March 1, 1986.

(C) *Specific rehabilitations.* See section 251(d)(3) and (4) of the Tax Reform Act of 1986 for additional rehabilitations that are exempted from the amendments made by sections 251 and 201 of the Tax Reform Act of 1986.

(b) *Definition of qualified rehabilitated building*—(1) *In general.* The term "qualified rehabilitated building" means any building and its structural components—

(i) That has been substantially rehabilitated (within the meaning of paragraph (b)(2) of this section) for the taxable year,

(ii) That was placed in service (within the meaning of § 1.46-3(d)) as a building by any person before the beginning of the rehabilitation, and

(iii) That meets the applicable existing external wall retention test or the existing external wall and internal structural framework reten-

Reg. § 1.48-12(b)(1)

tion test in accordance with paragraph (b)(3) of this section.

The requirement in paragraph (b)(1)(iii) of this section does not apply to a certified historic structure. See paragraph (b)(4) and (5) of this section for additional requirements related to the definition of a qualified rehabilitated building.

(2) *Substantially rehabilitated building*—(i) *Substantial rehabilitation test.* A building shall be treated as having been substantially rehabilitated for a taxable year only if the qualified rehabilitation expenditures (as defined in paragraph (c) of this section) incurred during any 24-month period selected by the taxpayer ending with or within the taxable year exceed the greater of—

    (A) the adjusted basis of the building (and its structural components), or

    (B) $5,000.

(ii) *Date to determine adjusted basis of the building*—(A) *In general.* The adjusted basis of the building (and its structural components) shall be determined as of the beginning of the first day of the 24-month period selected by the taxpayer or the first day of the taxpayer's holding period of the building (within the meaning of section 1250(e)), whichever is later. For purposes of determining the holding period under section 1250(e), any reconstruction that is part of the rehabilitation shall be disregarded.

(B) *Special rules.* In the event that a building is not owned by the taxpayer, the adjusted basis of the building shall be determined as of the date that would have been used if the owner had been the taxpayer. The adjusted basis of a building that is being rehabilitated by a taxpayer other than the owner shall thus be determined as of the beginning of the first day of the 24-month period selected by the taxpayer or the first day of the owner's holding period, whichever is later. Therefore, if a building that is being rehabilitated by a lessee is sold subject to the lease prior to the date that the lessee has substantially rehabilitated the building, the lessee's adjusted basis is determined as of the beginning of the first day of the new lessor's holding period or the beginning of the first day of the 24-month period selected by the lessee (the taxpayer), whichever is later. If, therefore, the first day of the new lessor's holding period were later than the first day of the 24-month period selected by the lessee (the taxpayer), the lessee's adjusted basis for purposes of the substantial rehabilitation test would be the same as the adjusted basis of the new lessor as determined under paragraph (b)(2)(vii) of this section. If a building is sold after the date that a lessee has substantially rehabilitated the building with respect to the original lessor's adjusted basis,

however, the lessee's basis may be determined as of the first day of the 24-month period selected by the lessee or the first day of the original lessor's holding period, whichever is later, and the transfer of the building will not affect the adjusted basis for purposes of the substantial rehabilitation test. The preceding sentence shall not apply, however, if the building is sold to the lessee or a related party within the meaning of section 267(b) or section 707(b)(1).

(iii) *Adjusted basis of the building*—(A) *In general.* The term "adjusted basis of the building" means the aggregate adjusted basis (within the meaning of section 1011(a)) in the building (and its structural components) of all the parties who have an interest in the building.

(B) *Special rules.* In the case of a building that is leased to one or more tenants in whole or in part, the adjusted basis of the building is determined by adding the adjusted basis of the owner (lessor) in the building to the adjusted basis of the lessee (or lessees) in the leasehold and any leasehold improvements that are structural components of the building. Similarly, in the case of a building that is divided into condominium units, the adjusted basis of the building means the aggregate adjusted basis of all of the respective condominium owners (including the basis of any lessee in the leasehold and leasehold improvements) in the building (and its structural components). If the adjusted basis of a building would be determined in whole or in part by reference to the adjusted basis of a person or persons other than the taxpayer (*e.g.,* a rehabilitation by a lessee) and the taxpayer is unable to obtain the required information, the taxpayer must establish by clear and convincing evidence that the adjusted basis of such person or persons in the building on the date specified in paragraph (b)(2)(ii) of this section is an amount that is less than the amount of qualified rehabilitation expenditures incurred by the taxpayer. If no such amount can be so established, the adjusted basis of the building will be deemed to be the fair market value of the building on the relevant date. For purposes of determining the adjusted basis of a building, the portion of the adjusted basis of a building that is allocable to an addition (within the meaning of paragraph (b)(4)(ii) of this section) to the building that does not meet the age requirement in paragraph (b)(4)(i) of this section shall be disregarded. (See paragraph (b)(2)(vii) of this section for the rule applicable to the determination of the adjusted basis of a building when qualified rehabilitation expenditures are treated as incurred by the taxpayer.)

Reg. § 1.48-12(b)(2)

(iv) *Rehabilitation.* Rehabilitation includes renovation, restoration, or reconstruction of a building, but does not include an enlargement (within the meaning of paragraph (c) (10) of this section) or new construction. The determination of whether expenditures are attributable to the rehabilitation of an existing building or to new construction shall be based upon all the facts and circumstances.

(v) *Special rule for phased rehabilitation.* In the case of any rehabilitation that may reasonably be expected to be completed in phases set forth in written architectural plans and specifications completed before the physical work on the rehabilitation begins, paragraphs (b) (2) (i), (ii), and (vii) of this section shall be applied by substituting "60-month period" for "24-month period." A rehabilitation may reasonably be expected to be completed in phases if it consists of two or more distinct stages of development. The determination of whether a rehabilitation consists of distinct stages and therefore may reasonably be expected to be completed in phases shall be made on the basis of all the relevant facts and circumstances in existence before physical work on the rehabilitation begins. For purposes of this paragraph and paragraph (a) (2) (iii) of this section, written plans that describe generally all phases of the rehabilitation process shall be treated as written architectural plans and specifications. Such written plans are not required to contain detailed working drawings or detailed specifications of the materials to be used. In addition, the taxpayer may include a description of work to be done by lessees in the written plans. For example, where the owner of a vacant four story building plans to rehabilitate two floors of the building and plans to require, as a condition of any lease, that tenants of the other two floors must rehabilitate those floors, the requirements of this paragraph (b) (2) (v) shall be met if the owner provides written plans for the rehabilitation work to be done by the owner and a description of the rehabilitation work that the tenants will be required to complete. The work required of the tenants may be described in the written plans in terms of minimum specifications (*e.g.,* as to lighting, wiring, materials, appearance) that must be met by such tenants. See paragraph (b) (6) (i) of this section for the definition of physical work on a rehabilitation.

(vi) *Treatment of expenses incurred by persons who have an interest in the building.* For purposes of the substantial rehabilitation test in paragraph (b) (2) (i) of this section, the taxpayer may take into account qualified rehabilitation expenditures incurred during the same rehabilitation process by any other person who has an interest in the building. Thus, for example, to determine whether a building has been substantially rehabilitated, a lessee may include the expenditures of the lessor and of other lessees; a condominium owner may include the expenditures incurred by other condominium owners; and an owner may include the expenditures of the lessees.

(vii) *Special rules when qualified rehabilitation expenditures are treated as incurred by the taxpayer.* In the case where qualified rehabilitation expenditures are treated as having been incurred by a taxpayer under paragraph (c) (3) (ii) of this section, the transferee shall be treated as having incurred the expenditures incurred by the transferor on the date that the transferor incurred the expenditures within the meaning of paragraph (c) (3) (i) of this section. For purposes of the substantial rehabilitation test in paragraph (b) (2) (i) of this section, the transferee's adjusted basis in the building shall be determined as of the beginning of the first day of a 24-month period, or the first day of the transferee's holding period, whichever is later, as provided in paragraph (b) (2) (ii) of this section. The transferee's basis as of the first day of the transferee's holding period for purposes of the substantial rehabilitation test in paragraph (b) (2) (i) of this section, however, shall be considered to be equal to the transferee's basis in the building on such date less—

(A) The amount of any qualified rehabilitation expenditures incurred (or treated as having been incurred) by the transferor during the 24-month period that are treated as having been incurred by the transferee under paragraph (c) (3) (ii) of this section, and

(B) The amount of qualified rehabilitation expenditures incurred before the transfer and during the 24-month period by any other person who has an interest in the building (*e.g.,* a lessee of the transferor).

The preceding sentence shall not apply, however, unless the transferee's basis in the building is determined with reference to (*1*) the transferee's cost of the building (including the rehabilitation expenditures), (*2*) the transferor's basis in the building (where such basis includes the amount of the expenditures), or (*3*) any other amount that includes the cost of the rehabilitation expenditures. In the event that the transferee's basis is determined with reference to an amount not described above (*e.g.,* transferee's basis in one building is determined with reference to the transferee's basis in another building under section 1031 (d)), the amount of the expenditures incurred by the transferor and treated as having been incurred by the transferee are not deducted from the transferee's basis for purposes of the substantial rehabilitation test. If a transferee's basis is determined under section 1014, any expenditures incurred by the decedent within the measuring period that are treated as having been incurred by the transferee under paragraph (c) (3) (ii) of this section shall decrease the transferee's basis for purposes of the substantial rehabilitation test.

(viii) *Statement of adjusted basis, measuring period, and qualified rehabilitation expenditures.* In the case of any tax return filed after August 27, 1985, on which an investment tax credit for property, described in section 48 (a) (1) (E) is claimed, the taxpayer shall indicate by way of a marginal notation on, or a supplemental statement attached to, Form 3468—

(A) The beginning and ending dates for the measuring period selected by the taxpayer under section 48 (g) (1) (C) (i) and paragraph (b) (2) of this section,

(B) The adjusted basis of the building (within the meaning of paragraph (b) (2) (iii) or (vii) of this section) as of the beginning of such measuring period, and

(C) The amount of qualified rehabilitation expenditures incurred, and treated as incurred, respectively, during such measuring period.

Furthermore, for returns filed after August 27, 1985, if the adjusted basis of the building for purposes of the substantial rehabilitation test is determined in whole or in part by reference to the adjusted basis of a person, or persons, other than the taxpayer, (*e.g.*, a rehabilitation by a lessee), the taxpayer must attach to the Form 3468 filed with the tax return on which the credit is claimed a statement addressed to the District Director, signed by such third party, that states the first day of the third party's holding period and the amount of the adjusted basis of such third party in the building at the beginning of the measuring period or the first day of the holding period, whichever is later. If the taxpayer is unable to obtain the required information, that fact should be indicated and the taxpayer should state the manner in which the adjusted basis was determined and, if different, the fair market value of the building on the relevant date.

(ix) *Partnerships and S corporations.* If a building is owned by a partnership (*i.e.*, the building is partnership property) or an S corporation, the substantial rehabilitation test shall be determined at the entity level. Thus, the entity shall compare the amount of qualified rehabilitation expenditures incurred during the measuring period against its basis in the building at the beginning of its holding period or the beginning of its measuring period, whichever is later. (See section

1223 (2) for rules concerning the determination of a partnership's holding period in the case of a contribution of property to the partnership meeting the requirements of section 721.) The adjusted basis of the building to a partnership shall be determined by taking into account any adjustments to the basis of the building made under section 743 and section 734. Any adjustments to the building's basis that are made under section 743 or section 734 after the beginning of the partnership's holding period, but before the end of the measuring period, shall be deemed for purposes of the substantial rehabilitation test to have been made on the first day of the partnership's holding period. However, in such case, the partnership's basis in the building shall be reduced by the amount of qualified rehabilitation expenditures incurred by the partnership. In the case of any tax return filed after January 9, 1989, on which a credit is claimed by a partner or a shareholder of an S corporation for rehabilitation expenditures incurred by a partnership or an S corporation, the partner or shareholder shall indicate on the Form 3468 on which the credit is claimed the name, address, and identification number of the partnership or S corporation that incurred the rehabilitation expenditures, and the partnership or S corporation shall, by way of a marginal notation on or a supplemental statement attached to the entity's return, provide the information required by paragraph (b) (2) (viii) of this section.

(x) *Examples.* The following examples illustrate the application of the substantial rehabilitation test in this paragraph (b) (2):

Example (1). Assume that A, a calendar year taxpayer, purchases a building for $140,000 on January 1, 1982, incurs qualified rehabilitation expenditures in the amount of $48,000 (at the rate of $4,000 per month) in 1982, $100,000 in 1983, and $20,000 (at the rate of $2,000 per month) in the first ten months of 1984, and places the rehabilitated building in service on October 31, 1984. Assume that A did not have written architectural plans and specifications describing a phased rehabilitation within the meaning of paragraph (b) (2) (v) of this section in existence prior to the beginning of physical work on the rehabilitation. For purposes of the substantial rehabilitation test in paragraph (b) (2) of this section, A may select any 24-consecutive-month measuring period that ends in 1984, the taxable year in which the rehabilitated building was placed in service. Assume that on A's 1984 return, A selects a measuring period beginning on February 1, 1982, and ending on January 31, 1984, and specifies that A's basis in the building (within the meaning of section 1011 (a)) was $144,000 on

February 1, 1982 ($140,000 + $4,000). (The $4,000 of rehabilitation expenditures incurred during January 1982 are included in A's basis under section 1011 even though such property has not been placed in service.) The amount of qualified rehabilitation expenditures incurred during the measuring period was $146,000 ($44,000 from February 1 to December 31, 1982, plus $100,000 in 1983, plus $2,000 in January 1984). The building shall be treated as "substantially rehabilitated" within the meaning of this paragraph (b) (2) for A's 1984 taxable year because the $146,000 of expenditures incurred by A during the measuring period exceeded A's adjusted basis of $144,000 at the beginning of the period. If the other requirements of section 48 (g) (1) and this paragraph are met, the building is treated as a qualified rehabilitated building, and A can treat as qualified rehabilitation expenditures the amount of $168,000 (i.e., $146,000 of expenditures incurred during the measuring period, $4,000 of expenditures incurred prior to the beginning of the measuring period as part of the rehabilitation process, and $18,000 of expenditures incurred after the measuring period during the taxable year within which the measuring period ends (See paragraph (c) (6) of this section.)). The result would generally be the same if the property attributable to the rehabilitation expenditures was placed in service as the expenditures were incurred, but A would have $148,000 of qualified rehabilitation expenditures for 1983 and $20,000 of qualified rehabilitation expenditures for 1984. (See paragraph (f) (2) of this section).

Example (2). Assume the same facts as in example (1), except that additional rehabilitation expenditures are incurred after the portion of the basis of the building attributable to qualified rehabilitation expenditures was placed in service on October 31, 1984. Such expenditures are incurred through the end of 1984 and in 1985 when the portion of the basis attributable to the additional expenditures is placed in service. The fact that the building qualified as a substantially rehabilitated building for A's 1984 taxable year has no effect on whether the building is a qualified rehabilitated building for property placed in service in A's 1985 taxable year. In order to determine whether the building is a qualified rehabilitated building for A's 1985 taxable year, A must select a measuring period that ends in 1985 and compare the expenditures incurred within that period with the adjusted basis as of the beginning of the period. Solely for the purpose of determining whether the building was substantially rehabilitated for A's 1985 taxable year, expenditures incurred during 1983 and 1984, even though considered in determining whether the building

was substantially rehabilitated in 1984, may also be used to determine whether the building was substantially rehabilitated for A's 1985 taxable year, provided the expenditures were incurred during any 24-month measuring period selected by A that ends in 1985.

Example (3). (i) Assume that B purchases a building for $100,000 on January 1, 1982, and leases the building to C who rehabilitates the building. Assume that C, a calendar year taxpayer, places the property with respect to which rehabilitation expenditures were made in service in 1982 and selects December 31, 1982, as the end of the measuring period for purposes of the substantial rehabilitation test. The beginning of the measuring period is January 2, 1982, the beginning of B's holding period under section 1250 (e), and the adjusted basis of the building is $100,000. Accordingly, if C incurred more than $100,000 of qualified rehabilitation expenditures during 1982, the building would be substantially rehabilitated within the meaning of paragraph (b) (2) (i) of this section.

(ii) Assume the facts of example (3) (i), except that after C begins physical work on the rehabilitation, but before C incurs $100,000 of expenditures, D acquires the building, subject to C's lease, from B for $200,000. D's holding period under section 1250 (e) begins on the day after D acquired the building, and C's adjusted basis for purposes of the substantial rehabilitation test is $200,000, less the amount of expenditures incurred by C before the transfer. (See paragraph (b) (2) (ii) and (vii) of this section.) Accordingly, if C incurred more than $200,000 (less the amount of expenditures incurred prior to the transfer) of qualified rehabilitation expenditures during 1982, the building would be substantially rehabilitated within the meaning of paragraph (b) (2) of this section. Under paragraph (b) (2) (ii) (B) of this section, however, C's adjusted basis for purposes of the substantial rehabilitation test would be $100,000 if C had substantially rehabilitated the building (i.e., incurred more than $100,000 in rehabilitation expenditures) prior to B's sale to D.

Example (4). E owns a building with a basis of $10,000 and E incurs $5,000 of rehabilitation expenditures. Before completing the rehabilitation project, E sells the building to F for $30,000. Assume that F is treated under paragraph (c) (3) (ii) of this section as having incurred the $5,000 of rehabilitation expenditures actually incurred by E. Because F's basis in the building is determined under section 1011 with reference to F's $30,000 cost of the building (which includes the property attributable to E's rehabilitation expenditures), F's basis for purposes of the substantial rehabilitation test is $25,000 ($30,000 cost basis less $5,000 rehabilitation expenditures treated as if incurred by F). (See paragraph (b)(2)(vii) of this section.) F would thus be required to incur more than $20,000 of rehabilitation expenditures (in addition to the $5,000 incurred by E and treated as having been incurred by F) during a measuring period selected by F to satisfy the substantial rehabilitation test.

Example (5). G owns Building I with a basis of $10,000 and a fair market value of $20,000. H owns Building II with a basis of $5,000 and a fair market value of $20,000, with respect to which H has incurred $1,000 of rehabilitation expenditures. G and H exchange their buildings in a transaction that qualifies for nonrecognition treatment under section 1031. Assume that G is treated under paragraph (c)(3)(ii) of this section as having incurred $1,000 of rehabilitation expenditures. G's basis in Building II, computed under section 1031 (d), is $10,000. G's basis in Building II is not determined with reference to (A) the cost of Building II, (B) H's basis in Building II (including the cost of the rehabilitation expenditures) or (C) any other amount that includes the cost of the expenditures, but is instead determined with reference to G's basis in other property (Building I). Therefore, G's basis in Building II for purposes of the substantial rehabilitation test is not reduced by the $1,000 of rehabilitation expenditures treated as if incurred by G. (See paragraph (b)(2)(vii) of this section.) Accordingly, G's basis in Building II for purposes of the substantial rehabilitation test is $10,000, and G must incur additional rehabilitation expenditures in excess of $9,000 within a measuring period selected by G to satisfy the test.

(3) *Retention of existing external walls and internal structural framework*—(i) *In general*—(A) *Property placed in service after December 31, 1986.* Except in the case of property that qualifies for the transition rules in paragraph (a)(2)(iv)(B) or (C) of this section, in the case of property that is placed in service after December 31, 1986, a building (other than a certified historic structure) meets the requirement in paragraph (b)(1)(iii) of this section only if in the rehabilitation process—

(*1*) 50 percent or more of the existing external walls of such building are retained in place as external walls;

(*2*) 75 percent or more of the existing external walls of such building are retained in place as internal or external walls, and

(*3*) 75 percent or more of the internal structural framework of such building (as defined

in paragraph (b)(3)(iii) of this section) is retained in place.

(B) *Expenditures incurred before January 1, 1984, for property placed in service before January 1, 1987.* With respect to rehabilitation expenditures incurred before January 1, 1984, for property that is either placed in service before January 1, 1987, or that qualifies for the transition rules in paragraph (a)(2)(iv)(B) or (C) of this section, a building meets the requirement in paragraph (b)(1)(iii) of this section only if 75 percent or more of the existing external walls of the building are retained in place as external walls in the rehabilitation process. If an addition to a building is not treated as part of a qualified rehabilitated building because it does not meet the 30-year requirement in paragraph (b)(4)(i)(B) of this section, then the external walls of such addition shall not be considered to be existing external walls of the building for purposes of section 48 (g)(1)(A)(iii) (as in effect prior to enactment of the Tax Reform Act of 1986), and this section.

(C) *Expenditures incurred after December 31, 1983, for property placed in service before January 1, 1987.* With respect to expenditures incurred after December 31, 1983, for property that is either placed in service before January 1, 1987, or that qualifies for the transition rules in paragraph (a)(2)(iv)(B) or (C) of this section, the requirement of paragraph (b)(1)(iii) of this section is satisfied only if in the rehabilitation process either the existing external wall retention requirement in paragraph (b)(3)(i)(B) of this section is satisfied, or:

(*1*) 50 percent or more of the existing external walls of the building are retained in place as external walls,

(*2*) 75 percent or more of the existing external walls are retained in place as internal or external walls, and

(*3*) 75 percent or more of the existing internal structural framework of such building is retained in place.

(D) *Area of external walls and internal structural framework.* The determinations required by paragraph (b)(3)(i)(A), (B), and (C) of this section shall be based upon the area of the external walls or internal structural framework that is retained in place compared to the total area of each prior to the rehabilitation. The area of the existing external walls and internal structural framework of a building shall be determined prior to any destruction, modification, or construction of external walls or internal structural framework that is undertaken by any party in anticipation of the rehabilitation.

Reg. § 1.48-12(b)(3)

(ii) *Definition of external wall.* For purposes of this paragraph (b), a wall includes both the supporting elements of the wall and the non-supporting elements (*e.g.*, a curtain, windows or doors) of the wall. Except as otherwise provided in this paragraph (b)(3), the term "external wall" includes any wall that has one face exposed to the weather, earth, or an abutting wall of an adjacent building. The term "external wall" also includes a shared wall (*i.e.*, a single wall shared with an adjacent building), generally referred to as a "party wall," provided that the shared wall has no windows or doors *in* any portion of the wall that does not have one face exposed to the weather, earth, or an abutting wall. In general, the term "external wall" includes only those external walls that form part of the outline or perimeter of the building or that surround an uncovered courtyard. Therefore, the walls of an uncovered internal shaft, designed solely to bring light or air into the center of a building, which are completely surrounded by external walls of the building and which enclose space not designated for occupancy or other use by people (other than for maintenance or emergency), are not considered external walls. Thus, for example, a wall of a light well in the center of a building is not an external wall. However, walls surrounding an outdoor space which is usable by people, such as a courtyard, are external walls.

(iii) *Definition of internal structural framework.* For purposes of this section, the term "internal structural framework" includes all load-bearing internal walls and any other internal structural supports, including the columns, girders, beams, trusses, spandrels, and all other members that are essential to the stability of the building.

(iv) *Retained in place.* An existing external wall is retained in place if the supporting elements of the wall are retained in place. An existing external wall is not retained in place if the supporting elements of the wall are replaced by new supporting elements. An external wall is retained in place, however, if the supporting elements are reinforced in the rehabilitation, provided that such supporting elements of the external wall are retained in place. An external wall also is retained in place if it is covered (*e.g.*, with new siding). Moreover, an external wall is retained in place if the existing curtain is replaced with a new curtain, provided that the structural framework that provides for the support of the existing curtain is retained in place. An external wall is retained in place notwithstanding that the existing doors and windows in the wall are modified, eliminated, or replaced. An external wall is retained in place if the wall is disassembled and reassembled, provided the same supporting elements are used when the wall is reassembled and the configuration of the external walls of the building after the rehabilitation is the same as it was before the rehabilitation process commenced. Thus, for example, a brick wall is considered retained in place even though the original bricks are removed (for cleaning, *etc.*) and replaced to form the wall. The principles of this paragraph (b)(3)(iv) shall also apply to determine whether internal structural framework of the building *is* retained in place.

(v) *Effect of additions.* If an existing external wall is converted into an internal wall (*i.e.*, a wall that is not an external wall), the wall is not retained in place as an external wall for purposes of this section.

(vi) *Examples.* The provisions of this paragraph (b)(3) may be illustrated by the following examples:

Example (1). Taxpayer A rehabilitated a building all of the walls of which consisted of wood siding attached to gypsum board sheets (which covered the supporting elements of the wall, *i.e.*, studs). A covered the existing wood siding with aluminum siding as part of a rehabilitation that otherwise qualified under this subparagraph. The addition of the aluminum siding does not affect the status of the existing external walls as external walls and they would be considered to have been retained in place.

Example (2). Taxpayer B rehabilitated a building, the external walls of which had a masonry curtain. The masonry on the wall face was replaced with a glass curtain. The steel beam and girders supporting the existing masonry curtain were retained in place. The walls of the building are considered to be retained in place as external walls, notwithstanding the replacement of the curtain.

Example (3). Taxpayer C rehabilitated a building that has two external walls measuring 75' × 20' and two other external walls measuring 100' × 20'. C demolished one of the larger walls, including its supporting elements and constructed a new wall. Because one of the larger walls represents more than 25 percent of the area of the building's external walls, C has not satisfied the requirement that 75 percent of the existing external walls must be retained in place as either internal or external walls. If however, C had not demolished the wall, but had converted it into an internal wall (*e.g.*, by building a new external wall), the building would satisfy the external wall requirements.

Example (4). The facts are the same as in example (3), except that C does not tear down any

Reg. § 1.48-12(b)(3)

walls, but builds an addition that results in one of the smaller walls becoming an internal wall. In addition, C enlarged 8 of the existing windows on one of the larger walls, increasing them from a size of 3' × 4' to 6' × 8'. Since the smaller wall accounts for less than 25 percent of the total wall area, C has satisfied the requirement that 75 percent of the existing external walls must be retained in place as external walls in the rehabilitation process. The enlargement of the existing windows on the larger wall does not affect its status as an external wall.

Example (5). Taxpayer D rehabilitated a building that was in the center of a row of three buildings. The building being rehabilitated by D shares its side walls with the buildings on either side. The shared walls measure 100' × 20' and the rear and front walls measure 75' × 20'. As part of a rehabilitation, D tears down and replaces the front wall. Because the shared walls as well as the front and back walls are considered external walls and the front wall accounts for less than 25 percent of the total external wall area (including the shared walls), D has satisfied the requirement that 75 percent of the existing external walls must be retained in place as external walls in the rehabilitation process.

(4) Age requirement—(i) In general—(A) Property placed in service after December 31, 1986. Except in the case of property that qualifies for the transition rules in paragraph (a)(2)(iv)(B) or (C) of this section, a building other than a certified historic structure shall not be considered a qualified rehabilitated building unless the building was first placed in service (within the meaning of § 1.46-3(d)) before January 1, 1936.

(B) Property placed in service before January 1, 1987, and property qualifying under a transition rule. In the case of property placed in service before January 1, 1987, and property that qualifies under the transition rules in paragraph (a)(2)(iv)(B) or (C) of this section, a building other than a certified historic structure is considered a qualified rehabilitated building only if a period of at least 30 years has elapsed between the date physical work on the rehabilitation of the building began and the date the building was first placed in service (within the meaning of § 1.46-3(d)) as a building by any person.

(ii) Additions. A building that was first placed in service before 1936 in the case described in paragraph (b)(4)(i)(A) of this section, or at least 30 years before physical work on the rehabilitation began in the case described in paragraph (b)(4)(i)(B) of this section, will not be disqualified because additions to such building have been added since 1936 in the case described in para-

graph (b)(4)(i)(A) of this section, or are less than 30 years old in the case described in paragraph (b)(4)(i)(B). Such additions, however, shall not be treated as part of the qualified rehabilitated building. The term "addition" means any construction that resulted in any portion of an external wall becoming an internal wall, that resulted in an increase in the height of the building, or that increased the volume of the building.

(iii) Vacant periods. The determinations required by paragraph (b)(4)(i) of this section include periods during which a building was vacant or devoted to a personal use and is computed without regard to the number of owners or the identity of owners during the period.

(5) Location at which the rehabilitation occurs. A building, other than a certified historic structure, is not a qualified rehabilitated building unless it has been located where it is rehabilitated since before 1936 in the case described in paragraph (b)(4)(i)(A) of this section. Similarly, in the case described in paragraph (b)(4)(i)(B) of this section, a building, other than a certified historic structure, is not a qualified rehabilitated building unless it has been located where it is rehabilitated for the thirty-year period immediately preceding the date physical work on the rehabilitation began in the case of a "30-year building" or the forty-year period immediately preceding the date physical work on the rehabilitation began in the case of a "40-year building." (See § 1.46-1 (q)(1)(iii) for the definitions of "30-year building" and "40-year building.")

(6) Definition and special rule—(i) Physical work on a rehabilitation. For purposes of this section, "physical work on a rehabilitation" begins when actual construction, or destruction in preparation for construction, begins. The term "physical work on a rehabilitation," however, does not include preliminary activities such as planning, designing, securing financing, exploring, researching, developing plans and specifications, or stabilizing a building to prevent deterioration (e.g., placing boards over broken windows).

(ii) Special rule for adjoining buildings that are combined. For purposes of this paragraph (b), if as part of a rehabilitation process two or more adjoining buildings are combined and placed in service as a single building after the rehabilitation process, then, at the election of the taxpayer, all of the requirements for a qualified rehabilitated building in section 48(g)(1) and this section may be applied to the constituent adjoining buildings in the aggregate. For example, if such requirements are applied in the aggregate, any shared walls or abutting walls between the constituent buildings that would otherwise be treated

Reg. § 1.48-12(b)(4)

as external walls (within the meaning of paragraph (b)(3) of this section) would not be treated as external walls of the building, and the substantial rehabilitation test in paragraph (b)(2) of this section would be applied to the aggregate expenditures with respect to all of the constituent buildings and to the aggregate adjusted basis of all of the constituent buildings. A taxpayer shall elect the special rule of this paragraph (b)(6)(ii) for adjoining buildings by indicating by way of a marginal notation on, or a supplemental statement attached to, the Form 3468 on which a credit is first claimed for qualified rehabilitation expenditures with respect to such buildings that such buildings are a single qualified rehabilitated building because of the application of the special rule in this paragraph (b)(6)(ii).

(c) *Definition of qualified rehabilitation expenditures*—(1) *In general.* Except as otherwise provided in paragraph (c)(7) of this section, the term "qualified rehabilitation expenditure" means any amount that is—

    (i) Properly chargeable to capital account (as described in paragraph (c)(2) of this section),

    (ii) Incurred by the taxpayer after December 31, 1981 (as described in paragraph (c)(3) of this section),

    (iii) For property for which depreciation is allowable under section 168 and which is real property described in paragraph (c)(4) of this section, and

    (iv) Made in connection with the rehabilitation of a qualified rehabilitated building (as described in paragraph (c)(5) of this section).

(2) *Chargeable to capital account.* For purposes of paragraph (c)(1) of this section, amounts are chargeable to capital account if they are properly includible in computing basis of real property under § 1.46-3(c). Amounts treated as an expense and deducted in the year they are paid or incurred or amounts that are otherwise not added to the basis of real property described in paragraph (c)(4) of this section do not qualify. For purposes of this paragraph (c), amounts incurred for architectural and engineering fees, site survey fees, legal expenses, insurance premiums, development fees, and other construction related costs, satisfy the requirement of this paragraph (c)(2) if they are added to the basis of real property that is described in paragraph (c)(4) of this section. Construction period interest and taxes that are amortized under section 189 (as in effect prior to its repeal by the Tax Reform Act of 1986) do not satisfy the requirement of this paragraph (c)(2). If, however, such interest and taxes are treated by the taxpayer as chargeable to capital account with respect to property described in paragraph

(c)(4) of this section, they shall be treated in the same manner as other costs described in this paragraph (c)(2). Any construction period interest or taxes or other fees or costs incurred in connection with the acquisition of a building, any interest in a building, or land, are subject to paragraph (c)(7)(ii) of this section. See paragraph (c)(9) of this section for additional rules concerning interest.

(3) *Incurred by the taxpayer*—(i) *In general.* Qualified rehabilitation expenditures are incurred by the taxpayer for purposes of this section on the date such expenditures would be considered incurred under an accrual method of accounting, regardless of the method of accounting used by the taxpayer with respect to other items of income and expense. If qualified rehabilitation expenditures are treated as having been incurred by a taxpayer under paragraph (c)(3)(ii) of this section, the taxpayer shall be treated as having incurred the expenditures on the date such expenditures were incurred by the transferor.

    (ii) *Qualified rehabilitation expenditures treated as incurred by the taxpayer*—(A) Where rehabilitation expenditures are incurred with respect to a building by a person (or persons) other than the taxpayer and the taxpayer subsequently acquires the building, or a portion of the building to which some or all of the expenditures are allocable (*e.g.,* a condominium unit to which rehabilitation expenditures have been allocated), the taxpayer acquiring such property shall be treated as having incurred the rehabilitation expenditures actually incurred by the transferor (or treated as incurred by the transferor under this paragraph (c)(3)(ii)) allocable to the acquired property, provided that—

        (*1*) The building, or the portion of the building, acquired by the taxpayer was not used (or, if later, was not placed in service (as defined in paragraph (f)(2) of this section)) after the rehabilitation expenditures were incurred and prior to the date of acquisition, and

        (*2*) No credit with respect to such qualified rehabilitation expenditures is claimed by anyone other than the taxpayer acquiring the property.

For purposes of this paragraph (c)(3)(ii), use shall mean actual use, whether personal or business. In the case of a building that is divided into condominium units, expenditures attributable to the common elements shall be allocable to the individual condominium units in accordance with the principles of paragraph (c)(10)(ii) of this section. Furthermore, for purpose of this paragraph (c)(3)(ii), a condominium unit's share of the common elements shall not be considered to have been

Reg. § 1.48-12(c)(3)

used (or placed in service) prior to the time that the particular condominium unit is used.

(B) The amount of rehabilitation expenditures described in paragraph (c)(3)(ii)(A) of this section treated as incurred by the taxpayer under this paragraph shall be the lesser of—

(1) The amount of rehabilitation expenditures incurred before the date on which the taxpayer acquired the building (or portion thereof) to which the rehabilitation expenditures are attributable, or

(2) The portion of the taxpayer's cost or other basis for the property that is properly allocable to the property resulting from the rehabilitation expenditures described in paragraph (c)(3)(ii)(B)(1) of this section.

(C) For purposes of this paragraph (c)(3)(ii), the amount of rehabilitation expenditures treated as incurred by the taxpayer under this paragraph (c) shall not be treated as costs for the acquisition of a building. The portion of the cost of acquiring a building (or an interest therein) that is not treated under this paragraph as qualified rehabilitation expenditures incurred by the taxpayer is not treated as section 38 property in the hands of the acquiring taxpayer. (See paragraph (c)(7)(ii) of this section.) (See paragraph (b)(2)(vii) for rules concerning the application of the substantial rehabilitation test when expenditures are treated as incurred by the taxpayer.)

(iii) *Examples.* The provisions of this paragraph (c) may be illustrated by the following examples:

Example (1). In 1981, A, a taxpayer using the cash receipts and disbursements method of accounting, commenced the rehabilitation of a 30-year old building. In June 1981, A signed a contract with a plumbing contractor for replacement of the plumbing in the building. A agreed to pay the contractor as soon as the work was completed. The work was completed in December 1981, but A did not pay the amount due until January 15, 1982. The expenditures for the plumbing are not qualified rehabilitation expenditures (within the meaning of this paragraph (c)) because they were not incurred under an accrual method of accounting after December 31, 1981.

Example (2). B incurred qualified rehabilitation expenditures of $300,000 with respect to an existing building between January 1, 1982, and May 15, 1982, and then sold the building to C on June 1, 1982. The portion of the building to which the expenditures were allocable was not used by B or any other person during the period from January 1, 1982, to June 1, 1982, and neither B nor any other person claimed the credit. Consequently, C will be treated as having incurred expenditures on the dates that B incurred the expenditures.

Example (3). D, a taxpayer using the cash receipts and disbursements method of accounting, begins the rehabilitation of a building on January 11, 1982. Prior to May 1, 1982, D makes rehabilitation expenditures of $16,000. On May 3, 1982, D sells the building, the land, and the property attributable to the rehabilitation expenditures to E for $35,000. The purchase price is properly allocable as follows:

land	$ 5,000
existing building	11,000
property attributable to rehabilitation expenditures	19,000
total purchase price	$35,000

The property attributable to the rehabilitation expenditures is placed in service by E on September 5, 1982. E may treat a portion of the $35,000 purchase price as rehabilitation expenditures paid or incurred by him. Since the rehabilitation expenditures paid by D ($16,000) are less than the portion of the purchase price properly allocable to property attributable to these expenditures ($19,000), E may treat only $16,000 as rehabilitation expenditures paid or incurred by him. The excess of the purchase price allocable to rehabilitation expenditures ($19,000) over the rehabilitation expenditures paid by D ($16,000), or $3,000, is treated as the cost of acquiring an interest in the building and is not a qualified rehabilitation expenditure treated as incurred by E.

Example (4). The facts are the same as in example (3), except that the purchase price prop-erly allocable to the property attributable to rehabilitation expenditures is $15,000. Under these circumstances, E may treat only $15,000 of D's $16,000 rehabilitation expenditures as rehabilitation expenditures paid by D. The excess of the rehabilitation expenditures paid by D ($16,000) over the purchase price allocable to rehabilitation expenditures ($15,000), or $1,000, is treated as the cost of acquiring an interest in the building and is not a qualified rehabilitation expenditure treated as incurred by E.

(4) *Incurred for depreciable real property—* (i) *Property placed in service after December 31, 1986.* Except as otherwise provided in paragraph (c)(4)(ii) of this section (relating to certain property that qualifies under a transition rule), in the case of property placed in service after December 31, 1986, an expenditure is incurred for deprecia-

Reg. § 1.48-12(c)(4)

ble real property for purposes of paragraph (c)(1)(iii) of this section, only if it is added to the depreciable basis of depreciable property which is—

    (A) Nonresidential real property,

    (B) Residential rental property,

    (C) Real property which has a class life of more than 12.5 years, or

    (D) An addition or improvement to property described in paragraph (c)(4)(i)(A), (B), or (C) of this section.

For purposes of this paragraph (c)(4)(i), the terms "nonresidential real property", "residential rental property", and "class life" have the respective meanings given to such terms by section 168 and the regulations thereunder.

    (ii) *Property placed in service before January 1, 1987, and property that qualifies under a transition rule.* In the case of property placed in service before January 1, 1987, and property placed in service after December 31, 1986, that qualifies for the transition rules in paragraph (a)(2)(iv)(B) or (C) of this section, an expenditure attributable to such property shall be a qualified rehabilitation expenditure only if such expenditure is incurred for property that is real property (or additions or improvements to real property) with a recovery period (within the meaning of section 168 as in effect prior to its amendment by the Tax Reform Act of 1986) of 19 years (15 years for low-income housing) and if the other requirements of this paragraph (c) are met. For purposes of this section, an expenditure is incurred for recovery property having a recovery period of 19 years only if the amount of the expenditure is added to the basis of property which is 19-year real property or 15-year real property in the case of low-income housing. For purposes of this section, the term "low-income housing" has the meaning given such term by section 168 (c)(2)(F) (as in effect prior to the amendments made by the Tax Reform Act of 1986).

    (5) *Made in connection with the rehabilitation of a qualified rehabilitated building.* In order for an expenditure to be a qualified rehabilitation expenditure, such expenditure must be incurred in connection with a rehabilitation (as defined in paragraph (b)(2)(iv) of this section) of a qualified rehabilitated building. Expenditures attributable to work done to facilities related to a building (*e.g.,* sidewalk, parking lot, landscaping) are not considered made in connection with the rehabilitation of a qualified rehabilitated building.

    (6) *When expenditures may be incurred.* An expenditure is a qualified rehabilitation expenditure only if the building with respect to which the expenditures are incurred is substantially rehabilitated (within the meaning of paragraph (b)(2) of this section) for the taxable year in which the property attributable to the expenditures is placed in service (*i.e.,* the building is substantially rehabilitated during a measuring period ending with or within the taxable year in which a credit is claimed). (See paragraph (f)(2) of this section for rules relating to when property is placed in service.) Once the substantial rehabilitation test is met for a taxable year, the amount of qualified rehabilitation expenditures upon which a credit can be claimed for the taxable year is limited to expenditures incurred:

    (i) Before the beginning of a measuring period during which the building was substantially rehabilitated that ends with or within the taxable year, provided that the expenditures were incurred in connection with the rehabilitation process that resulted in the substantial rehabilitation of the building;

    (ii) Within a measuring period during which the building was substantially rehabilitated that ends with or within the taxable year, and

    (iii) After the end of a measuring period during which the building was substantially rehabilitated but prior to the end of the taxable year with or within which the measuring period ends.

    (7) *Certain expenditures excluded from qualified rehabilitation expenditures.* The term "qualified rehabilitation expenditures" does not include the following expenditures:

    (i) Except as otherwise provided in paragraph (c)(8) of this section, any expenditure with respect to which the taxpayer does not use the straight line method over a recovery period determined under section 168 (c) and (g).

    (ii) The cost of acquiring a building, any interest in a building (including a leasehold interest), or land, except as provided in paragraph (c)(3)(ii) of this section.

    (iii) Any expenditure attributable to an enlargement of a building (within the meaning of paragraph (c)(10) of this section).

    (iv) Any expenditure attributable to the rehabilitation of a certified historic structure or a building located in a registered historic district, unless the rehabilitation is a certified rehabilitation. (See paragraph (d) of this section which contains definitions and special rules applicable to rehabilitations of certified historic structures and buildings located in registered historic districts.)

    (v) Any expenditure of a lessee of a building or a portion of a building, if, on the date the rehabilitation is completed with respect to property placed in service by such lessee, the remain-

Reg. § 1.48-12(c)(7)

ing term of the lease (determined without regard to any renewal period) is less than the recovery period determined under section 168(c) (or 19 years in the case of property placed in service before January 1, 1987, and property placed in service that qualifies under the transition rules in paragraph (a)(2)(iv)(B) or (C) of this section).

(vi) Any expenditure allocable to that portion of a building which is (or may reasonably be expected to be) tax-exempt use property (within the meaning of section 168 and the regulations thereunder), except that the exclusion in this paragraph (c)(7)(vi) shall not apply for purposes of determining whether the building is a substantially rehabilitated building under paragraph (b)(2) of this section.

(8) *Requirement to use straight line depreciation*—(i) *Property placed in service after December 31, 1986.* The requirement in section 48(g)(2)(B)(i) and paragraph (c)(7)(i) of this section to use straight line cost recovery does not apply to any expenditure to the extent that the alternative depreciation system of 168(g) applies to such expenditure by reason of section 168(g)(1)(B) or (C). In addition, the requirement in section 48(g)(2)(B)(i) and paragraph (c)(7)(i) of this section applies only to the depreciation of the portion of the basis of a qualified rehabilitated building that is attributable to qualified rehabilitation expenditures.

(ii) *Property placed in service before January 1, 1987, and property placed in service after December 31, 1986, that qualifies for a transition rule.* In the case of expenditures attributable to property placed in service before January 1, 1987, and property that qualifies for the transition rules in paragraph (a)(2)(iv)(B) or (C) of this section, the term "qualified rehabilitation expenditure" does not include an expenditure with respect to which an election was not made under section 168(b)(3) as in effect prior to its amendment by the Tax Reform Act of 1986, to use the straight line method of depreciation. In such case, the requirement that an election be made to use straight line cost recovery applies only to the cost recovery of the portion of the basis of a qualified rehabilitated building that is attributable to qualified rehabilitation expenditures. See section 168(f)(1), as in effect prior to its amendment by the Tax Reform Act of 1986, for rules relating to the use of different methods of cost recovery for different components of a building. In addition, such requirement shall not apply to any expenditure to the extent that section 168(f)(12) or (j), as in effect prior to the amendments made by the Tax Reform Act of 1986, applied to such expenditure.

(9) *Cost of acquisition.* For purposes of paragraph (c)(7)(ii) of this section, cost of acquisition includes any interest incurred on indebtedness the proceeds of which are attributable to the acquisition of a building, an interest in a building, or land upon which a building exists. Interest incurred on a construction loan the proceeds of which are used for qualified rehabilitation expenditures, however, is not treated as a cost of acquisition.

(10) *Enlargement defined*—(i) *In general.* A building is enlarged to the extent that the total volume of the building is increased. An increase in floor space resulting from interior remodelling is not considered an enlargement. The total volume of a building is generally equal to the product of the floor area of the base of the building and the height from the underside of the lowest floor (including the basement) to the average height of the finished roof (as it exists or existed). For this purpose, floor area is measured from the exterior faces of external walls (other than shared walls that are external walls) and from the centerline of shared walls that are external walls.

(ii) *Rehabilitation that includes enlargement.* If expenditures for property only partially qualify as qualified rehabilitation expenditures because some of the expenditures are attributable to the enlargement of the building, the expenditures must be apportioned between the original portion of the building and the enlargement. The expenditures must be specifically allocated between the original portion of the building and the enlargement to the extent possible. If it is not possible to make a specific allocation of the expenditures, the expenditures must be allocated to each portion on some reasonable basis. The determination of a reasonable basis for an allocation depends on factors such as the type of improvement and how the improvement relates functionally to the building. For example, in the case of expenditures for an air-conditioning system or a roof, a reasonable basis for allocating the expenditures among the two portions generally would be the volume of the building, excluding the enlargement, served by the air-conditioning system or the roof relative to the volume of the enlargement served by the improvement.

(d) *Rules applicable to rehabilitations of certified historic structures*—(1) *Definition of certified historic structure.* The term "certified historic structure" means any building (and its structural components) that is—

(i) Listed in the National Register of Historic Places ("National Register"); or

(ii) Located in a registered historic district and certified by the Secretary of the Interior to the Internal Revenue Service as being of historic significance to the district.

For purposes of this section, a building shall be considered to be a certified historic structure at the time it is placed in service if the taxpayer reasonably believes on that date the building will be determined to be a certified historic structure and has requested on or before that date a determination from the Department of Interior that such building is a certified historic structure within the meaning of this paragraph (d)(1)(i) or (ii) and the Department of Interior later determines that the building is a certified historic structure.

(2) *Definition of registered historic district.* The term "registered historic district" means any district that is—

(i) Listed in the National Register, or

(ii) (A) Designated under a statute of the appropriate State or local government that has been certified by the Secretary of the Interior to the Internal Revenue Service as containing criteria that will substantially achieve the purpose of preserving and rehabilitating buildings of historic significance to the district, and (B) certified by the Secretary of the Interior as meeting substantially all of the requirements for the listing of districts in the National Register.

(3) *Definition of certified rehabilitation.* The term "certified rehabilitation" means any rehabilitation of a certified historic structure that the Secretary of the Interior has certified to the Internal Revenue Service as being consistent with the historic character of the building and, where applicable, the district in which such building is located. The determination of the scope of a rehabilitation shall be made on the basis of all the facts and circumstances surrounding the rehabilitation and shall not be made solely on the basis of ownership. The Secretary of the Interior shall take all of the rehabilitation work performed as part of a single rehabilitation, including any post-certification work, into account in determining whether the rehabilitation complies with the Department of Interior standards for rehabilitation and whether the certification should be granted, revoked, or otherwise invalidated.

(4) *Revoked or invalidated certification.* If the Department of Interior revokes or otherwise invalidates a certification after it has been issued to a taxpayer, the basis attributable to rehabilitation of the decertified property shall cease to be section 38 property described in section 48(a)(1)(E). Such cessation shall be effective as of the date the activity giving rise to the revocation or invalidation commenced. See section 47 for the rules applicable to property that ceases to be section 38 property.

(5) *Special rule for certain buildings located in registered historic districts.* The exclusion in paragraph (c)(7)(iv) of this section does not apply to a building in a registered historic district if—

(i) Such building was not a certified historic structure during the rehabilitation process; and

(ii) The Secretary of the Interior certified to the Internal Revenue Service that such building was not of historic significance to the district.

In general, the certification referred to in paragraph (d)(5)(ii) of this section must be requested by the taxpayer prior to the time that physical work on the rehabilitation began. If, however, the certification referred to in paragraph (d)(5)(ii) of this section is requested by the taxpayer after physical work on the rehabilitation of the building has begun, the taxpayer must certify to the Internal Revenue Service that, prior to the date that physical work on the rehabilitation began, the taxpayer in good faith was not aware of the requirement of paragraph (d)(5)(ii) of this section. The certification referred to in the previous sentence must be attached to the Form 3468 filed with the tax return for the year in which the credit is claimed.

(6) *Special rule for certain rehabilitations begun before an area is designated as a registered historic district.* In general, the exclusion from the definition of qualified rehabilitation expenditure in paragraph (c)(7)(iv) of this section applies to any rehabilitation expenditures that are incurred after a building becomes a certified historic structure within the meaning of section 48(g)(3)(A) and paragraph (d)(1) of this section or the area in which a building is located becomes a registered historic district within the meaning of section 48(g)(3)(B) and paragraph (d)(2) of this section. Rehabilitation expenditures incurred prior to such date, however, are not disqualified. In addition, rehabilitation expenditures made after the date the area in which a building is located becomes a registered historic district shall not be disqualified under paragraph (c)(7)(iv) of this section in any case in which physical work on the rehabilitation of a building begins prior to the date the taxpayer knows or has reason to know of an intention to nominate the area in which such building is located as a registered historic district. For purposes of this paragraph (d)(6), the taxpayer knows or has reason to know of such an intention if there is (A) a communication (written or oral) to the owner of any building within the district from the Department of the Interior, or any agency or instrumentality of the appropriate state or local

Reg. § 1.48-12(d)(6)

government (or a designee of such agency or instrumentality) that the district in which the building is located is being considered for designation as a registered historic district, (B) a legal notice of such consideration published in a newspaper, or (C) a public meeting held to discuss such consideration. In order to take advantage of the special rule of this paragraph (d)(6), the taxpayer must attach to the Form 3468 filed for the taxable year in which the credit is claimed a statement that the taxpayer in good faith did not know, or have reason to know, of an intention to nominate the area in which the building is located as a registered historic district.

(7) *Notice of certification*—(i) *In general.* Except as otherwise provided in paragraph (d)(7)(ii) of this section, a taxpayer claiming the credit for rehabilitation of a certified historic structure (within the meaning of section 48(g)(3) and paragraph (d)(1) of this section) must attach to the Form 3468 filed with the tax return for the taxable year in which the credit is claimed a copy of the final certification of completed work by the Secretary of the Interior, and for returns filed after January 9, 1989, evidence that the building is a certified historic structure.

(ii) *Late certification.* If the final certification of completed work has not been issued by the Secretary of the Interior at the time the tax return is filed for a year in which the credit is claimed, a copy of the first page of the Historic Preservation Certification Application—Part 2—Description of Rehabilitation (NPS Form 10-168a), with an indication that it has been received by the Department of the Interior or its designate, together with proof that the building is a certified historic structure (or that such status has been requested), must be attached to the Form 3468 filed with the return. A notice from the Department of the Interior or the State Historic Preservation Officer, stating that the nomination or application has been received, or a date-stamped nomination or application shall be sufficient indication that the nomination or application has been received. The building need not be either listed in the National Register or be determined to be of historic significance to a registered historic district at the time the return is filed for the year in which the credit is claimed. (See paragraph (d)(1) of this section.) The taxpayer must submit a copy of the final certification as an attachment to Form 3468 with the first income tax return filed after the receipt by the taxpayer of the certification. If the final certification is denied by the Department of Interior, the credit will be disallowed for any taxable year in which it was claimed. If the taxpayer fails to receive final certification of completed work prior to the date

that is 30 months after the date that the taxpayer filed the tax return on which the credit was claimed, the taxpayer must submit a written statement to the District Director stating such fact prior to the last day of the 30th month, and the taxpayer shall be requested to consent to an agreement under section 6501(c)(4) extending the period of assessment for any tax relating to the time for which the credit was claimed. The procedure permitted by the preceding sentence shall be used whenever the entire rehabilitation project is not fully completed by the date that is 30 months after the taxpayer filed the tax return upon which the credit was claimed (*e.g.* a phased rehabilitation) and the Secretary of the Interior has thus not yet certified the rehabilitation.

(iii) *Effective dates.* Paragraph (d)(7)(i) of this section applies to returns for taxable years beginning before January 1, 2002. The requirement in the fourth sentence of paragraph (d)(7)(ii) of this section applies only if the first income tax return filed after receipt by the taxpayer of the certification is for a taxable year beginning before January 1, 2002. For rules applicable to returns for taxable years beginning after December 31, 2001, see § 1.48-12T(d)(7)(iii).

(e) *Adjustment to basis*—(1) *General rule.* Except as otherwise provided by this paragraph (e), if a credit is allowed with respect to property attributable to qualified rehabilitation expenditures incurred in connection with the rehabilitation of a qualified rehabilitated building, the increase in the basis of the rehabilitated property that would otherwise result from the qualified rehabilitation expenditures must be reduced by the amount of the credit allowed. See section 48(q) and the regulations thereunder for other rules concerning adjustments to basis in the case of section 38 property.

(2) *Special rule for certain property relating to certified historic structures.* If a rehabilitation investment credit is allowed with respect to property that is placed in service before January 1, 1987, or property that qualifies for the transition rules in paragraph (a)(2)(iv)(B) or (C) of this section, and such property is attributable to qualified rehabilitation expenditures incurred in connection with the rehabilitation of a certified historic structure, the increase in the basis of the rehabilitated property that would otherwise result from the qualified rehabilitation expenditures must be reduced by one-half of the amount of the credit allowed.

(3) *Recapture of rehabilitation investment credit.* If during any taxable year there is a recapture amount determined with respect to any credit that resulted in a basis adjustment under

Reg. § 1.48-12(d)(7)

paragraph (e)(1) or (2) of this section, the basis of such building (immediately before the event resulting in such recapture) shall be increased by an amount equal to such recapture amount. For purposes of the preceding sentence, the term "recapture amount" means any increase in tax (or adjustment in carrybacks or carryovers) determined under section 47(a)(5).

(f) *Coordination with other provisions of the Code*—(1) *Credit claimed by lessee for rehabilitation performed by lessor.* A lessee may take the credit for rehabilitation performed by the lessor if the requirements of this section and section 48(d) are satisfied. For purposes of applying section 48(d), the fair market value of section 38 property described in section 48(a)(1)(E) shall be limited to that portion of the lessor's basis in the qualified rehabilitated building that is attributable to qualified rehabilitation expenditures. In the case of a portion of a building that is divided into more than one leasehold interest, the qualified rehabilitation expenditures attributable to the common elements shall be allocated to the individual leasehold interests in accordance with the principles of paragraph (c)(10)(ii) of this section. Furthermore, a leasehold interest's share of the common elements shall not be considered to have been placed in service prior to the time that the particular leasehold interest is placed in service.

(2) *When the credit may be claimed*—(i) *In general.* The investment credit for qualified rehabilitation expenditures is generally allowed in the taxable year in which the property attributable to the expenditure is placed in service, provided the building is a qualified rehabilitated building for the taxable year. See paragraph (b) of this section and section 46(c) and § 1.46-3(d). Under certain circumstances, however, the credit may be available prior to the date the property is placed in service. See section 46(d) and § 1.46-5 (relating to qualified progress expenditures). Solely for purposes of section 46(c), property attributable to qualified rehabilitation expenditures will not be treated as placed in service until the building with respect to which the expenditures are made meets the definition of a qualified rehabilitated building (as defined in section 48(g)(1) and paragraph (b) of this section) for the taxable year. Accordingly, in the first taxable year for which the building becomes a qualified rehabilitated building, the property described in section 48(a)(1)(E) attributable to expenditures described in paragraph (c) of this section shall be considered to be placed in service, if such property was considered placed in service under section 46(c) and the regulations thereunder without regard to this paragraph (f)(2)(i) in that taxable year or a prior taxable year. For purposes of the preceding

sentence, the requirement in section 48(g)(1)(A)(iii) and paragraph (b)(3) of this section relating to the definition of a qualified rehabilitated building shall be deemed to be met if the taxpayer reasonably expects that no rehabilitation work undertaken during the remainder of the rehabilitation process will result in a failure to satisfy the requirements of paragraph (b)(3) of this section. If the requirements of paragraph (b)(3) are not satisfied, however, the credit shall be disallowed for the taxable year in which it was claimed. If a taxpayer fails to complete physical work on the rehabilitation prior to the date that is 30 months after the date that the taxpayer filed a tax return on which the credit is claimed, the taxpayer must submit a written statement to the District Director stating such fact prior to the last day of the 30th month, and shall be requested to consent to an agreement under section 6501(c)(4) extending the period of assessment for any tax relating to the item for which the credit was claimed.

(ii) *Section 38 property described in section 48(a)(1)(E).* In the case of section 38 property described in section 48(a)(1)(E), the section 38 property is not the building. Instead, the section 38 property is the portion of the basis of the building that is attributable to qualified rehabilitation expenditures. Therefore, for example, for purposes of the determination of when such section 38 property is placed in service, a determination must be made regarding when property attributable to the a portion of the basis of the building attributable to qualified rehabilitation expenditures is placed in service. The issue of when the building is placed in service is thus not relevant. In fact, under this test, the building itself may never have been taken out of service during the rehabilitation process. If the building is rehabilitated over several years in stages (*e.g.*, by floors), section 38 property attributable to qualified rehabilitation expenditures to a qualified rehabilitated building placed in service in each taxable year shall, generally, be treated as a separate item of section 38 property.

(iii) *Example.* The application of this paragraph (f)(2) may be illustrated by the following example:

Example. Assume that A, a calendar year taxpayer, purchases a four-story building on January 1, 1983, for $100,000, and incurs $10,000 of qualified rehabilitation expenditures in 1983 to rehabilitate floor one, $50,000 of qualified rehabilitation expenditures in 1984 to rehabilitate floor two, $70,000 of qualified rehabilitation expenditures in 1985 to rehabilitate floor three, and $60,000 of qualified rehabilitation expenditures in

Reg. § 1.48-12(f)(2)

1986 to rehabilitate floor four. Assume further that A places the property attributable to these expenditures in service on the last day of the year in which the respective expenditures were incurred and that the building is never taken out of service since as each floor is rehabilitated, the other three floors are occupied by tenants. Under the rule in this paragraph (f)(2), the portion of the basis of the building that is attributable to qualified rehabilitation expenditures incurred with respect to floor one and two are deemed to be placed in service in 1985, because that is the first year that the substantial rehabilitation test described in paragraph (b) of this section is met ($120,000 of expenditures incurred by A during a measuring period ending on December 31, 1985 is greater than the $110,000 basis at the beginning of the period). Assume that as of December 31, 1985, at least 75 percent of the external walls of the building have been retained during the rehabilitation process and that A has a reasonable expectation that no work during the remainder of the rehabilitation process will result in less than 75 percent of the external walls being retained. A may claim a credit for A's 1985 taxable year on $130,000 of qualified rehabilitation expenditures ($10,000 in 1983, $50,000 in 1984, and $70,000 in 1985). (See paragraph (c)(6) of this section for rules applicable to when qualified expenditures may be incurred. In addition, see section 46(d) and § 1.46-5 for rules relating to qualified progress expenditures.) The fact that the building was a qualified rehabilitated building for A's 1985 taxable year, however, has no effect on whether the building is a qualified rehabilitated building for A's 1986 taxable year. In order to determine whether A is entitled to claim a credit on A's 1986 return for the $60,000 of qualified rehabilitation expenditures incurred in 1986, A must select a measuring period ending in 1986 and must determine whether the building is a qualified rehabilitated building for that year. Solely for purposes of determining whether the building was substantially rehabilitated, expenditures incurred in 1984 and 1985, even though considered in determining whether the building was substantially rehabilitated for A's 1985 taxable year, may be used in addition to the expenditures incurred in 1986 to determine whether the building was substantially rehabilitated for A's 1986 taxable year, provided the expenditures were incurred during any measuring period selected by A that ends in 1986.

(3) *Coordination with section 47.* If property described in section 48(a)(1)(E) is disposed of by the taxpayer, or otherwise ceases to be "section 38 property," section 47 may apply. Property will cease to be section 38 property, and therefore section 47 may apply, in any case in which the

Department of Interior revokes or otherwise invalidates a certification of rehabilitation after the property is placed in service or a building (other than a certified historic structure) is moved from the place where it is rehabilitated after the property is placed in service. If, for example, the taxpayer made modifications to the building inconsistent with Department of Interior standards, the Secretary of the Interior might revoke the certification. In addition, if all or a portion of a substantially rehabilitated building becomes tax-exempt use property (see paragraph (c)(7)(vi) of this section) for the first time within five years after the credit is claimed, the credit will be recaptured under section 47 at that time as if the building or portion of the building which becomes tax-exempt use property had then been sold. [Reg. § 1.48-12.]

☐ [*T.D.* 8233, 10-7-88. *Amended by T.D.* 8989, 4-23-2002.]

[Reg. § 1.48-12T]

§ 1.48-12T. Qualified rehabilitated building; expenditures incurred after December 31, 1981 (temporary).—(a) through (d)(7)(ii) [Reserved] For further guidance, see § 1.48-12(a) through (d)(7)(ii).

(iii) *Returns for taxable years beginning after December 31, 2001—(A) In general.* Except as otherwise provided in § 1.48-12(d)(7)(ii) and this paragraph (d)(7)(iii), a taxpayer claiming the credit for rehabilitation of a certified historic structure (within the meaning of section 47(c)(3) and § 1.48-12(d)(1)) for a taxable year beginning after December 31, 2001, must provide with the return for the taxable year in which the credit is claimed, the NPS project number assigned by, and the date of the final certification of completed work received from, the Secretary of the Interior. If a credit (including a credit for a taxable year beginning before January 1, 2002) is claimed under the late certification procedures of § 1.48-12(d)(7)(ii) and the first income tax return filed by the taxpayer after receipt of the certification is for a taxable year beginning after December 31, 2001, the taxpayer must provide the NPS project number assigned by, and the date of the final certification of completed work received from, the Secretary of the Interior with that return.

(B) *Reporting and recordkeeping requirements.* The information required under paragraph (d)(7)(iii)(A) of this section must be provided on Form 3468 (or its successor) filed with the taxpayer's return. In addition, the taxpayer must retain a copy of the final certification of completed work for as long as its contents may become material in the administration of any internal revenue law.

(C) *Passthrough entities.* In the case of a credit for qualified rehabilitation expenditures of a partnership, S corporation, estate, or trust, the requirements of this paragraph (d)(7)(iii) apply only to the entity. Each partner, shareholder or beneficiary claiming a credit for such qualified rehabilitation expenditures from a passthrough entity must, however, provide the employer identification number of the entity on Form 3468 (or its successor).

(D) *Effective dates.* This paragraph (d)(7)(iii) applies to returns and records for taxable years beginning after December 31, 2001. For rules applicable to returns and records for taxable years beginning before January 1, 2002, see § 1.48-12(d)(7)(i) and the fourth sentence of § 1.48-12(d)(7)(ii).

(e) through (f)(3) [Reserved] For further guidance, see § 1.48-12(e) through (f)(3). [Temporary Reg. § 1.48-12T.]

☐ [T.D. 8033, 6-38-05. Amended by T.D. 8989, 4-23-2002.]

[Reg. § 1.51-1]

§ 1.51-1. Amount of credit.—(a) *Determination of amount*—(1) *General rule.* Except as provided in paragraph (a)(2) of this section, the amount of the targeted jobs credit for purposes of section 38 (formerly designated section 44B) for the taxable year equals 50 percent of the qualified first-year wages (minus any qualified first-year wages paid to individuals while such individuals are qualified summer youth employees) plus 25 percent of the qualified second-year wages.

(2) *Special rule for employment of qualified summer youth employees.* In the case of an employer who pays or incurs qualified wages after April 30, 1983, to a qualified summer youth employee beginning work for the employer after such date, the amount of the targeted jobs credit for the taxable year is equal to the amount determined under paragraph (a)(1) of this section plus an amount equal to 85 percent of the first $3,000 of qualified wages paid to each qualified summer youth employee during the taxable year. Such wages must be attributable to services rendered by the qualified summer youth employee during any 90-day period beginning on or after May 1 and ending on or before September 15.

(3) *Limitation.* See section 38(c) for rules limiting the amount of the credit to a percentage of the amount of the taxpayer's net tax liability.

(b) *Definitions*—(1) *Qualified wages.* The term "qualified wages" means wages (as defined in paragraph (b)(4)) paid or incurred by the employer during the taxable year to individuals who are members of a targeted group (within the meaning of section 51(d)).

(2) *Qualified first-year wages*—(i) *General rule.* Except in the case of qualified summer youth employees, the term "qualified first-year wages" means the first $6,000 of wages (as defined in paragraph (b)(4) of this section) attributable to service rendered by a member of a targeted group during the 1-year period beginning with the day the individual first begins work for the employer. In the case of a vocational rehabilitation referral (as defined in section 51(d)(2)) who begins work for the employer before July 19, 1984, the one-year period begins with the day the individual begins work for the employer on or after the beginning of such individual's rehabilitation plan. However, with the exception of vocational rehabilitation referrals for whom the employer claimed a credit under section 44B (as in effect prior to enactment of the Revenue Act of 1978) for a taxable year beginning before January 1, 1979, members of a targeted group who are first hired after September 26, 1978, and before January 1, 1979, will be treated as if they first began work for the employer on January 1, 1979. The date on which the wages are paid is not determinative of whether the wages are first-year wages; rather, the wages must be attributed to the period during which the work was performed. See paragraph (f)(1) of this section for an additional limitation on the term "qualified first-year wages". (See examples (1), (2), (3), (4), (5), and (6) in paragraph (j) of this section for examples illustrating the application of the rules in this paragraph (b)(2)).

(ii) *Special rule for qualified summer youth employees.* In the case of a qualified summer youth employee, qualified first-year wages for purposes of the 85 percent credit referred to in paragraph (a)(2) of this section include only wages attributable to services rendered by a qualified summer youth employee during any 90-day period beginning on or after May 1 and ending on or before September 15. If the individual is retained by the employer after the 90-day period and recertified as a member of another targeted group, the term "qualified first-year wages" for purposes of the 50 percent credit described by section 51(a)(1) has the meaning assigned that term in paragraph (b)(2)(i) of this section except that the $6,000 limitation for qualified first-year wages shall be reduced by wages up to, but not more than, $3,000 attributable to services rendered during the 90-day period.

(3) *Qualified second-year wages.* The term "qualified second-year wages" means the first

Reg. § 1.51-1(b)(3)

$6,000 of wages attributable to services rendered by a member of a targeted group, other than a qualified summer youth employee, during the 1-year period beginning on the day after the last day of the period for qualified first-year wages. The date on which the wages are paid is not determinative of whether the wages are second-year wages; rather, the wages must be attributed to the period during which the work was performed.

(4) *Wages*—(i) *General rule.* Except as otherwise provided in paragraph (b)(4)(ii) and (iii) of this section, the term "wages" shall only include amounts paid or incurred after December 31, 1978, for taxable years ending after December 31, 1978. For purposes of this section, the term "wages" has the meaning assigned such term by section 3306(b) (determined without regard to any dollar limitation contained in such subsection).

(ii) *Special rules.* In the case of agricultural labor or railway labor, the term "wages" means unemployment insurance wages within the meaning of subparagraph (A) or (B) of section 51(h)(1). The term "wages" shall not include any amounts paid or incurred by an employer for any pay period to any individual for whom the employer receives federally funded payments for on-the-job training for such individual for such pay period. (See example (7) in paragraph (j) of this section.) The amount of wages which would otherwise be qualified wages under this section with respect to an individual for a taxable year shall be reduced by an amount equal to the amount of payments made to the employer (however utilized by such employer) with respect to such individual for such taxable year under a program established under section 414 of the Social Security Act. In addition, the term "wages" shall not include any amount paid or incurred by the employer in a taxable year beginning before January 1, 1982, to an individual with respect to whom the employer claims a credit under section 40 (relating to expenses of work incentive programs). For youths participating in a qualified cooperative education program:

(A) Section 3306(c)(10)(C) (relating to the definition of employment for certain students) does not apply in determining wages under this section; and

(B) The term "wages" shall include only those amounts paid or incurred by the employer that are attributable to services rendered by the individual while he or she meets the conditions specified in section 51(d)(8)(A). For purposes of the preceding sentence, an employee who met the requirement in section 51(d)(8)(A)(iv), dealing

with economically disadvantaged status, when hired, shall be deemed to continuously meet the requirement in section 51(d)(8)(A)(iv) during the time the employee is in the cooperative education program. See also paragraph (e) of this section for rules relating to the exclusion of wages paid to certain individuals.

(iii) *Termination.* The term "wages" shall not include any amount paid or incurred to an individual who begins work for the emloyer after December 31, 1985.

(5) *Special rule for eligible work incentive employees.* In the case of an eligible work incentive employee (as defined in § 1.51-1(c)(4)), this paragraph (b) shall be applied for taxable years beginning after December 31, 1981, as if such employee had been a member of a targeted group for taxable years beginning before January 1, 1982. (See example (8) in paragraph (j) of this section.)

(c) *Members of targeted groups*—(1) *In general.* An individual is a member of a targeted group if the individual is certified as (i) a vocational rehabilitation referral, (ii) an economically disadvantaged youth, (iii) an economically disadvantaged Vietnam-era veteran, (iv) an SSI recipient, (v) a general assistance recipient, (vi) a youth participating in a cooperative education program, (vii) an economically disadvantaged ex-convict, (viii) an eligible work incentive employee, (ix) a qualified summer youth employee, or (x) an involuntarily terminated CETA employee. Except as provided below, see section 51(d) of this section for a definition of these groups. See paragraph (d) of this section for rules concerning the certification of individuals as members of one of these targeted groups.

(2) *Youths participating in a qualified cooperative education program*—(i) *Student requirements.* For an individual to qualify as a youth participating in a qualified cooperative education program, the individual must meet each of the following conditions (A) through (D)—

(A) The youth must have attained the age of 16 but not 20. (An individual reaching 19 will be treated as a youth participating in a qualified cooperative education program only for wages paid or incurred after November 26, 1979.)

(B) The youth must not have graduated from a high school or vocational school.

(C) The youth must be enrolled in and actively pursuing a qualified cooperative education program (as defined in paragraph (c)(2)(iii) of this section).

(D) With respect to wages paid or incurred after December 31, 1981, the youth must

Reg. § 1.51-1(b)(4)

be a member of an economically disadvantaged family when initially hired.

(ii) *Economically disadvantaged family.* See section 51(d)(11) for the rules relating to the determination of whether an individual is a member of an economically disadvantaged family.

(iii) *Qualified cooperative education program.* The term "qualified cooperative education program" means a program of vocational education for individuals who (through written cooperative arrangements between a qualified school and one or more employers) receive instruction (including required academic instruction) by alternation of study in school with a job in any occupational field (but only if these two experiences are planned by the school and employer so that each contributes to the student's education and employability). See section 51(d)(8)(C) for the definition of a "qualified school." For purposes of this paragraph, the term "program of vocational education" means an organized educational program which is directly related to the preparation of individuals for employment, or for additional preparation for a career requiring other than a baccalaureate or advanced degree. An "organized educational program" means only instruction related to the occupation or occupations for which the students are in training or instruction necessary for students to benefit from such training. The student's employment contributes to his or her education and employability only if it is related to the occupation, or a cluster of closely related occupations, for which the student is in training in school. However, the student's employment need not be directly related to or in the same technical field as the training the student receives in school. For example, a student studying carpentry does not have to work as a carpenter for the program to constitute a "qualified cooperative education program." The program will qualify if, for example, the student works at a hardware store because the student's work would familiarize the student with the materials and tools used by carpenters. The program would not qualify, however, if the student works at a restaurant and generally performs tasks in such employment not related to carpentry.

(iv) *Actively pursuing.* For purposes of this paragraph (c)(2), a youth will not be considered to be "actively pursuing" a school's qualified cooperative education program (within the meaning of paragraph (c)(2)(iii) of this section) during summer vacation unless that school program continues during the summer vacation. Whether the school program continues during the summer vacation will be determined by examining the written agreement between the school and the employer. Thus, if a written agreement specifically covers the summer vacation period and provides for a significant degree of involvement by school personnel to provide supervision for the students in the program during that period, the school program will be considered to continue during the summer, regardless of whether classes are held during the vacation period.

(3) *General assistance recipients.* In order for an individual to qualify as a general assistance recipient, the individual, or another member of the assistance unit (within the meaning of 45 CFR 205.40(a)(1)) that the individual is a member of, must receive assistance for a period of not less than 30 days ending within the preemployment period (as defined in section 51(d)(13)) from a qualified general assistance program. A qualified general assistance program is a program of a State or a political subdivision of a State that the Secretary (after consultation with the Secretary of Health and Human Services) has designated as providing general assistance (or similar assistance) which is based on need and consists of money payments or voucher or scrip. For purposes of the preceding sentences, a program qualifying as a general assistance program by reason of non-cash assistance (*i.e.,* voucher or scrip) shall be so treated only with respect to amounts paid or incurred after July 1, 1982, to individuals beginning work for the employer after such date. For purposes of this subparagraph, the term "money" means cash or an instrument convertible into cash (*e.g.,* a check).

(4) *Eligible work incentive employees.* An eligible work incentive employee means an individual who has been certified by the designated local agency (as defined in paragraph (d)(10) of this section) as—

(i) Being eligible for financial assistance under part A of title IV of the Social Security Act and as having continuously received such financial assistance during the 90-day period which immediately precedes the date on which such individual is hired by the employer, or

(ii) Having been placed in employment under a work incentive program established under section 432(b)(1) or 445 of the Social Security Act. The provisions of this paragraph (c)(4) are effective with respect to taxable years of the employer beginning after December 31, 1981. (See paragraph (b)(5) of this section for a special rule relating to eligible work incentive employees.)

(5) *Involuntarily terminated CETA employees*—(i) *In general.* An involuntarily terminated CETA employee is an individual who first began work for an employer after August 13, 1981, in taxable years of the employer ending after August

Reg. § 1.51-1(c)(5)

13, 1981, and is certified by the designated local agency (as defined in paragraph (d)(10) of this section) as having been involuntarily terminated after December 31, 1980, from employment financed in whole, or in part, under a program under part D of title II or title VI of the Comprehensive Employment and Training Act.

(ii) *Termination.* Section 51(d)(10) and this paragraph (c)(5) shall not apply to any individual who begins work for the employer after December 31, 1982.

(d) *Certification*—(1) *General rule.* Except as otherwise provided in this paragraph, an individual shall not be treated as a member of a targeted group unless, on or before the day on which such individual begins work for the employer, the employer has received, or has requested in writing, a certification that the individual is a member of a targeted group from the designated local agency (as defined in paragraph (d)(10) of this section). In addition, the employer must receive a certification before the targeted jobs credit can be claimed. However, with respect to individuals who began work for the employer on or before May 11, 1982, the certification will be timely only if requested or received before the day the individual began work for the employer. In the case of a request in writing mailed via the United States Postal Service, the request shall be deemed to be made on the date of the postmark stamped on the cover in which such request was mailed to the designated local agency provided the request is mailed in accordance with the mailing requirements in § 301.7502-1(c) and delivered in accordance with the delivery requirements in § 301.7502-1(d). In the case of a deadline that but for this sentence would fall on a Saturday, Sunday, or a legal holiday, the deadline for making a timely request in writing for a certification or receiving a timely certification shall be the next succeeding day which is not a Saturday, Sunday, or legal holiday. (See section 7503 for the definition of "legal holiday.") See paragraph (d)(2) of this section for transitional rules applicable to certain employees who began work for the employer before September 26, 1981. See paragraph (d)(3) of this section for special rules applicable to cooperative education students and paragraph (d)(4) of this section for special rules applicable to eligible work incentive employees.

(2) *Timeliness of certification in the case of an individual to whom a written preliminary eligibility determination has been issued.* If on or before the day on which an individual begins work for the employer, such individual has received from a designated local agency (or other agency or organization designated pursuant to a written

agreement with such designated local agency) a written preliminary determination that such individual is a member of a targeted group, then such individual may be treated as a member of a targeted group if on or before the fifth day after the day such individual begins work for the employer such employer receives, or requests in writing, from the designated local agency a certification that such individual is a member of a targeted group. This paragraph (d)(2) only applies to individuals who begin work for the employer after July 18, 1984.

(3) *Transitional rules for certain employees who began work for the employer on or before September 26, 1981.* In the case of an individual, other than a cooperative education student, who began work for the employer before June 29, 1981, the employer must either receive, or request in writing, a certification before July 23, 1981. In the case of an individual, other than a cooperative education student, who began work for the employer after June 28, 1981, and on or before September 26, 1981, the employer must either receive, or request in writing, a certification before September 26, 1981.

(4) *Cooperative education students.* In the case of cooperative education students, the school administering the cooperative education program must issue the certification. Form 6199 is provided for this purpose. If the student begins work for the employer after September 26, 1981, see the general rule in § 1.51-1(d)(1) for the date when this certification must be received or requested. If the student begins work for the employer on or before September 26, 1981, the employer must receive the certification or request it in writing before September 26, 1981. In order for an employer to claim a credit on wages paid or incurred to a cooperative education student after December 31, 1981, the employer must receive or request in writing a determination that the student is a member of an economically disadvantaged family. A request for economic eligibility determination for a cooperative education student must be made in writing by the employer to the participating school. If the student begins work for the employer on or before September 26, 1981, the employer must receive or request in writing such determination before September 26, 1981. However, a request in writing on or after August 13, 1981, to a participating school for certification will be deemed to include a request for an economic eligibility determination. In addition, any certification issued by a school after August 13, 1981, will be deemed to be issued in response to a request for certification which includes a request for an economic eligibility determination. The rule in the preceding sentence does not eliminate

Reg. § 1.51-1(d)(1)

the requirement that the employer receive a certification that includes an economic eligibility determination in order to claim a credit for wages paid or incurred after December 31, 1981. If a certification issued by a school after August 13, 1984, does not contain an economic eligibility determination and the employer wishes to claim a credit for wages paid or incurred after December 31, 1981, the employer must receive a completed certification before the date on which the credit is claimed.

(5) *Eligible work incentive employees.* In the case of eligible work incentive employees, the employer must either receive, or request in writing, a certification within the time requirements of paragraph (d)(1), (2), or (3) of this section, whichever is applicable. Before October 12, 1981 (the date the Economic Recovery Tax Act of 1981 codified the State employment security agency as the designated local agency for certifying targeted groups), a certificate may be received or requested in writing from either the designated local agency (as defined in paragraph (d)(10) of this section) or the office or agency that properly issued certifications under former section 50B(h)(1) (relating to the work incentive credit).

(6) *Certifications that are not timely.* Any certification that is not timely received or requested by the employer in accordance with the rules of this paragraph will be treated as invalid. Thus, the employer will not be allowed to claim a credit under section 51 with respect to any wages paid or incurred to an employee whose certification or request for certification is not timely. A timely request for certification does not eliminate the need for the employer to receive a certification before claiming the credit. In the case of a request for certification that was denied, resubmitted, and then approved, the timeliness of the request shall be determined by the timeliness of the first request.

(7) *Incorrect certification*—(i) *In general.* Except as otherwise provided in paragraph (d)(7)(ii) of this section, if an individual has been certified as a member of a targeted group, and such certification is based on false information provided by such individual, the certification shall be revoked and wages paid by the employer after the date on which notice of revocation is received by the employer shall not be treated as qualified wages. For purposes of this paragraph, a certification will be revoked only if the individual would not have been certified had correct information been provided to the issuer of the certification. Thus, false information that is not material to an individual's eligibility as a member

of a targeted group will not invalidate an otherwise valid certification.

(ii) *Employer's knowledge that the certification was incorrect.* In the case of an employer who knew, or had reason to know, at the time of certification that the information provided to the designated local agency was false, none of the wages paid by such employer to an individual to whom an incorrect certification has been issued will be qualified wages.

(8) *Certifications issued to certain rehires.* This paragraph (d)(8) applies in the case of an employee who first began work for the employer before August 13, 1981, and was dismissed and rehired by the employer. A certification received or requested by an employer with respect to such an employee will be considered timely only if there was a valid business reason, unrelated to the availability of the credit, for the dismissal and rehire and if the employer did not dismiss and then rehire the employee in order to meet the timing requirement with respect to certification. An individual who is dismissed and then rehired for the purpose described in the preceding sentence will be considered for purposes of section 51(d)(16) and this paragraph to have been continuously employed by the employer during the time between the dismissal and the rehire. Whether the employer was motivated by reason of the certification rules in section 51(d)(16) and this paragraph to dismiss and then rehire an employee is a question of fact to be determined from all the circumstances surrounding the dismissal and rehire. (See paragraph (e)(2) of this section for a separate rule disallowing the credit in the case of nonqualifying rehires.)

(9) *Individuals who continue to be employed by the same employer but as a member of another targeted group.* This paragraph (d)(9) applies in the case of an employee who continues to be employed by the same employer but no longer qualifies as a member of the targeted group for which such employee was first certified (*e.g.*, the employee was originally certified as a qualified summer youth employee with respect to a ninety-day period between May 1 and September 15, but such ninety-day period has ended). In such case, the employer may request a certification that the employee is a member of another targeted group, and if any wages paid to such individual are qualified first-year wages or qualified second-year wages, the employer may be entitled to a targeted jobs credit with respect to such wages. The second certification will not be invalid merely because it was requested or received after the individual began work for the employer; only the first certification (for example, the certification with respect

Reg. § 1.51-1(d)(9)

to an individual hired first as a qualified summer youth employee) must meet the requirement of section 51(d)(16) that a certification must be requested or received by an employer on or before the day on which the individual begins work for the employer. In the case of a former qualified summer youth employee or a youth participating in a qualified cooperative education program who is recertified as an economically disadvantaged youth, the term "hiring date" in section 51(d)(3)(B) does not mean the day the individual is hired by the employer but means the day the individual is certified as a member of the new targeted group. Accordingly, the age requirement of section 51(d)(3)(B) shall be applied as of the day the individual is certified as a member of the second targeted group. In addition, see section 51(d)(11) for rules concerning the viability of the original economic eligibility determination.

(10) *Certification where a trade or business has been transferred to a new employer.* In the case of a transfer of a trade or business in which an individual who is a member of a targeted group is retained as an employee in the trade or business, the certification obtained for such employee by the transferor-employer will apply with respect to the transferee-employer.

(11) *Designated local agency*—(i) *In general.* For the period before October 12, 1981, the term "designated local agency" means the agency for any locality designated jointly by the Secretary and the Secretary of Labor to perform certifications of employees for employers in that locality. On or after October 12, 1981, the term "designated local agency" means a State employment security agency established in accordance with the Act of June 6, 1933, as amended (29 U.S.C. 49-49n).

(ii) *Jurisdiction.* The designated local agency is the agency that has, pursuant to its charter, jurisdiction over the individual that is sought to be certified. Thus, any certification that is issued with respect to an individual who is not within the jurisdiction of the designated local agency that issued the certification will be invalid. Notwithstanding any other provision of this section, a request in writing for certification to the appropriate designated local agency that is made before January 23, 1984, will be considered to be timely if it is made after an otherwise timely request in writing for certification was made to a designated local agency that does not have jurisdiction over the individual sought to be certified.

(e) *Certain ineligible individuals*—(1) *Related individuals.* For purposes of section 51(a), "qualified wages" does not include any amounts paid or incurred by a taxpayer to any of the following individuals:

(i) An individual who is related (within the meaning of any of paragraphs (1) through (8) of section 152(a)) to the taxpayer;

(ii) An individual who is a dependent (within the meaning of section 152(a)(9)) of the taxpayer;

(iii) An individual who is related (within the meaning of any of paragraphs (1) through (8) of section 152(a)) to a shareholder who owns (within the meaning of section 267(c)) more than 50 percent in value of the outstanding stock of the taxpayer, if the taxpayer is a corporation;

(iv) An individual who is a dependent (within the meaning of section 152(a)(9)) of a shareholder described in paragraph (e)(1)(iii) of this section;

(v) An individual who is a grantor, beneficiary or fiduciary of the taxpayer, if the taxpayer is an estate or trust;

(vi) An individual who is a dependent (within the meaning of section 152(a)(9)) of an individual described in paragraph (e)(1)(v) of this section; or

(vii) An individual who is related (within the meaning of any of paragraphs (1) through (8) of section 152(a)) to an individual described in paragraph (e)(1)(v) of this section.

(2) *Nonqualifying rehires.* For purposes of section 51(a), "qualified wages" does not include wages paid to an employee who had been employed by the employer prior to the current hiring date of the employee if at any time during such prior employment the employee was not a member of a targeted group. The preceding sentence shall not apply to an employee who was previously timely certified as a member of a targeted group with respect to the same employer. An employee shall be treated as not having been a member of a targeted group if the certification requirements of section 51(d)(16) were not met. (See example (8) in paragraph (j) of this section.)

(3) *Effective date.* The provisions of this paragraph (e) are effective with respect to employees first beginning work for an employer after August 13, 1981.

(f) *Limitations.*—(1) *Limitation on qualified first-year wages.* With respect to taxable years beginning before January 1, 1982, the amount of the qualified first-year wages which may be taken into account for purposes of the targeted jobs credit for any taxable year shall not exceed 30 percent of the aggregate unemployment insurance wages paid by the employer during the calendar year ending in such taxable year. In the case of a

Reg. § 1.51-1(d)(10)

group of trades or businesses under common control (as defined in § 1.52-1(b)), the qualified first-year wages cannot exceed 30 percent of the aggregate unemployment insurance wages paid to all employees of that group of trades or businesses under common control during the calendar year ending in such taxable year. For this purpose, the term "unemployment insurance wages" has the same meaning given to the term "wages" as defined in § 1.51-1(b)(4). In this case of agricultural or railway labor, see section 51(h)(1) for the applicable definition of unemployment insurance wages. (See examples (13) and (14) in paragraph (j) of this section.)

(2) *Remuneration must be for trade or business employment.* Remuneration paid by an employer to an employee during any taxable year shall be taken into account only if more than one-half of the remuneration paid by the employer to an employee is for services in a trade or business of the employer. This determination shall be made by each employer without regard to section 52(a) or (b). Accordingly, employees of corporations that are members of a controlled group or employees of partnerships, proprietorships, and other trades or businesses (whether or not incorporated) which are under common control will be treated as being employed by each separate employer for this purpose. For this purpose, the term "year" means the taxable year of the employer. (See example (15) in paragraph (j) of this section.)

(g) *Election not to claim the targeted jobs credit.* The election under section 51(j) (as amended by section 474(p) of the Tax Reform Act of 1984) not to claim the targeted jobs credit is available for taxable years beginning after December 31, 1983, and shall be made for the taxable year in which such credit is available by not claiming such credit on an original return or amended return at any time before the expiration of the 3-year period beginning on the last date prescribed by law for filing the return for the taxable year (determined without regard to extensions). The election may be revoked within the 3-year period by filing an amended return on which the credit is claimed.

(h) *Treatment of successor-employers.* In the case of a successor-employer referred to in section 3306(b)(1), the determination of the amount of credit under this section with respect to wages paid by such successor-employer shall be made in the same manner as if such wages were paid by the predecessor-employer referred to in such section. Thus, the 1-year period referred to in § 1.51-1(b)(2)(i) will be considered to begin with the day the employee first began work for the transferor-employer, and the amount of qualified

first-year wages and qualified second-year wages paid or incurred with respect to the employee must be reduced by the amount of any such wages paid or incurred by the transferor-employer. (See examples (10) and (11) in paragraph (j) of this section.) Also, see paragraph (d)(10) of this section for rules concerning the viability of the employee's certification.

(i) *Treatment of employees performing services for other persons.* No credit shall be determined under this section with respect to remuneration paid by an employer to an employee for services performed by such employee for another person unless the amount reasonably expected to be received by the employer for such services from such other person exceeds the remuneration paid by the employer to such employee for such services.

(j) *Examples.* The application of this section may be illustrated by the following examples which, except as otherwise stated, assume that the limitations imposed by §§ 1.51-1(f)(2) and 1.53-3 are inapplicable:

Example (1). Corporation M is a calendar year, cash receipts and disbursements method taxpayer. A, an economically disadvantaged youth, first began work for Corporation M on October 1, 1978. Qualified first-year wages with respect to A are wages attributable to the period beginning on January 1, 1979 (since A was first hired after September 26, 1978, he is treated as having begun work on January 1, 1979) and ending on December 31, 1979. In the 1979 taxable year, Corporation M pays A $5,000 of qualified first-year wages attributable to services performed in 1979. Corporation M's allowable credit is equal to $2,500 (50 percent of $5,000).

Example (2). Assume the same facts as in example (1), except that in 1980 Corporation M pays to A $100 of wages attributable to services rendered in 1979. These wages will still be considered as qualified first-year wages, but the credit may not be claimed until the 1980 taxable year.

Example (3). Corporation O is a calendar year, cash receipts and disbursements method taxpayer. C, a vocational rehabilitation referral, first began work for Corporation O on July 1, 1978. Corporation O claimed a credit under section 44B (as in effect prior to enactment of the Revenue Act of 1978) for $3,000 of wages paid to C in the 1978 taxable year. Corporation O paid C $6,000 for services performed from January 1, 1979 to June 30, 1979. The period during which qualified first-year wages are determined begins on July 1, 1978, and ends on June 30, 1979. Amounts paid before January 1, 1979, however, are not taken into consideration in determining the amount of qualified first-year wages. Accordingly, only the wages attributable to services performed from January 1, 1979, through June 30, 1979, are considered as qualified first-year wages. Corporation O's allowable credit is equal to $3,000 (50 percent of $6,000).

Example (4). I first began work for Corporation Q, a cash receipts and disbursements method taxpayer, on January 1, 1981, and was not a member of a targeted group. On March 1, 1981, I was convicted of a felony and sentenced to prison. I quit work for Corporation Q, and served the prison sentence. On November 1, 1981, I again was hired by Corporation Q and began work on that date. On the November 1, 1981 hiring date, I was an economically disadvantaged ex-convict for whom Corporation Q received a certificate. Corporation Q paid I $500 of wages for services performed from November 1, 1981, to December 31, 1981, and $6,000 of wages for services performed during 1982. The $500 of wages paid for services performed from November 1, 1981, to December 31, 1981, would be qualified first-year wages because these qualified wages were paid for services performed during the 1-year period beginning on the date I first began work for Corporation Q (January 1, 1981). The $6,000 of wages paid for services performed during 1982 would be qualified second-year wages because these qualified wages were paid for services performed during the 1-year period beginning on the date after the first 1-year period. Accordingly, Corporation Q has an allowable credit of $250 attributable to qualified first-year wages and $1,500 attributable to qualified second-year wages.

Example (5). Assume the same facts as in example (4), except that all dates are 1 year later. Thus, I first began work for Corporation Q on January 1, 1982, was convicted on March 1, 1982, and was rehired on November 1, 1982. Under these facts, Q is not entitled to take a targeted jobs credit with respect to I's wages because I is a nonqualifying rehire.

Example (6). J, an economically disadvantaged youth, first began work for Corporation R, a calendar year cash receipts and disbursements method taxpayer, on December 1, 1979. On July 1, 1980, J was laid off by Corporation R and began work for Corporation S, which is unrelated to Corporation R, on July 2, 1980. On November 1, 1980, J again began work for Corporation R and continued working for Corporation R until January 1, 1982. At the time J first began work for Corporation S, J no longer met the qualifications of an economically disadvantaged youth. Corporation S may not claim a credit for wages paid to J because J was not a member of a

targeted group at the time he began work for Corporation S. Corporation R, however, may claim a credit for wages paid to J because J was a member of a targeted group when he was hired by Corporation R. Corporation R's qualified first-year wages paid to J are the wages paid for services performed by J from December 1, 1979, to July 1, 1980, and from November 1, 1980, to November 30, 1980. Corporation R's qualified second-year wages paid to J are wages paid for services performed by J from December 1, 1980, to November 30, 1981. Corporation R may not claim a credit for wages paid for services performed by J after November 30, 1981.

Example (7). K, a member of a targeted group, first began work for Corporation T on January 1, 1979. For the pay periods from January 1, 1979, to March 31, 1979, Corporation T received federally funded payments for on-the-job training for K and paid wages of $2,000 to K. During the remainder of 1979 Corporation T paid wages of $7,000 to K. Corporation T may claim a credit on $6,000 of qualified first-year wages. Amounts paid to K by Corporation T during the pay periods for which Corporation T received federally funded payments for on-the-job training for K are not considered wages for purposes of the credit. However, Corporation T may consider $6,000 of the total $7,000 of wages paid after March 31, 1979, as qualified first-year wages.

Example (8). P first began work for Corporation X on January 1, 1981, as an individual who was certified to be an eligible employee for purposes of the WIN credit provided in section 40. Corporation X paid P $6,000 in wages during its taxable year beginning on January 1, 1981, and $6,000 of wages during its taxable year beginning on January 1, 1982. X can claim a targeted jobs credit for the wages paid in 1982 if the requirements of section 51 are met. For purposes of section 51(a), P's qualified first-year wages are the wages paid from January 1, 1981, to December 31, 1981, and P's qualified second-year wages are the wages paid from January 1, 1982, to December 31, 1982. Thus, Corporation X is only entitled to claim a targeted job credit based on P's qualified second-year wages.

Example (9). (i) L, 15 years of age, first began work for Corporation U on August 1, 1979. On September 3, 1979, L began her junior year in high school and enrolled in a qualified cooperative education program that was to run for her junior and senior years. On October 1, 1979, when L turned 16, she met all the requirements of § 1.51-1(c)(2)(i) and qualified as a youth participating in a qualified cooperative education program. Corporation U is entitled to claim a credit

Reg. § 1.51-1(j)

on wages paid or incurred for services performed by L after September 30, 1979, so long as L meets the requisite requirements. L's summer vacation began on June 1, 1980. Assume that the cooperative education program L was enrolled in did not continue during the summer vacation (*i.e.*, the written agreement between the employer and the school did not cover the summer vacation). Thus, during her summer vacation, L did not meet the requirement of actively pursuing a qualified cooperative education program. Accordingly, Corporation U may not claim a credit on wages paid for services performed by L during L's summer vacation. On September 2, 1980, L began her senior year, and again met all the requirements of § 1.51-1(c)(2)(i). She continued to meet these requirements until June 5, 1981, when she graduated from high school. Accordingly, Corporation U may claim a credit on wages paid for services performed after September 1, 1980, and before June 5, 1981.

(ii) Assume the same facts as in (i), above, except that all dates are 3 years later. Under these facts, U is not entitled to claim a targeted jobs credit with respect to any of L's wages because L has not been timely certified under section 51(d)(16) and § 1.51-1(d)(3).

Example (10). D began work for a drugstore owned by E as a sole proprietor on January 1, 1979, and was certified as a member of a targeted group with respect to E. On June 1, 1979, E sold the drugstore where D worked to F, who continued to operate the drugstore with D as an employee. D's qualification as a member of a targeted group is not required to be redetermined in order for F to qualify for the targeted jobs credit. F will take into account the certification of D's eligibility that was provided to E. F will have qualified first-year wages consisting of the first $6,000 of wages paid or incurred to D by E and F from January 1, 1979 to December 31, 1979 (reduced by any qualified wages paid or incurred by E to D from January 1, 1979, to May 31, 1979). F's qualified second-year wages will consist of the first $6,000 of wages paid or incurred to D by F from January 1, 1980, to December 31, 1980.

Example (11). G began work in a machine shop owned by H as a sole proprietor on January 1, 1979, and was certified as a member of a targeted group with respect to H. On June 1, 1980, H transferred all the assets of the machine shop to newly formed Corporation P. Corporation P retained G as an employee in the machine shop. G's qualification as a member of a targeted group is not required to be redetermined in order for P to qualify for the targeted jobs credit. H has qualified first-year wages in the amount of the first $6,000 of wages paid or incurred to G by H from January 1, 1979, to December 31, 1979. Corporation P has qualified second-year wages in the amount of the first $6,000 of wages paid or incurred to G by H and Corporation P from January 1, 1980, to December 31, 1980 (reduced by any qualified second-year wages paid by H to G).

Example (12). W operates a retail store as a sole proprietor. On June 1, 1982, W hires S after receiving a written determination from a local community organization that S meets the requirements of an economically disadvantaged youth. W does not request a certification from the State employment security agency as to S's eligibility. W is not entitled to claim a credit with respect to wages paid to S because W did not receive, or request in writing, a certification from the State employment security agency as to S's eligibility on or before the day on which S began to work for W.

Example (13). Corporation V is a cash receipts and disbursements method taxpayer with a July 1 through June 30 taxable year. In the taxable year ending June 30, 1980, the aggregate unemployment insurance wages paid by V were $150,000. In calendar year 1979 the aggregate unemployment insurance wages paid by Corporation V were $110,000. Corporation V's qualified first-year wages are limited to 30 percent of the aggregate unemployment insurance wages paid by it in calendar year 1979 or $33,000 (30 percent of $110,000), even though the aggregate unemployment insurance wages paid by it in the taxable year ending June 30, 1980, were $150,000.

Example (14). Assume the same facts as in example (13), except that all dates are 3 years later. Since the limitation on qualified first-year wages does not apply to taxable years beginning after December 31, 1981, Corporation V's qualified first-year wages are $150,000.

Example (15). M operates a retail store as a sole proprietor. N and O, both members of a targeted group, first began work for M on January 1, 1979. M paid N total qualified first-year wages of $6,000 in 1979. Three thousand one hundred dollars of those wages were for services in M's retail store, and $2,900 of those wages were for services as M's maid. M paid O total qualified first-year wages of $6,000 in 1979. Three thousand dollars of those wages were for services in M's store and $3,000 of those wages were for services as M's chauffeur. M has an allowable credit of $3,000 in 1979 on all $6,000 of qualified first-year wages paid to N because more than one-half of the remuneration paid by M to N was for services in M's trade or business. M may not take into account the wages paid to O because not more than one-half of the remuneration paid by M to O was for services in M's trade or business. Accordingly, M may not claim a credit on wages paid to O. [Reg. § 1.51-1.]

☐ [T.D. 8062, 11-5-85.]

[Reg. § 1.52-1]

§ 1.52-1. Trades or businesses that are under common control.—(a) *Apportionment of new jobs credit among members of a group of trades or businesses that are under common control*—(1) *Targeted jobs credit.* (i) In the case of a group of trades or businesses that are under common control (within the meaning of paragraph (b) of this section) at any time during the calendar year, the amount of the targeted jobs credit (computed under section 51 as if all the organizations that are under common control are one trade or business) under section 4-1B must be apportioned among the members of the group on the basis of each member's proportionate share of the wages giving rise to such credit. If the group of trades or businesses that are under common control have different taxable years, the credit shall be computed as if all the organizations have the same taxable year as the organization for which a determination of the proportionate share of the credit

is being made. For taxable years beginning before January 1, 1982, the amount of the qualified first-year wages cannot exceed 30 percent of the aggregate unemployment insurance wages paid by the group of trades or businesses under common control during the calendar year ending in the taxable year of the organization for which a determination of the proportionate share of the credit is being made. The limitations in section 53 and the regulations thereunder apply to each organization individually (although, in applying these limitations, an affiliated group of corporations electing to make a consolidated return shall be treated as one organization).

(ii) The application of the subparagraph may be illustrated by the following examples:

Example (1). (a) Corporation M and its three subsidiaries, Corporations N, O, and P, are a group of businesses that are under common control and each uses the cash receipts and disbursements method of accounting and has a calendar year taxable year. Corporations M, N, O, and P paid out the following amounts in unemployment insurance wages, qualified first-year wages and qualified second-year wages during 1980.

Corporation:	Unemployment insurance wages	Qualified 1st-year wages	Qualified 2d-year wages
M	$ 600,000	$184,000	$ 75,000
N	300,000	85,000	90,000
O	360,000	120,000	115,000
P	24,000	24,000	0
Total	1,284,000	413,000	280,000

(b) Since Corporations M, N, O, and P are under common control, the amount of qualified first-year wages paid by the group is limited to 30 percent of the aggregate unemployment insurance wages paid by the group in the calendar year ending in the group's taxable year. Since the qualified first-year wages of $413,000 exceeds 30% of the aggregate unemployment insurance wages, the group is limited to qualified first-year wages of $385,200 (30% of $1,284,000). The amount of the targeted jobs credit attributable to qualified first-year wages is equal to $192,600

(50% of $385,200). The amount of the credit attributable to qualified second-year wages is equal to $70,000 (25% of $280,000).

(c) The credit is apportioned among Corporations M, N, O, and P on the basis of their proportionate share of the qualified first-year wages or qualified second-year wages giving rise to the credit. Each corporation's share of the credit attributable to qualified first-year wages would be computed as follows:

Corporation:

$$\text{M} \quad \$192,600 \times \frac{\$184,000}{\$413,000} = \$85,807.26$$

$$\text{N} \quad \$192,600 \times \frac{\$ 85,000}{\$413,000} = \$39,639.23$$

Reg. § 1.52-1(a)(1)

$$O \ldots\ldots\ldots\ldots\ldots\ldots\ldots\ldots\ldots \$192,600 \times \frac{\$120,000}{\$413,000} = \$55,961.26$$

$$P \ldots\ldots\ldots\ldots\ldots\ldots\ldots\ldots\ldots \$192,600 \times \frac{\$24,000}{\$413,000} = \$11,192.25$$

Each corporation's share of the credit attributable to qualified second-year wages is computed as follows:

Corporation:

Amount of credit

$$M \ldots\ldots\ldots\ldots\ldots\ldots\ldots\ldots\ldots \$70,000 \times \frac{\$75,000}{\$280,000} = \$18,750$$

$$N \ldots\ldots\ldots\ldots\ldots\ldots\ldots\ldots\ldots \$70,000 \times \frac{\$90,000}{\$280,000} = \$22,500$$

$$O \ldots\ldots\ldots\ldots\ldots\ldots\ldots\ldots\ldots \$70,000 \times \frac{\$115,000}{\$280,000} = \$28,750$$

$$P \ldots\ldots\ldots\ldots\ldots\ldots\ldots\ldots\ldots \$70,000 \times \frac{0}{\$280,000} = 0$$

Example (2). Assume the facts in example (1) with these additional facts. A, a member of a targeted group, worked for more than one of the members of the controlled group in the taxable year. A first began work for Corporation M on January 1, 1980, and later worked for Corporations N and O during 1980. For services rendered by A during 1980, the following wages were paid to A: Corporation M paid A $2,500 of qualified first-year wages; Corporation N paid A $1,500 of qualified first-year wages; Corporation O paid A $3,000 of qualified first-year wages. Corporations M, N, and O paid A a total of $7,000 of wages during 1980. Only $6,000 of qualified first-year wages per year per employee may be taken into account for purposes of the credit. See § 1.51-1(d)(1). Since Corporations M, N, and O are treated as a single employer under section 52(a), the maximum $6,000 of qualified first-year wages paid A by the group must be apportioned among Corporations M, N, and O as follows:

Corporation:

Qualified 1st-Year wages

$$M \ldots\ldots\ldots\ldots\ldots\ldots\ldots\ldots\ldots \$6,000 \times \frac{\$2,500}{\$7,000} = \$2,142.86$$

$$N \ldots\ldots\ldots\ldots\ldots\ldots\ldots\ldots\ldots \$6,000 \times \frac{\$1,500}{\$7,000} = \$1,285.71$$

$$O \ldots\ldots\ldots\ldots\ldots\ldots\ldots\ldots\ldots \$6,000 \times \frac{\$3,000}{\$7,000} = \$2,571.48$$

Example (3). (a) Corporation Q and its two subsidiaries, Corporations R and S, are a group of businesses that are under common control and each uses the cash receipts and disbursements method of accounting. Corporation Q has a calendar year taxable year. Corporation R has a July 1 through June 30 taxable year. Corporation S has an October 1 through September 30 taxable year. For purposes of determining Corporation R's proportionate share of the credit, the credit is computed as if Corporation Q and S have the same taxable year as Corporation R. Accordingly, Corporation R would compute its share of the credit for its 1979-1980 taxable year as set forth below.

Corporation:	Unemployment insurance wages, 1979	1st year wages	Qualified wages paid from July 1, 1979, to June 30, 1980 2nd year wages
Q	$500,000	$150,000	$ 80,000
R	300,000	110,000	50,000
S	100,000	25,000	10,000
Total	$900,000	$285,000	$140,000

Reg. § 1.52-1(a)(1)

(b) Since Corporations Q, R, and S are under common control, the amount of qualified first-year wages is limited to 30 percent of the aggregate unemployment insurance wages paid by the group during the calendar year ending in Corporation R's taxable year. Since the qualified first-year wages of $285,000 exceeds 30 percent of the aggregate unemployment insurance wages, the group is limited to qualified first-year wages of $270,000 (30% of $900,000). The amount of the targeted jobs credit attributable to qualified first-year wages paid by members of the group during the period of the taxpayer's taxable year is $135,000 (50% of $270,000). The amount of the credit attributable to qualified second-year wages paid or incurred by members of the group during the period of the taxpayer's taxable year is $35,000 (25% of $140,000).

(c) The credit is apportioned to Corporation R on the basis of its proportionate share of the qualified first-year wages and qualified second-year wages giving rise to the credit. Corporation R's share of the credit attributable to qualified first-year wages is $52,105.26

$$\$135,000 \times \frac{\$110,000}{\$285,000}$$

Corporation R's share of the credit attributable to qualified second-year wages is $12,500

$$\$35,000 \times \frac{\$50,000}{\$140,000}$$

Corporation R's share of the credit for its 1979-1980 taxable year is $64,605.26 ($52,105.26 + $12,500).

(2) *New jobs credit.* In the case of a group of trades or businesses that are under common control at any time during the calendar year, the amount of the new jobs credit (computed under section 51 as if all the organizations that are under common control are one trade or business) under section 44B (as in effect prior to enactment of the Revenue Act of 1978) must be apportioned among the members of the group on the basis of each member's proportionate contribution to the increase in unemployment insurance wages for the entire group. The limitations in section 53 (as in effect prior to enactment of the Revenue Act of 1978) and the regulations thereunder apply to each organization individually (although, in applying these limitations, an affiliated group of corporations electing to make a consolidated return shall be treated as one organization). The application of this subparagraph may be illustrated by the following example:

Example. (a) Corporation T and its three subsidiaries, U, V, and W, are a group of businesses that are under common control and each has a calendar year taxable year. Corporations T, U, V, and W have paid out the following amounts in unemployment insurance wages during 1976 and 1977:

Corporation:	1976	1977	Increase in FUTA wages in 1977 over 1976
T	$1,000,000	$1,015,000	+ $ 15,000
U	500,000	650,000	+150,000
V	600,000	580,000	− 20,000
W	40,000	100,000	+60,000
Total	$2,140,000	$2,345,000	$205,000

(b) Since all employees of trades or businesses that are under common control are treated as employed by a single employer, the computations in section 51 are performed as if all the organizations which are under common control are one trade or business. Consequently, the amounts of the total unemployment insurance wages of the group in 1976 (*i.e.*, $2,140,000) and 1977 (*i.e.*, $2,345,000) are used to determine the increase in unemployment insurance wages in 1977 over the 1976 wage base. Since the amount equal to 102 percent of the 1976 unemployment insurance wages ($2,182,800) is greater than the amount equal to 50 percent of the 1977 unemployment insurance wages ($1,172,500), the increase in unemployment insurance wages in 1977 over the 1976 wage basis is $162,200 ($2,345,000 − $2,182,800). The limitations in section 51(c), (d), and (g) (as in effect prior to enactment of the Revenue Act of 1978) must also be computed as though all the organizations under common control are one trade or business. For purposes of this example, it is assumed that none of those limitations reduce the amount of increase in unemployment insurance wages. As a result, the amount of the new jobs credit allowed to the group of business is $81,100 (50% of $162,200).

(c) The credit is apportioned among Corporations T, U, and W on the basis of their proportionate contributions to the increase in unemployment insurance wages. No credit would

Reg. § 1.52-1(a)(2)

be allowed to Corporation V because it did not contribute to the increase in the group's unemployment insurance wages. Corporation T's share of the credit would be $5,406.66 ($81,100 × ($15,000 ÷ $225,000 (*i.e.,* $15,000 + $150,000 + $60,000))), Corporation U's share would be $54,066.67 ($81,100 × ($150,000 ÷ 225,000)), and Corporation W's share would be $21,626.67 ($81,100 × ($60,000 ÷ $225,000)).

(b) *Trades or businesses that are under common control.* For purposes of this section, the term "trades or businesses that are under common control" means any group of trades or businesses that is either a "parent-subsidiary group under common control" as defined in paragraph (c) of this section, a "brother-sister group under common control" as defined in paragraph (d) of this section, or a "combined group under common control" as defined in paragraph (e) of this section. For purposes of this section and §§ 1.52-2 and 1.52-3, the term "organization" means a sole proprietorship, a partnership, a trust, an estate, or a corporation. An organization may be a member of only one group of trades or businesses under common control. If, without the application of this paragraph, an organization would be a member of more than one such group, that organization shall indicate in its timely filed return the group in which it is being included. If the organization does not so indicate, then the district director with audit jurisdiction of the organization's return will determine the group in which the organization is to be included.

(c) *Parent-subsidiary group under common control* — (1) *In general.* The term "parent-subsidiary group under common control" means one or more chains of organizations conducting trades or businesses that are connected through ownership of a controlling interest with a common parent organization if—

(i) A controlling interest in each of the organizations, except the common parent organization, is owned (directly and with the application of § 1.414(c)-4(b)(1), relating to options) by one or more of the other organizations; and

(ii) The common parent organization owns (directly and with the application of § 1.414(c)-4(b)(1), relating to options) a controlling interest in at least one of the other organizations, excluding, in computing the controlling interest, any direct ownership interest by the other organizations.

(2) *Controlling interest defined.* For purposes of this paragraph, the term "controlling interest" means:

(i) In the case of a corporation, ownership of stock possessing more than 50 percent of the total combined voting power of all classes of stock entitled to vote or more than 50 percent of the total value of the shares of all classes of stock of the corporation;

(ii) In the case of a trust or estate, ownership of an actuarial interest (determined under paragraph (f) of this section) of more than 50 percent of the trust or estate;

(iii) In the case of a partnership, ownership or more than 50 percent of the profit interest or capital interest of the partnership; and

(iv) In the case of a sole proprietorship, ownership of the sole proprietorship.

(d) *Brother-sister group under common control* —(1) *In general.* The term "brother-sister group under common control" means two or more organizations conducting trades or businesses if—

(i) The same five or fewer persons who are individuals, estates, or trusts own (directly and with the application of § 1.414(c)-4(b)(1)) [§ 1.414(c)-4], a controlling interest of each organization; and

(ii) Taking into account the ownership of each person only to the extent that person's ownership is identical with respect to each organization, such persons are in effective control of each organization.

The five or fewer persons whose ownership is considered for purposes of the controlling interest requirement for each organization must be the same persons whose ownership is considered for purposes of the effective control requirement.

(2) *Controlling interest defined.* For purposes of this paragraph, the term "controlling interest" means:

(i) In the case of a corporation, ownership of stock possessing at least 80 percent of the total combined voting power of all classes of stock entitled to vote or at least 80 percent of the total value of the shares of all classes of stock of the corporation;

(ii) In case of a trust or estate, ownership of an actuarial interest (determined under paragraph (f) of this section) of at least 80 percent of the trust or estate;

(iii) In the case of a partnership, ownership of at least 80 percent of the profit interest or capital interest of the partnership; and

(iv) In the case of a sole proprietorship, ownership of the sole proprietorship.

(3) *Effective control defined.* For purposes of this paragraph "effective control" means:

Reg. § 1.52-1(d)(3)

(i) In the case of a corporation, ownership of stock possessing more than 50 percent of the total combined voting power of all classes of stock entitled to vote or more than 50 percent of the total value of the shares of all classes of stock of the corporation;

(ii) In the case of a trust or estate, ownership of an actuarial interest (determined under paragraph (f) of this section) of more than 50 percent of the trust or estate;

(iii) In the case of a partnership, ownership of more than 50 percent of the profit interest or capital interest of the partnership; and

(iv) In the case of a sole proprietorship, ownership of the sole proprietorship.

(e) *Combined group under common control.* The term "combined group under common control" means a group of three or more organizations, in which (1) each organization is a member of either a parent-subsidiary group under common control or brother-sister group under common control, and (2) at least one organization is the common parent organization of a parent-subsidiary group under common control and also a member of a brother-sister group under common control.

(f) *Actuarial interest.* For purposes of this section, the actuarial interest of each beneficiary of a trust or estate shall be determined by assuming the maximum exercise of discretion by the fiduciary in favor of the beneficiary. The factors and method prescribed in § 20.2031-7 or, for certain prior periods, § 20.2031-7A of this chapter (Estate Tax Regulations) for use in ascertaining the value of an interest in property for estate tax purposes will be used to determine a beneficiary's actuarial interest.

(g) *Exclusion of certain interests and stock in determining control.* In determining control under this paragraph, the term "interest" and the term "stock" do not include an interest that is treated as not outstanding under § 1.414(c)-3. In addition, the term "stock" does not include treasury stock or nonvoting stock that is limited and preferred regarding dividends.

(h) *Transitional rule*—(1) *In general.* Paragraph (d) of this section, as amended by T.D. 8179, applies to all taxable years to which section 52(b) applies.

(2) *Election.* In the case of taxable years ending before March 2, 1988:

(i) If, pursuant to paragraph (b) of this section, an organization indicated in a timely filed return that it chose to be a member of a brother-sister group under common control, and it is not a member of such group because of the amendments to paragraph (d) of this section made by T.D.

8179 such organization may make the choice described in paragraph (b) of this section by filing an amended return on or before September 2, 1988 if such organization would otherwise still be a member of more than one group of trades or businesses under common control, and

(ii) If an organization

(A) Is a member of a brother-sister group of trades or businesses under common control under § 1.52-1(d)(1) as in effect before amendment by T.D. 8179 ("old group"), for such taxable year and

(B) Is not such a member for such taxable year because of the amendments made by such Treasury decision,

such organization (whether or not a corporation) nevertheless will be treated as a member of such old group if all the organizations (whether or not corporations) that are members of the old group meet all the requirements of § 1.1563-1(d)(3) with respect to such taxable year. [Reg. § 1.52-1.]

□ [*T.D. 7553, 7-20-78, Amended by T.D. 7921, 11-18-83, T.D. 7955, 5-10-84, T.D. 8179, 3-1-88 and T.D. 8540, 6-9-94.*]

[Reg. § 1.52-2]

§ 1.52-2. **Adjustments for acquisitions and dispositions.**—(a) *General rule.* The provisions in this section only apply to the computation of the new jobs credit. If, after December 31, 1975, an employer acquires the major portion of a trade or business or the major portion of a separate unit of a trade or business, then, for purposes of computing the new jobs credit for any calendar year ending after the acquisition, both the amount of unemployment insurance wages and the amount of total wages considered to have been paid by the acquiring employer, for both the year in which the acquisition occurred and the preceding year, must be increased, respectively, by the amount of unemployment insurance wages and the amount of total wages paid by the predecessor employer that are attributable to the acquired portion of the trade or business or separate unit. If the predecessor employer informs the acquiring employer in writing of the amount of unemployment insurance wages and the amount of total wages attributable to the acquired portion of the trade or business that have been paid during the periods preceding the acquisition, then, for purposes of computing the credit for any calendar year ending after the acquisition the amount of unemployment insurance wages and the amount of total wages considered paid by the predecessor employer shall be decreased by those amounts. Regardless of whether the predecessor employer so informs the acquiring employer, the predecessor employer

Reg. § 1.52-2(a)

shall not be allowed a credit for the amount of any increase in the employment insurance wages or the total wages in the calendar year of the acquisition attributable to the acquired portion of the trade or business over the amount of such wages in the calendar year preceding the acquisition.

(b) *Meaning of terms*—(1) *Acquisition.* (i) For purposes of this section, the term "acquisition" includes a lease agreement if the effect of the lease is to transfer the major portion of the trade or business or of a separate unit of the trade or business for the period of the lease. For instance, if one company leases a factory (including equipment) to another company for a two-year period, the employees are retained by the second company, and the factory is used for the same general purposes as before, then for purposes of this section the lessee has acquired the lessor's trade or business for the period of the lease.

(ii) Neither the major portion of a trade or business nor the major portion of a separate unit of a trade or business is acquired merely by acquiring physical assets. The acquisition must transfer a viable trade or business.

(iii) Subdivision (ii) of this subparagraph may be illustrated by the following examples:

Example (1). R Company, a restaurant, sells its building and all its restaurant equipment to S Company and moves into a larger, more modern building across the street. R Company purchases new equipment, retains its name and continues to operate as a restaurant. S Company opens a new restaurant in the old R Company building. S Company has merely acquired the old R Company assets; it has not acquired any portion of R Company's business.

Example (2). The facts are the same as in *Example (1),* except that R Company also sells its name and goodwill to S Company and ceases to operate a restaurant business. S Company operates its restaurant using the old R Company name. In this situation, S Company has acquired R Company's business.

(2) *Separate unit.* (i) A separate unit is a segment of a trade or business capable of operating as a self-sustaining enterprise with minor adjustments. The allocation of a portion of the goodwill of a trade or business to one of its segments is a strong indication that that segment is a separate unit.

(ii) The following examples are illustrations of the acquisition of a separate unit of a trade or business:

Example (1). The M Corporation, which has been engaged in the sale and repair of boats, leases the repair shop building and all the property used in its boat repair operations to the N Company for four years and gives the N Company a covenant not to compete in the boat repair business for the period of the lease. The N Company is considered to have acquired a separate unit of M Corporation's business for the period of the lease.

Example (2). (a) The P Company is engaged in the operation of a chain of department stores. There are eight divisions, each division is located in a different metropolitan area of the country, and each division operates under a different name. Although certain buying and merchandising functions are centralized, each division's day-to-day operations are independent of the others. The Q Corporation acquires all of the physical and intangible assets of one of the divisions, including the division's name. Other than making those minor adjustments necessary to give the division buying and merchandising departments, the Q Corporation allows the division to continue doing business in the same manner as it had been operating prior to the acquisition. The Q Corporation has acquired a separate unit of the P Company's business.

(b) The facts are the same as in (a) above, except that Q Corporation buys the division merely to obtain its store locations. Before the Q Corporation takes over, the division liquidates its inventory in a going-out-of-business sale. The Q Corporation has merely acquired assets in this transaction, not a separate unit of P Company's business.

Example (3). The R Company processes and distributes meat products. Both the processing division and the distributorship are self-sustaining, profitable operations. The acquisition of either the meat processing division or the distributorship would be an acquisition of a separate unit of the R Company's business.

Example (4). The S Corporation is engaged in the manufacture and sale of steel and steel products. S Corporation also owns a coal mine, which it operates for the sole purpose of supplying its coal requirements for its steel manufacturing operations. The acquisition of the coal mine would be an acquisition of a separate unit of the S Company's business.

Example (5). The T Company, which is engaged in the business of operating a chain of drug stores, sells its only downtown drug store to the V Company and agrees not to open another T Company store in the downtown area for five years. Included in the purchase price is an amount that is charged for the goodwill of the store location. The V Company has acquired a separate unit of the T Company's business.

Reg. § 1.52-2(b)(2)

Example (6). The W Company, which is engaged in the business of operating a chain of drug stores, sells one of its stores to the X Company, but continues to operate another drug store three blocks away. The X Company opens the store doing business under its own name. The X Company has not acquired a separate unit of the W Company's business.

Example (7). (a) The Y Corporation, which is engaged in the manufacture of mattresses, sells one of its three factories to the Z Company. At the time of the sale, the factory is capable of profitably manufacturing mattresses on its own. Z Company has acquired a separate unit of the Y Corporation.

(b) The facts are the same as in (a) above, except that a profitable manufacturing operation cannot be conducted in the factory standing on its own. Z Company has not acquired a separate unit of the Y Corporation.

Example (8). The O Construction Company is owned by A, B, and C, who are unrelated individuals. It owns equipment valued at 1.5 million dollars and construction contracts valued at 6 million dollars. A, wishing to start his own company, exchanges his interest in O Company for 2 million dollars of contracts and a sufficient amount of equipment to enable him to begin business immediately. A has acquired a separate unit of the O Company's business.

(3) *Major portion.* All the facts and circumstances surrounding the transaction shall be taken into account in determining what constitutes a major portion of a trade or business (or separate unit). Factors to be considered include:

(i) The fair market value of the assets in the portion relative to the fair market value of the other assets of the trade or business (or separate unit);

(ii) The proportion of goodwill attributable to the portion of the trade or business (or separate unit);

(iii) The proportion of the number of employees of the trade or business (or separate unit) attributable to the portion in the periods immediately preceding the transaction; and

(iv) The proportion of the sales or gross receipts, net income, and budget of the trade or business (or separate unit) attributable to the portion. [Reg. § 1.52-2.]

☐ [*T.D. 7553, 7-20-78. Amended by T.D. 7921, 11-18-83.*]

Reg. § 1.52-3(a)

[Reg. § 1.52-3]

§ 1.52-3. Limitations with respect to certain persons.—(a) *Mutual savings institutions.* In the case of an organization to which section 593 applies (that is, a mutual savings bank, a cooperative bank or a domestic building and loan association), the amount of the targeted jobs credit (new jobs credit in the case of wages paid before 1979) allowable under section 44B shall be 50 percent of the amount otherwise determined under section 51, or, in the case of an organization under common control, under § 1.52-1(a) and (b).

(b) *Regulated investment companies and real estate investment trusts.* In the case of a regulated investment company or a real estate investment trust subject to taxation under subchapter M, chapter 1 of the Code, the amount of the targeted jobs credit (new jobs credit in the case of wages paid before 1979) allowable under section 44B shall be reduced to the company's or trust's ratable share of the credit. The ratable share shall be determined in accordance with rules similar to the rules provided in section 46(e)(2)(B) and the regulations thereunder. For purposes of computing the ratable share, the reduction of the deduction for wage or salary expenses under § 1.280C-1 shall not be taken into account.

(c) *Cooperatives*—(1) *Taxable years ending after October 31, 1978.* For taxable years ending after October 31, 1978, in the case of a cooperative organization described in section 1381(a), rules similar to rules provided in section 46(h) and the regulations thereunder shall apply in determining the distribution of the amount of the targeted jobs credit (new jobs credit in the case of wages paid before 1979) allowable to the cooperative organization and its patrons under section 44B.

(2) *Taxable years ending before November 1, 1978.* For taxable years ending before November 1, 1978, in the case of a cooperative organization described in section 1381(a), the amount of new jobs credit allowable under section 44B shall be reduced to the cooperative's ratable share of the credit. The ratable share shall be the ratio which the taxable income of the cooperative for the taxable year bears to its taxable income increased by the amount of the deductions allowed under section 1382(b) and (c). For purposes of computing the ratable share, the reduction of the deduction for wage or salary expenses under § 1.280C-1 shall not be taken into account. [Reg. § 1.52-3.]

☐ [*T. D. 7553, 7-20-78. Amended by T. D. 7921, 11-18-83.*]

→ *Caution: Reg. § 1.53-1 was adopted under former Code Sec. 53 of the Internal Revenue Code of 1954. Current Code Sec. 38 contains provisions comparable to the former Code Sec. 53 limits on credits.*←

[Reg. § 1.53-1]

§ 1.53-1. Limitation based on amount of credit.—(a) *General rule*—(1) *Targeted jobs credit.* For taxable years beginning after December 31, 1978, the amount of the targeted jobs credit allowed by section 44B (as amended by the Revenue Act of 1978) shall not exceed 90 percent of the tax imposed by chapter 1, reduced by the credits enumerated in section 53(a).

(2) *New jobs credit.* For taxable years beginning before January 1, 1979, the amount of the new jobs credit allowed by section 44B (as in effect prior to enactment of the Revenue Act of 1978) shall not exceed the tax imposed by chapter 1, reduced by the credits enumerated in section 53(a).

(b) *Special rule for 1978-79 fiscal year.*—In the case of a taxable year beginning before January 1, 1979, and ending after that date, the sum of the targeted jobs credit (determined without regard to the tax liability limitation in paragraph (a)(1) of this section) and the new jobs credit (determined without regard to the tax liability limitation in paragraph (a)(2) of this section) shall not exceed the tax imposed by chapter 1, reduced by the credits enumerated in section 53(a). [Reg. § 1.53-1.]

☐ [*T.D. 7921, 11-18-83.*]

→ *Caution: Reg. § 1.53-2 was adopted under former Code Sec. 53 of the Internal Revenue Code of 1954. Current Code Sec. 39 contains provisions comparable to the former Code Sec. 53 limits on carryovers of unused credits.*←

[Reg. § 1.53-2]

§ 1.53-2. Carryback and carryover of unused credit.—(a) *Allowance of unused credit as a carryback or carryover*—(1) *In general.* Section 53(b) (formerly designated as section 53(c) for taxable years beginning before 1979) provides for carrybacks and carryovers of unused targeted jobs credit (new jobs credit in the case of wages paid before 1979). An unused credit is the excess of the credit determined under section 51 for the taxable year over the limitations provided by Sec. 1.53-1 for such taxable year. Subject to the limitations contained in paragraph (b) of this section and paragraph (f) of section 1.53-3, an unused credit shall be added to the amount allowable as a credit under section 44B for the years to which an unused credit can be carried. The year with respect to which an unused credit arises shall be referred to in this section as the "unused credit year."

(2) *Taxable years to which unused credit may be carried.* An unused targeted jobs credit (new jobs credit in the case of wages paid before 1979) shall be a new employee credit carryback to each of the 3 taxable years preceding the unused credit year and a new employee credit carryove to each of the 15 taxable years succeeding the unused credit year. An unused credit must be carried first to the earliest of the taxable years to which it may be carried, and then to each of the other taxable years (in order of time) to the extent that the unused credit may not be added (because of the limitation contained in paragraph (b) of this section) to the amount allowable as a credit under section 44B for a prior taxable year.

(b) *Limitations on allowance of unused credit*—(1) *In general.* The amount of the unused targeted jobs credit (new jobs credit in the case of wages paid before 1979) from any particular unused credit year which may be added under section 53(b)(1) (section 53(c)(1) in the case of a new jobs credit) to the amount allowable as a credit under section 44B for any of the preceding or succeeding taxable years to which such credit may be carried shall not exceed the amount by which the limitation in Sec 1.53-1 for such preceding or succeeding taxable year exceeds the sum of (i) the credit allowable under section 44B for such preceding or succeeding taxable year, and (ii) other unused credits carried to such preceding or succeeding taxable year which are attributable to unused credit years prior to the particular unused credit year. Thus, in determining the amount, if any, of an unused credit from a particular unused credit year which shall be added to the amount allowable as a credit for any preceding or succeeding taxable year, the credit earned for such preceding or succeeding taxable year, plus any unused credits originating in taxable years prior to the particular unused credit year, shall first be applied against the limitation based on amount of tax for such preceding or succeeding taxable year. To the extent the limitation based on amount of tax for the preceding or succeeding taxable year exceeds the sum of the credit earned for such year and other unused credits attributable to years prior to the particular unused credit year, the unused credit from the particular unused credit year shall be added to the amount allowable as a credit under section 44B for such preceding or suc-

→ *Caution: Reg. § 1.53-2 was adopted under former Code Sec. 53 of the Internal Revenue Code of 1954. Current Code Sec. 39 contains provisions comparable to the former Code Sec. 53 limits on carryovers of unused credits.*←

ceeding year. If any portion of the unused credit is a carryback to a taxable year beginning before January 1, 1977, section 44B shall be deemed to have been in effect for such taxable year for purposes of allowing such carryback as a credit under section 44B. To the extent that an unused credit cannot be added for a particular preceding or succeeding taxable year because of the limitation contained in this paragraph, such unused credit shall be available as a carryback or carryover to the next succeeding taxable year to which it may be carried.

(2) *Special rules for an electing small business corporation.* An unused targeted jobs credit (new jobs credit in the case of wages paid before 1979) under section 44B of a corporation which arises in an unused credit year for which the coporation is not an electing small business corporation (as defined in section 1371(b)) and which is a carryback or carryover to a taxable year for which the corporation is an electing small business corporation shall not be added to the amount allowable as a credit under section 44B to the shareholders of such corporation for any taxable year. However, a taxable year for which the corporation is an electing small business corporation shall be counted as a taxable year for purposes of determining the taxable years to which such unused credit may be carried.

(3) *Corporate acquisitions.* For the carryover of unused credits under section 44B in the case of certain corporate acquisitions, see section 381(c)(26) and Sec. 1.381(c)(26)-1.

(4) *Examples.* This paragraph may be illustrated by the following examples.

Example 1. In 1978, A, a calendar year taxpayer, had an unused new jobs credit of $2,000. In 1979, A has a targeted jobs credit of $2,000 and a tax liability imposed by chapter 1 of the Code of $4,000 after all credits listed in section 53(a) have

been taken into account. The amount of A's targeted jobs credit allowable under section 44B for 1979 is 90 percent of A's tax liability. The amount of the new jobs credit that may be carried to 1979 is limited to $1,600 ($3,600 [90% of $4,000] − $2,000).

Example 2. In 1979, B, a calendar year taxpayer, has a tax liability imposed by chapter 1 of the Code of $10,000 after all credits listed in section 53(a) have been taken. B's targeted jobs credit for that taxable year is limited to 90 percent of his income tax liability of $9,000. B has a $15,000 targeted jobs credit in 1979 resulting in an unused targeted jobs credit of $5,000 for that year. In 1976 and 1977 B had tax liabilities imposed by chapter 1 of the Code of $3,000 and $4,000 respectively after all credits listed in section 53(a) had been taken. For purposes of carrying back an unused targeted jobs credit to a taxable year beginning before January 1, 1977, section 44B as amended by the Revenue Act of 1978 is deemed to have been in effect for such taxable year. Accordingly, the applicable tax liability limitation for 1976 would be governed by section 53(a) (as amended by the Revenue Act of 1978) which limits the amount of targeted jobs credit allowed to 90 percent of the tax imposed by chapter 1 of the Code after all credits listed in section 53(a) have been taken. B may carry back $2,700 (90% of 3,000) of the 1979 unused targeted jobs credit to 1976. B may carry back $4,000 of the unused targeted jobs credit to 1977 because section 53(a) as it applied to the 1977 taxable year limited the amount of the credit to 100 percent of the taxpayer's tax liability imposed by chapter 1 of the Code after all credits listed in section 53(a) had been taken.

[Reg. § 1.53-2.]

□ [*T.D.* 7921, 11-18-83.]

→ *Caution: Reg. § 1.53-3 was adopted under former Code Sec. 53 of the Internal Revenue Code of 1954. Current Code Sec. 41 contains provisions comparable to the former Code Sec. 53 special rule for pass-through of credit.*←

[Reg. § 1.53-3]

§ 1.53-3. **Separate rule for pass-through of jobs credit.**—(a) *In general.* Under section 53(b), in the case of a new jobs credit or targeted jobs credit earned under section 44B by a partnership, estate or trust, or subchapter S corporation, the amount of the credit that may be taken into account by a partner, beneficiary, or shareholder may not exceed a limitation under section 53(b)

separately computed with respect to the partner's, beneficiary's, or shareholder's interest in the entity. A credit is subject to the limitation of section 53(b) with respect to a partner, beneficiary, or shareholder if it is earned by a partnership, estate or trust, or subchapter S corporation in a taxable year ending within, or ending before, a taxable year beginning before January 1, 1979 of the partner, beneficiary, or shareholder. See

Reg. § 1.53-3(a)

→ *Caution: Reg. § 1.53-3 was adopted under former Code Sec. 53 of the Internal Revenue Code of 1954. Current Code Sec. 41 contains provisions comparable to the former Code Sec. 53 special rule for pass-through of credit.*←

paragraph (f) of this section for rules on carryback or carryover of a credit subject to separate limitation. This section prescribes rules, under the authority of section 44B(b), relating to the computation of the separate limitation. For purposes of this section, references to section 53(a) and (b) are to that section as it existed before it was amended by the Revenue Act of 1978. This paragraph may be illustrated by the following examples:

Example 1. A, a calendar year taxpayer, is a partner in P, a calendar year partnership. A's pro rata portion of the credit earned by P in 1978 is $200. The $200 credit to be claimed on A's 1978 return is subject to the separate limitation in section 53(b) because the limitation applies to taxable years of the taxpayer beginning before January 1, 1979.

Example 2. B, a calendar year taxpayer, is a shareholder in Corporation M, a subchapter S corporation with a July to June fiscal year. B's pro rata portion of the credit earned by Corporation M in its taxable year beginning in 1978 is $100. The $100 credit to be claimed on B's 1979 return is not subject to the separate limitation requirement of section 53(b) because the limitation only applies to taxable years of the taxpayer beginning before 1979, notwithstanding the credit was earned by Corporation M before 1979.

(b) *Application of credit earned.* A credit earned under section 44B by a partnership, estate or trust, or subchapter S corporation shall be applied by a partner, beneficiary, or shareholder, to the extent allowed under section 53(b), before applying any other credit earned under section 44B. For example, if an individual has a new jobs credit from a proprietorship of $2,000 and from a partnership (after applying section 53(b)) of $1,800, but the credit must be limited under section 53(a) to $3,000, the entire $1,800 credit from the partnership would be applied before any part of the $2,000 amount is applied.

(c) *Amount of separate limitation.* The amount of the separate limitation is equal to the partner's, beneficiary's, or shareholder's limitation under section 53(a) for the taxable year multiplied by a fraction. The numerator of the fraction is the portion of the taxpayer's taxable income for the year attributable to the taxpayer's interest in the entity. The denominator of the fraction is the taxpayer's total taxable income for the year reduced by the zero bracket amount, if any.

(d) *Portion of taxable income attributable to an interest in a partnership, estate or trust, or sub-* chapter S corporation—(1) *General rule.* The portion of a taxpayer's taxable income attributable to an interest in a partnership, estate or trust, or subchapter S corporation is the amount of income from that entity the taxpayer is required to include in gross income, reduced by—

(i) The amount of the deductions allowed to the taxpayer that are attributable to the taxpayer's interest in the entity; and

(ii) A proportionate share of the deductions allowed to the taxpayer not attributable to a specific activity (as defined in paragraph (e)).

If a deduction comprises both an item that is attributable to the taxpayer's interest in the entity and an item or items that are not attributable to the interest in the entity, and if the deduction is limited by a provision of the Code (such as section 170(b), relating to limitations on charitable contributions), the deduction must be prorated among the items taken into account in computing the deduction. For example, if an individual makes a charitable contribution of $5,000 and his distributive share of a partnership includes $2,000 in charitable contributions made by the partnership, and if the charitable contribution deduction is limited to $3,500 under section 170(b), then the portion of the deduction allowed to the taxpayer that is not attributable to a specific activity is $2,500 ($3,500 × ($5,000 ÷ $7,000)) and the portion of the deduction allowed to the taxpayer that is attributable to the interest in the partnership is $1,000 ($3,500 × ($2,000 ÷ $7,000)).

(2) *Deductions attributable to an interest in an entity.* Examples of deductions that are attributable to the taxpayer's interest in an entity include (but are not limited to) a deduction under section 1202 attributable to a net capital gain passed through the entity, and a deduction attributable to a deductible item (such as a charitable contribution) that has been passed through the entity.

(3) *Computation of the proportionate share of deductions not attributable to a specific activity.* The proportionate share of a deduction of the taxpayer not attributable to a specific activity is obtained by multiplying the amount of the deduction by a fraction. The numerator of the fraction is the income from the entity that the taxpayer is required to include in gross income, reduced by the amount of the deductions of the taxpayer that are attributable to the taxpayer's interest in the entity. The denominator is the taxpayer's gross

Reg. § 1.53-3(d)(3)

→ *Caution: Reg. § 1.53-3 was adopted under former Code Sec. 53 of the Internal Revenue Code of 1954. Current Code Sec. 41 contains provisions comparable to the former Code Sec. 53 special rule for pass-through of credit.* ←

income reduced by the amount of all the deductions attributable to specific activities.

(4) *Examples.* The method of determining the amount of taxable income attributable to an interest in a partnership, estate or trust, or subchapter S corporation is illustrated by the following examples:

Example 1. (a) A, a single individual, is a shareholder in S Corporation, a subchapter S corporation. A is required to include the following amounts from S corporation is his gross income:

Salary	$ 3,000

Undistributed taxable income:

Ordinary income	8,000	
Net capital gain	2,000	
Total		10,000
Total		13,000

A has income from other activities:

Ordinary income	6,000	
Net capital gain	4,000	
Total		10,000

(b) In order to determine the taxable income attributable to A's interest in S Corporation, it is necessary to reduce the amount of income from S Corporation that A is required to include in gross income by the amount of A's deductions attributable to the interest in S Corporation and by a proportionate share of A's deductions not attributable to a specific activity. These computations are made in paragraph (c) of this example. However, before the computation reducing A's income by a proportionate share of the deductions not attributable to a specific activity can be made, the ratio described in subparagraph (3) of this paragraph (d) must be determined. The numerator of the ratio (the amount of income from S Corporation that A is required to include in gross income, reduced by the amount of the deductions attributable to A's interest in S Corporation) is obtained in paragraph (c) of this example in the process of computing A's taxable income attributable to the interest in S Corporation. The determination of the denominator (A's gross income reduced by the amount of all deductions attributable to specific activities), however, require a separate computation, which follows:

Gross income:

Income from S Corporation		$13,000
Income from other sources		10,000
Total		23,000

Less: Deductions attributable to specific activities:

Section 1202 deduction (50 percent of $6,000)	3,000

A's gross income reduced by the amount of the deductions attributable to specific activities (denominator of the ratio for determining the proportionate share of deductions not attributable to a specific activity)	20,000

(c) Computation of the amount of A's taxable income attributable to the interest in S Corporation:

Income from S Corporation that A is required to include in gross income:

Ordinary income		$11,000
Net capital gain		2,000
Total		13,000

Less: Deductions of the taxpayer attributable to the interest in S Corporation:

Section 1202 deduction (50 pct. of $2,000)	1,000
(Numerator of the ratio for determining the proportionate share of deductions not attributable to a specific activity)	12,000

Less: Proportionate share of the deductions of the taxpayer not attributable to a specific activity:

Personal exemption deduction ($750 × $12,000/$20,000)		450
Zero bracket amount ($2,200 × $12,000/$20,000)		1,320
Total		1,770

Portion of A's taxable income attributable to interest in S Corporation	10,230

Example 2. (a) C, a married individual with two children, is a partner in the CD Company. C's distributive share of the CD Company consists of the following:

Ordinary income (other than guaranteed payment)	$38,420
Guaranteed payment	20,000
Net long-term capital gain	6,000
Net short-term capital loss	2,000
Dividends qualifying for exclusion	100
Charitable contributions	500

Reg. § 1.53-3(d)(4)

→ *Caution: Reg. § 1.53-3 was adopted under former Code Sec. 53 of the Internal Revenue Code of 1954. Current Code Sec. 41 contains provisions comparable to the former Code Sec. 53 special rule for pass-through of credit.*←

C also has items of income from other sources and deductions, as follows:

Ordinary income	$21,680
Short-term capital gain	2,000
Dividends qualifying for exclusion	400
Deductions:	
Deductible medical expenses	16,000
Charitable contributions	4,000
Alimony	18,000
Interest and taxes on home	8,000
Loss relating to another specific activity	4,000

(b) In order to determine C's taxable income attributable to the interest in the partnership, it is necessary to reduce the amount of income from the partnership that C is required to include in gross income by the amount of C's deductions attributable to the interest in the partnership and by a proportionate share of C's deductions not attributable to a specific activity. These computations are made in paragraph (c) of this example. However, before the computation reducing C's income by a proportionate share of the deductions not attributable to a specific activity can be made, the ratio described in paragraph (d)(3) of this section must be determined. The numerator of the ratio is determined in paragraph (c) of this example in the process of computing C's taxable income attributable to the interest in the partnership. The denominator, however, requires a separate computation, reducing C's gross income by the amount of all deductions attributable to specific activities. This computation is as follows:

Gross income: Income from the partnership:

Ordinary income		$58,420
Net long-term capital gain		6,000
Dividends		100
Less: Proportionate share of dividend exclusion ($100 × $100/$500)		20
		80
		64,500

Income from other sources:

Ordinary income		21,680
Net short/term capital gain		2,000
Dividends		400
Less: Proportionate share of dividend exclusion ($100 × $400/$500)	$	80
		320
		24,000
		88,500

Less: Deductions attributable to specific activities:		
Net short-term capital loss passed through the partnership		2,000
Loss related to another specific activity		4,000
Section 1202 deduction attributable to the interest in the partnership		2,000
Charitable contribution deduction passed through the partnership		500
		8,500

C's gross income, reduced by the amount of the deductions attributable to specific activities (denominator of the ratio for determining the proportionate share of deductions not attributable to a specific activity)	80,000

(c) Computation of the amount of C's taxable income attributable to the interest in the partnership:

Reg. § 1.53-3(d)(4)

→ *Caution: Reg. § 1.53-3 was adopted under former Code Sec. 53 of the Internal Revenue Code of 1954. Current Code Sec. 41 contains provisions comparable to the former Code Sec. 53 special rule for pass-through of credit.*←

Distributive share of ordinary income (other than guaranteed payments) ...	$38,420
Guaranteed payment	20,000
Distributive share of dividends less share of exclusion	80
Distributive share of net long-term capital gain	6,000
	64,500

Section 1202 deduction (50 pct. of $4,000)	2,000
Charitable contribution passed through the partnership	500
Net short-term capital loss passed through the partnership	2,000
	4,500

(Numerator of the ratio for determining the proportionate share of deductions not attributable to a specific activity).	60,000

Section 1202 deduction ($1,000 × $60,000/$80,000)	750
Deductible medical expenses ($16,000 × $60,000/$80,000)	12,000
Charitable contributions ($4,000 × $60,000/$80,000)	3,000
Alimony ($18,000 × $60,000/$80,000) ..	13,500
Interest and taxes on home ($8,000 × $60,000/$80,000)	6,000
Personal exemption deduction ($3,000 × $60,000/$80,000)	2,250
Total	37,500

Portion of C's taxable income attributable to the interest in the partnership	22,500

C has a deduction under section 1202 of $3,000. Of that deduction, $2,000 is attributable directly to C's interest in the partnership (50 percent of the net capital gain that would result from offsetting the $6,000 net long-term capital gain and the $2,000 net short-term capital loss that are attributable to C's interest in the partnership). Since the remaining $1,000 deduction under section 1202 cannot be attributed directly to either C's income from the partnership or any other specific activity, it must be treated as a deduction not attributable to a specific activity.

(e) *Deductions not attributable to a specific activity*—(1) *Specific activity defined.* A specific activity means a course of continuous conduct involving a particular line of endeavor, whether or not the activity is carried on for profit. Examples of a specific activity are:

(i) A trade or business carried on by the taxpayer;

(ii) A trade or business carried on by an entity in which the taxpayer has an interest;

(iii) An activity with respect to which the taxpayer is entitled to a deduction under section 212;

(iv) The operation of a farm as a hobby.

(2) *Types of deductions not attributable to a specific activity.* Examples of deductions not attributable to a specific activity include charitable contributions made by the partner, beneficiary, or shareholder; medical expenses; alimony; interest on personal debts of the partner, beneficiary, or shareholder; and real estate taxes on the personal residence of the partner, beneficiary, or shareholder. For purposes of this section, in cases in which deductions are not itemized, the zero bracket amount is considered to be a deduction not attributable to a specific activity.

(f) *Carryback or carryover of credit subject to separate limitation.* A credit subject to the separate limitation under section 53(b) that is carried back or carried over to a taxable year beginning before January 1, 1979, is also subject to the separate limitation in the carryback or carryover year. For purposes of the preceding sentence, a credit that is earned by a partnership, a trust, or estate, or a subchapter S corporation in a taxable year of such entity ending within, or after, the taxable year of a partner beneficiary or shareholder beginning after December 31, 1978, will not be subject to the separate limitation in section 53(b) with respect to such partner, beneficiary, or shareholder. The taxpayer to whom the credit has been passed through shall not be prevented from applying the unused portion in a carryback or carryover year merely because the entity that earned the credit changes its form of conducting business if the nature of its trade or business essentially remains the same. The computation of the separate limitation in such a case shall reflect the income attributable to the taxpayer's interest in the entity in its revised form. Thus, a shareholder carrying over a credit from a subchapter S corporation may include dividends declared by that corporation after the subchapter S election had been terminated as income attributable to that person's interest in the entity. Similarly, if a partnership incorporates in a carryover year, any income attributable to an interest in the corporation will be regarded, for purposes of computing the separate limitation under section 53(b), as income attributable to an interest in the entity. This paragraph may be illustrated by the following examples:

Example 1. A, a calendar year taxpayer, is a shareholder in Corporation M, a subchapter S

Reg. § 1.53-3(e)(1)

→ *Caution: Reg. § 1.53-3 was adopted under former Code Sec. 53 of the Internal Revenue Code of 1954. Current Code Sec. 41 contains provisions comparable to the former Code Sec. 53 special rule for pass-through of credit.*←

corporation. In 1977, A's pro rata share of the new jobs credit earned by Corporation M was $10,000. A could only use $2,000 of the credit in 1977 because of the separate limitation under section 53(b). In 1978, A carries the unused credit over from 1977. The carryover credit is subject to the separate limitation under section 53(b).

Example 2. Assume the same facts as in example 1 except that the unused credit is carried over to 1979. The carryover credit is not subject to the separate limitation under section 53(b) because that limitation does not apply to taxable years of a taxpayer beginning after December 31, 1978.

Example 3. B, a calendar year taxpayer, is a shareholder in Corporation W, a subchapter S corporation. In 1979, B's pro rata share of the targeted jobs credit covered by Corporation W was $5,000 but B could only use $3,000 of the credit in 1979. B carries back the unused credit to 1978. The carryback credit is not subject to the separate limitation under section 53(b).

[Reg. § 1.53-3.]

☐ [*T.D.* 7560, 12-28-78. *Redesignated and amended by T.D.* 7921, 11-18-83.]

Alternative Minimum Tax

[Reg. § 1.55-1]

§ 1.55-1. Alternative minimum taxable income.—(a) *General rule for computing alternative minimum taxable income.* Except as otherwise provided by statute, regulations, or other published guidance issued by the Commissioner, all Internal Revenue Code provisions that apply in determining the regular taxable income of a taxpayer also apply in determining the alternative minimum taxable income of the taxpayer.

(b) *Items based on adjusted gross income or modified adjusted gross income.* In determining the alternative minimum taxable income of a taxpayer other than a corporation, all references to the taxpayer's adjusted gross income or modified adjusted gross income in determining the amount of items of income, exclusion, or deduction must be treated as references to the taxpayer's adjusted gross income or modified adjusted gross income as determined for regular tax purposes.

(c) *Effective date.* These regulations are effective for taxable years beginning after December 31, 1993. [Reg. § 1.55-1.]

☐ T.D. 8569, 11-23-94.]

[Reg. § 1.56-0]

§ 1.56-0. Table of contents to § 1.56-1, adjustment for book income of corporations.

(a) Computation of the book income adjustment.

(1) In general.

(2) Taxpayers subject to the book income adjustment.

(3) Consolidated returns.

(4) Examples.

(b) Adjusted net book income.

(1) In general.

(2) Net book income.

(i) In general.

(II) Measures of net book income.

(iii) Tax-free transactions and tax-free income.

(iv) Treatment of dividends and other amounts.

(3) Additional rules for consolidated groups.

(i) Consolidated adjusted net book income.

(ii) Consolidated net book income.

(iii) Consolidated pre-adjustment alternative minimum taxable income.

(iv) Cross references.

(4) Computation of adjusted net book income when taxable year and financial accounting year differ.

(i) In general.

(ii) Estimating adjusted net book income.

(iii) Election to compute adjusted net book income based on the financial statement for the year ending within the taxable year.

(A) In general.

(B) Time of making election.

(C) Eligibility to make and manner of making election.

(D) Election or revocation of election made on an amended return.

(iv) Quarterly statement filed with the Securities and Exchange Commission (SEC).

(5) Computation of net book income using current earnings and profits.

(i) In general.

(ii) Current earnings and profits of a consolidated group.

Reg. § 1.56-0

(6) Additional rules for computation of net book income of a foreign corporate taxpayer.

(i) Adjusted net book income of a foreign taxpayer.

(ii) Effectively connected net book income of a foreign taxpayer.

(A) In general.

(B) Certain exempt amounts.

(iii) Computation of net book income of a foreign taxpayer using current earnings and profits.

(7) Examples.

(c) Applicable financial statement.

(1) In general.

(i) Statement required to be filed with the Securities and Exchange Commission (SEC).

(ii) Certified audited financial statement.

(iii) Financial statement provided to a government regulator.

(iv) Other financial statements.

(v) Required use of current earnings and profits.

(2) Election to treat net book income as equal to current earnings and profits for the taxable year.

(i) In general.

(ii) Time of making election.

(iii) Eligibility to make and manner of making election.

(iv) Election by common parent of consolidated group.

(v) Election or revocation of election made on an amended return.

(3) Priority among statements.

(i) In general.

(ii) Special priority rules for use of certified audited financial statements and other financial statements.

(iii) Priority among financial statements provided to a government regulator.

(iv) Statements of equal priority.

(A) In general.

(B) Exceptions to the general rule in paragraph (c)(3)(iv)(A).

(4) Use of financial statement for a substantial non-tax purpose.

(5) Special rules.

(i) Applicable financial statement of related corporations.

(A) Applicable financial statement of a consolidated group.

(B) Special rule for statements of equal priority.

(C) Special rule for related corporations.

(D) Anti-abuse rule.

(ii) Applicable financial statement of a foreign corporation with a United States trade or business.

(A) In general.

(B) Special rules for applicable financial statement of a trade or business of a foreign taxpayer.

(C) Special rule for statements of equal priority.

(D) Anti-abuse rule.

(iii) Supplement or amendment to an applicable financial statement.

(A) Excluding a restatement of net book income.

(B) Restatement of net book income.

(6) Examples.

(d) Adjustments to net book income.

(1) In general.

(2) Definitions.

(i) Historic practice.

(ii) Accounting literature.

(3) Adjustments for certain taxes.

(i) In general.

(ii) Exception for certain foreign taxes.

(iii) Certain valuation adjustments.

(iv) Examples.

(4) Adjustments to prevent omission or duplication.

(i) In general.

(ii) Special rule for depreciating an asset below its cost.

(iii) Consolidated group using current earnings and profits.

(iv) Restatement of a prior year's applicable financial statement.

(A) In general.

(B) Reconciliation of owner's equity in applicable financial statements.

(C) Use of different priority applicable financial statements in consecutive taxable years.

(D) First successor year defined.

(E) Exceptions.

(v) Adjustment for items previously taxed as subpart F income.

(vi) Adjustment for pooling of interests.

(vii) Adjustment for certain deferred foreign taxes.

Reg. § 1.56-0

(viii) Examples.

(5) Adjustments resulting from disclosure.

(i) Adjustment for footnote disclosure or other supplementary information.

(A) In general.

(B) Disclosures not specifically authorized in the accounting literature.

(ii) Equity adjustments.

(A) In general.

(B) Definition of equity adjustment.

(iii) Amount disclosed in an accountant's opinion.

(iv) Accounting method changes that result in cumulative adjustments to the current year's applicable financial statement.

(A) In general.

(B) Exception.

(v) Examples.

(6) Adjustments applicable to related corporations.

(i) Consolidated returns.

(A) In general.

(B) Corporations included in the consolidated Federal income tax return but excluded from the applicable financial statement.

(C) Corporations included in the applicable financial statement but excluded from the consolidated tax return.

(ii) Adjustment under the principles of section 482.

(iii) Adjustment for dividends received from section 936 corporations.

(A) In general.

(B) Treatment as foreign taxes.

(C) Treatment of taxes imposed on section 936 corporations.

(iv) Adjustment to net book income on sale of certain investments.

(v) Examples.

(7) Adjustments for foreign taxpayers with a United States trade or business.

(i) In general.

(ii) Example.

(8) Adjustment for corporations subject to subchapter F.

(e) Special rules.

(1) Cooperatives.

(2) Alaska Native Corporations.

(3) Insurance companies.

(4) Estimating the net book income adjustment for purposes of estimated tax liability.

[Reg. § 1.56-0.]

☐ [*T.D.* 8138, 4-23-87. *Amended by T.D.* 8197, 4-27-88. *Redesignated and amended by T.D.* 8307, 8-16-90.]

[Reg. § 1.56-1]

§ 1.56-1. Adjustment for the book income of corporations—(a) *Computation of the book income adjustment*—(1) *In general.* For taxable years beginning in 1987, 1988, and 1989, the alternative minimum taxable income of any taxpayer is increased by the book income adjustment described in this paragraph (a)(1). The book income adjustment is 50 percent of the excess, if any, of—

(i) The adjusted net book income (as defined in paragraph (b) of this section) of the taxpayer, over

(ii) The pre-adjustment alternative minimum taxable income for the taxable year.

For purposes of this section, pre-adjustment alternative minimum taxable income is alternative minimum taxable income, determined without regard to the book income adjustment or the alternative tax net operating loss determined under section 56(a)(4). See paragraph (a)(4) of this section for examples relating to the computation of the book income adjustment.

(2) *Taxpayers subject to the book income adjustment.* The book income adjustment is applicable to any corporate taxpayer that is not an S corporation, regulated investment company (RIC), real estate investment trust (REIT), or real estate mortgage investment company (REMIC).

(3) *Consolidated returns.* In the case of a taxpayer that is a consolidated group, the book income adjustment equals 50 percent of the amount, if any, by which its consolidated adjusted net book income (as defined in paragraph (b)(3)(i) of this section) exceeds its consolidated pre-adjustment alternative minimum taxable income (as defined in paragraph (b)(3)(iii) of this section). See paragraph (a)(4), Example (4) of this section. For purposes of this section, with respect to any taxable year the term "consolidated group" has the same meaning as in § 1.1502-1T. See paragraph (d)(6) of this section for rules relating to adjustments attributable to related corporations.

(4) *Examples.* The provisions of this paragraph may be illustrated by the following examples.

Example (1). Corporation A has adjusted net book income of $200 and pre-adjustment alternative minimum taxable income of $100. A must increase its pre-adjustment alternative minimum taxable income by $50 (($200 − $100) × .50).

Example (2). Corporation B has adjusted net book income of $200 and pre-adjustment alternative minimum taxable income of $300. B does not have a book income adjustment for the taxable year because its adjusted net book income does not exceed its pre-adjustment alternative minimum taxable income.

Example (3). Corporation C has adjusted net book income of negative $200 and pre-adjustment alternative minimum taxable income of negative $300. C must increase its pre-adjustment alternative minimum taxable income by $50 ((− $200 − (− $300)) × .50). Thus, C's alternative minimum taxable income determined after the book income adjustment, but without regard to the alternative tax net operating loss, is negative $250 (− $300 + $50).

Example (4). Corporations D and E are a consolidated group for tax purposes. D and E do not have a consolidated financial statement. On their separate financial statements D and E have adjusted net book income of $100 and $50 respectively, and preadjustment alternative minimum taxable income of $50 and $80 respectively. Assuming there are no intercompany transactions, DE's consolidated adjusted net book income (as defined in paragraph (b)(3)(i) of this section) is $150 and its consolidated pre-adjustment alternative minimum taxable income (as defined in paragraph (b)(3)(iii) of this section) is $130. DE must increase its consolidated pre-adjustment alternative minimum taxable income by $10 (($150 − $130) × .50).

(b) *Adjusted net book income—*(1) *In general.* "Adjusted net book income" means the net book income (as defined in paragraph (b)(2) of this section) adjusted as provided in paragraph (d) of this section. Except as provided in paragraph (d) of this section, a taxpayer may not make any adjustments to net book income.

(2) *Net book income—*(i) *In general.* "Net book income" means the income or loss of a taxpayer reported in the taxpayer's applicable financial statement (as defined in paragraph (c) of this section). Net book income must take into account all items of income, expense, gain and loss for the taxable year, including extraordinary items, income or loss from discontinued operations, and cumulative adjustments resulting from accounting method changes. Net book income is not reduced by any distributions to shareholders. See paragraph (b)(5)(i) of this section for a similar rule for corporations using current earnings and profits to compute net book income.

(ii) *Measures of net book income.* Except as described in paragraph (b)(5) of this section, net book income is disclosed on the income state-

ment included in a taxpayer's applicable financial statement. Such income statement must reconcile with the balance sheet, if any, that is included in the applicable financial statement and must be used in computing changes in owner's equity reflected in the applicable financial statement. See paragraph (c) of this section for the definition of an applicable financial statement.

(iii) *Tax-free transactions and tax-free income.* Net book income includes income or loss that is reported on a taxpayer's applicable financial statement regardless of whether such income or loss is recognized, realized or otherwise taken into account for other Federal income tax purposes. See paragraph (b)(7), Examples (1), (2) and (3) of this section.

(iv) *Treatment of dividends and other amounts.* The adjusted net book income of a taxpayer shall include the earnings of other corporations not filing a consolidated Federal income tax return with the taxpayer only to the extent that amounts are required to be included in the taxpayer's gross income under chapter 1 of the Code with respect to the earnings of such other corporation (*e.g.,* dividends received from such corporation and amounts included under subpart A). See paragraph (b)(7), Examples (4) and (5) of this section.

(3) *Additional rules for consolidated groups—*(i) *Consolidated adjusted net book income.* "Consolidated adjusted net book income" means the consolidated net book income (as defined in paragraph (b)(3)(ii) of this section), after taking into account the adjustments under the rules of paragraph (d) of this section.

(ii) *Consolidated net book income.* Consolidated net book income is the income or loss of a consolidated group as reported on its applicable financial statement as defined in paragraph (c)(5) of this section.

(iii) *Consolidated pre-adjustment alternative minimum taxable income.* Consolidated pre-adjustment alternative minimum taxable income is the taxable income of the consolidated group for the taxable year, determined with the adjustments provided in sections 56 and 58 (except for the book income adjustment and the alternative tax net operating loss determined under section 56(a)(4)) and increased by the preference items described in section 57.

(iv) *Cross references.* See paragraph (c)(5) of this section for rules relating to the applicable financial statement of related corporations and paragraph (d)(6) of this section for rules relating to adjustments attributable to related corporations.

Reg. § 1.56-1(b)(1)

(4) *Computation of adjusted net book income when taxable year and financial accounting year differ*—(i) *In general.* If a taxpayer's applicable financial statement is prepared on the basis of a financial accounting year that differs from the year that the taxpayer uses for filing its Federal income tax return, adjusted net book income must be computed either—

(A) By including a pro rata portion of the adjusted net book income for each financial accounting year that includes any part of the taxpayer's taxable year (see paragraph (b)(7), Example (6) of this section), or

(B) In accordance with the election described in paragraph (b)(4)(iii) of this section.

(ii) *Estimating adjusted net book income.* If a taxpayer is using the pro rata approach described in paragraph (b)(4)(i)(A) of this section and an applicable financial statement for part of the taxpayer's taxable year is not available when the taxpayer files its Federal income tax return, the taxpayer must make a reasonable estimate of adjusted net book income for the pro rata portion of the taxable year. If the actual pro rata portion of adjusted net book income that results from the taxpayer's applicable financial statement for the financial accounting year exceeds the estimate of adjusted net book income used on the original tax return and results in additional tax liability, the taxpayer must file an amended Federal income tax return reflecting such additional liability. The amended return must be filed within 90 days of the date the previously unavailable applicable financial statement is available.

(iii) *Election to compute adjusted net book income based on the financial statement for the year ending within the taxable year*—(A) *In general.* If a taxpayer's accounting year ends five or more months after the end of its taxable year, the taxpayer may elect to compute adjusted net book income based on the net book income reported on the applicable financial statement prepared for the financial accounting year ending within the taxpayer's taxable year. See paragraph (b)(7), Examples (7) and (8) of this section. For purposes of this paragraph (b)(4)(iii)(A), if a taxpayer uses a 52-53 week year for financial accounting or Federal income tax purposes, the last day of such year shall be deemed to occur on the last day of the calendar month ending closest to the end of such year.

(B) *Time of making election.* An election under this paragraph (b)(4)(iii) is made by attaching the statement described in paragraph (b)(4)(iii)(C) of this section to the taxpayer's Federal income tax return for the first taxable year in which the taxpayer is eligible to make the elec-

tion. An election under this paragraph (b)(4)(iii) that is made prior to the first taxable year in which the taxpayer is eligible to make the election (as determined under paragraph (b)(4)(iii)(C) of this section) is valid unless revoked pursuant to paragraph (b)(4)(iii)(D) of this section.

(C) *Eligibility to make and manner of making election.* A taxpayer is eligible to make the election specified in paragraph (b)(4)(iii)(A) of this section in the first taxable year beginning after 1986 in which—

(1) The taxpayer has an accounting year ending five or more months after the end of its taxable year,

(2) The use of the pro rata approach described in paragraph (b)(4)(i)(A) of this section produces an excess of adjusted net book income over pre-adjustment alternative minimum taxable income, as defined in paragraph (a)(1) of this section, and

(3) The taxpayer has an excess of tentative minimum tax over regular tax for the taxable year, as defined in section 55(a), or is liable for the environmental tax imposed by section 59A.

Thus, a taxpayer is not required to evaluate the merits of an election to compute its adjusted net book income based on the applicable financial statement prepared for the financial accounting year ending within the taxpayer's taxable year unless the taxpayer, when using the pro rata approach described in paragraph (b)(4)(i)(A) of this section, either has an excess of tentative minimum tax over its regular tax or is liable for the environmental tax imposed by section 59A. The election statement must set forth the electing taxpayer's name, address, taxpayer identification number, taxable year and financial accounting year. An election under this paragraph (b)(4)(iii) will apply for the taxable year when initially made and for all subsequent years until revoked with the consent of the District Director.

(D) *Election or revocation of election made on an amended return.* An election under paragraph (b)(4)(iii) of this section may be made by attaching the statement described in paragraph (b)(4)(iii)(C) to an amended return for the first taxable year in which the taxpayer is eligible to make the election. An election under paragraph (b)(4)(iii) of this section that was made prior to the first taxable year in which the taxpayer was eligible to make the election, as determined under paragraph (b)(4)(iii)(C) of this section, may be revoked by filing an amended return for the taxable year in which the election was initially made. However, an election made or revoked on an amended return under paragraph (b)(4)(iii) of

Reg. § 1.56-1(b)(4)

this section will be allowed only if the amended return is filed no later than December 14, 1990.

(iv) *Quarterly statement filed with the Securities and Exchange Commission (SEC).* A taxpayer with different financial accounting and taxable years that is required to file both annual and quarterly financial statements with the SEC may not aggregate quarterly statements filed with the SEC in order to obtain a statement covering the taxpayer's taxable year. See paragraph (b)(7), Example (9) of this section. See paragraph (c)(3)(iv)(B)(*1*) of this section for priority rules relating to statements required to be filed with the SEC.

(5) *Computation of net book income using current earnings and profits*—(i) *In general.* If a taxpayer does not have an applicable financial statement, or only has a statement described in paragraph (c)(1)(iv) of this section and makes the election described in paragraph (c)(2) of this section, net book income for purposes of this section is equal to the taxpayer's current earnings and profits for its taxable year. Generally, a taxpayer's current earnings and profits is computed under the rules of section 312 and the regulations thereunder. Current earnings and profits therefore is reduced by Federal income tax expense and any foreign tax expense for foreign taxes eligible for the foreign tax credit under section 27 of the Code. Current earnings and profits is then adjusted as described in paragraph (d) of this section to arrive at adjusted net book income. No adjustment is made under paragraph (d) of this section, however, for any adjustment that is already reflected in current earnings and profits. See paragraph (d)(3) of this section for adjustments to net book income with respect to certain taxes. For purposes of this section, current earnings and profits is not reduced by any distribution to shareholders. See paragraph (d)(3)(iv), Example (5) of this section.

(ii) *Current earnings and profits of a consolidated group.*

For purposes of this paragraph (b)(5), the current earnings and profits of a consolidated group is the aggregate of the current earnings and profits of each member of the group, as determined pursuant to paragraph (d)(4)(iii) of this section.

(6) *Additional rules for computation of net book income of a foreign corporate taxpayer*—(i) *Adjusted net book income of a foreign taxpayer.* Adjusted net book income of a foreign corporate taxpayer ("foreign taxpayer") means the effectively connected net book income (as defined in paragraph (b)(6)(ii) of this section) of the foreign taxpayer, after taking into account the adjust-

ments under the rules of paragraph (d) of this section.

(ii) *Effectively connected net book income of a foreign taxpayer*—(A) *In general.* Effectively connected net book income of a foreign taxpayer is the income or loss reported in its applicable financial statement (as defined in paragraph (c)(5)(ii) of this section), but only to the extent that such amount is attributable to items of income or loss that would be treated as effectively connected with the conduct of a trade or business in the United States by the foreign taxpayer as determined under either the principles of section 864(c) and the regulations thereunder, or any other applicable provision of the Internal Revenue Code of 1986. Thus, if for tax purposes an item of income or loss is treated as effectively connected with the conduct of a trade or business in the United States, then the income or loss reported on the foreign taxpayer's applicable financial statement attributable to such item is effectively connected net book income. See paragraph (b)(7), Examples (11), (12) and (13) of this section.

(B) *Certain exempt amounts.* Effectively connected net book income does not include any amount attributable to an item that is exempt from United States taxation under sections 883, 892, 894 or 895 of the Internal Revenue Code of 1986. See paragraph (b)(7), Examples (14) and (15) of this section.

(iii) *Computation of net book income of a foreign taxpayer using current earnings and profits.* If a foreign taxpayer does not have an applicable financial statement or only has a statement described in paragraph (c)(1)(iv) of this section and makes the election described in paragraph (c)(2) of this section, net book income for purposes of this section is equal to the foreign taxpayer's current earnings and profits that are attributable to income or loss that is effectively connected (or treated as effectively connected) with the conduct of a trade or business in the United States. Effectively connected current earnings and profits are computed under the rules of section 884(d) and the regulations thereunder, relating to effectively connected earnings and profits for purposes of computing the branch profits tax, but without regard to the exceptions set forth under section 884(d)(2)(B) through (E). For purposes of this section, effectively connected current earnings and profits are not reduced by any remittances or distributions. Effectively connected current earnings and profits takes into account Federal income tax expense and any foreign tax expense; however, see paragraph (d)(3) of this section for adjustments to net book income with respect to certain taxes.

Reg. § 1.56-1(b)(5)

(7) Examples. The provisions of this paragraph may be illustrated by the following examples.

Example (1). Corporation A owns 100 percent of corporation B and the AB affiliated group files a consolidated Federal income tax return. AB uses a calendar year for both financial accounting and tax purposes. During 1987, A transfers all of its stock in B for stock of an acquiring corporation in a transaction described in section 368(a)(1)(B). Although AB recognizes no taxable gain on the transfer pursuant to section 354, gain from the transfer is reported on AB's 1987 applicable financial statement. Pursuant to paragraph (b)(2)(iii) of this section, AB's net book income includes the book gain attributable to the transfer.

Example (2). Corporation C uses a calendar year for both financial accounting and tax purposes. C adopted a plan of liquidation prior to August 1, 1986. On June 1, 1987, C makes a bulk sale of all of its assets subject to liabilities and completely liquidates. Pursuant to section 633(c) of the Tax Reform Act of 1986 (the Act), section 337, as in effect prior to its amendment by the Act, applies. Thus, C will generally not recognize taxable gain upon the bulk sale. However, C's applicable financial statement for the period January 1, 1987, through June 1, 1987, reports net book income of $500, $400 of which is attributable to the bulk sale of assets on June 1, 1987. Pursuant to paragraph (b)(2)(iii) of this section, C's net book income includes the amount attributable to the bulk sale. Thus, assuming C has no other adjustments to net book income, its adjusted net book income for the period January 1, 1987 through June 1, 1987, is $500.

Example (3). Corporation Z has a large inventory of marketable securities. On its applicable financial statement, Z marks these securities to market, i.e., as they appreciate in value, Z restates their value on its balance sheet to their fair market value, and increases the income on its income statement by that amount. Pursuant to paragraph (b)(2)(iii) of this section, the adjusted net book income of Z includes the income from the valuation adjustment.

Example (4). Corporation D owns 100 percent of E, a controlled foreign corporation as defined in section 957. Both D and E use a calendar year for financial accounting and tax purposes. D's applicable financial statement includes E. Pursuant to section 951, D includes $100 of E's subpart F income in its gross income for 1987. Although D's applicable financial statement is adjusted to eliminate E's income, pursuant to paragraph (b)(2)(iv) of this section, D's adjusted net book income for 1987 includes the $100 of gross income included under section 951.

Example (5). Corporation F owns 20 percent of G, a foreign corporation. Both F and G use a calendar year for financial accounting and tax purposes. During 1987, G pays F a $100 dividend. F's applicable financial statement accounts for F's investment in G by the equity method. F is eligible for a deemed paid foreign tax credit of $30 with respect to the dividend from G and must include the $130 in gross income pursuant to section 78 of the Code. Although F's applicable financial statement is adjusted to eliminate F's income from G under the equity method, pursuant to paragraph (b)(2)(iv) of this section, F's adjusted net book income for 1987 includes the $130 of gross income recognized with respect to the dividend from G.

Example (6). Corporation H files its Federal income tax return on a calendar year basis. However, its applicable financial statement is based on a fiscal year ending June 30. H does not make the election described in paragraph (b)(4)(iii) of this section. Pursuant to paragraph (b)(4)(i) of this section, H's adjusted net book income for calendar year 1987 is computed by adding 50 percent of adjusted net book income from the applicable financial statement for the year ending June 30, 1987 and 50 percent of adjusted net book income from the applicable financial statement for the year ending June 30, 1988.

Example (7). Corporation J files its Federal income tax returns for 1987, 1988, and 1989 on a calendar year basis. However, its applicable financial statement is based on a year ending May 31. Pursuant to paragraph (b)(4)(iii) of this section, J elects in 1987 to compute its adjusted net book income by using the applicable financial statement for the fiscal year ending May 31, 1987. Unless the District Director consents to revocation of the election, for calendar year 1988 or 1989, J's adjusted net book income for 1988 and 1989 is determined from its applicable financial statements for the years ending May 31, 1988 and May 31, 1989, respectively.

Example (8). The facts are the same as in Example (7), except that J's applicable financial statement is based on a year ending April 30. Since April 30, is less than 5 months after December 31, the end of J's taxable year, J is not permitted to make the election described in paragraph (b)(4)(iii) of this section.

Example (9). The facts are the same as in Example (8), except H files quarterly and annual financial statements with the Securities and Exchange Commission (SEC). The fourth quarter statement is included as a footnote to the annual

Reg. § 1.56-1(b)(7)

statement that it files with the SEC. Pursuant to paragraph (b)(4)(iv) of this section, H may not determine its net book income by aggregating its four quarterly statements for 1987. Thus, H's net book income is computed as described in Example (8).

Example (10). Corporation I is a United States corporation with a 100 percent owned subsidiary, J, a foreign sales corporation (FSC). I uses a calendar year for both financial accounting and tax purposes. Income from J is consolidated in I's applicable financial statement. I and J do not file a consolidated tax return. In 1987, J pays a dividend to I of $100 out of J's earnings and profits. For purposes of this example, it is assumed that the distribution is made out of the profits attributable solely to foreign trade income determined through use of the administrative pricing rules of section 925(a)(1) and (2). Accordingly, the distribution is eligible for the 100 percent dividends received deduction under section 245(c). Although I's applicable financial statement is adjusted to eliminate income or loss attributable to J, the entire amount of the dividend distribution must be included in I's adjusted net book income pursuant to paragraph (b)(2)(iv) of this section.

Example (11). Corporation K is a foreign corporation incorporated under the laws of country X. K uses a calendar year for both financial accounting and tax purposes. In 1987, K actively conducts a real estate business, L, in the United States. The financial statement that is used as K's applicable financial statement (as determined under paragraph (c)(5)(ii) of this section) discloses total net income of $150. Of this amount, $100 is attributable to L's real estate business and $50 is attributable to dividends paid to L from its investment in certain securities. The securities investment is not connected with L's real estate business. Under the rules of section 864, only $100 is effectively connected to the conduct of a trade or business in the United States. Thus, K's effectively connected net book income for 1987 equals $100.

Example (12). Assume the same facts as in Example (11) except that K's applicable financial statement also discloses $75 attributable to investment real property located in the United States, so that the net income amount reported on the financial statement equals $225. The $75 of income is not effectively connected with the conduct of a trade or business in the United States. K, for regular tax purposes, makes an election under section 882(d) to treat this income as effectively connected with the conduct of a trade or business in the United States. As a result, K's

effectively connected net book income for 1987 equals $175 ($100 + $75).

Example (13). Corporation M is a foreign corporation that actively conducts a manufacturing business, N, in the United States. M is a calendar year taxpayer for both financial accounting and tax purposes. In 1987, the financial statement that is used as M's applicable financial statement (as determined under paragraph (c)(5)(ii) of this section) reflects an anticipated loss from the sale of a division of N. For Federal income tax purposes the loss is not recognized in 1987, but rather is recognized in 1988 when M sells the division. In determining M's effectively connected net book income for 1987, the anticipated loss reported on M's 1987 applicable financial statement is taken into account because the reported loss is effectively connected to the conduct of a trade or business in the United States under the principles of section 864.

Example (14). Corporation O is a foreign corporation that is engaged in the international shipping business. O is incorporated under the laws of X. O is a calendar year taxpayer for both financial accounting and tax purposes. In 1987, O actively conducts a shipping business, P, within the United States. The statement that is used in 1987 as O's applicable financial statement (as determined under paragraph (c)(5)(ii) of this section) discloses income of $100 that is attributable to P's operation of ships in international traffic. Under section 864, $50 is effectively connected with the conduct of a trade or business in the United States. However, the United States income tax treaty with X exempts from United States income tax any income derived by a resident of X from the operation of ships in international traffic. Thus, pursuant to paragraph (b)(6)(ii) (B) of this section, no amount of P's income is includible in O's effectively connected net book income.

Example (15). Assume the same facts as in Example (14) except that there is no United States income tax treaty with X. However, X by statute exempts United States citizens and United States corporations from tax imposed by X on gross income derived from the operation of a ship or ships in international traffic. Under section 883(a), P's income of $50 that is effectively connected with the conduct of a trade or business in the United States is exempt from United States taxation. Thus, pursuant to paragraph (b)(6)(ii)(B) of this section, no amount of P's income is includible in O's effectively connected net book income.

(c) *Applicable financial statement*—(1) *In general.* A taxpayer's applicable financial statement is the statement described in this paragraph (c)(1)

Reg. § 1.56-1(c)(1)

that has the highest priority, as determined under paragraph (c)(3) of this section. Generally, an applicable financial statement includes an income statement, a balance sheet (listing assets, liabilities, and owner's equity including changes thereto), and other appropriate information. An income statement alone may constitute an applicable financial statement for purposes of this section if the other materials described in this paragraph are not prepared or used by the taxpayer. However, an income statement that does not reconcile with financial materials otherwise issued will not qualify as an applicable financial statement. For purposes of determining the book income adjustment, the following may be considered applicable financial statements (subject to the rules relating to priority among statements under paragraph (c)(3) of this section)—

(i) *Statement required to be filed with the Securities and Exchange Commission (SEC).* A financial statement that is required to be filed with the Securities and Exchange Commission.

(ii) *Certified audited financial statement.* A certified audited financial statement that is used for credit purposes, for reporting to shareholders or for any other substantial non-tax purpose. Such a statement must be accompanied by the report of an independent (as defined in the American Institute of Certified Public Accountants Professional Standards, Code of Professional Conduct, Rule 101 and its interpretations and rulings) Certified Public Accountant or, in the case of a foreign corporation, a similarly qualified and independent professional who is licensed in any foreign country. A financial statement is "certified audited" for purposes of this section if it is—

(A) Certified to be fairly presented (an unqualified or "clean" opinion),

(B) Subject to a qualified opinion that such financial statement is fairly presented subject to a concern about a contingency (a qualified "subject to" opinion),

(C) Subject to a qualified opinion that such financial statement is fairly presented, except for a method of accounting with which the accountant disagrees (a qualified "except for" opinion), or

(D) Subject to an adverse opinion, but only if the accountant discloses the amount of the disagreement with the statement.

Any other statement or report, such as a review statement or a compilation report that is not subject to a full audit is not a certified audited statement. See paragraph (c)(3)(iv)(B)(*2*) of this section for a special rule for a statement accompanied by a review report when there are statements

of equal priority. See also paragraph (d)(5)(iii) of this section for rules relating to adjustments for information disclosed in an accountant's opinion to a certified audited statement.

(iii) *Financial statement provided to a government regulator.* A financial statement that is required to be provided to the Federal government or any agency thereof (other than the Securities and Exchange Commission), a state government or any agency thereof, or a political subdivision of a state or any agency thereof. An income tax return, franchise tax return or other tax return prepared for the purpose of determining any tax liability that is filed with a Federal, state or local government or agency cannot be an applicable financial statement.

(iv) *Other financial statements.* A financial statement that is used for credit purposes, for reporting to shareholders, or for any other substantial non-tax purpose, even though such financial statement is not described in paragraphs (c)(1)(i) through (c)(1)(iii) of this section.

(v) *Required use of current earnings and profits.* If a taxpayer does not have a financial statement described in paragraphs (c)(1)(i) through (c)(1)(iv) of this section, the taxpayer does not have an applicable financial statement. In that case, net book income for the taxable year will be treated as being equal to the taxpayer's current earnings and profits for the taxable year. See paragraph (b)(5) of this section for rules relating to the computation of current earnings and profits for the taxable year. See paragraph (c)(4) of this section for rules relating to use of a financial statement for a substantial non-tax purpose.

(2) *Election to treat net book income as equal to current earnings and profits for the taxable year*—(i) *In general.* If a taxpayer's only financial statement is a statement described in paragraph (c)(1)(iv) of this section, the taxpayer may elect to treat net book income as equal to the taxpayer's current earnings and profits for all taxable years in which the taxpayer is eligible to make the election.

(ii) *Time of making election.* An election under this paragraph (c)(2) is made by attaching the statement described in paragraph (c)(2)(iii) of this section to the taxpayer's Federal income tax return for the first taxable year the taxpayer is eligible to make the election. An election under this paragraph (c)(2), which is made prior to the first taxable year in which the taxpayer is eligible to make the election, as determined under paragraph (c)(2)(iii) of this section, is valid unless revoked pursuant to paragraph (c)(2)(iv) of this section.

Reg. § 1.56-1(c)(2)

(iii) *Eligibility to make and manner of making election.* A taxpayer is eligible to make the election in the first taxable year in which—

(A) The taxpayer has an applicable financial statement described in paragraph (c)(1)(iv) of this section;

(B) The use of this applicable financial statement produces an excess of adjusted net book income over pre-adjustment alternative minimum taxable income, as defined in paragraph (a)(1) of this section, and

(C) The taxpayer has, as determined under section 55(a), an excess of tentative minimum tax over regular tax for the taxable year, or is liable for the environmental tax imposed by section 59A.

Thus, a taxpayer is not required to evaluate the merits of an election to use its current earnings and profits as its net book income unless the taxpayer, when using an applicable financial statement described in paragraph (c)(1)(iv) of this section, has an excess of tentative minimum tax over its regular tax or is liable for the environmental tax imposed by section 59A. The election statement must set forth the electing taxpayer's name, address and taxpayer identification number, state that the election is being made under the provisions of section 56(f)(3)(B), and state that the only financial statement of the taxpayer is a financial statement described in paragraph (c)(1)(iv) of this section. An election under this paragraph (c)(2) is effective for every taxable year in which the taxpayer does not have a financial statement described in paragraphs (c)(1)(i) through (c)(1)(iii) of this section and may be revoked only with the consent of the District Director. See paragraph (c)(6), Example (1) of this section.

(iv) *Election or revocation of election made on an amended return.* An election under paragraph (c)(2) of this section may be made by attaching the statement described in paragraph (c)(2)(iii) to an amended return for the first taxable year in which the taxpayer is eligible to make the election. An election under paragraph (c)(2) of this section that was made prior to the first taxable year in which the taxpayer was eligible to make the election, as determined under paragraph (c)(2)(iii) of this section, may be revoked by filing an amended return for the taxable year in which the election was initially made. However, an election made or revoked on an amended return will be allowed only if the amended return is filed no later than December 14, 1990.

(v) *Election by common parent of consolidated group.* The election by the common parent of a consolidated group to treat net book income

as equal to current earnings and profits shall bind all members of the group. This rule shall not apply in the case of any taxpayer that first, has made the election on a return filed before August 16, 1990, second, applied the election only to those members of the group that are themselves eligible to make the election, and third, properly consolidated the adjusted net book income of the group. In order to change its election to apply to all members of the group, a taxpayer must attach a statement to an amended return for the first taxable year the taxpayer is eligible to make the election. However, an election made on an amended return under this paragraph (c)(2)(iv) will be allowed only if the amended return is filed no later than December 14, 1990. See paragraph (b)(5)(ii) of this section regarding the current earnings and profits of a consolidated group. See paragraph (d)(4)(iii) of this section for adjustments that apply when a consolidated group uses current earnings and profits to compute its net book income.

(3) *Priority among statements—(i) In general.* If a taxpayer has more than one financial statement described in paragraph (c)(1)(i) through (c)(1)(iv) of this section, the taxpayer's applicable financial statement is the statement with the highest priority. Priority is determined in the following order—

(A) A financial statement described in paragraph (c)(1)(i) of this section.

(B) A certified audited statement described in paragraph (c)(1)(ii) of this section.

(C) A financial statement required to be provided to a Federal or other government regulator described in paragraph (c)(1)(iii) of this section.

(D) Any other financial statement described in paragraph (c)(1)(iv) of this section.

For example, corporation A, which uses a calendar year for both financial accounting and tax purposes, prepares a financial statement for calendar year 1987 that is provided to a state regulator and an unaudited financial statement that is provided to A's creditors. The statement provided to the state regulator is A's financial statement with the highest priority and thus is A's applicable financial statement.

(ii) *Special priority rules for use of certified audited financial statements and other financial statements.* In the case of financial statements described in paragraphs (c)(1)(ii) and (c)(1)(iv) of this section, within each of these categories the taxpayer's applicable financial statement is determined according to the following priority—

Reg. § 1.56-1(c)(3)

(A) A statement used for credit purposes,

(B) A statement used for disclosure to shareholders, and

(C) Any other statement used for other substantial non-tax purposes.

For example, corporation B uses a calendar year for both financial accounting and tax purposes. B prepares a financial statement for calendar year 1987 that it uses for credit purposes and prepares another financial statement for calendar year 1987 that it uses for disclosure to shareholders. Both financial statements are unaudited. The statement used for credit purposes is B's financial statement with the highest priority and thus is B's applicable financial statement.

(iii) *Priority among financial statements provided to a government regulator.* In the case of two or more financial statements described in paragraph (c)(1)(iii) of this section (relating to financial statements required to be provided to a Federal or other governmental regulator) that are of equal priority, the taxpayer's applicable financial statement is determined according to the following priority—

(A) A statement required to be provided to the Federal government or any of its agencies,

(B) A statement required to be provided to a State government or any of its agencies, and

(C) A statement required to be provided to any subdivision of a state or any agency of a subdivision.

(iv) *Statements of equal priority*—(A) *In general.* Except as provided in paragraph (c)(3)(iv)(B) and paragraph (c)(5)(i)(B) of this section, if a taxpayer has two or more financial statements of equal priority (determined under paragraphs (c)(3)(i), (c)(3)(ii) and (c)(3)(iii) of this section), the taxpayer's applicable financial statement is the statement that results in the greatest amount of adjusted net book income.

(B) *Exceptions to the general rule in paragraph (c)(3)(iv)(A)*—(1) In the case of two or more financial statements described in paragraph (c)(1)(i) of this section (relating to financial statements required to be filed with the SEC) that are of equal priority, a certified audited financial statement has a higher priority than an unaudited financial statement.

(2) In the case of two or more financial statements described in paragraph (c)(1)(iv) of this section (relating to other financial statements) that are of equal priority, a financial statement accompanied by an auditor's "review report" has a higher priority than another financial statement of otherwise equal priority. For

purposes of this section, an auditor's review report is defined in the American Institute of Certified Public Accountant Professional Standards, AR section 100.32. See paragraph (c)(6), Examples (2) and (3) of this section.

(4) *Use of financial statement for a substantial non-tax purpose.* In order to be an applicable financial statement for purposes of computing the book income adjustment, a financial statement described in paragraph (c)(1)(ii) or (c)(1)(iv) must be used by the taxpayer for credit purposes, for disclosure to shareholders, or for any other substantial non-tax purpose. A financial statement is used by a taxpayer if the taxpayer reasonably anticipates that users of the statement will rely on it for non-tax purposes. Thus, a financial statement used for the purpose of computing the book income adjustment is not an applicable financial statement even if it is provided to shareholders or creditors, unless the taxpayer reasonably anticipates that users of the statement will rely on it for nontax purposes. See paragraph (c)(6), Examples (4), (5), (19) and (20) of this section.

(5) *Special rules*—(i) *Applicable financial statement of related corporations*—(A) *Applicable financial statement of a consolidated group.* The applicable financial statement of a consolidated group (as defined in paragraph (a)(3) of this section) is the financial statement of the common parent (within the meaning of section 1504(a)(1)) of the consolidated group that has the highest priority under the rules of paragraphs (c)(3)(i), (c)(3)(ii) and (c)(5)(i)(B) of this section. See paragraph (d)(6)(i) of this section for rules relating to adjustments to net book income of a consolidated group. See paragraph (c)(6), Example (7) of this section. See paragraph (c)(2)(iv) of this section for rules relating to the election by the common parent of a consolidated group to use current earnings and profits to compute net book income.

(B) *Special rule for statements of equal priority.* If a consolidated group has two or more financial statements of equal priority (determined under paragraphs (c)(3)(i) and (c)(3)(ii) of this section and this paragraph (c)(5)), the consolidated group's applicable financial statement is determined under either paragraph (c)(5)(i)(B)(1) or (2), whichever is applicable.

(1) *Two or more financial statements reporting on the same corporations.* If two or more financial statements of equal priority report on the same corporations, the consolidated group's applicable financial statement is determined under the rules of paragraph (c)(3)(iv) of this section. Thus, the financial statement that results in the greatest consolidated adjusted net book

Reg. § 1.56-1(c)(5)

income is the consolidated group's applicable financial statement.

(*2*) *Two or more financial statements reporting on different corporations*. If two or more financial statements of equal priority report on different corporations, the consolidated group's applicable financial statement is—

(*i*) The statement that reflects the greatest amount of gross receipts attributable to members of the consolidated group, or

(*ii*) The statement that reflects the greatest amount of gross receipts (including gross receipts attributable to corporations that are not members of the consolidated group), but only if the consolidated group has financial statements of equal priority after applying the rules of paragraph (c)(5)(i)(B)(*2*)(*i*).

If after applying the rules of paragraphs (c)(5)(i)(B)(*2*)(*i*) and (*ii*) of this section, the consolidated group still has financial statements of equal priority, the rules of paragraph (c)(3)(iv) of this section apply. See paragraph (c)(6), Examples (7) and (8) of this section.

(C) *Special rule for related corporations.* If any portion of the net book income of a corporation (the "first corporation") is included on the applicable financial statement of a second corporation, but the first and second corporations are not members of the same consolidated group, the applicable financial statement of the second corporation is disregarded when determining the applicable financial statement of the first corporation. Thus, the applicable financial statement of the first corporation is the financial statement of highest priority determined under the rules of paragraph (c)(3) of this section without regard to the financial statement of the second corporation. Pursuant to paragraph (c)(1)(iv) of this section, if a separate financial statement is not prepared by the first corporation, the rules of paragraph (b)(5) (relating to current earnings and profits) apply. See paragraph (c)(6), Examples (9) and (10) of this section.

(D) *Anti-abuse rule.* The special rules of this paragraph (c)(5)(i) will not apply if the taxpayer rearranges its corporate structure or modifies its financial reporting and the principal purpose of such action is to use the special rules of this paragraph (c)(5)(i) to reduce the amount of the book income adjustment. In such cases, the District Director may, based upon all the facts and circumstances, determine the taxpayer's applicable financial statement. See paragraph (c)(6), Examples (13) and (14) of this section.

(ii) *Applicable financial statement of a foreign corporation with a United States trade or business*—(A) *In general.* The applicable financial

statement of a foreign taxpayer conducting one or more trades or businesses in the United States is the financial statement prepared by any such trade or business (or attributable to more than one such trades or businesses) that has the highest priority as determined under paragraph (c)(3) of this section. See paragraph (c)(6), Example (15) of this section.

(B) *Special rules for applicable financial statement of a trade or business of a foreign taxpayer*—(*1*) *Financial statement prepared under foreign generally accepted accounting principles.* Subject to the rules of this section, a financial statement prepared by a United States trade or business using generally accepted accounting principles of a foreign country may be an applicable financial statement under this paragraph (c). See paragraph (c)(6), Example (16) of this section.

(*2*) *Financial statement denominated in United States dollars.* Except as provided in paragraph (c)(5)(ii)(D) of this section, the financial statement of a United States trade or business must be denominated in United States dollars in order to be considered the applicable financial statement of the foreign taxpayer under this paragraph (c). See paragraph (c)(6), Example (17) of this section.

(C) *Special rule for statements of equal priority.* If a foreign taxpayer has two or more financial statements of equal priority (determined under paragraphs (c)(3)(i) and (c)(3)(ii) of this section and this paragraph (c)(5)(ii)), the foreign taxpayer's applicable financial statement is determined under either paragraph (c)(5)(ii)(C)(*1*) or (*2*) of this section, whichever is applicable.

(*1*) *Two or more financial statements reporting on the same trades or businesses.* If two or more financial statements of equal priority report on the same United States trades or businesses, the applicable financial statement of the foreign taxpayer is determined under the rule of paragraph (c)(3)(iv) of this section. In applying this rule, adjusted net book income (as defined under paragraph (b)(6) of this section) shall be used. Thus, the financial statement that results in the greatest amount of adjusted net book income is the foreign taxpayer's applicable financial statement.

(*2*) *Two or more financial statements reporting on different trades or businesses.* If two or more financial statements of equal priority report on different United States trades or businesses, the foreign taxpayer's applicable financial statement is—

(*i*) The financial statement that reflects the greatest amount of gross receipts at-

Reg. § 1.56-1(c)(5)

tributable to United States trades or businesses, or

(ii) If after applying the rules of paragraph (c)(5)(ii)(C)(2)(i) of this section, the foreign taxpayer still has financial statements of equal priority, the financial statement determined under the rules of paragraph (c)(3)(iv) of this section (using effectively connected adjusted net book income).

See paragraph (c)(6), Example (18) of this section.

(D) *Anti-abuse rule.* The special rules of this paragraph (c)(5)(ii) will not apply if a trade or business conducted in the United States by a foreign taxpayer modifies its financial reporting and the principal purpose of such action is to reduce the amount of the book income adjustment. In such cases, the District Director may, based upon all the facts and circumstances, determine the taxpayer's applicable financial statement. See paragraph (c)(6), Example (21), of this section.

(iii) *Supplement or amendment to an applicable financial statement—(A) Excluding a restatement of net book income.* An applicable financial statement includes any supplement or amendment thereto (excluding a restatement of net book income) for the taxable year that is prepared and used for a substantial non-tax purpose (within the meaning of paragraph (c)(4) of this section) prior to the date the taxpayer's Federal income tax return for the taxable year would be due if the time for filing were extended under section 6081. For example, a calendar year taxpayer's applicable financial statement includes any supplement or amendment prepared and used prior to September 15 of the year immediately following its taxable year. If a taxpayer files its Federal income tax return before the issuance of a supplement or amendment to the applicable financial statement and before the extended due date for filing under section 6081, the taxpayer must file an amended Federal income tax return reporting any additional tax that results from treating the supplement or amendment as part of the applicable financial statement. A supplement or amendment (excluding restatements of net book income) to an applicable financial statement after the date specified in section 6081 is disregarded for purposes of the book income adjustment.

(B) *Restatement of net book income.* If a taxpayer restates net book income in what otherwise would have been its applicable financial statement (its "original financial statement"), referred to in this section as a "restatement of net book income," prior to the date that the tax-

payer's Federal income tax return for such taxable year would be due if the time for filing were extended under section 6081, then—

(1) If the financial statement that includes the restated net book income is of a higher priority than the original financial statement, the restated financial statement is the taxpayer's applicable financial statement.

(2) If the financial statement that includes the restated net book income is of equal priority to the original financial statement and—

(i) The restatement is attributable to an error (as described in Accounting Principles Board Opinion No. 20, paragraph 13), the restated financial statement is the taxpayer's applicable financial statement, or

(ii) The restatement is not attributable to an error, the original and restated financial statements will be considered of equal priority, and paragraph (c)(3)(iv) will apply. Thus, the taxpayer's applicable financial statement is the financial statement that results in the greatest amount of adjusted net book income.

See paragraph (d)(4)(iv) of this section for rules that apply to restatements occurring after the due date (including the extension under section 6081) of the return for the taxable year to which the applicable financial statement relates. See paragraph (c)(6), Examples (11) and (12) of this section.

(6) *Examples.* The provisions of this paragraph may be illustrated by the following examples.

Example (1). In 1987, Corporation A only has a financial statement described in paragraph (c)(1)(iv) of this section and elects to treat net book income as equal to its current earnings and profits. In 1988, A has a certified audited financial statement (as described in paragraph (c)(1)(ii) of this section). In 1989, A only has a statement described in paragraph (c)(1)(iv) of this section. In 1988, A's certified audited financial statement is its applicable financial statement. However, in 1989, A is bound by the election it made in 1987 (unless revoked with the consent of the District Director) and must treat net book income as equal to its current earnings and profits.

Example (2). Corporation B prepares two unaudited financial statements. Both statements are distributed to creditors and are used for substantial non-tax purposes. The first financial statement is accompanied by an auditor's review report while the second statement has no auditor's review report. B has no other financial statement. Pursuant to paragraph (c)(3)(iv)(B)(2) of this

Reg. § 1.56-1(c)(6)

section, the financial statement accompanied by the auditor's review report is B's applicable financial statement.

Example (3). Assume the same facts as in Example (2), except the financial statement accompanied by an auditor's review report is distributed to shareholders while the other statement is distributed to creditors, and both statements are used for substantial non-tax purposes. Pursuant to paragraph (c)(3)(ii) of this section, B's applicable financial statement is the statement distributed to its creditors. Paragraph (c)(3)(iv)(B)(2) of this section does not apply because the two statements are not of equal priority after applying paragraphs (c)(3)(i) and (ii) of this section.

Example (4). Corporation C is a closely held corporation with two shareholders. Both shareholders participate in the business on a day-to-day basis and are aware of the financial status of the business. C prepares a financial statement that is used by C's two shareholders to calculate bonuses. The financial statement prepared by C is used for a substantial non-tax purpose.

Example (5). Corporation D prepares a financial statement that it only sends to banks with which D is neither currently doing business nor negotiating. D does not reasonably anticipate that the financial statement will be relied on by the banks for any non-tax purpose, and therefore, for purposes of computing net book income, the financial statement is not used for a substantial non-tax purpose. The result would be the same if D sent the statement to a bank whose only relationship to D is that it holds a mortgage on D's property and D's rights and obligations under the mortgage are not affected by changes in its financial condition. The result would also be the same if D sent the statement to a bank with which D is doing business, and the statement is not reasonably expected to come to the attention of the bank's employees who are responsible for D's account.

Example (6). Corporation E and its subsidiaries, F and G are a consolidated group. Certified audited financial statements are prepared by EF and by FG. Both statements are used for substantial non-tax purposes. Pursuant to paragraph (c)(5)(i)(A) of this section, the financial statement that is prepared by EF is the applicable financial statement of the consolidated group. However, pursuant to paragraph (d)(6)(i)(B) of this section, an adjustment will be required to include the adjusted net book income attributable to G. The result would be the same even if the financial statement prepared by FG is of higher priority

(under the rules of paragraph (c)(3) of this section) than the statement prepared by E and F.

Example (7). Corporation H and its subsidiaries I, J and K are a consolidated group. Certified audited financial statements are prepared by H and I and by H, J and K. Both statements are used for substantial non-tax purposes. The financial statement prepared by H, J, and K includes the greater amount of gross receipts attributable to members of the consolidated group and thus, pursuant to paragraph (c)(5)(i)(B)(2)(i) of this section, it is the consolidated group's applicable financial statement.

Example (8). Corporation L and its subsidiary M are a consolidated group. Corporation L, also owns 100 percent of N, a foreign corporation that is not part of the consolidated group. A certified audited financial statement prepared by L, M and N discloses gross receipts of $200, of which $150 is attributable to L and M, and a separate certified audited financial statement prepared by L and M discloses gross receipts of $150. Both statements are used for substantial non-tax purposes. Pursuant to paragraph (c)(5)(i)(B) of this section, the consolidated group's applicable financial statement is the statement prepared by L, M and N.

Example (9). Corporation O is 60 percent owned by corporation P and 40 percent owned by corporation Q. Both P and Q prepare financial statements that are required to be filed with the SEC reflecting their respective interests in O. O also separately prepares a certified audited financial statement, or uses a summary of its books and records for credit purposes. Under paragraph (c)(5)(i)(C), O's separate statement is its applicable financial statement.

Example (10). Assume the same facts as in Example (9) except that O does not prepare a separate financial statement or a summary of its books and records for credit purposes. Pursuant to paragraph (c)(5)(i)(C) of this section, O must treat its net book income as equal to its current earnings and profits.

Example (11). Corporation R uses a calendar year for both financial accounting and tax purposes. Initially, R issues its calendar year 1987 financial statement on March 1, 1988. R's adjusted net book income resulting from this statement is $80. This would be R's applicable financial statement for 1987, but for the restatement described in the next sentence. On September 1, 1988, R restates its 1987 financial statement to correct an error (as described in Accounting Principles Board Opinion No. 20, paragraph 13). The restated financial statement is of the same priority as the initial financial state-

Reg. § 1.56-1(c)(6)

ment. The restatement results in adjusted net book income for calendar year 1987 of $50. Pursuant to paragraph (c)(5)(iii)(B)(2)(i) of this section, the restated financial statement is treated as R's 1987 applicable financial statement.

Example (12). Assume the same facts as in Example (11), except that R restates its financial statement in order to reflect a change in accounting method. Since the restatement does not result from an error, paragraph (c)(5)(iii)(B)(2)(i) of this section does not apply. Pursuant to paragraph (c)(5)(iii)(B)(2)(ii) of this section, R's 1987 applicable financial statement is the financial statement for 1987 that results in the greater amount of adjusted net book income. Thus, R's March 1, 1988 financial statement is treated as its 1987 applicable financial statement.

Example (13). Corporation S, which is not a member of an affiliated group, uses a calendar year for both financial accounting and tax purposes. S's 1987 applicable financial statement is a certified audited financial statement. On January 1, 1988, S transfers all of its assets subject to liabilities to T, a newly created subsidiary that is 100 percent owned by S. The principal purpose of the transfer is to use the special rules of paragraph (c)(5)(i) of this section to reduce the adjusted net book income of S. For calendar year 1988, T prepares and uses a certified audited financial statement. Since S's only asset is its investment in T, S does not prepare a financial statement for calendar year 1988. In addition, since S is only a holding company, T's 1988 certified audited financial statement reports the same net book income that would have been reported on a consolidated ST financial statement. If paragraph (c)(5)(i)(D) of this section does not apply, ST's 1988 applicable financial statement is the financial statement of S (the parent of the consolidated group) with the highest priority. Under paragraph (c)(1) of this section, since S does not have a financial statement in 1988, the net book income of the ST consolidated group is ordinarily deemed to equal the aggregate earnings and profits of the members of the consolidated group. However, given these facts, the District Director may determine that the 1988 certified audited financial statement of T is the 1988 applicable financial statement of the ST consolidated group.

Example (14). The facts are the same as in Example 13, except that S has owned 100 percent of T for several years prior to calendar year 1987. In addition, prior to 1987, ST prepared a consolidated certified audited financial statement. For calendar year 1987, ST does not prepare a consolidated certified audited financial statement. Instead, T prepares and uses a certified audited

financial statement while S does not prepare a financial statement. The principal purpose of the change in financial reporting is to use the special rules of paragraph (c)(5)(i) of this section to reduce the adjusted net book income of the ST consolidated group. Given these facts, the District Director may determine that the 1987 certified audited financial statement of T is the 1987 applicable financial statement of the ST consolidated group.

Example (15). Corporation U is a foreign corporation incorporated in A. U is a calendar year taxpayer for both financial accounting and tax purposes. U actively conducts three real estate businesses, X, Y and Z, in the United States. In 1987, X prepares a certified audited financial statement that it provides to its United States creditor. In addition, in 1987, X, Y and Z each prepare unaudited financial statements that they provide to U for incorporation in U's worldwide financial statement. Under paragraph (c)(5)(ii)(A) of this section, U's applicable financial statement is the certified audited financial statement prepared by X. However, pursuant to paragraph (d)(7) of this section, an adjustment is required to include any of U's effectively connected net book income that is not included in X's certified audited financial statement (i.e., the effectively connected net book income attributable to Y and Z).

Example (16). Corporation A is a foreign corporation incorporated in Z. A is a calendar year taxpayer for both financial accounting and tax purposes. A actively conducts a real estate business, B, in the United States. B prepares a certified audited financial statement for 1987 using the accounting principles of Z that it provides to A for incorporation into A's worldwide financial statement. In addition, B prepares a review statement for 1987 using United States generally accepted accounting principles that it provides to its United States creditors. Both the certified statement and the review statement are denominated in United States dollars. Under paragraphs (c)(5)(ii)(A) and (c)(5)(ii)(B)(1) of this section, the financial statement prepared under the accounting principles of Z is the applicable financial statement.

Example (17). Assume the same facts as in Example (16) except that amounts are reported on B's certified audited financial statement in the currency of Z and amounts are reported on B's review statement in United States dollars. Since the review statement is denominated in United States dollars, under paragraph (c)(5)(ii)(B)(2) of this section, it is the applicable financial statement.

Reg. § 1.56-1(c)(6)

Example (18). Corporation C is a foreign corporation incorporated in Z. C is a calendar year taxpayer for both financial accounting and tax purposes. C actively conducts two real estate businesses, D and E, in the United States. D and E each separately prepare a certified audited financial statement for 1987 that they provide to their United States creditors. D's financial statement reports gross receipts of $100. E's financial statement reports gross receipts of $200. Under paragraph (c)(5)(ii)(C)(2) of this section, E's certified audited financial statement is the applicable financial statement and must be adjusted under the rules of paragraph (d)(7) of this section to include effectively connected book income attributable to D.

Example (19). F is a foreign corporation incorporated in X. F is a calendar year taxpayer for both financial accounting and tax purposes. F actively conducts a banking business, G, in the United States. G has been engaged in business in the United States since 1977. For the years 1977 through 1986, G did not prepare a separate financial statement. However, each year G provided F with its books, records and other raw financial data. F used this data in preparing its worldwide financial statement. G provides F with its 1987 books and records on January 5, 1988, in accordance with its historic practice. On February 15, 1988, G prepares an unaudited financial statement for calendar year 1987 that it provides to F. The principal purpose of creating this financial statement is to reduce net book income. Under these facts, the financial statement provided by G is not intended to be reasonably relied upon by F in preparing its worldwide financial statement. Therefore, for purposes of computing net book income, G's financial statement has not been used for a substantial non-tax purpose.

Example (20). Assume the same facts as in Example (19) except that for purposes of preparing F's 1987 worldwide financial statement, G does not provide F with any raw financial data, and G only provides F with an audited financial statement that is prepared for a substantial non-tax purpose. Under these facts, the financial statement provided by G is intended to be relied upon by F in preparing its worldwide financial statement. Therefore, for purposes of computing net book income, G's financial statement has been used for a substantial non-tax purpose.

Example (21). Corporation H is a foreign corporation incorporated in I. H is a calendar year taxpayer for both financial accounting and tax purposes. H actively conducts a real estate business, J, in the United States. For the years 1976 through 1986, J prepared a certified audited financial statement using United States dollars that it provided to H. In 1987, J prepares a certified audited financial statement using the currency of I. The principal purpose of the modification of J's financial reporting is to reduce the amount of the book income adjustment. Given these facts, the District Director may determine that J's 1987 certified audited financial statement prepared in the currency of I is J's applicable financial statement for 1987, and such statement must be converted into United States dollars based upon the translation used to prepare the certified audited financial statement in the currency of I. Accordingly, the effectively connected net book income of J for 1987 is the effectively connected net book income reported on the financial statement that has been converted into United States dollars.

(d) *Adjustments to net book income*—(1) *In general.* Adjusted net book income is computed by making the adjustments described in this paragraph (d) to net book income (as defined in paragraph (b)(2) of this section). No adjustment may be made to net book income except as provided in this paragraph (d).

(2) *Definitions*—(i) *Historic practice.* For purposes of this paragraph (d), historic practice is defined as an accounting practice that—

(A) Was used consistently by the taxpayer for each of the 2 years immediately preceding its first taxable year beginning after 1986, and

(B) Was used on the financial statement that would have been the taxpayer's applicable financial statement (as determined under paragraph (c) of this section) for each of the 2 years immediately preceding its first taxable year beginning after 1986 if section 56(f), as amended by the Tax Reform Act of 1986, had been in effect.

Thus, in order for a calendar year corporation to have an historic practice in 1987, the corporation must have used the accounting practice in its 1985 and 1986 financial statements. However, to be treated as used for purposes of this paragraph, an accounting practice must have been used prior to April 23, 1987. For example, an accounting practice that is first used after April 23, 1987 in a restatement of a taxpayer's 1985 and 1986 financial statements is not the taxpayer's historic practice.

(ii) *Accounting literature.* For purposes of this paragraph (d), the term "accounting literature" means—

(A) Generally accepted accounting principles (GAAP) as defined in the American Institute of Certified Public Accountants Professional

Reg. § 1.56-1(d)(1)

Standards, AU Sections 411.05, paragraphs (a) through (c), and

(B) Pronouncements by the SEC including, but not limited to, Regulation S-X, SEC Financial Reporting Releases, and SEC Staff Accounting Bulletins,

that are effective for the accounting period covered by the applicable financial statement.

(3) *Adjustments for certain taxes*—(i) *In general.* Net book income for purposes of this paragraph (d) must be adjusted to disregard (for example, by adding back) any Federal income taxes or income, war profits, or excess profits taxes imposed by any foreign country or possession of the United States that are directly or indirectly taken into account on the taxpayer's applicable financial statement. No adjustment is made for taxes not described in the preceding sentence. Taxes directly or indirectly taken into account consist of the taxpayer's total income tax expense that includes both current and deferred income tax expense. In addition, items of income and expense, including extraordinary items that are stated net of tax, must be adjusted to disregard the taxes described in this paragraph (d)(3)(i). See paragraph (d)(4)(vii) of this section for an adjustment for certain deferred foreign taxes.

(ii) *Exception for certain foreign taxes.* Net book income is not adjusted to disregard taxes imposed by a foreign country or possession of the United States if the taxpayer does not choose to take the benefits of section 901 (relating to the foreign tax credit) with respect to these taxes for the taxable year. The rule in the preceding sentence only applies to the amount of taxes the taxpayer deducts in the current taxable year under section 164(a). See paragraph (d)(3)(iv), Example (4) of this section. Net book income also is not adjusted to disregard foreign taxes that cannot be claimed as a credit (other than by virtue of a foreign tax credit limitation). Thus, a taxpayer does not add back to net book income any taxes it is not allowed to claim as a credit against its United States income tax liability because of sections 245(a)(8), 901(j), 907(b) or 908 of the Code.

(iii) *Certain valuation adjustments.* Income tax expense under paragraph (d)(3)(i) of this section does not include valuation adjustments such as the valuation adjustments related to purchase accounting described in Accounting Principles Board (APB) Opinion No. 16, paragraph 89. However, income tax expense does include the tax associated with any gain or loss on the sale or other disposition of any asset the basis of which was adjusted under paragraph 89 of

Opinion 16. See paragraph (d)(3)(iv), Example (6) of this section.

(iv) *Examples.* The provisions of this paragraph may be illustrated by the following examples.

Example (1). Corporation A has $120 of net book income. In calculating net book income, A has deducted $20 of state income tax expense and $60 of Federal income tax expense. Assuming there are no other adjustments to net book income, A's adjusted net book income is $180 ($120 of net book income + $60 of Federal income tax expense). Pursuant to paragraph (d)(3)(i) of this section, no adjustment is made for the state income tax expense.

Example (2). Assume the same facts as in Example (1), except that A also has a net extraordinary item of $40. Thus, A has net book income of $160 ($120 + $40). The $40 net extraordinary item is composed of a $70 gross extraordinary item less $30 of Federal income tax expense. Assuming there are no other adjustments to net book income, A's adjusted net book income is $250 ($160 of net book income + $60 of Federal income tax expense on book income other than the extraordinary item + $30 of Federal income tax expense on the extraordinary item).

Example (3). Assume the same facts as in Example (1), except that in calculating A's $120 of net book income, A has $50 of Federal income tax expense and $10 of foreign income tax expense. The $10 of foreign income tax expense results from a foreign branch and is composed of $7 of current foreign income tax expense and $3 of deferred foreign income tax expense. A chooses to take the benefits of the foreign tax credit under section 901 for the current taxable year. Assuming there are no other adjustments to net book income, A's adjusted net book income is $180 ($120 of net book income + $50 of Federal income tax expense + $10 of foreign income tax expense).

Example (4). Assume the same facts as in Example (3), except that A does not choose to take the benefits of the foreign tax credit in the current taxable year and instead deducts the $7 of current foreign income tax paid. Pursuant to paragraph (d)(3)(ii) of this section, net book income is not adjusted for the $7 of current foreign income tax expense. However, net book income is adjusted for the $3 of deferred foreign income tax expense. Thus, assuming there are no other adjustments to net book income, D's adjusted net book income is $173 ($120 of net book income + $50 of Federal income tax expense + $3 of deferred foreign income tax expense).

Example (5). In 1987, corporation B only has a financial statement described in paragraph

Reg. § 1.56-1(d)(3)

(c)(1)(iv) of this section. B elects pursuant to paragraph (c)(2) of this section to treat net book income as equal to its current earnings and profits. B's current earnings and profits in 1987 is $60, after reduction for $40 of Federal income tax (see paragraph (b)(5)(i) of this section). Pursuant to paragraph (d)(3) of this section, B must make a $40 adjustment to net book income. Thus, assuming no other adjustments to net book income, B's 1987 adjusted net book income is $100 ($60 of net book income + $40 adjustment for Federal income taxes).

Example (6). Corporation A acquires assets from corporation B in a transaction where the tax basis of B's assets will carry over to A. For financial accounting purposes, A will account for the acquisition in accordance with Accounting Principles Board (APB) Opinion No. 16. One of the assets acquired from B has an appraised value of $10,000. However, because the tax basis of B's assets will carry over to A, A's tax basis in the asset is only $7,000. Given these facts, APB Opinion No. 16, paragraph 89 requires that the asset be recorded at $10,000 less the tax effect of the difference between the appraised value and the tax basis. Assuming a 30 percent tax rate for A, the asset would be recorded at $9,100 ($10,000 appraised value − ($3,000 difference between the appraised value and the tax basis × 30 percent)). If A sells the asset for $10,000, A will recognize a book gain of $900 with respect to the sale (assuming the asset is not amortized for book purposes). However, A will also have income tax expense of $900 (($10,000 sales proceeds − $7,000 tax basis) × 30 percent) with respect to the sale. Thus, A will have no net book income from the sale. Pursuant to paragraph (d)(3)(iii) of this section, A's income tax expense includes the $900 of income tax expense attributable to the effects of the valuation adjustment made in accordance with APB Opinion No. 16, paragraph 89. As a result, A's adjusted net book income with respect to its asset sale is $900 ($0 of net book income + $900 adjustment for income tax expense).

(4) *Adjustments to prevent omission or duplication*—(i) *In general.* In order to prevent omissions or duplications, net book income must be adjusted for the items described in paragraph (d)(4)(ii) through (d)(4)(vii) of this section and for such other items as approved or required by the Commissioner in published guidance. Except as provided in this paragraph (d), a taxpayer may not adjust net book income to prevent omission or duplication of items. See paragraph (d)(4)(viii), Example (1) of this section.

(ii) *Special rule for depreciating an asset below its cost.* Net book income must be adjusted to exclude depreciation or amortization expense to the extent such expense exceeds the asset's financial accounting historical cost ("excess depreciation"). However, no adjustment is required if excess depreciation has been the taxpayer's historic practice (as defined in paragraph (d)(2)(i) of this section) or if the excess depreciation is properly attributable to negative salvage value (*i.e.*, where the cost of removal or clean-up exceeds the salvage value).

(iii) *Consolidated group using current earnings and profits.* In the case of a consolidated group that uses its aggregate current earnings and profits as net book income (as determined under the rules of paragraph (b)(5)(ii) of this section), the current earnings and profits of the group is the aggregate of the current earnings and profits of each member of the group. In determining aggregate current earnings and profits, the adjustments described in § 1.1502-33 apply except for the adjustment for intercompany distributions with respect to stock and obligations of members of the group described in § 1.1502-33(c)(1) and the investment adjustment described in § 1.1502-33(c)(4)(ii)(*a*).

(iv) *Restatement of a prior year's applicable financial statement*—(A) *In general.* If a taxpayer restates an applicable financial statement and as a result, the net book income for a taxable year is restated after the last date that the taxpayer could have filed its Federal income tax return for such taxable year (if it had obtained an extension of time under section 6081 of the Code), net book income for the first successor year (as defined in paragraph (d)(4)(iv)(D) of this section) must be adjusted by that part of the cumulative effect of the restatement on net book income attributable to taxable years beginning after 1986. To the extent that the cumulative effect of the restatement on net book income includes a tax component, paragraph (d)(3) of this section may apply. See paragraph (c)(5)(iii) of this section for rules relating to the restatement of an applicable financial statement prior to the date the taxpayer's return for the taxable year would be due if the time for filing the return is extended.

(B) *Reconciliation of owner's equity in applicable financial statements.* If—

(*1*) The beginning balance of owner's equity on the taxpayer's applicable financial statement for the current taxable year is different than the ending balance of owner's equity on the taxpayer's applicable financial statement for the preceding taxable year, and

(*2*) The taxpayer is not otherwise subject to the restatement rules in paragraph (d)(4)(iv)(A) of this section,

Reg. § 1.56-1(d)(4)

the taxpayer will be deemed to have restated its applicable financial statement for the preceding year and paragraph (d)(4)(iv)(A) of this section will apply.

(C) *Use of different priority applicable financial statements in consecutive taxable years.* If the priority of a taxpayer's applicable financial statement (as determined under the rules of paragraph (c)(3) of this section) for the current taxable year is different than the priority of the taxpayer's applicable financial statement for the preceding taxable year, the taxpayer shall be required to adjust net book income to the extent required under the rules of either paragraph (d)(4)(iv)(A) or (B) of this section.

(D) *First successor year defined.* The "first successor year" is the first taxable year for which the taxpayer could have timely filed a return if it had obtained an extension of time under section 6081 of the Code after the restatement occurs. For example, if a calendar year corporation restates and uses its 1987 applicable financial statement between September 16, 1988 and September 15, 1989, any adjustment resulting from the restatement will be made in the taxpayer's 1988 Federal income tax return. If the restatement occurs prior to September 15, 1988, the rules of paragraph (c)(5)(iii) of this section will apply.

(E) *Exceptions.* (1) No adjustment is made under paragraph (d)(4)(iv)(A) of this section for a restatement prepared in accordance with APB Opinion No. 16, paragraph 53, requiring restatements of financial statements to reflect the combined operation of corporations combined in a pooling transaction.

(2) In order to prevent duplication of an adjustment, an adjustment otherwise required under paragraph (d)(4)(iv)(A) of this section may be decreased to take into account an adjustment previously made under the disclosure rules described in paragraph (d)(5) of the section. See paragraph (d)(4)(viii), Example (3) of this section.

(v) *Adjustment for items previously taxed as subpart F income.* Net book income does not include any item excluded from regular taxable income under section 959 if the item was included in adjusted net book income in a prior taxable year under the provisions of paragraph (b)(2)(iv) of this section and due to section 951. A taxpayer may not adjust net book income under this paragraph (d)(4)(v) to the extent any portion of the subpart F income was recognized during taxable years beginning before 1987. See example (5) of paragraph (d)(4)(viii) of this section.

(vi) *Adjustment for poolings of interests.* In a business combination accounted for as a pooling of interests under paragraph 50 of APB Opinion 16, net book income does not include the income of a separate corporation for that part of the taxable year preceding the combination of that corporation with the taxpayer, to the extent the separate corporation included this income in its net book income for the taxable year preceding the business combination. A taxpayer may not adjust net book income under this paragraph (d)(4)(vi) to the extent the separate corporation's income is attributable to taxable years beginning before 1987.

(vii) *Adjustment for certain deferred foreign taxes.* In the case of deferred foreign taxes that were previously added back to net book income in accordance with paragraph (d)(3) of this section, a deduction is allowed in computing adjusted net book income for the taxable year in which the deferred foreign taxes are deducted under section 164(a). A taxpayer may not adjust net book income under this paragraph (d)(4)(vii) to the extent the foreign taxes were deferred during taxable years beginning before 1987.

(viii) *Examples.* The provisions of this paragraph may be illustrated by the following examples.

Example (1). Corporation A uses a calendar year for both financial accounting and tax purposes. In 1986, A's financial statement included a $100 financial accounting loss for a plant shutdown. A could not deduct the loss on its 1986 Federal income tax return. In 1987, A deducts the loss from the 1986 plant shutdown in its 1987 Federal income tax return. As a result, A's 1987 adjusted net book income exceeds its 1987 preadjustment alternative minimum taxable income by $100 (an amount equal to the deduction for the 1986 plant shutdown). Pursuant to paragraph (d)(4)(i) of this section, A cannot make an adjustment to net book income.

Example (2). Corporation B uses a calendar year for both financial accounting and tax purposes. B issues its calendar year 1987 applicable financial statement on March 1, 1988. The applicable financial statement reports net book income for the calendar years 1985 through 1987 of $50, $70, and $80, respectively. On March 1, 1989 when it issues its calendar year 1988 applicable financial statement, B restates its 1985, 1986 and 1987 applicable financial statements. The restatement results from a change in accounting method that is made during calendar year 1988. After restatement, B's net book income for 1985, 1986, and 1987 is $60, $80, and $90, respectively. Based upon these facts, the cumulative

Reg. § 1.56-1(d)(4)

effect of the restatement on B's net book income for years prior to 1988 is $30. However, since $20 of the cumulative effect is attributable to years beginning before 1987, B's 1988 net book income is increased by only $10 ($30 − $20). If the cumulative effect includes a tax adjustment, see paragraph (d)(3) of this section.

Example (3). Assume the same facts for Corporation B as in Example (2), except that B's 1987 net book income of $80 is increased by $10 for purposes of B's 1987 Federal income tax return. The $10 adjustment is made pursuant to paragraph (d)(5)(iii) of this section relating to disclosure in the accountant's opinion. Specifically, the accountant's opinion on B's 1987 applicable financial statement disclosed that if D had used a certain accounting method, B's 1987 net book income would have been $90 rather than $80. The restatement of B's 1987 applicable financial statement on March 1, 1988 results entirely from B changing to the accounting method referred to in the 1987 accountant's opinion. Pursuant to paragraph (d)(4)(iv)(E)(*2*) of this section, no adjustment is made to B's 1988 net book income as a result of the restatement of B's 1987 applicable financial statement.

Example (4). Assume the same facts as in Example (1), except that when A issues its 1987 applicable financial statement it also restates the net book income reported on its 1986 financial statement to exclude the $100 loss attributable to the plant shutdown. Furthermore, the $100 loss from the plant shutdown is included in A's 1987 net book income as reported on its 1987 applicable financial statement. Pursuant to paragraph (d)(4) of this section, no adjustment is made to A's 1987 net book income as a result of the restatement of A's 1986 net book income.

Example (5). Corporation D is a domestic corporation. D owns ten percent of the issued and outstanding stock of corporation F, a foreign corporation. D and F file separate financial statements and federal income tax returns, both on a calendar-year basis. F is a controlled foreign corporation as defined in section 957. In 1987, D includes ten percent of F's subpart F income in its income under section 951. F makes no actual distributions to D in that year, and D's applicable financial statement includes the earnings of F only when actual distributions are made. See paragraph (d)(6)(i)(A) of this section. In 1987, D must adjust its net book income under paragraph (b)(2)(iv) of this section to include ten percent of F's subpart F income. In 1988, F makes an actual distribution to D which qualifies for the exclusion of section 959. D includes this actual distribution as income on its applicable financial statement for

1987. Pursuant to paragraph (d)(4)(v) of this section, D must adjust its net book income for 1988 to exclude the actual distribution from F.

(5) *Adjustments resulting from disclosure—* (i) *Adjustment for footnote disclosure or other supplementary information—(A) In general.* Except as described in this paragraph (d)(5)(i), net book income must be increased by any amount disclosed in a footnote or other supplementary information to the applicable financial statement if the disclosure supports a calculation of a net book income amount that would be greater than the net book income reported on the taxpayer's applicable financial statement. However, net book income will not be increased if the disclosure—

(*1*) Is specifically authorized by the accounting literature described in paragraph (d)(2)(ii) of this section, or

(*2*) Is in accordance with the taxpayer's historic practice as defined in paragraph (d)(2)(i) of this section.

See paragraph (d)(5)(v), Examples (1) and (2) of this section.

(B) *Disclosures not specifically authorized in the accounting literature.* The following footnote or other supplementary disclosures will not be considered specifically authorized in the accounting literature—

(*1*) Disclosure of what the taxpayer's net book income would have been if GAAP had been used in preparing the applicable financial statement instead of tax accounting rules (or disclosure of the adjustment necessary to determine net book income on a GAAP basis), and

(*2*) Disclosure of what the taxpayer's net book income would have been if the accrual method had been used in preparing the applicable financial statement instead of the cash method (or disclosure of the adjustment necessary to determine net book income on the accrual method).

(ii) *Equity adjustments—(A) In general.* Except as described in this paragraph (d)(5)(ii), net book income must be increased by the amount of any equity adjustment (as defined in paragraph (d)(5)(ii)(B) of this section) included in the applicable financial statement if the equity adjustment increases owner's equity as reported on the taxpayer's applicable financial statement and the increase is attributable to the taxpayer or a member of the taxpayer's consolidated group. However, net book income will not be increased if the equity adjustment—

(*1*) Is specifically authorized by the accounting literature described in paragraph (d)(2)(ii) of this section, or

Reg. § 1.56-1(d)(5)

(2) Is in accordance with the taxpayer's historic practice, as defined in paragraph (d)(2)(i) of this section.

See paragraph (d)(5)(v), Examples (3) and (4) of this section.

(B) *Definition of equity adjustment.* An equity adjustment is any reconciling item between beginning and ending owner's equity as reported on the taxpayer's applicable financial statement for the current taxable year. However, if properly accounted for, the following reconciling items are not considered equity adjustments and do not require adjustment under paragraph (d)(5)(ii)(A) of this section—

(1) Net book income,

(2) Non-liquidating dividend distributions, and

(3) Contributions to capital.

(iii) *Amounts disclosed in an accountant's opinion.* Net book income must be increased by the amount of any item disclosed in the accountant's opinion (as described in paragraphs (c)(1)(ii)(C) and (c)(1)(ii)(D) of this section) if the disclosure supports a calculation of a net book income amount that would be greater than the net book income reported on the taxpayer's applicable financial statement. However, net book income will not be increased if the disclosure is in accordance with the taxpayer's historic practice, as defined in paragraph (d)(2)(i) of this section.

(iv) *Accounting method changes that result in cumulative adjustments to the current year's applicable financial statement—*(A) *In general.* If net book income for the current taxable year includes a cumulative adjustment attributable to an accounting method change and the amount of the cumulative adjustment may be determined upon review of the applicable financial statement (including footnotes) or other supplementary disclosure, net book income for the current taxable year shall be adjusted to exclude that portion of the cumulative adjustment attributable to taxable years beginning before 1987. To the extent the cumulative adjustment is reported net of a tax, paragraph (d)(3) of this section may apply. See paragraph (d)(5)(v), Example (5) of this section. If an accounting method change results in a restatement of an applicable financial statement, paragraphs (c)(5)(iii) or (d)(4)(iv)(A) of this section may apply.

(B) *Exception.* In order to prevent duplication of an adjustment, the adjustment required under paragraph (d)(5)(iv)(A) of this section may be decreased to take into account any adjustment for the accounting method change previously made under the rules described in paragraph (d)(5) of this section (relating to adjustments resulting from disclosure).

(v) *Examples.* The provisions of this paragraph may be illustrated by the following examples.

Example (1). Corporation A uses a calendar year for both financial accounting and tax purposes. For calendar years 1984 through 1986, A used the cash method of accounting on its financial statement and disclosed in a footnote the net income or loss that would have resulted if the accrual method of accounting had been used. A's 1987 net book income, as reported on its 1987 applicable financial statement, is $100 and is calculated on the cash method of accounting. In addition, a footnote in A's 1987 applicable financial statement states that A's 1987 net book income would have been $30 greater had the accrual method of accounting been used. Pursuant to paragraph (d)(5)(i)(B)(2) of this section, A's 1987 footnote disclosure is not considered specifically authorized by the accounting literature. However, since A made such disclosure for calendar years 1985 and 1986, the 1987 disclosure is in accordance with A's historic practice, as defined in paragraph (d)(2)(i) of this section. Since A satisfies the exception described in paragraph (d)(5)(i)(A)(2) of this section, no adjustment is made to A's 1987 net book income for the footnote disclosure.

Example (2). Assume the same facts for corporation B as in Example (1), except that B's 1985 and 1986 financial statements did not disclose the amount of income or loss that would result if the accrual method of accounting (rather than the cash method of accounting) were used. Since B does not satisfy either of the exceptions described in paragraph (d)(5)(i)(A) of this section, B's 1987 adjusted net book income is $130 ($100 of net book income plus $30 adjustment for footnote disclosure).

Example (3). Corporation C uses a calendar year for both financial accounting and tax purposes. C's 1987 net book income, as reported on its 1987 applicable financial statement, is $200. However, as specifically authorized in FASB Statement of Standards No. 52, C's 1987 applicable financial statement also includes a $50 equity adjustment (as defined in paragraph (d)(5)(ii)(B) of this section) for foreign currency translation gains. Since the equity adjustment is specifically authorized in the accounting literature, C satisfies the exception described in paragraph (d)(5)(ii)(A)(1) of this section, and no adjustment is made to C's 1987 net book income for the $50 equity adjustment.

Reg. § 1.56-1(d)(5)

Example (4). Assume the same facts for corporation D as in Example (3), except that D's equity adjustment is for foreign currency transaction gains instead of foreign currency translation gains. Pursuant to FASB Statement of Financial Accounting Standards No. 52, foreign currency transaction gains (as compared with foreign currency translation gains) are included in the income statement rather than in equity. In addition, in 1985 and 1986, D included foreign currency transaction gains in its income statement. Since D does not satisfy either of the exceptions described in paragraph (d)(5)(ii)(A) of this section, D's 1987 adjusted net book income is $250 ($200 of net book income plus $50 equity adjustment).

Example (5). Corporation E uses a calendar year for both financial accounting and tax purposes. E's net book income for 1988 is $100. The $100 of net book income includes $30 of financial accounting loss attributable to a cumulative adjustment as of January 1, 1988, resulting from a change in E's accounting method. The $30 cumulative loss is disclosed in E's 1988 applicable financial statement. If E had made the accounting method change in calendar year 1987, the cumulative loss as of January 1, 1987 would have been $20. Based upon the above facts, E must increase net book income by $20 to disregard that portion of the cumulative adjustment attributable to years beginning before 1987. Thus, assuming no other adjustments to net book income, E's adjusted net book income for 1988 is $120 ($100 plus $20).

(6) *Adjustments applicable to related corporations*—(i) *Consolidated returns*—(A) *In general.* Pursuant to paragraphs (a)(3) and (b)(3) of this section, the book income adjustment with respect to a consolidated group (as described under paragraph (a)(3) of this section) is computed based on the consolidated adjusted net book income (as defined in paragraph (b)(3)(i) of this section). In the case of any corporation that is not included in the consolidated group, consolidated adjusted net book income of the consolidated group shall include only the sum of the dividends received from such other corporation and other amounts includible in gross income under this chapter with respect to the earnings of such other corporation. See paragraph (d)(6)(v), Example (4) of this section.

(B) *Corporations included in the consolidated Federal income tax return but excluded from the applicable financial statement*—(1) *In general.* Consolidated net book income reported on the applicable financial statement (as determined under paragraph (c)(5) of this section) shall be adjusted to include net book income attributable to a corporation that is included in the consolidated group but is not included in the applicable financial statement. Net book income for the corporation not included in the applicable financial statement of the consolidated group is the net book income reported on such corporation's applicable financial statement (determined under the rules of paragraph (c) of this section and adjusted under the rules of this paragraph (d)). The adjusted net book income of such corporation must be consolidated with the adjusted net book income of other members of the consolidated group and appropriate adjustments, including consolidating elimination entries, must be made.

(2) *Adjustments to net book income for minority interests.* Consolidated net book income must be adjusted to include income or loss allocated to minority interests in members of the consolidated group. Failure to include income or loss allocated to minority interests shall be treated as an omission of net book income. See paragraph (d)(6)(v), Example (1) of this section.

(3) *Corporations included in the consolidated group that are accounted for under the equity method of accounting.* No adjustment is required to consolidated net book income for income or loss of a member of the consolidated group that is reported in the applicable financial statement under the equity method of accounting (as described in APB Opinion No. 18, paragraph (6)). However, consolidated adjusted net book income (as defined in paragraph (b)(3)(i) of this section) must include 100 percent of the net book income attributable to such member. See paragraph (d)(6)(i)(B)(2) of this section. For example, if consolidated net book income (as defined in paragraph (b)(3)(ii) of this section) only includes 85 percent of the equity income attributable to a member of the consolidated group, an adjustment will be required to include the 15 percent of equity income excluded from consolidated net book income. In addition, to the extent the equity income reflects an adjustment for tax expense or benefit, paragraph (d)(3) may apply. See paragraph (d)(6)(v), Examples (2) and (3) of this section.

(C) *Corporations included in the applicable financial statement but excluded from the consolidated tax return.* Net book income or consolidated net book income must be adjusted to eliminate the income or loss of a corporation that is included in the applicable financial statement, but is not included in the consolidated group. When net book income attributable to a corporation that is not a member of the consolidated group is removed from the computation of net book income in the applicable financial statement, consolidating elimination entries attributable to the excluded member must also be removed.

(ii) *Adjustment under the principles of section 482.* In order to fairly allocate items relating to intercompany transactions between corporations that are owned or controlled directly or indirectly by the same interests but are not members of a consolidated group, adjustments must be made to the net book income reported on the applicable financial statement of each corporation under the principles of section 482 and the regulations thereunder (relating to allocation of income and deductions among related taxpayers). For example, assume corporation A owns 100 percent of F, a foreign subsidiary, but A and F are not members of a consolidated group. However, A and F prepare a consolidated financial statement. In adjusting A's applicable financial statement to eliminate the net book income attributable to F, A must apply the principles of section 482. If a corporation fails to make appropriate adjustments to its applicable financial statement under the rules of this paragraph (d)(6)(ii), the District Director may make such adjustments under the principles of section 482 and the regulations thereunder.

(iii) *Adjustment for dividends received from section 936 corporations—(A) In general.* Any dividend received from a corporation eligible for the credit provided by section 936 (relating to the possession tax credit) shall be included in adjusted net book income. For example, assume corporation A owns 100 percent of B, a section 936 corporation, and B pays a $100 dividend to A. Furthermore, assume that of the $100 dividend, $15 of withholding tax is paid to a possession of the United States, so that A only receives $85 from the dividend. Given these facts, A's adjusted net book income includes $100 with respect to the dividend from B.

(B) *Treatment as foreign taxes.* Fifty percent of any withholding tax paid to a possession of the United States with respect to dividends referred to in paragraph (d)(6)(iii)(A) of this section may be treated for purposes of the alternative minimum foreign tax credit as a tax paid to foreign country by the corporation receiving the dividend. However, if the aggregate of these dividends exceeds the excess referred to in paragraph (a)(1) of this section, the amount treated as a tax paid to the foreign country shall not exceed 50 percent of the aggregate amount of the tax withheld multiplied by a fraction,

(*1*) the numerator of which is the excess referred to in paragraph (a)(1) of this section; and

(*2*) the denominator of which is the aggregate amount of these dividends.

(C) *Treatment of taxes imposed on section 936 corporations.* Taxes paid by any corporation eligible for the credit provided under section 936 shall be treated as a withholding tax paid with respect to any dividend paid by such corporation, and thus subject to the rules of this paragraph (d)(6)(iii), but only to the extent such taxes would be treated as paid by the corporation receiving the dividend under rules similar to the rules of section 902.

(iv) *Adjustment to net book income on sale of certain investments.* If a taxpayer accounts for an investment under any method equivalent to the equity method of accounting (as described in APB Opinion No. 18, paragraph 6) and pursuant to paragraphs (b)(2)(iv) or (d)(6)(i) of this section the taxpayer excludes net book income attributable to that investment, the taxpayer must adjust its net book income in the year the investment is sold (or partially sold). The adjustment equals the amount of net book income previously excluded under paragraphs (b)(2)(iv) or (d)(6)(i)(A) of this section). See paragraph (d)(6)(v), Example (4) of this section.

(v) *Examples.* The provisions of this paragraph may be illustrated by the following examples.

Example (1). Corporation A and its 100 percent owned subsidiary B and its 90 percent owned subsidiary C are a consolidated group. A also owns 100 percent of D, a foreign corporation. ABC's applicable financial statement is a certified audited financial statement that includes A, B, C and D. The net book income reported on the statement excludes $10 of C's net book income that is attributable to the 10 percent minority interest in C held outside of the consolidated group. Pursuant to paragraph (d)(6)(i)(B)(*2*) of this section, net book income of the consolidated group must be adjusted to include the $10 of net book income attributable to the minority interest in C. In addition, pursuant to paragraph (d)(6)(i)(C) of this section, net book income shown on the applicable financial statement must be adjusted to eliminate the net book income attributable to D.

Example (2). Corporation E owns 100 percent of F, a finance subsidiary, and EF are a consolidated group. Since F is a finance subsidiary, E's applicable financial statement accounts for F under the equity method of accounting. F also prepares a separate financial statement that is of equal or higher priority than E's applicable financial statement. In 1987, E's applicable financial statement includes $60 of equity income

Reg. § 1.56-1(d)(6)

from F. The $60 of equity income reflects a reduction for $40 of Federal income tax expense. Thus, E's equity income from F prior to the reduction for Federal income tax expense, is $100 ($60 + $40). Since E's applicable financial statement includes E's equity income in F, F's separate financial statement is not relevant for determining the adjusted net book income of the EF consolidated group. However, pursuant to paragraphs (d)(3) and (d)(6)(i)(B)(3) of this section, E is required to adjust its equity income in F by the $40 of Federal income tax expense attributable to F. Thus, assuming there are no other adjustments, E's adjusted net book income with respect to F is $100.

Example (3). The facts are the same as Example (2), except that E reports its equity income in F without reduction for F's Federal income tax expense. The $40 of Federal income tax expense attributable to F is combined with E's Federal income tax expense. Assuming no other adjustments, E's adjusted net book income with respect to F is $100. Thus, E's adjusted net book income with respect to F will be the same regardless of whether E's equity income in F is reported before or after taxes.

Example (4). A, a domestic corporation, uses a calendar year for both financial accounting and tax purposes. On January 1, 1987, A purchases 100 percent of F, a foreign corporation, for $100. F does not file a Federal income tax return and A does not recognize any taxable income with respect to F under section 951 (relating to controlled foreign corporations). In its applicable financial statement, A accounts for its investment in F under the equity method of accounting. Thus, A's initial investment in F is $100. During calendar year 1987, F has $50 of net book income but makes no dividend payments to A. Under the equity method of accounting, A's net book income includes the $50 of net book income attributable to A's net book investment in F. Thus, A's investment in F is increased to $150. Pursuant to paragraph (d)(6)(i)(C) of this section, A's net book income is adjusted to eliminate the $50 of net book income attributable to F. On January 1, 1988, A sells F for $150. Since A's investment in F under the equity method of accounting is $150, A's net book income for 1988 will not include any gain on the sale of F. However, pursuant to paragraph (d)(6)(iv), A's 1988 net book income must be increased by $50, the amount of net book income previously eliminated with respect to A's investment in F. The result would be the same if instead of accounting for its investment in F under the equity method of accounting, A and F prepare a consolidated financial statement.

(7) *Adjustments for foreign taxpayers with a United States trade or business*—(i) *In general.* Pursuant to paragraph (b)(6) of this section, the book income adjustment with respect to a foreign taxpayer with a United States trade or business is computed based on the effectively connected net book income of the foreign taxpayer (as defined in paragraph (b)(6)(ii) of this section). The net book income amount reported on the applicable financial statement of the foreign taxpayer (as determined under paragraph (c)(5)(ii) of this section) must be adjusted to—

(A) Include effectively connected net book income attributable to a trade or business conducted in the United States by the foreign taxpayer that is not reported on the applicable financial statement. Such amounts shall be determined from a financial statement (determined under paragraph (c) of this section and adjusted under the rules of this paragraph (d)) that would have qualified as an applicable financial statement of such excluded trade or business or upon effectively connected earnings and profits (if the rules of section (b)(6)(iii) of this section apply), and

(B) Exclude any amount reported on such applicable financial statement that does not qualify as effectively connected net book income.

See the example in paragraph (d)(7)(ii) of this section.

(ii) *Example.* The provisions of this paragraph may be illustrated by the following example.

Example. Foreign corporation A, a calendar year taxpayer for financial accounting and tax purposes, is incorporated in X. A actively conducts two real estate businesses, B and C, in the United States. B prepares a certified audited financial statement that it provides to its United States creditor. C does not prepare a financial statement. The certified audited financial statement prepared by B is treated as A's applicable financial statement under paragraph (c)(5)(ii) of this section. B's certified audited financial statement, in addition to amounts related to the conduct of its real estate business, also reports income received from its investment in United States securities, unrelated to its conduct of business in the United States that does not qualify as effectively connected net book income. In order to determine A's effectively connected net book income from the net book income reported on the applicable financial statement, such statement must be adjusted to exclude amounts attributable to the securities. In addition, book income or loss attributable to C, to the extent effectively connected to its business in the United States, must

Reg. § 1.56-1(d)(7)

be included in the effectively connected net book income reported on B's financial statement. Since C does not have a financial statement, C's effectively connected net book income is determined by computing its effectively connected earnings and profits under paragraph (b)(6)(iii) of this section.

(8) *Adjustment for corporations subject to subchapter F.* A corporation subject to tax under subchapter F of chapter 1 of the Code shall adjust its book income to exclude all items of income, loss or expense other than those relating to the calculation of unrelated business taxable income for purposes of section 512(a).

(e) *Special rules*—(1) *Cooperatives.* For purposes of computing the book income adjustment, net book income of a cooperative to which section 1381 applies is reduced by patronage dividends and per-unit retain allocations under section 1382(b) that are paid by the cooperative to the extent such amounts are deductible for regular income tax and general alternative minimum tax purposes under section 1382, and not otherwise taken into account in determining adjusted net book income.

(2) *Alaska Native Corporations.* In computing the net book income of an Alaska Native Corporation, cost recovery and depletion are computed using the asset basis determined under section 21(c) of the Alaska Native Claims Settlement Act (43 U.S.C. 1620(c)). In addition, net book income is reduced by expenses payable under either section 7(i) or section 7(j) of the Alaska Native Claims Settlement Act (43 U.S.C. 1606(i) and (j)) only when deductions for such expenses are allowed for tax purposes.

(3) *Insurance companies.* In the case of an insurance company whose applicable financial statement is a statement described in paragraph (c)(1)(iii) of this section (relating to statements provided to a government regulator), net book income for purposes of the book income adjustment is the net income or loss from operations, after reduction for dividends paid to policyholders, but without reduction for Federal income taxes.

(4) *Estimating the book income adjustment for purposes of the estimated tax liability.* See § 1.6655-7 for special rules for estimating the corporate alternative minimum tax book income adjustment under the annualization exception. [Reg. § 1.56-1.]

☐ [*T.D.* 8138, 4-23-87. *Amended by T.D.* 8197, 4-27-88. *Redesignated and amended by T.D.* 8307, 8-16-90.]

[Reg. § 1.56(g)-0]

§ 1.56(g)-0. **Table of Contents.**—This section lists the paragraphs contained in § 1.56(g)-1.

§ 1.56(g)-1 Adjusted current earnings.

(a) Adjustment for adjusted current earnings.

(1) Positive adjustment.

(2) Negative adjustment.

(i) In general.

(ii) Limitation on negative adjustments.

(iii) Example.

(3) Negative amounts.

(4) Taxpayers subject to adjustment for adjusted current earnings.

(5) General rule for applying Internal Revenue Code provisions in determining adjusted current earnings.

(i) In general.

(ii) Example.

(6) Definitions.

(i) Pre-adjustment alternative minimum taxable income.

(ii) Adjusted current earnings.

(iii) Earnings and profits.

(7) Application to foreign corporations.

(b) Depreciation allowed.

(1) Property placed in service after 1989.

(2) Property subject to new ACRS.

(i) In general.

(ii) Rules for computing the depreciation deduction.

(iii) Example.

(3) Property subject to original ACRS.

(i) In general.

(ii) Rules for computing the depreciation deduction.

(iii) Example.

(4) Special rule for certain section 168(f) property.

(5) Certain property not subject to ACRS.

(c) Inclusion in adjusted current earnings of items included in earnings and profits.

(1) In general.

(2) Certain amounts not taken into account in determining whether an item is permanently excluded.

(3) Allowance of offsetting deductions.

(4) Special rules.

(i) Income from the discharge of indebtedness.

(ii) Federal income tax refunds.

Reg. § 1.56(g)-0

(iii) Income earned on behalf of states and municipalities.

(5) Treatment of life insurance contracts.

(i) In general.

(ii) Inclusion of inside buildup.

(iii) Calculation of income on the contract.

(iv) Treatment of distributions under the life insurance contract.

(v) Treatment of death benefits.

(vi) Other rules.

(A) Term life insurance contracts without net surrender values.

(B) Life insurance contracts involving divided ownership.

(vii) Examples.

(6) Partial list of income items excluded from gross income but included in earnings and profits.

(7) Partial list of items excluded from both pre-adjustment alternative minimum taxable income and adjusted current earnings.

(d) Disallowance of items not deductible in computing earnings and profits.

(1) In general.

(2) Deductions for certain dividends received.

(i) Certain amounts deducted under sections 243 and 245.

(ii) Special rules.

(A) Dividends received from a foreign sales corporation.

(B) Dividends received from a section 936 corporation.

(iii) Special rule for certain dividends received by certain cooperatives.

(3) Partial list of items not deductible in computing earnings and profits.

(4) Partial list of items deductible for purposes of computing both pre-adjustment alternative minimum taxable income and adjusted current earnings.

(e) Treatment of income items included, and deduction items not allowed, in computing pre-adjustment alternative minimum taxable income.

(f) Certain other earnings and profits adjustments.

(1) Intangible drilling costs.

(2) Certain amortization provisions do not apply.

(3) LIFO recapture adjustment.

(i) In general.

(ii) Beginning LIFO and FIFO inventory.

(iii) Definitions.

(A) LIFO recapture amount.

(1) Definition.

(2) Assets included.

(B) FIFO method.

(C) LIFO method.

(D) Inventory amounts.

(iv) Exchanges under sections 351 and 721.

(v) Examples.

(vi) Effective date.

(4) Installment sales.

(i) In general.

(ii) Exception for prior dispositions.

(iii) Special rules for obligations to which section 453A applies.

(A) In general.

(B) Limitation on application of installment method.

(C) Treatment of the ineligible portion.

(D) Treatment of the eligible portion.

(E) Coordination with the pledge rule.

(F) Example.

(g) Disallowance of loss on exchange of debt pools. [RESERVED]

(h) Policy acquisition expenses of life insurance companies.

(1) In general.

(2) Reasonably estimated life.

(3) Reasonable allowance for amortization.

(4) Safe harbor for public financial statements.

(i) [RESERVED]

(j) Depletion.

(k) Treatment of certain ownership changes.

(1) In general.

(2) Definition of ownership change.

(3) Determination of net unrealized built-in loss immediately before an ownership change.

(4) Example.

(l) [RESERVED]

(m) Adjusted current earnings of foreign corporations.

(1) In general.

(2) Definitions.

(i) Effectively connected pre-adjustment alternative minimum taxable income.

(ii) Effectively connected adjusted current earnings.

(3) Rules to determine effectively connected pre-adjustment alternative minimum taxable in-

Reg. § 1.56(g)-0

come and effectively connected adjusted current earnings.

(4) Certain exempt amounts.

(n) Adjustment for adjusted current earnings of consolidated groups.

(1) Positive adjustments.

(2) Negative adjustments.

(i) In general.

(ii) Limitation on negative adjustments.

(3) Definitions.

(i) Consolidated pre-adjustment alternative minimum taxable income.

(ii) Consolidated adjusted current earnings.

(4) Example.

(o) [RESERVED]

(p) Effective dates for corporate partners in partnerships.

(1) In general.

(2) Application of effective dates.

(3) Example.

(q) Treatment of distributions of property to shareholders.

(1) In general.

(2) Examples.

(r) Elections to use simplified inventory methods to compute alternative minimum tax.

(1) In general.

(2) Effect of election.

(i) Inventories

(ii) Modifications required.

(A) In general.

(B) Negative modifications allowed.

(iii) LIFO recapture adjustment.

(3) Time and manner of making election.

(i) Prospective election.

(ii) Retroactive election.

(iii) Taxpayers under examination.

(A) In general.

(1) Year of change under examination.

(2) Other open years under examination.

(B) Statement required.

(C) Year of change.

(D) Treatment of additional tax liability.

(iv) Election as method of accounting.

(v) Untimely election to use simplified inventory method.

(4) Example.

(5) Election to use alternative minimum tax inventories to compute adjusted current earnings.

(s) Adjustment for alternative tax energy preference deduction.

(1) In general.

(2) Example.

[Reg. § 1.56(g)-0.]

☐ [*T.D.* 8340, 3-14-91. *Amended by* T.D. 8454, 12-18-92.]

[Reg. § 1.56(g)-1]

§ 1.56(g)-1. **Adjusted current earnings.**—(a) *Adjustment for adjusted current earnings*—(1) *Positive adjustment.* For taxable years beginning after December 31, 1989, the alternative minimum taxable income of any taxpayer described in paragraph (a)(4) of this section is increased by the adjustment for adjusted current earnings. The adjustment for adjusted current earnings is 75 percent of the excess, if any, of—

(i) The adjusted current earnings (as defined in paragraph (a)(6)(ii) of this section) of the taxpayer for the taxable year over

(ii) The pre-adjustment alternative minimum taxable income (as defined in paragraph (a)(6)(i) of this section) of the taxpayer for the taxable year.

(2) *Negative adjustment*—(i) *In general.* For taxable years beginning after December 31, 1989, the alternative minimum taxable income of any taxpayer is decreased, subject to the limitation of paragraph (a)(2)(ii) of this section, by 75 percent of the excess, if any, of pre-adjustment alternative minimum taxable income (as defined in paragraph (a)(6)(i) of this section), over adjusted current earnings (as defined in paragraph (a)(6)(ii) of this section).

(ii) *Limitation on negative adjustments.* The amount of the negative adjustment for any taxable year is limited to the excess, if any, of —

(A) The aggregate increases in alternative minimum taxable income in prior years under paragraph (a)(1) of this section over

(B) The aggregate decreases in alternative minimum taxable income in prior years under this paragraph (a)(2).

Any excess of pre-adjustment alternative minimum taxable income over adjusted current earnings that is not allowed as a negative adjustment for the taxable year because of the limitation in this paragraph (a)(2)(ii) is not applied to reduce any positive adjustment in any other taxable year.

Reg. § 1.56(g)-1(a)(2)

(iii) *Example.* The following example illustrates the provisions of this paragraph (a)(2):

(A) Corporation P is a calendar-year taxpayer and has pre-adjustment alternative minimum taxable income and adjusted current earnings in the following amounts for 1990 through 1993:

Year	Pre-adjustment alternative minimum taxable income	Adjusted current earnings
1990	$800,000	$700,000
1991	600,000	900,000
1992	500,000	400,000
1993	500,000	100,000

(B) Under these facts, corporation P has the following positive and negative adjustments for adjusted current earnings:

Year	Negative adjustment	Positive adjustment
1990	–0–	–0–
1991	–0–	$225,000
1992	$ 75,000	–0–
1993	150,000	–0–

(C) In 1990, P has a potential negative adjustment (before the cumulative limitation) of $75,000 (75 percent of the $100,000 excess of pre-adjustment alternative minimum taxable income over adjusted current earnings). Nonetheless, P is not permitted a negative adjustment because P had no prior increases in its alternative minimum taxable income due to an adjustment for adjusted current earnings.

(D) In 1991, P has a positive adjustment of $225,000 (75 percent of the $300,000 excess of adjusted current earnings over pre-adjustment alternative minimum taxable income). P is not allowed to use the prior year's excess of pre-adjustment alternative minimum taxable income over adjusted current earnings to reduce its 1991 positive adjustment.

(E) In 1992, P is permitted a negative adjustment of $75,000, the full amount of 75 percent of the $100,000 excess of pre-adjustment alternative minimum taxable income over adjusted current earnings for the taxable year. This is because P's prior cumulative increases in alternative minimum taxable income due to the positive adjustments for adjusted current earnings exceed the negative adjustment for the year.

(F) In 1993, P has a potential negative adjustment (before the cumulative limitation) of $300,000 (75 percent of the $400,000 excess of pre-adjustment alternative minimum taxable income over adjusted current earnings). P's net cumulative increases in alternative minimum taxable income due to the adjustment for adjusted current earnings are $150,000 ($225,000 increase in 1991, less $75,000 decrease in 1992). Thus, P's negative adjustment in 1993 is limited to $150,000. P may not use the remaining portion ($150,000) of the negative adjustment for 1993 to reduce positive adjustments in other taxable years.

(3) *Negative amounts.* In determining whether an excess exists under paragraph (a)(1) or (a)(2) of this section, a positive amount exceeds a negative amount by the sum of the absolute numbers, and a smaller negative amount exceeds a larger negative amount by the difference between the absolute numbers. Thus, for example, a positive amount of adjusted current earnings of $30 exceeds a negative amount (or loss) of pre-adjustment AMTI of $10 by the sum of the absolute numbers, or $40 (30 + 10). Accordingly, the adjustment for adjusted current earnings would be 75 percent of $40, or $30. In contrast, a negative amount of adjusted current earnings of $10 exceeds a negative amount (or loss) of pre-adjustment alternative minimum taxable income of $30 by the difference between the absolute numbers, or $20 (30 − 10). Accordingly, the adjustment for adjusted current earnings would be 75 percent of $20, or $15.

(4) *Taxpayers subject to adjustment for adjusted current earnings.* The adjustment for adjusted current earnings applies to any corporation other than—

(i) An S corporation as defined in section 1361,

(ii) A regulated investment company as defined in section 851,

(iii) A real estate investment trust as defined in section 856, or

(iv) A real estate mortgage investment conduit as defined in section 860A.

(5) *General rule for applying Internal Revenue Code provisions in determining adjusted current earnings—*(i) *In general.* Except as otherwise provided by regulations or other guidance issued by the Internal Revenue Service, all Internal Revenue Code provisions that apply in determining the regular taxable income of a taxpayer also apply in determining adjusted current earnings. For example, the rules of part V of subchapter P (relating to original issue discount and similar matters) of the Code apply in determining the amount (and the timing) of any interest income included in adjusted current earnings under this section. In applying Code provisions, however, the adjustments of section 56(g) and this section are also taken into account. For example, in applying the capitalization provisions of section 263A, the amount of depreciation to be capitalized is based

Reg. § 1.56(g)-1(a)(3)

on the amount of depreciation allowed in computing adjusted current earnings.

(ii) *Example.* The following example illustrates the provisions of this paragraph (a)(5):

(A) Corporation N is a calendar year manufacturer of golf clubs. N places new manufacturing equipment in service in 1990. The regular tax depreciation allowable for this equipment is $80,000; the pre-adjustment alternative minimum taxable income depreciation is $60,000; and the adjusted current earnings depreciation is $40,000. All of the golf clubs N produces in 1990 are unsold and are in ending inventory.

(B) Pursuant to section 263A and § 1.263A-1(e)(3)(ii)(I), N must capitalize the depreciation allowed for the year for the new manufacturing equipment in the ending inventory of golf clubs. Thus, when N sells the golf clubs (or is deemed to have sold them under its normal method of accounting), the cost of goods sold attributable to the capitalized depreciation will be $80,000 in computing regular taxable income; $60,000 in computing pre-adjustment alternative minimum taxable income; and $40,000 in computing adjusted current earnings.

(6) *Definitions.* The following terms have the following meanings for purposes of this section.

(i) *Pre-adjustment alternative minimum taxable income.* Pre-adjustment alternative minimum taxable income is the alternative minimum taxable income of the taxpayer for the taxable year, determined under section 55(b)(2), but without the adjustment for adjusted current earnings under section 56(g) and this section, without the alternative tax net operating loss deduction under section 56(a)(4), and without the alternative tax energy preference deduction under section 56(h).

(ii) *Adjusted current earnings.* Adjusted current earnings is the pre-adjustment alternative minimum taxable income of the taxpayer for the taxable year, adjusted as provided in section 56(g) and this section. To the extent an amount is included (or deducted) in computing pre-adjustment alternative minimum taxable income for the taxable year (whether because an adjustment is made under section 56 or 58, because of a tax preference item under section 57, or because the item is reflected in taxable income), that amount is not again included (or deducted) in computing adjusted current earnings for the taxable year.

(iii) *Earnings and profits.* Earnings and profits means current earnings and profits within the meaning of section 316(a)(2), that is, earnings and profits for the taxable year computed as of the close of the taxable year of the corporation without diminution by reason of any distributions made during the taxable year.

(7) *Application to foreign corporations.* See paragraph (m) of this section for rules relating to the application of this section to foreign corporations.

(b) *Depreciation allowed.* The depreciation deduction allowed in computing adjusted current earnings is determined under the rules of this paragraph (b). Generally, the rules for computing the adjusted current earnings depreciation deduction differ depending on the taxable year in which the property is placed in service and the method used in computing the depreciation deduction for taxable income purposes. See § 1.168(i)-1(k) for an election to use general asset accounts.

(1) *Property placed in service after 1989.* The depreciation deduction for property placed in service in a taxable year beginning after December 31, 1989, is the amount determined by using the alternative depreciation system of section 168(g). This paragraph (b)(1) does not apply to property to which paragraph (b)(4) of this section applies (relating to certain property described in sections 168(f)(1) through (f)(4)).

(2) *Property subject to new ACRS*—(i) *In general.* This paragraph (b)(2) provides the rules for computing the depreciation deduction for property to which the amendments made by section 201 of the Tax Reform Act of 1986 (new ACRS) apply (generally property placed in service after December 31, 1986), and that is placed in service in a taxable year beginning before January 1, 1990. This paragraph (b)(2) does not apply to property described in paragraph (b)(4) of this section (relating to certain property described in sections 168(f)(1) through (f)(4)) or to property described in paragraph (b)(5)(i) of this section (relating to certain churning transactions described in section 168(f)(5)).

(ii) *Rules for computing the depreciation deduction.* The depreciation deduction for property described in this paragraph (b)(2) is the amount determined by using—

(A) The adjusted basis of the property as determined in computing alternative minimum taxable income as of the close of the last taxable year beginning before January 1, 1990,

(B) The straight-line method, and

(C) The recovery period that consists of the remainder of the recovery period applicable to the property under the alternative depreciation system of section 168(g). Thus, the recovery period begins on the first day of the first taxable year beginning after December 31, 1989, and ends on the last day of the recovery period that would have applied had the recovery period for the property originally been determined under section 168(g). In determining the recovery period that would have applied, the property is deemed placed in service on the date it was considered placed in service under the depreciation convention that would have applied to the property under section 168(d).

(iii) *Example.* The following example illustrates the provisions of this paragraph (b)(2).

Example. Corporation X, a calendar-year taxpayer, purchases and places in service on August 1, 1987, computer-based telephone central office switching equipment. This is the only item of depreciable property X places in service during 1987. Thus, the applicable convention under section 168(d) is the half-year convention. As of December 31, 1989, the adjusted basis of the property used in computing alternative minimum taxable income is $42,000. The recovery period that would have applied to the property under section 168(g)(2) is 9.5 years (from July 1, 1987 to December 31, 1996). Thus, the recovery period for computing adjusted current earnings under section 56(g)(4)(A)(ii) and this paragraph (b)(2) begins on January 1, 1990, and ends on December 31, 1996. X's 1990 depreciation deduction for computing adjusted current earnings is $6,000, determined under the straight-line method by dividing $42,000 (adjusted basis) by 7 (recovery period).

(3) *Property subject to original ACRS—*(i) *In general.* This paragraph (b)(3) provides the rules for computing the depreciation deduction for property to which section 168 as in effect on the day before the date of enactment of the Tax Reform Act of 1986 (original ACRS) applies and that is placed in service in a taxable year beginning before January 1, 1990 (generally property that was placed in service after December 31, 1980 and before January 1, 1987). In determining whether original ACRS applies to property, the fact that the unadjusted basis of the property is reduced or eliminated under section 168(d)(4)(A)(i) of original ACRS is not taken into account. This paragraph (b)(3) does not apply to property described in paragraph (b)(4) or (b)(5)(i) of this section (relating to certain section 168(f) property).

(ii) *Rules for computing the depreciation deduction.* The depreciation deduction for property described in this paragraph (b)(3) is the amount determined by using—

(A) The adjusted basis of the property as determined in computing taxable income as of the close of the last taxable year beginning before January 1, 1990,

(B) The straight-line method, and

(C) The recovery period that consists of the remainder of the recovery period applicable to

the property under the alternative depreciation system of section 168(g). Thus, the recovery period begins on the first day of the first taxable year beginning after December 31, 1989, and ends on the last day of the recovery period that would have applied had the recovery period for the property originally been determined under section 168(g)(2). In determining the recovery period that would have applied, the property is deemed placed in service on the date it was considered placed in service under the depreciation convention that would have applied to the property under section 168(d) (without regard to section 168(d)(3)).

(iii) *Example.* The following example illustrates the provisions of this paragraph (b)(3).

Example. Corporation Y, a calendar-year taxpayer, purchases and places in service on December 1, 1986, computer-based telephone central office switching equipment. The depreciation convention that would have applied to this property under section 168(d) (without regard to section 168(d)(3)) is the half-year convention. As of December 31, 1989, the adjusted basis of the property used in computing taxable income is $21,000. The recovery period for the property under section 168(g)(2) is 9.5 years (from July 1, 1986 to December 31, 1995). Thus, the recovery period for computing adjusted current earnings under section 56(g)(4)(A)(iii) and this paragraph (b)(3) begins on January 1, 1990, and ends on December 31, 1995. Y's 1990 depreciation deduction for computing adjusted current earnings is $3,500, determined under the straight-line method by dividing $21,000 (adjusted basis) by 6 (recovery period).

(4) *Special rule for certain section 168(f) property.* The depreciation or amortization deduction for property described in section 168(f)(1) through (4) is determined in the same manner as used in computing taxable income, without regard to when the property is placed in service.

(5) *Certain property not subject to ACRS.* The depreciation or amortization deduction for property not described in paragraphs (b)(1) through (4) of this section is determined in the same manner as used in computing taxable income. Thus, this paragraph (b)(5) applies to—

(i) Property placed in service after December 31, 1980, in a taxable year beginning before January 1, 1990, and that is excluded from the application of original ACRS or new ACRS by section 168(e)(4) of original ACRS or section 168(f)(5)(A)(i) of new ACRS, and

(ii) Property placed in service before January 1, 1981.

Reg. § 1.56(g)-1(b)(3)

(c) *Inclusion in adjusted current earnings of items included in earnings and profits*—(1) *In general.* Except as otherwise provided in paragraph (c)(4) of this section, adjusted current earnings includes all income items that are permanently excluded from (*i.e.,* not taken into account in determining) pre-adjustment alternative minimum taxable income but that are taken into account in determining earnings and profits. An income item is considered taken into account in determining pre-adjustment alternative minimum taxable income without regard to the timing of its inclusion. Thus, this paragraph (c)(1) does not apply to any income item that is, has been, or will be included in pre-adjustment alternative minimum taxable income. For example, a taxpayer eligible to use the completed contract method of accounting for long-term construction contracts does not take income (or expenses) into account in determining pre-adjustment alternative minimum taxable income for taxable years before the taxable year the contract is completed. The taxpayer is required under section 312(n)(6) to include income (and expenses) in earnings and profits throughout the term of the contract under the percentage of completion method. This paragraph (c)(1) does not require the income on the contract to be included in adjusted current earnings, however, because the income will be taken into account in the taxable year the contract is completed and therefore is considered to be taken into account in determining pre-adjustment alternative minimum taxable income.

(2) *Certain amounts not taken into account in determining whether an item is permanently excluded.* The fact that proceeds from an income item may eventually be reflected in pre-adjustment alternative minimum taxable income of another taxpayer on the liquidation or disposal of a business, or similar circumstances, is not taken into account in determining whether the item is permanently excluded from pre-adjustment alternative minimum taxable income. Thus, for example, a corporation's adjusted current earnings include interest excluded from pre-adjustment alternative minimum taxable income under section 103 even though the interest might eventually be reflected in the pre-adjustment alternative minimum taxable income of a corporate shareholder as gain on the liquidation of the corporation.

(3) *Allowance of offsetting deductions.* In determining adjusted current earnings under this paragraph (c), a deduction is allowed for all items that relate to income required to be included in adjusted current earnings under this paragraph (c) and that would be deductible in computing pre-adjustment alternative minimum taxable income if the income items to which the items of deduction relate were included in pre-adjustment alternative minimum taxable income for any taxable year. For example, deductions disallowed under section 265(a)(2) for the costs of carrying tax-exempt obligations, the interest on which is excluded from pre-adjustment alternative minimum taxable income under section 103 but is included in adjusted current earnings under this paragraph (c), are generally allowed as deductions in computing adjusted current earnings. Amounts deductible under this paragraph (c)(3) are taken into account using the taxpayer's method of accounting and are subject to any provisions or limitations of the Code that would have applied if the amounts had been deductible in determining pre-adjustment alternative minimum taxable income. For example, section 267(a)(2) may affect the timing of a deduction otherwise disallowed under section 265(a)(2).

(4) *Special rules.* Adjusted current earnings does not include the following amounts.

(i) *Income from the discharge of indebtedness.* Amounts that are excluded from gross income under section 108 of the Internal Revenue Code of 1986 or any corresponding provision of prior law (including the Bankruptcy Tax Act of 1980, case law, income tax regulations and administrative pronouncements).

(ii) *Federal income tax refunds.* Refunds of federal income taxes.

(iii) *Income earned on behalf of states and municipalities.* Amounts that are excluded from gross income under section 115.

(5) *Treatment of life insurance contracts*—(i) *In general.* This paragraph (c)(5) addresses the treatment of life insurance contracts in determining adjusted current earnings. These rules apply to life insurance contracts as defined in section 7702. Generally, death benefits under a life insurance contract are included in adjusted current earnings, and all other distributions (including surrenders) are taxed in accordance with the principles of section 72(e), taking into account the taxpayer's basis in the contract for purposes of adjusted current earnings. If the adjusted basis in the contract for purposes of adjusted current earnings exceeds the amount of death benefits received or the amount received when the contract is surrendered (increased by the amount of any outstanding policy loan), the resulting loss is allowed as a deduction under paragraph (c)(3) of this section in computing adjusted current earnings for the taxable year. In addition, undistributed income on the contract is included in adjusted current earnings as provided in paragraph (c)(5)(ii) of this section. Paragraph (c)(5)(vi)(A) of this section provides special rules

for term insurance that has no net surrender value.

(ii) *Inclusion of inside buildup.* Income on a life insurance contract with respect to a taxable year (or any shorter period either ending or beginning with the date of a distribution from the contract) is included in adjusted current earnings for the taxable year. Thus, income on the contract is calculated from the beginning of a taxable year to the date of any distribution, from immediately after any distribution to the date of the next distribution, and from the last distribution during the taxable year through the end of the taxable year. Income on a life insurance contract is not included in adjusted current earnings for any taxable year in which the insured dies or the contract is completely surrendered for its entire net surrender value. Solely for purposes of computing adjusted current earnings, the taxpayer's adjusted basis in the contract (as determined under section 72(e)(6)) is increased to reflect any positive income on the contract included in adjusted current earnings under this paragraph (c)(5)(ii). The manner in which the income on the contract is determined for adjusted current earnings purposes is prescribed in paragraph (c)(5)(iii) of this section. If the income on the contract determined under paragraph (c)(5)(iii) of this section is a negative amount, income on the contract is not included in adjusted current earnings and no deduction from adjusted current earnings is allowed for the negative amount.

(iii) *Calculation of income on the contract.* For purposes of determining adjusted current earnings, the income on a life insurance contract for any period, including a taxable year, is the excess, if any, of—

(A) The sum of the contract's net surrender value (as defined in section 7702(f)(2)(B)) at the end of the period, and any distributions under the contract during the period that, in accordance with the principles of section 72(e), are not taxed because they represent recoveries of the taxpayer's basis in the contract for adjusted current earnings, over

(B) The sum of the contract's net surrender value at the end of the preceding period, and any premiums paid under the contract during the period.

(iv) *Treatment of distributions under the life insurance contract.* Any distribution under a life insurance contract (whether a partial withdrawal or an amount received on complete surrender of the contract) is included in adjusted current earnings in accordance with the principles of section 72(e), taking into account the taxpayer's basis in the contract for purposes of computing adjusted current earnings. The taxpayer's basis in the contract is equal to the basis at the end of the immediately preceding period, plus any premiums paid before the distribution. The taxpayer's basis in the contract for purposes of adjusted current earnings is reduced, in accordance with the principles of section 72(e), to the extent that the distribution is not included in adjusted current earnings because it represents a recovery of that basis.

(v) *Treatment of death benefits.* The excess of the contractual death benefit of a life insurance contract over the taxpayer's adjusted basis in the contract for purposes of computing adjusted current earnings at the time of the insured's death is included in adjusted current earnings as provided by paragraph (c)(6)(i) of this section. The amount of the death benefit that is taken into account for adjusted current earnings includes the amount of any outstanding policy loan treated as forgiven or discharged by the insurance company upon the death of the insured.

(vi) *Other rules—*(A) *Term life insurance contracts without net surrender values.* Except as provided in this paragraph (c)(5)(vi), the requirements of paragraph (c)(5) of this section do not apply to term life insurance contracts that provide no net surrender value. Adjusted current earnings are reduced by any premiums paid under such a contract that are allocable to the taxable year. Any premiums paid that are not allocable to the taxable year must be included in the basis of the contract. The death benefit under such a term insurance contract is included in adjusted current earnings as provided by paragraph (c)(5)(v) of this section.

(B) *Life insurance contracts involving divided ownership.* If the ownership of a life insurance contract is divided between different persons (for example, a split-dollar arrangement), the requirements of paragraph (c)(5) of this section apply to the separate ownership interests as though each interest were a separate contract.

(vii) *Examples.* The following examples illustrate the provisions of this paragraph (c)(5).

Example 1. (i) On January 1, 1987, corporation X, a calendar-year taxpayer, purchased a flexible premium life insurance contract with a death benefit of $100,000 and planned annual gross premiums of $2,200 payable on January 1 of each year. The net surrender value of the contract at the end of 1987 and subsequent years, together with the cumulative premiums for the contract at the end of each year, are set forth in the following table:

Year	Cumulative Premiums Paid	Year-End Net Surrender Value
1987	$ 2,200	$ 2,420
1988	4,400	5,082
1989	6,600	8,010
1990	8,800	11,231
1991	11,000	14,774

(ii) Under paragraph (c)(5)(ii) of this section, X must include $1,021 in adjusted current earnings for 1990. The inclusion is computed by subtracting from the net surrender value of the contract at the end of the taxable year ($11,231) the sum of the net surrender value of the contract at the end of the preceding taxable year ($8,010) plus the premiums paid during the taxable year ($2,200). See paragraph (c)(5)(iii) of this section. For purposes of determining adjusted current earnings, X's adjusted basis in the contract would be increased at the end of 1990 from $8,800 to $9,821 to reflect the $1,021 inclusion. See paragraph (c)(5)(ii) of this section. The income under the contract attributable to taxable years prior to 1990 does not increase X's adjusted basis in the contract.

(iii) For 1991, the income on the contract included in adjusted current earnings is determined in the same manner as the preceding year, and there is a corresponding increase in X's adjusted basis in the contract. Thus, for 1991, the income on the contract is $1,343, which is determined by subtracting from the net surrender value of the contract at the end of the taxable year ($14,774) the sum of the net surrender value at the end of the preceding taxable year ($11,231) plus the premiums paid during the taxable year ($2,200). At the end of 1991, X's adjusted basis in the contract for adjusted current earnings is $13,364, which reflects the basis of the contract at the beginning of 1991, increased by the premium paid during the year ($2,200) and the income on the contract that has been included in adjusted current earnings for the taxable year ($1,343).

Example 2. The facts are the same as in example 1, except that, after the payment of the premium for 1991, the insured dies and X receives the $100,000 death benefit under the contract. Under paragraph (c)(5)(ii) of this section, no amount is included in adjusted current earnings for income on the contract for the taxable year in which the insured dies. Instead, under paragraph (c)(5)(v) of this section, X must include in adjusted current earnings for 1991 the excess of the death benefit ($100,000) over the adjusted basis in the contract for purposes of computing adjusted current earnings at the time of the insured's death ($12,021), which equals X's adjusted basis in the contract at the end of 1990 ($9,821), increased by X's premium payment for 1991 ($2,200).

Example 3. (i) The facts are the same as in example 1, except that in addition to making the $2,200 planned premium payment for 1992, X receives a $16,200 distribution under the contract on February 1, 1992, leaving a net surrender value of $915 immediately following the distribution. On March 1, 1992, X pays an additional premium of $5,000 under the contract. The net surrender value of the contract at the end of 1992 is $6,417.

(ii) Treatment of the distribution. Under paragraph (c)(5)(iv) of this section, the $16,200 distribution in 1992 is included in adjusted current earnings as an amount taxable in accordance with the principles of section 72(e) to the extent that the distribution ($16,200) exceeds X's adjusted basis for adjusted current earnings, as determined at the end of the immediately preceding period, and including premiums paid through the period ending on the date of the distribution ($15,564). Thus, X must include $636 in adjusted current earnings for 1992 as an amount taxable in accordance with the principles of section 72(e).

(iii) Determination of the income on the contract. Under paragraph (c)(5)(iii) of this section, for 1992, the income on the contract must be separately determined for the period beginning with the first day of the taxable year to the date of the distribution and for the period beginning immediately after the distribution to the end of the taxable year, using the contract's net surrender values at the beginning and end of each of these periods. The income on the contract for the period beginning on January 1, 1992 and ending on February 1, 1992 (the date of the distribution) is equal to the excess, if any, of (A) the sum of the net surrender value at the end of the period ($915) and the amount of the distribution that is allocable to X's basis in the contract for adjusted current earnings ($15,564), over (B) the sum of the net surrender value at the end of the preceding taxable year ($14,774) plus any premiums paid on the contract during the period ($2,200). Because the net result of this computation is a negative amount (($915 + $15,564) − ($14,774 + $2,200) = − $495), no income on the contract for the period ending with the date of the distribution is included in adjusted current earnings for 1992.

(iv) Under paragraph (c)(5)(ii), X must also determine the income on the contract for the period beginning immediately after the distribution through the end of the taxable year. The income on the contract for this period is $502, which is equal to the excess of the net surrender value at the end of the taxable year ($6,417) over the sum of the net surrender value at the end of

Reg. § 1.56(g)-1(c)(5)

the preceding period ($915), plus any premiums paid during the period ($5,000). At the end of 1992, X's adjusted basis in the contract for adjusted current earnings is $5,502, determined by adding the income on the contract ($502) and the premiums paid during the period ($5,000) to the basis at the end of the preceding period ($0).

(v) Thus, X must include a total of $1,138 ($636 + 502) in adjusted current earnings for 1992. This inclusion reflects both the undistributed income on the contract for the taxable year plus the amount of income from distributions under the contract that is taxed in accordance with the principles of section 72(e) using X's adjusted basis in the contract for adjusted current earnings.

(6) *Partial list of income items excluded from gross income but included in earnings and profits.* The following is a partial list of items that are permanently excluded from pre-adjustment alternative minimum taxable income but that are included in earnings and profits, and are therefore included in adjusted current earnings under this paragraph (c).

(i) Proceeds of life insurance contracts that are excluded under section 101, to the extent provided in paragraph (c)(5)(v) or (c)(5)(vi) of this section.

(ii) Interest that is excluded under section 103.

(iii) Amounts received as compensation for injuries or sickness that are excluded under section 104.

(iv) Income taxes of a lessor of property that are paid by a lessee and are excluded under section 110.

(v) Income attributable to the recovery of an item deducted in computing earnings and profits in a prior year that is excluded under section 111.

(vi) Amounts received as proceeds from sports programs that are excluded under section 114.

(vii) Cost-sharing payments that are excluded under section 126, to the extent section 126(e) does not apply.

(viii) Interest on loans used to acquire employer securities that is excluded under section 133.

(ix) Financial assistance that is excluded under section 597.

(x) Amounts that are excluded from pre-adjustment alternative minimum taxable income as a result of an election under section 831(b) (allowing certain insurance companies to compute their pre-adjustment alternative minimum taxable income using only their investment income).

Items described in paragraph (c)(1) of this section must be included in earnings and profits (and therefore in adjusted current earnings) even if they are not identified in this paragraph (c)(6). The Commissioner may identify additional items described in paragraph (c)(1) in other published guidance.

(7) *Partial list of items excluded from both pre-adjustment alternative minimum taxable income and adjusted current earnings.* The following is a partial list of items that are excluded from both pre-adjustment alternative minimum taxable income and adjusted current earnings, and for which no adjustment is allowed under this section.

(i) The value of improvements made by a lessee to a lessor's property that is excluded from the lessor's income under section 109.

(ii) Contributions to the capital of a corporation by a non-shareholder that are excluded from the corporation's income under section 118.

The Commissioner may identify additional items described in this paragraph (c)(7) in other published guidance.

(d) *Disallowance of items not deductible in computing earnings and profits—*(1) *In general.* Except as otherwise provided in this paragraph (d), no deduction is allowed in computing adjusted current earnings for any items that are not taken into account in determining earnings and profits for any taxable year, even if the items are taken into account in determining pre-adjustment alternative minimum taxable income. These items therefore increase adjusted current earnings to the extent they are deducted in computing pre-adjustment alternative minimum taxable income. An item of deduction is considered taken into account without regard to the timing of its deductibility in computing earnings and profits. Thus, to the extent an item is, has been, or will be deducted for purposes of determining earnings and profits, it does not increase adjusted current earnings in the taxable year in which it is deducted for purposes of determining pre-adjustment alternative minimum taxable income. For example, a deduction allowed (in determining pre-adjustment alternative minimum taxable income) under section 196 for unused research credits allowable under section 41 is taken into account in computing earnings and profits because the costs that gave rise to the credit were deductible in computing earnings and profits when incurred. Therefore, the deduction does not increase adjusted current earnings. As a further example, payments by a United States parent corporation with respect to employees of certain foreign subsidiaries, which are de-

Reg. § 1.56(g)-1(c)(6)

ductible under section 176, are considered contributions to the capital of the foreign subsidiary for purposes of computing earnings and profits. Although the payments are not deductible in computing the earnings and profits of the United States parent corporation in the year incurred, the payments do increase the parent's basis in its stock in the foreign subsidiary. This basis increase will reduce any gain the parent may later realize for purposes of computing earnings and profits on the disposition of the stock of the foreign subsidiary. Therefore, the amount of the payment by the parent is considered taken into account in computing the earnings and profits of the parent and does not increase adjusted current earnings. Thus, only deduction items that are never taken into account in computing earnings and profits are disallowed in computing adjusted current earnings under this paragraph (d).

(2) *Deductions for certain dividends received*—(i) *Certain amounts deducted under sections 243 and 245.* Paragraph (d)(1) of this section does not apply to, and adjusted current earnings therefore are not increased by, amounts deducted under sections 243 and 245 that qualify as 100-percent deductible dividends under sections 243(a), 245(b) or 245(c), or to any dividend received from a 20-percent owned corporation (as defined in section 243(c)(2)), to the extent that the dividend giving rise to the deductions is attributable to earnings of the paying corporation that are subject to federal income tax. Earnings are considered subject to federal income tax if the earnings are included on the federal income tax return (that is filed or, if not, that should be filed) of an entity subject to United States taxation, even if there is no resulting United States tax liability (e.g., because of net operating losses or tax credits, other than the credit provided for in section 936).

(ii) *Special rules*—(A) *Dividends received from a foreign sales corporation.* The portion of a dividend received from a foreign sales corporation (FSC) that is classified as a 100-percent deductible dividend attributable to earnings of the FSC subject to federal income tax is that portion of the dividend distributed out of earnings and profits of the FSC attributable to non-exempt foreign trade income determined under either of the administrative pricing methods of section 925(a)(1) or (2), and to non-exempt foreign trade income determined under section 925(a)(3) that is effectively connected with the conduct of a trade or business in the United States (determined without regard to section 921). If the FSC is a 20-percent owned corporation (as defined in section 243(c)(2)), an additional portion of that dividend is classified as being attributable to earnings of the FSC subject to federal income tax to the extent that the divi-

dend is distributed out of earnings and profits of the FSC attributable to effectively connected income (as defined in section 245(c)(4)(B)). A FSC is defined in section 922 and, for purposes of this paragraph, includes a small FSC and a former FSC. The ordering rules for distributions from a FSC set forth in § 1.926(a)-1T(b)(1) apply to determine the classification of earnings and profits out of which a distribution has been made.

(B) *Dividends received from a section 936 corporation.* In the case of a dividend received from a corporation eligible for the credit provided by section 936, only that part of the dividend that is attributable to income that is not eligible for the credit is attributable to earnings of the paying corporation that are subject to federal income tax. Dividends are deemed to be distributed first out of earnings and profits for the current taxable year of the section 936 corporation, to the extent thereof, and then out of the most recently accumulated earnings and profits, under the principles of section 316. With respect to a distribution of less than all of the earnings and profits for the current or any prior taxable year, the amount of the distribution attributable to income not eligible for the section 936 credit is determined on a pro rata basis. For example, assume that a section 936 corporation earns $100 of taxable income in its current taxable year, $10 of which is not eligible for the credit under section 936. If the section 936 corporation makes a distribution of $50 during that year, $5 of that distribution ($10 of income not eligible for the section 936 credit divided by $100 of income, times $50 distributed) is deemed to be attributable to earnings of the paying corporation that are subject to federal income tax.

(iii) *Special rule for certain dividends received by certain cooperatives.* Paragraph (d)(1) of this section does not apply to, and adjusted current earnings do not include, any dividend received by any organization to which part I of subchapter T of the Code applies and that is engaged in the marketing of agricultural or horticultural products, if the dividend is paid by a FSC and is allowable as a deduction under section 245(c).

(3) *Partial list of items not deductible in computing earnings and profits.* The following is a partial list of items that are not taken into account in computing earnings and profits and thus are not deductible in computing adjusted current earnings.

(i) Unrecovered losses attributable to certain damages that are deductible under section 186, to the extent those damages were previously deducted in computing earnings and profits.

(ii) The deduction for small life insurance companies allowed under section 806.

(iii) Dividends deductible under the following sections of the Code:

(A) Dividends received by corporations that are deductible under section 243, to the extent paragraph (d)(2)(i) of this section does not apply.

(B) Dividends received on certain preferred stock that are deductible under section 244.

(C) Dividends received from certain foreign corporations that are deductible under section 245, to the extent neither paragraph (d)(2)(i) nor (d)(2)(iii) of this section applies.

(D) Dividends paid on certain preferred stock of public utilities that are deductible under section 247.

(E) Dividends paid to an employee stock ownership plan that are deductible under section 404(k).

(F) Non-patronage dividends that are paid and deductible under section 1382(c)(1).

Items described in paragraph (d)(1) of this section are not taken into account in computing earnings and profits (and thus are not deductible in computing adjusted current earnings) even if they are not identified in this paragraph (d)(3). The Commissioner may identify additional items described in paragraph (d)(1) of this section in other published guidance.

(4) *Partial list of items deductible for purposes of computing both pre-adjustment alternative minimum taxable income and adjusted current earnings.* The following is a partial list of items that are deductible for purposes of computing both pre-adjustment alternative minimum taxable income and adjusted current earnings, and for which no adjustment is allowed under this section.

(i) Payments by a United States corporation with respect to employees of certain foreign corporations that are deductible under section 176.

(ii) Dividends paid on deposits by thrift institutions that are deductible under section 591.

(iii) Life insurance policyholder dividends that are deductible under section 808.

(iv) Dividends paid by cooperatives that are deductible under sections 1382(b) or 1382(c)(2) and that are not paid with respect to stock.

The Commissioner may identify additional items described in this paragraph (d)(4) in other published guidance.

(e) *Treatment of income items included, and deduction items not allowed, in computing pre-*

adjustment alternative minimum taxable income. Adjusted current earnings includes any income item that is included in pre-adjustment alternative minimum taxable income, even if that income item is not included in earnings and profits for the taxable year. Except as specifically provided in paragraph (c)(3) or (c)(5) of this section, no deduction is allowed for an item in computing adjusted current earnings if the item is not deductible in computing pre-adjustment alternative minimum taxable income for the taxable year, even if the item is deductible in computing earnings and profits for the year. Thus, for example, capital losses in excess of capital gains for the taxable year are not deductible in computing adjusted current earnings for the taxable year.

(f) *Certain other earnings and profits adjustments*—(1) *Intangible drilling costs.* For purposes of computing adjusted current earnings, the amount allowable as a deduction for intangible drilling costs (as defined in section 263(c)) for amounts paid or incurred in taxable years beginning after December 31, 1989, is determined as provided in section 312(n)(2)(A). See section 56(h) for an additional adjustment to alternative minimum taxable income based on energy preferences for taxable years beginning after 1990.

(2) *Certain amortization provisions do not apply.* For purposes of computing adjusted current earnings, sections 173 (relating to circulation expenditures) and 248 (relating to organizational expenditures) do not apply to amounts paid or incurred in taxable years beginning after December 31, 1989. If an election is made under section 59(e) to amortize circulation expenditures described in section 173 over a three-year period, the expenditures to which the election applies are deducted ratably over the three-year period for purposes of computing taxable income, pre-adjustment alternative minimum taxable income, and adjusted current earnings.

(3) *LIFO recapture adjustment*—(i) *In general.* Adjusted current earnings are generally increased or decreased by the increase or decrease in the taxpayer's LIFO recapture amount (as defined in paragraph (f)(3)(iii)(A) of this section) as of the close of each taxable year.

(ii) *Beginning LIFO and FIFO inventory.* For purposes of computing the increase or decrease in the LIFO recapture amount, the beginning LIFO and FIFO inventory amounts for the first taxable year beginning after December 31, 1989, are—

(A) The ending LIFO inventory amount used in computing pre-adjustment alternative minimum taxable income for the last year beginning before January 1, 1990; and

Reg. § 1.56(g)-1(d)(4)

(B) The ending FIFO inventory amount for the last year beginning before January 1, 1990, computed with the adjustments described in section 56 (other than the adjustment described in section 56(g)) and section 58, the items of tax preference described in section 57 and using the methods used in computing pre-adjustment alternative minimum taxable income.

(iii) Definitions—(A) *LIFO recapture amount*—(*1*) *Definition.* The taxpayer's LIFO recapture amount is the excess, if any, of—

(*i*) the inventory amount of its assets under the FIFO method, computed using the rules of this section; over

(*ii*) the inventory amount of its assets under the LIFO method, computed using the rules of this section.

(*2*) *Assets included.* Only the assets for which the taxpayer uses the LIFO method to compute pre-adjustment alternative minimum taxable income are taken into account in determining the LIFO recapture amount.

(B) *FIFO Method.* For purposes of this paragraph, the FIFO method is the first in, first out method described in section 471, determined by using—

(*1*) The retail method if that is the method the taxpayer uses in computing pre-adjustment alternative minimum taxable income; or

(*2*) The lower of cost or market method for all other taxpayers.

(C) *LIFO method.* The LIFO method is the last in, first out method authorized by section 472.

(D) *Inventory amounts.* Except as otherwise provided, inventory amounts are computed using the methods used in computing pre-adjustment alternative minimum taxable income. To the extent inventory is treated as produced or acquired during taxable years beginning after December 31, 1989, the inventory amount is determined with the adjustments described in sections 56 and 58 and the items of tax preference described in section 57. Thus, for example, the amount of depreciation to be capitalized under section 263A with respect to inventory produced in taxable years beginning after December 31, 1989, is based on the depreciation allowed under the rules of paragraph (b) of this section. See paragraph (a)(5) of this section.

(iv) *Exchanges under sections 351 and 721.* For purposes of this section, any decrease in a transferor's LIFO recapture amount that occurs as a result of a transfer of inventories in an exchange to which section 351 or section 721 applies cannot be used to decrease the adjusted current earnings of the transferor. A decrease that is disallowed under the preceding sentence is instead carried over to reduce any LIFO recapture adjustment that the transferee (or its corporate partners, if section 721 applies) would otherwise make (in the absence of this paragraph (f)(3)(iv)) solely by reason of its carryover basis in inventories received in the section 351 or section 721 exchange. Nothing in this paragraph (f)(3)(iv), however, alters the computation of the LIFO recapture amount of the transferor or transferee as of the close of any taxable year.

(v) *Examples.* The following examples illustrate the provisions of this paragraph (f)(3).

Example 1. M Corporation, a calendar-year taxpayer, uses the LIFO method of accounting for its inventory for purposes of computing pre-adjustment alternative minimum taxable income. M's ending LIFO inventory for all of its pools for purposes of computing pre-adjustment alternative minimum taxable income on December 31, 1989, is $300. M computes a $500 FIFO inventory amount on that date, after applying the provisions of section 263A along with the adjustments and preferences required in computing pre-adjustment alternative minimum taxable income. M's FIFO and LIFO ending inventory amounts at the close of its taxable years, its LIFO reserves, and its adjustment under this paragraph (f)(3), are as follows:

	1989	1990	1991	1992
Ending inventory:				
A. FIFO	$ 500 [1]	$ 360	$ 560	$ 600
B. LIFO	300 [2]	180	320	440
LIFO recapture amount:				
A − B	$ 200	$ 180	$ 240	$ 160
Change in LIFO recapture amount and adjustment under paragraph (f)(3)	—	$ (20)	$ 60	$ (80)

[1] Beginning FIFO inventory amount under paragraph (f)(3)(ii).
[2] Beginning LIFO inventory amount under paragraph (f)(3)(ii).

Reg. § 1.56(g)-1(f)(3)

Example 2. (A) X Corporation, a calendar-year taxpayer, uses the LIFO method for purposes of computing pre-adjustment alternative minimum taxable income. X's LIFO recapture amount is $300 as of December 31, 1992, and is $200 as of December 31, 1993. Immediately prior to calculating its LIFO recapture amount as of December 31, 1993, X transfers inventory with an adjusted current earnings (ACE) basis of $500 to Y Corporation in an exchange to which section 351 applies. X determines that the $100 decrease in its LIFO recapture amount occurred as a result of its transfer of inventories to Y in the section 351 exchange. Thus, under paragraph (f)(3)(iv) of this section, X cannot decrease its adjusted current earnings by that amount. In computing its 1994 LIFO recapture adjustment, X will use $200 as its LIFO recapture amount as of December 31, 1993, even though it was not entitled to reduce adjusted current earnings by the $100 decrease in its LIFO recapture amount in 1993.

(B) For purposes of computing its ACE, Y takes a $500 carryover basis in the inventories received from X. If Y, a newly-formed calendar-year taxpayer, engages in no other inventory transactions in 1993 and adopts the LIFO inventory method on its 1993 tax return, it will have a LIFO recapture amount of $0 as of December 31, 1993 (because its FIFO inventory amount and its LIFO inventory amount are both $500). Assume that at December 31, 1994, Y has a LIFO recapture amount of $200 ($1,000 FIFO inventory amount—$800 LIFO inventory amount). Under paragraph (f)(3)(i) of this section, Y computes a LIFO recapture adjustment for 1994 of $200 ($200 − $0). If any portion of Y's $200 LIFO recapture adjustment occurs solely by reason of its carryover basis in the inventories it received from X, Y reduces its $200 LIFO recapture adjustment by that portion under paragraph (f)(3)(iv). In any event, however, Y will use its $200 LIFO recapture amount as of December 31, 1994, in computing its 1995 LIFO recapture adjustment.

(vi) *Effective date.* Paragraph (f)(3) is effective for taxable years beginning after December 18, 1992. A taxpayer may choose to apply this paragraph, however, to all taxable years beginning after December 31, 1989.

(4) *Installment sales*—(i) *In general.* Adjusted current earnings are computed without regard to the installment method, except as provided in this paragraph (f)(4).

(ii) *Exception for prior dispositions.* Paragraph (f)(4)(i) of this section does not apply to any disposition in a taxable year beginning before January 1, 1990, that is taken into account under the installment method for purposes of computing

pre-adjustment alternative minimum taxable income. Thus, for any disposition in a taxable year beginning before January 1, 1990, the installment method applies in computing adjusted current earnings for taxable years beginning after December 31, 1989, to the same extent it applies in determining pre-adjustment alternative minimum taxable income for the taxable year.

(iii) *Special rules for obligations to which section 453A applies*—(A) *In general.* The following special rules apply to any installment sale occurring in a taxable year beginning after December 31, 1989, that results in an installment obligation to which section 453A(a)(1) applies and with respect to which pre-adjustment alternative minimum taxable income is determined under the installment method. As explained in paragraph (f)(4)(iii)(B) of this section, for purposes of computing adjusted current earnings, a portion of the contract price is eligible for the installment method, and the remainder of the contract price is not eligible for the installment method. Payments under the obligation are allocated pro-rata between the two accounting methods.

(B) *Limitation on application of installment method.* Only a portion of the contract price of an installment sale described in paragraph (f)(4)(iii)(A) of this section is eligible to be accounted for under the installment method for purposes of computing adjusted current earnings. The portion eligible for the installment method is equal to the total contract price of the sale multiplied by the applicable percentage (as determined under section 453A(c)(4)) for the taxable year of the sale. The remainder of the contract price is not eligible to be accounted for under the installment method for purposes of computing adjusted current earnings. The gross profit ratio is determined without regard to this bifurcated treatment of the sale.

(C) *Treatment of the ineligible portion.* The gain on the sale that is taken into account in the taxable year of the sale for purposes of computing adjusted current earnings is equal to the gross profit ratio multiplied by the entire portion of the contract price that is ineligible for the installment method.

(D) *Treatment of the eligible portion.* For purposes of calculating adjusted current earnings, the amount of gain recognized in a taxable year on the portion of the contract price that is eligible for the installment method is equal to—

(*1*) The amount of payments received during the taxable year, multiplied by

(*2*) The applicable percentage for the taxable year of the sale, multiplied by

(*3*) The gross profit ratio.

Reg. § 1.56(g)-1(f)(4)

(E) *Coordination with the pledge rule.* For purposes of determining the amount of payments received during the taxable year under paragraph (f)(4)(iii)(D), the rules of section 453A(d) (relating to the treatment of certain pledge proceeds as payments) apply. This includes the rules under section 453A(d)(3) that relate to treating later payments as receipts of amounts on which tax has already been paid.

(F) *Example.* The following example illustrates the provisions of this paragraph (f)(4)(iii):

(*1*) On January 1, 1990, corporation A, a calendar-year taxpayer, sells a building with an adjusted basis for purposes of computing adjusted current earnings of $10 million, for $5 million and an installment obligation bearing adequate stated interest with a principal amount of $20 million. The installment obligation calls for 4 annual payments of $5 million on January 1 of 1991, 1992, 1993 and 1994. A does not elect out of the installment method, and disposes of no other property under the installment method during 1990. No gain with respect to the sale is recaptured pursuant to section 1250.

(*2*) The gross profit percentage for purposes of computing adjusted current earnings on the sale is 60 percent, computed as follows: gross profit of $15 million ($25 million contract price less $10 million adjusted basis) divided by $25 million contract price. The applicable percentage on the sale is 75 percent, computed as follows: $15 million ($20 million of installment obligations arising during and outstanding at the end of 1990 less $5 million) divided by $20 million of installment obligations arising during and outstanding at the end of 1990. See section 453A(c)(4). The portion of the contract price eligible for accounting under the installment method for purposes of computing adjusted current earnings is $18.75 million, or $25 million total contract price times applicable percentage of 75 percent. The portion of the contract price ineligible for the installment method is $6.25 million, or $25 million less $18.75 million.

(*3*) In computing adjusted current earnings for 1990, A must include $3.75 million of the gain on the sale. This amount is equal to the portion of the contract price that is ineligible for the installment method times the gross profit ratio, or $6.25 million times 60 percent. A must also include $2.25 million of gain from the $5 million payment received in 1990. This amount is computed as follows: the eligible portion of the payment, $3.75 million ($5 million payment times the applicable percentage of 75 percent), times the gross profit ratio of 60 percent. Thus, the total amount of gain from the sale that A must include

in adjusted current earnings for 1990 is $6 million ($3.75 million of gain from the portion of the contract price that is not eligible for the installment method, plus $2.25 million of gain from the 1990 payment).

(*4*) A does not pledge or otherwise accelerate payments on the note in any other taxable year. In computing adjusted current earnings for 1991, 1992, 1993 and 1994, A therefore includes $2.25 million of gain on the installment sale, computed as follows: $5 million payment times the applicable percentage of 75 percent, times the gross profit ratio of 60 percent.

(g) *Disallowance of loss on exchange of debt pools.* [RESERVED]

(h) *Policy acquisition expenses of life insurance companies*—(1) *In general.* This paragraph (h) addresses the treatment of policy acquisition expenses of life insurance companies in determining adjusted current earnings. Policy acquisition expenses are those expenses that, under generally accepted accounting principles in effect at the time the expenses are incurred, are considered to vary with and to be primarily related to the acquisition of new and renewal insurance policies. Generally, these acquisition expenses must be capitalized and amortized for purposes of adjusted current earnings over the reasonably estimated life of the acquired policy, using a method that provides a reasonable allowance for amortization. This method of amortization is treated as if it applied to all taxable years in determining the amount of policy acquisition expenses deducted for adjusted current earnings. The rules in this paragraph (h) apply to any life insurance company, as defined in section 816(a).

(2) *Reasonably estimated life.* The reasonably estimated life of an acquired policy is determined based on the facts with respect to each policy (such as the age, sex and health of the insured), and the company's experience (such as mortality, lapse rate and renewals) with similar policies. A company may treat as the reasonably estimated life of an acquired policy the period for amortizing expenses of the acquired policy that would be required by the Financial Accounting Standards Board (FASB) at the time the acquisition expenses are incurred. If the FASB has not established such a period, the period for amortizing acquisition expense of an acquired policy under guidelines issued by the American Institute of Certified Public Accountants in effect at the time the acquisition expenses are incurred may be treated as the reasonably estimated life of the acquired policy.

(3) *Reasonable allowance for amortization.* For purposes of determining a reasonable allowance for amortization, a company may use a

Reg. § 1.56(g)-1(h)(3)

method that amortizes acquisition expenses in the same proportion that gross premiums and gross investment income for the taxable year bear to total anticipated receipts of gross premiums (including anticipated renewal premiums) and gross investment income to be realized over the reasonably estimated life of the policy.

(4) *Safe harbor for public financial statements*. Any company that is required to file with the Securities and Exchange Commission (SEC) a financial statement with respect to the taxable year will be treated as having complied with paragraph (h)(1) of this section if it accounts for acquisition expenses for adjusted current earnings purposes in the same manner as it accounts for those expenses on its financial statements filed with the SEC.

(i) [RESERVED]

(j) *Depletion*. For purposes of computing adjusted current earnings, the allowance for depletion with respect to any property placed in service in a taxable year beginning after December 31, 1989 is determined under the cost depletion method of section 611.

(k) *Treatment of certain ownership changes*— (1) *In general*. In the case of any corporation that has an ownership change as defined in paragraph (k)(2) of this section in a taxable year beginning after December 31, 1989, and that also has a net unrealized built-in loss (as defined in paragraph (k)(3) of this section) immediately before the ownership change, the adjusted basis of each asset of the corporation for purposes of computing adjusted current earnings following the ownership change shall be its proportionate share (determined on the basis of the respective fair market values of each asset) of the fair market value of the assets of the corporation immediately before the ownership change. The rules of § 1.338-6(b), if otherwise applicable to the transaction, are applied in making this allocation of basis. If such rules apply, the limitations of § 1.338-6(c)(1) and (2) also apply in allocating basis under this paragraph (k)(1).

(2) *Definition of ownership change*. A corporation has an ownership change for purposes of section 56(g)(4)(G)(i) and this paragraph (k) if there is an ownership change under section 382(g) for purposes of computing the corporation's amount of taxable income that may be offset by pre-change losses or the regular tax liability that may be offset by pre-change credits. See § 1.382-2T for rules to determine whether a corporation has an ownership change. Accordingly, in order for an ownership change to occur for purposes of this paragraph (k), a corporation must be a loss corporation as defined in § 1.382-2(a)(1). In determining whether the corporation is a loss corporation, the determination of whether there is a net unrealized built-in loss is made by using the aggregate adjusted basis of the assets of the corporation used in computing taxable income. The aggregate adjusted basis of the corporation's assets for purposes of computing adjusted current earnings is not relevant in determining whether the corporation is a loss corporation. See part (iv) of the example in paragraph (k)(4) of this section.

(3) *Determination of net unrealized built-in loss immediately before an ownership change*. In order to determine whether it has a net unrealized built-in loss for purposes of section 56(g)(4)(G)(ii) and paragraph (k)(1) of this section, a corporation that has an ownership change as defined in paragraph (k)(2) of this section must use the aggregate adjusted basis of its assets that it uses in computing its adjusted current earnings. The rules of section 382 (including sections 382(h)(3)(B)(i) and 382(h)(8)) otherwise apply in determining whether the corporation has a net unrealized built-in loss.

(4) *Example*. The following example illustrates the provisions of this paragraph (k):

(i) Individual A has owned all the issued and outstanding stock of corporation L for the past 5 years. A sells all of his stock in L to unrelated individual B. On the date of the sale, L owns the following assets (all numbers are in millions):

Asset	Adjusted basis for computing taxable income	Adjusted basis for computing adjusted current earnings	Fair market value
x	$ 45	$ 50	$ 50
y	55	60	30
z	10	10	20
	$110	$120	$100

For purposes of computing taxable income, L has a $500 million net operating loss carryforward to the taxable year in which the sale occurs. Therefore, L is a loss corporation. As a result of the transfer of shares of L from A to B, L has had an ownership change.

(ii) L has no net unrealized built-in loss for purposes of computing taxable income because the amount by which the aggregate adjusted basis of its assets for that purpose exceeds their fair market value is $10 million, which is less than 15 percent of their fair market value and is not greater than $10 million. See section 382(h)(3)(B)(i). L, however, does have a net unrealized built-in loss for purposes of computing adjusted current earnings because the aggregate adjusted basis of its assets for that purpose exceeds their fair market value by $20 million, and that amount is greater than $10 million.

(iii) Under paragraph (k)(1) of this section, L must restate the adjusted basis of its assets for purposes of computing adjusted current earnings to their fair market values, as follows (all numbers are in millions):

Asset	New adjusted basis
x	$50
y	30
z	20

L must use these new adjusted bases for all purposes in determining adjusted current earnings, including computing depreciation and any gain or loss on disposition.

(iv) If L did not have the net operating loss carryforward, and had no other loss or credit carryovers or other attributes described in § 1.382-2(a)(1) for purposes of computing the amount of its taxable income that may be offset by pre-change losses or its regular tax liability that may be offset by pre-change credits, it would not have been a loss corporation on the date of the sale and therefore would not be treated as having had an ownership change for purposes of computing adjusted current earnings. This would be true even though L had a net unrealized built-in loss for purposes of computing adjusted current earnings. Therefore, this paragraph (k) would not have applied.

(l) [RESERVED]

(m) *Adjusted current earnings of a foreign corporation*—(1) *In general.* The alternative minimum taxable income of a foreign corporation is increased by 75 percent of the excess of—

(i) Its effectively connected adjusted current earnings for the taxable year; over

(ii) Its effectively connected pre-adjustment alternative minimum taxable income for the taxable year.

(2) Definitions—(i) *Effectively connected pre-adjustment alternative minimum taxable income.* Effectively connected preadjustment alternative minimum taxable income is the effectively connected taxable income of the foreign corporation for the taxable year, determined with the adjustments under sections 56 and 58 (except for the adjustment for adjusted current earnings, the alternative tax net operating loss and the alternative tax energy preference deduction) and increased by the tax preference items of section 57, but taking into account only items of income of the foreign corporation that are effectively connected (or treated as effectively connected) with the conduct of a trade or business in the United States, and any expense, loss or deduction that is properly allocated and apportioned to that income.

(ii) *Effectively connected adjusted current earnings.* Effectively connected adjusted current earnings is the effectively connected pre-adjustment alternative minimum taxable income of the foreign corporation for the taxable year, adjusted under section 56(g) and this section, but taking into account only items of income of the foreign corporation that are effectively connected (or treated as effectively connected) with the conduct of a trade or business in the United States, and any expense, loss or deduction that is properly allocated and apportioned to that income.

(3) *Rules to determine effectively connected pre-adjustment alternative minimum taxable income and effectively connected adjusted current earnings.* The principles of section 864(c) (and the regulations thereunder) and any other applicable provision of the Internal Revenue Code apply to determine whether items of income of the foreign corporation are effectively connected (or treated as effectively connected) with the conduct of a trade or business in the United States, and whether any expense, loss or deduction is properly allocated and apportioned to that income.

(4) *Certain exempt amounts.* Effectively connected adjusted current earnings and effectively connected pre-adjustment alternative minimum taxable income do not include any item of income, or any expense, loss or deduction that is properly allocated and apportioned to income that is exempt from United States taxation under section 883 or an applicable income tax treaty. See section 894.

(n) *Adjustment for adjusted current earnings of consolidated groups*—(1) *Positive adjustments.* For taxable years beginning after December 31, 1989, the alternative minimum taxable income of a consolidated group (as defined in § 1.1502-1T) is increased by 75 percent of the excess, if any, of—

(i) The consolidated adjusted current earnings for the taxable year, over

(ii) The consolidated pre-adjustment alternative minimum taxable income for the taxable year.

(2) *Negative adjustments*—(i) *In general.* The alternative minimum taxable income of a consolidated group is decreased, subject to the limitation of paragraph (n)(2)(ii) of this section, by 75 percent of the excess, if any, of the consolidated pre-adjustment alternative minimum taxable income over consolidated adjusted current earnings.

(ii) *Limitation on negative adjustments.* The amount of the negative adjustment for any taxable year shall be limited to the excess, if any, of—

(A) The aggregate increases in the alternative minimum taxable income of the group in prior years under this section, over

(B) The aggregate decreases in the alternative minimum taxable income of the group in prior years under this section.

(3) *Definitions*—(i) *Consolidated pre-adjustment alternative minimum taxable income.* Consolidated pre-adjustment alternative minimum taxable income is the consolidated taxable income (as defined in § 1.1502-11) of a consolidated group for the taxable year, determined with the adjustments provided in sections 56 and 58 (except for the adjustment for adjusted current earnings and the alternative tax net operating loss determined under section 56(a)(4)) and increased by the preference items described in section 57.

(ii) *Consolidated adjusted current earnings.* The consolidated adjusted current earnings of a consolidated group is the consolidated pre-adjustment alternative minimum taxable income of the consolidated group for the taxable year, adjusted as provided in section 56(g) and this section.

(4) *Example.* The following example illustrates the provisions of this paragraph (n):

(i) P is the common parent of a consolidated group. In 1990, the group has consolidated pre-adjustment alternative minimum taxable income of $1,400,000 and consolidated adjusted current earnings of $1,600,000. Thus, the group has a consolidated adjustment for adjusted current earnings for 1990 of $150,000 (75 percent of the $200,000 excess of consolidated adjusted current earnings over consolidated pre-adjustment alter-

native minimum taxable income), and alternative minimum taxable income of $1,550,000 ($1,400,000 plus $150,000).

(ii) In 1991, the group has consolidated pre-adjustment alternative minimum taxable income of $1,500,000 and consolidated adjusted current earnings of $1,100,000. Thus, the group can reduce its alternative minimum taxable income by $150,000. The potential negative adjustment of $300,000 (75 percent of the $400,000 excess of consolidated pre-adjustment alternative minimum taxable income over consolidated adjusted current earnings) is limited to the $150,000 consolidated adjustment for adjusted current earnings taken into account in 1990.

(o) [RESERVED]

(p) *Effective dates for corporate partners in partnerships*—(1) *In general.* The provisions of this section apply to a corporate partner's distributive share of items of income and expense from a partnership for any taxable year of the partnership ending within or with any taxable year of the corporate partner beginning after December 31, 1989.

(2) *Application of effective dates.* Solely for purposes of the effective date provisions of this section, a partnership event (such as placing property in service, paying or incurring a cost, or closing an installment sale) is deemed to occur on the last day of the partnership's taxable year.

(3) *Example.* The following example illustrates the provisions of this paragraph (p):

(i) X is a calendar-year corporation that is a partner in P, an accrual-basis partnership with a taxable year ending March 31. During P's taxable year ending March 31, 1990, P earned ratably throughout the year interest income on tax-exempt obligations. In addition, P incurred intangible drilling costs in November 1989 and in February 1990.

(ii) X's adjusted current earnings for 1990 includes X's distributive share of the interest on the tax-exempt obligations earned by P for its taxable year ending March 31, 1990. This is true even though P earned a portion of the interest prior to January 1, 1990.

(iii) For purposes of computing X's adjusted current earnings for 1990, the adjustment provided in paragraph (f)(1) of this section applies to

Reg. § 1.56(g)-1(n)(2)

X's distributive share of P's November 1989 and February 1990 intangible drilling costs.

(q) *Treatment of distributions of property to shareholders*—(1) *In general.* If a distribution of an item of property by a corporation with respect to its stock gives rise to more than one adjustment to earnings and profits under section 312, all of the adjustments with respect to that item of property (including the adjustment described in section 312(c) with respect to liabilities to which the item is subject or which are assumed in connection with the distribution) are combined for purposes of determining the corporation's adjusted current earnings for the taxable year. If the amount included in pre-adjustment alternative minimum taxable income with respect to a distribution of an item of property exceeds the net increase in earnings and profits caused by the distribution, pre-adjustment alternative minimum taxable income is not reduced in computing adjusted current earnings. If the net increase in earnings and profits caused by a distribution of an item of property exceeds the amount included in pre-adjustment alternative minimum taxable income with respect to the distribution, that excess is added to pre-adjustment alternative minimum taxable income in computing adjusted current earnings.

(2) *Examples.* The following examples illustrate the provisions of this paragraph (q).

(i) *Example 1.* K corporation distributes property with a fair market value of $150 and an adjusted basis of $100. The adjusted basis is the same for purposes of computing taxable income, pre-adjustment alternative minimum taxable income, adjusted current earnings, and earnings and profits. Under section 312(a)(3), as modified by section 312(b)(2), K decreases its earnings and profits by the fair market value of the property, or $150. Under section 312(b)(1), K increases its earnings and profits by the excess of the fair market value of the property over its adjusted basis, or $50. As a result of the distribution, there is a net decrease in K's earnings and profits of $100. K recognizes $50 of gain under section 311(b) as a result of the distribution as if K sold the property for $150. K thus has no amount permanently excluded from pre-adjustment alternative minimum taxable income that is taken into account in determining current earnings and profits, and thus has no adjustment under paragraph (c)(1) of this section.

(ii) *Example 2.* The facts are the same as in example 1, except that the distributee shareholder assumes a $190 liability in connection with the distribution. Under section 312(c)(1), K must adjust the adjustments to its earnings and profits under section 312(a) and (b) to account for the

liability the shareholder assumes. K adjusts the $100 net decrease in its earnings and profits to reflect the $190 liability, resulting in an increase in its earnings and profits of $90. Because section 311(b)(2) makes the rules of section 336(b) apply, the fair market value of the property is not less than the amount of the liability, or $190. K therefore is treated as if it sold the property for $190, recognizing $90 of gain. K thus has no amount permanently excluded from pre-adjustment alternative minimum taxable income that is taken into account in determining current earnings and profits, and thus has no adjustment under paragraph (c)(1) of this section.

(r) *Elections to use simplified inventory methods to compute alternative minimum tax*—(1) *In general.* If a taxpayer makes an election under this paragraph (r) (and does not make the election in paragraph (r)(5) of this section), the rules of paragraph (r)(2) of this section apply in computing the taxpayer's pre-adjustment alternative minimum taxable income and adjusted current earnings.

(2) *Effect of election*—(i) *Inventories.* The taxpayer's inventory amounts as determined for purposes of computing taxable income are used for purposes of computing pre-adjustment alternative minimum taxable income and adjusted current earnings. Subject to the further modification described in paragraph (r)(2)(ii) of this section, the taxpayer's cost of sales as determined for purposes of computing taxable income is also used for purposes of computing pre-adjustment alternative minimum taxable income and adjusted current earnings.

(ii) *Modifications required*—(A) *In general.* If a taxpayer makes an election under this paragraph (r), pre-adjustment alternative minimum taxable income and adjusted current earnings are computed with the modifications described in this paragraph. The items of adjustment under sections 56 and 58 and the items of tax preference under section 57 are computed without regard to the portion of those adjustments and preferences which, but for the election described in this paragraph, would have been capitalized in ending inventory. For example, pre-adjustment alternative minimum taxable income is increased by the excess of the depreciation allowable for the taxable year under section 168 for purposes of computing taxable income (determined without regard to section 263A) over the depreciation allowable for the taxable year under section 56(a)(1) and section 57 for purposes of computing pre-adjustment alternative minimum taxable income (determined without regard to section 263A). Similarly, adjusted current earnings is

Reg. § 1.56(g)-1(r)(2)

further increased by the excess of the depreciation allowable for the taxable year under section 56(a)(1) and section 57 for purposes of computing pre-adjustment alternative minimum taxable income (determined without regard to section 263A) over the depreciation allowable for the taxable year under section 56(g)(4)(A) for purposes of computing adjusted current earnings (determined without regard to section 263A). Thus, the modifications described in the preceding sentence do not duplicate amounts that are taken into account in computing pre-adjustment alternative minimum taxable income. See paragraph (a)(6)(ii) of this section.

(B) *Negative modifications allowed.* An election under this paragraph (r) does not affect the taxpayer's ability to make negative adjustments. Thus, if an election is made under this paragraph (r) and the amount of any adjustment under section 56 or 58, determined after modification under paragraph (r)(2)(ii)(A) of this section, is a negative amount, then this amount reduces pre-adjustment alternative minimum taxable income or adjusted current earnings. However, no negative adjustment under this paragraph (r)(2)(ii)(B) is allowed for the items of tax preference under section 57.

(iii) *LIFO recapture adjustment.* If a taxpayer makes an election under this paragraph (r) and uses the LIFO method for some assets, for purposes of computing the LIFO recapture adjustment under paragraph (f)(3) of this section for taxable years beginning after December 31, 1989—

(A) The LIFO inventory amount as determined for purposes of computing taxable income is used in lieu of the LIFO inventory amount as determined under paragraph (f)(3)(iii) of this section;

(B) The FIFO inventory amount is computed without regard to the adjustments under sections 56 (including the adjustments of section 56(g)(4)) and 58 and the items of tax preference of section 57; and

(C) The beginning LIFO and FIFO inventory amounts under paragraph (f)(3)(ii) of this section are the ending LIFO inventory amount as determined for purposes of computing taxable income and the ending FIFO inventory amount computed without regard to the adjustments under sections 56 (including the adjustments of section 56(g)(4)) and 58 and the items of tax preference of section 57 for the last taxable year beginning before January 1, 1990.

(3) *Time and manner of making election*—(i) *Prospective election.* (A) A prospective election

under this paragraph (r) may be made by any taxpayer—

(1) That has computed pre-adjustment alternative minimum taxable income and adjusted current earnings for all prior taxable years in accordance with the method described in this paragraph (r); or

(2) That has not computed pre-adjustment alternative minimum taxable income and adjusted current earnings for all prior tax years in accordance with the method described in this paragraph (r), but for which the use of the method described in this paragraph (r) for all prior taxable years would not have changed the taxpayer's tax liability (as shown on returns filed as of the date the election is made) for any prior taxable year for which the period of limitations under section 6501(a) has not expired (as of the date the election is made).

(B) A prospective election under this paragraph (r) may only be made by attaching a statement to the taxpayer's timely filed (including extensions) original Federal income tax return for any taxable year that is no later than its first taxable year to which this paragraph (r) applies and in which the taxpayer's tentative minimum tax (computed under the provisions of this paragraph (r)) exceeds its regular tax. However, in the case of a taxpayer described in paragraph (r)(3)(i)(A)(1) of this section that had tentative minimum tax in excess of its regular tax for any prior taxable year, the election may only be made by attaching a statement to its timely filed (including extensions) original Federal income tax return for the first taxable year ending after December 18, 1992. The statement must—

(1) Give the name, address and employer identification number of the taxpayer; and

(2) Identify the election as made under this paragraph (r).

(C) The determination of whether a taxpayer is described in paragraph (r)(3)(i)(A)(2) of this section is to be made as of the time the taxpayer makes a prospective election in accordance with the procedures in paragraph (r)(3)(i)(B) of this section.

(D) Any taxpayer described in paragraph (r)(3)(i)(A)(2) of this section that makes a prospective election will be deemed to have used the method described in this paragraph (r) in computing pre-adjustment alternative minimum taxable income and adjusted current earnings for all prior taxable years.

(ii) *Retroactive election*—(A) A retroactive election under this paragraph (r) may be made by any taxpayer not described in paragraph

Reg. § 1.56(g)-1(r)(3)

(r)(3)(i)(A)(*1*) or (*2*) of this section. Except as provided in paragraph (r)(3)(iii) of this section, a retroactive election may only be made by attaching a statement to the taxpayer's amended Federal income tax return for the earliest taxable year for which the period of limitations under section 6501(a) has not expired and which begins after December 31, 1986. The amended return to which the election under this paragraph (r)(3)(ii) is attached must be filed no later than June 19, 1993.

(B) The amended return must contain the statement described in paragraph (r)(3)(i)(B) of this section. In addition, the statement must contain a representation that the taxpayer will modify its pre-adjustment alternative minimum taxable income and adjusted current earnings for all open taxable years in accordance with paragraph (r)(2) of this section. Upon this change in method of accounting, the taxpayer must include the entire adjustment required under section 481(a), if any, in pre-adjustment alternative minimum taxable income and adjusted current earnings on the amended return for the year of the election. The taxpayer must also reflect the method of accounting described in paragraph (r)(2) of this section on amended returns filed for all taxable years after the year of the election for which returns were originally filed before making the election (and for which the period of limitations under section 6501(a) has not expired).

(C) Provided a taxpayer meets the requirements of this paragraph (r), any change in method of accounting arising as a result of making a retroactive election will be treated as made with the advance consent of the Commissioner.

(D) Any retroactive election under this paragraph (r) that is made without filing amended returns required under this paragraph (r)(3)(ii) shall constitute a change in method of accounting made without the consent of the Commissioner.

(iii) *Taxpayers under examination*—(A) *In general.* A taxpayer that wishes to make a retroactive election under section (r)(3)(ii) of this section may use the procedures in paragraph (r)(3)(iii)(A)(*1*) or (*2*) in lieu of filing an amended return for any taxable year that is under examination by the Internal Revenue Service.

(*1*) *Year of change under examination.* If the year of the change is under examination at the time the taxpayer timely makes the election, the taxpayer may (in lieu of filing an amended return for the year of the change) furnish the written statement described in paragraph (r)(3)(iii)(B) of this section to the revenue agent responsible for examining the taxpayer's return no

later than June 19, 1993. It is the taxpayer's responsibility to make a timely election either by furnishing the statement to the revenue agent or by filing amended returns by June 19, 1992.

(*2*) *Other open years under examination.* If any other year for which the taxpayer must modify its pre-adjustment alternative minimum taxable income and adjusted current earnings (see paragraph (r)(3)(ii)(B) of this section) is examined, the taxpayer may (in lieu of filing an amended return) furnish the amount of the conforming adjustment to the revenue agent responsible for examining the taxpayer's return. It is the taxpayer's responsibility to timely modify its pre-adjustment alternative minimum taxable income and adjusted current earnings for each year other than the year of change, either by furnishing the amount of the adjustment to the revenue agent or by filing amended returns.

(B) *Statement required.* The statement required under paragraph (r)(3)(iii)(A)(*1*) of this section must include all of the items required under paragraph (r)(3)(ii)(B) of this section, as well as—

(*1*) The caption "Election to use regular tax inventories for AMT purposes;"

(*2*) A description of the nature and amount of all items that would result in adjustments and that the taxpayer would have reported if the taxpayer had used the method described in this paragraph (r) for all prior taxable years for which the period of limitations under section 6501(a) has not expired and which begin after December 31, 1986; and

(*3*) The following declaration signed by the person authorized to sign the return for the taxpayer: "Under penalties of perjury, I declare that I have examined this written statement, and to the best of my knowledge and belief this written statement is true, correct, and complete."

(C) *Year of change.* The year of change is the earliest taxable year for which the period of limitations under section 6501(a) has not expired at the time the statement is submitted to the appropriate revenue agent and that begins after December 31, 1986. Thus, the adjustments required to be included on the statement must include any adjustment under section 481(a) determined as if the method described in this paragraph (r) had been used in all taxable years prior to the year of change that begin after December 31, 1986.

(D) *Treatment of additional tax liability.* Any additional tax liability that results from the adjustments identified in the written statement described in paragraph (r)(3)(iii)(B) of this section is treated as an additional amount of tax shown on an amended return.

(iv) *Election as method of accounting.* The elections provided in paragraphs (r)(3)(i) and (ii) of this section constitute either adoptions of, or changes in, methods of accounting. These elections, once made, may be revoked only with the consent of the Commissioner in accordance with the rules of section 446(e) and § 1.446-1(e).

(v) *Untimely election to use simplified inventory method.* If a taxpayer makes an election described in this paragraph (r) after the times set forth in paragraph (r)(3)(i) or (ii) of this section, the taxpayer must comply with the requirements of § 1.446-1(e)(3) in order to secure the consent of the Commissioner to change to the method of accounting prescribed in this paragraph (r). The taxpayer generally will be subject to terms and conditions designed to place the taxpayer in a position no more favorable than a taxpayer that timely complied with paragraph (r)(3)(i) or (ii) of this section, whichever is applicable.

(4) *Example.* The following example illustrates the provisions of this paragraph (r).

Example. (i) Corporation L is a calendar year manufacturer of baseball bats and uses the LIFO method of accounting for inventories. During 1987, 1988, and 1989, L's cost of goods sold in computing taxable income was as follows:

	1987	1988	1989
Beginning LIFO inventory	$ 3,000	$ 4,000	$ 5,000
Purchases and other costs	9,000	9,000	9,000
Ending LIFO inventory	(4,000)	(5,000)	(6,000)
Cost of goods sold	$ 8,000	$ 8,000	$ 8,000

(ii) L has no preferences under section 57 during 1987, 1988 and 1989. L's sole adjustment in computing alternative minimum tax during 1987, 1988, and 1989 was the depreciation adjustment under section 56(a)(1). Depreciation determined for both production and non-production assets under section 168 and under section 56(a)(1) during 1987, 1988, and 1989 was as follows:

	1987	1988	1989
Section 168 depreciation	$ 1,800	$ 1,800	$ 1,800
Section 56(a)(1) depreciation	(900)	(900)	(900)
Depreciation difference	$ 900	$ 900	$ 900
Portion of difference capitalized in the increase in inventory	(100)	(100)	$ (100)
Adjustment required under section 56(a)(1)	$ 800	$ 800	$ 800

(iii) In computing taxable income, a portion of each year's section 168 depreciation attributable to production assets is deducted currently and a portion is capitalized into the increase in ending inventory. For 1987, 1988, and 1989, L computed alternative minimum tax by deducting the cost of goods sold which was reflected in taxable income ($8,000) in accordance with paragraph (r)(2)(i) of this section. For 1987, 1988, and 1989, L also modified its adjustments under sections 56 and 58 and its preferences under section 57 to disregard the portion of any adjustment or preference that was capitalized in inventory. Thus, under section 56(a)(1), L increased alternative minimum taxable income during each year by $900.

(iv) L is eligible to make the election under paragraph (r)(1) of this section in accordance with paragraph (r)(3)(i) of this section (a prospective election).

(v) L must compute its LIFO recapture adjustment for each year by reference to—

(A) The FIFO inventory amount after applying the provisions of section 263A but before applying the adjustments of sections 56 and 58 and the items of preference in section 57; and

(B) The LIFO inventory amount used in computing taxable income.

(5) *Election to use alternative minimum tax inventories to compute adjusted current earnings.* A taxpayer may elect under this paragraph (r)(5) to use the inventory amounts used to compute pre-adjustment alternative minimum taxable income in computing its adjusted current earnings. Rules similar to those of paragraphs (r)(2) and (r)(3) of this section apply for purposes of this election.

(s) *Adjustment for alternative tax energy preference deduction—(1) In general.* For purposes of computing adjusted current earnings, any taxpayer claiming a deduction under section 56(h) must properly decrease basis by the portion of the deduction allowed under section 56(h) which is

Reg. § 1.56(g)-1(r)(4)

attributable to adjustments under section 56(g)(4). In taxable years following the taxable year in which the section 56(h) deduction is claimed, basis recovery (including amortization, depletion, and gain on sale) must properly take into account this basis reduction.

(2) *Example.* The following example illustrates the provisions of this paragraph (s):

Example. Corporation A, a calendar year taxpayer, incurs $100 of intangible drilling costs on January 1, 1994 and as a result of these intangible drilling costs A claims a deduction under section 56(h) of $40. Assume that $20 of A's deduction under section 56(h) is attributable to the adjustment under paragraph (f)(1) of this section. A must reduce by $20 the amount of intangible drilling costs to be amortized under paragraph (f)(1) of this section in 1995 through 1998 (the balance of the 60 month amortization period). [Reg. § 1.56(g)-1.]

☐ [*T.D.* 8340, 3-14-91. *Amended by T.D.* 8352, 6-26-91; *T.D.* 8454, 12-18-92; *T.D.* 8482, 8-6-93; *T.D.* 8566, 10-7-94; *T.D.* 8858, 1-5-2000 and *T.D.* 8940, 2-12-2001.]

Regulations Applicable to Taxable Years Beginning in 1969 and Ending in 1970

[Reg. § 1.56A-1]

§ 1.56A-1. Imposition of tax.—(a) *In general.* Section 56(a) imposes an income tax on the items of tax preference (as defined in § 1.57-1) of all persons other than persons specifically exempt from the taxes imposed by chapter 1. The items of tax preference represent income of a person which either is not subject to current taxation by reason of temporary exclusion (such as stock options) or by reason of an acceleration of deductions (such as accelerated depreciation) or is sheltered from full taxation by reason of certain deductions (such as percentage depletion) or by reason of a special rate of tax (such as the rate of tax on corporate capital gains). The tax imposed by section 56 is in addition to the other taxes imposed by chapter 1.

(b) *Computation of tax.* The amount of such tax is 10 percent of the excess (referred to herein as "the minimum tax base") of—

(1) The sum of the taxpayer's items of tax preference for such year in excess of the taxpayer's minimum tax exemption (determined under § 1.58-1) for such year, over

(2) The sum of:

(i) The taxes imposed for such year under chapter 1 other than the taxes imposed by section 56 (relating to minimum tax for tax preferences), by section 531 (relating to accumulated earnings tax), or by section 541 (relating to personal hold-

ing company tax), reduced by the sum of the credits allowable under—

(a) Section 33 (relating to taxes of foreign countries and possessions of the United States),

(b) Section 37 (relating to retirement income),

(c) Section 38 (relating to investment credit),

(d) Section 40 (relating to expenses of work incentive programs), and

(e) Section 41 (relating to contributions to candidates for public office), and

(ii) The tax carryovers to such taxable year (as described in § 1.56A-5).

(c) *Special rule.* For purposes of paragraph (b) of this section where for any taxable year in which a tax is imposed under section 667 (relating to treatment of amounts deemed distributed by a trust in preceding years), that portion of the section 667 tax representing an increase in an earlier year's chapter 1 taxes (as recomputed), which taxes are allowed as a reduction in any such earlier year's minimum tax base, is not allowable as a reduction in the minimum tax base for the current taxable year. The remaining portion of the section 667 tax, representing the taxes imposed by section 56, section 531, and section 541, is not allowable as a reduction in the minimum tax base for any taxable year. Similarly, taxes imposed under section 614(c)(4) (relating to increase in tax with respect to aggregation of certain mineral interests) or under section 1351(d) (relating to recoveries of foreign expropriation losses) for any taxable year are not allowed as a reduction in the minimum tax base for such taxable year to the extent they represent chapter 1 taxes which are allowable as a reduction in a minimum tax base for an earlier taxable year for purposes of the computations under section 614(c)(4) or section 1351(d) or to the extent they represent an increase in the tax imposed by section 56, section 531, or section 541 in an earlier taxable year. [Reg. § 1.56A-1.]

☐ [*T.D.* 7564, 9-11-78. *Amended by T.D.* 8138, 4-23-88.]

[Reg. § 1.56A-2]

§ 1.56A-2. Deferral of tax liability in case of certain net operating losses.—(a) *In general.* Section 56(b) provides for the deferral of liability for the minimum tax where, for the taxable year, the taxpayer has—

(1) A net operating loss for such taxable year any portion of which (under sec. 172) remains as a

net operating loss carryover to a succeeding taxable year, and

(2) Items of tax preference in excess of the minimum tax exemptions (hereinafter referred to as "excess tax preferences").

In such a case, an amount of tax equal to the lesser of the tax imposed under section 56(a) (after allowance of the retirement income credit to the extent that such credit cannot be used against the other taxes imposed by chapter 1) or 10 percent of the amount of the net operating loss carryover described in subparagraph (1) of this paragraph is deferred. Such amount is not treated as tax imposed in such taxable year, but is treated as tax imposed in the succeeding taxable year or years in which the net operating loss is used as provided in paragraphs (b) and (c) of this section. Deferral will result in the above case regardless of the character of the tax preference items. Thus, for example, if the taxpayer has $1,030,000 of items of tax preference, including the stock option item of tax preference, and a $750,000 net operating loss available for carryover to subsequent taxable years, the amount of tax imposed for the taxable year under section 56(a) is $100,000 and $75,000 is deferred by application of section 56(b). Therefore, only $25,000 is treated as tax imposed for the taxable year. The provisions of this section are applicable in the case of a net operating loss or comparable item such as an operations loss under section 812 and an unused loss as defined in section 825(b).

(b) *Year of liability.* In any taxable year in which any portion of a net operating loss carryover attributable to the amount of excess tax preferences reduces taxable income (in the form of a net operating loss deduction), section 56(b)(2) treats as tax liability imposed in such taxable year an amount equal to 10 percent of such reduction. For this purpose, the portion of such net operating loss which is considered attributable to the amount of excess tax preferences is an amount equal to the lesser of such excess or the amount of the net operating loss carryover described in paragraph (a)(1) of this section. In no case, however, shall the total amount of tax imposed by reason of section 56(b) in subsequent years exceed the amount of the tax that was deferred in the loss year.

(c) *Priority of reduction.* (1) If a portion of a net operating loss is attributable to an amount of excess tax preferences, such portion is considered to reduce taxable income in succeeding taxable years only after the other portion (if any) of such net operating loss is used to reduce taxable income. Accordingly, if the amount of a net operating loss which may be carried to succeeding

taxable years is reduced because of a modification required to be made pursuant to section 172(b)(2), such reduction is to be considered to be first from that portion of the net operating loss that is attributable to excess tax preferences. If a portion of a net operating loss carryover which is attributable to an amount of excess tax preferences is not used to reduce taxable income in any succeeding taxable year, no minimum tax will be imposed with respect to such portion.

(2) In the case of taxpayers with deductions attributable to foreign sources which are suspense preferences (as defined in paragraphs (c)(1)(ii) and (2)(ii) of sec. 1.58-7), the amount of such deductions is not included in the portion of the net operating loss not attributable to excess tax preferences. The portion of the net operating loss attributable to excess tax preferences is increased by the amount of suspense preferences which are, in accordance with the provisions of section 1.58-7(c), converted to actual items of tax preference (and not used against the minimum tax exemption of the loss year) in subsequent taxable years. The other portion of the net operating loss is increased by the amount of suspense preferences which reduce taxable income in subsequent taxable years but are not converted to actual items of tax preference (or are so converted but used against the minimum tax exemption of the loss year). See section 1.58-7(c)(1)(iii) example (4).

(d) *Multiple net operating loss carryovers.* In determining whether a net operating loss is used to reduce taxable income in a taxable year to which two or more net operating losses are carried, the ordering rules of section 172 (b) and the regulations thereunder are to be applied. Thus, for example, the portion of a net operating loss carried over from an earlier taxable year which is attributable to an amount of excess tax preference is used to reduce taxable income in the carryover year before any portion of any other net operating loss carried over or back from a taxable year subsequent to the earlier taxable year.

(e) *Examples.* The application of this section may be illustrated by the following examples:

Example (1). In 1970, A, a calendar year taxpayer, who is a single individual, has $180,000 of items of tax preference, a $150,000 net operating loss of which $100,000 may be carried forward, and no tax liability under chapter 1 without regard to the minimum tax. His minimum tax computed under section 56(a) is $15,000 (10 percent times ($180,000 minus $30,000)). Under section 56(b)(1) an amount equal to the lesser of the amount determined under section 56(a) ($15,000) or 10 percent of the net operating loss which may

Reg. § 1.56A-2(a)(2)

be carried forward ($10,000) is treated as a deferred liability. Thus, his minimum tax liability for 1970 is $5,000 ($15,000 minimum tax under section 56(a) minus $10,000 deferred tax liability under section 56(b)). If, in 1971, he has $80,000 of taxable income before the deduction for the 1970 net operating loss, his minimum tax liability is $8,000 (10 percent of the amount by which the net operating loss carryforward from 1970 reduces taxable income) plus any minimum tax liability resulting from items of tax preference arising in 1971. If, by any reason of the modifications provided by section 172(b)(2), no portion of the 1970 net operating loss remains as a carryover from 1971, no further minimum tax liability will result from the items of tax preference arising in 1970.

Example (2). In 1970, A, a calendar year taxpayer who is a single individual, has $90,000 of items of tax preference, a $100,000 net operating loss available for carryover to future taxable years, no net operating loss carryovers from prior taxable years, and no tax liability under chapter 1 without regard to the minimum tax. His minimum tax computed under section 56(a) is $6,000 (10 percent times ($90,000 minus $30,000)). Under section 56(b)(1) an amount equal to the lesser of the amount determined under section 56(a) ($6,000) or 10 percent of the net operating loss subject to carryforward ($10,000) is treated as a deferred liability. Thus, A owes no minimum tax in 1970 and the entire $6,000 of minimum tax liability is deferred. Under section 56(b)(2), the portion of the net operating loss attributable to the excess tax preferences described in section 56(b)(1)(B) is $60,000.

(a) In 1971, A has $25,000 of taxable income before the deduction for the 1970 net operating loss. Thus, in 1971, A has no minimum tax liability attributable to the items of tax preference arising in 1970 since, by application of section 56(b)(3), the portion of the 1970 net operating loss carryforward not attributable to the excess described in section 56(b)(1)(B), or $40,000, is considered applied against taxable income before the remaining portion.

(b) In 1972, A has $50,000 of taxable income before the deduction for the remaining 1970 net operating loss. Thus, the first $15,000 of reduction in taxable income is considered as from the portion of the 1970 net operating loss carryforward not attributable to the excess tax preferences described in section 56(b)(1)(B) and the remaining $35,000 of reduction in taxable income is considered attributable to such excess. A's 1972 minimum tax attributable to items of tax preference arising in 1970 is, therefore, $3,500 (10 percent times $35,000).

(c) In 1973, A has $80,000 of taxable income before the deduction for the 1970 net operating loss. The remaining $25,000 of the 1970 net operating loss carryforward is used to reduce taxable income in 1973. Thus, A's 1973 minimum tax liability attributable to items of tax preference arising in 1970 is $2,500 (10 percent times $25,000).

Example (3). In 1971, M Corporation, a Western Hemisphere trade corporation (as defined in sec. 921), reporting on a calendar year basis has $20,000 of taxable income after all deductions including the Western Hemisphere trade deduction allowable under section 922 in the amount of $30,000. In 1970, M Corporation had a net operating loss of $100,000 all of which was available for carryover to 1971 and $60,000 of which was attributable to excess tax preferences. In computing the amount of the 1970 net operating loss carried over to 1972 pursuant to section 172(b), the 1971 Western Hemisphere trade corporation deduction is not taken into account. Thus, M Corporation's recomputed income under section 172(b) is $50,000 ($20,000 taxable income plus $30,000 Western Hemisphere trade corporation deduction). Pursuant to paragraph (c)(1) of this section, $20,000 of the $40,000 portion of the 1970 net operating loss not attributable to excess tax preferences is considered to reduce taxable income in 1971 and $30,000 of the $60,000 portion of the 1970 net operating loss attributable to excess tax preferences is considered reduced pursuant to section 172(b)(2). Thus, M Corporation has no 1971 minimum tax attributable to items of tax preference arising in 1970. Of the $50,000 remaining of the 1970 net operating loss, $30,000 is attributable to excess tax preference.

Example (4). In 1972, A, a calendar year taxpayer who is a single individual, has $25,000 of taxable income resulting from $50,000 of net long-term capital gains. In 1971, A had a net operating loss of $100,000 all of which is available to carryover to 1972 and $60,000 of which is attributable to excess tax preferences. By application of section 172(b) only $50,000 of the 1971 net operating loss is carried over to 1973. Pursuant to paragraph (c) of this section, $25,000 of the $40,000 portion of the 1971 net operating loss not attributable to excess tax preferences is considered to reduce taxable income in 1972. Of the $50,000 remaining of the 1971 net operating loss, $15,000 is not attributable to excess tax preferences and $35,000 is attributable to excess tax preferences. Thus, the $25,000 section 1202 deduction, in effect, reduces the portion of the 1971 net operating loss attributable to excess tax preferences. Because a net operating loss carryover is reduced to the extent of any section 1202 deduction, section

Reg. § 1.56A-2(e)

1202 deductions do not normally produce a tax benefit in such circumstances and, pursuant to § 1.57-4, would not be treated as items of tax preference. However, in this case, to the extent the portion of the 1971 net operating loss carryover attributable to excess tax preferences is reduced by reason of the section 1202 deduction, such deduction does result in a tax benefit to the taxpayer and is, therefore, treated as an item of tax preference in 1971. See § 1.57-4(b)(2). [Reg. § 1.56A-2.]

☐ [*T.D. 7564, 9-11-78. Amended by T.D. 8138, 4-23-87.*]

[Reg. § 1.56A-3]

§ **1.56A-3. Effective date.**—(a) *In general.* The minimum tax is effective for taxable years ending after December 31, 1969.

[(b) Reg. § 1.56-3(b) deals with the application of minimum tax for tax years beginning in 1969 and ending in 1970. This regulation was last reported at 821 CCH ¶ 577H.] [Reg. § 1.56A-3.]

☐ [*T.D. 7564, 9-11-78. Amended by T.D. 8138, 4-23-87.*]

[Reg. § 1.56A-4]

§ **1.56A-4. Certain taxpayers.**—For application of the minimum tax in the case of estates and trusts, electing small business corporations, common trust funds, regulated investment companies, real estate investment trusts, and partnerships, see § § 1.58-2 through 1.58-6. [Reg. § 1.56A-4.]

☐ [*T.D. 7564, 9-11-78.*]

[Reg. § 1.56A-5]

§ **1.56A-5. Tax carryovers.**—(a) *In general.* Section 56(c) provides a 7-year carryover of the excess of the taxes described in paragraph (1) of such section imposed during the taxable year over the items of tax preference described in paragraph (2) of such section for such taxable year for the purpose of reducing the amount subject to tax under section 56(a) in subsequent taxable years.

(b) *Computation of amount of carryover.* The amount of tax carryover described in section 56(c) is the excess (if any) of—

(1) The taxes imposed for the taxable year under chapter 1 other than taxes imposed by section 56 (relating to minimum tax for tax preferences), by section 531 (relating to accumulated earnings tax), or by section 541 (relating to personal holding company tax), reduced by the sum of the credits allowable under—

(i) Section 33 (relating to taxes of foreign countries and possessions of the United States),

(ii) Section 37 (relating to retirement income),

(iii) Section 38 (relating to investment credit),

(iv) Section 40 (relating to expenses of work incentive programs), and

(v) Section 41 (relating to contributions to candidates for public office), over

(2) The sum of the taxpayer's items of tax preference for such year in excess of the taxpayer's minimum tax exemption (determined under § 1.58-1) for such year.

For purposes of section 56(c) and this section, taxes imposed in a taxable year ending on or before December 31, 1969, are not included in the taxes described in subparagraph (1) of this paragraph. In addition, the rules of paragraph (c) of § 1.56A-1 are applicable in determining the taxable year for which taxes are imposed under chapter 1 for purposes of paragraph (a)(1) of this section.

(c) *Operation of carryover.* Tax carryovers attributable to the taxable year shall be carried over to each of the 7 succeeding taxable years as follows:

(1) To the first such succeeding taxable year to reduce in the manner described in paragraph (d) of this section the amount subject to tax under section 56(a) for such first succeeding taxable year and

(2) To the extent such amount is not used as a reduction in the amount subject to tax under section 56(a) for such taxable year, such amount (if any) is carried over to each of the succeeding 6 taxable years but only to the extent such amount is not used to reduce the amount subject to tax under section 56(a) in taxable years intervening between the taxable year to which such amount is attributable and the taxable year to which such amount may otherwise be carried over.

(d) *Priority of reduction.* Where tax carryovers attributable to two or more taxable years are carried over to a subsequent taxable year such amounts attributable to the earliest taxable year shall be used to reduce the amount subject to tax under section 56(a) for such subsequent taxable year before any such amounts attributable to a later taxable year.

(e) *Special rules*—(1) *Periods of less than 12 months.* A fractional part of a year which is a taxable year under section 441(b) or 7701(a)(23) is a taxable year for purposes of section 56(c) and this section.

(2) *Electing small business corporations.* A taxable year for which a corporation is an electing small business corporation (as defined in section 1371(b)) shall be counted as a taxable year for purposes of determining the taxable years to

which amounts which are available as a carryover under paragraph (a) of this section may be carried whether or not such carryovers arose in a year in which an election was in effect.

(3) *Husband and wife*—(i) *From joint to separate return.* If a joint return is filed by a husband and wife in a taxable year or years to which a tax carryover is attributable but separate returns are filed in any subsequent taxable year to which such carryover may be carried over to reduce the amount subject to tax under section 56(a), such carryover described in paragraph (b) of this section shall be allocated between husband and wife for purposes of reducing the amount subject to tax under section 56(a) for such subsequent taxable year in accordance with the principles of § 1.172-7(d).

(ii) *From separate to joint return.* If separate returns are filed by a husband and wife in a taxable year or years in which a tax carryover is attributable but a joint return is filed in any subsequent taxable year to which such carryover may be carried over to reduce the amount subject to tax under section 56(a), such carryover shall be aggregated for purposes of reducing the amount subject to tax under section 56(a), for such subsequent taxable year.

(4) *Estates and trusts.* In the case of the termination of an estate or trust, tax carryovers attributable to the estate or trust shall not be allowed to the beneficiaries succeeding to the property of the estate or trust.

(5) *Corporate acquisitions.* In the case of a transaction to which section 381(a) applies, the acquiring corporation shall succeed to and take into account, as of the close of the date of distribution or transfer the tax carryovers attributable to the distributor or transferor corporation. The portion of such carryovers which may be taken into account under paragraph (b)(2)(ii) of § 1.56A-1 for any taxable year shall not exceed the excess of (i) the sum of the items of tax preference for such year resulting from the continuation of the business in which the distributor or transferor corporation was engaged at the time of such transaction and the items of tax preference not related to the continuation of such business which are directly attributable to the assets acquired from the distributor or transferor corporation over (ii) an amount which bears the same ratio to the acquiring corporation's minimum tax exemption for such year as the items of tax preference described in subdivision (i) of this subparagraph bear to all of the acquiring corporation's items of tax preference for such year. This item shall be taken into account by the acquiring corporation subject to the rules in section 381(b) and the regulations thereunder.

(f) *Suspense preferences.* Where an item of tax preference which is a suspense preference (as defined in § 1.58-7) arises in a taxable year in which tax carryovers may be used to reduce the minimum tax base (or in which such carryovers arise) the minimum tax liability for that year and the tax carryovers to subsequent taxable years shall be recomputed upon the conversion of the suspense preference in a subsequent year. In lieu of the above, in all cases, since there is no difference in tax consequence, the recomputation may be accomplished by recomputing the minimum tax liability of the taxable year in which the suspense preference arose without reduction of the minimum tax base for the tax carryovers which have been used as a reduction in the minimum tax base in intervening taxable years. If such method is used, the minimum tax liability of the intervening year is not recomputed and any tax carryovers carried from the taxable year in which the suspense preference arose which remain as a carryover in the year of conversion are reduced, in the priority provided in paragraph (d) of this section, to the extent used to reduce an increase in the minimum tax base for the earlier year resulting from the conversion of the suspense preference.

(g) *Taxes imposed in a taxable year beginning in 1969 and ending in 1970.* In the case of a taxable year beginning in 1969 and ending in 1970 the amount of the carryover determined under paragraph (b) of this section is reduced to an amount equal to the amount of such carryover (without regard to this paragraph) multiplied by the following fraction:

$$\frac{\text{Number of days in taxable year ending after December 31, 1969}}{\text{Number of days in the entire taxable year.}}$$

(h) *Examples.* The provisions of this section may be illustrated by the following examples:

Example (1). A is a single individual who uses a June 30 fiscal year. For fiscal 1968-1969, A had income tax liability under chapter 1 in the amount of $100,000. For fiscal 1969-1970, A had items of tax preference in the amount of $212,500 and income tax liability under chapter 1 (other than taxes imposed under sections 56, 531, and 541) of $365,000.

(a) The chapter 1 tax attributable to fiscal 1968-1969 is not available as a carryover under section 56(c) to reduce the amount subject to tax under section 56(a) since this tax arose in a taxable year ending on or before December 31, 1969.

Reg. § 1.56A-5(h)

(b) A portion of the excess of chapter 1 tax over the amount subject to tax under section 56(a) attributable to fiscal year 1969-1970 is available as a carryover as provided in section 56(c) to reduce the amount subject to tax under section 56(a). The amount of this carryover is $91,000 computed as follows:

1. Carryover under paragraph (b) of this section:

Chapter 1 taxes	$365,000
Items of tax preference in excess of exemption	182,500
	$182,500

2. Reduction pursuant to paragraph (g) of this section:

$$\frac{182}{365} \times \$182,500 = \dots\dots\dots\dots\dots\dots\dots\dots\quad \$\ 91,000$$

Example (2). A is a calendar year taxpayer who is a single individual. In 1972, A had chapter 1 income tax liability (other than taxes imposed under sections 56, 531, and 541) of $200,000 and $50,000 of items of tax preference. In 1973, A had chapter 1 income tax liability (other than taxes imposed under sections 56, 531, and 541) of $120,000 and $40,000 of items of tax preference. In 1974, A had $400,000 of items of tax preference and no liability for tax under chapter 1 other than under section 56(a). Under section 56(c), the excess of the taxes described in paragraph (1) of that section arising in an earlier taxable year not used to reduce the amount subject to tax under section 56(a) for such taxable year can be carried over as provided in section 56(c) to reduce the amount subject to tax under section 56(a).

(a) The amount of the carryover from 1972 is $180,000 computed as follows:

Carryover under paragraph (b) of this section:

Chapter 1 taxes	$200,000
Items of tax preference in excess of exemption	20,000
Total	$180,000

(b) The amount of the carryover from 1973 is $110,000 computed as follows:

Carryover under paragraph (b) of this section:

Chapter 1 taxes	$120,000
Items of tax preference in excess of exemption	10,000
	$110,000

(c) For 1974, the excess of taxes in the preceding taxable years is used to reduce the amount subject to tax under section 56(a). The amount of carryover attributable to excess taxes arising in 1972 is used before such excess arising in 1973. The amount of tax under section 56(a) is $8,000 computed as follows:

1974 tax preferences	$400,000
Less exemption	30,000
	370,000
Less 1972 carryover	180,000
	190,000
Less 1973 carryover	110,000
1974 minimum tax base	$ 80,000
1974 minimum tax ($80,000 × 10%)	$ 8,000

Example (3). The facts are the same as in example (2) except that in 1974 A had $300,000 of items of tax preference. The amount of the carryover for taxable years after 1974 is computed as follows:

1974 tax preferences	$300,000
Less exemption	30,000
	270,000
Less 1972 carryover	180,000

Reg. § 1.56A-5(h)

	90,000
Less 1973 carryover	$ 90,000
Minimum tax base	-0-
1973 carryover	110,000
Amount used in 1974	90,000
Amount available for taxable years after 1974	$ 20,000

The $20,000 remaining of the 1973 carryover is available to reduce the amount subject to tax under section 56(a) in 1975 or other future taxable years as provided in section 56(c).

Example (4). M Corporation is a calendar year taxpayer. N Corporation uses a June 30 fiscal year. For the fiscal year 1970-1971, N Corporation had excess chapter 1 tax liability as described in paragraph (a) of this section in the amount of $75,000. On January 1, 1972, M Corporation acquired N Corporation in a reorganization described in section 368(a)(1)(A). N Corporation does not use any of such excess chapter 1 tax liability to reduce the amount subject to tax under section 56(a) for the short taxable year beginning on July 1, 1971, and ending on December 31, 1971. Thus, the excess chapter 1 tax liability is available to M Corporation as a carryover under paragraph (a) of this section to reduce the amount subject to tax for the next 6 succeeding taxable years beginning with taxable year 1972 as provided in this section. In applying the carryover to 1972 and succeeding taxable years, the carryover of N Corporation subject to the limitation of § 1.56-5A(e)(4) is combined with any carryovers originating with M Corporation in 1970. [Reg. § 1.56A-5.]

☐ [T.D. 7564, 9-11-78. Amended by T.D. 8138, 4-23-87.]

→ *Caution: Reg. § 12.8 was issued under Code Sec. 57.*←

[Reg. § 12.8]

§12.8. **Elections with respect to net leases of real property.**—(a) *In general.* The elections described in this section are available for determining whether real property held by the taxpayer is subject to a net lease for purposes of section 57 (relating to items of tax preference for purposes of the minimum tax for tax preferences) or 163(d) (relating to limitation on interest on investment indebtedness). Under sections 57(c)(1)(A) and 163(d)(4)(A)(i), property will be considered to be subject to a net lease for a taxable year where the sum of the deductions of the lessor with respect to the property for the taxable year allowable solely by reason of section 162 (other than rents and reimbursed amounts with respect to the property) is less than 15 percent of the gross income from rents produced by the property (hereinafter referred to as the "expense test"). Under sections 57(c)(2) and 163(d)(7)(A), where a parcel of real property of the taxpayer is leased under two or more leases, the taxpayer may elect to apply the expense test set forth in sections 57(c)(1)(A) and 163(d)(4)(A)(i) by treating all leased portions of such property as subject to a single lease. Under sections 57(c)(3) and 163(d)(7)(B), at the election of the taxpayer, the expense test set forth in sections 57(c)(1)(A) and 163(d)(4)(A)(i) shall not apply with respect to real property of the taxpayer which has been in use for more than 5 years.

(b) *Election with respect to multiple leases of single parcel of real property.* If a parcel of real property of the taxpayer is leased under two or more leases, the expense test referred to in paragraph (a) of this section shall, at the election of the taxpayer, be applied by treating all leased portions of such property as subject to a single lease. For purposes of this paragraph, the term "parcel of real property" includes adjacent properties each of which is subject to lease.

(c) *Election with respect to real property in use for more than five years.* At the election of the taxpayer, the expense test referred to in paragraph (a) of this section shall not apply with respect to real property of the taxpayer which has been in use for more than five years. For this purpose, real property is in use only during the period that such property is both owned and used for commercial purposes by the taxpayer. If an improvement to the property was made during the time such property was owned by the taxpayer, and if, as a result of such improvement, the adjusted basis of such property was increased by 50 percent or more, use of such property for commercial purposes shall be deemed to have commenced for purposes of this paragraph as of the date such improvement was completed. An election under this paragraph shall apply to all real property of the taxpayer which has been in use for more than five years.

(d) *Procedure for making election—*(1) *Time and scope of election.* An election under paragraph (b) or (c) of this section shall be made for each taxable year to which such election is to apply. The election must be made before the later

→ *Caution: Reg. § 12.8 was issued under Code Sec. 57.*←

of (i) the time prescribed by law for filing the taxpayer's return for the taxable year for which the election is made (determined with regard to any extension of time) or (ii) August 31, 1973, but the election may not be made after the expiration of the time prescribed by law for the filing of a claim for credit or refund of tax with respect to the taxable year for which the election is to apply.

(2) *Manner of making election.* Except as provided in the following sentence, an election by the taxpayer with respect to a taxable year shall be made by a statement containing the information described in paragraph (d)(3) of this section which is—

(i) Attached to the taxpayer's return or amended return for such taxable year,

(ii) Attached to a timely filed claim by the taxpayer for credit or refund of tax for such taxable year, or

(iii) Filed by the taxpayer with the director of the Internal Revenue Service Center where the return for such taxable year was filed.

In the case of a taxable year ending before July 1, 1973, no formal statement of election is necessary if the taxpayer's return took into account an election under paragraph (b) or (c) of this section; the taxpayer will be considered to have made an election in accordance with the manner in which leases with respect to parcels of real property described in paragraph (b) of this section, or leases of property which has been in use for more than 5 years as described in paragraph (c) of this section, are treated in the return.

(3) *Statement.* The statement described in paragraph (d)(2) of this section shall contain the following information:

(i) The name, address, and taxpayer identification number of the taxpayer;

(ii) The taxable year to which the election is to apply if the statement is not attached to the return or a claim for credit or refund;

(iii) A description of any leases which are to be treated as a single lease; and

(iv) A description of any real property in use for more than five years to which the expense test is not to apply.

(4) *Revocation of election.* An election made pursuant to this paragraph may be revoked within the time prescribed in paragraph (d)(1) of this section for making an election and may not be revoked thereafter. Any such revocation shall be made in the manner prescribed by paragraph (d)(2) of this section for the making of an election.

(e) *Election by members of partnership.* Under section 703(b) (as amended by section 304(c) of the Revenue Act of 1971), any election under section 57(c) or 163(d)(7) with respect to property held by a partnership shall be made by each partner separately, rather than by the partnership. If an election made by a taxpayer under paragraph (b) of this section applies in whole or in part to property held by a partnership, the taxpayer shall, in applying the expense test referred to in paragraph (a) of this section, take into account his distributive share of the deductions of the partnership with respect to the property for the taxable year allowable solely by reason of section 162 (other than rents and reimbursed amounts with respect to the property) and also his distributive share of the partnership's rental income from such property for the taxable year. [Temporary Reg. § 12.8.]

☐ [*T.D.* 7271, 4-11-73.]

[Reg. § 1.57-0]

§ 1.57-0. Scope.—For purposes of the minimum tax for tax preferences (subtitle A, ch. I, pt. VI), the items of tax preference are:

(a) Excess investment interest,

(b) The excess of accelerated depreciation on section 1250 property over straight line depreciation,

(c) The excess of accelerated depreciation on section 1245 property subject to a net lease over straight line depreciation,

(d) The excess of the amortization deduction for certified pollution control facilities over the depreciation otherwise allowable,

(e) The excess of the amortization deduction for railroad rolling stock over the depreciation otherwise allowable,

(f) The excess of the fair market value of a share of stock received pursuant to a qualified or restricted stock option over the exercise price,

(g) The excess of the addition to the reserve for losses on bad debts of financial institutions over the amount which has been allowable based on actual experience,

(h) The excess of the percentage depletion deduction over the adjusted basis of the property, and

(i) The capital gains deduction allowable under section 1202 or an equivalent amount in the case of corporations.

Accelerated depreciation on section 1245 property subject to a net lease and excess investment interest are not items of tax preference in the case of a

Reg. § 1.57-0(a)

corporation, other than a personal holding company (as defined in section 542) and an electing small business corporation (as defined in section 1371(b)). In addition, excess investment interest is an item of tax preference only for taxable years beginning before January 1, 1972. Rules for the determination of the items of tax preference are contained in §§ 1.57-1 through 1.57-5. Generally, in the case of a nonresident alien or foreign corporation, the application of §§ 1.57-1 through 1.57-5 will be limited to cases in which the taxpayer has income effectively connected with the conduct of a trade or business within the United States. Special rules for the treatment of items of tax preference in the case of certain entities and the treatment of items of tax preference relating to income from sources outside the United States are provided in section 58 and in §§ 1.58-1 through 1.58-8. [Reg. § 1.57-0.]

☐ [*T.D. 7564, 9-11-78.*]

[Reg. § 1.57 1]

§ 1.57-1. Items of tax preference defined.—
(a) [Reserved]

(b) *Accelerated depreciation on section 1250 property*—(1) *In general.* Section 57(a)(2) provides that, with respect to each item of section 1250 property (as defined in section 1250(c)), there is to be included as an item of tax preference the amount by which the deduction allowable for the taxable year for depreciation or amortization exceeds the deduction which would have been allowable for the taxable year if the taxpayer had depreciated the property under the straight line method for each year of its useful life for which the taxpayer has held the property. The determination of the excess under section 57(a)(2) is made with respect to each separate item of section 1250 property. Accordingly, where the amount of depreciation which would have been allowable with respect to one item of section 1250 property if the taxpayer had originally used the straight line method exceeds the allowable depreciation or amortization with respect to such property, such excess may not be used to reduce the amount of the item of tax preference resulting from another item of section 1250 property.

(2) *Separate items of section 1250 property.* The determination of what constitutes a separate item of section 1250 property is to be made on the facts and circumstances of each individual case. In general, each building (or component thereof, if the taxpayer uses the component method of computing depreciation) is a separate item of section 1250 property. However, for purposes of this section, assets placed in a group, classified, or composite account are to be treated as a single item by a taxpayer, provided that such account contains only property placed in service during a single taxable year. In addition, two or more items may be treated as one item of section 1250 property for purposes of this paragraph where, with respect to each such item: (i) the period for which depreciation is taken begins on the same date, (ii) the same estimated useful life has continually been used for purposes of taking depreciation or amortization, and (iii) the same method (and rate) of depreciation or amortization has continually been used. For example, assume a taxpayer constructed a 40-unit rental townhouse development and began taking declining balance depreciation on all 40 units as of January 1, 1970, at a uniform rate and has consistently taken depreciation on all 40 units on this same basis. Although each townhouse is a separate item of section 1250 property, all 40 townhouses may be treated as one item of section 1250 property for purposes of the minimum tax since the conditions of subdivisions (i), (ii), and (iii) of this subparagraph are met. This would be true even if the 40 townhouses comprised two 20-unit developments located apart from each other. However, if the taxpayer constructed an additional development or new section on the existing development for which he began taking depreciation on July 1, 1970, at a uniform rate for all the additional units, the additional units and the original units may not be treated as one item of section 1250 property since the condition of subdivision (i) of this subparagraph is not met. Where a portion of an item of section 1250 property has been depreciated or amortized under a method (or rate) which is different from the method (or rate) under which the other portion or portions of such item have been depreciated or amortized, such portion is considered a separate item of section 1250 property for purposes of this paragraph.

(3) *Allowable depreciation or amortization.* The phrase "deduction allowable for the taxable year for exhaustion, wear and tear, obsolescence, or amortization" and references in this paragraph to "allowable depreciation or amortization" include deductions allowable for the taxable year under sections 162, 167, 212, or 611 for the depreciation or amortization of section 1250 property. Such phrase does not include depreciation allowable in the year in which section 1250 property is disposed of. For the determination of "allowable depreciation or amortization" for taxable years in which the taxpayer has taken no deduction, see § 1.1016-3(a)(2).

(4) *Straight line depreciation.* (i) For purposes of computing the depreciation which would have been allowable for the taxable year if the taxpayer had depreciated the property under the straight line method for each taxable year of its

Reg. § 1.57-1(b)(4)

useful life, the taxpayer must use the same useful life and salvage value as was used for the first taxable year in which the taxpayer depreciated or amortized the property (subject to redeterminations made pursuant to § 1.167(a)-1(b) and (c)). If, however, for any taxable year, no useful life was used under the method of depreciation or amortization used or an artificial period was used, such as, for example, by application of section 167(k), or salvage value was not taken into account in determining the annual allowances, such as, for example, under the declining balance method, then, for purposes of computing the depreciation which would have been allowable under the straight line method for the taxable year—

(a) There is to be used the useful life and salvage value which would have been proper if depreciation had actually been determined under the straight line method (without reference to an artificial life) throughout the period the property was held, and

(b) Such useful life and such salvage value is to be determined by taking into account for each taxable year the same facts and circumstances as would have been taken into account if the taxpayer had used such method throughout the period the property was held.

If an election under § 1.167(a)-11(f), § 1.167(a)-12(e), or § 1.167(a)-12(f) is applicable to the property, the salvage value of the property shall be determined in accordance with such election, and the asset depreciation period (or asset guideline period) applicable to the property pursuant to such election shall be considered to be the useful life of the property for the purposes of this section.

(ii) Where the taxpayer acquires property in a transaction to which section 381(a) applies or from another member of an affiliated group during a consolidated return year and an "accelerated" method of depreciation as described in section 167(b)(2), (3), or (4) or section 167(j)(1)(B) or (C) is permitted (see § 1.381(c)(6)-1 and § 1.1502-12(g)), the depreciation which would have been allowable under the straight line method is determined as if the property had been depreciated under the straight line method since depreciation was first taken on the property by the transferor of such property. In such cases, references in this paragraph to the

period for which the property is held or useful life of the property are treated as including the period beginning with the commencement of the original use of the property.

(iii) For purposes of section 57(a)(2), the straight line method includes the method of depreciation described in § 1.167(b)-1 or any other method which provides for a uniform proration of the cost or other basis (less salvage value) of the property over the estimated useful life of the property to the taxpayer (in terms of years, hours of use, or other similar time units) or estimated number of units to be produced over the life of the property to the taxpayer. If a method other than the method described in § 1.167(b)-1 is used, the estimated useful life or estimated units of production shall be determined in a manner consistent with subdivision (i) of this subparagraph.

(iv) In the case of property constructed by or improvements made by a lessee, the useful life is to be determined in accordance with § 1.167(a)-4.

(5) *Application for partial period.* If an item is section 1250 property for less than the entire taxable year, the allowable depreciation or amortization includes only the depreciation or amortization for that portion of the taxable year during which the item is section 1250 property and the amount of the depreciation which would have been allowable under the straight line method is determined only with regard to such portion of the taxable year.

(6) *No section 1250 and basis adjustment.* No adjustment is to be made as a result of the minimum tax either to the basis of section 1250 property or with respect to computations under section 1250.

(7) *Example.* The principles of this paragraph may be illustrated by the following example:

Example. The taxpayer's only item of section 1250 property is an office building with respect to which operations were commenced on January 1, 1971. The taxpayer depreciates the component parts of the building on the declining balance method. The useful life and costs of the component parts for depreciation purposes are as follows:

Asset	Useful Life	Cost	Salvage Value
Building shell	50	$400,000	$50,000
Partitions and walls	10	40,000	—0—
Ceilings	10	20,000	—0—
Electrical system	25	40,000	2,500
Heating and air-conditioning system	25	60,000	2,500

For purposes of computing the item of tax preference under this paragraph for the taxpayer, the partitions, walls, and ceilings may be grouped together and the electrical, heating, and air conditioning systems may be grouped together since the period for which depreciation is taken began with respect to the assets within these two groups

on the same date and the assets within each group have continually had the same useful life and have continually been depreciated under the same method (and rate).

(a) The taxpayer's 1971 item of tax preference under this paragraph would be determined as follows:

(1) Item of 1250 property	(2) Declining balance depreciation	(3) Straight line depreciation	(4) Excess of (2) over (3)
1. Shell	$12,000	$7,000	$ 5,000
2. Partitions, walls, ceilings	9,000	6,000	3,000
3. Electrical, heating and air-conditioning systems	6,000	3,800	2,200
1971 preference			$10,200

(b) Assuming the above facts are the same for 1974, the taxpayer's 1974 item of tax preference under this paragraph would be determined as follows:

(1) Item of 1250 property	(2) Declining balance depreciation	(3) Straight line depreciation	(4) Excess of (2) over (3)
1. Shell	$10,952	$7,000	$ 3,952
2. Partitions, walls, ceilings	5,529	8,000	None
3. Electrical, heating and air-conditioning systems	4,983	3,800	1,183
1974 preference			$ 5,135

(c) *Accelerated depreciation on section 1245 property subject to a net lease*—(1) *In general.* Section 57(a)(3) provides that, with respect to each item of section 1245 property (as defined in section 1245(a)(3)) which is the subject of a net lease for the taxable year, there is to be included as an item of tax preference the amount by which the deduction allowable for the taxable year for depreciation or amortization exceeds the deduction which would have been allowable for the taxable year if the taxpayer had depreciated the property under the straight line method for each year of its useful life for which the taxpayer has held the property. Except as provided in paragraph (b)(1)(ii) of this section the determination of the excess under section 57(a)(3) is made with respect to each separate item of section 1245 property. Accordingly, where the amount of depreciation which would have been allowable with respect to one item of section 1245 property if the taxpayer had originally used the straight line method exceeds the allowable depreciation or amortization with respect to such property, such excess may not be used to reduce the amount of the item of tax preference resulting from another item of section 1245 property.

(2) *Separate items of property.* The determination of what constitutes a separate item of section 1245 property must be made on the facts and circumstances of each individual case. Such determination shall be made in a manner consistent with the principles expressed in paragraph (b)(2) of this section.

(3) *Allowable depreciation or amortization.* The phrase "deduction allowable for the taxable year for exhaustion, wear and tear, obsolescence, or amortization" and references in this paragraph to "allowable depreciation or amortization" include deductions allowable for the taxable year under sections 162, 167 (including depreciation allowable under section 167 by reason of section 179), 169, 184, 185, 212, or 611 for the depreciation or amortization of section 1245 property. Such phrase does not include depreciation allowable in the year in which the section 1245 property is disposed of. Amortization of certified pollution control facilities under section 169, and amortization of railroad rolling stock under section 184 are not to be treated as amortization for purposes of section 57 (a)(3) to the extent such amounts are treated as an item of tax preference under section 57(a)(4) or (5) (see paragraphs (d) and (e) of this section). For the determination of "allowable depreciation or amortization" for taxable years in which the taxpayer has taken no deduction, see § 1.1016-3(a)(2).

(4) *Straight line method of depreciation.* The determination of the depreciation which would have been allowable under the straight line method shall be made in a manner consistent with paragraph(b)(4) of this section. Such amount shall include any amount allowable under section 167 by reason of section 179 (relating to additional first-year depreciation for small business).

(5) *Application for partial period.* If an item is section 1245 property for less than the entire taxable year or subject to a net lease for less than the entire taxable year the allowable depreciation or amortization includes only the depreciation or amortization for that portion of the taxable year during which the item was both section 1245 property and subject to a net lease and the amount of the depreciation which would have been allowable under the straight line method is to be determined only with regard to such portion of the taxable year.

(6) *Net lease.* Section 57(a)(3) applies only if the section 1245 property is the subject of a net lease for all or part of the taxable year. See § 1.57-3 for the determination of when an item is considered the subject of a net lease.

(7) *No section 1245 and basis adjustment.* No adjustment is to be made as a result of the minimum tax either to the basis of section 1245 property or with respect to computations under section 1245.

(8) *Nonapplicability to corporations.* Section 57(a)(3) does not apply to a corporation other than an electing small business corporation (as defined in section 1371(b)) and a personal holding company (as defined in section 542).

(d) *Amortization of certified pollution control facilities*—(1) *In general.* Section 57(a)(4) provides that, with respect to each certified pollution control facility for which an election is in effect under section 169, there is to be included as an item of tax preference the amount by which the deduction allowable for the taxable year under such section exceeds the depreciation deduction which would otherwise be allowable under section 167. The determination under section 57(a)(4) is made with respect to each separate certified pollution control facility. Accordingly, where the amount of the depreciation deduction which would otherwise be allowable under section 167 with respect to one facility exceeds the allowable amortization deduction under section 169 with respect to such facility, such excess may not be used to offset an item of tax preference resulting from another facility.

(2) *Separate facilities.* The determination of what constitutes a separate facility must be made on the facts and circumstances of each individual case. Generally, each facility with respect to which a separate election is in effect under section 169 shall be treated as a separate facility for purposes of this paragraph. However, if the depreciation or amortization which would have been allowable without regard to section 169 with respect to any part of a facility is based on a different useful life, date placed in service, or

method of depreciation or amortization from the other part or parts of such facility, such part is considered a separate facility for purposes of this paragraph. For example, if a building constitutes a certified pollution control facility and various component parts of the building have different useful lives, each group of component parts with the same useful life would be treated as a separate facility for purposes of this paragraph. Two or more facilities may be treated as one facility for purposes of this paragraph where, with respect to each such facility: (i) the initial amortization under section 169 commences on the same date, (ii) the facility is placed in service on the same date, (iii) the estimated useful life which would be the basis for depreciation or amortization other than section 169 has continually been the same, and (iv) the method of depreciation or amortization which could have been used without regard to section 169 could have continually been the same.

(3) *Amount allowable under section 169.* For purposes of the determination of the amount of the deduction allowable under section 169, see section 169 and the regulations thereunder. Such amount, however, shall not include amortization allowable in the year in which the pollution control facility is disposed of.

(4) *Otherwise allowable deduction.* (i) The determination of the amount of the depreciation deduction otherwise allowable under section 167 is made as if the taxpayer had depreciated the property under section 167 for each year of its useful life for which the property has been held. This amount may be determined under § 1.167(a)-11(c) if the property is eligible property (as defined in § 1.167(a)-11(b)(2)) and, during the taxable year in which the property was first placed in service, the taxpayer—

(*a*) Has made an election under § 1.167(a)-11(f) with respect to eligible property first placed in service in such taxable year, or

(*b*) Has placed no eligible property in service other than property described in § 1.167(a)-11(b)(5)(iii), (iv), or (v).

The amount determined pursuant to the preceding sentence shall be determined as if the taxpayer had depreciated the property in accordance with § 1.167(a)-11 for all years to which such section applies and during which the taxpayer held the property. This amount may be determined under § 1.167(a)-12(a)(5) if the property is qualified property (as defined in § 1.167(a)-12(a)(3)) and the taxpayer has made an election with respect to such property under § 1.167(a)-12(e). If the taxpayer has made an election under § 1.167(a)-12(f)(1) for a taxable year ending before January 1, 1971, this amount

Reg. § 1.57-1(c)(5)

shall be determined for such year in accordance with such election. For purposes of this determination, any method selected by the taxpayer which would have been permissible under section 167 for such taxable year, including accelerated methods, may be used. Any additional amount which would have been allowable by reason of section 179 (relating to additional first-year depreciation for small business) may be included provided such amount is reflected in the determination made under this paragraph in subsequent years.

(ii) If a deduction for depreciation has not been taken by the taxpayer in any taxable year under section 167 with respect to the facility—

(a) There is to be used the useful life and salvage value which would have been proper under section 167,

(b) Such useful life and salvage value is determined by taking into account for each taxable year the same facts and circumstances as would have been taken into account if the taxpayer had used such method throughout the period the property has been held, and

(c) The date the property is placed in service is, for purposes of this section, deemed to be the first day of the first month for which the amortization deduction is taken with respect to the facility under section 169.

If, prior to the date amortization begins under section 169, a deduction for depreciation has been taken by the taxpayer in any taxable year under section 167 with respect to the facility, the useful life, salvage value, etc., used for that purpose is deemed to be the appropriate useful life, salvage value, etc., for purposes of this paragraph, with such adjustments as are appropriate in light of the facts and circumstances which would have been taken into account since the time the last such depreciation deduction was taken, unless it is established by clear and convincing evidence that some other useful life, salvage value, or date the property is placed in service is more appropriate.

(iii) For purposes of section (57)(a)(4) and this paragraph, if the deduction for amortization or depreciation which would have been allowable had no election been made under section 169 would have been—

(a) An amortization deduction based on the term of a leasehold or

(b) A depreciation deduction determined by reference to section 611,

such deduction is to be deemed to be a deduction allowable under section 167.

(iv) If a facility is subject to amortization under section 169 for less than the entire taxable year, the otherwise allowable depreciation deduction under section 167 shall be determined only with regard to that portion of the taxable year during which the election under section 169 is in effect.

(v) If less than the entire adjusted basis of a facility is subject to amortization under section 169, the otherwise allowable depreciation deduction under section 167 shall be determined only with regard to that portion of the adjusted basis subject to amortization under section 169.

(5) *No section 1245 and basis adjustment.* No adjustment is to be made as a result of the minimum tax either to the basis of a certified pollution control facility or with respect to computations under section 1245.

(6) *Relationship to section 57(a)(3).* See paragraph (c)(3) with respect to an adjustment in the amount treated as amortization under that provision where both paragraphs (3) and (4) of section 57(a) are applicable to the same item of property.

(7) *Example.* The principles of this paragraph may be illustrated by the following example:

Example. A calendar year taxpayer has a certified pollution control facility on which an election is in effect under section 169 commencing with January 1, 1971. No part of the facility is section 1250 property. The original basis of the facility is $100,000 of which $75,000 constitutes amortizable basis. The useful life of the facility is 20 years. The taxpayer depreciates the $25,000 portion of the facility which is not amortizable basis under the double declining method and began taking depreciation on January 1, 1971.

(a) The taxpayer's 1971 item of tax preference under this paragraph would be determined as follows:

1. Amortization deduction	$15,000
2. Depreciation deduction on amortizable basis (double declining method)	7,500
1971 Preference (excess of 1 over 2)	$ 7,500

(b) If the taxpayer terminated his election under section 169 in 1972 effective as of July 1, 1972, the taxpayer's 1972 item of tax preference would be determined as follows:

1. Amortization deduction	$7,500
2. Depreciation deduction on amortizable basis:	
Full year ($75,000 (original basis) less $7,500 ("depreciation" to 1-1-72) equals adjusted basis of $67,500; multiplied by .10 (double declining rate))	$6,750
Portion of full year's depreciation attributable to amortization period (one-half) .	3,375
1972 Preference (excess of 1 over 2)	$4,125

(e) *Amortization of railroad rolling stock* —(1) *In general.* Section 57(a)(5) provides that, with respect to each unit of railroad rolling stock for which an election is in effect under section 184, there is to be included as an item of tax preference the amount by which the deduction allowable for the taxable year under such section exceeds the depreciation deduction which would otherwise be allowable under section 167. The determination under section 57(a)(5) is made with respect to each separate unit of rolling stock. Accordingly, where the amount of the depreciation deduction which would otherwise be allowable under section 167 with respect to one unit exceeds the allowable amortization deduction under section 184 with respect to such unit, such excess may not be used to offset an item of tax preference resulting from another unit.

(2) *Separate units of rolling stock.* The determination of what constitutes a separate unit of rolling stock must be made on the facts and circumstances of each individual case. Such determination shall be made in a manner consistent with the manner in which the comparable determination is made with respect to separate certified pollution control facilities under paragraph (d)(2) of this section.

(3) *Amount allowable under section 184.* For purposes of the determination of the amount of the deduction allowable under section 184, see section 184. Such amount, however, does not include amortization allowable in the year in which the rolling stock is disposed of.

(4) *Otherwise allowable deduction.* The determination of the amount of the depreciation deduction otherwise allowable under section 167 is to be made in a manner consistent with the manner in which the comparable deduction with respect to certified pollution control facilities is determined under paragraph (d)(4) of this section.

(5) *No section 1245 or basis adjustment.* No adjustment is to be made as a result of the minimum tax either to the basis of a unit of railroad rolling stock or with respect to computations under section 1245.

(6) *Relationship to section 57(a)(3).* See paragraph (c)(3) of this section with respect to an adjustment in the amount treated as amortization under that provision where both paragraphs (3) and (5) of section 57(a) are applicable to the same item.

(f) *Stock options*—(1) *In general.* Section 57(a)(6) provides that with respect to each transfer of a share of stock pursuant to the exercise of a qualified stock option or a restricted stock option, there shall be included by the transferee as an item of tax preference the amount by which the fair market value of the share at the time of exercise exceeds the option price. The stock option item of tax preference is subject to tax under section 56(a) in the taxable year of the transferee in which the transfer is made.

(2) *Definitions.* See generally § 1.421-7(e), (f), and (g) for the definitions of "option price," "exercise," and "transfer," respectively; however, in the case of a transfer of a share of stock pursuant to the exercise of a qualified stock option or a restricted stock option after the death of an employee by the estate of the decedent (or by a person who acquired the right to exercise such option by bequest or inheritance or by reason of the death of the decedent), the term "option price" shall, for purposes of this paragraph, include both the consideration paid by the estate (or such person) for such share of stock and so much of the basis of the option as is attributable to such share of stock. For the definition of a qualified stock option see section 422(b) and § 1.422-2. For the definition of a restricted stock option see section 424(b) and § 1.424-2. The definitions and special rules contained in section 425 and the regulations thereunder are applicable to this paragraph.

(3) *Fair market value.* In accordance with the principles of section 83(a)(1), the fair market value of a share of stock received pursuant to the exercise of a qualified or restricted stock option is to be determined without regard to restrictions (other than nonlapse restrictions within the meaning of § 1.83-3(h)). Notwithstanding any valuation date given in section 83(a)(1), for purposes of this section, fair market value is determined as of the date the option is exercised.

(4) *Foreign source options.* In the case of an option attributable to sources within any foreign country or possession, see section 58(g) and § 1.58-8.

(5) *Inapplicability in certain cases.* (i) Section 57(a)(6) is inapplicable if during the same

taxable year in which stock is transferred pursuant to the exercise of an option, the transferee makes a disposition (within the meaning of section 425(c)) of such stock. In the case of a nonresident alien, section 57(a)(6) is inapplicable to the extent the stock option is attributable (in accordance with the principles of sections 861 through 863 and the regulations thereunder) to sources without the United States.

(ii) Section 57(a)(6) is inapplicable if section 421(a) does not apply to the transfer because of employment requirements of section 422(a)(2) or section 424(a)(2).

(6) *Proportionate applicability*. Where, by reason of section 422(b)(7) and (c)(3) (relating to percentage ownership limitations), only a portion of a transfer qualifies for application of section 421, the fair market value and option price shall be determined only with regard to that portion of the transfer which so qualifies.

(7) *No basis adjustment*. No adjustment shall be made to the basis of the stock received pursuant to the exercise of a qualified or restricted stock option as a result of the minimum tax.

(g) *Reserves for losses on bad debts of financial institutions*—(1) *In general*. Section 57(a)(7) provides that, in the case of a financial institution to which section 585 or 593 (both relating to reserves for losses on loans) applies, there shall be included as an item of tax preference the amount by which the deduction allowable for the taxable year for a reasonable addition to a reserve for bad debts exceeds the amount that would have been allowable had the institution maintained its bad debt reserve for all taxable years on the basis of the institution's actual experience.

(2) *Taxpayers covered*. Section 57(a)(7) applies only to an institution (or organization) to which section 585 or 593 applies. See sections 585(a) and 593(a) and the regulations thereunder for a description of those institutions.

(3) *Allowable deduction*. For purposes of this paragraph, the amount of the deduction allowable for the taxable year for a reasonable addition to a reserve for bad debts is the amount of the deduction allowed under section 166(c) by reference to section 585 or 593.

(4) *Actual experience*. (i) For purposes of this paragraph, the determination of the amount which would have been allowable had the institution maintained its reserve for bad debts on the basis of actual experience is the amount determined under section 585(b)(3)(A) and the regulations thereunder. For this purpose, the beginning

balance for the first taxable year ending in 1970 is the amount which bears the same ratio to loans outstanding at the beginning of the taxable year as (*a*) the total bad debts sustained during the 5 preceding taxable years, adjusted for recoveries of bad debts during such period, bears to (*b*) the sum of the loans outstanding at the close of such 5 taxable years. The taxpayer may, however, select a more appropriate balance based on its actual experience during a shorter period subject to the approval of the district director upon examination of the return provided there are unusual circumstances which indicate that such period is more indicative of the taxpayer's actual loss experience. Any such selection and approval shall be made in a manner consistent with the selection and approval of a bad debt reserve method under § 1.166-1(b). In the case of an institution which has been in existence for less than 5 taxable years as of the beginning of the first taxable year ending in 1970, the above formula for determining the beginning balance is applied by substituting the number of taxable years for which the institution has been in existence as of the beginning of the taxable year for "5" each time it appears. If any taxable year utilized in the above formula for determining the beginning balance is a short taxable year the amount of the bad debts, adjusted for recoveries, for such taxable year is modified by dividing such amount by the number of days in the taxable year and multiplying the resulting amount by 365. The beginning balance for any subsequent taxable year is the amount of the beginning balance of the preceding taxable year, decreased by bad debt losses during such year and increased by recoveries of bad debts during such year and increased by the lower of the maximum amount determined under section 585(b)(3)(A) for such year or the amount of the deduction allowed for such year. The application of this subdivision (i) may be illustrated by the following example:

Example. The Y Bank, a calendar year taxpayer, uses the reserve method of accounting for bad debts. On December 31, 1969, Y determines the balance of its reserve for bad debts to the $70,000 under the percentage method. On the same date Y's 5-year moving average is $52,000. Y incurs net bad debt losses (bad debt losses less recoveries of bad debts) of $3,000 for each of the years 1970, 1971, and 1972, which it charges to its reserve for bad debts. Y's 6-year moving averages computed under section 585(b)(3)(A) at the close of 1970, 1971, and 1972 are $50,000, $49,000, and $51,000, respectively. Y's preference items are computed as follows based upon additional facts assumed:

Reg. § 1.57-1(g)(4)

	1970	1971	1972
1. Bad debt reserve—percentage method:			
(a) Balance beginning of year (closing balance prior year)...	$70,000	$70,000	$68,000
(b) Net bad debts charged to reserve	3,000	3,000	3,000
(c) Subtotal	$67,000	$67,000	$65,000
(d) Deduction allowed	3,000	1,000	4,000
(e) Balance end of year	$70,000	$68,000	$69,000
2. Bad debt reserve—"actual experience":			
(a) Beginning balance (for 1970, 5-year moving average; for other years, closing balance prior year)	$52,000	$50,000	$48,000
(b) Net bad debts charged to reserve	$ 3,000	$ 3,000	$ 3,000
(c) Subtotal	$49,000	$47,000	$45,000
(d) Maximum amount under section 585(b)(3)(A) (6-year moving average minus (c))	$ 1,000	$ 2,000	$ 6,000
(e) Deduction allowed (line 1(d))	3,000	1,000	4,000
(f) Lower of (d) or (e)	1,000	1,000	4,000
(g) Closing balance (line (c) + (f))	$50,000	$48,000	$49,000
3. Preference item under section 57(a)(7):			
(a) Deduction allowed	$ 3,000	$ 1,000	$ 4,000
(b) Maximum amount under section 585(b)(3)(A)	1,000	2,000	6,000
(c) Preference item (excess of (a) over (b))	$ 2,000	0	0

(ii) In the case of a new institution whose first taxable year ends after 1969, its beginning balance for its reserve for bad debts, for purposes of this paragraph, is zero and its reasonable addition to the reserve for such taxable year is determined on the basis of the actual experience of similar institutions located in the area served by the taxpayer.

(h) *Depletion*—(1) *In general.* Section 57(a)(8) provides that with respect to each property (as defined in section 614), there is to be included as an item of tax preference the amount by which the deduction allowable for the taxable year under section 611 for depletion for the property exceeds the adjusted basis of the property at the end of the taxable year (determined without regard to the depletion deduction for that taxable year). The determination under section 57(a)(8) is made with respect to each separate property. Thus, for example, if one mineral property has an adjusted basis remaining at the end of the taxable year, such basis may not be used to reduce the amount of an item of tax preference resulting from another mineral property.

(2) *Allowable depletion.* For the determination of the amount of the deduction for depletion allowable for the taxable year see section 611 and the regulations thereunder.

(3) *Adjusted basis.* For the determination of the adjusted basis of the property at the end of the taxable year see section 1016 and the regulations thereunder.

(4) *No basis adjustment.* No adjustment is to be made to the basis of property subject to depletion as a result of the minimum tax.

(i) *Capital gains*—(1) *Taxpayers other than corporations.* Section 57(a)(9)(A) provides that, in

the case of a taxpayer other than a corporation, there is to be included as an item of tax preference one-half of the amount by which the taxpayer's net long-term capital gain for the taxable year exceeds the taxpayer's net short-term capital loss for the taxable year. For this purpose, for taxable years beginning after December 31, 1971, the taxpayer's net long-term capital gain does not include an amount equal to the deduction allowable under section 163 (relating to interest expense) by reason of subsection (d)(1)(C) of that section, and the excess described in the preceding sentence is reduced by an amount equal to the reduction of disallowed interest expense by reason of section 163(d)(2)(B). Furthermore, the net long-term capital gain of an estate or trust does not include capital gains described in section 642(c)(4). Included in the computation of the taxpayer's capital gains item of tax preference are amounts reportable by the taxpayer as distributive shares of gain or loss from partnerships, estates or trusts, electing small business corporations, common trust funds, etc. See section 58 and the regulations thereunder with respect to the above entities.

Example. For 1971, A, a calendar year individual taxpayer, recognized $50,000 from the sale of securities held for more than 6 months. In addition, A received a $15,000 dividend from X Fund, a regulated investment company, $12,000 of which was designated as a capital gain dividend by the company pursuant to section 852(b)(3)(C). The AB partnership recognized a gain of $20,000 from the sale of section 1231 property held by the partnership. The AB partnership agreement provides that A is entitled to 50 percent of the income and gains of the partnership. A had net

Reg. § 1.57-1(h)(1)

short-term capital loss for the year of $10,000. A's 1971 capital gains item of tax preference is computed as follows:

Capital gain recognized from securities	$50,000
Capital gain dividend from regulated investment company	12,000
Distributive share of partnership capital gain	10,000
Total net long-term capital gain	$72,000
Less: net short-term capital loss	(10,000)
Excess of net long-term capital gain over net short-term capital loss	$62,000
One-half of above excess	$31,000

(2) *Corporations.* (i) Section 57(a)(9)(B) provides that in the case of corporations there is to be included as an item of tax preference with respect to a corporation's net section 1201 gain an amount equal to the product obtained by multiplying the excess of the net long-term capital gain over the net short-term capital loss by a fraction. The numerator of this fraction is the sum of the normal tax rate and the surtax rate under section 11 minus the alternative tax rate under section 1201(a) for the taxable year, and the denominator of the fraction is the sum of the normal tax rate and the surtax rate under section 11 for the taxable year. Included in the above computation are amounts reportable by the taxpayer as distributive shares of gain or loss from partnerships, estates or trusts, common trust funds, etc. In certain cases the amount of the net section 1201 gain which results in preferential treatment will be less than the amount determined by application of the statutory formula. Therefore, in lieu of the statutory formula, the capital gains item of tax preference for corporations may in all cases be determined by dividing—

(a) The amount of tax which would have been imposed under section 11 if section 1201 (a) did not apply minus—

(b) The amount of the taxes actually imposed

by the sum of the normal tax rate plus the surtax rate under section 11. In case of foreign source capital gains and losses which are not taken into account pursuant to sections 58(g)(2)(B) and 1.58-8, the amount determined in the preceding sentence shall be multiplied by a fraction the numerator of which is the corporation's net section 1201 gain without regard to such gains and losses which are not taken into account and the denominator of which is the corporation's net section 1201 gain. The computation of the corporate capital gains item of tax preference may be illustrated by the following examples:

Example (1). For 1971, A, a calendar year corporate taxpayer, has ordinary income of $10,000 and net section 1201 gain of $50,000, none of which is subsection (d) gain (as defined in sec. 1201(d)) and none of which is attributable to foreign sources. A's 1971 capital gain item of tax preference may be computed as follows:

1. Tax under section 11:		
Normal tax (0.22 × $60,000)		$13,200
Surtax (0.26 × $35,000)		9,100
		$22,300
2. Tax under section 1201(a)		
Normal tax on ordinary income (0.22 × $10,000)	$ 2,200	
Tax on net section 1201 gain (0.30 × $50,000)	15,000	17,200
3. Excess		$ 5,100
4. Normal tax rate plus surtax rate		.48
5. Capital gains preference (line 3 divided by line 4)		$10,625

Example (2). For 1971, A, a calendar year corporate taxpayer, has a loss from operations of $30,000 and net section 1201 gain of $150,000, none of which is subsection (d) gain (as defined in sec. 1201(d)) and none of which is attributable to foreign sources. A's 1971 capital gain item of tax preference may be computed as follows:

Reg. § 1.57-1(i)(2)

1. Tax under section 11:
   Normal tax (0.22 × $120,000) $26,400
   Surtax (0.26 × $95,000) 24,700
                                                       $51,100

2. Tax under section 1201(a)
   Normal tax on ordinary income .... None
   Tax on net section 1201 gain (0.30 × $150,000) $45,000   45,000

3. Excess .... $ 6,100

4. Normal tax rate plus surtax rate .... .48
5. Capital gain preference (line 3 divided by line 4) $12,708

(ii) In the case of organizations subject to the tax imposed by section 511(a), mutual savings banks conducting a life insurance business (see sec. 594), life insurance companies (as defined in sec. 801), mutual insurance companies to which part II of subchapter L applies, insurance companies to which part III of subchapter L applies, regulated investment companies subject to tax under part I of subchapter M, real estate investment trusts subject to tax under part II of subchapter M, or any other corporation not subject to the taxes imposed by sections 11 and 1201(a), the capital gains item of tax preference may be computed in accordance with subdivision (i) of this subparagraph except that, in lieu of references to section 11, there is to be substituted the section which imposes the tax comparable to the tax imposed by section 11 and, in lieu of references to section 1201(a), there is to be substituted the section which imposes the alternative or special tax applicable to the capital gains of such corporation.

(iii) For purposes of this paragraph, where the net section 1201 gain is not in any event subject to the tax comparable to the normal tax and the surtax under section 11, such as in the case of regulated investment companies subject to tax under subchapter M, such comparable tax shall be computed as if it were applicable to net section 1201 gain to the extent such gain is subject to the tax comparable to the alternative tax under section 1201(a). Thus, in the case of a regulated investment company subject to tax under subchapter M, the tax comparable to the normal tax and the surtax would be the tax computed under section 852(b)(1) determined as if the amount subject to tax under section 852(b)(3) were included in investment company taxable income. The principles of this subdivision (iii) may be illustrated by the following example:

Example. M, a calendar year regulated investment company, in 1971, has investment company taxable income (subject to tax under sec. 852(b)(1)) of $125,000 and net long-term capital gain of $800,000. M Company has no net short-term capital loss but has a deduction for dividends paid (determined with reference to capital gains only) of $700,000. M's 1971 capital gains item of tax reference is computed as follows:

1. Section 852(b)(1) tax computed as if it were applicable to all income including capital gains:
   Amount subject to section 852(b)(1) $125,000
   Net section 1201 gain $800,000
   Less: Dividends paid deduction 700,000

   Net section 1201 gain subject to tax at the
     company level 100,000
                                             $225,000
   Normal tax (0.22 × $225,000) .... $ 49,500
   Surtax (0.26 × 200,000) 52,000
                                                   $101,500

2. Tax comparable to section 1201(a) tax section 852(b)(1) tax:
   Normal tax (0.22 × 125,000) .... $ 27,500
   Surtax (0.26 × 100,000) .... 26,000 $ 53,500
   Section 852(b)(3) tax (0.30 × 100,000) .... 30,000 $ 83,500

3. Excess .... $ 18,000

4. Normal tax rate plus surtax rate .... .48
5. Capital gains preference (line 3 divided by line 4) .... $ 37,500

Reg. § 1.57-1(i)(2)

(iv) For the computation of the capital gains item of tax preference in the case of an electing small business corporation (as defined in sec. 1371(b)), see section 1.58-4(c).

(3) *Nonresident aliens, foreign corporations.* In the case of a nonresident alien individual or foreign corporation, there shall be included in computing the capital gains item of tax preference under section 57(a)(9) only those capital gains and losses included in the computation of income effectively connected with the conduct of a trade or business within the United States as provided in section 871(b) or 882. [Reg. § 1.57-1.]

☐ [*T.D.* 7564, 9-11-78.]

[Reg. § 1.57-5]

§ 1.57-5. Records to be kept.—(a) *In general.* The taxpayer shall have available permanent records of all the facts necessary to determine with reasonable accuracy the amounts described in § 1.57-1. Such records shall include:

(1) In the case of amounts described in paragraph (a) of § 1.57-1: the amount and nature of indebtedness outstanding for the taxable year and the date or dates on which each such indebtedness was incurred or renewed in any form; the amount expended for property held for investment during any taxable year during which such indebtedness was incurred or renewed; and the manner in which it was determined that property was or was not held for investment.

(2) In the case of amounts described in paragraphs (b), (c), (d), (e), and (h) of § 1.57-1:

(i) The dates, and manner in which the property was acquired and placed in service,

(ii) The taxpayer's basis on the date the property was acquired and the manner in which the basis was determined,

(iii) An estimate of the useful life (in terms of months, hours of use, etc., whichever is appropriate) of the property on the date placed in service or an estimate of the number of units to be produced by the property on the date the property is placed in service, whichever is appropriate, and the manner in which such estimate was determined,

(iv) The amount and date of all adjustments by the taxpayer to the basis of the property and an explanation of the nature of such adjustments, and

(v) In the case of property which has an adjusted basis reflecting adjustments taken by another taxpayer with respect to the property or taken by the taxpayer with respect to other property, the information described in subdivisions (i) through (iv) above, with respect to such other property or other taxpayer.

(3) In the case of amounts described in paragraph (f) of § 1.57-1, the fair market value of the shares of stock at the date of exercise of the option and the option price and the manner in which each was determined.

(4) In the case of amounts described in paragraph (g) of § 1.57-1, the amount of debts written off and the amount of the loans outstanding for the taxable year and the 5 preceding taxable years or such shorter or longer period as is appropriate.

(b) *Net operating losses.* The taxpayer shall have available permanent records for the first taxable year in which a portion of a net operating loss was attributable to items of tax preference (within the meaning of § 1.56A-2(b)) and each succeeding taxable year in which there is a net operating loss or a net operating loss carryover a portion of which is so attributable. Such records shall include all the facts necessary to determine with reasonable accuracy the amount of deferred tax liability under section 56, including the amount of the net operating loss in each taxable year in which there are items of tax preference in excess of the minimum tax exemption (as determined under § 1.58-1), the amount of the items of tax preference for each such taxable year, the amount by which each such net operating loss reduces taxable income in any taxable year, and the amount by which each such net operating loss is reduced in any taxable year. [Reg. § 1.57-5.]

☐ [*T.D.* 7564, 9-11-78. *Amended by T.D.* 8138, 4-23-87.]

[Reg. § 7.57(d)-1]

§ 7.57(d)-1. Election with respect to straight line recovery of intangibles.—(a) *Purpose.* This section prescribes rules for making the election permitted under section 57(d)(2), as added by the Tax Reform Act of 1976. Under this election taxpayers may use cost depletion to compute straight line recovery of intangibles.

(b) *Election.* The election under section 57(d) is subject to the following rules:

(1) The election is made within the time prescribed by law (including extensions thereof) for filing the return for the taxable year in which the intangible drilling costs are paid or incurred or, if later, by June 25, 1978.

(2) The election is made separately for each well. Thus, a taxpayer may make the election for only some of his or her wells.

(3) The election is made by using, for the well or wells to which the election applies, cost depletion to compute straight line recovery of in-

Reg. § 7.57(d)-1(b)(3)

tangibles for purposes of determining the amount of the preference under section 57(a)(11).

(4) The election may be made whether or not the taxpayer uses cost depletion in computing taxable income.

(5) The election is made by a partnership rather than by each partner.

(c) *Computation of cost depletion.* For purposes of computing straight line recovery of intangibles through cost depletion, both depletable and depreciable intangible drilling and development costs for the taxable year are taken into account. They are treated as if capitalized, added to basis, and recovered under § 1.611-2(a). Costs paid or incurred in other taxable years are not taken into account. [Temporary Reg. § 7.57(d)-1.]

☐ [*T.D.* 7541, 4-25-78. *Amended by T.D.* 8138, 4-23-87.]

[Reg. § 1.58-1]

§ 1.58-1. **Minimum tax exemption.**—(a) *In general.* For purposes of the minimum tax for tax preferences (subtitle A, chapter 1A, part VI), the minimum tax exemption is $30,000 except as otherwise provided in this section.

(b) *Husband and wife.* In the case of a married individual filing a separate return, section 58(a) provides that the minimum tax exemption is $15,000. This rule applies without regard to whether the married individual is living together with or apart from his spouse and without regard to whether or not his spouse has any items of tax preference.

(c) *Members of controlled groups*—(1) *Amount of exemption*—(i) *General rule.* Under section 58(b), if a corporation is a component member of a controlled group of corporations on a December 31 (as defined in section 1563(a) and (b) and the regulations thereunder), the minimum tax exemption for such taxable year which includes such December 31 is an amount equal to—

(a) $30,000 divided by the number of corporations which are component members of such group on December 31, or

(b) If an apportionment plan is adopted under subparagraph (3) of this paragraph, such portion of the $30,000 as is apportioned to such member in accordance with such plan.

(ii) *Consolidated returns.* The minimum tax exemption of a controlled group all of whose component members join in the filing of a consolidated return is $30,000. If there are component members of the controlled group which do not join in the filing of a consolidated return, and there is no apportionment plan effective under subparagraph (3) of this paragraph apportioning the

$30,000 among the component members filing the consolidated return and the other component members of the controlled group, each component member of the controlled group (including each component member which joins in filing the consolidated return) is treated as a separate corporation for purposes of equally apportioning the $30,000 amount under subdivision (i)(a) of this subparagraph. In such case, the minimum tax exemption of the corporations filing the consolidated return is the sum of the amounts apportioned to each component member which joins in the filing of the consolidated return.

(2) *Certain short taxable years.* If the return of a corporation is for a short period which does not include a December 31, and such corporation is a component member of a controlled group of corporations with respect to such short period, the minimum tax exemption of such corporation for such short period is an amount equal to $30,000 divided by the number of corporations which are component members of such group on the last day of such short period. The minimum tax exemption so determined is also subject to the rules of section 443(d) (relating to reduction in the amount of the exemption for short periods) and the regulations thereunder. For purposes of this subparagraph, the term "short period" does not include any period if the income for such period is required to be included in a consolidated return under § 1.1502-76(b). The determination of whether a corporation is a component member of a controlled group of corporations on the last day of a short period is made by applying the definition of "component member" contained in section 1563(b) and § 1.1563-1 as if the last day of such short period were a December 31.

(3) *Apportionment of minimum tax exemption*—(i) *Apportionment plan. (a)* (In general.) In the case of corporations which are component members of a controlled group of corporations on a December 31, a single minimum tax exemption may be apportioned among such members if all such members consent, in the manner provided in subdivision (ii) of this subparagraph, to an apportionment plan with respect to such December 31. Such plan must provide for the apportionment of a fixed dollar amount to one or more of such members, but in no event may the sum of the amount so apportioned exceed $30,000. An apportionment plan is not considered as adopted with respect to a particular December 31 until each component member which is required to consent to the plan under subdivision (ii)(a) of this subparagraph files the original of a statement described in such subdivision (or, the original of a statement incorporating its consent is filed on its behalf). In the case of a return filed before a plan

is adopted, the minimum tax exemption for purposes of such return is to be equally apportioned in accordance with subparagraph (1) of this paragraph. If a valid apportionment plan is adopted after the return is filed and within the time prescribed in (b) of this subdivision (i), such return must be amended (or a claim for refund should be made) to reflect the change from equal apportionment.

(b) (Time for adopting plan.) A controlled group may adopt an apportionment plan with respect to a particular December 31 only if, at the time such plan is sought to be adopted, there is at least one year remaining in the statutory period (including any extensions thereof) for the assessment of the deficiency against any corporation the tax liability of which would be increased by the adoption of such plan. If there is less than 1 year remaining with respect to any such corporation, the district director or the director of the service center with whom such corporation files its income tax return will ordinarily, upon request, enter into an agreement to extend such statutory period for the limited purpose of assessing any deficiency against such corporation attributable to the adoption of such apportionment plan.

(c) (Years for which effective.) (1) The amount apportioned to a component member of a controlled group of corporations in an apportionment plan adopted with respect to a particular December 31 constitutes such member's minimum tax exemption for its taxable year including the particular December 31, and for all taxable years including succeeding December 31's, unless the apportionment plan is amended in accordance with subdivision (iii) of this subparagraph or is terminated under (c)(2) of this subdivision (i). Thus, the apportionment plan (including any amendments thereof) has a continuing effect and need not be renewed annually.

(2) If an apportionment plan is adopted with respect to a particular December 31, such plan terminates with respect to a succeeding December 31, if: the controlled group goes out of existence with respect to such succeeding December 31 within the meaning of paragraph (b) of § 1.1562-5, any corporation which was a component member of such group on the particular December 31 is not a component member of such group on such succeeding December 31, or any corporation which was not a component member of such group on the particular December 31 is a component member of such group on such succeeding December 31. An apportionment plan, once terminated with respect to a December 31, is no longer effective. Accordingly, unless a new

apportionment plan is adopted, the minimum tax exemption of the component members of the controlled group for their taxable years which include such December 31 and all December 31's thereafter will be determined under subparagraph (1) of this paragraph.

(3) If an apportionment plan is terminated with respect to a particular December 31 by reason of the addition or withdrawal of a component member, each corporation which is a component member of the controlled group on such particular December 31 must, on or before the date it files its income tax return for the taxable year which includes such particular December 31, notify the district director or the director of the service center with whom it files such return of such termination. If an apportionment plan is terminated with respect to a particular December 31 by reason of the controlled group going out of existence, each corporation which was a component member of the controlled group on the preceding December 31 must, on or before the date it files its income tax return for the taxable year which includes such particular December 31, notify the district director or the director of the service center with whom it files such return of such termination.

(ii) Consents to plan—(a) General rule. (1) The consent of a component member (other than a wholly-owned subsidiary) to an apportionment plan with respect to a particular December 31 is to be made by means of a statement, signed by any person who is duly authorized to act on behalf of the consenting member, stating that such member consents to the apportionment plan with respect to such December 31. The statement must set forth the name, address, taxpayer identification number, and taxable year of the consenting component member, the amount apportioned to such member under the plan, and the internal revenue district or service center where the original of the statement is to be filed. The consent of more than one component member may be incorporated in a single statement. The original of a statement of consent is to be filed with the district director or the director of the service center with whom the component member of the group on such December 31 which has the taxable year ending first on or after such date filed its return for such taxable year. If two or more component members have the same such taxable year, a statement of consent may be filed with the district director or the director of the service center with whom the return for any such taxable year is filed. The original of a statement of consent is to have attached thereto information (referred to in this subdivision as "group identification") setting forth the name, address, taxpayer identification number, and taxable year of each component member of the controlled group on such December 31 (including wholly-owned subsidiaries) and the amount apportioned to each such member under the plan. If more than one original statement is filed, a statement may incorporate the group identification by reference to the name, address, taxpayer identification number, and taxable year of the component member of the group which has attached such group identification to the original of its statement.

(2) Each component member of the group on such December 31 (other than wholly-owned subsidiaries) must attach a copy of its consent (or a copy of the statement incorporating its consent) to the income tax return, amended return, or claim for refund filed with its district director or director of the service center for the taxable year including such date. Such copy must either have attached thereto information on group identification or must incorporate such information by reference to the name, address, taxpayer identification number, and taxable year of the component member of the group which has attached such information to its income tax return, amended return, or claim for refund filed with the same district director or director of the service center for the taxable year including such date.

(b) *Wholly-owned subsidiaries.* (1) Each component member of a controlled group which is a wholly-owned subsidiary of such group with respect to a December 31 is deemed to consent to an apportionment plan with respect to such December 31, provided each component member of the group which is not a wholly-owned subsidiary consents to the plan. For purposes of this paragraph, a component member of a controlled group is considered to be a wholly-owned subsidiary of the group with respect to a December 31, if, on each day preceding such date and during its taxable year which includes such date, all of its stock is owned directly by one or more corporations which are component members of the group on such December 31.

(2) Each wholly-owned subsidiary of a controlled group with respect to a December 31 must attach a statement containing the information which is required to be set forth in a statement of consent to an apportionment plan with respect to such December 31 to the income tax return, amended return, or claim for refund filed with its district director or director of the service center for the taxable year which includes such date. Such statement must either have attached thereto information on group identification or incorporate such information by reference to the name, address, taxpayer identification number,

and taxable year of a component member of the group which has attached such information to its income tax return, amended return, or claim for refund filed with the same district director or director of the service center for the taxable year including such date.

(iii) *Amendment of plan.* An apportionment plan adopted with respect to a December 31 by a controlled group of corporations may be amended with respect to such December 31 or with respect to any succeeding December 31 for which the plan is effective under subdivision (i)(c) of this subparagraph. An apportionment plan must be amended with respect to a particular December 31 and the amendments to the plan are effective only if adopted in accordance with the rules prescribed in this paragraph for the adoption of an original plan with respect to such December 31.

(iv) *Component members filing consolidated return.* If the component members of a controlled group of corporations on a December 31 include corporations which join the filing of a consolidated return, the corporations filing the consolidated return are treated as a single component member for purposes of this subparagraph. Thus, for example, only one consent executed by the common parent to an apportionment plan filed pursuant to this section is required on behalf of the component members filing the consolidated return.

(d) *Estates and trusts.* Section 58(c)(2) provides that, in the case of an estate or trust, the minimum tax exemption applicable to such estate or trust is an amount which bears the same ratio to $30,000 as the portion of the sum of the items of tax preference apportioned to the estate or trust bears to the full sum before apportionment. For example, if one-third of the sum of the items of tax preference of a trust are subject to tax at the trust level after apportionment under section 58(c)(1) and § 1.58-3, the trust's minimum tax exemption is $10,000. See § 1.58-3 for rules with respect to the apportionment of items of tax preference of an estate or trust.

(e) *Short taxable year.* See section 443(d) and § 1.443-1(d) with respect to reduction in the amount of the minimum tax exemption in the case of a short taxable year. [Reg. § 1.58-1.]

□ [*T.D.* 7564, 9-11-78.]

[Reg. § 1.58-2]

§ 1.58-2. General rules for conduit entities; partnerships and partners.—(a) *General rules for conduit entities.* Sections 1.58-3 through 1.58-6 provide rules under which items of tax preference of an estate, trust, electing small business corporation, common trust fund, regulated investment company, or real estate investment trust (referred to in this paragraph as the "conduit entity") are treated as items of tax preference of the beneficiaries, shareholders, participants, etc. (referred to in this paragraph as the "distributees"). Where an item of tax preference of a conduit entity is so apportioned to a distributee, the item of tax preference retains its character in the hands of the distributee and is adjusted to reflect: (1) the separate items of income and deduction of the distributee and (2) the tax status of the distributee as an individual, corporation, etc. For example, if a trust has $100,000 of capital gains for the taxable year, all of which are distributed to A, an individual, the item of tax preference apportioned to A under section 57(a)(9) (and § 1.57-1(i)(1)) is $50,000. If, however, A had a net capital loss for the taxable year of $60,000 without regard to the distribution from the trust, the trust tax preference would be adjusted in the hands of A to reflect the separate items of income and deduction passed through to the distributee, or, in this case, to reflect the net section 1201 gain to A of $40,000. Thus, A's capital gains items of tax preference would be $20,000. By application of this rule, A, in effect, treats capital gains distributed to him from the trust the same as his other capital gains in computing his capital gains item of tax preference. If A had been a corporation, the trust tax preference would be adjusted both to reflect the capital loss and to reflect A's tax status by recomputing the capital gains item of tax preference (after adjustment for the capital loss) under section 57(a)(9)(B) and § 1.57-1(i)(2). Similarly, if depreciation on section 1245 property subject to a net lease (as defined in section 57(a)(3) and § 1.57-1(c)) is apportioned from a conduit entity to a corporation (other than a personal holding company or electing small business corporation), the amount so apportioned to the corporation is not treated as an item of tax preference to such corporation since such item is not an item of tax preference in the case of a corporation (other than a personal holding company or an electing small business corporation).

(b) *Partnerships and partners.*—(1) Section 701 provides that a partnership as such is not subject to the income tax imposed by chapter 1. Thus, a partnership as such is not subject to the minimum tax for tax preferences. Section 702 provides that, in determining his income tax, each partner is to take into account separately his distributive share of certain items of income, deductions, etc. of the partnership and other items of income, gain, loss, deduction, or credit of the partnership to the extent provided by regulations prescribed by the Secretary or his delegate. Accordingly, each part-

ner, in computing his items of tax preference must take into account separately those items of income and deduction of the partnership which enter into the computation of the items of tax preference in accordance with subparagraph (2) of this paragraph.

(2) Pursuant to section 702, each partner must, solely for purposes of the minimum tax for tax preferences (to the extent not otherwise required to be taken into account separately under section 702 and the regulations thereunder), take into account separately in the manner provided in subchapter K and the regulations thereunder those items of income and deduction of the partnership which enter into the computation of the items of tax preference specified in section 57 and the regulations thereunder. A partner must, for this purpose, take into account separately his distributive share of:

(i) Investment interest expense (as defined in section 57(b)(2)(D)) determined at the partnership level;

(ii) Investment income (as defined in section 57(b)(2)(B)) determined at the partnership level;

(iii) Investment expenses (as defined in section 57(b)(2)(C)) determined at the partnership level;

(iv) With respect to each section 1250 property (as defined in section 1250(c)), the amount of the deduction allowable for the taxable year for exhaustion, wear and tear, obsolescence, or amortization and the deduction which would have been allowable for the taxable year had the property been depreciated under the straight line method each taxable year of its useful life (determined without regard to section 167(k)) for which the partnership has held the property;

(v) With respect to each item of section 1245 property (as defined in section 1245(a)(3)) which is subject to a net lease, the amount of the deduction allowable for exhaustion, wear and tear, obsolescence, or amortization and the deduction which would have been allowable for the taxable year had the property been depreciated under the straight line method for each taxable year of its useful life for which the partnership has held the property;

(vi) With respect to each certified pollution control facility for which an election is in effect under section 169, the amount of the deduction allowable for the taxable year under such section and the deduction which would have been allowable under section 167 had no election been in effect under section 169;

Reg. § 1.58-2(b)(2)

(vii) With respect to each unit of railroad rolling stock for which an election is in effect under section 184, the amount of the deduction allowable for the taxable year under such section and the deduction which would have been allowable under section 167 had no election been in effect under section 184;

(viii) In the case of a partnership which is a financial institution to which section 585 or 593 applies, the amount of the deduction allowable for the taxable year for a reasonable addition to a reserve for bad debts and the amount of the deduction that would have been allowable for the taxable year had the institution maintained its bad debt reserve for all taxable years on the basis of actual experience; and

(ix) With respect to each mineral property, the deduction for depletion allowable under section 611 for the taxable year and the adjusted basis of the property at the end of the taxable year (determined without regard to the depletion deduction for the taxable year).

If, pursuant to section 743 (relating to optional adjustment to basis), the basis of partnership property is adjusted with respect to a transferee partner due to an election being in effect under section 754 (relating to manner of electing optional adjustment), items representing amortization, depreciation, depletion, gain or loss, and the adjusted basis of property subject to depletion, described above, shall be adjusted to reflect the basis adjustment under section 743.

(3) The minimum tax is effective for taxable years ending after December 31, 1969. Thus, subparagraph (2) of this paragraph is inapplicable in the case of items of income or deduction paid or accrued in a partnership's taxable year ending on or before December 31, 1969. [Reg. § 1.58-2.]

☐ [*T.D. 7564, 9-11-78.*]

[Reg. § 1.58-3]

§ 1.58-3. Estates and trusts.—(a) *In general.* (1) Section 58(c)(1) provides that the sum of the items of tax preference of an estate or trust shall be apportioned between the estate or trust and the beneficiary on the basis of the income of the estate or trust allocable to each. Income for this purpose is the income received or accrued by the trust or estate which is not subject to current taxation either in the hands of the trust or estate or the beneficiary by reason of an item of tax preference. The character of the amounts distributed is determined under section 652(b) or 662(b) and the regulations thereunder.

(2) Additional computations required by reason of excess distributions are to be made in accordance with the principles of sections 665-669 and the regulations thereunder.

(3) In the case of a charitable remainder annuity trust (as defined in section 664(d)(1) and § 1.664-2) or a charitable remainder unitrust (as defined in section 664(d)(2) and § 1.664-3), the determination of the income not subject to current taxation by reason of an item of tax preference is to be made as if such trust were generally subject to taxation. Where income of such a trust is not subject to current taxation in accordance with this section and is distributed to a beneficiary in a taxable year subsequent to the taxable year in which the trust received or accrued such income, the items of tax preference relating to such income are apportioned to the beneficiary in such subsequent year (without credit for minimum tax paid by the trust with respect to items of tax preference which are subject to the minimum tax by reason of section 664(c)).

(4) Items of tax preference apportioned to a beneficiary pursuant to this section are to be taken into account by the beneficiary in his taxable year within or with which ends the taxable year of the estate or trust during which it has such items of tax preference.

(5) Where a trust or estate has items of income or deduction which enter into the computation of the excess investment interest item of tax preference, but such items do not result in an item of tax preference at the trust or estate level, each beneficiary must take into account, in computing his excess investment interest, the portion of such items distributed to him. The determination of the portion of such items distributed to each beneficiary is made in accordance with the character rules of section 652(b) or section 662(b) and the regulations thereunder.

(6) Where, pursuant to subpart E of part 1 of subchapter J (sections 671-678), the grantor of a trust or another person is treated as the owner of any portion of the trust, there shall be included in computing the items of tax preference of such person those items of income, deductions, and credits against tax of the trust which are attributable to that portion of the trust to the extent such items are taken into account under section 671 and the regulations thereunder. Any remaining portion of the trust is subject to the provisions of this section.

(b) *Examples.* The principles of this section may be illustrated by the following examples in each of which it is assumed that none of the distributions are accumulation distributions (see sections 665-669 and the regulations thereunder):

Example (1). Trust A, with one income beneficiary, has the following items of income and deduction without regard to the deduction for distributions:

Income:		
Business income		$200,000
Investment income		20,000
		$220,000
Deductions:		
Business deductions (nonpreference)		$100,000
Investment interest expense		80,000
		$180,000

Based on the above figures, the trust has $100,000 of taxable income without regard to items which enter into the computation of excess investment interest and the deduction for distributions. The trust also has $60,000 of excess investment interest, resulting in $40,000 of distributable net income. Thus, $60,000 of the $100,000 of noninvestment income is not subject to current taxation by reason of the excess investment interest.

(a) If $40,000 is distributed to the beneficiary, the beneficiary will normally be subject to tax on the full amount received and the "sheltered" portion of the income will remain at the trust level. Thus, none of the excess investment interest item of tax preference is apportioned to the beneficiary.

(b) If the beneficiary receives $65,000 from the trust, the beneficiary is still subject to tax on only $40,000 (the amount of the distributable net income) and, thus, is considered to have received $25,000 of business income "sheltered" by excess investment interest. Thus, $25,000 of the $60,000 of excess investment interest of the trust is apportioned to the beneficiary.

Example (2). Trust B has $150,000 of net section 1201 gain.

(a) If none of the gain is distributed to the beneficiaries, none of the capital gains item of tax preference is apportioned to the beneficiaries.

(b) If all or a part of the gain is distributed to the beneficiaries, a proportionate part of the capital gains item of tax preference is apportioned to the beneficiaries. If any of the beneficiaries are corporations the capital gains item of tax preference is adjusted in the hands of the corporations as provided in § 1.58-2(a).

Example (3). Trust C has taxable income of $200,000 computed without regard to depreciation on section 1250 property and the deduction for distributions. The depreciation on section 1250 property held by the trust is $160,000. The trust instrument provides for income to be retained by the trust in an amount equal to the depreciation on the property determined under the straight line method (which method has been used for this purpose for the entire period the trust has held the property) which, in this case, is equal to $100,000. The $60,000 excess of the accelerated depreciation of $160,000 over the straight line amount which would have resulted had the property been depreciated under that method for the entire period for which the trust has held the property is an item of tax preference pursuant to section 57(a)(2)). Of the remaining $100,000 of net income of the trust (after the reserve for depreciation), 80 percent is distributed to the beneficiaries. Pursuant to sections 167(h) and 642(e), 80 percent of the remaining $60,0000 of depreciation deduction (or $48,000) is taken as a deduction directly by the beneficiaries and "shelters" the income received by the beneficiaries. Thus, the full $48,000 deduction taken by the beneficiaries is "excess accelerated depreciation" on section 1250 property and is an item of tax preference in the hands of the beneficiaries. None of the remaining $12,000 of "excess accelerated depreciation" is apportioned to the beneficiaries since this amount "shelters" income retained at the trust level.

Example (4). G creates a trust the ordinary income of which is payable to his adult son. Ten years from the date of the transfer, corpus is to revert to G. G retains no other right or power which would cause him to be treated as an owner under subpart E of part 1 of subchapter J (section 671 and following). Under the terms of the trust instrument and applicable local law capital gains must be applied to corpus. During the taxable year 1970 the trust has $200,000 income from dividends and interest and a net long-term capital gain of $100,000. Since the capital gain is held or accumulated for future distribution to G, he is treated under section 677(a)(2) as an owner of a portion of the trust to which the gain is attributable. Therefore, he must include the capital gain in the computation of his taxable income in 1970 and the capital gain item of tax preference is treated as being directly received by G. Accordingly, no adjustment is made to the trust's minimum tax exemption by reason of the capital gain.

Reg. § 1.58-3(b)

Example (5). For its taxable year 1971 the trust referred to in example (4) has taxable income of $200,000 computed without regard to depreciation on section 1250 property and the deduction for distributions. The depreciation on section 1250 property held by the trust is $160,000. The trust instrument provides for income to be retained by the trust in an amount equal to the depreciation on the property determined for purposes of the Federal income tax. If the property had been depreciated under the straight line method for the entire period for which the trust held the property the resulting depreciation deduction would have been $100,000. The $60,000 excess is, therefore, an item of tax preference pursuant to section 57(a)(2) and § 1.57-1(d). Since this amount of "income" is held or accumulated for future distributions to G, he is treated under section 677(a)(2) as an owner of a portion of the trust to which such income is attributable. Therefore, section 671 requires that in computing the tax liability of the grantor the income, deductions, and credits against tax of the trust which are attributable to such portion shall be taken into account. Thus, the grantor has received $160,000 of income and is entitled to a depreciation deduction in the same amount. The $60,000 item of tax preference resulting from the excess depreciation is treated as being directly received by G as he has directly received the income sheltered by that preference. Accordingly, no adjustment is made to the trust's minimum tax exemption by reason of such depreciation. [Reg. § 1.58-3.]

☐ [*T.D.* 7564, 9-11-78.]

[Reg. § 1.58-3T]

§ 1.58-3T. Treatment of non-alternative tax itemized deductions by trusts and estates and their beneficiaries in taxable years beginning after December 31, 1982.—For purposes of section 58(c), in taxable years beginning after December 31, 1982, itemized deductions of a trust or estate which are not alternative tax itemized deductions (as defined in section 55(e)(1)), shall be treated as items of tax preference and apportioned between trusts and their beneficiaries, and estates and their beneficiaries. [Temporary Reg. § 1.58-3T.]

☐ [*T.D.* 8083, 4-22-86.]

[Reg. § 1.58-4]

§ 1.58-4. Electing small business corporations.—(a) *In general.* Section 58(d)(1) provides rules for the apportionment of the items of tax preference of an electing small business corporation among the shareholders of such corporation. Section 58(d)(2) provides rules for the imposition

of the minimum tax on an electing small business corporation with respect to certain capital gains. For purposes of section 58(d) and this section, the items of tax preference are computed at the corporate level as if section 57 generally applied to the corporation. However, the items of tax preference so computed are treated as items of tax preference of the shareholders of such corporation and not as items of tax preference of such corporation (except as provided in paragraph (c) of this section). The items of tax preference specified in section 57(a)(1) and § 1.57-1(a) (excess investment interest) and section 57(a)(3) and § 1.57-1(c) (accelerated depreciation on section 1245 property subject to a net lease), while generally inapplicable to corporations, are included as items of tax preference in the case of an electing small business corporation.

(b) *Apportionment to shareholders.* (1) The items of tax preference of an electing small business corporation, other than the capital gains item of tax preference described in paragraph (c) of this section, are apportioned pro rata among the shareholders of such corporation in a manner consistent with section 1374(c)(1). Thus, with respect to the items of tax preference of the electing small business corporation, there is to be treated as items of tax preference of each shareholder a pro rata share of such items computed as follows:

(i) Divide the total amount of such items of tax preference of the corporation by the number of days in the taxable year of the corporation, thus determining the daily amount of such items of tax preference.

(ii) Determine for each day the shareholder's portion of the daily amount of each such item of tax preference by applying to such amount the ratio which the stock owned by the shareholder on that day bears to the total stock outstanding on that day.

(iii) Total the shareholder's daily portions of each such item of tax preference of the corporation for its taxable year.

Amounts taken into account by shareholders in accordance with this paragraph are considered to consist of a pro rata share of each item of tax preference of the corporation. Thus, for example, if the corporation has $50,000 of excess investment interest and $150,000 of excess accelerated depreciation on section 1250 property and a shareholder, in accordance with this paragraph, takes into account $60,000 of the total $200,000 of tax preference items of the corporation, one-fourth ($50,000 ÷ $200,000) of the $60,000, or $15,000, taken into account by the shareholder is considered excess investment interest and three-fourths of the $60,000, or $45,000, is considered excess accelerated depreciation on section 1250 property.

(2) Items of tax preference apportioned to a shareholder pursuant to subparagraph (1) of this paragraph are taken into account by the shareholder for the shareholder's taxable year in which or with which the taxable year of the corporation ends, except that, in the case of the death of a shareholder during any taxable year of the corporation (during which the corporation is an electing small business corporation), the items of tax preference of the corporation for such taxable year are taken into account for the final taxable year of the shareholder.

(c) *Capital gains.* (1) Capital gains of an electing small business corporation, other than those capital gains subject to tax under section 1378, do not result in an item of tax preference at the corporate level since, in applying the formula specified in sections 57(a)(9)(B) and 1.57-1(i)(2), the rate of tax on capital gains (and the resulting tax) at the corporate level is zero. Under section 1375(a) shareholders of an electing small business corporation take into account the capital gains of the corporation (including capital gains subject to tax under sec. 1378). Therefore, the computation of the capital gains item of tax preference at the shareholder level, with respect to such capital gains, is taken into account automatically by the operation of sections 57(a)(9) and 1.57-1(i). To avoid double inclusion of the capital gains item of tax preference by a shareholder with respect to capital gains subject to tax under section 1378, the capital gains item of tax preference which results at the corporate level by reason of section 58(d)(2) is not treated under section 58(d)(1) as an item of tax preference of the shareholders of the corporation.

(2) The capital gains item of tax preference of an electing small business corporation subject to the tax imposed by section 1378 is the excess of the amount of tax computed under section 1378(b)(2) over the sum of—

(i) The amount of tax that would be computed under section 1378(b)(2) if the following amount were excluded:

(*a*) That portion of the net section 1201 gain of the corporation described in section 1378(b)(1), or

(*b*) If section 1378(c)(3) applies, that portion of the net section 1201 gain attributable to the property described in section 1378(c)(3), and

(ii) The amount of tax imposed under section 1378 divided by the sum of the normal tax rate and the surtax rate under section 11 for the taxable year.

(3) The principles of this paragraph may be illustrated by the following example.

Example. Corporation X is a calendar year taxpayer and an electing small business corporation. For its taxable year 1971 the corporation has net section 1201 gain of $650,000 and taxable income of $800,000 (including the net section 1201 gain). Although X's election under section 1372(a) has been in effect for its three immediately preceding taxable years, X is subject to the tax imposed by section 1378 for 1971 since it has net section 1201 gain (in the amount of $200,000) attributable to property with a substituted basis. The tax computed under section 1378(b)(1) is $187,500 (30 percent of $650,000 − $25,000) and under section 1378(b)(2) is $377,500 (22 percent of $800,000 plus 26 percent of $775,000). By reason of the limitation imposed by section 1378(c) the tax actually imposed by section 1378 is $60,000 (30 percent of $200,000, the net section 1201 gain). The tax computed under section 1378(b)(2) with the modification required under subparagraph (2)(i) of this paragraph is $281,500 (22 percent of $600,000 plus 26 percent of $575,000). Thus, the 1971 capital gains item of tax preference of X is $75,000 computed as follows:

1. Tax computed under 1378(b)(2)	$377,500
2. Tax computed under 1378(b)(2) with modification	281,500
3. Excess	96,000
4. Tax actually imposed under 1378	60,000
5. Difference	36,000
6. Normal tax rate plus surtax rate	.48
7. Tax preference (line 5 ÷ line 6)	$ 75,000

In addition, each shareholder of X will take into account his distributive share of the $650,000 of net section 1201 gain of X less the taxes paid by X under sections 56 and 1378 on the gain. [Reg. § 1.58-4.]

□ [*T.D.* 7564, 9-11-78.]

Reg. § 1.58-4(c)(3)

[Reg. § 1.58-5]

§ 1.58-5. Common trust funds.—Section 58(e) provides that each participant in a common trust fund (as defined in section 584 and the regulations thereunder) is to treat as items of tax preference his proportionate share of the items of tax preference of the fund computed as if the fund were an individual subject to the minimum tax. The participant's proportionate share of the items of tax preference of the fund is determined as if the participant had realized, or incurred, his pro rata share of items of income, gain, loss, or deduction of the fund directly from the source from which realized or incurred by the fund. The participant's pro rata share of such items is determined in a manner consistent with § 1.584-2(c). Items of tax preference apportioned to a participant pursuant to this paragraph are taken into account by the participant for the participant's taxable year in which or with which the taxable year of the trust ends. [Reg. § 1.58-5.]

☐ [*T.D.* 7564, 9-11-78.]

[Reg. § 1.58-6]

§ 1.58-6. Regulated investment companies; real estate investment trusts.—(a) *In general.* Section 58(f) provides rules with respect to the determination of the items of tax preference of regulated investment companies (as defined in section 851) and their shareholders and real estate investment trusts (as defined in section 856) and their shareholders, or holders of beneficial interest. In general, the items of tax preference of such companies and such trusts are determined at the company or trust level and the items of tax preference so determined (other than the capital gains item of tax preference (section 57(a)(9) and § 1.57-1(i)) and, in the case of a real estate investment trust, accelerated depreciation on section 1250 property (section 57(a)(2) and § 1.57-1(b))) are treated as items of tax preference of the shareholders or holders of beneficial interest, in the same proportion that the dividends (other than capital gains dividends) paid to each such shareholder, or holder of beneficial interest, bear to the taxable income of such company or such trust determined without regard to the deduction for dividends paid. In no case, however, is such proportion to be considered in excess of 100 percent. For example, if a regulated investment company has items of tax preference of $500,000 for the taxable year, none of which resulted from capital gains, and distributes dividends in an amount equal to 90 percent of its taxable income, each shareholder treats his share of 90 percent of the company's items of tax preference, or (a proportionate share of) $450,000, as items of tax preference of the shareholder. The remaining $50,000

constitutes items of tax preference of the company. Amounts treated under this paragraph as items of tax preference of the shareholders, or holders of beneficial interest, are deemed to be derived proportionately from each item of tax preference of the company or trust, other than the capital gains item of tax preference and, in the case of a real estate investment trust, accelerated depreciation on section 1250 property. Such amounts are taken into account by the shareholders, or holders of beneficial interest, in the same taxable year in which the dividends on which the apportionment is based are includible in income. The minimum tax exemption of the trust or company shall not be reduced because a portion of the trust's or company's items of tax preference are allocated to the shareholders or holders of beneficial interests.

(b) *Capital gains.* Section 58(g)(1) provides that a regulated investment company or real estate investment trust does not treat as an item of tax preference the capital gains item of tax preference under section 57(a)(9) (and § 1.57-1(i)) to the extent that such item is attributable to amounts taken into income by the shareholders of such company under section 852(b)(3) or by the shareholders or holders of beneficial interest of such trust under section 857(b)(3). Thus, such a company or trust computes its capital gains item of tax preference on the basis of its net section 1201 gain less the sum of (1) the capital gains dividend (as defined in section 852(b)(3)(C) or section 857(b)(3)(C)) for the taxable year of the company or trust plus (2), in the case of a regulated investment company, that portion of the undistributed capital gains designated, pursuant to section 852(b)(3)(D) and the regulations thereunder, by the company to be includible in the shareholder's return as long-term capital gains for the shareholder's taxable year in which the last day of the company's taxable year falls. Amounts treated under section 852(b)(3) or 857(b)(3) as long-term capital gains of shareholders, or holders of beneficial interest, are automatically included, pursuant to section 57(a)(9) and § 1.57-1(i), in the computation of the capital gains item of tax preference of the shareholders, or holders of beneficial interest.

(c) *Accelerated depreciation on section 1250 property.* In the case of a real estate investment trust, all of the items of tax preference resulting from accelerated depreciation on section 1250 property held by the trust (section 57(a)(2) and § 1.57-1(b)) are treated as items of tax preference of the trust, and, thus, none are treated as items of tax preference of the shareholder, or holder of beneficial interest. [Reg. § 1.58-6.]

☐ [*T.D.* 7564, 9-11-78.]

Reg. § 1.58-5

[Reg. § 1.58-7]

§ 1.58-7. Tax preferences attributable to foreign sources; preferences other than capital gains and stock options.—(a) *In general.* Section 58(g)(1) provides that, except in the case of the stock options item of tax preference (section 57(a)(6) and § 1.57-1 (f)) and the capital gains item of tax preference (section 57(a)(9) and § 1.57-1 (i)), items of tax preference which are attributable to sources within any foreign country or possession of the United States shall, for purposes of section 56, be taken into account only to the extent that such items reduce the tax imposed by chapter 1 (other than the minimum tax under section 56) on income derived from sources within the United States. Items of tax preference from sources within any foreign country or possession of the United States reduce the chapter 1 tax on income from sources within the United States to the extent the deduction relating to such preferences, in combination with other foreign deductions, exceed the income from such sources and, in effect, offset income from sources within the United States. Items of tax preference, for this purpose, are determined after application of § 1.57-4 (relating to limitation on amounts treated as items of tax preference). In the case of a taxpayer who deducted foreign taxes under section 164 for a taxable year, the provisions of this section shall be applied (without regard to section 275(a)(4)) as if he had elected the overall foreign tax credit limitation under section 904(a)(2) for such year.

(b) *Preferences attributable to foreign sources*—(1) *Preferences other than excess investment interest.* Except in the case of excess investment interest (see subparagraph (2) of this paragraph), an item of tax preference to which this section applies is attributable to sources within a foreign country or possession of the United States to the extent such item is attributable to a deduction properly allocable or apportionable to an item or class of gross income from sources within a foreign country or possession of the United States under the principles of section 862(b), or section 863, and the regulations thereunder. Where, in the case of income partly from sources within the United States and partly from sources within a foreign country or possession of the United States, taxable income is computed before apportionment to domestic and foreign sources, and is then apportioned by processes or formulas of general apportionment (pursuant to section 863(b) and the regulations thereunder), deductions attributable to such taxable income are considered to be proportionately from sources within the United States and within the foreign

country or possession of the United States on the same basis as taxable income.

(2) *Excess investment interest*—(i) *Per-country limitation.* (a) In the case of a taxpayer on the per-country foreign tax credit limitation under section 904(a) for the taxable year, excess investment interest (as defined in section 57(b)(1)), and the resulting item of tax preference, is attributable to sources within a foreign country or a possession of the United States to the extent that investment interest expense attributable to income from sources within such foreign country or possession of the United States exceeds the net investment income from sources within such foreign country or such possession. For this purpose, net investment income from within a foreign country or possession of the United States is the excess (if any) of the investment income from sources within such country or possession over the investment expenses attributable to income from sources within such country or such possession. For the definition of investment interest expense see section 57(b)(2)(D); for the definition of investment income see section 57(b)(2)(B); for the definition of investment expense see section 57(b)(2)(C).

(b) If the taxpayer's excess investment interest computed on a worldwide basis is less than the taxpayer's total separately determined excess investment interest (as defined in this subdivision (b)), the amount of the taxpayer's excess investment interest from each foreign country or possession is the amount which bears the same relationship to the taxpayer's excess investment interest from each such country or possession, determined without regard to this subdivision (b), as the taxpayer's worldwide excess investment interest bears to the taxpayer's total separately determined excess investment interest. For purposes of this subdivision (b), the taxpayer's total separately determined excess investment interest is the sum of the total excess investment interest determined without regard to this subdivision (b) plus the taxpayer's excess investment interest from sources within the United States determined in a manner consistent with (a) of this subdivision (i).

(ii) *Overall limitation.* In the case of a taxpayer who has elected the overall foreign tax credit limitation under section 904(a)(2) for the taxable year, excess investment interest (as defined in section 57(b)(1)), and the resulting item of tax preference, is attributable to sources within any foreign country or possession of the United States to the extent that investment interest expense attributable to income from such sources

Reg. § 1.58-7(b)(2)

..ceeds the sum of (a) the net investment income .rom such sources plus (b) the excess, if any, of net investment income from sources within the United States over investment interest expense attributable to sources within the United States. For this purpose, net investment income from sources within any foreign country or possession of the United States is the excess (if any) of the investment income from all such sources over the investment expenses attributable to income from such sources. For the definition of investment interest expense see section 57(b)(2)(D); for the definition of investment income see section 57(b)(2)(B); for the definition of investment expense see section 57(b)(2)(C).

(iii) *Allocation of expenses.* The determination of the investment interest expense and investment expenses attributable to a foreign country or possession of the United States is made in a manner consistent with subparagraph (1) of this paragraph.

(iv) *Attribution of certain interest deductions to foreign sources.* Where net investment income from sources within any foreign country or possession has the effect of offsetting investment interest expense attributable to income from sources within the United States, the deductions for the investment interest expense so offset are, for purposes of § 1.58-7(c) (relating to reduction in taxes on United States source income), treated as deductions attributable to income from sources within the foreign country or possession from which such net investment income is derived. Such an offset will occur where there is an excess of investment interest expense attributable to in-

come from sources within the United States over net investment income from such sources and (a) in the case of a taxpayer on the per-country foreign tax credit limitation, an excess of net investment income from sources within a foreign country or possession of the United States over investment interest expense from within such foreign country or possession, or (b) in the case of a taxpayer who has elected the overall foreign tax credit limitation, there is an excess of net investment income from sources within foreign countries or possessions of the United States over investment interest expense attributable to income from within such sources.

(v) *Separate limitation on interest income.* Where a taxpayer has income described in section 904 (f)(2) (relating to interest income subject to the separate foreign tax credit limitation) or expenses attributable to such income, the determination of the excess investment interest resulting therefrom must be determined separately with respect to such income and the expenses properly allocable or apportionable thereto in the same manner as such determination is made in the case of a taxpayer on the per-country foreign tax credit limitation for the taxable year (see subdivision (i) of this subparagraph).

(vi) *Examples.* The principles of this subparagraph may be illustrated by the following examples in each of which the taxpayer is an individual and a citizen of the United States:

Example (1). The taxpayer's only items of income and deduction relating to excess investment interest are as follows:

	United States	France	Germany	Total
Investment income from sources within	$150,000	$120,000	$180,000	$450,000
Investment expenses relating to income from sources within	(100,000)	(90,000)	(120,000)	(310,000)
Net investment income	$ 50,000	$ 30,000	$ 60,000	$140,000
Investment interest expense relating to income from sources within	($110,000)	($70,000)	($50,000)	($230,000)
(Excess) of investment interest expense over net investment income	($60,000)	($40,000)	* $ 10,000	($90,000)

* Excess of net investment income over investment interest expense.

(a) If the taxpayer has elected the overall foreign tax credit limitation, his excess investment interest from sources within any foreign

countries or possessions of the United States determined under subdivision (ii) of this subparagraph is computed as follows:

Investment interest:

French	($70,000)		
German	(50,000)		($120,000)

Net investment income:
Investment income:

French	$120,000	
German	180,000	$300,000

Less:
Investment expenses:

French	($ 90,000)		
German	(120,000)	(210,000)	90,000

Excess of U.S. net income over investment interest expenses 0

Total foreign excess investment interest .... ($30,000)

(b) If the taxpayer is on the per-country foreign tax credit limitation, his excess investment interest from France and Germany determined under subdivision (i)(a) of this subparagraph is $40,000 and zero, respectively. Since the taxpayer's worldwide excess investment interest ($90,000) is less than his total separately determined excess investment interest ($60,000 (U.S.) plus $40,000 (French) plus zero (German), or $100,000), the limitation in subdivision (i)(b) of this subparagraph applies and the excess investment interest attributable to France is limited as follows:

$$\frac{\text{Total worldwide excess (\$90,000)}}{\text{Total separately determined excess (\$100,000)}} \times \text{French excess (\$40,000)} = \$36,000$$

The taxpayer's total excess investment interest attributable to sources within any foreign country or possession of the United States is, thus, $36,000 ($36,000 (French) plus zero (German)). The taxpayer's excess investment interest attributable to sources within the United States is $54,000

$$\left(\frac{\$ 9,000}{\$100,000} \times \$60,000.\right).$$

Since, in making the latter determination, $6,000 of the $60,000 of U.S. investment interest expense in excess of U.S. net investment income is, in effect, offset by German net investment income, for purposes of § 1.58-7(c), $6,000 of interest deductions attributable to income from sources within the United States are, pursuant to subdivision (iv) of this subparagraph, treated as deductions attributable to income from sources within Germany.

Example (2). Assume the same facts as in example (1) except that the items of income and deduction in Germany and the United States are reversed. The worldwide excess investment interest, thus, remains $90,000 and the items of income and deduction relating to excess investment interest are as follows:

	U.S.	France	Germany	Total
Investment income from sources within:	$180,000	$120,000	$150,000	$450,000
Investment expenses relating to income from sources within:	(120,000)	(90,000)	(100,000)	(310,000)
Net investment income:	$ 60,000	$ 30,000	$ 50,000	$140,000
Investment interest expense relating to income from sources within:	($ 50,000)	($ 70,000)	($110,000)	($230,000)
(Excess) of investment interest expense over net investment income:	$ 10,000	($ 40,000)	($ 60,000)	($ 90,000)

(a) If the taxpayer has elected the overall limitation, his excess investment interest from sources within any foreign countries or possessions of the United States determined under subdivision (ii) of this subparagraph is determined as follows:

Reg. § 1.58-7(b)(2)

ıgn investment interest:		
French .... ($ 70,000)		
German .... (110,000)		($180,000)
ʾoreign net investment income:		
French $120,000		
German 150,000	$270,000	
Less:		
Investment expenses:		
French .... ($ 90,000)		
German .... (100,000)	(190,000)	80,000
Excess of U.S. net investment income over U.S. investment interest expense		$ 10,000
Excess investment interest attributable to foreign sources		($ 90,000)

(b) If the taxpayer has not elected the overall foreign tax credit limitation, his excess investment interest from France and Germany determined under subdivision (i) of this subparagraph (without regard to the limitation to worldwide excess investment interest) is $40,000 and $60,000, respectively, and his total separately determined excess investment interest is, thus, $100,000. Since the total separately determined excess would exceed the worldwide excess, the limitation to the worldwide excess in subdivision (i) applies and the excess investment interest is determined as follows:

France:
$$\frac{\$\,90,000}{\$100,000} \times \$40,000 = \$36,000$$

Germany:
$$\frac{\$\,90,000}{\$100,000} \times \$60,000 = \$54,000$$

Total excess investment interest attributable to sources within any foreign countries and possessions $90,000

Example (3). Assume the same facts as in example (1) except that the taxpayer, in addition has investment income, investment expenses, and investment interest subject to the separate limitation under section 904(f).

(a) If the taxpayer has elected the overall foreign tax credit limitation, his excess investment interest from sources within any foreign countries or possessions of the United States determined under subdivision (ii) of this subparagraph is the same as in (a) of example (1) of this subdivision (vi). He then treats such amount as separately determined excess investment interest attributable to a single foreign country as determined under subdivision (i) of this subparagraph and proceeds as in (b) of example (1) of this subdivision (vi) treating items of income and deduction subject to section 904(f) and from each

separate foreign country or possession separately in making the additional determinations under subdivisions (i) and (iv) of this subparagraph.

(b) If the taxpayer has not elected the overall foreign tax credit limitation, his excess investment interest from sources within any foreign country or possession of the United States would be determined in the same manner as in (b) of example (1) treating items of income and deduction which are subject to section 904(f) and from each separate foreign country or possession separately in making the determinations under subdivisions (i) and (iv) of this subparagraph.

(c) *Reduction in taxes on United States source income*—(1) *Overall limitation*—(i) *In general.* If a taxpayer is on the overall foreign tax credit limitation under section 904(a)(2), the items of tax preference determined to be attributable to foreign sources under paragraph (b) of this section reduce the tax imposed by chapter 1 (other than the minimum tax imposed under section 56) on income from sources within the United States for the taxable year to the extent of the smallest of the following three amounts:

(*a*) Items of tax preference (other than stock options and capital gains) attributable to sources within a foreign country or possession of the United States,

(*b*) The excess (if any) of the total deductions properly allocable or apportionable to items or classes of gross income from sources within foreign countries and possessions of the United States over the gross income from such sources, or

(*c*) Taxable income from sources within the United States. See § 1.58-7(b)(2)(iv) with respect to the attribution of certain interest deductions to foreign sources in cases involving the excess investment interest item of tax preference.

(ii) *Net operating loss.* Where there is an overall net operating loss for the taxable year, to the extent that the lesser of the amounts deter-

Reg. § 1.58-7(c)(1)

mined under (a) or (b) of subdivision (i) of this subparagraph exceeds the taxpayer's taxable income from sources within the United States (and, therefore do not offset taxable income from sources within the United States for the taxable year) the amount of such excess is treated as "suspense preferences." Suspense preferences are converted to actual items of tax preference, arising in the loss year and subject to the provisions of section 56, as the net operating loss is used in other taxable years, in the form of a net operating loss deduction under section 172, to offset taxable income from sources within the United States. Suspense preferences which, in other taxable years, reduce taxable income from sources within any foreign country or possession of the United States lose their character as suspense preferences and, thus, are never converted into actual items of tax preference. The amount of the suspense preferences which are converted into actual items of tax preference is equal to that portion of the net operating loss attributable to the suspense preferences which offset taxable income from sources within the United States in taxable years other than the loss year. The determination of the component parts of the net operating loss and the determination of the amount by which the portion of the net operating loss attributable to suspense preferences offsets taxable income from sources within the United States is made on a year-by-year basis in the same order as the net operating loss is used in accordance with section 172(b). Such determination is made by applying deductions attributable to U.S. source income first against such income and deductions attributable to foreign source income first against such foreign source income and in accordance with the following principles:

(a) Deductions attributable to items or classes of gross income from sources within the United States offset taxable income from sources within the United States before any remaining portion of the net operating loss;

(b) Deductions attributable to item classes of gross income from sources within fore countries or possessions of the United States offs taxable income from such sources before any re maining portion of the net operating loss;

(c) Deductions described in (b) of this subdivision (ii) which are not suspense preferences (referred to in this subparagraph as "other foreign deductions") offset taxable income from sources within foreign countries and possessions of the United States before suspense preferences; and

(d) Suspense preferences offset taxable income from sources within the United States before other foreign deductions.

For purposes of the above computations, taxable income is computed with the modifications specified in section 172(b)(2) or section 172(c), whichever is applicable. However, the amount of suspense preferences which are converted into actual items of tax preference in accordance with the above principles is reduced to the extent suspense preferences offset increases in taxable income from sources within the United States due to the modifications specified in section 172(b)(2) or section 172(c). For this purpose, suspense preferences are considered to offset an increase in taxable income due to the section 172(b)(2) modifications only after reducing taxable income computed before the section 172(b)(2) or section 172(c) modifications.

(iii) *Examples.* The principles of this subparagraph may be illustrated by the following examples. In each example the taxpayer is an individual citizen of the United States and has elected the overall foreign tax credit limitation. Personal deductions and exemptions are disregarded for purposes of these examples.

Example (1). In 1974, the taxpayer has the following items of income and deduction:

United States taxable income:			
Gross income		$750,000	
Deductions		(250,000)	$500,000
Foreign source loss:			
Gross income		$200,000	
Deductions:			
Preference items (excess of percentage depletion over basis)	$550,000		
Other	50,000	(600,000)	(400,000)
Overall taxable income			$100,000

Pursuant to subdivision (i) of this subparagraph the smallest of (a) the items of tax preference attributable to the foreign sources ($550,000), (b) the foreign source loss ($400,000), or (c) the taxable income from sources within the United States ($500,000) reduces the tax imposed by chapter 1 (other than the minimum tax) on income from sources within the United States. Thus, $400,000 of the $550,000 of excess depletion is treated as an item of tax preference in 1974 subject to the minimum tax.

Reg. § 1.58-7(c)(1)

Example (2). Assume the same facts as in ...mple (1) except that the gross income from ...urces within the United States is $350,000 re-...ulting in U.S. taxable income of $100,000 and an overall net operating loss of $300,000. Pursuant to subdivision (i) of this subparagraph, $100,000 of the $550,000 excess depletion would be treated as an item of tax preference in 1974 subject to the minimum tax. In addition, pursuant to subdivision (ii) of this subparagraph, the excess of the items of tax preference from foreign sources ($550,000) or the foreign source loss ($400,000), whichever is less, over the U.S. taxable income ($100,000), or, in this example, $300,000, is treated as suspense preferences.

(a) If, in 1971, the taxpayer's total items of income and deduction result in $350,000 of taxable income all of which is from sources within the United States, the entire $300,000 net

United States loss:
Gross income .... $ 75,000
Deductions .... (225,000)

($150,000)

Foreign loss:
Gross income $400,000
Deductions:
Preference items (excess of accelerated depreciation
on section 1250 property over straight-line
amount) $200,000
Other 550,000 ($750,000)

(350,000)

Overall net operating loss .... ($500,000)

Since the nonpreference deductions reduce the foreign source income before the preference portion, the $350,000 foreign source loss consists of $200,000 of suspense preferences and $150,000 of other deductions. In 1971, 1972, and 1973 the taxpayer had taxable income from sources within the United States of $100,000, $200,000, and

operating loss, all of which is attributable to suspense preferences, is used to offset U.S. taxable income. Accordingly, the full $300,000 of suspense preferences are converted into actual items of tax preference arising in 1974 and are subject to tax under section 56.

(b) If the $350,000 in 1971 is modified taxable income resulting from the denial of a section 1202 capital gains deduction of $175,000 by reason of section 172(b)(2), the $300,000, otherwise treated as actual items of tax preference, is reduced by $125,000, *i.e.*, the extent to which the suspense preferences offset U.S. taxable income attributable to the increase in taxable income resulting from the denial of the section 1202 deduction.

Example (3). In 1974, the taxpayer has the following items of income and deduction:

$300,000, respectively and taxable income from sources within foreign countries of $80,000 each year. Of the $200,000 of suspense preferences, $150,000 are converted into actual items of tax preference, subject to the minimum tax in 1974, determined as follows:

[In thousands of dollars]

	Taxable income			Foreign deductions	
Year—Explanation	U.S. source	Foreign source	U.S. deductions	Suspense preferences	Other
1971 End of year balance before section 58(g) computations	100	80	150	200	150
1. U.S. deductions against U.S. income	(100)	...	(100)	...	...
2. Other foreign deductions against foreign income	...	(80)	...	...	(80)
1972 End of year balance before section 58(g) computations	200	80	50	200	70
1. U.S. deductions against U.S. income	(50)	...	(50)	...	...
2. Other foreign deductions against foreign income	...	(70)	...	...	(70)
3. Suspense preferences against foreign income	...	(10)	...	(10)	...
4. Suspense preferences against U.S. income .	(150)	...	...	(150)	...

Reg. § 1.58-7(c)(1)

[In thousands of dollars]

		Taxable income			Foreign deduct
Year—Explanation		U.S. source	Foreign source	U.S. deductions	Suspense preferences	Oth.
1973	End of year balance before section 58(g) computations	300	80	...	40	...
	1. U.S. deductions against U.S. income			Not applicable.		
	2. Other foreign deductions against foreign income			Not applicable.		
	3. Suspense preferences against foreign income	...	(40)	...	(40)	
	4. Suspense preferences against U.S. income .			Not applicable.		
	Balances	300	40	...	...	...

* Suspense preferences converted to actual items of tax preference.

Example (4). In 1970, The taxpayer's total items of income and deduction, all of which are attributable to foreign sources, are as follows:

Foreign loss:		
Gross income		$400,000
Deductions:		
Preferences (excess of accelerated depreciation on section 1250 property over straight-line)	$200,000	
Other deductions	$550,000	($750,000)
Net operating loss		$350,000

Pursuant to subdivision (i) of this subparagraph, none of the preferences attributable to foreign sources reduce the tax imposed by chapter 1 (other than the minimum tax) on taxable income from sources within the United States. Pursuant to subdivision (ii) of this subparagraph, the $200,000 portion of the net operating loss result- ing from the excess accelerated depreciation con- stitutes suspense preferences. No part of the net operating loss that is carried back to previous years is reduced in such previous years. In 1971 and 1972, the taxpayer's income (before the net operating loss deduction) consists of the following:

1971 taxable income:	
United States	$160,000
Foreign	70,000
Total	$230,000
1972 taxable income:	
United States	$ 25,000
Foreign	105,000
Total	$130,000

(a) In 1971, the conversion of suspense preferences into actual items of tax preference under section 58(g) (and this paragraph) and the imposition of the minimum tax on 1970 items of tax preference under section 56(b) (and § 1.56A-2) are determined as follows:

Conversion of suspense preferences:

1970 NET OPERATING LOSS
(In thousands of dollars)

	U.S. Taxable Income	Foreign Taxable Income	U.S. Deduc- tions	Suspense Preferences	Other For- eign Deductions
	$ 160	$70	...	$200	$150
1. U.S. deductions against U.S. income			Not applicable		
2. Other foreign deductions against foreign income..		70			(70)
3. Suspense preference against foreign income			Not applicable		
4. Suspense preference against U.S. income	* (160)			(160)	
Balance to 1972.....................	...	...	...	$ 40	$ 80

* Suspense preferences converted into actual items of tax preference.

Reg. § 1.58-7(c)(1)

...sition of minimum tax on 1970 items of tax
...erence:

1970 NET OPERATING LOSS
(In thousands of dollars)

	1971 Taxable Income	Nonpreference portion	Preference portion	Suspense portion
	$230	$150	. . .	$200
1. 1971 Conversion of suspense preferences pursuant to section 58(g).		30[1]	$130	(160)
Adjusted NOL		$180	$130	$ 40
2. Nonpreference portion against taxable income	(180)	(180)		
3. Preference portion against taxable income	(50)[2]	. . .	(50)	. . .
Balance to 1972	. . .	. . .	$ 80	$ 40

[1] Represents the 1970 minimum tax exemption.

[2] Imposition of 1970 minimum tax (10% × $50,000 = $5,000).

(b) In 1972, the conversion of suspense preferences into actual items of tax preferences under section 58(g) (and this paragraph) and the imposition of the minimum tax on 1970 items of tax preference under section 56(b) (and § 1.56A-2) are determined as follows:

Conversion of suspense preferences:

1970 NET OPERATING LOSS
(In thousands of dollars)

	U.S. Taxable Income	Foreign Taxable Income	U.S. Deductions	Suspense Preferences	Other Foreign Deductions
	$25	$105	. . .	$40	$80
1. U.S. deduction against U.S. income			Not applicable		
2. Other foreign deductions against foreign income .		(80)			(80)
3. Suspense preferences against foreign income		(25)		(25)	
4. Suspense preferences against U.S. income	(15)[1]	. . .	. . .	(15)	. . .
Balance	10				

[1] Suspense preferences converted into actual items of tax preference.

Imposition of minimum tax on 1970 items of tax preference:

1970 NET OPERATING LOSS
(In thousands of dollars)

	1971 Taxable Income	Nonpreference portion	Preference portion	Suspense portion
	$130	. . .	$80	$40
1. 1972 Conversion of suspense preferences pursuant to section 58(g).	. . .	$25	15	(40)
Adjusted NOL		$25	$95	. . .
2. Nonpreference portion against taxable income	(25)	(25)	. . .	. . .
3. Preference portion against taxable income	(95)[1]	. . .	(95)	. . .
Balance	$ 10			

[1] Imposition of 1970 minimum tax (10% × $95,000 = $9,500).

(2) *Per-country limitation.* (i) *In general.* If a taxpayer is on the per-country foreign tax credit limitation for the taxable year, the amount by which the items of tax preference to which this section applies reduce the tax imposed by chapter 1 (other than the minimum tax under section 56) on income from sources within the United States is determined separately with respect to each foreign country or possession of the United States. Such determination is made in a manner consis-tent with subparagraph (1) of this paragraph as modified in subdivision (ii) of this subparagraph. In applying subparagraph (1)(i) of this paragraph to a taxpayer on the per-country limitation, if the total potential preference amounts (as defined in this subdivision (i)) exceed the taxpayer's taxable income from sources within the United States, then, for purposes of subparagraph (1)(i)(c) of this paragraph (relating to the U.S. taxable income limitation on the amount treated as a reduction of

Reg. § 1.58-7(c)(2)

U.S. taxable income), the taxable income from sources within the United States which is reduced by potential preference amounts with respect to each foreign country or possession is an amount which bears the same relationship to such income as the potential preference amount with respect to such foreign country or possession bears to the total of the potential preference amounts with respect to all foreign countries and possessions. For purposes of this subparagraph, the potential preference amount with respect to a foreign country or possession is the lesser of the amount of foreign source preference (described in subparagraph (1)(i)(a) of this paragraph) attributable to such country or possession or the amount of foreign source loss (described in subparagraph (1)(i)(b) of this paragraph) attributable to such country or possession.

(ii) *Net operating loss.* Where there is an overall net operating loss for the taxable year and the total of the potential preference amounts with respect to all foreign countries and possessions exceeds the taxpayer's taxable income from sources within the United States, the amount of such excess is treated as "suspense preferences". The suspense preferences are converted into actual items of tax preference, arising in the loss year and subject to the provisions of section 56, as the net operating loss is used in other taxable years, in the form of a net operating loss deduction under section 172, to offset taxable income from sources within the United States. Suspense preferences attributable to a foreign country or possession which, in other taxable years, reduce taxable income from sources within such country or possession or offset taxable income from sources within any other foreign country or possession lose their character as suspense preferences and, thus, are never converted into actual items of tax preference. The amount of the suspense preferences which are converted into actual items of tax preference is equal to that portion of the net operating loss attributable to the suspense preferences which offsets taxable income from sources within the United States in taxable years other than the loss year. The determination of the component parts of the net operating loss and the determination of the amount by which the portion of the net operating loss attributable to the suspense p referesces taxable income from sources basis the United States is made on a year-by-is used in the same order as the net operatingdetermi-in accordance with section 172(b). attributa-nation is made by applying deducirst against ble to United States source incs attributable such income and applying dedeign country or to income from sources withifirst against in-possession of the United

come from sources within such country or poss sion and in accordance with the followi principles:

(a) Deductions attributable to items or classes of gross income from sources within the United States offset taxable income from sources within the United States before any remaining deductions;

(b) Deductions attributable to items or classes of gross income from sources within any foreign country or possession of the United States which are not suspense preferences (referred to in this paragraph as "other foreign deductions") offset taxable income from sources within such country or possession before any remaining deductions;

(c) Suspense preferences attributable to items or classes of gross income from sources within a foreign country or possession offset any remaining taxable income from sources within such foreign country or possession after application of (b) of this subdivision (ii) before any remaining deductions;

(d) Suspense preferences from each foreign country and possession (remaining after application of (c) of this subdivision (ii)) offset taxable income from sources within the United States (remaining after application of (a) of this subdivision (ii)) before other foreign deductions pro rata on the basis of the total of such suspense preferences;

(e) Other foreign deductions from each foreign country and possession (remaining after application of (b) of this subdivision (ii)) offset taxable income from sources within the United States (remaining after application of (a) and (d) of this subdivision (ii) pro rata on the basis of the total of such other foreign deductions;

(f) ;eductions attributable to income from source within the United States (remaining ation of (a) of this subdivision (ii)) after ap, able income from sources within any offset country or possession before any foreign fore; ctions; de

(g) Other foreign deductions from each foreign country and possession (remaining after application of (b) and (e) of this subdivision (ii)) offset taxable income from sources within any other foreign countries or possessions (remaining after application of (f) of this subdivision (ii)) pro rata on the basis of the total of such other foreign deductions; and

(h) Suspense preferences (remaining after the application of (c) and (d) of this subdivision (ii)) offset taxable income from sources within any foreign country or possession (remaining after the application of (f) and (g) of this subdivision

Reg. § 1.58-7(c)(2)

)) pro rata on the basis of the total of such suspense preferences.

For purposes of the above computations, taxable income is computed with the modifications specified in section 172(b)(2) or section 172(c), whichever is applicable. However, the amount of suspense preferences which are converted into actual items of tax preference in accordance with the above principles is reduced to the extent the suspense preferences offset increases in taxable income from sources within the United States due to the modifications specified in section 172(b)(2) or section 172(c). For this purpose, suspense preferences are considered to offset an increase in taxable income due to section 172(b)(2) or section 172(c) modifications only after reducing taxable income computed before such modifications.

(iii) *Examples.* The principles of this subparagraph may be illustrated by the following examples in each of which the per-country foreign tax credit limitation is applicable. For purposes of these examples, personal deductions and exemptions are disregarded.

Example (1). The taxpayer has the following items of income and deduction for the taxable year 1971:

	United States	France	Germany	United Kingdom
Gross income	$180,000	$165,000	$50,000	$75,000
Deductions:				
Preferences	0	0	0	(45,000)
Other	(120,000)	(125,000)	(80,000)	(100,000)
Taxable income (or loss)	$ 60,000	$ 40,000	($30,000)	($70,000)

(a) Pursuant to subdivision (i) of this subparagraph, the potential preference amount in the case of the United Kingdom is the lesser of the preferences attributable to the United Kingdom ($45,000) or the excess of deductions over gross income from sources within the United Kingdom ($70,000) and the potential preference amounts in the case of France and Germany are zero in both cases since the preferences attributable to both countries are zero. Since the total potential preference amounts ($45,000) is less than the taxable income from sources within the United States ($60,000), no modification of U.S. taxable income is required. Thus, the amount by which the U.K. preferences reduce the tax or taxable income from sources within the United States, determined in a manner consistent with subparagraph (1)(i) of this paragraph, is the smallest of the items of tax preference attributable to the United Kingdom ($45,000), (2) the excess of deductions over gross income attributable to the United Kingdom ($70,000), or (3) taxable income from sources

within the United States ($60,000). The full $45,000 of U.K. preference items are, therefore, taken into account as items of tax preference in 1971 and subject to the minimum tax. Since there is no net operating loss, subdivision (ii) of this subparagraph does not apply.

(b) If the French taxable income is $15,000 instead of $40,000, a $25,000 net operating loss (on a worldwide basis) results. The determination of the foreign preference items taken into account pursuant to subdivision (i) of this subparagraph is the same as in (a) of this example. Subdivision (ii) of this subparagraph again does not apply since the total potential preference amounts ($45,000) is less than the U.S. taxable income ($60,000).

Example (2). For the taxable year 1972, the taxpayer has a net operating loss of $35,000 consisting of the following items of income and deduction:

	ited es	France	Germany	United Kingdom	Belgium
Gross income	$250,	$50,000	$60,000	$5,000	$45,000
Deductions:					
Preferences	(100,000)	35,000)	(70,000)	(95,000)	
Other	$150,000	75,000)	(30,000)		(40,000)
Taxable income (or loss)		=000)	($40,000)	($90,000)	$5,000

(a) Pursuant to subdivision (i) of this subparagraph the potential preference amount with respect to each country is the lesser of the amount shown as preferences with respect to such

country try. Thus, amount of the loss from such country this case are potential preference amounts in

France	$ 35,000
Germany	40,000
United Kingdom	90,000
Belgium	0
Total	$165,000

Since the total of the potential preference amounts exceeds the U.S. taxable income, in applying the principles of subparagraph (1)(i) of this paragraph, U.S. taxable income which is reduced by potential preference amounts with respect to each country is a pro rata amount based on the total potential preference amounts as follows:

$$\text{France} \quad \left\{ \frac{35,000}{165,000} \times \$150,000 \right\} \quad \ldots \ldots \ldots \quad \$\ 31,818$$

$$\text{Germany} \quad \left\{ \frac{40,000}{165,000} \times \$150,000 \right\} \quad \ldots \ldots \ldots \quad \$\ 36,364$$

$$\text{United Kingdom} \quad \left\{ \frac{90,000}{165,000} \times \$150,000 \right\} \quad \ldots \ldots \ldots \quad \$\ 81,818$$

$$\text{Belgium} \quad \left\{ \frac{0}{165,000} \times \$150,000 \right\} \quad \ldots \ldots \ldots \quad 0$$

$$\$150,000$$

The amount by which the foreign preference items offset U.S. taxable income pursuant to subdivision (i) of this subparagraph is then determined as follows:

	(a) Preferences	(b) Loss	(c) U.S. taxable income	(d) Smallest of (a), (b), or (c)
France	$35,000	$60,000	$31,818	$ 31,818
Germany	70,000	40,000	36,364	36,364
United Kingdom	95,000	90,000	81,818	81,818
Belgium	–0–	–0–	–0–	–0–
				$150,000

Thus, $150,000 of the total foreign preference items will be taken into account pursuant to subdivision (i) of this subparagraph as items of tax preference in 1972 and subject to the provisions of section 56.

   (b) Pursuant to subdivision (ii) of this subparagraph, the 1972 net operating loss of $35,000 will consist of suspense preferences of $15,000 and other foreign deductions of $20,000 attributable to each foreign country as shown below and determined as follows:

		Deductions					
		France		Germany		United Kingdom	
Explanation	United States	Preferences	Other	Preferences	Other	Kingdom preferences	Belgium other
	$100,000	$35,000	$75,000	$70,000	$30,000	$95,000	$40,000
1. U.S. deductions against U.S. income ($250,000)	(100,000)	....					
2. Other foreign deductions against foreign income (per- country)[1]			(50,000)	....	(30,000)	....	(40,000)
3. Suspense preferences against remaining foreign income (per-country)				(30,000)	....	(5,000)	......

Reg. § 1.58-7(c)(2)

4. Suspense preferences
against remaining U.S.
income:

     France (35,000 × $150,000) ....   (31,818)   ....

        ———————
       165,000

     Germany (40,000 × $150,000) ....   (36,364)   ....

        ———————
       165,000

     U.K. (90,000 × $150,000) ....   (81,818)   ......

        ———————
       165,000

5. Other foreign
deductions against
remaining U.S. income
(0) ....   Not applicable.

6. U.S. deductions against
other foreign income ..   Not applicable.

7. Other foreign deductions against remaining foreign
income ($5,000) ....   (5,000)   ....

8. Suspense preferences
against remaining
foreign income (0)   Not applicable.

     Balance (components of NOL)   3,182   20,000   3,636   8,182   ......

---

[1] Foreign income amounts before step 2 are; France—$50,000; Germany—$60,000; United Kingdom—$5,000; Belgium—$45,000.

Example (3). In 1973, the taxpayer has taxable income (computed without regard to the net operating loss deduction) from the following sources and in the following amounts:

United States	France	Germany	United Kingdom
$100,000	$60,000	$20,000	$30,000

In addition, the taxpayer has a net operating loss deduction of $235,000 resulting from a 1972 net operating loss consisting of the following amounts:

Deductions attributable to income from sources within the United States $25,000
Suspense preferences attributable to income from sources within France $75,000
Deductions other than suspense preferences attributable to income from sources within
    France $85,000
Deductions other than suspense preferences attributable to sources within the
    Netherlands $50,000

(a) Pursuant to subdivision (ii) of this subparagraph, the converted suspense preferences and the remaining portions of the 1972 net operating loss carried over to 1974 are computed as follows:

[In thousands of dollars]

	1973 income				1972 net operating loss			
	United States	France	Germany	United Kingdom	United States	French suspense preferences	French other deductions	Dutch other deductions
	100	60	20	30	25	75	85	50
U.S. deductions against U.S. income	(25)	....			(25)	....		
Other foreign deductions against foreign income (per-country) ...	.....	(60)	....				(60)	.....
Suspense preferences against remaining foreign income (per-country)			Not applicable.					
Suspense preferences against remaining U.S. income	([1] 75)	....			(75)	....		
Other foreign deductions against remaining U.S. income			Not applicable.					
U.S. deductions against remaining foreign income			Not applicable.					

Reg. § 1.58-7(c)(2)

Other foreign deductions against remaining foreign income:				
French (25,000 × $80,000)	(16.7)	....	(16.7)	.....
75,000				
Dutch 50,000 × $50,000	(33.3)	....	(33.3)	
75,000				
Suspense preferences against remaining foreign income		Not applicable.		
Balance (1972 carryover to 1974)			8.3	16.7

[1] Suspense preferences converted to actual items of tax preferences.

(b) If, in 1972, there had been no items of tax preference without regard to the suspense preferences, the conversion of the suspense preferences in 1973 would result in a 1972 minimum tax liability under section 56(a) of $4,500 (10 percent × ($75,000 − $30,000)), all of which would have been deferred by reason of section 56(b). Further, by application of section 56(b) and § 1.56A-2, $20,000 of the $45,000 preference portion of the 1972 net operating loss would be treated as having reduced taxable income in 1973 resulting in the imposition in 1973 of $2,000 of the deferred 1972 minimum tax liability.

(3) *Separate limitation under section 904(f).* In the case of a taxpayer subject to the separate limitation on interest income under section 904(f), the provisions of this paragraph shall be applied in the same manner as in subparagraph (2) of this paragraph. If the taxpayer has elected the overall foreign tax credit limitation, subparagraph (2) of this paragraph shall be applied as if all income from sources within any foreign countries or possessions of the United States and deductions relating to income from such sources other than income or deductions subject to the separate limitation under section 904(f) were from a single foreign country.

(4) *Carryover of excess taxes.* For rules relating to carryover of excess taxes described in paragraph (1) of section 56(c) when suspense preferences are converted to actual items of tax preference, see § 1.56A-5(f).

(5) *Character of amounts.* Where the amounts from sources within a foreign country or possession of the United States (or all such countries or possessions in the case of a taxpayer who has elected the overall foreign tax credit limitation) which are treated as reducing chapter 1 tax on income from sources within the United States or as suspense preferences are less than the total items of tax preference described in subparagraph (1)(i)(a) of this paragraph attributable to such sources, the amounts so treated are considered derived proportionately from each such item of tax preference. [Reg. § 1.58-7.]

☐ [*T.D. 7564, 9-11-78. Amended by T.D. 8138, 4-23-87.*]

[Reg. § 1.58-8]

§ 1.58-8. Capital gains and stock options.— (a) *In general.* Section 58(g)(2) provides that the items of tax preference specified in section 57 (a)(6), and § 1.57-1(b) (stock options), and section 57(a)(9), and § 1.57-1(i) (capital gains), which are attributable to sources within any foreign country or possession of the United States shall not be taken into account as items of tax preference if, under the tax laws of such country or possession, preferential treatment is not accorded:

(1) In the case of stock options, to the gain, profit, or other income realized from the transfer of shares of stock pursuant to the exercise of an option which is under United States tax law a qualified or restricted stock option (under section 422 or section 424); and

(2) In the case of capital gains, to gain from the sale or exchange of capital assets (or property treated as capital assets under United States tax law).

Where capital gains are not accorded preferential treatment within a foreign country, capital losses as well as capital gains from such country are not taken into account for purposes of the minimum tax.

(b) *Source of capital gains and stock options.* Generally, in determining whether the capital gain or stock option item of tax preference is attributable to sources within any foreign country or possession of the United States, the principles of sections 861-863 and the regulations thereunder are applied. Thus, the stock option item of tax preference, representing compensation for personal services, is attributable, in accordance with § 1.861-4, to sources within the country in which the personal services were performed. Where the capital gain item of tax preference represents gain from the purchase and sale of personal property, such gain is attributable, in accordance with § 1.861-7, entirely to sources within the country in which the property is sold. In accordance with paragraph (c) of § 1.861-7, in any case in which the sales transaction is arranged in a particular manner for the primary purpose of tax avoidance, all factors of the transaction, such as negotiations, the execution of the agreement, the location of the property, and the place of payment, will be considered, and the sale will be treated as having

Reg. § 1.58-8(b)

been consummated at the place where the substance of the sale occurred.

(c) *Preferential treatment.* For purposes of this section, gain, profit, or other income is accorded preferential treatment by a foreign country or possession of the United States if (1) recognition of the income, for foreign tax purposes, is deferred beyond the taxpayer's taxable year or comparable period for foreign tax purposes which coincide with the taxpayer's U.S. taxable year in cases where other items of profit, gain, or other income may not be deferred; (2) it is subject to tax at a lower effective rate (including no rate of tax) than other items of profit, gain, or other income, by means of a special rate of tax, artificial deductions, exemptions, exclusions, or similar reductions in the amount subject to tax; (3) it is subject to no significant amount of tax; or (4) the laws of the foreign country or possession by any other method provide tax treatment for such profit, gain, or other income more beneficial than the tax treatment otherwise accorded income by such country or possession. For the purpose of the preceding sentence, gain, profit, or other income is subject to no significant amount of tax if the amount of taxes imposed by the foreign country or possession of the United States is equal to less than 2.5 percent of the gross amount of such income.

(d) *Examples.* The principles of this section may be illustrated by the following examples:

Example (1). The Bahamas imposes no income tax on individuals or corporations, whether resident or nonresident. Since capital gains are subject to no tax in the Bahamas, capital gains are considered to be accorded preferential treatment and will be taken into account for purposes of the minimum tax.

Example (2). In France, except in certain cases involving the sale of large blocks of stock, a nonresident individual is not subject to tax on isolated capital gains transactions. Since such capital gains are not subject to tax in France, they are considered to be accorded preferential treatment irrespective of the treatment accorded other capital gains in France and such gains will be taken into account for purposes of the minimum tax.

Example (3). In Germany, in the case of the sale within one taxable year of 1 percent or more of the shares of a corporation in which an individual taxpayer is regarded as holding a substantial interest, the gains on the sale of the large block of stock will be taxed as extraordinary income at one-half the ordinary income tax rate. Since these gains are taxed at a reduced rate of tax in comparison to other income, they are considered to be accorded preferential treatment and will be taken into account for purposes of the minimum tax.

Example (4). In Belgium, gains derived by an individual in the course of regular speculative transactions are taxed as ordinary income, but with an upper limit of 30 percent. Rates of tax on individuals in Belgium range from approximately 30 percent to approximately 60 percent. Since the gains on speculative transactions are taxed at a maximum rate which is more beneficial than the rates accorded to other income, such gains are considered to be accorded preferential treatment and will be taken into account for purposes of the minimum tax.

Example (5). In France, gains derived by a company on the sale of fixed assets held for less than 2 years are treated as short-term gains. The excess of short-term gains in any fiscal year is taxed at the full company tax rate of 50 percent. However, this tax may be paid in equal portions over the 5 years immediately following the realization of such short-term gains. Since recognition of the short-term gains for tax purposes is subject to deferral over a 5-year period, such gains are considered to be accorded preferential treatment and will be taken into account for purposes of the minimum tax.

Example (6). Also in France, in the case of the sale or exchange by a company of depreciable assets and nondepreciable assets owned for at least 2 years, the excess of long-term capital gains over long-term capital losses in a fiscal year is subject to an immediate tax at the reduced rate of 10 percent. Such excess, reduced by the 10-percent tax, is carried in a special reserve account on the taxpayer's books. If the excess is reinvested in other fixed assets within a stated period, no further tax is due. If the amounts in the special reserve are distributed, they will be treated as ordinary income for the fiscal year in which the distribution is made. Since such gains (other than those distributed in the same fiscal year they are realized) are subject to deferral or a reduced rate of tax, they are (except to the extent distributed in the year of realization) considered to be accorded preferential treatment and are taken into account for purposes of the minimum tax.

Example (7). In Sweden, in the case of gains derived by an individual on the sale of shares or bonds held for 5 years or less, 25 percent of the gains are taxed if the holding period is 4 to 5 years, 50 percent of the gain is taxed if the holding period is 3 to 4 years, and 75 percent of the gain is taxed if the holding period is 2 to 3 years. The gain is fully taxable at ordinary income rates if held for less than 2 years. Thus, gains on shares or bonds held for 2 years or more are considered accorded preferential treatment in Sweden since they are either subject to exemption or treatment comparable to the United States capital gains deduction and are taxed at a reduced rate. Thus, such gains are taken into account for purposes of the minimum tax.

Example (8). Pursuant to Article XIV of the United States-United Kingdom Income Tax Convention, a resident of the United States is exempt from United Kingdom tax on most capital gains.

Reg. § 1.58-8(c)

Since such capital gains are exempt from United Kingdom taxation, they are considered to be accorded preferential treatment and are taken into account for purposes of the minimum tax.

Example (9). An individual resident of the United States is desirous of selling his stock in a corporation listed on the New York Stock Exchange. He requests the stock certificates from his broker in the United States, travels to a foreign country, delivers the certificates to a broker in that country, and has the foreign broker execute the sale which takes place on the New York Stock Exchange. Since the sale was consummated in the United States, pursuant to paragraph (b) of this section and § 1.861-7, the resulting capital gain item of tax preference is attributable to sources within the United States.

Example (10). Two individuals, both residing in the United States, negotiate and reach agreement in New York City for the sale of stock of a close corporation. Prior to the transfer of the stock, in order to avoid imposition of the minimum tax, both individuals travel to a foreign country which does not accord preferential treatment to capital gains, but imposes a 5 percent rate of income tax which would be fully creditable against United States tax under sections 901 and 904 if the capital gains were sourced in that country. The stock is actually transferred and consideration paid in the foreign country. Since the primary purpose of consummating the sale in the foreign country was the avoidance of tax, pursuant to paragraph (b) of this section, and § 1.861-7(c), the resulting capital gain item of tax preference will be considered attributable to sources within the country in which the substance of sale took place or, in this case, the United States. [Reg. § 1.58-8.]

☐ [*T.D. 7564, 9-11-78.*]

[Reg. § 1.58-9]

§ 1.58-9. Application of the tax benefit rule to the minimum tax for taxable years beginning prior to 1987.—(a) *In general.* For purposes of computing the minimum tax liability imposed under section 56 of the Internal Revenue Code of 1954 (Code), taxpayers are not liable for minimum tax on tax preference items that do not reduce the taxpayer's tax liability under subtitle A of the Code for the taxable year. In general, tax preference items that do not reduce tax liability under subtitle A for the taxable year are those from which no current tax benefit is derived because available credits would have reduced or eliminated the taxpayer's regular tax liability if the preference items had not been allowed in computing taxable income. However, any credits that, because of such preference items, are not needed for use against regular tax ("freed-up cred-

its"), are required to be reduced under the rules of paragraph (c) of this section. For purposes of this section, a taxpayer's regular tax is the Federal income tax liability under subchapter A of chapter 1 of the Code, not including the minimum tax imposed by section 56. Unless otherwise noted, all references to Internal Revenue Code sections refer to the Internal Revenue Code of 1954.

(b) *Effective date.* The rules of this section are effective May 5, 1992, but only as they affect tax preference items that arise in taxable years beginning after December 31, 1976, and before January 1, 1987.

(c) *Adjustment of carryover credits*—(1) *In general.* A taxpayer's freed-up credits must be reduced by the additional minimum tax that would have been imposed if a current tax benefit had been derived from preference items that did not actually produce a current tax benefit. The amount of this reduction shall be calculated in the following manner—

(i) Determine the amount of freed-up credits;

(ii) Determine the amount of tax preference items (if any) from which a current tax benefit was derived for the taxable year ("beneficial preferences"), and the amount of preferences from which no current tax benefit was derived for the taxable year ("non-beneficial preferences"); and

(iii) Determine the portion of the total minimum tax on all tax preference items for the taxable year that is attributable to the non-beneficial preferences.

The freed-up credits are then reduced by an amount equal to such portion of the minimum tax.

(2) *Determine freed-up credits.* (i) To determine the freed-up credits for the taxable year, first determine the regular tax that would have been imposed for the taxable year if preference items had not been allowed in computing taxable income ("non-preference regular tax"). In the case of a taxpayer with the capital gain preference described in section 57(a)(9)(B), non-preference regular tax is computed without regard to section 1201 and without adding the section 57(a)(9)(B) preference amount to taxable income. Second, compute the amount of credits that would have been allowed to reduce the non-preference regular tax. The credits available to reduce non-preference regular tax shall include any freed-up credits from other taxable years, as reduced under paragraph (c)(5) of this section, that are carried to the current taxable year. Third, subtract the amount of credits that were actually allowed to reduce the regular tax for such taxable year from the amount

Reg. § 1.58-9(c)(2)

of credits that would have been allowed to reduce non-preference regular tax. The result is the amount of the freed-up credits.

(ii) The following examples illustrate the determination of freed-up credits. The first two examples assume that the foreign tax credits being used do not exceed the limitation under section 904.

Example 1. In 1982 Corporation B has $17.6 million dollars in foreign tax credits available for the taxable year. If preference items were not allowed in determining regular tax, the regular tax would have been $10.2 million and foreign tax credits used to reduce regular tax would have been $10.2 million. Because of tax preference items, however, B's regular tax is $6.3 million and the amount of foreign tax credits actually used to reduce the regular tax is $6.3 million. The amount of freed-up foreign tax credits is $3.9 million ($10.2 million minus $6.3 million).

Example 2. Assume the same facts as in *Example 1* of paragraph (c)(2)(ii) of this section except that Corporation B has $7.2 million dollars in foreign tax credits. If preference items were not allowed, the non-preference regular tax would have been $10.2 million and the foreign tax credits used to reduce the regular tax would have been $7.2 million. Because of tax preference items, however, B's regular tax is $6.3 million, and the amount of foreign tax credits actually used to reduce the regular tax is $6.3 million. The amount of freed-up foreign tax credits is $.9 million ($7.2 million minus $6.3 million).

Example 3. In 1983 Corporation C has $500,000 of investment tax credits available. If preference items were not allowed, non-preference regular tax would have been $690,000 and all $500,000 of investment tax credits would have been allowed to reduce non-preference regular tax liability. Because of tax preferences, however, C's actual regular tax is $439,750. As a result of the limitation under section 38(c), only $377,537 of the investment tax credits are allowed to reduce the actual regular tax. Freed-up credits are $122,463 ($500,000 minus $377,537).

Example 4. In 1984 Corporation B has ordinary income of $20,000 and net section 1201 gain of $300,000, none of which is attributable to foreign sources. B has no other items of tax preference in 1984. B's non-preference regular tax for 1984 is $126,950, the amount of tax that would be imposed without regard to section 1201.

(3) *Determination of beneficial and non-beneficial preferences*—(i) *In general.* The amount of tax preferences from which a current tax benefit is derived ("beneficial preferences") and the amount from which no current tax benefit is de-

rived ("non-beneficial preferences") for the taxable year are determined as set forth below.

(ii) *Regular tax liability is the same regardless of preference items.* (A) If the taxpayer's tax liability (after credits) would be the same regardless of whether preference items were allowed to reduce taxable income, then all of the taxpayer's preference items are non-beneficial preference items.

(B) The following example illustrates the rule set forth in paragraph (c)(3)(ii)(A) of this section. This example assumes that foreign tax credits being used do not exceed the limitation under section 904.

Example. (i) In 1982 Corporation B has $17.6 million dollars in foreign tax credits available for the taxable year. If preference items were not allowed in determining regular tax, the regular tax would have been $10.2 million and foreign tax credits used to reduce regular tax would have been $10.2 million. Because of tax preference items, however, B's regular tax is $6.3 million and the amount of foreign tax credits actually used to reduce the regular tax is $6.3 million. The amount of freed-up foreign tax credits is $3.9 million ($10.2 million minus $6.3 million).

(ii) The total amount of B's tax preference items is $8.4 million. B's non-preference regular tax is $10.2 million and, reduced by foreign tax credits, is zero. B's actual regular tax is $6.3 million and, reduced by foreign tax credits, is zero. Since the amount of credits that would have been allowed to offset the non-preference regular tax would have reduced such tax to an amount ($0) equal to the actual regular tax liability ($0), B received a tax benefit from none of the $8.4 million of tax preferences and therefore all of these preferences are non-beneficial preferences.

(iii) *Regular tax liability differs because of preference items.* If tax liability (after credits) is less because preference items are allowed to reduce taxable income, then some of these preference items have provided a current tax benefit. In such cases, the amount of beneficial and non-beneficial preferences are determined as follows:

(A) *Non-beneficial preferences.*—(1) The non-beneficial preferences are determined by converting the freed-up credits for such taxable year into an amount of taxable income. To make this conversion, freed-up credits are "grossed up" (*i.e.,* divided by the regular tax marginal rate at which such credits would have offset non-preference regular tax) to determine the amount of tax preferences that freed up such credits. For purposes of this calculation, the 5-percent addition to tax provided by section 11(b) shall be included in determining the marginal rate. The aggregate of these grossed-up amounts is the total amount of non-beneficial preferences for the taxable year.

(2) The freed-up credits shall be grossed up beginning at the lowest marginal tax rate that would have applied to the additional taxable income arising if tax preferences were not allowed. Thus, the marginal tax rates at which the actual regular tax was imposed shall not be taken into account in grossing up freed-up credits, even if all or a portion of such tax is not offset by credits because of limitations on the allowance of such credits (such as the section 904 limit on foreign tax credits or the section 38(c) limit on investment tax credits). For example, if the first dollar of additional non-preference taxable income would have been taxed at a rate of 46 percent,

then freed-up credits shall be grossed up at 46 percent, even if regular tax imposed on taxable income at a 40-percent rate was not offset by credits because of the limitations on investment tax credits under section 38(c). See Examples 1 and 2 in paragraph (d) of this section for illustrations of the gross up of freed-up credits in cases where limitations apply to the amount of credit allowed to offset actual regular tax.

(3) The following example illustrates the gross up of freed-up credits to determine non-beneficial preferences. This example assumes that foreign tax credits being used do not exceed the limitation under section 904.

Example. (i) Corporation L has the following items for the 1985 taxable year:

Actual taxable income	$90,000
Regular tax	21,750
Available credits:	
Foreign tax credits for 1985	$15,000
Foreign tax credits carried forward from 1984	25,000
Investment tax credits carried forward from 1984	20,000
	60,000
Credit allowed to offset actual regular tax:	
Foreign tax credits for 1985	$15,000
Foreign tax credits carried forward from 1984	6,750
	21,750
Actual regular tax liability	-0-
Preferences	110,000
Taxable income for 1985 determined as though preferences were not allowed	200,000
Non-preference regular tax	71,750
Credits allowed to offset non-preference regular tax:	
Foreign tax credits for 1985	$15,000
Foreign tax credits carried forward from 1984	25,000
Investment tax credits carried forward from 1984	20,000
	60,000
Non-preference regular tax liability	11,750

(ii) The freed-up credits for 1985 are $38,250 ($60,000 minus $21,750). The non-preference regular tax of $71,750 is determined by applying the regular tax rates set forth in section 11(b) to the $200,000 of taxable income as follows:

Taxable Income	Rate		Tax
$ 25,000	× .15	=	$ 3,750
25,000	× .18	=	4,500
25,000	× .30	=	7,500
25,000	× .40	=	10,000
100,000	× .46	=	46,000
$200,000			$71,750

(iii) Thus, for purposes of determining the non-beneficial preferences, freed-up credits

are grossed up as follows: The credits allowed against the regular tax and the freed-up credits are treated as offsetting non-preference regular tax in the same order as such credits would have been allowed to offset such tax, beginning at the lowest marginal tax rate. The freed-up credits are grossed up beginning at the lowest marginal tax rate at which additional taxable income would have been taxed if preferences were not allowed. Thus, in this example freed-up credits are grossed up beginning at 40 percent, and the amount of L's non-beneficial preferences for the 1985 taxable year is $84,456.

Type	Credit allowed against regular tax	Freed-up credit	Divided by tax Rate	Non-beneficial preferences
FTC (85)	$ 3,750	—	.15	—
FTC (85)	4,500	—	.18	—
FTC (85)	6,750	—	.30	—
FTC (84)	750	—	.30	—

Reg. § 1.58-9(c)(3)

FTC (84)	6,000	—	.40		—
FTC (84)	—	$ 4,000	.40	=	$10,000
FTC (84)	—	14,250	.46	=	30,978
ITC (84)	—	20,000	.46	=	43,478
	$21,750	$38,250			$84,456

Foreign tax credit = FTC (year)
Investment tax credit = ITC (year)

(B) *Beneficial preferences.* The amount of beneficial preferences for the taxable year is computed by subtracting the non-beneficial preferences for the taxable year from the total amount of tax preferences for such year. This rule may be illustrated by the following example:

Example. Assume the same facts as in the *Example* in paragraph (c)(3)(iii)(A)(*3*) of this section. The amount of L's beneficial preferences for 1985 is $25,544 (total preferences of $110,000, minus non-beneficial preferences of $84,456).

(4) *Determine the minimum tax attributable to non-beneficial preferences.* (i) The portion of the minimum tax that is attributable to the non-beneficial preferences is computed as follows—

(A) Compute the minimum tax that would be imposed on all tax preference items for the taxable year if all of the preferences had produced a tax benefit.

(B) Compute the minimum tax that would be imposed on the beneficial preferences if these were the taxpayer's only preferences. (This is the amount of minimum tax actually imposed for the taxable year.)

(C) Subtract the amount computed in paragraph (c)(4)(i)(B) of this section from the amount computed in paragraph (c)(4)(i)(A) of this section. The result is the minimum tax attributable to the non-beneficial preferences for the taxable year. This amount is sometimes referred to hereinafter as the "credit reduction amount".

(ii) The following examples illustrate determination of the credit reduction amount. These examples assume that foreign tax credits being used do not exceed the limitation under section 904.

Example 1. (i) In 1982 Corporation B has $17.6 million dollars in foreign tax credits available for the taxable year. If preference items were not allowed in determining regular tax, the regular tax would have been $10.2 million and foreign tax credits used to reduce regular tax would have been $10.2 million. Because of tax preference items, however, B's regular tax is $6.3 million and the amount of foreign tax credits actually used to reduce the regular tax is $6.3 million. The amount of freed-up foreign tax credits is $3.9 million ($10.2 million minus $6.3 million).

(ii) The total amount of B's tax preference items is $8.4 million. B's non-preference regular tax is $10.2 million and, reduced by foreign tax credits, is zero. B's actual regular tax is $6.3 million and, reduced by foreign tax credits, is zero. Since the amount of credits that would have been allowed to offset the non-preference regular tax would have reduced such tax to an amount ($0) equal to the actual regular tax liability ($0), B received a tax benefit from none of the $8.4 million of tax preferences and therefore all of these preferences are non-beneficial preferences.

(iii) Since B has $8.4 million in total preference items and no regular tax liability, the minimum tax on that amount would be $1,258,500 (($8.4 million minus $10,000) multiplied by .15). None of the preference items is a beneficial preference. Thus, the minimum tax attributable to non-beneficial preferences (and therefore, the credit reduction amount) is $1,258,500.

Example 2. (i) Corporation L has the following items for the 1985 taxable year:

Actual taxable income		$ 90,000
Regular tax		21,750
Available credits:		
Foreign tax credits for 1985	$15,000	
Foreign tax credits carried forward from 1984	25,000	
Investment tax credits carried forward from 1984	20,000	
		$ 60,000
Credit allowed to offset actual regular tax:		
Foreign tax credits for 1985	$15,000	
Foreign tax credits carried forward from 1984	6,750	
		$ 21,750
Actual regular tax liability		–0–
Preferences		110,000

Reg. § 1.58-9(c)(4)

Taxable income for 1985 determined as though preferences were not allowed	200,000
Non-preference regular tax	71,750
Credits allowed to offset non-preference regular tax:	
Foreign tax credits for 1985 .... $15,000	
Foreign tax credits carried forward from 1984.................... 25,000	
Investment tax credits carried forward from 1984 20,000	
	$ 60,000
Non-preference regular tax liability	11,750

(ii) The freed-up credits for 1985 are $38,250 ($60,000 minus $21,750). The non-preference regular tax is $71,750. The amount of L's non-beneficial preferences for the 1985 taxable year is $84,456.

(iii) The minimum tax on L's total preference items of $110,000 would be $15,000 (($110,000 minus $10,000) multiplied by .15). Since the amount of non-beneficial preferences is $84,456, the amount of L's beneficial preferences for 1985 is $25,544 ($110,000 minus $84,456). The minimum tax on L's beneficial preferences of $25,544 is $2,332 (($25,544 minus $10,000) multiplied by .15). (This is the amount of minimum tax imposed for 1985.) The minimum tax attributable to non-beneficial preference items (and therefore, the credit reduction amount) is $12,668 ($15,000 minus $2,332).

(5) *Reduction of freed-up credits*—(i) *In general.* The freed-up credits are reduced by an amount equal to the minimum tax attributable to the non-beneficial preferences ("credit reduction amount"). If the taxpayer has only one type of freed-up credit (*i.e.,* only investment tax credit or only foreign tax credit) and that credit was earned in only one year (the current year or a carryover year), then the credit is reduced by the credit reduction amount. This rule may be illustrated by the following example. This example assumes that foreign tax credits being used do not exceed the limitation under section 904.

Example. (i) In 1982 Corporation B has $17.6 million dollars in foreign tax credits available for the taxable year. If preference items were not allowed in determining regular tax, the regular tax would have been $10.2 million and foreign tax credits used to reduce regular tax would have been $10.2 million. Because of tax preference items, however, B's regular tax is $6.3 million and the amount of foreign tax credits actually used to reduce the regular tax is $6.3 million. The amount of freed-up foreign tax credits is $3.9 million ($10.2 million minus $6.3 million).

(ii) The total amount of B's tax preference items is $8.4 million. B's non-preference regular tax is $10.2 million and, reduced by foreign tax credits, is zero. B's actual regular tax is $6.3 million and, reduced by foreign tax credits, is zero. Since the amount of credits that would have

been allowed to offset the non-preference regular tax would have reduced such tax to an amount ($0) equal to the actual regular tax liability ($0), B received a tax benefit from none of the $8.4 million of tax preferences and therefore all of these preferences are non-beneficial preferences.

(iii) Since B has $8.4 million in total preference items and no regular tax liability, the minimum tax on that amount would be $1,258,500 (($8.4 million minus $10,000) multiplied by .15). None of the preference items is a beneficial preference. Thus, the minimum tax attributable to non-beneficial preferences (and therefore, the credit reduction amount) is $1,258,500.

(iv) All of the $3.9 million of freed-up credits are foreign tax credits that arise in the same year and that otherwise would be carried forward. Since the entire amount of B's tax preferences are non-beneficial preferences, the minimum tax of $1,258,500 that would be imposed on the total tax preferences is the credit reduction amount. Thus, B's $3.9 million of freed-up foreign tax credits is reduced by $1,258,500. The foreign tax credit carryforward from 1982 is $10,041,500. This amount is the sum of $2,641,500 (the freed-up foreign tax credit of $3,900,000, reduced by the credit reduction amount of $1,258,500), plus $7.4 million (the foreign tax credit that would have been carried over even if tax preference items had not been allowed).

However, if the taxpayer has more than one type of freed-up credit, or the taxpayer's freed-up credits are from more than one taxable year, then the credit reduction amount must be allocated under the exact method described in paragraph (c)(5)(ii) of this section, unless an election is made under paragraph (c)(5)(iii) of this section to use the simplified method.

(ii) *Exact method.* For each type of freed-up credits and for each taxable year within such type from which any such credits are earned, the amount of credit reduction shall be equal to the amount of minimum tax attributable to the non-beneficial preferences that freed up the credits for that type and taxable year. The amount of the credit reduction is computed by multiplying the amount of non-beneficial preferences which freed up credits for each type and taxable year by the minimum tax rate. For purposes of this computa-

Reg. § 1.58-9(c)(5)

tion, if the amount of the taxpayer's minimum tax exemption for the taxable year (as determined under section 56(a)) exceeds the amount of the taxpayer's beneficial preferences, such excess exemption shall reduce the amount of non-beneficial preferences to be multiplied by the minimum tax rate. The non-beneficial preferences shall be reduced by any such excess exemption in the same order in which the credits that were freed up by such preferences would have been allowed to offset tax. Thus, for example, any excess exemption shall first reduce non-beneficial preferences that freed up foreign tax credits. Any such excess exemption remaining after reducing non-beneficial preferences that freed up foreign tax credits to zero would then be used to reduce the non-beneficial preferences that freed up investment tax credits.

(iii) *Simplified method*—(A) *Description of method.* In lieu of the exact credit reduction method described in paragraph (c)(5)(ii) of this section, taxpayers may elect to use the simplified credit reduction method. Under the simplified credit reduction method, the amount of freed-up credits for each type of credit and for each taxable year in which such credit is earned is multiplied by a fraction. The numerator of the fraction is the total credit reduction amount as determined in paragraph (c)(4)(i)(C) of this section. The denominator is the total amount of freed-up credits as determined in paragraph (c)(2)(i) of this section. The product of this multiplication is the amount of credit reduction for each type and taxable year of freed-up credit.

(B) *Election to use simplified method.* A taxpayer may elect to use the simplified credit reduction method for all taxable years to which this section applies by attaching a statement indicating such an election on the amended Federal income tax return or returns applying the adjustments of this section. If an election is made for any taxable year, it must be made for all taxable years. Once an election has been made, it can be revoked only with the permission of the Commissioner. Similarly, once returns have been filed applying the exact credit reduction method, an election to apply the simplified method can be made only with the consent of the Commissioner.

(iv) *Effect of credit reduction on credit carryovers.* Under both the exact method and the simplified method, the determination of credit carryovers to other taxable years is made on the basis of freed-up credits remaining after such reduction, plus any other unused credits. Thus, an amount of freed-up credits that is equal to the credit reduction amount shall not be allowed to reduce tax liability in any taxable year. Such disallowance is without regard to whether such credits would otherwise be allowed as a carryover. The freed-up credits, as reduced under this paragraph (c)(5), shall be carried over or carried back in applying this section in a carryover or carryback year. No minimum tax liability shall be due with respect to the non-beneficial preferences for any taxable year.

(v) *Examples.* The following examples illustrate reduction of freed-up credits.

Example 1. (i) Corporation L has the following items for the 1985 taxable year:

Actual taxable income		$ 90,000
Regular tax		21,750
Available credits:		
Foreign tax credits for 1985	$15,000	
Foreign tax credits carried forward		
from 1984	25,000	
Investment tax credits carried forward		
from 1984	20,000	
		60,000
Credit allowed to offset actual regular tax:		
Foreign tax credits for 1985	$15,000	
Foreign tax credits carried forward from 1984..................	6,750	
		21,750
Actual regular tax liability...		–0–
Preferences		110,000
Taxable income for 1985 determined as though preferences were not allowed		200,000
Non-preference regular tax		71,750
Credits allowed to offset non-preference regular tax:		
Foreign tax credits for 1985	$15,000	
Foreign tax credits carried forward		
from 1984	25,000	
Investment tax credits carried forward		
from 1984	20,000	
		60,000
Non-preference regular tax liability		11,750

Reg. § 1.58-9(c)(5)

(ii) The freed-up credits for 1985 are $38,250 ($60,000 minus $21,750). The non-preference regular tax is $71,750. The amount of L's non-beneficial preferences for the 1985 taxable year is $84,456.

(iii) The credit reduction amount for 1985 is $12,668, the amount of minimum tax attributable to L's non-beneficial preferences. This amount is allocated to reduce each category of freed-up credit and to each year from which such credit is carried over. L's $38,250 of freed-up credits consists of $18,250 of foreign tax credits carried for-

$$\frac{\text{Non-beneficial preferences}}{\text{that freed up 1984 FTC}} \times .15 = \frac{\text{Credit reduction}}{\text{of 1984 FTC}}$$

$$\$40,978 \times .15 = \underline{\$6,146}$$

(B) Investment tax credits carried forward from 1984:

$$\frac{\text{Non-beneficial preferences}}{\text{that freed up 1984 ITC}} \times .15 = \frac{\text{Credit reduction}}{\text{of 1984 ITC}}$$

$$\$43,478 \times .15 = \underline{\$6,522}$$

Thus, the foreign tax credits from 1984 that are carried forward to 1986 are $12,104 ($18,250 minus $6,146). The investment tax credits from 1984 that are carried forward to 1986 are $13,478 ($20,000 minus $6,522).

(v) The reduction of the freed-up credit under the simplified credit reduction method is as follows:

$$\frac{\text{Freed-up foreign tax}}{\text{credits from 1984}} \times \frac{\text{Credit}}{\text{reduction amount}}$$
$$\overline{\text{Total freed-up credit}}$$

$$= \frac{\text{Credit reduction allocated to freed-up}}{\text{foreign tax credits carried forward from 1984}}$$

$$\$18,250 \times \frac{\$12,668}{\$38,250} = \underline{\$6,044}$$

(B) Investment tax credits carried forward from 1984:

$$\frac{\text{Freed-up investment tax}}{\text{credits from 1984}} \times \frac{\text{Credit}}{\text{reduction amount}}$$
$$\overline{\text{Total freed-up credit}}$$

$$= \frac{\text{Credit reduction allocated to freed-up}}{\text{investment tax credits carried forward from 1984}}$$

$$\$20,000 \times \frac{\$12,668}{\$38,250} = \underline{\$6,624}$$

Thus, under the simplified credit reduction method, L has $12,206 of foreign tax credits for 1984 ($18,250 minus $6,044) that are carried forward to 1986, and $13,376 of investment tax credits for 1984 ($20,000 minus $6,624) that are carried forward to 1986.

Example 2. Assume the same facts as in *Example 1* of this paragraph (c)(5)(v), except that

ward from 1984, which were freed up by $40,978 of non-beneficial preferences, and $20,000 of investment tax credits carried forward from 1984, which were freed up by $43,478 of non-beneficial preferences.

(iv) The apportionment of this credit reduction amount to each category of freed-up credit and each taxable year from which such credits are carried over is determined as follows under the exact credit reduction method:

(A) Foreign tax credits carried forward from 1984:

(A) Foreign tax credit carried forward from 1984:

the foreign tax credits available for use in 1985 include $10,750 in credits carried forward from 1980 and $14,250 in credits carried forward from 1984, rather than $25,000 carried forward from 1984. Thus, $4,000 of the freed-up foreign tax credit is carried over from 1980. The other $14,250 of freed-up foreign tax credit is carried over from 1984. The non-beneficial preferences that freed up the 1980 foreign tax credit are $10,000. The non-beneficial preferences that freed up the 1984 foreign tax credit are $30,978. Under the exact credit reduction method, the credit reduction amounts for each of these credits are determined as follows:

(i) Foreign tax credit carried forward from 1980:

$$\$10,000 \times .15 = \underline{\$1,500}$$

(ii) Foreign tax credit carried forward from 1984:

$$\$30,978 \times .15 = \underline{\$4,646}$$

Thus, the foreign tax credit from 1984 that is carried forward to 1986 is $9,604 ($14,250 minus

$4,646). Since the foreign tax credit from 1980 expires after 1985, none of that credit is carried forward to 1986.

(d) *Examples.* The following examples are comprehensive illustrations of the adjustments described in paragraph (c) of this section:

Example 1. (i) This example illustrates the operation of the credit reduction adjustment when the amount of foreign tax credit allowed is subject to the overall limitation under section 904. For purposes of this example, assume that Corporation X has the following items for the 1984 taxable year:

Taxable income (determined as though preferences were not allowed)	$140,000
From foreign sources	70,000
Foreign tax credits from 1984	5,000
Foreign tax credits from 1983	7,000
Actual taxable income	50,000
From foreign sources	25,000

(ii) The credit reduction adjustment and minimum tax liability for the taxable year are determined as follows:

1. Taxable income (determined as though preferences were not allowed) ... $140,000
2. Tax preferences for 1984 ... 90,000
3. Taxable income (line 1 minus line 2) ... 50,000
4. Regular tax on line 3 amount (actual regular tax) before credits:

    $25,000   × .15 = $3,750

    25,000 × .18 =   4,500 ... 8,250
5. Foreign tax credits allowed against regular tax (limited to 50% of actual regular tax under sec. 904) — 1984 foreign tax credits ... 4,125
6. Regular tax after credits ... 4,125

    (line 4 minus line 5)
7. Regular tax on line 1 amount (non-preference regular tax) before credits:

    $25,000   × .15 = $ 3,750

    25,000 × .18 =   4,500

    25,000 × .3 =   7,500

    25,000 × .4 =   10,000

    40,000 × .46 = 18,400 ... 44,150
8. Foreign tax credits allowed against non-preference regular tax:

    $5,000 (1984 foreign tax credits)

    7,000 (1983 foreign tax credits) ... 12,000

    (the allowed credits do not exceed the section 904 limitation of $22,075)
9. Non-preference regular tax after credits (line 7 minus line 8) ... 32,150
10. Freed-up credits (line 8 minus line 5):

    1984 foreign tax credits ... $5,000

    (4,125)

                            $ 875

    1983 foreign tax credits ... $7,000

                        −0−

                         7,000

    Total ... $ 7,875
11. Non-beneficial preferences are computed as set forth in the table below. Under this computation, non-beneficial preferences are considered to free up credits that would have offset non-preference regular tax beginning at the lowest tax rates at which income that was offset by tax preferences otherwise would have been subject to regular tax. In this case, income that was offset by tax preferences would have been taxed beginning at the 30 percent marginal tax rate.

Reg. § 1.58-9(d)

Type	Freed-up Credit	Divided by tax Rate	Non-beneficial preferences
FTC (84)	$ 875	.30	$ 2,917
FTC (83)	6,625	.30	22,083
"	375	.40	938
	$ 7,875		$ 25,938

Total non-beneficial preferences 25,938
12. Beneficial preferences
(line 2 minus line 11)... 64,062
13. Minimum tax on total tax preferences
((line 2 minus the greater of line 6 or $10,000) × .15)..................... 12,000
14. Minimum tax on beneficial preferences
((line 12 minus the greater of line 6 or $10,000) × .15)................... 8,109
15. Credit reduction amount (line 13 minus line 14) 3,891
16. Reduction of freed-up credits under the exact method
(subtotals of line 11 multiplied by .15):

   (a) 1984 foreign tax credits:
   $2,917 × .15 = $438
   (b) 1983 foreign tax credits:
   ($22,083 + $938) × .15 = $3,453
   (c) Total credit reduction ....,.. 3,891

Note: If X had elected to use the simplified credit reduction method, the amount of credit reduction would be determined by multiplying the amount of freed-up credit in each category and taxable year by the following ratio:

$$\frac{\text{credit reduction amount}}{\text{total freed-up credit}} = \frac{\$3,891}{\$7,875} = .494$$

(d) Under this method, the 1984 freed-up foreign tax credits would be reduced by $433 ($875 × .494) and the 1983 freed-up foreign tax credits would be reduced by $3,458 ($7,000 × .494).

17. Freed-up credits after reduction under the exact method (line 10 subtotal minus line 16 subtotals).

   (a) 1984 foreign tax credits ($875 minus $438) 437
   (b) 1983 foreign tax credits ($7,000 minus $3,453) 3,547

Thus, assuming that Corporation X did not elect to use the simplified method, Corporation X will carryover $437 of 1984 foreign tax credits to 1985 and $3,547 of 1983 foreign tax credits to 1985.

Had Corporation X elected to use the simplified method, freed-up credits after reduction would be as follows:

   (a) 1984 foreign tax credits ($875 minus $433) 442
   (b) 1983 foreign tax credits ($7,000 minus $3,458) 3,542

Example 2. (i) Corporation X has the following items for its 1985 taxable year:

Taxable income (determined as though preferences were not allowed) $1,500,000
1984 investment tax credits 400,000
1985 investment tax credits 100,000
Actual taxable income 1,000,000

(ii) The credit reduction and minimum tax of X for 1985 are determined as follows:

1. Taxable income determined as though preferences were not allowed $1,500,000
2. Tax preferences for 1985 500,000
3. Taxable income (line 1 minus line 2) 1,000,000
4. Regular tax on line 3 amount (actual regular tax) before credits:
   $25,000 × .15 = $ 3,750
   25,000 × .18 =   4,500
   25,000 × .30 =   7,500
   25,000 × .40 =   10,000
   900,000 × .46 = 414,000 439,750
5. Investment tax credits allowed (limited under section 38(c) to $25,000 of net tax liability, plus 85 percent of net tax liability in excess of $25,000 377,537
6. Regular tax after credits (line 4 minus line 5) 62,212

Reg. § 1.58-9(d)

7. Regular tax on line 1 amount (non-preference regular tax) before credits:

$25,000 × .15 = $	3,750		
25,000 × .18 =	4,500		
25,000 × .30 =	7,500		
25,000 × .40 =	10,000		
900,000 × .46 =	414,000		
405,000 × .51 =	206,550		
95,000 × .46 =	43,700	....	690,000

8. Investment tax credits allowed against non-preference regular tax 500,000
9. Non-preference regular tax after credits (line 7 minus line 8) 190,000

10. Freed-up credits (line 8 minus line 5):

1984 investment tax credit	$400,000	
	(377,537)	
		22,463
1985 investment tax credit	$100,000	
	–0–	
		100,000
Total		$122,463

11. Non-beneficial preferences are computed as set forth in the table below. Under this computation, non-beneficial preferences are considered to free up credits that would have offset non-preference regular tax beginning at the lowest tax rates at which income that was offset by tax preferences otherwise would have been subject to regular tax. In this case, income that was offset by tax preferences would have been taxed beginning at the 51 percent marginal tax rate. Although some of the income offset by preferences would be taxed at the 46 percent marginal rate (because taxable income in excess of $1,405,000 is not subject to the 5 percent addition to tax on taxable income in excess of $1 million), the 51 percent marginal rate is taken into account first.

Type	Freed-up Credit	Divided by tax Rate	Non-beneficial preferences
ITC (84)	$ 22,463	.51	$ 44,045
ITC (85)	100,000	.51	196,078
	$ 122,463		$ 240,123

Total non-beneficial preferences 240,123

12. Beneficial preferences (line 2 minus line 11) 259,877
13. Minimum tax on total tax preferences
((line 2 minus the greater of line 6 or $10,000) × .15)................................ 65,668
14. Minimum tax on beneficial preferences
((line 12 minus the greater of line 6 or $10,000) × .15)............................... 29,650
15. Credit reduction amount (line 13 minus line 14) 36,018
16. Reduction of freed-up credits under the exact method (subtotals of line 11 multiplied by .15):
(a) 1984 investment tax credits:
$ 44,045 × .15 = $ 6,607
(b) 1985 investment tax credits:
$196,078   × .15 = $29,411
(c) Total credit reduction 36,018
17. Freed-up credits after reduction (assuming that Corporation X does not elect the simplified method):
(a) 1984 investment credit
($ 22,463 minus $ 6,607)... 15,856
(b) 1985 investment credit
($100,000   minus $29,411)... 70,589

(e) *Miscellaneous rules—*(1) *Investment Credit Recapture.* If during any taxable year property to which section 47 applies is disposed of, then for purposes of determining any increase in tax under section 47 for such year, the amount of any reduction under this section of freed-up section 38 credit which was earned in the year the property was placed in service shall be treated as a credit that was allowed in a prior taxable year.

Example. Corporation D places property in service in 1983 that generates investment tax credits of $10,000. D earns no other investment tax credits in 1983. None of the investment tax credits are used to reduce tax liability in 1983 or any prior years. In 1984, D uses $1,000 of this credit to reduce regular tax liability. In addition, D has items of tax preference in 1984. However, under section 58(h), D is not liable for minimum tax on any of these preference items because none of

Reg. § 1.58-9(e)(1)

these preference items produces a tax benefit in 1984. As a result, an adjustment is made under the provisions of § 1.58-9 and the investment tax credit carryforward from 1983 is reduced by $4,000. Thus, D has an investment tax credit carryforward of $5,000 that is attributable to the property placed in service in 1983. In 1986, the property is disposed of and the investment tax credits earned in 1983 are recomputed as required under section 47. This recomputation results in a reduction of $6,000 of the investment tax credits earned in 1983. D must now adjust its 1983 investment tax credit carryforward under section 47(a)(6) by reducing this carryforward to zero. In addition, D has an additional tax liability of $1,000 for 1986.

(2) *Period of limitations; adjustments to tax liability.* The adjustments described in this section shall, in general, apply for purposes of assessing deficiencies or claiming refunds of tax for any taxable year for which the tax liability is affected by the adjustments of this section, provided that the period of limitations under section 6501 has not expired for such taxable year. Therefore, these adjustments generally apply for purposes of assessing deficiencies and refunding any overpayment of tax for all years for which the period of limitations has not expired regardless of whether the period of limitations has expired for the taxable year in which the non-beneficial preferences arose. However, the adjustments of this section do not apply to reduce otherwise allowable credits that were freed up by such non-beneficial preferences where:

(i) The taxpayer paid minimum tax on all tax preference items arising in the taxable year in which the non-beneficial preferences arose;

(ii) The taxpayer has not made a claim for a credit or refund for such minimum tax; and

(iii) The period of limitations for claiming a credit or refund under section 6511 has expired for such taxable year.

(A) Further, if—

(*1*) the taxpayer never paid minimum tax attributable to non-beneficial preferences;

(*2*) credits that were freed up by such preferences were used to reduce tax liability for a taxable year for which the period of limitations has expired; and

(*3*) credits so used exceed the amount of credits that would have been available if the credit reduction required under this section with respect to such preferences had been made,

(B) Then, the taxpayer shall be liable for the minimum tax equal to the amount of credits

so used, provided the period of limitations has not expired for the taxable year in which preferences arose.

(3) *Claims for credit or refund.* A taxpayer may claim a credit or refund of minimum tax that was paid on nonbeneficial preferences. However, such a claim for a credit or refund shall be disallowed to the extent that the taxpayer has reduced tax liability in a taxable year for which the period of limitations has expired by using freed-up credits in excess of the amount that would have been available if the credit reduction required under this section had been made. Such claim must be made by filing an amended return for the taxable year for which such minimum tax was paid. Further, if a claim for credit or refund is filed, amended returns must also be filed for any taxable year for which tax liability would be affected as a result of the reduction, under this section, of credits freed up by such nonbeneficial preferences. See section 6511 and the regulations thereunder regarding the period of limitations for claiming a credit or refund.

(4) *Carryovers of foreign tax credit to taxable years after 1986.* In the case of foreign tax credit carryforwards to taxable years beginning after December 31, 1986, reductions in such credits required under this section shall apply for purposes of computing the alternative minimum tax foreign tax credit under section 59(a) of the Internal Revenue Code of 1986 as well as for purposes of computing the foreign tax credit for regular tax purposes.

(5) *Credit carrybacks.* If credit carrybacks increase the amount of credits for a taxable year, the adjustments described in this section shall be recomputed taking into account the additional credits. This rule may be illustrated by the following examples:

Example 1. (i) In 1981 corporation D has actual taxable income of $72,500 and regular tax before credits of $15,000. In computing actual regular taxable income, D made use of $36,739 of tax preference items, so that D's taxable income determined as though preference were not allowed would be $109,239. D's non-preference regular tax before credits is $30,000. D earns $25,000 of foreign tax credits in 1981, none of which exceed the limitation under section 904 determined using either actual regular taxable income or the non-preference taxable income. These credits reduce actual regular tax to zero ($0) and would have reduced non-preference regular tax to $5,000 ($30,000 minus $25,000). Thus, D has freed-up foreign tax credits from 1981 of $10,000 ($25,000 minus $15,000). Pursuant to the adjustments required under this section, D determines that its

Reg. § 1.58-9(e)(5)

credit reduction amount is $3,843 and reduces its freed-up credit (and its credit carryover) from 1981 to $6,157 ($10,000 minus $3,843). D also pays minimum tax of $167 on $11,114 of beneficial preferences (($11,114 minus $10,000) multiplied by .15).

(ii) In 1982 D earns additional foreign tax credits. After application of the foreign tax credit carryback rules, D would have $5,000 of 1982 foreign tax credits available for use in 1981. D must recalculate the adjustments required under this section by treating $5,000 of foreign tax credit from 1982 as carried back and (assuming that these credits do not exceed the limitation under section 904) used to reduce non-preference regular tax liability in 1981 to zero ($0). That is, $5,000 of the foreign tax credits earned in 1982 are treated as credits freed up because of D's tax preference items in 1981. Pursuant to the rules set forth herein, D must take into account the foreign tax credits from both 1981 and 1982 in determining to what extent a tax benefit was derived from the preference items used to determine actual regular tax liability in 1981 and in computing the credit reduction amount. When the $5,000 of foreign tax credits from 1982 are considered, all preferences become nonbeneficial preferences, and the credit reduction amount is $4,010. Assuming that D elects the simplified method, the 1981 freed-up credits and the 1982 freed-up credits will each be reduced by the following percentage:

$$\frac{\$4,010 \ \text{(credit reduction amount)}}{\$15,000 \ \text{(total freed-up credits)}} = .2673$$

The 1981 freed-up foreign tax credits of $10,000 are thus reduced by $2,673 ($10,000 multiplied by .2673), to $7,327 and the 1982 freed-up foreign tax credits of $5,000 are reduced by $1,334 ($5,000 multiplied by .2673) to $3,666. D also

files a claim for credit or refund of the $167 of minimum tax paid in 1981.

Example 2. In 1985 corporation E's non-preference regular taxable income was $25,000. E had no available credits. It paid zero in regular tax, however, because of $25,000 in preference items. E paid $2,250 of minimum tax on these preferences (($25,000 minus $10,000) multiplied by .15). In 1986, E has additional investment tax credits. After application of the investment tax credit carryback rules, E would have $1,000 investment tax credit from 1986 available for use in 1985. E must recompute the adjustments required under this section by treating $1,000 of these 1986 investment tax credits as carried back and used to reduce non-preference regular tax liability for 1985. Pursuant to the rules of this section, all of these $1,000 of credits are freed-up credits. Nonbeneficial preferences are $6,667 ($1,000 grossed up at a 15 percent regular tax rate). Beneficial preferences are $18,333 ($25,000 minus $6,667). Minimum tax on all preferences would be $2,250 (($25,000 minus $10,000) multiplied by .15); minimum tax on beneficial preferences would be $1,250 (($18,333 minus $10,000) multiplied by .15) Minimum tax attributable to the nonbeneficial preferences is thus $1,000 ($2,250 minus $1,250), which is the credit reduction amount. E thus reduces the $1,000 of credits carried back to 1985 to zero. Under the rules of this section, the amount of minimum tax due for 1985 is redetermined. It is equal to the minimum tax on beneficial preferences, which, as described above, is $1,250. Because E paid minimum tax of $2,250 in 1985, E files a claim for credit or refund for $1,000 of the minimum tax paid in 1985.

(f) *Treatment of net operating losses.* [Reserved] [Reg. § 1.58-9.]

□ [*T.D.* 8416, 5-4-92.]

[The next page is 24,001.]

COMPUTATION OF TAXABLE INCOME

Definition of Gross Income, Adjusted Gross Income, Taxable Income, Etc.

[Reg. § 1.61-1]

§ 1.61-1. **Gross income.**—(a) *General definition.* Gross income means all income from whatever source derived, unless excluded by law. Gross income includes income realized in any form, whether in money, property, or services. Income may be realized, therefore, in the form of services, meals, accommodations, stock, or other property, as well as in cash. Section 61 lists the more common items of gross income for purposes of illustration. For purposes of further illustration, § 1.61-14 mentions several miscellaneous items of gross income not listed specifically in section 61. Gross income, however, is not limited to the items so enumerated.

(b) *Cross references.* Cross references to other provisions of the Code are to be found throughout the regulations under section 61. The purpose of these cross references is to direct attention to the more common items which are included in or excluded from gross income entirely, or treated in some special manner. To the extent that another section of the Code or of the regulations thereunder, provides specific treatment for any item of income, such other provision shall apply notwithstanding section 61 and the regulations thereunder. The cross references do not cover all possible items.

(1) For examples of items specifically included in gross income, see part II (section 71 and following), subchapter B, chapter 1 of the Code.

(2) For examples of items specifically excluded from gross income, see part III (section 101 and following), subchapter B, chapter 1 of the Code.

(3) For general rules as to the taxable year for which an item is to be included in gross income, see section 451 and the regulations thereunder. [Reg. § 1.61-1.]

☐ [*T.D.* 6272, 11-25-57.]

[Reg. § 1.61-2]

§ 1.61-2. **Compensation for services, including fees, commissions, and similar items.**—(a) *In general.* (1) Wages, salaries, commissions paid salesmen, compensation for services on the basis of a percentage of profits, commissions on insurance premiums, tips, bonuses (including Christmas bonuses), termination or severance pay, rewards, jury fees, marriage fees and other contributions received by a clergyman for services, pay of persons in the military or naval forces of the United States, retired pay of employees, pensions, and retirement allowances are income to the recipients unless excluded by law. Several special rules apply to members of the Armed Forces, National Oceanic and Atmospheric Administration, and Public Health Service of the United States; see paragraph (b) of this section.

(2) The Internal Revenue Code provides special rules including the following items in gross income:

(i) Distributions from employees' trusts, see sections 72, 402, and 403, and the regulations thereunder;

(ii) Compensation for child's services (in child's gross income), see section 73 and the regulations thereunder;

(iii) Prizes and awards, see section 74 and the regulations thereunder.

(3) Similarly, the Code provides special rules excluding the following items from gross income in whole or in part:

(i) Gifts, see section 102 and the regulations thereunder;

(ii) Compensation for injuries or sickness, see section 104 and the regulations thereunder;

(iii) Amounts received under accident and health plans, see section 105 and the regulations thereunder;

(iv) Scholarship and fellowship grants, see section 117 and the regulations thereunder;

(v) Miscellaneous items, see section 122.

(b) *Members of the Armed Forces, National Oceanic and Atmospheric Administration, and Public Health Service.* (1) Subsistence and uniform allowances granted commissioned officers, chief warrant officers, warrant officers, and enlisted personnel of the Armed Forces, National Oceanic and Atmospheric Administration, and Public Health Service of the United States, and amounts received by them as commutation of quarters, are excluded from gross income. Similarly, the value of quarters or subsistence furnished to such persons is excluded from gross income.

(2) For purposes of this section, quarters or subsistence includes the following allowances for expenses incurred after December 31, 1993, by members of the Armed Forces, members of the commissioned corps of the National Oceanic and Atmospheric Administration, and members of the

Reg. § 1.61-2(b)(2)

commissioned corps of the Public Health Service, to the extent that the allowances are not otherwise excluded from gross income under another provision of the Internal Revenue Code: a dislocation allowance, authorized by 37 U.S.C. 407; a temporary lodging allowance, authorized by 37 U.S.C. 405; a temporary lodging expense, authorized by 37 U.S.C. 404a; and a move-in housing allowance, authorized by 37 U.S.C. 405. No deduction is allowed under this chapter for any expenses reimbursed by such excluded allowances. For the exclusion from gross income of—

(i) Disability pensions, see section 104(a)(4) and the regulations thereunder;

(ii) Miscellaneous items, see section 122.

(3) The per diem or actual expense allowance, the monetary allowance in lieu of transportation, and the mileage allowance received by members of the Armed Forces, National Oceanic and Atmospheric Administration, and the Public Health Service, while in a travel status or on temporary duty away fron their permanent stations, are included in their gross income except to the extent excluded under the accountable plan provisions of § 1.62-2.

(c) *Payment to charitable, etc., organization on behalf of person rendering services.* The value of services is not includible in gross income when such services are rendered directly and gratuitously to an organization described in section 170(c). Where, however, pursuant to an agreement or understanding, services are rendered to a person for the benefit of an organization described in section 170(c) and an amount for such services is paid to such organization by the person to whom the services are rendered, the amount so paid constitutes income to the person performing the services.

(d) *Compensation paid other than in cash* —(1) *In general.* Except as otherwise provided in paragraph (d)(6)(i) of this section (relating to certain property transferred after June 30, 1969), if services are paid for in property, the fair market value of the property taken in payment must be included in income as compensation. If services are paid for in exchange for other services, the fair market value of such other services taken in payment must be included in income as compensation. If the services are rendered at a stipulated price, such price will be presumed to be the fair market value of the compensation received in the absence of evidence to the contrary. For special rules relating to certain options received as compensation, see §§ 1.61-15, 1.83-7, and section 421 and the regulations thereunder. For special rules relating to premiums paid by an employer for an annuity contract which is not subject to section

403(a), see section 403(c) and the regulations thereunder and § 1.83-8(a). For special rules relating to contributions made to an employees' trust which is not exempt under section 501, see section 402(b) and the regulations thereunder and § 1.83-8(a).

(2) *Property transferred to employee or independent contractor.* (i) Except as otherwise provided in section 421 and the regulations thereunder and § 1.61-15 (relating to stock options), and paragraph (d)(6)(i) of this section, if property is transferred by an employer to an employee or if property is transferred to an independent contractor, as compensation for services, for an amount less than its fair market value, then regardless of whether the transfer is in the form of a sale or exchange, the difference between the amount paid for the property and the amount of its fair market value at the time of the transfer is compensation and shall be included in the gross income of the employee or independent contractor. In computing the gain or loss from the subsequent sale of such property, its basis shall be the amount paid for the property increased by the amount of such difference included in gross income.

(ii)*(a) Cost of life insurance on the life of the employee.* Generally, life insurance premiums paid by an employer on the life of his employee where the proceeds of such insurance are payable to the beneficiary of such employee are part of the gross income of the employee. However, the amount includible in the employee's gross income is determined with regard to the provisions of section 403 and the regulations thereunder in the case of an individual contract issued after December 31, 1962, or a group contract, which provides incidental life insurance protection and which satisfies the requirements of section 401(g) and § 1.401-9, relating to the nontransferability of annuity contracts. For the special rules relating to the includibility in an employee's gross income of an amount equal to the cost of certain group-term life insurance on the employee's life which is carried directly or indirectly by his employer, see section 79 and the regulations thereunder. For special rules relating to the exclusion of contributions by an employer to accident and health plans for the employees, see section 106 and the regulations thereunder.

(b) Cost of group-term life insurance on the life of an individual other than an employee. The cost (determined under paragraph (d)(2) of § 1.79-3) of group-term life insurance on the life of an individual other than an employee (such as the spouse or dependent of the employee) provided in connection with the performance of

services by the employee is includible in the gross income of the employee.

(3) *Meals and living quarters.* The value of living quarters or meals which an employee receives in addition to his salary constitutes gross income unless they are furnished for the convenience of the employer and meet the conditions specified in section 119 and the regulations thereunder. For the treatment of rental value of parsonages or rental allowance paid to ministers, see section 107 and the regulations thereunder; for the treatment of statutory subsistence allowances received by police, see section 120 and the regulations thereunder.

(4) *Stock and notes transferred to employee or independent contractor.* Except as otherwise provided by section 421 and the regulations thereunder and § 1.61-15 (relating to stock options), and paragraph (d)(6)(i) of this section, if a corporation transfers its own stock to an employee or independent contractor as compensation for services, the fair market value of the stock at the time of transfer shall be included in the gross income of the employee or independent contractor. Notes or other evidences of indebtedness received in payment for services constitute income in the amount of their fair market value at the time of the transfer. A taxpayer receiving as compensation a note regarded as good for its face value at maturity, but not bearing interest, shall treat as income as of the time of receipts its fair discounted value computed at the prevailing rate. As payments are received on such a note, there shall be included in income that portion of each payment which represents the proportionate part of the discount originally taken on the entire note.

(5) *Property transferred on or before June 30, 1969, subject to restrictions.* Notwithstanding paragraph (d)(1), (2), or (4) of this section, if any property is transferred after September 24, 1959, by an employer to an employee or independent contractor as compensation for services, and such property is subject to a restriction which has a significant effect on its value at the time of trans-

fer, the rules of § 1.421-6(d)(2) shall apply in determining the time and the amount of compensation to be included in the gross income of the employee or independent contractor. This (5) is also applicable to transfers subject to a restriction which has a significant effect on its value at the time of transfer and to which § 1.83-8(b) (relating to transitional rules with respect to transfers of restricted property) applies. For special rules relating to options to purchase stock or other property which are issued as compensation for services, see § 1.61-15 and section 421 and the regulations thereunder.

(6) *Certain property transferred, premiums paid, and contributions made in connection with the performance of services after June 30, 1969—* (i) *Exception.* Paragraph (d)(1), (2), (4), and (5) of this section and § 1.61-15 do not apply to the transfer of property (as defined in § 1.83-3(e)) after June 30, 1969, unless § 1.83-8 (relating to the applicability of section 83 and transitional rules) applies. If section 83 applies to a transfer of property, and the property is not subject to a restriction that has a significant effect on the fair market value of such property, then the rules contained in paragraph (d)(1), (2), and (4) of this section and § 1.61-15 shall also apply to such transfer to the extent such rules are not inconsistent with section 83.

(ii) *Cross references.* For rules relating to premiums paid by an employer for an annuity contract which is not subject to section 403(a), see section 403(c) and the regulations thereunder. For rules relating to contributions made to an employees' trust which is not exempt under section 501(a), see section 402(b) and the regulations thereunder. [Reg. § 1.61-2.]

☐ [*T.D. 6272, 11-25-57. Amended by T.D. 6416, 9-24-59; T.D. 6696, 12-11-63; T.D. 6856, 10-19-65; T.D. 6888, 7-5-66; T.D. 7554, 7-21-78; T.D. 7623, 5-14-79; T.D. 8256, 7-5-89 and T.D. 8607, 8-4-95.*]

→ *Caution: Temporary Reg. § 1.61-2T applies to the tax treatment of fringe benefits for 1985—1988. See Reg. § 1.61-21 for post-1988 rules.*←

[Reg. § 1.61-2T]

§ 1.61-2T. Taxation of fringe benefits—1985 through 1988 (Temporary).—(a) *Fringe benefits*—(1) *In general.* Section 61(a)(1) provides that, except as otherwise provided in subtitle A, gross income includes compensation for services, including fees, commissions, fringe benefits, and similar items. Examples of fringe benefits include: an employer-provided automobile, a flight on an employer-provided aircraft, an employer-provided

free or discounted commercial airline flight, an employer-provided vacation, an employer-provided discount on property or services, an employer-provided membership in a country club or other social club, and an employer-provided ticket to an entertainment or sporting event.

(2) *Fringe benefits excluded from income.* To the extent that a particular fringe benefit is specifically excluded from gross income pursuant to another section of subtitle A, that section shall

→ *Caution: Temporary Reg. § 1.61-2T applies to the tax treatment of fringe benefits for 1985—1988. See Reg. § 1.61-21 for post-1988 rules.←*

govern the treatment of that fringe benefit. Thus, if the requirements of the governing section are satisfied, the fringe benefits may be excludable from gross income. Examples of excludable fringe benefits are qualified tuition reductions provided to an employee (section 117(d)); meals and lodging furnished to an employee for the convenience of the employer (section 119); and benefits provided under a dependent care assistance program (section 129). Similarly, the value of the use by an employee of an employer-provided vehicle or a flight provided to an employee on an employer-provided aircraft may be excludable from income under section 105 (because, for example, the transportation is provided for medical reasons) if and to the extent that the requirements of that section are satisfied. Section 61 and the regulations thereunder shall apply, however, to the extent that they are not inconsistent with such other section. For example, many fringe benefits specifically addressed in other sections of subtitle A are excluded from gross income only to the extent that they do not exceed specific dollar or percentage limits, or only if certain other requirements are met. If the limits are exceeded or the requirements are not met, some or all of the fringe benefits may be includible in gross income. See paragraph (b)(3) of this section.

(3) *Compensation for services.* A fringe benefit provided in connection with the performance of services shall be considered to have been provided as compensation for services. Refraining from the performance of services (such as pursuant to a covenant not to compete) is deemed to be the performance of services for purposes of this section.

(4) *Recipient of a fringe benefit*—(i) *Definition.* A fringe benefit is included in the income of the "recipient" of the fringe benefit. The recipient of a fringe benefit is the person performing the services in connection with which the fringe benefit is provided. Thus, a person may be considered to be a recipient, even though that person did not actually receive the fringe benefit. For example, a fringe benefit provided to any person in connection with the performance of services by another person is considered to have been provided to the person who performs the services and not the person who receives the fringe benefit. In addition, if a fringe benefit is provided to a person, but taxable to a second person as the recipient, such benefit is referred to as provided to the second person and use by the first person is considered use by the second person. For example, provision of an automobile to an employee's spouse by the

employer is taxable to the employee as the recipient. The automobile is referred to as available to the employee and use by the employee's spouse is considered use by the employee.

(ii) *Recipient may be other than an employee.* The recipient of a fringe benefit need not be an employee of the provider of the fringe benefit, but may be a partner, director, or an independent contractor. For convenience, the term "employee" includes a reference to any recipient of a fringe benefit, unless otherwise specifically provided in this section.

(5) *Provider of a fringe benefit.* The "provider" of a fringe benefit is that person for whom the services are performed, regardless of whether that person actually provides the fringe benefit to the recipient. The provider of a fringe benefit need not be the employer of the recipient of the fringe benefit, but may be, for example, a client or customer of an independent contractor. For convenience, the term "employer" includes a reference to any provider of a fringe benefit, unless otherwise specifically provided in this section.

(6) *Effective date.* This section is effective from January 1, 1985, to December 31, 1988, with respect to fringe benefits furnished before January 1, 1989. No inference may be drawn from the promulgation of terms of this section concerning the application of law in effect prior to January 1, 1985.

(b) *Valuation of fringe benefits*—(1) *In general.* An employee must include in gross income the amount by which the fair market value of the fringe benefit exceeds the sum of (i) the amount, if any, paid for the benefit, and (ii) the amount, if any, specifically excluded from gross income by some other section of subtitle A. Therefore, for example, if the employee pays fair market value for what is received, no amount is includible in the gross income of the employee.

(2) *Fair market value.* In general, fair market value is determined on the basis of all the facts and circumstances. Specifically, the fair market value of a fringe benefit is that amount a hypothetical person would have to pay a hypothetical third party to obtain (i.e., purchase or lease) the particular fringe benefit. Thus, for example, the effect of any special relationship that may exist between the employer and the employee must be disregarded. This also means that an employee's subjective perception of the value of a fringe benefit is not relevant to the determination of a fringe benefit's fair market value. In addition, the cost incurred by the employer is not

Reg. § 1.61-2T(a)(3)

→ *Caution: Temporary Reg. § 1.61-2T applies to the tax treatment of fringe benefits for 1985—1988. See Reg. § 1.61-21 for post-1988 rules.←*

determinative of the fair market value of the fringe benefit. For special rules relating to the valuation of certain fringe benefits, see paragraph (c) of this section.

(3) *Exclusion from income based on cost.* If a statutory exclusion phrased in terms of cost applies to the provision of a fringe benefit, section 61 does not require the inclusion in the recipient's gross income of the difference between the fair market value and the excludable cost of that fringe benefit. For example, section 129 provides an exclusion from an employee's gross income for amounts paid or incurred by an employer to provide dependent care assistance to employees. Even if the fair market value of the dependent care assistance exceeds the employer's cost, the excess is not subject to inclusion under section 61 and this section. If the statutory cost exclusion is a limited amount, however, then the fair market value of the fringe benefit attributable to any excess cost is subject to inclusion.

(4) *Fair market value of the availability of an employer-provided vehicle.* If the vehicle special valuation rules of paragraphs (d), (e), or (f) of this section are not used by a taxpayer entitled to use such rules, the value of the availability of an employer-provided vehicle is determined under the general valuation principles set forth in this section. In general, such valuation must be determined by reference to the cost to a hypothetical person of leasing from a hypothetical third party the same or comparable vehicle on the same or comparable terms in the geographic area in which the vehicle is available for use. Unless the employee can substantiate that the same or comparable vehicle could have been leased on a cents-per-mile basis, the value of the availability of the vehicle cannot be determined by reference to a cents-per-mile rate applied to the number of miles the vehicle is driven. An example of a comparable lease term is the amount of time that the vehicle is available to the employee for use, e.g., a one-year period.

(5) *Fair market value of a flight on an employer-provided aircraft.* If the non-commercial flight special valuation rule of paragraph (g) of this section is not used (or is not properly used) by a taxpayer entitled to use such rule, the value of a flight on an employer-provided aircraft is determined under the general valuation principles set forth in this section. An example of how the general valuation principles would apply is that if an employee whose flight is primarily personal controls the use of an aircraft with respect to such flight, such flight is valued by reference to how

much it would cost a hypothetical person to charter the same or comparable aircraft for the same or comparable flight. The cost to charter the aircraft must be allocated among all employees on board the aircraft based on all the facts and circumstances, including which employee or employees controlled the use of the aircraft. Notwithstanding the allocation required by the preceding sentence, no additional amount shall be included in the income of any employee whose flight is properly valued under the special valuation rule of paragraph (g) of this section.

(c) *Special valuation rules—*(1) *In general.* Paragraphs (d) through (j) of this section provide special valuation rules that may be used under certain circumstances for certain commonly provided fringe benefits. Paragraph (d) provides a lease valuation rule relating to employer-provided automobiles. Paragraph (e) provides a cents-per-mile valuation rule relating to employer-provided vehicles. Paragraph (f) provides a commuting valuation rule relating to employer-provided vehicles. Paragraph (g) provides a flight valuation rule relating to flights on employer-provided aircraft. Paragraph (h) provides a flight valuation rule relating to flights on commercial airlines. Paragraph (i) is reserved. Paragraph (j) provides a meal valuation rule relating to employer-operated eating facilities for employees. For general rules relating to the valuation of fringe benefits not eligible for valuation under the special valuation rules, see paragraph (b) of this section.

(2) *Use of the special valuation rules—*(i) *In general.* The special valuation rules may be used for income, employment tax, and reporting purposes. Use of any of the special valuation rules is optional. An employer need not use the same vehicle special valuation rule for all vehicles provided to all employees. For example, an employer may use the automobile lease valuation rule for automobiles provided to some employees, and the commuting and vehicle cents-per-mile valuation rules for automobiles provided to other employees. Except as otherwise provided, however, if either the commercial flight valuation rule or the non-commercial flight valuation rule is used, such rule must be used by an employer to value all flights taken by employees in a calendar year. Effective January 1, 1986, if an employer uses one of the special rules to value the benefit provided to an employee, the employee may not use another special rule to value that benefit. The employer may, however, use general valuation rules based on facts and circumstances (see paragraph (b) of this section). Effective January 1, 1986, an employee

Reg. § 1.61-2T(c)(2)

→ *Caution: Temporary Reg. § 1.61-2T applies to the tax treatment of fringe benefits for 1985—1988. See Reg. § 1.61-21 for post-1988 rules.*←

may only use a special valuation rule if the employer uses the rule. If a special rule is used, it must be used for all purposes. If an employer properly uses a special rule and the employee uses the special rule, the employee must include in gross income the amount determined by the employer under the special rule less any amount reimbursed by the employee to the employer. The employer and the employee may use the special rules to determine the amount of the reimbursement due the employer by the employee. If an employer properly uses a special rule and properly determines the amount of an employee's working condition fringe under section 132 and § 1.132-1T (under the general rule or under a special rule), and the employee uses the special valuation rule, the employee must include in gross income the amount determined by the employer less any amount reimbursed by the employee to the employer.

(ii) *Transitional rules*—(A) *Use of vehicle special valuation rules for 1985 and 1986.* For purposes of valuing the use or availability of a vehicle, the consistency rules provided in paragraphs (d)(6) and (e) (5) of this section (relating to the automobile lease valuation rule and the vehicle cents-per-mile valuation rule, respectively) apply for 1987 and thereafter. Therefore, for 1985 and 1986 an employer (and employee, subject to paragraph (c)(2)(i) of this section) may use any applicable special valuation rule (or no special valuation rule) to value the use or availability of a vehicle, subject to paragraph (c)(2)(ii)(B) of this section.

(B) *Consistency Rules for 1985 and 1986.* If an employer uses the automobile lease valuation rule of paragraph (d) of this section in 1985 or 1986 with respect to an automobile, such rule must be used for the entire calendar year with respect to the automobile except for any period during which the commuting valuation rule of paragraph (f) of this section is properly used. If an employer uses the vehicle cents-per-mile valuation rule of paragraph (e) of this section in 1985 or 1986 with respect to a vehicle, such rule must be used for the entire calendar year with respect to the vehicle except for any period during which the commuting valuation rule of paragraph (f) of this section is properly used. The rules of this paragraph (c)(2)(ii)(B) also apply to employees using the special valuation rules of paragraphs (d) or (e) of this section.

(C) *Employee's use of special valuation rules for 1985.* An employee may use a special valuation rule (other than the rule in paragraph

(e) of this section relating to the vehicle cents-per-mile valuation rule) during 1985 even if the employer does not use the same special valuation rule during 1985. An employee's use of a special valuation rule in 1986 and thereafter must be consistent with his employer's use of the rule as required under paragraph (c)(2)(i) of this section.

(D) *Examples.* The following examples illustrate the rules of paragraph (c)(2)(ii) of this section:

Example (1). Assume that an employer properly uses the automobile lease valuation rule in 1985. The employer may use the vehicle cents-per-mile valuation rule in 1986 if the requirements of the vehicle cents-per-mile valuation rule are satisfied.

Example (2). Assume that an employer does not use a special valuation rule to value the availability of an automobile in 1985. The employer may use any of the special valuation rules in 1986 if the requirements of the rule chosen are satisfied. The same applies for 1987.

Example (3). Assume that an employer properly uses the vehicle cents-per-mile valuation rule in 1985. The employer may continue to use the rule or use any of the other special valuation rules to value the benefit provided in 1986 if the requirements of the rule chosen are satisfied. Alternatively, the employer may use none of the special valuation rules in 1986 but use any of the rules in 1987 if the requirements of the rule chosen are satisfied.

Example (4). Assume that an employee properly uses the automobile lease valuation rule in 1985. In 1986 and thereafter the employee may use a special valuation rule only if the employee's employer uses the same special valuation rule. The employee may use general valuation principles to value the benefit provided in 1986 and thereafter.

(3) *Election to use the special valuation rules.* A particular special valuation rule is deemed to have been elected by the employer (and, if applicable, by the employee), if the employer (and, if applicable, the employee) determines the value of the fringe benefit provided by applying the special valuation rule and treats such value as the fair market value of the fringe benefit for income, employment tax, and reporting purposes. Neither the employer nor the employee is required to notify the Internal Revenue Service of the election.

(4) *Application of section 414 to employers.* For purposes of paragraphs (c) through (j) of this

Reg. § 1.61-2T(c)(3)

→ *Caution: Temporary Reg. § 1.61-2T applies to the tax treatment of fringe benefits for 1985—1988. See Reg. § 1.61-21 for post-1988 rules.*←

section, except as otherwise provided therein, the term "employer" includes all entities required to be treated as a single employer under section 414(b), (c), or (m).

(5) *Valuation formulas contained in the special valuation rules.* The valuation formulas contained in the special valuation rules are provided only for use in connection with such rules. Thus, when a special valuation rule is properly applied to a fringe benefit, the Commissioner will accept the value calculated pursuant to the rule as the fair market value of that fringe benefit. However, when a special valuation rule is not properly applied to a fringe benefit (see, for example, paragraph (g)(11) of this section), or when a special valuation rule is not used to value a fringe benefit by a taxpayer entitled to use the rule, the fair market value of that fringe benefit may not be determined by reference to any value calculated under any special valuation rule. Under the circumstancs described in the preceding sentence, the fair market value of the fringe benefit must be determined pursuant to paragraph (b) of this section.

(6) *Modification of the special valuation rules.* The Commissioner may, if he deems it necessary, add, delete, or modify the special valuation rules, including the valuation formulas contained herein, on a prospective basis.

(7) *Special Accounting Period.* If the employer is using the special accounting rule provided in Announcement 85-113 (1985-31 I.R.B., August 5, 1985) (relating to the reporting of and withholding on the value of noncash fringe benefits), benefits which are deemed provided in a subsequent calendar year pursuant to such rule are considered as provided in such subsequent calendar year for purposes of the special valuation rules. Thus, if a particular special valuation rule is in effect for a calendar year, it applies to benefits deemed provided during such calendar year under the special accounting rule.

(d) *Automobile lease valuation rule*—(1) *In general*—(i) *Annual Lease Value.* Under the special valuation rule of this paragraph (d), if an employer provides an employee with an automobile that is available to the employee for an entire calendar year, the value of the benefit provided is the Annual Lease Value (determined under paragraph (d)(2) of this section) of that automobile. Except as otherwise provided, for an automobile that is available to an employee for less than an entire calendar year, the value of the benefit provided is either a pro-rated Annual Lease Value

or the Daily Lease Value (as defined in paragraph (d)(4) of this section), whichever is applicable. Absent any statutory exclusion relating to the employer-provided automobile (see, for example, section 132(a)(3) and § 1.132-5T(b)), the amount of the Annual Lease Value (or a pro-rated Annual Lease Value or the Daily Lease Value, as applicable) is included in the gross income of the employee.

(ii) *Definition of automobile.* For purposes of this paragraph (d), the term "automobile" means any four-wheeled vehicle manufactured primarily for use on public streets, roads, and highways.

(2) *Calculation of Annual Lease Value*—(i) *In general.* The Annual Lease Value of a particular automobile is calculated as follows:

(A) Determine the fair market value of the automobile as of the first date on which the automobile is made available to any employee of the employer for personal use. For an automobile first made available to any employee for personal use prior to January 1, 1985, determine the fair market value as of January 1, 1985. For rules relating to determination of the fair market value of an automobile for purposes of this paragraph (d), see paragraph (d)(5) of this section.

(B) Select the dollar range in column 1 of the Annual Lease Value Table, set forth in paragraph (d)(2)(iii) of this section, corresponding to the fair market value of the automobile. Except as otherwise provided in paragraphs (d)(2)(iv) and (v) of this section, the Annual Lease Value for each year of availability of the automobile is the corresponding amount in column 2 of the Table.

(ii) *Use by employee only in 1985.* If the employee, but not the employer, is using the special rule of this paragraph (d), the employee may calculate the Annual Lease Value in the same manner as described in paragraph (d)(2)(i)(A) of this section, except that the fair market value of the automobile is determined as of the first date on which the automobile is made available to the employee for personal use or, for an automobile made available to the employee for personal use prior to January 1, 1985, by determining the fair market value as of January 1, 1985. If the employer is also using the special rule of this paragraph (d), however, then the employee to whom the automobile is made available must use the special rule, if at all, by using the Annual Lease Value calculated by the employer. The rules of this paragraph (d)(2)(ii) apply only for 1985.

(iii) *Annual Lease Value Table.*

Reg. § 1.61-2T(d)(2)

→ *Caution: Temporary Reg. § 1.61-2T applies to the tax treatment of fringe benefits for 1985—1988. See Reg. § 1.61-21 for post-1988 rules.*←

Automobile fair market value (1)	Annual Lease Value (2)
$0 to 999	$ 600
1,000 to 1,999	850
2,000 to 2,999	1,100
3,000 to 3,999	1,350
4,000 to 4,999	1,600
5,000 to 5,999	1,850
6,000 to 6,999	2,100
7,000 to 7,999	2,350
8,000 to 8,999	2,600
9,000 to 9,999	2,850
10,000 to 10,999	3,100
11,000 to 11,999	3,350
12,000 to 12,999	3,600
13,000 to 13,999	3,850
14,000 to 14,999	4,100
15,000 to 15,999	4,350
16,000 to 16,999	4,600
17,000 to 17,999	4,850
18,000 to 18,999	5,100
19,000 to 19,999	5,350
20,000 to 20,999	5,600
21,000 to 21,999	5,850
22,000 to 22,999	6,100
23,000 to 23,999	6,350
24,000 to 24,999	6,600
25,000 to 25,999	6,850
26,000 to 27,999	7,250
28,000 to 29,999	7,750
30,000 to 31,999	8,250
32,000 to 33,999	8,750
34,000 to 35,999	9,250
36,000 to 37,999	9,750
38,000 to 39,999	10,250
40,000 to 41,999	10,750
42,000 to 43,999	11,250
44,000 to 45,999	11,750
46,000 to 47,999	12,250
48,000 to 49,999	12,750
50,000 to 51,999	13,250
52,000 to 53,999	13,750
54,000 to 55,999	14,250
56,000 to 57,999	14,750
58,000 to 59,999	15,250

For vehicles having a fair market value in excess of $59,999, the Annual Lease Value is equal to: (.25 × the fair market value of the automobile) + $500.

(iv) *Recalculation of Annual Lease Value.* The Annual Lease Values determined under the rules of this paragraph (d) are based on a four-year lease term. Therefore, except as otherwise provided in paragraph (d)(2)(v) of this section, the Annual Lease Value calculated by applying paragraph (d)(2)(i) or (ii) of this section shall remain in effect for the period that begins with the first date the special valuation rule of paragraph (d) of this section is applied by the employer to the automobile and ends on December 31 of the fourth full calendar year following that date. The Annual Lease Value for each subsequent four-year period is calculated by determining the fair market value of the automobile as of the January 1 following the period described in the previous sentence and selecting the amount in column 2 of the Annual Lease Value Table corresponding to the appropriate dollar range in column 1 of the Table. If, however, the employer is using the special accounting rule provided in Announcement 85-113 (1985-31 I.R.B., August 5, 1985) (relating to the reporting of and withholding on the value of noncash fringe benefits), the employer may calculate the Annual Lease Value for each subsequent four-year period as of the beginning of the special accounting period that begins immediately prior to the January 1 described in the previous sentence. For example, assume that pursuant to Announcement 85-113,

Reg. § 1.61-2T(d)(2)

→ *Caution: Temporary Reg. § 1.61-2T applies to the tax treatment of fringe benefits for 1985—1988. See Reg. § 1.61-21 for post-1988 rules.*←

an employer uses the special accounting rule. Assume further that beginning on November 1, 1985, the special accountng period is November 1 to October 31 and that the employer elects to use the special valuation rule of this paragraph (d) as of January 1, 1985. The employer may recalculate the Annual Lease Value as of November 1, 1988, rather than as of January 1, 1989.

(v) *Transfer of the automobile to another employee.* Unless the primary purpose of the transfer is to reduce Federal taxes, if an employer transfers an automobile from one employee to another employee, the employer may recalculate the Annual Lease Value based on the fair market value of the automobile as of January 1 of the year of transfer. If, however, the employer is using the special accounting rule provided in Announcement 85-113 (1985-31 I.R.B., August 5, 1985) (relating to the reporting of and withholding on the value of noncash fringe benefits), the employer may recalculate the Annual Lease Value based on the fair market value of the automobile as of the beginning of the special accounting period in which the transfer occurs. If the employer does not recalculate the Annual Lease Value, and the employee to whom the automobile is transferred uses the special valuation rule, the employee may not recalculate the Annual Lease Value.

(3) *Services included in, or excluded from, the Annual Lease Value Table*—(i) *Maintenance and insurance included.* The Annual Lease Values contained in the Annual Lease Value Table include the fair market value of maintenance of, and insurance for, the automobile. Neither an employer nor an employee may reduce the Annual Lease Value by the fair market value of any service included in the Annual Lease Value that is not provided by the employer, such as reducing the Annual Lease Value by the fair market value of a maintenance service contract or insurance. An employer or employee may take into account the services actually provided with respect to the automobile by valuing the availability of the automobile under the general valuation rules of paragragh (b) of this section.

(ii) *Fuel excluded*—(A) *In general.* The Annual Lease Values do not include the fair market value of fuel provided by the employer, regardless of whether fuel is provided in kind or its cost is reimbursed by or charged to the employer.

(B) *Valuation of fuel provided in kind.* The provision of fuel in kind may be valued at fair market value based on all the facts and circumstances or, in the alternative, it may be valued at 5.5 cents per mile for all miles driven by the employee. However, the provision of fuel in kind may not be valued at 5.5 cents per mile for miles driven outside the United States, Canada, and Mexico. For purposes of this section, the United States includes the United States and its territories.

(C) *Valuation of fuel where cost reimbursed by or charged to employer.* The fair market value of fuel, the cost of which is reimbursed by or charged to an employer, is generally the amount of the actual reimbursement of the amount charged, provided the purchase of the fuel is at arm's length. If an employer with a fleet of at least 20 automobiles that meet the requirements of paragraph (d)(5)(v)(C) of this section reimburses employees for the cost of fuel or allows employees to charge the employer for the cost of the fuel, however, the fair market value of fuel provided to those automobiles may be determined by reference to the employer's fleet-average cents-per-mile fuel cost. The fleet-average cents-per-mile fuel cost is equal to the fleet-average per-gallon fuel cost divided by the fleet-average miles-per-gallon rate. The averages described in the preceding sentence must be determined by averaging the per-gallon fuel costs and miles-per-gallon rates of a representative sample of the automobiles in the fleet equal to the greater of ten percent of the automobiles in the fleet or 20 automobiles for a representative period, such as a two month period.

(iii) *All other services excluded.* The fair market value of any service not specifically identified in paragraph (d)(3)(i) of this section that is provided by the employer with respect to an automobile (such as the services of a chauffeur) must be added to the Annual Lease Value of the automobile in determining the fair market value of the benefit provided.

(4) *Availability of an automobile for less than an entire calendar year*—(i) *Pro-rated Annual Lease Value used for continuous availability of 30 or more days.* Except as otherwise provided in paragraph (d)(4)(iv) of this section, for periods of continuous availability of 30 or more days, but less than an entire calendar year, the value of the availability of the employer-provided automobile is the pro-rated Annual Lease Value. The pro-rated Annual Lease Value is calaculated by multiplying the applicable Annual Lease Value by a fraction, the numerator of which is the number of days of availability and the denominator of which is 365.

Reg. § 1.61-2T(d)(4)

→ *Caution: Temporary Reg. § 1.61-2T applies to the tax treatment of fringe benefits for 1985—1988. See Reg. § 1.61-21 for post-1988 rules.*←

(ii) *Daily Lease Value used for continuous availability of less than 30 days.* Except as otherwise provided in paragraph (d)(4)(iii) of this section, for periods of continuous availability of one or more but less than 30 days, the value of the availability of the employer-provided automobile is the Daily Lease Value. The Daily Lease Value is calculated by multiplying the applicable Annual Lease Value by a fraction, the numerator of which is four times the number of days of availability and the denominator of which is 365.

(iii) *Election to treat all periods as periods of at least 30 days.* A pro-rated Annual Lease Value may be applied with respect to a period of continuous availability of less than 30 days, by treating the automobile as if it had been available for 30 days, if to do so would result in a lower valuation than applying the Daily Lease Value to the shorter period of actual availability.

(iv) *Periods of unavailability—(A) General rule.* In general, a pro-rated Annual Lease Value (as provided in paragraph (d)(4)(i) of this section) is used to value the availability of an employer-provided automobile when the automobile is available to an employee for a period of continuous availability of at least 30 days but less than the entire calendar year. Neither an employer nor an employee may use a pro-rated Annual Lease Value when the reduction of Federal taxes is the primary reason the automobile is unavailable to an employee during the calendar year.

(B) *Unavailability for personal reasons of the employee.* If an automobile is unavailable to an employee because of personal reasons of the employee, such as while the employee is on vacation, a pro-rated Annual Lease Value may not be used. For example, assume an automobile is available to an employee during the first five months of the year and during the last five months of the year. Assume further that the period of unavailability occurs because the employee is on vacation. The Annual Lease Value, if it is applied, must be applied with respect to the entire 12 month period. The Annual Lease Value may not be pro-rated to take into account the two-month period of unavailability.

(5) *Fair market value—(i) In general.* For purposes of determining the Annual Lease Value of an automobile under the Annual Lease Value Table, the fair market value of an automobile is that amount a hypothetical person would have to pay a hypothetical third party to purchase the particular automobile provided. Thus, for example, any special relationship that may exist between the employee and the employer must be disregarded. Also, the employee's subjective perception of the value of the automobile is not relevant to the determination of the automobile's fair market value. In addition, except as provided in paragraph (d)(5)(ii) of this section, the cost incurred by the employer of either purchasing or leasing the automobile is not determinative of the fair market value of the automobile.

(ii) *Safe-harbor valuation rule.* For purposes of calculating the Annual Lease Value of an automobile under this paragraph (d), the safe-harbor value of the automobile may be used as the fair market value of the automobile. For an automobile owned by the employer, the safe-harbor value of the automobile is the employer's cost of purchasing the automobile, provided the purchase is made at arm's length. For an automobile leased by the employer, the safe-harbor value of the automobile is the value determined under paragraph (d)(5)(iii) of this section.

(iii) *Use of nationally recognized pricing guides.* The fair market value of an automobile that is (A) provided to an employee prior to January 1, 1985, (B) being revalued pursuant to paragraphs (d)(2)(iv) or (v) of this section, or (C) is a leased automobile being valued pursuant to paragraph (d)(5)(ii) of this section, may be determined by using the retail value of such automobile as reported in a nationally recognized publication that regularly reports new or used automobile retail values, whichever is applicable. The values contained in (and obtained from) the publication must be reasonable with respect to the automobile being valued.

(iv) *Fair market value of special equipment—(A) Certain equipment excluded.* The fair market value of an automobile does not include the fair market value of any telephone or any specialized equipment that is added to or carried in the automobile if the presence of such equipment is necessitated by, and attributable to, the business needs of the employer.

(B) *Use of specialized equipment outside of employer's business.* The value of specialized equipment must be included, however, if the employee to whom the automobile is available uses the specialized equipment in a trade or business of the employee other than the employee's trade or business of being an employee of the employer.

(C) *Equipment susceptible to personal use.* The exclusion rule provided in this paragraph

Reg. § 1.61-2T(d)(5)

→ *Caution: Temporary Reg. § 1.61-2T applies to the tax treatment of fringe benefits for 1985—1988. See Reg. § 1.61-21 for post-1988 rules.*←

(d)(5)(iv) does not apply to specialized equipment susceptible to personal use.

(v) *Fleet-average valuation rule*—(A) *In general.* An employer with a fleet of 20 or more automobiles may use a fleet-average value for purposes of calculating the Annual Lease Values of the automobiles in the fleet. The fleet-average value is the average of the fair market values of each automobile in the fleet. The fair market value of each automobile in the fleet shall be determined, pursuant to the rules of paragraphs (d)(5)(i) through (iv) of this section, as of the later of January 1, 1985, or the first date on which the automobile is made available to any employee of the employer for personal use.

(B) *Period for use of rule.* The fleet-average valuation rule of this paragraph (d)(5)(v) may be used by an employer as of January 1 of any calendar year following the calendar year in which the employer acquires a fleet of 20 or more automobiles. The Annual Lease Value calculated for the automobiles in the fleet, based on the fleet-average value, shall remain in effect for the period that begins with the first January 1 the fleet-average valuation rule of this paragraph (d)(5)(v) is applied by the employer to the automobiles in the fleet and ends on December 31 of the subsequent calendar year. The Annual Lease Value for each subsequent two year period is calculated by determining the fleet-average value of the automobiles in the fleet as of the first January 1 of such period. An employer may cease using the fleet-average valuation rule as of any January 1. The fleet-average valuation rule does not apply as of January 1 of the year in which the number of automobiles in the employer's fleet declines to fewer than 20. If, however, the employer is using the special accounting rule provided in Announcement 85-113 (I.R.B. No. 31, August 5, 1985), the employer may apply the rules of this paragraph (d)(5)(v)(B) on the basis of the special accounting period rather than the calendar year. (This is accomplished by substituting (1) the beginning of the special accounting period that begins immediately prior to the January 1 described in this paragraph (d)(5)(v)(B) for January 1 wherever it appears in this paragraph (d)(5)(v)(B) and (2) the end of such accounting period for December 31.) The revaluation rules of paragraph (d)(2)(iv) and (v) of this section do not apply to automobiles valued under this paragraph (d)(5)(v).

(C) *Limitations on use of fleet-average rule.* The rule provided in this paragraph (d)(5)(v) may not be used for any automobile whose fair market value (determined pursuant to paragraphs (d)(5)(i) through (iv) of this section as of either the first date on which the automobile is made available to any employee of the employer for personal use or, if later, January 1, 1985) exceeds $16,500. In addition, the rule provided in this paragraph (d)(5)(v) may only be used for automobiles that the employer reasonably expects will regularly be used in the employer's trade or business. Infrequent use of the vehicle, such as for trips to the airport or between the employer's multiple business premises, does not constitute regular use of the vehicle in the employer's trade or business.

(D) *Additional automobiles added to the fleet.* If the rule provided in this paragraph (d)(5)(v) is used by an employer, it must be used for every automobile included in or added to the fleet that meets the requirements of paragraph (d)(5)(v)(C) of this section. The fleet-average value in effect at the time an automobile is added to the fleet is treated as the fair market value of the automobile for purposes of determining the Annual Lease Value of the automobile until the fleet-average value changes pursuant to paragraph (d)(5)(v)(B) of this section.

(E) *Use of the fleet-average rule by employees.* An employee can only use the fleet-average value if it is used by the employer. If an employer uses the fleet-average value, and the employee uses the special valuation rule of paragraph (d) of this section, the employee must use the fleet-average value.

(6) *Consistency rules*—(i) *Use of the automobile lease valuation rule by an employer.* Except as provided in paragraph (d)(5)(v)(B) of this section, an employer may adopt the automobile lease valuation rule of this paragraph (d) for an automobile only if the rule is adopted with respect to the later of the period that begins on January 1, 1987, or the first period in which the automobile is made available to an employee of the employer for personal use or, if the commuting valuation rule of paragraph (f) of this section is used when the automobile is first made available to an employee of the employer for personal use, the first period in which the commuting valuation rule is not used.

(ii) *An employer must use the automobile lease valuation rule for all subsequent periods.* Once the automobile lease valuation rule has been adopted for an automobile by an employer, the rule must be used by the employer for all subsequent periods in which the employer makes the automobile available to any employee, except that the employer may, for any period during which

Reg. § 1.61-2T(d)(6)

→ *Caution: Temporary Reg. § 1.61-2T applies to the tax treatment of fringe benefits for 1985—1988. See Reg. § 1.61-21 for post-1988 rules.←*

use of the automobile qualifies for the commuting valuation rule of paragraph (f) of this section, use the commuting valuation rule with respect to the automobile.

(iii) *Use of the automobile lease valuation rule by an employee.* Except as provided in paragraph (c)(2)(ii)(C) of this section, an employee may adopt the automobile lease valuation rule for an automobile only if the rule is adopted (A) by the employer and (B) with respect to the first period in which the automobile for which the employer (consistent with paragraph (d)(6)(i) of this section) adopted the rule is made available to that employee for personal use, or, if the commuting valuation rule of paragraph (f) of this section is used when the automobile is first made available to that employee for personal use, the first period in which the commuting valuation rule is not used.

(iv) *An employee must use the automobile lease valuation rule for all subsequent periods.* Once the automobile lease valuation rule has been adopted for an automobile by an employee, the rule must be used by the employee for all subsequent periods in which the automobile for which the rule is used is available to the employee, except that the employee may, for any period during which use of the automobile qualifies for use of the commuting valuation rule of paragraph (f) of this section and for which the employer uses the rule, use the commuting valuation rule with respect to the automobile.

(v) *Replacement automobiles.* Notwithstanding anything in this paragraph (d)(6) to the contrary, if the automobile lease valuation rule is used by an employer, or by an employer and an employee, with respect to a particular automobile, and a replacement automobile is provided to the employee for the primary purpose of reducing Federal taxes, then the employer, or the employer and the employee, using the rule must continue to use the rule with respect to the replacement automobile.

(e) *Vehicle cents-per-mile valuation rule—(1) In general—(i) General rule.* Under the vehicle cents-per-mile valuation rule of this paragraph (e), if an employer provides an employee with the use of a vehicle that (A) the employer reasonably expects will be regularly used in the employer's trade or business throughout the calendar year (or such shorter period as the vehicle may be owned or leased by the employer) or (B) satisfies the requirements of paragraph (e)(1)(ii) of this section, the value of the benefit provided in the calendar year is the standard mileage rate provided in the applicable Revenue Ruling or Revenue Procedure ("cents-per-mile rate") multiplied by the total number of miles the vehicle is driven by the employee for personal purposes. For 1985, the standard mileage rate is 21 cents per mile for the first 15,000 miles and 11 cents per mile for all miles over 15,000. See Rev. Proc. 85-49. The standard mileage rate must be applied to personal miles independent of business miles. Thus, for example, if an employee drives 20,000 personal miles and 35,000 business miles in 1985, the value of the personal use of the vehicle is \$3,700 (15,000 × \$.21 + 5,000 × \$.11). For purposes of this section, the use of a vehicle for personal purposes is any use of the vehicle other than use in the employee's trade or business of being an employee of the employer. Infrequent use of the vehicle, such as for trips to the airport or between the employer's multiple business premises, does not constitute regular use of the vehicle in the employer's trade or business.

(ii) *Mileage rule.* A vehicle satisfies the requirements of this paragraph (e)(1)(ii) in a calendar year if (A) it is actually driven at least 10,000 miles in that year, and (B) use of the vehicle during the year is primarily by employees. For example, if a vehicle is used by only one employee during the year and that employee drives a vehicle at least 10,000 miles in a calendar year, such vehicle satisfies the requirements of this paragraph (e)(1)(ii) even if all miles driven by the employee are personal. The requirements of this paragraph (e)(1)(ii), however, will not be satisfied if during the year the vehicle is transferred among employees in such a way which enables an employee whose use was at a rate significantly less than 10,000 miles per year to meet the 10,000 mile threshold. Assume that an employee uses a vehicle for the first six months of the year and drives 2,000 miles, and that vehicle is then used by other employees who drive the vehicle 8,000 miles in the last six months of the year. Because the rate at which miles were driven in the first six months of the year would result in only 4,000 miles being driven in the year, and because the first employee did not use the vehicle during the last six months of the year, the requirements of this paragraph (e)(1)(ii) are not satisfied. The requirement of paragraph (e)(1)(ii)(B) of this section is deemed satisfied if employees use the vehicle on a consistent basis for commuting. If the employer does not own or lease the vehicle during a portion of the year, the 10,000 mile threshold is to be reduced proportionately to reflect the periods when the employer owned or

→ *Caution: Temporary Reg. § 1.61-2T applies to the tax treatment of fringe benefits for 1985—1988. See Reg. § 1.61-21 for post-1988 rules.*←

leased the vehicle. For purposes of this paragraph (e)(1)(ii), use of the vehicle by an individual (other than the employee) whose use would be taxed to the employee is not considered use by the employee.

(iii) *Limitation on use of the vehicle cents-per-mile valuation rule.* The value of the use of an automobile (as defined in paragraph (d)(1)(ii) of this section) may not be determined under the vehicle cents-per-mile valuation rule of this paragraph (e) if the fair market value of the automobile (determined pursuant to paragraphs (d)(5)(i) through (iv) of this section as of the later of January 1, 1985, or the first date on which the automobile is made available to any employee of the employer for personal use) exceeds $12,800. No inference may be drawn from the promulgation or terms of this section concerning the application of law in effect prior to January 1, 1985.

(2) *Definition of vehicle.* For purposes of this paragraph (e), the term "vehicle" means any motorized wheeled vehicle manufactured primarily for use on public streets, roads, and highways. The term "vehicle" includes an automobile as defined in paragraph (d)(1)(ii) of this section.

(3) *Services included in, or excluded from, the cents-per-mile rate*—(i) *Maintenance and insurance included.* The cents-per-mile rate includes the fair market value of maintenance of, and insurance for, the vehicle. An employer may not reduce the cents-per-mile rate by the fair market value of any service included in the cents-per-mile rate but not provided by the employer. An employer or employee may take into account the services provided with respect to the automobile by valuing the availability of the automobile under the general valuation rules of paragraph (b) of this section.

(ii) *Fuel provided by the employer*—(A) *Miles driven in the United States, Canada, and Mexico.* With respect to miles driven in the United States, Canada, and Mexico, the cents-per-mile rate includes the fair market value of fuel provided by the employer. If fuel is not provided by the employer, the cents-per-mile rate may be reduced by no more than 5.5 cents or the amount specified in any applicable Revenue Ruling or Revenue Procedure. For purposes of this section, the United States includes the United States and its territories.

(B) *Miles driven outside the United States, Canada, and Mexico.* With respect to miles driven outside the United States, Canada, and Mexico, the fair market value of fuel provided by the employer is not reflected in the cents-per-mile

rate. Accordingly, the cents-per-mile rate may be reduced but by no more than 5.5 cents or the amount specified in any applicable Revenue Ruling or Revenue Procedure. If the employer provides the fuel in kind, it must be valued based on all the facts and circumstances. If the employer reimburses the employee for the cost of fuel or allows the employee to charge the employer for the cost of fuel, the fair market value of the fuel is generally the amount of the actual reimbursement or the amount charged, provided the purchase of the fuel is at arm's length.

(4) *Valuation of personal use only.* The vehicle cents-per-mile valuation rule of this paragraph (e) may only be used to value the miles driven for personal purposes. Thus, the employer must include an amount in an employee's income with respect to the use of a vehicle that is equal to the product of the number of personal miles driven by the employee and the appropriate cents-per-mile rate. The employer may not include in income a greater or lesser amount; for example, the employer may not include in income 100 percent (all business and personal miles) of the value of the use of the vehicle. The term "personal miles" means all miles driven by the employee except miles driven by the employee in the employee's trade or business of being an employee of the employer.

(5) *Consistency rules*—(i) *Use of the vehicle cents-per-mile valuation rule by an employer.* An employer must adopt the vehicle cents-per-mile valuation rule of this paragraph (e) for a vehicle by the later of the period that begins on January 1, 1987, or the first period in which the vehicle is used by an employee of the employer for personal use or, if the commuting valuation rule of paragraph (f) of this section is used when the vehicle is first used by an employee of the employer for personal use, the first period in which the commuting valuation rule is not used.

(ii) *An employer must use the vehicle cents-per-mile valuation rule for all subsequent periods.* Once the vehicle cents-per-mile valuation rule has been adopted for a vehicle by an employer, the rule must be used by the employer for all subsequent periods in which the vehicle qualifies for use of the rule, except that (A) the employer may, for any period during which use of the vehicle qualifies for the commuting valuation rule of paragraph (f) of this section, use the commuting valuation rule with respect to the vehicle, and (B) if the employer elects to use the automobile lease valuation rule of paragraph (d) of this section for a period in which the vehicle does not

→ *Caution: Temporary Reg. § 1.61-2T applies to the tax treatment of fringe benefits for 1985—1988. See Reg. § 1.61-21 for post-1988 rules.*←

qualify for use of the vehicle cents-per-mile valuation rule, then the employer must comply with the requirements of paragraph (d)(6) of this section. If the vehicle fails to qualify for use of the vehicle cents-per-mile valuation rule during a subsequent period, the employer may adopt for such subsequent period and thereafter any other special valuation rule for which the vehicle then qualifies. For purposes of paragraph (d)(6) of this section, the first day on which an automobile with respect to which the vehicle cents-per-mile rule had been used fails to qualify for use of the vehicle cents-per-mile valuation rule may be deemed to be the first day on which the automobile is available to an employee of the employer for personal use.

(iii) *Use of the vehicle cents-per-mile valuation rule by an employee.* An employee may adopt the vehicle cents-per-mile valuation rule for a vehicle only if the rule is adopted (A) by the employer and (B) with respect to the first period in which the vehicle for which the employer (consistent with paragraph (e)(5)(i) of this section) adopted the rule is available to that employee for personal use or, if the commuting valuation rule of paragraph (f) of this section is used by both the employer and the employee when the vehicle is first used by an employee for personal use, the first period in which the commuting valuation rule is not used.

(iv) *An employee must use the vehicle cents-per-mile valuation rule for all subsequent periods.* Once the vehicle cents-per-mile valuation rule has been adopted for a vehicle by an employee, the rule must be used by the employee for all subsequent periods of personal use of the vehicle by the employee for which the rule is used by the employer, except that the employee may, for any period during which use of the vehicle qualifies for use of the commuting valuation rule of paragraph (f) of this section and for which such rule is used by the employer, use the commuting valuation rule with respect to the vehicle.

(v) *Replacement vehicles.* Notwithstanding anything in this paragraph (e)(5) to the contrary, if the vehicle cents-per-mile valuation rule is used by an employer, or by an employer and an employee, with respect to a particular vehicle, and a replacement vehicle is provided to the employee for the primary purpose of reducing Federal taxes, then the employer, or the employer and the employee, using the rule must continue to use the rule with respect to the replacement vehicle if the replacement vehicle qualifies for use of the rule.

(f) *Commuting valuation rule*—(1) *In general.* Under the commuting valuation rule of this paragraph (f), the value of the commuting use of an employer-provided vehicle may be determined pursuant to paragraph (f)(3) of this section if the following criteria are met by the employer and employees with respect to the vehicle:

(i) the vehicle is owned or leased by the employer and is provided to one or more employees for use in connection with the employer's trade or business and is used in the employer's trade or business;

(ii) For bona fide noncompensatory business reasons, the employer requires the employee to commute to and/or from work in the vehicle;

(iii) The employer has established a written policy under which the employee may not use the vehicle for personal purposes, other than for commuting or de minimis personal use (such as a stop for a personal errand on the way between a business delivery and the employee's home);

(iv) Except for de minimis personal use, the employee does not use the vehicle for any personal purpose other than commuting; and

(v) The employee required to use the vehicle for commuting is not a control employee of the employer (as defined in paragraphs (f)(5) and (6) of this section).

If the vehicle is a chauffeur-driven vehicle, the commuting valuation rule of this paragraph (f) may not be used to value the commuting use of any passenger who commutes in the vehicle. The rule may be used, however, to value the commuting use of the chauffeur. Personal use of a vehicle is all use of the vehicle by the employee that is not use in the employee's trade or business of being an employee of the employer.

(2) *Special rules.* Notwithstanding anything in paragraph (f)(1) of this section to the contrary, the following special rules apply—

(i) *Written policy not required in 1985.* The policy described in paragraph (f)(1)(iii) of this section prohibiting personal use need not be written with respect to the commuting use which occurs prior to January 1, 1986;

(ii) *Commuting use during 1985.* For commuting use that occurs after December 31, 1984, but before January 1, 1986, the restrictions of paragraph (f)(1)(v) of this section shall be applied by substituting "an employee who is an officer or a five-percent owner of the employer" in lieu of "a control employee". For purposes of determining who is a five-percent owner, any individual who owns (or is considered as owning) five or more

Reg. § 1.61-2T(f)(1)

→ *Caution: Temporary Reg. § 1.61-2T applies to the tax treatment of fringe benefits for 1985—1988. See Reg. § 1.61-21 for post-1988 rules.*←

percent of the fair market value of an entity (the "owned entity") is considered a five-percent owner of all entities that would be aggregated with the owned entity under the rules of section 414(b), (c), or (m). An employee who is an officer of an employer shall be treated as an officer of all entities treated as a single employer pursuant to section 414(b), (c), or (m). The definitions provided in paragraphs (f)(5)(i) and (f)(6) of this section may be used to define an officer; and

(iii) *Control employee exception.* If the vehicle in which the employee is required to commute is not an automobile as defined in paragraph (d)(1)(ii) of this section, the restrictions of paragraph (f)(1)(v) of this section do not apply.

(3) *Commuting value—(i) $1.50 per one-way commute.* If the requirements of this paragraph (f) are satisfied, the value of the commuting use of an employer-provided vehicle is $1.50 per one-way commute (e.g., from home to work or from work to home).

(ii) *Value per employee.* If there is more than one employee who commutes in the vehicle, such as in the case of an employer-sponsored car pool, the amount includible in the income of each employee is $1.50 per one-way commute. Thus, the amount includible for each round-trip commute is $3.00 per employee.

(4) *Definition of vehicle.* For purposes of this paragraph (f), the term "vehicle" means any motorized wheeled vehicle manufactured primarily for use on public streets, roads, and highways. The term "vehicle" includes an automobile as defined in paragraph (d)(1)(ii) of this section.

(5) *Control employee defined—Non-government employer.* For purposes of this paragraph (f), a control employee of a non-government employer is any employee—

(i) Who is a Board- or shareholder- appointed, confirmed, or elected officer of the employer,

(ii) Who is a director of the employer, or

(iii) Who owns a one-percent or greater equity, capital, or profits interest in the employer. For purposes of determining who is a one-percent owner under paragraph (f)(5)(iii) of this section, any individual who owns (or is considered as owning under section 318(a) or principles similar to section 318(a) for entities other than corporations) one percent or more of the fair market value of an entity (the "owned entity") is considered a one-percent owner of all entities which would be aggregated with the owned entity under the rules of

section 414(b), (c), or (m). An employee who is an officer of an employer shall be treated as an officer of all entities treated as a single employer pursuant to section 414(b), (c) or (m).

(6) *Control employee defined—Government employer.* For purposes of this paragraph (f), a control employee of a government employer is any—

(i) Elected official,

(ii) Federal employee who is appointed by the President and confirmed by the Senate. In the case of commissioned officers of the United States Armed Forces, an officer is any individual with the rank of brigadier general or above or the rank of rear admiral (lower half) or above; or

(iii) State or local executive officer comparable to the individuals described in paragraph (f)(6)(i) and (ii) of this section.

For purposes of this paragraph (f), the term "government" includes any Federal, state, or local governmental unit, and any agency or instrumentality thereof.

(g) *Non-commercial flight valuation rule* —(1) *In general.* Under the non-commercial flight valuation rule of this paragraph (g), if an employee is provided with a flight on an employer-provided aircraft, the value of the flight is calculated using the aircraft valuation formula provided in paragraph (g)(5) of this section. Except as otherwise provided, for purposes of this paragraph (g), a flight provided to a person whose flight would be taxable to an employee as the recipient is referred to as provided to the employee, and a flight taken by such person is considered a flight taken by the employee.

(2) *Eligible flights and eligible aircraft.* The valuation rule of this paragraph (g) may be used to value flights on all employer-provided aircraft, including helicopters. The valuation rule of this paragraph (g) may be used to value international as well as domestic flights. The valuation rule of this paragraph (g) may not be used to value a flight on any commercial aircraft on which air transportation is sold to the public on a per-seat basis. For a special valuation rule relating to certain flights on commercial aircraft, see paragraph (h) of this section.

(3) *Definition of a flight* —(i) *General rule.* Except as otherwise provided in paragraph (g)(3)(iii) of this section (relating to intermediate stops), for purposes of this paragraph (g), an individual's flight is the distance (in statute miles) between the place at which the individual boards

Reg. § 1.61-2T(g)(3)

→ *Caution: Temporary Reg. § 1.61-2T applies to the tax treatment of fringe benefits for 1985—1988. See Reg. § 1.61-21 for post-1988 rules.*←

the aircraft and the place at which the individual deplanes.

(ii) *Valuation of each flight.* Under the valuation rule of this paragraph (g), value is determined separately for each flight. Thus, a round-trip is comprised of at least two flights. For example, an employee who takes a personal trip on an employer-provided aircraft from New York, New York to Denver, Colorado, Denver to Los Angeles, California, and Los Angeles to New York has taken three flights and must apply the aircraft valuation formula separately to each flight. The value of a flight must be determined on a passenger-by-passenger basis. For example, if an individual accompanies an employee and the flight taken by the individual would be taxed to the employee, the employee would be taxed on the special rule value of the flight by the employee and by the individual.

(iii) *Intermediate stop.* If the primary purpose of a landing is necessitated by weather conditions, by an emergency, for purposes of refueling or obtaining other services relating to the aircraft, or for purposes of the employer's business unrelated to the employee whose flight is being valued ("an intermediate stop"), the distance between the place at which the trip originates and the place at which the intermediate stop occurs is not considered a flight. For example, assume that an employee's trip originates in St. Louis, Missouri, on route to Seattle, Washington, but, because of weather conditions, the aircraft lands in Denver, Colorado, and the employee stays in Denver overnight. Assume further that the next day the aircraft flies to Seattle where the employee deplanes. The employee's flight is the distance between the airport in St. Louis and the airport in Seattle. Assume that a trip originates in New York, New York, with five passengers and makes an intermediate stop in Chicago, Illinois, before going on to Los Angeles, California. If one of the five passengers deplanes in Chicago, the distance of that passenger's flight would be the distance between the airport in New York and the airport in Chicago. The intermediate stop is disregarded when measuring the flights taken by each of the other passengers. Their flights would be the distance between the airport in New York and the airport in Los Angeles.

(4) *Personal and non-personal flights—(i) In general.* The valuation rule of this paragraph (g) applies to personal flights on employer-provided aircraft. A personal flight is one the value of which in not excludable under another section of subtitle A, such as under section 132(d) (relating

to a working condition fringe). However, solely for purposes of paragraphs (g)(4)(ii) and (g)(4)(iii) of this section, references to personal flights do not include flights a portion of which would not be excludable by reason of section 274(c).

(ii) *Trip primarily for employer's business.* If an employee combines, in one trip, personal and business flights on an employer-provided aircraft and the employee's trip is primarily for the employer's business (see § 1.162-2(b)(2)), the employee must include in income the excess of the value of all the flights that comprise the trip over the value of the flights that would have been taken had there been no personal flights but only business flights. For example, assume that an employee flies on an employer-provided aircraft from Chicago, Illinois to Miami, Florida, for the employer's business and that from Miami the employee flies on the employer-provided aircraft to Orlando, Florida, for personal purposes and then flies back to Chicago. Assume further that the primary purpose of the trip is for the employer's business. The amount includible in income is the excess of the value of the three flights (Chicago to Miami, Miami to Orlando, and Orlando to Chicago), over the value of the flights that would have been taken had there been no personal flights but only business flights (Chicago to Miami and Miami to Chicago).

(iii) *Primarily personal trip.* If an employee combines, in one trip, personal and business flights on an employer-provided aircraft and the employee's trip is primarily personal (see § 1.162-2(b)(2)), the amount includible in the employee's income is the value of the personal flights that would have been taken had there been no business flights but only personal flights. For example, assume that an employee flies on an employer-provided aircraft from San Francisco, California, to Los Angeles, California, for the employer's business and that from Los Angeles the employee flies on an employer-provided aircraft to Palm Springs, California, primarily for personal reasons and then flies back to San Francisco. Assume further that the primary purpose of the trip is personal. The amount includible in the employee's income is the value of personal flights that would have been taken had there been no business flights but only personal flights (San Francisco to Palm Springs and Palm Springs to San Francisco).

(iv) *Application of section 274(c).* The value of employer-provided travel outside the United States away from home may not be excluded from the employee's gross income as a

Reg. § 1.61-2T(g)(4)

→ *Caution: Temporary Reg. § 1.61-2T applies to the tax treatment of fringe benefits for 1985—1988. See Reg. § 1.61-21 for post-1988 rules.←*

working condition fringe, by either the employer or the employee, to the extent not deductible by reason of section 274(c). The valuation rule of this paragraph (g) applies to that portion of the value of any flight not excludable by reason of section 274(c). Such value must be included in income in addition to the amounts determined under paragraphs (g)(4)(ii) and (g)(4)(iii) of this section.

(v) *Flight by individuals who are not personal guests.* If an individual who is not an employee of the employer providing the aircraft is on a flight, and the individual is not the personal guest of any employee, the flight by the individual is not taxable to any employee of the employer providing the aircraft. The rule in the preceding sentence applies where the individual is provided the flight by the employer for noncompensatory business reasons of the employer. For example, assume that G, an employee of company Y, accompanies A, an employee of company X, on company X's aircraft for the purpose of inspecting land under consideration for purchase by company X from company Y. The flight by G is not taxable to A.

(5) *Aircraft valuation formula.* Under the valuation rule of this paragraph (g), the value of a flight is determined by multiplying the base aircraft valuation formula for the period during which the flight was taken by the appropriate aircraft multiple (as provided in paragraph (g)(7) of this section) and then adding the applicable terminal charge. The base aircraft valuation

formula (also known as the Standard Industry Fare Level formula or SIFL) in effect on June 30, 1985, is as follows: ($.1402 per mile for the first 500 miles, $.1069 per mile for miles between 501 and 1500, and $.1028 per mile for miles over 1500). The terminal charge in effect on June 30, 1985, is $25.62. The SIFL cents-per-mile rates in the formula and the terminal charge are calculated by the Department of Transportation and are revised semi-annually.

(6) *SIFL formula in effect for a particular flight.* For purposes of this paragraph (g), in determining the value of a particular flight during the first six months of a calendar year, the SIFL formula (and terminal charge) in effect on December 31 of the preceding year applies, and in determining the value of a particular flight during the last six months of a calendar year, the SIFL formula (and terminal charge) in effect on June 30 of that year applies. The following is the SIFL formula in effect on December 31, 1984: ($.1480 per mile for the first 500 miles, $.1128 per mile for miles between 501 and 1500, and $.1085 per mile for miles over 1500. The terminal charge in effect on December 31, 1984, is $27.05.

(7) *Aircraft multiples*—(i) *In general.* The aircraft multiples are based on the maximum certified takeoff weight of the aircraft. For purposes of applying the aircraft valuation formula described in paragraph (g)(5) of this section, the aircraft multiples are as follows:

Maximum Certified Takeoff Weight of the Aircraft	Aircraft multiple for a Control Employee	Aircraft multiple for a Non-Control Employee
6,000 lbs. or less	62.5 percent	15.6 percent
6,001 - 10,000 lbs.	125 percent	23.4 percent
10,001 - 25,000 lbs.	300 percent	31.3 percent
25,001 lbs. or more	400 percent	31.3 percent

(ii) *Flights treated as provided to a control employee.* Except as provided in paragraph (g)(10) of this section, any flight provided to an individual whose flight would be taxable to a control employee (as defined in paragraph (g)(8) and (9) of this section) as the recipient shall be valued as if such flight had been provided to that control employee. For example, assume that the chief executive officer of an employer, his spouse, and his two children fly on an employer-provided aircraft for personal purposes. Assume further that the maximum certified takeoff weight of the aircraft is 12,000 lbs. The amount includible in the employee's income is 4 × ((300 percent × base

aircraft valuation formula) plus the applicable terminal charge).

(8) *Control employee defined*—*Nongovernment employer.* For purposes of this paragraph (g), a control employee of a non-government employer is any employee—

(i) Who is a Board- or shareholder- appointed, confirmed, or elected officer of the employer, limited to the lesser of (A) one-percent of all employees (increased to the next highest integer, if not an integer) or (B) ten employees;

(ii) Whose compensation equals or exceeds the compensation of the top one percent most highly-paid employees of the employer (increased

Reg. § 1.61-2T(g)(8)

→ *Caution: Temporary Reg. § 1.61-2T applies to the tax treatment of fringe benefits for 1985—1988. See Reg. § 1.61-21 for post-1988 rules.*←

to the next highest integer, if not an integer) limited to a maximum of 25 employees;

(iii) Who owns a ten-percent or greater equity, capital or profits interest in the employer; or

(iv) Who is a director of the employer.

For purposes of this paragraph (g), any employee who is a family member (within the meaning of section 267(c)(4)) of a control employee is also a control employee. Pursuant to this paragraph (g)(8), an employee may be a control employee under more than one of the requirements listed in paragraphs (g)(8)(i) through (iv) of this section. For example, an employee may be both an officer under paragraph (g)(8)(i) of this section and a highly-paid employee under paragraph (g)(8)(ii) of this section. In this case, for purposes of the officer limitation rule of paragraph (g)(8)(i) of this section and the highly-paid employee limitation rule of paragraph (g)(8)(ii) of this section, the employee would be counted as reducing both such limitation rules. In no event shall an employee whose compensation is less than $50,000 be a control employee under paragraph (g)(8)(ii) of this section. For purposes of determining who is a ten-percent owner under paragraph (g)(8)(iii) of this section, any individual who owns (or is considered as owning under section 318(a) or principles similar to section 318(a) for entities other than corporations) ten percent or more of the fair market value of an entity (the "owned entity") is considered a ten-percent owner of all entities which would be aggregated with the owned entity under the rules of section 414(b), (c), or (m). For purposes of determining who is an officer under paragraph (g)(8)(i) of this section, notwithstanding anything in this section to the contrary, if the employer would be aggregated with other employers under the rules of section 414(b), (c), or (m), the officer definition and the limitations are applied to each separate employer rather than to the aggregated employer. If applicable, the officer limitation rule of paragraph (g)(8)(i) of this section is applied to employees in descending order of their compensation. Thus, if an employer has 11 board-appointed officers, the employee with the least compensation of those officers would not be an officer under paragraph (g)(8)(i) of this section. For purposes of this paragraph (g), the term "compensation" means the amount reported on a Form W-2 as income for the prior calendar year. Compensation includes all amounts received from all entities treated as a single employer under section 414(b), (c), or (m).

(9) *Control employee defined—Government.* For purposes of this paragraph (g), a control employee of a government employer is any—

(i) Elected official;

(ii) Federal employee who is appointed by the President and confirmed by the Senate. In the case of commissioned officers of the United States Armed Forces, an officer is any individual with the rank of brigadier general or above the or rank of rear admiral (lower half) or above; or

(iii) State or local executive officer comparable to the individuals in paragraph (g)(9)(i) and (ii) of this section.

For purposes of this paragraph (g), the term "government" includes any Federal, state, or local government unit, and any agency or instrumentality thereof.

(10) *Seating capacity rule* —(i) *In general.* Where 50 percent or more of the regular passenger seating capacity of an aircraft (as used by the employer) is occupied by individuals whose flights are primarily for the employer's business (and whose flights are excludable from income under section 132(d)), the value of a flight on that aircraft by any employee who is not flying primarily for the employer's business (or who is flying primarily for the employer's business but the value of whose flight is not excludable under section 132(d) by reason of section 274(c)) is deemed to be zero. See § 1.132-5T which limits the exclusion under section 132(d) to situations where the employee receives the flight in connection with the performance of services for the employer providing the aircraft. For purposes of this paragraph (g)(10), the term "employee" includes only employees and partners of the employer providing the aircraft and does not include independent contractors and directors of the employer. For purposes of this paragraph (g)(10), the second sentence of paragraph (g)(1) of this section will not apply. Instead, a flight taken by an individual who is either treated as an employee pursuant to section 132(f)(1) or whose flight is treated as a flight taken by an employee pursuant to section 132(f)(2) is considered a flight taken by an employee. If (A) a flight is considered taken by an individual other than an employee (as defined in this paragraph (g)(10)), (B) the value of that individual's flight is not excludable under section 132(d), and (C) the seating capacity rule of this paragraph (g)(10) otherwise applies, then the value of the flight provided to such an individual is the value of a flight provided to a non-control employee (even if the individual who would be

→ *Caution: Temporary Reg. § 1.61-2T applies to the tax treatment of fringe benefits for 1985—1988. See Reg. § 1.61-21 for post-1988 rules.*←

taxed on the value of such individual's flight is a control employee).

(ii) *Application of 50-percent test to multiple flights.* The seating capacity rule of this paragraph (g)(10) must be met both at the time the individual whose flight is being valued boards the aircraft and at the time the individual deplanes. For example, assume that employee A boards an employer-provided aircraft for personal purposes in New York, New York, and that at that time 80 percent of the regular passenger seating capacity of the aircraft is occupied by individuals whose flights are primarily for the employer's business (and whose flights are excludable from income under section 132(d)) ("the business passengers"). If the aircraft flies directly to Hartford, Connecticut, where all of the passengers, including A, deplane, the requirements of the seating capacity rule of this paragraph (g)(10) have been satisfied. If instead, some of the passengers, including A, remain on the aircraft in Hartford and the aircraft continues on to Boston, Massachusetts, where they all deplane, the requirements of the seating capacity rule of this paragraph (g)(10) will not be satisfied unless at least 50 percent of the seats comprising the aircraft's regular passenger seating capacity were occupied by the business passengers at the time A deplanes in Boston.

(iii) *Regular passenger seating capacity.* The regular passenger seating capacity of an aircraft is the maximum number of seats that have at any time been on the aircraft (while owned or leased by the employer). Except to the extent excluded pursuant to paragraph (g)(10)(v) of this section, regular seating capacity includes all seats which may be occupied by members of the flight crew. It is irrelevant that on a particular flight, less than the maximum number of seats are available for use, because, for example, some of the seats are removed. When determining the maximum number of seats, those seats that cannot at any time be legally used during takeoff and are not any time used during takeoff are not counted.

(iv) *Examples.* The rules of paragraph (g)(10)(iii) of this section are illustrated by the following examples:

Example (1). Employer A and employer B order the same aircraft, except that A orders it with 10 seats and B orders it with eight seats. A always uses its aircraft as a 10-seat aircraft; B always uses its aircraft as an eight-seat aircraft. The regular passenger seating capacity of A's aircraft is 10 and of B's aircraft is eight.

Example (2). Assume the same facts as in example (1), except that whenever A's chief exec-

utive officer and spouse use the aircraft eight seats are removed. Even if substantially all of the use of the aircraft is by the chief executive officer and spouse the regular passenger seating capacity of the aircraft is 10.

Example (3). Assume the same facts as in example (1), except that whenever more than eight people want to fly in B's aircraft, two extra seats are added. Even if substantially all of the use of the aircraft occurs with eight seats, the regular passenger seating capacity of the aircraft is 10.

(v) *Seats occupied by flight crew.* When determining the regular passenger seating capacity of an aircraft, any seat occupied by a member of the flight crew (whether or not such individual is an employee of the employer providing the aircraft) shall not be counted, unless the purpose of the flight by such individual is not primarily to serve as a member of the flight crew. If the seat occupied by a member of the flight crew is not counted as a passenger seat pursuant to the previous sentence, such member of the flight crew is disregarded in applying the 50 percent test described in the first sentence of paragraph (g)(10)(i) of this section. For example, assume that, prior to application of this paragraph (g)(10)(v), the regular passenger seating capacity of an aircraft is two seats. Assume further that an employee pilots the aircraft and that the employee's flight is not primarily for the employer's business. If the employee's spouse occupies the other seat for personal purposes, the seating capacity rule is not met and the value of both flights must be included in the employee's income. If, however, the employee's flight were primarily for the employer's business (unrelated to serving as a member of the flight crew), then the seating capacity rule is met and the value of the flight for the employee's spouse is deemed to be zero. If the employee's flight were primarily to serve as a member of the flight crew, then the seating capacity rule is not met and the value of a flight by any passenger for primarily personal reasons is not deemed to be zero.

(11) *Erroneous use of the non-commercial flight valuation rule*—(i) *In general.* If the non-commercial flight valuation rule of this paragraph (g) is used by an employer or a control employee, as the case may be, on a return as originally filed, on the grounds that either the control employee is not in fact a control employee, or that the aircraft is within a specific weight classification, and either position is subsequently determined to be erroneous, the valuation rule of this paragraph (g)

Reg. § 1.61-2T(g)(11)

→ *Caution: Temporary Reg. § 1.61-2T applies to the tax treatment of fringe benefits for 1985—1988. See Reg. § 1.61-21 for post-1988 rules.*←

(including paragraph (g)(13) of this section) is not available to value the flight taken by that control employee by the person or persons taking the erroneous position. With respect to the weight classifications, the previous sentence does not apply if the position taken is that the weight of the aircraft is greater than it is subsequently determined to be. If, with respect to a flight by a control employee, the seating capacity rule of paragraph (g)(10) of this section is used by an employer or the control employee, as the case may be, on a return as originally filed, and it is subsequently determined that the requirements of paragraph (g)(10) of this section were not met, the valuation rule of this paragraph (g) (including paragraph (g)(13) of this section) is not available to value the flight taken by that control employee by the person or persons taking the erroneous position.

(ii) *Value of flight excluded as a working condition fringe.* If either an employer or an employee, on a return as originally filed, excludes from the employee's income or wages the value of a flight on the grounds that the flight was excludable as a working condition fringe under section 132, and that position is subsequently determined to be erroneous, the valuation rule of this paragraph (g) (including paragraph (g)(13) of this section) is not available to value the flight taken by that employee by the person or persons taking the erroneous position.

(12) *Consistency rules—*(i) *Use by the employer.* Except as otherwise provided in paragraphs (g)(11) and (g)(13)(iv) of this section, if the non-commercial flight valuation rule of this paragraph (g) is used by an employer to value flights provided in a calendar year, the rule must be used to value all flights provided in the calendar year.

(ii) *Use by the employee.* Except as otherwise provided in paragraphs (g)(11) and (g)(13)(iv) of this section, if the non-commercial flight valuation rule of this paragraph (g) is used by an employee to value a flight taken in a calendar year, the rule must be used to value all flights taken in the calendar year.

(13) *Transitional valuation rule—* (i) *In general.* If the value of a flight determined under this paragraph (g)(13) is lower than the value of the flight otherwise determined under paragraph (g) of this section, the value of the flight is the lower amount. The transitional valuation rule of this paragraph (g)(13) is available only for flights provided after December 31, 1984, and before January 1, 1986.

(ii) *Transitional valuation rule aircraft multiples.* The appropriate aircraft multiples under the transitional valuation rule are as follows:

(A) 125 percent of the base aircraft valuation formula, plus the applicable terminal charge, for any flight by any employee who is not a key employee (as defined in paragraph (g)(13)(iii) of this section).

(B) 125 percent of the base aircraft valuation formula, plus the applicable terminal charge, for a flight by a key employee if there is a primary business purpose for the trip by the aircraft. For purposes of this paragraph (g)(13)(ii)(B), entertaining an employee or other individual is not a business purpose.

(C) 600 percent of the base aircraft valuation formula, plus the applicable terminal charge, for a flight by a key employee if there is no primary business purpose for the trip by the aircraft.

Where there is no business purpose for the trip by the aircraft, the alternative valuation rule may not be used to value a flight by a key employee. For purposes of this section, compensating an employee is not a business purpose.

(iii) *Key employee defined.* A "key employee" is any employee who is a five-percent owner or an officer of the employer, or who, with respect to a particular trip by the aircraft, controls the use of the aircraft. For purposes of determining who is a five-percent owner, any individual who owns (or is considered as owning) five or more percent of the fair market value of an entity (the "owned entity") is considered a five-percent owner of all entities that would be aggregated with the owned entity under the rules of section 414(b), (c), or (m).

(iv) *Erroneous use of transitional valuation rule.* If the transitional valuation rule is used by an employer or a key employee, as the case may be, on a return as originally filed, on the grounds that—

(A) The key employee is not in fact a key employee,

(B) An aircraft trip had a primary business purpose, or

(C) An aircraft trip had some business purpose,

and such position is subsequently determined to be erroneous, neither the transitional valuation rule nor the non-commercial flight valuation rule of this paragraph (g) is available to value such

Reg. § 1.61-2T(g)(12)

→ *Caution: Temporary Reg. § 1.61-2T applies to the tax treatment of fringe benefits for 1985—1988. See Reg. § 1.61-21 for post-1988 rules.*←

flight taken by that key employee by the person or persons taking the erroneous position.

(h) *Commercial flight valuation rule*—(1) *In general.* Under the commercial flight valuation rule of this paragraph (h), the value of a space-available flight (as defined in paragraph (h)(2) of this section) on a commercial aircraft is 25 percent of the actual carrier's highest unrestricted coach fare in effect for the particular flight taken.

(2) *Space-available flight.* The commercial flight valuation rule of this paragraph (h) is available to value a space-available flight. The term "space-available flight" means a flight on a commercial aircraft (i) for which the airline (the actual carrier) incurs no substantial additional cost (including forgone revenue) determined without regard to any amount paid for the flight and (ii) which is subject to the same types of restrictions customarily associated with flying on an employee "standby" or "space-available" basis. A flight may be a space-available flight even if the airline that is the actual carrier is not the employer of the employee.

(3) *Commercial aircraft.* If the actual carrier does not offer, in the ordinary course of its business, air transportation to customers on a per-seat basis, the commercial flight valuation rule of this paragraph (h) is not available. Thus, if, in the ordinary course of its line of business, the employer only offers air transportation to customers on a charter basis, the commercial flight valuation rule of this paragraph (h) may not be used to value a space-available flight on the employer's aircraft. Similarly, if, in the ordinary course of its line of business, an employer only offers air transportation to customers for the transport of cargo, the commercial flight valuation rule of this paragraph (h) may not be used to value a space-available flight on the employer's aircraft.

(4) *Timing of inclusion.* The date that the flight is taken is the relevant date for purposes of applying section 61(a)(1) and this section to a space-available flight on a commercial aircraft. The date of purchase or issuance of a pass or ticket is not relevant. Thus, this section applies to a flight taken on or after January 1, 1985, regardless of the date on which the pass or ticket for the flight was purchased or issued.

(5) *Consistency rules*—(i) *Use by employer.* If the commercial flight valuation rule of this paragraph (h) is used by an employer to value flights provided in a calendar year, the rule must be used to value all flights provided in the calendar year.

(ii) *Use by employee.* If the commercial flight valuation rule of this paragraph (h) is used by an employee to value a flight taken in a calendar year, the rule must be used to value all flights taken by such employee in the calendar year.

(i) [Reserved]

(j) *Valuation of meals provided at an employer-operated eating facility for employees*—(1) *In general.* The valuation rule of this paragraph (j) may be used to value a meal provided at an employer-operated eating facility for employees (as defined in § 1.132-7T). For rules relating to an exclusion for the value of meals provided at an employer-operated eating facility for employees, see § 1.132-7T.

(2) *Valuation formula*—(i) *In general.* The value of all meals provided at an employer-operated eating facility for employees during a calendar year is 150 percent of the direct operating costs of the eating facility ("total meal value"). For purposes of this paragraph (j), the definition of direct operating costs provided in § 1.132-7T applies. The taxable value of meals provided at an eating facility may be determined in two ways. The "individual meal subsidy" may be treated as the taxable value of a meal provided at the eating facility (see paragraph (j)(2)(ii) of this section). Alternatively, the employer may allocate the "total meal subsidy" among employees (see paragraph (j)(2)(iii) of this section).

(ii) *"Individual meal subsidy" defined.* The "individual meal subsidy" is determined by multiplying the price charged for a particular meal by a fraction, the numerator of which is the total meal value and the denominator of which is the gross receipts of the eating facility, and then subtracting the amount paid for the meal. The taxable value of meals provided to a particular employee during a calendar year, therefore, is the sum of the individual meal subsidies provided to the employee during the calendar year.

(iii) *Allocation of "total meal subsidy."* Instead of using the individual meal value method, the employer may allocate the "total meal subsidy" (total meal value less the gross receipts of the facility) among employees in any manner reasonable under the circumstances. [Temporary Reg. § 1.61-2T.]

☐ [*T.D.* 8063, 12-18-85. *Amended by T.D.* 8256, 7-5-89 *and T.D.* 8457, 12-29-92.]

Reg. § 1.61-2T(j)(2)

[Reg. § 1.61-3]

§ 1.61-3. **Gross income derived from business.**—(a) *In general.* In a manufacturing, merchandising, or mining business, "gross income" means the total sales, less the cost of goods sold, plus any income from investments and from incidental or outside operations or sources. Gross income is determined without subtraction of depletion allowances based on a percentage of income to the extent that it exceeds cost depletion which may be required to be included in the amount of inventoriable costs as provided in § 1.471-11 and without subtraction of selling expenses, losses or other items not ordinarily used in computing costs of goods sold or amounts which are of a type for which a deduction would be disallowed under section 162(c), (f), or (g) in the case of a business expense. The cost of goods sold should be determined in accordance with the method of accounting consistently used by the taxpayer. Thus, for example, an amount cannot be taken into account in the computation of cost of goods sold any earlier than the taxable year in which economic performance occurs with respect to the amount (see § 1.446-1(c)(1)(ii)).

(b) *State contracts.* The profit from a contract with a State or policitcal subdivision thereof must be included in gross income. If warrants are issued by a city, town, or other political subdivision of a State, and are accepted by the contractor in payment for public work done, the fair market value of such warrants should be returned as income. If, upon conversion of the warrants into cash, the contractor does not receive and cannot recover the full value of the warrants so returned, he may deduct any loss sustained from his gross income for the year in which the warrants are so converted. If, however, he realizes more than the value of the warrants so returned, he must include the excess in his gross income for the year in which realized. [Reg. § 1.61-3.]

☐ [T.D. 6272, 11-25-57. *Amended by T.D. 7207*, 10-3-72; *T.D. 7285*, 9-14-73 *and T.D. 8408*, 4-9-92.]

[Reg. § 1.61-4]

§ 1.61-4. **Gross income of farmers.**—(a) *Farmers using the cash method of accounting.* A farmer using the cash receipts and disbursements method of accounting shall include in his gross income for the taxable year—

(1) The amount of cash and the value of merchandise or other property received during the taxable year from the sale of livestock and produce which he raised,

(2) The profits from the sale of any livestock or other items which were purchased,

(3) All amounts received from breeding fees, fees from rent of teams, machinery, or land, and other incidental farm income,

(4) All subsidy and conservation payments received which must be considered as income, and

(5) Gross income from all other sources.

The profit from the sale of livestock or other items which were purchased is to be ascertained by deducting the cost from the sales price in the year in which the sale occurs, except that in the case of the sale of purchased animals held for draft, breeding, or dairy purposes, the profits shall be the amount of any excess of the sales price over the amount representing the difference between the cost and the depreciation allowed or allowable (determined in accordance with the rules applicable under section 1016(a) and the regulations thereunder). However, see section 162 and the regulations thereunder with respect of the computation of taxable income on other than the crop method where the cost of seeds or young plants purchased for further development and cultivation prior to the sale is involved. Crop shares (whether or not considered rent under State law) shall be included in gross income as of the year in which the crop shares are reduced to money or the equivalent of money. See section 263A for rules regarding costs that are required to be capitalized.

(b) *Farmers using an accrual method of accounting.* A farmer using an accrual method of accounting must use inventories to determine his gross income. His gross income on an accrual method is determined by adding the total of the items described in subparagraphs (1) through (5) of this paragraph and subtracting therefrom the total of the items described in subparagraphs (6) and (7) of this paragraph. These items are as follows:

(1) The sales price of all livestock and other products held for sale and sold during the year;

(2) The inventory value of livestock and products on hand and not sold at the end of the year;

(3) All miscellaneous items of income, such as breeding fees, fees from the rent of teams, machinery, or land, or other incidental farm income;

(4) Any subsidy or conservation payments which must be considered as income;

(5) Gross income from all other sources;

(6) The inventory value of the livestock and products on hand and not sold at the beginning of the year; and

Reg. § 1.61-3(a)

(7) The cost of any livestock or products purchased during the year (except livestock held for draft, dairy, or breeding purposes, unless included in inventory).

All livestock raised or purchased for sale shall be added in the inventory at their proper valuation determined in accordance with the method authorized and adopted for the purpose. Livestock acquired for draft, breeding, or dairy purposes and not for sale may be included in the inventory (see subparagraphs (2), (6), and (7) of this paragraph) instead of being treated as capital assets subject to depreciation, provided such practice is followed consistently from year to year by the taxpayer. When any livestock included in an inventory are sold, their cost must not be taken as an additional deduction in computing taxable income, because such deduction is reflected in the inventory. See the regulations under section 471. See section 263A for rules regarding costs that are required to be capitalized. Crop shares (whether or not considered rent under State law) shall be included in gross income as of the year in which the crop shares are reduced to money or the equivalent of money.

(c) *Special rules for certain receipts.* In the case of the sale of machinery, farm equipment, or any other property (except stock in trade of the taxpayer, or property of a kind which would properly be included in the inventory of the taxpayer if on hand at the close of the taxable year, or property held by the taxpayer primarily for sale to customers in the ordinary course of his trade or business), any excess of the proceeds of the sale over the adjusted basis of such property shall be included in the taxpayer's gross income for the taxable year in which such sale is made. See, however, section 453 and the regulations thereunder for special rules relating to certain installment sales. If farm produce is exchanged for merchandise, groceries, or the like, the market value of the article received in exchange is to be included in gross income. Proceeds of insurance, such as hail or fire insurance on growing crops, should be included in gross income to the extent of the amount received in cash or its equivalent for the crop injured or destroyed. See section 451(d) for special rule relating to election to include crop insurance proceeds in income for taxable year following taxable year of destruction. For taxable years beginning after July 12, 1972, where a farmer is engaged in producing crops and the process of gathering and disposing of such crops is not completed within the taxable year in which such crops are planted, the income therefrom may, with the consent of the Commissioner (see section 446 and the regulations thereunder), be computed upon the crop method. For taxable years beginning on or before July 12, 1972, where a farmer is engaged in producing crops which take more than a year from the time of planting to the time of gathering and disposing, the income therefrom may, with the consent of the Commissioner (see section 446 and the regulations thereunder), be computed upon the crop method. In any case in which the crop method is used, the entire cost of producing the crop must be taken as a deduction for the year in which the gross income from the crop is realized, and not earlier.

(d) *Definition of "farm".* As used in this section, the term "farm" embraces the farm in the ordinarily accepted sense, and includes stock, dairy, poultry, fruit, and truck farms; also plantations, ranches, and all land used for farming operations. All individuals, partnerships, or corporations that cultivate, operate, or manage farms for gain or profit, either as owners or tenants, are designated as farmers. For more detailed rules with respect to the determination of whether or not an individual is engaged in farming, see § 1.175-3. For rules applicable to persons cultivating or operating a farm for recreation or pleasure, see sections 162 and 165, and the regulations thereunder.

(e) *Cross references.* (1) For election to include Commodity Credit Corporation loans as income, see section 77 and regulations thereunder.

(2) For definition of gross income derived from farming for purposes of limiting deductibility of soil and water conservation expenditures, see section 175 and regulations thereunder.

(3) For definition of gross income from farming in connection with declarations of estimated income tax, see section 6073 and regulations thereunder. [Reg. § 1.61-4.]

☐ [*T.D.* 6272, *11-25-57. Amended by T.D.* 7198, *7-12-72 and T.D. 8729, 8-21-97.*]

[Reg. § 1.61-5]

§ 1.61-5. Allocations by cooperative associations; per-unit retain certificates—tax treatment as to cooperatives and patrons.—(a) *In general.* Amounts allocated on the basis of the business done with or for a patron by a cooperative association, whether or not entitled to tax treatment under section 522, in cash, merchandise, capital stock, revolving fund certificates, retain certificates, certificates of indebtedness, letters of advice or in some other manner disclosing to the patron the dollar amount allocated, shall be included in the computation of the gross income of such patron for the taxable year in which received to the extent prescribed in paragraph (b) of this section, regardless of whether the allocation is deemed, for the purpose of section

Reg. § 1.61-5(a)

522, to be made at the close of a preceding taxable year of the cooperative association. The determination of the extent of taxability of such amounts is in no way dependent upon the method of accounting employed by the patron or upon the method, cash, accrual, or otherwise, upon which the taxable income of such patron is computed.

(b) *Extent of taxability.* (1) Amounts allocated to a patron on a patronage basis by a cooperative association with respect to products marketed for such patron, or with respect to supplies, equipment, or services, the cost of which was deductible by the patron under section 162 or section 212, shall be included in the computation of the gross income of such patron, as ordinary income, to the following extent:

(i) If the allocation is in cash, the amount of cash received.

(ii) If the allocation is in merchandise, the amount of the fair market value of such merchandise at the time of receipt by the patron.

(iii) If the allocation is in the form of revolving fund certificates, retain certificates, certificates of indebtedness, letters of advice, or similar documents, the amount of the fair market value of such document at the time of its receipt by the patron. For the purposes of this subdivision, any document containing an unconditional promise to pay a fixed sum of money on demand or at a fixed or determinable time shall be considered to have a fair market value at the time of its receipt by the patron, unless it is clearly established to the contrary. However, for the purposes of this subdivision, any document which is payable only in the discretion of the cooperative association, or which is otherwise subject to conditions beyond the control of the patron, shall be considered not to have any fair market value at the time of its receipt by the patron, unless it is clearly established to the contrary.

(iv) If the allocation is in the form of capital stock, the amount of the fair market value, if any, of such capital stock at the time of its receipt by the patron.

(2) If any allocation to which subparagraph (1) of this paragraph applies is received in the form of a document of the type described in subparagraph (1) (iii) or (iv) of this paragraph and is redeemed in full or in part or is otherwise disposed of, there shall be included in the computation of the gross income of the patron, as ordinary income, in the year of redemption or other disposition, the excess of the amount realized on the redemption or other disposition over the amount previously included in the computation of gross income under such subparagraph.

(3)(i) Amounts which are allocated on a patronage basis by a cooperative association with respect to supplies, equipment, or services, the cost of which was not deductible by the patron under section 162 or section 212, are not includible in the computation of the gross income of such patron. However, in the case of such amounts which are allocated with respect to capital assets (as defined in section 1221) or property used in the trade or business within the meaning of section 1231, such amounts shall, to the extent set forth in subparagraph (1) of the paragraph, to be taken into account by such patron in determining the cost of the property to which the allocation relates. Notwithstanding the preceding sentence, to the extent that such amounts are in excess of the unrecovered cost of such property, and to the extent that such amounts relate to such property which the patron no longer owns, they shall be included in the computation of the gross income of such patron.

(ii) If any patronage dividend is allocated to the patron in the form of a document of the type described in subparagraph (1)(iii) or (iv) of this paragraph, and if such allocation is with respect to capital assets (as defined in section 1221) or property used in the trade or business within the meaning of section 1231, any amount realized on the redemption or other disposition of such document which is in excess of the amount which was taken into account upon the receipt of the document by the patron shall be taken into account by such patron in the year of redemption or other disposition as an adjustment to basis or as an inclusion in the computation of gross income, as the case may be.

(iii) Any adjustment to basis in respect of an amount to which subdivision (i) or (ii) of this subparagraph applies shall be made as of the first day of the taxable year in which such amount is received.

(iv) The application of the provisions of this subparagraph may be illustrated by the following examples:

Example (1). On July 1, 1959, P, a patron of a cooperative association, purchases a tractor for use in his farming business from such association for $2,200. The tractor has an estimated useful life of five years and an estimated salvage value of $200. P files his income tax returns on a calendar year basis and claims depreciation on the tractor for the year 1959 of $200 pursuant to his use of the straight-line method at the rate of $400 per year. On July 1, 1960, the cooperative association allocates to P with respect to his purchase of the tractor a dividend of $300 in cash. P will reduce his depreciation allowance with respect to the tractor for 1960 (and subsequent taxable years) to $333.33, determined as follows:

Cost of tractor, July 1, 1959		$2,200
Less: Depreciation for 1959 (6 mos.)	$200	
Adjustment as of January 1, 1960, for cash patronage dividend ..	300	
Salvage value	200	700
Basis for depreciation for the remaining 4½ years of estimated life		1,500
Basis for depreciation divided by the 4½ years of remaining life		333.33

Example (2). Assume the same facts as in example (1), except that on July 1, 1960, the cooperative association allocates a dividend to P with respect to his purchase of the tractor in the form of a revolving fund certificate having a face amount of $300. The certificate is redeemable in cash at the discretion of the directors of the association and is subject to diminution by any future losses of the association, and has no fair market value when received by P. Since the certificate had no fair market value when received by P, no amount with respect to such certificate was taken into account by him in the year 1960. In 1965, P receives $300 cash from the association in full redemption of the certificate. Prior to 1965, he

had recovered through depreciation $2,000 of the cost of the tractor, leaving an unrecovered cost of $200 (the salvage value). For the year 1965, the redemption proceeds of $300 are applied against the unrecovered cost of $200, reducing the basis to zero, and the balance of the redemption proceeds, $100, is includible in the computation of P's gross income.

Example (3). Assume the same facts as in example (2), except that the certificate is redeemed in full on July 1, 1962. The full $300 received on redemption of the certificate will be applied against the unrecovered cost of the tractor as of January 1, 1962, computed as follows:

Cost of tractor, July 1, 1959		$2,200
Less: Depreciation for 1959 (6 mos.)	$200	
Depreciation for 1960	400	
Depreciation for 1961	400	1,000
Unrecovered cost on January 1, 1962		$1,200
Adjustment as of January 1, 1962 for proceeds of the redemption of the revolving fund certificate		300
Unrecovered cost on January 1, 1962, after adjustment		$ 900
Less: Salvage value		200
Basis for depreciation on January 1, 1962		$ 700

If P uses the tractor in his business until June 30, 1964, he would be entitled to the following depreciation allowances with respect to the tractor:

For 1962	$280	
For 1963	280	
For 1964 (6 mos.)	$140	$ 700
Balance to be depreciated		0

Example (4). Assume the same facts as in example (3), except that P sells the tractor in 1961. The entire $300 received in 1962 in redemption of the revolving fund certificate is includible in the computation of P's gross income for the year 1962.

(c) *Special rule.* If, for any taxable year ending before December 3, 1959, a taxpayer treated any patronage dividend received in the form of a document described in paragraph (b)(1)(iii) or (iv) of this section in accordance with the regulations then applicable (whether such dividend is subject to paragraph (b)(1) or (3) of this section), such taxpayer is not required to change the treatment

of such patronage dividends for any such prior taxable year. On the other hand, the taxpayer may, if he so desires, amend his income tax returns to treat the receipt of such patronage dividend in accordance with the provisions of this section, but no provision in this paragraph shall be construed as extending the period of limitations within which a claim for credit or refund may be filed under section 6511.

(d) *Per-unit retain certificates; tax treatment of cooperative associations; distribution and reinvestment alternative.* (1)(i) In the case of a taxable year to which this paragraph applies to a cooperative association, such association shall, in computing the amount paid or returned to a patron with respect to products marketed for such patron, take into account the stated dollar amount of any per-unit retain certificate (as defined in paragraph (g) of this section)—

(a) Which is issued during the payment period for such year (as defined in subparagraph (3) of this paragraph) with respect to such products,

(b) With respect to which the patron is a qualifying patron (as defined in subparagraph (2) of this paragraph), and

(c) Which clearly states the fact that the patron has agreed to treat the stated dollar amount thereof as representing a cash distribution to him which he has reinvested in the cooperative association.

(ii) No amount shall be taken into account by a cooperative association by reason of the issuance of a per-unit retain certificate to a patron who was not a qualifying patron with respect to such certificate. However, any amount paid in redemption of a per-unit retain certificate which was issued to a patron who was not a qualifying patron with respect to such certificate shall be taken into account by the cooperative in the year of redemption, as an amount paid or returned to such patron with respect to products marketed for him. This subdivision shall apply only to per-unit retain certificates issued with respect to taxable years of the cooperative association to which this paragraph applied to the association (that is, taxable years with respect to which per-unit retain certificates were issued to one or more patrons who are qualifying patrons).

(2)(i) A patron shall be considered to be a "qualifying patron" with respect to a per-unit retain certificate if there is in effect an agreement between the cooperative association and such patron which clearly provides that such patron agrees to treat the stated dollar amounts of all per-unit retain certificates issued to him by the association as representing cash distributions which he has constructively received and which he has, of his own choice, reinvested in the cooperative association. Such an agreement may be included in a by-law of the cooperative which is adopted prior to the time the products to which the per-unit retain certificates relate are marketed. However, except where there is in effect a "written agreement" described in subdivision (ii) of this subparagraph, a patron shall not be considered to be a "qualifying patron" with respect to a per-unit retain certificate if it has been established by a determination of the Tax Court of the United States, or any other court of competent jurisdiction, which has become final, that the

stated dollar amount of such certificate, or of a similar certificate issued under similar circumstances, to such patron or any other patron by the cooperative association, is not required to be included (as ordinary income) in the gross income of such patron, or such other patron, for the taxable year of the patron in which received.

(ii) The "written agreement" referred to in subdivision (i) of this subparagraph is an agreement in writing, signed by the patron, on file with the cooperative association, and revocable as provided in this subdivision. Unless such an agreement specifically provides to the contrary, it shall be effective for per-unit retain certificates issued with respect to the taxable year of the cooperative association in which the agreement is received by the association, and, unless revoked, for per-unit retain certificates issued with respect to all subsequent taxable years. A "written agreement" must be revocable by the patron at any time after the close of the taxable year in which it is made. To be effective, a revocation must be in writing, signed by the patron, and furnished to the cooperative association. A revocation shall be effective only for per-unit retain certificates issued with respect to taxable years of the cooperative association following the taxable year in which it is furnished to the association. Notwithstanding the preceding sentence, a revocation shall not be effective for per-unit retain certificates issued with respect to products marketed for the patron under a pooling arrangement in which such patron participated before such revocation. The following is an example of an agreement which would meet the requirements of this subparagraph: I agree that, for purposes of determining the amount I have received from this cooperative in payment for my goods, I shall treat the face amount of any per-unit retain certificates issued to me on and after .. .. as representing a cash distribution which I have constructively received and which I have reinvested in the cooperative.

(3) For purposes of this paragraph and paragraph (e) of this section, the payment period for any taxable year of the cooperative is the period beginning with the first day of such taxable year and ending with the 15th day of the 9th month following the close of such year.

(4) This paragraph shall apply to any taxable year of a cooperative association if, with respect to such taxable year, the association has issued per-unit retain certificates to one or more of its patrons who are qualifying patrons with respect to such certificates within the meaning of subparagraph (2) of this paragraph.

Reg. § 1.61-5(d)(2)

(e) *Tax treatment of cooperative association; taxable years for which paragraph (d) does not apply.* (1) In the case of a taxable year to which paragraph (d) of this section does not apply to a cooperative association, such association shall, in computing the amount paid or returned to a patron with respect to products marketed for such patron, take into account the fair market value (at the time of issue) of any per-unit retain certificates which are issued by the association with respect to such products during the payment period for such taxable year.

(2) An amount paid in redemption of a per-unit retain certificate issued with respect to a taxable year of the cooperative association for which paragraph (d) of this section did not apply to the association, shall, to the extent such amount exceeds the fair market value of the certificate at the time of its issue, be taken into account by the association in the year of redemption, as an amount paid or returned to a patron with respect to products marketed for such patron.

(3) For purposes of this paragraph and paragraph (f)(2) of this section, any per-unit retain certificate containing an unconditional promise to pay a fixed sum of money on demand or at a fixed or determinable time shall be considered to have a fair market value at the time of its issue, unless it is clearly established to the contrary. On the other hand, any per-unit retain certificate (other than capital stock) which is redeemable only in the discretion of the cooperative association, or which is otherwise subject to conditions beyond the control of the patron, shall be considered not to have any fair market value at the time of its issue, unless it is clearly established to the contrary.

(f) *Tax treatment of patron.* (1) The following rules apply for purposes of computing the amount includible in gross income with respect to a per-unit retain certificate which was issued to a patron by a cooperative association with respect to a taxable year of such association for which paragraph (d) of this section applies.

(i) If the patron is a qualifying patron with respect to such certificate (within the meaning of paragraph (d)(2) of this section), he shall, in accordance with his agreement, include (as ordinary income) the stated dollar amount of the certificate in gross income for his taxable year in which the certificate is received by him.

(ii) If the patron is not a qualifying patron with respect to such certificate, no amount is includible in gross income on the receipt of the certificate; however, any gain on the redemption, sale, or other disposition of such certificate shall, to the extent of the stated dollar amount thereof, be considered as gain from the sale or exchange of property which is not a capital asset.

(2) The amount of the fair market value of a per-unit retain certificate which is issued to a patron by a cooperative association with respect to a taxable year of the association for which paragraph (d) of this section does not apply shall be included, as ordinary income, in the gross income of the patron for the taxable year in which the certificate is received. Any gain on the redemption, sale, or other disposition of such a per-unit retain certificate shall, to the extent its stated dollar amount exceeds its fair market value at the time of issue, be treated as gain on the redemption, sale, or other disposition of property which is not a capital asset.

(g) *"Per-unit retain certificate" defined.* For purposes of paragraphs (d), (e), and (f) of this section, the term "per-unit retain certificate" means any capital stock, revolving fund certificate, retain certificate, certificate of indebtedness, letter of advice, or other written notice—

(1) Which is issued to a patron with respect to products marketed for such patron;

(2) Which discloses to the patron the stated dollar amount allocated to him on the books of the cooperative association; and

(3) The stated dollar amount of which is fixed without reference to net earnings.

(h) *Effective date.* This section shall not apply to any amount the tax treatment of which is prescribed in section 1385 and § 1.1385-1. Paragraphs (d), (e), and (f) of this section shall apply to per-unit retain certificates as defined in paragraph (g) of this section issued by a cooperative association during taxable years of the association beginning after April 30, 1966, with respect to products marketed for patrons during such years. [Reg. § 1.61-5.]

☐ [*T.D.* 6272, 11-25-57. *Amended by T.D.* 6428, 12-2-59; *T.D.* 6643, 4-1-63; *and T.D.* 6855, 10-14-65.]

[Reg. § 1.61-6]

§ 1.61-6. Gains derived from dealings in property.—(a) *In general.* Gain realized on the sale or exchange of property is included in gross income, unless excluded by law. For this purpose property includes tangible items, such as a building, and intangible items, such as goodwill. Generally, the gain is the excess of the amount realized over the unrecovered cost or other basis for the property sold or exchanged. The specific rules for computing the amount of gain or loss are contained in section 1001 and the regulations thereunder. When a part of a larger property is sold, the cost or other basis of the entire property shall be equitably apportioned among the several parts, and the gain realized or loss sustained on the part of the entire property sold is the difference between the selling price and the cost or other basis allocated to such part. The sale of each part is treated as a separate transaction and gain or loss shall be computed separately on each part. Thus, gain or loss shall be determined at the time of sale of each part and not deferred until the entire property has been disposed of. This rule may be illustrated by the following examples:

Example (1). A, a dealer in real estate, acquires a 10-acre tract for $10,000, which he divides into 20 lots. The $10,000 cost must be equitably apportioned among the lots so that on the sale of each A can determine his taxable gain or deductible loss.

Example (2). B purchases for $25,000 property consisting of a used car lot and adjoining filling station. At the time, the fair market value of the filling station is $15,000 and the fair market value of the used car lot is $10,000. Five years later B sells the filling station for $20,000 at a time when $2,000 has been properly allowed as depreciation thereon. B's gain on this sale is $7,000, since $7,000 is the amount by which the selling price of the filling station exceeds the portion of the cost equitably allocable to the filling station at the time of purchase reduced by the depreciation properly allowed.

(b) *Nontaxable exchanges.* Certain realized gains or losses on the sale or exchange of property are not "recognized", that is, are not included in or deducted from gross income at the time the transaction occurs. Gain or loss from such sales or exchanges is generally recognized at some later time. Examples of such sales or exchanges are the following:

(1) Certain formations, reorganizations, and liquidations of corporations, see sections 331, 333, 337, 351, 354, 355, and 361;

(2) Certain formations and distributions of partnerships, see sections 721 and 731;

(3) Exchange of certain property held for productive use or investment for property of like kind, see section 1031;

(4) A corporation's exchange of its stock for property, see section 1032;

(5) Certain involuntary conversions of property if replaced, see section 1033;

(6) Sale or exchange of residence if replaced, see section 1034;

(7) Certain exchanges of insurance policies and annuity contracts, see section 1035; and

(8) Certain exchanges of stock for stock in the same corporation, see section 1036.

(c) *Character of recognized gain.* Under subchapter P, chapter 1 of the Code, relating to capital gains and losses, certain gains derived from dealings in property are treated specially, and under certain circumstances the maximum rate of tax on such gains is 25 percent, as provided in section 1201. Generally, the property subject to this treatment is a "capital asset," or treated as a "capital asset". For definition of such assets, see sections 1221 and 1231, and the regulations thereunder. For some of the rules either granting or denying this special treatment, see the following sections and the regulations thereunder:

(1) Transactions between partner and partnership, section 707;

(2) Sale or exchange of property used in the trade or business and involuntary conversions, section 1231;

(3) Payment of bonds and other evidences of indebtedness, section 1232;

(4) Gains and losses from short sales, section 1233;

(5) Options to buy or sell, section 1234;

(6) Sale or exchange of patents, section 1235;

(7) Securities sold by dealers in securities, section 1236;

(8) Real property subdivided for sale, section 1237;

(9) Amortization in excess of depreciation, section 1238;

(10) Gain from sale for certain property between spouses or between an individual and a controlled corporation, section 1239;

(11) Taxability to employee of termination payments, section 1240. [Reg. § 1.61-6.]

□ [*T.D.* 6272, 11-25-57.]

[Reg. § 1.61-7]

§ 1.61-7. Interest.—(a) *In general.* As a general rule, interest received by or credited to the taxpayer constitutes gross income and is fully taxable. Interest income includes interest on savings or other bank deposits; interest on coupon bonds; interest on an open account, a promissory note, a mortgage, or a corporate bond or debenture; the interest portion of a condemnation award; usurious interest (unless by State law it is automatically converted to a payment on the principal); interest on legacies; interest on life insurance proceeds held under an agreement to pay interest thereon; and interest on refunds of Federal taxes. For rules determining the taxable year in which interest, including interest accrued or constructively received, is included in gross income, see section 451 and the regulations thereunder. For the inclusion of interest in income for the purpose of the retirement income credit, see section 37 and the regulations thereunder. For credit of tax withheld at source on interest on tax-free covenant bonds, see section 32 and the regulations thereunder. For rules relating to interest on certain deferred payments, see section 483 and the regulations thereunder.

(b) *Interest on Government obligations* — (1) *Wholly tax-exempt interest.* Interest upon the obligations of a State, Territory, or a possession of the United States, or any political subdivision of any of the foregoing, or of the District of Columbia, is wholly exempt from tax. Interest on certain United States obligations issued before March 1, 1941, is exempt from tax to the extent provided in the acts of Congress authorizing the various issues. See section 103 and the regulations thereunder.

(2) *Partially tax-exempt interest.* Interest earned on certain United States obligations is partly tax exempt and partly taxable. For example, the interest on United States Treasury bonds issued before March 1, 1941, to the extent that the principal of such bonds exceeds $5,000, is exempt from normal tax but is subject to surtax. See sections 35 and 103, and the regulations thereunder.

(3) *Fully taxable interest.* In general, interest on United States obligations issued on or after March 1, 1941, and obligations issued by any agency or instrumentality of the United States after that date, is fully taxable; but see section 103 and the regulations thereunder. A taxpayer using the cash receipts and disbursements method of accounting who owns United States savings bonds issued at a discount has an election as to when he will report the interest; see section 454 and the regulations thereunder.

(c) *Obligations bought at a discount; bonds bought when interest defaulted or accrued.* When notes, bonds, or other certificates of indebtedness are issued by a corporation or the Government at a discount and are later redeemed by the debtor at the face amount, the original discount is interest, except as otherwise provided by law. See also paragraph (b) of this section for the rules relating to Government bonds. If a taxpayer purchases bonds when interest has been defaulted or when the interest has accrued but has not been paid, any interest which is in arrears but has accrued at the time of purchase is not income and is not taxable as interest if subsequently paid. Such payments are returns of capital which reduce the remaining cost basis. Interest which accrues after the date of purchase, however, is taxable interest income for the year in which received or accrued

(depending on the method of accounting used by the taxpayer).

(d) *Bonds sold between interest dates; amounts received in excess of original issue discount; interest on life insurance.* When bonds are sold between interest dates, part of the sales price represents interest accrued to the date of the sale and must be reported as interest income. Amounts received in excess of the original issue discount upon the retirement or sale of a bond or other evidence of indebtedness may under some circumstances constitute capital gain instead of ordinary income. See section 1232 and the regulations thereunder. Interest payments on amounts payable as employees' death benefits (whether or not section 101(b) applies thereto) and on the proceeds of life insurance policies payable by reason of the insured's death constitute gross income under some circumstances. See section 101 and the regulations thereunder for details. Where accrued interest on unwithdrawn insurance policy dividends is credited annually and is subject to withdrawal annually by the taxpayer, such interest credits constitute gross income to such taxpayer as of the year of credit. However, if under the terms of the insurance policy the interest on unwithdrawn policy dividends is subject to withdrawal only on the anniversary date of the policy (or some other date specified therein), then such interest shall constitute gross income to the taxpayer for the taxable year in which such anniversary date (or other specified date) falls. [Reg. § 1.61-7.]

☐ [*T.D. 6272*, 11-25-57. *Amended by T.D.* 6723, 4-20-64; *and T.D. 6873*, 1-24-66.]

[Reg. § 1.61-8]

§ 1.61-8. Rents and royalties.—(a) *In general.* Gross income includes rentals received or accrued for the occupancy of real estate or the use of personal property. For the inclusion of rents in income for the purpose of the retirement income credit, see section 37 and the regulations thereunder. Gross income includes royalties. Royalties may be received from books, stories, plays, copyrights, trademarks, formulas, patents, and from the exploitation of natural resources, such as coal, gas, oil, copper, or timber. Payments received as a result of the transfer of patent rights may under some circumstances constitute capital gain instead of ordinary income. See section 1235 and the regulations thereunder. For special rules for certain income from natural resources, see subchapter I (611 and following), chapter 1 of the Code, and the regulations thereunder.

(b) *Advance rentals; cancellation payments.* Except as provided in section 467 and the regulations thereunder, gross income includes advance rentals, which must be included in income for the year of receipt regardless of the period covered or the method of accounting employed by the taxpayer. An amount received by a lessor from a lessee for cancelling a lease constitutes gross income for the year in which it is received, since it is essentially a substitute for rental payments. As to amounts received by a lessee for the cancellation of a lease, see section 1241 and the regulations thereunder.

(c) *Expenditures by lessee.* As a general rule, if a lessee pays any of the expenses of his lessor such payments are additional rental income of the lessor. If a lessee places improvements on real estate which constitute, in whole or in part, a substitute for rent, such improvements constitute rental income to the lessor. Whether or not improvements made by a lessee result in rental income to the lessor in a particular case depends upon the intention of the parties, which may be indicated either by the terms of the lease or by the surrounding circumstances. For the exclusion from gross income of income (other than rent) derived by a lessor of real property on the termination of a lease, representing the value of such property attributable to buildings erected or other improvements made by a lessee, see section 109 and the regulations thereunder. For the exclusion from gross income of a lessor corporation of certain of its income taxes on rental income paid by a lessee corporation under a lease entered into before January 1, 1954, see section 110 and the regulations thereunder. [Reg. § 1.61-8.]

☐ *[T.D. 6272, 11-25-57. Amended by T.D. 8820, 5-17-99.]*

[Reg. § 1.61-9]

§ 1.61-9. **Dividends.**—(a) *In general.* Except as otherwise specifically provided, dividends are included in gross income under sections 61 and 301. For the principal rules with respect to dividends includible in gross income, see section 316 and the regulations thereunder. As to distributions made or deemed to be made by regulated investment companies, see sections 851 through 855, and the regulations thereunder. As to distributions made by real estate investment trusts, see sections 856 through 858, and the regulations thereunder. See section 116 for the exclusion from gross income of $100 ($50 for dividends received in taxable years beginning before January 1, 1964) of dividends received by an individual, except those from certain corporations. Furthermore, dividends may give rise to a credit against tax under section 34, relating to dividends received by individuals (for dividends received on or before December 31, 1964), and under section 37, relating to retirement income.

(b) *Dividends in kind; stock dividends; stock redemptions.* Gross income includes dividends in property other than cash, as well as cash dividends. For amounts to be included in gross income when distributions of property are made, see section 301 and the regulations thereunder. A distribution of stock, or rights to acquire stock, in the corporation making the distribution is not a dividend except under the circumstances described in section 305(b). However, the term "dividend" includes a distribution of stock, or rights to acquire stock, in a corporation other than the corporation making the distribution. For determining when distributions in complete liquidation shall be treated as dividends, see section 333 and the regulations thereunder. For rules determining when amounts received in exchanges under section 354 or exchanges and distributions under section 355 shall be treated as dividends, see section 356 and the regulations thereunder.

(c) *Dividends on stock sold.* When stock is sold, and a dividend is both declared and paid after the sale, such dividend is not gross income to the seller. When stock is sold after the declaration of a dividend and after the date as of which the seller becomes entitled to the dividend, the dividend ordinarily is income to the seller. When stock is sold between the time of declaration and the time of payment of the dividend, and the sale takes place at such time that the purchaser becomes entitled to the dividend, the dividend ordinarily is income to him. The fact that the purchaser may have included the amount of the dividend in his purchase price in contemplation of receiving the dividend does not exempt him from tax. Nor can the purchaser deduct the added amount he advanced to the seller in anticipation of the dividend. That added amount is merely part of the purchase price of the stock. In some cases, however, the purchaser may be considered to be the recipient of the dividend even though he has not received the legal title to the stock itself and does not himself receive the dividend. For example, if the seller retains the legal title to the stock as trustee solely for the purpose of securing the payment of the purchase price, with the understanding that he is to apply the dividends received from time to time in reduction of the purchase price, the dividends are considered to be income to the purchaser. [Reg. § 1.61-9.]

☐ *[T.D. 6272, 11-25-57. Amended by T.D. 6598, 4-25-62; and T.D. 6777, 12-15-64.]*

[Reg. § 1.61-10]

§ 1.61-10. **Alimony and separate maintenance payments; annuities; income from life insurance and endowment contracts.**—(a) *In general.* Alimony and separate maintenance payments, annuities, and income from life insurance and endowment contracts in general constitute gross income, unless excluded by law. Annuities paid by religious, charitable, and educational corporations are generally taxable to the same extent as other annuities. An annuity charged upon devised land is taxable to the donee-annuitant to the extent that it becomes payable out of the rents or other income of the land, whether or not it is a charge upon the income of the land.

(b) *Cross references.* For the detailed rules relating to—

(1) Alimony and separate maintenance payments, see section 71 and the regulations thereunder;

(2) Annuities, certain proceeds of endowment and life insurance contracts, see section 72 and the regulations thereunder;

(3) Life insurance proceeds paid by reason of death of insured, employees' death benefits, see section 101 and the regulations thereunder;

(4) Annuities paid by employees' trusts, see section 402 and the regulations thereunder;

(5) Annuities purchased for employee by employer, see section 403 and the regulations thereunder. [Reg. § 1.61-10.]

☐ [*T.D.* 6272, 11-25-57.]

[Reg. § 1.61-11]

§ 1.61-11. **Pensions.**—(a) *In general.* Pensions and retirement allowances paid either by the Government or by private persons constitute gross income unless excluded by law. Usually, where the taxpayer did not contribute to the cost of a pension and was not taxable on his employer's contributions, the full amount of the pension is to be included in his gross income. But see sections 72, 402, and 403, and the regulations thereunder. When amounts are received from other types of pensions, a portion of the payment may be excluded from gross income. Under some circumstances, amounts distributed from a pension plan in excess of the employee's contributions may constitute long-term capital gain, rather than ordinary income.

(b) *Cross references.* For the inclusion of pensions in income for the purpose of the retirement income credit, see section 37 and the regulations thereunder. Detailed rules concerning the extent to which pensions and retirement allowances are to be included in or excluded from gross income are contained in other sections of the Code and the regulations thereunder. Amounts received as pensions or annuities under the Social Security Act (42 U.S.C. ch. 7) or the Railroad Retirement Act (45 U.S.C. ch. 9) are excluded from gross

income. For other partial and total exclusions from gross income, see the following:

(1) Annuities in general, section 72 and the regulations thereunder;

(2) Employees' annuities, sections 402 and 403 and the regulations thereunder;

(3) References to other acts of Congress exempting veterans' pensions and railroad retirement annuities and pensions, section 122. [Reg. § 1.61-11.]

☐ [*T.D.* 6272, 11-25-57. *Amended by T.D.* 6598, 4-25-62; *and T.D.* 6777, 12-15-64.]

[Reg. § 1.61-12]

§ 1.61-12. **Income from discharge of indebtedness.**—(a) *In general.* The discharge of indebtedness, in whole or in part, may result in the realization of income. If, for example, an individual performs services for a creditor, who in consideration thereof cancels the debt, the debtor realizes income in the amount of the debt as compensation for his services. A taxpayer may realize income by the payment or purchase of his obligations at less than their face value. In general, if a shareholder in a corporation which is indebted to him gratuitously forgives the debt, the transaction amounts to a contribution to the capital of the corporation to the extent of the principal of the debt.

(b) *Proceedings under Bankruptcy Act.* (1) Income is not realized by a taxpayer by virtue of the discharge, under section 14 of the Bankruptcy Act (11 U.S.C. 32), of his indebtedness as the result of an adjudication in bankruptcy, or by virtue of an agreement among his creditors not consummated under any provision of the Bankruptcy Act, if immediately thereafter the taxpayer's liabilities exceed the value of his assets. Furthermore, unless one of the principal purposes of seeking a confirmation under the Bankruptcy Act is the avoidance of income tax, income is not realized by a taxpayer in the case of a cancellation or reduction of his indebtedness under—

(i) A plan of a corporate reorganization confirmed under Chapter X of the Bankruptcy Act (11 U.S.C., ch. 10);

(ii) An "arrangement" or a "real property arrangement" confirmed under Chapter XI or XII, respectively, of the Bankruptcy Act (11 U.S.C., ch. 11, 12); or

(iii) A "wage earner's plan" confirmed under Chapter XIII of the Bankruptcy Act (11 U.S.C., ch. 13).

(2) For adjustment of basis of certain property in the case of cancellation or reduction of indebtedness resulting from a proceeding under

the Bankruptcy Act, see the regulations under section 1016.

(c) *Issuance and repurchase of debt instruments*—(1) *Issuance.* An issuer does not realize gain or loss upon the issuance of a debt instrument. For rules relating to an issuer's interest deduction for a debt instrument issued with bond issuance premium, see § 1.163-13.

(2) *Repurchase*—(i) *In general.* An issuer does not realize gain or loss upon the repurchase of a debt instrument. However, if a debt instrument provides for payments denominated in, or determined by reference to, a nonfunctional currency, an issuer may realize a currency gain or loss upon the repurchase of the instrument. See section 988 and the regulations thereunder. For purposes of this paragraph (c)(2), the term *repurchase* includes the retirement of a debt instrument, the conversion of a debt instrument into stock of the issuer, and the exchange (including an exchange under section 1001) of a newly issued debt instrument for an existing debt instrument.

(ii) *Repurchase at a discount.* An issuer realizes income from the discharge of indebtedness upon the repurchase of a debt instrument for an amount less than its adjusted issue price (within the meaning of § 1.1275-1(b)). The amount of discharge of indebtedness income is equal to the excess of the adjusted issue price over the repurchase price. See section 108 and the regulations thereunder for additional rules relating to income from discharge of indebtedness. For example, to determine the repurchase price of a debt instrument that is repurchased through the issuance of a new debt instrument, see section 108(e)(10).

(iii) *Repurchase at a premium.* An issuer may be entitled to a repurchase premium deduction upon the repurchase of a debt instrument for an amount greater than its adjusted issue price (within the meaning of § 1.1275-1(b)). See § 1.163-7(c) for the treatment of repurchase premium.

(iv) *Effective date.* This paragraph (c)(2) applies to debt instruments repurchased on or after March 2, 1998.

(d) *Cross references.* For exclusion from gross income of—

(1) Income from discharge of indebtedness in certain cases, see sections 108 and 1017, and regulations thereunder;

(2) Forgiveness of Government payments to encourage exploration, development, and mining for defense purposes, see section 621 and regulations thereunder.

(e) *Cross reference.* For rules relating to the treatment of liabilities on the sale or other disposition of encumbered property, see § 1.1001-2. [Reg. § 1.61-12.]

☐ [*T.D.* 6272, 11-25-57. *Amended by T.D.* 6653, 5-22-63; *T.D.* 6984, 12-23-68; *T.D.* 7741, 12-11-80 *and T.D.* 8746, 12-30-97.]

[Reg. § 1.61-13]

§ 1.61-13. Distributive share of partnership gross income; income in respect of a decedent; income from an interest in an estate or trust.—(a) *In general.* A partner's distributive share of patnership gross income (under section 702(c)) constitutes gross income to him. Income in respect of a decedent (under section 691) constitutes gross income to the recipient. Income from an interest in an estate or trust constitutes gross income under the detailed rules of part I (section 641 and following), subchapter J, chapter 1 of the Code. In many cases, these sections also determine who is to include in his gross income the income from an estate or trust.

(b) *Creation of sinking fund by corporation.* If a corporation, for the sole purpose of securing the payment of its bonds or other indebtedness, places property in trust or sets aside certain amounts in a sinking fund under the control of a trustee who may be authorized to invest and reinvest such sums from time to time, the property or fund thus set aside by the corporation and held by the trustee is an asset of the corporation, and any gain arising therefrom is income of the corporation and shall be included as such in its gross income. [Reg. § 1.61-13.]

☐ [*T.D.* 6272, 11-25-57.]

[Reg. § 1.61-14]

§ 1.61-14. Miscellaneous items of gross income.—(a) *In general.* In addition to the items enumerated in section 61(a), there are many other kinds of gross income. For example, punitive damages such as treble damages under the antitrust laws and exemplary damages for fraud are gross income. Another person's payment of the taxpayer's income taxes constitutes gross income to the taxpayer unless excluded by law. Illegal gains constitute gross income. Treasure trove, to the extent of its value in United States currency, constitutes gross income for the taxable year in which it is reduced to undisputed possession.

(b) *Cross references.* (1) Prizes and awards, see section 74 and regulations thereunder;

(2) Damages for personal injury or sickness, see section 104 and the regulations thereunder;

(3) Income taxes paid by lessee corporation, see section 110 and regulations thereunder;

Reg. § 1.61-13(a)

(4) Scholarships and fellowship grants, see section 117 and regulations thereunder;

(5) Miscellaneous exemptions under other Acts of Congress, see section 122;

(6) Tax-free covenant bonds, see section 1451 and regulations thereunder.

(7) Notional principal contracts, see § 1.446-3. [Reg. § 1.61-14.]

☐ [*T.D. 6272, 11-25-57. Amended by T.D. 6856, 10-19-65 and T.D. 8491, 10-8-93.*]

[Reg. § 1.61-15]

§ 1.61-15. Options received as payment of income.—(a) *In general.* Except as otherwise provided in § 1.61-2(d)(6)(i) (relating to certain restricted property transferred after June 30, 1969), if any person receives an option in payment of an amount constituting compensation of such person (or any other person), such option is subject to the rules contained in § 1.421-6 for purposes of determining when income is realized in connection with such option and the amount of such income. In this regard, the rules of § 1.421-6 apply to an option received in payment of an amount constituting compensation regardless of the form of the transaction. Thus, the rules of § 1.421-6 apply to an option transferred for less than its fair market value in a transaction taking the form of a sale or exchange if the difference between the amount paid for the option and its fair market value at the time of transfer is the payment of an amount constituting compensation of the transferee or any other person. This section, for example, makes the rules of § 1.421-6 applicable to options granted in whole or partial payment for services of an independent contractor. If an amount money or property is paid for an option to which this paragraph applies, then the amount paid shall be part of the basis of such option.

(b) *Options to which paragraph (a) does not apply.* (1) Paragraph (a) of this section does not apply to:

(i) An option which is subject to the rules contained in section 421; and

(ii) An option which is not granted as the payment of an amount constituting compensation, such as an option which is acquired solely as an investment (including an option which is part of an investment unit described in paragraph (b) of § 1.1232-3). For rules relating to the taxation of options described in this subdivision, see section 1234 and the regulations thereunder.

(2) If a person acquires an option which is not subject to the rules contained in section 421, and if such option has a readily ascertainable fair market value, such person may establish that such option was not acquired as payment of an amount constituting compensation by showing that the amount of money or its equivalent paid for the option equaled the readily ascertainable fair market value of the option. If a person acquires an option which is not subject to the rules contained in section 421, and if such option does not have a readily ascertainable fair market value, then to establish that such option was not acquired as payment of an amount constituting compensation, such person must show that, from an examination of all the surrounding circumstances, there was no reason for the option to have been granted as the payment of an amount constituting compensation. For example, such person must show that he had neither rendered nor was obligated to render substantial services in consideration for the granting of the option. In determining whether an option, such as an option acquired in connection with an obligation as part of an investment unit, has been granted as compensation for services, the ordinary services performed by an investor in his own self-interest in connection with his investing activities will not be treated as the consideration for the grant of the option. For example, if a small business investment company takes an active part in the management of its debtor small business company, the rendering of such management services will not be treated as the consideration for the granting of the option, provided such services are rendered for an independent consideration, or are merely protective of the small business investment company's investment in the borrower. See paragraph (c) of § 1.421-6 for the meaning of the term "readily ascertainable fair market value."

(c) *Statement required in connection with certain options.* (1) Any person acquiring any option to purchase securities (other than an option described in subparagraph (2) of this paragraph) shall attach a statement to his income tax return for the taxable year in which the option was acquired. For the definition of the term "securities", see section 165(g)(2).

(2) The statement otherwise required by subparagraph (1) of this paragraph shall not be required with respect to the following options:

(i) Options subject to the rules contained in section 305(a) or section 421;

(ii) Options acquired as part of an investment unit consisting of an option and a debenture, note, or other similar obligation—

(a) If such unit is acquired as part of a public offering and the amount of money or its equivalent paid for such unit is not less than the public offering price, or

(b) If such unit is actively traded on an established market and the amount of money or

Reg. § 1.61-15(c)(2)

its equivalent paid for such unit is not less than the price paid for such unit in contemporaneous purchases of such unit by persons independent of both the seller and the taxpayer;

(iii) Options acquired as part of a public offering, if the amount of money or its equivalent paid for such option is not less than the public offering price; and

(iv) Options which are actively traded on an established market and which are acquired for money or its equivalent at a price not less than the price paid for such options in contemporaneous purchases of such options by persons independent of both the seller and the taxpayer.

(3) The statement required by subparagraph (1) of this paragraph shall contain the following information:

(i) Name and address of the taxpayer;

(ii) Description of the securities subject to the option (including number of shares of stock);

(iii) Period during which the option is exercisable;

(iv) Whether the option had a readily ascertainable fair market value at date of grant; and

(v) Whether the option is subject to paragraph (a) of this section.

(4) If the statement required by subparagraph (1) of this paragraph indicates either that the option is not subject to paragraph (a) of this section, or that the option is subject to paragraph (a) of this section but that such option had a readily ascertainable fair market value at date of grant, then such statement shall contain the following additional information:

(i) Option price;

(ii) Value at date of grant of securities subject to the option;

(iii) Restrictions (if any) on exercise or transfer of option;

(iv) Restrictions (if any) on transfer of securities subject to the option;

(v) Value of the option (if readily ascertainable);

(vi) How value of option was determined;

(vii) Amount of money (or its equivalent) paid for the option;

(viii) Person from whom the option was acquired;

(ix) A concise description of the circumstances surrounding the acquisition of the option and any other factors relied upon by the taxpayer to establish that the option is not subject to paragraph (a) of this section, or, if the option is treated by the taxpayer as subject to paragraph (a) of this section, that the option had a readily ascertainable fair market value at date of grant.

(d) *Effective date.* This section shall apply to options granted after July 11, 1963, other than options required to be granted pursuant to the terms of a written contract entered into on or before such date. [Reg. § 1.61-15.]

☐ [*T.D. 6696, 12-11-63. Amended by T.D. 6706, 3-2-64; T.D. 6984, 12-23-68* and *T.D. 7554, 7-21-78.*]

→ *Caution: Reg. § 1.61-21 applies to fringe benefits provided after 1988. See Temporary Reg. § 1.61-2T for tax treatment of fringe benefits for 1985— 1988.*←

[Reg. § 1.61-21]

§ 1.61-21. Taxation of fringe benefits.—(a) *Fringe benefits*—(1) *In general.* Section 61(a)(1) provides that, except as otherwise provided in subtitle A of the Internal Revenue Code of 1986, gross income includes compensation for services, including fees, commissions, fringe benefits, and similar items. For an outline of the regulations under this section relating to fringe benefits, see paragraph (a)(7) of this section. Examples of fringe benefits include: an employer-provided automobile, a flight on an employer-provided aircraft, an employer-provided free or discounted commercial airline flight, an employer-provided vacation, an employer-provided discount on property or services, an employer provided membership in a country club or other social club, and an employer-provided ticket to an entertainment or sporting event.

(2) *Fringe benefits excluded from income.* To the extent that a particular fringe benefit is specifically excluded from gross income pursuant to another section of subtitle A of the Internal Revenue Code of 1986, that section shall govern the treatment of that fringe benefit. Thus, if the requirements of the governing section are satisfied, the fringe benefits may be excludable from gross income. Examples of excludable fringe benefits include qualified tuition reductions provided to an employee (section 117(d)); meals or lodging furnished to an employee for the convenience of the employer (section 119); benefits provided under a dependent care assistance program (section 129); and no-additional-cost services, qualified employee discounts, working condition fringes, and de minimis fringes (section 132). Similarly, the value of the use by an employee of an employer-provided vehicle or a flight provided to an em-

Reg. § 1.61-21(a)(1)

→ *Caution: Reg. § 1.61-21 applies to fringe benefits provided after 1988. See Temporary Reg. § 1.61-2T for tax treatment of fringe benefits for 1985—1988.*←

ployee on an employer-provided aircraft may be excludable from income under section 105 (because, for example, the transportation is provided for medical reasons) if and to the extent that the requirements of that section are satisfied. Section 134 excludes from gross income "qualified military benefits." An example of a benefit that is not a qualified military benefit is the personal use of an employer-provided vehicle. The fact that another section of subtitle A of the Internal Revenue Code addresses the taxation of a particular fringe benefit will not preclude section 61 and the regulations thereunder from applying, to the extent that they are not inconsistent with such other section. For example, many fringe benefits specifically addressed in other sections of subtitle A of the Internal Revenue Code are excluded from gross income only to the extent that they do not exceed specific dollar or percentage limits, or only if certain other requirements are met. If the limits are exceeded or the requirements are not met, some or all of the fringe benefit may be includible in gross income pursuant to section 61. See paragraph (b)(3) of this section.

(3) *Compensation for services.* A fringe benefit provided in connection with the performance of services shall be considered to have been provided as compensation for such services. Refraining from the performance of services (such as pursuant to a covenant not to compete) is deemed to be the performance of services for purposes of this section.

(4) *Person to whom fringe benefit is taxable—*(i) *In general.* A taxable fringe benefit is included in the income of the person performing the services in connection with which the fringe benefit is furnished. Thus, a fringe benefit may be taxable to a person even though that person did not actually receive the fringe benefit. If a fringe benefit is furnished to someone other than the service provider such benefit is considered in this section as furnished to the service provider, and use by the other person is considered use by the service provider. For example, the provision of an automobile by an employer to an employee's spouse in connection with the performance of services by the employee is taxable to the employee. The automobile is considered available to the employee and use by the employee's spouse is considered use by the employee.

(ii) *All persons to whom benefits are taxable referred to as employees.* The person to whom a fringe benefit is taxable need not be an employee of the provider of the fringe benefit, but

may be, for example, a partner, director, or an independent contractor. For convenience, the term "employee" includes any person performing services in connection with which a fringe benefit is furnished, unless otherwise specifically provided in this section.

(5) *Provider of a fringe benefit referred to as an employer.* The "provider" of a fringe benefit is that person for whom the services are performed, regardless of whether that person actually provides the fringe benefit to the recipient. The provider of a fringe benefit need not be the employer of the recipient of the fringe benefit, but may be, for example, a client or customer of the employer or of an independent contractor. For convenience, the term "employer" includes any provider of a fringe benefit in connection with payment for the performance of services, unless otherwise specifically provided in this section.

(6) *Effective date.* Except as otherwise provided, this section is effective as of January 1, 1989 with respect to fringe benefits provided after December 31, 1988. See § 1.61-2T for rules in effect from January 1, 1985, to December 31, 1988.

(7) *Outline of this section.* The following is an outline of the regulations in this section relating to fringe benefits:

§ 1.61-21(a). *Fringe benefits.*

(1) In general.

(2) Fringe benefits excluded from income.

(3) Compensation for services.

(4) Person to whom fringe benefit is taxable.

(5) Provider of a fringe benefit referred to as an employer.

(6) Effective date.

(7) Outline of this section.

§ 1.61-21(b). *Valuation of fringe benefits.*

(1) In general.

(2) Fair market value.

(3) Exclusion from income based on cost.

(4) Fair market value of the availability of an employer-provided vehicle.

(5) Fair market value of chauffeur services.

(6) Fair market value of a flight on an employer-provided piloted aircraft.

(7) Fair market value of the use of an employer-provided aircraft for which the employer does not furnish a pilot.

§ 1.61-21(c). *Special valuation rules.*

Reg. § 1.61-21(a)(7)

→ *Caution: Reg. § 1.61-21 applies to fringe benefits provided after 1988. See Temporary Reg. § 1.61-2T for tax treatment of fringe benefits for 1985—1988.*←

(1) In general.

(2) Use of the special valuation rules.

(3) Additional rules for using special valuation.

(4) Application of section 414 to employers.

(5) Valuation formulae contained in the special valuation rules.

(6) Modification of the special valuation rules.

(7) Special accounting rule.

§ 1.61-21(d). *Automobile lease valuation rule.*

(1) In general.

(2) Calculation of Annual Lease Value.

(3) Services included in, or excluded from, the Annual Lease Value Table.

(4) Availability of an automobile for less than an entire calendar year.

(5) Fair market value.

(6) Special rules for continuous availability of certain automobiles.

(7) Consistency rules.

§ 1.61-21(e). *Vehicle cents-per-mile valuation rule.*

(1) In general.

(2) Definition of vehicle.

(3) Services included in, or excluded from, the cents-per-mile rate.

(4) Valuation of personal use only.

(5) Consistency rules.

§ 1.61-21(f). *Commuting valuation rule.*

(1) In general.

(2) Special rules.

(3) Commuting value.

(4) Definition of vehicle.

(5) Control employee defined—Non-government employer.

(6) Control employee defined—Government employer.

(7) "Compensation" defined.

§ 1.61-21(g). *Non-commercial flight valuation rule.*

(1) In general.

(2) Eligible flights and eligible aircraft.

(3) Definition of a flight.

(4) Personal and non-personal flights.

(5) Aircraft valuation formula.

(6) Discretion to provide new formula.

(7) Aircraft multiples.

(8) Control employee defined—Non-government employer.

(9) Control employee defined—Government employer.

(10) "Compensation" defined.

(11) Treatment of former employees.

(12) Seating capacity rule.

(13) Erroneous use of the non-commercial flight valuation rule.

(14) Consistency rules.

§ 1.61-21(h). *Commercial flight valuation rule.*

(1) In general.

(2) Space-available flight.

(3) Commercial aircraft.

(4) Timing of inclusion.

(5) Consistency rules.

§ 1.61-21(i). [*Reserved*]

§ 1.61-21(j). *Valuation of meals provided at an employer-operated eating facility for employees.*

(1) In general.

(2) Valuation formula.

§ 1.61-21(k). *Commuting valuation rule for certain employees.*

(1) In general.

(2) Trip-by-trip basis.

(3) Commuting value.

(4) Definition of employer-provided transportation.

(5) Unsafe conditions.

(6) Qualified employee defined.

(7) Examples.

(8) Effective date.

(b) *Valuation of fringe benefits—(1) In general.* An employee must include in gross income the amount by which the fair market value of the fringe benefit exceeds the sum of—

(i) The amount, if any, paid for the benefit by or on behalf of the recipient, and

(ii) The amount, if any, specifically excluded from gross income by some other section of subtitle A of the Internal Revenue Code of 1986.

Therefore, for example, if the employee pays fair market value for what is received, no amount is includible in the gross income of the employee. In general, the determination of the fair market value of a fringe benefit must be made before subtracting out the amount, if any, paid for the

Reg. § 1.61-21(b)(1)

→ *Caution: Reg. § 1.61-21 applies to fringe benefits provided after 1988. See Temporary Reg. § 1.61-2T for tax treatment of fringe benefits for 1985—1988.*←

benefit and the amount, if any, specifically excluded from gross income by another section of subtitle A. See paragraphs (d)(2)(ii) and (e)(1)(iii) of this section.

(2) *Fair market value.* In general, fair market value is determined on the basis of all the facts and circumstances. Specifically, the fair market value of a fringe benefit is the amount that an individual would have to pay for the particular fringe benefit in an arm's-length transaction. Thus, for example, the effect of any special relationship that may exist between the employer and the employee must be disregarded. Similarly, an employee's subjective perception of the value of a fringe benefit is not relevant to the determination of the fringe benefit's fair market value nor is the cost incurred by the employer determinative of its fair market value. For special rules relating to the valuation of certain fringe benefits, see paragraph (c) of this section.

(3) *Exclusion from income based on cost.* If a statutory exclusion phrased in terms of cost applies to the provision of a fringe benefit, section 61 does not require the inclusion in the recipient's gross income of the difference between the fair market value and the excludable cost of that fringe benefit. For example, section 129 provides an exclusion from an employee's gross income for amounts contributed by an employer to a dependent care assistance program for employees. Even if the fair market value of the dependent care assistance exceeds the employer's cost, the excess is not subject to inclusion under section 61 and this section. However, if the statutory cost exclusion is a limited amount, the fair market value of the fringe benefit attributable to any excess cost is subject to inclusion. This would be the case, for example, where an employer pays or incurs a cost of more than $5,000 to provide dependent care assistance to an employee.

(4) *Fair market value of the availability of an employer-provided vehicle*—(i) *In general.* If the vehicle special valuation rules of paragraphs (d), (e), or (f) of this section do not apply with respect to an employer-provided vehicle, the value of the availability of that vehicle is determined under the general valuation principles set forth in this section. In general, that value equals the amount that an individual would have to pay in an arm's-length transaction to lease the same or comparable vehicle on the same or comparable conditions in the geographic area in which the vehicle is available for use. An example of a comparable condition is the amount of time that the vehicle is available to the employee for use, e.g., a one-year period. Unless the employee can substantiate that the same or comparable vehicle could have been leased on a cents-per-mile basis, the value of the availability of the vehicle cannot be computed by applying a cents-per-mile rate to the number of miles the vehicle is driven.

(ii) *Certain equipment excluded.* The fair market value of a vehicle does not include the fair market value of any specialized equipment not susceptible to personal use or any telephone that is added to or carried in the vehicle, provided that the presence of that equipment or telephone is necessitated by, and attributable to, the business needs of the employer. However, the value of specialized equipment must be included, if the employee to whom the vehicle is available uses the specialized equipment in a trade or business of the employee other than the employee's trade or business of being an employee of the employer.

(5) *Fair market value of chauffeur services*—(i) *Determination of value*—(A) *In general.* The fair market value of chauffeur services provided to the employee by the employer is the amount that an individual would have to pay in an arm's-length transaction to obtain the same or comparable chauffeur services in the geographic area for the period in which the services are provided. In determining the applicable fair market value, the amount of time, if any, the chauffeur remains on-call to perform chauffeur services must be included. For example, assume that A, an employee of corporation M, needs a chauffeur to be on-call to provide services to A during a twenty-four hour period. If during that twenty-four hour period, the chauffeur actually drives A for only six hours, the fair market value of the chauffeur services would have to be the value of having a chauffeur on-call for a twenty-four hour period. The cost of taxi fare or limousine service for the six hours the chauffeur actually drove A would not be an accurate measure of the fair market value of chauffeur services provided to A. Moreover, all other aspects of the chauffeur's services (including any special qualifications of the chauffeur (e.g., training in evasive driving skills) or the ability of the employee to choose the particular chauffeur) must be taken into consideration.

(B) *Alternative valuation with reference to compensation paid.* Alternatively, the fair market value of the chauffeur services may be determined by reference to the compensation (as defined in paragraph (b)(5)(ii)) received by the chauffeur from the employer.

Reg. § 1.61-21(b)(5)

→ *Caution: Reg. § 1.61-21 applies to fringe benefits provided after 1988. See Temporary Reg. § 1.61-2T for tax treatment of fringe benefits for 1985— 1988.*←

(C) *Separate valuation for chauffeur services.* The value of chauffeur services is determined separately from the value of the availability of an employer-provided vehicle.

(ii) *Definition of compensation*—(A) *In general.* For purposes of this paragraph (b)(5)(ii), the term "compensation" means compensation as defined in section 414(q)(7) and the fair market value of nontaxable lodging (if any) provided by the employer to the chauffeur in the current year.

(B) *Adjustments to compensation*—For purposes of this paragraph (b)(5)(ii), a chauffeur's compensation is reduced proportionately to reflect the amount of time during which the chauffeur performs substantial services for the employer other than as a chauffeur and is not on-call as a chauffeur. For example, assume a chauffeur is paid $25,000 a year for working a ten-hour day, five days a week and also receives $5,000 in nontaxable lodging. Further assume that during four hours of each day, the chauffeur is not on-call to perform services as a chauffeur because that individual is performing secretarial functions for the employer. Then, for purposes of determining the fair market value of this chauffeur's services, the employer may reduce the chauffeur's compensation by $\frac{4}{10}$ or $12,000 (.4 × ($25,000 + $5,000) = $12,000). Therefore, in this example, the fair market value of the chauffeur's services is $18,000 ($30,000 − $12,000). However, for purposes of this paragraph (b)(5)(ii), a chauffeur's compensation is not to be reduced by any amounts paid to the chauffeur for time spent "on-call," even though the chauffeur actually performs other services for the employer during such time. For purposes of this paragraph (b)(5)(ii), a determination that a chauffeur is performing substantial services for the employer other than as a chauffeur is based upon the facts and circumstances of each situation. An employee will be deemed to be performing substantial services for the employer other than as a chauffeur if a certain portion of each working day is regularly spent performing other services for the employer.

(iii) *Calculation of chauffeur services for personal purposes of the employee.* The fair market value of chauffeur services provided to the employee for personal purposes may be determined by multiplying the fair market value of chauffeur services, as determined pursuant to paragraph (b)(5)(i)(A) or (B) of this section, by a fraction, the numerator of which is equal to the sum of the hours spent by the chauffeur actually providing personal driving services to the employee and the hours spent by the chauffeur in "personal on-call time," and the denominator of which is equal to all hours the chauffeur spends in driving services of any kind paid for by the employer, including all hours that are "on-call."

(iv) *Definition of on-call time.* For purposes of this paragraph, the term "on-call time" means the total amount of time that the chauffeur is not engaged in the actual performance of driving services, but during which time the chauffeur is available to perform such services. With respect to a round-trip, time spent by a chauffeur waiting for an employee to make a return trip is generally not treated as on-call time; rather such time is treated as part of the round-trip.

(v) *Definition of personal on-call time.* For purposes of this paragraph, the term "personal on-call time" means the amount of time outside the employee's normal working hours for the employer when the chauffeur is available to the employee to perform driving services.

(vi) *Presumptions.* (A) An employee's normal working hours will be presumed to consist of a ten hour period during which the employee usually conducts business activities for that employer.

(B) It will be presumed that if the chauffeur is on-call to provide driving services to an employee during the employee's normal working hours, then that on-call time will be performed for business purposes.

(C) Similarly, if the chauffeur is on-call to perform driving services to an employee after normal working hours, then that on-call time will be presumed to be "personal on-call time."

(D) The presumptions set out in paragraph (b)(5)(vi)(A), (B), and (C) of this section may be rebutted. For example, an employee may demonstrate by adequate substantiation that his or her normal working hours consist of more than ten hours. Furthermore, if the employee keeps adequate records and is able to substantiate that some portion of the driving services performed by the chauffeur after normal working hours is attributable to business purposes, then personal on-call time may be reduced by an amount equal to such personal on-call time multiplied by a fraction, the numerator of which is equal to the time spent by the chauffeur after normal working hours driving the employee for business purposes, and the denominator of which is equal to the total time spent by the chauffeur driving the employee after normal working hours for all purposes.

Reg. § 1.61-21(b)(5)

→ *Caution: Reg. § 1.61-21 applies to fringe benefits provided after 1988. See Temporary Reg. § 1.61-2T for tax treatment of fringe benefits for 1985— 1988.*←

(vii) *Examples.* The rules of this paragraph (b)(5) may be illustrated by the following examples:

Example (1). An employer makes available to employee A an automobile and a full-time chauffeur B (who performs no other services for A's employer) for an entire calendar year. Assume that the automobile lease valuation rule of paragraph (d) of this section is used and that the Annual Lease Value of the automobile is $9,250. Assume further that B's compensation for the year is $12,000 (as defined in section 414(q)(7)) and that B is furnished lodging with a value of $3,000 that is excludable from B's gross income. The maximum amount subject to inclusion in A's gross income for use of the automobile and chauffeur is therefore $24,250 ($12,000 + $3,000 + $9,250). If 70 percent of the miles placed on the automobile during the year are for A's employer's business, then $6,475 is excludable from A's gross income with respect to the automobile as a working condition fringe ($9,250 × .70). Thus, $2,775 is includible in A's gross income with respect to the automobile ($9,250 − $6,475). With respect to the chauffeur, if 20 percent of the chauffeur's time is spent actually driving A or being on-call to drive A for personal purposes, then $3,000 is includible in A's income (.20 × $15,000). Eighty percent of $15,000, or $12,000, is excluded from A's income as a working condition fringe.

Example (2). Assume the same facts as in example (1) except that in addition to providing chauffeur services, B is responsible for performing substantial non-chauffeur-related duties (such as clerical or secretarial functions) during which time B is not "on-call" as a chauffeur. If B spends only 75 percent of the time performing chauffeur services, then the maximum amount subject to inclusion in A's gross income for use of the automobile and chauffeur is $20,500 (($15,000 × .75) + $9,250). If B is actually driving A for personal purposes or is on-call to drive A for personal purposes for 20 percent of the time during which B is available to provide chauffeur services, then $2,250 is includible in A's gross income (.20 × $11,250). The income inclusion with respect to the automobile is the same as in example (1).

Example (3). Assume the same facts as in example (2) except that while B is performing non-chauffeur-related duties, B is on call as A's chauffeur. No part of B's compensation is excluded when determining the value of the benefit provided to A. Thus, as in example (1), $3,000 is includible in A's gross income with respect to the chauffeur.

(6) *Fair market value of a flight on an employer-provided piloted aircraft—*(i) *In general.* If the non-commercial flight special valuation rule of paragraph (g) of this section does not apply, the value of a flight on an employer-provided piloted aircraft is determined under the general valuation principles set forth in this paragraph.

(ii) *Value of flight.* If an employee takes a flight on an employer-provided piloted aircraft and that employee's flight is primarily personal (see § 1.162-2(b)(2)), the value of the flight is equal to the amount that an individual would have to pay in an arm's-length transaction to charter the same or a comparable piloted aircraft for that period for the same or a comparable flight. A flight taken under these circumstances may not be valued by reference to the cost of commercial airfare for the same or a comparable flight. The cost to charter the aircraft must be allocated among all employees on board the aircraft based on all the facts and circumstances unless one or more of the employees controlled the use of the aircraft. Where one or more employees control the use of the aircraft, the value of the flight shall be allocated solely among such controlling employees, unless a written agreement among all the employees on the flight otherwise allocates the value of such flight. Notwithstanding the allocation required by the preceding sentence, no additional amount shall be included in the income of any employee whose flight is properly valued under the special valuation rule of paragraph (g) of this section. For purposes of this paragraph (b)(6), "control" means the ability of the employee to determine the route, departure time and destination of the flight. The rules provided in paragraph (g)(3) of this section will be used for purposes of this section in defining a flight. Notwithstanding the allocation required by the preceding sentence, no additional amount shall be included in the income of an employee for that portion of any such flight which is excludible from income pursuant to section 132(d) or § 1.132-5 as a working condition fringe.

(iii) *Examples.* The rules of paragraph (b)(6) of this section may be illustrated by the following examples:

Example (1). An employer makes available to employees A and B a piloted aircraft in New York, New York. A wants to go to Los Angeles, California for personal purposes. B needs to go to Chicago, Illinois for business purposes,

Reg. § 1.61-21(b)(6)

→ *Caution: Reg. § 1.61-21 applies to fringe benefits provided after 1988. See Temporary Reg. § 1.61-2T for tax treatment of fringe benefits for 1985—1988.*←

and then wants to go to Los Angeles, California for personal purposes. Therefore, the aircraft first flies to Chicago, and B deplanes and then boards the plane again. The aircraft then flies to Los Angeles, California where A and B deplane. The value of the flight to employee A will be no more than the amount that an individual would have to pay in an arm's length transaction to charter the same or a comparable piloted aircraft for the same or comparable flight from New York City to Los Angeles. No amount will be imputed to employee A for the stop at Chicago. As to employee B, the value of the personal flight will be no more than the value of the flight from Chicago to Los Angeles. Pursuant to the rules set forth in § 1.132-5(k), the flight from New York to Chicago will not be included in employee B's income since that flight was taken solely for business purposes. The charter cost must be allocated between A and B, since both employees controlled portions of the flight. Assume that the employer allocates according to the relative value of each employee's flight. If the charter value of A's flight from New York City to Los Angeles is $1,000 and the value of B's flight from Chicago to Los Angeles is $600 and the value of the actual flight from New York to Chicago to Los Angeles is $1200, then the amount to be allocated to employee A is $750 ($1000/($1000 + $600) × $1200) and the amount to be allocated to employee B is $450 ($600/($1000 + $600) × $1200).

Example (2). Assume the same facts as in example (1), except that employee A also deplanes at Chicago, Illinois, but for personal purposes. The value of the flight to employee A then becomes the value of a flight from New York to Chicago to Los Angeles, i.e., $1200. Therefore, the amount to be allocated to employee A is $800 ($1200/($1200 + $600) × $1200) and the amount to be allocated to employee B is $400 ($600/($1200 + $600) × $1200).

(7) *Fair market value of the use of an employer-provided aircraft for which the employer does not furnish a pilot.* (i) *In general.* If the noncommercial flight special valuation rule of paragraph (g) of this section does not apply and if an employer provides an employee with the use of an aircraft without a pilot, the value of the use of the employer-provided aircraft is determined under the general valuation principles set forth in this paragraph (b)(7).

(ii) *Value of flight.* In general, if an employee takes a flight on an employer-provided aircraft for which the employer does not furnish a

pilot, the value of that flight is equal to the amount that an individual would have to pay in an arm's-length transaction to lease the same or comparable aircraft on the same or comparable terms for the same period in the geographic area in which the aircraft is used. For example, if an employer makes its aircraft available to an employee who will pilot the aircraft for a two-hour flight, the value of the use of the aircraft is the amount that an individual would have to pay in an arm's-length transaction to rent a comparable aircraft for that period in the geographic area in which the aircraft is used. As another example, assume that an employee uses an employer-provided aircraft to commute between home and work. The value of the use of the aircraft is the amount that an individual would have to pay in an arm's-length transaction to rent a comparable aircraft for commuting in the geographic area in which the aircraft is used. If the availability of the flight is of benefit to more than one employee, then such value shall be allocated among such employees on the basis of the relevant facts and circumstances.

(c) *Special valuation rules—*(1) *In general.* Paragraphs (d) through (k) of this section provide special valuation rules that may be used under certain circumstances for certain commonly provided fringe benefits. For general rules relating to the valuation of fringe benefits not eligible for valuation under the special valuation rules, or fringe benefits with respect to which the special valuation rules are not used, see paragraph (b) of this section.

(2) *Use of the special valuation rules—*(i) *For benefits provided before January 1, 1993.* The special valuation rules may be used for income tax, employment tax, and reporting purposes. The employer has the option to use any of the special valuation rules. However, an employee may only use a special valuation rule if the employer uses the rule. Moreover, an employee may only use the special rule that the employer uses to value the benefit provided; the employee may not use another special rule to value that benefit. The employee may always use general valuation rules based on facts and circumstances (see paragraph (b) of this section) even if the employer uses a special rule. If a special rule is used, it must be used for all purposes. If an employer properly uses a special rule and the employee uses the special rule, the employee must include in gross income the amount determined by the employer under the special rule reduced by the sum of—

Reg. § 1.61-21(b)(7)

→ *Caution: Reg. § 1.61-21 applies to fringe benefits provided after 1988. See Temporary Reg. § 1.61-2T for tax treatment of fringe benefits for 1985— 1988.*←

(A) Any amount reimbursed by the employee to the employer, and

(B) Any amount excludable from income under another section of subtitle A of the Internal Revenue Code of 1986. If an employer properly uses a special rule and properly determines the amount of an employee's working condition fringe under section 132 and § 1.132-5 (under the general rule or under a special rule), and the employee uses the special valuation rule, the employee must include in gross income the amount determined by the employer less any amount reimbursed by the employee to the employer. The employer and employee may use the special rules to determine the amount of the reimbursement due the employer by the employee. Thus, if an employee reimburses an employer for the value of a benefit as determined under a special valuation rule, no amount is includible in the employee's gross income with respect to the benefit. The provisions of this paragraph are effective for benefits provided before January 1, 1993.

(ii) *For benefits provided after December 31, 1992.* The special valuation rules may be used for income tax, employment tax, and reporting purposes. The employer has the option to use any of the special valuation rules. An employee may use a special valuation rule only if the employer uses that rule or the employer does not meet the condition of paragraph (c)(3)(ii)(A) of this section, but one of the other conditions of paragraph (c)(3)(ii) of this section is met. The employee may always use general valuation rules based on facts and circumstances (see paragraph (b) of this section) even if the employer uses a special rule. If a special rule is used, it must be used for all purposes. If an employer properly uses a special rule and the employee uses the special rule, the employee must include in gross income the amount determined by the employer under the special rule reduced by the sum of—

(A) Any amount reimbursed by the employee to the employer; and

(B) Any amount excludable from income under another section of subtitle A of the Internal Revenue Code of 1986. If an employer properly uses a special rule and properly determines the amount of an employee's working condition fringe under section 132 and § 1.132-5 (under the general rule or under a special rule), and the employee uses the special valuation rule, the employee must include in gross income the amount determined by the employer less any

amount reimbursed by the employee to the employer. The employer and employee may use the special rules to determine the amount of the reimbursement due the employer by the employee. Thus, if an employee reimburses an employer for the value of a benefit as determined under a special valuation rule, no amount is includible in the employee's gross income with respect to the benefit. The provisions of this paragraph are effective for benefits provided after December 31, 1992.

(iii) *Vehicle special valuation rules*—(A) *Vehicle by vehicle basis.* Except as provided in paragraphs (d)(7)(v) and (e)(5)(v) of this section, the vehicle special valuation rules of paragraphs (d), (e), and (f) of this section apply on a vehicle by vehicle basis. An employer need not use the same vehicle special valuation rule for all vehicles provided to all employees. For example, an employer may use the automobile lease valuation rule for automobiles provided to some employees, and the commuting and vehicle cents-per-mile valuation rules for automobiles provided to other employees. For purposes of valuing the use or availability of a vehicle, the consistency rules provided in paragraphs (d)(7) and (e)(5) of this section (relating to the automobile lease valuation rule and the vehicle cents-per-mile valuation rule, respectively) apply.

(B) *Shared vehicle usage.* If an employer provides a vehicle to employees for use by more than one employee at the same time, such as with an employer-sponsored vehicle commuting pool, the employer may use any of the special valuation rules that may be applicable to value the use of the vehicle by the employees. The employer must use the same special valuation rule to value the use of the vehicle by each employee who shares such use. The employer must allocate the value of the use of the vehicle based on the relevant facts and circumstances among the employees who share use of the vehicle. For example, assume that an employer provides an automobile to four of its employees and that the employees use the automobile in an employer-sponsored vehicle commuting pool. Assume further that the employer uses the automobile lease valuation rule of paragraph (d) of this section and that the Annual Lease Value of the automobile is $5,000. The employer must treat $5,000 as the value of the availability of the automobile to the employees, and must apportion the $5,000 value among the employees who share the use of the automobile based on the relevant facts and circumstances. Each em-

Reg. § 1.61-21(c)(2)

→ *Caution: Reg. § 1.61-21 applies to fringe benefits provided after 1988. See Temporary Reg. § 1.61-2T for tax treatment of fringe benefits for 1985— 1988.*←

ployee's share of the value of the availability of the automobile is then to be reduced by the amount, if any, of each employee's working condition fringe exclusion and the amount reimbursed by the employee to the employer.

(iv) *Commercial and noncommercial flight valuation rules.* Except as otherwise provided, if either the commercial flight valuation rule or the non-commercial flight valuation rule is used, that rule must be used by an employer to value all eligible flights taken by all employees in a calendar year. See paragraph (g)(14) of this section for the applicable consistency rules.

(3) *Additional rules for using special valuation*—(i) *Election to use special valuation rules for benefits provided before January 1, 1993.* A particular special valuation rule is deemed to have been elected by the employer (and, if applicable, by the employee), if the employer (and, if applicable, the employee) determines the value of the fringe benefit provided by applying the special valuation rule and treats that value as the fair market value of the fringe benefit for income, employment tax, and reporting purposes. Neither the employer nor the employee must notify the Internal Revenue Service of the election. The provisions of this paragraph are effective for benefits provided before January 1, 1993.

(ii) *Conditions on the use of special valuation rules for benefits provided after December 31, 1992.* Neither the employer nor the employee may use a special valuation rule to value a benefit provided after December 31, 1992, unless one of the following conditions is satisfied—

(A) The employer treats the value of the benefit as wages for reporting purposes within the time for filing the returns for the taxable year (including extensions) in which the benefit is provided;

(B) The employee includes the value of the benefit in income within the time for filing the returns for the taxable year (including extensions) in which the benefit is provided;

(C) The employee is not a control employee as defined in paragraphs (f)(5) and (f)(6) of this section; or

(D) The employer demonstrates a good faith effort to treat the benefit correctly for reporting purposes.

(4) *Application of section 414 to employers.* For purposes of paragraphs (c) through (k) of this section, except as otherwise provided therein, the term "employer" includes all entities required to

be treated as a single employer under section 414(b), (c), (m), or (o).

(5) *Valuation formulae contained in the special valuation rules.* The valuation formulae contained in the special valuation rules are provided only for use in connection with those rules. Thus, when a special valuation rule is properly applied to a fringe benefit, the Commissioner will accept the value calculated pursuant to the rule as the fair market value of that fringe benefit. However, when a special valuation rule is not properly applied to a fringe benefit (see, for example, paragraph (g)(13) of this section), or when a special valuation rule is used to value a fringe benefit by a taxpayer not entitled to use the rule, the fair market value of that fringe benefit may not be determined by reference to any value calculated under any special valuation rule. Under the circumstances described in the preceding sentence, the fair market value of the fringe benefit must be determined pursuant to the general valuation rules of paragraph (b) of this section.

(6) *Modification of the special valuation rules.* The Commissioner may, to the extent necessary for tax administration, add, delete, or modify any special valuation rule, including the valuation formulae contained herein, on a prospective basis by regulation, revenue ruling or revenue procedure.

(7) *Special accounting rule.* If the employer is using the special accounting rule provided in Announcement 85-113 (1985-31 I.R.B. 31, August 5, 1985) (*see* § 601.601(d)(2)(ii)(*b*) of this chapter) (relating to the reporting of and withholding on the value of noncash fringe benefits), benefits which are deemed provided in a subsequent calendar year pursuant to that rule are considered as provided in that subsequent calendar year for purposes of the special valuation rules. Thus, if a particular special valuation rule is in effect for a calendar year, it applies to benefits deemed provided during that calendar year under the special accounting rule.

(d) *Automobile lease valuation rule*—(1) *In general*—(i) *Annual Lease Value.* Under the special valuation rule of this paragraph (d), if an employer provides an employee with an automobile that is available to the employee for an entire calendar year, the value of the benefit provided is the Annual Lease Value (determined under paragraph (d)(2) of this section) of that automobile. Except as otherwise provided, for an automobile that is available to an employee for less than an entire calendar year, the value of the benefit

Reg. § 1.61-21(c)(3)

→ *Caution: Reg. § 1.61-21 applies to fringe benefits provided after 1988. See Temporary Reg. § 1.61-2T for tax treatment of fringe benefits for 1985— 1988.*←

provided is either a pro-rated Annual Lease Value or the Daily Lease Value (both as defined in paragraph (d)(4) of this section), whichever is applicable. Absent any statutory exclusion relating to the employer-provided automobile (see, for example, section 132(a)(3) and § 1.132-5(b)), the amount of the Annual Lease Value (or a pro-rated Annual Lease Value or the Daily Lease Value, as applicable) is included in the gross income of the employee.

(ii) *Definition of automobile.* For purposes of this paragraph (d), the term "automobile" means any four-wheeled vehicle manufactured primarily for use on public streets, roads, and highways.

(2) *Calculation of Annual Lease Value*—(i) *In general.* The Annual Lease Value of a particular automobile is calculated as follows:

(A) Determine the fair market value of the automobile as of the first date on which the automobile is made available to any employee of the employer for personal use. For an automobile first made available to any employee for personal use prior to January 1, 1985, determine the fair market value as of January 1 of the first year the special valuation rule of this paragraph (d) is used with respect to the automobile. For rules relating to determination of the fair market value of an automobile for purposes of this paragraph (d), see paragraph (d)(5) of this section.

(B) Select the dollar range in column 1 of the Annual Lease Value Table, set forth in paragraph (d)(2)(iii) of this section, corresponding to the fair market value of the automobile. Except as otherwise provided in paragraphs (d)(2)(iv) and (v) of this section, the Annual Lease Value for each year of availability of the automobile is the corresponding amount in column 2 of the Table.

(ii) *Calculation of Annual Lease Value of automobile owned or leased by both an employer and an employee*—(A) *Purchased automobiles.* Notwithstanding anything in this section to the contrary, if an employee contributes an amount toward the purchase price of an automobile in return for a percentage ownership interest in the automobile, the Annual Lease Value or the Daily Lease Value, whichever is applicable, is determined by reducing the fair market value of the employer-provided automobile by the lesser of—

(1) The amount contributed, or

(2) An amount equal to the employee's percentage ownership interest multiplied by the unreduced fair market value of the automobile.

If the automobile is subsequently revalued, the revalued amount (determined without regard to this paragraph (d)(2)(ii)(A)) is reduced by an amount which is equal to the employee's percentage ownership interest in the vehicle. If the employee does not receive an ownership interest in the employer-provided automobile, then the Annual Lease Value or the Daily Lease Value, whichever is applicable, is determined without regard to any amount contributed. For purposes of this paragraph (d)(2)(ii)(A), an employee's ownership interest in an automobile will not be recognized unless it is reflected in the title of the automobile. An ownership interest reflected in the title of an automobile will not be recognized if under the facts and circumstances the title does not reflect the benefits and burdens of ownership.

(B) *Leased automobiles.* Notwithstanding anything in this section to the contrary, if an employee contributes an amount toward the cost to lease an automobile in return for a percentage interest in the automobile lease, the Annual Lease Value or the Daily Lease Value, whichever is applicable, is determined by reducing the fair market value of the employer-provided automobile by the amount specified in the following sentence. The amount specified in this sentence is the unreduced fair market value of a vehicle multiplied by the lesser of—

(1) The employee's percentage interest in the lease, or

(2) A fraction, the numerator of which is the amount contributed and the denominator of which is the entire lease cost.

If the automobile is subsequently revalued, the revalued amount (determined without regard to this paragraph (d)(2)(ii)(B)) is reduced by an amount which is equal to the employee's percentage interest in the lease multiplied by the revalued amount. If the employee does not receive an interest in the automobile lease, then the Annual Lease Value or the Daily Lease Value, whichever is applicable, is determined without regard to any amount contributed. For purposes of this paragraph (d)(2)(ii)(B), an employee's interest in an automobile lease will not be recognized unless the employee is a named co-lessee on the lease. An interest in a lease will not be recognized if under the facts and circumstances the lease does not reflect the true obligations of the lessees.

Reg. § 1.61-21(d)(2)

→ *Caution: Reg. § 1.61-21 applies to fringe benefits provided after 1988. See Temporary Reg. § 1.61-2T for tax treatment of fringe benefits for 1985—1988.*←

(C) *Example.* The rules of paragraph (d)(2)(ii)(A) and (B) of this section are illustrated by the following example:

Example. Assume that an employer pays $15,000 and an employee pays $5,000 toward the purchase of an automobile. Assume further that the employee receives a 25 percent interest in the automobile and is named as a co-owner on the title to the automobile. Under the rule of paragraph (d)(2)(ii)(A) of this section, the Annual Lease Value of the automobile is determined by reducing the fair market value of the automobile ($20,000) by the $5,000 employee contribution. Thus, the Annual Lease Value of the automobile under the table in paragraph (d)(2)(iii) of this section is $4,350. If the employee in this example does not receive an ownership interest in the automobile and is provided the use of the automobile for two years, the Annual Lease Value would be determined without regard to the $5,000 employee contribution. Thus, the Annual Lease Value would be $5,600. The $5,000 employee contribution would reduce the amount includible in the employee's income after taking into account the amount, if any, excluded from income under another provision of subtitle A of the Internal Revenue Code, such as the working condition fringe exclusion. Thus, if the employee places 50 percent of the mileage on the automobile for the employer's business each year, then the amount includible in the employee's income in the first year would be ($5,600 − 2,800 − 2,800), or $0, the amount includible in the employee's income in the second year would be ($5,600 − 2,800 − 2,200 ($5,000 − 2,800)) or $600 and the amount includible in the third year would be ($5,600 − 2,800) or $2,800 since the employee's contribution has been completely used in the first two years.

(iii) *Annual Lease Value Table.*

Automobile fair market value	*Annual Lease Value*
(1)	(2)
$0 to 999	$ 600
1,000 to 1,999	850
2,000 to 2,999	1,100
3,000 to 3,999	1,350
4,000 to 4,999	1,600
5,000 to 5,999	1,850
6,000 to 6,999	2,100
7,000 to 7,999	2,350
8,000 to 8,999	2,600
9,000 to 9,999	2,850
10,000 to 10,999	3,100
11,000 to 11,999	3,350
12,000 to 12,999	3,600
13,000 to 13,999	3,850
14,000 to 14,999	4,100
15,000 to 15,999	4,350
16,000 to 16,999	4,600
17,000 to 17,999	4,850
18,000 to 18,999	5,100
19,000 to 19,999	5,350
20,000 to 20,999	5,600
21,000 to 21,999	5,850
22,000 to 22,999	6,100
23,000 to 23,999	6,350
24,000 to 24,999	6,600
25,000 to 25,999	6,850
26,000 to 27,999	7,250
28,000 to 29,999	7,750
30,000 to 31,999	8,250
32,000 to 33,999	8,750
34,000 to 35,999	9,250
36,000 to 37,999	9,750
38,000 to 39,999	10,250
40,000 to 41,999	10,750
42,000 to 43,999	11,250

Reg. § 1.61-21(d)(2)

→ *Caution: Reg. § 1.61-21 applies to fringe benefits provided after 1988. See Temporary Reg. § 1.61-2T for tax treatment of fringe benefits for 1985—1988.*←

44,000 to 45,999	11,750
46,000 to 47,999	12,250
48,000 to 49,999	12,750
50,000 to 51,999	13,250
52,000 to 53,999	13,750
54,000 to 55,999	14,250
56,000 to 57,999	14,750
58,000 to 59,999	15,250

For vehicles having a fair market value in excess of $59,999, the Annual Lease Value is equal to: (.25 × the fair market value of the automobile) + $500.

(iv) *Recalculation of Annual Lease Value.* The Annual Lease Values determined under the rules of this paragraph (d) are based on four-year lease terms. Therefore, except as otherwise provided in paragraph (d)(2)(v) of this section, the Annual Lease Value calculated by applying paragraph (d)(2)(i) or (ii) of this section shall remain in effect for the period that begins with the first date the special valuation rule of paragraph (d) of this section is applied by the employer to the automobile and ends on December 31 of the fourth full calendar year following that date. The Annual Lease Value for each subsequent four-year period is calculated by determining the fair market value of the automobile as of the first January 1 following the period described in the previous sentence and selecting the amount in column 2 of the Annual Lease Value Table corresponding to the appropriate dollar range in column 1 of the Table. If, however, the employer is using the special accounting rule provided in Announcement 85-113 (1985-31 I.R.B. 31, August 5, 1985) (relating to the reporting of and withholding on the value of noncash fringe benefits), the employer may calculate the Annual Lease Value for each subsequent four-year period as of the beginning of the special accounting period that begins immediately prior to the January 1 described in the previous sentence. For example, assume that pursuant to Announcement 85-113, an employer uses the special accounting rule. Assume further that beginning on November 1, 1988, the special accounting period is November 1 to October 31 and that the employer elects to use the special valuation rule of this paragraph (d) as of January 1, 1989. The employer may recalculate the Annual Lease Value as of November 1, 1992, rather than as of January 1, 1993.

(v) *Transfer of the automobile to another employee.* Unless the primary purpose of the transfer is to reduce Federal taxes, if an employer transfers the use of an automobile from one employee to another employee, the employer may recalculate the Annual Lease Value based on the fair market value of the automobile as of January 1 of the calendar year of transfer. If, however, the employer is using the special accounting rule provided in Announcement 85-113 (1985-31 I.R.B. 31, August 5, 1985) (relating to the reporting of and withholding on the value of noncash fringe benefits), the employer may recalculate the Annual Lease Value based on the fair market value of the automobile as of the beginning of the special accounting period in which the transfer occurs. If the employer does not recalculate the Annual Lease Value, and the employee to whom the automobile is transferred uses the special valuation rule, the employee may not recalculate the Annual Lease Value.

(3) *Services included in, or excluded from, the Annual Lease Value Table*—(i) *Maintenance and insurance included.* The Annual Lease Values contained in the Annual Lease Value Table include the fair market value of maintenance of, and insurance for, the automobile. Neither an employer nor an employee may reduce the Annual Lease Value by the fair market value of any service included in the Annual Lease Value that is not provided by the employer, such as reducing the Annual Lease Value by the fair market value of a maintenance service contract or insurance. An employer or employee who wishes to take into account only the services actually provided with respect to an automobile may value the availability of the automobile under the general valuation rules of paragraph (b) of this section.

(ii) *Fuel excluded*—(A) *In general.* The Annual Lease Values do not include the fair market value of fuel provided by the employer, whether fuel is provided in kind or its cost is reimbursed by or charged to the employer. Thus, if an employer provides fuel, the fuel must be valued separately for inclusion in income.

(B) *Valuation of fuel provided in kind.* The provision of fuel in kind may be valued at fair market value based on all the facts and circumstances or, in the alternative, it may be valued at 5.5 cents per mile for all miles driven by the employee. However, the provision of fuel in kind may not be valued at 5.5 cents per mile for miles

Reg. § 1.61-21(d)(3)

→ *Caution: Reg. § 1.61-21 applies to fringe benefits provided after 1988. See Temporary Reg. § 1.61-2T for tax treatment of fringe benefits for 1985—1988.* ←

driven outside the United States, Canada, or Mexico. For purposes of this section, the United States includes the United States, its possessions and its territories.

(C) *Valuation of fuel where cost reimbursed by or charged to an employer.* The fair market value of fuel, the cost of which is reimbursed by or charged to an employer, is generally the amount of the actual reimbursement or the amount charged, provided the purchase of the fuel is at arm's-length.

(D) *Fleet-average cents-per-mile fuel cost.* If an employer with a fleet of at least 20 automobiles that meets the requirements of paragraph (d)(5)(v)(D) of this section reimburses employees for the cost of fuel or allows employees to charge the employer for the cost of fuel, the fair market value of fuel provided to those automobiles may be determined by reference to the employer's fleet-average cents-per-mile fuel cost. The fleet-average cents-per-mile fuel cost is equal to the fleet-average per-gallon fuel cost divided by the fleet-average miles-per-gallon rate. The averages described in the preceding sentence must be determined by averaging the per-gallon fuel costs and miles-per-gallon rates of a representative sample of the automobiles in the fleet equal to the greater of ten percent of the automobiles in the fleet or 20 automobiles for a representative period, such as a two-month period. In lieu of determining the fleet-average cents-per-mile fuel cost, if an employer is using the fleet-average valuation rule of paragraph (d)(5)(v) of this section and if determining the amount of the actual reimbursement or the amount charged for the purchase of fuel would impose unreasonable administrative burdens on the employer, the provision of fuel may be valued under the rule provided in paragraph (d)(3)(ii)(B) of this section.

(iii) *Treatment of other services.* The fair market value of any service not specifically identified in paragraph (d)(3)(i) of this section that is provided by the employer with respect to an automobile (other than the services of a chauffeur) must be added to the Annual Lease Value of the automobile in determining the fair market value of the benefit provided. See paragraph (b)(5) of this section for rules relating to the valuation of chauffeur services.

(4) *Availability of an automobile for less than an entire calendar year*—(i) *Pro-rated Annual Lease Value used for continuous availability of at least 30 days*—(A) *In general.* Except as otherwise provided in paragraph (d)(4)(iv) of this section, for periods of continuous availability of at least 30 days, but less than an entire calendar year, the value of the availability of an automobile provided by an employer electing to use the automobile lease valuation rule of this paragraph (d) is the pro-rated Annual Lease Value. The pro-rated Annual Lease Value is calculated by multiplying the applicable Annual Lease Value by a fraction, the numerator of which is the number of days of availability and the denominator of which is 365.

(B) *Special rule for continuous availability of at least 30 days that straddles two reporting years.* If an employee is provided with the continuous availability of an automobile for at least 30 days, but the continuous period straddles two calendar years (or two special accounting periods if the special accounting rule of Announcement 85-113 (1985-31 I.R.B. 31, August 5, 1985) (relating to the reporting of and withholding on non-cash fringe benefits) is used), the pro-rated Annual Lease Value, rather than the Daily Lease Value, may be applied with respect to such period of continuous availability.

(ii) *Daily Lease Value used for continuous availability of less than 30 days.* Except as otherwise provided in paragraph (d)(4)(iii) of this section, for periods of continuous availability of one or more but less than 30 days, the value of the availability of the employer-provided automobile is the Daily Lease Value. The Daily Lease Value is calculated by multiplying the applicable Annual Lease Value by a fraction, the numerator of which is four times the number of days of availability and the denominator of which is 365.

(iii) *Election to treat all periods as periods of at least 30 days.* The value of the availability of an employer-provided automobile for a period of continuous availability of less than 30 days may be determined by applying the pro-rated Annual Lease Value by treating the automobile as if it had been available for 30 days, if doing so would result in a lower valuation than applying the Daily Lease Value to the shorter period of actual availability.

(iv) *Periods of unavailability*—(A) *General rule.* In general, a pro-rated Annual Lease Value (as provided in paragraph (d)(4)(i) of this section) is used to value the availability of an employer-provided automobile when the automobile is available to an employee for a continuous period of at least 30 days but less than the entire calendar year. Neither an employer nor an employee, however, may use a pro-rated Annual

Reg. § 1.61-21(d)(4)

→ *Caution: Reg. § 1.61-21 applies to fringe benefits provided after 1988. See Temporary Reg. § 1.61-2T for tax treatment of fringe benefits for 1985— 1988.*←

Lease Value when the reduction of Federal taxes is the primary reason the automobile is unavailable to an employee at certain times during the calendar year.

(B) *Unavailability for personal reasons of the employee.* If an automobile is unavailable to an employee because of personal reasons of the employee, such as while the employee is on vacation, a pro-rated Annual Lease Value, if used, must not take into account such periods of unavailability. For example, assume that an automobile is available to an employee during the first five months of the year and during the last five months of the year. Assume further that the period of unavailability occurs because the employee is on vacation. The Annual Lease Value, if it is applied, must be applied with respect to the entire 12-month period. The Annual Lease Value may not be pro-rated to take into account the two-month period of unavailability.

(5) *Fair market value*—(i) *In general.* For purposes of determining the Annual Lease Value of an automobile under the Annual Lease Value Table, the fair market value of an automobile is the amount that an individual would have to pay in an arm's-length transaction to purchase the particular automobile in the jurisdiction in which the vehicle is purchased or leased. That amount includes all amounts attributable to the purchase of an automobile such as sales tax and title fees as well as the purchase price of the automobile. Any special relationship that may exist between the employee and the employer must be disregarded. Also, the employee's subjective perception of the value of the automobile is not relevant to the determination of the automobile's fair market value, and, except as provided in paragraph (d)(5)(ii) of this section, the cost incurred by the employer in connection with the purchase or lease of the automobile is not determinative of the fair market value of the automobile.

(ii) *Safe-harbor valuation rule*—(A) *General rule.* For purposes of calculating the Annual Lease Value of an automobile under this paragraph (d), the safe-harbor value of the automobile may be used as the fair market value of the automobile.

(B) *Automobiles owned by the employer.* For an automobile owned by the employer, the safe-harbor value of the automobile is the employer's cost of purchasing the automobile (including sales tax, title, and other expenses attributable to such purchase), provided the purchase is made at arm's-length. Notwithstand-

ing the preceding sentence, the safe-harbor value of this paragraph (d)(5)(ii)(B) is not available with respect to an automobile manufactured by the employer. Thus, for example, if one entity manufactures an automobile and sells it to an entity with which it is aggregated pursuant to paragraph (c)(4) of this section, this paragraph (d)(5)(ii)(B) does not apply to value the automobile by the aggregated employer. In this case, value must be determined under paragraph (d)(5)(i) of this section.

(C) *Automobiles leased by the employer.* For an automobile leased but not manufactured by the employer, the safe-harbor value of the automobile is either the manufacturer's suggested retail price of the automobile less eight percent (including sales tax, title, and other expenses attributable to such purchase), or the value determined under paragraph (d)(5)(iii) of this section.

(iii) *Use of nationally recognized pricing sources.* The fair market value of an automobile that is—

(A) Provided to an employee prior to January 1, 1985,

(B) Being revalued pursuant to paragraphs (d)(2)(iv) or (v) of this section, or

(C) A leased automobile being valued pursuant to paragraph (d)(5)(ii) of this section,

may be determined by reference to the retail value of such automobile as reported by a nationally recognized pricing source that regularly reports new or used automobile retail values, whichever is applicable. That retail value must be reasonable with respect to the automobile being valued. Pricing sources consist of publications and electronic data bases.

(iv) *Fair market value of special equipment.* When determining the fair market value of an automobile, the employer may exclude the fair market value of any specialized equipment or telephone that is added to or carried in the automobile provided that the presence of that equipment or telephone is necessitated by, and attributable to, the business needs of the employer. The value of the specialized equipment must be included if the employee to whom the automobile is available uses the specialized equipment in a trade or business of the employee other than the employee's trade or business of being an employee of the employer.

(v) *Fleet-average valuation rule*—(A) *In general.* An employer with a fleet of 20 or more automobiles meeting the requirements of this par-

→ *Caution: Reg. § 1.61-21 applies to fringe benefits provided after 1988. See Temporary Reg. § 1.61-2T for tax treatment of fringe benefits for 1985— 1988.*←

agraph (d)(5)(v) (including the business-use and fair market value conditions of paragraph (d)(5)(v)(D) of this section) may use a fleet-average value for purposes of calculating the Annual Lease Values of the automobiles in the fleet. The fleet-average value is the average of the fair market values of all automobiles in the fleet. The fair market value of each automobile in the fleet shall be determined, pursuant to the rules of paragraphs (d)(5)(i) through (iv) of this section, as of the date described in paragraph (d)(2)(i)(A) of this section.

(B) *Period for use of rule.* The fleet-average valuation rule of this paragraph (d)(5)(v) may be used by an employer as of January 1 of any calendar year following the calendar year in which the employer acquires a sufficient number of automobiles to total a fleet of 20 or more automobiles. The Annual Lease Value calculated for the automobiles in the fleet, based on the fleet-average value, shall remain in effect for the period that begins with the first January 1 the fleet-average valuation rule of this paragraph (d)(5)(v) is applied by the employer to the automobiles in the fleet and ends on December 31 of the subsequent calendar year. The Annual Lease Value for each subsequent two-year period is calculated by determining the fleet-average value of the automobiles in the fleet as of the first January 1 of such period. An employer may cease using the fleet-average valuation rule as of any January 1. If, however, the employer is using the special accounting rule provided in Announcement 85-113 (1985-31 I.R.B. 31, August 5, 1985) (relating to the reporting of and withholding on non-cash fringe benefits), the employer may apply the rules of this paragraph (d)(5)(v)(B) on the basis of the special accounting period rather than the calendar year. (This is accomplished by substituting (*1*) the beginning of the special accounting period that begins immediately prior to the January 1 described in this paragraph (d)(5)(v)(B) for January 1 wherever it appears in this paragraph (d)(5)(v)(B) and (*2*) the end of such accounting period for December 31.) If the number of qualifying automobiles in the employer's fleet declines to fewer than 20 for more than 50 percent of the days in a year, then the fleet-average valuation rule does not apply as of January 1 of such year. In this case, the Annual Lease Value must be determined separately for each remaining automobile. The revaluation rules of paragraph (d)(2)(iv) and (v) of this section do not apply to

automobiles valued under this paragraph (d)(5)(v).

(C) *Automobiles included in the fleet.* An employer may include in a fleet any automobile that meets the requirements of this paragraph (d)(5)(v) and is available to any employee of the employer for personal use. An employer may include in the fleet only automobiles the availability of which is valued under the automobile lease valuation rule of this paragraph (d). An employer need not include in the fleet all automobiles valued under the automobile lease valuation rule. An employer may have more than one fleet for purposes of the fleet-average rule of this paragraph (d)(5)(v). For example, an employer may group automobiles in a fleet according to their physical type or use.

(D) *Limitations on use of fleet-average rule.* The rule provided in this paragraph (d)(5)(v) may not be used for any automobile the fair market value of which (determined pursuant to paragraphs (d)(5)(i) through (iv) of this section as of either the first date on which the automobile is made available to any employee of the employer for personal use or, if later, January 1, 1985) exceeds $16,500. The fair market value limitation of $16,500 shall be adjusted pursuant to section 280F(d)(7) of the Internal Revenue Code of 1986. The first such adjustment shall be for calendar year 1989 (substitute October 1986 for October 1987 in applying the formula). In addition, the rule provided in this paragraph (d)(5)(v) may only be used for automobiles that the employer reasonably expects will regularly be used in the employer's trade or business. For rules concerning when an automobile is regularly used in the employer's business, see paragraph (e)(1)(iv) of this section.

(E) *Additional automobiles added to the fleet.* The fleet-average value in effect at the time an automobile is added to a fleet is treated as the fair market value of the additional automobile for purposes of determining the Annual Lease Value of the automobile until the fleet-average value changes pursuant to paragraph (d)(5)(v)(B) of this section.

(F) *Use of the fleet-average rule by employees.* An employee may only use the fleet-average rule if it is used by the employer. If an employer uses the fleet-average rule, and the employee uses the special valuation rule of paragraph (d) of this section, the employee must use the fleet-average value determined by the employer.

Reg. § 1.61-21(d)(5)

→ *Caution: Reg. § 1.61-21 applies to fringe benefits provided after 1988. See Temporary Reg. § 1.61-2T for tax treatment of fringe benefits for 1985—1988.*←

(6) *Special rules for continuous availability of certain automobiles*—(i) *Fleet automobiles.* If an employer is using the fleet-average valuation rule of paragraph (d)(5)(v) of this section and the employer provides an employee with the continuous availability of an automobile from the same fleet during a period (though not necessarily the same fleet automobile for the entire period), the employee is treated as having the use of a single fleet automobile for the entire period, e.g., an entire calendar year. Thus, when applying the automobile lease valuation rule of this paragraph (d), the employer may treat the fleet-average value as the fair market value of the automobile deemed available to the employee for the period for purposes of calculating the Annual Lease Value (or pro-rated Annual Lease Value or Daily Lease Value, whichever is applicable) of the automobile. If an employer provides an employee with the continuous availability of more than one fleet automobile during a period, the employer may treat the fleet-average value as the fair market value of each automobile provided to the employee provided that the rules of paragraph (d)(5)(v)(D) of this section are satisfied.

(ii) *Demonstration automobiles*—(A) *In general.* If an automobile dealership provides an employee with the continuous availability of a demonstration automobile (as defined in § 1.132-5(o)(3)) during a period (though not necessarily the same demonstration automobile for the entire period), the employee is treated as having the use of a single demonstration automobile for the entire period, e.g., an entire calendar year. If an employer provides an employee with the continuous availability of more than one demonstration automobile during a period, the employer may treat the value determined under paragraph (d)(6)(ii)(B) of this section as the fair market value of each automobile provided to the employee. For rules relating to the treatment as a working condition fringe of the qualified automobile demonstration use of a demonstration automobile by a full-time automobile salesman, see § 1.132-5(o).

(B) *Determining the fair market value of a demonstration automobile.* When applying the automobile lease valuation rule of this paragraph (d), the employer may treat the average of the fair market values of the demonstration automobiles which are available to an employee and held in the dealership's inventory during the calendar year as the fair market value of the demonstration automobile deemed available to the employee for the period for purposes of calculating the Annual Lease Value of the automobile. If under the facts and circumstances it is inappropriate to take into account, with respect to an employee, certain models of demonstration automobiles, the value of the benefit is determined without reference to the fair market values of such models. For example, assume that an employee has the continuous availability for an entire calendar year of one demonstration automobile, although not the same one for the entire year. Assume further that the fair market values of the automobiles in the dealership's inventory during the year range from $8,000 to $20,000. If there is not a substantial period (such as three months) during the year when the employee uses demonstration automobiles valued at less than $16,000, then those automobiles are not considered in determining the value of the benefit provided to the employee. In this case, the average of the fair market values of the demonstration automobiles in the dealership's inventory valued at $16,000 or more is treated as the fair market value of the automobile deemed available to the employee for the calendar year for purposes of calculating the Annual Lease Value of the automobile.

(7) *Consistency rules*—(i) *Use of the automobile lease valuation rule by an employer.* Except as provided in paragraph (d)(5)(v)(B) of this section, an employer may adopt the automobile lease valuation rule of this paragraph (d) for an automobile only if the rule is adopted to take effect by the later of—

(A) January 1, 1989, or

(B) The first day on which the automobile is made available to an employee of the employer for personal use (or, if the commuting valuation rule of paragraph (f) of this section is used when the automobile is first made available to an employee of the employer for personal use, the first day on which the commuting valuation rule is not used).

(ii) *An employer must use the automobile lease valuation rule for all subsequent years.* Once the automobile lease valuation rule has been adopted for an automobile by an employer, the rule must be used by the employer for all subsequent years in which the employer makes the automobile available to any employee, except that the employer may, for any year during which (or for any employee for whom) use of the automobile qualifies for the commuting valuation rule of par-

Reg. § 1.61-21(d)(7)

→ *Caution: Reg. § 1.61-21 applies to fringe benefits provided after 1988. See Temporary Reg. § 1.61-2T for tax treatment of fringe benefits for 1985— 1988.*←

agraph (f) of this section, use the commuting valuation rule with respect to the automobile.

(iii) *Use of the automobile lease valuation rule by an employee.* An employee may adopt the automobile lease valuation rule for an automobile only if the rule is adopted—

(A) By the employer, and

(B) Beginning with the first day on which the automobile for which the employer (consistent with paragraph (d)(7)(i) of this section) adopted the rule is made available to that employee for personal use (or, if the commuting valuation rule of paragraph (f) of this section is used when the automobile is first made available to that employee for personal use, the first day on which the commuting valuation rule is not used).

(iv) *An employee must use the automobile lease valuation rule for all subsequent years.* Once the automobile lease valuation rule has been adopted for an automobile by an employee, the rule must be used by the employee for all subsequent years in which the automobile for which the rule is used is available to the employee. However, the employee may, for any year during which use of the automobile qualifies for use of the commuting valuation rule of paragraph (f) of this section and for which the employer uses such rule, use the commuting valuation rule with respect to the automobile.

(v) *Replacement automobiles.* Notwithstanding anything in this paragraph (d)(7) to the contrary, if the automobile lease valuation rule is used by an employer, or by an employer and an employee, with respect to a particular automobile, and a replacement automobile is provided to the employee for the primary purpose of reducing Federal taxes, then the employer, or the employer and the employee, using the rule must continue to use the rule with respect to the replacement automobile.

(e) *Vehicle cents-per-mile valuation rule—*(1) *In general—*(i) *General rule.* Under the vehicle cents-per-mile valuation rule of this paragraph (e), if an employer provides an employee with the use of a vehicle that—

(A) The employer reasonably expects will be regularly used in the employer's trade or business throughout the calendar year (or such shorter period as the vehicle may be owned or leased by the employer), or

(B) Satisfies the requirements of paragraph (e)(1)(ii) of this section,

the value of the benefit provided in the calendar year is the standard mileage rate provided in the applicable Revenue Ruling or Revenue Procedure ("cents-per-mile rate") multiplied by the total number of miles the vehicle is driven by the employee for personal purposes. The cents-per-mile rate is to be applied prospectively from the first day of the taxable year following the date of publication of the applicable Revenue Ruling or Revenue Procedure. An employee who uses an employer-provided vehicle, in whole or in part, for a trade or business other than the employer's trade or business, may take a deduction for such business use based upon the vehicle cents-per-mile rule as long as such deduction is at the same standard mileage rate as that used in calculating the employee's income inclusion. The standard mileage rate must be applied to personal miles independent of business miles. Thus, for example, if the standard mileage rate were 24 cents per mile for the first 15,000 miles and 11 cents per mile for all miles over 15,000 and an employee drives 20,000 personal miles and 45,000 business miles in a year, the value of the personal use of the vehicle is $4,150 ((15,000 × $.24) + (5,000 × $.11)). For purposes of this section, the use of a vehicle for personal purposes is any use of the vehicle other than use in the employee's trade or business of being an employee of the employer.

(ii) *Mileage rule.* A vehicle satisfies the requirements of this paragraph (e)(1)(ii) for a calendar year if—

(A) It is actually driven at least 10,000 miles in that year; and

(B) Use of the vehicle during the year is primarily by employees.

For example, if a vehicle is used by only one employee during the calendar year and that employee drives the vehicle at least 10,000 miles during the year, the vehicle satisfies the requirements of this paragraph (e)(1)(ii) even if all miles driven by the employee are personal. A vehicle is considered used during the year primarily by employees in accordance with the requirement of paragraph (e)(1)(ii)(B) of this section if employees use the vehicle on a consistent basis for commuting. If the employer does not own or lease the vehicle during a portion of the year, the 10,000 mile threshold is to be reduced proportionately to reflect the periods when the employer did not own or lease the vehicle. For purposes of this paragraph (e)(1)(ii), use of the vehicle by an individual (other than the employee) whose use would be

→ *Caution: Reg. § 1.61-21 applies to fringe benefits provided after 1988. See Temporary Reg. § 1.61-2T for tax treatment of fringe benefits for 1985—1988.*←

taxed to the employee is not considered use by the employee.

(iii) *Limitation on use of the vehicle cents-per-mile valuation rule*—(A) *In general.* Except as otherwise provided in the last sentence of this paragraph (e)(1)(iii)(A), the value of the use of an automobile (as defined in paragraph (d)(1)(ii) of this section) may not be determined under the vehicle cents-per-mile valuation rule of this paragraph (e) for a calendar year if the fair market value of the automobile (determined pursuant to paragraphs (d)(5)(i) through (iv) of this section as of the later of January 1, 1985, or the first date on which the automobile is made available to any employee of the employer for personal use) exceeds the sum of the maximum recovery deductions allowable under section 280F(a)(2) for a five-year period for an automobile first placed in service during that calendar year (whether or not the automobile is actually placed in service during that year) as adjusted by section 280F(d)(7). With respect to a vehicle placed in service prior to January 1, 1989, the limitation on value will be not less than $12,800. With respect to a vehicle placed in service in or after 1989, the limitation on value is $12,800 as adjusted by section 280F(d)(7).

(B) *Application of limitation with respect to a vehicle owned by both an employer and an employee.* If an employee contributes an amount towards the purchase price of a vehicle in return for a percentage ownership interest in the vehicle, for purposes of determining whether the limitation of this paragraph (e)(1)(iii) applies, the fair market value of the vehicle is reduced by the lesser of—

(*1*) The amount contributed, or

(*2*) An amount equal to the employee's percentage ownership interest multiplied by the unreduced fair market value of the vehicle. If the employee does not receive an ownership interest in the employer-provided vehicle, then the fair market value of the vehicle is determined without regard to any amount contributed. For purposes of this paragraph (e)(1)(iii)(B), an employee's ownership interest in a vehicle will not be recognized unless it is reflected in the title of the vehicle. An ownership interest reflected in the title of a vehicle will not be recognized if under the facts and circumstances the title does not reflect the benefits and burdens of ownership.

(C) *Application of limitation with respect to a vehicle leased by both an employer and*

employee. If an employee contributes an amount toward the cost to lease a vehicle in return for a percentage interest in the vehicle lease, for purposes of determining whether the limitation of this paragraph (e)(1)(iii) applies, the fair market value of the vehicle is reduced by the amount specified in the following sentence. The amount specified in this sentence is the unreduced fair market value of a vehicle multiplied by the lesser of—

(*1*) The employee's percentage interest in the lease, or

(*2*) A fraction, the numerator of which is the amount contributed and the denominator of which is the entire lease cost.

If the employee does not receive an interest in the vehicle lease, then the fair market value is determined without regard to any amount contributed. For purposes of this paragraph (e)(1)(iii)(C), an employee's interest in a vehicle lease will not be recognized unless the employee is a named co-lessee on the lease. An interest in a lease will not be recognized if under the facts and circumstances, the lease does not reflect the true obligations of the lessees.

(iv) *Regular use in an employer's trade or business.* Whether a vehicle is regularly used in an employer's trade or business is determined on the basis of all facts and circumstances. A vehicle is considered regularly used in an employer's trade or business for purposes of paragraph (e)(1)(i)(A) of this section if one of the following safe harbor conditions is satisfied:

(A) At least 50 percent of the vehicle's total annual mileage is for the employer's business; or

(B) The vehicle is generally used each workday to transport at least three employees of the employer to and from work in an employer-sponsored commuting vehicle pool. Infrequent business use of the vehicle, such as for occasional trips to the airport or between the employer's multiple business premises, does not constitute regular use of the vehicle in the employer's trade or business.

(v) *Application of rule to shared usage.* If an employer regularly provides a vehicle to employees for use by more than one employee at the same time, such as with an employer-sponsored vehicle commuting pool, the employer may use the vehicle cents-per-mile valuation rule to value the use of the vehicle by each employee who shares such use. See § 1.61-21(c)(2)(ii)(B) for pro-

Reg. § 1.61-21(e)(1)

→ *Caution: Reg. § 1.61-21 applies to fringe benefits provided after 1988. See Temporary Reg. § 1.61-2T for tax treatment of fringe benefits for 1985— 1988.*←

visions relating to the allocation of the value of an automobile to more than one employee.

(2) *Definition of vehicle.* For purposes of this paragraph (e), the term "vehicle" means any motorized wheeled vehicle manufactured primarily for use on public streets, roads, and highways. The term "vehicle" includes an automobile as defined in paragraph (d)(1)(ii) of this section.

(3) *Services included in, or excluded from, the cents-per-mile rate*—(i) *Maintenance and insurance included.* The cents-per-mile rate includes the fair market value of maintenance of, and insurance for, the vehicle. The cents-per-mile rate may not be reduced by the fair market value of any service included in the cents-per-mile rate but not provided by the employer. An employer or employee who wishes to take into account only the particular services provided with respect to a vehicle may value the availability of the vehicle under the general valuation rules of paragraph (b) of this section.

(ii) *Fuel provided by the employer*—(A) *Miles driven in the United States, Canada, or Mexico.* With respect to miles driven in the United States, Canada, or Mexico, the cents-per-mile rate includes the fair market value of fuel provided by the employer. If fuel is not provided by the employer, the cents-per-mile rate may be reduced by no more than 5.5 cents or the amount specified in any applicable Revenue Ruling or Revenue Procedure. For purposes of this section, the United States includes the United States, its possessions and its territories.

(B) *Miles driven outside the United States, Canada, or Mexico.* With respect to miles driven outside the United States, Canada, or Mexico, the fair market value of fuel provided by the employer is not reflected in the cents-per-mile rate. Accordingly, the cents-per-mile rate may be reduced but by no more than 5.5 cents or the amount specified in any applicable Revenue Ruling or Revenue Procedure. If the employer provides the fuel in kind, it must be valued based on all the facts and circumstances. If the employer reimburses the employee for the cost of fuel or allows the employee to charge the employer for the cost of fuel, the fair market value of the fuel is generally the amount of the actual reimbursement or the amount charged, provided the purchase of fuel is at arm's length.

(iii) *Treatment of other services.* The fair market value of any service not specifically identified in paragraph (e)(3)(i) of this section that is provided by the employer with respect to a vehicle is not reflected in the cents-per-mile rate. See paragraph (b)(5) of this section for rules relating to valuation of chauffeur services.

(4) *Valuation of personal use only.* The vehicle cents-per-mile valuation rule of this paragraph (e) may only be used to value the miles driven for personal purposes. Thus, the employer must include an amount in an employee's income with respect to the use of a vehicle that is equal to the product of the number of personal miles driven by the employee and the appropriate cents-per-mile rate. The term "personal miles" means all miles for which the employee used the automobile except miles driven in the employee's trade or business of being an employee of the employer. Unless additional services are provided with respect to the vehicle (see paragraph (e)(3)(iii) of this section), the employer may not include in income a greater amount; for example, the employer may not include in income 100 percent (all business and personal miles) of the value of the use of the vehicle.

(5) *Consistency rules*—(i) *Use of the vehicle cents-per-mile valuation rule by an employer.* An employer must adopt the vehicle cents-per-mile valuation rule of this paragraph (e) for a vehicle to take effect by the later of—

(A) January 1, 1989, or

(B) The first day on which the vehicle is used by an employee of the employer for personal use (or, if the commuting valuation rule of paragraph (f) of this section is used when the vehicle is first used by an employee of the employer for personal use, the first day on which the commuting valuation rule is not used).

(ii) *An employer must use the vehicle cents-per-mile valuation rule for all subsequent years.* Once the vehicle cents-per-mile valuation rule has been adopted for a vehicle by an employer, the rule must be used by the employer for all subsequent years in which the vehicle qualifies for use of the rule, except that the employer may, for any year during which use of the vehicle qualifies for the commuting valuation rule of paragraph (f) of this section, use the commuting valuation rule with respect to the vehicle. If the vehicle fails to qualify for use of the vehicle cents-per-mile valuation rule during a subsequent year, the employer may adopt for such subsequent year and thereafter any other special valuation rule for which the vehicle then qualifies. If the employer elects to use the automobile lease valuation rule of

Reg. § 1.61-21(e)(2)

→ *Caution: Reg. § 1.61-21 applies to fringe benefits provided after 1988. See Temporary Reg. § 1.61-2T for tax treatment of fringe benefits for 1985—1988.*←

paragraph (d) of this section for a period in which the automobile does not qualify for use of the vehicle cents-per-mile valuation rule, then the employer must comply with the requirements of paragraph (d)(7) of this section. For purposes of paragraph (d)(7) of this section, the first day on which the automobile with respect to which the vehicle cents-per-mile rule had been used fails to qualify for use of the vehicle cents-per-mile valuation rule may be deemed to be the first day on which the automobile is available to an employee of the employer for personal use.

(iii) *Use of the vehicle cents-per-mile valuation rule by an employee.* An employee may adopt the vehicle cents-per-mile valuation rule for a vehicle only if the rule is adopted—

(A) By the employer, and

(B) Beginning with respect to the first day on which the vehicle for which the employer (consistent with paragraph (e)(5)(i) of this section) adopted the rule is available to that employee for personal use (or, if the commuting valuation rule of paragraph (f) of this section is used when the vehicle is first used by an employee for personal use, the first day on which the commuting valuation rule is not used).

(iv) *An employee must use the vehicle cents-per-mile valuation rule for all subsequent years.* Once the vehicle cents-per-mile valuation rule has been adopted for a vehicle by an employee, the rule must be used by the employee for all subsequent years of personal use of the vehicle by the employee for which the rule is used by the employer. However, see paragraph (f) of this section for rules relating to the use of the commuting valuation rule for a subsequent year.

(v) *Replacement vehicles.* Notwithstanding anything in this paragraph (e)(5) to the contrary, if the vehicle cents-per-mile valuation rule is used by an employer, or by an employer and an employee, with respect to a particular vehicle, and a replacement vehicle is provided to the employee for the primary purpose of reducing Federal taxes, then the employer, or the employer and the employee, using the rule must continue to use the rule with respect to the replacement vehicle if the replacement vehicle qualifies for use of the rule.

(f) *Commuting valuation rule—(1) In general.* Under the commuting valuation rule of this paragraph (f), the value of the commuting use of an employer-provided vehicle may be determined pursuant to paragraph (f)(3) of this section if the following criteria are met by the employer and employees with respect to the vehicle:

(i) The vehicle is owned or leased by the employer and is provided to one or more employees for use in connection with the employer's trade or business and is used in the employer's trade or business;

(ii) For bona fide noncompensatory business reasons, the employer requires the employee to commute to and/or from work in the vehicle;

(iii) The employer has established a written policy under which neither the employee, nor any individual whose use would be taxable to the employee, may use the vehicle for personal purposes, other than for commuting or de minimis personal use (such as a stop for a personal errand on the way between a business delivery and the employee's home);

(iv) Except for de minimis personal use, the employee does not use the vehicle for any personal purpose other than commuting; and

(v) The employee required to use the vehicle for commuting is not a control employee of the employer (as defined in paragraphs (f)(5) and (6) of this section).

Personal use of a vehicle is all use of the vehicle by an employee that is not use in the employee's trade or business of being an employee of the employer. An employer-provided vehicle that is generally used each workday to transport at least three employees of the employer to and from work in an employer-sponsored commuting vehicle pool is deemed to meet the requirements of paragraphs (f)(1)(i) and (ii) of this section.

(2) *Special rules.* Notwithstanding anything in paragraph (f)(1) of this section to the contrary, the following special rules apply—

(i) *Chauffeur-driven vehicles.* If a vehicle is chauffeur-driven, the commuting valuation rule of this paragraph (f) may not be used to value the commuting use of any person (other than the chauffeur) who rides in the vehicle. (See paragraphs (d) and (e) of this section for other vehicle special valuation rules.) The special rule of this paragraph (f) may be used to value the commuting-only use of the vehicle by the chauffeur if the conditions of paragraph (f)(1) of this section are satisfied. For purposes of this paragraph (f)(2), an individual will not be considered a chauffeur if he or she performs non-driving services for the employer, is not available to perform driving services while performing such other services and whose only driving services consist of

Reg. § 1.61-21(f)(2)

→ *Caution: Reg. § 1.61-21 applies to fringe benefits provided after 1988. See Temporary Reg. § 1.61-2T for tax treatment of fringe benefits for 1985— 1988.*←

driving a vehicle used for commuting by other employees of the employer.

(ii) *Control employee exception.* If the vehicle in which the employee is required to commute is not an automobile as defined in paragraph (d)(1)(ii) of this section, the restriction of paragraph (f)(1)(v) of this section (relating to control employees) does not apply.

(3) *Commuting value—(i) $1.50 per one-way commute.* If the requirements of this paragraph (f) are satisfied, the value of the commuting use of an employer-provided vehicle is $1.50 per one-way commute (e.g., from home to work or from work to home). The value provided in this paragraph (f)(3) includes the value of any goods or services directly related to the vehicle (e.g., fuel).

(ii) *Value per employee.* If there is more than one employee who commutes in the vehicle, such as in the case of an employer-sponsored commuting vehicle pool, the amount includible in the income of each employee is $1.50 per one-way commute. Thus, the amount includible for each round-trip commute is $3.00 per employee. See paragraphs (d)(7)(vi) and (e)(5)(vi) of this section for use of the automobile lease valuation and vehicle cents-per-mile valuation special rules for valuing the use or availability of the vehicle in the case of an employer-sponsored vehicle or automobile commuting pool.

(4) *Definition of vehicle.* For purposes of this paragraph (f), the term "vehicle" means any motorized wheeled vehicle manufactured primarily for use on public streets, roads, and highways. The term "vehicle" includes an automobile as defined in paragraph (d)(1)(ii) of this section.

(5) *Control employee defined—Non-government employer.* For purposes of this paragraph (f), a control employee of a non-government employer is any employee—

(i) Who is a Board- or shareholder-appointed, confirmed, or elected officer of the employer whose compensation equals or exceeds $50,000,

(ii) Who is a director of the employer,

(iii) Whose compensation equals or exceeds $100,000, or

(iv) Who owns a one-percent or greater equity, capital, or profits interest in the employer.

For purposes of determining who is a one-percent owner under paragraph (f)(5)(iv) of this section, any individual who owns (or is considered as owning under section 318(a) or principles similar to

section 318(a) for entities other than corporations) one percent or more of the fair market value of an entity (the "owned entity") is considered a one-percent owner of all entities which would be aggregated with the owned entity under the rules of section 414(b), (c), (m), or (o). For purposes of determining who is an officer or director with respect to an employer under this paragraph (f)(5), notwithstanding anything in this section to the contrary, if an entity would be aggregated with other entities under the rules of section 414(b), (c), (m), or (o), the officer definition (but not the compensation requirement) and the director definition apply to each such separate entity rather than to the aggregated employer. An employee who is an officer or a director of an entity (the "first entity") shall be treated as an officer or a director of all entities aggregated with the first entity under the rules of section 414(b), (c), (m), or (o). Instead of applying the control employee definition of this paragraph (f)(5), an employer may treat all, and only, employees who are "highly compensated" employees (as defined in § 1.132-8(g)) as control employees for purposes of this paragraph (f).

(6) *Control employee defined—Government employer.* For purposes of this paragraph (f), a control employee of a government employer is any—

(i) Elected official, or

(ii) Employee whose compensation equals or exceeds the compensation paid to a Federal Government employee holding a position at Executive Level V, determined under Chapter 11 of title 2, United States Code, as adjusted by section 5318 of Title 5 United States Code.

For purposes of this paragraph (f), the term "government" includes any Federal, state or local governmental unit, and any agency or instrumentality thereof. Instead of applying the control employee definition of paragraph (f)(6), an employer may treat all and only employees who are "highly compensated" employees (as defined in § 1.132-8(f)) as control employees for purposes of this paragraph (f).

(7) *"Compensation" defined.* For purposes of this paragraph (f), the term "compensation" has the same meaning as in section 414(q)(7). Compensation includes all amounts received from all entities treated as a single employer under section 414(b), (c), (m), or (o). Levels of compensation shall be adjusted at the same time and in the same manner as provided in section 415(d). The

Reg. § 1.61-21(f)(3)

→ *Caution: Reg. § 1.61-21 applies to fringe benefits provided after 1988. See Temporary Reg. § 1.61-2T for tax treatment of fringe benefits for 1985—1988.*←

first such adjustment shall be for calendar year 1988.

(g) *Non-commercial flight valuation rule*—(1) *In general.* Under the non-commercial flight valuation rule of this paragraph (g), except as provided in paragraph (g)(12) of this section, if an employee is provided with a flight on an employer-provided aircraft, the value of the flight is calculated using the aircraft valuation formula of paragraph (g)(5) of this section. For purposes of this paragraph (g), the value of a flight on an employer-provided aircraft by an individual who is less than two years old is deemed to be zero. See paragraph (b)(1) of this section for rules relating to the amount includible in income when an employee reimburses the employee's employer for all or part of the fair market value of the benefit provided.

(2) *Eligible flights and eligible aircraft.* The valuation rule of this paragraph (g) may be used to value flights on all employer-provided aircraft, including helicopters. The valuation rule of this paragraph (g) may be used to value international as well as domestic flights. The valuation rule of this paragraph (g) may not be used to value a flight on any commercial aircraft on which air transportation is sold to the public on a per-seat basis. For a special valuation rule relating to certain flights on commercial aircraft, see paragraph (h) of this section.

(3) *Definition of a flight*—(i) *General rule.* Except as otherwise provided in paragraph (g)(3)(iii) of this section (relating to intermediate stops), for purposes of this paragraph (g), a flight is the distance (in statute miles, i.e., 5,280 feet per statute mile) between the place at which the individual boards the aircraft and the place at which the individual deplanes.

(ii) *Valuation of each flight.* Under the valuation rule of this paragraph (g), value is determined separately for each flight. Thus, a round-trip is comprised of at least two flights. For example, an employee who takes a personal trip on an employer-provided aircraft from New York City to Denver, then Denver to Los Angeles, and finally Los Angeles to New York City has taken three flights and must apply the aircraft valuation formula separately to each flight. The value of a flight must be determined on a passenger-by-passenger basis. For example, if an individual accompanies an employee and the flight taken by the individual would be taxed to the employee, the employee would be taxed on the special rule

value of the flight by the employee and the flight by the individual.

(iii) *Intermediate stop.* If a landing is necessitated by weather conditions, by an emergency, for purposes of refueling or obtaining other services relating to the aircraft, or for any other purpose unrelated to the personal purposes of the employee whose flight is being valued, that landing is an intermediate stop. Additional mileage attributable to an intermediate stop is not considered when determining the distance of an employee's flight.

(iv) *Examples.* The rules of paragraph (g)(3)(iii) of this section may be illustrated by the following examples:

Example (1). Assume that an employee's trip originates in St. Louis, Missouri, with Seattle, Washington as its destination, but, because of weather conditions, the aircraft lands in Denver, Colorado, and the employee stays in Denver overnight. Assume further that the next day the aircraft flies to Seattle where the employee deplanes. The employee's flight is the distance between the airport in St. Louis and the airport in Seattle.

Example (2). Assume that a trip originates in New York, New York, with five passengers and that the aircraft makes a stop in Chicago, Illinois, so that one of the passengers can deplane for a purpose unrelated to the personal purposes of the other passengers whose flights are being valued. The aircraft then goes on to Los Angeles, California, where the other four passengers will deplane. The flight of the passenger who deplaned in Chicago is the distance between the airport in New York and the airport in Chicago. The stop in Chicago is disregarded as an intermediate stop, however, when measuring the flights taken by each of the other four passengers. Their flights would be the distance between the airport in New York and the airport in Los Angeles.

(4) *Personal and non-personal flights*—(i) *In general.* The valuation rule of this paragraph (g) applies to personal flights on employer-provided aircraft. A personal flight is one the value of which is not excludable under another section of subtitle A of the Internal Revenue Code of 1986, such as under section 132(d) (relating to a working condition fringe). However, solely for purposes of paragraphs (g)(4)(ii) and (g)(4)(iii) of this section, references to personal flights do not include flights a portion of which would not be excludable from income by reason of section 274(c).

Reg. § 1.61-21(g)(4)

→ *Caution: Reg. § 1.61-21 applies to fringe benefits provided after 1988. See Temporary Reg. § 1.61-2T for tax treatment of fringe benefits for 1985— 1988.*←

(ii) *Trip primarily for employer's business.* If an employee combines, in one trip, personal and business flights on an employer-provided aircraft and the employee's trip is primarily for the employer's business (see § 1.162-2(b)(2)), the employee must include in income the excess of the value of all the flights that comprise the trip over the value of the flights that would have been taken had there been no personal flights but only business flights. For example, assume that an employee flies on an employer-provided aircraft from Chicago, Illinois, to Miami, Florida, for the employer's business and that from Miami the employee flies on the employer-provided aircraft to Orlando, Florida, for personal purposes and then flies back to Chicago. Assume further that the primary purpose of the trip is for the employer's business. The amount includible in income is the excess of the value of the three flights (Chicago to Miami, Miami to Orlando, and Orlando to Chicago), over the value of the flights that would have been taken had there been no personal flights but only business flights (Chicago to Miami and Miami to Chicago).

(iii) *Primarily personal trip.* If an employee combines, in one trip, personal and business flights on an employer-provided aircraft and the employee's trip is primarily personal (see § 1.162-2(b)(2)), the amount includible in the employee's income is the value of the personal flights that would have been taken had there been no business flights but only personal flights. For example, assume that an employee flies on an employer-provided aircraft from San Francisco, California, to Los Angeles, California, for the employer's business and that from Los Angeles the employee flies on an employer-provided aircraft to Palm Springs, California, primarily for personal reasons and then flies back to San Francisco. Assume further that the primary purpose of the trip is personal. The amount includible in the employee's income is the value of personal flights that would have been taken had there been no business flights but only personal flights (San Francisco to Palm Springs and Palm Springs to San Francisco).

(iv) *Application of section 274(c).* The value of employer-provided travel outside the United States away from home may not be excluded from the employee's gross income as a working condition fringe, by either the employer or the employee, to the extent not deductible by reason of section 274(c). The valuation rule of this paragraph (g) applies to that portion of the value of any flight not excludable by reason of section 274(c). Such value is includible in income in addition to the amounts determined under paragraphs (g)(4)(ii) and (g)(4)(iii) of this section.

(v) *Flights by individuals who are not personal guests.* If an individual who is not an employee of the employer providing the aircraft is on a flight, and the individual is not the personal guest of any employee of the employer, the flight by the individual is not taxable to any employee of the employer providing the aircraft. The rule in the preceding sentence applies where the individual is provided the flight by the employer for noncompensatory business reasons of the employer. For example, assume that G, an employee of company Y, accompanies A, an employee of company X, on company X's aircraft for the purpose of inspecting land under consideration for purchase by company X from company Y. The flight by G is not taxable to A. No inference may be drawn from this paragraph (g)(4)(v) concerning the taxation of a flight provided to an individual who is neither an employee of the employer nor a personal guest of any employee of the employer.

(5) *Aircraft valuation formula.* Under the valuation rule of this paragraph (g), the value of a flight is determined under the base aircraft valuation formula (also known as the Standard Industry Fare Level formula or SIFL) by multiplying the SIFL cents-per-mile rates applicable for the period during which the flight was taken by the appropriate aircraft multiple (as provided in paragraph (g)(7) of this section) and then adding the applicable terminal charge. The SIFL cents-per-mile rates in the formula and the terminal charge are calculated by the Department of Transportation and are revised semi-annually. The base aircraft valuation formula in effect from January 1, 1989 through June 30, 1989, is as follows: a terminal charge of $26.48 plus ($.1449 per mile for the first 500 miles, $.1105 per mile for miles between 501 and 1500, and $.1062 per mile for miles over 1500). For example, if a flight taken on January 15, 1989, by a non-control employee on an employer-provided aircraft with a maximum certified takeoff weight of 26,000 lbs. is 2,000 miles long, the value of the flight determined under this paragraph (g)(5) is $100.36 ((.313 × (($.1449 × 500) + ($.1105 × 1,000) + ($.1062 × 500))) + $26.48). The aircraft valuation formula applies separately to each flight being valued under this paragraph (g). Therefore, the number of miles an employee has flown on employer-provided aircraft

Reg. § 1.61-21(g)(5)

→ *Caution: Reg. § 1.61-21 applies to fringe benefits provided after 1988. See Temporary Reg. § 1.61-2T for tax treatment of fringe benefits for 1985—1988.*←

flights prior to the flight being valued does not affect the determination of the value of the flight.

(6) *Discretion to provide new formula.* The Commissioner may prescribe a different base aircraft valuation formula by regulation, Revenue Ruling or Revenue Procedure in the event that the calculation of the Standard Industry Fare Level is discontinued.

(7) *Aircraft multiples*—(i) *In general.* The aircraft multiples are based on the maximum certified takeoff weight of the aircraft. When applying the aircraft valuation formula to a flight, the appropriate aircraft multiple is multiplied by the product of the applicable SIFL cents-per-mile rates multiplied by the number of miles in the flight and then the terminal charge is added to the product. For purposes of applying the aircraft valuation formula described in paragraph (g)(5) of this section, the aircraft multiples are as follows:

Maximum Certified Takeoff Weight of the Aircraft	Aircraft Multiple for a Control Employee	Aircraft Multiple for a Non-Control Employee
6,000 lbs. or less	62.5 percent	15.6 percent
6,001—10,000 lbs.	125 percent	23.4 percent
10,001—25,000 lbs.	300 percent	31.3 percent
25,001 lbs. or more	400 percent	31.3 percent

(ii) *Flights treated as provided to a control employee.* Except as provided in paragraph (g)(12) of this section, any flight provided to an individual whose flight would be taxable to a control employee (as defined in paragraphs (g)(8) and (9) of this section) as the recipient shall be valued as if such flight had been provided to that control employee. For example, assume that the chief executive officer of an employer, his spouse, and his two children fly on an employer-provided aircraft for personal purposes. Assume further that the maximum certified takeoff weight of the aircraft is 12,000 lbs. The amount includible in the employee's income is 4 × ((300 percent × the applicable SIFL cents-per-mile rates provided in paragraph (g)(5) of this section multiplied by the number of miles in the flight) plus the applicable terminal charge).

(8) *Control employee defined—Non-government employer*—(i) *Definition.* For purposes of this paragraph (g), a control employee of a non-government employer is any employee—

(A) Who is a Board- or shareholder-appointed, confirmed, or elected officer of the employer, limited to the lesser of—

(*1*) One percent of all employees (increased to the next highest integer, if not an integer) or

(*2*) Ten employees;

(B) Who is among the top one percent most highly-paid employees of the employer (increased to the next highest integer, if not an integer) limited to a maximum of 50;

(C) Who owns a five-percent or greater equity, capital, or profits interest in the employer; or

(D) Who is a director of the employer.

(ii) *Special rules for control employee definition*—(A) *In general.* For purposes of this paragraph (g), any employee who is a family member (within the meaning of section 267(c)(4)) of a control employee is also a control employee. For purposes of paragraph (g)(8)(i)(B) of this section, the term "employee" does not include any individual unless such individual is a common-law employee, partner, or one-percent or greater shareholder of the employer. Pursuant to this paragraph (g)(8), an employee may be a control employee under more than one of the requirements listed in paragraphs (g)(8)(i)(A) through (D) of this section. For example, an employee may be both an officer under paragraph (g)(8)(i)(A) of this section and a highly-paid employee under paragraph (g)(8)(i)(B) of this section. In this case, for purposes of the officer limitation rule of paragraph (g)(8)(i)(A) of this section and the highly-paid employee limitation rule of paragraph (g)(8)(i)(B) of this section, the employee would be counted in applying both limitations. For purposes of determining the one-percent limitation under paragraphs (g)(8)(i)(A) and (B) of this section, an employer shall exclude from consideration employees described in § 1.132-8(b)(3). Instead of applying the control employee definition of this paragraph (g)(8), an employer may treat all (and only) employees who are "highly compensated"

Reg. § 1.61-21(g)(8)

→ *Caution: Reg. § 1.61-21 applies to fringe benefits provided after 1988. See Temporary Reg. § 1.61-2T for tax treatment of fringe benefits for 1985— 1988.*←

employees (as defined in § 1.132-8(f)) as control employees for purposes of this paragraph (g).

(B) *Special rules for officers, owners, and highly-paid control employees.* In no event shall an employee whose compensation is less than $50,000 be a control employee under paragraph (g)(8)(i)(A) or (B) of this section. For purposes of determining who is a five-percent (or one-percent) owner under this paragraph (g)(8), any individual who owns (or is considered as owning under section 318(a) or principles similar to section 318(a) for entities other than corporations) five percent (or one-percent) or more of the fair market value of an entity (the "owned entity") is considered a five-percent (or one-percent) owner of all entities which would be aggregated with the owned entity under the rules of section 414(b), (c), (m), or (o). For purposes of determining who is an officer or director with respect to an employer under this paragraph (g)(8), notwithstanding anything in this section to the contrary, if the employer would be aggregated with other employers under the rules of section 414(b), (c), (m), or (o), the officer definition and the limitations and the director definition are applied to each such separate employer rather than to the aggregated employer. An employee who is an officer or director of one employer (the "first employer") shall not be counted as an officer or a director of any other employer aggregated with the first employer under the rules of section 414(b), (c), or (m). If applicable, the officer limitation rule of paragraph (g)(8)(i)(A) of this section is applied to employees in descending order of their compensation. Thus, if an employer has 11 board-appointed officers and the limit imposed under paragraph (g)(8)(i)(A) of this section is 10 officers, the employee with the least compensation of those officers would not be a control employee under paragraph (g)(8)(i)(A) of this section.

(9) *Control employee defined—Government employer.* For purposes of this paragraph (g), a control employee of a government employer is any—

(i) Elected official, or

(ii) Employee whose compensation equals or exceeds the compensation paid to a Federal Government employee holding a position at Executive Level V, determined under Chapter 11 of title 2, United States Code, as adjusted by section 5318 of title 5 United States Code.

For purposes of paragraph (f), the term "government" includes any Federal, state or local govern-

mental unit, and any agency or instrumentality thereof. Instead of applying the control employee definition of paragraph (f)(6), an employer may treat all and only employees who are "highly compensated" employees (as defined in § 1.132-8(f)) as control employees for purposes of this paragraph (f).

(10) *"Compensation" defined.* For purposes of this paragraph (g), the term "compensation" has the same meaning as in section 414(q)(7). Compensation includes all amounts received from all entities treated as a single employer under section 414(b), (c), (m), or (o). Levels of compensation shall be adjusted at the same time and in the same manner as provided in section 415(d). The first such adjustment was for calendar year 1988.

(11) *Treatment of former employees.* For purposes of this paragraph (g), an employee who was a control employee of the employer (as defined in this paragraph (g)) at any time after reaching age 55, or within three years of separation from the service of the employer, is a control employee with respect to flights taken after separation from the service of the employer. An individual who is treated as a control employee under this paragraph (g)(11) is not counted when determining the limitations of paragraph (g)(8)(i)(A) and (B) of this section. Thus, the total number of individuals treated as control employees under such paragraphs may exceed the limitations of such paragraphs to the extent that this paragraph (g)(11) applies.

(12) *Seating capacity rule—(i) In general—* (A) *General rule.* Where 50 percent or more of the regular passenger seating capacity of an aircraft (as used by the employer) is occupied by individuals whose flights are primarily for the employer's business (and whose flights are excludable from income under section 132(d)), the value of a flight on that aircraft by any employee who is not flying primarily for the employer's business (or who is flying primarily for the employer's business but the value of whose flight is not excludable under section 132(d) by reason of section 274(c)) is deemed to be zero. See § 1.132-5 which limits the working condition fringe exclusion under section 132(d) to situations where the employee receives the flight in connection with the performance of services for the employer providing the aircraft.

(B) *Special rules—(1) Definition of "employee."* For purposes of this paragraph (g)(12), the term "employee" includes only employees of the employer, including a partner of a partner-

Reg. § 1.61-21(g)(9)

→ *Caution: Reg. § 1.61-21 applies to fringe benefits provided after 1988. See Temporary Reg. § 1.61-2T for tax treatment of fringe benefits for 1985— 1988.*←

ship, providing the aircraft and does not include independent contractors and directors of the employer. A flight taken by an individual other than an "employee" as defined in the preceding sentence is considered a flight taken by an employee for purposes of this paragraph (g)(12) only if that individual is treated as an employee pursuant to section 132(f)(1) or that individual's flight is treated as a flight taken by an employee pursuant to section 132(f)(2). If—

    (*i*) A flight by an individual is not considered a flight taken by an employee (as defined in this paragraph (g)(12)(i)),

    (*ii*) The value of that individual's flight is not excludable under section 132(d), and

    (*iii*) The seating capacity rule of this paragraph (g)(12) otherwise applies,

then the value of the flight provided to such an individual is the value of a flight provided to a non-control employee pursuant to paragraph (g)(5) of this section (even if the individual who would be taxed on the value of the flight is a control employee).

    (*2*) *Example.* The special rules of paragraph (g)(12)(i)(B)(*1*) of this section are illustrated by the following example:

    Example. Assume that 60 percent of the regular passenger seating capacity of an employer's aircraft is occupied by individuals whose flights are primarily for the employer's business and are excludable from income under section 132(d). If a control employee, his spouse, and his dependent child fly on the employer's aircraft for primarily personal reasons, the value of the three flights is deemed to be zero. If, however, the control employee's cousin were provided a flight on the employer's aircraft, the value of the flight taken by the cousin is determined by applying the aircraft valuation formula of paragraph (g)(5) of this section (including the terminal charge) and the non-control employee aircraft multiples of paragraph (g)(7) of this section.

    (ii) *Application of 50-percent test to multiple flights.* The seating capacity rule of this paragraph (g)(12) must be met both at the time the individual whose flight is being valued boards the aircraft and at the time the individual deplanes. For example, assume that employee A boards an employer-provided aircraft for personal purposes in New York, New York, and that at that time 80 percent of the regular passenger seating capacity of the aircraft is occupied by individuals whose flights is primarily for the employer's business

(and whose flights are excludable from income under section 132(d)) ("the business passengers"). If the aircraft flies directly to Hartford, Connecticut where all of the passengers, including A, deplane, the requirements of the seating capacity rule of this paragraph (g)(12) have been satisfied. If instead, some of the passengers, including A, remain on the aircraft in Hartford and the aircraft continues on to Boston, Massachusetts, where they all deplane, the requirements of the seating capacity rule of this paragraph (g)(12) will not be satisfied with respect to A's flight from New York to Boston unless at least 50 percent of the seats comprising the aircraft's regular passenger seating capacity were occupied by the business passengers at the time A deplanes in Boston.

    (iii) *Regular passenger seating capacity.* (A) *General rule.* Except as otherwise provided, the regular passenger seating capacity of an aircraft is the maximum number of seats that have at any time on or prior to the date of the flight been on the aircraft (while owned or leased by the employer). Except to the extent excluded pursuant to paragraph (g)(12)(v) of this section, regular seating capacity includes all seats which may be occupied by members of the flight crew. It is irrelevant that, on a particular flight, less than the maximum number of seats are available for use because, for example, some of the seats are removed.

    (B) *Special rules.* When determining the maximum number of seats that have at any time on or prior to the date of the flight been on the aircraft (while owned or leased by the employer), seats that could not at any time be legally used during takeoff and have not at any time been used during takeoff are not counted. As of the date an employer permanently reduces the seating capacity of an aircraft, the regular passenger seating capacity is the reduced number of seats on the aircraft. The previous sentence shall not apply if at any time within 24 months after such reduction any seats are added in the aircraft. Unless the conditions of this paragraph (g)(12)(iii)(B) are satisfied, jumpseats and removable seats used solely for purposes of flight crew training are counted for purposes of the seating capacity rule of this paragraph (g)(12).

    (iv) *Examples.* The rules of paragraph (g)(12)(iii) of this section are illustrated by the following examples:

    Example (1). Employer A and employer B order the same aircraft, except that A orders it with 10 seats and B orders it with eight seats. A

Reg. § 1.61-21(g)(12)

→ *Caution: Reg. § 1.61-21 applies to fringe benefits provided after 1988. See Temporary Reg. § 1.61-2T for tax treatment of fringe benefits for 1985— 1988.*←

always uses its aircraft as a 10-seat aircraft; B always uses its aircraft as an eight-seat aircraft. The regular passenger seating capacity of A's aircraft is 10 and of B's aircraft is eight.

Example (2). Assume the same facts as in example (1), except that whenever A's chief executive officer and spouse use the aircraft eight seats are removed. Even if substantially all of the use of the aircraft is by the chief executive officer and spouse, the regular passenger seating capacity of the aircraft is 10.

Example (3). Assume the same facts as in example (1), except that whenever more than eight people want to fly in B's aircraft, two extra seats are added. Even if substantially all of the use of the aircraft occurs with eight seats, the regular passenger seating capacity of the aircraft is 10.

Example (4). Employer C purchases an aircraft with 12 seats. Three months later C remodels the interior of the aircraft and permanently removes four of the seats. Upon completion of the remodeling, the regular passenger seating capacity of the aircraft is eight. If, however, any seats are added within 24 months after the remodeling, the regular seating capacity of the aircraft is treated as 12 throughout the entire period.

(v) *Seats occupied by flight crew.* When determining the regular passenger seating capacity of an aircraft, any seat occupied by a member of the flight crew (whether or not such individual is an employee of the employer providing the aircraft) shall not be counted, unless the purpose of the flight by such individual is not primarily to serve as a member of the flight crew. If the seat occupied by a member of the flight crew is not counted as a passenger seat pursuant to the previous sentence, such member of the flight crew is disregarded in applying the 50-percent test described in the first sentence of paragraph (g)(12)(i) of this section. For example, assume that prior to application of this paragraph (g)(12)(v) the regular passenger seating capacity of an aircraft is one. Assume further that an employee pilots the aircraft and that the employee's flight is not primarily for the employer's business. If the employee's spouse occupies the other seat for personal purposes, the seating capacity rule is not met and the value of both flights must be included in the employee's income. If, however, the employee's flight were primarily for the employer's business (unrelated to serving as a member of the flight crew), then the seating capacity rule is met and the value of the flight for

the employee's spouse is deemed to be zero. If the employee's flight were primarily to serve as a member of the flight crew, then the seating capacity rule is not met and the value of a flight by any passenger for primarily personal reasons is not deemed to be zero.

(13) *Erroneous use of the non-commercial flight valuation rule—*(i) *Certain errors in the case of a flight by a control employee.* If—

(A) The non-commercial flight valuation rule of this paragraph (g) is applied by an employer or a control employee, as the case may be, on a return as originally filed or on an amended return on the grounds that either—

(*1*) The control employee is not in fact a control employee, or

(*2*) The aircraft is within a specific weight classification, and

(B) Either position is subsequently determined to be erroneous,

the valuation rule of this paragraph (g) is not available to value the flight taken by that control employee by the person or persons taking the erroneous position. With respect to the weight classifications, the previous sentence does not apply if the position taken is that the weight of the aircraft is greater than it is subsequently determined to be. If, with respect to a flight by a control employee, the seating capacity rule of paragraph (g)(12) of this section is used by an employer or the control employee, as the case may be, on a return as originally filed or on an amended return, the valuation rule of this paragraph (g) is not available to value the flight taken by that control employee by the person or persons taking the erroneous position.

(ii) *Value of flight excluded as a working condition fringe.* If either an employer or an employee, on a return as originally filed or on an amended return, excludes from the employee's income or wages all or any part of the value of a flight on the grounds that the flight was excludable as a working condition fringe under section 132, and that position is subsequently determined to be erroneous, the valuation rule of this paragraph (g) is not available to value the flight taken by that employee by the person or persons taking the erroneous position. Instead, the general valuation rules of paragraph (b)(5) and (6) of this section apply.

(14) *Consistency rules—*(i) *Use by the employer.* Except as otherwise provided in paragraph (g)(13) of this section or § 1.132-5(m)(4), if

Reg. § 1.61-21(g)(13)

→ *Caution: Reg. § 1.61-21 applies to fringe benefits provided after 1988. See Temporary Reg. § 1.61-2T for tax treatment of fringe benefits for 1985—1988.*←

the non-commercial flight valuation rule of this paragraph (g) is used by an employer to value any flight provided to an employee in a calendar year, the rule must be used to value all flights provided to all employees in the calendar year.

(ii) *Use by the employee.* Except as otherwise provided in paragraph (g)(13) of this section or § 1.132-5(m)(4), if the non-commercial flight valuation rule of this paragraph (g) is used by an employee to value a flight provided by an employer in a calendar year, the rule must be used to value all flights provided to the employee by that employer in the calendar year.

(h) *Commercial flight valuation rule*—(1) *In general.* Under the commercial flight valuation rule of this paragraph (h), the value of a space-available flight (as defined in paragraph (h)(2) of this section) on a commercial aircraft is 25 percent of the actual carrier's highest unrestricted coach fare in effect for the particular flight taken. The rule of this paragraph (h) is available only to an individual described in § 1.132-1(b)(1).

(2) *Space-available flight.* The commercial flight valuation rule of this paragraph (h) is available to value a space-available flight. The term "space-available flight" means a flight on a commercial aircraft—

(i) Which is subject to the same types of restrictions customarily associated with flying on an employee "stand-by" or "space-available" basis, and

(ii) Which meets the definition of a no-additional-cost service under section 132(b), except that the flight is provided to an individual other than the employee or an individual treated as the employee under section 132(f). Thus, a flight is not a space-available flight if the employer guarantees the employee a seat on the flight or if the nondiscrimination requirements of section 132(h)(1) and § 1.132-8 are not satisfied. A flight may be a space-available flight even if the airline that is the actual carrier is not the employer of the employee.

(3) *Commercial aircraft.* If the actual carrier does not offer, in the ordinary course of its business, air transportation to customers on a per-seat basis, the commercial flight valuation rule of this paragraph (h) is not available. Thus, if, in the ordinary course of its line of business, the employer only offers air transportation to customers on a charter basis, the commercial flight valuation rule of this paragraph (h) may not be used to value a space-available flight on the employer's

aircraft. If the commercial flight valuation rule is not available, the flight may be valued under the non-commercial flight valuation rule of paragraph (g) of this section.

(4) *Timing of inclusion.* The date that the flight is taken is the relevant date for purposes of applying section 61(a)(1) and this section to a space-available flight on a commercial aircraft. The date of purchase or issuance of a pass or ticket is not relevant. Thus, this section applies to a flight taken on or after January 1, 1989, regardless of the date on which the pass or ticket for the flight was purchased or issued.

(5) *Consistency rules*—(i) *Use by employer.* If the commercial flight valuation rule of this paragraph (h) is used by an employer to value any flight provided in a calendar year, the rule must be used to value all flights eligible for use of the rule provided in the calendar year.

(ii) *Use by employee.* If the commercial flight valuation rule of this paragraph (h) is used by an employee to value a flight provided by an employer in a calendar year, the rule must be used to value all flights provided by that employer eligible for use of the rule taken by such employee in the calendar year.

(i) [Reserved.]

(j) *Valuation of meals provided at an employer-operated eating facility for employees*—(1) *In general.* The valuation rule of this paragraph (j) may be used to value a meal provided at an employer-operated eating facility for employees (as defined in § 1.132-7). For rules relating to an exclusion for the value of meals provided at an employer-operated eating facility for employees, see section 132(e)(2) and § 1.132-7.

(2) *Valuation formula*—(i) *In general.* The value of all meals provided at an employer-operated eating facility for employees during a calendar year ("total meal value") is 150 percent of the direct operating costs of the eating facility determined separately with respect to such eating facility whether or not the direct operating costs test is applied separately to such eating facility under § 1.132-7(b)(2). For purposes of this paragraph (j), the definition of direct operating costs provided in § 1.132-7(b) and the adjustments specified in § 1.132-7(a)(2) apply. The taxable value of meals provided at an eating facility may be determined in two ways. The "individual meal subsidy" may be treated as the taxable value of a meal provided at the eating facility (see paragraph (j)(2)(ii) of this section) to a particular

Reg. § 1.61-21(j)(2)

→ *Caution: Reg. § 1.61-21 applies to fringe benefits provided after 1988. See Temporary Reg. § 1.61-2T for tax treatment of fringe benefits for 1985—1988.*←

employee. Alternatively, the employer may allocate the "total meal subsidy" among employees (see paragraph (j)(2)(iii) of this section).

(ii) *"Individual meal subsidy" defined.* The "individual meal subsidy" is determined by multiplying the amount paid by the employee for a particular meal by a fraction, the numerator of which is the total meal value and the denominator of which is the gross receipts of the eating facility for the calendar year and then subtracting the amount paid by the employee for the meal. The taxable value of meals provided to a particular employee during a calendar year, therefore, is the sum of the individual meal subsidies provided to the employee during the calendar year. This rule is available only if there is a charge for each meal selection and if each employee is charged the same price for any given meal selection.

(iii) *Allocation of "total meal subsidy".* Instead of using the individual meal subsidy method provided in paragraph (j)(2)(ii) of this section, the employer may allocate the "total meal subsidy" (total meal value less the gross receipts of the facility) among employees in any manner reasonable under the circumstances. It will be presumed reasonable for an employer to allocate the total meal subsidy on a per-employee basis if the employer has information that would substantiate to the satisfaction of the Commissioner that each employee was provided approximately the same number of meals at the facility.

(k) *Commuting valuation rule for certain employees*—(1) *In general.* Under the rule of this paragraph (k), the value of the commuting use of employer-provided transportation may be determined under paragraph (k)(3) of this section if the following criteria are met by the employer and employee with respect to the transportation:

(i) The transportation is provided, solely because of unsafe conditions, to an employee who would ordinarily walk or use public transportation for commuting to or from work;

(ii) The employer has established a written policy (e.g., in the employer's personnel manual) under which the transportation is not provided for the employee's personal purposes other than for commuting due to unsafe conditions and the employer's practice in fact corresponds with the policy;

(iii) The transportation is not used for personal purposes other than commuting due to unsafe conditions; and

(iv) The employee receiving the employer-provided transportation is a qualified employee of the employer (as defined in paragraph (k)(6) of this section).

(2) *Trip-by-trip basis.* The special valuation rule of this paragraph (k) applies on a trip-by-trip basis. If an employer and employee fail to meet the criteria of paragraph (k)(1) of this section with respect to any trip, the value of the transportation for that trip is not determined under paragraph (k)(3) of this section and the amount includible in the employee's income is determined by reference to the fair market value of the transportation.

(3) *Commuting value*—(i) *$1.50 per one-way commute.* If the requirements of this paragraph (k) are satisfied, the value of the commuting use of the employer-provided transportation is $1.50 per one-way commute (i.e., from home to work or from work to home).

(ii) *Value per employee.* If transportation is provided to more than one qualified employee at the same time, the amount includible in the income of each employee is $1.50 per one-way commute.

(4) *Definition of employer-provided transportation.* For purposes of this paragraph (k), "employer-provided transportation" means transportation by vehicle (as defined in paragraph (f)(4) of this section) that is purchased by the employer (or that is purchased by the employee and reimbursed by the employer) from a party that is not related to the employer for the purpose of transporting a qualified employee to or from work. Reimbursements made by an employer to an employee to cover the cost of purchasing transportation (e.g., hiring cabs) must be made under a bona fide reimbursement arrangement.

(5) *Unsafe conditions.* Unsafe conditions exist if a reasonable person would, under the facts and circumstances, consider it unsafe for the employee to walk to or from home, or to walk to or use public transportation at the time of day the employee must commute. One of the factors indicating whether it is unsafe is the history of crime in the geographic area surrounding the employee's workplace or residence at the time of day the employee must commute.

(6) *Qualified employee defined*—(i) *In general.* For purposes of this paragraph (k), a qualified employee is one who meets the following requirements with respect to the employer:

Reg. § 1.61-21(k)(1)

→ *Caution: Reg. § 1.61-21 applies to fringe benefits provided after 1988. See Temporary Reg. § 1.61-2T for tax treatment of fringe benefits for 1985—1988.*←

(A) The employee performs services during the current year, is paid on an hourly basis, is not claimed under section 213(a)(1) of the Fair Labor Standards Act of 1938 (as amended), 29 U.S.C. §§ 201-219 (FLSA), to be exempt from the minimum wage and maximum hour provisions of the FLSA, and is within a classification with respect to which the employer actually pays, or has specified in writing that it will pay, compensation for overtime equal to or exceeding one and one-half times the regular rate as provided by section 207 of the FLSA; and

(B) The employee does not receive compensation from the employer in excess of the amount permitted by section 414(q)(1)(C) of the Code.

(ii) *"Compensation" and "paid on an hourly basis" defined.* For purposes of this paragraph (k), "compensation" has the same meaning as in section 414(q)(7). Compensation includes all amounts received from all entities treated as a single employer under section 414(b), (c), (m), or (o). Levels of compensation shall be adjusted at the same time and in the same manner as provided in section 415(d). If an employee's compensation is stated on an annual basis, the employee is treated as "paid on an hourly basis" for purposes of this paragraph (k) as long as the employee is not claimed to be exempt from the minimum wage and maximum hour provisions of the FLSA and is paid overtime wages either equal to or exceeding one and one-half the employee's regular hourly rate of pay.

(iii) *FLSA compliance required.* An employee will not be considered a qualified employee for purposes of this paragraph (k), unless the employer is in compliance with the recordkeeping requirements concerning that employee's wages, hours, and other conditions and practices of employment as provided in section 211(c) of the FLSA and 29 CFR part 516.

(iv) *Issues arising under the FLSA.* If questions arise concerning an employee's classification under the FLSA, the pronouncements and rulings of the Administrator of the Wage and Hour Division, Department of Labor are determinative.

(v) *Non-qualified employees.* If an employee is not a qualified employee within the meaning of this paragraph (k)(6), no portion of the value of the commuting use of employer-provided transportation is excluded under this paragraph (k).

(7) *Examples.* This paragraph (k) is illustrated by the following examples:

Example 1. A and B are word-processing clerks employed by Y, an accounting firm in a large metropolitan area, and both are qualified employees under paragraph (k)(6) of this section. The normal working hours for A and B are from 11:00 p.m. until 7:00 a.m. and public transportation, the only means of transportation available to A or B, would be considered unsafe by a reasonable person at the time they are required to commute from home to work. In response, Y hires a car service to pick up A and B at their homes each evening for purposes of transporting them to work. The amount includible in the income of both A and B is $1.50 for the one-way commute from home to work.

Example 2. Assume the same facts as in *Example 1*, except that Y also hires a car service to return A and B to their homes each morning at the conclusion of their shifts and public transportation would not be considered unsafe by a reasonable person at the time of day A and B commute to their homes. The value of the commute from work to home is includible in the income of both A and B by reference to fair market value since unsafe conditions do not exist for that trip.

Example 3. C is an associate for Z, a law firm in a metropolitan area. The normal working hours for C's law firm are from 9:00 a.m. until 6:00 p.m., but C's ordinary office hours are from 10:00 a.m. until 8:00 p.m. Public transportation, the only means of transportation available to C at the time C commutes from work to home during the evening, would be considered unsafe by a reasonable person. In response, Z hires a car service to take C home each evening. C does not receive annual compensation from Z in excess of the amount permitted by section 414(q)(1)(C) of the Code. However, C is treated as an employee exempt from the provisions of the FLSA and, accordingly, is not paid overtime wages. Therefore, C is not a qualified employee within the meaning of paragraph (k)(6) of this section. The value of the commute from work to home is includible in C's income by reference to fair market value.

(8) *Effective date.* This paragraph (k) applies to employer-provided transportation provided to a qualified employee on or after July 1, 1991. [Reg. § 1.61-21.]

☐ [*T.D. 8256, 7-5-89. Amended by T.D. 8389, 1-15-92 and T.D. 8457, 12-29-92.*]

Reg. § 1.61-21(k)(8)

[Reg. § 1.62-1]

§ 1.62-1. Adjusted gross income.—(a) [Reserved]

(b) [Reserved]

(c) *Deductions allowable in computing adjusted gross income.* The deductions specified in section 62(a) for purposes of computing adjusted gross income are—

(1) Deductions set forth in § 1.62-1T(c); and

(2) Deductions allowable under part VI, subchapter B, chapter 1 of the Internal Revenue Code, (section 161 and following) that consist of expenses paid or incurred by the taxpayer in connection with the performance of services as an employee under a reimbursement or other expense allowance arrangement (as defined in § 1.62-2) with his or her employer. For the rules pertaining to expenses paid or incurred in taxable years beginning before January 1, 1989, *see* paragraphs (c)(2) and (f) (*see* § 1.62-1T(c)(2) and (f) (as amended in 26 CFR part 1 §§ 1.61 to 1.169) revised April 1, 1992).

(d) through (h) [Reserved]

(i) *Effective date.* Paragraph (c) of this section is effective for taxable years beginning on or after January 1, 1989. [Reg. § 1.62-1.]

☐ [*T.D.* 8451, 12-4-92.]

[Reg. § 1.62-1T]

§ 1.62-1T. Adjusted gross income (temporary).—(a) *Basis for determining the amount of certain deductions.* The term "adjusted gross income" means the gross income computed under section 61 minus such of the deductions allowed by chapter 1 of the Code as are specified in section 62(a). Adjusted gross income is used as the basis for determining the following:

(1) The limitation on the amount of miscellaneous itemized deductions (under section 67).

(2) The limitation on the amount of the deduction for casualty losses (under section 165(h)(2)),

(3) The limitation on the amount of the deduction for charitable contributions (under section 170(b)(1)),

(4) The limitation on the amount of the deduction for medical and dental expenses (under section 213),

(5) The limitation on the amount of the deduction for qualified retirement contributions for active participants in certain pension plans (under section 219(g)), and

(6) The phase-out of the exemption from the disallowance of passive activity losses and credits (under section 469(i)(3)).

(b) *Double deduction not permitted.* Section 62(a) merely specifies which of the deductions provided in chapter 1 of the Code shall be allowed in computing adjusted gross income. It does not create any new deductions. The fact that a particular item may be described in more than one of the paragraphs under section 62(a) does not permit the item to be deducted twice in computing adjusted gross income or taxable income.

(c) *Deductions allowable in computing adjusted gross income.* The deductions specified in section 62(a) for purposes of computing adjusted gross income are:

(1) Deductions allowable under chapter 1 of the Code (other than by part VII (section 211 and following), subchapter B of such chapter) that are attributable to a trade or business carried on by the taxpayer not consisting of services performed as an employee;

(2) [Reserved]

(3) For taxable years beginning after December 31, 1986, deductions allowable under section 162 that consist of expenses paid or incurred by a qualified performing artist (as defined in section 62 (b)) in connection with the performance by him or her of services in the performing arts as an employee;

(4) Deductions allowable under part VI as losses from the sale or exchange of property;

(5) Deductions allowable under part VI, section 212, or section 611 that are attributable to property held for the production of rents or royalties;

(6) Deductions for depreciation or depletion allowable under sections 167 or 611 to a life tenant of property or to an income beneficiary of property held in trust or to an heir, legatee, or devisee of an estate;

(7) Deductions allowed by section 404 for contributions on behalf of a self-employed individual;

(8) Deductions allowed by section 219 for contributions to an individual retirement account described in section 408(a), or for an individual retirement annuity described in section 408(b);

(9) Deductions allowed by section 402(e)(3) with respect to a lump-sum distribution;

(10) For taxable years beginning after December 31, 1972, deductions allowed by section 165 for losses incurred in any transaction entered into for profit though not connected with a trade or business, to the extent that such losses include amounts forfeited to a bank, mutual savings bank,

savings and loan association, building and loan association, cooperative bank or homestead association as a penalty for premature withdrawal of funds from a time savings account, certificate of deposit, or similar class of deposit;

(11) For taxable years beginning after December 31, 1976, deductions for alimony and separate maintenance payments allowed by section 215;

(12) Deductions allowed by section 194 for the amortization of reforestation expenditures; and

(13) Deductions allowed by section 165 for the repayment (made in a taxable year beginning after December 28, 1980) to a trust described in paragraph (9) or (17) of section 501(c) of supplemental unemployment compensation benefits received from such trust if such repayment is required because of the receipt of trade readjustment allowances under section 231 or 232 of the Trade Act of 1974 (19 U.S.C. 2291 and 2292).

(d) *Expenses directly related to a trade or business.* For the purpose of the deductions specified in section 62, the performance of personal services as an employee does not constitute the carrying on of a trade or business, except as otherwise expressly provided. The practice of a profession, not as an employee, is considered the conduct of a trade or business within the meaning of such section. To be deductible for the purposes of determining adjusted gross income, expenses must be those directly, and not those merely remotely, connected with the conduct of a trade or business. For example, taxes are deductible in arriving at adjusted gross income only if they constitute expenditures directly attributable to a trade or business or to property from which rents or royalties are derived. Thus, property taxes paid or incurred on real property used in a trade or business are deductible, but state taxes on net income are not deductible even though the taxpayer's income is derived from the conduct of a trade or business.

(e) *Reimbursed and unreimbursed employee expenses*—(1) *In general.* Expenses paid or incurred by an employee that are deductible from gross income under part VI in computing taxable income (determined without regard to section 67) and for which the employee is reimbursed by the employer, its agent, or third party (for whom the employee performs a benefit as an employee of the employer) under an express agreement for reimbursement or pursuant to an *express* expense allowance arrangement may be deducted from gross income in computing adjusted gross income. Except as provided in paragraph (e)(2) and (e)(4) of this section, for taxable years beginning after December 31, 1986, if the amount of a reimburse-

ment made by an employer, its agent, or third party to an employee is less than the total amount of the business expenses paid or incurred by the employee, the determination of to which of the employee's business expenses the reimbursement applies and the amount of each expense that is covered by the reimbursement is made on the basis of all of the facts and circumstances of the particular case.

(2) *Facts and circumstances unclear on business expenses for meals and entertainment.* If—

(i) The facts and circumstances do not make clear—

(A) That a reimbursement does not apply to business expenses for meals or entertainment, or

(B) The amount of business expenses for meals or entertainment that is covered by the reimbursement, and

(ii) the employee pays or incurs business expenses for meals or entertainment,

the amount of the reimbursement that applies to such expenses (or portion thereof with respect to which the facts and circumstances are unclear) shall be determined by multiplying the amount of the employee's business expenses for meals and entertainment (or portion thereof with respect to which the facts and circumstances are unclear) by a fraction, the numerator of which is the total amount of the reimbursement (or portion thereof with respect to which the facts and circumstances are unclear) and the denominator of which is the aggregate amount of all the business expenses of the employee (or portion thereof with respect to which the facts and circumstances are unclear).

(3) *Deductibility of unreimbursed expenses.* The amount of expenses that is determined not to be reimbursed pursuant to paragraph (e)(1) or (2) of this section is deductible from adjusted gross income in determining the employee's taxable income subject to the limitations applicable to such expenses (*e.g.*, the 2-percent floor of section 67 and the 80-percent limitation on meal and entertainment expenses provided for in section 274(n)).

(4) *Unreimbursed expenses of State legislators.* For taxable years beginning after December 31, 1986, any portion of the amount allowed as a deduction to State legislators pursuant to section 162(h)(1)(B) that is not reimbursed by the State or a third party shall be allocated between lodging and meals in the same ratio as the amounts allowable for lodging and meals under the Federal per diem applicable to the legislator's State capital at the end of the legislator's taxable year (see Appendix 1-A of the Federal Travel Regulations (FTR),

which as of March 28, 1988, are contained in GSA Bulletin FPMR A-40, Supplement 20). For purposes of this paragraph (e)(4), the amount allowable for meals under the Federal per diem shall be the amount of the Federal per diem allowable for meals and incidental expenses reduced by $2 per legislative day (or other amount allocated to incidental expenses in 1-7.5(a)(2) of the FTR). The unreimbursed portion of each type of expense is deductible from adjusted gross income in determining the State legislator's taxable income subject to the limitations applicable to such expenses. For example, the unreimbursed portion allocable to meals shall be reduced by 20 percent pursuant to section 274(n) before being subjected to the 2-percent floor of section 67 for purposes of computing the taxable income of a State legislator. See § 1.67-1T(a)(2).

(5) *Expenses paid directly by an employer, its agent, or third party.* In the case of an employer, its agent, or a third party who provides property or services to an employee or who pays an employee's expenses directly instead of reimbursing the employee, see section 132 and the regulations thereunder for the income tax treatment of such expenses.

(6) *Examples.* The provisions of this paragraph (e) may be illustrated by the following examples:

Example (1). During 1987, A, an employee, while on business trips away form home pays $300 for travel fares, $200 for lodging and $100 for meals. In addition, A pays $50 for business meals in the area of his place of employment ("local meals"), $250 for continuing education courses, and $100 for business-related entertainment (other than meals). The total amount of the reimbursements received by A for his employee expenses from his employer is $750, and it is assumed that A's expenses meet the deductibility requirements of sections 162 and 274. A includes the amount of the reimbursement in his gross income. A's employer designates the reimbursement to cover in full A's expenses for travel fares, lodging, and meals while away from home, local meals, and entertainment, and no facts or circumstances indicate a contrary intention of the employer. Because the facts and circumstances make clear the amount of A's business expenses for meals and entertainment that is covered by the reimbursement, the reimbursement will be allocated to these expenses. In determining his adjusted gross income under section 62, A may deduct the full amount of the reimbursement for travel fares, lodging, and meals while away from home, local meals, and entertainment. In determining his taxable income under section 63, A

may deduct his expenses for continuing education courses to the extent allowable by sections 67 and 162.

Example (2). Assume the facts are the same as in example (1) except that the facts and circumstances make clear that the reimbursement covers all types of deductible expenses but they do not make clear the amount of each type of expense that is covered by the reimbursement. The amount of the reimbursement that is allocated to A's business expenses for meals and entertainment is $187.50. This amount is determined by multiplying the total amount of A's business expenses for meals and entertainment ($250) by the ratio of A's total reimbursement to A's total business expenses ($750/$1,000). The remaining amount of the reimbursement, $562.50 ($750 − $187.50), is allocated to A's business expenses other than meal and entertainment expenses. Therefore, in determining his adjusted gross income under section 62, A may deduct $750 for reimbursed business expenses (including meals and entertainment). In determining his taxable income under section 63, A may deduct (subject to the limitations and conditions of sections 67, 162, and 274) the unreimbursed portion of his expenses for meals and entertainment ($62.50 ($250 − $187.50)), and other employee business expenses ($187.50 ($750 − $562.50)).

Example (3). Assume the facts are the same as in example (1) except that the amount of the reimbursement is $500. Assume further that the facts and circumstances make clear that the reimbursement covers $100 of expenses for meals and that the remaining $400 of the reimbursement covers all types of deductible expenses (including any expenses for meals in excess of the $100 already designated) other than expenses for entertainment. The amount of the reimbursement that is allocated to A's business expenses for meals and entertainment is $125. This amount is equal to the sum of the amount of the reimbursement that clearly applies to meals ($100) and the amount of the reimbursement with respect to which the facts are unclear that is allocated to meals ($25). The latter amount is determined by multiplying the total amount of A's business expenses for meals and entertainment with respect to which the facts are unclear ($50) by the ratio of A's total reimbursement with respect to which the facts are unclear to A's total business expenses with respect to which the facts are unclear ($400/$800). The remaining amount of the reimbursement, $375 ($500 − $125) is allocated to A's business expenses other than meals and entertainment. Therefore, in determining his adjusted gross income under section 62, A may deduct $500 for reimbursed business expenses (including meals). In determining his taxable income under section 63, A may deduct (subject to the limitations and conditions of sections 67, 162, and 274) the unreimbursed portion of his expenses for meals ($25 ($150 − $125)), entertainment ($100), and other employee business expenses ($375 ($750 − $375)).

    Example (4). During 1987 B, a research scientist, is employed by Corporation X. B gives a speech before members of Association Y, a professional organization of scientists, describing her most recent research findings. Pursuant to a reimbursement arrangement, Y reimburses B for the full amount of her travel fares to the site of the speech and for the full amount of her expenses for lodging and meals while there. B includes the amount of the reimbursement in her gross income. B may deduct the full amount of her travel expenses pursuant to section 62(a)(2)(A) in computing her adjusted gross income.

    (f) [Reserved]

    (g) *Moving expenses.* For taxable years beginning after December 31, 1986, a taxpayer described in section 217(a) shall not take into account the deduction described in section 217 relating to moving expenses in computing adjusted gross income under section 62 even if the taxpayer is reimbursed for his or her moving expenses. Such a taxpayer shall include the amount of any reimbursement for moving expenses in income pursuant to section 82. The deduction described in section 217 shall be taken into account in computing the taxable income of the taxpayer under section 63. Pursuant to section 67(b)(6), the 2-percent floor described in section 67(a) does not apply to moving expenses.

    (h) *Cross-reference.* See 26 CFR 1.62-1 (Rev. as of April 1, 1986) with respect to pre-1987 deductions for travel, meal, lodging, transportation, and other trade or business expenses of an employee, reimbursed expenses of an employee, expenses of an outside salesperson, long-term capital gains, contributions described in section 405(c) to a bond purchase plan on behalf of a self-employed individual, moving expenses, amounts not received as benefits pursuant to section 1379(b)(3), and retirement bonds described in section 409 (allowed by section 219). [Temporary Reg. § 1.62-1T.]

    ☐ [*T.D. 8189, 3-25-88. Amended by T.D. 8276, 12-7-89; T.D. 8324, 12-14-90 and T.D. 8451, 12-4-92.*]

[Reg. § 1.62-2]

§ 1.62-2. Reimbursements and other expense allowance arrangements.—(a) *Table of contents.* The contents of this section are as follows:

    (a) *Table of contents.*

(m) *Effective dates.*

(b) *Scope.* For purposes of determining "adjusted gross income," section 62(a)(2)(A) allows an employee a deduction for expenses allowed by Part VI (section 161 and following), subchapter B, chapter 1 of the Code, paid by the employee, in connection with the performance of services as an employee of the employer, under a reimbursement or other expense allowance arrangement with a payor (the employer, its agent, or a third party). Section 62(c) provides that an arrangement will not be treated as a reimbursement or other expense allowance arrangement for purposes of section 62(a)(2)(A) if (1) such arrangement does not require the employee to substantiate the expenses covered by the arrangement to the payor, or (2) such arrangement provides the employee the right to retain any amount in excess of the substantiated expenses covered under the arrangement. This section prescribes rules relating to the requirements of section 62(c).

(c) *Reimbursement or other expense allowance arrangement*—(1) *Defined.* For purposes of §§ 1.62-1, 1.62-1T and 1.62-2, the phrase "reimbursement or other expense allowance arrangement" means an arrangement that meets the requirements of paragraphs (d) (business connection), (e) (substantiation), and (f) (returning amounts in excess of expenses) of this section. A payor may have more than one arrangement with respect to a particular employee, depending on the facts and circumstances. See paragraph (d)(2) of this section (payor treated as having two arrangements under certain circumstances).

(2) *Accountable plans*—(i) *In general.* Except as provided in paragraph (c)(2)(ii) of this section, if an arrangement meets the requirements of paragraphs (d), (e), and (f) of this section, all amounts paid under the arrangement are treated as paid under an "accountable plan."

(ii) *Special rule for failure to return excess.* If an arrangement meets the requirements of paragraphs (d), (e), and (f) of this section, but the employee fails to return, within a reasonable period of time, any amount in excess of the amount of the expenses substantiated in accordance with paragraph (e) of this section, only the amounts paid under the arrangement that are not in excess of the substantiated expenses are treated as paid under an accountable plan.

(3) *Nonaccountable plans*—(i) *In general.* If an arrangement does not satisfy one or more of the requirements of paragraphs (d), (e), or (f) of this section, all amounts paid under the arrangement are treated as paid under a "nonaccountable plan." If a payor provides a nonaccountable plan, an employee who receives payments under the plan cannot compel the payor to treat the payments as paid under an accountable plan by voluntarily substantiating the expenses and returning any excess to the payor.

(ii) *Special rule for failure to return excess.* If an arrangement meets the requirements of paragraphs (d), (e), and (f) of this section, but the employee fails to return, within a reasonable period of time, any amount in excess of the amount of the expenses substantiated in accordance with paragraph (e) of this section, the amounts paid under the arrangement that are in excess of the substantiated expenses are treated as paid under a nonaccountable plan.

(4) *Treatment of payments under accountable plans.* Amounts treated as paid under an accountable plan are excluded from the employee's gross income, are not reported as wages or other compensation on the employee's Form W-2, and are exempt from the withholding and payment of employment taxes (Federal Insurance Contributions Act (FICA), Federal Unemployment Tax Act (FUTA), Railroad Retirement Tax Act (RRTA), Railroad Unemployment Repayment Tax (RURT), and income tax). See paragraph (l) of this section for cross references.

(5) *Treatment of payments under nonaccountable plans.* Amounts treated as paid under a nonaccountable plan are included in the employee's gross income, must be reported as wages or other compensation on the employee's Form W-2, and are subject to withholding and payment of employment taxes (FICA, FUTA, RRTA, RURT, and income tax). See paragraph (h) of this section. Expenses attributable to amounts included in the employee's gross income may be deducted, provided the employee can substantiate the full amount of his or her expenses (i.e., the amount of the expenses, if any, the reimbursement for which is treated as paid under an accountable plan as well as those for which the employee is claiming the deduction) in accordance with § 1.274-5T and 1.274(d)-1 or § 1.162-17, but only as a miscellaneous itemized deduction subject to the limitations applicable to such expenses (e.g., the 80-percent limitation on meal and entertainment expenses provided in section 274(n) and the 2-percent floor provided in section 67).

(d) *Business connection*—(1) *In general.* Except as provided in paragraphs (d)(2) and (d)(3) of this section, an arrangement meets the requirements of this paragraph (d) if it provides advances, allowances (including per diem allowances, allowances only for meals and incidental expenses, and mileage allowances), or reimbursements only for business expenses that are allowable as deductions by Part VI (section 161 and the following), subchapter B, chapter 1 of the Code, and that are paid or incurred by the employee in connection with the performance of services as an employee of the employer. The payment may be actually received from the employer, its agent, or a third party for whom the employee performs a service as an employee of the employer, and may include amounts charged directly or indirectly to the payor through credit card systems or otherwise. In addition, if both wages and the reimbursement or other expense allowance are combined in a single payment, the reimbursement or other expense allowance must be identified either by making a separate payment or by specifically identifying the amount of the reimbursement or other expense allowance.

(2) *Other bona fide expenses.* If an arrangement provides advances, allowances, or reimbursements for business expenses described in paragraph (d)(1) of this section (i.e., deductible employee business expenses) and for other bona fide expenses related to the employer's business (e.g., travel that is not away from home) that are not deductible under Part VI (section 161 and the following), subchapter B, chapter 1 of the Code, the payor is treated as maintaining two arrangements. The portion of the arrangement that provides payments for the deductible employee business expenses is treated as one arrangement that satisfies this paragraph (d). The portion of the arrangement that provides payments for the nondeductible employee expenses is treated as a second arrangement that does not satisfy this paragraph (d) and all amounts paid under this second arrangement will be treated as paid under a nonaccountable plan. See paragraphs (c)(5) and (h) of this section.

(3) *Reimbursement requirement*—(i) *In general.* If a payor arranges to pay an amount to an employee regardless of whether the employee incurs (or is reasonably expected to incur) business expenses of a type described in paragraph (d)(1) or (d)(2) of this section, the arrangement does not satisfy this paragraph (d) and all amounts paid under the arrangement are treated as paid under a nonaccountable plan. See paragraphs (c)(5) and (h) of this section.

(ii) *Per diem allowances.* An arrangement providing a per diem allowance for travel expenses of a type described in paragraph (d)(1) or (d)(2) of this section that is computed on a basis similar to that used in computing the employee's wages or other compensation (e.g., the number of hours worked, miles traveled, or pieces produced) meets the requirements of this paragraph (d) only if, on December 12, 1989, the per diem allowance was identified by the payor either by making a

separate payment or by specifically identifying the amount of the per diem allowance, or a per diem allowance computed on that basis was commonly used in the industry in which the employee is employed. See section 274(d) and § 1.274(d)-1. A per diem allowance described in this paragraph (d)(3)(ii) may be adjusted in a manner that reasonably reflects actual increases in employee business expenses occurring after December 12, 1989.

(e) *Substantiation*—(1) *In general.* An arrangement meets the requirements of this paragraph (e) if it requires each business expense to be substantiated to the payor in accordance with paragraph (e)(2) or (e)(3) of this section, whichever is applicable, within a reasonable period of time. See § 1.274-5T or § 1.162-17.

(2) *Expenses governed by section 274(d).* An arrangement that reimburses travel, entertainment, use of a passenger automobile or other listed property, or other business expenses governed by section 274(d) meets the requirements of this paragraph (e)(2) if information sufficient to satisfy the substantiation requirements of section 274(d) and the regulations thereunder is submitted to the payor. See § 1.274-5. Under section 274(d), information sufficient to substantiate the requisite elements of each expenditure or use must be submitted to the payor. For example, with respect to travel away from home, § 1.274-5(b)(2) requires that information sufficient to substantiate the amount, time, place, and business purpose of the expense must be submitted to the payor. Similarly, with respect to use of a passenger automobile or other listed property, § 1.274-5(b)(6) requires that information sufficient to substantiate the amount, time, use, and business purpose of the expense must be submitted to the payor. See § 1.274-5(g), however, which grants the Commissioner authority to prescribe rules permitting the amount of certain expenses to be deemed substantiated to the payor (in lieu of substantiating the actual amount of such expenses) by means of per diem or mileage rates for travel away from home or transportation expenses. See also § 1.274-5(j)(1), which grants the Commissioner the authority to establish a method under which a taxpayer may use a specified amount for meals while traveling away from home in lieu of substantiating the actual cost of meals, and § 1.274-5(j)(2), which grants the Commissioner the authority to establish a method under which a taxpayer may use mileage rates to determine the amount of the ordinary and necessary expenses of using a vehicle for local transportation and transportation to, from, and at the destination while traveling away from home in lieu of substantiating the actual costs. Substantiation of the amount of a business expense in accordance

Reg. § 1.62-2(e)(2)

with rules prescribed pursuant to the authority granted by § 1.274-5(g) or (j) will be treated as substantiation of the amount of such expense for purposes of this section.

(3) *Expenses not governed by section 274(d).* An arrangement that reimburses business expenses not governed by section 274(d) meets the requirements of this paragraph (e)(3) if information is submitted to the payor sufficient to enable the payor to identify the specific nature of each expense and to conclude that the expense is attributable to the payor's business activities. Therefore, each of the elements of an expenditure or use must be substantiated to the payor. It is not sufficient if an employee merely aggregates expenses into broad categories (such as "travel") or reports individual expenses through the use of vague, nondescriptive terms (such as "miscellaneous business expenses"). See § 1.162-17(b).

(f) *Returning amounts in excess of expenses—* (1) *In general.* Except as provided in paragraph (f)(2) of this section, an arrangement meets the requirements of this paragraph (f) if it requires the employee to return to the payor within a reasonable period of time any amount paid under the arrangement in excess of the expenses substantiated in accordance with paragraph (e) of this section. The determination of whether an arrangement requires an employee to return amounts in excess of substantiated expenses will depend on the facts and circumstances. An arrangement whereby money is advanced to an employee to defray expenses will be treated as satisfying the requirements of this paragraph (f) only if the amount of money advanced is reasonably calculated not to exceed the amount of anticipated expenditures, the advance of money is made on a day within a reasonable period of the day that the anticipated expenditures are paid or incurred, and any amounts in excess of the expenses substantiated in accordance with paragraph (e) of this section are required to be returned to the payor within a reasonable period of time after the advance is received.

(2) *Per diem or mileage allowances.* The Commissioner may, in his discretion, prescribe rules in pronouncements of general applicability under which a reimbursement or other expense allowance arrangement that provides per diem allowances providing for ordinary and necessary expenses of traveling away from home (exclusive of transportation costs to and from destination) or mileage allowances providing for ordinary and necessary expenses of local travel and transportation while traveling away from home will be treated as satisfying the requirements of this paragraph (f), even though the arrangement does not require the employee to return the portion of such an allowance that relates to the days or miles of travel substantiated and that exceeds the amount of the employee's expenses deemed substantiated pursuant to rules prescribed under section 274(d), provided the allowance is paid at a rate for each day or mile of travel that is reasonably calculated not to exceed the amount of the employee's expenses or anticipated expenses and the employee is required to return to the payor within a reasonable period of time any portion of such allowance which relates to days or miles of travel not substantiated in accordance with paragraph (e) of this section.

(g) *Reasonable period—*(1) *In general.* The determination of a reasonable period of time will depend on the facts and circumstances.

(2) *Safe harbors—*(i) *Fixed date method.* An advance made within 30 days of when an expense is paid or incurred, an expense substantiated to the payor within 60 days after it is paid or incurred, or an amount returned to the payor within 120 days after an expense is paid or incurred will be treated as having occurred within a reasonable period of time.

(ii) *Periodic statement method.* If a payor provides employees with periodic statements (no less frequently than quarterly) stating the amount, if any, paid under the arrangement in excess of the expenses the employee has substantiated in accordance with paragraph (e) of this section, and requesting the employee to substantiate any additional business expenses that have not yet been substantiated (whether or not such expenses relate to the expenses with respect to which the original advance was paid) and/or to return any amounts remaining unsubstantiated within 120 days of the statement, an expense substantiated or an amount returned within that period will be treated as being substantiated or returned within a reasonable period of time.

(3) *Pattern of overreimbursements.* If, under a reimbursement or other expense allowance arrangement, a payor has a plan or practice to provide amounts to employees in excess of expenses substantiated in accordance with paragraph (e) of this section and to avoid reporting and withholding on such amounts, the payor may not use either of the safe harbors provided in paragraph (g)(2) of this section for any years during which such plan or practice exists.

(h) *Withholding and payment of employment taxes—*(1) *When excluded from wages.* If an arrangement meets the requirements of paragraphs (d), (e), and (f) of this section, the amounts paid under the arrangement that are not in excess of the expenses substantiated in accordance with

Reg. § 1.62-2(e)(3)

paragraph (e) of this section (i.e., the amounts treated as paid under an accountable plan) are not wages and are not subject to withholding and payment of employment taxes. If an arrangement provides advances, allowances, or reimbursements for meal and entertainment expenses and a portion of the payment is treated as paid under a nonaccountable plan under paragraph (d)(2) of this section due solely to section 274(n), then notwithstanding paragraph (h)(2)(ii) of this section, these nondeductible amounts are neither treated as gross income nor subject to withholding and payment of employment taxes.

(2) *When included in wages*—(i) *Accountable plans*—(A) *General rule.* Except as provided in paragraph (h)(2)(i)(B) of this section, if the expenses covered under an arrangement that meets the requirements of paragraphs (d), (e), and (f) of this section are not substantiated to the payor in accordance with paragraph (e) of this section within a reasonable period of time or if any amounts in excess of the substantiated expenses are not returned to the payor in accordance with paragraph (f) of this section within a reasonable period of time, the amount which is treated as paid under a nonaccountable plan under paragraph (c)(3)(ii) of this section is subject to withholding and payment of employment taxes no later than the first payroll period following the end of the reasonable period. A payor may treat any amount not substantiated or returned within the periods specified in paragraph (g)(2) of this section as not substantiated or returned within a reasonable period of time.

(B) *Per diem or mileage allowances*— (1) *In general.* If a payor pays a per diem or mileage allowance under an arrangement that meets the requirements of paragraphs (d), (e), and (f) of this section, the portion, if any, of the allowance paid that relates to days or miles of travel substantiated in accordance with paragraph (e) of this section and that exceeds the amount of the employee's expenses deemed substantiated for such travel pursuant to rules prescribed under section 274(d) and § 1.274(d)-1 or § 1.274-5T(j) is treated as paid under a nonaccountable plan. See paragraph (c)(3)(ii) of this section. Because the employee is not required to return this excess portion, the reasonable period of time provisions of paragraph (g) of this section (relating to the return of excess amounts) do not apply to this excess portion.

(2) *Reimbursements.* Except as provided in paragraph (h)(2)(i)(B)(4) of this section, in the case of a per diem or mileage allowance paid as a reimbursement at a rate for each day or mile of travel that exceeds the amount of the employee's expenses deemed substantiated for a day or mile of travel, the excess portion described in paragraph (h)(2)(i) of this section is subject to withholding and payment of employment taxes in the payroll period in which the payor reimburses the expenses for the days or miles of travel substantiated in accordance with paragraph (e) of this section.

(3) *Advances.* Except as provided in paragraph (h)(2)(i)(B)(4) of this section, in the case of a per diem or mileage allowance paid as an advance at a rate for each day or mile of travel that exceeds the amount of the employee's expenses deemed substantiated for a day or mile of travel, the excess portion described in paragraph (h)(2)(i) of this section is subject to withholding and payment of employment taxes no later than the first payroll period following the payroll period in which the expenses with respect to which the advance was paid (i.e., the days or miles of travel) are substantiated in accordance with paragraph (e) of this section. The expenses with respect to which the advance was paid must be substantiated within a reasonable period of time. See paragraph (g) of this section.

(4) *Special rules.* The Commissioner may, in his discretion, prescribe special rules in pronouncements of general applicability regarding the timing of withholding and payment of employment taxes on per diem and mileage allowances.

(ii) *Nonaccountable plans.* If an arrangement does not satisfy one or more of the requirements of paragraphs (d), (e), or (f) of this section, all amounts paid under the arrangement are wages and are subject to withholding and payment of employment taxes when paid.

(i) *Application.* The requirements of paragraphs (d)(business connection), (e)(substantiation), and (f)(returning amounts in excess of expenses) of this section will be applied on an employee-by-employee basis. Thus, for example, the failure by one employee to substantiate expenses under an arrangement in accordance with paragraph (e) of this section will not cause amounts paid to other employees to be treated as paid under a nonaccountable plan.

(j) *Examples.* The rules contained in this section may be illustrated by the following examples.

Example (1). Reimbursement requirement. Employer S pays its engineers $200 a day. On those days that an engineer travels away from home on business for Employer S, Employer S designates $50 of the $200 as paid to reimburse the engineer's travel expenses. Because Employer S would pay an engineer $200 a day regardless of whether the engineer was traveling away from

Reg. § 1.62-2(j)

home, the arrangement does not satisfy the reimbursement requirement of paragraph (d)(3)(i) of this section. Thus, no part of the $50 Employer S designated as a reimbursement is treated as paid under an accountable plan. Rather, all payments under the arrangement are treated as paid under a nonaccountable plan. Employer S must report the entire $200 as wages or other compensation on the employees' Forms W-2 and must withhold and pay employment taxes on the entire $200 when paid.

Example (2). Reimbursement requirement, multiple arrangements. Airline T pays all its employees a salary. Airline T also pays an allowance under an arrangement that otherwise meets the requirements of paragraphs (d), (e), and (f) of this section to its pilots and flight attendants who travel away from their home base airports, whether or not they are "away from home." Because the allowance is paid only to those employees who incur (or are reasonably expected to incur) expenses of a type described in paragraph (d)(1) or (d)(2) of this section, the arrangement satisfies the reimbursement requirement of paragraph (d)(3)(i) of this section. Under paragraph (d)(2) of this section, Airline T is treated as maintaining two arrangements. The portion of the arrangement providing the allowances for away from home travel is treated as an accountable plan. The portion of the arrangement providing the allowances for non-away from home travel is treated as a nonaccountable plan. Airline T must report the non-away from home allowances as wages or other compensation on the employees' Forms W-2 and must withhold and pay employment taxes on these payments when paid.

Example (3). Reimbursement requirement. Corporation R pays all its salespersons a salary. Corporation R also pays a travel allowance under an arrangement that otherwise meets the requirements of paragraphs (d), (e), and (f) of this section. This allowance is paid to all salespersons, including salespersons that Corporation R knows, or has reason to know, do not travel away from their offices on Corporation R business and would not be reasonably expected to incur travel expenses. Because the allowance is not paid only to those employees who incur (or are reasonably expected to incur) expenses of a type described in paragraph (d)(1) or (d)(2) of this section, the arrangement does not satisfy the reimbursement requirement of paragraph (d)(3)(i) of this section. Thus, no part of the allowance Corporation R designated as a reimbursement is treated as paid under an accountable plan. Rather, all payments under the arrangement are treated as paid under a nonaccountable plan. Corporation R must report all payments under the arrangement as

wages or other compensation on the employees' Forms W-2 and must withhold and pay employment taxes on the payments when paid.

Example (4). Separate arrangement, miscellaneous expenses. Under an arrangement that meets the requirements of paragraphs (d), (e), and (f) of this section, County U reimburses its employees for lodging and meal expenses incurred when they travel away from home on County U business. For its own convenience, County U also separately pays certain of its employees a $25 monthly allowance to cover the cost of small miscellaneous office expenses. County U does not require its employees to substantiate these miscellaneous expenses and does not require them to return the amounts by which the monthly allowance exceeds the miscellaneous expenses. The monthly allowance arrangement is a nonaccountable plan. County U must report the monthly allowances as wages or other compensation on the employees' Forms W-2 and must withhold and pay employment taxes on the monthly allowances when paid. The nonaccountable plan providing the monthly allowances is treated as separate from the accountable plan providing reimbursements for lodging and meal expenses incurred for travel away from home on County U business.

Example (5). Excessive advances. In anticipation of employee business expenses that Corporation V does not reasonably expect to exceed $400 in any quarter, Corporation V nonetheless advances $1,000 to Employee A for such expenses. Whenever Employee A substantiates an expense in accordance with paragraph (e) of this section, Corporation V provides an additional advance in an amount equal to the amount substantiated, thereby providing a continuing advance of $1,000. Because the amounts advanced under this arrangement are not reasonably calculated so as not to exceed the amount of anticipated expenditures and because the advance of money is not made on a day within a reasonable period of the day that the anticipated expenditures are paid or incurred, the arrangement is a nonaccountable plan. The arrangement fails to satisfy the requirements of paragraphs (d)(business connection) and (f) (reasonable calculation of advances) of this section. Thus, Corporation V must report the entire amount of each advance as wages or other compensation and must withhold and pay employment taxes on the entire amount of each advance when paid.

Example (6). Excess mileage advance. Under an arrangement that meets the requirements of paragraphs (d), (e), and (f) of this section, Employer W pays its employees a mileage allowance at a rate of 30 cents per mile (when the amount deemed substantiated for each mile of travel substantiated is 26 cents per mile) to cover automobile business expenses. The allowance is paid at a rate for each mile of travel that is reasonably calculated not to exceed the amount of the employee's expenses or anticipated expenses. Employer W does not require the return of the portion of the mileage allowance (4 cents) that exceeds the amount deemed substantiated for each mile of travel substantiated in accordance with paragraph (e) of this section. In June, Employer W advances Employee B $150 for 500 miles to be traveled by Employee B during the month. In July, Employee B substantiates 500 miles of business travel. The amount deemed substantiated by Employee B is $130. However, Employer W does not require Employee B to return the remaining $20 of the advance. No later than the first payroll period following the payroll period in which the business miles of travel are substantiated, Employer W must withhold and pay employment taxes on $20 (500 miles × 4 cents per mile).

Example (7). Excess per diem reimbursement. Under an arrangement that meets the requirements of paragraphs (d), (e), and (f) of this section, Employer X pays its employees a per diem allowance to cover lodging, meal, and incidental expenses incurred for travel away from home on Employer X business at a rate equal to 120 percent of the amount deemed substantiated for each day of travel to the localities to which the employees travel. Employer X does not require the employees to return the 20 percent by which the reimbursement for those expenses exceeds the amount deemed substantiated for each day of travel substantiated in accordance with paragraph (c) of this section. Employee C substantiates six days of business travel away from home: two days in a locality for which the amount deemed substantiated is $100 a day and four days in a locality for which the amount deemed substantiated is $125 a day. Employer X reimburses Employee C $840 for the six days of travel away from home (2 × (120% × $100) + 4 × (120% × $125)), and does not require Employee C to return the excess portion ($140 excess portion = (2 days × $20 ($120 − $100) + 4 days × $25 ($150 − $125)). For the payroll period in which Employer X reimburses the expenses, Employer X must withhold and pay employment taxes on $140.

Example (8). Return requirement. Employer Y provides expense allowances to certain of its employees to cover business expenses of a type described in paragraph (d)(1) of this section under an arrangement that requires the employees to substantiate their expenses within a reasonable period of time and to return any excess amounts within a reasonable period of time. Each time an employee returns an excess amount to Employer Y, however, Employer Y pays the employee a "bonus" equal to the amount returned by the employee. The arrangement fails to satisfy the requirements of paragraph (f)(returning amounts in excess of expenses) of this section. Thus, Employer Y must report the entire amount of the expense allowance payments as wages or other compensation and must withhold and pay employment taxes on the payments when paid. Compare example (6)(where the employee is not required to return the portion of the mileage allowance that exceeds the amount deemed substantiated for each mile of travel substantiated).

Example (9). Timely substantiation. Employer Z provides a $500 advance to Employee D for a trip away from home on Employer Z business. Employee D incurs $500 in business expenses on the trip. Employer Z uses the periodic statement method safe harbor. At the end of the quarter during which the trip occurred, Employer Z sends a quarterly statement to Employee D stating that $500 was advanced to Employee D during the quarter and that no expenses were substantiated and no excess amounts returned. The statement advises Employee D that Employee D must substantiate any additional business expenses within 120 days of the date of the statement, and must return any unsubstantiated excess within the 120-day period. Employee D fails to substantiate any expenses or to return the excess within the 120-day period. Employer Z treats the $500 as wages and withholds and pays employment taxes on the $500. After the 120-day period has expired, Employee D substantiates the $500 in travel expenses in accordance with paragraph (e) of this section. Employer Z properly reported and withheld and paid employment taxes on the $500 and no adjustments may be made. Employee D must include the $500 in gross income and may deduct the $500 of expenses as a miscellaneous itemized deduction subject to the 2-percent floor provided in section 67.

(k) *Anti-abuse provision.* If a payor's reimbursement or other expense allowance arrangement evidences a pattern of abuse of the rules of section 62(c) and this section, all payments made under the arrangement will be treated as made under a nonaccountable plan.

(l) *Cross references.* For employment tax regulations relating to reimbursement and expense allowance arrangements, see §§ 31.3121(a)-3, 31.3231(e)-3, 31.3306(b)-2, and 31.3401(a)-4, which generally apply to payments made under reimbursement or other expense allowance arrangements received by an employee on or after July 1, 1990 with respect to expenses paid or incurred on or after July 1, 1990. For reporting requirements, see § 1.6041-3(i), which generally applies to payments made under reimbursement or other expense allowance arrangements received by an employee on or after January 1, 1989 with respect to expenses paid or incurred on or after January 1, 1989.

(m) *Effective dates.* This section generally applies to payments made under reimbursement or other expense allowance arrangements received by an employee in taxable years of the employee beginning on or after January 1, 1989, with respect to expenses paid or incurred in taxable years beginning on or after January 1, 1989. Paragraph (h) of this section generally applies to payments made under reimbursement or other expense allowance arrangements received by an employee on or after July 1, 1990 with respect to expenses paid or incurred on or after July 1, 1990. Paragraphs (d)(3)(ii) and (h)(2)(i)(B) of this section apply to payments made under reimbursement or other expense allowance arrangements received by an employee on or after January 1, 1991 with respect to expenses paid or incurred on or after January 1, 1991. Paragraph (e)(2) of this section applies to payments made under reimbursement or other expense allowance arrangements received by an employee with respect to expenses paid or incurred after December 31, 1997. [Reg. § 1.62-2.]

☐ [*T.D. 8324, 12-14-90. Amended by T.D. 8451, 12-4-92; T.D. 8666, 5-29-96; T.D. 8784, 9-30-98 and T.D. 8864, 1-21-2000.*]

[Reg. § 1.63-1]

§ 1.63-1. Change of treatment with respect to the zero bracket amount and itemized deductions.—(a) *In general.* An individual who files a return on which the individual itemizes deductions in accordance with section 63(g) may later make a change of treatment by recomputing taxable income for the taxable year to which that return relates without itemizing deductions. Similarly, an individual who files a return on which the individual computes taxable income without itemizing deductions may later make a change of treatment by itemizing deductions in accordance with section 63(g) in recomputing taxable income for the taxable year to which that return relates.

(b) *No extension of time for claiming credit or refund.* A change of treatment described in paragraph (a) of this section does not extend the period of time prescribed in section 6511 within which the taxpayer may make a claim for credit or refund of tax.

(c) *Special requirements if spouse filed separate return*—(1) *Requirements.* If the spouse of the taxpayer filed a separate return for a taxable year corresponding to the taxable year of the taxpayer, the taxpayer may not make a change of treatment described in paragraph (a) of this section for that year unless—

(i) The spouse makes a change of treatment on the separate return consistent with the change of treatment sought by the taxpayer; and

(ii) The taxpayer and the taxpayer's spouse file a consent in writing to the assessment of any deficiency of either spouse to the extent attributable to the change of treatment, even though the assessment of the deficiency would otherwise be prevented by the operation of any law or rule of law. The consent must be filed with the district director for the district in which the taxpayer applies for the change of treatment, and the period during which a deficiency may be assessed shall be established by agreement of the spouses and the district director.

(2) *Corresponding taxable year.* A taxable year of one spouse corresponds to a taxable year of the other spouse if both taxable years end in the same calendar year. If the taxable year of one spouse ends with death, however, the corresponding taxable year of the surviving spouse is that in which the death occurs.

(d) *Inapplicable if tax liability has been compromised.* The taxpayer may not make a change of treatment described in paragraph (a) of this section for any taxable year if—

(1) The tax liability of the taxpayer for the taxable year has been compromised under section 7122; or

(2) The tax liability of the taxpayer's spouse for a taxable year corresponding to the taxable year of the taxpayer has been compromised under section 7122. See paragraph (c)(2) of this section for the determination of a corresponding taxable year.

(e) *Effective date.* This section applies to taxable years beginning after 1976. [Reg. § 1.63-1.]

☐ [*T.D. 7385, 1-3-79.*]

[Reg. § 1.63-2]

§ 1.63-2. Cross reference.—For rules with respect to charitable contribution deductions for nonitemizing taxpayers, see section 63(b)(1)(C) and (i) and section 170(i) of the Internal Revenue Code of 1954. [Reg. § 1.63-2.]

☐ [*T.D. 8002, 12-26-84.*]

Reg. § 1.63-1(a)

[Reg. § 1.67-1T]

§ 1.67-1T. 2-percent floor on miscellaneous itemized deductions (temporary).—(a) *Type of expenses subject to the floor*—(1) *In general.* With respect to individuals, section 67 disallows deductions for miscellaneous itemized deductions (as defined in paragraph (b) of this section) in computing taxable income (*i.e.,* so-called "below-the-line" deductions) to the extent that such otherwise allowable deductions do not exceed 2 percent of the individual's adjusted gross income (as defined in section 62 and the regulations thereunder). Examples of expenses that, if otherwise deductible, are subject to the 2-percent floor include but are not limited to—

(i) Unreimbursed employee expenses, such as expenses for transportation, travel fares and lodging while away from home, business meals and entertainment, continuing education courses, subscriptions to professional journals, union or professional dues, professional uniforms, job hunting, and the business use of the employee's home,

(ii) Expenses for the production or collection of income for which a deduction is otherwise allowable under section 212(1) and (2), such as investment advisory fees, subscriptions to investment advisory publications, certain attorneys' fees, and the cost of safe deposit boxes,

(iii) Expenses for the determination of any tax for which a deduction is otherwise allowable under section 212(3), such as tax counsel fees and appraisal fees, and

(iv) Expenses for an activity for which a deduction is otherwise allowable under section 183.

See section 62 with respect to deductions that are allowable in computing adjusted gross income (*i.e.,* so-called "above-the-line" deductions).

(2) *Other limitations.* Except as otherwise provided in paragraph (d) of this section, to the extent that any limitation or restriction is placed on the amount of a miscellaneous itemized deduction, that limitation shall apply prior to the application of the 2-percent floor. For example, in the case of an expense for food or beverages, only 80 percent of which is allowable as a deduction because of the limitations provided in section 274(n), the otherwise deductible 80 percent of the expense is treated as a miscellaneous itemized deduction and is subject to the 2-percent limitation of section 67.

(b) *Definition of miscellaneous itemized deductions.* For purposes of this section, the term "miscellaneous itemized deductions" means the deductions allowable from adjusted gross income in determining taxable income, as defined in section 63, other than—

(1) The standard deduction as defined in section 63(c),

(2) Any deduction allowable for impairment-related work expenses as defined in section 67(d),

(3) The deduction under section 72(b)(3) (relating to deductions if annuity payments cease before the investment is recovered),

(4) The deductions allowable under section 151 for personal exemptions,

(5) The deduction under section 163 (relating to interest),

(6) The deduction under section 164 (relating to taxes),

(7) The deduction under section 165(a) for losses described in subsection (c)(3) or (d) of section 165,

(8) The deduction under section 170 (relating to charitable contributions and gifts),

(9) The deduction under section 171 (relating to deductions for amortizable bond premiums),

(10) The deduction under section 213 (relating to medical and dental expenses),

(11) The deduction under section 216 (relating to deductions in connection with cooperative housing corporations),

(12) The deduction under section 217 (relating to moving expenses),

(13) The deduction under section 691(c) (relating to the deduction for estate taxes in the case of income in respect of the decedent),

(14) The deduction under 1341 (relating to the computation of tax if a taxpayer restores a substantial amount held under claim of right), and

(15) Any deduction allowable in connection with personal property used in a short sale.

(c) *Allocation of expenses.* If a taxpayer incurs expenses that relate to both a trade or business activity (within the meaning of section 162) and a production of income or tax preparation activity (within the meaning of section 212), the taxpayer shall allocate such expenses between the activities on a reasonable basis.

(d) *Members of Congress*—(1) *In general.* With respect to the deduction for living expenses of Members of Congress referred to in section 162(a), the 2-percent floor described in section 67 and paragraph (a) of this section shall be applied to the deduction before the application of the $3,000 limitation on deductions for living expenses referred to in section 162(a). (For purposes of this paragraph (d), the term "Member(s) of Congress" includes any Delegate or Resident Commissioner.)

Reg. § 1.67-1T(d)(1)

The amount of miscellaneous itemized deductions of a Member of Congress that is disallowed pursuant to section 67 and paragraph (a) of this section shall be allocated between deductions for living expenses (within the meaning of section 162(a)) and other miscellaneous itemized deductions. The amount of deductions for living expenses of a Member of Congress that is disallowed pursuant to section 67 and paragraph (a) of this section is determined by multiplying the aggregate amount of such living expenses (determined without regard to the $3,000 limitation of section 162(a) but with regard to any other limitations) by a fraction, the numerator of which is the aggregate amount disallowed pursuant to section 67 and paragraph (a) of this section with respect to miscellaneous itemized deductions of the Member of Congress and the denominator of which is the amount of miscellaneous itemized deductions (including deductions for living expenses) of the Member of Congress (determined without regard to the $3,000 limitation of section 162(a) but with regard to any other limitations). The amount of deductions for miscellaneous itemized deductions (other than deductions for living expenses) of a Member of Congress that are disallowed pursuant to section 67 and paragraph (a) of this section is determined by multiplying the amount of miscellaneous itemized deductions (other than deductions for living expenses) of the Member of Congress (determined with regard to any limitations) by the fraction described in the preceding sentence.

(2) *Example.* The provisions of this paragraph (d) may be illustrated by the following example:

Example. For 1987 A, a Member of Congress, has adjusted gross income of $100,000, and miscellaneous itemized deductions of $10,750 of which $3,750 is for meals, $3,000 is for other living expenses, and $4,000 is for other miscellaneous itemized deductions (none of which is subject to any percentage limitations other than the 2-percent floor of section 67). The amount of A's business meal expenses that are disallowed under section 274(n) is $750 ($3,750 × 20%). The amount of A's miscellaneous itemized deductions that are disallowed under section 67 is $2,000 ($100,000 × 2%). The portion of the amount disallowed under section 67 that is allocated to A's living expenses is $1,200. This portion is equal to the amount of A's deductions for living expenses allowable after the application of section 274(n) and before the application of section 67 ($6,000) multiplied by the ratio of A's total miscellaneous itemized deductions disallowed under section 67 to A's total miscellaneous itemized deductions, determined without regard to the $3,000 limita-

tion of section 162(a) ($2,000/$10,000). Thus, after application of section 274(n) and section 67, A's deduction for living expenses is $4,800 ($6,750 − $750 − $1,200). However, pursuant to section 162(a), A may deduct only $3,000 of such expenses. The amount of A's other miscellaneous itemized deductions that are disallowed under section 67 is $800 ($4,000 × $2,000/$10,000). Thus, $3,200 ($4,000 − $800) of A's miscellaneous itemized deductions (other than deductions for living expenses) are allowable after application of section 67. A's total allowable miscellaneous itemized deductions are $6,200 ($3,000 + $3,200).

(e) *State legislators.* See § 1.62-1T(e)(4) with respect to rules regarding state legislator's expenses. [Temporary Reg. § 1.67-1T.]

☐ [*T.D.* 8189, 3-25-88]

[Reg. § 1.67-2T]

§ 1.67-2T. **Treatment of pass-through entities (temporary).**—(a) *Application of section 67.* This section provides rules for the application of section 67 to partners, shareholders, beneficiaries, participants, and others with respect to their interests in pass-through entities (as defined in paragraph (g) of this section). In general, an affected investor (as defined in paragraph (h) of this section) in a pass-through entity shall separately take into account as an item of income and as an item of expense an amount equal to his or her allocable share of the affected expenses (as defined in paragraph (i) of this section) of the pass-through entity for purposes of determining his or her taxable income. Except as provided in paragraph (e)(1)(ii)(B) of this section, the expenses so taken into account shall be treated as paid or incurred by the affected investor in the same manner as paid or incurred by the pass-through entity. For rules regarding the application of section 67 to affected investors in—

(1) Partnerships, S corporations, and grantor trusts, see paragraph (b) of this section,

(2) Real estate mortgage investment conduits, see paragraph (c) of this section,

(3) Common trust funds, see paragraph (d) of this section,

(4) Nonpublicly offered regulated investment companies, see paragraph (e) of this section, and

(5) Publicly offered regulated investment companies, see paragraph (p) of this section.

(b) *Partnerships, S corporations, and grantor trusts*—(1) *In general.* Pursuant to sections 702(a) and 1366(a) of the Code and the regulations thereunder, each partner of a partnership or shareholder of an S corporation shall take into account separately his or her distributive or pro rata share of any items of deduction of such partnership or corporation that are defined as miscellaneous itemized deductions pursuant to section 67(b). The 2-percent limitation described in section 67 does not apply to the partnership or corporation with respect to such deductions, but such deductions shall be included in the deductions of the partner or shareholder to which that limitation applies. Similarly, the limitation applies to the grantor or other person treated as the owner of a grantor trust with respect to items that are paid or incurred by a grantor trust and are treated as miscellaneous itemized deductions of the grantor or other person pursuant to subpart E, part 1, subchapter J, chapter 1 of the Code, but not to the trust itself. The 2-percent limitation applies to amounts otherwise deductible in taxable years of partners, shareholders, or grantors beginning after December 31, 1986, regardless of the taxable year of the partnership, corporation, or trust.

(2) *Example.* The provisions of this paragraph (b) may be illustrated by the following example:

Example. P, a partnership, incurs $1,000 in expenses to which section 212 applies during its taxable year. A, an individual, is a partner in P. A's distributive share of the expenses to which section 212 applies is $20, determined without regard to the 2-percent limitation of section 67 Pursuant to section 702(a), A must take $20 of expenses to which section 212 applies into account in determining his income tax. Pursuant to section 67, in determining his taxable income A may deduct his miscellaneous itemized deductions (including his $20 distributive share of deductions from P) to the extent the total amount exceeds 2 percent of his adjusted gross income.

(c) *Real estate mortgage investment conduit.* See § 1.67-3T for rules regarding the application of section 67 to holders of interests in REMICs.

(d) *Common trust funds*—(1) *In general.* For purposes of determining the taxable income of an affected investor that is a participant in a common trust fund—

(i) The ordinary taxable income and ordinary net loss of the common trust fund shall be computed under section 584(d)(2) without taking into account any affected expenses, and

(ii) Each affected investor shall be treated as having paid or incurred an expense described in section 212 in an amount equal to the affected investor's proportionate share of the affected expenses.

The 2-percent limitation described in section 67 applies to amounts otherwise deductible in taxable years of participants beginning after December ber 31, 1986, regardless of the taxable year of the common trust fund.

(2) *Example.* The provisions of this paragraph (d) may be illustrated by the following example:

Example. During 1987, the gross income and deductions of common trust fund C, a calendar year taxpayer, consist of the following items: (i) $50,000 of short-term capital gains; (ii) $150,000 of long-term capital gains; (iii) $1,000,000 of dividend income; (iv) $10,000 of deductions that are not affected expenses; and (v) $60,000 of deductions that are affected expenses. The proportionate share of Trust T in the income and losses of C is one percent. In computing its taxable income for 1987, T, a calendar year taxpayer, shall take into account the following items: (A) $500 of short-term capital gains (one percent of $50,000, C's short-term capital gains); (B) $1,500 of long-term capital gains (one percent of $150,000, C's long-term capital gains); (C) $9,900 of ordinary taxable income (one percent of $990,000, the excess of $100,000, C's gross income after excluding capital gains and losses, over $10,000, C's deductions that are not affected expenses); (D) $600 of expenses described in section 212 (one percent of $60,000, C's affected expenses).

(e) *Nonpublicly offered regulated investment companies*—(1) *In general.* For purposes of determining the taxable income of an affected investor that is a shareholder of a nonpublicly offered regulated investment company (as defined in paragraph (g)(3) of this section) during a calendar year—

(i) The current earnings and profits of the nonpublicly offered regulated investment company shall be computed without taking into account any affected RIC expenses that are allocated among affected investors, and

(ii) The affected investor shall be treated—

(A) As having received or accrued a dividend in an amount equal to the affected investor's allocable share of the affected RIC expenses of the nonpublicly offered regulated investment company for the calendar year, and

(B) As having paid or incurred an expense described in section 212 (or section 162 in the case of an affected investor that is a nonpublicly offered regulated investment company) in an amount equal to the affected investor's allocable share of the affected RIC expenses of the nonpublicly offered regulated investment company for the calendar year

in the affected investor's taxable year with which (or within which) the calendar year with respect to which the expenses are allocated ends. An affected investor's allocable share of the affected RIC expenses is the amount allocated to that affected investor pursuant to paragraph (k) of this section.

(2) *Shareholders that are not affected investors.* A shareholder of a nonpublicly offered regulated investment company that is not an affected investor shall not take into account in computing its taxable income any amount of income or expense with respect to its allocable share of affected RIC expenses.

(3) *Example.* The provisions of this paragraph (e) may be illustrated by the following example:

Example. During calendar year 1987, nonpublicly offered regulated investment company M distributes to individual shareholder A, a calendar year taxpayer, capital gain dividends of $1,000 and other dividends of $5,000. A's allocable share of the affected RIC expenses of M is $200. In computing A's taxable income for 1987, A shall take into account the following items: (i) $1,000 of long-term capital gains (the capital gain dividends received by A); (ii) $5,200 of dividend income (the sum of the other dividends received by A and A's allocable share of the affected RIC expenses of M); and (iii) $200 of expenses described in section 212 (A's allocable share of the affected RIC expenses of M). A is allowed a deduction for miscellaneous itemized deductions (including A's $200 allocable share of the affected RIC expenses of M, which is treated as an expense described in section 212) for 1987 only to the extent the aggregate of such deductions exceeds 2 percent of A's adjusted gross income for 1987.

(f) *Cross-reference.* See § 1.67-1T with respect to limitations on deductions for expenses described in section 212 (including amounts treated as such expenses under this section).

(g) *Pass-through entity*—(1) *In general.* Except as provided in paragraph (g)(2) of this section, for purposes of section 67(c) and this section, a pass-through entity is—

(i) A trust (or any portion thereof) to which subpart E, part 1, subchapter J, chapter 1 of the Code applies,

(ii) A partnership,

(iii) An S corporation,

(iv) A common trust fund described in section 584,

(v) A nonpublicly offered regulated investment company,

(vi) A real estate mortgage investment conduit, and

(vii) Any other person—

(A) Which is not subject to the income tax imposed by subtitle A, chapter 1, or which is allowed a deduction in computing such tax for distributions to owners or beneficiaries, and

(B) The character of the income of which may affect the character of the income recognized with respect to that person by its owners or beneficiaries.

Entities that do not meet the requirements of paragraph (g)(1)(vii)(A) and (B), such as qualified pension plans, individual retirement accounts, and insurance companies holding assets in separate asset accounts to fund variable contracts defined in section 817(d), are not described in this paragraph (g)(1).

(2) *Exception.* For purposes of section 67(c) and this section, a pass-through entity does not include:

(i) An estate,

(ii) A trust (or any portion thereof) not described in paragraph (g)(1)(i) of this section,

(iii) A cooperative described in section 1381(a)(2), determined without regard to subparagraphs (A) and (C) thereof, or

(iv) A real estate investment trust.

(3) *Nonpublicly offered regulated investment company*—(i) *In general.* For purposes of this section, the term "nonpublicly offered regulated investment company" means a regulated investment company to which part I of subchapter M of the Code applies that is not a publicly offered regulated investment company.

(ii) *Publicly offered regulated investment company.* For purposes of this section, the term "publicly offered regulated investment company" means a regulated investment company to which part I of subchapter M of the Code applies the shares of which are—

(A) Continuously offered pursuant to a public offering (within the meaning of section 4 of the Securities Act of 1933, as amended (15 U.S.C. 77a to 77aa)),

(B) Regularly traded on an established securities market, or

(C) Held by or for no fewer than 500 persons at all times during the taxable year.

(h) *Affected investor*—(1) *In general.* For purposes of this section, the term "affected investor" means a partner, shareholder, beneficiary, participant, or other interest holder in a pass-through entity at any time during the pass-through entity's taxable year that is—

(i) An individual (other than a nonresident alien whose income with respect to his or her interest in the pass-through entity is not effec-

Reg. § 1.67-2T(e)(2)

tively connected with the conduct of a trade or business within the United States);

(ii) A person, including a trust or estate, that computes its taxable income in the same manner as in the case of an individual; or

(iii) A pass-through entity if one or more of its partners, shareholders, beneficiaries, participants, or other interest holders is (A) a pass-through entity or (B) a person described in paragraph (h)(1)(i) or (ii) of this section.

(2) *Examples.* The provisions of this paragraph (h) may be illustrated by the following examples:

Example (1). Corporation X holds shares of nonpublicly offered regulated investment company R in its capacity as a nominee or custodian for individual A, the beneficial owner of the shares. Because the owner of the shares for Federal income tax purposes is an individual, the shares are owned by an affected investor.

Example (2). Individual retirement account I owns shares of a nonpublicly offered regulated investment company. Because an individual retirement account is not a person described in paragraph (h)(1) of this section, the shares are not owned by an affected investor.

(i) *Affected expenses*—(1) *In general.* In general, for purposes of this section, the term "affected expenses" means expenses that, if paid or incurred by an individual, would be deductible, if at all, as miscellaneous itemized deductions as defined in section 67(b).

(2) *Special rule for nonpublicly offered regulated investment companies.* In the case of a nonpublicly offered regulated investment company, the term "affected expenses" means only affected RIC expenses.

(j) *Affected RIC expenses*—(1) *In general.* In general, for purposes of this section, the term "affected RIC expenses" means the excess of—

(i) The aggregate amount of the expenses (other than expenses described in sections 62(a)(3) and 67(b) and § 1.67-1T(b)) paid or incurred in the calendar year that are allowable as a deduction in determining the investment company taxable income (without regard to section 852(b)(2)(D)) of the nonpublicly offered regulated investment company for a taxable year that begins or ends with or within the calendar year, over

(ii) The amount of expenses taken into account under paragraph (j)(1)(i) of this section that are allocable to the following items (whether paid separately or included as part of a fee paid to an investment advisor or other person for a variety of services):

(A) Registration fees;

(B) Directors' or trustees' fees;

(C) Periodic meetings of directors, trustees, or shareholders;

(D) Transfer agent fees;

(E) Legal and accounting fees (other than fees for income tax return preparation or income tax advice); and

(F) Shareholder communications required by law (*e.g.*, the preparation and mailing of prospectuses and proxy statements).

Expenses described in paragraph (j)(1)(ii)(A) through (F) of this section do not include, for example, expenses allocable to investment advice, marketing activities, shareholder communications and other services not specifically described in paragraph (j)(1)(ii)(A) through (F) of this section, and custodian fees.

(2) *Safe harbor.* If a nonpublicly offered regulated investment company makes an election under this paragraph (j)(2), the affected RIC expenses for a calendar year shall be treated as equal to 40 percent of the amount determined under paragraph (j)(1)(i) of this section for that calendar year. The nonpublicly offered regulated investment company shall make the election by attaching to its income tax return for the taxable year that includes the last day of the first calendar year for which the nonpublicly offered regulated investment company makes the election a statement that it is making an election under paragraph (j)(2) of this section. An election made pursuant to this paragraph (j)(2) shall remain in effect for all subsequent calendar years unless revoked with the consent of the Commissioner.

(3) *Reduction for unused RIC expenses.* The amount determined under paragraph (j)(1)(i) of this section shall be reduced by the nonpublicly offered regulated investment company's net operating loss, if any, for the taxable year ending with or within the calendar year. In computing the nonpublicly offered regulated investment company's net operating loss for purposes of this section, the deduction for dividends paid shall not be allowed and any net capital gain for the taxable year shall be excluded.

(4) *Exception.* The affected RIC expenses of a nonpublicly offered regulated investment company will be treated as zero if the amount of its gross income for the calendar year (determined without regard to capital gain net income) is not greater than 1 percent of the sum of (i) such gross income and (ii) the amount of its interest income for the calendar year that is not includible in gross income pursuant to section 103.

(k) *Allocation of expenses among nonpublicly offered regulated investment company sharehold-*

Reg. § 1.67-2T(k)

ers—(1) *General rule.* A nonpublicly offered regulated investment company shall allocate to each of its affected investors that is a shareholder at any time during the calendar year, the affected investor's allocable share of the affected RIC expenses of the nonpublicly offered regulated investment company for that calendar year. (See paragraph (m) of this section for rules regarding estimates with respect to the amount of an affected investor's share of affected RIC expenses upon which certain persons can rely for certain purposes.) A nonpublicly offered regulated investment company may use any reasonable method to make the allocation. A method of allocation shall not be reasonable if—

(i) The method can be expected to have the effect, if applied to all affected RIC expenses and all shareholders (whether or not affected investors), of allocating to the shareholders an amount of affected RIC expenses that is less than the affected RIC expenses of the nonpublicly offered regulated investment company for the calendar year,

(ii) The method can be expected to have the effect of allocating a disproportionately high share of the affected RIC expenses of the nonpublicly offered regulated investment company to (A) shareholders that are not affected investors or (B) affected investors, the amount of whose miscellaneous itemized deductions (including their allocable share of affected RIC expenses) exceeds the 2-percent floor described in section 67, or

(iii) A principal purpose of the method of allocation is to avoid allocating affected RIC expenses to persons described in paragraph (h)(1)(i) or (ii) of this section whose miscellaneous itemized deductions (inclusive of their allocable share of affected RIC expenses) may not exceed the 2-percent floor described in section 67.

(2) *Reasonable allocation method described*—(i) *In general.* The allocation method described in this paragraph (k)(2) shall be treated as a reasonable allocation method. Under the method described in this paragraph, an affected investor's allocable share of the affected RIC expenses of a nonpublicly offered regulated investment company is the amount that bears the same ratio to the amount of affected RIC expenses of the nonpublicly offered regulated investment company for the calendar year as—

(A) The amount of dividends paid to the affected investor during the calendar year, bears to

(B) The sum of—

(*1*) The aggregate amount of dividends paid by the nonpublicly offered regulated investment company during the calendar year to all shareholders, and

(*2*) Any amount on which tax is imposed under section 852(b)(1) for any taxable year of the nonpublicly offered regulated investment company ending within or with the calendar year.

(ii) *Exception.* Paragraph (k)(2)(i) of this section does not apply if the amount of the deduction for dividends paid during the calendar year is zero.

(iii) *Dividends paid.* For purposes of this paragraph (k)(2)—

(A) Dividends that are treated as paid during a calendar year pursuant to section 852(b)(7) are treated as paid during that calendar year and not during the succeeding calendar year.

(B) The term "dividends paid" does not include capital gain dividends (as defined in section 852(b)(3)(C)), exempt-interest dividends (as defined in section 852(b)(5)(A)), or any amount to which section 302(a) applies.

(C) The dividends paid during a calendar year is determined without regard to section 855(a).

(3) *Reasonable allocation made by District Director.* If a nonpublicly offered regulated investment company does not make a reasonable allocation of affected RIC expenses to its affected investors as required by paragraph (k)(1) of this section, a reasonable allocation shall be made by the District Director of the internal revenue district in which the principal place of business or principal office or agency of the nonpublicly offered regulated investment company is located.

(4) *Examples.* The provisions of this paragraph (k) may be illustrated by the following examples:

Example (1). Nonpublicly offered regulated investment company M, in calculating its investment company taxable income, claims a dividends paid deduction for a portion of redemption distributions (to which section 302(a) applies) to shareholders, as well as for nonredemption distributions. M allocates affected expenses among shareholders who have received nonredemption distributions by multiplying the amount of nonredemption distributions distributed to each shareholder by a fraction, the numerator of which is the affected RIC expenses of M and the denominator of which is M's investment company taxable income, determined on a calendar year basis and without regard to deductions described in section 852(b)(2)(D). No affected RIC expenses are allocated with respect to the redemption distributions. This allocation method can be expected to have the effect of allocating

Reg. § 1.67-2T(k)(2)

among the shareholders an amount of expenses that is less than the total amount of affected RIC expenses of M. Accordingly, the allocation method is not reasonable.

Example (2). Nonpublicly offered regulated investment company N has two classes of stock, a "capital" class and an "income" class. Owners of the capital class receive the benefit of all capital appreciation on the stocks owned by N, and bear the burden of certain capital expenditures of N; owners of the income class receive the benefit of all other income of N, and bear the burden of all expenses of N that are deductible under section 162. M allocates all affected RIC expenses among shareholders of the income class shares under a method that would be reasonable if the income class were the only class of N stock. Corporations and other shareholders that are not affected investors own a higher proportion of income class shares than of capital class shares. The affected RIC expenses of N are properly allocated among the shareholders who bear the burden of those expenses. Accordingly, the allocation method does not have the effect of allocating a disproportionately high share of the affected RIC expenses of N to shareholders that are not affected investors merely because a disproportionate share of income class shares are owned by shareholders that are not affected investors. The allocation method is reasonable.

Example (3). Nonpublicly offered regulated investment company O has two classes of stock, Class A and Class B. Shares of Class A, which may be purchased without payment of a sales or brokerage commission, are charged with the expenses of a Rule 12b-1 distribution plan of O. Shares of Class B, which may be purchased only upon payment of a sales or brokerage commission, are not charged with the expenses of the Rule 12b-1 distribution plan of O. O allocates all affected RIC expenses among shareholders of Class A and Class B shares under a method that would be reasonable if Class A or Class B shares, respectively, were the only class of O stock. The affected RIC expenses attributable to the Rule 12b-1 plan are allocated to the shareholders of Class A shares. Shareholders that are not affected investors own a higher proportion of Class A shares than of Class B shares. The affected RIC expenses of O are properly allocated among the shareholders who bear the burden of those expenses. Accordingly, the allocation method does not have the effect of allocating a disproportionately high share of the affected RIC expenses of O to shareholders that are not affected investors merely because a disproportionately high share of Class A shares are owned by persons that are not affected investors. The allocation method is reasonable.

Example (4). Assume the facts are the same as in example (3) except that a portion of the affected RIC expenses attributable to the Rule 12b-1 plan are allocated to the shareholders of Class B shares, and shareholders that are not affected investors own a higher proportion of Class B shares than of Class A shares. Thus, the affected RIC expenses are not allocated among the class of shareholders that bear the burden of the expenses. Accordingly, the allocation method has the effect of allocating a disproportionate share of the affected RIC expenses of O to the shareholders of Class B shares. Because shareholders that are not affected investors own a higher proportion of Class B shares than Class A shares, the method can be expected to allocate a disproportionately high share of the affected RIC expenses of O to shareholders that are not affected investors. Accordingly, the allocation method is not reasonable.

(l) *Affected RIC expenses not subject to backup withholding.* The amount of dividend income that an affected investor in a nonpublicly offered regulated investment company is treated as having received or accrued under paragraph (e)(1)(ii) of this section is not subject to backup withholding under section 3406.

(m) *Reliance by nominees and pass-through investors on notices*—(1) *General rule.* Persons described in paragraph (m)(3) of this section may, for the purposes described in that paragraph (m)(3), treat an affected investor's allocable share of the affected RIC expenses of a nonpublicly offered regulated investment company as being equal to an amount determined by the nonpublicly offered regulated investment company on the basis of a reasonable estimate (*e.g.,* of allocable expenses as a percentage of dividend distributions or allocable expenses per share) that is (i) reported in writing by the nonpublicly offered regulated investment company to the person or (ii) reported in a newspaper or financial publication having a nationwide circulation (*e.g.,* the *Wall Street Journal* or *Standard and Poor's Weekly Dividend Record*).

(2) *Estimates must be reasonable.* In general, for purposes of paragraph (m)(1) of this section, estimates of affected RIC expenses of a nonpublicly offered regulated investment company will be treated as reasonable only if the nonpublicly offered regulated investment company makes a reasonable effort to offset material understatements (or overstatements) of affected RIC expenses for a period by increasing (or decreasing) estimates of affected RIC expenses for a subsequent period. Understatements or overstatements of affected RIC expenses that are not material

Reg. § 1.67-2T(m)(2)

may be corrected by making offsetting adjustments in future periods, provided that understatements and overstatements are treated consistently.

(3) *Application.* Paragraph (m)(1) of this section shall apply to the following persons for the following purposes:

(i) A nominee who, pursuant to section 6042(a)(1)(B) and paragraph (n)(2) of this section, is required to report dividends paid by a nonpublicly offered regulated investment company to the Internal Revenue Service and to the person to whom the payment is made, for purposes of reporting to the Internal Revenue Service and the person to whom the payment is made the amount of affected RIC expenses allocated to such person.

(ii) An affected investor to whom a nominee (to which paragraph (m)(3)(i) of this section applies) reports, for purposes of calculating the affected investor's taxable income and the amount of its affected expenses.

(iii) A shareholder that is a pass-through entity, for purposes of calculating its taxable income and the amount of its affected expenses.

(n) *Return of information and reporting to affected investors by a nonpublicly offered regulated investment company*—(1) *In general*—(i) *Return of information.* A nonpublicly offered regulated investment company shall make an information return (*e.g.,* Form 1099-DIV, Dividends and Distributions, for 1987) with respect to each affected investor to which an allocation of affected RIC expenses is required to be made pursuant to paragraph (k) of this section and for which the nonpublicly offered regulated investment company is required to make an information return to the Internal Revenue Service pursuant to section 6042 (or would be required to make such information return but for the $10 threshold described in section 6042(a)(1)(A) and (B)). The nonpublicly offered regulated investment company shall make the information return for each calendar year and shall state separately on such return—

(A) The amount of affected RIC expenses required to be allocated to the affected investor for the calendar year pursuant to paragraph (k) of this section,

(B) The sum of—

(*1*) The aggregate amount of the dividends paid to the affected investor during the calendar year, and

(*2*) The amount of the affected RIC expenses required to be allocated to the affected

investor for the calendar year pursuant to paragraph (k) of this section, and

(C) Such other information as may be specified by the form or its instructions.

(ii) *Statement to be furnished to affected investors.* A nonpublicly offered regulated investment company shall provide to each affected investor for each calendar year (whether or not the nonpublicly offered regulated investment company is required to make an information return with respect to the affected investor pursuant to section 6042), a written statement showing the following information:

(A) The information described in paragraph (n)(1)(i) of this section with respect to the affected investor;

(B) The name and address of the nonpublicly offered regulated investment company;

(C) The name and address of the affected investor; and

(D) If the nonpublicly offered regulated investment company is required to report the amount of the affected investor's allocation of affected RIC expenses to the Internal Revenue Service pursuant to paragraph (n)(1)(i) of this section, a statement to that effect.

(iii) *Affected investor's shares held by a nominee.* If an affected investor's shares in a nonpublicly offered regulated investment company are held in the name of a nominee, the nonpublicly offered regulated investment company may make the information return described in paragraph (n)(1)(i) of this section with respect to the nominee in lieu of the affected investor and may provide the written statement described in paragraph (n)(1)(ii) of this section to such nominee in lieu of the affected investor.

(2) *By a nominee*—(i) *In general.* Except as otherwise provided for in paragraph (n)(2)(iii) of this section, in any case in which a nonpublicly offered regulated investment company provides, pursuant to paragraph (n)(1)(iii) of this section, a written statement to the nominee of an affected investor for a calendar year, the nominee shall—

(A) If the nominee is required to make an information return pursuant to section 6042 (or would be required to make an information return but for the $10 threshold described in section 6042(a)(1)(A) and (B)), make an information return (*e.g.,* Form 1099-DIV, Dividends and Distributions, for 1987) for the calendar year with respect to each affected investor and state separately on such information return the information described in paragraph (n)(1)(i) of this section, and

Reg. § 1.67-2T(m)(3)

(B) Furnish each affected investor with a written statement for the calendar year showing the information required by paragraph (n)(2)(ii) of this section (whether or not the nominee is required to make an information return with respect to the affected investor pursuant to section 6042).

(ii) *Form of statement.* The written statement required to be furnished for a calendar year pursuant to paragraph (n)(2)(i)(B) of this section shall show the following information:

(A) The affected investor's proportionate share of the items described in paragraph (n)(1)(i) of this section for the calendar year,

(B) The name and address of the nominee,

(C) The name and address of the affected investor, and

(D) If the nominee is required to report the affected investor's share of the allocable investment expenses to the Internal Revenue Service pursuant to paragraph (n)(2)(i)(A) of this section, a statement to that effect.

(iii) *Return not required.* A nominee is not required to make an information return with respect to an affected investor pursuant to paragraph (n)(2)(i)(A) of this section if the nominee is excluded from the requirements of section 6042 pursuant to § 1.6042-2(a)(1)(ii) or (iii).

(iv) *Statement not required.* A nominee is not required to furnish a written statement to an affected investor pursuant to paragraph (n)(2)(i)(B) of this section if the nonpublicly offered regulated investment company furnishes the written statement to the affected investor pursuant to an agreement with the nominee described in § 1.6042-2(a)(1)(iii).

(v) *Special rule.* Paragraph (n)(1)(i) and (ii) of this section applies to a nonpublicly offered regulated investment company that agrees with the nominee to satisfy the requirements of section 6042 as described in § 1.6042-2(a)(1)(iii) with respect to the affected investor.

(3) *Time and place for furnishing returns.* The returns required by paragraph (n)(1)(i) and (2)(i)(A) of this section for any calendar year shall be filed at the time and place that a return required under section 6042 is required to be filed. See § 1.6042-2(c).

(4) *Time for furnishing statements.* The statements required by paragraph (n)(1)(ii) and (2)(i)(B) of this section to be furnished by a nonpublicly offered regulated investment company and a nominee, respectively, to an affected investor for a calendar year shall be furnished to such affected investor on or before January 31 of the following year.

(5) *Duplicative returns and statements not required—*(i) *Information return.* The requirements of paragraph (n)(1)(i) and (2)(i)(A) of this section for the making of an information return shall be met by the timely filing of an information return pursuant to section 6042 that contains the information required by paragraph (n)(1)(i).

(ii) *Written statement.* The requirements of paragraph (n)(1)(ii) and (2)(i)(B) of this section for the furnishing of a written statement (including the statement required by paragraph (n)(1)(ii)(D) and (2)(ii)(D) of this section) shall be met by furnishing the affected investor a copy of the information return to which section 6042 applies (whether or not the nonpublicly offered regulated investment company or nominee is required to file an information return with respect to the affected investor pursuant to section 6042) that contains the information required by paragraph (n)(1)(ii) or (2)(ii), whichever is applicable, of this section. Nonpublicly offered regulated investment companies and nominees may use a substitute form that contains provisions substantially similar to those of the prescribed form if the nonpublicly offered regulated investment company or nominee complies with all revenue procedures relating to substitute forms in effect at the time. The statement shall be furnished either in person or in a statement mailed by first-class mail that includes adequate notice that the statement is enclosed. A statement shall be considered to be furnished to an affected investor within the meaning of this section if it is mailed to such affected investor at its last known address.

(o) *Return of information by a common trust fund.* With respect to each affected investor to which paragraph (d) of this section applies, the common trust fund shall state on the return it is required to make pursuant to section 6032 for its taxable year, the following information:

(1) The amount of the affected investor's proportionate share of the affected expenses for the taxable year as described in paragraph (d)(1)(ii) of this section,

(2) The amount of the affected investor's proportionate share of ordinary taxable income or ordinary net loss for the taxable year determined pursuant to paragraph (d)(1)(i) of this section, and

(3) Such other information as may be specified by the form or its instructions.

(p) *Publicly offered regulated investment companies.* [Reserved]

[Temporary Reg. § 1.67-2T.]

☐ [*T.D.* 8189, 3-25-88.]

Reg. § 1.67-2T(p)

[Reg. § 1.67-3]

§ 1.67-3. Allocation of expenses by real estate mortgage investment conduits.—(a) *Allocation of allocable investment expenses.* [Reserved]

(b) *Treatment of allocable investment expenses.* [Reserved]

(c) *Computation of proportionate share.* [Reserved]

(d) *Example.* [Reserved]

(e) *Allocable investment expenses not subject to backup withholding.* [Reserved]

(f) *Notice to pass-through interest holders*—(1) *Information required.* A REMIC must provide to each pass-through interest holder to which an allocation of allocable investment expense is required to be made under § 1.67-3T(a)(1) notice of the following—

(i) If, pursuant to paragraph (f)(2)(i) or (ii) of this section, notice is provided for a calendar quarter, the aggregate amount of expenses paid or accrued during the calendar quarter for which the REMIC is allowed a deduction under section 212;

(ii) If, pursuant to paragraph (f)(2)(ii) of this section, notice is provided to a regular interest holder for a calendar year, the aggregate amount of expenses paid or accrued during each calendar quarter that the regular interest holder held the regular interest in the calendar year and for which the REMIC is allowed a deduction under section 212; and

(iii) The proportionate share of these expenses allocated to that pass-through interest holder, as determined under § 1.67-3T(c).

(2) *Statement to be furnished*—(i) *To residual interest holder.* For each calendar quarter, a REMIC must provide to each pass-through interest holder who holds a residual interest during the calendar quarter the notice required under paragraph (f)(1) of this section on Schedule Q (Form 1066), as required in § 1.860F-4(e).

(ii) *To regular interest holder.* For each calendar year, a single-class REMIC (as described in § 1.67-3T(a)(2)(ii)(B)) must provide to each pass-through interest holder who held a regular interest during the calendar year the notice required under paragraph (f)(1) of this section. Quarterly reporting is not required. The information required to be included in the notice may be separately stated on the statement described in § 1.6049-7(f) instead of on a separate statement provided in a separate mailing. See § 1.6049-7(f)(4). The separate statement provided in a separate mailing must be furnished to each pass-through interest holder no later than the last day of the month following the close of the calendar year.

(3) *Returns to the Internal Revenue Service*—(i) *With respect to residual interest holders.* Any REMIC required under paragraphs (f)(1) and (2)(i) of this section to furnish information to any pass-through interest holder who holds a residual interest must also furnish such information to the Internal Revenue Service as required in § 1.860F-4(e)(4).

(ii) *With respect to regular interest holders.* A single-class REMIC (as described in § 1.67-3T(a)(2)(ii)(B)) must make an information return on Form 1099 for each calendar year, with respect to each pass-through interest holder who holds a regular interest to which an allocation of allocable investment expenses is required to be made pursuant to § 1.67-3T(a)(1) and (2)(ii). The preceding sentence applies with respect to a holder for a calendar year only if the REMIC is required to make an information return to the Internal Revenue Service with respect to that holder for that year pursuant to section 6049 and § 1.6049-7(b)(2)(i) (or would be required to make an information return but for the $10 threshold described in section 6049(a)(1) and § 1.6049-7(b)(2)(i)). The REMIC must state on the information return—

(A) The sum of—

(*1*) The aggregate amounts includible in gross income as interest (as defined in § 1.6049-7(a)(1)(i) and (ii)), for the calendar year; and

(*2*) The sum of the amount of allocable investment expenses required to be allocated to the pass-through interest holder for each calendar quarter during the calendar year pursuant to § 1.67-3T(a); and

(B) Any other information specified by the form or its instructions.

(4) *Interest held by nominees and other specified persons*— (i) *Pass-through interest holder's interest held by a nominee.* If a pass-through interest holder's interest in a REMIC is held in the name of a nominee, the REMIC may make the information return described in paragraphs (f)(3)(i) and (ii) of this section with respect to the nominee in lieu of the pass-through interest holder and may provide the written statement described in paragraphs (f)(2)(i) and (ii) of this section to that nominee in lieu of the pass-through interest holder.

(ii) *Regular interests in a single-class REMIC held by certain persons.* If a person specified in § 1.6049-7(e)(4) holds a regular interest in a single-class REMIC (as described in § 1.67-3T(a)(2)(ii)(B)), then the single-class REMIC must provide the information described in paragraphs (f)(1) and (f)(3)(ii)(A) and (B) of this section to that person with the information specified in § 1.6049-7(e)(2) as required in § 1.6049-7(e).

(5) *Nominee reporting*—(i) *In general.* In any case in which a REMIC provides information pursuant to paragraph (f)(4) of this section to a nominee of a pass-through interest holder for a calendar quarter or, as provided in paragraph (f)(2)(ii) of this section, for a calendar year—

(A) The nominee must furnish each pass-through interest holder with a written statement described in paragraph (f)(2)(i) or (ii) of this section, whichever is applicable, showing the information described in paragraph (f)(1) of this section; and

(B) The nominee must make an information return on Form 1099 for each calendar year, with respect to the pass-through interest holder and state on this information return the information described in paragraphs (f)(3)(ii)(A) and (B) of this section, if—

(*1*) The nominee is a nominee for a pass-through interest holder who holds a regular interest in a single-class REMIC (as described in § 1.67-3T(a)(2)(ii)(B)); and

(*2*) The nominee is required to make an information return pursuant to section 6049 and § 1.6049-7(b)(2)(i) and (b)(2)(ii)(B) (or would be required to make an information return but for the $10 threshold described in section 6049(a)(2) and § 1.6049-7(b)(2)(i)) with respect to the pass-through interest holder.

(ii) *Time for furnishing statement.* The statement required by paragraph (f)(5)(i)(A) of this section to be furnished by a nominee to a pass-through interest holder for a calendar quarter or calendar year must be furnished to this holder no later than 30 days after receiving the written statement described in paragraph (f)(2)(i) or (ii) of this section from the REMIC. If, however, pursuant to paragraph (f)(2)(ii) of this section, the information is separately stated on the statement described in § 1.6049-7(f), then the information must be furnished to the pass-through interest holder in the time specified in § 1.6049-7(f)(5).

(6) *Special rules*—(i) *Time and place for furnishing returns.* The returns required by paragraphs (f)(3)(ii) and (f)(5)(i)(B) of this section for any calendar year must be filed at the time and place that a return required under section 6049 and § 1.6049-7(b)(2) is required to be filed. See § 1.6049-4(g) and § 1.6049-7(b)(2)(iv).

(ii) *Duplicative returns not required.* The requirements of paragraphs (f)(3)(ii) and (f)(5)(i)(B) of this section for the making of an information return are satisfied by the timely filing of an information return pursuant to section 6049 and § 1.6049-7(b)(2) that contains the information required by paragraph (f)(3)(ii) of this section. [Reg. § 1.67-3.]

☐ [*T.D. 8431, 9-2-92.*]

[Reg. § 1.67-3T]

§ 1.67-3T. Allocation of expenses by real estate mortgage investment conduits (temporary).—(a) *Allocation of allocable investment expenses*—(1) *In general.* A real estate mortgage investment conduit or REMIC (as defined in section 860D) shall allocate to each of its pass-through interest holders that holds an interest at any time during the calendar quarter the holder's proportionate share (as determined under paragraph (c) of this section) of the aggregate amount of allocable investment expenses of the REMIC for the calendar quarter.

(2) *Pass-through interest holder*—(i) *In general*—(A) *Meaning of term.* Except as provided in paragraph (a)(?)(ii) of this section, the term "pass-through interest holder" means any holder of a REMIC residual interest (as defined in section 860G (a)(2)) that is—

(*1*) An individual (other than a nonresident alien whose income with respect to his or her interest in the REMIC is not effectively connected with the conduct of a trade or business within the United States),

(*2*) A person, including a trust or estate, that computes its taxable income in the same manner as in the case of an individual, or

(*3*) A pass-through entity (as defined in paragraph (a)(3) of this section) if one or more of its partners, shareholders, beneficiaries, participants, or other interest holders is (*i*) a pass-through entity or (*ii*) a person described in paragraph (a)(2)(i)(A)(*1*) or (*2*) of this section.

(B) *Examples.* The provisions of this paragraph (a)(2)(i) may be illustrated by the following examples:

Example (1). Corporation X holds a residual interest in REMIC R in its capacity as a nominee or custodian for individual A, the beneficial owner of the interest. Because the owner of the interest for Federal income tax purposes is an individual, the interest is owned by a pass-through interest holder.

Reg. § 1.67-3T(a)(2)

Example (2). Individual retirement account I holds a residual interest in a REMIC. Because an individual retirement account is not a person described in paragraph (a)(2)(i)(A) of this section, the interest is not held by a pass-through interest holder.

(ii) *Single-class REMIC—(A) In general.* In the case of a single-class REMIC, the term "pass-through interest holder" means any holder of either—

(1) A REMIC regular interest (as defined in section 860G(a)(1)), or

(2) A REMIC residual interest,

that is described in paragraph (a)(2)(i)(A)(1), (2), or (3) of this section.

(B) *Single-class REMIC.* For purposes of paragraph (a)(2)(ii)(A) of this section, a single-class REMIC is either—

(1) A REMIC that would be classified as an investment trust under § 301.7701-4(c)(1) but for its qualification as a REMIC under section 860D and § 1.860D-1T, or

(2) A REMIC that—

(*i*) Is substantially similar to an investment trust under § 301.7701-4(c)(1), and

(*ii*) Is structured with the principal purposes of avoiding the requirement of paragraph (a)(1) and (2)(ii)(A) of this section to allocate allocable investment expenses to pass-through interest holders that hold regular interests in the REMIC.

For purposes of this paragraph (a)(2)(ii)(B), in determining whether a REMIC would be classified as an investment trust or is substantially similar to an investment trust, all interests in the REMIC shall be treated as ownership interests in the REMIC, without regard to whether or not they would be classified as debt for Federal income tax purposes in the absence of a REMIC election.

(C) *Examples.* The provisions of paragraph (a)(2)(ii) of this section may be illustrated by the following examples:

Example (1). Corporation M transfers mortgages to a bank under a trust agreement as described in Example (2) of § 301.7701-4(c)(2). There are two classes of certificates. Holders of class C certificates are entitled to receive 90 percent of the payments of principal and interest on the mortgages; holders of class D certificates are entitled to receive the remaining 10 percent. The two classes of certificates are identical except that, in the event of a default on the underlying mortgages, the payment rights of class D certificate holders are subordinated to the rights of class C certificate holders. M sells the class C certifi-

cates to investors and retains the class D certificates. The trust would be classified as an investment trust under § 301.7701-4(c)(1) but for its qualification as a REMIC under section 860D. The class C certificates represent regular interests in the REMIC and the class D certificates represent residual interests in the REMIC. The REMIC is a single-class REMIC within the meaning of paragraph (a)(2)(ii)(B)(1) of this section and, accordingly, holders of both the class C and class D certificates who are described in paragraph (a)(2)(i)(A)(1), (2), or (3) of this section are treated as pass-through interest holders.

Example (2). Assume that the facts are the same as in Example (1) except that M structures the REMIC to include a second regular interest represented by class E certificates. The principal purpose of M in structuring the REMIC to include class E certificates is to avoid allocating allocable investment expenses to class C certificate holders. The class E certificate holders are entitled to receive the payments otherwise due the class D certificate holders until they have been paid a stated amount of principal plus interest. The fair market value of the class E certificate is ten percent of the fair market value of the class D certificate and, therefore, less than one percent of the fair market value of the REMIC. The REMIC would not be classified as an investment trust under § 301.7701-4(c)(1) because the existence of the class E certificates is not incidental to the trust's purpose of facilitating direct investment in the assets of the trust. Nevertheless, because the fair market value of the class E certificates is de minimis, the REMIC is substantially similar to an investment trust under § 301.7701-4(c)(1). In addition, avoidance of the requirement to allocate allocable investment expenses to regular interest holders is the principal purpose of M in structuring the REMIC to include class E certificates. Therefore, the REMIC is a single-class REMIC within the meaning of paragraph (a)(2)(ii)(B)(2) of this section, and, accordingly, holders of both residual and regular interests who are described in paragraph (a)(2)(i)(A)(1), (2), or (3) of this section are treated as pass-through interest holders.

(3) *Pass-through entity—(i) In general.* Except as provided in paragraph (a)(3)(ii) of this section, for purposes of this section, a pass-through entity is—

(A) A trust (or any portion thereof) to which subpart E, part 1, subchapter J, chapter 1 of the Code applies,

(B) A partnership,

(C) An S corporation,

Reg. § 1.67-3T(a)(3)

(D) A common trust fund described in section 584,

(E) A nonpublicly offered regulated investment company (as defined in paragraph (a)(5)(i) of this section),

(F) A REMIC, and

(G) Any other person—

(1) Which is not subject to income tax imposed by subtitle A, chapter 1, or which is allowed a deduction in computing such tax for distributions to owners or beneficiaries, and

(2) The character of the income of which may affect the character of the income recognized with respect to that person by its owners or beneficiaries.

Entities that do not meet the requirements of paragraph (a)(3)(i)(G)(1) and (2), such as qualified pension plans, individual retirement accounts, and insurance companies holding assets in separate asset accounts to fund variable contracts defined in section 817(d), are not described in this paragraph (a)(3)(i).

(ii) *Exception.* For purposes of this section, a pass-through entity does not include—

(A) An estate,

(B) A trust (or any portion thereof) not described in paragraph (a)(3)(i)(A) of this section,

(C) A cooperative described in section 1,381(a)(2), determined without regard to subparagraphs (A) and (C) thereof, or

(D) A real estate investment trust.

(4) *Allocable investment expenses.* The term "allocable investment expenses" means the aggregate amount of the expenses paid or accrued in the calendar quarter for which a deduction is allowable under section 212 in determining the taxable income of the REMIC for the calendar quarter.

(5) *Nonpublicly offered regulated investment company*—(i) *In general.* For purposes of this section, the term "nonpublicly offered regulated investment company" means a regulated investment company to which part I of subchapter M of the Code applies that is not a publicly offered regulated investment company.

(ii) *Publicly offered regulated investment company.* For purposes of this section, the term "publicly offered regulated investment company" means a regulated investment company to which part I of subchapter M of the Code applies, the shares of which are—

(A) Continuously offered pursuant to a public offering (within the meaning of section 4 of the Securities Act of 1933, as amended (15 U.S.C. 77a to 77aa)),

(B) Regularly traded on an established securities market, or

(C) Held by or for no fewer than 500 persons at all times during the taxable year.

(b) *Treatment of allocable investment expenses*—(1) *By pass-through interest holders*—(i) *Taxable year ending with calendar quarter.* A pass-through interest holder whose taxable year is the calendar year or ends with a calendar quarter shall be treated as having—

(A) Received or accrued income, and

(B) Paid or incurred an expense described in section 212 (or section 162 in the case of a pass-through interest holder that is a regulated investment company), in an amount equal to the pass-through interest holder's proportionate share of the allocable investment expenses of the REMIC for those calendar quarters that fall within the holder's taxable year.

(ii) *Taxable year not ending with calendar quarter.* A pass-through interest holder whose taxable year does not end with a calendar quarter shall be treated as having—

(A) Received or accrued income, and

(B) Paid or incurred an expense described in section 212 (or section 162 in the case of a pass-through interest holder that is a regulated investment company),

in an amount equal to the sum of—

(C) The pass-through interest holder's proportionate share of the allocable investment expenses of the REMIC for those calendar quarters that fall within the holder's taxable year, and

(D) For each calendar quarter that overlaps the beginning or end of the taxable year, the sum of the daily amounts of the allocable investment expenses allocated to the holder pursuant to paragraph (c)(1)(ii) of this section for the days in the quarter that fall within the holder's taxable year.

(2) *Proportionate share of allocable investment expenses.* For purposes of paragraph (b) of this section, a pass-through interest holder's proportionate share of the allocable investment expenses is the amount allocated to the pass-through interest holder pursuant to paragraph (a)(1) of this section.

(3) *Cross-reference.* See § 1.67-1T with respect to limitations on deductions for expenses described in section 212 (including amounts treated as such expenses under this section).

(4) *Interest income to holders of regular interests in certain REMICs.* Any amount allocated under this section to the holder of a regular inter-

Reg. § 1.67-3T(b)(4)

est in a single-class REMIC (as described in paragraph (a)(2)(ii)(B) of this section) shall be treated as interest income.

(5) *No adjustment to basis.* The basis of any holder's interest in a REMIC shall not be increased or decreased by the amount of the holder's proportionate share of allocable investment expenses.

(6) *Interest holders other than pass-through interest holders.* An interest holder of a REMIC that is not a pass-through interest holder shall not take into account in computing its taxable income any amount of income or expense with respect to its proportionate share of allocable investment expenses.

(c) *Computation of proportionate share*—(1) *In general.* For purposes of paragraph (a)(1) of this section, a REMIC shall compute a pass-through interest holder's proportionate share of the REMIC's allocable investment expenses by—

(i) Determining the daily amount of the allocable investment expenses for the calendar quarter by dividing the total amount of such expenses by the number of days in that calendar quarter,

(ii) Allocating the daily amount of the allocable investment expenses to the pass-through interest holder in proportion to its respective holdings on that day, and

(iii) Totaling the interest holder's daily amount of allocable investment expenses for the calendar quarter.

(2) *Other holders taken into account.* For purposes of paragraph (c)(1)(ii) of this section, a pass-through interest holder's proportionate share of the daily amount of the allocable investment expenses is determined by taking into account all holders of residual interests in the REMIC, whether or not pass-through interest holders.

(3) *Single-class REMIC*—(i) *Daily allocation.* In lieu of the allocation specified in paragraph (c)(1)(ii) of this section, a single-class REMIC (as described in paragraph (a)(2)(ii)(B) of this section) shall allocate the daily amount of the allocable investment expenses to each pass-through interest holder in proportion to the amount of income accruing to the holder with respect to its interest in the REMIC on that day.

(ii) *Other holders taken into account.* For purposes of paragraph (c)(3)(i) of this section, the amount of the allocable investment expenses that is allocated on any day to each pass-through interest holder shall be determined by multiplying the daily amount of allocable investment expenses (determined pursuant to paragraph (c)(1)(i) of this section by a fraction, the numerator of which

is equal to the amount of income that accrues (but not less than zero) to the pass-through interest holder on that day and the denominator of which is the total amount of income (as determined under paragraph (c)(3)(iii) of this section) that accrues to all regular and residual interest holders, whether or not pass-through interest holders, on that day.

(iii) *Total income accruing.* The total amount of income that accrues to all regular and residual interest holders is the sum of—

(A) The amount includible under section 860B in the gross income (but not less than zero) of the regular interest holders, and

(B) The amount of REMIC taxable income (but not less than zero) taken into account under section 860C by the residual interest holders.

(4) *Dates of purchase and disposition.* For purposes of this section, a pass-through interest holder holds an interest on the date of its purchase but not on the date of its disposition.

(d) *Example.* The provisions of this section may be illustrated by the following example:

Example. (i) During the calendar quarter ending March 31, 1989, REMIC X, which is not a single-class REMIC, incurs $900 of allocable investment expenses. At the beginning of the calendar quarter, X has 4 residual interest holders, who hold equal proportionate shares, and 10 regular interest holders. The residual interest holders, all of whom have calendar-year taxable years, are as follows:

A, an individual,

C, a C corporation that is a nominee for individual I,

S, an S corporation, and

M, a C corporation that is not a nominee.

(ii) Except for A, all of the residual interest holders hold their interests in X for the entire calendar quarter. On January 31, 1989, A sells his interest to S. Thus, for the first month of the calendar quarter, each residual interest holder holds a 25 percent interest (100%/4 interest holders) in X. For the last two months, S's holding is increased to 50 percent and A's holding is decreased to zero. The daily amount of allocable investment expenses for the calendar quarter is $10 ($900/90 days).

(iii) The amount of allocable investment expenses apportioned to the residual interest holders is as follows:

(A) $75 ($10 × 25% × 30 days) is allocated to A for the 30 days that A holds an interest in X during the calendar quarter. A includes $75 in gross income in calendar year 1989. The amount of A's expenses described in section 212 is increased by $75 in calendar year 1989. A's deduction under section 212 (including the $75 amount of the allocation) is subject to the limitations contained in section 67.

(B) $225 ($10 × 25% × 90 days) is allocated to C. Because C is a nominee for I, C does not include $225 in gross income or increase its deductible expenses by $225. Instead, I includes $225 in gross income in calendar year 1989, her taxable year. The amount of I's expenses described in section 212 is increased by $225. I's deduction under section 212 (including the $225 amount of the allocation) is subject to the limitations contained in section 67.

(C) $375 (($10 × 25% × 30 days) + ($10 × 50% × 60 days)) is allocated to S. S includes in gross income $375 of allocable investment expenses in calendar year 1989. The amount of S's expenses described in section 212 for that taxable year is increased by $375. S allocates the $375 to its shareholders in accordance with the rules described in sections 1366 and 1377 in calendar year 1989 Thus, each shareholder of S includes its pro rata share of the $375 in gross income in its taxable year in which or with which calendar year 1989 ends. The amount of each shareholder's expenses described in section 212 is increased by the amount of the shareholder's allocation for the shareholder's taxable year in which or with which calender year 1989 ends. The shareholder's deduction under section 212 (including the allocation under this section) is subject to the limitations contained in section 67.

(D) No amount is allocated to M. However, M's interest is taken into account for purposes of determining the proportionate share of those residual interest holders to whom an allocation is required to be made.

(iv) No allocation is made to the 10 regular interest holders pursuant to paragraph (a) of this section. In addition, the interests held by these interest holders are not taken into account for purposes of determining the proportionate share of the residual interest holders to whom an allocation is required to be made.

(e) *Allocable investment expenses not subject to backup withholding.* The amount of allocable investment expenses required to be allocated to a pass-through interest holder pursuant to paragraph (a)(1) of this section is not subject to backup withholding under section 3406.

(f) *Notice to pass-through interest holders*—(1) *Information required.* A REMIC must provide to each pass-through interest holder to which an allocation of allocable investment expense is re-

quired to be made under paragraph (a)(1) of this section notice of the following—

(i) If, pursuant to paragraph (f)(2)(i) or (ii) of this section, notice is provided for a calendar quarter, the aggregate amount of expenses paid or accrued during the calendar quarter for which the REMIC is allowed a deduction under section 212;

(ii) If, pursuant to paragraph (f)(2)(ii) of this section, notice is provided to a regular interest holder for a calendar year, the aggregate amount of expenses paid or accrued during each calendar quarter that the regular interest holder held the regular interest in the calendar year and for which the REMIC is allowed a deduction under section 212; and

(iii) The proportionate share of these expenses allocated to that pass-through interest holder, as determined under paragraph (c) of this section.

(2) *Statement to be furnished*—(i) *To residual interest holder.* For each calendar quarter, a REMIC shall provide to each pass-through interest holder who holds a residual interest during the calendar quarter the notice required under paragraph (f)(1) of this section on Schedule Q (Form 1066), as required in § 1.860F-4(e).

(ii) *To regular interest holder*—(A) *In general.* For each calendar year, a single-class REMIC (as described in paragraph (a)(2)(ii)(B) of this section) must provide to each pass-through interest holder who held a regular interest during the calendar year the notice required under paragraph (f)(1) of this section. Quarterly reporting is not required. The information required to be included in the notice may be separately stated on the statement described in § 1.6049-7(f) instead of on a separate statement provided in a separate mailing. See § 1.6049-7(f)(4). The separate statement provided in a separate mailing must be furnished to each pass-through interest holder no later than the last day of the month following the close of the calendar year.

(B) *Special rule for 1987.* The information required under paragraph (f)(2)(ii)(A) of this section for any calendar quarter of 1987 shall be mailed (or otherwise delivered) to each pass-through interest holder who holds a regular interest during that calendar quarter no later than March 28, 1988.

(3) *Returns to the Internal Revenue Service*—(i) *With respect to residual interest holders.* Any REMIC required under paragraphs (f)(1) and (2)(i) of this section to furnish information to any pass-through interest holder who holds a residual interest shall also furnish such informa-

tion to the Internal Revenue Service as required in § 1.860F-4(e)(4).

(ii) *With respect to regular interest holders.* A single-class REMIC (as described in paragraph (a)(2)(ii)(B) of this section) shall make an information return on Form 1099 for each calendar year beginning after December 31, 1987, with respect to each pass-through interest holder who holds a regular interest to which an allocation of allocable investment expenses is required to be made pursuant to paragraphs (a)(1) and (2)(ii) of this section. The preceding sentence applies with respect to a holder for a calendar year only if the REMIC is required to make an information return to the Internal Revenue Service with respect to that holder for that year pursuant to section 6049 and § 1.6049-7(b)(2)(i) (or would be required to make an information return but for the $10 threshold described in section 6049(a)(1) and § 1.6049-7(b)(2)(i)). The REMIC shall state on the information return—

(A) The sum of—

(*1*) The aggregate amounts includible in gross income as interest (as defined in § 1.6049-7(a)(1)(i) and (ii)), for the calendar year, and

(*2*) The sum of the amount of allocable investment expenses required to be allocated to the pass-through interest holder for each calendar quarter during the calendar year pursuant to paragraph (a) of this section, and

(B) Any other information specified by the form or its instructions.

(4) *Interest held by nominees and other specified persons*—(i) *Pass-through interest holder's interest held by a nominee.* If a pass-through interest holder's interest in a REMIC is held in the name of a nominee, the REMIC may make the information return described in paragraphs (f)(3)(i) and (ii) of this section with respect to the nominee in lieu of the pass-through interest holder and may provide the written statement described in paragraphs (f)(2)(i) and (ii) of this section to that nominee in lieu of the pass-through interest holder.

(ii) *Regular interests in a single-class REMIC held by certain persons.* For calendar quarters and calendar years after December 31, 1991, if a person specified in § 1.6049-7(e)(4) holds a regular interest in a single-class REMIC (as described in paragraph (a)(2)(ii)(B) of this section), then the single-class REMIC must provide the information described in paragraphs (f)(1) and (f)(3)(ii)(A) and (B) of this section to that person with the information specified in § 1.6049-7(e)(2) as required in § 1.6049-7(e).

(5) *Nominee reporting*—(i) *In general.* In any case in which a REMIC provides information pursuant to paragraph (f)(4) of this section to a nominee of a pass-through interest holder for a calendar quarter or, as provided in paragraph (f)(2)(ii) of this section, for a calendar year—

(A) The nominee shall furnish each pass-through interest holder with a written statement described in paragraph (f)(2)(i) or (ii) of this section, whichever is applicable, showing the information described in paragraph (f)(1) of this section, and

(B) If—

(*1*) The nominee is a nominee for a pass-through interest holder who holds a regular interest in a single-class REMIC (as described in paragraph (a)(2)(ii)(B) of this section), and

(*2*) The nominee is required to make an information return pursuant to section 6049 and § 1.6049-7(b)(2)(i) and (b)(2)(ii)(B) (or would be required to make an information return but for the $10 threshold described in section 6049(a)(2) and § 1.6049-7(b)(2)(i)) with respect to the pass-through interest holder,

the nominee shall make an information return on Form 1099 for each calendar year beginning after December 31, 1987, with respect to the pass-through interest holder and state on this information return the information described in paragraph (f)(3)(ii)(A) and (B) of this section.

(ii) *Time for furnishing statement.* The statement required by paragraph (f)(5)(i)(A) of this section to be furnished by a nominee to a pass-through interest holder for a calendar quarter or calendar year shall be furnished to this holder no later than 30 days after receiving the written statement described in paragraph (f)(2)(i) or (ii) of this section from the REMIC. If, however, pursuant to paragraph (f)(2)(ii) of this section, the information is separately stated on the statement described in § 1.6049-7(f), then the information must be furnished to the pass-through interest holder in the time specified in § 1.6049-7(f)(5).

(6) *Special rules*—(i) *Time and place for furnishing returns.* The returns required by paragraphs (f)(3)(ii) and (f)(5)(i)(B) of this section for any calendar year shall be filed at the time and place that a return required under section 6049 and § 1.6049-7(b)(2) is required to be filed. See § 1.6049-4(g) and § 1.6049-7(b)(2)(iv).

(ii) *Duplicative returns not required.* The requirements of paragraphs (f)(3)(ii) and (f)(5)(i)(B) of this section for the making of an information return shall be met by the timely filing of an information return pursuant to section

Reg. § 1.67-3T(f)(4)

6049 and § 1.6049-7(b)(2) that contains the information required by paragraph (f)(3)(ii) of this section. [Temporary Reg. § 1.67-3T.]

☐ [*T.D. 8186, 3-4-88. Amended by T.D. 8259, 9-6-89 and T.D. 8366, 9-27-91.*]

Items Specifically Included in Gross Income
[Reg. § 1.71-1]

§ 1.71-1. Alimony and separate maintenance payments; income to wife or former wife.—(a) *In general.* Section 71 provides rules for treatment in certain cases of payments in the nature of or in lieu of alimony or an allowance for support as between spouses who are divorced or separated. For convenience, the payee spouse will hereafter in this section be referred to as the "wife" and the spouse from whom she is divorced or separated as the "husband." See section 7701(a)(17). For rules relative to the deduction by the husband of periodic payments not attributable to transferred property, see section 215 and the regulations thereunder. For rules relative to the taxable status of income of an estate or trust in case of divorce, etc., see section 682 and the regulations thereunder.

(b) *Alimony or separate maintenance payments received from the husband.* (1) *Decree of divorce or separate maintenance.* (i) In the case of divorce or legal separation, paragraph (1) of section 71(a) requires the inclusion in the gross income of the wife of periodic payments (whether or not made at regular intervals) received by her after a decree of divorce or of separate maintenance. Such periodic payments must be made in discharge of a legal obligation imposed upon or incurred by the husband because of the marital or family relationship under a court order or decree divorcing or legally separating the husband and wife or a written instrument incident to such divorce status or legal separation status.

(ii) For treatment of payments attributable to property transferred (in trust or otherwise), see paragraph (c) of this section.

(2) *Written separation agreement.* (i) Where the husband and wife are separated and living apart and do not file a joint income tax return for the taxable year, paragraph (2) of section 71(a) requires the inclusion in the gross income of the wife of periodic payments (whether or not made at regular intervals) received by her pursuant to a written separation agreement executed after August 16, 1954. The periodic payments must be made under the terms of the written separation agreement after its execution and because of the marital or family relationship. Such payments are includible in the wife's gross income whether or not the agreement is a legally enforceable instru-

[Reg. § 1.67-4T]

§ 1.67-4T. Allocation of expenses by non-grantor trusts and estates (temporary). [Reserved]

ment. Moreover, if the wife is divorced or legally separated subsequent to the written separation agreement, payments made under such agreement continue to fall within the provisions of section 71(a)(2).

(ii) For purposes of section 71(a)(2), any written separation agreement executed on or before August 16, 1954, which is altered or modified in writing by the parties in any material respect after that date will be treated as an agreement executed after August 16, 1954, with respect to payments made after the date of alteration or modification.

(iii) For treatment of payments attributable to property transferred (in trust or otherwise), see paragraph (c) of this section.

(3) *Decree for support.* (i) Where the husband and wife are separated and living apart and do not file a joint income tax return for the taxable year, paragraph (3) of section 71(a) requires the inclusion in the gross income of the wife of periodic payments (whether or not made at regular intervals) received by her after August 16, 1954, from her husband under any type of court order or decree (including an interlocutory decree of divorce or a decree of alimony pendente lite) entered after March 1, 1954, requiring the husband to make the payments for her support or maintenance. It is not necessary for the wife to be legally separated or divorced from her husband under a court order or decree; nor is it necessary for the order or decree for support to be for the purpose of enforcing a written separation agreement.

(ii) For purposes of section 71(a)(3), any decree which is altered or modified by a court order entered after March 1, 1954, will be treated as a decree entered after such date.

(4) *Scope of section 71(a).* Section 71(a) applies only to payments made because of the family or marital relationship in recognition of the general obligation to support which is made specific by the decree, instrument, or agreement. Thus, section 71(a) does not apply to that part of any periodic payment which is attributable to the repayment by the husband of, for example, a bona fide loan previously made to him by the wife, the satisfaction of which is specified in the decree, instrument, or agreement as a part of the general settlement between the husband and wife.

Reg. § 1.71-1(b)(4)

(5) *Year of inclusion.* Periodic payments are includible in the wife's income under section 71(a) only for the taxable year in which received by her. As to such amounts, the wife is to be treated as if she makes her income tax returns on the cash receipts and disbursements method, regardless of whether she normally makes such returns on the accrual method. However, if the periodic payments described in section 71(a) are to be made by an estate or trust, such periodic payments are to be included in the wife's taxable year in which they are includible according to the rules as to income of estates and trusts provided in sections 652, 662, and 682, whether or not such payments are made out of the income of such estates or trusts.

(6) *Examples.* The foregoing rules are illustrated by the following examples in which it is assumed that the husband and wife file separate income tax returns on the calendar year basis:

Example (1). W files suit for divorce from H in 1953. In consideration of W's promise to relinquish all marital rights and not to make public H's financial affairs, H agrees in writing to pay $200 a month to W during her lifetime if a final decree of divorce is granted without any provision for alimony. Accordingly, W does not request alimony and no provision for alimony is made under a final decree of divorce entered December 31, 1953. During 1954, H pays W $200 a month, pursuant to the promise. The $2,400 thus received by W is includible in her gross income under the provisions of section 71(a)(1). Under section 215, H is entitled to a deduction of $2,400 from his gross income.

Example (2). During 1945, H and W enter into an antenuptial agreement, under which, in consideration of W's relinquishment of all marital rights (including dower) in H's property, and, in order to provide for W's support and household expenses, H promises to pay W $200 a month during her lifetime. Ten years after their marriage, W sues H for divorce but does not ask for or obtain alimony because of the provision already made for her support in the antenuptial agreement. Likewise, the divorce decree is silent as to such agreement and H's obligation to support W. Section 71(a) does not apply to such a case. If, however, the decree were modified so as to refer to the antenuptial agreement, or if reference had been made to the antenuptial agreement in the court's decree or in a written instrument incident to the divorce status, section 71(a)(1) would require the inclusion in W's gross income of the payments received by her after the decree. Similarly, if a written separation agreement were executed after August 16, 1954, and incorporated the payment provisions of the antenuptial agreement, section 71(a)(2) would require the inclusion in W's income of payments received by W after W begins living apart from H, whether or not the divorce decree was subsequently entered and whether or not W was living apart from H when the separation agreement was executed, provided that such payments were made after such agreement was executed and pursuant to its terms. As to including such payments in W's income, if made by a trust created under the antenuptial agreement, regardless of whether referred to in the decree or a later instrument, or created pursuant to the written separation agreement, see section 682 and the regulations thereunder.

Example (3). H and W are separated and living apart during 1954. W sues H for support and on February 1, 1954, the court enters a decree requiring H to pay $200 a month to W for her support and maintenance. No part of the $200 a month support payments is includible in W's income under section 71(a)(3) or deductible by H under section 215. If, however, the decree had been entered after March 1, 1954, or had been altered or modified by a court order entered after March 1, 1954, the payments received by W after August 16, 1954, under the decree as altered or modified would be includible in her income under sections 71(a)(3) and deductible by H under section 215.

Example (4). W sues H for divorce in 1954. On January 15, 1954, the court awards W temporary alimony of $25 a week pending the final decree. On September 1, 1954, the court grants W a divorce and awards her $200 a month permanent alimony. No part of the $25 a week temporary alimony received prior to the decree is includible in W's income under section 71(a), but the $200 a month received during the remainder of 1954 by W is includible in her income for 1954. Under section 215, H is entitled to deduct such $200 payments from his income. If, however, the decree awarding W temporary alimony had been entered after March 1, 1954, or had been altered or modified by a court order entered after March 1, 1954, temporary alimony received by her after August 16, 1954, would be includible in her income under section 71(a)(3) and deductible by H under section 215.

(c) *Alimony and separate maintenance payments attributable to property.* (1)(i) In the case of divorce or legal separation, paragraph (1) of section 71(a) requires the inclusion in the gross income of the wife of periodic payments (whether or not made at regular intervals) attributable to property transferred, in trust or otherwise, and received by her after a decree of divorce or of separate maintenance. Such property must have been transferred in discharge of a legal obligation imposed upon or incurred by the husband because of the marital or family relationship under a decree of divorce or separate maintenance or under a written instrument incident to such divorce status or legal separation status.

(ii) Where the husband and wife are separated and living apart and do not file a joint income tax return for the taxable year, paragraph (2) of section 71(a) requires the inclusion in the gross income of the wife of periodic payments (whether or not made at regular intervals) received by her which are attributable to property transferred, in trust or otherwise, under a written separation agreement executed after August 16, 1954. The property must be transferred because of the marital or family relationship. The periodic payments attributable to the property must be received by the wife after the written separation agreement is executed.

(iii) The periodic payments received by the wife attributable to property transferred under subdivisions (i) and (ii) of this subparagraph and includible in her gross income are not to be included in the gross income of the husband.

(2) The full amount of periodic payments received under the circumstances described in section 71(a)(1), (2), and (3) is required to be included in the gross income of the wife regardless of the source of such payments. Thus, it matters not that such payments are attributable to property in trust, to life insurance, endowment, or annuity contracts, or to any other interest in property, or are paid directly or indirectly by the husband from his income or capital. For example, if in order to meet an alimony or separate maintenance obligation of $500 a month the husband purchases or assigns for the benefit of his wife a commercial annuity contract paying such amount, the full $500 a month received by the wife is includible in her income, and no part of such amount is includible in the husband's income or deductible by him. See section 72(k) and the regulations thereunder. Likewise, if property is transferred by the husband, subject to an annual charge of $5,000, payable to his wife in discharge of his alimony or separate maintenance obligation under the divorce or separation decree or written instrument incident to the divorce status or legal separation status or if such property is transferred pursuant to a written separation agreement and subject to a similar annual charge, the $5,000 received annually is, under section 71(a)(1) or (2), includible in the wife's income, regardless of whether such amount is paid out of income or principal of the property.

(3) The same rule applies to periodic payments attributable to property in trust. The full amount of periodic payments to which section 71(a)(1) and (2) applies is includible in the wife's income regardless of whether such payments are made out of trust income. Such periodic payments are to be included in the wife's income under section 71(a)(1) or (2) and are to be excluded from the husband's income even though the income of the trust would otherwise be includible in his income under subpart E, part I, subchapter J, chapter 1 of the Code, relating to trust income attributable to grantors and others as substantial owners. As to periodic payments received by a wife attributable to property in trust in cases to which section 71(a)(1) or (2) does not apply because the husband's obligation is not specified in the decree or an instrument incident to the divorce status or legal separation status or the property was not transferred under a written separation agreement, see section 682 and the regulations thereunder.

(4) Section 71(a)(1) or (2) does not apply to that part of any periodic payment attributable to that portion of any interest in property transferred in discharge of the husband's obligation under the decree or instrument incident to the divorce status or legal separation status, or transferred pursuant to the written separation agreement, which interest originally belonged to the wife. It will apply, however, if she received such interest from her husband in contemplation of or as an incident to the divorce or separation without adequate and full consideration in money or money's worth, other than the release of the husband or his property from marital obligations. An example of the first rule is a case where the husband and wife transfer securities, which were owned by them jointly, in trust to pay an annuity to the wife. In this case, the full amount of that part of the annuity received by the wife attributable to the husband's interest in the securities transferred in discharge of his obligation under the decree, or instrument incident to the divorce status or legal separation status, or transferred under the written separation agreement, is taxable to her under section 71(a)(1) or (2), while that portion of the annuity attributable to the wife's interest in the securities so transferred is taxable to her only to the extent it is out of trust income as provided in part I (sections 641 and following), subchapter J, chapter 1 of the Code. If, however, the husband's transfer to his wife is made before such property is transferred in discharge of his obligation under the decree or written instrument, or pursuant to the separation agreement in an attempt to avoid the application of section 71(a)(1) or (2) to part of such payments received

Reg. § 1.71-1(c)(4)

by his wife, such transfers will be considered as a part of the same transfer by the husband of his property in discharge of his obligation or pursuant to such agreement. In such a case, section 71(a)(1) or (2) will be applied to the full amount received by the wife. As to periodic payments received under a joint purchase of a commercial annuity contract, see section 72 and the regulations thereunder.

(d) *Periodic and installment payments.*—(1) In general, installment payments discharging a part of an obligation the principal sum of which is, in terms of money or property, specified in the decree, instrument, or agreement are not considered "periodic payments" and therefore are not to be included under section 71(a) in the wife's income.

(2) An exception to the general rule stated in subparagraph (1) of this paragraph is provided, however, in cases where such principal sum, by the terms of the decree, instrument, or agreement, may be or is to be paid over a period ending more than 10 years from the date of such decree, instrument, or agreement. In such cases, the installment payment is considered a periodic payment for the purposes of section 71(a) but only to the extent that the installment payment, or sum of the installment payments, received during the wife's taxable year does not exceed 10 percent of the principal sum. This 10-percent limitation applies to installment payments made in advance but does not apply to delinquent installment payments for a prior taxable year of the wife made during her taxable year.

(3)(i) Where payments under a decree, instrument, or agreement are to be paid over a period ending 10 years or less from the date of such decree, instrument, or agreement, such payments are not installment payments discharging a part of an obligation the principal sum of which is, in terms of money or property, specified in the decree, instrument, or agreement (and are considered periodic payments for the purposes of section 71(a)) only if such payments meet the following two conditions:

(a) Such payments are subject to any one or more of the contingencies of death of either spouse, remarriage of the wife, or change in the economic status of either spouse, and

(b) Such payments are in the nature of alimony or an allowance for support.

(ii) Payments meeting the requirements of subdivision (i) are considered periodic payments for the purposes of section 71(a) regardless of whether—

(a) The contingencies described in subdivision (i)(a) are set forth in the terms of the

decree, instrument, or agreement, or are imposed by local law, or

(b) The aggregate amount of the payments to be made in the absence of the occurrence of the contingencies described in subdivision (i)(a) of this subparagraph is explicitly stated in the decree, instrument, or agreement or may be calculated from the face of the decree, instrument, or agreement, or

(c) The total amount which will be paid may be calculated actuarially.

(4) Where payments under a decree, instrument, or agreement are to be paid over a period ending more than ten years from the date of such decree, instrument, or agreement, but where such payments meet the conditions set forth in subparagraph (3)(i) of this paragraph, such payments are considered to be periodic payments for the purpose of section 71 without regard to the rule set forth in subparagraph (2) of this paragraph. Accordingly, the rules set forth in subparagraph (2) of this paragraph are not applicable to such payments.

(5) The rules as to periodic and installment payments are illustrated by the following examples:

Example (1). Under the terms of a written instrument, H is required to make payments to W which are in the nature of alimony, in the amount of $100 a month for nine years. The instrument provides that if H or W dies the payments are to cease. The payments are periodic.

Example (2). The facts are the same as in example (1) except that the written instrument explicitly provides that H is to pay W the sum of $10,080 in monthly payments of $100 over a period of nine years. The payments are periodic.

Example (3). Under the terms of a written instrument, H is to pay W $100 a month over a period of nine years. The monthly payments are not subject to any of the contingencies of death of H or W, remarriage of W, or change in the economic status of H or W under the terms of the written instrument or by reason of local law. The payments are not periodic.

Example (4). A divorce decree in 1954 provides that H is to pay W $20,000 each year for the next five years, beginning with the date of the decree, and then $5,000 each year for the next ten years. Assuming the wife makes her returns on the calendar year basis, each payment received in the years 1954 to 1958, inclusive, is treated as a periodic payment under section 71(a)(1), but only to the extent of 10 percent of the principal sum of $150,000. Thus, for such taxable years, only $15,000 of the $20,000 received is includible

Reg. § 1.71-1(d)(1)

under section 71(a)(1) in the wife's income and is deductible by the husband under section 215. For the years 1959 to 1968, inclusive, the full $5,000 received each year by the wife is includible in her income and is deductible from the husband's income.

(e) *Payments for support of minor children.* Section 71(a) does not apply to that part of any periodic payment which, by the terms of the decree, instrument, or agreement under section 71(a), is specifically designated as a sum payable for the support of minor children of the husband. The statute prescribes the treatment in cases where an amount or portion is so fixed but the amount of any periodic payment is less than the amount of the periodic payment specified to be made. In such cases, to the extent of the amount which would be payable for the support of such children out of the originally specified periodic payment, such periodic payment is considered a payment for such support. For example, if the husband is by terms of the decree, instrument, or agreement required to pay $200 a month to his divorced wife, $100 of which is designated by the decree, instrument, or agreement to be for the support of their minor children, and the husband pays only $150 to his wife, $100 is nevertheless considered to be a payment by the husband for the support of his children. If, however, the periodic payments are received by the wife for the support and maintenance of herself and of minor children of the husband without such specific designation of the portion for the support of such children, then the whole of such amounts is includible in the income of the wife as provided in section 71(a). Except in cases of a designated amount or portion for the support of the husband's minor children, periodic payments described in section 71(a) received by the wife for herself and any other person or persons are includible in whole in the wife's income, whether or not the amount or portion for such other person or persons is designated. [Reg. § 1.71-1.]

☐ [*T.D.* 6270, 11-16-57.]

[Reg. § 1.71-1T]

§ 1.71-1T. **Alimony and separate maintenance payments (temporary).**—(a) *In general.*

Q-1. What is the income tax treatment of alimony or separate maintenance payments?

A-1. Alimony or separate maintenance payments are, under section 71, included in the gross income of the payee spouse and, under section 215, allowed as a deduction from the gross income of the payor spouse.

Q-2. What is an alimony or separate maintenance payment?

A-2. An alimony or separate maintenance payment is any payment received by or on behalf of a spouse (which for this purpose includes a former spouse) of the payor under a divorce or separation instrument that meets all of the following requirements:

(a) The payment is in cash (see A-5).

(b) The payment is not designated as a payment which is excludible from the gross income of the payee and nondeductible by the payor (see A-8).

(c) In the case of spouses legally separated under a decree of divorce or separate maintenance, the spouses are not members of the same household at the time the payment is made (see A-9).

(d) The payor has no liability to continue to make any payment after the death of the payee (or to make any payment as a substitute for such payment) and the divorce or separation instrument states that there is no such liability (see A-10).

(e) The payment is not treated as child support (see A-15).

(f) To the extent that one or more annual payments exceed $10,000 during any of the 6-post-separation years, the payor is obligated to make annual payments in each of the post-separation years (see A-19).

Q-3. In order to be treated as alimony or separate maintenance payments, must the payments be "periodic" as that term was defined prior to enactment of the Tax Reform Act of 1984 or be made in discharge of a legal obligation of the payor to support the payee arising out of a marital or family relationship?

A-3. No. The Tax Reform Act of 1984 replaces the old requirements with the requirements described in A-2 above. Thus, the requirements that alimony or separate maintenance payments be "periodic" and be made in discharge of a legal obligation to support arising out of a marital or family relationship have been eliminated.

Q-4. Are the instruments described in section 71(a) of prior law the same as divorce or separation instruments described in section 71, as amended by the Tax Reform Act of 1984?

A-4. Yes.

(b) *Specific requirements.*

Q-5. May alimony or separate maintenance payments be made in a form other than cash?

A-5. No. Only cash payments (including checks and money orders payable on demand) qualify as alimony or separate maintenance payments. Transfers of services or property (including a debt

Reg. § 1.71-1T(b)

instrument of a third party or an annuity contract), execution of a debt instrument by the payor, or the use of property of the payor do not qualify as alimony or separate maintenance payments.

Q-6. May payments of cash to a third party on behalf of a spouse qualify as alimony or separate maintenance payments if the payments are pursuant to the terms of a divorce or separation instrument?

A-6. Yes. Assuming all other requirements are satisfied, a payment of cash by the payor spouse to a third party under the terms of the divorce or separation instrument will qualify as a payment of cash which is received "on behalf of a spouse". For example, cash payments of rent, mortgage, tax, or tuition liabilities of the payee spouse made under the terms of the divorce or separation instrument will qualify as alimony or separate maintenance payments. Any payments to maintain property owned by the payor spouse and used by the payee spouse (including mortgage payments, real estate taxes and insurance premiums) are not payments on behalf of a spouse even if those payments are made pursuant to the terms of the divorce or separation instrument. Premiums paid by the payor spouse for term or whole life insurance on the payor's life made under the terms of the divorce or separation instrument will qualify as payments on behalf of the payee spouse to the extent that the payee spouse is the owner of the policy.

Q-7. May payments of cash to a third party on behalf of a spouse qualify as alimony or separate maintenance payments if the payments are made to the third party at the written request of the payee spouse?

A-7. Yes. For example, instead of making an alimony or separate maintenance payment directly to the payee, the payor spouse may make a cash payment to a charitable organization if such payment is pursuant to the written request, consent or ratification of the payee spouse. Such request, consent or ratification must state that the parties intend the payment to be treated as an alimony or separate maintenance payment to the payee spouse subject to the rules of section 71, and must be received by the payor spouse prior to the date of filing of the payor's first return of tax for the taxable year in which the payment was made.

Q-8. How may spouses designate that payments otherwise qualifying as alimony or separate maintenance payments shall be excludible from the gross income of the payee and nondeductible by the payor?

A-8. The spouses may designate that payments otherwise qualifying as alimony or separate maintenance payments shall be nondeductible by the payor and excludible from gross income by the payee by so providing in a divorce or separation instrument (as defined in section 71(b)(2)). If the spouses have executed a written separation agreement (as described in section 71(b)(2)(B)), any writing signed by both spouses which designates otherwise qualifying alimony or separate maintenance payments as nondeductible and excludible and which refers to the written separation agreement will be treated as a written separation agreement (and thus a divorce or separation instrument) for purposes of the preceding sentence. If the spouses are subject to temporary support orders (as described in section 71(b)(2)(C)), the designation of otherwise qualifying alimony or separate payments as nondeductible and excludible must be made in the original or a subsequent temporary support order. A copy of the instrument containing the designation of payments as not alimony or separate maintenance payments must be attached to the payee's first filed return of tax (Form 1040) for each year in which the designation applies.

Q-9. What are the consequences if, at the time a payment is made, the payor and payee spouses are members of the same household?

A-9. Generally, a payment made at the time when the payor and payee spouses are members of the same household cannot qualify as an alimony or separate maintenance payment if the spouses are legally separated under a decree of divorce or of separate maintenance. For purposes of the preceding sentence, a dwelling unit formerly shared by both spouses shall not be considered two separate households even if the spouses physically separate themselves within the dwelling unit. The spouses will not be treated as members of the same household if one spouse is preparing to depart from the household of the other spouse, and does depart not more than one month after the date the payment is made. If the spouses are not legally separated under a decree of divorce or separate maintenance, a payment under a written separation agreement or a decree described in section 71(b)(2)(C) may qualify as an alimony or separate maintenance payment notwithstanding that the payor and payee are members of the same household at the time the payment is made.

Q-10. Assuming all other requirements relating to the qualification of certain payments as alimony or separate maintenance payments are met, what are the consequences if the payor spouse is required to continue to make the payments after the death of the payee spouse?

Reg. § 1.71-1T(b)

A-10. None of the payments before (or after) the death of the payee spouse qualify as alimony or separate maintenance payments.

Q-11. What are the consequences if the divorce or separation instrument fails to state that there is no liability for any period after the death of the payee spouse to continue to make any payments which would otherwise qualify as alimony or separate maintenance payments?

A-11. If the instrument fails to include such a statement, none of the payments, whether made before or after the death of the payee spouse, will qualify as alimony or separate maintenance payments.

Example (1). A is to pay B $10,000 in cash each year for a period of 10 years under a divorce or separation instrument which does not state that the payments will terminate upon the death of B. None of the payments will qualify as alimony or separate maintenance payments.

Example (2). A is to pay B $10,000 in cash each year for a period of 10 years under a divorce or separation instrument which states that the payments will terminate upon the death of B. In addition, under the instrument, A is to pay B or B's estate $20,000 in cash each year for a period of 10 years. Because the $20,000 annual payments will not terminate upon the death of B, these payments will not qualify as alimony or separate maintenance payments. However, the separate $10,000 annual payments will qualify as alimony or separate maintenance payments.

Q-12. Will a divorce or separation instrument be treated as stating that there is no liability to make payments after the death of the payee spouse if the liability to make such payments terminates pursuant to applicable local law or oral agreement?

A-12. No. Termination of the liability to make payments must be stated in the terms of the divorce or separation instrument.

Q-13. What are the consequences if the payor spouse is required to make one or more payments (in cash or property) after the death of the payee spouse as a substitute for the continuation of pre-death payments which would otherwise qualify as alimony or separate maintenance payments?

A-13. If the payor spouse is required to make any such substitute payments, none of the otherwise qualifying payments will qualify as alimony or separate maintenance payments. The divorce or separation instrument need not state, however, that there is no liability to make any such substitute payment.

Q-14. Under what circumstances will one or more payments (in cash or property) which are to occur after the death of the payee spouse be treated as a substitute for a continuation of payments which would otherwise qualify as alimony or separate maintenance payments?

A-14. To the extent that one or more payments are to begin to be made, increase in amount, or become accelerated in time as a result of the death of the payee spouse, such payments may be treated as a substitute for the continuation of payments terminating on the death of the payee spouse which would otherwise qualify as alimony or separate maintenance payments. The determination of whether or not such payments are a substitute for the continuation of payments which would otherwise qualify as alimony or separate maintenance payments, and of the amount of the otherwise qualifying alimony or separate maintenance payments for which any such payments are a substitute, will depend on all of the facts and circumstances.

Example (1). Under the terms of a divorce decree, A is obligated to make annual alimony payments to B of $30,000, terminating on the earlier of the expiration of 6 years or the death of B. B maintains custody of the minor children of A and B. The decree provides that at the death of B, if there are minor children of A and B remaining, A will be obligated to make annual payments of $10,000 to a trust, the income and corpus of which are to be used for the benefit of the children until the youngest child attains the age of majority. These facts indicate that A's liability to make annual $10,000 payments in trust for the benefit of his minor children upon the death of B is a substitute for $10,000 of the $30,000 annual payments to B. Accordingly, $10,000 of each of the $30,000 annual payments to B will not qualify as alimony or separate maintenance payments.

Example (2). Under the terms of a divorce decree, A is obligated to make annual alimony payments to B of $30,000, terminating on the earlier of the expiration of 15 years or the death of B. The divorce decree provides that if B dies before the expiration of the 15 year period, A will pay to B's estate the difference between the total amount that A would have paid had B survived, minus the amount actually paid. For example, if B dies at the end of the 10th year in which payments are made, A will pay to B's estate $150,000 ($450,000 − $300,000). These facts indicate that A's liability to make a lump sum payment to B's estate upon the death of B is a substitute for the full amount of each of the annual $30,000 payments to B. Accordingly, none of the annual $30,000 payments to B will qualify as alimony or separate maintenance payments. The result would be the same if the lump sum payable

Reg. § 1.71-1T(b)

at B's death were discounted by an appropriate interest factor to account for the prepayment.

(c) *Child support payments.*

Q-15. What are the consequences of a payment which the terms of the divorce or separation instrument fix as payable for the support of a child of the payor spouse?

A-15. A payment which under the terms of the divorce or separation instrument is fixed (or treated as fixed) as payable for the support of a child of the payor spouse does not qualify as an alimony or separate maintenance payment. Thus, such a payment is not deductible by the payor spouse or includible in the income of the payee spouse.

Q-16. When is a payment fixed (or treated as fixed) as payable for the support of a child of the payor spouse?

A-16. A payment is fixed as payable for the support of a child of the payor spouse if the divorce or separation instrument specifically designates some sum or portion (which sum or portion may fluctuate) as payable for the support of a child of the payor spouse. A payment will be treated as fixed as payable for the support of a child of the payor spouse if the payment is reduced (a) on the happening of a contingency relating to a child of the payor, or (b) at a time which can clearly be associated with such a contingency. A payment may be treated as fixed as payable for the support of a child of the payor spouse even if other separate payments specifically are designated as payable for the support of a child of the payor spouse.

Q-17. When does a contingency relate to a child of the payor?

A-17. For this purpose, a contingency relates to a child of the payor if it depends on any event relating to that child, regardless of whether such event is certain or likely to occur. Events that relate to a child of the payor include the following: the child's attaining a specified age or income level, dying, marrying, leaving school, leaving the spouse's household, or gaining employment.

Q-18. When will a payment be treated as to be reduced at a time which can clearly be associated with the happening of a contingency relating to a child of the payor?

A-18. There are two situations, described below, in which payments which would otherwise qualify as alimony or separate maintenance payments will be presumed to be reduced at a time clearly associated with the happening of a contingency relating to a child of the payor. In all other situations, reductions in payments will not be treated as clearly associated with the happening of a contingency relating to a child of the payor.

The first situation referred to above is where the payments are to be reduced not more than 6 months before or after the date the child is to attain the age of 18, 21, or local age of majority. The second situation is where the payments are to be reduced on two or more occasions which occur not more than one year before or after a different child of the payor spouse attains a certain age between the ages of 18 and 24, inclusive. The certain age referred to in the preceding sentence must be the same for each such child, but need not be a whole number of years.

The presumption in the two situations described above that payments are to be reduced at a time clearly associated with the happening of a contingency relating to a child of the payor may be rebutted (either by the Service or by taxpayers) by showing that the time at which the payments are to be reduced was determined independently of any contingencies relating to the children of the payor. The presumption in the first situation will be rebutted conclusively if the reduction is a complete cessation of alimony or separate maintenance payments during the sixth post-separation year (described in A-21) or upon the expiration of a 72-month period. The presumption may also be rebutted in other circumstances, for example, by showing that alimony payments are to be made for a period customarily provided in the local jurisdiction, such as a period equal to one-half the duration of the marriage.

Example: A and B are divorced on July 1, 1985, when their children, C (born July 15, 1970) and D (born September 23, 1972), are 14 and 12, respectively. Under the divorce decree, A is to make alimony payments to B of $2,000 per month. Such payments are to be reduced to $1,500 per month on January 1, 1991 and to $1,000 per month on January 1, 1995. On January 1, 1991, the date of the first reduction in payments, C will be 20 years 5 months and 17 days old. On January 1, 1995, the date of the second reduction in payments, D will be 22 years 3 months and 9 days old. Each of the reductions in payments is to occur not more than one year before or after a different child of A attains the age of 21 years and 4 months. (Actually, the reductions are to occur not more than one year before or after C and D attain *any* of the ages 21 years 3 months and 9 days through 21 years 5 months and 17 days.) Accordingly, the reductions will be presumed to clearly be associated with the happening of a contingency relating to C and D. Unless this presumption is rebutted, payments under the divorce decree equal to the sum of the reductions ($1,000 per month) will be treated as fixed for the support of the children of A and therefore will not quaify as alimony or separate maintenance payments.

(d) *Excess front-loading rules.*

Q-19. What are the excess front-loading rules?

A-19. The excess front-loading rules are two special rules which may apply to the extent that payments in any calendar year exceed $10,000. The first rule is a minimum term rule, which must be met in order for any annual payment, to the extent in excess of $10,000, to qualify as an alimony or separate maintenance payment (see A-2(f)). This rule requires that alimony or separate maintenance payments be called for, at a minimum, during the 6 "post-separation years". The second rule is a recapture rule which characterizes payments retrospectively by requiring a recalculation and inclusion in income by the payor and deduction by the payee of previously paid alimony or separate maintenance payments to the extent that the amount of such payments during any of the 6 "post-separation years" falls short of the amount of payments during a prior year by more than $10,000.

Q-20. Do the excess front-loading rules apply to payments to the extent that annual payments never exceed $10,000?

A-20. No. For example, A is to make a single $10,000 payment to B. Provided that the other requirements of section 71 are met, the payment will qualify as an alimony or separate maintenance payment. If A were to make a single $15,000 payment to B, $10,000 of the payment would qualify as an alimony or separate maintenance payment and $5,000 of the payment would be disqualified under the minimum term rule because payments were not to be made for the minimum period.

Q-21. Do the excess front-loading rules apply to payments received under a decree described in section 71(b)(2)(C)?

A-21. No. Payments under decrees described in section 71(b)(2)(C) are to be disregarded entirely for purposes of applying the excess front-loading rules.

Q-22. Both the minimum term rule and the recapture rule refer to 6 "post-separation years". What are the 6 "post-separation years"?

A-22. The 6 "post-separation years" are the 6 consecutive calendar years beginning with the first calendar year in which the payor pays to the payee an alimony or separate maintenance payment (except a payment made under a decree described in section 71(b)(2)(C)). Each year within this period is referred to as a "post-separation year". The 6-year period need not commence with the year in which the spouses separate or divorce, or with the year in which payments under the divorce or separation instrument are made, if no payments during such year qualify as alimony or separate maintenance payments. For example, a decree for the divorce of A and B is entered in October, 1985. The decree requires A to make monthly payments to B commencing November 1, 1985, but A and B are members of the same household until February 15, 1986 (and as a result, the payments prior to January 16, 1986, do not qualify as alimony payments). For purposes of applying the excess front-loading rules to payments from A to B, the 6 calendar years 1986 through 1991 are post-separation years. If a spouse has been making payments pursuant to a divorce or separation instrument described in section 71(b)(2)(A) or (B), a modification of the instrument or the substitution of a new instrument (for example, the substitution of a divorce decree for a written separation agreement) will not result in the creation of additional post-separation years. However, if a spouse has been making payments pursuant to a divorce or separation instrument described in section 71(b)(2)(C), the 6-year period does not begin until the first calendar year in which alimony or separate maintenance payments are made under a divorce or separation instrument described in section 71(b)(2)(A) or (B).

Q-23. How does the minimum term rule operate?

A-23. The minimum term rule operates in the following manner. To the extent payments are made in excess of $10,000, a payment will qualify as an alimony or separate maintenance payment only if alimony or separate maintenance payments are to be made in each of the 6 post-separation years. For example, pursuant to a divorce decree, A is to make alimony payments to B of $20,000 in each of the 5 calendar years 1985 through 1989. A is to make no payment in 1990. Under the minimum term rule, only $10,000 will qualify as an alimony payment in each of the calendar years 1985 through 1989. If the divorce decree also required A to make a $1 payment in 1990, the minimum term rule would be satisfied and $20,000 would be treated as an alimony payment in each of the calendar years 1985 through 1989. The recapture rule would, however, apply for 1990. For purposes of determining whether alimony or separate maintenance payments are to be made in any year, the possible termination of such payments upon the happening of a contingency (other than the passage of time) which has not yet occurred is ignored (unless such contingency may cause all or a portion of the payment to be treated as a child support payment).

Reg. § 1.71-1T(d)

Q-24. How does the recapture rule operate?

A-24. The recapture rule operates in the following manner. If the amount of alimony or separate maintenance payments paid in any post-separation year (referred to as the "computation year") falls short of the amount of alimony or separate maintenance payments paid in any prior post-separation year by more than $10,000, the payor must compute an "excess amount" for the computation year. The excess amount for any computation year is the sum of excess amounts determined with respect to each prior post-separation year. The excess amount determined with respect to a prior post-separation year is the excess of (1) the amount of alimony or separate maintenance payments paid by the payor spouse during such prior post-separation year, over (2) the amount of the alimony or separate maintenance payments paid by the payor spouse during the computation year plus $10,000. For purposes of this calculation, the amount of alimony or separate maintenance payments made by the payor spouse during any post-separation year preceding the computation year is reduced by any excess amount previously determined with respect to such year. The rules set forth above may be illustrated by the following example. A makes alimony payments to B of $25,000 in 1985 and $12,000 in 1986. The excess amount with respect to 1985 that is recaptured in 1986 is $3,000 ($25,000 − ($12,000 + $10,000)). For purposes of subsequent computation years, the amount deemed paid in 1985 is $22,000. If A makes alimony payments to B of $1,000 in 1987, the excess amount that is recaptured in 1987 will be $12,000. This is the sum of an $11,000 excess amount with respect to 1985 ($22,000 − ($1,000 + $10,000)) and a $1,000 excess amount with respect to 1986 ($12,000 − ($1,000 + $10,000)). If, prior to the end of 1990, payments decline further, additional recapture will occur. The payor spouse must include the excess amount in gross income for his/her taxable year beginning with or in the computation year. The payee spouse is allowed a deduction for the excess amount in computing adjusted gross income for his/her taxable year beginning with or in the computation year. However, the payee spouse must compute the excess amount by reference to the date when payments were made and not when payments were received.

Q-25. What are the exceptions to the recapture rule?

A-25. Apart from the $10,000 threshold for application of the recapture rule, there are three exceptions to the recapture rule. The first exception is for payments received under temporary support orders described in section 71(b)(2)(C)

(see A-21). The second exception is for any payment made pursuant to a continuing liability over the period of the post-separation years to pay a fixed portion of the payor's income from a business or property or from compensation for employment or self-employment. The third exception is where the alimony or separate maintenance payments in any post-separation year cease by reason of the death of the payor or payee or the remarriage (as defined under applicable local law) of the payee before the close of the computation year. For example, pursuant to a divorce decree, A is to make cash payments to B of $30,000 in each of the calendar years 1985 through 1990. A makes cash payments of $30,000 in 1985 and $15,000 in 1986, in which year B remarries and A's alimony payments cease. The recapture rule does not apply for 1986 or any subsequent year. If alimony or separate maintenance payments made by A decline or cease during a post-separation year for any other reason (including a failure by the payor to make timely payments, a modification of the divorce or separation instrument, a reduction in the support needs of the payee, or a reduction in the ability of the payor to provide support) excess amounts with respect to prior post-separation years will be subject to recapture.

(e) *Effective dates.*

Q-26. When does section 71, as amended by the Tax Reform Act of 1984, become effective?

A-26. Generally, section 71, as amended, is effective with respect to divorce or separation instruments (as defined in section 71(b)(2)) executed after December 31, 1984. If a decree of divorce or separate maintenance executed after December 31, 1984, incorporates or adopts without change the terms of the alimony or separate maintenance payments under a divorce or separation instrument executed before January 1, 1985, such decree will be treated as executed before January 1, 1985. A change in the amount of alimony or separate maintenance payments or the time period over which such payments are to continue, or the addition or deletion of any contingencies or conditions relating to such payments is a change in the terms of the alimony or separate maintenance payments. For example, in November 1984, A and B executed a written separation agreement. In February 1985, a decree of divorce is entered in substitution for the written separation agreement. The decree of divorce does not change the terms of the alimony A pays to B. The decree of divorce will be treated as executed before January 1, 1985 and hence alimony payments under the decree will be subject to the rules of section 71 prior to amendment by the Tax Reform Act of 1984. If the amount or time period

Reg. § 1.71-1T(e)

of the alimony or separate maintenance payments are not specified in the pre-1985 separation agreement or if the decree of divorce changes the amount or term of such payments, the decree of divorce will not be treated as executed before January 1, 1985, and alimony payments under the decree will be subject to the rules of section 71, as amended by the Tax Reform Act of 1984.

Section 71, as amended, also applies to any divorce or separation instrument executed (or treated as executed) before January 1, 1985 that has been modified on or after January 1, 1985, if such modification expressly provides that section 71, as amended by the Tax Reform Act of 1984, shall apply to the instrument as modified. In this case, section 71, as amended, is effective with respect to payments made after the date the instrument is modified [Temporary Reg. § 1.71-1T.]

☐ [*T.D.* 7973, 8-30 84.]

[Reg. § 1.71-2]

§ 1.71-2. Effective date; taxable years ending after March 31, 1954, subject to the Internal Revenue Code of 1939.—Pursuant to section 7851(a)(1)(C), the regulations prescribed in § 1.71-1, to the extent that they relate to payments under a written separation agreement executed after August 16, 1954, and to the extent that they relate to payments under a decree for support received after August 16, 1954, under a decree entered after March 1, 1954, shall also apply to taxable years beginning before January 1, 1954, and ending after August 16, 1954, although such years are subject to the Internal Revenue Code of 1939. [Reg. § 1.71-2.]

☐ [*T.D.* 6270, 11-16-57.]

[Reg. § 1.72-1]

§ 1.72-1. Introduction.—(a) *General principle.* Section 72 prescribes rules relating to the inclusion in gross income of amounts received under a life insurance, endowment, or annuity contract unless such amounts are specifically excluded from gross income under other provisions of chapter 1 of the Code. In general, these rules provide that amounts subject to the provisions of section 72 are includible in the gross income of the recipient except to the extent that they are considered to represent a reduction or return of premiums or other consideration paid.

(b) *Amounts to be considered as a return of premiums.* For the purpose of determining the extent to which amounts received represent a reduction or return of premiums or other consideration paid, the provisions of section 72 distinguish between "amounts received as an annuity" and "amounts not received as an annuity". In general,

"amounts received as an annuity" are amounts which are payable at regular intervals over a period of more than one full year from the date on which they are deemed to begin, provided the total of the amounts so payable or the period for which they are to be paid can be determined as of that date. See paragraph (b)(2) and (3) of § 1.72.2. Any other amounts to which the provisions of section 72 apply are considered to be "amounts not received as an annuity." See § 1.72-11.

(c) *"Amounts received as an annuity."* (1) In the case of "amounts received as an annuity" (other than certain employees' annuities described in section 72(d) and in § 1.72-13), a proportionate part of each amount so received is considered to represent a return of premiums or other consideration paid. The proportionate part of each annuity payment which is thus excludable from gross income is determined by the ratio which the investment in the contract as of the date on which the annuity is deemed to begin bears to the expected return under the contract as of that date. See § 1.72-4.

(2) In the case of employees' annuities of the type described in section 72(d), no amount received as an annuity in a taxable year to which the Internal Revenue Code of 1954 applies is includible in the gross income of a recipient until the aggregate of all amounts received thereunder and excluded from gross income under the applicable income tax law exceeds the consideration contributed (or deemed contributed) by the employee under § 1.72-8. Thereafter, all amounts so received are includible in the gross income of the recipient. See § 1.72-13.

(d) *"Amounts not received as an annuity".* In the case of "amounts not received as an annuity", if such amounts are received after an annuity has begun and during its continuance, amounts so received are generally includible in the gross income of the recipient. Amounts not received as an annuity which are received at any other time are generally includible in the gross income of the recipient only to the extent that such amounts, when added to all amounts previously received under the contract which were excludable from the gross income of the recipient under the income tax law applicable at the time of receipt, exceed the premiums or other consideration paid (see § 1.72-11). However, if the aggregate of premiums or other consideration paid for the contract includes amounts for which a deduction was allowed under section 404 as contributions on behalf of an owner-employee, the amounts received under the circumstances of the preceding sentence shall be includible in gross income until the amount so included equals the amount for which the deduction was so allowed. See paragraph (b) of § 1.72-17.

(e) *Classification of recipients.* For the purpose of the regulations under section 72, a recipient shall be considered an "annuitant" if he receives amounts under an annuity contract during the period that the annuity payments are to continue, whether for a term certain or during the continuing life or lives of the person or persons whose lives measure the duration of such annuity. However, a recipient shall be considered a "beneficiary" rather than an "annuitant" if the amounts he receives under a contract are received after the term of the annuity for a life or lives has expired and such amounts are paid by reason of the fact that the contract guarantees that payments of some minimum amount or for some minimum period shall be made. For special rules with respect to beneficiaries, see paragraphs (a)(1)(ii) and (c) of § 1.72-11. [Reg. § 1.72-1.]

☐ [*T.D. 6211, 11-14-56. Amended by T.D. 6676, 9-16-63.*]

[Reg. § 1.72-2]

§ 1.72-2. **Applicability of section.**—(a) *Contracts.* (1) The contracts under which amounts paid will be subject to the provisions of section 72 include contracts which are considered to be life insurance, endowment, and annuity contracts in accordance with the customary practice of life insurance companies. For the purposes of section 72, however, it is immaterial whether such contracts are entered into with an insurance company. The term "endowment contract" also includes the "face-amount certificates" described in section 72(l).

(2) If two or more annuity obligations or elements to which section 72 applies are acquired for a single consideration, such as an obligation to pay an annuity to A for his life accompanied by an obligation to pay an annuity to B for his life, there being a single consideration paid for both obligations (whether paid by one or more persons in equal or different amounts, and whether paid in a single sum or otherwise), such annuity elements shall be considered to comprise a single contract for the purpose of the application of section 72 and the regulations thereunder. For rules relating to the allocation of investment in the contract in the case of annuity elements payable to two or more persons, see § 1.72-6(b).

(3)(i) Sections 402 and 403 provide that certain distributions by employees' trusts and certain payments under employee plans are taxable under section 72. For taxable years beginning before January 1, 1964, section 72(e)(3), as in effect before such date, does not apply to such distributions or payments. For purposes of applying section 72 to such distributions and payments (other than those described in subdivision (iii) of this subparagraph), each separate program of the employer consisting of interrelated contributions and benefits shall be considered a single contract. Therefore, all distributions or payments (other than those described in subdivision (iii) of this subparagraph) which are attributable to a separate program of interrelated contributions and benefits are considered as received under a single contract. A separate program of interrelated contributions and benefits may be financed by the purchase from an insurance company of one or more group contracts or one or more individual contracts, or may be financed partly by the purchase of contracts from an insurance company and partly through an investment fund, or may be financed completely through an investment fund. A program may be considered separate for purposes of section 72 although it is only a part of a plan which qualifies under section 401. There may be several trusts under one separate program, or several separate programs may make use of a single trust. See, however, subdivision (iii) of this subparagraph for rules relating to what constitutes a "contract" for purposes of applying section 72 to distributions commencing before October 20, 1960.

(ii) The following types of benefits, and the contributions used to provide them, are examples of separate programs of interrelated contributions and benefits:

(a) Definitely determinable retirement benefits.

(b) Definitely determinable benefits payable prior to retirement in case of disability.

(c) Life insurance.

(d) Accident and health insurance.

However, retirement benefits and life insurance will be considered part of a single separate program of interrelated contributions and benefits to the extent they are provided under retirement income, endowment, or other contracts providing life insurance protection. See examples (6), (7), and (8) contained in subdivision (iv) of this subparagraph for illustrations of the principles of this subdivision. See, also, § 1.72-15 for rules relating to the taxation of amounts received under an employee plan which provides both retirement benefits and accident and health benefits.

(iii) If any amount which is taxable under section 72 by reason of section 402 or 403 is actually distributed or made available to any person under an employees' trust or plan (other than the Civil Service Retirement Act (5 U.S.C. ch.14)) before October 20, 1960, section 72 shall, notwithstanding any other provisions in this subparagraph, be applied to all the distributions with respect to such person (or his beneficiaries) under such trust or plan (whether received before or after October 20, 1960) as though such distributions were provided under a single contract. For purposes of applying section 72 to distributions to which this subdivision applies, therefore, the term "contract" shall be considered to include the entire interest of an employee in each trust or plan described in sections 402 and 403 to the extent that distributions thereunder are subject to the provisions of section 72. Section 72 shall be applied to distributions received under the Civil Service Retirement Act in the manner prescribed in subdivision (i) of this subparagraph (see example (4) in subdivision (iv) of this subparagraph).

(iv) The application of this subparagraph may be illustrated by the following examples:

Example (1). On January 1, 1961, X Corporation established a noncontributory profit-sharing plan for its employees providing that the amount standing to the account of each participant will be paid to him at the time of his retirement and also established a contributory pension plan for its employees providing for the payment to each participant of a lifetime pension after retirement. The profit-sharing plan is designed to enable the employees to participate in the profits of X Corporation; the amount of the contributions to it are determined by reference to the profits of X Corporation; and the amount of any distribution is determined by reference to the amount of contributions made on behalf of any participant and the earnings thereon. On the other hand, the pension plan is designed to provide a lifetime pension for a retired employee; the amount of the pension is to be determined by a formula set forth in the plan; and the amount of contributions to the plan is the amount necessary to provide such pensions. In view of the fact that each of these plans constitutes a separate program of interrelated contributions and benefits, the distributions from each shall be treated as received under a separate contract. If these plans had been established before October 20, 1960, then, in the case of an employee who receives a distribution under the plans before October 20, 1960, the determination as to whether that distribution and all subsequent distributions to such employee are received under a single contract or under more than one contract shall be made by applying the rules in subdivision (iii) of this subparagraph. On the other hand, in the case of an employee who does not receive any distribution under these plans before October 20, 1960, the determination as to whether distributions to him are received under a single contract

or under more than one contract shall be made in accordance with the rules illustrated by this example.

Example (2). On January 1, 1961, Z Corporation established a profit-sharing plan for its employees providing that any employee may make contributions, not in excess of 6 percent of his compensation, to a trust and that the employer would make matching contributions out of profits. Under the plan, a participant may receive a periodic distribution of the amount standing in his account during any period that he is absent from work due to a personal injury or sickness. On separation from service, the participant is entitled to receive a distribution of the balance standing in his account in accordance with one of several options. One option provides for the immediate distribution of one-half of the account and for the periodic distribution of the remaining one-half of the account. In addition, any participant may, after the completion of five years of participation, withdraw any part of his account, but in the case of such a withdrawal, the participant forfeits his rights to participate in the plan for a period of two years. Thus, a participant may receive distributions before separation from service; he may receive a distribution of a lump sum upon separation from service; he may also receive periodic distributions upon separation from service. However, since it is the total amount received under all the options that is interrelated with the contributions to the plan and not the amount received under any one option, this profit-sharing plan consists of only one separate program of interrelated contributions and benefits and all distributions under the plan (regardless of the option under which received) are treated as received under one contract. However, if, instead of providing that the amount standing in an employee's account would be paid to him during any period that he is absent from work due to a personal injury or sickness, the plan provided that a portion of the amount in the employee's account would be used to purchase incidental accident and health insurance, this plan would consist of two separate programs of interrelated contributions and benefits. The accident and health insurance, and the contributions used to purchase it, would be considered as one separate program of interrelated contributions and benefits and, therefore, a separate contract; whereas, the remaining contributions and benefits would be considered another separate program of interrelated contributions and benefits and, consequently, another separate contract.

Example (3). On January 1, 1961, N Corporation established a profit-sharing plan for its employees providing that the employees may

Reg. § 1.72-2(a)(3)

make contributions, not in excess of 6 percent of their compensation, to a trust and that N Corporation would make matching contributions out of its profits. Under the plan, the employee may elect each year to have his and the employer's contributions for such year placed in either a savings arrangement or a retirement arrangement. Such an election is irrevocable. Under the savings arrangement, contributions to such arrangement for any one year and the earnings thereon will be distributed five years later. The retirement arrangement provides that all contributions thereto and the earnings thereon will be distributed when the employee is separated from the service of N Corporation. Since the distributions under the retirement arrangement are attributable solely to the contributions made to such arrangement and are not affected in any manner by contributions or distributions under the savings arrangement or any other plan, such distributions are treated as received under a separate program of interrelated contributions and benefits. Similarly, since distributions during any year under the savings arrangement are attributable only to contributions to such arrangement made during the fifth preceding year and not affected in any manner by any other contributions to or distributions from such arrangement or any other plan, the savings arrangement constitutes a series of separate programs of interrelated contributions and benefits. The contributions to the savings arrangement for any year and the distribution in a subsequent year based thereon constitute a separate contract for purposes of section 72.

Example (4). The Civil Service Retirement Act (5 U.S.C. ch. 14) which provides retirement benefits for participating employees, consists of a compulsory program and a voluntary program. Under the compulsory program, all participating employees are required to make certain contributions and, upon retirement, are provided retirement benefits computed on the basis of compensation and length of service. Under the voluntary program, such participating employees are permitted to make contributions in addition to those required under the compulsory program and, upon retirement, are provided additional retirement benefits computed on the basis of their voluntary contributions. Distributions received under the Act constitute distributions from two separate contracts for purposes of section 72. Distributions received under the compulsory program are considered as received under a separate program of interrelated contributions and benefits since they are computed solely under the compulsory program and are not affected by any contributions or distributions under the voluntary program or under any other plan. For similar

reasons, distributions which are attributable to the voluntary contributions are considered as received under a separate program of interrelated contributions and benefits.

Example (5). On January 1, 1961, M Corporation established a contributory pension plan for its employees and created a trust to which it makes contributions to fund such plan. The plan provides that each participant will receive after age 65 a pension of 1½ percent of his compensation for each year of service performed subsequent to the establishment of such plan. In order to fund part of the benefits under the plan, the trustee purchased a group annuity contract. The remaining part of the benefits are to be paid out of a separate investment fund. This pension plan constitutes a single program of interrelated contributions and benefits and, therefore, all distributions received by an employee under the plan are considered as received under a single contract for purposes of section 72.

Example (6). On January 1, 1961, Y Corporation established a noncontributory pension plan (including incidental death benefits) for its employees and created a trust to which it makes contributions to fund such plan. The plan provides that each participant will receive after age 65 a pension of 1½ percent of his compensation for each year of service performed subsequent to the establishment of such plan. In addition, such plan provides for the payment of a death benefit if the employee dies before age 65. The trustee funded the death benefits through the purchase of a group term insurance policy and funded the retirement benefits through the purchase of a group annuity contract. Because of a subsequent change in funding from the deferred annuity method to the deposit administration method, the trustee purchased a second group annuity contract to provide the retirement benefits under the plan accruing after the effective date of the change in method of funding. Thus, retirement benefits distributed to an employee whose service with Y Corporation commenced before the effective date of the change in method of funding will be attributable to both group annuity contracts. This pension plan includes two separate programs of interrelated contributions and benefits. The death benefits, and the contributions required to provide them, are considered as one separate program of interrelated contributions and benefits; whereas, the retirement benefits, and the contributions required to provide them, are considered as another separate program of interrelated contributions and benefits. Therefore, any retirement benefits received by an employee, whether attributable to one or both of the group annuity contracts, shall be considered as received under a single contract for purposes of section 72. In determining the tax treatment of any such retirement benefits under section 72, no amount of the premiums used to purchase the group term insurance policy shall be taken into account, since such premiums, and the death benefits which they purchased, constitute a separate program of interrelated contributions and benefits.

Example (7). Assume the same facts as in example (6) except that, in lieu of funding the benefits in the manner described in that example, the trustee purchased individual retirement income contracts from an insurance company. Additional individual retirement income contracts are purchased in order to fund any increase in benefits resulting from increases in salary. Therefore, distributions to a particular employee may be attributable to a single retirement income contract or to more than one such contract. All distributions received by an employee under the pension plan, whether attributable to one or more retirement income contracts and whether made directly from the insurance company to the employee or made through the trustee, are considered as received under a single contract for purposes of section 72. For rules relating to the tax treatment of contributions and distributions under retirement income, endowment, or other life insurance contracts purchased by a trust described in section 401(a) and exempt under section 501(a), see paragraph (a)(2), (3), and (4) of § 1.402(a)-1.

Example (8). Assume the same facts as in example (6) except that, in lieu of funding the benefits in the manner described in that example, the trustee funded the death benefits and part of the retirement benefits by purchasing individual retirement income contracts from an insurance company. The remaining part of the retirement benefits (such as any increase in benefits resulting from increases in salary) are to be paid out of a separate investment fund. This pension plan includes, with respect to each participant, two separate contracts for purposes of section 72. The retirement income contract purchased by the trust for each participant is a separate program of interrelated contributions and benefits and all distributions attributable to such contract (whether made directly from the insurance company to the employee or made through the trustee) are considered as received under a single contract. For rules relating to the tax treatment of contributions and distributions under retirement income, endowment, or other life insurance contracts purchased by a trust described in section 401(a) and exempt under section 501(a), see paragraph (a)(2), (3), and (4) of § 1.402(a)-1. The remaining distributions under the plan are considered as received

under another separate program of interrelated contributions and benefits.

(b) Amounts. (1)(i) In general, the amounts to which section 72 applies are any amounts received under the contracts described in paragraph (a)(1). However, if such amounts are specifically excluded from gross income under other provisions of chapter 1 of the Internal Revenue Code, section 72 shall not apply for the purpose of including such amounts in gross income. For example, section 72 does not apply to amounts received under a life insurance contract if such amounts are paid by reason of the death of the insured and are excludable from gross income under section 101(a) of the Code. See also sections 101(d), relating to proceeds of life insurance paid at a date later than death, and 104(a)(4), relating to compensation for injuries or sickness.

(ii) Section 72 does not exclude from gross income any amounts received under an agreement to hold an amount and pay interest thereon. See § 1.72-14(a). However, section 72 does apply to amounts received by a surviving annuitant under a joint and survivor annuity contract since such amounts are not considered to be paid by reason of the death of an insured. For a special deduction for the estate tax attributable to the inclusion of the value of the interest of a surviving annuitant under a joint and survivor annuity contract in the estate of the deceased primary annuitant, see section 691(d) and the regulations thereunder.

(2) Amounts subject to section 72 in accordance with subparagraph (1) are considered "amounts received as an annuity" only in the event that all of the following tests are met:

(i) They must be received on or after the "annuity starting date" as that term is defined in § 1.72-4(b);

(ii) They must be payable in periodic installments at regular intervals (whether annually, semiannually, quarterly, monthly, weekly, or otherwise) over a period of more than one full year from the annuity starting date; and

(iii) Except as indicated in subparagraph (3), the total of the amounts payable must be determinable at the annuity starting date either directly from the terms of the contract or indirectly by the use of either mortality tables or compound interest computations, or both, in conjunction with such terms and in accordance with sound actuarial theory.

For the purpose of determining whether amounts subject to section 72(d) and § 1.72-13 are "amounts received as an annuity," however, the provisions of subdivision (i) shall be disregarded. In addition, the term "amounts received as an annuity" does not include amounts received to

Reg. § 1.72-2(b)(2)

which the provisions of § 1.72-11(b) or (c) apply, relating to dividends and certain amounts received by a beneficiary in the nature of a refund. If an amount is to be paid periodically until a fund plus interest at a fixed rate is exhausted, but further payments may be made thereafter because of earnings at a higher interest rate, the requirements of subdivision (iii) are met with respect to the payments determinable at the outset by means of computations involving the fixed interest rate, but any payments received after the expiration of the period determinable by such computations shall be taxable as dividends received after the annuity starting date in accordance with § 1.72-11(b)(2).

(3)(i) Notwithstanding the requirement of subdivision (iii) of subparagraph (2), if amounts are to be received for a definite or determinable time (whether for a period certain or for a life or lives) under a contract which provides—

(a) That the amount of the periodic payments may vary in accordance with investment experience (as in certain profit-sharing plans), cost of living indices, or similar fluctuating criteria, or

(b) For specified payments the value of which may vary for income tax purposes, such as in the case of any annuity payable in foreign currency,

each such payment received shall be considered as an amount received as an annuity only to the extent that it does not exceed the amount computed by dividing the investment in the contract, as adjusted for any refund feature, by the number of periodic payments anticipated during the time that the periodic payments are to be made. If payments are to be made more frequently than annually, the amount so computed shall be multiplied by the number of periodic payments to be made during the taxable year for the purpose of determining the total amount which may be considered received as an annuity during such year. To this extent, the payments received shall be considered to represent a return of premiums or other consideration paid and shall be excludable from gross income in the taxable year in which received. See § 1.72-4(d)(2), and (3). To the extent that the payments received under the contract during the taxable year exceed the total amount thus considered to be received as an annuity during such year, they shall be considered to be amounts not received as an annuity and shall be included in the gross income of the recipient. See section 72(e) and § 1.72-11(b)(2).

(ii) For purposes of subdivision (i), the number of periodic payments anticipated during the time payments are to be made shall be determined by multiplying the number of payments to be made each year (a) by the number of years payments are to be made, or (b) if payments are to be made for a life or lives, by the multiple found by the use of the appropriate tables contained in § 1.72-9, as adjusted in accordance with the table in § 1.72-5(a)(2).

(iii) For an example of the computation to be made in accordance with this subparagraph and a special election which may be made in a taxable year subsequent to a taxable year in which the total payments received under a contract described in this subparagraph are less than the total of the amounts excludable from gross income in such year under subdivision (i), see § 1.72-4(d)(3). [Reg. § 1.72-2.]

☐ [*T.D. 6211*, 11-14-56. *Amended by T.D. 6497*, 10-19-60, *and by T.D. 6885*, 6-1-66.]

[Reg. § 1.72-3]

§ 1.72-3. Excludable amounts not income.— In general, amounts received under contracts described in paragraph (a)(1) of § 1.72-2 are not to be included in the income of the recipient to the extent that such amounts are excludable from gross income as the result of the application of section 72 and the regulations thereunder. [Reg. § 1.72-3.]

☐ [*T.D.* 6211, 11-14-56.]

[Reg. § 1.72-4]

§ 1.72-4. Exclusion ratio.—(a) *General rule.* (1)(i) To determine the proportionate part of the total amount received each year as an annuity which is excludable from the gross income of a recipient in the taxable year of receipt (other than amounts received under (a) certain employee annuities described in section 72(d) and § 1.72-13, or (b) certain annuities described in section 72(o) and § 1.122-1), an exclusion ratio is to be determined for each contract. In general, this ratio is determined by dividing the investment in the contract as found under § 1.72-6 by the expected return under such contract as found under § 1.72-5. Where a single consideration is given for a particular contract which provides for two or more annuity elements, an exclusion ratio shall be determined for the contract as a whole by dividing the investment in such contract by the aggregate of the expected returns under all the annuity elements provided thereunder. However, where the provisions of paragraph (b)(3) of § 1.72-2 apply to payments received under such a contract, see paragraph (b)(3) of § 1.72-6. In the case of a contract to which § 1.72-6(d) (relating to contracts in which amounts were invested both before July 1, 1986, and after June 30, 1986) applies, the exclusion ratio for purposes of this paragraph (a) is determined in accordance with § 1.72-6(d) and, in particular, § 1.72-6(d)(5)(i).

(ii) The exclusion ratio for the particular contract is then applied to the total amount received as an annuity during the taxable year by each recipient. See, however, paragraph (e)(3) of § 1.72-5. Any excess of the total amount received as an annuity during the taxable year over the amount determined by the application of the exclusion ratio to such total amount shall be included in the gross income of the recipient for the taxable year of receipt.

(2) The principles of subparagraph (1) may be illustrated by the following example:

Example. Taxpayer A purchased an annuity contract providing for payments of $100 per month for a consideration of $12,650. Assuming that the expected return under this contract is $16,000 the exclusion ratio to be used by A is $12,650 ÷ [$]16,000; or 79.1 percent (79.06 rounded to the nearest tenth). If 12 such monthly payments are received by A during his taxable year, the total amount he may exclude from his gross income in such year is $949.20 ($1,200 × 79.1 percent). The balance of $250.80 ($1,200 less $949.20) is the amount to be included in gross income. If A instead received only five such payments during the year, he should exclude $395.50 ([$]500 × 79.1 percent) of the total amounts received.

For examples of the computation of the exclusion ratio in cases where two annuity elements are acquired for a single consideration, see paragraph (b)(1) of § 1.72-6.

(3) The exclusion ratio shall be applied only to amounts received as an annuity within the meaning of that term under paragraph (b)(2) and (3) of § 1.72-2. Where the periodic payments increase in amount after the annuity starting date in a manner not provided by the terms of the contract at such date, the portion of such payments representing the increase is not an amount received as an annuity. For the treatment of amounts not received as an annuity, see section 72(e) and § 1.72-11. For special rules where paragraph (b)(3) of § 1.72-2 applies to amounts received, see paragraph (d)(3) of this section.

(4) After an exclusion ratio has been determined for a particular contract, it shall be applied to any amounts received as an annuity thereunder unless or until one of the following occurs:

(i) The contract is assigned or transferred for a valuable consideration (see section 72(g) and paragraph (a) of § 1.72-10);

(ii) The contract matures or is surrendered, redeemed, or discharged in accordance with the provisions of paragraph (c) or (d) of § 1.72-11;

(iii) The contract is exchanged (or is considered to have been exchanged) in a manner described in paragraph (e) of § 1.72-11.

(b) *Annuity starting date.* (1) Except as provided in subparagraph (2) of this paragraph, the annuity starting date is the first day of the first period for which an amount is received as an annuity, except that if such date was before January 1, 1954, then the annuity starting date is January 1, 1954. The first day of the first period for which an amount is received as an annuity shall be whichever of the following is the later:

(i) The date upon which the obligations under the contract became fixed, or

(ii) The first day of the period (year, half-year, quarter, month, or otherwise, depending on whether payments are to be made annually, semiannually, quarterly, monthly, or otherwise) which ends on the date of the first annuity payment.

(2) Notwithstanding the provisions of paragraph (b)(1) of this section, the annuity starting date shall be determined in accordance with whichever of the following provisions is appropriate:

(i) In the case of a joint and survivor annuity contract described in section 72(i) and paragraph (b)(3) of § 1.72-5, the annuity starting date is January 1, 1954, or the first day of the first period for which an amount is received as an annuity by the surviving annuitant, whichever is the later;

(ii) In the case of the transfer of an annuity contract for a valuable consideration, as described in section 72(g) and paragraph (a) of § 1.72-10, the annuity starting date shall be January 1, 1954, or the first day of the first period for which the transferee received an amount as an annuity, whichever is the later;

(iii) If the provisions of paragraph (e) of § 1.72-11 apply to an exchange of one contract for another, or to a transaction deemed to be such an exchange, the annuity starting date of the contract received (or deemed received) in exchange shall be January 1, 1954, or the first day of the first period for which an amount is received as an annuity under such contract, whichever is the later; and

(iv) In the case of an employee who has retired from work because of personal injuries or sickness, and who is receiving amounts under a plan that is a wage continuation plan under section 105(d) and § 1.105-4, the annuity starting date shall be the date the employee reaches mandatory retirement age, as defined in § 1.105-4(a)(3)(i)(B). (See, also §§ 1.72-15 and 1.105-6 for transitional and other special rules.)

(c) *Fiscal year taxpayers.* Fiscal year taxpayers receiving amounts as annuities in a taxable year to which the Internal Revenue Code of 1954 applies shall determine the annuity starting date in accordance with section 72(c)(4) and this section. The annuity starting date for fiscal year taxpayers receiving amounts as an annuity in a taxable year to which the Internal Revenue Code of 1939 applies shall be January 1, 1954, except where the first day of the first period for which an amount is received by such a taxpayer as an annuity is subsequent thereto and before the end of a fiscal year to which the Internal Revenue Code of 1939 applied. In such case, the latter date shall be the annuity starting date. In all cases where a fiscal year taxpayer received an amount as an annuity in a taxable year to which the Internal Revenue Code of 1939 applied and subsequent to the annuity starting date determined in accordance with the provisions of this paragraph, such amount shall be disregarded for the purposes of section 72 and the regulations thereunder.

(d) *Exceptions to the general rule.* (1) Where the provisions of section 72 would otherwise require an exclusion ratio to be determined, but the investment in the contract (determined under § 1.72-6) is an amount of zero or less, no exclusion ratio shall be determined and all amounts received under such a contract shall be includible in the gross income of the recipient for the purposes of section 72.

(2) Where the investment in the contract is equal to or greater than the total expected return under such contract found under § 1.72-5, the exclusion ratio shall be considered to be 100 percent and all amounts received as an annuity under such contract shall be excludable from the recipient's gross income. See, for example, paragraph (f)(1) of § 1.72-5. In the case of a contract to which § 1.72-6(d) (relating to contracts in which amounts were invested both before July 1, 1986, and after June 30, 1986) applies, this paragraph (d)(2) is applied in the manner prescribed in § 1.72-6(d) and, in particular, § 1.72-6(d)(5)(ii).

(3)(i) If a contract provides for payments to be made to a taxpayer in the manner described in paragraph (b)(3) of § 1.72-2, the investment in the contract shall be considered to be equal to the expected return under such contract and the resulting exclusion ratio (100%) shall be applied to all amounts received as an annuity under such contract. For any taxable year, payments received under such a contract shall be considered to be amounts received as an annuity only to the

extent that they do not exceed the portion of the investment in the contract which is properly allocable to that year and hence excludable from gross income as a return of premiums or other consideration paid for the contract. The portion of the investment in the contract which is properly allocable to any taxable year shall be determined by dividing the investment in the contract (adjusted for any refund feature in the manner described in paragraph (d) of § 1.72-7) by the applicable multiple (whether for a term certain, life, or lives) which would otherwise be used in determining the expected return for such a contract under § 1.72-5. The multiple shall be adjusted in accordance with the provisions of the table in paragraph (a)(2) of § 1.72-5, if any adjustment is necessary, before making the above computation. If payments are to be made more frequently than annually and the number of payments to be made in the taxable year in which the annuity begins are less than the number of payments to be made each year thereafter, the amounts considered received as an annuity (as otherwise determined under this subdivision) shall not exceed, for such taxable year (including a short taxable year), an amount which bears the same ratio to the portion of the investment in the contract considered allocable to each taxable year as the number of payments to be made in the first year bears to the number of payments to be made in each succeeding year. Thus, if payments are to be made monthly, only seven payments will be made in the first taxable year, and the portion of the investment in the contract allocable to a full year of payments is $600, the amounts considered received as an annuity in the first taxable year cannot exceed $350 ($600 × 7/12). See subdivision (iii) of this subparagraph for an example illustrating the determination of the portion of the investment in the contract allocable to one taxable year of the taxpayer.

(ii) if subdivision (i) of this subparagraph applies to amounts received by a taxpayer and the total amount of payments he receives in a taxable year is less than the total amount excludable for such year under subdivision (i) of this subparagraph, the taxpayer may elect, in a succeeding taxable year in which he receives another payment, to redetermine the amounts to be received as an annuity during the current and succeeding taxable years. This shall be computed in accordance with the provisions of subdivision (i) of this subparagraph except that:

(a) The difference between the portion of the investment in the contract allocable to a taxable year, as found in accordance with subdivision (i) of this subparagraph, and the total payments actually received in the taxable year prior

Reg. § 1.72-4(c)

to the election shall be divided by the applicable life expectancy of the annuitant (or annuitants), found in accordance with the appropriate table in § 1.72-9 (and adjusted in accordance with paragraph (a)(2) of § 1.72-5), or by the remaining term of a term certain annuity, computed as of the first day of the first period for which an amount is received as an annuity in the taxable year of the election; and

(b) The amount determined under (a) of this subdivision shall be added to the portion of the investment in the contract allocable to each taxable year (as otherwise found). To the extent that the total periodic payments received under the contract in the taxable year of the election or any succeeding taxable year does not equal this total sum, such payments shall be excludable from the gross income of the recipient. To the extent such payments exceed the sum so found, they shall be fully includible in the recipient's gross income. See subdivision (iii) of this subparagraph for an example illustrating the redetermination of amounts to be received as an annuity and subdivision (iv) of this subparagraph for the method of making the election provided by this subdivision.

(iii) The application of the principles of paragraph (d)(3)(i) and (ii) of this section may be illustrated by the following example:

Example. Taxpayer A, a 64 year old male, files his return on a calendar year basis and has a life expectancy of 15.6 years on June 30, 1954, the annuity starting date of a contract to which § 1.72-2(b)(3) applies and which he purchased for $20,000. The contract provides for variable annual payments for his life. He receives a payment of $1,000 on June 30, 1955, but receives no other payment until June 30, 1957. He excludes the $1,000 payment from his gross income for the year 1955 since this amount is less than $1,324.50, the amount determined by dividing his investment in the contract ($20,000) by his life expectancy adjusted for annual payments, 15.1 (15.6-0.5), as of the original annuity starting date. Taxpayer A may elect, in his return for the taxable year 1957, to redetermine amounts to be received as an annuity under his contract as of June 30, 1956. For the purpose of determining the extent to which amounts received in 1957 or thereafter shall be considered amounts received as an annuity (to which a 100 percent exclusion ratio shall apply) he shall add $118.63 to the $1,324.50 originally determined to be receivable as an annuity under the contract, making a total of $1,443.13. This is determined by dividing the difference between what was excludable in 1955 and 1956, $2,649 (2 × $1,324.50) and what he actually received in those years ($1,000) by his

life expectancy adjusted for annual payments, 13.9 (14.4 − 0.5), as of his age at his nearest birthday (66) on the first day of the first period for which he received an amount as an annuity in the taxable year of election (June 30, 1956). The result, $1,443.13, is excludable in that year and each year thereafter as an amount received as an annuity to which the 100% exclusion ratio applies. It will be noted that in this example the taxpayer received amounts less than the excludable amounts in two successive years and deferred making his election until the third year, and thus was able to accumulate the portion of the investment in the contract allocable to each taxable year to the extent he failed to receive such portion in both years. Assuming that he received $1,500 in the taxable year of his election, he would include $56.87 in his gross income and exclude $1,443.13 therefrom for that year.

(iv) If the taxpayer chooses to make the election described in subdivision (ii) of this subparagraph, he shall file with his return a statement that he elects to make a redetermination of the amounts excludable from gross income under his annuity contract in accordance with the provisions of paragraph (d)(3) of § 1.72-4. This statement shall also contain the following information:

(a) The original annuity starting date and his age on that date,

(b) The date of the first day of the first period for which he received an amount in the current taxable year,

(c) The investment in the contract originally determined (as adjusted for any refund feature), and

(d) The aggregate of all amounts received under the contract between the date indicated in (a) of this subdivision and the day after the date indicated in (b) of this subdivision to the extent such amounts were excludable from gross income.

He shall include in gross income any amounts received during the taxable year for which the return is made in accordance with the redetermination made under this subparagraph.

(v) In the case of a contract to which § 1.72-6(d) (relating to contracts in which amounts were invested both before July 1, 1986, and after June 30, 1986) applies, this paragraph (d)(3) is applied in the manner prescribed in § 1.72-6(d) and, in particular, § 1.72-6(d)(5)(iii). This application may be illustrated by the following example:

Example. B, a male calendar year taxpayer, purchases a contract which provides for variable annual payments for life and to which

Reg. § 1.72-4(d)(3)

§ 1.72-2(b)(3) applies. The annuity starting date of the contract is June 30, 1990, when B is 64 years old. B receives a payment of $1,000 on June 30, 1991, but receives no other payment until June 30, 1993. B's total investment in the contract is $25,000. B's pre-July 1986 investment in the contract is $12,000. If B makes the election described in § 1.72-6(d)(6), separate computations are required to determine the amounts received as an annuity and excludable from gross income with respect to the pre-July 1986 investment in the contract and the post-June 1986 investment in the contract. In the separate computations, B first determines the applicable portions of the total payment received which are allocable to the pre-July 1986 investment in the contract and the post-June 1986 investment in the contract. The portion of the payment received allocable to the pre-July 1986 investment in the contract is $480 ($12,000/$25,000 × $1,000). The portion of the payment received allocable to the post-June 1986 investment in the contract is $520 ($13,000/$25,000 × $1,000).

Second, B determines the pre-July 1986 investment in the contract and the post-June 1986 investment in the contract allocable to the taxable year by dividing the pre-July 1986 and post-June 1986 investments in the contract by the applicable life expectancy multiple. The life expectancy multiple applicable to pre-July 1986 investment in the contract is B's life expectancy as

of the original annuity starting date adjusted for annual payments and is determined under Table I of § 1.72-9 [15.1 (15.6 − 0.5)]. The life expectancy multiple applicable to post-June 1986 investment in the contract is determined under Table V of § 1.72-9 (20.3 (20.8 − 0.5)). Thus, the pre-July 1986 investment in the contract allocable to each taxable year is $794.70 ($12,000 ÷ 15.1) and the post-June 1986 investment in the contract so allocable is $640.39 ($13,000 ÷ 20.3). Because the applicable portions of the total payment received in 1991 under the contract ($480 allocable to the pre-July 1986 investment in the contract and $520 allocable to the post-June 1986 investment in the contract) are treated as amounts received as an annuity and are excludable from gross income to the extent they do not exceed the portion of the corresponding investment in the contract allocable to 1991 ($794.70 pre-July 1986 investment in the contract and $640.39 post-June 1986 investment in the contract), the entire amount of each applicable portion of the total payment is excludable from gross income. B may elect, in the return filed for taxable year 1993, to redetermine amounts to be received as an annuity under the contract as of June 30, 1992. The extent to which the amounts received in 1993 or thereafter shall be considered amounts received as an annuity is determined as follows:

Pre-July 1986 investment in the contract allocable to taxable years 1991 and 1992 ($794.70 × 2)	$1,589.40
Less: Portion of total payments allocable to pre-July 1986 investment in the contract actually received as an annuity in taxable years 1991 and 1992	480.00
	1,109.40
Divided by: Life expectancy multiple applicable to pre-July 1986 investment in the contract for B, age 66 (14.4 − 0.5)	13.9
	79.81
Plus: Amount originally determined with respect to pre-July 1986 investment in the contract..	794.70
Pre-July 1986 amount	874.51
Post-June 1986 investment in the contract allocable to taxable years 1991 and 1992 ($640.39 × 2)	$1,280.78
Less: Portion of total payments allocable to post-June 1986 investment in the contract actually received as an annuity in taxable years 1991 and 1992	520.00
	760.78
Divided by: Life expectancy multiple applicable to post-June 1986 investment in the contract for B, age 66 (19.2 − 0.5)	18.7
	40.68
Plus: Amount originally determined with respect to post-June 1986 investment in the contract..	640.39
Post-June 1986 amount	681.07

(vi) The method of making an election to perform the separate computations illustrated in paragraph (d)(3)(v) of this section is described in § 1.72-6(d)(6).

Reg. § 1.72-4(d)(3)

(e) *Exclusion ratio in the case of two or more annuity elements acquired for a single consideration.* (1)(i) Where two or more annuity elements are provided under a contract described in paragraph (a)(2) of § 1.72-2, an exclusion ratio shall be determined for the contract as a whole and applied to all amounts received as an annuity under any of the annuity elements. To obtain this ratio, the investment in the contract determined in accordance with § 1.72-6 shall be divided by the aggregate of the expected returns found with respect to each of the annuity elements in accordance with § 1.72-5. For this purpose, it is immaterial that payments under one or more of the annuity elements involved have not commenced at the time when an amount is first received as an annuity under one or more of the other annuity elements.

(ii) The exclusion ratio found under subdivision (i) of this subparagraph does not apply to:

(a) An annuity element payable to a surviving annuitant under a joint and survivor annuity contract to which section 72(i) and paragraphs (b)(3) and (e)(3) of § 1.72-5 apply, or to

(b) A contract under which one or more of the constituent annuity elements provides for payments described in paragraph (b)(3) of § 1.72-2.

For rules with respect to a contract providing for annuity elements described in (b) of this subdivision, see subparagraph (2) of this paragraph.

(2) If one or more of the annuity elements under a contract described in paragraph (a)(2) of § 1.72-2 provides for payments to which paragraph (b)(3) of § 1.72-2 applies:

(i) With respect to the annuity elements to which paragraph (b)(3) of § 1.72-2 does not apply, an exclusion ratio shall be determined by dividing the portion of the investment in the entire contract which is properly allocable to all such elements (in the manner provided in paragraph (b)(3)(ii) of § 1.72-6) by the aggregate of the expected returns thereunder and such ratio shall be applied in the manner described in subdivision (i) of subparagraph (1); and

(ii) With respect to the annuity elements to which paragraph (b)(3) of § 1.72-2 does apply, the investment in the entire contract shall be reduced by the portion thereof found in subdivision (i) of this subparagraph and the resulting amount shall be used to determine the extent to which the aggregate of the payments received during the taxable year under all such elements is excludable from gross income. The amount so excludable shall be allocated to each recipient under such elements in the same ratio that the total of payments he receives each year bears to the total of the payments received by all such recipients during the year. The exclusion ratio with respect to the amounts so allocated shall be 100 percent. See paragraph (f)(2) of § 1.72-5 and paragraph (b)(3) of § 1.72-6.

(iii) In the case of a contract to which § 1.72-6(d) (relating to contracts in which amounts were invested both before July 1, 1986, and after June 30, 1986) applies, this paragraph (e) is applied in the manner prescribed in § 1.72-6(d) and, in particular, § 1.72-6(d)(5)(iv). [Reg. § 1.72-4.]

□ [*T.D. 6211, 11-14-56. Amended by T.D. 7043, 6-1-70, T.D. 7352, 4-9-75, and T.D. 8115, 12-16-86.*]

[Reg. § 1.72-5]

§ 1.72-5. **Expected return.**—(a) *Expected return for but one life.* (1) If a contract to which section 72 applies provides that one annuitant is to receive a fixed monthly income for life, the expected return is determined by multiplying the total of the annuity payments to be received annually by the multiple shown in Table I or V (whichever is applicable) of § 1.72-9 under the age (as of the annuity starting date) and, if applicable, sex of the measuring life (usually the annuitant's). Thus, where a male purchases a contract before July 1, 1986, providing for an immediate annuity of $100 per month for his life and, as of the annuity starting date (in this case the date of purchase), the annuitant's age at his nearest birthday is 66, the expected return is computed as follows:

Monthly payment of $100 × 12 months equals annual payment of .... $ 1,200
Multiple shown in Table I, male, age 66 .... 14.4

Expected return ($1,200 × 14.4) 17,280

If, however, the taxpayer had purchased the contract after June 30, 1986, the expected return would be $23,040, determined by multiplying 19.2 (multiple shown in Table V, age 66) by $1,200.

(2)(i) If payments are to be made quarterly, semiannually, or annually, an adjustment of the applicable multiple shown in Table I or V (whichever is applicable) may be required. A further adjustment may be required where the interval between the annuity starting date and the date of the first payment is less than the interval between future payments. Neither adjustment shall be made, however, if the payments are to be made more frequently than quarterly. The amount of the adjustment, if any, is to be found in accordance with the following table:

If the number of whole months from the annuity starting date to the first payment date is—	0-1	2	3	4	5	6	7	8	9	10	11	12
And payments under the contract are to be made:												
Annually	+0.5	+0.4	+0.3	+0.2	+0.1	0	0	−0.1	−0.2	−0.3	−0.4	−0.5
Semiannually	+ .2	+ .1	0	0	− .1	− .2	...	...	...	...	...	...
Quarterly	+ .1	0	− .1	...	...	...	...	...	...	...	...	...

Thus, for a male, age 66, the multiple found in Table I, adjusted for quarterly payments the first of which is to be made one full month after the annuity starting date, is 14.5 (14.4 + 0.1); for semiannual payments the first of which is to be made six full months from the annuity starting date, the adjusted multiple is 14.2 (14.4 − 0.2); for annual payments the first of which is to be made one full month from the annuity starting date, the adjusted multiple is 14.9 (14.4 + 0.5). If the annuitant in the example shown in subparagraph (1) of this paragraph were to receive an annual payment of $1,200 commencing 12 full months after his annuity starting date, the amount of the expected return would be $16,680 ($1,200 × 13.9 [14.4 − 0.5]). Similarly, for an annuitant, age 50, the multiple found in Table V, adjusted for quarterly payments the first of which is to be made one full month after the annuity starting date, is 33.2 (33.1 + 0.1); for semiannual payments the first of which is to be made six full months from the annuity starting date, the adjusted multiple is 32.9 (33.1 − 0.2); for annual payments the first of which is to be made one full month from the annuity starting date, the adjusted multiple is 33.6 (33.1 + 0.5).

(ii) Notwithstanding the table in subdivision (i) of this subparagraph, adjustments of multiples for early or other than monthly payments determined prior to February 19, 1956, under the table prescribed in paragraph 1(b)(4) of T.D. 6118 (19 FR 9897, C.B. 1955-1, 699), approved December 30, 1954, need not be redetermined.

(3) If the contract provides for fixed payments to be made to an annuitant until death or until the expiration of a specified limited period, whichever occurs earlier, the expected return of such temporary life annuity is determined by multiplying the total of the annuity payments to be received annually by the multiple shown in Table IV or VII (whichever is applicable) of § 1.72-9 for the age (as of the annuity starting date) and, if applicable, sex of the annuitant and the nearest whole number of years in the specified period. For example, if a male annuitant, age 60 (at his nearest birthday), is to receive $60 per month for five years or until he dies, whichever is earlier, and there is no post-June 1986, investment in the contract, the expected return under such a contract is $3,456, computed as follows:

Monthly payments of $60 × 12 months equals annual payment of	$ 720
Multiple shown in Table IV for male, age 60, for term of 5 years	4.8
Expected return for 5-year temporary life annuity of $720 per year ($720 × 4.8)	$3,456

If the annuitant purchased the same contract after June 30, 1986, the expected return under the contract would be $3,528, computed as follows:

Monthly payments of $60 × 12 months equals annual payment of	$ 720.00
Multiple shown in Table VIII for annuitant, age 60, for term of 5 years	4.9
Expected return for 5-year temporary life annuity of $720 per year ($720 × 4.9)	$3,528.00

The adjustment provided by subparagraph (2) of this paragraph shall not be made with respect to the multiple found in Table IV or VIII (whichever is applicable).

(4) If the contract provides for payments to be made to an annuitant for the annuitant's lifetime, but the amount of the annual payments is to be decreased after the expiration of a specified

Reg. § 1.72-5(a)(3)

limited period, the expected return is computed by considering the contract as a combination of a whole life annuity for the smaller amount plus a temporary life annuity for an amount equal to the difference between the larger and the smaller amount. For example, if a male annuitant, age 60, is to receive $150 per month for five years or until his earlier death, and is to receive $90 per month for the remainder of his lifetime after such five years, the expected return is computed as if the annuitant's contract consisted of a whole life annuity for $90 per month plus a five-year temporary life annuity of $60 per month. In such circumstances, the expected return if there is no post-June 1986 investment in the contract is computed as follows:

Monthly payments of $90 × 12 months equals annual payment of	$ 1,080
Multiple shown in Table I for male, age 60	18.2
Expected return for whole life annuity of $1,080 per year	$19,656
Expected return for 5-year temporary life annuity of $720 per year (as found in subparagraph (3) of this paragraph (a))	$ 3,456
Total expected return	$23,112

If the annuitant purchased the same contract after June 30, 1986, the expected return would be $29,664, computed as follows:

Monthly payments of $90 × 12 months equals annual payment of	$ 1,080
Multiple shown in Table V for annuitant, age 60	24.2
Expected return for whole life annuity of $1,080 per year	$26,136
Plus: Expected return for 5-year temporary life annuity of $720 per year (as found in subparagraph (3) of this paragraph (a))	$ 3,528
Total expected return	$29,664

If payments are to be made quarterly, semiannually, or annually, an appropriate adjustment of the multiple found in Table I or V (whichever is applicable) for the whole life annuity should be made in accordance with subparagraph (2) of this paragraph.

(5) If the contract described in subparagraph (4) of this paragraph provided that the amount of the annual payments to the annuitant were to be increased (instead of decreased) after the expiration of a specified limited period, the expected return would be computed as if the annuitant's contract consisted of a whole life annuity for the larger amount minus a temporary life annuity for an amount equal to the difference between the larger and smaller amount. Thus, if the annuitant described in subparagraph (4) of this paragraph were to receive $90 per month for five years or until his earlier death, and to receive $150 per month for the remainder of his lifetime after such five years, the expected return would be computed by subtracting the expected return under a five year temporary life annuity of $60 per month from the expected return under a whole life annuity of $150 per month. In such circumstances, the expected return if there is no post-June 1986 investment in the contract is computed as follows:

Monthly payments of $150 × 12 months equals annual payment of	$ 1,800
Multiple shown in Table I (male, age 60)	18.2
Expected return for annuity for whole life of $1,800 per year	$32,760
Less expected return for 5-year temporary life annuity of $720 per year (as found in subparagraph (3))	$ 3,456
Net expected return	$29,304

If the annuitant purchased the same contract after June 30, 1986, the expected return would be $40,032, computed as follows:

Monthly payments of $150 × 12 months equals annual payments of	$ 1,800
Multiple shown in Table V (age 60)	24.2
Expected return for annuity for whole life of $1,800 per year	$43,560
Less expected return for 5-year temporary life annuity of $720 per year (as found in subparagraph (3) of this paragraph (a))	$ 3,528
Net expected return	$40,032

If payments are to be made quarterly, semiannually, or annually, an appropriate adjustment of the multiple found in Table I or V (whichever is applicable) for the whole life annuity should be made in accordance with subparagraph (2) of this paragraph.

(b) *Expected return under joint and survivor and joint annuities.* (1) In the case of a joint and survivor annuity contract involving two annuitants which provides the first annuitant with a fixed monthly income for life and, after the death of the first annuitant, provides an identical monthly income for life to a second annuitant, the expected return shall be determined by multiplying the total amount of the payments to be received annually by the multiple obtained from

Table II or VI (whichever is applicable) of § 1.72-9 under the ages (as of the annuity starting date) and, if applicable, sexes of the living annuitants. For example, a husband purchases a joint and survivor annuity contract providing for payments of $100 per month for life and, after his death, for the same amount to his wife for the remainder of her life. As of the annuity starting date his age at his nearest birthday is 70 and that of his wife at her nearest birthday is 67. If there is no post-June 1986 investment in the contract, the expected return is computed as follows:

Monthly payments of $100 × 12 months equals annual payment of	$ 1,200
Multiple shown in Table II (male, age 70, female, age 67)	19.7
Expected return ($1,200 × 19.7)	$23,640

If the annuitants purchased the same contract after June 30, 1986, the expected return would be $26,400, computed as follows:

Monthly payments of $100 × 12 months equals annual payment of	$ 1,200
Multiple shown in Table VI (ages 70, 67)	22.0
Expected return ($1,200 × 22.0)	$26,400

If payments are to be made quarterly, semiannually, or annually, an appropriate adjustment of the multiple found in Table II or VI (whichever is applicable) should be made in accordance with paragraph (a)(2) of this section.

(2) If a contract of the type described in subparagraph (1) of this paragraph provides that a different (rather than an identical) monthly income is payable to the second annuitant, the expected return is computed in the following manner. The applicable multiple in Table II or VI (whichever is applicable) is first found as in the example in subparagraph (1) of this paragraph. The multiple applicable to the first annuitant is then found in Table I or V (whichever is applicable) as though the contract were for a single life annuity. The multiple from Table I or V is then subtracted from the multiple obtained from Table II or VI and the resulting multiple is applied to the total payments to be received annually under

the contract by the second annuitant. The result is the expected return with respect to the second annuitant. The portion of the expected return with respect to payments to be made during the first annuitant's life is then computed by applying the multiple found in Table I or V to the total annual payments to be received by such annuitant under the contract. The expected returns with respect to each of the annuitants separately are then aggregated to obtain the expected return under the entire contract.

Example (1). A husband purchases a joint and survivor annuity providing for payments of $100 per month for his life and, after his death, payments to his wife of $50 per month for her life. As of the annuity starting date his age at his nearest birthday is 70 and that of his wife at her nearest birthday is 67. There is no post-June 1986 investment in the contract.

Multiple from Table II (male, age 70, female, age 67)	19.7
Multiple from Table I (male, age 70)	12.1
Difference (multiple applicable to second annuitant)	7.6
Portion of expected return, second annuitant ($600 × 7.6)	$ 4,560
Portion of expected return, first annuitant ($1,200 × 12.1)	$14,520
Expected return under the contract	$19,080

The expected return thus found, $19,080, is to be used in computing the amount to be excluded from gross income. Thus, if the investment in the contract in this example is $14,310, the exclusion ratio is $14,310 ÷ $19,080, or 75 percent. The amount excludable from each monthly payment made to the husband is 75 percent of $100, or $75,

and the remaining $25 of each payment received by him shall be included in his gross income. After the husband's death, the amount excludable by the second annuitant (the surviving wife) would be 75 percent of each monthly payment of $50, or $37.50, and the remaining $12.50 of each payment shall be included in her gross income.

Reg. § 1.72-5(b)(2)

Example (2). If the same contract were purchased after June 30, 1986, the expected return would be $22,800, computed as follows:

Multiple from Table VI (ages 70, 67)	22.0
Multiple from Table V (age 70)	16.0
Difference (multiple applicable to second annuitant)	6.0
Portion of expected return, second annuitant ($600 × 6.0)	$ 3,600
Plus: Portion of expected return, first annuitant ($1,200 × 16.0)	$19,200
Expected return under the contract	$22,800

If the investment in the contract is $14,310, the exclusion ratio is $14,310 ÷ $22,800, or 62.8 percent. Thus, the husband would exclude $62.80 of each $100 payment received by him. After his death, his wife would exclude 62.8 percent, or $31.40, of each $50 monthly payment.

Example (3). If amounts were invested in the same contract both before July 1, 1986, and after June 30, 1986, and the election described in § 1.72-6(d)(6) were made, two exclusion ratios would be determined pursuant to § 1.72-6(d). Assume that the husband's total investment in the contract is $14,310 and that $7,310 is the pre-July 1986 investment in the contract. The pre-July 1986 exclusion ratio would be $7,310 ÷ $19,080, or 38.3 percent. The post-June 1986 exclusion ratio would be $7,000 ÷ $22,800, or 30.7 percent. The husband would exclude $69.00 ($38.30 + $30.70) of the $100 monthly payment received by him. The remaining $31.00 would be included in his gross income. After the husband's death, the amount excludable by his wife would be $34.50 (38.3 percent of $50 plus 30.7 percent of $50). The remaining $15.50 would be included in gross income.

The same method is used if the payments are to be increased after the death of the first annuitant. Thus, if the payments to be made until the husband's death were $50 per month and his widow were to receive $100 per month thereafter until her death, the 7.6 multiple in example (1) above would be applied to the $100 payments, yielding an expected return with respect to this portion of the annuity contract of $9,120 ($1,200 × 7.6). An expected return of $7,260 ($600 × 12.1) would be obtained with respect to the payments to be made to the husband, yielding a total expected return under the contract of $16,380 ($9,120 plus $7,260). If payments are to be made quarterly, semiannually, or annually, an appropriate adjustment of the multiples found in Tables I and II or Tables V and VI (whichever are applicable) should be made in accordance with paragraph (a)(2) of this section.

(3) In the case of a joint and survivor annuity contract in respect of which the first annuitant died in 1951, 1952, or 1953, and the basis of the surviving annuitant's interest in the contract was determinable under section 113(a)(5) of the Internal Revenue Code of 1939, such basis shall be considered the "aggregate of premiums or other consideration paid" by the surviving annuitant for the contract. (For rules governing this determination, see 26 CFR (1939) 39.22(b)(2) 2 and 39.113(a)(5)-1 (Regulations 118).) In determining such an annuitant's investment in the contract, such aggregate shall be reduced by any amounts received under the contract by the surviving annuitant before the annuity starting date, to the extent such amounts were excludable from his gross income at the time of receipt. The expected return of the surviving annuitant in such cases shall be determined in the manner prescribed in paragraph (a) of this section, as though the surviving annuitant alone were involved. For this purpose, the appropriate multiple for the survivor shall be obtained from Table I as of the annuity starting date determined in accordance with paragraph (b)(2)(i) of § 1.72-4.

(4) If a contract involving two annuitants provides for fixed monthly payments to be made as a joint life annuity until the death of the first annuitant to die (in other words, only as long as both remain alive), the expected return under such contract shall be determined by multiplying the total of the annuity payments to be received annually under the contract by the multiple obtained from Table IIA or VIA (whichever is applicable) of § 1.72-9 under the ages (as of the annuity starting date) and, if applicable, sexes of the annuitants. If, however, payments are to be made under the contract quarterly, semiannually, or annually, an appropriate adjustment of the multiple found in Table IIA or VIA shall be made in accordance with paragraph (a)(2) of this section.

(5) If a joint and survivor annuity contract involving two annuitants provides that a specified amount shall be paid during their joint lives and a different specified amount shall be paid to the survivor upon the death of whichever of the annuitants is the first to die, the following preliminary computation shall be made in all cases preparatory to determining the expected return under the contract:

Reg. § 1.72-5(b)(5)

(i) From Table II or VI (whichever is applicable), obtain the multiple under both of the annuitants' ages (as of the annuity starting date) and, if applicable, their appropriate sexes;

(ii) From Table IIA or VIA (whichever is applicable), obtain the multiple applicable to both annuitants' ages (as of the annuity starting date) and, if applicable, their appropriate sexes;

(iii) Apply the multiple found in subdivision (i) of this subparagraph to the total of the amounts to be received annually after the death of the first to die; and

(iv) Apply the multiple found in subdivision (ii) of this subparagraph to the difference between the total of amounts to be received annually before and the total of the amounts to be received annually after the death of the first to die.

If the original annual payment is in excess of the annual payment to be made after the death of the first to die, the expected return is the sum of the amounts determined under subdivisions (iii) and (iv) of this subparagraph. This may be illustrated by the following examples:

Example (1). A husband purchases a joint and survivor annuity providing for payments of $100 per month for as long as both he and his wife live, and, after the death of the first to die, payments to the survivor of $75 a month for life. As of the annuity starting date, his age at his nearest birthday is 70 and that of his wife at her nearest birthday is 67. If there is no post-June 1986 investment in the contract, the expected return under the contract is computed as follows:

Multiple from Table II (male age 70, female age 67)	19.7
Multiple from Table IIA (male age 70, female age 67)	9.3
Portion of expected return ($900 × 19.7—sum per year after first death)	$17,730
Plus: Portion of expected return ($300 × 9.3—amount of change in sum at first death) . . .	$ 2,790
Expected return under the contract	$20,520

The total expected return in this example, $20,520, is to be used in computing the amount to be excluded from gross income. Thus, if the investment in the contract is $17,887, the exclusion ratio is $17,887 ÷ $20,520, or 87.2 percent. The amount excludable from each monthly payment made while both are alive is 87.2 percent of $100, or $87.20, and the remaining $12.80 of each payment shall be included in gross income. After the death of the first to die, the amount excludable by

the survivor shall be 87.2 percent of each monthly payment of $75, or $65.40, and the remaining $9.60 of each payment shall be included in gross income.

Example (2). Assume the same facts as in example (1), except that the contract is purchased after June 30, 1986.

The expected return under the contract is computed as follows:

Multiple from Table VI (ages 70, 67)	22.0
Multiple from Table VIA (ages 70, 67)	12.4
Portion of expected return ($900 × 22.0—sum per year after first death)	$19,800
Plus: Portion of expected return ($300 × 12.4—amount of change in sum at first death) . .	$ 3,720
Expected return under the contract	$23,520

Thus, if the investment in the contract is $17,887, the exclusion ratio is $17,887 ÷ $23,520, or 76.1 percent. The amount excludable from each monthly payment made while both are alive would be 76.1 percent of $100, or $76.10, and the remaining $23.90 of each payment would be included in gross income. After the death of the first to die, the amount excludable by the survivor would be 76.1 percent of each monthly payment of $75, or $57.08, and the remaining $17.92 of each payment would be included in gross income.

Example (3). Assume the same facts as in examples (1) and (2), except that the total investment in the contract is $17,887, and that the pre-July 1986 investment in the contract is $8,000. Assume also that one of the annuitants makes the election described in § 1.72-6(d)(6). Separate computations shall be performed pursuant to § 1.72-6(d) to determine the amount excludable from gross income. The pre-July 1986 exclusion ratio would be $8,000 ÷ $20,520, or 39 percent. The post-June 1986 exclusion ratio would be $9,887 ÷ $23,520, or 42 percent. The amount excludable from each monthly payment made while both are alive would be $81 ((.39 × 100) + (.42 × 100)), and the remaining $19 would be included in gross income. After the death of the first to die, the amount excludable by the survivor would be $60.75 ((.39 × 75) + (.42 × 75)), and the remaining $14.25 would be included in gross income.

If the original annual payment is less than the annual payment to be made after the death of the first to die, the expected return is the difference

Reg. § 1.72-5(b)(5)

between the amounts determined under subdivisions (iii) and (iv) of this subparagraph. If, however, payments are to be made quarterly, semiannually, or annually under the contract, the multiples obtained from both Tables II and IIA or Tables VI and VIA (whichever are applicable) shall first be adjusted in a manner prescribed in paragraph (a)(2) of this section.

(6) If a contract provides for the payment of life annuities to two persons during their respective lives and, after the death of one (without regard to which one dies first), provides that the survivor shall receive for life both his own annuity payments and the payments made formerly to the deceased person, the expected return shall be determined in accordance with paragraph (e)(4) of this section.

(7) If paragraph (b)(3) of § 1.72-2 applies to payments provided under a contract and this paragraph applies to such payments, the principles of this paragraph shall be used in making the computations described in paragraph (d)(3) of § 1.72-4. This may be illustrated by the following examples, examples (1) through (3) of which assume that there is no post-June 1986 investment in the contract:

Example (1). Taxpayer A, a male age 63, pays $24,000 for a contract which provides that the proceeds (both income and return of capital) from eight units of an investment fund shall be paid monthly to him for his life and that after his death the proceeds from six such units shall be paid monthly to B, a female age 55, for her life. The portion of the investment in the contract allocable to each taxable year of A is $955.20 and that allocable to each taxable year of B is $716.40. This is determined in the following manner:

Multiple from Table II (male, age 63, and female, age 55)	38.1
Number of units to be paid, in effect, as a joint and survivor annuity	× 6
Number of total annual unit payments anticipatable with respect to the joint and survivor annuity element	168.6
Multiple from Table I (male, age 63)	16.2
Number of units to be paid, in effect, as a single life annuity	× 2
Number of total annual unit payments anticipatable with respect to A alone	32.4
Total number of unit payments anticipatable	201
Portion of investment in the contract allocable to unit payments ($24,000 ÷ 201) on an annual basis	$119.40
Number of units payable to A while he continues to live	× 8
Portion of the investment in the contract allocable to each taxable year of A	$955.20
Portion of investment in the contract allocable to unit payments ($24,000 ÷ 201) on an annual basis	$119.40
Number of units payable to B for her life after A's death	× 6
Portion of the investment in the contract allocable to each taxable year of B	$716.40

For the purpose of the above computation it is immaterial whether or not A lives to or beyond the life expectancy shown for him in Table I.

Example (2). Assume that Taxpayer A in example (1) receives payments for five years which are at least as large as the portion of the investment in the contract allocable to such years, but in the sixth year he receives a total of only $626.40 rather than the $955.20 allocable to such year. A is 69 and B is 61 at the beginning of the first monthly period for which an amount is payable in the seventh taxable year. A makes the election in that year provided under paragraph (d)(3) of § 1.72-4. The difference between the portion of the investment in the contract allocable to the sixth year and the amount actually received in that year is $328.80 ($955.20 less $626.40). In this case, 139.2 unit payments are anticipatable (on an annual basis), since the appropriate multiple from Table II of § 1.72-9, 23.2, multiplied by the number of units payable, in effect, as a joint and survivor annuity yields this result (6 × 23.2). A's appropriate multiple from Table I of § 1.72-9 for the two units which will cease to be paid at his death is 12.6, and the total number of unit payments anticipatable (on an annual basis) is, therefore, 164.4 (2 × 12.6 plus 139.2). Dividing the difference previously found ($328.80) by the total number of unit payments thus determined (164.4) indicates that A will have an additional allocation of the investment in the contract of $16 to the seventh and every succeeding full taxable year (8 units × $2), and B will have an additional allocation of the investment in the contract of $12 (6 units × $2) to each taxable year in which she received 12 monthly payments subsequent to the death of A. The total allocable to each taxable year of A is, therefore, $971.20, and that allocable to each taxable year of B will be $728.40.

Reg. § 1.72-5(b)(7)

Example (3). If, in example (2), A had died at the end of the fifth year, in the sixth year B would have received a payment of $469.80 (that portion of the $626.40 that A would have received which is in the same ratio that 6 units bear to 8 units) and would thus have received $246.60 less than the portion of the investment in the contract originally determined to be allocable to each of her taxable years. In these circumstances, B would be entitled to elect to redetermine the portion of the investment in the contract allocable to the taxable year of election and all subsequent years. The new amount allocable thereto would be found by dividing the $246.60 difference by her life expectancy as of the first day of the first period for which she received an amount as an annuity in the seventh year of the annuity contract, and adding the result to her originally determined allocation of $716.40.

Example (4). On July 1, 1986, Taxpayer C, age 60, pays $28,000 for a contract which provides that the proceeds (both income and return of capital) from 10 units of an investment fund shall be paid monthly to C for C's life and that after C's death the proceeds from 4 such units shall be paid monthly to D, age 57, for D's life. The portion of the investment in the contract allocable to each taxable year of C is $1,037.00 and that allocable to each taxable year of D is $414.80. This is determined as follows:

Multiple for Table VI (ages 60, 57)	31.2
Number of units to be paid, in effect, as a joint and survivor annuity	× 4
Number of total annual unit payments anticipatable with respect to the joint and survivor annuity element	124.8
Multiple from Table V (age 60)	24.2
Number of units to be paid, in effect, as a single life annuity	× 6
Number of total annual unit payments anticipatable with respect to C alone	145.2
Total number of unit payments anticipatable	270
Portion of investment in the contract allocable to unit payments ($28,000 ÷ 270) on an annual basis	103.70
Number of units payable to C while C continues to live	× 10
Portion of the investment in the contract allocable to each taxable year of C	$1,037.00
Portion of investment in the contract allocable to unit payments ($28,000 ÷ 270) on an annual basis	$ 103.70
Number of units payable to D for D's life after C's death	× 4
Portion of the investment in the contract allocable to each taxable year of D	$ 414.80

For purposes of the above computation it is immaterial whether or not C lives to or beyond the life expectancy shown in Table V.

Example (5). Assume the same facts as in example (4), except that C's total investment in the contract is $28,000, and C's pre-July 1986 investment in the contract is $16,000. If C makes the election described in § 1.72-6(d)(6), separate computations are required to determine the amount excludable from gross income with respect to the pre-July 1986 investment in the contract and the post-June 1986 investment in the contract. The annuitant shall apply the appropriate pre-July 1986 and post-June 1986 life expectancy multiples to the applicable portions of the units to be paid as a joint and survivor annuity, and as a single life annuity.

Pre-July 1986 Computation (all references to unit payments are to the pre-July 1986 applicable portion of such payments):

Multiple from Table II (male, age 60, female, age 57)	27.6
Number of units to be paid, in effect, as a joint and survivor annuity	× 4
Number of total annual unit payments anticipatable with respect to the joint and survivor annuity element	110.40
Multiple from Table I (male, age 60)	18.2
Number of units to be paid, in effect, as a single life annuity	× 6
Number of total annual unit payments anticipatable with respect to C alone	109.20
Total number of unit payments anticipatable	219.6
Portion of pre-July 1986 investment in the contract allocable to unit payments ($16,000 ÷ 219.60) on an annual basis	$ 72.86

Reg. § 1.72-5(b)(7)

Number of units payable to C while C continues to live	× 10
Portion of pre-July 1986 investment in the contract allocable to each taxable year of C . . .	728.60
Portion of pre-July 1986 investment in the contract allocable to unit payments ($16,000 ÷ 219.60) on an annual basis	72.86
Number of units payable to D for D's life after C's death	× 4
Portion of pre-July 1986 investment in the contract allocable to each taxable year of D . . .	$291.44

Post-June 1986 Computation (all references to unit payments are to the post-June 1986 applicable portion of such payments):

Multiple from Table VI (ages 60, 57)	31.2
Number of units to be paid, in effect, as a joint and survivor annuity	× 4
Number of total annual unit payments anticipatable with respect to the joint and survivor annuity element	$ 124.80
Multiple from Table V (age 60)	24.2
Number of units to be paid, in effect, as a single life annuity	× 6
Number of total annual unit payments anticipatable with respect to C alone	145.20
Total number of unit payments anticipatable	270
Portion of post-June 1986 investment in the contract allocable to unit payments ($12,000 ÷ 270) on an annual basis	$ 44.44
Number of units payable to C while C continues to live	× 10
Portion of post-June 1986 investment in the contract allocable to each taxable year of C	$ 444.40
Portion of post-June 1986 investment in the contract allocable to unit payments ($12,000 ÷ 270) on an annual basis	44.44
Number of units payable to D for D's life after C's death	× 4
Portion of post-June 1986 investment in the contract allocable to each taxable year of D	$ 177.78

Total computation:

Total portion of the investment in the contract allocable to each taxable year of C ($728.60 + $444.40)	$1,173.00
Total portion of the investment in the contract allocable to each taxable year of D ($291.44 + $177.78)	$ 469.22

Example (6). Assume that taxpayer C in example (4) receives payments for four years which are at least as large as the portion of the investment in the contract allocable to such years, but in the fifth year receives a total of only $600 rather than the $1,037 allocable to such year. C is 65 and D is 62 at the beginning of the first monthly period for which an amount is payable in the sixth taxable year. C makes the election in that year provided under paragraph (d)(3) of § 1.72-4. The difference between the portion of the investment in the contract allocable to the fifth year and the amount actually received in that year is $437 ($1,037 − $600). In this case, 106 unit payments are anticipatable with respect to the joint and survivor annuity element, since the appropriate multiple from Table VI of § 1.72-9, 26.5, multiplied by the number of units payable, in effect, as a joint and survivor annuity yields this result (4 × 26.5). C's appropriate multiple from Table V of § 1.72-9 for the six units which

will cease to be paid at C's death is 20.0, and the number of unit payments anticipatable with respect to C alone is 120 (6 × 20). The total number of unit payments anticipatable is, therefore, 226 (120 plus 106). Dividing the difference previously found ($437) by the total number of unit payments thus determined (226) indicates that C will have an additional allocation of the investment in the contract of $19.30 to the sixth and every succeeding full taxable year (10 units × $1.93), and D will have an additional allocation of the investment in the contract of $7.72 (4 units × $1.93) to each taxable year in which D receives 12 monthly payments subsequent to the death of C. The total allocable to each taxable year of C is, therefore, $1,056.30, and that allocable to each taxable year of D will be $422.52.

Example (7). If, in example (6), C had died at the end of the fourth year, in the fifth year D would have received a payment of $240 (that portion of the $600 that C would have received which is in the same ratio that 4 units bear to 10 units) and would thus have received $174.80 less than the portion of the investment in the contract allocable to each of D's taxable years. In these circumstances, D would be entitled to elect to redetermine the portion of the investment in the contract allocable to the taxable year of election and all subsequent years. The new amount allocable thereto would be found by dividing the $174.80 difference by D's life expectancy as of the first day of the first period for which D received an amount as an annuity in the sixth year of the annuity contract, and adding the result to D's originally determined allocation of $414.80.

(c) *Expected return for term certain.* In the case of a contract providing for specific periodic payments which are to be paid for a term certain such as a fixed number of months or years, without regard to life expectancy, the expected return is determined by multiplying the fixed number of years or months for which payments are to be on or after the annuity starting date by the amount of the payment provided in the contract for each such period.

(d) *Expected return with respect to amount certain.* In the case of contracts involving no life or lives as a measurement of their duration, but under which a determinable total amount is to be paid in installments of lesser amounts paid at periodic intervals, the expected return shall be the total amount guaranteed. If an amount is to be paid periodically until a fund plus interest at a fixed rate is exhausted, but further payments may be made thereafter because of earnings at a higher interest rate, this paragraph shall apply to the total amount anticipatable as a result of the amount of the fund plus the fixed interest thereon. Any amount which may be paid as the result of earnings at a greater interest rate shall be disregarded in determining the expected return. If such an amount is later received, it shall be considered an amount not received as an annuity after the annuity starting date. See paragraph (b)(2) of § 1.72-11.

(e) *Expected return where two or more annuity elements providing for fixed payments are acquired for a single consideration.* (1) In the case of a contract described in paragraph (a)(2) of § 1.72-2, which provides for specified payments to be made under two or more annuity elements, the expected return shall be found for the contract as a whole by aggregating the expected returns found with respect to each annuity element. If individual life annuity elements are involved (including joint and survivor annuities where the primary annuitant died before January 1, 1954)

the expected return for each of them shall be determined in the manner prescribed in paragraph (a) of this section. If joint and survivor annuity elements are involved, the expected return for such elements shall be determined under the appropriate subparagraph of paragraph (b) of this section. If terms certain or amounts certain are involved, the expected returns for such elements shall be determined under paragraph (c) or (d) of this section, respectively.

(2) The aggregate expected return found in accordance with the rules set forth in subparagraph (1) of this paragraph shall constitute the expected return for the contract as a whole. The investment in the contract shall be divided by the amount thus determined to obtain the exclusion ratio for the contract as a whole. This exclusion ratio shall be applied to all amounts received as a annuity under the contract by any recipient (in accordance with the provisions of § 1.72-4), except in the case of amounts received by a surviving annuitant under a joint and survivor annuity element to which the provisions of section 72(i) and paragraph (b)(3) of this section would apply if it were a separate contract. See subparagraph (3) of this paragraph.

(3) In the case of a contract providing two or more annuity elements, one of which is a joint and survivor annuity element of the type described in section 72(i) and paragraph (b)(3) of this section, the general exclusion ratio for the contract as a whole, for the purpose of computations with respect to all the other annuity elements shall be determined in accordance with the principles of subparagraphs (1) and (2) of this paragraph. A special exclusion ratio shall thereafter be determined for the surviving annuitant receiving payments under the annuity element described in section 72(i) and paragraph (b)(3) of this section by using the investment in the contract and the expected return determined in accordance with the provisions of paragraph (b)(3) of this section.

(4) In the case of a contract providing for payments to be made to two persons in the manner described in paragraph (b)(6) of this section, the expected return is to be computed as though there were two joint and survivor annuities under the same contract, in the following manner. First, the multiple appropriate to the ages (as of the annuity starting date) and, if applicable, sexes of the annuitants involved shall be found in Table II or VI (whichever is applicable) of § 1.72-9 and adjusted, if necessary, in the manner described in paragraph (a)(2) of this section. Second, the multiple so found shall be applied to the sum of the payments to be made each year to both annui-

Reg. § 1.72-5(c)

tants. The result is the expected return for the contract as a whole.

(5) For rules relating to expected return where two or more annuity elements are acquired for a single consideration and one or more of such elements does not specify a fixed payment for each period, see paragraph (f) of this section.

(f) *Expected return with respect to obligations providing for payments described in paragraph (b)(3) of § 1.72-2.* (1) If a contract to which section 72 applies provides only for payments to be made in a manner described in paragraph (b)(3) of § 1.72-2, the expected return for such contract as a whole shall be an amount equal to the investment in the contract found in accordance with section 72(c)(1) and § 1.72-6, as adjusted for any refund feature in accordance with § 1.72-7.

(2) If a contract to which section 72 applies provides for annuity elements, one or more of which (but not all) provide for payments to be made in a manner described in paragraph (b)(3) of § 1.72-2:

(i) With respect to the portion of the contract providing for annuity elements to which paragraph (b)(3) of § 1.72-2 does not apply, the expected return shall be the aggregate of the expected returns found for each of such elements in accordance with the appropriate paragraph of this section; and

(ii) With respect to all annuity elements to which paragraph (b)(3) of § 1.72-2 does apply, the expected return for all such elements shall be an amount equal to the portion of the investment in the contract allocable to such elements in accordance with the provisions of paragraph (e)(2)(ii) of § 1.72-4 and paragraph (b)(3)(ii)(*b*) of § 1.72-6.

(g) *Expected return with respect to contracts subject to § 1.72-6(d).* In the case of a contract to which § 1.72-6(d) (relating to contracts in which amounts were invested both before July 1, 1986, and after June 30, 1986) applies, an expected return is computed using the multiples in Tables I through IV of § 1.72-9 with respect to the pre-July 1986 investment in the contract and a second expected return is computed using the multiples in Tables V through VIII of § 1.72-9 with respect to the post-June 1986 investment in the contract. [Reg. § 1.72-5.]

☐ [*T.D. 6211, 11-14-56. Amended by T.D. 8115, 12-16-86.*]

[Reg. § 1.72-6]

§ 1.72-6. Investment in the contract.—(a) *General rule.* (1) For the purpose of computing the "investment in the contract", it is first necessary to determine the "aggregate amount of premiums or other consideration paid" for such

contract. See section 72(c)(1). This determination is made as of the later of the annuity starting date of the contract or the date on which an amount is first received thereunder as an annuity. The amount so found is then reduced by the sum of the following amounts in order to find the investment in the contract:

(i) The total amount of any return of premiums or dividends received (including unrepaid loans or dividends applied against the principal or interest on such loans) on or before the date on which the foregoing determination is made, and

(ii) The total of any other amounts received with respect to the contract on or before such date which were excludable from the gross income for the recipient under the income tax law applicable at the time of receipt.

Amounts to which subdivision (ii) of this subparagraph applies shall include, for example, amounts considered to be return of premiums or other consideration paid under section 22(b)(2) of the Internal Revenue Code of 1939 and amounts considered to be an employer-provided death benefit under section 22(b)(1)(B) of such Code. For rules relating to the extent to which an employee or his beneficiary may include employer contributions in the aggregate amount of premiums or other consideration paid, see § 1.72-8. If the aggregate amount of premiums or other consideration paid for the contract includes amounts for which deductions were allowed under section 404 as contributions on behalf of a self-employed individual, such amounts shall not be included in the investment in the contract.

(2) For the purpose of subparagraph (1) of this paragraph, amounts received subsequent to the receipt of an amount as an annuity or subsequent to the annuity starting date, whichever is the later, shall be disregarded. See, however, § 1.72-11.

(3) The application of this paragraph may be illustrated by the following examples:

Example (1). In 1950, B purchased an annuity contract for $10,000 which was to provide him with an annuity of $1,000 per year for life. He received $1,000 in each of the years 1950, 1951, 1952, and 1953, prior to the annuity starting date (January 1, 1954). Under the Internal Revenue Code of 1939, $300 of each of these payments (3% of $10,000) was includible in his gross income, and the remaining $700 was excludable therefrom during each of the taxable years mentioned. In computing B's investment in the contract as of January 1, 1954, the total amount excludable from his gross income during the years 1950 through 1953 ($2,800) must be subtracted from the consideration paid ($10,000). Accordingly, B's investment in the contract as of January 1, 1954, is $7,200 ($10,000 less $2,800).

Example (2). In 1945, C contracted for an annuity to be paid to him beginning December 31, 1960. In 1945 and in each successive year until 1960, he paid a premium of $5,000. Assuming he receives no payments of any kind under the contract until the date on which he receives the first annual payment as an annuity (December 31, 1960), his investment in the contract as of the annuity starting date (December 31, 1959) will be $75,000 ($5,000 paid each year for the 15 years from 1945 to 1959, inclusive).

Example (3). Assume the same facts as in example (2), except that prior to the annuity starting date C has already received from the insurer dividends of $1,000 each in 1949, 1954, and 1959, such dividends not being includible in his gross income in any of those years. C's investment in the contract, as of the annuity starting date, will then be $72,000 ($75,000 − $3,000).

(b) *Allocation of the investment in the contract where two or more annuity elements are acquired for a single consideration.* (1) In the case of a contract described in § 1.72-2(a)(2) which pro-

vides for two or more annuity elements, the investment in the contract determined under paragraph (a) shall be allocated to each of the annuity elements in the ratio that the expected return under each annuity element bears to the aggregate of the expected returns under all the annuity elements. The exclusion ratio for the contract as a whole shall be determined by dividing the investment in the contract (after adjustment for the present value of any or all refund features) by the aggregate of the expected returns under all the annuity elements. This may be illustrated by the following examples:

Example (1). If a contract provides for annuity payments of $1,000 per year for life (with no refund feature) to both A and B, a male and female, respectively, each 70 years of age as of the annuity starting date, such contract is acquired for consideration of $19,575 (without regard to whether paid by A, B, or both), and there is no post-June 1986 investment in the contract, the investment in the contract shall be allocated by determining the exclusion ratio for the contract as a whole in the following manner:

Expectancy of A under Table I and § 1.72-5(a)(2), 11.6 (12.1 − 0.5), multiplied by $1,000
.... $11,600
Plus: Expectancy of B computed in a similar manner ($1,000 × 14.5 [15.0 − 0.5]) 14,500

Total expected return 26,100

The exclusion ratio for both A and B is then $19,575, $26,100, or 75 percent. A and B shall each exclude from gross income three-fourths ($750) of each $1,000 annual payment received and shall include the remaining one-fourth ($250) of each $1,000 annual payment received in gross income.

Example (2). Assume the same facts as in example (1) except that of the total investment in the contract of $19,575, the pre-July 1986 invest-

ment in the contract is $10,000. If the election described in § 1.72-6(d)(6) is made with respect to the contract, the investment in the contract shall be allocated by determining an exclusion ratio for the contract as a whole based on separately computed exclusion ratios with respect to the pre-July 1986 investment in the contract and the post-June 1986 investment in the contract in the following manner:

Expectancy of A under Table I and § 1.72-5(a)(2), 11.6 (12.1 − 0.5), multiplied by $1,000
.... $11,600
Plus: Expectancy of B under Table I and § 1.72-5(a)(2), 14.5 (15.0 − 0.5), multiplied by
$1,000 .... $14,500
Pre-July 1986 expected return $26,100
Expectancy of A under Table V and § 1.72-5(a)(2), 15.5 (16.0 − 0.5), multiplied by $1,000
.... $15,500
Plus: Expectancy of B under Table V and § 1.72-5(a)(2), 15.5 (16.0 − 0.5), multiplied by
$1,000 .... $15,500
Post-June 1986 expected return $31,000

Pre-July 1986 exclusion ratio ($10,000 ÷ $26,100)................................ 38.3
Post-June 1986 exclusion ratio ($9,575 ÷ 31,000)................................ 30.9

A and B shall each exclude from gross income $692 (38.3 percent of $1,000 + 30.9 percent of $1,000) of each $1,000 payment and include the remaining $308 in gross income.

(2) In the case of a contract providing for specified annual annuity payments to be made to two persons during their joint lives and the payment of the aggregate of the two individual pay-

ments to the survivor for his life, the investment in the contract shall be allocated in accordance with the provisions of subparagraph (1) of this paragraph. For this purpose, the investment in the contract (without regard to the fact that differing amounts may have been contributed by the two annuitants) shall be divided by the expected return determined in accordance with paragraph (e)(4) of § 1.72-5. The resulting exclusion ratio shall then be applied to any amounts received as an annuity by either annuitant.

(3) In the case of a contract providing two or more annuity elements, one or more of which provides for payments to be made in a manner described in paragraph (b)(3) of § 1.72-2, the investment in the contract shall be allocated to the various annuity elements in the following manner.

(i) If all the annuity elements provide for payments to be made in the manner described in paragraph (b)(3) of § 1.72-2, the investment in the contract shall be allocated on the basis of the amounts received by each recipient by apportioning the amount determined to be excludable under that section to each recipient in the same ratio as the total of the amounts received by him in the taxable year bears to the total of the amounts received by all recipients during the same period; and

(ii) If one or more, but not all, of the annuity elements provide for payments to be made in a manner described in paragraph (b)(3) of § 1.72-2:

(a) With respect to all annuity elements to which that section does not apply, the investment in the contract for all such elements shall be the portion of the investment in the contract as a whole (found in accordance with the provisions of this section) which is properly allocable to all such elements; and

(b) With respect to all annuity elements to which paragraph (b)(3) of § 1.72-2 does apply, the investment in the contract for all such elements shall be the investment in the contract as a whole (found in accordance with the provisions of this section) as reduced by the portion thereof determined under (a) of this subdivision.

For the purpose of determining, pursuant to (a) of this subdivision, the portion of the investment in the contract as a whole properly allocable to a particular annuity element, reference shall be made to the present value of such annuity element determined in accordance with paragraph (e)(1)(iii)(b) of § 1.101-2.

(iii) In the case of a contract to which paragraph (d) of this section applies, this paragraph (b) is applied in the manner prescribed in paragraph (d) and, in particular, paragraph (d)(5)(v) of this section.

(c) *Special rules.* (1) For the special rule for determining the investment in the contract for a surviving annuitant in cases where the prior annuitant of a joint and survivor annuity contract died in 1951, 1952, or 1953, see paragraph (b)(3) of § 1.72-5.

(2) For special rules relating to the determination of the investment in the contract where employer contributions are involved, see § 1.72-8. See also paragraph (b) of § 1.72-16 for a special rule relating to the determination of the premiums or other consideration paid for a contract where an employee is taxable on the premiums paid for life insurance protection that is purchased by and considered to be a distribution from an exempt employees' trust.

(3) For the determination of an adjustment in investment in the contract in cases where a contract contains a refund feature, see § 1.72-7.

(4) In the case of "face-amount certificates" described in section 72(1), the amount of consideration paid for purposes of computing the investment in the contract shall include any amount added to the holder's basis by reason of section 1232(a)(3)(F) (relating to basis adjustment for amount of original issue discount ratably included in gross income as interest under section 1232(a)(3)).

(d) *Pre-July 1986 and post June 1986 investment in the contract.* (1) This paragraph (d) applies to an annuity contract if—

(i) The investment in the contract includes a pre-July 1986 investment in the contract and a post-June 1986 investment in the contract (both as defined in § 1.72-6(d)(3));

(ii) The use of a multiple found in Tables I through VIII of § 1.72-9 is required to determine the expected return under the contract; and

(iii) The election described in paragraph (d)(6) of this section is made with respect to the contract.

(2) In the case of an annuity contract to which this paragraph (d) applies—

(i) All computations required to determine the amount excludable from gross income shall be performed separately with respect to the pre-July 1986 investment in the contract and the post-June 1986 investment in the contract as if each such amount were the entire investment in the contract;

(ii) The multiples in Tables I through IV shall be used for computations involving the pre-July 1986 investment in the contract and the multiples in Tables V through VIII shall be used for computations involving the post-June 1986 investment in the contract; and

(iii) The amount excludable from gross income shall be the sum of the amounts determined

Reg. § 1.72-6(d)(2)

under the separate computations required by paragraph (d)(2)(i) of this section.

(3) For purposes of the regulations under section 72, the pre-July 1986 investment in the contract and post-June 1986 investment in the contract are determined in accordance with the following rules:

(i)(A) Except as provided in § 1.72-9, if the annuity starting date of the contract occurs before July 1, 1986, the pre-July 1986 investment in the contract is the total investment in the contract as of the annuity starting date;

(B) Except as provided in § 1.72-9, if the annuity starting date of the contract occurs after June 30, 1986, and the contract does not provide for a disqualifying form of payment or settlement, the pre-July 1986 investment in the contract is the investment in the contract computed as of June 30, 1986, as if June 30, 1986, had been the later of the annuity starting date of the contract or the date on which an amount is first received thereunder as an annuity;

(C) If the annuity starting date of the contract occurs after June 30, 1986, and the contract provides, at the option of the annuitant or of any other person (including, in the case of an employee's annuity, an option exercisable only by, or with the consent of, the employer), for a disqualifying form of payment or settlement, the pre-July 1986 investment in the contract is zero (i.e., the total investment in the contract is post-June 1986 investment in the contract).

(ii) The post-June 1986 investment in the contract is the amount by which the total investment in the contract as of the annuity starting date exceeds the pre-July 1986 investment in the contract.

(iii) For purposes of paragraph (d)(3)(i) of this section, a disqualifying form of payment or settlement is any form of payment or settlement (whether or not selected) that permits the receipt of amounts under the contract in a form other than a life annuity. For example, each of the following options provides for a disqualifying form of payment or settlement:

(A) An option to receive a lump sum in full discharge of the obligation under the contract.

(B) An option to receive an amount under the contract after June 30, 1986, and before the annuity starting date.

(C) An option to receive an annuity for a period certain.

(D) An option to receive payments under a refund feature (within the meaning of paragraphs (b) and (c) of this section) that is substantially equivalent to an annuity for a period certain.

(E) An option to receive a temporary life annuity (within the meaning of § 1.72-5(a)(3)) that is substantially equivalent to an annuity for a period certain.

An option to receive alternative forms of life annuity is not a disqualifying option for purposes of paragraph (d)(3)(i) of this section. Thus, if the sole options provided under a contract are a single life annuity and a joint and survivor life annuity, paragraph (d)(3)(i)(C) of this section does not apply to such contract.

(iv) For purposes of paragraph (d)(3)(iii) of this section, a refund feature is substantially equivalent to an annuity for a period certain if its value determined under Table VII of § 1.72-9 exceeds 50 percent. Similarly, a temporary life annuity is substantially equivalent to an annuity for a period certain if the multiple determined under Table VIII of § 1.72-9 exceeds 50 percent of the maximum duration of the annuity.

(4) In any separate computation under this paragraph (d), only the applicable portion of other amounts (such as the total expected return under the contract, or the total amount guaranteed under the contract as of the annuity starting date) shall be taken into account if the use of the entire amount in such computation is inconsistent with the use in the computation of only a portion of the investment in the contract. For example, such use is generally inconsistent if the computation requires a comparison of the investment in the contract and such other amount for the purpose of using the greater (or lesser) amount or the difference between the two. For purposes of the first sentence of this paragraph (d)(4), the applicable portion is the amount that bears the same ratio to the entire amount as the pre-July 1986, investment in the contract or the post-June 1986 investment in the contract, whichever is applicable, bears to the total investment in the contract as of the annuity starting date.

(5) *Application to particular computations.* (i) In the case of a contract to which this paragraph (d) applies, the exclusion ratio for purposes of § 1.72-4(a) is the sum of the exclusion ratios separately computed in accordance with this paragraph (d). The exclusion ratio with respect to the pre-July 1986 investment in the contract is determined by dividing the pre-July 1986 investment in the contract by the expected return as found under § 1.72-5 by applying the appropriate multiples of Tables I through IV of § 1.72-9. Similarly, the exclusion ratio with respect to the post-June 1986 investment in the contract is determined by dividing the post-June 1986 investment in the

Reg. § 1.72-6(d)(3)

contract by the expected return as found under § 1.72-5 by applying the appropriate multiples in Tables V through VIII of § 1.72-9.

(ii) The applicability of § 1.72-4(d)(2) to a contract to which this paragraph (d) applies shall be determined separately with respect to the post-June 1986 investment in the contract and the pre-July 1986 investment in the contract and in each such determination only the applicable portion of the total expected return under the contract shall be taken into account. If § 1.72-4(d)(2) applies with respect to either such investment in the contract, the separately computed exclusion ratio shall be considered to be the applicable portion of 100 percent.

(iii) If § 1.72-4(d)(3) applies to a contract to which this paragraph (d) applies—

(A) The applicable portions (as defined in paragraph (d)(4) of this section) of payments received under the contract for a taxable year shall be separately computed;

(B) The pre-July 1986 investment in the contract and the post-June 1986 investment in the contract shall be separately allocated to the taxable year; and

(C) The separate applicable portions of the payments received under the contract for the taxable year shall be considered to be amounts received as an annuity (for which the exclusion ratio is 100 percent) only to the extent they do not exceed the portions of the corresponding investments in the contract which are properly allocable to that year.

See the example in § 1.72-4(d)(3)(v).

(iv) If § 1.72-4(e) applies to a contract to which this paragraph (d) applies, the exclusion ratio shall be separately computed with respect to the pre-July 1986 investment in the contract and the post-June 1986 investment in the contract. For purposes of the separate computations under § 1.72-4(e)(2)(ii), only the applicable portion of payments received shall be taken into account and the exclusion ratio (100%) shall be applied to the separately computed portion allocated to each participant.

(v) If paragraph (b)(3) of this section applies to a contract to which this paragraph (d) applies, separate allocations are required with respect to the pre-July 1986 investment in the contract and the post-June 1986 investment in the contract. For purposes of the separate computations required to determine the portion of the investment in the contract properly allocable to a particular annuity element, only the applicable portion of the present value of the annuity ele-

ment determined in accordance with § 1.101-2(e)(1)(iii)(b) is taken into account.

(vi) If § 1.72-7 applies to a contract to which this paragraph (d) applies, separate computations are required to determine the adjustment to the pre-July 1986 investment in the contract and the post-June 1986 investment in the contract. For purposes of such separate computations, only the applicable portions of the amounts described in § 1.72-7(b)(3)(ii), (c)(1)(ii)(B), (c)(2)(vii)(B), and (d)(1)(ii) are taken into account. Similarly, in the case of computations with respect to the guarantee of a specified amount under § 1.72-7(d)(1), only the applicable portion of such amount is taken into account.

(6) This paragraph (d) applies to a contract only if the first taxpayer to receive an amount as an annuity under the contract elects to perform separate computations with respect to the pre-July 1986 investment in the contract and the post-June 1986 investment in the contract as if each such amount were the entire investment in contract. If two or more annuitants receive an amount as an annuity under the contract at the same time (such as under a joint-and-last-survivorship annuity contract), an election by one of the annuitants is treated as an election by each of the annuitants. The election is made by attaching a statement to the first return filed by the taxpayer for the first taxable year in which an amount is received as an annuity under the contract. The statement must indicate that the taxpayer is electing to apply the provisions of paragraph (d) of § 1.72-6, and must also contain the name, address, and taxpayer identification number of each annuitant under the contract, and the amount of the pre-July 1986 investment in the contract.

(7) If the investment in the contract includes a post-June 1986 investment in the contract and the election described in paragraph (d)(6) of this section is not made—

(i) The amount excludable from gross income shall be determined without regard to the separate computations described in this paragraph (d); and

(ii) Only the multiples found in Tables V through VIII shall be used in determining the amount excludable from gross income. [Reg. § 1.72-6.]

□ [*T.D.* 6211, 11-14-56. *Amended by T.D.* 6676, 9-16-63, *T.D.* 7311, 3-29-74 *and T.D.* 8115, 12-16-86.]

[Reg. § 1.72-7]

§ 1.72-7. Adjustment in investment where a contract contains a refund feature.—(a) *Defini-*

tion of a contract containing a refund feature. A contract to which section 72 applies, contains a refund feature if:

(1) The total amount receivable as an annuity under such contract depends, in whole or in part, on the continuing life of one or more persons,

(2) The contract provides for payments to be made to a beneficiary or the estate of an annuitant on or after the death of the annuitant if a specified amount or a stated number of payments has not been paid to the annuitant or annuitants prior to death, and

(3) Such payments are in the nature of a refund of the consideration paid. See paragraph (c)(1) of § 1.72-11.

(b) *Adjustment of investment for the refund feature in the case of a single life annuity.* Where a single life annuity contract to which section 72 applies contains a refund feature and the special rule of paragraph (d) of this section does not apply, the investment in the contract shall be adjusted in the following manner:

(1) Determine the number of years necessary for the guaranteed amount to be fully paid by dividing the maximum amount guaranteed as of the annuity starting date by the amount to be received annually under the contract to the extent such amount reduces the guaranteed amount. The number of years should be stated in terms of the nearest whole year, considering for this purpose a fraction of one-half or more as an additional whole year.

(2) Consult Table III or VII (whichever is applicable) of § 1.72-9 for the appropriate per-

centage under the whole number of years found in subparagraph (1) of this paragraph and the age (as of the annuity starting date) and, if applicable, sex of the annuitant.

(3) Multiply the percentage found in subparagraph (2) of this paragraph by whichever of the following is the smaller: (i) the investment in the contract found in accordance with § 1.72-6 or (ii) the total amount guaranteed as of the annuity starting date.

(4) Subtract the amount found in subparagraph (3) of this paragraph from the investment in the contract found in accordance with § 1.72-6.

The resulting amount is the investment in the contract adjusted for the present value of the refund feature without discount for interest and is to be used in determining the exclusion ratio to be applied to the payments received as an annuity. The percentage found in Table III or VII shall not be adjusted in a manner described in paragraph (a)(2) of § 1.72-5. These principles may be illustrated by the following examples:

Example (1). On January 1, 1954, a husband, age 65, purchased for $21,053, an immediate installment refund annuity payable $100 per month for life. The contract provided that in the event the husband did not live long enough to recover the full purchase price, payments were to be made to his wife until the total payments under the contract equaled the purchase price. The investment in the contract adjusted for the purpose of determining the exclusion ratio is computed in the following manner:

Cost of the annuity contract (investment in the contract, unadjusted)	$21,053
Amount to be received annually	$ 1,200
Number of years for which payment guaranteed ($21,053 divided by $1,200)	17.5
Rounded to nearest whole number of years	18
Percentage located in Table III for age 65 (age of the annuitant as of the annuity starting date) and 18 (the number of whole years) (percent)	30
Subtract value of the refund feature to the nearest dollar (30% of $21,053)	$ 6,316
Investment in the contract adjusted for the present value of the refund feature without discount for interest	$14,737

Example (2). Assume the same facts as in example (1), except that the total investment in the contract was made after June 30, 1986. The investment in the contract adjusted for the purpose of determining the exclusion ratio is computed as follows:

Cost of the annuity contract (investment in the contract, unadjusted)	$21,053
Amount to be received annually	$ 1,200
Number of years for which payment guaranteed ($21,053÷$1,200)	17.5
Rounded to nearest whole number of years	18
Percentage in Table VII for age 65 and 18 years (percent)	15
Subtract value of the refund feature to the nearest dollar (15 percent of $21,053)	$ 3,158
Investment in the contract adjusted for the present value of the refund feature without discount for interest	$17,895

Example (3). Assume the same facts as in example (1), except that the pre-July 1986 investment in the contract is $10,000 and the post-June 1986 investment in the contract is $11,053. If the annuitant makes the election described in § 1.72-6(d)(6), separate computations must be performed pursuant to § 1.72-6(d) to determine the adjusted investment in the contract. The pre-July 1986 investment in the contract and the post-June 1986 investment in the contract ad-justed for the purpose of determining the exclusion ratios are, respectively, $7,000 and $9,395, determined as follows:

Pre-July 1986 investment in the contract (unadjusted) $10,000
Pre-July 1986 portion of the amount to be received annually ($10,000/$21,053×$1,200).. $570.00
Number of years for which payment guaranteed ($10,000÷$570) 17.50
Rounded to nearest whole number of years 18
Percentage in Table III for age 65 and 18 years (percent) 30
Subtract value of the refund feature to the nearest dollar (30 percent of $10,000)........ $ 3,000
Pre-July 1986 investment in the contract adjusted for the present value of the refund
   feature without discount for interest .... $ 7,000

Post-June 1986 investment in the contract (unadjusted) $11,053
Post-June 1986 portion of the amount to be received annually ($11,053/$21,053×$1,200). $ 630
Number of years for which payment guaranteed ($11,053÷$630) 17.54
Rounded to nearest whole number of years 18
Percentage in Table VII for age 65 and 18 years (percent) 15
Subtract value of the refund feature to the nearest dollar (15 percent of $11,053)........ $ 1,658

Post-June 1986 investment in the contract adjusted for the present value of the refund
   feature without discount for interest .... $ 9,395

If, in the above examples, the guaranteed amount had exceeded the investment in the contract (or applicable portion thereof), the percentage found in Table III or VII (whichever is applicable) should have been applied to the lesser of these amounts since any excess of the guaranteed amount over the investment in the contract (as found under § 1.72-6) would not have constituted a refund of premiums or other consideration paid. In such a case, however, a different multiple might have been obtained from Table III or VII (whichever is applicable) since the number of years for which payments were guaranteed would have been greater.

(c) *Adjustment of investment for the refund feature in the case of a joint and survivor annuity.*—(1) Except as provided in paragraph (c)(2) of this section, if a joint and survivor annuity contract described in paragraph (b)(1), (2) or (6) of § 1.72-5 contains a refund feature and the special rule of paragraph (d) of this section does not apply, the investment in the contract shall be adjusted in the following manner:

(i) Find the percentage determined under the following formula:

$$V = \frac{\displaystyle\sum_{t=0}^{N-1} \frac{d_{x+t}}{l_x}\left[(N-\tfrac{1}{2}-t)-P\left(\frac{T_{y+t+1}-T_{y+t+M+1}}{l_y}\right)\right]}{N}$$

In which:

V = The percentage, rounded to the nearest whole percent,

x = The age at the nearest birthday of the primary annuitant,

y = The age at the nearest birthday of the survivor annuitant,

N = The guaranteed amount divided by the annual annuity payable to the primary annuitant, rounded to the nearest integer,

P = The annual annuity continued to the survivor annuitant divided by the annual annuity payable to the primary annuitant,

$$M = \frac{N-\tfrac{1}{2}-t}{P}$$

$$l_x = \text{The number of survivors at age x, } d = l_x - l_{x+1}, \text{ and}$$

$$T_x = \sum_{s=0}^{\infty} \tfrac{1}{2}\,(l_{x+s} + l_{x+s+1}).$$

(ii) Multiply the percentage found in paragraph (c)(1)(i) of this section by the lesser of (A) the investment in the contract found in accordance with § 1.72-6, or (B) the total amount guaranteed as of the annuity starting date.

(iii) Subtract the amount found in paragraph (c)(1)(ii) of this section from the investment in the contract found in accordance with § 1.72-6.

In the case of a contract providing for payments to be made to two persons in the manner described in paragraph (b)(6) of § 1.72-5, this paragraph (c)(1) is applied as though the older person were the primary annuitant and the younger person were the survivor annuitant. For purposes of this paragraph (c)(1), the number of survivors at age$_x$ (l_x) is determined under the following table:

x	lx	x	lx	x	lx
5	1000000.	42	982230.	79	665977.
6	999729.	43	981046.	80	637260.
7	999493.	44	979742.	81	607339.
8	999284.	45	978302.	82	575531.
9	999069.	46	976709.	83	541919.
10	998849.	47	974945.	84	506647.
11	998620.	48	972992.	85	469931.
12	998382.	49	970832.	86	432459.
13	998135.	50	968447.	87	394138.
14	997876.	51	966000.	88	355393.
15	997606.	52	963313.	89	316712.
16	997322.	53	960375.	90	278663.
17	997025.	54	957175.	91	242020.
18	996714.	55	953705.	92	207150.
19	996387.	56	949954.	93	174602.
20	996044.	57	945912.	94	144828.
21	995684.	58	941568.	95	118151.
22	995304.	59	936908.	96	94871.7
23	994905.	60	931903.	97	74863.6
24	994484.	61	926451.	98	58042.2
25	994041.	62	920540.	99	44176.1
26	993573.	63	914090.	100	32956.4
27	993080.	64	907011.	101	24044.8
28	992563.	65	899221.	102	17104.1
29	992024.	66	890428.	103	11815.5
30	991461.	67	880797.	104	7886.75
31	990876.	68	870298.	105	5054.94
32	990269.	69	858904.	106	3086.95
33	989638.	70	846565.	107	1778.82
34	988984.	71	832316.	108	955.465
35	988303.	72	816861.	109	470.955
36	987593.	73	800078.	110	208.668
37	986846.	74	781837.	111	80.7899
38	986055.	75	762012.	112	26.2340
39	985210.	76	740743.	113	6.69620
40	984298.	77	717689.	114	1.19385
41	983310.	78	692780.	115	.111460

(2) If the multiples in Tables I through IV of § 1.72-9 are used to determine any portion of the expected return under a contract described in paragraph (c)(1) of this section, only the post-June 1986 investment in the contract (if any) shall be adjusted in the manner described in paragraph (c)(1) of this section, and the pre-July 1986 investment in the contract shall, in the case of a

contract described in paragraph (b)(1) or (6) of § 1.72-5, be adjusted in the following manner:

(i) Determine the number of years necessary for the guaranteed amount to be fully paid by dividing the maximum amount guaranteed as of the annuity starting date by the amount to be received annually under the contract. The number of years should be stated in terms of the nearest whole year, considering for this purpose a

Reg. § 1.72-7(c)(2)

fraction of one-half or more as an additional whole year.

(ii) Consult Table III of § 1.72-9 for the appropriate percentages under the whole number of years found in subdivision (i) of this subparagraph and the age (as of the annuity starting date) and sex of each annuitant. If the annuitants are not of the same sex, substitute for the female annuitant a male annuitant 5 years younger, or for the male annuitant a female annuitant 5 years older, so that Table III will be entered in both cases with the ages of annuitants of the same sex.

(iii) Find the sum of the two percentages found in accordance with subdivision (ii) of this subparagraph.

(iv) To the age of the elder of the two annuitants (as determined under subdivision (ii) of this subparagraph), add the number of years (indicated in the table below) opposite the number of years by which such annuitants' ages differ:

Number of years difference in age (2 male annuitants or 2 female annuitants)	Addition to older age in years
0 to 1, inclusive	9
2 to 3, inclusive	8
4 to 5, inclusive	7
6 to 8, inclusive	6
9 to 11, inclusive	5
12 to 15, inclusive	4
16 to 20, inclusive	3
21 to 27, inclusive	2
28 to 42, inclusive	1
Over 42	0

(v) Consult Table III for the appropriate percentage under the whole number of years found in subdivision (i) of this subparagraph and the age and sex of the elder annuitant as adjusted under subdivision (iv) of this subparagraph.

(vi) Subtract the percentage obtained in subdivision (v) of this subparagraph from the sum of the percentages found under subdivision (iii) of this subparagraph. If the result is less than one, subdivisions (vii) and (viii) of this subparagraph shall be disregarded and no adjustment made to the investment in the contract.

(vii) Multiply the percentage found in subdivision (vi) of this subparagraph by whichever of the following is the smaller: (A) the investment in the contract found in accordance with § 1.72-6 or (B) the total amount guaranteed as of the annuity starting date.

(viii) Subtract the amount found in subdivision (vii) of this subparagraph from the invest-ment in the contract found in accordance with § 1.72-6.

(3) The principles of this paragraph (c) may be illustrated by the following examples:

Example (1). Prior to July 1, 1986, Taxpayer A, a 70-year old male, purchases a joint and last survivor annuity for $33,050. The contract provides for payments of $100 a month to be paid first to himself for life and then to B, his 40-year old daughter, if she survives him. The contract further provides that in the event both die before ten years' payments have been made, payments will be continued to C, a beneficiary, or to C's estate, until ten years' payments have been made. If there is no post-June 1986 investment in the contract, the investment in the contract adjusted for the purpose of determining the exclusion ratio is computed in the following manner:

Cost of the annuity contract (investment in the contract unadjusted)	$33,050
Guaranteed amount ($1,200 × 10)	$12,000
Percentage in Table III for male, age 70 (for female, age 75) for duration of the guarantee (10)	21
Percentage in Table III for female, age 40 (or male, age 35) for duration of the guarantee (10)	2
Sum of percentages obtained	23
Difference in years of age between two males, aged 70 and 35 (or 2 females, aged 75 and 40)	35
Addition, in years, to older age	1
Percentage in Table III for male one year older than A	22
Difference between percentages obtained (23 percent less 22 percent)	1
Value of the refund feature to the nearest dollar (1 percent of $12,000)	$ 120
Investment in the contract adjusted for present value of the refund feature	$32,930

Reg. § 1.72-7(c)(3)

Example (2). The facts are the same as in example (1), except that the total investment in the contract was made after June 30, 1986. A is 73 years of age, and B is A's 70 year old spouse. The percentage determined under the formula in paragraph (c)(1)(i) of this section is two percent. Thus, the amount determined under paragraph (c)(1)(ii) of this section is $240 (2 percent of $12,000), and the investment in the contract adjusted for the present value of the refund feature is $32,810 ($33,050 − $240).

(4) If an annuity described in paragraph (b) of § 1.72-5 contains a refund feature and the manner of determining the adjustment to the investment in the contract (or to any part of such investment) is not prescribed or requires use of the formula in paragraph (c)(1)(i) of this section, the Commissioner will determine the amount of the adjustment upon request. The request must contain the date of birth of each annuitant, the guaranteed amount, the annual annuity payable to each annuitant, and the annuity starting date. Send the request to the Commissioner of Internal Revenue, Attention: OP:E:EP:GA, Washington, D.C. 20224.

(d) *Adjustment of investment in the contract where paragraph (b)(3) of § 1.72-2 applies to payments.* (1) If paragraph (b)(3) of § 1.72-2 applies to payments to be made under a contract and this section also applies because of the provision for a refund feature, an adjustment shall be made to the investment in the contract in accordance with this paragraph before making the computations required by paragraph (d)(3) of § 1.72-4 and paragraph (b)(7) of § 1.72-5. In the case of the guarantee of a specified amount, the adjustment shall be made by applying the appropriate multiple from Table III or VII (whichever is applicable), as otherwise determined under this section, to the investment in the contract or the guaranteed amount, whichever is the lesser. The guarantee period shall be found by dividing the amount guaranteed by an amount determined by placing the payments received during the first taxable year (to the extent such payments reduce the guaranteed amount) on an annual basis. Thus, if monthly payments are first received by a taxpayer on a calendar year basis in August, his total payments (to the extent that they reduce the guaranteed amount) for the taxable year would be divided by 5 and multiplied by 12. The guaranteed amount would then be divided by the result of this computation to obtain the guarantee period. If the contract merely guarantees that proceeds from a unit or units of a fund shall be paid for a fixed number of years or the life (or lives) of an annuitant (or annuitants), whichever is the longer, the fixed number of years is the guarantee

period. The appropriate percentage in Table III or VII shall be applied to whichever of the following is the smaller: (i) the investment in the contract; or (ii) the product of the payments received in the first taxable year, placed on an annual basis, multiplied by the number of years for which payment of the proceeds of a unit or units is guaranteed.

(2) The principles of this paragraph may be illustrated by the following examples:

Example (1). Taxpayer A, a 50-year-old male, purchases for $25,000 a contract which provides for variable monthly payments to be paid to him for his life. The contract also provides that if he should die before receiving payments for fifteen years, payments shall continue according to the original formula to his estate or beneficiary until payments have been made for that period. Beginning with the month of September, A receives payments which total $450 for the first taxable year of receipt. This amount, placed on an annual basis, is $1,350 ($450 divided by 4, or $112.50; $112.50 multiplied by 12, or $1,350). If there is no post-June 1986 investment in the contract, the guaranteed amount is considered to be $20,250 ($1,350 × 15), and the multiple from Table III (found in the same manner as in paragraph (b) of this section), 9 percent, applied to $20,250 (since this amount is less than the investment in the contract), results in a refund adjustment of $1,822.50. The latter amount, subtracted from the investment in the contract of $25,000, results in an adjusted investment in the contract of $23,177.50. If A dies before receiving payments for 15 years and the remaining payments are made to B, his beneficiary, B shall exclude the entire amount of such payments from his gross income until the amounts so received by B, together with the amounts received by A and excludable from A's gross income, equal or exceed $25,000. Any excess and any payments thereafter received by B shall be fully includible in gross income.

Example (2). Assume the same facts as in example (1), except that the total investment in the contract was made after June 20, 1986. The applicable multiple found in Table VII is 3 percent. When this is applied to the guaranteed amount of $20,250, it results in a refund adjustment of $607.50. The adjusted investment in the contract is $24,392.50 ($25,000 − $607.50).

(e) *Adjustment of the investment in the contract where more than one annuity element is provided for a single consideration.* In the case of contracts to which paragraph (b) of § 1.72-6 applies for the purpose of allocating the investment in the contract to two or more annuity elements which are provided for a single consideration, if

Reg. § 1.72-7(c)(4)

one or more of such elements involves a refund feature, the portion of the investment in the contract properly allocable to each such element shall be adjusted for the refund feature before aggregating all the investments in order to obtain the exclusion ratio which is to apply to the contract as a whole.

Example (1). If taxpayer A, an insured 70 years of age, upon maturity of an endowment policy which cost him a net amount of $86,000, elected a dual settlement consisting of (1) monthly payments for his life aggregating $4,146 per year with 10 years' payments certain, and (2) monthly payments for his 60 year old brother, B, aggregating $2,820 per year with 20 years' payments certain, the exclusion ratio to be used by both A and B if there is no post-June 1988 investment in the contract would be determined in the following manner:

A's expected return (A's payments per year of $4,146 multiplied by his life expectancy from Table 1 of 12.1)	$ 50,166.60
B's expected return (B's payments per year of $2,820 multiplied by his life expectancy from Table 1 of 18.2)	$ 51,324.00
Sum of expected returns to be used in determining exclusion ratio	$101,490.60
Percentage of total expected return attributable to A's expectancy of life ($50,166.60 ÷ $101,490.60)	49.4
Percentage of total expected return attributable to B's expectancy of life ($51,324/$101,490.60)	50.6
Portion of investment in the contract allocable to A's annuity (49.4 percent of $86,000)	$ 42,484.00
Portion of investment in the contract allocable to B's annuity (50.6 percent of $86,000)	$ 43,516.00
Value of the refund feature with respect ot A's annuity (percentage from Table III for male, age 70, and duration 10, or 21 percent, multiplied by lesser of guaranteed amount and allocable portion of investment in the contract, $41,460)	$ 8,707.00
A's allocable portion of the investment in the contract adjusted for refund feature ($42,484 less $8,707.00)	$ 33,777.00
Value of the refund feature with respect to B's annuity (percentage from Table III for male, age 60, and duration 20, or 25 percent, multiplied by lesser of guaranteed amount and allocable portion of investment in the contract, $43,516)	$ 10,879.00
B's allocable portion of the investment in the contract adjusted for refund feature ($43,516 less $10,879.00)	$ 32,637.00
Sum of A's and B's allocable portions of the investment in the contract after adjustment for the refund feature	$ 66,414.00
Exclusion ratio for the contract as a whole (total adjusted investment in the contract, $66,414, divided by the total expected return from above, $101,490.60) (percent) ..	65.4

Example (2). Assume the same facts as in example (1) except that the total investment in the contract was made after June 30, 1986. The exclusion ratio to be used by both A and B would be 56.9 percent, determined as follows:

A's expected return (A's payments per year of $41,146 multiplied by his life expectancy from Table V of 16.0)	$ 66,336.00
B's expected return (B's payments per year of $2,820 multiplied by his life expectancy from Table V of 24.2)	$ 68,244.00
Sum of expected returns to be used in determining exclusion ratio	$134,580.00
Percentage of total expected return attributable to A's expectancy of life ($66,336.00 ÷ $134,580.00)	49.3
Percentage of total expected return attributable to B's expectancy of life ($68,244.00 ÷ $134,580.00)	50.7
Portion of investment in the contract allocable to A's annuity (49.3 percent of $86,000)	$ 42,398.00
Portion of investment in the contract allocable to B's annuity (50.7 percent of $86,000)	$ 43,602.00
Value of the refund feature with respect to A's annuity (percentage from Table VII for age 70 and duration 10, or 11 percent, multiplied by lesser of the guaranteed amount and allocable portion of investment in the contract, $41,460)	$ 4,560.60
A's allocable portion of the investment in the contract adjusted for refund feature ($42,398 less $4,560.60)	$ 37,837.40

Reg. § 1.72-7(e)

Value of the refund feature with respect to B's annuity (percentage from Table VII for age 60 and duration 20, or 11 percent, multiplied by lesser of guaranteed amount and allocable portion of investment in the contract, $43,602) .... $ 4,796.22

B's allocable portion of the investment in the contract adjusted for refund feature ($43,602 less $4,796.22) .... $ 38,805.78

Sum of A's and B's allocable portions of the investment in the contract after adjustment for the refund feature .... $ 76,643.18

Exclusion ratio for the contract as a whole (total adjusted investment in the contract, $76,643.18, divided by the total expected return from above, $134,580.00) (percent) 56.9

(f) *Adjustment of investment in the contract with respect to contracts subject to § 1.72-6(d).* In the case of a contract to which § 1.72-6(d) (relating to contracts in which amounts were invested both before July 1, 1986, and after June 30, 1986) applies, this section is applied in the manner prescribed in § 1.72-6(d) and, in particular, § 1.72-6(d)(5)(vi).

[Reg. § 1.72-7.]

☐ [T.D. 6211, 11-14-56. *Amended by T.D.* 8115, 12-16-86.]

[Reg. § 1.72-8]

§ 1.72-8. Effect of certain employer contributions with respect to premiums or other consideration paid or contributed by an employee.—(a) *Contributions in the nature of compensation*—(1) *Amounts includible in gross income of employee under subtitle A of the Code or prior income tax laws.* Section 72(f) provides that for the purposes of section 72(c), (d), and (e), amounts contributed by an employer for the benefit of an employee or his beneficiaries shall constitute consideration paid or contributed by the employee to the extent that such amounts were includible in the gross income of the employee under subtitle A of the Code or prior income tax laws. Amounts to which this paragraph applies include, for example, contributions made by an employer to or under a trust or plan which fails to qualify under the provisions of section 401(a), provided that the employee's rights to such contributions are nonforfeitable at the time the contributions are made. See sections 402(b) and 403(c) and the regulations thereunder. This subparagraph also applies to premiums paid by an employer (other than premiums paid on behalf of an owner-employee) for life insurance protection for an employee if such premiums are includible in the gross income of the employee when paid. See § 1.72-16. However, such premiums shall only be considered as premiums and other consideration paid by the employee with respect to any benefits attributable to the contract providing the life insurance protection. See § 1.72-16.

(2) *Amounts not includible in gross income of employee at time contributed if paid directly to employee at that time.* Except as provided in subparagraph (3) of this paragraph, section 72(f) provides that for the purposes of section 72(c), (d), and (e), amounts contributed by an employer for the benefit of an employee or his beneficiaries shall constitute consideration paid or contributed by the employee to the extent that such amounts would not have been includible in the gross income of the employee at the time contributed had they been paid directly to the employee at that time. Amounts to which this subparagraph applies include, for example, contributions made by an employer after December 31, 1950, and before January 1, 1963, if made on account of foreign services rendered by an employee during a period in which the employee qualified as a bona fide resident of a foreign country under section 911(a) of the Internal Revenue Code of 1954, or under section 116(a) of the Internal Revenue Code of 1939. In such a case, it would be immaterial whether such contributions were made under a qualified plan or otherwise. See subparagraph (4) of this paragraph for rules governing the determination of the amount of employer foreign service contributions to which this subparagraph applies. On the other hand, if contributions are made by an employer to a qualified plan at a time when compensation paid directly to the employee concerned with respect to the same services rendered would have been includible in the gross income of the employee, such as in the case of an employee of a State government where contributions are made in 1955 with respect to services rendered by the employee prior to the year 1939, this subparagraph does not apply to such contributions.

(3) *Limitation*—(i) *In general.* Except as provided in subdivision (ii) of this subparagraph, the provisions of subparagraph (2) of this paragraph shall not apply to amounts which were contributed by the employer after December 31, 1962, and which would not have been includible in the gross income of the employee by reason of the application of section 911, if such amounts had been paid directly to the employee at the time of contribution. Employer contributions attributable to foreign services performed by the employee after December 31, 1962, do not constitute, for purposes of section 72(c), (d), and (e), consideration paid or contributed by the employee.

(ii) *Exception.* The provisions of subdivision (i) of this subparagraph shall not apply to amounts which were contributed by the employer to provide pension or annuity credits (determined in accordance with the provisions of subparagraph (4) of this paragraph) to the extent such credits are—

(a) Attributable to foreign services performed before January 1, 1963, with respect to which the employee qualified for the benefits of section 911(a) (or corresponding provisions of prior revenue laws), and

(b) Provided pursuant to pension or annuity plan provisions in existence on March 12, 1962, and on that date applicable to such services. Amounts described in this subdivision constitute, for purposes of section 72(c), (d), and (e), consideration paid or contributed by the employee even though such amounts are contributed by the employer after December 31, 1962.

(4) *Determination of employer foreign service contributions which constitute consideration paid or contributed by the employee.* For purposes of subparagraphs (2) and (3)(ii) of this paragraph, employer foreign service contributions which constitute, for purposes of section 72(c), (d), and (e), consideration paid or contributed by the employee shall be determined as follows:

(i) *Treatment of identifiable contributions.* If, under the terms of the pension or annuity plan under which employer contributions were made, such contributions may be identified as—

(a) Attributable to foreign services performed before January 1, 1963, with respect to which the employee qualified for the benefits of section 911(a) (or corresponding provisions of prior revenue laws), and

(b) Made under pension or annuity plan provisions in existence on March 12, 1962, which were applicable to the services referred to in (a) of this subdivision on that date,

the amount of employer contributions so identified shall be considered paid or contributed by the employee.

(ii) *Alternative rule for unidentifiable contributions.* If employer contributions may not be identified in the manner described in subdivision (i) of this subparagraph, the amount of employer contributions attributable to foreign services performed before January 1, 1963, and considered paid or contributed by the employee shall be determined on the basis of an estimated allocation which is reasonable and consistent with the circumstances and the provisions of the pension or annuity plan under which such contributions are made. For example, if an employee's benefits

under a pension or annuity plan, which is unchanged after March 12, 1962, are determined with respect to his basic compensation during his entire period of credited service, the amount of employer contributions considered paid or contributed by the employee shall be an amount which bears the same ratio to total employer contributions for such employee under the pension or annuity plan as his basic compensation attributable to foreign services performed before January 1, 1963, with respect to which he qualified for the benefits of section 911(a) (or corresponding provisions of prior revenue laws) bears to his total basic compensation. On the other hand, if an employee's benefits under a pension or annuity plan, which is unchanged after March 12, 1962, are determined with respect to his basic compensation during his final five years of credited service, the amount of employer contributions considered paid or contributed by the employee shall be an amount which bears the same ratio to total employer contributions for such employee as his number of years of credited service before January 1, 1963, with respect to which he qualified for the benefits of section 911(a) (or corresponding provisions of prior revenue laws) bears to his total number of years of credited service.

(5) *Amounts not includible in gross income of employee under subtitle A of the Code or prior income tax laws.* Amounts contributed by an employer which were not includible in the gross income of the employee under subtitle A of the Code or prior income tax laws, but which would have been includible therein had they been paid directly to the employee, do not constitute consideration paid or contributed by the employee for the purposes of section 72. For example, contributions made by an employer under a qualified employees' trust or plan, which contributions would have been includible in the gross income of the employee had such contributions been paid to him directly as compensation, do not constitute consideration paid or contributed by the employee. Accordingly, the aggregate amount of premiums or other consideration paid or contributed by an employee, insofar as compensatory employer contributions are concerned, consists solely of the (i) sum of all amounts actually contributed by the employee, plus (ii) contributions in the nature of compensation which are deemed to be paid or contributed by the employee under this paragraph.

(b) *Contributions in the nature of death benefits.* In the case of an employee's beneficiary, the aggregate amount of premiums or other consideration paid or deemed to be paid or contributed by the employee shall also include:

Reg. § 1.72-8(b)

(1) Amounts (other than amounts paid as an annuity) to the extent such amounts are excludable from the beneficiary's gross income as a death benefit under section 101(b), and

(2) Any amount or amounts of death benefits which are treated as additional consideration contributed by the employee under section 101(b)(2)(D) and the regulations thereunder, or which were excludable from the beneficiary's gross income as a death benefit under section 22(b)(1)(B) of the Internal Revenue Code of 1939 and the regulations thereunder.

Accordingly, in the case of an employee's beneficiary, any such amount shall be added to any amount or amounts deemed paid or contributed by the employee under paragraph (a)(1) of this section and to any amounts actually contributed by the employee for the purpose of finding the aggregate amount of premiums or other consideration paid or contributed by the employee.

(c) *Amounts "made available" to an employee or his beneficiary.* Any amount which, although not actually paid, is made available to and includible in the gross income of an employee or his beneficiary under the rules of sections 402 and 403 and the regulations thereunder, shall be considered an amount contributed by the employee and shall be aggregated with amounts, if any, to which paragraphs (a) and (b) of this section apply for the purpose of determining the aggregate amount of premiums or other consideration paid by the employee.

(d) *Amounts includible in gross income of employee when his rights under annuity contract change to nonforfeitable rights.* Any amount which, by reason of section 403(d) and after the application of paragraph (b) of § 1.403(b)-1, is required to be included in an employee's gross income for the year when his rights under an annuity contract change from forfeitable to nonforfeitable rights shall be considered an amount contributed by the employee and shall be aggregated with amounts, if any, to which paragraphs (a), (b), and (c) of this section apply for the purpose of determining the aggregate amount of premiums or other consideration paid or contributed by the employee for such annuity contract. In other words, if, under section 403(d), an employee of an organization exempt from tax under section 501(a) or 521(a) is required to include an amount in gross income by reason of his rights under an annuity contract changing from forfeitable to nonforfeitable rights, such amount, to the extent it is not excludable from gross income under paragraph (b) of § 1.403(b)-1, shall be con-

sidered an amount contributed by such employee for the annuity contract. [Reg. § 1.72-8.]

☐ [*T.D. 6211, 11-14-56. Amended by T.D. 6665, 7-15-63 and T.D. 6783, 12-23-64.*]

[Reg. § 1.72-9]

§ **1.72-9. Tables.**—The following tables are to be used in connection with computations under section 72 and the regulations thereunder. Tables I, II, IIA, III, and IV are to be used if the investment in the contract does not include a post-June 1986 investment in the contract (as defined in § 1.72-6(d)(3)). Tables V, VI, VIA, VII, and VIII are to be used if the investment in the contract includes a post-June 1986 investment in the contract (as defined in § 1.72-6(d)(3)).

In the case of a contract under which amounts are received as an annuity after June 30, 1986, a taxpayer receiving such amounts may elect to treat the entire investment in the contract as post-June 1986 investment in the contract and thus apply Tables V through VIII. A taxpayer may make the election for any taxable year in which such amounts are received by attaching to the taxpayer's return for such taxable year a statement that the taxpayer is electing under § 1.72-9 to treat the entire investment in the contract as post-June 1986 investment in the contract. The statement must contain the taxpayer's name, address, and taxpayer identification number. The election is irrevocable and applies with respect to all amounts that the taxpayer receives as an annuity under the contract in the taxable year for which the election is made or in any subsequent taxable year. (Note that for purposes of the examples in §§ 1.72-4 through 1.72-11 the election described in this section is disregarded, (i.e., it is assumed that the taxpayer does not make an election under this section).)

See also § 1.72-6(d)(3) for rules treating the entire investment in a contract as post-June 1986 investment in a contract if the annuity starting date of the contract is after June 30, 1986, and the contract provides for a disqualifying form of payment or settlement, such as an option to receive a lump sum in full discharge of the obligation under the contract. In addition, see § 1.72-6(d) for special rules concerning the tables to be used and the separate computations required if the investment in the contract includes both a pre-July 1986 investment in the contract and a post-June 1986 investment in the contract and the election described in § 1.72-6(d)(6) is made with respect to the contract.

Reg. § 1.72-9

See p. 20,601 for regulations not amended to reflect law changes

TABLE I.—ORDINARY LIFE ANNUITIES—ONE LIFE—EXPECTED RETURN MULTIPLES

Male	Female	Multiples	Male	Female	Multiples	Male	Female	Multiples
6	11	65.0	41	46	33.0	76	81	9.1
7	12	64.1	42	47	32.1	77	82	8.7
8	13	63.2	43	48	31.2	78	83	8.3
9	14	62.3	44	49	30.4	79	84	7.8
10	15	61.4	45	50	29.6	80	85	7.5
11	16	60.4	46	51	28.7	81	86	7.1
12	17	59.5	47	52	27.9	82	87	6.7
13	18	58.6	48	53	27.1	83	88	6.3
14	19	57.7	49	54	26.3	84	89	6.0
15	20	56.7	50	55	25.5	85	90	5.7
16	21	55.8	51	56	24.7	86	91	5.4
17	22	54.9	52	57	24.0	87	92	5.1
18	23	53.9	53	58	23.2	88	93	4.8
19	24	53.0	54	59	22.4	89	94	4.5
20	25	52.1	55	60	21.7	90	95	4.2
21	26	51.1	56	61	21.0	91	96	4.0
22	27	50.2	57	62	20.3	92	97	3.7
23	28	49.3	58	63	19.6	93	98	3.5
24	29	48.3	59	64	18.9	94	99	3.3
25	30	47.4	60	65	18.2	95	100	3.1
26	31	46.5	61	66	17.5	96	101	2.9
27	32	45.6	62	67	16.9	97	102	2.7
28	33	44.6	63	68	16.2	98	103	2.5
29	34	43.7	64	69	15.6	99	104	2.3
30	35	42.8	65	70	15.0	100	105	2.1
31	36	41.9	66	71	14.4	101	106	1.9
32	37	41.0	67	72	13.8	102	107	1.7
33	38	40.0	68	73	13.2	103	108	1.5
34	39	39.1	69	74	12.6	104	109	1.3
35	40	38.2	70	75	12.1	105	110	1.2
						106	111	1.0
36	41	37.3	71	76	11.6	107	112	.8
37	42	36.5	72	77	11.0	108	113	.7
38	43	35.6	73	78	10.5	109	114	.6
39	44	34.7	74	79	10.1	110	115	.5
40	45	33.8	75	80	9.6	111	116	0

TABLE II.—ORDINARY JOINT LIFE AND LAST SURVIVOR ANNUITIES—TWO LIVES—EXPECTED RETURN MULTIPLES

Male	Male	6	7	8	9	10	11	12	13	14	15	16	17	18	19	20
Male	Female	11	12	13	14	15	16	17	18	19	20	21	22	23	24	25
6	11	73.5	73.0	72.6	72.2	71.8	71.4	71.0	70.7	70.4	70.0	69.7	69.5	69.2	68.9	68.7
7	12	73.0	72.6	72.1	71.7	71.3	70.9	70.5	70.1	69.8	69.4	69.1	68.8	68.5	68.3	68.0
8	13	72.6	72.1	71.6	71.2	70.8	70.4	70.0	69.6	69.2	68.9	68.5	68.2	67.9	67.6	67.3
9	14	72.2	71.7	71.2	70.7	70.3	69.9	69.4	69.0	68.7	68.3	67.9	67.6	67.3	67.0	66.7
10	15	71.8	71.3	70.8	70.3	69.8	69.4	68.9	68.5	68.1	67.7	67.4	67.0	66.7	66.4	66.1
11	16	71.4	70.9	70.4	69.9	69.4	68.9	68.5	68.0	67.6	67.2	66.8	66.5	66.1	65.8	65.4
12	17	71.0	70.5	70.0	69.4	68.9	68.5	68.0	67.5	67.1	66.7	66.3	65.9	65.5	65.2	64.8
13	18	70.7	70.1	69.6	69.0	68.5	68.0	67.5	67.1	66.6	66.2	65.8	65.4	65.0	64.6	64.2
14	19	70.4	69.8	69.2	68.7	68.1	67.6	67.1	66.6	66.1	65.7	65.3	64.8	64.4	64.0	63.7
15	20	70.0	69.4	68.9	68.3	67.7	67.2	66.7	66.2	65.7	65.2	64.8	64.3	63.9	63.5	63.1
16	21	69.7	69.1	68.5	67.9	67.4	66.8	66.3	65.8	65.3	64.8	64.3	63.8	63.4	63.0	62.6
17	22	69.5	68.8	68.2	67.6	67.0	66.5	65.9	65.4	64.8	64.3	63.8	63.4	62.9	62.5	62.0
18	23	69.2	68.5	67.9	67.3	66.7	66.1	65.5	65.0	64.4	63.9	63.4	62.9	62.4	62.0	61.5
19	24	68.9	68.3	67.6	67.0	66.4	65.8	65.2	64.6	64.0	63.5	63.0	62.5	62.0	61.5	61.0
20	25	68.7	68.0	67.3	66.7	66.1	65.4	64.8	64.2	63.7	63.1	62.6	62.0	61.5	61.0	60.6

TABLE II.—ORDINARY JOINT LIFE AND LAST SURVIVOR ANNUITIES—TWO LIVES—
EXPECTED RETURN MULTIPLES—Continued

Ages															
	Male	21	22	23	24	25	26	27	28	29	30	31	32	33	34
Male	Female	26	27	28	29	30	31	32	33	34	35	36	37	38	39
6	11	68.4	68.2	68.0	67.8	67.6	67.5	67.3	67.1	67.0	66.8	66.7	66.6	66.5	66.4
7	12	67.8	67.5	67.3	67.1	66.9	66.7	66.5	66.4	66.2	66.1	65.9	65.8	65.7	65.6
8	13	67.1	66.8	66.6	66.4	66.2	66.0	65.8	65.6	65.4	65.3	65.1	65.0	64.9	64.7
9	14	66.4	66.2	65.9	65.7	65.4	65.2	65.0	64.8	64.7	64.5	64.3	64.2	64.1	63.9
10	15	65.8	65.5	65.2	65.0	64.7	64.5	64.3	64.1	63.9	63.7	63.6	63.4	63.3	63.1
11	16	65.1	64.8	64.6	64.3	64.1	63.8	63.6	63.4	63.2	63.0	62.8	62.6	62.5	62.3
12	17	64.5	64.2	63.9	63.6	63.4	63.1	62.9	62.7	62.4	62.2	62.0	61.9	61.7	61.5
13	18	63.9	63.6	63.3	63.0	62.7	62.4	62.2	61.9	61.7	61.5	61.3	61.1	60.9	60.8
14	19	63.3	63.0	62.7	62.3	62.0	61.8	61.5	61.2	61.0	60.8	60.6	60.4	60.2	60.0
15	20	62.7	62.4	62.0	61.7	61.4	61.1	60.8	60.6	60.3	60.1	59.8	59.6	59.4	59.2
16	21	62.2	61.8	61.4	61.1	60.8	60.5	60.2	59.9	59.6	59.4	59.1	58.9	58.7	58.5
17	22	61.6	61.2	60.9	60.5	60.2	59.8	59.5	59.2	58.9	58.7	58.4	58.2	57.9	57.7
18	23	61.1	60.7	60.3	59.9	59.6	59.2	58.9	58.6	58.3	58.0	57.7	57.5	57.2	57.0
19	24	60.6	60.2	59.7	59.4	59.0	58.6	58.3	57.9	57.6	57.3	57.0	56.8	56.5	56.3
20	25	60.1	59.6	59.2	58.8	58.4	58.0	57.7	57.3	57.0	56.7	56.4	56.1	55.8	55.6
21	26	59.6	59.1	58.7	58.3	57.9	57.5	57.1	56.7	56.4	56.0	55.7	55.4	55.1	54.9
22	27	59.1	58.7	58.2	57.7	57.3	56.9	56.5	56.1	55.8	55.4	55.1	54.8	54.5	54.2
23	28	58.7	58.2	57.7	57.2	56.8	56.4	55.9	55.5	55.2	54.8	54.4	54.1	53.8	53.5
24	29	58.3	57.7	57.2	56.8	56.3	55.8	55.4	55.0	54.6	54.2	53.8	53.5	53.2	52.8
25	30	57.9	57.3	56.8	56.3	55.8	55.3	54.9	54.4	54.0	53.6	53.2	52.9	52.5	52.2
26	31	57.5	56.9	56.4	55.8	55.3	54.8	54.4	53.9	53.5	53.1	52.7	52.3	51.9	51.6
27	32	57.1	56.5	55.9	55.4	54.9	54.4	53.9	53.4	53.0	52.5	52.1	51.7	51.3	50.9
28	33	56.7	56.1	55.5	55.0	54.4	53.9	53.4	52.9	52.4	52.0	51.6	51.1	50.7	50.3
29	34	56.4	55.8	55.2	54.6	54.0	53.5	53.0	52.4	52.0	51.5	51.0	50.6	50.2	49.8
30	35	56.0	55.4	54.8	54.2	53.6	53.1	52.5	52.0	51.5	51.0	50.5	50.1	49.6	49.2
31	36	55.7	55.1	54.4	53.8	53.2	52.7	52.1	51.6	51.0	50.5	50.0	49.5	49.1	48.7
32	37	55.4	54.8	54.1	53.5	52.9	52.3	51.7	51.1	50.6	50.1	49.5	49.1	48.6	48.1
33	38	55.1	54.5	53.8	53.2	52.5	51.9	51.3	50.7	50.2	49.6	49.1	48.6	48.1	47.6
34	39	54.9	54.2	53.5	52.8	52.2	51.6	50.9	50.3	49.8	49.2	48.7	48.1	47.6	47.1

Ages															
	Male	35	36	37	38	39	40	41	42	43	44	45	46	47	48	49
Male	Female	40	41	42	43	44	45	46	47	48	49	50	51	52	53	54
6	11	66.3	66.2	66.1	66.0	65.9	65.9	65.8	65.7	65.7	65.6	65.6	65.5	65.5	65.5	65.4
7	12	65.4	65.3	65.3	65.2	65.1	65.0	64.9	64.9	64.8	64.8	64.7	64.7	64.6	64.6	64.5
8	13	64.6	64.5	64.4	64.3	64.2	64.2	64.1	64.0	64.0	63.9	63.8	63.8	63.7	63.7	63.7
9	14	63.8	63.7	63.6	63.5	63.4	63.3	63.2	63.2	63.1	63.0	63.0	62.9	62.9	62.8	62.8
10	15	63.0	62.9	62.8	62.7	62.6	62.5	62.4	62.3	62.2	62.2	62.1	62.0	62.0	61.9	61.9
11	16	62.2	62.1	61.9	61.8	61.7	61.6	61.5	61.4	61.3	61.3	61.2	61.1	61.1	61.0	61.0
12	17	61.4	61.3	61.1	61.0	60.9	60.8	60.7	60.6	60.5	60.4	60.4	60.3	60.2	60.2	60.1
13	18	60.6	60.5	60.3	60.2	60.1	60.0	59.9	59.8	59.7	59.6	59.5	59.4	59.4	59.3	59.2
14	19	59.8	59.7	59.5	59.4	59.3	59.1	59.0	58.9	58.8	58.7	58.6	58.6	58.5	58.4	58.4
15	20	59.0	58.9	58.7	58.6	58.4	58.3	58.2	58.1	58.0	57.9	57.8	57.7	57.6	57.6	57.5
16	21	58.3	58.1	57.9	57.8	57.6	57.5	57.4	57.2	57.1	57.0	56.9	56.8	56.8	56.7	56.6
17	22	57.5	57.3	57.2	57.0	56.8	56.7	56.6	56.4	56.3	56.2	56.1	56.0	55.9	55.8	55.7
18	23	56.8	56.6	56.4	56.2	56.0	55.9	55.7	55.6	55.5	55.4	55.2	55.1	55.1	55.0	54.9
19	24	56.0	55.8	55.6	55.4	55.3	55.1	54.9	54.8	54.7	54.5	54.4	54.3	54.2	54.1	54.0
20	25	55.3	55.1	54.9	54.7	54.5	54.3	54.1	54.0	53.8	53.7	53.6	53.5	53.4	53.3	53.2
21	26	54.6	54.4	54.1	53.9	53.7	53.5	53.4	53.2	53.0	52.9	52.8	52.6	52.5	52.4	52.3
22	27	53.9	53.6	53.4	53.2	53.0	52.8	52.6	52.4	52.2	52.1	51.9	51.8	51.7	51.6	51.5
23	28	53.2	52.9	52.7	52.5	52.2	52.0	51.8	51.6	51.5	51.3	51.1	51.0	50.9	50.7	50.6
24	29	52.5	52.3	52.0	51.7	51.5	51.3	51.1	50.9	50.7	50.5	50.3	50.2	50.0	49.9	49.8
25	30	51.9	51.6	51.3	51.0	50.8	50.5	50.3	50.1	49.9	49.7	49.6	49.4	49.2	49.1	49.0
26	31	51.2	50.9	50.6	50.3	50.1	49.8	49.6	49.4	49.2	49.0	48.8	48.6	48.4	48.3	48.1
27	32	50.6	50.3	50.0	49.7	49.4	49.1	48.9	48.6	48.4	48.2	48.0	47.8	47.6	47.5	47.3
28	33	50.0	49.6	49.3	49.0	48.7	48.4	48.2	47.9	47.7	47.5	47.2	47.1	46.9	46.7	46.5
29	34	49.4	49.0	48.7	48.3	48.0	47.7	47.5	47.2	47.0	46.7	46.5	46.3	46.1	45.9	45.7
30	35	48.8	48.4	48.1	47.7	47.4	47.1	46.8	46.5	46.2	46.0	45.8	45.5	45.3	45.2	45.0
31	36	48.2	47.8	47.5	47.1	46.8	46.4	46.1	45.8	45.6	45.3	45.0	44.8	44.6	44.4	44.2
32	37	47.7	47.3	46.9	46.5	46.1	45.8	45.5	45.2	44.9	44.6	44.3	44.1	43.9	43.7	43.4
33	38	47.2	46.7	46.3	45.9	45.5	45.2	44.8	44.5	44.2	43.9	43.7	43.4	43.2	42.9	42.7
34	39	46.7	46.2	45.8	45.4	45.0	44.6	44.2	43.9	43.6	43.3	43.0	42.7	42.5	42.2	42.0

Reg. § 1.72-9

TABLE II.—ORDINARY JOINT LIFE AND LAST SURVIVOR ANNUITIES—TWO LIVES—
EXPECTED RETURN MULTIPLES—Continued

Ages															
	Male	50	51	52	53	54	55	56	57	58	59	60	61	62	63
Male	Female	55	56	57	58	59	60	61	62	63	64	65	66	67	68
6	11	65.4	65.4	65.3	65.3	65.3	65.3	65.3	65.2	65.2	65.2	65.2	65.2	65.2	65.2
7	12	64.5	64.5	64.4	64.4	64.4	64.4	64.4	64.3	64.3	64.3	64.3	64.3	64.3	64.2
8	13	63.6	63.6	63.5	63.5	63.5	63.5	63.4	63.4	63.4	63.4	63.4	63.4	63.3	63.3
9	14	62.7	62.7	62.7	62.6	62.6	62.6	62.6	62.5	62.5	62.5	62.5	62.5	62.4	62.4
10	15	61.8	61.8	61.8	61.7	61.7	61.7	61.6	61.6	61.6	61.6	61.6	61.6	61.5	61.5
11	16	61.0	60.9	60.9	60.8	60.8	60.8	60.7	60.7	60.7	60.7	60.7	60.6	60.6	60.6
12	17	60.1	60.0	60.0	59.9	59.9	59.9	59.8	59.8	59.8	59.8	59.7	59.7	59.7	59.7
13	18	59.2	59.1	59.1	59.0	59.0	59.0	58.9	58.9	58.9	58.9	58.8	58.8	58.8	58.8
14	19	58.3	58.2	58.2	58.2	58.1	58.1	58.0	58.0	58.0	57.9	57.9	57.9	57.9	57.9
15	20	57.4	57.4	57.3	57.3	57.2	57.2	57.1	57.1	57.1	57.0	57.0	57.0	57.0	56.9
16	21	56.5	56.5	56.4	56.4	56.3	56.3	56.2	56.2	56.2	56.1	56.1	56.1	56.1	56.0
17	22	55.7	55.6	55.5	55.5	55.4	55.4	55.3	55.3	55.3	55.2	55.2	55.2	55.1	55.1
18	23	54.8	54.7	54.7	54.6	54.6	54.5	54.5	54.4	54.4	54.3	54.3	54.3	54.2	54.2
19	24	53.9	53.9	53.8	53.7	53.7	53.6	53.6	53.5	53.5	53.4	53.4	53.4	53.3	53.3
20	25	53.1	53.0	52.9	52.8	52.8	52.7	52.7	52.6	52.6	52.5	52.5	52.5	52.4	52.4
21	26	52.2	52.1	52.0	52.0	51.9	51.8	51.8	51.7	51.7	51.6	51.6	51.5	51.5	51.5
22	27	51.4	51.3	51.2	51.1	51.0	51.0	50.9	50.8	50.8	50.7	50.7	50.6	50.6	50.6
23	28	50.5	50.4	50.3	50.2	50.2	50.1	50.0	50.0	49.9	49.8	49.8	49.7	49.7	49.7
24	29	49.7	49.6	49.5	49.4	49.3	49.2	49.2	49.1	49.1	49.0	49.0	48.9	48.8	48.8
25	30	48.8	48.7	48.6	48.5	48.4	48.3	48.3	48.2	48.1	48.1	48.1	48.0	47.9	47.9
26	31	48.0	47.9	47.8	47.7	47.6	47.5	47.4	47.3	47.3	47.2	47.1	47.1	47.0	47.0
27	32	47.2	47.1	46.9	46.8	46.7	46.6	46.6	46.5	46.5	46.4	46.3	46.2	46.1	46.1
28	33	46.4	46.3	46.1	46.0	45.9	45.8	45.7	45.6	45.5	45.4	45.4	45.3	45.2	45.2
29	34	45.6	45.4	45.3	45.2	45.1	44.9	44.8	44.7	44.7	44.6	44.5	44.4	44.4	44.3
30	35	44.8	44.6	44.5	44.4	44.2	44.1	44.0	43.9	43.8	43.7	43.6	43.6	43.5	43.4
31	36	44.0	43.9	43.7	43.6	43.4	43.3	43.2	43.1	43.0	42.9	42.8	42.7	42.6	42.6
32	37	43.3	43.1	42.9	42.8	42.6	42.5	42.4	42.2	42.1	42.0	41.9	41.9	41.8	41.7
33	38	42.5	42.3	42.1	42.0	41.8	41.7	41.5	41.4	41.3	41.2	41.1	41.0	40.9	40.8
34	39	41.8	41.6	41.4	41.2	41.0	40.9	40.7	40.6	40.5	40.4	40.3	40.2	40.1	40.0

Ages															
	Male	64	65	66	67	68	69	70	71	72	73	74	75	76	77	78
Male	Female	69	70	71	72	73	74	75	76	77	78	79	80	81	82	83
6	11	65.1	65.1	65.1	65.1	65.1	65.1	65.1	65.1	65.1	65.1	65.1	65.1	65.1	65.1	65.1
7	12	64.2	64.2	64.2	64.2	64.2	64.2	64.2	64.2	64.2	64.2	64.2	64.2	64.2	64.1	64.1
8	13	63.3	63.3	63.3	63.3	63.3	63.3	63.3	63.3	63.3	63.2	63.2	63.2	63.2	63.2	63.2
9	14	62.4	62.4	62.4	62.4	62.4	62.4	62.3	62.3	62.3	62.3	62.3	62.3	62.3	62.3	62.3
10	15	61.5	61.5	61.5	61.5	61.4	61.4	61.4	61.4	61.4	61.4	61.4	61.4	61.4	61.4	61.4
11	16	60.6	60.6	60.6	60.5	60.5	60.5	60.5	60.5	60.5	60.5	60.5	60.5	60.5	60.5	60.5
12	17	59.7	59.6	59.6	59.6	59.6	59.6	59.6	59.6	59.6	59.6	59.6	59.6	59.6	59.5	59.5
13	18	58.8	58.7	58.7	58.7	58.7	58.7	58.7	58.7	58.7	58.6	58.6	58.6	58.6	58.6	58.6
14	19	57.8	57.8	57.8	57.8	57.8	57.8	57.8	57.7	57.7	57.7	57.7	57.7	57.7	57.7	57.7
15	20	56.9	56.9	56.9	56.9	56.9	56.8	56.8	56.8	56.8	56.8	56.8	56.8	56.8	56.8	56.8
16	21	56.0	56.0	56.0	56.0	55.9	55.9	55.9	55.9	55.9	55.9	55.9	55.9	55.9	55.9	55.8
17	22	55.1	55.1	55.1	55.0	55.0	55.0	55.0	55.0	55.0	55.0	55.0	54.9	54.9	54.9	54.9
18	23	54.2	54.2	54.1	54.1	54.1	54.1	54.1	54.1	54.0	54.0	54.0	54.0	54.0	54.0	54.0
19	24	53.3	53.2	53.2	53.2	53.2	53.2	53.2	53.1	53.1	53.1	53.1	53.1	53.1	53.1	53.1
20	25	52.4	52.3	52.3	52.3	52.3	52.2	52.2	52.2	52.2	52.2	52.2	52.2	52.2	52.1	52.1
21	26	51.4	51.4	51.4	51.4	51.3	51.3	51.3	51.3	51.3	51.3	51.3	51.2	51.2	51.2	51.2
22	27	50.5	50.5	50.5	50.5	50.4	50.4	50.4	50.4	50.4	50.3	50.3	50.3	50.3	50.3	50.3
23	28	49.6	49.6	49.6	49.5	49.5	49.5	49.5	49.5	49.4	49.4	49.4	49.4	49.4	49.4	49.4
24	29	48.7	48.7	48.7	48.6	48.6	48.6	48.6	48.6	48.5	48.5	48.5	48.5	48.5	48.4	48.4
25	30	47.8	47.8	47.8	47.7	47.7	47.7	47.6	47.6	47.6	47.6	47.6	47.5	47.5	47.5	47.5
26	31	46.9	46.9	46.8	46.8	46.8	46.8	46.7	46.7	46.7	46.7	46.6	46.6	46.6	46.6	46.6
27	32	46.0	46.0	45.9	45.9	45.9	45.8	45.8	45.8	45.8	45.7	45.7	45.7	45.7	45.7	45.7
28	33	45.1	45.1	45.1	45.0	45.0	44.9	44.9	44.9	44.9	44.8	44.8	44.8	44.8	44.8	44.8
29	34	44.3	44.2	44.2	44.1	44.1	44.0	44.0	44.0	44.0	43.9	43.9	43.9	43.9	43.9	43.8
30	35	43.4	43.3	43.3	43.2	43.2	43.1	43.1	43.1	43.1	43.0	43.0	43.0	43.0	42.9	42.9
31	36	42.5	42.4	42.4	42.3	42.3	42.3	42.2	42.2	42.2	42.1	42.1	42.1	42.1	42.0	42.0
32	37	41.6	41.6	41.5	41.5	41.4	41.4	41.3	41.3	41.3	41.2	41.2	41.2	41.2	41.1	41.1
33	38	40.8	40.7	40.7	40.6	40.6	40.5	40.5	40.4	40.4	40.3	40.3	40.3	40.3	40.2	40.2
34	39	39.9	39.9	39.8	39.7	39.7	39.6	39.6	39.5	39.5	39.5	39.4	39.4	39.4	39.3	39.3

TABLE II.—ORDINARY JOINT LIFE AND LAST SURVIVOR ANNUITIES—TWO LIVES—
EXPECTED RETURN MULTIPLES—Continued

Ages Male	Ages Female	79 / 84	80 / 85	81 / 86	82 / 87	83 / 88	84 / 89	85 / 90	86 / 91	87 / 92	88 / 93	89 / 94	90 / 95	91 / 96	92 / 97
6	11	65.1	65.1	65.1	65.1	65.1	65.1	65.1	65.1	65.1	65.0	65.0	65.0	65.0	65.0
7	12	64.1	64.1	64.1	64.1	64.1	64.1	64.1	64.1	64.1	64.1	64.1	64.1	64.1	64.1
8	13	63.2	63.2	63.2	63.2	63.2	63.2	63.2	63.2	63.2	63.2	63.2	63.2	63.2	63.2
9	14	62.3	62.3	62.3	62.3	62.3	62.3	62.3	62.3	62.3	62.3	62.3	62.3	62.3	62.3
10	15	61.4	61.4	61.4	61.4	61.4	61.4	61.4	61.4	61.4	61.4	61.4	61.4	61.4	61.4
11	16	60.5	60.5	60.5	60.5	60.5	60.5	60.4	60.4	60.4	60.4	60.4	60.4	60.4	60.4
12	17	59.5	59.5	59.5	59.5	59.5	59.5	59.5	59.5	59.5	59.5	59.5	59.5	59.5	59.5
13	18	58.6	58.6	58.6	58.6	58.6	58.6	58.6	58.6	58.6	58.6	58.6	58.6	58.6	58.6
14	19	57.7	57.7	57.7	57.7	57.7	57.7	57.7	57.7	57.7	57.7	57.7	57.7	57.7	57.7
15	20	56.8	56.8	56.8	56.8	56.8	56.8	56.7	56.7	56.7	56.7	56.7	56.7	56.7	56.7
16	21	55.8	55.8	55.8	55.8	55.8	55.8	55.8	55.8	55.8	55.8	55.8	55.8	55.8	55.8
17	22	54.9	54.9	54.9	54.9	54.9	54.9	54.9	54.9	54.9	54.9	54.9	54.9	54.9	54.9
18	23	54.0	54.0	54.0	54.0	54.0	54.0	54.0	54.0	54.0	54.0	54.0	54.0	54.0	53.9
19	24	53.1	53.1	53.1	53.0	53.0	53.0	53.0	53.0	53.0	53.0	53.0	53.0	53.0	53.0
20	25	52.1	52.1	52.1	52.1	52.1	52.1	52.1	52.1	52.1	52.1	52.1	52.1	52.1	52.1
21	26	51.2	51.2	51.2	51.2	51.2	51.2	51.2	51.2	51.2	51.2	51.2	51.2	51.2	51.2
22	27	50.3	50.3	50.3	50.3	50.3	50.2	50.2	50.2	50.2	50.2	50.2	50.2	50.2	50.2
23	28	49.4	49.3	49.3	49.3	49.3	49.3	49.3	49.3	49.3	49.3	49.3	49.3	49.3	49.3
24	29	48.4	48.4	48.4	48.4	48.4	48.4	48.4	48.4	48.4	48.4	48.4	48.4	48.4	48.4
25	30	47.5	47.5	47.5	47.5	47.5	47.5	47.5	47.5	47.4	47.4	47.4	47.4	47.4	47.4
26	31	46.6	46.6	46.6	46.6	46.5	46.5	46.5	46.5	46.5	46.5	46.5	46.5	46.5	46.5
27	32	45.7	45.6	45.6	45.6	45.6	45.6	45.6	45.6	45.6	45.6	45.6	45.6	45.6	45.6
28	33	44.7	44.7	44.7	44.7	44.7	44.7	44.7	44.7	44.7	44.7	44.7	44.7	44.7	44.7
29	34	43.8	43.8	43.8	43.8	43.8	43.8	43.8	43.8	43.8	43.7	43.7	43.7	43.7	43.7
30	35	42.9	42.9	42.9	42.9	42.9	42.9	42.8	42.8	42.8	42.8	42.8	42.8	42.8	42.8
31	36	42.0	42.0	42.0	42.0	42.0	41.9	41.9	41.9	41.9	41.9	41.9	41.9	41.9	41.9
32	37	41.1	41.1	41.1	41.1	41.0	41.0	41.0	41.0	41.0	41.0	41.0	41.0	41.0	41.0
33	38	40.2	40.2	40.2	40.2	40.1	40.1	40.1	40.1	40.1	40.1	40.1	40.1	40.1	40.1
34	39	39.3	39.3	39.3	39.3	39.2	39.2	39.2	39.2	39.2	39.2	39.2	39.2	39.2	39.2

Ages Male	Ages Female	93 / 98	94 / 99	95 / 100	96 / 101	97 / 102	98 / 103	99 / 104	100 / 105	101 / 106	102 / 107	103 / 108	104 / 109	105 / 110	106 / 111	107 / 112	108 / 113
6	11	65.0	65.0	65.0	65.0	65.0	65.0	65.0	65.0	65.0	65.0	65.0	65.0	65.0	65.0	65.0	65.0
7	12	64.1	64.1	64.1	64.1	64.1	64.1	64.1	64.1	64.1	64.1	64.1	64.1	64.1	64.1	64.1	64.1
8	13	63.2	63.2	63.2	63.2	63.2	63.2	63.2	63.2	63.2	63.2	63.2	63.2	63.2	63.2	63.2	63.2
9	14	62.3	62.3	62.3	62.3	62.3	62.3	62.3	62.3	62.3	62.3	62.3	62.3	62.3	62.3	62.3	62.3
10	15	61.4	61.4	61.4	61.4	61.4	61.4	61.4	61.4	61.4	61.4	61.4	61.4	61.4	61.4	61.4	61.4
11	16	60.4	60.4	60.4	60.4	60.4	60.4	60.4	60.4	60.4	60.4	60.4	60.4	60.4	60.4	60.4	60.4
12	17	59.5	59.5	59.5	59.5	59.5	59.5	59.5	59.5	59.5	59.5	59.5	59.5	59.5	59.5	59.5	59.5
13	18	58.6	58.6	58.6	58.6	58.6	58.6	58.6	58.6	58.6	58.6	58.6	58.6	58.6	58.6	58.6	58.6
14	19	57.7	57.7	57.7	57.7	57.7	57.7	57.7	57.7	57.7	57.7	57.7	57.7	57.7	57.7	57.7	57.7
15	20	56.7	56.7	56.7	56.7	56.7	56.7	56.7	56.7	56.7	56.7	56.7	56.7	56.7	56.7	56.7	56.7
16	21	55.8	55.8	55.8	55.8	55.8	55.8	55.8	55.8	55.8	55.8	55.8	55.8	55.8	55.8	55.8	55.8
17	22	54.9	54.9	54.9	54.9	54.9	54.9	54.9	54.9	54.9	54.9	54.9	54.9	54.9	54.9	54.9	54.9
18	23	53.9	53.9	53.9	53.9	53.9	53.9	53.9	53.9	53.9	53.9	53.9	53.9	53.9	53.9	53.9	53.9
19	24	53.0	53.0	53.0	53.0	53.0	53.0	53.0	53.0	53.0	53.0	53.0	53.0	53.0	53.0	53.0	53.0
20	25	52.1	52.1	52.1	52.1	52.1	52.1	52.1	52.1	52.1	52.1	52.1	52.1	52.1	52.1	52.1	52.1
21	26	51.2	51.2	51.2	51.2	51.2	51.1	51.1	51.1	51.1	51.1	51.1	51.1	51.1	51.1	51.1	51.1
22	27	50.2	50.2	50.2	50.2	50.2	50.2	50.2	50.2	50.2	50.2	50.2	50.2	50.2	50.2	50.2	50.2
23	28	49.3	49.3	49.3	49.3	49.3	49.3	49.3	49.3	49.3	49.3	49.3	49.3	49.3	49.3	49.3	49.3
24	29	48.4	48.4	48.4	48.4	48.4	48.4	48.4	48.4	48.4	48.4	48.4	48.4	48.4	48.4	48.3	48.3
25	30	47.4	47.4	47.4	47.4	47.4	47.4	47.4	47.4	47.4	47.4	47.4	47.4	47.4	47.4	47.4	47.4
26	31	46.5	46.5	46.5	46.5	46.5	46.5	46.5	46.5	46.5	46.5	46.5	46.5	46.5	46.5	46.5	46.5
27	32	45.6	45.6	45.6	45.6	45.6	45.6	45.6	45.6	45.6	45.6	45.6	45.6	45.6	45.6	45.6	45.6
28	33	44.7	44.6	44.6	44.6	44.6	44.6	44.6	44.6	44.6	44.6	44.6	44.6	44.6	44.6	44.6	44.6
29	34	43.7	43.7	43.7	43.7	43.7	43.7	43.7	43.7	43.7	43.7	43.7	43.7	43.7	43.7	43.7	43.7
30	35	42.8	42.8	42.8	42.8	42.8	42.8	42.8	42.8	42.8	42.8	42.8	42.8	42.8	42.8	42.8	42.8
31	36	41.9	41.9	41.9	41.9	41.9	41.9	41.9	41.9	41.9	41.9	41.9	41.9	41.9	41.9	41.9	41.9
32	37	41.0	41.0	41.0	41.0	41.0	41.0	41.0	41.0	41.0	41.0	41.0	41.0	41.0	41.0	41.0	41.0
33	38	40.1	40.1	40.1	40.1	40.1	40.1	40.1	40.1	40.1	40.1	40.1	40.1	40.1	40.0	40.0	40.0
34	39	39.2	39.2	39.2	39.2	39.2	39.2	39.2	39.2	39.2	39.2	39.2	39.2	39.1	39.1	39.1	39.1

TABLE II.—ORDINARY JOINT LIFE AND LAST SURVIVOR ANNUITIES—TWO LIVES—
EXPECTED RETURN MULTIPLES—Continued

Ages														
	Male	35	36	37	38	39	40	41	42	43	44	45	46	47
Male	Female	40	41	42	43	44	45	46	47	48	49	50	51	52
35	40	46.2	45.7	45.3	44.8	44.4	44.0	43.6	43.3	43.0	42.6	42.3	42.0	41.8
36	41	45.7	45.2	44.8	44.3	43.9	43.5	43.1	42.7	42.3	42.0	41.7	41.4	41.1
37	42	45.3	44.8	44.3	43.8	43.4	42.9	42.5	42.1	41.8	41.4	41.1	40.7	40.4
38	43	44.8	44.3	43.8	43.3	42.9	42.4	42.0	41.6	41.2	40.8	40.5	40.1	39.8
39	44	44.4	43.9	43.4	42.9	42.4	41.9	41.5	41.0	40.6	40.2	39.9	39.5	39.2
40	45	44.0	43.5	42.9	42.4	41.9	41.4	41.0	40.5	40.1	39.7	39.3	38.9	38.6
41	46	43.6	43.1	42.5	42.0	41.5	41.0	40.5	40.0	39.6	39.2	38.8	38.4	38.0
42	47	43.3	42.7	42.1	41.6	41.0	40.5	40.0	39.6	39.1	38.7	38.2	37.8	37.5
43	48	43.0	42.3	41.8	41.2	40.6	40.1	39.6	39.1	38.6	38.2	37.7	37.3	36.9
44	49	42.6	42.0	41.4	40.8	40.2	39.7	39.2	38.7	38.2	37.7	37.2	36.8	36.4
45	50	42.3	41.7	41.1	40.5	39.9	39.3	38.8	38.2	37.7	37.2	36.8	36.3	35.9
46	51	42.0	41.4	40.7	40.1	39.5	38.9	38.4	37.8	37.3	36.8	36.3	35.9	35.4
47	52	41.8	41.1	40.4	39.8	39.2	38.6	38.0	37.5	36.9	36.4	35.9	35.4	35.0

Ages														
	Male	48	49	50	51	52	53	54	55	56	57	58	59	60
Male	Female	53	54	55	56	57	58	59	60	61	62	63	64	65
35	40	41.5	41.3	41.0	40.8	40.6	40.4	40.3	40.1	40.0	39.8	39.7	39.6	39.5
36	41	40.8	40.6	40.3	40.1	39.9	39.7	39.5	39.3	39.2	39.0	38.9	38.8	38.6
37	42	40.2	39.9	39.6	39.4	39.2	39.0	38.8	38.6	38.4	38.3	38.1	38.0	37.9
38	43	39.5	39.2	39.0	38.7	38.5	38.3	38.1	37.9	37.7	37.5	37.3	37.2	37.1
39	44	38.9	38.6	38.3	38.0	37.8	37.6	37.3	37.1	36.9	36.8	36.6	36.4	36.3
40	45	38.3	38.0	37.7	37.4	37.1	36.9	36.6	36.4	36.2	36.0	35.9	35.7	35.5
41	46	37.7	37.3	37.0	36.7	36.5	36.2	36.0	35.7	35.5	35.3	35.1	35.0	34.8
42	47	37.1	36.8	36.4	36.1	35.8	35.6	35.3	35.1	34.8	34.6	34.4	34.2	34.1
43	48	36.5	36.2	35.8	35.5	35.2	34.9	34.7	34.4	34.2	33.9	33.7	33.5	33.3
44	49	36.0	35.6	35.3	34.9	34.6	34.3	34.0	33.8	33.5	33.3	33.0	32.8	32.6
45	50	35.5	35.1	34.7	34.4	34.0	33.7	33.4	33.1	32.9	32.6	32.4	32.2	31.9
46	51	35.0	34.6	34.2	33.8	33.5	33.1	32.8	32.5	32.2	32.0	31.7	31.5	31.3
47	52	34.5	34.1	33.7	33.3	32.9	32.6	32.2	31.9	31.6	31.4	31.1	30.9	30.6
48	53	34.0	33.6	33.2	32.8	32.4	32.0	31.7	31.4	31.1	30.8	30.5	30.2	30.0
49	54	33.6	33.1	32.7	32.3	31.9	31.5	31.2	30.8	30.5	30.2	29.9	29.6	29.4
50	55	33.2	32.7	32.3	31.8	31.4	31.0	30.6	30.3	29.9	29.6	29.3	29.0	28.8
51	56	32.8	32.3	31.8	31.4	30.9	30.5	30.1	29.8	29.4	29.1	28.8	28.5	28.2
52	57	32.4	31.9	31.4	30.9	30.5	30.1	29.7	29.3	28.9	28.6	28.2	27.9	27.6
53	58	32.0	31.5	31.0	30.5	30.1	29.6	29.2	28.8	28.4	28.1	27.7	27.4	27.1
54	59	31.7	31.2	30.6	30.1	29.7	29.2	28.8	28.3	27.9	27.6	27.2	26.9	26.5
55	60	31.4	30.8	30.3	29.8	29.3	28.8	28.3	27.9	27.5	27.1	26.7	26.4	26.0
56	61	31.1	30.5	29.9	29.4	28.9	28.4	27.9	27.5	27.1	26.7	26.3	25.9	25.5
57	62	30.8	30.2	29.6	29.1	28.6	28.1	27.6	27.1	26.7	26.2	25.8	25.4	25.1
58	63	30.5	29.9	29.3	28.8	28.2	27.7	27.2	26.7	26.3	25.8	25.4	25.0	24.6
59	64	30.2	29.6	29.0	28.5	27.9	27.1	26.9	26.4	25.9	25.4	25.0	24.6	24.2
60	65	30.0	29.4	28.8	28.2	27.6	27.1	26.5	26.0	25.5	25.1	24.6	24.2	23.8

TABLE II.—ORDINARY JOINT LIFE AND LAST SURVIVOR ANNUITIES—TWO LIVES—
EXPECTED RETURN MULTIPLES—Continued

Ages														
	Male	61	62	63	64	65	66	67	68	69	70	71	72	73
Male	Female	66	67	68	69	70	71	72	73	74	75	76	77	78
35	40	39.4	39.3	39.2	39.1	39.0	38.9	38.9	38.8	38.8	38.7	38.7	38.6	38.6
36	41	38.5	38.4	38.3	38.2	38.2	38.1	38.0	38.0	37.9	37.9	37.8	37.8	37.7
37	42	37.7	37.6	37.5	37.4	37.3	37.3	37.2	37.1	37.1	37.0	36.9	36.9	36.9
38	43	36.9	36.8	36.7	36.6	36.5	36.4	36.4	36.3	36.2	36.2	36.1	36.0	36.0
39	44	36.2	36.0	35.9	35.8	35.7	35.6	35.5	35.5	35.4	35.3	35.3	35.2	35.2
40	45	35.4	35.3	35.1	35.0	34.9	34.8	34.7	34.6	34.6	34.5	34.4	34.4	34.3
41	46	34.6	34.5	34.4	34.2	34.1	34.0	33.9	33.8	33.8	33.7	33.6	33.5	33.5
42	47	33.9	33.7	33.6	33.5	33.4	33.2	33.1	33.0	33.0	32.9	32.8	32.7	32.7
43	48	33.2	33.0	32.9	32.7	32.6	32.5	32.4	32.3	32.2	32.1	32.0	31.9	31.9
44	49	32.5	32.3	32.1	32.0	31.8	31.7	31.6	31.5	31.4	31.3	31.2	31.1	31.1
45	50	31.8	31.6	31.4	31.3	31.1	31.0	30.8	30.7	30.6	30.5	30.4	30.4	30.3
46	51	31.1	30.9	30.7	30.5	30.4	30.2	30.1	30.0	29.9	29.8	29.7	29.6	29.5
47	52	30.4	30.2	30.0	29.8	29.7	29.5	29.4	29.3	29.1	29.0	28.9	28.8	28.7
48	53	29.8	29.5	29.3	29.2	29.0	28.8	28.7	28.5	28.4	28.3	28.2	28.1	28.0
49	54	29.1	28.9	28.7	28.5	28.3	28.1	28.0	27.8	27.7	27.6	27.5	27.4	27.3
50	55	28.5	28.3	28.1	27.8	27.6	27.5	27.3	27.1	27.0	26.9	26.7	26.6	26.5
51	56	27.9	27.7	27.4	27.2	27.0	26.8	26.6	26.5	26.3	26.2	26.0	25.9	25.8
52	57	27.3	27.1	26.8	26.6	26.4	26.2	26.0	25.8	25.7	25.5	25.4	25.2	25.1
53	58	26.8	26.5	26.2	26.0	25.8	25.6	25.4	25.2	25.0	24.8	24.7	24.6	24.4
54	59	26.2	25.9	25.7	25.4	25.2	25.0	24.7	24.6	24.4	24.2	24.0	23.9	23.8
55	60	25.7	25.4	25.1	24.9	24.6	24.4	24.1	23.9	23.8	23.6	23.4	23.3	23.1
56	61	25.2	24.9	24.6	24.3	24.1	23.8	23.6	23.4	23.2	23.0	22.8	22.6	22.5
57	62	24.7	24.4	24.1	23.8	23.5	23.3	23.0	22.8	22.6	22.4	22.2	22.0	21.9
58	63	24.3	23.9	23.6	23.3	23.0	22.7	22.5	22.2	22.0	21.8	21.6	21.4	21.3
59	64	23.8	23.5	23.1	22.8	22.5	22.2	21.9	21.7	21.5	21.2	21.0	20.9	20.7
60	65	23.4	23.0	22.7	22.3	22.0	21.7	21.4	21.2	20.9	20.7	20.5	20.3	20.1
61	66	23.0	22.6	22.2	21.9	21.6	21.3	21.0	20.7	20.4	20.2	20.0	19.8	19.6
62	67	22.6	22.2	21.8	21.5	21.1	20.8	20.5	20.2	19.9	19.7	19.5	19.2	19.0
63	68	22.2	21.8	21.4	21.1	20.7	20.4	20.1	19.8	19.5	19.2	19.0	18.7	18.5
64	69	21.9	21.5	21.1	20.7	20.3	20.0	19.6	19.3	19.0	18.7	18.5	18.2	18.0
65	70	21.6	21.1	20.7	20.3	19.9	19.6	19.2	18.9	18.6	18.3	18.0	17.8	17.5
66	71	21.3	20.8	20.4	20.0	19.6	19.2	18.8	18.5	18.2	17.9	17.6	17.3	17.1
67	72	21.0	20.5	20.1	19.6	19.2	18.8	18.5	18.1	17.8	17.5	17.2	16.9	16.7
68	73	20.7	20.2	19.8	19.3	18.9	18.5	18.1	17.8	17.4	17.1	16.8	16.5	16.2
69	74	20.4	19.9	19.5	19.0	18.6	18.2	17.8	17.4	17.1	16.7	16.4	16.1	15.8
70	75	20.2	19.7	19.2	18.7	18.3	17.9	17.5	17.1	16.7	16.4	16.1	15.8	15.5
71	76	20.0	19.5	19.0	18.5	18.0	17.6	17.2	16.8	16.4	16.1	15.7	15.4	15.1
72	77	19.8	19.2	18.7	18.2	17.8	17.3	16.9	16.5	16.1	15.8	15.4	15.1	14.8
73	78	19.6	19.0	18.5	18.0	17.5	17.1	16.7	16.2	15.8	15.5	15.1	14.8	14.4

See p. 20,601 for regulations not amended to reflect law changes

TABLE II.—ORDINARY JOINT LIFE AND LAST SURVIVOR ANNUITIES—TWO LIVES—
EXPECTED RETURN MULTIPLES—Continued

Ages Male	Male	74	75	76	77	78	79	80	81	82	83	84	85
Male	Female	79	80	81	82	83	84	85	86	87	88	89	90
35	40	38.6	38.5	38.5	38.5	38.4	38.4	38.4	38.4	38.4	38.4	38.3	38.3
36	41	37.7	37.6	37.6	37.6	37.6	37.5	37.5	37.5	37.5	37.5	37.5	37.4
37	42	36.8	36.8	36.7	36.7	36.7	36.7	36.6	36.6	36.6	36.6	36.6	36.6
38	43	36.0	35.9	35.9	35.9	35.8	35.8	35.8	35.8	35.7	35.7	35.7	35.7
39	44	35.1	35.1	35.0	35.0	35.0	34.9	34.9	34.9	34.9	34.8	34.8	34.8
40	45	34.3	34.2	34.2	34.1	34.1	34.1	34.1	34.0	34.0	34.0	34.0	34.0
41	46	33.4	33.4	33.3	33.3	33.3	33.3	33.2	33.2	33.2	33.2	33.1	33.1
42	47	32.6	32.6	32.5	32.5	32.4	32.4	32.4	32.3	32.3	32.3	32.3	32.3
43	48	31.8	31.8	31.7	31.7	31.6	31.6	31.5	31.5	31.5	31.5	31.4	31.4
44	49	31.0	30.9	30.9	30.8	30.8	30.8	30.8	30.7	30.7	30.7	30.6	30.6
45	50	30.2	30.1	30.1	30.0	30.0	29.9	29.9	29.9	29.8	29.8	29.8	29.8
46	51	29.4	29.4	29.3	29.2	29.2	29.2	29.1	29.1	29.0	29.0	29.0	28.9
47	52	28.7	28.6	28.5	28.5	28.4	28.4	28.3	28.3	28.2	28.2	28.2	28.1
48	53	27.9	27.8	27.8	27.7	27.6	27.6	27.5	27.5	27.5	27.4	27.4	27.4
49	54	27.2	27.1	27.0	26.9	26.9	26.8	26.8	26.7	26.7	26.6	26.6	26.6
50	55	26.4	26.3	26.3	26.2	26.1	26.1	26.0	26.0	25.9	25.9	25.8	25.8
51	56	25.7	25.6	25.5	25.5	25.4	25.3	25.3	25.2	25.2	25.1	25.1	25.0
52	57	25.0	24.9	24.8	24.7	24.7	24.6	24.5	24.5	24.4	24.4	24.3	24.3
53	58	24.3	24.2	24.1	24.0	23.9	23.9	23.8	23.7	23.7	23.6	23.6	23.5
54	59	23.6	23.5	23.4	23.3	23.2	23.2	23.1	23.0	23.0	22.9	22.9	22.8
55	60	23.0	22.9	22.8	22.7	22.6	22.5	22.4	22.3	22.3	22.2	22.2	22.1
56	61	22.3	22.2	22.1	22.0	21.9	21.8	21.7	21.6	21.6	21.5	21.5	21.4
57	62	21.7	21.6	21.5	21.3	21.2	21.1	21.1	21.0	20.9	20.8	20.8	20.7
58	63	21.1	21.0	20.8	20.7	20.6	20.5	20.4	20.3	20.2	20.2	20.1	20.0
59	64	20.5	20.4	20.2	20.1	20.0	19.9	19.8	19.7	19.6	19.5	19.4	19.4
60	65	19.9	19.8	19.6	19.5	19.4	19.3	19.1	19.0	19.0	18.9	18.8	18.7
61	66	19.4	19.2	19.1	18.9	18.8	18.7	18.5	18.4	18.3	18.3	18.2	18.1
62	67	18.8	18.7	18.5	18.3	18.2	18.1	18.0	17.8	17.7	17.7	17.6	17.5
63	68	18.3	18.1	18.0	17.8	17.6	17.5	17.4	17.3	17.2	17.1	17.0	16.9
64	69	17.8	17.6	17.4	17.3	17.1	17.0	16.8	16.7	16.6	16.5	16.4	16.3
65	70	17.3	17.1	16.9	16.7	16.6	16.4	16.3	16.2	16.0	15.9	15.8	15.8
66	71	16.9	16.6	16.4	16.3	16.1	15.9	15.8	15.6	15.5	15.4	15.3	15.2
67	72	16.4	16.2	16.0	15.8	15.6	15.4	15.3	15.1	15.0	14.9	14.8	14.7
68	73	16.0	15.7	15.5	15.3	15.1	15.0	14.8	14.6	14.5	14.4	14.3	14.2
69	74	15.5	15.3	15.1	14.9	14.7	14.5	14.3	14.2	14.0	13.9	13.8	13.7
70	75	15.2	14.9	14.7	14.5	14.3	14.1	13.9	13.7	13.6	13.4	13.3	13.2
71	76	14.8	14.5	14.3	14.1	13.8	13.6	13.5	13.3	13.1	13.0	12.8	12.7
72	77	14.5	14.2	13.9	13.7	13.5	13.2	13.0	12.9	12.7	12.5	12.4	12.3
73	78	14.1	13.8	13.6	13.3	13.1	12.9	12.7	12.5	12.3	12.1	12.0	11.9
74	79	13.8	13.5	13.2	13.0	12.7	12.5	12.3	12.1	11.9	11.7	11.6	11.4
75	80	13.5	13.2	12.9	12.6	12.4	12.2	11.9	11.7	11.5	11.4	11.2	11.0
76	81	13.2	12.9	12.6	12.3	12.1	11.8	11.6	11.4	11.2	11.0	10.8	10.7
77	82	13.0	12.6	12.3	12.1	11.8	11.5	11.3	11.1	10.8	10.7	10.5	10.3
78	83	12.7	12.4	12.1	11.8	11.5	11.2	11.0	10.7	10.5	10.3	10.1	10.0
79	84	12.5	12.2	11.8	11.5	11.2	11.0	10.7	10.5	10.2	10.0	9.8	9.6
80	85	12.3	11.9	11.6	11.3	11.0	10.7	10.4	10.2	10.0	9.7	9.5	9.3
81	86	12.1	11.7	11.4	11.1	10.7	10.5	10.2	9.9	9.7	9.5	9.3	9.1
82	87	11.9	11.5	11.2	10.8	10.5	10.2	10.0	9.7	9.4	9.2	9.0	8.8
83	88	11.7	11.4	11.0	10.7	10.3	10.0	9.7	9.5	9.2	9.0	8.7	8.5
84	89	11.6	11.2	10.8	10.5	10.1	9.8	9.5	9.3	9.0	8.7	8.5	8.3
85	90	11.4	11.0	10.7	10.3	10.0	9.6	9.3	9.1	8.8	8.5	8.3	8.1

Reg. § 1.72-9

TABLE II.—ORDINARY JOINT LIFE AND LAST SURVIVOR ANNUITIES—TWO LIVES—
EXPECTED RETURN MULTIPLES—Continued

Ages													
Male	Male	86	87	88	89	90	91	92	93	94	95	96	97
Male	Female	91	92	93	94	95	96	97	98	99	100	101	102
35	40	38.3	38.3	38.3	38.3	38.3	38.3	38.3	38.3	38.3	38.3	38.3	38.3
36	41	37.4	37.4	37.4	37.4	37.4	37.4	37.4	37.4	37.4	37.4	37.4	37.4
37	42	36.5	36.5	36.5	36.5	36.5	36.5	36.5	36.5	36.5	36.5	36.5	36.5
38	43	35.7	35.7	35.6	35.6	35.6	35.6	35.6	35.6	35.6	35.6	35.6	35.6
39	44	34.8	34.8	34.8	34.8	34.8	34.8	34.7	34.7	34.7	34.7	34.7	34.7
40	45	33.9	33.9	33.9	33.9	33.9	33.9	33.9	33.9	33.9	33.9	33.9	33.9
41	46	33.1	33.1	33.1	33.0	33.0	33.0	33.0	33.0	33.0	33.0	33.0	33.0
42	47	32.2	32.2	32.2	32.2	32.2	32.2	32.2	32.2	32.2	32.1	32.1	32.1
43	48	31.4	31.4	31.4	31.3	31.3	31.3	31.3	31.3	31.3	31.3	31.3	31.3
44	49	30.6	30.5	30.5	30.5	30.5	30.5	30.5	30.5	30.5	30.5	30.5	30.4
45	50	29.7	29.7	29.7	29.7	29.7	29.7	29.7	29.6	29.6	29.6	29.6	29.6
46	51	28.9	28.9	28.9	28.9	28.9	28.8	28.8	28.8	28.8	28.8	28.8	28.8
47	52	28.1	28.1	28.1	28.1	28.0	28.0	28.0	28.0	28.0	28.0	28.0	28.0
48	53	27.3	27.3	27.3	27.3	27.2	27.2	27.2	27.2	27.2	27.2	27.2	27.2
49	54	26.5	26.5	26.5	26.5	26.5	26.4	26.4	26.4	26.4	26.4	26.4	26.4
50	55	25.8	25.7	25.7	25.7	25.7	25.7	25.6	25.6	25.6	25.6	25.6	25.6
51	56	25.0	25.0	24.9	24.9	24.9	24.9	24.9	24.9	24.8	24.8	24.8	24.8
52	57	24.3	24.2	24.2	24.2	24.1	24.1	24.1	24.1	24.1	24.1	24.1	24.0
53	58	23.5	23.5	23.4	23.4	23.4	23.4	23.4	23.3	23.3	23.3	23.3	23.3
54	59	22.8	22.7	22.7	22.7	22.7	22.6	22.6	22.6	22.6	22.6	22.6	22.5
55	60	22.1	22.0	22.0	22.0	21.9	21.9	21.9	21.9	21.8	21.8	21.8	21.8
56	61	21.4	21.3	21.3	21.3	21.2	21.2	21.2	21.2	21.1	21.1	21.1	21.1
57	62	20.7	20.6	20.6	20.6	20.5	20.5	20.5	20.4	20.4	20.4	20.4	20.4
58	63	20.0	19.9	19.9	19.9	19.8	19.8	19.8	19.8	19.7	19.7	19.7	19.7
59	64	19.3	19.3	19.2	19.2	19.2	19.1	19.1	19.1	19.0	19.0	19.0	19.0

Ages													
Male	Male	98	99	100	101	102	103	104	105	106	107	108	
Male	Female	103	104	105	106	107	108	109	110	111	112	113	
35	40	38.3	38.3	38.3	38.3	38.3	38.3	38.2	38.2	38.2	38.2	38.2	
36	41	37.4	37.4	37.4	37.4	37.4	37.4	37.4	37.4	37.4	37.4	37.3	
37	42	36.5	36.5	36.5	36.5	36.5	36.5	36.5	36.5	36.5	36.5	36.5	
38	43	35.6	35.6	35.6	35.6	35.6	35.6	35.6	35.6	35.6	35.6	35.6	
39	44	34.7	34.7	34.7	34.7	34.7	34.7	34.7	34.7	34.7	34.7	34.7	
40	45	33.9	33.8	33.8	33.8	33.8	33.8	33.8	33.8	33.8	33.8	33.8	
41	46	33.0	33.0	33.0	33.0	33.0	33.0	33.0	33.0	33.0	33.0	33.0	
42	47	32.1	32.1	32.1	32.1	32.1	32.1	32.1	32.1	32.1	32.1	32.1	
43	48	31.3	31.3	31.3	31.3	31.3	31.3	31.3	31.3	31.3	31.3	31.3	
44	49	30.4	30.4	30.4	30.4	30.4	30.4	30.4	30.4	30.4	30.4	30.4	
45	50	29.6	29.6	29.6	29.6	29.6	29.6	29.6	29.6	29.6	29.6	29.6	
46	51	28.8	28.8	28.8	28.8	28.8	28.8	28.8	28.8	28.8	28.8	28.7	
47	52	28.0	28.0	28.0	28.0	28.0	28.0	28.0	27.9	27.9	27.9	27.9	
48	53	27.2	27.2	27.2	27.2	27.2	27.1	27.1	27.1	27.1	27.1	27.1	
49	54	26.4	26.4	26.4	26.4	26.4	26.3	26.3	26.3	26.3	26.3	26.3	
50	55	25.6	25.6	25.6	25.6	25.6	25.6	25.6	25.6	25.5	25.5	25.5	
51	56	24.8	24.8	24.8	24.8	24.8	24.8	24.8	24.8	24.8	24.8	24.7	
52	57	24.0	24.0	24.0	24.0	24.0	24.0	24.0	24.0	24.0	24.0	24.0	
53	58	23.3	23.3	23.3	23.3	23.3	23.3	23.2	23.2	23.2	23.2	23.2	
54	59	22.5	22.5	22.5	22.5	22.5	22.5	22.5	22.5	22.5	22.5	22.5	
55	60	21.8	21.8	21.8	21.8	21.8	21.8	21.8	21.8	21.8	21.7	21.7	
56	61	21.1	21.1	21.1	21.1	21.1	21.1	21.0	21.0	21.0	21.0	21.0	
57	62	20.4	20.4	20.4	20.3	20.3	20.3	20.3	20.3	20.3	20.3	20.3	
58	63	19.7	19.7	19.7	19.6	19.6	19.6	19.6	19.6	19.6	19.6	19.6	
59	64	19.0	19.0	19.0	19.0	19.0	18.9	18.9	18.9	18.9	18.9	18.9	

See p. 20,601 for regulations not amended to reflect law changes

TABLE II.—ORDINARY JOINT LIFE AND LAST SURVIVOR ANNUITIES—TWO LIVES—
EXPECTED RETURN MULTIPLES—Continued

Ages													
	Male	86	87	88	89	90	91	92	93	94	95	96	97
Male	Female	91	92	93	94	95	96	97	98	99	100	101	102
60	65	18.7	18.6	18.6	18.5	18.5	18.5	18.4	18.4	18.4	18.4	18.3	18.3
61	66	18.1	18.0	17.9	17.9	17.9	17.8	17.8	17.8	17.7	17.7	17.7	17.7
62	67	17.4	17.4	17.3	17.3	17.2	17.2	17.1	17.1	17.1	17.1	17.0	17.0
63	68	16.8	16.8	16.7	16.7	16.6	16.6	16.5	16.5	16.5	16.5	16.4	16.4
64	69	16.2	16.2	16.1	16.1	16.0	16.0	15.9	15.9	15.9	15.8	15.8	15.8
65	70	15.7	15.6	15.5	15.5	15.4	15.4	15.3	15.3	15.3	15.2	15.2	15.2
66	71	15.1	15.0	15.0	14.9	14.8	14.8	14.7	14.7	14.7	14.6	14.6	14.6
67	72	14.6	14.5	14.4	14.4	14.3	14.2	14.2	14.2	14.1	14.1	14.1	14.0
68	73	14.1	14.0	13.9	13.8	13.8	13.7	13.6	13.6	13.6	13.5	13.5	13.5
69	74	13.6	13.5	13.4	13.3	13.2	13.2	13.1	13.1	13.0	13.0	13.0	12.9
70	75	13.1	13.0	12.9	12.8	12.7	12.7	12.6	12.5	12.5	12.5	12.4	12.4
71	76	12.6	12.5	12.4	12.3	12.2	12.2	12.1	12.1	12.0	12.0	11.9	11.9
72	77	12.1	12.0	11.9	11.8	11.8	11.7	11.6	11.6	11.5	11.5	11.4	11.4
73	78	11.7	11.6	11.5	11.4	11.3	11.2	11.2	11.1	11.0	11.0	11.0	10.9
74	79	11.3	11.2	11.1	11.0	10.9	10.8	10.7	10.7	10.6	10.6	10.5	10.5
75	80	10.9	10.8	10.7	10.5	10.5	10.4	10.3	10.2	10.2	10.1	10.1	10.0
76	81	10.5	10.4	10.3	10.2	10.1	10.0	9.9	9.8	9.7	9.7	9.7	9.6
77	82	10.2	10.0	9.9	9.8	9.7	9.6	9.5	9.4	9.3	9.3	9.2	9.2
78	83	9.8	9.7	9.5	9.4	9.3	9.2	9.1	9.0	9.0	8.9	8.9	8.8
79	84	9.5	9.3	9.2	9.1	8.9	8.8	8.8	8.7	8.6	8.5	8.5	8.4
80	85	9.2	9.0	8.9	8.7	8.6	8.5	8.4	8.3	8.3	8.2	8.1	8.1
81	86	8.9	8.7	8.6	8.4	8.3	8.2	8.1	8.0	7.9	7.9	7.8	7.7
82	87	8.6	8.4	8.3	8.1	8.0	7.9	7.8	7.7	7.6	7.5	7.5	7.4
83	88	8.3	8.2	8.0	7.9	7.7	7.6	7.5	7.4	7.3	7.2	7.2	7.1
84	89	8.1	7.9	7.8	7.6	7.5	7.3	7.2	7.1	7.0	7.0	6.9	6.8

Ages													
	Male	98	99	100	101	102	103	104	105	106	107	108
Male	Female	103	104	105	106	107	108	109	110	111	112	113
60	65	18.3	18.3	18.3	18.3	18.3	18.3	18.3	18.2	18.2	18.2	18.2
61	66	17.7	17.7	17.6	17.6	17.6	17.6	17.6	17.6	17.6	17.6	17.5
62	67	17.0	17.0	17.0	17.0	17.0	17.0	16.9	16.9	16.9	16.9	16.9
63	68	16.4	16.4	16.4	16.3	16.3	16.3	16.3	16.3	16.3	16.3	16.2
64	69	15.8	15.8	15.7	15.7	15.7	15.7	15.7	15.7	15.7	15.7	15.6
65	70	15.2	15.2	15.1	15.1	15.1	15.1	15.1	15.1	15.1	15.0	15.0
66	71	14.6	14.6	14.5	14.5	14.5	14.5	14.5	14.5	14.5	14.4	14.4
67	72	14.0	14.0	14.0	14.0	13.9	13.9	13.9	13.9	13.9	13.9	13.8
68	73	13.5	13.4	13.4	13.4	13.4	13.4	13.3	13.3	13.3	13.3	13.2
69	74	12.9	12.9	12.9	13.0	12.8	12.8	12.8	12.8	12.8	12.7	12.7
70	75	12.4	12.4	12.3	12.3	12.3	12.3	12.3	12.2	12.2	12.2	12.1
71	76	11.9	11.9	11.8	11.8	11.8	11.8	11.7	11.7	11.7	11.7	11.6
72	77	11.4	11.4	11.3	11.3	11.3	11.3	11.2	11.2	11.2	11.2	11.1
73	78	10.9	10.9	10.9	10.8	10.8	10.8	10.7	10.7	10.7	10.7	10.6
74	79	10.5	10.4	10.4	10.4	10.3	10.3	10.3	10.3	10.2	10.2	10.1
75	80	10.0	10.0	9.9	9.9	9.9	9.8	9.8	9.8	9.8	9.7	
76	81	9.6	9.5	9.5	9.5	9.4	9.4	9.4	9.4	9.3	9.3	
77	82	9.2	9.1	9.1	9.1	9.0	9.0	9.0	8.9	8.9	8.9	
78	83	8.8	8.7	8.7	8.7	8.6	8.6	8.5	8.5	8.5	8.4	
79	84	8.4	8.4	8.3	8.3	8.2	8.2	8.2	8.1	8.1	8.0	
80	85	8.0	8.0	7.9	7.9	7.9	7.8	7.8	7.7	7.7	7.6	
81	86	7.7	7.6	7.6	7.6	7.5	7.5	7.4	7.4	7.3	7.3	
82	87	7.4	7.3	7.3	7.2	7.2	7.1	7.1	7.0	7.0	6.9	
83	88	7.1	7.0	6.9	6.9	6.8	6.8	6.7	6.7	6.7	6.6	
84	89	6.8	6.7	6.6	6.6	6.5	6.5	6.4	6.4	6.3		

Reg. § 1.72-9

TABLE II.—ORDINARY JOINT LIFE AND LAST SURVIVOR ANNUITIES—TWO LIVES—
EXPECTED RETURN MULTIPLES—Continued

Ages			86	87	88	89	90	91	92	93	94	95	96
		Male											
Male		Female	91	92	93	94	95	96	97	98	99	100	101
85		90	7.9	7.7	7.5	7.4	7.2	7.1	7.0	6.9	6.8	6.7	6.6
86		91	7.7	7.5	7.3	7.1	7.0	6.8	6.7	6.6	6.5	6.4	6.4
87		92	7.5	7.3	7.1	6.9	6.8	6.6	6.5	6.4	6.3	6.2	6.1
88		93	7.3	7.1	6.9	6.7	6.6	6.4	6.3	6.2	6.1	6.0	5.9
89		94	7.1	6.9	6.7	6.5	6.4	6.2	6.1	6.0	5.9	5.8	5.7
90		95	7.0	6.8	6.6	6.4	6.2	6.1	5.9	5.8	5.7	5.6	5.5
91		96	6.8	6.6	6.4	6.2	6.1	5.9	5.8	5.7	5.5	5.4	5.3
92		97	6.7	6.5	6.3	6.1	5.9	5.8	5.6	5.5	5.4	5.3	5.2
93		98	6.6	6.4	6.2	6.0	5.8	5.7	5.5	5.4	5.2	5.1	5.0
94		99	6.5	6.3	6.1	5.9	5.7	5.5	5.4	5.2	5.1	5.0	4.9
95		100	6.4	6.2	6.0	5.8	5.6	5.4	5.3	5.1	5.0	4.9	4.7
96		101	6.4	6.1	5.9	5.7	5.5	5.3	5.2	5.0	4.9	4.7	4.6
97		102	6.3	6.1	5.8	5.6	5.4	5.2	5.1	4.9	4.8	4.6	4.5
98		103	6.2	6.0	5.8	5.5	5.3	5.1	5.0	4.8	4.7	4.5	4.4
99		104	6.2	5.9	5.7	5.5	5.2	5.1	4.9	4.7	4.6	4.4	4.3

Ages			97	98	99	100	101	102	103	104	105	106
		Male										
Male		Female	102	103	104	105	106	107	108	109	110	111
85		90	6.6	6.5	6.4	6.4	6.3	6.2	6.2	6.1	6.1	6.0
86		91	6.3	6.2	6.2	6.1	6.0	6.0	5.9	5.9	5.8	5.7
87		92	6.1	6.0	5.9	5.8	5.8	5.7	5.6	5.6	5.5	5.4
88		93	5.8	5.8	5.7	5.6	5.5	5.5	5.4	5.3	5.3	5.1
89		94	5.6	5.5	5.5	5.4	5.3	5.2	5.2	5.1	5.0	
90		95	5.4	5.3	5.2	5.2	5.1	5.0	4.9	4.9	4.8	
91		96	5.2	5.1	5.1	5.0	4.9	4.8	4.7	4.6	4.5	
92		97	5.1	5.0	4.9	4.8	4.7	4.6	4.5	4.4		
93		98	4.9	4.8	4.7	4.6	4.5	4.4	4.3	4.2		
94		99	4.8	4.7	4.6	4.5	4.4	4.3	4.1			
95		100	4.6	4.5	4.4	4.3	4.2	4.1	4.0			
96		101	4.5	4.4	4.3	4.2	4.1	3.9				
97		102	4.4	4.3	4.1	4.0	3.9	3.7				
98		103	4.3	4.1	4.0	3.9	3.7					
99		104	4.1	4.0	3.9	3.7						

TABLE IIA.—ANNUITIES FOR JOINT LIFE ONLY—TWO LIVES—
EXPECTED RETURN MULTIPLES

Ages			6	7	8	9	10	11	12	13	14	15	16	17	18	19	20
		Male															
Male		Female	11	12	13	14	15	16	17	18	19	20	21	22	23	24	25
6		11	56.6	56.1	55.7	55.1	54.6	54.1	53.5	52.9	52.3	51.7	51.1	50.5	49.8	49.1	48.4
7		12	56.1	55.7	55.2	54.7	54.2	53.7	53.1	52.6	52.0	51.4	50.8	50.2	49.5	48.9	48.2
8		13	55.7	55.2	54.8	54.3	53.8	53.3	52.8	52.2	51.6	51.1	50.5	49.9	49.2	48.6	47.9
9		14	55.1	54.7	54.3	53.8	53.3	52.9	52.3	51.8	51.3	50.7	50.1	49.5	48.9	48.3	47.7
10		15	54.6	54.2	53.8	53.3	52.9	52.4	51.9	51.4	50.9	50.3	49.8	49.2	48.6	48.0	47.4
11		16	54.1	53.7	53.3	52.9	52.4	52.0	51.5	51.0	50.5	50.0	49.4	48.8	48.3	47.7	47.1
12		17	53.5	53.1	52.8	52.3	51.9	51.5	51.0	50.6	50.1	49.6	49.0	48.5	47.9	47.3	46.7
13		18	52.9	52.6	52.2	51.8	51.4	51.0	50.6	50.1	49.6	49.1	48.6	48.1	47.5	47.0	46.4
14		19	52.3	52.0	51.6	51.3	50.9	50.5	50.1	49.6	49.2	48.7	48.2	47.7	47.2	46.6	46.1
15		20	51.7	51.4	51.1	50.7	50.3	50.0	49.6	49.1	48.7	48.2	47.8	47.3	46.8	46.2	45.7
16		21	51.1	50.8	50.5	50.1	49.8	49.4	49.0	48.6	48.2	47.8	47.3	46.8	46.3	45.8	45.3
17		22	50.5	50.2	49.9	49.5	49.2	48.8	48.5	48.1	47.7	47.3	46.8	46.4	45.9	45.4	44.9
18		23	49.8	49.5	49.2	48.9	48.6	48.3	47.9	47.5	47.2	46.8	46.3	45.9	45.4	45.0	44.5
19		24	49.1	48.9	48.6	48.3	48.0	47.7	47.3	47.0	46.6	46.2	45.8	45.4	45.0	44.5	44.0
20		25	48.4	48.2	47.9	47.7	47.4	47.1	46.7	46.4	46.1	45.7	45.3	44.9	44.5	44.0	43.6

TABLE IIA.—ANNUITIES FOR JOINT LIFE ONLY—TWO LIVES—
EXPECTED RETURN MULTIPLES—Continued

Ages			21	22	23	24	25	26	27	28	29	30	31	32	33	34
	Male		21	22	23	24	25	26	27	28	29	30	31	32	33	34
Male	Female		26	27	28	29	30	31	32	33	34	35	36	37	38	39
6	11		47.7	47.0	46.3	45.6	44.8	44.1	43.3	42.5	41.8	41.0	40.2	39.4	38.6	37.8
7	12		47.5	46.8	46.1	45.4	44.6	43.9	43.2	42.4	41.6	40.9	40.1	39.3	38.5	37.7
8	13		47.3	46.6	45.9	45.2	44.5	43.7	43.0	42.2	41.5	40.7	39.9	39.2	38.4	37.6
9	14		47.0	46.3	45.6	45.0	44.2	43.5	42.8	42.1	41.3	40.6	39.8	39.0	38.3	37.5
10	15		46.7	46.1	45.4	44.7	44.0	43.3	42.6	41.9	41.1	40.4	39.7	38.9	38.1	37.4
11	16		46.4	45.8	45.1	44.5	43.8	43.1	42.4	41.7	41.0	40.2	39.5	38.8	38.0	37.2
12	17		46.1	45.5	44.9	44.2	43.6	42.9	42.2	41.5	40.8	40.1	39.3	38.6	37.9	37.1
13	18		45.8	45.2	44.6	43.9	43.3	42.6	42.0	41.3	40.6	39.9	39.2	38.4	37.7	37.0
14	19		45.5	44.9	44.3	43.7	43.0	42.4	41.7	41.0	40.4	39.7	39.0	38.3	37.5	36.8
15	20		45.1	44.6	44.0	43.4	42.7	42.1	41.5	40.8	40.1	39.5	38.8	38.1	37.4	36.6
16	21		44.8	44.2	43.6	43.0	42.4	41.8	41.2	40.5	39.9	39.2	38.6	37.9	37.2	36.5
17	22		44.4	43.8	43.3	42.7	42.1	41.5	40.9	40.3	39.6	39.0	38.3	37.7	37.0	36.3
18	23		44.0	43.5	42.9	42.4	41.8	41.2	40.6	40.0	39.4	38.7	38.1	37.4	36.8	36.1
19	24		43.6	43.1	42.5	42.0	41.4	40.9	40.3	39.7	39.1	38.5	37.8	37.2	36.5	35.9
20	25		43.1	42.6	42.1	41.6	41.1	40.5	40.0	39.4	38.8	38.2	37.6	36.9	36.3	35.7
21	26		42.7	42.2	41.7	41.2	40.7	40.2	39.6	39.1	38.5	37.9	37.3	36.7	36.1	35.4
22	27		42.2	41.8	41.3	40.8	40.3	39.8	39.3	38.7	38.2	37.6	37.0	36.4	35.8	35.2
23	28		41.7	41.3	40.8	40.4	39.9	39.4	38.9	38.4	37.8	37.3	36.7	36.1	35.5	34.9
24	29		41.2	40.8	40.4	39.9	39.5	39.0	38.5	38.0	37.5	36.9	36.4	35.8	35.2	34.6
25	30		40.7	40.3	39.9	39.5	39.0	38.6	38.1	37.6	37.1	36.6	36.0	35.5	34.9	34.4
26	31		40.2	39.8	39.4	39.0	38.6	38.1	37.7	37.2	36.7	36.2	35.7	35.2	34.6	34.1
27	32		39.6	39.3	38.9	38.5	38.1	37.7	37.2	36.8	36.3	35.8	35.3	34.8	34.3	33.7
28	33		39.1	38.7	38.4	38.0	37.6	37.2	36.8	36.3	35.9	35.4	34.9	34.5	33.9	33.4
29	34		38.5	38.2	37.8	37.5	37.1	36.7	36.3	35.9	35.5	35.0	34.6	34.1	33.6	33.1
30	35		37.9	37.6	37.3	36.9	36.6	36.2	35.8	35.4	35.0	34.6	34.1	33.7	33.2	32.7
31	36		37.3	37.0	36.7	36.4	36.0	35.7	35.3	34.9	34.6	34.1	33.7	33.3	32.8	32.3
32	37		36.7	36.4	36.1	35.8	35.5	35.2	34.8	34.5	34.1	33.7	33.3	32.9	32.4	32.0
33	38		36.1	35.8	35.5	35.2	34.9	34.6	34.3	33.9	33.6	33.2	32.8	32.4	32.0	31.6
34	39		35.4	35.2	34.9	34.6	34.4	34.1	33.7	33.4	33.1	32.7	32.3	32.0	31.6	31.1

Ages			35	36	37	38	39	40	41	42	43	44	45	46	47	48	49
	Male		35	36	37	38	39	40	41	42	43	44	45	46	47	48	49
Male	Female		40	41	42	43	44	45	46	47	48	49	50	51	52	53	54
6	11		37.0	36.2	35.4	34.6	33.8	33.0	32.2	31.4	30.6	29.8	29.0	28.2	27.5	26.7	25.9
7	12		36.9	36.1	35.3	34.5	33.7	32.9	32.1	31.3	30.5	29.8	29.0	28.2	27.4	26.7	25.9
8	13		36.8	36.0	35.2	34.4	33.7	32.9	32.1	31.3	30.5	29.7	28.9	28.2	27.4	26.6	25.9
9	14		36.7	35.9	35.1	34.4	33.6	32.8	32.0	31.2	30.4	29.7	28.9	28.1	27.3	26.6	25.8
10	15		36.6	35.8	35.1	34.3	33.5	32.7	31.9	31.2	30.4	29.6	28.8	28.1	27.3	26.5	25.8
11	16		36.5	35.7	34.9	34.2	33.4	32.6	31.9	31.1	30.3	29.5	28.8	28.0	27.3	26.5	25.7
12	17		36.4	35.6	34.8	34.1	33.3	32.5	31.8	31.0	30.2	29.5	28.7	28.0	27.2	26.4	25.7
13	18		36.2	35.5	34.7	34.0	33.2	32.4	31.7	30.9	30.2	29.4	28.7	27.9	27.1	26.4	25.7
14	19		36.1	35.3	34.6	33.8	33.1	32.3	31.6	30.8	30.1	29.3	28.6	27.8	27.1	26.3	25.6
15	20		35.9	35.2	34.5	33.7	33.0	32.2	31.5	30.7	30.0	29.3	28.5	27.8	27.0	26.3	25.6
16	21		35.8	35.0	34.3	33.6	32.9	32.1	31.4	30.6	29.9	29.2	28.4	27.7	27.0	26.2	25.5
17	22		35.6	34.9	34.2	33.4	32.7	32.0	31.3	30.5	29.8	29.1	28.3	27.6	26.9	26.2	25.4
18	23		35.4	34.7	34.0	33.3	32.6	31.9	31.2	30.4	29.7	29.0	28.3	27.5	26.8	26.1	25.4
19	24		35.2	34.5	33.8	33.1	32.4	31.7	31.0	30.3	29.6	28.9	28.2	27.4	26.7	26.0	25.3
20	25		35.0	34.3	33.7	33.0	32.3	31.6	30.9	30.2	29.5	28.8	28.1	27.3	26.6	25.9	25.2
21	26		34.8	34.1	33.5	32.8	32.1	31.4	30.7	30.0	29.3	28.6	27.9	27.2	26.5	25.8	25.1
22	27		34.5	33.9	33.3	32.6	31.9	31.3	30.6	29.9	29.2	28.5	27.8	27.1	26.4	25.7	25.1
23	28		34.3	33.7	33.0	32.4	31.7	31.1	30.4	29.7	29.1	28.4	27.7	27.0	26.3	25.6	25.0
24	29		34.0	33.4	32.8	32.2	31.5	30.9	30.2	29.6	28.9	28.2	27.6	26.9	26.2	25.5	24.9
25	30		33.8	33.2	32.6	32.0	31.3	30.7	30.1	29.4	28.8	28.1	27.4	26.8	26.1	25.4	24.8
26	31		33.5	32.9	32.3	31.7	31.1	30.5	29.9	29.2	28.6	27.9	27.3	26.6	26.0	25.3	24.6
27	32		33.2	32.6	32.1	31.5	30.9	30.3	29.6	29.0	28.4	27.8	27.1	26.5	25.8	25.2	24.5
28	33		32.9	32.3	31.8	31.2	30.6	30.0	29.4	28.8	28.2	27.6	27.0	26.3	25.7	25.0	24.4
29	34		32.6	32.0	31.5	30.9	30.4	29.8	29.2	28.6	28.0	27.4	26.8	26.2	25.5	24.9	24.3
30	35		32.2	31.7	31.2	30.6	30.1	29.5	29.0	28.4	27.8	27.2	26.6	26.0	25.4	24.7	24.1
31	36		31.9	31.4	30.9	30.3	29.8	29.3	28.7	28.1	27.6	27.0	26.4	25.8	25.2	24.6	24.0
32	37		31.5	31.0	30.5	30.0	29.5	29.0	28.4	27.9	27.3	26.8	26.2	25.6	25.0	24.4	23.8
33	38		31.1	30.7	30.2	29.7	29.2	28.7	28.2	27.6	27.1	26.5	26.0	25.4	24.8	24.2	23.6
34	39		30.7	30.3	29.8	29.3	28.9	28.4	27.9	27.3	26.8	26.3	25.7	25.2	24.6	24.0	23.5

Reg. § 1.72-9

TABLE IIA.—ANNUITIES FOR JOINT LIFE ONLY—TWO LIVES—
EXPECTED RETURN MULTIPLES—Continued

Ages															
	Male	50	51	52	53	54	55	56	57	58	59	60	61	62	63
Male	Female	55	56	57	58	59	60	61	62	63	64	65	66	67	68
6	11	25.2	24.4	23.7	22.9	22.2	21.5	20.8	20.1	19.4	18.7	18.0	17.4	16.7	16.1
7	12	25.1	24.4	23.6	22.9	22.2	21.5	20.8	20.1	19.4	18.7	18.0	17.4	16.7	16.1
8	13	25.1	24.4	23.6	22.9	22.2	21.4	20.7	20.0	19.4	18.7	18.0	17.4	16.7	16.1
9	14	25.1	24.3	23.6	22.9	22.1	21.4	20.7	20.0	19.3	18.7	18.0	17.3	16.7	16.1
10	15	25.0	24.3	23.6	22.8	22.1	21.4	20.7	20.0	19.3	18.6	18.0	17.3	16.7	16.1
11	16	25.0	24.3	23.5	22.8	22.1	21.4	20.7	20.0	19.3	18.6	18.0	17.3	16.7	16.1
12	17	25.0	24.2	23.5	22.8	22.1	21.4	20.7	20.0	19.3	18.6	18.0	17.3	16.7	16.0
13	18	24.9	24.2	23.5	22.7	22.0	21.3	20.6	19.9	19.3	18.6	17.9	17.3	16.7	16.0
14	19	24.9	24.1	23.4	22.7	22.0	21.3	20.6	19.9	19.2	18.6	17.9	17.3	16.6	16.0
15	20	24.8	24.1	23.4	22.7	22.0	21.3	20.6	19.9	19.2	18.5	17.9	17.3	16.6	16.0
16	21	24.8	24.0	23.3	22.6	21.9	21.2	20.5	19.9	19.2	18.5	17.9	17.2	16.6	16.0
17	22	24.7	24.0	23.3	22.6	21.9	21.2	20.5	19.8	19.2	18.5	17.8	17.2	16.6	16.0
18	23	24.7	23.9	23.2	22.5	21.8	21.1	20.5	19.8	19.1	18.5	17.8	17.2	16.6	15.9
19	24	24.6	23.9	23.2	22.5	21.8	21.1	20.4	19.8	19.1	18.4	17.8	17.2	16.5	15.9
20	25	24.5	23.8	23.1	22.4	21.7	21.1	20.4	19.7	19.1	18.4	17.8	17.1	16.5	15.9
21	26	24.4	23.7	23.1	22.4	21.7	21.0	20.3	19.7	19.0	18.4	17.7	17.1	16.5	15.9
22	27	24.4	23.7	23.0	22.3	21.6	21.0	20.3	19.6	19.0	18.3	17.7	17.1	16.5	15.9
23	28	24.3	23.6	22.9	22.2	21.6	20.9	20.2	19.6	18.9	18.3	17.7	17.0	16.4	15.8
24	29	24.2	23.5	22.8	22.2	21.5	20.8	20.2	19.5	18.9	18.3	17.6	17.0	16.4	15.8
25	30	24.1	23.4	22.8	22.1	21.4	20.8	20.1	19.5	18.8	18.2	17.6	17.0	16.4	15.8
26	31	24.0	23.3	22.7	22.0	21.4	20.7	20.1	19.4	18.8	18.2	17.5	16.9	16.3	15.7
27	32	23.9	23.2	22.6	21.9	21.3	20.6	20.0	19.4	18.7	18.1	17.5	16.9	16.3	15.7
28	33	23.8	23.1	22.5	21.8	21.2	20.6	19.9	19.3	18.7	18.1	17.4	16.8	16.2	15.6
29	34	23.6	23.0	22.4	21.7	21.1	20.5	19.8	19.2	18.6	18.0	17.4	16.8	16.2	15.6
30	35	23.5	22.9	22.3	21.6	21.0	20.4	19.8	19.1	18.5	17.9	17.3	16.7	16.1	15.6
31	36	23.4	22.7	22.1	21.5	20.9	20.3	19.7	19.1	18.5	17.9	17.3	16.7	16.1	15.5
32	37	23.2	22.6	22.0	21.4	20.8	20.2	19.6	19.0	18.4	17.8	17.2	16.6	16.0	15.5
33	38	23.1	22.5	21.9	21.3	20.7	20.1	19.5	18.9	18.3	17.7	17.1	16.5	16.0	15.4
34	39	22.9	22.3	21.7	21.1	20.5	20.0	19.4	18.8	18.2	17.6	17.0	16.5	15.9	15.3

Ages															
	Male	64	65	66	67	68	69	70	71	72	73	74	75	76	77	78
Male	Female	69	70	71	72	73	74	75	76	77	78	79	80	81	82	83
6	11	15.5	14.9	14.3	13.7	13.1	12.6	12.0	11.5	11.0	10.5	10.0	9.6	9.1	8.7	8.2
7	12	15.5	14.9	14.3	13.7	13.1	12.6	12.0	11.5	11.0	10.5	10.0	9.6	9.1	8.7	8.2
8	13	15.5	14.9	14.3	13.7	13.1	12.6	12.0	11.5	11.0	10.5	10.0	9.6	9.1	8.7	8.2
9	14	15.5	14.9	14.3	13.7	13.1	12.6	12.0	11.5	11.0	10.5	10.0	9.5	9.1	8.7	8.2
10	15	15.4	14.8	14.3	13.7	13.1	12.6	12.0	11.5	11.0	10.5	10.0	9.5	9.1	8.7	8.2
11	16	15.4	14.8	14.2	13.7	13.1	12.6	12.0	11.5	11.0	10.5	10.0	9.5	9.1	8.7	8.2
12	17	15.4	14.8	14.2	13.7	13.1	12.5	12.0	11.5	11.0	10.5	10.0	9.5	9.1	8.6	8.2
13	18	15.4	14.8	14.2	13.6	13.1	12.5	12.0	11.5	11.0	10.5	10.0	9.5	9.1	8.6	8.2
14	19	15.4	14.8	14.2	13.6	13.1	12.5	12.0	11.5	11.0	10.5	10.0	9.5	9.1	8.6	8.2
15	20	15.4	14.8	14.2	13.6	13.1	12.5	12.0	11.5	11.0	10.5	10.0	9.5	9.1	8.6	8.2
16	21	15.4	14.8	14.2	13.6	13.1	12.5	12.0	11.5	11.0	10.5	10.0	9.5	9.1	8.6	8.2
17	22	15.4	14.8	14.2	13.6	13.0	12.5	12.0	11.5	10.9	10.5	10.0	9.5	9.1	8.6	8.2
18	23	15.3	14.7	14.2	13.6	13.0	12.5	12.0	11.4	10.9	10.4	10.0	9.5	9.1	8.6	8.2
19	24	15.3	14.7	14.1	13.6	13.0	12.5	12.0	11.4	10.9	10.4	10.0	9.5	9.1	8.6	8.2
20	25	15.3	14.7	14.1	13.6	13.0	12.5	11.9	11.4	10.9	10.4	10.0	9.5	9.0	8.6	8.2
21	26	15.3	14.7	14.1	13.5	13.0	12.5	11.9	11.4	10.9	10.4	9.9	9.5	9.0	8.6	8.2
22	27	15.3	14.7	14.1	13.5	13.0	12.4	11.9	11.4	10.9	10.4	9.9	9.5	9.0	8.6	8.2
23	28	15.2	14.6	14.1	13.5	13.0	12.4	11.9	11.4	10.9	10.4	9.9	9.5	9.0	8.6	8.2
24	29	15.2	14.6	14.0	13.5	12.9	12.4	11.9	11.4	10.9	10.4	9.9	9.5	9.0	8.6	8.2
25	30	15.2	14.6	14.0	13.5	12.9	12.4	11.9	11.4	10.9	10.4	9.9	9.5	9.0	8.6	8.2
26	31	15.1	14.6	14.0	13.4	12.9	12.4	11.9	11.3	10.8	10.4	9.9	9.4	9.0	8.6	8.2
27	32	15.1	14.5	14.0	13.4	12.9	12.4	11.8	11.3	10.8	10.4	9.9	9.4	9.0	8.6	8.2
28	33	15.1	14.5	13.9	13.4	12.9	12.3	11.8	11.3	10.8	10.3	9.9	9.4	9.0	8.6	8.1
29	34	15.0	14.5	13.9	13.4	12.8	12.3	11.8	11.3	10.8	10.3	9.9	9.4	9.0	8.5	8.1
30	35	15.0	14.4	13.9	13.3	12.8	12.3	11.8	11.3	10.8	10.3	9.8	9.4	9.0	8.5	8.1
31	36	14.9	14.4	13.8	13.3	12.8	12.2	11.7	11.2	10.8	10.3	9.8	9.4	8.9	8.5	8.1
32	37	14.9	14.3	13.8	13.3	12.7	12.2	11.7	11.2	10.7	10.3	9.8	9.4	8.9	8.5	8.1
33	38	14.8	14.3	13.8	13.2	12.7	12.2	11.7	11.2	10.7	10.2	9.8	9.3	8.9	8.5	8.1
34	39	14.8	14.2	13.7	13.2	12.7	12.2	11.7	11.2	10.7	10.2	9.8	9.3	8.9	8.5	8.1

TABLE IIA.—ANNUITIES FOR JOINT LIFE ONLY—TWO LIVES—
EXPECTED RETURN MULTIPLES—Continued

Ages Male		79	80	81	82	83	84	85	86	87	88	89	90	91	92	93
Male	Female	84	85	86	87	88	89	90	91	92	93	94	95	96	97	98
6	11	7.8	7.4	7.1	6.7	6.3	6.0	5.7	5.4	5.1	4.8	4.5	4.2	4.0	3.7	3.5
7	12	7.8	7.4	7.1	6.7	6.3	6.0	5.7	5.4	5.1	4.8	4.5	4.2	4.0	3.7	3.5
8	13	7.8	7.4	7.0	6.7	6.3	6.0	5.7	5.4	5.1	4.8	4.5	4.2	4.0	3.7	3.5
9	14	7.8	7.4	7.0	6.7	6.3	6.0	5.7	5.4	5.1	4.8	4.5	4.2	4.0	3.7	3.5
10	15	7.8	7.4	7.0	6.7	6.3	6.0	5.7	5.4	5.1	4.8	4.5	4.2	4.0	3.7	3.5
11	16	7.8	7.4	7.0	6.7	6.3	6.0	5.7	5.4	5.1	4.8	4.5	4.2	4.0	3.7	3.5
12	17	7.8	7.4	7.0	6.7	6.3	6.0	5.7	5.4	5.1	4.8	4.5	4.2	4.0	3.7	3.5
13	18	7.8	7.4	7.0	6.7	6.3	6.0	5.7	5.3	5.1	4.8	4.5	4.2	4.0	3.7	3.5
14	19	7.8	7.4	7.0	6.7	6.3	6.0	5.7	5.3	5.0	4.8	4.5	4.2	4.0	3.7	3.5
15	20	7.8	7.4	7.0	6.7	6.3	6.0	5.7	5.3	5.0	4.8	4.5	4.2	4.0	3.7	3.5
16	21	7.8	7.4	7.0	6.7	6.3	6.0	5.7	5.3	5.0	4.8	4.5	4.2	4.0	3.7	3.5
17	22	7.8	7.4	7.0	6.7	6.3	6.0	5.7	5.3	5.0	4.8	4.5	4.2	4.0	3.7	3.5
18	23	7.8	7.4	7.0	6.7	6.3	6.0	5.7	5.3	5.0	4.8	4.5	4.2	4.0	3.7	3.5
19	24	7.8	7.4	7.0	6.7	6.3	6.0	5.7	5.3	5.0	4.8	4.5	4.2	4.0	3.7	3.5
20	25	7.8	7.4	7.0	6.7	6.3	6.0	5.6	5.3	5.0	4.8	4.5	4.2	4.0	3.7	3.5
21	26	7.8	7.4	7.0	6.7	6.3	6.0	5.6	5.3	5.0	4.8	4.5	4.2	4.0	3.7	3.5
22	27	7.8	7.4	7.0	6.7	6.3	6.0	5.6	5.3	5.0	4.8	4.5	4.2	4.0	3.7	3.5
23	28	7.8	7.4	7.0	6.6	6.3	6.0	5.6	5.3	5.0	4.8	4.5	4.2	4.0	3.7	3.5
24	29	7.8	7.4	7.0	6.6	6.3	6.0	5.6	5.3	5.0	4.7	4.5	4.2	4.0	3.7	3.5
25	30	7.8	7.4	7.0	6.6	6.3	6.0	5.6	5.3	5.0	4.7	4.5	4.2	4.0	3.7	3.5
26	31	7.8	7.4	7.0	6.6	6.3	6.0	5.6	5.3	5.0	4.7	4.5	4.2	4.0	3.7	3.5
27	32	7.7	7.4	7.0	6.6	6.3	5.9	5.6	5.3	5.0	4.7	4.5	4.2	4.0	3.7	3.5
28	33	7.7	7.4	7.0	6.6	6.3	5.9	5.6	5.3	5.0	4.7	4.5	4.2	4.0	3.7	3.5
29	34	7.7	7.3	7.0	6.6	6.3	5.9	5.6	5.3	5.0	4.7	4.5	4.2	4.0	3.7	3.5
30	35	7.7	7.3	7.0	6.6	6.3	5.9	5.6	5.3	5.0	4.7	4.5	4.2	4.0	3.7	3.5
31	36	7.7	7.3	7.0	6.6	6.3	5.9	5.6	5.3	5.0	4.7	4.5	4.2	4.0	3.7	3.5
32	37	7.7	7.3	7.0	6.6	6.3	5.9	5.6	5.3	5.0	4.7	4.5	4.2	4.0	3.7	3.5
33	38	7.7	7.3	6.9	6.6	6.2	5.9	5.6	5.3	5.0	4.7	4.5	4.2	3.9	3.7	3.5
34	39	7.7	7.3	6.9	6.6	6.2	5.9	5.6	5.3	5.0	4.7	4.4	4.2	3.9	3.7	3.5

Ages Male		94	95	96	97	98	99	100	101	102	103	104	105	106	107	108
Male	Female	99	100	101	102	103	104	105	106	107	108	109	110	111	112	113
6	11	3.3	3.1	2.9	2.7	2.5	2.3	2.1	1.9	1.7	1.5	1.3	1.2	1.0	0.8	0.7
7	12	3.3	3.1	2.9	2.7	2.5	2.3	2.1	1.9	1.7	1.5	1.3	1.2	1.0	0.8	0.7
8	13	3.3	3.1	2.9	2.7	2.5	2.3	2.1	1.9	1.7	1.5	1.3	1.2	1.0	0.8	0.7
9	14	3.3	3.1	2.9	2.7	2.5	2.3	2.1	1.9	1.7	1.5	1.3	1.2	1.0	0.8	0.7
10	15	3.3	3.1	2.9	2.7	2.5	2.3	2.1	1.9	1.7	1.5	1.3	1.2	1.0	0.8	0.7
11	16	3.3	3.1	2.9	2.7	2.5	2.3	2.1	1.9	1.7	1.5	1.3	1.2	1.0	0.8	0.7
12	17	3.3	3.1	2.9	2.7	2.5	2.3	2.1	1.9	1.7	1.5	1.3	1.2	1.0	0.8	0.7
13	18	3.3	3.1	2.9	2.7	2.5	2.3	2.1	1.9	1.7	1.5	1.3	1.2	1.0	0.8	0.7
14	19	3.3	3.1	2.9	2.7	2.5	2.3	2.1	1.9	1.7	1.5	1.3	1.2	1.0	0.8	0.7
15	20	3.3	3.1	2.9	2.7	2.5	2.3	2.1	1.9	1.7	1.5	1.3	1.2	1.0	0.8	0.7
16	21	3.3	3.1	2.9	2.7	2.5	2.3	2.1	1.9	1.7	1.5	1.3	1.2	1.0	0.8	0.7
17	22	3.3	3.1	2.9	2.7	2.5	2.3	2.1	1.9	1.7	1.5	1.3	1.2	1.0	0.8	0.7
18	23	3.3	3.1	2.9	2.7	2.5	2.3	2.1	1.9	1.7	1.5	1.3	1.2	1.0	0.8	0.7
19	24	3.3	3.1	2.9	2.7	2.5	2.3	2.1	1.9	1.7	1.5	1.3	1.2	1.0	0.8	0.7
20	25	3.3	3.1	2.9	2.7	2.5	2.3	2.1	1.9	1.7	1.5	1.3	1.2	1.0	0.8	0.7
21	26	3.3	3.1	2.9	2.7	2.5	2.3	2.1	1.9	1.7	1.5	1.3	1.2	1.0	0.8	0.7
22	27	3.3	3.1	2.9	2.7	2.5	2.3	2.1	1.9	1.7	1.5	1.3	1.2	1.0	0.8	0.7
23	28	3.3	3.1	2.9	2.7	2.5	2.3	2.1	1.9	1.7	1.5	1.3	1.2	1.0	0.8	0.7
24	29	3.3	3.1	2.9	2.7	2.5	2.3	2.1	1.9	1.7	1.5	1.3	1.2	1.0	0.8	0.7
25	30	3.3	3.1	2.9	2.7	2.5	2.3	2.1	1.9	1.7	1.5	1.3	1.2	1.0	0.8	0.7
26	31	3.3	3.1	2.9	2.7	2.5	2.3	2.1	1.9	1.7	1.5	1.3	1.2	1.0	0.8	0.7
27	32	3.3	3.1	2.9	2.7	2.5	2.3	2.1	1.9	1.7	1.5	1.3	1.2	1.0	0.8	0.7
28	33	3.3	3.1	2.9	2.7	2.5	2.3	2.1	1.9	1.7	1.5	1.3	1.2	1.0	0.8	0.7
29	34	3.3	3.1	2.9	2.7	2.5	2.3	2.1	1.9	1.7	1.5	1.3	1.2	1.0	0.8	0.7
30	35	3.3	3.1	2.9	2.7	2.5	2.3	2.1	1.9	1.7	1.5	1.3	1.2	1.0	0.8	0.7
31	36	3.3	3.1	2.9	2.7	2.5	2.3	2.1	1.9	1.7	1.5	1.3	1.2	1.0	0.8	0.7
32	37	3.3	3.1	2.9	2.7	2.5	2.3	2.1	1.9	1.7	1.5	1.3	1.2	1.0	0.8	0.7
33	38	3.3	3.1	2.9	2.7	2.5	2.3	2.1	1.9	1.7	1.5	1.3	1.2	1.0	0.8	0.7
34	39	3.3	3.1	2.9	2.7	2.5	2.3	2.1	1.9	1.7	1.5	1.3	1.2	1.0	0.8	0.7

TABLE IIA.—ANNUITIES FOR JOINT LIFE ONLY—TWO LIVES—
EXPECTED RETURN MULTIPLES—Continued

Ages														
	Male	35	36	37	38	39	40	41	42	43	44	45	46	47
Male	Female	40	41	42	43	44	45	46	47	48	49	50	51	52
35	40	30.3	29.9	29.4	29.0	28.5	28.0	27.5	27.0	26.5	26.0	25.5	24.9	24.4
36	41	29.9	29.5	29.0	28.6	28.2	27.7	27.2	26.7	26.2	25.7	25.2	24.7	24.2
37	42	29.4	29.0	28.6	28.2	27.8	27.3	26.9	26.4	25.9	25.5	25.0	24.4	23.9
38	43	29.0	28.6	28.2	27.8	27.4	27.0	26.5	26.1	25.6	25.2	24.7	24.2	23.7
39	44	28.5	28.2	27.8	27.4	27.0	26.6	26.2	25.8	25.3	24.8	24.4	23.9	23.4
40	45	28.0	27.7	27.3	27.0	26.6	26.2	25.8	25.4	25.0	24.5	24.1	23.6	23.1
41	46	27.5	27.2	26.9	26.5	26.2	25.8	25.4	25.0	24.6	24.2	23.8	23.3	22.9
42	47	27.0	26.7	26.4	26.1	25.8	25.4	25.0	24.6	24.2	23.8	23.4	23.0	22.6
43	48	26.5	26.2	25.9	25.6	25.3	25.0	24.6	24.2	23.9	23.5	23.1	22.7	22.2
44	49	26.0	25.7	25.5	25.2	24.8	24.5	24.2	23.8	23.5	23.1	22.7	22.3	21.9
45	50	25.5	25.2	25.0	24.7	24.4	24.1	23.8	23.4	23.1	22.7	22.4	22.0	21.6
46	51	24.9	24.7	24.4	24.2	23.9	23.6	23.3	23.0	22.7	22.3	22.0	21.6	21.2
47	52	24.4	24.2	23.9	23.7	23.4	23.1	22.9	22.6	22.2	21.9	21.6	21.2	20.9

Ages														
	Male	48	49	50	51	52	53	54	55	56	57	58	59	60
Male	Female	53	54	55	56	57	58	59	60	61	62	63	64	65
35	40	23.8	23.3	22.7	22.1	21.6	21.0	20.4	19.8	19.3	18.7	18.1	17.5	17.0
36	41	23.6	23.1	22.5	22.0	21.4	20.8	20.3	19.7	19.1	18.6	18.0	17.4	16.9
37	42	23.4	22.9	22.3	21.8	21.2	20.7	20.1	19.6	19.0	18.4	17.9	17.3	16.8
38	43	23.2	22.6	22.1	21.6	21.1	20.5	20.0	19.4	18.9	18.3	17.8	17.2	16.7
39	44	22.9	22.4	21.9	21.4	20.9	20.3	19.8	19.3	18.7	18.2	17.7	17.1	16.6
40	45	22.7	22.2	21.7	21.2	20.7	20.1	19.6	19.1	18.6	18.0	17.5	17.0	16.5
41	46	22.4	21.9	21.4	20.9	20.4	19.9	19.4	18.9	18.4	17.9	17.4	16.9	16.3
42	47	22.1	21.6	21.2	20.7	20.2	19.7	19.2	18.7	18.2	17.7	17.2	16.7	16.2
43	48	21.8	21.4	20.9	20.5	20.0	19.5	19.0	18.6	18.1	17.6	17.1	16.6	16.1
44	49	21.5	21.1	20.6	20.2	19.8	19.3	18.8	18.4	17.9	17.4	16.9	16.4	15.9
45	50	21.2	20.8	20.4	19.9	19.5	19.1	18.6	18.1	17.7	17.2	16.7	16.3	15.8
46	51	20.9	20.5	20.1	19.7	19.2	18.8	18.4	17.9	17.5	17.0	16.6	16.1	15.6
47	52	20.5	20.1	19.8	19.4	19.0	18.5	18.1	17.7	17.3	16.8	16.4	15.9	15.5
48	53	20.2	19.8	19.4	19.1	18.7	18.3	17.9	17.5	17.0	16.6	16.2	15.7	15.3
49	54	19.8	19.5	19.1	18.8	18.4	18.0	17.6	17.2	16.8	16.4	16.0	15.5	15.1
50	55	19.4	19.1	18.8	18.4	18.1	17.7	17.3	16.9	16.6	16.2	15.8	15.3	14.9
51	56	19.1	18.8	18.4	18.1	17.8	17.4	17.0	16.7	16.3	15.9	15.5	15.1	14.7
52	57	18.7	18.4	18.1	17.8	17.4	17.1	16.8	16.4	16.0	15.7	15.3	14.9	14.5
53	58	18.3	18.0	17.7	17.4	17.1	16.8	16.4	16.1	15.8	15.4	15.1	14.7	14.3
54	59	17.9	17.6	17.3	17.0	16.8	16.4	16.1	15.8	15.5	15.1	14.8	14.4	14.1
55	60	17.5	17.2	16.9	16.7	16.4	16.1	15.8	15.5	15.2	14.9	14.5	14.2	13.9
56	61	17.0	16.8	16.6	16.3	16.0	15.8	15.5	15.2	14.9	14.6	14.3	13.9	13.6
57	62	16.6	16.4	16.3	15.9	15.7	15.4	15.1	14.9	14.6	14.3	14.0	13.7	13.4
58	63	16.2	16.0	15.8	15.5	15.3	15.1	14.8	14.5	14.3	14.0	13.7	13.4	13.1
59	64	15.7	15.5	15.3	15.1	14.9	14.7	14.4	14.2	13.9	13.7	13.4	13.1	12.8
60	65	15.3	15.1	14.9	14.7	14.5	14.3	14.1	13.9	13.6	13.4	13.1	12.8	12.6

Reg. § 1.72-9

See p. 20,601 for regulations not amended to reflect law changes

TABLE IIA.—ANNUITIES FOR JOINT LIFE ONLY—TWO LIVES—
EXPECTED RETURN MULTIPLES—Continued

Ages														
	Male	61	62	63	64	65	66	67	68	69	70	71	72	73
Male	Female	66	67	68	69	70	71	72	73	74	75	76	77	78
35	40	16.4	15.8	15.3	14.7	14.2	13.7	13.1	12.6	12.1	11.6	11.1	10.7	10.2
36	41	16.3	15.8	15.2	14.7	14.1	13.6	13.1	12.6	12.1	11.6	11.1	10.6	10.2
37	42	16.2	15.7	15.1	14.6	14.1	13.6	13.0	12.5	12.0	11.5	11.1	10.6	10.1
38	43	16.1	15.6	15.1	14.5	14.0	13.5	13.0	12.5	12.0	11.5	11.0	10.6	10.1
39	44	16.0	15.5	15.0	14.5	13.9	13.4	12.9	12.4	11.9	11.5	11.0	10.5	10.1
40	45	15.9	15.4	14.9	14.4	13.9	13.4	12.9	12.4	11.9	11.4	11.0	10.5	10.0
41	46	15.8	15.3	14.8	14.3	13.8	13.3	12.8	12.3	11.8	11.4	10.9	10.5	10.0
42	47	15.7	15.2	14.7	14.2	13.7	13.2	12.7	12.3	11.8	11.3	10.9	10.4	10.0
43	48	15.6	15.1	14.6	14.1	13.6	13.1	12.7	12.2	11.7	11.3	10.8	10.4	9.9
44	49	15.5	15.0	14.5	14.0	13.5	13.1	12.6	12.1	11.7	11.2	10.8	10.3	9.9
45	50	15.3	14.8	14.4	13.9	13.4	13.0	12.5	12.0	11.6	11.1	10.7	10.3	9.8
46	51	15.2	14.7	14.2	13.8	13.3	12.9	12.4	12.0	11.5	11.1	10.6	10.2	9.8
47	52	15.0	14.6	14.1	13.7	13.2	12.8	12.3	11.9	11.4	11.0	10.6	10.1	9.7
48	53	14.9	14.4	14.0	13.5	13.1	12.6	12.2	11.8	11.3	10.9	10.5	10.1	9.7
49	54	14.7	14.3	13.8	13.4	13.0	12.5	12.1	11.7	11.3	10.8	10.4	10.0	9.6
50	55	14.5	14.1	13.7	13.3	12.8	12.4	12.0	11.6	11.2	10.7	10.3	9.9	9.5
51	56	14.3	13.9	13.5	13.1	12.7	12.3	11.9	11.5	11.1	10.7	10.3	9.9	9.5
52	57	14.1	13.7	13.3	12.9	12.5	12.1	11.7	11.3	10.9	10.6	10.2	9.8	9.4
53	58	13.9	13.6	13.2	12.8	12.4	12.0	11.6	11.2	10.8	10.5	10.1	9.7	9.3
54	59	13.7	13.4	13.0	12.6	12.2	11.9	11.5	11.1	10.7	10.3	10.0	9.6	9.2
55	60	13.5	13.2	12.8	12.4	12.1	11.7	11.3	11.0	10.6	10.2	9.9	9.5	9.1
56	61	13.3	12.9	12.6	12.2	11.9	11.5	11.2	10.8	10.5	10.1	9.8	9.4	9.0
57	62	13.0	12.7	12.4	12.1	11.7	11.4	11.0	10.7	10.3	10.0	9.6	9.3	8.9
58	63	12.8	12.5	12.2	11.8	11.5	11.2	10.9	10.5	10.2	9.8	9.5	9.2	8.8
59	64	12.6	12.3	11.9	11.6	11.3	11.0	10.7	10.4	10.0	9.7	9.4	9.1	8.7
60	65	12.3	12.0	11.7	11.4	11.1	10.8	10.5	10.2	9.9	9.6	9.3	8.9	8.6
61	66	12.0	11.8	11.5	11.2	10.9	10.6	10.3	10.0	9.7	9.4	9.1	8.8	8.5
62	67	11.8	11.5	11.2	11.0	10.7	10.4	10.1	9.8	9.6	9.3	9.0	8.7	8.4
63	68	11.5	11.2	11.0	10.7	10.5	10.2	9.9	9.7	9.4	9.1	8.8	8.5	8.2
64	69	11.2	11.0	10.7	10.5	10.2	10.0	9.7	9.5	9.2	8.9	8.7	8.4	8.1
65	70	10.9	10.7	10.5	10.2	10.0	9.8	9.5	9.3	9.0	8.8	8.5	8.2	8.0
66	71	10.6	10.4	10.2	10.0	9.8	9.5	9.3	9.1	8.8	8.6	8.3	8.1	7.8
67	72	10.3	10.1	9.9	9.7	9.5	9.3	9.1	8.9	8.6	8.4	8.1	7.9	7.7
68	73	10.0	9.8	9.7	9.5	9.3	9.1	8.9	8.6	8.4	8.2	8.0	7.7	7.5
69	74	9.7	9.6	9.4	9.2	9.0	8.8	8.6	8.4	8.2	8.0	7.8	7.6	7.3
70	75	9.4	9.3	9.1	8.9	8.8	8.6	8.4	8.2	8.0	7.8	7.6	7.4	7.2
71	76	9.1	9.0	8.8	8.7	8.5	8.3	8.1	8.0	7.8	7.6	7.4	7.2	7.0
72	77	8.8	8.7	8.5	8.4	8.2	8.1	7.9	7.7	7.6	7.4	7.2	7.0	6.8
73	78	8.5	8.4	8.2	8.1	8.0	7.8	7.7	7.5	7.3	7.2	7.0	6.8	6.7

Items Specifically Included in Gross Income

See p. 20,601 for regulations not amended to reflect law changes

TABLE IIA.—ANNUITIES FOR JOINT LIFE ONLY—TWO LIVES—
EXPECTED RETURN MULTIPLES—Continued

Ages														
	Male	74	75	76	77	78	79	80	81	82	83	84	85	86
Male	Female	79	80	81	82	83	84	85	86	87	88	89	90	91
35	40	9.7	9.3	8.9	8.5	8.1	7.7	7.3	6.9	6.6	6.2	5.9	5.6	5.3
36	41	9.7	9.3	8.9	8.4	8.0	7.7	7.3	6.9	6.6	6.2	5.9	5.6	5.3
37	42	9.7	9.3	8.8	8.4	8.0	7.6	7.3	6.9	6.5	6.2	5.9	5.6	5.3
38	43	9.7	9.2	8.8	8.4	8.0	7.6	7.2	6.9	6.5	6.2	5.9	5.6	5.3
39	44	9.6	9.2	8.8	8.4	8.0	7.6	7.2	6.9	6.5	6.2	5.9	5.6	5.3
40	45	9.6	9.2	8.8	8.4	8.0	7.6	7.2	6.9	6.5	6.2	5.9	5.5	5.2
41	46	9.6	9.2	8.7	8.3	7.9	7.6	7.2	6.8	6.5	6.2	5.8	5.5	5.2
42	47	9.5	9.1	8.7	8.3	7.9	7.5	7.2	6.8	6.5	6.2	5.8	5.5	5.2
43	48	9.5	9.1	8.7	8.3	7.9	7.5	7.2	6.8	6.5	6.1	5.8	5.5	5.2
44	49	9.5	9.0	8.6	8.2	7.9	7.5	7.1	6.8	6.4	6.1	5.8	5.5	5.2
45	50	9.4	9.0	8.6	8.2	7.8	7.5	7.1	6.8	6.4	6.1	5.8	5.5	5.2
46	51	9.4	9.0	8.6	8.2	7.8	7.4	7.1	6.7	6.4	6.1	5.8	5.5	5.2
47	52	9.3	8.9	8.5	8.1	7.8	7.4	7.1	6.7	6.4	6.1	5.8	5.5	5.2
48	53	9.3	8.9	8.5	8.1	7.7	7.4	7.0	6.7	6.4	6.0	5.7	5.4	5.1
49	54	9.2	8.8	8.4	8.1	7.7	7.3	7.0	6.7	6.3	6.0	5.7	5.4	5.1
50	55	9.1	8.8	8.4	8.0	7.7	7.3	7.0	6.6	6.3	6.0	5.7	5.4	5.1
51	56	9.1	8.7	8.3	8.0	7.6	7.3	6.9	6.6	6.3	6.0	5.7	5.4	5.1
52	57	9.0	8.6	8.3	7.9	7.6	7.2	6.9	6.6	6.2	5.9	5.6	5.4	5.1
53	58	8.9	8.6	8.2	7.9	7.5	7.2	6.9	6.5	6.2	5.9	5.6	5.3	5.1
54	59	8.9	8.5	8.2	7.8	7.5	7.1	6.8	6.5	6.2	5.9	5.6	5.3	5.0
55	60	8.8	8.4	8.1	7.7	7.4	7.1	6.8	6.4	6.1	5.8	5.6	5.3	5.0
56	61	8.7	8.4	8.0	7.7	7.3	7.0	6.7	6.4	6.1	5.8	5.5	5.3	5.0
57	62	8.6	8.3	7.9	7.6	7.3	7.0	6.7	6.4	6.1	5.8	5.5	5.2	5.0
58	63	8.5	8.2	7.9	7.5	7.2	6.9	6.6	6.3	6.0	5.7	5.5	5.2	4.9
59	64	8.4	8.1	7.8	7.5	7.1	6.8	6.5	6.3	6.0	5.7	5.4	5.2	4.9
60	65	8.3	8.0	7.7	7.4	7.1	6.8	6.5	6.2	5.9	5.6	5.4	5.1	4.9
61	66	8.2	7.9	7.6	7.3	7.0	6.7	6.4	6.1	5.9	5.6	5.3	5.1	4.8
62	67	8.1	7.8	7.5	7.2	6.9	6.6	6.4	6.1	5.8	5.5	5.3	5.0	4.8
63	68	8.0	7.7	7.4	7.1	6.8	6.6	6.3	6.0	5.7	5.5	5.2	5.0	4.7
64	69	7.8	7.6	7.3	7.0	6.7	6.5	6.2	5.9	5.7	5.4	5.2	4.9	4.7
65	70	7.7	7.4	7.2	6.9	6.6	6.4	6.1	5.9	5.6	5.4	5.1	4.9	4.7
66	71	7.6	7.3	7.1	6.8	6.5	6.3	6.0	5.8	5.5	5.3	5.1	4.8	4.6
67	72	7.4	7.2	6.9	6.7	6.4	6.2	6.0	5.7	5.5	5.2	5.0	4.8	4.6
68	73	7.3	7.0	6.8	6.6	6.3	6.1	5.9	5.6	5.4	5.2	4.9	4.7	4.5
69	74	7.1	6.9	6.7	6.4	6.2	6.0	5.8	5.5	5.3	5.1	4.9	4.7	4.5
70	75	7.0	6.8	6.5	6.3	6.1	5.9	5.7	5.4	5.2	5.0	4.8	4.6	4.4
71	76	6.8	6.6	6.4	6.2	6.0	5.8	5.6	5.3	5.1	4.9	4.7	4.5	4.3
72	77	6.6	6.4	6.3	6.1	5.9	5.7	5.5	5.3	5.0	4.9	4.7	4.5	4.3
73	78	6.5	6.3	6.1	5.9	5.7	5.5	5.3	5.1	5.0	4.8	4.6	4.4	4.2
74	79	6.3	6.1	6.0	5.8	5.6	5.4	5.2	5.0	4.9	4.7	4.5	4.3	4.1
75	80	6.1	6.0	5.8	5.6	5.5	5.3	5.1	4.9	4.8	4.6	4.4	4.2	4.1
76	81	6.0	5.8	5.6	5.5	5.3	5.2	5.0	4.8	4.7	4.5	4.3	4.1	4.0
77	82	5.8	5.6	5.5	5.3	5.2	5.0	4.9	4.7	4.5	4.4	4.2	4.1	3.9
78	83	5.6	5.5	5.3	5.2	5.0	4.9	4.7	4.6	4.4	4.3	4.1	4.0	3.8
79	84	5.4	5.3	5.2	5.0	4.9	4.7	4.6	4.5	4.3	4.2	4.0	3.9	3.7
80	85	5.2	5.1	5.0	4.9	4.7	4.6	4.5	4.3	4.2	4.1	3.9	3.8	3.6
81	86	5.0	4.9	4.8	4.7	4.6	4.5	4.3	4.2	4.1	3.9	3.8	3.7	3.6
82	87	4.9	4.8	4.7	4.5	4.4	4.3	4.2	4.1	4.0	3.8	3.7	3.6	3.5
83	88	4.7	4.6	4.5	4.4	4.3	4.2	4.1	3.9	3.8	3.7	3.6	3.5	3.4
84	89	4.5	4.4	4.3	4.2	4.1	4.0	3.9	3.8	3.7	3.6	3.5	3.4	3.3
85	90	4.3	4.2	4.1	4.1	4.0	3.9	3.8	3.7	3.6	3.5	3.4	3.3	3.2
86	91	4.1	4.1	4.0	3.9	3.8	3.7	3.6	3.6	3.5	3.4	3.3	3.2	3.1

See p. 20,601 for regulations not amended to reflect law changes

TABLE IIA.—ANNUITIES FOR JOINT LIFE ONLY—TWO LIVES—
EXPECTED RETURN MULTIPLES—Continued

Ages Male		87	88	89	90	91	92	93	94	95	96	97
Male	Female	92	93	94	95	96	97	98	99	100	101	102
35	40	5.0	4.7	4.4	4.2	3.9	3.7	3.5	3.3	3.1	2.9	2.7
36	41	5.0	4.7	4.4	4.2	3.9	3.7	3.5	3.3	3.1	2.9	2.7
37	42	5.0	4.7	4.4	4.2	3.9	3.7	3.5	3.3	3.1	2.9	2.7
38	43	5.0	4.7	4.4	4.2	3.9	3.7	3.5	3.3	3.1	2.8	2.6
39	44	5.0	4.7	4.4	4.2	3.9	3.7	3.5	3.3	3.0	2.8	2.6
40	45	5.0	4.7	4.4	4.2	3.9	3.7	3.5	3.3	3.0	2.8	2.6
41	46	5.0	4.7	4.4	4.2	3.9	3.7	3.5	3.2	3.0	2.8	2.6
42	47	4.9	4.7	4.4	4.2	3.9	3.7	3.5	3.2	3.0	2.8	2.6
43	48	4.9	4.7	4.4	4.1	3.9	3.7	3.5	3.2	3.0	2.8	2.6
44	49	4.9	4.7	4.4	4.1	3.9	3.7	3.4	3.2	3.0	2.8	2.6
45	50	4.9	4.6	4.4	4.1	3.9	3.7	3.4	3.2	3.0	2.8	2.6
46	51	4.9	4.6	4.4	4.1	3.9	3.7	3.4	3.2	3.0	2.8	2.6
47	52	4.9	4.6	4.4	4.1	3.9	3.7	3.4	3.2	3.0	2.8	2.6
48	53	4.9	4.6	4.4	4.1	3.9	3.6	3.4	3.2	3.0	2.8	2.6
49	54	4.9	4.6	4.3	4.1	3.9	3.6	3.4	3.2	3.0	2.8	2.6
50	55	4.8	4.6	4.3	4.1	3.9	3.6	3.4	3.2	3.0	2.8	2.6
51	56	4.8	4.6	4.3	4.1	3.8	3.6	3.4	3.2	3.0	2.8	2.6
52	57	4.8	4.5	4.3	4.1	3.8	3.6	3.4	3.2	3.0	2.8	2.6
53	58	4.8	4.5	4.3	4.0	3.8	3.6	3.4	3.2	3.0	2.8	2.6
54	59	4.8	4.5	4.3	4.0	3.8	3.6	3.4	3.2	3.0	2.8	2.6
55	60	4.7	4.5	4.3	4.0	3.8	3.6	3.4	3.2	3.0	2.8	2.6
56	61	4.7	4.5	4.2	4.0	3.8	3.6	3.3	3.1	2.9	2.8	2.6
57	62	4.7	4.5	4.2	4.0	3.8	3.5	3.3	3.1	2.9	2.7	2.6
58	63	4.7	4.4	4.2	4.0	3.7	3.5	3.3	3.1	2.9	2.7	2.5
59	64	4.6	4.4	4.2	3.9	3.7	3.5	3.3	3.1	2.9	2.7	2.5

Ages Male		98	99	100	101	102	103	104	105	106	107	108
Male	Female	103	104	105	106	107	108	109	110	111	112	113
35	40	2.5	2.3	2.1	1.9	1.7	1.5	1.3	1.2	1.0	0.8	0.7
36	41	2.5	2.3	2.1	1.9	1.7	1.5	1.3	1.2	1.0	0.8	0.7
37	42	2.5	2.3	2.1	1.9	1.7	1.5	1.3	1.1	1.0	0.8	0.7
38	43	2.5	2.3	2.1	1.9	1.7	1.5	1.3	1.1	1.0	0.8	0.7
39	44	2.4	2.3	2.1	1.9	1.7	1.5	1.3	1.1	1.0	0.8	0.7
40	45	2.4	2.2	2.1	1.9	1.7	1.5	1.3	1.1	1.0	0.8	0.7
41	46	2.4	2.2	2.1	1.9	1.7	1.5	1.3	1.1	1.0	0.8	0.7
42	47	2.4	2.2	2.0	1.9	1.7	1.5	1.3	1.1	1.0	0.8	0.7
43	48	2.4	2.2	2.0	1.9	1.7	1.5	1.3	1.1	1.0	0.8	0.7
44	49	2.4	2.2	2.0	1.9	1.7	1.5	1.3	1.1	1.0	0.8	0.7
45	50	2.4	2.2	2.0	1.8	1.7	1.5	1.3	1.1	1.0	0.8	0.7
46	51	2.4	2.2	2.0	1.8	1.7	1.5	1.3	1.1	1.0	0.8	0.7
47	52	2.4	2.2	2.0	1.8	1.7	1.5	1.3	1.1	1.0	0.8	0.7
48	53	2.4	2.2	2.0	1.8	1.7	1.5	1.3	1.1	1.0	0.8	0.7
49	54	2.4	2.2	2.0	1.8	1.7	1.5	1.3	1.1	1.0	0.8	0.7
50	55	2.4	2.2	2.0	1.8	1.6	1.5	1.3	1.1	1.0	0.8	0.7
51	56	2.4	2.2	2.0	1.8	1.6	1.5	1.3	1.1	1.0	0.8	0.7
52	57	2.4	2.2	2.0	1.8	1.6	1.5	1.3	1.1	1.0	0.8	0.7
53	58	2.4	2.2	2.0	1.8	1.6	1.5	1.3	1.1	1.0	0.8	0.7
54	59	2.4	2.2	2.0	1.8	1.6	1.5	1.3	1.1	1.0	0.8	0.7
55	60	2.4	2.2	2.0	1.8	1.6	1.4	1.3	1.1	1.0	0.8	0.7
56	61	2.4	2.2	2.0	1.8	1.6	1.4	1.3	1.1	1.0	0.8	0.7
57	62	2.4	2.2	2.0	1.8	1.6	1.4	1.3	1.1	0.9	0.8	0.7
58	63	2.4	2.2	2.0	1.8	1.6	1.4	1.3	1.1	0.9	0.8	0.7
59	64	2.3	2.2	2.0	1.8	1.6	1.4	1.3	1.1	0.9	0.8	0.7

Reg. § 1.72-9

TABLE IIA.—ANNUITIES FOR JOINT LIFE ONLY—TWO LIVES—
EXPECTED RETURN MULTIPLES—Continued

Ages												
Male	87	88	89	90	91	92	93	94	95	96	97
Male	Female	92	93	94	95	96	97	98	99	100	101	102
60	65	4.6	4.4	4.1	3.9	3.7	3.5	3.3	3.1	2.9	2.7	2.5
61	66	4.6	4.3	4.1	3.9	3.7	3.5	3.3	3.1	2.9	2.7	2.5
62	67	4.5	4.3	4.1	3.9	3.7	3.5	3.3	3.1	2.9	2.7	2.5
63	68	4.5	4.3	4.1	3.8	3.6	3.4	3.2	3.0	2.9	2.7	2.5
64	69	4.5	4.2	4.0	3.8	3.6	3.4	3.2	3.0	2.8	2.7	2.5
65	70	4.4	4.2	4.0	3.8	3.6	3.4	3.2	3.0	2.8	2.6	2.5
66	71	4.4	4.2	4.0	3.8	3.6	3.4	3.2	3.0	2.8	2.6	2.4
67	72	4.3	4.1	3.9	3.7	3.5	3.3	3.1	3.0	2.8	2.6	2.4
68	73	4.3	4.1	3.9	3.7	3.5	3.3	3.1	2.9	2.8	2.6	2.4
69	74	4.2	4.0	3.8	3.6	3.5	3.3	3.1	2.9	2.7	2.6	2.4
70	75	4.2	4.0	3.8	3.6	3.4	3.2	3.1	2.9	2.7	2.5	2.4
71	76	4.1	3.9	3.8	3.6	3.4	3.2	3.0	2.9	2.7	2.5	2.3
72	77	4.1	3.9	3.7	3.5	3.3	3.2	3.0	2.8	2.7	2.5	2.3
73	78	4.0	3.8	3.7	3.5	3.3	3.1	3.0	2.8	2.6	2.5	2.3
74	79	3.9	3.8	3.6	3.4	3.3	3.1	2.9	2.8	2.6	2.4	2.3
75	80	3.9	3.7	3.5	3.4	3.2	3.0	2.9	2.7	2.6	2.4	2.2
76	81	3.8	3.6	3.5	3.3	3.2	3.0	2.8	2.7	2.5	2.4	2.2
77	82	3.7	3.6	3.4	3.3	3.1	3.0	2.8	2.6	2.5	2.3	2.2
78	83	3.7	3.5	3.4	3.2	3.1	2.9	2.7	2.6	2.4	2.3	2.1
79	84	3.6	3.4	3.3	3.1	3.0	2.8	2.7	2.5	2.4	2.2	2.1
80	85	3.5	3.4	3.2	3.1	2.9	2.8	2.6	2.5	2.3	2.2	2.0
81	86	3.4	3.3	3.1	3.0	2.9	2.7	2.6	2.4	2.3	2.1	2.0
82	87	3.3	3.2	3.1	2.9	2.8	2.7	2.5	2.4	2.2	2.1	2.0
83	88	3.2	3.1	3.0	2.9	2.7	2.6	2.5	2.3	2.2	2.0	1.9
84	89	3.1	3.0	2.9	2.8	2.7	2.5	2.4	2.3	2.1	2.0	1.9

Ages												
Male	98	99	100	101	102	103	104	105	106	107	108
Male	Female	103	104	105	106	107	108	109	110	111	112	113
60	65	2.3	2.1	2.0	1.8	1.6	1.4	1.3	1.1	0.9	0.8	0.7
61	66	2.3	2.1	2.0	1.8	1.6	1.4	1.2	1.1	0.9	0.8	0.7
62	67	2.3	2.1	1.9	1.8	1.6	1.4	1.2	1.1	0.9	0.8	0.7
63	68	2.3	2.1	1.9	1.7	1.6	1.4	1.2	1.1	0.9	0.8	0.7
64	69	2.3	2.1	1.9	1.7	1.6	1.4	1.2	1.1	0.9	0.8	0.7
65	70	2.3	2.1	1.9	1.7	1.6	1.4	1.2	1.1	0.9	0.8	0.7
66	71	2.3	2.1	1.9	1.7	1.5	1.4	1.2	1.1	0.9	0.8	0.7
67	72	2.2	2.1	1.9	1.7	1.5	1.4	1.2	1.0	0.9	0.7	0.7
68	73	2.2	2.0	1.9	1.7	1.5	1.4	1.2	1.0	0.9	0.7	0.7
69	74	2.2	2.0	1.8	1.7	1.5	1.3	1.2	1.0	0.9	0.7	0.6
70	75	2.2	2.0	1.8	1.7	1.5	1.3	1.2	1.0	0.9	0.7	0.6
71	76	2.2	2.0	1.8	1.6	1.5	1.3	1.2	1.0	0.9	0.7	0.6
72	77	2.1	2.0	1.8	1.6	1.5	1.3	1.1	1.0	0.8	0.7	0.6
73	78	2.1	1.9	1.8	1.6	1.4	1.3	1.1	1.0	0.8	0.7	0.6
74	79	2.1	1.9	1.7	1.6	1.4	1.3	1.1	1.0	0.8	0.7	0.6
75	80	2.1	1.9	1.7	1.6	1.4	1.3	1.1	1.0	0.8	0.7	
76	81	2.0	1.9	1.7	1.5	1.4	1.2	1.1	0.9	0.8	0.7	
77	82	2.0	1.8	1.7	1.5	1.4	1.2	1.1	0.9	0.8	0.7	
78	83	2.0	1.8	1.6	1.5	1.3	1.2	1.0	0.9	0.8	0.7	
79	84	1.9	1.8	1.6	1.5	1.3	1.2	1.0	0.9	0.8	0.7	
80	85	1.9	1.7	1.6	1.4	1.3	1.1	1.0	0.9	0.7	0.7	
81	86	1.8	1.7	1.5	1.4	1.3	1.1	1.0	0.8	0.7	0.6	
82	87	1.8	1.7	1.5	1.4	1.2	1.1	1.0	0.8	0.7	0.6	
83	88	1.8	1.6	1.5	1.3	1.2	1.1	0.9	0.8	0.7	0.6	
84	89	1.7	1.6	1.4	1.3	1.2	1.0	0.9	0.8	0.7		

Reg. § 1.72-9

TABLE IIA.—ANNUITIES FOR JOINT LIFE ONLY—TWO LIVES—
EXPECTED RETURN MULTIPLES—Continued

Ages											
	Male	87	88	89	90	91	92	93	94	95	96
Male	Female	92	93	94	95	96	97	98	99	100	101
85	90	3.1	2.9	2.8	2.7	2.6	2.5	2.3	2.2	2.1	1.9
86	91	3.0	2.8	2.7	2.6	2.5	2.4	2.3	2.1	2.0	1.9
87	92	2.9	2.8	2.6	2.5	2.4	2.3	2.2	2.1	1.9	1.8
88	93	2.8	2.7	2.6	2.4	2.3	2.2	2.1	2.0	1.9	1.7
89	94	2.6	2.6	2.5	2.4	2.2	2.1	2.0	1.9	1.8	1.7
90	95	2.5	2.4	2.4	2.3	2.2	2.0	1.9	1.8	1.7	1.6
91	96	2.4	2.3	2.2	2.2	2.1	2.0	1.9	1.7	1.6	1.5
92	97	2.3	2.2	2.1	2.0	2.0	1.9	1.8	1.7	1.6	1.5
93	98	2.2	2.1	2.0	1.9	1.9	1.8	1.7	1.6	1.5	1.4
94	90	2.1	2.0	1.9	1.8	1.7	1.7	1.6	1.5	1.4	1.3
95	100	1.9	1.9	1.8	1.7	1.6	1.6	1.5	1.4	1.3	1.2
96	101	1.8	1.7	1.7	1.6	1.5	1.5	1.4	1.3	1.2	1.1
97	102	1.7	1.6	1.6	1.5	1.4	1.4	1.3	1.2	1.1	1.1
98	103	1.6	1.5	1.4	1.4	1.3	1.3	1.2	1.1	1.0	1.0
99	104	1.4	1.4	1.3	1.3	1.2	1.1	1.1	1.0	1.0	0.9

Ages											
	Male	97	98	99	100	101	102	103	104	105	106
Male	Female	102	103	104	105	106	107	108	109	110	111
85	90	1.8	1.7	1.5	1.4	1.3	1.1	1.0	0.9	0.8	0.7
86	91	1.7	1.6	1.5	1.3	1.2	1.1	1.0	0.8	0.7	0.7
87	92	1.7	1.6	1.4	1.3	1.2	1.1	0.9	0.8	0.7	0.6
88	93	1.6	1.5	1.4	1.3	1.1	1.0	0.9	0.8	0.7	0.6
89	94	1.6	1.4	1.3	1.2	1.1	1.0	0.9	0.7	0.7	
90	95	1.5	1.4	1.3	1.2	1.0	0.9	0.8	0.7	0.6	
91	96	1.4	1.3	1.2	1.1	1.0	0.9	0.8	0.7	0.6	
92	97	1.4	1.3	1.1	1.0	0.9	0.8	0.7	0.7		
93	98	1.3	1.2	1.1	1.0	0.9	0.8	0.7	0.6		
94	99	1.2	1.1	1.0	0.9	0.8	0.7	0.7			
95	100	1.1	1.0	1.0	0.9	0.8	0.7	0.6			
96	101	1.1	1.0	0.9	0.8	0.7	0.7				
97	102	1.0	0.9	0.8	0.7	0.7	0.6				
98	103	0.9	0.8	0.7	0.7	0.6					
99	104	0.8	0.7	0.7	0.6						

See p. 20,601 for regulations not amended to reflect law changes

TABLE III.—PERCENT VALUE OF REFUND FEATURE

Ages		Duration of guaranteed amount												
Male	Female	1 year	2 years	3 years	4 years	5 years	6 years	7 years	8 years	9 years	10 years	11 years	12 years	13 years
		Per-cent	Per-cent	Per-cent	Per-cent	Per-cent	Per-cent	Per-cent	Per-cent	Per-cent	Per-cent	Per-cent	Per-cent	Per-cent
6	11									1	1	1	1	1
7	12									1	1	1	1	1
8	13								1	1	1	1	1	1
9	14								1	1	1	1	1	1
10	15								1	1	1	1	1	1
11	16								1	1	1	1	1	1
12	17								1	1	1	1	1	1
13	18								1	1	1	1	1	1
14	19								1	1	1	1	1	1
15	20								1	1	1	1	1	1
16	21								1	1	1	1	1	1
17	22								1	1	1	1	1	1
18	23								1	1	1	1	1	1
19	24								1	1	1	1	1	1
20	25								1	1	1	1	1	1
21	26								1	1	1	1	1	1
22	27							1	1	1	1	1	1	1
23	28							1	1	1	1	1	1	1
24	29							1	1	1	1	1	1	1
25	30							1	1	1	1	1	1	1
26	31						1	1	1	1	1	1	1	1
27	32						1	1	1	1	1	1	1	1
28	33						1	1	1	1	1	1	1	1
29	34						1	1	1	1	1	1	1	2
30	35					1	1	1	1	1	1	1	2	2
31	36					1	1	1	1	1	1	1	2	2
32	37					1	1	1	1	1	1	1	2	2
33	38				1	1	1	1	1	1	1	2	2	2
34	39				1	1	1	1	1	1	2	2	2	2
35	40				1	1	1	1	1	1	2	2	2	2
36	41				1	1	1	1	1	2	2	2	2	3
37	42			1	1	1	1	1	2	2	2	2	3	3
38	43			1	1	1	1	1	2	2	2	2	3	3
39	44			1	1	1	1	2	2	2	2	3	3	3
40	45			1	1	1	1	2	2	2	3	3	3	4
41	46			1	1	1	1	2	2	2	3	3	3	4
42	47			1	1	1	2	2	2	3	3	3	4	4
43	48		1	1	1	1	2	2	2	3	3	4	4	4
44	49		1	1	1	1	2	2	3	3	3	4	4	5
45	50		1	1	1	2	2	2	3	3	4	4	5	5
46	51		1	1	1	2	2	3	3	3	4	4	5	5
47	52		1	1	1	2	2	3	3	4	4	5	5	6
48	53		1	1	2	2	2	3	3	4	5	5	6	6
49	54		1	1	2	2	3	3	4	4	5	5	6	7
50	55		1	1	2	2	3	3	4	5	5	6	7	7
51	56		1	1	2	3	3	4	4	5	6	6	7	8
52	57	1	1	2	2	3	3	4	5	5	6	7	8	8
53	58	1	1	2	2	3	4	4	5	6	7	7	8	9
54	59	1	1	2	2	3	4	5	5	6	7	8	9	10
55	60	1	1	2	3	3	4	5	6	7	8	8	9	10
56	61	1	1	2	3	4	4	5	6	7	8	9	10	11
57	62	1	1	2	3	4	5	6	7	8	9	10	11	12
58	63	1	2	2	3	4	5	6	7	8	9	10	12	13
59	64	1	2	3	4	5	6	7	8	9	10	11	12	14
60	65	1	2	3	4	5	6	7	8	10	11	12	13	15
61	66	1	2	3	4	5	6	8	9	10	12	13	14	16
62	67	1	2	3	4	6	7	8	10	11	12	14	15	17
63	68	1	2	4	5	6	7	9	10	12	13	15	16	18
64	69	1	3	4	5	7	8	9	11	13	14	16	17	19
65	70	1	3	4	6	7	9	10	12	13	15	17	19	20

TABLE III.—PERCENT VALUE OF REFUND FEATURE—Continued

Male	Female	1 year	2 years	3 years	4 years	5 years	6 years	7 years	8 years	9 years	10 years	11 years	12 years	year
		Percent	Percent	Percent	Percent	Percent	Percent	Percent	Percent	Percent	Percent	Percent	Percent	Percent
66	71	1	3	4	6	8	9	11	13	14	16	18	20	22
67	72	2	3	5	6	8	10	12	14	15	17	19	21	23
68	73	2	3	5	7	9	11	13	14	16	18	21	23	25
69	74	2	4	6	7	9	11	13	16	18	20	22	24	26
70	75	2	4	6	8	10	12	14	17	19	21	23	26	28
71	76	2	4	6	9	11	13	15	18	20	22	25	27	29
72	77	2	5	7	9	12	14	16	19	21	24	26	29	31
73	78	2	5	7	10	12	15	18	20	23	25	28	30	33
74	79	3	5	8	11	13	16	19	22	24	27	30	32	35
75	80	3	6	8	11	14	17	20	23	26	29	31	34	37
76	81	3	6	9	12	15	18	21	24	27	30	33	36	39
77	82	3	7	10	13	16	20	23	26	29	32	35	38	41
78	83	4	7	11	14	17	21	24	28	31	34	37	40	43
79	84	4	8	11	15	19	22	26	29	33	36	39	42	45
80	85	4	8	12	16	20	24	27	31	34	38	41	44	47
81	86	4	9	13	17	21	25	29	33	36	40	43	46	49
82	87	5	9	14	18	23	27	31	35	38	42	45	48	51
83	88	5	10	15	19	24	28	33	37	40	44	47	50	53
84	89	5	11	16	21	26	30	34	38	42	46	49	52	55
85	90	6	11	17	22	27	32	36	41	44	48	51	55	57

Male	Female	14 years	15 years	16 years	17 years	18 years	19 years	20 years	21 years	22 years	23 years	24 years	25 years	26 years
		Percent	Percent	Percent	Percent	Percent	Percent	Percent	Percent	Percent	Percent	Percent	Percent	Percent
6	11	1	1	1	1	1	1	1	1	1	1	2	2	2
7	12	1	1	1	1	1	1	1	1	1	1	2	2	2
8	13	1	1	1	1	1	1	1	1	1	1	2	2	2
9	14	1	1	1	1	1	1	1	1	1	1	2	2	2
10	15	1	1	1	1	1	1	1	1	1	2	2	2	2
11	16	1	1	1	1	1	1	1	1	1	2	2	2	2
12	17	1	1	1	1	1	1	1	1	1	2	2	2	2
13	18	1	1	1	1	1	1	1	1	2	2	2	2	2
14	19	1	1	1	1	1	1	1	1	2	2	2	2	2
15	20	1	1	1	1	1	1	1	1	2	2	2	2	2
16	21	1	1	1	1	1	1	1	2	2	2	2	2	2
17	22	1	1	1	1	1	1	1	2	2	2	2	2	2
18	23	1	1	1	1	1	1	2	2	2	2	2	2	2
19	24	1	1	1	1	1	2	2	2	2	2	2	2	2
20	25	1	1	1	1	1	2	2	2	2	2	2	2	3
21	26	1	1	1	1	2	2	2	2	2	2	2	3	3
22	27	1	1	1	1	2	2	2	2	2	2	3	3	3
23	28	1	1	1	2	2	2	2	2	2	2	3	3	3
24	29	1	1	2	2	2	2	2	2	2	3	3	3	3
25	30	1	1	2	2	2	2	2	2	3	3	3	3	3
26	31	1	2	2	2	2	2	2	3	3	3	3	3	4
27	32	2	2	2	2	2	2	3	3	3	3	3	4	4
28	33	2	2	2	2	2	3	3	3	3	3	4	4	4
29	34	2	2	2	2	2	3	3	3	3	4	4	4	5
30	35	2	2	2	2	3	3	3	3	4	4	4	5	5
31	36	2	2	2	3	3	3	3	4	4	4	5	5	5
32	37	2	2	3	3	3	3	4	4	4	5	5	5	6
33	38	2	3	3	3	3	4	4	4	5	5	5	6	6
34	39	3	3	3	3	4	4	4	5	5	5	6	6	7
35	40	3	3	3	4	4	4	5	5	5	6	6	7	7

Reg. § 1.72-9

Items Specifically Included in Gross Income

See p. 20,601 for regulations not amended to reflect law changes

TABLE III.—PERCENT VALUE OF REFUND FEATURE—Continued

Ages		Duration of guaranteed amount												
Male	Female	14 years	15 years	16 years	17 years	18 years	19 years	20 years	21 years	22 years	23 years	24 years	25 years	26 years
		Percent	Percent	Percent	Percent	Percent	Percent	Percent	Percent	Percent	Percent	Percent	Percent	Percent
36	41	3	3	4	4	4	5	5	5	6	6	7	7	8
37	42	3	3	4	4	4	5	5	6	6	7	7	8	8
38	43	3	4	4	4	5	5	6	6	7	7	8	8	9
39	44	4	4	4	5	5	6	6	7	7	8	8	9	9
40	45	4	4	5	5	6	6	7	7	8	8	9	9	10
41	46	4	5	5	6	6	7	7	8	8	9	9	10	11
42	47	5	5	5	6	6	7	8	8	9	9	10	11	12
43	48	5	5	6	6	7	8	8	9	9	10	11	12	12
44	49	5	6	6	7	7	8	9	9	10	11	12	12	13
45	50	6	6	7	7	8	9	9	10	11	12	12	13	14
46	51	6	7	7	8	9	9	10	11	12	12	13	14	15
47	52	7	7	8	9	9	10	11	12	12	13	14	15	16
48	53	7	8	8	9	10	11	12	12	13	14	15	16	17
49	54	8	8	9	10	11	11	12	13	14	15	16	17	18
50	55	8	9	10	11	11	12	13	14	15	16	17	18	20
51	56	9	10	10	11	12	13	14	15	16	17	18	20	21
52	57	9	10	11	12	13	14	15	16	17	18	20	21	22
53	58	10	11	12	13	14	15	16	17	19	20	21	22	24
54	59	11	12	13	14	15	16	17	18	20	21	22	24	25
55	60	11	13	14	15	16	17	18	20	21	22	24	25	26
56	61	12	13	15	16	17	18	20	21	22	24	25	27	28
57	62	13	14	16	17	18	20	21	22	24	25	27	28	30
58	63	14	15	17	18	19	21	22	24	25	27	28	30	31
59	64	15	16	18	19	21	22	24	25	27	28	30	31	33
60	65	16	18	19	20	22	24	25	27	28	30	32	33	35
61	66	17	19	20	22	23	25	27	28	30	32	33	35	37
62	67	18	20	22	23	25	27	28	30	32	33	35	37	38
63	68	20	21	23	25	26	28	30	32	33	35	37	39	40
64	69	21	23	24	26	28	30	32	33	35	37	39	41	42
65	70	22	24	26	28	30	32	33	35	37	39	41	42	44
66	71	24	26	28	29	31	33	35	37	39	41	43	44	46
67	72	25	27	29	31	33	35	37	39	41	43	45	46	48
68	73	27	29	31	33	35	37	39	41	43	45	47	48	50
69	74	28	30	33	35	37	39	41	43	45	47	48	50	52
70	75	30	32	34	37	39	41	43	45	47	49	50	52	54
71	76	32	34	36	39	41	43	45	47	49	51	52	54	56
72	77	34	36	38	41	43	45	47	49	51	53	54	56	58
73	78	35	38	40	43	45	47	49	51	53	55	56	58	59
74	79	37	40	42	45	47	49	51	53	55	57	58	60	61
75	80	39	42	44	47	49	51	53	55	57	58	60	62	63
76	81	41	44	46	49	51	53	55	57	59	60	62	63	65
77	82	43	46	48	51	53	55	57	59	61	62	64	65	66
78	83	45	48	50	53	55	57	59	61	62	64	65	67	68
79	84	48	50	53	55	57	59	61	63	64	66	67	68	70
80	85	50	52	55	57	59	61	63	64	66	67	69	70	71
81	86	52	54	57	59	61	63	65	66	68	69	70	72	73
82	87	54	56	59	61	63	65	66	68	69	71	72	73	74
83	88	56	58	61	63	65	66	68	70	71	72	73	74	75
84	89	58	60	63	65	67	68	70	71	73	74	75	76	77
85	90	60	62	65	67	68	70	71	73	74	75	76	77	

Reg. § 1.72-9

TABLE III.—PERCENT VALUE OF REFUND FEATURE—Continued

Ages		Duration of guaranteed amount								
Male	Female	27 years	28 years	29 years	30 years	31 years	32 years	33 years	34 years	years
		Percent	Percent	Percent	Percent	Percent	Percent	Percent	Percent	Percent
6	11	2	2	2	2	2	2	2	2	
7	12	2	2	2	2	2	2	2	2	3
8	13	2	2	2	2	2	2	2	3	3
9	14	2	2	2	2	2	2	2	3	3
10	15	2	2	2	2	2	2	3	3	3
11	16	2	2	2	2	2	2	3	3	3
12	17	2	2	2	2	2	3	3	3	3
13	18	2	2	2	2	2	2	3	3	3
14	19	2	2	2	2	2	3	3	3	3
15	20	2	2	2	2	3	3	3	3	3
16	21	2	2	3	3	3	3	3	3	4
17	22	2	2	3	3	3	3	3	4	4
18	23	2	3	3	3	3	3	4	4	4
19	24	3	3	3	3	3	4	4	4	4
20	25	3	3	3	3	4	4	4	4	5
21	26	3	3	3	4	4	4	4	5	5
22	27	3	3	4	4	4	4	5	5	5
23	28	3	3	4	4	4	5	5	5	5
24	29	3	4	4	4	5	5	5	6	6
25	30	4	4	4	5	5	5	6	6	6
26	31	4	4	5	5	5	6	6	6	7
27	32	4	5	5	5	6	6	6	7	7
28	33	5	5	5	6	6	6	7	7	8
29	34	5	5	6	6	6	7	7	8	8
30	35	5	6	6	6	7	7	8	8	9
31	36	6	6	6	7	7	8	8	9	9
32	37	6	7	7	7	8	8	9	10	10
33	38	7	7	7	8	8	9	10	10	11
34	39	7	7	8	8	9	9	10	11	12
35	40	8	8	9	9	10	10	11		12
36	41	8	9	9	10	10	11	12	13	13
37	42	9	9	10	11	11	12	13		14
38	43	9	10	11	11	12	13	13	14	15
39	44	10	11	11	12	13	14	14		16
40	45	11	11	12	13	14	15	15		17
41	46	11	12	13	14	15	16	16		18
42	47	12	13	14	15	16	17	18		19
43	48	13	14	15	16	17	18	19		21
44	49	14	15	16	17	18	19	20		22
45	50	15	16	17	18	19	20	21		23
46	51	16	17	18	19	20	21	22	24	25
47	52	17	18	19	20	21	23	24	25	26
48	53	18	19	20	22	23	24	25	26	28
49	54	19	21	22	23	24	25	27	28	29
50	55	21	22	23	24	26	27	28	29	31
51	56	22	23	25	26	27	28	30	31	32
52	57	23	25	26	27	29		31	33	34
53	58	25	26	28	29	30		33	35	36
54	59	26	28	29	31	32	37	35	36	38
55	60	28	29	31	32	34	39	36	40	39
56	61	29	31	32	34	36	40		41	41
57	62	31	33	34	36	37	42		43	43
58	63	33	34	36	37		44		45	45
59	64	35	36	38	39	46			47	47
60	65	36	38	40	48	48		47		48
61	66	38	40	41	50	50	50	49	49	50
62	67	40	42	43	52	52	52	51	51	52
63	68	42	44	45			53	53	52	54
64	69	44	46	47	54	55	55		54	55
65	70	46	47		56	55		56	56	57
					57	57	56	58	58	
66	71	48	49		59	59	58	59	59	59
67	72	50	51		60	60	60	61	61	61
68	73	52	53		61	62	62		63	62
69	74	53	55				63		64	64
70	75	55							65	65

Reg. § 1.72-9

TABLE III.—PERCENT VALUE OF REFUND FEATURE—Continued

| Ages | | Duration of guaranteed amount | | | | | | | | |
Male	Female	27 years	28 years	29 years	30 years	31 years	32 years	33 years	34 years	35 years
		Percent	Percent	Percent	Percent	Percent	Percent	Percent	Percent	Percent
71	76	57	59	60	61	63	64	65	66	67
72	77	59	60	62	63	64	65	66	67	68
73	78	61	62	64	65	66	67	68	69	70
74	79	63	64	65	66	67	68	69	70	71
75	80	64	66	67	68	69	70	71	72	72
76	81	66	67	68	69	70	71	72	73	
77	82	68	69	70	71	72	73	74		
78	83	69	70	71	72	73	74			
79	84	71	72	73	74	75				
80	85	72	73	74	75					
81	86	74	75	75						
82	87	75	76							
83	88	76								
84	89									
85	90									

| Ages | | Duration of guaranteed amount | | | | | | | | | | | | | |
Male	Female	1 year	2 years	3 years	4 years	5 years	6 years	7 years	8 years	9 years	10 years	11 years	12 years	13 years	14 years
		Per-cent	Per-cent	Per-cent	Per-cent	Per-cent	Per-cent	Per-cent	Per-cent	Per-cent	Per-cent	Per-cent	Per-cent	Per-cent	Per-cent
86	91	6	12	18	24	29	34	38	43	47	50	54	57	59	62
87	92	7	13	19	25	31	36	40	45	49	52	56	59	61	64
88	93	7	14	21	27	32	38	42	47	51	55	58	61	63	66
89	94	8	15	22	28	34	40	45	49	53	57	60	63	65	68
90	95	8	16	23	30	36	42	47	51	55	59	62	65	67	70
91	96	9	17	25	32	38	44	49	53	57	61	64	67	69	71
92	97	9	18	26	34	40	46	51	55	59	63	66	69	71	73
93	98	10	20	28	36	42	48	53	58	62	65	68	70	73	75
94	99	11	21	30	37	44	50	55	60	64	67	70	72	74	76
95	100	12	22	31	39	46	52	58	62	66	69	72	74	76	78
96	101	12	24	33	42	49	55	60	64	68	71	73	76	78	79
97	102	13	25	35	44	51	57	62	66	70	73	75	77	79	
98	103	14	27	37	46	54	60	65	69	72	75	77	79		
99	104	15	29	40	49	56	62	67	71	74	77	79			
100	105	17	31	43	52	59	65	70	74	76	79				
101	106	18	33	46	55	63	68	73	76	79					
102	107	20	36	49	59	66	71	75	78						
103	108	22	40	53	62	69	74	78							
104		24	43	57	68	73	77								
105		27	48	61	70	76									
106		31	53	66	74										
107		35	58	71											
108		40	64												

| Ages | | Duration of guaranteed amount | | | | | | | | | |
Male	Female	16 years	17 years	18 years	19 years	20 years	21 years	22 years	23 years	24 years	25 years
		Per-cent	Per-cent	Per-cent	Per-cent	Per-cent	Per-cent	Per-cent	Per-cent	Per-cent	Per-cent
86	91	66	68	70	72	73	74	75	76	77	
87	92	68	70	72	73	74	76	77	78		
88	93	70	72	73	75	76	77	78			
89	94	72	73	75	76	77	78				
90	95	73	75	76	77	79					
91	96	75	76	78	79						
92	97	76	78	79							
93	98	78	79								
94	99	79									
95	100										

Reg. § 1.72-9

TABLE IV.—TEMPORARY LIFE ANNUITIES [1]—ONE LIFE—EXPECTED RETURN MULTIPLES

| Ages | | Temporary period—maximum duration of annuity | | | | | | | | | |
Male	Female	1	2	3	4	5	6	7	8	9	10
0 to 8	0 to 13	1.0	2.0	3.0	4.0	5.0	6.0	7.0	8.0	8.9	9.9
9	14	1.0	2.0	3.0	4.0	5.0	6.0	7.0	8.0	8.9	9.9
10	15	1.0	2.0	3.0	4.0	5.0	6.0	7.0	8.0	8.9	9.9
11	16	1.0	2.0	3.0	4.0	5.0	6.0	7.0	8.0	8.9	9.9
12	17	1.0	2.0	3.0	4.0	5.0	6.0	7.0	8.0	8.9	9.9
13	18	1.0	2.0	3.0	4.0	5.0	6.0	7.0	8.0	8.9	9.9
14	19	1.0	2.0	3.0	4.0	5.0	6.0	7.0	8.0	8.9	9.9
15	20	1.0	2.0	3.0	4.0	5.0	6.0	7.0	8.0	8.9	9.9
16	21	1.0	2.0	3.0	4.0	5.0	6.0	7.0	8.0	8.9	9.9
17	22	1.0	2.0	3.0	4.0	5.0	6.0	7.0	8.0	8.9	9.9
18	23	1.0	2.0	3.0	4.0	5.0	6.0	7.0	8.0	8.9	9.9
19	24	1.0	2.0	3.0	4.0	5.0	6.0	7.0	8.0	8.9	9.9
20	25	1.0	2.0	3.0	4.0	5.0	6.0	7.0	8.0	8.9	9.9
21	26	1.0	2.0	3.0	4.0	5.0	6.0	7.0	8.0	8.9	9.9
22	27	1.0	2.0	3.0	4.0	5.0	6.0	7.0	8.0	8.9	9.9
23	28	1.0	2.0	3.0	4.0	5.0	6.0	7.0	8.0	8.9	9.9
24	29	1.0	2.0	3.0	4.0	5.0	6.0	7.0	7.9	8.9	9.9
25	30	1.0	2.0	3.0	4.0	5.0	6.0	7.0	7.9	8.9	9.9
26	31	1.0	2.0	3.0	4.0	5.0	6.0	7.0	7.9	8.9	9.9
27	32	1.0	2.0	3.0	4.0	5.0	6.0	7.0	7.9	8.9	9.9
28	33	1.0	2.0	3.0	4.0	5.0	6.0	7.0	7.9	8.9	9.9
29	34	1.0	2.0	3.0	4.0	5.0	6.0	6.9	7.9	8.9	9.9
30	35	1.0	2.0	3.0	4.0	5.0	6.0	6.9	7.9	8.9	9.9
31	36	1.0	2.0	3.0	4.0	5.0	6.0	6.9	7.9	8.9	9.9
32	37	1.0	2.0	3.0	4.0	5.0	6.0	6.9	7.9	8.9	9.9
33	38	1.0	2.0	3.0	4.0	5.0	6.0	6.9	7.9	8.9	9.9
34	39	1.0	2.0	3.0	4.0	5.0	5.9	6.9	7.9	8.9	9.8
35	40	1.0	2.0	3.0	4.0	5.0	5.9	6.9	7.9	8.9	9.8
36	41	1.0	2.0	3.0	4.0	5.0	5.9	6.9	7.9	8.9	9.8
37	42	1.0	2.0	3.0	4.0	5.0	5.9	6.9	7.9	8.8	9.8
38	43	1.0	2.0	3.0	4.0	5.0	5.9	6.9	7.9	8.8	9.8
39	44	1.0	2.0	3.0	4.0	4.9	5.9	6.9	7.9	8.8	9.8
40	45	1.0	2.0	3.0	4.0	4.9	5.9	6.9	7.8	8.8	9.7
41	46	1.0	2.0	3.0	4.0	4.9	5.9	6.9	7.8	8.8	9.7
42	47	1.0	2.0	3.0	4.0	4.9	5.9	6.9	7.8	8.8	9.7
43	48	1.0	2.0	3.0	4.0	4.9	5.9	6.9	7.8	8.8	9.7
44	49	1.0	2.0	3.0	4.0	4.9	5.9	6.8	7.8	8.7	9.7
45	50	1.0	2.0	3.0	3.9	4.9	5.9	6.8	7.8	8.7	9.6
46	51	1.0	2.0	3.0	3.9	4.9	5.9	6.8	7.8	8.7	9.6
47	52	1.0	2.0	3.0	3.9	4.9	5.9	6.8	7.7	8.7	9.6
48	53	1.0	2.0	3.0	3.9	4.9	5.9	6.8	7.7	8.6	9.5
49	54	1.0	2.0	3.0	3.9	4.9	5.8	6.8	7.7	8.6	9.5
50	55	1.0	2.0	3.0	3.9	4.9	5.8	6.8	7.7	8.6	9.5
51	56	1.0	2.0	3.0	3.9	4.9	5.8	6.7	7.7	8.6	9.4
52	57	1.0	2.0	3.0	3.9	4.9	5.8	6.7	7.6	8.5	9.4
53	58	1.0	2.0	2.9	3.9	4.9	5.8	6.7	7.6	8.5	9.3
54	59	1.0	2.0	2.9	3.9	4.8	5.8	6.7	7.6	8.4	9.3
55	60	1.0	2.0	2.9	3.9	4.8	5.8	6.7	7.5	8.4	9.2
56	61	1.0	2.0	2.9	3.9	4.8	5.7	6.6	7.5	8.4	9.2
57	62	1.0	2.0	2.9	3.9	4.8	5.7	6.6	7.5	8.3	9.1
58	63	1.0	2.0	2.9	3.9	4.8	5.7	6.6	7.4	8.3	9.1
59	64	1.0	2.0	2.9	3.9	4.8	5.7	6.5	7.4	8.2	9.0
60	65	1.0	2.0	2.9	3.8	4.8	5.6	6.5	7.3	8.1	8.9
61	66	1.0	2.0	2.9	3.8	4.7	5.6	6.5	7.3	8.1	8.8
62	67	1.0	2.0	2.9	3.8	4.7	5.6	6.4	7.2	8.0	8.8
63	68	1.0	2.0	2.9	3.8	4.7	5.6	6.4	7.2	7.9	8.7
64	69	1.0	1.9	2.9	3.8	4.7	5.5	6.3	7.1	7.9	8.6
65	70	1.0	1.9	2.9	3.8	4.6	5.5	6.3	7.1	7.8	8.5
66	71	1.0	1.9	2.9	3.8	4.6	5.4	6.2	7.0	7.7	8.4
67	72	1.0	1.9	2.9	3.7	4.6	5.4	6.2	6.9	7.6	8.3
68	73	1.0	1.9	2.8	3.7	4.6	5.4	6.1	6.8	7.5	8.2
69	74	1.0	1.9	2.8	3.7	4.5	5.3	6.1	6.8	7.4	8.0
70	75	1.0	1.9	2.8	3.7	4.5	5.3	6.0	6.7	7.3	7.9
71	76	1.0	1.9	2.8	3.7	4.5	5.2	5.9	6.6	7.2	7.8
72	77	1.0	1.9	2.8	3.6	4.4	5.2	5.8	6.5	7.1	7.6
73	78	1.0	1.9	2.8	3.6	4.4	5.1	5.8	6.4	7.0	7.5
74	79	1.0	1.9	2.8	3.6	4.3	5.0	5.7	6.3	6.8	7.3
75	80	1.0	1.9	2.7	3.5	4.3	5.0	5.6	6.2	6.7	7.1
76	81	1.0	1.9	2.7	3.5	4.2	4.9	5.5	6.1	6.5	7.0
77	82	1.0	1.9	2.7	3.5	4.2	4.8	5.4	5.9	6.4	6.8
78	83	1.0	1.9	2.7	3.4	4.1	4.7	5.3	5.8	6.2	6.6
79	84	1.0	1.8	2.7	3.4	4.1	4.7	5.2	5.7	6.1	6.4
80	85	1.0	1.8	2.6	3.4	4.0	4.6	5.1	5.5	5.9	6.2
81	86	1.0	1.8	2.6	3.3	3.9	4.5	5.0	5.4	5.7	6.0
82	87	1.0	1.8	2.6	3.3	3.9	4.4	4.8	5.2	5.6	5.8
83	88	.9	1.8	2.6	3.2	3.8	4.3	4.7	5.1	5.4	5.6
84	89	.9	1.8	2.5	3.2	3.7	4.2	4.6	4.9	5.2	5.4
85	90	.9	1.8	2.5	3.1	3.6	4.1	4.5	4.8	5.0	5.2
86	91	.9	1.8	2.5	3.1	3.6	4.0	4.3	4.6	4.8	5.0

[1] See footnote at end of table.

TABLE IV.—TEMPORARY LIFE ANNUITIES [1]—ONE LIFE—EXPECTED RETURN MULTIPLES—Continued

Ages		Temporary period—maximum duration of annuity									
Male	Female	Years									
		11	12	13	14	15	16	17	18	19	20
0 to 8	0 to 13	10.9	11.9	12.9	13.9	14.9	15.8	16.8	17.8	18.8	19.7
9	14	10.9	11.9	12.9	13.9	14.9	15.8	16.8	17.8	18.8	19.7
10	15	10.9	11.9	12.9	13.9	14.9	15.8	16.8	17.8	18.8	19.7
11	16	10.9	11.9	12.9	13.9	14.9	15.8	16.8	17.8	18.8	19.7
12	17	10.9	11.9	12.9	13.9	14.9	15.8	16.8	17.8	18.8	19.7
13	18	10.9	11.9	12.9	13.9	14.9	15.8	16.8	17.8	18.8	19.7
14	19	10.9	11.9	12.9	13.9	14.9	15.8	16.8	17.8	18.8	19.7
15	20	10.9	11.9	12.9	13.9	14.9	15.8	16.8	17.8	18.7	19.7
16	21	10.9	11.9	12.9	13.9	14.8	15.8	16.8	17.8	18.7	19.7
17	22	10.9	11.9	12.9	13.9	14.8	15.8	16.8	17.8	18.7	19.7
18	23	10.9	11.9	12.9	13.9	14.8	15.8	16.8	17.8	18.7	19.7
19	24	10.9	11.9	12.9	13.9	14.8	15.8	16.8	17.7	18.7	19.7
20	25	10.9	11.9	12.9	13.9	14.8	15.8	16.8	17.7	18.7	19.7
21	26	10.9	11.9	12.9	13.8	14.8	15.8	16.8	17.7	18.7	19.6
22	27	10.9	11.9	12.9	13.8	14.8	15.8	16.7	17.7	18.7	19.6
23	28	10.9	11.9	12.9	13.8	14.8	15.8	16.7	17.7	18.7	19.6
24	29	10.9	11.9	12.9	13.8	14.8	15.8	16.7	17.7	18.6	19.6
25	30	10.9	11.9	12.8	13.8	14.8	15.7	16.7	17.7	18.6	19.6
26	31	10.9	11.9	12.8	13.8	14.8	15.7	16.7	17.6	18.6	19.5
27	32	10.9	11.9	12.8	13.8	14.8	15.7	16.7	17.6	18.6	19.5
28	33	10.9	11.8	12.8	13.8	14.7	15.7	16.6	17.6	18.5	19.5
29	34	10.9	11.8	12.8	13.8	14.7	15.7	16.6	17.6	18.5	19.4
30	35	10.9	11.8	12.8	13.7	14.7	15.6	16.6	17.5	18.4	19.4
31	36	10.8	11.8	12.8	13.7	14.7	15.6	16.5	17.5	18.4	19.3
32	37	10.8	11.8	12.7	13.7	14.6	15.6	16.5	17.4	18.4	19.3
33	38	10.8	11.8	12.7	13.7	14.6	15.6	16.5	17.4	18.3	19.2
34	39	10.8	11.8	12.7	13.6	14.6	15.5	16.4	17.4	18.3	19.2
35	40	10.8	11.7	12.7	13.6	14.6	15.5	16.4	17.3	18.2	19.1
36	41	10.8	11.7	12.7	13.6	14.5	15.4	16.3	17.2	18.1	19.0
37	42	10.8	11.7	12.6	13.6	14.5	15.4	16.3	17.2	18.1	18.9
38	43	10.7	11.7	12.6	13.5	14.4	15.3	16.2	17.1	18.0	18.9
39	44	10.7	11.6	12.6	13.5	14.4	15.3	16.2	17.1	17.9	18.8
40	45	10.7	11.6	12.5	13.5	14.4	15.2	16.1	17.0	17.8	18.7
41	46	10.7	11.6	12.5	13.4	14.3	15.2	16.1	16.9	17.8	18.6
42	47	10.6	11.6	12.5	13.4	14.3	15.1	16.0	16.8	17.7	18.5
43	48	10.6	11.5	12.4	13.3	14.2	15.1	15.9	16.7	17.6	18.4
44	49	10.6	11.5	12.4	13.3	14.1	15.0	15.8	16.7	17.5	18.3
45	50	10.5	11.4	12.3	13.2	14.1	14.9	15.7	16.6	17.4	18.1
46	51	10.5	11.4	12.3	13.2	14.0	14.8	15.7	16.5	17.2	18.0
47	52	10.5	11.4	12.2	13.1	13.9	14.7	15.6	16.3	17.1	17.8
48	53	10.4	11.3	12.2	13.0	13.8	14.7	15.4	16.2	17.0	17.7
49	54	10.4	11.3	12.1	12.9	13.8	14.6	15.3	16.1	16.8	17.5
50	55	10.3	11.2	12.0	12.9	13.7	14.5	15.2	16.0	16.7	17.4
51	56	10.3	11.1	12.0	12.8	13.6	14.3	15.1	15.8	16.5	17.2
52	57	10.2	11.1	11.9	12.7	13.5	14.2	14.9	15.6	16.3	17.0
53	58	10.2	11.0	11.8	12.6	13.4	14.1	14.8	15.5	16.1	16.8
54	59	10.1	10.9	11.7	12.5	13.2	14.0	14.6	15.3	15.9	16.5
55	60	10.1	10.9	11.6	12.4	13.1	13.8	14.5	15.1	15.7	16.3
56	61	10.0	10.8	11.5	12.3	13.0	13.7	14.3	14.9	15.5	16.1
57	62	9.9	10.7	11.4	12.2	12.8	13.5	14.1	14.7	15.3	15.8
58	63	9.8	10.6	11.3	12.0	12.7	13.3	13.9	14.5	15.0	15.5
59	64	9.8	10.5	11.2	11.9	12.5	13.2	13.7	14.3	14.8	15.3
60	65	9.7	10.4	11.1	11.7	12.4	13.0	13.5	14.0	14.5	15.0
61	66	9.6	10.3	11.0	11.6	12.2	12.8	13.3	13.8	14.2	14.7
62	67	9.5	10.2	10.8	11.4	12.0	12.5	13.1	13.5	14.0	14.3
63	68	9.4	10.0	10.7	11.3	11.8	12.3	12.8	13.2	13.7	14.0
64	69	9.3	9.9	10.5	11.1	11.6	12.1	12.5	13.0	13.3	13.7
65	70	9.1	9.8	10.3	10.9	11.4	11.9	12.3	12.7	13.0	13.3
66	71	9.0	9.6	10.2	10.7	11.2	11.6	12.0	12.4	12.7	13.0
67	72	8.9	9.5	10.0	10.5	10.9	11.3	11.7	12.0	12.3	12.6
68	73	8.7	9.3	9.8	10.3	10.7	11.1	11.4	11.7	12.0	12.2
69	74	8.6	9.1	9.6	10.0	10.4	10.8	11.1	11.4	11.6	11.8
70	75	8.4	8.9	9.4	9.8	10.2	10.5	10.8	11.0	11.2	11.4
71	76	8.3	8.7	9.2	9.6	9.9	10.2	10.4	10.7	10.9	11.0
72	77	8.1	8.6	8.9	9.3	9.6	9.9	10.1	10.3	10.5	10.6
73	78	7.9	8.3	8.7	9.0	9.3	9.6	9.8	9.9	10.1	10.2
74	79	7.7	8.1	8.5	8.8	9.0	9.2	9.4	9.6	9.7	9.8
75	80	7.6	7.9	8.2	8.5	8.7	8.9	9.1	9.2	9.3	9.4
76	81	7.4	7.7	8.0	8.2	8.4	8.6	8.7	8.8	8.9	9.0
77	82	7.1	7.5	7.7	7.9	8.1	8.3	8.4	8.5	8.5	8.6
78	83	6.9	7.2	7.4	7.6	7.8	7.9	8.0	8.1	8.2	8.2
79	84	6.7	7.0	7.2	7.3	7.5	7.6	7.7	7.7	7.8	7.8
80	85	6.5	6.7	6.9	7.1	7.2	7.3	7.3	7.4	7.4	7.4
81	86	6.3	6.5	6.6	6.8	6.9	6.9	7.0	7.0	7.1	
82	87	6.0	6.2	6.4	6.5	6.5	6.6	6.7	6.7		
83	88	5.8	6.0	6.1	6.2	6.2	6.3	6.3			
84	89	5.6	5.7	5.8	5.9	5.9	6.0				
85	90	5.3	5.5	5.5	5.6	5.6					
86	91	5.1	5.2	5.3	5.3						

[1] See footnote at end of table

Reg. § 1.72-9

TABLE IV.—TEMPORARY LIFE ANNUITIES [1]—ONE LIFE—EXPECTED RETURN MULTIPLES—Continued

Ages		Temporary period—maximum duration of annuity									
		Years									
Male	Female	21	22	23	24	25	26	27	28	29	30
0 to 8	0 to 13	20.7	21.7	22.7	23.6	24.6	25.6	26.5	27.5	28.4	29.4
9	14	20.7	21.7	22.7	23.6	24.6	25.5	26.5	27.5	28.4	29.4
10	15	20.7	21.7	22.7	23.6	24.6	25.5	26.5	27.5	28.4	29.4
11	16	20.7	21.7	22.6	23.6	24.6	25.5	26.5	27.4	28.4	29.3
12	17	20.7	21.7	22.6	23.6	24.6	25.5	26.5	27.4	28.4	29.3
13	18	20.7	21.7	22.6	23.6	24.6	25.5	26.5	27.4	28.4	29.3
14	19	20.7	21.7	22.6	23.6	24.5	25.5	26.4	27.4	28.3	29.3
15	20	20.7	21.6	22.6	23.6	24.5	25.5	26.4	27.4	28.3	29.2
16	21	20.7	21.6	22.6	23.6	24.5	25.5	26.4	27.3	28.3	29.2
17	22	20.7	21.6	22.6	23.5	24.5	25.4	26.4	27.3	28.2	29.2
18	23	20.7	21.6	22.6	23.5	24.5	25.4	26.3	27.3	28.2	29.1
19	24	20.6	21.6	22.5	23.5	24.4	25.4	26.3	27.2	28.1	29.1
20	25	20.6	21.6	22.5	23.5	24.4	25.3	26.3	27.2	28.1	29.0
21	26	20.6	21.5	22.5	23.4	24.4	25.3	26.2	27.1	28.0	28.9
22	27	20.6	21.5	22.5	23.4	24.3	25.3	26.2	27.1	28.0	28.9
23	28	20.6	21.5	22.4	23.4	24.3	25.2	26.1	27.0	27.9	28.8
24	29	20.5	21.5	22.4	23.3	24.2	25.2	26.1	27.0	27.8	28.7
25	30	20.5	21.4	22.4	23.3	24.2	25.1	26.0	26.9	27.8	28.6
26	31	20.5	21.4	22.3	23.2	24.1	25.0	25.9	26.8	27.7	28.5
27	32	20.4	21.3	22.3	23.2	24.1	25.0	25.8	26.7	27.6	28.4
28	33	20.4	21.3	22.2	23.1	24.0	24.9	25.8	26.6	27.5	28.3
29	34	20.3	21.2	22.1	23.0	23.9	24.8	25.7	26.5	27.4	28.2
30	35	20.3	21.2	22.1	23.0	23.8	24.7	25.6	26.4	27.2	28.1
31	36	20.2	21.1	22.0	22.9	23.8	24.6	25.5	26.3	27.1	27.9
32	37	20.2	21.1	21.9	22.8	23.7	24.5	25.4	26.2	27.0	27.8
33	38	20.1	21.0	21.9	22.7	23.6	24.4	25.2	26.0	26.8	27.6
34	39	20.0	20.9	21.8	22.6	23.5	24.3	25.1	25.9	26.7	27.4
35	40	20.0	20.8	21.7	22.5	23.3	24.2	25.0	25.7	26.5	27.2
36	41	19.9	20.7	21.6	22.4	23.2	24.0	24.8	25.6	26.3	27.0
37	42	19.8	20.6	21.5	22.3	23.1	23.9	24.6	25.4	26.1	26.8
38	43	19.7	20.5	21.4	22.2	23.0	23.7	24.5	25.2	25.9	26.6
39	44	19.6	20.4	21.2	22.0	22.8	23.6	24.3	25.0	25.7	26.4
40	45	19.5	20.3	21.1	21.9	22.6	23.4	24.1	24.8	25.5	26.1
41	46	19.4	20.2	21.0	21.7	22.5	23.2	23.9	24.6	25.2	25.9
42	47	19.3	20.1	20.8	21.6	22.3	23.0	23.7	24.3	25.0	25.6
43	48	19.2	19.9	20.7	21.4	22.1	22.8	23.4	24.1	24.7	25.3
44	49	19.0	19.8	20.5	21.2	21.9	22.6	23.2	23.8	24.4	25.0
45	50	18.9	19.6	20.3	21.0	21.7	22.3	22.9	23.5	24.1	24.6
46	51	18.7	19.4	20.1	20.8	21.5	22.1	22.7	23.2	23.8	24.3
47	52	18.6	19.3	19.9	20.6	21.2	21.8	22.4	22.9	23.4	23.9
48	53	18.4	19.1	19.7	20.4	21.0	21.5	22.1	22.6	23.1	23.5
49	54	18.2	18.9	19.5	20.1	20.7	21.2	21.7	22.2	22.7	23.1
50	55	18.0	18.7	19.3	19.8	20.4	20.9	21.4	21.9	22.3	22.7
51	56	17.8	18.4	19.0	19.6	20.1	20.6	21.0	21.5	21.9	22.3
52	57	17.6	18.2	18.7	19.3	19.8	20.2	20.7	21.1	21.5	21.8
53	58	17.4	17.9	18.5	19.0	19.4	19.9	20.3	20.7	21.0	21.3
54	59	17.1	17.7	18.2	18.7	19.1	19.5	19.9	20.2	20.6	20.8
55	60	16.9	17.4	17.9	18.3	18.7	19.1	19.5	19.8	20.1	20.3
56	61	16.6	17.1	17.5	18.0	18.4	18.7	19.0	19.3	19.6	19.8
57	62	16.3	16.8	17.2	17.6	18.0	18.3	18.6	18.9	19.1	19.3
58	63	16.0	16.5	16.9	17.2	17.6	17.9	18.1	18.4	18.6	18.8
59	64	15.7	16.1	16.5	16.8	17.1	17.4	17.7	17.9	18.1	18.2
60	65	15.4	15.8	16.1	16.4	16.7	17.0	17.2	17.4	17.5	17.7
61	66	15.1	15.4	15.7	16.0	16.3	16.5	16.7	16.9	17.0	17.1
62	67	14.7	15.0	15.3	15.6	15.8	16.0	16.2	16.3	16.4	16.5
63	68	14.4	14.6	14.9	15.1	15.3	15.5	15.7	15.8	15.9	16.0
64	69	14.0	14.3	14.5	14.7	14.9	15.0	15.2	15.3	15.3	15.4
65	70	13.6	13.8	14.1	14.2	14.4	14.5	14.6	14.7	14.8	14.9
66	71	13.2	13.4	13.6	13.8	13.9	14.0	14.1	14.2	14.2	14.3
67	72	12.8	13.0	13.2	13.3	13.4	13.5	13.6	13.7	13.7	13.7
68	73	12.4	12.6	12.7	12.8	12.9	13.0	13.1	13.1	13.2	13.2
69	74	12.0	12.1	12.3	12.4	12.4	12.5	12.6	12.6	12.6	12.6
70	75	11.6	11.7	11.8	11.9	12.0	12.0	12.0	12.1	12.1	12.1
71	76	11.2	11.3	11.3	11.4	11.5	11.5	11.5	11.6	11.6	
72	77	10.7	10.8	10.9	10.9	11.0	11.0	11.0	11.0		
73	78	10.3	10.4	10.4	10.5	10.5	10.5	10.5			
74	79	9.9	9.9	10.0	10.0	10.1	10.1				
75	80	9.5	9.5	9.6	9.6	9.6					
76	81	9.1	9.1	9.1	9.1						
77	82	8.6	8.7	8.7							
78	83	8.2	8.3								
79	84	7.8									

[1] The multiples in this table are not applicable to annuities for a term certain; for such cases see § 1.72-5(c).

TABLE V.—ORDINARY LIFE ANNUITIES; ONE LIFE—EXPECTED RETURN MULTIPLES

Age	Multiple	Age	Multiple
5	76.6	61	23.3
6	75.6	62	22.5
7	74.7	63	21.6
8	73.7	64	20.8
9	72.7	65	20.0
10	71.7	66	19.2
11	70.7	67	18.4
12	69.7	68	17.6
13	68.8	69	16.8
14	67.8	70	16.0
15	66.8	71	15.3
16	65.8	72	14.6
17	64.8	73	13.9
18	63.9	74	13.2
19	62.9	75	12.5
20	61.9	76	11.9
21	60.9	77	11.2
22	59.9	78	10.6
23	59.0	79	10.0
24	58.0	80	9.5
25	57.0	81	8.9
26	56.0	82	8.4
27	55.1	83	7.9
28	54.1	84	7.4
29	53.1	85	6.9
30	52.2	86	6.5
31	51.2	87	6.1
32	50.2	88	5.7
33	49.3	89	5.3
34	48.3	90	5.0
35	47.3	91	4.7
36	46.4	92	4.4
37	45.4	93	4.1
38	44.4	94	3.9
39	43.5	95	3.7
40	42.5	96	3.4
41	41.5	97	3.2
42	40.6	98	3.0
43	39.6	99	2.8
44	38.7	100	2.7
45	37.7	101	2.5
46	36.8	102	2.3
47	35.9	103	2.1
48	34.9	104	1.9
49	34.0	105	1.8
50	33.1	106	1.6
51	32.2	107	1.4
52	31.3	108	1.3
53	30.4	109	1.1
54	29.5	110	1.0
55	28.6	111	.9
56	27.7	112	.8
57	26.8	113	.7
58	25.9	114	.6
59	25.0	115	.5
60	24.2		

Reg. § 1.72-9

TABLE VI.—ORDINARY JOINT LIFE AND LAST SURVIVOR ANNUITIES; TWO LIVES—EXPECTED RETURN MULTIPLES

Ages	5	6	7	8	9	10	11	12	13	14
5	83.8	83.3	82.8	82.4	82.0	81.6	81.2	80.9	80.6	80.3
6	83.3	82.8	82.3	81.8	81.4	81.0	80.6	80.3	79.9	79.6
7	82.8	82.3	81.8	81.3	80.9	80.4	80.0	79.6	79.3	78.9
8	82.4	81.8	81.3	80.8	80.3	79.9	79.4	79.0	78.6	78.3
9	82.0	81.4	80.9	80.3	79.8	79.3	78.9	78.4	78.0	77.6
10	81.6	81.0	80.4	79.9	79.3	78.8	78.3	77.9	77.4	77.0
11	81.2	80.6	80.0	79.4	78.9	78.3	77.8	77.3	76.9	76.4
12	80.9	80.3	79.6	79.0	78.4	77.9	77.3	76.8	76.3	75.9
13	80.6	79.9	79.3	78.6	78.0	77.4	76.9	76.3	75.8	75.3
14	80.3	79.6	78.9	78.3	77.6	77.0	76.4	75.9	75.3	74.8
15	80.0	79.3	78.6	77.9	77.3	76.6	76.0	75.4	74.9	74.3
16	79.8	79.0	78.3	77.6	76.9	76.3	75.6	75.0	74.4	73.9
17	79.5	78.8	78.0	77.3	76.6	75.9	75.3	74.6	74.0	73.4
18	79.3	78.5	77.8	77.0	76.3	75.6	74.9	74.3	73.6	73.0
19	79.1	78.3	77.5	76.8	76.0	75.3	74.6	73.9	73.3	72.6
20	78.9	78.1	77.3	76.5	75.8	75.0	74.3	73.6	72.9	72.3
21	78.7	77.9	77.1	76.3	75.5	74.8	74.0	73.3	72.6	71.9
22	78.6	77.7	76.9	76.1	75.3	74.5	73.8	73.0	72.3	71.6
23	78.4	77.6	76.7	75.9	75.1	74.3	73.5	72.8	72.0	71.3
24	78.3	77.4	76.6	75.7	74.9	74.1	73.3	72.6	71.8	71.1
25	78.2	77.3	76.4	75.6	74.8	73.9	73.1	72.3	71.6	70.8
26	78.0	77.2	76.3	75.4	74.6	73.8	72.9	72.1	71.3	70.6
27	77.9	77.1	76.2	75.3	74.4	73.6	72.8	71.9	71.1	70.3
28	77.8	76.9	76.1	75.2	74.3	73.4	72.6	71.8	70.9	70.1
29	77.7	76.8	76.0	75.1	74.2	73.3	72.5	71.6	70.8	70.0
30	77.7	76.8	75.9	75.0	74.1	73.2	72.3	71.5	70.6	69.8
31	77.6	76.7	75.8	74.9	74.0	73.1	72.2	71.3	70.5	69.6
32	77.5	76.6	75.7	74.8	73.9	73.0	72.1	71.2	70.3	69.5
33	77.5	76.5	75.6	74.7	73.8	72.9	72.0	71.1	70.2	69.3
34	77.4	76.5	75.5	74.6	73.7	72.8	71.9	71.0	70.1	69.2
35	77.3	76.4	75.5	74.5	73.6	72.7	71.8	70.9	70.0	69.1
36	77.3	76.3	75.4	74.5	73.5	72.6	71.7	70.8	69.9	69.0
37	77.2	76.3	75.4	74.4	73.5	72.6	71.6	70.7	69.8	68.9
38	77.2	76.2	75.3	74.4	73.4	72.5	71.6	70.6	69.7	68.8
39	77.2	76.2	75.3	74.3	73.4	72.4	71.5	70.6	69.6	68.7
40	77.1	76.2	75.2	74.3	73.3	72.4	71.4	70.5	69.6	68.6
41	77.1	76.1	75.2	74.2	73.3	72.3	71.4	70.4	69.5	68.6
42	77.0	76.1	75.1	74.2	73.2	72.3	71.3	70.4	69.4	68.5
43	77.0	76.1	75.1	74.1	73.2	72.2	71.3	70.3	69.4	68.5
44	77.0	76.0	75.1	74.1	73.1	72.2	71.2	70.3	69.3	68.4
45	77.0	76.0	75.0	74.1	73.1	72.2	71.2	70.2	69.3	68.4
46	76.9	76.0	75.0	74.0	73.1	72.1	71.2	70.2	69.3	68.3
47	76.9	75.9	75.0	74.0	73.1	72.1	71.1	70.2	69.2	68.3
48	76.9	75.9	74.9	74.0	73.0	72.1	71.1	70.1	69.2	68.2
49	76.9	75.9	74.9	74.0	73.0	72.0	71.1	70.1	69.1	68.2
50	76.9	75.9	74.9	73.9	73.0	72.0	71.0	70.1	69.1	68.2
51	76.8	75.9	74.9	73.9	73.0	72.0	71.0	70.1	69.1	68.1
52	76.8	75.9	74.9	73.9	72.9	72.0	71.0	70.0	69.1	68.1
53	76.8	75.8	74.9	73.9	72.9	71.9	71.0	70.0	69.0	68.1
54	76.8	75.8	74.8	73.9	72.9	71.9	71.0	70.0	69.0	68.1
55	76.8	75.8	74.8	73.9	72.9	71.9	70.9	70.0	69.0	68.0
56	76.8	75.8	74.8	73.8	72.9	71.9	70.9	69.9	69.0	68.0

Reg. § 1.72-9

TABLE VI.—ORDINARY JOINT LIFE AND LAST SURVIVOR ANNUITIES; TWO LIVES—EXPECTED RETURN MULTIPLES—Continued

Ages	5	6	7	8	9	10	11	12	13	14
57	76.8	75.8	74.8	73.8	72.9	71.9	70.9	69.9	69.0	68.0
58	76.8	75.8	74.8	73.8	72.8	71.9	70.9	69.9	68.9	68.0
59	76.7	75.8	74.8	73.8	72.8	71.9	70.9	69.9	68.9	68.0
60	76.7	75.8	74.8	73.8	72.8	71.8	70.9	69.9	68.9	67.9
61	76.7	75.7	74.8	73.8	72.8	71.8	70.9	69.9	68.9	67.9
62	76.7	75.7	74.8	73.8	72.8	71.8	70.8	69.9	68.9	67.9
63	76.7	75.7	74.8	73.8	72.8	71.8	70.8	69.9	68.9	67.9
64	76.7	75.7	74.7	73.8	72.8	71.8	70.8	69.8	68.9	67.9
65	76.7	75.7	74.7	73.8	72.8	71.8	70.8	69.8	68.9	67.9
66	76.7	75.7	74.7	73.7	72.8	71.8	70.8	69.8	68.9	67.9
67	76.7	75.7	74.7	73.7	72.8	71.8	70.8	69.8	68.8	67.9
68	76.7	75.7	74.7	73.7	72.8	71.8	70.8	69.8	68.8	67.9
69	76.7	75.7	74.7	73.7	72.7	71.8	70.8	69.8	68.8	67.8
70	76.7	75.7	74.7	73.7	72.7	71.8	70.8	69.8	68.8	67.8
71	76.7	75.7	74.7	73.7	72.7	71.8	70.8	69.8	68.8	67.8
72	76.7	75.7	74.7	73.7	72.7	71.8	70.8	69.8	68.8	67.8
73	76.7	75.7	74.7	73.7	72.7	71.7	70.8	69.8	68.8	67.8
74	76.7	75.7	74.7	73.7	72.7	71.7	70.8	69.8	68.8	67.8
75	76.7	75.7	74.7	73.7	72.7	71.7	70.8	69.8	68.8	67.8
76	76.6	75.7	74.7	73.7	72.7	71.7	70.8	69.8	68.8	67.8
77	76.6	75.7	74.7	73.7	72.7	71.7	70.8	69.8	68.8	67.8
78	76.6	75.7	74.7	73.7	72.7	71.7	70.7	69.8	68.8	67.8
79	76.6	75.7	74.7	73.7	72.7	71.7	70.7	69.8	68.8	67.8
80	76.6	75.7	74.7	73.7	72.7	71.7	70.7	69.8	68.8	67.8
81	76.6	75.7	74.7	73.7	72.7	71.7	70.7	69.8	68.8	67.8
82	76.6	75.7	74.7	73.7	72.7	71.7	70.7	69.8	68.8	67.8
83	76.6	75.7	74.7	73.7	72.7	71.7	70.7	69.8	68.8	67.8
84	76.6	75.7	74.7	73.7	72.7	71.7	70.7	69.8	68.8	67.8
85	76.6	75.7	74.7	73.7	72.7	71.7	70.7	69.8	68.8	67.8
86	76.6	75.7	74.7	73.7	72.7	71.7	70.7	69.8	68.8	67.8
87	76.6	75.7	74.7	73.7	72.7	71.7	70.7	69.8	68.8	67.8
88	76.6	75.7	74.7	73.7	72.7	71.7	70.7	69.7	68.8	67.8
89	76.6	75.7	74.7	73.7	72.7	71.7	70.7	69.7	68.8	67.8
90	76.6	75.6	74.7	73.7	72.7	71.7	70.7	69.7	68.8	67.8
91	76.6	75.6	74.7	73.7	72.7	71.7	70.7	69.7	68.8	67.8
92	76.6	75.6	74.7	73.7	72.7	71.7	70.7	69.7	68.8	67.8
93	76.6	75.6	74.7	73.7	72.7	71.7	70.7	69.7	68.8	67.8
94	76.6	75.6	74.7	73.7	72.7	71.7	70.7	69.7	68.8	67.8
95	76.6	75.6	74.7	73.7	72.7	71.7	70.7	69.7	68.8	67.8
96	76.6	75.6	74.7	73.7	72.7	71.7	70.7	69.7	68.8	67.8
97	76.6	75.6	74.7	73.7	72.7	71.7	70.7	69.7	68.8	67.8
98	76.6	75.6	74.7	73.7	72.7	71.7	70.7	69.7	68.8	67.8
99	76.6	75.6	74.7	73.7	72.7	71.7	70.7	69.7	68.8	67.8
100	76.6	75.6	74.7	73.7	72.7	71.7	70.7	69.7	68.8	67.8
101	76.6	75.6	74.7	73.7	72.7	71.7	70.7	69.7	68.8	67.8
102	76.6	75.6	74.7	73.7	72.7	71.7	70.7	69.7	68.8	67.8
103	76.6	75.6	74.7	73.7	72.7	71.7	70.7	69.7	68.8	67.8
104	76.6	75.6	74.7	73.7	72.7	71.7	70.7	69.7	68.8	67.8
105	76.6	75.6	74.7	73.7	72.7	71.7	70.7	69.7	68.8	67.8
106	76.6	75.6	74.7	73.7	72.7	71.7	70.7	69.7	68.8	67.8
107	76.6	75.6	74.7	73.7	72.7	71.7	70.7	69.7	68.8	67.8
108	76.6	75.6	74.7	73.7	72.7	71.7	70.7	69.7	68.8	67.8
109	76.6	75.6	74.7	73.7	72.7	71.7	70.7	69.7	68.8	67.8
110	76.6	75.6	74.7	73.7	72.7	71.7	70.7	69.7	68.8	67.8
111	76.6	75.6	74.7	73.7	72.7	71.7	70.7	69.7	68.8	67.8
112	76.6	75.6	74.7	73.7	72.7	71.7	70.7	69.7	68.8	67.8
113	76.6	75.6	74.7	73.7	72.7	71.7	70.7	69.7	68.8	67.8
114	76.6	75.6	74.7	73.7	72.7	71.7	70.7	69.7	68.8	67.8
115	76.6	75.6	74.7	73.7	72.7	71.7	70.7	69.7	68.8	67.8

Reg. § 1.72-9

TABLE VI.—ORDINARY JOINT LIFE AND LAST SURVIVOR ANNUITIES; TWO LIVES—EXPECTED RETURN MULTIPLES—Continued

Ages	15	16	17	18	19	20	21	22	23	24
15	73.8	73.3	72.9	72.4	72.0	71.6	71.3	70.9	70.6	70.3
16	73.3	72.8	72.3	71.9	71.4	71.0	70.7	70.3	70.0	69.6
17	72.9	72.3	71.8	71.3	70.9	70.5	70.0	69.7	69.3	69.0
18	72.4	71.9	71.3	70.8	70.4	69.9	69.5	69.0	68.7	68.3
19	72.0	71.4	70.9	70.4	69.8	69.4	68.9	68.5	68.1	67.7
20	71.6	71.0	70.5	69.9	69.4	68.8	68.4	67.9	67.5	67.1
21	71.3	70.7	70.0	69.5	68.9	68.4	67.9	67.4	66.9	66.5
22	70.9	70.3	69.7	69.0	68.5	67.9	67.4	66.9	66.4	65.9
23	70.6	70.0	69.3	68.7	68.1	67.5	66.9	66.4	65.9	65.4
24	70.3	69.6	69.0	68.3	67.7	67.1	66.5	65.9	65.4	64.9
25	70.1	69.3	68.6	68.0	67.3	66.7	66.1	65.5	64.9	64.4
26	69.8	69.1	68.3	67.6	67.0	66.3	65.7	65.1	64.5	63.9
27	69.6	68.8	68.1	67.3	66.7	66.0	65.3	64.7	64.1	63.5
28	69.3	68.6	67.8	67.1	66.4	65.7	65.0	64.3	63.7	63.1
29	69.1	68.4	67.6	66.8	66.1	65.4	64.7	64.0	63.3	62.7
30	69.0	68.2	67.4	66.6	65.8	65.1	64.4	63.7	63.0	62.3
31	68.8	68.0	67.2	66.4	65.6	64.8	64.1	63.4	62.7	62.0
32	68.6	67.8	67.0	66.2	65.4	64.6	63.8	63.1	62.4	61.7
33	68.5	67.6	66.8	66.0	65.2	64.4	63.6	62.8	62.1	61.4
34	68.3	67.5	66.6	65.8	65.0	64.2	63.4	62.6	61.9	61.1
35	68.2	67.4	66.5	65.6	64.8	64.0	63.2	62.4	61.6	60.9
36	68.1	67.2	66.4	65.5	64.7	63.8	63.0	62.2	61.4	60.6
37	68.0	67.1	66.2	65.4	64.5	63.7	62.8	62.0	61.2	60.4
38	67.9	67.0	66.1	65.2	64.4	63.5	62.7	61.8	61.0	60.2
39	67.8	66.9	66.0	65.1	64.2	63.4	62.5	61.7	60.8	60.0
40	67.7	66.8	65.9	65.0	64.1	63.3	62.4	61.5	60.7	59.9
41	67.7	66.7	65.8	64.9	64.0	63.1	62.3	61.4	60.5	59.7
42	67.6	66.7	65.7	64.8	63.9	63.0	62.2	61.3	60.4	59.6
43	67.5	66.6	65.7	64.8	63.8	62.9	62.1	61.2	60.3	59.4
44	67.5	66.5	65.6	64.7	63.8	62.9	62.0	61.1	60.2	59.3
45	67.4	66.5	65.5	64.6	63.7	62.8	61.9	61.0	60.1	59.2
46	67.4	66.4	65.4	64.6	63.6	62.7	61.8	60.9	60.0	59.1
47	67.3	66.4	65.4	64.5	63.6	62.6	61.7	60.8	59.9	59.0
48	67.3	66.3	65.4	64.4	63.5	62.6	61.6	60.7	59.8	58.9
49	67.2	66.3	65.3	64.4	63.5	62.5	61.6	60.7	59.7	58.8
50	67.2	66.2	65.3	64.3	63.4	62.5	61.5	60.6	59.7	58.8
51	67.2	66.2	65.3	64.3	63.4	62.4	61.5	60.5	59.6	58.7
52	67.1	66.2	65.2	64.3	63.3	62.4	61.4	60.5	59.6	58.6
53	67.1	66.2	65.2	64.2	63.3	62.3	61.4	60.4	59.5	58.6
54	67.1	66.1	65.2	64.2	63.2	62.3	61.3	60.4	59.5	58.5
55	67.1	66.1	65.1	64.2	63.2	62.3	61.3	60.4	59.4	58.5
56	67.0	66.1	65.1	64.1	63.2	62.2	61.3	60.3	59.4	58.4
57	67.0	66.1	65.1	64.1	63.2	62.2	61.2	60.3	59.3	58.4
58	67.0	66.0	65.1	64.1	63.1	62.2	61.2	60.3	59.3	58.4
59	67.0	66.0	65.0	64.1	63.1	62.1	61.2	60.2	59.3	58.3
60	67.0	66.0	65.0	64.1	63.1	62.1	61.2	60.2	59.2	58.3
61	67.0	66.0	65.0	64.0	63.1	62.1	61.1	60.2	59.2	58.3
62	66.9	66.0	65.0	64.0	63.1	62.1	61.1	60.2	59.2	58.2
63	66.9	66.0	65.0	64.0	63.0	62.1	61.1	60.1	59.2	58.2
64	66.9	65.9	65.0	64.0	63.0	62.1	61.1	60.1	59.2	58.2
65	66.9	65.9	65.0	64.0	63.0	62.0	61.1	60.1	59.1	58.2
66	66.9	65.9	64.9	64.0	63.0	62.0	61.1	60.1	59.1	58.2
67	66.9	65.9	64.9	64.0	63.0	62.0	61.1	60.1	59.1	58.1

Reg. § 1.72-9

TABLE VI.—ORDINARY JOINT LIFE AND LAST SURVIVOR ANNUITIES; TWO LIVES—EXPECTED RETURN MULTIPLES—Continued

Ages	15	16	17	18	19	20	21	22	23	24
68.	66.9	65.9	64.9	64.0	63.0	62.0	61.0	60.1	59.1	58.1
69.	66.9	65.9	64.9	63.9	63.0	62.0	61.0	60.0	59.1	58.1
70.	66.9	65.9	64.9	63.9	63.0	62.0	61.0	60.0	59.1	58.1
71.	66.9	65.9	64.9	63.9	62.9	62.0	61.0	60.0	59.1	58.1
72.	66.9	65.9	64.9	63.9	62.9	62.0	61.0	60.0	59.0	58.1
73.	66.8	65.9	64.9	63.9	62.9	62.0	61.0	60.0	59.0	58.1
74.	66.8	65.9	64.9	63.9	62.9	62.0	61.0	60.0	59.0	58.1
75.	66.8	65.9	64.9	63.9	62.9	61.9	61.0	60.0	59.0	58.1
76.	66.8	65.9	64.9	63.9	62.9	61.9	61.0	60.0	59.0	58.0
77.	66.8	65.9	64.9	63.9	63.9	62.9	61.0	60.0	59.0	58.0
78.	66.8	65.8	64.9	63.9	62.9	61.9	61.0	60.0	59.0	58.0
79.	66.8	65.8	64.9	63.9	62.9	61.9	61.0	60.0	59.0	58.0
80.	66.8	65.9	64.9	63.9	62.9	61.9	60.9	60.0	59.0	58.0
81.	66.8	65.8	64.9	63.9	62.9	61.9	60.9	60.0	59.0	58.0
82.	66.8	65.8	64.9	63.9	62.9	61.9	60.9	60.0	59.0	58.0
83.	66.8	65.8	64.9	63.9	62.9	61.9	60.9	60.0	59.0	58.0
84.	66.8	65.8	64.8	63.9	62.9	61.9	60.9	60.0	59.0	58.0
85.	66.8	65.8	64.8	63.9	62.9	61.9	60.9	60.0	59.0	58.0
86.	66.8	65.8	64.8	63.9	62.9	61.9	60.9	60.0	59.0	58.0
87.	66.8	65.8	64.8	63.9	62.9	61.9	60.9	60.0	59.0	58.0
88.	66.8	65.8	64.8	63.9	62.9	61.9	60.9	60.0	59.0	58.0
89.	66.8	65.8	64.8	63.9	62.9	61.9	60.9	60.0	59.0	58.0
90.	66.8	65.8	64.8	63.9	62.9	61.9	60.9	60.0	59.0	58.0
91.	66.8	65.8	64.8	63.9	62.9	61.9	60.9	60.0	59.0	58.0
92.	66.8	65.8	64.8	63.9	62.9	61.9	60.9	59.9	59.0	58.0
93.	66.8	65.8	64.8	63.9	62.9	61.9	60.9	59.9	59.0	58.0
94.	66.8	65.8	64.8	63.9	62.9	61.9	60.9	59.9	59.0	58.0
95.	66.8	65.8	64.8	63.9	62.9	61.9	60.9	59.9	59.0	58.0
96.	66.8	65.8	64.8	63.9	62.9	61.9	60.9	59.9	59.0	58.0
97.	66.8	65.8	64.8	63.9	62.9	61.9	60.9	59.9	59.0	58.0
98.	66.8	65.8	64.8	63.9	62.9	61.9	60.9	59.9	59.0	58.0
99.	66.8	65.8	64.8	63.9	62.9	61.9	60.9	59.9	59.0	58.0
100.	66.8	65.8	64.8	63.9	62.9	61.9	60.9	59.9	59.0	58.0
101.	66.8	65.8	64.8	63.9	62.9	61.9	60.9	59.9	59.0	58.0
102.	66.8	65.8	64.8	63.9	62.9	61.9	60.9	59.9	59.0	58.0
103.	66.8	65.8	64.8	63.9	62.9	61.9	60.9	59.9	59.0	58.0
104.	66.8	65.8	64.8	63.9	62.9	61.9	60.9	59.9	59.0	58.0
105.	66.8	65.8	64.8	63.9	62.9	61.9	60.9	59.9	59.0	58.0
106.	66.8	65.8	64.8	63.9	62.9	61.9	60.9	59.9	59.0	58.0
107.	66.8	65.8	64.8	63.9	62.9	61.9	60.9	59.9	59.0	58.0
108.	66.8	65.8	64.8	63.9	62.9	61.9	60.9	59.9	59.0	58.0
109.	66.8	65.8	64.8	63.9	62.9	61.9	60.9	59.9	59.0	58.0
110.	66.8	65.8	64.8	63.9	62.9	61.9	60.9	59.9	59.0	58.0
111.	66.8	65.8	64.8	63.9	62.9	61.9	60.9	59.9	59.0	58.0
112.	66.8	65.8	64.8	63.9	62.9	61.9	60.9	59.9	59.0	58.0
113.	66.8	65.8	64.8	63.9	62.9	61.9	60.9	59.9	59.0	58.0
114.	66.8	65.8	64.8	63.9	62.9	61.9	60.9	59.9	59.0	58.0
115.	66.8	65.8	64.8	63.9	62.9	61.9	60.9	59.9	59.0	58.0

Reg. § 1.72-9

See p. 20,601 for regulations not amended to reflect law changes

TABLE VI.—ORDINARY JOINT LIFE AND LAST SURVIVOR ANNUITIES; TWO LIVES—EXPECTED RETURN MULTIPLES—Continue

Ages	25	26	27	28	29	30	31	32	33	34
25	63.9	63.4	62.9	62.5	62.1	61.7	61.3	61.0	60.7	60.4
26	63.4	62.9	62.4	61.9	61.5	61.1	60.7	60.4	60.0	59.7
27	62.9	62.4	61.9	61.4	60.9	60.5	60.1	59.7	59.4	59.0
28	62.5	61.9	61.4	60.9	60.4	60.0	59.5	59.1	58.7	58.4
29	62.1	61.5	60.9	60.4	59.9	59.4	59.0	58.5	58.1	57.7
30	61.7	61.1	60.5	60.0	59.4	58.9	58.4	58.0	57.5	57.1
31	61.3	60.7	60.1	59.5	59.0	58.4	57.9	57.4	57.0	56.5
32	61.0	60.4	59.7	59.1	58.5	58.0	57.4	56.9	56.4	56.0
33	60.7	60.0	59.4	58.7	58.1	57.5	57.0	56.4	55.9	55.5
34	60.4	59.7	59.0	58.4	57.7	57.1	56.5	56.0	55.5	54.9
35	60.1	59.4	58.7	58.0	57.4	56.7	56.1	55.6	55.0	54.5
36	59.9	59.1	58.4	57.7	57.0	56.4	55.8	55.1	54.6	54.0
37	59.6	58.9	58.1	57.4	56.7	56.0	55.4	54.8	54.2	53.6
38	59.4	58.6	57.9	57.1	56.4	55.7	55.1	54.4	53.8	53.2
39	59.2	58.4	57.7	56.9	56.2	55.4	54.7	54.1	53.4	52.8
40	59.0	58.2	57.4	56.7	55.9	55.2	54.5	53.8	53.1	52.4
41	58.9	58.0	57.2	56.4	55.7	54.9	54.2	53.5	52.8	52.1
42	58.7	57.9	57.1	56.2	55.5	54.7	53.9	53.2	52.5	51.8
43	58.6	57.7	56.9	56.1	55.3	54.5	53.7	52.9	52.2	51.5
44	58.4	57.6	56.7	55.9	55.1	54.3	53.5	52.7	52.0	51.2
45	58.3	57.4	56.6	55.7	54.9	54.1	53.3	52.5	51.7	51.0
46	58.2	57.3	56.5	55.6	54.8	53.9	53.1	52.3	51.5	50.7
47	58.1	57.2	56.3	55.5	54.6	53.8	52.9	52.1	51.3	50.5
48	58.0	57.1	56.2	55.3	54.5	53.6	52.8	51.9	51.1	50.3
49	57.9	57.0	56.1	55.2	54.4	53.5	52.6	51.8	51.0	50.1
50	57.8	56.9	56.0	55.1	54.2	53.4	52.5	51.7	50.8	50.0
51	57.8	56.9	55.9	55.0	54.1	53.3	52.4	51.5	50.7	49.8
52	57.7	56.8	55.9	55.0	54.1	53.2	52.3	51.4	50.5	49.7
53	57.6	56.7	55.8	54.9	54.0	53.1	52.2	51.3	50.4	49.6
54	57.6	56.7	55.7	54.8	53.9	53.0	52.1	51.2	50.3	49.4
55	57.5	56.6	55.7	54.7	53.8	52.9	52.0	51.1	40.2	49.3
56	57.5	56.5	55.6	54.7	53.8	52.8	51.9	51.0	50.1	49.2
57	57.4	56.5	55.6	54.6	53.7	52.8	51.9	50.9	50.0	49.1
58	57.4	56.5	55.5	54.6	53.6	52.7	51.8	50.9	50.0	49.1
59	57.4	56.4	55.5	54.5	53.6	52.7	51.7	50.8	49.9	49.0
60	57.3	56.4	55.4	54.5	53.6	52.6	51.7	50.8	49.8	48.9
61	57.3	56.4	55.4	54.5	53.5	52.6	51.6	50.7	49.8	48.9
62	57.3	56.3	55.4	54.4	53.5	52.5	51.6	50.7	49.7	48.8
63	57.3	56.3	55.3	54.4	53.4	52.5	51.6	50.6	49.7	48.7
64	57.2	56.3	55.3	54.4	53.4	52.5	51.5	50.6	49.6	48.7
65	57.2	56.3	55.3	54.3	53.4	52.4	51.5	50.5	49.6	48.7
66	57.2	56.2	55.3	54.3	53.4	52.4	51.5	50.5	49.6	48.6
67	57.2	56.2	55.3	54.3	53.3	52.4	51.4	50.5	49.5	48.6
68	57.2	56.2	55.2	54.3	53.3	52.4	51.4	50.4	49.5	48.6
69	57.1	56.2	55.2	54.3	53.3	52.3	51.4	50.4	49.5	48.5

Reg. § 1.72-9

ABLE VI.—ORDINARY JOINT LIFE AND LAST SURVIVOR ANNUITIES; TWO LIVES—EXPECTED RETURN MULTIPLES—Continued

Ages	25	26	27	28	29	30	31	32	33	34
70	57.1	56.2	55.2	54.2	53.3	52.3	51.4	50.4	49.4	48.5
71	57.1	56.2	55.2	54.2	53.3	52.3	51.3	50.4	49.4	48.5
72	57.1	56.1	55.2	54.2	53.2	52.3	51.3	50.4	49.4	48.5
73	57.1	56.1	55.2	54.2	53.2	52.3	51.3	50.3	49.4	48.4
74	57.1	56.1	55.2	54.2	53.2	52.3	51.3	50.3	49.4	48.4
75	57.1	56.1	55.1	54.2	53.2	52.2	51.3	50.3	49.4	48.4
76	57.1	56.1	55.1	54.2	53.2	52.2	51.3	50.3	49.3	48.4
77	57.1	56.1	55.1	54.2	53.2	52.2	51.3	50.3	49.3	48.4
78	57.1	56.1	55.1	54.2	53.2	52.2	51.3	50.3	49.3	48.4
79	57.1	56.1	55.1	54.1	53.2	52.2	51.2	50.3	49.3	48.4
80	57.1	56.1	55.1	54.1	53.2	52.2	51.2	50.3	49.3	48.3
81	57.0	56.1	55.1	54.1	53.2	52.2	51.2	50.3	49.3	48.3
82	57.0	56.1	55.1	54.1	53.2	52.2	51.2	50.3	49.3	48.3
83	57.0	56.1	55.1	54.1	53.2	52.2	51.2	50.3	49.3	48.3
84	57.0	56.1	55.1	54.1	53.2	52.2	51.2	50.3	49.3	48.3
85	57.0	56.1	55.1	54.1	53.2	52.2	51.2	50.2	49.3	48.3
86	57.0	56.1	55.1	54.1	53.1	52.2	51.2	50.2	49.3	48.3
87	57.0	56.1	55.1	54.1	53.1	52.2	51.2	50.2	49.3	48.3
88	57.0	56.1	55.1	54.1	53.1	52.2	51.2	50.2	49.3	48.3
89	57.0	56.1	55.1	54.1	53.1	52.2	51.2	50.2	49.3	48.3
90	57.0	56.1	55.1	54.1	53.1	52.2	51.2	50.2	49.3	48.3
91	57.0	56.1	55.1	54.1	53.1	52.2	51.2	50.2	49.3	48.3
92	57.0	56.1	55.1	54.1	53.1	52.2	51.2	50.2	49.3	48.3
93	57.0	56.1	55.1	54.1	53.1	52.2	51.2	50.2	49.3	48.3
94	57.0	56.0	55.1	54.1	53.1	52.2	51.2	50.2	49.3	48.3
95	57.0	56.0	55.1	54.1	53.1	52.2	51.2	50.2	49.3	48.3
96	57.0	56.0	55.1	54.1	53.1	52.2	51.2	50.2	49.3	48.3
97	57.0	56.0	55.1	54.1	53.1	52.2	51.2	50.2	49.3	48.3
98	57.0	56.0	55.1	54.1	53.1	52.2	51.2	50.2	49.3	48.3
99	57.0	56.0	55.1	54.1	53.1	52.2	51.2	50.2	49.3	48.3
100	57.0	56.0	55.1	54.1	53.1	52.2	51.2	50.2	49.3	48.3
101	57.0	56.0	55.1	54.1	53.1	52.2	51.2	50.2	49.3	48.3
102	57.0	56.0	55.1	54.1	53.1	52.2	51.2	50.2	49.3	48.3
103	57.0	56.0	55.1	54.1	53.1	52.2	51.2	50.2	49.3	48.3
104	57.0	56.0	55.1	54.1	53.1	52.2	51.2	50.2	49.3	48.3
105	57.0	56.0	55.1	54.1	53.1	52.2	51.2	50.2	49.3	48.3
106	57.0	56.0	55.1	54.1	53.1	52.2	51.2	50.2	49.3	48.3
107	57.0	56.0	55.1	54.1	53.1	52.2	51.2	50.2	49.3	48.3
108	57.0	56.0	55.1	54.1	53.1	52.2	51.2	50.2	49.3	48.3
109	57.0	56.0	55.1	54.1	53.1	52.2	51.2	50.2	49.3	48.3
110	57.0	56.0	55.1	54.1	53.1	52.2	51.2	50.2	49.3	48.3
111	57.0	56.0	55.1	54.1	53.1	52.2	51.2	50.2	49.3	48.3
112	57.0	56.0	55.1	54.1	53.1	52.2	51.2	50.2	49.3	48.3
113	57.0	56.0	55.1	54.1	53.1	52.2	51.2	50.2	49.3	48.3
114	57.0	56.0	55.1	54.1	53.1	52.2	51.2	50.2	49.3	48.3
115	57.0	56.0	55.1	54.1	53.1	52.2	51.2	50.2	49.3	48.3

TABLE VI.—ORDINARY JOINT LIFE AND LAST SURVIVOR ANNUITIES; TWO LIVES—EXPECTED RETURN MULTIPLES—Continu

Ages	35	36	37	38	39	40	41	42	43	44
35	54.0	53.5	53.0	52.6	52.2	51.8	51.4	51.1	50.8	50.5
36	53.5	53.0	52.5	52.0	51.6	51.2	50.8	50.4	50.1	49.8
37	53.0	52.5	52.0	51.5	51.0	50.6	50.2	49.8	49.5	49.1
38	52.6	52.0	51.5	51.0	50.5	50.0	49.6	49.2	48.8	48.5
39	52.2	51.6	51.0	50.5	50.0	49.5	49.1	48.6	48.2	47.8
40	51.8	51.2	50.6	50.0	49.5	49.0	48.5	48.1	47.6	47.2
41	51.4	50.8	50.2	49.6	49.1	48.5	48.0	47.5	47.1	46.7
42	51.1	50.4	49.8	49.2	48.6	48.1	47.5	47.0	46.6	46.1
43	50.8	50.1	49.5	48.8	48.2	47.6	47.1	46.6	46.0	45.6
44	50.5	49.8	49.1	48.5	47.8	47.2	46.7	46.1	45.6	45.1
45	50.2	49.5	48.8	48.1	47.5	46.9	46.3	45.7	45.1	44.6
46	50.0	49.2	48.5	47.8	47.2	46.5	45.9	45.3	44.7	44.1
47	49.7	49.0	48.3	47.5	46.8	46.2	45.5	44.9	44.3	43.7
48	49.5	48.8	48.0	47.3	46.6	45.9	45.2	44.5	43.9	43.3
49	49.3	48.5	47.8	47.0	46.3	45.6	44.9	44.2	43.6	42.9
50	49.2	48.4	47.6	46.8	46.0	45.3	44.6	43.9	43.2	42.6
51	49.0	48.2	47.4	46.6	45.8	45.1	44.3	43.6	42.9	42.2
52	48.8	48.0	47.2	46.4	45.6	44.8	44.1	43.3	42.6	41.9
53	48.7	47.9	47.0	46.2	45.4	44.6	43.9	43.1	42.4	41.7
54	48.6	47.7	46.9	46.0	45.2	44.4	43.6	42.9	42.1	41.4
55	48.5	47.6	46.7	45.9	45.1	44.2	43.4	42.7	41.9	41.2
56	48.3	47.5	46.6	45.8	44.9	44.1	43.3	42.5	41.7	40.9
57	48.3	47.4	46.5	45.6	44.8	43.9	43.1	42.3	41.5	40.7
58	48.2	47.3	46.4	45.5	44.7	43.8	43.0	42.1	41.3	40.5
59	48.1	47.2	46.3	45.4	44.5	43.7	42.8	42.0	41.2	40.4
60	48.0	47.1	46.2	45.3	44.4	43.6	42.7	41.9	41.0	40.2
61	47.9	47.0	46.1	45.2	44.3	43.5	42.6	41.7	40.9	40.0
62	47.9	47.0	46.0	45.1	44.2	43.4	42.5	41.6	40.8	39.9
63	47.8	46.9	46.0	45.1	44.2	43.3	42.4	41.5	40.6	39.8
64	47.8	46.8	45.9	45.0	44.1	43.2	42.3	41.4	40.5	39.7
65	47.7	46.8	45.9	44.9	44.0	43.1	42.2	41.3	40.4	39.6
66	47.7	46.7	45.8	44.9	44.0	43.1	42.2	41.3	40.4	39.5
67	47.6	46.7	45.8	44.8	43.9	43.0	42.1	41.2	40.3	39.4
68	47.6	46.7	45.7	44.8	43.9	42.9	42.0	41.1	40.2	39.3
69	47.6	46.6	45.7	44.8	43.8	42.9	42.0	41.1	40.2	39.3
70	47.5	46.6	45.7	44.7	43.8	42.9	41.9	41.0	40.1	39.2
71	47.5	46.6	45.6	44.7	43.8	42.8	41.9	41.0	40.1	39.1
72	47.5	46.6	45.6	44.7	43.7	42.8	41.9	40.9	40.0	39.1
73	47.5	46.5	45.6	44.6	43.7	42.8	41.8	40.9	40.0	39.0
74	47.5	46.5	45.6	44.6	43.7	42.7	41.8	40.9	39.9	39.0
75	47.4	46.5	45.5	44.6	43.6	42.7	41.8	40.8	39.9	39.0

Reg. § 1.72-9

ABLE VI.—ORDINARY JOINT LIFE AND LAST SURVIVOR ANNUITIES; TWO LIVES—EXPECTED RETURN MULTIPLES—Continued

Ages	35	36	37	38	39	40	41	42	43	44
76	47.4	46.5	45.5	44.6	43.6	42.7	41.7	40.8	39.9	38.9
77	47.4	46.5	45.5	44.6	43.6	42.7	41.7	40.8	39.8	38.9
78	47.4	46.4	45.5	44.5	43.6	42.6	41.7	40.7	39.8	38.9
79	47.4	46.4	45.5	44.5	43.6	42.6	41.7	40.7	39.8	38.9
80	47.4	46.4	45.5	44.5	43.6	42.6	41.7	40.7	39.8	38.8
81	47.4	46.4	45.5	44.5	43.5	42.6	41.6	40.7	39.8	38.8
82	47.4	46.4	45.4	44.5	43.5	42.6	41.6	40.7	39.7	38.8
83	47.4	46.4	45.4	44.5	43.5	42.6	41.6	40.7	39.7	38.8
84	47.4	46.4	45.4	44.5	43.5	42.6	41.6	40.7	39.7	38.8
85	47.4	46.4	45.4	44.5	43.5	42.6	41.6	40.7	39.7	38.8
86	47.3	46.4	45.4	44.5	43.5	42.5	41.6	40.6	39.7	38.8
87	47.3	46.4	45.4	44.5	43.5	42.5	41.6	40.6	39.7	38.7
88	47.3	46.4	45.4	44.5	43.5	42.5	41.6	40.6	39.7	38.7
89	47.3	46.4	45.4	44.4	43.5	42.5	41.6	40.6	39.7	38.7
90	47.3	46.4	45.4	44.4	43.5	42.5	41.6	40.6	39.7	38.7
91	47.3	46.4	45.4	44.4	43.5	42.5	41.6	40.6	39.7	39.7
92	47.3	46.4	45.4	44.4	44.4	43.5	42.5	41.6	40.6	38.7
93	47.3	46.4	45.4	43.5	42.5	41.6	40.6	39.7	39.7	38.7
94	47.3	46.4	45.4	44.4	43.5	42.5	41.6	40.6	39.7	38.7
95	47.3	46.4	45.4	44.4	43.5	42.5	41.6	40.6	39.7	38.7
96	47.3	46.4	45.4	44.4	43.5	42.5	41.6	40.6	39.7	38.7
97	47.3	46.4	45.4	44.4	43.5	42.5	41.6	40.6	39.6	38.7
98	47.3	46.4	45.4	44.4	43.5	42.5	41.6	40.6	39.6	38.7
99	47.3	46.4	45.4	44.4	43.5	42.5	41.5	40.6	39.6	38.7
100	47.3	46.4	45.4	44.4	43.5	42.5	41.5	40.6	39.6	38.7
101	47.3	46.4	45.4	44.4	43.5	42.5	41.5	40.6	39.6	38.7
102	47.3	46.4	45.4	44.4	43.5	42.5	41.5	40.6	39.6	38.7
103	47.3	46.4	45.4	44.4	43.5	42.5	41.5	40.6	39.6	38.7
104	47.3	46.4	45.4	44.4	43.5	42.5	41.5	40.6	39.6	38.7
105	47.3	46.4	45.4	44.4	43.5	42.5	41.5	40.6	39.6	38.7
106	47.3	46.4	45.4	44.4	43.5	42.5	41.5	40.6	39.6	38.7
107	47.3	46.4	45.4	44.4	43.5	42.5	41.5	40.6	39.6	38.7
108	47.3	46.4	45.4	44.4	43.5	42.5	41.5	40.6	39.6	38.7
109	47.3	46.4	45.4	44.4	43.5	42.5	41.5	40.6	39.6	38.7
110	47.3	46.4	45.4	44.4	43.5	42.5	41.5	40.6	39.6	38.7
111	47.3	46.4	45.4	44.4	43.5	42.5	41.5	40.6	39.6	38.7
112	47.3	46.4	45.4	44.4	43.5	42.5	41.5	40.6	39.6	38.7
113	47.3	46.4	45.4	44.4	43.5	42.5	41.5	40.6	39.6	38.7
114	47.3	46.4	45.4	44.4	43.5	42.5	41.5	40.6	39.6	38.7
115	47.3	46.4	45.4	44.4	43.5	42.5	41.5	40.6	39.6	38.7

Reg. § 1.72-9

TABLE VI.—ORDINARY JOINT LIFE AND LAST SURVIVOR ANNUITIES; TWO LIVES—EXPECTED RETURN MULTIPLES—Continued

Ages	45	46	47	48	49	50	51	52	53	54
45	44.1	43.6	43.2	42.7	42.3	42.0	41.6	41.3	41.0	40.7
46	43.6	43.1	42.6	42.2	41.8	41.4	41.0	40.6	40.3	40.0
47	43.2	42.6	42.1	41.7	41.2	40.8	40.4	40.0	39.7	39.3
48	42.7	42.2	41.7	41.2	40.7	40.2	39.8	39.4	39.0	38.7
49	42.3	41.8	41.2	40.7	40.2	39.7	39.3	38.8	38.4	38.1
50	42.0	41.4	40.8	40.2	39.7	39.2	38.7	38.3	37.9	37.5
51	41.6	41.0	40.4	39.8	39.3	38.7	38.2	37.8	37.3	36.9
52	41.3	40.6	40.0	39.4	38.8	38.3	37.8	37.3	36.8	36.4
53	41.0	40.3	39.7	39.0	38.4	37.9	37.3	36.8	36.3	35.8
54	40.7	40.0	39.3	38.7	38.1	37.5	36.9	36.4	35.8	35.3
55	40.4	39.7	39.0	38.4	37.7	37.1	36.5	35.9	35.4	34.9
56	40.2	39.5	38.7	38.1	37.4	36.8	36.1	35.6	35.0	34.4
57	40.0	39.2	38.5	37.8	37.1	36.4	35.8	35.2	34.6	34.0
58	39.7	39.0	38.2	37.5	36.8	36.1	35.5	34.8	34.2	33.6
59	39.6	38.8	38.0	37.3	36.6	35.9	35.2	34.5	33.9	33.3
60	39.4	38.6	37.8	37.1	36.3	35.6	34.9	34.2	33.6	32.9
61	39.2	38.4	37.6	36.9	36.1	35.4	34.6	33.9	33.3	32.6
62	39.1	38.3	37.5	36.7	35.9	35.1	34.4	33.7	33.0	32.3
63	38.9	38.1	37.3	36.5	35.7	34.9	34.2	33.5	32.7	32.0
64	38.8	38.0	37.2	36.3	35.5	34.8	34.0	33.2	32.5	31.8
65	38.7	37.9	37.0	36.2	35.4	34.6	33.8	33.0	32.3	31.6
66	38.6	37.8	36.9	36.1	35.2	34.4	33.6	32.9	32.1	31.4
67	38.5	37.7	36.8	36.0	35.1	34.3	33.5	32.7	31.9	31.2
68	38.4	37.6	36.7	35.8	35.0	34.2	33.4	32.5	31.8	31.0
69	38.4	37.5	36.6	35.7	34.9	34.1	33.2	32.4	31.6	30.8
70	38.3	37.4	36.5	35.7	34.8	34.0	33.1	32.3	31.5	30.7
71	38.2	37.3	36.5	35.6	34.7	33.9	33.0	32.2	31.4	30.5
72	38.2	37.3	36.4	35.5	34.6	33.8	32.9	32.1	31.2	30.4
73	38.1	37.2	36.3	35.4	34.6	33.7	32.8	32.0	31.1	30.3
74	38.1	37.2	36.3	35.4	34.5	33.6	32.8	31.9	31.1	30.2
75	38.1	37.1	36.2	35.3	34.5	33.6	32.7	31.8	31.0	30.1
76	38.0	37.1	36.2	35.3	34.4	33.5	32.6	31.8	30.9	30.1
77	38.0	37.1	36.2	35.3	34.4	33.5	32.6	31.7	30.8	30.0
78	38.0	37.0	36.1	35.2	34.3	33.4	32.5	31.7	30.8	29.9
79	37.9	37.0	36.1	35.2	34.3	33.4	32.5	31.6	30.7	29.9
80	37.9	37.0	36.1	35.2	34.2	33.4	32.5	31.6	30.7	29.8
81	37.9	37.0	36.0	35.1	34.2	33.3	32.4	31.5	30.7	29.8
82	37.9	36.9	36.0	35.1	34.2	33.3	32.4	31.5	30.6	29.7
83	37.9	36.9	36.0	35.1	34.2	33.3	32.4	31.5	30.6	29.7
84	37.8	36.9	36.9	35.0	34.2	33.2	32.3	31.4	30.6	29.7
85	37.8	36.9	36.0	35.1	34.1	33.2	32.3	31.4	30.5	29.6
86	38.8	36.9	36.0	35.0	34.1	33.2	32.3	31.4	30.5	29.6
87	37.8	36.9	35.9	35.0	34.1	33.2	32.3	31.4	30.5	29.6
88	37.8	36.9	35.9	35.0	34.1	33.2	32.3	31.4	30.5	29.6
89	37.8	36.9	35.9	35.0	34.1	33.2	32.3	31.4	30.5	29.6
90	37.8	36.9	35.9	35.0	34.1	33.2	32.3	31.3	30.5	29.6
91	37.8	36.8	35.9	35.0	34.1	33.2	32.2	31.3	30.4	29.5
92	37.8	36.8	35.9	35.0	34.1	33.2	32.2	31.3	30.4	29.5
93	37.8	36.8	35.9	35.0	34.1	33.1	32.2	31.3	30.4	29.5
94	37.8	36.8	35.9	35.0	34.1	33.1	32.2	31.3	30.4	29.5
95	37.8	36.8	35.9	35.0	34.0	33.1	32.2	31.3	30.4	29.5
96	37.8	36.8	35.9	35.0	34.0	33.1	32.2	31.3	30.4	29.5
97	37.8	36.8	35.9	35.0	34.0	33.1	32.2	31.3	30.4	29.5
98	37.8	36.8	35.9	35.0	34.0	33.1	32.2	31.3	30.4	29.5
99	37.8	36.8	35.9	35.0	34.0	33.1	32.2	31.3	30.4	29.5
101	37.8	36.8	35.9	35.0	34.0	33.1	32.2	31.3	30.4	29.5
102	37.8	36.8	35.9	35.0	34.0	33.1	32.2	31.3	30.4	29.5
103	37.7	36.8	35.9	34.9	34.0	33.1	32.2	31.3	30.4	29.5
104	37.7	36.8	35.9	34.9	34.0	33.1	32.2	31.3	30.4	29.5
105	37.7	36.8	35.9	34.9	34.0	33.1	32.2	31.3	30.4	29.5
106	37.7	36.8	35.9	34.9	34.0	33.1	32.2	31.3	30.4	29.5
107	37.7	36.8	35.9	34.9	34.0	33.1	32.2	31.3	30.4	29.5
108	37.7	36.8	35.9	34.9	34.0	33.1	32.2	31.3	30.4	29.5
109	37.7	36.8	35.9	34.9	34.0	33.1	32.2	31.3	30.4	29.5
110	37.7	36.8	35.9	34.9	34.0	33.1	32.2	31.3	30.4	29.5
111	37.7	36.8	35.9	34.9	34.0	33.1	32.2	31.3	30.4	29.5
112	37.7	36.8	35.9	34.9	34.0	33.1	32.2	31.3	30.4	29.5
113	37.7	36.8	35.9	34.9	34.0	33.1	32.2	31.3	30.4	29.5
114	37.7	36.8	35.9	34.9	34.0	33.1	32.2	31.3	30.4	29.5
115	37.7	36.8	35.9	34.9	34.0	33.1	32.2	31.3	30.4	29.5

Reg. § 1.72-9

TABLE VI.—ORDINARY JOINT LIFE AND LAST SURVIVOR ANNUITIES; TWO LIVES—EXPECTED RETURN MULTIPLES—Continued

Ages	55	56	57	58	59	60	61	62	63	64
55	34.4	33.9	33.5	33.1	32.7	32.3	32.0	31.7	31.4	31.1
56	33.9	33.4	33.0	32.5	32.1	31.7	31.4	31.0	30.7	30.4
57	33.5	33.0	32.5	32.0	31.6	31.2	30.8	30.4	30.1	29.8
58	33.1	32.5	32.0	31.5	31.1	30.6	30.2	29.9	29.5	29.2
59	32.7	32.1	31.6	31.1	30.6	30.1	29.7	29.3	28.9	28.6
60	32.3	31.7	31.2	30.6	30.1	29.7	29.2	28.8	28.4	28.0
61	32.0	31.4	30.8	30.2	29.7	29.2	28.7	28.3	27.8	27.4
62	31.7	31.0	30.4	29.9	29.3	28.8	28.3	27.6	27.3	26.9
63	31.4	30.7	30.1	29.5	28.9	28.4	27.6	27.3	26.9	26.4
64	31.1	30.4	29.8	29.2	28.6	28.0	27.4	26.9	26.4	25.9
65	30.9	30.2	29.5	28.9	28.2	27.6	27.1	26.5	26.0	25.5
66	30.6	29.9	29.2	28.6	27.9	27.3	26.7	26.1	25.6	25.1
67	30.4	29.7	29.0	28.3	27.6	27.0	26.4	25.8	25.2	24.7
68	30.2	29.5	28.8	28.1	27.4	26.7	26.1	25.5	24.9	24.3
69	30.1	29.3	28.6	27.8	27.1	26.5	25.8	25.2	24.6	24.0
70	29.9	29.1	28.4	27.6	26.9	26.2	25.6	24.9	24.3	23.7
71	29.7	29.0	28.2	27.5	26.7	26.0	25.3	24.7	24.0	23.4
72	29.6	28.8	28.1	27.3	26.5	25.8	25.1	24.4	23.8	23.1
73	29.5	28.7	27.9	27.1	26.4	25.6	24.9	24.2	23.5	22.9
74	29.4	28.6	27.8	27.0	26.2	25.5	24.7	24.0	23.3	22.7
75	29.3	28.5	27.7	26.9	26.1	25.3	24.6	23.8	23.1	22.4
76	29.2	28.4	27.6	26.8	26.0	25.2	24.4	23.7	23.0	22.3
77	29.1	28.3	27.5	26.7	25.9	25.1	24.3	23.6	22.8	22.1
78	29.1	28.2	27.4	26.6	25.8	25.0	24.2	23.4	22.7	21.9
79	29.0	28.2	27.3	26.5	25.7	24.9	24.1	23.3	22.6	21.8
80	29.0	28.1	27.3	26.4	25.6	24.8	24.0	23.2	22.4	21.7
81	28.9	28.1	27.2	26.4	25.5	24.7	23.9	23.1	22.3	21.6
82	28.9	28.0	27.2	26.3	25.5	24.6	23.8	23.0	22.3	21.5
83	28.8	28.0	27.1	26.3	25.4	24.6	23.8	23.0	22.2	21.4
84	28.8	27.9	27.1	26.2	25.4	24.5	23.7	22.9	22.1	21.3
85	28.8	27.9	27.0	26.2	25.3	24.5	23.7	22.8	22.0	21.3
86	28.7	27.9	27.0	26.1	25.3	24.5	23.6	22.8	22.0	21.2
87	28.7	27.8	27.0	26.1	25.3	24.4	23.6	22.8	21.9	21.1
88	28.7	27.8	27.0	26.1	25.2	24.4	23.5	22.7	21.9	21.1
89	28.7	27.8	26.9	26.1	25.2	24.4	23.5	22.7	21.9	21.1
90	28.7	27.8	26.9	26.1	25.2	24.3	23.5	22.7	21.8	21.0
91	28.7	27.8	26.9	26.0	25.2	24.3	23.5	22.6	21.8	21.0
92	28.6	27.8	26.9	26.0	25.2	24.3	23.5	22.6	21.8	21.0
93	28.6	27.8	26.9	26.0	25.1	24.3	23.4	22.6	21.8	20.9
94	28.6	27.7	26.9	26.0	25.1	24.3	23.4	22.6	21.7	20.9
95	28.6	27.7	26.9	26.0	25.1	24.3	23.4	22.6	21.7	20.9
96	28.6	27.7	26.9	26.0	25.1	24.2	23.4	22.6	21.7	20.9
97	28.6	27.7	26.8	26.0	25.1	24.2	23.4	22.5	21.7	20.9
98	28.6	27.7	26.8	26.0	25.1	24.2	23.4	22.5	21.7	20.9
99	28.6	27.7	26.8	26.0	25.1	24.2	23.4	22.5	21.7	20.9
100	28.6	27.7	26.8	26.0	25.1	24.2	23.4	22.5	21.7	20.8
101	28.6	27.7	26.8	25.9	25.1	24.2	23.4	22.5	21.7	20.8
102	28.6	27.7	26.8	25.9	25.1	24.2	23.3	22.5	21.7	20.8
103	28.6	27.7	26.8	25.9	25.1	24.2	23.3	22.5	21.7	20.8
104	28.6	27.7	26.8	25.9	25.1	24.2	23.3	22.5	21.6	20.8
105	28.6	27.7	26.8	25.9	25.1	24.2	23.3	22.5	21.6	20.8
106	28.6	27.7	26.8	25.9	25.1	24.2	23.3	22.5	21.6	20.8
107	28.6	27.7	26.8	25.9	25.1	24.2	23.3	22.5	21.6	20.8
108	28.6	27.7	26.8	25.9	25.1	24.2	23.3	22.5	21.6	20.8
109	28.6	27.7	26.8	25.9	25.1	24.2	23.3	22.5	21.6	20.8
110	28.6	27.7	26.8	25.9	25.1	24.2	23.3	22.5	21.6	20.8
111	28.6	27.7	26.8	25.9	25.0	24.2	23.3	22.5	21.6	20.8
112	28.6	27.7	26.8	25.9	25.0	24.2	23.3	22.5	21.6	20.8
113	28.6	27.7	26.8	25.9	25.0	24.2	23.3	22.5	21.6	20.8
114	28.6	27.7	26.8	25.9	25.0	24.2	23.3	22.5	21.6	20.8
115	28.6	27.7	26.8	25.9	25.0	24.2	23.3	22.5	21.6	20.8

Reg. § 1.72-9

TABLE VI.—ORDINARY JOINT LIFE AND LAST SURVIVOR ANNUITIES; TWO LIVES—EXPECTED RETURN MULTIPLES—Continued

Ages	65	66	67	68	69	70	71	72	73	74
65	25.0	24.6	24.2	23.8	23.4	23.1	22.8	22.5	22.2	22.0
66	24.6	24.1	23.7	23.3	22.9	22.5	22.2	21.9	21.6	21.4
67	24.2	23.7	23.2	22.8	22.4	22.0	21.7	21.3	21.0	20.8
68	23.8	23.3	22.8	22.3	21.9	21.5	21.2	20.8	20.5	20.2
69	23.4	22.9	22.4	21.9	21.5	21.1	20.7	20.3	20.0	19.6
70	23.1	22.5	22.0	21.5	21.1	20.6	20.2	19.8	19.4	19.1
71	22.8	22.2	21.7	21.2	20.7	20.2	19.8	19.4	19.0	18.6
72	22.5	21.9	21.3	20.8	20.3	19.8	19.4	18.9	18.5	18.2
73	22.2	21.6	21.0	20.5	20.0	19.4	19.0	18.5	18.1	17.7
74	22.0	21.4	20.8	20.2	19.6	19.1	18.6	18.2	17.7	17.3
75	21.8	21.1	20.5	19.9	19.3	18.8	18.3	17.8	17.3	16.9
76	21.6	20.9	20.3	19.7	19.1	18.5	18.0	17.5	17.0	16.5
77	21.4	20.7	20.1	19.4	18.8	18.3	17.7	17.2	16.7	16.2
78	21.2	20.5	19.9	19.2	18.6	18.0	17.5	16.9	16.4	15.9
79	21.1	20.4	19.7	19.0	18.4	17.8	17.2	16.7	16.1	15.6
80	21.0	20.2	19.5	18.9	18.2	17.6	17.0	16.4	15.9	15.4
81	20.8	20.1	19.4	18.7	18.1	17.4	16.8	16.2	15.7	15.1
82	20.7	20.0	19.3	18.6	17.9	17.3	16.6	16.0	15.5	14.9
83	20.6	19.9	19.2	18.5	17.8	17.1	16.5	15.9	15.3	14.7
84	20.5	19.8	19.1	18.4	17.7	17.0	16.3	15.7	15.1	14.5
85	20.5	19.7	19.0	18.3	17.6	16.9	16.2	15.6	15.0	14.4
86	20.4	19.6	18.9	18.2	17.5	16.8	16.1	15.5	14.8	14.2
87	20.4	19.6	18.8	18.1	17.4	16.7	16.0	15.4	14.7	14.1
88	20.3	19.5	18.8	18.0	17.3	16.6	15.9	15.3	14.6	14.0
89	20.3	19.5	18.7	18.0	17.2	16.5	15.8	15.2	14.5	13.9
90	20.2	19.4	18.7	17.9	17.2	16.5	15.8	15.1	14.5	13.8
91	20.2	19.4	18.6	17.9	17.1	16.4	15.7	15.0	14.4	13.7
92	20.2	19.4	18.6	17.8	17.1	16.4	15.7	15.0	14.3	13.7
93	20.1	19.3	18.6	17.8	17.1	16.3	15.6	14.9	14.3	13.6
94	20.1	19.3	18.5	17.8	17.0	16.3	15.6	14.9	14.2	13.6
95	20.1	19.3	18.5	17.8	17.0	16.3	15.6	14.9	14.2	13.5
96	20.1	19.3	18.5	17.7	17.0	16.2	15.5	14.8	14.2	13.5
97	20.1	19.3	18.5	17.7	17.0	16.2	15.5	14.8	14.1	13.5
98	20.1	19.3	18.5	17.7	16.9	16.2	15.5	14.8	14.1	13.4
99	20.0	19.2	18.5	17.7	16.9	16.2	15.5	14.7	14.1	13.4
100	20.0	19.2	18.4	17.7	16.9	16.2	15.4	14.7	14.0	13.4
101	20.0	19.2	18.4	17.7	16.9	16.1	15.4	14.7	14.0	13.3
102	20.0	19.2	18.4	17.6	16.9	16.1	15.4	14.7	14.0	13.3
103	20.0	19.2	18.4	17.6	16.9	16.1	15.4	14.7	14.0	13.3
104	20.0	19.2	18.4	17.6	16.9	16.1	15.4	14.7	14.0	13.3
105	20.0	19.2	18.4	17.6	16.8	16.1	15.4	14.6	13.9	13.3
106	20.0	19.2	18.4	17.6	16.8	16.1	15.3	14.6	13.9	13.3
107	20.0	19.2	18.4	17.6	16.8	16.1	15.3	14.6	13.9	13.2
108	20.0	19.2	18.4	17.6	16.8	16.1	15.3	14.6	13.9	13.2
109	20.0	19.2	18.4	17.6	16.8	16.1	15.3	14.6	13.9	13.2
110	20.0	19.2	18.4	17.6	16.8	16.1	15.3	14.6	13.9	13.2
111	20.0	19.2	18.4	17.6	16.8	16.0	15.3	14.6	13.9	13.2
112	20.0	19.2	18.4	17.6	16.8	16.0	15.3	14.6	13.9	13.2
113	20.0	19.2	18.4	17.6	16.8	16.0	15.3	14.6	13.9	13.2
114	20.0	19.2	18.4	17.6	16.8	16.0	15.3	14.6	13.9	13.2
115	20.0	19.2	18.4	17.6	16.8	16.0	15.3	14.6	13.9	13.2

Reg. § 1.72-9

TABLE VI.—ORDINARY JOINT LIFE AND LAST SURVIVOR ANNUITIES; TWO LIVES—EXPECTED RETURN MULTIPLES—Continued

Ages	75	76	77	78	79	80	81	82	83	84
75	16.5	16.1	15.8	15.4	15.1	14.9	14.6	14.4	14.2	14.0
76	16.1	15.7	15.4	15.0	14.7	14.4	14.1	13.9	13.7	13.5
77	15.8	15.4	15.0	14.6	14.3	14.0	13.7	13.4	13.2	13.0
78	15.4	15.0	14.6	14.2	13.9	13.5	13.2	13.0	12.7	12.5
79	15.1	14.7	14.3	13.9	13.5	13.2	12.8	12.5	12.3	12.0
80	14.9	14.4	14.0	13.5	13.2	12.8	12.5	12.2	11.9	11.6
81	14.6	14.1	13.7	13.2	12.8	12.5	12.1	11.8	11.5	11.2
82	14.4	13.9	13.4	13.0	12.5	12.2	11.8	11.5	11.1	10.9
83	14.2	13.7	13.2	12.7	12.3	11.9	11.5	11.1	10.8	10.5
84	14.0	13.5	13.0	12.5	12.0	11.6	11.2	10.9	10.5	10.2
85	13.8	13.3	12.8	12.3	11.8	11.4	11.0	10.6	10.2	9.9
86	13.7	13.1	12.6	12.1	11.6	11.2	10.8	10.4	10.0	9.7
87	13.5	13.0	12.4	11.9	11.4	11.0	10.6	10.1	9.8	9.4
88	13.4	12.8	12.3	11.8	11.3	10.8	10.4	10.0	9.6	9.2
89	13.3	12.7	12.2	11.6	11.1	10.7	10.2	9.8	9.4	9.0
90	13.2	12.6	12.1	11.5	11.0	10.5	10.1	9.6	9.2	8.8
91	13.1	12.5	12.0	11.4	10.9	10.4	9.9	9.5	9.1	8.7
92	13.1	12.5	11.9	11.3	10.8	10.3	9.8	9.4	8.9	8.5
93	13.0	12.4	11.8	11.3	10.7	10.2	9.7	9.3	8.8	8.4
94	12.9	12.3	11.7	11.2	10.6	10.1	9.6	9.2	8.7	8.3
95	12.9	12.3	11.7	11.1	10.6	10.1	9.6	9.1	8.6	8.2
96	12.9	12.2	11.6	11.1	10.5	10.0	9.5	9.0	8.5	8.1
97	12.8	12.2	11.6	11.0	10.5	9.9	9.4	8.9	8.5	8.0
98	12.8	12.2	11.5	11.0	10.4	9.9	9.4	8.9	8.4	8.0
99	12.7	12.1	11.5	10.9	10.4	9.8	9.3	8.8	8.3	7.9
100	12.7	12.1	11.5	10.9	10.3	9.8	9.2	8.7	8.3	7.8
101	12.7	12.1	11.4	10.8	10.3	9.7	9.2	8.7	8.2	7.8
102	12.7	12.0	11.4	10.8	10.2	9.7	9.2	8.7	8.2	7.7
103	12.6	12.0	11.4	10.8	10.2	9.7	9.1	8.6	8.1	7.7
104	12.6	12.0	11.4	10.8	10.2	9.6	9.1	8.6	8.1	7.6
105	12.6	12.0	11.3	10.7	10.2	9.6	9.1	8.5	8.0	7.6
106	12.6	11.9	11.3	10.7	10.1	9.6	9.0	8.5	8.0	7.5
107	12.6	11.9	11.3	10.7	10.1	9.6	9.0	8.5	8.0	7.5
108	12.6	11.9	11.3	10.7	10.1	9.5	9.0	8.5	8.0	7.5
109	12.6	11.9	11.3	10.7	10.1	9.5	9.0	8.4	7.9	7.5
110	12.6	11.9	11.3	10.7	10.1	9.5	9.0	8.4	7.9	7.4
111	12.5	11.9	11.3	10.7	10.1	9.5	8.9	8.4	7.9	7.4
112	12.5	11.9	11.3	10.6	10.1	9.5	8.9	8.4	7.9	7.4
113	12.5	11.9	11.2	10.6	10.0	9.5	8.9	8.4	7.9	7.4
114	12.5	11.9	11.2	10.6	10.0	9.5	8.9	8.4	7.9	7.4
115	12.5	11.9	11.2	10.6	10.0	9.5	8.9	8.4	7.9	7.4

Ages	85	86	87	88	89	90	91	92	93	94
85	9.6	9.3	9.1	8.9	8.7	8.5	8.3	8.2	8.0	7.9
86	9.3	9.1	8.8	8.6	8.3	8.2	8.0	7.8	7.7	7.6
87	9.1	8.8	8.5	8.3	8.1	7.9	7.7	7.5	7.4	7.2
88	8.9	8.6	8.3	8.0	7.8	7.6	7.4	7.2	7.1	6.9
89	8.7	8.3	8.1	7.8	7.5	7.3	7.1	6.9	6.8	6.6
90	8.5	8.2	7.9	7.6	7.3	7.1	6.9	6.7	6.5	6.4
91	8.3	8.0	7.7	7.4	7.1	6.9	6.7	6.5	6.3	6.2
92	8.2	7.8	7.5	7.2	6.9	6.7	6.5	6.3	6.1	5.9
93	8.0	7.7	7.4	7.1	6.8	6.5	6.3	6.1	5.9	5.8
94	7.9	7.6	7.2	6.9	6.6	6.4	6.2	5.9	5.8	5.6
95	7.8	7.5	7.1	6.8	6.5	6.3	6.0	5.8	5.6	5.4
96	7.7	7.3	7.0	6.7	6.4	6.1	5.9	5.7	5.5	5.3
97	7.6	7.3	6.9	6.6	6.3	6.0	5.8	5.5	5.3	5.1
98	7.6	7.2	6.8	6.5	6.2	5.9	5.6	5.4	5.2	5.0
99	7.5	7.1	6.7	6.4	6.1	5.8	5.5	5.3	5.1	4.9
100	7.4	7.0	6.6	6.3	6.0	5.7	5.4	5.2	5.0	4.8
101	7.3	6.9	6.6	6.2	5.9	5.6	5.3	5.1	4.9	4.7
102	7.3	6.9	6.5	6.2	5.8	5.5	5.3	5.0	4.8	4.6
103	7.2	6.8	6.4	6.1	5.8	5.5	5.2	4.9	4.7	4.5
104	7.2	6.8	6.4	6.0	5.7	5.4	5.1	4.8	4.6	4.4
105	7.1	6.7	6.3	6.0	5.6	5.3	5.0	4.8	4.5	4.3
106	7.1	6.7	6.3	5.9	5.6	5.3	5.0	4.7	4.5	4.2
107	7.1	6.6	6.2	5.9	5.5	5.2	4.9	4.6	4.4	4.2
108	7.0	6.6	6.2	5.8	5.5	5.2	4.9	4.6	4.3	4.1
109	7.0	6.6	6.2	5.8	5.5	5.1	4.8	4.5	4.3	4.1
110	7.0	6.6	6.2	5.8	5.4	5.1	4.8	4.5	4.3	4.0
111	7.0	6.5	6.1	5.7	5.4	5.1	4.8	4.5	4.2	4.0
112	7.0	6.5	6.1	5.7	5.4	5.0	4.7	4.4	4.2	3.9
113	6.9	6.5	6.1	5.7	5.4	5.0	4.7	4.4	4.2	3.9
114	6.9	6.5	6.1	5.7	5.3	5.0	4.7	4.4	4.1	3.9
115	6.9	6.5	6.1	5.7	5.3	5.0	4.7	4.4	4.1	3.9

Reg. § 1.72-9

TABLE VI.—ORDINARY JOINT LIFE AND LAST SURVIVOR ANNUITIES; TWO LIVES—EXPECTED RETURN MULTIPLES—Continued

Ages	95	96	97	98	99	100	101	102	103	104
95	5.3	5.1	5.0	4.8	4.7	4.6	4.5	4.4	4.3	4.2
96	5.1	5.0	4.8	4.7	4.5	4.4	4.3	4.2	4.1	4.0
97	5.0	4.8	4.7	4.5	4.4	4.3	4.1	4.0	3.9	3.8
98	4.8	4.7	4.5	4.4	4.2	4.1	4.0	3.9	3.8	3.7
99	4.7	4.5	4.4	4.2	4.1	4.0	3.8	3.7	3.6	3.5
100	4.6	4.4	4.3	4.1	4.0	3.8	3.7	3.6	3.5	3.3
101	4.5	4.3	4.1	4.0	3.8	3.7	3.6	3.4	3.3	3.2
102	4.4	4.2	4.0	3.9	3.7	3.6	3.4	3.3	3.2	3.1
103	4.3	4.1	3.9	3.8	3.6	3.5	3.3	3.2	3.0	2.9
104	4.2	4.0	3.8	3.7	3.5	3.3	3.2	3.1	2.9	2.8
105	4.1	3.9	3.7	3.6	3.4	3.2	3.1	2.9	2.8	2.7
106	4.0	3.8	3.6	3.5	3.3	3.1	3.0	2.8	2.7	2.5
107	4.0	3.8	3.6	3.4	3.2	3.1	2.9	2.7	2.6	2.4
108	3.9	3.7	3.5	3.3	3.1	3.0	2.8	2.7	2.5	2.3
109	3.8	3.6	3.4	3.3	3.1	2.9	2.7	2.6	2.4	2.3
110	3.8	3.6	3.4	3.2	3.0	2.8	2.7	2.5	2.3	2.2
111	3.8	3.5	3.3	3.2	3.0	2.8	2.6	2.4	2.3	2.1
112	3.7	3.5	3.3	3.1	2.9	2.8	2.6	2.4	2.2	2.1
113	3.7	3.5	3.3	3.1	2.9	2.7	2.5	2.4	2.2	2.0
114	3.7	3.5	3.3	3.1	2.9	2.7	2.5	2.3	2.1	2.0
115	3.7	3.4	3.2	3.0	2.8	2.7	2.5	2.3	2.1	1.9

Ages	105	106	107	108	109	110	111	112	113	114	115
105	2.5	2.4	2.3	2.2	2.1	2.0	2.0	1.9	1.8	1.8	1.8
106	2.4	2.3	2.2	2.1	2.0	1.9	1.8	1.7	1.7	1.6	1.6
107	2.3	2.2	2.1	1.9	1.8	1.7	1.7	1.6	1.5	1.5	1.4
108	2.2	2.1	1.9	1.8	1.7	1.6	1.5	1.5	1.4	1.3	1.3
109	2.1	2.0	1.8	1.7	1.6	1.5	1.4	1.3	1.3	1.2	1.1
110	2.0	1.9	1.7	1.6	1.5	1.4	1.3	1.2	1.1	1.1	1.0
111	2.0	1.8	1.7	1.5	1.4	1.3	1.2	1.1	1.0	.9	.9
112	1.9	1.7	1.6	1.5	1.3	1.2	1.1	1.0	.9	.8	.8
113	1.8	1.7	1.5	1.4	1.3	1.1	1.0	.9	.8	.7	.7
114	1.8	1.6	1.5	1.3	1.2	1.1	.9	.8	.7	.6	.6
115	1.8	1.6	1.4	1.3	1.1	1.0	.9	.8	.7	.6	.5

TABLE VIA.—ANNUITIES FOR JOINT LIFE ONLY; TWO LIVES—EXPECTED RETURN MULTIPLES

Ages	5	6	7	8	9	10	11	12	13	14
5	69.5	69.0	68.4	67.9	67.3	66.7	66.1	65.5	64.8	64.1
6	69.0	68.5	68.0	67.5	66.9	66.4	65.8	65.1	64.5	63.8
7	68.4	68.0	67.5	67.0	66.5	66.0	65.4	64.8	64.2	63.5
8	67.9	67.5	67.0	66.6	66.1	65.5	65.0	64.4	63.8	63.2
9	67.3	66.9	66.5	66.1	65.6	65.1	64.6	64.0	63.4	62.8
10	66.7	66.4	66.0	65.5	65.1	64.6	64.1	63.6	63.0	62.5
11	66.1	65.8	65.4	65.0	64.6	64.1	63.6	63.1	62.6	62.1
12	65.5	65.1	64.8	64.4	64.0	63.6	63.1	62.7	62.2	61.7
13	64.8	64.5	64.2	63.8	63.4	63.0	62.6	62.2	61.7	61.2
14	64.1	63.8	63.5	63.2	62.8	62.5	62.1	61.7	61.2	60.7
15	63.4	63.1	62.9	62.6	62.2	61.9	61.5	61.1	60.7	60.2
16	62.7	62.4	62.2	61.9	61.6	61.3	60.9	60.5	60.1	59.7
17	61.9	61.7	61.5	61.2	60.9	60.6	60.3	59.9	59.6	59.2
18	61.2	61.0	60.7	60.5	60.2	60.0	59.7	59.3	59.0	58.6
19	60.4	60.2	60.0	59.8	59.5	59.3	59.0	58.7	58.4	58.0
20	59.6	59.4	59.2	59.0	58.8	58.6	58.3	58.0	57.7	57.4
21	58.8	58.7	58.5	58.3	58.1	57.8	57.6	57.3	57.1	56.8
22	58.0	57.8	57.7	57.5	57.3	57.1	56.9	56.6	56.4	56.1
23	57.2	57.0	56.9	56.7	56.5	56.4	56.1	55.9	55.7	55.4
24	56.3	56.2	56.1	55.9	55.8	55.6	55.4	55.2	55.0	54.7
25	55.5	55.4	55.2	55.1	55.0	54.8	54.6	54.4	54.2	54.0
26	54.6	54.5	54.4	54.3	54.1	54.0	53.8	53.7	53.5	53.3
27	53.8	53.7	53.6	53.4	53.3	53.2	53.0	52.9	52.7	52.5
28	52.9	52.8	52.7	52.6	52.5	52.4	52.2	52.1	51.9	51.7
29	52.0	51.9	51.8	51.7	51.6	51.5	51.4	51.3	51.1	51.0
30	51.1	51.0	51.0	50.9	50.8	50.7	50.6	50.4	50.3	50.2
31	50.2	50.2	50.1	50.0	49.9	49.8	49.7	49.6	49.5	49.3
32	49.3	49.3	49.2	49.1	49.0	49.0	48.9	48.8	48.6	48.5
33	48.4	48.4	48.3	48.2	48.2	48.1	48.0	47.9	47.8	47.7
34	47.5	47.5	47.4	47.4	47.3	47.2	47.1	47.0	47.0	46.8
35	46.6	46.6	46.5	46.5	46.4	46.3	46.3	46.2	46.1	46.0
36	45.7	45.7	45.6	45.6	45.5	45.4	45.4	45.3	45.2	45.1
37	44.8	44.7	44.7	44.6	44.6	44.5	44.5	44.4	44.3	44.3
38	43.9	43.8	43.8	43.7	43.7	43.6	43.6	43.5	43.5	43.4
39	42.9	42.9	42.9	42.8	42.8	42.7	42.7	42.6	42.6	42.5
40	42.0	42.0	42.0	41.9	41.9	41.8	41.8	41.7	41.7	41.6
41	41.1	41.1	41.0	41.0	41.0	40.9	40.9	40.8	40.8	40.7
42	40.2	40.1	40.1	40.1	40.1	40.0	40.0	39.9	39.9	39.8

Reg. § 1.72-9

TABLE VIA.—ANNUITIES FOR JOINT LIFE ONLY; TWO LIVES—EXPECTED RETURN MULTIPLES—Continued

Ages	5	6	7	8	9	10	11	12	13	14
43	39.2	39.2	39.2	39.2	39.1	39.1	39.1	39.0	39.0	39.0
44	38.3	38.3	38.3	38.3	38.2	38.2	38.2	38.1	38.1	38.1
45	37.4	37.4	37.4	37.3	37.3	37.3	37.3	37.2	37.2	37.2
46	36.5	36.5	36.5	36.4	36.4	36.4	36.4	36.3	36.3	36.3
47	35.6	35.6	35.5	35.5	35.5	35.5	35.5	35.4	35.4	35.4
48	34.7	34.7	34.6	34.6	34.6	34.6	34.6	34.5	34.5	34.5
49	33.8	33.8	33.7	33.7	33.7	33.7	33.7	33.7	33.6	33.6
50	32.9	32.9	32.8	32.8	32.8	32.8	32.8	32.8	32.7	32.7
51	32.0	32.0	31.9	31.9	31.9	31.9	31.9	31.9	31.9	31.8
52	31.1	31.1	31.1	31.0	31.0	31.0	31.0	31.0	31.0	30.9
53	30.2	30.2	30.2	30.2	30.1	30.1	30.1	30.1	30.1	30.1
54	29.3	29.3	29.3	29.3	29.3	29.2	29.2	29.2	29.2	29.2
55	28.4	28.4	28.4	28.4	28.4	28.4	28.4	28.3	28.3	28.3
56	27.5	27.5	27.5	27.5	27.5	27.5	27.5	27.5	27.5	27.5
57	26.7	26.7	26.7	26.6	26.6	26.6	26.6	26.6	26.6	26.6
58	25.8	25.8	25.8	25.8	25.8	25.8	25.8	25.7	25.7	25.7
59	24.9	24.9	24.9	24.9	24.9	24.9	24.9	24.9	24.9	24.9
60	24.1	24.1	24.1	24.1	24.1	24.0	24.0	24.0	24.0	24.0
61	23.2	23.2	23.2	23.2	23.2	23.2	23.2	23.2	23.2	23.2
62	22.4	22.4	22.4	22.4	22.4	22.4	22.3	22.3	22.3	22.3
63	21.5	21.5	21.5	21.5	21.5	21.5	21.5	21.5	21.5	21.5
64	20.7	20.7	20.7	20.7	20.7	20.7	20.7	20.7	20.7	20.7
65	19.9	19.9	19.9	19.9	19.9	19.9	19.9	19.9	19.9	19.9
66	19.1	19.1	19.1	19.1	19.1	19.1	19.1	19.1	19.1	19.1
67	18.3	18.3	18.3	18.3	18.3	18.3	18.3	18.3	18.3	18.3
68	17.5	17.5	17.5	17.5	17.5	17.5	17.5	17.5	17.5	17.5
69	16.8	16.8	16.8	16.7	16.7	16.7	16.7	16.7	16.7	16.7
70	16.0	16.0	16.0	16.0	16.0	16.0	16.0	16.0	16.0	16.0
71	15.3	15.3	15.3	15.3	15.3	15.3	15.3	15.3	15.3	15.2
72	14.6	14.6	14.5	14.5	14.5	14.5	14.5	14.5	14.5	14.5
73	13.9	13.9	13.8	13.8	13.8	13.8	13.8	13.8	13.8	13.8
74	13.2	13.2	13.2	13.2	13.2	13.2	13.2	13.2	13.2	13.2
75	12.5	12.5	12.5	12.5	12.5	12.5	12.5	12.5	12.5	12.5
76	11.9	11.9	11.8	11.8	11.8	11.8	11.8	11.8	11.8	11.8
77	11.2	11.2	11.2	11.2	11.2	11.2	11.2	11.2	11.2	11.2
78	10.6	10.6	10.6	10.6	10.6	10.6	10.6	10.6	10.6	10.6
79	10.0	10.0	10.0	10.0	10.0	10.0	10.0	10.0	10.0	10.0
80	9.5	9.5	9.5	9.5	9.5	9.5	9.5	9.5	9.4	9.4
81	8.9	8.9	8.9	8.9	8.9	8.9	8.9	8.9	8.9	8.9
82	8.4	8.4	8.4	8.4	8.4	8.4	8.4	8.4	8.4	8.4
83	7.9	7.9	7.9	7.9	7.9	7.9	7.9	7.9	7.9	7.9
84	7.4	7.4	7.4	7.4	7.4	7.4	7.4	7.4	7.4	7.4
85	6.9	6.9	6.9	6.9	6.9	6.9	6.9	6.9	6.9	6.9
86	6.5	6.5	6.5	6.5	6.5	6.5	6.5	6.5	6.5	6.5
87	6.1	6.1	6.1	6.1	6.1	6.1	6.1	6.1	6.1	6.1
88	5.7	5.7	5.7	5.7	5.7	5.7	5.7	5.7	5.7	5.7
89	5.3	5.3	5.3	5.3	5.3	5.3	5.3	5.3	5.3	5.3
90	5.0	5.0	5.0	5.0	5.0	5.0	5.0	5.0	5.0	5.0
91	4.7	4.7	4.7	4.7	4.7	4.7	4.7	4.7	4.7	4.7
92	4.4	4.4	4.4	4.4	4.4	4.4	4.4	4.4	4.4	4.4
93	4.1	4.1	4.1	4.1	4.1	4.1	4.1	4.1	4.1	4.1
94	3.9	3.9	3.9	3.9	3.9	3.9	3.9	3.9	3.9	3.9
95	3.7	3.7	3.7	3.7	3.7	3.7	3.7	3.6	3.6	3.6
96	3.4	3.4	3.4	3.4	3.4	3.4	3.4	3.4	3.4	3.4
97	3.2	3.2	3.2	3.2	3.2	3.2	3.2	3.2	3.2	3.2
98	3.0	3.0	3.0	3.0	3.0	3.0	3.0	3.0	3.0	3.0
99	2.8	2.8	2.8	2.8	2.8	2.8	2.8	2.8	2.8	2.8
100	2.7	2.7	2.7	2.7	2.7	2.7	2.7	2.7	2.7	2.7
101	2.5	2.5	2.5	2.5	2.5	2.5	2.5	2.5	2.5	2.5
102	2.3	2.3	2.3	2.3	2.3	2.3	2.3	2.3	2.3	2.3
103	2.1	2.1	2.1	2.1	2.1	2.1	2.1	2.1	2.1	2.1
104	1.9	1.9	1.9	1.9	1.9	1.9	1.9	1.9	1.9	1.9
105	1.8	1.8	1.8	1.8	1.8	1.8	1.8	1.8	1.8	1.8
106	1.6	1.6	1.6	1.6	1.6	1.6	1.6	1.6	1.6	1.6
107	1.4	1.4	1.4	1.4	1.4	1.4	1.4	1.4	1.4	1.4
108	1.3	1.3	1.3	1.3	1.3	1.3	1.3	1.3	1.3	1.3
109	1.1	1.1	1.1	1.1	1.1	1.1	1.1	1.1	1.1	1.1
110	1.0	1.0	1.0	1.0	1.0	1.0	1.0	1.0	1.0	1.0
111	.9	.9	.9	.9	.9	.9	.9	.9	.9	.9
112	.8	.8	.8	.8	.8	.8	.8	.8	.8	.8
113	.7	.7	.7	.7	.7	.7	.7	.7	.7	.7
114	.6	.6	.6	.6	.6	.6	.6	.6	.6	.6
115	.5	.5	.5	.5	.5	.5	.5	.5	.5	.5

Reg. § 1.72-9

See p. 20,601 for regulations not amended to reflect law changes

TABLE VIA.—ANNUITIES FOR JOINT LIFE ONLY; TWO LIVES—EXPECTED RETURN MULTIPLES

Ages	15	16	17	18	19	20	21	22	23	24
15	59.8	59.3	58.8	58.2	57.6	57.0	56.4	55.8	55.1	54.5
16	59.3	58.8	58.3	57.8	57.2	56.7	56.1	55.5	54.8	54.2
17	58.8	58.3	57.8	57.3	56.8	56.3	55.7	55.1	54.5	53.9
18	58.2	57.8	57.3	56.9	56.4	55.9	55.3	54.7	54.2	53.5
19	57.6	57.2	56.8	56.4	55.9	55.4	54.9	54.4	53.8	53.2
20	57.0	56.7	56.3	55.9	55.4	54.9	54.5	53.9	53.4	52.8
21	56.4	56.1	55.7	55.3	54.9	54.5	54.0	53.5	53.0	52.4
22	55.8	55.5	55.1	54.7	54.4	53.9	53.5	53.0	52.5	52.0
23	55.1	54.8	54.5	54.2	53.8	53.4	53.0	52.6	52.1	51.6
24	54.5	54.2	53.9	53.5	53.2	52.8	52.4	52.0	51.6	51.1
25	53.8	53.5	53.2	52.9	52.6	52.2	51.9	51.5	51.1	50.6
26	53.0	52.8	52.5	52.3	52.0	51.6	51.3	50.9	50.5	50.1
27	52.3	52.1	51.8	51.6	51.3	51.0	50.7	50.3	50.0	49.6
28	51.5	51.3	51.1	50.9	50.6	50.3	50.0	49.7	49.4	49.0
29	50.8	50.6	50.4	50.2	49.9	49.7	49.4	49.1	48.8	48.4
30	50.0	49.8	49.6	49.4	49.2	49.0	48.7	48.4	48.1	47.8
31	49.2	49.0	48.9	48.7	48.5	48.3	48.0	47.8	47.5	47.2
32	48.4	48.2	48.1	47.9	47.7	47.5	47.3	47.1	46.8	46.5
33	47.6	47.4	47.3	47.1	47.0	46.8	46.6	46.3	46.1	45.9
34	46.7	46.6	46.5	46.3	46.2	46.0	45.8	45.6	45.4	45.2
35	45.9	45.8	45.7	45.5	45.4	45.2	45.1	44.9	44.7	44.4
36	45.0	44.9	44.8	44.7	44.6	44.4	44.3	44.1	43.9	43.7
37	44.2	44.1	44.0	43.9	43.8	43.6	43.5	43.3	43.2	43.0
38	43.3	43.2	43.1	43.0	42.9	42.8	42.7	42.5	42.4	42.2
39	42.4	42.4	42.3	42.2	42.1	42.0	41.9	41.7	41.6	41.4
40	41.6	41.5	41.4	41.3	41.2	41.1	41.0	40.9	40.8	40.6
41	40.7	40.6	40.5	40.5	40.4	40.3	40.2	40.1	40.0	39.8
42	39.8	39.7	39.7	39.6	39.5	39.4	39.4	39.3	39.1	39.0
43	38.9	38.9	38.8	38.7	38.7	38.6	38.5	38.4	38.3	38.2
44	38.0	38.0	37.9	37.9	37.8	37.7	37.7	37.6	37.5	37.4
45	37.1	37.1	37.0	37.0	36.9	36.9	36.8	36.7	36.6	36.5
46	36.2	36.2	36.2	36.1	36.1	36.0	35.9	35.9	35.8	35.7
47	35.3	35.3	35.3	35.2	35.2	35.1	35.1	35.0	34.9	34.9
48	34.5	34.4	34.4	34.4	34.3	34.3	34.2	34.2	34.1	34.0
49	33.6	33.5	33.5	33.5	33.4	33.4	33.4	33.3	33.2	33.2
50	32.7	32.7	32.6	32.6	32.6	32.6	32.5	32.4	32.4	32.3
51	31.8	31.8	31.8	31.7	31.7	31.7	31.6	31.6	31.5	31.5
52	30.9	30.9	30.9	30.9	30.8	30.8	30.8	30.7	30.7	30.6
53	30.0	30.0	30.0	30.0	30.0	29.9	29.9	29.9	29.8	29.8
54	29.2	29.2	29.1	29.1	29.1	29.1	29.0	29.0	29.0	28.9
55	28.3	28.3	28.3	28.3	28.2	28.2	28.2	28.2	28.1	28.1
56	27.4	27.4	27.4	27.4	27.4	27.3	27.3	27.3	27.3	27.2
57	26.6	26.6	26.5	26.5	26.5	26.5	26.5	26.5	26.4	26.4
58	25.7	25.7	25.7	25.7	25.7	25.6	25.6	25.6	25.6	25.6
59	24.9	24.8	24.8	24.8	24.8	24.8	24.8	24.8	24.7	24.7
60	24.0	24.0	24.0	24.0	24.0	23.9	23.9	23.9	23.9	23.9
61	23.2	23.2	23.1	23.1	23.1	23.1	23.1	23.1	23.1	23.0
62	22.3	22.3	22.3	22.3	22.3	22.3	22.3	22.2	22.2	22.2
63	21.5	21.5	21.5	21.5	21.5	21.4	21.4	21.4	21.4	21.4
64	20.7	20.7	20.7	20.6	20.6	20.6	20.6	20.6	20.6	20.6
65	19.9	19.8	19.8	19.8	19.8	19.8	19.8	19.8	19.8	19.8

Reg. § 1.72-9

TABLE VIA.—ANNUITIES FOR JOINT LIFE ONLY; TWO LIVES—EXPECTED RETURN MULTIPLES—Continued

Ages	15	16	17	18	19	20	21	22	23	24
66	19.1	19.0	19.0	19.0	19.0	19.0	19.0	19.0	19.0	19.0
67	18.3	18.3	18.3	18.3	18.2	18.2	18.2	18.2	18.2	18.2
68	17.5	17.5	17.5	17.5	17.5	17.5	17.5	17.5	17.4	17.4
69	16.7	16.7	16.7	16.7	16.7	16.7	16.7	16.7	16.7	16.7
70	16.0	16.0	16.0	16.0	16.0	16.0	15.9	15.9	15.9	15.9
71	15.2	15.2	15.2	15.2	15.2	15.2	15.2	15.2	15.2	15.2
72	14.5	14.5	14.5	14.5	14.5	14.5	14.5	14.5	14.5	14.5
73	13.8	13.8	13.8	13.8	13.8	13.8	13.8	13.8	13.8	13.8
74	13.2	13.1	13.1	13.1	13.1	13.1	13.1	13.1	13.1	13.1
75	12.5	12.5	12.5	12.5	12.5	12.5	12.5	12.5	12.5	12.5
76	11.8	11.8	11.8	11.8	11.8	11.8	11.8	11.8	11.8	11.8
77	11.2	11.2	11.2	11.2	11.2	11.2	11.2	11.2	11.2	11.2
78	10.6	10.6	10.6	10.6	10.6	10.6	10.6	10.6	10.6	10.6
79	10.0	10.0	10.0	10.0	10.0	10.0	10.0	10.0	10.0	10.0
80	9.4	9.4	9.4	9.4	9.4	9.4	9.4	9.4	9.4	9.4
81	8.9	8.9	8.9	8.9	8.9	8.9	8.9	8.9	8.9	8.9
82	8.4	8.4	8.4	8.4	8.4	8.4	8.4	8.4	8.4	8.4
83	7.9	7.9	7.9	7.9	7.9	7.9	7.9	7.9	7.8	7.8
84	7.4	7.4	7.4	7.4	7.4	7.4	7.4	7.4	7.4	7.4
85	6.9	6.9	6.9	6.9	6.9	6.9	6.9	6.9	6.9	6.9
86	6.5	6.5	6.5	6.5	6.5	6.5	6.5	6.5	6.5	6.5
87	6.1	6.1	6.1	6.1	6.1	6.1	6.1	6.1	6.1	6.1
88	5.7	5.7	5.7	5.7	5.7	5.7	5.7	5.7	5.7	5.7
89	5.3	5.3	5.3	5.3	5.3	5.3	5.3	5.3	5.3	5.3
90	5.0	5.0	5.0	5.0	5.0	5.0	5.0	5.0	5.0	5.0
91	4.7	4.7	4.7	4.7	4.7	4.7	4.7	4.7	4.7	4.7
92	4.4	4.4	4.4	4.4	4.4	4.4	4.4	4.4	4.4	4.4
93	4.1	4.1	4.1	4.1	4.1	4.1	4.1	4.1	4.1	4.1
94	3.9	3.9	3.9	3.9	3.9	3.9	3.9	3.9	3.9	3.9
95	3.6	3.6	3.6	3.6	3.6	3.6	3.6	3.6	3.6	3.6
96	3.4	3.4	3.4	3.4	3.4	3.4	3.4	3.4	3.4	3.4
97	3.2	3.2	3.2	3.2	3.2	3.2	3.2	3.2	3.2	3.2
98	3.0	3.0	3.0	3.0	3.0	3.0	3.0	3.0	3.0	3.0
99	2.8	2.8	2.8	2.8	2.8	2.8	2.8	2.8	2.8	2.8
100	2.7	2.7	2.7	2.7	2.7	2.7	2.7	2.7	2.7	2.7
101	2.5	2.5	2.5	2.5	2.5	2.5	2.5	2.5	2.5	2.5
102	2.3	2.3	2.3	2.3	2.3	2.3	2.3	2.3	2.3	2.3
103	2.1	2.1	2.1	2.1	2.1	2.1	2.1	2.1	2.1	2.1
104	1.9	1.9	1.9	1.9	1.9	1.9	1.9	1.9	1.9	1.9
105	1.8	1.8	1.8	1.8	1.8	1.8	1.8	1.8	1.8	1.8
106	1.6	1.6	1.6	1.6	1.6	1.6	1.6	1.6	1.6	1.6
107	1.4	1.4	1.4	1.4	1.4	1.4	1.4	1.4	1.4	1.4
108	1.3	1.3	1.3	1.3	1.3	1.3	1.3	1.3	1.3	1.3
109	1.1	1.1	1.1	1.1	1.1	1.1	1.1	1.1	1.1	1.1
110	1.0	1.0	1.0	1.0	1.0	1.0	1.0	1.0	1.0	1.0
111	.9	.9	.9	.9	.9	.9	.9	.9	.9	.9
112	.8	.8	.8	.8	.8	.8	.8	.8	.8	.8
113	.7	.7	.7	.7	.7	.7	.7	.7	.7	.7
114	.6	.6	.6	.6	.6	.6	.6	.6	.6	.6
115	.5	.5	.5	.5	.5	.5	.5	.5	.5	.5

See p. 20,601 for regulations not amended to reflect law changes

TABLE VIA.—ANNUITIES FOR JOINT LIFE ONLY; TWO LIVES—EXPECTED RETURN MULTIPLES

Ages	25	26	27	28	29	30	31	32	33	34
25	50.2	49.7	49.2	48.6	48.1	47.5	46.9	46.2	45.6	44.9
26	49.7	49.2	48.7	48.2	47.7	47.1	46.5	45.9	45.3	44.6
27	49.2	48.7	48.3	47.8	47.3	46.7	46.2	45.6	45.0	44.3
28	48.6	48.2	47.8	47.3	46.8	46.3	45.8	45.2	44.6	44.0
29	48.1	47.7	47.3	46.8	46.4	45.9	45.4	44.8	44.3	43.7
30	47.5	47.1	46.7	46.3	45.9	45.4	44.9	44.4	43.9	43.3
31	46.9	46.5	46.2	45.8	45.4	44.9	44.5	44.0	43.5	42.9
32	46.2	45.9	45.6	45.2	44.8	44.4	44.0	43.5	43.0	42.5
33	45.6	45.3	45.0	44.6	44.3	43.9	43.5	43.0	42.6	42.1
34	44.9	44.6	44.3	44.0	43.7	43.3	42.9	42.5	42.1	41.6
35	44.2	44.0	43.7	43.4	43.1	42.7	42.4	42.0	41.6	41.1
36	43.5	43.3	43.0	42.7	42.4	42.1	41.8	41.4	41.0	40.6
37	42.8	42.5	42.3	42.1	41.8	41.5	41.2	40.8	40.5	40.1
38	42.0	41.8	41.6	41.4	41.1	40.8	40.6	40.2	39.9	39.5
39	41.3	41.1	40.9	40.7	40.4	40.2	39.9	39.6	39.3	39.0
40	40.5	40.3	40.1	39.9	39.7	39.5	39.2	39.0	38.7	38.4
41	39.7	39.5	39.4	39.2	39.0	38.8	38.5	38.3	38.0	37.7
42	38.9	38.8	38.6	38.4	38.3	38.1	37.8	37.6	37.4	37.1
43	38.1	38.0	37.8	37.7	37.5	37.3	37.1	36.9	36.7	36.4
44	37.3	37.2	37.0	36.9	36.7	36.6	36.4	36.2	36.0	35.8
45	36.5	36.3	36.2	36.1	36.0	35.8	35.6	35.5	35.3	35.1
46	35.6	35.5	35.4	35.3	35.2	35.0	34.9	34.7	34.5	34.4
47	34.8	34.7	34.6	34.5	34.4	34.3	34.1	34.0	33.8	33.6
48	34.0	33.9	33.8	33.7	33.6	33.5	33.4	33.2	33.1	32.9
49	33.1	33.0	33.0	32.9	32.8	32.7	32.6	32.4	32.3	32.2
50	32.3	32.2	32.1	32.1	32.0	31.9	31.8	31.7	31.5	31.4
51	31.4	31.4	31.3	31.2	31.2	31.1	31.0	30.9	30.8	30.6
52	30.6	30.5	30.5	30.4	30.3	30.3	30.2	30.1	30.0	29.9
53	29.7	29.7	29.6	29.6	29.5	29.5	29.4	29.3	29.2	29.1
54	28.9	28.9	28.8	28.8	28.7	28.6	28.6	28.5	28.4	28.3
55	28.1	28.0	28.0	27.9	27.9	27.8	27.8	27.7	27.6	27.5
56	27.2	27.2	27.1	27.1	27.0	27.0	26.9	26.9	26.8	26.7
57	26.4	26.3	26.3	26.3	26.2	26.2	26.1	26.1	26.0	25.9
58	25.5	25.5	25.5	25.4	25.4	25.4	25.3	25.3	25.2	25.1
59	24.7	24.7	24.6	24.6	24.6	24.5	24.5	24.5	24.4	24.3
60	23.9	23.8	23.8	23.8	23.8	23.7	23.7	23.6	23.6	23.5
61	23.0	23.0	23.0	23.0	22.9	22.9	22.9	22.8	22.8	22.7
62	22.2	22.2	22.2	22.1	22.1	22.1	22.1	22.0	22.0	21.9
63	21.4	21.4	21.3	21.3	21.3	21.3	21.3	21.2	21.2	21.2
64	20.6	20.6	20.5	20.5	20.5	20.5	20.5	20.4	20.4	20.4
65	19.8	19.8	19.7	19.7	19.7	19.7	19.7	19.6	19.6	19.6
66	19.0	19.0	19.0	18.9	18.9	18.9	18.9	18.9	18.8	18.8
67	18.2	18.2	18.2	18.2	18.2	18.1	18.1	18.1	18.1	18.1
68	17.4	17.4	17.4	17.4	17.4	17.4	17.4	17.3	17.3	17.3
69	16.7	16.7	16.7	16.6	16.6	16.6	16.6	16.6	16.6	16.6
70	15.9	15.9	15.9	15.9	15.9	15.9	15.9	15.9	15.8	15.8

Reg. § 1.72-9

TABLE VIA.—ANNUITIES FOR JOINT LIFE ONLY; TWO LIVES—EXPECTED RETURN MULTIPLES—Continued

Ages	25	26	27	28	29	30	31	32	33	34
71	15.2	15.2	15.2	15.2	15.2	15.2	15.2	15.1	15.1	15.1
72	14.5	14.5	14.5	14.5	14.5	14.5	14.5	14.4	14.4	14.4
73	13.8	13.8	13.8	13.8	13.8	13.8	13.8	13.8	13.7	13.7
74	13.1	13.1	13.1	13.1	13.1	13.1	13.1	13.1	13.1	13.1
75	12.5	12.5	12.5	12.4	12.4	12.4	12.4	12.4	12.4	12.4
76	11.8	11.8	11.8	11.8	11.8	11.8	11.8	11.8	11.8	11.8
77	11.2	11.2	11.2	11.2	11.2	11.2	11.2	11.2	11.2	11.1
78	10.6	10.6	10.6	10.6	10.6	10.6	10.6	10.6	10.6	10.5
79	10.0	10.0	10.0	10.0	10.0	10.0	10.0	10.0	10.0	10.0
80	9.4	9.4	9.4	9.4	9.4	9.4	9.4	9.4	9.4	9.4
81	8.9	8.9	8.9	8.9	8.9	8.9	8.9	8.9	8.9	8.9
82	8.4	8.4	8.3	8.3	8.3	8.3	8.3	8.3	8.3	8.3
83	7.8	7.8	7.8	7.8	7.8	7.8	7.8	7.8	7.8	7.8
84	7.4	7.4	7.4	7.4	7.4	7.4	7.4	7.4	7.4	7.4
85	6.9	6.9	6.9	6.9	6.9	6.9	6.9	6.9	6.9	6.9
86	6.5	6.5	6.5	6.5	6.5	6.5	6.5	6.5	6.5	6.5
87	6.1	6.1	6.1	6.1	6.1	6.1	6.1	6.1	6.1	6.1
88	5.7	5.7	5.7	5.7	5.7	5.7	5.7	5.7	5.7	5.7
89	5.3	5.3	5.3	5.3	5.3	5.3	5.3	5.3	5.3	5.3
90	5.0	5.0	5.0	5.0	5.0	5.0	5.0	5.0	5.0	5.0
91	4.7	4.7	4.7	4.7	4.7	4.7	4.7	4.7	4.7	4.7
92	4.4	4.4	4.4	4.4	4.4	4.4	4.4	4.4	4.4	4.4
93	4.1	4.1	4.1	4.1	4.1	4.1	4.1	4.1	4.1	4.1
94	3.9	3.9	3.9	3.9	3.9	3.9	3.9	3.9	3.9	3.9
95	3.6	3.6	3.6	3.6	3.6	3.6	3.6	3.6	3.6	3.6
96	3.4	3.4	3.4	3.4	3.4	3.4	3.4	3.4	3.4	3.4
97	3.2	3.2	3.2	3.2	3.2	3.2	3.2	3.2	3.2	3.2
98	3.0	3.0	3.0	3.0	3.0	3.0	3.0	3.0	3.0	3.0
99	2.8	2.8	2.8	2.8	2.8	2.8	2.8	2.8	2.8	2.8
100	2.7	2.7	2.7	2.7	2.7	2.7	2.7	2.7	2.7	2.7
101	2.5	2.5	2.5	2.5	2.5	2.5	2.5	2.5	2.5	2.5
102	2.3	2.3	2.3	2.3	2.3	2.3	2.3	2.3	2.3	2.3
103	2.1	2.1	2.1	2.1	2.1	2.1	2.1	2.1	2.1	2.1
104	1.9	1.9	1.9	1.9	1.9	1.9	1.9	1.9	1.9	1.9
105	1.8	1.8	1.8	1.8	1.8	1.8	1.8	1.8	1.8	1.8
106	1.6	1.6	1.6	1.6	1.6	1.6	1.6	1.6	1.6	1.6
107	1.4	1.4	1.4	1.4	1.4	1.4	1.4	1.4	1.4	1.4
108	1.3	1.3	1.3	1.3	1.3	1.3	1.3	1.3	1.3	1.3
109	1.1	1.1	1.1	1.1	1.1	1.1	1.1	1.1	1.1	1.1
110	1.0	1.0	1.0	1.0	1.0	1.0	1.0	1.0	1.0	1.0
111	.9	.9	.9	.9	.9	.9	.9	.9	.9	.9
112	.8	.8	.8	.8	.8	.8	.8	.8	.8	.8
113	.7	.7	.7	.7	.7	.7	.7	.7	.7	.7
114	.6	.6	.6	.6	.6	.6	.6	.6	.6	.6
115	.5	.5	.5	.5	.5	.5	.5	.5	.5	.5

Reg. § 1.72-9

TABLE VIA.—ANNUITIES FOR JOINT LIFE ONLY; TWO LIVES—EXPECTED RETURN MULTIPLES

Ages	35	36	37	38	39	40	41	42	43	44
35	40.7	40.2	39.7	39.2	38.6	38.0	37.4	36.8	36.2	35.5
36	40.2	39.7	39.3	38.7	38.2	37.7	37.1	36.5	35.9	35.2
37	39.7	39.3	38.8	38.3	37.8	37.3	36.7	36.2	35.6	34.9
38	39.2	38.7	38.3	37.9	37.4	36.9	36.3	35.8	35.2	34.6
39	38.6	38.2	37.8	37.4	36.9	36.4	35.9	35.4	34.9	34.3
40	38.0	37.7	37.3	36.9	36.4	36.0	35.5	35.0	34.5	34.0
41	37.4	37.1	36.7	36.3	35.9	35.5	35.1	34.6	34.1	33.6
42	36.8	36.5	36.2	35.8	35.4	35.0	34.6	34.1	33.7	33.2
43	36.2	35.9	35.6	35.2	34.9	34.5	34.1	33.7	33.2	32.8
44	35.5	35.2	34.9	34.6	34.3	34.0	33.6	33.2	32.8	32.3
45	34.8	34.6	34.3	34.0	33.7	33.4	33.0	32.7	32.3	31.8
46	34.1	33.9	33.7	33.4	33.1	32.8	32.5	32.1	31.8	31.4
47	33.4	33.2	33.0	32.8	32.5	32.2	31.9	31.6	31.2	30.8
48	32.7	32.5	32.3	32.1	31.8	31.6	31.3	31.0	30.7	30.3
49	32.0	31.8	31.6	31.4	31.2	30.9	30.7	30.4	30.1	29.8
50	31.3	31.1	30.9	30.7	30.5	30.3	30.0	29.8	29.5	29.2
51	30.5	30.4	30.2	30.0	29.8	29.6	29.4	29.2	28.9	28.6
52	29.7	29.6	29.5	29.3	29.1	28.9	28.7	28.5	28.3	28.0
53	29.0	28.9	28.7	28.6	28.4	28.2	28.1	27.9	27.6	27.4
54	28.2	28.1	28.0	27.8	27.7	27.5	27.4	27.2	27.0	26.8
55	27.4	27.3	27.2	27.1	27.0	26.8	26.7	26.5	26.3	26.1
56	26.7	26.6	26.5	26.3	26.2	26.1	26.0	25.8	25.6	25.4
57	25.9	25.8	25.7	25.6	25.5	25.4	25.2	25.1	24.9	24.8
58	25.1	25.0	24.9	24.8	24.7	24.6	24.5	24.4	24.2	24.1
59	24.3	24.2	24.1	24.1	24.0	23.9	23.8	23.6	23.5	23.4
60	23.5	23.4	23.4	23.3	23.2	23.1	23.0	22.9	22.8	22.7
61	22.7	22.6	22.6	22.5	22.4	22.4	22.3	22.2	22.1	22.0
62	21.9	21.9	21.8	21.7	21.7	21.6	21.5	21.4	21.3	21.2
63	21.1	21.1	21.0	21.0	20.9	20.8	20.8	20.7	20.6	20.5
64	20.3	20.3	20.2	20.2	20.1	20.1	20.0	20.0	19.9	19.8
65	19.6	19.5	19.5	19.4	19.4	19.3	19.3	19.2	19.1	19.1
66	18.8	18.8	18.7	18.7	18.6	18.6	18.5	18.5	18.4	18.4
67	18.0	18.0	18.0	17.9	17.9	17.9	17.8	17.8	17.7	17.6
68	17.3	17.3	17.2	17.2	17.2	17.1	17.1	17.0	17.0	16.9
69	16.5	16.5	16.5	16.5	16.4	16.4	16.4	16.3	16.3	16.2
70	15.8	15.8	15.8	15.7	15.7	15.7	15.6	15.6	15.6	15.5
71	15.1	15.1	15.1	15.0	15.0	15.0	15.0	14.9	14.9	14.9
72	14.4	14.4	14.4	14.3	14.3	14.3	14.3	14.2	14.2	14.2
73	13.7	13.7	13.7	13.7	13.7	13.6	13.6	13.6	13.6	13.5
74	13.1	13.0	13.0	13.0	13.0	13.0	13.0	12.9	12.9	12.9
75	12.4	12.4	12.4	12.4	12.3	12.3	12.3	12.3	12.3	12.2
76	11.8	11.8	11.7	11.7	11.7	11.7	11.7	11.7	11.6	11.6
77	11.1	11.1	11.1	11.1	11.1	11.1	11.1	11.1	11.0	11.0
78	10.5	10.5	10.5	10.5	10.5	10.5	10.5	10.5	10.5	10.4
79	10.0	10.0	9.9	9.9	9.9	9.9	9.9	9.9	9.9	9.9
80	9.4	9.4	9.4	9.4	9.4	9.4	9.4	9.3	9.3	9.3
81	8.9	8.8	8.8	8.8	8.8	8.8	8.8	8.8	8.8	8.8
82	8.3	8.3	8.3	8.3	8.3	8.3	8.3	8.3	8.3	8.3
83	7.8	7.8	7.8	7.8	7.8	7.8	7.8	7.8	7.8	7.8
84	7.3	7.3	7.3	7.3	7.3	7.3	7.3	7.3	7.3	7.3
85	6.9	6.9	6.9	6.9	6.9	6.9	6.9	6.9	6.9	6.9
86	6.5	6.5	6.5	6.5	6.4	6.4	6.4	6.4	6.4	6.4
87	6.1	6.0	6.0	6.0	6.0	6.0	6.0	6.0	6.0	6.0
88	5.7	5.7	5.7	5.7	5.7	5.7	5.7	5.6	5.6	5.6
89	5.3	5.3	5.3	5.3	5.3	5.3	5.3	5.3	5.3	5.3
90	5.0	5.0	5.0	5.0	5.0	5.0	5.0	5.0	5.0	5.0
91	4.7	4.7	4.7	4.7	4.7	4.7	4.7	4.7	4.6	4.6
92	4.4	4.4	4.4	4.4	4.4	4.4	4.4	4.4	4.4	4.4
93	4.1	4.1	4.1	4.1	4.1	4.1	4.1	4.1	4.1	4.1
94	3.9	3.9	3.9	3.9	3.9	3.9	3.9	3.9	3.9	3.9
95	3.6	3.6	3.6	3.6	3.6	3.6	3.6	3.6	3.6	3.6
96	3.4	3.4	3.4	3.4	3.4	3.4	3.4	3.4	3.4	3.4
97	3.2	3.2	3.2	3.2	3.2	3.2	3.2	3.2	3.2	3.2
98	3.0	3.0	3.0	3.0	3.0	3.0	3.0	3.0	3.0	3.0
99	2.8	2.8	2.8	2.8	2.8	2.8	2.8	2.8	2.8	2.8
100	2.7	2.7	2.7	2.7	2.7	2.7	2.7	2.7	2.6	2.6
101	2.5	2.5	2.5	2.5	2.5	2.5	2.5	2.5	2.5	2.5
102	2.3	2.3	2.3	2.3	2.3	2.3	2.3	2.3	2.3	2.3
103	2.1	2.1	2.1	2.1	2.1	2.1	2.1	2.1	2.1	2.1
104	1.9	1.9	1.9	1.9	1.9	1.9	1.9	1.9	1.9	1.9
105	1.8	1.8	1.8	1.8	1.8	1.8	1.8	1.8	1.8	1.8
106	1.6	1.6	1.6	1.6	1.6	1.6	1.6	1.6	1.6	1.6
107	1.4	1.4	1.4	1.4	1.4	1.4	1.4	1.4	1.4	1.4
108	1.3	1.3	1.3	1.3	1.3	1.3	1.3	1.3	1.3	1.3
109	1.1	1.1	1.1	1.1	1.1	1.1	1.1	1.1	1.1	1.1
110	1.0	1.0	1.0	1.0	1.0	1.0	1.0	1.0	1.0	1.0
111	.9	.9	.9	.9	.9	.9	.9	.9	.9	.9
112	.8	.8	.8	.8	.8	.8	.8	.8	.8	.8
113	.7	.7	.7	.7	.7	.7	.7	.7	.7	.7
114	.6	.6	.6	.6	.6	.6	.6	.6	.6	.6
115	.5	.5	.5	.5	.5	.5	.5	.5	.5	.5

Reg. § 1.72-9

TABLE VIA.—ANNUITIES FOR JOINT LIFE ONLY; TWO LIVES—EXPECTED RETURN MULTIPLES—Continued

Ages	45	46	47	48	49	50	51	52	53	54
45	31.4	30.9	30.5	30.0	29.4	28.9	28.3	27.7	27.1	26.5
46	30.9	30.5	30.0	29.6	29.1	28.5	28.0	27.4	26.9	26.3
47	30.5	30.0	29.6	29.2	28.7	28.2	27.7	27.1	26.6	26.0
48	30.0	29.6	29.2	28.7	28.3	27.8	27.3	26.8	26.3	25.7
49	29.4	29.1	28.7	28.3	27.9	27.4	26.9	26.5	25.9	25.4
50	28.9	28.5	28.2	27.4	27.4	27.0	26.5	26.1	25.6	25.1
51	28.3	28.0	27.7	27.3	26.9	26.5	26.1	25.7	25.2	24.7
52	27.7	27.4	27.1	26.8	26.5	26.1	25.7	25.3	24.8	24.4
53	27.1	26.9	26.6	26.3	25.9	25.6	25.2	24.8	24.4	24.0
54	26.5	26.3	26.0	25.7	25.4	25.1	24.7	24.4	24.0	23.6
55	25.9	25.7	25.4	25.1	24.9	24.6	24.2	23.9	23.5	23.2
56	25.2	25.0	24.8	24.6	24.3	24.0	23.7	23.4	23.1	22.7
57	24.6	24.4	24.2	24.0	23.7	23.5	23.2	22.9	22.6	22.2
58	23.9	23.7	23.5	23.3	23.1	22.9	22.6	22.4	22.1	21.7
59	23.2	23.1	22.9	22.7	22.5	22.3	22.1	21.8	21.5	21.2
60	22.5	22.4	22.2	22.1	21.9	21.7	21.5	21.2	21.0	20.7
61	21.8	21.7	21.6	21.4	21.2	21.1	20.9	20.6	20.4	20.2
62	21.1	21.0	20.9	20.7	20.6	20.4	20.2	20.0	19.8	19.6
63	20.4	20.3	20.2	20.1	19.9	19.8	19.6	19.4	19.2	19.0
64	19.7	19.6	19.5	19.4	19.3	19.1	19.0	18.8	18.6	18.5
65	19.0	18.9	18.8	18.7	18.6	18.5	18.3	18.2	18.0	17.9
66	18.3	18.2	18.1	18.0	17.9	17.8	17.7	17.6	17.4	17.3
67	17.6	17.5	17.4	17.3	17.3	17.2	17.1	16.9	16.8	16.7
68	16.9	16.8	16.7	16.7	16.6	16.5	16.4	16.3	16.2	16.1
69	16.2	16.1	16.1	16.0	15.9	15.8	15.8	15.7	15.6	15.4
70	15.5	15.4	15.4	15.3	15.3	15.2	15.1	15.0	14.9	14.8
71	14.8	14.8	14.7	14.7	14.6	14.5	14.5	14.4	14.3	14.2
72	14.1	14.1	14.1	14.0	14.0	13.9	13.8	13.8	13.7	13.6
73	13.5	13.5	13.4	13.4	13.3	13.3	13.2	13.2	13.1	13.0
74	12.8	12.8	12.8	12.7	12.7	12.7	12.6	12.6	12.5	12.4
75	12.2	12.2	12.2	12.1	12.1	12.1	12.0	12.0	11.9	11.9
76	11.6	11.6	11.6	11.5	11.5	11.5	11.4	11.4	11.3	11.3
77	11.0	11.0	11.0	10.9	10.9	10.9	10.8	10.8	10.8	10.7
78	10.4	10.4	10.4	10.4	10.3	10.3	10.3	10.2	10.2	10.2
79	9.9	9.8	9.8	9.8	9.8	9.8	9.7	9.7	9.7	9.6
80	9.3	9.3	9.3	9.3	9.2	9.2	9.2	9.2	9.1	9.1
81	8.8	8.8	8.7	8.7	8.7	8.7	8.7	8.7	8.6	8.6
82	8.3	8.2	8.2	8.2	8.2	8.2	8.2	8.2	8.1	8.1
83	7.8	7.8	7.7	7.7	7.7	7.7	7.7	7.7	7.7	7.6
84	7.3	7.3	7.3	7.3	7.3	7.2	7.2	7.2	7.2	7.2
85	6.8	6.8	6.8	6.8	6.8	6.8	6.8	6.8	6.8	6.7
86	6.4	6.4	6.4	6.4	6.4	6.4	6.4	6.4	6.3	6.3
87	6.0	6.0	6.0	6.0	6.0	6.0	6.0	6.0	6.0	5.9
88	5.6	5.6	5.6	5.6	5.6	5.6	5.6	5.6	5.6	5.6
89	5.3	5.3	5.3	5.3	5.3	5.3	5.2	5.2	5.2	5.2
90	5.0	4.9	4.9	4.9	4.9	4.9	4.9	4.9	4.9	4.9
91	4.6	4.6	4.6	4.6	4.6	4.6	4.6	4.6	4.6	4.6
92	4.4	4.4	4.4	4.3	4.3	4.3	4.3	4.3	4.3	4.3
93	4.1	4.1	4.1	4.1	4.1	4.1	4.1	4.1	4.1	4.1
94	3.9	3.9	3.8	3.8	3.8	3.8	3.8	3.8	3.8	3.8
95	3.6	3.6	3.6	3.6	3.6	3.6	3.6	3.6	3.6	3.6
96	3.4	3.4	3.4	3.4	3.4	3.4	3.4	3.4	3.4	3.4
97	3.2	3.2	3.2	3.2	3.2	3.2	3.2	3.2	3.2	3.2
98	3.0	3.0	3.0	3.0	3.0	3.0	3.0	3.0	3.0	3.0
99	2.8	2.8	2.8	2.8	2.8	2.8	2.8	2.8	2.8	2.8
100	2.6	2.6	2.6	2.6	2.6	2.6	2.6	2.6	2.6	2.6
101	2.5	2.5	2.5	2.5	2.5	2.5	2.5	2.5	2.5	2.5
102	2.3	2.3	2.3	2.3	2.3	2.3	2.3	2.3	2.3	2.3
103	2.1	2.1	2.1	2.1	2.1	2.1	2.1	2.1	2.1	2.1
104	1.9	1.9	1.9	1.9	1.9	1.9	1.9	1.9	1.9	1.9
105	1.8	1.8	1.8	1.8	1.8	1.8	1.8	1.8	1.8	1.8
106	1.6	1.6	1.6	1.6	1.6	1.6	1.6	1.6	1.6	1.6
107	1.4	1.4	1.4	1.4	1.4	1.4	1.4	1.4	1.4	1.4
108	1.3	1.3	1.3	1.3	1.3	1.3	1.3	1.3	1.3	1.3
109	1.1	1.1	1.1	1.1	1.1	1.1	1.1	1.1	1.1	1.1
110	1.0	1.0	1.0	1.0	1.0	1.0	1.0	1.0	1.0	1.0
111	.9	.9	.9	.9	.9	.9	.9	.9	.9	.9
112	.8	.8	.8	.8	.8	.8	.8	.8	.8	.8
113	.7	.7	.7	.7	.7	.7	.7	.7	.7	.7
114	.6	.6	.6	.6	.6	.6	.6	.6	.6	.6
115	.5	.5	.5	.5	.5	.5	.5	.5	.5	.5

Reg. § 1.72-9

TABLE VIA.—ANNUITIES FOR JOINT LIFE ONLY; TWO LIVES—EXPECTED RETURN MULTIPLES

Ages	55	56	57	58	59	60	61	62	63	64
55	22.7	22.3	21.9	21.4	20.9	20.4	19.9	19.4	18.8	18.3
56	22.3	21.9	21.5	21.1	20.6	20.1	19.6	19.1	18.6	18.0
57	21.9	21.5	21.1	20.7	20.3	19.8	19.3	18.8	18.3	17.8
58	21.4	21.1	20.7	20.3	19.9	19.5	19.0	18.5	18.0	17.5
59	20.9	20.6	20.3	19.9	19.5	19.1	18.7	18.2	17.7	17.3
60	20.4	20.1	19.8	19.5	19.1	18.7	18.3	17.9	17.4	17.0
61	29.9	19.6	19.3	19.0	18.7	18.3	17.9	17.5	17.1	16.7
62	19.4	19.1	18.8	18.5	18.2	17.9	17.5	17.1	16.8	16.3
63	18.8	18.6	18.3	18.0	17.7	17.4	17.1	16.8	16.4	16.0
64	18.3	18.0	17.8	17.5	17.3	17.0	16.7	16.3	16.0	15.6
65	17.7	17.5	17.3	17.0	16.8	16.5	16.2	15.9	15.6	15.3
66	17.1	16.9	16.7	16.5	16.3	16.0	15.8	15.5	15.2	14.9
67	16.5	16.3	16.2	16.0	15.8	15.5	15.3	15.0	14.7	14.5
68	15.9	15.8	15.6	15.4	15.2	15.0	14.8	14.6	14.3	14.0
69	15.3	15.2	15.0	14.9	14.7	14.5	14.3	14.1	13.9	13.6
70	14.7	14.6	14.5	14.3	14.2	14.0	13.8	13.6	13.4	13.2
71	14.1	14.0	13.9	13.8	13.6	13.5	13.3	13.1	12.9	12.7
72	13.5	13.4	13.3	13.2	13.1	12.9	12.8	12.6	12.4	12.3
73	13.0	12.9	12.8	12.7	12.5	12.4	12.3	12.1	12.0	11.8
74	12.4	12.3	12.2	12.1	12.0	11.9	11.8	11.6	11.5	11.3
75	11.8	11.7	11.7	11.6	11.5	11.4	11.3	11.1	11.0	10.9
76	11.2	11.2	11.1	11.0	10.9	10.9	10.8	10.6	10.5	10.4
77	10.7	10.6	10.6	10.5	10.4	10.3	10.3	10.2	10.0	9.9
78	10.1	10.1	10.0	10.0	9.9	9.8	9.8	9.7	9.6	9.5
79	9.6	9.6	9.5	9.5	9.4	9.3	9.3	9.2	9.1	9.0
80	9.1	9.0	9.0	9.0	8.9	8.9	8.8	8.7	8.7	8.6
81	8.6	8.5	8.5	8.5	8.4	8.4	8.3	8.3	8.2	8.1
82	8.1	8.1	8.0	8.0	8.0	7.9	7.9	7.8	7.8	7.7
83	7.6	7.6	7.6	7.5	7.5	7.5	7.4	7.4	7.3	7.3
84	7.2	7.1	7.1	7.1	7.1	7.0	7.0	7.0	6.9	6.9
85	6.7	6.7	6.7	6.7	6.6	6.6	6.6	6.5	6.5	6.5
86	6.3	6.3	6.3	6.3	6.2	6.2	6.2	6.2	6.1	6.1
87	5.9	5.9	5.9	5.9	5.9	5.8	5.8	5.8	5.8	5.7
88	5.6	5.5	5.5	5.5	5.5	5.5	5.5	5.4	5.4	5.4
89	5.2	5.2	5.2	5.2	5.2	5.1	5.1	5.1	5.1	5.1
90	4.9	4.9	4.9	4.9	4.9	4.8	4.8	4.8	4.8	4.8
91	4.6	4.6	4.6	4.6	4.6	4.5	4.5	4.5	4.5	4.5
92	4.3	4.3	4.3	4.3	4.3	4.3	4.3	4.2	4.2	4.2
93	4.1	4.1	4.0	4.0	4.0	4.0	4.0	4.0	4.0	4.0
94	3.8	3.8	3.8	3.8	3.8	3.8	3.8	3.8	3.8	3.7
95	3.6	3.6	3.6	3.6	3.6	3.6	3.6	3.6	3.5	3.5
96	3.4	3.4	3.4	3.4	3.4	3.4	3.4	3.3	3.3	3.3
97	3.2	3.2	3.2	3.2	3.2	3.2	3.2	3.2	3.1	3.1
98	3.0	3.0	3.0	3.0	3.0	3.0	3.0	3.0	3.0	3.0
99	2.8	2.8	2.8	2.8	2.8	2.8	2.8	2.8	2.8	2.8
100	2.6	2.6	2.6	2.6	2.6	2.6	2.6	2.6	2.6	2.6
101	2.5	2.4	2.4	2.4	2.4	2.4	2.4	2.4	2.4	2.4
102	2.3	2.3	2.3	2.3	2.3	2.3	2.3	2.3	2.3	2.2
103	2.1	2.1	2.1	2.1	2.1	2.1	2.1	2.1	2.1	2.1
104	1.9	1.9	1.9	1.9	1.9	1.9	1.9	1.9	1.9	1.9
105	1.8	1.8	1.8	1.8	1.8	1.8	1.7	1.7	1.7	1.7
106	1.6	1.6	1.6	1.6	1.6	1.6	1.6	1.6	1.6	1.6
107	1.4	1.4	1.4	1.4	1.4	1.4	1.4	1.4	1.4	1.4
108	1.3	1.3	1.3	1.3	1.3	1.3	1.3	1.3	1.3	1.3
109	1.1	1.1	1.1	1.1	1.1	1.1	1.1	1.1	1.1	1.1
110	1.0	1.0	1.0	1.0	1.0	1.0	1.0	1.0	1.0	1.0
111	.9	.9	.9	.9	.9	.9	.9	.9	.9	.9
112	.8	.8	.8	.8	.8	.8	.8	.8	.8	.8
113	.7	.7	.7	.7	.7	.7	.7	.7	.7	.7
114	.6	.6	.6	.6	.6	.6	.6	.6	.6	.6
115	.5	.5	.5	.5	.5	.5	.5	.5	.5	.5

Reg. § 1.72-9

TABLE VIA.—ANNUITIES FOR JOINT LIFE ONLY; TWO LIVES—EXPECTED RETURN MULTIPLES—Continued

Ages	65	66	67	68	69	70	71	72	73	74
65	14.9	14.5	14.1	13.7	13.3	12.9	12.5	12.0	11.6	11.2
66	14.5	14.2	13.8	13.4	13.1	12.6	12.2	11.8	11.4	11.0
67	14.1	13.8	13.5	13.1	12.8	12.4	12.0	11.6	11.2	10.8
68	13.7	13.4	13.1	12.8	12.5	12.1	11.7	11.4	11.0	10.6
69	13.3	13.1	12.8	12.5	12.1	11.8	11.4	11.1	10.7	10.4
70	12.9	12.6	12.4	12.1	11.8	11.5	11.2	10.8	10.5	10.1
71	12.5	12.2	12.0	11.7	11.4	11.2	10.9	10.5	10.2	9.9
72	12.0	11.8	11.6	11.4	11.1	10.8	10.5	10.2	9.9	9.6
73	11.6	11.4	11.2	11.0	10.7	10.5	10.2	9.9	9.7	9.4
74	11.2	11.0	10.8	10.6	10.4	10.1	9.9	9.6	9.4	9.1
75	10.7	10.5	10.4	10.2	10.0	9.8	9.5	9.3	9.1	8.8
76	10.3	10.1	9.9	9.8	9.6	9.4	9.2	9.0	8.8	8.5
77	9.8	9.7	9.5	9.4	9.2	9.0	8.8	8.6	8.4	8.2
78	9.4	9.2	9.1	9.0	8.8	8.7	8.5	8.3	8.1	7.9
79	8.9	8.8	8.7	8.6	8.4	8.3	8.1	8.0	7.8	7.6
80	8.5	8.4	8.3	8.2	8.0	7.9	7.8	7.6	7.5	7.3
81	8.0	8.0	7.9	7.9	7.7	7.5	7.4	7.3	7.1	7.0
82	7.6	7.5	7.5	7.4	7.3	7.2	7.1	6.9	6.8	6.7
83	7.2	7.1	7.1	7.0	6.9	6.8	6.7	6.6	6.5	6.4
84	6.8	6.7	6.7	6.6	6.5	6.4	6.4	6.3	6.2	6.0
85	6.4	6.4	6.3	6.2	6.2	6.1	6.0	5.9	5.8	5.7
86	6.0	6.0	5.9	5.9	5.8	5.8	5.7	5.6	5.5	5.4
87	5.7	5.6	5.6	5.6	5.5	5.4	5.4	5.3	5.2	5.2
88	5.3	5.3	5.3	5.2	5.2	5.1	5.1	5.0	5.0	4.9
89	5.0	5.0	5.0	4.9	4.9	4.8	4.8	4.7	4.7	4.6
90	4.7	4.7	4.7	4.6	4.6	4.6	4.5	4.5	4.4	4.4
91	4.5	4.4	4.4	4.4	4.3	4.3	4.3	4.2	4.2	4.1
92	4.2	4.2	4.1	4.1	4.1	4.1	4.0	4.0	3.9	3.9
93	3.9	3.9	3.9	3.9	3.9	3.8	3.8	3.8	3.7	3.7
94	3.7	3.7	3.7	3.7	3.6	3.6	3.6	3.6	3.5	3.5
95	3.5	3.5	3.5	3.5	3.4	3.4	3.4	3.4	3.3	3.3
96	3.3	3.3	3.3	3.3	3.3	3.2	3.2	3.2	3.2	3.1
97	3.1	3.1	3.1	3.1	3.1	3.1	3.0	3.0	3.0	3.0
98	2.9	2.9	2.9	2.9	2.9	2.9	2.9	2.9	2.8	2.8
99	2.8	2.8	2.8	2.7	2.7	2.7	2.7	2.7	2.7	2.6
100	2.6	2.6	2.6	2.6	2.6	2.5	2.5	2.5	2.5	2.5
101	2.4	2.4	2.4	2.4	2.4	2.4	2.4	2.4	2.3	2.3
102	2.2	2.2	2.2	2.2	2.2	2.2	2.2	2.2	2.2	2.2
103	2.1	2.1	2.1	2.1	2.1	2.0	2.0	2.0	2.0	2.0
104	1.9	1.9	1.9	1.9	1.9	1.9	1.9	1.9	1.9	1.9
105	1.7	1.7	1.7	1.7	1.7	1.7	1.7	1.7	1.7	1.7
106	1.6	1.6	1.6	1.6	1.6	1.6	1.6	1.6	1.5	1.5
107	1.4	1.4	1.4	1.4	1.4	1.4	1.4	1.4	1.4	1.4
108	1.3	1.3	1.3	1.3	1.3	1.3	1.3	1.3	1.3	1.3
109	1.1	1.1	1.1	1.1	1.1	1.1	1.1	1.1	1.1	1.1
110	1.0	1.0	1.0	1.0	1.0	1.0	1.0	1.0	1.0	1.0
111	.9	.9	.9	.9	.9	.9	.9	.9	.9	.9
112	.8	.8	.8	.8	.8	.8	.8	.8	.8	.8
113	.7	.7	.7	.7	.7	.6	.6	.6	.6	.6
114	.6	.6	.6	.6	.6	.6	.5	.5	.5	.5
115	.5	.5	.5	.5	.5	.5	.5	.5	.5	.5

Reg. § 1.72-9

TABLE VIA.—ANNUITIES FOR JOINT LIFE ONLY; TWO LIVES—EXPECTED RETURN MULTIPLES

Ages	75	76	77	78	79	80	81	82	83	84
75	8.6	8.3	8.0	7.7	7.4	7.1	6.6	6.5	6.2	5.9
76	8.3	8.0	7.8	7.5	7.2	6.9	6.7	6.4	6.1	5.8
77	8.0	7.8	7.6	7.3	7.0	6.8	6.5	6.2	5.9	5.7
78	7.7	7.5	7.3	7.0	6.8	6.6	6.3	6.0	5.8	5.5
79	7.4	7.2	7.0	6.8	6.6	6.3	6.1	5.9	5.6	5.4
80	7.1	6.9	6.8	6.6	6.3	6.1	5.9	5.7	5.5	5.2
81	6.8	6.7	6.5	6.3	6.1	5.9	5.7	5.5	5.3	5.1
82	6.5	6.4	6.2	6.0	5.9	5.7	5.5	5.3	5.1	4.9
83	6.2	6.1	5.9	5.8	5.6	5.5	5.3	5.1	4.9	4.7
84	5.9	5.8	5.7	5.5	5.4	5.2	5.1	4.9	4.7	4.6
85	5.6	5.5	5.4	5.3	5.2	5.0	4.9	4.7	4.6	4.4
86	5.4	5.3	5.1	5.0	4.9	4.8	4.7	4.5	4.4	4.2
87	5.1	5.0	4.9	4.8	4.7	4.6	4.4	4.3	4.2	4.1
88	4.8	4.7	4.6	4.5	4.4	4.3	4.2	4.1	4.0	3.9
89	4.5	4.5	4.4	4.3	4.2	4.1	4.0	3.9	3.8	3.7
90	4.3	4.2	4.2	4.1	4.0	3.9	3.8	3.8	3.7	3.5
91	4.1	4.0	4.0	3.9	3.8	3.7	3.7	3.6	3.5	3.4
92	3.9	3.8	3.7	3.7	3.6	3.6	3.5	3.4	3.3	3.2
93	3.7	3.6	3.6	3.5	3.4	3.4	3.3	3.2	3.2	3.1
94	3.5	3.4	3.4	3.3	3.3	3.2	3.2	3.1	3.0	3.0
95	3.3	3.2	3.2	3.2	3.1	3.1	3.0	3.0	2.9	2.8
96	3.1	3.1	3.0	3.0	3.0	2.9	2.9	2.8	2.8	2.7
97	2.9	2.9	2.9	2.9	2.8	2.8	2.7	2.7	2.6	2.6
98	2.8	2.8	2.7	2.7	2.7	2.6	2.6	2.6	2.5	2.5
99	2.6	2.6	2.6	2.6	2.5	2.5	2.5	2.4	2.4	2.3
100	2.5	2.5	2.4	2.4	2.4	2.4	2.3	2.3	2.3	2.2
101	2.3	2.3	2.3	2.3	2.2	2.2	2.2	2.2	2.1	2.1
102	2.2	2.1	2.1	2.1	2.1	2.1	2.0	2.0	2.0	2.0
103	2.0	2.0	2.0	2.0	1.9	1.9	1.9	1.9	1.9	1.8
104	1.8	1.8	1.8	1.8	1.8	1.8	1.8	1.7	1.7	1.7
105	1.7	1.7	1.7	1.7	1.6	1.6	1.6	1.6	1.6	1.6
106	1.5	1.5	1.5	1.5	1.5	1.5	1.5	1.5	1.5	1.4
107	1.4	1.4	1.4	1.4	1.4	1.4	1.3	1.3	1.3	1.3
108	1.3	1.2	1.2	1.2	1.2	1.2	1.2	1.2	1.2	1.2
109	1.1	1.1	1.1	1.1	1.1	1.1	1.1	1.1	1.1	1.1
110	1.0	1.0	1.0	1.0	1.0	1.0	1.0	1.0	1.0	1.0
111	.9	.9	.9	.9	.9	.9	.9	.9	.8	.8
112	.8	.8	.8	.7	.7	.7	.7	.7	.7	.7
113	.6	.6	.6	.6	.6	.6	.6	.6	.6	.6
114	.5	.5	.5	.5	.5	.5	.5	.5	.5	.5
115	.5	.5	.5	.5	.5	.5	.5	.5	.5	.5

Ages	85	86	87	88	89	90	91	92	93	94
85	4.2	4.1	3.9	3.8	3.6	3.4	3.3	3.2	3.0	2.9
86	4.1	3.9	3.8	3.6	3.5	3.3	3.2	3.1	2.9	2.8
87	3.9	3.8	3.6	3.5	3.4	3.2	3.1	3.0	2.8	2.7
88	3.8	3.6	3.5	3.4	3.2	3.1	3.0	2.9	2.8	2.6
89	3.6	3.5	3.4	3.2	3.1	3.0	2.9	2.8	2.7	2.6
90	3.4	3.3	3.2	3.1	3.0	2.9	2.8	2.7	2.6	2.5
91	3.3	3.2	3.1	3.0	2.9	2.8	2.7	2.6	2.5	2.4
92	3.2	3.1	3.0	2.9	2.8	2.7	2.6	2.5	2.4	2.3
93	3.0	2.9	2.8	2.8	2.7	2.6	2.5	2.4	2.3	2.3
94	2.9	2.8	2.7	2.6	2.6	2.5	2.4	2.3	2.3	2.2
95	2.8	2.7	2.6	2.5	2.5	2.4	2.3	2.2	2.2	2.1
96	2.6	2.6	2.5	2.4	2.4	2.3	2.2	2.2	2.1	2.0
97	2.5	2.5	2.4	2.3	2.3	2.2	2.2	2.1	2.0	2.0
98	2.4	2.4	2.3	2.2	2.2	2.1	2.1	2.0	2.0	1.9
99	2.3	2.2	2.2	2.1	2.1	2.0	2.0	1.9	1.9	1.8
100	2.2	2.1	2.1	2.0	2.0	1.9	1.9	1.9	1.8	1.8
101	2.1	2.0	2.0	1.9	1.9	1.9	1.8	1.8	1.7	1.7
102	1.9	1.9	1.9	1.8	1.8	1.8	1.7	1.7	1.6	1.6
103	1.8	1.8	1.8	1.7	1.7	1.7	1.6	1.6	1.5	1.5
104	1.7	1.7	1.6	1.6	1.6	1.5	1.5	1.5	1.5	1.4
105	1.6	1.5	1.5	1.5	1.5	1.4	1.4	1.4	1.4	1.3
106	1.4	1.4	1.4	1.4	1.4	1.3	1.3	1.3	1.3	1.2
107	1.3	1.3	1.3	1.3	1.2	1.2	1.2	1.2	1.2	1.2
108	1.2	1.2	1.2	1.1	1.1	1.1	1.1	1.1	1.1	1.1
109	1.1	1.1	1.0	1.0	1.0	1.0	1.0	1.0	1.0	1.0
110	.9	.9	.9	.9	.9	.9	.9	.9	.9	.9
111	.8	.8	.8	.8	.8	.8	.8	.8	.8	.8
112	.7	.7	.7	.7	.7	.7	.7	.7	.7	.7
113	.6	.6	.6	.6	.6	.6	.6	.6	.6	.6
114	.5	.5	.5	.5	.5	.5	.5	.5	.5	.5
115	.5	.5	.5	.5	.5	.5	.5	.5	.5	.5

TABLE VIA.—ANNUITIES FOR JOINT LIFE ONLY; TWO LIVES—EXPECTED RETURN MULTIPLES—Continued

Ages	95	96	97	98	99	100	101	102	103	104
95	2.0	2.0	1.9	1.8	1.8	1.7	1.6	1.6	1.5	1.4
96	2.0	1.9	1.9	1.8	1.7	1.7	1.6	1.5	1.5	1.4
97	1.9	1.9	1.8	1.7	1.7	1.6	1.6	1.5	1.4	1.3
98	1.8	1.8	1.7	1.7	1.6	1.6	1.5	1.5	1.4	1.3
99	1.8	1.7	1.7	1.6	1.6	1.5	1.5	1.4	1.4	1.3
100	1.7	1.7	1.6	1.6	1.5	1.5	1.4	1.4	1.3	1.3
101	1.6	1.6	1.6	1.5	1.5	1.4	1.4	1.3	1.3	1.2
102	1.6	1.5	1.5	1.5	1.4	1.4	1.3	1.3	1.2	1.2
103	1.5	1.5	1.4	1.4	1.4	1.3	1.3	1.2	1.2	1.1
104	1.4	1.4	1.3	1.3	1.3	1.3	1.2	1.2	1.1	1.1
105	1.3	1.3	1.3	1.2	1.2	1.2	1.2	1.1	1.1	1.0
106	1.2	1.2	1.2	1.2	1.1	1.1	1.1	1.1	1.0	1.0
107	1.1	1.1	1.1	1.1	1.1	1.0	1.0	1.0	1.0	.9
108	1.0	1.0	1.0	1.0	1.0	1.0	1.0	.9	.9	.9
109	1.0	.9	.9	.9	.9	.9	.9	.9	.8	.8
110	.9	.9	.8	.8	.8	.8	.8	.8	.8	.8
111	.8	.8	.8	.8	.8	.7	.7	.7	.7	.7
112	.7	.7	.7	.7	.7	.7	.7	.7	.6	.6
113	.6	.6	.6	.6	.6	.6	.6	.6	.6	.6
114	.5	.5	.5	.5	.5	.5	.5	.5	.5	.5
115	.5	.5	.5	.5	.5	.5	.5	.5	.5	.5

Ages	105	106	107	108	109	110	111	112	113	114	115
105	1.0	1.0	.9	.9	.8	.7	.7	.6	.6	.5	.5
106	1.0	.9	.9	.8	.8	.7	.7	.6	.6	.5	.5
107	.9	.9	.8	.8	.7	.7	.7	.6	.6	.5	.5
108	.9	.8	.8	.8	.7	.7	.6	.6	.5	.5	.5
109	.8	.8	.7	.7	.7	.7	.6	.6	.5	.5	.5
110	.7	.7	.7	.7	.7	.6	.6	.6	.5	.5	.5
111	.7	.7	.7	.6	.6	.6	.6	.5	.5	.5	.5
112	.6	.6	.6	.6	.6	.6	.5	.5	.5	.5	.5
113	.6	.6	.6	.5	.5	.5	.5	.5	.5	.5	.5
114	.5	.5	.5	.5	.5	.5	.5	.5	.5	.5	.5
115	.5	.5	.5	.5	.5	.5	.5	.5	.5	.5	.5

TABLE VII.—PERCENT VALUE OF REFUND FEATURE; DURATION OF GUARANTEED AMOUNT

Age	Years—									
	1	2	3	4	5	6	7	8	9	10
5	0	0	0	0	0	0	0	0	0	0
6	0	0	0	0	0	0	0	0	0	0
7	0	0	0	0	0	0	0	0	0	0
8	0	0	0	0	0	0	0	0	0	0
9	0	0	0	0	0	0	0	0	0	0
10	0	0	0	0	0	0	0	0	0	0
11	0	0	0	0	0	0	0	0	0	0
12	0	0	0	0	0	0	0	0	0	0
13	0	0	0	0	0	0	0	0	0	0
14	0	0	0	0	0	0	0	0	0	0
15	0	0	0	0	0	0	0	0	0	0
16	0	0	0	0	0	0	0	0	0	0
17	0	0	0	0	0	0	0	0	0	0
18	0	0	0	0	0	0	0	0	0	0
19	0	0	0	0	0	0	0	0	0	0
20	0	0	0	0	0	0	0	0	0	0
21	0	0	0	0	0	0	0	0	0	0
22	0	0	0	0	0	0	0	0	0	0
23	0	0	0	0	0	0	0	0	0	0
24	0	0	0	0	0	0	0	0	0	0
25	0	0	0	0	0	0	0	0	0	0

Reg. § 1.72-9

TABLE VII.—PERCENT VALUE OF REFUND FEATURE; DURATION OF GUARANTEED AMOUNT

Age	Years—									
	1	2	3	4	5	6	7	8	9	10
26	0	0	0	0	0	0	0	0	0	0
27	0	0	0	0	0	0	0	0	0	0
28	0	0	0	0	0	0	0	0	0	0
29	0	0	0	0	0	0	0	0	0	0
30	0	0	0	0	0	0	0	0	0	0
31	0	0	0	0	0	0	0	0	0	0
32	0	0	0	0	0	0	0	0	0	0
33	0	0	0	0	0	0	0	0	0	0
34	0	0	0	0	0	0	0	0	0	0
35	0	0	0	0	0	0	0	0	0	0
36	0	0	0	0	0	0	0	0	0	0
37	0	0	0	0	0	0	0	0	0	1
38	0	0	0	0	0	0	0	0	0	1
39	0	0	0	0	0	0	0	0	1	1
40	0	0	0	0	0	0	0	1	1	1
41	0	0	0	0	0	0	0	1	1	1
42	0	0	0	0	0	0	1	1	1	1
43	0	0	0	0	0	0	1	1	1	1
44	0	0	0	0	0	1	1	1	1	1
45	0	0	0	0	0	1	1	1	1	1
46	0	0	0	0	1	1	1	1	1	1
47	0	0	0	0	1	1	1	1	1	1
48	0	0	0	0	1	1	1	1	1	1
49	0	0	0	1	1	1	1	1	1	2
50	0	0	0	1	1	1	1	1	1	2
51	0	0	0	1	1	1	1	1	2	2
52	0	0	0	1	1	1	1	1	2	2
53	0	0	1	1	1	1	1	2	2	2
54	0	0	1	1	1	1	1	2	2	2
55	0	0	1	1	1	1	2	2	2	3
56	0	0	1	1	1	1	2	2	2	3
57	0	0	1	1	1	2	2	2	3	3
58	0	1	1	1	1	2	2	2	3	3
59	0	1	1	1	1	2	2	2	3	4
60	0	1	1	1	2	2	2	3	3	4
61	0	1	1	1	2	2	2	3	3	4
62	0	1	1	2	2	2	3	4	4	5
63	0	1	1	2	2	2	3	4	5	5
64	0	1	1	2	2	3	4	4	5	6
65	0	1	2	2	3	3	4	5	6	6
66	1	1	2	2	3	4	5	5	6	7
67	1	1	2	3	3	4	5	6	7	8
68	1	1	2	3	4	5	6	7	8	9
69	1	1	2	3	4	5	6	7	8	10
70	1	2	3	4	5	6	7	8	9	11
71	1	2	3	4	5	6	8	9	10	12
72	1	2	3	4	6	7	8	10	11	13
73	1	2	4	5	6	8	9	11	13	14
74	1	3	4	5	7	9	10	12	14	16
75	1	3	4	6	8	9	11	13	15	17
76	2	3	5	7	9	10	12	15	17	19
77	2	4	5	7	9	12	14	16	18	21
78	2	4	6	8	10	13	15	18	20	23
79	2	4	7	9	11	14	17	19	22	25
80	2	5	7	10	13	15	18	21	24	27
81	3	5	8	11	14	17	20	23	26	29
82	3	6	9	12	15	19	22	25	28	32
83	3	7	10	13	17	20	24	27	31	34
84	4	7	11	15	19	22	26	30	33	37
85	4	8	12	16	20	24	28	32	36	40
86	4	9	13	18	22	27	31	35	39	42
87	5	10	15	20	24	29	33	37	41	45
88	5	11	16	21	26	31	36	40	44	48
89	6	12	18	23	28	33	38	43	47	50
90	7	13	19	25	31	36	41	45	49	53
91	7	14	21	27	33	38	43	48	52	55
92	8	15	22	29	35	40	45	50	54	58
93	9	17	24	31	37	43	48	52	56	60
94	9	18	26	33	39	45	50	54	58	62
95	10	19	27	35	41	47	52	57	60	64
96	11	20	29	36	43	49	54	59	62	66
97	11	21	30	38	45	51	56	61	64	68
98	12	23	32	40	47	53	58	63	66	69
99	13	24	34	42	49	55	60	65	68	71

Reg. § 1.72-9

TABLE VII.—PERCENT VALUE OF REFUND FEATURE; DURATION OF GUARANTEED AMOUNT—Continued

Age	Years—									
	1	2	3	4	5	6	7	8	9	10
100...............	14	26	36	44	52	58	63	67	70	73
101...............	14	27	38	47	54	60	65	69	72	75
102...............	15	29	40	49	56	62	67	71	74	77
103...............	17	31	42	52	59	65	69	73	76	78
104...............	18	33	45	55	62	67	72	75	78	80
105...............	19	36	48	58	65	70	74	77	80	82
106...............	21	38	51	61	68	73	77	79	82	84
107...............	23	42	55	64	71	75	79	81	84	85
108...............	25	45	58	67	73	78	81	83	85	87
109...............	28	49	62	71	76	80	83	85	87	88
110...............	31	52	66	74	79	82	85	87	88	89
111...............	34	57	70	77	82	85	87	88	90	91
112...............	37	61	73	80	84	87	88	90	91	92
113...............	41	66	77	83	86	88	90	91	92	93
114...............	45	70	80	85	88	90	92	93	93	94
115...............	50	75	83	88	90	92	93	94	94	95

Reg. § 1.72-9

TABLE VII.—PERCENT VALUE OF REFUND FEATURE; DURATION OF GUARANTEED AMOUNT

Age	Years—									
	11	12	13	14	15	16	17	18	19	20
5	0	0	0	0	0	0	0	0	0	0
6	0	0	0	0	0	0	0	0	0	0
7	0	0	0	0	0	0	0	0	0	0
8	0	0	0	0	0	0	0	0	0	0
9	0	0	0	0	0	0	0	0	0	0
10	0	0	0	0	0	0	0	0	0	0
11	0	0	0	0	0	0	0	0	0	0
12	0	0	0	0	0	0	0	0	0	0
13	0	0	0	0	0	0	0	0	0	0
14	0	0	0	0	0	0	0	0	0	0
15	0	0	0	0	0	0	0	0	0	0
16	0	0	0	0	0	0	0	0	0	0
17	0	0	0	0	0	0	0	0	0	0
18	0	0	0	0	0	0	0	0	0	0
19	0	0	0	0	0	0	0	0	0	0
20	0	0	0	0	0	0	0	0	0	1
21	0	0	0	0	0	0	0	0	0	1
22	0	0	0	0	0	0	0	0	1	1
23	0	0	0	0	0	0	0	1	1	1
24	0	0	0	0	0	0	0	1	1	1
25	0	0	0	0	0	0	1	1	1	1
26	0	0	0	0	0	0	1	1	1	1
27	0	0	0	0	0	1	1	1	1	1
28	0	0	0	0	1	1	1	1	1	1
29	0	0	0	0	1	1	1	1	1	1
30	0	0	0	1	1	1	1	1	1	1
31	0	0	0	1	1	1	1	1	1	1
32	0	0	1	1	1	1	1	1	1	1
33	0	0	1	1	1	1	1	1	1	1
34	0	1	1	1	1	1	1	1	1	1
35	0	1	1	1	1	1	1	1	1	1
36	1	1	1	1	1	1	1	1	1	1
37	1	1	1	1	1	1	1	1	1	1
38	1	1	1	1	1	1	1	1	1	2
39	1	1	1	1	1	1	1	1	2	2
40	1	1	1	1	1	1	1	2	2	2
41	1	1	1	1	1	1	2	2	2	2
42	1	1	1	1	1	2	2	2	2	2
43	1	1	1	1	2	2	2	2	2	3
44	1	1	1	2	2	2	2	2	3	3
45	1	1	2	2	2	2	2	3	3	3
46	1	2	2	2	2	2	3	3	3	3
47	1	2	2	2	2	2	3	3	3	4
48	2	2	2	2	2	3	3	3	4	4
49	2	2	2	2	3	3	3	4	4	4
50	2	2	2	3	3	3	3	4	4	5
51	2	2	3	3	3	3	4	4	4	5
52	2	2	3	3	3	4	4	5	5	5
53	2	3	3	3	4	4	5	5	5	6
54	3	3	3	4	4	4	5	5	6	7
55	3	3	4	4	4	5	5	6	7	7
56	3	3	4	4	5	5	6	7	7	8
57	3	4	4	5	5	6	6	7	8	9
58	4	4	5	5	6	6	7	8	9	9
59	4	5	5	6	6	7	8	9	9	10
60	4	5	6	6	7	8	9	10	10	11
61	5	6	6	7	8	9	10	10	11	13
62	5	6	7	8	9	10	11	12	13	14
63	6	7	8	9	10	11	12	13	14	15
64	7	8	8	9	10	12	13	14	15	17
65	7	8	9	10	12	13	14	15	17	18
66	8	9	10	12	13	14	15	17	18	20
67	9	10	11	13	14	15	17	18	20	22
68	10	11	13	14	15	17	19	20	22	24
69	11	12	14	15	17	19	20	22	24	26
70	12	14	15	17	19	20	22	24	26	28
71	13	15	17	18	20	22	24	26	28	30
72	15	17	18	20	22	24	26	28	30	32
73	16	18	20	22	24	26	28	31	33	35
74	18	20	22	24	26	28	31	33	35	37
75	19	22	24	26	28	31	33	35	38	40
76	21	24	26	28	31	33	36	38	40	43
77	23	26	28	31	33	36	38	41	43	45
78	25	28	31	33	36	38	41	43	46	48
79	28	30	33	36	38	41	44	46	48	51
80	30	33	36	38	41	44	46	49	51	53
81	32	35	38	41	44	47	49	51	54	56
82	35	38	41	44	47	49	52	54	56	58
83	38	41	44	47	49	52	54	57	59	61
84	40	44	47	49	52	55	57	59	61	63
85	43	46	49	52	55	57	59	62	63	65

TABLE VII.—PERCENT VALUE OF REFUND FEATURE; DURATION OF GUARANTEED AMOUNT—Continued

Age	Years— 11	12	13	14	15	16	17	18	19	20
86	46	49	52	55	57	60	62	64	66	67
87	48	52	55	57	60	62	64	66	68	69
88	51	54	57	60	62	64	66	68	70	71
89	54	57	60	62	65	67	68	70	72	73
90	56	59	62	64	67	69	70	72	74	75
91	59	62	64	67	69	71	72	74	75	76
92	61	64	66	69	71	72	74	75	77	78
93	63	66	68	70	72	74	75	77	78	79
94	65	68	70	72	74	75	77	78	79	80
95	67	69	72	74	75	77	78	79	81	82
96	69	71	73	75	77	78	80	81	82	83
97	70	73	75	77	78	80	81	82	83	84
98	72	74	76	78	79	81	82	83	84	85
99	74	76	78	79	81	82	83	84	85	86
100	75	78	79	81	82	83	84	85	86	86
101	77	79	81	82	83	84	85	86	87	87
102	79	81	82	83	84	85	86	87	88	88
103	80	82	83	85	86	87	87	88	89	89
104	82	84	85	86	87	88	88	89	90	90
105	84	85	86	87	88	89	89	90	90	91
106	85	86	87	88	89	90	90	91	91	92
107	87	88	89	89	90	91	91	92	92	93
108	88	89	90	90	91	92	92	93	93	93
109	89	90	91	92	92	93	93	93	94	94
110	90	91	92	92	93	93	94	94	94	95
111	92	92	93	93	94	94	95	95	95	95
112	93	93	94	94	95	95	95	96	96	96
113	94	94	95	95	95	96	96	96	96	97
114	95	95	95	96	96	96	97	97	97	97
115	95	96	96	96	97	97	97	97	97	98

Age	Years— 21	22	23	24	25	26	27	28	29	30
5	0	0	0	0	0	0	0	0	0	0
6	0	0	0	0	0	0	0	0	0	0
7	0	0	0	0	0	0	0	0	0	0
8	0	0	0	0	0	0	0	0	0	1
9	0	0	0	0	0	0	0	0	1	1
10	0	0	0	0	0	0	0	1	1	1
11	0	0	0	0	0	0	1	1	1	1
12	0	0	0	0	0	0	1	1	1	1
13	0	0	0	0	0	1	1	1	1	1
14	0	0	0	0	1	1	1	1	1	1
15	0	0	0	1	1	1	1	1	1	1
16	0	0	1	1	1	1	1	1	1	1
17	0	0	1	1	1	1	1	1	1	1
18	0	1	1	1	1	1	1	1	1	1
19	1	1	1	1	1	1	1	1	1	1
20	1	1	1	1	1	1	1	1	1	1
21	1	1	1	1	1	1	1	1	1	1
22	1	1	1	1	1	1	1	1	1	1
23	1	1	1	1	1	1	1	1	1	1
24	1	1	1	1	1	1	1	1	1	1
25	1	1	1	1	1	1	1	1	1	1
26	1	1	1	1	1	1	1	1	1	1
27	1	1	1	1	1	1	1	1	1	2
28	1	1	1	1	1	1	1	1	2	2
29	1	1	1	1	1	1	1	2	2	2
30	1	1	1	1	1	1	2	2	2	2
31	1	1	1	1	1	2	2	2	2	2
32	1	1	1	1	2	2	2	2	2	2
33	1	1	1	2	2	2	2	2	2	2
34	1	1	2	2	2	2	2	2	2	3
35	1	2	2	2	2	2	2	2	3	3
36	2	2	2	2	2	2	3	3	3	3
37	2	2	2	2	2	2	3	3	3	3
38	2	2	2	2	2	3	3	3	3	4
39	2	2	2	2	3	3	3	3	4	4
40	2	2	3	3	3	3	3	4	4	4
41	2	3	3	3	3	3	4	4	4	5
42	3	3	3	3	3	4	4	4	5	5
43	3	3	3	4	4	4	4	5	5	6
44	3	3	4	4	4	4	5	5	6	6
45	3	4	4	4	5	5	5	6	6	7
46	4	4	4	5	5	5	6	6	7	7
47	4	4	5	5	5	6	6	7	7	8
48	4	5	5	5	6	6	7	7	8	9
49	5	5	5	6	6	7	8	8	9	10
50	5	5	6	6	7	8	8	9	10	10
51	5	6	6	7	8	8	9	10	11	11
52	6	7	7	8	8	9	10	11	11	12
53	7	7	8	8	9	10	11	12	13	14
54	7	8	8	9	10	11	12	13	14	15

Reg. § 1.72-9

TABLE VII.—PERCENT VALUE OF REFUND FEATURE; DURATION OF GUARANTEED AMOUNT

Age	Years—									
	21	22	23	24	25	26	27	28	29	30
55	8	9	9	10	11	12	13	14	15	16
56	9	9	10	11	12	13	14	15	16	18
57	9	10	11	12	13	14	15	17	18	19
58	10	11	12	13	14	16	17	18	19	21
59	11	12	13	15	16	17	18	20	21	22
60	12	14	15	16	17	19	20	21	23	24
61	14	15	16	17	19	20	22	23	25	26
62	15	16	18	19	20	22	23	25	27	28
63	16	18	19	21	22	24	25	27	29	30
64	18	19	21	23	24	26	28	29	31	33
65	20	21	23	25	26	28	30	31	33	35
66	21	23	25	27	28	30	32	34	35	37
67	23	25	27	29	31	32	34	36	38	40
68	25	27	29	31	33	35	37	38	40	42
69	28	29	31	33	35	37	39	41	43	44
70	30	32	34	36	38	40	42	43	45	47
71	32	34	36	38	40	42	44	46	47	49
72	35	37	39	41	43	45	46	48	50	51
73	37	39	41	43	45	47	49	51	52	54
74	40	42	44	46	48	50	51	53	54	56
75	42	44	46	48	50	52	54	55	57	58
76	45	47	49	51	53	54	56	58	59	60
77	47	50	51	53	55	57	58	60	61	62
78	50	52	54	56	57	59	61	62	63	64
79	53	55	56	58	60	61	63	64	65	66
80	55	57	59	60	62	63	65	66	67	68
81	58	59	61	63	64	66	67	68	69	70
82	60	62	63	65	66	68	69	70	71	72
83	62	64	66	67	68	70	71	72	73	74
84	65	66	68	69	70	71	72	73	74	75
85	67	68	70	71	72	73	74	75	76	77
86	69	70	72	73	74	75	76	77	77	78
87	71	72	73	75	76	76	77	78	79	80
88	73	74	75	76	77	78	79	80	80	81
89	74	76	77	78	79	79	80	81	81	82
90	76	77	78	79	80	81	81	82	83	83
91	78	79	79	80	81	82	83	83	84	84
92	79	80	81	82	82	83	84	84	85	85
93	80	81	82	83	83	84	85	85	86	86
94	81	82	83	84	84	85	85	86	86	87
95	82	83	84	85	85	86	86	87	87	88
96	83	84	85	86	86	87	87	88	88	88
97	84	85	86	86	87	87	88	88	89	89
98	85	86	87	87	88	88	89	89	89	90
99	86	87	87	88	88	89	89	90	90	90
100	87	88	88	89	89	90	90	90	91	91
101	88	89	89	90	90	90	91	91	91	92
102	89	89	90	90	91	91	91	92	92	92
103	90	90	91	91	91	92	92	92	93	93
104	91	91	91	92	92	92	93	93	93	93
105	91	92	92	92	93	93	93	94	94	94
106	92	93	93	93	93	94	94	94	94	95
107	93	93	94	94	94	94	95	95	95	95
108	94	94	94	94	95	95	95	95	95	96
109	94	95	95	95	95	95	96	96	96	96
110	95	95	95	96	96	96	96	96	96	96
111	96	96	96	96	96	96	97	97	97	97
112	96	96	96	97	97	97	97	97	97	97
113	97	97	97	97	97	97	97	98	98	98
114	97	97	97	98	98	98	98	98	98	98
115	98	98	98	98	98	98	98	98	98	98

Reg. § 1.72-9

TABLE VII.—PERCENT VALUE OF REFUND FEATURE; DURATION OF GUARANTEED AMOUNT—Continued

Age	Years—									
	31	32	33	34	35	36	37	38	39	40
5	0	1	1	1	1	1	1	1	1	1
6	0	1	1	1	1	1	1	1	1	1
7	1	1	1	1	1	1	1	1	1	1
8	1	1	1	1	1	1	1	1	1	1
9	1	1	1	1	1	1	1	1	1	1
10	1	1	1	1	1	1	1	1	1	1
11	1	1	1	1	1	1	1	1	1	1
12	1	1	1	1	1	1	1	1	1	1
13	1	1	1	1	1	1	1	1	1	1
14	1	1	1	1	1	1	1	1	1	1
15	1	1	1	1	1	1	1	1	1	1
16	1	1	1	1	1	1	1	1	1	1
17	1	1	1	1	1	1	1	1	1	1
18	1	1	1	1	1	1	1	1	1	2
19	1	1	1	1	1	1	1	1	2	2
20	1	1	1	1	1	1	1	2	2	2
21	1	1	1	1	1	1	2	2	2	2
22	1	1	1	1	1	2	2	2	2	2
23	1	1	1	2	2	2	2	2	2	2
24	1	1	2	2	2	2	2	2	2	3
25	1	2	2	2	2	2	2	2	2	3
26	2	2	2	2	2	2	2	2	3	3
27	2	2	2	2	2	2	2	3	3	3
28	2	2	2	2	2	2	3	3	3	3
29	2	2	2	2	2	3	3	3	3	4
30	2	2	2	3	3	3	3	3	4	4
31	2	2	3	3	3	3	3	4	4	4
32	2	3	3	3	3	3	4	4	4	5
33	3	3	3	3	3	4	4	4	5	5
34	3	3	3	3	4	4	4	5	5	5
35	3	3	3	4	4	4	5	5	5	6
36	3	4	4	4	4	5	5	5	6	6
37	4	4	4	4	5	5	6	6	6	7
38	4	4	5	5	5	6	6	7	7	8
39	4	5	5	5	6	6	7	7	8	8
40	5	5	5	6	6	7	7	8	8	9
41	5	5	6	6	7	7	8	9	9	10
42	6	6	6	7	7	8	9	9	10	11
43	6	7	7	8	8	9	9	10	11	12
44	7	7	8	8	9	10	10	11	12	13
45	7	8	8	9	10	10	11	12	13	14
46	8	9	9	10	11	11	12	13	14	15
47	9	9	10	11	12	12	13	14	15	16
48	9	10	11	12	13	14	15	16	17	18
49	10	11	12	13	14	15	16	17	18	19
50	11	12	13	14	15	16	17	18	20	21
51	12	13	14	15	16	17	19	20	21	22
52	13	14	15	17	18	19	20	21	23	24
53	15	16	17	18	19	20	22	23	24	26
54	16	17	18	19	21	22	23	25	26	28
55	17	18	20	21	22	24	25	27	28	30
56	19	20	21	23	24	26	27	29	30	32
57	20	22	23	25	26	28	29	31	32	34
58	22	24	25	27	28	30	31	33	34	36
59	24	25	27	28	30	32	33	35	36	38

Reg. § 1.72-9

See p. 20,601 for regulations not amended to reflect law changes

TABLE VII.—PERCENT VALUE OF REFUND FEATURE; DURATION OF GUARANTEED AMOUNT

Age	Years—									
	31	32	33	34	35	36	37	38	39	40
60	26	27	29	31	32	34	35	37	38	40
61	28	29	31	33	34	36	37	39	40	42
62	30	32	33	35	36	38	40	41	42	44
63	32	34	35	37	39	40	42	43	45	46
64	34	36	38	39	41	42	44	45	47	48
65	37	38	40	42	43	45	46	47	49	50
66	39	41	42	44	45	47	48	50	51	52
67	41	43	45	46	48	49	50	52	53	54
68	44	45	47	48	50	51	52	54	55	56
69	46	48	49	51	52	53	54	56	57	58
70	48	50	51	53	54	55	57	58	59	60
71	51	52	54	55	56	57	59	60	61	62
72	53	54	56	57	58	59	60	62	62	63
73	55	57	58	59	60	61	62	63	64	65
74	57	59	60	61	62	63	64	65	66	67
75	59	61	62	63	64	65	66	67	68	69
76	62	63	64	65	66	67	68	69	69	70
77	64	65	66	67	68	69	70	70	71	72
78	66	67	68	69	70	70	71	72	73	73
79	67	68	69	70	71	72	73	73	74	75
80	69	70	71	72	73	74	74	75	76	76
81	71	72	73	74	74	75	76	76	77	78
82	73	74	74	75	76	77	77	78	78	79
83	74	75	76	77	77	78	79	79	80	80
84	76	77	77	78	79	79	80	80	81	81
85	78	78	79	79	80	81	81	82	82	83
86	79	80	80	81	81	82	82	83	83	84
87	80	81	81	82	83	83	83	84	84	85
88	82	82	83	83	84	84	85	85	85	86
89	83	83	84	84	85	85	85	86	86	87
90	84	84	85	85	86	86	86	87	87	87
91	85	85	86	86	87	87	87	88	88	88
92	86	86	87	87	87	88	88	88	89	89
93	87	87	87	88	88	88	89	89	89	90
94	87	88	88	88	89	89	89	90	90	90
95	88	88	89	89	89	90	90	90	91	91
96	89	89	89	90	90	90	91	91	91	91
97	89	90	90	90	91	91	91	91	92	92
98	90	90	91	91	91	91	92	92	92	92
99	91	91	91	92	92	92	92	92	93	93
100	91	92	92	92	92	92	93	93	93	93
101	92	92	92	93	93	93	93	93	94	94
102	92	93	93	93	93	94	94	94	94	94
103	93	93	93	94	94	94	94	94	94	95
104	94	94	94	94	94	95	95	95	95	95
105	94	94	95	95	95	95	95	95	95	95
106	95	95	95	95	95	95	96	96	96	96
107	95	95	96	96	96	96	96	96	96	96
108	96	96	96	96	96	96	96	96	97	97
109	96	96	96	97	97	97	97	97	97	97
110	97	97	97	97	97	97	97	97	97	97
111	97	97	97	97	97	97	98	98	98	98
112	97	97	98	98	98	98	98	98	98	98
113	98	98	98	98	98	98	98	98	98	98
114	98	98	98	98	98	98	98	98	98	99
115	98	98	98	99	99	99	99	99	99	99

Reg. § 1.72-9

TABLE VIII.—TEMPORARY LIFE ANNUITIES; [1] ONE LIFE—EXPECTED RETURN MULTIPLES
(See footnote at end of tables)
Temporary Period—Maximum Duration of Annuity

Age	Years—									
	1	2	3	4	5	6	7	8	9	10
5	1.0	2.0	3.0	4.0	5.0	6.0	7.0	8.0	9.0	10.0
6	1.0	2.0	3.0	4.0	5.0	6.0	7.0	8.0	9.0	10.0
7	1.0	2.0	3.0	4.0	5.0	6.0	7.0	8.0	9.0	10.0
8	1.0	2.0	3.0	4.0	5.0	6.0	7.0	8.0	9.0	10.0
9	1.0	2.0	3.0	4.0	5.0	6.0	7.0	8.0	9.0	10.0
10	1.0	2.0	3.0	4.0	5.0	6.0	7.0	8.0	9.0	10.0
11	1.0	2.0	3.0	4.0	5.0	6.0	7.0	8.0	9.0	10.0
12	1.0	2.0	3.0	4.0	5.0	6.0	7.0	8.0	9.0	10.0
13	1.0	2.0	3.0	4.0	5.0	6.0	7.0	8.0	9.0	10.0
14	1.0	2.0	3.0	4.0	5.0	6.0	7.0	8.0	9.0	10.0
15	1.0	2.0	3.0	4.0	5.0	6.0	7.0	8.0	9.0	10.0
16	1.0	2.0	3.0	4.0	5.0	6.0	7.0	8.0	9.0	10.0
17	1.0	2.0	3.0	4.0	5.0	6.0	7.0	8.0	9.0	10.0
18	1.0	2.0	3.0	4.0	5.0	6.0	7.0	8.0	9.0	10.0
19	1.0	2.0	3.0	4.0	5.0	6.0	7.0	8.0	9.0	10.0
20	1.0	2.0	3.0	4.0	5.0	6.0	7.0	8.0	9.0	10.0
21	1.0	2.0	3.0	4.0	5.0	6.0	7.0	8.0	9.0	10.0
22	1.0	2.0	3.0	4.0	5.0	6.0	7.0	8.0	9.0	10.0
23	1.0	2.0	3.0	4.0	5.0	6.0	7.0	8.0	9.0	10.0
24	1.0	2.0	3.0	4.0	5.0	6.0	7.0	8.0	9.0	10.0
25	1.0	2.0	3.0	4.0	5.0	6.0	7.0	8.0	9.0	10.0
26	1.0	2.0	3.0	4.0	5.0	6.0	7.0	8.0	9.0	10.0
27	1.0	2.0	3.0	4.0	5.0	6.0	7.0	8.0	9.0	10.0
28	1.0	2.0	3.0	4.0	5.0	6.0	7.0	8.0	9.0	10.0
29	1.0	2.0	3.0	4.0	5.0	6.0	7.0	8.0	9.0	10.0
30	1.0	2.0	3.0	4.0	5.0	6.0	7.0	8.0	9.0	10.0
31	1.0	2.0	3.0	4.0	5.0	6.0	7.0	8.0	9.0	10.0
32	1.0	2.0	3.0	4.0	5.0	6.0	7.0	8.0	9.0	10.0
33	1.0	2.0	3.0	4.0	5.0	6.0	7.0	8.0	9.0	10.0
34	1.0	2.0	3.0	4.0	5.0	6.0	7.0	8.0	9.0	10.0
35	1.0	2.0	3.0	4.0	5.0	6.0	7.0	8.0	9.0	10.0
36	1.0	2.0	3.0	4.0	5.0	6.0	7.0	8.0	9.0	9.9
37	1.0	2.0	3.0	4.0	5.0	6.0	7.0	8.0	9.0	9.9
38	1.0	2.0	3.0	4.0	5.0	6.0	7.0	8.0	9.0	9.9
39	1.0	2.0	3.0	4.0	5.0	6.0	7.0	8.0	9.0	9.9
40	1.0	2.0	3.0	4.0	5.0	6.0	7.0	8.0	8.9	9.9
41	1.0	2.0	3.0	4.0	5.0	6.0	7.0	8.0	8.9	9.9
42	1.0	2.0	3.0	4.0	5.0	6.0	7.0	8.0	8.9	9.9
43	1.0	2.0	3.0	4.0	5.0	6.0	7.0	7.9	8.9	9.9
44	1.0	2.0	3.0	4.0	5.0	6.0	7.0	7.9	8.9	9.9
45	1.0	2.0	3.0	4.0	5.0	6.0	7.0	7.9	8.9	9.9
46	1.0	2.0	3.0	4.0	5.0	6.0	6.9	7.9	8.9	9.9
47	1.0	2.0	3.0	4.0	5.0	6.0	6.9	7.9	8.9	9.9
48	1.0	2.0	3.0	4.0	5.0	6.0	6.9	7.9	8.9	9.9
49	1.0	2.0	3.0	4.0	5.0	6.0	6.9	7.9	8.9	9.8
50	1.0	2.0	3.0	4.0	5.0	5.9	6.9	7.9	8.9	9.8
51	1.0	2.0	3.0	4.0	5.0	5.9	6.9	7.9	8.9	9.8
52	1.0	2.0	3.0	4.0	5.0	5.9	6.9	7.9	8.8	9.8
53	1.0	2.0	3.0	4.0	5.0	5.9	6.9	7.9	8.8	9.8
54	1.0	2.0	3.0	4.0	4.9	5.9	6.9	7.9	8.8	9.8
55	1.0	2.0	3.0	4.0	4.9	5.9	6.9	7.8	8.8	9.7
56	1.0	2.0	3.0	4.0	4.9	5.9	6.9	7.8	8.8	9.7
57	1.0	2.0	3.0	4.0	4.9	5.9	6.9	7.8	8.8	9.7
58	1.0	2.0	3.0	4.0	4.9	5.9	6.9	7.8	8.7	9.7
59	1.0	2.0	3.0	4.0	4.9	5.9	6.8	7.8	8.7	9.6
60	1.0	2.0	3.0	3.9	4.9	5.9	6.8	7.8	8.7	9.6
61	1.0	2.0	3.0	3.9	4.9	5.9	6.8	7.7	8.7	9.6
62	1.0	2.0	3.0	3.9	4.9	5.8	6.8	7.7	8.6	9.5
63	1.0	2.0	3.0	3.9	4.9	5.8	6.8	7.7	8.6	9.5
64	1.0	2.0	3.0	3.9	4.9	5.8	6.7	7.6	8.5	9.4
65	1.0	2.0	3.0	3.9	4.9	5.8	6.7	7.6	8.5	9.3
66	1.0	2.0	2.9	3.9	4.8	5.8	6.7	7.6	8.4	9.3
67	1.0	2.0	2.9	3.9	4.8	5.7	6.6	7.5	8.4	9.2
68	1.0	2.0	2.9	3.9	4.8	5.7	6.6	7.5	8.3	9.1
69	1.0	2.0	2.9	3.9	4.8	5.7	6.6	7.4	8.2	9.0
70	1.0	2.0	2.9	3.9	4.8	5.6	6.5	7.3	8.1	8.9
71	1.0	2.0	2.9	3.8	4.7	5.6	6.5	7.3	8.1	8.8
72	1.0	2.0	2.9	3.8	4.7	5.6	6.4	7.2	8.0	8.7
73	1.0	2.0	2.9	3.8	4.7	5.5	6.3	7.1	7.9	8.6
74	1.0	1.9	2.9	3.8	4.6	5.5	6.3	7.0	7.7	8.4
75	1.0	1.9	2.9	3.8	4.6	5.4	6.2	6.9	7.6	8.3
76	1.0	1.9	2.8	3.7	4.6	5.4	6.1	6.8	7.5	8.1
77	1.0	1.9	2.8	3.7	4.5	5.3	6.0	6.7	7.3	7.9
78	1.0	1.9	2.8	3.7	4.5	5.2	5.9	6.6	7.2	7.7
79	1.0	1.9	2.8	3.6	4.4	5.1	5.8	6.4	7.0	7.5
80	1.0	1.9	2.8	3.6	4.4	5.1	5.7	6.3	6.8	7.3
81	1.0	1.9	2.8	3.6	4.3	5.0	5.6	6.1	6.6	7.0
82	1.0	1.9	2.7	3.5	4.2	4.9	5.4	6.0	6.4	6.8
83	1.0	1.9	2.7	3.5	4.1	4.8	5.3	5.8	6.2	6.5
84	1.0	1.8	2.7	3.4	4.1	4.6	5.2	5.6	6.0	6.3

Reg. § 1.72-9

TABLE VIII.—TEMPORARY LIFE ANNUITIES; [1] ONE LIFE—EXPECTED RETURN MULTIPLES—Continued
(See footnote at end of tables)
Temporary Period—Maximum Duration of Annuity

Age	Years—									
	1	2	3	4	5	6	7	8	9	10
85	1.0	1.8	2.6	3.3	4.0	4.5	5.0	5.4	5.7	6.0
86	1.0	1.8	2.6	3.3	3.9	4.4	4.8	5.2	5.5	5.7
87	.9	1.8	2.5	3.2	3.8	4.3	4.7	5.0	5.3	5.5
88	.9	1.8	2.5	3.1	3.7	4.1	4.5	4.8	5.0	5.2
89	.9	1.8	2.5	3.1	3.6	4.0	4.3	4.6	4.8	4.9
90	.9	1.7	2.4	3.0	3.4	3.8	4.1	4.4	4.5	4.7
91	.9	1.7	2.4	2.9	3.3	3.7	4.0	4.2	4.3	4.4
92	.9	1.7	2.3	2.8	3.2	3.5	3.8	4.0	4.1	4.2
93	.9	1.7	2.3	2.7	3.1	3.4	3.6	3.8	3.9	4.0
94	.9	1.6	2.2	2.7	3.0	3.3	3.5	3.6	3.7	3.8
95	.9	1.6	2.2	2.6	2.9	3.1	3.3	3.4	3.5	3.6
96	.9	1.6	2.1	2.5	2.8	3.0	3.2	3.3	3.3	3.4
97	.9	1.6	2.1	2.4	2.7	2.9	3.0	3.1	3.2	3.2
98	.9	1.5	2.0	2.4	2.6	2.8	2.9	3.0	3.0	3.0
99	.9	1.5	2.0	2.3	2.5	2.6	2.7	2.8	2.8	2.8
100	.9	1.5	1.9	2.2	2.4	2.5	2.6	2.6	2.6	2.7
101	.8	1.4	1.8	2.1	2.3	2.4	2.4	2.5	2.5	2.5
102	.8	1.4	1.8	2.0	2.1	2.2	2.3	2.3	2.3	2.3
103	.8	1.4	1.7	1.9	2.0	2.1	2.1	2.1	2.1	2.1
104	.8	1.3	1.6	1.8	1.9	1.9	1.9	1.9	1.9	1.9
105	.8	1.3	1.5	1.7	1.7	1.8	1.8	1.8	1.8	1.8
106	.8	1.2	1.4	1.5	1.6	1.6	1.6	1.6	1.6	1.6
107	.7	1.1	1.3	1.4	1.4	1.4	1.4	1.4	1.4	1.4
108	.7	1.1	1.2	1.3	1.3	1.3	1.3	1.3	1.3	1.3
109	.7	1.0	1.1	1.1	1.1	1.1	1.1	1.1	1.1	1.1
110	.7	.9	1.0	1.0	1.0	1.0	1.0	1.0	1.0	1.0
111	.6	.8	.9	.9	.9	.9	.9	.9	.9	.9
112	.6	.7	.8	.8	.8	.8	.8	.8	.8	.8
113	.6	.6	.7	.7	.7	.7	.7	.7	.7	.7
114	.5	.6	.6	.6	.6	.6	.6	.6	.6	.6
115	.5	.5	.5	.5	.5	.5	.5	.5	.5	.5

Age	Years—									
	11	12	13	14	15	16	17	18	19	20
5	11.0	12.0	13.0	14.0	15.0	16.0	17.0	18.0	19.0	19.9
6	11.0	12.0	13.0	14.0	15.0	16.0	17.0	18.0	19.0	19.9
7	11.0	12.0	13.0	14.0	15.0	16.0	17.0	18.0	19.0	19.9
8	11.0	12.0	13.0	14.0	15.0	16.0	17.0	18.0	18.9	19.9
9	11.0	12.0	13.0	14.0	15.0	16.0	17.0	18.0	18.9	19.9
10	11.0	12.0	13.0	14.0	15.0	16.0	17.0	18.0	18.9	19.9
11	11.0	12.0	13.0	14.0	15.0	16.0	17.0	17.9	18.9	19.9
12	11.0	12.0	13.0	14.0	15.0	16.0	17.0	17.9	18.9	19.9
13	11.0	12.0	13.0	14.0	15.0	16.0	17.0	17.9	18.9	19.9
14	11.0	12.0	13.0	14.0	15.0	16.0	16.9	17.9	18.9	19.9
15	11.0	12.0	13.0	14.0	15.0	16.0	16.9	17.9	18.9	19.9
16	11.0	12.0	13.0	14.0	15.0	16.0	16.9	17.9	18.9	19.9
17	11.0	12.0	13.0	14.0	15.0	15.9	16.9	17.9	18.9	19.9
18	11.0	12.0	13.0	14.0	15.0	15.9	16.9	17.9	18.9	19.9
19	11.0	12.0	13.0	14.0	15.0	15.9	16.9	17.9	18.9	19.9
20	11.0	12.0	13.0	14.0	14.9	15.9	16.9	17.9	18.9	19.9
21	11.0	12.0	13.0	14.0	14.9	15.9	16.9	17.9	18.9	19.9
22	11.0	12.0	13.0	14.0	14.9	15.9	16.9	17.9	18.9	19.9
23	11.0	12.0	13.0	13.9	14.9	15.9	16.9	17.9	18.9	19.9
24	11.0	12.0	13.0	13.9	14.9	15.9	16.9	17.9	18.9	19.9
25	11.0	12.0	13.0	13.9	14.9	15.9	16.9	17.9	18.9	19.9
26	11.0	12.0	12.9	13.9	14.9	15.9	16.9	17.9	18.9	19.9
27	11.0	12.0	12.9	13.9	14.9	15.9	16.9	17.9	18.9	19.9
28	11.0	12.0	12.9	13.9	14.9	15.9	16.9	17.9	18.9	19.8
29	11.0	12.0	12.9	13.9	14.9	15.9	16.9	17.9	18.9	19.8
30	11.0	11.9	12.9	13.9	14.9	15.9	16.9	17.9	18.8	19.8
31	11.0	11.9	12.9	13.9	14.9	15.9	16.9	17.9	18.8	19.8
32	11.0	11.9	12.9	13.9	14.9	15.9	16.9	17.8	18.8	19.8
33	11.0	11.9	12.9	13.9	14.9	15.9	16.9	17.8	18.8	19.8
34	10.9	11.9	12.9	13.9	14.9	15.9	16.8	17.8	18.8	19.8
35	10.9	11.9	12.9	13.9	14.9	15.9	16.8	17.8	18.8	19.7
36	10.9	11.9	12.9	13.9	14.9	15.8	16.8	17.8	18.8	19.7
37	10.9	11.9	12.9	13.9	14.9	15.8	16.8	17.8	18.7	19.7
38	10.9	11.9	12.9	13.9	14.8	15.8	16.8	17.8	18.7	19.7
39	10.9	11.9	12.9	13.9	14.8	15.8	16.8	17.7	18.7	19.6
40	10.9	11.9	12.9	13.8	14.8	15.8	16.7	17.7	18.7	19.6
41	10.9	11.9	12.9	13.8	14.8	15.8	16.7	17.6	18.6	19.6
42	10.9	11.9	12.8	13.8	14.8	15.7	16.7	17.6	18.6	19.5
43	10.9	11.9	12.8	13.8	14.8	15.7	16.7	17.6	18.6	19.5
44	10.9	11.8	12.8	13.8	14.7	15.7	16.6	17.6	18.5	19.4
45	10.9	11.8	12.8	13.8	14.7	15.7	16.6	17.5	18.5	19.4
46	10.9	11.8	12.8	13.7	14.7	15.6	16.6	17.5	18.4	19.3
47	10.8	11.8	12.8	13.7	14.7	15.6	16.5	17.5	18.4	19.3
48	10.8	11.8	12.7	13.7	14.6	15.6	16.5	17.4	18.3	19.2

Reg. § 1.72-9

TABLE VIII.—TEMPORARY LIFE ANNUITIES; [1] ONE LIFE—EXPECTED RETURN MULTIPLES—Continued
(See footnote at end of tables)
Temporary Period—Maximum Duration of Annuity

Age	Years—									
	11	12	13	14	15	16	17	18	19	20
49	10.8	11.8	12.7	13.7	14.6	15.5	16.4	17.4	18.3	19.2
50	10.8	11.7	12.7	13.6	14.6	15.5	16.4	17.3	18.2	19.1
51	10.8	11.7	12.7	13.6	14.5	15.4	16.3	17.2	18.1	19.0
52	10.8	11.7	12.6	13.6	14.5	15.4	16.3	17.2	18.0	18.9
53	10.7	11.7	12.6	13.5	14.4	15.3	16.2	17.1	18.0	18.8
54	10.7	11.6	12.6	13.5	14.4	15.3	16.2	17.0	17.9	18.7
55	10.7	11.6	12.5	13.4	14.3	15.2	16.1	16.9	17.8	18.6
56	10.7	11.6	12.5	13.4	14.3	15.1	16.0	16.8	17.6	18.4
57	10.6	11.5	12.4	13.3	14.2	15.1	15.9	16.7	17.5	18.3
58	10.6	11.5	12.4	13.3	14.1	15.0	15.8	16.6	17.4	18.1
59	10.6	11.4	12.3	13.2	14.0	14.9	15.7	16.4	17.2	17.9
60	10.5	11.4	12.3	13.1	13.9	14.7	15.5	16.3	17.0	17.7
61	10.5	11.3	12.2	13.0	13.8	14.6	15.4	16.1	16.8	17.5
62	10.4	11.3	12.1	12.9	13.7	14.5	15.2	15.9	16.6	17.2
63	10.3	11.2	12.0	12.8	13.6	14.3	15.0	15.7	16.3	17.0
64	10.3	11.1	11.9	12.7	13.4	14.1	14.8	15.5	16.1	16.7
65	10.2	11.0	11.8	12.5	13.2	13.9	14.6	15.2	15.8	16.3
66	10.1	10.9	11.6	12.4	13.1	13.7	14.4	14.9	15.5	16.0
67	10.0	10.8	11.5	12.2	12.9	13.5	14.1	14.7	15.2	15.6
68	9.9	10.6	11.4	12.0	12.7	13.3	13.8	14.3	14.8	15.3
69	9.8	10.5	11.2	11.8	12.4	13.0	13.5	14.0	14.4	14.8
70	9.6	10.3	11.0	11.6	12.2	12.7	13.2	13.7	14.0	14.4
71	9.5	10.2	10.8	11.4	11.9	12.4	12.9	13.3	13.6	13.9
72	9.4	10.0	10.6	11.2	11.7	12.1	12.5	12.9	13.2	13.5
73	9.2	9.8	10.4	10.9	11.4	11.8	12.1	12.5	12.7	13.0
74	9.0	9.6	10.1	10.6	11.0	11.4	11.7	12.0	12.3	12.5
75	8.8	9.4	9.9	10.3	10.7	11.0	11.3	11.6	11.8	12.0
76	8.6	9.1	9.6	10.0	10.3	10.6	10.9	11.1	11.3	11.4
77	8.4	8.9	9.3	9.7	10.0	10.2	10.5	10.6	10.8	10.9
78	8.2	8.6	9.0	9.3	9.6	9.8	10.0	10.2	10.3	10.4
79	7.9	8.3	8.7	9.0	9.2	9.4	9.5	9.7	9.8	9.8
80	7.7	8.0	8.3	8.6	8.8	9.0	9.1	9.2	9.3	9.3
81	7.4	7.7	8.0	8.2	8.4	8.5	8.6	8.7	8.8	8.8
82	7.1	7.4	7.6	7.8	8.0	8.1	8.2	8.2	8.3	8.3
83	6.8	7.1	7.3	7.4	7.5	7.6	7.7	7.8	7.8	7.8
84	6.5	6.7	6.9	7.0	7.1	7.2	7.3	7.3	7.3	7.4
85	6.2	6.4	6.6	6.7	6.7	6.8	6.8	6.9	6.9	6.9
86	5.9	6.1	6.2	6.3	6.4	6.4	6.4	6.5	6.5	6.5
87	5.6	5.8	5.9	5.9	6.0	6.0	6.0	6.1	6.1	6.1
88	5.3	5.4	5.5	5.6	5.6	5.6	5.7	5.7	5.7	5.7
89	5.1	5.1	5.2	5.3	5.3	5.3	5.3	5.3	5.3	5.3
90	4.8	4.9	4.9	4.9	5.0	5.0	5.0	5.0	5.0	5.0
91	4.5	4.6	4.6	4.6	4.7	4.7	4.7	4.7	4.7	4.7
92	4.3	4.3	4.3	4.4	4.4	4.4	4.4	4.4	4.4	4.4
93	4.0	4.1	4.1	4.1	4.1	4.1	4.1	4.1	4.1	4.1
94	3.8	3.8	3.9	3.9	3.9	3.9	3.9	3.9	3.9	3.9
95	3.6	3.6	3.6	3.6	3.7	3.7	3.7	3.7	3.7	3.7
96	3.4	3.4	3.4	3.4	3.4	3.4	3.4	3.4	3.4	3.4
97	3.2	3.2	3.2	3.2	3.2	3.2	3.2	3.2	3.2	3.2
98	3.0	3.0	3.0	3.0	3.0	3.0	3.0	3.0	3.0	3.0
99	2.8	2.8	2.8	2.8	2.8	2.8	2.8	2.8	2.8	2.8
100	2.7	2.7	2.7	2.7	2.7	2.7	2.7	2.7	2.7	2.7
101	2.5	2.5	2.5	2.5	2.5	2.5	2.5	2.5	2.5	2.5
102	2.3	2.3	2.3	2.3	2.3	2.3	2.3	2.3	2.3	2.3
103	2.1	2.1	2.1	2.1	2.1	2.1	2.1	2.1	2.1	2.1
104	1.9	1.9	1.9	1.9	1.9	1.9	1.9	1.9	1.9	1.9
105	1.8	1.8	1.8	1.8	1.8	1.8	1.8	1.8	1.8	1.8
106	1.6	1.6	1.6	1.6	1.6	1.6	1.6	1.6	1.6	1.6
107	1.4	1.4	1.4	1.4	1.4	1.4	1.4	1.4	1.4	1.4
108	1.3	1.3	1.3	1.3	1.3	1.3	1.3	1.3	1.3	1.3
109	1.1	1.1	1.1	1.1	1.1	1.1	1.1	1.1	1.1	1.1
110	1.0	1.0	1.0	1.0	1.0	1.0	1.0	1.0	1.0	1.0
111	.9	.9	.9	.9	.9	.9	.9	.9	.9	.9
112	.8	.8	.8	.8	.8	.8	.8	.8	.8	.8
113	.7	.7	.7	.7	.7	.7	.7	.7	.7	.7
114	.6	.6	.6	.6	.6	.6	.6	.6	.6	.6
115	.5	.5	.5	.5	.5	.5	.5	.5	.5	.5

Age	Years—									
	21	22	23	24	25	26	27	28	29	30
5	20.9	21.9	22.9	23.9	24.9	25.9	26.9	27.9	28.9	29.9
6	20.9	21.9	22.9	23.9	24.9	25.9	26.9	27.9	28.9	29.9
7	20.9	21.9	22.9	23.9	24.9	25.9	26.9	27.9	28.9	29.9
8	20.9	21.9	22.9	23.9	24.9	25.9	26.9	27.9	28.9	29.8
9	20.9	21.9	22.9	23.9	24.9	25.9	26.9	27.9	28.9	29.8
10	20.9	21.9	22.9	23.9	24.9	25.9	26.9	27.9	28.8	29.8
11	20.9	21.9	22.9	23.9	24.9	25.9	26.9	27.9	28.8	29.8
12	20.9	21.9	22.9	23.9	24.9	25.9	26.9	27.8	28.8	29.8

Reg. § 1.72-9

TABLE VIII.—TEMPORARY LIFE ANNUITIES; [1] ONE LIFE—EXPECTED RETURN MULTIPLES—Continued
(See footnote at end of tables)
Temporary Period—Maximum Duration of Annuity

Age	Years—									
	21	22	23	24	25	26	27	28	29	30
13	20.9	21.9	22.9	23.9	24.9	25.9	26.9	27.8	28.8	29.8
14	20.9	21.9	22.9	23.9	24.9	25.9	26.8	27.8	28.8	29.8
15	20.9	21.9	22.9	23.9	24.9	25.9	26.8	27.8	28.8	29.8
16	20.9	21.9	22.9	23.9	24.9	25.8	26.8	27.8	28.8	29.8
17	20.9	21.9	22.9	23.9	24.9	25.8	26.8	27.8	28.8	29.8
18	20.9	21.9	22.9	23.9	24.8	25.8	26.8	27.8	28.8	29.7
19	20.9	21.9	22.9	23.9	24.8	25.8	26.8	27.8	28.8	29.7
20	20.9	21.9	22.9	23.8	24.8	25.8	26.8	27.8	28.7	29.7
21	20.9	21.9	22.9	23.8	24.8	25.8	26.8	27.8	28.7	29.7
22	20.9	21.9	22.8	23.8	24.8	25.8	26.8	27.7	28.7	29.7
23	20.9	21.9	22.8	23.8	24.8	25.8	26.7	27.7	28.7	29.7
24	20.9	21.8	22.8	23.8	24.8	25.8	26.7	27.7	28.7	29.6
25	20.9	21.8	22.8	23.8	24.8	25.7	26.7	27.7	28.6	29.6
26	20.8	21.8	22.8	23.8	24.8	25.7	26.7	27.7	28.6	29.6
27	20.8	21.8	22.8	23.8	24.7	25.7	26.7	27.6	28.6	29.5
28	20.8	21.8	22.8	23.7	24.7	25.7	26.6	27.6	28.6	29.5
29	20.8	21.8	22.8	23.7	24.7	25.7	26.6	27.6	28.5	29.5
30	20.8	21.8	22.7	23.7	24.7	25.6	26.6	27.5	28.5	29.4
31	20.8	21.8	22.7	23.7	24.6	25.6	26.6	27.5	28.4	29.4
32	20.8	21.7	22.7	23.7	24.6	25.6	26.5	27.5	28.4	29.3
33	20.8	21.7	22.7	23.6	24.6	25.5	26.5	27.4	28.4	29.3
34	20.7	21.7	22.7	23.6	24.6	25.5	26.4	27.4	28.3	29.2
35	20.7	21.7	22.6	23.6	24.5	25.5	26.4	27.3	28.2	29.2
36	20.7	21.6	22.6	23.5	24.5	25.4	26.3	27.3	28.2	29.1
37	20.7	21.6	22.6	23.5	24.4	25.4	26.3	27.2	28.1	29.0
38	20.6	21.6	22.5	23.4	24.4	25.3	26.2	27.1	28.0	28.9
39	20.6	21.5	22.5	23.4	24.3	25.2	26.1	27.0	27.9	28.8
40	20.6	21.5	22.4	23.3	24.3	25.1	26.1	27.0	27.8	28.7
41	20.5	21.4	22.4	23.3	24.2	25.1	26.0	26.9	27.7	28.6
42	20.5	21.4	22.3	23.2	24.1	25.0	25.9	26.8	27.6	28.5
43	20.4	21.3	22.2	23.2	24.0	24.9	25.8	26.6	27.5	28.3
44	20.4	21.3	22.2	23.1	24.0	24.8	25.7	26.5	27.3	28.2
45	20.3	21.2	22.1	23.0	23.9	24.7	25.6	26.4	27.2	28.0
46	20.2	21.1	22.0	22.9	23.8	24.6	25.4	26.2	27.0	27.8
47	20.2	21.1	21.9	22.8	23.6	24.5	25.3	26.1	26.8	27.6
48	20.1	21.0	21.8	22.7	23.5	24.3	25.1	25.9	26.6	27.4
49	20.0	20.9	21.7	22.6	23.4	24.2	25.0	25.7	26.4	27.1
50	19.9	20.8	21.6	22.4	23.2	24.0	24.8	25.5	26.2	26.9
51	19.8	20.7	21.5	22.3	23.1	23.8	24.6	25.3	25.9	26.6
52	19.7	20.6	21.4	22.1	22.9	23.6	24.3	25.0	25.7	26.3
53	19.6	20.4	21.2	22.0	22.7	23.4	24.1	24.7	25.3	25.9
54	19.5	20.3	21.0	21.8	22.5	23.2	23.8	24.4	25.0	25.6
55	19.3	20.1	20.8	21.6	22.2	22.9	23.5	24.1	24.6	25.2
56	19.2	19.9	20.6	21.3	22.0	22.6	23.2	23.7	24.3	24.7
57	19.0	19.7	20.4	21.1	21.7	22.3	22.8	23.4	23.8	24.3
58	18.8	19.5	20.2	20.8	21.4	21.9	22.5	22.9	23.4	23.8
59	18.6	19.3	19.9	20.5	21.1	21.6	22.0	22.5	22.9	23.2
60	18.4	19.0	19.6	20.2	20.7	21.2	21.6	22.0	22.4	22.7
61	18.1	18.7	19.3	19.8	20.3	20.7	21.1	21.5	21.8	22.1
62	17.8	18.4	18.9	19.4	19.9	20.3	20.6	21.0	21.2	21.5
63	17.5	18.1	18.5	19.0	19.4	19.8	20.1	20.4	20.6	20.8
64	17.2	17.7	18.1	18.6	18.9	19.3	19.5	19.8	20.0	20.2
65	16.8	17.3	17.7	18.1	18.4	18.7	18.9	19.2	19.3	19.5
66	16.5	16.9	17.3	17.6	17.9	18.1	18.3	18.5	18.7	18.8
67	16.1	16.4	16.8	17.1	17.3	17.5	17.7	17.9	18.0	18.1
68	15.6	16.0	16.3	16.5	16.7	16.9	17.1	17.2	17.3	17.4
69	15.2	15.5	15.7	16.0	16.1	16.3	16.4	16.5	16.6	16.7
70	14.7	15.0	15.2	15.4	15.5	15.7	15.8	15.8	15.9	15.9
71	14.2	14.4	14.6	14.8	14.9	15.0	15.1	15.2	15.2	15.2
72	13.7	13.9	14.1	14.2	14.3	14.4	14.4	14.5	14.5	14.5
73	13.2	13.3	13.5	13.6	13.7	13.7	13.8	13.8	13.8	13.9
74	12.6	12.8	12.9	13.0	13.0	13.1	13.1	13.1	13.2	13.2
75	12.1	12.2	12.3	12.4	12.4	12.5	12.5	12.5	12.5	12.5
76	11.5	11.6	11.7	11.8	11.8	11.8	11.8	11.9	11.9	11.9
77	11.0	11.1	11.1	11.2	11.2	11.2	11.2	11.2	11.2	11.2
78	10.4	10.5	10.5	10.6	10.6	10.6	10.6	10.6	10.6	10.6
79	9.9	9.9	10.0	10.0	10.0	10.0	10.0	10.0	10.0	10.0
80	9.4	9.4	9.4	9.4	9.5	9.5	9.5	9.5	9.5	9.5
81	8.8	8.9	8.9	8.9	8.9	8.9	8.9	8.9	8.9	8.9
82	8.3	8.4	8.4	8.4	8.4	8.4	8.4	8.4	8.4	8.4
83	7.8	7.9	7.9	7.9	7.9	7.9	7.9	7.9	7.9	7.9
84	7.4	7.4	7.4	7.4	7.4	7.4	7.4	7.4	7.4	7.4
85	6.9	6.9	6.9	6.9	6.9	6.9	6.9	6.9	6.9	6.9
86	6.5	6.5	6.5	6.5	6.5	6.5	6.5	6.5	6.5	6.5
87	6.1	6.1	6.1	6.1	6.1	6.1	6.1	6.1	6.1	6.1
88	5.7	5.7	5.7	5.7	5.7	5.7	5.7	5.7	5.7	5.7
89	5.3	5.3	5.3	5.3	5.3	5.3	5.3	5.3	5.3	5.3
90	5.0	5.0	5.0	5.0	5.0	5.0	5.0	5.0	5.0	5.0
91	4.7	4.7	4.7	4.7	4.7	4.7	4.7	4.7	4.7	4.7
92	4.4	4.4	4.4	4.4	4.4	4.4	4.4	4.4	4.4	4.4
93	4.1	4.1	4.1	4.1	4.1	4.1	4.1	4.1	4.1	4.1
94	3.9	3.9	3.9	3.9	3.9	3.9	3.9	3.9	3.9	3.9

TABLE VIII.—TEMPORARY LIFE ANNUITIES; [1] ONE LIFE—EXPECTED RETURN MULTIPLES—Continued

(See footnote at end of tables)

Temporary Period—Maximum Duration of Annuity

Age	Years—									
	21	22	23	24	25	26	27	28	29	30
95	3.7	3.7	3.7	3.7	3.7	3.7	3.7	3.7	3.7	3.7
96	3.4	3.4	3.4	3.4	3.4	3.4	3.4	3.4	3.4	3.4
97	3.2	3.2	3.2	3.2	3.2	3.2	3.2	3.2	3.2	3.2
98	3.0	3.0	3.0	3.0	3.0	3.0	3.0	3.0	3.0	3.0
99	2.8	2.8	2.8	2.8	2.8	2.8	2.8	2.8	2.8	2.8
100	2.7	2.7	2.7	2.7	2.7	2.7	2.7	2.7	2.7	2.7
101	2.5	2.5	2.5	2.5	2.5	2.5	2.5	2.5	2.5	2.5
102	2.3	2.3	2.3	2.3	2.3	2.3	2.3	2.3	2.3	2.3
103	2.1	2.1	2.1	2.1	2.1	2.1	2.1	2.1	2.1	2.1
104	1.9	1.9	1.9	1.9	1.9	1.9	1.9	1.9	1.9	1.9
105	1.8	1.8	1.8	1.8	1.8	1.8	1.8	1.8	1.8	1.8
106	1.6	1.6	1.6	1.6	1.6	1.6	1.6	1.6	1.6	1.6
107	1.4	1.4	1.4	1.4	1.4	1.4	1.4	1.4	1.4	1.4
108	1.3	1.3	1.3	1.3	1.3	1.3	1.3	1.3	1.3	1.3
109	1.1	1.1	1.1	1.1	1.1	1.1	1.1	1.1	1.1	1.1
110	1.0	1.0	1.0	1.0	1.0	1.0	1.0	1.0	1.0	1.0
111	.9	.9	.9	.9	.9	.9	.9	.9	.9	.9
112	.8	.8	.8	.8	.8	.8	.8	.8	.8	.8
113	.7	.7	.7	.7	.7	.7	.7	.7	.7	.7
114	.6	.6	.6	.6	.6	.6	.6	.6	.6	.6
115	.5	.5	.5	.5	.5	.5	.5	.5	.5	.5

TABLE VIII.—TEMPORARY LIFE ANNUITIES; [1] ONE LIFE—EXPECTED RETURN MULTIPLES

(See footnote at end of tables)

Temporary Period—Maximum Duration of Annuity

Age	Years—									
	31	32	33	34	35	36	37	38	39	40
5	30.8	31.8	32.8	33.8	34.8	35.8	36.8	37.7	38.7	39.7
6	30.8	31.8	32.8	33.8	34.8	35.8	36.8	37.7	38.7	39.7
7	30.8	31.8	32.8	33.8	34.8	35.8	36.7	37.7	38.7	39.7
8	30.8	31.8	32.8	33.8	34.8	35.7	36.7	37.7	38.7	39.7
9	30.8	31.8	32.8	33.8	34.8	35.7	36.7	37.7	38.7	39.6
10	30.8	31.8	32.8	33.8	34.7	35.7	36.7	37.7	38.6	39.6
11	30.8	31.8	32.8	33.8	34.7	35.7	36.7	37.7	38.6	39.6
12	30.8	31.8	32.8	33.7	34.7	35.7	36.7	37.6	38.6	39.6
13	30.8	31.8	32.7	33.7	34.7	35.7	36.6	37.6	38.6	39.5
14	30.8	31.8	32.7	33.7	34.7	35.7	36.6	37.6	38.6	39.5
15	30.8	31.7	32.7	33.7	34.7	35.6	36.6	37.6	38.5	39.5
16	30.8	31.7	32.7	33.7	34.6	35.6	36.6	37.5	38.5	39.4
17	30.7	31.7	32.7	33.7	34.6	35.6	36.5	37.5	38.5	39.4
18	30.7	31.7	32.7	33.6	34.6	35.6	36.5	37.5	38.4	39.4
19	30.7	31.7	32.6	33.6	34.6	35.5	36.5	37.4	38.4	39.3
20	30.7	31.7	32.6	33.6	34.5	35.5	36.4	37.4	38.3	39.3
21	30.7	31.6	32.6	33.6	34.5	35.5	36.4	37.4	38.3	39.2
22	30.6	31.6	32.6	33.5	34.5	35.4	36.4	37.3	38.2	39.2
23	30.6	31.6	32.5	33.5	34.4	35.4	36.3	37.3	38.2	39.1
24	30.6	31.5	32.5	33.5	34.4	35.3	36.3	37.2	38.1	39.0
25	30.6	31.5	32.5	33.4	34.3	35.3	36.2	37.1	38.1	39.0
26	30.5	31.5	32.4	33.4	34.3	35.2	36.2	37.1	38.0	38.9
27	30.5	31.4	32.4	33.3	34.2	35.2	36.1	37.0	37.9	38.8
28	30.5	31.4	32.3	33.3	34.2	35.1	36.0	36.9	37.8	38.7
29	30.4	31.4	32.3	33.2	34.1	35.0	35.9	36.8	37.7	38.6
30	30.4	31.3	32.2	33.1	34.1	35.0	35.8	36.7	37.6	38.5
31	30.3	31.2	32.2	33.1	34.0	34.9	35.8	36.6	37.5	38.3
32	30.3	31.2	32.1	33.0	33.9	34.8	35.6	36.5	37.4	38.2
33	30.2	31.1	32.0	32.9	33.8	34.7	35.5	36.4	37.2	38.0
34	30.1	31.0	31.9	32.8	33.7	34.6	35.4	36.2	37.1	37.9
35	30.1	31.0	31.8	32.7	33.6	34.4	35.3	36.1	36.9	37.7
36	30.0	30.9	31.7	32.6	33.5	34.3	35.1	35.9	36.7	37.4
37	29.9	30.8	31.6	32.5	33.3	34.1	34.9	35.7	36.5	37.2
38	29.8	30.7	31.5	32.3	33.2	34.0	34.7	35.5	36.2	37.0
39	29.7	30.5	31.4	32.2	33.0	33.8	34.5	35.3	36.0	36.7
40	29.6	30.4	31.2	32.0	32.8	33.6	34.3	35.0	35.7	36.4
41	29.4	30.2	31.0	31.8	32.6	33.3	34.1	34.7	35.4	36.0
42	29.3	30.1	30.9	31.6	32.4	33.1	33.8	34.4	35.1	35.7
43	29.1	29.9	30.7	31.4	32.1	33.8	33.6	34.1	34.7	35.3
44	28.9	29.7	30.5	31.2	31.9	32.5	33.2	33.8	34.3	34.9
45	28.8	29.5	30.2	30.9	31.6	32.2	32.8	33.4	33.9	34.4
46	28.5	29.3	30.0	30.6	31.3	31.9	32.4	33.0	33.5	33.9
47	28.3	29.0	29.7	30.3	30.9	31.5	32.0	32.5	33.0	33.4
48	28.1	28.7	29.4	30.0	30.6	31.1	31.6	32.1	32.5	32.9
49	27.8	28.4	29.0	29.6	30.2	30.7	31.1	31.5	31.9	32.3
50	27.5	28.1	28.7	29.2	29.7	30.2	30.6	31.0	31.4	31.7
51	27.2	27.8	28.3	28.8	29.3	29.7	30.1	30.4	30.7	31.0
52	26.8	27.4	27.9	28.4	28.8	29.2	29.5	29.8	30.1	30.3
53	26.5	27.0	27.4	27.9	28.3	28.6	28.9	29.2	29.4	29.6
54	26.1	26.5	27.0	27.4	27.7	28.0	28.3	28.5	28.7	28.9
55	25.6	26.1	26.5	26.8	27.1	27.4	27.6	27.8	28.0	28.1
56	25.2	25.6	25.9	26.2	26.5	26.7	26.9	27.1	27.2	27.3
57	24.7	25.0	25.3	25.6	25.8	26.0	26.2	26.3	26.5	26.5
58	24.1	24.4	24.7	25.0	25.2	25.3	25.5	25.6	25.7	25.7
59	23.6	23.8	24.1	24.3	24.4	24.6	24.7	24.8	24.9	24.9
60	23.0	23.2	23.4	23.6	23.7	23.8	23.9	24.0	24.0	24.1

Reg. § 1.72-9

TABLE VIII.—TEMPORARY LIFE ANNUITIES; [1] ONE LIFE—EXPECTED RETURN MULTIPLES—Continued

(See footnote at end of tables)

Temporary Period—Maximum Duration of Annuity

Age	Years—									
	31	32	33	34	35	36	37	38	39	40
61...............	22.3	22.5	22.7	22.9	23.0	23.1	23.1	23.2	23.2	23.3
62...............	21.7	21.9	22.0	22.1	22.2	22.3	22.3	22.4	22.4	22.4
63...............	21.0	21.1	21.3	21.4	21.4	21.5	21.5	21.6	21.6	21.6
64...............	20.3	20.4	20.5	20.6	20.6	20.7	20.7	20.7	20.8	20.8
65...............	19.6	19.7	19.8	19.8	19.9	19.9	19.9	19.9	19.9	20.0
66...............	18.9	19.0	19.0	19.1	19.1	19.1	19.1	19.1	19.1	19.1
67...............	18.2	18.2	18.3	18.3	18.3	18.3	18.3	18.3	18.4	18.4
68...............	17.4	17.5	17.5	17.5	17.5	17.6	17.6	17.6	17.6	17.6
69...............	16.7	16.7	16.8	16.8	16.8	16.8	16.8	16.8	16.8	16.8
70...............	16.0	16.0	16.0	16.0	16.0	16.0	16.0	16.0	16.0	16.0
71...............	15.3	15.3	15.3	15.3	15.3	15.3	15.3	15.3	15.3	15.3
72...............	14.6	14.6	14.6	14.6	14.6	14.6	14.6	14.6	14.6	14.6
73...............	13.9	13.9	13.9	13.9	13.9	13.9	13.9	13.9	13.9	13.9
74...............	13.2	13.2	13.2	13.2	13.2	13.2	13.2	13.2	13.2	13.2
75...............	12.5	12.5	12.5	12.5	12.5	12.5	12.5	12.5	12.5	12.5
76...............	11.9	11.9	11.9	11.9	11.9	11.9	11.9	11.9	11.9	11.9
77...............	11.2	11.2	11.2	11.2	11.2	11.2	11.2	11.2	11.2	11.2
78...............	10.6	10.6	10.6	10.6	10.6	10.6	10.6	10.6	10.6	10.6
79...............	10.0	10.0	10.0	10.0	10.0	10.0	10.0	10.0	10.0	10.0
80...............	9.5	9.5	9.5	9.5	9.5	9.5	9.5	9.5	9.5	9.5
81...............	8.9	8.9	8.9	8.9	8.9	8.9	8.9	8.9	8.9	8.9
82...............	8.4	8.4	8.4	8.4	8.4	8.4	8.4	8.4	8.4	8.4
83...............	7.9	7.9	7.9	7.9	7.9	7.9	7.9	7.9	7.9	7.9
84...............	7.4	7.4	7.4	7.4	7.4	7.4	7.4	7.4	7.4	7.4
85...............	6.9	6.9	6.9	6.9	6.9	6.9	6.9	6.9	6.9	6.9
86...............	6.5	6.5	6.5	6.5	6.5	6.5	6.5	6.5	6.5	6.5
87...............	6.1	6.1	6.1	6.1	6.1	6.1	6.1	6.1	6.1	6.1
88...............	5.7	5.7	5.7	5.7	5.7	5.7	5.7	5.7	5.7	5.7
89...............	5.3	5.3	5.3	5.3	5.3	5.3	5.3	5.3	5.3	5.3
90...............	5.0	5.0	5.0	5.0	5.0	5.0	5.0	5.0	5.0	5.0
91...............	4.7	4.7	4.7	4.7	4.7	4.7	4.7	4.7	4.7	4.7
92...............	4.4	4.4	4.4	4.4	4.4	4.4	4.4	4.4	4.4	4.4
93...............	4.1	4.1	4.1	4.1	4.1	4.1	4.1	4.1	4.1	4.1
94...............	3.9	3.9	3.9	3.9	3.9	3.9	3.9	3.9	3.9	3.9
95...............	3.7	3.7	3.7	3.7	3.7	3.7	3.7	3.7	3.7	3.7
96...............	3.4	3.4	3.4	3.4	3.4	3.4	3.4	3.4	3.4	3.4
97...............	3.2	3.2	3.2	3.2	3.2	3.2	3.2	3.2	3.2	3.2
98...............	3.0	3.0	3.0	3.0	3.0	3.0	3.0	3.0	3.0	3.0
99...............	2.8	2.8	2.8	2.8	2.8	2.8	2.8	2.8	2.8	2.8
100...............	2.7	2.7	2.7	2.7	2.7	2.7	2.7	2.7	2.7	2.7
101...............	2.5	2.5	2.5	2.5	2.5	2.5	2.5	2.5	2.5	2.5
102...............	2.3	2.3	2.3	2.3	2.3	2.3	2.3	2.3	2.3	2.3
103...............	2.1	2.1	2.1	2.1	2.1	2.1	2.1	2.1	2.1	2.1
104...............	1.9	1.9	1.9	1.9	1.9	1.9	1.9	1.9	1.9	1.9
105...............	1.8	1.8	1.8	1.8	1.8	1.8	1.8	1.8	1.8	1.8
106...............	1.6	1.6	1.6	1.6	1.6	1.6	1.6	1.6	1.6	1.6
107...............	1.4	1.4	1.4	1.4	1.4	1.4	1.4	1.4	1.4	1.4
108...............	1.3	1.3	1.3	1.3	1.3	1.3	1.3	1.3	1.3	1.3
109...............	1.1	1.1	1.1	1.1	1.1	1.1	1.1	1.1	1.1	1.1
110...............	1.0	1.0	1.0	1.0	1.0	1.0	1.0	1.0	1.0	1.0
111...............	.9	.9	.9	.9	.9	.9	.9	.9	.9	.9
112...............	.8	.8	.8	.8	.8	.8	.8	.8	.8	.8
113...............	.7	.7	.7	.7	.7	.7	.7	.7	.7	.7
114...............	.6	.6	.6	.6	.6	.6	.6	.6	.6	.6
115...............	.5	.5	.5	.5	.5	.5	.5	.5	.5	.5

[1] The multiples in this table are not applicable to annuities for a term certain; for such cases see paragraph (c) of § 1.72-5.

If (a) the terms of the contract involve a life or lives, and are such that the above tables cannot be correctly applied, and (b) the amounts received under the contract are at least partly "amounts received as an annuity" under a contract to which section 72 applies, the taxpayer may submit with his return an actuarial computation based upon the applicable annuity table (described below) with ages set back one year, showing the appropriate factors applied in his case, subject to the approval of the Commissioner upon examination of such return. The applicable annuity table is the 1937 Standard Annuity Table (if the investment in the contract does not include a post-June 1986 investment in the contract) or the gender-neutral version of the 1983 Basic Table (if the investment

in the contract includes a post-June 1986 investment in the contract). In the case of a contract to which § 1.72-6(d) (relating to contracts in which amounts were invested both before July 1, 1986, and after June 30, 1986) applies, the actuarial computation shall be based on both tables in accordance with the principles of § 1.72-6(d). Computations involving factors to compensate for the effects of contingencies other than mortality, such as marriage or remarriage, re-employment, recovery from disability, or the like, will not be approved. [Reg. § 1.72-9.]

□ [*T.D.* 6211, 11-14-56. *Amended by T.D.* 6233, 5-14-57 *and T.D.* 8115, 12-16-86.]

[Reg. § 1.72-10]

§ 1.72-10. Effect of transfer of contracts on investment in the contract.—(a) If a contract to which section 72 applies, or any interest therein, is transferred for a valuable consideration, by assignment or otherwise, only the actual value of the consideration given for such transfer and the amount of premiums or other consideration subsequently paid by the transferee shall be included in the transferee's aggregate of premiums or other consideration paid. In accordance with the provisions of section 72(g)(3) and paragraph (b) of § 1.72-4, an annuity starting date shall be determined for the transferee without regard to the annuity starting date, if any, of the transferor. In determining the transferee's investment in the contract, the aggregate amount of premiums or other consideration paid shall be reduced by all amounts received by the transferee before the receipt of an amount as an annuity or before the annuity starting date, whichever is the later, to the extent that such amounts were excludable from his gross income under the applicable income tax law at the time of receipt. For the treatment of amounts received by the transferee subsequent to both the annuity starting date and the date of receipt of a payment as an annuity, but not received as annuity payments, see § 1.72-11. For a limitation on adjustments to the basis of annuity contracts sold, see section 1021.

(b) In the case of a transfer of such a contract without valuable consideration, the annuity starting date and the expected return under the contract shall be determined as though no such transfer had taken place. See paragraph (b) of § 1.72-4. The transferee shall include the aggregate of premiums or other consideration paid or deemed to have been paid by his transferor in the aggregate of premiums or other consideration as though paid by him. In determining the transferee's investment in the contract, the transferee's aggregate amount of premiums or other consideration paid (as so found) shall be reduced by all amounts either received or deemed to have been received by himself or his transferor before the annuity starting date, or before the date on which an amount is first received as an annuity, whichever is the later, to the extent that such amounts were excludable from the gross income of the actual recipient under the applicable income tax law at the time of receipt. For treatment of amounts received subsequent to both the above dates by such transferee, but not received as annuity payments, see § 1.72-11. [Reg. § 1.72-10.]

☐ [*T.D.* 6211, 11-14-56.]

Reg. § 1.72-10(a)

[Reg. § 1.72-11]

§ 1.72-11. Amounts not received as annuity payments.—(a) *Introductory.* (1) This section applies to amounts received under a contract to which section 72 applies if either:

(i) Paragraph (b) of § 1.72-2 is inapplicable to such amounts.

(ii) Paragraph (b) of § 1.72-2 is applicable but the annuity payments received differ either in amount, duration, or both, from those originally provided under the contract, or

(iii) Paragraph (b) of § 1.72-2 is applicable, but such annuity payments are received by a beneficiary after the death of an annuitant (or annuitants) in full discharge of the obligation under the contract and solely because of a guarantee.

The payments referred to in subdivision (i) of this subparagraph include all amounts other than "amounts received as an annuity" as that term is defined in paragraph (b)(2) and (3) of § 1.72-2. If such amounts are received as dividends or payments in the nature of dividends, or as a return of premiums, see paragraph (b) of this section. If such amounts are paid in full discharge of the obligation under the contract and are in the nature of a refund of the consideration, see paragraph (c) of this section. If such amounts are paid upon the surrender, redemption, or maturity of the contract, see paragraph (d) of this section. The payments referred to in subdivision (ii) of this subparagraph include all annuity payments which are paid as the result of a modification or an exchange of the annuity obligations originally provided under a contract for different annuity obligations (whether or not such modification or exchange is accompanied by the payment of an amount to which subdivision (i) of this subparagraph applies). If the duration of the new annuity obligations differs from the duration of the old annuity obligations, paragraph (e) of this section applies to the new annuity obligations and paragraph (d) of this section applies to any lump sum payment received. If, however, the duration of the new annuity obligations is the same as the duration of the old obligations, paragraph (f) of this section applies to the new obligations and to any lump sum received in connection therewith. The annuity payments referred to in subdivision (iii) of this subparagraph are annuity payments which are made to a beneficiary after the death of annuitant (or annuitants) in full discharge of the obligations under a contract because of a provision in the contract requiring the payment of a guaranteed amount or minimum number of payments for a fixed period; see paragraph (c) of this section.

(2) The principles of this section apply, to the extent appropriate thereto, to amounts paid which are taxable under section 72 (except, for taxable years beginning before January 1, 1964, section 72(e)(3)) in accordance with sections 402 and 403 and the regulations thereunder. However, if contributions used to purchase the contract include amounts for which a deduction was allowed under section 404 as contributions on behalf of an owner-employee, the rules of this section are modified by the rules of paragraph (b) of § 1.72-17. Further, in applying the provisions of this section, the aggregate premiums or other consideration paid shall not include contributions on behalf of self-employed individuals to the extent that deductions were allowed under section 404 for such contributions. Nor shall the aggregate of premiums or other consideration paid include amounts used to purchase life, accident, health, or other insurance protection for an owner-employee. See paragraph (b)(4) of § 1.72-16 and paragraph (c) of § 1.72-17. The principles of this section also apply to payments made in the manner described in paragraph (b)(3)(i) of § 1.72-2.

(b) *Amounts received in the nature of dividends or similar distributions.* (1) if dividends (or payments in the nature of dividends or a return of premiums or other consideration) are received under a contract to which section 72 applies and such payments are received before the annuity starting date or before the date on which an amount is first received as an annuity, whichever is the later, such payments are includible in the gross income of the recipient only to the extent that they, taken together with all previous payments received under the contract which were excludable from the gross income of the recipient under the applicable income tax law, exceed the aggregate of premiums or other consideration paid or deemed to have been paid by the recipient. Such payments shall also be subtracted from the consideration paid (or deemed paid) both for the purpose of determining an exclusion ratio to be applied to subsequent amounts paid as an annuity and for the purpose of determining the applicability of section 72(d) and § 1.72-13, relating to employee contributions recoverable in three years.

(2) If dividends or payments in the nature of dividends are paid under a contract to which section 72 applies and such payments are received on or after the annuity starting date or the date on which an amount is first received as an annuity, whichever is later, such payments shall be fully includible in the gross income of the recipient. The receipt of such payments shall not affect the aggregate of premiums or other consideration paid nor the amounts contributed or deemed to have been contributed by an employee as otherwise calculated for purposes of section 72. Since the investment in the contract and the expected return are not affected by a payment which is fully includible in the gross income of the recipient under this rule, the exclusion ratio will not be affected by such payment and will continue to be applied to amounts received as annuity payments in the future as though such payment had not been made. This subparagraph shall apply to amounts received under a contract described in paragraph (b)(3)(i) of § 1.72-2 to the extent that the amounts received exceed the portion of the investment in the contract allocable to each taxable year in accordance with paragraph (d)(3) of § 1.72-4. Hence, such excess is fully includible in the gross income of the recipient.

(c) *Amounts received in the nature of a refund of the consideration under a contract and in full discharge of the obligation thereof* (1) Any amount received under a contract to which section 72 applies, if it is at least in part a refund of the consideration paid, including amounts payable to a beneficiary after the death of an annuitant by reason of a provision in the contract for a life annuity with minimum period of payments certain or with a minimum amount which must be paid in any event, shall be considered an amount received in the nature of a refund of the consideration paid for such contract. If such an amount is in full discharge of an obligation to pay a fixed amount (whether in a lump sum or otherwise) or to pay amounts for a fixed number of years (including amounts described in paragraph (b)(3)(i) of § 1.72-2), it shall be included in the gross income of the recipient only to the extent that it, when added to amounts previously received under the contract which were excludable from gross income under the law applicable at the time of receipt, exceeds the aggregate of premiums or other consideration paid. See section 73(e)(2)(A). This paragraph shall not apply if the total of the amounts to be paid in discharge of the obligation can in any event exceed the total of the annuity payments which would otherwise fully discharge the obligation. For rules to be applied in such a case, see paragraph (e) of this section.

(2) The principles of subparagraph (1) of this paragraph may be illustrated by the following examples:

Example (1). A, a male employee, retired on December 31, 1954, at the age of 60. A life annuity of $75 per month was payable to him beginning January 31, 1955. The annuity contract guaranteed that if A did not live for at least ten years after his retirement his beneficiary, B, would receive the monthly payments for any balance of such ten year period which remained at the date of A's death. Under section 72, A was deemed to have paid $3,600 toward the cost of the annuity. A lived for five years after his retirement receiving a total of $4,500 in annuity payments. After A's death, B began receiving the monthly payments of $75 beginning with the January 31, 1960 payment. B will exclude such payments

from his gross income throughout 1960, 1961, and 1962, and will exclude only $18 of the first payment in 1963 from his gross income for that year. Thereafter, B will include the entire amount of all such payments in his gross income for the taxable year of receipt. This result is determined as follows:

A's investment in the contract (unadjusted)	$3,600
Multiple from Table III of § 1.72-9 for male, age 60, where duration of guaranteed amount is 10 years (percent) 11	
Subtract value of the refund feature to the nearest dollar (11 percent of $3,600)	396
Investment in the contract adjusted for the present value of the refund feature without discount for interest	3,204
Aggregate of premiums or other consideration paid	3,600
A's exclusion ratio ($3,204 ÷ $16,380 [$900 × 18.2]) (percent) 19.6	
Subtract amount excludable during five years A received payments (19.6 percent of $4,500 [$900 × 5])	882
Remainder of aggregate of premiums or other consideration paid excludable from gross income of B under section 72(e)	2,718

As a result of the above computation, the number of payments to B which will exhaust the remainder of consideration paid which is excludable from gross income of the recipient is 36⁶/25 ($2,718 ÷ $75) and B will exclude the payments from his gross income for three years, then exclude only $18 of the first payment for the fourth year from his gross income, and thereafter include the entire amount of all payments he receives in his gross income.

Example (2). The facts are the same as in example (1), except that B, the beneficiary, elects to receive $50 per month for his life in lieu of the payments guaranteed under the original contractual obligation. Since such amounts will be received as an annuity and may, because of the length of time B may live, exceed the amount guaranteed, they are not amounts to which this paragraph applies. See paragraph (e) of this section.

Example (3). The facts are the same as in example (1), except that B, the beneficiary, elects to receive the remaining guaranteed amount in installments which are larger or smaller than the $75 per month provided until, under the terms of the contract, the guaranteed amount is exhausted. The rule of subparagraph (1) of this paragraph and the computation illustrated in example (1) apply to such installments since the total of such installments will not exceed the original amount guaranteed to be paid at A's death in any event.

Example (4). C pays $12,000 for a contract providing that he is to be paid an annuity of $1,000 per year for 15 years. His exclusion ratio is therefore 80 percent ($12,000 ÷ $15,000). He directs that the annuity is to be paid to D, his beneficiary, if he should die before the full 15 year period has expired. C dies after 5 years and D is

paid $1,000 in 1960. D will include $200 ($1,000 − $800 [80 percent of $1,000]) in his gross income for the taxable year in which he receives the $1,000 since section 72(e) and this section do not apply to the annuity payments made in accordance with the provisions and during the term of the contract. D will continue with the same exclusion ratio used by C (80 percent).

Example (5). In 1954, E paid $50,000 into a fund and was promised an annual income for life the amount of which would depend in part upon the earnings realized from the investment of the fund in accordance with an agreed formula. The contract also specified that if E should die before ten years had elapsed, his beneficiary, F, would be paid the amounts determined annually under the formula until ten payments had been received by E and F together. E died in 1960, having received five payments totaling $30,000. Assuming that $22,000 of this amount was properly excludable from E's gross income prior to his death, F will exclude from his gross income the payments he receives until the taxable year in which his total receipts from the fund exceed $28,000 ($50,000 − $22,000). F will include any excess over the $28,000 in his gross income for that taxable year. Thereafter, F will include in his gross income the entire amount of any payments made to him from the fund.

Example (6). Assume the facts are the same as in example (1), except that the total investment in the contract is made after June 30, 1986, that A is to receive payments under the life annuity contract beginning on January 31, 1987, and that B will begin to receive the monthly payments on January 31, 1992. B will exclude the $75 monthly payments from gross income throughout 1992, 1993, and 1994. B will exclude only the first

Reg. § 1.72-11(c)(2)

two monthly payments and $21 of the third monthly payment in 1995. This is determined as follows:

A's investment in the contract (unadjusted)	$	3,600
Multiple from Table VII, age 60, 10 years (percent)		4
Subtract value of the refund feature (4 percent of $3,600)	$	144
Investment in the contract adjusted for the present value of the refund feature without discount for interest	$	3,456
Aggregate of premiums or other consideration paid		$3,600.00
A's exclusion ratio ($3,456 ÷ $21,780 [$900 × 24.2]) (percent)		15.9
Subtract amount excludable during five years A received payments (15.9 percent of $4,500 [$900 × 5])	$	715.50
Remainder of aggregate of premiums or other consideration paid excludable from gross income of B under section 72(e)		$2,884.50

As a result of the above computation, the number of payments to B which will exhaust the remainder of consideration paid which is excludable from gross income of the recipient is 38²³/₅₀ ($2,884.50 ÷ 75) and B will exclude the payments from gross income for three years, then exclude only the first two monthly payments and $34.50 of the third. Thereafter B shall include the entire amount of all payments received in gross income.

(3) For the purpose of applying the rule contained in subparagraph (1) of this paragraph, it is immaterial whether the recipient of the amount received in full discharge of the obligation is the same person as the recipient of amounts previously received under the contract which were excludable from gross income, except in the case of a contract transferred for a valuable consideration, with respect to which see paragraph (a) of § 1.72-10. For the limit on the tax, for taxable years beginning before January 1, 1964, attributable to the receipt of a lump sum to which this paragraph applies, see paragraph (g) of this section.

(d) *Amounts received upon the surrender, redemption, or maturity of a contract.* (1) Any amount received upon the surrender, redemption, or maturity of a contract to which section 72 applies, which is not received as an annuity under the rules of paragraph (b) of § 1.72-2, shall be included in the gross income of the recipient to the extent that it, when added to amounts previously received under the contract and which were excludable from the gross income of the recipient under the law applicable at the time of receipt, exceeds the aggregate of premiums or other consideration paid. See section 72(e)(2)(B). If amounts are to be received as an annuity, whether in lieu of or in addition to amounts described in the preceding sentence, such amounts shall be included in the gross income of the recipient in accordance with the provisions of paragraph (e) or (f) of this section, whichever is applicable. The rule stated in the first sentence of this paragraph shall not apply to payments received as an annu-

ity or otherwise after the date of the first receipt of an amount as an annuity subsequent to the maturity, redemption, or surrender of the original contract. If amounts are so received and are other than amounts received as an annuity, they are includible in the gross income of the recipient. See section 72(e)(1)(A) and paragraph (b)(2).

(2) For the purpose of applying the rule contained in subparagraph (1) of this paragraph, it is immaterial whether the recipient of the amount received upon the surrender, redemption, or maturity of the contract is the same as the recipient of amounts previously received under the contract which were excludable from gross income, except in the case of a contract transferred for a valuable consideration, with respect to which see paragraph (a) of § 1.72-10. For the limit on the amount of tax, for taxable years beginning before January 1, 1964, attributable to the receipt of certain lump sums to which this paragraph applies, see paragraph (g) of this section.

(e) *Periodic payments received for a different term.* If, after the date on which an amount is first received as an annuity under a contract to which section 72 applies, the terms of the contract are modified or the annuity obligations are exchanged so that periodic payments are to be received for a different term than originally provided under the contract (whether or not accompanied by the receipt of a lump sum to which paragraph (d) of this section applies), the rules of this paragraph shall apply to such payments. Hence, the provisions of section 72(e) and paragraphs (b), (c), (d), and (f) of this section are inapplicable for the purpose of determining the includibility of such payments in gross income and the general principles of section 72 with respect to the use of an exclusion ratio shall be applied to such payments as if they were provided under a new contract received in exchange for the contract providing the original annuity payments. If such payments are received as the result of the surrender, redemption, or discharge of a contract to which section 72 applies, they shall be considered to be received as an annuity under a contract exchanged for the contract whose redemption, surrender, or discharge was involved. For the purpose of determining the extent to which the payments so received are to be included in the gross income of the recipient, an exclusion ratio shall be determined for such contract as of the later of January 1, 1954, or the first day of the first period for which an amount is received as an annuity thereunder, whichever is the later. See paragraph (b) of § 1.72-4. In determining the investment in the contract for this purpose, any lump sum amount received at the time of the exchange shall not be considered an amount to which paragraph (a)(2) of § 1.72-6 applies. However, such lump sum shall be subtracted from the aggregate of premiums or other consideration paid to the extent it is excludable as an amount not received as an annuity under this section as if it were an amount received before the annuity starting date of the contract obtained in exchange.

(f) *Periodic payments received for the same term after a lump sum withdrawal.* (1) If, after the date of the first receipt of a payment as an annuity, the annuitant receives a lump sum and is thereafter to receive annuity payments in a reduced amount under the contract for the same term, life, or lives as originally specified in the contract, a portion of the contract shall be considered to have been surrendered or redeemed in consideration of the payment of such lump sum and the exclusion ratio originally determined for the contract shall continue to apply to the amounts received as an annuity without regard to the fact that such amounts are less than the original amounts which were to be paid periodically. The lump sum shall be includible in the gross income of the recipient in accordance with the provisions of subparagraph (2) of this paragraph. However, except in the case of amounts to which sections 402 and 403 apply, the tax, for taxable years beginning before January 1, 1964, attributable to the inclusion of all or part of the lump sum in gross income shall not exceed the amount determined under section 72(e)(3) and

paragraph (g) of this section. For taxable years beginning after December 31, 1963, such amounts may be taken into account in computations under sections 1301 through 1305 (relating to income averaging).

(2) There shall be excluded from gross income that portion of the lump sum which bears the same ratio to the aggregate premiums or other consideration paid for the contract, as reduced by all amounts previously received under the contract and excludable from the gross income of the recipient under the applicable income tax law, as:

(i) In the case of payments to be made in the manner described in paragraph (b)(2) of § 1.72-2, the amount of the reduction in the annuity payments to be made thereafter bears to the annuity payments originally provided under the contract, or

(ii) In the case of a contract providing for payments to be made in the manner described in paragraph (b)(3)(i) of § 1.72-2, the amount of the reduction in the number of units per period to be paid thereafter bears to the number of units per period payable under the contract immediately before the lump sum withdrawal.

(3) This paragraph may be illustrated by the following examples:

Example (1). Taxpayer A pays $20,000 for an annuity contract providing for payments to him of $100 per month for his life. At the annuity starting date he has a life expectancy of 20 years. His expected return is therefore $24,000 and the exclusion ratio is five-sixths. He continues to receive the original annuity payments for 5 years, receiving a total of $6,000, and properly excludes a total of $5,000 from his gross income in his income tax returns for those years. At the beginning of the next year, A agrees with the insurer to take a reduced annuity of $75 per month and a lump sum payment of $4,000 in cash. Of the lump sum he receives, he will include $250 and exclude $3,750 from his gross income for his taxable year of receipt, determined as follows:

Aggregate of premiums or other consideration paid	$20,000
Less amounts received as an annuity to the extent they were excludable from A's income	5,000
Remainder of the consideration	$15,000
Ratio of the reduction in the amount of the annuity payments to the original annuity payments	25/$100 or ¼
Lump sum received	$4,000
Less one-fourth of the remainder of the consideration (¼ of $15,000)	3,750
Portion of the lump sum includible in gross income	$250

For taxable years beginning before January 1, 1964, the limit on tax of section 72(e)(3), as in effect before such date, applies to the portion of

the lump sum includible in gross income. For taxable years beginning after December 31, 1963, such portion may be taken into account in computations under sections 1301 through 1305 (relating to income averaging). If, in this example, the annuity were a pension payable to A as a retired employee, but the facts were otherwise the same (assuming that, for instance, the $20,000 aggregate of premiums or other consideration paid were A's contributions as determined under section 72(f) and § 1.72-8) the result would be the same except that the tax attributable to the inclusion of the $250 in A's gross income, for taxable years beginning before January 1, 1964, would not be limited by section 72(e)(3), as in effect before such date. If such a lump sum is received in a taxable year beginning after December 31, 1963, the portion of such sum includible in gross income may be taken into account in computations under sections 1301 through 1305 (relating to income averaging)

Example (2). Taxpayer B pays $30,000 for a contract providing for monthly payments to be made to him for 15 years with respect to the principal and earnings of 10 units of an investment fund. B receives $12,000 during the first 5 years of participation and of this amount he has properly excluded a total of $10,000 from his gross income in his income returns for the taxable years, since $2,000 of $2,400 he received in each such year represented his investment divided by the term of the annuity ($30,000 ÷ 15). At the beginning of the 6th year, B agrees to take $11,000 in a lump sum and thereafter to accept the payments arising with respect to five units for the remaining 10 years of payments in full discharge of the original obligations of the contract. B shall include $1,000 in his gross income for the 6th year as the result of the lump sum he receives and allocates $1,000 of his original investment in the contract to each of the remaining 10 years with respect to the payments which will continue, determined as follows:

Aggregate of premiums or other consideration paid	$30,000
Total amount received and excludable from gross income	10,000
Remainder of the consideration	$20,000
Ratio of units discontinued to the total units originally provided	5/10, or 1/2
Lump sum received at the time of reduction in the number of units to be paid	$11,000
Less one-half of the remainder of the consideration (1/2 of $20,000)	10,000
Portion of the lump sum received and includible in gross income	$1,000
Remainder of the consideration less the portion of such remainder attributable to the excludable portion of the lump sum ($20,000 − $10,000)	$10,000
Remainder of the consideration properly allocable to each taxable year for the remaining 10 years ($10,000 ÷ 10)	1,000

For the taxable years beginning before January 1, 1964, the limit on tax of section 72(e)(3), as in effect before such date, applies to the portion of the lump sum received and includible in gross income. For taxable years beginning after December 31, 1963, such portion may be taken into account in computations under sections 1301 through 1305 (relating to income averaging).

(g) *Limit on tax attributable to the receipt of a lump sum.* (1) For taxable years beginning before January 1, 1964, if the entire amount of the proceeds received upon the redemption, maturity, surrender, or discharge of a contract to which section 72 applies is received in a lump sum and paragraph (c), (d), or (f) of this section is applicable in determining the portion of such amount which is includible in gross income, the tax attributable to such portion shall not exceed the tax which would have been attributable thereto had such portion been received ratably in the taxable year in which received and the 2 preceding taxable years. The amount of tax attributable to the includible portion of the lump sum received shall be the lessor of:

(i) The difference between the amount of tax for the taxable year of receipt computed by including such portion in gross income and the amount of tax for such taxable year computed by excluding such portion from gross income; or

(ii) The difference between the total amount of tax for the taxable year of receipt and the 2 preceding taxable years computed by including one-third of such portion in gross income for each of the 3 taxable years, and the total amount of the tax for the taxable year of receipt and the 2 preceding taxable years computed by entirely excluding such portion from the gross income of all 3 taxable years.

For the definition of "taxable year", see section 441(b). This subparagraph shall not apply, for taxable years beginning before January 1, 1964, to payments excepted from the application of section 72(e)(3), as in effect before such date, under the provisions of section 402 or 403. See paragraph (a) of § 1.72-2 and paragraph (d) of § 1.72-14.

(2) For taxable years beginning after December 31, 1963, any amount includible in gross income to which this section relates may be taken

Reg. § 1.72-11(g)(2)

into account in computations under sections 1301 through 1305 (relating to income averaging).

(h) *Amounts deemed to be paid or received by a transferee.* Amounts deemed to have been paid or received by a transferee for the purposes of § 1.72-10 shall also be deemed to have been so paid or received by such transferee for the purposes of this section. Thus, if a donee is deemed to have paid the premiums or other consideration actually paid by his transferor for the purposes of section 72(g) and paragraph (b) of § 1.72-10, such consideration shall be deemed premiums or other consideration paid by the donee for the purposes of this section. [Reg. § 1.72-11.]

□ [*T.D. 6211, 11-14-56. Amended by T.D. 6676, 9-16-63, T.D. 6885, 6-1-66 and T.D. 8115, 12-16-86.*]

[Reg. § 1.72-12]

§ 1.72-12. Effect of taking an annuity in lieu of a lump sum upon the maturity of a contract.—If a contract to which section 72 applies provides for the payment of a lump sum in full discharge of the obligation thereunder and the obligee entitled thereto, prior to receiving any portion of such lump sum and within 60 days after the date on which such lump sum first becomes payable, exercises an option or irrevocably agrees with the obligor to take, in lieu thereof, payments which will constitute "amounts received as an annuity", as that term is defined in paragraph (b) of § 1.72-2, no part of such lump sum shall be deemed to have been received by the obligee at the time he was first entitled thereto merely because he would have been entitled to such amount had he not exercised the option or made such an agreement with the obligor. [Reg. § 1.72-12.]

□ [*T.D. 6211, 11-14-56.*]

[Reg. § 1.72-13]

§ 1.72-13. Special rule for employee contributions recoverable in three years.—(a) *Amounts received as an annuity.* (1) Section 72(d) provides a special rule for the treatment of amounts received as an annuity by an employee (or by the beneficiary or beneficiaries of an employee) under a contract to which section 72 applies. This special rule is applicable only in the event that:

(i) At least part of the consideration paid for the contract is contributed by the employer, and

(ii) The aggregate amount receivable as an annuity under such contract by the employee (or by his beneficiary or beneficiaries if the employee died before any amount was received as an annu-

ity under the contract) within the 3-year period beginning on the date (whether or not before January 1, 1954) on which an amount is first received as an annuity equals or exceeds the total consideration contributed (or deemed contributed under section 72 (f) and § 1.72-8) by the employee as of such date as reduced by all amounts previously received and excludable from the gross income of the recipient under the applicable income tax law.

In such an event, section 72(d) provides that all amounts received as an annuity under the contract during a taxable year to which the Code applies shall be excluded from gross income until the total of the amounts excluded under that section plus all amounts excluded under prior income tax laws equals or exceeds the consideration contributed (or deemed contributed) by the employee. The excess, if any, and all amounts received by any recipient thereafter (whether or not received as an annuity), shall be fully included in gross income. See paragraph (b) of this section.

(2) If the aggregate amount receivable as an annuity under the contract within three years from the date on which an amount is first received as an annuity thereunder will not equal or exceed the consideration contributed (or deemed contributed) by the employee in accordance with the provisions of § 1.72-8, computed as of such date, the special rule of section 72(d) shall not apply to amounts received as an annuity under the contract and the general rules of section 72 shall apply thereto.

(3) The aggregate of the amounts receivable as an annuity within the prescribed 3-year period shall be the total of all annuity payments anticipatable by an employee (or a beneficiary or beneficiaries of an employee, if the employee died before any amount was received as an annuity) under the contract as a whole as defined in paragraph (a) of § 1.72-2. See paragraph (a)(3) of § 1.72-2 for rules for determining what constitutes "the contract" in the case of distributions from an employees' trust or plan.

(4) If subparagraphs (1) and (3) of this paragraph apply to amounts received as an annuity under a contract, the rule prescribed in subparagraph (1) of this paragraph shall apply to all amounts so received thereunder regardless of the fact that they may be payable (i) to more than one beneficiary, (ii) for the same or different intervals, (iii) in different sums, or (iv) for a different period certain, life, or lives.

(5) For purposes of section 72(d), contributions which are made with respect to a self-employed individual and which are allowed as a deduction under section 404(a) are not considered

contributions by the employee, but such contributions are considered contributions by the employer. A contribution which is deemed paid in a prior taxable year under the provisions of section 404(a)(6) shall be considered made with respect to a self-employed individual if the individual on whose behalf the contribution is made was self-employed for the taxable year in which the contribution is deemed paid, whether or not such individual is self-employed at the time the contribution is actually paid. Contributions with respect to a self-employed individual who is an owner-employee used to purchase life, accident, health, or other insurance protection for such owner-employee shall not be treated as consideration for the contract contributed by the employee in computing the employee contributions for purposes of section 72(d).

(b) *Amounts not received as an annuity.* If the rule of paragraph (a) applies to a contract and, after the date on which an annuity payment is first received, amounts are received other than as an annuity under such contract in a taxable year to which the Code applies, they shall be included in the gross income of the recipient in accordance with the provisions of § 1.72-11. Thus, if such amounts are received as a dividend or a similar distribution after the date on which an amount is first received as an annuity under the contract, they shall be included in the gross income of the recipient (in accordance with section 72(e)(1)(A) and paragraph (b)(2) of § 1.72-11). All other amounts not received as an annuity shall be included in the gross income of the recipient in accordance with the provisions of section 72(e)(1)(B) and paragraph (c), (d), or (f), whichever is applicable, of § 1.72-11. See section 72(e)(2).

(c) *Amounts received after the exhaustion of employee contributions.* (1) Amounts received under a contract to which the rule of paragraph (a) of this section applies (whether or not such amounts are received as an annuity) shall be included in the gross income of the recipient if such amounts are received after the date on which the aggregate of all amounts excluded from gross income by the recipients under section 72(d) and prior income tax laws equalled or exceeded the consideration contributed (or deemed contributed) by the employee.

(2) If the rule of paragraph (a) of this section applies to amounts received by an employee (or his beneficiary or beneficiaries) under a joint and survivor annuity contract, payments made to a prior annuitant may entirely exhaust the amounts excludable from gross income. In such case, amounts paid to the surviving annuitant (or annuitants) shall be included in gross income by such recipients.

(d) *Application of section 72(d) to a contract, trust, or plan providing for payments in a manner described in paragraph (b)(3)(i) of § 1.72-2.* For the purpose of applying section 72(d) and this section, any amount received in the nature of a periodic payment under a contract, trust, or plan which provides for the payment of amounts in a manner described in paragraph (b)(3)(i) of § 1.72-2 shall be considered an amount received as an annuity notwithstanding the provisions of any other section of the regulations under section 72. The special exclusion rule of section 72(d) and paragraph (a) of this section shall apply to all amounts so received if the first amount received, when multiplied by the number of periodic payments to be made within the three years beginning on the date of its receipt, results in an amount in excess of the aggregate premiums or other consideration contributed (or deemed contributed) by the employee as of that date. If more than one series of periodic payments is to be paid under the same contract, trust, or plan, all payments anticipatable, whether because fixed in amount or determinable in the manner described in the preceding sentence, shall be aggregated for the purpose of determining the applicability of section 72(d) to the contract, trust, or plan as a whole.

(e) *Inapplicability of section 72(d) and this section.* Section 72(d) and this section do not apply to:

(1) Amounts received as proceeds of a life insurance contract to which section 101(a) applies, nor to

(2) Amounts paid to a surviving annuitant under a joint and survivor annuity contract to which paragraph (b)(3) of § 1.72-5 applies, nor to

(3) Amounts paid to an annuitant under chapter 73 of title 10 of the United States Code with respect to which section 72(o) and § 1.122-1 apply.

See also paragraph (d) of § 1.72-14. [Reg. § 1.72-13.]

☐ [*T.D.* 6211, 11-14-56. *Amended by T.D.* 6497, 10-19-60, *T.D.* 6676, 9-16-63 *and T.D.* 7043, 6-1-70.]

[Reg. § 1.72-14]

§ 1.72-14. **Exceptions from application of principles of section 72.**—(a) *Payments of interest.* If any amount is received under an agreement to pay interest on a sum or sums held by the obligor, such amount shall not be excludable from the gross income of the recipient under the provisions of section 72 to the extent that it is an actual interest payment. See section 72(j). An amount shall be considered to be held under an agreement to pay interest thereon if the amount payable after the term of the annuity (whether for a term certain or for a life or lives) is substantially equal to or larger than the aggregate amount of premiums or other consideration paid therefor. For this purpose, however, the aggregate amount of premiums or other consideration paid shall include all contributions made by an employer and not merely those to which section 72(f) applies.

(b) *Alimony payments.* To the extent that payments made to a wife are includible in her gross income by reason of either or both sections 71 and 682, they shall not be excluded from the wife's gross income under the principles of section 72 although made under a contract to which that section applies. However, section 72 shall apply in the case of amounts received under such a contract if a husband and wife are entitled to make and do make a single return jointly.

(c) *Certain "face-amount certificates."* The principles of section 72 do not apply to "face-amount certificates" described in section 72(l) which were issued before January 1, 1955.

(d) *Employer plans.* The provisions of §§ 1.72-1 to 1.72-13, inclusive, shall be disregarded to the extent that they are inconsistent with the treatment of amounts received provided in section 402 (relating to the taxability of a beneficiary of an employee's trust), section 403 (relating to the taxation of employee annuities), or the regulations under either of such sections. [Reg. § 1.72-14.]

☐ [*T.D. 6211, 11-14-56.*]

[Reg. § 1.72-15]

§ 1.72-15. Applicability of section 72 to accident or health plans.—(a) *Applicability of section.* This section provides the rules for determining the taxation of amounts received from an employer-established plan which provides for distributions that are taxable under section 72 (or for distributions that are taxable under section 402(a)(2) or (e), or section 403(a)(2), in the case of lump sum distributions) and which also provides for distributions that may be excludable from gross income under section 104 or 105 as accident or health benefits. For example, this section will apply to a pension plan described in section 401 and exempt under section 501 which provides for the payment of pensions at retirement and the payment of an earlier pension in the event of permanent disability. This section will also apply to a profit-sharing plan described in section 401 and exempt under section 501 which provides for periodic distribution of the amount standing to the account of a participant during any period

that the participant is absent from work due to a personal injury or sickness and for the distribution of any balance standing to the account of the participant upon his separation from service. For purposes of this section, the term "contributions of the employee" includes contributions by the employer which were includible in the employee's gross income. For special rules for taxable years ending before January 27, 1975, relating to certain accident or health benefits which were treated as distributions to which section 72 applied, see paragraph (i) of this section.

(b) *General rule.* Section 72 does not apply to any amount received as an accident or health benefit, and the tax treatment of any such amount shall be determined under sections 104 and 105. See paragraphs (c) and (d) of this section, paragraph (d) of § 1.104-1, and §§ 1.105-1 through 1.105-5. Section 72 (or, in the case of certain total distributions, section 402(a)(2) or section 403(a)(2)) does apply to any amount which is received under a plan to which this section applies and which is not an accident or health benefit. See paragraph (e) of this section.

(c) *Accident or health benefits attributable to employee contributions.* (1) If a plan to which this section applies provides that any portion of the accident or health benefits is attributable to the contributions of the employee to such plan, then such portion of such benefits is excludable from gross income under section 104(a)(3) and paragraph (d) of § 1.104-1. Neither section 72 nor section 105 applies to any accident or health benefits (whether paid before or after retirement) attributable to contributions of the employee. Since such portion is excludable under section 104(a)(3), such portion is not subject to the dollar limitation of section 105(d) and if such portion is payable after the retirement of the employee, it is excludable without regard to the provisions of § 1.105-4 and section 72.

(2) In determining the taxation of any amounts received as accident or health benefits from a plan to which this section applies, the first step is to determine the portion, if any, of the contributions of the employee which is used to provide the accident or health benefits and the portion of the accident or health benefits attributable to such portion of the employee's contributions. If such a plan expressly provides that the accident or health benefits are provided in whole or in part by employee contributions and the portion of employee contributions to be used for such purpose, the contributions so used will be treated as used to provide accident or health benefits. However, if the plan does not expressly provide that the accident or health benefits are to

Reg. § 1.72-15(a)

be provided with employee contributions and the portion of employee contributions to be used for such purpose, it will be presumed that none of the employee contributions is used to provide such benefits. Thus, in the case of a contributory pension plan, it will be presumed that the disability pension is provided by employer contributions, unless the plan expressly provides otherwise, or in the case of a contributory profit-sharing plan providing that a portion of the amount standing to the account of each participant will be used to purchase accident or health insurance, it will be presumed that such insurance is purchased with employer contributions, unless the plan expressly provides otherwise. Similarly, unless the plan expressly provides otherwise, it will be presumed that if a contributory profit-sharing plan provides for periodic distributions from the account of a participant during any absence from work because of a personal injury or sickness, all such distributions which do not exceed the contributions of the employer plus earnings thereon are provided by employer contributions.

(3) Any employee contributions that are treated under subparagraph (2) of this paragraph as used to provide accident or health benefits shall not be included for any purpose under section 72 as employee contributions or as aggregate premiums or other consideration paid. Thus, in the case of a pension plan, or in the case of a profit-sharing plan providing that a portion of the amount standing to the account of each participant will be used to purchase accident or health insurance, any employee whose contributions are so used must make the adjustment provided by this subparagraph irrespective of whether such employee receives any accident or health benefits under such plan. However, in the case of a profit-sharing plan providing for periodic distributions from the account of a participant during any absence from work because of a personal injury or sickness, and adjustment under this subparagraph is required only when an employee receives distributions in excess of the employer contributions and earnings thereon or receives distributions consisting in whole or in part of his own contributions.

(4) If any of the employee contributions are treated under subparagraph (2) of this paragraph as used to provide any of the accident or health benefits, the portion of the benefits attributable to employee contributions shall be determined in accordance with § 1.105-1. Any accident or health benefits that are excludable under section 104(a)(3) shall not be included in the expected return for purposes of section 72.

(d) *Accident or health benefits attributable to employer contributions.* Any amounts received as accident or health benefits and not attributable to contributions of the employee are includible in gross income except to the extent that such amounts are excludable from gross income under section 105(b), (c), or (d) and the regulations thereunder. Thus, such amounts may be excludable under section 105(d) as payments under a wage continuation plan. However, if such payments, when added to other such payments attributable to employer contributions, exceed the limitations of section 105(d), then the excess is includible in gross income under section 105(a). Such excess is not excludable under section 72. See, however, paragraph (i) of this section, for special rules for taxable years ending before January 27, 1975, relating to certain accident or health benefits which were treated as distributions to which section 72 applied.

(c) *Other benefits under the plan.* The taxability of amounts that are received under a plan to which this section applies and that are not accident or health benefits is determined under section 72 (or, in the case of certain total distributions, under section 402(a)(2) or section 403(a)(2)) without regard to any exclusion or inclusion of accident or health benefits under sections 104 and 105. For example, the investment in the contract or aggregate premiums paid is determined without regard to the exclusion of any amount under section 104 or 105, and the annuity starting date is determined without regard to the receipt of any accident or health benefits. However, if any employee contributions are used to provide any accident or health benefits, the investment in the contract or aggregate premiums paid must be adjusted as provided in paragraph (c)(3) of this section.

(f) *Examples.* The principles of this section may be illustrated by the following examples:

Example (1). A, an employee, is a participant in a contributory pension plan described in section 401(a) and exempt under section 501(a). Such plan provides for the payment of a pension to each participant when he retires at age 65 or when he retires earlier if the retirement is due to permanent and total disability. In 1964, A, who was age 52, became totally and permanently disabled because of an injury, was hospitalized, and commenced to receive a pension of $74 a week under this plan. The weekly amounts received by A do not exceed 75 percent of his "regular weekly rate of wages" under section 105(d). A had contributed $11,500 to the plan. The plan does not expressly provide that any portion of the disability pension is purchased with employee contributions. Accordingly, it is presumed that no portion of the disability pension is purchased with A's contributions. The disability pension which A receives qualifies as payments under a wage continuation plan for purposes of section 105(d) and § 1.105-4, and if such payments are the only accident or health benefits which are attributable to the contributions of his employer, such payments are entirely excludable under section 105(d) until A reaches age 65, his mandatory retirement age under the plan. The payments which A receives after he becomes age 65 are taxable under section 72. The payments which A receives do constitute an annuity as defined in paragraph (b) of § 1.72-2, but since the amounts which he will receive during the first three years after attaining age 65 exceed his contributions, he shall exclude under § 1.72-13 the entire amount of all payments that he receives as an annuity after attaining age 65 until such amounts equal his contributions to the plan, or $11,500. Thereafter, the payments that he receives under the plan are includible in gross income.

Example (2). B, an employee, is a participant in a contributory profit-sharing plan described in section 401(a) and exempt under section 501(a). Such plan provides that, in the event a participant is absent from work because of a personal injury or sickness, he will be paid $125 a week out of his account in such plan. Such weekly amount does not exceed 75 percent of B's "regular weekly rate of wages" under section 105(d). Any amount standing to the account of a participant at the time of his separation from service will be paid to him at such time. During 1964, B incurred a personal injury, was hospitalized, and as a result was absent from work for nine weeks. He received nine weekly payments of $125, or a total of $1,125, on account of such absence from work. At the time B was injured, he had contributed $5,000 to the plan. The plan did not expressly provide that a participant's contributions are to be used to provide for the distributions during disability. Accordingly, it is presumed that B's contributions were not used to provide the accident or health benefits under the plan. Since these weekly payments are paid because of B's absence from work due to the injury, and since such payments are considered as attributable to contributions of his employer, such payments are required under section 105(a) to be included in B's gross income except to the extent that they are excludable under section 105(d). If B receives no other payments under a wage continuation plan attributable to contributions of his employer, during the first 30 days in the period of absence $75 of each weekly payment is excludable from gross income under section 105(d), but $50 of each weekly payment is includible in gross income under section 105(a). Amounts attributable to the period of absence in excess of 30 days are excludable from gross income under section 105(d) to the extent of $100 a week and includible in gross income under section 105(a) to the extent of $25 a week. The excludable portion of payments does not reduce B's investment in the contract or the amount of premiums considered to have been paid by B for purposes of any subsequent computations under section 72.

Example (3). The facts are the same as in example (2) except that B was absent from work for 130 weeks. At the time B was injured, his employer had contributed $10,000 to the plan on his account, and $6,000 of earnings of the plan had been allocated to his account. Thus, at the time he was injured, B's account included $21,000, and $14,000 of such amount consists of employer contributions of $10,000 plus earnings of $4,000 thereon. The first 112 weekly payments (totaling $14,000) which B receives are treated in the manner set forth in example (2). However, since the remaining payments exceed the employer contributions plus earnings thereon, such remaining payments are considered to be distributions of B's contributions plus earnings thereon. Since the total of such payments, or $2,250, is less than B's contributions to the plan, $5,000, the entire amount of such payments is excludable from B's gross income, but a corresponding adjustment with respect to the return of B's contributions shall be made to his consideration in determining the taxation of any lump sum paid to B upon separation from service.

(g) *Payments to or on behalf of a self-employed individual.* A self-employed individual is not considered an employee for purposes of section 105, relating to amounts received by employees under accident and health plans, nor for purposes of excluding under section 104(a)(3) amounts received by him under an accident and health plan as referred to in section 105(e). See section 105(g) and paragraph (a) of § 1.105-1. Therefore, the other paragraphs of this section are not applicable to amounts received by or on behalf of a self-employed individual. Except where accident or health benefits are provided through an insurance contract or an arrangement having the effect of insurance, all amounts received by or on behalf of a self-employed individual from a plan described in section 401(a) and exempt under section 501(a) or a plan described in section 403(a) shall be taxed as otherwise provided in section 72, 402, or 403. If the accident or health benefits are paid under an insurance contract or under an arrangement having the effect of insurance, section 104(a)(3) shall apply. Section 72 shall not apply to any amounts received under such circumstances. For the treatment of the amounts paid

Reg. § 1.72-15(g)

for such accident or health benefits, see section 404(e)(3) and paragraph (b) of § 1.404(e)-1.

(h) *Medical benefits for retired employees, etc.* Employer contributions to provide medical benefits described in section 401(h) under a qualified pension or annuity plan are not includible in the gross income of the employee on whose behalf such contributions were made. Similarly, if the trustee of a trust forming a part of a qualified pension plan applies employer contributions which have been contributed to provide medical benefits described in section 401(h) or earnings thereon, to purchase insurance contracts which provide such benefits, the amount so applied is not includible in the gross income of the employee on whose behalf such insurance was purchased. The payment of medical benefits described in section 401(h) as defined in paragraph (a) of § 1.401-14 under a plan established by an employer shall be treated in the same manner as the payment of any other accident or health benefits under an employer-established plan. See paragraphs (b), (c), and (d) of this section.

(i) *Special rules*—(1) *Special rule for taxable years ending before January 27, 1975.* A taxpayer who has reached retirement age, as defined in § 1.79-2(b)(3) (hereinafter referred to as "initial retirement age"), before January 27, 1975, and who has received payments under a plan described in paragraph (a) of this section, which are wage continuation benefits to which section 105(d) and this section apply, or which are treated as such by reason of the employee having so agreed under § 1.105-6, shall be entitled to an exclusion, in taxable years ending before January 27, 1975, with respect to payments received after initial retirement age but before mandatory retirement age, as defined in § 1.105-4(a)(3)(i)(B), which is the greater of:

(i) the amount actually excluded on an original return under section 72(b) or (d) with respect to payments received after initial retirement age, to the extent such amount does not exceed an amount properly excludable under section 72(b) or (d) if this paragraph and paragraph (b) of this section did not apply; or

(ii) the amount that would have been properly excludable under section 105(d) during the same period.

(2) *Investment in the annuity contract.* A taxpayer described in paragraph (i)(1) of this section shall redetermine his investment in, consideration for, or basis of his annuity contract (hereinafter referred to in this paragraph as the "investment in the contract") in accordance with the applicable rules of section 72 and the regulations thereunder, and the rules of this paragraph. In making such redetermination the taxpayer's

investment in his contract shall be decreased, by the excess (if any) of the amount which the taxpayer is entitled to exclude under paragraph (i)(1) of this section over the amount which could have been excluded under section 105(d) (subject to the limitations contained in such provision). Such investment in the contract shall be decreased only by the excess of the amount excluded under section 72 in taxable years ending before January 27, 1975, over the amount which could have been excluded under section 105(d) during the same period. For example, the investment in the contract shall not be decreased in the case of an individual who was retired from work on account of injury or sickness for a full taxable year, if the amount excluded under section 72 was less than $5,200, since the entire amount could have been excluded under section 105(d). On the other hand, if the amount excluded under section 72 was equal to or greater than $5,200 for a full taxable year, for example, $6,000 for the full taxable year, then $5,200 shall be treated as excluded under section 105(d) and the investment in the contract shall be reduced by $800 ($6,000 − $5,200).

(3) *Surviving annuitants and beneficiaries.* (i) The rights of a surviving annuitant or beneficiary, with respect to the application of the rules of section 72, shall be based on the employee's investment in his annuity contract, as adjusted in accordance with the provisions of this paragraph. Thus, where an employee dies after having recomputed his investment as provided in paragraph (i)(2) of this section, and his contract provided a survivorship element, the survivor would assume the employee' recomputed investment for purposes of determining excludability of amounts under section 72.

(ii) Where a beneficiary failed to increase the amount treated as an employee's contribution toward his annuity contract to reflect the employee death benefit under section 101(b) and § 1.72-8(b), because the employee had treated his initial retirement age as his annuity starting date, such beneficiary may apply section 101(b) as if the appropriate addition to basis had been made in the year of the employee's death, but only if the employee had not reached his mandatory retirement age (as defined in section 105-4(a)(3)(i)(B)). For purposes of this paragraph, the amount treated as the section 101(b) death benefit would be valued as of the date of the employee's death.

(4) *Records.* (i) For purposes of section 72(b) and (d), and this section, the taxpayer shall maintain such records as are necessary to substantiate the amount treated as his investment in his annuity contract.

(ii) The Commissioner may prescribe a form and instructions with respect to the taxpayer's past and current treatment of amounts received under section 72 or 105, and the tax-payer's computation, or recomputation, of his investment in his annuity contract. Such form may be required to be filed with the taxpayer's return for years in which amounts are excluded under section 72 or 105.

(5) *Cross references.* (i) See section 72(b)(4) and § 1.72-4(b) with respect to annuity starting dates.

(ii) See §§ 1.72-8(b) and 1.101-2(a)(2) with respect to treating certain amounts received by an estate or beneficiary as employee death benefits.

(iii) See § 1.105-4(a)(3)(i)(B) for the definition of "mandatory retirement age."

(iv) See § 1.105-6 with respect to the application of section 105(d) to certain amounts received as retirement annuities before January 27, 1975, where the employee would otherwise have been eligible for benefits to which section 105(d) applies.

(6) *Examples.* The provisions of this paragraph may be illustrated by the following examples. In such examples assume that the plan does not expressly provide that any portion of the disability pension is purchased with employee contributions. Accordingly, it is presumed that no portion of the disability pension is purchased with employee contributions. Also, assume that in each case the taxpayer retired only after he had been absent from work for at least 30 days on account of personal injuries or sickness.

Example (1). A, a calendar year taxpayer, retired because of disability on January 1, 1968, his 58th birthday, receiving $80 per week ($4,160 per year) under a plan which qualifies as a wage continuation plan under section 105(d) and § 1.105-4. Under the plan, A's initial retirement age is age 60 (January 1, 1970), and his mandatory retirement age is 65 (January 1, 1975). A's consideration for the contract was $10,000. For payments received in 1968 and 1969 A excluded the entire amount under section 105(d). Payments received with respect to periods after A's initial retirement age (January 1, 1970) were excluded under section 72(d) until his entire $10,000 consideration for his contract had been excluded. Thus, A applied section 72(d) to exclude

$4,160 each year for taxable years 1970 and 1971, and $1,680 ($10,000 − ($4,160 + $4,160)) for 1972. In late 1974 A realized that he was entitled to treat the full amount received under his annuity as excludable under section 105(d) rather than section 72 for the taxable years 1970 through 1974. Consequently, A filed amended returns for 1972 and 1973 excluding an additional $2,480 ($4,160 − $1,680) and $4,160, respectively, claiming refunds based upon such additional exclusions. Moreover, A's annuity starting date is January 1, 1975 (A's mandatory retirement age), and he excludes under section 72(d) for 1975, 1976, and 1977, $4,160, $4,160 and $1,680 ($10,000 − ($4,160 + $4,160)), respectively.

Example (2). B, a calendar year taxpayer retired because of disability, July 1, 1970, on his 58th birthday, receiving $1,000 per month under a plan which qualifies as a wage continuation plan for purposes of section 105(d) and § 1.105-4. Under the plan, B's initial retirement age is age 60 (July 1, 1972), and his mandatory retirement age is 65 (July 1, 1977). B's consideration for the contract was $25,000. For payments received in 1970 and 1971 B excluded under section 105(d) $2,600 and $5,200, respectively, of the $6,000 (6 × $1,000) and $12,000 (12 × $1,000) received under the plan. For the period January 1, 1972, through June 30, 1972, B excluded an additional $2,600 under section 105(d). For the period July 1, 1972 through December 31, 1972, B excluded under section 72(d)(1) the entire $6,000 in payments received under the plan. Similarly, under section 72(d)(1), B excluded the entire $12,000 in payments received under the plan in 1973, and in 1974 B excluded the remaining $7,000 of his annuity basis. In 1975, B realized that he will be entitled to take full advantage of the exclusion under section 105(d) for periods through June 30, 1977, when he would reach age 65. B need not file amended returns for 1972, 1973, and 1974, even though the amounts he excluded under section 72(d) exceeded the amount he was entitled to exclude under section 105(d). He must, however, recompute the amount that will be treated as his investment in his annuity contract. Thus, on July 1, 1977, B's annuity starting date, his investment in his annuity contract would be $13,000, recomputed as follows:

B's original investment	$25,000
Less amounts excluded under section 72 to the extent they exceed amounts that would have been excludable during the same period uner section 105(d):	
1972 ($6,000 − 2,600) . . . . $ 3,400	
1973 ($12,000 − 5,200) 6,800	
1974 ($7,000 − 5,200) 1,800	
Total	$12,000
B's recomputed investment in his annuity contract	$13,000

Reg. § 1.72-15(i)(5)

Example (3). Assume the same facts as in example (2) except that B's investment in his annuity contract is $37,000, and he excluded under section 72(b) 16.9 percent, or $2,028, of the $12,000 received per year. Thus, for the period July 1, 1972 through December 31, 1972, B excluded under section 72(b) $1,014 (16.9 percent of $6,000), and $2,028 in both 1973 and 1974. B files amended returns for 1972, 1973, and 1974 claiming the exclusion under section 105(d). Thus, B restored to income $1,014 for 1972, and $2,028 for both 1973 and 1974, claiming $2,600 ($5,200 − $2,600) exclusion under section 105(d) for 1972 and a $5,200 exclusion in both 1973 and 1974. Thus, for 1972 B is entitled to an additional exclusion of $1,586 ($2,600 − $1,014), and, for both 1973 and 1974, an additional exclusion of $3,172 ($5,200 − $2,028). On July 1, 1977, B's investment in the contract is $37,000.

Example (4). C, a calendar year taxpayer, retired because of disability on January 1, 1965, his 58th birthday, receiving payments of $500 per month under a plan which qualifies as a wage continuation plan for purposes of section 105(d) and § 1.105-4. C had contributed $18,000 toward the cost of his annuity contract. Under the plan, C's initial retirement age is age 60 (January 1, 1967) and C's mandatory retirement age is age 70 (January 1, 1977). For taxable years 1965 and 1966 C excluded from gross income under section 105(d) $5,200 of the $6,000 (12 × $500) he received from his employer as wage continuation benefits. On January 1, 1967, C began excluding all of the benefits C received in accordance with the rules of section 72(d). Thus, for 1967, 1968 and 1969, C excluded 100 percent of the annuity payments. For his taxable years 1970 through 1973, C included in his gross income all annuity payments. In 1974, C realized that he will be entitled to use the exclusion under section 105(d) through December 31, 1976 (until he reaches age 70). In 1974, C filed a timely claim for refund for his taxable years 1971, 1972 and 1973 (refunds for taxable year 1970 and prior years were barred by the statute of limitations), and continues to claim the exclusion under section 105(d) for 1974, 1975 and 1976. For 1977, C treats January 1, 1977, as the annuity starting date, and treats $15,600 as the investment in the contract. The $15,600 represents the $18,000 original investment in the contract reduced by the excess, $2,400, of the amount excluded under section 72 for 1967, 1968 and 1969 ($18,000) over the amount excludable under section 105(d) ($5,200 × 3) for such years.

Example (5). (i) D, a calendar year taxpayer, retired because of disability on June 30, 1965, receiving $100 per month under a plan which qualifies as a wage continuation plan for purposes of section 105(d) and § 1.105-4. Under the plan, the initial retirement age of D, whose birthday is January 1, is age 60 (January 1, 1967), and D's mandatory retirement age is age 70 (January 1, 1977). D had contributed $6,000 toward the cost of the annuity contract under such plan. For 1965 and 1966, D excluded under section 105(d) the entire amount received under the plan ($600 and $1,200 respectively). For 1967 through 1973, D excluded $330 per year under section 72(b), or 27.5 percent of the $1,200 payment received under the plan per year.

(ii) In 1974, D realized that he will be entitled to use the exclusion provided in section 105(d) up until January 1, 1977, when he reaches his mandatory retirement age, and that he improperly applied section 72 to payments received in the years 1967 through 1973. In 1974, D filed a timely claim for refund with respect to the section 105(d) wage continuation benefits, for 1971, 1972 and 1973 (refunds for taxable year 1970 and prior years were barred by the statute of limitations), and continues to claim the section 105(d) exclusion for 1974, 1975 and 1976. D is entitled to an additional exclusion of $870 ($1,200 − $330) for each of the years 1971, 1972 and 1973.

(iii) Upon reaching mandatory retirement age on January 1, 1977, D treats such date as the annuity starting date, and treats $6,000 as the investment in the contract. The investment in the contract is not reduced, because the amount excluded under section 72(b) for 1967 through 1970 ($330 per year) does not exceed the amount excludable under section 105(d) ($1,200 per year), and the $330 per year excluded for 1971, 1972, and 1973 were restored to the investment in the contract. Therefore, assuming that D would be entitled to exclude 41.3 percent of the payments under the plan if the annuity starting date is January 1, 1977, D would be entitled to exclude $495.60 (41.3 percent of $1,200) per annum.

Example (6). Assume the facts stated in example (5) except that D's investment in his annuity contract is $100,000 and he received payments equaling $10,000 per year. Assume also, that D had excluded under section 72(b) 54.9 percent of the payments received under the plan through 1974. Consequently, he excluded $5,490 (54.9 percent of $10,000) from his gross income for the years 1967 through 1974. D need not file amended returns for 1971, 1972, 1973, and 1974, even though the amount he excluded under section 72(b) exceeded the amounts he was entitled to exclude under section 105(d). He must, however, recompute the amount that will be treated as his investment in his annuity contract. Thus, on January 1, 1977, D's annuity starting date, his investment in his annuity contract would be $97,680. This figure represents the original investment ($100,000) reduced by the amount excluded under section 72(b) for the years 1967-1974 (8 × $5,490 = $43,920) over the amount properly excludable during those years under section 105(d) ($5,200 × 8 = $41,600).

Example (7). Assume the same facts as in example (6) except that D's mandatory retirement age is 63 (January 1, 1970). D would redetermine his exclusion ratio for purposes of section 72(b) as of January 1, 1970, since D's mandatory retirement age is D's annuity starting date. D would treat $99,130 as his investment in his annuity contract as of such date for purposes of section 72(b). Assuming refunds for 1970 and prior taxable years were barred by the statute of limitations, the $99,130 represents the original investment of $100,000 reduced by the excess of the amount excluded under section 72(b) for 1967, 1968, and 1969 ($5,490 × 3 = $16,470) over the amount otherwise excludable during those years under section 105(d) ($5,200 × 3 = $15,600). Therefore, assuming that D would be entitled to exclude 61.2 of the payments received under the plan if the annuity starting date is January 1, 1970, D would be entitled to exclude $6,120 (61.2 percent of the $10,000 received under the plans) per annum for 1971 and subsequent years. However, D is not entitled to exclude the additional $630 ($6,120 − $5,490) for 1970, because credit or refund for 1970 and prior years is barred by the statute of limitations. [Reg. § 1.72-15.]

□ [*T.D. 6485, 7-29-60. Amended by T.D. 6676, 9-16-63, T.D. 6722, 4-13-64, T.D. 6770, 11-16-64 and T.D. 7352, 4-9-75.*]

[Reg. § 1.72-16]

§ 1.72-16. Life insurance contracts purchased under qualified employee plans.—(a) *Applicability of section.* This section provides rules for the tax treatment of premiums paid under qualified pension, annuity, or profit-sharing plans for the purchase of life insurance contracts and rules for the tax treatment of the proceeds of such a life insurance contract and of annuity contracts purchased under such plans. For purposes of this section, the term "life insurance contract" means a retirement income, an endowment, or other contract providing life insurance protection. The rules of this section apply to plans covering only common-law employees as well as to plans covering self-employed individuals.

(b) *Treatment of cost of life insurance protection.* (1) The rules of this paragraph are applicable to any life insurance contract—

(i) Purchased as a part of a plan described in section 403(a), or

(ii) Purchased by a trust described in section 401(a) which is exempt from tax under section 501(a) if the proceeds of such contract are payable directly or indirectly to a participant in such trust or to a beneficiary of such participant.

The proceeds of a contract described in subdivision (ii) of this subparagraph will be considered payable indirectly to a participant or beneficiary of such participant where they are payable to the trustee but under the terms of the plan the trustee is required to pay over all of such proceeds to the beneficiary.

(2) If under a plan or trust described in subparagraph (1) of this paragraph, amounts which were allowed as a deduction under section 404, or earnings of the trust, are applied toward the purchase of a life insurance contract described in subparagraph (1) of this paragraph, the cost of the life insurance protection under such contract shall be included in the gross income of the participant for the taxable year or years in which such contributions or earnings are so applied.

(3) If the amount payable upon death at any time during the year exceeds the cash value of the insurance policy at the end of the year, the entire amount of such excess is considered current life insurance protection. The cost of such insurance will be considered to be a reasonable net premium cost, as determined by the Commissioner, for such amount of insurance for the appropriate period.

(4) The amount includible in the gross income of the employee under this paragraph shall be considered as premiums or other consideration paid or contributed by the employee only with respect to any benefits attributable to the contract (within the meaning of paragraph (a)(3) of § 1.72-2) providing the life insurance protection. However, if under the rules of this paragraph an owner-employee is required to include any amounts in his gross income, such amounts shall not in any case be treated as part of his investment in the contract.

(5) The determination of the cost of life insurance protection may be illustrated by the following example:

Example. An annual premium policy purchased by a qualified trust for a common-law employee provides an annuity of $100 per month upon retirement at age 65, with a minimum death benefit of $10,000. The insurance payable if death occurred in the first year would be $10,000. The cash value at the end of the first year is 0. The net insurance is therefore $10,000 minus 0, or $10,000. Assuming that the Commissioner has determined that a reasonable net premium cost for the employee's age is $5.85 per $1,000, the premium for $10,000 of life insurance is therefore $58.50, and this is the amount to be reported as income by the employee for his taxable year in which the premium is paid. The balance of the premium is the amount contributed for the annuity, which is not taxable to the employee under a plan meeting the requirements of section 401(a), except as provided under section 402(a). Assuming that the cash value at the end of the second year is $500, the net insurance would then be $9,500 for the second year. With a net 1-year term rate of $6.30 for the employee's age in the second year, the amount to be reported as income to the employee would be $59.85.

(6) This paragraph shall not apply if the trust has a right under any circumstances to retain any part of the proceeds of the life insurance contract. But see paragraph (c)(4) of this section relating to the taxability of the distribution of such proceeds to a beneficiary.

(c) *Treatment of proceeds of life insurance and annuity contracts.* (1) If under a qualified pension, annuity, or profit-sharing plan, there is purchased either—

(i) A life insurance contract described in paragraph (b)(1) of this section, and the employee either paid the cost of the insurance or was taxable on the cost of the insurance under paragraph (b) of this section, or

(ii) An annuity contract,

the amounts payable under any such contract by reason of the death of the employee are taxable under the rules of subparagraph (2) of this paragraph, except in the case of a joint and survivor annuity.

(2)(i) In the case of an annuity contract, the death benefit is the accumulation of the premiums (plus earnings thereon) which is intended to fund pension or other deferred benefits under a pension, annuity, or profit-sharing plan. Such death benefits are not in the nature of life insurance and are not excludable from gross income under section 101(a).

(ii) In the case of a life insurance contract under which there is a reserve accumulation which is intended to fund pension or other deferred benefits under a pension, annuity, or profit-sharing plan, such reserve accumulation constitutes the source of the cash value of the contract and approximates the amount of such cash value. The portion of the proceeds paid upon the death of the insured employee which is equal to the cash value immediately before death is not excludable from gross income under section 101(a). The remaining portion, if any, of the proceeds paid to the beneficiary by reason of the death of the insured employee—that is, the amount in excess of the cash value—constitutes current insurance protection and is excludable under section 101(a).

(iii) The death benefit under an annuity contract, or the portion of the death proceeds under a life insurance contract which is equal to the cash value of the contract immediately before death, constitutes a distribution under the plan consisting in whole or in part of deferred compensation and is taxable to the beneficiary in accordance with section 72(m)(3) and the provisions of this paragraph, except to the extent that the limited exclusion from income provided in section 101(b) is applicable.

(iv) In the case of a life insurance contract under which the benefits are paid at a date or dates later than the death of the employee, section 101(d) is applicable only to the portion of the benefits which is attributable to the amount excludable under section 101(a). The portion of such benefits which is attributable to the cash value of the contract immediately before death is taxable under section 72, and in such case, any amount excludable under section 101(b) is treated as additional consideration paid by the employee in accordance with section 101(b)(2)(D).

(3) The application of the rules under subparagraph (2) of this paragraph with respect to the taxability of proceeds of a life insurance contract paid by reason of the death of an insured common-law employee who has paid no contributions under the plan is illustrated by the following examples:

Example (1).

Total face amount of the contract payable in a lump sum at time of death	$25,000
Cash value of the contract immediately before death	11,000
Excess over cash value, excludable under section 101(a)	$14,000
Cash value subject to limited exclusion under section 101(b)	$11,000
Excludable under section 101(b) (assuming that there is no other death benefit paid by or on behalf of any employer with respect to the employee)	5,000

Balance taxable in accordance with section 402(a)(2) or 403(a)(2) (assuming a total distribution in one taxable year of the distributee) .... $ 6,000

Portion of premiums taxed to employee under the provisions of paragraph (b) of this section and considered as contributions of the employee 940

Balance taxable as long-term capital gain .... $ 5,060

Example (2). The facts are the same as in example (1), except that the contract provides that the beneficiary may elect within 60 days after the death of the employee either to take the $25,000 or to receive 10 annual installments of $3,000 each, and the beneficiary elects to receive the 10 installments. In addition, the employee's rights to the cash value immediately before his death were forfeitable at least to the extent of $5,000. Section 101(d) is applicable to the amount excludable under section 101(a), that is, $14,000. The portion of each annual installment of $3,000 which is attributable to this $14,000 is determined by allocating each installment in accordance with the ratio which this $14,000 bears to

the total amount which was payable at death ($25,000). Accordingly, the portion of each annual installment which is subject to section 101(d) is $1,680 (14/25 of $3,000), of which $1,400 (1/10 of $14,000) is excludable under section 101(a), and the remaining $280 is includable in the gross income of the beneficiary. However, if the beneficiary is a surviving spouse as defined in section 101(d)(3), the exclusion provided by section 101(d)(1)(B) is applicable to such $280. The remaining portion of each annual $3,000 installment, $1,320, is attributable to the cash value of the contract and is treated under section 72, as follows:

Amount actually contributed by the employee .... $ 0

Amount considered contributed by employee by reason of section 101(b) 5,000

Portion of premiums taxed to employee under the provisions of paragraph (b) of this section and considered as contributions of the employee 940

Investment in the contract .... $ 5,940

Expected return, 10 × $1,320 .... $13,200

Exclusion ratio, $5,940 ÷ $13,200 .... 0.45

Annual exclusion, 0.45 × $1,320 .... $ 594

Accordingly, $594 of the $1,320 portion of each annual installment is excludable each year under section 72, and the remaining $726 is includible. Thus, if the beneficiary is not a surviving spouse, a total of $1,006 ($280 plus $726) of each annual $3,000 installment is includible in income each year. If the beneficiary is a surviving spouse, and can exclude all of the $280 under section 101(d)(1)(B), the amount includible in gross income each year is $726 of each annual $3,000 installment.

(4) If an employee neither paid the total cost of the life insurance protection provided under a life insurance contract, nor was taxable under paragraph (b) of this section with respect thereto, no part of the proceeds of such a contract which are paid to the beneficiaries of the employee as a death benefit is excludable under section 101(a). The entire distribution is taxable to the beneficiaries under section 402(a) or 403(a) except to the extent that a limited exclusion may be allowable under section 101(b). [Reg. § 1.72-16.]

☐ [*T.D.* 6676, 9-16-63.]

[Reg. § 1.72-17]

§ 1.72-17. Special rules applicable to owner-employees.—(a) *In general.* Under section 401(c) and section 403(a), certain self-employed individ-

uals may participate in qualified pension, annuity, and profit-sharing plans, and the amounts received by such individuals from such plans are taxable under section 72. Section 72(m) and this section contain special rules for the taxation of amounts received from qualified pension, profit-sharing, or annuity plans covering an owner-employee. For purposes of section 72 and the regulations thereunder, the term "employee" shall include the self-employed individual who is treated as an employee by section 401(c)(1) (see paragraph (b) of § 1.401-10), and the term "owner-employee" has the meaning assigned to it in section 401(c)(3) (see paragraph (d) of § 1.401-10). See also paragraph (a)(2) of § 1.401-10 for the rule for determining when a plan covers an owner-employee. For purposes of this section, a self-employed individual may not treat as consideration for the contract contributed by the employee any contributions under the plan for which deductions were allowed under section 404 and which, consequently, are considered employer contributions.

(b) *Certain amounts received before annuity starting date.*—(1) The rules of this paragraph are applicable to amounts received from a qualified pension, profit-sharing, or annuity plan by an employee (or his beneficiary) who is or was an owner-employee with respect to such plan when such amounts—

    (i) Are received before the annuity starting date; and

    (ii) Are not received as an annuity.

For the definition of annuity starting date, see paragraph (b) of § 1.72-4 and subparagraph (4) of this paragraph. As to what constitutes amounts not received as an annuity, see paragraphs (c) and (d) of § 1.72-11.

    (2) Amounts to which this paragraph applies shall be included in the recipient's gross income for the taxable year in which received. However, the sum of the amounts so included under this subparagraph in all taxable years shall not exceed the aggregate deductions allowed under section 404 for premiums or other consideration paid under the plan on behalf of the employee while he was an owner-employee, including any such deductions taken in the taxable year of receipt.

    (3) Any amounts to which this paragraph applies and which are not includible in gross income under the rules of subparagraph (2) of this paragraph shall be subject to the provisions of section 72(e) and § 1.72-11. However, for taxable years beginning before January 1, 1964, section 72(e)(3), as in effect before such date, shall not apply to such amounts. For taxable years beginning after December 31, 1963, such amounts (other than amounts subject to a penalty under section 72(m)(5) and paragraph (e) of this section) may be taken into account in computations under sections 1301 through 1305 (relating to income averaging).

    (4) Under section 401(d)(4), a qualified pension, profit sharing, or annuity plan may not provide for distributions to an owner-employee before he reaches age 59½ years, except in the case of his earlier disability. Therefore, in the case of a distribution from a qualified plan to an individual for whom contributions have been made to the plan as an owner-employee, the annuity starting date cannot be prior to the time such individual attains the age 59½ years unless he is entitled to benefits before reaching such age because of his disability. For taxable years beginning after December 31, 1966, see section 72(m)(7) and paragraph (f) of this section for the meaning of disabled. For taxable years beginning before January 1, 1967, see section 213(g)(3) for the meaning of disabled.

    (5) The rules of this paragraph are not applicable to amounts credited to an individual in his capacity as a policyholder of an annuity, endowment, or life insurance contract which are in the nature of a dividend or refund of premium, and which are applied in accordance with paragraph (a)(4) of § 1.404(a)-8 towards the purchase of benefits under the policy.

    (6) The rules of this paragraph may be illustrated by the following example:

    Example. B, a self-employed individual, received $8,000 as a distribution under a qualified pension plan before the annuity starting date. At the time of such distribution, $10,000 had been contributed (the whole amount being allowed as a deduction) under the plan on behalf of such individual while he was a common-law employee and $5,000 had been contributed under the plan on his behalf while he was an owner-employee, of which $2,500 was allowed as a deduction. In addition, B had contributed $1,000 on his own behalf as an employee under the plan. Of the $8,000, $2,500 (the amount allowed as a deduction with respect to contributions on behalf of the individual while he was an owner-employee) is includible in gross income under subparagraph (2) of this paragraph. With respect to the remaining $5,500, B has a basis of $3,500, consisting of the $2,500 contributed on his behalf while he was an owner-employee which was not allowed as a deduction and the $1,000 which B contributed as an employee. The difference between the $5,500 and B's basis of $3,500, or $2,000, is includible in gross income under section 72(e).

    (c) *Amounts paid for life, accident, health, or other insurance.* Amounts used to purchase life, accident, health, or other insurance protection for an owner-employee shall not be taken into account in computing the following:

    (1) The aggregate amount of premiums or other consideration paid for the contract for purposes of determining the investment in the contract under section 72(c)(1)(A) and § 1.72-6;

    (2) The consideration for the contract contributed by the employee for purposes of section 72(d)(1) and § 1.72-13, which provide the method of taxing employees' annuities where the employees's contributions will be recoverable within 3 years; and

    (3) The aggregate premiums or other consideration paid for purposes of section 72(e)(1)(B) and § 1.72-11, which provide the rules for taxing amounts not received as annuities prior to the annuity starting date.

The cost of such insurance protection will be considered to be a reasonable net premium cost, as determined by the Commissioner, for the appropriate period.

    (d) *Amounts constructively received.* (1) If during any taxable year an owner-employee assigns or pledges (or agrees to assign or pledge) any portion of his interest in a trust described in section 401(a) which is exempt from tax under section 501(a), or any portion of the value of a contract purchased as part of a plan described in section 403(a), such portion shall be treated as having been received by such owner-employee as a distribution from the trust or as an amount received under the contract during such taxable year.

(2) If during any taxable year an owner-employee receives, either directly or indirectly, any amount from any insurance company as a loan under a contract purchased by a trust described in section 401(a) which is exempt from tax under section 501(a) or purchased as part of a plan described in section 403(a), and issued by such insurance company, such amount shall be treated as an amount received under the contract during such taxable year. An owner-employee will be considered to have received an amount under a contract if a premium, which is otherwise in default, is paid by the insurance company in the form of a loan against the cash surrender value of the contract. Further, an owner-employee will be considered to have received an amount to which this subparagraph applies if an amount is received from the issuer of a face-amount certificate as a loan under such a certificate purchased as part of a qualified trust or plan.

(e) *Penalties applicable to certain amounts received by owner-employees.* (1)(i) The rules of this paragraph are applicable to amounts, to the extent includible in gross income, received from a trust described in section 401(a) or under a plan described in section 403(a) by or on behalf of an individual who is or has been an owner-employee with respect to such plan or trust—

(a) Which are received before the owner-employee reaches the age 59½ years and which are attributable to contributions paid on behalf of such owner-employee (whether or not paid by him) while he was an owner-employee (see subdivision (ii) of this subparagraph),

(b) Which are in excess of the benefits provided for such owner-employee under the plan formula (see subdivision (iii) of this subparagraph), or

(c) Which are received by reason of a distribution of the owner-employee's entire interest under the provisions of section 401(e)(2)(E), relating to excess contributions on behalf of an owner-employee which are willfully made.

(ii) The amounts referred to in subdivision (i)(a) of this subparagraph do not include—

(a) Amounts received by reason of the owner-employee becoming disabled, or

(b) Amounts received by the owner-employee in his capacity as a policyholder of an annuity, endowment, or life insurance contract which are in the nature of a dividend or similar distribution.

Amounts attributable to contributions paid on behalf of an owner-employee and which are paid to a person other than the owner-employee before the owner-employee dies or reaches the age 59½ shall be considered received by the owner-employee for purposes of this paragraph. For taxable years beginning after December 31, 1966, see section 72(m)(7) and paragraph (f) of this section for the meaning of disabled. For taxable years beginning before January 1, 1967, see section 213(g)(3) for the meaning of disabled. For taxable years beginning after December 31, 1968, if an amount is not included in the amounts referred to in subdivision (i)(a) of this subparagraph solely by reason of the owner-employee becoming disabled and if a penalty would otherwise be applicable with respect to all or a portion of such amount, then for the taxable year in which such amount is received, there must be submitted with the owner-employee's income tax return a doctor's statement as to the impairment, and a statement by the owner-employee with respect to the effect of such impairment upon his substantial gainful activity and the date such impairment occurred. For taxable years which are subsequent to the first taxable year beginning after December 31, 1968, with respect to which the statements referred to in the preceding sentence are submitted, the owner-employee may, in lieu of such statements, submit a statement declaring the continued existence (without substantial diminution) of the impairment and its continued effect upon his substantial gainful activity.

(iii) This paragraph applies to amounts described in subdivision (i) (b) of this subparagraph (relating to excess benefits) even though a portion of such amounts may be attributable to contributions made on behalf of an individual while he was not an owner-employee and even though the amounts are received by his successor. However, these amounts do not include the portion of a distribution to which section 402(a)(2) or 403(a)(2) (relating to certain total distributions in one taxable year) applies.

(iv)(a) For purposes of subdivision (i) (a) of this subparagraph, the portion of any distribution or payment attributable to contributions on behalf of an employee-participant while he was an owner-employee includes the contributions made on his behalf while he was an owner-employee and the increments in value attributable to such contributions.

Reg. § 1.72-17(d)(2)

(b) The increments in value of an individual's account may be allocated to contributions on his behalf while he was an owner-employee either by maintaining a separate account, or an accounting, which reflects the actual increment attributable to such contributions, or by the method described in (c) of this subdivision.

(c) Where an individual is covered under the same plan both as an owner-employee and as a nonowner-employee, the portion of the increment in value of his interest attributable to contributions made on his behalf while he was an owner-employee may be determined by multiplying the total increment in value in his account by a fraction. The numerator of the fraction is the total contributions made on behalf of the individual as an owner-employee, weighted for the number of years that each contribution was in the plan. The denominator is the total contributions made on behalf of the individual, whether or not an owner-employee, weighted for the number of years each contribution was in the plan. The contributions are weighted for the number of years in the plan by multiplying each contribution by the number of years it was in the plan. For purposes

of this computation, any forfeiture allocated to the account of the individual is treated as a contribution to the account made at the time so allocated.

(d) The method described in (c) of this subdivision may be illustrated by the following example:

Example. B was a member of the XYZ Partnership and a participant in the partnership's profit-sharing plan which was created in 1963. Until the end of 1967, B's interest in the partnership was less than 10 percent. On January 1, 1968, B obtained an interest in excess of 10 percent in the partnership and continued to participate in the profit-sharing plan until 1972. During 1972, prior to the time he attained the age of $59\frac{1}{2}$ years and during a time when he was not disabled, B withdrew his entire interest in the profit-sharing plan. At that time his interest was $15,000, $9,600 contributions and $5,400 increment attributable to the contributions. The portion of the increment attributable to contributions while B was an owner-employee is $667.80, determined as follows:

	A	B	C
	Contribution	No. of years contribution was in trust	Contribution weighted for years In trust (A × B)
1972	$1,000	0	0
1971	800	1	$ 800
1970	1,200	2	2,400
1969	600	3	1,800
1968	200	4	800
1967	400	5	2,000
1966	2,000	6	12,000
1965	1,000	7	7,000
1964	1,500	8	12,000
1963	900	9	8,100
	$9,600		$46,900

Total weighted contributions as owner-employee
(1968-1972) — $5,800
Total weighted contributions — $46,900

$$\frac{5,400 \times 5,800}{46,900} = 667.80$$

(2)(i) If the aggregate of the amounts to which this paragraph applies received by any person in his taxable year equals or exceeds $2,500, the tax with respect to such amount shall be the greater of—

(a) The increase in tax attributable to the inclusion of the amounts so received in his gross income for the taxable year in which received, or

(b) 110 percent of the aggregate increase in taxes, for such taxable year and the four immediately preceding taxable years, which

would have resulted if such amounts had been included in such person's gross income ratably over such taxable years. However, if deductions were allowed under section 404 for contributions to the plan on behalf of the individual as an owner-employee for less than four prior taxable years (whether or not consecutive), the number of immediately preceding taxable years taken into account shall be the number of prior taxable years in which such deductions were allowed.

(ii) If the aggregate of the amounts to which this paragraph applies received by any person in his taxable year is less than $2,500, the

Reg. § 1.72-17(e)(2)

tax with respect to such amounts shall be 110 percent of the increase in tax which results from including such amounts in the person's gross income for the taxable year in which received.

(3)(i) For purposes of making the ratable inclusion computations of subparagraph (2) (i) of this paragraph, the taxable income of the recipient for each taxable year involved (notwithstanding section 63, relating to definition of taxable income) shall be treated as being not less than the amount required to be treated as includible in the taxable year pursuant to the ratable inclusion.

(ii) For purposes of subparagraph (2) (i) (a) and (ii) of this paragraph, the recipient's taxable income (notwithstanding section 63, relating to definition of taxable income) shall be treated as being not less than the aggregate of the amounts to which this paragraph applies reduced by the deductions allowed the recipient for such taxable year under section 151 (relating to deductions for personal exemptions).

(iii) In any case in which the application of subdivision (i) or (ii) of this subparagraph results in an increase in taxable income for any taxable year, the resulting increase in taxes imposed by section 1 or 3 for such taxable year shall be reduced by the credits against tax provided by section 31 (tax withheld on wages) and section 39 (certain uses of gasoline and lubricating oil), but shall not be reduced by any other credits against tax.

(4) The application of the rules of subparagraphs (2) (i) and (3) of this paragraph may be illustrated by the following example:

Example. B, a sole proprietor and a calendar-year basis taxpayer, established a qualified pension trust to which he made annual contributions for 10 years of 10 percent of his earned income. B withdrew his entire interest in the trust during 1973 when he was 55 years old and not disabled and for which, without regard to the distribution, he had a net operating loss and for which he is allowed under section 151 a deduction for one personal exemption. The portion of the distribution includible in B's gross income is $25,750. In addition, B had a net operating loss for 1972. The other three taxable years involved in the computation under subparagraph (2)(i) of this paragraph were years of substantial income. For purposes of determining B's increase in tax attributable to the receipt of the $25,750 (before the application of the provisions of subparagraph (2)(i)(b) of this paragraph), B's taxable income for the year he received the $25,750 is treated, under subparagraph (3)(ii) of this paragraph, as being $25,000 ($25,750 minus $750, the amount of the deduction allowed for each personal exemp-

tion under section 151 for 1973). For purposes of determining whether 110 percent of the aggregate increase in taxes which would have resulted if 20 percent of the amount of the withdrawal had been included in B's gross income for the year of receipt and for each of the 4 preceding taxable years is greater (and thus is the amount of his increase in tax attributable to the receipt of the $25,750), B's taxable income for the taxable year of receipt, and for the immediately preceding taxable year, is treated, under subparagraph (3)(i) of this paragraph, as being $5,150 ($25,750 divided by 5).

(f) *Meaning of disabled.* (1) For taxable years beginning after December 31, 1966, section 72(m)(7) provides that an individual shall be considered to be disabled if he is unable to engage in any substantial gainful activity by reason of any medically determinable physical or mental impairment which can be expected to result in death or to be of long-continued and indefinite duration. In determining whether an individual's impairment makes him unable to engage in any substantial gainful activity, primary consideration shall be given to the nature and severity of his impairment. Consideration shall also be given to other factors such as the individual's education, training, and work experience. The substantial gainful activity to which section 72(m)(7) refers is the activity, or a comparable activity, in which the individual customarily engaged prior to the arising of the disability (or prior to retirement if the individual was retired at the time the disability arose).

(2) Whether or not the impairment in a particular case constitutes a disability is to be determined with reference to all the facts in the case. The following are examples of impairments which would ordinarily be considered as preventing substantial gainful activity:

(i) Loss of use of two limbs;

(ii) Certain progressive diseases which have resulted in the physical loss or atrophy of a limb, such as diabetes, multiple sclerosis, or Buerger's disease;

(iii) Diseases of the heart, lungs, or blood vessels which have resulted in major loss of heart or lung reserve as evidenced by X-ray, electrocardiogram, or other objective findings, so that despite medical treatment breathlessness, pain, or fatigue is produced on slight exertion, such as walking several blocks, using public transportation, or doing small chores;

(iv) Cancer which is inoperable and progressive;

(v) Damage to the brain or brain abnormality which has resulted in severe loss of judgment, intellect, orientation, or memory;

Reg. § 1.72-17(e)(3)

(vi) Mental diseases (e.g. psychosis or severe psychoneurosis) requiring continued institutionalization or constant supervision of the individual;

(vii) Loss or diminution of vision to the extent that the affected individual has a central visual acuity of no better than 20/200 in the better eye after best correction, or has a limitation in the fields of vision such that the widest diameter of the visual fields subtends an angle no greater than 20 degrees;

(viii) Permanent and total loss of speech;

(ix) Total deafness uncorrectible by a hearing aid.

The existence of one or more of the impairments described in this subparagraph (or of an impairment of greater severity) will not, however, in and of itself always permit a finding that an individual is disabled as defined in section 72(m)(7). Any impairment, whether of lesser or greater severity, must be evaluated in terms of whether it does in fact prevent the individual from engaging in his customary or any comparable substantial gainful activity.

(3) In order to meet the requirements of section 72(m)(7), an impairment must be expected either to continue for a long and indefinite period or to result in death. Ordinarily, a terminal illness because of disease or injury would result in disability. Indefinite is used in the sense that it cannot reasonably be anticipated that the impairment will, in the foreseeable future, be so diminished as no longer to prevent substantial gainful activity. For example, an individual who suffers a bone fracture which prevents him from working for an extended period of time will not be considered disabled, if his recovery can be expected in the foreseeable future; if the fracture persistently fails to knit, the individual would ordinarily be considered disabled.

(4) An impairment which is remediable does not constitute a disability within the meaning of section 72(m)(7). An individual will not be deemed disabled if, with reasonable effort and safety to himself, the impairment can be diminished to the extent that the individual will not be prevented by the impairment from engaging in his customary or any comparable substantial gainful activity.

(g) *Years to which this section applies.* This section applies to taxable years ending before September 3, 1974. For taxable years ending after September 2, 1974, see § 1.72-17A. [Reg. § 1.72-17.]

□ [*T.D.* 6676, 9-16-63. *Amended by T.D.* 6885, 6-1-66, *T.D.* 6985, 12-26-68, *T.D.* 7114, 5-17-71 and *T.D.* 7636, 8-9-79.]

[Reg. § 1.72-17A]

§ 1.72-17A. Special rules applicable to employee annuities and distributions under deferred compensation plans to self-employed individuals and owner-employees.—(a) *In general.* Section 72(m) and this section contain special rules for the taxation of amounts received from qualified pension, profit-sharing, or annuity plans covering an owner-employee. This section applies to such amounts for taxable years of the recipient ending after September 2, 1974, unless another date is specified. For purposes of this section, the term "employee" shall include the self-employed individual who is treated as an employee by section 401(c)(1), and the term "owner-employee" has the meaning assigned to it in section 401(c)(3). Paragraph (b) of this section provides rules dealing with the computation of consideration paid by self-employed individuals and paragraph (c) of this section provides rules dealing with such computation when insurance is purchased for owner-employees. Paragraph (d) of this section provides rules for constructive receipt and, for purposes of these rules, treats as an owner-employee an individual for whose benefit an individual retirement account or annuity described in section 408(a) or (b) is maintained after December 31, 1974. Paragraph (e) of this section provides rules for penalties provided by section 72(m)(5) with respect to certain distributions received by owner-employees or their successors. Paragraph (f) of this section provides rules for determining whether a person is disabled within the meaning of section 72(m)(7). See § 1.72-16, relating to life insurance contracts purchased under qualified employee plans, for rules under section 72(m)(3).

(b) *Computation of consideration paid by self-employed individuals.* Under section 72(m)(2), consideration paid or contributed for the contract by any self-employed individual shall for purposes of section 72 be deemed not to include any contributions paid or contributed under a plan described in paragraph (a), or any other plan of deferred compensation described in section 404(a) (whether or not qualified), if the contributions are—

(1) Paid under such plan with respect to a time during which the employee was an employee only by reason of sections 401(c)(1) and 404(a)(8), and

(2) Deductible under section 404 by the employer, including an employer within the meaning of sections 401(c)(4) and 404(a)(8), of such self-

employed individual at the time of such payment, or subsequent to such time of payment.

For purposes of this paragraph the term "consideration paid or contributed for the contract" has the same meaning as under subparagraphs (1), (2), and (3) of paragraph (c) of this section.

(c) *Amounts paid for life, accident, health, or other insurance.* Under section 72(m)(2), amounts used to purchase life, accident, health, or other insurance protection for an owner-employee shall not be taken into account in computing the following:

(1) The aggregate amount of premiums or other consideration paid for the contract for purposes of determining the investment in the contract under section 72(c)(1)(A) and § 1.72-6;

(2) The consideration for the contract contributed by the employee for purposes of section 72(d)(1) and § 1.72-13, which provide the method of taxing employee's annuities where the employee's contributions will be recoverable within 3 years; and

(3) The aggregate premiums or other consideration paid for purposes of section 72(e)(1)(B) and § 1.72-11, which provide the rules for taxing amounts not received as annuities prior to the annuity starting date.

The cost of such insurance protection will be considered to be a reasonable net premium cost, as determined by the Commissioner, for the appropriate period.

(d) *Amounts constructively received.*—(1) The references in this paragraph (d) to section 72(m)(4) are to that section as in effect on August 13, 1982. Section 236(b)(1) of the Tax Equity and Fiscal Responsibility Act of 1982 (96 Stat. 324) repealed section 72(m)(4), generally effective for assignments, pledges and loans made after August 13, 1982, and added section 72(p). See section 72(p) and § 1.72(p)-1 for rules governing the income tax treatment of certain assignments, pledges and loans from qualified employer plans made after August 13, 1982.

(2) Under section 72(m)(4)(A), if during any taxable year an owner-employee assigns or pledges (or agrees to assign or pledge) any portion of his interest in a trust described in section 401(a) which is exempt from tax under section 501(a), or any portion of the value of a contract purchased as part of a plan described in section 403(a), such portion shall be treated as having been received by such owner-employee as a distribution from the trust or as an amount received under the contract during such taxable year.

(3)(i) Under paragraphs (4)(A) and (6) of section 72(m), if after December 31, 1974, during any taxable year an individual for whose benefit an individual retirement account or annuity described in section 408(a) or (b) is maintained assigns or pledges (or agrees to assign or pledge) any portion of his interest in such account or annuity, such portion shall be treated as having been received by such individual as a distribution from such account or trust during such taxable year. See subsections (d) and (f) of section 408 and the regulations thereunder for the tax treatment of an amount treated as a distribution under this subparagraph.

(ii) Notwithstanding subdivision (i) of this subparagraph, if an individual retirement account or annuity, or portion thereof, is subject to the additional tax imposed by section 408(f), that amount shall be deemed not to be a distribution under section 72(m)(4)(A) and subdivision (i) of this subparagraph.

(4) Under section 72(m)(4)(B), if during any taxable year an owner-employee receives, either directly or indirectly, any amount from any insurance company as a loan under a contract purchased by a trust described in section 401(a) which is exempt from tax under section 501(a) or purchased as part of a plan described in section 403(a), and issued by such insurance company, such amount shall be treated as an amount received under the contract during such taxable year. An owner-employee will be considered to have received an amount under a contract if a premium, which is otherwise in default, is paid by the insurance company in the form of a loan against the cash surrender value of the contract. Further, an owner-employee will be considered to have received an amount to which this subparagraph applies if an amount is received from the issuer of a face-amount certificate as a loan under such a certificate purchased as part of a qualified trust or plan.

(e) *Penalties applicable to certain amounts received with respect to owner-employees under section 72(m)(5).*—(1)(i) For taxable years of the recipient beginning after December 31, 1975, if any person receives an amount to which subparagraph (2) of this paragraph applies, his tax under chapter 1 for the taxable year in which such amount is received shall be increased by an amount equal to 10 percent of the portion of the amount so received which is includible in his gross income for such taxable year.

(ii) For taxable years of the recipient beginning before January 1, 1976, see subparagraph (3) of this paragraph.

(2)(i) This subparagraph is applicable to amounts, to the extent includible in gross income, received from a qualified trust described in sec-

Reg. § 1.72-17A(c)(1)

tion 401(a) or under a plan described in section 403(a) by or on behalf of an individual who is or has been an owner-employee with respect to such trust or plan—

(A) Which are received before the owner-employee reaches the age of 59½ years, and which are attributable to contributions paid on behalf of such owner-employee by his employer (that is employer contributions within the meaning of section 401(c)(5)(A) and the increments in value attributable to such employer contributions) and the increments in value attributable to contributions made by him as an owner-employee while he was an owner-employee (that is, the increments attributable to owner-employee contributions within the meaning of section 401(c)(5)(B), but not such contributions; see subdivision (ii) of this subparagraph).

(B) Which are in excess of the benefits provided for such owner-employee under the plan formula (see subdivision (iii) of this subparagraph), or

(C) Which are subject to the transitional rules with respect to willful excess contributions made on behalf of an owner-employee in his employer's taxable years which begin before January 1, 1976 (see subdivision (v) of this subparagraph).

(ii) The amounts referred to in subdivision (i)(A) of this subparagraph do not include—

(A) Amounts received by reason of the owner-employee becoming disabled (see paragraph (f) of this section).

(B) Amounts received by the owner-employee in his capacity as a policyholder of an annuity, endowment, or life insurance contract which are in the nature of a dividend or similar distribution, or

(C) Amounts attributable to contributions (and increments in value thereon) made for years for which the recipient was not an owner-employee.

If an amount is not included in the amounts referred to in subdivision (i)(A) of this subparagraph solely by reason of the owner-employee's becoming disabled and if a penalty would otherwise be applicable with respect to all or a portion of such amount, then for the owner-employee's taxable year in which such amount is received, there must be submitted with his income tax return a doctor's statement as to the impairment, and a statement by the owner-employee with re-

spect to the effect of such impairment upon his substantial gainful activity and the date such impairment occurred. For taxable years which are subsequent to the first taxable year with respect to which the statements referred to in the preceding sentence are submitted, the owner-employee may, in lieu of such statements, submit a statement declaring the continued existence (without substantial diminution) of the impairment and its continued effect upon his substantial gainful activity.

(iii) This subparagraph applies to amounts described in subdivision (i)(B) of this subparagraph (relating to benefits in excess of the plan formula) even though a portion of such amounts may be attributable to contributions made on behalf of an individual while he was not an owner-employee and even if he is deceased and the amounts are received by his successor.

(iv)(A) The rules described in subdivisions (i)(A) and (iii) of this subparagraph, relating to the treatment under section 72(m)(5)(A)(i) of certain premature distributions, may be illustrated by the following example:

Example. (1) A was a member of the X partnership, consisting of partners A through I, and a participant in the partnership's qualified profit-sharing plan which was established on January 1, 1972. A's taxable years, the X partnership's taxable years, the plan years, and other relevant years are all calendar years at all relevant times. For the three calendar years 1972 through 1974, A was an owner-employee in the X partnership. On January 1, 1975, new partners J and K became partners in the X partnership, and as of that date, each of partners A through K held a 1/11 interest in the capital and profits of the X partnership. On that date, A became a partner who was not an owner-employee. A continued in this status for the 2 calendar years 1975 and 1976. On January 1, 1977, when A was 50 years old and not disabled, he liquidated his interest in the X partnership and became an employee of an unrelated employer. On that date, A received a distribution representing his entire interest in the X partnership's plan of $54,000 cash in violation of the plan provision required by section 401(d)(4)(B). As of that date, the distribution was attributable to the following sources and times, computed by the plan in a manner consistent with the subparagraph:

Calendar years	X contributions on behalf of A deductible under sec. 404	A's contributions made as an employee	Increments in value attributable to column A yearly contributions	Increments in value attributable to column B yearly contributions
	A	B	C	D
1977	0	0	0	0
1976	$ 7,500	$ 2,500	$ 900	$ 300
1975	7,500	2,500	4,000	1,300
1974	7,500	2,500	1,800	700
1973	2,500	2,500	1,200	1,200
1972	2,500	2,500	1,300	1,300
Totals	$27,500	$12,500	$9,200	$4,800

(2) The amount of the $54,000 distribution to which subdivision (i)(A) of this subparagraph applies is $20,000, computed as follows:

1974	$ 7,500
1973	2,500
1972	2,500
Total	$12,500

Increments in value attributable to such contributions:

1974	1,800
1973	1,200
1972	1,300
Total	$ 4,300

Increments in value attributable to contributions made by A as an employee for years in which he was an owner-employee:

1974	700
1973	1,200
1972	1,300
Total	$ 3,200
Grand Total	$20,000

X contributions on behalf of A made in years A was an owner-employee:

In this example, the $20,000 amount computed above would be includible in A's gross income for 1977 and would be subject to the 10 percent tax described in subparagraph (1)(i) of this paragraph.

(3) Subdivision (i)(A) of this subparagraph does not apply to the contributions made by X on behalf of A for 1976 and 1975 ($7,500 each year, totaling $15,000) nor to the increments in value attributable to those contributions ($900 for 1976 and $4,000 for 1975, totaling $4,900) because A was not an owner-employee with respect to these two years 1976 and 1975, on account of which these employer contributions were made. For the same reason, subdivision (i)(A) of this subparagraph does not apply to the increments in value attributable to A's contributions for 1976 and 1975 ($300 and $1,300, respectively, totaling $1,600).

See section 4972(c) for the amount of employee contributions which is permitted to be contributed by an owner-employee (as an employee) without subjecting an owner-employee to the tax on excess contributions.

(4) Subdivision (i)(A) of this subparagraph does not apply to the contributions made by A, as an employee during the years when he was an owner-employee ($2,500 during each of the years 1972, 1973, and 1974, totaling $7,500), because the distribution was received in a taxable year of A ending after September 2, 1974; see subparagraph (3) of this paragraph. Furthermore, because the distribution of the amount of A's contributions ($12,500) constitutes consideration for the contract paid by A for purposes of section 72, the $7,500 amount described in the preceding sentence is not includible in his gross income, and that amount is not subject to the rules of this

Reg. § 1.72-17A(e)(2)

subparagraph; see subdivision (i) of this subparagraph, and paragraphs (b) and (c) of this section.

(B) The increments in value of an individual's account may be allocated to contributions on his behalf, by his employer or by such individual as an owner-employee, while he was an owner-employee either by maintaining a separate account, or an accounting, which reflects the actual increment attributable to such contributions, or by the method described in (C) of this subdivision.

(C) Where an individual is covered under the same plan both as an owner-employee and as a non-owner-employee, the portion of the increment in value of his interest attributable to contributions made on his behalf while he was an owner-employee may be determined by multiplying the total increment in value in his account by a fraction. The numerator of the fraction is the total contributions made on behalf of the individual as an owner-employee, weighted for the number of years that each contribution was in the plan. The denominator is the total contributions made on behalf of the individual, whether or not as an owner-employee, weighted for the number of years each contribution was in the plan. The contributions are weighted for the number of years in the plan by multiplying each contribution by the number of years it was in the plan. For purposes

of this computation, any forfeiture allocated to the account of the individual is treated as a contribution to the account made at the time so allocated. For purposes of this computation, where the individual has received a prior distribution from such account, an appropriate adjustment must be made to reflect such prior distribution.

(D) The method described in (C) of this subdivision may be illustrated by the following example:

Example. B was a member of the XYZ Partnership and a participant in the partnership's profit-sharing plan which was created in 1973. Until the end of 1977, B's interest in the partnership was less than 10 percent. On January 1, 1978, B obtained an interest in excess of 10 percent in the partnership and continued to participate in the profit-sharing plan until 1982. During 1982, prior to the time he attained the age of 59½ years and during a time when he was not disabled, B, who had not received any prior plan distributions, withdrew his entire interest in the profit-sharing plan. At the time his interest was $15,000, $9,600 contributions and $5,400 increment attributable to the contributions. The portion of the increment attributable to contributions while B was an owner-employee is $667.80, determined as follows:

	Contribution A	Number of years contribution was in trust B	Contribution weighted for years in trust (A × B) C
1982	$1,000	0	0
1981	800	1	800
1980	1,200	2	2,400
1979	600	3	1,800
1978	200	4	800
1977	400	5	2,000
1976	2,000	6	12,000
1975	1,000	7	7,000
1974	1,500	8	12,000
1973	900	9	8,100
Total	9,600		46,900

Total weighted contributions as owner-employee (1978-1982) = $5,800.

Total weighted contributions = $46,900.

$$\$5,400 \times \frac{\$5,800}{\$46,900} = \$667.80$$

(E)(1) The rules set forth in subdivision (iv)(E)(2) of this subparagraph shall be used to determine the amounts to which subdivision (i)(A) of this subparagraph applies in the case of a distribution of less than the entire balance of the employee's account from a plan in which he has been covered at different times as owner-employee or as an employee other than an owner-employee.

(2) Distributions or payments from a plan for any employee taxable year shall be

deemed to be attributable to contributions to the plan, and increments thereon, in the following order—

(i) Excess contributions, within the meaning of section 4972(b), designated as such by the trustee;

(ii) Employee contributions;

(iii) Employer contributions, other than those described in (i), and the increments in value attributable to the employee's own contri-

Reg. § 1.72-17A(e)(2)

butions and his employer's contributions on the basis of the taxable years of his employer in succeeding order of time whether or not the employee was an owner-employee for any such year.

For purposes of (*iii*) of this subdivision, the time of contributions made on the basis of any employer taxable year shall take into account the rule specified in section 404(a)(6), relating to time when contributions deemed made.

(v) The amounts referred to in subdivision (i)(C) of this subparagraph are amounts which are received by reason of a distribution of the owner-employee's entire interest under the provisions of section 401(e)(2)(E), as in effect on September 1, 1974, relating to excess contributions on behalf of an owner-employee which are willfully made. Notwithstanding the preceding sentence, an owner-employee's entire interest in all plans with respect to which he is an owner-employee (within the meaning of subsections (d)(8)(C) and (e)(2)(E)(ii) of section 401, as in effect on September 1, 1974) does not include any distribution or payment attributable to his employer's contributions or his own contributions made with respect to his employer's taxable years beginning after December 31, 1975. However, his entire interest in all plans does include all of the distribution or payment attributable to his employer's contributions and his own contributions made with respect to all of his employer's taxable years beginning before January 1, 1976, if any portion thereof is attributable in whole or in part to such a willful excess contribution and such entire interest is received because of a willful excess contribution pursuant to section 401(e)(2)(E)(ii). A distribution or payment is described in the preceding sentence even though it is received in an owner-employee's taxable year beginning after December 31, 1975. For purposes of computing the increments in value attributable to employer taxable years which begin before January 1, 1976, and such increments attributable to such years beginning after December 31, 1975, the rules specified in subdivision (iv)(B), (C), (D), and (E) of this subparagraph shall be applied to the extent applicable. See § 1.401(e)-4(c) for transitional rules with respect to contributions described in this subdivision.

(3)(i) For taxable years of the recipient beginning before January 1, 1976, the tax with respect to amounts to which subparagraph (2) of this paragraph applies shall be computed under subparagraphs (B), (C), (D), and (E) of section 72(m)(5) as such subparagraphs were in effect prior to the amendments made by subsections (g)(1) and (2)(A) of section 2001 of the Employee Retirement Income Security Act of 1974 (88 Stat. 957) except as provided in subdivisions (ii) and (iii) of this subparagraph (see paragraph (e) of

§ 1.72-17). For purposes of the preceding sentence, amounts to which subparagraph (2) of this paragraph applies in the case of an amount described in section 72(m)(5)(A)(i) shall be determined under subdivisions (i)(*a*) and (ii) of § 1.72-17(e)(1), except as provided in subdivision (ii) of this subparagraph. For purposes of the first sentence of this subdivision, amounts to which subparagraph (2) of this paragraph applies in the case of an amount described in section 72(m)(5)(A)(ii) shall be determined under subdivisions (i)(*b*) and (iii) of § 1.72-17(e)(1), except as provided in subdivision (iii) of this subparagraph.

(ii) For purposes of applying section 72(m)(5)(A)(i), after the amendment made by section 2001(h)(3) of such Act, and subdivisions (i)(*a*) and (ii) of § 1.72-17(e)(1), to a distribution or payment received in recipient taxable years ending after September 2, 1974, and beginning before January 1, 1976, with respect to contributions made on behalf of an owner-employee which were made by him as an owner-employee (that is, employee contributions within the meaning of section 401(c)(5)(B)) the portion of any distribution or payment attributable to such contributions shall not include such contributions but shall include the increments in value attributable to such contributions.

(iii) For purposes of applying section 72(m)(5)(D) and subdivisions (i)(*b*) and (iii) of § 1.72-17(e)(1) to recipient taxable years beginning after December 31, 1973, and beginning before January 1, 1976, in the case of distributions or payments made after December 31, 1973, the amounts to which section 402(a)(2) or 403(a)(2) applies after the amendments made by section 2005(b)(1) and (2) of such Act (88 Stat. 990 and 991) (which are amounts to which subdivision (i)(*b*) of § 1.72-17(e)(1) does not apply) shall be deemed to be the amount which is treated as a gain from the sale or exchange of a capital asset held for more than 6 months under either of such sections.

(f) *Meaning of disabled.*—(1) Section 72(m)(7) provides that an individual shall be considered to be disabled if he is unable to engage in any substantial gainful activity by reason of any medically determinable physical or mental impairment which can be expected to result in death or to be of long-continued and indefinite duration. In determining whether an individual's impairment makes him unable to engage in any substantial gainful activity, primary consideration shall be given to the nature and severity of his impairment. Consideration shall also be given to other factors such as the individual's education, training, and work experience. The substantial gainful activity to which section 72(m)(7) refers is the

Reg. § 1.72-17A(e)(3)

activity, or a comparable activity, in which the individual customarily engaged prior to the arising of the disability or prior to retirement if the individual was retired at the time the disability arose.

(2) Whether or not the impairment in a particular case constitutes a disability is to be determined with reference to all the facts in the case. The following are examples of impairments which would ordinarily be considered as preventing substantial gainful activity:

(i) Loss of use of two limbs;

(ii) Certain progressive diseases which have resulted in the physical loss or atrophy of a limb, such as diabetes, multiple sclerosis, or Buerger's disease;

(iii) Diseases of the heart, lungs, or blood vessels which have resulted in major loss of heart or lung reserve as evidenced by X-ray, electrocardiogram, or other objective findings, so that despite medical treatment breathlessness, pain, or fatigue is produced on slight exertion, such as walking several blocks, using public transportation, or doing small chores;

(iv) Cancer which is inoperable and progressive;

(v) Damage to the brain or brain abnormality which has resulted in severe loss of judgment, intellect, orientation, or memory;

(vi) Mental diseases (e.g., psychosis or severe psychoneurosis) requiring continued institutionalization or constant supervision of the individual,

(vii) Loss or diminution of vision to the extent that the affected individual has a central visual acuity of no better than 20/200 in the better eye after best correction, or has a limitation in the fields of vision such that the widest diameter of the visual fields subtends an angle no greater than 20 degrees;

(viii) Permanent and total loss of speech;

(ix) Total deafness uncorrectible by a hearing aid.

The existence of one or more of the impairments described in this subparagraph (or of an impairment of greater severity) will not, however, in and of itself always permit a finding that an individual is disabled as defined in section 72(m)(7). Any impairment, whether of lesser or greater severity, must be evaluated in terms of whether it does in fact prevent the individual from engaging in his customary or any comparable substantial gainful activity.

(3) In order to meet the requirements of section 72(m)(7), an impairment must be expected either to continue for a long and indefinite period or to result in death. Ordinarily, a terminal illness because of disease or injury would result in

disability. The term "indefinite" is used in the sense that it cannot reasonably be anticipated that the impairment will, in the foreseeable future, be so diminished as no longer to prevent substantial gainful activity. For example, an individual who suffers a bone fracture which prevents him from working for an extended period of time will not be considered disabled, if his recovery can be expected in the foreseeable future; if the fracture persistently fails to knit, the individual would ordinarily be considered disabled.

(4) An impairment which is remediable does not constitute a disability within the meaning of section 72(m)(7). An individual will not be deemed disabled if, with reasonable effort and safety to himself, the impairment can be diminished to the extent that the individual will not be prevented by the impairment from engaging in his customary or any comparable substantial gainful activity. [Reg. § 1.72-17A.]

☐ [T.D. 7636, 8-9-79. Amended by T.D. 8894, 7-28-2000.]

[Reg. § 1.72-18]

§ 1.72-18. Treatment of certain total distributions with respect to self-employed individuals.—(a) In general. The Self-Employed Individuals Tax Retirement Act of 1962 permits self-employed individuals to be treated as employees for purposes of participation in pension, profit-sharing, and annuity plans described in sections 401(a) and 403(a). In general, amounts received by a distributee or payee which are attributable to contributions made on behalf of a participant while he was self-employed are taxed in the same manner as amounts which are attributable to contributions made on behalf of a common-law employee. However, such amounts which are paid in one taxable year representing the total distributions payable to a distributee or payee with respect to an employee, are not eligible for the capital gains treatment of section 402(a)(2) or 403(a)(2). This section sets forth the treatment of such distributions, except where such a distribution is subject to the penalties of section 72(m)(5) and paragraph (3) of § 1.72-17.

. (b) Distributions to which this section applies.—(1)(i) Except as provided in subparagraphs (2) and (3) of this paragraph, this section applies to amounts distributed to a distributee in one taxable year of the distributee in the case of an employees' trust described in section 401 (a) which is exempt under section 501 (a), or to amounts paid to a payee in one taxable year of the payee in the case of an annuity plan described in section 403 (a), which constitute the total distributions payable, or the total amounts payable, to the distributee or payee with respect to an employee.

(ii) For the total distributions or amounts payable to a distributee or payee to be considered paid within one taxable year of the distributee or payee for purposes of this section, all amounts to the credit of the employee-participant through the end of such taxable year which are payable to the distributee or payee must be distributed or paid within such taxable year. Thus, the provisions of this section are not applicable to a distribution or payment to a distributee or payee if the trust or plan retains any amounts after the close of such taxable year which are payable to the same distributee or payee even though the amounts retained may be attributable to contributions on behalf of the employee-participant while he was a common-law employee in the business with respect to which the plan was established.

(iii) For purposes of this section, the total amounts payable to a distributee or the amounts to the credit of the employee do not include United States Retirement Plan Bonds held by a trust to the credit of the employee. Thus, a distribution to a distributee by a qualified trust may constitute a distribution to which this section applies even though the trust retains retirement plan bonds registered in the name of the employee on whose behalf the distribution is made which are to be distributed to the same distributee. Moreover, the proceeds of a retirement bond received as part of a distribution which constitutes the total distributions payable to the distributee are not entitled to the special tax treatment of this section. See section 405(d) and paragraph (a)(1) of § 1.405-3.

(iv) If the amounts payable to a distributee from a qualified trust with respect to an employee-participant includes an annuity contract, such contract must be distributed along with all other amounts payable to the distributee in order to have a distribution to which this section applies. However, the proceeds of an annuity contract received in a total distribution will not be entitled to the tax treatment of this section unless the contract is surrendered in the taxable year of the distributee in which the total distribution was received.

(v) In the case of a qualified annuity plan, the term "total amounts" means all annuities payable to a payee. If more than one annuity contract is received under the plan by a distributee, this section shall not apply to an amount received on surrender of any such contracts unless all contracts under the plan payable to the payee are surrendered within one taxable year of the payee.

(vi)(a) The provisions of this section are applicable where the total amounts payable to a distributee or payee are paid within one taxable year of the distributee or payee whether or not a portion of the employee-participant's interest which is payable to another distributee or payee is paid within the same taxable year. However, a distributee or payee who, in prior taxable years received amounts (except amounts described in (b) of this subdivision) after the employee-participant ceases to be eligible for additional contributions to be made on his behalf, does not receive a distribution or payment to which this section applies, even though the total amount remaining to be paid to such distributee or payee with respect to such employee is paid within one taxable year. On the other hand, a distribution to a distributee or payee prior to the time that the employee-participant ceases to be eligible for additional contributions on his behalf does not preclude the application of this section to a later distribution to the same distributee or payee.

(b) The receipt of an amount which constitutes—

(1) A payment in the nature of a dividend or similar distribution to an individual in his capacity as a policyholder of an annuity, endowment, or life insurance contract, or

(2) A return of excess contributions which were not willfully made,

does not prevent the application of this section to a total distribution even though the amount is received after the employee-participant ceases to be eligible for additional contributions and in a taxable year other than the taxable year in which the total amount is received.

(vii) For purposes of this section, the total amounts payable to a distributee or payee, or the amounts to the credit of the employee, do not include any amounts which have been placed in a separate account for the funding of medical benefits described in section 401(h) as defined in paragraph (a) of § 1.401-14. Thus, a distribution by a qualified trust or annuity plan may constitute a distribution to which this section applies even though amount attributable to the funding of section 401(h) medical benefits as defined in paragraph (a) of § 1.401-14 are not so distributed.

(2) This section shall apply—

(i) Only if the distribution or payment is made—

(a) On account of the employee's death at any time,

(b) After the employee has attained the age 59½ years, or

Reg. § 1.72-18(b)(2)

(c) After the employee has become disabled; and

(ii) Only to so much of the distribution or payment as is attributable to contributions made on behalf of an employee while he was a self-employed individual in the business with respect to which the plan was established. Any distribution or payment, or any portion thereof, which is not so attributable shall be subject to the rules of taxation which apply to any distribution or payment that is attributable to contributions on behalf of common-law employees.

For taxable years beginning after December 31, 1966, see section 72(m)(7) and paragraph (f) of § 1.72-17 for the meaning of disabled. For taxable years beginning before January 1, 1967, see section 213(g)(3) for the meaning of disabled. For taxable years beginning after December 31, 1968, if this section is applicable by reason of the distribution or payment being made after the employee has become disabled, then for the taxable year in which the amounts to which this section applies are distributed or paid, there shall be submitted with the recipient's income tax return a doctor's statement as to the nature and effect of the employee's impairment.

(3) This section shall not apply to—

(i) Distributions or payments to which the penalty provisions of section 72(m)(5) and paragraph (e) of § 1.72-17 apply,

(ii) Distributions or payments from a trust or plan made to or on behalf of an individual prior to the time such individual ceases to be eligible for additional contributions (except the contribution attributable to the last year of service) to be made to the trust or plan on his behalf as a self-employed individual, and

(iii) Distributions or payments made to the employee from a plan or trust unless contributions which were allowed as a deduction under section 404 have been made on behalf of such employee as a self-employed individual under such trust or plan for 5 or more taxable years (whether or not consecutive) prior to the taxable year in which such distributions or payments are made. Distributions or payments to which this section does not apply by reason of this subdivision are taxed as otherwise provided in section 72. However, for taxable years beginning before January 1, 1964, section 72(e)(3), as in effect before such date, is not applicable. For taxable years beginning after December 31, 1963, such distributions or payments may be taken into account in computations under sections 1301 through 1305 (relating to income averaging).

(4) The portion of any distribution or payment attributable to contributions on behalf of an employee-participant while he was self-employed includes the contributions made on his behalf while he was self-employed and the increments in value attributable to such contributions. Where the amounts to the credit of an employee-participant include amounts attributable to contributions on his behalf while he was a self-employed individual and amounts attributable to contributions on his behalf while he was a common-law employee, the increment in value attributable to the employee-participant's interest shall be allocated to the contributions on his behalf while he was self-employed either by maintaining a separate account, or an accounting, which reflects the actual increment attributable to such contributions, or by the method described in paragraph (e)(1)(iv)(c) of § 1.72-17. However, if the latter method is used, the numerator of the fraction is the total contributions made on behalf of the individual as a self-employed individual, weighted for the number of years that each contribution was in the plan.

(c) *Amounts includible in gross income.*—(1) Where a total distribution or payment to which this section applies is made to one distributee or payee and includes the total amount remaining to the credit of the employee-participant on whose behalf the distribution or payment was made, the distributee or payee shall include in gross income an amount equal to the portion of the distribution or payment which exceeds the employee-participant's investment in the contract. For purposes of this paragraph, the investment in the contract shall be reduced by any amounts previously received from the plan or trust by or on behalf of the employee-participant which were excludable from gross income as a return of the investment in the contract.

(2) In the case of a distribution to which this section applies and which is made to more than one distributee or payee, each element of the amounts to the credit of an employee-participant shall be allocated among the several distributees or payees on the basis of the ratio of the value of the distributee's or payee's distribution or payment to the total amount to the credit of the employee-participant. The elements to be so allocated include the investment in the contract, the increments in value, and the portion of the amounts to the credit of the employee-participant which is attributable to the contributions on behalf of the employee-participant while he was a self-employed individual.

(d) *Computation of tax.*—(1) The tax attributable to the amounts to which this section applies for the taxable year in which such amounts are received is the greater of—

Reg. § 1.72-18(d)(1)

(i) 5 times the increase in tax which would result from the inclusion in gross income of the recipient of 20 percent of so much of the amount so received as is includible in gross income, or

(ii) 5 times the increase which would result if the taxable income of the recipient for such taxable year equaled 20 percent of the excess of the aggregate of the amounts so received and includible in gross income over the amount of the deductions allowed the recipient for such taxable year under section 151 (relating to deduction for personal exemptions).

In any case in which the application of subdivision (ii) of this subparagraph results in an increase in taxable income for any taxable year, the resulting increase in taxes imposed by section 1 or 3 for such taxable year shall be reduced by the credit against tax provided by section 31 (tax withheld on wages), but shall not be reduced by any other credits against tax.

(2) The application of the rules of this paragraph may be illustrated by the following example:

Example. B, a sole proprietor and a calendar-year basis taxpayer, established a qualified pension trust to which he made annual contributions for 10 years of 10 percent of his earned income. B withdrew his entire interest in the trust during 1973, for which year, without regard to the distribution, he had a net operating loss and is allowed under section 151 a deduction for one personal exemption. At the time of the withdrawal, B was 64 years old. The amount of the distribution that is includible in his gross income is $25,750. Because of B's net operating loss, the tax attributable to the distribution is determined under the rule of subparagraph (1)(ii) of this paragraph. For purposes of determining the tax attributable to the $25,750, B's taxable income for 1973 is treated, under subparagraph (1)(ii) of this paragraph, as being 20 percent of $25,000 ($25,750 minus $750, the amount of the deduction allowed for each personal exemption under section 151 for 1973). Thus, under subparagraph (1) of this paragraph, the tax attributable to the $25,750 would be 5 times the increase which would result if the taxable income of B for the taxable year he received such amount equaled $5,000. B has had no amounts withheld from wages and thus is not entitled to reduce the increase in taxes by the credit against tax provided in section 31 and may not reduce the increase in taxes by any other credits against tax. [Reg. § 1.72-18.]

☐ [*T.D. 6676, 9-16-63. Amended by T.D. 6722, 4-13-64, T.D. 6885, 6-1-66, T.D. 6985, 12-26-68 and T.D. 7114, 5-17-71.*]

[Reg. § 1.72(e)-1T]

§ 1.72(e)-1T. Treatment of distributions where substantially all contributions are employee contributions (Temporary).

Q-1: How did the Tax Reform Act (TRA) of 1984 change the law with regard to the treatment of non-annuity distributions (i.e., amounts distributed prior to the annuity starting date and not received as annuities) from a qualified plan that is treated as a single contract under section 72 and under which substantially all of the contributions are employee contributions?

A-1: (a) Prior to the amendment of section 72(e) by the TRA of 1984, non-annuity distributions from such a qualified plan generally were allocable, first, to nondeductible employee contributions and thus were not includible in gross income. After distributions equaled the balance of nondeductible employee contributions, further non-annuity distributions generally were includible in gross income.

(b) Pursuant to section 72(e)(7), as added by the TRA of 1984, non-annuity distributions from such a qualified plan that are allocable to investment in the plan after August 13, 1982 (as determined in accordance with section 72(e)(5)(B)), generally will be treated, first, as allocable to income and, second, as allocable to nondeductible employee contributions. Distributions allocable to income are includible in gross income. Distributions allocable to nondeductible employee contributions are not includible in gross income.

Q-2: To which qualified plans and contracts does section 72(e)(7) apply?

A-2: Section 72 (e)(7) applies to any plan or contract under which substantially all of the contributions are employee contributions if—

(a) Such plan is described in section 401(a) and the related trust or trusts are exempt from tax under section 501(a); or

(b) Such contract is—

(1) Purchased by a trust described in (a) above,

(2) Purchased as part of a plan described in section 403(a), or

(3) Described in section 403(b).

Q-3: What is the definition of a qualified plan or contract under which substantially all of the contributions are employee contributions?

A-3: (a) A qualified plan or contract under which substantially all of the contributions are employee contributions is a plan or contract with respect to which 85 percent or more of the total contributions during the "representative period" are employee contributions. The "representative period" means the five-plan-year period preceding the plan year during which a distribution occurs. However, if less than 85 percent of the total contributions for all plan years during which the plan or contract is in existence prior to the plan year of distribution are employee contributions, then the plan or contract is not one with respect to which substantially all of the contributions are employee contributions.

(b) For purposes of the 85 percent test, contributions made to a predecessor plan or contract are aggregated with contributions made to the plan or contract to which the 85 percent test is being applied (the successor plan or contract). For purposes of the preceding sentence, a predecessor plan or contract is a plan or contract the terms of which are substantially the same as the successor plan or contract.

Q-4: What is the definition of employee contributions for purposes of section 72(e)(7)?

A-4: For purposes of section 72(e)(7), employee contributions are those amounts contributed by the employee and those amounts considered contributed by the employee under section 72(f). For example, amounts contributed to a section 401(k) qualified cash or deferred arrangement, pursuant to an employee's election to defer such amounts, are employer contributions to the extent that such amounts are not currently includible in gross income. In addition, deductible employee contributions under section 72(o) are disregarded in their entirety (i.e., treated as neither employee contributions nor employer contributions) in determining whether substantially all the contributions are employee contributions.

Q-5: How is the 85 percent test of section 72(e)(7) applied to a qualified plan or contract?

A-5: (a) Except as provided in paragraphs (b), (c), and (d), the 85 percent test is applied separately with respect to each contract under section 72.

(b) If a single qualified plan described in section 401(a) or section 403(a) comprises more than one contract under section 72, regardless of whether such plan includes multiple trusts or combinations of profit-sharing and pension features, these contracts are aggregated for purposes of applying the 85 percent test. Thus, if substantially all of the contributions under a qualified plan comprising two contracts under section 72 are employee contributions, section 72(e)(5)(D) shall not apply to non-annuity distributions under either of the contracts.

(c) With respect to the plans maintained by the Federal Government or by instrumentalities of the Federal Government, the 85 percent test shall be applied by aggregating all such plans. This aggregation rule applies only to those plans that are actively administered by the Federal Government or an instrumentality thereof. Thus, if a plan of the Federal Government is administered by a commercial financial institution, it would not be aggregated with other plans of the Federal Government and its instrumentalities for purposes of applying the 85 percent test.

(d) In the case of a contract described in section 403(b), the 85 percent test is applied separately to each such contract.

Q-6: Is a loan from a qualified plan or contract described in section 72(e)(7) treated as a distribution under section 72(e)(4)(A)?

A-6: Yes. Pursuant to section 72(e)(4)(A), if an employee receives, either directly or indirectly, any amount as a loan from a qualified plan or contract described in section 72(e)(7), such amount shall be treated as a distribution from the plan or contract of an amount not received as an annuity. Similarly, if an employee assigns or pledges, or agrees to assign or pledge, any portion of the value of any qualified plan or contract, such portion shall be treated as a distribution from the plan or contract of an amount not received as an annuity.

Q-7: Does the five percent penalty for premature distributions from annuity contracts, as described in section 72(q), apply to distributions from a qualified plan or contract described in section 72(e)(7)?

A-7: No.

Q-8: When is section 72(e)(7) effective?

A-8: Section 72(e)(7) is effective for amounts received or loans made on or after October 17, 1984. For purposes of this effective date provision, loan amounts outstanding on October 16, 1984, which are renegotiated, extended, renewed, or revised after that date generally are treated as loans made on the date of the renegotiation, etc. [Temporary Reg. § 1.72(e)-1T.]

☐ [*T.D.* 8073, 1-29-86.]

[Reg. § 1.72(p)-1]

§ 1.72(p)-1. Loans treated as distributions.— The questions and answers in this section provide guidance under section 72(p) pertaining to loans from qualified employer plans (including government plans and tax-sheltered annuities and employer plans that were formerly qualified). The examples included in the questions and answers in this section are based on the assumption that a bona fide loan is made to a participant from a qualified defined contribution plan pursuant to an enforceable agreement (in accordance with paragraph (b) of Q&A-3 of this section), with adequate security and with an interest rate and repayment terms that are commercially reasonable. (The particular interest rate used, which is solely for illustration, is 8.75 percent compounded annually.) In addition, unless the contrary is specified, it is assumed in the examples that the amount of the loan does not exceed 50 percent of the participant's nonforfeitable account balance, the participant has no other outstanding loan (and had no prior loan) from the plan or any other plan maintained by the participant's employer or any other person required to be aggregated with the employer under section 414(b), (c) or (m), and the loan is not excluded from section 72(p) as a loan made in the ordinary course of an investment program as described in Q&A-18 of this section. The regulations and examples in this section do not provide guidance on whether a loan from a plan would result in a prohibited transaction under section 4975 of the Internal Revenue Code or on whether a loan from a plan covered by Title I of the Employee Retirement Income Security Act of 1974 (88 Stat. 829) (ERISA) would be consistent with the fiduciary standards of ERISA or would result in a prohibited transaction under section 406 of ERISA. The questions and answers are as follows:

Q-1: In general, what does section 72(p) provide with respect to loans from a qualified employer plan?

A-1: (a) *Loans.* Under section 72(p), an amount received by a participant or beneficiary as a loan from a qualified employer plan is treated as having been received as a distribution from the plan (a deemed distribution), unless the loan satisfies the requirements of Q&A-3 of this section. For purposes of section 72(p) and this section, a loan made from a contract that has been purchased under a qualified employer plan (including a contract that has been distributed to the participant or beneficiary) is considered a loan made under a qualified employer plan.

(b) *Pledges and assignments.* Under section 72(p), if a participant or beneficiary assigns or pledges (or agrees to assign or pledge) any portion of his or her interest in a qualified employer plan as security for a loan, the portion of the individual's interest assigned or pledged (or subject to an agreement to assign or pledge) is treated as a loan from the plan to the individual, with the result that such portion is subject to the deemed distribution rule described in paragraph (a) of this Q&A-1. For purposes of section 72(p) and this section, any assignment or pledge of (or agreement to assign or to pledge) any portion of a participant's or beneficiary's interest in a contract that has been purchased under a qualified employer plan (including a contract that has been

distributed to the participant or beneficiary) is considered an assignment or pledge of (or agreement to assign or pledge) an interest in a qualified employer plan. However, if all or a portion of a participant's or beneficiary's interest in a qualified employer plan is pledged or assigned as security for a loan from the plan to the participant or the beneficiary, only the amount of the loan received by the participant or the beneficiary, not the amount pledged or assigned, is treated as a loan.

Q-2: What is a qualified employer plan for purposes of section 72(p)?

A-2: For purposes of section 72(p) and this section, a qualified employer plan means—

(a) A plan described in section 401(a) which includes a trust exempt from tax under section 501(a);

(b) An annuity plan described in section 403(a);

(c) A plan under which amounts are contributed by an individual's employer for an annuity contract described in section 403(b);

(d) Any plan, whether or not qualified, established and maintained for its employees by the United States, by a State or political subdivision thereof, or by an agency or instrumentality of the United States, a State or a political subdivision of a State; or

(e) Any plan which was (or was determined to be) described in paragraph (a), (b), (c), or (d) of this Q&A-2.

Q-3: What requirements must be satisfied in order for a loan to a participant or beneficiary from a qualified employer plan not to be a deemed distribution?

A-3: (a) *In general.* A loan to a participant or beneficiary from a qualified employer plan will not be a deemed distribution to the participant or beneficiary if the loan satisfies the repayment term requirement of section 72(p)(2)(B), the level amortization requirement of section 72(p)(2)(C), and the enforceable agreement requirement of paragraph (b) of this Q&A-3, but only to the extent the loan satisfies the amount limitations of section 72(p)(2)(A).

(b) *Enforceable agreement requirement.* A loan does not satisfy the requirements of this paragraph unless the loan is evidenced by a legally enforceable agreement (which may include more than one document) and the terms of the agreement demonstrate compliance with the requirements of section 72(p)(2) and this section. Thus, the agreement must specify the amount and date of the loan and the repayment schedule. The agreement does not have to be signed if the agreement is enforceable under applicable law without

Reg. § 1.72(p)-1

being signed. The agreement must be set forth either—

(1) In a written paper document;

(2) In an electronic medium that is reasonably accessible to the participant or the beneficiary and that is provided under a system that satisfies the following requirements:

(i) The system must be reasonably designed to preclude any individual other than the participant or the beneficiary from requesting a loan.

(ii) The system must provide the participant or the beneficiary with a reasonable opportunity to review and to confirm, modify, or rescind the terms of the loan before the loan is made.

(iii) The system must provide the participant or the beneficiary, within a reasonable time after the loan is made, a confirmation of the loan terms either through a written paper document or through an electronic medium that is reasonably accessible to the participant or the beneficiary and that is provided under a system that is reasonably designed to provide the confirmation in a manner no less understandable to the participant or beneficiary than a written document and, under which, at the time the confirmation is provided, the participant or the beneficiary is advised that he or she may request and receive a written paper document at no charge, and, upon request, that document is provided to the participant or beneficiary at no charge.

or

(3) In such other form as may be approved by the Commissioner.

Q-4: If a loan from a qualified employer plan to a participant or beneficiary fails to satisfy the requirements of Q&A-3 of this section, when does a deemed distribution occur?

A-4: (a) *Deemed distribution.* For purposes of section 72, a deemed distribution occurs at the first time that the requirements of Q&A-3 of this section are not satisfied, in form or in operation. This may occur at the time the loan is made or at a later date. If the terms of the loan do not require repayments that satisfy the repayment term requirement of section 72(p)(2)(B) or the level amortization requirement of section 72(p)(2)(C), or the loan is not evidenced by an enforceable agreement satisfying the requirements of paragraph (b) of Q&A-3 of this section, the entire amount of the loan is a deemed distribution under section 72(p) at the time the loan is made. If the loan satisfies the requirements of Q&A-3 of this section except that the amount loaned exceeds the limitations of section 72(p)(2)(A), the amount of the loan in excess of the applicable limitation is a deemed distribution

under section 72(p) at the time the loan is made. If the loan initially satisfies the requirements of section 72(p)(2)(A), (B) and (C) and the enforceable agreement requirement of paragraph (b) of Q&A-3 of this section, but payments are not made in accordance with the terms applicable to the loan, a deemed distribution occurs as a result of the failure to make such payments. See Q&A-10 of this section regarding when such a deemed distribution occurs and the amount thereof and Q&A-11 of this section regarding the tax treatment of a deemed distribution.

(b) *Examples.* The following examples illustrate the rules in paragraph (a) of this Q&A-4 and are based upon the assumptions described in the introductory text of this section:

Example 1. (i) A participant has a nonforfeitable account balance of $200,000 and receives $70,000 as a loan repayable in level quarterly installments over five years.

(ii) Under section 72(p), the participant has a deemed distribution of $20,000 (the excess of $70,000 over $50,000) at the time of the loan, because the loan exceeds the $50,000 limit in section 72(p)(2)(A)(i). The remaining $50,000 is not a deemed distribution.

Example 2. (i) A participant with a nonforfeitable account balance of $30,000 borrows $20,000 as a loan repayable in level monthly installments over five years.

(ii) Because the amount of the loan is $5,000 more than 50% of the participant's nonforfeitable account balance, the participant has a deemed distribution of $5,000 at the time of the loan. The remaining $15,000 is not a deemed distribution. (Note also that, if the loan is secured solely by the participant's account balance, the loan may be a prohibited transaction under section 4975 because the loan may not satisfy 29 CFR 2550.408b-1(f)(2).)

Example 3. (i) The nonforfeitable account balance of a participant is $100,000 and a $50,000 loan is made to the participant repayable in level quarterly installments over seven years. The loan is not eligible for the section 72(p)(2)(B)(ii) exception for loans used to acquire certain dwelling units.

(ii) Because the repayment period exceeds the maximum fiveyear period in section 72(p)(2)(B)(i), the participant has a deemed distribution of $50,000 at the time the loan is made.

Example 4. (i) On August 1, 2002, a participant has a nonforfeitable account balance of $45,000 and borrows $20,000 from a plan to be repaid over five years in level monthly installments due at the end of each month. After making monthly payments through July 2003, the participant fails to make any of the payments due thereafter.

(ii) As a result of the failure to satisfy the requirement that the loan be repaid in level monthly installments, the participant has a deemed distribution. See paragraph (c) of Q&A10 of this section regarding when such a deemed distribution occurs and the amount thereof.

Q-5: What is a principal residence for purposes of the exception in section 72(p)(2)(B)(ii) from the requirement that a loan be repaid in five years?

A-5: Section 72(p)(2)(B)(ii) provides that the requirement in section 72(p)(2)(B)(i) that a plan loan be repaid within five years does not apply to a loan used to acquire a dwelling unit which will within a reasonable time be used as the principal residence of the participant (a principal residence plan loan). For this purpose, a principal residence has the same meaning as a principal residence under section 121.

Q-6: In order to satisfy the requirements for a principal residence plan loan, is a loan required to be secured by the dwelling unit that will within a reasonable time be used as the principal residence of the participant?

A-6: A loan is not required to be secured by the dwelling unit that will within a reasonable time be used as the participant's principal residence in order to satisfy the requirements for a principal residence plan loan.

Q-7: What tracing rules apply in determining whether a loan qualifies as a principal residence plan loan?

A-7: The tracing rules established under section 163(h)(3)(B) apply in determining whether a loan is treated as for the acquisition of a principal residence in order to qualify as a principal residence plan loan.

Q-8: Can a refinancing qualify as a principal residence plan loan?

A-8: (a) *Refinancings.* In general, no, a refinancing cannot qualify as a principal residence plan loan. However, a loan from a qualified employer plan used to repay a loan from a third party will qualify as a principal residence plan loan if the plan loan qualifies as a principal residence plan loan without regard to the loan from the third party.

(b) *Example.* The following example illustrates the rules in paragraph (a) of this Q&A-8 and is based upon the assumptions described in the introductory text of this section:

Example. (i) On July 1, 2003, a participant requests a $50,000 plan loan to be repaid in level monthly installments over 15 years. On August 1,

2003, the participant acquires a principal residence and pays a portion of the purchase price with a $50,000 bank loan. On September 1, 2003, the plan loans $50,000 to the participant, which the participant uses to pay the bank loan.

(ii) Because the plan loan satisfies the requirements to qualify as a principal residence plan loan (taking into account the tracing rules of section 163(h)(3)(B)), the plan loan qualifies for the exception in section 72(p)(2)(B)(ii).

Q-9: Does the level amortization requirement of section 72(p)(2)(C) apply when a participant is on a leave of absence without pay?

A-9: (a) *Leave of absence.* The level amortization requirement of section 72(p)(2)(C) does not apply for a period, not longer than one year (or such longer period as may apply under section 414(u) and paragraph (b) of this Q&A-9), that a participant is on a bona fide leave of absence, either without pay from the employer or at a rate of pay (after applicable employment tax withholdings) that is less than the amount of the installment payments required under the terms of the loan. However, the loan (including interest that accrues during the leave of absence) must be repaid by the latest permissible term of the loan and the amount of the installments due after the leave ends must not be less than the amount required under the terms of the original loan.

(b) *Military service.* In accordance with section 414(u)(4), if a plan suspends the obligation to repay a loan made to an employee from the plan for any part of a period during which the employee is performing service in the uniformed services (as defined in 38 U.S.C. chapter 43), whether or not qualified military service, such suspension shall not be taken into account for purposes of section 72(p) or this section. Thus, if a plan suspends loan repayments for any part of a period during which the employee is performing military service described in the preceding sentence, such suspension shall not cause the loan to be deemed distributed even if the suspension exceeds one year and even if the term of the loan is extended. However, the loan will not satisfy the repayment term requirement of section 72(p)(2)(B) and the level amortization requirement of section 72(p)(2)(C) unless loan repayments resume upon the completion of such period of military service and the loan is repaid thereafter by amortization in substantially level installments over a period that ends not later than the latest permissible term of the loan.

(c) *Latest permissible term of a loan.* For purposes of this Q&A-9, the latest permissible term of a loan is the latest date permitted under section 72(p)(2)(B) (i.e., five years from the date of the loan, assuming that the replacement loan does not qualify for the exception at section 72(p)(2)(B)(ii) for principal residence plan loans) plus any additional period of suspension permitted under paragraph (b) of this Q&A-9.

(d) *Examples.* The following examples illustrate the rules of this Q&A-9 and are based upon the assumptions described in the introductory text of this section:

Example 1. (i) On July 1, 2003, a participant with a nonforfeitable account balance of $80,000 borrows $40,000 to be repaid in level monthly installments of $825 each over 5 years. The loan is not a principal residence plan loan. The participant makes 9 monthly payments and commences an unpaid leave of absence that lasts for 12 months. The participant was not performing military service during this period. Thereafter, the participant resumes active employment and resumes making repayments on the loan until the loan is repaid. The amount of each monthly installment is increased to $1,130 in order to repay the loan by June 30, 2008.

(ii) Because the loan satisfies the requirements of section 72(p)(2), the participant does not have a deemed distribution. Alternatively, section 72(p)(2) would be satisfied if the participant continued the monthly installments of $825 after resuming active employment and on June 30, 2008 repaid the full balance remaining due.

Example 2. (i) The facts are the same as in *Example 1,* except the participant was on leave of absence performing service in the uniformed services (as defined in chapter 43 of title 38, United States Code) for two years and the rate of interest charged during this period of military service is reduced to 6 percent compounded annually under 50 App. Section 526 (relating to the Soldiers' and Sailors' Civil Relief Act Amendments of 1942). After the military service ends on April 2, 2006, the participant resumes active employment on April 19, 2006, continues the monthly installments of $825 thereafter, and on June 30, 2010 repays the full balance remaining due ($6,487).

(ii) Because the loan satisfies the requirements of section 72(p)(2) and paragraph (b) of this Q&A-9, the participant does not have a deemed distribution. Alternatively, section 72(p)(2) would also be satisfied if the amount of each monthly installment after April 19, 2006, is increased to $930 in order to repay the loan by June 30, 2010 (without any balance remaining due then).

Q-10: If a participant fails to make the installment payments required under the terms of a loan that satisfied the requirements of Q&A-3 of this section when made, when does a deemed distribu-

tion occur and what is the amount of the deemed distribution?

A-10: (a) *Timing of deemed distribution.* Failure to make any installment payment when due in accordance with the terms of the loan violates section 72(p)(2)(C) and, accordingly, results in a deemed distribution at the time of such failure. However, the plan administrator may allow a cure period and section 72(p)(2)(C) will not be considered to have been violated if the installment payment is made not later than the end of the cure period, which period cannot continue beyond the last day of the calendar quarter following the calendar quarter in which the required installment payment was due.

(b) *Amount of deemed distribution.* If a loan satisfies Q&A-3 of this section when made, but there is a failure to pay the installment payments required under the terms of the loan (taking into account any cure period allowed under paragraph (a) of this Q&A-10), then the amount of the deemed distribution equals the entire outstanding balance of the loan (including accrued interest) at the time of such failure.

(c) *Example.* The following example illustrates the rules in paragraphs (a) and (b) of this Q&A-10 and is based upon the assumptions described in the introductory text of this section:

Example. (i) On August 1, 2002, a participant has a nonforfeitable account balance of $45,000 and borrows $20,000 from a plan to be repaid over 5 years in level monthly installments due at the end of each month. After making all monthly payments due through July 31, 2003, the participant fails to make the payment due on August 31, 2003 or any other monthly payments due thereafter. The plan administrator allows a threemonth cure period.

(ii) As a result of the failure to satisfy the requirement that the loan be repaid in level installments pursuant to section 72(p)(2)(C), the participant has a deemed distribution on November 30, 2003, which is the last day of the threemonth cure period for the August 31, 2003 installment. The amount of the deemed distribution is $17,157, which is the outstanding balance on the loan at November 30, 2003. Alternatively, if the plan administrator had allowed a cure period through the end of the next calendar quarter, there would be a deemed distribution on December 31, 2003 equal to $17,282, which is the outstanding balance of the loan at December 31, 2003.

Q-11: Does section 72 apply to a deemed distribution as if it were an actual distribution?

A-11: (a) *Tax basis.* If the employee's account includes after-tax contributions or other investment in the contract under section 72(e), section 72 applies to a deemed distribution as if it were an actual distribution, with the result that all or a portion of the deemed distribution may not be taxable.

(b) *Section 72(t) and (m)*. Section 72(t) (which imposes a 10 percent tax on certain early distributions) and section 72(m)(5) (which imposes a separate 10 percent tax on certain amounts received by a 5-percent owner) apply to a deemed distribution under section 72(p) in the same manner as if the deemed distribution were an actual distribution.

Q-12: Is a deemed distribution under section 72(p) treated as an actual distribution for purposes of the qualification requirements of section 401, the distribution provisions of section 402, the distribution restrictions of section 401(k)(2)(B) or 403(b)(11), or the vesting requirements of § 1.411(a)-7(d)(5) (which affects the application of a graded vesting schedule in cases involving a prior distribution)?

A-12: No; thus, for example, if a participant in a money purchase plan who is an active employee has a deemed distribution under section 72(p), the plan will not be considered to have made an in-service distribution to the participant in violation of the qualification requirements applicable to money purchase plans. Similarly, the deemed distribution is not eligible to be rolled over to an eligible retirement plan and is not considered an impermissible distribution of an amount attributable to elective contributions in a section 401(k) plan. See also § 1.402(c)-2, Q&A-4(d) and § 1.401(k)-1(d)(6)(ii).

Q-13: How does a reduction (offset) of an account balance in order to repay a plan loan differ from a deemed distribution?

A-13: (a) *Difference between deemed distribution and plan loan offset amount.*—(1) Loans to a participant from a qualified employer plan can give rise to two types of taxable distributions—

(i) A deemed distribution pursuant to section 72(p); and

(ii) A distribution of an offset amount.

(2) As described in Q&A-4 of this section, a deemed distribution occurs when the requirements of Q&A-3 of this section are not satisfied, either when the loan is made or at a later time. A deemed distribution is treated as a distribution to the participant or beneficiary only for certain tax purposes and is not a distribution of the accrued benefit. A distribution of a plan loan offset amount (as defined in § 1.402(c)-2, Q&A-9(b)) occurs when, under the terms governing a plan loan, the accrued benefit of the participant or benefici-

ary is reduced (offset) in order to repay the loan (including the enforcement of the plan's security interest in the accrued benefit). A distribution of a plan loan offset amount could occur in a variety of circumstances, such as where the terms governing the plan loan require that, in the event of the participant's request for a distribution, a loan be repaid immediately or treated as in default.

(b) *Plan loan offset*. In the event of a plan loan offset, the amount of the account balance that is offset against the loan is an actual distribution for purposes of the Internal Revenue Code, not a deemed distribution under section 72(p). Accordingly, a plan may be prohibited from making such an offset under the provisions of section 401(a), 401(k)(2)(B) or 403(b)(11) prohibiting or limiting distributions to an active employee. See § 1.402(c)-2, Q&A-9(c), *Example 6*. See also Q&A-19 of this section for rules regarding the treatment of a loan after a deemed distribution.

Q-14: How is the amount includible in income as a result of a deemed distribution under section 72(p) required to be reported?

A-14: The amount includible in income as a result of a deemed distribution under section 72(p) is required to be reported on Form 1099-R (or any other form prescribed by the Commissioner).

Q-15: What withholding rules apply to plan loans?

A-15: To the extent that a loan, when made, is a deemed distribution or an account balance is reduced (offset) to repay a loan, the amount includible in income is subject to withholding. If a deemed distribution of a loan or a loan repayment by benefit offset results in income at a date after the date the loan is made, withholding is required only if a transfer of cash or property (excluding employer securities) is made to the participant or beneficiary from the plan at the same time. See § § 35.3405-1, f-4, and 31.3405(c)-1, Q&A-9 and Q&A11, of this chapter for further guidance on withholding rules.

Q-16: If a loan fails to satisfy the requirements of Q&A-3 of this section and is a prohibited transaction under section 4975, is the deemed distribution of the loan under section 72(p) a correction of the prohibited transaction?

A-16: No, a deemed distribution is not a correction of a prohibited transaction under section 4975. See § § 141.4975-13 and 53.4941(e)-1(c)(1) of this chapter for guidance concerning correction of a prohibited transaction.

Q-17: What are the income tax consequences if an amount is transferred from a qualified employer plan to a participant or beneficiary as a

Reg. § 1.72(p)-1

loan, but there is an express or tacit understanding that the loan will not be repaid?

A-17: If there is an express or tacit understanding that the loan will not be repaid or, for any reason, the transaction does not create a debtor-creditor relationship or is otherwise not a bona fide loan, then the amount transferred is treated as an actual distribution from the plan for purposes of the Internal Revenue Code, and is not treated as a loan or as a deemed distribution under section 72(p).

Q-18: If a qualified employer plan maintains a program to invest in residential mortgages, are loans made pursuant to the investment program subject to section 72(p)?

A-18: (a) Residential mortgage loans made by a plan in the ordinary course of an investment program are not subject to section 72(p) if the property acquired with the loans is the primary security for such loans and the amount loaned does not exceed the fair market value of the property. An investment program exists only if the plan has established, in advance of a specific investment under the program, that a certain percentage or amount of plan assets will be invested in residential mortgages available to persons purchasing the property who satisfy commercially customary financial criteria. A loan will not be considered as made under an investment program if—

(1) Any of the loans made under the program matures upon a participant's termination from employment;

(2) Any of the loans made under the program is an earmarked asset of a participant's or beneficiary's individual account in the plan; or

(3) The loans made under the program are made available only to participants or beneficiaries in the plan.

(b) Paragraph (a)(3) of this Q&A-18 shall not apply to a plan which, on December 20, 1995, and at all times thereafter, has had in effect a loan program under which, but for paragraph (a)(3) of this Q&A-18, the loans comply with the conditions of paragraph (a) of this Q&A-18 to constitute residential mortgage loans in the ordinary course of an investment program.

(c) No loan that benefits an officer, director, or owner of the employer maintaining the plan, or

their beneficiaries, will be treated as made under an investment program.

(d) This section does not provide guidance on whether a residential mortgage loan made under a plan's investment program would result in a prohibited transaction under section 4975, or on whether such a loan made by a plan covered by Title I of ERISA would be consistent with the fiduciary standards of ERISA or would result in a prohibited transaction under section 406 of ERISA. See 29 CFR 2550.408b-1.

Q-19: If there is a deemed distribution under section 72(p), is the interest that accrues thereafter on the amount of the deemed distribution an indirect loan for income tax purposes and what effect does the deemed distribution have on subsequent loans?

A-19: (a) *General rule.* Except as provided in paragraph (b) of this Q&A-19, a deemed distribution of a loan is treated as a distribution for purposes of section 72. Therefore, a loan that is deemed to be distributed under section 72(p) ceases to be an outstanding loan for purposes of section 72, and the interest that accrues thereafter under the plan on the amount deemed distributed is disregarded for purposes of applying section 72 to the participant or the beneficiary. Even though interest continues to accrue on the outstanding loan (and is taken into account for purposes of determining the tax treatment of any subsequent loan in accordance with paragraph (b) of this Q&A-19), this additional interest is not treated as an additional loan (and thus, does not result in an additional deemed distribution) for purposes of section 72(p). However, a loan that is deemed distributed under section 72(p) is not considered distributed for all purposes of the Internal Revenue Code. See Q&A-16 of this section.

(b) *Effect on subsequent loans*—(1) *Application of section 72(p)(2)(A).* A loan that is deemed distributed under section 72(p) (including interest accruing thereafter) and that has not been repaid (such as by a plan loan offset) is considered outstanding for purposes of applying section 72(p)(2)(A) to determine the maximum amount of any subsequent loan to the participant or beneficiary.

→ *Caution: Reg. § 1.72(p)-1, Q&A-19(b)(2), below, applies to assignments, pledges, and loans made on or after January 1, 2004.*←

(2) *Additional security for subsequent loans.* If a loan is deemed distributed to a participant or beneficiary under section 72(p) and has not been repaid (such as by a plan loan offset), then no

payment made thereafter to the participant or beneficiary is treated as a loan for purposes of section 72(p)(2) unless the loan otherwise satisfies

Reg. § 1.72(p)-1

→ *Caution: Reg. § 1.72(p)-1, Q&A-19(b)(2), below, applies to assignments, pledges, and loans made on or after January 1, 2004.*←

section 72(p)(2) and this section and either of the following conditions is satisfied:

(i) There is an arrangement among the plan, the participant or beneficiary, and the employer, enforceable under applicable law, under which repayments will be made by payroll withholding. For this purpose, an arrangement will not fail to be enforceable merely because a party has the right to revoke the arrangement prospectively.

(ii) The plan receives adequate security from the participant or beneficiary that is in addition to the participant's or beneficiary's accrued benefit under the plan.

(3) *Condition no longer satisfied.* If, following a deemed distribution that has not been repaid, a payment is made to a participant or beneficiary that satisfies the conditions in paragraph (b)(2) of this Q&A-19 for treatment as a plan loan and, subsequently, before repayment of the second loan, the conditions in paragraph (b)(2) of this Q&A-19 are no longer satisfied with respect to the second loan (for example, if the loan recipient revokes consent to payroll withholding), the amount then outstanding on the second loan is treated as a deemed distribution under section 72(p).

→ *Caution: Reg. § 1.72(p)-1, Q&A-20, below, applies to assignments, pledges, and loans made on or after January 1, 2004.*←

Q-20: May a participant refinance an outstanding loan or have more than one loan outstanding from a plan?

A-20: (a) *Refinancings and multiple loans*—(1) *General rule.* A participant who has an outstanding loan that satisfies section 72(p)(2) and this section may refinance that loan or borrow additional amounts if, under the facts and circumstances, the loans collectively satisfy the amount limitations of section 72(p)(2)(A) and the prior loan and the additional loan each satisfy the requirements of section 72(p)(2)(B) and (C) and this section. For this purpose, a refinancing includes any situation in which one loan replaces another loan.

(2) *Loans that repay a prior loan and have a later repayment date.* For purposes of section 72(p)(2) and this section (including paragraph (a)(3) of this Q&A-20 and the amount limitations of section 72(p)(2)(A)), if a loan that satisfies section 72(p)(2) is replaced by a loan (a replacement loan) and the term of the replacement loan ends after the latest permissible term of the loan it replaces (the replaced loan), then the replacement loan and the replaced loan are both treated as outstanding on the date of the transaction. For purposes of the preceding sentence, the latest permissible term of the replaced loan is the latest date permitted under section 72(p)(2)(C) (i.e., five years from the original date of the replaced loan, assuming that the replaced loan does not qualify for the exception at section 72(p)(2)(B)(ii) for principal residence plan loans and that no additional period of suspension applied to the replaced loan under Q&A-9(b) of this section). Thus, for example, if the term of the replacement loan ends after the latest permissible term of the replaced loan and the sum of the amount of the

replacement loan plus the outstanding balance of all other loans on the date of the transaction, including the replaced loan, fails to satisfy the amount limitations of section 72(p)(2)(A), then the replacement loan results in a deemed distribution. This paragraph (a)(2) does not apply to a replacement loan if the terms of the replacement loan would satisfy section 72(p)(2) and this section determined as if the replacement loan consisted of two separate loans, the replaced loan (amortized in substantially level payments over a period ending not later than the last day of the latest permissible term of the replaced loan) and, to the extent the amount of the replacement loan exceeds the amount of the replaced loan, a new loan that is also amortized in substantially level payments over a period ending not later than the last day of the latest permissible term of the replaced loan.

(b) *Examples.* The following examples illustrate the rules of this Q&A-20 and are based on the assumptions described in the introductory text of this section:

Example 1. (i) A participant with a vested account balance that exceeds $100,000 borrows $40,000 from a plan on January 1, 2005, to be repaid in 20 quarterly installments of $2,491 each. Thus, the term of the loan ends on December 31, 2009. On January 1, 2006, when the outstanding balance on the loan is $33,322, the loan is refinanced and is replaced by a new $40,000 loan from the plan to be repaid in 20 quarterly installments. Under the terms of the refinanced loan, the loan is to be repaid in level quarterly installments (of $2,491 each) over the next 20 quarters. Thus, the term of the new loan ends on December 31, 2010.

Reg. § 1.72(p)-1

→ *Caution: Reg. § 1.72(p)-1, Q&A-20, below, applies to assignments, pledges, and loans made on or after January 1, 2004.*←

(ii) Under section 72(p)(2)(A), the amount of the new loan, when added to the outstanding balance of all other loans from the plan, must not exceed $50,000 reduced by the excess of the highest outstanding balance of loans from the plan during the 1-year period ending on December 31, 2005 over the outstanding balance of loans from the plan on January 1, 2006, with such outstanding balance to be determined immediately prior to the new $40,000 loan. Because the term of the new loan ends later than the term of the loan it replaces, under paragraph (a)(2) of this Q&A-20, both the new loan and the loan it replaces must be taken into account for purposes of applying section 72(p)(2), including the amount limitations in section 72(p)(2)(A). The amount of the new loan is $40,000, the outstanding balance on January 1, 2006 of the loan it replaces is $33,322, and the highest outstanding balance of loans from the plan during 2005 was $40,000. Accordingly, under section 72(p)(2)(A), the sum of the new loan and the outstanding balance on January 1, 2006 of the loan it replaces must not exceed $50,000 reduced by $6,678 (the excess of the $40,000 maximum outstanding loan balance during 2005 over the $33,322 outstanding balance on January 1, 2006, determined immediately prior to the new loan) and, thus, must not exceed $43,322. The sum of the new loan ($40,000) and the outstanding balance on January 1, 2006 of the loan it replaces ($33,322) is $73,322. Since $73,322 exceeds the $43,322 limit under section 72(p)(2)(A) by $30,000, there is a deemed distribution of $30,000 on January 1, 2006.

(iii) However, no deemed distribution would occur if, under the terms of the refinanced loan, the amount of the first 16 installments on the refinanced loan were equal to $2,907, which is the sum of the $2,491 originally scheduled quarterly installment payment amount under the first loan, plus $416 (which is the amount required to repay, in level quarterly installments over 5 years beginning on January 1, 2006, the excess of the refinanced loan over the January 1, 2006 balance of the first loan ($40,000 minus $33,322 equals $6,678)), and the amount of the 4 remaining installments was equal to $416. The refinancing would not be subject to paragraph (a)(2) of this Q&A-20 because the terms of the new loan would satisfy section 72(p)(2) and this section (including the substantially level amortization requirements of section 72(p)(2)(B) and (C)) determined as if the new loan consisted of 2 loans, one of which is in the amount of the first loan ($33,322) and is amortized in substantially level payments over a

period ending December 31, 2009 (the last day of the term of the first loan) and the other of which is in the additional amount ($6,678) borrowed under the new loan. Similarly, the transaction also would not result in a deemed distribution (and would not be subject to paragraph (a)(2) of this Q&A-20) if the terms of the refinanced loan provided for repayments to be made in level quarterly installments (of $2,990 each) over the next 16 quarters.

Example 2. (i) The facts are the same as in *Example 1*(i), except that the applicable interest rate used by the plan when the loan is refinanced is significantly lower due to a reduction in market rates of interest and, under the terms of the refinanced loan, the amount of the first 16 installments on the refinanced loan is equal to $2,848 and the amount of the next 4 installments on the refinanced loan is equal to $406. The $2,848 amount is the sum of $2,442 to repay the first loan by December 31, 2009 (the term of the first loan), plus $406 (which is the amount to repay, in level quarterly installments over 5 years beginning on January 1, 2006 the $6,678 excess of the refinanced loan over the January 1, 2006 balance of the first loan).

(ii) The transaction does not result in a deemed distribution (and is not subject to paragraph (a)(2) of this Q&A-20) because the terms of the new loan would satisfy section 72(p)(2) and this section (including the substantially level amortization requirements of section 72(p)(2)(B) and (C)) determined as if the new loan consisted of 2 loans, one of which is in the amount of the first loan ($33,322) and is amortized in substantially level payments over a period ending December 31, 2009 (the last day of the term of the first loan) and the other of which is in the additional amount ($6,678) borrowed under the new loan. The transaction would also not result in a deemed distribution (and not be subject to paragraph (a)(2) of this Q&A-20) if the terms of the new loan provided for repayments to be made in level quarterly installments (of $2,931 each) over the next 16 quarters.

Q-21: Is a participant's tax basis under the plan increased if the participant repays the loan after a deemed distribution?

A-21: (a) *Repayments after deemed distribution.* Yes, if the participant or beneficiary repays the loan after a deemed distribution of the loan under section 72(p), then, for purposes of section 72(e), the participant's or beneficiary's investment in the contract (tax basis) under the plan increases by the amount of the cash repayments that the participant or beneficiary makes on the loan after the deemed distribution. However, loan repayments are not treated as aftertax contributions for other purposes, including sections 401(m) and 415(c)(2)(B).

(b) *Example.* The following example illustrates the rules in paragraph (a) of this Q&A-21 and is based on the assumptions described in the introductory text of this section:

Example. (i) A participant receives a $20,000 loan on January 1, 2003, to be repaid in 20 quarterly installments of $1,245 each. On December 31, 2003, the outstanding loan balance ($19,179) is deemed distributed as a result of a failure to make quarterly installment payments that were due on September 30, 2003 and December 31, 2003. On June 30, 2004, the participant repays $5,147 (which is the sum of the three installment payments that were due on September 30, 2003, December 31, 2003, and March 31, 2004, with interest thereon to June 30, 2004, plus the installment payment due on June 30, 2004). Thereafter, the participant resumes making the installment payments of $1,245 from September 30, 2004 through December 31, 2007. The loan repayments made after December 31, 2003 through December 31, 2007 total $22,577.

(ii) Because the participant repaid $22,577 after the deemed distribution that occurred on December 31, 2003, the participant has investment in the contract (tax basis) equal to $22,577 (14 payments of $1,245 each plus a single payment of $5,147) as of December 31, 2007.

Q-22: When is the effective date of section 72(p) and the regulations in this section?

A-22: (a) *Statutory effective date.* Section 72(p) generally applies to assignments, pledges, and loans made after August 13, 1982.

(b) *Regulatory effective date.* This section applies to assignments, pledges, and loans made on or after January 1, 2002.

(c) *Loans made before the regulatory effective date*—(1) *General rule.* A plan is permitted to apply Q&A-19 and Q&A-21 of this section to a loan made before the regulatory effective date in paragraph (b) of this Q&A-22 (and after the statutory effective date in paragraph (a) of this Q&A-22) if there has not been any deemed distribution of the loan before the transition date or if the conditions of paragraph (c)(2) of this Q&A-22 are satisfied with respect to the loan.

(2) *Consistency transition rule for certain loans deemed distributed before the regulatory effective date.*—(i) The rules in this paragraph (c)(2) of this Q&A-22 apply to a loan made before the regulatory effective date in paragraph (b) of this Q&A-22 (and after the statutory effective date in

paragraph (a) of this Q&A-22) if there has been any deemed distribution of the loan before the transition date.

(ii) The plan is permitted to apply Q&A-19 and Q&A-21 of this section to the loan beginning on any January 1, but only if the plan reported, in Box 1 of Form 1099-R, for a taxable year no later than the latest taxable year that would be permitted under this section (if this section had been in effect for all loans made after the statutory effective date in paragraph (a) of this Q&A-22), a gross distribution of an amount at least equal to the initial default amount. For purposes of this section, the initial default amount is the amount that would be reported as a gross distribution under Q&A-4 and Q&A-10 of this section and the transition date is the January 1 on which a plan begins applying Q&A-19 and Q&A-21 of this section to a loan.

(iii) If a plan applies Q&A-19 and Q&A-21 of this section to such a loan, then the plan, in its reporting and withholding on or after the transition date, must not attribute investment in the contract (tax basis) to the participant or beneficiary based upon the initial default amount.

(iv) This paragraph (c)(2)(iv) of this Q&A-22 applies if—

(A) The plan attributed investment in the contract (tax basis) to the participant or beneficiary based on the deemed distribution of the loan;

(B) The plan subsequently made an actual distribution to the participant or beneficiary before the transition date; and

(C) Immediately before the transition date, the initial default amount (or, if less, the amount of the investment in the contract so attributed) exceeds the participant's or beneficiary's investment in the contract (tax basis). If this paragraph (c)(2)(iv) of this Q&A-22 applies, the plan must treat the excess (the loan transition amount) as a loan amount that remains outstanding and must include the excess in the participant's or beneficiary's income at the time of the first actual distribution made on or after the transition date.

(3) *Examples.* The rules in paragraph (c)(2) of this Q&A-22 are illustrated by the following examples, which are based on the assumptions described in the introductory text of this section (and, except as specifically provided in the examples, also assume that no distributions are made to the participant and that the participant has no investment in the contract with respect to the plan). *Example 1, Example 2,* and *Example 4* of this paragraph (c)(3) of this Q&A-22 illustrate the application of the rules in paragraph (c)(2) of this Q&A-22 to a plan that, before the transition date, did not treat interest accruing after the initial

Reg. § 1.72(p)-1

deemed distribution as resulting in additional deemed distributions under section 72(p). *Example 3* of this paragraph (c)(3) of this Q&A-22 illustrates the application of the rules in paragraph (c)(2) of this Q&A-22 to a plan that, before the transition date, treated interest accruing after the initial deemed distribution as resulting in additional deemed distributions under section 72(p). The examples are as follows:

Example 1. (i) In 1998, when a participant's account balance under a plan is $50,000, the participant receives a loan from the plan. The participant makes the required repayments until 1999 when there is a deemed distribution of $20,000 as a result of a failure to repay the loan. For 1999, as a result of the deemed distribution, the plan reports, in Box 1 of Form 1099-R, a gross distribution of $20,000 (which is the initial default amount in accordance with paragraph (c)(2)(ii) of this Q&A-22) and, in Box 2 of Form 1099-R, a taxable amount of $20,000. The plan then records an increase in the participant's tax basis for the same amount ($20,000). Thereafter, the plan disregards, for purposes of section 72, the interest that accrues on the loan after the 1999 deemed distribution. Thus, as of December 31, 2001, the total taxable amount reported by the plan as a result of the deemed distribution is $20,000 and the plan's records show that the participant's tax basis is the same amount ($20,000). As of January 1, 2002, the plan decides to apply Q&A-19 of this section to the loan. Accordingly, it reduces the participant's tax basis by the initial default amount of $20,000, so that the participant's remaining tax basis in the plan is zero. Thereafter, the amount of the outstanding loan is not treated as part of the account balance for purposes of section 72. The participant attains age 59-1/2 in the year 2003 and receives a distribution of the full account balance under the plan consisting of $60,000 in cash and the loan receivable. At that time, the plan's records reflect an offset of the loan amount against the loan receivable in the participant's account and a distribution of $60,000 in cash.

(ii) For the year 2003, the plan must report a gross distribution of $60,000 in Box 1 of Form 1099-R and a taxable amount of $60,000 in Box 2 of Form 1099-R.

Example 2. (i) The facts are the same as in *Example 1,* except that in 1999, immediately prior to the deemed distribution, the participant's account balance under the plan totals $50,000 and the participant's tax basis is $10,000. For 1999, the plan reports, in Box 1 of Form 1099-R, a gross distribution of $20,000 (which is the initial default amount in accordance with paragraph

(c)(2)(ii) of this Q&A-22) and reports, in Box 2 of Form 1099-R, a taxable amount of $16,000 (the $20,000 deemed distribution minus $4,000 of tax basis ($10,000 times ($20,000/$50,000)) allocated to the deemed distribution). The plan then records an increase in tax basis equal to the $20,000 deemed distribution, so that the participant's remaining tax basis as of December 31, 1999, totals $26,000 ($10,000 minus $4,000 plus $20,000). Thereafter, the plan disregards, for purposes of section 72, the interest that accrues on the loan after the 1999 deemed distribution. Thus, as of December 31, 2001, the total taxable amount reported by the plan as a result of the deemed distribution is $16,000 and the plan's records show that the participant's tax basis is $26,000. As of January 1, 2002, the plan decides to apply Q&A19 of this section to the loan. Accordingly, it reduces the participant's tax basis by the initial default amount of $20,000, so that the participant's remaining tax basis in the plan is $6,000. Thereafter, the amount of the outstanding loan is not treated as part of the account balance for purposes of section 72. The participant attains age 59-1/2 in the year 2003 and receives a distribution of the full account balance under the plan consisting of $60,000 in cash and the loan receivable. At that time, the plan's records reflect an offset of the loan amount against the loan receivable in the participant's account and a distribution of $60,000 in cash.

(ii) For the year 2003, the plan must report a gross distribution of $60,000 in Box 1 of Form 1099-R and a taxable amount of $54,000 in Box 2 of Form 1099-R.

Example 3. (i) In 1993, when a participant's account balance in a plan is $100,000, the participant receives a loan of $50,000 from the plan. The participant makes the required loan repayments until 1995 when there is a deemed distribution of $28,919 as a result of a failure to repay the loan. For 1995, as a result of the deemed distribution, the plan reports, in Box 1 of Form 1099-R, a gross distribution of $28,919 (which is the initial default amount in accordance with paragraph (c)(2)(ii) of this Q&A-22) and, in Box 2 of Form 1099-R, a taxable amount of $28,919. For 1995, the plan also records an increase in the participant's tax basis for the same amount ($28,919). Each year thereafter through 2001, the plan reports a gross distribution equal to the interest accruing that year on the loan balance, reports a taxable amount equal to the interest accruing that year on the loan balance reduced by the participant's tax basis allocated to the gross distribution, and records a net increase in the participant's tax basis equal to that taxable amount. As of December 31, 2001, the taxable amount reported by the plan as a result of the loan totals $44,329 and the plan's records for purposes of section 72 show that the participant's tax basis totals the same amount ($44,329). As of January 1, 2002, the plan decides to apply Q&A-19 of this section. Accordingly, it reduces the participant's tax basis by the initial default amount of $28,919, so that the participant's remaining tax basis in the plan is $15,410 ($44,329 minus $28,919). Thereafter, the amount of the outstanding loan is not treated as part of the account balance for purposes of section 72. The participant attains age 59-1/2 in the year 2003 and receives a distribution of the full account balance under the plan consisting of $180,000 in cash and the loan receivable equal to the $28,919 outstanding loan amount in 1995 plus interest accrued thereafter to the payment date in 2003. At that time, the plan's records reflect an offset of the loan amount against the loan receivable in the participant's account and a distribution of $180,000 in cash.

(ii) For the year 2003, the plan must report a gross distribution of $180,000 in Box 1 of Form 1099-R and a taxable amount of $164,590 in Box 2 of Form 1099-R ($180,000 minus the remaining tax basis of $15,410).

Example 4. (i) The facts are the same as in *Example 1*, except that in 2000, after the deemed distribution, the participant receives a $10,000 hardship distribution. At the time of the hardship distribution, the participant's account balance under the plan totals $50,000. For 2000, the plan reports, in Box 1 of Form 1099-R, a gross distribution of $10,000 and, in Box 2 of Form 1099-R, a taxable amount of $6,000 (the $10,000 actual distribution minus $4,000 of tax basis ($10,000 times ($20,000/$50,000)) allocated to this actual distribution). The plan then records a decrease in tax basis equal to $4,000, so that the participant's remaining tax basis as of December 31, 2000, totals $16,000 ($20,000 minus $4,000). After 1999, the plan disregards, for purposes of section 72, the interest that accrues on the loan after the 1999 deemed distribution. Thus, as of December 31, 2001, the total taxable amount reported by the plan as a result of the deemed distribution plus the 2000 actual distribution is $26,000 and the plan's records show that the participant's tax basis is $16,000. As of January 1, 2002, the plan decides to apply Q&A-19 of this section to the loan. Accordingly, it reduces the participant's tax basis by the initial default amount of $20,000, so that the participant's remaining tax basis in the plan is reduced from $16,000 to zero. However, because the $20,000 initial default amount exceeds $16,000, the plan records a loan transition amount of $4,000 ($20,000 minus $16,000). Thereafter, the amount of the outstanding loan,

other than the $4,000 loan transition amount, is not treated as part of the account balance for purposes of section 72. The participant attains age 59-1/2 in the year 2003 and receives a distribution of the full account balance under the plan consisting of $60,000 in cash and the loan receivable. At that time, the plan's records reflect an offset of the loan amount against the loan receivable in the participant's account and a distribution of $60,000 in cash.

(ii) In accordance with paragraph (c)(2)(iv) of this Q&A22, the plan must report in Box 1 of Form 1099-R a gross distribution of $64,000 and in Box 2 of Form 1099-R a taxable amount for the participant for the year 2003 equal to $64,000 (the sum of the $60,000 paid in the year 2003 plus $4,000 as the loan transition amount).

(d) *Effective date for Q&A-19(b)(2) and Q&A-20.* Q&A-19(b)(2) and Q&A-20 of this section apply to assignments, pledges, and loans made on or after January 1, 2004. [Reg. § 1.72(p)-1.]

☐ [*T.D. 8894, 7-28-2000. Amended by T.D. 9021, 12-2-2002.*]

[Reg. § 1.73-1]

§ 1.73-1. **Services of child.**—(a) Compensation for personal services of a child shall, regardless of the provisions of State law relating to who is entitled to the earnings of the child, and regardless of whether the income is in fact received by the child, be deemed to be the gross income of the child and not the gross income of the parent of the child. Such compensation, therefore, shall be included in the gross income of the child and shall be reflected in the return rendered by or for such child. The income of a minor child is not required to be included in the gross income of the parent for income tax purposes. For requirements for making the return by such child, or for such child by his guardian, or other person charged with the care of his person or property, see section 6012.

(b) In the determination of taxable income or adjusted gross income, as the case may be, all expenditures made by the parent or the child attributable to amounts which are includible in the gross income of the child and not of the parent solely by reason of section 73 are deemed to have been paid or incurred by the child. In such determination, the child is entitled to take deductions not only for expenditures made on his behalf by his parent which would be commonly considered as business expenses, but also for other expenditures such as charitable contributions made by the parent in the name of the child and out of the child's earnings.

(c) For purposes of section 73, the term "parent" includes any individual who is entitled to the services of the child by reason of having parental rights and duties in respect of the child. See section 6201(c) and the regulations in Part 301 of this chapter (Regulations on Procedure and Administration) for assessment of tax against the parent in certain cases. [Reg. § 1.73-1.]

☐ [*T.D.* 6211, 11-14-56.]

[Reg. § 1.74-1]

§ 1.74-1. Prizes and awards.—(a) *Inclusion in gross income.* (1) Section 74(a) requires the inclusion in gross income of all amounts received as prizes and awards, unless such prizes or awards qualify as an exclusion from gross income under subsection (b), or unless such prize or award is a scholarship or fellowship grant excluded from gross income by section 117. Prizes and awards which are includible in gross income include (but are not limited to) amounts received from radio and television giveaway shows, door prizes, and awards in contests of all types, as well as any prizes and awards from an employer to an employee in recognition of some achievement in connection with his employment.

(2) If the prize or award is not made in money but is made in goods or services, the fair market value of the goods or services is the amount to be included in income.

(b) *Exclusion from gross income.* Section 74(b) provides an exclusion from gross income of any amount received as a prize or award, if (1) such prize or award was made primarily in recognition of past achievements of the recipient in religious, charitable, scientific, educational, artistic, literary, or civic fields; (2) the recipient was selected without any action on his part to enter the contest or proceedings; and (3) the recipient is not required to render substantial future services as a condition to receiving the prize or award. Thus, such awards as the Nobel prize and the Pulitzer prize would qualify for the exclusion. Section 74(b) does not exclude prizes or awards from an employer to an employee in recognition of some achievement in connection with his employment.

(c) *Scholarships and fellowship grants.* See section 117 and the regulations thereunder for provisions relating to scholarships and fellowship grants. [Reg. § 1.74-1.]

☐ [*T.D.* 6137, 7-6-55.]

[Reg. § 1.75-1]

§ 1.75-1. Treatment of bond premiums in case of dealers in tax-exempt securities.—(a) *In general.* (1) Section 75 requires certain adjustments to be made by dealers in securities with respect to premiums paid on municipal bonds which are held for sale to customers in the ordinary course of the trade or business. The adjustments depend upon the method of accounting used by the taxpayer in computing the gross income from the trade or business. See paragraphs (b) and (c) of this section.

(2) The term "municipal bond" under section 75 means any obligation issued by a government or political subdivision thereof if the interest on the obligation is excludable from gross income under section 103. However, such term does not include an obligation—

(i) If the earliest maturity or call date of the obligation is more than 5 years from the date of acquisition by the taxpayer or the obligation is sold or otherwise disposed of by the taxpayer within 30 days after the date of acquisition by him, and

(ii) If, in case of an obligation acquired after December 31, 1957, the amount realized upon its sale (or, in the case of any other disposition, its fair market value at the time of disposition) is higher than its adjusted basis.

For purposes of this subparagraph, the amount realized on the sale of the obligation, or the fair market value of the obligation, shall not include any amount attributable to interest, and the adjusted basis shall be computed without regard to any adjustment for amortization of bond premium required under section 75 and section 1016(a)(6). For purposes of determining whether the obligation is sold or otherwise disposed of by the taxpayer within 30 days after the date of its acquisition by him, it is immaterial whether or not such 30-day period is entirely within one taxable year.

(3) The term "cost of securities sold" means the amount ascertained by subtracting the inventory value of the closing inventory of a taxable year from the sum of the inventory value of the opening inventory for such year and the cost of securities and other property purchased during such year which would properly be included in the inventory of the taxpayer if on hand at the close of the taxable year.

(b) *Inventories not valued at cost.* (1) In the case of a dealer in securities who computes gross income from his trade or business by the use of inventories and values such inventories on any basis other than cost, the adjustment required by section 75 is, except as provided in subparagraph (2) of this paragraph, the reduction of "cost of securities sold" by the amount equal to the amortizable bond premium which would be disallowed as a deduction under section 171(a)(2) with respect to the municipal bond if the dealer were an ordinary investor holding such bond. Such amortizable bond premium is computed under section

171(b) by reference to the cost or other original basis of the bond on the date of acquisition (determined without regard to section 1013, relating to inventory value on a subsequent date).

(2) With respect to an obligation acquired after December 31, 1957, which has as its earliest maturity or call date a date more than five years from the date on which it was acquired by the taxpayer, the following rules shall apply:

(i) If the taxpayer holds the obligation at the end of the taxable year, he is not required by section 75 to reduce the "cost of securities sold" for such year with respect to the obligation.

(ii) If the taxpayer sells or otherwise disposes of the obligation during the taxable year, he shall reduce the "cost of securities sold" for the taxable year of the sale or disposition unless he sold the obligation for more than its adjusted basis or otherwise disposed of it when its fair market value was more than its adjusted basis. For purposes of determining whether or not the taxpayer sold the obligation for more than its adjusted basis, or otherwise disposed of it when its fair market value was more than its adjusted basis, the amount realized on the sale of the obligation, or the fair market value of the obligation, shall not include any amount attributable to interest, and the adjusted basis shall be computed without regard to any adjustment for amortization of bond

premium required under sections 75 and 1016(a)(6). The amount of the reduction referred to in the first sentence of this subdivision is the total amount by which the adjusted basis of the obligation would be required to be reduced under section 1016(a)(5) were the obligation subject to the amortizable bond premium provisions of section 171; that is, the amount of the amortizable bond premium attributable to the period during which the obligation was held which would be disallowed as a deduction under section 171(a)(2) if the taxpayer were an ordinary investor.

(3) This paragraph may be illustrated by the following examples:

Example (1). X, a dealer in securities who values his inventories on a basis other than cost, makes his income tax returns on the calendar year basis. On July 1, 1954, he bought, for $1,060 each, three municipal bonds (A, B, and C) having a face obligation of $1,000, and maturing on July 1, 1959. Bond A is sold on December 31, 1954, bond B is sold on December 31, 1955, and bond C is sold on June 30, 1956. For each bond the amortizable bond premium to maturity is $60, the period from date of acquisition to maturity is 60 months, and the amortizable bond premium per month is $1. The adjustment for each of the years 1954, 1955, and 1956 is as follows:

			Adjustment to "cost of securities sold" for—		
Bond	Date acquired	Date Sold	1954	1955	1956
A	July 1, 1954	Dec. 31, 1954	$ 6	—	—
B	July 1, 1954	Dec. 31, 1955	6	$12	—
C	July 1, 1954	June 30, 1956	6	12	$6
		Total	$18	$24	$6

Example (2). Y is a dealer in securities who values his inventories on a basis other than cost. He makes his income tax returns on the calendar year basis. On January 1, 1958, Y bought five bonds (D, E, F, G, and H) issued by various municipalities. Each bond has a face obligation of $1,000 and was purchased for $1,060. The interest on each is excludable from gross income under section 103. Bonds D, E, and F mature on December 31, 1962, and bonds G and H mature on December 31, 1967. The amortizable bond premium per month is $1 with respect to bonds D, E, and F, and is $.50 with respect to bonds G and H. The following table indicates the reduction in "cost of securities sold" which Y should make for the years shown, assuming that he sells the bonds on the dates and for the prices set forth:

			Adjustment to "cost of securities sold" for—		
Bond	Date sold	Sale price	1958	1959	1960
D	Feb. 1, 1959	$1,090	$ 12	$ 1	...
E	Jan. 30, 1958	1,100	None	...	...
F	Jan. 30, 1958	1,000	1	...	...
G	Dec. 31, 1960	1,065	None	None	None
H	Dec. 31, 1960	1,050	None	None	$ 18
			$ 13	$ 1	$ 18

Reg. § 1.75-1(b)(2)

An adjustment to "cost of securities sold" must be made with respect to bond D (even though it was ultimately sold at a gain) because the bond neither had an earliest maturity or call date of more than 5 years from the date on which Y acquired it, nor was it disposed of within 30 days after such date. An adjustment must be made for the years 1958 and 1959 since section 75(a)(1) requires that an adjustment be made with respect to such a bond at the close of each taxable year in which it is held. On the other hand, since bonds E, F, G, and H either were disposed of within 30 days after the date of such acquisition or had an earliest maturity or call date more than 5 years from the date of acquisition, and were acquired after December 31, 1957, it is necessary to determine whether Y disposed of them at a loss so as to require an adjustment under section 75. No adjustment is necessary with respect to bonds E and G because they were sold at a gain. An adjustment to "cost of securities sold" is required with respect to bonds F and H because they were sold at a loss. As in the case of bond D, an adjustment with respect to bond F is made in 1958 in accordance with section 75(a)(1); however, the adjustment with respect to bond H is made entirely in 1960, the taxable year in which Y sold that bond, in accordance with the last sentence of section 75(a). If Y had acquired bonds before January 1, 1958, it would be unnecessary to determine whether they were disposed of at a loss since that factor is significant only with respect to bonds acquired on or after that date.

(c) *Inventories not used or inventories at cost.* (1) In the case of a dealer in securities who computes gross income from his trade business without the use of inventories or by of inventories valued at cost, the adjustment required by section 75 is a reduction of the adjusted basis of each municipal bond sold or otherwise disposed of during the taxable year. The amount of such reduction is the total amount by which the adjusted basis of the bond would be required to be reduced under section 1016(a)(5) were the bond subject to the amortizable bond premium provisions of section 171; that is, the amount of the amortizable bond premium attributable to the period during which the bond was held which would be disallowed as a deduction under section 171(a)(2) if the taxpayer were an ordinary investor.

(2) Subparagraph (1) of this paragraph may be illustrated by the following example:

Example. Z, a dealer in securities who values his inventories on the basis of cost, makes his income tax returns on the calendar year basis. On January 1, 1954, he buys, for $1,060 each, three municipal bonds (I, J, and K) having a face obligation of $1,000, and maturing on January 1, 1959. Bond I is sold on December 31, 1954, bond J is sold on June 30, 1955, and bond K is sold on December 31, 1956. For each bond, the amortizable bond premium to maturity is $60, the period from the date of acquisition to maturity is 60 months, and the amortizable bond premium per month is $1.

Bond	Date acquired	Date sold	Adjustment for—		
			1954	1955	1956
I	Jan. 1, 1954	Dec. 31, 1954	$12	...	...
J	Jan. 1, 1954	June 30, 1955	None	$18	...
K	Jan. 1, 1954	Dec. 31, 1956	None	None	$36

(d) *Bonds acquired before July 1, 1950.* Under section 203(c) of the Revenue Act of 1950, adjustment is required for a municipal bond acquired before July 1, 1950, only with respect to taxable years beginning on or after that date. Accordingly, if the municipal bond was acquired before July 1, 1950, then for purposes of section 75 the amortizable bond premium under section 171 must be computed after adjusting the bond premium to the extent proper to reflect unamortized bond premium for so much of the holding period (as determined under section 1223) as precedes

the taxable year of the dealer beginning on or after July 1, 1950. Thus, in example (1) of paragraph (b) and in the example in paragraph (c) of this section, the first taxable year beginning on or after July 1, 1950, is, for each dealer, the taxable year beginning January 1, 1951. If each dealer had purchased for $1,060 on April 1, 1950, a municipal bond having a face obligation of $1,000 and maturing April 1, 1955, and had sold such bond on February 28, 1955, the adjustment under section 75 would be computed as follows:

	Dealer X	Dealer Z
Bond premium	$ 60	$ 60
Adjustment for holding period prior to January 1, 1951	9	9
Amortizable bond premium to maturity, as adjusted	$ 51	$ 51
Amortizable bond premium per month	$ 1	$ 1
Total adjustments under sec. 22(o), 1939 Code, for years 1951-1953	36	None
Adjustment under sec. 75 for 1954	12	None
Adjustment under sec. 75 for 1955	2	50

[Reg. § 1.75-1.]

☐ [*T.D.* 6137, 7-6-55. *Amended by T.D.* 6647, 4-10-63.]

[Reg. § 1.77-1]

§ 1.77-1. **Election to consider Commodity Credit Corporation loans as income.**—A taxpayer who receives a loan from the Commodity Credit Corporation may, at his election, include the amount of such loan in his gross income for the taxable year in which the loan is received. If a taxpayer makes such an election (or has made such an election under section 123 of the Internal Revenue Code of 1939 or under section 223(d) of the Revenue Act of 1939 (53 Stat. 897)), then for subsequent taxable years he shall include in his gross income all amounts received during those years as loans from the Commodity Credit Corporation, unless he secures the permission of the Commissioner to change to a different method of accounting. Application for permission to change such method of accounting and the basis upon which the return is made shall be filed with the Commissioner of Internal Revenue, Washington 25, D.C., within 90 days after the beginning of the taxable year to be covered by the return. [Reg. § 1.77-1.]

☐ [*T.D.* 6137, 7-6-55.]

[Reg. § 1.77-2]

§ 1.77-2. **Effect of election to consider commodity credit loans as income.**—(a) If a taxpayer elects or has elected under section 77, section 123 of the Internal Revenue Code of 1939, or section 223(d) of the Revenue Act of 1939 (53 Stat. 897), as amended, to include in his gross income the amount of a loan from the Commodity Credit Corporation for the taxable year in which it is received, then—

(1) No part of the amount realized by the Commodity Credit Corporation upon the sale or other disposition of the commodity pledged for such loan shall be recognized as income to the taxpayer, unless the taxpayer receives an amount in addition to that advanced to him as the loan, in which event such additional amount shall be in-

cluded in the gross income of the taxpayer for the taxable year in which it is received, and

(2) No deductible loss to the taxpayer shall be recognized on account of any deficiency realized by the Commodity Credit Corporation on such loan if the taxpayer was relieved from liability for such deficiency.

(b) The application of paragraph (a) of this section may be illustrated by the following example:

Example. A, a taxpayer who elected for his taxable year 1952 to include in gross income amounts received as loans from the Commodity Credit Corporation, received as loans $500 in 1952, $700 in 1953, and $900 in 1954. In 1956 all the pledged commodity was sold by the Commodity Credit Corporation for an amount $100 and $200 less than the loans with respect to the commodity pledged in 1952 and 1953, respectively, and for an amount $150 greater than the loan with respect to the commodity pledged in 1954. A, in making his return for 1956, shall include in gross income the sum of $150 if it is received during that year, but will not be allowed a deduction for the deficiencies of $100 and $200 unless he is required to satisfy such deficiencies and does satisfy them during that year. [Reg. § 1.77-2.]

☐ [*T.D.* 6137, 7-6-55.]

[Reg. § 1.78-1]

§ 1.78-1. **Dividends received from certain foreign corporations by certain domestic corporations choosing the foreign tax credit.**—(a) *Taxes deemed paid by certain domestic corporations treated as a section 78 dividend.* If a domestic corporation chooses to have the benefits of the foreign tax credit under section 901 for any taxable year, an amount which is equal to the foreign income taxes deemed to be paid by such corporation for such year under section 902(a) in accordance with § § 1.902-1 and 1.902-2, or under section 960(a)(1) in accordance with § 1.960-7, shall, to the extent provided by this section, be treated as a dividend (hereinafter referred to as a section 78 dividend) received by such domestic

Reg. § 1.77-1

corporation from the foreign corporation described in section 902(a) in accordance with §§ 1.902-1 and 1.902-2 or section 960(a)(1) in accordance with § 1.960-7, as the case may be. Any reduction under section 907(a) of the foreign income taxes deemed to be paid with respect to foreign oil and gas extraction income does not affect the amount treated as a section 78 dividend. A section 78 dividend shall be treated as a dividend for all purposes of the Code, except that it shall not be treated as a dividend under section 245, relating to dividends received from certain foreign corporations, or increase the earnings and profits of the domestic corporation. For purposes of determining the source of a section 78 dividend in computing the limitation on the foreign tax credit under section 904, see § 1.902-1(h)(1) and the regulations under section 960. For special rules relating to the determination of the foreign tax credit under section 902 with respect to certain minimum distributions received from controlled foreign corporations and the effect of such rules upon the gross-up under section 78, see paragraph (c) of § 1.963-4. For rules respecting the reduction of foreign income taxes under section 6038(b) in applying section 902(a) in accordance with §§ 1.902-1 and 1.902-2 and section 960(a)(1) in accordance with § 1.960-7 where there has been a failure to furnish certain information and for an illustration of the effect of such reduction upon the amount of a section 78 dividend, see paragraph (1) of § 1.6038-2.

(b) *Certain taxes not treated as a section 78 dividend.* Foreign income taxes deemed paid by a domestic corporation under section 902(a) in accordance with §§ 1.902-1 and 1.902-2 or section 960(a)(1) in accordance with § 1.960-7 shall not, to the extent provided by paragraph (b) of § 1.960-3, be treated as a section 78 dividend where such taxes are imposed on certain distributions from the earnings and profits of a controlled foreign corporation attributable to an amount which is, or has been, included in gross income of the domestic corporation under section 951.

(c) *United Kingdom income tax included in gross income under treaty.* Any amount of United Kingdom income tax appropriate to a dividend paid by a corporation which is a resident of the United Kingdom shall not be treated as a section 78 dividend by a domestic corporation to the extent that such tax is included in the gross income of such domestic corporation in accordance with Article XIII (1) of the income tax convention between the United States and the United Kingdom, as amended by Article II of the supplementary protocol between such Governments signed on August 19, 1957 (9 UST 1331). See § 507.117

of this chap...
States tax lia...
to have been p...

(c) *Taxable* ... received. A sec... ered received in... corporation in wh...

(1) The corp... reason of which ... 902(a) in accordan... the foreign income ... section 78 dividend, ...

(2) The corporat... under section 951(a) ... which there are dee... 960(a)(1) in accordance... income taxes which give... dividend,

notwithstanding that such foreign... may be carried back or carried over to... taxable year under section 904(d) and are deem... to be paid or accrued in such other taxable year.

(e) *Effective dates for the application of section 78*—(1) *In general.* This section shall apply to amounts of foreign income taxes deemed paid under section 902(a) in accordance with §§ 1.902-1 and 1.902-2, or under section 960(a)(1) in accordance with § 1.960-7 by reason of a distribution received by a domestic corporation—

(i) After December 31, 1964, or

(ii) Before January 1, 1965, in a taxable year of such domestic corporation beginning after December 31, 1962, but only to the extent that such distribution is made out of the accumulated profits of a foreign corporation for a taxable year of such foreign corporation beginning after December 31, 1962.

For special rules relating to determination of accumulated profits for such purposes, see regulations under section 902.

(2) *Amounts under section 951 treated as distributions.* For purposes of this paragraph, any amount attributable to the earnings and profits for the taxable year of a first-tier corporation (as defined in paragraph (b)(1) of § 1.960-1) which is included in the gross income of a domestic corporation under section 951(a) shall be treated as a distribution received by such domestic corporation on the last day in such taxable year on which such first-tier corporation is a controlled foreign corporation.

(f) *Illustrations.* The application of this section may be illustrated by the examples provided in § 1.902-1, § 1.904-5, § 1.960-3, § 1.960-4 and § 1.963-4. [Reg. § 1.78-1.]

24,250

...ed by T.D. 7120, ...e.D. 7490, 6-10-77, ... 7961, 6-20-84.]

[1.79-0]

☐[ITE... ...n life insurance—defini-
...ms.—The following defini-
...ses of section 79, this section,
6-3-2, and 1.79-3.

...ly or indirectly. A policy of life
...arried directly or indirectly" by an

...employer pays any part of the cost of
...surance directly or through another per-

The employer or two or more employers
...ange for payment of the cost of the life insur-
...ce by their employees and charge at least one
employee less than the cost of his or her insurance,
as determined under Table I of § 1.79-3(d)(2), and
at least one other employee more than the cost of
his or her insurance, determined in the same way.

Employee. An "employee" is—

(a) A person who performs services if his or her
relationship to the person for whom services are
performed is the legal relationship of employer
and employee described in § 31.3401(c)-1; or

(b) A full-time life insurance salesperson described in section 7701(a)(20); or

(c) A person who formerly performed services
as an employee.

A person who formerly performed services as an
employee and currently performs services for the
same employer as an independent contractor is
considered an employee only with respect to insurance provided because of the person's former services as an employee.

Group of employees. A "group of employees" is
all employees of an employer, or less than all
employees if membership in the group is determined solely on the basis of age, marital status, or
factors related to employment. Examples of factors related to employment are membership in a
union some or all of whose members are employed
by the employer, duties performed, compensation
received, and length of service. Ordinarily the
purchase of something other than group-term life
insurance is not a factor related to employment.
For example, if an employer provides credit life
insurance to all employees who purchase automobiles, these employees are not a "group of employees" because membership is not determined solely
on the basis of age, marital status, or factors
related to employment. On the other hand, participation in an employer's pension, profit-sharing,
or accident and health plan is considered a factor

related to employment even if employees are required to contribute to the cost of the plan. Ownership of stock in the employer corporation is not
a factor related to employment. However, participation in an employer's stock bonus plan may be
a factor related to employment and a "group of
employees" may include employees who own stock
in the employer corporation.

Permanent benefit. A "permanent benefit" is
an economic value extending beyond one policy
year (for example, a paid-up or cash surrender
value) that is provided under a life insurance
policy. However, the following features are not
permanent benefits:

(a) A right to convert (or continue) life insurance after group life insurance coverage
terminates;

(b) Any other feature that provides no economic benefit (other than current insurance protection) to the employee; or

(c) A feature under which term life insurance is
provided at a level premium for a period of five
years or less.

Policy. The term "policy" includes two or more
obligations of an insurer (or its affiliates) that are
sold in conjunction. Obligations that are offered or
available to members of a group of employees are
sold in conjunction if they are offered or available
because of the employment relationship. The actuarial sufficiency of the premium charged for
each obligation is not taken into account in determining whether the obligations are sold in conjunction. In addition, obligations may be sold in
conjunction even if the obligations are contained
in separate documents, each document is filed
with and approved by the applicable state insurance commission, or each obligation is independent of any other obligation. Thus, a group of
individual contracts under which life insurance is
provided to a group of employees may be a policy.
Similarly, two benefits provided to a group of
employees, one term life insurance and the other a
permanent benefit, may be a policy, even if one of
the benefits is provided only to employees who
decline the other benefit. However, an employer
may elect to treat two or more obligations each of
which provides no permanent benefits as separate
policies if the premiums are properly allocated
among such policies. An employer also may elect
to treat an obligation which provides permanent
benefits as a separate policy if—

(1) The insurer sells the obligation directly to
the employee who pays the full cost thereof;

(2) The participation of the employer with
respect to sales of the obligation to employees is
limited to selection of the insurer and the type of
coverage and to sales assistance activities such as

providing employee lists to the insurer, permitting the insurer to use the employer's premises for solicitation, and collecting premiums through payroll deduction;

(3) The insurer sells the obligation on the same terms and in substantial amounts to individuals who do not purchase (and whose employers do not purchase) any other obligation from the insurer; and

(4) No employer-provided benefit is conditioned on purchase of the obligation. [Reg. § 1.79-0.]

☐ [*T.D. 7623, 5-14-79. Amended by T.D. 7917, 10-6-83.*]

[Reg. § 1.79-1]

§ 1.79-1. Group-term life insurance—general rules.—(a) *What is group-term life insurance?* Life insurance is not group-term life insurance for purposes of section 79 unless it meets the following conditions:

(1) It provides a general death benefit that is excludable from gross income under section 101(a).

(2) It is provided to a group of employees.

(3) It is provided under a policy carried directly or indirectly by the employer.

(4) The amount of insurance provided to each employee is computed under a formula that precludes individual selection. This formula must be based on factors such as age, years of service, compensation, or position. This condition may be satisfied even if the amount of insurance provided is determined under a limited number of alternative schedules that are based on the amount each employee elects to contribute. However, the amount of insurance provided under each schedule must be computed under a formula that precludes individual selection.

(b) *May group-term life insurance be combined with other benefits?* No part of the life insurance provided under a policy that provides a permanent benefit is group-term life insurance unless—

(1) The policy or the employer designates in writing the part of the death benefit provided to each employee that is group-term life insurance; and

(2) The part of the death benefit that is provided to an employee and designated as the group-term life insurance benefit for any policy year is not less than the difference between the total death benefit provided under the policy and the employee's deemed death benefit (DDB) at the end of the policy year determined under paragraph (d)(3) of this section.

(c) *May a g~~roup of employ~~ees?* (1) As a ge~~neral rule~~, ~~fewer than 10 employ~~ees? to a group of e~~mployees~~. term life insura~~nce... life insurance provided~~ unless, at some ti~~me... not qualify as group-~~ is provided to at le~~ast... es of section 79~~ are members of the ~~... lendar year, it~~ poses of this rule, all ~~... ployees who~~ policies carried direct~~... For pur-~~ ployer is taken into a~~ccount... ... under~~ number of employees to~~... ~~ provided.

(2) The general rule ~~... em~~ this section does not apply ~~... tions are met:

(i) The insurance is p~~rovided to full-~~time employees of the employe~~r... insurability affects eligibility, to a~~ll em~~ployees who provide evidence of insurab~~ility satis~~factory to the insurer.

(ii) The amount of insurance provided is computed either as a uniform percentage of compensation or on the basis of coverage brackets established by the insurer. However, the amount computed under either method may be reduced in the case of employees who do not provide evidence of insurability satisfactory to the insurer. In general, no bracket may exceed 2½ times the next lower bracket and the lowest bracket must be at least 10 percent of the highest bracket. However, the insurer may establish a separate schedule of coverage brackets for employees who are over age 65, but no bracket in the over-65 schedule may exceed 2½ times the next lower bracket and the lowest bracket in the over-65 schedule must be at least 10 percent of the highest bracket in the basic schedule.

(iii) Evidence of insurability affecting an employee's eligibility for insurance or the amount of insurance provided to that employee is limited to a medical questionnaire completed by the employee that does not require a physical examination.

(3) The general rule of paragraph (c)(1) of this section does not apply if the following conditions are met:

(i) The insurance is provided under a common plan to the employees of two or more unrelated employers.

(ii) The insurance is restricted to, but mandatory for, all employees of the employer who belong to or are represented by an organization (such as a union) that carries on substantial activities in addition to obtaining insurance.

Items S...

See p. 2...

24,252

...bility does not af-
...for insurance or the
...d to that employee.

(iii) Evid... ...aragraphs (c)(2) and (3)
...es are not taken into ac-
fect an empl... ...d insurance for the follow-
amount o... ...

...re not eligible for insurance
of the policy because they have
...yed for a waiting period, specified
which does not exceed six months.

They are part-time employees. Em-
...hose customary employment is for not
...an 20 hours in any week, or 5 months in
...lendar year, are presumed to be part-time
...oyees.

(iii) They have reached the age of 65.

(5) For purposes of paragraph (c)(1) and (2)
of this section, insurance is considered to be provided to an employee who elects not to receive
insurance unless, in order to receive the insurance,
the employee is required to contribute to the cost
of benefits other than term life insurance. Thus, if
an employee could receive term life insurance by
contributing to its cost, the employee is taken into
account in determining whether the insurance is
provided to 10 or more employees even if such
employee elects not to receive the insurance. However, an employee who must contribute to the cost
of permanent benefits to obtain term life insurance is not taken into account in determining
whether the term life insurance is provided to 10
or more employees unless the term life insurance
is actually provided to such employee.

(d) *How much must an employee receiving permanent benefits include in income?*—(1) *In general.* If an insurance policy that meets the
requirements of this section provides permanent
benefits to an employee, the cost of the permanent
benefits reduced by the amount paid for permanent benefits by the employee is included in the
employee's income. The cost of the permanent
benefits is determined under the formula in paragraph (d)(2) of this section.

(2) *Formula for determining cost of the permanent benefits.* In each policy year the cost of
the permanent benefits for any particular employee must be no less than—

$$X \, (DDB_2 - DDB_1)$$

where—

DDB_2 is the employee's deemed death benefit
at the end of the policy year;

DDB_1 is the employee's deemed death benefit
at the end of the preceding policy year; and

X is the net single premium for insurance (the
premium for one dollar of paid-up, whole-life in-

surance) at the employee's attained age at the
beginning of the policy year.

(3) *Formula for determining deemed death
benefit.* The deemed death benefit (DDB) at the
end of any policy year for any particular employee is equal to—

$$R/Y$$

where—

R is the net level premium reserve at the end of
that policy year for all benefits provided to the
employee by the policy or, if greater, the cash
value of the policy at the end of that policy year;
and

Y is the net single premium for insurance (the
premium for one dollar of paid-up, whole life
insurance) at the employee's age at the end of
that policy year.

(4) *Mortality tables and interest rates used.*
For purposes of paragraphs (d)(2) and (d)(3) of
this section, the net level premium reserve (R)
and the net single premium (X or Y) shall be
based on the 1958 CSO mortality Table and 4
percent interest.

(5) *Dividends.* If an insurance policy that
meets the requirements of this section provides
permanent benefits, part or all of the dividends
under the policy may be includible in the employee's income. If the employee pays nothing for
the permanent benefits, all dividends under the
policy that are actually or constructively received
by the employee are includible in the employee's
income. In all other cases, the amount of dividends included in the employee's income is equal
to—

$$(D + C) - (PI + DI + AP)$$

where—

D is the total amount of dividends actually or
constructively received under the policy by the
employee in the current and all preceding taxable
years of the employee;

C is the total cost of the permanent benefits for
the current and all preceding taxable years of the
employee determined under the formulas in
paragraphs (d)(2) and (6) of this section;

PI is the total amount of premium included in
the employee's income under paragraph (d)(1) of
this section for the current and all preceding taxable years of the employee;

DI is the total amount of dividends included in
the employee's income under this paragraph
(d)(5) in all preceding taxable years of the employee; and

AP is the total amount paid for permanent
benefits by the employee in the current and all
preceding taxable years of the employee.

Reg. § 1.79-1(c)(4)

(6) *Different policy and taxable years.* (i) If a policy year begins in one employee taxable year and ends in another employee taxable year, the cost of the permanent benefits, determined under the formula in paragraph (d)(2) of this section, is allocated between the employee taxable years.

(ii) The cost of permanent benefits for a policy year is allocated first to the employee taxable year in which the policy year begins. The cost of permanent benefits allocated to that policy year is equal to—

$$F \times C$$

where—

F is the fraction of the premium for that policy year that is paid on or before the last day of the employee taxable year; and

C is the cost of permanent benefits for the policy year determined under the formula in paragraph (d)(2) of this section.

(iii) Any part of the cost of permanent benefits that is not allocated to the employee taxable year in which the policy year begins is allocated to the subsequent employee taxable year.

(iv) The cost of permanent benefits for an employee taxable year is the sum of the costs of

permanent ... paragraphs (a...

(7) *Exampl*ocated to that year under graph may be ...(iii) of this section. example:

Example. An empl...ons of this para-employee A under a polic...the following ments of this section. Und... 47 years old, received $70,0... ce to insurance and elects to receive ... fit under the policy. A pays $2 ... group-term life insurance through ... tions and the employer pays the rem... premium for the group-term life insu... employer also pays one half of the premi... fied in the policy for the permanent benefit. A pays the other half of the premium for the permanent benefit through payroll deductions. The policy specifies that the annual premium paid for the permanent benefit is $300. However, the amount of premium allocated to the permanent benefit by the formula in paragraph (d)(2) of this section is $350. A is a calendar year taxpayer; the policy year begins January 1. In year 2000, $200 is includible in A's income because of insurance provided by the employer. This amount is computed as follows:

(1)	Cost of permanent benefits	$350
(2)	Amounts considered paid by A for permanent benefits ($\frac{1}{2} \times \$300$).................	150
(3)	Line (1) minus line (2)...	200
(4)	Cost of $70,000 of group-term life insurance under Table I of § 1.79-3	126
(5)	Cost of $50,000 of group-term life insurance under Table I of § 1.79-3	90
(6)	Cost of group-term insurance in excess of $50,000 (line (4) minus line (5))	36
(7)	Amount considered paid by A for group-term life insurance ($70 \times \$2$)	140
(8)	Line (6) minus line (7) (but not less than 0)	0
(9)	Amount includible in income (line (3) plus line (8))	200

(e) *What is the effect of state law limits?* Section 79 does not apply to life insurance in excess of the limits under applicable state law on the amount of life insurance that can be provided to an employee under a single contract of group-term life insurance.

(f) *Cross references.*—(1) See section 79(b) and § 1.79-2 for rules relating to group-term life insurance provided to certain retired individuals.

(2) See section 61(a) and the regulations thereunder for rules relating to life insurance not meeting the requirements of section 79, this section, or § 1.79-2, such as insurance provided on the life of a non-employee (for example, an employee's spouse), insurance not provided as compensation for personal services performed as an employee, insurance not provided under a policy carried directly or indirectly by the employer, or permanent benefits.

(3) See section 106 and § 1.106-1 for rules relating to certain insurance that does not provide general death benefits, such as travel insurance or accident and health insurance (including amounts payable under a double indemnity clause or rider).

(g) [Reserved]

(h) *Effective date.* Section 1.79-0 applies to insurance provided in employee taxable years beginning on or after January 1, 1977 (except as provided in 26 CFR 1.79-1(g) (revised as of April 1, 1983) with respect to insurance provided in employee taxable years beginning in 1977). Sections 1.79-1 through 1.79-3 apply to insurance provided in employee taxable years beginning after December 31, 1982. See 26 CFR 1.79-1 through 1.79-3 (revised as of April 1, 1983) for rules applicable to insurance provided in employee taxable years beginning before January 1, 1983. [Reg. § 1.79-1.]

24,254

Items Specified by T.D. 6999,
See p. 20,69 .D. 7236, 12-27-72,
7917, 10-6-83; T.D.
~521, 5-28-99.]

□ [T.D. 6888,
1-17-69, T. Pg. § 1.79-2]

...ceptions to the rule of inclu-
T.D. general.—(1) Section 79(b) provides
7for the cost of group-term life insur-
ovided under certain policies otherwise
...bed in section 79(a). The policy or policies of
...up-term life insurance which are described in
section 79(a) but which qualify for one of the
exceptions set forth in section 79(b) are described
in paragraphs (b) through (d) of this section.
Paragraph (b) of this section discusses the exception provided in section 79(b)(1); paragraph (c) of
this section discusses the exception provided in
section 79(b)(2); and paragraph (d) of this section
discusses the exception provided in section
79(b)(3).

(2)(i) If a policy of group-term life insurance
qualifies for an exception provided by section
79(b), then the amount equal to the cost of such
insurance is excluded from the application of the
provisions of section 79(a).

(ii) If a policy, or portion of a policy of
group-term life insurance qualifies for an exception provided by section 79(d), the amount (if
any) paid by the employee toward the purchase of
such insurance is not to be taken into account as
an amount referred to in section 79(a)(2). In the
case of a policy or policies of group-term life
insurance which qualify for an exception provided
by section 79(b)(1) or (3), the amount paid by the
employee which is not to be taken into account as
an amount referred to in section 79(a)(2) is the
amount paid by the employee for the particular
policy or policies of group-term life insurance
which qualify for an exception provided under
such section. If the exception provided in section
79(b)(2) is applicable only to a portion of the
group-term life insurance on the employee's life,
the amount considered to be paid by the employee
toward the purchase of such portion is the amount
equal to the excess of the cost of such portion of
the insurance over the amount otherwise includible in the employee's gross income with respect to
the group-term life insurance on his life carried
directly or indirectly by such employer.

(iii) The rules of this subparagraph may be
illustrated by the following example:

Example. A is an employee of X Corporation and is also an employee of Y Corporation, a
subsidiary of X Corporation. A is provided, under
a separate plan arranged by each of his employers, group-term life insurance on his life. During
his taxable year, under the group-term life insurance plan of X Corporation, A is provided $60,000
of group-term life insurance on his life, and A
pays $360.00 toward the purchase of such insur-
ance. Under the group-term life insurance plan of
Y Corporation, A is provided $65,000 of group-
term life insurance on his life, but does not pay
any part of the cost of such insurance. At the
beginning of his taxable year, A terminates his
employment with the X Corporation after he has
reached the retirement age with respect to such
employer, and the policy carried by the X Corporation qualifies for the exception provided by section 79(b)(1). For that taxable year, the cost of
the group-term life insurance on A's life which is
provided under the plan of X Corporation is not
taken into account in determining the amount
includible in A's gross income under section 79(a),
and A may not take into account as an amount
described in section 79(a)(2) the $360.00 he pays
toward the purchase of such insurance.

(b) *Retired and disabled employees*—(1) *In
general.* Section 79(b)(1) provides an exception for
the cost of group-term life insurance on the life of
an individual which is provided under a policy or
policies otherwise described in section 79(a) if the
individual has terminated his employment (as defined in subparagraph (2) of this paragraph) with
such employer and either has reached the retirement age with respect to such employer (as defined in subparagraph (3) of this paragraph, or
has become disabled (as defined in subparagraph
(4)(i) of this paragraph). If an individual who has
terminated his employment attains retirement
age or has become disabled during his taxable
year, or if an employee who has attained retirement age or has become disabled terminates his
employment during the taxable year, the exception provided by section 79(b)(1) applies only to
the portion of the cost of group-term life insurance
which is provided subsequent to the happening of
the last event which qualifies the policy of insurance on the employee's life for the exception provided in such section.

(2) *Termination of employment.* For purposes of section 79(b)(1), an individual has terminated his employment with an employer
providing such individual group-term life insurance when such individual no longer renders services to that employer as an employee of such
employer.

(3) *Retirement age.* For purposes of section
79(b)(1) and this section, the meaning of the term
"retirement age" is determined in accordance
with the following rules—

(i)(a) If the employee is covered under a
written pension or annuity plan of the employer

Reg. § 1.79-2(a)(1)

providing such individual group-term life insurance on his life (whether or not such plan is qualified under section 401(a) or 403(a)), then his retirement age shall be considered to be the earlier of

 (1) The earliest age indicated by such plan at which an active employee has the right (or an inactive individual would have the right had he continued in employment) to retire without disability and without the consent of his employer and receive immediate retirement benefits computed at either the full rate or a rate proportionate to completed service as set forth in the normal retirement formula of the plan, i.e., without actuarial or similar reduction because of retirement before some later specified age, or

 (2) The age at which it has been the practice of the employer to terminate, due to age, the services of the class of employees to which he last belonged.

 (b) For purposes of *(a)* of this subdivision, if an employee is covered under more than one pension or annuity plan of the employer, his retirement age shall be determined with regard to that plan which covers that class of employees of the employer to which the employee last belonged. If the class of employees to which the employee last belonged is covered under more than one pension or annuity plan, then the employee's retirement age shall be determined with regard to that plan which covers the greatest number of the employer's employees.

 (ii) In the absence of a written employee's pension or annuity plan described in subdivision (i) of this subparagraph, retirement age is the age, if any, at which it has been the practice of the employer to terminate, due to age, the services of the class of employees to which the particular employee last belonged, provided such age is reasonable in view of all the pertinent facts and circumstances.

 (iii) If neither subdivision (i) or (ii) of this subparagraph applies, the retirement age is considered to be age 65.

 (4) Disabled. (i) For taxable years beginning after December 31, 1966, an individual is considered disabled for purposes of section 79(b)(1) and subparagraph (1) of this paragraph if he is disabled within the meaning of section 72(m)(7) and paragraph (f) of § 1.72-17. For taxable years beginning before January 1, 1967, an individual is considered disabled for purposes of section 79(b)(1) and subparagraph (1) of this paragraph if he is disabled within the meaning of section 213(g)(3), relating to the meaning of disabled, but the determination of the individual's status shall be made without regard to the provisions of section 213(g)(4), ... status.

 (ii)*(a)* In an... individual seeks to a... in section 79(b)(1) by re...year in which an... within the meaning of s...exception set forth paragraph, and in which ti...being disabled insurance on the individua... of this subrule of inclusion set forth i... amount of determined without regard to ... insurance subject to any except to the section 79(b), is greater than $... but insurance, the substantiation requir... *(c)* of this subdivision must be submitt... individual's tax return.

 (b) For the first taxable year fo... the individual seeks to apply the exceptio... forth in section 79(b)(1) by reason of his being disabled within the meaning of subdivision (i) of this subparagraph, there must be submitted with his income tax return a doctor's statement as to his impairment. There must also be submitted with the return a statement by the individual with respect to the effect of the impairment upon his substantial gainful activity, and the date such impairment occurred. For subsequent taxable years, the taxpayer may, in lieu of such statements, submit a statement declaring the continued existence (without substantial diminution) of the impairment and its continued effect upon his substantial gainful activity.

 (c) In lieu of the substantiation required to be submitted by *(b)* of this subdivision for the taxable year, the individual may submit a signed statement issued to him by the insurer to the effect that the individual is disabled within the meaning of subdivision (i) of this paragraph. Such statement must set forth the basis for the insurer's determination that the individual was so disabled, and, for the first taxable year in which the individual is so disabled, the date such disability occurred.

 (c) Employer or charity a beneficiary.—*(1) General rule.* Section 79(b)(2) provides an exception with respect to the amounts referred to in section 79(a) for the cost of any portion of the group-term life insurance on the life of an employee provided during part or all of the taxable year of the employee under which the employer is directly or indirectly the beneficiary, or under which a person described in section 170(c) (relating to definition of charitable contributions) is the sole beneficiary, for the entire period during such taxable year for which the employee receives such insurance.

 (2) Employer is a beneficiary. For purposes of section 79(b)(2) and subparagraph (1) of this

Reg. § 1.79-2(c)(2)

...of whether the em-
...ctly the beneficiary
...group-term life insur-
paragraph, the determi acts and circumstances of
ployer is directly such determination is not
under a policy gard to whether the employer
ance depend incidents of ownership in the
the part example, if the employer is the
made iciary under a policy of group-term
...ce on the life of his employee but there
...angement whereby the employer is re-
...to pay over all (or a portion) of the pro-
...of such policy to the employee's estate or his
...eficiary, the employer is not considered a ben-
...iciary under such policy (or such portion of the
policy).

(3) *Charity a beneficiary.* (i) For purposes of
section 79(b)(2) and subparagraph (1) of this paragraph, a person described in section 170(c) is a
beneficiary under a policy providing group-term
life insurance if such person is designated the
beneficiary under the policy by any assignment or
designation of beneficiary under the policy which,
under the law of the jurisdiction which is applicable to the policy, has the effect of making such
person the beneficiary under such policy (whether
or not such designation is revocable during the
taxable year). Such a designation may be made by
the employee with respect to any portion of the
group-term life insurance on his life. However, no
deduction is allowed under section 170, relating to
charitable, etc., contributions and gifts, with respect to any such assignment or designation.

(ii) A person described in section 170(c)
must be designated the sole beneficiary under the
policy or portion of the policy. Such requirement
is satisfied if the person described in section
170(c) is the beneficiary under such policy or
portion of the policy, and there is no contingent or
similar beneficiary under such policy or such portion other than a person described in section
170(c). A general "preference beneficiary clause"
in a policy governing payment where there is no
designated beneficiary in existence at the death of
the employee will not of itself be considered to
create a contingent or similar beneficiary. A person described in section 170(c) may be designated
the beneficiary under a portion of the policy if
such person is designated the sole beneficiary
under a beneficiary designation which is expressed, for example, as a fraction of the amount
of insurance on the insured's life.

(iii) If a person described in section 170(c)
is designated, before May 1, 1964, the beneficiary
under the policy (or portion thereof) and such
person remains the beneficiary for the period beginning May 1, 1964, and ending with the close of

the first taxable year of the employee ending after
April 30, 1964, such person shall be treated as the
beneficiary under the policy (or the portion
thereof) for the period beginning January 1, 1964,
and ending April 30, 1964.

(d) *Insurance contracts purchased under qualified employee plans.*—(1) Section 79(b)(3) provides an exception with respect to the cost of any
group-term life insurance which is provided under
a life insurance contract purchased as a part of a
plan described in section 403(a), or purchased by
a trust described in section 401(a) which is exempt from tax under section 501(a) if the proceeds of such contract are payable directly or
indirectly to a participant in such trust or to a
beneficiary of such participant. The provisions of
sections 72(m)(3) and § 1.72-16 apply to the cost
of such group-term life insurance, and, therefore,
no part of such cost is excluded from the gross
income of the employee by reason of the provisions of section 79.

(2) Whether the life insurance protection on
an employee's life is provided under a qualified
employee plan referred to in subparagraph (1) of
this paragraph depends upon the provisions of
such plan. In determining whether a pension,
profit-sharing, stock bonus, or annuity plan satisfies the requirements for qualification set forth in
sections 401(a) or 403(a), only group-term life
insurance which is provided under such plan is
taken into account. [Reg. § 1.79-2.]

☐ [*T.D.* 6888, 7-5-66. *Amended by T.D.* 6919,
5-17-67, *T.D.* 6985, 12-26-68 *and T.D.* 7623,
5-14-79.]

[Reg. § 1.79-3]

**§ 1.79-3. Determination of amount equal to
cost of group-term life insurance.**—(a) *In general.* This section prescribes the rules for determining the amount equal to the cost of group-
term life insurance on an employee's life which is
to be included in his gross income pursuant to the
rule of inclusion set forth in section 79(a). Such
amount is determined by—

(1) Computing the cost of the portion of the
group-term life insurance on the employee's life to
be taken into account (determined in accordance
with the rules set forth in paragraph (b) of this
section) for each "period of coverage" (as defined
in paragraph (c) of this section) and aggregating
the costs so determined, then

(2) Reducing the amount determined under
subparagraph (1) of this paragraph by the
amount determined in accordance with the rules
set forth in paragraph (e) of this section, relating
to the amount paid by the employee toward the
purchase of group-term life insurance.

Reg. § 1.79-3(a)(1)

(b) *Determination of the portion of the group-term life insurance on the employee's life to be taken into account.*—(1) For each "period of coverage" (as defined in paragraph (c) of this section), the portion of the group-term life insurance to be taken into account in computing the amount includible in an employee's gross income for purposes of paragraph (a)(1) of this section is the sum of the proceeds payable upon the death of the employee under each policy, or portion of a policy, of group-term life insurance on such employee's life to which the rule of inclusion set forth in section 79(a) applies, less $50,000 of such insurance. Thus, the amount of any proceeds payable under a policy, or portion of a policy, which qualifies for one of the exceptions to the rule of inclusion provided by section 79(b) is not taken into account. For the regulations relating to such exceptions to the rule of inclusion, see § 1.79-2.

(2) For purposes of making the computation required by subparagraph (1) of this paragraph in any case in which the amount payable under the policy, or portion thereof, varies during the period of coverage, the amount payable under such policy during such period is considered to be the average of the amount payable under such policy at the beginning and the end of such period.

(3)(i) For purposes of making the computation required by subparagraph (1) of this paragraph in any case in which the amount payable under the policy is not payable as a specific amount upon the death of the employee in full discharge of the liability of the insurer, and such form of payment is not one of alternative methods of payment, the amount payable under such policy is the present value of the agreement by the insurer under the policy to make the payments to the beneficiary or beneficiaries entitled to such amounts upon the employee's death. For each period of coverage, such present value is to be determined as if the first and last day of such period is the date of death of the employee.

(ii) The present value of the agreement by the insurer under the policy to make payments shall be determined by the use of the mortality tables and interest rate employed by the insurer with respect to such a policy in calculating the amount held by the insurer (as defined in section 101(d)(2)), unless the Commissioner otherwise determines that a particular mortality table and interest rate, representative of the mortality table and interest rate used by commercial insurance companies with respect to such policies, shall be used to determine the present value of the policy for purposes of this subdivision.

(iii) For purposes of making the computation required by subdivision (i) of this subparagraph in any case in which it is necessary to determine the age of an employee's beneficiary and such beneficiary remains the same (under the policy, or the portion of the policy, with respect to which the determination of the present value of the agreement of the insurer to pay benefits is being made) for the entire period during the employee's taxable year for which such policy is in effect, the age of such beneficiary is such beneficiary's age at his nearest birthday on June 30th of the calendar year.

(iv) If the policy of group-term life insurance on the employee's life is such that the present value of the agreement by the insurer under the policy to pay benefits cannot be determined by the rules prescribed in this subparagraph, the taxpayer may submit with his return a computation of such present value, consistent with the actuarial and other assumptions set forth in this subparagraph, showing the appropriate factors applied in his case. Such computation shall be subject to the approval of the Commissioner upon examination of such return.

(c) *Period of coverage.* For purposes of this section, the phrase "period of coverage" means any one calendar month period, or part thereof, during the employee's taxable year during which the employee is provided group-term life insurance on his life to which the rule of inclusion set forth in section 79(a) applies. The phrase "part thereof" as used in the preceding sentence means any continuous period which is less than the one calendar month period referred to in the preceding sentence for which premiums are charged by the insurer.

(d) *The cost of the portion of the group-term life insurance on an employee's life.*—(1) This paragraph sets forth the rules for determining the cost, for each period of coverage, of the portion of the group-term life insurance on the employee's life to be taken into account in computing the amount includible in the employee's gross income for purposes of paragraph (a)(1) of this section. The portion of the group-term life insurance on the employee's life to be taken into account is determined in accordance with the provisions of paragraph (b) of this section. Table I, which is set forth in subparagraph (2) of this paragraph, determines the cost for each $1,000 of such portion of the group-term life insurance on the employee's life for each one-month period. The cost of the portion of the group-term life insurance on the employee's life for each period of coverage of one month is obtained by multiplying the number of thousand dollars of such insurance computed to the nearest tenth which is provided during such period by the appropriate amount set forth in

Reg. § 1.79-3(d)(1)

Table 1. In any case in which group-term life insurance is provided for a period of coverage of less than one month, the amount set forth in Table I is prorated over such period of coverage.

→ *Caution: Reg. § 1.79-3(d)(2), below, is effective before July 1, 1999.*←

(2) For the cost of group-term life insurance provided after December 31, 1988, the following table sets forth the cost of $1,000 of group-term life insurance provided for one month, computed on the basis of 5-year age brackets. For purposes of Table I, the age of the employee is the employee's attained age on the last day of the employee's taxable year.

TABLE I.—UNIFORM PREMIUMS FOR $1,000 OF GROUP-TERM LIFE INSURANCE PROTECTION

5-year age bracket	Cost per $1,000 of protection for one month
Under 30	$0.08
30 to 34	.09
35 to 39	.11
40 to 44	.17
45 to 49	.29
50 to 54	.48
55 to 59	.75
60 to 64	1.17
65 to 69	2.10
70 and above	3.76

→ *Caution: Reg. § 1.79-3(d)(2), below, is effective July 1, 1999.*←

(2) For the cost of group-term life insurance provided after June 30, 1999, the following table sets forth the cost of $1,000 of group-term life insurance provided for one month, computed on the basis of 5-year age brackets. See 26 CFR 1.79-3(d)(2) in effect prior to July 1, 1999, and contained in the 26 CFR part 1 edition revised as of April 1, 1999, for a table setting forth the cost of group-term life insurance provided before July 1, 1999. For purposes of Table I, the age of the employee is the employee's attained age on the last day of the employee's taxable year.

TABLE I.—UNIFORM PREMIUMS FOR $1,000 OF GROUP-TERM LIFE INSURANCE PROTECTION

5-year age bracket	Cost per $1,000 of protection for one month
Under 25	$0.05
25 to 29	.06
30 to 34	.08
35 to 39	.09
40 to 44	.10
45 to 49	.15
50 to 54	.23
55 to 59	.43
60 to 64	.66
65 to 69	1.27
70 and above	2.06

(3) The net premium cost of group-term life insurance as provided in Table I of subparagraph (2) of this paragraph applies only to the cost of group-term life insurance subject to the rule of inclusion set forth in section 79(a). Therefore, such net premium cost is not applicable to the determination of the cost of group-term life insurance provided under a policy which is not subject to such rule of inclusion.

(e) *Effective date*—(1) *General effective date for table.* Except as provided in paragraph (e)(2) of this section, the table in paragraph (d)(2) of this section is applicable July 1, 1999. Until January 1, 2000, an employer may calculate imputed income for all its employees under age 30 using the 5-year age bracket for ages 25 to 29.

(2) *Effective date for table for purposes of § 1.79-0.* For a policy of life insurance issued under a plan in existence on June 30, 1999, which would not be treated as carried directly or indirectly by an employer under § 1.79-0 (taking into account the Table I in effect on that date), until January 1, 2003, an employer may use either the table in paragraph (d)(2) of this section or the table in effect prior to July 1, 1999 (as described in paragraph (d)(2) of this section) for determin-

Reg. § 1.79-3(d)(2)

ing if the policy is carried directly or indirectly by the employer.

(f) *Amount paid by the employee toward the purchase of group-term life insurance.*—(1) Except as otherwise provided in subparagraph (2) of this paragraph, if an employee pays any amount toward the purchase of group-term life insurance provided for a taxable year which is subject to the rule of inclusion set forth in section 79(a), the sum of all such amounts is the amount referred to in section 79(a)(2) and paragraph (a)(2) of this section. The rule of the preceding sentence applies even though the payments made by the employee are made with respect to a period of coverage during which no portion of the group-term life insurance on his life is taken into account under paragraph (b)(1) of this section.

(2) In determining the amount paid by the employee for purposes of section 79(a)(2) and paragraph (a)(2) of this section, there is not taken into account any amounts paid by the employee for group-term life insurance provided (or to be provided) for a different taxable year (other than amounts applicable to regular pay periods extending into the next taxable year). Thus, for example, if part of an employee's payment during a taxable year represents a prepayment for insurance to be provided after his retirement, such part does not reduce the amount includible in his gross income for the current taxable year. Furthermore, in determining such amount, there is not taken into account any amount paid by an employee toward the purchase of group-term life insurance which qualifies for one of the exceptions described in section 79(b). The amount paid by an employee toward the purchase of group-term life insurance which qualifies for one of the exceptions described in section 79(b) is determined under the rules of paragraph (a)(2) of § 1.79-2.

(3) If payments are made by the employer and his employees to provide group-term life insurance which is subject to the rule of inclusion set forth in section 79(a) as well as to provide other benefits for the employees, and if the amount paid by the employee toward the purchase of such insurance cannot be determined by the provisions of the policy or plan under which such benefits are provided, then the determination of the portion of the cost of group-term life insurance (computed in accordance with the provisions of this section) which is attributable to the contributions of the employee shall be made in accordance with the provisions of this subparagraph. The amount paid by the employee toward the purchase of all the group-term life insurance on his life for his taxable year (or for the portion of his taxable year if such portion is the basis of

the computation) under such group policy shall be an amount determined first by ascertaining the total amount paid by all employees who are covered for multiple benefits which is allocable toward the purchase of group-term life insurance on their lives for the year, and then by ascertaining the pro rata portion of such total amount attributable to the individual employee. The total amount paid by all employees who are covered for multiple benefits which is allocable toward the purchase of group-term life insurance on their lives with respect to such year shall be an amount which bears the same ratio to the total amount paid by all employees for multiple benefits with respect to such year as the aggregate premiums paid to the insurer for group-term life insurance on such employees' lives with respect to such year bears to the aggregate premiums paid to the insurer for such multiple benefits with respect to such year. The pro rata portion of such total amount attributable to the individual employee for the cost of group-term life insurance on his life shall be an amount which bears the same ratio to the total amount paid by all employees which is allocable towards the purchase of group-term insurance on their lives with respect to such year as the amount of group-term life insurance on the life of the employee at a specified time during the year, as determined by the employer, bears to the total amount of group-term life insurance on the lives of all employees insured for such multiple benefits at such time.

(g) *Effect of provision of other benefits*—(1) *In general.* This paragraph discusses the effect of the provision of certain benefits other than group-term life insurance on the life of the employee if the provision of such benefits is contingent upon the underwriting of group-term life insurance on the employee's life to which the rule of inclusion set forth in section 79(a) applies.

(2) *Dependent coverage.* An amount equal to the cost of group-term life insurance on the life of the spouse or other family member of the employee which is provided under a policy of group-term life insurance carried directly or indirectly by his employer is not subject to the provisions of section 79 since it is not on the life of the employee. See paragraph (d)(2)(ii)(b) of § 1.61-2 for rules regarding the tax treatment of such insurance.

(3) *Disability provisions.* Payments made for disability benefits provided under a group-term life insurance contract are considered to constitute payments made for accident and health insurance. Thus, employer contributions to provide such benefits are excluded from gross income by reason of the provisions of section 106.

Reg. § 1.79-3(g)(3)

(4) *Cost of other benefits.* If a benefit described in this paragraph is provided under a policy under which both the employer and his employees contribute, then, except as otherwise provided in this subparagraph, the employer and the employees will be treated as contributing toward the payment of such benefit at the same rate as they contribute toward the cost of group-term life insurance on the employees' lives. A separate allocation of employer and employee contributions for such benefits is permissible only if—

(i) Such separate allocation is set forth in the group policy and is applicable to all the employees covered under such policy;

(ii) Such separate allocation is followed in transactions between the insurer and the group-policyholder; and

(iii) The allocation set forth in the policy satisfies the requirements of the law of the jurisdiction which is applicable to the contract regarding any minimum or maximum contribution rate by the employer or the employees. [Reg. § 1.79-3.]

☐ [*T.D.* 6888, 7-5-66. *Amended by T.D.* 7623, 5-14-79; *T.D.* 7924, 12-1-83; *T.D.* 8273, 11-17-89; *T.D.* 8424, 7-29-92 *and T.D.* 8821, 5-28-99.]

[Reg. § 1.79-4T]

§ 1.79-4T. Questions and answers relating to the nondiscrimination requirements for group-term life insurance (Temporary).

Q-1: When does section 79, as amended by the Tax Reform Act of 1984, become effective?

A-1: (a) Generally, section 79, as amended, applies to taxable years (of the employee receiving insurance coverage) beginning after December 31, 1983. There are, however, several exceptions to this effective date where there is coverage under a group-term life insurance plan of the employer that was in existence on January 1, 1984, or a comparable successor to such a plan maintained by the employer or a successor employer.

(b) First, the new rules of section 79(b) and (e), that require the inclusion in income of a retired employee of amounts attributable to the cost of group-term life insurance in excess of $50,000 and that include former employees within the definition of the term "employee" will not apply to any employee who retired from employment on or before January 1, 1984.

(c) Second, in the case of an individual who retires after January 1, 1984, and before January 1, 1987, the new rules of section 79(b) and (e) do not apply if (1) the individual attained age 55 on or before January 1, 1984, and (2) the plan was maintained by the same employer who employed the individual during 1983, or by a successor employer.

(d) Third, in the case of an individual who retires after December 31, 1986, the new rules of section 79(b) and (e) do not apply if (1) the individual attained age 55 on or before January 1, 1984, (2) the plan was maintained by the same employer who employed the individual during 1983, or by a successor employer, and (3) the plan is not, after December 31, 1986, a discriminatory group-term life insurance plan (not taking into account any group-term life insurance coverage provided to employees who retired before January 1, 1987).

(e) For purposes of determining whether a plan is, after December 31, 1986, a discriminatory group-term life insurance plan, there shall be ignored any insurance coverage provided pursuant to a state law requirement that an insurer continue to provide insurance coverage for a period of time not in excess of two months following the termination of a policy.

Q-2: What is meant by a "group-term life insurance plan of the employer that was in existence on January 1, 1984"?

A-2: A group-term life insurance plan of the employer was in existence on January 1, 1984, only if the group policy or policies providing group-term life insurance benefits under the plan were executed on or before January 1, 1984, and were not terminated prior to such date. The applicability of section 79, as amended, to an employee will not be affected by the transfer of the employee between employers treated as a single employer under section 79(d)(7) if the employee continues, after the transfer, to be provided with group-term life insurance benefits under a plan that is comparable (determined under the principles set forth in Q&A 3) to the plan provided by the former employer.

Q-3: When is a plan of group-term life insurance a "comparable successor" to another such plan?

A-3: A plan of group-term life insurance will be a comparable successor to another plan of group-term life insurance (the first plan) only if the plan does not differ from the first plan in any significant aspect with respect to individuals who are potentially eligible for benefits provided under the grandfather provisions in Q&A 1. These individuals consist of those persons who are covered under a plan of group-term life insurance of the employer that was in existence on January 1, 1984, or a comparable successor to such a plan maintained by the employer or a successor employer, and who either retired on or before January 1, 1984, or who both attained age 55 on or before

Reg. § 1.79-4T

January 1, 1984, and were employed by the employer maintaining the plan (or a predecessor of that employer) during the year 1983. Accordingly, if significant additional or reduced benefits are provided only to individuals who are not described in the preceding sentence, the plan will be considered a comparable successor plan. A plan will not fail to be a comparable successor plan merely because the employer purchases a policy or policies identical to the employer's first plan from a different insurance company. If the new plan provides significant additional or reduced benefits (either as to the type or amount available) to employees, or provides benefits to a category of employees that was formerly excluded from participating in the plan, the plan is generally not a comparable successor to the first plan. However, a plan will not be considered as providing significant additional or reduced benefits merely because a participant's coverage is based on a percentage of compensation and the participant's compensation for the taxable year has been increased or decreased. Furthermore, a plan will not be considered a non-comparable successor plan merely because it is amended, either to decrease benefits provided to key employees or to increase benefits provided to non-key employees, solely in order to comply with the nondiscrimination requirements of section 79(d). Finally, a plan will not be considered a non-comparable successor plan merely because a policy that is part of a discriminatory plan is terminated in order to end discriminatory coverage.

Q-4: For purposes of determining the effective date of section 79, as amended by the Tax Reform Act of 1984, what is a "successor employer"?

A-4: A successor employer is an employer who employs a group of individuals formerly employed by another employer as a result of a business merger, acquisition or division.

Q-5: Under what circumstances will separate policies of group-term life insurance of an employer be considered to be a single plan in determining whether the employer's plan of group-term life insurance is discriminatory?

A-5: All policies providing group-term life insurance to a common key employee or key employees (as defined in this Q&A) carried directly or indirectly by an employer (or by a group of employers described in section 79(d)(7)) will be considered as a single plan for purposes of determining whether an employer's group-term life insurance plan is discriminatory. For example, if a key employee receives $50,000 of group-term life insurance coverage under one policy and the same key employee receives an additional $250,000 of coverage under a separate group-term life insur-

ance policy, ... single plan in ... term life insura... discriminatory. ... employees cover... ceive the benefi... 79(c) for either p... if each policy, co... criminatory. A p... life insurance to ... under which the sa... receive group-term l... from service will be ... term life insurance to ... addition, an employer ... policies that do not provide group... ance to a common key employee. In ... single plan for purposes ... more ... crimination provisions of ... sur... ple, if the employer pre... insurance coverage for no... a... one policy and provides gr... coverage for key employees ... the two policies may be c... determining whether the req... 79(d) are satisfied with rega... ...w, (2) ...icy. For purposes of this sec... ...employee... employee" has the meaning giv... ...aph ... paragraph (1) of section 416(i), ...premium ... paragraph (A)(iv) of such parag... ...mium ... plied by not taking into acc... age ... described in section 79(d)(3)(B) w... ...pre... ticipants in the plan. For purposes ...miu... all references to "plan year" or "p... section 416(g)(4)(C) and section 416... ...pr... ...eleted and replaced with "taxable ye... employer" or "taxable years of the emp... respectively.

Q-6: In the case of a discriminatory group-term life insurance plan, what amounts should be included in the gross income of a key employee?

A-5: (a) In the case of a discriminatory group-term life insurance plan, each key employee must include in gross income for the taxable year the cost of his or her insurance benefit for that year provided by the employer under the plan.

(b) The cost of group-term life insurance coverage provided by an employer for a key employee during the employee's taxable year is determined by apportioning the net premium (group premium less policy dividends, premium refunds or experience rating credits) allocable to the group-term life insurance coverage during the key employee's taxable year, less the actual cost allocated to other key employees pursuant to the method described in the subparagraph (d) of this answer, if applicable, among the covered employees. In the event

Reg. § 1.79-4T

24,262

See P. 20...

...ns and types of ...er, the employer ...ation of the total ... for example, where ... insurance coverage ...e insurance with the ... volume discount, the ...group-term life insur- ...ess, if any, of the pay- ...makes for the health ...r the payments the em- ...uch coverage if the plan of ...nce for which this calcula- ...not exist.

...e portion of the net premium ...insurance that should be ap- ...y employee, other than a key ...m the method in subparagraph ...er is applicable, is determined by ...a "tabular" premium for the entire ...e exception of all key employees to ...ethod in subparagraph (d) of this ...pplicable), in the manner described ...etermining the ratio of the total actual ...m (less the actual cost allocated to key ...s pursuant to the method in the subpara- ...) of this answer) to the total tabular ...n and (3) multiplying the tabular pre- ...or the key employee at his or her attained ...y such ratio. Thus, if the total actual net ...ium is 125 percent of the total tabular pre- ...m for all covered employees and the tabular ...mium at the key employee's attained age is ...00 per thousand per month, the cost for such ...mployee would be $2.50 per thousand per month ...$2.00 times 125 percent). For these purposes the table used to calculate tabular premiums will be determined as follows:

(i) If the group policy contains a reasonable table (based on recognized mortality assumptions) of premium rates on an attained age basis (which table may use age brackets not exceeding five years) with reference to which the group premium is determined, such table will be used;

(ii) If such table is not available, the 1960 Basic Group Table published by the Society of Actuaries will be used.

(d) In cases where the mortality charge for group-term life insurance coverage provided to a key employee is calculated separately by the insurer (for example, where the charge for the coverage provided to a key employee is based on a medical examination) and the amount of such mortality charge plus a proportionate share of the loading charge for the coverage provided to the group is higher than the amount that would be allocable to such employee under the allocation method in subparagraph (c) the cost of group-term life insurance coverage for that employee shall be that higher amount.

Q-7: Must all active and former employees be considered in applying the coverage tests in section 79(d)(3) to determine whether or not a plan of group-term life insurance is discriminatory with respect to coverage?

A-7: No. Generally, a plan of group-term life insurance which covers both active and former employees will not satisfy the nondiscrimination requirements of section 79(d) unless the coverage tests in section 79(d)(3) are satisfied with respect to both the active and the former employees of the employer, except to the extent they are excluded from tests for discrimination by application of the grandfather provisions set forth in Q&A 1. However, for purposes of determining whether a plan is discriminatory with respect to coverage, the coverage tests must be applied separately to active and former employees. In addition, if the plan limits participation by former employees to employees who retired from employment with the employer, then only retired employees must be considered in applying the coverage tests to former employees. Also, in applying the coverage tests in section 79(d)(3), the employer may make reasonable mortality assumptions regarding former employees who are not covered under the plan but must be considered in applying the coverage tests. Furthermore, only those former employees who terminated employment on or after the earliest date of termination from employment for any former employee covered by the plan must be considered. Finally, for purposes of determining whether a plan of group-term life insurance of the employer (or a successor employer) that was in existence on January 1, 1984 (or a comparable successor to such a plan) is discriminatory, after December 31, 1986, with respect to group-term life insurance coverage for former employees, coverage provided to employees who retired on or before December 31, 1986, shall not be taken into account.

Q-8: Will a group-term life insurance plan be considered discriminatory if active employees receive greater benefits as a percentage of compensation than former employees, or vice versa?

A-8: No. For purposes of determining whether a plan is discriminatory with respect to the type and amount of benefits available, insurance coverage for former employees must be tested separately from insurance coverage for active employees. For example, a group-term life insurance plan that provides group-term life insurance benefits equal to 200 percent of compensation for all active employees and 100 percent of final

Reg. § 1.79-4T

compensation (based on the average annual compensation for the final five years) for all former employees would satisfy the nondiscrimination requirements of section 79(d). However, a group-term life insurance plan that provides group-term life insurance benefits equal to 200 percent of compensation for all active employees and 100 percent of final compensation (based on the average annual compensation for the final five years) only for key employees who are no longer employed by the employer (or a successor employer) would not satisfy the nondiscrimination requirement of section 79(d)(2)(A).

Q-9: Under what circumstances will the amount of benefits available under a plan of group-term life insurance be considered not to discriminate in favor of participants who are key employees?

A-9: A plan of group-term life insurance will be considered not to discriminate in favor of participants who are key employees, as to the amount of benefits available, if the plan provides a fixed amount of insurance which is the same for all covered employees. In other circumstances, the determination of whether a plan is nondiscriminatory will be based on all of the facts and circumstances. Such plans will be considered not to discriminate in favor of participants who are key employees, as to the amount of benefits available, if the plan contains no group of employees described in the following sentence that, if tested separately, would fail to satisfy the requirements of section 79(d)(2)(A). The group subject to separate testing under the preceding sentence consists of a key employee and all other participants (including other key employees) who receive, under the plan, an amount of insurance (as a multiple of compensation (either total compensation or the basic or regular rate of compensation)) that is equal to or greater than the amount of insurance received by such key employee. As described in Q&As 7&8, active and former employees are tested separately under section 79(d)(2)(A).

Example: Assume that a plan of group-term life insurance has 500 participants, 10 of whom are key employees. Under the plan, 400 of the non-key employees receive an amount of insurance equal to 100 percent of compensation, while all of the key employees and 90 of the non-key employees receive an amount of insurance equal to 200 percent of compensation. The plan will be considered not to discriminate in favor of the participants who are key employees because, tested separately, the group of participants receiving an amount of insurance equal to or greater then 200 percent of compensation would satisfy the requirements of section 79(d)(2)(A) (by reason of section 79(d)(3)(A)(ii)). If one of the key employ-

ees received an amount of insurance equal to 300 percent of compensation, the plan would be considered to discriminate in favor of participants who are key employees, because, tested separately, the group consisting of the single key employee receiving an amount of insurance equal to or greater than 300 percent of compensation would fail to satisfy the requirements of section 79(d)(2)(A).

In determining the groups of employees that are tested separately for this purpose, allowance shall be made for reasonable differences in amount of insurance (as a multiple of compensation) due to rounding, the use of compensation brackets or other similar factors. Thus, if a plan bases group-term life insurance coverage on "compensation brackets," it is not intended that any participants will be treated as receiving an amount of insurance (as a multiple of compensation) that is greater (or less) than that of any other participant merely because the first participant's compensation is at the lower (or higher) end of a compensation bracket while the second participant's compensation is at the higher (or lower) end of a compensation bracket. However, any compensation brackets utilized by a plan will be examined to determine if the brackets, or compensation groupings, result in discrimination in favor of key employees. In addition, a plan does not meet the requirements for nondiscrimination as to the type and amount of benefits available under the plan unless all types of benefits (including permanent benefits) and all terms and conditions with respect to such benefits which are available to any participant who is a key employee are also available on a nondiscriminatory basis to non-key employee participants.

Q-10: How is additional coverage purchased by employees under a plan of group-term life insurance treated for purposes of determining whether a plan of group-term life insurance is discriminatory?

A-10: (a) The extent to which employees purchase additional coverage under a plan of group-term life insurance is not taken into account for purposes of determining whether a plan of group-term life insurance is discriminatory. For example, a plan providing insurance to all employees of 1 times annual compensation, which gives all employees the option to purchase additional insurance of 1 times annual compensation at their own expense, would not be considered discriminatory as to the type and amount of benefits available, even if the group (or groups) of participants who purchase additional insurance, if tested separately, would not satisfy the requirements of section 79(d)(2)(A). Solely for this purpose, the choice of an amount of group-term life insurance as a benefit under a cafeteria plan will be treated as the purchase of additional insurance surance by an employee any key employee that is coverage is available nondiscriminatory basis, to not available, or, the plan will be considered non-key employee if the full cost of such additional discriminary ice coverage is paid by the employer ecting such benefits.

plow the employer bears a part of the expense y additional coverage that is purchased by employee under a plan of group-term life insurance, the additional insurance shall be treated, in part, as an amount of insurance provided by the employer under the plan and, in part, as an amount of insurance purchased by the employee. Except to the extent provided in subparagraph (a) above, the portion of insurance treated as an amount of insurance purchased by the employee is not taken into account for purposes of determining whether the plan is discriminatory. Whether such insurance (together with any other insurance provided by the employer under the plan) will cause the plan to be considered to discriminate in favor of participants who are key employees is determined under the rules of Q&A 9.

Q-11: What effect do the provisions of section 79(d)(1) have if a plan of group-term life insurance is discriminatory for only part of a year?

A-11: If a plan of group-term life insurance is discriminatory at any time during the key employee's taxable year, then it is a discriminatory group-term life insurance plan for that taxable year and the provisions of section 79(d)(1) will be applicable with respect to all group-term life insurance costs allocable to that employee for that year.

Q-12: Are the section 79(d) provisions independent from the requirements contained in Treas. Reg. § 1.79-1?

A-12: Yes. Treas. Reg. § 1.79-1(c)(1) provides that life insurance provided to a group of employees cannot qualify as group-term life insurance if it is provided to less than ten full-time employees unless certain requirements are satisfied. The satisfaction of these requirements does not guarantee that the plan will be nondiscriminatory, and vice versa. Treas. Reg. § 1.79-1(a)(4) provides that life insurance is not group-term life insurance unless the amount of insurance provided to each employee is computed under a formula that precludes individual selection. The mere fact that a life insurance policy is nondiscriminatory is not determinative as to whether the policy precludes individual selection, and vice versa. [Temporary Reg. § 1.79-4T.]

□ [*T.D. 8073*, 1-29-86.]

[Reg. § 1.82-1]

§ 1.82-1. Payments for or reimbursements of expenses of moving from one residence to another residence attributable to employment or self-employment.—(a) *Reimbursements in gross income*—(1) *In general.* Any amount received or accrued, directly or indirectly, by an individual as a payment for or reimbursement of expenses of moving from one residence to another residence attributable to employment or self-employment is includible in gross income under section 82 as compensation for services in the taxable year received or accrued. For rules relating to the year a deduction may be allowed for expenses of moving from one residence to another residence, see section 217 and the regulations thereunder.

(2) *Amounts received or accrued as reimbursement or payment.* For purposes of this section, amounts are considered as being received or accrued by an individual as reimbursement or payment whether received in the form of money, property, or services. A cash basis taxpayer will include amounts in gross income under section 82 when they are received or treated as received by him. Thus, for example, if an employer moves an employee's household goods and personal effects from the employee's old residence to his new residence using the employer's facilities, the employee is considered as having received a payment in the amount of the fair market value of the services furnished at the time the services are furnished by the employer. If the employer pays a mover for moving the employee's household goods and personal effects, the employee is considered as having received the payment at the time the employer pays the mover, rather than at the time the mover moves the employee's household goods and effects. Where an employee receives a loan or advance from an employer to enable him to pay his moving expenses, the employee will not be deemed to have received a reimbursement of moving expenses until such time as he accounts to his employer if he is not required to repay such loan or advance and if he makes such accounting within a reasonable time. Such loan or advance will be deemed to be a reimbursement of moving expenses at the time of such accounting to the extent used by the employee for such moving expenses.

(3) *Direct or indirect payments or reimbursements.* For purposes of this section amounts are considered as being received or accrued whether received directly (paid or provided to an individual by an employer, a client, a customer, or similar person) or indirectly (paid to a third party on behalf of an individual by an employer, a client, a

customer, or similar person). Thus, if an employer pays a mover for the expenses of moving an employee's household goods and personal effects from one residence to another residence, the employee has indirectly received a payment which is includible in his gross income under section 82.

(4) *Expenses of moving from one residence to another residence.* An expense of moving from one residence to another residence is any expenditure, cost, loss, or similar item paid or incurred in connection with a move from one residence to another residence. Moving expenses include (but are not limited to) any expenditure, cost, loss, or similar item directly or indirectly resulting from the acquisition, sale, or exchange of property, the transportation of goods or property, or travel (by the taxpayer or any other person) in connection with a change in residence. Such expenses include items described in section 217(b) (relating to the definition of moving expenses), irrespective of the dollar limitations contained in section 217(b)(3) and the conditions contained in section 217(c), as well as items not described in section 217(b), such as a loss sustained on the sale or exchange of personal property, storage charges, taxes, or expenses of refitting rugs or draperies.

(5) *Attributable to employment or self-employment.* Any amount received or accrued from an employer, a client, a customer, or similar person in connection with the performance of services for such employer, client, customer, or similar person, is attributable to employment or self-employment. Thus, for example, if an employer reimburses an employee for a loss incurred on the sale of the employee's house, reimbursement is attributable to the performance of services if made because of the employer-employee relationship. Similarly, if an employer in order to prevent an employee's sustaining a loss on a sale of a house acquires the property from the employee at a price in excess of fair market value, the employee is considered to have received a payment attributable to employment to the extent that such payment exceeds the fair market value of the property.

(b) *Effective date*—(1) *In general.* Except as provided in subparagraph (2) of this paragraph, paragraph (a) of this section is applicable only to amounts received or accrued in taxable years beginning after December 31, 1969.

(2) *Election with respect to payments or reimbursements for expenses paid or incurred before January 1, 1971.* Paragraph (a) of this section does not apply with respect to moving expenses paid or incurred before January 1, 1971, in connection with the commencement of work by an employee at a new principal place of work where

such employee had been notified by his employer on or before December 19, 1969, of such move and the employee makes an election under paragraph (h) of § 1.217-2. [Reg. § 1.82-1.]

☐ [*T.D. 7195, 7-10-72. Amended by T.D. 7578, 12-19-78.*]

[Reg. § 1.83-1]

§ 1.83-1. **Property transferred in connection with the performance of services.**—(a) *Inclusion in gross income*—(1) *General rule.* Section 83 provides rules for the taxation of property transferred to an employee or independent contractor (or beneficiary thereof) in connection with the performance of services by such employee or independent contractor. In general, such property is not taxable under section 83(a) until it has been transferred (as defined in § 1.83-3(a)) to such person and become substantially vested (as defined in § 1.83-3(b)) in such person. In that case, the excess of—

(i) The fair market value of such property (determined without regard to any lapse restriction, as defined in § 1.83-3(i)) at the time that the property becomes substantially vested, over

(ii) The amount (if any) paid for such property,

shall be included as compensation in the gross income of such employee or independent contractor for the taxable year in which the property becomes substantially vested. Until such property becomes substantially vested, the transferor shall be regarded as the owner of such property, and any income from such property received by the employee or independent contractor (or beneficiary thereof) or the right to the use of such property by the employee or independent contractor constitutes additional compensation and shall be included in the gross income of such employee or independent contractor for the taxable year in which such income is received or such use is made available. This paragraph applies to a transfer of property in connection with the performance of services even though the transferor is not the person for whom such services are performed.

(2) *Life insurance.* The cost of life insurance protection under a life insurance contract, retirement income contract, endowment contract, or other contract providing life insurance protection is taxable generally under section 61 and the regulations thereunder during the period such contract remains substantially nonvested (as defined in § 1.83-3(b)). The cost of such life insurance protection is the reasonable net premium cost, as determined by the Commissioner, of the current life insurance protection (as defined in § 1.72-16(b)(3)) provided by such contract.

Reg. § 1.83-1(a)(2)

(3) *Cross references.* For rules concerning the treatment of employers and other transferors of property in connection with the performance of services, see section 83(h) and § 1.83-6. For rules concerning the taxation of beneficiaries of an employees' trust that is not exempt under section 501(a), see section 402(b) and the regulations thereunder.

(b) *Subsequent sale, forfeiture, or other disposition of nonvested property.* (1) If substantially nonvested property (that has been transferred in connection with the performance of services) is subsequently sold or otherwise disposed of to a third party in an arm's length transaction while still substantially nonvested, the person who performed such services shall realize compensation in an amount equal to the excess of—

(i) The amount realized on such sale or other disposition, over

(ii) The amount (if any) paid for such property.

Such amount of compensation is includible in his gross income in accordance with his method of accounting. Two preceding sentences also apply when the person disposing of the property has received it in a non-arm's length transaction described in paragraph (c) of this section. In addition, section 83(a) and paragraph (a) of this section shall thereafter cease to apply with respect to such property.

(2) If substantially nonvested property that has been transferred in connection with the performance of services to the person performing such services is forfeited while still substantially nonvested and held by such person, the difference between the amount paid (if any) and the amount received upon forfeiture (if any) shall be treated as an ordinary gain or loss. This paragraph (b)(2) does not apply to property to which § 1.83-2(a) applies.

(3) This paragraph (b) shall not apply to, and no gain shall be recognized on, any sale, forfeiture, or other disposition described in this paragraph to the extent that any property received in exchange therefor is substantially nonvested. Instead, section 83 and this section shall apply with respect to such property received (as if it were substituted for the property disposed of).

(c) *Dispositions of nonvested property not at arm's length.* If substantially nonvested property (that has been transferred in connection with the performance of services) is disposed of in a transaction which is not at arm's length and the property remains substantially nonvested, the person who performed such services realizes compensation equal in amount to the sum of any money

and the fair market value of any substantially vested property received in such disposition. Such amount of compensation is includible in his gross income in accordance with his method of accounting. However, such amount of compensation shall not exceed the fair market value of the property disposed of at the time of disposition (determined without regard to any lapse restriction), reduced by the amount paid for such property. In addition, section 83 and these regulations shall continue to apply with respect to such property, except that any amount previously includible in gross income under this paragraph (c) shall thereafter be treated as an amount paid for such property. For example, if in 1971 an employee pays $50 for a share of stock which has a fair market value of $100 and is substantially nonvested at that time and later in 1971 (at a time when the property still has a fair market value of $100 and is still substantially nonvested) the employee disposes of, in a transaction not at arm's length, the share of stock to his wife for $10, the employee realizes compensation of $10 in 1971. If in 1972, when the share of stock has a fair market value of $120, it becomes substantially vested, the employee realizes additional compensation in 1972 in the amount of $60 (the $120 fair market value of the stock less both the $50 price paid for the stock and the $10 taxed as compensation in 1971). For purposes of this paragraph, if substantially nonvested property has been transferred to a person other than the person who performed the services, and the transferee dies holding the property while the property is still substantially nonvested and while the person who performed the services is alive, the transfer which results by reason of the death of such transferee is a transfer not at arm's length.

(d) *Certain transfers upon death.* If substantially nonvested property has been transferred in connection with the performance of services and the person who performed such services dies while the property is still substantially nonvested, any income realized on or after such death with respect to such property under this section is income in respect of a decedent to which the rules of section 691 apply. In such a case the income in respect of such property shall be taxable under section 691 (except to the extent not includible under section 101(b)) to the estate or beneficiary of the person who performed the services, in accordance with section 83 and the regulations thereunder. However, if an item of income is realized upon such death before July 21, 1978, because the property became substantially vested upon death, the person responsible for filing decedent's income tax return for decedent's last taxable year may elect to treat such item as includible in gross

Reg. § 1.83-1(a)(3)

income for decedent's last taxable year by including such item in gross income on the return or amended return filed for decedent's last taxable year.

(e) *Forfeiture after substantial vesting.* If a person is taxable under section 83(a) when the property transferred becomes substantially vested and thereafter the person's beneficial interest in such property is nevertheless forfeited pursuant to a lapse restriction, any loss incurred by such person (but not by a beneficiary of such person) upon such forfeiture shall be an ordinary loss to the extent the basis in such property has been increased as a result of the recognition of income by such person under section 83(a) with respect to such property.

(f) *Examples.* The provisions of this section may be illustrated by the following examples:

Example (1). On November 1, 1978, X corporation sells to E, an employee, 100 shares of X corporation stock at $10 per share. At the time of such sale the fair market value of the X corporation stock is $100 per share. Under the terms of the sale each share of stock is subject to a substantial risk of forfeiture which will not lapse until November 1, 1988. Evidence of this restriction is stamped on the face of E's stock certificates, which are therefore nontransferable (within the meaning of § 1.83-3(d)). Since in 1978 E's stock is substantially nonvested, E does not include any of such amount in his gross income as compensation in 1978. On November 1, 1988, the fair market value of the X corporation stock is $250 per share. Since the X corporation stock becomes substantially vested in 1988, E must include $24,000 (100 shares of X corporation stock × $250 fair market value per share less $10 price paid by E for each share) as compensation for 1988. Dividends paid by X to E on E's stock after it was transferred to E on November 1, 1973, are taxable to E as additional compensation during the period E's stock is substantially nonvested and are deductible as such by X.

Example (2). Assume the facts are the same as in example (1), except that on November 1, 1985, each share of stock of X corporation in E's hands could as a matter of law be transferred to a bona fide purchaser who would not be required to forfeit the stock if the risk of forfeiture materialized. In the event, however, that the risk materializes, E would be liable in damages to X. On November 1, 1985, the fair market value of the X corporation stock is $230 per share. Since E's stock is transferable within the meaning of § 1.83-3(d) in 1985, the stock is substantially vested and E must include $22,000 (100 shares of X corporation stock × $230 fair market value per share less $10

price paid by E for each share) as compensation for 1985.

Example (3). Assume the facts are the same as in example (1) except that, in 1984 E sells his 100 shares of X corporation stock in an arm's length sale to I, an investment company, for $120 per share. At the time of this sale each share of X corporation's stock has a fair market value of $200. Under paragraph (b) of this section, E must include $11,000 (100 shares of X corporation stock × $120 amount realized per share less $10 price paid by E per share) as compensation for 1984 notwithstanding that the stock remains nontransferable and is still subject to a substantial risk of forfeiture at the time of such sale. Under § 1.83-4(b)(2), I's basis in the X corporation stock is $120 per share. [Reg. § 1.83-1.]

□ [T.D. 7554, 7-21-78.]

[Reg. § 1.83-2]

§ 1.83-2. **Election to include in gross income in year of transfer.**—(a) *In general.* If property is transferred (within the meaning of § 1.83-3(a)) in connection with the performance of services, the person performing such services may elect to include in gross income under section 83(b) the excess (if any) of the fair market value of the property at the time of transfer (determined without regard to any lapse restriction, as defined in § 1.83-3(i)) over the amount (if any) paid for such property, as compensation for services. The fact that the transferee has paid full value for the property transferred, realizing no bargain element in the transaction, does not preclude the use of the election as provided for in this section. If this election is made, the substantial vesting rules of section 83(a) and the regulations thereunder do not apply with respect to such property, and except as otherwise provided in section 83(d)(2) and the regulations thereunder (relating to the cancellation of a nonlapse restriction), any subsequent appreciation in the value of the property is not taxable as compensation to the person who performed the services. Thus, property with respect to which this election is made shall be includible in gross income as of the time of transfer, even though such property is substantially nonvested (as defined in § 1.83-3(b)) at the time of transfer, and no compensation will be includible in gross income when such property becomes substantially vested (as defined in § 1.83-3(b)). In computing the gain or loss from the subsequent sale or exchange of such property, its basis shall be the amount paid for the property increased by the amount included in gross income under section 83(b). If property for which a section 83(b) election is in effect is forfeited while substantially nonvested, such forfeiture shall be treated as a sale or exchange upon which there is realized a loss equal to the excess (if any) of—

(1) The amount paid (if any) for such property, over,

(2) The amount realized (if any) upon such forfeiture.

If such property is a capital asset in the hands of the taxpayer, such loss shall be a capital loss. A sale or other disposition of the property that is in substance a forfeiture, or is made in contemplation of a forfeiture, shall be treated as a forfeiture under the two immediately preceding sentences.

(b) *Time for making election.* Except as provided in the following sentence, the election referred to in paragraph (a) of this section shall be filed not later than 30 days after the date the property was transferred (or, if later, January 29, 1970) and may be filed prior to the date of transfer. Any statement filed before February 15, 1970, which was amended not later than February 16, 1970, in order to make it conform to the requirements of paragraph (e) of this section, shall be deemed a proper election under section 83(b).

(c) *Manner of making election.* The election referred to in paragraph (a) of this section is made by filing one copy of a written statement with the internal revenue officer with whom the person who performed the services files his return. In addition, one copy of such statement shall be submitted with his income tax return for the taxable year in which such property was transferred.

(d) *Additional copies.* The person who performed the services shall also submit a copy of the statement referred to in paragraph (c) of this section to the person for whom the services are performed. In addition, if the person who performs the services and the transferee of such property are not the same person, the person who performs the services shall submit a copy of such statement to the transferee of the property.

(e) *Content of statement.* The statement shall be signed by the person making the election and shall indicate that it is being made under section 83(b) of the Code, and shall contain the following information:

(1) The name, address and taxpayer identification number of the taxpayer;

(2) A description of each property with respect to which the election is being made;

(3) The date or dates on which the property is transferred and the taxable year (for example, "calendar year 1970" or "fiscal year ending May 31, 1970") for which such election was made;

(4) The nature of the restriction or restrictions to which the property is subject;

(5) The fair market value at the time of transfer (determined without regard to any lapse restriction, as defined in § 1.83-3(i)) of each property with respect to which the election is being made;

(6) The amount (if any) paid for such property; and

(7) With respect to elections made after July 21, 1978, a statement to the effect that copies have been furnished to other persons as provided in paragraph (d) of this section.

(f) *Revocability of election.* An election under section 83(b) may not be revoked except with the consent of the Commissioner. Consent will be granted only in the case where the transferee is under a mistake of fact as to the underlying transaction and must be requested within 60 days of the date on which the mistake of fact first became known to the person who made the election. In any event, a mistake as to the value, or decline in the value, of the property with respect to which an election under section 83(b) has been made or a failure to perform an act contemplated at the time of transfer of such property does not constitute a mistake of fact. [Reg. § 1.83-2.]

☐ [*T.D.* 7554, 7-21-78.]

[Reg. § 1.83-3]

§ **1.83-3. Meaning and use of certain terms.**—(a) *Transfer*—(1) *In general.* For purposes of section 83 and the regulations thereunder, a transfer of property occurs when a person acquires a beneficial ownership interest in such property (disregarding any lapse restriction, as defined in § 1.83-3(i)).

(2) *Option.* The grant of an option to purchase certain property does not constitute a transfer of such property. However, see § 1.83-7 for the extent to which the grant of the option itself is subject to section 83. In addition, if the amount paid for the transfer of property is an indebtedness secured by the transferred property, on which there is no personal liability to pay all or a substantial part of such indebtedness, such transaction may be in substance the same as the grant of an option. The determination of the substance of the transaction shall be based upon all the facts and circumstances. The factors to be taken into account include the type of property involved, the extent to which the risk that the property will decline in value has been transferred, and the likelihood that the purchase price will, in fact, be paid. See also § 1.83-4(c) for the treatment of forgiveness of indebtedness that has constituted an amount paid.

(3) *Requirement that property be returned.* Similarly, no transfer may have occurred where

Reg. § 1.83-3(a)(1)

property is transferred under conditions that require its return upon the happening of an event that is certain to occur, such as the termination of employment. In such a case, whether there is, in fact, a transfer depends upon all the facts and circumstances. Factors which indicate that no transfer has occurred are described in paragraph (a)(4), (5) and (6) of this section.

(4) *Similarity to option.* An indication that no transfer has occurred is the extent to which the conditions relating to a transfer are similar to an option.

(5) *Relationship to fair market value.* An indication that no transfer has occurred is the extent to which the consideration to be paid the transferee upon surrendering the property does not approach the fair market value of the property at the time of surrender. For purposes of paragraph (a)(5) and (6) of this section, fair market value includes fair market value determined under the rules of § 1.83-5(a)(1), relating to the valuation of property subject to nonlapse restrictions. Therefore, the existence of a nonlapse restriction referred to in § 1.83-5(a)(1) is not a factor indicating no transfer has occurred.

(6) *Risk of loss.* An indication that no transfer has occurred is the extent to which the transferee does not incur the risk of a beneficial owner that the value of the property at the time of transfer will decline substantially. Therefore, for purposes of this (6), risk of decline in property value is not limited to the risk that any amount paid for the property may be lost.

(7) *Examples.* The provisions of this paragraph may be illustrated by the following examples:

Example (1). On January 3, 1971, X corporation sells for $500 to S, a salesman of X, 10 shares of stock in X corporation with a fair market value of $1,000. The stock is nontransferable and subject to return to the corporation (for $500) if S's sales do not reach a certain level by December 31, 1971. Disregarding the restriction concerning S's sales (since the restriction is a lapse restriction), S's interest in the stock is that of a beneficial owner and therefore a transfer occurs on January 3, 1971.

Example (2). On November 17, 1972, W sells to E 100 shares of stock in W corporation with a fair market value of $10,000 in exchange for a $10,000 note without personal liability. The note requires E to make yearly payments of $2,000 commencing in 1973. E collects the dividends, votes the stock and pays the interest on the note. However, he makes no payments towards the face amount of the note. Because E has no personal liability on the note, and since E is making no

payments towards the face amount of the note, the likelihood of E paying the full purchase price is in substantial doubt. As a result, E has not incurred the risks of a beneficial owner that the value of the stock will decline. Therefore, no transfer of the stock has occurred on November 17, 1972, but an option to purchase the stock has been granted to E.

Example (3). On January 3, 1971, X corporation purports to transfer to E, an employee, 100 shares of stock in X corporation. The X stock is subject to the sole restriction that E must sell such stock to X on termination of employment for any reason for an amount which is equal to the excess (if any) of the book value of the X stock at termination of employment over book value on January 3, 1971. The stock is not transferable by E and the restrictions on transfer are stamped on the certificate. Under these facts and circumstances, there is no transfer of the X stock within the meaning of section 83.

Example (4). Assume the same facts as in example (3) except that E paid $3,000 for the stock and that the restriction required E upon termination of employment to sell the stock to M for the total amount of dividends that have been declared on the stock since September 2, 1971, or $3,000 whichever is higher. Again, under the facts and circumstances, no transfer of the X stock has occurred.

Example (5). On July 4, 1971, X corporation purports to transfer to G an employee, 100 shares of X stock. The stock is subject to the sole restriction that upon termination of employment G must sell the stock to X for the greater of its fair market value at such time or $100, the amount G paid for the stock. On July 4, 1971 the X stock has a fair market value of $100. Therefore, G does not incur the risk of a beneficial owner that the value of the stock at the time of transfer ($100) will decline substantially. Under these facts and circumstances, no transfer has occurred.

(b) *Substantially vested and substantially nonvested property.* For purposes of section 83 and the regulations thereunder, property is substantially nonvested when it is subject to a substantial risk of forfeiture, within the meaning of paragraph (c) of this section, and is nontransferable, within the meaning of paragraph (d) of this section. Property is substantially vested for such purposes when it is either transferable or not subject to a substantial risk of forfeiture.

(c) *Substantial risk of forfeiture*—(1) *In general.* For purposes of section 83 and the regulations thereunder, whether a risk of forfeiture is substantial or not depends upon the facts and circumstances. A substantial risk of forfeiture ex-

Reg. § 1.83-3(c)(1)

ists where rights in property that are transferred are conditioned, directly or indirectly, upon the future performance (or refraining from performance) of substantial services by any person, or the occurrence of a condition related to a purpose of the transfer, and the possibility of forfeiture is substantial if such condition is not satisfied. Property is not transferred subject to a substantial risk of forfeiture to the extent that the employer is required to pay the fair market value of a portion of such property to the employee upon the return of such property. The risk that the value of property will decline during a certain period of time does not constitute a substantial risk of forfeiture. A nonlapse restriction, standing by itself, will not result in a substantial risk of forfeiture.

(2) *Illustrations of substantial risks of forfeiture.* The regularity of the performance of services and the time spent in performing such services tend to indicate whether services required by a condition are substantial. The fact that the person performing services has the right to decline to perform such services without forfeiture may tend to establish that services are insubstantial. Where stock is transferred to an underwriter prior to a public offering and the full enjoyment of such stock is expressly or impliedly conditioned upon the successful completion of the underwriting, the stock is subject to a substantial risk of forfeiture. Where an employee receives property from an employer subject to a requirement that it be returned if the total earnings of the employer do not increase, such property is subject to a substantial risk of forfeiture. On the other hand, requirements that the property be returned to the employer if the employee is discharged for cause or for committing a crime will not be considered to result in a substantial risk of forfeiture. An enforceable requirement that the property be returned to the employer if the employee accepts a job with a competing firm will not ordinarily be considered to result in a substantial risk of forfeiture unless the particular facts and circumstances indicate to the contrary. Factors which may be taken into account in determining whether a covenant not to compete constitutes a substantial risk of forfeiture are the age of the employee, the availability of alternative employment opportunities, the likelihood of the employee's obtaining such other employment, the degree of skill possessed by the employee, the employee's health, and the practice (if any) of the employer to enforce such covenants. Similarly, rights in property transferred to a retiring employee subject to the sole requirement that it be returned unless he renders consulting services upon the request of his former employer will not be considered subject to a sub-

stantial risk of forfeiture unless he is in fact expected to perform substantial services.

(3) *Enforcement of forfeiture condition.* In determining whether the possibility of forfeiture is substantial in the case of rights in property transferred to an employee of a corporation who owns a significant amount of the total combined voting power or value of all classes of stock of the employer corporation or of its parent corporation, there will be taken into account (i) the employee's relationship to other stockholders and the extent of their control, potential control and possible loss of control of the corporation, (ii) the position of the employee in the corporation and the extent to which he is subordinate to other employees, (iii) the employee's relationship to the officers and directors of the corporation, (iv) the person or persons who must approve the employee's discharge, and (v) past actions of the employer in enforcing the provisions of the restrictions. For example, if an employee would be considered as having received rights in property subject to a substantial risk of forfeiture, but for the fact that the employee owns 20 percent of the single class of stock in the transferor corporation, and if the remaining 80 percent of the class of stock is owned by an unrelated individual (or members of such an individual's family) so that the possibility of the corporation enforcing a restriction on such rights is substantial, then such rights are subject to a substantial risk of forfeiture. On the other hand, if 4 percent of the voting power of all the stock of a corporation is owned by the president of such corporation and the remaining stock is so diversely held by the public that the president, in effect, controls the corporation, then the possibility of the corporation enforcing a restriction on rights in property transferred to the president is not substantial, and such rights are not subject to a substantial risk of forfeiture.

(4) *Examples.* The rules contained in paragraph (c)(1) of this section may be illustrated by the following examples. In each example it is assumed that, if the conditions on transfer are not satisfied, the forfeiture provision will be enforced.

Example (1). On November 1, 1971, corporation X transfers in connection with the performance of services to E, an employee, 100 shares of corporation X stock for $90 per share. Under the terms of the transfer, E will be subject to a binding commitment to resell the stock to corporation X at $90 per share if he leaves the employment of corporation X for any reason prior to the expiration of a 2-year period from the date of such transfer. Since E must perform substantial services for corporation X and will not be paid more than $90 for the stock, regardless of its value, if he

Reg. § 1.83-3(c)(2)

fails to perform such services during such 2-year period, E's rights in the stock are subject to a substantial risk of forfeiture during such period.

Example (2). On November 10, 1971, corporation X transfers in connection with the performance of services to a trust for the benefit of employees, $100x. Under the terms of the trust any child of an employee who is an enrolled full-time student at an accredited educational institution as a candidate for a degree will receive an annual grant of cash for each academic year the student completes as a student in good standing, up to a maximum of four years. E, an employee, has a child who is enrolled as a full-time student at an accredited college as a candidate for a degree. Therefore, E has a beneficial interest in the assets of the trust equalling the value of four cash grants. Since E's child must complete one year of college in order to receive a cash grant, E's interest in the trust assets are subject to a substantial risk of forfeiture to the extent E's child has not become entitled to any grants.

Example (3). On November 25, 1971, corporation X gives to E, an employee, in connection with his performance of services to corporation X, a bonus of 100 shares of corporation X stock. Under the terms of the bonus arrangement E is obligated to return the corporation X stock to corporation X if he terminates his employment for any reason. However, for each year occurring af-

ter November 25, 1971, during which E remains employed with corporation X, E ceases to be obligated to return 10 shares of the corporation X stock. Since in each year occurring after November 25, 1971, for which E remains employed he is not required to return 10 shares of corporation X's stock, E's rights in 10 shares each year for 10 years cease to be subject to a substantial risk of forfeiture for each year he remains so employed.

Example (4). (a) Assume the same facts as in example (3) except that for each year occurring after November 25, 1971, for which E remains employed with corporation X, X agrees to pay, in redemption of the bonus shares given to E if he terminates employment for any reason, 10 percent of the fair market value of each share of stock on the date of such termination of employment. Since corporation X will pay E 10 percent of the value of his bonus stock for each of the 10 years after November 25, 1971, in which he remains employed by X, and the risk of a decline in value is not a substantial risk of forfeiture, E's interest in 10 percent of such bonus stock becomes substantially vested in each of those years.

(b) The following chart illustrates the fair market value of the bonus stock and the fair market value of the portion of bonus stock that becomes substantially vested on November 25, for the following years:

Year	(I) All stock	Fair market value of: (II) Portion of stock that becomes vested
1972	$200	$20
1973	300	30
1974	150	15
1975	150	15
1976	100	10

If E terminates his employment on July 1, 1977, when the fair market value of the bonus stock is $100, E must return the bonus stock to X, and X must pay, in redemption of the bonus stock, $50 (50 percent of the value of the bonus stock on the date of termination of employment). E has recognized income under section 83(a) and § 1.83-1(a) with respect to 50 percent of the bonus stock, and E's basis in that portion of the stock equals the amount of income recognized, $90. Under § 1.83-1(e), the $40 loss E incurred upon forfeiture ($90 basis less $50 redemption payment) is an ordinary loss.

Example (5). On January 7, 1971, corporation X, a computer service company, transfers to E, 100 shares of corporation X stock for $50. E is a highly compensated salesman who sold X's prod-

ucts in a three-state area since 1960. At the time of transfer each share of X stock has a fair market value of $100. The stock is transferred to E in connection with his termination of employment with X. Each share of X stock is subject to the sole condition that E can keep such share only if he does not engage in competition with X for a 5-year period in the three-state area where E had previously sold X's products. E, who is 45 years old, has no intention of retiring from the work force. In order to earn a salary comparable to his current compensation, while preventing the risk of forfeiture from arising, E will have to expend a substantial amount of time and effort in another industry or market to establish the necessary business contacts. Thus, under these facts and circumstances E's rights in the stock are subject to a substantial risk of forfeiture.

Reg. § 1.83-3(c)(4)

(d) *Transferability of property.* For purposes of section 83 and the regulations thereunder, the rights of a person in property are transferable if such person can transfer any interest in the property to any person other than the transferor of the property, but only if the rights in such property of such transferee are not subject to a substantial risk of forfeiture. Accordingly, property is transferable if the person performing the services or receiving the property can sell, assign, or pledge (as collateral for a loan, or as security for the performance of an obligation, or for any other purpose) his interest in the property to any person other than the transferor of such property and if the transferee is not required to give up the property or its value in the event the substantial risk of forfeiture materializes. On the other hand, property is not considered to be transferable merely because the person performing the services or receiving the property may designate a beneficiary to receive the property in the event of his death.

(e) *Property.* For purposes of section 83 and the regulations thereunder, the term "property" includes real and personal property other than either money or an unfunded and unsecured promise to pay money or property in the future. The term also includes a beneficial interest in assets (including money) which are transferred or set aside from the claims of creditors of the transferor, for example, in a trust or escrow account. See, however, § 1.83-8(a) with respect to employee trusts and annuity plans subject to section 402(b) and section 403(c). In the case of a transfer of a life insurance contract, retirement income contract, endowment contract, or other contract providing life insurance protection, only the cash surrender value of the contract is considered to be property. Where rights in a contract providing life insurance protection are substantially nonvested, see § 1.83-1(a)(2) for rules relating to the taxation of the cost of life insurance protection.

(f) *Property transferred in connection with the performance of services.* Property transferred to an employee or an independent contractor (or beneficiary thereof) in recognition of the performance of, or the refraining from performance of, services is considered transferred in connection with the performance of services within the meaning of section 83. The existence of other persons entitled to buy stock on the same terms and conditions as an employee, whether pursuant to a public or private offering may, however, indicate that in such circumstances a transfer to the employee is not in recognition of the performance of, or the refraining from performance of, services. The transfer of property is subject to section 83 whether such transfer is in respect of past, present, or future services.

(g) *Amount paid.* For purposes of section 83 and the regulations thereunder, the term "amount paid" refers to the value of any money or property paid for the transfer of property to which section 83 applies, and does not refer to any amount paid for the right to use such property or to receive the income therefrom. Such value does not include any stated or unstated interest payments. For rules regarding the calculation of the amount of unstated interest payments, see § 1.483-1(c). When section 83 applies to the transfer of property pursuant to the exercise of an option, the term "amount paid" refers to any amount paid for the grant of the option plus any amount paid as the exercise price of the option. For rules regarding the forgiveness of indebtedness treated as an amount paid, see § 1.83-4(c).

(h) *Nonlapse restriction.* For purposes of section 83 and the regulations thereunder, a restriction which by its terms will never lapse (also referred to as a "nonlapse restriction") is a permanent limitation on the transferability of property—

(i) Which will require the transferee of the property to sell, or offer to sell, such property at a price determined under a formula, and

(ii) Which will continue to apply to and be enforced against the transferee or any subsequent holder (other than the transferor).

A limitation subjecting the property to a permanent right of first refusal in a particular person at a price determined under a formula is a permanent nonlapse restriction. Limitations imposed by registration requirements of State or Federal security laws or similar laws imposed with respect to sales or other dispositions of stock or securities are not nonlapse restrictions. An obligation to resell or to offer to sell property transferred in connection with the performance of services to a specific person or persons at its fair market value at the time of such sale is not a nonlapse restriction. See § 1.83-5(c) for examples of nonlapse restrictions.

(i) *Lapse restriction.* For purposes of section 83 and the regulations thereunder, the term "lapse restriction" means a restriction other than a nonlapse restriction as defined in paragraph (h) of this section, and includes (but is not limited to) a restriction that carries a substantial risk of forfeiture.

(j) *Sales which may give rise to suit under section 16(b) of the Securities Exchange Act of 1934* —(1) *In general.* For purposes of section 83 and the regulations thereunder if the sale of property at a profit within six months after the purchase of the property could subject a person to

Reg. § 1.83-3(d)

suit under section 16(b) of the Securities Exchange Act of 1934, the person's rights in the property are treated as subject to a substantial risk of forfeiture and as not transferable until the earlier of (i) the expiration of such six-month period, or (ii) the first day on which the sale of such property at a profit will not subject the person to suit under section 16(b) of the Securities Exchange Act of 1934. However, whether an option is "transferable by the optionee" for purposes of § 1.83-7(b)(2)(i) is determined without regard to section 83(c)(3) and this paragraph (j).

(2) *Examples.* The provisions of this paragraph may be illustrated by the following examples:

Example (1). On January 1, 1983, X corporation sells to P, a beneficial owner of 12% of X corporation stock, in connection with P's performance of services, 100 shares of X corporation stock at $10 per share. At the time of the sale the fair market value of the X corporation stock is $100 per share. P, as a beneficial owner of more than 10% of X corporation stock, is liable to suit under section 16(b) of the Securities Exchange Act of 1934 for recovery of any profit from any sale and purchase or purchase and sale of X corporation stock within a six-month period, but no other restrictions apply to the stock. Because the section 16(b) restriction is applicable to P, P's rights in the 100 shares of stock purchased on January 1, 1983, are treated as subject to a substantial risk of forfeiture and as not transferable through June 29, 1983. P chooses not to make an election under section 83(b) and therefore does not include any amount with respect to the stock purchase in gross income as compensation on the date of purchase. On June 30, 1983, the fair market value of X corporation stock is $250 per share. P must include $24,000 (100 shares of X corporation stock × $240 ($250 fair market value per share less $10 price paid by P for each share)) in gross income as compensation on June 30, 1983. If, in this example, restrictions other than section 16(B) applied to the stock, such other restrictions (but not section 16(b)) would be taken into account in determining whether the stock is subject to a substantial risk of forfeiture and is nontransferable for periods after June 29, 1983.

Example (2). Assume the same facts as in example (1) except that P is not an insider on or after May 1, 1983, and the section 16(b) restriction does not apply beginning on that date. On May 1, 1983, P must include in gross income as compensation the difference between the fair market value of the stock on that date and the amount paid for the stock.

Example (3). Assume the same facts as in example (1) except that on June 1, 1983, X corporation sells to P an additional 100 shares of X corporation stock at $20 per share. At the time of the sale the fair market value of the X corporation stock is $150 per share. On June 30, 1983, P must include $24,000 in gross income as compensation with respect to the January 1, 1983 purchase. On November 30, 1983, the fair market value of X corporation stock is $200 per share. Accordingly, on that date P must include $18,000 (100 shares of X corporation stock × $180 ($200 fair market value per share less $20 price paid for P each share)) in gross income as compensation with respect to the June 1, 1983 purchase.

(3) *Effective date.* This paragraph applies to property transferred after December 31, 1981.

(k) *Special rule for certain accounting rules.* (1) For purposes of section 83 and the regulations thereunder, property is subject to substantial risk of forfeiture and is not transferable so long as the property is subject to a restriction on transfer to comply with the "Pooling-of-Interests Accounting" rules set forth in Accounting Series Release Numbered 130 ((10/5/72) 37 FR 20937; 17 CFR 211.130) and Accounting Series Release Numbered 135 ((1/18/73) 38 FR 1734; 17 CFR 211.135).

(2) *Effective date.* This paragraph applies to property transferred after December 31, 1981. [Reg. § 1.83-3.]

□ *T.D. 7554, 7-21-78. Amended by T.D. 8042, 8-5-85.*]

[Reg. § 1.83-4]

§ 1.83-4. **Special rules.**—(a) *Holding period.* Under section 83(f), the holding period of transferred property to which section 83(a) applies shall begin just after such property is substantially vested. However, if the person who has performed the services in connection with which property is transferred has made an election under section 83(b), the holding period of such property shall begin just after the date such property is transferred. If property to which section 83 and the regulations thereunder apply is transferred at arm's length, the holding period of such property in the hands of the transferee shall be determined in accordance with the rules provided in section 1223.

(b) *Basis.* (1) Except as provided in paragraph (b)(2) of this section, if property to which section 83 and the regulations thereunder apply is acquired by any person (including a person who acquires such property in a subsequent transfer which is not at arm's length), while such property is still substantially nonvested, such person's basis

Reg. § 1.83-4(b)

for the property shall reflect any amount paid for such property and any amount includible in the gross income of the person who performed the services (including any amount so includible as a result of a disposition by the person who acquired such property). Such basis shall also reflect any adjustments to basis provided under sections 1015 and 1016.

(2) If property to which § 1.83-1 applies is transferred at arm's length, the basis of the property in the hands of the transferee shall be determined under section 1012 and the regulations thereunder.

(c) *Forgiveness of indebtedness treated as an amount paid.* If an indebtedness that has been treated as an amount paid under § 1.83-1 (a) (1) (ii) is subsequently cancelled, forgiven or satisfied for an amount less than the amount of such indebtedness, the amount that is not, in fact, paid shall be includible in the gross income of the service provider in the taxable year in which such cancellation, forgiveness or satisfaction occurs. [Reg. § 1.83-4.]

☐ [*T.D.* 7554, 7-21-78.]

[Reg. § 1.83-5]

§ 1.83-5. **Restrictions that will never lapse.**—(a) *Valuation.* For purposes of section 83 and the regulations thereunder, in the case of property subject to a nonlapse restriction (as defined in § 1.83-3(h)), the price determined under the formula price will be considered to be the fair market value of the property unless established to the contrary by the Commissioner, and the burden of proof shall be on the Commissioner with respect to such value. If stock in a corporation is subject to a nonlapse restriction which requires the transferee to sell such stock only at a formula price based on book value, a reasonable multiple of earnings or a reaasonable combination thereof, the price so determined will ordinarily be regarded as determinative of the fair market value of such property for purposes of section 83. However, in certain circumstances the formula price will not be considered to be the fair market value of property subject to such a formula price restriction, even though the formula price restriction is a substantial factor in determining such value. For example, where the formula price is the current book value of stock, the book value of the stock at some time in the future may be a more accurate measure of the value of the stock than the current book value of the stock for purposes of determining the fair market value of the stock at the time the stock becomes substantially vested.

(b) *Cancellation*—(1) *In general.* Under section 83(d) (2), if a nonlapse restriction imposed on

property that is subject to section 83 is cancelled, then, unless the taxpayer establishes—

(i) That such cancellation was not compensatory, and

(ii) That the person who would be allowed a deduction, if any, if the cancellation were treated as compensatory, will treat the transaction as not compensatory, as provided in paragraph (c) (2) of this section, the excess of the fair market value of such property (computed without regard to such restriction) at the time of cancellation, over the sum of—

(iii) The fair market value of such property (computed by taking the restriction into account) immediately before the cancellation, and

(iv) The amount, if any, paid for the cancellation,

shall be treated as compensation for the taxable year in which such cancellation occurs. Whether there has been a noncompensatory cancellation of a nonlapse restriction under section 83 (d) (2) depends upon the particular facts and circumstances. Ordinarily the fact that the employee or independent contractor is required to perform additional services or that the salary or payment of such a person is adjusted to take the cancellation into account indicates that such cancellation has a compensatory purpose. On the other hand, the fact that the original purpose of a restriction no longer exists may indicate that the purpose of such cancellation is noncompensatory. Thus, for example, if a so-called "buy-sell" restriction was imposed on a corporation's stock to limit ownership of such stock and is being cancelled in connection with a public offering of the stock, such cancellation will generally be regarded as noncompensatory. However, the mere fact that the employer is willing to forego a deduction under section 83(h) is insufficient evidence to establish a noncompensatory cancellation of a nonlapse restriction. The refusal by a corporation or shareholder to repurchase stock of the corporation which is subject to a permanent right of first refusal will generally be treated as a cancellation of a nonlapse restriction. The preceding sentence shall not apply where there is no nonlapse restriction, for example, where the price to be paid for the stock subject to the right of first refusal is the fair market value of the stock. Section 83 (d) (2) and this (1) do not apply where immediately after the cancellation of a nonlapse restriction the property is still substantially nonvested and no section 83 (b) election has been made with respect to such property. In such a case the rules of section 83 (a) and § 1.83-1 shall apply to such property.

(2) *Evidence of noncompensatory cancellation.* In addition to the information necessary to

establish the factors described in paragraph (b) (1) of this section, the taxpayer shall request the employer to furnish the taxpayer with a written statement indicating that the employer will not treat the cancellation of the nonlapse restriction as a compensatory event, and that no deduction will be taken with respect to such cancellation. The taxpayer shall file such written statement with his income tax return for the taxable year in which or with which such cancellation occurs.

(c) *Examples.* The provisions of this section may be illustrated by the following examples:

Example (1). On November 1, 1971, X corporation whose shares are closely held and not regularly traded, transfers to E, an employee, 100 shares of X corporation stock subject to the condition that, if he desires to dispose of such stock during the period of his employment, he must resell the stock to his employer at its then existing book value. In addition, E or E's estate is obligated to offer to sell the stock at his retirement or death to his employer at its then existing book value. Under these facts and circumstances, the restriction to which the shares of X corporation stock are subject is a nonlapse restriction. Consequently, the fair market value of the X stock is includible in E's gross income as compensation for taxable year 1971. However, in determining the fair market value of the X stock, the book value formula price will ordinarily be regarded as being determinative of such value.

Example (2). Assume the facts are the same as in example (1), except that the X stock is subject to the condition that if E desires to dispose of the stock during the period of his employment he must resell the stock to his employer at a multiple of earnings per share that is in this case a reasonable approximation of value at the time of transfer to E. In addition, E or E's estate is obligated to offer to sell the stock at his retirement or death to his employer at the same multiple of earnings. Under these facts and circumstances, the restriction to which the X corporation stock is subject is a nonlapse restriction. Consequently, the fair market value of the X stock is includible in E's gross income for taxable year 1971. However, in determining the fair market value of the X stock, the multiple-of-earnings formula price will ordinarily be regarded as determinative of such value.

Example (3). On January 4, 1971, X corporation transfers to E, an employee, 100 shares of stock in X corporation. Each such share of stock is subject to an agreement between X and E whereby E agrees that such shares are to be held solely for investment purposes and not for resale (a so-called investment letter restriction). E's rights in such stock are substantially vested upon transfer, causing the fair market value of each share of X corporation stock to be includible in E's gross income as compensation for taxable year 1971. Since such an investment letter restriction does not constitute a nonlapse restriction, in determining the fair market value of each share, the investment letter restriction is disregarded.

Example (4). On September 1, 1971, X corporation transfers to B, an independent contractor, 500 shares of common stock in X corporation in exchange for B's agreement to provide services in the construction of an office building on property owned by X corporation. X corporation has 100 shares of preferred stock outstanding and an additional 500 shares of common stock outstanding. The preferred stock has a liquidation value of $1,000x, which is equal to the value of all assets owned by X. Therefore, the book value of the common stock in X corporation is $0. Under the terms of the transfer, if B wishes to dispose of the stock, B must offer to sell the stock to X for 150 percent of the then existing book value of B's common stock. The stock is also subject to a substantial risk of forfeiture until B performs the agreed-upon services. B makes a timely election under section 83(b) to include the value of the stock in gross income in 1971. Under these facts and circumstances, the restriction to which the shares of X corporation common stock are subject is a nonlapse restriction. In determining the fair market value of the X common stock at the time of transfer, the book value formula price would ordinarily be regarded as determinative of such value. However, the fair market value of X common stock at the time of transfer, subject to the book value restriction, is greater than $0 since B was willing to agree to provide valuable personal services in exchange for the stock. In determining the fair market value of the stock, the expected book value after construction of the office building would be given great weight. The likelihood of completion of construction would be a factor in determining the expected book value after completion of construction. [Reg. § 1.83-5.]

☐ *T.D. 7554, 7-21-78.]*

[Reg. § 1.83-6]

§ 1.83-6. Deduction by employer.—(a) *Allowance of deduction*—(1) *General rule.* In the case of a transfer of property in connection with the performance of services, or a compensatory cancellation of a nonlapse restriction described in section 83(d) and § 1.83-5, a deduction is allowable under section 162 or 212 to the person for whom the services were performed. The amount of the deduction is equal to the amount included as compensation in the gross income of the service provider under section 83(a), (b), or (d)(2), but only to the extent the amount meets the requirements of section 162 or 212 and the regulations thereunder. The deduction is allowed only for the taxable year of that person in which or with which ends the taxable year of the service provider in which the amount is included as compensation. For purposes of this paragraph, any amount excluded from gross income under section 79 or section 101(b) or subchapter N is considered to have been included in gross income.

(2) *Special rule.* For purposes of paragraph (a)(1) of this section, the service provider is deemed to have included the amount as compensation in gross income if the person for whom the services were performed satisfies in a timely manner all requirements of section 6041 or section 6041A, and the regulations thereunder, with respect to that amount of compensation. For purposes of the preceding sentence, whether a person for whom services were performed satisfies all requirements of section 6041 or section 6041A, and the regulations thereunder, is determined without regard to § 1.6041-3(c) (exception for payments to corporations). In the case of a disqualifying disposition of stock described in section 421(b), an employer that otherwise satisfies all requirements of section 6041 and the regulations thereunder will be considered to have done so timely for purposes of this paragraph (a)(2) if Form W-2 or Form W-2c, as appropriate, is furnished to the employee or former employee, and is filed with the federal government, on or before the date on which the employer files the tax return claiming the deduction relating to the disqualifying disposition.

(3) *Exceptions.* Where property is substantially vested upon transfer, the deduction shall be allowed to such person in accordance with his method of accounting (in conformity with sections 446 and 461). In the case of a transfer to an employee benefit plan described in § 1.162-10(a) or a transfer to an employees' trust or annuity plan described in section 404(a)(5) and the regulations thereunder, section 83(h) and this section do not apply.

(4) *Capital expenditure, etc.* No deduction is allowed under section 83(h) to the extent that the transfer of property constitutes a capital expenditure, an item of deferred expense, or an amount properly includible in the value of inventory items. In the case of a capital expenditure, for example, the basis of the property to which such capital expenditure relates shall be increased at the same time and to the same extent as any amount includible in the employee's gross income in respect of such transfer. Thus, for example, no deduction is allowed to a corporation in respect of

a transfer of its stock to a promoter upon its organization, notwithstanding that such promoter must include the value of such stock in his gross income in accordance with the rules under section 83.

(5) *Effective date.* Paragraphs (a)(1) and (2) of this section apply to deductions for taxable years beginning on or after January 1, 1995. However, taxpayers may also apply paragraphs (a)(1) and (2) of this section when claiming deductions for taxable years beginning before that date if the claims are not barred by the statute of limitations. Paragraphs (a)(3) and (4) of this section are effective as set forth in § 1.83-8(b).

(b) *Recognition of gain or loss.* Except as provided in section 1032, at the time of a transfer of property in connection with the performance of services the transferor recognizes gain to the extent that the transferor receives an amount that exceeds the transferor's basis in the property. In addition, at the time a deduction is allowed under section 83(h) and paragraph (a) of this section, gain or loss is recognized to the extent of the difference between (i) the sum of the amount paid plus the amount allowed as a deduction under section 83(h), and (ii) the sum of the taxpayer's basis in the property plus any amount recognized pursuant to the previous sentence.

(c) *Forfeitures.* If, under section 83(h) and paragraph (a) of this section, a deduction, an increase in basis, or a reduction of gross income was allowable (disregarding the reasonableness of the amount of compensation) in respect of a transfer of property and such property is subsequently forfeited, the amount of such deduction, increase in basis or reduction of gross income shall be includible in the gross income of the person to whom it was allowable for the taxable year of forfeiture. The basis of such property in the hands of the person to whom it is forfeited shall include any such amount includible in the gross income of such person, as well as any amount such person pays upon forfeiture.

(d) *Special rules for transfers by shareholders—* (1) *Transfers.* If a shareholder of a corporation transfers property to an employee of such corporation or to an independent contractor (or to a beneficiary thereof), in consideration of services performed for the corporation, the transaction shall be considered to be a contribution of such property to the capital of such corporation by the shareholder, and immediately thereafter a transfer of such property by the corporation to the employee or independent contractor under paragraphs (a) and (b) of this section. For purposes of this (1), such a transfer will be considered to be in consideration for services performed for

Reg. § 1.83-6(a)(2)

the corporation if either the property transferred is substantially nonvested at the time of transfer or an amount is includible in the gross income of the employee or independent contractor at the time of transfer under § 1.83-1(a)(1) or § 1.83-2(a). In the case of such a transfer, any money or other property paid to the shareholder for such stock shall be considered to be paid to the corporation and transferred immediately thereafter by the corporation to the shareholder as a distribution to which section 3C2 applies. For special rules that may apply to a corporation's transfer of its own stock to any person in consideration of services performed for another corporation or partnership, see § 1.1032-3. The preceding sentence applies to transfers of stock and amounts paid for such stock occurring on or after May 16, 2000.

(2) *Forfeiture.* If, following a transaction described in paragraph (d)(1) of this section, the transferred property is forfeited to the shareholder, paragraph (c) of this section shall apply both with respect to the shareholder and with respect to the corporation. In addition, the corporation shall, in the taxable year of forfeiture be allowed a loss (or realize a gain) to offset any gain (or loss) realized under paragraph (b) of this section. For example, if a shareholder transfers property to an employee of the corporation as compensation, and as a result the shareholder's basis of $200x in such property is allocated to his stock in such corporation and such corporation recognizes a short-term capital gain of $800x, and is allowed a deduction of $1,000x on such transfer, upon a subsequent forfeiture of the property to the shareholder, the shareholder shall take $200x into gross income, and the corporation shall take $1,000x into gross income and be allowed a short-term capital loss of $800x.

(e) *Options.* [Reserved.]

(f) *Reporting requirements.* [Reserved.]

[Reg. § 1.83-6.]

☐ [*T.D.* 7554, 7-21-78. Amended by *T.D.* 8599, 7-18-95 and *T.D.* 8883, 5-11-2000.]

[Reg. § 1.83-7]

§ 1.83-7. **Taxation of nonqualified stock options.**—(a) *In general.* If there is granted to an employee or independent contractor (or beneficiary thereof) in connection with the performance of services, an option to which section 421 (relating generally to certain qualified and other options) does not apply, section 83(a) shall apply to such grant if the option has a readily ascertainable fair market value (determined in accordance with paragraph (b) of this section) at the time the option is granted. The person who performed such

services realizes compensation upon such grant at the time and in the amount determined under section 83(a). If section 83(a) does not apply to the grant of such an option because the option does not have a readily ascertainable fair market value at the time of grant, sections 83(a) and 83(b) shall apply at the time the option is exercised or otherwise disposed of, even though the fair market value of such option may have become readily ascertainable before such time. If the option is exercised, sections 83(a) and 83(b) apply to the transfer of property pursuant to such exercise, and the employee or independent contractor realizes compensation upon such transfer at the time and in the amount determined under section 83(a) or 83(b). If the option is sold or otherwise disposed of in an arm's length transaction, sections 83(a) and 83(b) apply to the transfer of money or other property received in the same manner as sections 83(a) and 83(b) would have applied to the transfer of property pursuant to an exercise of the option.

(b) *Readily ascertainable defined*—(1) *Actively traded on an established market.* Options have a value at the time they are granted, but that value is ordinarily not readily ascertainable unless the option is actively traded on an established market. If an option is actively traded on an established market, the fair market value of such option is readily ascertainable for purposes of this section by applying the rules of valuation set forth in § 20.2031-2.

2) *Not actively traded on an established market.* When an option is not actively traded on an established market, it does not have a readily ascertainable fair market value unless its fair market value can otherwise be measured with reasonable accuracy. For purposes of this section, if an option is not actively traded on an established market, the option does not have a readily ascertainable fair market value when granted unless the taxpayer can show that all of the following conditions exist:

(i) The option is transferable by the optionee;

(ii) The option is exercisable immediately in full by the optionee;

(iii) The option or the property subject to the option is not subject to any restriction or condition (other than a lien or other condition to secure the payment of the purchase price) which has a significant effect upon the fair market value of the option; and

(iv) The fair market value of the option privilege is readily ascertainable in accordance with paragraph (b)(3) of this section.

(3) *Option privilege.* The option privilege in the case of an option to buy is the opportunity to benefit during the option's exercise period from any increase in the value of property subject to the option during such period, without risking any capital. Similarly, the option privilege in the case of an option to sell is the opportunity to benefit during the exercise period from a decrease in the value of property subject to the option. For example, if at some time during the exercise period of an option to buy, the fair market value of the property subject to the option is greater than the option's exercise price, a profit may be realized by exercising the option and immediately selling the property so acquired for its higher fair market value. Irrespective of whether any such gain may be realized immediately at the time an option is granted, the fair market value of an option to buy includes the value of the right to benefit from any future increase in the value of the property subject to the option (relative to the option exercise price), without risking any capital. Therefore, the fair market value of an option is not merely the difference that may exist at a particular time between the option's exercise price and the value of the property subject to the option, but also includes the value of the option privilege for the remainder of the exercise period. Accordingly, for purposes of this section, in determining whether the fair market value of an option is readily ascertainable, it is necessary to consider whether the value of the entire option privilege can be measured with reasonable accuracy. In determining whether the value of the option privilege is readily ascertainable, and in determining the amount of such value when such value is readily ascertainable, it is necessary to consider—

(i) Whether the value of the property subject to the option can be ascertained;

(ii) The probability of any ascertainable value of such property increasing or decreasing; and

(iii) The length of the period during which the option can be exercised.

(c) *Reporting requirements.* [Reserved]

[Reg. § 1.83-7.]

□ [*T.D.* 7554, 7-21-78.]

[Reg. § 1.83-8]

§ 1.83-8. **Applicability of section and transitional rules.**— (a) *Scope of section 83.* Section 83 is not applicable to—

(1) A transaction concerning an option to which section 421 applies;

(2) A transfer to or from a trust described in section 401(a) for the benefit of employees or their

beneficiaries, or a transfer under an annuity plan that meets the requirements of section 404(a)(2) for the benefit of employees or their beneficiaries;

(3) The transfer of an option without a readily ascertainable fair market value (as defined in § 1.83-7(b)(1)); or

(4) The transfer of property pursuant to the exercise of an option with a readily ascertainable fair market value at the date of grant.

Section 83 applies to a transfer to or from a trust or under an annuity plan for the benefit of employees, independent contractors, or their beneficiaries (except as provided in paragraph (a)(2) of this section), but to the extent a transfer is subject to section 402(b) or 403(c), section 83 applies to such a transfer only as provided for in section 402(b) or 403(c).

(b) *Transitional rules*—(1) *In general.* Except as otherwise provided in this paragraph, section 83 and the regulations thereunder shall apply to property transferred after June 30, 1969.

(2) *Binding written contracts.* Section 83 and the regulations thereunder shall not apply to property transferred pursuant to a binding written contract entered into before April 22, 1969. For purposes of this paragraph, a binding written contract means only a written contract under which the employee or independent contractor has an enforceable right to compel the transfer of property or to obtain damages upon the breach of such contract. A contract which provides that a person's right to such property is contingent upon the happening of an event (including the passage of time) may satisfy the requirements of this paragraph. However, if the event itself, or the determination of whether the event has occurred, rests with the board of directors or any other individual or group acting on behalf of the employer (other than an arbitrator), the contract will not be treated as giving the person an enforceable right for purposes of this paragraph. The fact that the board of directors has the power (either expressly or impliedly) to terminate employment of an officer pursuant to a contract that contemplates the completion of services over a fixed or ascertainable period does not negate the existence of a binding written contract. Nor will the binding nature of the contract be negated by a provision in such contract which allows the employee or independent contractor to terminate the contract for any year and receive cash instead of property if such election would cause a substantial penalty, such as a forfeiture of part or all of the property received in connection with the performance of services in an earlier year.

(3) *Options granted before April 22, 1969.* Section 83 shall not apply to property received

upon the exercise of an option granted before April 22, 1969.

(4) *Certain written plans.* Section 83 shall not apply to property transferred (whether or not by the exercise of an option) before May 1, 1970, pursuant to a written plan adopted and approved before July 1, 1969. A plan is to be considered as having been adopted and approved before July 1, 1969, only if prior to such date the transferor of the property undertook an ascertainable course of conduct which under applicable State law does not require further approval by the board of directors or the stockholders of any corporation. For example, if a corporation transfers property to an employee in connection with the performance of services pursuant to a plan adopted and approved before July 1, 1969, by the board of directors of such corporation, it is not necessary that the stockholders have adopted or approved such plan if State law does not require such approval. However, such approval is necessary if required by the articles of incorporation or the by-laws or if, by its terms, such plan will not become effective without such approval.

(5) *Certain options granted pursuant to a binding written contract.* Section 83 shall not apply to property transferred before January 1, 1973, upon the exercise of an option granted pursuant to a binding written contract (as defined in paragraph (b)(2) of this section) entered into before April 22, 1969, between a corporation and the transferor of such property requiring the transferor to grant options to employees of such corporation (or a subsidiary of such corporation) to purchase a determinable number of shares of stock of such corporation, but only if the transferee was an employee of such corporation (or a subsidiary of such corporation) on or before April 22, 1969.

(6) *Certain tax free exchanges.* Section 83 shall not apply to property transferred in exchange for (or pursuant to the exercise of a conversion privilege contained in) property transferred before July 1, 1969, or in exchange for property to which section 83 does not apply (by reason of paragraphs (1), (2) (3), or (4) of section 83(i)), if section 354, 355, 356, or 1036 (or so much of section 1031 as relates to section 1036) applies, or if gain or loss is not otherwise required to be recognized upon the exercise of such conversion privilege, and if the property received in such exchange is subject to restrictions and conditions substantially similar to those to which the property given in such exchange was subject. [Reg. § 1.83-8.]

☐ [*T.D.* 7554, 7-21-78.]

[Reg. § 1.84-1]

§ 1.84-1. Transfer of appreciated property to political organizations.—(a) *Transfer defined.* A transfer after May 7, 1974, of property to a political organization (as defined in section 527(e)(1), and including a newsletter fund to the extent provided under section 527(g)) is treated as a sale of the property to the political organization if the fair market value of the property exceeds its adjusted basis. The transferor is treated as having realized an amount equal to the fair market value of the property on the date of the transfer. For purposes of this section, a transfer is any assignment, conveyance, or delivery of property other than a bona fide sale for an adequate and full consideration in money or money's worth, whether the transfer is in trust or otherwise, whether the transfer is direct or indirect and whether the property is real or personal, tangible or intangible. Thus, for example, a sale at less than fair market value (other than an ordinary trade discount), or a receipt of property by a political organization under an agency agreement entitling the organization to sell the property and retain all or a portion of the proceeds of the sale, is a transfer within the meaning of this section. The term "transfer" also includes an illegal contribution of property.

(b) *Amount realized.* A transferor to whom this section applies realizes an amount equal to the fair market value of the property on the date of the transfer. For purposes of this section, the definition of fair market value set forth in § 1.170A-1(c)(2) and (3) is incorporated by reference.

(c) *Amount recognized.* A transferor to whom this section applies is treated as having sold the property to the political organization on the date of the transfer. Therefore, the rules of chapter 1 of subtitle A (relating to income tax) apply to the gain realized under this section as if this gain were an amount realized upon the sale of the property. These rules include those of section 55 and section 56 (relating to minimum tax for tax preference), section 306 (relating to disposition of certain stock), section 1201 (relating to the alternative tax on certain capital gains), section 1245 (relating to gain from dispositions of certain depreciable property), and section 1250 (relating to gain from dispositions of certain depreciable realty).

(d) *Holding period.* The holding period of property transferred to a political organization to which this section applies begins on the day after the date of acquisition of the property by the political organization. [Reg. § 1.84-1.]

☐ [*T.D.* 7671, 2-5-80.]

[Reg. § 1.85-1]

§ 1.85-1. Unemployment compensation.— (a) *Introduction.* Section 85 prescribes rules relating to the inclusion in gross income of unemployment compensation (as defined in paragraph (b)(1) of this section) paid in taxable years beginning after December 31, 1978 pursuant to governmental programs. In general, these rules provide that unemployment compensation paid pursuant to governmental programs is includible in the gross income of a taxpayer if the taxpayer's modified adjusted gross income (as defined in paragraph (b)(2) of this section) exceeds a statutory base amount (as defined in paragraph (b)(3) of this section). If there is such an excess, however, the amount included in gross income is limited under paragraph (c)(1) of this section to the lesser of one-half of such excess or the amount of the unemployment compensation. If such taxpayer's modified adjusted gross income does not exceed the applicable statutory base amount, none of the unemployment compensation is included in the taxpayer's gross income.

(b) *Definitions*—(1) *Unemployment compensation*—(i) *General rule.* Except as provided in paragraph (b)(1)(iii) of this section, the term "unemployment compensation" means any amount received under a law of the United States, or of a State, which is in the nature of unemployment compensation. Thus, section 85 applies only to unemployment compensation paid pursuant to governmental programs and does not apply to amounts paid pursuant to private nongovernmental unemployment compensation plans (which are includible in income without regard to section 85). Generally, unemployment compensation programs are those designed to protect taxpayers against the loss of income caused by involuntary layoff. Ordinarily, unemployment compensation is paid in cash and on a periodic basis. The amount of the payments is usually computed in accordance with a formula based on the taxpayer's length of prior employment and wages. Such payments, however, may be made in a lump sum or other than in cash or on some other basis.

(ii) *Disability and worker's compensation payments.* Amounts in the nature of unemployment compensation also include cash disability payments made pursuant to a governmental program as a substitute for cash unemployment payments to an unemployed taxpayer who is ineligible for such payments solely because of the disability. Usually these disability payments are paid in the same weekly amount and for the same period as the unemployed compensation benefits to which the unemployed taxpayer otherwise would have been entitled. Amounts received under workmen's compensation acts as compensation for personal injuries or sickness are not amounts in the nature of unemployment compensation. See section 104(a)(1) relating to the exclusion from gross income of such amounts.

(iii) *Employee contributions to a governmental plan.* If a governmental unemployment compensation program is funded in part by an employee's contribution which is not deductible by the employee, an amount paid to such employee under the program is not to be considered unemployment compensation until an amount equal to the total nondeductible contributions paid by the employee to such program has been paid to such employee.

(iv) *Examples of governmental unemployment compensation programs.* Governmental unemployment compensation programs include (but are not limited to) programs established under:

(A) A State law approved by the Secretary of Labor pursuant to section 3304 of the Internal Revenue Code of 1954.

(B) Chapter 85 of Title 5, United States Code, relating to unemployment compensation for Federal employees generally and for ex-servicemen.

(C) Trade Act of 1974, sections 231 and 232 (19 U.S.C. 2291 and 2292).

(D) Disaster Relief Act of 1974, section 407 (42 U.S.C. 5177).

(E) The Airline Deregulation Act of 1978 (49 U.S.C. 1552 (b)).

(F) The Railroad Unemployment Insurance Act, section 2 (45 U.S.C. 352).

(2) *Modified adjusted gross income.* The term "modified adjusted gross income" means the sum of the following amounts:

(i) Adjusted gross income (as defined in section 62);

(ii) All disability payments of the type that are eligible for exclusion from gross income under section 105(d); and

(iii) All amounts of unemployment compensation as (defined in paragraph (b)(1) of this section).

(3) *Base amount.* The term "base amount" means—

(i) $25,000 in the case of a joint return under section 6013.

(ii) Zero in the case of a taxpayer who—

(A) Is married (within the meaning of section 143) at the close of the taxable year,

(B) Does not file a joint return for such taxable year, and

Reg. § 1.85-1(a)

(C) Does not live apart (as defined in paragraph (b)(4) of this section) from his or her spouse at all times during the taxable year.

(iii) $20,000 in the case of all other taxpayers.

(4) *Living apart.* A taxpayer does not "live apart" from his or her spouse at all times during a taxable year if for any period during the taxable year the taxpayer is a member of the same household as such taxpayer's spouse. A taxpayer is a member of a household for any period, including temporary absences due to special circumstances, during which the household is the taxpayer's place of abode. A temporary absence due to special circumstances includes a nonpermanent absence caused by illness, education, business, vacation, or military service.

(c) *Limitations*—(1) *General rule.* If for a taxable year, a taxpayer's modified adjusted gross income does not exceed the applicable statutory base amount, no amount of unemployment compensation is included in gross income for the taxable year. If there is such an excess, the taxpayer includes in gross income for the taxable year the lesser of the following:

(i) One-half of the excess of the taxpayer's modified adjusted gross income over such taxpayer's base amount, or

(ii) The amount of unemployment compensation.

(2) *Exception for fraudulently received unemployment compensation.* If a taxpayer fraudulently receives unemployment compensation under any governmental unemployment compensation program, then the entire amount of such fraudulently received unemployment compensation must be included in the taxpayer's gross income for the taxable year in which the benefits were received. Thus, the limitation in section 85 and in paragraph (c)(1) of this section, does not apply to such amounts.

(3) *Examples.* The application of this paragraph may be illustrated by the following examples:

Example (1). H and W are married taxpayers who for calendar year 1979 file a joint income tax return. During 1979 H receives $4,500 of disability income that is eligible for an exclusion under section 105(d). W works for part of 1979 and receives $20,000 as compensation and also receives $5,000 of unemployment compensation in 1979. Assume that H and W's adjusted gross income is $20,000. The modified adjusted gross income of H & W is $29,500 ($4,500 + $20,000 + $5,000). Since their modified adjusted gross income ($29,500) is greater than their base amount

($25,000), some of the unemployment compensation received by W must be included in their gross income on their 1979 joint income tax return. Under paragraph (c)(1) of this section, of the $5,000 which is unemployment compensation, the lesser of $2,250 (($29,500 − 25,000) ÷ 2) or $5,000 must be included in their gross income. Thus, $2,250 of the $5,000 received by F in 1979 is included in the gross income of H and W on their joint income tax return for 1979.

Example (2). Assume the same facts in example (1) except H receives $5,000 of disability income that is eligible for an exclusion under section 105(d) and W receives $28,000 as compensation, and $4,000 which is unemployment compensation. Assume that H and W's adjusted gross income is $28,000. The modified adjusted gross income of H and W is $37,000 ($4,000 + $28,000 + $5,000). Since their modified adjusted gross income ($37,000) is greater than their base amount ($25,000), all of the unemployment compensation received by W must be included in their gross income on their 1979 joint income tax return. Under paragraph (c)(1) of this section, of the $4,000 which is unemployment compensation, the lesser of $6,000 (($37,000 − $25,000) ÷ 2) or $4,000 must be included in their gross income. Thus, all of the $4,000 unemployment compensation received by W is included in the gross income of H and W on their joint income tax return for 1979.

(d) *Cross reference.* See section 6050B, relating to the requirement that every person who makes payments of unemployment compensation aggregating $10 or more to any individual during any calendar year file an information return with the Internal Revenue Service. [Reg. § 1.85-1.]

☐ [*T.D.* 7705, 7-8-80.]

[Reg. § 1.88-1]

§ 1.88-1. **Nuclear decommissioning costs.**— (a) *In general.* Section 88 provides that the amount of nuclear decommissioning costs directly or indirectly charged to the customers of a taxpayer that is engaged in the furnishing or sale of electric energy generated by a nuclear power plant must be included in the gross income of such taxpayer in the same manner as amounts charged for electric energy. For this purpose, decommissioning costs directly or indirectly charged to the customers of a taxpayer include all decommissioning costs that consumers are liable to pay by reason of electric energy furnished by the taxpayer during the taxable year, whether payable to the taxpayer, a trust, State government, or other entity, and even though the taxpayer may not control the investment or current expenditure of the amount and the amount may not be paid to the taxpayer at the time decommissioning costs are incurred. However, decommissioning costs payable to a taxpayer holding a qualified leasehold interest (as described in paragraph (b)(2)(ii) of § 1.468A-1) are included in the gross income of such taxpayer, and not in the gross income of the lessor.

(b) *Examples.* The following examples illustrate the application of the principles of paragraph (a) of this section:

Example (1). X corporation, an accrual method taxpayer engaged in the sale of electric energy generated by a nuclear power plant owned by X, is authorized by the public utility commission of State A to collect nuclear decommissioning costs from ratepayers residing in State A. With respect to the sale of electric energy, X includes in income amounts that have been billed to customers as well as estimated unbilled amounts that relate to energy provided by X after the previous billing but before the end of the taxable year ("accrued unbilled amounts"). The decommissioning costs are included in the monthly bills provided by X to its ratepayers and the entire amount billed is remitted directly to X. Under paragraph (a) of this section, the decommissioning costs must be included in the gross income of X in the same manner as amounts charged for electric energy (*i.e.,* by including in income decommissioning costs that relate to amounts billed as well as decommissioning costs that relate to accrued unbilled amounts). The same rule would apply if the decommissioning costs charged to ratepayers were separately billed and the amounts billed were remitted to State A to be held in trust for the purpose of decommissioning the nuclear power plant owned by X. In that case, X must include in gross income decommissioning costs that relate to

amounts billed as well as decommissioning costs that relate to accrued unbilled amounts.

Example (2). Assume the same facts as in Example (1), except that X and M, a municipality located in State A, have entered into a life-of-unit contract pursuant to which (i) M is entitled to 20 percent of the electric energy generated by the nuclear power plant owned by X, and (ii) M is obligated to pay 20 percent of the plant operating costs, including decommissioning costs, incurred by X. Under paragraph (a) of this section, the decommissioning costs that relate to electric energy consumed or distributed by M during any taxable year must be included in the gross income of X for such taxable year. The result contained in this example would be the same if M was a State or an agency or instrumentality of a State or a political subdivision thereof.

(c) *Cross reference.* For special rules relating to the deduction for amounts paid to a nuclear decommissioning fund, see § 1.468A-1 through § 1.468A-8.

(d) *Effective date.* (1) Section 88 and this section apply to nuclear decommissioning costs directly or indirectly charged to the customers of a taxpayer on or after July 18, 1984, and with respect to taxable years ending on or after such date.

(2) If the amount of nuclear decommissioning costs directly or indirectly charged to the customers of a taxpayer before July 18, 1984, was includible in gross income in a different manner than amounts charged for electric energy, such amounts must be included in gross income for the taxable year in which includible in gross income under the method of accounting of the taxpayer that was in effect when such amount was charged to customers. [Reg. § 1.88-1.]

☐ [*T.D.* 8184, 2-29-88.]

[The next page is 25,011.]

Reg. § 1.88-1(b)

Items Specifically Excluded from Gross Income

[Reg. § 1.101-1]

§ 1.101-1. Exclusion from gross income of proceeds of life insurance contracts payable by reason of death.—(a)(1) *In general.* Section 101(a)(1) states the general rule that the proceeds of life insurance policies, if paid by reason of the death of the insured, are excluded from the gross income of the recipient. Death benefit payments having the characteristics of life insurance proceeds payable by reason of death under contracts, such as workmen's compensation insurance contracts, endowment contracts, or accident and health insurance contracts, are covered by this provision. For provisions relating to death benefits paid by or on behalf of employers, see section 101(b) and § 1.101-2. The exclusion from gross income allowed by section 101(a) applies whether payment is made to the estate of the insured or to any beneficiary (individual, corporation, or partnership) and whether it is made directly or in trust. The extent to which this exclusion applies in cases where life insurance policies have been transferred for a valuable consideration is stated in section 101(a)(2) and in paragraph (b) of this section. In cases where the proceeds of a life insurance policy, payable by reason of the death of the insured, are paid other than in a single sum at the time of such death, the amounts to be excluded from gross income may be affected by the provisions of section 101(c) (relating to amounts held under agreements to pay interest) or section 101(d) (relating to amounts payable at a date later than death). See §§ 1.101-3 and 1.101-4. However, neither section 101(c) nor section 101(d) applies to a single sum payment which does not exceed the amount payable at the time of death even though such amount is actually paid at a date later than death.

(2) *Cross references.* For rules governing the taxability of insurance proceeds constituting benefits payable on the death of an employee—

(i) Under pension, profit-sharing, or stock bonus plans described in section 401(a) and exempt from tax under section 501(a), or under annuity plans described in section 403(a), see section 72(m)(3) and paragraph (c) of § 1.72-16;

(ii) Under annuity contracts to which paragraph (a) or (b) of § 1.403(b)-1 applies, see paragraph (c)(3) of § 1.403(b)-1; or

(iii) Under eligible State deferred compensation plans described in section 457(b), see paragraph (c) of § 1.457-1.

For the definition of a life insurance company, see section 801.

(b) *Transfers of life insurance policies.* (1) In the case of a transfer, by assignment or otherwise, of a life insurance policy or any interest therein for a valuable consideration, the amount of the proceeds attributable to such policy or interest which is excludable from the transferee's gross income is generally limited to the sum of (i) the actual value of the consideration for such transfer, and (ii) the premiums and other amounts subsequently paid by the transferee (see section 101(a)(2) and example (1) of subparagraph (5) of this paragraph). However, this limitation on the amount excludable from the transferee's gross income does not apply (except in certain special cases involving a series of transfers), where the basis of the policy or interest transferred, for the purpose of determining gain or loss with respect to the transferee, is determinable, in whole or in part, by reference to the basis of such policy or interest in the hands of the transferor (see section 101(a)(2)(A) and examples (2) and (4) of subparagraph (5) of this paragraph). Neither does the limitation apply where the policy or interest therein is transferred to the insured, to a partner of the insured, to a partnership in which the insured is a partner, or to a corporation in which the insured is a shareholder or officer (See section 101(a)(2)(B)). For rules relating to gratuitous transfers, see subparagraph (2) of this paragraph. For special rules with respect to certain cases where a series of transfers is involved, see subparagraph (3) of this paragraph.

(2) In the case of a gratuitous transfer, by assignment or otherwise, of a life insurance policy or any interest therein, as a general rule the amount of the proceeds attributable to such policy or interest which is excludable from the transferee's gross income under section 101(a) is limited to the sum of (i) the amount which would have been excludable by the transferor (in accordance with this section) if no such transfer had taken place, and (ii) any premiums and other amounts subsequently paid by the transferee. See example (6) of subparagraph (5) of this paragraph. However, where the gratuitous transfer in question is made by or to the insured, a partner of the insured, a partnership in which the insured is a partner, or a corporation in which the insured is a shareholder or officer, the entire amount of the proceeds attributable to the policy or interest transferred shall be excludable from the transferee's gross income (see section 101(a)(2)(B) and example (7) of subparagraph (5) of this paragraph).

Reg. § 1.101-1(b)(2)

(3) In the case of a series of transfers, if the last transfer of a life insurance policy or an interest therein is for a valuable consideration—

(i) The general rule is that the final transferee shall exclude from gross income, with respect to the proceeds of such policy or interest therein, only the sum of—

(a) The actual value of the consideration paid by him, and

(b) The premiums and other amounts subsequently paid by him;

(ii) If the final transfer is to the insured, to a partner of the insured, to a partnership in which the insured is a partner, or to a corporation in which the insured is a shareholder or officer, the final transferee shall exclude the entire amount of the proceeds from gross income;

(iii) Except where subdivision (ii) of this subparagraph applies, if the basis of the policy or interest transferred, for the purpose of determining gain or loss with respect to the final transferee, is determinable, in whole or in part, by reference to the basis of such policy or interest therein in the hands of the transferor, the amount of the proceeds which is excludable by the final transferee is limited to the sum of—

(a) The amount which would have been excludable by his transferor if no such transfer had taken place, and

(b) Any premiums and other amounts subsequently paid by the final transferee himself.

(4) For the purposes of section 101(a)(2) and subparagraphs (1) and (3) of this paragraph, a "transfer for a valuable consideration" is any absolute transfer for value of a right to receive all or a part of the proceeds of a life insurance policy. Thus, the creation, for value, of an enforceable contractual right to receive all or a part of the proceeds of a policy may constitute a transfer for a valuable consideration of the policy or an interest therein. On the other hand, the pledging or assignment of a policy as collateral security is not a transfer for a valuable consideration of such policy or an interest therein, and section 101 is inapplicable to any amounts received by the pledgee or assignee.

(5) The application of this paragraph may be illustrated by the following examples:

Example (1). A pays premiums of $500 for an insurance policy in the face amount of $1,000 upon the life of B, and subsequently transfers the policy to C for $600. C receives the proceeds of $1,000 upon the death of B. The amount which C can exclude from his gross income is limited to $600 plus any premiums paid by C subsequent to the transfer.

Example (2). The X Corporation purchases for a single premium of $500 an insurance policy in the face amount of $1,000 upon the life of A, one of its employees, naming the X Corporation as beneficiary. The X Corporation transfers the policy to the Y Corporation in a tax-free reorganization (the policy having a basis for determining gain or loss in the hands of the Y Corporation determined by reference to its basis in the hands of the X Corporation). The Y Corporation receives the proceeds of $1,000 upon the death of A. The entire $1,000 is to be excluded from the gross income of the Y Corporation.

Example (3). The facts are the same as in example (2) except that, prior to the death of A, the Y Corporation transfers the policy to the Z Corporation for $600. The Z Corporation receives the proceeds of $1,000 upon the death of A. The amount which the Z Corporation can exclude from its gross income is limited to $600 plus any premiums paid by the Z Corporation subsequent to the transfer of the policy to it.

Example (4). The facts are the same as in example (3) except that, prior to the death of A, the Z Corporation transfers the policy to the M Corporation in a tax-free reorganization (the policy having a basis for determining gain or loss in the hands of the M Corporation determined by reference to its basis in the hands of the Z Corporation). The M Corporation receives the proceeds of $1,000 upon the death of A. The amount which the M Corporation can exclude from its gross income is limited to $600 plus any premiums paid by the Z Corporation and the M Corporation subsequent to the transfer of the policy to the Z Corporation.

Example (5). The facts are the same as in example (3) except that, prior to the death of A, the Z Corporation transfers the policy to the N Corporation, in which A is a shareholder. The N Corporation receives the proceeds of $1,000 upon the death of A. The entire $1,000 is to be excluded from the gross income of the N Corporation.

Example (6). A pays premiums of $500 for an insurance policy in the face amount of $1,000 upon his own life, and subsequently transfers the policy to his wife B for $600. B later transfers the policy without consideration to C, who is the son of A and B. C receives the proceeds of $1,000 upon the death of A. The amount which C can exclude from his gross income is limited to $600 plus any premiums paid by B and C subsequent to the transfer of the policy to B.

Example (7). The facts are the same as in example (6) except that, prior to the death of A, C transfers the policy without consideration to A, the insured. A's estate receives the proceeds of

Reg. § 1.101-1(b)(3)

$1,000 upon the death of A. The entire $1,000 is to be excluded from the gross income of A's estate. [Reg. § 1.101-1.]

☐ [*T.D. 6280, 12-16-57. Amended by T.D. 6783, 12-23-64 and T.D. 7836, 9-23-82.*]

[Reg. § 1.101-2]

§ 1.101-2. Employees' death benefits.—(a) *In general.* (1) Section 101(b) states the general rule that amounts up to $5,000 which are paid to the beneficiaries or the estate of an employee, or former employee, by or on behalf of an employer and by reason of the death of the employee shall be excluded from the gross income of the recipient. This exclusion from gross income applies whether payment is made to the estate of the employee or to any beneficiary (individual, corporation, or partnership), whether it is made directly or in trust, and whether or not it is made pursuant to a contractual obligation of the employer. The exclusion applies whether payment is made in a single sum or otherwise, subject to the provisions of section 101(c), relating to amounts held under an agreement to pay interest thereon (see § 1.101-3). The exclusion from gross income also applies to any amount not actually paid which is otherwise taxable to a beneficiary of an employee because it was made available as a distribution from an employee's trust.

(2) The exclusion does not apply to amounts constituting income payable to the employee during his life as compensation for his services, such as bonuses or payments for unused leave or uncollected salary, nor to certain other amounts with respect to which the deceased employee possessed, immediately before his death, a nonforfeitable right to receive the amounts while living (see section 101(b)(2)(B) and paragraph (d) of this section). Further, the exclusion does not apply to amounts received as an annuity under a joint and survivor annuity obligation where the employee was the primary annuitant and the annuity starting date occurred before the death of the employee (see section 101(b)(2)(C) and paragraph (e)(1)(ii) of this section). In the case of amounts received by a beneficiary as an annuity (but not as a survivor under a joint and survivor annuity with respect to which the employee was the primary annuitant), the exclusion is applied indirectly by means of the provisions of section 72 and the regulations thereunder (see section 101(b)(2)(D) and paragraph (e)(1)(iii) and (iv) of this section). Thus, for example, the exclusion applies to amounts which are received by a survivor of an employee retired on disability under the provisions of the Civil service retirement law (5 U.S.C. 8301 or any former corresponding provisions of law) or the Retired Serviceman's Family

Protection Plan or Survivor Benefit Plan (10 U.S.C. 1431 et seq.), provided such employee dies before attaining mandatory retirement age (as defined in § 1.105-4(a)(3)(i)(B)).

(3) The total amount excludable with respect to any employee may not exceed $5,000, regardless of the number of employers or the number of beneficiaries. For allocation of the exclusion among beneficiaries, see paragraph (c) of this section. For rules governing the taxability of benefits payable on the death of an employee under pension, profit-sharing, or stock bonus plans described in section 401(a) and exempt under section 501(a), under annuity plans described in section 403(a), or under annuity contracts to which paragraph (a) or (b) of § 1.403(b)-1 applies, see sections 72(m)(3), 402(a), and 403 and the regulations thereunder.

(b) *Payments under certain employee benefit plans*—(1) *In general.* Where a payment is made by reason of the death of an employee by an employer-provided welfare fund or a trust, including a stock bonus, pension, or profit-sharing trust described in section 401(a), or by an insurance company (if such payment does not constitute "life insurance" within the purview of section 101(a)), the payment shall be considered to have been made by or on behalf of the employer to the extent that it exceeds amounts contributed by, or deemed contributed by, the deceased employee.

(2) *Cross references.* For provisions governing the taxability of distributions payable on the death of an employee participant—

(i) Under a trust described in section 401(a) and exempt from tax under section 501(a), see paragraph (c) of § 1.72-16 and paragraph (a)(5) of § 1.402(a)-1;

(ii) Under an annuity plan described in section 403(a), see paragraph (c) of § 1.72-16 and paragraph (c) of § 1.403(a)-1;

(iii) Under annuity contracts to which paragraph (a) or (b) of § 1.403(b)-1 applies, see paragraph (c)(2) and (3) of § 1.403(b)-1;

(iv) Under eligible State deferred compensation plans described in section 457(b), see paragraph (c) of § 1.457-1.

(c) *Allocation of the exclusion.*—(1) Where the aggregate payments by or on behalf of an employer or employers as death benefits to the beneficiaries or the estate of the deceased employee exceed $5,000, the $5,000 exclusion shall be apportioned among them in the same proportion as the amount received by or the present value of the amount payable to each bears to the total death benefits paid or payable by or on behalf of the employer or employers.

Reg. § 1.101-2(c)(1)

(2) The application of the rule in subparagraph (1) of this paragraph may be illustrated by the following example:

Example. The M Corporation, the employer of A, a deceased employee who died November 30, 1954, makes payments in 1955 to the beneficiaries of A as follows: $5,000 to W, A's widow, $2,000 to B, the son of A, and $3,000 to C, the daughter of A. No other amounts are paid by any other employer of A to his estate or beneficiaries. By application of the apportionment rule stated above, W, the widow, will exclude $2,500 ($5,000/$10,000, or one-half, of $5,000); B, the son, will exclude $1,000 ($2,000/$10,000, or one-fifth, of $5,000); and C, the daughter, will exclude $1,500 ($3,000/$10,000 or three-tenths, of $5,000).

(d) *Nonforfeitable rights.* (1) Except as provided in subparagraphs (3) and (4) of this paragraph, the exclusion provided by section 101(b) does not apply to amounts with respect to which the deceased employee possessed, immediately before his death, a nonforfeitable right to receive the amounts while living. Section 101(b)(2)(B). For the purpose of section 101(b) and this paragraph, an employee shall be considered to have had a nonforfeitable right with respect to—

(i) Any amount to which he would have been entitled—

(a) If he had made an appropriate election or demand, or

(b) Upon termination of his employment (see examples (5) and (6) of subparagraph (2) of this paragraph); or

(ii) The present value (immediately before his death) of—

(a) Amounts payable as an annuity (as defined in paragraph (b) of § 1.72-2, whether immediate or deferred) by or on behalf of the employer (see example (1) of subparagraph (2) of this paragraph), or

(b) Amounts which would have been so payable if the employee had terminated his employment and continued to live;

or

(iii) Any amount to the extent it is paid in lieu of amounts described in either subdivision (i) or (ii) of this subparagraph. See examples (2), (3), and (4) of subparagraph (2) of this paragraph.

For purposes of subdivision (iii) of this subparagraph, any amount paid in discharge of an obligation which arose solely because of the existence of a particular fact or circumstance subsequent to the employee's death shall not be considered an amount paid in lieu of amounts described in subdivision (i) or (ii) of this subparagraph. Subdivi-

sion (iii) of this subparagraph shall apply, however, to the extent indicated therein, to amounts payable without regard to any such contingency (to the extent that such amounts are equal to or less than those described in subdivisions (i) and (ii) of this subparagraph which are not paid). See paragraph (e)(1)(iii)(b) of this section for rules with respect to finding the present value of an annuity immediately before the employee's death.

(2) The application of paragraph (d)(1) of this section may be illustrated by the following examples, in which it is assumed that the plans are not "qualified plans" and that no employer is an organization referred to in section 170(b)(1)(A)(ii) or (vi) or a religious organization (other than a trust) which is exempt from tax under section 501(a):

Example (1). A, who was a participant under the X Company pension plan, retired on December 31, 1953. He had made no contributions to the plan. Upon his retirement, he became entitled to monthly payments of $100 payable for life, or 120 months certain. A died on October 31, 1954, having received 10 monthly payments of $100 each. After his death, the monthly payments became payable to his estate for the remaining 110 months certain. No exclusion from gross income is allowed to A's estate (or any beneficiary who receives the right to such payments from the estate), since the employee's right to the monthly payments was nonforfeitable at the date of his death. It will be noted that in this example it is unnecessary to consider the present value of the annuity to A just before his death since the payments to be made include only those certain to be made in any event under the plan whether or not A continued to live.

Example (2). C, a participant under the Y Company pension plan, died on December 15, 1954, while actively in the employment of the company, survived by a widow and minor children. Because of his years of service, he would have been entitled to an annuity for life, his own contributions to the plan and interest thereon being guaranteed, if he had retired or terminated his employment at a time immediately before his death. The plan further provides that—(a) if, but only if, an employee is survived by a widow and minor children, his widow is to receive an annuity for her life without regard to whether or not the employee had begun his annuity; (b) any payments made with respect to his widow's annuity are to reduce the guaranteed amount to an equal extent; and (c) if the employee is not so survived, the guaranteed amount is payable to his beneficiary or estate, but no amount is payable to anyone

Reg. § 1.101-2(c)(2)

with respect to what would have been the widow's annuity. In view of these provisions, that portion of the present value of the annuity payable to C's widow which exceeds the guaranteed amount shall be considered paid neither as an amount, nor in lieu of an amount, which C had a nonforfeitable right to receive while living. The reason for this result is that the payment of such excess is contingent upon C's begin survived by a widow and minor children, a circumstance existing subsequent to his death. Conversely, to the extent that the present value of the annuity payable to C's widow does not exceed the guaranteed amount, annuity payments attributable to such present value shall be considered paid in lieu of an amount which C had a nonforfeitable right to receive while living.

Example (3). D, a participant under the Y Company pension plan, died on January 1, 1955, while actively in the employment of the company. The Y Company plan provides that where an employee dies in service, the present value of the accumulated credits which he could have obtained at that time if he had instead separated from the service shall be paid in a single sum to his surviving spouse or to his estate if no widow survives him. The present value of D's accumulated credits, at the time of his death, was $10,000. However, the plan also provides that a surviving spouse may elect to take, in lieu of a single sum, an annuity the present value of which exceeds such sum by $2,500. D's widow elects to receive an annuity (the present value of which is $12,500). Therefore, $2,500 is an amount to which the exclusion of section 101(b) and this section shall apply.

Example (4). A, an employee of the X Company, continues to work after reaching the normal retirement age of 60 years, although he could have retired at that age and obtained an annuity of $3,000 per year for his life. A is not entitled to any part of the annuity while he is employed and receiving compensation. A dies at the age of 67 while still in active employment. Since he had passed normal retirement age, his additional years of service did not entitle him to a larger annuity at age 67 than that which he could have obtained at age 60. However, the plan of the X Company provides that in the event of an employee's death prior to separation from the service, his widow is to be paid an annuity for her life in the same amount per year as that which the employee could have obtained if he had instead retired but if no widow survives him, the present value of the annuity which the employee could have obtained at a time just before his death is to be paid to a named beneficiary or the estate of the employee. Assuming that the present value of the annuity to A's widow, whose age is 61, is $36,000 and the present value of the annuity which would have been payable to A at age 67 if he had then retired is $23,500, the present value of the widow's annuity, to the extent of $23,500, is an amount which is payable in lieu of amounts which the employee had a nonforfeitable right to receive while living because it does not exceed the value of his nonforfeitable rights and is not otherwise paid. On the other hand, the $12,500 excess of the value of the widow's annuity ($36,000) over the value of the employee's annuity ($23,500) is an amount to which section 101(b) applies since the employee had no right to any part of it. If no other death benefits are payable, a $5,000 exclusion is available (see section 101(b)(2)(D) and paragraph (e) of this section).

Example (5). The trustee of the X Corporation noncontributory profit-sharing plan is required under the provisions of the plan to pay to the beneficiary of B, an employee of the X Corporation who died on July 1, 1955, the benefit due on account of the death of B. The provisions of the profit-sharing plan give each participating employee in case of termination of employment a 10-percent vested interest in the amount accumulated in his account for each year of participation in the plan. In case of death, the entire credit in the participant's account is to be paid to his beneficiary. At the time of B's death, he had been a participant for three years and the accumulation in his account was $8,000. After his death this amount is paid to his beneficiary. At the time of B's death, the amount distributable to him on account of termination of employment would have been $2,400 (30 percent of $8,000). The difference of $5,600 ($8,000 minus $2,400), payable to the beneficiary of B, is an amount payable solely by reason of B's death. Accordingly, $5,000 of the $5,600 may be excluded from the gross income of the beneficiary receiving such payment (assuming no other death benefits are involved). However, if it is assumed that the facts are the same as above, except that at the time of his death B has been a participant for 6 years, the amount distributable to him on account of termination of employment would have been $4,800 (60 percent of $8,000). The difference of $3,200 ($8,000 minus $4,800), payable to B's beneficiary, is an amount payable solely by reason of B's death. Accordingly, only $3,200 may be excluded from the gross income of the beneficiary receiving such payment (assuming no other death benefits are involved).

Example (6). The X Corporation instituted a trust, forming part of a pension plan, for its employees, the cost thereof being borne entirely by the corporation. The plan provides, in part, that after 10 or more years of service and attain-

Reg. § 1.101-2(d)(2)

ing the age of 55, an employee can elect to retire and receive benefits before the normal retirement date contingent upon the employer's approval. If he retires without the employer's consent, or voluntarily leaves the company, no benefits are or will be payable. The plan further provides that if the employee is involuntarily separated or dies before retirement, he or his beneficiary, respectively, will receive a percentage of the reserve provided for the employee in the trust fund on the following basis: 10 to 15 years of service, 25 percent; 15 to 20 years of service, 50 percent; 20 to 25 years of service, 75 percent; 25 or more years of service, 100 percent. A, an employee of the X Corporation for 17 years, died at the age of 56 while in the employ of the corporation. At the time of his death, $15,000 was the reserve provided for him in the trust. His beneficiary receives $7,500, an amount equal to 50 percent of the reserve provided for A's retirement; accordingly, $5,000 of the $7,500 may be excluded from the gross income of the beneficiary receiving such payment (assuming no other death benefits are involved) since A, prior to his death, had only a forfeitable right to receive $7,500.

(3)(i) Notwithstanding the rule stated in subparagraph (1) of this paragraph and illustrated in subparagraph (2) of this paragraph, the exclusion from gross income provided by section 101(b) applies to the receipt of certain amounts, paid under "qualified" plans, with respect to which the deceased employee possessed, immediately before his death, a nonforfeitable right to receive the amounts while living (see section 101(b)(2)(B)(i) and (ii)). The payments to which this exclusion applies are—

(a) "Total distributions payable" by a stock bonus, pension, or profit-sharing trust described in section 401(a) which is exempt from tax under section 501(a), and

(b) "Total amounts" paid under an annuity contract under a plan described in section 403(a),

provided such distributions or amounts are paid in full within one taxable year of the distributee (see example (3) of subdivision (ii) of this subparagraph). For the purposes of applying section 101(b), "total distributions payable" means the balance to the credit of an employee which becomes payable to a distributee on account of the employee's death, either before or after separation from the service (see section 402(a)(3)(C), the regulations thereunder, and examples (2) and (4) of subdivision (ii) of this subparagraph); and "total amounts" means the balance to the credit of an employee which becomes payable to the payee by reason of the employee's death, either before or

after separation from the service (see section 403(a)(2)(B), the regulations thereunder, and example (1) of subdivision (ii) of this subparagraph). See subparagraph (4) of this paragraph relating to the exclusion of amounts which are received under annuity contracts purchased by certain exempt organizations and with respect to which the deceased employee possessed, immediately before his death, a nonforfeitable right to receive the amounts while living.

(ii) The application of the provisions of subdivision (i) of this subparagraph may be illustrated by the following examples:

Example (1). The widow of an employee elects, under a noncontributory "qualified" plan, to receive in a lump sum the present value of the annuity which C, the deceased employee, could have obtained at a time just before his death if he had retired at that time. Such present value is $6,000. Of this amount, $5,000 is excludable from the widow's gross income despite the fact that C had a nonforfeitable right to the amount in lieu of which the payment is made, since such payment is an amount to which subdivision (i) of this subparagraph applies (assuming no other death benefits are involved).

Example (2). The trustee of the X Corporation noncontributory, "qualified", profit-sharing plan is required under the provisions of the plan to pay to the beneficiary of B, an employee of the X Corporation who died on July 1, 1955, the benefit due on account of the death of B. The provisions of the profit-sharing plan give each participating employee, in case of termination of employment, a 10 percent vested interest in the amount accumulated in his account for each year of participation in the plan, but, in case of death, the entire credit to the participant's account is to be paid to his beneficiary. At the time of B's death, he had been a participant for five years. The accumulation in his account was $8,000, and the amount which would have been distributable to him in the event of termination of employment was $4,000 (50 percent of $8,000). After his death, $8,000 is paid to his beneficiary in a lump sum. (It may be noted that these are the same facts as in example (5) of subparagraph (2) of this paragraph except that the employee has been a participant for five years instead of three and the plan is a "qualified" plan.) It is immaterial that the employee had a nonforfeitable right to $4,000, because the payment of the $8,000 to the beneficiary is the payment of the "total distributions payable" within one taxable year of the distributee to which subdivision (i) of this subparagraph applies. Assuming no other death benefits are

Reg. § 1.101-2(d)(3)

involved, the beneficiary may exclude $5,000 of the $8,000 payment from gross income.

Example (3). The facts are the same as in example (2) except that the beneficiary is entitled to receive only the $4,000 to which the employee had a nonforfeitable right and elects, 30 days after B's death, to receive it over a period of ten years. Since the "total distributions payable" are not paid within one taxable year of the distributee, no exclusion from gross income is allowable with respect to the $4,000.

Example (4). The X Corporation instituted a trust, forming part of a "qualified" profit-sharing plan for its employees, the cost thereof being borne entirely by the corporation. The plan provides, in part, that if, after 10 or more years of service, an employee leaves the employ of the corporation, either voluntarily or involuntarily, before retirement, a percentage of the reserve provided for the employee in the trust fund will be paid to the employee as follows: 10 to 15 years of service, 25 percent; 15 to 20 years of service, 50 percent; 20 to 25 years of service, 75 percent; 25 or more years of service, 100 percent. The plan further provides that if an employee dies before reaching retirement age, his beneficiary will receive a percentage of the reserve provided for the employee in the trust fund, on the same basis as shown in the preceding sentence. A, an employee of the X Corporation for 17 years, died before attaining retirement age while in the employ of the corporation. At the time of his death, $15,000 was the reserve provided for him in the trust fund. His beneficiary receives $7,500 in a lump sum, an amount equal to 50 percent of the reserve provided for A's retirement. The beneficiary may exclude from gross income (assuming no other death benefits are involved) $5,000 of the $7,500, since the latter amount constitutes "total distributions payable" paid within one taxable year of the distributee, to which subdivision (i) of this subparagraph applies.

(4)(i) Notwithstanding the rule stated in subparagraph (1) of this paragraph and illustrated in subparagraph (2) of this paragraph, the exclusion from gross income under section 101(b) also applies (but only to the extent provided in the next sentence) to amounts with respect to which the deceased employee possessed, immediately before his death, a nonforfeitable right to receive the amounts while living—

(a) If such amounts are paid under an annuity contract purchased by an employer which is an organization referred to in section 170(b)(1)(A)(ii) or (vi) or which is a religious organization (other than a trust) and which is exempt from tax under section 501(a);

(b) If such amounts are paid as part of a "total payment" with respect to the deceased employee; and

(c) If such "total payment" is paid in full within one taxable year of the payee beginning after December 31, 1957.

However, the amount that is excludable under section 101(b) by reason of this subparagraph shall not exceed an amount which bears the same ratio to the amount which would be includible in the payee's gross income if it were not for the second sentence of section 101(b)(2)(B) and this subparagraph, as the amount contributed by the employer for the annuity contract that was excludable from the deceased employee's gross income under paragraph (b) of § 1.403(b)-1 bears to the total amount contributed by the employer for the annuity contract. See section 101(b)(2)(B)(iii). For purposes of this subparagraph, a "total payment" means a payment of the balance to the credit of an employee with respect to all "section 403(b) annuities" purchased by the employer which becomes payable to the payee by reason of the employee's death, either before or after separation from the service. An annuity contract will be regarded as a "section 403(b) annuity" if any amount contributed (or considered as contributed under paragraph (b)(2) of § 1.403(b)-1) by the employer for such contract was excludable from the employee's gross income under paragraph (b) of § 1.403(b)-1. Under this definition, therefore, an annuity contract may be regarded as a "section 403(b) annuity" even though some of the employer's contributions for the contract were not excludable from the employee's gross income under paragraph (b) of § 1.403(b)-1 because, for example, the employer was not an exempt organization when such contributions were paid. For purposes of computing the ratio described in this subdivision in such a case, the total amount contributed by the employer for the contract includes the amounts contributed by the employer when it was not an exempt organization.

(ii) This subparagraph does not relate to any amounts with respect to which the deceased employee did not possess, immediately before his death, a nonforfeitable right to receive the amounts while living. Such amounts are excludable under the provisions of section 101(b) without regard to section 101(b)(2)(B) and this subparagraph. Thus, if a "total payment" received by a beneficiary of a deceased employee under an annuity contract purchased by an organization described in subdivision (i)(a) of this subparagraph consists both of amounts with respect to which the deceased employee possessed, immediately before his death, a nonforfeitable right to receive the amounts while living and of amounts with respect to which the deceased employee did not possess such a nonforfeitable right, only those amounts with respect to which the deceased employee possessed such a nonforfeitable right are amounts to which this subparagraph applies. Therefore, for purposes of computing the ratio described in subdivision (i) of this subparagraph in such a case, there shall be taken into account only the employer contributions attributable to those amounts with respect to which the deceased employee possessed, immediately before his death, a nonforfeitable right to receive the amounts while living. See example (e) of subdivision (v) of this subparagraph. In no event, however, may the total amount excludable under section 101(b) with respect to any employee exceed $5,000 (see paragraph (a)(3) of this section).

(iii)(*a*) In any case when the deceased employee's interest in the employer's contributions for an annuity contract was forfeitable at the time the contributions were made but, at a subsequent date prior to his death, such interest changed to a nonforfeitable interest, then, for purposes of computing the ratio described in subdivision (i) of this subparagraph, the cash surrender value of the contract on the date of the change (except to the extent attributable to employee contributions) shall be considered as the amount contributed by the employer for the contract. In such a case, if only part of the deceased employee's interest in the annuity changed from a forfeitable to a nonforfeitable interest, then only the corresponding part of the case surrender value of the contract on the date of the change shall be considered as the amount contributed by the employer for the contract. Similarly, if part of the deceased employee's interest in the annuity contract changed from a forfeitable to a nonforfeitable interest on a particular date and another part of his interest so changed on a subsequent date, it is necessary, in order to compute the amount contributed by the employer for the contract, to first determine (under the rules in the preceding sentence) the amount that is considered as the amount contributed by the employer with respect to each change, and then to add these amounts together. For purposes of computing the ratio described in subdivision (i) of this subparagraph in all of the above cases, the amount contributed by the employer that was excludable from the employee's gross income under paragraph (b) of § 1.403(b)-1 is that amount which, under paragraph (b)(2) of such section, was considered as employer contributions and which, under such paragraph (b) of § 1.403-1, was excludable from the deceased employee's gross income for the taxable year in which the change occurred.

(*b*) This subdivision (iii) may be illustrated by the following examples:

Example (1). X Organization contributed $4,000 toward the purchase of an annuity contract for A, an employee who died in 1970. At the time they were made, A's interest in such contributions was forfeitable. A made no contributions toward the purchase of the annuity contract. On January 1, 1960, A's entire interest in the annuity contract changed to a nonforfeitable interest. At the time of such change, the cash surrender value of the contract was $5,000. For purposes of the ratio described in subdivision (i) of this subparagraph, the total amount contributed by X Organization for the annuity contract is $5,000. If any part of such $5,000 was excludable under paragraph (b) of § 1.403(b)-1 from A's gross income for his taxable year in which the change occurred, the amount so excludable shall be considered as the amount contributed for the contract by the employer that was excludable from the employee's gross income under paragraph (b) of § 1.403(b)-1.

Example (2). Assume the same facts as in example (1) except that only one-half of A's interest in the annuity contract changed to a nonforfeitable interest on January 1, 1960, and that no other part of his interest so changed during his lifetime. For purposes of the ratio described in subdivision (i) of this subparagraph, the total amount contributed by X Organization for the annuity contract is $2,500 ($\frac{1}{2}$ of the cash surrender value of the annuity contract on the date of the change). To the extent such $2,500 was, under paragraph (b) of § 1.403(b)-1, excludable from A's gross income for the taxable year of the change, it is considered as the amount contributed by the employer that was excludable under paragraph (b) of § 1.403(b)-1.

Example (3). Assume the same facts as in example (1) except that one-half of A's interest in the annuity contract changed to a nonforfeitable interest on January 1, 1960, and the other half of his interest changed to a nonforfeitable interest on January 1, 1965. On January 1, 1965, the cash surrender value of the annuity contract was $6,000. For purposes of the ratio described in subdivision (i) of this subparagraph, the total amount contributed by X organization for the annuity contract is $5,500 (*i.e.*, $\frac{1}{2} \times$ $5,000 plus $\frac{1}{2} \times$ $6,000). The amount contributed by the employer that was excludable from A's gross income under paragraph (b) of § 1.403(b)-1 is an amount equal to the sum of the amount that was, under such paragraph, excludable from A's gross income for the taxable year during which the first change occurred and the amount that was, under

Reg. § 1.101-2(d)(4)

such paragraph, excludable from A's gross income for the taxable year in which the second change occurred.

(iv) For purposes of this subparagraph, an annuity contract will be considered to have been purchased by an employer which is an organization referred to in section 170(b)(1)(A)(ii) or (vi) or which is a religious organization (other than a trust) and which is exempt from tax under section 501(a), if any of the contributions paid toward the purchase price of such contract by the employer were paid at a time when the employer was such an organization. Thus an annuity contract may be regarded as purchased by such an organization even though part of the organization's contributions for such annuity contract were paid at a time when the organization was not such an exempt organization.

(v) The application of this subparagraph may be illustrated by the following examples:

Example (1). The widow of A, a deceased employee, elects, under an annuity contract purchased for A by X Organization, to receive in a lump sum the present value of such annuity contract as of the date of A's death. Such present value is $6,000 and is received by the widow in a taxable year beginning after December 31, 1957. X Organization contributed $3,000 toward the purchase of the annuity contract and A contributed $2,000 toward such purchase. A's interest in X Organization's contributions was nonforfeitable at the time such contributions were made. Thus, just before his death, A's entire interest in the annuity contract was a nonforfeitable interest and, if he had retired at that time, he could have received the present value of $6,000. The whole amount of the $3,000 contributed by X Organization for the annuity contract was excludable from A's gross income under paragraph (b) of § 1.403(b)-1. This annuity contract was the only annuity contract purchased by X Organization for A and was not purchased as part of a qualified plan. However, all the contributions paid by X Organization were paid at a time when X Organization was an organization referred to in section 170(b)(1)(A)(ii) and exempt from tax under section 501(a). The amount that A's widow may exclude from gross income (assuming no other death benefits) is computed in the following manner:

(a) Amount includible in gross income without regard to second sentence of section 101(b)(2)(B) ($6,000 minus $2,000 contributed for contract by A) ... $4,000
(b) Total employer contributions for the contract $3,000

(c) Amount of employer contributions for the contract that was excludable under paragraph (b) of § 1.403(b)-1.. $3,000
(d) Percent of total employer contributions for the contract that were excludable under paragraph (b) of § 1.403(b)-1 ((c) ÷ (b)) 100%
(e) Amount to which section 101(b) exclusion applies ((d) × (a)) $4,000

Example (2). The facts are the same as in example (1) except that only $2,000 of X Organization's contributions for the annuity contract was excludable from A's gross income under paragraph (b) of § 1.403(b)-1 and that the remaining $1,000 was includible in A's gross income for the taxable years during which such amounts were contributed by X Organization. The amount that A's widow may exclude from gross income (assuming no other death benefits) is computed in the following manner:

(a) Amount includible in gross income without regard to second sentence of section 101(b)(2)(B) ($6,000 minus $2,000 contributed for contract by A and $1,000 of X organization's contributions includible in A's gross income)........................ $3,000
(b) Total employer contributions for the contract $3,000
(c) Amount of employer contributions for the contract that was excludable under paragraph (b) of § 1.403(b)-1.. $2,000
(d) Percent of total employer contributions for the contract that were excludable under paragraph (b) of § 1.403(b)-1 ((c) ÷ (b)) 67%
(e) Amount to which section 101(b) exclusion applies ((d) × (a)) $2,000

Example (3). The widow of B, a deceased employee, elects, under an annuity contract purchased for B by Y Organization, to receive in a lump sum the present value of such annuity contract as of the date of B's death. Such present value is $6,000 and is received by the widow in a taxable year beginning after December 31, 1957. Y Organization contributed $4,000 toward the purchase of the contract; whereas B made no contributions toward the purchase of the contract. This annuity contract was the only annuity contract purchased by Y Organization for B and was not purchased as part of a "qualified" plan. However, all the contributions paid by Y Organization were paid at a time when it was an organization referred to in section 170(b)(1)(A)(ii) and exempt from tax under section 501(a). B's interest in Y Organization's contributions was, at the time they were paid, forfeitable. However, prior to his death, one-half of B's interest in the annuity contract changed from a forfeitable to a nonforfeitable interest. Therefore, just before his death, B could have obtained $3,000 under the annuity

Reg. § 1.101-2(d)(4)

contract if he had retired at that time. On the date of the change, the cash surrender value of the annuity contract was $5,000. As a result of the change, $1,500 was, under paragraph (b) of § 1.403(b)-1, excludable from B's gross income, and $600 was includible in his gross income for the taxable year in which the change occurred. Part of the value of the annuity contract on the date of the change was attributable to contributions made by Y Organization prior to January 1, 1958, and, consequently, was neither excludable from B's gross income under paragraph (b) of § 1.403(b)-1 nor includible in B's gross income (see paragraph (b) of § 1.403(d)-1). The amount that B's widow may exclude from gross income (assuming no other death benefits) is computed in the following manner:

(a) Amount of "total payment" with respect to which A had a forfeitable right at time of death. (½ × $6,000) $3,000
(b) Amount includible in gross income without regard to second sentence of section 101(b)(2)(B) (½ × $6,000 less $600 includible in B's gross income for year when his rights changed to nonforfeitable rights) ... $2,400
(c) Total employer contributions for the contract (½ of cash surrender value of contract on date B's rights changed to nonforfeitable rights) ... $2,500
(d) Amount of employer contributions for the contract that was excludable under paragraph (b) of § 1.403(b)-1 . $1,500
(e) Percent of total employer contributions for the contract that were excludable under paragraph (b) of § 1.403(b)-1 ((d) ÷ (c)) 60%
(f) Amount to which section 101(b) exclusion applies by reason of the second sentence of section 101(b)(2)(B) ((e) × (b)) $1,440
(g) Total amount to which section 101(b) exclusion applies ((a) + (f)) $4,440

(e) *Annuity payments.*—(1) Where death benefits are paid in the form of annuity payments, the following rules shall govern for purposes of the exclusion provided in section 101(b):

(i) The exclusion from gross income provided by section 101(b) does not apply to amounts, paid as an annuity, with respect to which the employee possessed, immediately before his death, a nonforfeitable right to receive the amounts while living, or to amounts paid as an annuity in lieu thereof. See paragraph (d) of this section.

(ii) Under section 101(b)(2)(C), no exclusion is allowable for amounts received by a surviving annuitant under a joint and survivor's annuity contract if the annuity starting date (as defined in section 72(c)(4) and paragraph (b) of § 1.72-4) occurs before the death of the employee.

If the annuity starting date occurs after the death of the employee, the joint and survivor's annuity contract shall be treated as an annuity to which section 101(b)(2)(D) applies. See subdivision (iii) of this subparagraph.

(iii)(a) Subject to the other limitations stated in section 101(b) and in this section (see section 101(b)(2)(D)), the amount to which the exclusion of section 101(b) shall apply, with respect to "amounts received as an annuity" (as defined in paragraph (b) of § 1.72-2), shall be the amount by which the present value of the annuity to be paid to the beneficiary, computed as of the date of the employee's death, exceeds the value (if any) of whichever of the following is the larger:

(1) Amounts contributed by the employee (determined in accordance with the provisions of section 72 and the regulations thereunder), or

(2) Amounts with respect to which the employee possessed, immediately before his death, a nonforfeitable right to receive the amounts while living, or amounts paid in lieu thereof (see paragraph (d) of this section).

(b) The present value of an annuity (immediately before the death of the employee), to the employee, or (immediately after the death of the employee), to his estate or beneficiary, shall be determined as follows:

(1) In the case of an annuity paid by an insurance company or by an organization (other than an insurance company) regularly engaged in issuing annuity contracts with an insurance company as the coinsurer or reinsurer of the obligations under the contract, by use of the discount interest rates and mortality tables used by the insurance company involved to determine the installment benefits; and

(2) In the case of an annuity issued after November 23, 1984, to which paragraph (e)(1)(iii)(b)(1) of this section is not applicable, by use of the appropriate tables in § 20.2031-7 of this chapter (Estate Tax Regulations).

(iv) Any amount subject to section 101(b)(2)(D) which is excludable under section 101(b) (see subdivision (iii) of this subparagraph) shall, for purposes of section 72, be treated as additional consideration paid by the employee. See paragraph (b) of § 1.72-8.

(v) Where more than one beneficiary, or more than one death benefit, is involved, the exclusion provided by section 101(b) shall be apportioned to the various beneficiaries and benefits in accordance with the proportion that the present value of each benefit bears to the total present value of all the benefits.

Reg. § 1.101-2(e)(1)

(2) The application of the principles of this paragraph may be illustrated by the following examples:

Example (1). (i) A died on January 1, 1969. Under the plan of the X Corporation, W, who is the widow of employee A, and who is 55 years old at the time of A's death, is entitled to an immediate annuity of $2,000 per year during her life and C, the minor child of A, is entitled to receive $1,000 per year for 15 years. A made no contributions under the plan and died while still employed by the X Corporation. At the time of A's death, the amount in his account is $18,000. Under the terms of the plan, this amount would have been distributable to him on account of voluntary termination of employment, but would not have been payable after his death except in the form of the annuities just described. This amount, accordingly, constitutes a nonforfeitable interest in lieu of which the annuities are paid. The exclusion does not apply, except to the extent that the present value of the annuities exceeds $18,000, whether or not the plan is "qualified", since the total of the amount in A's account will not be paid within one taxable year of the distributees. See subparagraph (1)(i) of this paragraph.

(ii) The computation of the exclusion applicable to the interests of W and C (assuming that the payments will not be made by an insurance company or some other organization regularly engaged in issuing annuity contracts) is, by application of the tables in § 20.2031-7 of this chapter (Estate Tax Regulations) [Reg. § 20.2031-7 of this chapter is reproduced at ¶ 2391.05 and Reg. § 20.2031-10 is reproduced at ¶ 2391.10.—CCH.], as follows: The present value of W's interest is $26,243.60, determined by multiplying the annual payment of $2,000 by 13.1218 (the factor in Table I for a person aged 55); the present value of C's interest is $11,517.40, determined by multiplying the yearly payment of $1,000 by 11.5174 (the factor in Table II for payments for a term certain of 15 years). The present value of both annuities is $37,761 and (assuming no other death benefits are involved), the total amount excludable is $5,000, because the total present value of the annuities exceeds the employee's nonforfeitable interest by more than $5,000 ($37,761 minus $18,000 equal $19,761). The exclusion allocable to W's interest is $26,243.60/$37,761 times $5,000 or $3,474.96; the exclusion allocable to C's interest is $11,517.40/$37,761 times $5,000, or $1,525.04. That portion of the death benefit exclusion as so determined for each beneficiary is to be treated as consideration paid by the employee for purposes of section 72.

Example (2). The facts are the same as in example (1), except that the nonforfeitable interest of A, at the time of his death, amounted to $33,761. Since the present value of both annuities ($37,761) exceeds the value of such nonforfeitable interest by only $4,000, the latter amount is the total amount excludable from the gross income of the beneficiaries. This $4,000 exclusion is to be divided in the same proportions as those indicated in example (1). Thus, the exclusion allocable to W's interest is $26,243.60/$37,761 times $4,000, or $2,779.97; and the exclusion allocable to the interest of C is $11,517.40/$37,761 times $4,000, or $1,220.03. That portion of the death benefit exclusion as so determined for each beneficiary is to be treated as consideration paid by the employee for purposes of section 72.

(f) *Distributions on behalf of a self-employed individual.* (1) Under sections 401(c)(1) and 403(a)(3), certain self-employed individuals may be covered by a pension or profit-sharing plan described in section 401(a) and exempt under section 501(a) or under an annuity plan described in section 403(a). However, a payment pursuant to the provisions of any such plan by reason of the death of an individual who participated in such a plan as a self-employed individual immediately before his retirement or death to the beneficiary or estate of such individual does not qualify for the exclusion provided by section 101(b).

(2) The application of this paragraph may be illustrated by the following examples:

Example (1). From 1950 to 1965, A was an employee of B, a sole proprietor. In 1963, B established a qualified pension plan covering A and all other persons who had been employed by B for more than 3 years. In 1965, A acquired from B a 40-percent interest in the capital and profits of the business. A continued to participate in the pension plan as a self-employed individual. In 1970, A died and his widow, in compliance with one of the provisions of the pension plan, elected to receive all of the benefits accrued to A prior to his death in a lump-sum distribution. As A participated in the plan as a self-employed individual immediately prior to his death, A's widow may not exclude any portion of such distribution from her gross income under section 101(b).

Example (2). A, an attorney, is employed by the X Company in their legal department. He is covered by the pension plan that X has established for its employees. Under the terms of A's contract of employment with X, A is permitted to carry on the private practice of law in his off-duty hours. A establishes his own pension plan with respect to his earnings from his private practice. On A's death, his widow elected to receive a lump-

Reg. § 1.101-2(f)(2)

sum distribution with respect to any benefits accrued to A under both X's pension plan and A's own pension plan. To the extent that such payment otherwise complies with the requirements of section 101(b), up to $5,000 of the amount paid by X may be excluded from her gross income. No part of the distribution from A's own pension plan may be excluded from her gross income under section 101(b) because A participated in the plan as a self-employed individual immediately before his death. [Reg. § 1.101-2.]

□ [T.D. 6280, 12-16-57. Amended by T.D. 6722, 4-13-64, T.D. 6783, 12-23-64, T.D. 7043, 6-1-70, T.D. 7352, 4-9-75, T.D. 7428, 8-13-76, T.D. 7836, 9-23-82, T.D. 7955, 5-10-84 and T.D. 8540, 6-9-94.]

[Reg. § 1.101-3]

§ 1.101-3. Interest payments.—(a) *Applicability of section 101(c)*. Section 101(c) provides that if any amount excluded from gross income by section 101(a) (relating to life insurance proceeds) or section 101(b) (relating to employees' death benefits) is held under an agreement to pay interest thereon, the interest payments shall be included in gross income. This provision applies to payments made (either by an insurer or by or on behalf of an employer) of interest earned on any amount so excluded from gross income which is held without substantial diminution of the principal amount during the period when such interest payments are being made or credited to the beneficiaries or estate of the insured or the employee. For example, if a monthly payment is $100, of which $99 represents interest and $1 represents diminution of the principal amount, the principal amount shall be considered held under an agreement to pay interest thereon and the interest payment shall be included in the gross income of the recipient. Section 101(c) applies whether the election to have an amount held under an agreement to pay interest thereon is made by the insured or employee or by his beneficiaries or estate, and whether or not an interest rate is explicitly stated in the agreement. Section 101(d), relating to the payment of life insurance proceeds at a date later than death, shall not apply to any amount to which section 101(c) applies. See section 101(d)(4). However, both section 101(c) and section 101(d) may apply to payments received under a single life insurance contract. For provisions relating to the application of this rule to payments received under a permanent life insurance policy with a family income rider attached, see paragraph (h) of § 1.101-4.

(b) *Determinations of "present value"*. For the purpose of determining whether section 101(c) or section 101(d) applies, the present value (at the time of the insured's death) of any amount which is to be paid at a date later than death shall be determined by the use of the interest rate and mortality tables used by the insurer in determining the size of the payments to be made. [Reg. § 1.101-3.]

□ [T.D. 6280, 12-16-57. Amended by T.D. 6577, 10-27-61.]

[Reg. § 1.101-4]

§ 1.101-4. Payment of life insurance proceeds at a date later than death.—(a) *In general*. (1) (i) Section 101(d) states the provisions governing the exclusion from gross income of amounts (other than those to which section 101(c) applies) received under a life insurance contract and paid by reason of the death of the insured which are paid to a beneficiary on a date or dates later than the death of the insured. However, if the amounts payable as proceeds of life insurance to which section 101(a)(1) applies cannot in any event exceed the amount payable at the time of the insured's death, such amounts are fully excludable from the gross income of the recipient (or recipients) without regard to the actual time of payment and no further determination need be made under this section. Section 101(d)(1)(A) provides an exclusion from gross income of any amount determined by a proration, under applicable regulations, of "an amount held by an insurer with respect to any beneficiary". The quoted phrase is defined in section 101(d)(2). For the regulations governing the method of computation of this proration, see paragraphs (c) through (f) of this section. The prorated amounts are to be excluded from the gross income of the beneficiary regardless of the taxable year in which they are actually received (see example (2) of subparagraph (2) of this paragraph).

(ii) Section 101(d)(1)(B) provides an additional exclusion where life insurance proceeds are paid to the surviving spouse of an insured. For purposes of this exclusion, the term "surviving spouse" means the spouse of the insured as of the date of death, including a spouse legally separated, but not under a decree of absolute divorce (section 101(d)(3)). To the extent that the total payments, under one or more agreements, made in excess of the amounts determined by proration under section 101(d)(1)(A) do not exceed $1,000 in the taxable year of receipt, they shall be excluded from the gross income of the surviving spouse (whether or not payment of any part of such amounts is guaranteed by the insurer). Amounts excludable under section 101(d)(1)(B) are not "prorated" amounts.

(2) The principles of this paragraph may be illustrated by the following examples:

Reg. § 1.101-3(a)

Example (1). A surviving spouse elects to receive all of the life insurance proceeds with respect to one insured, amounting to $150,000, in ten annual installments of $16,500 each, based on a certain guaranteed interest rate. The prorated amount is $15,000 ($150,000 ÷ 10). As the second payment, the insurer pays $17,850, which exceeds the guaranteed payment by $1,350 as the result of earnings of the insurer in excess of those required to pay the guaranteed installments. The surviving spouse shall include $1,850 in gross income and exclude $16,000—determined in the following manner:

Fixed payment (including guaranteed interest) ..	$16,500
Excess interest	1,350
Total payment	17,850
Prorated amount	15,000
Excess over prorated amount .	2,850
Annual excess over prorated amount excludable under section 101(d)(1)(B) ..	$ 1,000
Amount includible in gross income	1,850

Example (2). Assume the same facts as in example (1), except that the third and fourth annual installments, totalling $33,000 (2 × $16,500), are received in a single subsequent taxable year of the surviving spouse. The prorated amount of $15,000 of each annual installment, totalling $30,000, shall be excluded even though the spouse receives more than one annual installment in the single subsequent taxable year. However, the surviving spouse is entitled to only one exclusion of $1,000 under section 101(d)(1)(B) for each taxable year of receipt. The surviving spouse shall include $2,000 in her gross income for the taxable year with respect to the above installment payments ($33,000 less the sum of $30,000 plus $1,000).

Example (3). Assume the same facts as in example (1), except that the surviving spouse dies before receiving all ten annual installments and the remaining installments are paid to her estate or beneficiary. In such a case, $15,000 of each installment would continue to be excludable from the gross income of the recipient, but any amounts received in excess thereof would be fully includible.

(b) *Amount held by an insurer.* (1) For the purpose of the proration referred to in section 101(d)(1), an "amount held by an insurer with respect to any beneficiary" means an amount equal to the present value to such beneficiary (as of the date of death of the insured) of an agreement by the insurer under a life insurance policy (whether as an option or otherwise) to pay such beneficiary an amount or amounts at a date or

dates later than the death of the insured (section 101(d)(2)). The present value of such agreement is to be computed as if the agreement under the life insurance policy had been entered into on the date of death of the insured, except that such value shall be determined by the use of the mortality table and interest rate used by the insurer in calculating payments to be made to the beneficiary under such agreement. Where an insurance policy provides an option for the payment of a specific amount upon the death of the insured in full discharge of the contract, such lump sum is the amount held by the insurer with respect to all beneficiaries (or their beneficiaries) under the contract. See, however, paragraph (e) of this section.

(2) In the case of two or more beneficiaries, the "amount held by the insurer" with respect to each beneficiary depends on the relationship of the different benefits payable to such beneficiaries. Where the amounts payable to two or more beneficiaries are independent of each other, the "amount held by the insurer with respect to each beneficiary" shall be determined and prorated over the periods involved independently. Thus, if a certain amount per month is to be paid to A for his life, and, concurrently, another amount per month is to be paid to B for his life, the "amount held by the insurer" shall be determined and prorated for both A and B independently, but the aggregate shall not exceed the total present value of such payments to both. On the other hand, if the obligation to pay B was contingent on his surviving A, the "amount held by the insurer" shall be considered an amount held with respect to both beneficiaries simultaneously. Furthermore, it is immaterial whether B is a named beneficiary or merely the ultimate recipient of payments for a term of years. For the special rules governing the computation of the proration of the "amount held by an insurer" in determining amounts excludable under the provisions of section 101(d), see paragraphs (c) to (f), inclusive, of this section.

(3) Notwithstanding any other provision of this section, if the policy was transferred for a valuable consideration, the total "amount held by an insurer" cannot exceed the sum of the consideration paid plus any premiums or other consideration paid subsequent to the transfer if the provisions of section 101(a)(2) and paragraph (b) of § 1.101-1 limit the excludability of the proceeds to such total.

(c) *Treatment of payments for life to a sole beneficiary.* If the contract provides for the payment of a specified lump sum, but, pursuant to an agreement between the beneficiary and the insurer, payments are to be made during the life of

Reg. § 1.101-4(c)

the beneficiary in lieu of such lump sum, the lump sum shall be divided by the life expectancy of the beneficiary determined in accordance with the mortality table used by the insurer in determining the benefits to be paid. Moreover, if payments are to be made to the estate or beneficiary of the primary beneficiary in the event that the primary beneficiary dies before receiving a certain number of payments or a specified total amount, such lump sum shall be reduced by the present value (at the time of the insured's death) of amounts which may be paid by reason of the guarantee, in accordance with the provisions of paragraph (e) of this section, before making this calculation. To the extent that payments received in each taxable year do not exceed the amount found from the above calculation, they are "prorated amounts" of the "amount held by an insurer" and are excludable from the gross income of the beneficiary without regard to whether he lives beyond the life expectancy used in making the calculation. If the contract in question does not provide for the payment of a specific lump sum upon the death of the insured as one of the alternative methods of payment, the present value (at the time of the death of the insured) of the payments to be made the beneficiary, determined in accordance with the interest rate and mortality table used by the insurer in determining the benefits to be paid, shall be used in the above calculation in lieu of a lump sum.

(d) *Treatment of payments to two or more beneficiaries*—(1) *Unrelated payments.* If payments are to be made to two or more beneficiaries, but the payments to be made to each are to be made without regard to whether or not payments are made or continue to be made to the other beneficiaries, the present value (at the time of the insured's death) of such payments to each beneficiary shall be determined independently for each such beneficiary. The present value so determined shall then be divided by the term for which the payments are to be made. If the payments are to be made for the life of the beneficiary, the divisor shall be the life expectancy of the beneficiary. To the extent that payments received by a beneficiary do not exceed the amount found from the above calculation, they are "prorated amounts" of the "amount held by an insurer" with respect to such beneficiary and are excludable from the gross income of the beneficiary without regard to whether he lives beyond any life expectancy used in making the calculation. For the purpose of the calculation described above, both the "present value" of the payments to be made periodically and the "life expectancy" of a beneficiary shall be determined in accordance with the interest rate and mortality table used by the insurer in deter-

mining the benefits to be paid. If payments are to be made to the estate or beneficiary of a primary beneficiary in the event that such beneficiary dies before receiving a certain number of payments or a specified total amount, the "present value" of payments to such beneficiary shall not include the present value (at the time of the insured's death) of amounts which may be paid by reason of such a guarantee. See paragraph (e) of this section.

(2) *Related payments.* If payments to be made to two or more beneficiaries are in the nature of a joint and survivor annuity (as described in paragraph (b) of § 1.72-5), the present value (at the time of the insured's death) of the payments to be made to all such beneficiaries shall be divided by the life expectancy of such beneficiaries as a group. To the extent that the payments received by a beneficiary do not exceed the amount found from the above calculation, they are "prorated amounts" of the "amount held by an insurer" with respect to such beneficiary and are excludable from the gross income of the beneficiary without regard to whether all the beneficiaries involved live beyond the life expectancy used in making the calculation. For the purpose of the calculation described above, both the "present value" of the payments to be made periodically and the "life expectancy" of all the beneficiaries as a group shall be determined in accordance with the interest rate and mortality table used by the insurer in determining the benefits to be paid. If the contract provides that certain payments are to be made in the event that all the beneficiaries of the group die before a specified number of payments or a specified total amount is received by them, the present value of payments to be made to the group shall not include the present value (at the time of the insured's death) of amounts which may be paid by reason of such a guarantee. See paragraph (e) of this section.

(3) *Payments to secondary beneficiaries.* Payments made by reason of the death of a beneficiary (or beneficiaries) under a contract providing that such payments shall be made in the event that the beneficiary (or beneficiaries) die before receiving a specified number of payments or a specified total amount shall be excluded from the gross income of the recipient to the extent that such payments are made solely by reason of such guarantee.

(e) *Treatment of present value of guaranteed payments.* In the case of payments which are to be made for a life or lives under a contract providing that further amounts shall be paid upon the death of the primary beneficiary (or beneficiaries) in the event that such beneficiary (or beneficiaries) die before receiving a specified number of

Reg. § 1.101-4(d)(1)

payments or a specified total amount, the present value (at the time of the insured's death) of all payments to be made under the contract shall not include, for purposes of prorating the amount held by the insurer, the present value of the payments which may be made to the estate or beneficiary of the primary beneficiary. In such a case, any lump sum amount used to measure the value of the amount held by an insurer with respect to the primary beneficiary must be reduced by the value at the time of the insured's death of any amounts which may be paid by reason of the guarantee provided for a secondary beneficiary or the estate of the primary beneficiary before prorating such lump sum over the life or lives of the primary beneficiaries. Such present value (of the guaranteed payment) shall be determined by the use of the interest rate and mortality tables used by the insurer in determining the benefits to be paid.

(f) *Treatment of payments not paid periodically.* Payments made to beneficiaries other than periodically shall be included in the gross income of the recipients, but only to the extent that they exceed amounts payable at the time of the death of the insured to each such beneficiary or, where no such amounts are specified, the present value of such payments at that time.

(g) *Examples.* The principles of this section may be illustrated by the following examples:

Example (1). A life insurance policy provides for the payment of $20,000 in a lump sum to the beneficiary at the death of the insured. Upon the death of the insured, the beneficiary elects an option to leave the proceeds with the company for five years and then receive payment of $24,000, having no claim of right to any part of such sum before the entire five years have passed. Upon the payment of the larger sum, $24,000, the beneficiary shall include $4,000 in gross income and exclude $20,000 therefrom. If it is assumed that the same insurer has determined the benefits to be paid, the same result would obtain if no lump sum amount were provided for at the death of the insured and the beneficiary were to be paid $24,000 five years later. In neither of these cases would the surviving spouse be able to exclude any additional amount from gross income since both cases involve an amount held by an insurer under an agreement to pay interest thereon to which section 101(c) applies, rather than an amount to be paid periodically after the death of the insured to which section 101(d) applies.

Example (2). A life insurance policy provides that $1,200 per year shall be paid the sole beneficiary (other than a surviving spouse) until a fund of $20,000 and interest which accrues on the remaining balance is exhausted. A guaranteed rate

of interest is specified, but excess interest may be credited according to the earnings of the insurer. Assuming that the fund will be exhausted in 20 years if only the guaranteed interest is actually credited, the beneficiary shall exclude $1,000 of each installment received ($20,000 divided by 20) and any installments received, whether by the beneficiary or his estate or beneficiary, in excess of 20 shall be fully included in the gross income of the recipient. If, instead, the excess interest were to be paid each year, any portion of each installment representing an excess over $1,000 would be fully includible in the recipient's gross income. Thus, if an installment of $1,350 were received, $350 of it would be included in gross income.

Example (3). Assume that the sole life insurance policy of a decedent provides only for the payment of $5,000 per year for the life of his surviving spouse, beginning with the insured's death. If the present value of the proceeds, determined by reference to the interest rate and the mortality table used by the insurance company, is $60,000, and such beneficiary's life expectancy is 20 years, $3,000 of each $5,000 payment ($60,000 divided by 20) is excludable as the prorated portion of the "amount held by an insurer". For each taxable year in which a payment is made, an additional $1,000 is excludable from the gross income of the surviving spouse. Hence, if she receives only one $5,000 payment in her taxable year, only $1,000 is includible in her gross income in that year with respect to such payment ($5,000 less the total amount excludable, $4,000). Assuming that the policy also provides for payments of $2,000 per year for 10 years to the daughter of the insured, the present value of the payments to the daughter is to be computed separately for the purpose of determining the excludable portion of each payment to her. Assuming that such present value is $15,000, $1,500 of each payment of $2,000 received by the daughter is excludable from her gross income ($15,000 divided by 10). The remaining $500 shall be included in the gross income of the daughter.

Example (4). Beneficiaries A and B, neither of whom is the surviving spouse of the insured, are each to receive annual payments of $1,800 for each of their respective lives upon the death of the insured. The contract does not provide for payments to be made in any other manner. Assuming that the present value of the payments to be made to A, whose life expectancy according to the insurer's mortality table is 30 years, is $36,000, A shall exclude $1,200 of each payment received ($36,000 divided by 30). Assuming that the present value of the payments to be made to B, whose life expectancy according to the insurer's mortality table is 20 years, is $27,000, B shall exclude

Reg. § 1.101-4(g)

$1,350 of each payment received ($27,000 divided by 20).

Example (5). A life insurance policy provides for the payment of $76,500 in a lump sum to the beneficiary, A, at the death of the insured. Upon the insured's death, however, A selects an option for the payment of $2,000 per year for her life and for the same amount to be paid after her death to B, her daughter, for her life. Assuming that since A is 51 years of age and her daughter is 28 years of age, the insurer determined the amount of the payments by reference to a mortality table under which the life expectancy for the lives of both A and B, joint and survivor, is 51 years, $1,500 of each $2,000 payment to either A or B ($76,500 divided by 51, or $1,500) shall be excluded from the gross income of the recipient. However, if A is the surviving spouse of the insured and no other contracts of insurance whose proceeds are to be paid to her at a date later than death are involved, A shall exclude the entire payment of $2,000 in any taxable year in which she receives but one such payment because of the additional exclusion under section 101(d)(1)(B).

Example (6). Beneficiaries A and B, neither of whom is the surviving spouse of the insured, are each to receive annual payments of $1,800 for each of their respective lives upon the death of the insured, but after the death of either, the survivor is to receive the payments formerly made to the deceased beneficiary until the survivor dies. Assuming that the life expectancy, joint and survivor, of A and B in accordance with the mortality table used by the insurer is 32 years and assuming that the total present value of the benefits to both (determined in accordance with the interest rate used by the insurer), is $80,000. A and B shall each exclude $1,250 of each installment of $1,800 ($80,000 divided by the life expectancy, 32, multiplied by the fraction of the annual payment payable to each, one-half) until the death of either. Thereafter, the survivor shall exclude $2,500 of each installment of $3,600 ($80,000 divided by 32).

Example (7). A life insurance policy provides for the payment of $75,000 in a lump sum to the beneficiary, A, at the death of the insured. A, upon the insured's death, however, selects an option for the payment of $4,000 per year for life, with a guarantee that any part of the $75,000 lump sum not paid to A before his death shall be paid to B (or his estate), A's beneficiary. Assuming that, under the criteria used by the insurer in determining the benefits to be paid, the present value of the guaranteed amount to B is $13,500 and that A's life expectancy is 25 years, the lump sum shall be reduced by the present value of the

guarantee to B ($75,000 less $13,500 or $61,500) and divided by A's life expectancy ($61,500 divided by 25, or $2,460). Hence, $2,460 of each $4,000 payment is excludable from A's gross income. If A is the surviving spouse of the insured and no other contracts of insurance whose proceeds are to be paid to her at a date later than death are involved, A shall exclude $3,460 of each $4,000 payment from gross income in any taxable year in which but one such payment is received. Under these facts, if any amount is paid to B by reason of the fact that A dies before receiving a total of $75,000, the residue of the lump sum paid to B shall be excluded from B's gross income since it is wholly in lieu of the present value of such guarantee plus the present value of the payments to be made to the first beneficiary, and is therefore entirely an "amount held by an insurer" paid at a date later than death (see paragraph (d)(3) of this section).

Example (8). Assume that an insurance policy does not provide for the payment of a lump sum, but provides for the payment of $1,200 per year for a beneficiary's life upon the death of the insured, and also provides that if ten payments are not made to the beneficiary before death a secondary beneficiary (whether named by the insured or by the first beneficiary) shall receive the remainder of the ten payments in similar installments. If, according to the criteria used by the insurance company in determining the benefits, the present value of the payments to the first beneficiary is $12,000 and the life expectancy of such beneficiary is 15 years, $800 of each payment received by the first beneficiary is excludable from gross income. Assuming that the same figures obtain even though the payments are to be made at the rate of $100 per month, the yearly exclusion remains the same unless more or less than twelve months' installments are received by the beneficiary in a particular taxable year. In such a case two-thirds of the total received in the particular taxable year with respect to such beneficiary shall be excluded from gross income. Under either of the above alternatives, any amount received by the second beneficiary by reason of the guarantee of ten payments is fully excludable from the beneficiary's gross income since it is wholly in lieu of the present value of such guarantee plus the present value of the payments to be made to the first beneficiary and is therefore entirely an "amount held by an insurer" paid at a date later than death (see paragraph (d)(3) of this section).

(h) *Applicability of both section 101(c) and 101(d) to payments under a single life insurance contract*—(1) *In general.* Section 101(d) shall not apply to interest payments on any amount held

Reg. § 1.101-4(h)

by an insurer under an agreement to pay interest thereon (see sections 101(c) and 101(d)(4) and § 1.101-3). On the other hand, both section 101(c) and section 101(d) may be applicable to payments received under a single life insurance contract, if such payments consist both of interest on an amount held by an insurer under an agreement to pay interest thereon and of amounts held by the insurer and paid on a date or dates later than the death of the insured. One instance when both section 101(c) and section 101(d) may be applicable to payments received under a single life insurance contract is in the case of a permanent life insurance policy with a family income rider attached. A typical family income rider is one which provides additional term insurance coverage for a specified number of years from the register date of the basic policy. Under the policy with such a rider, ith B) nsured dies at any time during the term period, the beneficiary is entitled to receive (i) monthly payments of a specified amount commencing as of the date of death and continuing for the balance of the term period, and (ii) a lump sum payment of the proceeds under the basic policy to be paid at the end of the term period. If the insured dies after the expiration of the term period, the beneficiary receives only the proceeds under the basic policy. If the insured dies before the expiration of the term period, part of each monthly payment received by the beneficiary during the term period consists of interest on the proceeds of the basic policy (such proceeds being retained by the insurer until the end of the term period). The remaining part consists of an installment (principal plus interest) of the proceeds of the term insurance purchased under the family income rider. The amount of term insurance which is provided under the family income rider is, therefore, that amount which, at the date of the insured's death, will provide proceeds sufficient to fund such remaining part of each monthly payment. Since the proceeds under the basic policy are held by the insurer until the end of the term period, that portion of each monthly payment which consists of interest on such proceeds is interest on an amount held by an insurer under an agreement to pay interest thereon and is includible in gross income under section 101(c). On the

other hand, since the remaining portion of each monthly payment consists of an installment payment (principal plus interest) of the proceeds of the term insurance, it is a payment of an amount held by the insurer and paid on a date later than the death of the insured to which section 101(d) and this section applies (including the $1,000 exclusion allowed the surviving spouse under section 101(d)(1)(B)). The proceeds of the basic policy, when received in a lump sum at the end of the term period, are excludable from gross income under section 101(a).

(2) *Example of tax treatment of amounts received under a family income rider.* The following example illustrates the application of the principles contained in subparagraph (1) of this paragraph to payments received under a permanent life insurance policy with a family income rider attached:

Example. The sole life insurance policy of the insured provides for the payment of $100,000 to the beneficiary (the insured's spouse) on his death. In addition, there is attached to the policy a family income rider which provides that, if the insured dies before the 20th anniversary of the basic policy, the beneficiary shall receive (i) monthly payments of $1,000 commencing on the date of the insured's death and ending with the payment prior to the 20th anniversary of the basic policy, and (ii) a single payment of $100,000 payable on the 20th anniversary of the basic policy. On the date of the insured's death, the beneficiary (surviving spouse of the insured) is entitled to 36 monthly payments of $1,000 and to the single payment of $100,000 on the 20th anniversary of the basic policy. The value of the proceeds of the term insurance at the date of the insured's death is $28,409.00 (the present value of the portion of the monthly payments to which section 101(d) applies computed on the basis that the interest rate used by the insurer in determining the benefits to be paid under the contract is 2¼ percent). The amount of each monthly payment of $1,000 which is includible in the beneficiary's gross income is determined in the following manner:

(a) Total amount of monthly payment $1,000.00	
(b) Amount includible in gross income under section 101(c) as interest on the $100,000 proceeds under the basic policy held by the insurer until 20th anniversary of the basic policy (computed on the basis that the interest rate used by the insurer in determining the benefits to be paid under the contract is 2¼ percent) 185.00	
(c) Amount to which section 101(d) applies ((a) minus (b)) 815.00	
(d) Amount excludable from gross income under section 101(d) ($28,409 ÷ 36) 789.14	

Reg. § 1.101-4(h)(2)

(*e*) Amount includible in gross income under section 101(d) without taking into account the $1,000 exclusion allowed the beneficiary as the surviving spouse (((*c*) minus (*d*)) 25.86

The beneficiary, as the surviving spouse of the insured, is entitled to exclude the amounts otherwise includible in gross income under section 101(d) (item (*e*)) to the extent such amounts do not exceed $1,000 in the taxable year of receipt. This exclusion is not applicable, however, with respect to the amount of each payment which is includible in gross income under section 101(c) (item (*b*)). In this example, therefore, the beneficiary must include $185 of each monthly payment in gross income (amount includible under section 101(c)), but may exclude the $25.86 which is otherwise includible under section 101(d). The payment of $100,000 which is payable to the beneficiary on the 20th anniversary of the basic policy will be entirely excludable from gross income under section 101(a).

(3) *Limitation on amount considered to be an "amount held by an insurer".* See paragraph (b)(3) of this section for a limitation on the amount which shall be considered an "amount held by an insurer" in the case of proceeds of life insurance which are paid subsequent to the transfer of the policy for a valuable consideration.

(4) *Effective date.* The provisions of this paragraph are applicable only with respect to amounts received during the taxable years beginning after October 28, 1961, irrespective of the date of the death of the insured. [Reg. § 1.101-4.]

☐ [*T.D. 6280, 12-16-57. Amended by T.D. 6577, 10-27-61.*]

[Reg. § 1.101-5]

§ 1.101-5. **Alimony, etc., payments.**—Proceeds of life insurance policies paid by reason of the death of the insured to his separated wife, or payments excludable as death benefits under section 101(b) paid to a deceased employee's separated wife, if paid to discharge legal obligations imposed by a decree of divorce or separate maintenance, by a written separation agreement executed after August 16, 1954, or by a decree of support entered after March 1, 1954, shall be included in the gross income of the separated wife if section 71 or 682 is applicable to the payments made. For definition of "wife", see section 7701(a)(17) and the regulations thereunder. [Reg. § 1.101-5.]

☐ [*T.D. 6280, 12-16-57.*]

[Reg. § 1.101-6]

§ 1.101-6. **Effective date.**—(a) Except as otherwise provided in paragraph (h)(4) of § 1.101-4, the provisions of section 101 of the Internal Revenue Code of 1954 and §§ 1.101-1, 1.101-2, 1.101-3, 1.101-4, and 1.101-5 are applicable only with respect to amounts received by reason of the death of an insured or an employee occurring after August 16, 1954. In the case of such amounts, these sections are applicable even though the receipt of such amounts occurred in a taxable year beginning before January 1, 1954, to which the Internal Revenue Code of 1939 applies.

(b) Section 22(b)(1) of the Internal Revenue Code of 1939 and the regulations pertaining thereto shall apply to amounts received by reason of the death of an insured or an employee occurring before August 17, 1954, regardless of the date of receipt. [Reg. § 1.101-6.]

☐ [*T.D. 6280, 12-16-57. Amended by T.D. 6577, 10-27-61.*]

[Reg. § 1.101-7]

§ 1.101-7. **Mortality table used to determine exclusion for deferred payments of life insurance proceeds.**—(a) *Mortality Table.* Notwithstanding any provision of § 1.101-4 that otherwise would permit the use of a mortality table not described in this section, the mortality table set forth in § 1.72-7(c)(1) must be used to determine—

(1) The amount held by an insurer with respect to a beneficiary for purposes of section 101(d)(2) and § 1.101-4; and

(2) The period or periods with respect to which payments are to be made for purposes of section 101(d)(1) and § 1.101-4.

(b) *Examples.* The principles of this section may be illustrated by the following examples:

Example (1). A life insurance policy provides only for the payment of $5,000 per year for the life of the beneficiary, A, beginning with the insured's death. If A is 59 years of age at the time of the insured's death, the period with respect to which the payments are to be made is 25 years. This period is determined by using the mortality table set forth in § 1.72-7(c)(1), and is shown in Table V of § 1.72-9 (which contains life expectancy tables determined using this mortality table). If the present value of the proceeds, determined by reference to the interest rate used by the insurance company and the mortality table set forth in § 1.72-7(c)(1), is $75,000, $3,000 of each $5,000 payment ($75,000 divided by 25) is excluded from the gross income of A.

Example (2). A life insurance policy provides for the payment of $82,500 in a lump sum to the beneficiary, A, at the death of the insured. Upon the insured's death, however, A selects an option for the payment of $2,000 per year for life and for the same amount to be paid after A's death to B for B's life. If A is 51 years of age and B is 28 years of age at the death of the insured, the period with respect to which the payments are to be made is 55 years. This period is determined by using the mortality table set forth in § 1.72-7(c)(1), and is shown in Table VI of § 1.72-9 (which contains life expectancy tables determined using this mortality table). Accordingly, $1,500 of each $2,000 payment ($82,500 divided by 55) is excluded from the gross income of the recipient.

(c) *Effective date.* This section applies to amounts received with respect to deaths occurring after October 22, 1986, in taxable years ending after October 22, 1986. [Reg. § 1.101-7.]

□ [*T.D.* 8161, 9-18-87. *Amended by T.D.* 8272, 11-17-89.]

[Reg. § 1.102-1]

§ 1.102-1. Gifts and inheritances.—(a) *General rule.* Property received as a gift, or received under a will or under statutes of descent and distribution, is not includible in gross income, although the income from such property is includible in gross income. An amount of principal paid under a marriage settlement is a gift. However, see section 71 and the regulations thereunder for rules relating to alimony or allowances paid upon divorce or separation. Section 102 does not apply to prizes and awards (see section 74 and § 1.74-1) nor to scholarships and fellowship grants (see section 117 and the regulations thereunder).

(b) *Income from gifts and inheritances.* The income from any property received as a gift, or under a will or statute of descent and distribution shall not be excluded from gross income under paragraph (a) of this section.

(c) *Gifts and inheritances of income.* If the gift, bequest, devise, or inheritance is of income from property, it shall not be excluded from gross income under paragraph (a) of this section. Section 102 provides a special rule for the treatment of certain gifts, bequests, devises, or inheritances which by their terms are to be paid, credited, or distributed at intervals. Except as provided in section 663(a)(1) and paragraph (d) of this section, to the extent any such gift, bequest, devise, or inheritance is paid, credited, or to be distributed out of income from property, it shall be considered a gift, bequest, devise, or inheritance of income from property. Section 102 provides the same treatment for amounts of income from property which is paid, credited, or to be distributed under a gift or bequest whether the gift or bequest is in terms of a right to payments at intervals (regardless of income) or is in terms of a right to income. To the extent the amounts in either case are paid, credited, or to be distributed at intervals out of income, they are not to be excluded under section 102 from the taxpayer's gross income.

(d) *Effect of subchapter J.* Any amount required to be included in the gross income of a beneficiary under sections 652, 662, or 668 shall be treated for purposes of this section as a gift, bequest, devise, or inheritance of income from property. On the other hand, any amount excluded from the gross income of a beneficiary under section 663(a)(1) shall be treated for purposes of this section as property acquired by gift, bequest, devise, or inheritance.

(e) *Income taxed to grantor or assignor.* Section 102 is not intended to tax a donee upon the same income which is taxed to the grantor of a trust or assignor of income under section 61 or sections 671 through 677, inclusive. [Reg. § 1.102-1.]

□ [*T.D.* 6220, 12-28-56.]

→ *Caution: Code Sec. 103 has been amended to remove special exempt bond issue rules and provide similar rules in Code Secs. 141–150.*←

[Reg. § 1.103-1]

§ 1.103-1. Interest upon obligations of a State, Territory, etc.—(a) Interest upon obligations of a State, territory, a possession of the United States, the District of Columbia, or any political subdivision thereof (hereinafter collectively or individually referred to as "State or local governmental unit") is not includable in gross income except as provided under section 103(c) and (d) and the regulations thereunder.

(b) Obligations issued by or on behalf of any State or local governmental unit by constituted authorities empowered to issue such obligations

are the obligations of such a unit. However, section 103(a)(1) and this section do not apply to industrial development bonds except as otherwise provided in section 103(c). See section 103(c) and §§ 1.103-7 through 1.103-12 for the rules concerning interest paid on industrial development bonds. See section 103(d) for rules concerning interest paid on arbitrage bonds. Certificates issued by a political subdivision for public improvements (such as sewers, sidewalks, streets, etc.) which are evidence of special assessments against specific property, which assessments become a lien against such property and which the political

→ *Caution: Code Sec. 103 has been amended to remove special exempt bond issue rules and provide similar rules in Code Secs. 141–150.*←

subdivision is required to enforce, are, for purposes of this section, obligations of the political subdivision even though the obligations are to be satisfied out of special funds and not out of general funds or taxes. The term "political subdivision", for purposes of this section denotes any division of any State or local governmental unit which is a municipal corporation or which has been delegated the right to exercise part of the sovereign power of the unit. As thus defined, a political subdivision of any State or local governmental unit may or may not, for purposes of this section, include special assessment districts so created, such as road, water, sewer, gas, light, reclamation, drainage, irrigation, levee, school, harbor, port improvement, and similar districts and divisions of any such unit. [Reg. § 1.103-1.]

☐ [*T.D. 6220, 12-28-56. Amended by T.D. 7199, 7-31-72.*]

[Reg. § 5c.103-1]

§ 5c.103-1. Leases and capital expenditures (Temporary).—For purposes of section 103(b)(6)(D) and § 1.103-10(b)(2)(iv)(*b*), the determination of whether property is leased and whether property is of a type that is ordinarily subject to a lease shall be made without regard to the characterization of the transaction as a lease under section 168(f)(8). [Temporary Reg. § 5c.103-1.]

☐ [*T.D. 7791, 10-20-81.*]

[Reg. § 5f.103-1]

§ 5f.103-1. Obligations issued after December 31, 1982, required to be in registered form (Temporary).—(a) *Registration; general rule.* Interest on a registration-required obligation (as defined in paragraph (b) of this section) shall not be exempt from tax notwithstanding section 103(a) or any other provision of law, exclusive of any treaty obligation of the United States, unless the obligation is issued in registered form (as defined in paragraph (c) of this section).

(b) *Registration-required obligation.* For purposes of this section, the term "registration-required obligation" means any obligation except any one of the following:

(1) An obligation not of a type offered to the public. The determination as to whether an obligation is not of a type offered to the public shall be based on whether similar obligations are in fact publicly offered or traded.

(2) An obligation that has a maturity at the date of issue of not more than 1 year.

(3) An obligation issued before January 1, 1983. An obligation first issued before January 1, 1983, shall not be considered to have been issued on or after that date merely as a result of the existence of a right on the part of the holder of such obligation to convert the obligation from registered form into bearer form, or as a result of the exercise of such a right.

(4) An obligation described in § 5f.163-1(c) (relating to certain obligations issued to foreign persons).

(c) *Registered form*—(1) *General rule.* An obligation issued after January 20, 1987, pursuant to a binding contract entered into after January 20, 1987, is in registered form if—

(i) The obligation is registered as to both principal and any stated interest with the issuer (or its agent) and transfer of the obligation may be effected only by surrender of the old instrument and either the reissuance by the issuer of the old instrument to the new holder or the issuance by the issuer of a new instrument to the new holder,

(ii) The right to the principal of, and stated interest on, the obligation may be transferred only through a book entry system maintained by the issuer (or its agent) (as described in paragraph (c)(2) of this section), or

(iii) The obligation is registered as to both principal and any stated interest with the issuer (or its agent) and may be transferred through both of the methods described in subdivisions (i) and (ii).

(2) *Special rule for registration of a book entry obligation.* An obligation shall be considered transferable through a book entry system if the ownership of an interest in the obligation is required to be reflected in a book entry, whether or not physical securities are issued. A book entry is a record of ownership that identifies the owner of an interest in the obligation.

(d) *Effective date.* The provisions of this section shall apply to obligations issued after December 31, 1982, unless issued on an exercise of a warrant for the conversion of a convertible obligation if such warrant or obligation was offered or sold outside the United States without registration under the Securities Act of 1933 and was issued before August 10, 1982.

(e) *Special rules.* The following special rules apply to obligations issued after January 20, 1987, pursuant to a binding contract entered into after January 20, 1987.

→ *Caution: Code Sec. 103 has been amended to remove special exempt bond issue rules and provide similar rules in Code Secs. 141–150.*←

(1) An obligation that is not in registered form under paragraph (c) of this section is considered to be in bearer form.

(2) An obligation is not considered to be in registered form as of a particular time if it can be transferred at that time or at any time until its maturity by any means not described in paragraph (c) of this section.

(3) An obligation that as of a particular time is not considered to be in registered form by virtue of subparagraph (2) of this paragraph (e) and that, during a period beginning with a later time and ending with the maturity of the obligation, can be transferred only by a means described in paragraph (c) of this section, is considered to be in registered form at all times during such period.

(f) *Examples.* The application of this section may be illustrated by the following examples:

Example (1). Municipality X publicly offers its general debt obligations to United States persons. The obligations have a maturity at issue exceeding 1 year. The obligations are registration-required obligations under § 5f.103-1(b). When individual A buys an obligation, X issues an obligation in A's name evidencing A's ownership of the principal and interest under the obligation. A can transfer the obligation only by surrendering the obligation to X and by X issuing a new instrument to the new holder. The obligation is issued in registered form.

Example (2). Municipality Y issues a single obligation on January 4, 1983 to Bank M provided that (i) Bank M will not at any time transfer any interest in the obligation to any person unless the transfer is recorded on Municipality Y's records (except by means of a transfer permitted in (ii) of this example) and (ii) interests in the obligation that are sold by Bank M (and any persons who acquire interests from M) will be reflected in book entries. C, an individual, buys an interest in Y's obligation from Bank M. Bank M receives the interest or principal payments with respect to C's interest in the obligation as agent for C. Bank M records interests in the Municipality Y obligation as agent of Municipality Y. Any transfer of C's interest must be reflected in a book entry in accordance with Bank M's agreement with Municipality Y. Since C's interest can only be transferred through a book entry system maintained by the issuer (or its agent), the obligation is considered issued in registered form. Interest received by C is excludable from gross income under section 103(a).

Example (3). Municipality Z wishes to sell its debt obligations having a maturity in excess of 1 year. The obligations are sold to Bank N, O, and P, all of which are located in Municipality Z. By their terms the obligations are freely transferable, although each of the banks has stated that it acquired the obligations for purposes of investment and not for resale. Obligations similar to the obligations sold by Municipality Z are traded in the market for municipal securities. The obligations issued by Municipality Z are of a type offered to the public and are therefore registration-required under § 5f.103-1(b).

Example (4). Corporation A issues an obligation that is registered with the corporation as to both principal and any stated interest. Transfer may be effected by the surrender of the old instrument and either the reissuance by the issuer of the old instrument to the new holder or the issuance by the issuer of a new instrument to the new holder. The obligation can be converted into a form in which the right to the principal of, or stated interest on, the obligation may be effected by physical transfer of the obligation. Under § 5f.103-1(c) and (e), the obligation is not considered to be in registered form and is considered to be in bearer form.

Example (5). Corporation B issues its obligations in a public offering in bearer definitive form. Beginning at X months after the issuance of the obligations, a purchaser (either the original purchaser or a purchaser in the secondary market) may deliver the definitive bond in bearer form to the issuer in exchange for a registration receipt evidencing a book entry record of the ownership of the obligation. The issuer maintains the book entry system. The purchaser identified in the book entry as the owner of record has the right to receive a definitive bearer obligation at any time. Under § 5f.103-1(c) and (e), the obligation is not considered to be issued in registered form and is considered to be issued in bearer form. All purchasers of the obligation are considered to hold an obligation in bearer form.

Example (6). Corporation C issues obligations in bearer form. A foreign person purchases a definitive bearer obligation and then sells it to a United States person. At the time of the sale, the United States person delivers the bearer obligation to Corporation C and receives an obligation that is identical except that the obligation is registered as to both principal and any stated interest with the issuer or its agent and may be transferred at all times until its maturity only through a means described in § 5f.103-1(c). Under

→ *Caution: Code Sec. 103 has been amended to remove special exempt bond issue rules and provide similar rules in Code Secs. 141–150.*←

§ 5f.103-1(e), the obligation is considered to be in registered form from the time it is delivered to Corporation C until its maturity.

(g) *Cross-references.* See section 103A(j)(1), for the registration requirement of certain mortgage subsidy bonds issued after December 31, 1981, and § 6a.103A-1(a)(5) for the definition of registered form for such obligations issued after December 31, 1981, and on or before December 31, 1982. See also section 103(h) (requiring registration of certain energy bonds issued on or after October 18, 1979). [Temporary Reg. § 5f.103-1.]

☐ [*T.D. 7852, 11-9-82. Amended by T.D. 8111, 12-16-86.*]

[Reg. § 1.103-2]

§ 1.103-2. **Dividends from shares and stock of Federal agencies or instrumentalities.**—(a) *Issued before March 28, 1942.*—(1) Section 26 of the Federal Farm Loan Act of July 17, 1916 (12 U.S.C. 931), provides that Federal land banks and Federal land bank associations, including the capital and reserve or surplus therein and the income derived therefrom, shall be exempt from taxation, except taxes upon real estate. Section 7 of the Federal Reserve Act of December 23, 1913 (12 U.S.C. 531), provides that Federal reserve banks, including the capital stock and surplus therein and the income derived therefrom, shall be exempt from taxation, except taxes upon real estate. Section 13 of the Federal Home Loan Bank Act (12 U.S.C. 1433) provides that the Federal Home Loan Bank including its franchise, its capital, reserves, and surplus, its advances, and its income shall be exempt from all taxation, except taxes upon real estate. Section 5(h) of the Home Owner's Loan Act of 1933 (12 U.S.C. 1464(h)) provides that shares of Federal savings and loan associations shall, both as to their value and the income therefrom, be exempt from all taxation (except surtaxes, estate, inheritance, and gift taxes) imposed by the United States. Under the above-mentioned provisions, income consisting of dividends on stock of Federal land banks, Federal land bank associations, Federal home loan banks, and Federal reserve banks is not, in the case of stock issued before March 28, 1942, includible in gross income. Income consisting of dividends on share accounts of Federal savings and loan associations is includible in gross income but, in the case of shares issued before March 28, 1942, is not subject to the normal tax on income. For taxability of such income in the case of such stock or shares issued on or after March 28, 1942, see section 6 of the Public Debt Act of 1942 (31

U.S.C. 742a) and paragraph (b) of this section. For the time at which a stock or share is issued within the meaning of this section, see paragraph (b) of this section.

(2) Regardless of the exemption from income tax of dividends paid on the stock of Federal reserve banks, dividends paid by member banks are treated like dividends of ordinary corporations.

(3) Dividends on the stock of the central bank for cooperatives, the production credit corporations, production credit associations, and banks for cooperatives, organized under the provisions of the Farm Credit Act of 1933 (12 U.S.C. 1138), constitute income to the recipients, subject to both the normal tax and surtax (see section 63 of the Farm Credit Act of 1933 (12 U.S.C. 1138c)).

(b) *Issued on or after March 28, 1942.* (1) By virtue of the provisions of section 6 of the Public Debt Act of 1942 (31 U.S.C. 742(a)), the tax exemption provisions set forth in paragraph (a) of this section with respect to income consisting of dividends on stock of the Federal land banks, Federal land bank associations, and Federal reserve banks, or on share accounts of Federal savings and loan associations, are not applicable in the case of dividends on such stock or shares issued on or after March 28, 1942.

(2) For the purposes of this section, a stock or share is deemed to be issued at the time and to the extent that payment therefor is made to the agency or instrumentality. The date of issuance of the certificate or other evidence of ownership of such stock or share is not determinative if payment is made at an earlier or later date. Where old stock is retired in exchange for new stock of a different character or preference, the new stock shall be deemed to have been issued at the time of the exchange rather than when the old stock was paid for. These rules may be illustrated by the following examples:

Example (1). A, the owner of an investment share account, consisting of 10 shares, in a Federal savings and loan association, has a single certificate issued before March 28, 1942, evidencing such ownership. In order that A may dispose of half of such shares, the association at his request issues, after March 27, 1942, two 5-share certificates in substitution for the 10-share certificate. The shares evidenced by the two new certificates are deemed to have been issued before March 28, 1942, the shares having been paid for before such date.

Reg. § 1.103-2(a)(1)

→ *Caution: Code Sec. 103 has been amended to remove special exempt bond issue rules and provide similar rules in Code Secs. 141–150.*←

Example (2). The X Bank, a member of a Federal reserve bank, owns 50 shares of Federal reserve bank stock, evidenced by a single stock certificate issued before March 28, 1942. On December 31, 1942, the X Bank reduces the amount of its capital stock, as a result of which it is required to reduce the amount of its Federal reserve bank stock to 40 shares. It surrenders the 50-share certificate to the Federal reserve bank and receives a new 40-share certificate. The 40 shares evidenced by such certificate are deemed to have been issued before March 28, 1942. On December 31, 1943, the X Bank increases the amount of its capital stock, as a result of which it is required to purchase 10 additional shares of the Federal reserve bank stock. The Federal reserve bank issues a 10-share certificate evidencing ownership of the new shares. Of the 50 shares then owned by the X Bank, 40 were issued prior to March 28, 1942, and 10 were issued after March 27, 1942.

Example (3). A, the owner of a savings share account in the amount of $100 in a Federal savings and loan association, has a passbook containing a certificate issued prior to March 28, 1942, evidencing such ownership. Subsequent to March 27, 1942, A deposits $10,000 in the account. With respect to the $10,000 deposit, the share is deemed to have been issued after March 27, 1942. [Reg. § 1.103-2.]

□ [*T.D. 6220, 12-28-56. Amended by T.D. 8129, 3-10-87.*]

[Reg. § 5c.103-2]

§ 5c.103-2. Leases and industrial development bonds (Temporary).—For purposes of section 103(b)(2), the determination of whether an obligation constitutes an industrial development bond shall be made without regard to the characterization of the transaction as a lease under section 168(f)(8). [Temporary Reg. § 5c.103-2.]

□ [*T.D. 7800, 12-28-81.*]

[Reg. § 5f.103-2]

§ 5f.103-2. Public approval of industrial development bonds (Temporary).—(a) *General rule.* An industrial development bond (within the meaning of § 1.103-7(b)(1)) issued after December 31, 1982, shall be treated as an obligation not described in section 103(a) unless it is issued as part of an issue which satisfies the public approval requirement of section 103(k) and paragraph (c) of this section or is described in the exceptions set forth in paragraph (b) of this section.

(b) *Exceptions*—(1) *No extension of maturity.* Paragraph (a) of this section does not apply to a refunding obligation if—

(i) It refunds an obligation which was approved under section 103(k) and this section (or which is treated as approved pursuant to paragraph (f) of this section), and

(ii) It has a maturity date which is not later than the maturity date of the obligation to be refunded.

(2) *Refunding of pre-July 1, 1982, obligation.* Paragraph (a) of this section does not apply to an obligation issued solely to refund an obligation which—

(i) Was issued before July 1, 1982, and

(ii) Has a term which does not exceed 3 years.

The term of an obligation is determined without regard to whether it is a refunding obligation. With respect to the refunding of an issue also containing obligations with terms which exceed 3 years, paragraph (b)(2) applies only if the refunding issue proceeds are used solely to refund obligations with terms not exceeding 3 years and to pay reasonable incidental costs of the refunding (*e.g.,* legal and accounting fees, printing costs, and rating fees) attributable thereto. Paragraph (b)(2) applies only to issues issued after December 31, 1982, the proceeds of which are used to refund issues issued prior to July 1, 1982. Thus, subsequent refundings of such refunding issues must satisfy the public approval requirement of section 103(k) and paragraph (c) of this section.

(c) *Public approval requirement*—(1) *In general.* An issue is publicly approved if prior to the date of issue the governmental unit(s) described in subparagraphs (2) and (3) this paragraph (c) approve the issue, in the manner described in paragraph (d) of this section. See paragraph (f) for rules pertaining to determining the scope of an approval and paragraph (g)(1) for the definition of "governmental unit".

(2) *Issuer approval.* The governmental unit (i) which will issue the obligations or (ii) on behalf of which the issue is to be issued must approve the issue ("issuer approval"). If the issuer is not a governmental unit, the governmental unit on behalf of which the issuer acts shall be determined in a manner consistent with determinations under § 1.103-1, and such unit must approve the issue. However, in the case of an issuer which issues obligations on behalf of more than one governmental unit (*e.g.,* an authority which acts for two

→ *Caution: Code Sec. 103 has been amended to remove special exempt bond issue rules and provide similar rules in Code Secs. 141–150.*←

countries), any one of such units may give the issuer approval required by this paragraph (c)(2).

(3) *Host approval.* Each governmental unit the geographic jurisdiction (as defined in paragraph (g)(4)) of which contains the site of a facility to be financed by the issue must approve the issue ("host approval"). However, if the entire site of a facility to be financed by the issue is within the geographic jurisdiction of more than one governmental unit within a State (counting the State as a governmental unit within such State), then any one of such units may provide host approval for the issue with respect to that facility. For purposes of this paragraph (c)(3), if property to be financed by the issue is located within two or more governmental units but not entirely within either of such units, each portion of the property which is located entirely within the smallest respective governmental units may be treated as a separate facility. The issuer approval (as described in paragraph (c)(2)) may be treated as a host approval if the governmental unit giving the issuer approval is also a governmental unit described in this paragraph (c)(3). See paragraph (e)(2) with respect to host approval by a governmental unit with no applicable elected representative.

(d) *Method of public approval.* For purposes of this section, an issue is approved by a governmental unit only if—

(1) An applicable elected representative (as defined in paragraph (e)) of such unit approves the issue following a public hearing (as defined in paragraph (g)(2)) held in a location which, under the facts and circumstances, is convenient for residents of the unit, and for which there was reasonable public notice (as defined in paragraph (g)(3)), or

(2) A referendum of the voters of the unit (as defined in paragraph (g)(5)) approves the issue.

An approval may satisfy the requirements of this section without regard to the authority under State or local law for the acts constituting such approval. The location of hearing will be presumed convenient for residents of the unit if it is located in the approving governmental unit's capital or seat of government. If more than one governmental unit is required to provide a public hearing, such hearings may be combined as long as the combined hearing is a joint undertaking that provides all of the residents of the participating governmental units (*i.e.,* those relying on such hearing as an element of public approval) a reasonable opportunity to be heard. The location of any combined hearing is presumed to provide a reasonable opportunity to be heard provided it is no farther than 100 miles from the seat of government of each participating governmental unit beyond whose geographic jurisdiction the hearing is conducted.

(e) *Applicable elected representative*—(1) *In general.* The applicable elected representative of a governmental unit means—

(i) Its elected legislative body,

(ii) Its chief elected executive officer,

(iii) In the case of a State, the chief elected legal officer of the State's executive branch of government, or

(iv) Any official elected by the voters of the unit and designated for purposes of this section by the unit's chief elected executive officer of by State or local law to approve issues for the unit.

For purposes of subdivisions (ii), (iii), and (iv) of this paragraph (e)(1), an official shall be considered elected by the voters of the unit only if he is popularly elected at-large by the voters of the governmental unit. If an official popularly elected at-large by the voters of a governmental unit is appointed or selected pursuant to State or local law to be the chief executive officer of the unit, such official is deemed to be an elected chief executive officer for purposes of this section but for no longer than his tenure as an official elected at-large. In the case of a bicameral legislature which is popularly elected, both chambers together constitute an applicable elected representative, but neither chamber does independently, unless so designated under paragraph (e)(1)(iv). If multiple elected legislative bodies of a governmental unit have independent legislative authority, however, the body with the more specific authority relating to the issue is the only legislative body described in paragraph (e)(1)(i) of this section. See paragraph (h), Example (7) of this section.

(2) *Governmental unit with no applicable elected representative.* (i) The applicable elected representatives of a governmental unit with no representative (but for this paragraph (e)(2) and section 103(k)(2)(E)(ii)) are deemed to be those of the next higher governmental unit (with an applicable elected representative) from which the governmental unit derives its authority. For purposes of this subparagraph (2), a governmental unit derives its authority from another unit which—

(A) Enacts a specific (*e.g.,* a provision in a State constitution, charter or statute) by or under which the governmental unit is created,

→ *Caution: Code Sec. 103 has been amended to remove special exempt bond issue rules and provide similar rules in Code Secs. 141–150.*←

(B) Otherwise empowers or approves the creation of the governmental unit, or

(C) Appoints members to the governing body of the governmental unit.

In the case of a governmental unit with no applicable elected representative (but for this paragraph (e)(2)), any unit described in subdivision (A), (B), or (C) of this paragraph (e)(2)(i) may be treated as the next higher unit, without regard to the relative status of all of such units under State law.

(ii) In the case of a host approval (as required under paragraph (e)(3) of this section), a unit may be treated as the next higher unit, only if—

(A) The facility is located within its geographic jurisdiction, and

(B) Eligible individuals, if any, residing at the site of the facility are entitled to vote for the applicable elected representative of that unit (as determined under this paragraph (e)).

(3) *On behalf of issuers.* In the case of an issuer which is not a governmental unit but which issues bonds on behalf of a governmental unit, the applicable elected representative is any applicable elected representative of the unit on behalf of which the bonds are issued. If the unit on behalf of which the bonds are issued has no applicable elected representative (but for paragraph (e)(2) of this section), the applicable elected representative of the governmental unit is determined in the manner described in paragraph (e)(2).

(f) *Scope of approval*—(1) *In general.* Public approval is required by section 103(x) and this section for issues of industrial development bonds, except as otherwise provided in paragraph (a) and (b) of this section. An issue is treated as approved if the governmental units (described in paragraph (c) of this section in relation to the issue) have approved either—

(i) The issue (by approving each facility to be financed), not more than one year before the date of issue, or

(ii) A plan of financing for each facility financed by the issue pursuant to which the issue in question is timely issued (as required in paragraph (f)(3) of this section).

In either case, the scope of the approval is determined by the information, as specified in paragraph (f)(2), contained in the notice of hearing (when required) and the approval.

(2) *Information required.* A facility is within the scope of an approval if the notice of hearing (when required) and the approval contain—

(i) A general, functional description of the type and use of the facility to be financed (*e.g.*, "a 10,000 square foot machine shop and hardware manufacturing plant", "400-room airport hotel building", "dock facility for supertankers", "convention center auditorium and sports arena with 25,000 seating capacity", "air and water pollution control facilities for oil refinery"),

(ii) The maximum aggregate face amount of obligations to be issued with respect to the facility,

(iii) The initial owner, operator, or manager of the facility,

(iv) The prospective location of the facility by its street address or, if none, by a general description designed to inform readers of its specific location.

An approval is valid for purposes of this section with respect to any issue used to provide publicly approved facilities, notwithstanding insubstantial deviations with respect to the maximum aggregate face amount of the bonds issued under the approval for the facility, the name of its initial owner, manager, or operator, or the type or location of the facility from that described in the approval. An approval or notice of public hearing will not be considered to be adequate if any of the items in subdivisions (i) through (iv) of this subparagraph (2), with respect to the facility to be financed, are unknown on the date of the approval or the date of the public notice.

(3) *Timely issuance pursuant to a plan of financing.* An issue is timely issued pursuant to a plan of financing for a facility if—

(i) The issue is issued no later than 3 years after the first issue pursuant to the plan, and

(ii) The first such issue in whole or in part issued pursuant to the plan was issued no later than 1 year after the date of approval.

(4) *Facility—definition.* For purposes of this paragraph (f), the term "facility" includes a tract or adjoining tracts of land, the improvements thereon and any personal property used in connection with such real property. Separate tracts of land (including improvements and connected personal property) may be treated as one facility only if they are used in an integrated operation.

(g) *Definitions.* For purposes of this section—
(1) *Governmental unit.* Governmental unit has the same meaning as in § 1.103-1. Thus, a govern-

Reg. § 5f.103-2(g)(1)

→ *Caution: Code Sec. 103 has been amended to remove special exempt bond issue rules and provide similar rules in Code Secs. 141–150.*←

mental unit is a State, territory, a possession of the United States, the District of Columbia, or any political subdivision thereof. The term "political subdivision" denotes any division of any State or local governmental unit which is a municipal corporation or which has been delegated the right to exercise part of the sovereign power of the unit.

(2) *Public hearing.* Public hearing means a forum providing a reasonable opportunity for interested individuals to express their views, both orally and in writing, on the proposed issue of bonds and the location and nature of a proposed facility to be financed. In general, a governmental unit may select its own procedure for the hearing, provided that interested individuals have a reasonable opportunity to express their views. Thus, it may impose reasonable requirements on persons who wish to participate in the hearing, such as a requirement that persons desiring to speak at the hearing so request in writing at least 24 hours before the hearing or that they limit their oral remarks to 10 minutes. For purposes of this public hearing requirement, it is not necessary, for example, that the applicable elected representative who will approve the bonds be present at the hearing, that a report on the hearing be submitted to that official, or that State administrative procedural requirements for public hearings in general be observed. However, compliance with such State procedural requirements (except those at variance with a specific requirement set forth in this section) will generally assure that the hearing satisfies the requirements of this section. The hearing may be conducted by any individual appointed or employed to perform such function by the governmental unit or its agencies, or by the issuer (if and on behalf of issuer). Thus, for example, for bonds to be issued by an authority that acts on behalf of a county, the hearing may be conducted by the authority, the county, or an appointee or employee of either.

(3) *Reasonable public notice.* Reasonable public notice means published notice which is reasonably designed to inform residents of the affected governmental units, including residents of the issuing unit and the governmental unit where a facility is to be located, of the proposed issue. The notice must state the time and place for the hearing and contain the information contained in paragraph (f)(2) of this section. Notice is presumed reasonable if published no fewer than 14 days before the hearing. Except in the locality of the facility, publication is presumed to be reasonably designed to inform residents of the approving governmental unit if given in the same manner and same locations as required of the approving governmental unit for any other purposes for which applicable State or local law specifies a notice of public hearing requirement (including laws relating to notice of public meetings of the governmental unit). Notice is presumed reasonably designed to inform affected residents in the locality of the facility only if published in one or more newspapers of general circulation available to residents of that locality or if announced by radio or television broadcast to those residents.

(4) *Geographic jurisdiction.* Geographic jurisdiction is the area encompassed by the boundaries prescribed by State or local law for a governmental unit or, if there are no such boundaries, the area in which a unit may exercise such sovereign powers that make that unit a governmental unit for purposes of § 1.103-1 and this section.

(5) *Voter referendum.* A voter referendum is a vote by the voters of the affected governmental unit conducted in the manner and at such a time as voter referenda on matters relating to governmental spending or bond issuances by the governmental unit under applicable State and local law.

(h) *Examples.* The provisions of this section may be illustrated by the following examples:

Example (1). State X proposes to issue an industrial development bond the proceeds of which are to finance a facility located entirely within the geographic jurisdiction of City Y (which is located in State X). Under the provisions of paragraph (c), only State X must approve the issue because State X is the issuer and the facility is to be located entirely within the State's geographic jurisdiction. Its applicable elected representative must approve the issue after the public notice and public hearing requirements are satisfied.

Example (2). (i) Industrial Development Authority X proposes to issue an industrial development bond the proceeds of which are to finance a facility located entirely within the geographic jurisdiction of City Y (which is located in State Z). Authority X acts on behalf of State Z. Under the provisions of paragraph (c), only State Z must approve the issue because State Z is the governmental unit on behalf of which Authority X, the issuer, is acting and the facility is to be located entirely within its geographic jurisdiction.

(ii) State Z has a governor, an elected bicameral legislature and an appointed attorney general who is the chief legal officer of State Z. Under the laws of State Z, the attorney general must approve any issue of industrial development

→ *Caution: Code Sec. 103 has been amended to remove special exempt bond issue rules and provide similar rules in Code Secs. 141–150.*←

bonds. The approval by the attorney general is not a sufficient approval under this section, since the attorney general is not an applicable elected representative within the meaning of this section. Under the provisions of paragraphs (d) and (e), either the governor, both chambers of the legislature or any popularly elected official of the State who is designated for this purpose by the governor or by State law must approve the issue after the public notice and public hearing requirements are satisfied.

Example (3). (i) County Y, a county in State X, proposes to issue an industrial development bond, the proceeds of which are to finance a facility located entirely within its jurisdiction. Under the provisions of paragraph (c), only County Y must approve the issue because County Y is the issuer and the facility is to be located entirely within the geographic jurisdiction of County Y.

(ii) County Y has no elected officials or legislature. County Y derives its authority from State X which is the next higher governmental unit with an applicable elected representative. The laws of State X designate the attorney general, who is an official of State X elected at-large, as the official who must approve any issue of industrial development bonds for the State. Under this section, State X's attorney general is an applicable elected representative who may approve the issue after the public notice and public hearing requirements are satisfied.

Example (4). (i) City X, a city located in County Y and State Z, proposes to issue an industrial development bond, the proceeds of which are to finance a facility located entirely within the geographic jurisdiction of City X. Under the provisions of paragraph (c), only City X must approve the issue because it is the issuer and the facility is to be located entirely within the geographic jurisdiction of City X.

(ii) Mayor A, the chief elected executive officer of City X, has designated, for purposes of this section, Deputy Mayor B, an official of City X elected at-large, to approve industrial development bond issues for the city. Under the provisions of paragraph (e), Deputy Mayor B may approve the issue, since he is an applicable elected representative, after the public notice and public hearing requirements are satisfied.

Example (5). (i) County M proposes to issue an industrial development bond to finance a project located partly within the geographic jurisdiction of County M and partly within the geographic jurisdiction of County N. Both counties are located in State X. The part of the project in

County N is also located partly within the geographic jurisdiction of City O and partly within the geographic jurisdiction of City P. Under the provisions of paragraph (c)(2), County M must give issuer approval. Additionally, under the provisions of paragraph (c)(3), either State X, County N, or both Cities O and P, must give host approval.

(ii) Counties M and N will approve the issue, but neither has any officials who are elected at-large by the voters of the respective governmental units. Both governmental units derive their authority from State X which is the next higher governmental unit with an applicable elected representative. Under the provisions of paragraph (e), an applicable elected representative of State X must approve the issue for Counties M and N after the public notice and public hearing requirements are satisfied.

Example (6). (i) County M proposes to issue an industrial development bond to finance two facilities. One facility is located entirely within the geographic jurisdiction of County M and the second facility is located partly within the geographic jurisdiction of County M and partly within the geographic jurisdiction of County N. The second facility is also located within the geographic jurisdictions of Cities O and P, which cities are located within the geographic jurisdiction of County N. Under the provisions of paragraph (c)(2), County M must give issuer approval. Additionally, under the provisions of paragraph (c)(3), either State X, County N, or both Cities O and P, must give host approval.

(ii) Counties M and N will approve the issue. Each has a chief elected executive officer. Under the provisions of paragraphs (d) and (e), the chief elected executive officer of each county may approve the issue, after the public notice and public hearing requirements are satisfied.

Example (7). (i) State X proposes to issue an industrial development bond to finance a facility located partly within the geographic jurisdiction of State X and partly within the geographic jurisdiction of State Y. That portion of the facility located in State Y is located entirely within the geographic jurisdiction of City Z. State X must give issuer approval. Additionally, either State Y or City Z must give host approval as that part of the facility to be located outside State X will be entirely within the geographic jurisdiction of each unit.

(ii) Under the provisions of paragraphs (d) and (e), the governor of State X may approve the issue after the public notice and public hearing

→ *Caution: Code Sec. 103 has been amended to remove special exempt bond issue rules and provide similar rules in Code Secs. 141–150.*←

requirements are satisfied. City Z (assuming that it gives host approval for the bond) has a city council and a school board, both of which are elected legislative bodies with independent jurisdiction. The authority of the school board is limited under State law to matters directly concerning the provision of public education. Under paragraph (e) the school board is not an applicable elected representative of City Z but the city council is an applicable elected representative of City Z. The city council may approve the issue after the public hearing and public notice requirements are satisfied.

Example (8). (i) Public Housing Authority M, a governmental unit, proposes to issue an industrial development bond to finance several housing projects with known sites located entirely within its geographic jurisdiction. M's geographic jurisdiction is coextensive with the combined geographic jurisdictions of Counties N and O. The projects are separately owned and managed. They are not adjacent to each other. The projects also are located in County N. Under the provisions of paragraph (c), M must give issuer approval.

(ii) M, which has no elected officials or legislature, was created by both Counties N and O pursuant to a special statute of State Q permitting such a joint undertaking. Both Counties N and O have an applicable elected representative. Under the provisions of paragraph (e)(2), either County N, County O, or State Q is deemed to be the next higher governmental unit with an applicable elected representative, and an applicable elected representative from any of these units may give the issuer approval for Authority M. Therefore, either the applicable representative of County N, County O, or State Q can give the issuer approval for Authority M.

(iii) For purposes of the host approval, the issuer approval by M will satisfy the host approval requirement only if the applicable elected representative of County N or State Q gives issuer approval for M. Under the provisions of paragraph (e)(2), the host approval requirement is satisfied only if qualified persons residing at the site of the facility are entitled to vote for the applicable elected representative who gave the approval (*i.e.*, the representative of State Q or County N). However, if the applicable elected representative of O gave issuer approval for Authority M, a separate host approval would be required because the residents of the sites where the projects are located (*i.e.*, County N) could not vote for the applicable elected representative of County O.

(iv) Public Housing Authority M conducts a public hearing concerning prospective housing projects following notice thereof published in a newspaper of general circulation in County N. Additionally, M provides notice to the residents of O (which are also within M's jurisdiction) in the manner required for notice of public hearing for other purposes under State Q law. Following the public hearing, the chief elected executive officer of County N approves for Authority M prospective issues for the project. M issues two $7 million issues, one for each project. One issue is issued six months after the date of approval; the second issue is issued thirteen months thereafter. On these facts, only the first issue satisfied the public approval requirement of this section. [Temporary Reg. § 5f.103-2.]

☐ [*T.D.* 7892, 5-6-83.]

[Reg. § 1.103-3]

§ 1.103-3. Interest upon notes secured by mortgages executed to Federal agencies or instrumentalities.—Section 26 of the Federal Farm Loan Act (12 U.S.C. 931), and section 210 of such act, as added by section 2 of the act of March 4, 1923 (12 U.S.C. 1111), provide that first mortgages executed to Federal land banks, joint-stock land banks, or Federal intermediate credit banks, and the income derived therefrom, shall be exempt from taxation. Accordingly, income consisting of interest on promissory notes held by such banks and secured by such first mortgages is not subject to the income tax. [Reg. § 1.103-3.]

☐ [*T.D.* 6220, 12-28-56.]

[Reg. § 5c.103-3]

§ 5c.103-3. Leases and arbitrage.—In the case of a sale and leaseback transaction qualifying under section 168(f)(8), where the lessee's rental payments are substantially equal in timing and amount to the principal and interest payments on the lessor's note, the arbitrage provisions of section 103(c) and §§ 1.103-13, 1.103-14, and 1.103-15 shall apply to any obligations of the lessee (or party related to the lessee) without regard to the section 168(f)(8) lease transaction. [Temporary Reg. § 5c.103-3]

☐ [*T.D.* 7800, 12-28-81.]

[Reg. § 5f.103-3]

§ 5f.103-3. Information reporting requirements for certain bonds (Temporary).—(a) *General rule.* Under section 103(l), any private purpose bond issued after December 31, 1982 (including any obligation issued thereafter to re-

Reg. § 1.103-3

→ *Caution: Code Sec. 103 has been amended to remove special exempt bond issue rules and provide similar rules in Code Secs. 141–150.*←

fund private purpose bonds issued before December 31, 1982) shall be treated as an obligation not described in section 103(a) unless the information reporting requirement (as described in paragraph (c) of this section) is substantially satisfied with respect to the issue of which the bond is a part. For rules concerning bonds issued after December 31, 1986, see § 1.149(e)-1 of this chapter.

(b) *Private purpose bonds.* For purposes of this section, the term "private purpose bond" means—

(1) Any industrial development bond (as defined in section 103(b)(2) and § 1.103-7(b)(1)), or

(2) Any obligation which is issued as part of an issue all or a major portion of the proceeds of which are to be used directly or indirectly—

(i) To finance loans to individuals for educational or related expenses (hereinafter referred to as a "student loan bond"), or

(ii) By an organization described in section 501(c)(3) which is exempt from taxation by reason of section 501(a) (hereinafter referred to as "private exempt entity bond").

The meaning of the terms "major portion" and "directly or indirectly" shall be the same as under § 1.103-7. Student loan bonds include, but are not limited to, qualified scholarship funding bonds (as defined in section 103(e)).

(c) *Information required.* An obligation satisfies the requirements of section 103(l) and this section only if it is issued as part of an issue with respect to which the issuer, based on information and reasonable expectations determined as of the date of issue, submits on Form 8038 the information required therein, including—

(1) The name, address, and employer identification number of the issuer,

(2) The date of issue (as defined in paragraph (g)(1)),

(3) The face amount of the issue,

(4) The total purchase price of the issue,

(5) The amount allocated to a reasonably required reserve or replacement fund,

(6) The amount of lendable proceeds (as defined in paragraph (g)(4) of this section),

(7) The stated interest rate of each maturity (as defined in paragraph (g)(2) of this section) or, if the interest rate is variable, a description of the method under which the interest rate is computed,

(8) The term (as defined in paragraph (g)(3)) of each maturity,

(9) A general description of the property to be financed by the issue (including property financed by an obligation that will be refunded with the issue proceeds) which includes—

(i) The type of bond issued, that is, a student loan bond, a private exempt entity bond, or an industrial development bond and in the case of an industrial development bond described in section 103(b)(4), the subparagraph of section 103(b)(4) that describes the property, *e.g.,* for a football stadium, that the property is described in section 103(b)(4)(B),

(ii) The recovery classes (as defined in section 168(c)(2)), if applicable, of the various items of financed property and the approximate amount of lendable proceeds attributable thereto,

(iii) The approximate amount of lendable proceeds attributable to land or other property not described in subdivision (ii),

(iv) In the case of obligations described in section 103(b)(6) or private exempt entity bonds, the four-digit Standard Industrial Classification Code of the facilities financed.

(10) If section 103(k) (relating to public approval requirement for industrial development bonds) applies to such issue, the name(s) of the approving governmental unit(s) and of the applicable elected representative(s) (as defined in section 103(k)(2)(E) and § 5f.103-2(e)) or a description of the voter referendum that approved the issue for such unit(s).

(11) The name, address, and employer identification number of—

(i) Each initial principal user (as defined in paragraph (g)(5) of this section) of any facilities provided with the proceeds of the issue,

(ii) The common parent, if any, of any affiliated group of corporations (as defined in section 1504(a) but determined without regard to the exceptions of section 1504(b)) of which such initial principal user is a member, and

(iii) Any person (not included under paragraph (c)(11)(i)) that is treated as a principal user under section 103(b)(6)(L), but only if the issue is treated as a separate issue under section 103(b)(6)(K).

The information to be supplied must be determined based on information and reasonable expectations as of the date of issue. Therefore, such statement need not be amended to report information learned subsequent to the date of issue. However, if the statement is filed after the date of issue it may reflect such information and the

Reg. § 5f.103-3(c)(11)

→ *Caution: Code Sec. 103 has been amended to remove special exempt bond issue rules and provide similar rules in Code Secs. 141–150.*←

reasonable expectations of the issuer as of that date.

(d) *Additional information.* An issuer may supply the following information—

(1) The average maturity of the issue (as defined in section 103(b)(14)), and

(2) The average reasonably expected economic life (as defined in section 103(b)(14)) of the facility which is financed with the issue.

(e) *Time for filing.* The statement required by section 103(l) and this section shall be filed not later than the 15th day of the 2nd calendar month after the close of the calendar quarter in which the obligation is issued. It may be filed at any time before such date but must be complete based on facts and reasonable expectations as of the date of issue. The Secretary may grant an extension of time for filing the statement required under section 103(l) and this section if there is reasonable cause for the failure to file such statement in a timely fashion.

(f) *Place for filing.* Form 8038 is to be mailed to the Internal Revenue Service Center, Philadelphia, Pennsylvania 19255.

(g) *Definitions.* For purposes of this section—

(1) The term "date of issue" means the date on which the issuer physically exchanges the first of the obligations which are part of the issue for the underwriter's (or other purchaser's) funds. In the event that amounts are periodically advanced with respect to an issue, the date of issue is when the first of such obligations under the issue is created and the funds are advanced.

(2) The term "maturity" means those obligations of the issue having both the same maturity date and the same stated interest rate.

(3) The term "term of an issue" means the duration of the period beginning on the date of issue and ending on the latest maturity date of any obligation of the issue without regard to optional redemption dates.

(4) The term "lendable proceeds" means the amount of the original proceeds, net of amounts allocated to a reasonably required reserve or replacement fund. See generally § 1.103-13(b) and § 1.103-14(d) for further definitions.

(5) The term "initial principal user" means each person who as of the date of issue is obligated to use the facility to such an extent that under section 103(b)(6) such person would be treated as a principal user. With respect to organizations described in section 501(c)(3), however, such determination is made without regard to whether

such organization is treated as an exempt organization under section 103(b)(3) and § 1.103-7(b)(2). [Temporary Reg. § 5f.103-3.]

☐ [*T.D. 7892, 5-6-83. Amended by T.D. 8129, 3-10-87 and T.D. 8425, 8-11-92.*]

[Reg. § 1.103-4]

§ 1.103-4. Interest upon United States obligations.—(a) *Issued before March 1, 1941.* (1) Interest upon obligations of the United States issued on or before September 1, 1917, is exempt from tax. In the case of obligations issued by the United States after September 1, 1917, and in the case of obligations of a corporation organized under act of Congress, if such corporation is an instrumentality of the United States, the interest is exempt from tax only if and to the extent provided in the acts authorizing the issue thereof, as amended and supplemented.

(2) Interest on Treasury bonds issued before March 1, 1941, is exempt from Federal income taxes except surtaxes imposed upon the income or profits of individuals, associations, or corporations. However, interest on an aggregate of not exceeding $5,000 principal amount of such bonds is also exempt from surtaxes. Interest in excess of the interest on an aggregate of not exceeding $5,000 principal amount of such bonds is subject to surtax and must be included in gross income.

(3) Interest credited to postal savings accounts upon moneys deposited before March 1, 1941, in postal savings banks is wholly exempt from income tax.

(b) *Issued on or after March 1, 1941.* (1) Under the provisions of sections 4 and 5 of the Public Debt Act of 1941 (31 U.S.C. 742(a)), interest upon obligations issued on or after March 1, 1941, by the United States, or any agency or instrumentality thereof, shall not have any exemption, as such, from Federal income tax except in respect of any such obligations which the Federal Maritime Board and Maritime Administration (formerly United States Maritime Commission) or the Federal Housing Administration has, before March 1, 1941, contracted to issue at a future date. The interest on such obligations so contracted to be issued shall bear such tax-exemption privileges as were at the time of such contract provided in the law authorizing their issuance. For the purposes hereof, under section 4(a) of the Public Debt Act of 1941, a Territory and a possession of the United States (or any political subdivisions thereof), and the District of Columbia, and any agency or instrumentality of any one or more of

→ *Caution: Code Sec. 103 has been amended to remove special exempt bond issue rules and provide similar rules in Code Secs. 141–150.*←

the foregoing, shall not be considered as an agency or instrumentality of the United States.

(2) In the case of obligations issued as the result of a refunding operation, as, for example, where a corporation exchanges bonds for previously issued bonds, the refunding obligations are deemed, for the purposes of this section, to have been issued at the time of the exchange rather than at the time the original bonds were issued. [Reg. § 1.103-4.]

☐ [*T.D.* 6220, 12-28-56.]

[Reg. § 1.103-5]

§ 1.103-5. Treasury bond exemption in the case of trusts or partnerships.—(a) When the income of a trust is taxable to beneficiaries, as in the case of a trust the income of which is to be distributed to the beneficiaries currently, each beneficiary is entitled to exemption as if he owned directly a proportionate part of the Treasury bonds held in trust. When, on the other hand, income is taxable to the trustee, as in the case of a trust the income of which is accumulated for the benefit of unborn or unascertained persons, the trust, as the owner of the bonds held in trust, is entitled to the exemption on account of such ownership. In general, see sections 552(b) and 662(b) and the regulations thereunder.

(b) As the income of a partnership is taxable to the individual partners, each partner is entitled to exemption as if he owned directly a proportionate part of the bonds held by the partnership. For rules relating to partially tax-exempt interest see section 702(a)(7) and the regulations thereunder. [Reg. § 1.103-5.]

☐ [*T.D.* 6220, 12-28-56.]

[Reg. § 1.103-6]

§ 1.103-6. Interest upon United States obligations in the case of nonresident aliens and foreign corporations, not engaged in business in the United States.—By virtue of section 4 of the Victory Liberty Loan Act of March 3, 1919 (31 U.S.C. 750), amending section 3 of the Fourth Liberty Bond Act of July 9, 1918 (31 U.S.C. 750), the interest received on and after March 3, 1919, on bonds, notes, and certificates of indebtedness of the United States while beneficially owned by a nonresident alien individual, or a foreign corporation, partnership, or association, if such individual, corporation, partnership, or association is not engaged in business in the United States, is exempt from income taxes. Such exemption applies only to such bonds, notes, or certificates as have been issued before March 1, 1941. Interest de-

rived by a nonresident alien individual, or by a foreign corporation, partnership, or association on such bonds, notes, or certificates issued on or after March 1, 1941, is subject to tax as in the case of taxpayers generally as provided in paragraph (b) of § 1.103-4. [Reg. § 1.103-6.]

☐ [*T.D.* 6220, 12-28-56.]

[Reg. § 1.103-7]

§ 1.103-7. Industrial development bonds.—(a) *In general.* Under section 103(c)(1) and this section an industrial development bond issued after April 30, 1968, shall be treated as an obligation not described in section 103(a)(1) and § 1.103-1. Accordingly, interest paid on such a bond is includable in gross income unless the bond was issued by a State or local governmental unit to finance certain exempt facilities (see section 103(c)(4) and § 1.103-8), to finance an industrial park (see section 103(c)(5) and § 1.103-9), or as part of an exempt small issue (see section 103(c)(6) and § 1.103-10). For applicable rules when an industrial development bond is held by a substantial user (or a person related to a substantial user) of such an exempt facility, or an industrial park, or a facility financed with the proceeds of such an exempt small issue, see section 103(c)(7) and § 1.103-11. See also § 1.103-12 for the transitional provisions concerning the interest paid on certain industrial development bonds issued before January 1, 1969, and certain other industrial development bonds. Even if section 103(c) does not prevent a bond from being treated as an obligation described in section 103(a)(1) and § 1.103-1, such bond shall nevertheless be treated as an obligation which is not described in section 103(a)(1) and § 1.103-1 if under section 103(d) it is an arbitrage bond. For purposes of section 103(c), the term "issue" includes a single obligation such as a single note issued in connection with a bank loan as well as a series of notes or bonds.

(b) *Industrial development bonds*—(1) *Definition.* For purposes of this section, the term "industrial development bond" means any obligation—

(i) Which is issued as part of an issue all or a major portion of the proceeds of which are to be used directly or indirectly in any trade or business carried on by any person who is not an exempt person (as defined in subparagraph (2) of this paragraph), and

(ii) The payment of the principal or interest on which, under the terms of such obligation or any underlying arrangement (as described in sub-

Reg. § 1.103-7(b)(1)

→ *Caution: Code Sec. 103 has been amended to remove special exempt bond issue rules and provide similar rules in Code Secs. 141–150.*←

paragraph (4) of this paragraph), is in whole or in major part (*i.e.*, major portion)—

(*a*) Secured by any interest in property used or to be used in a trade or business,

(*b*) Secured by any interest in payments in respect of property used or to be used in a trade or business, or

(*c*) To be derived from payments in respect of property, or borrowed money, used or to be used in a trade or business.

See subparagraphs (3) and (4) of this paragraph for the trade or business test and the security interest test respectively, See § 1.103-8(a)(6) to determine the amount of proceeds of an issue for which the amount payable during each annual period over the term of the issue is less than the amount of interest accruing thereon in such period, *e.g.*, in the case of an issue sold by the issuer for less than its face amount.

(2) *Exempt person.* The term "exempt person" means a governmental unit as defined in this subparagraph, or an organization which is described in section 501(c)(3) and this subparagraph and is exempt from taxation under section 501(a). For purposes of this subparagraph, the term "governmental unit" means a State or local governmental unit (as defined in § 1.103-1). For purposes of this subparagraph, the term "governmental unit" also includes the United States of America (or an agency or instrumentality of the United States of America), but only in the case of obligations (i) issued on or before August 3, 1972, or (ii) issued after August 3, 1972, with respect to which a bond resolution or any other official action was taken and in reliance on such action either (*a*) construction of such facility to be financed with such obligations commenced or (*b*) a binding contract was entered into, or an irrevocable bid was submitted, prior to August 3, 1972, or (iii) issued after August 3, 1972, with respect to a program approved by Congress prior to such date but only if (*a*) a portion of such program has been financed by obligations issued prior to such date, to which section 103(a) applied pursuant to a ruling issued by the Commissioner or his delegate prior to such date and (*b*) construction of one or more facilities comprising a part of such program commenced prior to such date. For purposes of this subparagraph, a tax-exempt organization is an exempt person only with respect to a trade or business it carries on which is not an unrelated trade or business. Whether a particular trade or business carried on by a tax-exempt organization is an unrelated trade or business is determined by

applying the rules of section 513(a) (relating to general rule for unrelated trade or business) and the regulations thereunder to the tax-exempt organization without regard to whether the organization is an organization subject to the tax imposed by section 511 (relating to imposition of tax on unrelated business income of charitable, etc., organizations).

(3) *Trade or business test.* (i) The trade or business test relates to the use of the proceeds of a bond issue. The test is met if all or a major portion of the proceeds of a bond issue is used in a trade or business carried on by a nonexempt person. For example, if all or a major portion of the proceeds of a bond issue is to be loaned to one or more private business users, or is to be used to acquire, construct, or reconstruct facilities to be leased or sold to such private business users, and such proceeds or facilities are to be used in trades or businesses carried on by them, such proceeds are to be used in a trade or business carried on by persons who are not exempt persons, and the debt obligations comprising the bond issue satisfy the trade or business test. If, however, less than a major portion of the proceeds of an issue is to be loaned to nonexempt persons or is to be used to acquire or construct facilities which will be used in a trade or business carried on by a nonexempt person, the debt obligations will not be industrial development bonds. Also, when publicly-owned facilities which are intended for general public use, such as toll roads or bridges, are constructed with the proceeds of a bond issue and used by nonexempt persons in their trades or businesses on the same basis as other members of the public, such use does not constitute a use in the trade or business of a nonexempt person for purposes of the trade or business test.

(ii) In determining whether a debt obligation meets the trade or business test, the indirect, as well as the direct, use of the proceeds is to be taken into account. For example, the debt obligations comprising a bond issue do not fail to satisfy the trade or business test merely because the State or local governmental unit uses the proceeds to engage in a series of financing transactions for property to be used by private business users in trades or businesses carried on by them. Similarly, if such proceeds are to be used to construct facilities to be leased or sold to any nonexempt person for use in a trade or business it carries on, such proceeds are to be used in a trade or business carried on by a nonexempt person and the debt obligations comprising such issue satisfy the trade or business test. If such proceeds are to be used to

Reg. § 1.103-7(b)(2)

→ *Caution: Code Sec. 103 has been amended to remove special exempt bond issue rules and provide similar rules in Code Secs. 141–150.*←

construct facilities to be leased or sold to an exempt person who will, in turn, lease or sell the facilities to a nonexempt person for use in a trade or business, such proceeds are to be used in a trade or business carried on by a nonexempt person and the debt obligations comprising such issue satisfy the trade or business test. In addition, proceeds will be treated as being used in the trade or business of a nonexempt person in situations involving other arrangements, whether in a single transaction or in a series of transactions, whereby a nonexempt person uses property acquired with the proceeds of a bond issue in its trade or business.

(iii) The use of more than 25 percent of the proceeds of an issue of obligations in the trades or businesses of nonexempt persons will constitute the use of a major portion of such proceeds in such manner. In the case of the direct or indirect use of the proceeds of an issue of obligations or the direct or indirect use of a facility constructed, reconstructed, or acquired with such proceeds, the use by all nonexempt persons in their trades or businesses must be aggregated to determine whether the trade or business test is satisfied. If more than 25 percent of the proceeds of a bond issue is used in the trades or businesses of nonexempt persons, the trade or business test is satisfied. For special rules with respect to the acquisition of the output of facilities, see subparagraph (5) of this paragraph.

(4) *Security interest test.* The security interest test relates to the nature of the security for, and the source of, the payment of either the principal or interest on a bond issue. The nature of the security for, and the source of, the payment may be determined from the terms of the bond indenture or on the basis of an underlying arrangement. An underlying arrangement to provide security for, or the source of, the payment of the principal or interest on an obligation may result from separate agreements between the parties or may be determined on the basis of all the facts and circumstances surrounding the issuance of the bonds. The property which is the security for, or the source of, the payment of either the principal or interest on a debt obligation need not be property acquired with bond proceeds. The security interest test is satisfied if, for example, a debt obligation is secured by unimproved land or investment securities used, directly or indirectly, in any trade or business carried on by any private business user. A pledge of the full faith and credit of a State or local governmental unit will not prevent a debt obligation from otherwise satisfying the security interest test. For example, if the payment of either the principal or interest on a bond issue is secured by both a pledge of the full faith and credit of a State or local governmental unit and any interest in property used or to be used in a trade or business, the bond issue satisfies the security interest test. For rules with respect to the acquisition of the output of facilities, see subparagraph (5) of this paragraph.

(5) *Trade or business test and security interest test with respect to certain output contracts.* (i) The use by one or more nonexempt persons of a major portion of the subparagraph (5) output of facilities such as electric energy, gas, or water facilities constructed, reconstructed, or acquired with the proceeds of an issue satisfies the trade or business test and the security interest test if such use has the effect of transferring to nonexempt persons the benefits of ownership of such facilities, and the burdens of paying the debt service on governmental obligations used directly or indirectly to finance such facilities, so as to constitute the indirect use by them of a major portion of such proceeds. Such benefits and burdens are transferred and a major portion of the proceeds of an issue is used indirectly by the users of the subparagraph (5) output of such a facility which is owned and operated by an exempt person where—

(a)(1) One nonexempt person agrees pursuant to a contract to take, or to take or pay for, a major portion (more than 25 percent) of the subparagraph (5) output (within the meaning of subdivision (ii) of this subparagraph) of such a facility (whether or not conditional upon the production of such output) or (2) two or more nonexempt persons, each of which pays annually a guaranteed minimum payment exceeding 3 percent of the average annual debt service with respect to the obligations in question, agree, pursuant to contracts, to take, or to take or pay for, a major portion (more than 25 percent) of the subparagraph (5) output of such a facility (whether or not conditioned upon the production of such output), and

(b) Payment made or to be made with respect to such contract or contracts by such nonexempt person or persons exceeds a major part (more than 25 percent) of the total debt service with respect to such issue of obligations.

(ii) For purposes of this subparagraph—

(a) Where a contract described in subdivision (i) of this subparagraph may be extended by the issuer of obligations described therein, the term of the contract shall be considered to include

Reg. § 1.103-7(b)(5)

→ *Caution: Code Sec. 103 has been amended to remove special exempt bond issue rules and provide similar rules in Code Secs. 141–150.*←

the period for which such contract may be so extended.

(*b*) The subparagraph (5) output of a facility shall be determined by multiplying the number of units produced or to be produced by the facility in one year by the number of years in the contract term of the issue of obligations issued to provide such facility. The number of units produced or to be produced by a facility in one year shall be determined by reference to its nameplate capacity (or where there is no nameplate capacity, its maximum capacity) without any reduction for reserves or other unutilized capacity. The contract term of an issue begins on the date the output of a facility is first taken, pursuant to a take or a take or pay contract, by a nonexempt person and ends on the latest maturity date of any obligation of the issue (determined without regard to any optional redemption dates). If, however, on or before the date of issue of a prior issue of governmental obligations issued to provide a facility, the issuer makes a commitment in the bond indenture or related document to refinance such prior issue with one or more subsequent issues of governmental obligations, then the contract term of the issue shall be determined with regard to the latest redemption date of any obligation of the last such refinancing issue with respect to such facility (determined without regard to any optional redemption dates). Where it appears that the term of an issue (or the terms of 2 or more issues) is extended for purposes of extending the contract term of an issue and thereby increasing the subparagraph (5) output of the facility provided by such issue, the subparagraph (5) output of such facility shall be determined by the Commissioner without regard to the provisions of this subdivision (*b*).

(c) The total debt service with respect to an issue of obligations shall be the total dollar amount (excluding any penalties) payable with respect to such issue over its entire term. The entire term of an issue begins on its date of issue and ends on the latest maturity date of any obligation of the issue (determined without regard to any optional redemption dates). If, however, on or before the date of issue of a prior issue of governmental obligations the issuer makes a commitment of the bond indenture or related document to refinance such prior issue with one or more subsequent issues of governmental obligations, the entire term of the issue shall be determined with regard to the latest redemption date of any obligation of the last such refinancing issue (determined without regard to any optional redemption dates).

(*d*) Two or more nonexempt persons who are related persons (within the meaning of section 103(c)(6)(C)) shall be treated as one nonexempt person.

(c) *Examples.* The application of the rules contained in section 103(c)(2) and (3) and paragraph (b) of this section are illustrated by the following examples:

Example (1). State A and corporation X enter into an arrangement under which A is to provide a factory which X will lease for 20 years. The arrangement provides (1) that A will issue $10 million of bonds, (2) that the proceeds of the bond issue will be used to purchase land and to construct and equip a factory in accordance with X's specifications, (3) that X will rent the facility (land, factory, and equipment) for 20 years at an annual rental equal to the amount necessary to amortize the principal and pay the interest on the outstanding bonds, and (4) that such payments by X and the facility itself will be the security for the bonds. The bonds are industrial development bonds since they are part of an issue of obligations (1) all of the proceeds of which are to be used (by purchasing land and constructing and equipping the factory) in a trade or business by a nonexempt person, and (2) the payment of the principal and interest on which is secured by the facility and payments to be made with respect thereto.

Example (2). The facts are the same as in example (1) except that (1) X will purchase the facility, and (2) annual payments equal to the amount necessary to amortize the principal and pay the interest on the outstanding bonds will be made by X. The bonds are industrial development bonds for the reasons set forth in example (1).

Example (3). State B and corporation X enter into an arrangement under which B is to loan $10 million to X. The arrangement provides (1) that B will issue $10 million of bonds, (2) that the proceeds of the bond issue will be loaned to X to provide additional working capital and to finance the acquisition of certain new machinery, (3) that X will repay the loan in annual installments equal to the amount necessary to amortize the principal and pay the interest on the outstanding bonds, and (4) that the payments on the loan and the machinery will be the security for only the payment of the principal on the bonds. The bonds are industrial development bonds since they are part of an issue of obligations (1) all of the proceeds of which are to be used in a trade or business by a nonexempt person, and (2) the payment of the principal on which is secured by payments to be made in respect of property to be used in a trade

Reg. § 1.103-7(c)

→ *Caution: Code Sec. 103 has been amended to remove special exempt bond issue rules and provide similar rules in Code Secs. 141–150.*←

or business. The result would be the same if only the payment of the interest on the bonds were secured by payments on the loan and machinery.

Example (4). The facts are the same as in example (1), (2), or (3) except that the annual payments required to be made by corporation X exceed the amount necessary to amortize the principal and pay the interest on the outstanding bonds. The bonds are industrial development bonds for the reasons set forth in such examples. The fact that corporation X is required to pay an amount in excess of the amount necessary to pay the principal and interest on the bonds does not affect their status as industrial development bonds. Similarly, if the annual payments required to be made by corporation X were sufficient to pay only a major portion of either the principal or the interest on the outstanding bonds, the bonds would be industrial development bonds for the reasons set forth in such examples.

Example (5). The facts are the same as in example (1), (2), (3), or (4) except that the issuer is a political subdivision which has taxing power and the bonds are general obligation bonds. Since both the trade or business and the security interest tests are met, the bonds are industrial development bonds notwithstanding the fact that they constitute an unconditional obligation of the issuer payable from its general revenues.

Example (6). (a) State C issues its general obligation bonds to purchase land and construct a hotel for use by the general public (*i.e.,* tourists, visitors, travelers on business, etc.). The bond indenture provides (1) that C will own and operate the project for the period required to redeem the bonds, and (2) that the project itself and the revenues derived therefrom are the security for the bonds. The bonds are not industrial development bonds since (1) the proceeds are to be used by an exempt person in a trade or business carried on by such person, and (2) a major portion of such proceeds is not to be used, directly or indirectly, in a trade or business carried on by a nonexempt person. Use of the hotel by hotel guests who are travelling in connection with trades or businesses of nonexempt persons is not an indirect use of the hotel by such nonexempt persons for purposes of section 103(c).

(b) The facts are the same as in paragraph (a) of this example except that corporation Y enters into a long-term agreement with C that Y will rent more than one-fourth of the rooms on an annual basis for a period approximately equal to one half of the term of the bonds. The bonds are industrial development bonds because (1) a major

portion of the proceeds used to construct the hotel is to be used in the trade or business of corporation Y (a nonexempt person), and (2) a major portion of the principal and interest on such issue will be derived from payments in respect of the property used in the trade or business of Y.

Example (7). (a) State D and corporation Y enter into an agreement under which Y will lease for 20 years three floors of a 12-story office building to be constructed by D on land which it will acquire. D will occupy the grade floor and the remaining eight floors of the building. The portion of the costs of acquiring the land and constructing the building which are allocated to the space to be leased by Y is not in excess of 25 percent of the total costs of acquiring the land and constructing the building. Such costs, whether attributable to the acquisition of land or the construction of the building, were allocated to leased space in the same proportion that the reasonable rental value of such leased space bears to the reasonable rental value of the entire building. From the facts and circumstances presented, it is determined that such allocation was reasonable. The arrangement between D and Y provides that D will issue $10 million of bonds, that the proceeds of the bond issue will be used to purchase land and construct an office building, that Y will lease the designated floor space for 20 years at its reasonable rental value, and that such rental payments and the building itself shall be security for the bonds. The bonds are not industrial development bonds since a major portion of the proceeds is not to be used, directly or indirectly, in the trade or business of a nonexempt person.

(b) The facts are the same as in paragraph (a) of this example except that corporation Y will lease 4 floors, and the costs allocated to these floors are in excess of 25 percent of D's investment in the land and building. The bonds are industrial development bonds because (1) a major portion of the building is to be used in the trade or business of a nonexempt person, and (2) a major portion of the principal and interest on such issue is secured by the rental payments on the building.

Example (8). The facts are the same as in paragraph (b) of example (7) except that, instead of leasing any space to corporation Y, State D will lease the 4 floors to numerous unrelated private business users to be used in their trades or businesses. No lease will have a term exceeding 2 years. A major portion of the principal and interest will be paid from the revenues that D will derive from such leases. The fact that the activities of D, an exempt person, may amount to a

→ *Caution: Code Sec. 103 has been amended to remove special exempt bond issue rules and provide similar rules in Code Secs. 141–150.*←

trade or business of leasing property is not material, and the bonds are industrial development bonds for the reasons set forth in paragraph (b) of example (7). The result would be the same in the case of long-term leases.

Example (9). State E issues its obligations to finance the construction of dormitories for educational institution Z which is an organization described in section 501(c)(3) and exempt from tax under section 501(a). The dormitories are to be owned and operated by Z and their operation does not constitute an unrelated trade or business. The bonds are not industrial development bonds since the proceeds are to be used by an exempt person in a trade or business carried on by such person which is not an unrelated trade or business, as determined by applying section 513(a) to Z.

Example (10). State F issues its obligations to finance the construction of a toll road and the cost of erecting related facilities such as gasoline service stations and restaurants. Such related facilities represent less than 25 percent of the total cost of the project and are to be leased or sold to nonexempt persons. The toll road is to be owned and operated by F. The revenues from the toll road and from the rental of related facilities are the security for the bonds. The bonds are not industrial development bonds since a major portion of the proceeds is not to be used, directly or indirectly, in the trades or businesses of nonexempt persons. The fact that vehicles owned by nonexempt persons engaged in their trades or businesses may use the road in common with, or as a part of, the general public is not material.

Example (11). City G issues its obligations to finance the construction of a municipal auditorium which it will own and operate. The use of the auditorium will be open to anyone who wishes to use it for a short period of time on a rate-scale basis. The rights of such a user are only those of a transient occupant rather than the full legal possessory interests of a lessee. It is anticipated that the auditorium will be used by schools, church groups, and fraternities, and numerous commercial organizations. The revenues from the rentals of the auditorium and the auditorium building itself will be the security for the bonds. The bonds are not industrial development bonds because such use is not a use in the trade or business of a nonexempt person.

Example (12). The facts are the same as in example (11) except that one nonexempt person will have a 20-year rental agreement providing for exclusive use of the entire auditorium for more than three months of each year at a rental comparable to that charged short-term users. The bonds are industrial development bonds since such use is a use in the trade or business of a nonexempt person and, therefore, a major portion of the proceeds of the issue will be used in the trade or business of a nonexempt person and a major portion of the principal or interest on such issue will be secured by a facility used in such trade or business and by payments with respect to such facility.

Example (13). In order to construct an electric generating facility of a size sufficient to take advantage of the economies of scale: (1) City H will issue $50 million of its 25-year bonds and Z (a privately owned electric utility) will use $100 million of its funds for construction of a facility they will jointly own as tenants in common. (2) Each of the participants will share in the ownership, output, and operating expenses of the facility in proportion to its contribution to the cost of the facility, that is, one-third by H and two-thirds by Z. (3) H's bonds will be secured by H's ownership in the facility and by revenues to be derived from the sale of H's share of the annual output of the facility. (4) Because H will need only 50 percent of its share of the annual output of the facility, it agrees to sell to Z 25 percent of its share of such annual output for a period of 20 years pursuant to a contract under which Z agrees to take or pay for such power in all events. The facility will begin operation, and Z will begin to receive power, 4 years after the City H obligations are issued. The contract term of the issue will, therefore, be 21 years. (5) H also agrees to sell the remaining 25 percent of its share of the annual output to numerous other private utilities under a prevailing rate schedule including demand charges. (6) No contracts will be executed obligating any person other than Z to purchase any specified amount of the power for any specified period of time and no one such person (other than Z) will pay a demand charge or other minimum payment under conditions which, under paragraph (b)(5) of this section, result in a transfer of the benefits of ownership and the burdens of paying the debt service on obligations used directly or indirectly to provide such facilities. The bonds are not industrial development bonds because H's one-third interest in the facility (financed with bond proceeds) shall be treated as a separate property interest and, although 25 percent of H's interest in the annual output of the facility will be used directly or indirectly in the trade or business of Z, a nonexempt person, under the rule of paragraph (b)(5) of this section, such portion consti-

Reg. § 1.103-7(c)

→ *Caution: Code Sec. 103 has been amended to remove special exempt bond issue rules and provide similar rules in Code Secs. 141–150.*←

tutes less than a major portion of the subparagraph (5) output of the facility. If more than 25 percent of the subparagraph (5) output of the facility were to be sold to Z pursuant to the take or pay contract, the bonds would be industrial development bonds since they would be secured by H's ownership in the facility and revenues therefrom, and under the rules of paragraph (b)(5) of this section a major portion of the proceeds of the bond issue would be used in the trade or business of Z, a nonexempt person.

Example (14). J, a political subdivision of a State, will issue several series of bonds from time to time and will use the proceeds to rehabilitate urban areas. More than 25 percent of the proceeds of each issue will be used for the rehabilitation and construction of buildings which will be leased or sold to nonexempt persons for use in their trades or businesses. There is no limitation either on the number of issues or the aggregate amount of bonds which may be outstanding. No group of bondholders has any legal claim prior to any other bondholders or creditors with respect to specific revenues of J, and there is no arrangement whereby revenues from a particular project are paid into a trust or constructive trust, or sinking fund, or are otherwise segregated or restricted for the benefit of any group of bondholders. There is, however, an unconditional obligation by J to pay the principal and interest on each issue of bonds. Further, it is apparent that J requires the revenues from the lease or sale of buildings to nonexempt persons in order to pay in full the principal and interest on the bonds in question. The bonds are industrial development bonds because a major portion of the proceeds will be used in the trades or businesses of nonexempt persons and, pursuant to an underlying arrangement, payment of the principal and interest is, in major part, to be derived from payments in respect of property or borrowed money used in the trades or businesses of nonexempt persons.

Example (15). Power Authority K, a political subdivision created by the legislature in state X to own and operate certain power generating facilities, sells all of the power from its existing facilities to four private utility systems under contracts executed in 1970, whereby such four systems are required to take or pay for specified portions of the total power output until the year 2000. Currently, existing facilities supply all of the present needs of the four utility systems but their future power requirements are expected to increase substantially. K issues 20-year general obligation bonds to construct a large nuclear gen-

erating facility. A fifth private utility system contracts with K to take or pay for 30 percent of the subparagraph (5) output of the new facility. The balance of the power output of the new facility will be available for sale as required, but initially it is not anticipated there will be any need for such power. The revenues from the contract with the fifth private utility system will be sufficient to pay less than 25 percent of the principal or interest on the bonds. The balance, which will exceed 25 percent of the principal or interest on such bonds, will be paid from revenue from the contracts with the four systems from sale of power produced by the old facilities. The bonds will be industrial development bonds because a major portion of the proceeds will be used in the trade or business of a nonexempt person, and payment of the principal and interest, pursuant to an underlying arrangement, will be derived in major part from payments in respect of property used in the trades or businesses of nonexempt persons.

(d) *Certain refunding issues*—(1) *General rule.* In the case of an issue of obligations issued to refund the outstanding face amount of an issue of obligations, the proceeds of the refunding issue will be considered to be used for the purpose for which the proceeds of the issue to be refunded were used. The rules of this subparagraph shall apply regardless of the date of issuance of the issue to be refunded and shall apply to refunding issues to be issued to refund prior refunding issues.

(2) *Obligations issued prior to effective date.* In the case of an issue of obligations issued to refund the outstanding face amount of an issue of obligations issued on or before April 30, 1968 (or before January 1, 1969, if the transitional rules of § 1.103-12 are applicable) which would have been industrial development bonds within the meaning of section 103(c)(2) had they been issued after such date, the refunding issue shall not be considered to be an issue of industrial development bonds if it does not make funds available for any purpose other than the debt service on the obligations. For rules as to arbitrage bonds, see section 103(d).

(3) *Examples.* The provisions of this paragraph may be illustrated by the following examples:

Example (1). In 1969, State A issued $20 million of 20-year revenue bonds the proceeds of which were used to construct a sports facility which qualifies as an exempt facility described in section 103(c)(4)(B) and paragraph (c) of § 1.103-8. The sports facility will be owned and

Reg. § 1.103-7(d)(3)

→ *Caution: Code Sec. 103 has been amended to remove special exempt bond issue rules and provide similar rules in Code Secs. 141–150.*←

operated by X, a nonexempt person, for the use of the general public. In 1975, A issues $15 million of revenue bonds in order to refund the outstanding face amount of the 1969 issue. Since the proceeds of the 1969 issue were used for an exempt facility, the proceeds of the 1975 refunding issue will be considered to be used for the same purposes and section 103(c)(1) shall not apply to the 1975 refunding issue. The result would have been the same if the original issue had been issued in 1965. For rules as to a refunding obligation held by substantial users of facilities constructed with the proceeds of the issue refunded, see section 103(c)(7) and § 1.103-11.

Example (2). In 1967, prior to the effective date of section 103(c), City B issued $10 million of revenue bonds the proceeds of which were used to construct a manufacturing facility for corporation Y, a nonexempt person. Lease payments by Y were security for the bonds. In 1975, B issues $7 million of revenue bonds in order to retire the outstanding face amount of the 1967 issue. The interest rate of the 1975 issue is one and one-half percentage points lower than the interest rate on the 1967 issue. Both issues sold at par. All of the terms of the 1975 issue are the same as the terms of the 1967 issue with the exception of the interest rate. The 1975 refunding issue will not be considered to be an issue of industrial development bonds since the refunding issue will not make funds available for any purpose other than the debt service on the outstanding obligations.

Example (3). The facts are the same as in example (2) except that the interest rate on the refunding issue is the same as the interest rate on the issue to be refunded. Assume further that City B issued the 1975 refunding issue in order to extend the term of the obligations issued in 1967 as the result of its inability to pay such obligations due to insufficient revenues. The results will be the same as in example (2) for the reasons stated therein. [Reg. § 1.103-7.]

☐ [*T.D. 7199, 7-31-72. Amended by T.D. 7869,* 1-12-83.]

[Reg. § 1.103-8]

§ 1.103-8. Interest on bonds to finance certain exempt facilities.—(a) *In general* —(1) *General rule.* (i) Under section 103(b)(4), interest paid on an issue of obligations issued by a State or local governmental unit (as defined in § 1.103-1) is not includable in gross income if substantially all of the proceeds of such issue is to be used to provide one or more of the exempt facilities listed in subparagraphs (A) through (G) of section

103(b)(4) and in this section. However, interest on an obligation of such issue is includable in gross income if the obligation is held by a substantial user or a related person (as described in section 103(b)(8) and § 1.103-11). If substantially all of the proceeds of a bond issue is to be used to provide such exempt facilities, the debt obligations are treated as obligations described in section 103(a)(1) and § 1.103-1 even though such obligations are industrial development bonds as defined in section 103(b)(2) and § 1.103-7. Substantially all of the proceeds of an issue of governmental obligations are used to provide an exempt facility if 90 percent or more of such proceeds are so used. For purposes of this "substantially all" test, two rules apply. First, proceeds are reduced by amounts properly allocable on a pro rata basis between providing the exempt facility and other uses of the proceeds. Second, amounts used to provide an exempt facility include amounts paid or incurred which are chargeable to the facility's capital account or would be so chargeable either with a proper election by a taxpayer (for example, under section 266) or but for a proper election by a taxpayer to deduct such amounts. In the event the amount payable with respect to an issue during each annual period over its term is less than the amount of interest accruing thereon in such period, *e.g.*, in the case of an issue sold by the issuer for less than its face amount, see paragraph (a)(6) of this section to determine the amount of proceeds of the issue.

(ii) The provisions of subdivision (i) of this subparagraph shall also apply to an issue of obligations substantially all of the proceeds of which is to be used to provide exempt facilities described in this section and for either or both of the following purposes: (*a*) to acquire or develop land as the site for an industrial park described in section 103(b)(5) and § 1.103-9, (*b*) to provide facilities to be used by an exempt person.

(iii) Section 103(b)(4) only becomes applicable where the bond issue meets both the trade or business and the security interest tests so that obligations are industrial development bonds within the meaning of section 103(b)(2). For rules as to exempt facilities including property functionally related and subordinate to such facilities, see subparagraph (3) of this paragraph. For rules with respect to the ultimate use of proceeds of obligations, see paragraph (4) of this subparagraph. For rules which limit the application of the provisions of this section see subparagraph (5) of this paragraph. For the interrelationship of the rules provided in this section and the exemption

→ *Caution: Code Sec. 103 has been amended to remove special exempt bond issue rules and provide similar rules in Code Secs. 141–150.*←

for certain small issues provided in section 103(b)(6), see § 1.103-10.

(2) *Public use requirement.* To qualify under section 103(b)(4) and this section as an exempt facility, a facility must serve or be available on a regular basis for general public use, or be a part of a facility so used, as contrasted with similar types of facilities which are constructed for the exclusive use of a limited number of nonexempt persons in their trades or businesses. For example, a private dock or wharf owned by or leased to, and serving only a single manufacturing plant would not qualify as a facility for general public use, but a hangar or repair facility at a municipal airport, or a dock or a wharf, would qualify even if it is owned by, or leased or permanently assigned to, a nonexempt person provided that such nonexempt person directly serves the general public, such as a common passenger carrier or freight carrier. Similarly, an airport owned or operated by a nonexempt person for general public use is a facility for public use, as is a dock or wharf which is part of a public port. However, a landing strip which, by reason of a formal or informal agreement or by reason of geographic location, will not be available for general public use does not satisfy the public use requirement. Sewage or solid waste disposal facilities and air or water pollution control facilities, described in sections 103(b)(4)(E) and (F) and paragraphs (f) and (g) of this section, will be treated in all events as serving a general public use although they may be part of a nonpublic facility such as a manufacturing facility used in the trade or business of a nonexempt user.

(3) *Functionally related and subordinate.* An exempt facility includes any land, building, or other property functionally related and subordinate to such facility. Property is not functionally related and subordinate to a facility if it is not of a character and size commensurate with the character and size of such facility. Since substantially all of the proceeds of a bond issue must be used for the exempt facility (or for any combination of exempt facilities, industrial parks, and facilities to be used by exempt persons), including property functionally related and subordinate thereto, an insubstantial amount of the proceeds of a bond issue may be used for facilities which are neither exempt facilities (or a combination of exempt facilities, industrial parks and facilities to be used by exempt persons) nor functionally related and subordinate to exempt facilities. Thus, for example, where substantially all of the proceeds of an urban redevelopment bond issue are to be used by a State urban redevelopment agency

for residential real property for family units within the meaning of section 103(b)(4)(A) and paragraph (b) of this section, an insubstantial amount may be used for an industrial or commercial project or for any other purpose that is not functionally related and subordinate to the residential real property for family units.

(4) *Ultimate use of proceeds.* The question whether substantially all of the proceeds of an issue of obligations are to be used to provide one or more of the exempt facilities listed in subparagraphs (A) through (G) of section 103(b)(4) and in this section is to be resolved by reference to the ultimate use of such proceeds. For example, such proceeds will be treated as used to provide residential rental property whether the State or local governmental unit (i) constructs such property and leases or sells it to any person who is not an exempt person for use in such person's trade or business or leasing such property; (ii) lends the proceeds to any such person for such purpose; or (iii) lends the proceeds to banks or other financial institutions in order to increase the supply of funds for mortgage lending under conditions requiring such banks or other financial institutions to use such proceeds only for further lending for residential rental property.

(5) *Limitation.* (i) A facility qualifies under this section only to the extent that there is a valid reimbursement allocation under § 1.150-2 with respect to expenditures that are incurred before the issue date of the bonds to provide the facility and that are to be paid with the proceeds of the issue. In addition, if the original use of the facility begins before the issue date of the bonds, the facility does not qualify under this section if any person that was a substantial user of the facility at any time during the 5-year period before the issue date or any related person to that user receives (directly or indirectly) 5 percent or more of the proceeds of the issue for the user's interest in the facility and is a substantial user of the facility at any time during the 5-year period after the issue date, unless—

(A) An official intent for the facility is adopted under § 1.150-2 within 60 days after the date on which acquisition, construction, or reconstruction of that facility commenced; and

(B) For an acquisition, no person that is a substantial user or related person after the acquisition date was also a substantial user more than 60 days before the date on which the official intent was adopted.

(ii) A facility, the original use of which commences (or the acquisition of which occurs) on

Reg. § 1.103-8(a)(5)

→ *Caution: Code Sec. 103 has been amended to remove special exempt bond issue rules and provide similar rules in Code Secs. 141–150.←*

or after the issue date of bonds to provide that facility, qualifies under this section only to the extent that an official intent for the facility is adopted under § 1.150-2 by the issuer of the bonds within 60 days after the commencement of the construction, reconstruction, or acquisition of that facility. Temporary construction or other financing of a facility prior to the issuance of the bonds to provide that facility will not cause that facility to be one that does not qualify under this paragraph (a)(5)(ii).

(iii) For purposes of paragraph (a)(5)(i) of this section, *substantial user* has the meaning used in section 147(a)(1), *related person* has the meaning used in section 144(a)(3), and a user that is a governmental unit within the meaning of § 1.103-1 is disregarded.

(iv) Except to the extent provided in §§ 1.142-4(d), 1.148-11A(i), and 1.150-2(j), this paragraph (a)(5) applies to bonds issued after June 30, 1993, and sold before July 8, 1997. See § 1.142-4(d) for rules relating to bonds sold on or after July 8, 1997.

(6) *Deep discount obligations.* (i) Except as otherwise provided in paragraph (a)(7) of this section, the proceeds of any issue of obligations sold by the issuer after June 4, 1982, shall include any imputed proceeds of the issue. The imputed proceeds of an issue equal the sum of the amounts of imputed proceeds for each annual period (hereinafter, bond year) over the term of the issue.

(ii) The amount of imputed proceeds for a bond year equals—

(a) The sum of the amounts of interest that will accrue with respect to each obligation that is part of the issue in such year, reduced (but not below zero) by

(b) The sum of the amounts of principal and interest that become payable with respect to the issue in that bond year.

(iii) Interest will be deemed to accrue with respect to an obligation on an amount that, as of the commencement of that year, is equal to the sum of—

(a) The purchase price (as defined in § 1.103-13(d)(2)) allocable to the obligation and

(b) The aggregate of the amounts of interest accruing in each prior bond year with respect to the obligation, reduced by all amounts that became payable with respect to the obligation in prior bond years. Any amount that becomes payable during the 30 day period following any bond year will be deemed to have become payable in such bond year. Thus, to the extent

interest on an obligation accruing during a bond year does not become payable within 30 days from the end of such year, it is treated as reinvested under the same terms as the obligation. For purposes of this subparagraph (6), the rate at which such interest accrues is equal to the yield of the obligation. Yield is computed in the same manner as set forth in § 1.103-13(c)(1)(ii) for computing yield on governmental obligations (assuming annual compounding of interest). Such computations shall be made without regard to optional call dates.

(7) *Deep discount obligations; special rules.* (i) There are no imputed proceeds with respect to an obligation if—

(a) The obligation does not have a stated interest rate (determinable at the date of issue) that increases over the term of the obligation, and

(b) The purchase price of the obligation is at least 95 percent of its face amount.

At the option of the issuer, any obligation described in the preceeding sentence may be disregarded in computing the imputed proceeds of the issue. Payments with respect to such obligations are also disregarded in determining the amount payable with respect to the issue in that bond year. If each obligation which is part of an issue is described in this subdivision (i), there are no imputed proceeds with respect to the issue.

(ii) If the actual rate at which interest is to accrue over the term of an obligation is indeterminable at the date of issue then, in computing the yield of the obligation for purposes of this paragraph, such rate shall be determined as if the conditions as of the date of issue will not change over the term of the obligation. Thus, for example, if interest on an obligation is to be paid semiannually at a rate equal to 80 percent of the yield on six month Treasury bills at the most recent public sale immediately prior to the corresponding interest payment date and the yield on six month Treasury bills sold immediately preceding the issue date is 10 percent, then the six month Treasury bill rate is deemed to be a constant 10 percent for purposes of determining the amount of imputed proceeds of the issue. Therefore, all interest payments on the obligation would be deemed to be made at a rate of 8 percent.

(8) *Examples.* The principles of this paragraph may be illustrated by the following examples:

Example (1). State A issues its bonds and plans to use substantially all of the proceeds from such bond issue to purchase land and build a

→ *Caution: Code Sec. 103 has been amended to remove special exempt bond issue rules and provide similar rules in Code Secs. 141–150.*←

facility which will be used for one of the purposes described in section 103(b)(4) and this section. The arrangement provides that (1) A will issue bonds with a face amount of $21 million and with all accrued interest payable annually, the proceeds of which (after deducting bond election costs, costs of publishing notices, attorneys' fees, printing costs, trustees' fees for fiscal agents, and similar expenses) will be $20 million; (2) $18 million of the proceeds of the bond issue will be used to purchase land and to construct such facility; (3) $2 million of the proceeds will be used for an unrelated facility which will be used by X, a nonexempt person, in a separate trade or business and for a purpose not described in section 103(b)(4) or (5); (4) X will rent both facilities for 20 years at an annual rental equal to the amount necessary to amortize the principal and pay the interest annually on the outstanding bonds; and (5) such payments by X and the facilities will be the security for the bonds. On these facts, substantially all of the proceeds will be used in connection with an exempt facility described in section 103(b)(4) and this section. Accordingly,

section 103(b)(1) does not apply to the bonds unless such bonds are thereafter held by a person who is a substantial user of the facilities or a related person within the meaning of section 103(b)(13) and § 1.103-11.

Example (2). On July 1, 1982, State B sells an issue of its obligations to an underwriter in anticipation of a public offering. The initial offering price is $18,627,639.69 of which $17,000,000 is to be used to construct a pollution control facility described in section 103(b)(4)(F). X Corporation, a nonexempt person, is to use the facility and, in exchange, is obligated to pay an amount equal to the face amount of the issue when it becomes due. The obligations are issued on August 1, 1982. The face amount of the issue is $30,000,000. The issue is a term issue with all obligations maturing on August 1, 1987. The issue bears no stated rate of interest; there are no interest coupons on the obligations. The bonds are industrial development bonds with a yield (based upon annual compounding) of ten percent. Based on these facts, the amount of imputed proceeds with respect to the issue is determined as follows:

Date	Purchase price plus accumulated interest	Interest	Imputed proceeds
Aug. 1, 1983	$18,627,639.69	$1,862,763.97	$1,862,763.97
Aug. 1, 1984	20,490,403.68	2,049,040.37	2,049,040.37
Aug. 1, 1985	22,539,444.03	2,253,944.40	2,253,944.40
Aug. 1, 1986	24,793,388.43	2,479,338.84	2,479,338.84
Aug. 1, 1987	27,272,727.27	2,727,272.73	0
Total imputed proceeds			$8,645,087.58

Therefore, proceeds of the issue equal $27,272,727.27 less issuance costs. Substantially all of the bond proceeds are not used to provide an exempt facility, and section 103(b)(1) applies to the issue.

Example (3). The facts are the same as example (2) except that the issue has a face amount and purchase price of $18,500,000. The issue also provides for one payment in addition to the redemption payment, in the amount of $10,267,668 payable on or after August 1, 1986, one year before maturity. Section 103(b)(1) applies to the issue.

Example (4). On July 1, 1982, City E sells an issue of industrial development bonds to provide for a convention facility, as described in section 103(b)(4)(C). Assume that the bonds are issued on that date as well. The issue has a face amount of $15,240,000 and a purchase price of $11,929,382.53. The estimated cost of the facility is $11,000,000. The bonds are "zero coupon" bonds, i.e., there are no interest coupons. Each series is initially offered for less than 95 percent of its face amount. The issue matures serially over a five year period, with each series being allocated a part of the purchase price of the issue. The following chart indicates the purchase price and yield for each series and debt service for the issue:

Reg. § 1.103-8(a)(8)

→ *Caution: Code Sec. 103 has been amended to remove special exempt bond issue rules and provide similar rules in Code Secs. 141–150.*←

[Amount allocable to each series]

Date	1983 series at 8 percent	1984 series at 8.5 percent	1985 series at 8.75 percent	1986 series at 9.25 percent	1987 series at 9.75 percent	Interest accruing on issue*	Amount due	Imputed proceeds
July 1, 1983	2,939,814.82	2,697,020.54	2,468,629.60	2,228.732.51	1,595,185.06	.....	.....	0
	235,185.18	229,246.75	216,005.09	206,157.76	155,530.54	1,042,125.32	3,175,000	.....
July 1, 1984	.....	2,926,267.29	2,684,634.69	2,434,890.27	1,750,715.60	.....	.....	0
	.....	248,732.71	234,905.54	225,227.35	170,694.77	879,560.37	3,175,000	.....
July 1, 1985	.....	.....	2,919,540.23	2,660,117.62	1,921,410.37	.....	.....	0
	.....	.....	255,459.77	246,060.88	187,337.51	688,858.16	3,175,000	.....
July 1, 1986	.....	.....	.....	2,906,178.50	2,108,747.88	.....	.....	0
	.....	.....	.....	266,821.50	205,602.92	474,424.42	3,175,000	.....
July 1, 1987	.....	.....	.....	.....	2,314,350.80	.....	.....	0
	.....	.....	.....	.....	225,649.20	* 225,649.20	2,540,000	.....
Total							15,240,000	

* This column (Interest accruing on the issue) contains the sums of the interest that accrues on each series in each bond year. The amount of interest accruing on the issue is computed by adding the amount of interest accruing on each series outstanding for that bond year (the bottom number in the line for each bond year). The amount of interest annually accruing on each series also is added to the purchase price of the series to determine the amount of interest accruing in subsequent year, inasmuch as there are no payments with respect to the outstanding series prior to maturity. Thus, the "principal" amount, of the top of the two numbers given in such line for each bond year, is the purchase price allocable to that series plus the amount of interest that accrued on that series in prior years.

There are no imputed proceeds because the amount payable on the issue in each bond year exceeds the total amount of interest accruing on the issue during such bond year. Section 103(b)(1) does not apply to the bonds unless such bonds are held by a person who is a substantial user of the facility or a related person within the meaning of section 103(b)(13) and § 1.103-11.

Example (5). On July 1, 1982, City C issues industrial development bonds in the face amount of $30 million to construct a sports facility described in section 103(b)(4)(B) to be leased to D, a nonexempt person, with payments on the bonds secured by the lease. C receives $30 million in exchange for the bonds which will be used to provide the facility. The bonds mature on July 1, 2002. Each bond provides for an annual interest payment equal to ten percent of the face amount of the bond, with the last payment thereon (on July 1, 2002) including a return of the principal amount of the bond. The proceeds of the issue are $30 million. Section 103(b)(1) does not apply to the bonds unless such bonds are held by a person who is a substantial user of the facility or a related person within the meaning of section 103(b)(13) and § 1.103-11.

Example (6). The facts are the same as example (5) except that each bond provides for an annual interest payment equal to nine percent of its face amount and is sold with the option to tender the bond to D for purchase at par 5 years after the sale date of July 1, 1982 (i.e., the bonds are sold with a "put" option). Such bonds also provide a put option annually thereafter. There are no imputed proceeds (without regard to

§ 1.103-8(a)(7)), and the result is the same as example (5).

Example (7). On July 1, 1982, City F sells an issue of industrial development bonds in the face amount of $20 million to acquire a parking facility as described in section 103(b)(4)(D). The estimated cost of the facility is $17,800,000. The issue is issued on the same date and will mature serially over the following ten years. Each bond that is part of the issue bears annual interest coupons, each of which is in an amount equal to ten percent of the face amount of the bond. Each maturity has a face amount of $2,000,000. The issue is initially offered to the public for $19,700,000, allocable to each maturity as follows:

Maturity	Purchase price
July 1, 1983	$1,990,000
July 1, 1984	$1,980,000
July 1, 1985	$1,980,000
July 1, 1986	$1,970,000
July 1, 1987	$1,970,000
July 1, 1988	$1,970,000
July 1, 1989	$1,960,000
July 1, 1990	$1,960,000
July 1, 1991	$1,960,000
July 1, 1992	$1,960,000

Based on the foregoing issue proceeds equal $19,700,000 less issuance costs. There are no imputed proceeds with respect to this issue inasmuch as each bond pays interest at a constant rate in each bond year and the purchase price of each bond is at least 95 percent of its face amount. Substantially all of the proceeds are to be used to provide the exempt facility. Accordingly, section 103(b)(1) does not apply to the bonds

Reg. § 1.103-8(a)(8)

→ *Caution: Code Sec. 103 has been amended to remove special exempt bond issue rules and provide similar rules in Code Secs. 141–150.*←

unless such bonds are thereafter held by a person who is a substantial user of the facility or a related person within the meaning of section 103(b)(13) and § 1.103-11.

(b) *Residential rental property*—(1) *General rule for obligations issued after April 24, 1979.* Section 103(b)(1) shall not apply to any obligation which is issued after April 24, 1979, and is part of an issue substantially all of the proceeds of which are to be used to provide a residential rental project in which 20 percent or more of the units are to be occupied by individuals or families of low or moderate income (as defined in paragraph (b)(8)(v) of this section). In the case of a targeted area project, the minimum percentage of units which are to be occupied by individuals of low or moderate income is 15 percent. See generally § 1.103-7 for rules relating to refunding issues.

(2) *Registration requirement.* Any obligation (including any refunding obligation) issued after December 31, 1981, to provide a residential rental project must be issued as part of an issue, each obligation of which is in registered form (as defined in paragraph (b)(8)(ii) of this section).

(3) *Transitional rule.* For purposes of this section, obligations issued after April 24, 1979, may be treated as issued before April 25, 1979, if the transitional requirements of section 1104 of the Mortgage Subsidy Bond Tax Act of 1980 (94 Stat. 2670) are satisfied.

(4) *Residential rental project.*—(i) *In general.* A residential rental project is a building or structure, together with any functionally related and subordinate facilities, containing one or more similarly constructed units—

(a) Which are used on other than a transient basis, and

(b) Which satisfy the requirements of paragraph (b)(5)(i) of this section and are available to members of the general public in accordance with the requirement of paragraph (a)(2) of this section.

Substantially all of each project must contain such units and functionally related and subordinate facilities. Hotels, motels, dormitories, fraternity and sorority houses, rooming houses, hospitals, nursing homes, sanitariums, rest homes, and trailer parks and courts for use on a transient basis are not residential rental projects.

(ii) *Multiple buildings.* (a) Proximate buildings or structures (hereinafter "buildings")

which have similarly constructed units are treated as part of the same project if they are owned for Federal tax purposes by the same person and if the buildings are financed pursuant to a common plan.

(b) Buildings are proximate if they are located on a single tract of land. The term "tract" means any parcel or parcels of land which are contiguous except for the interposition of a road, street, stream or similar property. Otherwise, parcels are contiguous if their boundaries meet at one or more points.

(c) A common plan of financing exists if, for example, all such buildings are provided by the same issue or several issues subject to a common indenture.

(iii) *Functionally related and subordinate facilities.* Under paragraph (a)(3) of this section, facilities that are functionally related and subordinate to residential rental projects include facilities for use by the tenants, for example, swimming pools, other recreational facilities, parking areas, and other facilities which are reasonably required for the project, for example, heating and cooling equipment, trash disposal equipment or units for resident managers or maintenance personnel.

(iv) *Owner-occupied residences.* For purposes of section 103(b)(4)(A) and this paragraph (b), the term "residential rental project" does not include any building or structure which contains fewer than five units, one unit of which is occupied by an owner of the units.

(5) *Requirements must be continuously satisfied*—(i) *Rental requirement.* Once available for occupancy, each unit (as defined in paragraph (b)(8)(i) of this section) in a residential rental project must be rented or available for rental on a continuous basis during the longer of—

(a) the remaining term of the obligation, or

(b) the qualified project period (as defined in paragraph (b)(7) of this section).

(ii) *Low or moderate income occupancy requirement.* Individuals or families of low or moderate income must occupy that percentage of completed units in such project applicable to the project under paragraph (b)(1) of this section continuously during the qualified project period. For this purpose, a unit occupied by an individual or

Reg. § 1.103-8(b)(5)

→ *Caution: Code Sec. 103 has been amended to remove special exempt bond issue rules and provide similar rules in Code Secs. 141–150.*←

family who at the commencement of the occupancy is of low or moderate income is treated as occupied by such an individual or family during their tenancy in such unit, even though they subsequently cease to be of low or moderate income. Moreover, such unit is treated as occupied by an individual or family of low or moderate income until reoccupied, other than for a temporary period, at which time the character of the unit shall be redetermined. In no event shall such temporary period exceed 31 days.

(6) *Effect of post-issuance noncompliance.*— (i) *In general.* Unless corrected within a reasonable period, noncompliance with the requirements of this paragraph (b) shall cause the project to be treated as other than a project described in section 103(b)(4)(A) and this paragraph (b) as of the date of issue. After an issue to provide such project ceases to qualify, subsequent conformity with the requirements will not alter the taxable status of such issue.

(ii) *Correction of noncompliance.* If the issuer corrects any noncompliance arising from events occurring after the issuance of the obligation within a reasonable period, such noncompliance (*e.g.*, an unauthorized sublease) shall not cause the project to be a project not described in this paragraph (b). A reasonable period is at least 60 days after such error is first discovered or would have been discovered by the exercise of reasonable diligence.

(iii) *Involuntary loss.* (a) The requirements of paragraph (b) shall cease to apply to a project in the event of involuntary noncompliance caused by fire, seizure, requisition, foreclosure, transfer of title by deed in lieu of foreclosure, change in a Federal law or an action of a Federal agency after the date of issue which prevents an issuer from enforcing the requirements of this paragraph, or condemnation or similar event but only if, within a reasonable period, either the obligation used to provide such project is retired or amounts received as a consequence of such event are used to provide a project which meets the requirements of section 103(b)(4)(A) and this paragraph (b).

(*b*) The provisions of paragraph (b)(6)(iii)(*a*) of this section shall cease to apply to a project subject to foreclosure, transfer of title by deed in lieu of foreclosure or similar event if, at anytime during that part of the qualified project period subsequent to such event, the obligor on the acquired purpose obligation (as defined in § 1.103-13(b)(4)(iv)(*a*)) or a related person (as defined in § 1.103-10(e)) obtains an ownership interest in such project for tax purposes.

(7) *Qualified project period.* The term "qualified project period" means—

(i) For obligations issued after April 24, 1979, and prior to September 4, 1982, a period of 20 years commencing on the later of the date that the project becomes available for occupancy or the date of issue of the obligations. The requirement of paragraph (b)(5)(ii) of this section shall be deemed met if the owner of the project contracts with a Federal or state agency to maintain at least 20 percent (or 15 percent in the case of targeted areas) of the units for low or moderate income individuals or families (as defined in paragraph (b)(8)(v) of this section) for 20 years in consideration for rent subsidies for such individuals or families for such period.

(ii) For obligations issued after September 3, 1982, a period beginning on the later of the first day on which at least 10 percent of the units in the project are first occupied or the date of issue of an obligation described in section 103(b)(4)(A) and this paragraph and ending on the later of the date—

(*a*) Which is 10 years after the date on which at least 50 percent of the units in the project are first occupied,

(*b*) Which is a qualified number of days after the date on which any of the units in the project is first occupied, or

(*c*) On which any assistance provided with respect to the project under section 8 of the United States Housing Act of 1937 terminates. For purposes of this paragraph (b)(7)(ii), the term "qualified number of days" means 50 percent of the total number of days comprising the term of the obligation with the longest maturity in the issue used to provide the project. In the case of a refunding of such an issue, the longest maturity is equal to the sum of the period the prior issue was outstanding and the longest term of any refunding obligations.

(8) *Other definitions.* For purposes of this paragraph—

(i) *Unit.* The term "unit" means any accommodation containing separate and complete facilities for living, sleeping, eating, cooking, and sanitation. Such accommodations may be served by centrally located equipment, such as air conditioning or heating. Thus, for example, an apartment containing a living area, a sleeping area, bathing and sanitation facilities, and cooking facilities equipped with a cooking range, refrigerator, and sink, all of which are separate and

Reg. § 1.103-8(b)(6)

→ *Caution: Code Sec. 103 has been amended to remove special exempt bond issue rules and provide similar rules in Code Secs. 141–150.*←

distinct from other apartments, would constitute a unit.

(ii) *In registered form.* The term "in registered form" has the same meaning as in section 6049. With respect to obligations issued after December 31, 1982, such term shall have the same meaning as prescribed in section 103(j) (including the regulations thereunder).

(iii) *Targeted area project.* The term "targeted area project" means a project located in a qualified census tract (as defined in § 6a.103A-2(b)(4)) or in an area of chronic economic distress (as defined in § 6a.103A-2(b)(5)).

(iv) *Building or structure.* The term "building or structure" generally means a discrete edifice or other man-made construction consisting of an independent foundation, outer walls, and roof. A single unit which is not an entire building but is merely a part of a building is not a building or structure within the meaning of this section. As such, while single townhouses are not buildings if their foundation, outer walls, and roof are not independent, detached houses and rowhouses are buildings.

(v) *Low or moderate income.* Individuals and families of low or moderate income shall be determined in a manner consistent with determinations of lower income families under section 8 of the United States Housing Act of 1937, as amended, except that the percentage of median gross income which qualifies as low or moderate income shall be 80 percent. Therefore, occupants of a unit are considered individuals or families of low or moderate income only if their adjusted income (computed in the manner prescribed with § 1.167(k)-3(b)(3)) does not exceed 80 percent of the median gross income for the area. Notwithstanding the foregoing, the occupants of a unit shall not be considered to be of low or moderate income if all the occupants are students (as defined in section 151(e)(4)), no one of whom is entitled to file a joint return under section 6013. The method of determining low or moderate income in effect on the date of issue will be determinative for such issue, even if such method is subsequently changed. In the event programs under § 8(f) of the Housing Act of 1937, as amended, are terminated prior to the date of issue, the applicable method shall be that in effect immediately prior to the date of such termination.

(9) *Examples.* The following examples illustrate the application of this paragraph (b).

Example (1). In August 1982, City X issues $10 million of registered bonds with a term of 20 years to be used to finance the construction of an apartment building to be available to members of the general public. X loans the proceeds of the bonds to Corporation M, the tax owner of the project. The loan is secured by a promissory note from M and a mortgage on the project. The mortgage requires annual payments sufficient to amortize the principal and interest on the bonds. Corporation M maintains 20 percent of the units in the project for low or moderate income individuals and meets all of the requirements of this section until 2002, at which time M converts the project to offices. The bonds are industrial development bonds, but because the proceeds are used for construction of residential rental property, which is an exempt facility under section 103(b)(4)(A) and paragraph (b) of this section, section 103(b)(1) does not apply.

Example (2). The facts are the same as in example (1), except that the building is constructed adjacent to a factory, and the factory employees are to be given preference in selecting tenants. The bonds are industrial development bonds and the facility is not an exempt facility under section 103(b)(4)(A) and paragraph (b) of this section because it is not a facility constructed for use by the general public.

Example (3). The facts are the same as in example (1), except that the proceeds of the obligation are provided to N, a cooperative housing corporation, to finance the construction of a cooperative housing project. N sells stock in such cooperative to shareholders, some of whom occupy the units in the cooperative and some of whom rent the units to other persons. Such project is not a residential rental project within the meaning of section 103(b)(4)(A) and § 1.103-8(b) because less than all of the units in the building are used for rental. Further, the bonds are mortgage subsidy bonds under section 103A because more than a significant portion of the proceeds are used to provide financing for residences, some of which are owner-occupied and some of which are used in the trade or business of rental.

Example (4). On February 1, 1984, County Z issues registered obligations with a term of 3 years and loans the proceeds to Corporation V to construct a garden apartment project for tenants who are 65 years or older. The mortgage on the project secures the loan. At the end of 3 years, V obtains permanent financing for the project from a commercial lender. The project is not a targeted area project. V has not contracted with any Federal or state agency to provide rental assistance under section 8 of the United States Housing Act of

Reg. § 1.103-8(b)(9)

→ *Caution: Code Sec. 103 has been amended to remove special exempt bond issue rules and provide similar rules in Code Secs. 141–150.*←

1937. As a condition for providing financing for construction, Z requires that the deed to the project contain a covenant that requires the project be used for elderly tenants and restricts occupancy of 20 percent of the units in the project to individuals or families of low or moderate income. Further, the deed provides that "Such covenant shall run with and bind the land, from the date that ten percent of the units in the project are first occupied until ten years after the date that at least half the units are first occupied. The right to enforce these restrictions is vested in County Z." In 1990, however, less than 20 percent of the units are occupied by families or individuals of low or moderate incomes, and three months after learning of this condition County Z had not commenced enforcement of the covenant. Although on the date of issue the proceeds of the obligation were used to provide a residential rental project, the obligation will not be treated as providing a residential rental project within the meaning of section 103(b)(4)(A) as of February 1, 1984, because the project did not meet the requirements of this paragraph for at least 10 years after at least 50 percent of the units are first occupied.

Example (5). On January 15, 1983, State X issues registered obligations with a term of 15 years, the proceeds of which are loaned to Corporation P to construct an apartment building. The project will be a "targeted area project", within the meaning of § 1.103-8(b)(8)(iii). Corporation P intends to rent all the units to individuals for their residences, maintaining 15 percent of the units in the project for individuals having low or moderate incomes, for 15 years. In 1988, however, Corporation P converts 80 percent of the units to condominiums. Corporation P repays the loan to State X which, in turn, redeems the obligations. The obligations are not used to provide a residential rental project within the meaning of section 103(b)(4)(A), and all the interest paid or to be paid on such obligations will be includible in gross income.

Example (6). On January 15, 1984, State Z issues registered obligations with a term of 15 years the proceeds of which will be used to acquire and renovate a residential apartment building. Z sells the project to Corporation U and receives a 30-year mortgage. On June 1, 1985, the first occupants of the project commence their tenancies. At least 50 percent of the units in the project are occupied on July 1, 1985. On January 15, 1988, Z issues 35-year refunding bonds the proceeds of which are used to retire the obligations issued in 1984. The prior issue will be discharged by March

15, 1988. In order to meet the requirement of § 1.103-8(b)(5)(ii), at least 20 percent of such units must be occupied by individuals of low or moderate income until January 1, 2005.

Example (7). The facts are the same as in example (6) except that in 1987, the apartment building is substantially destroyed by fire. The building was insured at its fair market value. U does not intend to reconstruct the building but uses a portion of the insurance proceeds to repay the unpaid balance of the mortgage. Z uses this amount to redeem the outstanding bonds at the first available call date. Since the project was substantially destroyed by fire and the outstanding bonds are retired at the first available call date, the requirements of section 103(b)(4)(A) and this paragraph (b) are satisfied with respect to the obligations.

Example (8). The facts are the same as in example (6) except that in 1987 U defaults on the mortgage, and Z obtains title to the project without instituting foreclosure proceedings. Z sells the project to S and uses the proceeds to retire the outstanding bonds. Since S did not obtain the project with obligations described in section 103(b)(4), S is not required to meet the requirements of section 103(b)(4)(A) and this paragraph. Further, the 1984 obligations are obligations described in section 103(b)(4)(A).

Example (9). In September 1983, State W issues $10 million of registered bonds with a term of 3 years, the proceeds of which are to be loaned to Corporation V to finance the construction of an apartment building in a rural community. At the end of 3 years, V obtains permanent financing from Federal Agency T. Agency T will not allow the deed to contain any restrictive covenant relating to the use of the project. Under Federal law, however, T requires that V maintain all of the units in the project for rental to low-income farmworkers for the term of the mortgage, which is 20 years. Further, the mortgage between T and V provides that if T determines that low-income housing is no longer required in the community in which the project is constructed then the repayment of the mortgage may be accelerated. T determines as of the date of issue that low-income housing will be needed in the community for at least 20 years. In 1987, the project fails to meet the requirements of section 1.103-8(b)(5)(ii), relating to occupancy by individuals or families of low or moderate income. Further, T does not require V to correct the failure. Based on the foregoing, the bonds issued by W will be treated as described in section 103(b)(4)(A).

Reg. § 1.103-8(b)(9)

→ *Caution: Code Sec. 103 has been amended to remove special exempt bond issue rules and provide similar rules in Code Secs. 141–150.*←

Example (10). The facts are the same as in example (9) except that in 1987, the Federal law is amended to provide that Agency T may not enforce its low-income occupancy requirement. The result is the same.

Example (11). The facts are the same as in example (9) except that in 1987 Agency T determines that due to a change in circumstances in the community in which the project is located low-income rental housing is no longer required. As such, T requires V to repay the mortgage. Since the obligations have been repaid, W has no legal right to enforce the requirements of paragraph (b) with respect to the project. Subsequent nonconformity of the project with the requirements of § 1.103-8(b) under these circumstances will not cause the obligations issued by W to be industrial development bonds within the meaning of section 103(b)(1).

(10) *Obligations issued before April 25, 1979*—(i) *General rules.* Section 103(b)(1) shall not apply to obligations issued before April 25, 1979, which are part of an issue substantially all of the proceeds of which are to be used to provide residential real property for family units. In order to qualify under this paragraph (b) as an exempt facility, the facility must satisfy the public use requirement of paragraph (a)(2) of this section by being available for use by members of the general public.

(ii) *Family units defined.* For purposes of this paragraph (b) the term "family unit" means a building or any portion thereof which contains complete living facilities which are to be used on other than a transient basis by one or more persons, and facilities functionally related and subordinate thereto. Thus, an apartment which is to be used on other than a transient basis as a residence by a single person or by a family and which contains complete facilities for living, sleeping, eating, cooking, and sanitation, constitutes a family unit. Such a unit may be served by centrally located machinery and equipment as in a typical apartment building. To qualify as a family unit, the living facilities must be a separate, self-contained building or constitute one unit in a building substantially all of which consists of similar units, together with functionally related and subordinate facilities and areas. Hotels, motels, dormitories, fraternity and sorority houses, rooming houses, hospitals, sanitariums, rest homes, and trailer parks and courts for use on a transient basis do not constitute residential real property for family units.

(iii) *Functionally related and subordinate facilities.* Under paragraph (a)(3) of this section, facilities which are functionally related and subordinate to residential real property actually used for family units include, for example, facilities for use by the occupants such as a swimming pool, a parking area, and recreational facilities.

(c) *Sports facilities*—(1) *General rule.* Section 103(b)(4)(B) provides that section 103(b)(1) shall not apply to obligations issued by a State or local governmental unit which are part of an issue substantially all of the proceeds of which are to be used to provide sports facilities. In order to qualify as an exempt facility under section 103(b)(4)(B) and this paragraph, the facility must satisfy the public use requirement of paragraph (a)(2) of this section by being available for use by members of the general public either as participants or as spectators.

(2) *Sports facility defined.* (i) For purposes of section 103(b)(4)(B) and this paragraph, the term "sport facilities" includes both outdoor and indoor facilities. The facility may be designed either as a spectator or as a participation facility. For example, the term includes both indoor and outdoor stadiums for baseball, football, ice hockey, or other sports events, as well as facilities for the participation of the general public in sports activities, such as golf courses, ski slopes, swimming pools, tennis courts, and gymnasiums. The term does not include, however, facilities such as a golf course, swimming pool, or tennis court, which are constructed for use by members of a private club or as integral or subordinate parts of a hotel or motel, or the use of which will be restricted to a special class or group or to guests of a particular hotel or motel, since they are not facilities for the use of the general public as required by paragraph (a)(2) of this section.

(ii) Under paragraph (a)(3) of this section, facilities which are functionally related and subordinate to a sports facility, such as a parking lot, clubhouse, ski slope warming house, bath house, or ski tow, are considered to be part of a sports facility. A ski lodge which consists primarily of overnight accommodations is not functionally related and subordinate to a sports facility.

(d) *Convention or trade show facilities*—(1) *General rule.* Section 103(b)(4)(C) provides that section 103(b)(1) shall not apply to obligations issued by a State or local governmental unit which are a part of an issue substantially all of the proceeds of which are to be used to provide convention or trade show facilities. In order to qualify under section 103(b)(4)(C) and this paragraph

→ *Caution: Code Sec. 103 has been amended to remove special exempt bond issue rules and provide similar rules in Code Secs. 141–150.*←

as an exempt facility, the facility must satisfy the public use requirement of paragraph (a)(2) of this section by being available for an appropriate charge or rental, on a rate scale basis, for use by members of the general public. The public use requirement is not satisfied if the use of a convention or trade show facility is limited by long-term leases to a single user or group of users.

(2) *Convention or trade show facilities defined.* For purposes of section 103(b)(4)(C) and this paragraph, the term "convention or trade show facilities" means special-purpose buildings or structures, such as meeting halls and display areas, which are generally used to house a convention or trade show, including, under paragraph (a)(3) of this section, facilities functionally related and subordinate to such facilities such as parking lots or railroad sidings. A hotel or motel which is available to the general public, whether or not it is intended primarily to house persons attending or participating in a convention or trade show, is neither a convention or trade show facility nor functionally related and subordinate thereto.

(e) *Certain transportation facilities*—(1) *General rule.* Section 103(b)(4)(D) provides that section 103(b)(1) shall not apply to obligations issued by a State or local governmental unit which are part of an issue substantially all of the proceeds of which are to be used to provide (i) airports, docks, wharves, mass commuting facilities, or public parking facilities, or (ii) storage or training facilities directly related to any such facility. In order to qualify under section 103(b)(4)(D) and this paragraph as an exempt facility, the facility must satisfy the public use requirement of paragraph (a)(2) of this section by being available for use by members of the general public or for use by common carriers or charter carriers which serve members of the general public. A dock or wharf which is part of a public port (or a public port to be constructed in accordance with a plan which has been finally adopted on the date the obligations in question are issued) satisfies the public use test. A parking lot will be availabe for use by the general public unless more than an insubstantial portion thereof will be used exclusively by or for the benefit of a nonexempt person by reason of a formal or informal agreement or by reason of the remote geographic location of the facility.

(2) *Definitions.* For purposes of section 103(b)(4)(D) and this paragraph—

(i) With respect to bonds sold at or before 5:00 p.m. EST on December 29, 1978, an airport includes service accommodations for the public such as terminals, retail stores in such terminals,

runways, hangars, loading facilities, repair shops, parking areas, and facilities which, under paragraph (a)(3) of this section, are functionally related and subordinate to the airport, such as facilities for the preparation of in-flight meals, restaurants, and accommodations for temporary or overnight use by passengers, and other facilities functionally related to the needs or convenience of passengers, shipping companies, and airlines. The term "airport" does not include a landing strip which, by reason of a formal or informal agreement, or by reason of geographic location, will not be available for general public use.

(ii) With respect to bonds sold after 5:00 p.m. EST on December 29, 1978—

(*a*) An airport includes facilities which are directly related and essential to—

(*1*) Servicing aircraft or enabling aircraft to take off and land, or

(*2*) Transferring passengers or cargo to or from aircraft.

A facility does not satisfy either of the foregoing requirements if the facility need not be located at, or in close proximity to, the take-off and landing area in order to perform its function. Examples of facilities which satisfy those requirements are terminals, runways, hangars, loading facilities, repair shops, and land-based navigation aids such as radar installations.

(*b*) Under paragraph (a)(3) of this section, an airport includes facilities other than those described in paragraph (e)(2)(ii)(*a*) only if they are functionally related and subordinate to an airport (as defined in paragraph (e)(2)(ii)(*a*)). A facility (or part thereof) is not functionally related and subordinate to an airport if the facility (or part thereof)—

(*1*) Is not of a character and size commensurate with the character and size of the airport at or adjacent to which the facility is located, or

(*2*) Is not located at or adjacent to that airport.

A facility may satisfy the character and size requirement although it provides minimal benefits to other airports. For example, a facility for the preparation of in-flight meals which has capacity sufficient to prepare all in-flight meals for aircraft departing the airport where the facility is located qualifies although some meals may be consumed in transit between other airports. Other examples of facilities functionally related and subordinate to an airport are restaurants and

Reg. § 1.103-8(d)(2)

→ *Caution: Code Sec. 103 has been amended to remove special exempt bond issue rules and provide similar rules in Code Secs. 141–150.←*

retail stores located in terminals, ground transportation parking areas, and accommodations for temporary or overnight use by passengers. Unimproved land (including agricultural land) that is adjacent to an airport and that is impaired by a significant level of airport noise is functionally related and subordinate to the airport if after its acquisition that land will not be converted to a use that is incompatible with the level of airport noise. Adjacent land with existing improvements also may be functionally related and subordinate to an airport by reason of impairment by a significant level of airport noise but only if the use of such land before its acquisition is incompatible with the airport noise level, its use after acquisition is to be compatible, and the post-acquisition use will be essentially different from the pre-acquisition use. Notwithstanding the foregoing, an interest in such improved land acquired solely to mitigate damages attributable to airport noise is treated as functionally related and subordinate to the airport. Thus, for example, amounts allocated to imposing a servitude on improved land adjacent to an airport restricting its future use to uses compatible with airport noise are treated as amounts allocated to property functionally related and subordinate to an airport. For the purpose of determining whether land is impaired by a significant level of airport noise, any generally accepted noise estimating methodology may be used. For example, a Noise Exposure Forecast (NEF), a method for composite noise rating recommended by the Federal Aviation Administration to measure the impact of airport noise, may be used for this purpose. Compatibility may be determined by reference to regulations or general guidelines published by the Federal Aviation Administration under section 102 of the Aviation Safety and Noise Abatement Act of 1979 (49 U.S.C. 2102), or sections 11(3)(C) and 18(a)(4) of the Airport and Airway Development Act of 1970, as amended (49 U.S.C. 1711(3)(C) and 1718 (a)(4)), concerning uses of land impaired by a significant level of airport noise, or, where available, by reference to the airport compatibility plan specifically addressing what constitutes a compatible use of that land.

(c) As an illustration of the rules of this paragraph (e)(2)(ii), an office building (or office space within a building) or a computer facility, either of which serves a system-wide or regional function of an airline, is not considered part of an airport since that facility is not described in either paragraph (e)(2)(ii)(a) or (b). However, a maintenance or overhaul facility which services aircraft is considered part of an airport under paragraph (e)(2)(ii)(a) since that facility is directly related and essential to servicing aircraft and must be located where aircraft take off and land in order to perform its function.

(d) A hotel located at or adjacent to an airport satisfies the requirements of paragraph (e)(2)(ii)(b), that is, it is of a character and size commensurate with the character and size of the airport at or adjacent to which it is located, if the number of guest rooms in the hotel is reasonable for the size of the airport, taking into account the current and projected passenger usage of the terminal facility. If the hotel contains meeting rooms, the number and size of these rooms must be in reasonable proportion to the number of guest rooms in the hotel. Limited recreational facilities will not prevent the hotel from being of a character and size commensurate with the character and size of the airport.

(iii) A dock or wharf includes property which, under paragraph (a)(3) of this section, is functionally related and subordinate to a dock or wharf such as the structure alongside which a vessel docks, the equipment needed to receive and to discharge cargo and passengers from the vessel, such as cranes and conveyors, related storage, handling, office, and passenger areas, and similar facilities.

(iv) A mass commuting facility includes real property together with improvements and personal property used therein, such as machinery, equipment, and furniture, serving the general public commuting on a day-to-day basis by bus, subway, rail, ferry, or other conveyance which moves over prescribed routes. Such property also includes terminals and facilities which, under paragraph (a)(3) of this section, are functionally related and subordinate to the mass commuting facility, such as parking garages, car barns, and repair shops. Use of mass commuting facilities by noncommuters in common with commuters is immaterial. Thus, a terminal leased to a common carrier bus line which serves both commuters and long distance travellers would qualify as an exempt facility.

(3) *Related storage and training facility.* Section 103(b)(4)(D) includes only those storage and training facilities which are both (i) directly related to a facility to which subparagraph (1)(i) or (ii) of this paragraph applies and (ii) physically located on or adjacent to such a facility. For example, a storage facility would include a grain elevator, silo, warehouse, or oil and gas storage tank used in connection with a dock or wharf and

Reg. § 1.103-8(e)(3)

→ *Caution: Code Sec. 103 has been amended to remove special exempt bond issue rules and provide similar rules in Code Secs. 141–150.*←

located on or adjacent to such dock or wharf. Similarly, a training facility would include a building located at or adjacent to an airport for the training of flight personnel or a paved area immediately adjoining a bus garage used to train bus drivers.

(4) *Examples.* The principles of this paragraph may be illustrated by the following examples:

Example (1). B Airport Authority, a political subdivision of State A, owns and operates B Airport. B Airport Authority adds several runways. In view of the expanded area impaired by significant levels of airport noise, the Authority proposes to issue bonds the proceeds of which are to be used to acquire a hospital located adjacent to the airport. The noise level on the acquired property is 40 NEF. By reference to a noise exposure map setting forth noncompatible land uses and by reference to guidelines published by the Federal Aviation Administration, it is established that continued use of the land for a hospital is not compatible with the noise level. Prior to issuing the bonds, B contracts to lease the property to Corporation C to be used for warehouse space. Within 18 months of the bonds' issuance C will remodel the hospital (previously owned by D, who is unrelated to C) with its own funds and rent the facility as a warehouse. Use as a warehouse is determined to be compatible with the level of airport noise impairing the land. The improved land and prospective revenues from the facility's rental are security for the proposed issuance. Based on the foregoing, the acquired land satisfies the public use test. Furthermore, it is functionally related and subordinate to the airport because the improvements are to be used in an essentially different manner than prior to the land's acquisition. The bonds are industrial development bonds. However, section 103(b)(1) does not apply unless the provisions of section 103(b)(8) and § 1.103-11 apply.

Example (2). The facts are the same as in Example (1) except that a substantial portion of the proceeds of the bond issue is allocated to the acquisition of a limited interest in an additional tract of land (also impaired by airport noise measured at 40 NEF) on which an office building stands. The limited interest holds B harmless for damages caused by airport noise and restricts uses of the tract after the building is retired to those compatible with noise levels caused by the airport. Based on the foregoing, such interest satisfies the public use test. Furthermore, the interest is functionally related and subordinate to the air-

port because it is solely to mitigate damage attributable to airport noise, in part by restricting future land uses. The bonds are industrial development bonds. However, section 103(b)(1) does not apply unless the provisions of section 103(b)(8) or § 1.103-11 apply.

Example (3). On June 1, 1980, M Airport Authority, a political subdivision of State O, issues obligations, the proceeds of which are loaned to X Corporation, a nonexempt person. X uses the proceeds to construct a hotel adjacent to the main terminal building at M Airport. X will be unconditionally liable for repayment of the proposed obligations. The hotel will be used to provide temporary and overnight accommodations for airline passengers using M Airport. The number of rooms in the hotel is reasonable for an airport of M's size, taking into account the current and projected passenger usage of the terminal facility. In addition to guest rooms, the hotel will contain a restaurant, small retail stores (such as a gift shop and newsstand), and limited recreation facilities (such as a swimming pool). The hotel will also contain several multipurpose rooms suitable for use as meeting rooms. The number and size of these rooms will be in reasonable proportion to the number and size of the guest rooms in the hotel. Use of the guest rooms, restaurant and stores, recreational facilities, and meeting rooms by air passengers arriving at or departing from M Airport will be incidental to the use of the hotel by air passengers for temporary and overnight accommodations. The hotel is of a character and size commensurate with the character and size of M Airport. Consequently, applying the provisions of § 1.103-8(e)(2) the hotel is functionally related and subordinate to M Airport. The obligations are industrial development bonds. Section 103(b)(1) does not apply to the obligations, however, unless the provisions of section 103(b)(10) and § 1.103-11 apply.

Example (4). On June 1, 1980, N Airport Authority, a political subdivision of State P, issues obligations, the proceeds of which are loaned to Y Corporation, a nonexempt person. Y uses the proceeds to construct a hotel adjacent to the main terminal building at N Airport. Y Corporation will be unconditionally liable for repayment of the proposed obligations. The hotel will contain extensive recreational facilities, including a large rooftop swimming pool, tennis courts, and a health club. In addition, facilities for conferences consisting of a ballroom-sized meeting room capable of being partitioned by movable panels and several smaller meeting rooms will be constructed. The

Reg. § 1.103-8(e)(4)

→ *Caution: Code Sec. 103 has been amended to remove special exempt bond issue rules and provide similar rules in Code Secs. 141–150.*←

number of rooms in the hotel will substantially exceed the number which is reasonable based on the current and projected passenger usage of the terminal facility. Because of the presence of extensive recreational and conference facilities, as well as the presence of an excessive number of rooms at the hotel, the hotel fails to be of a character and size commensurate with the character and size of N Airport. The result would be the same if the hotel did not have extensive recreational facilities. Consequently, the hotel is not functionally related and subordinate to N Airport under § 1.103-8(e)(2). The obligations are industrial development bonds and interest thereon is not excluded from gross income by reason of subsection (a)(1) or (b)(4) of section 103.

(f) *Certain public utility facilities*—(1) *General rule.* (i) Section 103 (b)(4)(E) provides that section 103(c)(1) shall not apply to obligations issued by a State or local governmental unit which are part of an issue substantially all of the proceeds of which are to be used to provide sewage disposal facilities, solid waste disposal facilities, or facilities for the local furnishing of electric energy or gas. In order to qualify under section 103(b)(4)(E) as an exempt facility, the facility must satisfy the public use requirement of paragraph (a)(2) of this section. A public utility facility described in this subparagraph (with the exception of sewage and solid waste disposal facilities which will be treated in all events as serving the general public) will satisfy the public use requirement only if such facility, or the output thereof, is available for use by members of the general public.

(ii) A facility for the local furnishing of electric energy or gas is, for purposes of applying the public use test in paragraph (a)(2) of this section, available for use by members of the general public if (a) the owner or operator of the facility is obligated, by a legislative enactment, local ordinance, regulation, or the equivalent thereof, to furnish electric energy or gas to all persons who desire such services and who are within the service area of the owner or operator of such facility, and (b) it is reasonably expected that such facility will serve or be available to a large segment of the general public in such service area. For rules with respect to facilities for furnishing of water, see paragraph (h) of this section.

(2) *Definitions.* For purposes of section 103(b)(4)(E) and this paragraph—

(i) The term "sewage disposal facilities" means any property used for the collection, storage, treatment, utilization, processing, or final disposal of sewage.

(ii) (a) The term "solid waste disposal facilities" means any property or portion thereof used for the collection, storage, treatment, utilization, processing, or final disposal of solid waste. Only expenditures for that portion of property which is a solid waste disposal facility qualify as expenditures for solid waste disposal facilities. The fact that a facility which otherwise qualifies as a solid waste disposal facility operates at a profit will not, of itself, disqualify the facility as an exempt facility. However, whether a collection or storage facility qualifies as a solid waste disposal facility depends upon all of the facts and circumstances. Thus, land and facilities for the collection of materials to form a slag heap which is not preliminary to the recycling or other final disposal of such materials within a reasonable period of time will not qualify. The term does not include facilities for collection, storage, or disposal of liquid or gaseous waste except where such facilities are facilities which, under paragraph (a)(3) of this section, are functionally related and subordinate to a solid waste disposal facility.

(b) The term "solid waste" shall have the same meaning as in section 203(4) of the Solid Waste Disposal Act (42 U.S.C. § 3252(4)), except that for purposes of this paragraph, material will not qualify as solid waste unless, on the date of issue of the obligations issued to provide the facility to dispose of such waste material, it is property which is useless, unused, unwanted, or discarded solid material which has no market or other value at the place where it is located. Thus, where any person is willing to purchase such property, at any price, such material is not waste. Where any person is willing to remove such property at his own expense but is not willing to purchase such property at any price, such material is waste. Section 203(4) of the Solid Waste Disposal Act provides that:

"(4) The term 'solid waste' means garbage, refuse, and other discarded solid materials, including solid-waste materials resulting from industrial, commercial, and agricultural operations, and from community activities, but does not include solids or dissolved material in domestic sewage or other significant pollutants in water resources, such as silt, dissolved or suspended solids in industrial waste water effluents, dissolved materials in irrigation return flows or other common water pollutants."

(c) A facility which disposes of solid waste by reconstituting, converting, or otherwise recycling it into material which is not waste shall also qualify as a solid waste disposal facility if

→ *Caution: Code Sec. 103 has been amended to remove special exempt bond issue rules and provide similar rules in Code Secs. 141–150.*←

solid waste (within the meaning of (b) of this subdivision (ii) constitutes at least 65 percent, by weight or volume, of the total materials introduced into the recycling process. Such a recycling facility shall not fail to qualify as a solid waste disposal facility solely because it operates at a profit.

(d) For rules relating to property which has both a solid waste disposal function and a function other than the disposal of solid waste, see § 17.1 of this chapter.

(iii) The term "facilities for the local furnishing of electric energy or gas" means property which—

(a) Is either property of a character subject to the allowance for depreciation provided in section 167 or land,

(b) Is used to produce, collect, generate, transmit, store, distribute, or convey electric energy or gas,

(c) Is used in the trade or business of furnishing electric energy or gas, and

(d) Is a part of a system providing service to the general populace of one or more communities or municipalities, but in no event more than 2 contiguous counties (or a political equivalent) whether or not such counties are located in one state.

For purposes of this subdivision, a city which is not within, or does not consist of, one or more counties (or a political equivalent) shall be treated as a county (or a political equivalent). A facility for the generation of electric energy otherwise qualifying under this subdivision will not be disqualified because it is connected to a system for interconnection with other public utility systems for the emergency transfer of electric energy. The facilities need not be located in the area served by them. Also, the term "facilities for the local furnishing of electric energy or gas" does not include coal, oil, gas, nuclear cores, or other materials performing a similar function.

(g) *Air or water pollution control facilities—(1) General rule.* Section 103(b)(4)(F) provides that section 103(b)(1) shall not apply to obligations issued by a State or local governmental unit which are part of an issue substantially all of the proceeds of which are to be used to provide air or water pollution control facilities. Such facilities are in all events treated as serving the general public and, thus, satisfy the public use requirement of paragraph (a)(2) of this section.

(2) *Definitions.* (i) For purposes of section 103(b)(4)(F) and this paragraph, property is a pollution control facility to the extent that the test of either subdivision (iii) or (iv) of this subparagraph is satisfied, but only if—

(a) It is property which is described in subdivision (ii) of this subparagraph and is either of a character subject to the allowance for depreciation provided in section 167 or land, and

(b) Either (1) a Federal, State, or local agency exercising jurisdiction has certified that the facility, as designed, is in furtherance of the purpose of abating or controlling atmospheric pollutants or contaminants, or water pollution, as the case may be, or (2) the facility is designed to meet or exceed applicable Federal, State, and local requirements for the control of atmospheric pollutants or contaminants, or water pollution, as the case may be, in effect at the time the obligations, the proceeds of which are to be used to provide such facilities, are issued.

(ii) Property is described in this subdivision if it is property to be used, in whole or in part, to abate or control water or atmospheric pollution or contamination by removing, altering, disposing, or storing pollutants, contaminants, wastes, or heat. In the case of property to be used to control water pollution, such property includes the necessary intercepting sewers, pumping, power, and other equipment, and their appurtenances. For rules relating to facilities which remove pollutants from fuel or certain other items, see subdivision (vi) of this subparagraph.

(iii) In the case of an expenditure for property which is designed for no significant purpose other than the control of pollution, the total expenditure for such property satisfies the test of this subdivision. Thus, where property which is to serve no function other than the control of pollution is to be added to an existing manufacturing or production facility, the total expenditure for such property satisfies the test of this subdivision. Also, if an expenditure for property would not be made but for the purpose of controlling pollution, and if the expenditure has no significant purpose other than the purpose of pollution control, the total expenditure for such property satisfies the test of this subdivision even though such property serves one or more functions in addition to its function as a pollution control facility.

(iv) In the case of property to be placed in service for the purpose of controlling pollution and for a significant purpose other than controlling pollution, only the incremental cost of such facility satisfies the test of this subdivision. The "incremental cost" of property is the excess of its

→ *Caution: Code Sec. 103 has been amended to remove special exempt bond issue rules and provide similar rules in Code Secs. 141–150.*←

total cost over that portion of its cost expended for a purpose other than the control of pollution.

(v) An expenditure has a significant purpose other than the control of pollution if it results in an increase in production or capacity, or in a material extension of the useful life of a manufacturing or production facility of a part thereof.

(vi) [Reserved]

(h) *Water facilities*—(1) *General rule.* Section 103(b)(4)(G) provides that section 103(b)(1) shall not apply to obligations issued by a State or local governmental unit which are part of an issue substantially all of the proceeds of which are to be used to provide facilities for the furnishing of water which are available, on reasonable demand, to members of the general public. A water facility will satisfy the public use test of paragraph (a)(2) of this section if it will provide water, on reasonable demand, to any member of the general public within the service area of the water system of which such facility is a part.

(2) *Definition.* For purposes of section 103(b)(4)(G) and this paragraph, the "water facilities" include artesian wells, reservoirs, dams, related equipment and pipelines, and other facilities used to furnish water for domestic, industrial, irrigation, or other purposes.

(3) *Effective date.* The provisions of this paragraph apply in the case of facilities provided by obligations issued after January 1, 1969. In the case of facilities provided by obligations issued on or before such date to which section 103(b) is applicable, the provisions of paragraph (f) of this section shall apply. For such purposes, wherever the term "local furnishing of electric energy or gas" appears in paragraph (f) of this section, such term shall be deemed to read "local furnishing of electric energy, gas, or water."

(i) *Examples.* The application of section 103(b)(4) and this section are illustrated by the following examples:

Example (1). City B plans to issue $10 million of bonds to be used to construct a sports stadium. The revenues from the facility and the facility itself will be the security for the bonds. A professional football team rents the facility on a long-term lease for part of the year and a professional baseball team rents the sports facility for the remainder of the year. Tickets are sold by the teams to the general public. The bonds are industrial development bonds, but since the proceeds are used for a spectator facility for general public use, which is an exempt facility under section 103(b)(4)(B) and paragraph (c) of this section,

section 103(b)(1) does not apply unless the provisions of section 103(b)(8) and § 1.103-11 apply.

Example (2). City C plans to issue $10 million of bonds to be used to construct a convention hall which it will own. City C plans to lease the convention hall for 25 years to corporation Y, a nonexempt person, which will operate and maintain it. The terms of the lease obligate Y to make the convention hall generally available for civic, business, and recreational shows, meetings, performances, and similar activities serving or benefiting the community. Lease payments from Y and the facility will be security for the bonds. The bonds are industrial development bonds, but since the proceeds are to be used for a facility for general public use, which is an exempt facility under section 103(b)(4)(C) and paragraph (d) of this section, section 103(b)(1) does not apply unless the provisions of section 103(b)(8) and § 1.103-11 apply.

Example (3). City D issues $100 million of its bonds and uses the proceeds to finance construction of an airport for the use of the general public. D will own and operate the airport. A major portion of the rentable space in the terminal building is leased on a long-term basis to common carrier and non-scheduled airlines. The bonds will be secured by the airport landing and runway charges and by payments with respect to such long-term leases from such commercial airlines. Such commercial airline payments are expected to constitute more than 50 percent of the total revenues from the airport. The bonds are industrial development bonds, but since the proceeds are to be used for an airport for use by the general public and by carriers serving the general public, which is an exempt facility under section 103(b)(4)(D) and paragraph (e) of this section, section 103(b)(1) does not apply unless the provisions of section 103(b)(8) and § 1.103-11 apply. The result would be the same if D hired an airport management firm to operate the airport.

Example (4). City E issues $6 million of its bonds and uses the proceeds to finance construction of a landing strip for airplanes to be located adjacent to the factories of corporations Y and Z. The landing strip will be used in the trades or businesses of Y and Z and by any member of the general public wishing to use it. However, due to its location, general public use will be negligible. The lease payments by Y and Z for the use of the facility are the security for the bonds. The bonds are industrial development bonds and the facility is not an exempt facility under section 103(b)(4)(D) and paragraph (c) of this section

→ *Caution: Code Sec. 103 has been amended to remove special exempt bond issue rules and provide similar rules in Code Secs. 141–150.*←

because it is not a facility constructed for general public use.

Example (5). State F and corporation Z enter into an arrangement which provides that F will issue $10 million of its bonds and use the proceeds to construct a facility for Z the only purpose of which is to control air and water pollution at Z's plant. The principal and interest on the bonds will be secured by the charges which F will impose on Z. The bonds are industrial development bonds, but since the proceeds are to be used for air and water pollution facilities designed to abate pollution by private persons, such facilities are for the benefit of the general public and are exempt facilities under section 103(b)(4)(F) and paragraph (g) of this section. Accordingly, section 103(b)(1) does not apply unless the provisions of section 103(b)(8) and § 1.103-11 apply.

Example (6). City G issues $20 million of its bonds and will use $6 million to finance residential rental property which qualifies as an exempt facility under section 103(b)(4)(A) and paragraph (b) of this section, $9 million to finance construction of a stadium which qualifies as an exempt facility under section 103(b)(4)(B) and paragraph (c) of this section, and $5 million for convention facilities which qualify as exempt facilities under section 103(b)(4)(C) and paragraph (d) of this section. The facilities will be used in the trades or businesses of nonexempt persons and rental payments with respect to such facilities and the facilities themselves will be the security for the bonds. The bonds are industrial development bonds, but since all the proceeds are to be used for facilities which are exempt facilities under section 103(b)(4), section 103(b)(1) does not apply unless the provisions of section 103(b)(10) and § 1.103-11 apply. The result would be the same, if; instead of using $9 million to finance construction of a stadium, the $9 million were used to finance construction of a capitol building. [Reg. § 1.103-8].

☐ [T.D. 7199, 7-31-72. Amended by T.D. 7362, 6-17-75; T.D. 7511, 9-30-77; T.D. 7737, 11-14-80; T.D. 7840, 10-12-82; T.D. 7848, 11-10-82; T.D. 7869, 1-12-83; T.D. 8476, 6-14-93; T.D. 8538, 5-5-94 and T.D. 8718, 5-8-97.]

[Reg. § 17.1]

§ 17.1. **Industrial development bonds used to provide solid waste disposal facilities; temporary rules (Temporary).**—(a) *In general.* Section 103(c)(4)(E) provides that section 103(c)(1) shall not apply to obligations issued by a State or local governmental unit which are part of an issue substantially all the proceeds of which are used to provide solid waste disposal facilities. Section 1.103-8(f) of this chapter provides general rules with respect to such facilities and defines such facilities. In the case of property which has both a solid waste disposal function and a function other than the disposal of solid waste, only the portion of the cost of the property allocable to the function of solid waste disposal (as determined under paragraph (b) of this section) is taken into account as an expenditure to provide solid waste disposal facilities. A facility which otherwise qualifies as a solid waste disposal facility will not be treated as having a function other than solid waste disposal merely because material or heat which has utility or value is recovered or results from the disposal process. Where materials or heat are recovered, the waste disposal function includes the processing of such materials or heat which occurs in order to put them into the form in which the materials or heat are in fact sold or used, but does not include further processing which converts the materials or heat into other products.

(b) *Allocation.* The portion of the cost of property allocable to solid waste disposal is determined by allocating the cost of such property between the property's solid waste disposal function and any other functions by any method which, with reference to all the facts and circumstances with respect to such property, reasonably reflects a separation of costs for each function of the property.

(c) *Example.* The principles of this paragraph may be illustrated by the following example:

Example. Company A intends to construct a new facility to process solid waste which City X will deliver to the facility. City X will pay a disposal fee for each ton of solid waste that City X dumps at the facility. The waste will be processed by A in a manner which separates metals, glass, and similar materials. As separated, some of such items are commercially saleable; but A does not intend to sell the metals and glass until the metals are further separated, sorted, sized and cleaned and the glass is pulverized. The metals and pulverized glass will then be sold to commercial users. The waste disposal function includes such processing of the metals and glass, but no further processing is included.

The remaining waste will be burned in an incinerator. Gases generated by the incinerator will be cleaned by use of an electrostatic precipitator. To reduce the size and cost of the electrostatic precipitator, the incinerator exhaust gases will be

→ *Caution: Code Sec. 103 has been amended to remove special exempt bond issue rules and provide similar rules in Code Secs. 141–150.*←

cooled and reduced in volume by means of a heat exchange process using boilers. The precipitator is functionally related and subordinate to disposal of the waste residue and is therefore property used in solid waste disposal. The heat can be used by A to produce steam. Company B operates an adjacent electric generating facility and B can use steam to power its turbine-generator. B needs steam with certain physical characteristics and as a result A's boilers, heat exchanger and related equipment are somewhat more costly than might be required to produce steam for some other uses. The disposal function includes the equipment actually used to put the heat into the form in which it is sold.

Company A intends to construct pipes to carry the steam from A's boiler to B's facility. When converted to such steam the heat is in the form in which sold, and therefore the disposal function does not include subsequent transporting of the steam by pipes. Similarly, if A installed generating equipment and used the steam to generate electricity, the disposal function would not include the generating equipment, since such equipment transforms the commercially saleable steam into another form of energy. [Temporary Reg. § 17.1.]

□ [*T.D.* 7362, 6-17-75.]

[Reg. § 1.103-9]

§ 1.103-9. Interest on bonds to finance industrial parks.—(a) *General rule.*—(1) Under section 103(c)(5), interest paid on an issue of obligations issued by a State or local governmental unit (as defined in § 1.103-1) is not includable in gross income if substantially all of the proceeds of such issue is to be used to finance the acquisition or development of land as the site for an industrial park (referred to in this section as "industrial park bonds"). However, interest on an obligation of such an issue is includable in gross income if the obligation is held by a substantial user or a related person (as described in section 103(c)(7) and § 1.103-11). If substantially all of the proceeds of a bond issue is to be so used to finance an industrial park, the debt obligations are treated as obligations described in section 103(a)(1) and § 1.103-1 even though such obligations are industrial development bonds within the meaning of section 103(c)(2) and § 1.103-7. Whether substantially all of the proceeds of an issue of governmental obligations are used to finance an industrial park is determined consistently with the rules for exempt facilities in § 1.103-8 (a)(1)(i).

(2) The provisions of subparagraph (1) of this paragraph shall also apply to an issue of obligations substantially all of the proceeds of which is to be used to acquire or develop land as the site for an industrial park described in section 103(c)(5) and this section and for either or both of the following purposes: (i) to finance exempt facilities described in section 103(c)(4) and § 1.103-8, (ii) to finance facilities to be used by an exempt person.

(3) Section 103(c)(5) only becomes applicable where the bond issue meets both the trade or business and the security interest tests so that the obligations are industrial development bonds within the meaning of section 103(c)(2). For the interrelationship of the rules provided in this section and the exemption for certain small issues provided in section 103(c)(6), see § 1.103-10.

(b) *Definition of an industrial park.* For purposes of section 103(c)(5) and this section, the term "industrial park" means a tract of land, other than a tract of land intended for use by a single enterprise, suitable primarily for use as building sites by a group of enterprises engaged in industrial, distribution, or wholesale businesses if either—

(1) The control and administration of the tract is vested in an exempt person (within the meaning of paragraph (b)(2) of § 1.103-7), or

(2) The uses of the tract are normally (i) regulated by protective minimum restrictions, ordinarily including the size of individual sites, parking and loading regulations, and building setback lines, and (ii) designed to be compatible, under a comprehensive plan, with the community in which the industrial park is located and with the uses of the surrounding land.

(c) *Development of land defined.* For purposes of section 103(c)(5) and this section, the term "development of land" includes the provision of certain improvements to an industrial park site if such improvements are incidental to the use of the land as an industrial park. Such incidental improvements include the building or installation of incidental water, sewer, sewage and waste disposal, drainage, or similar facilities (whether surface, subsurface, or both). Such incidental improvements include the provision of incidental transportation facilities, such as hard-surface roads (including curbs and gutters) and railroad spurs and sidings; power distribution facilities, such as gas and electric lines; and communication facilities. The provision of structures or buildings of any kind is not included within the meaning of the term "development of land," except for those

Reg. § 1.103-9(c)

→ *Caution: Code Sec. 103 has been amended to remove special exempt bond issue rules and provide similar rules in Code Secs. 141–150.*←

structures or buildings which are necessary in connection with the incidental improvements encompassed by the term, such as, for example, a water pumphouse and storage tank needed in connection with the incidental provision of water facilities in an industrial park.

(d) *Examples.* The applications of the rules contained in section 103(c)(5) and this section are illustrated by the following examples:

Example (1). City A and corporation X, Y, and Z (unrelated companies) enter into an arrangement under which A is to acquire a tract of land suitable for use as an industrial park. The arrangement provides that: (1) A will issue $10 million of bonds to be used for the acquisition and development of a suitable tract of land; (2) the tract will be controlled and administered by A, pursuant to a comprehensive zoning plan, for the use of a group of enterprises; (3) A will install necessary water, sewer, and drainage facilities on the tract; (4) A will sell substantial portions of the developed tract to X for use as a factory site and to Y for use as a warehouse site; (5) A will lease a sizeable portion of the tract to Z for 20 years as a distribution center site; and (6) the developed tract and the proceeds from the sale or lease of parts of the tract will be the security for the bonds. The bonds are industrial development bonds. Since, however, the proceeds of the issue are to be used for the acquisition and development of a tract of land as the site for an industrial park under section 103(c)(5), section 103(c)(1) does not apply unless the provisions of section 103(c)(7) and § 1.103-11 apply.

Example (2). The facts are the same as in example (1) except that $1 million of the proceeds of the $10 million issue are to be used for the construction of a factory by corporation W or X. The bonds are industrial development bonds. Under these circumstances, substantially all of the proceeds are treated as used or to be used for the acquisition and development of a tract of land as the site for an industrial park described in section 103(c)(5). Accordingly, section 103(c)(1) does not apply unless the provisions of section 103(c)(7) and § 1.103-11 apply. [Reg. § 1.103-9.]

☐ [*T.D. 7199, 7-31-72. Amended by T.D. 7511, 9-30-77.*]

[Reg. § 1.103-10]

§ 1.103-10. Exemption for certain small issues of industrial development bonds.—(a) *In general.* Section 103(b)(6) applies to certain industrial development bond issues (referred to in this section as "exempt small issues") and bonds issued to refund certain issues (referred to in this section as "exempt small refunding issues"). If an issue is an exempt small issue or an exempt small refunding issue, then under the requirements of section 103(b)(6) and this section the interest paid on the debt obligations is not includable in gross income, and the obligations are treated as obligations described in section 103(a)(1) and § 1.103-1, even though such obligations are industrial development bonds as defined in section 103(b)(2) and § 1.103-7. However, interest on an obligation of such an issue is includable in gross income if the obligation is held by a substantial user of the financial facilities or a related person (as described in section 103(b)(7) and § 1.103-11). Section 103(b)(6) only becomes applicable where the bond issue meets both the trade or business and the security interest tests so that the obligations are industrial development bonds within the meaning of section 103(b)(2). For bonds issued before January 1, 1979, in taxable years ending before such date, and for capital expenditures made before January 1, 1979, with respect to such bonds, paragraphs (b), (c), and (d) of this section shall be applied by substituting $5 million for $10 million.

(b) *Small issue exemption*—(1) *$1 million or less.* Section 103(b)(6)(A) provides that section 103(b)(1) shall not apply to any debt obligation issued by a State or local governmental unit as part of an issue where—

(i) The aggregate authorized face amount of such issue (determined by aggregating the outstanding face amount of any prior exempt small issues described in paragraph (d) of this section and the face amount of the issue of obligations in question) is $1 million or less; and

(ii) Substantially all of the proceeds of such issue is to be used for the acquisition, construction, reconstruction, or improvement of land or property of a character subject to the allowance for depreciation under section 167. Proceeds which are loaned to a borrower for use as working capital or to finance inventory are not used in the manner described in the preceding sentence. Whether substantially all of the proceeds of an issue of governmental obligations are used in such manner is determined consistently with the rules for exempt facilities in § 1.103-8(a)(1)(i). Any obligation which is an industrial development bond within the meaning of section 103(b)(2) and which satisfies the $1 million small issue exemption requirements is an exempt small issue. See paragraph (c)(1) of this section for the treatment of refunding issues of $1 million or less.

Reg. § 1.103-10(a)

→ *Caution: Code Sec. 103 has been amended to remove special exempt bond issue rules and provide similar rules in Code Secs. 141–150.*←

(2) *$10 million or less.* (i) Under section 103(b)(6)(D), the issuing State or local governmental unit may elect to have an aggregate authorized face amount of $10 million or less, in lieu of the $1 million exemption otherwise provided for in section 103(b)(6)(A), with respect to issues of obligations that are industrial development bonds (within the meaning of section 103(b)(2)) issued after October 24, 1968. If the election s made in a timely manner, the bonds will be treated as obligations of a State or local governmental unit described in section 103(a)(1) and § 1..03-1 if the sum of—

(a) The aggregate face amount of the issue including the aggregate outstanding face amount of any prior $1 million or $10 million exempt small issues taken into account under section 103(b)(6)(B) and paragraph (d) of this section, and

(b) The aggregate amount of "section 103(b)(6)(D) capital expenditures" (within the meaning of paragraph (b)(2)(ii) of this section),

is $10 million or less. In the case of an issue of obligations that qualified for exemption uner section 103(b)(6)(A) and this paragraph, if a section 103(b)(6)(D) capital expenditure made after the date of issue has the effect of making taxable the interest on the issue, under section 103(b)(6)(G) the loss of tax exemption for the interest shall begin only with the date on which the expenditure that caused the issue to cease to qualify under the $10 million limit was paid or incurred. See paragraph (b)(2)(vi) of this section for the time and manner in which the issuer may elect the $10 million exemption. See section 103(b)(6)(H) and paragraph (c)(2) of this section for the treatment of certain refinancing issues of $10 million or less.

(ii) The term "section 103(b)(6)(D) capital expenditure" is defined in this subdivision. Special rules for applying such definition in the case of certain expenditures paid or incurred by a State or local governmental unit are prescribed in subdivision (iii) of this subparagraph. Except as excluded by subdivision (iv) or (v) of this subparagraph, an expenditure (regardless of how paid, whether in cash, notes, or stock in a taxable or nontaxable transaction) is a section 103(b)(6)(D) capital expenditure if—

(a) The capital expenditure was financed other than out of the proceeds of issues to the extent such issues are taken into account under paragraph (b)(2)(i)(a) of this section.

(b) The capital expenditures were paid or incurred during the 6-year period which begins

3 years before the date of issuance of the issue in question and ends 3 years after such date,

(c) The principal user of the facility in connection with which the property resulting from the capital expenditures is used and the principal user of the facility financed by the proceeds of the issue in question is the same person or are two or more related persons (as defined in section 103(b)6)(C) and paragraph (e) of this section),

(d) Both facilities referred to in (c) of this subdivision were (during the period described in (b) of this subdivision or a part thereof) located in the same incorporated municipality or in the same county (outside of the incorporated municipalities in such county), and

(e) The capital expenditures were properly chargeable to the capital account of any person or State or local governmental unit (whether or not such person is the principal user of the facility or a related person) determined, for this purpose, without regard to any rule of the Code which permits expenditures properly chargeable to capital account to be treated as current expenses. With respect to obligations issued on or after August 8, 1972, determinations under the preceding sentence shall be made by including any expenditure which may, under any rule or election under the Code, be treated as a capital expenditure (whether or not such expenditure is so treated). With respect to obligations issued on or after August 8, 1972, for purposes of this subparagraph, capital expenditures made with respect to a contiguous or integrated facility which is located on both sides of a border between two or more political jurisdictions are made with respect to a facility located in all such jurisdictions and, therefore, shall be treated as if they were made in each such political jurisdiction.

(iii) Amounts properly chargeable to capital account under subdivision (ii)(e) of this subparagraph include capital expenditures made by a State or local governmental unit with respect to an exempt facility or an industrial park, within the 6-year period described in subdivision (ii)(b) of this subparagraph, out of the proceeds of bond issues to which section 103(b)(1) did not apply by reason of section 103(b)(4) or (5) (relating to certain exempt activities and industrial parks). Thus, for example, the cost to the lessor of a leased plant site financed out of the proceeds of an issue for an exempt air pollution control facility under section 103(b)(4)(F) and paragraph (g) of § 1.103-8 would constitute a section 103(b)(6)(D) capital expenditure. However, in the case of an industrial park, only the land costs allocated on

→ *Caution: Code Sec. 103 has been amended to remove special exempt bond issue rules and provide similar rules in Code Secs. 141–150.*←

an area basis to the plant site and the actual cost of any improvements made on the plant site, or to be used principally in connection with the actual plant site occupied by a principal user or a related person, shall be taken into account as capital expenditures. Where the actual amount of capital expenditures made with respect to a facility by a person (including a State or local governmental unit) other than the user of such facility (or a related person) cannot be ascertained, the fair market value of the property with respect to which the capital expenditures were made, at the time of such capital expenditures, shall be deemed to be the amount of such capital expenditures. In the case of a transaction which is not in form a purchase but which is treated as a purchase for Federal income tax purposes, the purchase price for Federal income tax purposes shall constitute a capital expenditure.

(iv) A section 103(b)(6)(D) capital expenditure shall not include any "excluded expenditure" described in subdivision (a) through (e) of this subdivision (iv):

(a) A capital expenditure is an excluded expenditure if either it is made by a public utility company which is not the principal user of the facility financed by the proceeds of the issue in question (or a related person) with respect to property of such company, or it is made by a State or local governmental unit with respect to property of such unit, and if in either case it meets all of the following three conditions: Such property of such company or unit (as the case may be) must be used to provide gas, water, sewage disposal services, electric energy, or telephone service. Such property must be installed in, or connected to, the facility but must not consist of property which is such an integral part of the facility that the cost of such property is ordinarily included as part of the acquisition, construction, or reconstruction cost of such facility. Such property must be of a type normally paid for by the user (or a related person) in the form of periodic fees based upon time or use.

(b) A capital expenditure is an excluded expenditure if it is made by a person other than the user, a related person, or a State or local governmental unit and if it is made with respect to tangible personal property (within the meaning of paragraph (c) of § 1.48-1), or intangible personal property, leased to the user (or a related person) of a facility. However, the preceding sentence shall apply only if such personal property is leased by the manufacturer of such tangible or intangible personal property, or by a person in the

trade or business of leasing property the same as, or similar to, such personal property, and only if, pursuant to general business practice, property of such type is ordinarily the subject of a lease.

(c) A capital expenditure is an excluded expenditure if it is made to replace property damaged or destroyed by fire, storm, or other casualty, to the extent that these expenditures do not exceed in dollar amount the fair market value (determined immediately before the casualty) of the property replaced.

(d) A capital expenditure is an excluded expenditure if it is required by a change made after the date of issue in a Federal or State law, or a local ordinance which has general application, or if it is required by a change made after such date in rules and regulations of general application issued under such law or ordinance.

(e) A capital expenditure is an excluded expenditure if it is required by or arises out of circumstances which could not reasonably be foreseen on the date of issue or which arise out of a mistake of law or fact. However, the aggregate dollar amount taken into account under this subdivision (e) with respect to any issue may not exceed $1,000,000. With respect to expenditures incurred prior to December 11, 1971, the dollar amount specified in the preceding sentence shall be $250,000.

(v)(a) If the assets of a corporation are acquired by another corporation in a transaction to which section 381(a) (relating to carryovers in certain corporate acquisitions) applies, the exchange of consideration by the acquiring corporation for such assets is not a section 103(b)(6)(D) capital expenditure by such acquiring corporation.

(b) However, if an exchange referred to in (a) of this subdivision occurs during the 6-year period beginning 3 years before the date of issuance of an issue of obligations and ending 3 years after such date, the transferor and transferee shall be treated as having been related persons for the portion of such 6-year period preceding the date of the exchange for purposes of determining whether section 103(b)(6)(D) capital expenditures have been made. For purposes of this subdivision (b), the date of an exchange to which section 381 applies shall be the date of distribution or transfer within the meaning of paragraph (b) of § 1.381(b)-1.

(c) If section 351 (a) applies to a transfer of property to a corporation solely in exchange for its stock or securities, the issuance of such

→ *Caution: Code Sec. 103 has been amended to remove special exempt bond issue rules and provide similar rules in Code Secs. 141–150.*←

stock or securities in such exchange is not a section 103(b)(6)(D) capital expenditure by such corporation.

(d) However, if such a transfer referred to in *(c)* of this subdivision occurs during the 6-year period beginning 3 years before the date of issuance of an issue of obligations and ending 3 years after such date, and if, with respect to the property transferred, expenditures made within such period would have been section 103(b)(6)(D) capital expenditures if the transferor and transferee had been related persons for such period, then such expenditures shall be considered to be section 103(b)(6)(D) capital expenditures made by the transferee. In addition, if a transferor and transferee are related persons immediately following such transfer, such transferor and transferee shall also be treated as having been related persons for the portion of such 6-year period preceding the date of such transfer.

(e) For purposes of this subdivision (v), the term "issue of obligations" means an issue being tested for purposes of qualifying or continuing to qualify under an election pursuant to section 103(b)(6)(D) as to which an amount which would be a section 103(b)(6)(D) capital expenditure solely by reason of *(b)* or *(d)* of the subdivision must be taken into account.

(f) If with respect to an issue of obligations an expenditure would not have been a section 103(b)(6)(D) capital expenditure but for the application of *(b)* or *(d)* of this subdivision, and if such section 103(b)(6)(D) capital expenditure has the effect of making taxable the interest on an issue of obligations which qualified for exemption under section 103(b)(6)(A) and this paragraph, the loss of tax exemption for such interest shall begin not earlier than the date of such exchange or transfer referred to in this subdivision (v).

(vi) The issuer may make the election provided by section 103(b)(6)(D) and this paragraph (b)(2) (assuming that the bonds otherwise qualify under section 103(b)(6)) by noting the election affirmatively at or before the time of issuance of the issue in question on its books or records with respect to the issue. The term "books or records" includes the bond resolution or other similar legislation for the issue in question as well as the bond transcript or other compilation of bond and bond-related documents. If the issuer fails to make an election at the time and in the manner prescribed in this paragraph (b)(2), the issue will not be treated as described in section 103(b)(6)(D), and interest thereon will be includible in gross income.

(c) *Refunding or refinancing issue exemption*—(1) *$1 million or less refunding issue.* Section 103(b)(6)(A) also provides that section 103(b)(1) shall not apply to any debt obligation issued by a State or local governmental unit as part of an issue the aggregate authorized face amount of which is $1 million or less, if substantially all of the proceeds of such issue are to be used—

(i) To redeem part or all of a prior issue substantially all of the proceeds of which were used to acquire, construct, reconstruct, or improve land or property of a character subject to the allowance for depreciation, or

(ii) To redeem part or all of a prior exempt small refunding issue.

(2) *$10 million or less refinancing issue.* Section 103(b)(6)(H) provides that section 103(b)(1) shall not apply to any debt obligation issued by a governmental unit as part of an issue which is $10 million or less if the condition of section 103(b)(6)(H) is met and if substantially all of the proceeds are to be used—

(i) To redeem part or all of one or more prior exempt small issues, or

(ii) To redeem part or all of one or more prior exempt small refunding issues.

The condition of section 103(b)(6)(H) is that an election by the issuer of the $10 million exemption in lieu of the $1 million limit for a refunding issue may be made only if each prior issue being redeemed is an issue which qualified either for the $1 million exemption or, by reason of an election under section 103(b)(6)(D), for the $10 million exemption. In addition, in applying the capital expenditures test under section 103(b)(6)(D)(ii) and paragraph (b)(2)(i)(*b*) of this section to refinancing issues, section 103(b)(6)(D) capital expenditures are taken into account only for purposes of determining whether prior issues which were made under the section 103(b)(6)(D) election qualified under section 103(b)(6)(A) and would have continued to qualify under that section but for the redemption.

(d) *Certain prior issues taken into account*—(1) *In general.* Section 103(b)(6)(B) provides, in effect, that if (i) a prior issue specified in subparagraph (2) of this paragraph is an exempt small issue (including for this purpose an exempt small refunding issue) under section 103(b)(6)(A) and this section, and (ii) such prior issue is outstanding at the time of issuance of a subsequent issue, then in determining the aggregate face amount of such subsequent issue (for purposes of determining whether such issue is a $1 million or $10

Reg. § 1.103-10(d)(1)

→ *Caution: Code Sec. 103 has been amended to remove special exempt bond issue rules and provide similar rules in Code Secs. 141–150.*←

million exempt small issue under section 103(b)(6)(A) and this section) there shall be taken into account the outstanding face amount of such prior exempt small issue. For purposes of this paragraph, the outstanding face amount of a prior exempt small issue does not include the face amount of any obligation which is to be redeemed from the proceeds of such subsequent issue.

(2) *Prior issues specified.* The face amount of an outstanding prior exempt small issue is taken into account under subparagraph (1) of this paragraph if—

(i) The proceeds of both the prior exempt small issue and of the subsequent issue (whether or not the State or local governmental unit issuing such obligation is the same unit for each such issue) are or will be used primarily with respect to facilities located or to be located in the same incorporated municipality or located or to be located in the same county outside of an incorporated municipality in such county (and for purposes of this subdivision, on or after August 8, 1972, a contiguous or integrated facility which is located on both sides of a border between two or more political jurisdictions shall be treated as if it is entirely within each such political jurisdiction), and

(ii) The principal user of the financed facilities referred to in subdivision (i) of this subparagraph is or will be the same person or two or more related persons (as defined in section 103(b)(6)(C) and paragraph (e) of this section).

(3) *Rules of application.* The rules of this paragraph shall apply—

(i) Only in the case of outstanding prior exempt small issues which are industrial development bonds to which section 103(b)(1) would have applied but for the provisions of section 103(b)(6). Thus, for example, the provisions of this paragraph do not apply in respect of a prior issue of obligations issued on or before April 30, 1968. In addition, the provisions of this paragraph do not apply in respect of a prior issue for an exempt facility under section 103(b)(4) and § 1.103-8, or for an industrial park under section 103(b)(5) and § 1.103-9, whether or not the issue might also have qualified as an exempt small issue under section 103(b)(6)(A) and this section.

(ii) To all prior exempt small issues which meet the requirements of this paragraph. Thus, for example, in determining the aggregate face amount of an issue under section 103(b)(6)(A), the outstanding face amount of prior $1 million or $10 million exempt small issues which meet the

requirements of this paragraph shall be taken into account in determining the aggregate face amount of a subsequent issue being tested for the $1 million small issue exemption. Similarly, in determining the aggregate face amount of an issue under section 103(b)(6)(A) and (D), the outstanding face amount of prior $1 million or $10 million exempt small issues which meet the requirements of this paragraph shall be taken into account in determining the aggregate face amount of a subsequent issue being tested for the $10 million small issue exemption.

(e) *Related persons.* For purposes of section 103(b) and § § 1.103-7 through 1.103-11, the term "related person" means a person who is related to another person if, on the date of issue of an issue of obligations—

(1) The relationship between such persons would result in a disallowance of losses under section 267 (relating to disallowance of losses, etc., between related taxpayers) and section 707(b) (relating to losses disallowed, etc., between partners and controlled partnerships) and the regulations thereunder, or

(2) Such persons are members of the same controlled group of corporations, as defined in section 1563(a), relating to definition of controlled group of corporations (except that "more than 50 percent" shall be substituted for "at least 80 percent" each place it appears in section 1563(a)) and the regulations thereunder.

(f) *Disqualification of certain small issues.* (1) Section 103(b)(6) shall not apply to any obligation issued after April 24, 1979, which is part of an issue, a significant portion of the proceeds of which are to be used directly or indirectly to provide residential real property for family units. For purposes of the preceding sentence, the term "residential real property for family units" means residential rental projects (within the meaning of § 1.103-8(b)) and owner-occupied residences (within the meaning of section 103A).

(2) For purposes of paragraph (f)(1), a significant portion of the proceeds of an issue are used to provide residential real property for family units if 5 percent or more of the proceeds are so used.

(g) *Examples.* The application of the rules contained in section 103(b)(6) and this section are illustrated by the following examples:

Example (1). County A and corporation X enter into an arrangement under which the county will provide a factory which X will lease for 25 years. The arrangement provides (1) that A will issue $1

Reg. § 1.103-10(d)(2)

→ *Caution: Code Sec. 103 has been amended to remove special exempt bond issue rules and provide similar rules in Code Secs. 141–150.*←

million of bonds on March 1, 1970, (2) that the proceeds of the bond issue will be used to acquire land in County A (but not in an incorporated municipality) and to construct and equip a factory on such land in accordance with X's specifications, (3) that X will rent the facility for 25 years at an annual rental equal to the amount necessary to amortize the principal and pay the interest on the outstanding bonds, and (4) that such payments by X and the facility itself shall be the security for the bonds. Although the bonds issued are industrial development bonds, the bonds are an exempt small issue under section 103(b)(6)(A) and this section since the aggregate authorized face amount of the bond issue is $1 million or less and all of the proceeds of the bond issue are to be used to acquire and improve land and acquire and construct depreciable property. The result would be the same if the arrangement provided that X would purchase the facility from A.

Example (2). The facts are the same as in example (1) except that, instead of acquiring land and constructing a new factory, the arrangement provides that A will acquire a vacant existing factory building and rebuild and equip the building in accordance with X's specifications. The bonds are an exempt small issue for the same reasons as in example (1).

Example (3). The facts are the same as in example (1) or (2) except that the financed facilities are additions to facilities which were financed by an issue of bonds to which section 103(c)(1) does not apply because such bonds were issued prior to May 1, 1968, or were subject to the transitional provisions of § 1.103-12. The bonds are an exempt small issue since neither of the prior bond issues are taken into account under section 103(b)(6)(B) and this section in determining the status of industrial development bonds which are issued after April 30, 1968, and which are not subject to the transitional provisions of § 1.103-12.

Example (4). The facts are the same as in example (1) except that, subsequently, corporation X proposes to County A that A built a $400,000 warehouse located in Town M (an unincorporated town located in County A) for X under terms similar to the factory arrangement described in example (1). On the proposed issue date of the subsequent bond issue, $600,000 of the first exempt small issue will be outstanding. If A issues $400,000 of bonds for such purposes, the bonds will be an exempt small issue under section 103(b)(6) and this section since, under the rules of

section 103(b)(6)(B) and paragraph (d) of this section, if the aggregate authorized face amount of the new issue and the outstanding prior exempt small issue will be $1 million or less, the new issue will be an exempt small issue. If, however, the aggregate authorized face amount of the prior issue outstanding on the date of the subsequent issue were in excess of $600,000, the subsequent issue would not qualify as an exempt small issue because (1) the combined aggregate face amount of the outstanding prior issue and the new issue would be in excess of $1 million, (2) the facilities financed by both issues are to be located in unincorporated areas in the same county, (3) the same taxpayer will be the principal user of both facilities, and (4) but for the rules of section 103(b)(6)(B) and paragraph (d) of this section the prior issue would be an exempt small issue.

Example (5). The facts are the same as in example (1) except that subsequently corporation X proposes to City P and City R (incorporated municipalities located in County A) that P and R each issue bonds and each build $1 million facilities to be located in Cities P and R for the use of X under terms similar to the arrangement in example (1). Each of the $1 million issues will be an exempt small issue because each proposed facility is located within a different incorporated municipality and the proceeds of the prior outstanding exempt small issue were used to construct facilities outside of an incorporated area.

Example (6). The facts are the same as in example (1) except that $95,000 of the $1 million will be used by the corporation as working capital. The bonds are an exempt small issue for the same reason as in example (1) since substantially all of the proceeds will be used for the acquisition of land and the construction of depreciable property.

Example (7). The facts are the same as in example (1) except that on November 1, 1969, County A issued $10 million of industrial development bonds, all of the proceeds of which were issued for the acquisition of land as the site for an industrial park within the meaning of section 103(c)(5) and § 1.103-9. The proceeds of the $1 million of bonds issued in 1970 will be used to construct a factory for corporation X to be located in the industrial park. The bonds issued in 1970 are industrial development bonds within the meaning of section 103(b)(2) and § 1.103-7. Since, however, the prior 1969 issue is not an issue to which section 103(b)(6)(A) applied (see paragraph (d)(3)(i) of this section), the bonds issued in 1970 are an exempt small issue for the reasons stated in example (1).

Reg. § 1.103-10(g)

25,072   **Items Specifically Excluded from Gross Income**

See p. 20,601 for regulations not amended to reflect law changes .

→ *Caution: Code Sec. 103 has been amended to remove special exempt bond issue rules and provide similar rules in Code Secs. 141–150.*←

Example (8). County B enters into three separate arrangements with three unrelated corporations whereby the county will provide separate storage facilities for each corporation. The arrangement provides (1) that the county will issue bonds and loan to each corporation $250,000 of the proceeds which will be used to acquire land in the county and to construct the facilities, (2) that the rental payments by the corporations will be equal to the amount necessary to amortize the principal and pay the interest on any outstanding bonds issued by the county, and (3) that the payments by the corporations and the facilities themselves shall be the security for the industrial development bonds. For convenience, the county issues one series of bonds in the face amount of $750,000 rather than three separate series of bonds of $250,000 each. The issue is an exempt small issue under section 103(c)(6)(A) and paragraph (b)(1) of this section since the aggregate authorized face amount of the bond issue is $1 million or less, and all of the proceeds of the bond issue are to be used to acquire and improve land and acquire and construct depreciable property.

Example (9). City C and corporation Y enter into an arrangement under which C will provide a factory which Y will lease for 25 years. The arrangement provides (1) that C will issue $4 million of bonds on March 1, 1969, after making the election under section 103(b)(6)(D) and paragraph (b)(2) of this section, (2) that the proceeds of the bond issue will be used to acquire land in the city and to construct and equip a factory on such land in accordance with Y's specifications, (3) that Y will rent the facilities for 25 years at an annual rental equal to the amount necessary to amortize the principal and pay the interest on the outstanding bonds, (4) that such payments by Y and the facility itself shall be the security for the bonds, and (5) that, if corporation Y pays or incurs capital expenditures in excess of $1 million within 3 years from the date of issue which disqualify the bonds as an exempt small issue under section 103(b)(6)(D), it will either furnish funds to C to redeem such bonds at par or at a premium, or increase the rental payments to C in an amount sufficient to pay a premium interest rate. Although the bonds issued are industrial development bonds, they are an exempt small issue under section 103(b)(6)(A) by reason of the election under section 103(b)(6)(D) and paragraph (b)(2) of this section, since the aggregate authorized face amount of the bond issue is $5 million or less and all of the proceeds of the bond issue are to be used to acquire and improve land and acquire and construct depreciable property. The provisions for redemption of the bonds or an increase in rental if the bonds are disqualified as an exempt small issue under section 103(b)(6)(A) will not disqualify an otherwise valid election under section 103(b)(6)(D) and paragraph (b)(2) of this section.

Example (10). The facts are the same as in example (9) except that corporation Y subsequently proposed to the city that it build a $1 million warehouse next to the plant for the use of Y under terms similar to the factory arrangement. Assume further that the factory building was completed by March 1, 1970, and that on January 15, 1972, the proposed issue date of the subsequent bond issue, $2 million of the first exempt small issue will be outstanding. In determining the aggregate authorized face amount of the new issue, the original face amount of a prior outstanding issue must be reduced by that portion which is to be redeemed before it is added to the face amount of the new issue. Therefore, if the city issues $3 million of bonds to redeem the remaining $2 million of bonds and to construct the warehouse, the bonds will be an exempt small issue under section 103(b)(6)(A) if an election is made under section 103(b)(6)(D) and paragraph (b)(2) of this section since (1) the face amount of the new issue ($3 million), plus (2) the face amount of the prior outstanding exempt small issue minus the amount of such issue to be refunded ($2 million minus $2 million), plus (3) capital expenditures during the preceding three years financed other than out of the proceeds of outstanding issues to which section 103(b)(6)(A) and paragraph (b) of this section applied ($2 million), do not exceed $5 million. If, however, the amount of the January 15, 1972, issue were $3½ million, the issue would not qualify as an exempt small issue under section 103(b)(6)(A) and paragraph (b)(2) of this section.

Example (11). The facts are the same as in example (9), except that on June 15, 1971, Y purchases from an unrelated motor carrier business a warehouse terminal in the same city at a cost of $250,000 and tractor-trailers and other automotive equipment based at the terminal at a cost of $1 million. This subsequent expenditure by Y has the effect of making the interest on the city C bonds includible in the gross income of the holders of such bonds as of June 15, 1971, because the face amount of the March 1, 1969, issue ($4 million) plus the subsequent capital expenditures within three years of the date of issue ($1,250,000) exceed $5 million. (See section

Reg. § 1.103-10(g)

→ *Caution: Code Sec. 103 has been amended to remove special exempt bond issue rules and provide similar rules in Code Secs. 141–150.*←

103(b)(6)(D) and paragraph (b)(2)(i) of this section.)

Example (12). The facts are the same as in example (9), except that in March, 1970, Y will move $3 million of additional used machinery and equipment into the factory from its factory in another city. The expenditures for such machinery and equipment were incurred by Y more than 3 years prior to the date of issue of the bonds. The transfer of such used equipment into city C does not constitute a section 103(c)(6)(D) capital expenditure within the meaning of paragraph (b)(2)(ii) of this section since the expenditures with respect to such property were incurred more than three years prior to the date of issue of the bonds. Had the capital expenditures with respect to such property been incurred during the 6-year period beginning 3 years before the date of issue of the bonds and in the 3 years after such date, they would constitute section 103(b)(6)(D) capital expenditures.

Example (13). The facts are the same as in example (9), except that in March, 1970, corporation Y enters into an arrangement with respect to machinery and equipment to be used in the facility. The arrangement is labeled by the parties as a lease but is treated as a sale for Federal income tax purposes. The amount treated as the purchase price of the machinery and equipment is a section 103(b)(6)(D) capital expenditure.

Example (14). On February 1, 1970, city D issues $5 million of its bonds to finance construction of an addition to the manufacturing plant of corporation Z. The bonds will be secured by the facility and lease payments to be made by Z which will be sufficient to pay the principal and interest on such bonds. Assume that the bonds qualify as an exempt small issue under section 103(b)(6)(A) pursuant to an election under section 103(b)(6)(D) and paragraph (b)(2) of this section. On February 1, 1971, D plans to issue $1 million of its bonds to construct a pollution control facility to be leased to Z for use at its manufacturing plant. The rental payments from the lease will be sufficient to pay the principal and interest on the bonds. The bonds will be secured by such facility and the lease payments. Capital expenditures for the pollution control facility will be paid or incurred beginning before February 1, 1973. Although the pollution control facility is an exempt facility under section 103(b)(4)(F) and paragraph (g) of § 1.103-8, amounts used for the pollution control facility shall be considered to be a section 103(b)(6)(D) capital expenditure and the interest on the February 1, 1970, issue will become taxable

as of the date such capital expenditure began to be paid or incurred. See section 103(b)(6)(G) and paragraph (b)(2)(i) of this section.

Example (15). On February 1, 1970, city E issues $500,000 of its bonds to acquire and develop an industrial park within the meaning of section 103(b)(5) and paragraph (b) of § 1.103-9. The park consists of 100 acres and is divided into one 50 acre plant site and 4 smaller sites. The aggregate acquisition cost of the undeveloped land is $150,000 or an average per acre cost of $1,500. Roads, sidewalks, sewers, utilities, sewage, and waste disposal facilities serving the entire industrial park cost $300,000. On September 1, 1970, E leases to corporation Y for 30 years the 50 acre plant site (with an allocated cost of $75,000) and a railroad spur track from the railroad right of way to Y's plant site for Y's exclusive use. The spur track was constructed using $50,000 of the proceeds of the industrial park bond issue. E also proposes to issue on September 1, 1970, $4,875,000 of its bonds to construct and equip a building on the leased plant site to be leased to Y at an additional rental sufficient to pay the principal and interest on this issue of bonds. The September 1, 1970, issue will be an exempt small issue under section 103(c)(6)(A) pursuant to an election under section 103(b)(6)(D) and paragraph (b)(2) of this section since the sum of the amount of the second issue ($4,875,000) and the capital expenditures allocated to the plant site ($75,000 for 50 acres of land plus $50,000 for the railroad spur tract, totalling $125,000) does not exceed $5 million. The sum of $300,000 which was spent in development of the industrial park provided facilities which will serve or benefit the users generally and hence under paragraph (b)(2)(ii) of this section is not considered to have provided facilities as to which Y will be the principal user.

Example (16). On June 1, 1970, corporation Z simultaneously enters into separate arrangements with city F and city G under which each city will issue a $5 million exempt small issue of bonds the proceeds of which will be used by Z to construct separate facilities in each city. By June 1, 1971, the facilities have been completed in the respective cities. On January 1, 1972, cities F and G, through a valid legal proceeding, merge into a new city FG. Since in this case F and G were separate cities on June 1, 1970 (the date of the bond issues), the factories are not considered to be located in the same incorporated municipality. Accordingly, each $5 million issue by city F and G will continue to qualify as an exempt small issue.

Reg. § 1.103-10(g)

→ *Caution: Code Sec. 103 has been amended to remove special exempt bond issue rules and provide similar rules in Code Secs. 141–150.*←

Example (17). On June 1, 1973, city H issues an exempt small issue of $4.75 million to finance a facility of corporation S to be located in city H. On October 1, 1974, S and corporation T, previously unrelated to S, consummated a statutory merger which qualifies as a reorganization described in section 368(a)(1)(A) and thus as a transaction described in section 381(a). In the transaction, T transferred to S assets with a fair market value of $1.5 million in exchange for stock of S, $300,000 of securities of S, and $100,000 cash. On March 23, 1971, T made $400,000 of capital expenditures for an addition to its factory located in city H. For purposes of testing the H issue of June 1, 1973, such expenditures would have been section 103(b)(6)(D) capital expenditures if T and S had been related persons. Under the provisions of paragraph (b)(2)(v)(a) of this section, the exchange of $1.5 million of stock, securities, and cash by S does not constitute a section 103(b)(6)(D) capital expenditure. Since, however, S and T are treated as related persons starting three years prior to the date of issue of the obligations, the $400,000 of expenditures by T constitute section 103(b)(6)(D) capital expenditures. Thus, the interest on the June 1, 1973, issue of obligations would become taxable (since the $5 million limit would be exceeded) on the date of the merger.

Example (18). In 1965 City I issues $10 million of industrial development bonds to construct and equip a factory for corporation Z. In 1975 the remaining principal amount of the bonds outstanding is $4.1 million. If I issues $4.5 million of bonds to redeem the balance of the prior issue, and for other purposes, such issue cannot qualify as an exempt small issue under section 103(b)(6)(D) and paragraph (b)(2) of this section even though at the time of issue the interest on the 1965 bonds was tax-exempt since the prior issue must be one which qualified under section 103(b)(6)(A) and this section. Further, the 1975 issue will be an issue of industrial development bonds notwithstanding the provisions of paragraph (d)(2) of § 1.103-7 which provides that certain bonds issued to refund an issue of obligations issued on or before April 30, 1968 (or January 1, 1969, in certain cases) will not be so treated. Paragraph (d)(2) of § 1.103-7 is not applicable because the 1975 issue makes funds available for a purpose other than the debt service obligation on the 1965 bonds.

Example (19). In 1969 City J issues $4 million of industrial development bonds which qualify as an exempt small issue under section 103(b)(6)(A)

pursuant to an election under section 103(b)(6)(D) and paragraph (b)(2) of this section. In 1971, by reason of a $2 million addition to the factory built with the proceeds of the issue, the 1969 exempt small issue loses its tax-exempt status. In 1972, the city issues a $5 million issue to redeem the prior 1969 issue. The redemption issue will not qualify as an exempt small issue since the prior 1969 issue did not continue to qualify under section 103(b)(6)(A) and this section. [Reg. § 1.103-10.]

☐ [*T.D. 7199, 7-31-72. Amended by T.D. 7511, 9-30-77, T.D. 7840, 10-12-82 and T.D. 8086, 5-1-86.*]

[Reg. § 1.103-11]

§ 1.103-11. Bonds held by substantial users.—(a) *In general.* Section 103(c)(4), (5), or (6) (relating respectively to interest on bonds to finance certain exempt facilities, interest on bonds to finance industrial parks, and the exemption for certain small issues of industrial development bonds) does not apply, as provided in section 103(c)(7), with respect to any obligation for any period during which such obligation is held either by a person who is a substantial user of the facilities with respect to which the proceeds of such obligation were used or by a related person (within the meaning of section 103(c)(6)(C) and paragraph (e) of § 1.103-10). Therefore, in such a case, interest paid on such an obligation is includable in the gross income of a substantial user (or related person) for any period during which such obligation is held by such user (or related person).

(b) *Substantial user.* In general, a substantial user of a facility includes any nonexempt person who regularly uses a part of such facility in his trade or business. However, unless a facility, or a part thereof, is constructed, reconstructed, or acquired specifically for a nonexempt person or persons, such a nonexempt person shall be considered to be a substantial user of a facility only if (1) the gross revenue derived by such user with respect to such facility is more than 5 percent of the total revenue derived by all users of such facility or (2) the amount of area of the facility occupied by such user is more than 5 percent of the entire usable area of the facility. Under certain facts and circumstances, where a nonexempt person has a contractual or preemptive right to the exclusive use of property or a portion of property, such person may be a substantial user of such property. A substantial user may also be a lessee or sublessee of all or any portion of the facility. A licensee or similar person may also be a substantial user

Reg. § 1.103-11(a)

→ *Caution: Code Sec. 103 has been amended to remove special exempt bond issue rules and provide similar rules in Code Secs. 141–150.*←

where his use is regular and is not merely a casual, infrequent, or sporadic use of the facility. Absent special circumstances, individuals who are physically present on or in the facility as employees of a substantial user shall not be deemed to be substantial users.

(c) *Examples.* The application of section 103(c)(7) and this section are illustrated by the following examples:

Example (1). Pursuant to an arrangement with corporation X, county A issues $4 million of its bonds (an exempt small issue under section 103(c)(6)(A) pursuant to an election under section 103(c)(6)(D) and paragraph (b)(2) of § 1.103-10) and will use the proceeds to finance construction of a manufacturing facility which is to be leased to X for an annual rental of $500,000. X subleases space to a restaurant operator at an annual rental of $25,000 for the operation of a canteen and lunch counter for the convenience of X's employees. The canteen is required to be open at least five days each week (except holidays) from 8:30 A.M. to 5:00 P.M., and the lunch counter must be in operation during the noon hour. The canteen regularly sells cigarettes, candy, and soft drinks, and uses advertising displays and dispensers with product names. The space physically occupied and the amount of revenue derived by the restaurant operator are more than 5 percent of the respective amounts with respect to the entire facility. Both X and the restaurant operator are substantial users. However, absent special circumstances none of X's employees, the employees of the restaurant operator, or the customers or salesmen who regularly visit the premises to do business either with X or the restaurant operator are substantial users. Similarly, the manufacturers, distributors, and dealers of products sold in the canteen ordinarily are not substantial users.

Example (2). The facts are the same as in example (1) except that X rents food and beverage vending machines from a local dealer. The machines are regularly serviced by the local dealer under a contract with X. Title to and ownership of the machines are retained by the dealer. The local dealer is not deemed to be a substantial user if the revenue derived by such dealer from, and the space occupied by, such machines do not exceed 5 percent of the respective amounts with respect to the entire facility.

Example (3). City B proposes to issue $2 million of bonds which qualify as an exempt small issue under section 103(c)(6)(A) pursuant to an election under section 103(c)(6)(D) and paragraph (b)(2) of § 1.103-10 in order to construct a medical building for certain physicians and dentists. The facility will contain thirty offices to be leased on equal terms and for the same rental rates to each physician or dentist for use in his trade or business. Each physician or dentist will be a substantial user of the facility since the facility is being constructed specifically for such physicians and dentists. The result would be the same in the case of an office building for general commercial use.

Example (4). City C proposes to expand the airport it owns and operates with the proceeds of its bonds which qualify as bonds issued for an exempt facility under section 103(c)(4)(D) and paragraph (e) of § 1.103-8 and which are secured by a pledge of airport revenues. The airport is serviced by several commercial airlines which have long-term agreements with C for the use of runways, terminal space, and hangar and storage facilities. Each of the airlines either occupies more than 5 percent of the usable space of, or derives more than 5 percent of the revenue derived with respect to, the airport. C also leases counter and vehicle servicing and parking areas to car rental companies, space for restaurants, kiosks for the sale of newspapers and magazines, and space for the operations of a charter plane company. The latter operates its own planes, offers flying lessons and services, and stores private planes for local businesses and individuals. An airport limousine company has an exclusive franchise for passenger pick-up at the terminal. Other taxi, transfer, freight, and express companies regularly deliver passengers and freight to the terminal but do not have space regularly assigned to them, nor do they have operating agreements with C. Various business concerns have advertising product displays in the terminal building. In addition to regular telephone service, coin-operated telephones, provided by the telephone company, are located throughout the terminal, at locations specified by C. None of the above exceed the 5 percent limitations of paragraph (b) of this section and the bond proceeds will not be specifically used for any of them. Only the commercial airlines, which violate the 5 percent limitations, are substantial users of the airport.

Example (5). City D issues $25 million of its revenue bonds and will use $10 million of the proceeds to finance construction of a sports facility which qualifies as an exempt facility under section 103(c)(4)(B) and paragraph (c) of § 1.103-8, $8 million to acquire and develop land as the site for an industrial park within the meaning of section 103(c)(5) and § 1.103-9, and $7

Reg. § 1.103-11(c)

→ *Caution: Code Sec. 103 has been amended to remove special exempt bond issue rules and provide similar rules in Code Secs. 141–150.*←

million to finance the construction of an office building to be used exclusively by the city, an exempt person. The revenues from the sports facility and the industrial park and all the facilities themselves will be the security for the bonds. The sports facility and the industrial park sites will be used in the trades or businesses of nonexempt persons. The bonds are industrial development bonds, but under the provisions of paragraph (a)(1) of § 1.103-8 and paragraph (a) of § 1.103-9, the interest on the $25 million issue will not be includable in gross income. However, the interest on bonds held shall be includable in the gross income of a substantial user of either the sports facility or the industrial park if such substantial user holds any of the obligations of the $25 million issue. The 5 percent limitations of paragraph (b) of this section are applied separately with respect to each facility.

Example (6). Authority E issues $4 million of bonds which qualify as an exempt small issue under section 103(c)(6)(A) pursuant to an election under section 103(c)(6)(D) and paragraph (b)(2) of § 1.103-10 in order to construct a bank building on the grounds of an airport. In addition, E issues $40 million to expand the airport. The bank will not derive revenue in excess of 5 percent of the revenue derived with respect to the airport nor will it occupy more than 5 percent of the usable area of such airport. The bank will be a substantial user of the bank building constructed with the proceeds of the $4 million issue since the facility was constructed specifically for the bank. However, the bank will not be a substantial user with respect to the airport because it does not exceed the 5 percent limitations of paragraph (b) of this section. Had E issued one issue of $44 million in order to expand the airport and construct a bank building, the bank would be a substantial user of the entire facility since the $44 million issue was being used to construct a facility a portion of which was specifically for the bank. [Reg. § 1.103-11.]

☐ [*T.D.* 7199, 7-31-72.]

[Reg. § 1.103-16]

§ 1.103-16. Obligations of certain volunteer fire departments.—(a) *General rule.* An obligation of a volunteer fire department issued after December 31, 1980, shall be treated as an obligation of a political subdivision of a State for purposes of section 103(a)(1) of—

(1) The volunteer fire department is a qualified volunteer fire department within the meaning of paragraph (b) of this section, and

(2) Substantially all of the proceeds of the issue of which the obligation is a part are to be used for the acquisition, construction, reconstruction, or improvement of a fire house or fire truck used or to be used by the qualified volunteer fire department.

An obligation of a volunteer fire department shall not be treated as an obligation of a political subdivision of a State for purposes of section 103(a)(1) unless both conditions set forth in this paragraph (a) are satisfied. Thus, for example, if an obligation is issued by an ambulance and rescue squad that is a qualified volunteer fire department as required by paragraph (a)(1) of this section, but substantially all of the proceeds of the issue of which the obligation is a part are to be used for the furnishing of emergency medical services, rather than for the purposes specified in paragraph (a)(2) of this section, the obligation shall not be treated as an obligation of a political subdivision of a State for purposes of section 103(a)(1).

(b) *Definition of qualified volunteer fire department.* For purposes of this section, the term "qualified volunteer fire department" means an organization—

(1) That is organized and operated to provide firefighting services or emergency medical services in an area within the jurisdiction of a political subdivision, and

(2) That is required to furnish firefighting services by written agreement with the political subdivision, and

(3) That serves persons in an area within the jurisdiction of the political subdivision that is not provided with any other firefighting services. The requirement of paragraph (b)(2) of this section that a qualified volunteer fire department be required to furnish firefighting services by written agreement with the political subdivision may be satisfied by an ordinance or statute of the political subdivision that establishes, regulates, or funds the volunteer fire department. A volunteer fire department does not fail to satisfy the requirement of paragraph (b)(3) of this section by furnishing or receiving firefighting services on an emergency basis, or by cooperative agreement with other fire departments, to or from areas outside of the area that the volunteer fire department is organized and operated to serve. The fact that tax revenues of a political subdivision served by a volunteer fire department contribute toward the support of the volunteer fire department in the form of salary, purchase of equipment, or other defrayment of expenses will not prevent the

→ *Caution: Code Sec. 103 has been amended to remove special exempt bond issue rules and provide similar rules in Code Secs. 141–150.*←

volunteer fire department from being a "qualified volunteer fire department" within the meaning of this paragraph (b). Moreover, an obligation of a volunteer fire department receiving such support may qualify as an obligation of a political subdivision within the meaning of section 103(a)(1) independently of section 103(i) and this section if the requirements of section 103(a)(1) are satisfied. See § 1.103-1(b) for rules relating to qualification under section 103(a)(1).

(c) *"Substantially all" test.* Substantially all of the proceeds of an issue are used for the purposes specified in paragraph (a)(2) of this section if 90 percent or more of the proceeds are so used. Thus, for example, if more than 10 percent of the proceeds of an obligation issued by a qualified volunteer fire department are used for the purchase of an ambulance or for rescue equipment not to be used in providing fire fighting services, interest on the obligation is not exempt from tax under section 103(i) and this section. In computing this percentage—

(1) Costs are allocated between providing a firehouse or firetruck and other uses of the proceeds on a pro rata basis; and

(2) The rules set forth in § 1.103-8(a)(1)(i), relating to amounts allocable to exempt and nonexempt uses and amounts chargeable to capital account, apply.

(d) *Refunding issues.* An obligation which is part of an issue issued by a qualified volunteer fire department after December 31, 1980, part or all of the proceeds of which issue are used directly or indirectly to pay principal, interest, call premium, or reasonable incidental costs of refunding a prior issue qualifies as an obligation of a political subdivision under section 103(i) and this section only if—

(1) The prior issue was issued by a qualified volunteer fire department;

(2) Substantially all of the proceeds of the prior issue were used for the purposes described in paragraph (a)(2) of this section;

(3) The prior issue was issued after December 31, 1980; and

(4) The refunding issue is issued not more than 180 days before the date on which the last obligation of the prior issue is discharged (within the meaning of § 1.103-13(b)(11)).

(e) *Examples.* The provisions of this section may be illustrated by the following examples:

Example (1). The County M Volunteer Fire and Rescue Association provides firefighting, ambu-

lance, and emergency medical services in County M. The board of county commissioners of County M contracts with the County M Volunteer Fire and Rescue Association for these services, and County M is not served by any other firefighting association. On August 1, 1981, the Association issues an obligation for funds to purchase a new fire truck, a new ambulance, and rescue equipment not to be used for fighting fires. Funds to be used for the purchase of the ambulance and rescue equipment constitute more than 10 percent of the proceeds of the obligation. Thus, substantially all of the proceeds of the obligations are not used for one of the purposes described in paragraph (a)(2) of this section. Although the County M Volunteer Fire and Rescue Association is a qualified volunteer fire department under paragraph (b) of this section because it provides firefighting and emergency medical services in an area within County M which is not provided with any other firefighting services and is required to provide these services by written agreement with County M, the August 1, 1981, obligation of County M Volunteer Fire and Rescue Association will not be treated as an obligation of a political subdivision of a State under section 103(i) and paragraph (a) of this section because substantially all of the proceeds of the obligation are not to be used for a purpose described in section 103(i)(1)(B) and paragraph (a)(2) of this section. Accordingly, interest on the August 1, 1981, obligation of County M Volunteer Fire and Rescue Association is not exempt from gross income under section 103(a)(1).

Example (2). County N Volunteer Fire Department provides firefighting services in County N by contract with the county, which is not served by any other firefighting association. On June 15, 1982, County N Volunteer Fire Department issues its obligation for funds to construct an addition to its firehouse to house a rescue squad, the rescue squad's vehicle, and rescue equipment not to be used in firefighting. Although the County N Volunteer Fire Department is a qualified volunteer fire department under paragraph (b) of this section, interest on its June 15, 1982, obligation will not be exempt from tax under section 103(i) and this section because the proceeds of this obligation will not be used for the purposes described in paragraph (a) of this section.

Example (3). The County O Volunteer Fire and Rescue Association provides firefighting, ambulance, and emergency medical services in County O. The board of county commissioners of County O contracts with the County O Volunteer Fire and Rescue Association for these services, and County

Reg. § 1.103-16(e)

→ *Caution: Code Sec. 103 has been amended to remove special exempt bond issue rules and provide similar rules in Code Secs. 141–150.*←

O is not served by any other firefighting association. On September 1, 1983, the Association issues its obligations for funds to construct a new building to house its firefighting, ambulance, and rescue functions. Although the ambulance and rescue equipment will occupy space in the projected facility, the cost allocable on a pro rata basis to providing housing for the ambulance and rescue equipment represents less than 10 percent of the proceeds of the obligations. Thus, substantially all of the proceeds of the obligations are used for one of the purposes described in paragraph (a)(2) of this section. The County O Volunteer Fire and Rescue Association is a qualified volunteer fire department under paragraph (b) of this section because it provides firefighting and emergency medical services in an area within County O which is not provided with any other firefighting

services and is required to provide these services by written agreement with County O. The obligations of County O Volunteer Fire and Rescue Association will be treated as obligations of a political subdivision of a State under section 103(i) and paragraph (a) of this section because the obligations are those of a qualified volunteer fire department and because substantially all of the proceeds of the obligations are to be used for a purpose described in section 103(i)(1)(B) and paragraph (a)(2) of this section. Accordingly, interest on the September 1, 1983, issue of obligations of County O Volunteer Fire and Rescue Association is exempt from gross income under section 103(a)(1). [Reg. § 1.103-16.]

☐ [*T.D.* 7901, 7-19-83.]

→ *Caution: Code Sec. 103 has been amended to remove special exempt bond issue rules and provide similar rules in Code Secs. 141—150.*←

[Reg. § 1.103(n)-1T]

§ 1.103(n)-1T. Limitation on aggregate amount of private activity bonds (Temporary).—Q-1: What does section 103(n) provide?

A-1: Interest on an issue of private activity bonds will not be tax exempt unless the aggregate amount of bonds issued pursuant to that issue, when added to (i) the aggregate amount of private activity bonds previously issued by the issuing authority during the calendar year and (ii) the portion of that year's private activity bond limit that the issuing authority has elected to carry forward to a future year, does not exceed the issuing authority's private activity bond limit for that calendar year. See A-4 of § 1.103(n)-4T with respect to private activity bonds issued under a carryforward election.

Q-2: What is the effective date of section 103(n)?

A-2: In general, section 103(n) applies to private activity bonds issued after December 31, 1983. Section 103(n) does not apply to any issue of obligations, however, if there was an inducement resolution (or other comparable preliminary approval) for the project before June 19, 1984, and the issue for such project is issued before January 1, 1985. An issue of obligations will be considered to be issued for the project pursuant to the inducement resolution in existence before June 19, 1984, to the extent that the nature, character, and purpose of the facility has not changed in any material way, and to the extent that the capacity of the facility has not increased materially; in addition, the issue of obligations must be for the

same or a related initial owner, manager, or operator. See § 1.103-10(e) for the definition of related persons. See A-16 of § 1.103(n)-3T with respect to certain projects preliminarily approved before October 19, 1983. The transitional rules provided by section 631(c) of the Tax Reform Act of 1984 do not apply to section 103(n). See § 1.103-13(b)(6) for the rules relating to the date of issue of obligations.

Q-3: If an issue of private activity bonds causes the issuer's private activity bond limit to be exceeded, what is the effect on that issue?

A-3: If an issue of private activity bonds causes the issuing authority's private activity bond limit to be exceeded, no portion of that issue will be treated as obligations described in section 103(a), and interest paid on the issue will be subject to Federal income taxation.

Q-4: If an issue of private activity bonds causes the issuer's private activity bond limit to be exceeded, what is the effect on previous issues of private activity bonds that met the requirements of section 103(n) when issued?

A-4: Private activity bonds issued as part of an issue that met the private activity bond limit when issued continue to meet the requirements of section 103(n) even though a subsequent issue causes the aggregate amount of private activity bonds issued by an issuing authority to exceed the authority's private activity bond limit for the calendar year.

Example. The following example illustrates the provisions of A-3 and A-4 of this § 1.103(n)-1T:

→ *Caution: Code Sec. 103 has been amended to remove special exempt bond issue rules and provide similar rules in Code Secs. 141—150.*←

Example. The State ceiling for State Z for 1986 is $200 million. City M, within the State, and State Z itself are authorized to issue private activity bonds. Under the allocation formula provided by the Governor of State Z, City M has a private activity bond limit of $50 million; the balance of the State ceiling is allocated to State Z. On June 1, 1986, City M issues a $75 million issue of private activity bonds. On September 1, 1986, State Z issues a $150 million issue of private activity bonds. Based on these facts, the obligations of City M do not meet the requirements of section 103(n) since the aggregate amount of private activity bonds issued by City M in 1986 exceeded its private activity bond limit for such year; thus, such obligations are not described in section 103(a). That the State Z issue caused the aggregate amount of private activity bonds issued in the State during 1986 to exceed the State ceiling does not cause such obligations to fail to meet the requirements of section 103(n).

Q-5: What is the aggregate amount of private activity bonds issued as part of an issue?

A-5: The aggregate amount of private activity bonds issued as part of an issue is the face amount of the issue. [Temporary Reg. § 1.103(n)-1T.]

☐ [*T.D.* 7981, 10-2-84.]

[Reg. § 1.103(n)-2T]

§ 1.103(n)-2T. Private activity bond defined (Temporary).—Q-1: What is the definition of the term "private activity bond"?

A-1: In general, for purposes of § § 1.103(n)-1T through 1.103(n)-6T, the term "private activity bond" means any industrial development bond or student loan bond the interest on which is exempt from tax under section 103(a) (without application of section 103(n)). See § 1.103-7(b) for the definition of the term "industrial development bond." See A-17 of this § 1.103(n)-2T for the definition of the term "student loan bond." There are five exceptions to the general definition of the term "private activity bond"; the exceptions include the exception for the Texas Veterans' Bond Program, the residential rental property exception, the exception for certain facilities described in section 103(b)(4)(C) or (D), and the refunding obligation exception. These exceptions are described in A-2 through A-16 of this § 1.103(n)-2T. In addition, the term "private activity bond" does not include any issue of obligations if there was an inducement resolution (or other comparable preliminary approval) for the project before June 19, 1984, and the issue for that project is issued before January 1, 1985. See A-2 of § 1.103(n)-1T.

Q-2: To which obligations does the exception for the Texas Veterans' Bond Program apply?

A-2: The term "private activity bond" does not include general obligation bonds issued under the Texas Veterans' Bond Program if the proceeds of the issue, other than an amount that is not a major portion of the proceeds, are used to make loans of up to $20,000 for the purchase of land for purposes authorized by such program as in effect on June 19, 1984. The use of the proceeds may be established by the affidavit of the veteran receiving the loan. For purposes of this exception to the definition of the term "private activity bond," the use of more than 25 percent of the proceeds of an issue of obligations will constitute the use of a major portion of such proceeds.

Q-3: To which obligations does the residential rental property exception apply?

A-3: The term "private activity bond" does not include any obligation issued to provide projects for residential rental property (including property functionally related and subordinate to any such facility), as described in section 103(b)(4)(A) and § 1.103-8(b). In addition, the term "private activity bond" does not include any housing program obligation under section 11(b) of the United States Housing Act of 1937.

Q-4: To which obligations does the exception for certain facilities described in section 103(b)(4)(C) or (D) apply?

A-4: Section 103(n)(7)(C) provides that the term "private activity bond" does not include any obligation issued as part of an issue to provide convention or trade show facilities, as described in section 103(b)(4)(C) and § 1.103-8(d) (including property functionally related and subordinate to any such facilities), if the property so described is owned by, or on behalf of, a governmental unit. In addition, the term "private activity bond" does not include any obligation issued as part of an issue to provide airports, docks, wharfs, mass commuting facilities, or storage or training facilities directly related to any of the foregoing facilities, as described in section 103(b)(4)(D) and § 1.103-8(e) (including property functionally related and subordinate to any such facilities), if the property so described is owned by, or on behalf of, a governmental unit. See § 1.103-8(a)(3), in general, for the definition of the term "functionally related and subordinate." For purposes of this exception to the definition of the term "private activity bond," the term "mass commuting facilities" includes "qualified mass commuting vehicles," as defined in section 103(d)(9), that are associated with a mass com-

→ *Caution: Code Sec. 103 has been amended to remove special exempt bond issue rules and provide similar rules in Code Secs. 141—150.*←

muting facility described in § 1.103-8(e)(2)(iv). Obligations issued as part of an issue to provide parking facilities, as described in section 103(b)(4)(D), are not excepted from the definition of the term "private activity bond;" however, parking facilities may be functionally related and subordinate to another facility described in section 103(b)(4)(C) or (D).

Q-5: When is property described in section 103(b)(4)(C) or (D) owned by, or on behalf of, a governmental unit?

A-5: In general, property described in section 103(b)(4)(C) or (D) will be considered to be owned by a governmental unit if a governmental unit is the owner of the property for Federal income tax purposes generally. See A-5 of § 1.103(n)-3T for the definition of the term "governmental unit". In general, property described in section 103(b)(4)(C) or (D) will be considered to be owned on behalf of a governmental unit if a constituted authority empowered to issue obligations on behalf of a governmental unit is the owner of the property for Federal income tax purposes generally. Whether the property is owned by, or on behalf of, a governmental unit will be determined on the basis of the facts and circumstances of each particular case. The fact that the governmental unit's or constituted authority's obligation to pay principal and interest on an obligation is limited to revenues from fees collected from users of the property provided with the proceeds of such obligation will not, in itself, cause such property to be treated as not owned by, or on behalf of, the governmental unit. In order to qualify for the exception described in section 103(n)(7)(C), the property must be owned by, or on behalf of, the governmental unit throughout the term of the issues. See A-10 of this § 1.103(n)-2T with respect to the consequences of a transfer of ownership.

Q-6: Will property described in section 103(b)(4)(C) or (D) that is leased to a non-governmental entity be treated as owned by, or on behalf of, a governmental unit if the lessee is the owner of the property for Federal income tax purposes generally solely by reason of the length of the lease?

A-6: If property, or any portion thereof, is leased to a non-governmental entity and if, for Federal income tax purposes generally, the lessee is the owner of the property solely by reason of the length of the lease, then, for purposes of § § 1.103(n)-1T through 1.103(n)-6T (but not for other Federal income tax purposes, such as whether payments under the lease constitute deductible rental payments), the governmental unit

will be treated as the owner of the property if the lessee elects not to claim depreciation or an investment credit with respect to such property. See A-7 of this § 1.103(n)-2T for the rules describing the method of making this election. For purposes of § § 1.103(n)-1T through 1.103(n)-6T, the term "non-governmental entity" means a person other than a governmental unit or a constituted authority empowered to issue obligations on behalf of a governmental unit. The fact that a non-governmental entity lessee elects not to claim depreciation or an investment credit with respect to property does not, however, ensure that the property will be treated as owned by, or on behalf of a governmental unit for purposes of § § 1.103(n)-1T through 1.103(n)-6T. Thus, for example, if the lessee is the owner of the property for Federal income tax purposes generally other than solely because of the length of the lease, the obligations issued as part of the issue are private activity bonds notwithstanding that the lessee elected not to claim depreciation or an investment credit with respect to the property. Similarly, even if a governmental unit is the owner of property for Federal income tax purposes generally, the property will not be treated as owned by, or on behalf of, a governmental unit for purposes of § § 1.103(n)-1T through 1.103(n)-6T if the lease under which such property is leased to a non-governmental entity provides for significant front end loading of rental accruals or payments. See A-12 of this § 1.103(n)-2T with respect to significant front end loading of rental accruals or payments.

Q-7: What must a lessee do in order to elect not to take depreciation or an investment credit with respect to property described in section 103(b)(4)(C) or (D)?

A-7: The lessee must make the election at the time the lease is executed. The election must include a description of the property with respect to which the election is being made; the name, address, and TIN of the issuing authority; the name, address, and TIN of the lessee; and the date and face amount of the issue the proceeds of which are to be used to provide the property. The election must be signed by the lessee, if a natural person, or by a duly authorized official of the lessee. The issuing authority must be provided with a copy of the election. The issuing authority and the lessee must retain copies of the election in their respective records for the entire term of the lease. In addition, the lease, and any publicly recorded document recorded in lieu of such lease, must state that neither the lessee nor any successor in interest under the lease may claim depreci-

Reg. § 1.103(n)-2T

→ *Caution: Code Sec. 103 has been amended to remove special exempt bond issue rules and provide similar rules in Code Secs. 141—150.*←

ation or an investment credit with respect to such property. This election may be made with respect to property whether or not such property otherwise would be eligible for depreciation or an investment tax credit. See section 7701(a)(41) for the definition of the term "TIN."

Q-8: Is the election not to claim depreciation or an investment credit revocable?

A-8: No, the election is irrevocable. In addition, the election is binding on all successors in interest under the lease regardless of whether the obligations remain outstanding. If a successor in interest claims depreciation or an investment credit with respect to property for which such an election has been made, such property will be considered transferred to a non-governmental entity. See A-10 of this § 1.103(n)-2T with respect to the consequences of such a transfer.

Q-9: Where obligations are issued to provide all or any portion of a facility described in section 103(b)(4)(C) or (D), must all of the property described in section 103(b)(4)(C) or (D) that is part of such facility be owned by, or on behalf of, a governmental unit in order for such obligations to qualify for the exception to the definition of the term "private activity bond" provided in section 103(n)(7)(C)?

A-9: Generally, yes. If obligations are issued to provide all or any portion of a facility described in section 103(b)(4)(C) or (D), the obligations comprising such issue will not qualify for the exception to the definition of the term "private activity bond" provided in section 103(n)(7)(C) unless all of the property described in section 103(b)(4)(C) or (D) that is part of (or functionally related and subordinate to) the facility being financed is owned by, or on behalf of, a governmental unit throughout the term of the issue. For this purpose, the facility being financed will be construed to include the entire airport, dock, etc., under consideration and not merely the part of the facility being provided with the proceeds of the issue. For example, the term facility, when used in reference to an airport, will be considered to include all property that is part of, or included in, that airport under § 1.103-8(e)(2)(ii)(a), including all property functionally related and subordinate thereto under § 1.103-8(a)(3) and (e)(2)(ii)(b). Thus, if the proceeds of an issue are used to provide a hanger at an airport described in section 103(b)(4)(D), that airport is considered as being financed with such issue, and if any portion of that airport, including property functionally related and subordinate thereto, is treated as owned by a non-governmental entity, that issue

does not qualify for the exception to the definition of the term "private activity bond" provided in section 103(n)(7)(C).

There are three exceptions to this rule, however. First, if any property otherwise would be considered part of the facility being financed and such property was not provided with proceeds of any obligation described in section 103(a), such property will not be considered part of the facility being financed.

Second, if any property otherwise would be considered part of the facility being financed and such property was part of such facility on or before October 5, 1984, such property will not be considered part of the facility being financed. For this purpose, property will be considered part of the facility on or before October 5, 1984 if any person was under a binding contract to acquire or construct such property to be a part of such facility on October 5, 1984.

Third, property will not be considered part of the facility being financed if such property (i) is land, a building, a structural component of a building, or other structure (other than tangible personal property (other than an air conditioning or heating unit)) and such property is not physically supported by, does not physically support, and is not physically connected to any property provided with the proceeds of obligations that qualify for the exception to the definition of the term "private activity bond" provided in section 103(n)(7)(C), or (ii) is tangible personal property (other than an air conditioning or heating unit). For this purpose, contiguous parcels of land will not be considered to support, to be supported by, or to be physically connected to each other, and insignificant physical connections (such as a connection by a sidewalk) will be disregarded. For purposes of this A-9, the term "tangible personal property" shall have the meaning given to it under section 48(a)(1)(A) and § 1.48-1(c).

Examples. The following examples illustrate the provisions of A-9 of this § 1.103(n)-2T:

Example (1). On January 1, 1986, Governmental Unit M issues industrial development bonds to provide an airport, as described in section 103(b)(4)(D), which will consist of land, runways, a terminal and a functionally related and subordinate hotel. The hotel will be leased to N, a non-governmental entity. The lease does not call for significant front end loading of rental accruals or payments. For Federal income tax purposes generally, M will own the entire airport except that N will be the owner of the hotel solely by reason of the length of the lease. N properly elects

Reg. § 1.103(n)-2T

→ *Caution: Code Sec. 103 has been amended to remove special exempt bond issue rules and provide similar rules in Code Secs. 141—150.*←

not to claim depreciation or an investment credit with respect to the hotel. The industrial development bonds are not private activity bonds.

Example (2). The facts are the same as in Example (1) except that N does not make the election and claims depreciation with respect to the hotel. The entire issue of industrial development bonds is treated as an issue of private activity bonds.

Example (3). The facts are the same as in Example (2) except that the hotel is provided other than with the proceeds of an obligation described in section 103(a). The issue for the remainder of the airport qualifies for the exception to the definition of the term "private activity bond" provided in section 103(n)(7)(C).

Example (4). The facts are the same as in Example (2) except that the hotel, including the hotel parking lot, the hotel grounds, and the parcel of land on which they rest, are provided with a separate issue of industrial development bonds. There are no significant connections between the hotel and the airport. The issue for the hotel is an issue of private activity bonds. The issue for the remainder of the airport qualifies for the exception to the definition of the term "private activity bonds" provided in section 103(n)(7)(C).

Example (5). The facts are the same as Example (4) except that the hotel is constructed upon land provided with the proceeds of the issue used to provide the remainder of the airport. Both issues are treated as issues of private activity bonds.

Example (6). On June 30, 1983, construction began on the City NN airport, which consists of land, runways, a terminal, and hangars. Corporation XX (a non-governmental entity) owns for Federal income tax purposes generally several of the hangars, which it financed with obligations described in section 103(a) issued on June 30, 1983. On March 1, 1985, at a time when XX still owns the hangars, City NN issues an issue of obligations described in section 103(b)(4)(D) to enlarge the terminal at the City NN airport. City NN will own the addition to the terminal for Federal income tax purposes generally. The obligations comprising the March 1, 1985, issue will not be private activity bonds.

Q-10: What are the consequences if a governmental unit ceases to be treated as owning property described in section 103(b)(4)(C) or (D) where the property was provided by obligations that were not private activity bonds on the date

of issue due to the exception provided in section 103(n)(7)(C)?

A-10: The obligations outstanding on the date such ownership ceases are private activity bonds and are treated as if they are the last private activity bonds issued by the issuer in the calendar year in which the transfer of ownership occurs. Thus, if the aggregate amount of bonds issued pursuant to such issue, when added to the aggregate amount of other private activity bonds actually issued or treated as issued under this A-10 by the issuer during such year and the amount of any carryforward elections made during the year, exceeds the issuer's private activity bond limit for such year, the obligations are not described in section 103(a) as of the date on which transfer of ownership occurs; if such obligations do not comply with the requirements of section 103(n), the obligations will be treated as not described in section 103(a) as of the date such ownership ceases. However, if on the date of issue the issuer intended to transfer ownership of such property to a non-governmental entity during the term of the issue, then the obligations are treated as the last private activity bonds actually issued or treated as issued under this A-10 by the issuer during the year in which such obligations were actually issued; if such obligations do not comply with the requirements of section 103(n), the obligations will be treated as not described in section 103(a) as of the date of issue. The exception to the definition of the term "private activity bond" for facilities described in section 103(b)(4)(C) and (D) only applies if the property is owned by, or on behalf of, a governmental unit while all or any part of the issue or any refunding issue remains outstanding. If all or a portion of the property is sold to a non-governmental entity for its fair market value and all of the proceeds from the sale (except for a de minimis amount less than $5,000) are used within six months to redeem outstanding obligations, the obligations will not be treated as private activity bonds.

Q-11: What are the consequences if private activity bonds are issued to provide additions to a facility that was provided with obligations that were not private activity bonds when issued by virtue of the exception provided in section 103(n)(7)(C) and such additions are not treated as owned by a governmental unit?

A-11: In order to qualify for the exception to the definition of the term "private activity bond" for obligations described in section 103(b)(4)(C) or (D), all of the property described in section 103(b)(4)(C) or (D) that is part of the facility

Reg. § 1.103(n)-2T

→ *Caution: Code Sec. 103 has been amended to remove special exempt bond issue rules and provide similar rules in Code Secs. 141—150.*←

provided with the proceeds generally must be owned by, or on behalf of, a governmental unit. See A-9 of this § 1.103(n)-2T. However, if the proceeds of an issue of private activity bonds are used to make additions to a facility (other than additions that are not considered to be part of the facility under A-9 of this § 1.103(n)-2T) that was provided with another issue of industrial development bonds that were not private activity bonds when issued by virtue of the exception provided in section 103(n)(7)(C), then the prior issue will not cease to qualify for that exception. Nevertheless, for purposes of determining the aggregate amount of private activity bonds issued during the year that the issue to provide the addition to the previously financed facility is issued, the portion of the prior issue outstanding on the date of issue of the issue to provide the addition will be treated as part of the issue to provide the addition.

Example. The following example illustrates the provisions of A-11 of this § 1.103(n)-2T:

Example. On March 1, 1986, City P issues a $100 million issue of industrial development bonds to provide an airport, as described in section 103(b)(4)(D). City P uses substantially all of the proceeds to acquire land and to construct runways and a terminal on that land. No other property is constructed on the land. City P is the owner of the land and the terminal for Federal income tax purposes generally. Thus, the obligations comprising the March 1, 1986, issue are not private activity bonds when issued. On September 1, 1988, City P leases a portion of the land adjacent to the terminal to Corporation V (a non-governmental entity) under a true lease for Federal income tax purposes. City P's private activity bond limit for 1988 is $100 million, and as of September 30, 1988, City P has not issued any private activity bonds during 1988. On September 30, 1988, City P issues a $20 million issue of industrial development bonds, the proceeds of which are to be used to construct a hotel that is functionally related and subordinate to the airport. The hotel is to be constructed on the land that P leased to Corporation V. The hotel will be owned by Corporation V for Federal income tax purposes generally. On September 30, 1988, the outstanding face amount of the March 1, 1986, issue is 100 million. Although the obligations comprising the March 1, 1986, issue will not become private activity bonds as a result of the subsequent issue, on September 30, 1988, City P is treated as issuing a $120 million issue of private activity bonds. Since that amount exceeds City P's private activity bond limit, the 20 million

issue of private activity bonds issued on September 30 1988, does not meet the requirements of section 103(n). In addition, any subsequent issuance of private activity bonds by City P during 1988 will fail to meet the requirements of section 103(n). The March 1, 1986, issue continues to be described in section 103(a).

Q-12 Section 103(n)(7)(C)(iv) provides that the exception for certain facilities described in section 103(b)(4)(C) or (D) shall not apply in any case where the facility is leased under a lease that has significant front end loading of rental accruals or payments. What does "significant front end loading of rental accruals or payments" mean?

A-12 Where a lease requires rental payments that are significantly higher in the early years of the lease than in later years, the lease calls for significant front end loading of rental accruals or payments. A lease that provides for flat rental payments during the entire lease term does not violate the prohibition against significant front end loading of rent. In addition, a lease may provide for adjustments in rent for inflation or deflation, provided that such adjustments are to be made on the basis of a generally recognized price index. In addition, a lease may provide that rental payments are to be determined, in whole or part, based on a percentage of income, production, etc., provided that the percentage rate is kept constant (or increases) over the term of the lease and that the threshold, if any, above which the percentage applies is kept constant (or decreases) over the term of the lease. Thus, for example, a lease that requires rental payments throughout the term of the lease of $100,000 per year plus 5 percent of the gross income from the facility in excess of $500,000 does not violate the prohibition against significant front end loading of rent.

Examples. The following examples illustrate the provisions of A-4 through A-12 of this § 1.103(n)-2T:

Example (1). On February 1, 1985, County Z issues obligations with a term of 30 years. Substantially all of the proceeds of the obligations are to be used to provide a trade show facility as described in section 103(b)(4)(C). Z leases the entire facility to Corporation S. For Federal income tax purposes generally, S is treated as the owner of the facility solely by reason of the length of the lease. The lease provides that the lessee will elect not to claim depreciation or an investment credit with respect to the facility and that S will provide Z with a copy of the election. S makes the election retains it in its records, and provides County Z with a copy. The lease provides that

→ *Caution: Code Sec. 103 has been amended to remove special exempt bond issue rules and provide similar rules in Code Secs. 141—150.←*

neither the lessee nor any successor in interest will claim a deduction for depreciation or an investment credit with respect to such facility. The obligations are not private activity bonds on the date of issue, provided that the lease does not call for significant front end loading of rental accruals or payments.

Example (2). The facts are the same as in Example (1) except that on February 1, 1986, S assigns the lease to Corporation T. For its taxable year ending March 31, 1986, Corporation T claims depreciation with respect to the trade show facility. The obligations outstanding on the date Corporation T claims depreciation on its Federal income tax return are treated as the last private activity bonds actually issued or treated as issued by County Z during 1986, and such obligations must comply with the requirements of section 103(n). In addition, Corporation T is not entitled to claim depreciation or an investment credit with respect to the trade show facility during the balance of the term of the lease and will be subject to the applicable penalties for so claiming depreciation.

Example (3). The facts are the same as in Example (1) except that the obligations are redeemed on January 31, 1998; on January 31, 1999, S assigns the lease to Corporation X; and on its Federal income tax return for calendar year 1999, Corporation X claims depreciation with respect to the facility. The obligations are not private activity bonds provided that the lease does not call for significant front end loading of rental accruals or payments. However, X is not entitled to claim depreciation or an investment credit with respect to the trade show facility during the balance of the term of the lease and will be subject to the applicable penalties for so claiming those items.

Q-13: To which obligations does the refunding obligation exception apply?

A-13: The term "private activity bond" does not include any refunding obligation to the extent specified in this A-13. The term "refunding obligation" means an obligation that is part of an issue of obligations the proceeds of which are used to pay any principal or interest on any other issue of obligations described in section 103(a) (referred to as the prior issue). The term "refunding obligation" does not include any obligations issued more than 180 days before the prior issue is discharged ("advanced refundings"). The exception for refunding obligations only applies to the extent that the aggregate amount of the refunding issue does not exceed the outstanding face amount of the

prior issue, or portion thereof, being refunded. Thus, for example, in the case of an obligation part of the proceeds of which are to be used to refund a prior issue of private activity bonds and part of the proceeds of which are to be used to provide a pollution control facility under section 103(b)(4)(F), those proceeds to be used to refund all or any part of the principal amount of the prior issue are not the proceeds of a private activity bond; the balance of the proceeds are the proceeds of a private activity bond. The refunding obligation exception does not apply to obligations to the extent that amounts are used to pay the costs of issuing refunding obligations. If an issue of obligations consists of both obligations that qualify for the refunding obligation exception and private activity bonds that do not meet the requirements of section 103(n), the entire issue is treated as consisting of obligations not described in section 103(a).

Q-14: Does the refunding obligation exception apply to obligations issued to refund a prior issue of student loan bonds?

A-14: In the case of any student loan bond, the refunding obligation exception applies only if, in addition to the requirements stated in A-13 of this § 1.103(n)-2T, the maturity date of the refunding obligation is not later than the later of (i) the maturity date of the obligation to be refunded, or (ii) the date 17 years after the date on which the refunded obligation was issued (or, in the case of a series of refundings, the date on which the original obligation was issued).

Q-15: What is the "maturity date" of an obligation?

A-15: For purposes of section 103(n), the "maturity date" of an obligation is the date on which interest ceases to accrue and the obligation may either be paid or redeemed without penalty. The date is determined without regard to optional redemption dates (including those at the option of holders). If the issuer is required by the obligations or the indenture to redeem portions of obligations or to make payments of principal with respect to obligations in specified amounts and at specified times, such mandatory redemptions or payments shall be treated as separate obligations.

Q-16: Where private activity bonds are refunded with other obligations described in section 103(a), does the refunding obligation exception apply to the extent that the aggregate amount of the refunding obligations exceeds the outstanding principal amount of the prior issue due to the use of a portion of the proceeds of the refunding issue

Reg. § 1.103(n)-2T

→ *Caution: Code Sec. 103 has been amended to remove special exempt bond issue rules and provide similar rules in Code Secs. 141—150.*←

to fund a reasonably required reserve or replacement fund?

A-16: Whether the prior issue was issued prior to January 1, 1984, or thereafter, the refunding obligation exception to the definition of the term "private activity bond" only applies to the extent that the aggregate amount of the refunding obligation does not exceed the outstanding principal amount of the prior issue. Thus, the additional obligations issued to provide for a reasonably required reserve or replacement fund are private activity bonds.

Q-17: What is a "student loan bond'?

A-17: The term "student loan bond" means an obligation that is issued as part of an issue all or a major portion of the proceeds of which are to be used directly or indirectly to finance loans to individuals for educational expenses. For purposes of this A-17, the use of more than 25 percent of the proceeds of an issue of obligations to finance loans to individuals for educational expenses will constitute the use of a major portion of such proceeds in such manner. [Temporary Reg. § 1.103(n)-2T.]

☐ [*T.D.* 7981, 10-2-84.]

[Reg. § 1.103(n)-3T]

§ 1.103(n)-3T. **Private activity bond limit (Temporary).**—Q-1: What is the "State ceiling"?

A-1: In general, the State ceiling applicable to each State and the District of Columbia for any calendar year prior to 1987 shall be the greater of $200 million or an amount equal to $150 multiplied by the State's (or the District of Columbia's) population. In the case of any territory or possession of the United States, the State ceiling for any calendar year prior to 1987 shall be an amount equal to $150 multiplied by the population of such territory or possession. In the case of calendar years after 1986, the two preceding sentences shall be applied by substituting '$100" for "$150." In the case of any State that had an excess bond amount for 1983, the State ceiling for calendar year 1984 shall be the sum of the State ceiling determined under the general rule plus 50 percent of the excess bond amount for 1983. The excess bond amount for 1983 is the excess (if any) of (i) the aggregate amount of private activity bonds issued by issuing authorities in such State during the first 9 months of calendar year 1983 multiplied by 4/3, over (ii) the State ceiling determined under the general rule for 1984. For purposes of determining the State ceiling amount applicable to any State for calendar year 1984, an issuer may rely upon the State ceiling amount

published by the Treasury Department for such calendar year. However, an issuer may compute a different excess bond amount for 1983 where the issuer or the State in which the issuer is located has made a more accurate determination of the amount of private activity bonds issued by issuing authorities in the issuer's State during 1983. See A-7 of this § 1.103(n)-3T for rules regarding a State containing constitutional home rule cities.

Q-2: What is the private activity bond limit for a State agency?

A-2 Under section 103(n)(2) the private activity bond limit for any agency of the State authorized to issue private activity bonds for any calendar year shall be 50 percent of the State ceiling for such year unless the State provides for a different allocation. For this purpose, the State is considered an agency. See, however, A-17 of this § 1.103(n)-3T with respect to the penalty for failure to comply with the requirements of section 631(a)(3) of the Tax Reform Act of 1984.

Q-3: How is the private activity bond limit determined where a State has more than one agency?

A-3: If any State has more than one agency (including the State) authorized to issue private activity bonds, all such agencies shall be treated as a single agency for purposes of determining the aggregate private activity bond limit available for all of such agencies. Each of the State agencies is treated as having jurisdiction over the entire State. Therefore, under A-8 of this § 1.103(n)-3T the aggregate private activity bond limit for all the State agencies is allocated to the State since it possesses the broadest sovereign powers of any of the State agencies. Each other State agency's private activity bond limit is zero until it is assigned part of the private activity bond limit of another governmental unit pursuant to these regulations.

Q-4: What is a State agency?

A-4: A State agency is an agency authorized by a State to issue private activity bonds on behalf of the State. In addition, a special purpose governmental unit that derives its sovereign powers from the State and may exercise its sovereign powers throughout the State is a State agency. See A-5 of this § 1.103(n)-3T for the definition of the term "special purpose governmental unit." The term "State agency" does not include issuing authorities empowered by a State at the request of another governmental unit within the State to issue private activity bonds to provide facilities within the jurisdiction of such other governmental unit. For example, if County O requests the legislature

→ *Caution: Code Sec. 103 has been amended to remove special exempt bond
issue rules and provide similar rules in Code Secs. 141—150.*←

of State P to create an issuing authority empowered to issue obligations to provide pollution control facilities in County O, the authority is not a State agency.

Examples. The following examples illustrate the provisions of A-3 and A-4 of this § 1.103(n)-3T:

Example (1). For 1987 State Q has a State ceiling of $200 million. Neither the Governor nor the legislature of State Q has provided a formula for allocating the State ceiling different from that provided by section 103(n)(2) and (3). State Q has authorized the following State agencies to issue private activity bonds on its behalf: Authority M, Authority N, and Authority O. The aggregate private activity bond limit available for State agencies of State Q is $100 million. As of January 1, 1987, none of this aggregate private activity bond limit has been assigned to any of Authorities M, N, or O. On January 1, 1987, Authority M issues $25 million of private activity bonds. During 1987, the duly authorized official designated by State Q to allocate the aggregate private activity bond limit among the three authorities does not allocate any of the State's private activity bond limit to Authority M. The January 1, 1987, issue does not meet the requirements of section 103(n) since Authority M has no private activity bond limit for 1987.

Example (2). Under the laws of State U, only the State legislature can create constituted authorities empowered to issue private activity bonds on behalf of governmental units within State U. Authority R was created by the State U legislature at the request of County X. Authority R is a constituted authority empowered to issue private activity bonds on behalf of County X to provide facilities located in County X. Authority S was created by the legislature to issue private activity bonds to provide pollution control facilities throughout the State. Authority S is a State agency as defined in A-4 of this § 1.103(n)-3T. Authority R is not a State agency.

Q-5: What is a governmental unit?

A-5: The term "governmental unit" has the meaning given such term by § 1.103-1. For purposes of §§ 1.103(n)-1T through 1.103(n)-6T, a governmental unit is either a general purpose governmental unit or a special purpose governmental unit. The term "general purpose governmental unit" means a State, territory, possession of the United States, the District of Columbia, or any general purpose political subdivision thereof. The term "general purpose political subdivision"

denotes any division of government that possesses the right to exercise police powers, the power to tax, and the power of eminent domain and that is governed, at least in part, by popularly elected officials (*e.g.*, county, city, town, township, parish, village). The term "special purpose governmental unit" means any governmental unit as defined in § 1.103-1 other than a general purpose governmental unit. For example, a sewer authority with the power of eminent domain but without police powers is a special purpose governmental unit. A constituted authority empowered to issue private activity bonds on behalf of a governmental unit is not a governmental unit.

Q-6: What is the private activity bond limit for a general purpose governmental unit other than a State, the District of Columbia, a territory, or a possession?

A-6: The private activity bond limit for any such general purpose governmental unit for any calendar year is an amount equal to the general purpose governmental unit's proportionate share of 50 percent of the State ceiling amount for such calendar year. See A-10 of this § 1.103(n)-3T with respect to the rules for providing a different allocation. The proportionate share of a general purpose governmental unit is an amount that bears the same ratio to 50 percent of the State ceiling for such year as the population of the jurisdiction of such general purpose governmental unit bears to the population of the entire State, District of Columbia, territory, or possession in which its jurisdiction falls. See, however, A-17 of this § 1.103(n)-3T with respect to the penalty for failure to comply with the requirements of section 631(a)(3) of the Tax Reform Act of 1984. See A-9 of this § 1.103(n)-3T with respect to the private activity bond limit of issuing authorities other than general purpose governmental units.

Q-7: What is the private activity bond limit for a general purpose governmental unit in a State with one or more constitutional home rule cities?

A-7: The private activity bond limit for a constitutional home rule city for any calendar year is an amount equal to the constitutional home rule city's proportionate share of 100 percent of the State ceiling amount for the calendar year. The proportionate share of a constitutional home rule city is an amount that bears the same ratio to the State ceiling for such year as the population of the jurisdiction of such constitutional home rule city bears to the population of the entire State. The private activity bond limit for issuers other than constitutional home rule cities is computed in the manner described in A-2 through A-6 of this

Reg. § 1.103(n)-3T

→ *Caution: Code Sec. 103 has been amended to remove special exempt bond issue rules and provide similar rules in Code Secs. 141—150.*←

§ 1.103(n)-3T, except that in computing the private activity bond limit for issuers other than such constitutional home rule cities, the State ceiling amount for any calendar year shall be reduced by the aggregate private activity bond limit for all constitutional home rule cities in the State. The term "constitutional home rule city" means, with respect to any calendar year, any political subdivision of a State that, under a State constitution that was adopted in 1970 and effective on July 1, 1971, had home rule powers on the first day of the calendar year. See, however, A-17 of this § 1.103(n)-3T with respect to the penalty for failure to comply with the requirements of section 631(a)(3) of the Tax Reform Act of 1984.

Q-8: How is the private activity bond limit of an issuing authority determined under section 103(n)(3) when there are overlapping jurisdictions?

A-8: If an area is within the jurisdiction of two or more governmental units, that area will be treated as only within the jurisdiction of the governmental unit having jurisdiction over the smallest geographical area. However, the governmental unit with jurisdiction over the smallest geographical area may enter into a written agreement to allocate all or a designated portion of such overlapping area to the governmental unit having jurisdiction over the next smallest geographical area. Where two or more issuing authorities, whether governmental units or constituted authorities, have authority to issue private activity bonds and both issuing authorities have jurisdiction over the identical geographical area, that area will be treated as only within the jurisdiction of the one having the broadest sovereign powers. However, the issuing authority having the broadest sovereign powers may enter into a written agreement to allocate all or a designated portion of such area to the one with the narrower sovereign powers. All written agreements entered into pursuant to this A-8 must be retained by the assignee in its records for the term of all private activity bonds it issues in each calendar year to which such agreements applies. See A-9 of this § 1.103(n)-3T with respect to the private activity bond limit of issuing authorities other than general purpose governmental units.

Q-9: What is the private activity bond limit of an issuing authority (other than a State agency) that is not a general purpose governmental unit?

A-9: A constituted authority empowered to issue private activity bonds on behalf of a governmental unit is treated as having jurisdiction over the same geographical area as the governmental unit on behalf of which it is empowered to issue private activity bonds. Since a governmental unit has broader sovereign powers than a constituted authority empowered to issue private activity bonds on its behalf, a constituted authority has a private activity bond limit under section 103(n)(2) and (3) of zero. Similarly, a special purpose governmental unit is treated for purposes of section 103(n) as having jurisdiction over the same geographical area as that of the general purpose governmental unit or units from which the special purpose governmental unit derives its sovereign powers. Since a general purpose governmental unit has broader sovereign powers than a special purpose governmental unit, a special purpose governmental unit has a private activity bond limit under section 103(n)(2) and (3) of zero. An issuer of qualified scholarship funding bonds, as defined in section 103(e), is treated for purposes of section 103(n) as issuing on behalf of the State or political subdivision or subdivisions that requested its organization or its exercise of power to issue bonds. See A-13 and A-14 of this § 1.103(n)-3T with respect to assignments of private activity bond limit. For purposes of §§ 1.103(n)-1T through 1.103(n)-6T, a special purpose governmental unit shall be considered to derive its authority from the smallest general purpose governmental unit that—

(i) Enacts a specific law (e.g., a provision of a State constitution, charter, or statute) by or under which the special purpose governmental unit is created, or

(ii) Otherwise empowers, approves, or requests the creation of the special purpose governmental unit, or

(iii) Appoints members to the governing body of the special governmental unit,

and within which general purpose governmental unit falls the entire area in which such special purpose governmental unit may exercise its sovereign powers. If no one general purpose governmental unit meets such criteria (e.g., a regional special purpose governmental unit that exercises its sovereign powers within three counties pursuant to a separate ordinance adopted by each such county), such special purpose governmental unit shall be considered to derive its sovereign powers from each of the general purpose governmental units comprising the combination of smallest general purpose governmental units within which falls the entire area in which such special purpose governmental unit may exercise its sovereign powers and each of which meets (i), (ii), or (iii) above.

Reg. § 1.103(n)-3T

→ *Caution: Code Sec. 103 has been amended to remove special exempt bond issue rules and provide similar rules in Code Secs. 141—150.*←

Q-10: Does the issue comply with the requirements of section 103(n) under the following circumstances? Based on the most recent estimate of the resident population of State Y published by the Bureau of the Census before the beginning of 1988, the State ceiling for State Y is $200 million. Based on the same estimate, the population of City Q is one-fourth of the population of State Y. No part of the geographical area within the jurisdiction of City Q is within the jurisdiction of any other governmental unit with jurisdiction over a smaller geographical area. There are no constitutional home rule cities in State Y. Neither the Governor nor the legislature of State Y has provided a different formula for allocating the State ceiling than that provided by section 103(n)(2) and (3); thus, City Q's private activity bond limit for 1988 is $25 million (.25 × .50 × $200 million). As of March 1, 1988, City Q has issued $15 million of private activity bonds during calendar year 1988, none of which were issued pursuant to a carryforward election made in a prior year. On March 1, 1988, City Q will issue $5 million of private activity bonds to provide a pollution control facility as described in section 103(b)(4)(F). C, a duly authorized official of City Q responsible for issuing the bonds, provides a statement that will be included in the bond indenture or a related document providing that—

(i) Under section 103(n)(2) and (3) of the Internal Revenue Code, City Q has a private activity bond limit of $25 million for calendar year 1988 (.25 × .50 × $200 million), none of which has been assigned to it by another governmental unit,

(ii) State Y has not provided a different method of allocating the State ceiling,

(iii) City Q has not assigned any portion of its private activity bond limit to a constituted authority empowered to issue private activity bonds on its behalf, or to any other governmental unit,

(iv) City Q has not elected to carry forward any of its private activity bond limit for 1988 to another calendar year, nor has City Q in any prior year made a carryforward election for the pollution control facility,

(v) The aggregate amount of private activity bonds issued by City Q during 1988 is $15 million, and

(vi) The issuance of $5 million of private activity bonds on March 1, 1988, will not violate the requirements of section 103(n) and the regulations thereunder.

In addition, C provides the certification described in section 103(n)(12)(A).

A-10: Based on these facts, the issue meets the requirements of section 103(n) and §§ 1.103(n)-1T through 1.103(n)-6T. See § 1.103-13(b)(8) for the definition of the terms "bond indenture" and "related documents."

Q-11: May a State provide a different formula for allocating the State ceiling?

A-11: A State, by law enacted at any time, may provide a different formula for allocating the State ceiling among the governmental units in the State (other than constitutional home rule cities) having authority to issue private activity bonds, subject to the limitation provided in A-12 of this § 1.103(n)-3T. The governor of a State may proclaim a different formula for allocating the State ceiling among the governmental units in such State having authority to issue private activity bonds. The authority of the governor to proclaim a different formula shall not apply after the earlier of (i) the first day of the first calendar year beginning after the legislature of the State has met in regular session for more than 60 days after July 18, 1984, and (ii) the effective date of any State legislation dealing with the allocation of the State ceiling. If, on or before either date, the governor of any State exercises the authority to provide a different allocation, such allocation shall be effective until the date specified in (ii) of the immediately preceding sentence. Unless otherwise provided in a State constitutional amendment or by a law changing the home rule provisions adopted in the manner provided by the State constitution, the allocation of that portion of the State ceiling that is allocated to any constitutional home rule city may not be changed by the governor or State legislature unless such city agrees to such different allocation.

Q-12: Where a State provides an allocation formula different from that provided in section 103(n)(2) and (3), which allocation formula applies to obligations issued prior to the adoption of the different allocation formula?

A-12: Where a State provides a different allocation formula, the determination as to whether a particular bond issue meets the requirements of section 103(n) will be based upon the allocation formula in effect at the time such bonds were issued. The amount that may be reallocated pursuant to the later allocation formula is limited to the State ceiling for such year reduced by the amount of private activity bonds issued under the prior allocation formula in effect for such year.

Reg. § 1.103(n)-3T

→ *Caution: Code Sec. 103 has been amended to remove special exempt bond issue rules and provide similar rules in Code Secs. 141—150.*←

Q-13: May an issuing authority assign a portion of its private activity bond limit to another issuing authority if the governor or legislature has not provided for an allocation formula different from that provided in section 103(n)(2) and (3)?

A-13: Except as provided in this A-13 or in A-8, A-14, or A-15 of this § 1.103(n)-3T, no issuing authority may assign, directly or indirectly, all or any portion of its private activity bond limit to any other issuing authority, and no such attempted assignment will be effective. However, a general purpose governmental unit may assign a portion of its private activity bond limit to (i) a constituted authority empowered to issue private activity bonds on behalf of the assigning governmental unit, and (ii) a special purpose governmental unit deriving sovereign powers from the governmental unit making the assignment. In addition, a State may assign a portion of its private activity bond limit to a constituted authority empowered to issue private activity bonds on behalf of any governmental unit within such State and to any governmental unit within such State. Finally, an issuing authority that is assigned all or a portion of the private activity bond limit of a governmental unit pursuant to the immediately preceding two sentences may assign such amount or any part thereof to the governmental unit from which it received the assignment. None of these permissible types of assignments shall be effective, however, unless made in writing by a duly authorized official of the governmental unit making the assignment and a record of the assignment is maintained by the assignee for the term of all private activity bonds it issues in each calendar year to which such assignment applies. None of these permissible types of assignments shall be effective if made retroactively; provided, however, that retroactive assignments may be made during 1984. In addition, except as provided in A-15 of this § 1.103(n)-3T, a purported assignment by a governmental unit of a portion of its private activity bond limit to an issuing authority will be ineffective to the extent that private activity bonds issued by such authority provide facilities not located within the jurisdiction of the governmental unit making the assignment, unless the sole beneficiary of the facility is the governmental unit attempting to make the assignment. Similarly, except as provided in A-15 of this § 1.103(n)-3T, a governmental unit may not allocate a portion of its private activity bond limit to an issue of obligations to provide a facility not located within the jurisdiction of that governmental unit unless the sole beneficiary of the facility

is the governmental unit attempting to allocate its private activity bond limit to the issue. If an issuing authority issues an issue of obligations a portion of the proceeds of which are to be used to provide a facility not within its jurisdiction other than one described in the immediately preceding sentence, that issue will not meet the requirements of section 103(n) unless an issuing authority within the jurisdiction of which the facility is to be located specifically allocates a portion of its private activity bond limit to such issue equal to the amount of proceeds to be used to provide such facility.

Q-14: May an issuing authority assign a portion of its private activity bond limit to another issuing authority if the governor or legislature has provided for an allocation formula different from that provided in section 103(n)(2) and (3)?

A-14: Yes, under certain conditions. In providing a different formula for allocating the State ceiling, a State may permit an issuing authority to assign all or a portion of its private activity bond limit to other issuing authorities within the State, provided that such assignment is made in writing and a record of that assignment is maintained by the assignee in its records for the term of all private activity bonds it issues in each calendar year to which such assignment applies and a record of that assignment is maintained during such period by the public official responsible for making allocations of the State ceiling to issuing authorities within the State. The preceding sentence will only apply where the different formula expressly permits such assignments. Notwithstanding this A-14, no assignments may be made to regional authorities without compliance with the provisions of A-15 of this § 1.103(n)-3T.

Q-15: May a general purpose governmental unit assign a portion of its private activity bond limit to a regional authority empowered to issue private activity bonds on behalf of two or more general purpose governmental units?

A-15: Yes, under certain conditions. In order for an issue of private activity bonds issued by such a regional authority to meet the requirements of section 103(n), each of the governmental units on behalf of which the regional authority issues private activity bonds must assign to the regional authority a portion of its private activity bond limit based on the ratio of its population to the aggregate population of all such governmental units. The governmental unit within the jurisdiction of which the facility to be provided by the private activity bonds will be located, however, may elect to treat the regional authority as if it

Reg. § 1.103(n)-3T

→ *Caution: Code Sec. 103 has been amended to remove special exempt bond issue rules and provide similar rules in Code Secs. 141—150.*←

were a constituted authority empowered to issue such obligations solely on behalf of that governmental unit and, therefore, may assign a portion of its limit to the authority solely to provide the facility within its jurisdiction. Similarly, if a facility will solely benefit one governmental unit, that governmental unit may make the election described in the preceding sentence. In addition, any of the governmental units on behalf of which the regional authority issues private activity bonds, other than the governmental unit within the jurisdiction of which the facility will be located, may elect to be treated as if it had not empowered the authority to issue that issue of private activity bonds on its behalf. In providing a different formula for allocating the State ceiling, a State may permit a governmental unit to assign all or a portion of its private activity bond limit to a constituted authority empowered to issue private activity bonds on behalf of two or more governmental units, all of which are located within the State. The preceding sentence will only apply where the different formula expressly so provides. The principles of this A-15 shall not apply to any regional authority created with a principal purpose of avoiding the restrictions provided in A-13 or A-14 of this § 1.103(n)-3T. The principles of this A-15 shall also apply to a special purpose governmental unit providing facilities located within the jurisdiction of two or more general purpose governmental units from which it derives sovereign powers.

Examples. The following examples illustrate the provisions of A-8 through A-15 of this section:

Example (1). Authority ZZ is empowered by City Y to issue obligations on its behalf to provide financing for pollution control facilities located within the jurisdiction of City Y and the geographical area within 10 miles of the limits of City Y. Authority ZZ has no sovereign powers. Although the authority of Authority ZZ to issue obligations enables it to provide facilities located outside of the jurisdiction of City Y, Authority ZZ is treated as having jurisdiction over the same geographical area as City Y. Since City Y has broader sovereign powers than Authority ZZ, under section 103(n)(3) Authority ZZ has a private activity bond limit of zero. On March 31, 1985, Authority ZZ issues $5 million of private activity bonds. City Y has not assigned any portion of its private activity bond limit to Authority ZZ. Thus, the March 31, 1985, issue of private activity bonds is treated as an issue of obligations not described in section 103(a), and the interest

on such obligations is subject to Federal income taxation.

Example (2). In 1972, State S, State T, and State V empowered Authority Z to issue industrial development bonds on behalf of the three States and to provide port facilities in a harbor serving residents of all three States. S, T, and V have populations of 1,000,000, 2,000,000, and 7,000,000, respectively. Authority Z will issue $100 million of private activity bonds on September 1, 1985, to finance construction of a dock to be located in State S. The obligations will not meet the requirements of section 103(n) unless S, T, and V assign a portion of their private activity bond limits to Authority Z pursuant to one of three methods. First, S, T, and V may assign $10 million, $20 million, and $70 million, respectively, of their private activity bond limits to Authority Z for this issue. Second, S, T, and V may assign $100 million, $0, and $0, respectively, of their private activity bond limits to Authority Z for this issue. Third, either T or V (but not S) may allocate $0 of its private activity bond limit to Authority Z for purposes of this issue, and the remaining two States may allocate the $100 million based upon their respective populations. For instance, if T were to allocate $0 for purposes of this issue, S and V must allocate $12.5 million and $87.5 million, respectively, of their private activity bond limits to Authority Z.

Q-16: Must an issuing authority allocate any of its private activity bond limit to certain preliminarily approved projects?

A-16. Yes. Section 631(a)(3) of the Tax Reform Act of 1984 provides that, with respect to certain projects preliminarily approved by an issuing authority before October 19, 1983, the issuing authority shall allocate its share of the private activity bond limit for the calendar year during which the obligations are to be issued first to those projects. For purposes of this A-16 and A-17 and A-18 of this § 1.103(n)-3T, a general purpose governmental unit will be treated as having preliminarily approved a project if the project was preliminarily approved by it, by a constituted authority empowered to issue private activity bonds on its behalf, or by a special purpose governmental unit treated as having jurisdiction over the same geographical area as the general purpose governmental unit. Thus, if a project was approved by a constituted authority, the governmental unit on behalf of which such issue is to be issued must assign a portion of its private activity bond limit to the authority pursuant to section 631(a)(3) of the Act. If a project was prelimina-

Reg. § 1.103(n)-3T

→ *Caution: Code Sec. 103 has been amended to remove special exempt bond issue rules and provide similar rules in Code Secs. 141—150.*←

rily approved by a constituted authority empowered to issue private activity bonds on behalf of more than one general purpose governmental unit or a special purpose governmental unit that derives its sovereign powers from more than one general purpose governmental unit, the project will be considered approved by each of such general purpose governmental units in proportion to their relative populations. The projects that receive priority under section 631(a)(3) of the Act and this A-16 are those with respect to which—

(i) There was an inducement resolution (or other comparable preliminary approval) for a project before October 19, 1983, by an issuing authority,

(ii) A substantial user of the project notified such issuing authority—

(A) By August 17, 1984, that it intended to claim its rights under section 631(a)(3) of the Tax Reform Act of 1984, and

(B) By December 31, 1984, as to the calendar year in which it expects the obligations to provide the project to be issued, and

(iii) Construction of such project began before October 19, 1983, or a substantial user was under a binding obligation on that date to incur significant expenditures with respect to the project.

For purposes of the preceding sentence, the term "significant expenditures" means expenditures that equal or exceed the lesser of $15 million or 20 percent of the estimated cost of the facilities. An issuing authority may require, as part of the submission required by (ii)(B) of this A-16, that a substantial user specify the aggregate amount of private activity bonds necessary for the project. Section 631(a)(3) does not apply to a project to the extent that the aggregate amount of obligations required for such project exceeds the amount, if any, provided for in the inducement resolution or resolutions in existence with respect to such project before October 19, 1983, or in the statement that may be required by the issuing authority as part of the submission required by (ii)(B) of this A-16. Similarly, section 631(a)(3) does not apply to a project to the extent of any material change in its nature, character, purpose, or capacity. Section 631(a)(3) does not apply to a project if the owner, operator, or manager of such project is not the same (or a related person) as the owner, operator, or manager named in the latest inducement resolution with respect to such project in existence before October 19, 1983. Section 631(a)(3) of the Act does not apply to any project

if the obligations to provide the project are not issued in the year specified in the submission required by (ii)(B) of this A-16. In addition, section 631(a)(3) of the Act does not apply to any project to the extent that the amount of obligations to be issued for such project exceeds the share of the State ceiling to which the issuing authority that authorized the project is entitled as determined under section 103(n)(2) and (3) without regard to any alternative formula for allocating the State ceiling. The requirements of section 631(a)(3) will not apply where a State statute specifically so provides.

Q-17: What is the penalty for failure to comply with the requirements of section 631(a)(3) of the Act?

A-17: If any issuing authority fails to comply with the requirements of section 631(a)(3) of the Act, its private activity bond limit for the calendar year following the year in which the failure occurs shall be reduced by the amount of private activity bonds with respect to which the failure occurs. This penalty applies whether the issuing authority's private activity bond limit is determined under the formula provided under section 103(n)(2) and (3) or a different formula provided under section 103(n)(6). The penalty is imposed on the issuing authority that failed to comply with the requirements of section 631(a)(3) or, if in the year in which the penalty is imposed the issuing authority does not have a sufficient private activity bond limit to absorb the entire penalty, on the general purpose governmental unit treated as having jurisdiction over the same geographical area as the issuing authority. For purposes of this A-17, the general purpose governmental unit's private activity bond limit includes the private activity bond limit of each issuing authority treated as having preliminarily approved the project under A-16 of this § 1.103(n)-3T. Thus, for example, if a governmental unit failed to comply with the requirements of section 631(a)(3) of the Act with respect to a $5 million issue to be issued in 1985, and that governmental unit is assigned $15 million of the State ceiling for 1986 pursuant to a formula provided under section 103(n)(6), that governmental unit has a private activity bond limit of $10 million for 1986. Similarly, where a project that was preliminarily approved by an issuing authority that is not a governmental unit qualifies for $10 million of priority under section 631(a)(3) of the Act is not allocated a total of $10 million by the governmental unit on behalf of which the issuing authority is empowered to issue private activity bonds,

Reg. § 1.103(n)-3T

→ *Caution: Code Sec. 103 has been amended to remove special exempt bond issue rules and provide similar rules in Code Secs. 141—150.*←

the issuing authority's private activity bond limit, if any, for the year following this failure is reduced by $10 million; if the issuing authority's private activity bond limit for the year following the failure is less than $10 million, the private activity bond limit of the governmental unit on behalf of which the private activity bonds would have been issued had the failure not occurred (including if necessary, on a proportionate basis, the private activity bond limit purported to have been assigned to each of the other constituted authorities empowered to issue private activity bonds on behalf of the governmental unit and each special purpose governmental unit deriving all or part of its sovereign powers from the governmental unit) is reduced by the difference between $10 million and the reduction made in the issuing authority's private activity bond limit with respect to such failure.

Q-18: Will a penalty be assessed for failure to allocate private activity bond limit to all projects that meet the requirements of section 631(a)(3) if the amount of obligations required by all such projects preliminarily approved by (or treated as having been preliminarily approved by) an issuing authority exceeds the private activity bond limit of such issuing authority?

A-18: No penalty will be assessed if priority is given to those eligible projects for which substantial expenditures were incurred before October 19, 1983. An issuer may define the term "substantial expenditures" in any reasonable manner based on the relevant facts and circumstances and its private activity bond limit.

Examples. The following examples illustrate the provisions of A-16 through A-18:

Example (1). On October 1, 1983, County S approved an inducement resolution for the issuance of up to $30 million of industrial development bonds to provide a pollution control facility described in section 103(b)(4)(F) for Corporation R. On October 5, 1983, R contracted with Corporation Q to begin construction of the pollution control facility immediately, and construction began on October 10, 1983. Not later than August 17, 1984, Corporation R notified County S that it intended to seek priority under section 631(a)(3) of the Tax Reform Act of 1984. In addition, prior to December 31, 1984, Corporation R notified County S that it expected the County to issue $25 million of industrial development bonds for its project during calendar year 1985. Under section 103(n)(3), County S has a private activity bond limit of $50 million for calendar year 1985, and neither the Governor nor the legislature of the

State has provided a different allocation formula under section 103(n)(6). There are no other projects approved by County S that have rights under section 631(a)(3). On March 1, 1985, County S issues $25 million of industrial development bonds for the pollution control facility for Corporation R. If County S allocates less than $25 million of its private activity bond limit to that project, its private activity bond limit for 1986 will be reduced by the difference between $25 million and the amount County S actually allocates to the project.

Example (2). The facts are the same as in Example (1) except that during 1984 Corporation R fails to notify County S of the year in which it expects the obligations to be issued. Upon such failure the pollution control facility no longer qualifies for priority under section 631(a)(3), and County S will not be penalized if it does not allocate any of its private activity bond limit for 1985, or any future year, to that project.

Example (3). The facts are the same as in Example (1) except that under section 103(n)(3) County S has a private activity bond limit of $10 million for 1985. County S will not be penalized if it allocates $10 million of its private activity bond limit to the project.

Example (4). The facts are the same as in Example (3) except that on December 31, 1984, the Governor of the State provides a different allocation from that provided under section 103(n)(2) and (3). (The State has not enacted a statute specifically providing that section 631(a)(3) does not apply.) The different allocation provides that the entire State ceiling is allocated to the State and that the State will allocate the State ceiling to issuing authorities for specific projects on a first-come, first-served basis. Corporation R qualifies for the special rights granted by section 631(a)(3) of the Tax Reform Act to the extent of County S's private activity bond limit as determined under section 103(n)(3), i.e., $10 million. If the State fails to assign to County S $10 million of the State ceiling or if County S, after receiving such assignment, fails to allocate $10 million of private activity bond limit to the project, County S's private activity bond limit (if any) for 1986 will be reduced by the difference between $10 million and the amount of private activity bond limit allocated to the project.

Example (5). The facts are the same as in Example (1) except that Corporation R notifies County S that it only requires $15 million for the pollution control facility, County S only issues $15 million of private activity bonds for the pollution

Reg. § 1.103(n)-3T

→ *Caution: Code Sec. 103 has been amended to remove special exempt bond issue rules and provide similar rules in Code Secs. 141—150.*←

control facility, and County S only allocates $15 million of its private activity bond limit to such obligations. County S will not be penalized for not allocating more than $15 million of its private activity bond limit to Corporation R even though the original inducement resolution provided for up to $25 million. [Temporary Reg. § 1.103(n)-3T.]

☐ [T.D. 7981, 10-2-84.]

[Reg. § 1.103(n)-4T]

§ 1.103(n)-4T. Elective carryforward of unused private activity bond limit (Temporary).—Q-1: May an issuing authority carry forward any of its unused private activity bond limit for a calendar year?

A-1: In any calendar year after 1983 in which an issuing authority's private activity bond limit exceeds the aggregate amount of private activity bonds issued during such calendar year by such issuing authority, such issuing authority may elect to treat all, or any portion, of such excess as a carryforward for any one or more projects described in A-5 of this § 1.103(n)-4T (carryforward projects).

Q-2: How is the election to carry forward an issuing authority's unused private activity bond limit made?

A-2: (i) An issuing authority may make the election by means of a statement, signed by an authorized public official responsible for making allocations of such issuing authority's private activity bond limit, that the issuing authority elects to carry forward its unused private activity bond limit. The statement shall be filed with the Internal Revenue Service Center, Philadelphia, Pennsylvania 19255. Except with respect to elections to carry forward any unused private activity bond limit for calendar year 1984, the election must be filed prior to the end of the calendar year with respect to which the issuing authority has unused private activity bond limit; elections with respect to unused private activity bond limit for calendar year 1984 must be filed prior to February 26, 1985. The statement is to be titled "Carryforward election under section 103(n)."

(ii) The statement required by (i) of this A-2 shall contain the following information:

(A) The name, address, and TIN of the issuing authority,

(B) The issuing authority's private activity bond limit for the calendar year,

(C) The aggregate amount of private activity bonds issued by the issuing authority dur-

ing the calendar year for which the election is being made,

(D) The unused private activity bond limit of the issuing authority, and

(E) For each carryforward project—

(1) A description of the project, including its address (by its street address or, if none, by a general description designed to indicate its specific location) and the general type of facility (e.g., an airport described in section 103(b)(4)(D)),

(2) The name, address, and TIN of the initial owner, operator, or manager, and

(3) The amount to be carried forward for the project.

(iii) For purposes of (ii)(E) of this A-2, in the case of a carryforward project for which the initial owner, operator, or manager is to be selected pursuant to a competitive bidding process, the election may include up to 3 prospective addresses for the project and the name, address, and TIN of more than one prospective initial owner, operator, or manager, if prior to the end of the calendar year for which the election is made—

(A) In the case of elections for calendar years other than 1984, the issuing authority has taken preliminary official action approving the undertaking of the carryforward project,

(B) All persons included as prospective owners, operators, or managers have met all applicable conditions (if any) to submit proposals to provide the project, and

(C) The issuing authority has expended (or has entered into binding contracts to expend) in connection with the planning and construction of the carryforward project the lesser of $500,000 or $2\frac{1}{2}$ percent of the carryforward amount.

(iv) For purposes of (ii) of this A-2, in the case of a carryforward election for the purpose of issuing student loan bonds, the statement need not include the address of a facility or the name, address, and TIN of an initial owner, operator, or manager of a project but shall state that the carryforward election is for the purpose of issuing student loan bonds.

Q-3: Is a carryforward election revocable?

A-3: Any carryforward election, and any specification contained therein, shall be irrevocable after the last day of the calendar year in which the election is made. Thus, for example, obligations issued to finance a carryforward project with a different initial owner, operator, or manager from the owner, operator, or manager specified in

→ *Caution: Code Sec. 103 has been amended to remove special exempt bond issue rules and provide similar rules in Code Secs. 141—150.*←

the carryforward election shall not be issued pursuant to such carryforward election. An insubstantial deviation from a specification contained in a carryforward election shall not prevent obligations from being issued pursuant to such carryforward election. In addition, where a carryforward election is made with respect to more than one carryforward project, a substantial deviation with respect to one carryforward project shall not prevent obligations from being issued pursuant to such carryforward election with respect to the other carryforward projects.

Q-4: How is a carryforward used?

A-4: Any private activity bonds issued during the three calendar years (six calendar years in the case of a project described in section 103(b)(4)(F)) following the calendar year in which the carryforward election was first made with respect to a carryforward project shall not be taken into account in determining whether the issue meets the requirements of section 103(n). If, however, the amount of private activity bonds issued for the carryforward project exceeds the amount of the carryforward elected with respect to the project, then the portion of the issue that exceeds the carryforward shall be taken into account in determining whether the issue meets the requirements of section 103(n); if that portion of the issue does not meet the requirements of section 103(n) then the entire issue is treated as consisting of obligations not described in section 103(a). Carryforwards elected with respect to any project shall be used in the order of the calendar years in which they arose. Thus, for example, if an issuing authority makes carryforward elections in 1986 and 1988 for a carryforward project and issues private activity bonds for that project in 1989 and 1990, the obligations issued in 1989 will be applied to the 1986 carryforward election to the extent thereof.

Q-5: For what projects may a carryforward election be made?

A-5: A carryforward election may be made for any project described in section 103(b)(4) or (5), and for the purpose of issuing student loan bonds. Thus, for example, an issuing authority may elect to carry forward its unused private activity bond limit in order to provide a sports facility described in section 103(b)(4)(B). In addition, a governmental unit may elect to carry forward its unused private activity bond limit in order to issue qualified scholarship funding bonds. An issuing authority may not, however, elect to carry forward its unused private activity bond limit in order to issue an exempt small issue of industrial develop-

ment bonds under section 103(b)(6). [Temporary Reg. § 1.103(n)-4T.]

☐ *[T.D. 7981, 10-2-84. Amended by T.D. 8001, 12-26-84.]*

[Reg. § 1.103(n)-5T]

§ 1.103(n)-5T. Certification of no consideration for allocation (Temporary).—Q-1: Who must certify that there was no consideration for an allocation?

A-1: Section 103(n)(12)(A) provides that, with respect to any private activity bond allocated any portion of the State ceiling, the private activity bond will not be described under section 103(a) unless the public official, if any, responsible for such allocation ("responsible public official") certifies under penalties of perjury that to the best of his knowledge the allocation of the State ceiling to that private activity bond was not made in consideration of any bribe, gift, gratuity, or direct or indirect contribution to any political campaign. With respect to any issue of private activity bonds, the responsible public official is the official or officer of the issuing authority that in fact is responsible for choosing which individual projects will be allocated a portion of the State ceiling. If a body of several individuals is responsible for such choices, any one member of such body qualifies as the responsible public official.

Q-2: What is the penalty for willfully making an allocation in consideration of any bribe, gift, gratuity, or direct or indirect contribution to any political campaign?

A-2: Section 103(n)(12)(B) provides that any person willfully making an allocation of any portion of the State ceiling in consideration of any bribe, gift, gratuity, or direct or indirect contribution to any political campaign will be subject to criminal penalty as though the allocation were a willful attempt to evade tax imposed by the Internal Revenue Code. [Temporary Reg. § 1.103(n)-5T.]

☐ *[T.D. 7981, 10-2-84.]*

[Reg. § 1.103(n)-6T]

§ 1.103(n)-6T. Determination of population (Temporary).—Q-1: What is the proper method for determining population?

A-1: All determinations of population must be made with respect to any calendar year on the basis of the most recent census estimate (whether final or provisional) of the resident population of the State or other governmental unit published by the Bureau of the Census in the "Current Popula-

→ *Caution: Code Sec. 103 has been amended to remove special exempt bond issue rules and provide similar rules in Code Secs. 141—150.←*

tion Reports" series before the beginning of the calendar year.

However, determinations of the population of a general purpose governmental unit (other than a State, territory, or possession) within a State, territory, or possession may not be based on estimates that do not contain estimates for all of the general purpose governmental units within such State, territory, or possession. Thus, a county may not determine its population on the basis of a census estimate that does not provide an estimate of the population of the other general purpose governmental units within the State (*e.g.*, cities, towns). If no census estimate is available for all such general purpose governmental units, the most recent decennial census of population may be relied on.

Example: The following example illustrates the provisions of A-1 of this § 1.103(n)-6T:

Example. County Q is located within State R. There are no constitutional home rule cities in State R. State R has not adopted a formula for allocating the State ceiling different from the formula provided in section 103(n)(2) and (3). The geographical area within the jurisdiction of County Q is not within the jurisdiction of any other governmental unit having jurisdiction over a smaller geographical area. As of December 31, 1984, the Bureau of the Census has published the following estimates of resident population: "Current Population Reports; Series P-25: Population Estimates and Projections, Estimates of the Population of States: July 1, 1981-1983" and "Current Population Reports; Series P-26: Local Population Estimates: Population of State R, Counties, Incorporated Places, and Minor Civil Divisions: July 1, 1981-1982." The most recent population estimate for State R available prior to 1985 provides population estimates as of July 1, 1983. The most recent population estimates for County Q available prior to 1985 is the estimate for July 1, 1982. Assuming that the State ceiling for State R for 1985 is in excess of $200 million (*i.e.*, $150 multiplied by the estimated population of State R as of July 1, 1983, exceeds $200 million), County Q may determine its private activity bond limit by using the following formula:

$P = \$150 \times .5 \times W \times Y/Z$, where

P = County Q's private activity bond limit,

W = the July 1, 1983, population estimate for State R,

Y = the July 1, 1982, population estimate for County Q, and

Z = the July 1, 1982, population estimate for State R.

If the State ceiling for State R is not in excess of $200 million, County Q may determine its private activity bond limit by using the following formula:

$P = \$200,000,000 \times .5 \times Y/Z$, where

P, Y, and Z have the same meaning as above.

[Temporary Reg. § 1.103(n)-6T.]

□ [*T.D.* 7981, 10-2-84.]

[Reg. § 1.103(n)-7T]

§ 1.103(n)-7T. Election to allocate State ceiling to certain facilities for local furnishing of electricity (Temporary).—(a) *Election*—(1) *In general.* The issuing authorities of the State of New York ("New York") may elect to use in 1984 up to one-half of the amount that would have been New York's State ceiling (as defined in section 103(n)(4) and A-1 of § 1.103(n)-3T) for calendar years 1985, 1986, and 1987 for the purpose of issuing obligations to provide facilities for the local furnishing of electric energy described in section 644(a) of the Tax Reform Act of 1984 (the "Act"). For purposes of this paragraph, New York's State ceiling for calendar years 1985, 1986, and 1987 is considered equal to the State ceiling for 1984 (without taking into account any increase in the State ceiling for 1984 as a result of an election under section 644(b) and this section).

(2) *Procedure.* The election shall be made by filing the statement described in this paragraph (a)(2) with the Internal Revenue Service Center, Philadelphia, Pennsylvania, on or before December 31, 1984. The statement shall be titled "Allocation election under section 644 of the Tax Reform Act of 1984," shall be signed by the Governor of New York or his authorized representative, and shall contain the following information:

(i) The name, address, and TIN of the issuing authority (or authorities) that is expected to issue the obligations for the facilities described in section 644(a) of the Act pursuant to the election described in section 644(b) of the Act and this section, and

(ii) The amount of the State ceiling for each of calendar years 1985, 1986, and 1987 with respect to which the election is made.

(b) *Effect of election*—(1) *In 1984.* The amount of the State ceiling for calendar years 1985, 1986, and 1987 with respect to which the election is made will be considered part of New York's State ceiling for calendar year 1984. For purposes of section 644(b) of the Act, such amount will be

Reg. § 1.103(n)-7T(b)(1)

→ *Caution: Code Sec. 103 has been amended to remove special exempt bond issue rules and provide similar rules in Code Secs. 141—150.*←

considered used in 1984 only to the extent that obligations are issued in 1984 to provide facilities for the local furnishing of electric energy described in section 644(a) of the Act, or to the extent that a proper election is made on or before December 31, 1984 (and is not revoked or amended between the time it is made and the end of 1984), pursuant to section 103(n)(10) and § 1.103(n)-4T to carry forward all or part of such amount to provide such facilities during the carryforward period applicable to calendar year 1984 State ceiling.

(2) *In 1985, 1986, and 1987.* An election under section 644(b) of the Act and this section to use in calendar year 1984 an amount of New York's State ceiling for a subsequent calendar year reduces the State ceiling for such subsequent calendar year by the amount with respect to which the election is made, whether or not such amount is considered used in 1984 pursuant to this paragraph (b). Thus, no obligations may be issued pursuant to the election described in section 644(b) of the Act and this section to provide a facility other than the facilities for the furnishing of electric energy described in section 644(a) of the Act.

(3) *Other effects.* An election or the failure to make an election under section 644(b) of the Act and this section shall not affect any otherwise applicable rule that permits an issuing authority, for any calendar year, to—

(i) Allocate a portion of its private activity bond limit,

(ii) Issue obligations within its private activity bond limit, or

(iii) Elect under section 103(n)(10) and § 1.103(n)-4T to carry forward any portion of its private activity bond limit,

in order to issue obligations to provide a facility described in section 644(a) of the Act.

(c) *Revocation of election.* An election made under section 644(b) of the Act and this section may not be revoked or amended. An insubstantial deviation from a specification contained in an election under section 644(b) of the Act and this section shall not prevent obligations from being issued pursuant to such election. [Temporary Reg. § 1.103(n)-7T.]

☐ [*T.D. 8001, 12-26-84.*]

→ *Caution: Code Sec. 103A has been repealed. Similar exempt bond issue rules have been provided in Code Secs. 141–150.*←

[Reg. § 6a.103A-1]

§ 6a.103A-1. **Interest on mortgage subsidy bonds (Temporary).**—(a) *In general*—(1) *Mortgage subsidy bond.* A mortgage subsidy bond shall be treated as an obligation not described in section 103(a)(1) or (a)(2). Thus, the interest on a mortgage subsidy bond is includible in gross income and subject to Federal income taxation.

(2) *Exceptions.* Any qualified mortgage bond and any qualified veterans' mortgage bond shall not be treated as a mortgage subsidy bond. See § 6a.103A-2 with respect to requirements of qualified mortgage bonds and § 6a.103A-3 with respect to requirements of qualified veterans' mortgage bonds.

(3) *Additional requirement.* In addition to the requirements of § 6a.103A-2, § 6a.103A-3, and this section, qualified mortgage bonds and qualified veterans' mortgage bonds shall be subject to the requirements of section 103(c) and the regulations thereunder.

(4) *Advance refunding.* On or after December 5, 1980, no tax-exempt obligation may be issued for the advance refunding of a mortgage subsidy bond (determined without regard to section

103A(b)(2) or § 6a.103A-1(a)(2)). An obligation issued for the refunding of a mortgage subsidy bond will be considered to be an advance refunding obligation if it is issued more than 180 days before the prior issue is discharged.

(5) *Registration.* Any obligation that is part of a qualified mortgage bond issue or qualified veterans' mortgage bond issue and which is issued after December 31, 1981, must be in registered form. The term "in registered form" has the same meaning as in § 1.6049-2(d). Thus, in general, an obligation is issued in registered form if it is registered as to both principal and interest and if its transfer must be effected by the surrender of the old instrument to the issuer and by either the reissuance of the old instrument to a new holder or the issuance of a new instrument to a new holder.

(b) *Definitions.* For purposes of § 6a.103A-2, § 6a.103A-3, and this section the following definitions apply:

(1) *Mortgage subsidy bond.* (i) The term "mortgage subsidy bond" means any obligation which is issued as part of an issue a significant portion of the proceeds of which is to be used

Reg. § 6a.103A-1(a)(1)

→ *Caution: Code Sec. 103A has been repealed. Similar exempt bond issue rules have been provided in Code Secs. 141–150.*←

directly or indirectly to provide mortgages on owner-occupied residences.

(ii) For purposes of subdivision (i), a significant portion of the proceeds of an issue is used to provide mortgages if 5 percent or more of the proceeds are so used.

(2) *Mortgage.* The term "mortgage" includes deeds of trust, conditional sales contracts, pledges, agreements to hold title in escrow, and any other form of owner financing.

(3) *Bond.* The term "bond" means any obligation. The term "obligation" means any evidence of indebtedness.

(4) *State.* (i) The term "State" includes a possession of the United States and the District of Columbia.

(ii) For purposes of subdivision (i), obligations issued by or on behalf of any State or local governmental unit by constituted authorities empowered to issue such obligations are the obligations of such governmental unit. See § 1.103-1(b).

(5) *Proceeds.* The term "proceeds" includes original proceeds and investment proceeds. The terms "original proceeds" and "investment proceeds" shall have the same meaning as in § 1.103-13(b)(2). Unless otherwise provided in § 6a.103A-2 or this section, however, amounts earned from the investment of proceeds which are derived from qualified mortgage bonds in nonmortgage investments may not be commingled for the purposes of accounting for expenditures with other non-bond amounts, and such proceeds are investment proceeds even though not treated as investment proceeds for purposes of section 103(c). Repayments of principal on mortgages shall be treated as proceeds of an issue. Amounts (such as State appropriations or surplus funds) which are provided by the issuer or a private lender in conjunction with a qualified mortgage bond or a qualified veterans' mortgage bond shall not be treated as proceeds of a mortgage subsidy bond under this section. However, fees which are paid by a participating financial institution pursuant to an agreement with the issuer whereby such institution receives the right to originate or service mortgages and which are retained by an issuer are treated as original proceeds of the issue. Amounts provided by the issuer or a private lender may be treated as proceeds of an issue for purposes of section 103(c).

(6) *Single-family and owner-occupied residences.* Except for purposes of § 6a.103A-2(g) and (h)(2)(ii), the terms "single-family" and "owner-

occupied," when used with respect to residences, include two-, three-, and four-family residences—

(i) One unit of which is occupied by the owner of the units, and

(ii) Which were first occupied as a residence at least 5 years before the mortgage is executed. [Temporary Reg. § 6a.103A-1.]

□ [*T.D. 7780, 6-29-81. Amended by T.D. 7794, 11-5-81.*]

[Reg. § 1.103A-2]

§ 1.103A-2. **Qualified mortgage bond.—**

(a)–(j) [Reserved]

(k) *Information reporting requirement*—(1) *In general.* An issue meets the requirements of this paragraph only if the issuer in good faith attempted to meet the information reporting requirements of this paragraph. Except as otherwise provided in paragraph (k)(5)(iv), the requirements of this paragraph apply to qualified veterans mortgage bonds issued after July 18, 1984, and to qualified mortgage bonds issued after December 31, 1984. With respect to bonds issued after December 31, 1986, see the regulations under section 149(e).

(2) *Information required.* (i) The issuer must, based on information and reasonable expectations determined as of the date of issue, submit on Form 8038 the information required therein; the issuer need not, however, include the information required by Form 8038 that is relevant only to obligations described in section 103(l)(1) and the regulations thereunder. The information that must be submitted includes—

(A) The name, address, and employer identification number of the issuer,

(B) The date of issue,

(C) The face amount of each obligation which is part of the issue,

(D) The total purchase price of the issue,

(E) The amount allocated to a reasonably required reserve or replacement fund,

(F) The amount of lendable proceeds,

(G) The stated interest rate of each maturity,

(H) The term of each maturity,

(I) In the case of an issue of qualified mortgage bonds, whether the issuer has elected under section § 6a.103A-2(i)(4)(v) to pay arbitrage to the United States,

Reg. § 1.103A-2(k)(2)

→ *Caution: Code Sec. 103A has been repealed. Similar exempt bond issue rules have been provided in Code Secs. 141–150.*←

(J) In the case of an issue of qualified mortgage bonds, the issuer's market limitation as of the date of issue (as defined in § 6a.103A-2(g)), the amount of qualified mortgage bonds that the issuer has elected not to issue under section 25(c)(2) and the regulations thereunder, and the aggregate amount of qualified mortgage bonds issued to date by the issuer during the calendar year, and

(K) In the case of an issue of qualified veterans' mortgage bonds, the issuer's State veterans limit (as defined in section 103A(o)(3)(B) and the regulations thereunder) and the aggregate amount of qualified veterans' mortgage bonds issued to date by the issuer during the calendar year and prior to the date of issue of the issue for which the Form 8038 is being submitted.

(ii) With respect to issues issued after December 31, 1984, the issuer must submit a report containing information on the borrowers of the original proceeds of such issues. The report must be filed for each reporting period in which the original proceeds of any of such issues are used to provide mortgages. The issuer is not responsible for false information provided by a borrower if the issuer did not know or have reason to know that the information was false. The report must be filed on the form prescribed by the Internal Revenue Service. If no form is prescribed, or if the form prescribed is not readily available, the issuer may use its own form provided that such form is in the format set forth in paragraph (k)(3) and contains the information required by this paragraph (k)(2)(ii). The report must be titled "Qualified Mortgage Bond Information Report" or "Qualified Veterans' Mortgage Bond Information Report", and must include the name, address, and TIN of the issuer, the reporting period for which the information is provided, and the following tables containing information concerning the borrowers of the original proceeds of the issues subject to the requirements of this paragraph (k)(2)(ii) with respect to mortgages provided during the reporting period for which the report is filed:

(A) A table titled "Number of Mortgage Loans by Income and Acquisition Cost" showing the number of mortgage loans (other than those issued in connection with qualified home improvement and rehabilitation loans) made during the reporting period according to the annualized gross income of the borrowers (categorized in the following intervals of income: $0 - $9,999; $10,000 - $19,999; $20,000 - $29,999; $30,000 - $39,999; $40,000 - $49,999; $50,000 - $74,999; and $75,000

or more) and according to the acquisition cost of each residence being financed (categorized in the following intervals of acquisition cost: $0 - $19,999; $20,000 - $39,999; $40,000 - $59,999; $60,000 - $79,999; $80,000 - $99,999; $100,000 - $119,999; $120,000 - $149,999; $150,000 - $199,999; and $200,000 or more). For each interval of income and acquisition cost the table must also be categorized according to the number of borrowers that—

(1) Did not have a present ownership interest in a principal residence at any time during the 3-year period ending on the date the mortgage is executed (i.e., satisfied the 3-year requirement) and purchased residences in targeted areas,

(2) Satisfied the 3-year requirement and purchased residences not located in targeted areas,

(3) Did have a present ownership interest in a principal residence at any time during the 3-year period ending on the date the mortgage is executed (i.e., did not satisfy the 3-year requirement) and purchased residences in targeted areas, and

(4) Did not satisfy the 3-year requirement and purchased residences not located in targeted areas.

With respect to issues of qualified veterans' mortgage bonds, for each interval of income and acquisition cost the table need only be categorized according to the number of borrowers that satisfied the 3-year requirement and the number of borrowers that failed to satisfy the 3-year requirement.

(B) A table titled "Volume of Mortgage Loans by Income and Acquisition Cost" showing the total principal amount of the mortgage loans (other than qualified home improvement and rehabilitation loans) provided during the reporting period according to annualized gross income (categorized in the same intervals of income as the preceding table) and according to the acquisition cost of the residences acquired (categorized in the same acquisition cost intervals as the preceding table). For each interval of income and acquisition cost the table must also be categorized according to the total principal amount of the mortgage loans of borrowers that—

(1) Satisfied the 3-year requirement and purchased residences in targeted areas,

(2) Satisfied the 3-year requirement and purchased residences not located in targeted areas,

Reg. § 1.103A-2(k)(2)

→ *Caution: Code Sec. 103A has been repealed. Similar exempt bond issue rules have been provided in Code Secs. 141–150.*←

(*3*) Did not satisfy the 3-year requirement and purchased residences in targeted areas, and

(*4*) Did not satisfy the 3-year requirement and purchased residences not located in targeted areas.

With respect to issues of qualified veterans' mortgage bonds, for each interval of income and acquisition cost the table need only be categorized according to the total principal amount of the mortgage loans of borrowers that satisfied the 3-year requirement and the total principal amount of the mortgage loans of borrowers that did not satisfy the 3-year requirement.

(C) For issues other than qualified veterans' mortgage bonds, a table titled "Mortgage Subsidy Bonds for Qualified Home Improvement and Rehabilitation Loans" showing the number of borrowers obtaining qualified home improvement loans and qualified rehabilitation loans and the total of the principal amounts of such loans; the information contained in the table must also be categorized according to whether the residences with respect to which the loans were provided are located in targeted areas.

(3) *Format.* (i) With respect to the report required by paragraph (k)(2)(ii), if no form is prescribed by the Internal Revenue Service, or if the prescribed form is not readily available, the issuer must submit the report in the format specified in this paragraph (k)(3).

(ii) With respect to issues of qualified mortgage bonds, the format of the report specified in paragraph (k)(3) is the following:

QUALIFIED MORTGAGE BOND INFORMATION REPORT

Name of issuer:

Address of issuer:

TIN of issuer:

Reporting period:

NUMBER OF MORTGAGE LOANS BY INCOME AND ACQUISITION COST

3-year Requirement: Annualized Gross Monthly Income of Borrowers	Satisfied		Not Satisfied		Totals
	Nontargeted Area	Targeted Area	Nontargeted Area	Targeted Area	
$ 0 — 9,999					
$ 10,000—19,999					
$ 20,000—29,999					
$ 30,000—39,999					
$ 40,000—49,999					
$ 50,000—74,999					
$ 75,000 or more					
Total					
Acquisition Cost					
$ 0 — 19,999					
$ 20,000— 39,999					
$ 40,000— 59,999					
$ 60,000— 79,999					
$ 80,000— 99,999					
$100,000—119,999					
$120,000—149,999					
$150,000—199,999					
$200,000 or more					
Total					

Reg. § 1.103A-2(k)(3)

→ *Caution: Code Sec. 103A has been repealed. Similar exempt bond issue rules have been provided in Code Secs. 141–150.←*

VOLUME OF MORTGAGE LOANS BY INCOME AND ACQUISITION COST

3-year Requirement: Annualized Gross Monthly Income of Borrowers	Satisfied		Not Satisfied		Totals
	Nontargeted Area	Targeted Area	Nontargeted Area	Targeted Area	
$ 0 — 9,999					
$ 10,000—19,999					
$ 20,000—29,999					
$ 30,000—39,999					
$ 40,000—49,999					
$ 50,000—74,999					
$ 75,000 or more					
Total					
Acquisition Cost					
$ 0 — 19,999					
$ 20,000— 39,999					
$ 40,000— 59,999					
$ 60,000— 79,999					
$ 80,000— 99,999					
$100,000—119,999					
$120,000—149,999					
$150,000—199,999					
$200,000 or more					
Total					

MORTGAGE SUBSIDY BONDS FOR QUALIFIED HOME IMPROVEMENT AND REHABILITATION LOANS

	Nontargeted Area	Targeted Area	Totals
Number of qualified home improvement loans			
Volume of qualified home improvement loans			
Number of qualified rehabilitation loans			
Volume of qualified rehabilitation loans			

(iii) The format of the report specified in paragraph (k)(3) for qualified veterans' mortgage bonds is the following:

QUALIFIED VETERANS' MORTGAGE BOND INFORMATION REPORT

Name of issuer:

Address of issuer:

TIN of issuer:

Reporting period:

NUMBER OF MORTGAGE LOANS BY INCOME AND ACQUISITION COST

3-year Requirement: Annualized Gross Monthly Income of Borrowers	Satisfied	Not Satisfied	Totals
$ 0 — 9,999			
$ 10,000— 19,999			
$ 20,000— 29,999			
$ 30,000— 39,999			
$ 40,000— 49,999			
$ 50,000— 74,999			
$ 75,000 or more			
Total			
Acquisition Cost			

Reg. § 1.103A-2(k)(3)

→ *Caution: Code Sec. 103A has been repealed. Similar exempt bond issue rules have been provided in Code Secs. 141–150.*←

	Satisfied	Not Satisfied	Totals
$ 0 — 19,999			
$ 20,000 — 39,999			
$ 40,000— 59,999			
$ 60,000— 79,999			
$ 80,000— 99,999			
$100,000—119,999			
$120,000—149,999			
$150,000—199,999			
$200,000 or more			
Total			

VOLUME OF MORTGAGE LOANS BY INCOME AND ACQUISITION COST

3-year Requirement:	Satisfied	Not Satisfied	Totals
Annualized Gross Monthly Income of Borrowers			
$ 0 — 9,999			
$ 10,000— 19,999			
$ 20,000— 29,999			
$ 30,000— 39,999			
$ 40,000— 49,999			
$ 50,000— 74,999			
$ 75,000 or more			
Total			
Acquisition Cost			
$ 0 — 19,999			
$ 20,000— 39,999			
$ 40,000— 59,999			
$ 60,000— 79,999			
$ 80,000— 99,999			
$100,000—119,999			
$120,000—149,999			
$150,000—199,999			
$200,000 or more			
Total			

(4) *Definitions and special rules.* (i) For purposes of this paragraph the term "annualized gross income" means the borrower's gross monthly income multiplied by 12. Gross monthly income is the sum of monthly gross pay, any additional income from investments, pensions, Veterans Administration (VA) compensation, part-time employment, bonuses, dividends, interest, current overtime pay, net rental income, etc., and other income (such as alimony and child support, if the borrower has chosen to disclose such income). Information with respect to gross monthly income may be obtained from available loan documents, e.g., the sum of lines 23D and 23E on the Application for VA or FmHA Home Loan Guaranty or or HUD/FHA Insured Mortgage (VA Form 26-1802a, HUD 92900, Jan. 1982), or the total line from the Gross Monthly Income section of FHLMC Residential Loan Application form (FHLMC 65 Rev. 8/78). With respect to obligations issued prior to October 1, 1985, issuers may submit data based on annualized gross income or, instead, based on the adjusted income (as defined in § 1.167(k)-3(o)(3)) of the mortgagor's family for the previous calendar year. If data is submitted based on adjusted income, the issuer must note this fact in the report.

(ii) For purposes of this paragraph, the term "reporting period" means the following periods:

(A) The period beginning January 1, 1985, and ending on September 30, 1985,

(B) The period beginning on October 1, 1985, and ending on June 30, 1986, and

(C) After June 30, 1986, each 1-year period beginning July 1 and ending June 30.

(iii) See the regulations under section 103(l) for the definitions of the terms "date of issue", "maturity", and "term of issue".

(iv) For purposes of this paragraph, verification of information concerning a borrower's gross monthly income with other available information concerning the borrower's income (e.g., Federal income tax returns) is not required. In determining whether a borrower acquiring a residence in a targeted area satisfies the 3-year requirement, the issuer may rely on a statement signed by the borrower.

(5) *Time for filing.* (i) The report required by paragraph (k)(2)(i) shall be filed not later than

Reg. § 1.103A-2(k)(5)

→ *Caution: Code Sec. 103A has been repealed. Similar exempt bond issue rules have been provided in Code Secs. 141–150.*←

the 15th day of the second calendar month after the close of the calendar quarter in which the obligation is issued. The statement may be filed at any time before such date but must be complete based on facts and reasonable expectations as of the date of issue. The statement need not be amended to report information learned subsequent to the date of issue or to reflect changed circumstances with respect to the issuer.

(ii) The report required by paragraph (k)(2)(ii) (relating to use of proceeds) shall be filed not later than the 15th day of the second calendar month after the close of the reporting period, except that the report for the reporting period ending September 30, 1985, is due not later than February 15, 1986. The report may be filed at any time before such date but must be complete based on facts and reasonable expectations as of the date the report is filed. The report need not be amended to reflect information learned subsequent to the date the report is filed or to reflect changed circumstances with respect to any borrower.

(iii) The Commissioner may grant an extension of time for the filing of a report required by paragraph (k)(2)(i) or (ii) if there is reasonable cause for the failure to file such report in a timely fashion.

(iv) An issue of qualified veterans' mortgage bonds issued after July 18, 1984, and prior to January 1, 1985, will be treated as satisfying the information reporting requirement of this paragraph if a Form 8038 with respect to the issue is properly filed not later than February 15, 1985; the report described in paragraph (k)(2)(ii) need not be filed with respect to such issues.

(6) *Place for filing.* The reports required by paragraph (k)(2)(i) and (ii) are to be filed at the Internal Revenue Service Center, Philadelphia, Pennsylvania 19255.

(l) *Policy statement* —(1) *In general.* (i) For obligations issued after December 31, 1984, an issue meets the requirements of this paragraph only if the applicable elected representative of the governmental unit which is the issuer (or on behalf of which the issuing authority is empowered to issue qualified mortgage bonds) has published (after a public hearing following reasonable public notice) the report described in paragraph (l)(3) by the last day of the year preceding the year in which such issue is issued and a copy of such report has been submitted to the Commissioner on or before such last day. The Commissioner may grant an extension of time for publishing and filing the report if there is reasonable cause for the failure to publish or file such report in a

timely fashion. The requirements of this paragraph will be treated as met if the issuer in good faith attempted to meet the policy statement requirements of this paragraph.

(ii) With respect to reports required by paragraph (l)(1)(i) to be published and submitted to the Commissioner not later than December 31, 1984, the Commissioner has determined that there is reasonable cause for the failure to publish or file such reports in a timely fashion; such a report will be considered published and filed in a timely fashion if, not later than March 11, 1985, the report is published (after a public hearing following reasonable public notice) and a copy is submitted to the Commissioner. In addition, any report submitted not later than December 31, 1984, with respect to which an issuer in good faith attempted to satisfy the requirements of section 103A(j)(5) shall be treated as substantially satisfying the requirements of this paragraph. For example, with respect to a report submitted not later than December 31, 1984, an issuer shall not be treated as failing to satisfy the requirements of section 103A(j)(5) based on the fact that (A) the notice of public hearing failed to state the manner in which affected residents may obtain copies of the proposed report prior to the hearing, or (B) the proposed report was not available prior to or at the public hearing. With respect to reports required to be published and submitted to the Commissioner not later than December 31, 1986, the Commissioner has determined that there is a reasonable cause for the failure to publish and file such reports in a timely fashion; such reports will be considered published and filed in a timely fashion if, not later than December 31, 1987, the report is published (after having a public hearing following reasonable public notice) and a copy is submitted to the Commissioner.

(2) *Definitions and special rules.* (i) In the case of an issuer that issues qualified mortgage bonds on behalf of one or more governmental units, a single report may be filed provided that such report is signed (A) by the applicable elected representative of each governmental unit on whose behalf obligations have been issued during any preceding calendar year or (B) by the Governor of the State in which the issuer is located.

(ii) See section 103(k)(2)(E) and the regulations thereunder for the definition of the term "applicable elected representative".

(iii) In the case of qualified mortgage bonds issued by, or on behalf of, a governmental unit that did not reasonably expect during the preceding calendar year to issue (or have issued on its behalf by any other issuer) qualified mortgage bonds during the current calendar year, the

Reg. § 1.103A-2(k)(6)

→ *Caution: Code Sec. 103A has been repealed. Similar exempt bond issue rules have been provided in Code Secs. 141–150.*←

requirements of this paragraph will be treated as met if the applicable governmental unit which is the issuer (or on behalf of which the issuing authority is empowered to issue qualified mortgage bonds) has published (after a public hearing following reasonable public notice) the report described in paragraph (l)(3) prior to the issuance of any qualified mortgage bonds and a copy of such report has been submitted to the Commissioner prior to such issuance.

(iv) For purposes of this paragraph a report will be considered to be "published" when the applicable elected representative of the governmental unit has made copies of the report available for distribution to the public. Reasonable public notice of the manner in which copies of the report may be obtained must be provided; such notice may be included as part of the public notice required by paragraph (l)(4).

(3) *Report.* (i) A report is described in this paragraph (l)(3) if it contains the issuer's name, TIN, and the title "Policy Report Under Section 103A" stated on the cover page of the report and if it includes—

(A) A statement of the policies of the issuer with respect to housing, development, and low-income housing assistance which such issuer is to follow in issuing qualified mortgage bonds and mortgage credit certificates, and

(B) An assessment of the compliance of such issuer during the 1-year period preceding the date of the report with—

(1) The statement of policy on qualified mortgage bonds and mortgage credit certificates that was set forth in the previous report, if any, of the issuer, and

(2) The intent of Congress that State and local governments are expected to use their authority to issue qualified mortgage bonds and mortgage credit certificates to the greatest extent feasible (taking into account prevailing interest rates and conditions in the housing market) to assist lower income families to afford home ownership before assisting higher income families.

(ii) For example, a report described in this paragraph (l)(3) may (but is not required to) contain—

(A) A specific statement of the policies with respect to housing, development, and low-income housing assistance which the issuer is to follow in issuing qualified mortgage bonds and mortgage credit certificates, including, for example, a statement as to—

(1) With respect to housing policies, (i) whether the proceeds will be used to provide financing for the acquisition of residences, to provide qualified home improvement loans, or to provide qualified rehabilitation loans; (ii) whether all or a portion of the proceeds will be targeted to new existing, or any other particular class or type of housing; (iii) how the existence of a need or absence of a need for such targeting has been determined; (iv) the method by which the proceeds will be targeted; (v) any other pertinent information relating to the issuer's housing policies; and (vi) how the housing policies relate to the issuer's development and low-income housing assistance policies;

(2) With respect to development policies, (i) whether all or a portion of the proceeds will be targeted to specific areas (including targeted areas as described in § 6a.103A-2(b)(3)); (ii) a description of the areas to which the proceeds will be targeted; (iii) the reasons for selecting such areas; (iv) whether proceeds targeted to each area are to be used to finance redevelopment of existing housing or new construction; (v) any other pertinent information relating to the issuer's development policies; and (vi) how the development policies relate to the issuer's low-income housing assistance policies; and

(3) With respect to low-income housing assistance policies, (i) whether all or a portion of the proceeds will be targeted to low-income (i.e., 80 percent of median income), moderate-income (i.e., 100 percent of median income), or any other class of borrowers; (ii) the method by which the proceeds will be targeted to such borrowers; and (iii) any other pertinent information relating to the issuer's low-income housing assistance policies;

(B) An assessment of the compliance of the governmental unit or issuing authority during the twelve-month period ending with the date of the report with the statement of housing, development, and low-income housing assistance policies with respect to qualified mortgage bonds and mortgage credit certificates that were set forth in the report, if any, published in the preceding year with respect to such governmental unit, including, for example, a statement as to whether the governmental unit or issuing authority successfully implemented its policies and, if not, an analysis of the reasons for such failure; and

(C) An assessment of the compliance of the governmental unit or issuing authority during the twelve-month period ending with the date of the report with the intent of Congress that State

Reg. § 1.103A-2(l)(3)

→ *Caution: Code Sec. 103A has been repealed. Similar exempt bond issue rules have been provided in Code Secs. 141–150.* ←

and local governments are expected to use their authority to issue qualified mortgage bonds and mortgage credit certificates to the greatest extent feasible (taking into account prevailing interest rates and conditions in the housing market) to assist lower income families to afford home ownership before assisting higher income families, including, for example, a description of (1) the method used by the governmental unit or issuing authority to distribute proceeds, (2) whether and how that method enabled the governmental unit or issuing authority to assist lower income families before higher income families, and (3) any income levels that have been defined and used by the governmental unit or issuing authority in connection with distribution of the proceeds (no specific definition of lower income and higher income is imposed on governmental units or issuing authorities).

(iii) For purposes of the assessments of compliance required by paragraph (l)(3)(i)(B) to be included in the report, the "date of the report" means June 30. For purposes of the report required to be filed prior to January 1, 1986, an issuer need not perform these assessments of compliance with respect to any period prior to January 1, 1985.

(iv) An issuer that fails to establish policies with respect to the criteria provided in paragraph (l)(3)(i) will not be treated as failing to satisfy the requirements of this paragraph. Thus, for example, an issuer may state in its report that none of the proceeds of the issue will be targeted to specific areas. Similarly, an issuer that fails to successfully implement its policies will not be treated as failing to satisfy the requirements of this paragraph.

(4) *Public hearing.* The public hearing required by paragraph (l)(1) means a forum providing a reasonable opportunity for interested individuals to express their views, both orally and in writing, on the report that the applicable representative proposes to publish to satisfy the requirements of this paragraph (l). A public hearing held prior to January 1, 1985, will not fail to satisfy the requirements of this paragraph (l)(4) merely because the proposed policy statement was not available prior to the public hearing. In general, a governmental unit may select its own procedure for the hearing, provided that interested individuals have a reasonable opportunity to express their views. Thus, it may impose reasonable requirements on persons who wish to participate in the hearing, such as a requirement that persons desiring to speak at the hearing so request in

writing at least 24 hours before the hearing or that they limit their oral remarks to 10 minutes. For purposes of this public hearing requirement, it is not necessary that the applicable elected representative who will publish the report be present at the hearing, that a report on the hearing be submitted to that official, or that State administrative procedural requirements for public hearings in general be observed. However, compliance with such State procedural requirements (except those at variance with a specific requirement set forth in this paragraph) will generally assure that the hearing satisfies the requirements of this paragraph. The hearing may be conducted by any individual appointed or employed to perform such function by the governmental unit, its agencies, or by the issuer. Thus, for example, for a report to be issued by an issuing authority that acts on behalf of a county, the hearing may be conducted by the issuing authority, the county, or an appointee or employee of either.

(5) *Reasonable public notice.* (i) The reasonable public notice required by paragraph (l)(1) means published notice which is reasonably designed to inform residents of the geographical area within the jurisdiction of the governmental unit that will publish the report. The notice must state the time and place for the hearing and contain the information required by paragraph (l)(5)(ii). Notice is presumed reasonable if published no fewer than 14 days before the hearing. Notice is presumed reasonably designed to inform affected residents only if published in one or more newspapers of general circulation available to residents of that locality or if announced by radio or television broadcast to those residents.

(ii) The notice of hearing described in this paragraph (l)(5) must state—

(A) The time and place for the hearing,

(B) Any applicable limitations regarding participation in the hearing,

(C) With respect to any notice of hearing published after December 31, 1984, the manner in which affected residents may obtain copies of the proposed report prior to the hearing, and

(D) With respect to any notice of hearing published after December 31, 1984, that the hearing will involve the issuer's policies with respect to housing, development, and low-income housing assistance which the issuer is to follow in issuing qualified mortgage bonds and mortgage credit certificates.

(6) *Procedure for public hearings of multiple jurisdiction issuers.* In the case of an issuer that

Reg. § 1.103A-2(l)(4)

→ *Caution: Code Sec. 103A has been repealed. Similar exempt bond issue rules have been provided in Code Secs. 141–150.*←

issues qualified mortgage bonds on behalf of two or more governmental units ("multiple jurisdiction issuer"), each governmental unit on whose behalf the issuer reasonably expects to issue qualified mortgage bonds during the succeeding calendar year must hold a public hearing following reasonable public notice prior to the publication of the report required by this paragraph. A multiple jurisdiction issuer may hold a combined hearing as long as the combined hearing is a joint undertaking that provides all residents of the participating governmental units (*i.e.*, each governmental unit on whose behalf qualified mortgage bonds were issued by the authority and each governmental unit on whose behalf the authority reasonably expects to issue qualified mortgage bonds during the succeeding calendar year) a reasonable opportunity to be heard. The location of any combined hearing is presumed to provide a reasonable opportunity for all affected residents to be heard if it is no farther than 100 miles from the seat of government of each participating governmental unit beyond whose geographic jurisdiction the hearing is conducted.

(7) *Place for filing.* The report is to be filed with the Internal Revenue Service Center, Philadelphia, Pennsylvania 19255.

(m) *State certification requirements*—(1) *In general.* An issue meets the requirements of this paragraph only if the issuer in good faith attempted to meet the State certification requirements of this paragraph. The requirements of this paragraph apply to obligations issued after December 31, 1984; see section 149(e) and the regulations thereunder with respect to obligations issued after December 31, 1986.

(2) *Certification.* (i) An issue satisfies the requirements of section 103A(j)(4) and this paragraph (m)(2) only if the State official designated by law (or, if there is no State official, the Governor) certifies on or before the later of the date of issue or October 3, 1985, following a request for such certification by the issuer, that, as of the date the certification is executed, the issue meets the requirements of section 103A(g) and the regulations thereunder (relating to volume limitation). In the case of any constitutional home rule city, the certification shall be made by the chief executive officer of the city. To the extent consistent with State and local law, the Governor (or the chief executive officer of any constitutional home rule city) may delegate the responsibility to execute the certification required by this paragraph.

(ii) The certifying official need not perform an independent investigation in order to

determine whether the issue meets the requirements of section 103A(g). In determining the aggregate amount of qualified mortgage bonds previously issued by an issuer during a calendar year, the certifying official may rely on copies of the reports submitted, to date, by the issuer pursuant to section 103A(j)(3) for other issues of qualified mortgage bonds issued during that year and copies of any elections previously made pursuant to section 25(c)(2) not to issue qualified mortgage bonds, together with an affidavit executed by an officer of the issuer responsible for issuing the bonds stating that the issuer has not, to date during the calendar year, issued any other qualified mortgage bonds, the amount, if any, of the issuer's market limitation that it has, to date during the calendar year, surrendered to other issuing authorities, and that it has not, to date during the calendar year, made any other elections not to issue qualified mortgage bonds. If, based on such information, the certifying official determines that, as of the date the certification is executed, the issue will not exceed the issuer's market limitation for the year, the official may certify that the issue meets the requirements of section 103A(g).

(3) *Special rule.* If 15 days elapse after the issuer files a proper request for the certification described in paragraph (m)(2) and the issuer has not received from the State official designated by law (or, if there is no State official, the Governor) certification that the issue meets the requirements of section 103A(g) and § 6a.103A-2(g) or, in the alternative, a statement that the issue does not meet such requirements, the issuer may, instead, submit an affidavit executed by an officer of the issuer responsible for issuing the bonds stating that—

(i) The issue meets the requirements of section 103(A)(g) and § 6a.103A-2(g),

(ii) At least 15 days before the execution of the affidavit the issuer filed a proper request for the certification described in paragraph (m)(2), and

(iii) The State official designated by law (or, if there is no State official, the Governor) has not provided the certification described in paragraph (m)(2).

In the case of obligations issued prior to October 4, 1985, the preceding sentence shall be applied by substituting "30 days" for "15 days". For purposes of this paragraph, a request for certification is proper if the request includes the reports and affidavits described in paragraph (m)(2)(ii).

Reg. § 1.103A-2(m)(3)

→ *Caution: Code Sec. 103A has been repealed. Similar exempt bond issue rules have been provided in Code Secs. 141–150.←*

(4) *Filing.* The certification (or affidavit) required by this paragraph shall be filed with the Internal Revenue Service Center, Philadelphia, PA 19255. The certification (or affidavit) shall be submitted with the Form 8038 required to be filed by section 103A(j)(3) and paragraph (k) of this § 1.103A-2. The Commissioner may grant an extension of time for filing the certification (or affidavit) if there is a reasonable cause for the failure to file such statement in a timely fashion.

(5) *Effect of certification.* The fact that an issuer obtains the certification (or affidavit) described in this paragraph does not ensure that the requirements of paragraph (g) of this section are met. Obligations that do not meet the requirements of paragraph (g) are not described in section 103(a). [Reg. § 1.103A-2.]

☐ [*T.D.* 8049, 8-29-85. *Amended by T.D.* 8129, 3-10-87.]

[Reg. § 6a.103A-2]

§ 6a.103A-2. **Qualified mortgage bond (Temporary).**—(a) *In general*—(1) *Qualified mortgage bond.* A qualified mortgage bond shall not be treated as a mortgage subsidy bond, and the interest on a qualified mortgage bond will be exempt from Federal income taxation.

(2) *Termination date.* No obligation issued after December 31, 1983, shall be treated as part of a qualified mortgage bond issue.

(b) *Definitions and special rules.* For purposes of this section and § 6a.103A-1, the following definitions apply:

(1) *Qualified mortgage bond.* The term "qualified mortgage bond" means one or more obligations issued by a State or any political subdivision thereof (hereinafter referred to as "governmental unit") as part of an issue—

(i) All of the original proceeds of which, net of the costs of issuing the obligations and proceeds invested in a reasonably required reserve fund (such net amount hereinafter in this section referred to as "lendable proceeds"), are to be used to finance owner-occupied residences, and

(ii) Which meets each of the requirements of § 6a.103A-1 and this section.

A qualified mortgage bond does not include any bond that is an industrial development bond under section 103(b).

(2) *Constitutional home rule city.* The term "constitutional home rule city" means, with respect to any calendar year, any political subdivision of a State which, under a State constitution which was adopted in 1970 and effective on July 1, 1971, had home rule powers on the 1st day of the calendar year.

(3) *Targeted area residence.* The term "targeted area residence" means a residence in an area which is either—

(i) A qualified census tract, or

(ii) An area of chronic economic distress.

(4) *Qualified census tract.* (i) The term "qualified census tract" means a census tract in which 70 percent or more of the families have an income which is 80 percent or less of the State-wide median family income.

(ii) The determination under subdivision (i) shall be made on the basis of the most recent decennial census for which data are available. With respect to any particular bond issue, such determination may be based upon the decennial census data available 3 months prior to the date of issuance and shall not be affected by official changes to such data during or after such 3-month period.

(iii) The term "census tract" means a census tract as defined by the Secretary of Commerce.

(5) *Areas of chronic economic distress.* (i) The term "area of chronic economic distress" means an area designated by a State as meeting the standards established by that State for purposes of this subparagraph and approved by the Secretary and by the Secretary of Housing and Urban Development in accordance with the criteria set forth in (iii) of this subparagraph. A State may withdraw such designation at any time, with reasonable cause. Such withdrawal shall be effective upon notification by the State to the Assistant Secretary for Housing/Federal Housing Commissioner of the Department of Housing and Urban Development. Such withdrawal shall not affect the tax-exempt status of any outstanding issue of obligations.

(ii) For purposes of making a designation under this subparagraph, withdrawing a designation, or making any other submission, "State" means the governor of a State, or a State official commissioned by the governor or by State statute for such purposes.

(iii) The following criteria will be used in evaluating a proposed designation of an area of chronic economic distress:

(A) The condition of the housing stock, including the age of the housing and the number of abandoned and substandard residential units. Data pertinent to this criterion include the num-

→ *Caution: Code Sec. 103A has been repealed. Similar exempt bond issue rules have been provided in Code Secs. 141–150.* ←

ber and percentage of housing units that were constructed prior to 1940, the average age of the housing stock, the number and percentage of abandoned housing units, and the number and percentage of substandard residential units.

(B) The need of area residents for owner financing under a qualified mortgage bond issue as indicated by low per capita income, a high percentage of families in poverty, a high number of welfare recipients, and high unemployment rates. Data pertinent to this criterion include the per capita income of the population in the area, the number and percentage of families eligible to receive food stamps from a program pursuant to 7 U.S.C. 2011, the number and percentage of families eligible to receive payments under the Aid to Families with Dependent Children program, and the unemployment rate.

(C) The potential for use of owner financing under a qualified mortgage bond issue to improve housing conditions in the area. Data pertinent to this criterion include the number and percentage of owner-occupied homes that are substandard, the number and percentage of families that are low- or moderate-income renters, and the number and percentage of sub-standard units in the area that will be improved through the use of owner financing provided by the proceeds of a qualified mortgage bond issue.

(D) The existence of a housing assistance plan which provides a displacement program and a public improvements and services program (similar to the Housing Assistance Plan (HAP) required by the Department of Housing and Urban Development under the Community Development Block Grant program (42 U.S.C. section 5301 *et seq.*)).

This determination shall be based upon the most recent data available. The certification described in subdivision (iv)(C) shall satisfy the criteria set forth in subdivisions (C) and (D). A certification described in (iv)(D) shall satisfy the criteria set forth in subdivisions (A) and (B), provided that the majority of the households in the proposed area have incomes less than 80 percent of the median income for the standard metropolitan statistical area (SMSA) in which the proposed area is located or, if the proposed area is not within a SMSA, less than 80 percent of the median income for the State.

(iv) A proposal by the State that an area be approved as an area of chronic economic distress shall contain the following information:

(A) A description of the proposed area by its geographical limits.

(B) Maps of the State and of areas within the State that are qualified census tracts and existing or proposed areas of chronic economic distress.

(C) Where applicable, a certification of the local Area Manager of the Department of Housing and Urban Development in which the proposed area is located that the proposed area is a Neighborhood Strategy Area (NSA) under 24 CFR 570.301(c) promulgated pursuant to the Community Development Block Grant program or an area comparable to a NSA which has been reviewed and approved by the Area Manager as meeting the standards for an NSA.

(D) Where applicable, a certification from the HUD Area Manager with jurisdiction over the proposed area that the proposed area is within a geographic area which has been declared eligible for grants under the Urban Development Action Grant Program, pursuant to 24 CFR 570.452, by the Secretary of Housing and Urban Development.

(E) Statistical and descriptive information pertinent to the criteria enumerated in subdivision (iii) of this section, and a succinct statement of how the information furnished satisfies those criteria. Such statistical information shall be based upon the most recent data available.

(F) If the State so desires, a written request for a conference prior to any adverse decision on the proposed designation.

(G) A certification by the Governor or designated official that the proposed designation conforms to these regulations.

(v) The proposed designation and the information furnished with it as required by subdivision (iv) shall be submitted in triplicate to the Assistant Secretary for Housing/Federal Housing Commissioner of the Department of Housing and Urban Development (Attention: Office of State Agency and Bond Financed Programs, Rm. 6138, 451 7th Street, S.W., Washington, D.C. 20410).

(vi) Only those areas of chronic economic distress that have been previously designated by the State and approved in accordance with this subparagraph at least 3 months prior to the date of issuance need to be taken into account for any particular bond issue. Residences located in areas designated as areas of chronic economic distress approved in accordance with this subparagraph within such 3-month period or after the date of

Reg. § 6a.103A-2(b)(5)

→ *Caution: Code Sec. 103A has been repealed. Similar exempt bond issue rules have been provided in Code Secs. 141–150.*←

issue, however, may be treated as targeted area residences. However, for purposes of paragraph (h) (2), relating to the specified portion of proceeds to be placed in targeted areas, and paragraph (i)(3)(ii)(A), relating to the 1½ year temporary period, only areas approved as areas of chronic economic distress in accordance with this subparagraph at the time of issue may be taken into consideration.

(6) *Standard metropolitan statistical area.* A standard metropolitan statistical area ("SMSA") is an area in and around a city of 50,000 inhabitants or more (or equivalent area) and defined by the Secretary of Commerce as an SMSA.

(7) *Statistical area.* The term "statistical area" means—

(i) An SMSA,

(ii) Any county (or portion thereof) which is not within an SMSA, or

(iii) If there is insufficient recent statistical information with respect to a county (or portion thereof) described in subdivision (ii), such other area as may be designated by the Commissioner, upon proper application, as a substitute for such county (or portion thereof).

For purposes of subdivisions (ii) and (iii), in Alaska, the entire State, and in Louisiana, a parish, shall be treated in a manner similar to a county.

(8) *Acquisition cost.* (i) The term "acquisition cost" means the cost of acquiring a residence from the seller as a completed residential unit. Acquisition cost includes the following:

(A) All amounts paid, either in cash or in kind, by the purchaser (or a related party or for the benefit of the purchaser) to the seller (or a related party or for the benefit of the seller) as consideration for the residence.

(B) If a residence is incomplete, the reasonable cost of completing the residence whether or not the cost of completing construction is to be financed with bond proceeds. For example, where a mortgagor purchases a building which is so incomplete that occupancy of the building is not permitted under local law, the acquisition cost includes the cost of completing the building so that occupancy of the building is permitted.

(C) Where a residence is purchased subject to a ground rent, the capitalized value of the ground rent. Such value shall be calculated using a discount rate equal to the yield on the issue (as defined in § 6a.103A-2(i)(2)(vi)).

(ii) The term "acquisition cost" does not include the following:

(A) The usual and reasonable settlement or financing costs. Settlement costs include titling and transfer costs, title insurance, survey fees, or other similar costs. Financing costs include credit reference fees, legal fees, appraisal expenses, "points" which are paid by the buyer (but not the seller, even though borne by the mortgagor through a higher purchase price) or other costs of financing the residence. However, such amounts will be excluded in determining acquisition cost only to the extent that the amounts do not exceed the usual and reasonable costs which would be paid by the buyer where financing is not provided through a qualified mortgage bond issue. For example, if the purchaser agrees to pay to the seller more than a pro rata share of property taxes, such excess shall be treated as part of the acquisition cost of a residence.

(B) The value of services performed by the mortgagor or members of the mortgagor's family in completing the residence. For purposes of the preceding sentence, the family of an individual shall include only the individual's brothers and sisters (whether by the whole or half blood), spouse, ancestors, and lineal descendants. For example, where the mortgagor builds a home alone or with the help of family members, the acquisition cost includes the cost of materials provided and work performed by subcontractors (whether or not related to the mortgagor) but does not include the imputed cost of any labor actually performed by the mortgagor or a member of the mortgagor's family in constructing the residence. Similarly, where the mortgagor purchases an incomplete residence, the acquisition cost includes the cost of material and labor paid by the mortgagor to complete the residence but does not include the imputed value of the mortgagor's labor or the labor of the mortgagor's family in completing the residence.

(C) The cost of land which has been owned by the mortgagor for at least 2 years prior to the date on which construction of the residence begins.

(iii) The following examples illustrate the provisions of subparagraph (8):

Example (1). A contracts with B, a builder of single-family residences, for the purchase of a residence. Under the terms of the contract, B will deliver a residential unit to A that contains an uncompleted recreation room and an unfinished third floor and which lacks a garage. Normally, a

Reg. § 6a.103A-2(b)(6)

→ *Caution: Code Sec. 103A has been repealed. Similar exempt bond issue rules have been provided in Code Secs. 141–150.*←

completed recreation room, a finished third floor and a garage are provided as part of the residence built by B. The contract price for the residence is $58,000. At the same time, A contracts with C, an affiliate of B, to complete the recreation room and third floor and to construct the garage for a contract price of $10,000. C will perform this work after A receives title to the unit from B. Under § 6a.103A-2(b)(8)(i)(A), the acquisition cost of A's completed residential unit is $68,000, which represents the contract price of the residence plus the cost of completion of the recreation room and third floor and construction of the garage.

Example (2). E owns a single-family residence which E has listed for sale. D contracts to purchase E's residence, and the contract provides for a selling price of $30,000. D also agrees to pay an unsecured debt in the amount of $5,000, which E owes to X, a local bank. D further agrees to purchase from E the refrigerator, stove, washer, and dryer located in E's residence for $500. Such amount is equal to the fair market value of such personalty. D also agrees to purchase the light fixtures, curtain rods, and wall-to-wall carpeting for a fair market value price of $700. Under § 6a.103A-2(b)(8)(i)(A), the acquisition cost of D's completed residential unit is $35,700. Such amount includes the $5,000 unsecured debt paid off by D. The $500 paid for the refrigerator, stove, washer, and dryer are not included because such items are not included within the definition of a residence under § 6a.103A-2(d)(4). Such definition does include, however, the light fixtures, curtain rods, and wall-to-wall carpeting purchased by D.

Example (3). F contracts with G to purchase G's home for $40,000. After purchasing the residence, F pays a party unrelated to G $3,000 for painting, minor repairs, and refinishing the floors. Under § 6a.103A-2(b)(8)(i)(A), the acquisition cost of the residence is $40,000. Such fix-up expenses are not treated as part of the acquisition costs. If G had incurred such fix-up expenses, however, F may not reduce his acquisition cost of the residence by such amounts.

(9) *Qualified home improvement loan.* (i) The term "qualified home improvement loan" means the financing (whether or not secured by a mortgage), in an amount which does not exceed $15,000 with respect to any residence, of alterations, repairs, and improvements on, or in connection with, an existing single-family, owner-occupied residence by the owner thereof, but only if such items substantially protect or improve the basic livability or energy efficiency of the residence.

(ii) Alterations, repairs, or improvements that satisfy the requirement of subdivision (i) include the renovation of plumbing or electric systems, the installation of improved heating or air conditioning systems, the addition of living space, or the renovation of a kitchen area. Items that will not be considered to substantially protect or improve the basic livability of the residence include swimming pools, tennis courts, saunas, or other recreational or entertainment facilities.

(iii) If—

(A) Two or more qualified home improvement loans are provided for the same residence, whether or not by the same lender, and

(B) Any person who had a present ownership interest in such residence at the time the previous qualified home improvement loan or loans were made has a present ownership interest in the residence at the time the subsequent qualified home improvement loan is made,

then the allowable amount of the subsequent qualified home improvement loan shall be reduced by the amount, at origination, of any previous qualified home improvement loan, so that the sum of such loans does not exceed $15,000.

(iv) The following example illustrates the provisions of subparagraph (9):

Example. A and B jointly own a residence located in Town M. They obtain a qualified home improvement loan for $10,000 from Town M. A acquires B's interest in the residence. A applies to State X for a qualified home improvement loan. The maximum amount of a qualified home improvement loan which may be made by State X is $5,000, the amount that when added to the $10,000 previous loan from Town M does not exceed $15,000.

(10) *Qualified rehabilitation loans.* (i) The term "qualified rehabilitation loan" means any owner financing provided in connection with—

(A) A qualified rehabilitation, or

(B) the acquisition of a residence with respect to which there has been a qualified rehabilitation,

but only if the mortgagor to whom such financing is provided is the first resident of the residence after completion of the rehabilitation. Where there are two or more mortgagors of a rehabilitation loan, the first residency requirement is met if any of the mortgagors meets the first residency requirement.

Reg. § 6a.103A-2(b)(10)

→ *Caution: Code Sec. 103A has been repealed. Similar exempt bond issue rules have been provided in Code Secs. 141–150.*←

(ii) The term "qualified rehabilitation" means any rehabilitation of a residence if—

(A) There is a period of at least 20 years between the date on which the building was first used and the date on which physical work on such rehabilitation begins,

(B) 75 percent or more of the existing external walls of such building are retained in place as external walls in the rehabilitation process, and

(C) The expenditures for such rehabilitation are 25 percent or more of the mortgagor's adjusted basis in the residence (including the land on which the residence is located).

(iii) For purposes of (A) and (B), the rules applicable to the investment tax credit for qualified rehabilitated buildings under section 48(g)(1)(A)(iii) and (B) shall apply. However, unlike section 48(g)(1)(B), once a building meets the 20-year test, more than one rehabilitation of that building within a 20-year period may qualify as a qualified rehabilitation.

(iv) The adjusted basis to the mortgagor is the mortgagor's adjusted basis for purposes of determining gain or loss on the sale or exchange of a capital asset (as defined in section 1221). The mortgagor's adjusted basis shall be determined as of the date of completion of the rehabilitation, or, if later, the date the mortgagor acquires the residence, *i.e.,* the date on which the mortgagor includes in basis any amounts expended for rehabilitation that are expended for capital assets.

(v) The amounts expended by the mortgagor for rehabilitation include all amounts expended for rehabilitation regardless of whether the amounts expended were financed from the proceeds of the loan or from other sources, and regardless of whether the expenditure is a capital expenditure, so long as the expenditure is made during the rehabilitation of the residence and is reasonably related to the rehabilitation of the residence. The value of services performed by the mortgagor or members of the mortgagor's family (as used in § 6a.103A-2(b)(8)(ii)(B)) in rehabilitating the residence will not be included in determining the rehabilitation expenditures for purposes of the 25-percent test.

(vi) Where a mortgagor purchases a residence that has been substantially rehabilitated, the 25-percent test is determined by comparing the total expenditures made by the seller for the rehabilitation of the residence with the acquisition cost of the residence to the mortgagor. The total expenditures made by the seller for rehabilitation do not include the cost of acquiring the building or land but do include all amounts directly expended by the seller in rehabilitating the building (excluding overhead and other indirect charges).

(c) *Good faith compliance efforts—*(1) *Mortgage eligibility requirements.* An issue of qualified mortgage bonds which fails to meet one or more of the requirements of paragraphs (d), (e), (f), and (i) shall be treated as meeting such requirements if each of the following provisions is met.

(i) The issue in good faith attempted to meet all such requirements before the mortgages were executed. Good faith requires that the trust indenture, participation agreements with loan originators, and other relevant instruments contain restrictions that permit the financing of mortgages only in accordance with such requirements. In addition, the issuer must establish reasonable procedures to ensure compliance with such requirements. Such procedures include reasonable investigations by the issuer or its agent to determine that the mortgages satisfy such requirements.

(ii) Ninety-five percent or more of the lendable proceeds (as defined in § 6a.103A-2(b)(1)) that were devoted to owner financing were devoted to residences with respect to which, at the time the mortgages were executed or assumed, all such requirements were met. In determining whether the proceeds are devoted to owner financing which meets such requirements, the issuer may rely on an affidavit of the mortgagor that the property is located within the issuer's jurisdiction and an affidavit of the mortgagor and the seller that the requirements of § 6a.103A-2(f) are met. The issuer may also rely on his own or his agent's examination of copies of income tax returns which were filed with the Internal Revenue Service and which are provided by the mortgagor or obtained by the issuer or loan originator in accordance with the procedures set forth in § 301.6103(c)-1 which indicate that, during the preceding 3 years, the mortgagor did not claim deductions for taxes or interest on indebtedness with respect to real property constituting his principal residence, in addition to an affidavit of the mortgagor that the requirements of § 6a.103A-2(e) are met. The mortgagor may also provide the issuer or his agent with an affidavit that the mortgagor was not required to file such return in accordance with section 6012 during one or all of the preceding 3 years. Where a particular mortgage fails to meet more than one of these

Reg. § 6a.103A-2(c)(1)

→ *Caution: Code Sec. 103A has been repealed. Similar exempt bond issue rules have been provided in Code Secs. 141–150.*←

requirements, the amount of the mortgage will be taken into account only once in determining whether the 95-percent requirement is met. However, all of the defects in the mortgage must be corrected pursuant to subdivision (iii).

(iii) Any failure to meet such requirements is corrected within a reasonable period after such failure is discovered. For example, where a mortgage fails to meet one or more of such requirements those failures can be corrected by calling the nonqualifying mortgage or by replacing the nonqualifying mortgage with a qualifying mortgage.

(iv) *Examples.* The following examples illustrate the application of this subparagraph (1):

Example (1). State X issues obligations to be used to provide mortgages for owner-occupied residences. X contracts with bank M to originate and service the mortgages. The trust indenture and participation agreement require that the mortgages meet the mortgage eligibility requirements referred to in paragraph (c)(1). In addition, pursuant to procedures established by X, M obtains a signed affidavit from each applicant that the applicant intends to occupy the property as his or her principal residence within 60 days after the final closing and thereafter to maintain the property as his or her principal residence. Further, M obtains from each applicant copies certified by the Internal Revenue Service of the applicant's Federal tax returns for the preceding 3 years and examines each statement to determine whether the applicant has claimed a deduction for taxes on real property which was the applicant's principal residence pursuant to section 164(a)(1) or a deduction pursuant to section 163 for interest paid on a mortgage secured by real property which was the applicant's principal residence. Also in accordance with X's procedures, M obtains from each applicant a signed affidavit as to facts that are sufficient for M to determine whether the residence is located within X's jurisdiction and affidavits from the seller and the buyer that the purchase price and the new mortgage requirements have been met, and neither M nor X knows or has reason to believe that such affidavits are false. The mortgage instrument provides that the mortgage may not be assumed by another person unless X determines that the principal residence, 3-year, and purchase price requirements are met at the time of the assumption. These facts are sufficient evidence of the good faith of the issuer and meet the requirements of paragraph (c)(1)(i). Further, if 95 percent of the lendable proceeds are devoted to owner financing

which according to these procedures meet the requirements of paragraphs (d), (e), (f), and (i), then the issue meets the requirements of paragraph (c)(1)(ii).

Example (2). State Y issues obligations to be used to provide mortgages for owner-occupied residences. Y contracts with bank N to originate and service the mortgages. The trust indenture and participation agreement require that the mortgagor certify compliance with the requirements referred to in paragraph (c)(1). By itself, this certification is not sufficient evidence of the good faith of the issuer to meet the requirements referred to in paragraph (c)(1).

Example (3). The facts are the same as in Example 1, except that M discovers through a verification procedure required by X that, at the time of closing, A fraudulently executed the residency affidavit. Instead of occupying the property as a principal residence, A leased the property to B for one year. A did not use the property as his residence during the lease term. Thus, at the time that A's mortgage was executed the residence failed to meet the requirements of paragraph (d) of this section.

More than 95 percent of the lendable proceeds of the issue were devoted to residences which met all the requirements referred to in paragraph (c)(1) at the time the mortgages were executed. Furthermore, pursuant to a provision in the mortgage instrument M called the loan. Any failures with respect to other mortgages are corrected by M. Based on these facts, the issue meets the requirements of subparagraph (c)(1).

Example (4). The facts are the same as in Example (1), except that the issuer requires copies of the applicant's signed tax returns that were filed with the Internal Revenue Service for the preceding 3 years but does not require that such returns be certified. If 95 percent of the lendable proceeds are devoted to owner financing which according to these procedures meet the requirements of paragraphs (d), (e), (f), and (i), then the issue meets the requirements of paragraph (c)(1)(ii).

(2) *Nonmortgage eligibility requirements.* An issue of qualified mortgage bonds which fails to meet one or more of the requirements of paragraphs (g), (h), and (i) of this section and § 6a.103A-1(a)(5) shall be treated as meeting such requirements if each of the following provisions is met.

(i) The issuer in good faith attempted to meet all such requirements. This good faith re-

Reg. § 6a.103A-2(c)(2)

→ *Caution: Code Sec. 103A has been repealed. Similar exempt bond issue rules have been provided in Code Secs. 141–150.*←

quirement will be met if all reasonable steps are taken by the issuer to ensure that the issue complies with these requirements.

(ii) Any failure to meet such requirements is due to inadvertent error, *e.g.,* mathematical error, after taking reasonable steps to comply with such requirements.

(iii) The following examples illustrate the application of this subparagraph (2):

Example (1). City X issues obligations to finance owner-occupied residences. However, despite taking all reasonable steps to determine accurately the size of the market share limitation, as provided in paragraph (g)(3), the limit is exceeded because the amount of the mortgages originated in the area during the past 3 years is incorrectly computed as a result of mathematical error. Such facts are sufficient evidence of the good faith of the issuer to meet the requirements of paragraph (c)(2).

Example (2). City Y issues $25 million of bonds to finance single-family, owner-occupied homes. Attorney A gives an opinion that the bonds satisfy the arbitrage requirements of § 6a.103A-2(i) and § 6a.103A-1(a)(3). In fact, however, the legal conclusion reached by A is erroneous, and the bonds do not meet the requirements of § 6a.103A-2(i). The issue does not meet the requirements of subparagraph (c)(2) because the erroneous opinion does not constitute inadvertent error.

(d) *Residence requirements*—(1) *In general.* An issue meets the requirements of this paragraph only if all of the residences for which owner financing is provided under the issue meet the requirements of this paragraph. A residence meets the requirements of this paragraph only if—

(i) It is a single-family residence (as defined in § 6a.103A-1(b)(6)) which, at the time the mortgage is executed or assumed, can reasonably be expected by the issuer to become the principal residence of the mortgagor within a reasonable time after the financing is provided; and

(ii) It is located within the jurisdiction of the authority issuing the obligation.

(2) *Affidavit.* The requirements of subparagraph (1)(i) may normally be met if the mortgagor executes an affidavit of his intent to use the residence as his principal residence within a reasonable time (*e.g.,* 60 days) after the financing is provided.

(3) *Principal residence.* Whether a residence is used as a principal residence depends upon all the facts and circumstances of each case, includ-

ing the good faith of the mortgagor. A residence which is primarily intended to be used in a trade or business shall not satisfy the requirements of this subparagraph. For purposes of the preceding sentence, any use of a residence which does not qualify for a deduction allowable for certain expenses incurred in connection with the business use of a home under section 280A shall not be considered as a use in a trade or business. Except for certain owner-occupied residences described in paragraph (b)(6) of § 6a.103A-1, a residence more than 15 percent of the total area of which is reasonably expected to be used primarily in a trade or business does not satisfy the requirements of this subparagraph. Further, a residence used as an investment property or a recreational home does not satisfy the requirements of this subparagraph.

(4) *Residence.* (i) The term "residence" includes stock held by a tenant-stockholder in a cooperative housing corporation (as those terms are defined in section 216(b)(1) and (2)). It does not include property such as an appliance, a piece of furniture, a radio, etc., which, under applicable local law, is not a fixture. The term also includes factory-made housing which is permanently fixed to real property. The determination of whether factory-made housing is permanently fixed to real property shall be made on the basis of the facts and circumstances of each particular case.

(ii) *Land.* Land appurtenant to a residence shall be considered as part of the residence only if such land reasonably maintains the basic livability of the residence and does not provide, other than incidentally, a source of income to the mortgagor.

(5) *Examples.* The following examples illustrate the application of this paragraph (d):

Example (1). A contracts to purchase a new residence from B. Since B is unable to move from the residence until 1 month after the scheduled closing date, A agrees to lease the residence to B for 1 month at a rent equal to the fair rental value. A applies for a mortgage to be provided from the proceeds of a qualified mortgage bond. In light of all the facts and circumstances in the case, the fact that A temporarily leases the residence to B does not prevent the residence from being considered as property that can reasonably be expected to be used as A's principal residence within a reasonable period of time after financing is provided.

Example (2). C contracts to purchase a new residence located on 2 acres of land in city X. City

Reg. § 6a.103A-2(d)(1)

→ *Caution: Code Sec. 103A has been repealed. Similar exempt bond issue rules have been provided in Code Secs. 141–150.*←

X has a zoning regulation which prevents the subdividing of any lot in that part of the city for use as a private residence into parcels of less than 2 acres. In light of all the facts and circumstances in the case, the fact that the residence is located on 2 acres of land appurtenant to the residence does not prevent the entire property from being considered as property to be used by C as a residence.

Example (3). D contracts to purchase a new residence located on 40 acres of land that D intends to farm. Any financing provided for the purchase of that portion of the property intended to be farmed will not be considered as financing provided for an owner-occupied residence.

(e) *3-year requirement* —(1) *In general.* An issue meets the requirements of this paragraph only if each of the mortgagors to whom owner financing is provided under the issue meets the requirements of this paragraph. A mortgagor meets the requirements of this paragraph only if the mortgagor had no present ownership interest in a principal residence at any time during the 3-year period prior to the date on which the mortgage is executed. For purposes of the preceding sentence, the mortgagor's interest in the residence with respect to which the financing is being provided shall not be taken into account.

(2) *Exceptions.* Subparagraph (1) shall not apply with respect to—

(i) Any financing provided with respect to a targeted area residence (as defined in § 6a.103A-2(b)(3)),

(ii) Any qualified home improvement loan (as defined in § 6a.103A-2(b)(9)), and

(iii) Any qualified rehabilitation loan (as defined in § 6a.103A-2(b)(10)).

(3) *Multiple mortgagors.* In the event that there is more than one mortgagor with respect to a particular residence, each of such mortgagors must meet the 3-year requirement. A person who is liable under a note secured by the mortgage but who does not have a present ownership interest in a residence subject to the mortgage need not meet the 3-year requirement. For example, where a parent of a home purchaser cosigns the note for a child but the parent takes no interest in the residence, it is not necessary that the parent meet the 3-year requirement since the parent is not a mortgagor of the residence.

(4) *Included interests.* Examples of interests which constitute present ownership interests are the following:

(i) A fee simple interest;

(ii) A joint tenancy, a tenancy in common, or tenancy by the entirety;

(iii) The interest of a tenant-shareholder in a cooperative;

(iv) A life estate;

(v) A land contract (*i.e.,* a contract pursuant to which possession and the benefits and burdens of ownership are transferred although legal title is not transferred until some later time); and

(vi) An interest held in trust for the mortgagor (whether or not created by the mortgagor) that would constitute a present ownership interest if held directly by the mortgagor.

(5) *Excluded interests.* Examples of interests which do not constitute present ownership interests are the following:

(i) A remainder interest;

(ii) A lease with or without an option to purchase;

(iii) A mere expectancy to inherit an interest in a principal residence;

(iv) The interest that a purchaser of a residence acquires on the execution of a purchase contract; and

(v) An interest in other than a principal residence during the previous 3 years.

(f) *Purchase price requirements*—(1) *In general.* An issue meets the requirements of this paragraph only if the acquisition cost (as defined in § 6a.103A-2(b)(8)) of each residence, other than a targeted area residence, for which owner financing is provided does not exceed 90 percent of the average area purchase price applicable to such residence. In the case of a targeted area residence (as defined in § 6a.103A-2(b)(3)), the acquisition cost may not exceed 110 percent of the average area purchase price applicable to such residence.

(2) *Exception.* Paragraph (1) shall not apply with respect to any qualified home improvement loan (as defined in § 6a.103A-2(b)(9)).

(3) *Average area purchase price.* The term "average area purchase price" means, with respect to any residence, the average purchase price of all single-family residences in the statistical area (as defined in § 6a.103A-2(b)(7)) in which the residence being financed is located for the most recent 12-month period for which sufficient statistical information is available. The determination whether a particular residence meets the purchase price requirement shall be made as of the date on which the commitment to provide the financing is made or, if earlier, the date of purchase of the residence.

Reg. § 6a.103A-2(f)(3)

→ *Caution: Code Sec. 103A has been repealed. Similar exempt bond issue rules have been provided in Code Secs. 141–150.*←

(4) *Special rules.* (i) In the case of a qualified rehabilitation loan, the requirements of this paragraph are met if the mortgagor's adjusted basis in the property as of the completion of the rehabilitation (including the cost of the rehabilitation) meets the requirements of paragraph (f)(1). For this purpose, a rehabilitated residence is to be treated as a residence which has been previously occupied.

(ii) The determination of average area purchase price shall be made separately with respect to—

(A) Residences which have not been previously occupied;

(B) Residences which have been previously occupied; and

(C) One-family, two-family, three-family, and four-family residences.

(5) *Safe harbor limitation.* (i) For purposes of meeting the requirements of this paragraph, an issuer may rely upon average area purchase price limitations published by the Treasury Department for the statistical area in which a residence is located. These safe harbor limitations will be effective for the period stated at the time of publication. An issuer may use a limitation different from such safe harbor limitation for any statistical area (as defined in § 6a.103A-2(b)(7)) for which the issuer has more accurate and comprehensive data.

(ii) The following example illustrates the application of subparagraph (5)(i):

Example. The average area purchase price safe harbor limitation for new single-family residences published by the Treasury Department for the second half of 1981 for the jurisdiction of governmental unit X is $41,500. However, on July 1, 1981, X determines that its average area purchase price for new single-family residences is actually $43,000. Such determination is based on a comprehensive survey of residential housing sales in the jurisdiction over the previous calendar year. The data accumulated are based on records maintained by the county clerk's office in X's jurisdiction, which enables X to compute average area purchase prices separately for new and used residences and for one-, two-, three-, and four-family residences. X cannot reasonably update such data more often than once a year. X may use average area purchase prices computed from these data for mortgages made from July 1, 1981, through June 30, 1982, rather than the safe harbor published by the Treasury Department.

(g) *Limitation on aggregate amount of qualified mortgage bonds issued during any calendar year*—(1) *In general.* An issue meets the requirements of this section only if the aggregate amount of bonds issued pursuant thereto, when added to the sum of (i) the aggregate amount of qualified mortgage bonds previously issued by the issuing authority during the calendar year and (ii) the amount of qualified mortgage bonds which the issuing authority previously elected not to issue under section 25(c)(2)(A)(ii) and the regulations thereunder during the calendar year, does not exceed the applicable limit ("market limitation") for such authority for such calendar year.

(2) *State housing finance agency.* Except as provided in paragraph (g)(4), the market limitation for any State housing finance agency for any calendar year shall be 50 percent of the State ceiling for such year. For purposes of the preceding sentence, if any State has more than one housing finance agency all such agencies shall be treated as a single agency.

(3) *Other issuers.* Except as provided in paragraph (g)(4), the market limitation for any issuing authority (other than a State housing finance agency) for any calendar year is an amount equal to that authority's proportionate share of 50 percent of the State ceiling amount for such calendar year. The proportionate share is an amount which bears the same ratio to 50 percent of the State ceiling for such year as—

(i) The average annual aggregate principal amount of mortgages executed during the immediately preceding 3 calendar years for single-family, owner-occupied residences located within the jurisdiction of such issuing authority bears to

(ii) An average determined in the same way for the entire State.

(4) *Constitutional home rule city.* (i) In determining the market limitation for any constitutional home rule city (as defined in paragraph (b)(2)), subparagraph (3) shall be applied by substituting "100 percent" for "50 percent."

(ii) In a State with one or more constitutional home rule cities, in computing the market limitation for issuers other than constitutional home rule cities, the State ceiling amount for any calendar year shall be reduced by the aggregate market limitation for such year for all constitutional home rule cities in the State.

(5) *Overlapping jurisdictions.* (i) For purposes of subparagraph (3), if an area is within the jurisdiction of two or more governmental units, such area shall be treated as only within the

→ *Caution: Code Sec. 103A has been repealed. Similar exempt bond issue rules have been provided in Code Secs. 141–150.* ←

jurisdiction of the unit having jurisdiction over the smallest geographical area. However, the governmental unit with jurisdiction over the smallest geographical area may enter into a written agreement to allocate all or a designated portion of such overlapping area to the governmental unit having jurisdiction over the next smallest geographical area.

(ii) Where two governmental units have authority to issue mortgage subsidy bonds and both governmental units have jurisdiction over the identical geographical area, the aggregate principal amount of mortgages on residences located within that area shall be allocated to the governmental unit having broader sovereign powers.

(6) *State ceiling.* (i) Except as provided in paragraph (g)(6)(v), the State ceiling applicable to any State for any calendar year shall be the greater of—

(A) 9 percent of the average annual aggregate principal amount of mortgages executed during the immediately preceding 3 calendar years for single-family, owner-occupied residences located within the jurisdiction of such State, or

(B) $200,000,000.

Only single-family owner-occupied residences (without regard to the definition of such term under § 6a.103A-1(b)(6)) may be used in determining the market limitation regardless of whether or not residences with up to four family units are to be financed by the program. First and second mortgages or mortgages used to refinance an existing mortgage shall be used in making such determination. Liens, special assessments, and similar encumbrances may not be taken into consideration.

(ii) For mortgages on residences with more than one family unit, the full amount of the mortgage shall be applied toward the market limitation and not merely that portion allocable to the owner-occupied unit.

(iii) For purposes of determining the State ceiling amount applicable to any State for any calendar year an issuer may rely upon the State ceiling amount published by the Treasury Department for such calendar year. An issuer may rely on different State ceiling amount than such safe harbor limitation where the issuer has made a more accurate and comprehensive determination of such amount.

(iv) The following example illustrates the application of subparagraphs (3) and (6) of paragraph (g):

Example. Pursuant to the allocation rule provided in subparagraph (3), City Y determines that its maximum market limitation in 1981 is $15,000,000. This determination is based on records maintained by the county clerk's office from which data for the preceding 3 years have been accumulated by City Y as to the number of sales of single-family homes in City Y's jurisdiction, the purchase price in each such sales transaction, the number of such sales that were financed by mortgages and the volume of second mortgages and refinancing on previously purchased owner-occupied single-family residences. This information, combined with estimates made by City Y of the average mortgage-loan-to-purchase-price ratio and the ratio of sales of single-family, owner-occupied residences to all sales of single-family residences from a representative sample of sales transactions, enables Y to estimate the preceding 3 years' annual aggregate mortgage volume by using the following formula:

→ *Caution: Code Sec. 103A has been repealed. Similar exempt bond issue rules have been provided in Code Secs. 141–150.*←

$$v = 1/3 \sum_{i=t-3}^{t-1} (u_i \cdot w_i \cdot x_i \cdot y_i \cdot z_i) + a_i,$$

where

v = the preceding 3 years' average annual aggregate volume of mortgages on single-family, owner-occupied residences in City Y,

u_i = number of sales of single-family residences,

w_i = average purchase price of all sales,

x_i = percent of all sales transactions that were financed with mortgages,

y_i = estimated average mortgage-loan-to-purchase-price ratio,

z_i = estimated percent of sales that were owner-occupied residences,

a_i = total volume of second mortgages and refinancing on previously purchased owner-occupied, single-family residences,

i = the annual period of calculation, and

t = the current year.

City Y determines its applicable limit for 1981 based on the following formula:

L = 0.5 $(v/s)r$, where

L = market limitation for City Y for the current year,

s = the preceding 3 years' average annual aggregate volume of mortgages on single-family, owner-occupied residences in State X, and

r = ceiling for State X (*i.e.*, r = the greater of .09s or $200,000,000).

City Y may use the Treasury estimate of s which will be published with the mortgage volume safe harbor limitation. City Y may rely on its determination of its market limitation for obligations issued during 1981.

(v) *Reduction in State ceiling.* If for any calendar year an issuer of mortgage credit certificates, as defined in section 25 and the regulations thereunder, fails to meet the requirements of section 25(d)(2) and the regulations thereunder, relating to the limit on the aggregate amount of mortgage credit certificates that may be issued, the applicable State ceiling under paragraph (g)(6)(i) of this section for the State in which that program operates will be reduced by 1.25 times the correction amount (as defined in section 25(f)(2) and the regulations thereunder) with respect to that failure for the calendar year following the calendar year in which the Commissioner determines the correction amount with respect to that failure.

(7) *Excess obligations.* Where an issue of obligations when added to the aggregate amount of bonds issued by the same issuing authority in the same calendar year exceeds the market limitation determined in accordance with this paragraph (g), no portion of the issue will be treated as a qualified mortgage bond issue, and interest on such obligations shall be subject to Federal income taxation. However, previously issued qualified mortgage bond issues which met the market limitation at the time of their issuance will not cease to be qualified mortgage bond issues even though a subsequent issue causes the aggregate amount of obligations to exceed such limitation for a calendar year.

(8) *Transitional rule obligations.* In applying this paragraph (g) to any calendar year, there shall not be taken into account any bond which, by reason of section 1104 of the Mortgage Subsidy Bond Tax Act of 1980 (94 Stat. 2670) (relating to transitional rules), receives the same tax treatment as bonds issued on or before April 24, 1979.

(9) *Procedure for providing a different allocation.* (i) A State may, by law enacted after December 5, 1980, provide a different formula for allocating the State ceiling amount among the governmental units in such State (other than constitutional home rule jurisdictions) having authority to issue qualified mortgage bonds.

(ii) The governor of any State may proclaim a different formula than provided in subparagraphs (g)(2) and (g)(3) for allocating the State ceiling amount among the governmental units in such State having authority to issue qualified mortgage bonds. The authority of the governor to proclaim a different formula shall not apply after the earlier of—

(A) The 1st day of the 1st calendar year beginning after the 1st calendar year after 1980

Reg. § 6a.103A-2(g)(7)

→ *Caution: Code Sec. 103A has been repealed. Similar exempt bond issue rules have been provided in Code Secs. 141–150.*←

during which the legislature of the State met in regular session, or

(B) The effective date of any State legislation dealing with such ceiling enacted after December 5, 1980.

If, on or before either date, the governor of any State exercises the authority to provide a different allocation, such allocation shall be effective until the date specified in (B).

(iii) Unless otherwise provided in a State constitutional amendment or by law changing the home rule provisions adopted in the manner provided by the State constitution, the allocation of that portion of the State ceiling which is allocated to any constitutional home rule city may not be changed by the governor or State legislature unless such city agrees to such different allocation.

(iv) Where a State elects to make a different allocation in accordance with subdivision (i) or (ii) of this subparagraph, the determination as to whether a particular bond issue meets the requirements of paragraph (g) will be based upon the allocation in effect at the time such bonds were issued. Moreover, the authority to provide for a different allocation may not be used directly or indirectly to increase the State ceiling amount.

(v) An issuing authority located in a State with one or more constitutional home rule cities may use an alternative method to those provided in subparagraphs (2), (3), and (4) for determining such issuing authority's market limitation if, prior to issuing any obligations for the calendar year, it demonstrates to the satisfaction of the Commissioner that—

(1) The use of the methods provided in subparagraph (2), (3), or (4) would impose an unreasonable hardship on the issuing authority, and

(2) Such alternative method is reasonable.

$$P = 2(X/Y \times Z),$$

where
P = Required portion to be made available in targeted areas,
X = Average annual aggregate principal amount of mortgages executed during the immediately preceding 3 calendar years for single-family, owner-occupied residences within the State in which the issuing jurisdiction is located,
Y = The total population within the State, based on the most recent decennial census for which data are available, and
Z = The total population in the targeted areas located within the issuer's jurisdiction, based on the most recent decennial census for which data are available.

The issuing jurisdiction may use the Treasury Department estimate of X which will be pub-

(h) *Portion of loans required to be placed in targeted areas*—(1) *In general.* An issue meets the requirements of this paragraph only if—

(i) The portion of the lendable proceeds (as defined in § 6a.103A-2(b)(1)) of the issue specified in subparagraph (2) is made available for owner financing of targeted area residences (as defined in § 6a.103A-2(b)(3)) for at least 1 year after the date on which owner financing is first made available with respect to targeted area residences, and

(ii) The issuer attempts with reasonable diligence to place such proceeds in qualified mortgages.

Proceeds are considered first made available with respect to targeted area residences on the date on which any financing of mortgages with the lendable proceeds of an issue first becomes available. Reasonable diligence requires that the issuer and the loan originators use reasonable efforts in trying to place mortgages in targeted areas, such as by advertising that mortgage funds are available for targeted areas. Reasonable diligence is not shown by merely providing in the governing instruments that the required amount be set aside for targeted areas.

(2) *Specified portion.* The specified portion of lendable proceeds of an issue required to be made available in targeted areas is the lesser of—

(i) 20 percent of the lendable proceeds, or

(ii) 40 percent of the average annual aggregate principal amount of mortgages executed during the immediately preceding 3 calendar years for single-family, owner-occupied residences in targeted areas within the jurisdiction of the issuing authority.

(3) *Safe harbor.* For purposes of computing the required portion of proceeds specified in subparagraph (2)(ii), where such provision is applicable, an issuer may rely upon the amount produced by the following formula:

lished with the mortgage volume safe harbor limitation.

Reg. § 6a.103A-2(h)(3)

→ *Caution: Code Sec. 103A has been repealed. Similar exempt bond issue rules have been provided in Code Secs. 141–150.*←

(4) *Minimum amount.* (i) The specified portion required to be made available in targeted areas is a minimum amount. More than the minimum amount may be (but need not be) made available in targeted areas.

(ii) With respect to any proceeds not required to be made available in targeted areas, the requirements of this paragraph do not abrogate the requirement of the arbitrage rules that due diligence be used in placing lendable proceeds into mortgages.

(i) *Arbitrage and investment gain*—(1) *In general.* An issue meets the requirements of this paragraph only if such issue meets the requirements of subparagraphs (2), (3), and (4). For purposes of these requirements, all determinations of yield, effective interest rates, and amounts required to be paid or credited to mortgagors under subparagraph (i)(4)(i) shall be made on an actuarial basis taking into account the present value of money. The requirements of section 103A(i) and this paragraph are applicable in addition to the requirements of section 103(c) and § § 1.103-13, 1.103-14, and 1.103-15.

(2) *Effective rate of mortgage interest not to exceed bond yield by more than 1 percentage point*—(i) *Maximum yield.* An issue of qualified mortgage bonds shall be treated as meeting the requirements of this subparagraph only if the excess of—

(A) The effective rate of interest on the mortgages financed by the issue, over

(B) The yield on the issue,

is not greater over the term of the issue than 1 percentage point.

(ii) *Effective rate of interest.* (A) In determining the effective rate of interest on any mortgage for purposes of this subparagraph, there shall be taken into account all fees, charges, and other amounts borne by the mortgagor which are attributable to the mortgage or to the bond issue. Such amounts include points, commitment fees, origination fees, servicing fees, and prepayment penalties paid by the mortgagor.

(B) Items that shall be treated as borne by the mortgagor and shall be taken into account in calculating the effective rate of interest also include—

(1) All points, commitment fees, origination fees, or similar charges borne by the seller of the property;

(2) The excess of any amounts received from any person other than the mortgagor by any person in connection with the acquisition of the mortgagor's interest in the property over the usual and reasonable costs incurred by a person acquiring like property where owner financing is not provided through the use of qualified mortgage bonds.

(C) The following items shall not be treated as borne by the mortgagor and shall not be taken into account in calculating the effective rate of interest:

(1) Any expected rebate of arbitrage profit (as required by § 6a.103A-2(i)(4)).

(2) Any application fee, survey fee, credit report fee, insurance fee or similar settlement or financing cost to the extent such amount does not exceed amounts charged in such area in cases where owner financing is not provided through the use of qualified mortgage bonds. For example, amounts paid for FHA, VA, or similar private mortgage insurance on an individual's mortgage need not be taken into account so long as such amounts do not exceed the amounts charged in the area with respect to a similar mortgage that is not financed with qualified mortgage bonds. Premiums charged for pool mortgage insurance will be considered amounts in excess of the usual and reasonable amounts charged for insurance in cases where owner financing is not provided through the use of qualified mortgage bonds.

(D)(1) Where amounts other than those derived from the proceeds of a mortgage subsidy bond are used to finance single-family residences such amounts will not be treated as the proceeds of a qualified mortgage bond issue and will not be subject to the limitations set forth in subparagraphs (2), (3), and (4) of this paragraph (i). Such amounts may, however, be treated as proceeds for purposes of the requirements of section 103(c) and the regulations thereunder. Thus, the portion of the mortgage pool financed by the proceeds of a qualified mortgage bond issue will be subject to the limitations of subparagraphs (2), (3), and (4) of this paragraph (i), while the portion not provided with bond proceeds will not be subject to such limitations. The interest rate, points, origination fees, servicing fees, and other amounts charged with respect to that portion of a mortgage loan financed with non-bond amounts may not exceed the reasonable and customary amount which would be charged where financing is not provided through a qualified mortgage bond issue. Where the charge does exceed such reasonable and customary amount, any excess will be taken into account in computing the effective interest rate

→ *Caution: Code Sec. 103A has been repealed. Similar exempt bond issue rules have been provided in Code Secs. 141–150.* ←

on the portion of the loan provided with the proceeds of the qualified mortgage bond issue. Furthermore, where such fees and other charges are less than the reasonable and customary charges, the issuer may not allocate that portion of the charges on the loan amounts made with bond proceeds which is equal to such differential to loan amounts made with non-bond proceeds.

(2) If any mortgage is allocated to two or more sources of funds, the receipt of amounts which are described in paragraph (i)(2)(ii)(A) and (B), repayments of principal, or payments of interest on such mortgage must be allocated to each source of funds.

(E) The effective rate of interest on any mortgage shall be determined in a manner consistent with actuarial methods and shall take into account the discounted value of all amounts from the time received to an amount equal to the "purchase price" of the mortgage. Such discount rate is the effective rate of interest on the mortgages. The "purchase price" of a mortgage means the net amount loaned to the mortgagor. For example, if a mortgage loan is in the amount of $30,000 and the mortgagor is charged one point ($300) as an origination fee which amount is deducted from loan proceeds available to the mortgagor, the purchase price is $29,700. If interest on an issue is paid semiannually, all regular monthly mortgage payments and prepayments of principal may be treated as being received at the end of each semiannual debt service period.

(1) If interest on an issue is paid semiannually, all regular monthly mortgage payments may be treated as being received at the end of each semiannual debt service period.

(2) Prepayments of principal shall be treated as being received on the last day of the month in which the issuer reasonably expects to receive such prepayments.

(F) The rate shall be determined on a composite basis for all mortgages financed by the issue.

(iii) *Example*. The following example illustrates the provisions of subparagraph (2)(ii):

Example. Purchaser A contracts with seller B, who is represented by real estate agent C, for the purchase of B's residence for $65,000. A applies to County X for a mortgage provided by the proceeds of a qualified mortgage bond. County X requires that agent C provide it with a principal residence affidavit as well as verify the purchase price of the residence and the location of the purchaser's previous residences. Due to the increased administrative burden imposed on agent C by County X, C charges B a real estate commission of 8 percent ($5,200), rather than 6 percent ($3,900). The normal real estate commission is 6 percent. Since the 8 percent commission charged by C and paid by B is in excess of the usual and reasonable real estate commission where owner financing is not provided through the use of qualified mortgage bonds, 2 percent ($1,300) shall be treated as borne by A and taken into account in calculating the effective rate of interest on the mortgage.

(iv) *Prepayment assumption*. In determining the effective rate of interest on mortgages, it shall be assumed that the mortgage prepayment rate for mortgages made out of both original proceeds and mortgages that the issuer expects with reasonable certainty to be made out of prepayments of principal will be equal to 100 percent of the rate set forth in the most recent mortgage maturity experience table for mortgages having the same term insured under section 203 of the National Housing Act and published by the Federal Housing Administration in "Survivorship and Decrement Tables for HUD/FHA Home Mortgage Insurance Program" for the region, or, if available, the State in which the residence is located. For purposes of applying these tables, either the original balance method or the declining balance method of calculating mortgage loan prepayments may be used. For proceeds used to finance qualified home improvement loans or shorter term qualified rehabilitation loans for which there are no comparable FHA mortgage maturity experience tables, the assumption used by the issuer as to the rate of prepayment shall be based upon the reasonable expectations of the issuer, as reflected, where applicable, by the issuer's prior experience with such loans.

(v) *Net losses.* The projected net losses on the mortgage pool (after foreclosure and payment of insurance proceeds), based on the most recent default experience for the area in which the residences are located, shall be taken into consideration in calculating the effective rate of interest on the mortgages. However, where mortgages provided under an issue are insured with FHA, VA, or private mortgage insurance, in conjunction with pool mortgage insurance, the expected net losses will be presumed to be zero. In the event that the actual losses on the mortgage pool exceed the projected net losses which were taken into consideration in calculating the effective rate of interest on the mortgages, investment proceeds earned from nonmortgage assets may be used to

→ *Caution: Code Sec. 103A has been repealed. Similar exempt bond issue rules have been provided in Code Secs. 141–150.*←

recover the excess losses and need not be paid or credited to the mortgagors under § 6a.103A-2(i)(4).

(vi) *Yield on the issue.* (A) The yield on an issue of qualified mortgage bonds shall be calculated on the basis of—

(*1*) The issue price, and

(*2*) An expected maturity for the bonds which is consistent with the prepayment assumption required under subparagraph (2)(iv). The expected maturity will be considered consistent with such prepayment assumption if all prepayments are assumed to be used to call bonds proportionately (*i.e.*, a "strip" call). The preceding sentence shall not apply to prepayments of mortgages provided from original proceeds to the extent such prepayments are used to provide mortgages.

(B) For purposes of (1) of this subdivision (vi), the term "issue price" shall have the same meaning as in section 1232(b)(2). Thus, in general, such term means the initial offering price to the public, not including bond houses and brokers, or similar persons or organizations acting in the capacity of underwriters or wholesalers, at which price a substantial amount of such obligations were sold or, if privately placed, the price paid by the first buyer of such obligations or the acquisition cost of the first buyer.

(3) *Nonmortgage investments*—(i) *Maximum investment.* Except as provided in (ii), an issue meets the requirements of this subparagraph only if—

(A) At no time during any bond year does the aggregate amount invested in nonmortgage investments, *e.g.*, reasonably required reserve funds, with a yield materially higher than the yield on the issue exceed 150 percent of the debt service on the issue for the current bond year, and

(B) Such aggregate amount invested in nonmortgage assets with a yield materially higher than the yield on the issue is promptly and appropriately reduced as mortgages are repaid.

The amount subject to the maximum investment rule in (i)(A) includes the original bond proceeds, investment proceeds and repayments of principal on the mortgages. For purposes of subdivision (B), the amount described in subdivision (A) shall be considered promptly and appropriately reduced if beginning in the first bond year after the expiration of the temporary period for original proceeds described in subdivision (ii)(A), such amount is reduced within 30 days of the beginning of each

bond year by an amount equal to the difference between the average scheduled monthly mortgage receipts for the bond year (excluding any receipts that were scheduled with respect to mortgages that were discharged in the preceding bond year) and the average scheduled monthly mortgage receipts for the preceding bond year.

(ii) *Temporary periods.* Subparagraph (3)(i) shall not apply to—

(A) Proceeds (including prepayments of principal designated to be used to acquire additional mortgages) of the issue invested for an initial temporary period not to exceed 1 year (1½ years for proceeds required to be set aside for placing mortgages in targeted areas) until such proceeds are needed for mortgages, and

(B) Repayments of principal and interest on mortgages that are contributed to a bona fide debt service fund (as defined in § 1.103-13(b)(12)) and invested for a 13-month temporary period as provided in § 1.103-14(b)(10).

(iii) *Debt service defined.* For purposes of subparagraph (3)(i)(A), the debt service on the issue for any bond year is the scheduled amount of interest and amortization of principal payable for such year with respect to such issue. There shall not be taken into account amounts scheduled with respect to any bond which has been retired before the beginning of the bond year.

(iv) *Nonmortgage investments.* A nonmortgage investment is any investment other than an investment in a qualified mortgage. For example, a mortgage-secured certificate or obligation is a nonmortgage investment. Investment earnings from participation fees (described in § 6a.103A-1(b)(5)) are treated as investment proceeds on nonmortgage investments unless such fees are used to pay debt service or to finance owner occupied residences.

(v) *Bonds issued after June 30, 1993.* Section 1.148-2(f)(2)(iv) applies to bonds issued after June 30, 1993, in lieu of this paragraph (i)(3).

(4) *Arbitrage and investment gains to be used to reduce costs of owner financing*—(i) *Rebate requirement.* An issue shall be treated as meeting the requirements of this subparagraph only if an amount equal to the sum of

(A) The excess of—

(*1*) The net amount earned on all nonmortgage investments pursuant to subparagraph (3)(i) and (ii) (other than investments attributable to an excess described in this subdivision (A)) over

Reg. § 6a.103A-2(i)(3)

→ *Caution: Code Sec. 103A has been repealed Similar exempt bond issue rules have been provided in Code Secs. 141–150.*←

(2) The amount which would have been earned if the investments were invested at a rate equal to the yield on the issue, plus

(B) Any income attributable to the excess described in subdivision (A),

shall be paid or credited to the mortgagors as rapidly as practicable. Such amount may be disproportionately distributed to the mortgagors if the larger portion of such amount is distributed to lower income mortgagors. The determination of the excess described in subdivision (A) shall take into account any reinvestment of nonmortgage investment receipts and any gain or loss realized on the disposition of nonmortgage investments. In addition, where nonmortgage investments are retained by the issuer after retirement of an issue, any unrealized gains or losses as of the date of retirement of such issue must be taken into account, in calculating the amount to be rebated to the mortgagors. The amount described in subdivision (A)(2) is the amount that would have been earned if the investments in nonmortgage obligations were invested at a rate equal to the yield on the issue calculated in the same manner as provided in § 6a.103A-2(i)(2)(vi) and by using the same compounding method. For purposes of subdivision (B), any income attributable to the excess described in subdivision (A) shall be taken into account whether or not such income exceeds the yield on the bonds.

(ii) *Computation period.* Whether earnings are amounts described in subdivision (i)(A) or (B) shall be determined by making computations on an annual basis. For example, if at the end of the first year the earnings on nonmortgage investments exceed the amount that could have been earned if such investments were invested at the bond yield, the amount of earnings equal to such difference constitutes an excess described in subdivision (i)(A). In the following year, investment proceeds earned on such excess must be taken into account, whether or not such earnings exceed the yield on the bonds, and may not be treated as "negative arbitrage".

(iii) *Paid or credited.* For purposes of subdivision (i), amounts are paid or credited to mortgagors as rapidly as practicable if such amounts are paid or credited to such mortgagors at the time the mortgagor discharges the mortgage, for example, through prepayment of the entire principal amount or through making the last regular payment on the mortgage. The amount paid or credited to the mortgagors must have a present value at least equal to the present value of the amount described in subdivision (i), using the

yield on the bonds as the discount rate. In the case of prepayments, the cumulative amount required to be rebated under subparagraph (4)(i) may be determined as of a date before the actual prepayment but not more than 1 year earlier than the date of prepayment. Except as provided in subparagraph (2)(v) or subparagraph (4)(iv), such amount may not be subject to the claim of any party, *e.g.,* a bondholder, and may not be paid over to any party other than the mortgagor or the United States.

(iv) *Reduction where issuer does not use full 1 percentage point.* (A) The amount required to be paid or credited to mortgagors under subparagraph (4)(i) shall be reduced by the amount which (if it were treated as an interest payment made by mortgagors) would result in the excess referred to in subparagraph (2)(i) being equal to 1 percentage point. Such amount shall be fixed and determined as of the yield determination date. This fixed dollar amount may be received by the issuer at any time but may not be adjusted for the time of payment. Such fixed dollar amount shall be equal to the difference between the purchase price of mortgages financed by the proceeds of the issue and the present value of expected payments of principal and interest on such mortgages, using a discount rate equal to the bond yield plus 1 percentage point.

(B) The following example illustrates the provisions of subparagraph (4)(iv)(A):

Example. In 1981, County X issues obligations to provide mortgages for owner-occupied residences. The yield paid on the obligations is 10 percent, and the effective rate of interest on the mortgages provided by the proceeds of such obligations is 9.75 percent. X maintains a reasonably required reserve fund which is invested at 15 percent and intends to recover that additional amount computed in the manner described in subparagraph (4)(iv) which could have been earned from investment of the proceeds in mortgages with an effective interest rate of 11 percent from the arbitrage earned from the reserve fund nonmortgage assets. X plans to recover such amount from the arbitrage over a period of 3 years; thus, X will not recover such amount until 1984. X may not adjust the amount to be received to account for the time when such amount will be received.

(v) *Election to pay United States.* Subparagraph (4)(i) shall be satisfied with respect to any issue if the issuer elects in writing before issuing the obligations to pay over to the United States—

Reg. § 6a.103A-2(i)(4)

→ *Caution: Code Sec. 103A has been repealed. Similar exempt bond issue rules have been provided in Code Secs. 141–150.*←

(A) Not less frequently than once each 5 years after the date of issue, an amount equal to 90 percent of the aggregate amount described in subdivision (i) earned during such period (and not theretofore paid to the United States), and

(B) Not later than 30 days after the redemption of the last obligation, 100 percent of such aggregate amount not theretofore paid to the United States.

(j) *New mortgages*—(1) *In general.* An issue meets the requirements of this paragraph only if no part of the proceeds of such issue is to be used to acquire or replace an existing mortgage. All of the lendable proceeds must be used to provide mortgage loans to persons who did not have a mortgage (whether or not paid off) on the residence securing the mortgage note at any time prior to the execution of the mortgage.

(2) *Exceptions.* For purposes of this paragraph (j), the replacement of—

(i) Construction period loans,

(ii) Bridge loans or similar temporary initial financing, and

(iii) In the case of a qualified rehabilitation, an existing mortgage, shall not be treated as the acquisition or replacement of an existing mortgage. Generally, temporary initial financing is any financing which has a term of 24 months or less.

(3) *Assumptions.* An issue meets the requirement of this paragraph only if a mortgage with respect to which owner financing has been provided under such issue may be assumed only if the requirements of paragraphs (d), (e), and (f) are met with respect to such assumption. The determination of whether these requirements are met is based upon the facts as they exist at the time of the assumption as if the loan were being made for the first time. For example, the purchase price requirement is to be determined by reference to the average area purchase price at the time of the assumption and not when the mortgage was originally placed. If the bond documents and relevant mortgage instruments provide that a mortgage may be assumed only if the issuer has determined that the conditions stated in this subparagraph are satisfied, the good faith and 95-percent requirements of paragraph (c)(1)(i) and (ii) will be considered satisfied with respect to the requirements of this subparagraph at the time the mortgages were executed. However, any failure to meet the requirements of this subparagraph at the time a mortgage is assumed is subject to the remedy requirement in paragraph (c)(1)(iii).

(4) *Examples.* The following examples illustrate the application of this paragraph (j):

Example (1). In June 1981 mortgagor A obtained a mortgage from a private lending institution in order to construct a house on land which A purchased without a mortgage in May 1981. In January 1982 A applies to obtain permanent financing on the residence from a program sponsored by State housing finance agency Y. Such program is funded with the proceeds of qualified mortgage bonds. If A meets the other requirements of this section, A qualifies for such permanent financing since the replacing of construction financing is not treated as the acquisition or replacement of an existing mortgage.

Example (2). In June 1981 mortgagor B purchased a new residence in a targeted area but was unable to sell his former residence. Therefore, B obtained temporary financing for his new residence until his former residence was sold. In October 1981 B applies to County Z to obtain financing from a program funded with proceeds of qualified mortgage bonds. Such financing is needed by B to replace the temporary financing for his new residence. If B meets the other requirements of this section, the mortgage qualifies for such permanent financing since the permanent financing replaces temporary initial financing.

Example (3). In 1979 mortgagor C purchased a residence but was unable to obtain financing from a program sponsored by County W because such program prohibited loans from the program which were in excess of 80 percent of the fair market value of the property. Therefore, in 1979 C obtained financing from a private lending institution with the intention of refinancing when he accumulated sufficient equity in the property. In 1981 C has accumulated sufficient equity in the property so as to comply with the requirements of the program. C applies to County W to refinance under the program, which is funded with the proceeds of qualified mortgage bonds. Even if C met the other requirements of this section, the mortgage would fail to meet the requirement of paragraph (j) since such a mortgage would replace an existing mortgage.

Example (4). In 1969 mortgagor D purchased a residence and obtained financing from a private lending institution. In 1981 D applies to County U for a loan for the rehabilitation of the property and for the refinancing of the existing mortgage. The program is funded with qualified mortgage bonds. If D meets the other requirements of this section the mortgage qualifies for

Reg. § 6a.103A-2(j)(1)

→ *Caution: Code Sec. 103A has been repealed. Similar exempt bond issue rules have been provided in Code Secs. 141–150.*←

such permanent financing since the replacement of the mortgage is not treated as the replacement or acquisition of an existing mortgage.

Example (5). In 1950 mortgagor E purchased a residence, obtaining a mortgage from a private lending institution to finance the purchase price. In 1980 E completed repaying the mortgage. In 1981 E applies for a loan from a program sponsored by State housing finance agency X and funded with the proceeds of qualified mortgage bonds. The mortgage does not meet the requirements of paragraph (j) since E had a previous mortgage on his residence, even though such mortgage was previously released.

(k) *Information reporting requirement.* See § 1.103A-2(k) for rules relating to section 103A(j)(3).

(l) *Policy statement.* See § 1.103A-2(l) for rules relating to section 103A(j)(5).

(m) *State certification.* See § 1.103A-2(m) for rules relating to section 103A(j)(4). [Temporary Reg. § 6a.103A-2.]

☐ [*T.D. 7780, 6-29-81. Amended by T.D. 7794, 11-5-81; T.D. 7817, 5-19-82; T.D. 7819, 6-3-82; T.D. 7821, 6-24-82; T.D. 7995, 12-7-84; T.D. 8023, 5-3-85; T.D. 8049, 8-29-85 and T.D. 8476, 6-14-93.*]

[Reg. § 6a.103A-3]

§ 6a.103A-3. Qualified veteran's mortgage bonds (Temporary).—(a) *In general.* A qualified veterans' mortgage bond shall not be treated as a mortgage subsidy bond and the interest shall be exempt from Federal income taxation.

(b) *Qualified veterans' mortgage bond.* (1) With respect to obligations issued prior to July 19, 1984, the term "qualified veterans' mortgage bond" means any issue of obligations—

(i) Which meets the requirements of § 6a.103A-1, § 6a.103A-2(j)(1) and (2), and this section;

(ii) Substantially all of the proceeds of which are to be used to provide financing for single-family, owner-occupied residences (which meet the requirements of § 6a.103A-1(b)(6) and § 6a.103A-2(d)) for veterans; and

(iii) Payment of the principal and interest on which is secured by a pledge of the full faith and credit of the issuing State.

A qualified veterans' mortgage bond does not include any bond that is an industrial development bond under section 103(b).

(2) With respect to obligations issued after July 18, 1984, the term "qualified veterans' mortgage bond" means any issue of obligations—

(i) Which meets the requirements of § 6a.103A-1, § 6a.103A-2(d) (relating to residence requirements), (j)(1) and (2) (relating to new mortgage requirement), and (k) (relating to information reporting requirement), and this section;

(ii) Substantially all of the proceeds of which are to be used to provide financing for qualified veterans; and

(iii) Payment of the principal and interest on which is secured by a pledge of the full faith and credit of the issuing State.

A qualified veterans' mortgage bond does not include any bond that is an industrial development bond under section 103(b).

(c) *Qualified veteran.* (1) An issue meets the requirements of this paragraph only if each of the mortgagors to whom owner financing is provided is a qualified veteran.

(2) With respect to obligations issued prior to July 19, 1984, the term "qualified veteran" means any veteran.

(3) With respect to obligations issued after July 18, 1984, the term "qualified veteran" means any veteran who—

(i) Served on active duty at some time before January 1, 1977, and

(ii) Applied for financing before the later of—

(A) The date 30 years after the date on which such veteran left active service, or

(B) January 1, 1985.

(4) The term "veteran" shall have the same meaning as in 38 U.S.C. 101(2), that is, a person who served in the active military, naval, or air service, and who was discharged or released therefrom under conditions other than dishonorable.

(d) *Husband and wife.* For purposes of this section, if a residence is to be owned by a husband and wife as joint tenants, as tenants by the entirety, or as community property, and if one spouse is a veteran, then both spouses shall be treated as satisfying the requirements of paragraph (c).

(e) *Substantially all.* For purposes of this section, the term "substantially all" shall have the same meaning as in § 1.103-8.

(f) *Qualified home improvement loan.* The term "qualified home improvement loan" means the financing (whether or not secured by a mortgage)

→ *Caution: Code Sec. 103A has been repealed. Similar exempt bond issue rules have been provided in Code Secs. 141–150.*←

of alterations, repairs, and improvements on, or in connection with, an existing single-family, owner-occupied residence by a veteran who is the owner thereof. The alterations, repairs, and improvements, however, must substantially protect or improve the basic livability or energy efficiency of the property, such as the renovation of plumbing or electric systems, the installation of improved heating or air conditioning systems, the addition of living space, or the renovation of a kitchen area. Items that will not be considered to substantially protect or improve the basic livability of the property include swimming pools, tennis courts, saunas, or other recreational or entertainment facilities.

(g) *Volume limitation*—(1) *In general.* In the case of obligations issued after June 22, 1984, an issue meets the requirements of this paragraph only if the aggregate amount of obligations issued pursuant thereto, when added to the aggregate amount of qualified veterans' mortgage bonds previously issued by the State during the calendar year, does not exceed the State veterans limit for such calendar year. In determining the aggregate amount of qualified veterans' mortgage bonds issued in calendar year 1984, obligations issued prior to June 23, 1984, shall not be taken into account.

(2) *State veterans limit.* (i) The State veterans limit for any State is the amount equal to—

(A) The aggregate amount of qualified veterans' mortgage bonds issued by the State during the period beginning on January 1, 1979, and ending on June 22, 1984 (not including the amount of any qualified veterans' mortgage bonds actually issued during the calendar year, or the applicable portion of 1984, in such period for which the amount of such bonds was the lowest), divided by

(B) The number (not to exceed 5) of calendar years after 1978 and before 1985 during which the State issued qualified veterans' mortgage bonds.

In determining the number of calendar years after 1978 and before 1985 during which the State issued qualified veterans' mortgage bonds, any qualified veterans' mortgage bonds issued after June 22, 1984, shall not be taken into account. A State that did not issue qualified veterans' mortgage bonds during the period beginning on January 1, 1979, and ending on June 22, 1984, may not issue qualified veterans' mortgage bonds after June 22, 1984.

(ii) In the case of any obligation which has a term of 1 year or less and which was issued to provide financing for property taxes, the amount taken into account under this paragraph with respect to such obligation shall be 1/15 of its principal amount.

(3) *Examples.* The following examples illustrate the provisions of this paragraph:

Example (1). State R issued the following issues of qualified veterans' mortgage bonds: a $200 million issue on March 31, 1979, a $150 million issue on May 1, 1980, a $75 million issue on September 1, 1981, a $200 million issue on June 5, 1982, a $125 million issue on March 1, 1983, a $60 million issue on April 1, 1984, and a $100 million issue on September 1, 1984. R issued no other issues of qualified veterans' mortgage bonds during the period beginning January 1, 1979, and ending on December 31, 1984. The aggregate amount of qualified veterans' mortgage bonds issued during the period January 1, 1984, through June 22, 1984 ($60 million), is not taken into account in determining R's State veterans limit because that is the lowest aggregate amount of qualified veterans' mortgage bonds issued during the calendar year or the applicable portion of 1984, in the period beginning on January 1, 1979, and ending on June 22, 1984. Thus, R's State veterans limit is $150 million ($750 million (which is the sum of $200 million, $150 million, $75 million, $200 million, and $125 million) divided by 5). The September 1, 1984, issue is not included in determining the State veterans limit because that issue was issued after June 22, 1984. The September 1, 1984, issue of qualified veterans' mortgage bonds meets the requirements of § 6a.103A-3(g) since the aggregate amount of qualified veterans' mortgage bonds issued in calendar year 1984 (not including obligations issued prior to June 23, 1984), does not exceed the State veterans limit.

Example (2). State S issued a $100 million issue of qualified veterans' mortgage bonds on March 31, 1984. S issued no other issues of qualified veterans' mortgage bonds during the period beginning on January 1, 1979, and ending on June 22, 1984. The aggregate amount of qualified veterans' mortgage bonds issued in the calendar year, or the applicable portion of 1984, in the period January 1, 1979, through June 22, 1984, for which the amount of bonds was the lowest is zero. Thus, the State veterans limit for S is $100 million ($100 million minus $0) divided by 1).

(h) *Good faith compliance efforts*—(1) *Mortgage eligibility requirements.* An issue of qualified

Reg. § 6a.103A-3(g)(1)

→ *Caution: Code Sec. 103A has been repealed Similar exempt bond issue rules have been provided in Code Secs. 141–150.*←

veterans' mortgage bonds issued after July 18, 1984, which fails to meet the requirements of section 103A(o)(1), § 6a.103A-2(d) (relating to residence requirements), and § 6a.103A-2(j)(1) and (2) (relating to new mortgage requirement) shall be treated as meeting such requirements if each of the following provisions is complied with:

(i) The issuer in good faith attempted to meet all such requirements before the mortgages were executed. Good faith requires that the trust indenture, participation agreements with loan originators, and other relevant instruments contain restrictions that permit the financing of residences only in accordance with such requirements. In addition, the issuer must establish reasonable procedures to ensure compliance with such requirements. Such procedures include reasonable investigations by the issuer to satisfy such requirements.

(ii) Ninety-five percent or more of the lendable proceeds (as defined in § 6a.103A-2(b)(1)) that were devoted to owner-financing were devoted to residences with respect to which, at the time the mortgages were executed, all such requirements were met. In determining whether a person is a qualified veteran the issuer may rely on copies of the mortgagor's certificate of discharge indicating that the mortgagor served on active duty at some time before January 1, 1977, and stating the date on which the mortgagor left active service provided that neither the issuer nor its agent knows or has reason to believe that such affidavit is false. Where a particular mortgage fails to meet more than one of these requirements, the amount of the mortgage will be taken into account only once in determining whether the 95-percent requirement is met. However, all of the defects in the mortgage must be corrected pursuant to subdivision (iii).

(iii) Any failure to meet such requirements is corrected within a reasonable period after such failure is discovered. For example, failures can be corrected by calling the nonqualifying mortgage or by replacing the nonqualifying mortgage with a qualifying mortgage.

(2) *Nonmortgage eligibility requirements.* An issue of qualified veterans' mortgage bonds issued after July 18, 1984, which fails to meet the requirements of paragraph (g) of this section shall be treated as meeting such requirements if each of the requirements of § 6a.103A-2(c)(2)(i) and (ii) is met. [Temporary Reg. § 6a.103A-3.]

☐ [*T.D. 7780, 6-29-81. Amended by T.D. 7995, 12-7-84.*]

[Reg. § 1.104-1]

§ 1.104-1. **Compensation for injuries or sickness.**—(a) *In general.*—Section 104(a) provides an exclusion from gross income with respect to certain amounts described in paragraphs (b), (c), (d) and (e) of this section, which are received for personal injuries or sickness, except to the extent that such amounts are attributable to (but not in excess of) deductions allowed under section 213 (relating to medical, etc., expenses) for any prior taxable year. See section 213 and the regulations thereunder.

(b) *Amounts received under workmen's compensation acts.*—Section 104(a)(1) excludes from gross income amounts which are received by an employee under a workmen's compensation act (such as the Longshoremen's and Harbor Workers' Compensation Act, 33 U.S.C., c. 18), or under a statute in the nature of a workmen's compensation act which provides compensation to employees for personal injuries or sickness incurred in the course of employment. Section 104(a)(1) also applies to compensation which is paid under a workmen's compensation act to the survivor or survivors of a deceased employee. However, section 104(a)(1) does not apply to a retirement pension or annuity to the extent that it is determined by reference to the employee's age or length of service, or the employee's prior contributions, even though the employee's retirement is occasioned by an occupational injury or sickness. Section 104(a)(1) also does not apply to amounts which are received as compensation for a nonoccupational injury or sickness nor to amounts received as compensation for an occupational injury or sickness to the extent that they are in excess of the amount provided in the applicable workmen's compensation act or acts. See, however, §§ 1.105-1 through 1.105-5 for rules relating to exclusion of such amounts from gross income.

(c) *Damages received on account of personal injuries or sickness.*—Section 104(a)(2) excludes from gross income the amount of any damages received (whether by suit or agreement) on account of personal injuries or sickness. The term "damages received (whether by suit or agreement)" means an amount received (other than workmen's compensation) through prosecution of a legal suit or action based upon tort or tort type rights, or through a settlement agreement entered into in lieu of such prosecution.

(d) *Accident or health insurance.*—Section 104(a)(3) excludes from gross income amounts received through accident or health insurance for personal injuries or sickness (other than amounts received by an employee, to the extent that such amounts (1) are attributable to contributions of the employer which were not includible in the gross income of the employee, or (2) are paid by the employer). Similar treatment is also accorded to amounts received under accident or health plans and amounts received from sickness or disability funds. See section 105(e) and § 1.105-5. If, therefore, an individual purchases a policy of accident or health insurance out of his own funds, amounts received thereunder for personal injuries or sickness are excludable from his gross income under section 104(a)(3). See, however, section 213 and the regulations thereunder as to the inclusion in gross income of amounts attributable to deductions allowed under section 213 for any prior taxable year. Section 104(a)(3) also applies to amounts received by an employee for personal injuries or sickness from a fund which is maintained exclusively by employee contributions. Conversely, if an employer is either the sole contributor to such a fund, or is the sole purchaser of a policy of accident or health insurance for his employees (on either a group or individual basis), the exclusion provided under section 104(a)(3) does not apply to any amounts received by his employees through such fund or insurance. If the employer and his employees contribute to a fund or purchase insurance which pays accident or health benefits to employees, section 104(a)(3) does not apply to amounts received thereunder by employees to the extent that such amounts are attributable to the employer's contributions. See § 1.105-1 for rules relating to the determination of the amount attributable to employer contributions. Although amounts paid by or on behalf of an employer to an employee for personal injuries or sickness are not excludable from the employee's gross income under section 104(a)(3), they may be excludable therefrom under section 105. See §§ 1.105-1 through 1.105-5 , inclusive. For treatment of accident or health benefits paid to or on behalf of a self-employed individual by a trust described in section 401(a) which is exempt under section 501(a) or under a plan described in section 403(a), see paragraph (g) of § 1.72-15.

(e) *Amounts received as pensions, etc., for certain personal injuries or sickness.* (1) Section 104(a)(4) excludes from gross income amounts which are received as a pension, annuity, or similar allowance for personal injuries or sickness resulting from active service in the armed forces of any country, or in the Coast and Geodetic Survey, or the Public Health Service. For purposes of this section, that part of the retired pay of a member of an armed force, computed under formula No. 1 or 2 of 10 U.S.C. 1401, or under 10 U.S.C.

1402(d), on the basis of years of service, which exceeds the retired pay that he would receive if it were computed on the basis of percentage of disability is not considered as a pension, annuity, or similar allowance for personal injury or sickness, resulting from active service in the armed forces of any country, or in the Coast and Geodetic Survey, or the Public Health Service (see 10 U.S.C. 1403 (formerly 37 U.S.C. 272(h), section 402(h) of the Career Compensation Act of 1949)). See paragraph (a)(3)(i)(a) of § 1.105-4 for the treatment of retired pay in excess of the part computed on the basis of percentage of disability as amounts received through a wage continuation plan. For the rules relating to certain reduced uniformed services retirement pay, see paragraph (c)(2) of § 1.122-1. For rules relating to a waiver by a member or former member of the uniformed services of a portion of disability retired pay in favor of a pension or compensation receivable under the laws administered by the Veterans Administration (38 U.S.C. 3105), see section 1.122-1(c)(3). For rules relating to a reduction of the disability retired pay of a member or former member of the uniformed services under the Dual Compensation Act of 1964 (5 U.S.C. 5531) by reason of Federal employment, see section 1.122-1(c)(4).

(2) Section 104(a)(4) excludes from gross income amounts which are received by a participant in the Foreign Service Retirement and Disability System in a taxable year of such participant ending after September 8, 1960, as a disability annuity payable under the provisions of section 831 of the Foreign Service Act of 1946, as amended (22 U.S.C. 1081; 60 Stat. 1021). However, if any amount is received by a survivor of a disabled or incapacitated participant, such amount is not excluded from gross income by reason of the provisions of section 104(a)(4).

(3) Section 104(a)(4) excludes from gross income amounts which are received by a participant in the Retired Serviceman's Family Protection Plan as a disability annuity payable under the provisions of 10 U.S.C. 1431. However, if any amount is received by a survivor of a disabled or incapacitated participant, such amount is not excluded from gross income by reason of the provisions of section 104(a)(4). [Reg. § 1.104-1.]

□ [*T.D.* 6169, 4-13-56. *Amended by T.D.* 6722, 4-13-64 *and T.D.* 7043, 6-1-70.]

[Reg. § 1.105-1]

§ 1.105-1. Amounts attributable to employer contributions.—(a) *In general.*—Under section 105(a), amounts received by an employee through accident or health insurance for personal injuries or sickness must be included in his gross income to the extent that such amounts (1) are attributable to contributions of the employer which were not includible in the gross income of the employee, or (2) are paid by the employer, unless such amounts are excluded therefrom under section 105(b), (c), or (d). For purposes of this section, the term "amounts received by an employee through an accident or health plan" refers to any amounts received through accident or health insurance, and also to any amounts which, under section 105(e), are treated as being so received. See § 1.105-5. In determining the extent to which amounts received for personal injuries or sickness by an employee through an accident or health plan are subject to the provisions of section 105(a), rather than section 104(a)(3), the provisions of paragraphs (b), (c), (d), and (e) of this section shall apply. A self-employed individual is not an employee for purposes of section 105 and § § 1.105-1 through 1.105-5. See paragraph (g) of § 1.72-15. Thus, such an individual will not be treated as an employee with respect to benefits described in section 105 received from a plan in which he participates as an employee within the meaning of section 401(c)(1) at the time he, his spouse, or any of his dependents becomes entitled to receive such benefits.

(b) *Noncontributory plans.*—All amounts received by employees through an accident or health plan which is financed solely by their employer, either by payment of premiums on an accident or health insurance policy (whether on a group or individual basis), by contributions to a fund which pays accident or health benefits, or by direct payment of the benefits under the plan, are subject to the provisions of section 105(a), except to the extent that they are excludable under section 105(b), (c), or (d). This rule may be illustrated by the following examples:

Example (1). Employer A maintains a plan for his employees which provides that he will continue to pay regular wages to employees who are absent from work due to sickness or personal injuries. Employees make no contributions to the plan and all benefits are paid by the employer. Amounts received by employees under the plan are subject to section 105(a), and must be included in gross income unless excluded therefrom under section 150(b), (c), or (d).

Example (2). Pursuant to a State nonoccupational disability benefits law, employer B maintains an accident and health plan for his employees. Although under the State law B is authorized to withhold from his employees' wages a specified amount for employee contributions to the State fund, in actual practice B does not so withhold and makes all contributions out of his own funds. All amounts received by B's employees from the State fund are subject to section 105(a), and must be included in gross income unless excluded therefrom under section 105(b), (c), or (d).

(c) *Contributory plans.*—(1) In the case of amounts received by an employee through an accident or health plan which is financed partially by his employer and partially by contributions of the employee, section 105(a) applies to the extent that such amounts are attributable to contributions of the employer which were not includible in the employee's gross income. The portion of such amounts which is attributable to such contributions of the employer shall be determined in accordance with paragraph (d) of this section in the case of an insured plan, or paragraph (e) of this section in the case of a noninsured plan. As used in this section, the phrase "contributions of the employer" means employer contributions which are not includible in the gross income of the employee. See section 106 for the exclusion from an employee's gross income of employer contributions to accident or health plans.

(2) A separate determination of the portion of the amounts received under the accident or health plan which is attributable to the contributions of the employer shall be made with respect to each class of employees in any case where the plan provides that some classes of covered employees contribute but others do not, or that the employer will make different contributions for different classes of employees, or that different classes of employees will make different contributions, and where in any such case both the contributions of the employer on account of each such class of employees and the contributions of such class of employees can be ascertained. For example, if employees contribute during the first year of employment but not thereafter, there will have to be a separate determination for first-year employees, provided that the amount of the contributions of the employer on account of first-year employees and the contributions of such first-year employees can be ascertained for the required period to apply the rules of paragraph (d) or (e) of this section. If in such a case the contributions of the employer to the plan on account of first-year employees are not distinguishable from his other contributions to the plan, then the determination shall be made for all employees under the plan, and such determination shall be used by all employees under the plan.

(3) Except as provided in paragraph (c)(2) of § 1.72-15, if the plan provides accident or health benefits as well as other benefits for the employees, and if the respective contributions made by

Reg. § 1.105-1(c)(3)

the employer and the employees to provide the accident or health benefits cannot be ascertained, the determination of the portion of the accident or health benefits received under such plan which is attributable to the contributions of the employer shall be made in accordance with the rules of paragraph (d) or (e) of this section on the basis of the contributions of the employer and of the employees to the entire plan.

(4) A determination of the portion attributable to the contributions of the employer, once made in accordance with the rules of this section, shall as to such portion be used for all purposes. For example, if an employee receives amounts under a wage continuation plan during the month of January and terminates his services during February, the portion of such amounts which is attributable to the contributions of the employer may be determined in order to provide the employee with such information at the time he is provided his Form W-2. The determination made for such purpose will also be used by the employee to report his income for his taxable year in which such amounts are received, without regard to the experience under the plan for the rest of the year.

(d) *Insured plans*—(1) *Individual policies.* If an amount is received from an insurance company by an employee under an individual policy of accident or health insurance purchased by contributions of the employer and the employee, the portion of the amount received which is attributable to the employer's contributions shall be an amount which bears the same ratio to the amount received as the portion of the premiums paid by the employer for the current policy year bears to the total premiums paid by the employer and the employee for that year. This rule may be illustrated by the following example:

Example. Employer A maintains a plan whereby he pays two-thirds of the annual premium cost on individual policies of accident and health insurance for his employees. The remainder of each employee's premium is paid by a payroll deduction from the wages of the employee. The annual premium for employee X is $24, of which $16 is paid by the employer. Thus, 16/24 or two-thirds of all amounts received by X under such insurance policy are attributable to the contributions of the employer and are subject to section 105(a), and the remaining one-third of such amounts is excludable from X's gross income under section 104(a)(3).

(2) *Group policies.* If the accident or health coverage is provided under or is a part of a group insurance policy purchased by contributions of

the employer and of the employees, and the net premiums for such coverage for a period of at least three policy years are known at the beginning of the calendar year, the portion of any amount received by an employee which is attributable to the contributions of the employer for such coverage shall be an amount which bears the same ratio to the amount received as the portion of the net premiums contributed by the employer for the last three policy years which are known at the beginning of the calendar year bears to the total of the net premiums contributed by the employer and all employees for such policy years. If the net premiums for such coverage for a period of at least three policy years are not known at the beginning of the calendar year but are known for at least one policy year, such determination shall be made by using the net premiums for such coverage which are known at the beginning of the calendar year. If the net premiums for such coverage are not known at the beginning of the calendar year for even one policy year, such determination shall be made by using either (i) a reasonable estimate of the net premiums for the first policy year, or (ii) if the net premiums for a policy year are ascertained during the calendar year, by using such net premiums. These rules may be illustrated by the following example:

Example. An employer maintains a plan under which a portion of the cost of a group policy of accident and health insurance for his employees is paid through payroll deductions from wages of the employees. The remainder of the cost is borne by the employer. The policy year begins on November 1, and ends on October 31. The net premium for the policy year ended October 31, 1954, is not known on January 1, 1955, because retroactive premium adjustments, such as dividends and credits, are not determinable until after January 1. Therefore, for purposes of this computation the last three policy years are the policy years ended October 31, 1951, 1952, and 1953. The net premium for the policy year ended October 31, 1953, was $8,000, of which the employer contributed $3,000; the net premium for the policy year ended October 31, 1952, was $9,000, of which the employer contributed $3,500; and the net premium for the policy year ended October 31, 1951, was $7,000, of which the employer contributed $1,500. The portion of any amount received under the policy by an employee at any time during 1955 which is attributable to the contributions of the employer is to be determined by using the ratio of $8,000 ($3,000 plus $3,500 plus $1,500) to $24,000 ($8,000 plus $9,000 plus

Reg. § 1.105-1(c)(4)

$7,000$). Thus, $\dfrac{\$\,8,000}{\$24,000}$ or one-third, of the amounts received by an employee

at any time during 1955 is attributable to contributions of the employer.

(e) *Noninsured plans.*—If the accident or health benefits are a part of a noninsured plan to which the employer and the employees contribute, and such plan has been in effect for at least three years before the beginning of the calendar year, the portion of the amount received which is attributable to the employer's contributions shall be an amount which bears the same ratio to the amount received as the contributions of the employer for the period of three calendar years next preceding the year of receipt bear to the total contributions of the employer and all the employees for such period. If, at the beginning of the calendar year of receipt, such plan has not been in effect for three years but has been in effect for at least one year, such determination shall be based upon the contributions made during the 1-year or 2-year period during which the plan has been in effect. If such plan has not been in effect for one full year at the beginning of the calendar year of receipt, such determination may be based upon the portion of the year of receipt preceding the time when the determination is made, or such determination may be made periodically (such as monthly or quarterly) and used throughout the succeeding period. For example if an employee terminates his services on April 15, 1955, and 1955 is the first year the plan has been in effect, such determination may be based upon the contributions of the employer and the employees during the period beginning with January 1, and ending with April 15, or during the month of March, or during the quarter consisting of January, February, and March. [Reg. § 1.105-1.]

☐ [*T.D.* 6169, 4-13-56. *Amended by T.D.* 6485, 7-29-60 and T.D. 6722, 4-13-64]

[Reg. § 1.105-2]

§ 1.105-2. Amounts expended for medical care.—Section 105(b) provides an exclusion from gross income with respect to the amounts referred to in section 105(a) (see § 1.105-1) which are paid, directly or indirectly, to the taxpayer to reimburse him for expenses incurred for the medical care (as defined in section 213(e)) of the taxpayer, his spouse, and his dependents (as defined in section 152). However, the exclusion does not apply to amounts which are attributable to (and not in excess of) deductions allowed under section 213 (relating to medical, etc., expenses) for any prior taxable year. See section 213 and the regulations thereunder. Section 105(b) applies only to amounts which are paid specifically to reimburse

the taxpayer for expenses incurred by him for the prescribed medical care. Thus, section 105(b) does not apply to amounts which the taxpayer would be entitled to receive irrespective of whether or not he incurs expenses for medical care. For example, if under a wage continuation plan the taxpayer is entitled to regular wages during a period of absence from work due to sickness or injury, amounts received under such plan are not excludable from his gross income under section 105(b) even though the taxpayer may have incurred medical expenses during the period of illness. Such amounts may, however, be excludable from his gross income under section 105(d). See § 1.105-4. If the amounts are paid to the taxpayer solely to reimburse him for expenses which he incurred for the prescribed medical care, section 105(b) is applicable even though such amounts are paid without proof of the amount of the actual expenses incurred by the taxpayer, but section 105(b) is not applicable to the extent that such amounts exceed the amount of the actual expenses for such medical care. If the taxpayer incurs an obligation for medical care, payment to the obligee in discharge of such obligation shall constitute indirect payment to the taxpayer as reimbursement for medical care. Similarly, payment to or on behalf of the taxpayer's spouse or dependents shall constitute indirect payment to the taxpayer. [Reg. § 1.105-2.]

☐ [*T.D.* 6169, 4-13-56.]

[Reg. § 1.105-3]

§ 1.105-3. Payments unrelated to absence from work.—Section 105(c) provides an exclusion from gross income with respect to the amounts referred to in section 105(a) to the extent that such amounts (a) constitute payments for the permanent loss or permanent loss of use of a member or function of the body, or the permanent disfigurement, of the taxpayer, his spouse, or a dependent (as defined in section 152), and (b) are computed with reference to the nature of the injury without regard to the period the employee is absent from work. Loss of use or disfigurement shall be considered permanent when it may reasonably be expected to continue for the life of the individual. For purposes of section 105(c), loss or loss of use of a member or function of the body includes the loss or loss of use of an appendage of the body, the loss of an eye, the loss of substantially all of the vision of an eye, and the loss of substantially all of the hearing in one or both ears. The term "disfigurement" shall be given a reasonable interpretation in the light of all the particular facts and circumstances. Section 105(c) does not apply if the amount of the benefits is determined by reference to the period the employee is absent from work. For example, if an employee is absent from work as a result of the loss of an arm, and under the accident and health plan established by his employer, he is to receive $125 a week so long as he is absent from work for a period not in excess of 52 weeks, section 105(c) is not applicable to such payments. See, however, section 105(d) and § 1.105-4. However, for purposes of section 105(c), it is immaterial whether an amount is paid in a lump sum or in installments. Section 105(c) does not apply to amounts which are treated as workmen's compensation under paragraph (b) of § 1.104-1, or to amounts paid by reason of the death of the employee (see section 101). [Reg. § 1.105-3.]

☐ [*T.D.* 6169, 4-13-56.]

[Reg. § 1.105-4]

§ 1.105-4. **Wage continuation plans.**—(a) *In general.*—(1) Subject to the limitations provided in this section, section 105(d) provides an exclusion from gross income with respect to amounts referred to in section 105(a) which are paid to an employee through a wage continuation plan and which constitute wages or payments in lieu of wages for a period during which the employee is absent from work on account of personal injuries or sickness.

(2)(i) Section 105(d) is applicable only if the wages or payments in lieu of wages are paid pursuant to a wage continuation plan. (See § 1.105-6 for special rules for employees retired before January 27, 1975.) The term "wage continuation plan" means an accident or health plan, as defined in § 1.105-5, under which wages, or payments in lieu of wages, are paid to an employee for a period during which he is absent from work on account of a personal injury or sickness. Such term includes plans under which payments are continued as long as the employee is absent from work on account of personal injury or sickness. It includes plans under which there is a limitation on the period for which benefits will be paid, such as 13 or 26 weeks, and also plans under which benefits are continued until the employee is either able to return to work or reaches mandatory retirement age. Such term also includes a plan under which wages or payments in lieu of wages are paid to an employee who is absent from work on account of personal injury or sickness, even though the plan also provides that wages or payments in lieu of wages may be paid to an employee who is absent from work for reasons other than a personal injury or sickness.

(ii) Section 105(d) is applicable if, and only if, the employee is absent from work and

such absence is due to a personal injury or sickness. Thus, if an employer has a plan for continuing the wages of employees when they are absent from work, regardless of the cause of the absence from work, section 105(d) is applicable to any payments made under this plan to an employee whose absence from work is in fact due to a personal injury or sickness. On the other hand, although the terms of a plan provide that benefits are to be continued only as long as the employee is absent from work on account of a personal injury or sickness, section 105(d) does not apply to payments made to an employee for a period of absence from work where such absence is not in fact due to a personal injury or sickness.

(3)(i)(A) Section 105(d) applies only to amounts attributable to periods during which the employee would be at work were it not for a personal injury or sickness. Thus, an employee is not absent from work if he is not expected to work because, for example, he has reached mandatory retirement age. If a plan provides that an employee, who is absent from work on account of a personal injury or sickness, will receive a disability pension or annuity as long as he is disabled, section 105(d) is applicable to any payments that he receives under this plan before reaching mandatory retirement age, as defined in paragraph (a)(3)(i)(B) of this section. Thus, section 105(d) would not apply to the payments that an employee receives after reaching mandatory retirement age. The disability retired pay received by a member on the retired list pursuant to section 402 of the Career Compensation Act of 1949 (63 Stat. 802) or chapter 61 of title 10, United States Code (10 U.S.C. 1201 *et seq.*) which is in excess of the amounts excludable under section 104(a)(4) and paragraph (e) of § 1.104-1 shall be excluded from gross income subject to the limitations of section 105(d) and this section, if such pay is received before the member reaches mandatory retirement age. See § 1.72-15 for additional rules relating to the tax treatment of disability pensions. For the rules relating to certain reduced uniformed services retirement pay, see paragraph (c)(2) of § 1.122-1. For rules relating to a waiver by a member or former member of the uniformed services of a portion of disability retired pay in favor of a pension or compensation receivable under the laws administered by the Veterans Administration (38 U.S.C. 3105), see § 1.122-1(c)(3).

(B) The term "mandatory retirement age" as used in paragraph (a)(3)(i)(A) of this section means the age set by an employer for the mandatory retirement of employees in the class to which the taxpayer last belonged, unless such age has been set at an age higher than that at which it has been the practice of the employer to terminate, due to age, the services of such employees, or for purposes of tax avoidance. Where no age is set for mandatory retirement, such term means age 65, or, if higher, the age at which it has been the practice of the employer to terminate, due to age, the services of the class of employees to which the taxpayer last belonged.

(ii) Similarly, an employee who incurs a personal injury or sickness during his paid vacation is not allowed to exclude under section 105(d) any of the vacation pay which he receives, since he is not absent from work on account of the personal injury or sickness. Likewise, a teacher who becomes sick during the summer or other vacation period when he is not expected to teach, is not entitled to any exclusion under section 105(d) for the summer or vacation period. However, if an employee who would otherwise be at work during a particular period is absent from work and his absence is in fact due to a personal injury or sickness, a payment which he receives for such period under a wage continuation plan is subject to section 105(d).

(4) A period of absence from work shall commence the moment the employee first becomes absent from work and shall end the moment the employee first returns to work. However, the exclusion provided under section 105(d) is applicable only to payments attributable to a period of absence from work which is due to a personal injury or sickness, and to payments attributable to a period when the employee would have been at work but for such personal injury or sickness.

(5) For the purpose of section 105(d), whether an employee is absent from work depends upon all the circumstances. For example, an employee, who is a farm hand and who lives upon the premises of his employer, is absent from work when he is unable to work even though he remains on the premises of his employer. A member of the Armed Forces, who on a particular day has no assigned duties but to stand ready for duty, is absent from work if he is unable to answer any duty call that may be made upon him. An employee is not absent from work when he performs any services for his employer at his usual place or places of employment, whether or not the services are the usual services performed by the employee. Furthermore, the employee is not absent from work when he performs substantial services for his employer, even though they are performed at a place other than his usual place of employment. Thus, if an employee returns to his usual place or places of employment and performs any services for his employer, he has returned to work, but if he merely holds occasional short conferences concerning his work with other employees or clients while hospitalized or at home recuperating, such conferences do not constitute a return to work.

(b) *Determination of amount attributable to period of absence.*—The amount which is paid to an employee as wages or payments in lieu of wages for a period of absence from work due to a personal injury or sickness shall be determined by reference to the plan under which the amount is paid, and to the contract, statute, or regulation which provides the terms of the employment. However, unless the plan, contract, statute, or regulation provides otherwise, it will be presumed that no wages or plan benefits are attributable to days (or portions of days) which are not normal working days for the particular employee. Also, section 105(d) does not apply to amounts earned prior to or subsequent to the period of absence from work, even though received during such period. These rules may be illustrated by the following examples:

Example (1). Employee A, who receives regular wages of $70 per week, normally works five days (Monday through Friday) during each week. A is absent from work on a Friday and the succeeding Monday (two working days) on account of a personal injury, but receives his regular wages with respect to such period of absence under his employer's accident and health plan. Unless the plan of A's employer, or the contract, statute, or regulation under which A is employed, provides otherwise, it will be presumed that A is not paid with respect to nonworking days (Saturday and Sunday). Therefore, the amount received by A with respect to his period of absence from work due to injury is $28, which is two days regular wages. If the plan, or the employment contract, statute, or regulation had provided that wages were paid on a 7-day per week basis and that A must be available for call to work on Saturday and Sunday, A's daily wage would have been $10, and the amount attributable to the period of absence would have been $40 ($10 per day for four days).

Example (2). Employee B is a salesman who is paid on a commission basis. The employer purchases for B an accident and health insurance policy which provides that B shall receive $50 per week during any period (after a 7-day waiting period) that he is unable to work due to personal injuries or sickness. B incurs a personal injury and is incapacitated for two weeks. He receives $50 under the insurance policy with respect to the second week of absence. In addition, during the 2-week period of absence he receives a check for $40 from his employer as his commission on a sale which he made before becoming incapacitated. Section 105(d) applies to the $50 received through

Reg. § 1.105-4(b)

the insurance policy, but does not apply to the $40 commission which B earned prior to the period of absence from work.

(c) *Limitation in the case of absence from work due to sickness for periods commencing prior to January 1, 1964.* (1) In the case of a period of absence from work on account of sickness commencing prior to January 1, 1964, the exclusion provided by section 105(d) does not apply to amounts attributable to the first seven calendar days of each such period, unless the employee is hospitalized on account of sickness for at least one day during the period of absence from work. This 7-day rule applies to each period of absence from work because of sickness, regardless of the frequency of such absences or the closeness in time to any prior period of absence from work because of sickness. For example, employee A becomes absent from work because of sickness on Friday, October 4, 1963, and returns to work on the morning of Monday, October 14, 1963. He suffers a relapse and again becomes absent from work on the afternoon of Monday, October 14, 1963. A's return to work on the morning of Monday, October 14, 1963, terminates the first period of absence from work because of sickness, and a new period of absence from work because of sickness begins on the afternoon of Monday, October 14, 1963. The 7-day limitation does not apply if the absence from work is due to personal injury. These rules may be illustrated by the following examples:

Example (1). Employee C normally works five days (Monday through Friday) during each week. On Saturday, October 5, 1963 (a non-working day), C becomes sick and as a result, he does not return to work until Thursday, October 17, 1963. The period of absence from work due to sickness commences on Monday, October 7, 1963, and terminates when C returns to work on Thursday, October 17, 1963. If C is not hospitalized during such period of absence from work, section 105(d) does not apply to amounts which C receives under his employer's wage continuation plan attributable to the 7-day period commencing Monday, October 7, 1963, and ending Sunday, October 13, 1963, inclusive.

Example (2). Employee D incurs a personal injury which causes him to be absent from work two days. His regular wages are continued during this period in accordance with the wage continuation plan of his employer. Since D's absence from work was due to a personal injury, rather than a sickness, the 7-day waiting period does not apply, and, subject to the other requirements of section 105(d), D is entitled to an exclusion with respect

to the amounts received under the employer's plan attributable to the 2-day period of absence.

(2) For the purpose of starting the 7-day waiting period, if the period of absence due to sickness commences after the start of a working day, the amount received with respect to the portion of such day that the employee is absent from work shall be considered the amount attributable to the first calendar day of the period of absence from work due to sickness. This rule may be illustrated by the following example:

Example. Employee E normally works from 9 a.m. until 5:30 p.m. on five days (Monday through Friday) during each week. From noon on Friday, September 6, 1963, until noon on Monday, September 16, 1963, E is absent from work on account of sickness but is not hospitalized at any time during this period. Section 105(d) does not apply to amounts received by E under his employer's wage continuation plan which are attributable to the calendar period beginning September 6, 1963, and ending September 12, 1963, inclusive. However, if the other requirements of section 105(d) are met, E may exclude from gross income amounts attributable to the period beginning September 13, 1963, and ending at noon on September 16, 1963, inclusive.

(3) If the absence from work is due to sickness, the amount attributable to the first seven calendar days of such absence includes all amounts paid for such seven calendar days, regardless of the number of work days included in such seven calendar days. For example, if on one of such seven calendar days an employee would have worked two 8-hour shifts, the amount he is paid for the two shifts is considered to be an amount attributable to only one calendar day.

(4) An employee is considered to be hospitalized for one day only if he is admitted to and confined in a hospital as a bed patient for at least one hospital day. Entry into a hospital as an in-and-out patient does not constitute hospitalization for purposes of section 105(d). The same applies to mere entry into the out-patient ward or the emergency ward of a hospital.

(d) *Exclusion not applicable to the extent that amounts exceed a weekly rate of $100 for periods of absence commencing prior to January 1, 1964*—(1) *In general.* Amounts received under a wage continuation plan, attributable to periods of absence commencing before January 1, 1964, which are not excludable from gross income as being attributable to contributions of the employee (see § 1.105-1) must be included in gross income under section 105(d) to the extent that the weekly rate of such amounts exceeds $100. Thus, an employee, who receives $50 under his employer's wage continuation plan on account of his being absent from work for two days due to a personal injury, cannot exclude the entire $50 under section 105(d) if the weekly rate of such benefits exceeds $100. If an employee receives payments under a wage continuation plan for less than a full pay period, the excludability of such payments shall be determined under subparagraph (2) of this paragraph. In all other cases, the weekly rate and excludability of such payments under a wage continuation plan shall be determined under subparagraph (3) of this paragraph. If, with respect to any pay period or portion thereof, the employee receives amounts under two or more wage continuation plans (whether such plans are maintained by or for the same employer or by different employers), the weekly rate and excludability of amounts received under each plan shall be determined under subparagraph (3) of this paragraph and the weekly rate for purposes of section 105(d) shall be the sum of all such weekly rates. This rule may be illustrated by the following examples:

Example (1). An employee whose weekly salary is $120 is covered by two wage continuation plans maintained by his employer. Plan A is a contributory insured plan to which the employee contributes 60 percent of the premiums and which provides a weekly payment of $30. Plan B is a salary continuation plan completely financed by the employer. Since 60 percent of the cost of plan A is contributed by the employee, 60 percent of the weekly payment of $30 ($18) is excluded from gross income under section 104(a)(3). The remainder of each weekly payment ($12) is the weekly rate of plan A. Since the employer pays the entire cost of plan B, the weekly rate of this plan is the total amount paid per week. In the case of an employee whose weekly wages of $120 are continued under plan B, the weekly rate for the employee for purposes of section 105(d) is $132 ($120 from plan B, plus $12 from plan A).

Example (2). Assume, in example (1), that plan A provides a waiting period of four calendar days while plan B is effective immediately. For the first four days of absence the weekly rate for purposes of section 105(d) is $120, and for periods after the first four days the weekly rate for purposes of section 105(d) is $132.

(2) *Daily exclusion.* If an employee receives payments under a wage continuation plan for less than a full pay period, the extent to which such benefits are excludable under section 105(d) shall be determined by computing the daily rate of the benefits which can be excluded under section 105(d). Such daily rate is determined by dividing the weekly rate at which wage continuation payments are excludable ($100) by the number of work days in a normal work week. This rule may be illustrated by the following example:

Example. Employee E is covered by a wage continuation plan maintained by his employer providing that E's regular salary of $220 semimonthly will be continued in case he is absent from work on account of a personal injury or sickness. E is absent from work on account of a personal injury for three days and under the plan he received $66 as wage continuation payments. The extent to which the $66 is excludable under section 105(d) shall be determined by dividing $100 by 5, the number of work days in a normal work week for E, resulting in a daily exclusion of $20 and a total exclusion of $60.

(3) *Determination of weekly rate at which amounts are paid under a wage continuation plan.* (i) For purposes of this subparagraph the pay period of a particular wage continuation plan shall be determined by reference to such plan. If, in the usual operation of the plan, benefits are paid for the same periods as regular wages, then the pay period of such benefits shall be the period for which a payment of wages is ordinarily made to the employee by the employer. If plan benefits are ordinarily paid for different periods than regular wages then the pay period of such benefits shall be the period for which payment of such benefits is ordinarily made.

(ii) The weekly rate shall be determined in accordance with the following rules:

(a) *Weekly pay period.* If benefits are paid on the basis of a weekly pay period, the weekly rate at which such benefits are paid shall be the weekly amount of such benefits.

(b) *Biweekly pay period.* If benefits are paid on the basis of a biweekly pay period, the weekly rate at which such benefits are paid shall be one-half of the biweekly rate.

(c) *Semimonthly pay period.* If benefits are paid on the basis of a semimonthly pay period, the weekly rate at which such benefits are paid shall be the semimonthly rate multiplied by 24 and divided by 52.

(d) *Monthly pay period.* If benefits are paid on the basis of a monthly pay period, the weekly rate at which such benefits are paid shall be the monthly rate multiplied by 12 and divided by 52.

(e) *Other pay periods.* If benefits are paid on the basis of a period other than a period described in (a) through (d) of this subdivision, the weekly rate at which such benefits are paid shall be determined by ascertaining the annual rate at which such benefits are paid and dividing such annual rate by 52.

(f) *Examples.* The operation of the rules of this subdivision may be illustrated by the following examples:

Example (1). A's employer maintains a noncontributory plan which provides for the continuation of regular salary during periods of absence from work due to personal injury or sickness. A, an office employee, receives regular salary of $520 per month, and he is paid on the basis of a monthly pay period. Since benefits under the salary continuation plan are paid for the same periods as regular salary, the pay period of the plan is monthly. For purposes of section 105(d), the weekly rate at which benefits are paid to A under the plan is $120, determined as follows:

$ 520 (monthly rate) × 12 . . . $6,240 (annual rate)

$$\frac{\$6,240}{52} \dots \dots \dots \dots \dots \$ \ 120 \ (\text{weekly rate})$$

Example (2). B, a factory employee of the same employer, is paid regular wages on the basis of a 10-day pay period. B's regular wages are $200 per pay period. If B is absent from work for 15 days, the weekly rate of the amount he receives under his employer's plan will be determined as follows:

$$\frac{365 \times \$200}{10} \dots \dots \dots \dots \dots \$ \ 7,300 \ (\text{annual rate})$$

$$\frac{\$7,300}{52} \dots \dots \dots \dots \dots \$140.38 \ (\text{weekly rate})$$

(iii) If the weekly rate for purposes of section 105(d) (as determined in subdivision (ii) of this subparagraph) does not exceed $100, the amount received which is not attributable to the 7-day waiting period described in paragraph (c) of this subsection is fully excludable from gross income. If the weekly rate for purposes of section 105(d) (as determined in subdivision (ii) of this subparagraph) exceeds $100, the amount received which is not attributable to the 7-day waiting period provided in paragraph (c) of this subsection is only partially excludable. The excludable portion of such amount shall bear the same ratio to such amount as $100 bears to the weekly rate for purposes of section 105(d). This rule may be illustrated by the following example:

Example. The weekly rate of benefits in the case of employee A in example (1) of subdivision (ii) of this subparagraph was $120. If A does not receive amounts under any other plan, this is the weekly rate for purposes of section 105(d). Assume that A is absent from work on account of a personal injury for one full month and receives full pay of $520 for such period of absence. Since

there is no waiting period requirement, the exclusion is $433.33, computed as follows:

$$\frac{\$100}{\$120} \times \$520 \text{ or } \$433.33.$$

(e) *Limitation in the case of absence from work on account of personal injury or sickness for periods commencing after December 31, 1963.* (1) In the case of periods of absence from work on account of sickness or personal injury commencing after December 31, 1963, the exclusion provided by section 105(d) does not apply to amounts attributable to the first 30 calendar days of each such period, if such amounts are at a rate which exceeds 75 percent of the employee's "regular weekly rate of wages," as determined under subparagraph (5) of this paragraph. If the amounts are at a rate of 75 percent or less of the employee's "regular weekly rate of wages," the exclusion provided by section 105(d) does not apply to amounts attributable to the first 7 calendar days of each such period, unless the employee is hospitalized on account of personal injury or sickness for at least one day during the period of absence from work. The 7- or 30-day waiting period (whichever is applicable) applies to each period of absence from work because of personal injury or sickness, regardless of the frequency of such absences or the closeness in time to any prior period of absence from work because of personal injury or sickness. The waiting period is to be counted by beginning with the first work day for which the employee was absent. These rules may be illustrated by the following examples:

Example (1). Employee A is absent from work because of sickness on Tuesday, January 7, 1964, and returns to work on the morning of Thursday, February 13, 1964. He suffers a relapse and again becomes absent from work on the afternoon of Thursday, February 13, 1964. A's return to work on the morning of Thursday, February 13, 1964, terminates the first period of absence from work because of sickness, and a new period of absence from work because of sickness begins on the afternoon of Thursday, February 13, 1964.

Example (2). Employee B normally works five days (Monday through Friday) during each week. On Saturday, January 11, 1964 (a nonworking day), B becomes sick or injured and as a result he does not return to work until Monday, February 17, 1964. The period of absence from work commences on Monday, January 13, 1964, and terminates when B returns to work on Monday, February 17, 1964. Assuming B receives amounts under his employer's wage continuation plan at a rate exceeding 75 percent of his "regular weekly rate of wages" (as determined under subparagraph (5) of this paragraph), the exclusion

Reg. § 1.105-4(e)

provided by section 105(d) does not apply to amounts B receives under his employer's wage continuation plan which are attributable to the 30-day period commencing Monday, January 13, 1964, and ending Tuesday, February 11, 1964, inclusive. If B receives amounts under his employer's wage continuation plan at a rate which is 75 percent or less of his "regular weekly rate of wages" and he is not hospitalized during the period of absence from work, the exclusion provided by section 105(d) does not apply to amounts B receives which are attributable to the 7-day period commencing Monday, January 13, 1964, and ending Sunday, January 19, 1964, inclusive.

Example (3). Employee C is sick or incurs a personal injury which causes him to be absent from work for two weeks. He receives amounts under his employer's wage continuation plan at a rate which is 75 percent or less of his "regular weekly rate of wages" (as determined under subparagraph (5) of this paragraph) and is hospitalized from the eighth through the eleventh day of his absence. Since C was hospitalized on account of personal injury or sickness for at least one day during the period of absence, the 7-day waiting period does not apply, and, subject to the other requirements of section 105(d), C is entitled to an exclusion with respect to the amounts received under his employer's plan attributable to the two-week period of absence. If C were receiving amounts under his employer's wage continuation plan at a rate exceeding 75 percent of his "regular weekly rate of wages", he would not be entitled to an exclusion under section 105(d).

(2) For the purpose of starting the 7- or 30-day waiting period, whichever is applicable, if the period of absence commences after the start of a working day, the amount received with respect to the portion of such day that the employee is absent from work shall be considered an amount attributable to the first calendar day of the period of absence from work This rule may be illustrated by the following example:

Example. Employee D normally works from 9 a.m. until 5:30 p.m. on five days (Monday through Friday) during each week. From noon on Wednesday, January 8, 1964, until noon on Monday, February 17, 1964, D is absent from work on account of personal injury or sickness but is not hospitalized at any time during this period. D receives amounts under his employer's wage continuation plan at a rate not exceeding 75 percent of his "regular weekly rate of wages" (as determined under subparagraph (5) of this paragraph). Section 105(d) does not apply to amounts received by D under his employer's wage continuation plan which are attributable to the calendar period beginning January 8, 1964, and continuing through January 14, 1964, inclusive. However, if the other requirements of section 105(d) are met, D may exclude from gross income amounts attributable to the remainder of the period of absence, ending at noon on Monday, February 17, 1964.

(3) If the exclusion is subject to a 7- or 30-calendar-day waiting period, any amount attributable to such 7- or 30-calendar-day waiting period includes all amounts paid therefor, regardless of the number of work days included in such 7 or 30 calendar days. For example, if on one of the days included in the waiting period, an employee would have worked two 8-hour shifts, the amount he is paid for the two shifts is considered to be attributable to only one calendar day.

(4) An employee is considered to be hospitalized for one day only if he is admitted to and confined in a hospital as a bed patient for at least one hospital day. Entry into a hospital as an in- and out-patient does not constitute hospitalization for purpose of section 105(d). The same applies to mere entry into the out-patient ward or the emergency ward of a hospital.

(5)(i) In general, the "regular weekly rate of wages", for purposes of section 105(d), shall be the average weekly wages paid for the last four weekly periods falling within a full pay period or full pay periods immediately preceding the commencement of the period of absence. If the employee was absent from work for three or more normal working days during any such pay period, and the amount of wages paid for such pay period was less than the amount of wages paid for the immediately preceding pay period during which the employee was not absent from work for three or more normal working days, then the amount of wages paid for the weekly period or weekly periods falling wholly or partly within the pay period during which each such absence occurred shall not be used in the determination of "regular weekly rate of wages." In such a case, there shall be substituted the amount of wages paid for the last weekly period or weekly periods falling within the pay period or pay periods immediately preceding the pay period or pay periods in which such absence or absences occurred during which the employee was not absent from work for three or more normal working days.

(a) In order to compute wages paid for the last four weekly periods falling within a full pay period or full pay periods immediately preceding the commencement of the period of absence, or any substituted weekly periods therefor, it will be necessary to convert the wages paid for any pay period other than a weekly pay period into a weekly rate or weekly rates of payment of

Reg. § 1.105-4(e)(5)

such wages in accordance with the rules stated in subdivision (iv) of this subparagraph. Such weekly rate or weekly rates of wage payments are then used in determining the wages for the last four weekly periods falling within a full pay period or full pay periods immediately preceding the commencement of the period of absence, or any substituted weekly periods therefor.

(*b*) If the employee does not have four weekly periods falling with a full pay period or full pay periods preceding his absence during which he was not absent from work or three or more normal working days, then the greatest number of available weekly periods shall be used, consistent with the rules set forth in this subdivision (i), in determining the "regular weekly rate of wages".

(*c*) If the employee has been employed for a full pay period or more preceding his absence, and has worked for the number of days in a normal work week, but was absent from work for three or more normal working days during each of the pay periods preceding his absence, then the "regular weekly rate of wages" shall be determined by multiplying the employee's actual wages paid for the total number of normal working days in the pay period immediately preceding the employee's absence by the number of days that the employee is expected to work in a normal work week, and by dividing the product by the number of normal work days in such pay period for which wages were paid.

(*d*) If the employee has not been employed for a full pay period preceding his absence, and has worked for the number of days in a normal work week, the "regular weekly rate of wages" shall be determined by multiplying the employee's actual wages paid for the total number of normal working days preceding the employee's absence by the number of days that the employee is expected to work in a normal work week, and by dividing the product by the number of normal work days for which wages were paid.

(*e*) If the employee has not worked the number of days in a normal work week, then there is no "regular weekly rate of wages", and the employee will not be permitted an exclusion under section 105(d) for amounts attributable to the first 30 calendar days in the period of absence.

(*f*) Wages paid by a former employer shall not be used in the determination of "regular weekly rate of wages" as described in this subparagraph.

(ii) In the case of a wage continuation plan of an employer under which the benefits are computed as a specified percentage of average wages, the formula for computing the employee's average

wages included in the plan may be used (in lieu of the formula provided in subdivision (i) of this subparagraph) for determining the "regular weekly rate of wages" for purposes of section 105(d), if under the plan—

(*a*) The definition of wages does not include any items which are not considered "wages" as defined in subdivision (iii) of this subparagraph,

(*b*) The period for computing average wages is not less than twenty-eight successive calendar days, does not end earlier than five months preceding the date on which the period of absence commences, and is one in which the employee was at work at least 35 percent of the normal working time, and

(*c*) The period and formula for computing average wages are applied uniformly with respect to all employees eligible to receive benefits under the plan.

A plan will not fail to meet the conditions of this subdivision merely because different portions of the employee's wages are averaged over different periods for purposes of computing his average wages, so long as each such period meets the requirements in (*b*) and (*c*) of this subdivision.

(iii) For the purpose of determining "regular weekly rate of wages" under subdivision (i) or (ii) of this subparagraph, whichever is applicable, an employee's wages shall comprise basic salary, fees, commissions, tips, gratuities, overtime, and any other type of taxable compensation which is normally paid for services. However, wages shall not include any type of compensation which is not normally paid, such as bonuses and incentive payments. An employee's compensation, for the purpose of determining his "regular weekly rate of wages", will not include any compensation which is not currently includible in gross income. For example, an employee's wages for the purpose of this subdivision shall not include deferred compensation paid by the employer which is not includible in gross income until received by the employee, such as employer contributions to a qualified annuity under section 403(a), or employer contributions to an accident or health plan excluded under section 106.

(iv) The following rules shall be used to convert wages for pay periods other than weekly pay periods into weekly rates of wage payments to be used in determining "regular weekly rate of wages" as described in subdivision (i) of this subparagraph.

(*a*) If wages are paid biweekly, the weekly rate of wage payments shall be one-half of the biweekly wages paid.

Reg. § 1.105-4(e)(5)

(*b*) If the employee is paid semimonthly, the weekly rate of wage payments shall be the semimonthly wages paid multiplied by 24 and divided by 52.

(*c*) If wages are paid monthly, the weekly rate of wage payments shall be the monthly wages paid multiplied by 12 and divided by 52.

(*d*) If wages are paid on the basis of a pay period other than a period described in (*a*) through (*c*) of this subdivision, the weekly rate of wage payments shall be determined by ascertaining the annual rate of wage payments and dividing by 52.

(*e*) For the purpose of this subparagraph, if separate portions of an employee's wages are paid on the basis of different pay periods, the weekly rate or weekly rate of wage payments of each portion of wages paid with respect to each

pay period shall first be determined under the rules set forth in (*a*) through (*d*) of this subdivision and the average weekly rate of each portion of wages, determined in accordance with the rules set forth in subdivision (i) of this subparagraph, shall be aggregated to determine the employee's "regular weekly rate of wages" for purposes of section 105(d).

(v) The provisions of subdivisions (i), (iii) and (iv) of this subparagraph may be illustrated by the following examples:

Example (1). Employee A is a salesman who is paid a basic salary of $60 per week and, in addition, is paid commissions on a weekly basis. A became ill and did not report for work beginning Monday, February 17, 1964. For the four-week period preceding the commencement of the period of absence, A was paid the following:

Week of	Basic Salary	Commissions	Total Weekly Wages
Jan. 20, 1964	$60	$10	$ 70
Jan. 27, 1964	60	50	110
Feb. 3, 1964	60	30	90
Feb. 10, 1964	60	40	100
Total four-week wages			$370

A's wages, under the rules set forth in subdivision (iii) of this subparagraph, consist of basic salary plus commissions. Since the amount of A's average weekly wages paid for the last four weekly periods falling within the four pay periods immediately preceding the commencement of his period of absence from work is $92.50 ($370 ÷ 4), such amount is considered as the "regular weekly rate of wages" (as computed under subdivision (i) of this subparagraph) for purposes of section 105(d).

Example (2). Assume, in example (1), that A normally works five days during each week (Monday through Friday) and that he was also absent from work for any reason from Monday, February 3, 1964, through Wednesday, February 5, 1964. Since A was absent from work for three normal working days during the pay period of February 3, 1964, and was paid a lesser amount of wages for such pay period than in the immediately preceding pay period during which he was not absent from work (week of January 27), the weekly pay period beginning January 27, 1964 is substituted for the weekly pay period beginning February 3, 1964 in the determination of "regular weekly rate of wages" (as computed under subdivision (i) of this subparagraph) for purposes of

section 105(d). The regular weekly rate of wages" is calculated to be $97.50, as follows:

Week of:	Total Wages
February 10	$100
January 27 (substitute for week of Feb. 3)	110
January 27	110
January 20	70

$390 ÷ 4 = $97.50

Example (3). Employee B is a salesman who is paid a basic salary of $75 and, in addition, is paid commissions for semimonthly periods ending on the 15th day and the last day of each month. He was absent from work on account of a personal injury beginning Monday, February 17, 1964. He was paid the following amounts:

Pay Period	Salary	Commissions	Total Wages
Feb. 1-15, 1964	$75	$60	$135
Jan. 16-31, 1964	75	50	125

The four weekly periods falling within full pay periods preceding the commencement of the period of absence are the weeks beginning February 9, February 2, January 26, and January 19. B's wages are converted to weekly rates of wage payments per pay period in accordance with the rule set forth in subdivision (iv)(*b*) of this subparagraph as follows:

Reg. § 1.105-4(e)(5)

From February 1, 1964—February 15, 1964, inclusive:

135×24 =   \$3,240.00   (annual rate)

$$\frac{\$3,240.00}{52} = \$62.31 \text{ (weekly rate)}$$

From January 16-31, inclusive:

125×24 =   \$3,000.00   (annual rate)

$$\frac{\$3,000.00}{52} = \$57.69 \text{ (weekly rate)}$$

The weekly rates are then used in determining the wages for four weekly periods falling within the pay periods immediately preceding the commencement of B's absence. B's "regular weekly rate of wages" (as computed under subdivision (i) of this subparagraph) is calculated to be \$60.17, as follows:

February 9-15, inclusive \$62.31
February 2-8, inclusive 62.31
January 26-February 1,
inclusive
(6/7 × \$57.69 + 1/7 ×
\$62.31) 58.35
January 19-25, inclusive 57.69

$$\$240.66 \div 4 = \$60.17$$

Example (4). Employee C is paid semimonthly on the 5th and 20th of each month and he began working for his present employer at the beginning of the semimonthly pay period commencing Tuesday, January 21, 1964. C received total wages of \$200 for the pay period of January 21, 1964 through February 5, 1964, inclusive. He was not absent during that pay period. C became sick and was absent from work beginning February 7, 1964. Since employee C does not have four weekly periods falling within a full pay period or full pay periods preceding his absence, the average wages for the last two weekly periods falling within such full pay period will be C's "regular weekly rate of wages" (as computed under subdivision (i) of this subparagraph) for purposes of section 105(d), determined to be \$92.31, as follows:

200×24 = \$4,800   (annual rate)

$$\frac{\$4,800}{52} = \$92.31 \text{ (weekly rate)}$$

Example (5). Employee D, an office worker, is paid weekly and is expected to work five days during each week. He has been employed by his present employer for three weeks, but has been absent from work for three normal work days in each of the weeks preceding his illness. He became ill and was absent from work on Monday, February 17, 1964. During the weekly pay period immediately preceding his absence (week of February 10) D was paid \$48 salary. He was paid for two working days during such weekly pay period. D's "regular weekly rate of wages" (as computed under subdivision (i) of this subparagraph), is calculated to be \$120.00, determined as follows:

$$\frac{\$48 \text{ (total wages)} \times 5 \text{ (normal work days in week)}}{2 \text{ (number of work days for which wages were paid)}} = \$120.00$$

Example (6). Employee E is an hourly worker who is paid a salary of \$1.25 per hour. E is paid basic salary on a biweekly basis for the periods beginning every other Thursday and ending every other Wednesday. E is also paid monthly for his overtime work and is compensated for such work at one and one-half times the hourly rate. E worked 16 hours of overtime for his employer during the month of January. E was injured and could not report for work on Friday, February 21, 1964. E returned to work on Monday, March 16, 1964. E was paid as follows for the pay periods indicated:

Pay Period	Reg.	Over-time	Reg.	Over-time	Total Salary
		Hours		*Salary Per Hour*	
Month of Jan. 1964	—	16	—	\$1.875	\$ 30.00
Jan. 23-Feb. 5, 1964, inclusive	80	—	\$1.25	—	100.00
Feb. 6-19, 1964, inclusive	80	—	1.25	—	100.00

Under the rule set forth in subdivision (iv)(e) of this subparagraph, the weekly rates of payment of salary and overtime must be determined separately. Since basic salary is paid biweekly, the weekly rate of payment is determined to be one-half of \$100.00, or \$50.00. The full pay period immediately preceding the commencement of E's absence for overtime compensation ended on January 31, 1964. E's overtime earnings are converted to a weekly rate for such period, as follows:

$ 30.00   (overtime pay) × 12 =   \$360.00   (annual rate)

$$\frac{\$360.00}{52} = \$ 6.93 \text{ (weekly rate)}$$

Reg. § 1.105-4(e)(5)

The average wages for the last four weekly periods falling within pay periods immediately preceding the commencement of E's absence with respect to basic salary (weeks of February 13, 6, January 30, and 23) is $50.00. The average wages for the last four weekly periods falling within the pay period immediately preceding the commencement of E's absence with respect to overtime compensation (weeks of January 25, 18, 11, and 4) is $6.93. Accordingly, E's "regular weekly rate of wages" (as computed under subdivision (i) of this subparagraph) for the purpose of section 105(d) is $56.93.

(6)(i) Amounts paid under a wage continuation plan must be converted to a weekly rate in order to determine the percentage of benefits paid in relation to the employee's "regular weekly rate of wages", since such percentage is used in determining the waiting period, if any, after which an exclusion is allowable under section 105(d). In order to calculate the weekly rate at which benefits are being paid, reference is made to the particular wage continuation plan. If, in the usual operation of the plan, benefits are paid for the same periods as regular wages, then the pay period of such benefits shall be the period for which a payment of wages is ordinarily made to the employee by the employer. If plan benefits are ordinarily paid for different periods than regular wages, then the pay period of such benefits shall be the period for which payment of such benefits is ordinarily made.

(ii) The weekly rate at which the benefits are paid under a wage continuation plan shall be determined in accordance with the following rules:

(a) If benefits are paid on the basis of a weekly pay period, the weekly rate at which such benefits are paid shall be the weekly amount of such benefits.

(b) If benefits are paid on the basis of a biweekly pay period, the weekly rate at which such benefits are paid shall be one-half of the biweekly rate.

(c) If benefits are paid on the basis of a semimonthly pay period, the weekly rate at which such benefits are paid shall be the semimonthly rate multiplied by 24 and divided by 52.

(d) If benefits are paid on the basis of a monthly pay period, the weekly rate at which such benefits are paid shall be the monthly rate multiplied by 12 and divided by 52.

(e) If benefits are paid on the basis of a period other than a period described in (a) through (d) of this subdivision the weekly rate at which such benefits are paid shall be determined by ascertaining the annual rate at which such benefits are paid and dividing such annual rate by 52.

(iii) The principles of subdivisions (i) and (ii) of this subparagraph may be illustrated by the following example:

Example. A's employer maintains a noncontributory plan which provides for a monthly benefit of $400 during periods of absence from work due to personal injury or sickness. A, a salesman, receives regular salary of $520 per calendar month plus commissions, depending upon the amount of sales made by A during the month. During the month of January 1964, A was paid commissions of $180. A received a total benefit of $200 for an absence of two weeks because of illness occurring in February 1964. He was not hospitalized. Since benefits under the salary continuation plan are paid for the same period as regular wages, the pay period of the plan is monthly. A's "regular weekly rate of wages", determined in accordance

with the rules set forth in subparagraph (5)(i) is $161.54 $\frac{(\$700 \times 12)}{52}$. For

purposes of determining the percentage of benefits paid in relation to A's "regular weekly rate of wages", the weekly rate of the benefits is calculated to be $92.31, as follows:

$400   (monthly rate) × 12 = $4,800 annual rate)

$$\frac{\$4800}{52} = \$92.31 \text{ (weekly rate)}$$

Since $92.31 does not exceed 75 percent of A's "regular weekly rate of wages", A is entitled to an exclusion under section 105(d) for the second week of absence, subject to the other limitations provided in this section.

(iv) For the purpose of determining whether or not the rate of benefits paid under a wage continuation plan for a period of absence exceeds 75 percent of the employee's "regular weekly rate of wages" (as determined under subparagraph (5) of this paragraph), it is necessary

to ascertain the average percentage of benefits paid in relation to the employee's "regular weekly rate of wages" for the first 30 calendar days in the period of absence. Such percentage is derived from a fraction, the numerator of which is the sum of benefits paid (attributable to employer contributions) for the period of absence occurring within the first 30 calendar days, and the denominator of which is the collective sum of the employee's "regular weekly rate of wages" during such period. This rule may be illustrated by the following examples:

Example (1). Employee A is paid a semi-monthly basic salary of $150 plus commissions. He normally works five days during each week (Monday through Friday). During the month of January 1964, A received wages of $150 plus commissions of $66.67 for each of the semi-monthly pay periods. A became ill on Monday, February 3, 1964, and as a result was absent from work until Monday, February 17, 1964, but was not hospitalized. Under the noncontributory wage continuation plan of A's employer, A received no benefits for the first three working days' absence (Monday through Wednesday) and was paid benefits at the rate of $100 a week thereafter. A's "regular weekly rate of wages", determined under the rules set forth in subparagraph (5) of this paragraph, is $100. A is considered to have received average benefits at a rate of 70 percent of his "regular weekly rate of wages", computed as follows:

(1) Week of absence	(2) Benefits paid	(3) Regular weekly rate of wages
1—Feb. 3	$ 40	$100
2—Feb. 10	100	100
Totals	$140	$200

Average percentage of benefits paid— $\dfrac{140}{200}$ = 70%. Accordingly, A may exclude amounts attributable to the second week of absence, subject to the other limitations of section 105(d).

Example (2). Assume, in example (1), that A did not return to work until Thursday, February 20, 1964. A is considered to have received average weekly benefits at the rate of 76.92 percent of his "regular" weekly rate of wages", computed as follows:

(1) Week of absence	(2) Benefits paid	(3) Regular weekly rate of wages
1—Feb. 3	$ 40	$100
2—Feb. 10	100	100
2³⁄₅—Feb. 17	¹ 60	¹ 60
Totals	$200	$260

¹ Three-fifths of 100.

Average percentage of benefits paid— $\dfrac{200}{260}$ = 76.92%. Accordingly, A would not be permitted any exclusion under section 105(d).

(v) If with respect to any pay period or portion thereof the employee receives amounts under two or more wage continuation plans (whether such plans are maintained by or for the same employers or by different employers), the weekly rate for purposes of section 105(d) shall be the sum of the weekly rates received under all plans. This rule may be illustrated by the following example:

Example. An employee who is absent because of personal injuries or sickness receives $100 biweekly under wage continuation plan A maintained by his employer. He contributes one-half of the premiums for maintenance of the plan. Under wage continuation plan B maintained by his employer the employee receives $400 monthly. Plan B is noncontributory. The weekly rate at which benefits are paid for the purpose of section 105(d) is computed as follows:

Plan A— $\dfrac{\$100}{2}$ =	$ 50.00	(weekly rate)
	25.00	(less amount attributable to employee contributions (½))
	$ 25.00	(weekly rate of Plan A)
Plan B— $\dfrac{\$400 \times 12}{52}$ =	$ 92.31	(weekly rate of Plan B)
	$117.31	(combined weekly rate at which benefits are paid)

Reg. § 1.105-4(e)(6)

The $25 attributable to contributions made by the employee under Plan A would be subject to section 104(a)(3).

(f) *Amount of exclusion for periods of absence commencing after December 31, 1963* —(1) *In general.* Amounts received under a wage continuation plan attributable to periods of absence commencing after December 31, 1963, and which are not excludable from gross income as being attributable to contributions of the employee (see § 1.105-1) are excludable from gross income of the employee to the extent that such amounts do not exceed—

(i) A weekly rate of $75, during the first 30 calendar days in the period of absence; and

(ii) A weekly rate of $100, after the first 30 calendar days in the period of absence.

For example, an employee who normally works five days during each week is absent from work for two days, is hospitalized during his absence, and receives $75 under his employer's wage continuation plan, which amount is at a rate of 75 percent of his "regular weekly rate of wages". The employee cannot exclude the entire $75 under section 105(d), if the weekly rate of such benefits exceeds $75.

(2) *Daily exclusion.* An employee receiving payments under a wage continuation plan must, in order to determine the amount of the exclusion under section 105(d), compute the daily rate of the benefits. Such daily rate is determined, for amounts attributable to the first 30 calendar days in the period of absence, by dividing the weekly rate at which benefits are paid (as determined under paragraph (e)(6)(ii) of this section), or the maximum weekly rate at which wage continuation payments are excludable ($75), whichever is lower, by the number of work days in a normal work week. In the case of amounts attributable to days in a period of absence in excess of 30 calendar days, the daily rate for such period is determined by dividing the weekly rate at which benefits are paid (as determined under paragraph (e)(6)(ii) of this section), or the maximum weekly rate at which wage continuation payments are excludable ($100), whichever is lower, by the number of work days in a normal work week. The daily rate or daily rates of exclusion are then multiplied by the number of normal work days in the period of absence for which an exclusion is allowable in order to determine the total allowable exclusion. These rules may be illustrated by the following examples:

Example (1). Employee A is a salesman receiving salary and commissions on a weekly basis.

His employer maintains a noncontributory wage continuation plan which provides for the continuation of A's basic salary of $80 per week during periods of absence. A was absent from work on account of sickness from Monday, February 3, 1964, through Sunday, March 15, 1964, but was not hospitalized. His normal work week is from Monday through Friday. The weekly amount of benefits paid to A ($80) does not exceed 75 percent of his "regular weekly rate of wages" as defined in paragraph (e)(5) of this section. Under section 105(d), the daily rate of exclusion for amounts attributable to the first 30 calendar days in the period of absence, excluding the first 7 days thereof (Monday, February 10, 1964, through Tuesday, March 3, 1964, inclusive) is limited to $15 ($75, maximum weekly rate of exclusion divided by 5 (number of normal work days in week)). The daily rate of exclusion for amounts attributable to the period of absence in excess of 30 calendar days (Wednesday, March 4, 1964, through Sunday, March 15, 1964, inclusive) is limited to $16 ($80, weekly rate of benefits divided by 5). Thus, the total exclusion permitted to employee A by section 105(d) is $383.00 ($15 × 17 work days ($255) + $16 × 8 work days ($128)).

Example (2). Assume the facts in example (1) except that A is paid benefits at the rate of $500 a month during periods of absence. The weekly rate of the benefits computed under the rules stated in paragraph (e)(6)(ii) of this section is $115.38, which amount does not exceed 75 percent of his "regular weekly rate of wages" as defined in paragraph (e)(5) of this section. Under section 105(d), the daily rate of exclusion for amounts attributable to the first 30 calendar days in the period of absence, excluding the first 7 days thereof (Monday, February 10, 1964, through Tuesday, March 3, 1964, inclusive) is limited to $15 ($75, maximum weekly rate of exclusion divided by 5). The daily rate of exclusion for amounts attributable to the period of absence in excess of 30 calendar days (Wednesday, March 4, 1964, through Sunday, March 15, 1964, inclusive) is limited to $20 ($100, maximum weekly rate of exclusion divided by 5). Thus, the total exclusion permitted to employee A by section 105(d) is $415.00 ($15 × 17 work days ($255) + $20 × 8 work days ($160)).

Example (3). Employee B, an office worker works five days during each week (Monday through Friday) and receives a salary of $85 per week. His employer maintains a noncontributory wage continuation plan which provides for no benefits during the first three days of absence, the continuation of full salary for one week thereafter and benefits at the rate of $65 per week thereafter. B was absent from work on account of sickness from Monday, March 16, 1964, through Tuesday, March 31, 1964, and was hospitalized from Wednesday, March 18, through Tuesday,

Period of Absence	Weekly Rate of Benefits
March 16-18	0
March 19-25	$85
March 26-31	65

(g) *Definitions.* The term "personal injury" as used in this section, means an externally caused sudden hurt or damage to the body brought about by an identifiable event. The term "sickness" as used in this section, means mental illnesses and all bodily infirmities and disorders other than "personal injuries". Diseases, whether resulting from the occupation or otherwise, are not considered personal injuries, but they are treated as a sickness. [Reg. § 1.105-4.]

☐ [*T.D. 6169, 4-13-56. Amended by T.D. 6177, 5-29-56, T.D. 6485, 7-29-60, T.D. 6770, 11-16-64, T.D. 6888, 7-5-66, T.D. 7043, 6-1-70 and T.D. 7352, 4-9-75.*]

[Reg. § 1.105-5]

§ 1.105-5. **Accident and health plans.**—(a) *In general.* Sections 104(a)(3) and 105(b), (c), and (d) exclude from gross income certain amounts received through accident or health insurance. Section 105(e) provides that for purposes of sections 104 and 105 amounts received through an accident or health plan for employees, and amounts received from a sickness and disability fund for employees maintained under the law of a State, a Territory, or the District of Columbia, shall be treated as amounts received through accident or health insurance. In general, an accident or health plan is an arrangement for the payment of amounts to employees in the event of personal injuries or sickness. A plan may cover one or more employees, and there may be different plans for different employees or classes of employees. An accident or health plan may be either insured or noninsured, and it is not necessary that the plan be in writing or that the employee's rights to benefits under the plan be enforceable. However, if the employee's rights are not enforceable, an amount will be deemed to be received under a plan only if, on the date the employee became sick or injured, the employee was covered by a plan (or a program, policy, or custom having the effect of a plan) providing for the payment of amounts to the employee in the event of personal injuries or

March 24. B received total benefits of $137 for the period of absence, which does not exceed 75 percent of his "regular weekly rate of wages" as determined under paragraph (e)(5) of this section. B is permitted an exclusion under section 105(d) of $127 calculated as follows:

Maximum Weekly Rate of Exclusion	Daily Rate of Exclusion	Days of Absence in Period	Maximum Exclusion
$75	0	3	0
75	$15.00	5	$ 75
75	13.00	4	52

Total Exclusion $127

sickness, and notice or knowledge of such plan was reasonably available to the employee. It is immaterial who makes payment of the benefits provided by the plan. For example, payment may be made by the employer, a welfare fund, a State sickness or disability benefits fund, an association of employers or employees, or by an insurance company.

(b) *Self-employed individuals.* Under section 105(g), a self-employed individual is not treated as an employee for purposes of section 105. Therefore, for example, benefits paid under an accident or health plan as referred to in section 105(e) to or on behalf of an individual who is self-employed in the business with respect to which the plan is established will not be treated as received through accident and health insurance for purposes of sections 104(a)(3) and 105. [Reg. § 1.105-5.]

☐ [*T.D. 6169, 4-13-56. Amended by T.D. 6722, 4-13-64.*]

[Reg. § 1.105-6]

§ 1.105-6. **Special rules for employees retired before January 27, 1975.**—(a) *Application of section 105(d) to amounts received as retirement annuities.* An employee who retired from work before January 27, 1975, receiving payments under his employer-established plan (to which § 1.72-15(a) applies) [,] which payments were not treated as amounts received under a wage continuation plan for purposes of section 105(d), may, as of the date the employee retired, treat such plan as such a wage continuation plan to the extent such payments are received prior to mandatory retirement age (as described in § 1.105-4(a)(3)(i)(B)), if—

(1) His employer had in operation at the time of his retirement a program providing accident and health benefits under a wage continuation plan to which section 105(d) would apply;

(2) The employer certifies, under procedures approved in advance under paragraph (c) of this section, that the employee would have been eligible for wage continuation benefits, under the

Reg. § 1.105-5(a)

terms and conditions of his employer's plan, because of personal injuries or sickness;

(3) At the time of the employee's retirement there was no substantive difference between the benefits being actually received and the benefits he would have received had he retired under his employer's wage continuation plan; and

(4) The employee agrees to the adjustments and conditions required by the Commissioner with respect to amounts excluded under section 72(b) or (d) in taxable years ending before January 27, 1975.

(b) *Filing requirements.* (1) The certification required in paragraph (a)(2) and the agreement required in paragraph (a)(4) of this section shall be filed on or before April 15, 1977, with the return, or timely amended return or claim, made for the taxable year in which the employee reached retirement age as described in § 1.79-2(b)(3), or, for the first taxable year for which the taxpayer files an income tax return claiming an exclusion under section 105(d), as provided in paragraph (a) of this section.

(2) The Commissioner may prescribe a form and instructions with respect to the agreement provided for in paragraph (a)(4) of this section.

(c) *Employer certification*—(1) *Advance approval of procedures.* Any reasonable and consistently applied procedures, approved in advance by the Internal Revenue Service, which require the employee to provide the employer or the insurer with medical documentation sufficient to show that an illness or disability existed as of the date of the employee's retirement, which would have entitled him to retire on account of personal injuries or sickness alone, are sufficient for purposes of this paragraph.

(2) *Place of submission.* Request for advance approval of procedures for certification shall be submitted to the district director.

(d) *Cross reference.* For special rules pertaining to taxpayers retired on disability before January 27, 1975, see § 1.72-15(i). [Reg. § 1.105-6.]

□ [*T.D. 7352, 4-9-75.*]

[Reg. § 1.105-11]

§ 1.105-11. Self-insured medical reimbursement plan.—(a) *In general.* Under section 105(a), amounts received by an employee through a self-insured medical reimbursement plan which are attributable to contributions of the employer, or are paid by the employer, are included in the employee's gross income unless such amounts are excludable under section 105(b). For amounts reimbursed to a highly compensated individual to be fully excludable from such individual's gross income under section 105(b), the plan must sat-

isfy the requirements of section 105(h) and this section. Section 105(h) is not satisfied if the plan discriminates in favor of highly compensated individuals as to eligibility to participate or benefits. All or a portion of the reimbursements or payments on behalf of such individuals under a discriminatory plan are not excludable from gross income under section 105(b). However, benefits paid to participants who are not highly compensated individuals may be excluded from gross income if the requirements of section 105(b) are satisfied, even if the plan is discriminatory.

(b) *Self-insured medical reimbursement plan*—(1) *General rule*—(i) *Definition.* A self-insured medical reimbursement plan is a separate written plan for the benefit of employees which provides for reimbursement of employee medical expenses referred to in section 105(b). A plan or arrangement is self-insured unless reimbursement is provided under an individual or group policy of accident or health insurance issued by a licensed insurance company or under an arrangement in the nature of a prepaid health care plan that is regulated under federal or state law in a manner similar to the regulation of insurance companies. Thus, for example, a plan of a health maintenance organization, established under the Health Maintenance Organization Act of 1973, would qualify as a prepaid health care plan. In addition, this section applies to a self-insured medical reimbursement plan, determined in accordance with the rules of this section, maintained by an employee organization described in section 501(c)(9).

(ii) *Shifting of risk.* A plan underwritten by a policy of insurance or a prepaid health care plan that does not involve the shifting of risk to an unrelated third party is considered self-insured for purposes of this section. Accordingly, a cost-plus policy or a policy which in effect merely provides administrative or bookkeeping services is considered self-insured for purposes of this section. However, a plan is not considered self-insured merely because one factor the insurer uses in determining the premium is the employer's prior claims experience.

(iii) *Captive insurance company.* A plan underwritten by a policy of insurance issued by a captive insurance company is not considered self-insured for purposes of this section if for the plan year the premiums paid by companies unrelated to the captive insurance company equal or exceed 50 percent of the total premiums received and the policy of insurance is similar to policies sold to such unrelated companies.

(2) *Other rules.* The rules of this section apply to a self-insured portion of an employer's medical plan or arrangement even if the plan is in

Reg. § 1.105-11(b)(2)

part underwritten by insurance. For example, if an employer's medical plan reimburses employees for benefits not covered under the insured portion of an overall plan, or for deductible amounts under the insured portions, such reimbursement is subject to the rules of this section. However, a plan which reimburses employees for premiums paid under an insured plan is not subject to this section. In addition, medical expense reimbursements not described in the plan are not paid pursuant to a plan for the benefit of employees, and therefore are not excludable from gross income under section 105(b). Such reimbursements will not affect the determination of whether or not a plan is discriminatory.

(c) *Prohibited discrimination*—(1) *In general.* A self-insured medical reimbursement plan does not satisfy the requirements of section 105(h) and this paragraph for a plan year unless the plan satisfies subparagraphs (2) and (3) of this paragraph. However, a plan does not fail to satisfy the requirements of this paragraph merely because benefits under the plan are offset by benefits paid under a self-insured or insured plan of the employer or another employer, or by benefits paid under Medicare or other Federal or State law or similar foreign law. A self-insured plan may take into account the benefits provided under another plan only to the extent that the type of benefit subject to reimbursement is the same under both plans. For example, an amount reimbursed to an employee for a hospital expense under a medical plan maintained by the employer of the employee's spouse may be offset against the self-insured benefit where the self-insured plan covering the employee provides the same type of hospital benefit.

(2) *Eligibility to participate*—(i) *Percentage test.* A plan satisfies the requirements of this subparagraph if it benefits—

(A) Seventy percent or more of all employees, or

(B) Eighty percent or more of all the employees who are eligible to benefit under the plan if 70 percent or more of all employees are eligible to benefit under the plan.

(ii) *Classification test.* A plan satisfies the requirements of this subparagraph if it benefits such employees as qualify under a classification of employees set up by the employer which is found by the Internal Revenue Service not to be discriminatory in favor of highly compensated individuals. In general, this determination will be made based upon the facts and circumstances of each case, applying the same standards as are applied under section 410(b)(1)(B) (relating to qualified pension, profit-sharing and stock bonus

plans), without regard to the special rules in section 401(a)(5) concerning eligibility to participate.

(iii) *Exclusion of certain employees.* Under section 105(h)(3), for purposes of this subparagraph (2), there may be excluded from consideration:

(A) Employees who have not completed 3 years of service prior to the beginning of the plan year. For purposes of this section years of service may be determined by any method that is reasonable and consistent. A determination made in the same manner as (and not requiring service in excess of how) a year of service is determined under section 410 (a)(3) shall be deemed to be reasonable. For purposes of the 3-year rule, all of an employee's years of service with the employer prior to a separation from service are not taken into account. For purposes of the 3-year rule, an employee's years of service prior to age 25, as a part-time or seasonal employee, as a member of a collective bargaining unit, or as a nonresident alien, as each is described in this subdivision, are not excluded by reason of being so described from counting towards satisfaction of the rule. In addition, if the employer is a predecessor employer (determined in a manner consistent with section 414(a)), service for such predecessor is treated as service for the employer.

(B) Employees who have not attained age 25 prior to the beginning of the plan year.

(C) Part-time employees whose customary weekly employment is less than 35 hours, if other employees in similar work with the same employer (or, if no employees of the employer are in similar work, in similar work in the same industry and location) have substantially more hours, and seasonal employees whose customary annual employment is less than 9 months, if other employees in similar work with the same employer (or, if no employees of the employer are in similar work, in similar work in the same industry and location) have substantially more months. Notwithstanding the preceding sentence, any employee whose customary weekly employment is less than 25 hours or any employee whose customary annual employment is less than 7 months may be considered as a part-time or seasonal employee.

(D) Employees who are included in a unit of employees covered by an agreement between employee representatives and one or more employers which the Commissioner finds to be a collective bargaining agreement, if accident and health benefits were the subject of good faith bargaining between such employee representatives and such employer or employers. For purposes of determining whether such bargaining

Reg. § 1.105-11(c)(1)

occurred, it is not material that such employees are not covered by another medical plan or that the plan was not considered in such bargaining.

(E) Employees who are nonresident aliens and who receive no earned income (within the meaning of section 911(b) and the regulations thereunder) from the employer which constitutes income from sources within the United States (within the meaning of section 861(a)(3) and the regulations thereunder).

(3) *Nondiscriminatory benefits*—(i) *In general.* In general, benefits subject to reimbursement under a plan must not discriminate in favor of highly compensated individuals. Plan benefits will not satisfy the requirements of this subparagraph unless all the benefits provided for participants who are highly compensated individuals are provided for all other participants. In addition, all the benefits available for the dependents of employees who are highly compensated individuals must also be available on the same basis for the dependents of all other employees who are participants. A plan that provides optional benefits to participants will be treated as providing a single benefit with respect to the benefits covered by the option provided that (A) all eligible participants may elect any of the benefits covered by the option and (B) there are either no required employee contributions or the required employee contributions are the same amount. This test is applied to the benefits subject to reimbursement under the plan rather than the actual benefit payments of claims under the plan. The presence or absence of such discrimination will be determined by considering the type of benefit subject to reimbursement provided highly compensated individuals, as well as the amount of the benefit subject to reimbursement. A plan may establish a maximum limit for the amount of reimbursement which may be paid a participant for any single benefit, or combination of benefits. However, any maximum limit attributable to employer contributions must be uniform for all participants and for all dependents of employees who are participants and may not be modified by reason of a participant's age or years of service. In addition, if a plan covers employees who are highly compensated individuals, and the type or the amount of benefits subject to reimbursement under the plan are in proportion to employee compensation, the plan discriminates as to benefits.

(ii) *Discriminatory operation.* Not only must a plan not discriminate on its face in providing benefits in favor of highly compensated individuals, the plan also must not discriminate in favor of such employees in actual operation. The determination of whether plan benefits discriminate in operation in favor of highly compensated individuals is made on the basis of the facts and circumstances of each case. A plan is not considered discriminatory merely because highly compensated individuals participating in the plan utilize a broad range of plan benefits to a greater extent than do other employees participating in the plan. In addition, if a plan (or a particular benefit provided by a plan) is terminated, the termination would cause the plan benefits to be discriminatory if the duration of the plan (or benefit) has the effect of discriminating in favor of highly compensated individuals. Accordingly, the prohibited discrimination may occur where the duration of a particular benefit coincides with the period during which a highly compensated individual utilizes the benefit.

(iii) *Retired employees.* To the extent that an employer provides benefits under a self-insured medical reimbursement plan to a retired employee that would otherwise be excludible from gross income under section 105(b), determined without regard to section 105(h), such benefits shall not be considered a discriminatory benefit under this paragraph (c). The preceding sentence shall not apply to a retired employee who was a highly compensated individual unless the type, and the dollar limitations, of benefits provided retired employees who were highly compensated individuals are the same for all other retired participants. If this subdivision applies to a retired participant, that individual is not considered an employee for purposes of determining the highest paid 25 percent of all employees under paragraph (d) of this section solely by reason of receiving such plan benefits.

(4) *Multiple plans, etc.*—(i) *General rule.* An employer may designate two or more plans as constituting a single plan that is intended to satisfy the requirements of section 105(h)(2) and paragraph (c) of this section, in which case all plans so designated shall be considered as a single plan in determining whether the requirements of such section are satisfied by each of the separate plans. A determination that the combination of plans so designated does not satisfy such requirements does not preclude a determination that one or more of such plans, considered separately, satisfies such requirements. A single plan document may be utilized by an employer for two or more separate plans provided that the employer designates the plans that are to be considered separately and the applicable provisions of each separate plan.

(ii) *Other rules.* If the designated combined plan discriminates as to eligibility to participate or benefits, the amount of the excess

Reg. § 1.105-11(c)(4)

reimbursement will be determined under the rules of section 105(h)(7) and paragraph (e) of this section by taking into account all reimbursements made under the combined plan.

(iii) *H.M.O. participants.* For purposes of section 105(h)(2)(A) and paragraph (c)(2) of this section, a self-insured plan will be deemed to benefit an employee who has enrolled in a health maintenance organization (HMO) that is offered on an optional basis by the employer in lieu of coverage under the self-insured plan if, with respect to that employee, the employer's contributions to the HMO plan equal or exceed those that would be made to the self-insured plan, and if the HMO plan is designated in accordance with subdivision (i) with the self-insured plan as a single plan. For purposes of section 105(h) and this section, except as provided in the preceding sentence, employees covered by, and benefits under, the HMO plan are not treated as part of the self-insured plan.

(d) *Highly compensated individuals defined.* For purposes of section 105(h) and this section, the term "highly compensated individuals" means an individual who is—

(1) One of the 5 highest paid officers,

(2) A shareholder who owns (with the application of section 318) more than 10 percent in value of the stock of the employer, or

(3) Among the highest paid 25 percent of all employees (including the 5 highest paid officers, but not including employees excludable under paragraph (c)(2)(iii) of this section who are not participants in any self-insured medical reimbursement plan of the employer, whether or not designated as a single plan under paragraph (c)(4) of this section, or in a health maintenance organization plan).

The status of an employee as an officer or stockholder is determined with respect to a particular benefit on the basis of the employee's officer status or stock ownership at the time during the plan year at which the benefit is provided. In calculating the highest paid 25 percent of all employees, the number of employees included will be rounded to the next highest number. For example, if there are 5 employees, the top two are in the highest paid 25 percent. The level of an employee's compensation is determined on the basis of the employee's compensation for the plan year. For purposes of the preceding sentence, fiscal year plans may determine employee compensation on the basis of the calendar year ending within the plan year.

(e) *Excess reimbursement of highly compensated individual* —(1) *In general.* For purposes of section 105(h) and this section, a reimbursement paid to a highly compensated individual is an excess reimbursement if it is paid pursuant to a plan that fails to satisfy the requirements of paragraph (c)(2) or (c)(3) for the plan year. The amount reimbursed to a highly compensated individual which constitutes an excess reimbursement is not excludable from such individual's gross income under section 105(b).

(2) *Discriminatory benefit.* In the case of a benefit available to highly compensated individuals but not to all other participants (or which otherwise discriminates in favor of highly compensated individuals as opposed to other participants), the amount of excess reimbursement equals the total amount reimbursed to the highly compensated individual with respect to the benefit.

(3) *Discriminatory coverage.* In the case of benefits (other than discriminatory benefits described in subparagraph (2)) paid to a highly compensated individual under a plan which fails to satisfy the requirements of paragraph (c)(2) relating to nondiscrimination in eligibility to participate, the amount of excess reimbursement is determined by multiplying the total amount reimbursed to the individual by a fraction. The numerator of the fraction is the total amount reimbursed during that plan year to all highly compensated individuals. The denominator of the fraction is the total amount reimbursed during that plan year to all participants. In computing the fraction and the total amount reimbursed to the individual, discriminatory benefits described in subparagraph (2) are not taken into account. Accordingly, any amount which is included in income by reason of the benefit's not being available to all other participants will not be taken into account.

(4) *Examples.* The provisions of this paragraph are illustrated by the following examples:

Example (1). Corporation M maintains a self-insured medical reimbursement plan which covers all employees. The plan provides the following maximum limits on the amount of benefits subject to reimbursement: $5,000 for officers and $1,000 for all other participants. During a plan year Employee A, one of the 5 highest paid officers, received reimbursements in the amount of $4,000. Because the amount of benefits provided for highly compensated individuals is not provided for all other participants, the plan benefits are discriminatory. Accordingly, Employee A received an excess reimbursement of $3,000 ($4,000 − $1,000) which constitutes a benefit available to highly compensated individuals, but not to all other participants.

Reg. § 1.105-11(d)(1)

Example (2). Corporation N maintains a self-insured medical reimbursement plan which covers all employees. The plan provides a broad range of medical benefits subject to reimbursement for all participants. However, only the 5 highest paid officers are entitled to dental benefits. During the plan year Employee B, one of the 5 highest paid officers, received dental payments under the plan in the amount of $300. Because dental benefits are provided for highly compensated individuals, and not for all other participants, the plan discriminates as to benefits. Accordingly, Employee B received an excess reimbursement in the amount of $300.

Example (3). Corporation O maintains a self-insured medical reimbursement plan which discriminates as to eligibility by covering only the highest paid 40% of all employees. Benefits subject to reimbursement under the plan are the same for all participants. During a plan year Employee C, a highly compensated individual, received benefits in the amount of $1,000. The amount of excess reimbursement paid Employee C during the plan year will be calculated by multiplying the $1,000 by a fraction determined under subparagraph (3).

Example (4). Corporation P maintains a self-insured medical reimbursement plan for its employees. Benefits subject to reimbursement under the plan are the same for all plan participants. However, the plan fails the eligibility tests of section 105(h)(3)(A) and thereby discriminates as to eligibility. During the 1980 plan year Employee D, a highly compensated individual, was hospitalized for surgery and incurred medical expenses of $4,500 which were reimbursed to D under the plan. During that plan year the Corporation P medical plan paid $50,000 in benefits under the plan, $30,000 of which constituted benefits paid to highly compensated individuals. The amount of excess reimbursement not excludable by D under section 105(b) is $2,700

$$\left(\$4,500 \times \frac{\$30,000}{\$50,000} \right).$$

Example (5). Corporation Q maintains a self-insured medical reimbursement plan for its employees. The plan provides a broad range of medical benefits subject to reimbursement for participants. However, only the five highest paid officers are entitled to dental benefits. In addition, the plan fails the eligibility test of section 105(h)(3)(A) and thereby discriminates as to eligibility. During the calendar 1981 plan year, Employee E, a highly compensated individual, received dental benefits under the plan in the amount of $300, and no other employee received

dental benefits. In addition, Employee E was hospitalized for surgery and incurred medical expenses, reimbursement for which was available to all participants, of $4,500 which were reimbursed to E under the plan. Because dental benefits are only provided for highly compensated individuals, Employee E received an excess reimbursement under paragraph (e)(2) above in the amount of $300. For the 1981 plan year, the Corporation Q medical plan paid $50,300 in total benefits under the plan, $30,300 of which constituted benefits paid to highly compensated individuals. In computing the fraction under paragraph (e)(3), discriminatory benefits described in paragraph (e)(2) are not taken into account. Therefore, the amount of excess reimbursement not excludable to Employee E with respect to the $4,500 of medical expenses incurred is $2,700,

$$\left(\$4,500 \times \frac{\$30,000}{\$50,000} \right)$$

and the total amount of excess reimbursements includable in E's income for 1981 is $3,000.

Example (6). (i) Corporation R maintains a calendar year self-insured medical reimbursement plan which covers all employees. The type of benefits subject to reimbursement under the plan include all medical care expenses as defined in section 213(e). The amount of reimbursement available to any employee for any calendar year is limited to 5 percent of the compensation paid to each employee during the calendar year. The amount of compensation and reimbursement paid to Employees A—F for the calendar year is as follows:

Employee	Compensation	Reimbursable Amount Paid
A	$100,000	$5,000
B	25,000	1,250
C	15,000	750
D	10,000	500
E	10,000	500
F	8,000	400
		$8,400

(ii) Because the amount of benefits subject to reimbursement under the plan is in proportion to employee compensation, the plan discriminates as to benefits. In addition, Employees A and B are highly compensated individuals. The amount of excess reimbursement paid Employees A and B during the year will be determined under paragraph (e)(2). Because benefits in excess of $400 (Employee F's maximum benefit) are provided for highly compensated individuals and not for all other participants, Employees A and B received, respectively, an excess reimbursement of $4,600 and $850.

Reg. § 1.105-11(e)(4)

(f) *Certain controlled groups.* For purposes of applying the provisions of section 105(h) and this section, all employees who are treated as employed by a single employer under section 414(b) and (c), and the regulations thereunder (relating to special rules for qualified pension, profit-sharing and stock bonus plans), shall be treated as employed by a single employer.

(g) *Exception for medical diagnostic procedures*—(1) *In general.* For purposes of applying section 105(h) and this section, reimbursements paid under a plan for medical diagnostic procedures for an employee, but not a dependent, are not considered to be a part of a plan described in this section. The medical diagnostic procedures include routine medical examinations, blood tests, and X-rays. Such procedures do not include expenses incurred for the treatment, cure or testing of a known illness or disability, or treatment or testing for a physical injury, complaint or specific symptom of a bodily malfunction. For example, a routine dental examination with X-rays is a medical diagnostic procedure, but X-rays and treatment for a specific complaint are not. In addition, such procedures do not include any activity undertaken for exercise, fitness, nutrition, recreation, or the general improvement of health unless they are for medical care as defined in section 213(e). The diagnostic procedures must be performed at a facility which provides no services (directly or indirectly) other than medical, and ancillary, services. For purposes of the preceding sentence, physical proximity between a medical facility and nonmedical facilities will not for that reason alone cause the medical facility not to qualify. For example, an employee's annual physical examination conducted at the employee's personal physician's office is not considered a part of the medical reimbursement plan and therefore is not subject to the nondiscrimination requirements. Accordingly, the amount reimbursed may be excludable from the employee's income if the requirements of section 105(b) are satisfied.

(2) *Transportation, etc. expenses.* Transportation expenses primarily for an allowable diagnostic procedure are included within the exception described in this paragraph, but only to the extent they are ordinary and necessary. Transportation undertaken merely for the general improvement of health, or in connection with a vacation, is not within the scope of this exception, nor are any incidental expenses for food or lodging; therefore, amounts reimbursed for such expenses may be excess reimbursements under paragraph (e).

(h) *Time of inclusion.* Excess reimbursements (determined under paragraph (e)) paid to a highly compensated individual for a plan year will be considered as received in the taxable year of the individual in which (or with which) the plan year ends. The particular plan year to which reimbursements relate shall be determined under the plan provisions. In the absence of plan provisions reimbursements shall be attributed to the plan year in which payment is made. For example, under a calendar year plan an excess reimbursement paid to A in 1981 on account of an expense incurred and subject to reimbursement for the 1980 plan year under the terms of the plan will be considered as received in 1980 by A.

(i) *Self-insured contributory plan.* A medical plan subject to this section may provide for employer and employee contributions. See § 1.105-1(c). The tax treatment of reimbursements attributable to employee contributions is determined under section 104(a)(3). The tax treatment of reimbursements attributable to employer contributions is determined under section 105. The amount of reimbursements which are attributable to contributions of the employer shall be determined in accordance with § 1.105-1(e).

(j) *Effective date.* Section 105(h) and this section are effective for taxable years beginning after December 31, 1979 and for amounts reimbursed after December 31, 1979. In determining plan discrimination and the taxability of excess reimbursements made for a plan year beginning in 1979 and ending in 1980, a plan's eligibility and benefit requirements as well as actual reimbursements made in the plan year during 1979, will not be taken into account. In addition, this section does not apply to expenses which are incurred in 1979 and paid in 1980.

(k) *Special rules*—(1) *Relation to cafeteria plans.* If a self-insured medical reimbursement plan is included in a cafeteria plan as described in section 125, the rules of this section will determine the status of a benefit as a taxable or nontaxable benefit, and the rules of section 125 will determine whether an employee is taxed as though he elected all available taxable benefits (including taxable benefits under a discriminatory medical reimbursement plan). This rule is illustrated by the following example:

Example. Corporation M maintains a cafeteria plan described in section 125. Under the plan an officer of the corporation may elect to receive medical benefits provided by a self-insured medical reimbursement plan which is subject to the rules of this section. However, the self-insured medical reimbursement plan fails the nondiscrimination rules under paragraph (c) of this section. Accordingly, the amount of excess reimbursement is taxable to the officer participating in the medical reimbursement plan pursuant to section

105(h) and this section. Therefore, the self-insured medical reimbursement plan will be considered a taxable benefit under section 125 and the regulations thereunder.

(2) *Benefit subject to reimbursement.* For purposes of this section, a benefit subject to reimbursement is a benefit described in the plan under which a claim for reimbursement or for a payment directly to the health service provider may be filed by a plan participant. It does not refer to actual claims or benefit reimbursements paid under a plan. [Reg. § 1.105-11.]

☐ [*T.D.* 7754, 1-13-81.]

[Reg. § 1.106-1]

§ 1.106-1. **Contributions by employer to accident and health plans.**—The gross income of an employee does not include contributions which his employer makes to an accident or health plan for compensation (through insurance or otherwise) to the employee for personal injuries or sickness incurred by him, his spouse, or his dependents, as defined in section 152. The employer may contribute to an accident or health plan either by paying the premium (or a portion of the premium) on a policy of accident or health insurance covering one or more of his employees, or by contributing to a separate trust or fund (including a fund referred to in section 105(e)) which provides accident or health benefits directly or through insurance to one or more of his employees. However, if such insurance policy, trust, or fund provides other benefits in addition to accident or health benefits, section 106 applies only to the portion of the employer's contribution which is allocable to accident or health benefits. See paragraph (d) of § 1.104-1 and §§ 1.105-1 through 1.105-5, inclusive, for regulations relating to exclusion from an employee's gross income of amounts received through accident or health insurance and through accident or health plans. [Reg. § 1.106-1.]

☐ [*T.D.* 6169, 4-13-56.]

[Reg. § 1.107-1]

§ 1.107-1. **Rental value of parsonages.**—(a) In the case of a minister of the gospel, gross income does not include (1) the rental value of a home, including utilities, furnished to him as a part of his compensation, or (2) the rental allowance paid to him as part of his compensation to the extent such allowance is used by him to rent or otherwise provide a home. In order to qualify for the exclusion, the home or rental allowance must be provided as remuneration for services which are ordinarily the duties of a minister of the gospel. In general, the rules provided in § 1.1402(c)-5 will be applicable to such determination. Examples of specific services the perform-

ance of which will be considered duties of a minister for purposes of section 107 include the performance of sacerdotal functions, the conduct of religious worship, the administration and maintenance of religious organizations and their integral agencies, and the performance of teaching and administrative duties at theological seminaries. Also, the service performed by a qualified minister as an employee of the United States (other than as a chaplain in the Armed Forces, whose service is considered to be that of a commissioned officer in his capacity as such, and not as a minister in the exercise of his ministry), or a State, Territory, or possession of the United States, or a political subdivision of any of the foregoing, or the District of Columbia, is in the exercise of his ministry provided the service performed includes such services as are ordinarily the duties of a minister.

(b) For purposes of section 107, the term "home" means a dwelling place (including furnishings) and the appurtenances thereto, such as a garage. The term "rental allowance" means an amount paid to a minister to rent or otherwise provide a home if such amount is designated as rental allowance pursuant to official action taken prior to January 1, 1958, by the employing church or other qualified organization, or if such amount is designated as rental allowance pursuant to official action taken in advance of such payment by the employing church or other qualified organization when paid after December 31, 1957. The designation of an amount as rental allowance may be evidenced in an employment contract, in minutes of or in a resolution by a church or other qualified organization or in its budget, or in any other appropriate instrument evidencing such official action. The designation referred to in this paragraph is a sufficient designation if it permits a payment or a part thereof to be identified as a payment of rental allowance as distinguished from salary or other remuneration.

(c) A rental allowance must be included in the minister's gross income in the taxable year in which it is received, to the extent that such allowance is not used by him during such taxable year to rent or otherwise provide a home. Circumstances under which a rental allowance will be deemed to have been used to rent or provide a home will include cases in which the allowance is expended (1) for rent of a home, (2) for purchase of a home, and (3) for expenses directly related to providing a home. Expenses for food and servants are not considered for this purpose to be directly related to providing a home. Where the minister rents, purchases, or owns a farm or other business property in addition to a home, the portion of the rental allowance expended in connection with the farm or business property shall not be excluded from his gross income. [Reg. § 1.107-1.]

□ [*T.D. 6239, 6-14-57. Amended by T.D. 6691,* 12-2-63.]

[Reg. § 1.108-1]

§ 1.108-1. Stock-for-debt exception not to apply in de minimis cases.—(a) *Overview.* Section 108(e)(8) provides that the common law stock-for-debt exception does not apply if stock issued for indebtedness is nominal or token or if a proportionality test is not met. Paragraph (b) of this section provides rules for the nominal or token determination under section 108(e)(8)(A). Paragraph (c) of this section provides rules for the proportionality test under section 108(e)(8)(B). Paragraph (d) of this section provides certain general rules and definitions. Paragraph (e) of this section provides an effective date.

(b) *Issuance of nominal or token stock.* Under section 108(e)(8)(A), the common law stock-for-debt exception does not apply to indebtedness discharged for stock that is nominal or token. All relevant facts and circumstances must be considered in making this determination. If common and preferred stock are issued for indebtedness, the determination is made separately with respect to the common stock and the preferred stock. The determination of whether common stock issued for unsecured indebtedness is nominal or token is made on an aggregate basis with respect to all common stock issued for unsecured indebtedness in the title 11 case or insolvency workout. Preferred stock issued for unsecured indebtedness is also tested on an aggregate basis with respect to all preferred stock issued for unsecured indebtedness in the title 11 case or insolvency workout.

(c) *Issuance of a disproportionately small amount of stock for unsecured indebtedness*—(1) *Common stock issued for unsecured indebtedness*—(i) *In general.* The common law stock-for-debt exception does not apply to an unsecured indebtedness discharged for common stock in a title 11 case or insolvency workout if the individual common stock ratio does not equal at least one-half of the group common stock ratio.

(ii) *Individual common stock ratio defined.* The individual common stock ratio is the ratio of the value of the common stock issued for an unsecured indebtedness to the amount of the unsecured indebtedness allocated to that common stock. The amount of unsecured indebtedness allocated to the common stock is the amount of the indebtedness for which the common stock is issued (as defined in paragraph (d)(5) of this section), reduced by the amount of other consideration, if

any, transferred in exchange for the indebtedness, including—

(A) The amount of any money;

(B) The issue price (determined under section 1273 or 1274) of any new indebtedness;

(C) With respect to any preferred stock, the amount of indebtedness allocated to the preferred stock under paragraph (c)(2)(ii) of this section; and

(D) The value of any other property, including any disqualified stock.

(iii) *Group common stock ratio defined.* The group common stock ratio is the ratio of the aggregate value of all common stock issued for unsecured indebtedness in the title 11 case or insolvency workout to the aggregate amount of unsecured indebtedness allocated to that common stock. The amount of unsecured indebtedness allocated to the common stock is the aggregate amount of all unsecured indebtedness exchanged for stock or cancelled in the title 11 case or insolvency workout, reduced by the amount of other consideration, if any, issued for that indebtedness, including—

(A) The amount of any money;

(B) The issue price (determined under section 1273 or 1274) of any new indebtedness;

(C) With respect to any preferred stock, the amount of indebtedness allocated to the preferred stock under paragraph (c)(2)(iii) of this section; and

(D) The value of any other property, including any disqualified stock.

(iv) *Example.* The following example illustrates these provisions.

Example. (A) X Corporation has three outstanding debts, Debt 1, Debt 2, and Debt 3. Debts 1 and 2 are unsecured and each has an adjusted issue price of $100,000. Debt 3 is also unsecured, and it has an adjusted issue price of $90,000 and accrued but unpaid interest of $10,000. In a title 11 case, Debt 1 is exchanged for $50,000 cash and $20,000 of common stock, Debt 2 is exchanged for $10,000 cash, and Debt 3 is exchanged for $5,000 common stock. The individual common stock ratio for Debt 1 is 40 percent, which is determined by comparing the value of the common stock issued for the indebtedness ($20,000) to the amount of unsecured indebtedness allocated to that stock ($100,000 adjusted issue price less $50,000 cash received). The individual common stock ratio for Debt 2 is 0 percent because no stock is received in exchange for the indebtedness. The individual common stock ratio for Debt 3 is 5 percent, which is determined by comparing the value of the common stock issued for the indebtedness ($5,000) to the amount of unsecured indebtedness allocated to that stock ($100,000 = $90,000 adjusted issue price and $10,000 of accrued but unpaid interest).

(B) The group common stock ratio is 10.4 percent, which is determined by comparing the value of all of the common stock issued for unsecured indebtedness in the title 11 case ($25,000) to the amount of unsecured indebtedness allocated to the stock ($290,000 aggregate adjusted issue price of all indebtedness exchanged for stock or cancelled in the title 11 case plus $10,000 accrued but unpaid interest less $60,000 cash received). Accordingly, section 108(e)(8)(B) is satisfied only with respect to the common stock issued for Debt 1. The stock-for-debt exception does not apply to Debt 2 or Debt 3.

(2) *Preferred stock issued for unsecured indebtedness*—(i) *In general.* The common law stock-for-debt exception does not apply to an unsecured indebtedness discharged for preferred stock in a title 11 case or insolvency workout if the individual preferred stock ratio does not equal at least one-half of the group preferred stock ratio.

(ii) *Individual preferred stock ratio defined.* The individual preferred stock ratio is the ratio of the value of the preferred stock issued for an unsecured indebtedness to the amount of the unsecured indebtedness allocated to the preferred stock. The amount of the unsecured indebtedness allocated to preferred stock is equal to the lesser of the lowest redemption price (if any) or lowest liquidation preference (if any) of the preferred stock (determined at issuance). However, the allocable indebtedness may not be less than the fair market value of the preferred stock or greater than the amount of the unsecured indebtedness.

(iii) *Group preferred stock ratio defined.* The group preferred stock ratio is the ratio of the aggregate value of all preferred stock issued for unsecured indebtedness in the title 11 case or insolvency workout to the aggregate amount of unsecured indebtedness allocated to the preferred stock under paragraph (c)(2)(ii) of this section.

(d) *Definitions and special rules.* For purposes of this section:

(1) *Common stock.* Common stock is all stock other than disqualified stock and preferred stock.

(2) *Disqualified stock.* Disqualified stock is disqualified stock as defined in section 108(e)(10)(B)(ii).

(3) *Liquidation preference.* A liquidation preference exists if the stock's right to share in liquidation proceeds is limited and preferred.

(4) *Preferred stock.* Preferred stock is any stock (other than disqualified stock) that has a limited or fixed redemption price or liquidation

preference and does not upon issuance have a right to participate in corporate growth to a meaningful extent. Preferred stock that is convertible into common stock is not treated as preferred stock if the conversion right represents, in substance, a meaningful right to participate in corporate growth. Solely for purposes of this paragraph (d)(4), a right to participate in corporate growth is not established by the fact that the redemption price or liquidation preference exceeds the fair market value of the preferred stock.

(5) *Amount of indebtedness.* Generally, the amount of indebtedness is the adjusted issue price of the indebtedness. Appropriate adjustments are made for accrued but unpaid stated interest. (See the example in paragraph (c)(1)(iv) of this section.)

(6) *Undersecured indebtedness*—(i) *General rule.* If an indebtedness is secured by property with a value less than its adjusted issue price, the indebtedness is considered to be two separate debts: a secured indebtedness with an adjusted issue price equal to the value of the property, and an unsecured indebtedness with an adjusted issue price equal to the remainder. Absent strong evidence to the contrary, the value of the property securing the indebtedness is presumed to be equal to the issue price of any new secured indebtedness received for the indebtedness plus the value of any other consideration (except stock or new unsecured indebtedness) received for the indebtedness. A valuation of that property by a court in a title 11 case is a factor in determining value, but is not controlling.

(ii) *Example.* The following example illustrates these provisions:

Example. Corporation X owes an indebtedness with an adjusted issue price of $100,000. The indebtedness is secured by certain property owned by Corporation X. Corporation X exchanges the indebtedness for $10,000 of stock and new secured indebtedness with an issue price of $70,000. Under paragraph (d)(6)(i) of this section, the indebtedness is bifurcated into a secured indebtedness of $70,000 (the issue price of the new secured indebtedness received in exchange therefor) and an unsecured indebtedness of $30,000 (the remainder of the adjusted issue price of the indebtedness).

(e) *Effective date.* This section is effective with respect to any issuance of stock for indebtedness on or before December 31, 1994, or any issuance of stock for indebtedness in a title 11 or similar case (as defined in section 368(a)(3)(A) of the Internal Revenue Code) that was filed on or before December 31, 1993—

Reg. § 1.108-1(e)

(1) Pursuant to a plan confirmed by the court in a title 11 case after May 17, 1994, or

(2) If there is no title 11 case, pursuant to an insolvency workout in which all issuances of stock for indebtedness occur after May 17, 1994. [Reg. § 1.108-1.]

☐ [T.D. 8532, 3-17-94.]

[Reg. § 1.108-2]

§ 1.108-2. **Acquisition of indebtedness by a person related to the debtor**—(a) *General rules.* The acquisition of outstanding indebtedness by a person related to the debtor from a person who is not related to the debtor results in the realization by the debtor of income from discharge of indebtedness (to the extent required by section 61(a)(12) and section 108) in an amount determined under paragraph (f) of this section. Income realized pursuant to the preceding sentence is excludible from gross income to the extent provided in section 108(a). The rules of this paragraph apply if indebtedness is acquired directly by a person related to the debtor in a direct acquisition (as defined in paragraph (b) of this section) or if a holder of indebtedness becomes related to the debtor in an indirect acquisition (as defined in paragraph (c) of this section).

(b) *Direct acquisition.* An acquisition of outstanding indebtedness is a direct acquisition under this section if a person related to the debtor (or a person who becomes related to the debtor on the date the indebtedness is acquired) acquires the indebtedness from a person who is not related to the debtor. Notwithstanding the foregoing, the Commissioner may provide by Revenue Procedure or other published guidance that certain acquisitions of indebtedness described in the preceding sentence are not direct acquisitions for purposes of this section.

(c) *Indirect acquisition*—(1) *In general.* An indirect acquisition is a transaction in which a holder of outstanding indebtedness becomes related to the debtor, if the holder acquired the indebtedness in anticipation of becoming related to the debtor.

(2) *Proof of anticipation of relationship.* In determining whether indebtedness was acquired by a holder in anticipation of becoming related to the debtor, all relevant facts and circumstances will be considered. Such facts and circumstances include, but are not limited to, the intent of the parties at the time of the acquisition, the nature of any contacts between the parties (or their respective affiliates) before the acquisition, the period of time for which the holder held the indebtedness, and the significance of the indebtedness in proportion to the total assets of the

holder group (as defined in paragraph (c)(5) of this section). For example, if a holder acquired the indebtedness in the ordinary course of its portfolio investment activities and the holder's acquisition of the indebtedness preceded any discussions concerning the acquisition of the holder by the debtor (or by a person related to the debtor) or the acquisition of the debtor by the holder (or by a person related to the holder), as the case may be, these facts, taken together, would ordinarily establish that the holder did not acquire the indebtedness in anticipation of becoming related to the debtor. The absence of discussions between the debtor and the holder (or their respective affiliates), however, does not by itself establish that the holder did not acquire the indebtedness in anticipation of becoming related to the debtor (if, for example, the facts and circumstances show that the holder was considering a potential acquisition of or by the debtor, or the relationship is created within a relatively short period of time of the acquisition, or the indebtedness constitutes a disproportionate portion of the holder group's assets).

(3) *Indebtedness acquired within 6 months of becoming related.* Notwithstanding any other provision of this paragraph (c), a holder of indebtedness is treated as having acquired the indebtedness in anticipation of becoming related to the debtor if the holder acquired the indebtedness less than 6 months before the date the holder becomes related to the debtor.

(4) *Disclosure of potential indirect acquisition*—(i) *In General.* If a holder of outstanding indebtedness becomes related to the debtor under the circumstances described in paragraph (c)(4)(ii) or (iii) of this section, the debtor is required to attach the statement described in paragraph (c)(4)(iv) of this section to its tax return (or to a qualified amended return within the meaning of § 1.6664-2(c)(3)) for the taxable year in which the debtor becomes related to the holder, unless the debtor reports its income on the basis that the holder acquired the indebtedness in anticipation of becoming related to the debtor. Disclosure under this paragraph (c) (4) is in addition to, and is not in substitution for, any disclosure required to be made under section 6662, 6664 or 6694.

(ii) *Indebtedness represents more than 25 percent of holder group's assets*—(A) *In general.* Disclosure under this paragraph (c)(4) is required if, on the date the holder becomes related to the debtor, indebtedness of the debtor represents more than 25 percent of the fair market value of the total gross assets of the holder group (as defined in paragraph (c)(5) of this section).

(B) *Determination of total gross assets.* In determining the total gross assets of the holder group, total gross assets do not include any cash, cash item, marketable stock or security, short-term indebtedness, option, futures contract, notional principal contract, or similar item (other than indebtedness of the debtor), nor do total gross assets include any asset in which the holder has substantially reduced its risk of loss. In addition, total gross assets do not include any ownership interest in or indebtedness of a member of the holder group.

(iii) *Indebtedness acquired within 6 to 24 months of becoming related.* Disclosure under this paragraph (c)(4) is required if the holder acquired the indebtedness 6 months or more before the date the holder becomes related to the debtor, but less than 24 months before that date.

(iv) *Contents of statement.* A statement under this paragraph (c)(4) must include the following—

(A) A caption identifying the statement as disclosure under § 1.108-2(c);

(B) An identification of the indebtedness with respect to which disclosure is made;

(C) The amount of such indebtedness and the amount of income from discharge of indebtedness if section 108(e)(4) were to apply;

(D) Whether paragraph (c)(4)(ii) or (iii) of this section applies to the transaction; and

(E) A statement describing the facts and circumstances supporting the debtor's position that the holder did not acquire the indebtedness in anticipation of becoming related to the debtor.

(v) *Failure to disclose.* In addition to any other penalties that may apply, if a debtor fails to provide a statement required by this paragraph (c)(4), the holder is presumed to have acquired the indebtedness in anticipation of becoming related to the debtor unless the facts and circumstances clearly establish that the holder did not acquire the indebtedness in anticipation of becoming related to the debtor.

(5) *Holder group.* For purposes of this paragraph (c), the holder group consists of the holder of the indebtedness and all persons who are both—

(i) Related to the holder before the holder becomes related to the debtor; and

(ii) Related to the debtor after the holder becomes related to the debtor.

(6) *Holding period*—(i) *Suspensions.* The running of the holding periods set forth in paragraphs (c)(3) and (c)(4)(iii) of this section is suspended during any period in which the holder

or any person related to the holder is protected (directly or indirectly) against risk of loss by an option, a short sale, or any other device or transaction.

(ii) *Tacking.* For purposes of paragraphs (c)(3) and (c)(4)(iii) of this section, the period for which a holder held the debtor's indebtedness includes—

(A) The period for which the indebtedness was held by a corporation to whose attributes the holder succeeded pursuant to section 381; and

(B) The period (ending on the date on which the holder becomes related to the debtor) for which the indebtedness was held continuously by members of the holder group (as defined in paragraph (c)(5) of this section).

(d) *Definitions*—(1) *Acquisition date.* For purposes of this section, the acquisition date is the date on which a direct acquisition of indebtedness or an indirect acquisition of indebtedness occurs.

(2) *Relationship.* For purposes of this section, persons are considered related if they are related within the meaning of sections 267(b) or 707(b)(1). However—

(i) Sections 267(b) and 707(b)(1) are applied as if section 267(c)(4) provided that the family of an individual consists of the individual's spouse, the individual's children, grandchildren, and parents, and any spouse of the individual's children or grandchildren; and

(ii) Two entities that are treated as a single employer under subsection (b) or (c) of section 414 are treated as having a relationship to each other that is described in section 267(b).

(e) *Exceptions*—(1) *Indebtedness retired within one year.* This section does not apply to a direct or indirect acquisition of indebtedness with a stated maturity date on or before the date that is one year after the acquisition date, if the indebtedness is, in fact, retired on or before its stated maturity date.

(2) *Acquisitions by securities dealers.* (i) This section does not apply to a direct acquisition or an indirect acquisition of indebtedness by a dealer that acquires and disposes of such indebtedness in the ordinary course of its business of dealing in securities if—

(A) The dealer accounts for the indebtedness as a security held primarily for sale to customers in the ordinary course of business;

(B) The dealer disposes of the indebtedness (or it matures while held by the dealer) within a period consistent with the holding of the indebtedness for sale to customers in the ordinary course of business, taking into account the terms of the indebtedness and the conditions and prac-

Reg. § 1.108-2(e)(2)

tices prevailing in the markets for similar indebtedness during the period in which it is held; and

(C) The dealer does not sell or otherwise transfer the indebtedness to a person related to the debtor (other than in a sale to a dealer that in turn meets the requirements of this paragraph (e)(2)).

(ii) A dealer will continue to satisfy the conditions of this paragraph (e)(2) with respect to indebtedness that is exchanged for successor indebtedness in a transaction in which unrelated holders also exchange indebtedness of the same issue, provided that the conditions of this paragraph (e)(2) are met with respect to the successor indebtedness.

(iii) For purposes of this paragraph (e)(2), if the period consistent with the holding of indebtedness for sale to customers in the ordinary course of business is 30 days or less, the dealer is considered to dispose of indebtedness within that period if the aggregate principal amount of indebtedness of that issue sold by the dealer to customers in the ordinary course of business (or that mature and are paid while held by the dealer) in the calendar month following the month in which the indebtedness is acquired equals or exceeds the aggregate principal amount of indebtedness of that issue held in the dealer's inventory at the close of the month in which the indebtedness is acquired. If the period consistent with the holding of indebtedness for sale to customers in the ordinary course of business is greater than 30 days, the dealer is considered to dispose of the indebtedness within that period if the aggregate principal amount of indebtedness of that issue sold by the dealer to customers in the ordinary course of business (or that mature and are paid while held by the dealer) within that period equals or exceeds the aggregate principal amount of indebtedness of that issue held in inventory at the close of the day on which the indebtedness was acquired.

(f) *Amount of discharge of indebtedness income realized*—(1) *Holder acquired the indebtedness by purchase on or less than six months before the acquisition date.* Except as otherwise provided in this paragraph (f), the amount of discharge of indebtedness income realized under paragraph (a) of this section is measured by reference to the adjusted basis of the related holder (or of the holder that becomes related to the debtor) in the indebtedness on the acquisition date if the holder acquired the indebtedness by purchase on or less than six months before the acquisition date. For purposes of this paragraph (f), indebtedness is acquired "by purchase" if the indebtedness in the hands of the holder is not substituted basis property within the meaning of section 7701(a)(42).

However, indebtedness is also considered acquired by purchase within six months before the acquisition date if the holder acquired the indebtedness as transferred basis property (within the meaning of section 7701(a)(43)) from a person who acquired the indebtedness by purchase on or less than six months before the acquisition date.

(2) *Holder did not acquire the indebtedness by purchase on or less than six months before the acquisition date.* Except as otherwise provided in this paragraph (f), the amount of discharge of indebtedness income realized under paragraph (a) of this section is measured by reference to the fair market value of the indebtedness on the acquisition date if the holder (or the transferor to the holder in a transferred basis transaction) did not acquire the indebtedness by purchase on or less than six months before the acquisition date.

(3) *Acquisitions of indebtedness in nonrecognition transactions.* [Reserved]

(4) *Avoidance transactions.* The amount of discharge of indebtedness income realized by the debtor under paragraph (a) of this section is measured by reference to the fair market value of the indebtedness on the acquisition date if the indebtedness is acquired in a direct or an indirect acquisition in which a principal purpose for the acquisition is the avoidance of federal income tax.

(g) *Correlative adjustments*—(1) *Deemed issuance.* For income tax purposes, if a debtor realizes income from discharge of its indebtedness in a direct or an indirect acquisition under this section (whether or not the income is excludible under section 108(a)), the debtor's indebtedness is treated as new indebtedness issued by the debtor to the related holder on the acquisition date (the deemed issuance). The new indebtedness is deemed issued with an issue price equal to the amount used under paragraph (f) of this section to compute the amount realized by the debtor under paragraph (a) of this section (*i.e.*, either the holder's adjusted basis or the fair market value of the indebtedness, as the case may be). Under section 1273(a)(1), the excess of the stated redemption price at maturity (as defined in section 1273(a)(2)) of the indebtedness over its issue price is original issue discount (OID) which, to the extent provided in sections 163 and 1272, is deductible by the debtor and includible in the gross income of the related holder. Notwithstanding the foregoing, the Commissioner may provide by Revenue Procedure or other published guidance that the indebtedness is not treated as newly issued indebtedness for purposes of designated provisions of the income tax laws.

(2) *Treatment of related holder.* The related holder does not recognize any gain or loss on the

Reg. § 1.108-2(f)(1)

deemed issuance described in paragraph (g)(1) of this section. The related holder's adjusted basis in the indebtedness remains the same as it was immediately before the deemed issuance. The deemed issuance is treated as a purchase of the indebtedness by the related holder for purposes of section 1272(a)(7) (pertaining to reduction of original issue discount where a subsequent holder pays acquisition premium) and section 1276 (pertaining to acquisitions of debt at a market discount).

(3) *Loss deferral on disposition of indebtedness acquired in certain exchanges.* (i) Any loss otherwise allowable to a related holder on the disposition at any time of indebtedness acquired in a direct or indirect acquisition (whether or not any discharge of indebtedness income was realized under paragraph (a) of this section) is deferred until the date the debtor retires the indebtedness if—

(A) The related holder acquired the debtor's indebtedness in exchange for its own indebtedness; and

(B) The issue price of the related holder's indebtedness was not determined by reference to its fair market value (*e.g.*, the issue price was determined under section 1273(b)(4) or 1274(a) or any other provision of applicable law).

(ii) Any comparable tax benefit that would otherwise be available to the holder, debtor, or any person related to either, in any other transaction that directly or indirectly results in the disposition of the indebtedness is also deferred until the date the debtor retires the indebtedness.

(4) *Examples.* The following examples illustrate the application of this paragraph (g). In each example, all taxpayers are calendar-year taxpayers, no taxpayer is insolvent or under the jurisdiction of a court in a title 11 case and no indebtedness is qualified farm indebtedness described in section 108(g).

Example 1. (i) P, a domestic corporation, owns 70 percent of the single class of stock of S, a domestic corporation. S has outstanding indebtedness that has an issue price of $10,000,000 and provides for monthly interest payments of $80,000 payable at the end of each month and a payment at maturity of $10,000,000. The indebtedness has a stated maturity date of December 31, 1994. On January 1, 1992, P purchases S's indebtedness from I, an individual not related to S within the meaning of paragraph (d)(2) of this section, for cash in the amount of $9,000,000. S repays the indebtedness in full at maturity.

(ii) Under section 61(a)(12), section 108(e)(4), and paragraphs (a) and (f) of this sec-

tion, S realizes $1,000,000 of income from discharge of indebtedness on January 1, 1992.

(iii) Under paragraph (g)(1) of this section, the indebtedness is treated as issued to P on January 1, 1992, with an issue price of $9,000,000. Under section 1273(a), the $1,000,000 excess of the stated redemption price at maturity of the indebtedness ($10,000,000) over its issue price ($9,000,000) is original issue discount, which is includible in gross income by P and deductible by S over the remaining term of the indebtedness under sections 163(e) and 1272(a).

(iv) Accordingly, S deducts and P includes in income original issue discount, in addition to stated interest, as follows: in 1992, $289,144.88; in 1993, $331,286.06; and in 1994, $379,569.06.

Example 2. The facts are the same as in *Example 1*, except that on January 1, 1993, P sells S's indebtedness to J, who is not related to S within the meaning of paragraph (d)(2) of this section, for $9,400,000 in cash. J holds S's indebtedness to maturity. On January 1, 1993, P's adjusted basis in S's indebtedness is $9,289,144.88. Accordingly, P realizes gain in the amount of $110,855.12 upon the disposition. S and J continue to deduct and include the original issue discount on the indebtedness in accordance with *Example 1*. The amount of original issue discount includible by J is reduced by the $110,855.12 acquisition premium as provided in section 1272(a)(7).

Example 3. The facts are the same as in *Example 1*, except that on February 1, 1992 (one month after P purchased S's indebtedness), S retires the indebtedness for an amount of cash equal to the fair market value of the indebtedness. Assume that the fair market value of the indebtedness is $9,022,621.41, which in this case equals the issue price of the indebtedness determined under paragraph (g)(1) of this section ($9,000,000) plus the accrued original issue discount through February 1 ($22,621.41). Section 1.61-12(c)(3) provides that if indebtedness is repurchased for a price that is exceeded by the issue price of the indebtedness plus the amount of discount already deducted, the excess is income from discharge of indebtedness. Therefore, S does not realize income from discharge of indebtedness. The result would be the same if P had contributed the indebtedness to the capital of S. Under section 108(e)(6), S would be treated as having satisfied the indebtedness with an amount of money equal to P's adjusted basis and, under section 1272(d)(2), P's adjusted basis is equal to $9,022,621.41.

Example 4. (i) P, a domestic corporation, owns 70 percent of the single class of stock of S, a domestic corporation. On January 1, 1986, P issued indebtedness that has an issue price of $5,000,000 and provides for no stated interest payments and a payment at maturity of $10,000,000. The indebtedness has a stated maturity date of December 31, 1995. On January 1, 1992, S purchases P's indebtedness from K, a partnership not related to P within the meaning of paragraph (d)(2) of this section, for cash in the amount of $6,000,000. The sum of the debt's issue price and previously deducted original issue discount is $7,578,582.83. P repays the indebtedness in full at maturity.

(ii) Under section 61(a)(12), section 108(e)(4), and paragraphs (a) and (f) of this section, P realizes $1,578,582.83 in income from discharge of indebtedness ($7,578,582.83 minus $6,000,000) on January 1, 1992.

(iii) Under paragraph (g)(1) of this section, the indebtedness is treated as issued to S on January 1, 1992, with an issue price of $6,000,000. Under section 1273(a), the $4,000,000 excess of the stated redemption price at maturity of the indebtedness ($10,000,000) over its issue price ($6,000,000) is original issue discount, which is includible in gross income by S and deductible by P over the remaining term of the indebtedness under sections 163(e) and 1272(a).

(iv) Accordingly, P deducts and S includes in income original issue discount as follows: in 1992, $817,316.20; in 1993, $928,650.49; in 1994, $1,055,150.67; and in 1995, $1,198,882.64.

(h) *Effective date.* This section applies to any transaction described in paragraph (a) and in either paragraph (b) or (c) of this section with an acquisition date on or after March 21, 1991. Although this section does not apply to direct or indirect acquisitions occurring before March 21, 1991, section 108(e)(4) is effective for any transaction after December 31, 1980, subject to the rules of section 7 of the Bankruptcy Tax Act of 1980 (Pub. L. 96-589, 94 Stat. 3389, 3411). Taxpayers may use any reasonable method of determining the amount of discharge of indebtedness income realized and the treatment of correlative adjustments under section 108(e)(4) for acquisitions of indebtedness before March 21, 1991, if such method is applied consistently by both the debtor and related holder. [Reg. § 1.108-2.]

☐ [*T.D. 8460*, 12-28-92.]

[Reg. § 1.108-3]

§ 1.108-3. **Intercompany losses and deductions.**—(a) *General rule.* This section applies to certain losses and deductions from the sale, exchange, or other transfer of property between corporations that are members of a consolidated

group or a controlled group (an intercompany transaction). See section 267(f) (controlled groups) and § 1.1502-13 (consolidated groups) for applicable definitions. For purposes of determining the attributes to which section 108(b) applies, a loss or deduction not yet taken into account under section 267(f) or § 1.1502-13 (an intercompany loss or deduction) is treated as basis described in section 108(b) that the transferor retains in property. To the extent a loss not yet taken into account is reduced under this section, it cannot subsequently be taken into account under this section, it cannot subsequently be taken into account under 267(f) or § 1.1502-13. For example, if S and B are corporations filing a consolidated return, and S sells land with a $100 basis to B for $90 and the $10 loss is deferred under section 267(f) and § 1.1502-13, the deferred loss is treated for purposes of section 108(b) as $10 of basis that S has in land (even though S has no remaining interest in the land sold to B) and is subject to reduction under section 108(b)(2)(E). Similar principles apply, with appropriate adjustments, if S and B are members of a controlled group and S's loss is deferred only under Section 267(f).

(b) *Effective date.* This section applies with respect to discharges of indebtedness occurring on or after September 11, 1995. [Reg. § 1.108-3.]

☐ [*T.D. 8597*, 7-12-95.]

[Reg. § 1.108-4]

§ 1.108-4. **Election to reduce basis of depreciable property under section 108(b)(5) of the Internal Revenue Code.**—(a) *Description.* An election under section 108(b)(5) is available whenever a taxpayer excludes discharge of indebtedness income (COD income) from gross income under sections 108(a)(1)(A), (B), or (C) (concerning title 11 cases, insolvency, and qualified farm indebtedness, respectively). See sections 108(d)(2) and (3) for the definitions of *title 11 case* and *insolvent.* See section 108(g)(2) for the definition of *qualified farm indebtedness.*

(b) *Time and manner.* To make an election under section 108(b)(5), a taxpayer must enter the appropriate information on Form 982, *Reduction of Tax Attributes Due to Discharge of Indebtedness (and Section 1082 Basis Adjustment),* and attach the form to the timely filed (including extensions) Federal income tax return for the taxable year in which the taxpayer has COD income that is excluded from gross income under section 108(a). An election under this section may be revoked only with the consent of the Commissioner.

Reg. § 1.108-3(a)

(c) *Effective date.* This section applies to elections concerning discharges of indebtedness occurring on or after October 22, 1998. [Reg. § 1.108-4.]

☐ [*T.D.* 8787, 10-21-98.]

[Reg. § 1.108-5]

§ 1.108-5. Time and manner for making election under the Omnibus Budget Reconciliation Act of 1993.—(a) *Description.* Section 108(c)(3)(C), as added by section 13150 of the Omnibus Budget Reconciliation Act of 1993 (Public Law 103-66, 107 Stat. 446), allows certain noncorporate taxpayers to elect to treat certain indebtedness described in section 108(c)(3) that is discharged after December 31, 1992, as qualified real property business indebtedness. This discharged indebtedness is excluded from gross income to the extent allowed by section 108.

(b) *Time and manner for making election.* The election described in this section must be made on the timely-filed (including extensions) Federal income tax return for the taxable year in which the taxpayer has discharge of indebtedness income that is excludible from gross income under section 108(a). The election is to be made on a completed Form 982, in accordance with that Form and its instructions.

(c) *Revocability of election.* The election described in this section is revocable with the consent of the Commissioner.

(d) *Effective date.* The rules set forth in this section are effective December 27, 1993. [Reg. § 1.108-5.]

☐ [*T.D.* 8688, 12-11-96. Redesignated by *T.D.* 8787, 10-21-98.]

[Reg. § 1.108-6]

§ 1.108-6. Limitations on the exclusion of income from the discharge of qualified real property business indebtedness.—(a) *Indebtedness in excess of value.* With respect to any qualified real property business indebtedness that is discharged, the amount excluded from gross income under section 108(a)(1)(D) (concerning discharges of qualified real property business indebtedness) shall not exceed the excess, if any, of the outstanding principal amount of that indebtedness immediately before the discharge over the net fair market value of the qualifying real property, as defined in § 1.1017-1(c)(1), immediately before the discharge. For purposes of this section, *net fair market value* means the fair market value of the qualifying real property (notwithstanding section 7701(g)), reduced by the outstanding principal amount of any qualified real property business indebtedness (other than

the discharged indebtedness) that is secured by such property immediately before and after the discharge. Also, for purposes of section 108(c)(2)(A) and this section, outstanding principal amount means the principal amount of indebtedness together with all additional amounts owed that, immediately before the discharge, are equivalent to principal, in that interest on such amounts would accrue and compound in the future, except that outstanding principal amount shall not include amounts that are subject to section 108(e)(2) and shall be adjusted to account for unamortized premium and discount consistent with section 108(e)(3).

(b) *Overall limitation.* The amount excluded from gross income under section 108(a)(1)(D) shall not exceed the aggregate adjusted bases of all depreciable real property held by the taxpayer immediately before the discharge (other than depreciable real property acquired in contemplation of the discharge) reduced by the sum of any—

(1) Depreciation claimed for the taxable year the taxpayer excluded discharge of indebtedness from gross income under section 108(a)(1)(D); and

(2) Reductions to the adjusted bases of depreciable real property required under section 108(b) or section 108(g) for the same taxable year.

(c) *Effective date.* This section applies to discharges of qualified real property business indebtedness occurring on or after, October 22, 1998. [Reg. § 1.108-6.]

☐ [*T.D.* 8787, 10-21-98.]

[Reg. § 1.109-1]

§ 1.109-1. Exclusion from gross income of lessor of real property of value of improvements erected by lessee.—(a) Income derived by a lessor of real property upon the termination, through forfeiture or otherwise, of the lease of such property and attributable to buildings erected or other improvements made by the lessee upon the leased property is excluded from gross income. However, where the facts disclose that such buildings or improvements represent in whole or in part a liquidation in kind of lease rentals, the exclusion from gross income shall not apply to the extent that such buildings or improvements represent such liquidation. The exclusion applies only with respect to the income realized by the lessor upon the termination of the lease and has no application to income, if any, in the form of rent, which may be derived by a lessor during the period of the lease and attributable to buildings erected or other improvements made by the lessee. It has no application to income which may be realized by the lessor upon the termination of the lease but not attributable to the value of such buildings or improvements. Neither does it apply to income derived by the lessor subsequent to the termination of the lease incident to the ownership of such buildings or improvements.

(b) The provisions of this section may be illustrated by the following example:

Example. The A Corporation leased in 1945 for a period of 50 years unimproved real property to the B Corporation under a lease providing that the B Corporation erect on the leased premises an office building costing $500,000, in addition to paying the A Corporation a lease rental of $10,000 per annum beginning on the date of completion of the improvements, the sum of $100,000 being placed in escrow for the payment of the rental. The building was completed on January 1, 1950. The lease provided that all improvements made by the lessee on the leased property would become the absolute property of the A Corporation on the termination of the lease by forfeiture or otherwise and that the lessor would become entitled on such termination to the remainder of the sum, if any, remaining in the escrow fund. The B Corporation forfeited its lease on January 1, 1955, when the improvements had a value of $100,000. Under the provisions of section 109, the $100,000 is excluded from gross income. The amount of $50,000 representing the remainder in the escrow fund is forfeited to the A Corporation and is included in the gross income of that taxpayer. As to the basis of the property in the hands of the A Corporation, see § 1.1019-1. [Reg. § 1.109-1.]

☐ [*T.D.* 6220, 12-28-56.]

[Reg. § 1.110-1]

§ 1.110-1. Qualified lessee construction allowances.—(a) *Overview.* Amounts provided to a lessee by a lessor for property to be constructed and used by the lessee pursuant to a lease are not includible in the lessee's gross income if the amount is a qualified lessee construction allowance under paragraph (b) of this section.

(b) *Qualified lessee construction allowance*—(1) *In general.* A qualified lessee construction allowance means any amount received in cash (or treated as a rent reduction) by a lessee from a lessor—

(i) Under a short-term lease of retail space;

(ii) For the purpose of constructing or improving qualified long-term real property for use in the lessee's trade or business at that retail space; and

(iii) To the extent the amount is expended by the lessee in the taxable year received on the construction or improvement of qualified long-

term real property for use in the lessee's trade or business at that retail space.

(2) *Definitions*—(i) *Qualified long-term real property* is nonresidential real property under section 168(e)(2)(B) that is part of, or otherwise present at, the retail space referred to in paragraph (b)(1)(i) of this section and which reverts to the lessor at the termination of the lease. Thus, qualified long-term real property does not include property qualifying as section 1245 property under section 1245(a)(3).

(ii) *Short-term lease* is a lease (or other agreement for occupancy or use) of retail space for 15 years or less (as determined pursuant to section 168(i)(3)).

(iii) *Retail space* is nonresidential real property under section 168(e)(2)(B) that is leased, occupied, or otherwise used by the lessee in its trade or business of selling tangible personal property or services to the general public. The term *retail space* includes not only the space where the retail sales are made, but also space where activities supporting the retail activity are performed (such as an administrative office, a storage area, and employee lounge). Examples of services typically sold to the general public include services provided by hair stylists, tailors, shoe repairmen, doctors, lawyers, accountants, insurance agents, stock brokers, securities dealers (including dealers who sell securities out of inventory), financial advisors and bankers. For purposes of this paragraph (b)(2)(iii), a taxpayer is selling to the general public if the products or services for sale are made available to the general public, even if the product or service is targeted to certain customers or clients.

(3) *Purpose requirement.* An amount will meet the requirement in paragraph (b)(1)(ii) of this section only to the extent that the lease agreement for the retail space expressly provides that the construction allowance is for the purpose of constructing or improving qualified long-term real property for use in the lessee's trade or business at the retail space. An ancillary agreement between the lessor and the lessee providing for a construction allowance, executed contemporaneously with the lease or during the term of the lease, is considered a provision of the lease agreement for purposes of the preceding sentence, provided the agreement is executed before payment of the construction allowance.

(4) *Expenditure requirement*—(i) *In general.* Expenditures referred to in paragraph (b)(1)(iii) of this section may be treated as being made first from the lessee's construction allowance. Tracing of the construction allowance to the actual lessee expenditures for the construction or improvement

Reg. § 1.110-1(a)

of qualified long-term real property is not required. However, the lessee should maintain accurate records of the amount of the qualified lessee construction allowance received and the expenditures made for qualified long-term real property.

(ii) *Time when expenditures deemed made.* For purposes of paragraph (b)(1)(iii) of this section, an amount is deemed to have been expended by a lessee in the taxable year in which the construction allowance was received by the lessee if—

(A) The amount is expended by the lessee within 8½ months after the close of the taxable year in which the amount was received; or

(B) The amount is a reimbursement from the lessor for amounts expended by the lessee in a prior year and for which the lessee has not claimed any depreciation deductions.

(5) *Consistent treatment by lessor.* Qualified long-term real property constructed or improved with any amount excluded from a lessee's gross income by reason of paragraph (a) of this section must be treated as nonresidential real property owned by the lessor (for purposes of depreciation under 168(e)(2)(B) and determining gain or loss under section 168(i)(8)(B)). For purposes of the preceding sentence, the lessor must treat the construction allowance as fully expended in the manner required by paragraph (b)(1)(iii) of this section unless the lessor is notified by the lessee in writing to the contrary. General tax principles apply for purposes of determining when the lessor may begin depreciation of its nonresidential real property. The lessee's exclusion from gross income under paragraph (a) of this section, however, is not dependent upon the lessor's treatment of the property as nonresidential real property.

(c) *Information required to be furnished*—(1) *In general.* The lessor and the lessee described in paragraph (b) of this section who are paying and receiving a qualified lessee construction allowance, respectively, must furnish the information described in paragraph (c)(3) of this section in the time and manner prescribed in paragraph (c)(2) of this section.

(2) *Time and manner for furnishing information.* The requirement to furnish information under paragraph (c)(1) of this section is met by attaching a statement with the information described in paragraph (c)(3) of this section to the lessor's or the lessee's, as applicable, timely filed (including extensions) Federal income tax return for the taxable year in which the construction allowance was paid by the lessor or received by the lessee (either in cash or treated as a rent reduction), as applicable. A lessor or a lessee may report the required information for several qualified lessee construction allowances on a combined statement. However, a lessor's or a lessee's failure to provide information with respect to each lease will be treated as a separate failure to provide information for purposes of paragraph (c)(4) of this section.

(3) *Information required*—(i) *Lessor.* The statement provided by the lessor must contain the lessor's name (and, in the case of a consolidated group, the parent's name), employer identification number, taxable year and the following information for each lease:

(A) The lessee's name (in the case of a consolidated group, the parent's name).

(B) The address of the lessee.

(C) The employer identification number of the lessee.

(D) The location of the retail space (including mall or strip center name, if applicable, and store name).

(E) The amount of the construction allowance.

(F) The amount of the construction allowance treated by the lessor as nonresidential real property owned by the lessor.

(ii) *Lessee.* The statement provided by the lessee must contain the lessee's name (and, in the case of a consolidated group, the parent's name), employer identification number, taxable year and the following information for each lease:

(A) The lessor's name (in the case of a consolidated group, the parent's name).

(B) The address of the lessor.

(C) The employer identification number of the lessor.

(D) The location of the retail space (including mall or strip center name, if applicable, and store name).

(E) The amount of the construction allowance.

(F) The amount of the construction allowance that is a qualified lessee construction allowance under paragraph (b) of this section.

(4) *Failure to furnish information.* A lessor or a lessee that fails to furnish the information required in this paragraph (c) may be subject to a penalty under section 6721.

(d) *Effective date.* This section is applicable to leases entered into on or after October 5, 2000. [Reg. § 1.110-1.]

□ [T.D. 8901, 9-1-2000.]

[Reg. § 1.111-1]

§ 1.111-1. **Recovery of certain items previously deducted or credited.**—(a) *General.* Section 111 provides that income attributable to the recovery during any taxable year of bad debts, prior taxes, and delinquency amounts shall be excluded from gross income to the extent of the "recovery exclusion" with respect to such items. The rule of exclusion so prescribed by statute applies equally with respect to all other losses, expenditures, and accruals made the basis of deductions from gross income for prior taxable years, including war losses referred to in section 127 of the Internal Revenue Code of 1939, but not including deductions with respect to depreciation, depletion, amortization, or amortizable bond premiums. The term "recovery exclusion" as used in this section means an amount equal to the portion of the bad debts, prior taxes, and delinquency amounts (the items specifically referred to in section 111), and of all other items subject to the rule of exclusion which, when deducted or credited for a prior taxable year, did not result in a reduction of any tax of the taxpayer under subtitle A (other than the accumulated earnings tax imposed by section 531 or the personal holding company tax imposed by section 541) of the Internal Revenue Code of 1954 or corresponding provisions of prior income tax laws (other than the World War II excess profits tax imposed under subchapter E of chapter 2 of the Internal Revenue Code of 1939.

(1) *Section 111 items.* The term "section 111 items" as used in this section means bad debts, prior taxes, delinquency amounts, and all other items subject to the rule of exclusion, for which a deduction or credit was allowed for a prior taxable year. If a bad debt was previously charged against a reserve by a taxpayer on the reserve method of treating bad debts, it was not deducted, and it is, therefore, not considered a section 111 item. Bad debts, prior taxes, and delinquency amounts are defined in section 111(b)(1), (2), and (3), respectively. An example of a delinquency amount is interest on delinquent taxes. An example of the other items not expressly referred to in section 111 but nevertheless subject to the rule of exclusion is a loss sustained upon the sale of stock and later recovered, in whole or in part, through an action against the party from whom such stock had been purchased.

(2) *Definition of "recovery."* Recoveries result from the receipt of amounts in respect of the previously deducted or credited section 111 items, such as from the collection or sale of a bad debt, refund or credit of taxes paid, or cancellation of taxes accrued. Care should be taken in the case of bad debts which were treated as only partially worthless in prior years to distinguish between the item described in section 111, that is, the part of such debt which was deducted, and the part not previously deducted, which is not a section 111

item and is considered the first part collected. The collection of the part not deducted is not considered a "recovery." Furthermore, the term "recovery" does not include the gain resulting from the receipt of an amount on account of a section 111 item which, together with previous such receipts, exceeds the deduction or credit previously allowed for such item. For instance, a $100 corporate bond purchased for $40 and later deducted as worthless is subsequently collected to the extent of $50. The $10 gain (excess of $50 collection over $40 cost) is not a recovery of a section 111 item. Such gain is in no case excluded from gross income under section 111, regardless of whether the $40 recovery is or is not included.

(3) *Treatment of debt deducted in more than one year by reason of partial worthlessness.* In the case of a bad debt deducted in part for two or more prior years, each such deduction of a part of the debt is considered a separate section 111 item. A recovery with respect to such debt is considered first a recovery of those items (or portions thereof), resulting from such debt, for which there are recovery exclusions. If there are recovery exclusions for two or more items resulting from the same bad debt, such items are considered recovered in the order of the taxable years for which they were deducted, beginning with the latest. The recovery exclusion for any such item is determined by considering the recovery exclusion with respect to the prior year for which such item was deducted as being first used to offset all other applicable recoveries in the year in which the bad debt is recovered.

(4) *Special provisions as to worthless bonds, etc., which are treated as capital losses.* Certain bad debts arising from the worthlessness of securities and certain nonbusiness bad debts are treated as losses from the sale or exchange of capital assets. See sections 165(g) and 166(d). The amounts of the deductions allowed for any year under section 1211 on account of such losses for such year are considered to be section 111 items. Any part of such losses which, under section 1211, is a deduction for a subsequent year through the capital loss carryover (any later receipt of an amount with respect to such deducted loss is a recovery) is considered a section 111 item for the year in which such loss was sustained.

(b) *Computation of recovery exclusion*—(1) *Amount of recovery exclusion allowable for year of recovery.* For the year of any recovery, the section 111 items which were deducted or credited for one prior year are considered as a group and the recovery thereon is considered separately from recoveries of any items which were deducted or credited for other years. This recovery is excluded

Reg. § 1.111-1(a)(1)

from gross income to the extent of the recovery exclusion with respect to this group of items as (i) determined for the original year for which such items were deducted or credited (see subparagraph (2) of this paragraph) and (ii) reduced by the excludable recoveries in intervening years on account of all section 111 items for such original year. A taxpayer claiming a recovery exclusion shall submit, at the time the exclusion is claimed, the computation of the recovery exclusion claimed for the original year for which the items were deducted or credited, and computations showing the amount recovered in intervening years on account of the section 111 items deducted or credited for the original year.

(2) *Determination of recovery exclusion for original year for which items were deducted or credited.* (i) The recovery exclusion for the taxable year for which section 111 items were deducted or credited (that is, the "original taxable year") is the portion of the aggregate amount of such deductions and credits which could be disallowed without causing an increase in any tax of the taxpayer imposed under subtitle A (other than the accumulated earnings tax imposed by section 531 or the personal holding company tax imposed by section 541) of the Internal Revenue Code of 1954 or corresponding provisions of prior income tax laws (other than the World War II excess profits tax imposed under subchapter E of chapter 2 of the Internal Revenue Code of 1939). For the purpose of such recovery exclusion, consideration must be given to the effect of net operating loss carryovers and carrybacks or capital loss carryovers.

(ii) This rule shall be applied by determining the recovery exclusion as the aggregate amount of the section 111 items for the original year for which such items were deducted or credited reduced by whichever of the following amounts is the greater:

(a) The difference between (1) the taxable income for such original year and (2) the taxable income computed without regard to the section 111 items for such original year.

(b) In the case of a taxpayer subject to any income tax in lieu of normal tax or surtax or both (except the alternative tax on capital gains imposed by section 1201, which is disregarded), the difference between (1) the income subject to such tax for such original year and (2) the income subject to such tax computed without regard to the section 111 items for such original year.

(Neither the amount determined under (1) nor the amount under (2) of (a) or (b) of this subdivision shall in any case be considered less than zero.) For this determination of the recovery exclusion the aggregate of the section 111 items must be further decreased by the portion thereof which caused a reduction in tax in preceding or succeeding taxable years through any net operating loss carryovers or carrybacks or capital loss carryovers affected by such items. This decrease is the aggregate of the largest amount determined for each of such preceding and succeeding years under (a) and (b) of this subdivision, the computation of each carryover or carryback to the preceding or succeeding year being made under (1) of (a) and (b) of this subdivision with regard to the section 111 items for the original year and such computation being made under (2) of (a) and (b) of this subdivision without regard to such items. For the purpose of the preceding sentence, the computations under both (1) and (2) of (a) and (b) of this subdivision shall be made without regard to any section 111 items for such preceding or succeeding year and the carryovers and carrybacks to such year shall be determined without regard to any section 111 items for years subsequent to the original year.

(iii) The determination of the recovery exclusion for original taxable years subject to the provisions of the Internal Revenue Code of 1939 shall be made under 26 CFR (1939) 39.22(b)(12)-1(b)(2) of Regulations 118.

(3) *Example.* The provisions of this paragraph may be illustrated by the following example:

Example. A single individual with no dependents has for his 1954 taxable year the following income and deductions:

	With deduction of section 111 items		Without deduction of section 111 items	
Gross income		$25,000		$25,000
Less deductions:				
Depreciation	$20,000		$20,000	
Business bad debts and taxes...	6,300			
Personal exemption	600	26,900	600	20,600
Taxable income or (loss)		(1,900)		4,400
Adjustment under section 172(d)(3)		600		
Net operating loss		(1,300)		

Reg. § 1.111-1(b)(3)

The full amount of the net operating loss of $1,300 is carried back and allowed as a deduction for 1952. The aggregate of the section 111 items for 1954 is $6,300 (bad debts and taxes). The recovery exclusion on account of section 111 items for 1954 is $600, determined by reducing the $6,300 aggregate of the section 111 items by $5,700, i.e., the sum of (1) the difference between the amount of the taxable income for 1954 computed without regard to the section 111 items ($4,400) and the amount of the taxable income for 1954 (not less than zero) computed by taking such items into account, and (2) the amount of the net operating loss ($1,300) which caused the reduction in tax for 1952 by reason of the carryback provisions. If in 1956 the taxpayer recovers $400 of the bad debts, all of the recovery is excluded from the income by reason of the recovery exclusion of $600 determined for the original year 1954. If in 1957 the taxpayer recovers an additional $300 of the bad debts, only $200 is excluded from gross income. That is, the recovery exclusion of $600 determined for the original year 1954 is reduced by the $400 recovered in 1956, leaving a balance of $200 which is used in 1957. The balance of the amount recovered in 1957, $100 ($300 less $200), is included in gross income for 1957.

(c) *Provisions as to taxes imposed by section 531 (relating to the accumulated earnings tax) and section 541 (relating to the tax on personal holding companies).* A recovery exclusion allowed for purposes of subtitle A (other than section 531 or section 541) of the Internal Revenue Code of 1954 shall also be allowed for the purpose of determining the accumulated earnings tax under section 531 or the personal holding company tax under section 541 regardless of whether or not the section 111 items on which such recovery exclusion is based resulted in a reduction of the tax under section 531 or section 541 of the Internal Revenue Code of 1954 (or corresponding provisions of prior income tax laws) for the prior taxable year. Furthermore, if there is recovery of a section 111 item which was not allowable as a deduction or credit for the prior taxable year for purposes of subtitle A (not including section 531 or section 541) or corresponding provisions of prior income tax laws (other than subchapter E of chapter 2 of the Internal Revenue Code of 1939, relating to World War II excess profits tax), but was allowable for such prior taxable year in determining the tax under section 531 or section 541 (or corresponding provisions of prior income tax laws) then for the purpose of determining the tax under section 531 or section 541 a recovery exclusion shall be allowable with respect to such recovery if the section 111 item did not result in a reduction of the tax under section 531 or section 541 (or corresponding provisions of prior income tax laws). [Reg. § 1.111-1.]

□ [*T.D.* 6220, 12-28-56.]

[Reg. § 1.112-1]

§ 1.112-1. Combat zone compensation of members of the Armed Forces.—(a) *Combat zone compensation exclusion*—(1) *Amount excluded.* In addition to the exemptions and credits otherwise applicable, section 112 excludes from gross income the following compensation of members of the Armed Forces:

(i) *Enlisted personnel.* Compensation received for active service as a member below the grade of commissioned officer in the Armed Forces of the United States for any month during any part of which the member served in a combat zone or was hospitalized at any place as a result of wounds, disease, or injury incurred while serving in the combat zone.

(ii) *Commissioned officers.* Compensation not exceeding the monthly dollar limit received for active service as a commissioned officer in the Armed Forces of the United States for any month during any part of which the officer served in a combat zone or was hospitalized at any place as a result of wounds, disease, or injury incurred while serving in the combat zone. The monthly dollar limit is the monthly amount excludable from the officer's income under section 112(b) as amended. Beginning in 1966, the monthly dollar limit for periods of active service after 1965 became $500. As of September 10, 1993, the monthly dollar limit continues to be $500.

(2) *Time limits on exclusion during hospitalization.* Compensation received for service for any month of hospitalization that begins more than 2 years after the date specified by the President in an Executive Order as the date of the termination of combatant activities in the combat zone cannot be excluded under section 112. Furthermore, compensation received while hospitalized after January 1978 for wounds, disease, or injury incurred in the Vietnam combat zone designated by Executive Order 11216 cannot be excluded under section 112.

(3) *Special terms.* A commissioned warrant officer is not a *commissioned officer* under section 112(b) and is entitled to the exclusion allowed to enlisted personnel under section 112(a). *Compensation,* for the purpose of section 112, does not include pensions and retirement pay. *Armed Forces of the United States* is defined (and members of the Armed Forces are described) in section 7701(a)(15).

Reg. § 1.112-1(a)(1)

(4) *Military compensation only.* Only compensation paid by the Armed Forces of the United States to members of the Armed Forces can be excluded under section 112, except for compensation paid by an agency or instrumentality of the United States or by an international organization to a member of the Armed Forces whose military active duty status continues during the member's assignment to the agency or instrumentality or organization on official detail. Compensation paid by other employers (whether private enterprises or governmental entities) to members of the Armed Forces cannot be excluded under section 112 even if the payment is made to supplement the member's military compensation or is labeled by the employer as compensation for active service in the Armed Forces of the United States. Compensation paid to civilian employees of the federal government, including civilian employees of the Armed Forces, cannot be excluded under section 112, except as provided in section 112(d)(2) (which extends the exclusion to compensation of civilian employees of the federal government in missing status due to the Vietnam conflict).

(b) *Service in combat zone*—(1) *Active service.* The exclusion under section 112 applies only if active service is performed in a combat zone. A member of the Armed Forces is in active service if the member is actually serving in the Armed Forces of the United States. Periods during which a member of the Armed Forces is absent from duty on account of sickness, wounds, leave, internment by the enemy, or other lawful cause are periods of active service. A member of the Armed Forces in active service in a combat zone who becomes a prisoner of war or missing in action in the combat zone is deemed, for the purpose of section 112, to continue in active service in the combat zone for the period for which the member is treated as a prisoner of war or as missing in action for military pay purposes.

(2) *Combat zone status.* Except as provided in paragraphs (e) and (f) of this section, service is performed in a combat zone only if it is performed in an area which the President of the United States has designated by Executive Order, for the purpose of section 112, as an area in which Armed Forces of the United States are or have been engaged in combat, and only if it is performed on or after the date designated by the President by Executive Order as the date of the commencing of combatant activities in that zone and on or before the date designated by the President by Executive Order as the date of the termination of combatant activities in that zone.

(3) *Partial month service.* If a member of the Armed Forces serves in a combat zone for any part of a month, the member is entitled to the exclusion for that month to the same extent as if the member has served in that zone for the entire month. If a member of the Armed Forces is hospitalized for a part of a month as a result of wounds, disease, or injury incurred while serving in that zone, the member is entitled to the exclusion for the entire month.

(4) *Payment time and place.* The time and place of payment are irrelevant in considering whether compensation is excludable under section 112; rather, the time and place of the entitlement to compensation determine whether the compensation is excludable under section 112. Thus, compensation can be excluded under section 112 whether or not it is received outside a combat zone, or while the recipient is hospitalized, or in a year different from that in which the service was rendered for which the compensation is paid, provided that the member's entitlement to the compensation fully accrued in a month during which the member served in the combat zone or was hospitalized as a result of wounds, disease, or injury incurred while serving in the combat zone. For this purpose, entitlement to compensation fully accrues upon the completion of all actions required of the member to receive the compensation. Compensation received by a member of the Armed Forces for services rendered while in active service can be excluded under section 112 even though payment is received subsequent to discharge or release from active service. Compensation credited to a deceased member's account for a period subsequent to the established date of the member's death and received by the member's estate can be excluded from the gross income of the estate under section 112 to the same extent that it would have been excluded from the gross income of the member had the member lived and received the compensation.

(5) *Examples of combat zone compensation.* The rules of this section are illustrated by the following examples:

Example 1. On January 5, outside of a combat zone, an enlisted member received basic pay for active duty services performed from the preceding December 1 through December 31. On December 4 (and no other date), the member performed services within a combat zone. The member may exclude from income the entire payment received on January 5, although the member served in the combat zone only one day during December, received the payment outside of the combat zone, and received the payment in a year other than the year in which the combat zone services were performed.

Example 2. From March through December, an enlisted member became entitled to 25 days of annual leave while serving in a combat zone. The member used all 25 days of leave in the following year. The member may exclude from income the compensation received for those 25 days, even if the member performs no services in the combat zone in the year the compensation is received.

Example 3. From March through December, a commissioned officer became entitled to 25 days of annual leave while serving in a combat zone. During that period the officer also received basic pay of $1,000 per month from which the officer excluded from income $500 per month (exhausting the monthly dollar limit under section 112 for that period). The officer used all 25 days of leave in the following year. The officer may not exclude from income any compensation received in the following year related to those 25 days of leave, since the officer had already excluded from income the maximum amount of combat zone compensation for the period in which the leave was earned.

Example 4. In November, while serving in a combat zone, an enlisted member competing for a cash award submitted an employee suggestion. After November, the member neither served in a combat zone nor was hospitalized for wounds incurred in the combat zone. In June of the following year, the member's suggestion was selected as the winner of the competition and the award was paid. The award can be excluded from income as combat zone compensation although granted and received outside of the combat zone, since the member completed the necessary action to win the award (submission of the suggestion) in a month during which the member served in the combat zone.

Example 5. In July, while serving in a combat zone, an enlisted member voluntarily reenlisted. After July, the member neither served in a combat zone nor was hospitalized for wounds incurred in the combat zone. In February of the following year, the member received a bonus as a result of the July reenlistment. The reenlistment bonus can be excluded from income as combat zone compensation although received outside of the combat zone, since the member completed the necessary action for entitlement to the reenlistment bonus in a month during which the member served in the combat zone.

Example 6. In July, while serving outside a combat zone, an enlisted member voluntarily reenlisted. In February of the following year, the member, while performing services in a combat zone, received a bonus as a result of the July reenlistment. The reenlistment bonus cannot be excluded from income as combat zone compensation although received while serving in the combat zone, since the member completed the necessary action for entitlement to the reenlistment bonus in a month during which the member had neither served in the combat zone nor was hospitalized for wounds incurred while serving in a combat zone.

(c) *Hospitalization*—(1) *Presumption of combat zone injury.* If an individual is hospitalized for [a] wound, disease, or injury while serving in a combat zone, the wound, disease, or injury will be presumed to have been incurred while serving in a combat zone, unless the contrary clearly appears. In certain cases, however, a wound, disease, or injury may have been incurred while serving in a combat zone even though the individual was not hospitalized for it while so serving. In exceptional cases, a wound, disease, or injury will not have been incurred while serving in a combat zone even though the individual was hospitalized for it while so serving.

(2) *Length of hospitalization.* An individual is hospitalized only until the date the individual is discharged from the hospital.

(3) *Examples of combat zone injury.* The rules of this paragraph (c) are illustrated by the following examples:

Example 1. An individual is hospitalized for a disease in the combat zone where the individual has been serving for three weeks. The incubation period of the disease is two to four weeks. The disease is incurred while serving in the combat zone.

Example 2. The facts are the same as in *Example 1* except that the incubation period of the disease is one year. The disease is not incurred while serving in the combat zone.

Example 3. A member of the Air Force, stationed outside the combat zone, is shot while participating in aerial combat over the combat zone, but is not hospitalized until returning to the home base. The injury is incurred while serving in a combat zone.

Example 4. An individual is hospitalized for a disease three weeks after having departed from a combat zone. The incubation period of the disease is two to four weeks. The disease is incurred while serving in a combat zone.

(d) *Married members.* The exclusion under section 112 applies without regard to the marital status of the recipient of the compensation. If both spouses meet the requirements of the statute, then each spouse is entitled to the benefit of

Reg. § 1.112-1(c)(1)

an exclusion. In the case of a husband and wife domiciled in a State recognized for Federal income tax purposes as a community property State, any exclusion from gross income under section 112 operates before apportionment of the gross income of the spouses under community property law. For example, a husband and wife are domiciled in a community property State and the member spouse is entitled, as a commissioned officer, to the benefit of the exclusion under section 112(b) of $500 for each month. The member receives $7,899 as compensation for active service for 3 months in a combat zone. Of that amount, $1,500 is excluded from gross income under section 112(b) and $6,399 is taken into account in determining the gross income of both spouses.

(e) *Service in area outside combat zone*—(1) *Combat zone treatment.* For purposes of section 112, a member of the Armed Forces who performs military service in an area outside the area designated by Executive Order as a combat zone is deemed to serve in that combat zone while the member's service is in direct support of military operations in that zone and qualifies the member for the special pay for duty subject to hostile fire or imminent danger authorized under section 310 of title 37 of the United States Code, as amended (37 U.S.C. 310) (hostile fire/imminent danger pay).

(2) *Examples of combat zone treatment.* The examples in this paragraph (e)(2) are based on the following circumstances: Certain areas, airspace, and adjacent waters are designated as a combat zone for purposes of section 112 as of May 1. Some members of the Armed Forces are stationed in the combat zone; others are stationed in two foreign countries outside the combat zone, named Nearby Country and Destination Country.

Example 1. B is a member of an Armed Forces ground unit stationed in the combat zone. On May 31, B's unit crosses into Nearby Country. B performs military service in Nearby Country in direct support of the military operations in the combat zone from June 1 through June 8 that qualifies B for hostile fire/imminent danger pay. B does not return to the combat zone during June. B is deemed to serve in the combat zone from June 1 through June 8. Accordingly, B is entitled to the exclusion under section 112 for June. Of course, B is also entitled to the exclusion for any month (May, in this example) in which B actually served in the combat zone.

Example 2. B is a member of an Armed Forces ground unit stationed in the combat zone. On May 31, B's unit crosses into Nearby Country. On June 1, B is wounded while performing military service in Nearby Country in direct support

of the military operations in the combat zone that qualifies B for hostile fire/imminent danger pay. On June 2, B is transferred for treatment to a hospital in the United States. B is hospitalized from June through October for those wounds. B is deemed to have incurred the wounds while serving in the combat zone on June 1. Accordingly, B is entitled to the exclusion under section 112 for June through October. Of course, B is also entitled to the exclusion for any month (May, in this example) in which B actually served in the combat zone.

Example 3. B is stationed in Nearby Country for the entire month of June as a member of a ground crew servicing combat aircraft operating in the combat zone. B's service in Nearby Country during June does not qualify B for hostile fire/imminent danger pay. Accordingly, B is not deemed to serve in the combat zone during June and is not entitled to the exclusion under section 112 for that month.

Example 4. B is assigned to an air unit stationed in Nearby Country for the entire month of June. In June, members of air units of the Armed Forces stationed in Nearby Country fly combat and supply missions into and over Destination Country in direct support of military operations in the combat zone. B flies combat missions over Destination Country from Nearby Country from June 1 through June 8. B's service qualifies B for hostile fire/imminent danger pay. Accordingly, B is deemed to serve in the combat zone during June and is entitled to the exclusion under section 112. The result would be the same if B were to fly supply missions into Destination Country from Nearby Country in direct support of operations in the combat zone qualifying B for hostile fire/imminent danger pay.

Example 5. Assigned to an air unit stationed in Nearby Country, B was killed in June when B's plane crashed on returning to the airbase in Nearby Country. B was performing military service in direct support of the military operations in the combat zone at the time of B's death. B's service also qualified B for hostile fire/imminent danger pay. B is deemed to have died while serving in the combat zone or to have died as a result of wounds, disease, or injury incurred while serving in the combat zone for purposes of section 692(a) and section 692(b) (providing relief from certain income taxes for members of the Armed Forces dying in a combat zone or as a result of wounds, disease, or injury incurred while serving in a combat zone) and section 2201 (providing relief from certain estate taxes for members of the Armed Forces dying in a combat zone or by reason of combat-zone-incurred wounds). The result

Reg. § 1.112-1(e)(2)

would be the same if B's mission had been a supply mission instead of a combat mission.

Example 6. In June, B was killed as a result of an off-duty automobile accident while leaving the airbase in Nearby Country shortly after returning from a mission over Destination Country. At the time of B's death, B was not performing military duty qualifying B for hostile fire/imminent danger pay. B is not deemed to have died while serving in the combat zone or to have died as the result of wounds, disease, or injury incurred while serving in the combat zone. Accordingly, B does not qualify for the benefits of section 692(a), section 692(b), or section 2201.

Example 7. B performs military service in Nearby Country from June 1 through June 8 in direct support of the military operations in the combat zone. Nearby Country is designated as an area in which members of the Armed Forces qualify for hostile fire/imminent danger pay due to imminent danger, even though members in Nearby Country are not subject to hostile fire. B is deemed to serve in the combat zone from June 1 through June 8. Accordingly, B is entitled to the exclusion under section 112 for June.

(f) *Nonqualifying presence in combat zone*—(1) *Inapplicability of exclusion.* The following members of the Armed Forces are not deemed to serve in a combat zone within the meaning of section 112(a)(1) or section 112(b)(1) or to be hospitalized as a result of wounds, disease, or injury incurred while serving in a combat zone within the meaning of section 112(a)(2) or section 112(b)(2)—

(i) Members present in a combat zone while on leave from a duty station located outside a combat zone;

(ii) Members who pass over or through a combat zone during the course of a trip between two points both of which lie outside a combat zone; or

(iii) Members present in a combat zone solely for their own personal convenience.

(2) *Exceptions for temporary duty or special pay.* Paragraph (f)(1) of this section does not apply to members of the Armed Forces who—

(i) Are assigned on official temporary duty to a combat zone (including official temporary duty to the airspace of a combat zone); or

(ii) Qualify for hostile fire/imminent danger pay.

(3) *Examples of nonqualifying presence and its exceptions.* The examples in this paragraph (f)(3) are based on the following circumstances: Certain areas, airspace, and adjacent waters are designated as a combat zone for purposes of section 112 as of May 1. Some members of the Armed Forces are stationed in the combat zone; others are stationed in two foreign countries outside the combat zone, named Nearby Country and Destination Country.

Example 1. B is a member of the Armed Forces assigned to a unit stationed in Nearby Country. On June 1, B voluntarily visits a city within the combat zone while on leave. B is not deemed to serve in a combat zone since B is present in a combat zone while on leave from a duty station located outside a combat zone.

Example 2. B is a member of the Armed Forces assigned to a unit stationed in Nearby Country. During June, B takes authorized leave and elects to spend the leave period by visiting a city in the combat zone. While on leave in the combat zone, B is subject to hostile fire qualifying B for hostile fire/imminent danger pay. Although B is present in the combat zone while on leave from a duty station outside the combat zone, B qualifies for the exclusion under section 112 because B qualifies for hostile fire/imminent danger pay while in the combat zone.

Example 3. B is a member of the Armed Forces assigned to a ground unit stationed in the combat zone. During June, B takes authorized leave and elects to spend the leave period in the combat zone. B is not on leave from a duty station located outside a combat zone, nor is B present in a combat zone solely for B's own personal convenience. Accordingly, B's combat zone tax benefits continue while B is on leave in the combat zone.

Example 4. B is assigned as a navigator to an air unit stationed in Nearby Country. On June 4, during the course of a flight between B's home base in Nearby Country and another base in Destination Country, the aircraft on which B serves as a navigator flies over the combat zone. B is not on official temporary duty to the airspace of the combat zone and does not qualify for hostile fire/imminent danger pay as a result of the flight. Accordingly, B is not deemed to serve in a combat zone since B passes over the combat zone during the course of a trip between two points both of which lie outside the combat zone without either being on official temporary duty to the combat zone or qualifying for hostile fire/imminent danger pay.

Example 5. B is a member of the Armed Forces assigned to a unit stationed in Nearby Country. B enters the combat zone on a 3-day pass. B is not on official temporary duty and does not qualify for hostile fire/imminent danger pay while present in the combat zone. Accordingly, B is not deemed to serve in a combat zone since B is present in the combat zone solely for B's own personal convenience.

Reg. § 1.112-1(f)(1)

Example 6. B, stationed in Nearby Country, is a military courier assigned on official temporary duty to deliver military pouches in the combat zone and in Destination Country. On June 1, B arrives in the combat zone from Nearby Country, and on June 2, B departs for Destination Country. Although B passes through the combat zone during the course of a trip between two points outside the combat zone, B is nevertheless deemed to serve in a combat zone while in the combat zone because B is assigned to the combat zone on official temporary duty.

Example 7. B is a member of an Armed Forces ground unit stationed in Nearby Country. On June 1, B took authorized leave and elected to spend the leave period by visiting a city in the combat zone. On June 2, while on leave in the combat zone, B was wounded by hostile fire qualifying B for hostile fire/imminent danger pay. On June 3, B was transferred for treatment to a hospital in the United States. B is hospitalized from June through October for those wounds. Although B was present in the combat zone while on leave from a duty station outside the combat zone, B is deemed to have incurred the wounds while serving in the combat zone on June 2, because B qualified for hostile fire/imminent danger pay while in the combat zone. Accordingly, B is entitled to the exclusion under section 112 for June through October.

Example 8. The facts are the same as in *Example 7* except that B dies on September 1 as a result of the wounds incurred in the combat zone. B is deemed to have died as a result of wounds, disease, or injury incurred while serving in the combat zone for purposes of section 692(a) and section 692(b) (providing relief from certain income taxes for members of the Armed Forces dying in a combat zone or as a result of wounds, disease, or injury incurred while serving in a combat zone) and section 2201 (providing relief from certain estate taxes for members of the Armed Forces dying in a combat zone or by reason of combat-zone-incurred wounds). [Reg. § 1.112-1.]

☐ [*T.D.* 6220, 12-28-56. *Amended by T.D.* 6906, 12-28-66; *T.D.* 7066, 11-10-70 *and T.D.* 8489, 9-9-93.]

[Reg. § 1.113-1]

§ 1.113-1. Mustering-out payments for members of the Armed Forces.—For the purposes of the exclusion from gross income under section 113 of mustering-out payments with respect to service in the Armed Forces, mustering-out payments are payments made to any recipients pursuant to the provisions of 38 U.S.C. 2105 (formerly section 5 of the Mustering-Out Payment

Act of 1944 and section 505 of the Veterans Readjustment Assistance Act of 1952). [Reg. § 1.113-1.]

☐ [*T.D.* 6220, 12-28-58.]

[Reg. § 1.117-1]

§ 1.117-1. Exclusion of amounts received as a scholarship or fellowship grant.—(a) *In general.* Any amount received by an individual as a scholarship at an educational institution or as a fellowship grant, including the value of contributed services and accommodations, shall be excluded from the gross income of the recipient, subject to the limitations set forth in section 117(b) and § 1.117-2. The exclusion from gross income of an amount which is a scholarship or fellowship grant is controlled solely by section 117. Accordingly, to the extent that a scholarship or a fellowship grant exceeds the limitations of section 117(b) and § 1.117-2, it is includible in the gross income of the recipient notwithstanding the provisions of section 102 relating to exclusion from gross income of gifts, or section 74(b) relating to exclusion from gross income of certain prizes and awards. For definitions, see § 1.117-3.

(b) *Exclusion of amounts received to cover expenses.* (1) Subject to the limitations provided in subparagraph (2) of this paragraph, any amount received by an individual to cover expenses for travel (including meals and lodging while traveling and an allowance for travel of the individual's family), research, clerical help, or equipment is excludable from gross income provided that such expenses are incident to a scholarship or fellowship grant which is excludable from gross income under section 117(a)(1). If, however, only a portion of a scholarship or fellowship grant is excludable from gross income under section 117(a)(1) because of the part-time employment limitation contained in section 117(b)(1) or because of the expiration of the 36-month period described in section 117(b)(2)(B), only the amount received to cover expenses incident to such excludable portion is excludable from gross income. The requirement that these expenses be incident to the scholarship or the fellowship grant means that the expenses of travel, research, clerical help, or equipment must be incurred by the individual in order to effectuate the purpose for which the scholarship or the fellowship grant was awarded.

(2)(i) In the case of a scholarship or fellowship grant which is awarded after July 28, 1956, the exclusion provided under subparagraph (1) of this paragraph is not applicable unless the amount received by the individual is specifically designated to cover expenses for travel, research, clerical help, or equipment.

(ii) In the case of a scholarship or fellowship grant awarded before July 29, 1956, the exclusion provided under subparagraph (1) of this paragraph is not applicable unless the recipient establishes, by competent evidence, that the amount was received to cover expenses for travel, research, clerical help, or equipment, but such amount need not be specifically designated. The fact that the recipient actually incurred expenses for travel, research, clerical help, or equipment is not sufficient to establish that the amount was received to cover such expenses.

(iii) The exclusion provided under subparagraph (1) of this paragraph is applicable only to the extent that the amount received for travel, research, clerical help, or equipment is actually expended for such expenses by the recipient during the term of the scholarship or fellowship grant and within a reasonable time before and after such term.

(3) The portion of any amount received to cover the expenses described in subparagraph (1) of this paragraph which is not actually expended for such expenses within the exclusion period described in subparagraph (2) of this paragraph shall, if not returned to the grantor within this period, be included in the gross income of the recipient for the taxable year in which such exclusion period expires. [Reg. § 1.117-1.]

☐ [*T.D. 6186, 6-29-56. Amended by T.D. 6456, 3-22-60.*]

[Reg. § 1.117-2]

§ 1.117-2. **Limitations.**—(a) *Individuals who are candidates for degrees*—(1) *In general.* Under the limitations provided by section 117(b)(1) in the case of an individual who is a candidate for a degree at an educational institution, the exclusion from gross income shall not apply (except as otherwise provided in subparagraph (2) of this paragraph) to that portion of any amount received as payment for teaching, research, or other services in the nature of part-time employment required as a condition to receiving a scholarship or fellowship grant. Payments for such part-time employment shall be included in the gross income of the recipient in an amount determined by reference to the rate of compensation ordinarily paid for similar services performed by an individual who is not the recipient of a scholarship or a fellowship grant. A typical example of employment under this subparagraph is the case of an individual who is required, as a condition to receiving the scholarship or the fellowship grant, to perform part-time teaching services. A requirement that the individual shall furnish periodic reports to the grantor of the scholarship or the fellowship grant for the purpose of keeping the grantor informed as to the general progress of the individual shall not be deemed to constitute the performance of services in the nature of part-time employment.

(2) *Exception.* If teaching, research, or other services are required of all candidates (whether or not recipients of scholarships or fellowship grants) for a particular degree as a condition to receiving the degree, such teaching, research, or other services on the part of the recipient of a scholarship or fellowship grant who is a candidate for such degree shall not be regarded as part-time employment within the meaning of this paragraph. Thus, if all candidates for a particular education degree are required, as part of their regular course of study or curriculum, to perform part-time practice teaching services, such services are not to be regarded as part-time employment within the meaning of this paragraph.

(b) *Individuals who are not candidates for degrees*—(1) *Conditions for exclusion.* In the case of an individual who is not a candidate for a degree at an educational institution, the exclusion from gross income of an amount received as a scholarship or a fellowship grant shall apply (to the extent provided in subparagraph (2) of this paragraph) only if the grantor of the scholarship or fellowship grant is—

(i) An organization described in section 501(c)(3) which is exempt from tax under section 501(a),

(ii) The United States or an instrumentality or agency thereof, or a State, a territory, or a possession of the United States, or any political subdivision thereof, or the District of Columbia, or

(iii) For taxable years beginning after December 31, 1961, a foreign government, an international organization, or a binational or multinational educational and cultural foundation or commission created or continued pursuant to section 103 of the Mutual Educational and Cultural Exchange Act of 1961 (22 U.S.C. 2453).

(2) *Extent of exclusion.* (i) In the case of an individual who is not a candidate for a degree, the amount received as a scholarship or a fellowship grant which is excludable from gross income under section 117(a)(1) shall not exceed an amount equal to $300 times the number of months for which the recipient received amounts under the scholarship or fellowship grant during the taxable year. In determining the number of months during the period for which the recipient received amounts under a scholarship or fellowship grant, computation shall be made on the basis of whole calendar months. A whole calendar month means a period of time terminating with the day of the succeeding month numerically corresponding to

the day of the month of its beginning, less one, except that if there be no corresponding day of the succeeding month the period terminates with the last day of the succeeding month. For purposes of this computation a fractional part of a calendar month consisting of a period of time including 15 days or more shall be considered to be a whole calendar month and a fractional part of a calendar month consisting of a period of time including 14 days or less shall be disregarded. For example, if an individual receives a fellowship grant on September 13 which is to expire on June 12 of the following year, the grant shall be considered to have extended for a period of 9 months. If in the preceding example the grant expired on June 27, instead of June 12, the grant shall be considered to have extended for a period of 10 months.

(ii) No exclusion shall be allowed under section 117(a)(1) to an individual who is not a candidate for a degree after the recipient has, as an individual who is not a candidate for a degree, been entitled to an exclusion under that section for a period of 36 months. This limitation applies if the individual has received any amount which was either excluded or excludable from his gross income under section 117(a)(1) for any prior 36 months, whether or not consecutive. For example, if the individual received a fellowship grant of $7,200 for 3 years (which he elects to receive in 36 monthly installments of $200), his exclusion period would be exhausted even though he did not in any of the 36 months make use of the maximum exclusion. Accordingly, such individual would be entitled to no further exclusion from gross income with respect to any additional grants which he may receive as an individual who is not a candidate for a degree.

(iii) If an individual who is not a candidate for degree receives amounts from more than one scholarship or fellowship grant during the taxable year, the total amounts received in the taxable year shall be aggregated for the purpose of computing the amount which may be excludable from gross income for such taxable year. If amounts are received from more than one scholarship or fellowship grant during the same month or months within the taxable year, such month or months shall be counted only once for the purpose of determining the number of months for which the individual received such amounts under the scholarships or fellowship grants during the taxable year. For example, if an individual receives a fellowship grant from one source for the months of January to June of the taxable year and also receives a fellowship grant from another source for the months of March through December of the same taxable year, he shall be considered to have received amounts for 12 months of the taxable

year. See example (4) in subparagraph (3) of this paragraph for further illustration.

(3) *Examples.* The application of this paragraph may be further illustrated by the following examples, it being assumed that in each example the grantor is a grantor who is described in section 117(b)(2)(A) and subparagraph (1) of this paragraph.

Example (1). B, an individual who files his return on the calendar year basis, is awarded a post-doctorate fellowship grant in March 1955. The grant is to commence on September 1, 1955, and is to end on May 31, 1956, so that it will extend over a period of 9 months. The amount of the fellowship grant is $4,500 and B receives this amount in monthly installments of $500 on the first day of each month commencing September 1, 1955. During the taxable year 1955, B receives a total of $2,000 with respect to the 4-month period September through December, inclusive. He may exclude $1,200 from gross income in the taxable year 1955 ($300 × 4) and must include the remaining $800 in gross income for that year. For the year 1956, he will exclude $1,500 ($300 × 5) from gross income with respect to the $2,500 which he receives in that year and must include in gross income $1,000.

Example (2). Assume the same facts as in example (1) except that B receives the full amount of the grant ($4,500) on September 1, 1955. Since the amount received in the taxable year 1955 is for the full term of the fellowship grant (9 months), B may exclude $2,700 ($300 × 9) from gross income for the taxable year 1955. The remaining $1,800 must be included in gross income for that year.

Example (3). C, an individual who files his return on the calendar year basis, is awarded a post-doctorate fellowship grant in March 1955. The amount of the grant is $4,500 for a period commencing on September 1, 1955, and ending 24 months thereafter. C receives the full amount of the grant on September 1, 1955. C may exclude from gross income for the taxable year 1955, the full amount of the grant ($4,500) since this amount does not exceed an amount equal to $300 times the number of months (24) for which he received the amount of the grant during that taxable year.

Example (4). (i) F, an individual who files his return on the calendar year basis, is awarded a post-doctorate fellowship grant (Grant A) for two years commencing June 1, 1955, in the amount of $4,800. He elects to receive his grant in monthly installments of $200 commencing June 1, 1955. On March 1, 1956, F is awarded another post-doctorate fellowship grant (Grant B) for two years commencing September 1, 1956, in the amount of $7,200. He elects to receive this grant in monthly installments of $300 commencing September 1, 1956.

(ii) For the calendar year 1955, F receives $1,400 from Grant A which he is entitled to exclude from gross income since it does not exceed an amount equal to $300 times the number of months (7) for which he received amounts under the grant in the taxable year.

(iii) For the calendar year 1956, F receives $3,600 as the aggregate of amounts received under fellowship grants ($2,400 from Grant A and $1,200 from Grant B). F will be entitled to exclude the entire amount of $3,600 from gross income for the calendar year 1956 since such amount does not exceed an amount equal to $300 times the number of months (12) for which he received amounts under the grants in the taxable year.

(iv) For the calendar year 1957, F receives $4,600 as the aggregate of amounts received under fellowship grants ($1,000 from Grant A and $3,600 from Grant B). F will be entitled to exclude $3,600 ($300 × 12) from gross income for the calendar year 1957 and he will have to include $1,000 in gross income.

(v) For the calendar year 1958, F receives $2,400 from Grant B. F is entitled to exclude $1,500 ($300 × 5) from gross income for the calendar year 1958 and he will have to include $900 in gross income. While F receives amounts under fellowship Grant B for 8 months during the calendar year 1958, he is limited to an amount equal to $300 times 5 (months) because of the fact that he has already been entitled to exclude (and has in fact excluded) amounts received as a fellowship grant for a period of 31 months. Accordingly, he can only exclude amounts received under the fellowship grant for 5 months during the calendar year 1958, because of the 36-month limitation period. The fact that he was entitled to exclude only $1,400 ($200 a month for 7 months) instead of the maximum amount of $2,100 ($300 × 7) in 1955, is immaterial and the limitation period of 36 months is applicable.

(vi) The following chart illustrates the computation of the number of months for which F received amounts under the fellowship grants during the respective taxable years and the computation of the total amount received under the fellowship grants during each taxable year:

Period for which received and source	Number of months	Amounts received
1955:		
June 1 to December 31....	7	
Grant A............	...	$1,400
Grant B............	...	None
Aggregate	7	1,400
1956:		
January 1 to August 31 ...	8	
Grant A............	...	$1,600
Grant B............	...	None
September 1 to December 31	4	....
Grant A............	...	800
Grant B............	...	1,200
Aggregate	12	3,600
1957:		
January 1 to May 31	5	....
Grant A............	...	1,000
Grant B............	...	1,500
June 1 to December 31....	7	....
Grant A............	...	None
Grant B............	...	2,100
Aggregate	12	4,600
1958:		
January 1 to August 31 ...	8	....
Grant A............	...	None
Grant B............	...	2,400
Aggregate	8	2,400

[Reg. § 1.117-2.]

□ [T.D. 6186, 6-29-56. Amended by T.D. 6782, 12-23-64.]

[Reg. § 1.117-3]

§ 1.117-3. Definitions.—(a) Scholarship. A scholarship generally means an amount paid or allowed to, or for the benefit of, a student, whether an undergraduate or a graduate, to aid such individual in pursuing his studies. The term includes the value of contributed services and accommodations (see paragraph (d) of this section) and the amount of tuition, matriculation, and other fees which are furnished or remitted to a student to aid him in pursuing his studies. The term also includes any amount received in the nature of a family allowance as a part of a scholarship. However, the term does not include any amount provided by an individual to aid a relative, friend, or other individual in pursuing his studies where the grantor is motivated by family or philanthropic considerations. If an educational institution maintains or participates in a plan whereby the tuition of a child of a faculty member of such institution is remitted by any other participating educational institution attended by such child, the amount of the tuition so remitted shall be considered to be an amount received as a scholarship.

(b) Educational organization. For definition of "educational organization" paragraphs (a) and (b) of § 117 adopt the definition of that term which is prescribed in section 151(e)(4). Accordingly, for purposes of section 117 the term "educational organization" means only an educational organization which normally maintains a regular faculty and curriculum and normally has a regularly organized body of students in attendance at the place where its educational activities are carried on. See section 151(e)(4) and regulations thereunder.

(c) *Fellowship grant.* A fellowship grant generally means an amount paid or allowed to, or for the benefit of, an individual to aid him in the pursuit of study or research. The term includes the value of contributed services and accommodations (see paragraph (d) of this section) and the amount of tuition, matriculation, and other fees which are furnished or remitted to an individual to aid him in the pursuit of study or research. The term also includes any amount received in the nature of a family allowance as a part of a fellowship grant. However, the term does not include any amount provided by an individual to aid a relative, friend, or other individual in the pursuit of study or research where the grantor is motivated by family or philanthropic considerations.

(d) *Contributed services and accommodations.* The term "contributed services and accommodations" means such services and accommodations as room, board, laundry service, and similar services or accommodations which are received by an individual as part of a scholarship or fellowship grant.

(e) *Candidate for a degree.* The term "candidate for a degree" means an individual, whether an undergraduate or a graduate, who is pursuing studies or conducting research to meet the requirements for an academic or professional degree conferred by colleges or universities. It is not essential that such study or research be pursued or conducted at an educational institution which confers such degrees if the purpose thereof is to meet the requirements for a degree of a college or university which does confer such degrees. A student who receives a scholarship for study at a secondary school or other educational institution is considered to be a "candidate for a degree". [Reg. § 1.117-3.]

☐ *[T.D. 6186, 6-29-56. Amended by T.D. 8032, 7-1-85.]*

[Reg. § 1.117-4]

§ 1.117-4. **Items not considered as scholarships or fellowship grants.**—The following payments or allowances shall not be considered to be amounts received as a scholarship or a fellowship grant for the purpose of section 117:

(a) *Educational and training allowances to veterans.* Educational and training allowances to a veteran pursuant to section 400 of the Service-

men's Readjustment Act of 1944 (58 Stat. 287) or pursuant to 38 U.S.C. 1631 (formerly section 231 of the Veterans Readjustment Assistance Act of 1952).

(b) *Allowances to members of the Armed Forces of the United States.* Tuition and subsistence allowances to members of the Armed Forces of the United States who are students at an educational institution operated by the United States or approved by the United States for their education and training, such as the United States Naval Academy and the United States Military Academy.

(c) *Amounts paid as compensation for services or primarily for the benefit of the grantor.*

(1) Except as provided in paragraph (a) of § 1.117-2 and § 1.117-5, any amount paid or allowed to, or on behalf of, an individual to enable him to pursue studies or research, if such amount represents either compensation for past, present, or future employment services or represents payment for services which are subject to the direction or supervision of the grantor.

(2) Any amount paid or allowed to, or on behalf of, an individual to enable him to pursue studies or research primarily for the benefit of the grantor.

However, amounts paid or allowed to, or on behalf of, an individual to enable him to pursue studies or research are considered to be amounts received as a scholarship or fellowship grant for the purpose of section 117 if the primary purpose of the studies or research is to further the education and training of the recipient in his individual capacity and the amount provided by the grantor for such purpose does not represent compensation or payment for the services described in subparagraph (1) of this paragraph. Neither the fact that the recipient is required to furnish reports of his progress to the grantor, nor the fact that the results of his studies or research may be of some incidental benefit to the grantor shall, of itself, be considered to destroy the essential character of such amount as a scholarship or fellowship grant. [Reg. § 1.117-4.]

☐ *[T.D. 6186, 6-29-56. Amended by T.D. 8032, 7-1-85.]*

[Reg. § 1.117-5]

§ 1.117-5. **Federal grants requiring future service as a federal employee.**—(a) *In general.* Under section 117(c), amounts received by an individual under a federal program as a scholarship or grant for qualified tuition and expenses at an institution of higher education are excluded from the gross income of the recipient even though the recipient is required to perform future

Reg. § 1.117-5(a)

service as a federal employee. See paragraph (c) of this section for the definitions of the terms "qualified tuition and expenses" and "institution of higher education."

(b) *Exception for uniformed services scholarship programs.* The requirements of this section do not apply to amounts received before 1985 by a member of a uniformed service who entered training before 1981 under the Armed Forces Health Professions Scholarship Program, National Public Health Service Corps Scholarship Training Program, or other substantially similar federal programs requiring the recipient to work for a uniformed federal service after completion of studies. These awards are governed by section 4 of Pub. L. 93-483 as amended by Pub. L. 95-171, Pub. L. 95-600 and Pub. L. 96-167. See section 101(3) of title 37, United States Code for the definition of the term "uniformed service."

(c) *Definitions.* (1) *Qualified tuition and related expenses.* For purposes of section 117(c) and this section, qualified tuition and related expenses are those amounts which under the terms of the federal program are required to be used and in fact are used for payment of:

(i) Tuition and fees that are required for the recipient's enrollment or attendance at an institution of higher education; and

(ii) Those amounts used for payment of fees, books, supplies and equipment required for courses of instruction at such an institution.

Incidental expenses are not considered related expenses and thus are not excludable from gross income under section 117(c). Incidental expenses include room and board at an institution of higher education, expenses for travel (including expenses for meals and lodging incurred during travel and allowances for travel of the recipient's family), research, clerical help, equipment and other expenses which are not required for enrollment at the institution or in a course of instruction at such institution.

(2) *Institution of higher education.* To qualify as an institution of higher education under this section, the institution must be a public or other nonprofit institution in any state which—

(i) Admits as regular students only individuals who have a certificate of graduation from a high school or the recognized equivalent of such a certificate;

(ii) Is legally authorized within the state to provide a program of education beyond high school; and

(iii) Provides an education program for which it awards a bachelor's or higher degree or which is acceptable for full credit towards such a degree, or which trains and prepares students for

gainful employment in a recognized health profession. For purposes of this section, recognized health professions are those health professions which are supervised or monitored by appropriate state or federal agencies or governing professional associations and which require members to be currently licensed or certified in order to practice.

(3) *Service as a federal employee*—(i) *In general.* Except as otherwise provided in paragraph (c)(3)(ii) of this section, service as a federal employee refers to employment of the recipient by the federal government to work directly for the federal government. Thus, federal grants or scholarships which do not require the recipient to work directly for the federal government are not governed by the rules of this section.

(ii) *Service in a health manpower shortage area.* For purposes of this section an obligation under a grant for the recipient to serve in a health related field in a health manpower shortage area as designated by the Secretary of Health and Human Services according to the criteria of the Public Health Services Act (42 U.S.C. 254(e)) and the regulations promulgated thereunder (42 CFR 5.1-5.4) will be considered an obligation to serve as a federal employee.

(d) *Records required for exclusion from gross income.* To exclude amounts received under federal programs requiring future services as a federal employee, the recipient must maintain records that establish that the amounts received under such programs were used for qualified tuition and related expenses as defined in paragraph (c)(1) of this section. Qualifying uses may be established by providing to the Service, upon request, copies of relevant bills, receipts, cancelled checks or other convenient documentation or records which clearly reflect the use of the money received under the grant. The recipient must also submit, upon request, documentation establishing receipt of the grant and setting out the terms and requirements of the particular grant.

(e) *Applicability of rules of §§ 117(a) and 117(b).* Except where a different rule has been expressly provided in this section, amounts received under federal grants requiring future service as a federal employee, and which meet the requirements for exclusion from gross income under this section, are subject to the rules, limitations and definitions specified in §§ 117(a) and (b) of the Code and §§ 1.117-1 through 1.117-4.

(f) *Effective date.* Except as provided in paragraph (b) of this section, this section will apply to amounts received after December 31, 1980 under federal programs which meet the requirements of this section. [Reg. § 1.117-5.]

☐ [*T.D.* 8032, 7-1-85.]

Reg. § 1.117-5(b)

[Reg. § 1.118-1]

§ **1.118-1. Contributions to the capital of a corporation.**—In the case of a corporation, section 118 provides an exclusion from gross income with respect to any contribution of money or property to the capital of the taxpayer. Thus, if a corporation requires additional funds for conducting its business and obtains such funds through voluntary pro rata payments by its shareholders, the amounts so received being credited to its surplus account or to a special account, such amounts do not constitute income, although there is no increase in the outstanding shares of stock of the corporation. In such a case the payments are in the nature of assessments upon, and represent an additional price paid for, the shares of stock held by the individual shareholders, and will be treated as an addition to and as a part of the operating capital of the company. Section 118 also applies to contributions to capital made by persons other than shareholders. For example, the exclusion applies to the value of land or other property contributed to a corporation by a governmental unit or by a civic group for the purpose of inducing the corporation to locate its business in a particular community, or for the purpose of enabling the corporation to expand its operating facilities. However, the exclusion does not apply to any money or property transferred to the corporation in consideration for goods or services rendered, or to subsidies paid for the purpose of inducing the taxpayer to limit production. See section 362 for the basis of property acquired by a corporation through a contribution to its capital by its stockholders or by nonstockholders. [Reg. § 1.118-1.]

☐ [*T.D.* 6220, 12-28-56.]

[Reg. § 1.118-2]

§ **1.118-2. Contribution in aid of construction.**—(a) *Special rule for water and sewerage disposal utilities*—(1) *In general.* For purposes of section 118, the term *contribution to the capital of the taxpayer* includes any amount of money or other property received from any person (whether or not a shareholder) by a regulated public utility that provides water or sewerage disposal services if—

(i) The amount is a contribution in aid of construction under paragraph (b) of this section;

(ii) In the case of a contribution of property other than water or sewerage disposal facilities, the amount satisfies the expenditure rule under paragraph (c) of this section; and

(iii) The amount (or any property acquired or constructed with the amount) is not included in the taxpayer's rate base for ratemaking purposes.

(2) *Definitions*—(i) *Regulated public utility* has the meaning given such term by section 7701(a)(33), except that such term does not include any utility which is not required to provide water or sewerage disposal services to members of the general public in its service area.

(ii) *Water or sewerage disposal facility* is defined as tangible property described in section 1231(b) that is used predominately (80% or more) in the trade or business of furnishing water or sewerage disposal services.

(b) *Contribution in aid of construction*—(1) *In general.* For purposes of section 118(c) and this section, the term *contribution in aid of construction* means any amount of money or other property contributed to a regulated public utility that provides water or sewerage disposal services to the extent that the purpose of the contribution is to provide for the expansion, improvement, or replacement of the utility's water or sewerage disposal facilities.

(2) *Advances.* A contribution in aid of construction may include an amount of money or other property contributed to a regulated public utility for a water or sewerage disposal facility subject to a contingent obligation to repay the amount, in whole or in part, to the contributor (commonly referred to as an advance). For example, an amount received by a utility from a developer to construct a water facility pursuant to an agreement under which the utility will pay the developer a percentage of the receipts from the facility over a fixed period may constitute a contribution in aid of construction. Whether an advance is a contribution or a loan is determined under general principles of federal tax law based on all the facts and circumstances. For the treatment of any amount of a contribution in aid of construction that is repaid by the utility to the contributor, see paragraphs (c)(2)(ii) and (d)(2) of this section.

(3) *Customer connection fee*—(i) *In general.* Except as provided in paragraph (b)(3)(ii) of this section, a customer connection fee is not a contribution in aid of construction under this paragraph (b) and generally is includible in income. The term *customer connection fee* includes any amount of money or other property transferred to the utility representing the cost of installing a connection or service line (including the cost of meters and piping) from the utility's main water or sewer lines to the line owned by the customer or potential customer. A customer connection fee

Reg. § 1.118-2(b)(3)

also includes any amount paid as a service charge for starting or stopping service.

(ii) *Exceptions*—(A) *Multiple customers.* Money or other property contributed for a connection or service line from the utility's main line to the customer's or the potential customer's line is not a customer connection fee if the connection or service line serves, or is designed to serve, more than one customer. For example, a contribution for a split service line that is designed to serve two customers is not a customer connection fee. On the other hand, if a water or sewerage disposal utility treats an apartment or office building as one utility customer, then the cost of installing a connection or service line from the utility's main water or sewer lines serving that single customer is a customer connection fee.

(B) *Fire protection services.* Money or other property contributed for public and private fire protection services is not a customer connection fee.

(4) *Reimbursement for a facility previously placed in service*—(i) *In general.* If a water or sewerage disposal facility is placed in service by the utility before an amount is contributed to the utility, the contribution is not a contribution in aid of construction under this paragraph (b) with respect to the cost of the facility unless, no later than 8 1/2 months after the close of the taxable year in which the facility was placed in service, there is an agreement, binding under local law, that the utility is to receive the amount as reimbursement for the cost of acquiring or constructing the facility. An order or tariff, binding under local law, that is issued or approved by the applicable public utility commission requiring current or prospective utility customers to reimburse the utility for the cost of acquiring or constructing the facility, is a binding agreement for purposes of the preceding sentence. If an agreement exists, the basis of the facility must be reduced by the amount of the expected contributions. Appropriate adjustments must be made if actual contributions differ from expected contributions.

(ii) *Example.* The application of paragraph (b)(4)(i) of this section is illustrated by the following example:

Example. M, a calendar year regulated public utility that provides water services, spent $1,000,000 for the construction of a water facility that can serve 200 customers. M placed the facility in service in 2000. In June 2001, the public utility commission that regulates M approves a tariff requiring new customers to reimburse M for the cost of constructing the facility by paying a service availability charge of $5,000 per lot. Pursuant to the tariff, M expects to receive reim-

bursements for the cost of the facility of $100,000 per year for the years 2001 through 2010. The reimbursements are contributions in aid of construction under paragraph (b) of this section because no later than 8 1/2 months after the close of the taxable year in which the facility was placed in service there was a tariff, binding under local law, approved by the public utility commission requiring new customers to reimburse the utility for the cost of constructing the facility. The basis of the $1,000,000 facility is zero because the expected contributions equal the cost of the facility.

(5) *Classification by ratemaking authority.* The fact that the applicable ratemaking authority classifies any money or other property received by a utility as a contribution in aid of construction is not conclusive as to its treatment under this paragraph (b).

(c) *Expenditure rule*—(1) *In general.* An amount satisfies the expenditure rule of section 118(c)(2) if the amount is expended for the acquisition or construction of property described in section 118(c)(2)(A), the amount is paid or incurred before the end of the second taxable year after the taxable year in which the amount was received as required by section 118(c)(2)(B), and accurate records are kept of contributions and expenditures as provided in section 118(c)(2)(C).

(2) *Excess amount*—(i) *Includible in the utility's income.* An amount received by a utility as a contribution in aid of construction that is not expended for the acquisition or construction of water or sewerage disposal facilities as required by paragraph (c)(1) of this section (the excess amount) is not a contribution to the capital of the taxpayer under paragraph (a) of this section. Except as provided in paragraph (c)(2)(ii) of this section, such excess amount is includible in the utility's income in the taxable year in which the amount was received.

(ii) *Repayment of excess amount.* If the excess amount described in paragraph (c)(2)(i) of this section is repaid, in whole or in part, either —

(A) Before the end of the time period described in paragraph (c)(1) of this section, the repayment amount is not includible in the utility's income; or

(B) After the end of the time period described in paragraph (c)(1) of this section, the repayment amount may be deducted by the utility in the taxable year in which it is paid or incurred to the extent such amount was included in income.

(3) *Example.* The application of this paragraph (c) is illustrated by the following example:

Reg. § 1.118-2(b)(4)

Example. M, a calendar year regulated public utility that provides water services, received a $1,000,000 contribution in aid of construction in 2000 for the purpose of constructing a water facility. To the extent that the $1,000,000 exceeded the actual cost of the facility, the contribution was subject to being returned. In 2001, M built the facility at a cost of $700,000 and returned $200,000 to the contributor. As of the end of 2002, M had not returned the remaining $100,000. Assuming accurate records are kept, the requirement under section 118(c)(2) is satisfied for $700,000 of the contribution. Because $200,000 of the contribution was returned within the time period during which qualifying expenditures could be made, this amount is not includible in M's income. However, the remaining $100,000 is includible in M's income for its 2000 taxable year (the taxable year in which the amount was received) because the amount was neither spent nor repaid during the prescribed time period. To the extent M repays the remaining $100,000 after year 2002, M would be entitled to a deduction in the year such repayment is paid or incurred.

(d) *Adjusted basis*—(1) *Exclusion from basis.* Except for a repayment described in paragraph (d)(2) of this section, to the extent that a water or sewerage disposal facility is acquired or constructed with an amount received as a contribution to the capital of the taxpayer under paragraph (a) of this section, the basis of the facility is reduced by the amount of the contribution. To the extent the water or sewerage disposal facility is acquired as a contribution to the capital of the taxpayer under paragraph (a) of this section, the basis of the contributed facility is zero.

(2) *Repayment of contribution.* If a contribution to the capital of the taxpayer under paragraph (a) of this section is repaid to the contributor, either in whole or in part, then the repayment amount is a capital expenditure in the taxable year in which it is paid or incurred, resulting in an increase in the property's adjusted basis in such year. Capital expenditures allocated to depreciable property under paragraph (d)(3) of this section may be depreciated over the remaining recovery period for that property.

(3) *Allocation of contributions.* An amount treated as a capital expenditure under this paragraph (d) is to be allocated proportionately to the adjusted basis of each property acquired or constructed with the contribution based on the relative cost of such property.

(4) *Example.* The application of this paragraph (d) is illustrated by the following example:

Example. A, a calendar year regulated public utility that provides water services, received a $1,000,000 contribution in aid of construction in 2000 as an advance from B, a developer, for the purpose of constructing a water facility. To the extent that the $1,000,000 exceeds the actual cost of the facility, the contribution is subject to being returned. Under the terms of the advance, A agrees to pay to B a percentage of the receipts from the facility over a fixed period, but limited to the cost of the facility. In 2001, A builds the facility at a cost of $700,000 and returns $300,000 to B. In 2002, A pays $20,000 to B out of the receipts from the facility. Assuming accurate records are kept, the $700,000 advance is a contribution to the capital of A under paragraph (a) of this section and is excludable from A's income. The basis of the $700,000 facility constructed with this contribution to capital is zero. The $300,000 excess amount is not a contribution to the capital of A under paragraph (a) of this section because it does not meet the expenditure rule described in paragraph (c)(1) of this section. However, this excess amount is not includible in A's income pursuant to paragraph (c)(2)(ii) of this section since the amount is repaid to B within the required time period. The repayment of the $300,000 excess amount to B in 2001 is not treated as a capital expenditure by A. The $20,000 payment to B in 2002 is treated as a capital expenditure by A in 2002 resulting in an increase in the adjusted basis of the water facility from zero to $20,000.

(e) *Statute of limitations*—(1) *Extension of statute of limitations.* Under section 118(d)(1), the statutory period for assessment of any deficiency attributable to a contribution to capital under paragraph (a) of this section does not expire before the expiration of 3 years after the date the taxpayer notifies the Secretary in the time and manner prescribed in paragraph (e)(2) of this section.

(2) *Time and manner of notification.* Notification is made by attaching a statement to the taxpayer's federal income tax return for the taxable year in which any of the reportable items in paragraphs (e)(2)(i) through (iii) of this section occur. The statement must contain the taxpayer's name, address, employer identification number, taxable year, and the following information with respect to contributions of property other than water or sewerage disposal facilities that are subject to the expenditure rule described in paragraph (c) of this section—

(i) The amount of contributions in aid of construction expended during the taxable year for property described in section 118(c)(2)(A) (qualified property) as required under paragraph (c)(1)

Reg. § 1.118-2(e)(2)

of this section, identified by taxable year in which the contributions were received;

(ii) The amount of contributions in aid of construction that the taxpayer does not intend to expend for qualified property as required under paragraph (c)(1) of this section, identified by taxable year in which the contributions were received; and

(iii) The amount of contributions in aid of construction that the taxpayer failed to expend for qualified property as required under paragraph (c)(1) of this section, identified by taxable year in which the contributions were received.

(f) *Effective date.* This section is applicable for any money or other property received by a regulated public utility that provides water or sewerage disposal services on or after January 11, 2001. [Reg. § 1.118-2.]

☐ [*T.D.* 8936, 1-10-2001.]

[Reg. § 1.119-1]

§ 1.119-1. Meals and lodging furnished for the convenience of the employer.—(a) *Meals—* (1) *In general.* The value of meals furnished to an employee by his employer shall be excluded from the employee's gross income if two tests are met: (i) The meals are furnished on the business premises of the employer, and (ii) the meals are furnished for the convenience of the employer. The question of whether meals are furnished for the convenience of the employer is one of fact to be determined by analysis of all the facts and circumstances in each case. If the tests described in subdivisions (i) and (ii) of this subparagraph are met, the exclusion shall apply irrespective of whether under an employment contract or a statute fixing the terms of employment such meals are furnished as compensation.

(2) *Meals furnished without a charge.* (i) Meals furnished by an employer without charge to the employee will be regarded as furnished for the convenience of the employer if such meals are furnished for a substantial noncompensatory business reason of the employer. If an employer furnishes meals as a means of providing additional compensation to his employee (and not for a substantial noncompensatory business reason of the employer), the meals so furnished will not be regarded as furnished for the convenience of the employer. Conversely, if the employer furnishes meals to his employee for a substantial noncompensatory business reason, the meals so furnished will be regarded as furnished for the convenience of the employer, even though such meals are also furnished for a compensatory reason. In determining the reason of an employer for furnishing meals, the mere declaration that meals are fur-

nished for a noncompensatory business reason is not sufficient to prove that meals are furnished for the convenience of the employer, but such determination will be based upon an examination of all the surrounding facts and circumstances. In subdivision (ii) of this subparagraph, there are set forth some of the substantial noncompensatory business reasons which occur frequently and which justify the conclusion that meals furnished for such a reason are furnished for the convenience of the employer. In subdivision (iii) of this subparagraph, there are set forth some of the business reasons which are considered to be compensatory and which, in the absence of a substantial noncompensatory business reason, justify the conclusion that meals furnished for such a reason are not furnished for the convenience of the employer. Generally, meals furnished before or after the working hours of the employee will not be regarded as furnished for the convenience of the employer, but see subdivision (ii)(*d*) and (*f*) of this subparagraph for some exceptions to this general rule. Meals furnished on nonworking days do not qualify for the exclusion under section 119. If the employee is required to occupy living quarters on the business premises of his employer as a condition of his employment (as defined in paragraph (b) of this section), the exclusion applies to the value of any meal furnished without charge to the employee on such premises.

(ii) (*a*) Meals will be regarded as furnished for a substantial noncompensatory business reason of the employer when the meals are furnished to the employee during his working hours to have the employee available for emergency call during his meal period. In order to demonstrate that meals are furnished to the employee to have the employee available for emergency call during the meal period, it must be shown that emergencies have actually occurred, or can reasonably be expected to occur, in the employer's business which have resulted, or will result, in the employer calling on the employee to perform his job during his meal period.

(*b*) Meals will be regarded as furnished for a substantial noncompensatory business reason of the employer when the meals are furnished to the employee during his working hours because the employer's business is such that the employee must be restricted to a short meal period, such as 30 or 45 minutes, and because the employee could not be expected to eat elsewhere in such a short meal period. For example, meals may qualify under this subdivision when the employer is engaged in a business in which the peak workload occurs during the normal lunch hours. However, meals cannot qualify under this subdivision (*b*) when the reason for restricting the time of the meal period is so that the employee can be let off earlier in the day.

(c) Meals will be regarded as furnished for a substantial noncompensatory business reason of the employer when the meals are furnished to the employee during his working hours because the employee could not otherwise secure proper meals within a reasonable meal period. For example, meals may qualify under this subdivision (c) when there are insufficient eating facilities in the vicinity of the employer's premises.

(d) A meal furnished to a restaurant employee or other food service employee for each meal period in which the employee works will be regarded as furnished for a substantial noncompensatory business reason of the employer, irrespective of whether the meal is furnished during, immediately before, or immediately after the working hours of the employee.

(e) If the employer furnishes meals to employees at a place of business and the reason for furnishing the meals to each of substantially all of the employees who are furnished the meals is a substantial noncompensatory business reason of the employer, the meals furnished to each other employee will also be regarded as furnished for a substantial noncompensatory business reason of the employer.

(f) If an employer would have furnished a meal to an employee during his working hours for a substantial noncompensatory business reason, a meal furnished to such an employee immediately after his working hours because his duties prevented him from obtaining a meal during his working hours will be regarded as furnished for a substantial noncompensatory business reason.

(iii) Meals will be regarded as furnished for a compensatory business reason of the employer when the meals are furnished to the employee to promote the morale or goodwill of the employee, or to attract prospective employees.

(3) *Meals furnished with a charge.* (i) If an employer provides meals which an employee may or may not purchase, the meals will not be regarded as furnished for the convenience of the employer. Thus, meals for which a charge is made by the employer will not be regarded as furnished for the convenience of the employer if the employee has a choice of accepting the meals and paying for them or of not paying for them and providing his meals in another manner.

(ii) If an employer furnishes an employee meals for which the employee is charged an unvarying amount (for example, by subtraction from his stated compensation) irrespective of whether he accepts the meals, the amount of such flat charge made by the employer for such meals is

not, as such, part of the compensation includible in the gross income of the employee; whether the value of the meals so furnished is excludable under section 119 is determined by applying the rules of subparagraph (2) of this paragraph. If meals furnished for an unvarying amount are not furnished for the convenience of the employer in accordance with the rules of subparagraph (2) of this paragraph, the employee shall include in gross income the value of the meals regardless of whether the value exceeds or is less than the amount charged for such meals. In the absence of evidence to the contrary, the value of the meals may be deemed to be equal to the amount charged for them.

(b) *Lodging.* The value of lodging furnished to an employee by the employer shall be excluded from the employee's gross income if three tests are met—

(1) The lodging is furnished on the business premises of the employer,

(2) The lodging is furnished for the convenience of the employer, and

(3) The employee is required to accept such lodging as a condition of his employment.

The requirement of subparagraph (3) of this paragraph that the employee is required to accept such lodging as a condition of his employment means that he be required to accept the lodging in order to enable him properly to perform the duties of his employment. Lodging will be regarded as furnished to enable the employee properly to perform the duties of his employment when, for example, the lodging is furnished because the employee is required to be available for duty at all times or because the employee could not perform the services required of him unless he is furnished such lodging. If the tests described in subparagraphs (1), (2), and (3) of this paragraph are met, the exclusion shall apply irrespective of whether a charge is made, or whether, under an employment contract or statute fixing the terms of employment, such lodging is furnished as compensation. If the employer furnishes the employee lodging for which the employee is charged an unvarying amount irrespective of whether he accepts the lodging, the amount of the charge made by the employer for such lodging is not, as such, part of the compensation includible in the gross income of the employee; whether the value of the lodging is excludable from gross income under section 119 is determined by applying the other rules of this paragraph. If the tests described in subparagraphs (1), (2), and (3) of this paragraph are not met, the employee shall include in gross income the value of the lodging regardless of whether it exceeds or is less than the amount

Reg. § 1.119-1(b)(3)

charged. In the absence of evidence to the contrary, the value of the lodging may be deemed to be equal to the amount charged.

(c) *Business premises of the employer*—(1) *In general.* For purposes of this section, the term "business premises of the employer" generally means the place of employment of the employee. For example, meals and lodging furnished in the employer's home to a domestic servant would constitute meals and lodging furnished on the business premises of the employer. Similarly, meals furnished to cowhands while herding their employer's cattle on leased land would be regarded as furnished on the business premises of the employer.

(2) *Certain camps.* For taxable years beginning after December 31, 1981, in the case of an individual who is furnished lodging by or on behalf of his employer in a camp (as defined in paragraph (d) of this section) in a foreign country (as defined in § 1.911-2(h)), the camp shall be considered to be part of the business premises of the employer.

(d) *Camp defined*—(1) *In general.* For the purposes of paragraph (c)(2) of this section, a camp is lodging that is all of the following:

(i) Provided by or on behalf of the employer for the convenience of the employer because the place at which the employee renders services is in a remote area where satisfactory housing is not available to the employee on the open market within a reasonable commuting distance of that place;

(ii) Located, as near as practicable, in the vicinity of the place at which the employee renders services; and

(iii) Furnished in a common area or enclave which is not available to the general public for lodging or accommodations and which normally accommodates ten or more employees.

(2) *Satisfactory housing.* For purposes of paragraph (d)(1)(i) of this section, facts and circumstances that may be relevant in determining whether housing available to the employee is satisfactory include, but are not limited to, the size and condition of living space and the availability and quality of utilities such as water, sewers or other waste disposal facilities, electricity, or heat. The general environment in which housing is located (*e.g.* climate, prevalence of insects, etc.) does not of itself make housing unsatisfactory. The general environment is relevant, however, if housing is inadequate to protect the occupants from environmental conditions. The individual employee's income level is not relevant in determining whether housing is satisfactory; it may,

however, be relevant in determining whether satisfactory housing is available to the employee (see paragraph (d)(3)(i)(B) of this section).

(3) *Availability of satisfactory housing*—(i) *Facts and circumstances.* For purposes of paragraph (d)(1)(i) of this section, facts and circumstances to be considered in determining whether satisfactory housing is available to the employee on the open market include but are not limited to:

(A) The number of housing units available on the open market in relation to the number of housing units required for the employer's employees;

(B) The cost of housing available on the open market;

(C) The quality of housing available on the open market; and

(D) The presence of warfare or civil insurrection within the area where housing would be available which would subject U.S. citizens to unusual risk of personal harm or property loss.

(ii) *Presumptions.* Satisfactory housing will generally be considered to be unavailable to the employee on the open market if either of the following conditions is satisfied:

(A) The foreign government requires the employer to provide housing for its employees other than housing available on the open market; or

(B) An unrelated person awarding work to the employer requires that the employer's employees occupy housing specified by such unrelated person.

The condition of either paragraph (d)(3)(ii)(A) or (B) of this section is not satisfied if the requirement described therein and imposed either by a foreign government or unrelated person applies primarily to U.S. employers and not to a significant number of third country employers or applies primarily to employers of U.S. employees and not to a significant number of employers of third country employees.

(4) *Reasonable commuting distance.* For purposes of paragraph (d)(1)(i) of this section, in determining whether a commuting distance is reasonable, the accessibility of the place at which the employee renders services due to geographic factors, the quality of the roads, the customarily available transportation, and the usual travel time (at the time of day such travel would be required) to the place at which the employee renders services shall be taken into account.

(5) *Common area or enclave.* A cluster of housing units does not satisfy paragraph (d)(1)(iii) of this section if it is adjacent to or surrounded by substantially similar housing avail-

Reg. § 1.119-1(c)(1)

able to the general public. Two or more common areas or enclaves that house employees who work on the same project (for example, a highway project) are considered to be one common area or enclave in determining whether they normally accommodate ten or more employees.

(e) *Rules.* The exclusion provided by section 119 applies only to meals and lodging furnished in kind by or on behalf of an employer to his employee. If the employee has an option to receive additional compensation in lieu of meals or lodging in kind, the value of such meals and lodging is not excludable from gross income under section 119. However, the mere fact that an employee, at his option, may decline to accept meals tendered in kind will not of itself require inclusion of the value thereof in gross income. Cash allowances for meals or lodging received by an employee are includible in gross income to the extent that such allowances constitute compensation.

(f) *Examples.* The provisions of section 119 may be illustrated by the following examples:

Example (1). A waitress who works from 7 a.m. to 4 p.m. is furnished without charge two meals a work day. The employer encourages the waitress to have her breakfast on his business premises before starting work, but does not require her to have breakfast there. She is required, however, to have her lunch on such premises. Since the waitress is a food service employee and works during the normal breakfast and lunch periods, the waitress is permitted to exclude from her gross income both the value of the breakfast and the value of the lunch.

Example (2). The waitress in example (1) is allowed to have meals on the employer's premises without charge on her days off. The waitress is not permitted to exclude the value of such meals from her gross income.

Example (3). A bank teller who works from 9 a.m. to 5 p.m. is furnished his lunch without charge in a cafeteria which the bank maintains on its premises. The bank furnishes the teller such meals in order to limit his lunch period to 30 minutes since the bank's peak work load occurs during the normal lunch period. If the teller had to obtain his lunch elsewhere, it would take him considerably longer than 30 minutes for lunch, and the bank strictly enforces the 30-minute time limit. The bank teller may exclude from his gross income the value of such meals obtained in the bank cafeteria.

Example (4). Assume the same facts as in example (3), except that the bank charges the bank teller an unvarying rate per meal regardless of whether he eats in the cafeteria. The bank teller is not required to include in gross income such flat amount charged as part of his compensation, and he is entitled to exclude from his gross income the value of the meals he receives for such flat charge.

Example (5). A Civil Service employee of a State is employed at an institution and is required by his employer to be available for duty at all times. The employer furnishes the employee with meals and lodging at the institution without charge. Under the applicable State statute, his meals and lodging are regarded as part of the employee's compensation. The employee would nevertheless be entitled to exclude the value of such meals and lodging from his gross income.

Example (6). An employee of an institution is given the choice of residing at the institution free of charge, or of residing elsewhere and receiving a cash allowance in addition to his regular salary. If he elects to reside at the institution, the value to the employee of the lodging furnished by the employer will be includible in the employee's gross income because his residence at the institution is not required in order for him to perform properly the duties of his employment.

Example (7). A construction worker is employed at a construction project at a remote job site in Alaska. Due to the inaccessibility of facilities for the employees who are working at the job site to obtain food and lodging and the prevailing weather conditions, the employer is required to furnish meals and lodging to the employee at the camp site in order to carry on the construction project. The employee is required to pay $40 a week for the meals and lodging. The weekly charge of $40 is not, as such, part of the compensation includible in the gross income of the employee, and under paragraphs (a) and (b) of this section the value of the meals and lodging is excludable from his gross income.

Example (8). A manufacturing company provides a cafeteria on its premises at which its employees can purchase their lunch. There is no other eating facility located near the company's premises, but the employee can furnish his own meal by bringing his lunch. The amount of compensation which any employee is required to include in gross income is not reduced by the amount charged for the meals, and the meals are not considered to be furnished for the convenience of the employer.

Example (9). A hospital maintains a cafeteria on its premises where all of its 230 employees may obtain a meal during their working hours. No charge is made for these meals. The hospital furnishes such meals in order to have each of 210 of the employees available for any emergencies that may occur, and it is shown that each such employee is at times called upon to perform services

Reg. § 1.119-1(f)

during his meal period. Although the hospital does not require such employees to remain on the premises during meal periods, they rarely leave the hospital during their meal period. Since the hospital furnishes meals to each of substantially all of its employees in order to have each of them available for emergency call during his meal period, all of the hospital employees who obtain their meals in the hospital cafeteria may exclude from their gross income the value of such meals. [Reg. § 1.119-1.]

☐ [*T.D. 6220, 12-28-56. Amended by T.D. 6745, 7-8-64 and T.D. 8006, 1-17-85.*]

[Reg. § 1.120-3]

§ 1.120-3. Notice of application for recognition of status of qualified group legal services plan.—(a) *In general.* In order for a plan to be a qualified group legal services plan for purposes of the exclusion from gross income provided by section 120(a), the plan must give notice to the Internal Revenue Service that it is applying for recognition of its status as a qualified plan. Paragraph (b) of this section describes how the notice is to be filed for the plan. Paragraph (c) of this section describes the action that the Internal Revenue Service will take in response to the notice submitted for the plan. Paragraph (d) of this section describes the period of plan qualification.

(b) *Filing of notice*—(1) *In general.* A notice of application for recognition of the status of a qualified group legal services plan must be filed with the key district director of internal revenue as described in § 601.201(n). The notice must be filed on Form 1024, Application for Recognition of Exemption Under Section 501(a) or for Determination Under Section 120, with the accompanying Schedule L, and must contain the information required by the form and any accompanying instructions. The form may be filed by either the employer adopting the plan or the person administering the plan. No Form 1024 and Schedule L may be filed for a plan before an employer adopts the plan, or proposes to adopt the plan contingent only upon the recognition of the plan as a qualified plan.

(2) *Plans to which more than one employer contributes.* In general, for purposes of section 120 the adoption of a plan by an employer constitutes the adoption of a separate plan to which that employer alone contributes, notwithstanding that, in form, the employer purports to adopt a plan with respect to which the employer is one of two or more contributing employers. Accordingly, a separate Schedule L must be filed pursuant to the instructions accompanying Form 1024 for each employer adopting a plan.

(3) *Certain collectively bargained plans.* Notwithstanding subparagraph (2) of this paragraph, if a plan to which more than one employer contributes is a plan to which this subparagraph (3) applies, the plan is treated as a single plan for purposes of section 120. Accordingly, only one Form 1024 and Schedule L is required to be filed for the plan, regardless of the number of employers originally adopting the plan. In addition, once a Form 1024 and Schedule L is filed, no additional filing is required with respect to an employer who thereafter adopts the plan. In general, this subparagraph (3) applies to any plan that is maintained pursuant to a collective bargaining agreement between employee representatives and more than one employer who is required by the plan instrument or other agreement to contribute to the plan with respect to employees (or their spouses or dependents) participating in the plan. This subparagraph does not apply, however, if all employers required to contribute to the plan are corporations which are members of a controlled group of corporations within the meaning of section 1563(a), determined without regard to section 1563(e)(3)(C). If all employers required to contribute to the plan are corporations which are members of such a controlled group, the filing requirements described in subparagraph (2) of this paragraph apply, notwithstanding that the plan is maintained pursuant to a collective bargaining agreement.

(c) *Internal Revenue Service action on notice of application for recognition.* The Internal Revenue Service will issue to the person submitting Form 1024 and Schedule L a ruling or determination letter stating that the plan is or is not a qualified group legal services plan. For general procedural rules, see § 601.201(a) through (n), as that section relates to rulings and determination letters.

(d) *Period of plan qualification*—(1) *In general.* In the case of a favorable determination, the plan will be considered a qualified group legal services plan. If a Form 1024 and Schedule L required to be filed by or on behalf of an employer is filed before—

(i) The end of the first plan year (as determined under the plan),

(ii) The end of the plan year within which the employer adopts the plan, or

(iii) July 29, 1980,

the period of plan qualification with respect to the employer will begin on the date the plan is adopted by the employer (or, if later, January 1, 1977). If the form and schedule are not filed before the latest of the dates described in subdivisions (i), (ii) and (iii), the period of plan qualification with respect to the employer will begin on the

Reg. § 1.120-3(a)

date of filing. In any case in which either the Form 1024 or Schedule L filed by or on behalf of an employer is incomplete, the date of filing is the date on which the incomplete form or schedule is filed, if the necessary additional information is provided at the request of the Commissioner within the additional time period allowed by the Commissioner. If the additional information is not provided within the additional time period allowed, the date of filing is the date on which the additional information is filed. If no separate Form 1024 and Schedule L are required to be filed by or on behalf of an employer (see paragraph (b)(3) of this section), the period of plan qualification with respect to the employer will begin on the date the plan is adopted by the employer (or, if later, January 1, 1977). In any case in which a plan is materially modified to conform to the requirements of section 120, either before or after a Form 1024 and Schedule L are filed, the period of plan qualification will not include any period before the effective date of the modification.

(2) *Plans in existence on June 4, 1976.* (i) Notwithstanding paragraph (d)(1) of this section, a written group legal services plan providing for employer contributions which was in existence on June 4, 1976, will be considered a qualified group legal services plan for the period January 1, 1977, through April 2, 1977. However, if the plan is maintained pursuant to one or more agreements which were in effect on October 4, 1976, and which the Secretary of Labor finds to be collective bargaining agreements, the period of deemed qualification will extend beyond April 2, 1977, and end on the date on which the last of the collective bargaining agreements relating to the plan terminates. Extensions of a bargaining agreement which are agreed to after October 4, 1976, are to be disregarded. The period of deemed qualification for a plan maintained pursuant to a collective bargaining agreement will not, however, extend beyond December 31, 1981.

(ii) A written group legal services plan will be considered to have been in existence on June 4, 1976, if on or before that date the plan was reduced to writing and adopted by one or more employers. No amounts need have been contributed under the plan as of June 4, 1976.

(iii) Notwithstanding that a plan is a qualified plan for the period of deemed qualification described in this paragraph (d)(2), the rules of paragraphs (c) and (d)(1) of this section still apply with respect to a Form 1024 and Schedule L filed for the plan. For example, if a Form 1024 and Schedule L filed by or on behalf of an employer are filed before the latest of the 3 dates described in paragraph (d)(1) of this section, in

the case of a favorable determination the plan will be a qualified plan from the date the plan is adopted by the employer (or, if later, January 1, 1977), and any period of deemed qualification and the period of qualification based upon the favorable determination will overlap. However, in the case of a plan to which this paragraph (d)(2) applies, if a Form 1024 and Schedule L required to be filed by or on behalf of an employer is not filed before the latest of the 3 dates described in paragraph (d)(1) of this section, the following rules shall apply. In general, if Form 1024 and Schedule L are filed before the end of the plan year following the plan year with or within which the plan's period of deemed qualification expires, in the event of a favorable determination the plan will be a qualified plan with respect to the employer beginning on the earlier of the day following the date on which the period of deemed qualification expires or the date on which the Form 1024 and Schedule L are filed. The period of plan qualification with respect to an employer cannot, however, include any period before the employer adopts the plan. If the Form 1024 and Schedule L are not filed before the end of the plan year following the plan year with or within which the plan's period of deemed qualification expires, in the case of a favorable determination the plan will be a qualified plan with respect to an employer from the later of the date of filing or adoption of the plan by the employer. The rules described in paragraph (d)(1) of this section relating to incomplete filings and plan modifications apply with respect to a filing described in this paragraph (d)(2).

(e) *Effective date.* This section is effective for notices of application for recognition of the status of a qualified group legal services plan filed after May 29, 1980. [Reg. § 1.120-3.]

□ [*T.D.* 7696, 4-28-80.]

[Reg. § 1.121-1]

§ 1.121-1. **Exclusion of gain from sale or exchange of a principal residence.**—(a) *In general.* Section 121 provides that, under certain circumstances, gross income does not include gain realized on the sale or exchange of property that was owned and used by a taxpayer as the taxpayer's principal residence. Subject to the other provisions of section 121, a taxpayer may exclude gain only if, during the 5-year period ending on the date of the sale or exchange, the taxpayer owned and used the property as the taxpayer's principal residence for periods aggregating 2 years or more.

(b) *Residence*—(1) *In general.* Whether property is used by the taxpayer as the taxpayer's residence depends upon all the facts and circumstances. A property used by the taxpayer as the taxpayer's residence may include a houseboat, a house trailer, or the house or apartment that the taxpayer is entitled to occupy as a tenant-stock-holder in a cooperative housing corporation (as those terms are defined in section 216(b)(1) and (2)). Property used by the taxpayer as the tax-payer's residence does not include personal property that is not a fixture under local law.

(2) *Principal residence.* In the case of a tax-payer using more than one property as a resi-dence, whether property is used by the taxpayer as the taxpayer's principal residence depends upon all the facts and circumstances. If a tax-payer alternates between 2 properties, using each as a residence for successive periods of time, the property that the taxpayer uses a majority of the time during the year ordinarily will be considered the taxpayer's principal residence. In addition to the taxpayer's use of the property, relevant fac-tors in determining a taxpayer's principal resi-dence, include, but are not limited to—

(i) The taxpayer's place of employment;

(ii) The principal place of abode of the taxpayer's family members;

(iii) The address listed on the taxpayer's federal and state tax returns, driver's license, au-tomobile registration, and voter registration card;

(iv) The taxpayer's mailing address for bills and correspondence;

(v) The location of the taxpayer's banks; and

(vi) The location of religious organizations and recreational clubs with which the taxpayer is affiliated.

(3) *Vacant land*—(i) *In general.* The sale or exchange of vacant land is not a sale or exchange of the taxpayer's principal residence unless—

(A) The vacant land is adjacent to land containing the dwelling unit of the taxpayer's principal residence;

(B) The taxpayer owned and used the vacant land as part of the taxpayer's principal residence;

(C) The taxpayer sells or exchanges the dwelling unit in a sale or exchange that meets the requirements of section 121 within 2 years before or 2 years after the date of the sale or exchange of the vacant land; and

(D) The requirements of section 121 have otherwise been met with respect to the va-cant land.

(ii) *Limitations*—(A) *Maximum limitation amount.* For purposes of section 121(b)(1) and (2) (relating to the maximum limitation amount of

the section 121 exclusion), the sale or exchange of the dwelling unit and the vacant land are treated as one sale or exchange. Therefore, only one maxi-mum limitation amount of $250,000 ($500,000 for certain joint returns) applies to the combined sales or exchanges of vacant land and the dwelling unit. In applying the maximum limitation amount to sales or exchanges that occur in differ-ent taxable years, gain from the sale or exchange of the dwelling unit, up to the maximum limita-tion amount under section 121(b)(1) or (2), is excluded first and each spouse is treated as ex-cluding one-half of the gain from a sale or ex-change to which section 121(b)(2)(A) and § 1.121-2(a)(3)(i) (relating to the limitation for certain joint returns) apply.

(B) *Sale or exchange of more than one principal residence in 2-year period.* If a dwelling unit and vacant land are sold or exchanged in separate transactions that qualify for the section 121 exclusion under this paragraph (b)(3), each of the transactions is disregarded in applying section 121(b)(3) (restricting the application of section 121 to only 1 sale or exchange every 2 years) to the other transactions but is taken into account as a sale or exchange of a principal residence on the date of the transaction in applying section 121(b)(3) to that transaction and the sale or ex-change of any other principal residence.

(C) *Sale or exchange of vacant land before dwelling unit.* If the sale or exchange of the dwelling unit occurs in a later taxable year than the sale or exchange of the vacant land and after the date prescribed by law (including extensions) for the filing of the return for the taxable year of the sale or exchange of the vacant land, any gain from the sale or exchange of the vacant land must be treated as taxable on the taxpayer's return for the taxable year of the sale or exchange of the vacant land. If the taxpayer has reported gain from the sale or exchange of the vacant land as taxable, after satisfying the requirements of this paragraph (b)(3) the taxpayer may claim the sec-tion 121 exclusion with regard to the sale or ex-change of the vacant land (for any period for which the period of limitation under section 6511 has not expired) by filing an amended return.

(4) *Examples.* The provisions of this para-graph (b) are illustrated by the following examples:

Example 1. Taxpayer A owns 2 residences, one in New York and one in Florida. From 1999 through 2004, he lives in the New York residence for 7 months and the Florida residence for 5 months of each year. In the absence of facts and circumstances indicating otherwise, the New York residence is A's principal residence. A would be

Reg. § 1.121-1(b)(2)

eligible for the section 121 exclusion of gain from the sale or exchange of the New York residence, but not the Florida residence.

Example 2. Taxpayer B owns 2 residences, one in Virginia and one in Maine. During 1999 and 2000, she lives in the Virginia residence. During 2001 and 2002, she lives in the Maine residence. During 2003, she lives in the Virginia residence. B's principal residence during 1999, 2000, and 2003 is the Virginia residence. B's principal residence during 2001 and 2002 is the Maine residence. B would be eligible for the 121 exclusion of gain from the sale or exchange of either residence (but not both) during 2003.

Example 3. In 1991 Taxpayer C buys property consisting of a house and 10 acres that she uses as her principal residence. In May 2005 C sells 8 acres of the land and realizes a gain of $110,000. C does not sell the dwelling unit before the due date for filing C's 2005 return, therefore C is not eligible to exclude the $110,000 of gain. In March 2007 C sells the house and remaining 2 acres realizing a gain of $180,000 from the sale of the house. C may exclude the $180,000 of gain. Because the sale of the 8 acres occurred within 2 years from the date of the sale of the dwelling unit, the sale of the 8 acres is treated as a sale of the taxpayer's principal residence under paragraph (b)(3) of this section. C may file an amended return for 2005 to claim an exclusion for $70,000 ($250,000 − $180,000 gain previously excluded) of the $110,000 gain from the sale of the 8 acres.

Example 4. In 1998 Taxpayer D buys a house and 1 acre that he uses as his principal residence. In 1999 D buys 29 acres adjacent to his house and uses the vacant land as part of his principal residence. In 2003 D sells the house and 1 acre and the 29 acres in 2 separate transactions. D sells the house and 1 acre at a loss of $25,000. D realizes $270,000 of gain from the sale of the 29 acres. D may exclude the $245,000 gain from the 2 sales.

(c) *Ownership and use requirements*—(1) *In general.* The requirements of ownership and use for periods aggregating 2 years or more may be satisfied by establishing ownership and use for 24 full months or for 730 days (365 × 2). The requirements of ownership and use may be satisfied during nonconcurrent periods if both the ownership and use tests are met during the 5-year period ending on the date of the sale or exchange.

(2) *Use*—(i) In establishing whether a taxpayer has satisfied the 2-year use requirement, occupancy of the residence is required. However, short temporary absences, such as for vacation or other seasonal absence (although accompanied with rental of the residence), are counted as periods of use.

(ii) *Determination of use during periods of out-of-residence care.* If a taxpayer has become physically or mentally incapable of self-care and the taxpayer sells or exchanges property that the taxpayer owned and used as the taxpayer's principal residence for periods aggregating at least 1 year during the 5-year period preceding the sale or exchange, the taxpayer is treated as using the property as the taxpayer's principal residence for any period of time during the 5-year period in which the taxpayer owns the property and resides in any facility (including a nursing home) licensed by a State or political subdivision to care for an individual in the taxpayer's condition.

(3) *Ownership*—(i) *Trusts.* If a residence is owned by a trust, for the period that a taxpayer is treated under sections 671 through 679 (relating to the treatment of grantors and others as substantial owners) as the owner of the trust or the portion of the trust that includes the residence, the taxpayer will be treated as owning the residence for purposes of satisfying the 2-year ownership requirement of section 121, and the sale or exchange by the trust will be treated as if made by the taxpayer.

(ii) *Certain single owner entities.* If a residence is owned by an eligible entity (within the meaning of § 301.7701-3(a) of this chapter) that has a single owner and is disregarded for federal tax purposes as an entity separate from its owner under § 301.7701-3 of this chapter, the owner will be treated as owning the residence for purposes of satisfying the 2-year ownership requirement of section 121, and the sale or exchange by the entity will be treated as if made by the owner.

(4) *Examples.* The provisions of this paragraph (c) are illustrated by the following examples. The examples assume that § 1.121-3 (relating to the reduced maximum exclusion) does not apply to the sale of the property. The examples are as follows:

Example 1. Taxpayer A has owned and used his house as his principal residence since 1986. On January 31, 1998, A moves to another state. A rents his house to tenants from that date until April 18, 2000, when he sells it. A is eligible for the section 121 exclusion because he has owned and used the house as his principal residence for at least 2 of the 5 years preceding the sale.

Example 2. Taxpayer B owns and uses a house as her principal residence from 1986 to the end of 1997. On January 4, 1998, B moves to another state and ceases to use the house. B's son moves into the house in March 1999 and uses the residence until it is sold on July 1, 2001. B may not exclude gain from the sale under section 121 because she did not use the property as her principal residence for at least 2 years out of the 5 years preceding the sale.

Example 3. Taxpayer C lives in a townhouse that he rents from 1993 through 1996. On January 18, 1997, he purchases the townhouse. On February 1, 1998, C moves into his daughter's home. On May 25, 2000, while still living in his daughter's home, C sells his townhouse. The section 121 exclusion will apply to gain from the sale because C owned the townhouse for at least 2 years out of the 5 years preceding the sale (from January 19, 1997 until May 25, 2000) and he used the townhouse as his principal residence for at least 2 years during the 5-year period preceding the sale (from May 25, 1995 until February 1, 1998).

Example 4. Taxpayer D, a college professor, purchases and moves into a house on May 1, 1997. He uses the house as his principal residence continuously until September 1, 1998, when he goes abroad for a 1-year sabbatical leave. On October 1, 1999, 1 month after returning from the leave, D sells the house. Because his leave is not considered to be a short temporary absence under paragraph (c)(2) of this section, the period of the sabbatical leave may not be included in determining whether D used the house for periods aggregating 2 years during the 5-year period ending on the date of the sale. Consequently, D is not entitled to exclude gain under section 121 because he did not use the residence for the requisite period.

Example 5. Taxpayer E purchases a house on February 1, 1998, that he uses as his principal residence. During 1998 and 1999, E leaves his residence for a 2-month summer vacation. E sells the house on March 1, 2000. Although, in the 5-year period preceding the date of sale, the total time E used his residence is less than 2 years (21 months), the section 121 exclusion will apply to gain from the sale of the residence because, under paragraph (c)(2) of this section, the 2-month vacations are short temporary absences and are counted as periods of use in determining whether E used the residence for the requisite period.

(d) *Depreciation taken after May 6, 1997*—(1) *In general.* The section 121 exclusion does not apply to so much of the gain from the sale or exchange of property as does not exceed the portion of the depreciation adjustments (as defined in section 1250(b)(3)) attributable to the property for periods after May 6, 1997. Depreciation adjustments allocable to any portion of the property to which the section 121 exclusion does not apply under paragraph (e) of this section are not taken into account for this purpose.

(2) *Example.* The provisions of this paragraph (d) are illustrated by the following example:

Example. On July 1, 1999, Taxpayer A moves into a house that he owns and had rented to tenants since July 1, 1997. A took depreciation deductions totaling $14,000 for the period that he rented the property. After using the residence as his principal residence for 2 full years, A sells the property on August 1, 2001. A's gain realized from the sale is $40,000. A has no other section 1231 or capital gains or losses for 2001. Only $26,000 ($40,000 gain realized − $14,000 depreciation deductions) may be excluded under section 121. Under section 121(d)(6) and paragraph (d)(1) of this section, A must recognize $14,000 of the gain as unrecaptured section 1250 gain within the meaning of section 1(h).

(e) *Property used in part as a principal residence*—(1) *Allocation required.* Section 121 will not apply to the gain allocable to any portion (separate from the dwelling unit) of property sold or exchanged with respect to which a taxpayer does not satisfy the use requirement. Thus, if a portion of the property was used for residential purposes and a portion of the property (separate from the dwelling unit) was used for non-residential purposes, only the gain allocable to the residential portion is excludable under section 121. No allocation is required if both the residential and non-residential portions of the property are within the same dwelling unit. However, section 121 does not apply to the gain allocable to the residential portion of the property to the extent provided by paragraph (d) of this section.

(2) *Dwelling unit.* For purposes of this paragraph (e), the term *dwelling unit* has the same meaning as in section 280A(f)(1), but does not include appurtenant structures or other property.

(3) *Method of allocation.* For purposes of determining the amount of gain allocable to the residential and non-residential portions of the property, the taxpayer must allocate the basis and the amount realized between the residential and the non-residential portions of the property using the same method of allocation that the taxpayer used to determine depreciation adjustments (as defined in section 1250(b)(3)), if applicable.

(4) *Examples.* The provisions of this paragraph (e) are illustrated by the following examples:

Example 1. Non-residential use of property not within the dwelling unit. (i) Taxpayer A owns a property that consists of a house, a stable and 35 acres. A uses the stable and 28 acres for non-residential purposes for more than 3 years during the 5-year period preceding the sale. A uses the

Reg. § 1.121-1(d)(1)

entire house and the remaining 7 acres as his principal residence for at least 2 years during the 5-year period preceding the sale. For periods after May 6, 1997, A claims depreciation deductions of $9,000 for the non-residential use of the stable. A sells the entire property in 2004, realizing a gain of $24,000. A has no other section 1231 or capital gains or losses for 2004.

(ii) Because the stable and the 28 acres used in the business are separate from the dwelling unit, the allocation rules under this paragraph (e) apply and A must allocate the basis and amount realized between the portion of the property that he used as his principal residence and the portion of the property that he used for non-residential purposes. A determines that $14,000 of the gain is allocable to the non-residential-use portion of the property and that $10,000 of the gain is allocable to the portion of the property used as his residence. A must recognize the $14,000 of gain allocable to the non-residential-use portion of the property ($9,000 of which is unrecaptured section 1250 gain within the meaning of section 1(h), and $5,000 of which is adjusted net capital gain). A may exclude $10,000 of the gain from the sale of the property.

Example 2. Non-residential use of property not within the dwelling unit and rental of the entire property. (i) In 1998 Taxpayer B buys a property that includes a house, a barn, and 2 acres. B uses the house and 2 acres as her principal residence and the barn for an antiques business. In 2002, B moves out of the house and rents it to tenants. B sells the property in 2004, realizing a gain of $21,000. Between 1998 and 2004 B claims depreciation deductions of $4,800 attributable to the antiques business. Between 2002 and 2004 B claims depreciation deductions of $3,000 attributable to the house. B has no other section 1231 or capital gains or losses for 2004.

(ii) Because the portion of the property used in the antiques business is separate from the dwelling unit, the allocation rules under this paragraph (e) apply. B must allocate basis and amount realized between the portion of the property that she used as her principal residence and the portion of the property that she used for non-residential purposes. B determines that $4,000 of the gain is allocable to the non-residential portion of the property and that $17,000 of the gain is allocable to the portion of the property that she used as her principal residence.

(iii) B must recognize the $4,000 of gain allocable to the non-residential portion of the property (all of which is unrecaptured section 1250 gain within the meaning of section 1(h)). In addition, the section 121 exclusion does not apply

to the gain allocable to the residential portion of the property to the extent of the depreciation adjustments attributable to the residential portion of the property for periods after May 6, 1997 ($3,000). Therefore, B may exclude $14,000 of the gain from the sale of the property.

Example 3. Non-residential use of a separate dwelling unit. (i) In 2002 Taxpayer C buys a 3-story townhouse and converts the basement level, which has a separate entrance, into a separate apartment by installing a kitchen and bathroom and removing the interior stairway that leads from the basement to the upper floors. After the conversion, the property constitutes 2 dwelling units within the meaning of paragraph (e)(2) of this section. C uses the first and second floors of the townhouse as his principal residence and rents the basement level to tenants from 2003 to 2007. C claims depreciation deductions of $2,000 for that period with respect to the basement apartment. C sells the entire property in 2007, realizing gain of $18,000. C has no other section 1231 or capital gains or losses for 2007.

(ii) Because the basement apartment and the upper floors of the townhouse are separate dwelling units, C must allocate the gain between the portion of the property that he used as his principal residence and the portion of the property that he used for non-residential purposes under paragraph (e) of this section. After allocating the basis and the amount realized between the residential and non-residential portions of the property, C determines that $6,000 of the gain is allocable to the non-residential portion of the property and that $12,000 of the gain is allocable to the portion of the property used as his residence. C must recognize the $6,000 of gain allocable to the non-residential portion of the property ($2,000 of which is unrecaptured section 1250 gain within the meaning of section 1(h), and $4,000 of which is adjusted net capital gain). C may exclude $12,000 of the gain from the sale of the property.

Example 4. Separate dwelling unit converted to residential use. The facts are the same as in *Example 3* except that in 2007 C incorporates the basement of the townhouse into his principal residence by eliminating the kitchen and building a new interior stairway to the upper floors. C uses all 3 floors of the townhouse as his principal residence for 2 full years and sells the townhouse in 2010, realizing a gain of $20,000. Under section 121(d)(6) and paragraph (d) of this section, C must recognize $2,000 of the gain as unrecaptured section 1250 gain within the meaning of section 1(h). Because C used the entire 3 floors of the townhouse as his principal residence for 2 of the 5 years preceding the sale of the property, C may exclude the remaining $18,000 of the gain from the sale of the house.

Example 5. Non-residential use within the dwelling unit, property depreciated. Taxpayer D, an attorney, buys a house in 2003. The house constitutes a single dwelling unit but D uses a portion of the house as a law office. D claims depreciation deductions of $2,000 during the period that she owns the house. D sells the house in 2006, realizing a gain of $13,000. D has no other section 1231 or capital gains or losses for 2006. Under section 121(d)(6) and paragraph (d) of this section, D must recognize $2,000 of the gain as unrecaptured section 1250 gain within the meaning of section 1(h). D may exclude the remaining $11,000 of the gain from the sale of her house because, under paragraph (e)(1) of this section, she is not required to allocate gain to the business use within the dwelling unit.

Example 6. Non-residential use within the dwelling unit, property not depreciated. The facts are the same as in *Example 5*, except that D is not entitled to claim any depreciation deductions with respect to her business use of the house. D may exclude $13,000 of the gain from the sale of her house because, under paragraph (e)(1) of this section, she is not required to allocate gain to the business use within the dwelling unit.

(f) *Effective date.* This section is applicable for sales and exchanges on or after December 24, 2002. For rules on electing to apply the provisions of this section retroactively, see § 1.121-4(j). [Reg. § 1.121-1.]

☐ [*T.D.* 6856, 10-19-65. *Amended by T.D.* 7614, 4-26-79 *and T.D.* 9030, 12-23-2002.]

[Reg. § 1.121-2]

§ 1.121-2. Limitations.—(a) *Dollar limitations*—(1) *In general.* A taxpayer may exclude from gross income up to $250,000 of gain from the sale or exchange of the taxpayer's principal residence. A taxpayer is eligible for only one maximum exclusion per principal residence.

(2) *Joint owners.* If taxpayers jointly own a principal residence but file separate returns, each taxpayer may exclude from gross income up to $250,000 of gain that is attributable to each taxpayer's interest in the property, if the requirements of section 121 have otherwise been met.

(3) *Special rules for joint returns*—(i) *In general.* A husband and wife who make a joint return for the year of the sale or exchange of a principal residence may exclude up to $500,000 of gain if—

(A) Either spouse meets the 2-year ownership requirements of § 1.121-1(a) and (c);

(B) Both spouses meet the 2-year use requirements of § 1.121-1(a) and (c); and

(C) Neither spouse excluded gain from a prior sale or exchange of property under section 121 within the last 2 years (as determined under paragraph (b) of this section).

(ii) *Other joint returns.* For taxpayers filing jointly, if either spouse fails to meet the requirements of paragraph (a)(3)(i) of this section, the maximum limitation amount to be claimed by the couple is the sum of each spouse's limitation amount determined on a separate basis as if they had not been married. For this purpose, each spouse is treated as owning the property during the period that either spouse owned the property.

(4) *Examples.* The provisions of this paragraph (a) are illustrated by the following examples. The examples assume that § 1.121-3 (relating to the reduced maximum exclusion) does not apply to the sale of the property. The examples are as follows:

Example 1. Unmarried Taxpayers A and B own a house as joint owners, each owning a 50 percent interest in the house. They sell the house after owning and using it as their principal residence for 2 full years. The gain realized from the sale is $256,000. A and B are each eligible to exclude $128,000 of gain because the amount of realized gain allocable to each of them from the sale does not exceed each taxpayer's available limitation amount of $250,000.

Example 2. The facts are the same as in *Example 1*, except that A and B are married taxpayers who file a joint return for the taxable year of the sale. A and B are eligible to exclude the entire amount of realized gain ($256,000) from gross income because the gain realized from the sale does not exceed the limitation amount of $500,000 available to A and B as taxpayers filing a joint return.

Example 3. During 1999, married Taxpayers H and W each sell a residence that each had separately owned and used as a principal residence before their marriage. Each spouse meets the ownership and use tests for his or her respective residence. Neither spouse meets the use requirement for the other spouse's residence. H and W file a joint return for the year of the sales. The gain realized from the sale of H's residence is $200,000. The gain realized from the sale of W's residence is $300,000. Because the ownership and use requirements are met for each residence by each respective spouse, H and W are each eligible to exclude up to $250,000 of gain from the sale of their individual residences. However, W may not use H's unused exclusion to exclude gain in excess of her limitation amount. Therefore, H and W must recognize $50,000 of the gain realized on the sale of W's residence.

Example 4. Married Taxpayers H and W sell their residence and file a joint return for the year of the sale. W, but not H, satisfies the requirements of section 121. They are eligible to exclude up to $250,000 of the gain from the sale of the residence because that is the sum of each spouse's dollar limitation amount determined on a separate basis as if they had not been married ($0 for H, $250,000 for W).

Example 5. Married Taxpayers H and W have owned and used their principal residence since 1998. On February 16, 2001, H dies. On September 24, 2001, W sells the residence and realizes a gain of $350,000. Pursuant to section 6013(a)(3), W and H's executor make a joint return for 2001. All $350,000 of the gain from the sale of the residence may be excluded.

Example 6. Assume the same facts as *Example 5*, except that W does not sell the residence until January 31, 2002. Because W's filing status for the taxable year of the sale is single, the special rules for joint returns under paragraph (a)(3) of this section do not apply and W may exclude only $250,000 of the gain.

(b) *Application of section 121 to only 1 sale or exchange every 2 years*—(1) *In general.* Except as otherwise provided in § 1.121-3 (relating to the reduced maximum exclusion), a taxpayer may not exclude from gross income gain from the sale or exchange of a principal residence if, during the 2-year period ending on the date of the sale or exchange, the taxpayer sold or exchanged other property for which gain was excluded under section 121. For purposes of this paragraph (b)(1), any sale or exchange before May 7, 1997, is disregarded.

(2) *Example.* The following example illustrates the rules of this paragraph (b). The example assumes that § 1.121-3 (relating to the reduced maximum exclusion) does not apply to the sale of the property. The example is as follows:

Example. Taxpayer A owns a townhouse that he uses as his principal residence for 2 full years, 1998 and 1999. A buys a house in 2000 that he owns and uses as his principal residence. A sells the townhouse in 2002 and excludes gain realized on its sale under section 121. A sells the house in 2003. Although A meets the 2-year ownership and use requirements of section 121, A is not eligible to exclude gain from the sale of the house because A excluded gain within the last 2 years under section 121 from the sale of the townhouse.

(c) *Effective date.* This section is applicable for sales and exchanges on or after December 24, 2002. For rules on electing to apply the provisions

of this section retroactively, see § 1.121-4(j). [Reg. § 1.121-2.]

☐ [*T.D. 6856, 10-19-65. Amended by T.D. 7614, 4-26-79 and T.D. 9030, 12-23-2002.*]

[Reg. § 1.121-3]

§ 1.121-3. Reduced maximum exclusion for taxpayers failing to meet certain requirements.—(a) *In general.* In lieu of the limitation under section 121(b) and § 1.121-2, a reduced maximum exclusion limitation may be available for a taxpayer who sells or exchanges property used as the taxpayer's principal residence but fails to satisfy the ownership and use requirements described in § 1.121-1(a) and (c) or the 2-year limitation described in § 1.121-2(b).

(b) through (f) [Reserved]. For further guidance, see § 1.121-3T(b) through (f).

(g) *Computation of reduced maximum exclusion*—(1) The reduced maximum exclusion is computed by multiplying the maximum dollar limitation of $250,000 ($500,000 for certain joint filers) by a fraction. The numerator of the fraction is the shortest of the period of time that the taxpayer owned the property during the 5-year period ending on the date of the sale or exchange; the period of time that the taxpayer used the property as the taxpayer's principal residence during the 5-year period ending on the date of the sale or exchange; or the period of time between the date of a prior sale or exchange of property for which the taxpayer excluded gain under section 121 and the date of the current sale or exchange. The numerator of the fraction may be expressed in days or months. The denominator of the fraction is 730 days or 24 months (depending on the measure of time used in the numerator).

(2) *Examples.* The following examples illustrate the rules of this paragraph (g):

Example 1. Taxpayer A purchases a house that she uses as her principal residence. Twelve months after the purchase, A sells the house due to a change in place of her employment. A has not excluded gain under section 121 on a prior sale or exchange of property within the last 2 years. A is eligible to exclude up to $125,000 of the gain from the sale of her house (12/24 × $250,000).

Example 2. (i) Taxpayer H owns a house that he has used as his principal residence since 1996. On January 15, 1999, H and W marry and W begins to use H's house as her principal residence. On January 15, 2000, H sells the house due to a change in W's place of employment. Neither H nor W has excluded gain under section 121 on a prior sale or exchange of property within the last 2 years.

(ii) Because H and W have not each used the house as their principal residence for at least 2 years during the 5-year period preceding its sale, the maximum dollar limitation amount that may be claimed by H and W will not be $500,000, but the sum of each spouse's limitation amount determined on a separate basis as if they had not been married. (See § 1.121-2(a)(3)(ii).)

(iii) H is eligible to exclude up to $250,000 of gain because he meets the requirements of section 121. W is not eligible to exclude the maximum dollar limitation amount. Instead, because the sale of the house is due to a change in place of employment, W is eligible to claim a reduced maximum exclusion of up to $125,000 of the gain (365/730 × $250,000). Therefore, H and W are eligible to exclude up to $375,000 of gain ($250,000 + $125,000) from the sale of the house.

(h) [Reserved]. For further guidance, see § 1.121-3T(h).

(i) through (k) [Reserved].

(l) *Effective date.* This section is applicable for sales and exchanges on or after December 24, 2002. For rules on electing to apply the provisions of this section retroactively, see § 1.121-4(j). [Reg. § 1.121-3.]

☐ [*T.D.* 6856, 10-19-65. *Amended by T.D.* 7614, 4-26-79 *and T.D.* 9030, 12-23-2002.]

[Reg. § 1.121-3T]

§ 1.121-3T. Reduced maximum exclusion for taxpayers failing to meet certain requirements (temporary).—(a) [Reserved]. For further guidance, see § 1.121-3(a).

(b) *Primary reason for sale or exchange.* In order for a taxpayer to claim a reduced maximum exclusion under section 121(c), the sale or exchange must be by reason of a change in place of employment, health, or unforeseen circumstances. A sale or exchange is by reason of a change in place of employment, health, or unforeseen circumstances only if the primary reason for the sale or exchange is a change in place of employment (within the meaning of paragraph (c) of this section), health (within the meaning of paragraph (d) of this section), or unforeseen circumstances (within the meaning of paragraph (e) of this section). Whether the requirements of this section are satisfied depends upon all the facts and circumstances. If the taxpayer qualifies for a safe harbor described in this section, the taxpayer's primary reason is deemed to be a change in place of employment, health, or unforeseen circumstances. If the taxpayer does not qualify for a safe harbor, factors that may be relevant in determining the taxpayer's primary reason for the sale or

exchange include (but are not limited to) the extent to which—

(1) The sale or exchange and the circumstances giving rise to the sale or exchange are proximate in time;

(2) The suitability of the property as the taxpayer's principal residence materially changes;

(3) The taxpayer's financial ability to maintain the property materially changes;

(4) The taxpayer uses the property as the taxpayer's residence during the period of the taxpayer's ownership of the property;

(5) The circumstances giving rise to the sale or exchange are not reasonably foreseeable when the taxpayer begins using the property as the taxpayer's principal residence; and

(6) The circumstances giving rise to the sale or exchange occur during the period of the taxpayer's ownership and use of the property as the taxpayer's principal residence.

(c) *Sale or exchange by reason of a change in place of employment*—(1) *In general.* A sale or exchange is by reason of a change in place of employment if, in the case of a qualified individual described in paragraph (f) of this section, the primary reason for the sale or exchange is a change in the location of the individual's employment.

(2) *Distance safe harbor.* The primary reason for the sale or exchange is deemed to be a change in place of employment (within the meaning of paragraph (c)(1) of this section) if—

(i) The change in place of employment occurs during the period of the taxpayer's ownership and use of the property as the taxpayer's principal residence; and

(ii) The individual's new place of employment is at least 50 miles farther from the residence sold or exchanged than was the former place of employment, or, if there was no former place of employment, the distance between the individual's new place of employment and the residence sold or exchanged is at least 50 miles.

(3) *Employment.* For purposes of this paragraph (c), *employment* includes the commencement of employment with a new employer, the continuation of employment with the same employer, and the commencement or continuation of self-employment.

(4) *Examples.* The following examples illustrate the rules of this paragraph (c):

Example 1. A is unemployed and owns a townhouse that she has owned and used as her principal residence since 2002. In 2003 A obtains a job that is 54 miles from her townhouse, and she

Reg. § 1.121-3T(a)

sells the townhouse. Because the distance between A's new place of employment and the townhouse is at least 50 miles, the sale is within the safe harbor of paragraph (c)(2) of this section and A is entitled to claim a reduced maximum exclusion under section 121(c)(2).

Example 2. B is an officer in the United States Air Force stationed in Florida. B purchases a house in Florida in 2001. In May 2002 B moves out of his house to take a 3-year assignment in Germany. B sells his house in January 2003. Because B's new place of employment in Germany is at least 50 miles farther from the residence sold than is B's former place of employment in Florida, the sale is within the safe harbor of paragraph (c)(2) of this section and B is entitled to claim a reduced maximum exclusion under section 121(c)(2).

Example 3. C is employed by Employer R at R's Philadelphia office. C purchases a house in February 2001 that is 35 miles from R's Philadelphia office. In May 2002 C begins a temporary assignment at R's Wilmington office that is 72 miles from C's house, and moves out of the house. In June 2004 C is assigned to work in R's London office, and as a result, sells her house in August 2004. The sale of the house is not within the safe harbor of paragraph (c)(2) of this section by reason of the change in place of employment from Philadelphia to Wilmington because the Wilmington office is not 50 miles farther from C's house than is the Philadelphia office. Furthermore, the sale is not within the safe harbor by reason of the change in place of employment to London because C is not using the house as her principal residence when she moves to London. However, C is entitled to claim a reduced maximum exclusion under section 121(c)(2) because, under the facts and circumstances, the primary reason for the sale is the change in C's place of employment.

Example 4. In July 2002 D buys a condominium that is 5 miles from her place of employment and uses it as her principal residence. In February 2003 D, who works as an emergency medicine physician, obtains a job that is located 51 miles from D's condominium. D may be called in to work unscheduled hours and, when called, must be able to arrive at work quickly. Therefore, D sells her condominium and buys a townhouse that is 4 miles from her new place of employment. Because D's new place of employment is only 46 miles farther from the condominium than is D's former place of employment, the sale is not within the safe harbor of paragraph (c)(2) of this section. However, D is entitled to claim a reduced maximum exclusion under section 121(c)(2) because, under the facts and circumstances, the primary

reason for the sale is the change in D's place of employment.

(d) *Sale or exchange by reason of health*—(1) *In general.* A sale or exchange is by reason of health if the primary reason for the sale or exchange is to obtain, provide, or facilitate the diagnosis, cure, mitigation, or treatment of disease, illness, or injury of a qualified individual described in paragraph (f) of this section, or to obtain or provide medical or personal care for a qualified individual suffering from a disease, illness, or injury. A sale or exchange that is merely beneficial to the general health or well-being of the individual is not a sale or exchange by reason of health.

(2) *Physician's recommendation safe harbor.* The primary reason for the sale or exchange is deemed to be health if a physician (as defined in section 213(d)(4)) recommends a change of residence for reasons of health (as defined in paragraph (d)(1) of this section).

(3) *Examples.* The following examples illustrate the rules of this paragraph (d):

Example 1. In 2002 A buys a house that she uses as her principal residence. A is injured in an accident and is unable to care for herself. As a result, A sells her house in 2003 and moves in with her daughter so that the daughter can provide the care that A requires as a result of her injury. Because, under the facts and circumstances, the primary reason for the sale of A's house is A's health, A is entitled to claim a reduced maximum exclusion under section 121(c)(2).

Example 2. H's father has a chronic disease. In 2002 H and W purchase a house that they use as their principal residence. In 2003 H and W sell their house in order to move into the house of H's father so that they can provide the care he requires as a result of his disease. Because, under the facts and circumstances, the primary reason for the sale of their house is the health of H's father, H and W are entitled to claim a reduced maximum exclusion under section 121(c)(2).

Example 3. H and W purchase a house in 2002 that they use as their principal residence. Their son suffers from a chronic illness that requires regular medical care. Later that year their doctor recommends that their son begin a new treatment that is available at a medical facility 100 miles away from their residence. In 2003 H and W sell their house to be closer to the medical facility. Because, under the facts and circumstances, the primary reason for the sale is to facilitate the treatment of their son's chronic illness, H and W are entitled to claim a reduced maximum exclusion under section 121(c)(2).

Example 4. B, who has chronic asthma, purchases a house in Minnesota in 2002 that he

Reg. § 1.121-3T(d)(3)

uses as his principal residence. B's doctor tells B that moving to a warm, dry climate would mitigate B's asthma symptoms. In 2003 B sells his house and moves to Arizona to relieve his asthma symptoms. The sale is within the safe harbor of paragraph (d)(2) of this section and B is entitled to claim a reduced maximum exclusion under section 121(c)(2).

Example 5. In 2002 H and W purchase a house in Michigan that they use as their principal residence. H's doctor tells H that he should get more exercise, but H is not suffering from any disease that can be treated or mitigated by exercise. In 2003 H and W sell their house and move to Florida so that H can increase his general level of exercise by playing golf year-round. Because the sale of the house is merely beneficial to H's general health, the sale of the house is not by reason of H's health. H and W are not entitled to claim a reduced maximum exclusion under section 121(c)(2).

(e) *Sale or exchange by reason of unforeseen circumstances*—(1) *In general.* A sale or exchange is by reason of unforeseen circumstances if the primary reason for the sale or exchange is the occurrence of an event that the taxpayer does not anticipate before purchasing and occupying the residence.

(2) *Specific event safe harbors.* The primary reason for the sale or exchange is deemed to be unforeseen circumstances (within the meaning of paragraph (e)(1) of this section) if any of the events specified in paragraphs (e)(2)(i) through (iii) of this section occur during the period of the taxpayer's ownership and use of the residence as the taxpayer's principal residence—

(i) The involuntary conversion of the residence;

(ii) Natural or man-made disasters or acts of war or terrorism resulting in a casualty to the residence (without regard to deductibility under section 165(h));

(iii) In the case of a qualified individual described in paragraph (f) of this section—

(A) Death;

(B) The cessation of employment as a result of which the individual is eligible for unemployment compensation (as defined in section 85(b));

(C) A change in employment or self-employment status that results in the taxpayer's inability to pay housing costs and reasonable basic living expenses for the taxpayer's household (including amounts for food, clothing, medical expenses, taxes, transportation, court-ordered payments, and expenses reasonably necessary to the production of income, but not for the maintenance of an affluent or luxurious standard of living);

(D) Divorce or legal separation under a decree of divorce or separate maintenance; or

(E) Multiple births resulting from the same pregnancy; or

(iv) An event determined by the Commissioner to be an unforeseen circumstance to the extent provided in published guidance of general applicability or in a ruling directed to a specific taxpayer.

(3) *Examples.* The following examples illustrate the rules of this paragraph (e):

Example 1. In 2003 A buys a house in California. After A begins to use the house as her principal residence, an earthquake causes damage to A's house. A sells the house in 2004. The sale is within the safe harbor of paragraph (e)(2)(ii) of this section and A is entitled to claim a reduced maximum exclusion under section 121(c)(2).

Example 2. H works as a teacher and W works as a pilot. In 2003 H and W buy a house that they use as their principal residence. Later that year W is furloughed from her job for six months. H and W are unable to pay their mortgage during the period W is furloughed. H and W sell their house in 2004. The sale is within the safe harbor of paragraph (e)(2)(iii)(C) of this section and H and W are entitled to claim a reduced maximum exclusion under section 121(c)(2).

Example 3. In 2003 H and W buy a two-bedroom condominium that they use as their principal residence. In 2004 W gives birth to twins and H and W sell their condominium and buy a four-bedroom house. The sale is within the safe harbor of paragraph (e)(2)(iii)(E) of this section, and H and W are entitled to claim a reduced maximum exclusion under section 121(c)(2).

Example 4. B buys a condominium in 2003 and uses it as his principal residence. B's monthly condominium fee is $X. Three months after B moves into the condominium, the condominium association decides to replace the building's roof and heating system. Six months later, B's monthly condominium fee doubles. B sells the condominium in 2004 because B is unable to pay the new condominium fee along with the monthly mortgage payment. The safe harbors of paragraph (e)(2) of this section do not apply. However, under the facts and circumstances, the primary reason for the sale is unforeseen circumstances, and B is entitled to claim a reduced maximum exclusion under section 121(c)(2).

Example 5. In 2003 C buys a house that he uses as his principal residence. The property is located on a heavily trafficked road. C sells the

Reg. § 1.121-3T(e)(1)

property in 2004 because the traffic is more disturbing than he expected. C is not entitled to claim a reduced maximum exclusion under section 121(c)(2) because the safe harbors of paragraph (e)(2) of this section do not apply and, under the facts and circumstances, the traffic is not an unforeseen circumstance.

Example 6. In 2003 D and her fiancé E buy a house and live in it as their principal residence. In 2004 D and E cancel their wedding plans and E moves out of the house. Because D cannot afford to make the monthly mortgage payments alone, D and E sell the house in 2004. The safe harbors of paragraph (e)(2) of this section do not apply. However, under the facts and circumstances, the primary reason for the sale is unforeseen circumstances, and D and E are each entitled to claim a reduced maximum exclusion under section 121(c)(2).

(f) *Qualified individual.* For purposes of this section, *qualified individual* means—

(1) The taxpayer;

(2) The taxpayer's spouse;

(3) A co-owner of the residence;

(4) A person whose principal place of abode is in the same household as the taxpayer; or

(5) For purposes of paragraph (d) of this section, a person bearing a relationship specified in sections 152(a)(1) through 152(a)(8) (without regard to qualification as a dependent) to a qualified individual described in paragraphs (f)(1) through (4) of this section, or a descendant of the taxpayer's grandparent.

(g) [Reserved]. For further guidance, see § 1.121-3(g).

(h) *Election to apply regulations retroactively.* Taxpayers who would otherwise qualify under this section to exclude gain from a sale or exchange before December 24, 2002 but on or after May 7, 1997, may elect to apply all of the provisions of this section for any years for which the period of limitations under section 6511 has not expired. The taxpayer makes the election under this paragraph (h) by filing a return for the taxable year of the sale or exchange that does not include the gain from the sale or exchange of the taxpayer's principal residence in the taxpayer's gross income. Taxpayers who have filed a return for the taxable year of the sale or exchange may elect to apply all the provisions of this section for any years for which the period of limitations under section 6511 has not expired by filing an amended return.

(i) through (j) [Reserved]. See § 1.121-3(i) through (j).

(k) *Audit protection.* The Internal Revenue Service will not challenge a taxpayer's position that a sale or exchange of a principal residence that occurred before December 24, 2002 but on or after May 7, 1997, qualifies for the reduced maximum exclusion under section 121(c) if the taxpayer has made a reasonable, good faith effort to comply with the requirements of section 121(c) and if the sale or exchange otherwise qualifies under section 121.

(l) *Effective date.* For the applicability of this section, see § 1.121-3(l). [Temporary Reg. § 1.121-3T.]

☐ [*T.D.* 9031, 12-23-2002.]

[Reg. § 1.121-4]

§ 1.121-4. **Special rules.**—(a) *Property of deceased spouse*—(1) *In general.* For purposes of satisfying the ownership and use requirements of section 121, a taxpayer is treated as owning and using property as the taxpayer's principal residence during any period that the taxpayer's deceased spouse owned and used the property as a principal residence before death if—

(i) The taxpayer's spouse is deceased on the date of the sale or exchange of the property; and

(ii) The taxpayer has not remarried at the time of the sale or exchange of the property.

(2) *Example.* The provisions of this paragraph (a) are illustrated by the following example. The example assumes that § 1.121-3 (relating to the reduced maximum exclusion) does not apply to the sale of the property. The example is as follows:

Example. Taxpayer H has owned and used a house as his principal residence since 1987. H and W marry on July 1, 1999 and from that date they use H's house as their principal residence. H dies on August 15, 2000, and W inherits the property. W sells the property on September 1, 2000, at which time she has not remarried. Although W has owned and used the house for less than 2 years, W will be considered to have satisfied the ownership and use requirements of section 121 because W's period of ownership and use includes the period that H owned and used the property before death.

(b) *Property owned by spouse or former spouse*—(1) *Property transferred to individual from spouse or former spouse.* If a taxpayer obtains property from a spouse or former spouse in a transaction described in section 1041(a), the period that the taxpayer owns the property will include the period that the spouse or former spouse owned the property.

(2) *Property used by spouse or former spouse.* A taxpayer is treated as using property as the taxpayer's principal residence for any period that

the taxpayer has an ownership interest in the property and the taxpayer's spouse or former spouse is granted use of the property under a divorce or separation instrument (as defined in section 71(b)(2)), provided that the spouse or former spouse uses the property as his or her principal residence.

(c) *Tenant-stockholder in cooperative housing corporation.* A taxpayer who holds stock as a tenant-stockholder in a cooperative housing corporation (as those terms are defined in section 216(b)(1) and (2)) may be eligible to exclude gain under section 121 on the sale or exchange of the stock. In determining whether the taxpayer meets the requirements of section 121, the ownership requirements are applied to the holding of the stock and the use requirements are applied to the house or apartment that the taxpayer is entitled to occupy by reason of the taxpayer's stock ownership.

(d) *Involuntary conversions*—(1) *In general.* For purposes of section 121, the destruction, theft, seizure, requisition, or condemnation of property is treated as a sale of the property.

(2) *Application of section 1033.* In applying section 1033 (relating to involuntary conversions), the amount realized from the sale or exchange of property used as the taxpayer's principal residence is treated as being the amount determined without regard to section 121, reduced by the amount of gain excluded from the taxpayer's gross income under section 121.

(3) *Property acquired after involuntary conversion.* If the basis of the property acquired as a result of an involuntary conversion is determined (in whole or in part) under section 1033(b) (relating to the basis of property acquired through an involuntary conversion), then for purposes of satisfying the requirements of section 121, the taxpayer will be treated as owning and using the acquired property as the taxpayer's principal residence during any period of time that the taxpayer owned and used the converted property as the taxpayer's principal residence.

(4) *Example.* The provisions of this paragraph (d) are illustrated by the following example:

Example. (i) On February 18, 1999, fire destroys Taxpayer A's house which has an adjusted basis of $80,000. A had owned and used this property as her principal residence for 20 years prior to its destruction. A's insurance company pays A $400,000 for the house. A realizes a gain of $320,000 ($400,000 − $80,000). On August 27, 1999, A purchases a new house at a cost of $100,000.

(ii) Because the destruction of the house is treated as a sale for purposes of section 121, A will

exclude $250,000 of the realized gain from A's gross income. For purposes of section 1033, the amount realized is then treated as being $150,000 ($400,000 − $250,000) and the gain realized is $70,000 ($150,000 amount realized − $80,000 basis). A elects under section 1033 to recognize only $50,000 of the gain ($150,000 amount realized − $100,000 cost of new house). The remaining $20,000 of gain is deferred and A's basis in the new house is $80,000 ($100,000 cost − $20,000 gain not recognized).

(iii) A will be treated as owning and using the new house as A's principal residence during the 20-year period that A owned and used the destroyed house.

(e) *Sales or exchanges of partial interests*—(1) *Partial interests other than remainder interests*—(i) *In general.* Except as provided in paragraph (e)(2) of this section (relating to sales or exchanges of remainder interests), a taxpayer may apply the section 121 exclusion to gain from the sale or exchange of an interest in the taxpayer's principal residence that is less than the taxpayer's entire interest if the interest sold or exchanged includes an interest in the dwelling unit. For rules relating to the sale or exchange of vacant land, see § 1.121-1(b)(3).

(ii) *Limitations*—(A) *Maximum limitation amount.* For purposes of section 121(b)(1) and (2) (relating to the maximum limitation amount of the section 121 exclusion), sales or exchanges of partial interests in the same principal residence are treated as one sale or exchange. Therefore, only one maximum limitation amount of $250,000 ($500,000 for certain joint returns) applies to the combined sales or exchanges of the partial interests. In applying the maximum limitation amount to sales or exchanges that occur in different taxable years, a taxpayer may exclude gain from the first sale or exchange of a partial interest up to the taxpayer's full maximum limitation amount and may exclude gain from the sale or exchange of any other partial interest in the same principal residence to the extent of any remaining maximum limitation amount, and each spouse is treated as excluding one-half of the gain from a sale or exchange to which section 121(b)(2)(A) and § 1.121-2(a)(3)(i) (relating to the limitation for certain joint returns) apply.

(B) *Sale or exchange of more than one principal residence in 2-year period.* For purposes of applying section 121(b)(3) (restricting the application of section 121 to only 1 sale or exchange every 2 years), each sale or exchange of a partial interest is disregarded with respect to other sales or exchanges of partial interests in the same principal residence, but is taken into account as of the

Reg. § 1.121-4(c)

date of the sale or exchange in applying section 121(b)(3) to that sale or exchange and the sale or exchange of any other principal residence.

(2) *Sales or exchanges of remainder interests*—(i) *In general.* A taxpayer may elect to apply the section 121 exclusion to gain from the sale or exchange of a remainder interest in the taxpayer's principal residence.

(ii) *Limitations*—(A) *Sale or exchange of any other interest.* If a taxpayer elects to exclude gain from the sale or exchange of a remainder interest in the taxpayer's principal residence, the section 121 exclusion will not apply to a sale or exchange of any other interest in the residence that is sold or exchanged separately.

(B) *Sales or exchanges to related parties.* This paragraph (e)(2) will not apply to a sale or exchange to any person that bears a relationship to the taxpayer that is described in section 267(b) or 707(b).

(iii) *Election.* The taxpayer makes the election under this paragraph (e)(2) by filing a return for the taxable year of the sale or exchange that does not include the gain from the sale or exchange of the remainder interest in the taxpayer's gross income. A taxpayer may make or revoke the election at any time before the expiration of a 3-year period beginning on the last date prescribed by law (determined without regard to extensions) for the filing of the return for the taxable year in which the sale or exchange occurred.

(4) *Example.* The provisions of this paragraph (e) are illustrated by the following example:

Example. In 1991 Taxpayer A buys a house that A uses as his principal residence. In 2004 A's friend B moves into A's house and A sells B a 50% interest in the house realizing a gain of $136,000. A may exclude the $136,000 of gain. In 2005 A sells his remaining 50% interest in the home to B realizing a gain of $138,000. A may exclude $114,000 ($250,000 − $136,000 gain previously excluded) of the $138,000 gain from the sale of the remaining interest.

(f) *No exclusion for expatriates.* The section 121 exclusion will not apply to any sale or exchange by an individual if the provisions of section 877(a) (relating to the treatment of expatriates) applies to the individual.

(g) *Election to have section not apply.* A taxpayer may elect to have the section 121 exclusion not apply to a sale or exchange of property. The taxpayer makes the election by filing a return for the taxable year of the sale or exchange that includes the gain from the sale or exchange of the taxpayer's principal residence in the taxpayer's gross income. A taxpayer may make an election under this paragraph (g) to have section 121 not apply (or revoke an election to have section 121 not apply) at any time before the expiration of a 3-year period beginning on the last date prescribed by law (determined without regard to extensions) for the filing of the return for the taxable year in which the sale or exchange occurred.

(h) *Residences acquired in rollovers under section 1034.* If a taxpayer acquires property in a transaction that qualifies under section 1034 (section 1034 property) for the nonrecognition of gain realized on the sale or exchange of another property and later sells or exchanges such property, in determining the period of the taxpayer's ownership and use of the property under section 121 the taxpayer may include the periods that the taxpayer owned and used the section 1034 property as the taxpayer's principal residence (and each prior residence taken into account under section 1223(7) in determining the holding period of the section 1034 property).

(i) [Reserved].

(j) *Election to apply regulations retroactively.* Taxpayers who would otherwise qualify under §§ 1.121-1 through 1.121-4 to exclude gain from a sale or exchange of a principal residence before December 24, 2002 but on or after May 7, 1997, may elect to apply §§ 1.121-1 through 1.121-4 for any years for which the period of limitation under section 6511 has not expired. The taxpayer makes the election under this paragraph (j) by filing a return for the taxable year of the sale or exchange that does not include the gain from the sale or exchange of the taxpayer's principal residence in the taxpayer's gross income. Taxpayers who have filed a return for the taxable year of the sale or exchange may elect to apply the provisions of these regulations for any years for which the period of limitation under section 6511 has not expired by filing an amended return.

(k) *Audit protection.* The Internal Revenue Service will not challenge a taxpayer's position that a sale or exchange of a principal residence occurring before December 24, 2002 but on or after May 7, 1997, qualifies for the section 121 exclusion if the taxpayer has made a reasonable, good faith effort to comply with the requirements of section 121. Compliance with the provisions of the regulations project under section 121 (REG-105235-99 (2000-2 C.B. 447)) generally will be considered a reasonable, good faith effort to comply with the requirements of section 121.

(l) *Effective date.* This section is applicable for sales and exchanges on or after December 24, 2002. For rules on electing to apply the provisions retroactively, see paragraph (j) of this section. [Reg. § 1.121-4.]

☐ [*T.D.* 6856, 10-19-65. *Amended by T.D. 7614, 4-26-79; T.D. 7927, 12-15-83 and T.D. 9030, 12-23-2002.*]

[Reg. § 1.122-1]

§ 1.122-1. Applicable rules relating to certain reduced uniformed services retirement pay.—(a) *Rule applicable prior to January 1, 1966.* In the case of a member or former member of the uniformed services of the United States (as defined in 37 U. S. C. 101(3)) who has made an election under subchapter I of chapter 73 of title 10 of the United States Code (also referred to in this section as the Retired Serviceman's Family Protection Plan (10 U. S. C. 1431)) to receive a reduced amount of retired or retainer pay, gross income shall include the amount of any reduction made in his retired or retainer pay before January 1, 1966, by reason of such election, unless such reduction, or portion thereof, is otherwise excluded from gross income under part III of subchapter B of chapter 1 of the Internal Revenue Code of 1954 or any other provision of law.

(b) *Rule applicable after December 31, 1965.*—(1) In a case of a member or former member of the uniformed services of the United States (as defined in 37 U. S. C. 101(3)), gross income shall not include the amount of any reduction made in his or her retired or retainer pay after December 31, 1965, by reason of—

(i) An election made under the Retired Serviceman's Family Protection Plan (10 U. S. C. 1431), or

(ii) The provisions of subchapter II of chapter 73 of title 10 of the United States Code (also referred to in this section as the Survivor Benefit Plan (10 U. S. C. 1447)).

(2)(i) In a case where a member or former member of the uniformed services has, pursuant to the election described in paragraph (a) of this section, received before January 1, 1966, a reduced amount of retired or retainer pay, he shall, after December 31, 1965, exclude from gross income under section 122(b) and this subdivision all amounts received as uniformed services retired or retainer pay until there has been so excluded an amount of retired or retainer pay equal to the "consideration for the contract" (as described in subdivision (iii) of this subparagraph).

(ii) Upon the death of a member or former member of the uniformed services, where the "consideration for the contract" (as described in subdivision (iii) of this subparagraph) has not been excluded in whole or in part from gross income under section 122(b) and subdivision (i) of

this subparagraph, the survivor of such member who is receiving an annuity under chapter 73 of title 10 of the United States Code shall, after December 31, 1965, exclude from gross income under section 72(o) and this subdivision such annuity payments received after December 31, 1965, until there has been so excluded annuity payments equalling the portion of the "consideration for the contract" not previously excluded under subdivision (i) of this subparagraph.

(iii) The term "consideration for the contract" as used in this subparagraph means—

(*a*) The total amount of the reductions, if any, before January 1, 1966, in retired or retainer pay by reason of an election under subchapter I of chapter 73 of title 10 of the United States Code, plus

(*b*) The total amount, if any, deposited by the serviceman at any time pursuant to the provisions of sections 1438 or 1452(d) of title 10 of the United States Code, plus

(*c*) The total amount, if any, excludable from income under section 101(b)(2)(D) and paragraph (a)(2) of § 1.101-2 with respect to a survivor annuity provided by such retired or retainer pay, minus

(*d*) The total amount, if any, excluded from income before January 1, 1966, pursuant to the provisions of section 72(b) and (d) with respect to a survivor annuity provided by such retired or retainer pay.

(iv) In determining whether there has been a recovery of the "consideration for the contract" under subdivision (i) of this subparagraph, the exclusion of retired pay from income after December 31, 1965, under sections 104(a)(4) and 105(d) shall not be considered as recovery of all or part of the "consideration for the contract."

(c) *Special rules.* In any of the following situations, the computation of the excludable portion of disability retired pay received by the member or former member of the uniformed services shall be governed by the following rules:

(1) An exclusion under section 122(a) and paragraph (b)(1) of this section is applicable only in the taxable year in which a reduction in retired pay is made under the Retired Serviceman's Family Protection Plan (10 U. S. C. 1431) or the Survivor Benefit Plan (10 U. S. C. 1447).

(2) Where the member or former member of the uniformed services is entitled to exclude the whole or a portion of his retired pay under the provisions of section 104(a)(4) or section 105(d) and under section 122(a) and paragraph (b)(1) of this section, the exclusion under section 122(a) and paragraph (b)(1) of this section shall be ap-

plied prior to the exclusions under sections 104(a)(4) and 105(d).

(3) Where the member or former member of the uniformed services waives a portion of his disability retired pay, or such retired pay reduced under the Retired Serviceman's Family Protection Plan (10 U.S.C. 1431) or the Survivor Benefit Plan (10 U.S.C. 1447), in favor of a nontaxable pension or compensation receivable under laws administered by the Veterans Administration (38 U.S.C. 3105), the waived amount of such disability retired pay or reduced amount thereof, shall first be subtracted from any amounts which are excludable under the provisions of sections 104(a)(4) or 105(d) so as to reduce the amounts otherwise excludable under those sections.

(4) Where the member or former member of the uniformed services receives (before any forfeiture) disability retired pay (whether or not reduced under the Retired Serviceman's Family Protection Plan or Survivor Benefit Plan) which is partially excludable under section 104(a)(4), and also forfeits a portion of such disability retired pay under the Dual Compensation Act of 1964 (5 U.S.C. 5531 or any former corresponding provision of law), the amount of the forfeiture under such Act shall be applied against disability retired pay (before any forfeiture) in the same proportion that the excludable portion of such pay under section 104(a)(4) bears to the total amount of such pay after subtraction of any reduction under the Retired Serviceman's Family Protection Plan (10 U.S.C. 1431) or the Survivor Benefit Plan (10 U.S.C. 1447).

(5) The exclusion provided by section 122(b) and paragraph (b)(2)(i) of this section shall be available with respect to repayments made upon removal from the temporary disability retired list even though such repayments were previously excluded from gross income under section 104(a)(4) or 105(d).

However, the exclusion permitted by the prior sentence will apply only to the extent the repaid amount has not been previously excluded under section 122(b) and paragraph (b)(2)(i) of this section.

(d) *Examples with respect to the Retired Serviceman's Family Protection Plan.* The rules discussed in this section relating to the Retired Serviceman's Family Protection Plan (10 U.S.C. 1431) may be illustrated by the following examples:

Example (1). A, a member of the uniformed services, retires on January 1, 1963, and receives nondisability retired pay computed to be 60 percent of his active duty pay of $10,000 per year, or $6,000 per year, based upon 24 years of service.

He elects, under the Retired Serviceman's Family Protection Plan (10 U.S.C. 1431), to provide his survivor with an annuity equal to one-fourth of his reduced retired pay. His retired pay of $6,000 is reduced by $600, to $5,400, in order to provide a survivor annuity of $1,350 per year or $112.50 per month. For 1963, 1964, and 1965, A must include in gross income the unreduced amount of retired pay, or $6,000. For 1966 and subsequent years, he may exclude under section 122(a) and paragraph (b)(1) of this section the $600 total annual reductions to provide the survivor annuity, and may, for 1966, further exclude from gross income under section 122(b) and paragraph (b)(2)(i) of this section the $1,800 "consideration for the contract," *i.e.*, the total reductions which were made in 1963, 1964, and 1965, to provide the survivor annuity. Accordingly, A will include $3,600 of retired pay in gross income for 1966 ($6,000 minus the sum of $600 and $1,800).

Example (2). Assume the facts in Example (1) except that A retires on disability resulting from active service and his disability is rated at 40 percent. The entire amount of disability retirement pay, prior to and including 1966, is excludable from gross income under sections 104(a)(4) and 105(d), and in 1966, section 122(a). Assume further that A attains retirement age on December 31, 1966, dies on January 1, 1967, and his widow then begins receiving a survivor annuity under the Retired Serviceman's Family Protection Plan (10 U.S.C. 1431). A's widow may exclude from gross income in 1967 and 1968 under section 72(o) and paragraph (b)(2)(ii) of this section, the $1,800 of "consideration for the contract," *i.e.*, the reductions in 1963, 1964, and 1965 to provide the survivor annuity. Thus, A's widow will exclude all of the survivor annuity she receives in 1967 ($1,350) and $450 of the $1,350 annuity received in 1968. In addition, if A had not attained retirement age at the time of his death, his widow would, under section 101 and paragraph (a)(2) of § 1.101-2, exclude up to $5,000 subject to the limitations of paragraph (b)(2)(ii) of this section.

Example (3). Assume, in the previous example, that A dies on January 1, 1965, and his widow then begins receiving a survivor annuity. Assume further that A's widow is entitled to exclude under section 72(b) $1,000 of the $1,350 she received in 1965. Under section 72(o) and paragraph (b)(2)(ii) of this section, A's widow for 1966 will exclude the $200 remaining consideration for the contract ($1,200 − $1,000) and will include $1,150 of the survivor annuity in gross income.

Example (4). B, a member of the uniformed services, retires on January 1, 1966, after 32 years

Reg. § 1.122-1(d)

of active military service, and receives disability retirement pay under section 1401 of title 10, limited to 75 percent of his active duty pay of $15,000 per year, or $11,250. His disability rating is 30 percent. B has not reached retirement age (as defined in § 1.79-2(b)(3)). He elects under the Retired Serviceman's Family Protection Plan (10 U.S.C. 1431) to provide his survivor with an annuity equal to one-half of his reduced retired pay and, for that purpose, his retired pay of $11,250 is reduced by $1,250 to provide an annuity of $5,000 per year. B also elects to waive retired pay

in the amount of $1,000 in order to receive disability compensation in like amount under laws administered by the Veterans Administration. In addition, B is required to forfeit $4,088 of his retired pay under the Dual Compensation Act of 1964, 5 U.S.C. 5532 ($11,250 − $1,000 = $10,250 less one-half of excess thereof over $2,074) and by reason of his Federal employment is not entitled to an exclusion of his retired pay under section 105(d). B's taxable retired pay for 1966 is $3,002, computed as follows:

Gross retired pay	$11,250
Less: Section 122(a) exclusion	(1,250)
Reduced retired pay	$10,000
Less: Retired pay waived to receive V.A. compensation	(1,000)
Adjusted retired pay—	$ 9,000
Less:	
(i) Excludable retired pay computed under section 104(a)(4) as limited by 10 U.S.C. 1403 .... $4,500	
(ii) Less: Retired pay, not to exceed (i), waived to receive V.A. compensation .... ($1,000)	
(iii) Net disability exclusion	($ 3,500)
Taxable retired pay before adjustment for Dual Compensation forfeiture	$ 5,500
Less: Adjustment for Dual Compensation forfeiture of $4,088	
$\dfrac{5500}{9000} \times \$4,088 = \$2,498$ (rounded)	(2,498)
Net taxable retired pay	$3,002

Example (5). C, a member of the uniformed services retires on January 1, 1966, and receives disability retirement pay of $11,250 per year, which is reduced by $1,250 to provide a survivor annuity, and $1,000 of which is waived in order to receive disability compensation in like amount under laws administered by the Veterans Admin-

istration. C has not reached retirement age for purposes of section 105(d) and is not employed by the Federal Government. C's taxable disability retirement pay for 1966 is $300 computed as follows:

Adjusted retired pay	$ 9,000
Less:	
(i) Excludable retired pay under section 104(a)(4) as limited by 10 U.S.C. 1403 .... $ 4,500	
(ii) Excludable retired pay under section 105(d) 5,200	
(iii) Total .... $ 9,700	
(iv) Less: Retired pay, not to exceed (iii), waived to receive V.A. compensation .... (1,000)	
(v) Net disability and "sick pay" exclusion	(8,700)
Net taxable retired pay	$ 300

Example (6). D, a member of the uniformed services, retires for physical disability resulting from active service on January 1, 1966, after 35 years of service and with a disability rated at 20 percent. His active duty pay is $4,000 per year and he attained retirement age prior to retirement. He had an election in effect under the Retired Serviceman's Family Protection Plan to

provide his survivor with an annuity and his retired pay is reduced therefor by $500 per year. He waives $1,300 of his retired pay in order to receive compensation from the Veterans Administration in like amount. His taxable retired pay for 1966 is $1,200 computed as follows:

Gross retired pay (75% × $4,000)	$3,000
Less: Section 122(a) exclusion	(500)
Reduced retired pay	$2,500

Reg. § 1.122-1(d)

Less: V.A. waiver		(1,300)
Adjusted retired pay		$1,200
Less:		
(i) Section 104(a)(4) exclusion	$800	
(ii) Less: Retired pay, not to exceed (i), waived to receive V.A. compensation	(800)	
(iii) Net disability exclusion		0
Net taxable retired pay		$1,200

(e) *Principles applicable to the Survivor Benefit Plan.* The principles illustrated by the examples set forth in paragraph (d) of this section apply to an annuity under the Survivor Benefit Plan (10 U.S.C. 1447). [Reg. § 1.122-1.]

☐ [*T.D. 7043, 6-1-70. Amended by T.D. 7562, 8-30-78.*]

[Reg. § 1.123-1]

§ 1.123-1. Exclusion of insurance proceeds for reimbursement of certain living expenses.—(a) *In general.—*(1) Gross income does not include insurance proceeds received by an individual on or after January 1, 1969, pursuant to the terms of an insurance contract for indemnification of the temporary increase in living expenses resulting from the loss of use or occupancy of his principal residence, or a part thereof, due to damage or destruction by fire, storm, or other casualty. The term "other casualty" has the same meaning assigned to such term under section 165(c)(3). The exclusion also applies in the case of an individual who is denied access to his principal residence by governmental authorities because of the occurrence (or threat of occurrence) of such a casualty. The amount excludable under this section is subject to the limitation set forth in paragraph (b) of this section.

(2) This exclusion applies to amounts received as reimbursement or compensation for the reasonable and necessary increase in living expenses incurred by the insured and members of his household to maintain their customary standard of living during the loss period.

(3) This exclusion does not apply to an insurance recovery for the loss of rental income. Nor does the exclusion apply to any insurance recovery which compensates for the loss of, or damage to, real or personal property. See section 165(c)(3) relating to casualty losses; section 1231 relating to gain on an involuntary conversion of a capital asset held for more than 1 year (6 months for taxable years beginning before 1977; 9 months for taxable years beginning in 1977); and section 1033 relating to recognition of gain on an involuntary conversion. In the case of property used by an insured partially as a principal residence and partially for other purposes, the exclusion does not apply to the amount of insurance proceeds which compensates for the portion of increased expenses attributable to the nonresidential use of temporary replacement property during the loss period. In the case of denial of access to a principal residence by governmental authority, the exclusion provided by this section does not apply to an insurance recovery received by an individual as reimbursement for living expenses incurred by reason of a governmental condemnation or order not related to a casualty or the threat of a casualty.

(4)(i) Subject to the limitation set forth in paragraph (b), the amount excludable is the amount which is identified by the insurer as being paid exclusively for increased living expenses resulting from the loss of use or occupancy of the principal residence and pursuant to the terms of the insurance contract.

(ii) When a lump-sum insurance settlement includes, but does not specifically identify, compensation for property damage, loss of rental income, and increased living expenses, the amount of such settlement allocable to living expenses shall, in the case of uncontested claims, be that portion of the settlement which bears the same ratio to the total recovery as the amount of claimed increased living expense bears to the total amount of claimed losses and expenses, to the extent not in excess of the coverage limitations specified in the contract for such losses and expenses.

(iii) In the case of a lump-sum settlement involving contested claims, the insured shall establish the amount reasonably allocable to increased living expenses, consistent with the terms of the contract and other facts of the particular case.

(iv) In no event may the amount of a lump-sum settlement which is allocable to increased living expenses exceed the coverage limitation specified in the contract for increased living expenses. Where, however, a coverage limitation is applicable to the total amount payable for increased living expenses and, for example, loss of rental income, the amount of an unitemized settlement which is allocable to increased living expenses may not exceed the portion of the applicable coverage limitation which bears the same ratio to such limitation as the amount of increased living expenses bears to the sum of the amount of such increased living expenses and the amount, if any, of lost rental income.

(5) The portion of any insurance recovery for increased living expenses which exceeds the limitation set forth in paragraph (b) shall be included in gross income under section 61 of the Code.

(b) *Limitation*—(1) *Amount excludable.* The amount excludable under this section is limited to amounts received which are not in excess of the amount by which (i) total actual living expenses incurred by the insured and members of his household which result from the loss of use or occupancy of their residence exceed (ii) the total normal living expenses which would have been incurred during the loss period but are not incurred as a result of the loss of use or occupancy of the principal residence. Generally, the excludable amount represents such excess expenses acutally incurred by reason of a casualty, or threat thereof, for renting suitable housing and for extraordinary expenses for transportation, food, utilities, and miscellaneous services during the period of repair or replacement of the damaged principal residence or denial of access by governmental authority.

(2) *Actual living expenses.* For purposes of this section, actual living expenses are the reasonable and necessary expenses incurred as a result of the loss of use or occupancy of the principal residence to maintain the insured and members of his household in accordance with their customary standard of living. Actual living expenses must be of such a nature as to qualify as a reimbursable expense under the terms of the applicable insurance contract without regard to monetary limitations upon coverage. Generally, actual living expenses include the costs during the loss period of temporary housing, utilities furnished at the place of temporary housing, meals obtained at restaurants which customarily would have been prepared in the residence, transportation, and other miscellaneous services. To the extent that the loss of use or occupancy of the principal residence results merely in an increase in the amount expended for items of living expenses normally incurred, such as food and transportation, only the increase in such costs shall be considered as actual living expenses in computing the limitation.

(3) *Normal living expenses not incurred.* Normal living expenses consist of the same categories of expenses comprising actual living expenses which would have been incurred but are not incurred as a result of the casualty or threat thereof. If the loss of use of the residence results in a decrease in the amount normally expended for a living expense item during the loss period, the item of normal living expense is considered not to have been incurred to the extent of the decrease for purposes of computing the limitation.

(4) *Examples.* The application of this paragraph (b) may be illustrated by the following examples:

Example (1). On March 1, 1970, A's principal residence, a dwelling owned by A no part of which was rented to others or used for nonresidential purposes, was extensively damaged by fire. The damaged residence was under repair during the entire month of March making it necessary for A and his spouse to obtain temporary lodging and to take their meals at a restaurant. A and his spouse incur expenses of $200 for lodging at a motel, $180 for meals which customarily would have been prepared in his residence, and $25 for commercial laundry service which customarily would have been done by A's wife. A makes (directly or through mortgage insurance) or remains liable for, the required March payment of $190 on the mortgage note on his residence. The mortgage payment results from a contractual obligation having no causal relationship to the occurrence of the casualty and is not considered as an actual living expense resulting from the loss of use of the residence. A's customary commuting expense of $40 for bus fares to and from work is decreased by $20 for the month because of the motel's closer proximity to his place of employment. Other transportation expenses remain stable. Since there has been a decrease in the amount of A's customary bus fares, normal transportation expenses are considered not to have been incurred to the extent of the decrease. Finally, A does not incur customary expenses of $150 for food obtained for home preparation, $75 for utilities expenses, and $10 for laundry cleansers. The limitation upon the excludable amount of an insurance recovery for excess living expenses is $150, computed as follows:

| | Living Expenses | | |
	Actual resulting from casualty	Normal not incurred	Increase (decrease)
Housing	$200.00	$ —	$200.00
Utilities	—	75.00	(75.00)
Meals	180.00	150.00	30.00
Transportation . . .	—	20.00	(20.00)
Laundry	25.00	10.00	15.00
Total	$405.00	$255.00	$150.00

Example (2). Assume the same facts as in example (1) except that the damaged residence is not owned by A but is rented to him for $100 per month and that the risk of loss is upon the lessor. Since A would not have incurred the normal rental of $100 for March, the excludable amount

Reg. § 1.123-1(a)(5)

is limited to $50 ($150 as in previous example less $100 normal rent not incurred).

(c) *Principal residence.* Whether or not property is used by the insured taxpayer and members of his household as their principal residence depends upon all the facts and circumstances in each case. For purposes of this section a principal residence may be a dwelling or an apartment leased to the insured as well as a dwelling or apartment owned by the insured. [Reg. § 1.123-1.]

☐ [*T.D.* 7118, 6-1-71. *Amended by T.D.* 7728, 10-31-80.]

[Reg. § 1.125–2T]

§ 1.125-2T. Question and answer relating to the benefits that may be offered under a cafeteria plan (Temporary).

Q-1: What benefits may be offered to participants under a cafeteria plan?

A-1: (a) Generally, for cafeteria plan years beginning on or after January 1, 1985, a cafeteria plan is a written plan under which participants may choose among two or more benefits consisting of cash and certain other permissible benefits. In general, benefits that are excludable from the gross income of an employee under a specific section of the Internal Revenue Code may be offered under a cafeteria plan. However, scholarships and fellowships under section 117, vanpooling under section 124, educational assistance under section 127 and certain fringe benefits under section 132 may not be offered under a cafeteria plan. In addition, meals and lodging under section 119, because they are furnished for the convenience of the employer and thus are not elective in lieu of other benefits or compensation provided by the employer, may not be offered under a cafeteria plan. Thus, a cafeteria plan may offer coverage under a group-term life insurance plan of up to $50,000 (section 79) coverage under an accident or health plan (sections 105 and 106), coverage under a qualified group legal services plan (section 120), coverage under a dependent care assistance program (section 129), and participation in a qualified cash or deferred arrangement that is part of a profit-sharing or stock bonus plan (section 401(k)). In addition, a cafeteria plan may offer group-term life insurance coverage which is includible in gross income only because it is in excess of $50,000 or is on the lives of the participant's spouse and/or children. In addition, a cafeteria plan may offer participants the opportunity to purchase, with after-tax employee contributions, coverage under a group-term life insurance plan (section 79), coverage under an accident or health plan (section 105(e)), coverage

under a qualified group legal services plan (section 120), or coverage under a dependent care assistance program (section 129). Finally, a cafeteria plan may offer paid vacation days if the plan precludes any participant from using, or receiving cash for, in a subsequent plan year, any of such paid vacation days remaining unused as of the end of the plan year. For purposes of the preceding sentence, elective vacation days provided under a cafeteria plan are not considered to be used until all nonelective paid vacation days have been used.

(b) Note that benefits that may be offered under a cafeteria plan may or may not be taxable depending upon whether such benefits qualify for an exclusion from gross income. However, a cafeteria plan may not offer a benefit that is taxable because such benefit fails to satisfy any applicable eligibility, coverage, or nondiscrimination requirement. Similarly, a plan may not offer a benefit for purchase with after-tax employee contributions if such benefit would fail to satisfy any eligibility, coverage, or nondiscrimination requirement that would apply if such benefit were designed to be provided on a nontaxable basis with employer contributions. Also, note that section 125(d)(2) provides that a cafeteria plan may not offer a benefit that defers the receipt of compensation (other than the opportunity to make elective contributions under a qualified cash or deferred arrangement) and may not operate in a manner that enables participants to defer the receipt of compensation. [Temporary Reg. § 1.125-2T.]

☐ [*T.D.* 8073, 1-29-86.]

[Reg. § 1.125–3]

§ 1.125-3. Effect of the Family and Medical Leave Act (FMLA) on the operation of cafeteria plans.—The following questions and answers provide guidance on the effect of the Family and Medical Leave Act (FMLA), 29 U.S.C. 2601 et seq., on the operation of cafeteria plans:

Q-1: May an employee revoke coverage or cease payment of his or her share of group health plan premiums when taking unpaid FMLA, 29 U.S.C. 2601 et seq., leave?

A-1: Yes. An employer must either allow an employee on unpaid FMLA leave to revoke coverage, or continue coverage but allow the employee to discontinue payment of his or her share of the premium for group health plan coverage (including a health flexible spending arrangement (FSA)) under a cafeteria plan for the period of the FMLA leave. See 29 CFR 825.209(e). FMLA does not require that an employer allow an employee to revoke coverage if the employer pays the employee's share of premiums. As discussed in Q&A-3, if the employer continues coverage during an FMLA leave, the employer may recover the employee's share of the premiums when the employee returns to work. FMLA also provides the employee a right to be reinstated in the group health plan coverage (including a health FSA) provided under a cafeteria plan upon returning from FMLA leave if the employee's group health plan coverage terminated while on FMLA leave (either by revocation or due to nonpayment of premiums). Such an employee is entitled, to the extent required under FMLA, to be reinstated on the same terms as prior to taking FMLA leave (including family or dependent coverage), subject to any changes in benefit levels that may have taken place during the period of FMLA leave as provided in 29 CFR 825.215(d)(1). See 29 CFR 825.209(e) and 825.215(d). In addition, such an employee has the right to revoke or change elections under § 1.125-4 (e.g., because of changes in status or cost or coverage changes as provided under § 1.125-4) under the same terms and conditions as are available to employees participating in the cafeteria plan who are working and not on FMLA leave.

Q-2: Who is responsible for making premium payments under a cafeteria plan when an employee on FMLA leave continues group health plan coverage?

A-2: FMLA provides that an employee is entitled to continue group health plan coverage during FMLA leave whether or not that coverage is provided under a health FSA or other component of a cafeteria plan. See 29 CFR 825.209(b). FMLA permits an employer to require an employee who chooses to continue group health plan coverage while on FMLA leave to be responsible for the share of group health premiums that would be allocable to the employee if the employee were working, and, for this purpose, treats amounts paid pursuant to a pre-tax salary reduction agreement as amounts allocable to the employee. However, FMLA requires the employer to continue to contribute the share of the cost of the employee's coverage that the employer was paying before the employee commenced FMLA leave. See 29 CFR 825.100(b) and 825.210(a).

Q-3: What payment options are required or permitted to be offered under a cafeteria plan to an employee who continues group health plan coverage while on unpaid FMLA leave, and what is the tax treatment of these payments?

A-3: (a) *In general.* Subject to the limitations described in paragraph (b) of this Q&A-3, a cafeteria plan may offer one or more of the following payment options, or a combination of these op-

tions, to an employee who continues group health plan coverage (including a health FSA) while on unpaid FMLA leave; provided that the payment options for employees on FMLA leave are offered on terms at least as favorable as those offered to employees not on FMLA leave. These options are referred to in this section as pre-pay, pay-as-you-go, and catch-up. See also the FMLA notice requirements at 29 CFR 825.301(b)(1)(iv).

(1) *Pre-pay.* (i) Under the pre-pay option, a cafeteria plan may permit an employee to pay, prior to commencement of the FMLA leave period, the amounts due for the FMLA leave period. However, FMLA provides that the employer may not mandate that an employee pre-pay the amounts due for the leave period. See 29 CFR 825.210(c)(3) and (4).

(ii) Contributions under the pre-pay option may be made on a pre-tax salary reduction basis from any taxable compensation (including from unused sick days or vacation days). However, see Q&A-5 of this section regarding additional restrictions on pre-tax salary reduction contributions when an employee's FMLA leave spans two cafeteria plan years.

(iii) Contributions under the pre-pay option may also be made on an after-tax basis.

(2) *Pay-as-you-go.* (i) Under the pay-as-you-go option, employees may pay their share of the premium payments on the same schedule as payments would have been made if the employee were not on leave or under any other payment schedule permitted by the Labor Regulations at 29 CFR 825.210(c) (e.g., on the same schedule as payments are made under section 4980B (relating to coverage under the Consolidated Omnibus Budget Reconciliation Act (COBRA), 26 U.S.C. 4980B), under the employer's existing rules for payment by employees on leave without pay, or under any other C6/ROP 10-12-01 system voluntarily agreed to between the employer and the employee that is not inconsistent with this section or with 29 CFR 825.210(c)).

(ii) Contributions under the pay-as-you-go option are generally made by the employee on an after-tax basis. However, contributions may be made on a pre-tax basis to the extent that the contributions are made from taxable compensation (e.g., from unused sick days or vacation days) that is due the employee during the leave period.

(iii) An employer is not required to continue the group health coverage of an employee who fails to make required premium payments while on FMLA leave, provided that the employer follows the notice procedures required under FMLA. See 29 CFR 825.212. However, if the employer chooses to continue the health coverage of an employee who fails to pay his or her share of the premium payments while on FMLA leave, FMLA permits the employer to recoup the premiums (to the extent of the employee's share). See 29 CFR 825.212(b). Such recoupment may be made as set forth in paragraphs (a)(3)(i) and (ii) of this Q&A-3. See also Q&A-6 of this section regarding coverage under a health FSA when an employee fails to make the required premium payments while on FMLA leave.

(3) *Catch-up.* (i) Under the catch-up option, the employer and the employee may agree in advance that the group coverage will continue during the period of unpaid FMLA leave, and that the employee will not pay premiums until the employee returns from the FMLA leave. Where an employee is electing to use the catch-up option, the employer and the employee must agree in advance of the coverage period that: the employee elects to continue health coverage while on unpaid FMLA leave; the employer assumes responsibility for advancing payment of the premiums on the employee's behalf during the FMLA leave; and these advance amounts are to be paid by the employee when the employee returns from FMLA leave.

(ii) When an employee fails to make required premium payments while on FMLA leave, an employer is permitted to utilize the catch-up option to recoup the employee's share of premium payments when the employee returns from FMLA leave. See, e.g., 29 CFR 825.212(b). If the employer chooses to continue group coverage under these circumstances, the prior agreement of the employee, as set forth in paragraph (a)(3)(i) of this Q&A-3, is not required.

(iii) Contributions under the catch-up option may be made on a pre-tax salary reduction basis from any available taxable compensation (including from unused sick days and vacation days) after the employee returns from FMLA leave. The cafeteria plan may provide for the catch-up option to apply on a pre-tax salary reduction basis if premiums have not been paid on any other basis (i.e., have not been paid under the pre-pay or pay-as-you-go options or on a catch-up after-tax basis).

(iv) Contributions under the catch-up option may also be made on an after-tax basis.

(b)*Exceptions.* Whatever payment options are offered to employees on non-FMLA leave must be offered to employees on FMLA leave. In accordance with 29 CFR 825.210(c), cafeteria plans may offer one or more of the payment options described in paragraph (a) of this Q&A-3, with the following exceptions:

(1) FMLA does not permit the pre-pay option to be the sole option offered to employees on FMLA leave. However, the cafeteria plan may include pre-payment as an option for employees on FMLA leave, even if such option is not offered to employees on non-FMLA leave-without-pay.

(2) FMLA allows the catch-up option to be the sole option offered to employees on FMLA leave if and only if the catch-up option is the sole option offered to employees on non-FMLA leave-without-pay.

(3) If the pay-as-you-go option is offered to employees on non-FMLA leave-without-pay, the option must also be offered to employees on FMLA leave. The employer may also offer employees on FMLA leave the pre-pay option and/or the catch-up option.

(c) *Voluntary waiver of employee payments.* In addition to the foregoing payment options, an employer may voluntarily waive, on a nondiscriminatory basis, the requirement that employees who elect to continue group health coverage while on FMLA leave pay the amounts the employees would otherwise be required to pay for the leave period.

(a) *Example.* The following example illustrates this Q&A-3:

Example. (i) Employer Y allows employees to pay premiums for group health coverage during an FMLA leave on an after-tax basis while the employee is on unpaid FMLA leave. Under the terms of Y's cafeteria plan, if an employee elects to continue health coverage during an unpaid FMLA leave and fails to pay one or more of the after-tax premium payments due for that coverage, the employee's salary after the employee returns from FMLA leave is reduced to cover unpaid premiums (i.e. the premiums that were to be paid by the employee on an after-tax basis during the FMLA leave, but were paid by the employer instead).

(ii) In this *Example*, Y's cafeteria plan satisfies the conditions in this Q&A-3. Y's cafeteria plan would also satisfy the conditions in this Q&A-3 if the plan provided for coverage to cease in the event the employee fails to make a premium payment when due during an unpaid FMLA leave.

Q-4: Do the special FMLA requirements concerning payment of premiums by an employee who continues group health plan coverage under a cafeteria plan apply if the employee is on paid FMLA leave?

A-4: No. The Labor Regulations provide that, if an employee's FMLA leave is paid leave as described at 29 CFR 825.207 and the employer mandates that the employee continue group health plan coverage while on FMLA leave, the employee's share of the premiums must be paid by the method normally used during any paid leave (e.g., by pre-tax salary reduction if the employee's share of premiums were paid by pre-tax salary reduction before the FMLA leave began). See 29 CFR 825.210(b).

Q-5: What restrictions apply to contributions when an employee's FMLA leave spans two cafeteria plan years?

A-5: (a) No amount will be included in an employee's gross income due to participation in a cafeteria plan during FMLA leave, provided that the plan complies with other generally applicable cafeteria plan requirements. Among other requirements, a plan may not operate in a manner that enables employees on FMLA leave to defer compensation from one cafeteria plan year to a subsequent cafeteria plan year. See section 125(d)(2).

(b) The following example illustrates this Q&A-5:

Example. (i) Employee A elects group health coverage under a calendar year cafeteria plan maintained by Employer X. Employee A's premium for health coverage is $100 per month throughout the 12-month period of coverage. Employee A takes FMLA leave for 12 weeks beginning on October 31 after making 10 months of premium payments totaling $1,000 (10 months × $100 = $1,000). Employee A elects to continue health coverage while on FMLA leave and utilizes the pre-pay option by applying his or her unused sick days in order to make the required premium payments due while he or she is on FMLA leave.

(ii) Because A cannot defer compensation from one plan year to a subsequent year, A may pre-pay the premiums due in November and December (i.e., $100 per month) on a pre-tax basis, but A cannot pre-pay the premium payment due in January on a pre-tax basis. If A participates in the cafeteria plan in the subsequent plan year, A must either pre-pay for January on an after-tax basis or use another option (e.g., pay-as-you-go, catch-up, reduction in unused sick days, etc.) to make the premium payment due in January.

Q-6: Are there special rules concerning employees taking FMLA leave who participate in health FSAs offered under a cafeteria plan?

A-6: (a) *In general.* (1) A group health plan that is a flexible spending arrangement (FSA) offered under a cafeteria plan must conform to the generally applicable rules in this section concerning employees who take FMLA leave. Thus, to the extent required by FMLA (see 29 CFR 825.209(b)), an employer must—

(i) Permit an employee taking FMLA leave to continue coverage under a health FSA while on FMLA leave; and

(ii) If an employee is on unpaid FMLA leave, either—

(A) Allow the employee to revoke coverage; or

(B) Continue coverage, but allow the employee to discontinue payment of his or her share of the premium for the health FSA under the cafeteria plan during the unpaid FMLA leave period.

(2) Under FMLA, the plan must permit the employee to be reinstated in health coverage upon return from FMLA leave on the same terms as if the employee had been working throughout the leave period, without a break in coverage. See 29 CFR 825.214(a) and 825.215(d)(1) and paragraph (b)(2) of this Q&A-6. In addition, under FMLA, a plan may require an employee to be reinstated in health coverage upon return from a period of unpaid FMLA leave, provided that employees who return from a period of unpaid leave not covered by the FMLA are also required to resume participation upon return from leave.

(b) *Coverage.* (1) Regardless of the payment option selected under Q&A-3 of this section, for so long as the employee continues health FSA coverage (or for so long as the employer continues the health FSA coverage of an employee who fails to make the required contributions as described in Q&A-3(a)(2)(iii) of this section), the full amount of the elected health FSA coverage, less any prior reimbursements, must be available to the employee at all times, including the FMLA leave period.

(2)(i) If an employee's coverage under the health FSA terminates while the employee is on FMLA leave, the employee is not entitled to receive reimbursements for claims incurred during the period when the coverage is terminated. If an employee subsequently elects or the employer requires the employee to be reinstated in the health FSA upon return from FMLA leave for the remainder of the plan year, the employee may not retroactively elect health FSA coverage for claims incurred during the period when the coverage was terminated. Upon reinstatement into a health FSA upon return from FMLA leave (either because the employee elects reinstatement or because the employer requires reinstatement), the employee has the right under FMLA: to resume coverage at the level in effect before the FMLA leave and make up the unpaid premium payments, or to resume coverage at a level that is reduced and resume premium payments at the level in effect before the FMLA leave. If an employee chooses to resume health FSA coverage at a level that is reduced, the coverage is prorated for the period during the FMLA leave for which no premiums were paid. In both cases, the coverage level is reduced by prior reimbursements.

Reg. § 1.125-3

(ii) FMLA requires that an employee on FMLA leave have the right to revoke or change elections (because of events described in § 1.125-4) under the same terms and conditions that apply to employees participating in the cafeteria plan who are not on FMLA leave. Thus, for example, if a group health plan offers an annual open enrollment period to active employees, then, under FMLA, an employee on FMLA leave when the open enrollment is offered must be offered the right to make election changes on the same basis as other employees. Similarly, if a group health plan decides to offer a new benefit package option and allows active employees to elect the new option, then, under FMLA, an employee on FMLA leave must be allowed to elect the new option on the same basis as other employees.

(3) The following examples illustrate the rules in this Q&A-6:

Example 1. (i) Employee B elects $1,200 worth of coverage under a calendar year health FSA provided under a cafeteria plan, with an annual premium of $1,200. Employee B is permitted to pay the $1,200 through pre-tax salary reduction amounts of $100 per month throughout the 12-month period of coverage. Employee B incurs no medical expenses prior to April 1. On April 1, B takes FMLA leave after making three months of contributions totaling $300 (3 months × $100 = $300). Employee B's coverage ceases during the FMLA leave. Consequently, B makes no premium payments for the months of April, May, and June, and B is not entitled to submit claims or receive reimbursements for expenses incurred during this period. Employee B returns from FMLA leave and elects to be reinstated in the health FSA on July 1.

(ii) Employee B must be given a choice of resuming coverage at the level in effect before the FMLA leave (i.e., $1,200) and making up the unpaid premium payments ($300), or resuming health FSA coverage at a level that is reduced on a prorata basis for the period during the FMLA leave for which no premiums were paid (i.e., reduced for 3 months or 1/4 of the plan year) less prior reimbursements (i.e., $0) with premium payments due in the same monthly amount payable before the leave (i.e., $100 per month). Consequently, if B chooses to resume coverage at the level in effect before the FMLA leave, B's coverage for the remainder of the plan year would equal $1,200 and B's monthly premiums would be increased to $150 per month for the remainder of the plan year, to make up the $300 in premiums missed ($100 per month plus $50 per month ($300 divided by the remaining 6 months)). If B chooses prorated coverage, B's coverage for the remainder

of the plan year would equal $900, and B would resume making premium payments of $100 per month for the remainder of the plan year.

Example 2. (i) Assume the same facts as *Example 1* except that B incurred medical expenses totaling $200 in February and obtained reimbursement of these expenses.

(ii) The results are the same as in *Example 1*, except that if B chooses to resume coverage at the level in effect before the FMLA leave, B's coverage for the remainder of the year would equal $1,000 ($1,200 reduced by $200) and the monthly payments for the remainder of the year would still equal $150. If instead B chooses prorated coverage, B's coverage for the remainder of the plan year would equal $700 ($1,200 prorated for 3 months, and then reduced by $200) and the monthly payments for the remainder of the year would still equal $100.

Example 3. (i) Assume the same facts as *Example 1* except that, prior to taking FMLA leave, B elects to continue health FSA coverage during the FMLA leave. The plan permits B (and B elects) to use the catch-up payment option described in Q&A-3 of this section, and as further permitted under the plan, B chooses to repay the $300 in missed payments on a ratable basis over the remaining 6-month period of coverage (i.e., $50 per month).

(ii) Thus, B's monthly premium payments for the remainder of the plan year will be $150 ($100 + $50).

Q-7: Are employees entitled to non-health benefits while taking FMLA leave?

A-7: FMLA does not require an employer to maintain an employee's non-health benefits (e.g., life insurance) during FMLA leave. An employee's entitlement to benefits other than group health benefits under a cafeteria plan during a period of FMLA leave is to be determined by the employer's established policy for providing such benefits when the employee is on non-FMLA leave (paid or unpaid). See 29 CFR 825.209(h). Therefore, an employee who takes FMLA leave is entitled to revoke an election of non-health benefits under a cafeteria plan to the same extent as employees taking non-FMLA leave are permitted to revoke elections of non-health benefits under a cafeteria plan. For example, election changes are permitted due to changes of status or upon enrollment for a new plan year. See § 1.125-4. However, FMLA provides that, in certain cases, an employer may continue an employee's non-health benefits under the employer's cafeteria plan while the employee is on FMLA leave in order to ensure that the employer can meet its responsibility to provide equivalent benefits to the employee upon return from unpaid FMLA. If the employer continues an employee's non-health benefits during FMLA leave, the employer is entitled to recoup the costs incurred for paying the employee's share of the premiums during the FMLA leave period. See 29 CFR 825.213(b). Such recoupment may be on a pre-tax basis. A cafeteria plan must, as required by FMLA, permit an employee whose coverage terminated while on FMLA leave (either by revocation or nonpayment of premiums) to be reinstated in the cafeteria plan on return from FMLA leave. See 29 CFR 825.214(a) and 825.215(d).

Q-8: What is the applicability date of the regulations in this section?

A-8: This section is applicable for cafeteria plan years beginning on or after January 1, 2002. [Reg. § 1.125-3.]

☐ [T.D. 8966, 10-16-2001.]

[Reg. § 1.125-4]

§ 1.125-4. Permitted election changes.—(a) *Election changes*. A cafeteria plan may permit an employee to revoke an election during a period of coverage and to make a new election only as provided in paragraphs (b) through (g) of this section. Section 125 does not require a cafeteria plan to permit any of these changes. See paragraph (h) of this section for special provisions relating to qualified cash or deferred arrangements, and paragraph (i) of this section for special definitions used in this section.

(b) *Special enrollment rights*—(1) *In general*. A cafeteria plan may permit an employee to revoke an election for coverage under a group health plan during a period of coverage and make a new election that corresponds with the special enrollment rights provided in section 9801(f).

(2) *Examples*. The following examples illustrate the application of this paragraph (b):

Example 1. (i) Employer M provides health coverage for its employees pursuant to a plan that is subject to section 9801(f). Under the plan, employees may elect either employee-only coverage or family coverage. M also maintains a calendar year cafeteria plan under which qualified benefits, including health coverage, are funded through salary reduction. M's employee, A, is married to B and they have a child, C. In accordance with M's cafeteria plan, Employee A elects employee-only health coverage before the beginning of the calendar year. During the year, A and

B adopt a child, D. Within 30 days thereafter, A wants to revoke A's election for employee-only health coverage and obtain family health coverage for A's spouse, C, and D as of the date of D's adoption. Employee A satisfies the conditions for special enrollment of an employee with a new dependent under section 9801(f)(2), so that A may enroll in family coverage under M's accident or health plan in order to provide coverage effective as of the date of D's adoption.

(ii) M's cafeteria plan may permit A to change A's salary reduction election to family coverage for salary not yet currently available. The increased salary reduction is permitted to reflect the cost of family coverage from the date of adoption. (A's adoption of D is also a change in status, and the election of family coverage is consistent with that change in status. Thus, under paragraph (c) of this section, M's cafeteria plan could permit A to elect family coverage prospectively in order to cover B, C, and D for the remaining portion of the period of coverage.)

Example 2. (i) The employer plans and permissible coverage are the same as in *Example 1*. Before the beginning of the calendar year, Employee E elects employee-only health coverage under M's cafeteria plan. Employee E marries F during the plan year. F's employer, N, offers health coverage to N's employees, and, prior to the marriage, F had elected employee-only coverage. Employee E wants to revoke the election for employee-only coverage under M's cafeteria plan, and is considering electing family health coverage under M's plan or obtaining family health coverage under N's plan.

(ii) M's cafeteria plan may permit E to change E's salary reduction election to reflect the change to family coverage under M's accident or health plan because the marriage would result in special enrollment rights under section 9801(f), pursuant to which an election of family coverage under M's accident or health plan would be required to be effective no later than the first day of the first calendar month beginning after the completed request for enrollment is received by the plan. Since no retroactive coverage is required in the event of marriage under section 9801(f), E's salary reduction election may only be changed on a prospective basis. (E's marriage to F is also a change in status under paragraph (c) of this section, as illustrated in *Example 1* of paragraph (c)(4) of this section.)

→ *Caution: Reg. § 1.125-4(c), below, prior to amendment by T.D. 8921, is generally applicable for cafeteria plans beginning on or after January 1, 2001, and before January 1, 2002.*←

(c) *Changes in status*—(1) *In general*—(i) *Change in status rule.* A cafeteria plan may permit an employee to revoke an election during a period of coverage with respect to a qualified benefits plan to which this paragraph (c) applies and make a new election for the remaining portion of the period (referred to in this section as an election change) if, under the facts and circumstances—

(A) A change in status described in paragraph (c)(2) of this section occurs; and

(B) The election change satisfies the consistency rule of paragraph (c)(3) of this section.

(ii) *Application to accident or health plans and group-term life insurance plans.* This paragraph (c) applies to plans providing accident or health coverage and plans providing group-term life insurance coverage.

(iii) *Application to other qualified benefits.* [Reserved]

(2) *Change in status events.* The following events are changes in status for purposes of this paragraph (c):

(i) *Legal marital status.* Events that change an employee's legal marital status, including the following: marriage; death of spouse; divorce; legal separation; and annulment.

(ii) *Number of dependents.* Events that change an employee's number of dependents, including the following: birth; death; adoption; and placement for adoption.

(iii) *Employment status.* Any of the following events that change the employment status of the employee, the employee's spouse, or the employee's dependent: a termination or commencement of employment a strike or lockout; a commencement of or return from an unpaid leave of absence; and a change in worksite. In addition, if the eligibility conditions of the cafeteria plan or other employee benefit plan of the employer of the employee, spouse, or dependent depend on the employment status of that individual and there is a change in that individual's employment status with the consequence that the individual becomes (or ceases to be) eligible under the plan, then that change constitutes a change in employment under this paragraph (c) (e.g., if a plan only applies to salaried employees and an employee switches from salaried to hourly-paid with the consequence that the employee ceases to be eligible for the plan, then that change constitutes a change in

employment status under this paragraph (c)(2)(iii)).

(iv) *Dependent satisfies or ceases to satisfy eligibility requirements.* Events that cause an employee's dependent to satisfy or cease to satisfy eligibility requirements for coverage on account of attainment of age, student status, or any similar circumstance.

(v) *Residence.* A change in the place of residence of the employee, spouse, or dependent.

(3) *Consistency rule*—(i) *Application to accident or health coverage and group-term life insurance.* An election change satisfies the requirements of this paragraph (c)(3) with respect to accident or health coverage or group-term life insurance only if the election change is on account of and corresponds with a change in status that affects eligibility for coverage under an employer's plan.

(ii) *Application to other qualified benefits.* [Reserved]

(iii) *Application of consistency rule.* If the change in status is the employee's divorce, annulment or legal separation from a spouse, the death of a spouse or dependent, or a dependent ceasing to satisfy the eligibility requirements for coverage, an employee's election under the cafeteria plan to cancel accident or health insurance coverage for any individual other than the spouse involved in the divorce, annulment or legal separation, the deceased spouse or dependent, or the dependent that ceased to satisfy the eligibility requirements for coverage, respectively, fails to correspond with that change in status. Thus, if a dependent dies or ceases to satisfy the eligibility requirements for coverage, the employee's election to cancel accident or health coverage for any other dependent, for the employee, or for the employee's spouse fails to correspond with that change in status. In addition, if an employee, spouse, or dependent gains eligibility for coverage under a family member plan (as defined in paragraph (i)(5) of this section) as a result of a change in marital status under paragraph (c)(2)(i) of this section or a change in employment status under paragraph (c)(2)(iii) of this section, an employee's election under the cafeteria plan to cease or decrease coverage for that individual under the cafeteria plan corresponds with that change in status only if coverage for that individual becomes applicable or is increased under the family member plan. However, if the change in status is a change in the employee's marital status under paragraph

→ *Caution: Reg. § 1.125-4(c), below, prior to amendment by T.D. 8921, is generally applicable for cafeteria plans beginning on or after January 1, 2001, and before January 1, 2002.*←

(c)(2)(i) of this section or a change in the employment status of the employee's spouse or dependents under paragraph (c)(2)(iii) of this section, an election to increase, or an election to decrease, group-term life insurance or disability income coverage corresponds with that change in status.

(iv) *Exception for COBRA.* If the employee, spouse, or dependent becomes eligible for continuation coverage under the group health plan of the employee's employer as provided in section 4980B or any similar state law, a cafeteria plan may permit the employee to elect to increase payments under the employer's cafeteria plan in order to pay for the continuation coverage.

(4) *Examples.* The following examples illustrate the application of this paragraph (c):

Example 1. (i) Employer *M* provides health coverage (including a health FSA) for its employees through its cafeteria plan. Before the beginning of the calendar year, Employee *A* elects employee-only health coverage under *M*'s cafeteria plan and elects salary reduction contributions to fund coverage under the health FSA. Employee *A* marries *B* during the year. Employee *B*'s employer, *N*, offers health coverage to *N*'s employees (but not including any health FSA), and, prior to the marriage, *B* had elected employee-only coverage. Employee *A* wants to revoke the election for employee-only coverage, and is considering electing family health coverage under *M*'s plan or obtaining family health coverage under *N*'s plan.

(ii) Employee *A*'s marriage to *B* is a change in status under paragraph (c)(2)(i) of this section, pursuant to which *B* has become eligible for coverage under *M*'s health plan under paragraph (c)(3)(i) of this section. Two possible election changes by *A* correspond with the change in status: Employee *A* may elect family health coverage under *M*'s plan to cover *A* and *B*; or *A* may cancel coverage under *M*'s plan, if *B* elects family health coverage under *N*'s plan to cover *A* and *B*. Thus, *M*'s cafeteria plan may permit *A* to make either election change.

(iii) Employee *A* may also increase salary reduction contributions to fund coverage for *B* under the health FSA.

Example 2. (i) Employee *C*, a single parent, elects family health coverage under a calendar year cafeteria plan maintained by Employer *O*. Employee *C* and *C*'s 21-year old child, *D*, are covered under *O*'s health plan. During the year, *D* graduates from college. Under the terms of the health plan, dependents over the age of 19 must be full-time students to receive coverage. Employee *C* wants to revoke *C*'s election for family health coverage and obtain employee-only coverage under *O*'s cafeteria plan.

(ii) *D*'s loss of eligibility for coverage under the terms of the health plan is a change in status under paragraph (c)(2)(iv) of this section. A revocation of *C*'s election for family coverage and new election for employee-only coverage corresponds with the change in status. Thus, *O*'s cafeteria plan may permit *C* to elect employee-only coverage.

Example 3. (i) Employee *E* is married to *F* and they have one child, *G*. Employee *E* is employed by Employer *P*, and *P* maintains a calendar year cafeteria plan that allows employees to elect no health coverage, employee-only coverage, employee-plus-one-dependent coverage, or family coverage. Under the plan, before the beginning of the calendar year, *E* elects family health coverage for *E*, *F*, and *G*. *E* and *F* divorce during the year and *F* loses eligibility for coverage under *P*'s plan. *G* does not lose eligibility for health coverage under *P*'s plan upon the divorce. *E* now wants to revoke *E*'s election under the cafeteria plan and elect no coverage.

(ii) The divorce is a change in status under paragraph (c)(2)(i). A change in the cafeteria plan election to cancel health coverage for *F* is consistent with that change in status. However, an election change to cancel *E*'s or *G*'s health coverage does not satisfy the consistency rule under paragraph (c)(3)(iii) of this section regarding cancellation of coverage for an employee's other dependents in the event of divorce. Therefore, the cafeteria plan may not permit *E* to elect no coverage. However, an election to change to employee-plus-one-dependent health coverage would correspond with the change in status, and thus the cafeteria plan may permit *E* to elect employee-plus-one-dependent health coverage.

Example 4. (i) Employer *R* maintains a calendar year cafeteria plan under which full-time employees may elect coverage under one of three benefit package options provided under an accident or health plan: an indemnity option or either of two HMO options for employees who work in the respective service areas of the two HMOs. Employee *A*, who works in the service area of HMO #1, elects the HMO #1 option. During the year, *A* is transferred to another work location which is outside the HMO #1 service area and inside the HMO #2 service area.

Reg. § 1.125-4(c)(4)

→ *Caution: Reg. § 1.125-4(c), below, prior to amendment by T.D. 8921, is generally applicable for cafeteria plans beginning on or after January 1, 2001, and before January 1, 2002.←*

(ii) The transfer is a change in status under paragraph (c)(2)(iii) of this section (relating to a change in worksite), and, under the consistency rule in paragraph (c)(3) of this section, the cafeteria plan may permit *A* to make an election change to either the indemnity option or HMO #2.

Example 5. (i) Employer *S* maintains a calendar year cafeteria plan that allows employees to elect coverage under an accident or health plan providing indemnity coverage and coverage under a health FSA. Prior to the beginning of the calendar year, Employee *B* elects employee-only indemnity coverage, and elects salary reduction contributions of $600 during the year to fund coverage under the health FSA for up to $600 of reimbursements for the year. Employee *B*'s spouse, *C*, has employee-only coverage under an accident or health plan maintained by *C*'s employer. During the year, *C* terminates employment and loses coverage under that plan. *B* now wants to elect family coverage under *S*'s accident or health plan and increase *B*'s FSA election.

(ii) *C*'s termination of employment is a change in status under paragraph (c)(2)(iii) of this section, and the election change satisfies the consistency rule of paragraph (c)(3) of this section. Therefore, the cafeteria plan may permit *B* to elect family coverage under *S*'s accident or health plan and to increase *B*'s FSA coverage.

Example 6. (i) Employer *T* provides group-term life insurance coverage as described under section 79. Under *T*'s plan, an employee may elect life insurance coverage in an amount up to $50,000. *T* also maintains a calendar year cafeteria plan under which qualified benefits, including the group-term life insurance coverage, are funded through salary reduction. Employee *D* has a spouse and a child. Before the beginning of the year, *D* elects $10,000 of group-term life insurance coverage. During the year, *D* is divorced.

(ii) The divorce is a change in status under paragraph (c)(2)(i) of this section. Under paragraph (c)(3)(iii) of this section, either an increase or a decrease in coverage is consistent with this change in status. Thus, *T*'s cafeteria plan may permit *D* to increase or to decrease *D*'s group-term life insurance coverage.

Example 7. (i) Employee *E* is married to *F* and they have one child, *G*. Employee *E*'s employer, *U*, maintains a cafeteria plan under which employees may elect no coverage, employee-only coverage, or family coverage under a group health plan maintained by *U*, and may make a separate

vision coverage election under the plan. Before the beginning of the calendar year, *E* elects family health coverage and no vision coverage under *U*'s cafeteria plan. Employee *F*'s employer, *V*, maintains a cafeteria plan under which employees may elect no coverage, employee-only coverage, or family coverage under a group health plan maintained by *V*, and may make a separate vision coverage election under the plan. Before the beginning of the calendar year, *F* elects no health coverage and employee-only vision coverage under *V*'s plan. During the year, *F* terminates employment with *V* and loses vision coverage under *V*'s plan. Employee *E* now wants to elect family vision coverage under *U*'s group health plan.

(ii) *F*'s termination of employment is a change in status under paragraph (c)(2)(iii) of this section, and the election change satisfies the consistency rule of paragraph (c)(3) of this section. Therefore, *U*'s cafeteria plan may permit *E* to elect family vision coverage (covering *E* and *G* as well as *F*) under *U*'s group health plan.

Example 8. (i) Before the beginning of the year, Employee *H* elects to participate in a cafeteria plan maintained by *H*'s employer, *W*. However, in order to change the election during the year so as to cancel coverage, and by prior understanding with *W*, *H* terminates employment and resumes employment one week later.

(ii) In this *Example 8*, under the facts and circumstances, a principal purpose of the termination of employment was to alter the election, and reinstatement of employment was understood at the time of termination. Accordingly, *H* does not have a change in status under paragraph (c)(2)(iii) of this section.

(iii) However, *H*'s termination of employment would constitute a change in status, permitting a cancellation of coverage during the period of unemployment, if *H*'s original cafeteria plan election for the period of coverage was reinstated upon resumption of employment (for example, if *W*'s cafeteria plan contains a provision requiring an employee who resumes employment within 30 days, without any other intervening event that would permit a change in election, to return to the election in effect prior to termination of employment).

(iv) If, instead, *H* terminates employment and cancels coverage during a period of unemployment, and then returns to work more than 30 days following termination of employment, the cafeteria plan may permit *H* the option of re-

→ *Caution: Reg. § 1.125-4(c), below, prior to amendment by T.D. 8921, is generally applicable for cafeteria plans beginning on or after January 1, 2001, and before January 1, 2002.*←

turning to the election in effect prior to termination of employment or making a new election under the plan. Alternatively, the cafeteria plan may prohibit *H* from returning to the plan during that plan year.

→ *Caution: Reg. § 1.125-4(c), below, as amended by T.D. 8921, is generally applicable for cafeteria plans beginning on or after January 1, 2002.*←

(c) *Changes in status*—(1) *Change in status rule.* A cafeteria plan may permit an employee to revoke an election during a period of coverage with respect to a qualified benefits plan (defined in paragraph (i)(8) of this section) to which this paragraph (c) applies and make a new election for the remaining portion of the period (referred to in this section as an election change) if, under the facts and circumstances—

(i) change in status described in paragraph (c)(2) of this section occurs; and

(ii) The election change satisfies the consistency rule of paragraph (c)(3) of this section.

(2) *Change in status events.* The following events are changes in status for purposes of this paragraph (c):

(i) *Legal marital status.* Events that change an employee's legal marital status, including the following: marriage; death of spouse; divorce; legal separation; and annulment.

(ii) *Number of dependents.* Events that change an employee's number of dependents, including the following: birth; death; adoption; and placement for adoption.

(iii) *Employment status.* Any of the following events that change the employment status of the employee, the employee's spouse, or the employee's dependent: a termination or commencement of employment; a strike or lockout; a commencement of or return from an unpaid leave of absence; and a change in worksite. In addition, if the eligibility conditions of the cafeteria plan or other employee benefit plan of the employer of the employee, spouse, or dependent depend on the employment status of that individual and there is a change in that individual's employment status with the consequence that the individual becomes (or ceases to be) eligible under the plan, then that change constitutes a change in employment under this paragraph (c) (e.g., if a plan only applies to salaried employees and an employee switches from salaried to hourly-paid with the consequence that the employee ceases to be eligible for the plan, then that change constitutes a change in employment status under this paragraph (c)(2)(iii)).

(iv) *Dependent satisfies or ceases to satisfy eligibility requirements.* Events that cause an employee's dependent to satisfy or cease to satisfy eligibility requirements for coverage on account of attainment of age, student status, or any similar circumstance.

(v) *Residence.* A change in the place of residence of the employee, spouse, or dependent.

(vi) *Adoption assistance.* For purposes of adoption assistance provided through a cafeteria plan, the commencement or termination of an adoption proceeding.

(3) *Consistency rule*—(i) *Application to accident or health coverage and group-term life insurance.* An election change satisfies the requirements of this paragraph (c)(3) with respect to accident or health coverage or group-term life insurance only if the election change is on account of and corresponds with a change in status that affects eligibility for coverage under an employer's plan. A change in status that affects eligibility under an employer's plan includes a change in status that results in an increase or decrease in the number of an employee's family members or dependents who may benefit from coverage under the plan.

(ii) *Application to other qualified benefits.* An election change satisfies the requirements of this paragraph (c)(3) with respect to other qualified benefits if the election change is on account of and corresponds with a change in status that affects eligibility for coverage under an employer's plan. An election change also satisfies the requirements of this paragraph (c)(3) if the election change is on account of and corresponds with a change in status that effects expenses described in section 129 (including employment-related expenses as defined in section 21(b)(2)) with respect to dependent care assistance, or expenses described in section 137 (including qualified adoption expenses as defined in section 137(d)) with respect to adoption assistance.

(iii) *Application of consistency rule.* If the change in status is the employee's divorce, annulment or legal separation from a spouse, the death of a spouse or dependent, or a dependent ceasing to satisfy the eligibility requirements for cover-

Reg. § 1.125-4(c)(1)

→ *Caution: Reg. § 1.125-4(c), below, as amended by T.D. 8921, is generally applicable for cafeteria plans beginning on or after January 1, 2002.*←

age, an employee's election under the cafeteria plan to cancel accident or health insurance coverage for any individual other than the spouse involved in the divorce, annulment or legal separation, the deceased spouse or dependent, or the dependent that ceased to satisfy the eligibility requirements for coverage, respectively, fails to correspond with that change in status. Thus, if a dependent dies or ceases to satisfy the eligibility requirements for coverage, the employee's election to cancel accident or health coverage for any other dependent, for the employee, or for the employee's spouse fails to correspond with that change in status. In addition, if an employee, spouse, or dependent gains eligibility for coverage under a family member plan (as defined in paragraph (i)(5) of this section) as a result of a change in marital status under paragraph (c)(2)(i) of this section or a change in employment status under paragraph (c)(2)(iii) of this section, an employee's election under the cafeteria plan to cease or decrease coverage for that individual under the cafeteria plan corresponds with that change in status only if coverage for that individual becomes applicable or is increased under the family member plan. With respect to group-term life insurance and disability coverage (as defined in paragraph (i)(4) of this section), an election under a cafeteria plan to increase coverage (or an election to decrease coverage) in response to a change in status described in paragraph (c)(2) of this section is deemed to correspond with that change in status as required by paragraph (c)(3)(i) of this section.

(iv) *Exception for COBRA.* If the employee, spouse, or dependent becomes eligible for continuation coverage under the group health plan of the employee's employer as provided in section 4980B or any similar state law, a cafeteria plan may permit the employee to elect to increase payments under the employer's cafeteria plan in order to pay for the continuation coverage.

(4) *Examples.* The following examples illustrate the application of this paragraph (c):

Example 1. (i) Employer *M* provides health coverage (including a health FSA) for its employees through its cafeteria plan. Before the beginning of the calendar year, Employee *A* elects employee-only health coverage under *M's* cafeteria plan and elects salary reduction contributions to fund coverage under the health FSA. Employee *A* marries *B* during the year. Employee *B's* employer, *N*, offers health coverage to *N's* employees (but not including any health FSA), and, prior to the marriage, *B* had elected employee-only coverage. Employee *A* wants to revoke the election for

employee-only coverage, and is considering electing family health coverage under *M's* plan or obtaining family health coverage under *N's* plan.

(ii) Employee *A's* marriage to *B* is a change in status under paragraph (c)(2)(i) of this section, pursuant to which *B* has become eligible for coverage under *M's* health plan under paragraph (c)(3)(i) of this section. Two possible election changes by *A* correspond with the change in status: Employee *A* may elect family health coverage under *M's* plan to cover *A* and *B*; or *A* may cancel coverage under *M's* plan, if *B* elects family health coverage under *N's* plan to cover *A* and *B*. Thus, *M's* cafeteria plan may permit *A* to make either election change.

(iii) Employee *A* may also increase salary reduction contributions to fund coverage for *B* under the health FSA.

Example 2. (i) Employee *C*, a single parent, elects family health coverage under a calendar year cafeteria plan maintained by Employer *O*. Employee *C* and *C's* 21-year old child, *D*, are covered under *O's* health plan. During the year, *D* graduates from college. Under the terms of the health plan, dependents over the age of 19 must be full-time students to receive coverage. Employee *C* wants to revoke *C's* election for family health coverage and obtain employee-only coverage under *O's* cafeteria plan.

(ii) *D's* loss of eligibility for coverage under the terms of the health plan is a change in status under paragraph (c)(2)(iv) of this section. A revocation of *C's* election for family coverage and new election for employee-only coverage corresponds with the change in status. Thus, *O's* cafeteria plan may permit *C* to elect employee-only coverage.

Example 3. (i) Employee *E* is married to *F* and they have one child, *G*. Employee *E* is employed by Employer *P*, and *P* maintains a calendar year cafeteria plan that allows employees to elect no health coverage, employee-only coverage, employee-plus-one-dependent coverage, or family coverage. Under the plan, before the beginning of the calendar year, *E* elects family health coverage for *E*, *F*, and *G*. *E* and *F* divorce during the year and *F* loses eligibility for coverage under *P's* plan. *G* does not lose eligibility for health coverage under *P's* plan upon the divorce. *E* now wants to revoke *E's* election under the cafeteria plan and elect no coverage.

(ii) The divorce is a change in status under paragraph (c)(2)(i). A change in the cafeteria plan election to cancel health coverage for *F* is consistent with that change in status. However, an

→ *Caution: Reg. § 1.125-4(c), below, as amended by T.D. 8921, is generally applicable for cafeteria plans beginning on or after January 1, 2002.*←

election change to cancel E's or G's health coverage does not satisfy the consistency rule under paragraph (c)(3)(iii) of this section regarding cancellation of coverage for an employee's other dependents in the event of divorce. Therefore, the cafeteria plan may not permit E to elect no coverage. However, an election to change to employee-plus-one-dependent health coverage would correspond with the change in status, and thus the cafeteria plan may permit E to elect employee-plus-one-dependent health coverage.

(iii) In addition, under paragraph (f)(4) of this section, if F makes an election change to cover G under F's employer's plan, then E may make a corresponding change to elect employee-only coverage under P's cafeteria plan.

Example 4. (i) Employer R maintains a calendar year cafeteria plan under which full-time employees may elect coverage under one of three benefit package options provided under an accident or health plan: an indemnity option or either of two HMO options for employees who work in the respective service areas of the two HMOs. Employee A, who works in the service area of HMO #1, elects the HMO #1 option. During the year, A is transferred to another work location which is outside the HMO #1 service area and inside the HMO #2 service area.

(ii) The transfer is a change in status under paragraph (c)(2)(iii) of this section (relating to a change in worksite), and, under the consistency rule in paragraph (c)(3) of this section, the cafeteria plan may permit A to make an election change to elect the indemnity option or HMO #2 or to cancel accident or health coverage.

(iii) The change in work location has no effect on A's eligibility under R's health FSA, so no change in A's health FSA is authorized under this paragraph (c).

Example 5. (i) Employer S maintains a calendar year cafeteria plan that allows employees to elect coverage under an accident or health plan providing indemnity coverage and coverage under a health FSA. Prior to the beginning of the calendar year, Employee B elects employee-only indemnity coverage, and elects salary reduction contributions of $600 during the year to fund coverage under the health FSA for up to $600 of reimbursements for the year. Employee B's spouse, C, has employee-only coverage under an accident or health plan maintained by C's employer. During the year, C terminates employment and loses coverage under that plan. B now

wants to elect family coverage under S's accident or health plan and increase B's FSA election.

(ii) C's termination of employment is a change in status under paragraph (c)(2)(iii) of this section, and the election change satisfies the consistency rule of paragraph (c)(3) of this section. Therefore, the cafeteria plan may permit B to elect family coverage under S's accident or health plan and to increase B's FSA coverage.

Example 6. (i) Employer T provides group-term life insurance coverage as described under section 79. Under T's plan, an employee may elect life insurance coverage in an amount up to $50,000. T also maintains a calendar year cafeteria plan under which qualified benefits, including the group-term life insurance coverage, are funded through salary reduction. Employee D has a spouse and a child. Before the beginning of the year, D elects $10,000 of group-term life insurance coverage. During the year, D is divorced.

(ii) The divorce is a change in status under paragraph (c)(2)(i) of this section. Under paragraph (c)(3)(iii) of this section, either an increase or a decrease in coverage is consistent with this change in status. Thus, T's cafeteria plan may permit D to increase or to decrease D's group-term life insurance coverage.

Example 7. (i) Employee E is married to F and they have one child, G. Employee E's employer, U, maintains a cafeteria plan under which employees may elect no coverage, employee-only coverage, or family coverage under a group health plan maintained by U, and may make a separate vision coverage election under the plan. Before the beginning of the calendar year, E elects family health coverage and no vision coverage under U's cafeteria plan. Employee F's employer, V, maintains a cafeteria plan under which employees may elect no coverage, employee-only coverage, or family coverage under a group health plan maintained by V, and may make a separate vision coverage election under the plan. Before the beginning of the calendar year, F elects no health coverage and employee-only vision coverage under V's plan. During the year, F terminates employment with V and loses vision coverage under V's plan. Employee E now wants to elect family vision coverage under U's group health plan.

(ii) F's termination of employment is a change in status under paragraph (c)(2)(iii) of this section, and the election change satisfies the consistency rule of paragraph (c)(3) of this section. Therefore, U's cafeteria plan may permit E

Reg. § 1.125-4(c)(4)

→ *Caution: Reg. § 1.125-4(c), below, as amended by T.D. 8921, is generally applicable for cafeteria plans beginning on or after January 1, 2002.*←

to elect family vision coverage (covering *E* and *G* as well as *F*) under *U*'s group health plan.

Example 8. (i) Before the beginning of the year, Employee *H* elects to participate in a cafeteria plan maintained by *H*'s employer, *W*. However, in order to change the election during the year so as to cancel coverage, and by prior understanding with *W*, *H* terminates employment and resumes employment one week later.

(ii) In this *Example 8*, under the facts and circumstances, a principal purpose of the termination of employment was to alter the election, and reinstatement of employment was understood at the time of termination. Accordingly, *H* does not have a change in status under paragraph (c)(2)(iii) of this section.

(iii) However, *H*'s termination of employment would constitute a change in status, permitting a cancellation of coverage during the period of unemployment, if *H*'s original cafeteria plan election for the period of coverage was reinstated upon resumption of employment (for example, if *W*'s cafeteria plan contains a provision requiring an employee who resumes employment within 30 days, without any other intervening event that would permit a change in election, to return to the election in effect prior to termination of employment).

(iv) If, instead, *H* terminates employment and cancels coverage during a period of unemployment, and then returns to work more than 30 days following termination of employment, the cafeteria plan may permit *F* the option of returning to the election in effect prior to termination of employment or making a new election under the plan. Alternatively, the cafeteria plan may prohibit *H* from returning to the plan during that plan year.

Example 9. (i) Employee *A* has one child, *B*. Employee *A*'s employer, *X*, maintains a calendar year cafeteria plan that allows employees to elect coverage under a dependent care FSA. Prior to the beginning of the calendar year, *A* elects salary reduction contributions of $4,000 during the year to fund coverage under the dependent care FSA for up to $4,000 of reimbursements for the year. During the year, *B* reaches the age of 13, and *A* wants to cancel coverage under the dependent care FSA.

(ii) When *B* turns 13, *B* ceases to satisfy the definition of qualifying individual under section 21(b)(1) of the Internal Revenue Code. Accordingly, *B*'s attainment of age 13 is a change in status under paragraph (c)(2)(iv) of this section that affects *A*'s employment-related expenses as defined in section 21(b)(2). Therefore, *A* may make a corresponding change under *X*'s cafeteria plan to cancel coverage under the dependent care FSA.

Example 10. (i) Employer *Y* maintains a calendar year cafeteria plan under which full-time employees may elect coverage under either an indemnity option or an HMO. Employee *C* elects the employee-only indemnity option. During the year, *C* marries *D*. *D* has two children from a previous marriage, and has family group health coverage in a cafeteria plan sponsored by *D*'s employer, *Z*. *C* wishes to change from employee-only indemnity coverage to HMO coverage for the family. *D* wishes to cease coverage in *Z*'s group health plan and certifies to *Z* that *D* will have family coverage under *C*'s plan (and *Z* has no reason to believe the certification is incorrect).

(ii) The marriage is a change in status under paragraph (c)(2)(i) of this section. Under the consistency rule in paragraph (c)(3) of this section, *Y*'s cafeteria plan may permit *C* to change his or her salary reduction contributions to reflect the change from employee-only indemnity to HMO family coverage, and *Z* may permit *D* to revoke coverage under *Z*'s cafeteria plan.

(d) *Judgment, decree, or order*—(1) *Conforming election change.* This paragraph (d) applies to a judgment, decree, or order (order) resulting from a divorce, legal separation, annulment, or change in legal custody (including a qualified medical child support order as defined in section 609 of the Employee Retirement Income Security Act of 1974 (Public Law 93-406 (88 Stat. 829))) that requires accident or health coverage for an employee's child or for a foster child who is a dependent of the employee . A cafeteria plan will not fail to satisfy section 125 if it—

(i) Changes the employee's election to provide coverage for the child if the order requires coverage for the child under the employee's plan; or

Reg. § 1.125-4(d)(1)

→ *Caution: Reg. § 1.125-4(d)(1)(ii), below, prior to amendment by T.D. 8921, is generally applicable for cafeteria plans beginning on or after January 1, 2001, and before January 1, 2002.*←

(ii) Permits the employee to make an election change to cancel coverage for the child if the order requires the spouse, former spouse, or other individual to provide coverage for the child.

→ *Caution: Reg. § 1.125-4(d)(1)(ii), below, as amended by T.D. 8921, is generally applicable for cafeteria plans beginning on or after January 1, 2002.*←

(ii) Permits the employee to make an election change to cancel coverage for the child if:

(A) The order requires the spouse, former spouse, or other individual to provide coverage for the child; and

(B) That coverage is, in fact, provided.

(2) *Example.* The following example illustrates the application of this paragraph (d):

Example. (i) Employer *M* maintains a calendar year cafeteria plan that allows employees to elect no health coverage, employee-only coverage, employee-plus-one-dependent coverage, or family coverage. *M*'s employee, *A*, is married to *B* and they have one child, *C*. Before the beginning of the year, *A* elects employee-only health coverage. Employee *A* divorces *B* during the year and, pursuant to *A*'s divorce agreement with B, *M*'s health plan receives a qualified medical child support order (as defined in section 609 of the Employee Retirement Income Security Act of 1974) during the plan year. The order requires *M*'s health plan to cover *C*.

(ii) Under this paragraph (d), *M*'s cafeteria plan may change *A*'s election from employee-only health coverage to employee-plus-one-dependent coverage in order to cover *C*.

(e) *Entitlement to Medicare or Medicaid.* If an employee, spouse, or dependent who is enrolled in an accident or health plan of the employer becomes entitled to coverage (i.e., becomes enrolled) under Part A or Part B of Title XVIII of the Social Security Act (Medicare) (Public Law 89-97 (79 Stat. 291)) or Title XIX of the Social Security Act (Medicaid) (Public Law 89-97 (79 Stat. 343)), other than coverage consisting solely of benefits under section 1928 of the Social Security Act (the program for distribution of pediatric vaccines), a cafeteria plan may permit the employee to make a prospective election change to cancel or reduce coverage of that employee, spouse, or dependent under the accident or health plan. In addition, if an employee, spouse, or dependent who has been entitled to such coverage under Medicare or Medicaid loses eligibility for such coverage, the cafeteria plan may permit the employee to make a prospective election to commence or increase coverage of that employee, spouse, or dependent under the accident or health plan.

→ *Caution: Reg. § 1.125-4(f), below, as amended by T.D. 8921, is generally applicable for cafeteria plans beginning on or after January 1, 2002.*←

(f) *Significant cost or coverage changes*—(1) *In general.* Paragraphs (f)(2) through (5) of this section set forth rules for election changes as a result of changes in cost or coverage. This paragraph (f) does not apply to an election change with respect to a health FSA (or on account of a change in cost or coverage under a health FSA).

(2) *Cost changes*—(i) *Automatic changes.* If the cost of a qualified benefits plan increases (or decreases) during a period of coverage and, under the terms of the plan, employees are required to make a corresponding change in their payments, the cafeteria plan may, on a reasonable and consistent basis, automatically make a prospective increase (or decrease) in affected employees' elective contributions for the plan.

(ii) *Significant cost changes.* If the cost charged to an employee for a benefit package option (as defined in paragraph (i)(2) of this section) significantly increases or significantly decreases during a period of coverage, the cafeteria plan may permit the employee to make a corresponding change in election under the cafeteria plan. Changes that may be made include commencing participation in the cafeteria plan for the option with a decrease in cost, or, in the case of an increase in cost, revoking an election for that coverage and, in lieu thereof, either receiving on a prospective basis coverage under another benefit package option providing similar coverage or dropping coverage if no other benefit package option providing similar coverage is available. For example, if the cost of an indemnity option under an accident or health plan significantly increases during a period of coverage, employees who are covered by the indemnity option may make a

Reg. § 1.125-4(d)(2)

→ *Caution: Reg. § 1.125-4(f), below, as amended by T.D. 8921, is generally applicable for cafeteria plans beginning on or after January 1, 2002.*←

corresponding prospective increase in their payments or may instead elect to revoke their election for the indemnity option and, in lieu thereof, elect coverage under another benefit package option including an HMO option (or drop coverage under the accident or health plan if no other benefit package option is offered).

(iii) *Application of cost changes.* For purposes of paragraphs (f)(2)(i) and (ii) of this section, a cost increase or decrease refers to an increase or decrease in the amount of the elective contributions under the cafeteria plan, whether that increase or decrease results from an action taken by the employee (such as switching between full-time and part-time status) or from an action taken by an employer (such as reducing the amount of employer contributions for a class of employees).

(iv) *Application to dependent care.* This paragraph (f)(2) applies in the case of a dependent care assistance plan only if the cost change is imposed by a dependent care provider who is not a relative of the employee. For this purpose, a relative is an individual who is related as described in section 152(a)(1) through (8), incorporating the rules of section 152(b)(1) and (2).

(3) *Coverage changes*—(i) *Significant curtailment without loss of coverage.* If an employee (or an employee's spouse or dependent) has a significant curtailment of coverage under a plan during a period of coverage that is not a loss of coverage as described in paragraph (f)(3)(ii) of this section (for example, there is a significant increase in the deductible, the copay, or the out-of-pocket cost sharing limit under an accident or health plan), the cafeteria plan may permit any employee who had been participating in the plan and receiving that coverage to revoke his or her election for that coverage and, in lieu thereof, to elect to receive on a prospective basis coverage under another benefit package option providing similar coverage. Coverage under a plan is significantly curtailed only if there is an overall reduction in coverage provided under the plan so as to constitute reduced coverage generally. Thus, in most cases, the loss of one particular physician in a network does not constitute a significant curtailment.

(ii) *Significant curtailment with loss of coverage.* If an employee (or the employee's spouse or dependent) has a significant curtailment that is a loss of coverage, the plan may permit that employee to revoke his or her election under the Cafeteria plan and, in lieu thereof, to elect either to receive on a prospective basis coverage under another benefit package option providing similar coverage or to drop coverage if no similar benefit package option is available. For purposes of this paragraph (f)(3)(ii), a loss of coverage means a complete loss of coverage under the benefit package option or other coverage option (including the elimination of a benefits package option, an HMO ceasing to be available in the area where the individual resides, or the individual losing all coverage under the option by reason of an overall lifetime or annual limitation). In addition, the cafeteria plan may, in its discretion, treat the following as a loss of coverage—

(A) A substantial decrease in the medical care providers available under the option (such as a major hospital ceasing to be a member of a preferred provider network or a substantial decrease in the physicians participating in a preferred provider network or an HMO);

(B) A reduction in the benefits for a specific type of medical condition or treatment with respect to which the employee or the employee's spouse or dependent is currently in a course of treatment; or

(C) Any other similar fundamental loss of coverage.

(iii) *Addition or improvement of a benefit package option.* If a plan adds a new benefit package option or other coverage option, or if coverage under an existing benefit package option or other coverage option is significantly improved during a period of coverage, the cafeteria plan may permit eligible employees (whether or not they have previously made an election under the cafeteria plan or have previously elected the benefit package option) to revoke their election under the cafeteria plan and, in lieu thereof, to make an election on a prospective basis for coverage under the new or improved benefit package option.

(4) *Change in coverage under another employer plan.* A cafeteria plan may permit an employee to make a prospective election change that is on account of and corresponds with a change made under another employer plan (including a plan of the same employer or of another employer) if—

(i) The other cafeteria plan or qualified benefits plan permits participants to make an election change that would be permitted under paragraphs (b) through (g) of this section (disregarding this paragraph (f)(4)); or

(ii) The cafeteria plan permits participants to make an election for a period of coverage

→ *Caution: Reg. § 1.125-4(f), below, as amended by T.D. 8921, is generally applicable for cafeteria plans beginning on or after January 1, 2002.←*

that is different from the period of coverage under the other cafeteria plan or qualified benefits plan.

(5) *Loss of coverage under other group health coverage.* A cafeteria plan may permit an employee to make an election on a prospective basis to add coverage under a cafeteria plan for the employee, spouse, or dependent if the employee, spouse, or dependent loses coverage under any group health coverage sponsored by a governmental or educational institution, including the following—

(i) A State's children's health insurance program (SCHIP) under Title XXI of the Social Security Act;

(ii) A medical care program of an Indian Tribal government (as defined in section 7701(a)(40)), the Indian Health Service, or a tribal organization;

(iii) A State health benefits risk pool; or

(iv) A Foreign government group health plan.

(6) *Examples.* The following examples illustrate the application of this paragraph (f):

Example 1. (i) A calendar year cafeteria plan is maintained pursuant to a collective bargaining agreement for the benefit of Employer *M*'s employees. The cafeteria plan offers various benefits, including indemnity health insurance and a health FSA. As a result of mid-year negotiations, premiums for the indemnity health insurance are reduced in the middle of the year, insurance co-payments for office visits are reduced under the indemnity plan by an amount which constitutes a significant benefit improvement, and an HMO option is added.

(ii) Under these facts, the reduction in health insurance premiums is a reduction in cost. Accordingly, under paragraph (f)(2)(i) of this section, the cafeteria plan may automatically decrease the amount of salary reduction contributions of affected participants by an amount that corresponds to the premium change. However, the plan may not permit employees to change their health FSA elections to reflect the mid-year change in copayments under the indemnity plan.

(iii) Also, the decrease in co-payments is a significant benefit improvement and the addition of the HMO option is an addition of a benefit package option. Accordingly, under paragraph (f)(3)(ii) of this section, the cafeteria plan may permit eligible employees to make an election change to elect the indemnity plan or the new HMO option. However, the plan may not permit employees to change their health FSA elections to reflect differences in co-payments under the HMO option.

Example 2. (i) Employer *N* sponsors an accident or health plan under which employees may elect either employee-only coverage or family health coverage. The 12-month period of coverage under *N*'s cafeteria plan begins January 1, 2001. *N*'s employee, *A*, is married to *B*. Employee *A* elects employee-only coverage under *N*'s plan. *B*'s employer, *O*, offers health coverage to *O*'s employees under its accident or health plan under which employees may elect either employee-only coverage or family coverage. *O*'s plan has a 12-month period of coverage beginning September 1, 2001. *B* maintains individual coverage under *O*'s plan at the time *A* elects coverage under *N*'s plan, and wants to elect no coverage for the plan year beginning on September 1, 2001, which is the next period of coverage under *O*'s accident or health plan. *A* certifies to *N* that *B* will elect no coverage under *O*'s accident or health plan for the plan year beginning on September 1, 2001 and *N* has no reason to believe that *A*'s certification is incorrect.

(ii) Under paragraph (f)(4)(ii) of this section, *N*'s cafeteria plan may permit *A* to change *A*'s election prospectively to family coverage under that plan effective September 1, 2001.

Example 3. (i) Employer *P* sponsors a calendar year cafeteria plan under which employees may elect either employee-only or family health coverage. Before the beginning of the year, *P*'s employee, *C*, elects family coverage under *P*'s cafeteria plan. *C* also elects coverage under the health FSA for up to $200 of reimbursements for the year to be funded by salary reduction contributions of $200 during the year. *C* is married to *D*, who is employed by Employer *Q*. *Q* does not maintain a cafeteria plan, but does maintain an accident or health plan providing its employees with employee-only coverage. During the calendar year, *Q* adds family coverage as an option under its health plan. *D* elects family coverage under *Q*'s plan, and *C* wants to revoke *C*'s election for health coverage and elect no health coverage under *P*'s cafeteria plan for the remainder of the year.

(ii) *Q*'s addition of family coverage as an option under its health plan constitutes a new coverage option described in paragraph (f)(3)(ii) of this section. Accordingly, pursuant to paragraph (f)(4)(i) of this section, *P*'s cafeteria plan may permit *C* to revoke *C*'s health coverage election if *D* actually elects family health coverage under *Q*'s accident or health plan. Employer *P*'s

Reg. § 1.125-4(f)(5)

→ *Caution: Reg. § 1.125-4(f), below, as amended by T.D. 8921, is generally applicable for cafeteria plans beginning on or after January 1, 2002.←*

plan may not permit C to change C's health FSA election.

Example 4. (i) Employer R maintains a cafeteria plan under which employees may elect accident or health coverage under either an indemnity plan or an HMO. Before the beginning of the year, R's employee, E elects coverage under the HMO at a premium cost of $100 per month. During the year, E decides to switch to the indemnity plan, which charges a premium of $140 per month.

(ii) E's change from the HMO to indemnity plan is not a change in cost or coverage under this paragraph (f), and none of the other election change rules under paragraphs (b) through (e) of this section apply.

(iii) Although R's health plan may permit E to make the change from the HMO to the indemnity plan, R's cafeteria plan may not permit E to make an election change to reflect the increased premium. Accordingly, if E switches from the HMO to the indemnity plan, E may pay the $40 per month additional cost on an after-tax basis.

Example 5. (i) Employee A is married to Employee B and they have one child, C. Employee A's employer, M, maintains a calendar year cafeteria plan that allows employees to elect coverage under a dependent care FSA. Child C attends X's on site child care center at an annual cost of $3,000. Prior to the beginning of the year, A elects salary reduction contributions of $3,000 during the year to fund coverage under the dependent care FSA for up to $3,000 of reimbursements for the year. Employee A now wants to revoke A's election of coverage under the dependent care FSA, because A has found a new child care provider.

(ii) The availability of dependent care services from the new child care provider (whether the new provider is a household employee or family member of A or B or a person who is independent of A and B) is a significant change in coverage similar to a benefit package option becoming available. Because the FSA is a dependent care FSA rather than a health FSA, the coverage rules of this section apply and M's cafeteria plan may permit A to elect to revoke A's previous election of coverage under the dependent care FSA, and make a corresponding new election to reflect the cost of the new child care provider.

Example 6. (i) Employee D is married to Employee E and they have one child, F. Employee D's employer, N, maintains a calendar year cafeteria plan that allows employees to elect coverage under a dependent care FSA. Child F is cared for by Y, D's household employee, who provides child care services five days a week from 9 a.m. to 6 p.m. at an annual cost in excess of $5,000. Prior to the beginning of the year, D elects salary reduction contributions of $5,000 during the year to fund coverage under the dependent care FSA for up to $5,000 of reimbursements for the year. During the year, F begins school and, as a result, Y's regular hours of work are changed to five days a week from 3 p.m. to 6 p.m. Employee D now wants to revoke D's election under the dependent care FSA, and make a new election under the dependent care FSA to an annual cost of $4,000 to reflect a reduced cost of child care due to Y's reduced hours.

(ii) The change in the number of hours of work performed by Y is a change in coverage. Thus, N's cafeteria plan may permit D to reduce D's previous election under the dependent care FSA to $4,000.

Example 7. (i) Employee G is married to Employee H and they have one child, J. Employee G's employer, O, maintains a calendar year cafeteria plan that allows employees to elect coverage under a dependent care FSA. Child J is cared for by Z, G's household employee, who is not a relative of G and who provides child care services at an annual cost of $4,000. Prior to the beginning of the year, G elects salary reduction contributions of $4,000 during the year to fund coverage under the dependent care FSA for up to $4,000 of reimbursements for the year. During the year, G raises Z's salary. Employee G now wants to revoke G's election under the dependent care FSA, and make a new election under the dependent care FSA to an annual amount of $4,500 to reflect the raise.

(ii) The raise in Z's salary is a significant increase in cost under paragraph (f)(2)(ii) of this section, and an increase in election to reflect the raise corresponds with that change in status. Thus, O's cafeteria plan may permit G to elect to increase G's election under the dependent care FSA.

Example 8. (i) Employer P maintains a calendar year cafeteria plan that allows employees to elect employee-only, employee plus one dependent, or family coverage under an indemnity plan. During the middle of the year, Employer P gives its employees the option to select employee-only or family coverage from an HMO plan. P's employee, J, who had elected employee plus one dependent coverage under the indemnity plan, decides to switch to family coverage under the HMO plan.

Reg. § 1.125-4(f)(6)

→ *Caution: Reg. § 1.125-4(f), below, as amended by T.D. 8921, is generally applicable for cafeteria plans beginning on or after January 1, 2002.*←

(ii) Employer *P*'s midyear addition of the HMO option is an addition of a benefit package option. Under paragraph (f) of this section, Employee *J* may change his or her salary reduction contributions to reflect the change from indemnity to HMO coverage, and also to reflect the change from employee plus one dependent to family coverage (however, an election of employee-only coverage under the new option would not correspond with the addition of a new option). Employer *P* may not permit *J* to change *J*'s health FSA election.

(g) *Special requirements relating to the Family and Medical Leave Act.* An employee taking leave under the Family and Medical Leave Act (FMLA) (Public Law 103-3 (107 Stat. 6)) may revoke an existing election of accident or health plan coverage and make such other election for the remaining portion of the period of coverage as may be provided for under the FMLA. See § 1.125-3 for additional rules.

(h) *Elective contributions under a qualified cash or deferred arrangement.* The provisions of this section do not apply with respect to elective contributions under a qualified cash or deferred arrangement (within the meaning of section 401(k)) or employee contributions subject to section 401(m). Thus, a cafeteria plan may permit an employee to modify or revoke elections in accordance with section 401(k) and (m) and the regulations thereunder.

(i) *Definitions.* Unless otherwise provided, the definitions in paragraphs (i)(1) though (8) of this section apply for purposes of this section.

(1) *Accident or health coverage.* Accident or health coverage means coverage under an accident or health plan as defined in regulations under section 105.

(2) *Benefit package option.* A benefit package option means a qualified benefit under section 125(f) that is offered under a cafeteria plan, or an option for coverage under an underlying accident or health plan (such as an indemnity option, an HMO option, or a PPO option under an accident or health plan).

(3) *Dependent.* A dependent means a dependent as defined in section 152, except that, for purposes of accident or health coverage, any child to whom section 152(e) applies is treated as a dependent of both parents, and, for purposes of dependent care assistance provided through a cafeteria plan, a dependent means a qualifying individual (as defined in section 21(b)(1)) with respect to the employee.

(4) *Disability coverage.* Disability coverage means coverage under an accident or health plan that provides benefits due to personal injury or sickness, but does not reimburse expenses incurred for medical care (as defined in section 213(d)) of the employee or the employee's spouse and dependents. For purposes of this section, disability coverage includes payments described in section 105(c).

(5) *Family member plan.* A family member plan means a cafeteria plan or qualified benefit plan sponsored by the employer of the employee's spouse or the employee's dependent.

(6) *FSA, health FSA.* An FSA means a qualified benefits plan that is a flexible spending arrangement as defined in section 106(c)(2) . A health FSA means a health or accident plan that is an FSA.

(7) *Placement for adoption.* Placement for adoption means placement for adoption as defined in regulations under section 9801.

(8) *Qualified benefits plan.* A qualified benefits plan means an employee benefit plan governing the provision of one or more benefits that are qualified benefits under section 125(f). A plan does not fail to be a qualified benefits plan merely because it includes an FSA, assuming that the FSA meets the requirements of section 125 and the regulations thereunder.

→ *Caution: Reg. § 1.125-4(i)(9), below, as added by T.D. 8921, is generally applicable for cafeteria plans beginning on or after January 1, 2002.*←

(9) *Similar coverage.* Coverage for the same category of benefits for the same individuals (e.g., family to family or single to single). For example, two plans that provide coverage for major medical are considered to be similar coverage. For purposes of this definition, a health FSA is not similar coverage with respect to an accident or health plan that is not a health FSA. A plan may treat coverage by another employer, such as a spouse's or dependent's employer, as similar coverage.

(j) *Effective date*—(1) *General rule.* Except as provided in paragraph (j)(2) of this section, this section is applicable for cafeteria plan years beginning on or after January 1, 2001.

(2) *Delayed effective date for certain provisions.* The following provisions are applicable for cafeteria plan years beginning on or after January

1, 2002: paragraph (c) of this section to the extent applicable to qualified benefits other than an accident or health plan or a group-term life insurance plan; paragraph (d)(1)(ii)(B) of this section (relating to a spouse, former spouse, or other individual obtaining accident or health coverage for an employee's child in response to a judgment, decree, or order); paragraph (f) of this section (rules for election changes as a result of cost or coverage changes); and paragraph (i)(9) of this section (defining similar coverage). [Reg. § 1.125-4.]

☐ [*T.D.* 8878, 3-22-2000. *Amended by T.D.* 8921, 1-9-2001 (*corrected* 3-1-2001) *and T.D.* 8966, 10-16-2001.]

[Reg. § 16A.126-0]

§ 16A.126-0. Effective dates (Temporary).— These temporary regulations shall apply to any payments received under the contract signed by the taxpayer and the appropriate agency after September 30, 1979. [Temporary Reg. § 16A.126-0.]

☐ [*T.D.* 7778, 5-18-81.]

[Reg. § 16A.126-1]

§ 16A.126-1. Certain cost sharing payments—In general (Temporary).—(a) *Introduction.* In general, section 126 provides that recipients of payments made after September 30, 1979 under certain conservation, reclamation and restoration programs may exclude all or a portion of those payments from income if the payments do not substantially increase the annual income derived by the taxpayer from the affected property. For purposes of this section, the term "payment" as used in section 126 means payment of the economic benefit, if any, conferred upon the taxpayer upon receipt of the improvement. An increase in annual income is substantial if it exceeds the greater of 10 percent of the average annual income derived from the affected property prior to receipt of the improvement or an amount equal to $2.50 times the number of affected acres. The amount of gross income which a taxpayer realizes upon the receipt of a section 126 payment is the value of the section 126 improvement, reduced by the sum of the excludable portion and the taxpayer's share of the cost of the improvement (if any).

(b) *Definitions.* For purposes of this section, the term:

(1) "Cost of the improvement" means the sum of amounts paid by a government and the taxpayer, whether or not with borrowed funds, for the improvement.

(2) "Section 126 cost" means the cost of the improvement less the sum of

(i) Any government payments under a program which is not listed in section 126(a),

(ii) Any portion of a government payment under a program which is listed in section 126(a) which the Secretary of Agriculture has not certified is primarily for purposes of conservation.

(iii) Any government payment to the taxpayer which is in the nature of rent or compensation for services.

(3) "Value of the section 126 improvement" means the fair market value of the improvement multiplied by a fraction, the numerator of which is the section 126 cost and the denominator of which is the cost of the improvement.

(4) "Affected acreage" means the acres affected by the improvement.

(5) "Excludable portion" means the present fair market value of the right to receive annual income from the affected acreage of the greater of 10 percent of the prior average annual income from the affected acreage or $2.50 times the number of affected acres.

(6) "Prior average annual income" means the average of the gross receipts from the affected acreage for the last three taxable years preceding the taxable year in which installation of the improvement is commenced.

(7) "Section 126 improvement" means the portion of the improvement equal to the percentage which government payments made to the taxpayer, which the Secretary of Agriculture has certified were made primarily for the purpose of conservation, bear to the cost of the improvement.

(c) *Income realized upon receipt of a section 126 improvement*—(1) *Section 126 exclusion applied.* Unless a taxpayer elects not to have section 126 apply, the amount of gross income realized on receipt of the section 126 improvement is the value of the section 126 improvement less the sum of the taxpayer's share of the cost of the improvement and the excludable portion.

(2) *Section 126 exclusion not applied.* If a taxpayer elects under section 126(c) not to have section 126 apply in whole or in part, the amount realized on the receipt of the section 126 improvement is the value of the section 126 improvement less the sum of the taxpayer's share of the cost of the improvement and the excludable portion that applies, if any.

(d) *Payments under watershed programs*—(1) *Programs within section 126(a)(9).* Section 126(a)(9) covers certain programs affecting small watersheds. These programs must be administered by the Secretary of Agriculture and be determined by the Commissioner to be substantially similar to the type of program described in section

126(a)(1) through (8). The Commissioner has determined that section 126 improvements made in connection with small watersheds are within the scope of section 126(a)(9) if they are made under one of the following programs:

(A) The Watershed Protection and Flood Prevention Act, Pub. L. 566, 68 Stat. 666, as amended (16 U.S.C. 1001, et. seq.), as funded by the Act of November 9, 1979, Pub. L. 96-108, 93 Stat. 834.

(B) Flood Prevention Projects, Pub. L. 86-468, sec. 1, 74 Stat. 131, as amended (16 U.S.C. 1006a); Publ. L. 78-534, sec. 2, 58 Stat. 889 (33 U.S.C. 701a-1); Pub. L. 78-534, sec. 13, 58 Stat. 905;

(C) Emergency Watershed Protection, Pub. L. 81-516, sec. 216, 64 Stat. 184 (33 U.S.C. 701b-1), and

(D) Colorado River Basin Salinity Control Act, Pub. L. 93-320, 88 Stat. 266:

(1) Title 1—Programs downstream from Imperial Dam, and

(2) Title 2—Measures upstream from Imperial Dam.

(2) *Other programs.* The Commissioner may announce further determinations under section 126(a)(9) from time to time in the Internal Revenue Bulletin.

(3) *Small watershed defined.* A watershed is a "small watershed" under this paragraph and section 126(a)(9) if the watershed or subwatershed does not exceed 250,000 acres and does not include any single structure providing more than 12,500 acre-feet of floodwater detention capacity, nor more than 25,000 acre-feet of total capacity.

(e) *Basis of property not increased by reason of excludable amounts.* Notwithstanding any provision of section 1016 (relating to adjustments to basis) to the contrary, basis of any property does not include any amount which is excludable from gross income under section 126.

(f) *Cross reference.* For rules relating to the recapture as ordinary income of the gain from the disposition (within 20 years of the date of receipt) of property for which an exclusion is claimed for a section 126 improvement, see section 1255 and the regulations thereunder.

(g) *Examples.* The provisions of this section are illustrated by the following examples:

Example (1). In 1981, 100 acres of the taxpayer's land is reclaimed under a Rural Abandoned Mine Program contract with the Soil Conservation Service of the U.S. Department of Agriculture. The total cost of the improvement is $700,000. USDA pays $690,000, the taxpayer

$10,000. The Secretary of Agriculture certifies that 95% of the $690,000 USDA payment was primarily for the purpose of conservation. Therefore, $34,500 ($690,000 × .05) is a nonsection 126 payment, $150,000 of USDA's payment is compensation for the taxpayer's service in the reclamation project and is includible in gross income as compensation for services. The taxpayer has $20,000 of allowable deductions in 1981, $15,500 of which are properly attributable to the USDA payment. Based on all the facts and circumstances, the value of the improvement is $21,000. The taxpayer elects not to have section 126 apply. The taxpayer computes the amount which is included in gross income as a result of receipt of the improvement as follows:

(1)

Cost of improvement	$700,000
Nonsection 126 payment	(34,500)
Compensation for services	(150,000)
Current deductions	(15,500)
Section 126 cost	500,000

(2)

Value of improvement	21,000
Multiplied by section 126 cost	× 500,000
Cost of improvement	700,000
Value of section 126 improvement	15,000

(3)

Value of section 126 improvement	15,000
Taxpayer's contribution	10,000
Amount included in gross income	5,000

Example (2). The facts are the same as example (1) except that section 126 applies. Based on all the facts and circumstances, the present fair market value of the right to receive annual income from the property of 10 percent of the prior average annual income of the affected acreage prior to the receipt of the improvement is $1,380 and the present fair market value of the right to receive $250 ($2.50 × 100 acres) is $1,550. The excludable portion is, therefore, $1,550. The taxpayer computes the amount included in gross income as follows:

value of section 126 improvement	$ 15,000
(taxpayer's contribution)	(10,000)
(excludable portion)	(1,550)
amount included in income	$ 3,450

Example (3). The facts are the same as example (2) except that the present value of 10 percent of the prior average annual income is $5,600. The taxpayer realizes no income as a result of receipt of the section 126 project.

Reg. § 16A.126-1(d)(2)

value of section 126
improvement .... $ 15,000
(taxpayer's contribution) .... (10,000)
(excludable portion) .... (5,600)

amount included in income .... —0—

Example (4). In 1983, the taxpayer signs a contract under the water bank program under which he will maintain 20 acres of undistributed wetlands as a wildfowl preserve. In return he will receive $90 an acre as rent from the government. Although the payment is made under a program listed in section 126(a) and the Secretary of Agriculture has certified that the entire amount of payment was made primarily for the purpose of conservation, there is no income eligible for section 126 exclusion because the full payment is rent. The rent is included in full in gross income.

Example (5). In 1980, the taxpayer reforests 200 acres of nonindustrial private forest land by planting tree seedlings. The taxpayer pays the full cost of the reforestation, $15,000. Under the cost-sharing provisions of the forestry incentives program, the taxpayer receives a reimbursement from USDA of $12,000. The Secretary of Agriculture certifies that 100% of the USDA payment is primarily for the purpose of conservation. Assume that the excludable portion is $3,500 and that based on all the facts and circumstances, the value of the improvement is $15,000. The amount which is includible in income is the value of the section 126 improvement, reduced by the excludable portion and the taxpayer's share of the cost of the improvement. Therefore the taxpayer includes $8,500 in gross income as a result of the USDA payment, computed as follows:

value of section 126
improvement $15,000
(excludable portion) .... ($3,500)
(taxpayer's contribution) .... ($5,000)

amount included in gross income .... $ 8,500

[Temporary Reg. § 16A.126-1.]

☐ [*T.D.* 7778, 5-18-81.]

[Reg. § 16A.126-2]

§ 16A.126-2. Section 126 elections (temporary).—(a) *Election for section 126 not to apply in whole or in part.* A taxpayer may elect under section 126(c) not to have section 126 apply to all or any part of an improvement described in section 126.

(b) *Application of the section 126 exclusion.* To the extent the section 126 exclusion applies, the taxpayer should so indicate on an attachment to the tax return (or amended return) for the taxable year in which the taxpayer received the last payment made by a government for the improvement. The attachment should state the dollar amount of the section 126 cost funded by a government payment, the value of the section 126 improvement, and the amount that the taxpayer is excluding under section 126. [Temporary Reg. § 16A.126-2.]

☐ [*T.D.* 7778, 5-18-81.]

[Reg. § 1.127-1]

§ 1.127-1. Amounts received under a qualified educational assistance program.—(a) *Exclusion from gross income.* The gross income of an employee does not include—

(1) Amounts paid to, or on behalf of the employee under a qualified educational assistance program described in § 1.127-2, or

(2) The value of education provided to the employee under such a program.

(b) *Disallowance of excluded amounts as credit or deduction.* Any amount excluded from the gross income of an employee under paragraph (a) of this section shall not be allowed as a credit or deduction to such employee under any other provision of this part.

(c) *Amounts received under a nonqualified program.* Any amount received under an educational assistance program that is not a "qualified program" described in § 1.127-2 will not be excluded from gross income under paragraph (a) of this section. All or part of the amounts received under such a non-qualified program may, however, be excluded under section 117 or deducted under section 162 or section 212 (as the case may be), if the requirements of such section are satisfied.

(d) *Definitions.* For rules relating to the meaning of the terms "employee" and "employer", see paragraph (h) of § 1.127-2.

(e) *Effective date.* This section is effective for taxable years of the employee beginning after December 31, 1978, and before January 1, 1984. [Reg. § 1.127-1.]

☐ [*T.D.* 7898, 7-5-83.]

[Reg. § 1.127-2]

§ 1.127-2. Qualified educational assistance program.—(a) *In general.* A qualified educational assistance program is a plan established and maintained by an employer under which the employer provides educational assistance to employees. To be a qualified program, the requirements described in paragraphs (b) through (g) of this section must be satisfied. It is not required that a program be funded or that the employer apply to the Internal Revenue Service for a determination that the plan is a qualified program. However, under § 601.201 (relating to rulings and determination letters), an employer may request

Reg. § 1.127-2(a)

that the Service determine whether a plan is a qualified program.

(b) *Separate written plan.* The program must be a separate written plan of the employer. This requirement means that the terms of the program must be set forth in a separate document or documents providing only educational assistance within the meaning of paragraph (c) of this section. The requirement for a separate plan does not, however, preclude an educational assistance program from being part of a more comprehensive employer plan that provides a choice of nontaxable benefits to employees.

(c) *Educational assistance*—(1) *In general.* The benefits provided under the program must consist solely of educational assistance. The term "educational assistance" means—

(i) The employer's payment of expenses incurred by or on behalf of an employee for education, or

(ii) The employer's provision of education to an employee.

(2) *Alternative benefits.* Benefits will not be considered to consist solely of educational assistance if the program, in form or in actual operation, provides employees with a choice between educational assistance and other remuneration includible in the employee's gross income.

(3) *Certain benefits not considered educational assistance.* The term "educational assistance" does not include the employer's payment for, or provision of—

(i) Tools or supplies (other than textbooks) that the employee may retain after completing a course of instruction,

(ii) Meals, lodging, or transportation, or

(iii) Education involving sports, games, or hobbies, unless such education involves the business of the employer or is required as part of a degree program. The phrase "sports, games, or hobbies" does not include education that instructs employees how to maintain and improve health so long as such education does not involve the use of athletic facilities or equipment and is not recreational in nature.

(4) *Education defined.* As used in section 127, § 1.127-1, and this section, the term "education" includes any form of instruction or training that improves or develops the capabilities of an individual. Education paid for or provided under a qualified program may be furnished directly by the employer, either alone or in conjunction wuth other employers, or through a third party such as an educational institution. Education is not limited to courses that are job related or part of a degree program.

(d) *Exclusive benefit.* The program may benefit only the employees of the employer, including, at the employer's option, individuals who are employees within the meaning of paragraph (h)(1) of this section. A program that provides benefits to spouses or dependents of employees is not a qualified program within the meaning of this section.

(e) *Prohibited discrimination*—(1) *Eligibility for benefits.* The program must benefit the employer's employees generally. Among those benefited may be employees who are officers, shareholders, self-employed or highly compensated. A program is not for the benefit of employees generally, however, if the program discriminates in favor of employees described in the preceding sentence (or in favor of their spouses and dependents who are themselves employees) in requirements relating to eligibility for benefits. Thus, although a program need not provide benefits for all employees, it must benefit those employees who qualify under a classification of employees that does not discriminate in favor of the employees with respect to whom discrimination is prohibited. The classification of employees to be considered benefited will consist of that group of employees who are actually eligible for educational assistance under the program, taking into account the eligibility requirements set forth in the written plan, the eligibility requirements reflected in the types of educational assistance available under the program, and any other conditions that may affect the availability of benefits under the program. Thus, for example, if an employer's plan provides that all employees are eligible for educational assistance, yet limits that assistance to courses of study leading to postgraduate degrees in fields relating to the employer's business, then only those employees able to pursue such a course of study are considered actually eligible for educational assistance under the program. Whether any classification of employees discriminates in favor of employees with respect to whom discrimination is prohibited will generally be determined by applying the same standards as are applied under section 410(b)(1)(B) (relating to qualified pension, profit-sharing and stock bonus plans), without regard to section 401(a)(5). For purposes of making this determination, there shall be excluded from consideration employees not covered by the program who are included in a unit of employees covered by an agreement which the Secretary of Labor finds to be a collective bargaining agreement between employee representatives and one or more employers, if the Internal Revenue Service finds that educational assistance benefits were the subject of good faith bargaining between the employee representatives and the employer or

Reg. § 1.127-2(b)

employers. For purposes of determining whether such bargaining occurred, it is not material that the employees are not covered by another educational assistance program or that the employer's present program was not considered in the bargaining.

(2) *Factors not considered in determining the existence of prohibited discrimination.* A program shall not be considered discriminatory under this paragraph (e) merely because—

(i) Different types of educational assistance available under the program are utilized to a greater degree by employees with respect to whom discrimination is prohibited than by other employees, or

(ii) With respect to a course of study for which benefits are otherwise available, successful completion of the course, attaining a particular course grade, or satisfying a reasonable condition subsequent (such as remaining employed for one year after completing the course) are required or considered in determining the availability of benefits.

(f) *Benefit limitation*—(1) *In general.* Under section 127(b)(3), a program is a qualified program for a program year only if no more than 5% of the amounts paid or incurred by the employer for educational assistance benefits during the year are provided to the limitation class described in subparagraph (2). For purposes of this paragraph (f), the program year must be specified in the written plan as either the calendar year or the taxable year of the employer.

(2) *Limitation class.* The limitation class consists of—

(i) *Shareholders.* Individuals who, on any day of the program year, own more than 5% of the total number of shares of outstanding stock of the employer, or

(ii) *Owners.* In the case of an employer's trade or business which is not incorporated, individuals who, on any day of the program year, own more than 5% of the capital or profits interest in the employer, and

(iii) *Spouses or dependents.* Individuals who are spouses or dependents of shareholders or owners described in subdivision (i) or (ii). For purposes of determining stock ownership, the attribution rules described in paragraph (h)(4) of this section apply. The regulations prescribed under section 414(c) are applicable in determining an individual's interest in the capital or profits of an unincorporated trade or business.

(g) *Notification of employees.* A program is not a qualified program unless employees eligible to participate in the program are given reasonable notice of the terms and availability of the program.

(h) *Definitions.* For purposes of this section and § 1.127-1—

(1) *Employee.* The term "employee" includes—

(i) A retired, disabled or laid-off employee,

(ii) A present employee who is on leave, as, for example, in the Armed Forces of the United States, or

(iii) An individual who is self-employed within the meaning of section 401(c)(1).

(2) *Employer.* An individual who owns the entire interest in an unincorporated trade or business shall be treated as his or her own employer. A partnership is treated as the employer of each partner who is an employee within the meaning of section 401(c)(1).

(3) *Officer.* An officer is an individual who is an officer within the meaning of regulations prescribed under section 414(c).

(4) *Shareholder.* The term "shareholder" includes an individual who is a shareholder as determined by the attribution rules under section 1563(d) and (e), without regard to section 1563(e)(3)(C).

(5) *Highly compensated.* The term "highly compensated" has the same meaning as it does for purposes of section 410(b)(1)(B).

(i) *Substantiation.* An employee receiving payments under a qualified educational assistance program must be prepared to provide substantiation to the employer such that it is reasonable to believe that payments or reimbursements made under the program constitute educational assistance within the meaning of paragraph (c) of this section. [Reg. § 1.127-2.]

☐ [T.D. 7898, 7-5-83.]

[Reg. § 1.132-0]

§ 1.132-0. **Outline of regulations under section 132.**—The following is an outline of regulations in this section relating to exclusions from gross income for certain fringe benefits:

§ 1.132-0. *Outline of regulations under section 132.*

§ 1.132-1. *Exclusion from gross income for certain fringe benefits.*

§ 1.132-1(a) In general.

§ 1.132-1(b) Definition of employee.

(1) No-additional-cost services and qualified employee discounts.

(2) Working condition fringes.

(3) On-premises athletic facilities.

Reg. § 1.132-0

§ 1.132-5(f) Safe harbor substantiation rule for vehicles not available to employees for personal use other than commuting.

§ 1.132-5(g) Safe harbor substantiation rule for vehicles used in connection with the business of farming that are available to employees for personal use.

   (1) In general.

   (2) Vehicles available to more than one individual.

   (3) Examples.

§ 1.132-5(h) Qualified nonpersonal use vehicles.

   (1) In general.

   (2) Shared usage of qualified nonpersonal use vehicles.

§ 1.132-5(i) [Reserved].

§ 1.132-5(j) Application of section 280F.

§ 1.132-5(k) Aircraft allocation rule.

§ 1.132-5(l) [Reserved].

§ 1.132-5(m) Employer-provided transportation for security concerns.

   (1) In general.

   (2) Demonstration of bona fide business-oriented security concerns.

   (3) Application of security rules to spouses and dependents.

   (4) Working condition safe harbor for travel on employer-provided aircraft.

   (5) Bodyguard/chauffeur provided for a bona fide business-oriented security concern.

   (6) Special valuation rule for government employees.

   (7) Government employer and employee defined.

   (8) Examples.

§ 1.132-5(n) Product testing.

   (1) In general.

   (2) Employer-imposed limits.

   (3) Discriminating classifications.

   (4) Factors that negate the existence of a product testing program.

   (5) Failure to meet the requirements of this paragraph (n).

   (6) Example.

§ 1.132-5(o) Qualified automobile demonstration use.

   (1) In general.

   (2) Full-time automobile salesman.

   (3) Demonstration automobile.

   (4) Substantial restrictions on personal use.

   (5) Sales area.

   (5) Applicability of substantiation requirements of sections 162 and 274(d).

   (7) Special valuation rules.

§ 1.132-5(p) Parking.

   (1) In general.

   (2) Reimbursement of parking expenses.

   (3) Parking on residential property.

   (4) Dates of applicability.

§ 1.132-5(q) Nonapplicability of nondiscrimination rules.

§ 1.132-5(r) Volunteers.

   (1) In general.

   (2) Limit on application of this paragraph.

   (3) Definitions.

   (4) Example.

§ 1.132-6. De minimis fringes.

§ 1.132-6(a) In general.

§ 1.132-6(b) Frequency.

   (1) Employee-measured frequency.

   (2) Employer-measured frequency.

§ 1.132-6(c) Administrability.

§ 1.132-6(d) Special rules.

   (1) Transit passes.

   (2) Occasional meal money or local transportation fare.

   (3) Use of special rules or examples to establish a general rule.

   (4) Benefits exceeding value and frequency limits.

§ 1.132-6(e) Examples.

   (1) Benefits excludable from income.

   (2) Benefits not excludable as de minimis fringes.

§ 1.132-6(f) Nonapplicability of nondiscrimination rules.

§ 1.132-7. Employer-operated eating facilities.

§ 132-7(a) In general.

   (1) Conditions for exclusion.

   (2) Employer-operated eating facility for employees.

   (3) Operation by the employer.

   (4) Example.

§ 1.132-7(b) Direct operating costs.

   (1) In general.

   (2) Multiple dining rooms or cafeterias.

   (3) Payment to operator of facility.

§ 1.132-7(c) Valuation of non-excluded meals provided at an employer-operated eating facility for employees.

§ 1.132-8. Fringe benefit nondiscrimination rules.

Reg. § 1.132-0

§ 1.132-8(a) Application of nondiscrimination rules.

(1) General rule.

(2) Consequences of discrimination.

(3) Scope of the nondiscrimination rules provided in this section.

§ 1.132-8(b) Aggregation of employees.

(1) Section 132(a)(1) and (2).

(2) Section 132(e)(2).

(3) Classes of employees who may be excluded.

§ 1.132-8(c) Availability on substantially the same terms.

(1) General rule.

(2) Certain terms relating to priority.

§ 1.132-8(d) Testing for discrimination.

(1) Classification test.

(2) Classifications that are per se discriminatory.

(3) Former employees.

(4) Restructuring of benefits.

(5) Employer-operated eating facilities for employees.

§ 1.132-8(e) Cash bonuses or rebates.

§ 1.132-8(f) Highly compensated employee.

(1) Government and non-government employees.

(2) Former employees.

§ 1.132-9. Qualified transportation fringes.

§ 1.132-9(a) Table of contents.

§ 1.132-9(b) Questions and answers.

[Reg § 1.132-0.]

☐ [*T.D. 8256, 7-5-89. Amended by T.D. 8457, 12-29-92 and T.D. 8933, 1-10-2001.*]

[Reg. § 1.132-1]

§ 1.132-1. Exclusion from gross income for certain fringe benefits.—(a) *In general.* Gross income does not include any fringe benefit which qualifies as a—

(1) No-additional-cost service,

(2) Qualified employee discount,

(3) Working condition fringe, or

(4) De minimis fringe.

Special rules apply with respect to certain on-premises gyms and other athletic facilities (§ 1.132-1(e)), demonstration use of employer-provided automobiles by full-time automobile salesmen (§ 1.132-5(o)), parking provided to an employee on or near the business premises of the employer (§ 1.132-5(p)), and on-premises eating facilities (§ 1.132-7).

(b) *Definition of employee*—(1) *No-additional-cost services and qualified employee discounts.* For purposes of section 132(a)(1) (relating to no-additional-cost services) and section 132(a)(2) (relating to qualified employee discounts), the term "employee" (with respect to a line of business of an employer) means—

(i) Any individual who is currently employed by the employer in the line of business,

(ii) Any individual who was formerly employed by the employer in the line of business and who separated from service with the employer in the line of business by reason of retirement or disability, and

(iii) Any widow or widower of an individual who died while employed by the employer in the line of business or who separated from service with the employer in the line of business by reason of retirement or disability.

For purposes of this paragraph (b)(1), any partner who performs services for a partnership is considered employed by the partnership. In addition, any use by the spouse or dependent child (as defined in paragraph (b)(5) of this section) of the employee will be treated as use by the employee. For purposes of section 132(a)(1) (relating to no-additional-cost services), any use of air transportation by a parent of an employee (determined without regard to section 132(f)(1)(B) and paragraph (b)(1)(iii) of this section) will be treated as use by the employee.

(2) *Working condition fringes.* For purposes of section 132(a)(3) (relating to working condition fringes), the term "employee" means—

(i) Any individual who is currently employed by the employer,

(ii) Any partner who performs services for the partnership,

(iii) Any director of the employer, and

(iv) Any independent contractor who performs services for the employer.

Notwithstanding anything in this paragraph (b)(2) to the contrary, an independent contractor who performs services for the employer cannot exclude the value of parking or the use of consumer goods provided pursuant to a product testing program under § 1.132-5(n); in addition, any director of the employer cannot exclude the value of the use of consumer goods provided pursuant to a product testing program under § 1.132-5(n).

(3) *On-premises athletic facilities.* For purposes of section 132(h)(5) (relating to on-premises athletic facilities), the term "employee" means—

(i) Any individual who is currently employed by the employer,

(ii) Any individual who was formerly employed by the employer and who separated from service with the employer by reason of retirement or disability, and

(iii) Any widow or widower of an individual who died while employed by the employer or who separated from service with the employer by reason of retirement or disability.

For purposes of this paragraph (b)(3), any partner who performs services for a partnership is considered employed by the partnership. In addition, any use by the spouse or dependent child (as defined in paragraph (b)(5) of this section) of the employee will be treated as use by the employee.

(4) *De minimis fringes.* For purposes of section 132(a)(4) (relating to de minimis fringes), the term "employee" means any recipient of a fringe benefit.

(5) *Dependent child.* The term "dependent child" means any son, stepson, daughter, or stepdaughter of the employee who is a dependent of the employee, or both of whose parents are deceased and who has not attained age 25. Any child to whom section 152(e) applies will be treated as the dependent of both parents.

(c) *Special rules for employers—Effect of section 414.* All employees treated as employed by a single employer under section 414(b), (c), (m), or (o) will be treated as employed by a single employer for purposes of this section. Thus, employees of one corporation that is part of a controlled group of corporations may under certain circumstances be eligible to receive section 132 benefits from the other corporations that comprise the controlled group. However, the aggregation of employers described in this paragraph (c) does not change the other requirements for an exclusion, such as the line of business requirement. Thus, for example, if a controlled group of corporations consists of two corporations that operate in different lines of business, the corporations are not treated as operating in the same line of business even though the corporations are treated as one employer.

(d) *Customers not to include employees.* For purposes of section 132 and the regulations thereunder, the term "customer" means any customer who is not an employee. However, the preceding sentence does not apply to section 132(c)(2) (relating to the gross profit percentage for determining a qualified employee discount). Thus, an employer that provides employee discounts cannot exclude sales made to employees in determining the aggregate sales to customers.

(e) *Treatment of on-premises athletic facilities—(1) In general.* Gross income does not include the value of any on-premises athletic facility provided by an employer to its employees. For purposes of section 132(h)(5) and this paragraph (e), the term "on-premises athletic facility" means any gym or other athletic facility (such as a pool, tennis court, or golf course)—

(i) Which is located on the premises of the employer,

(ii) Which is operated by the employer, and

(iii) Substantially all of the use of which during the calendar year is by employees of the employer, their spouses, and their dependent children.

For purposes of paragraph (e)(1)(iii) of this section, the term "dependent children" has the same meaning as the plural of the term "dependent child" in paragraph (b)(5) of this section. The exclusion of this paragraph (e) does not apply to any athletic facility if access to the facility is made available to the general public through the sale of memberships, the rental of the facility, or a similar arrangement.

(2) *Premises of the employer.* The athletic facility need not be located on the employer's business premises. However, the athletic facility must be located on premises of the employer. The exclusion provided in this paragraph (e) applies whether the premises are owned or leased by the employer; in addition, the exclusion is available even if the employer is not a named lessee on the lease so long as the employer pays reasonable rent. The exclusion provided in this paragraph (e) does not apply to any athletic facility that is a facility for residential use. Thus, for example, a resort with accompanying athletic facilities (such as tennis courts, pool, and gym) would not qualify for the exclusion provided in this paragraph (e). An athletic facility is considered to be located on the employer's premises if the facility is located on the premises of a voluntary employees' beneficiary association funded by the employer.

(3) *Application of rules to membership in an athletic facility.* The exclusion provided in this paragraph (e) does not apply to any membership in an athletic facility (including health clubs or country clubs) unless the facility is owned (or leased) and operated by the employer and substantially all the use of the facility is by employees of the employer, their spouses, and their dependent children. Therefore, membership in a health club or country club not meeting the rules provided in this paragraph (e) would not qualify for the exclusion.

(4) *Operation by the employer.* An employer is considered to operate the athletic facility if the employer operates the facility through its own employees, or if the employer contracts out to

another to operate the athletic facility. For example, if an employer hires an independent contractor to operate the athletic facility for the employer's employees, the facility is considered to be operated by the employer. In addition, if an athletic facility is operated by more than one employer, it is considered to be operated by each employer. For purposes of paragraph (e)(1)(iii) of this section, substantially all of the use of a facility that is operated by more than one employer must be by employees of the various employers, their spouses, and their dependent children. Where the facility is operated by more than one employer, an employer that pays rent either directly to the owner of the premises or to a sublessor of the premises is eligible for the exclusion. If an athletic facility is operated by a voluntary employees' beneficiary association funded by an employer, the employer is considered to operate the facility.

(5) *Nonapplicability of nondiscrimination rules.* The nondiscrimination rules of section 132 and § 1.132-8 do not apply to on-premises athletic facilities.

(f) *Nonapplicability of section 132 in certain cases*—(1) *Tax treatment provided for in another section.* If the tax treatment of a particular fringe benefit is expressly provided for in another section of Chapter 1 of the Internal Revenue Code of 1986, section 132 and the applicable regulations (except for section 132(e) and the regulations thereunder) do not apply to such fringe benefit. For example, because section 129 provides an exclusion from gross income for amounts paid or incurred by an employer for dependent care assistance for an employee, the exclusions under section 132 and this section do not apply to the provision by an employer to an employee of dependent care assistance. Similarly, because section 117(d) applies to tuition reductions, the exclusions under section 132 do not apply to free or discounted tuition provided to an employee by an organization operated by the employer,

whether the tuition is for study at or below the graduate level. Of course, if the amounts paid by the employer are for education relating to the employee's trade or business of being an employee of the employer so that, if the employee paid for the education, the amount paid could be deducted under section 162, the costs of the education may be eligible for exclusion as a working condition fringe.

(2) *Limited statutory exclusions.* If another section of Chapter 1 of the Internal Revenue Code of 1986 provides an exclusion from gross income based on the cost of the benefit provided to the employee and such exclusion is a limited amount, section 132 and the regulations thereunder may apply to the extent the cost of the benefit exceeds the statutory exclusion.

(g) *Effective date.* Sections 1.132-0, 1.132-1, 1.132-2, 1.132-3, 1.132-4, 1.132-5, 1.132-6, 1.132-7 and 1.132-8 are effective as of January 1, 1989, except that §§ 1.132-1(b)(1) with respect to the use of air transportation by a parent of an employee and 1.132-4(d) are effective as of January 1, 1985. Furthermore, in § 1.132-5, the eleventh sentence of paragraph (m)(1), *Examples 6* and *7* in paragraph (m)(8), and paragraphs (m)(2)(i), (m)(2)(v), (m)(3)(iv), (m)(6), (m)(7), and (r) are effective December 30, 1992; however, taxpayers may treat the rules as applicable to benefits provided on or after January 1, 1989. For the applicable rules relating to employer-provided transportation for security concerns prior to December 30, 1992, *see* § 1.132-5(m) (as contained in 26 CFR part 1 (§§ 1.61 to 1.169) revised April 1, 1992). See §§ 1.132-1T, 1.132-2T, 1.132-3T, 1.132-4T, 1.132-5T, 1.132-6T, 1.132-7T and 1.132-8T for rules in effect for benefits received from January 1, 1985, to December 31, 1988. [Reg. § 1.132-1.]

☐ [*T.D.* 8256, 7-5-89. *Amended by T.D.* 8457, 12-29-92.]

→ *Caution: Temporary Reg. § 1.132-1T applies to the tax treatment of fringe benefits for 1985—1988. See Reg. §§ 1.132-0—1.132-8 for post-1988 rules.*←

[Reg. § 1.132-1T]

§ 1.132-1T. **Exclusion from gross income of certain fringe benefits—1985 through 1988 (Temporary).**—(a) *In general.* Gross income does not include any fringe benefit which qualifies as a—

(1) no-additional-cost service,

(2) qualified employee discount,

(3) working condition fringe, or

(4) de minimis fringe.

Special rules apply with respect to certain on-premises gyms and other athletic facilities (§ 1.132-1T(e)), demonstration use of employer-provided automobiles by full-time automobile salesmen (§ 1.132-5T(n)), parking provided to an employee on or near the business premises of the employer (§ 1.132-5T(o)), and on-premises eating facilities (§ 1.132-7T).

(b) *Definition of employee*—(1) *No-additional-cost services and qualified employee discounts.* For purposes of section 132(a)(1) (relating to no-

Reg. § 1.132-1T(a)(1)

→ *Caution: Temporary Reg. § 1.132-1T applies to the tax treatment of fringe benefits for 1985—1988. See Reg. § § 1.132-0—1.132-8 for post-1988 rules.*←

additional-cost services) and section 132(a)(2) (relating to qualified employee discounts), the term "employee" (with respect to a line of business of an employer) means—

(i) any individual who is currently employed by the employer in the line of business,

(ii) any individual who was formerly employed by the employer in the line of business and who separated from service with the employer in the line of business by reason of retirement or disability, and

(iii) any widow or widower of an individual who died while employed by the employer in the line of business or who separated from service with the employer in the line of business by reason of retirement or disability.

For purposes of this paragraph (b)(1), any partner who performs services for a partnership is considered employed by the partnership. In addition, any use by the spouse or dependent child (as defined in this paragraph (b)) of the employee will be treated as use by the employee.

(2) *Working condition fringes.* For purposes of section 132(a)(3) (relating to working condition fringes), the term "employee" means—

(i) any individual who is currently employed by the employer,

(ii) any partner who performs services for the partnership,

(iii) any director of the employer, and

(iv) any independent contractor who performs services for the employer.

Notwithstanding anything in this paragraph (b)(2) to the contrary, any independent contractor who performs services for the employer cannot exclude the value of parking or the use of consumer goods provided pursuant to a product testing program under § 1.132-5T(n); in addition, any director of the employer cannot exclude the value of the use of consumer goods provided pursuant to a product testing program under § 1.132-5T(n).

(3) *De minimis fringe.* For purposes of section 132(a)(4) (relating to de minimis fringes), the term "employee" means any recipient of a fringe benefit.

(4) *Dependent child.* For purposes of this paragraph (b), the term "dependent child" means any son, stepson, daughter, or stepdaughter of the employee who is a dependent of the employee, or both of whose parents are deceased. Any child to whom section 152(e) applies will be treated as the dependent of both parents.

(c) *Special rules for employers—Effect of section 414.* All employees treated as employed by a single employer under section 414(b), (c), or (m) will be treated as employed by a single employer for purposes of this section. Thus, employees of one corporation that is part of a controlled group of corporations may under certain circumstances be eligible to receive section 132 benefits from the other corporations that comprise the controlled group. However, the aggregation of employers described in this paragraph (c) does not change the other requirements for an exclusion, such as the line of business requirement. Thus, for example, if a controlled group of corporations consists of two corporations that operate in different lines of business, the corporations are not treated as operating in the same line of business even though the corporations are treated as one employer.

(d) *Customers not to include employees.* For purposes of section 132 and the regulations thereunder, the term "customer" means customers who are not employees. However, the preceding sentence does not apply to section 132(c)(2) (relating to the gross profit percentage for determining a qualified employee discount). Thus, an employer that provides employee discounts cannot exclude sales made to employees in determining the aggregate sales to customers.

(e) *Treatment of on-premises athletic facilities—*(1) *In general.* Gross income does not include the value of any on-premises athletic facility provided by the employer to its employees. For purposes of section 132 and this paragraph (e), the term "on-premises athletic facility" means any gym or other athletic facility (such as a pool, tennis court, or golf course)—

(i) which is located on the premises of the employer,

(ii) which is operated by the employer, and

(iii) where substantially all of the use of which is, during the calendar year, by employees of the employer, their spouses, and their dependent children.

For purposes of this paragraph (e)(1)(iii), the term "dependent children" has the same meaning as the plural of the term "dependent child" in paragraph (b)(4) of this section. The exclusion of this paragraph (e) does not apply to any athletic facility if access to the facility is made available to the general public through the sale of memberships, the rental of the facility, etc.

(2) *Premises of the employer.* The athletic facility need not be located on the employer's business premises. However, the athletic facility

Reg. § 1.132-1T(e)(2)

→ *Caution: Temporary Reg. § 1.132-1T applies to the tax treatment of fringe benefits for 1985—1988. See Reg. § § 1.132-0—1.132-8 for post-1988 rules.←*

must be located on premises of the employer. The exclusion provided in this paragraph (e) applies whether the premises are owned or leased by the employer; in addition, the exclusion is available even if the employer is not a named lessee on the lease so long as the employer pays reasonable rent. The exclusion provided in this paragraph (e) does not apply to any athletic facility that is a facility for residential use. Thus, for example, a resort with accompanying athletic facilities (such as tennis courts, pool, and gym) would not qualify for the exclusion provided in this paragraph (e).

(3) *Application of rules to membership in an athletic facility.* The exclusion provided in this paragraph (e) does not apply to any membership in an athletic facility (including health clubs or country clubs) unless the facility is owned (or leased) and operated by the employer and substantially all the use of the facility is by employees of the employer, their spouses, and their dependent children. Therefore, membership in a health club or country club not meeting the rules provided in this paragraph (e) would not qualify for the exclusion.

(4) *Operation by the employer.* An employer is considered to operate the athletic facility if the employer itself operates the facility through its own employees, or if the employer contracts out to another to operate the athletic facility. For example, if an employer hires an independent contractor to operate the athletic facility for the employer's employees, the facility is considered to be operated by the employer. In addition, if an athletic facility is operated by more than one employer, it is considered to be operated by each employer. For purposes of paragraph (e)(1)(iii) of this section, substantially all the use of a facility operated by more than one employer must be by employees of all of the employers, their spouses, and their dependent children. Where the facility is operated by more than one employer, an employer that either pays rent directly to the owner of the premises or pays rent to a named lessor of the premises is eligible for the exclusion.

(5) *Nonapplicability of nondiscrimination rules.* The nondiscrimination rules of section 132 and § 1.132-8T do not apply to on-premises athletic facilities.

(f) *Nonapplicability of section 132.* If the tax treatment of a particular fringe benefit is expressly provided for in another section of Chapter 1, section 132 and the applicable regulations (except for section 132(e) and the regulations thereunder) do not apply to such fringe benefit. For example, since section 129 provides an exclusion

from gross income for amounts paid or incurred by the employer for dependent care assistance for an employee, the exclusions under section 132 and this section do not apply to the provision by an employer to an employee of dependent care assistance. [Temporary Reg. § 1.132-1T.]

□ [*T.D. 8004, 1-2-85. Amended by T.D. 8009, 2-18-85; T.D. 8061, 11-1-85; T.D. 8063, 12-18-85 and T.D. 8256, 7-5-89.*]

[Reg. § 1.132-2]

§ 1.132-2. No-additional-cost services.—(a) *In general*—(1) *Definition.* Gross income does not include the value of a no-additional-cost service. A "no-additional-cost service" is any service provided by an employer to an employee for the employee's personal use if—

(i) The service is offered for sale by the employer to its customers in the ordinary course of the line of business of the employer in which the employee performs substantial services, and

(ii) The employer incurs no substantial additional cost in providing the service to the employee (including foregone revenue and excluding any amount paid by or on behalf of the employee for the service).

For rules relating to the line of business limitation, see § 1.132-4. For purposes of this section, a service will not be considered to be offered for sale by the employer to its customers if that service is primarily provided to employees and not to the employer's customers.

(2) *Excess capacity services.* Services that are eligible for treatment as no-additional-cost services include excess capacity services such as hotel accommodations; transportation by aircraft, train, bus, subway, or cruise line; and telephone services. Services that are not eligible for treatment as no-additional-cost services are non-excess capacity services such as the facilitation by a stock brokerage firm of the purchase of stock. Employees who receive non-excess capacity services may, however, be eligible for a qualified employee discount of up to 20 percent of the value of the service provided. See § 1.132-3.

(3) *Cash rebates.* The exclusion for a no-additional-cost service applies whether the service is provided at no charge or at a reduced price. The exclusion also applies if the benefit is provided through a partial or total cash rebate of an amount paid for the service.

(4) *Applicability of nondiscrimination rules.* The exclusion for a no-additional-cost service applies to highly compensated employees only if the

Reg. § 1.132-2(a)(1)

service is available on substantially the same terms to each member of a group of employees that is defined under a reasonable classification set up by the employer that does not discriminate in favor of highly compensated employees. See § 1.132-8.

(5) *No substantial additional cost*—(i) *In general.* The exclusion for a no-additional-cost service applies only if the employer does not incur substantial additional cost in providing the service to the employee. For purposes of the preceding sentence, the term "cost" includes revenue that is forgone because the service is provided to an employee rather than a nonemployee. (For purposes of determining whether any revenue is forgone, it is assumed that the employee would not have purchased the service unless it were available to the employee at the actual price charged to the employee.) Whether an employer incurs substantial additional cost must be determined without regard to any amount paid by the employee for the service. Thus, any reimbursement by the employee for the cost of providing the service does not affect the determination of whether the employer incurs substantial additional cost.

(ii) *Labor intensive services.* An employer must include the cost of labor incurred in providing services to employees when determining whether the employer has incurred substantial additional cost. An employer incurs substantial additional cost, whether non-labor costs are incurred, if a substantial amount of time is spent by the employer or its employees in providing the service to employees. This would be the result whether the time spent by the employer or its employees in providing the services would have been "idle," or if the services were provided outside normal business hours. An employer generally incurs no substantial additional cost, however, if the services provided to the employee are merely incidental to the primary service being provided by the employer. For example, the in-flight services of a flight attendant and the cost of in-flight meals provided to airline employees traveling on a space-available basis are merely incidental to the primary service being provided (i.e., air transportation). Similarly, maid service provided to hotel employees renting hotel rooms on a space-available basis is merely incidental to the primary service being provided (i.e., hotel accommodations).

(6) *Payments for telephone service.* Payment made by an entity subject to the modified final judgment (as defined in section 559(c)(5) of the Tax Reform Act of 1984) of all or part of the cost of local telephone service provided to an employee by a person other than an entity subject to the modified final judgment shall be treated as telephone service provided to the employee by the entity making the payment for purposes of this section. The preceding sentence also applies to a rebate of the amount paid by the employee for the service and a payment to the person providing the service. This paragraph (a)(6) applies only to services and employees described in § 1.132-4(c). For a special line of business rule relating to such services and employees, see § 1.132-4(c).

(b) *Reciprocal agreements.* For purposes of the exclusion from gross income for a no-additional-cost service, an exclusion is available to an employee of one employer for a no-additional-cost service provided by an unrelated employer only if all of the following requirements are satisfied—

(1) The service provided to such employee by the unrelated employer is the same type of service generally provided to nonemployee customers by both the line of business in which the employee works and the line of business in which the service is provided to such employee (so that the employee would be permitted to exclude from gross income the value of the service if such service were provided directly by the employee's employer);

(2) Both employers are parties to a written reciprocal agreement under which a group of employees of each employer, all of whom perform substantial services in the same line of business, may receive no-additional-cost services from the other employer; and

(3) Neither employer incurs any substantial additional cost (including forgone revenue) in providing such service to the employees of the other employer, or pursuant to such agreement. If one employer receives a substantial payment from the other employer with respect to the reciprocal agreement, the paying employer will be considered to have incurred a substantial additional cost pursuant to the agreement, and consequently services performed under the reciprocal agreement will not qualify for exclusion as no-additional-cost services.

(c) *Example.* The rules of this section are illustrated by the following example:

Example. Assume that a commercial airline permits its employees to take personal flights on the airline at no charge and receive reserved seating. Because the employer forgoes potential revenue by permitting the employees to reserve seats, employees receiving such free flights are not eligible for the no-additional-cost exclusion. [Reg. § 1.132-2.]

☐ *[T.D. 8256, 7-5-89.]*

→ *Caution: Temporary Reg. § 1.132-2T applies to the tax treatment of fringe benefits for 1985—1988. See Reg. §§ 1.132-0—1.132-8 for post-1988 rules.←*

[Reg. § 1.132-2T]

§ 1.132-2T. **No-additional-cost service— 1985—1988 (Temporary).**—(a) *In general*—(1) *Definition.* Gross income does not include the value of a no-additional-cost service. The term "no-additional-cost service" means any service provided by an employer to an employee for the employee's personal use if—

(i) the service is offered for sale to customers in the ordinary course of the line of business of the employer in which the employee performs substantial services, and

(ii) the employer incurs no substantial additional cost in providing the service to the employee (including foregone revenue and excluding any amount paid by or on behalf of the employee for the service).

For rules relating to the line of business limitation, see § 1.132-4T.

(2) *Examples.* Services that are eligible for treatment as no-additional-cost services are excess capacity services such as hotel accommodations; transportation by aircraft, train, bus, subway, or cruise line; and telephone services. Services that are not eligible for treatment as no-additional-cost services are non-excess capacity services such as the facilitation by a stock brokerage firm of the purchase of stock. Employees who receive non-excess capacity services may, however, be eligible for a qualified employee discount of up to 20 percent of the value of the service provided. See § 1.132-3T.

(3) *Cash rebates.* The exclusion for a no-additional-cost service applies whether the service is provided at no charge or at a reduced price. The exclusion also applies if the benefit is provided through a partial or total cash rebate of an amount paid for the service.

(4) *Applicability of nondiscrimination rules.* The exclusion for a no-additional-cost service applies to officers, owners, and highly compensated employees only if the service is available on substantially the same terms to each member of a group of employees that is defined under a reasonable classification set up by the employer that does not discriminate in favor of officers, owners, or highly compensated employees. See § 1.132-8T.

(5) *No substantial additional cost*—(i) *In general.* The exclusion for a no-additional-cost service applies only if the employer does not incur substantial additional cost in providing the service to the employee. For purposes of the preceding sentence, the term "cost" includes revenue that is foregone because the service is provided to

an employee rather than a nonemployee. (For purposes of determining whether any revenue is foregone, it is assumed that the employee would not have purchased the service unless it were available to the employee at the actual price charged to the employee.) Whether an employer incurs substantial additional cost must be determined without regard to any amount paid by the employee for the service. Thus, any reimbursement by the employee for the cost of providing the service does not affect the determination of whether the employer incurs substantial additional cost.

(ii) *Labor intensive services.* An employer must include the cost of labor incurred in providing services to employees when determining whether the employer has incurred substantial additional cost. An employer incurs substantial additional cost, whether or not nonlabor costs are incurred, if a substantial amount of time is spent by the employer or its employees in providing the service to employees. This would be the result whether or not the time spent by the employer or its employees in providing the services would have been "idle", or if the services were provided outside normal business hours. An employer generally incurs no substantial additional cost, however, if the employee services provided are merely incidental to the primary service being provided by the employer. For example, the in-flight services of a flight attendant provided to airline employees traveling on a space-available basis are merely incidental to the primary service being provided (i.e., air transportation). In addition, the cost of in-flight meals provided to airline employees is not considered substantial in relation to the air transportation being provided.

(b) *Reciprocal agreements.* For purposes of the exclusion for a no-additional-cost service, any service provided by an employer to an employee of another employer shall be treated as provided by the employer of such employee if all of the following requirements are satisfied:

(1) The service is provided pursuant to a written reciprocal agreement between the employers under which a group of employees of each employer, all of whom perform substantial services in the same line of business, may receive no-additional-cost services from the other employer;

(2) The service provided pursuant to the agreement to the employees of both employers is the same type of service provided by the employers to customers both in the line of business in which the employees perform substantial services

→ *Caution: Temporary Reg. § 1.132-2T applies to the tax treatment of fringe benefits for 1985—1988. See Reg. § § 1.132-0—1.132-8 for post-1988 rules.*←

and the line of business in which the service is provided to customers; and

(3) Neither employer incurs substantial additional cost (including foregone revenue) in providing the service to the employees of the other employer or pursuant to the agreement.

If one employer receives a substantial payment from the other employer with respect to the reciprocal agreement, the paying employer will be considered to have incurred a substantial additional cost pursuant to the agreement [Temporary Reg. § 1.132-2T.]

☐ [*T.D.* 8063, 12-18-85. *Amended by T.D.* 8256, 7-5-89.]

[Reg. § 1.132-3]

§ 1.132-3. Qualified employee discounts.— (a) *In general*—(1) *Definition.* Gross income does not include the value of a qualified employee discount. A "qualified employee discount" is any employee discount with respect to qualified property or services provided by an employer to an employee for use by the employee to the extent the discount does not exceed—

(i) The gross profit percentage multiplied by the price at which the property is offered to customers in the ordinary course of the employer's line of business, for discounts on property, or

(ii) Twenty percent of the price at which the service is offered to customers, for discounts on services.

(2) *Qualified property or services*—(i) *In general.* The term "qualified property or services" means any property or services that are offered for sale to customers in the ordinary course of the line of business of the employer in which the employee performs substantial services. For rules relating to the line of business limitation, see § 1.132-4.

(ii) *Exception for certain property.* The term "qualified property" does not include real property and it does not include personal property (whether tangible or intangible) of a kind commonly held for investment. Thus, an employee may not exclude from gross income the amount of an employee discount provided on the purchase of securities, commodities, or currency, or of either residential or commercial real estate, whether or not the particular purchase is made for investment purposes.

(iii) *Property and services not offered in ordinary course of business.* The term "qualified property or services" does not include any property or services of a kind that is not offered for

sale to customers in the ordinary course of the line of business of the employer. For example, employee discounts provided on property or services that are offered for sale primarily to employees and their families (such as merchandise sold at an employee store or through an employer-provided catalog service) may not be excluded from gross income. For rules relating to employer-operated eating facilities, see § 1.132-7, and for rules relating to employer-operated on-premises athletic facilities, see § 1.132-1(e).

(3) *No reciprocal agreement exception.* The exclusion for a qualified employee discount does not apply to property or services provided by another employer pursuant to a written reciprocal agreement that exists between employers to provide discounts on property and services to employees of the other employer.

(4) *Property or services provided without charge, at a reduced price, or by rebates.* The exclusion for a qualified employee discount applies whether the property or service is provided at no charge (in which case only part of the discount may be excludable as a qualified employee discount) or at a reduced price. The exclusion also applies if the benefit is provided through a partial or total cash rebate of an amount paid for the property or service.

(5) *Property or services provided directly by the employer or indirectly through a third party.* A qualified employee discount may be provided either directly by the employer or indirectly through a third party. For example, an employee of an appliance manufacturer may receive a qualified employee discount on the manufacturer's appliances purchased at a retail store that offers such appliances for sale to customers. The employee may exclude the amount of the qualified employee discount whether the employee is provided the appliance at no charge or purchases it at a reduced price, or whether the employee receives a partial or total cash rebate from either the employer-manufacturer or the retailer. If an employee receives additional rights associated with the property that are not provided by the employee's employer to customers in the ordinary course of the line of business in which the employee performs substantial services (such as the right to return or exchange the property or special warranty rights), the employee may only receive a qualified employee discount with respect to the property and not the additional rights. Receipt of such additional rights may occur, for example, when an employee of a manufacturer purchases

property manufactured by the employee's employer at a retail outlet.

(6) *Applicability of nondiscrimination rules.* The exclusion for a qualified employee discount applies to highly compensated employees only if the discount is available on substantially the same terms to each member of a group of employees that is defined under a reasonable classification set up by the employer that does not discriminate in favor of highly compensated employees. See § 1.132-8.

(b) *Employee discount*—(1) *Definition.* The term "employee discount" means the excess of—

(i) The price at which the property or service is being offered by the employer for sale to customers, over

(ii) The price at which the property or service is provided by the employer to an employee for use by the employee. A transfer of property by an employee without consideration is treated as use by the employee for purposes of this section. Thus, for example, if an employee receives a discount on property offered for sale by his employer to customers and the employee makes a gift of the property to his parent, the property will be considered to be provided for use by the employee; thus, the discount will be eligible for exclusion as a qualified employee discount.

(2) *Price to customers*—(i) *Determined at time of sale.* In determining the amount of an employee discount, the price at which the property or service is being offered to customers at the time of the employee's purchase is controlling. For example, assume that an employer offers a product to customers for $20 during the first six months of a calendar year, but at the time the employee purchases the product at a discount, the price at which the product is being offered to customers is $25. In this case, the price from which the employee discount is measured is $25. Assume instead that, at the time the employee purchases the product at a discount, the price at which the product is being offered to customers is $15 and the price charged the employee is $12. The employee discount is measured from $15, the price at which the product is offered for sale to customers at the time of the employee purchase. Thus, the employee discount is $15 − $12, or $3.

(ii) *Quantity discount not reflected.* The price at which a property or service is being offered to customers cannot reflect any quantity discount unless the employee actually purchases the requisite quantity of the property or service.

(iii) *Price to employer's customers controls.* In determining the amount of an employee discount, the price at which a property or service is offered to customers of the employee's employer is controlling. Thus, the price at which the property is sold to the wholesale customers of a manufacturer will generally be lower than the price at which the same property is sold to the customers of a retailer. However, see paragraph (a)(5) of this section regarding the effect of a wholesaler providing to its employees additional rights not provided to customers of the wholesaler in the ordinary course of its business.

(iv) *Discounts to discrete customer or consumer groups.* Subject to paragraph (2)(ii) of this section, if an employer offers for sale property or services at one or more discounted prices to discrete customer or consumer groups, and sales at all such discounted prices comprise at least 35 percent of the employer's gross sales for a representative period, then in determining the amount of an employee discount, the price at which such property or service is being offered to customers for purposes of this section is a discounted price. The applicable discounted price is the current undiscounted price, reduced by the percentage discount at which the greatest percentage of the employer's discounted gross sales are made for such representative period. If sales at different percentage discounts equal the same percentage of the employer's gross sales, the price at which the property or service is being provided to customers may be reduced by the average of the discounts offered to each of the two groups. For purposes of this section, a representative period is the taxable year of the employer immediately preceding the taxable year in which the property or service is provided to the employee at a discount. If more than one employer would be aggregated under section 414(b), (c), (m), or (o), and not all of the employers have the same taxable year, the employers required to be aggregated must designate the 12-month period to be used in determining gross sales for a representative period. The 12-month period designated, however, must be used on a consistent basis.

(v) *Examples.* The rules provided in this paragraph (b)(2) are illustrated by the following examples:

Example (1). Assume that a wholesale employer offers property for sale to two discrete customer groups at differing prices. Assume further that during the prior taxable year of the employer, 70 percent of the employer's gross sales are made at a 15 percent discount and 30 percent at no discount. For purposes of this paragraph (b)(2), the current undiscounted price at which the property or service is being offered by the employer for sale to customers may be reduced by the 15 percent discount.

Reg. § 1.132-3(a)(6)

Example (2). Assume that a retail employer offers a 20 percent discount to members of the American Bar Association, a 15 percent discount to members of the American Medical Association, and a ten percent discount to employees of the Federal Government. Assume further that during the prior taxable year of the employer, sales to American Bar Association members equal 15 percent of the employer's gross sales, sales to American Medical Association members equal 20 percent of the employer's gross sales, and sales to Federal Government employees equal 25 percent of the employer's gross sales. For purposes of this paragraph (b)(2), the current undiscounted price at which the property or service is being offered by the employer for sale to customers may be reduced by the ten percent Federal Government discount.

(3) *Damaged, distressed, or returned goods.* If an employee pays at least fair market value for damaged, distressed, or returned property, such employee will not have income attributable to such purchase.

(c) *Gross profit percentage*—(1) *In general*—(i) *General rule.* An exclusion from gross income for an employee discount on qualified property is limited to the price at which the property is being offered to customers in the ordinary course of the employer's line of business, multiplied by the employer's gross profit percentage The term "gross profit percentage" means the excess of the aggregate sales price of the property sold by the employer to customers (including employees) over the employer's aggregate cost of the property, then divided by the aggregate sales price.

(ii) *Calculation of gross profit percentage.* The gross profit percentage must be calculated separately for each line of business based on the aggregate sales price and aggregate cost of property in that line of business for a representative period. For purposes of this section, a representative period is the taxable year of the employer immediately preceding the taxable year in which the discount is available. For example, if the aggregate amount of sales of property in an employer's line of business for the prior taxable year was $800,000, and the aggregate cost of the property for the year was $600,000, the gross profit percentage would be 25 percent ($800,000 minus $600,000, then divided by $800,000) If two or more employers are required to aggregate under section 414(b), (c), (m), or (o) (aggregated employer), and if all of the aggregated employers do not share the same taxable year, then the aggregated employers must designate the 12-month period to be used in determining the gross profit percentage. The 12-month period designated,

however, must be used on a consistent basis. If an employee performs substantial services in more than one line of business, the gross profit percentage of the line of business in which the property is sold determines the amount of the excludable employee discount.

(iii) *Special rule for employers in their first year of existence.* An employer in its first year of existence may estimate the gross profit percentage of a line of business based on its mark-up from cost. Alternatively, an employer in its first year of existence may determine the gross profit percentage by reference to an appropriate industry average.

(iv) *Redetermination of gross profit percentage.* If substantial changes in an employer's business indicate at any time that it is inappropriate for the prior year's gross profit percentage to be used for the current year, the employer must, within a reasonable period, redetermine the gross profit percentage for the remaining portion of the current year as if such portion of the year were the first year of the employer's existence.

(2) *Line of business.* In general, an employer must determine the gross profit percentage on the basis of all property offered to customers (including employees) in each separate line of business. An employer may instead select a classification of property that is narrower than the applicable line of business. However, the classification must be reasonable. For example, if an employer computes gross profit percentage according to the department in which products are sold, such classification is reasonable. Similarly, it is reasonable to compute gross profit percentage on the basis of the type of merchandise sold (such as high mark-up and low mark-up classifications). It is not reasonable, however, for an employer to classify certain low mark-up products preferred by certain employees (such as highly compensated employees) with high mark-up products or to classify certain high mark-up products preferred by other employees with low mark-up products.

(3) *Generally accepted accounting principles.* In general, the aggregate sales price of property must be determined in accordance with generally accepted accounting principles. An employer must compute the aggregate cost of property in the same manner in which it is computed for the employer's Federal income tax liability; thus, for example, section 263A and the regulations thereunder apply in determining the cost of property.

(d) *Treatment of leased sections of department stores*—(1) *In general*—(i) *General rule.* For purposes of determining whether employees of a leased section of a department store may receive qualified employee discounts at the department store and whether employees of the department store may receive qualified employee discounts at the leased section of the department store, the leased section is treated as part of the line of business of the person operating the department store, and employees of the leased section are treated as employees of the person operating the department store as well as employees of their employer. The term "leased section of a department store" means a section of a department store where substantially all of the gross receipts of the leased section are from over-the-counter sales of property made under a lease, license, or similar arrangement where it appears to the general public that individuals making such sales are employed by the department store. A leased section of a department store which, in connection with the offering of beautician services, customarily makes sales of beauty aids in the ordinary course of business is deemed to derive substantially all of its gross receipts from over-the-counter sales of property.

(ii) *Calculation of gross profit percentage.* For purposes of paragraph (d) of this section, when calculating the gross profit percentage of property and services sold at a department store, sales of property and services sold at the department store, as well as sales of property and services sold at the leased section, are considered. The rule provided in the preceding sentence does not apply, however, if it is more reasonable to calculate the gross profit percentage for the department store and leased section separately, or if it would be inappropriate to combine them (such as where either the department store or the leased section but not both provides employee discounts).

(2) *Employees of the leased section*—(i) *Definition.* For purposes of this paragraph (d), "employees of the leased section" means all employees who perform substantial services at the leased section of the department store regardless of whether the employees engage in over-the-counter sales of property or services. The term "employee" has the same meaning as in section 132(f) and § 1.132-1(b)(1).

(ii) *Discounts offered to either department store employees or employees of the leased section.* If the requirements of this paragraph (d) are satisfied, employees of the leased section may receive qualified employee discounts at the department store whether or not employees of the department store are offered discounts at the leased section. Similarly, employees of the department store may receive a qualified employee discount at the leased section whether or not employees of the leased section are offered discounts at the department store.

(e) *Excess discounts.* Unless excludable under a provision of the Internal Revenue Code of 1986 other than section 132(a)(2), an employee discount provided on property is excludable to the extent of the gross profit percentage multiplied by the price at which the property is being offered for sale to customers. If an employee discount exceeds the gross profit percentage, the excess discount is includible in the employee's income. For example, if the discount on employer-purchased property is 30 percent and the employer's gross profit percentage for the period in the relevant line of business is 25 percent, then 5 percent of the price at which the property is being offered for sale to customers is includible in the employee's income. With respect to services, an employee discount of up to 20 percent may be excludable. If an employee discount exceeds 20 percent, the excess discount is includible in the employee's income. For example, assume that a commercial airline provides a pass to each of its employees permitting the employees to obtain a free roundtrip coach ticket with a confirmed seat to any destination the airline services. Neither the exclusion of section 132(a)(1) (relating to no-additional-cost services) nor any other statutory exclusion applies to a flight taken primarily for personal purposes by an employee under this program. However, an employee discount of up to 20 percent may be excluded as a qualified employee discount. Thus, if the price charged to customers for the flight taken is $300 (under restrictions comparable to those actually placed on travel associated with the employee airline ticket), $60 is excludible from gross income as a qualified employee discount and $240 is includible in gross income. [Reg. § 1.132-3.]

☐ [*T.D.* 8256, 7-5-89.]

→ **Caution: Temporary Reg. § 1.132-3T applies to the tax treatment of fringe benefits for 1985—1988. See Reg. §§ 1.132-0—1.132-8 for post-1988 rules.←**

[Reg. § 1.132-3T]

§1.132-3T. Qualified employee discount— 1985 through 1988 (Temporary).—(a) *In general*—(1) *Definition.* Gross income does not include the value of a qualified employee discount.

The term "qualified employee discount" means any employee discount with respect to qualified property or services provided by an employer to an employee for the employee's personal use to the extent the discount does not exceed—

Reg. § 1.132-3T(a)(1)

→ *Caution: Temporary Reg. § 1.132-3T applies to the tax treatment of fringe benefits for 1985—1988. See Reg. § § 1.132-0—1.132-8 for post-1988 rules.*←

(i) the gross profit percentage of the price at which the property is offered to customers, for discounts on property, or

(ii) 20 percent of the price at which the services are offered to customers, for discounts on services.

(2) *Qualified property or services*—(i) *In general.* The term "qualified property or services" means any property or services that are offered for sale to customers in the ordinary course of the line of business of the employer in which the employee performs substantial services. For rules relating to the line of business limitation, see § 1.132-4T.

(ii) *Exception for certain property.* The term "qualified property" does not include real property and it does not include personal property (whether tangible or intangible) of a kind commonly held for investment. Thus, an employee may not exclude from gross income the amount of an employee discount provided on the purchase of either residential or commercial real estate, securities, commodities, or currency, whether or not the particular purchase is made for investment purposes.

(iii) *Property and services not offered in ordinary course of business.* The term "qualified property or services" does not include any property or services of a kind that is not offered for sale to customers in the ordinary course of the line of business of the employer. For example, employee discounts provided on property or services that are offered for sale only to employees and their families (such as merchandise sold at an employee store or through an employer-provided catalog service) may not be excluded from gross income.

(3) *No reciprocal agreement exception.* The exclusion for a qualified employee discount does not apply to property or services provided by another employer pursuant to a written reciprocal agreement that exists between employers to provide discounts on property and services to employees of the other employer.

(4) *Cash or third-party rebates*—i) *Property or services provided without charge or at a reduced price.* The exclusion for a qualified employee discount applies whether the property or service is provided at no charge (in which case only part of the discount may be excludable as a qualified employee discount) or at a reduced price. The exclusion also applies if the benefit is provided through a partial or total cash rebate of an amount paid for the property or service.

(ii) *Property or services provided directly by the employer or indirectly through a third party.* A qualified employee discount may be provided either directly by the employer or indirectly through a third party. For example, an employee of an appliance manufacturer may receive a qualified employee discount on the manufacturer's appliances purchased at a retail store that offers such appliances for sale to customers. The employee may exclude the amount of the qualified employee discount whether the employee is provided the appliance at no charge or purchases it at a reduced price, or whether the employee receives a partial or total cash rebate from either the employer-manufacturer or the retailer. If an employee receives additional rights associated with the property that are not provided by the employee's employer to customers in the ordinary course of the line of business in which the employee performs substantial services (such as the right to return or exchange the property or special warranty rights), the employee may only receive a qualified employee discount with respect to the property and not the additional rights. Receipt of such additional rights may occur, for example, when an employee of a manufacturer purchases property manufactured by the employee's employer at a retail outlet.

(5) *Applicability of nondiscrimination rules.* The exclusion for a qualified employee discount applies to officers, owners, and highly compensated employees only if the discount is available on substantially the same terms to each member of a group of employees that is defined under a reasonable classification set up by the employer that does not discriminate in favor of officers, owners or highly compensated employees. See § 1.132-8T.

(b) *Employee discount*—(1) *Definition.* The term "employee discount" means the excess of—

(i) the price at which the property or service is being offered by the employer for sale to customers, over

(ii) the price at which the property or service is provided by the employer to an employee for use by the employee.

A transfer of property by an employee without consideration is considered use by the employee for purposes of this section. Thus, for example, if an employee receives a discount on property offered for sale by his employer to customers and the employee makes a gift of the property to his parent, the property will be considered to be provided for use by the employee, thus enabling the

Reg. § 1.132-3T(b)(1)

→ *Caution: Temporary Reg. § 1.132-3T applies to the tax treatment of fringe benefits for 1985—1988. See Reg. § § 1.132-0—1.132-8 for post-1988 rules.*←

discount to be eligible for exclusion as a qualified employee discount.

(2) *Price to customers*—(i) *Determined at time of sale.* In determining the amount of an employee discount, the price at which the property or service is being offered to customers at the time of the employee's purchase is controlling. For example, assume that an employer offers a product to customers for $20 during the first six months of a calendar year, but at the time the employee purchases the product at a discount, the price at which the product is being offered to customers is $25. In this case, the price from which the employee discount is measured is $25.

(ii) *Quantity discount not reflected.* The price referred to in paragraph (b)(2)(i) of this section cannot reflect any quantity discount unless the employee actually purchases the requisite quantity of the property or service.

(iii) *Customers of employee's employer controls.* In determining the amount of an employee discount, the price at which the property or service is offered to customers of the employee's employer is controlling. Thus, the price at which property is sold to the wholesale customers of a manufacturer will generally be lower than the price at which the same property is sold to the customers of a retailer. However, see paragraph (a)(4)(ii) of this section regarding the effect of a wholesaler providing to its employees additional rights not provided to customers of the wholesaler in the ordinary course of its business.

(iv) *Discounts to discrete customer or consumer groups.* In determining the amount of an employee discount, if an employer offers for sale property or services at one or more discounted prices to discrete customer or consumer groups, and sales at all such discounted prices comprise at least 35 percent of the employer's gross sales for a representative period, then the price at which property or service is being offered to customers is a discounted price. The applicable discounted price is the current undiscounted price, reduced by the percentage discount at which the greatest percentage of the employer's gross sales are made for such representative period. If sales at different percentage discounts equal the same percentage of the employer's gross sales, the price at which the property or service is being provided to customers may be reduced by the average of the two group discounts. For purposes of this section, a representative period is the taxable year of the employer immediately preceding the taxable year in which the property or service is provided to the employee at a discount. If more than one employer would be aggregated under section 414(b), (c), or (m), and all of the employers do not have the same taxable year, the employers required to be aggregated must designate the 12-month period to be used in determining gross sales for a representative period.

(v) *Examples.* The rules provided in this paragraph (b)(2) are illustrated by the following examples:

Example (1). Assume that a wholesale employer offers property for sale to two discrete customer groups at differing prices. Assume further that during the prior taxable year of the employer, 70 percent of the employer's gross sales are made at a 15-percent discount and 30 percent at no discount. The current undiscounted price at which the property or service is being offered by the employer for sale to customers may be reduced by the 15-percent discount.

Example (2). Assume that a retail employer offers a 20 percent discount to members of the American Bar Association, a 15 percent discount to members of the American Medical Association, and a ten percent discount to employees of the Federal Government. Assume further that during the prior taxable year of the employer, sales to American Bar Association members equal 15 percent of the employer's gross sales, sales to American Medical Association members equal 20 percent of the employer's gross sales, and sales to Federal Government employees equal 25 percent of the employer's gross sales. The current undiscounted price at which the property or service is being offered by the employer for sale to customers may be reduced by the ten percent Federal Government discount.

(3) *Damaged, distressed, or returned goods.* If an employee pays at least fair market value for damaged, distressed, or returned property, such employee will not have income attributable to such purchase.

(c) *Gross profit percentage*—(1) *In general*—(i) *General rule.* An exclusion from gross income for an employee discount on qualified property is limited to the price at which the property is being offered to customers in the ordinary course of the employer's line of business, multiplied by the employer's gross profit percentage. The term "gross profit percentage" means the excess of the aggregate sales price of the property sold by the employer to customers (including employees) over the employer's aggregate cost of the property, then divided by the aggregate sales price.

→ *Caution: Temporary Reg. § 1.132-3T applies to the tax treatment of fringe benefits for 1985—1988. See Reg. § § 1.132-0—1.132-8 for post-1988 rules.*←

(ii) *Calculation of gross profit percentage.* The gross profit percentage must be calculated separately for each line of business based on the aggregate sales price and aggregate cost of property in that line of business for a representative period. For purposes of this section, a representative period is the taxable year of the employer immediately preceding the taxable year in which the discount is available. For example, if the aggregate sales of property in an employer's line of business for the prior taxable year were $800,000, and the aggregate cost of the property for the year were $600,000, the gross profit percentage would be 25 percent ($800,000 minus $600,000, then divided by $800,000). If more than one employer would be aggregated under section 414(b), (c), or (m), and all of the employers do not have the same taxable year, the employers required to be aggregated must designate the 12-month period to be used in determining the gross profit percentage. If an employee performs substantial services in more than one line of business, the gross profit percentage of the line of business in which the property is sold determines the amount of the excludable employee discount.

(iii) *Special rule for employers in their first year of existence.* An employer in its first year of existence may estimate the gross profit percentage of a line of business based on its mark-up from cost. Alternatively, an employer in its first year of existence may determine the gross profit percentage by reference to an appropriate industry average.

(iv) *Redetermination of gross profit percentage.* If substantial changes in an employer's business indicate at any time that it is inappropriate for the prior years' gross profit percentage to be used for the current year, the employer must, within a reasonable period, redetermine the gross profit percentage for the remaining portion of the current year as if such portion of the year were the first year of the employer's existence.

(2) *Line of business.* In general, an employer must determine the gross profit percentage on the basis of all property offered to customers (including employees) in each separate line of business. An employer may instead select a classification of property that is narrower than the applicable line of business. However, such classification must be reasonable. For example, if an employer computes gross profit percentage according to the department in which products are sold, such classification is reasonable. Similarly, it is reasonable to compute gross profit percentage on the basis of the type of merchandise sold (such as high mark-

up and low mark-up classifications). It is not reasonable, however, for an employer to classify certain low mark-up products preferred by certain employees (such as officers, owners, and highly compensated employees) with high mark-up products or to classify certain high mark-up products preferred by other employees with low mark-up products.

(3) *Generally accepted accounting principles.* In general, the aggregate sales price of property must be determined in accordance with generally accepted accounting principles. An employer must compute the aggregate cost of property in the same manner in which it is computed for the employer's Federal income tax liability, pursuant to the inventory rules in section 471 and regulations thereunder.

(d) *Treatment of leased sections of department stores—(1) In general—(i) General rule.* For purposes of determining whether employees of a leased section of a department store may receive qualified employee discounts at the department store and whether employees of the department store may receive qualified employee discounts at the leased section of the department store, the leased section is treated as part of the line of business of the person operating the department store, and employees of the leased section are treated as employees of the person operating the department store as well as employees of their employer. The term "leased section of a department store" means a section of a department store where substantially all of the gross receipts of the leased section are over-the-counter sales of property made under a lease, license, or similar arrangement where it appears to the general public that individuals making such sales are employed by the department store. An example of a leased section of a department store is a cosmetics firm that leases floor space from a department store.

(ii) *Calculation of gross profit percentage.* When calculating the gross profit percentage of property and services sold at the department store under paragraph (c) of this section, sales of property and services sold at the department store, as well as sales of property and services sold at the leased section, are considered. The rule provided in the preceding sentence does not apply, however, if it is reasonable to calculate the gross profit percentage for the department store and leased section separately, or if it would be inappropriate to combine them (such as where either the department store or the leased section, but not both, provides employee discounts).

Reg. § 1.132-3T(d)(1)

→ *Caution: Temporary Reg. § 1.132-3T applies to the tax treatment of fringe benefits for 1985—1988. See Reg. § § 1.132-0—1.132-8 for post-1988 rules.*←

(2) *Employees of the leased section*—(i) *Definition*. For purposes of this paragraph (d), "employees of the leased section" means all employees who perform substantial services at the leased section regardless of whether the employees engage in over-the-counter sales of property or services. The term "employee" has the same meaning as in section 132(f).

(ii) *Discounts offered to either department store employees or employees of the leased section*. If the requirements of this paragraph (d) are satisfied, employees of the leased section may receive qualified employee discounts at the department store regardless of whether employees of the department store are offered discounts at the leased section. Similarly, regardless of whether employees of the leased section are offered discounts at the department store, employees of the department store may receive qualified employee discounts at the leased section.

(e) *Excess discounts*. Unless excludable under a statutory provision other than section 132(a)(2), an employee discount provided on property is excludable to the extent of the gross profit percentage multiplied by the price at which the property is being offered for sale to customers. If an employee discount exceeds the gross profit percentage, the excess discount is includible in the employee's income. For example, if the discount on property is 30 percent and the employer's gross profit percentage for the period in the relevant line of business is 25 percent, then 5 percent of the price at which the property is being offered for sale to customers is includible in the employee's income. With respect to services, an employee discount of up to 20 percent may be excludable. If an employee discount exceeds 20 percent, the excess discount is includible in the employee's income. [Temporary Reg. § 1.132-3T.]

☐ [*T.D.* 8063, 12-18-85. *Amended by T.D.* 8256, 7-5-89.]

[Reg. § 1.132-4]

§ 1.132-4. Line of business limitation.—(a) *In general*—(1) *Applicability*—(i) *General rule*. A no-additional-cost service or a qualified employee discount provided to an employee is only available with respect to property or services that are offered for sale to customers in the ordinary course of the same line of business in which the employee receiving the property or service performs substantial services. Thus, an employee who does not perform substantial services in a particular line of business of the employer may not exclude from income under section 132(a)(1) or (a)(2) the value

of services or employee discounts received on property or services in that line of business. For rules that relax the line of business requirement, see paragraphs (b) through (g) of this section.

(ii) *Property and services sold to employees rather than customers*. Because the property or services must be offered for sale to customers in the ordinary course of the same line of business in which the employee performs substantial services, the line of business limitation is not satisfied if the employer's products or services are sold primarily to employees of the employer, rather than to customers. Thus, for example, an employer in the banking line of business is not considered in the variety store line of business if the employer establishes an employee store that offers variety store items for sale to the employer's employees. See § 1.132-7 for rules relating to employer-operated eating facilities, and see § 1.132-1(e) for rules relating to employer-operated on-premises athletic facilities.

(iii) *Performance of substantial services in more than one line of business*. An employee who performs services in more than one of the employer's lines of business may only exclude no-additional-cost services and qualified employee discounts in the lines of business in which the employee performs substantial services.

(iv) *Performance of services that directly benefit more than one line of business*—(A) *In general*. An employee who performs substantial services that directly benefit more than one line of business of an employer is treated as performing substantial services in all such lines of business. For example, an employee who maintains accounting records for an employer's three lines of business may receive qualified employee discounts in all three lines of business. Similarly, if an employee of a minor line of business of an employer that is significantly interrelated with a major line of business of the employer performs substantial services that directly benefit both the major and the minor lines of business, the employee is treated as performing substantial services for both the major and the minor lines of business.

(B) *Examples*. The rules provided in this paragraph (a)(1)(iv) are illustrated by the following examples:

Example (1). Assume that employees of units of an employer provide repair or financing services, or sell by catalog, with respect to retail merchandise sold by the employer. Such employees may be considered to perform substantial ser-

Reg. § 1.132-4(a)(1)

vices for the retail merchandise line of business under paragraph (a)(1)(iv)(A) of this section.

Example (2). Assume that an employer operates a hospital and a laundry service. Assume further that some of the gross receipts of the laundry service line of business are from laundry services sold to customers other than the hospital employer. Only the employees of the laundry service who perform substantial services which directly benefit the hospital line of business (through the provision of laundry services to the hospital) will be treated as performing substantial services for the hospital line of business. Other employees of the laundry service line of business will not be treated as employees of the hospital line of business.

Example (3). Assume the same facts as in example (2), except that the employer also operates a chain of dry cleaning stores. Employees who perform substantial services which directly benefit the dry cleaning stores but who do not perform substantial services that directly benefit the hospital line of business will not be treated as performing substantial services for the hospital line of business.

(2) *Definition*—(i) *In general.* An employer's line of business is determined by reference to the Enterprise Standard Industrial Classification Manual (ESIC Manual) prepared by the Statistical Policy Division of the U.S. Office of Management and Budget. An employer is considered to have more than one line of business if the employer offers for sale to customers property or services in more than one two-digit code classification referred to in the ESIC Manual.

(ii) *Examples.* Examples of two-digit classifications are general retail merchandise stores; hotels and other lodging places; auto repair, services, and garages; and food stores.

(3) *Aggregation of two-digit classifications.* If, pursuant to paragraph (a)(2) of this section, an employer has more than one line of business, such lines of business will be treated as a single line of business where and to the extent that one or more of the following aggregation rules apply:

(i) If it is uncommon in the industry of the employer for any of the separate lines of business of the employer to be operated without the others, the separate lines of business are treated as one line of business.

(ii) If it is common for a substantial number of employees (other than those employees who work at the headquarters or main office of the employer) to perform substantial services for more than one line of business of the employer, so that determination of which employees perform substantial services for which line or lines of business would be difficult, then the separate lines of business of the employer in which such employees perform substantial services are treated as one line of business. For example, assume that an employer operates a delicatessen with an attached service counter at which food is sold for consumption on the premises. Assume further that most but not all employees work both at the delicatessen and at the service counter. Under the aggregation rule of this paragraph (a)(3)(ii), the delicatessen and the service counter are treated as one line of business.

(iii) If the retail operations of an employer that are located on the same premises are in separate lines of business but would be considered to be within one line of business under paragraph (a)(2) of this section if the merchandise offered for sale in such lines of business were offered for sale at a department store, then the operations are treated as one line of business. For example, assume that on the same premises an employer sells both women's apparel and jewelry. Because, if sold together at a department store, the operations would be part of the same line of business, the operations are treated as one line of business.

(b) *Grandfather rule for certain retail stores*—(1) *In general.* The line of business limitation may be relaxed under the special grandfather rule of this paragraph (b). Under this special grandfather rule, if—

(i) On October 5, 1983, at least 85 percent of the employees of one member of an affiliated group (as defined in section 1504 without regard to subsections (b)(2) and (b)(4) thereof) ("first member") were entitled to receive employee discounts at retail department stores operated by another member of the affiliated group ("second member"), and

(ii) More than 50 percent of the previous year's sales of the affiliated group are attributable to the operation of retail department stores,

then, for purposes of the exclusion from gross income of a qualified employee discount, the first member is treated as engaged in the same line of business as the second member (the operator of the retail department stores). Therefore, employees of the first member of the affiliated group may exclude from income qualified employee discounts received at the retail department stores operated by the second member. However, employees of the second member of the affiliated group may not under this paragraph (b)(1) exclude any discounts received on property or services offered for sale to customers by the first member of the affiliated group.

(2) *Taxable year of affiliated group.* If not all of the members of an affiliated group have the

same taxable year, the affiliated group must designate the 12-month period to be used in determining the "previous year's sales" (as referred to in the grandfather rule of this paragraph (b)). The 12-month period designated, however, must be used on a consistent basis.

(3) *Definition of "sales".* For purposes of this paragraph (b), the term "sales" means the gross receipts of an affiliated group, based upon the accounting methods used by its members.

(4) *Retired and disabled employees.* For purposes of this paragraph (b), an employee includes any individual who was, or whose spouse was, formerly employed by the first member of an affiliated group and who separated from service with the member by reason of retirement or disability if the second member of the group provided employee discounts to that individual on October 5, 1983.

(5) *Increase of employee discount.* If, after October 5, 1983, the employee discount described in this paragraph (b) is increased, the grandfather rule of this paragraph (b) does not apply to the amount of the increase. For example, if on January 1, 1989, the employee discount is increased from ten percent to 15 percent, the grandfather rule will not apply to the additional five percent discount.

(c) *Grandfather rule for telephone service provided to predivestiture retirees.* All entities subject to the modified final judgment (as defined in section 559(c)(5) of the Tax Reform Act of 1984) shall be treated as a single employer engaged in the same line of business for purposes of determining whether telephone service provided to certain employees is a no-additional-cost service. The preceding sentence applies only in the case of an employee who by reason of retirement or disability separated before January 1, 1984, from the service of an entity subject to the modified final judgment. This paragraph (c) only applies to services provided to such employees as of January 1, 1984. For a special no-additional-cost service rule relating to such employees and such services, see § 1.132-2(a)(6).

(d) *Special rule for certain affiliates of commercial airlines*—(1) *General rule.* If a qualified affiliate is a member of an airline affiliated group and employees of the qualified affiliate who are directly engaged in providing airline-related services are entitled to no-additional-cost service with respect to air transportation provided by such other member, then, for purposes of applying § 1.132-2 (relating to no-additional-cost services with respect to such air transportation), such qualified affiliate shall be treated as engaged in the same line of business as such other member.

(2) *"Airline affiliated group" defined.* An "airline affiliated group" is an affiliated group (as defined in section 1504(a)) one of whose members operates a commercial airline that provides air transportation to customers on a per-seat basis.

(3) *"Qualified affiliate" defined.* A "qualified affiliate" is any corporation that is predominantly engaged in providing airline-related services. The term "airline-related services" means any of the following services provided in connection with air transportation:

    (i) Catering,

    (ii) Baggage handling,

    (iii) Ticketing and reservations,

    (iv) Flight planning and weather analysis, and

    (v) Restaurants and gift shops located at an airport.

(e) *Grandfather rule for affiliated groups operating airlines.* The line of business limitation may be relaxed under the special grandfather rule of this paragraph (e). Under this special grandfather rule, if, as of September 12, 1984—

    (1) An individual—

        (i) Was an employee (within the meaning of § 1.132-1(b)) of one member of an affiliated group (as defined in section 1504(a)) ("first corporation"), and

        (ii) Was eligible for no-additional-cost services in the form of air transportation provided by another member of such affiliated group ("second corporation"),

    (2) At least 50 percent of the individuals performing services for the first corporation were, or had been employees of, or had previously performed services for, the second corporation, and

    (3) The primary business of the affiliated group was air transportation of passengers,

then, for purposes of applying sections 132(a)(1) and (2), with respect to no-additional-cost services and qualified employee discounts provided after December 31, 1984, for that individual by the second corporation, the first corporation is treated as engaged in the same air transportation line of business as the second corporation. For purposes of the preceding sentence, an employee of the second corporation who is performing services for the first corporation is also treated as an employee of the first corporation.

(f) *Special rule for qualified air transportation organizations.* A qualified air transportation organization is treated as engaged in the line of business of providing air transportation with respect to any individual who performs services for the organization if those services are performed

Reg. § 1.132-4(b)(3)

primarily for persons engaged in providing air transportation, and are of a kind which (if performed on September 12, 1984) would qualify the individual for no-additional-cost services in the form of air transportation. The term "qualified air transportation organization" means any organization—

(1) If such organization (or a predecessor) was in existence on September 12, 1984,

(2) If such organization is—

(i) A tax-exempt organization under section 501(c)(6) whose membership is limited to entities engaged in the transportation by air of individuals or property for compensation or hire, or

(ii) Is a corporation all the stock of which is owned entirely by entities described in paragraph (f)(2)(i) of this section, and

(3) If such organization is operated in furtherance of the activities of its members or owners.

(g) *Relaxation of line of business requirement.* The line of business requirement may be relaxed under an elective grandfather rule provided in section 4977. For rules relating to the section 4977 election, see § 54.4977-1T.

(h) *Line of business requirement does not expand benefits eligible for exclusion.* The line of business requirement limits the benefits eligible for the no-additional-cost service and qualified employee discount exclusions to property or services provided by an employer to its customers in the ordinary course of the line of business of the employer in which the employee performs substantial services. The requirement is intended to ensure that employers do not offer, on a tax-free or reduced basis, property or services to employees that are not offered to the employer's customers, even if the property or services offered to the customers and the employees are within the same line of business (as defined in this section). [Reg. § 1.132-4.]

☐ [*T.D.* 8256, 7-5-89.]

→ *Caution: Temporary Reg § 1.132-4T applies to the tax treatment of fringe benefits for 1985—1988. See Reg. § § 1.132-0—1.132-8 for post-1988 rules.*←

[Reg. § 1.132-4T]

§ **1.132-4T. Line of business limitation— 1985 through 1988 (Temporary).**—(a) *In general*—(1) *Applicability*—(i) *General rule.* A no-additional-cost service or qualified employee discount provided to an employee must be for property or services that are offered for sale to customers in the ordinary course of the same line of business in which the employee receiving the property or service performs substantial services. Thus, an employee who does not perform substantial services in a particular line of business of the employer may not exclude the value of services or employee discounts received on property or services in that line of business.

(ii) *Property and services sold to employees rather than customers.* Since the property or services must be offered for sale to customers in the ordinary course of the same line of business in which the employee performs substantial services, the line of business limitation is not satisfied if the employer's products or services are sold to employees of the employer, rather than to customers. Thus, for example, an employer in the banking line of business is not considered in the variety store line of business if the employer establishes an employee store that offers variety store items for sale to the employer's employees.

(iii) *Performance of substantial services in more than one line of business.* An employee who performs services in more than one of the employer's lines of business may only exclude no-additional-cost services and qualified employee discounts in the lines of business in which the employee performs substantial services.

(iv) *Performance of services that directly benefit more than one line of business*—(A) *In general.* An employee who performs substantial services that directly benefit more than one line of business of an employer is treated as performing substantial services in all such lines of business. For example, an employee who maintains accounting records for an employer's three lines of business may receive qualified employee discounts in all three lines of business.

(B) *Significantly interrelated minor line of business.* The employees of a minor line of business of an employer that is significantly interrelated with a major line of business of the employer who perform substantial services that directly benefit both the major and the minor lines of business are treated as employees of both the major and the minor lines of business. Employees of the minor line of business who do not perform substantial services which directly benefit the major line of business are not treated as employees of the major line of business. A minor line of business is significantly interrelated with a major line of business when, for example, the activity of the minor line of business is directly related to but is a minor part of the major line of business (such as laundry services provided at a hospital).

Reg. § 1.132-4T(a)(1)

→ *Caution: Temporary Reg. § 1.132-4T applies to the tax treatment of fringe benefits for 1985—1988. See Reg. § § 1.132-0—1.132-8 for post-1988 rules.*←

(C) *Examples.* The rules provided in this paragraph are illustrated in the following examples:

Example (1). Assume that employees of units of an employer provide repair or financing services, or sell by catalog, with respect to retail merchandise sold by the employer. Such employees may be considered as employees of the retail merchandise line of business under this paragraph (a)(1)(iv).

Example (2). Assume that an employer operates a hospital and a laundry service. Assume further that some of the gross receipts of the laundry service line of business are from laundry services sold to customers other than the hospital employer. Only the employees of the laundry service who perform substantial services which directly benefit the hospital line of business (through the provision of laundry services to the hospital) will be treated as employees of the hospital line of business. Other employees of the laundry service line of business will not be treated as employees of the hospital line of business.

Example (3). Assume the same facts as in example (2), except that the minor line of business also operates a chain of dry cleaning stores. Employees who perform substantial services which directly benefit the dry cleaning stores but who do not perform substantial services that directly benefit the hospital line of business will not be treated as employees of the hospital line of business.

(2) *Definition*—(i) *In general.* An employer's line of business is determined by reference to the Enterprise Standard Industrial Classification Manual (ESIC Manual) prepared by the Statistical Policy Division of the U.S. Office of Management and Budget. An employer is considered to have more than one line of business if the employer offers for sale to customers property or services in more than one two-digit code classification referred to in the ESIC Manual.

(ii) *Examples.* Examples of two-digit classifications are general retail merchandise stores; hotels and other lodging places; auto repair, services, and garages; and food stores.

(3) *Aggregation of two-digit classifications.* If, pursuant to paragraph (a)(2) of this section, an employer has more than one line of business, such lines of business will be treated as a single line of business where and to the extent that one or more of the following aggregation rules apply:

(i) If it is uncommon in the industry of the employer for any of the separate lines of business

of the employer to be operated without the others, the separate lines of business are treated as one line of business.

(ii) If it is common for a substantial number of employees (other than those employees who work at the headquarters or main office of the employer) to perform substantial services for more than one line of business of the employer, so that determination of which employees perform substantial services for which line of business would be difficult, then the separate lines of business of the employer in which such employees perform substantial services are treated as one line of business. For example, assume that an employer operates a delicatessen with an attached service counter at which food is sold for consumption on the premises. Assume further that most but not all employees work both at the delicatessen and at the service counter. The delicatessen and the service counter are treated as one line of business.

(iii) If the retail operations of an employer that are located on the same premises are in separate lines of business but would be considered to be within one line of business under paragraph (a)(2) of this section if the merchandise offered for sale in such lines of business were offered for sale at a department store, then the operations are treated as one line of business. For example, assume that on the same premises an employer sells both women's apparel and jewelry. Since, if sold together at a department store, the operations would be part of the same line of business, the operations are treated as one line of business.

(b) *Grandfather rule for certain retail stores*—(1) *In general.* The line of business limitation may be relaxed under a special grandfather rule. If—

(i) on October 5, 1983, 85 percent of the employees of one member of an affiliated group (as defined in section 1504 without regard to subsections (b)(2) and (b)(4) thereof) were entitled to employee discounts at retail department stores operated by another member of the affiliated group, and

(ii) more than 50 percent of the current year's sales of the affiliated group are attributable to the operation of retail department stores,

then for purposes of the exclusion from gross income of a qualified employee discount, the first member is treated as engaged in the same line of business as the second member (the operator of the retail department stores). Therefore, employees of the first member of the affiliated group may exclude qualified employee discounts received at

Reg. § 1.132-4T(a)(2)

→ *Caution: Temporary Reg. § 1.132-4T applies to the tax treatment of fringe benefits for 1985—1988. See Reg. §§ 1.132-0—1.132-8 for post-1988 rules.*←

the retail department stores operated by the second member. However, employees of the second member of the affiliated group may not exclude any discounts received on property or services offered for sale to customers by the first member of the affiliated group.

(2) *Taxable year of affiliated group.* If all of the members do not have the same taxable year, the affiliated group must designate the 12-month period to be used in determining the "current year's sales" (as referred to in this paragraph (b)). The 12-month period designated, however, must be used consistently.

(3) *Definition of "sales".* For purposes of this paragraph (b), the term "sales" means the gross receipts of the affiliated group, based upon the accounting methods used by its members.

(4) *Retired and disabled employees.* For purposes of this paragraph (b), an employee includes any individual who was, or whose spouse was, formerly employed by the first member of the affiliated group and who separated from service with the member by reason of retirement or disability if the second member of the group provided employee discounts to such individuals on October 5, 1983.

(5) *Increase of employee discount.* If, after October 5, 1983, the employee discount described in this paragraph (b) is increased, the grandfather rule of this paragraph (b) does not apply to the amount of the increase. For example, if on January 1, 1985, the employee discount is increased from ten percent to 15 percent, the grandfather rule will not apply to the additional five percent discount.

(c) *Relaxation of line of business requirement.* The line of business requirement may be relaxed under an elective grandfather rule provided in section 4977. For rules relating to the section 4977 election, see § 54.4977-1. [Temporary Reg. § 1.132-4T.]

☐ [*T.D. 8063, 12-18-85. Amended by T.D. 8256, 7-5-89.*]

[Reg. § 1.132-5]

§ 1.132-5. Working condition fringes.—(a) *In general*—(1) *Definition.* Gross income does not include the value of a working condition fringe. A "working condition fringe" is any property or service provided to an employee of an employer to the extent that, if the employee paid for the property or service, the amount paid would be allowable as a deduction under section 162 or 167.

(i) A service or property offered by an employer in connection with a flexible spending account is not excludable from gross income as a working condition fringe. For purposes of the preceding sentence, a flexible spending account is an agreement (whether or not written) entered into between an employer and an employee that makes available to the employee over a time period a certain level of unspecified non-cash benefits with a pre-determined cash value.

(ii) If, under section 274 or any other section, certain substantiation requirements must be met in order for a deduction under section 162 or 167 to be allowable, then those substantiation requirements apply when determining whether a property or service is excludable as a working condition fringe.

(iii) An amount that would be deductible by the employee under a section other than section 162 or 167, such as section 212, is not a working condition fringe.

(iv) A physical examination program provided by the employer is not excludable as a working condition fringe even if the value of such program might be deductible to the employee under section 213. The previous sentence applies without regard to whether the employer makes the program mandatory to some or all employees.

(v) A cash payment made by an employer to an employee will not qualify as a working condition fringe unless the employer requires the employee to—

(A) Use the payment for expenses in connection with a specific or pre-arranged activity or undertaking for which a deduction is allowable under section 162 or 167,

(B) Verify that the payment is actually used for such expenses, and

(C) Return to the employer any part of the payment not so used.

(vi) The limitation of section 67(a) (relating to the two-percent floor on miscellaneous itemized deductions) is not considered when determining the amount of a working condition fringe. For example, assume that an employer provides a $1,000 cash advance to Employee A and that the conditions of paragraph (a)(1)(v) of this section are not satisfied. Even to the extent A uses the allowance for expenses for which a deduction is allowable under section 162 or 167, because such cash payment is not a working condition fringe, section 67(a) applies. The $1,000 payment is includible in A's gross income and subject to income and employment tax withholding. If, however, the conditions of paragraph (a)(1)(v) of this section are satisfied with respect to the payment, then the amount of A's working condition fringe is determined without regard to section 67(a). The $1,000 payment is excludible from A's gross income and not subject to income and employment tax reporting and withholding.

(2) *Trade or business of the employee*—(i) *General.* If the hypothetical payment for a property or service would be allowable as a deduction with respect to a trade or business of an employee other than the employee's trade or business of being an employee of the employer, it cannot be taken into account for purposes of determining the amount, if any, of the working condition fringe.

(ii) *Examples.* The rule of paragraph (a)(2)(i) of this section may be illustrated by the following examples:

Example (1). Assume that, unrelated to company X's trade or business and unrelated to employee A's trade or business of being an employee of company X, A is a member of the board of directors of company Y. Assume further that company X provides A with air transportation to a company Y board of director's meeting. A may not exclude from gross income the value of the air transportation to the meeting as a working condition fringe. A may, however, deduct such amount under section 162 if the section 162 requirements are satisfied. The result would be the same whether the air transportation was provided in the form of a flight on a commercial airline or a seat on a company X airplane.

Example (2). Assume the same facts as in example (1) except that A serves on the board of directors of company Z and company Z regularly purchases a significant amount of goods and services from company X. Because of the relationship between Company Z and A's employer, A's membership on Company Z's board of directors is related to A's trade or business of being an employee of Company X. Thus, A may exclude from gross income the value of air transportation to board meetings as a working condition fringe.

Example (3). Assume the same facts as in example (1) except that A serves on the board of directors of a charitable organization. Assume further that the service by A on the charity's board is substantially related to company X's trade or business. In this case, A may exclude from gross income the value of air transportation to board meetings as a working condition fringe.

Example (4). Assume the same facts as in example (3) except that company X also provides A with the use of a company X conference room which A uses for monthly meetings relating to the charitable organization. Also assume that A uses company X's copy machine and word processor each month in connection with functions of the charitable organization. Because of the substantial business benefit that company X derives from A's service on the board of the charity, A may exclude as a working condition fringe the value of the use of company X property in connection with the charitable organization.

(b) *Vehicle allocation rules*—(1) *In general*—(i) *General rule.* In general, with respect to an employer-provided vehicle, the amount excludable as a working condition fringe is the amount that would be allowable as a deduction under section 162 or 167 if the employee paid for the availability of the vehicle. For example, assume that the value of the availability of an employer-provided vehicle for a full year is $2,000, without regard to any working condition fringe (i.e., assuming all personal use). Assume further that the employee drives the vehicle 6,000 miles for his employer's business and 2,000 miles for reasons other than the employer's business. In this situation, the value of the working condition fringe is $2,000 multiplied by a fraction, the numerator of which is the business-use mileage (6,000 miles) and the denominator of which is the total mileage (8,000 miles). Thus, the value of the working condition fringe is $1,500. The total amount includible in the employee's gross income on account of the availability of the vehicle is $500 ($2,000 − $1,500). For purposes of this section, the term "vehicle" has the meaning given the term in § 1.61-21(e)(2). Generally, when determining the amount of an employee's working condition fringe, miles accumulated on the vehicle by all employees of the employer during the period in which the vehicle is available to the employee are considered. For example, assume that during the year in which the vehicle is available to the employee in the above example, other employees accumulate 2,000 additional miles on the vehicle (while the employee is not in the automobile). In this case, the value of the working condition fringe is $2,000 multiplied by a fraction, the numerator of which is the business-use mileage by the employee (including all mileage (business and personal) accumulated by other employees) (8,000 miles) and the denominator of which is the total mileage (including all mileage accumulated by other employees) (10,000 miles). Thus, the value of the working condition fringe is $1,600; the total amount includible in the employee's gross income on account of the availability of the vehicle is $400 ($2,000 − $1,600). If, however, substantially all of the use of the automobile by other employees in the employer's business is limited to a certain period, such as the last three months of

Reg. § 1.132-5(a)(2)

the year, the miles driven by the other employees during that period would not be considered when determining the employee's working condition fringe exclusion. Similarly, miles driven by other employees are not considered if the pattern of use of the employer-provided automobiles is designed to reduce Federal taxes. For example, assume that an employer provides employees A and B each with the availability of an employer-provided automobile and that A uses the automobile assigned to him 80 percent for the employer's business and that B uses the automobile assigned to him 30 percent for the employer's business. If A and B alternate the use of their assigned automobiles each week in such a way as to achieve a reduction in federal taxes, then the employer may count only miles placed on the automobile by the employee to whom the automobile is assigned when determining each employee's working condition fringe.

(ii) *Use by an individual other than the employee.* For purposes of this section, if the availability of a vehicle to an individual would be taxed to an employee, use of the vehicle by the individual is included in references to use by the employee.

(iii) *Provision of an expensive vehicle for personal use.* If an employer provides an employee with a vehicle that an employee may use in part for personal purposes, there is no working condition fringe exclusion with respect to the personal miles driven by the employee; if the employee paid for the availability of the vehicle, he would not be entitled to deduct under section 162 or 167 any part of the payment attributable to personal miles. The amount of the inclusion is not affected by the fact that the employee would have chosen the availability of a less expensive vehicle. Moreover, the result is the same even though the decision to provide an expensive rather than an inexpensive vehicle is made by the employer for bona fide noncompensatory business reasons.

(iv) *Total value inclusion.* In lieu of excluding the value of a working condition fringe with respect to an automobile, an employer using the automobile lease valuation rule of § 1.61-21(d) may include in an employee's gross income the entire Annual Lease Value of the automobile. Any deduction allowable to the employee under section 162 or 167 with respect to the automobile may be taken on the employee's income tax return. The total inclusion rule of this paragraph (b)(1)(iv) is not available if the employer is valuing the use or availability of a vehicle under general valuation principles or a special valuation rule other than the automobile lease valuation rule. See

§§ 1.162-25 and 1.162-25T for rules relating to the employee's deduction.

(v) *Shared usage.* In calculating the working condition fringe benefit exclusion with respect to a vehicle provided for use by more than one employee, an employer shall compute the working condition fringe in a manner consistent with the allocation of the value of the vehicle under § 1.61-21(c)(2)(ii)(B).

(2) *Use of different employer-provided vehicles.* The working condition fringe exclusion must be applied on a vehicle-by-vehicle basis. For example, assume that automobile Y is available to employee D for 3 days in January and for 5 days in March, and automobile Z is available to D for a week in July. Assume further that the Daily Lease Value, as defined in § 1.61-21(d)(4)(ii), of each automobile is $50. For the eight days of availability of Y in January and March, D uses Y 90 percent for business (by mileage). During July, D uses Z 60 percent for business (by mileage). The value of the working condition fringe is determined separately for each automobile. Therefore, the working condition fringe for Y is $360 ($400 × .90) leaving an income inclusion of $40. The working condition fringe for Z is $210 ($350 × .60), leaving an income inclusion of $140. If the value of the availability of an automobile is determined under the Annual Lease Value rule for one period and Daily Lease Value rule for a second period (see § 1.61-21(d)), the working condition fringe exclusion must be calculated separately for the two periods.

(3) *Provision of a vehicle and chauffeur services—*(i) *General rule.* In general, with respect to the value of chauffeur services provided by an employer, the amount excludable as a working condition fringe is the amount that would be allowable as a deduction under section 162 or 167 if the employee paid for the chauffeur services. The working condition fringe with respect to a chauffeur is determined separately from the working condition fringe with respect to the vehicle. An employee may exclude from gross income the excess of the value of the chauffeur services over the value of the chauffeur services for personal purposes (such as commuting) as determined under § 1.61-21(b)(5). See § 1.61-21(b)(5) for additional rules and examples concerning the valuation of chauffeur services. See § 1.132-5(m)(5) for rules relating to an exclusion from gross income for the value of bodyguard/chauffeur services. When determining whether miles placed on the vehicle are for the employer's business, miles placed on the vehicle by a chauffeur between the chauffeur's residence and the place at which the chauffeur picks up (or drops off) the employee are with

respect to the employee (but not the chauffeur) considered to be miles placed on the vehicle for the employer's business and thus eligible for the working condition fringe exclusion. Thus, because miles placed on the vehicle by a chauffeur between the chauffeur's residence and the place at which the chauffeur picks up (or drops off) the employee are not considered business miles with respect to the chauffeur, the value of the availability of the vehicle for commuting is includible in the gross income of the chauffeur. For general and special rules concerning the valuation of the use of employer-provided vehicles, see paragraphs (b) through (f) of § 1.61-21.

(ii) *Examples.* The rules of paragraph (b)(3)(i) of this section are illustrated by the following examples:

Example (1). Assume that an employer makes available to an employee an automobile and a chauffeur. Assume further that the value of the chauffeur services determined in accordance with § 1.61-21 is $30,000 and that the chauffeur spends 30 percent of each workday driving the employee for personal purposes. There may be excluded from the employee's income 70 percent of $30,000, or $21,000, leaving an income inclusion with respect to the chauffeur services of $9,000.

Example (2). Assume that the value of the availability of an employer-provided vehicle for a year is $4,850 and that the value of employer-provided chauffeur services with respect to the vehicle for the year is $20,000. Assume further that 40 percent of the miles placed on the vehicle are for the employer's business and that 60 percent are for other purposes. In addition, assume that the chauffeur spends 25 percent of each workday driving the employee for personal purposes (i.e., 2 hours). The value of the chauffeur services includible in the employee's income is 25 percent of $20,000, or $5,000. The excess of $20,000 over $5,000 or $15,000 is excluded from the employee's income as a working condition fringe. The amount excludable as a working condition fringe with respect to the vehicle is 40 percent of $4,850, or $1,940 and the amount includible is $4,850 − $1,940, or $2,910.

(c) *Applicability of substantiation requirements of sections 162 and 274 (d)*—(1) *In general.* The value of property or services provided to an employee may not be excluded from the employee's gross income as a working condition fringe, by either the employer or the employee, unless the applicable substantiation requirements of either section 274 (d) or section 162 (whichever is applicable) and the regulations thereunder are satisfied. The substantiation requirements of section

274(d) apply to an employee even if the requirements of section 274 do not apply to the employee's employer for deduction purposes (such as when the employer is a tax-exempt organization or a governmental unit).

(2) *Section 274(d) requirements.* The substantiation requirements of section 274(d) are satisfied by "adequate records or sufficient evidence corroborating the [employee's] own statement". Therefore, such records or evidence provided by the employee, and relied upon by the employer to the extent permitted by the regulations promulgated under section 274(d), will be sufficient to substantiate a working condition fringe exclusion.

(d) *Safe harbor substantiation rules*—(1) *In general.* Section 1.274-6T provides that the substantiation requirements of section 274(d) and the regulations thereunder may be satisfied, in certain circumstances, by using one or more of the safe harbor rules prescribed in § 1.274-6T. If the employer uses one of the safe harbor rules prescribed in § 1.274-6T during a period with respect to a vehicle (as defined in § 1.61-21(e)(2)), that rule must be used by the employer to substantiate a working condition fringe exclusion with respect to that vehicle during the period. An employer that is exempt from Federal income tax may still use one of the safe harbor rules (if the requirements of that section are otherwise met during a period) to substantiate a working condition fringe exclusion with respect to a vehicle during the period. If the employer uses one of the methods prescribed in § 1.274-6T during a period with respect to an employer-provided vehicle, that method may be used by an employee to substantiate a working condition fringe exclusion with respect to the same vehicle during the period, as long as the employee includes in gross income the amount allocated to the employee pursuant to § 1.274-6T and this section. (See § 1.61-21(c)(2) for other rules concerning when an employee must include in income the amount determined by the employer.) If, however, the employer uses the safe harbor rule prescribed in § 1.274-6T(a)(2) or (3) and the employee without the employer's knowledge uses the vehicle for purposes other than de minimis personal use (in the case of the rule prescribed in § 1.274-6T(a)(2)), or for purposes other than de minimis personal use and commuting (in the case of the rule prescribed in § 1.274-6T(a)(3)), then the employee must include an additional amount in income for the unauthorized use of the vehicle.

(2) *Period for use of safe harbor rules.* The rules prescribed in this paragraph (d) assume that the safe harbor rules prescribed in § 1.274-6T are used for a one-year period. Accordingly, references

Reg. § 1.132-5(c)(1)

to the value of the availability of a vehicle, amounts excluded as a working condition fringe, etc., are based on a one-year period. If the safe harbor rules prescribed in § 1.274-6T are used for a period of less than a year, the amounts referred to in the previous sentence must be adjusted accordingly. For purposes of this section, the term "personal use" has the same meaning as prescribed in § 1.274-6T(e)(5).

(e) *Safe harbor substantiation rule for vehicles not used for personal purposes* For a vehicle described in § 1.274-6T(a)(2) (relating to certain vehicles not used for personal purposes), the working condition fringe exclusion is equal to the value of the availability of the vehicle if the employer uses the method prescribed in § 1.274-5T(a)(2).

(f) *Safe harbor substantiation rule for vehicles not available to employees for personal use other than commuting.* For a vehicle described in § 1.274-6T(a)(3) (relating to certain vehicles not used for personal purposes other than commuting), the working condition fringe exclusion is equal to the value of the availability of the vehicle for purposes other than commuting if the employer uses the method prescribed in § 1.274-6T(a)(3). This rule applies only if the special rule for valuing commuting use, as prescribed in § 1.61-21(f), is used and the amount determined under the special rule is either included in the employee's income or reimbursed by the employee.

(g) *Safe harbor substantiation rule for vehicles used in connection with the business of farming that are available to employees for personal use—* (1) *In general.* For a vehicle described in § 1.274-6T(b) (relating to certain vehicles used in connection with the business of farming), the working condition fringe exclusion is calculated by multiplying the value of the availability of the vehicle by 75 percent.

(2) *Vehicles available to more than one individual.* If the vehicle is available to more than one individual, the employer must allocate the gross income inclusion attributable to the vehicle (25 percent of the value of the availability of the vehicle) among the employees (and other individuals whose use would not be attributed to an employee) to whom the vehicle was available. This allocation must be done in a reasonable manner to reflect the personal use of the vehicle by the individuals. An amount that would be allocated to a sole proprietor reduces the amounts that may be allocated to employees but is otherwise to be disregarded for purposes of this paragraph (g). For purposes of this paragraph (g), the value of the availability of a vehicle may be calculated as if the vehicle were available to only one employee

continuously and without regard to any working condition fringe exclusion.

(3) *Examples.* The following examples illustrate a reasonable allocation of gross income with respect to an employer-provided vehicle between two employees:

Example (1). Assume that two farm employees share the use of a vehicle that for a calendar year is regularly used directly in connection with the business of farming and qualifies for use of the rule in § 1.274-6T(b). Employee A uses the vehicle in the morning directly in connection with the business of farming and employee B uses the vehicle in the afternoon directly in connection with the business of farming. Assume further that employee B takes the vehicle home in the evenings and on weekends. The employer should allocate all the income attributable to the availability of the vehicle to employee B.

Example (2). Assume that for a calendar year, farm employees C and D share the use of a vehicle that is regularly used directly in connection with the business of farming and qualifies for use of the rule in § 1.274-6T(b). Assume further that the employees alternate taking the vehicle home in the evening and alternate the availability of the vehicle for personal purposes on weekends. The employer should allocate the income attributable to the availability of the vehicle for personal use (25 percent of the value of the availability of the vehicle) equally between the two employees.

Example (3). Assume the same facts as in example (2) except that C is the sole proprietor of the farm. Based on these facts, C should allocate the same amount of income to D as was allocated to D in example (2). No other income attributable to the availability of the vehicle for personal use should be allocated.

(h) *Qualified nonpersonal use vehicles—*(1) *In general.* Except as provided in paragraph (h)(2) of this section, 100 percent of the value of the use of a qualified nonpersonal use vehicle (as described in § 1.274-5T(k)) is excluded from gross income as a working condition fringe, provided that, in the case of a vehicle described in paragraph (k)(3) through (8) of that section, the use of the vehicle conforms to the requirements of that paragraph.

(2) *Shared usage of qualified nonpersonal use vehicles.* In general, a working condition fringe under paragraph (h) of this section is available to the driver and all passengers of a qualified nonpersonal use vehicle. However, a working condition fringe under this paragraph (h) is available only with respect to the driver and not with respect to any passengers of a qualified nonpersonal use vehicle described in § 1.274-5T(k)(2)(ii)(L) or (P). In this case, the

Reg. § 1.132-5(h)(2)

passengers must comply with provisions of this section (excluding this paragraph (h)) to determine the applicability of the working condition fringe exclusion. For example, if an employer provides a passenger bus with a capacity of 25 passengers to its employees for purposes of transporting employees to and/or from work, the driver of the bus may exclude from gross income as a working condition fringe 100 percent of the value of the use of the vehicle. The value of the commuting use of the employer-provided bus by the employee-passengers is includible in their gross incomes. See § 1.61-21(f) for a special rule to value the commuting-only use of employer-provided vehicles.

(i) [Reserved.]

(j) *Application of section 280F.* In determining the amount, if any, of an employee's working condition fringe, section 280F and the regulations thereunder do not apply. For example, assume that an employee has available for a calendar year an employer-provided automobile with a fair market value of $28,000. Assume further that the special rule provided in § 1.61-21(d) is used yielding an Annual Lease Value, as defined in § 1.61-21(d), of $7,750, and that all of the employee's use of the automobile is for the employer's business. The employee would be entitled to exclude as a working condition fringe the entire Annual Lease Value, despite the fact that if the employee paid for the availability of the automobile, an income inclusion would be required under § 1.280F-6(d)(1). This paragraph (j) does not affect the applicability of section 280F to the employer with respect to such employer-provided automobile, nor does it affect the applicability of section 274 to either the employer or the employee. For rules concerning substantiation of an employee's working condition fringe, see paragraph (c) of this section.

(k) *Aircraft allocation rule.* In general, with respect to a flight on an employer-provided aircraft, the amount excludable as a working condition fringe is the amount that would be allowable as a deduction under section 162 or 167 if the employee paid for the flight on the aircraft. For example, if employee P and P's spouse fly on P's employer's airplane primarily for business reasons of P's employer so that P could deduct the expenses relating to the trip to the extent of P's payments, the value of the flights is excludable from gross income as a working condition fringe. However, if P's children accompany P on the trip primarily for personal reasons, the value of the flights by P's children are includible in P's gross income. See § 1.61-21(g) for special rules for valuing personal flights on employer-provided aircraft.

(l) [Reserved.]

(m) *Employer-provided transportation for security concerns—(1) In general.* The amount of a working condition fringe exclusion with respect to employer-provided transportation is the amount that would be allowable as a deduction under section 162 or 167 if the employee paid for the transportation. Generally, if an employee pays for transportation taken for primarily personal purposes, the employee may not deduct any part of the amount paid. Thus, the employee may not generally exclude the value of employer-provided transportation as a working condition fringe if such transportation is primarily personal. If, however, for bona fide business-oriented security concerns, the employee purchases transportation that provides him or her with additional security, the employee may generally deduct the excess of the amount actually paid for the transportation over the amount the employee would have paid for the same mode of transportation absent the bona fide business-oriented security concerns. This is the case whether or not the employee would have taken the same mode of transportation absent the bona fide business-oriented security concerns. With respect to a vehicle, the phrase "the same mode of transportation" means use of the same vehicle without the additional security aspects, such as bulletproof glass. With respect to air transportation, the phrase "the same mode of transportation" means comparable air transportation. These same rules apply to the determination of an employee's working condition fringe exclusion. For example, if an employer provides an employee with a vehicle for commuting and, because of bona fide business-oriented security concerns, the vehicle is specially designed for security, then the employee may exclude from gross income the value of the special security design as a working condition fringe. The employee may not exclude the value of the commuting from income as a working condition fringe because commuting is a nondeductible personal expense. However, if an independent security study meeting the requirements of paragraph (m)(2)(v) of this section has been performed with respect to a government employee, the government employee may exclude the value of the personal use (other than commuting) of the employer-provided vehicle that the security study determines to be reasonable and necessary for local transportation. Similarly, if an employee travels on a personal trip in an employer-provided aircraft for bona fide business-oriented security concerns, the employee may exclude the excess, if any, of the value of the flight over the amount the employee would have paid for the same mode of transportation, but for the bona fide business-

Reg. § 1.132-5(i)

oriented security concerns. Because personal travel is a nondeductible expense, the employee may not exclude the total value of the trip as a working condition fringe.

(2) *Demonstration of bona fide business-oriented security concerns*—(i) *In general.* For purposes of this paragraph (m), a bona fide business-oriented security concern exists only if the facts and circumstances establish a specific basis for concern regarding the safety of the employee. A generalized concern for an employee's safety is not a bona fide business-oriented security concern. Once a bona fide business-oriented security concern is determined to exist with respect to a particular employee, the employer must periodically evaluate the situation for purposes of determining whether the bona fide business-oriented security concern still exists. Example[s] of factors indicating a specific basis for concern regarding the safety of an employee are—

(A) A threat of death or kidnapping of, or serious bodily harm to, the employee or a similarly situated employee because of either employee's status as an employee of the employer; or

(B) A recent history of violent terrorist activity (such as bombings) in the geographic area in which the transportation is provided, unless that activity is focused on a group of individuals which does not include the employee (or a similarly situated employee of an employer), or occurs to a significant degree only in a location within the geographic area where the employee does not travel.

(ii) *Establishment of overall security program.* Notwithstanding anything in paragraph (m)(2)(i) of this section to the contrary, no bona fide business-oriented security concern will be deemed to exist unless the employee's employer establishes to the satisfaction of the Commissioner that an overall security program has been provided with respect to the employee involved. An overall security program is deemed to exist if the requirements of paragraph (m)(2)(iv) of this section are satisfied (relating to an independent security study).

(iii) *Overall security program*—(A) *Defined.* An overall security program is one in which security is provided to protect the employee on a 24-hour basis. The employee must be protected while at the employee's residence, while commuting to and from the employee's workplace, and while at the employee's workplace. In addition, the employee must be protected while traveling both at home and away from home, whether for business or personal purposes. An overall security program must include the provision of a bodyguard/chauffeur who is trained in evasive driving

techniques; an automobile specially equipped for security; guards, metal detectors, alarms, or similar methods of controlling access to the employee's workplace and residence; and, in appropriate cases, lights on the employer's aircraft for business and personal reasons.

(B) *Application.* There is no overall security program when, for example, security is provided at the employee's workplace but not at the employee's residence. In addition, the fact that an employer requires an employee to travel on the employer's aircraft, or in an employer-provided vehicle that contains special security features, does not alone constitute an overall security program. The preceding sentence applies regardless of the existence of a corporate or other resolution requiring the employee to travel in the employer's aircraft or vehicle for personal as well as business reasons.

(iv) *Effect of an independent security study.* An overall security program with respect to an employee is deemed to exist if the conditions of this paragraph (m)(2)(iv) are satisfied:

(A) A security study is performed with respect to the employer and the employee (or a similarly situated employee of the employer) by an independent security consultant;

(B) The security study is based on an objective assessment of all facts and circumstances;

(C) The recommendation of the security study is that an overall security program (as defined in paragraph (m)(2)(iii) of this section) is not necessary and the recommendation is reasonable under the circumstances; and

(D) The employer applies the specific security recommendations contained in the security study to the employee on a consistent basis.

The value of transportation-related security provided pursuant to a security study that meets the requirements of this paragraph (m)(2)(iv) may be excluded from income if the security study conclusions are reasonable and, but for the bona fide business-oriented security concerns, the employee would not have had such security. No exclusion from income applies to security provided by the employer that is not recommended in the security study. Security study conclusions may be reasonable even if, for example, it is recommended that security be limited to certain geographic areas, as in the case in which air travel security is provided only in certain foreign countries.

(v) *Independent security study with respect to government employees.* For purposes of establishing the existence of an overall security program under paragraph (m)(2)(ii) of this sec-

Reg. § 1.132-5(m)(2)

tion with respect to a particular government employee, a security study conducted by the government employer (including an agency or instrumentality thereof) will be treated as a security study pursuant to paragraph (m)(2)(iv) of this section if, in lieu of the conditions of paragraphs (m)(2)(iv)(A) through (D) of this section, the following conditions are satisfied:

(A) The security study is conducted by a person expressly designated by the government employer as having the responsibility and independent authority to determine both the need for employer-provided security and the appropriate protective services in response to that determination;

(B) The security study is conducted in accordance with written internal procedures that require an independent and objective assessment of the facts and circumstances, such as the nature of the threat to the employee, the appropriate security response to that threat, an estimate of the length of time protective services will be necessary, and the extent to which employer-provided transportation may be necessary during the period of protection;

(C) With respect to employer-provided transportation, the security study evaluates the extent to which personal use, including commuting, by the employee and the employee's spouse and dependents may be necessary during the period of protection and makes a recommendation as to what would be considered reasonable personal use during that period; and

(D) The employer applies the specific security recommendations contained in the study to the employee on a consistent basis.

(3) *Application of security rules to spouses and dependents*—(i) *In general.* If a bona fide business-oriented security concern exists with respect to an employee (because, for example, threats are made on the life of an employee), the bona fide business-oriented security concern is deemed to exist with respect to the employee's spouse and dependents to the extent provided in this paragraph (m)(3).

(ii) *Certain transportation.* If a working condition fringe exclusion is available under this paragraph (m) for transportation in a vehicle or aircraft provided for a bona fide business-oriented security concern with respect to an employee, the requirements of this paragraph (m) are deemed to be satisfied with respect to transportation in the same vehicle or aircraft provided at the same time to the employee's spouse and dependent children.

(iii) *Other.* Except as provided in paragraph (m)(3)(ii) of this section, a bona fide business oriented security concern is deemed to exist for the spouse and dependent children of the employer only if the requirements of paragraph (m)(2)(iii) or (iv) of this section are applied independently to such spouse and dependent children.

(iv) *Spouses and dependents of government employees.* The security rules of this paragraph (m)(3) apply to the spouse and dependents of a government employee. However, the value of local vehicle transportation provided to the government employee's spouse and dependents for personal purposes, other than commuting, during the period that a bona fide business-oriented security concern exists with respect to the government employee will not be included in the government employee's gross income if the personal use is determined to be reasonable and necessary by the security study described in paragraph (m)(2)(v) of this section.

(4) *Working condition safe harbor for travel on employer-provided aircraft.* Under the safe harbor rule of this paragraph (m)(4), if, for a bona fide business-oriented security concern, the employer requires that an employee travel on an employer-provided aircraft for a personal trip, the employer and the employee may exclude from the employee's gross income, as a working condition fringe, the excess value of the aircraft trip over the safe harbor airfare without having to show what method of transportation the employee would have flown but for the bona fide business-oriented security concern. For purposes of the safe harbor rule of this paragraph (m)(4), the value of the safe harbor airfare is determined under the non-commercial flight valuation rule of § 1.61-21(g) (regardless of whether the employer or employee elects to use such valuation rule) by multiplying an aircraft multiple of 200-percent by the applicable cents-per-mile rates and the number of miles in the flight and then adding the applicable terminal charge. The value of the safe harbor airfare determined under this paragraph (m)(4) must be included in the employee's income (to the extent not reimbursed by the employee) regardless of whether the employee or the employer uses the special valuation rule of § 1.61-21(g). The excess of the value of the aircraft trip over this amount may be excluded from gross income as a working condition fringe. If, for a bona fide business-oriented security concern, the employer requires that an employee's spouse and dependents travel on an employer-provided aircraft for a personal trip, the special rule of this paragraph (m)(4) is available to exclude the excess value of the aircraft trips over the safe harbor airfares.

Reg. § 1.132-5(m)(3)

(5) *Bodyguard/chauffeur provided for a bona fide business-oriented security concern.* If an employer provides an employee with vehicle transportation and a bodyguard/chauffeur for a bona fide business-oriented security concern, and but for the bona fide business-oriented security concern the employee would not have had a bodyguard or a chauffeur, then the entire value of the services of the bodyguard/chauffeur is excludable from gross income as a working condition fringe. For purposes of this section, a bodyguard/chauffeur must be trained in evasive driving techniques. An individual who performs services as a driver for an employee is not a bodyguard/chauffeur if the individual is not trained in evasive driving techniques. Thus, no part of the value of the services of such an individual is excludable from gross income under this paragraph (m)(5). (See paragraph (b)(3) of this section for rules relating to the determination of the working condition fringe exclusion for chauffeur services.)

(6) *Special valuation rule for government employees.* If transportation is provided to a government employee for commuting during the period that a bona fide business-oriented security concern under § 1.132-5(m) exists, the commuting use may be valued by reference to the values set forth in § 1.61-21(e)(1)(i) or (f)(3) (vehicle cents-per-mile or commuting valuation of $1.50 per one-way commute, respectively) without regard to the additional requirements contained in § 1.61-21(e) or (f) and is deemed to have met the requirements of § 1.61-21(c).

(7) *Government employer and employee defined.* For purposes of this paragraph (m), "government employer" includes any Federal, state, or local government unit, and any agency or instrumentality thereof. A "government employee" is any individual who is employed by the government employer.

(8) *Examples.* The provisions of this paragraph (m) may be illustrated by the following examples:

Example (1). Assume that in response to several death threats on the life of A, the president of X a multinational company, X establishes an overall security program for A, including an alarm system at A's home and guards at A's workplace, the use of a vehicle that is specially equipped with alarms, bulletproof glass, and armor plating, and a bodyguard/chauffeur. Assume further that A is driven for both personal and business reasons in the vehicle. Also, assume that but for the bona fide business-oriented security concerns, no part of the overall security program would have been provided to A. With respect to the transportation provided for security reasons,

A may exclude as a working condition fringe the value of the special security features of the vehicle and the value attributable to the bodyguard/chauffeur. Thus, if the value of the specially equipped vehicle is $40,000, and the value of the vehicle without the security features is $25,000, A may determine A's inclusion in income attributable to the vehicle as if the vehicle were worth $25,000. A must include in income the value of the availability of the vehicle for personal use.

Example (2). Assume that B is the chief executive officer of Y, a multinational corporation. Assume further that there have been kidnapping attempts and other terrorist activities in the foreign countries in which B performs services and that at least some of such activities have been directed against B or similarly situated employees. In response to these activities, Y provides B with an overall security program, including an alarm system at B's home and bodyguards at B's workplace, a bodyguard/chauffeur, and a vehicle specially designed for security during B's overseas travels. In addition, assume that Y requires B to travel in Y's airplane for business and personal trips taken to, from, and within these foreign countries. Also, assume that but for bona fide business-oriented security concerns, no part of the overall security program would have been provided to B. B may exclude as a working condition fringe the value of the special security features of the automobile and the value attributable to the bodyguards and the bodyguard/chauffeur. B may also exclude the excess, if any, of the value of the flights over the amount A would have paid for the same mode of transportation but for the security concerns. As an alternative to the preceding sentence, B may use the working condition safe harbor described in paragraph (m)(4) of this section and exclude as a working condition fringe the excess, if any, of the value of personal flights in the Y airplane over the safe harbor airfare determined under the method described in paragraph (m)(4) of this section. If this alternative is used, B must include in income the value of the availability of the vehicle for personal use and the value of the safe harbor.

Example (3). Assume the same facts as in example (2) except that Y also requires B to travel in Y's airplane within the United States, and provides B with a chauffeur-driven limousine for business and personal travel in the United States. Assume further that Y also requires B's spouse and dependents to travel in Y's airplane for personal flights in the United States. If no bona fide business-oriented security concern exists with respect to travel in the United States, B may not exclude from income any portion of the value of the availability of the chauffeur or limousine

Reg. § 1.132-5(m)(8)

for personal use in the United States. Thus, B must include in income the value of the availability of the vehicle and chauffeur for personal use. In addition, B may not exclude any portion of the value attributable to personal flights by B or B's spouse and dependents on Y's airplane. Thus, B must include in income the value attributable to the personal use of Y's airplane. See § 1.61-21 for rules relating to the valuation of an employer-provided vehicle and chauffeur, and personal flights on employer-provided airplanes.

Example (4). Assume that company Z retains an independent security consultant to perform a security study with respect to its chief executive officer. Assume further that, based on an objective assessment of the facts and circumstances, the security consultant reasonably recommends that 24-hour protection is not necessary but that the employee be provided security at his workplace and for ground transportation, but not for air transportation. If company Z follows the recommendations on a consistent basis, an overall security program will be deemed to exist with respect to the workplace and ground transportation security only.

Example (5). Assume the same facts as in example (4) except that company Z only provides the employee security while commuting to and from work, but not for any other ground transportation. Because the recommendations of the independent security study are not applied on a consistent basis, an overall security program will not be deemed to exist. Thus, the value of commuting to and from work is not excludable from income. However, the value of a bodyguard with professional security training who does not provide chauffeur or other personal services to the employee or any member of the employee's family may be excludable as a working condition fringe if such expense would be otherwise allowable as a deduction by the employee under section 162 or 167.

Example (6). J is a United States District Judge. At the beginning of a 3-month criminal trial in J's court, a member of J's family receives death threats. M, the division (within government agency W) responsible for evaluating threats and providing protective services to the Federal judiciary, directs its threat analysis unit to conduct a security study with respect to J and J's family. The study is conducted pursuant to internal written procedures that require an independent and objective assessment of any threats to members of the federal judiciary and their families, a statement of the requisite security response, if any, to a particular threat (including the form of transportation to be furnished to the employee as part

of the security program), and a description of the circumstances under which local transportation for the employee and the employee's spouse and dependents may be necessary for personal reasons during the time protective services are provided. M's study concludes that a bona fide business-oriented security concern exists with respect to J and J's family and determines that 24-hour protection of J and J's family is not necessary, but that protection is necessary during the course of the criminal trial whenever J or J's family is away from home. Consistent with that recommendation, J is transported every day in a government vehicle for both personal and business reasons and is accompanied by two bodyguard/chauffeurs who have been trained in evasive driving techniques. In addition, J's spouse is driven to and from work and J's children are driven to and from school and occasional school activities. Shortly after the trial is concluded, M's threat analysis unit determines that J and J's family no longer need special protection because the danger posed by the threat no longer exists and, accordingly, vehicle transportation is no longer provided. Because the security study conducted by M complies with the conditions of § 1.132-5(m)(2)(v), M has satisfied the requirement for an independent security study and an overall security program with respect to J is deemed to exist. Thus, with respect to the transportation provided for security concerns, J may exclude as a working condition fringe the value of any special security features of the government vehicle and the value attributable to the two bodyguard/chauffeurs. *See Example (1)* of this paragraph (m)(8). The value of vehicle transportation provided to J and J's family for personal reasons, other than commuting, may also be excluded during the period of protection, because its provision was consistent with the recommendation of the security study.

Example (7). Assume the same facts as in *Example (6)* and that J's one-way commute between home and work is 10 miles. Under paragraph (m)(6) of this section, the Federal government may value transportation provided to J for commuting purposes pursuant to the value set forth in either the vehicle cents-per-mile rule of § 1.61-21(e) or the commuting valuation rule of § 1.61-21(f). Because the commuting valuation rule yields the least amount of taxable income to J under the circumstances, W values the transportation provided to J for commuting at $1.50 per one-way commute, even though J is a control employee within the meaning of § 1.61-21(f)(6).

(n) *Product testing*—(1) *In general.* The fair market value of the use of consumer goods, which are manufactured for sale to nonemployees, for product testing and evaluation by an employee of

Reg. § 1.132-5(n)(1)

the manufacturer outside the employer's workplace, is excludable from gross income as a working condition fringe if—

(i) Consumer testing and evaluation of the product is an ordinary and necessary business expense of the employer;

(ii) Business reasons necessitate that the testing and evaluation of the product be performed off the employer's business premises by employees (i.e., the testing and evaluation cannot be carried out adequately in the employer's office or in laboratory testing facilities);

(iii) The product is furnished to the employee for purposes of testing and evaluation;

(iv) The product is made available to the employee for no longer than necessary to test and evaluate its performance and (to the extent not exhausted) must be returned to the employer at completion of the testing and evaluation period;

(v) The employer imposes limits on the employee's use of the product that significantly reduce the value of any personal benefit to the employee; and

(vi) The employee must submit detailed reports to the employer on the testing and evaluation. The length of the testing and evaluation period must be reasonable in relation to the product being tested.

(2) *Employer-imposed limits.* The requirement of paragraph (n)(1)(v) of this section is satisfied if—

(i) The employer places limits on the employee's ability to select among different models or varieties of the consumer product that is furnished for testing and evaluation purposes; and

(ii) The employer generally prohibits use of the product by persons other than the employee and, in appropriate cases, requires the employee, to purchase or lease at the employee's own expense the same type of product as that being tested (so that personal use by the employee's family will be limited). In addition, any charge by the employer for the personal use by an employee of a product being tested shall be taken into account in determining whether the requirement of paragraph (n)(1)(v) of this section is satisfied.

(3) *Discriminating classifications.* If an employer furnishes products under a testing and evaluation program only, or presumably, to certain classes of employees (such as highly compensated employees, as defined in § 1.132-8(g)), this fact may be relevant when determining whether the products are furnished for testing and evaluation purposes or for compensation purposes, unless the employer can show a business reason for the classification of employees to whom the products

are furnished (e.g., that automobiles are furnished for testing and evaluation by an automobile manufacturer to its design engineers and supervisory mechanics).

(4) *Factors that negate the existence of a product testing program.* If an employer fails to tabulate and examine the results of the detailed reports submitted by employees within a reasonable period of time after expiration of the testing period, the program will not be considered a product testing program for purposes of the exclusion of this paragraph (n). Existence of one or more of the following factors may also establish that the program is not a bona fide product testing program for purposes of the exclusion of this paragraph (n):

(i) The program is in essence a leasing program under which employees lease the consumer goods from the employer for a fee;

(ii) The nature of the product and other considerations are insufficient to justify the testing program; or

(iii) The expense of the program outweighs the benefits to be gained from testing and evaluation.

(5) *Failure to meet the requirements of this paragraph (n).* The fair market value of the use of property for product testing and evaluation by an employee outside the employee's workplace, under a product testing program that does not meet all of the requirements of this paragraph (n), is not excludable from gross income as a working condition fringe under this paragraph (n).

(5) *Example.* The rules of this paragraph (n) may be illustrated by the following example:

Example. Assume that an employer that manufactures automobiles establishes a product testing program under which 50 of its 5,000 employees test and evaluate the automobiles for 30 days. Assume further that the 50 employees represent a fair cross-section of all of the employees of the employer, such employees submit detailed reports to the employer on the testing and evaluation, the employer tabulates and examines the test results within a reasonable time, and the use of the automobiles is restricted to the employees. If the employer imposes the limits described in paragraph (n)(2) of this section, the employees may exclude the value of the use of the automobile during the testing and evaluation period.

(o) *Qualified automobile demonstration use—* (1) *In general.* The value of qualified automobile demonstration use is excludable from gross income as a working condition fringe. "Qualified automobile demonstration use" is any use of a demonstration automobile by a full-time automobile salesman in the sales area in which the automobile dealer's sales office is located if—

(i) Such use is provided primarily to facilitate the salesman's performance of services for the employer; and

(ii) There are substantial restrictions on the personal use of the automobile by the salesman.

(2) *Full-time automobile salesman*—(i) *Defined.* The term "full-time automobile salesman" means any individual who—

(A) Is employed by an automobile dealer;

(B) Customarily spends at least half of a normal business day performing the functions of a floor salesperson or sales manager;

(C) Directly engages in substantial promotion and negotiation of sales to customers;

(D) Customarily works a number of hours considered full-time in the industry (but at a rate not less than 1,000 hours per year); and

(E) Derives at least 25 percent of his or her gross income from the automobile dealership directly as a result of the activities described in paragraphs (o)(2)(i)(B) and (C) of this section.

For purposes of paragraph (o)(2)(i)(E) of this section, income is not considered to be derived directly as a result of activities described in paragraphs (o)(2)(i)(B) and (C) of this section to the extent that the income is attributable to an individual's ownership interest in the dealership. An individual will not be considered to engage in direct sales activities if the individual's sales-related activities are substantially limited to review of sales price offers from customers. An individual, such as the general manager of an automobile dealership, who receives a sales commission on the sale of an automobile is not a full-time automobile salesman unless the requirements of this paragraph (o)(2)(i) are met. The exclusion provided in this paragraph (o) is available to an individual who meets the definition of this paragraph (o)(2)(i) whether the individual performs services in addition to those described in this paragraph (o)(2)(i). For example, an individual who is an owner of the automobile dealership but who otherwise meets the requirements of this paragraph (o)(2)(i) may exclude from gross income the value of qualified automobile demonstration use. However, the exclusion of this paragraph (o) is not available to owners of large automobile dealerships who do not customarily engage in significant sales activities.

(ii) *Use by an individual other than a full-time automobile salesman.* Personal use of a demonstration automobile by an individual other than

a full-time automobile salesman is not treated as a working condition fringe. Therefore, any personal use, including commuting use, of a demonstration automobile by a part-time salesman, automobile mechanic, or other individual who is not a full-time automobile salesman is not "qualified automobile demonstration use" and thus not excludable from gross income. This is the case whether or not the personal use is within the sales area (as defined in paragraph (o)(5) of this section).

(3) *Demonstration automobile.* The exclusion provided in this paragraph (o) applies only to qualified use of a demonstration automobile. A demonstration automobile is an automobile that is—

(i) Currently in the inventory of the automobile dealership; and

(ii) Available for test drives by customers during the normal business hours of the employee.

(4) *Substantial restrictions on personal use.* Substantial restrictions on the personal use of a demonstration automobile exist when all of the following conditions are satisfied:

(i) Use by individuals other than the full-time automobile salesmen (e.g., the salesman's family) is prohibited;

(ii) Use for personal vacation trips is prohibited;

(iii) The storage of personal possessions in the automobile is prohibited; and

(iv) The total use by mileage of the automobile by the salesman outside the salesman's normal working hours is limited.

(5) *Sales area*—(i) *In general.* Qualified automobile demonstration use consists of use in the sales area in which the automobile dealer's sales office is located. The sales area is the geographic area surrounding the automobile dealer's sales office from which the office regularly derives customers.

(ii) *Sales area safe harbor.* With respect to a particular full-time salesman, the automobile dealer's sales area may be treated as the area within a radius of the larger of—

(A) 75 miles or

(B) The one-way commuting distance (in miles) of the particular salesman from the dealer's sales office.

(6) *Applicability of substantiation requirements of sections 162 and 274 (d).* Notwithstanding anything in this section to the contrary, the value of the use of a demonstration automobile may not be excluded from gross income as a working condition fringe, by either the employer or the employee, unless, with respect to the re-

Reg. § 1.132-5(o)(2)

strictions of paragraph (o)(4) cf this section, the substantiation requirements of section 274(d) and the regulations thereunder are satisfied. See § 1.132-5(c) for general and safe harbor rules relating to the applicability of the substantiation requirements of section 274(d).

(7) *Special valuation rules.* See § 1.61-21(d)(6)(ii) for special rules that may be used to value the availability of demonstration automobiles.

(p) *Parking*—(1) *In general.* The value of parking provided to an employee on or near the business premises of the employer is excludable from gross income as a working condition fringe under the special rule of this paragraph (p). If the rules of this paragraph (p) are satisfied, the value of parking is excludable from gross income whether the amount paid by the employee for parking would be deductible under section 162. The working condition fringe exclusion applies whether the employer owns or rents the parking facility or parking space.

(2) *Reimbursement of parking expenses.* A reimbursement to the employee of the ordinary and necessary expenses of renting a parking space on or near the business premises of the employer is excludable from gross income as a working condition fringe, if, but for the parking expense, the employee would not have been entitled to receive and retain such amount from the employer. If, however an employee is entitled to retain a general transportation allowance or a similar benefit whether or not the employee has parking expenses, no portion of that allowance is excludable from gross income under this paragraph (p) even if it is used for parking expenses.

(3) *Parking on residential property.* With respect to an employee, this paragraph (p) does not apply to any parking facility or space located on property owned or leased by the employee for residential purposes.

(4) *Dates of applicability.* This paragraph (p) applies to benefits provided before January 1, 1993. For benefits provided after December 31, 1992, see § 1.132-9.

(q) *Nonapplicability of nondiscrimination rules.* Except to the extent provided in paragraph (n)(3) of this section (relating to discriminating classifications of a product testing program), the nondiscrimination rules cf section 132(h)(1) and § 1.132-8 do not apply in determining the amount, if any, of a working condition fringe.

(r) *Volunteers*—(1) *In general.* Solely for purposes of section 132(d) and paragraph (a)(1) of this section, a bona fide volunteer (including a director or officer) who performs services for an organization exempt from tax under section 501(a), or for a government employer (as defined in paragraph (m)(7) of this section), is deemed to have a profit motive under section 162.

(2) *Limit on application of this paragraph.* This paragraph (r) shall not be used to support treatment of the bona fide volunteer as having a profit motive for purposes of any provision of the Internal Revenue Code of 1986 (Code) other than section 132(d). Nothing in this paragraph (r) shall be interpreted as determining the employment status of a bona fide volunteer for purposes of any section of the Code other than section 132(d).

(3) *Definitions*—(i) *Bona fide volunteer.* For purposes of this paragraph (r), an individual is considered a "bona fide volunteer" if the individual does not have a profit motive for purposes of section 162. For example, an individual is considered a "bona fide volunteer" if the total value of the benefits provided with respect to the volunteer services is substantially less than the total value of the volunteer services the individual provides to an exempt organization or government employer.

(ii) *Liability insurance coverage for a bona fide volunteer.* For purposes of this paragraph (r), the receipt of liability insurance coverage by a volunteer, or an exempt organization or government employer's undertaking to indemnify the volunteer for liability, does not by itself confer a profit motive on the volunteer, provided the insurance coverage or indemnification relates to acts performed by the volunteer in the discharge of duties, or the performance of services, on behalf of the exempt organization or government employer.

(4) *Example.* The following example illustrates the provisions of paragraph (r) of this section.

Example. A is a manager and full-time employee of P, a tax-exempt organization described in section 501(c)(3). B is a member of P's board of directors. Other than $25 to defray expenses for attending board meetings, B receives no compensation for serving as a director and does not have a profit motive. Therefore, B is a bona fide volunteer by application of paragraph (r)(3)(i) of this section and is deemed to have a profit motive under paragraph (r)(1) of this section for purposes of section 132(d). In order to provide liability insurance coverage, P purchases a policy that covers actions arising from A's and B's activities performed as part of their duties to P. The value of the policy and payments made to or on behalf of A under the policy are excludable from A's gross income as a working condition fringe, because A has a profit motive under section 162 and would be able to deduct payments for liability insurance coverage had he paid for it himself. The receipt of liability insurance coverage by B does not confer a profit motive on B by application of paragraph (r)(3)(ii) of this section. Thus, the value of the policy and payments made to or on behalf of B under the policy are excludable from B's income as a working condition fringe. For the year in which the liability insurance coverage is provided to A and B, P may exclude the value of the benefit on the Form W-2 it issues to A or on any Form 1099 it might otherwise issue to B.

(s) *Application of section 274(a)(3)*—(1) *In general.* If an employer's deduction under section 162(a) for dues paid or incurred for membership in any club organized for business, pleasure, recreation, or other social purpose is disallowed by section 274(a)(3), the amount, if any, of an employee's working condition fringe benefit relating to an employer-provided membership in the club is determined without regard to the application of section 274(a) to the employee. To be excludible as a working condition fringe benefit, however, the amount must otherwise qualify for deduction by the employee under section 162(a). If an employer treats the amount paid or incurred for membership in any club organized for business, pleasure, recreation, or other social purpose as compensation under section 274(e)(2), then the expense is deductible by the employer as compensation and no amount may be excluded from the employee's gross income as a working condition fringe benefit. See § 1.274-2(f)(2)(iii)(A).

(2) *Treatment of tax-exempt employers.* In the case of an employer exempt from taxation under subtitle A of the Internal Revenue Code, any reference in this paragraph (s) to a deduction disallowed by section 274(a)(3) shall be treated as a reference to the amount which would be disallowed as a deduction by section 274(a)(3) to the employer if the employer were not exempt from taxation under subtitle A of the Internal Revenue Code.

(3) *Examples.* The following examples illustrate this paragraph (s):

Example 1. Assume that Company X provides Employee B with a country club membership for which it paid $20,000. B substantiates, within the meaning of paragraph (c) of this section, that the club was used 40 percent for business purposes. The business use of the club (40 percent) may be considered a working condition fringe benefit, notwithstanding that the employer's deduction for the dues allocable to the business use is disallowed by section 274(a)(3), if X does not treat the club membership as compensation under section 274(e)(2). Thus, B may exclude from gross income $8,000 (40 percent of the club dues, which reflects B's business use). X must report $12,000 as wages subject to withholding and payment of employment taxes (60 percent of the value of the club dues, which reflects B's personal use). B must include $12,000 in gross incme. X may deduct as compensation the amount it paid for the club dues which reflects B's personal use provided the amount satisfies the other requirements for a salary or compensation deduction under section 162.

Example 2. Assume the same facts as *Example 1* except that Company X treats the $20,000 as compensation to B under section 274(e)(2). No portion of the $20,000 will be considered a working condition fringe benefit because the section 274(a)(3) disallowance will apply to B. Therefore, B must include $20,000 in gross income.

(t) *Application of section 274(m)(3)*—(1) *In general.* If an employer's deduction under section 162(a) for amounts paid or incurred for the travel expenses of a spouse, dependent, or other individual accompanying an employee is disallowed by section 274(m)(3), the amount, if any, of the employee's working condition fringe benefit relating to the employer-provided travel is determined without regard to the application of section 274(m)(3). To be excludible as a working condition fringe benefit, however, the amount must otherwise qualify for deduction by the employee under section 162(a). The amount will qualify for deduction and for exclusion as a working condition benefit benefit if it can be adequately shown that the spouse's, dependent's, or other accompanying individual's presence on the employee's business trip has a bona fide business purpose and if the employee substantiates the travel within the meaning of paragraph (c) of this section. If the travel does not qualify as a working condition fringe benefit, the employee must include in gross income as a fringe benefit the value of the employer's payment of travel expenses with respect to a spouse, dependent, or other individual accompanying the employee on business travel. See § § 1.61-21(a)(4) and 1.162-2(c). If an employer treats as compensation under section 274(e)(2) the amount paid or incurred for the travel expenses of a spouse, dependent, or other individual accompanying an employee, then the expense is deductible by the employer as compensation and no amount may be excluded from the employee's gross income as a working condition fringe benefit. See § 1.274-2(f)(2)(iii)(A).

(2) *Treatment of tax-exempt employers.* In the case of an employer exempt from taxation under subtitle A of the Internal Revenue Code, any reference in this paragraph (t) to a deduction disallowed by section 274(m)(3) shall be treated as a reference to the amount which would be

disallowed as a deduction by section 274 (m)(3) to the employer if the employer were not exempt from taxation under subtitle A of the Internal Revenue Code. [Reg. § 1.132-5.]

→ *Caution: Temporary Reg. § 1.132-5T applies to the tax treatment of fringe benefits for 1985—1988. See Reg. § § 1.132-0—1.132-8 for post-1988 rules.*←

[Reg. § 1.132-5T]

§ 1.132-5T. Working condition fringe—1985 through 1988 (Temporary).—(a) In general— (1) *Definition.* Gross income does not include the value of a working condition fringe. The term "working condition fringe" means any property or service provided to an employee of an employer to the extent that, if the employee paid for the property or service, the amount paid would be allowable as a deduction under section 162 or 167. If, under section 274 or any other section, certain substantiation requirements must be met in order for a deduction under section 162 or 167 to be allowable, those substantiation requirements apply to the determination of a working condition fringe. An amount that would be deductible by the employee under, for example, section 212 is not a working condition fringe.

(2) *Trade or business of the employee.* If the hypothetical payment for the property or service would be allowable as a deduction with respect to a trade or business of the employee other than the employee's trade or business of being an employee of the employer, it cannot be taken into account for purposes of determining the amount, if any, of the working condition fringe. For example, assume that, unrelated to company X's trade or business and unrelated to company X's employee's trade or business of being an employee of company X, the employee is a member of the board of directors of company Y. Assume further that company X provides the employee with air transportation to a company Y board of director's meeting. The employee may not exclude the value of the air transportation to the meeting as a working condition fringe. The employee may, however, deduct such amount under section 162 if the section 162 requirements are satisfied. The result would be the same whether the air transportation was provided in the form of a flight on a commercial airline or a seat on a company X airplane.

(b) *Vehicle allocation rules*—(1) *In general*—(i) *General rule.* In general, with respect to an employer-provided vehicle, the amount excludable as a working condition fringe is the amount that would be allowable as a deduction under section 162 or 167 if the employee paid for the availability of the vehicle. For example, assume that the value of the availability of an employer-provided vehicle for a full year is $2,000, without regard to

any working condition fringe (i.e., assuming all personal use). Assume further that the employee drives the vehicle 6,000 miles for his employer's business and 2,000 miles for reasons other than the employer's business. In this situation, the value of the working condition fringe is $2,000 multiplied by a fraction, the numerator of which is the business-use mileage (6,000 miles) and the denominator of which is the total mileage (8,000 miles). Thus, the value of the working condition fringe is $1,500. The total amount includible in the employee's gross income on account of the availability of the vehicle is $500. For purposes of this section, the term "vehicle" has the same meaning given the term in § 1.61-2T (e)(2). Generally, when determining the amount of an employee's working condition fringe, miles accumulated on the vehicle by all employees of the employer during the period in which the vehicle is available to the employee must be considered. For example, assume that an employee of the employer is provided the availability of an automobile for one year. Assume further that during the year, the automobile is regularly used in the employer's business by other employees. All miles accumulated on the automobile by all employees of the employer during the year must be considered. If, however, substantially all the use of the automobile by other employees in the employer's business is permitted during a certain period, such as the last three months of the year, the miles driven by the other employees during that period would not be considered when determining the employee's working condition fringe exclusion.

(ii) *Use by an individual other than the employee.* For purposes of this section, if the availability of a vehicle to an individual would be taxed to an employee, use of the vehicle by the individual is included in references to use by the employee.

(iii) *Provision of an expensive vehicle for personal use.* Assume an employer provides an employee with an expensive vehicle that an employee may use in part for personal purposes. Even though the decision to provide an expensive rather than an inexpensive vehicle is made by the employer for bona fide noncompensatory business reasons, there is no working condition fringe exclusion with respect to the personal miles driven by the employee. If the employee paid for the availa-

☐ [*T.D.* 8256, 7-5-89. *Amended by T.D.* 8451, 12-4-92; *T.D.* 8457, 12-29-92; *T.D.* 8666, 5-29-96 and *T.D.* 8933, 1-10-2001.]

→ *Caution: Temporary Reg. § 1.132-5T applies to the tax treatment of fringe benefits for 1985—1988. See Reg. § § 1.132-0—1.132-8 for post-1988 rules.*←

bility of the vehicle, he would not be entitled to deduct any part of the payment attributable to personal miles.

(2) *Use of different employer-provided automobiles.* The working condition fringe exclusion must be applied on an automobile by automobile basis. For example, assume that automobile Y is available to employee D for 3 days in January and for 5 days in March, and automobile Z is available to D for a week in July. Assume further that the Daily Lease Value, as defined in § 1.61-2T, of each automobile is $50. For the eight days of availability of Y in January and March, D uses Y 90 percent for business (by mileage). During July, D uses Z 60 percent for business (by mileage). The value of the working condition fringe is determined separately for each automobile. Therefore, the working condition fringe for Y is $360 ($400 × .90) leaving an income inclusion of $40. The working condition fringe for Z is $210 ($350 × .60) leaving an income inclusion of $140. If the value of the availability of an automobile is determined under the Annual Lease Value rule for one period and Daily Lease Value rule for a second period (see § 1.61-2T), the working condition fringe exclusion must be calculated separately for the two periods.

(c) *Applicability of sections 162 and 274(d)—* (1) *In general.* The value of property or services provided to an employee may not be excluded from the employee's gross income as a working condition fringe, by either the employer or the employee, unless the applicable substantiation requirements of either section 274(d) or section 162 (whichever is applicable) and the regulations thereunder are satisfied. With respect to listed property, the substantiation requirements of section 274(d) and the regulations thereunder do not apply to the determination of an employee's working condition fringe exclusion prior to the date that those requirements apply to the first taxable year of the employer beginning after December 31, 1985. For example, if an employer's first taxable year beginning after December 31, 1985, begins on July 1, 1986, with respect to listed property, the substantiation requirements of section 274(d) apply as of that date. The substantiation requirements of section 274(d) apply to an employee even if the requirements of section 274 do not apply to the employee's employer for deduction purposes (such as when the employer is a tax-exempt organization or a governmental unit); in these cases, the requirements of section 274(d) apply to the employee as to January 1, 1986.

(2) *Section 274(d) requirements.* The substantiation requirements of section 274(d) are satisfied by "adequate records or sufficient evidence corroborating the [employee's] own statement". Therefore, such records or evidence provided by the employee, and relied upon by the employer to the extent permitted by the regulations promulgated under section 274(d), will be sufficient to substantiate a working condition fringe exclusion.

(d) *Safe harbor rules—*(1) *In general.* Section 1.274-6T provides that the substantiation requirements of section 274(d) and the regulations thereunder may be satisfied, in certain circumstances, by using one or more of the safe harbor rules prescribed in § 1.274-6T. If the employer uses one of the safe harbor rules prescribed in § 1.274-6T during a period with respect to a vehicle (as defined in § 1.61-2T), that rule must be used by the employer to substantiate a working condition fringe exclusion with respect to that vehicle during the period. An employer that is exempt from Federal income tax may still use one of the safe harbor rules (if the requirements of that section are otherwise met during a period) to substantiate a working condition fringe exclusion with respect to a vehicle during the period. If the employer uses one of the methods prescribed in § 1.274-6T during a period with respect to an employer-provided vehicle, that method may be used by an employee to substantiate a working condition fringe exclusion with respect to the same vehicle during the period, as long as the employee includes in gross income the amount allocated to the employee pursuant to § 1.274-6T and this section. (See § 1.61-2T(c)(2)(i) for other rules concerning when an employee must include in income the amount determined by the employer.) If, however, the employer uses the safe harbor rule prescribed in § 1.274-6T(a)(2) or (3) and the employee without the employer's knowledge uses the vehicle for purposes other than de minimis personal use (in the case of the rule prescribed in § 1.274-6T(a)(2)), or for purposes other than de minimis personal use and commuting (in the case of the rule prescribed in § 1.274-6T(a)(3)), then the employee must include additional income for the unauthorized use of the vehicle.

(2) *Period for use of safe harbor rules.* The rules prescribed in this paragraph (d) assume that the safe harbor rules prescribed in § 1.274-6T are used for a one-year period. Accordingly, references to the value of the availability of a vehicle, amounts excluded as a working condition fringe, etc., are based on a one-year period. If the safe harbor rules prescribed in § 1.274-6T are used for

Reg. § 1.132-5T(b)(2)

→ *Caution: Temporary Reg. § 1.132-5T applies to the tax treatment of fringe benefits for 1985—1988. See Reg. § § 1.132-0—1.132-8 for post-1988 rules.←*

a period of less than a year, the amounts referenced in the previous sentence must be adjusted accordingly. For purposes of this section, the term "personal use" has the same meaning as prescribed in § 1.274-6T(e)(5).

(e) *Vehicles not available to employees for personal use.* For a vehicle described in § 1.274-6T(a)(2) (relating to certain vehicles not used for personal purposes), the working condition fringe exclusion is equal to the value of the availability of the vehicle if the employer uses the method prescribed in § 1.274-6T(a)(2).

(f) *Vehicles not available to employees for personal use other than commuting.* For a vehicle described in § 1.274-6T(a)(3) (relating to certain vehicles not used for personal purposes other than commuting), the working condition fringe exclusion is equal to the value of the availability of the vehicle for purposes other than commuting if the employer uses the method prescribed in § 1.274-6T(a)(3). This rule applies only if the special rule for valuing commuting use, as prescribed in § 1.61-2T, is used and the amount determined under the special rule is either included in the employee's income or reimbursed by the employee.

(g) *Vehicles used in connection with the business of farming that are available to employees for personal use*—(1) *In general.* For a vehicle described in § 1.274-6T(b) (relating to certain vehicles used in connection with the business of farming), the working condition fringe exclusion is calculated by multiplying the value of the availability of the vehicle by 75 percent.

(2) *Vehicles available to more than one individual.* If the vehicle is available to more than one individual, the employer must allocate the gross income attributable to the vehicle (25 percent of the value of the availability of the vehicle) among the employees (and other individuals whose use would not be attributed to an employee) to whom the vehicle was available. This allocation must be done in a reasonable manner to reflect the personal use of the vehicle by the individuals. An amount that would be allocated to a sole proprietor reduces the amounts that may be allocated to employees but are otherwise to be disregarded for purposes of this paragraph (g). For purposes of this paragraph (g), the value of the availability of a vehicle may be calculated as if the vehicle were available to only one employee continuously and without regard to any working condition fringe exclusion.

(3) *Examples.* The following examples illustrate a reasonable allocation of gross income with respect to an employer-provided vehicle between two employees:

Example (1). Assume that two farm employees share the use of a vehicle which for a calendar year is regularly used directly in connection with the business of farming and qualifies for use of the rule in § 1.274-6T(b). Employee A uses the vehicle in the morning directly in connection with the business of farming and employee B uses the vehicle in the afternoon directly in connection with the business of farming. Assume further that employee B takes the vehicle home in the evenings and on weekends. The employer should allocate all the income attributable to the availability of the vehicle to employee B.

Example (2). Assume that for a calendar year, farm employees C and D share the use of a vehicle that is regularly used directly in connection with the business of farming and qualifies for use of the rule in § 1.274-6T(b). Assume further that the employees alternate taking the vehicle home in the evening and alternate the availability of the vehicle for personal purposes on weekends. The employer should allocate the income attributable to the availability of the vehicle for personal use (25 percent of the value of the availability of the vehicle) equally between the two employees.

Example (3). Assume the same facts as in example (2) except that C is the sole proprietor of the farm. Based on these facts, C should allocate the same amount of income to D as was allocated to D in example (2). No other income attributable to the availability of the vehicle for personal use should be allocated.

(h) *Qualified non-personal use vehicles.* Effective January 1, 1985, 100 percent of the value of the use of a qualified nonpersonal use vehicle (as described in § 1.274-5T(k)) is excluded from gross income as a working condition fringe, provided that, in the case of a vehicle described in paragraph (k)(3) through (7) of that section, the use of the vehicles conforms to the requirements of that paragraph.

(i) [Reserved].

(j) *Application of section 280F.* In determining the amount, if any, of an employee's working condition fringe, section 280F and the regulations thereunder do not apply. For example, assume that an employee has available for a calendar year an employer-provided automobile with a fair market value of $28,000. Assume further that the special rule provided in § 1.61-2T is used and that the Annual Lease Value, as defined in § 1.61-2T, is $7,750, and that all of the employee's use of the

Reg. § 1.132-5T(j)

→ *Caution: Temporary Reg. § 1.132-5T applies to the tax treatment of fringe benefits for 1985—1988. See Reg. § § 1.132-0—1.132-8 for post-1988 rules.←*

automobile is in the employer's business. The employee would be entitled to exclude the entire Annual Lease Value as a working condition fringe, despite the fact that if the employee paid for the availability of the automobile, an income inclusion would be required under § 1.280F-5T(d)(1). This paragraph (j) does not affect the applicability of section 280F to the employer with respect to such employer-provided automobile, nor does it affect the applicability of section 274. For rules concerning substantiation of an employee's working condition fringe, see paragraph (c) of this section.

(k) *Aircraft allocation rule.* In general, with respect to a flight on an employer-provided aircraft, the amount excludable as a working condition fringe is the amount that would be allowable as a deduction under section 162 or 167 if the employee paid for the flight on the aircraft. For example, if employee P flies on P's employer's airplane primarily for business reasons of P's employer, the value of P's flight is excludable as a working condition fringe. However, if P's spouse and children accompany P on such airplane trip primarily for personal reasons, the value of the flights by P's spouse and children are includible in P's gross income. See § 1.61-2T(g) for special rules for valuing personal flights.

(l) [Reserved].

(m) *Employer-provided transportation for security concerns*—(1) *In general.* The amount of a working condition fringe exclusion with respect to employer-provided transportation is the amount that would be allowable as a deduction under section 162 or 167 if the employee paid for the transportation. Generally, if an employee pays for transportation taken for primarily personal purposes, the employee may not deduct any part of the amount paid. Thus, the employee may not generally exclude the value of employer-provided transportation as a working condition fringe if such transportation is primarily personal. If, however, for bona fide business-oriented security concerns, the employee purchases transportation that provides him or her with additional security, the employee may generally deduct the excess of the amount paid for the transportation over the lesser amount the employee would have paid for the same mode of transportation absent the bona fide business-oriented security concerns. With respect to a vehicle, the phrase "the same mode of transportation" means use of the same vehicle without the additional security aspects, such as bulletproof glass. With respect to air transportation, the phrase "the same mode of transportation" means

comparable air transportation. These same rules apply to the determination of an employee's working condition fringe exclusion. For example, if an employer provides an employee with an automobile for commuting and, for bona fide business-oriented security concerns, the automobile is specially designed for security, then the employee may exclude the value of the special security design as a working condition fringe if the employee's automobile would not have had such security design but for the bona fide business-oriented security concerns. The employee may not exclude the value of the commuting from income as a working condition fringe because commuting is a nondeductible personal expense. Similarly, if an employee travels on a personal trip in an employer-provided aircraft for bona fide business-oriented security concerns, the employee may exclude the excess, if any, of the value of the flight over the amount the employee would have paid for comparable air transportation, but for the bona fide business-oriented security concerns. Because personal travel is a nondeductible expense, the employee may not exclude the total value of the trip as a working condition fringe.

(2) *Demonstration of bona fide business-oriented security concerns*—(i) *In general.* For purposes of this paragraph (m), the existence of a bona fide business-oriented security concern for the furnishing of a specific form of transportation to an employee is determined on the basis of all the facts and circumstances within the following guidelines:

(A) *Services performed outside the United States.* With respect to an employee performing services for an employer in a geographic area other than the United States, a factor indicating a bona fide business-oriented security concern is a recent history of violent terrorist activity in such geographic area (such as bombings or abductions for ransom), unless such activity is focused on a group of individuals which does not include the employee or a similarly situated employee or on a section of the geographic area which does not include the employee.

(B) *Services performed in the United States.* With respect to an employee performing services for an employer in the United States, a factor indicating a bona fide business-oriented security concern is threats on the life of the employee or on the life of a similarly situated employee because of the employee's status as an employee of the employer.

(ii) *Establishment of overall security program.* Notwithstanding anything in paragraph

Reg. § 1.132-5T(k)

→ *Caution: Temporary Reg. § 1.132-5T applies to the tax treatment of fringe benefits for 1985—1988. See Reg. § § 1.132-0—1.132-8 for post-1988 rules.* ←

(m)(2)(i) of this section to the contrary, *no* bona fide business-oriented security concern will be deemed to exist unless the employee's employer establishes an overall security program with respect to the employee involved.

(iii) *Overall security program*—(A) *Definition.* An overall security program is one in which security is provided to protect the employee on a 24-hour basis. The employee must be protected while at the employee's residence, while commuting to and from the employee's workplace, and while at the employee's workplace. In addition, the employee must be protected while traveling, whether for business or personal purposes. An overall security program would include the provision of a bodyguard/driver who is trained in evasive driving techniques; an automobile specially equipped for security; guards, metal detectors, alarms, or similar methods of controlling access to the employee's workplace and residence; and, in appropriate cases, flights on the employer's aircraft for business and personal reasons.

(B) *Application.* There is no overall security program when, for example, security is provided at the employee's workplace but not at the employee's residence. In addition, the fact that an employer requires an employee to travel on the employer's aircraft, or in an employer-provided vehicle that contains special security features, does not alone constitute an overall security program. The preceding sentence applies regardless of the existence of a corporate or other resolution requiring the employee to travel in the employer's airplane or vehicle for personal as well as business reasons. Similarly, the existence of an independent security study particular to the employer and its employees, or to the employee involved, does not alone constitute an overall security program.

(iv) *Effect of an independent security study.* An overall security program with respect to an employee is deemed to exist even though security is not provided to an employee on a 24-hour basis if the conditions of this paragraph (m)(2)(iv) are satisfied:

(A) A security study is performed with respect to the employer and the employee (or a similarly situated employee) by an independent security consultant;

(B) The security study is based on an objective assessment of all the facts and circumstances;

(C) The recommendation of the security study is that an overall security program (as defined in paragraph (m)(2)(iii) of this section) is not necessary and such recommendation is reasonable under the circumstances; and

(D) The employer applies the specific security recommendations contained in the security study to the employee on a consistent basis.

The value of the security provided pursuant to a security study that meets the requirements of this paragraph (m)(2)(iv) may be excluded from income, if the security study conclusions are reasonable and, but for the bona fide business-oriented security concerns, the employee would not have had such security. No exclusion from income applies to security provided by the employer that is not recommended in the security study. Security study conclusions may be reasonable even if, for example, it is recommended that security be limited to certain geographic areas, as in the case where air travel security is provided only in certain foreign countries.

(v) *Application of security rules to spouses and dependents.* The availability of a working condition fringe exclusion based on the existence of a bona fide business-oriented security concern with respect to the spouse and dependents of an employee is determined separately for such spouse and dependents under the rules established in this paragraph (m).

(vi) *Working condition safe harbor.* Under the special rule of this paragraph (m)(2)(vi), if, for a bona fide business-oriented security concern, the employer requires that the employee travel on an employer-provided aircraft for a personal trip, the employer and the employee may exclude, as a working condition fringe, the excess value of the trip over comparable first-class airfare without having to show that but for the bona fide business-oriented security concerns, the employee would have flown first-class on a commercial aircraft. If the special valuation rule provided in § 1.61-2T is used, the excess over the amount determined by multiplying an aircraft multiple of 200-percent by the base aircraft valuation formula may be excluded as a working condition fringe.

(3) *Examples.* The provisions of this paragraph (m) may be illustrated by the following examples:

Example (1). Assume that in response to several death threats on the life of A, the president of a multinational company (company X), company X establishes an overall security program for A, including an alarm system at A's home and guards at A's workplace, the use of a

Reg. § 1.132-5T(m)(3)

→ *Caution: Temporary Reg. § 1.132-5T applies to the tax treatment of fringe benefits for 1985—1988. See Reg. § § 1.132-0—1.132-8 for post-1988 rules.*←

vehicle that is specially equipped with alarms, bulletproof glass, and armor plating and a bodyguard/driver who is trained in evasive driving techniques. Assume further that A is driven for both personal and business reasons in the vehicle. Also, assume that but for the bona fide business-oriented security concerns, no part of the overall security program would have been provided to A. With respect to the transportation provided for security reasons, A may exclude as a working condition fringe the value of the special security features of the vehicle and the value attributable to the bodyguard/driver. Thus, if the value of the specially equipped vehicle is $40,000, and the value of the vehicle without the security features is $25,000, A may determine A's income attributable to the vehicle as if the vehicle were worth $25,000. A must include in income the value of the availability of the vehicle for personal use.

Example (2). Assume that B is the chief executive officer of a multinational corporation (company Y). Assume further that there have been kidnapping attempts and other terrorist activities in the foreign countries in which B performs services and that at least some of such activities have been directed against B or similarly situated employees. In response to these activities, company Y provides B with an overall security program, including an alarm system at B's home and bodyguards at B's workplace, a bodyguard/driver who is trained in evasive driving techniques, and a vehicle specially designed for security during B's overseas travels. In addition, assume that company Y requires B to travel in company Y's airplane for business and personal trips taken to, from, and within these foreign countries. Also, assume that but for bona fide business-oriented security concerns, no part of the overall security program would have been provided to B. B may exclude as a working condition fringe the value of the special security features of the automobile and the value attributable to the bodyguards and the bodyguard/driver. B may also exclude as a working condition fringe the excess, if any, of the value of personal flights in the company Y airplane over first-class airfare (as determined under the special valuation rule provided in § 1.61-2T if the safe harbor described in paragraph (m)(2)(vi) of this section is used). B must include in income the value of the availability of the vehicle for personal use and the lesser of the value of first-class airfare or the value of the flight determined under § 1.61-2T for each personal flight taken by B in company Y's airplane.

Example (3). Assume the same facts as in example (2) except that company Y also requires B to travel in company Y's airplane within the United States, and provides B with a chauffeur-driven limousine for business and personal travel in the United States. Assume further that company Y also requires B's spouse and dependents to travel in company Y's airplane for personal flights in the United States. If no bona fide business-oriented security concern exists with respect to travel in the United States, B may not exclude any portion of the value of the availability of the driver or limousine for personal use in the United States. Thus, B must include in income the value of the availability of the vehicle and driver for personal use. In addition, B may not exclude any portion of the value attributable to personal flights by B or B's spouse and dependents on company Y's airplane. Thus, B must include in income the value attributable to the personal use of company Y's airplane. See § 1.61-2T for rules relating to the valuation of personal flights on employer-provided airplanes.

Example (4). Assume that company Z retains an independent security consultant to perform a security study with respect to its chief executive officer. Assume further that, based on an objective assessment of the facts and circumstances, the security consultant reasonably recommends that the employee be provided security at his workplace and for ground transportation, but not for air transportation. If company Z follows the recommendations on a consistent basis, an overall security program will be deemed to exist with respect to the workplace and ground transportation security only.

Example (5). Assume the same facts as in example (4) except that company Z only provides the employee security while commuting to and from work, but not for any other ground transportation. Since the recommendations of the independent security study are not applied on a consistent basis, an overall security program will not be deemed to exist.

(n) *Product testing*—(1) *In general.* The fair market value of the use of consumer goods, which are manufactured for sale to nonemployees, for product testing and evaluation by an employee outside the employer's workplace is excludable as a working condition fringe if—

(i) Consumer testing and evaluation of the product is an ordinary and necessary business expense of the employer,

Reg. § 1.132-5T(n)(1)

→ *Caution: Temporary Reg. § 1.132-5T applies to the tax treatment of fringe benefits for 1985—1988. See Reg. § § 1.132-0—1.132-8 for post-1988 rules.*←

(ii) Business reasons necessitate that the testing and evaluation of the product be performed off the employer's business premises by employees (i.e., the testing and evaluation cannot be carried out adequately in the employer's office or in laboratory testing facilities),

(iii) The product is furnished to the employee for purposes of testing and evaluation,

(iv) The product is made available to the employee for no longer than necessary to test and evaluate its performance and must be returned to the employer at completion of the testing and evaluation period,

(v) The employer imposes limitations of the employee's use of the product which significantly reduce the value of any personal benefit to the employee, and

(vi) The employee must submit detailed reports to the employer on the testing and evaluation.

The length of the testing and evaluation period must be reasonable in relation to the product being tested.

(2) *Employer-imposed limitations.* The requirement of paragraph (n)(1)(v) of this section is satisfied if—

(i) The employer places limitations on the employee's ability to select among different models or varieties of the consumer product that is furnished for testing and evaluation purposes,

(ii) The employer's policy provides for the employee, in appropriate cases, to purchase or lease at his or her own expense the same type of product as that being tested (so that personal use by the employee's family will be limited), and

(iii) The employer generally prohibits use of the product by members of the employee's family.

(3) *Discriminating classifications.* If an employer furnishes products under a testing and evaluation program only to officers, owners, or highly compensated employees, this fact may be considered in a determination of whether the products are furnished for testing and evaluation purposes or for compensation purposes, unless the employer can show a business reason for the classification of employees to whom the products are furnished (e.g., that automobiles are furnished for testing and evaluation by an automobile manufacturer to its design engineers and supervisory mechanics).

(4) *Factors that negate the existence of a product testing program.* If an employer fails to tabulate and examine the results of the detailed reports within a reasonable period of time after expiration of the testing period, the program will not be considered a product testing program. Existence of one or more of the following factors may also establish that the program is not a bona fide product testing program:

(i) The program is in essence a leasing program under which employees lease the consumer goods from the employer for a fee;

(ii) The nature of the product and other considerations are insufficient to justify the testing program; or

(iii) The expense of the program outweighs the benefits to be gained from testing and evaluation.

(5) *Failure to meet the requirements of this paragraph (n).* The fair market value of the use of property for product testing and evaluation by an employee outside the employee's workplace, under a product testing program that does not meet all of the requirements of this paragraph (n), is not excludable as a working condition fringe.

(6) *Example.* Assume that an employer that manufactures automobiles establishes a product testing program under which 50 of its 5,000 employees test and evaluate the automobiles for 30 days. Assume further that the 50 employees represent a fair cross section of all of the employees of the employer, such employees submit detailed reports to the employer on the testing and evaluation, the employer tabulates and examines the test results within a reasonable time, and the use of the automobile is restricted to the employees. If the rules of paragraph (n)(2) of this section are also met, the employees may exclude the value of the use of the automobile during the testing and evaluation period.

(o) *Qualified automobile demonstration use—* (1) *In general.* The value of qualified automobile demonstration use is excludable from gross income as a working condition fringe. The term "qualified automobile demonstration use" means any use of a demonstration automobile by a full-time automobile salesman in the sales area in which the automobile dealer's sales office is located if—

(i) Such use is provided primarily to facilitate the salesman's performance of services for the employer, and

(ii) There are substantial restrictions on the personal use of the automobile by the salesman.

(2) *Full-time automobile salesman—(i) Definition.* The term "full-time automobile salesman" means any individual who—

Reg. § 1.132-5T(o)(2)

→ *Caution: Temporary Reg. § 1.132-5T applies to the tax treatment of fringe benefits for 1985—1988. See Reg. § § 1.132-0—1.132-8 for post-1988 rules.*←

(A) Is employed by an automobile dealer,

(B) Customarily spends substantially all of a normal business day on the sales floor selling automobiles to customers of the automobile dealership,

(C) Customarily works a number of hours considered full-time in the industry (but at a rate not less than 1,000 hours per year), and

(D) Derives at least 85 percent of his or her gross income from the automobile dealership directly as a result of such automobile sales activities.

An individual, such as the general manager of an automobile dealership, who receives a sales commission on the sale of an automobile is not a full-time automobile salesman unless the requirements of this paragraph (o)(2)(i) are met. The exclusion provided in this paragraph (o) is available to an individual who meets the definition of this paragraph (o)(2)(i) regardless of whether the individual performs services in addition to those described in this paragraph (o)(2)(i). For example, an individual who is an owner of the automobile dealership but who otherwise meets the requirements of this paragraph (o)(2)(i) may exclude from gross income the value of qualified automobile demonstration use.

(ii) *Use by an individual other than a full-time automobile salesman.* Personal use of a demonstration automobile by an individual other than a full-time automobile salesman is not treated as a working condition fringe. Therefore, any personal use, including commuting use, of a demonstration automobile by a part-time salesman, automobile mechanic, manager, or other individual is not "qualified automobile demonstration use" and thus not excludable from gross income.

(3) *Demonstration Automobile.* The exclusion provided in this paragraph (o) applies only to qualified use of a demonstration automobile. A demonstration automobile is an automobile that is—

(i) Currently in the inventory of the automobile dealership, and

(ii) Available for test drives by customers during the normal business hours of the employee.

(4) *Substantial restrictions on personal use.* Substantial restrictions on the personal use of demonstration automobiles exist when all of the following conditions are satisfied:

(i) Use by individuals other than the full-time automobile salesmen (e.g., the salesman's family) is prohibited,

(ii) Use for personal vacation trips is prohibited,

(iii) The storage of personal possessions in the automobile is prohibited, and

(iv) The total use by mileage of the automobile by the salesman outside the salesman's normal working hours is limited.

(5) *Sales area*—(i) *In general.* Qualified automobile demonstration use must be use in the sales area in which the automobile dealer's sales office is located. The sales area is the geographic area surrounding the automobile dealer's sales office from which the office regularly derives customers.

(ii) *Sales area safe harbor.* With respect to a particular full-time salesman, the automobile dealer's sales area may be treated as the larger of the area within a 75 mile radius of the dealer's sales office, or the one-way commuting distance (in miles) of the particular salesman.

(p) *Parking*—(1) *In general.* The value of parking provided to an employee on or near the business premises of the employer is excludable from gross income as a working condition fringe. The working condition fringe exclusion applies whether the employer owns or rents the parking facility or parking space.

(2) *Reimbursement of parking expenses.* Any reimbursement to the employee of the ordinary and necessary expenses of renting a parking space on or near the business premises of the employer is excludable as a working condition fringe. The preceding sentence does not apply, however, to cash payments that are not actually used for renting a parking space. Thus, that part of a general transportation allowance that is not used for parking is not excludable as a working condition fringe under this paragraph (p).

(3) *Parking on residential property.* With respect to an employee, this paragraph (p) does not apply to any parking facility or space located on property owned or leased for residential purposes by the employee.

(q) *Nonapplicability of nondiscrimination rules.* Except to the extent provided in paragraph (n)(3) of this section, the nondiscrimination rules of section 132(h)(1) and § 1.132-8T do not apply in determining the amount, if any, of a working condition fringe. [Temporary Reg. § 1.132-5T.]

☐ [*T.D.* 8063, 12-18-85. *Amended by T.D.* 8256, 7-5-89.]

Reg. § 1.132-5T(o)(3)

[Reg. § 1.132-6]

§ 1.132-6. De minimis fringes.—(a) *In general.* Gross income does not include the value of a de minimis fringe provided to an employee. The term "de minimis fringe" means any property or service the value of which is (after taking into account the frequency with which similar fringes are provided by the employer to the employer's employees) so small as to make accounting for it unreasonable or administratively impracticable.

(b) *Frequency*—(1) *Employee-measured frequency.* Generally, the frequency with which similar fringes are provided by the employer to the employer's employees is determined by reference to the frequency with which the employer provides the fringes to each individual employee. For example, if an employer provides a free meal in kind to one employee on a daily basis, but not to any other employee, the value of the meals is not de minimis with respect to that one employee even though with respect to the employer's entire workforce the meals are provided "infrequently."

(2) *Employer-measured frequency.* Notwithstanding the rule of paragraph (b)(1) of this section, except for purposes of applying the special rules of paragraph (d)(2) of this section, where it would be administratively difficult to determine frequency with respect to individual employees, the frequency with which similar fringes are provided by the employer to the employer's employees is determined by reference to the frequency with which the employer provides the fringes to the workforce as a whole. Therefore, under this rule, the frequency with which any individual employee receives such a fringe benefit is not relevant and in some circumstances, the de minimis fringe exclusion may apply with respect to a benefit even though a particular employee receives the benefit frequently. For example, if an employer exercises sufficient control and imposes significant restrictions on the personal use of a company copying machine so that at least 85 percent of the use of the machine is for business purposes, any personal use of the copying machine by particular employees is considered to be a de minimis fringe.

(c) *Administrability.* Unless excluded by a provision of chapter 1 of the Internal Revenue Code of 1986 other than section 132(a)(4), the value of any fringe benefit that would not be unreasonable or administratively impracticable to account for is includible in the employee's gross income. Thus, except as provided in paragraph (d)(2) of this section, the provision of any cash fringe benefit is never excludable under section 132(a) as a de minimis fringe benefit. Similarly except as otherwise provided in paragraph (d) of this section, a cash equivalent fringe benefit (such as a fringe benefit provided to an employee through the use of a gift certificate or charge or credit card) is generally not excludable under § 132(a) even if the same property or service acquired (if provided in kind) would be excludable as a de minimis fringe benefit. For example, the provision of cash to an employee for a theatre ticket that would itself be excludable as a de minimis fringe (see paragraph (e)(1) of this section) is not excludable as a de minimis fringe.

(d) *Special rules*—(1) *Transit passes.* A public transit pass provided at a discount to defray an employee's commuting costs may be excluded from the employee's gross income as a de minimis fringe if such discount does not exceed $21 in any month. The exclusion provided in this paragraph (d)(1) also applies to the provision of tokens or fare cards that enable an individual to travel on the public transit system if the value of such tokens and fare cards in any month does not exceed by more than $21 the amount the employee paid for the tokens and fare cards for such month. Similarly, the exclusion of this paragraph (d)(1) applies to the provision of a voucher or similar instrument that is exchangeable solely for tokens, fare cards, or other instruments that enable the employee to use the public transit system if the value of such vouchers and other instruments in any month does not exceed $21. The exclusion of this paragraph (d)(1) also applies to reimbursements made by an employer to an employee after December 31, 1988, to cover the cost of commuting on a public transit system, provided the employee does not receive more than $21 in such reimbursements for commuting costs in any given month. The reimbursement must be made under a bona fide reimbursement arrangement. A reimbursement arrangement will be treated as bona fide if the employer establishes appropriate procedures for verifying on a periodic basis that the employee's use of public transportation for commuting is consistent with the value of the benefit provided by the employer for that purpose. The amount of in-kind public transit commuting benefits and reimbursements provided during any month that are excludible under this paragraph (d)(1) is limited to $21. For months ending before July 1, 1991, the amount is $15 per month. The exclusion provided in this paragraph (d)(1) does not apply to the provision of any benefit to defray public transit expenses incurred for personal travel other than commuting.

(2) *Occasional meal money or local transportation fare*—(i) *General rule.* Meals, meal money or local transportation fare provided to an employee is excluded as a de minimis fringe benefit if

the benefit provided is reasonable and is provided in a manner that satisfies the following three conditions:

(A) *Occasional basis.* The meals, meal money or local transportation fare is provided to the employee on an occasional basis. Whether meal money or local transportation fare is provided to an employee on an occasional basis will depend upon the frequency i.e. the availability of the benefit and regularity with which the benefit is provided by the employer to the employee. Thus, meals, meal money, or local transportation fare or a combination of such benefits provided to an employee on a regular or routine basis is not provided on an occasional basis.

(B) *Overtime.* The meals, meal money or local transportation fare is provided to an employee because overtime work necessitates an extension of the employee's normal work schedule. This condition does not fail to be satisfied merely because the circumstances giving rise to the need for overtime work are reasonably foreseeable.

(C) *Meal money.* In the case of a meal or meal money, the meal or meal money is provided to enable the employee to work overtime. Thus, for example, meals provided on the employer's premises that are consumed during the period that the employee works overtime or meal money provided for meals consumed during such period satisfy this condition.

In no event shall meal money or local transportation fare calculated on the basis of the number of hours worked (e.g., $1.00 per hour for each hour over eight hours) be considered a de minimis fringe benefit.

(ii) *Applicability of other exclusions for certain meals and for transportation provided for security concerns.* The value of meals furnished to an employee, an employee's spouse, or any of the employee's dependents by or on behalf of the employee's employer for the convenience of the employer is excluded from the employee's gross income if the meals are furnished on the business premises of the employer (see section 119). (For purposes of the exclusion under section 119, the definitions of an employee under § 1.132-1(b) do not apply.) If, for a bona fide business-oriented security concern, an employer provides an employee vehicle transportation that is specially designed for security (for example, the vehicle is equipped with bulletproof glass and armor plating), and the conditions of § 1.132-5(m) are satisfied, the value of the special security design is excludable from gross income as a working condition fringe if the employee would not have had

such special security design but for the bona fide business-oriented security concern.

(iii) *Special rule for employer-provided transportation provided in certain circumstances.*—(A) *Partial exclusion of value.* If an employer provides transportation (such as taxi fare) to an employee for use in commuting to and/or from work because of unusual circumstances and because, based on the facts and circumstances, it is unsafe for the employee to use other available means of transportation, the excess of the value of each one-way trip over $1.50 per one-way commute is excluded from gross income. The rule of this paragraph (d)(2)(iii) is not available to a control employee as defined in § 1.61-21(f)(5) and (6).

(B) *"Unusual circumstances".* Unusual circumstances are determined with respect to the employee receiving the transportation and are based on all facts and circumstances. An example of unusual circumstances would be when an employee is asked to work outside of his normal work hours (such as being called to the workplace at 1:00 am when the employee normally works from 8:00 am to 4:00 pm). Another example of unusual circumstances is a temporary change in the employee's work schedule (such as working from 12 midnight to 8:00 am rather than from 8:00 am to 4:00 pm for a two-week period).

(C) *"Unsafe conditions".* Factors indicating whether it is unsafe for an employee to use other available means of transportation are the history of crime in the geographic area surrounding the employee's workplace or residence and the time of day during which the employee must commute.

(3) *Use of special rules or examples to establish a general rule.* The special rules provided in this paragraph (d) or examples provided in paragraph (e) of this section may not be used to establish any general rule permitting exclusion as a de minimis fringe. For example, the fact that $252 (i.e., $21 per month for 12 months) worth of public transit passes can be excluded from gross income as a de minimis fringe in 1992 does not mean that any fringe benefit with a value equal to or less than $252 may be excluded as a de minimis fringe. As another example, the fact that the commuting use of an employer-provided vehicle more than one day a month is an example of a benefit not excludable as a de minimis fringe (see paragraph (e)(2) of this section) does not mean that the commuting use of a vehicle up to 12 times per year is excludable from gross income as a de minimis fringe.

(4) *Benefits exceeding value and frequency limits.* If a benefit provided to an employee is not de minimis because either the value or frequency exceeds a limit provided in this paragraph (d), no amount of the benefit is considered to be a de minimis fringe. For example, if, in 1992, an employer provides a $50 monthly public transit pass, the entire $50 must be included in income, not just the excess value over $21.

(e) *Examples*—(1) *Benefits excludable from income.* Examples of de minimis fringe benefits are occasional typing of personal letters by a company secretary; occasional personal use of an employer's copying machine, provided that the employer exercises sufficient control and imposes significant restrictions on the personal use of the machine so that at least 85 percent of the use of the machine is for business purposes; occasional cocktail parties, group meals, or picnics for employees and their guests; traditional birthday or holiday gifts of property (not cash) with a low fair market value; occasional theater or sporting event tickets; coffee, doughnuts, and soft drinks; local telephone calls; and flowers, fruit, books, or similar property provided to employees under special circumstances (e.g., on account of illness, outstanding performance, or family crisis).

(2) *Benefits not excludable as de minimis fringes.* Examples of fringe benefits that are not excludable from gross income as de minimis fringes are: season tickets to sporting or theatrical events; the commuting use of an employer-provided automobile or other vehicle more than one day a month; membership in a private country club or athletic facility, regardless of the frequency with which the employee uses the facility; employer-provided group-term life insurance on the life of the spouse or child of an employee; and use of employer-owned or leased facilities (such as an apartment, hunting lodge, boat, etc.) for a weekend. Some amount of the value of certain of these fringe benefits may be excluded from income under other statutory provisions, such as the exclusion for working condition fringes. See § 1.132-5.

(f) *Nonapplicability of nondiscrimination rules.* Except to the extent provided in § 1.132-7, the nondiscrimination rules of section 132(h)(1) and § 1.132-8 do not apply in determining the amount, if any, of a de minimis fringe. Thus, a fringe benefit may be excludable as a de minimis fringe even if the benefit is provided exclusively to highly compensated employees of the employer. [Reg. § 1.132-6.]

❑ [*T.D.* 8256, 7-5-89. *Amended by T.D.* 8389, 1-15-92.]

→ *Caution: Temporary Reg § 1.132-6T applies to the tax treatment of fringe benefits for 1985—1988. See Reg. §§ 1.132-0—1.132-8 for post-1988 rules.*←

[Reg. § 1.132-6T]

§ 1.132-6T. De minimis fringe—1985 through 1988 (Temporary).—(a) *In general.* Gross income does not include the value of a de minimis fringe provided to an employee. The term "de minimis fringe" means any property or service the value of which is (after taking into account the frequency with which similar fringes are provided by the employer to the employer's employees) so small as to make accounting for it unreasonable or administratively impracticable.

(b) *Frequency.* Generally, the frequency with which similar fringes are provided by the employer to the employer's employees is determined by reference to the frequency with which the employer provides the fringe to each individual employee. For example, if an employer provides a free meal to one employee on a daily basis, but not to any other employee, the value of the meals is not de minimis with respect to that one employee even though with respect to the employer's entire workforce the meals are provided "infrequently." However, where it would be administratively difficult to determine frequency with respect to individual employees, the frequency with which similar fringes are provided by the employer to the employer's employees is determined by reference to the frequency with which the employer provides the fringes to the employees and not the frequency with which individual employees receive them. In these cases, if an employer occasionally provides a fringe benefit of de minimis value to the employer's employees, the de minimis fringe exclusion may apply even though a particular employee receives the benefit frequently. For example, if an employer exercises sufficient control and imposes significant restrictions on the personal use of a company copying machine so that at least 85 percent of the use of the machine is for business purposes, any personal use of the copying machine by particular employees is considered to be a de minimis fringe.

(c) *Administrability.* Unless excluded by a statutory provision other than section 132(a)(4), the value of any fringe benefit that would not be unreasonable or administratively impracticable to account for must be included in the employee's gross income. Thus, except as otherwise provided

→ *Caution: Temporary Reg. § 1.132-6T applies to the tax treatment of fringe benefits for 1985—1988. See Reg. §§ 1.132-0—1.132-8 for post-1988 rules.*←

in this section, the provision of any cash fringe benefit (or any fringe benefit provided to an employee through the use of a charge or credit card) is not excludable as a de minimis fringe. For example, the provision of cash to an employee for personal entertainment is not excludable as a de minimis fringe.

(d) *Special rules*—(1) *Transit passes.* A transit pass provided to an employee at a discount not exceeding $15 per month may be excluded as a de minimis fringe. The exclusion provided in this paragraph (d) also applies to the provision of $15 in tokens or fare cards that enable an individual to travel on the transit system. The exclusion provided in this paragraph (d) does not apply to any provision of cash or other benefit to defray transit expenses incurred for personal travel.

(2) *Occasional meal money or local transportation fare.* Occasional meal money or local transportation fare provided to an employee because overtime work necessitates an extension of the employee's normal workday is excluded as a de minimis fringe.

(3) *Use of special rules to establish a general rule.* The special rules provided in this paragraph (d) may not be used to establish any general rule. For example, the fact that $180 ($15 per month for 12 months) worth of transit passes can be excluded in a year does not mean that any fringe benefit with a value equal to or less than $180 may be excluded as a de minimis fringe.

(4) *Benefits exceeding value and frequency limitations.* If the benefit provided to an employee is not de minimis because either the value or frequency exceeds a limit provided in this paragraph (d), no amount of the benefit is considered to be de minimis. For example, if an employer provides a $20 monthly transit pass, the entire $20 must be included in income, not just the excess value over $15.

(e) *Nonapplicability of nondiscrimination rules.* Except to the extent provided in § 1.132-7T, the nondiscrimination rules of section 132(h)(1) and § 1.132-8T do not apply. Thus, for example, a fringe benefit may be a de minimis fringe even if the benefit is provided exclusively to officers of the employer.

(f) *Examples*—(1) *Benefits excludable from income.* Examples of de minimis fringe benefits are occasional typing of personal letters by a company secretary; occasional personal use of an employer's copying machine, provided that the employer exercises sufficient control and imposes significant restrictions on the personal use of the

machine so that at least 85 percent of the use of the machine is for business purposes; occasional cocktail parties or picnics for employees and their guests; traditional holiday gifts of property (not cash) with a low fair market value; occasional theatre or sporting event tickets; and coffee and doughnuts.

(2) *Benefits not excludable as de minimis fringes.* Examples of fringe benefits that are not excludable from income as de minimis fringes are: season tickets to sporting or theatrical events; the commuting use of an employer-provided automobile or other vehicle more than once a month; membership in a private country club or athletic facility, regardless of the frequency with which the employee uses the facility; and use of employer-owned or leased facilities (such as an apartment, hunting lodge, boat, etc.) for a weekend. Some amount of the value of these fringe benefits may be excluded under other statutory provisions, such as the exclusion for working condition fringes. See § 1.132-5T. [Temporary Reg. § 1.132-6T.]

☐ [T.D. 8063, 12-18-85. Amended by T.D. 8256, 7-5-89.]

[Reg. § 1.132-7]

§ 1.132-7. **Employer-operated eating facilities.**—(a) *In general*—(1) *Condition for exclusion*—(i) *General rule.* The value of meals provided to employees at an employer-operated eating facility for employees is excludable from gross income as a de minimis fringe only if on an annual basis, the revenue from the facility equals or exceeds the direct operating costs of the facility.

(ii) *Additional condition for highly compensated employees.* With respect to any highly compensated employee, an exclusion is available under this section only if the condition set out in paragraph (a)(1)(i) of this section is satisfied and access to the facility is available on substantially the same terms to each member of a group of employees that is defined under a reasonable classification set up by the employer that does not discriminate in favor of highly compensated employees. See § 1.132-8. For purposes of this paragraph (a)(1)(ii), each dining room or cafeteria in which meals are served is treated as a separate eating facility, whether each such dining room or cafeteria has its own kitchen or other food-preparation area.

(2) *Employer-operated eating facility for employees.* An employer-operated eating facility for

employees is a facility that meets all of the following conditions—

(i) The facility is owned or leased by the employer,

(ii) The facility is operated by the employer,

(iii) The facility is located on or near the business premises of the employer, and

(iv) The meals furnished at the facility are provided during, or immediately before or after, the employee's workday.

For purposes of this section, the term "meals" means food, beverages, and related services provided at the facility. If an employer can reasonably determine the number of meals that are excludable from income by the recipient employees under section 119, the employer may, in determining whether the requirement of paragraph (a)(1)(i) of this section is satisfied, disregard all costs and revenues attributable to such meals provided to such employees. If an employer can reasonably determine the number of meals received by volunteers who receive food and beverages at a hospital, free or at a discount, the employer may, in determining whether the requirement of paragraph (a)(1)(i) of this section is satisfied, disregard all costs and revenues attributable to such meals provided to such volunteers. If an employer charges nonemployees a greater amount than employees, in determining whether the requirement of paragraph (a)(1)(i) of this section is satisfied, the employer must disregard all costs and revenues attributable to such meals provided to such nonemployees.

(3) *Operation by the employer.* If an employer contracts with another to operate an eating facility for its employees, the facility is considered to be operated by the employer for purposes of this section. If an eating facility is operated by more than one employer, it is considered to be operated by each employer.

(4) *Example.* The provisions of this paragraph (a)(2) may be illustrated by the following example:

Example (1). Assume that a not-for-profit hospital system maintains cafeterias for the use of its employees and volunteers. Only the employees are charged for food service at the cafeteria and the policy of the hospital is to charge the employees only for the costs of food, beverage and labor directly attributable to the meal. Most of the cafeterias within the system furnish more free meals to volunteers than they serve paid meals to employees. For purposes of this paragraph, as long as the employer can accurately determine the number of meals received free or at a discount by

volunteers, the employer may disregard all the costs and revenues attributable to such meals provided to volunteers. Therefore, for purposes of this paragraph, the costs of the hospital system for furnishing meals to employees who pay for them are the costs to be compared to determine if the revenues from the facility equal or exceed direct operating costs of the facility's service to employees.

(b) *Direct operating costs*—(1) *In general.* For purposes of this section, the direct operating costs of an eating facility are—

(i) The cost of food and beverages, and

(ii) The cost of labor for personnel whose services relating to the facility are performed primarily on the premises of the eating facility.

Direct operating costs do not include the labor cost attributable to personnel whose services relating to the facility are not performed primarily on the premises of the eating facility. Thus, for example, the labor costs attributable to cooks, waiters, and waitresses are included in direct operating costs, but the labor cost attributable to a manager of an eating facility whose services relating to the facility are not primarily performed on the premises of the eating facility is not included in direct operating costs. If an employee performs services relating to the facility both on and off the premises of the eating facility, only the portion of the total labor cost of the employee relating to the facility that bears the same proportion to such total labor cost as time spent on the premises bears to total time spent performing services relating to the facility is included in direct operating costs. For example, assume that 60 percent of the services of a cook in the above example are not related to the eating facility. Only 40 percent of the total labor cost of the cook is includible in direct operating costs. For purposes of this section, labor costs include all compensation required to be reported on a Form W-2 for income tax purposes and related employment taxes paid by the employer. In determining the direct operating costs of an eating facility, the employer may include as part of the facility, vending machines that are provided by the employer and located on the same premises as the other eating facilities operated by the employer.

(2) *Multiple dining rooms or cafeterias.* The direct operating costs test may be applied separately for each dining room or cafeteria. Alternatively, the direct operating costs test may be applied with respect to all the eating facilities operated by the employer.

(3) *Payment to operator of facility.* If an employer contracts with another to operate an eating facility for its employees, the direct operat-

ing costs of the facility consist both of direct operating costs, if any, incurred by the employer and the amount paid to the operator of the facility to the extent that such amount is attributable to what would be direct operating costs if the employer operated the facility directly.

(c) *Valuation of non-excluded meals provided at an employer-operated eating facility for employees.* If the exclusion for meals provided at an employer-operated eating facility for employees is not available, the recipient of meals provided at such facility must include in income the amount by which the fair market value of the meals provided exceeds the sum of—

(1) the amount, if any, paid for the meals, and

(2) the amount, if any, specifically excluded by another section of chapter 1 of this subtitle.

For special valuation rules relating to such meals, see § 1.61-21(j). [Reg. § 1.132-7.]

☐ [*T.D.* 8256, 7-5-89.]

→ *Caution: Temporary Reg. § 1.132-7T applies to the tax treatment of fringe benefits for 1985—1988. See Reg. § § 1.132-0—1.132-8 for post-1988 rules.*←

[Reg. § 1.132-7T]

§ 1.132-7T. Treatment of employer-operated eating facilities—1985 through 1988 (Temporary).—(a) *In general*—(1) *General rule.* The value of meals provided to employees at an employer-operated eating facility for employees is excludable from gross income as a de minimis fringe only if—

(i) On an annual basis, the revenue from the facility equals or exceeds the direct operating costs of the facility, and

(ii) With respect to any officer, owner or highly compensated employee, access to the facility is available on substantially the same terms to each member of a group of employees that is defined under a reasonable classification set up by the employer that does not discriminate in favor of officers, owners, and highly compensated employees. See § 1.132-8T.

(2) *Employer-operated eating facility for employees.* An employer-operated eating facility for employees is a facility that meets all of the following conditions—

(i) The facility is owned or leased by the employer,

(ii) The facility is operated by the employer,

(iii) The facility is located on or near the business premises of the employer,

(iv) Substantially all of the use of the facility is by employees of the employer operating the facility, and

(v) The meals furnished at the facility are provided during, or immediately before or after, the employee's workday.

For purposes of this section, the term "meals" means food, beverages, and related services provided at the facility. If an employer can determine the number of employees who receive meals that are excludable from income under section 119, the employer may, in determining whether the requirement of paragraph (a)(1)(i) of this section is satisfied, disregard all costs and revenues attributable to such meals provided to such employees. For purposes of this section, each dining room or cafeteria in which meals are served is treated as a separate eating facility, regardless of whether each such dining room or cafeteria has its own kitchen or other food-preparation area.

(3) *Operation by the employer.* If an employer contracts with another to operate an eating facility for its employees, the facility is considered to be operated by the employer for purposes of this section. If an eating facility is operated by more than one employer, it is considered to be operated by each employer.

(b) *Direct operating costs.* The direct operating costs test must be applied separately for each dining room or cafeteria. For purposes of this section, the direct operating costs of an eating facility are (1) the cost of food and beverages and (2) the cost of labor for personnel whose services relating to the facility are performed primarily on the premises of the eating facility. Direct operating costs do not include the cost of labor for personnel whose services relating to the facility are not performed primarily on the premises of the eating facility. Thus, for example, the labor cost for cooks, waiters, and waitresses is included in direct operating costs, but the labor cost for a manager of an eating facility whose services relating to the facility are not primarily performed on the premises of the eating facility is not included in direct operating costs. If an employee performs services both on and off the premises of the eating facility, only the applicable percentage of the total labor cost of the employee that bears the same proportion as time spent on the premises bears to total time is included in direct operating costs. For example, assume that 60 percent of the services of the cooks in the above example are not related to the eating facility. Only 40 percent of the total labor cost of the cooks is includible in

→ *Caution: Temporary Reg. § 1.132-7T applies to the tax treatment of fringe benefits for 1985—1988. See Reg. § § 1.132-0—1.132-8 for post-1988 rules.*←

direct operating costs. For purposes of this section, labor costs include all compensation required to be reported on a Form W-2 for income tax purposes and related employment taxes paid by the employer.

(c) *Valuation of non-excluded meals provided at an employer-operated eating facility for employees.* If the exclusion for meals provided at an employer-operated eating facility for employees is not available, the recipient of meals provided at such facility must include in income the amount by which the fair market value of the meals provided exceeds the sum of (1) the amount, if any, paid for the meals, and (2) the amount, if any, specifically excluded by another section of the Code. For special valuation rules relating to such meals see § 1.61-2T(j). [Temporary Reg. § 1.132-7T.]

☐ *[T.D. 8063, 12-18-85. Amended by T.D. 8256, 7-5-89.]*

[Reg. § 1.132-8]

§ 1.132-8. Fringe benefit nondiscrimination rules.—(a) *Application of nondiscrimination rules*—(1) *General rule.* A highly compensated employee who receives a no-additional cost service, a qualified employee discount or a meal provided at an employer-operated eating facility for employees shall not be permitted to exclude such benefit from his or her income unless the benefit is available on substantially the same terms to:

(i) All employees of the employer; or

(ii) A group of employees of the employer which is defined under a reasonable classification set up by the employer that does not discriminate in favor of highly compensated employees. See paragraph (f) of this section for the definition of a highly compensated employee.

(2) *Consequences of discrimination*—(i) *In general.* If an employer maintains more than one fringe benefit program, i.e.. either different fringe benefits being provided to the same group of employees, or different classifications of employees or the same fringe benefit being provided to two or more classifications of employees, the nondiscrimination requirements of section 132 will generally be applied separately to each such program. Thus, a determination that one fringe benefit program discriminates in favor of highly compensated employees generally will not cause other fringe benefit programs covering the same highly compensated employees to be treated as discriminatory. If the fringe benefits provided to a highly

compensated individual do not satisfy the nondiscrimination rules provided in this section, such individual shall be unable to exclude from gross income any portion of the benefit. For example, if an employer offers a 20 percent discount (which otherwise satisfies the requirements for a qualified employee discount) to all non-highly compensated employees and a 35 percent discount to all highly compensated employees, the entire value of the 35 percent discount (not just the excess over 20 percent) is includible in the gross income and wages of the highly compensated employees who make purchases at a discount.

(ii) *Exception*—(A) *Related fringe benefit programs.* If one of a group of fringe benefit programs discriminates in favor of highly compensated employees, no related fringe benefit provided to such highly compensated employees under any other fringe benefit program may be excluded from the gross income of such highly compensated employees. For example, assume a department store provides a 20 percent merchandise discount to all employees under one fringe benefit program. Assume further that under a second fringe benefit program, the department store provides an additional 15 percent merchandise discount to a group of employees defined under a classification which discriminates in favor of highly compensated employees. Because the second fringe benefit program is discriminatory, the 15 percent merchandise discount provided to the highly compensated employees is not a qualified employee discount. In addition, because the 20 percent merchandise discount provided under the first fringe benefit program is related to the fringe benefit provided under the second fringe benefit program, the 20 percent merchandise discount provided the highly compensated employees is not a qualified employee discount. Thus, the entire 35 percent merchandise discount provided to the highly compensated employees is includible in such employees' gross incomes.

(B) *Employer-operated eating facilities for employees.* For purposes of paragraph (a)(2)(ii)(A) of this section, meals at different employer-operated eating facilities for employees are not related fringe benefits, so that a highly compensated employee may exclude from gross income the value of a meal at a nondiscriminatory facility even though any meals provided to him or her at a discriminatory facility cannot be excluded.

(3) *Scope of the nondiscrimination rules provided in this section.* The nondiscrimination rules provided in this section apply only to fringe bene-

fits provided pursuant to section 132(a)(1), (a)(2), and (e)(2). These rules have no application to any other employee benefit that may be subject to nondiscrimination requirements under any other section of the Code.

(b) *Aggregation of employees—(1) Section 132(a)(1) and (2).* For purposes of determining whether the exclusions for no-additional-cost services and qualified employee discounts are available to highly compensated employees, the nondiscrimination rules of this section are applied by aggregating the employees of all related employers (as defined in § 1.132-1(c)), except that employees in different lines of business (as defined in § 1.132-4) are not to be aggregated. Thus, in general, for purposes of this section, the term "employees of the employer" refers to all employees of the employer and any other entity that is a member of a group described in sections 414(b), (c), (m), or, (o) and that performs services within the same line of business as the employer which provides the particular fringe benefit. Employees in different lines of business will be aggregated, however, if the line of business limitation has been relaxed pursuant to paragraphs (b) through (g) of § 1.132-4.

(2) *Section 132(e)(2).* For purposes of determining whether the exclusions for meals provided at employer-operated eating facilities are available to highly compensated employees, the nondiscrimination rules of this section are applied by aggregating the employees of all related employers (as defined in section § 1.132-1(c)) who regularly work at or near the premises on which the eating facility is located, except that employees in different lines of business (as defined in § 1.132-4) are not to be aggregated. The nondiscrimination rules of this section are applied separately to each eating facility. Each dining room or cafeteria in which meals are served is treated as a separate eating facility, regardless of whether each such dining room or cafeteria has its own kitchen or other food-preparation area.

(3) *Classes of employees who may be excluded.* For purposes of applying the nondiscrimination rules of this section to a particular fringe benefit program, there may be excluded from consideration employees who may be excluded from consideration under section 89(h), as enacted by the Tax Reform Act of 1986, Public Law 99-514, 100 Stat. 2085 (1986) and amended by the Technical and Miscellaneous Revenue Act of 1988, Public Law 100-647, 102 Stat. 3342 (1988).

(c) *Availability on substantially the same terms—(1) General rule.* The determination of whether a benefit is available on substantially the same terms shall be made upon the basis of the

facts and circumstances of each situation. In general, however, if any one of the terms or conditions governing the availability of a particular benefit to one or more employees varies from any one of the terms or conditions governing the availability of a benefit made available to one or more other employees, such benefit shall not be considered to be available on substantially the same terms except to the extent otherwise provided in paragraph (2) below. For example, if a department store provides a 20 percent qualified employee discount to all of its employees on all merchandise, then substantially the same terms requirement will be satisfied. Similarly, if the discount provided to all employees is 30 percent on certain merchandise (such as apparel), and 20 percent on all other merchandise, then substantially the same terms requirement will be satisfied. However, if a department store provides a 20 percent qualified employee discount to all employees, but as to the employees in certain departments, the discount is available upon hire, and as to the remaining departments, the discount is only available when an employee has completed a specified term of services, the 20 percent discount is not available on substantially the same terms to all of the employees of the employer. Similarly, if a greater discount is given to employees with more seniority, full-time work status, or a particular job description, such benefit (i.e., the discount) would not be available to all employees eligible for the discount on substantially the same terms, except to the extent otherwise provided in paragraph (2) below. These examples also apply to no-additional-cost services. Thus, if an employer charges non-highly compensated employees for a no-additional-cost service and does not charge highly compensated employees (or charges highly compensated employees a lesser amount), then substantially the same terms requirement will not be satisfied.

(2) *Certain terms relating to priority.* Certain fringe benefits made available to employees are available only in limited quantities that may be insufficient to meet employee demand. This situation may occur either because of employer policy (such as where an employer determines that only a certain number of units of a specific product will be made available to employees each year) or because of the nature of the fringe benefit (such as where an employer provides a no-additional-cost transportation service that is limited to the number of seats available just before departure). Under these circumstances, an employer may find it necessary to establish some method of allocating the limited fringe benefits among the employees eligible to receive the fringe benefits.

Reg. § 1.132-8(b)(1)

The employer may establish the priorities described below.

(i) *Priority on a first come, first served, or similar basis.* A benefit shall not fail to be treated as available to a group of employees on substantially the same terms merely because the employer allocates the benefit among such employees on a "first come, first served" or lottery basis, provided that the same notice of the terms of availability is given to all employees in the group and the terms under which the benefit is provided to employees within the group are otherwise the same with respect to all employees. For purposes of the preceding sentence, a program that gives priority to employees who are the first to submit written requests for the benefit will constitute priority on a "first come, first served" basis. Similarly, if the employer regularly engages in the practice of allocating benefits on a priority basis to employees demonstrating a critical need, such benefit shall not fail to be treated as available on substantially the same terms to all of the employees with respect to whom such priority status is available as long as the determination is based upon uniform and objective criteria which have been communicated to all employees in the group of eligible employees. An example of a critical need would be priority transportation given to an employee in the event of a medical emergency involving the employee (or a member of the employee's immediate family) or a recent death in the employee's immediate family. Frustrated vacation plans or forfeited deposits would not be treated as giving rise to particularly critical needs.

(ii) *Priority on the basis of seniority.* Solely for purposes of section 1.132-8, a benefit shall not fail to be treated as available to a group of employees of the employer on substantially the same terms merely because the employer allocates the benefit among such employees on a seniority basis provided that:

(A) the same notice of the terms of availability is given to all employees in the group; and

(B) the average value of the benefit provided for each nonhighly compensated employee is at least 75% of that provided for each highly compensated employee. For purposes of this test, the average value of the benefit provided for each nonhighly compensated (highly compensated) employee is determined by taking the sum of the fair market values of such benefit provided to all the nonhighly compensated (highly compensated) employees, determined in accordance with section 1.61-21, and then dividing that sum by the total number of nonhighly compensated (highly com-

pensated) employees of the employer. For purposes of determining the average value of the benefit provided for each employee, all employees of the employer are counted, including those who are not eligible to receive the benefit from the employer.

(d) *Testing for discrimination.*—(1) *Classification test.* In the event that a benefit described in section 132(a)(1), (a)(2) or (e)(2) is not available on substantially the same terms to all of the employees of the employer, no exclusion shall be available to a highly compensated employee for such benefit unless the program under which the benefit is provided satisfies the nondiscrimination standards set forth in this section. The nondiscrimination standard of this section will be satisfied only if the benefit is available on substantially the same terms to a group of employees of the employer which is defined under a reasonable classification established by the employer that does not discriminate in favor of highly compensated employees. The determination of whether a particular classification is discriminatory will generally depend upon the facts and circumstances involved, based upon principles similar to those applied for purposes of section 410(b)(2)(A)(i) or, for years commencing prior to January 1, 1988, section 410(b)(1)(B). Thus, in general, except as otherwise provided in this section, if a benefit is available on substantially the same terms to a group of employees which, when compared with all of the other employees of the employer, constitutes a nondiscriminatory classification under section 410(b)(2)(A)(i) (or, if applicable, section 410(b)(1)(B)), it shall be deemed to be nondiscriminatory.

(2) *Classifications that are per se discriminatory.* A classification that, on its face, makes fringe benefits available principally to highly compensated employees is per se discriminatory. In addition, a classification that is based on either an amount or rate of compensation is per se discriminatory if it favors those with the higher amount or rate of compensation. On the other hand, a classification that is based on factors such as seniority, full-time vs. part-time employment, or job description is not per se discriminatory but may be discriminatory as applied to the workforce of a particular employer.

(3) *Former employees.* When determining whether a classification is discriminatory, former employees shall be tested separately from other employees of the employer. Therefore, a classification is not discriminatory solely because the employer does not make fringe benefits available to any former employee. Whether a classification of

Reg. § 1.132-8(d)(3)

former employees discriminates in favor of highly compensated employees will depend upon the particular facts and circumstances.

(4) *Restructuring of benefits.* For purposes of testing whether a particular group of employees would constitute a discriminatory classification for purposes of this section, an employer may restructure its fringe benefit program as described in this paragraph. If a fringe benefit is provided to more than one group of employees, and one or more such groups would constitute a discriminatory classification if considered by itself, then for purposes of this section, the employer may restructure its fringe benefit program so that all or some of the members of such group may be aggregated with another group, provided that each member of the restructured group will have available to him or her the same benefit upon the same terms and conditions. For example, assume that all highly compensated employees of an employer have fewer than five years of service and all nonhighly compensated employees have over five years of service. If the employer provided a five percent discount to employees with under five years of service and a ten percent discount to employees with over five years of service, the discount program available to the highly compensated employees would not satisfy the nondiscriminatory classification test; however, as a result of the rule described in this paragraph (d)(4), the employer could structure the program to consist of a five percent discount for all employees and a five percent additional discount for nonhighly compensated employees.

(5) *Employer-operated eating facilities for employees*—(i) *General rule.* If access to an employer-operated eating facility for employees is available to a classification of employees that discriminates in favor of highly compensated employees, then the classification will not be treated as discriminating in favor of highly compensated employees unless the facility is used by one or more executive group employees more than a de minimis amount.

(ii) *Executive group employee.* For purposes of this paragraph (d)(5), an employee is an "executive group employee" if the definition of paragraph (f)(1) of this section is satisfied. For purposes of identifying such employees, the phrase "top one percent of the employees" is substituted for the phrase "top ten percent of the employees" in section 414(q)(4) (relating to the definition of "top-paid group").

(e) *Cash bonuses or rebates.* A cash bonus or rebate provided to an employee by an employer that is determined with reference to the value of employer-provided property or services purchased by the employee, is treated as an equivalent employee discount. For example, assume a department store provides a 20 percent merchandise discount to all employees under a fringe benefit program. In addition, assume that the department store provides cash bonuses to a group of employees defined under a classification which discriminates in favor of highly compensated employees. Assume further that such cash bonuses equal 15 percent of the value of merchandise purchased by each employee. This arrangement is substantively identical to the example described in paragraph (e)(2)(i) of this section concerning related fringe benefit programs. Thus, both the 20 percent merchandise discount and the 15 percent cash bonus provided to the highly compensated employees are includible in such employees' gross incomes.

(f) *Highly compensated employee*—(1) *Government and nongovernment employees.* A highly compensated employee of any employer is any employee who, during the year or the preceding year—

(i) Was a 5-percent owner,

(ii) Received compensation from the employer in excess of $75,000,

(iii) Received compensation from the employer in excess of $50,000 and was in the top-paid group of employees for such year, or

(iv) Was at any time an officer and received compensation greater than 150 percent of the amount in effect under section 415(c)(1)(A) for such year.

For purposes of determining whether an employee is a highly compensated employee, the rules of sections 414(q), (s), and (t) apply.

(2) *Former employees.* A former employee shall be treated as a highly compensated employee if—

(i) The employee was a highly compensated employee when the employee separated from service, or

(ii) The employee was a highly compensated employee at any time after attaining age 55. [Reg. § 1.132-8.]

□ [*T.D. 8256, 7-5-89.*]

Reg. § 1.132-8(d)(4)

→ *Caution: Temporary Reg. § 1.132-8T applies to the tax treatment of fringe benefits for 1985—1988. See Reg. § § 1.132-0—1.132-8 for post-1988 rules.←*

[Reg. § 1.132-8T]

§ 1.132-8T. **Nondiscrimination rules—1985 through 1988 (Temporary).**—(a) *Application of nondiscrimination rules*—(1) *General rule.* To qualify under section 132 for the exclusions for no-additional-cost services, qualified employee discounts, or meals provided at employer-operated eating facilities for employees, the fringe benefit must be available on substantially the same terms to each member of a group of employees which is defined under a reasonable classification set up by the employer that does not discriminate in favor of officers, owners, or highly compensated employees (the "prohibited group employees").

(2) *Consequences of discrimination.* If the availability of or the provision of the fringe benefit does not satisfy the nondiscrimination rules provided in this section, the exclusion applies only to those employees (if any) who receive the benefit and who are not prohibited group employees. For example, if an employer offers a 20 percent discount (which otherwise satisfies the requirements for a qualified employee discount) to all nonprohibited group employees and a 35 percent discount to all prohibited group employees, the entire value of the 35 percent discount (not just the excess over 20 percent) is includible in the gross income and wages of the prohibited group employees who make purchases at a discount.

(3) *Scope of the nondiscrimination rules provided in this section.* The nondiscrimination rules provided in this section apply only to fringe benefits provided pursuant to section 132(a)(1), (a)(2), and (e)(2). These rules have no application to any other employee benefit that may be subject to nondiscrimination requirements under any other section of the Code.

(b) *Coverage requirement*—(1) *Section 132(a)(1) and (2).* For purposes of the exclusions for no-additional-cost services and qualified employee discounts, the nondiscrimination rules of this section are applied by aggregating the employees of all related employers (as defined in § 1.132-1T(c)), but without aggregating employees in different lines of business (as defined in § 1.132-4T). Employees in different lines of business will be aggregated, however, if the line of business limitation has been relaxed pursuant to either section 1.132-4T(b) or (c). Except as provided in paragraph (e) of this section, the nondiscrimination rules of this section are generally applied separately to each fringe benefit program of an employer.

(2) *Section 132(e)(2).* For purposes of the exclusion for meals provided at employer-operated eating facilities for employees, the nondiscrimination rules of this section are applied by aggregating the employees of all related employers, without regard to different lines of business, who regularly work at or near the premises on which the eating facility is located. The nondiscrimination rules of this section are applied separately to each eating facility. Each dining room or cafeteria in which meals are served is treated as a separate eating facility, regardless of whether each such dining room or cafeteria has its own kitchen or other food-preparation area.

(3) *Classes of employees who may be excluded.* Except as otherwise provided in this section, for purposes of applying the nondiscrimination rules of this section to a particular fringe benefit program, there may be excluded from consideration the following classes of employees provided that, with respect to each class (other than the class described in paragraph (b)(3)(iii) of this section), all employees in the class are excluded from participating in the particular fringe benefit program—

(i) all part-time or seasonal employees who are (or who are reasonably expected to be) credited with less than 1,000 hours (or such lesser number required for the program) of service during a calendar year;

(ii) all employees who are included in a unit of employees covered by an agreement which the Secretary of Labor finds to be a collective bargaining agreement between employee representatives and one or more employers, if there is evidence that the particular fringe benefit program was the subject of good faith bargaining between such employee representatives and such employer or employers (and if, after March 31, 1984, the additional condition of section 7701(a)(46) is satisfied);

(iii) all employees who are nonresident aliens and who receive no earned income (within the meaning of section 911(d)(2)) from the employer which constitutes income from services within the United States (within the meaning of section 861(a)(3));

(iv) all employees who have not completed at least one year (or such lesser period required for the program) of service with the employer;

(v) all employees who have separated from the service of the employer in a year prior to the current year (regardless of the reason for the separation);

Reg. § 1.132-8T(b)(3)

→ *Caution: Temporary Reg. § 1.132-8T applies to the tax treatment of fringe benefits for 1985—1988. See Reg. § § 1.132-0—1.132-8 for post-1988 rules.*←

(vi) all employees who have separated from the service of the employer in a year prior to the current year except for retired and/or disabled employees (either with or without a time limit based on a set number of years since separation from the service of the employer); and

(vii) all employees of a leased section of a department store.

(c) *Classification requirement*—(1) *General rule.* The determination of whether a particular classification established by an employer discriminates in favor of the prohibited group will depend on the facts and circumstances involved, based on principles similar to those applied in the qualified plan area (see section 410(b)(1)(B) and the regulations thereunder). In general, except as otherwise provided in this section, a classification that would be determined to be nondiscriminatory pursuant to the application of the nondiscrimination standards that are applied in the qualified plan area shall be deemed to be nondiscriminatory for purposes of section 132.

(2) *Classifications that are per se discriminatory.* A classification that, on its face, makes fringe benefits available only to prohibited group employees is per se discriminatory, and no exclusion from gross income is available to any prohibited group employee under section 132. In addition, a classification that is based on either an amount or rate of compensation is per se discriminatory if it favors those with the higher amount or rate of compensation. On the other hand, a classification that is based on factors such as seniority, full-time vs. part-time employment, or job description is not per se discriminatory but may be discriminatory as applied to the workforce of a particular employer.

(3) *Former employees.* When determining whether a classification is discriminatory, former employees shall not be considered together with other employees of the employer. Therefore, a classification is not discriminatory if the employer does not make the fringe benefits available to any former employee. Whether a classification of former employees discriminates in favor of prohibited group employees will depend on the facts and circumstances. The rules of this section shall apply separately to the former employee classification.

(4) *Employer-operated eating facilities for employees*—(i) *General rule.* If access to an employer-operated eating facility for employees is available to a classification of employees that discriminates in favor of highly compensated employees, the classification will not be treated as discriminating in favor of the prohibited group employees unless the facility is used, more than a de minimis amount, by any executive group employee.

(ii) *Executive group employees.* For purposes of this paragraph (c)(4), the term "executive group employees" has the same meaning as the term "prohibited group employees" (as defined in paragraph (g) of this section), except that for purposes of identifying highly compensated employees—

(A) The exception provided in paragraph (g)(1)(i)(A) of this section does not apply, and

(B) The phrase "highest-paid one percent of all employees of an employer" is substituted for the phrase "highest-paid ten percent of all employees of an employer" in paragraph (g)(1)(ii)(A) of this section.

(d) *Substantially-the-same-terms requirement*—(1) *General rule.* Fringe benefits available to a particular classification of employees must be available to each employee in the classification on substantially the same terms. The determination of whether this requirement is met shall depend on the facts and circumstances involved. For example, if a department store provides a 20 percent qualified employee discount to its employees on all merchandise, the substantially-the-same-terms requirement will be satisfied. Similarly, if the discount provided to all employees is 30 percent on certain merchandise (such as apparel), and 20 percent on all other merchandise, the substantially-the-same-terms requirement will be satisfied. However, if the discount provided is 20 percent on all merchandise for hourly employees and 30 percent on all merchandise for salaried employees, the substantially-the-same-terms requirement will not be satisfied. In addition, if the percentage discount varies depending on either an employee's amount or rate of compensation, or volume of purchases, the substantially-the-same-terms requirement will not be satisfied. In order to determine whether such a discount program satisfies the nondiscrimination requirements of section 132, each group of employees that does receive fringe benefits on substantially the same terms must be treated as a separate classification. However, subject to the rules of paragraph (e)(2) of this section, an employer may divide a fringe benefit program into two programs for purposes of aggregating groups of employees. See Example (1) of paragraph (d)(3) of this section.

Reg. § 1.132-8T(c)(1)

→ *Caution: Temporary Reg. § 1.132-8T applies to the tax treatment of fringe benefits for 1985—1988. See Reg. § § 1.132-0—1.132-8 for post-1988 rules.*←

(2) *Terms relating to priority.* Certain fringe benefits made available to employees are available only in limited quantities that may be insufficient to meet employee demand. This may occur either because of employer policy (such as where an employer determines that only a certain number of units of a specific product will be made available to employees each year) or because of the nature of the fringe benefit (such as where an employer provides a no-additional-cost transportation service that is limited to the number of seats available just before departure). Under these circumstances, an employer may find it necessary to establish some method of allocating the limited fringe benefits among the employees eligible to receive the fringe benefits. An allocation among employees on a "first-come, first-served" basis will not violate the substantially-the-same-terms requirement provided that such an allocation is not discriminatory in practice. In addition, an allocation among employees on a lottery basis will not violate the substantially-the-same-terms requirement provided that such an allocation is nondiscriminatory in practice. For example, assume that an employer has a limited number of a particular benefit to offer to its employees. Assume further that the employees interested in receiving the benefit submit their names to the employer who then selects a number of names, at random, equal to the number of fringe benefits available. This lottery system would not violate the substantially-the-same-terms requirement. An allocation among employees on other than a "first-come, first-served", lottery, or similar basis will violate the substantially-the-same-terms requirement. Therefore, an allocation based on seniority, full-time vs. part-time employment, or job description will violate the substantially-the-same-terms requirement. In order to determine whether such a fringe benefit program satisfies the nondiscrimination requirements of section 132, each group of employees that does receive fringe benefits on substantially the same terms must be treated as a separate classification. For purposes of this rule, the last two sentences of paragraph (d)(1) of this section apply.

(3) *Examples.* The following examples illustrate the provisions of this paragraph (d):

Example 1. Assume that with respect to a benefit available in limited quantities an employer provides priority to employees based on seniority. Assume further that all non-prohibited group employees have ten years of seniority and all prohibited group employees have nine years seniority. If each of these groups were tested separately, the benefits offered to prohibited group employees would be discriminatory under this section. In this case, the employer could divide the fringe benefit program provided to non-prohibited group employees into two parts: one relating to nine years of seniority and one relating to an additional year of seniority. As restructured in this manner, all employees receive the benefit relating to nine years seniority and only non-prohibited group employees receive the benefit relating to an additional year of seniority. Both groups (all employees and all non-prohibited group employees) are nondiscriminatory groups.

Example 2. Assume that prices charged to prohibited group employees at an employer-operated eating facility for employees are lower than prices charged to non-prohibited group employees. The substantially-the-same requirement is not satisfied.

(4) *Disproportionate use of eating facility.* If access to an employer-operated eating facility for employees is technically available on substantially-the-same-terms to (i) all employees who regularly work at or near the premises on which the eating facility is located (the employee group), or (ii) a nondiscriminatory classification of the employee group, but in practice a highly disproportionate number of the prohibited group employees in the employee group, compared to the non-prohibited group employees in the employee group, use the facility, the substantially-the-same-terms requirement will not be satisfied unless no member of the executive group eats there more than a de minimis amount.

(e) *Aggregation of separate fringe benefit programs*—(1) *General rule.* If an employer maintains more than one fringe benefit program, i.e., two or more classifications of employees providing either identical or different fringe benefits, the nondiscrimination requirements of section 132 will generally be applied separately to each such program. Thus, a determination that one fringe benefit program discriminates in favor of prohibited group employees generally will not cause other fringe benefit programs covering the same prohibited group employees to be treated as discriminatory.

(2) *Exception*—(i) *Related fringe benefit programs.* If one of a group of fringe benefit programs discriminates in favor of prohibited group employees, no related fringe benefit provided to such prohibited group employees under any other fringe benefit program may be excluded from the gross income of such prohibited group

Reg. § 1.132-8T(e)(2)

→ *Caution: Temporary Reg. § 1.132-8T applies to the tax treatment of fringe benefits for 1985—1988. See Reg. § § 1.132-0—1.132-8 for post-1988 rules.*←

employees. For example, assume a department store provides a 20 percent merchandise discount to all employees under one fringe benefit program. Assume further that under a second fringe benefit program, the department store provides an additional 15 percent merchandise discount to a group of employees defined under a classification which discriminates in favor of the prohibited group. Because the second fringe benefit program is discriminatory, the 15 percent merchandise discount provided to the prohibited group employees is not a qualified employee discount. In addition, because the 20 percent merchandise discount provided under the first fringe benefit program is related to the fringe benefit provided under the second fringe benefit program, the 20 percent merchandise discount provided the prohibited group employees is not a qualified employee discount. Thus, the entire 35 percent merchandise discount provided to the prohibited group employees is includible in such employees' gross incomes.

(ii) *Employer-operated eating facilities for employees.* For purposes of paragraph (e)(2)(i) of this section, meals at different employer-operated eating facilities for employees are not related fringe benefits, so that a prohibited group employee may exclude the value of a meal at a nondiscriminatory facility even though any meals provided to him or her at the discriminatory facility cannot be excluded.

(f) *Cash bonuses or rebates.* A cash bonus or rebate provided to an employee by an employer that is determined pursuant to the value of employer-provided property or services purchased by the employee, is treated as an equivalent employee discount. For example, assume a department store provides a 20 percent merchandise discount to all employees under a fringe benefit program. In addition, assume that the department store provides cash bonuses to a group of employees defined under a classification which discriminates in favor of the prohibited group. Assume further that such cash bonuses equal 15 percent of the value of merchandise purchased by each employee. This arrangement is substantively identical to the example described in paragraph (e)(2) of this section. Thus, both the 20 percent merchandise discount and the 15 percent cash bonus provided to the prohibited group employees are includible in such employees' gross incomes.

(g) *Prohibited group employees*—(1) *Highly compensated*—(i) *General rule.* Except as otherwise provided in this paragraph (g)(1)(i), any employee of an employer who has (or is reasonably expected to have) compensation during a cal-endar year equal to or greater than the employer's base compensation amount is highly compensated. There are two exceptions to this rule:

(A) any employee who has (or is reasonably expected to have) compensation during a calendar year equal to or greater than $50,000 is highly compensated, regardless of whether such compensation is in excess of the base compensation amount, and

(B) any employee who is reasonably expected to have compensation during a calendar year equal to or less than $20,000 is not highly compensated, unless no employee of the employer is reasonably expected to have compensation equal to or greater than $35,000.

The determination of whether an employee is a highly compensated employee will be determined based on the entire employee workforce of all employers aggregated pursuant to the rules of section 414(b), (c), or (m) without regard to the regular workplace of the employees.

(ii) *Base compensation amount*—(A) *General rule.* The term "base compensation amount" is defined as that amount corresponding to the lowest annual compensation amount received by the highest-paid ten percent of all employees of an employer (the number of employees in the top ten percent will be increased to the next highest integer if necessary), determined on the basis of the preceding calendar year. For purposes of this paragraph (g)(1)(ii), the term "employer" includes all entities that would be aggregated pursuant to the rules of section 414(b), (c), or (m).

(B) *Employees that are excluded.* For purposes of determining the base compensation amount with respect to a fringe benefit program, employees described in paragraph (b)(3) of this section are excluded whether or not they are covered under the fringe benefit program, except that (1) employees described in paragraph (b)(3)(ii) of this section are taken into account with respect to the program even if they are excluded under paragraph (b)(3), and (2) employees described in paragraph (b)(3)(i) and (iv) of this section are taken into account with respect to the program unless they are excluded under paragraph (b)(3).

(C) *Exception to preceding calendar year rule.* In the case of an employer's first year of operation, or where an employer's business has changed significantly from the prior calendar year (e.g., due to an acquisition or merger), the employer must make a good faith attempt to either determine or adjust the base compensation

→ **Caution: Temporary Reg. § 1.132-8T applies to the tax treatment of fringe benefits for 1985—1988. See Reg. §§ 1.132-0—1.132-8 for post-1988 rules.←**

amount for the current year based on reasonable estimates of current year compensation.

(iii) *Compensation.* The term "compensation" is defined as the amount reportable on a Form W-2 as income. Amounts that would be excluded from income but for section 132(h)(1) are not included in compensation for purposes of this paragraph (g)(1). Compensation includes amounts received from all entities which would be treated as a single employer under section 414(b), (c), or (m) and is not restricted to amounts received with respect to any one line of business.

(iv) *Employee.* Generally, for purposes of determining whether an employee is highly compensated under this paragraph (g)(1), the term "employee" does not include any individual who does not perform services for the employer as an employee during the calendar year. For example, if an employer has active employees, retired or disabled employees, and widows or widowers who are "employees" under section 132(f)(1)(B), the general rule (described in paragraph (g)(1)(i) of this section) applies only to the active employees.

(2) *Owner*—(i) *General Rule.* For purposes of this section, the term "owner" means any employee who owns a one percent or greater interest in either the employer or in any entity that would be aggregated with the employer pursuant to the rules of section 414(b), (c), or (m). In addition, such an employee shall be treated as an owner of all entities that would be aggregated with the employer pursuant to the rules of section 414(b), (c), or (m).

(ii) *Determining ownership.* Ownership in a corporation shall be determined pursuant to the rules of section 318(a). For purposes of determining ownership in an entity other than a corporation, the rules of section 318(a) shall apply in a manner similar to the way in which they apply for purposes of determining ownership in a corporation. For non-corporate interests, capital or profits interest must be substituted for stock.

(3) *Officer.*—(i) *Non-government.* For purposes of this section, an officer of a non-government employer is any employee who is appointed, confirmed, or elected by the Board or shareholders of the employer. An employee who is an officer of an employer shall be treated as an officer of all entities treated as a single employer pursuant to section 414(b), (c), or (m). The number of officers is not to exceed one-percent of the total number of employees of all entities treated as a single employer pursuant to section 414(b), (c), or (m) (increased to the next highest integer, if necessary). If the number of officers exceeds one-per-

cent of all employees, then the limitation is to be applied to employees in descending order of compensation (as defined in paragraph (g)(1)(iii) of this section). Thus, if an employer with 1,000 employees has 11 board-appointed officers, the employee with the least compensation of those officers would not be an officer under this paragraph (g)(3)(i). In determining the total number of employees with respect to a fringe benefit program, employees described in paragraph (b)(3) of this section are excluded whether or not they are covered under the fringe benefit program, except that (A) employees described in paragraph (b)(3)(ii) of this section are taken into account with respect to the program even if they are excluded under paragraph (b)(3), and (B) employees described in paragraph (b)(3)(i) and (iv) of this section are taken into account with respect to the program unless they are excluded under paragraph (b)(3).

(ii) *Government.* For purposes of this section, an officer of a government employer is any—

(A) Elected official,

(B) Federal employee appointed by the President and confirmed by the Senate. However, in the case of any commissioned officer of the United States Armed Forces, an officer is any employee with the rank of brigadier general or rear admiral (lower half) or above, and

(C) State or local executive officer comparable to individuals described in paragraphs (g)(3)(ii)(A) and (B) of this section.

For purposes of this paragraph (g)(3)(ii), the term "government" includes any Federal, state, or local governmental unit, and any agency or instrumentality thereof.

(4) *Former employees.* [Reserved] [Temporary Reg. § 1.132-8T.]

☐ [T.D. 8063, 12-18-85. *Amended by* T.D. 8256, 7-5-89.]

[Reg. § 1.132-9]

§ 1.132-9.   Qualified   transportation fringes.—(a) *Table of contents.* This section contains a list of the questions and answers in § 1.132-9.

(1) *General rules.*

Q-1. What is a qualified transportation fringe?

Q-2. What is transportation in a commuter highway vehicle?

Q-3. What are transit passes?

Q-4. What is qualified parking?

Q-5. May qualified transportation fringes be provided to individuals who are not employees?

Q-6. Must a qualified transportation fringe benefit plan be in writing?

(2) *Dollar limitations.*

Q-7. Is there a limit on the value of qualified transportation fringes that may be excluded from an employee's gross income?

Q-8. What amount is includible in an employee's wages for income and employment tax purposes if the value of the qualified transportation fringe exceeds the applicable statutory monthly limit?

Q-9. Are excludable qualified transportation fringes calculated on a monthly basis?

Q-10. May an employee receive qualified transportation fringes from more than one employer?

(3) *Compensation reduction.*

Q-11. May qualified transportation fringes be provided to employees pursuant to a compensation reduction agreement?

Q-12. What is a compensation reduction election for purposes of section 132(f)?

Q-13. Is there a limit to the amount of the compensation reduction?

Q-14. When must the employee have made a compensation reduction election and under what circumstances may the amount be paid in cash to the employee?

Q-15. May an employee whose qualified transportation fringe costs are less than the employee's compensation reduction carry over this excess amount to subsequent periods?

(4) *Expense reimbursements.*

Q-16. How does section 132(f) apply to expense reimbursements?

Q-17. May an employer provide nontaxable cash reimbursement under section 132(f) for periods longer than one month?

Q-18. What are the substantiation requirements if an employer distributes transit passes?

Q-19. May an employer choose to impose substantiation requirements in addition to those described in this regulation?

(5) *Special rules for parking and vanpools.*

Q-20. How is the value of parking determined?

Q-21. How do the qualified transportation fringe rules apply to van pools?

(6) *Reporting and employment taxes.*

Q-22. What are the reporting and employment tax requirements for qualified transportation fringes?

(7) *Interaction with other fringe benefits.*

Q-23. How does section 132(f) interact with other fringe benefit rules?

(8) *Application to individuals who are not employees.*

Q-24. May qualified transportation fringes be provided to individuals who are partners, 2-percent shareholders of S-corporations, or independent contractors?

(9) *Effective date.*

Q-25. What is the effective date of this section?

(b) *Questions and answers.*

Q-1. What is a qualified transportation fringe?

A-1. (a) The following benefits are qualified transportation fringe benefits:

(1) Transportation in a commuter highway vehicle.

(2) Transit passes.

(3) Qualified parking.

(b) An employer may simultaneously provide an employee with any one or more these three benefits.

Q-2. What is transportation in a commuter highway vehicle?

A-2. Transportation in a commuter highway vehicle is transportation provided by an employer to an employee in connection with travel between the employee's residence and place of employment. A commuter highway vehicle is a highway vehicle with a seating capacity of at least 6 adults (excluding the driver) and with respect to which at least 80 percent of the vehicle's mileage for a year is reasonably expected to be—

(a) For transporting employees in connection with travel between their residences and their place of employment; and

(b) On trips during which the number of employees transported for commuting is at least one-half of the adult seating capacity of the vehicle (excluding the driver).

Q-3. What are transit passes?

A-3. A transit pass is any pass, token, farecard, voucher, or similar item (including an item exchangeable for fare media) that entitles a person to transportation—

(a) On mass transit facilities (whether or not publicly owned); or

(b) Provided by any person in the business of transporting persons for compensation or hire in a highway vehicle with a seating capacity of at least 6 adults (excluding the driver).

Q-4. What is qualified parking?

A-4. (a) Qualified parking is parking provided to an employee by an employer—

Reg. § 1.132-9(b)

(1) On or near the employer's business premises; or

(2) At a location from which the employee commutes to work (including commuting by carpool, commuter highway vehicle, mass transit facilities, or transportation provided by any person in the business of transporting persons for compensation or hire).

(b) For purposes of section 132(f), parking on or near the employer's business premises includes parking on or near a work location at which the employee provides services for the employer. However, qualified parking does not include—

(1) The value of parking provided to an employee that is excludable from gross income under section 132(a)(3) (as a working condition fringe), or

(2) Reimbursement paid to an employee for parking costs that is excludable from gross income as an amount treated as paid under an accountable plan. See § 1.62-2.

(c) However, parking on or near property used by the employee for residential purposes is not qualified parking.

(d) Parking is provided by an employer if—

(1) The parking is on property that the employer owns or leases;

(2) The employer pays for the parking; or

(3) The employer reimburses the employee for parking expenses (see Q/A-16 of this section for rules relating to cash reimbursements).

Q-5. May qualified transportation fringes be provided to individuals who are not employees?

A-5. An employer may provide qualified transportation fringes only to individuals who are currently employees of the employer at the time the qualified transportation fringe is provided. The term employee for purposes of qualified transportation fringes is defined in § 1.132-1(b)(2)(i). This term includes only common law employees and other statutory employees, such as officers of corporations. See Q/A-24 of this section for rules regarding partners, 2-percent shareholders, and independent contractors.

Q-6. Must a qualified transportation fringe benefit plan be in writing?

A-6. No. Section 132(f) does not require that a qualified transportation fringe benefit plan be in writing.

Q-7. Is there a limit on the value of qualified transportation fringes that may be excluded from an employee's gross income?

A-7. (a) *Transportation in a commuter highway vehicle and transit passes.* Before January 1, 2002, up to $65 per month is excludable from the gross income of an employee for transportation in a commuter highway vehicle and transit passes provided by an employer. On January 1, 2002, this amount is increased to $100 per month.

(b) *Parking.* Up to $175 per month is excludable from the gross income of an employee for qualified parking.

(c) *Combination.* An employer may provide qualified parking benefits in addition to transportation in a commuter highway vehicle and transit passes.

(d) *Cost-of-living adjustments.* The amounts in paragraphs (a) and (b) of this Q/A-7 are adjusted annually, beginning with 2000, to reflect cost-of-living. The adjusted figures are announced by the Service before the beginning of the year.

Q-8. What amount is includible in an employee's wages for income and employment tax purposes if the value of the qualified transportation fringe exceeds the applicable statutory monthly limit?

A-8. (a) Generally, an employee must include in gross income the amount by which the fair market value of the benefit exceeds the sum of the amount, if any, paid by the employee and any amount excluded from gross income under section 132(a)(5). Thus, assuming no other statutory exclusion applies, if an employer provides an employee with a qualified transportation fringe that exceeds the applicable statutory monthly limit and the employee does not make any payment, the value of the benefits provided in excess of the applicable statutory monthly limit is included in the employee's wages for income and employment tax purposes. See § 1.61-21(b)(1).

(b) The following examples illustrate the principles of this Q/A-8:

Example 1. (i) For each month in a year in which the statutory monthly transit pass limit is $100 (i.e., a year after 2001), Employer M provides a transit pass valued at $110 to Employee D, who does not pay any amount to Employer M for the transit pass.

(ii) In this *Example 1*, because the value of the monthly transit pass exceeds the statutory monthly limit by $10, $120 ($110 − $100, times 12 months) must be included in D's wages for income and employment tax purposes for the year with respect to the transit passes.

Example 2. (i) For each month in a year in which the statutory monthly qualified parking limit is $175, Employer M provides qualified parking valued at $195 to Employee E, who does not pay any amount to M for the parking.

(ii) In this *Example 2*, because the fair market value of the qualified parking exceeds the statutory monthly limit by $20, $240 ($195 − $175, times 12 months) must be included in Employee E's wages for income and employment tax purposes for the year with respect to the qualified parking.

Example 3. (i) For each month in a year in which the statutory monthly qualified parking limit is $175, Employer P provides qualified parking with a fair market value of $220 per month to its employees, but charges each employee $45 per month.

(ii) In this *Example 3*, because the sum of the amount paid by an employee ($45) plus the amount excludable for qualified parking ($175) is not less than the fair market value of the monthly benefit, no amount is includible in the employee's wages for income and employment tax purposes with respect to the qualified parking.

Q-9. Are excludable qualified transportation fringes calculated on a monthly basis?

A-9. (a) *In general.* Yes. The value of transportation in a commuter highway vehicle, transit passes, and qualified parking is calculated on a monthly basis to determine whether the value of the benefit has exceeded the applicable statutory monthly limit on qualified transportation fringes. Except in the case of a transit pass provided to an employee, the applicable statutory monthly limit applies to qualified transportation fringes used by the employee in a month. Monthly exclusion amounts are not combined to provide a qualified transportation fringe for any month exceeding the statutory limit. A month is a calendar month or a substantially equivalent period applied consistently.

(b) *Transit passes.* In the case of transit passes provided to an employee, the applicable statutory monthly limit applies to the transit passes provided by the employer to the employee in a month for that month or for any previous month in the calendar year. In addition, transit passes distributed in advance for more than one month, but not for more than twelve months, are qualified transportation fringes if the requirements in paragraph (c) of this Q/A-9 are met (relating to the income tax and employment tax treatment of advance transit passes). The applicable statutory monthly limit under section 132(f)(2) on the combined amount of transportation in a commuter highway vehicle and transit passes may be calculated by taking into account the monthly limits for all months for which the transit passes are distributed. In the case of a pass that is valid for more than one month, such as an annual pass, the value of the pass may be divided by the number of months for which it is valid for purposes of determining whether the value of the pass exceeds the statutory monthly limit.

(c) *Rule if employee's employment terminates*—(1) *income tax treatment.* The value of transit passes provided in advance to an employee with respect to a month in which the individual is not an employee is included in the employee's wages for income tax purposes.

(2) *Reporting and employment tax treatment.* Transit passes distributed in advance to an employee are excludable from wages for employment tax purposes under sections 3121, 3306, and 3401 (FICA, FUTA, and income tax withholding) if the employer distributes transit passes to the employee in advance for not more than three months and, at the time the transit passes are distributed, there is not an established date that the employee's employment will terminate (for example, if the employee has given notice of retirement) which will occur before the beginning of the last month of the period for which the transit passes are provided. If the employer distributes transit passes to an employee in advance for not more than three months and at the time the transit passes are distributed there is an established date that the employee's employment will terminate, and the employee's employment does terminate before the beginning of the last month of the period for which the transit passes are provided, the value of transit passes provided for months beginning after the date of termination during which the employee is not employed by the employer is included in the employee's wages for employment tax purposes. If transit passes are distributed in advance for more than three months, the value of transit passes provided for the months during which the employee is not employed by the employer is includible in the employee's wages for employment tax purposes regardless of whether at the time the transit passes were distributed there was an established date of termination of the employee's employment.

(d) *Examples.* The following examples illustrate the principles of this Q/A-9:

Example 1. (i) Employee E incurs $150 for qualified parking used during the month of June of a year in which the statutory monthly parking limit is $175, for which E is reimbursed $150 by Employer R. Employee E incurs $180 in expenses for qualified parking used during the month of July of that year, for which E is reimbursed $180 by Employer R.

(ii) In this *Example 1*, because monthly exclusion amounts may not be combined to provide a benefit in any month greater than the applicable statutory limit, the amount by which the amount reimbursed for July exceeds the applicable statutory monthly limit ($180 minus $175 equals $5) is includible in Employee E's wages for income and employment tax purposes.

Example 2. (i) Employee F receives transit passes from Employer G with a value of $195 in March of a year (for which the statutory monthly transit pass limit is $65) for January, February, and March of that year. F was hired during January and has not received any transit passes from G.

(ii) In this *Example 2*, the value of the transit passes (three months times $65 equals $195) is excludable from F's wages for income and employment tax purposes.

Example 3. (1) Employer S has a qualified transportation fringe benefit plan under which its employees receive transit passes near the beginning of each calendar quarter for that calendar quarter. All employees of Employer S receive transit passes from Employer S with a value of $195 on March 31 for the second calendar quarter covering the months April, May, and June (of a year in which the statutory monthly transit pass limit is $65).

(ii) In this *Example 3*, because the value of the transit passes may be calculated by taking into account the monthly limits for all months for which the transit passes are distributed, the value of the transit passes (three months times $65 equals $195) is excludable from the employees' wages for income and employment tax purposes.

Example 4. (i) Same facts as in *Example 3*, except that Employee T, an employee of Employer S, terminates employment with S on May 31. There was not an established date of termination for Employee T at the time the transit passes were distributed.

(ii) In this *Example 4*, because at the time the transit passes were distributed there was not an established date of termination for Employee T, the value of the transit passes provided for June ($65) is excludable from T's wages for employment tax purposes. However, the value of the transit passes distributed to Employee T for June ($65) is not excludable from T's wages for income tax purposes.

(iii) If Employee T's May 31 termination date was established at the time the transit passes were provided, the value of the transit passes provided for June ($65) is included in T's wages for both income and employment tax purposes.

Example 5. (i) Employer F has a qualified transportation fringe benefit plan under which its employees receive transit passes semi-annually in advance of the months for which the transit

passes are provided. All employees of Employer F, including Employee X, receive transit passes from F with a value of $390 on June 30 for the 6 months of July through December (of a year in which the statutory monthly transit pass limit is $65). Employee X's employment terminates and his last day of work is August 1. Employer F's other employees remain employed throughout the remainder of the year.

(ii) In this *Example 5*, the value of the transit passes provided to Employee X for the months September, October, November, and December ($65 times 4 months equals $260) of the year is included in X's wages for income and employment tax purposes. The value of the transit passes provided to Employer F's other employees is excludable from the employees' wages for income and employment tax purposes.

Example 6. (i) Each month during a year in which the statutory monthly transit pass limit is $65, Employer R distributes transit passes with a face amount of $70 to each of its employees. Transit passes with a face amount of $70 can be purchased from the transit system by any individual for $65.

(ii) In this *Example 6*, because the value of the transit passes distributed by Employer R does not exceed the applicable statutory monthly limit ($65), no portion of the value of the transit passes is included as wages for income and employment tax purposes.

Q-10. May an employee receive qualified transportation fringes from more than one employer?

A-10. (a) *General rule.* Yes. The statutory monthly limits described in Q/A-7 of this section apply to benefits provided by an employer to its employees. For this purpose, all employees treated as employed by a single employer under section 414(b), (c), (m), or (o) are treated as employed by a single employer. See section 414(t) and § 1.132-1(c). Thus, qualified transportation fringes paid by entities under common control under section 414(b), (c), (m), or (o) are combined for purposes of applying the applicable statutory monthly limit. In addition, an individual who is treated as a leased employee of the employer under section 414(n) is treated as an employee of that employer for purposes of section 132. See section 414(n)(3)(C).

(b) *Examples.* The following examples illustrate the principles of this Q/A-10:

Example 1. (i) During a year in which the statutory monthly qualified parking limit is $175, Employee E works for Employers M and N, who are unrelated and not treated as a single employer under section 414(b), (c), (m), or (o). Each month,

M and N each provide qualified parking benefits to E with a value of $100.

(ii) In this *Example 1*, because M and N are unrelated employers, and the value of the monthly parking benefit provided by each is not more than the applicable statutory monthly limit, the parking benefits provided by each employer are excludable as qualified transportation fringes assuming that the other requirements of this section are satisfied.

Example 2. (i) Same facts as in Example 1, except that Employers M and N are treated as a single employer under section 414(b).

(ii) In this *Example 2*, because M and N are treated as a single employer, the value of the monthly parking benefit provided by M and N must be combined for purposes of determining whether the applicable statutory monthly limit has been exceeded. Thus, the amount by which the value of the parking benefit exceeds the monthly limit ($200 minus the monthly limit amount of $175 equals $25) for each month in the year is includible in E's wages for income and employment tax purposes.

Q-11. May qualified transportation fringes be provided to employees pursuant to a compensation reduction agreement?

A-11. Yes. An employer may offer employees a choice between cash compensation and any qualified transportation fringe. An employee who is offered this choice and who elects qualified transportation fringes is not required to include the cash compensation in income if—

(a) The election is pursuant to an arrangement described in Q/A-12 of this section;

(b) The amount of the reduction in cash compensation does not exceed the limitation in Q/A-13 of this section;

(c) The arrangement satisfies the timing and reimbursement rules in Q/A-14 and 16 of this section; and

(d) The related fringe benefit arrangement otherwise satisfies the requirements set forth elsewhere in this section.

Q-12. What is a compensation reduction election for purposes of section 132(f)?

A-12. (a) *Election requirements generally.* A compensation reduction arrangement is an arrangement under which the employer provides the employee with the right to elect whether the employee will receive either a fixed amount of cash compensation at a specified future date or a fixed amount of qualified transportation fringes to be provided for a specified future period (such as qualified parking to be used during a future calendar month). The employee's election must be in

writing or another form, such as electronic, that includes, in a permanent and verifiable form, the information required to be in the election. The election must contain the date of the election, the amount of the compensation to be reduced, and the period for which the benefit will be provided. The election must relate to a fixed dollar amount or fixed percentage of compensation reduction. An election to reduce compensation for a period by a set amount for such period may be automatically renewed for subsequent periods.

(b) *Automatic election permitted.* An employer may provide under its qualified transportation fringe benefit plan that a compensation reduction election will be deemed to have been made if the employee does not elect to receive cash compensation in lieu of the qualified transportation fringe, provided that the employee receives adequate notice that a compensation reduction will be made and is given adequate opportunity to choose to receive the cash compensation instead of the qualified transportation fringe.

Q-13. Is there a limit to the amount of the compensation reduction?

A-13. Yes. Each month, the amount of the compensation reduction may not exceed the combined applicable statutory monthly limits for transportation in a commuter highway vehicle, transit passes, and qualified parking. For example, for a year in which the statutory monthly limit is $65 for transportation in a commuter highway vehicle and transit passes, and $175 for qualified parking, an employee could elect to reduce compensation for any month by no more than $240 ($65 plus $175) with respect to qualified transportation fringes. If an employee were to elect to reduce compensation by $250 for a month, the excess $10 ($250 minus $240) would be includible in the employee's wages for income and employment tax purposes.

Q-14. When must the employee have made a compensation reduction election and under what circumstances may the amount be paid in cash to the employee?

A-14. (a) The compensation reduction election must satisfy the requirements set forth under paragraphs (b), (c), and (d) of this Q/A-14.

(b) *Timing of election.* The compensation reduction election must be made before the employee is able currently to receive the cash or other taxable amount at the employee's discretion. The determination of whether the employee is able currently to receive the cash does not depend on whether it has been constructively received for purposes of section 451. The election must specify that the period (such as a calendar month) for which the qualified transportation

Reg. § 1.132-9(b)

fringe will be provided must not begin before the election is made. Thus, a compensation reduction election must relate to qualified transportation fringes to be provided after the election. For this purpose, the date a qualified transportation fringe is provided is—

(1) The date the employee receives a voucher or similar item; or

(2) In any other case, the date the employee uses the qualified transportation fringe.

(c) *Revocability of elections.* The employee may not revoke a compensation reduction election after the employee is able currently to receive the cash or other taxable amount at the employee's discretion. In addition, the election may not be revoked after the beginning of the period for which the qualified transportation fringe will be provided.

(d) *Compensation reduction amounts not refundable.* Unless an election is revoked in a manner consistent with paragraph (c) of this Q/A-14, an employee may not subsequently receive the compensation (in cash or any form other than by payment of a qualified transportation fringe under the employer's plan). Thus, an employer's qualified transportation fringe benefit plan may not provide that an employee who ceases to participate in the employer's qualified transportation fringe benefit plan (such as in the case of termination of employment) is entitled to receive a refund of the amount by which the employee's compensation reductions exceed the actual qualified transportation fringes provided to the employee by the employer.

(e) *Examples.* The following examples illustrate the principles of this Q/A-14:

Example 1. (i) Employer P maintains a qualified transportation fringe benefit arrangement during a year in which the statutory monthly limit is $100 for transportation in a commuter highway vehicle and transit passes (2002 or later) and $180 for qualified parking. Employees of P are paid cash compensation twice per month, with the payroll dates being the first and the fifteenth day of the month. Under P's arrangement, an employee is permitted to elect at any time before the first day of a month to reduce his or her compensation payable during that month in an amount up to the applicable statutory monthly limit ($100 if the employee elects coverage for transportation in a commuter highway vehicle or a mass transit pass, or $180 if the employee chooses qualified parking) in return for the right to receive qualified transportation fringes up to the amount of the election. If such an election is made, P will provide a mass transit pass for that month with a value not exceeding the compensa-

tion reduction amount elected by the employee or will reimburse the cost of other qualified transportation fringes used by the employee on or after the first day of that month up to the compensation reduction amount elected by the employee. Any compensation reduction amount elected by the employee for the month that is not used for qualified transportation fringes is not refunded to the employee at any future date.

(ii) In this *Example 1*, the arrangement satisfies the requirements of this Q/A-14 because the election is made before the employee is able currently to receive the cash and the election specifies the future period for which the qualified transportation fringes will be provided. The arrangement would also satisfy the requirements of this C/A-14 and Q/A-13 of this section if employees are allowed to elect to reduce compensation up to $280 per month ($100 plus $180).

(iii) The arrangement would also satisfy the requirements of this Q/A-14 (and Q/A-13 of this section) if employees are allowed to make an election at any time before the first or the fifteenth day of the month to reduce their compensation payable on that payroll date by an amount not in excess of one-half of the applicable statutory monthly limit (depending on the type of qualified transportation fringe elected by the employee) and P provides a mass transit pass on or after the applicable payroll date for the compensation reduction amount elected by the employee for the payroll date or reimburses the cost of other qualified transportation fringes used by the employee on or after the payroll date up to the compensation reduction amount elected by the employee for that payroll date.

Example 2. (i) Employee Q elects to reduce his compensation payable on March 1 of a year (for which the statutory monthly mass transit limit is $65) by $195 in exchange for a mass transit voucher to be provided in March. The election is made on the preceding February 27. Employee Q was hired in January of the year. On March 10 of the year, the employer of Employee Q delivers to Employee Q a mass transit voucher worth $195 for the months of January, February, and March.

(ii) In this *Example 2*, $65 is included in Employee Q's wages for income and employment tax purposes because the compensation reduction election fails to satisfy the requirement in this Q/A-14 and Q/A-12 of this section that the period for which the qualified transportation fringe will be provided not begin before the election is made to the extent the election relates to $65 worth of transit passes for January of the year. The $65 for February is not taxable because the election was for a future period that includes at least one day in February.

(iii) However, no amount would be included in Employee Q's wages as a result of the election if $195 worth of mass transit passes were instead provided to Q for the months of February, March, and April (because the compensation reduction would relate solely to fringes to be provided for a period not beginning before the date of the election and the amount provided does not exceed the aggregate limit for the period, i.e., the sum of $65 for each of February, March, and April). See Q/A-9 of this section for rules governing transit passes distributed in advance for more than one month.

Example 3. (i) Employee R elects to reduce his compensation payable on March 1 of a year (for which the statutory monthly parking limit is $175) by $185 in exchange for reimbursement by Employer T of parking expenses incurred by Employee R for parking on or near Employer T's business premises during the period beginning after the date of the election through March. The election is made on the preceding February 27. Employee R incurs $10 in parking expenses on February 28 of the year, and $175 in parking expenses during the month of March. On April 5 of the year, Employer T reimburses Employee R $185 for the parking expenses incurred on February 28, and during March, of the year.

(ii) In this *Example 3*, no amount would be includible in Employee R's wages for income and employment tax purposes because the compensation reduction related solely to parking on or near Employer R's business premises used during a period not beginning before the date of the election and the amount reimbursed for parking used in any one month does not exceed the statutory monthly limitation.

Q-15. May an employee whose qualified transportation fringe costs are less than the employee's compensation reduction carry over this excess amount to subsequent periods?

A-15. (a) Yes. An employee may carry over unused compensation reduction amounts to subsequent periods under the plan of the employee's employer.

(b) The following example illustrates the principles of this Q/A-15:

Example. (i) By an election made before November I of a year for which the statutory monthly mass transit limit is $65, Employee E elects to reduce compensation in the amount of $65 for the month of November. E incurs $50 in employee-operated commuter highway vehicle expenses during November for which E is reimbursed $50 by Employer R, E's employer. By an election made

before December, E elects to reduce compensation by $65 for the month of December. E incurs $65 in employee-operated commuter highway vehicle expenses during December for which E is reimbursed $65 by R. Before the following January, E elects to reduce compensation by $50 for the month of January. E incurs $65 in employee-operated commuter highway vehicle expenses during January for which E is reimbursed $65 by R because R allows E to carry over to the next year the $15 amount by which the compensation reductions for November and December exceeded the employee-operated commuter highway vehicle expenses incurred during those months.

(ii) In this *Example*, because Employee E is reimbursed in an amount not exceeding the applicable statutory monthly limit, and the reimbursement does not exceed the amount of employee-operated commuter highway vehicle expenses incurred during the month of January, the amount reimbursed ($65) is excludable from E's wages for income and employment tax purposes.

Q-16. How does section 132(f) apply to expense reimbursements?

A-16. (a) *In general.* The term qualified transportation fringe includes cash reimbursement by an employer to an employee for expenses incurred or paid by an employee for transportation in a commuter highway vehicle or qualified parking. The term qualified transportation fringe also includes cash reimbursement for transit passes made under a bona fide reimbursement arrangement, but, in accordance with section 132(f)(3), only if permitted under paragraph (b) of this Q/A-16. The reimbursement must be made under a bona fide reimbursement arrangement which meets the rules of paragraph (c) of this Q/A-16. A payment made before the date an expense has been incurred or paid is not a reimbursement. In addition, a bona fide reimbursement arrangement does not include an arrangement that is dependent solely upon an employee certifying in advance that the employee will incur expenses at some future date.

(b) *Special rule for transit passes—*(1) *In general.* The term *qualified transportation fringe* includes cash reimbursement for transit passes made under a bona fide reimbursement arrangement, but, in accordance with section 132(f)(3), only if no voucher or similar item that may be exchanged only for a transit pass is readily available for direct distribution by the employer to employees. If a voucher is readily available, the requirement that a voucher be distributed in-kind by the employer is satisfied if the voucher is distributed by the employer or by another person on behalf of the employer (for example, if a

Reg. § 1.132-9(b)

transit operator credits amounts to the employee's fare card as a result of payments made to the operator by the employer).

(2) *Voucher or similar item.* For purposes of the special rule in paragraph (b) of this Q/A-16, a transit system voucher is an instrument that may be purchased by employers from a voucher provider that is accepted by one or more mass transit operators (e.g., train, subway, and bus) in an area as fare media or in exchange for fare media. Thus, for example, a transit pass that may be purchased by employers directly from a voucher provider is a transit system voucher.

(3) *Voucher provider.* The term voucher provider means any person in the trade or business of selling transit system vouchers to employers, or any transit system or transit operator that sells vouchers to employers for the purpose of direct distribution to employees. Thus, a transit opera-

tor might or might not be a voucher provider. A voucher provider is not, for example, a third-party employee benefits administrator that administers a transit pass benefit program for an employer using vouchers that the employer could obtain directly.

(4) *Readily available.* For purposes of this paragraph (b), a voucher or similar item is readily available for direct distribution by the employer to employees if and only if an employer can obtain it from a voucher provider that—

(i) does not impose fare media charges that cause vouchers to not be readily available as described in paragraph (b)(5) of this section; and

(ii) does not impose other restrictions that cause vouchers to not be readily available as described in paragraph (b)(6) of this section.

→ *Caution: The last sentence of Reg. § 1.132-9, Q/A-16(b)(5), below, is applicable for employee tax years beginning after December 31, 2003.*←

(5) *Fare media charges.* For purposes of paragraph (b)(4) of this section, fare media charges relate only to fees paid by the employer to voucher providers for vouchers. The determination of whether obtaining a voucher would result in fare media charges that cause vouchers to not be readily available as described in this paragraph (b) is made with respect to each transit system voucher. If more than one transit system voucher is available for direct distribution to employees, the employer must consider the fees imposed for the lowest cost monthly voucher for purposes of determining whether the fees imposed by the voucher provider satisfy this paragraph. However, if transit system vouchers for multiple transit systems are required in an area to meet the transit needs of the individual employees in that area, the employer has the option of averaging the costs applied to each transit system voucher for purposes of determining whether the fare media charges for transit system vouchers satisfy this paragraph. Fare media charges are described in this paragraph (b)(5), and therefore cause vouchers to not be readily available, if and only if the average annual fare media charges that the employer reasonably expects to incur for transit system vouchers purchased from the voucher provider (disregarding reasonable and customary delivery charges imposed by the voucher provider, e.g., not in excess of $15) are more than 1 percent of the average annual value of the vouchers for a transit system.

(6) *Other restrictions.* For purposes of paragraph (b)(4) of this section, restrictions that cause vouchers to not be readily available are restric-

tions imposed by the voucher provider other than fare media charges that effectively prevent the employer from obtaining vouchers appropriate for distribution to employees. Examples of such restrictions include—

(i) *Advance purchase requirements.* Advance purchase requirements cause vouchers to not be readily available only if the voucher provider does not offer vouchers at regular intervals or fails to provide the voucher within a reasonable period after receiving payment for the voucher. For example, a requirement that vouchers may be purchased only once per year may effectively prevent an employer from obtaining vouchers for distribution to employees. An advance purchase requirement that vouchers be purchased not more frequently than monthly does not effectively prevent the employer from obtaining vouchers for distribution to employees.

(ii) *Purchase quantity requirements.* Purchase quantity requirements cause vouchers to not be readily available if the voucher provider does not offer vouchers in quantities that are reasonably appropriate to the number of the employer's employees who use mass transportation (for example, the voucher provider requires a $1,000 minimum purchase and the employer seeks to purchase only $200 of vouchers).

(iii) *Limitations on denominations of vouchers that are available.* If the voucher provider does not offer vouchers in denominations appropriate for distribution to the employer's employees, vouchers are not readily available. For example, vouchers provided in $5 increments up to the monthly limit are appropriate for distribution to

Reg. § 1.132-9(b)

employees, while vouchers available only in a denomination equal to the monthly limit are not appropriate for distribution to employees if the amount of the benefit provided to the employer's employees each month is normally less than the monthly limit.

(7) *Example.* The following example illustrates the principles of this paragraph (b):

Example. (i) Company C in City X sells mass transit vouchers to employers in the metropolitan area of X in various denominations appropriate for distribution to employees. Employers can purchase vouchers monthly in reasonably appropriate quantities. Several different bus, rail, van pool, and ferry operators service X, and a number of the operators accept the vouchers either as fare media or in exchange for fare media. To cover its operating expenses, C imposes on each voucher a 50 cents charge, plus a reasonable and customary $15 charge for delivery of each order of vouchers. Employer M disburses vouchers purchased from C to its employees who use operators that accept the vouchers and M reasonably expects that $55 is the average value of the voucher it will purchase from C for the next calendar year.

(ii) In this *Example,* vouchers for X are readily available for direct distribution by the employer to employees because the expected cost of the vouchers disbursed to M's employees for the next calendar year is not more than 1 percent of the value of the vouchers (50 cents divided by $55 equals 0.91 percent), the delivery charges are disregarded because they are reasonable and customary, and there are no other restrictions that cause the vouchers to not be readily available. Thus, any reimbursement of mass transportation costs in X would not be a qualified transportation fringe.

(c) *Substantiation requirements.* Employers that make cash reimbursements must establish a bona fide reimbursement arrangement to establish that their employees have, in fact, incurred expenses for transportation in a commuter highway vehicle, transit passes, or qualified parking. For purposes of section 132(f), whether cash reimbursements are made under a bona fide reimbursement arrangement may vary depending on the facts and circumstances, including the method or methods of payment utilized within the mass transit system. The employer must implement reasonable procedures to ensure that an amount equal to the reimbursement was incurred for transportation in a commuter highway vehicle, transit passes, or qualified parking. The expense must be substantiated within a reasonable period of time. An expense substantiated to the payor within 180 days after it has been paid will be treated as having been substantiated within a reasonable period of time. An employee certification at the time of reimbursement in either written or electronic form may be a reasonable reimbursement procedure depending on the facts and circumstances. Examples of reasonable reimbursement procedures are set forth in paragraph (d) of this Q/A-16.

(d) *Illustrations of reasonable reimbursement procedures.* The following are examples of reasonable reimbursement procedures for purposes of paragraph (c) of this Q/A-16. In each case, the reimbursement is made at or within a reasonable period after the end of the events described in paragraphs (d)(1) through (d)(3) of this section.

(1) An employee presents to the employer a parking expense receipt for parking on or near the employer's business premises, the employee certifies that the parking was used by the employee, and the employer has no reason to doubt the employee's certification.

(2) An employee either submits a used time-sensitive transit pass (such as a monthly pass) to the employer and certifies that he or she purchased it or presents an unused or used transit pass to the employer and certifies that he or she purchased it and the employee certifies that he or she has not previously been reimbursed for the transit pass. In both cases, the employer has no reason to doubt the employee's certification.

(3) If a receipt is not provided in the ordinary course of business (e.g., if the employee uses metered parking or if used transit passes cannot be returned to the user), the employee certifies to the employer the type and the amount of expenses incurred, and the employer has no reason to doubt the employee's certification.

Q-17. May an employer provide nontaxable cash reimbursement under section 132(f) for periods longer than one month?

A-17. (a) *General rule.* Yes. Qualified transportation fringes include reimbursement to employees for costs incurred for transportation in more than one month, provided the reimbursement for each month in the period is calculated separately and does not exceed the applicable statutory monthly limit for any month in the period. See Q/A-8 and 9 of this section if the limit for a month is exceeded.

(b) *Example.* The following example illustrates the principles of this Q/A-17:

Example. (i) Employee R pays $100 per month for qualified parking used during the period from April 1 through June 30 of a year in which the statutory monthly qualified parking limit is $175. After receiving adequate substantiation from Em-

Reg. § 1.132-9(b)

ployee R, R's employer reimburses R $300 in cash on June 30 of that year.

(ii) In this *Example*, because the value of the reimbursed expenses for each month did not exceed the applicable statutory monthly limit, the $300 reimbursement is excludable from R's wages for income and employment tax purposes as a qualified transportation fringe.

Q-18. What are the substantiation requirements if an employer distributes transit passes?

A-18. There are no substantiation requirements if the employer distributes transit passes. Thus, an employer may distribute a transit pass for each month with a value not more than the statutory monthly limit without requiring any certification from the employee regarding the use of the transit pass.

Q-19. May an employer choose to impose substantiation requirements in addition those described in this regulation?

A-19. Yes.

Q-20. How is the value of parking determined?

A-20. Section 1.61-21(b)(2) applies for purposes of determining the value of parking.

Q-21. How do the qualified transportation fringe rules apply to van pools?

A-21. (a) *Van pools generally.* Employer and employee-operated van pools, as well as private or public transit-operated van pools, may qualify as qualified transportation fringes. The value of van pool benefits which are qualified transportation fringes may be excluded up to the applicable statutory monthly limit for transportation in a commuter highway vehicle and transit passes, less the value of any transit passes provided by the employer for the month.

(b) *Employer-operated van pools.* The value of van pool transportation provided by or for an employer to its employees is excludable as a qualified transportation fringe, provided the van qualifies as a commuter highway vehicle as defined in section 132(f)(5)(B) and Q/A-2 of this section. A van pool is operated by or for the employer if the employer purchases or leases vans to enable employees to commute together or the employer contracts with and pays a third party to provide the vans and some or all of the costs of operating the vans, including maintenance, liability insurance and other operating expenses.

(c) *Employee-operated van pools.* Cash reimbursement by an employer to employees for expenses incurred for transportation in a van pool operated by employees independent of their employer are excludable as qualified transportation fringes, provided that the van qualifies as a commuter highway vehicle as defined in section

132(f)(5)(B) and Q/A-2 of this section. See Q/A-16 of this section for the rules governing cash reimbursements.

(d) *Private or public transit-operated van pool transit passes.* The qualified transportation fringe exclusion for transit passes is available for travel in van pools owned and operated either by public transit authorities or by any person in the business of transporting persons for compensation or hire. In accordance with paragraph (b) of Q/A-3 of this section, the van must seat at least 6 adults (excluding the driver). See Q/A-16(b) and (c) of this section for a special rule for cash reimbursement for transit passes and the substantiation requirements for cash reimbursement.

(e) *Value of van pool transportation benefits.* Section 1.61-21(b)(2) provides that the fair market value of a fringe benefit is based on all the facts and circumstances. Alternatively, transportation in an employer-provided commuter highway vehicle may be valued under the automobile lease valuation rule in § 1.61-21(d), the vehicle cents-per-mile rule in § 1.61-21(e), or the commuting valuation rule in § 11.61-21(f). If one of these special valuation rules is used, the employer must use the same valuation rule to value the use of the commuter highway vehicle by each employee who share the use. See § 1.61-21(c)(2)(i)(B).

(f) *Qualified parking prime member.* If an employee obtains a qualified parking space as a result of membership in a car or van pool, the applicable statutory monthly limit for qualified parking applies to the individual to whom the parking space is assigned. This individual is the prime member. In determining the tax consequences to the prime member, the statutory monthly limit amounts of each car pool member may not be combined. If the employer provides access to the space and the space is not assigned to a particular individual, then the employer must designate one of its employees as the prime member who will bear the tax consequences. The employer may not designate more than one prime member for a car or van pool during a month. The employer of the prime member is responsible for including the value of the qualified parking in excess of the statutory monthly limit in the prime member's wages for income and employment tax purposes.

Q-22. What are the reporting and employment tax requirements for qualified transportation fringes?

A-22. (a) *Employment tax treatment generally.* Qualified transportation fringes not exceeding the applicable statutory monthly limit described in Q/A-7 of this section are not wages for purposes of the Federal Insurance Contributions Act (FICA),

Reg. § 1.132-9(b)

the Federal Unemployment Tax Act (FUTA), and federal income tax withholding. Any amount by which an employee elects to reduce compensation as provided in Q/A-11 of this section is not subject to the FICA, the FUTA, and federal income tax withholding. Qualified transportation fringes exceeding the applicable statutory monthly limit described in Q/A-7 of this section are wages for purposes of the FICA, the FUTA, and federal income tax withholding and are reported on the employee's Form W-2, Wage and Tax Statement.

(b) *Employment tax treatment of cash reimbursement exceeding monthly limits.* Cash reimbursement to employees (for example, cash reimbursement for qualified parking) in excess of the applicable statutory monthly limit under section 132(f) is treated as paid for employment tax purposes when actually or constructively paid. See § § 31.3121(a)-2(a), 31.3301-4, 31.3402(a)-1(b) of this chapter. Employers must report and deposit the amounts withheld in addition to reporting and depositing other employment taxes. See Q/A-16 of this section for rules governing cash reimbursements.

(c) *Noncash fringe benefits exceeding monthly limits.* If the value of noncash qualified transportation fringes exceeds the applicable statutory monthly limit, the employer may elect, for purposes of the FICA, the FUTA, and federal income tax withholding, to treat the noncash taxable fringe benefits as paid on a pay period, quarterly, semi-annual, annual, or other basis, provided that the benefits are treated as paid no less frequently than annually.

Q-23. How does section 132(f) interact with other fringe benefit rules?

A-23. For purposes of section 132, the terms working condition fringe and de minimis fringe do not include any qualified transportation fringe under section 132(f). If, however, an employer provides local transportation other than transit passes (without any direct or indirect compensation reduction election), the value of the benefit may be excludable, either totally or partially, under fringe benefit rules other than the qualified transportation fringe rules under section 132(f). See § § 1.132-6(d)(2)(i) (occasional local transportation fare), 1.132-6(d)(2)(iii) (transportation provided under unusual circumstances), and 1.61-21(k) (valuation of local transportation provided to qualified employees). See also Q/A-4(b) of this section.

Q-24. May qualified transportation fringes be provided to individuals who are partners, 2-percent shareholders of S-corporations, or independent contractors?

A-24. (a) *General rule.* Section 132(f)(5)(E) states that self-employed individuals who are employees within the meaning of section 401(c)(1) are not employees for purposes of section 132(f). Therefore, individuals who are partners, sole proprietors, or other independent contractors are not employees for purposes of section 132(f). In addition, under section 1372(a), 2-percent shareholders of S corporations are treated as partners for fringe benefit purposes. Thus, an individual who is both a 2-percent shareholder of an S corporation and a common law employee of that S corporation is not considered an employee for purposes of section 132(f). However, while section 132(f) does not apply to individuals who are partners, 2-percent shareholders of S corporations, or independent contractors, other exclusions for working condition and de minimis fringes may be available as described in paragraphs (b) and (c) of this Q/A-24. See § § 1.132-1(b)(2) and 1.132-1(b)(4).

(b) *Transit passes.* The working condition and de minimis fringe exclusions under section 132(a)(3) and (4) are available for transit passes provided to individuals who are partners, 2-percent shareholders, and independent contractors. For example, tokens or farecards provided by a partnership to an individual who is a partner that enable the partner to commute on a public transit system (not including privately-operated van pools) are excludable from the partner's gross income if the value of the tokens and farecards in any month does not exceed the dollar amount specified in § 1.132-6(d)(1). However, if the value of a pass provided in a month exceeds the dollar amount specified in § 1.132-6(d)(1), the full value of the benefit provided (not merely the amount in excess of the dollar amount specified in § 1.132-6(d)(1)) is includible in gross income.

(c) *Parking.* The working condition fringe rules under section 132(d) do not apply to commuter parking. See § 1.132-5(a)(1). However, the de minimis fringe rules under section 132(e) are available for parking provided to individuals who are partners, 2-percent shareholders, or independent contractors that qualifies under the de minimis rules. See § 1.132-6(a) and (b).

(d) *Example.* The following example illustrates the principles of this Q/A-24:

Example. (i) Individual G is a partner in partnership P. Individual G commutes to and from G's office every day and parks free of charge in P's lot.

(ii) In this *Example*, the value of the parking is not excluded under section 132(f), but may be excluded under section 132(e) if the parking is a de minimis fringe under § 1.132-6.

Q-25. What is the effective date of this section?

Reg. § 1.132-9(b)

A-25. (a) Except as provided in paragraph (b) of this Q/A-25, this section is applicable for employee taxable years beginning after December 31, 2001. For this purpose, an employer may assume that the employee taxable year is the calendar year.

(b) The last sentence of paragraph (b)(5) of Q/A-16 of this section (relating to whether transit system vouchers for transit passes are readily available) is applicable for employee taxable years beginning after December 31, 2003. For this purpose, an employer may assume that the employee taxable year is the calendar year.

[Reg. § 1.132-9.]

□ [*T.D.* 8933, 1-10-2001 (*corrected* 4-5-2001).]

[Reg. § 1.133-1T]

§ 1.133-1T. Questions and answers relating to interest on certain loans used to acquire employer securities (Temporary).

Q-1: What does section 133 provide?

A-1: In general, section 133 provides that certain commercial lenders may exclude from gross income fifty percent of the interest received with respect to securities acquisition loans. A securities acquisition loan is any loan to an employee stock ownership plan (ESOP) (as defined in section 4975(e)(7)) that qualifies as an exempt loan under § 54.4975-7 and -11 to the extent that the proceeds are used to acquire employer securities (within the meaning of section 409 (l)) for the ESOP. A loan made to a corporation sponsoring an ESOP (or to a person related to such corporation under section 133(b)(2)) may also qualify as a securities acquisition loan to the extent and for the period that the proceeds are (a) loaned to the corporation's ESOP under a loan that qualifies as an exempt loan under § 54.4975-7 and -11 and that has substantially similar terms as the loan from the commercial lender to the sponsoring corporation, and (b) used to acquire employer securities for the ESOP. The terms of the loan between the commercial lender and the sponsoring corporation (or a related corporation) and the loan between such corporation and the ESOP shall be treated as substantially similar only if the timing and rate at which employer securities would be released from encumbrance if the loan from the commercial lender were the exempt loan under the applicable rule of § 54.4975-7(b)(8) are substantially similar to the timing and rate at which employer securities will actually be released from encumbrance in accordance with such rule. For this purpose, if the loan from the commercial lender to the sponsoring corporation states a variable rate of interest and the loan between the corporation and the ESOP states a fixed rate of interest, whether the terms of the loans are substantially similar shall be determined at the time the obligations are initially issued by taking into account the adjustment interval on the variable rate loan and the maturity of the fixed rate loan. For example, if the rate on the loan from the commercial lender to the sponsoring corporation adjusts each six months and the loan from the corporation to the ESOP has a ten year term, the initial interest rate on the variable rate loan could be compared to the rate on the fixed rate loan by comparing the yields on 6 month and ten year Treasury obligations. Similarly, if the rates on the two loans are based on different compounding assumptions, whether the terms of the loans are substantially similar shall be determined by taking into account the different compounding assumptions. A securities acquisition loan may be evidenced by any note, bond, debenture, or certificate. Also, section 133(b)(2) provides that certain loans between related persons are not securities acquisition loans. In addition, a loan from a commercial lender to an ESOP or sponsoring corporation to purchase employer securities will not be treated as a securities acquisition loan to the extent that such loan is used, either directly or indirectly, to purchase employer securities from any other qualified plan, including any other ESOP, maintained by the employer or any other corporation which is a member of the same controlled group (as defined in section 409(l)(4).

Q-2: What lenders are eligible to receive the fifty percent interest exclusion?

A-2: Under section 133(a), a bank (within the meaning of section 581), an insurance company to which subchapter L applies, or a corporation (other than a subchapter S corporation) actively engaged in the business of lending money may exclude from gross income fifty percent of the interest received with respect to a securities acquisition loan (as defined in Q&A-1 of § 1.133-1T). For purposes of section 133(a)(3), a corporation is actively engaged in the business of lending money if it lends money to the public on a regular and continuing basis (other than in connection with the purchase by the public of goods and services from the lender or a related party). A corporation is not actively engaged in the business of lending money if a predominant share of the original value of the loans it makes to unrelated parties (other than in connection with the purchase by the public of goods and services from the lender or a related party) are securities acquisition loans.

Q-3: May loans which qualify for the fifty percent interest exclusion under section 133 be syndicated to other lending institutions?

25,292   Tax Exempt. Requirements: State/Local Bonds

See p. 20,601 for regulations not amended to reflect law changes

A-3: Securities acquisition loans under section 133 may be syndicated to other lending institutions provided that such lending institutions are described in section 133(a)(1), (2) or (3) and the loan was originated by a qualified holder. Subsequent holders of the debt instrument may qualify for the partial interest exclusion of section 133 if such holders satisfy the requirements of section 133 and such loan does not fail to be a securities acquisition loan under section 133(b)(2).

Q-4: When is section 133 effective?

A-4: Section 133 applies to securities acquisition loans made after July 18, 1984, and used to acquire employer securities after July 18, 1984. The provision does not apply to loans made after July 18, 1984, to the extent that such loans are renegotiations, directly or indirectly, of loans outstanding on such date. A loan extended to an ESOP or sponsoring corporation after July 18, 1984, will be treated as a renegotiation of an outstanding loan if the loan proceeds are used to refinance acquisitions of employer securities made prior to July 19, 1984. For example, if an ESOP borrowed money prior to July 19, 1984, to purchase employer securities and after July 18, 1984, borrows other funds from the same or a different commercial lender to repay the first loan, the second loan will be treated as a renegotiation of an outstanding loan to the extent of the repaid amount. Similarly, if, after July 18, 1984, an ESOP sells employer securities, uses the proceeds to retire a pre-July 19, 1984, loan and obtains a second loan to acquire replacement employer securities, the second loan will be treated as a renegotiation of an outstanding loan. [Temporary Reg. § 1.133-1T.]

☐ [*T.D.* 8073, 1-29-86.]

Tax Exemption Requirements for State and Local Bonds

[Reg. § 1.141-0]

§ 1.141-0. Table of contents.—This section lists the captioned paragraphs contained in §§ 1.141-1 through 1.141-16.

§ 1.141-1 Definitions and rules of general application.

(a) In general.

(b) Certain general definitions.

(c) Elections.

(d) Related parties.

§ 1.141-2 Private activity bond tests.

(a) Overview.

(b) Scope.

(c) General definition of private activity bond.

(d) Reasonable expectations and deliberate actions.

(1) In general.

(2) Reasonable expectations test.

(3) Deliberate action defined.

(4) Special rule for dispositions of personal property in the ordinary course of an established governmental program.

(5) Special rule for general obligation bond programs that finance a large number of separate purposes.

(e) When a deliberate action occurs.

(f) Certain remedial actions.

(g) Examples.

§ 1.141-3 Definition of private business use.

(a) General rule.

(1) In general.

(2) Indirect use.

(3) Aggregation of private business use.

(b) Types of private business use arrangements.

(1) In general.

(2) Ownership.

(3) Leases.

(4) Management contracts.

(5) Output contracts.

(6) Research agreements.

(7) Other actual or beneficial use.

(c) Exception for general public use.

(1) In general.

(2) Use on the same basis.

(3) Long-term arrangements not treated as general public use.

(4) Relation to other use.

(d) Other exceptions.

(1) Agents.

(2) Use incidental to financing arrangements.

(3) Exceptions for arrangements other than arrangements resulting in ownership of financed property by a nongovernmental person.

(4) Temporary use by developers.

(5) Incidental use.

(6) Qualified improvements.

(e) Special rule for tax assessment bonds.

(f) Examples.

(g) Measurement of private business use.

(1) In general.

(2) Measurement period.

Reg. § 1.141-0

Tax Exempt. Requirements: State/Local Bonds 25,293

See p. 20,601 for regulations not amended to reflect law changes

(3) Determining average percentage of private business use.

(4) Determining the average amount of private business use for a 1-year period.

(5) Common areas.

(6) Allocation of neutral costs.

(7) Commencement of measurement of private business use.

(8) Examples.

§ 1.141-4 *Private security or payment test.*

(a) General rule.

(1) Private security or payment.

(2) Aggregation of private payments and security.

(3) Underlying arrangement.

(b) Measurement of private payments and security.

(1) Scope.

(2) Present value measurement.

(c) Private payments.

(1) In general.

(2) Payments taken into account.

(3) Allocation of payments.

(d) Private security.

(1) In general.

(2) Security taken into account.

(3) Pledge of unexpended proceeds.

(4) Secured by any interest in property or payments.

(5) Payments in respect of property.

(6) Allocation of security among issues.

(e) Generally applicable taxes.

(1) General rule.

(2) Definition of generally applicable taxes.

(3) Special charges.

(4) Manner of determination and collection.

(5) Payments in lieu of taxes.

(f) Certain waste remediation bonds.

(1) Scope.

(2) Persons that are not private users.

(3) Persons that are private users.

(g) Examples.

§ 1.141-5 *Private loan financing test.*

(a) In general.

(b) Measurement of test.

(c) Definition of private loan.

(1) In general.

(2) Application only to purpose investments.

(3) Grants.

(4) Hazardous waste remediation bonds.

(d) Tax assessment loan exception.

(1) General rule.

(2) Tax assessment loan defined.

(3) Mandatory tax or other assessment.

(4) Specific essential governmental function.

(5) Equal basis requirement.

(6) Coordination with private business tests.

(e) Examples.

§ 1.141-6 *Allocation and accounting rules.*

(a) Allocation of proceeds to expenditures.

(b) Allocation of proceeds to property. [Reserved]

(c) Special rules for mixed use facilities. [Reserved]

(d) Allocation of proceeds to common areas. [Reserved]

(e) Allocation of proceeds to bonds. [Reserved]

(f) Treatment of partnerships. [Reserved]

(g) Examples. [Reserved]

§ 1.141-7 *Special rules for output facilities.*

(a) Overview.

(b) Definitions.

(1) Available output.

(2) Measurement period.

(3) Sale at wholesale.

(4) Take contract and take or pay contract.

(5) Requirements contract.

(6) Nonqualified amount.

(c) Output contracts.

(1) General rule.

(2) Take contract or take or pay contract.

(3) Requirements contract.

(4) Output contract properly characterized as a lease.

(d) Measurement of private business use.

(e) Measurement of private security or payment.

(f) Exceptions for certain contracts.

(1) Small purchases of output.

(2) Swapping and pooling arrangements.

(3) Short-term output contracts.

(4) Certain conduit parties disregarded.

(g) Special rules for electric output facilities used to provide open access.

(1) Operation of transmission facilities by nongovernmental persons.

(2) Certain use by nongovernmental persons under output contracts.

Reg. § 1.141-0

25,294   **Tax Exempt. Requirements: State/Local Bonds**

See p. 20,601 for regulations not amended to reflect law changes

(3) Ancillary services.

(4) Exceptions to deliberate action rules.

(5) Additional transactions as permitted by the Commissioner.

(h) Allocations of output facilities and systems.

(1) Facts and circumstances analysis.

(2) Illustrations.

(3) Transmission and distribution contracts.

(4) Allocation of payments.

(i) Examples.

§ 1.141-8 $15 million limitation for output facilities.

(a) In general.

(1) General rule.

(2) Reduction in $15 million output limitation for outstanding issues.

(3) Benefits and burdens test applicable.

(b) Definition of project.

(1) General rule.

(2) Separate ownership.

(3) Generating property.

(4) Transmission and distribution.

(5) Subsequent improvements.

(6) Replacement property.

(c) Examples.

§ 1.141-9 Unrelated or disproportionate use test.

(a) General rules.

(1) Description of test.

(2) Application of unrelated or disproportionate use test.

(b) Unrelated use.

(1) In general.

(2) Use for the same purpose as government use.

(c) Disproportionate use.

(1) Definition of disproportionate use.

(2) Aggregation of related uses.

(3) Allocation rule.

(d) Maximum use taken into account.

(e) Examples.

§ 1.141-10 Coordination with volume cap.

[Reserved]

§ 1.141-11 Acquisition of nongovernmental output property.

[Reserved]

§ 1.141-12 Remedial actions.

(a) Conditions to taking remedial action.

(1) Reasonable expectations test met.

(2) Maturity not unreasonably long.

(3) Fair market value consideration.

(4) Disposition proceeds treated as gross proceeds for arbitrage purposes.

(5) Proceeds expended on a governmental purpose.

(b) Effect of a remedial action.

(1) In general.

(2) Effect on bonds that have been advance refunded.

(c) Disposition proceeds.

(1) Definition.

(2) Allocating disposition proceeds to an issue.

(3) Allocating disposition proceeds to different sources of funding.

(d) Redemption or defeasance of nonqualified bonds.

(1) In general.

(2) Special rule for dispositions for cash.

(3) Notice of defeasance.

(4) Special limitation.

(5) Defeasance escrow defined.

(e) Alternative use of disposition proceeds.

(1) In general.

(2) Special rule for use by 501(c)(3) organizations.

(f) Alternative use of facility.

(g) Rules for deemed reissuance.

(h) Authority of Commissioner to provide for additional remedial actions.

(i) Effect of remedial action on continuing compliance.

(j) Nonqualified bonds.

(1) Amount of nonqualified bonds.

(2) Allocation of nonqualified bonds.

(k) Examples.

§ 1.141-13 Refunding issues.

[Reserved]

§ 1.141-14 Anti-abuse rules.

(a) Authority of Commissioner to reflect substance of transactions.

(b) Examples.

§ 1.141-15 Effective dates.

(a) Scope.

(b) Effective dates.

(c) Refunding bonds.

(d) Permissive application of regulations.

(e) Permissive retroactive application of certain sections.

Reg. § 1.141-0

(f) Effective dates for certain regulations relating to output facilities.

(1) General rule.

(2) Transition rule for requirements contracts.

(g) Refunding bonds for output facilities.

(h) Permissive retroactive application.

(i) Permissive application of certain regulations relating to output facilities.

§ 1.141-16 Effective dates for qualified private activity bond provisions.

(a) Scope.

(b) Effective dates.

(c) Permissive application.

[Reg. § 1.141-0.]

☐ [T.D. 8712, 1-10-97. Amended by T.D. 8757, 1-21-98; T.D. 8941, 1-17-2001 and T.D. 9016, 9-19-2002.]

[Reg. § 1.141-1]

§ 1.141-1. Definitions and rules of general application.—(a) In general. For purposes of §§ 1.141-0 through 1.141-16, the following definitions and rules apply: the definitions in this section, the definitions in § 1.150-1, the definition of placed in service under § 1.150-2(c), the definition of grant under § 1.148-6(d)(4)(iii), the definition of reasonably required reserve or replacement fund in § 1.148-2(f), and the following definitions under § 1.148-1: bond year, commingled fund, fixed yield issue, higher yielding investments, investment, investment proceeds, issue price, issuer, nonpurpose investment, purpose investment, qualified guarantee, qualified hedge, reasonable expectations or reasonableness, rebate amount, replacement proceeds, sale proceeds, variable yield issue, and yield.

(b) Certain general definitions.

Common areas means portions of a facility that are equally available to all users of a facility on the same basis for uses that are incidental to the primary use of the facility. For example, hallways and elevators generally are treated as common areas if they are used by the different lessees of a facility in connection with the primary use of that facility.

Consistently applied means applied uniformly to account for proceeds and other amounts.

Deliberate action is defined in § 1.141-2(d)(3).

Discrete portion means a portion of a facility that consists of any separate and discrete portion of a facility to which use is limited, other than common areas. A floor of a building and a portion of a building separated by walls, partitions, or other physical barriers are examples of a discrete portion.

Disposition is defined in § 1.141-12(c)(1).

Disposition proceeds is defined in § 1.141-12(c)(1).

Essential governmental function is defined in § 1.141-5(d)(4)(ii).

Financed means constructed, reconstructed, or acquired with proceeds of an issue.

Governmental bond means a bond issued as part of an issue no portion of which consists of private activity bonds.

Governmental person means a state or local governmental unit as defined in § 1.103-1 or any instrumentality thereof. It does not include the United States or any agency or instrumentality thereof.

Hazardous waste remediation bonds is defined in § 1.141-4(f)(1).

Measurement period is defined in § 1.141-3(g)(2).

Nongovernmental person means a person other than a governmental person.

Output facility means electric and gas generation, transmission, distribution, and related facilities, and water collection, storage, and distribution facilities.

Private business tests means the private business use test and the private security or payment test of section 141(b).

Proceeds means the sale proceeds of an issue (other than those sale proceeds used to retire bonds of the issue that are not deposited in a reasonably required reserve or replacement fund). Proceeds also include any investment proceeds from investments that accrue during the project period (net of rebate amounts attributable to the project period). Disposition proceeds of an issue are treated as proceeds to the extent provided in § 1.141-12. The Commissioner may treat any replaced amounts as proceeds.

Project period means the period beginning on the issue date and ending on the date that the project is placed in service. In the case of a multipurpose issue, the issuer may elect to treat the project period for the entire issue as ending on either the expiration of the temporary period described in § 1.148-2(e)(2) or the end of the fifth bond year after the issue date.

Public utility property means public utility property as defined in section 168(i)(10).

Qualified bond means a qualified bond as defined in section 141(e).

Renewal option means a provision under which either party has a legally enforceable right to

Reg. § 1.141-1(b)

25,296   **Tax Exempt. Requirements: State/Local Bonds**

See p. 20,601 for regulations not amended to reflect law changes

renew the contract. Thus, for example, a provision under which a contract is automatically renewed for 1-year periods absent cancellation by either party is not a renewal option (even if it is expected to be renewed).

Replaced amounts means replacement proceeds other than amounts that are treated as replacement proceeds solely because they are sinking funds or pledged funds.

Weighted average maturity is determined under section 147(b).

Weighted average reasonably expected economic life is determined under section 147(b). The reasonably expected economic life of property may be determined by reference to the class life of the property under section 168.

(c) *Elections.* Elections must be made in writing on or before the issue date and retained as part of the bond documents, and, once made, may not be revoked without the permission of the Commissioner.

(d) *Related parties.* Except as otherwise provided, all related parties are treated as one person and any reference to "person" includes any related party. [Reg. § 1.141-1.]

□ [Reg. § 1.141-1, issued under Code Sec. 141 as it existed prior to repeal by P.L. 95-30, was removed from the CFR, and Reg. § 1.141-1, above, was adopted by *T.D.* 8712, 1-10-97.]

[Reg. § 1.141-2]

§ 1.141-2. Private activity bond tests.—(a) *Overview.* Interest on a private activity bond is not excludable from gross income under section 103(a) unless the bond is a qualified bond. The purpose of the private activity bond tests of section 141 is to limit the volume of tax-exempt bonds that finance the activities of nongovernmental persons, without regard to whether a financing actually transfers benefits of tax-exempt financing to a nongovernmental person. The private activity bond tests serve to identify arrangements that have the potential to transfer the benefits of tax-exempt financing, as well as arrangements that actually transfer these benefits. The regulations under section 141 may not be applied in a manner that is inconsistent with these purposes.

(b) *Scope.* Sections 1.141-0 through 1.141-16 apply generally for purposes of the private activity bond limitations under section 141.

(c) *General definition of private activity bond.* Under section 141, bonds are private activity bonds if they meet either the private business use test and private security or payment test of section 141(b) or the private loan financing test of section 141(c). The private business use and private security or payment tests are described in §§ 1.141-3 and 1.141-4. The private loan financing test is described in § 1.141-5.

(d) *Reasonable expectations and deliberate actions*—(1) *In general.* An issue is an issue of private activity bonds if the issuer reasonably expects, as of the issue date, that the issue will meet either the private business tests or the private loan financing test. An issue is also an issue of private activity bonds if the issuer takes a deliberate action, subsequent to the issue date, that causes the conditions of either the private business tests or the private loan financing test to be met.

(2) *Reasonable expectations test*—(i) *In general.* In general, the reasonable expectations test must take into account reasonable expectations about events and actions over the entire stated term of an issue.

(ii) *Special rule for issues with mandatory redemption provisions.* An action that is reasonably expected, as of the issue date, to occur after the issue date and to cause either the private business tests or the private loan financing test to be met may be disregarded for purposes of those tests if—

(A) The issuer reasonably expects, as of the issue date, that the financed property will be used for a governmental purpose for a substantial period before the action;

(B) The issuer is required to redeem all nonqualifying bonds (regardless of the amount of disposition proceeds actually received) within 6 months of the date of the action;

(C) The issuer does not enter into any arrangement with a nongovernmental person, as of the issue date, with respect to that specific action; and

(D) The mandatory redemption of bonds meets all of the conditions for remedial action under § 1.141-12(a).

(3) *Deliberate action defined*—(i) *In general.* Except as otherwise provided in this paragraph (d)(3), a deliberate action is any action taken by the issuer that is within its control. An intent to violate the requirements of section 141 is not necessary for an action to be deliberate.

(ii) *Safe harbor exceptions.* An action is not treated as a deliberate action if—

(A) It would be treated as an involuntary or compulsory conversion under section 1033; or

(B) It is taken in response to a regulatory directive made by the federal government. See § 1.141-7(g)(4).

Reg. § 1.141-2(a)

(4) *Special rule for dispositions of personal property in the ordinary course of an established governmental program*—(i) *In general.* Dispositions of personal property in the ordinary course of an established governmental program are not treated as deliberate actions if—

(A) The weighted average maturity of the bonds financing that personal property is not greater than 120 percent of the reasonably expected actual use of that property for governmental purposes;

(B) The issuer reasonably expects on the issue date that the fair market value of that property on the date of disposition will be not greater than 25 percent of its cost; and

(C) The property is no longer suitable for its governmental purposes on the date of disposition.

(ii) *Reasonable expectations test.* The reasonable expectation that a disposition described in paragraph (d)(4)(i) of this section may occur in the ordinary course while the bonds are outstanding will not cause the issue to meet the private activity bond tests if the issuer is required to deposit amounts received from the disposition in a commingled fund with substantial tax or other governmental revenues and the issuer reasonably expects to spend the amounts on governmental programs within 6 months from the date of commingling.

(iii) *Separate issue treatment.* An issuer may treat the bonds properly allocable to the personal property eligible for this exception as a separate issue under § 1.150-1(c)(3).

(5) *Special rule for general obligation bond programs that finance a large number of separate purposes.* The determination of whether bonds of an issue are private activity bonds may be based solely on the issuer's reasonable expectations as of the issue date if all of the requirements of paragraphs (d)(5)(i) through (vii) of this section are met.

(i) The issue is an issue of general obligation bonds of a general purpose governmental unit that finances at least 25 separate purposes (as defined in § 1.150-1(c)(3)) and does not predominantly finance fewer than 4 separate purposes.

(ii) The issuer has adopted a fund method of accounting for its general governmental purposes that makes tracing the bond proceeds to specific expenditures unreasonably burdensome.

(iii) The issuer reasonably expects on the issue date to allocate all of the net proceeds of the issue to capital expenditures within 6 months of the issue date and adopts reasonable procedures to verify that net proceeds are in fact so ex-

pended. A program to randomly spot check that 10 percent of the net proceeds were so expended generally is a reasonable verification procedure for this purpose.

(iv) The issuer reasonably expects on the issue date to expend all of the net proceeds of the issue before expending proceeds of a subsequent issue of similar general obligation bonds.

(v) The issuer reasonably expects on the issue date that it will not make any loans to nongovernmental persons with the proceeds of the issue.

(vi) The issuer reasonably expects on the issue date that the capital expenditures that it could make during the 6-month period beginning on the issue date with the net proceeds of the issue that would not meet the private business tests are not less than 125 percent of the capital expenditures to be financed with the net proceeds of the issue.

(vii) The issuer reasonably expects on the issue date that the weighted average maturity of the issue is not greater than 120 percent of the weighted average reasonably expected economic life of the capital expenditures financed with the issue. To determine reasonably expected economic life for this purpose an issuer may use reasonable estimates based on the type of expenditures made from a fund.

(e) *When a deliberate action occurs.* A deliberate action occurs on the date the issuer enters into a binding contract with a nongovernmental person for use of the financed property that is not subject to any material contingencies.

(f) *Certain remedial actions.* See § 1.141-12 for certain remedial actions that prevent a deliberate action with respect to property financed by an issue from causing that issue to meet the private business use test or the private loan financing test.

(g) *Examples.* The following examples illustrate the application of this section:

Example 1. Involuntary action. City B issues bonds to finance the purchase of land. On the issue date, B reasonably expects that it will be the sole user of the land for the entire term of the bonds. Subsequently, the federal government acquires the land in a condemnation action. B sets aside the condemnation proceeds to pay debt service on the bonds but does not redeem them on their first call date. The bonds are not private activity bonds because B has not taken a deliberate action after the issue date. See, however, § 1.141-14(b), *Example 2.*

Example 2. Reasonable expectations test—involuntary action. The facts are the same as in

Reg. § 1.141-2(g)

25,298   Tax Exempt. Requirements: State/Local Bonds

See p. 20,601 for regulations not amended to reflect law changes

Example 1, except that, on the issue date, B reasonably expects that the federal government will acquire the land in a condemnation action during the term of the bonds. On the issue date, the present value of the amount that B reasonably expects to receive from the federal government is greater than 10 percent of the present value of the debt service on the bonds. The terms of the bonds do not require that the bonds be redeemed within 6 months of the acquisition by the federal government. The bonds are private activity bonds because the issuer expects as of the issue date that the private business tests will be met.

Example 3. Reasonable expectations test—mandatory redemption. City C issues bonds to rehabilitate an existing hospital that it currently owns. On the issue date of the bonds, C reasonably expects that the hospital will be used for a governmental purpose for a substantial period. On the issue date, C also plans to construct a new hospital, but the placed in service date of that new hospital is uncertain. C reasonably expects that, when the new hospital is placed in service, it will sell or lease the rehabilitated hospital to a private hospital corporation. The bond documents require that the bonds must be redeemed within 6 months of the sale or lease of the rehabilitated hospital (regardless of the amount actually received from the sale). The bonds meet the reasonable expectations requirement of the private activity bond tests if the mandatory redemption of bonds meets all of the conditions for a remedial action under § 1.141-12(a).

Example 4. Dispositions in the ordinary course of an established governmental program. City D issues bonds with a weighted average maturity of 6 years for the acquisition of police cars. D reasonably expects on the issue date that the police cars will be used solely by its police department, except that, in the ordinary course of its police operations, D sells its police cars to a taxicab corporation after 5 years of use because they are no longer suitable for police use. Further, D reasonably expects that the value of the police cars when they are no longer suitable for police use will be no more than 25 percent of cost. D subsequently sells 20 percent of the police cars after only 3 years of actual use. At that time, D deposits the proceeds from the sale of the police cars in a commingled fund with substantial tax revenues and reasonably expects to spend the proceeds on governmental programs within 6 months of the date of deposit. D does not trace the actual use of these commingled amounts. The sale of the police cars does not cause the private activity bond tests to be met because the requirements of paragraph (d)(4) of this section are met.

[Reg. § 1.141-2.]

□ [*T.D.* 8712, 1-10-97. *Amended by T.D.* 8757, 1-21-98 *and T.D.* 9016, 9-19-2002.]

[Reg. § 1.141-3]

§ 1.141-3. Definition of private business use.—(a) *General rule*—(1) *In general.* The private business use test relates to the use of the proceeds of an issue. The 10 percent private business use test of section 141(b)(1) is met if more than 10 percent of the proceeds of an issue is used in a trade or business of a nongovernmental person. For this purpose, the use of financed property is treated as the direct use of proceeds. Any activity carried on by a person other than a natural person is treated as a trade or business. Unless the context or a provision clearly requires otherwise, this section also applies to the private business use test under sections 141(b)(3) (unrelated or disproportionate use), 141(b)(4) ($15 million limitation for certain output facilities), and 141(b)(5) (the coordination with the volume cap where the nonqualified amount exceeds $15 million).

(2) *Indirect use.* In determining whether an issue meets the private business use test, it is necessary to look to both the indirect and direct uses of proceeds. For example, a facility is treated as being used for a private business use if it is leased to a nongovernmental person and subleased to a governmental person or if it is leased to a governmental person and then subleased to a nongovernmental person, provided that in each case the nongovernmental person's use is in a trade or business. Similarly, the issuer's use of the proceeds to engage in a series of financing transactions for property to be used by nongovernmental persons in their trades or businesses may cause the private business use test to be met. In addition, proceeds are treated as used in the trade or business of a nongovernmental person if a nongovernmental person, as a result of a single transaction or a series of related transactions, uses property acquired with the proceeds of an issue.

(3) *Aggregation of private business use.* The use of proceeds by all nongovernmental persons is aggregated to determine whether the private business use test is met.

(b) *Types of private business use arrangements*—(1) *In general.* Both actual and beneficial use by a nongovernmental person may be treated as private business use. In most cases, the private business use test is met only if a nongovernmental person has special legal entitlements to use the financed property under an arrangement with the issuer. In general, a nongovernmental person is treated as a private business user of proceeds and financed property as a result of ownership; actual

Reg. § 1.141-3(a)(1)

or beneficial use of property pursuant to a lease, or a management or incentive payment contract; or certain other arrangements such as a take or pay or other output-type contract.

(2) *Ownership.* Except as provided in paragraph (d)(1) or (d)(2) of this section, ownership by a nongovernmental person of financed property is private business use of that property. For this purpose, ownership refers to ownership for federal income tax purposes.

(3) *Leases.* Except as provided in paragraph (d) of this section, the lease of financed property to a nongovernmental person is private business use of that property. For this purpose, any arrangement that is properly characterized as a lease for federal income tax purposes is treated as a lease. In determining whether a management contract is properly characterized as a lease, it is necessary to consider all of the facts and circumstances, including the following factors—

(i) The degree of control over the property that is exercised by a nongovernmental person; and

(ii) Whether a nongovernmental person bears risk of loss of the financed property.

(4) *Management contracts*—(i) *Facts and circumstances test.* Except as provided in paragraph (d) of this section, a management contract (within the meaning of paragraph (b)(4)(ii) of this section) with respect to financed property may result in private business use of that property, based on all of the facts and circumstances. A management contract with respect to financed property generally results in private business use of that property if the contract provides for compensation for services rendered with compensation based, in whole or in part, on a share of net profits from the operation of the facility.

(ii) *Management contract defined.* For purposes of this section, a management contract is a management, service, or incentive payment contract between a governmental person and a service provider under which the service provider provides services involving all, a portion of, or any function of, a facility. For example, a contract for the provision of management services for an entire hospital, a contract for management services for a specific department of a hospital, and an incentive payment contract for physician services to patients of a hospital are each treated as a management contract.

(iii) *Arrangements generally not treated as management contracts.* The arrangements described in paragraphs (b)(4)(iii)(A) through (D) of this section generally are not treated as management contracts that give rise to private business use.

(A) Contracts for services that are solely incidental to the primary governmental function or functions of a financed facility (for example, contracts for janitorial, office equipment repair, hospital billing, or similar services).

(B) The mere granting of admitting privileges by a hospital to a doctor, even if those privileges are conditioned on the provision of de minimis services, if those privileges are available to all qualified physicians in the area, consistent with the size and nature of its facilities.

(C) A contract to provide for the operation of a facility or system of facilities that consists predominantly of public utility property, if the only compensation is the reimbursement of actual and direct expenses of the service provider and reasonable administrative overhead expenses of the service provider.

(D) A contract to provide for services, if the only compensation is the reimbursement of the service provider for actual and direct expenses paid by the service provider to unrelated parties.

(iv) *Management contracts that are properly treated as other types of private business use.* A management contract with respect to financed property results in private business use of that property if the service provider is treated as the lessee or owner of financed property for federal income tax purposes, unless an exception under paragraph (d) of this section applies to the arrangement.

(5) *Output contracts.* See § 1.141-7 for special rules for contracts for the purchase of output of output facilities.

(6) *Research agreements*—(i) *Facts and circumstances test.* Except as provided in paragraph (d) of this section, an agreement by a nongovernmental person to sponsor research performed by a governmental person may result in private business use of the property used for the research, based on all of the facts and circumstances.

(ii) *Research agreements that are properly treated as other types of private business use.* A research agreement with respect to financed property results in private business use of that property if the sponsor is treated as the lessee or owner of financed property for federal income tax purposes, unless an exception under paragraph (d) of this section applies to the arrangement.

(7) *Other actual or beneficial use*—(i) *In general.* Any other arrangement that conveys special legal entitlements for beneficial use of bond proceeds or of financed property that are comparable to special legal entitlements described in paragraphs (b)(2), (3), (4), (5), or (6) of this section results in private business use. For example,

Reg. § 1.141-3(b)(7)

25,300   Tax Exempt. Requirements: State/Local Bonds

See p. 20,601 for regulations not amended to reflect law changes

an arrangement that conveys priority rights to the use or capacity of a facility generally results in private business use.

(ii) *Special rule for facilities not used by the general public.* In the case of financed property that is not available for use by the general public (within the meaning of paragraph (c) of this section), private business use may be established solely on the basis of a special economic benefit to one or more nongovernmental persons, even if those nongovernmental persons have no special legal entitlements to use of the property. In determining whether special economic benefit gives rise to private business use it is necessary to consider all of the facts and circumstances, including one or more of the following factors—

(A) Whether the financed property is functionally related or physically proximate to property used in the trade or business of a nongovernmental person;

(B) Whether only a small number of nongovernmental persons receive the special economic benefit; and

(C) Whether the cost of the financed property is treated as depreciable by any nongovernmental person.

(c) *Exception for general public use*—(1) *In general.* Use as a member of the general public (general public use) is not private business use. Use of financed property by nongovernmental persons in their trades or businesses is treated as general public use only if the property is intended to be available and in fact is reasonably available for use on the same basis by natural persons not engaged in a trade or business.

(2) *Use on the same basis.* In general, use under an arrangement that conveys priority rights or other preferential benefits is not use on the same basis as the general public. Arrangements providing for use that is available to the general public at no charge or on the basis of rates that are generally applicable and uniformly applied do not convey priority rights or other preferential benefits. For this purpose, rates may be treated as generally applicable and uniformly applied even if—

(i) Different rates apply to different classes of users, such as volume purchasers, if the differences in rates are customary and reasonable; or

(ii) A specially negotiated rate arrangement is entered into, but only if the user is prohibited by federal law from paying the generally applicable rates, and the rates established are as comparable as reasonably possible to the generally applicable rates.

(3) *Long-term arrangements not treated as general public use.* An arrangement is not treated as general public use if the term of the use under the arrangement, including all renewal options, is greater than 200 days. For this purpose, a right of first refusal to renew use under the arrangement is not treated as a renewal option if—

(i) The compensation for the use under the arrangement is redetermined at generally applicable, fair market value rates that are in effect at the time of renewal; and

(ii) The use of the financed property under the same or similar arrangements is predominantly by natural persons who are not engaged in a trade or business.

(4) *Relation to other use.* Use of financed property by the general public does not prevent the proceeds from being used for a private business use because of other use under this section.

(d) *Other exceptions*—(1) *Agents.* Use of proceeds by nongovernmental persons solely in their capacity as agents of a governmental person is not private business use. For example, use by a nongovernmental person that issues obligations on behalf of a governmental person is not private business use to the extent the nongovernmental person's use of proceeds is in its capacity as an agent of the governmental person.

(2) *Use incidental to financing arrangements.* Use by a nongovernmental person that is solely incidental to a financing arrangement is not private business use. A use is solely incidental to a financing arrangement only if the nongovernmental person has no substantial rights to use bond proceeds or financed property other than as an agent of the bondholders. For example, a nongovernmental person that acts solely as an owner of title in a sale and leaseback financing transaction with a city generally is not a private business user of the property leased to the city, provided that the nongovernmental person has assigned all of its rights to use the leased facility to the trustee for the bondholders upon default by the city. Similarly, bond trustees, servicers, and guarantors are generally not treated as private business users.

(3) *Exceptions for arrangements other than arrangements resulting in ownership of financed property by a nongovernmental person*—(i) *Arrangements not available for use on the same basis by natural persons not engaged in a trade or business.* Use by a nongovernmental person pursuant to an arrangement, other than an arrangement resulting in ownership of financed property by a nongovernmental person, is not private business use if—

Reg. § 1.141-3(c)(1)

(A) The term of the use under the arrangement, including all renewal options, is not longer than 100 days;

(B) The arrangement would be treated as general public use, except that it is not available for use on the same basis by natural persons not engaged in a trade or business because generally applicable and uniformly applied rates are not reasonably available to natural persons not engaged in a trade or business; and

(C) The property is not financed for a principal purpose of providing that property for use by that nongovernmental person.

(ii) *Negotiated arm's-length arrangements.* Use by a nongovernmental person pursuant to an arrangement, other than an arrangement resulting in ownership of financed property by a nongovernmental person, is not private business use if—

(A) The term of the use under the arrangement, including all renewal options, is not longer than 50 days;

(B) The arrangement is a negotiated arm's-length arrangement, and compensation under the arrangement is at fair market value; and

(C) The property is not financed for a principal purpose of providing that property for use by that nongovernmental person.

(4) *Temporary use by developers.* Use during an initial development period by a developer of an improvement that carries out an essential governmental function is not private business use if the issuer and the developer reasonably expect on the issue date to proceed with all reasonable speed to develop the improvement and property benefited by that improvement and to transfer the improvement to a governmental person, and if the improvement is in fact transferred to a governmental person promptly after the property benefited by the improvement is developed.

(5) *Incidental use*—(i) *General rule.* Incidental uses of a financed facility are disregarded, to the extent that those uses do not exceed 2.5 percent of the proceeds of the issue used to finance the facility. A use of a facility by a nongovernmental person is incidental if—

(A) Except for vending machines, pay telephones, kiosks, and similar uses, the use does not involve the transfer to the nongovernmental person of possession and control of space that is separated from other areas of the facility by walls, partitions, or other physical barriers, such as a night gate affixed to a structural component of a building (a nonpossessory use);

(B) The nonpossessory use is not functionally related to any other use of the facility by the same person (other than a different nonpossessory use); and

(C) All nonpossessory uses of the facility do not, in the aggregate, involve the use of more than 2.5 percent of the facility.

(ii) *Illustrations.* Incidental uses may include pay telephones, vending machines, advertising displays, and use for television cameras, but incidental uses may not include output purchases.

(6) *Qualified improvements.* Proceeds that provide a governmentally owned improvement to a governmentally owned building (including its structural components and land functionally related and subordinate to the building) are not used for a private business use if—

(i) The building was placed in service more than 1 year before the construction or acquisition of the improvement is begun;

(ii) The improvement is not an enlargement of the building or an improvement of interior space occupied exclusively for any private business use;

(iii) No portion of the improved building or any payments in respect of the improved building are taken into account under section 141(b)(2)(A) (the private security test); and

(iv) No more than 15 percent of the improved building is used for a private business use.

(e) *Special rule for tax assessment bonds.* In the case of a tax assessment bond that satisfies the requirements of § 1.141-5(d), the loan (or deemed loan) of the proceeds to the borrower paying the assessment is disregarded in determining whether the private business use test is met. However, the use of the loan proceeds is not disregarded in determining whether the private business use test is met.

(f) *Examples.* The following examples illustrate the application of paragraphs (a) through (e) of this section. In each example, assume that the arrangements described are the only arrangements with nongovernmental persons for use of the financed property.

Example 1. Nongovernmental ownership. State A issues 20-year bonds to purchase land and equip and construct a factory. A then enters into an arrangement with Corporation X to sell the factory to X on an installment basis while the bonds are outstanding. The issue meets the private business use test because a nongovernmental person owns the financed facility. See also § 1.141-2 (relating to the private activity bond tests), and § 1.141-5 (relating to the private loan financing test).

Reg. § 1.141-3(f)

25,302   **Tax Exempt. Requirements: State/Local Bonds**

See p. 20,601 for regulations not amended to reflect law changes

Example 2. Lease to a nongovernmental person.
(i) The facts are the same as in *Example 1*, except
that A enters into an arrangement with X to lease
the factory to X for 3 years rather than to sell it
to X. The lease payments will be made annually
and will be based on the tax-exempt interest rate
on the bonds. The issue meets the private business
use test because a nongovernmental person leases
the financed facility. See also § 1.141-14 (relating
to anti-abuse rules).

(ii) The facts are the same as in *Example 2(i)*,
except that the annual payments made by X will
equal fair rental value of the facility and exceed
the amount necessary to pay debt service on the
bonds for the 3 years of the lease. The issue meets
the private business use test because a nongovernmental person leases the financed facility and the
test does not require that the benefits of tax-
exempt financing be passed through to the nongovernmental person.

*Example 3. Management contract in substance
a lease.* City L issues 30-year bonds to finance the
construction of a city hospital. L enters into a
15-year contract with M, a nongovernmental person that operates a health maintenance organization relating to the treatment of M's members at
L's hospital. The contract provides for reasonable
fixed compensation to M for services rendered
with no compensation based, in whole or in part,
on a share of net profits from the operation of the
hospital. However, the contract also provides that
30 percent of the capacity of the hospital will be
exclusively available to M's members and M will
bear the risk of loss of that portion of the capacity
of the hospital so that, under all of the facts and
circumstances, the contract is properly characterized as a lease for federal income tax purposes.
The issue meets the private business use test
because a nongovernmental person leases the financed facility.

*Example 4. Ownership of title in substance a
leasehold interest.* Nonprofit corporation R issues
bonds on behalf of City P to finance the construction of a hospital. R will own legal title to the
hospital. In addition, R will operate the hospital,
but R is not treated as an agent of P in its
capacity as operator of the hospital. P has certain
rights to the hospital that establish that it is
properly treated as the owner of the property for
federal income tax purposes. P does not have
rights, however, to directly control operation of
the hospital while R owns legal title to it and
operates it. The issue meets the private business
use test because the arrangement provides a nongovernmental person an interest in the financed
facility that is comparable to a leasehold interest.
See paragraphs (a)(2) and (b)(7)(i) of this section.

*Example 5. Rights to control use of property
treated as private business use—parking lot.* Corporation C and City D enter into a plan to finance
the construction of a parking lot adjacent to C's
factory. Pursuant to the plan, C conveys the site
for the parking lot to D for a nominal amount,
subject to a covenant running with the land that
the property be used only for a parking lot. In
addition, D agrees that C will have the right to
approve rates charged by D for use of the parking
lot. D issues bonds to finance construction of the
parking lot on the site. The parking lot will be
available for use by the general public on the basis
of rates that are generally applicable and uniformly applied. The issue meets the private business use test because a nongovernmental person
has special legal entitlements for beneficial use of
the financed facility that are comparable to an
ownership interest. See paragraph (b)(7)(i) of this
section.

*Example 6. Other actual or beneficial use—
hydroelectric enhancements.* J, a political subdivision, owns and operates a hydroelectric generation
plant and related facilities. Pursuant to a take or
pay contract, J sells 15 percent of the output of
the plant to Corporation K, an investor-owned
utility. K is treated as a private business user of
the plant. Under the license issued to J for operation of the plant, J is required by federal regulations to construct and operate various facilities for
the preservation of fish and for public recreation.
J issues its obligations to finance the fish preservation and public recreation facilities. K has no
special legal entitlements for beneficial use of the
financed facilities. The fish preservation facilities
are functionally related to the operation of the
plant. The recreation facilities are available to
natural persons on a short-term basis according to
generally applicable and uniformly applied rates.
Under paragraph (c) of this section, the recreation
facilities are treated as used by the general public.
Under paragraph (b)(7) of this section, K's use is
not treated as private business use of the recreation facilities because K has no special legal entitlements for beneficial use of the recreation
facilities. The fish preservation facilities are not
of a type reasonably available for use on the same
basis by natural persons not engaged in a trade or
business. Under all of the facts and circumstances
(including the functional relationship of the fish
preservation facilities to property used in K's
trade or business) under paragraph (b)(7)(ii) of
this section, K derives a special economic benefit
from the fish preservation facilities. Therefore,
K's private business use may be established solely
on the basis of that special economic benefit, and
K's use of the fish preservation facilities is treated
as private business use.

Reg. § 1.141-3(f)

Example 7. Other actual or beneficial use—pollution control facilities. City B issues obligations to finance construction of a specialized pollution control facility on land that it owns adjacent to a factory owned by Corporation N. B will own and operate the pollution control facility, and N will have no special legal entitlements to use the facility. B, however, reasonably expects that N will be the only user of the facility. The facility will not be reasonably available for use on the same basis by natural persons not engaged in a trade or business. Under paragraph (b)(7)(ii) of this section, because under all of the facts and circumstances the facility is functionally related and is physically proximate to property used in N's trade or business, N derives a special economic benefit from the facility. Therefore, N's private business use may be established solely on the basis of that special economic benefit, and N's use is treated as private business use of the facility. See paragraph (b)(7)(ii) of this section.

Example 8. General public use—airport runway. (i) City I issues bonds and uses all of the proceeds to finance construction of a runway at a new city-owned airport. The runway will be available for take-off and landing by any operator of an aircraft desiring to use the airport, including general aviation operators who are natural persons not engaged in a trade or business. It is reasonably expected that most of the actual use of the runway will be by private air carriers (both charter airlines and commercial airlines) in connection with their use of the airport terminals leased by those carriers. These leases for the use of terminal space provide no priority rights or other preferential benefits to the air carriers for use of the runway. Moreover, under the leases the lease payments are determined without taking into account the revenues generated by runway landing fees (that is, the lease payments are not determined on a "residual" basis). Although the lessee air carriers receive a special economic benefit from the use of the runway, this economic benefit is not sufficient to cause the air carriers to be private business users, because the runway is available for general public use. The issue does not meet the private business use test. See paragraphs (b)(7)(ii) and (c) of this section.

(ii) The facts are the same as in *Example 8(i)*, except that the runway will be available for use only by private air carriers. The use by these private air carriers is not general public use, because the runway is not reasonably available for use on the same basis by natural persons not engaged in a trade or business. Depending on all of the facts and circumstances, including whether there are only a small number of lessee private air carriers, the issue may meet the private business

use test solely because the private air carriers receive a special economic benefit from the runway. See paragraph (b)(7)(ii) of this section.

(iii) The facts are the same as in *Example 8(i)*, except that the lease payments under the leases with the private air carriers are determined on a residual basis by taking into account the net revenues generated by runway landing fees. These leases cause the private business use test to be met with respect to the runway because they are arrangements that convey special legal entitlements to the financed facility to nongovernmental persons. See paragraph (b)(7)(i) of this section.

Example 9. General public use—airport parking garage. City S issues bonds and uses all of the proceeds to finance construction of a city-owned parking garage at the city-owned airport. S reasonably expects that more than 10 percent of the actual use of the parking garage will be by employees of private air carriers (both charter airlines and commercial airlines) in connection with their use of the airport terminals leased by those carriers. The air carriers' use of the parking garage, however, will be on the same basis as passengers and other members of the general public using the airport. The leases for the use of the terminal space provide no priority rights to the air carriers for use of the parking garage, and the lease payments are determined without taking into account the revenues generated by the parking garage. Although the lessee air carriers receive a special economic benefit from the use of the parking garage, this economic benefit is not sufficient to cause the air carriers to be private business users, because the parking garage is available for general public use. The issue does not meet the private business use test. See paragraphs (b)(7)(ii) and (c) of this section.

Example 10. Long-term arrangements not treated as general public use—insurance fund. Authority T deposits all of the proceeds of its bonds in its insurance fund and invests all of those proceeds in tax-exempt bonds. The insurance fund provides insurance to a large number of businesses and natural persons not engaged in a trade or business. Each participant receives insurance for a term of 1 year. The use by the participants, other than participants that are natural persons not engaged in a trade or business, is treated as private business use of the proceeds of the bonds because the participants have special legal entitlements to the use of bond proceeds, even though the contractual rights are not necessarily properly characterized as ownership, leasehold, or similar interests listed in paragraph (b) of this section. Use of the bond proceeds is not treated as general public use because the term of the insurance is

Reg. § 1.141-3(f)

25,304   **Tax Exempt. Requirements: State/Local Bonds**

See p. 20,601 for regulations not amended to reflect law changes

greater than 200 days. See paragraphs (b)(7)(i) and (c)(3) of this section.

Example 11. General public use—port road. Highway Authority W uses all of the proceeds of its bonds to construct a 25-mile road to connect an industrial port owned by Corporation Y with existing roads owned and operated by W. Other than the port, the nearest residential or commercial development to the new road is 12 miles away. There is no reasonable expectation that development will occur in the area surrounding the new road. W and Y enter into no arrangement (either by contract or ordinance) that conveys special legal entitlements to Y for the use of the road. Use of the road will be available without restriction to all users, including natural persons who are not engaged in a trade or business. The issue does not meet the private business use test because the road is treated as used only by the general public.

Example 12. General public use of governmentally owned hotel. State Q issues bonds to purchase land and construct a hotel for use by the general public (that is, tourists, visitors, and business travelers). The bond documents provide that Q will own and operate the project for the term of the bonds. Q will not enter into a lease or license with any user for use of rooms for a period longer than 200 days (although users may actually use rooms for consecutive periods in excess of 200 days). Use of the hotel by hotel guests who are travelling in connection with trades or businesses of nongovernmental persons is not a private business use of the hotel by these persons because the hotel is intended to be available and in fact is reasonably available for use on the same basis by natural persons not engaged in a trade or business. See paragraph (c)(1) of this section.

Example 13. General public use with rights of first refusal. Authority V uses all of the proceeds of its bonds to construct a parking garage. At least 90 percent of the spaces in the garage will be available to the general public on a monthly first-come, first-served basis. V reasonably expects that the spaces will be predominantly leased to natural persons not engaged in a trade or business who have priority rights to renew their spaces at then current fair market value rates. More than 10 percent of the spaces will be leased to nongovernmental persons acting in a trade or business. These leases are not treated as arrangements with a term of use greater than 200 days. The rights to renew are not treated as renewal options because the compensation for the spaces is redetermined at generally applicable, fair market value rates that will be in effect at the time of renewal and the use of the spaces under similar arrangements

is predominantly by natural persons who are not engaged in a trade or business. The issue does not meet the private business use test because at least 90 percent of the use of the parking garage is general public use. See paragraph (c)(3) of this section.

Example 14. General public use with a specially negotiated rate agreement with agency of United States. G, a sewage collection and treatment district, operates facilities that were financed with its bonds. F, an agency of the United States, has a base located within G. Approximately 20 percent of G's facilities are used to treat sewage produced by F under a specially negotiated rate agreement. Under the specially negotiated rate agreement, G uses its best efforts to charge F as closely as possible the same amount for its use of G's services as its other customers pay for the same amount of services, although those other customers pay for services based on standard district charges and tax levies. F is prohibited by federal law from paying for the services based on those standard district charges and tax levies. The use of G's facilities by F is on the same basis as the general public. See paragraph (c)(2)(ii) of this section.

Example 15. Arrangements not available for use by natural persons not engaged in a trade or business—federal use of prisons. Authority E uses all of the proceeds of its bonds to construct a prison. E contracts with federal agency F to house federal prisoners on a space-available, first-come, first-served basis, pursuant to which F will be charged approximately the same amount for each prisoner as other persons that enter into similar transfer agreements. It is reasonably expected that other persons will enter into similar agreements. The term of the use under the contract is not longer than 100 days, and F has no right to renew, although E reasonably expects to renew the contract indefinitely. The prison is not financed for a principal purpose of providing the prison for use by F. It is reasonably expected that during the term of the bonds, more than 10 percent of the prisoners at the prison will be federal prisoners. F's use of the facility is not general public use because this type of use (leasing space for prisoners) is not available for use on the same basis by natural persons not engaged in a trade or business. The issue does not meet the private business use test, however, because the leases satisfy the exception of paragraph (d)(3)(i) of this section.

Example 16. Negotiated arm's-length arrangements—auditorium reserved in advance. (i) City Z issues obligations to finance the construction of a municipal auditorium that it will own and operate. The use of the auditorium will be open to anyone who wishes to use it for a short period of time on a rate-scale basis. Z reasonably expects that the auditorium will be used by schools, church groups, sororities, and numerous commercial organizations. Corporation H, a nongovernmental person, enters into an arm's-length arrangement with Z to use the auditorium for 1 week for each year for a 10-year period (a total of 70 days), pursuant to which H will be charged a specific price reflecting fair market value. On the date the contract is entered into, Z has not established generally applicable rates for future years. Even though the auditorium is not financed for a principal purpose of providing use of the auditorium to H, H is not treated as using the auditorium as a member of the general public because its use is not on the same basis as the general public. Because the term of H's use of the auditorium is longer than 50 days, the arrangement does not meet the exception under paragraph (d)(3)(ii) of this section.

(ii) The facts are the same as in *Example 16(i)*, except that H will enter into an arm's-length arrangement with Z to use the auditorium for 1 week for each year for a 4-year period (a total of 28 days), pursuant to which H will be charged a specific price reflecting fair market value. H is not treated as a private business user of the auditorium because its contract satisfies the exception of paragraph (d)(3)(ii) of this section for negotiated arm's-length arrangements.

(g) *Measurement of private business use*—(1) *In general.* In general, the private business use of proceeds is allocated to property under § 1.141-6. The amount of private business use of that property is determined according to the average percentage of private business use of that property during the measurement period.

(2) *Measurement period*—(i) *General rule.* Except as provided in this paragraph (g)(2), the measurement period of property financed by an issue begins on the later of the issue date of that issue or the date the property is placed in service and ends on the earlier of the last date of the reasonably expected economic life of the property or the latest maturity date of any bond of the issue financing the property (determined without regard to any optional redemption dates). In general, the period of reasonably expected economic life of the property for this purpose is based on reasonable expectations as of the issue date.

(ii) *Special rule for refundings of short-term obligations.* For an issue of short-term obligations that the issuer reasonably expects to refund with a long-term financing (such as bond anticipation notes), the measurement period is

based on the latest maturity date of any bond of the last refunding issue with respect to the financed property (determined without regard to any optional redemption dates).

(iii) *Special rule for reasonably expected mandatory redemptions.* If an issuer reasonably expects on the issue date that an action will occur during the term of the bonds to cause either the private business tests or the private loan financing test to be met and is required to redeem bonds to meet the reasonable expectations test of § 1.141-2(d)(2), the measurement period ends on the reasonably expected redemption date.

(iv) *Special rule for ownership by a nongovernmental person.* The amount of private business use resulting from ownership by a nongovernmental person is the greatest percentage of private business use in any 1-year period.

(v) *Anti-abuse rule.* If an issuer establishes the term of an issue for a period that is longer than is reasonably necessary for the governmental purposes of the issue for a principal purpose of increasing the permitted amount of private business use, the Commissioner may determine the amount of private business use according to the greatest percentage of private business use in any 1-year period.

(3) *Determining average percentage of private business use.* The average percentage of private business use is the average of the percentages of private business use during the 1-year periods within the measurement period. Appropriate adjustments must be made for beginning and ending periods of less than 1 year.

(4) *Determining the average amount of private business use for a 1-year period*—(i) *In general.* The percentage of private business use of property for any 1-year period is the average private business use during that year. This average is determined by comparing the amount of private business use during the year to the total amount of private business use and use that is not private business use (government use) during that year. Paragraphs (g)(4)(ii) through (v) of this section apply to determine the average amount of private business use for a 1-year period.

(ii) *Uses at different times.* For a facility in which actual government use and private business use occur at different times (for example, different days), the average amount of private business use generally is based on the amount of time that the facility is used for private business use as a percentage of the total time for all actual use. In determining the total amount of actual use, periods during which the facility is not in use are disregarded.

Reg. § 1.141-3(g)(4)

25,306   **Tax Exempt. Requirements: State/Local Bonds**

See p. 20,601 for regulations not amended to reflect law changes

(iii) *Simultaneous use.* In general, for a facility in which government use and private business use occur simultaneously, the entire facility is treated as having private business use. For example, a governmentally owned facility that is leased or managed by a nongovernmental person in a manner that results in private business use is treated as entirely used for a private business use. If, however, there is also private business use and actual government use on the same basis, the average amount of private business use may be determined on a reasonable basis that properly reflects the proportionate benefit to be derived by the various users of the facility (for example, reasonably expected fair market value of use). For example, the average amount of private business use of a garage with unassigned spaces that is used for government use and private business use is generally based on the number of spaces used for private business use as a percentage of the total number of spaces.

(iv) *Discrete portion.* For purposes of this paragraph (g), measurement of the use of proceeds allocated to a discrete portion of a facility is determined by treating that discrete portion as a separate facility.

(v) *Relationship to fair market value.* For purposes of paragraphs (g)(4)(ii) through (iv) of this section, if private business use is reasonably expected as of the issue date to have a significantly greater fair market value than government use, the average amount of private business use must be determined according to the relative reasonably expected fair market values of use rather than another measure, such as average time of use. This determination of relative fair market value may be made as of the date the property is acquired or placed in service if making this determination as of the issue date is not reasonably possible (for example, if the financed property is not identified on the issue date). In general, the relative reasonably expected fair market value for a period must be determined by taking into account the amount of reasonably expected payments for private business use for the period in a manner that properly reflects the proportionate benefit to be derived from the private business use.

(5) *Common areas.* The amount of private business use of common areas within a facility is based on a reasonable method that properly reflects the proportionate benefit to be derived by the users of the facility. For example, in general, a method that is based on the average amount of private business use of the remainder of the entire facility reflects proportionate benefit.

(6) *Allocation of neutral costs.* Proceeds that are used to pay costs of issuance, invested in a reserve or replacement fund, or paid as fees for a qualified guarantee or a qualified hedge must be allocated ratably among the other purposes for which the proceeds are used.

(7) *Commencement of measurement of private business use.* Generally, private business use commences on the first date on which there is a right to actual use by the nongovernmental person. However, if an issuer enters into an arrangement for private business use a substantial period before the right to actual private business use commences and the arrangement transfers ownership or is an arrangement for other long-term use (such as a lease for a significant portion of the remaining economic life of financed property), private business use commences on the date the arrangement is entered into, even if the right to actual use commences after the measurement period. For this purpose, 10 percent of the measurement period is generally treated as a substantial period.

(8) *Examples.* The following examples illustrate the application of this paragraph (g):

Example 1. Research facility. University U, a state owned and operated university, owns and operates a research facility. U proposes to finance general improvements to the facility with the proceeds of an issue of bonds. U enters into sponsored research agreements with nongovernmental persons that result in private business use because the sponsors will own title to any patents resulting from the research. The governmental research conducted by U and the research U conducts for the sponsors take place simultaneously in all laboratories within the research facility. All laboratory equipment is available continuously for use by workers who perform both types of research. Because it is not possible to predict which research projects will be successful, it is not reasonably practicable to estimate the relative revenues expected to result from the governmental and nongovernmental research. U contributed 90 percent of the cost of the facility and the nongovernmental persons contributed 10 percent of the cost. Under this section, the nongovernmental persons are using the facility for a private business use on the same basis as the government use of the facility. The portions of the costs contributed by the various users of the facility provide a reasonable basis that properly reflects the proportionate benefit to be derived by the users of the facility. The nongovernmental persons are treated as using 10 percent of the proceeds of the issue.

Example 2. Stadium. (i) City L issues bonds and uses all of the proceeds to construct a sta-

Reg. § 1.141-3(g)(5)

dium. L enters into a long-term contract with a professional sports team T under which T will use the stadium 20 times during each year. These uses will occur on nights and weekends. L reasonably expects that the stadium will be used more than 180 other times each year, none of which will give rise to private business use. This expectation is based on a feasibility study and historical use of the old stadium that is being replaced by the new stadium. There is no significant difference in the value of T's uses when compared to the other uses of the stadium, taking into account the payments that T is reasonably expected to make for its use. Assuming no other private business use, the issue does not meet the private business use test because not more than 10 percent of the use of the facility is for a private business use.

(ii) The facts are the same as in *Example 2(i)*, except that L reasonably expects that the stadium will be used not more than 60 other times each year, none of which will give rise to private business use. The issue meets the private business use test because 25 percent of the proceeds are used for a private business use.

Example 3. Airport terminal areas treated as common areas. City N issues bonds to finance the construction of an airport terminal. Eighty percent of the leasable space of the terminal will be leased to private air carriers. The remaining 20 percent of the leasable space will be used for the term of the bonds by N for its administrative purposes. The common areas of the terminal, including waiting areas, lobbies, and hallways are treated as 80 percent used by the air carriers for purposes of the private business use test.

[Reg. § 1.141-3.]

□ [*T.D. 8712, 1-10-97. Amended by T.D. 8967, 11-19-2001.*]

[Reg. § 1.141-4]

§ 1.141-4. **Private security or payment test.**—(a) *General rule*—(1) *Private security or payment.* The private security or payment test relates to the nature of the security for, and the source of, the payment of debt service on an issue. The private payment portion of the test takes into account the payment of the debt service on the issue that is directly or indirectly to be derived from payments (whether or not to the issuer or any related party) in respect of property, or borrowed money, used or to be used for a private business use. The private security portion of the test takes into account the payment of the debt service on the issue that is directly or indirectly secured by any interest in property used or to be used for a private business use or payments in respect of property used or to be used for a pri-

vate business use. For additional rules for output facilities, see § 1.141-7.

(2) *Aggregation of private payments and security.* For purposes of the private security or payment test, payments taken into account as private payments and payments or property taken into account as private security are aggregated. However, the same payments are not taken into account as both private security and private payments.

(3) *Underlying arrangement.* The security for, and payment of debt service on, an issue is determined from both the terms of the bond documents and on the basis of any underlying arrangement. An underlying arrangement may result from separate agreements between the parties or may be determined on the basis of all of the facts and circumstances surrounding the issuance of the bonds. For example, if the payment of debt service on an issue is secured by both a pledge of the full faith and credit of a state or local governmental unit and any interest in property used or to be used in a private business use, the issue meets the private security or payment test.

(b) *Measurement of private payments and security*—(1) *Scope.* This paragraph (b) contains rules that apply to both private security and private payments.

(2) *Present value measurement*—(i) *Use of present value.* In determining whether an issue meets the private security or payment test, the present value of the payments or property taken into account is compared to the present value of the debt service to be paid over the term of the issue.

(ii) *Debt service*—(A) *Debt service paid from proceeds.* Debt service does not include any amount paid or to be paid from sale proceeds or investment proceeds. For example, debt service does not include payments of capitalized interest funded with proceeds.

(B) *Adjustments to debt service.* Debt service is adjusted to take into account payments and receipts that adjust the yield on an issue for purposes of section 148(f). For example, debt service includes fees paid for qualified guarantees under § 1.148-4(f) and is adjusted to take into account payments and receipts on qualified hedges under § 1.148-4(h).

(iii) *Computation of present value*—(A) *In general.* Present values are determined by using the yield on the issue as the discount rate and by discounting all amounts to the issue date. See, however, § 1.141-13 for special rules for refunding bonds.

(B) *Fixed yield issues.* For a fixed yield issue, yield is determined on the issue date and is not adjusted to take into account subsequent events.

(C) *Variable yield issues.* The yield on a variable yield issue is determined over the term of the issue. To determine the reasonably expected yield as of any date, the issuer may assume that the future interest rate on a variable yield bond will be the then-current interest rate on the bonds determined under the formula prescribed in the bond documents. A deliberate action requires a recomputation of the yield on the variable yield issue to determine the present value of payments under that arrangement. In that case, the issuer must use the yield determined as of the date of the deliberate action for purposes of determining the present value of payments under the arrangement causing the deliberate action. See paragraph (g) of this section, *Example 3.*

(iv) *Application to private security.* For purposes of determining the present value of debt service that is secured by property, the property is valued at fair market value as of the first date on which the property secures bonds of the issue.

(c) *Private payments*—(1) *In general.* This paragraph (c) contains rules that apply to private payments.

(2) *Payments taken into account*—(i) *Payments for use*—(A) *In general.* Both direct and indirect payments made by any nongovernmental person that is treated as using proceeds of the issue are taken into account as private payments to the extent allocable to the proceeds used by that person. Payments are taken into account as private payments only to the extent that they are made for the period of time that proceeds are used for a private business use. Payments for a use of proceeds include payments (whether or not to the issuer) in respect of property financed (directly or indirectly) with those proceeds, even if not made by a private business user. Payments are not made in respect of financed property if those payments are directly allocable to other property being directly used by the person making the payment and those payments represent fair market value compensation for that other use. See paragraph (g) of this section, *Example 4* and *Example 5.* See also paragraph (c)(3) of this section for rules relating to allocation of payments to the source or sources of funding of property.

(B) *Payments not to exceed use.* Payments with respect to proceeds that are used for a private business use are not taken into account to the extent that the present value of those payments exceeds the present value of debt service on those proceeds. Payments need not be directly

derived from a private business user, however, to be taken into account. Thus, if 7 percent of the proceeds of an issue is used by a person over the measurement period, payments with respect to the property financed with those proceeds are taken into account as private payments only to the extent that the present value of those payments does not exceed the present value of 7 percent of the debt service on the issue.

(C) *Payments for operating expenses.* Payments by a person for a use of proceeds do not include the portion of any payment that is properly allocable to the payment of ordinary and necessary expenses (as defined under section 162) directly attributable to the operation and maintenance of the financed property used by that person. For this purpose, general overhead and administrative expenses are not directly attributable to those operations and maintenance. For example, if an issuer receives $5,000 rent during the year for use of space in a financed facility and during the year pays $500 for ordinary and necessary expenses properly allocable to the operation and maintenance of that space and $400 for general overhead and general administrative expenses properly allocable to that space, $500 of the $5,000 received would not be considered a payment for the use of the proceeds allocable to that space (regardless of the manner in which that $500 is actually used).

(ii) *Refinanced debt service.* Payments of debt service on an issue to be made from proceeds of a refunding issue are taken into account as private payments in the same proportion that the present value of the payments taken into account as private payments for the refunding issue bears to the present value of the debt service to be paid on the refunding issue. For example, if all the debt service on a note is paid with proceeds of a refunding issue, the note meets the private security or payment test if (and to the same extent that) the refunding issue meets the private security or payment test. This paragraph (c)(2)(ii) does not apply to payments that arise from deliberate actions that occur more than 3 years after the retirement of the prior issue that are not reasonably expected on the issue date of the refunding issue. For purposes of this paragraph (c)(2)(ii), whether an issue is a refunding issue is determined without regard to § 1.150-1(d)(2)(i) (relating to certain payments of interest).

(3) *Allocation of payments*—(i) *In general.* Private payments for the use of property are allocated to the source or different sources of funding of property. The allocation to the source or different sources of funding is based on all of the facts and circumstances, including whether an

Tax Exempt. Requirements: State/Local Bonds 25,309

See p. 20,601 for regulations not amended to reflect law changes

allocation is consistent with the purposes of section 141. In general, a private payment for the use of property is allocated to a source of funding based upon the nexus between the payment and both the financed property and the source of funding. For this purpose, different sources of funding may include different tax-exempt issues, taxable issues, and amounts that are not derived from a borrowing, such as revenues of an issuer (equity).

(ii) *Payments for use of discrete property.* Payments for the use of a discrete facility (or a discrete portion of a facility) are allocated to the source or different sources of funding of that discrete property.

(iii) *Allocations among two or more sources of funding.* In general, except as provided in paragraphs (c)(3)(iv) and (v) of this section, if a payment is made for the use of property financed with two or more sources of funding (for example, equity and a tax-exempt issue), that payment must be allocated to those sources of funding in a manner that reasonably corresponds to the relative amounts of those sources of funding that are expended on that property. If an issuer has not retained records of amounts expended on the property (for example, records of costs of a building that was built 30 years before the allocation), an issuer may use reasonable estimates of those expenditures. For this purpose, costs of issuance and other similar neutral costs are allocated ratably among expenditures in the same manner as in § 1.141-3(g)(6). A payment for the use of property may be allocated to two or more issues that finance property according to the relative amounts of debt service (both paid and accrued) on the issues during the annual period for which the payment is made, if that allocation reasonably reflects the economic substance of the arrangement. In general, allocations of payments according to relative debt service reasonably reflect the economic substance of the arrangement if the maturity of the bonds reasonably corresponds to the reasonably expected economic life of the property and debt service payments on the bonds are approximately level from year to year.

(iv) *Payments made under an arrangement entered into in connection with issuance of bonds.* A private payment for the use of property made under an arrangement that is entered into in connection with the issuance of the issue that finances that property generally is allocated to that issue. Whether an arrangement is entered into in connection with the issuance of an issue is determined on the basis of all of the facts and circumstances. An arrangement is ordinarily treated as entered into in connection with the issuance of an issue if—

(A) The issuer enters into the arrangement during the 3-year period beginning 18 months before the issue date; and

(B) The amount of payments reflects all or a portion of debt service on the issue.

(v) *Allocations to equity.* A private payment for the use of property may be allocated to equity before payments are allocated to an issue only f—

(A) Not later than 60 days after the date of the expenditure of those amounts, the issuer adopts an official intent (in a manner comparable to § 1.150-2(e)) indicating that the issuer reasonably expects to be repaid for the expenditure from a specific arrangement; and

(B) The private payment is made not later than 18 months after the later of the date the expenditure is made or the date the project is placed in service.

d) *Private security*—(1) *In general.* This paragraph (d) contains rules that relate to private security.

(2) *Security taken into account.* The property that is the security for, or the source of, the payment of debt service on an issue need not be property financed with proceeds. For example, unimproved land or investment securities used, directly or indirectly, in a private business use that secures an issue provides private security. Private security (other than financed property and private payments) for an issue is taken into account under section 141(b), however, only to the extent it is provided, directly or indirectly, by a user of proceeds of the issue.

(3) *Pledge of unexpended proceeds.* Proceeds qualifying for an initial temporary period under § 1.148-2(e)(2) or (3) or deposited in a reasonably required reserve or replacement fund (as defined in § 1.148-2(f)(2)(i)) are not taken into account under this paragraph (d) before the date on which those amounts are either expended or loaned by the issuer to an unrelated party.

(4) *Secured by any interest in property or payments.* Property used or to be used for a private business use and payments in respect of that property are treated as private security if any interest in that property or payments secures the payment of debt service on the bonds. For this purpose, the phrase any interest in is to be interpreted broadly and includes, for example, any right, claim, title, or legal share in property or payments.

(5) *Payments in respect of property.* The payments taken into account as private security are payments in respect of property used or to be used for a private business use. Except as other-

Reg. § 1.141-4(d)(5)

25,310   Tax Exempt. Requirements: State/Local Bonds

See p. 20,601 for regulations not amended to reflect law changes

wise provided in this paragraph (d)(5) and paragraph (d)(6) of this section, the rules in paragraphs (c)(2)(i)(A) and (B) and (c)(2)(ii) of this section apply to determine the amount of payments treated as payments in respect of property used or to be used for a private business use. Thus, payments made by members of the general public for use of a facility used for a private business use (for example, a facility that is the subject of a management contract that results in private business use) are taken into account as private security to the extent that they are made for the period of time that property is used by a private business user.

(6) *Allocation of security among issues.* In general, property or payments from the disposition of that property that are taken into account as private security are allocated to each issue secured by the property or payments on a reasonable basis that takes into account bondholders' rights to the payments or property upon default.

(e) *Generally applicable taxes*—(1) *General rule.* For purposes of the private security or payment test, generally applicable taxes are not taken into account (that is, are not payments from a nongovernmental person and are not payments in respect of property used for a private business use).

(2) *Definition of generally applicable taxes.* A generally applicable tax is an enforced contribution exacted pursuant to legislative authority in the exercise of the taxing power that is imposed and collected for the purpose of raising revenue to be used for governmental purposes. A generally applicable tax must have a uniform tax rate that is applied to all persons of the same classification in the appropriate jurisdiction and a generally applicable manner of determination and collection.

(3) *Special charges.* A payment for a special privilege granted or service rendered is not a generally applicable tax. Special assessments paid by property owners benefiting from financed improvements are not generally applicable taxes. For example, a tax or a payment in lieu of tax that is limited to the property or persons benefited by an improvement is not a generally applicable tax.

(4) *Manner of determination and collection*—(i) *In general.* A tax does not have a generally applicable manner of determination and collection to the extent that one or more taxpayers make any impermissible agreements relating to payment of those taxes. An impermissible agreement relating to the payment of a tax is taken into account whether or not it is reasonably expected to result in any payments that would not

otherwise have been made. For example, if an issuer uses proceeds to make a grant to a taxpayer to improve property, agreements that impose reasonable conditions on the use of the grant do not cause a tax on that property to fail to be a generally applicable tax. If an agreement by a taxpayer causes the tax imposed on that taxpayer not to be treated as a generally applicable tax, the entire tax paid by that taxpayer is treated as a special charge, unless the agreement is limited to a specific portion of the tax.

(ii) *Impermissible agreements.* The following are examples of agreements that cause a tax to fail to have a generally applicable manner of determination and collection: an agreement to be personally liable on a tax that does not generally impose personal liability, to provide additional credit support such as a third party guarantee, or to pay unanticipated shortfalls; an agreement regarding the minimum market value of property subject to property tax; and an agreement not to challenge or seek deferral of the tax.

(iii) *Permissible agreements.* The following are examples of agreements that do not cause a tax to fail to have a generally applicable manner of determination and collection: an agreement to use a grant for specified purposes (whether or not that agreement is secured); a representation regarding the expected value of the property following the improvement; an agreement to insure the property and, if damaged, to restore the property; a right of a grantor to rescind the grant if property taxes are not paid; and an agreement to reduce or limit the amount of taxes collected to further a bona fide governmental purpose. For example, an agreement to abate taxes to encourage a property owner to rehabilitate property in a distressed area is a permissible agreement.

(5) *Payments in lieu of taxes.* A tax equivalency payment and any other payment in lieu of a tax is treated as a generally applicable tax if—

(i) The payment is commensurate with and not greater than the amounts imposed by a statute for a tax of general application; and

(ii) The payment is designated for a public purpose and is not a special charge (as described in paragraph (e)(3) of this section). For example, a payment in lieu of taxes made in consideration for the use of property financed with tax-exempt bonds is treated as a special charge.

(f) *Certain waste remediation bonds*—(1) *Scope.* This paragraph (f) applies to bonds issued to finance hazardous waste clean-up activities on privately owned land (hazardous waste remediation bonds).

(2) *Persons that are not private users.* Payments from nongovernmental persons who are not (other than coincidentally) either users of the site being remediated or persons potentially responsible for disposing of hazardous waste on that site are not taken into account as private security. This paragraph (f)(2) applies to payments that secure (directly or indirectly) the payment of principal of, or interest on, the bonds under the terms of the bonds. This paragraph (f)(2) applies only if the payments are made pursuant to either a generally applicable state or local taxing statute or a state or local statute that regulates or restrains activities on an industry-wide basis of persons who are engaged in generating or handling hazardous waste, or in refining, producing, or transporting petroleum, provided that those payments do not represent, in substance, payment for the use of proceeds. For this purpose, a state or local statute that imposes payments that have substantially the same character as those described in Chapter 38 of the Code are treated as generally applicable taxes.

(3) *Persons that are private users.* If payments from nongovernmental persons who are either users of the site being remediated or persons potentially responsible for disposing of hazardous waste on that site do not secure (directly or indirectly) the payment of principal of, or interest on, the bonds under the terms of the bonds, the payments are not taken into account as private payments. This paragraph (f)(3) applies only if at the time the bonds are issued the payments from those nongovernmental persons are not material to the security for the bonds. For this purpose, payments are not material to the security for the bonds if—

(i) The payments are not required for the payment of debt service on the bonds;

(ii) The amount and timing of the payments are not structured or designed to reflect the payment of debt service on the bonds;

(iii) The receipt or the amount of the payment is uncertain (for example, as of the issue date, no final judgment has been entered into against the nongovernmental person);

(iv) The payments from those nongovernmental persons, when and if received, are used either to redeem bonds of the issuer or to pay for costs of any hazardous waste remediation project; and

(v) In the case when a judgment (but not a final judgment) has been entered by the issue date against a nongovernmental person, there are, as of the issue date, costs of hazardous waste remediation other than those financed with the bonds that may be financed with the payments.

(g) *Examples.* The following examples illustrate the application of this section:

Example 1. Aggregation of payments. State B issues bonds with proceeds of $10 million. B uses $9.7 million of the proceeds to construct a 10-story office building. B uses the remaining $300,000 of proceeds to make a loan to Corporation Y. In addition, Corporation X leases 1 floor of the building for the term of the bonds. Under all of the facts and circumstances, it is reasonable to allocate 10 percent of the proceeds to that 1 floor. As a percentage of the present value of the debt service on the bonds, the present value of Y's loan repayments is 3 percent and the present value of X's lease payments is 8 percent. The bonds meet the private security or payment test because the private payments taken into account are more than 10 percent of the present value of the debt service on the bonds.

Example 2. Indirect private payments. J, a political subdivision of a state, will issue several series of bonds from time to time and will use the proceeds to rehabilitate urban areas. Under all of the facts and circumstances, the private business use test will be met with respect to each issue that will be used for the rehabilitation and construction of buildings that will be leased or sold to nongovernmental persons for use in their trades or businesses. Nongovernmental persons will make payments for these sales and leases. There is no limitation either on the number of issues or the aggregate amount of bonds that may be outstanding. No group of bondholders has any legal claim prior to any other bondholders or creditors with respect to specific revenues of J, and there is no arrangement whereby revenues from a particular project are paid into a trust or constructive trust, or sinking fund, or are otherwise segregated or restricted for the benefit of any group of bondholders. There is, however, an unconditional obligation by J to pay the principal of, and the interest on, each issue. Although not directly pledged under the terms of the bond documents, the leases and sales are underlying arrangements. The payments relating to these leases and sales are taken into account as private payments to determine whether each issue of bonds meets the private security or payment test.

Example 3. Computation of payment in variable yield issues. (i) City M issues general obligation bonds with proceeds of $10 million to finance a 5-story office building. The bonds bear interest at a variable rate that is recomputed monthly according to an index that reflects current market yields. The yield that the interest index would produce on the issue date is 6 percent. M leases 1 floor of the office building to Corporation T, a

25,312   **Tax Exempt. Requirements: State/Local Bonds**

See p. 20,601 for regulations not amended to reflect law changes

nongovernmental person, for the term of the bonds. Under all of the facts and circumstances, T is treated as using more than 10 percent of the proceeds. Using the 6 percent yield as the discount rate, M reasonably expects on the issue date that the present value of lease payments to be made by T will be 8 percent of the present value of the total debt service on the bonds. After the issue date of the bonds, interest rates decline significantly, so that the yield on the bonds over their entire term is 4 percent. Using this actual 4 percent yield as the discount rate, the present value of lease payments made by T is 12 percent of the present value of the actual total debt service on the bonds. The bonds are not private activity bonds because M reasonably expected on the issue date that the bonds would not meet the private security or payment test and because M did not take any subsequent deliberate action to meet the private security or payment test.

(ii) The facts are the same as *Example 3(i)*, except that 5 years after the issue date M leases a second floor to Corporation S, a nongovernmental person, under a long-term lease. Because M has taken a deliberate action, the present value of the lease payments must be computed. On the date this lease is entered into, M reasonably expects that the yield on the bonds over their entire term will be 5.5 percent, based on actual interest rates to date and the then-current rate on the variable yield bonds. M uses this 5.5 percent yield as the discount rate. Using this 5.5 percent yield as the discount rate, as a percentage of the present value of the debt service on the bonds, the present value of the lease payments made by S is 3 percent. The bonds are private activity bonds because the present value of the aggregate private payments is greater than 10 percent of the present value of debt service.

Example 4. Payments not in respect of financed property. In order to further public safety, City Y issues tax assessment bonds the proceeds of which are used to move existing electric utility lines underground. Although the utility lines are owned by a nongovernmental utility company, that company is under no obligation to move the lines. The debt service on the bonds will be paid using assessments levied by City Y on the customers of the utility. Although the utility lines are privately owned and the utility customers make payments to the utility company for the use of those lines, the assessments are payments in respect of the cost of relocating the utility line. Thus, the assessment payments are not made in respect of property used for a private business use. Any direct or indirect payments to Y by the utility company for the undergrounding are, however, taken into account as private payments.

Example 5. Payments from users of proceeds that are not private business users taken into account. City P issues general obligation bonds to finance the renovation of a hospital that it owns. The hospital is operated for P by D, a nongovernmental person, under a management contract that results in private business use under § 1.141-3. P will use the revenues from the hospital (after the required payments to D and the payment of operation and maintenance expenses) to pay the debt service on the bonds. The bonds meet the private security or payment test because the revenues from the hospital are payments in respect of property used for a private business use.

Example 6. Limitation of amount of payments to amount of private business use not determined annually. City Q issues bonds with a term of 15 years and uses the proceeds to construct an office building. The debt service on the bonds is level throughout the 15-year term. Q enters into a 5-year lease with Corporation R under which R is treated as a user of 11 percent of the proceeds. R will make lease payments equal to 20 percent of the annual debt service on the bonds for each year of the lease. The present value of R's lease payments is equal to 12 percent of the present value of the debt service over the entire 15-year term of the bonds. If, however, the lease payments taken into account as private payments were limited to 11 percent of debt service paid in each year of the lease, the present value of these payments would be only 8 percent of the debt service on the bonds over the entire term of the bonds. The bonds meet the private security or payment test, because R's lease payments are taken into account as private payments in an amount not to exceed 11 percent of the debt service of the bonds.

Example 7. Allocation of payments to funds not derived from a borrowing. City Z purchases property for $1,250,000 using $1,000,000 of proceeds of its tax increment bonds and $250,000 of other revenues that are in its redevelopment fund. Within 60 days of the date of purchase, Z declared its intent to sell the property pursuant to a redevelopment plan and to use that amount to reimburse its redevelopment fund. The bonds are secured only by the incremental property taxes attributable to the increase in value of the property from the planned redevelopment of the property. Within 18 months after the issue date, Z sells the financed property to Developer M for $250,000, which Z uses to reimburse the redevelopment fund. The property that M uses is financed both with the proceeds of the bonds and Z's redevelopment fund. The payments by M are properly allocable to the costs of property financed with the amounts in Z's redevelopment

Reg. § 1.141-4(g)

fund. See paragraphs (c)(3)(i) and (v) of this section.

Example 8. Allocation of payments to different sources of funding—improvements. In 1997, City L issues bonds with proceeds of $8 million to finance the acquisition of a building. In 2002, L spends $2 million of its general revenues to improve the heating system and roof of the building. At that time, L enters into a 10-year lease with Corporation M for the building providing for annual payments of $1 million to L. The lease payments are at fair market value, and the lease payments do not otherwise have a significant nexus to either the issue or to the expenditure of general revenues. Eighty percent of each lease payment is allocated to the issue and is taken into account under the private payment test because each lease payment is properly allocated to the sources of funding in a manner that reasonably corresponds to the relative amounts of the sources of funding that are expended on the building.

Example 9. Security not provided by users of proceeds not taken into account. County W issues certificates of participation in a lease of a building that W owns and covenants to appropriate annual payments for the lease. A portion of each payment is specified as interest. More than 10 percent of the building is used for private business use. None of the proceeds of the obligations are used with respect to the building. W uses the proceeds of the obligations to make a grant to Corporation Y for the construction of a factory that Y will own. Y makes no payments to W, directly or indirectly, for its use of proceeds, and Y has no relationship to the users of the leased building. If W defaults under the lease, the trustee for the holders of the certificates of participation has a limited right of repossession under which the trustee may not foreclose but may lease the property to a new tenant at fair market value. The obligations are secured by an interest in property used for a private business use. However, because the property is not provided by a private business user and is not financed property, the obligations do not meet the private security or payment test.

Example 10. Allocation of payments among issues. University L, a political subdivision, issued three separate series of revenue bonds during 1989, 1991, and 1993 under the same bond resolution. L used the proceeds to construct facilities exclusively for its own use. Bonds issued under the resolution are equally and ratably secured and payable solely from the income derived by L from rates, fees, and charges imposed by L for the use of the facilities. The bonds issued in 1989, 1991, and 1993 are not private activity bonds. In 1997,

L issues another series of bonds under the resolution to finance additional facilities. L leases 20 percent of the new facilities for the term of the 1997 bonds to nongovernmental persons who will use the facilities in their trades or businesses. The present value of the lease payments from the nongovernmental users will equal 15 percent of the present value of the debt service on the 1997 bonds. L will commingle all of the revenues from all its bond-financed facilities in its revenue fund. The present value of the portion of the lease payments from nongovernmental lessees of the new facilities allocable to the 1997 bonds under paragraph (d) of this section is less than 10 percent of the present value of the debt service on the 1997 bonds because the bond documents provide that the bonds are equally and ratably secured. Accordingly, the 1997 bonds do not meet the private security test. The 1997 bonds meet the private payment test, however, because the private lease payments for the new facility are properly allocated to those bonds (that is, because none of the proceeds of the prior issues were used for the new facilities). See paragraph (c) of this section.

Example 11. Generally applicable tax. (i) Authority N issues bonds to finance the construction of a stadium. Under a long-term lease, Corporation X, a professional sports team, will use more than 10 percent of the stadium. X will not, however, make any payments for this private business use. The security for the bonds will be a ticket tax imposed on each person purchasing a ticket for an event at the stadium. The portion of the ticket tax attributable to tickets purchased by persons attending X's events will, on a present value basis, exceed 10 percent of the present value of the debt service on N's bonds. The bonds meet the private security or payment test. The ticket tax is not a generally applicable tax and, to the extent that the tax receipts relate to X's events, the taxes are payments in respect of property used for a private business use.

(ii) The facts are the same as *Example 11(i)*, except that the ticket tax is imposed by N on tickets purchased for events at a number of large entertainment facilities within the N's jurisdiction (for example, other stadiums, arenas, and concert halls), some of which were not financed with tax-exempt bonds. The ticket tax is a generally applicable tax and therefore the revenues from this tax are not payments in respect of property used for a private business use. The receipt of the ticket tax does not cause the bonds to meet the private security or payment test.

[Reg. § 1.141-4.]

☐ [*T.D.* 8712, 1-10-97.]

25,314   Tax Exempt. Requirements: State/Local Bonds

See p. 20,601 for regulations not amended to reflect law changes

[Reg. § 1.141-5]

§ 1.141-5. Private loan financing test.—(a) *In general.* Bonds of an issue are private activity bonds if more than the lesser of 5 percent or $5 million of the proceeds of the issue is to be used (directly or indirectly) to make or finance loans to persons other than governmental persons. Section 1.141-2(d) applies in determining whether the private loan financing test is met. In determining whether the proceeds of an issue are used to make or finance loans, indirect, as well as direct, use of the proceeds is taken into account.

(b) *Measurement of test.* In determining whether the private loan financing test is met, the amount actually loaned to a nongovernmental person is not discounted to reflect the present value of the loan repayments.

(c) *Definition of private loan*—(1) *In general.* Any transaction that is generally characterized as a loan for federal income tax purposes is a loan for purposes of this section. In addition, a loan may arise from the direct lending of bond proceeds or may arise from transactions in which indirect benefits that are the economic equivalent of a loan are conveyed. Thus, the determination of whether a loan is made depends on the substance of a transaction rather than its form. For example, a lease or other contractual arrangement (for example, a management contract or an output contract) may in substance constitute a loan if the arrangement transfers tax ownership of the facility to a nongovernmental person. Similarly, an output contract or a management contract with respect to a financed facility generally is not treated as a loan of proceeds unless the agreement in substance shifts significant burdens and benefits of ownership to the nongovernmental purchaser or manager of the facility.

(2) *Application only to purpose investments*—(i) *In general.* A loan may be either a purpose investment or a nonpurpose investment. A loan that is a nonpurpose investment does not cause the private loan financing test to be met. For example, proceeds invested in loans, such as obligations of the United States, during a temporary period, as part of a reasonably required reserve or replacement fund, as part of a refunding escrow, or as part of a minor portion (as each of those terms are defined in § 1.148-1 or § 1.148-2) are generally not treated as loans under the private loan financing test.

(ii) *Certain prepayments treated as loans.* Except as otherwise provided, a prepayment for property or services is treated as a loan for purposes of the private loan financing test if a principal purpose for prepaying is to provide a benefit of tax-exempt financing to the seller. A prepay-

ment is not treated as a loan for purposes of the private loan financing test if—

(A) The prepayment is made for a substantial business purpose other than providing a benefit of tax-exempt financing to the seller and the issuer has no commercially reasonable alternative to the prepayment; or

(B) Prepayments on substantially the same terms are made by a substantial percentage of persons who are similarly situated to the issuer but who are not beneficiaries of tax-exempt financing.

(3) *Grants*—(i) *In general.* A grant of proceeds is not a loan. Whether a transaction may be treated as a grant or a loan depends on all of the facts and circumstances.

(ii) *Tax increment financing*—(A) *In general.* Generally, a grant using proceeds of an issue that is secured by generally applicable taxes attributable to the improvements to be made with the grant is not treated as a loan, unless the grantee makes any impermissible agreements relating to the payment that results in the taxes imposed on that taxpayer not to be treated as generally applicable taxes under § 1.141-4(e).

(B) *Amount of loan.* If a grant is treated as a loan under this paragraph (c)(3), the entire grant is treated as a loan unless the impermissible agreement is limited to a specific portion of the tax. For this purpose, an arrangement with each unrelated grantee is treated as a separate grant.

(4) *Hazardous waste remediation bonds.* In the case of an issue of hazardous waste remediation bonds, payments from nongovernmental persons that are either users of the site being remediated or persons potentially responsible for disposing of hazardous waste on that site do not establish that the transaction is a loan for purposes of this section. This paragraph (c)(4) applies only if those payments do not secure the payment of principal of, or interest on, the bonds (directly or indirectly), under the terms of the bonds and those payments are not taken into account under the private payment test pursuant to § 1.141-4(f)(3).

(d) *Tax assessment loan exception*—(1) *General rule.* For purposes of this section, a tax assessment loan that satisfies the requirements of this paragraph (d) is not a loan for purposes of the private loan financing test.

(2) *Tax assessment loan defined.* A tax assessment loan is a loan that arises when a governmental person permits or requires property owners to finance any governmental tax or assessment of general application for an essential governmental function that satisfies each of the

Tax Exempt. Requirements: State/Local Bonds   25,315

See p. 20,601 for regulations not amended to reflect law changes

requirements of paragraphs (d)(3) through (5) of this section.

(3) *Mandatory tax or other assessment.* The tax or assessment must be an enforced contribution that is imposed and collected for the purpose of raising revenue to be used for a specific purpose (that is, to defray the capital cost of an improvement). Taxes and assessments do not include fees for services. The tax or assessment must be imposed pursuant to a state law of general application that can be applied equally to natural persons not acting in a trade or business and persons acting in a trade or business. For this purpose, taxes and assessments that are imposed subject to protest procedures are treated as enforced contributions.

(4) *Specific essential governmental function*—(i) *In general.* A mandatory tax or assessment that gives rise to a tax assessment loan must be imposed for one or more specific, essential governmental functions.

(ii) *Essential governmental functions.* For purposes of paragraph (d) of this section, improvements to utilities and systems that are owned by a governmental person and that are available for use by the general public (such as sidewalks, streets and street-lights; electric, telephone, and cable television systems; sewage treatment and disposal systems; and municipal water facilities) serve essential governmental functions. For other types of facilities, the extent to which the service provided by the facility is customarily performed (and financed with governmental bonds) by governments with general taxing powers is a primary factor in determining whether the facility serves an essential governmental function. For example, parks that are owned by a governmental person and that are available for use by the general public serve an essential governmental function. Except as otherwise provided in this paragraph (d)(4)(ii), commercial or industrial facilities and improvements to property owned by a nongovernmental person do not serve an essential governmental function. Permitting installment payments of property taxes or other taxes is not an essential governmental function.

(5) *Equal basis requirement*—(i) *In general.* Owners of both business and nonbusiness property benefiting from the financed improvements must be eligible, or required, to make deferred payments of the tax or assessment giving rise to a tax assessment loan on an equal basis (the equal basis requirement). A tax or assessment does not satisfy the equal basis requirement if the terms for payment of the tax or assessment are not the same for all taxed or assessed persons. For example, the equal basis requirement is not met if certain prop-

erty owners are permitted to pay the tax or assessment over a period of years while others must pay the entire tax or assessment immediately or if only certain property owners are required to prepay the tax or assessment when the property is sold.

(ii) *General rule for guarantees.* A guarantee of debt service on bonds, or of taxes or assessments, by a person that is treated as a borrower of bond proceeds violates the equal basis requirement if it is reasonable to expect on the date the guarantee is entered into that payments will be made under the guarantee.

(6) *Coordination with private business tests.* See §§ 1.141-3 and 1.141-4 for rules for determining whether tax assessment loans cause the bonds financing those loans to be private activity bonds under the private business use and the private security or payment tests.

(e) *Examples.* The following examples illustrate the application of this section:

Example 1. Turnkey contract not treated as a loan. State agency Z and federal agency H will each contribute to rehabilitate a project owned by Z. H can only provide its funds through a contribution to Z to be used to acquire the rehabilitated project on a turnkey basis from an approved developer. Under H's turnkey program, the developer must own the project while it is rehabilitated. Z issues its notes to provide funds for construction. A portion of the notes will be retired using the H contribution, and the balance of the notes will be retired through the issuance by Z of long-term bonds. Z lends the proceeds of its notes to Developer B as construction financing and transfers title to B for a nominal amount. The conveyance is made on condition that B rehabilitate the property and reconvey it upon completion, with Z retaining the right to force reconveyance if these conditions are not satisfied. B must name Z as an additional insured on all insurance. Upon completion, B must transfer title to the project back to Z at a set price, which price reflects B's costs and profit, not fair market value. Further, this price is adjusted downward to reflect any cost-underruns. For purposes of section 141(c), this transaction does not involve a private loan.

Example 2. Essential government function requirement not met. City D creates a special taxing district consisting of property owned by nongovernmental persons that requires environmental clean-up. D imposes a special tax on each parcel within the district in an amount that is related to the expected environmental clean-up costs of that parcel. The payment of the tax over a 20-year period is treated as a loan by the prop-

25,316   Tax Exempt. Requirements: State/Local Bonds

See p. 20,601 for regulations not amended to reflect law changes

erty owners for purposes of the private loan financing test. The special district issues bonds, acting on behalf of D, that are payable from the special tax levied within the district, and uses the proceeds to pay for the costs of environmental clean-up on the property within the district. The bonds meet the private loan financing test because more than 5 percent of the proceeds of the issue are loaned to nongovernmental persons. The issue does not meet the tax assessment loan exception because the improvements to property owned by a nongovernmental person are not an essential governmental function under section 141(c)(2). The issue also meets the private business tests of section 141(b).

[Reg. § 1.141-5.]

□ [*T.D. 8712*, 1-10-97.]

[Reg. § 1.141-6]

§ 1.141-6. **Allocation and accounting rules.**—(a) *Allocation of proceeds to expenditures.*

For purposes of § § 1.141-1 through 1.141-15, the provisions of § 1.148-6(d) apply for purposes of allocating proceeds to expenditures. Thus, allocations generally may be made using any reasonable, consistently applied accounting method, and allocations under section 141 and section 148 must be consistent with each other.

(b) *Allocation of proceeds to property.* [Reserved]

(c) *Special rules for mixed use facilities.* [Reserved]

(d) *Allocation of proceeds to common areas.* [Reserved]

(e) *Allocation of proceeds to bonds.* [Reserved]

(f) *Treatment of partnerships.* [Reserved]

(g) *Examples.* [Reserved]

[Reg. § 1.141-6.]

□ [*T.D. 8712*, 1-10-97.]

→ *Caution: Reg. § 1.141-7, below, is generally applicable to bonds sold on or after November 22, 2002.* ←

[Reg. § 1.141-7]

§ 1.141-7. **Special rules for output facilities.**—(a) *Overview.* This section provides special rules to determine whether arrangements for the purchase of output from an output facility cause an issue of bonds to meet the private business tests. For this purpose, unless otherwise stated, water facilities are treated as output facilities. Sections 1.141-3 and 1.141-4 generally apply to determine whether other types of arrangements for use of an output facility cause an issue to meet the private business tests.

(b) *Definitions.* For purposes of this section and § 1.141-8, the following definitions and rules apply:

(1) *Available output.* The available output of a facility financed by an issue is determined by multiplying the number of units produced or to be produced by the facility in one year by the number of years in the measurement period of that facility for that issue.

(i) *Generating facilities.* The number of units produced or to be produced by a generating facility in one year is determined by reference to its nameplate capacity or the equivalent (or where there is no nameplate capacity or the equivalent, its maximum capacity), which is not reduced for reserves, maintenance or other unutilized capacity.

(ii) *Transmission and other output facilities*—(A) *In general.* For transmission, distribution, cogeneration, and other output facilities,

available output must be measured in a reasonable manner to reflect capacity.

(B) *Electric transmission facilities.* Measurement of the available output of all or a portion of electric transmission facilities may be determined in a manner consistent with the reporting rules and requirements for transmission networks promulgated by the Federal Energy Regulatory Commission (FERC). For example, for a transmission network, the use of aggregate load and load share ratios in a manner consistent with the requirements of the FERC may be reasonable. In addition, depending on the facts and circumstances, measurement of the available output of transmission facilities using thermal capacity or transfer capacity may be reasonable.

(iii) *Special rule for facilities with significant unutilized capacity.* If an issuer reasonably expects on the issue date that persons that are treated as private business users will purchase more than 30 percent of the actual output of the facility financed with the issue, the Commissioner may determine the number of units produced or to be produced by the facility in one year on a reasonable basis other than by reference to nameplate or other capacity, such as the average expected annual output of the facility. For example, the Commissioner may determine the available output of a financed peaking electric generating unit by reference to the reasonably expected annual output of that unit if the issuer reasonably expects, on the issue date of bonds that finance the unit, that an investor-owned utility will

→ *Caution: Reg. § 1.141-7, below, is generally applicable to bonds sold on or after November 22, 2002.*←

purchase more than 30 percent of the actual output of the facility during the measurement period under a take or pay contract, even if the amount of output purchased is less than 10 percent of the available output determined by reference to nameplate capacity. The reasonably expected annual output of the generating facility must be consistent with the capacity reported for prudent reliability purposes.

(iv) *Special rule for facilities with a limited source of supply.* If a limited source of supply constrains the output of an output facility, the number of units produced or to be produced by the facility must be determined by reasonably taking into account those constraints. For this purpose, a limited source of supply shall include a physical limitation (for example, flow of water), but not an economic limitation (for example, cost of coal or gas). For example, the available output of a hydroelectric unit must be determined by reference to the reasonably expected annual flow of water through the unit.

(2) *Measurement period.* The measurement period of an output facility financed by an issue is determined under § 1.141-3(g).

(3) *Sale at wholesale.* A sale at wholesale means a sale of output to any person for resale.

(4) *Take contract and take or pay contract.* A *take contract* is an output contract under which a purchaser agrees to pay for the output under the contract if the output facility is capable of providing the output. A *take or pay contract* is an output contract under which a purchaser agrees to pay for the output under the contract, whether or not the output facility is capable of providing the output.

(5) *Requirements contract.* A *requirements contract* is an output contract, other than a take contract or a take or pay contract, under which a nongovernmental person agrees to purchase all or part of its output requirements.

(6) *Nonqualified amount.* The nonqualified amount with respect to an issue is determined under section 141(b)(8).

(c) *Output contracts*—(1) *General rule.* The purchase pursuant to a contract by a nongovernmental person of available output of an output facility (output contract) financed with proceeds of an issue is taken into account under the private business tests if the purchase has the effect of transferring the benefits of owning the facility and the burdens of paying the debt service on bonds used (directly or indirectly) to finance the facility (the benefits and burdens test). See para-

graph (c)(4) of this section for the treatment of an output contract that is properly characterized as a lease for Federal income tax purposes. See paragraphs (d) and (e) of this section for rules regarding measuring the use of, and payments of debt service for, an output facility for determining whether the private business tests are met. See also § 1.141-8 for rules for when an issue that finances an output facility (other than a water facility) meets the private business tests because the nonqualified amount of the issue exceeds $15 million.

(2) *Take contract or take or pay contract.* The benefits and burdens test is met if a nongovernmental person agrees pursuant to a take contract or a take or pay contract to purchase available output of a facility.

(3) *Requirements contract*—(i) *In general.* A requirements contract may satisfy the benefits and burdens test under paragraph (c)(3)(ii) or (iii) of this section. See § 1.141-15(f)(2) for special effective dates for the application of this paragraph (c)(3) to issues financing facilities subject to requirements contracts.

(ii) *Requirements contract similar to take contract or take or pay contract.* A requirements contract generally meets the benefits and burdens test to the extent that it contains contractual terms that obligate the purchaser to make payments that are not contingent on the output requirements of the purchaser or that obligate the purchaser to have output requirements. For example, a requirements contract with an industrial purchaser meets the benefits and burdens test if the purchaser enters into additional contractual obligations with the issuer or another governmental unit not to cease operations. A requirements contract does not meet the benefits and burdens test, however, by reason of a provision that requires the purchaser to pay reasonable and customary damages (including liquidated damages) in the event of a default, or a provision that permits the purchaser to pay a specified amount to terminate the contract while the purchaser has requirements, in each case if the amount of the payment is reasonably related to the purchaser's obligation to buy requirements that is discharged by the payment.

(iii) *Wholesale requirements contract*—(A) *In general.* A requirements contract that is a sale at wholesale (a *wholesale requirements contract*) may satisfy the benefits and burdens test, depending on all the facts and circumstances.

(B) *Significant factors.* Significant factors that tend to establish that a wholesale re-

Reg. § 1.141-7(c)(3)

25,318   Tax Exempt. Requirements: State/Local Bonds

See p. 20,601 for regulations not amended to reflect law changes

→ *Caution: Reg. § 1.141-7, below, is generally applicable to bonds sold on or after November 22, 2002.*←

quirements contract meets the benefits and burdens test include, but are not limited to—

(1) The term of the contract is substantial relative to the term of the issue or issues that finance the facility; and

(2) The amount of output to be purchased under the contract represents a substantial portion of the available output of the facility.

(C) *Safe harbors.* A wholesale requirements contract does not meet the benefits and burdens test if—

(1) The term of the contract, including all renewal options, does not exceed the lesser of 5 years or 30 percent of the term of the issue; or

(2) The amount of output to be purchased under the contract (and any other requirements contract with the same purchaser or a related party with respect to the facility) does not exceed 5 percent of the available output of the facility.

(iv) *Retail requirements contract.* Except as otherwise provided in this paragraph (c)(3), a requirements contract that is not a sale at wholesale does not meet the benefits and burdens test.

(4) *Output contract properly characterized as a lease.* Notwithstanding any other provision of this section, an output contract that is properly characterized as a lease for Federal income tax purposes shall be tested under the rules contained in §§ 1.141-3 and 1.141-4 to determine whether it is taken into account under the private business tests.

(d) *Measurement of private business use.* If an output contract results in private business use under this section, the amount of private business use generally is the amount of output purchased under the contract.

(e) *Measurement of private security or payment.* The measurement of payments made or to be made by nongovernmental persons under output contracts as a percent of the debt service of an issue is determined under the rules provided in § 1.141-4.

(f) *Exceptions for certain contracts*—(1) *Small purchases of output.* An output contract for the use of a facility is not taken into account under the private business tests if the average annual payments to be made under the contract do not exceed I percent of the average annual debt service on all outstanding tax-exempt bonds issued to finance the facility, determined as of the effective date of the contract.

(2) *Swapping and pooling arrangements.* An agreement that provides for swapping or pooling of output by one or more governmental persons and one or more nongovernmental persons does not result in private business use of the output facility owned by the governmental person to the extent that—

(i) The swapped output is reasonably expected to be approximately equal in value (determined over periods of three years or less); and

(ii) The purpose of the agreement is to enable each of the parties to satisfy different peak load demands, to accommodate temporary outages, to diversify supply, or to enhance reliability in accordance with prudent reliability standards.

(3) *Short-term output contracts.* An output contract with a nongovernmental person is not taken into account under the private business tests if—

(i) The term of the contract, including all renewal options, is not longer than 3 years;

(ii) The contract either is a negotiated, arm's-length arrangement that provides for compensation at fair market value, or is based on generally applicable and uniformly applied rates; and

(iii) The output facility is not financed for a principal purpose of providing that facility for use by that nongovernmental person.

(4) *Certain conduit parties disregarded.* A nongovernmental person acting solely as a conduit for the exchange of output among governmentally owned and operated utilities is disregarded in determining whether the private business tests are met with respect to financed facilities owned by a governmental person.

(g) *Special rules for electric output facilities used to provide open access*—(1) *Operation of transmission facilities by nongovernmental persons*—(i) *In general.* The operation of an electric transmission facility by a nongovernmental person may result in private business use of the facility under § 1.141-3 and this section based on all the facts and circumstances. For example, a transmission facility is generally used for a private business use if a nongovernmental person enters into a contract to operate the facility and receives compensation based, in whole or in part, on a share of net profits from the operation of the facility.

(ii) *Certain use by independent transmission operators.* A contract for the operation of an electric transmission facility by an independent entity, such as a regional transmission organiza-

Reg. § 1.141-7(c)(4)

→ *Caution: Reg. § 1.141-7, below, is generally applicable to bonds sold on or after November 22, 2002.* ←

tion or an independent system operator (*independent transmission operator*), does not constitute private business use of the facility if—

(A) The facility is owned by a governmental person;

(B) The operation of the facility by the independent transmission operator is approved by the FERC under one or more provisions of the Federal Power Act (16 U.S.C. 791a through 825r) (or by a state authority under comparable provisions of state law);

(C) No portion of the compensation of the independent transmission operator is based on a share of net profits from the operation of the facility; and

(D) The independent transmission operator does not bear risk of loss of the facility.

(2) *Certain use by nongovernmental persons under output contracts*—(i) *Transmission facilities.* The use of an electric transmission facility by a nongovernmental person pursuant to an output contract does not constitute private business use of the facility if—

(A) The facility is owned by a governmental person;

(B) The facility is operated by an independent transmission operator in a manner that satisfies paragraph (g)(1)(ii) of this section; and

(C) The facility is not financed for a principal purpose of providing that facility for use by that nongovernmental person.

(ii) *Distribution facilities.* The use of an electric distribution facility by a nongovernmental person pursuant to an output contract does not constitute private business use of the facility if—

(A) The facility is owned by a governmental person;

(B) The facility is available for use on a nondiscriminatory, open access basis by buyers and sellers of electricity in accordance with rates that are generally applicable and uniformly applied within the meaning of § 1.141-3(c)(2); and

(C) The facility is not financed for a principal purpose of providing that facility for use by that nongovernmental person (other than a retail end-user).

(3) *Ancillary services.* The use of an electric output facility to provide ancillary services required to be offered as part of an open access transmission tariff under rules promulgated by the FERC under the Federal Power Act (16 U.S.C. 791a through 825r) (or by a state regula-

tory authority under comparable provisions of state law) does not result in private business use.

(4) *Exceptions to deliberate action rules*—(i) *Mandated wheeling.* Entering into a contract for the use of electric transmission or distribution facilities is not treated as a deliberate action under § 1.141-2(d) if—

(A) The contract is entered into in response to (or in anticipation of) an order by the United States under sections 211 and 212 of the Federal Power Act (16 U.S.C. 824j and 824k) (or a state regulatory authority under comparable provisions of state law); and

(B) The terms of the contract are bona fide and arm's-length, and the consideration paid is consistent with the provisions of section 212(a) of the Federal Power Act.

(ii) *Actions taken to implement non-discriminatory, open access.* An action is not treated as a deliberate action under § 1.141-2(d) if it is taken to implement the offering of non-discriminatory, open access tariffs for the use of electric transmission or distribution facilities in a manner consistent with rules promulgated by the FERC under sections 205 and 206 of the Federal Power Act (16 U.S.C. 824d and 824e) (or comparable provisions of state law). This paragraph (g)(4)(ii) does not apply, however, to the sale, exchange, or other disposition (within the meaning of section 1001(a)) of transmission or distribution facilities to a nongovernmental person.

(iii) *Application of reasonable expectations test to certain current refunding bonds.* An action taken or to be taken with respect to electric transmission or distribution facilities refinanced by an issue is not taken into account under the reasonable expectations test of § 1.141-2(d) if—

(A) The action is described in paragraph (g)(4)(i) or (ii) of this section;

(B) The bonds of the issue are current refunding bonds that refund bonds originally issued before February 23, 1998; and

(C) The weighted average maturity of the refunding bonds is not greater than the remaining weighted average maturity of the prior bonds.

(5) *Additional transactions as permitted by the Commissioner.* The Commissioner may, by published guidance, set forth additional circumstances in which the use of electric output facilities in a restructured electric industry does not constitute private business use.

Reg. § 1.141-7(g)(5)

25,320   Tax Exempt. Requirements: State/Local Bonds

See p. 20,601 for regulations not amended to reflect law changes

→ *Caution: Reg. § 1.141-7, below, is generally applicable to bonds sold on or after November 22, 2002.*←

(h) *Allocations of output facilities and systems*—(1) *Facts and circumstances analysis.* Whether output sold under an output contract is allocated to a particular facility (for example, a generating unit), to the entire system of the seller of that output (net of any uses of that system output allocated to a particular facility), or to a portion of a facility is based on all the facts and circumstances. Significant factors to be considered in determining the allocation of an output contract to financed property are the following:

(i) The extent to which it is physically possible to deliver output to or from a particular facility or system.

(ii) The terms of a contract relating to the delivery of output (such as delivery limitations and options or obligations to deliver power from additional sources).

(iii) Whether a contract is entered into as part of a common plan of financing for a facility.

(iv) The method of pricing output under the contract, such as the use of market rates rather than rates designed to pay debt service of tax-exempt bonds used to finance a particular facility.

(2) *Illustrations.* The following illustrate the factors set forth in paragraph (h)(1) of this section:

(i) *Physical possibility.* Output from a generating unit that is fed directly into a low voltage distribution system of the owner of that unit and that cannot physically leave that distribution system generally must be allocated to those receiving electricity through that distribution system. Output may be allocated without regard to physical limitations, however, if exchange or similar agreements provide output to a purchaser where, but for the exchange agreements, it would not be possible for the seller to provide output to that purchaser.

(ii) *Contract terms relating to performance.* A contract to provide a specified amount of electricity from a system, but only when at least that amount of electricity is being generated by a particular unit, is allocated to that unit. For example, a contract to buy 20 MW of system power with a right to take up to 40 percent of the actual output of a specific 50 MW facility whenever total system output is insufficient to meet all of the seller's obligations generally is allocated to the specific facility rather than to the system.

(iii) *Common plan of financing.* A contract entered into as part of a common plan of financing for a facility generally is allocated to the facility if debt service for the issue of bonds is reasonably expected to be paid, directly or indirectly, from payments under the contract.

(iv) *Pricing method.* Pricing based on the capital and generating costs of a particular turbine tends to indicate that output under the contract is properly allocated to that turbine.

(3) *Transmission and distribution contracts.* Whether use under an output contract for transmission or distribution is allocated to a particular facility or to a transmission or distribution network is based on all the facts and circumstances, in a manner similar to paragraphs (h)(1) and (2) of this section. In general, the method used to determine payments under a contract is a more significant contract term for this purpose than nominal contract path. In general, if reasonable and consistently applied, the determination of use of transmission or distribution facilities under an output contract may be based on a method used by third parties, such as reliability councils.

(4) *Allocation of payments.* Payments for output provided by an output facility financed with two or more sources of funding are generally allocated under the rules in § 1.141-4(c).

(i) *Examples.* The following examples illustrate the application of this section:

Example 1. Joint ownership. Z, an investor-owned electric utility, and City H agree to construct an electric generating facility of a size sufficient to take advantage of the economies of scale. H will issue $50 million of its 24-year bonds, and Z will use $100 million of its funds for construction of a facility they will jointly own as tenants in common. Each of the participants will share in the ownership, output, and operating expenses of the facility in proportion to its contribution to the cost of the facility, that is, one-third by H and two-thirds by Z. H's bonds will be secured by H's ownership interest in the facility and by revenues to be derived from its share of the annual output of the facility. H will need only 50 percent of its share of the annual output of the facility during the first 20 years of operations. It agrees to sell 10 percent of its share of the annual output to Z for a period of 20 years pursuant to a contract under which Z agrees to take that power if available. The facility will begin operation, and Z will begin to receive power, 4 years after the H bonds are issued. The measurement period for the property financed by the issue is 20 years. H also will sell the remaining 40 percent of its share of the annual output to numerous other private utilities under contracts of three years or less that

→ *Caution: Reg. § 1.141-7, below, is generally applicable to bonds sold on or after November 22, 2002.*←

satisfy the exception under paragraph (f)(3) of this section. No other contracts will be executed obligating any person to purchase any specified amount of the power for any specified period of time. No person (other than Z) will make payments that will result in a transfer of the burdens of paying debt service on bonds used directly or indirectly to provide H's share of the facilities. The bonds are not private activity bonds, because H's one-third interest in the facility is not treated as used by the other owners of the facility. Although 10 percent of H's share of the annual output of the facility will be used in the trade or business of Z, a nongovernmental person, under this section, that portion constitutes not more than 10 percent of the available output of H's ownership interest in the facility.

Example 2. Wholesale requirements contract. (i) City J issues 20-year bonds to acquire an electric generating facility having a reasonably expected economic life substantially greater than 20 years and a nameplate capacity of 100 MW. The available output of the facility under paragraph (b)(1) of this section is approximately 17,520,000 MWh (100 MW X 24 hours X 365 days X 20 years). On the issue date, J enters into a contract with T, an investor-owned utility, to provide T with all of its power requirements for a period of 10 years, commencing on the issue date. J reasonably expects that T will actually purchase an average of 30 MW over the 10-year period. The contract is taken into account under the private business tests pursuant to paragraph (c)(3) of this section because the term of the contract is substantial relative to the term of the issue and the amount of output to be purchased is a substantial portion of the available output.

(ii) Under paragraph (d) of this section, the amount of reasonably expected private business use under this contract is approximately 15 percent (30 MW X 24 hours X 365 days X 10 years, or 2,628,000 MWh) of the available output. Accordingly, the issue meets the private business use test. J reasonably expects that the amount to be paid for an average of 30 MW of power (less the operation and maintenance costs directly attributable to generating that 30 MW of power), will be more than 10 percent of debt service on the issue on a present-value basis. Accordingly, the issue meets the private security or payment test because J reasonably expects that payment of more than 10 percent of the debt service will be indirectly derived from payments by T. The bonds are private activity bonds under paragraph (c) of this section. Further, if 15 percent of the sale proceeds

of the issue is greater than $15 million and the issue meets the private security or payment test with respect to the $15 million output limitation, the bonds are also private activity bonds under section 141(b)(4). See § 1.141-8.

Example 3. Retail contracts. (i) State Agency M, a political subdivision, issues bonds in 2003 to finance the construction of a generating facility that will be used to furnish electricity to M's retail customers. In 2007, M enters into a 10-year contract with industrial corporation I. Under the contract, M agrees to supply I with all of its power requirements during the contract term, and I agrees to pay for that power at a negotiated price as it is delivered. The contract does not require I to pay for any power except to the extent I has requirements. In addition, the contract requires I to pay reasonable and customary liquidated damages in the event of a default by I, and permits I to terminate the contract while it has requirements by paying M a specified amount that is a reasonable and customary amount for terminating the contract. Any damages or termination payment by I will be reasonably related to I's obligation to buy requirements that is discharged by the payment. Under paragraph (c)(3) of this section, the contract does not meet the benefits and burdens test. Thus, it is not taken into account under the private business tests.

(ii) The facts are the same as in paragraph (i) of this *Example 3,* except that the contract requires I to make guaranteed minimum payments, regardless of I's requirements, in an amount such that the contract does not meet the exception for small purchases in paragraph (f)(1) of this section. Under paragraph (c)(3)(ii) of this section, the contract meets the benefits and burdens test because it obligates I to make payments that are not contingent on its output requirements. Thus, it is taken into account under the private business tests.

Example 4. Allocation of existing contracts to new facilities. Power Authority K, a political subdivision created by the legislature in State X to own and operate certain power generating facilities, sells all of the power from its existing facilities to four private utility systems under contracts executed in 1999, under which the four systems are required to take or pay for specified portions of the total power output until the year 2029. Existing facilities supply all of the present needs of the four utility systems, but their future power requirements are expected to increase substantially beyond the capacity of K's current generating system. K issues 20-year bonds in 2004 to

25,322   **Tax Exempt. Requirements: State/Local Bonds**

See p. 20,601 for regulations not amended to reflect law changes

→ *Caution: Reg. § 1.141-7, below, is generally applicable to bonds sold on or after November 22, 2002.*←

construct a large generating facility. As part of the financing plan for the bonds, a fifth private utility system contracts with K to take or pay for 15 percent of the available output of the new facility. The balance of the output of the new facility will be available for sale as required, but initially it is not anticipated that there will be any need for that power. The revenues from the contract with the fifth private utility system will be sufficient to pay less than 10 percent of the debt service on the bonds (determined on a present value basis). The balance, which will exceed 10 percent of the debt service on the bonds, will be paid from revenues derived from the contracts with the four systems initially from sale of power produced by the old facilities. The output contracts with all the private utilities are allocated to K's entire generating system. See paragraphs (h)(1) and (2) of this section. Thus, the bonds meet the private business use test because more than 10 percent of the proceeds will be used in the trade or business of a nongovernmental person. In addition, the bonds meet the private security or payment test because payment of more than 10 percent of the debt service, pursuant to underlying arrangements, will be derived from payments in respect of property used for a private business use.

Example 5. Allocation to displaced resource. Municipal utility MU, a political subdivision, purchases all of the electricity required to meet the needs of its customers (1,000 MW) from B, an investor-owned utility that operates its own electric generating facilities, under a 50-year take or pay contract. MU does not anticipate that it will require additional electric resources, and any new resources would produce electricity at a higher cost to MU than its cost under its contract with B. Nevertheless, B encourages MU to construct a new generating plant sufficient to meet MU's requirements. MU issues obligations to construct facilities that will produce 1,000 MW of electricity. MU, B, and I, another investor-owned utility, enter into an agreement under which MU assigns to I its rights under MU's take or pay contract with B. Under this arrangement, I will pay MU, and MU will continue to pay B, for the 1,000 MW. I's payments to MU will at least equal the amounts required to pay debt service on MU's bonds. In addition, under paragraph (h)(1)(iii) of this section, the contract among MU, B, and I is entered into as part of a common plan of financing of the MU facilities. Under all the facts and circumstances, MU's assignment to I of its rights under the original take or pay contract is alloca-

ble to MU's new facilities under paragraph (h) of this section. Because I is a nongovernmental person, MU's bonds are private activity bonds.

Example 6. Operation of transmission facilities by regional transmission organization. (i) Public Power Agency D is a political subdivision that owns and operates electric generation, transmission and distribution facilities. In 2003, D transfers operating control of its transmission system to a regional transmission organization (RTO), a nongovernmental person, pursuant to an operating agreement that is approved by the FERC under sections 205 and 206 of the Federal Power Act. D retains ownership of its facilities. No portion of the RTO's compensation is based on a share of net profits from the operation of D's facilities, and the RTO does not bear any risk of loss of those facilities. Under paragraph (g)(1)(ii) of this section, the RTO's use of D's facilities does not constitute a private business use.

(ii) Company A is located in D's service territory. In 2004, Power Supplier E, a nongovernmental person, enters into a 10-year contract with A to supply A's electricity requirements. The electricity supplied by E to A will be transmitted over D's transmission and distribution facilities. D's distribution facilities are available for use on a nondiscriminatory, open access basis by buyers and sellers of electricity in accordance with rates that are generally applicable and uniformly applied within the meaning of § 1.141-3(c)(2). D's facilities are not financed for a principal purpose of providing the facilities for use by E. Under paragraph (g)(2) of this section, the contract between A and E does not result in private business use of D's facilities.

Example 7. Certain actions not treated as deliberate actions. The facts are the same as in *Example 6* of this paragraph (i), except that the RTO's compensation is based on a share of net profits from operating D's facilities. In addition, D had issued bonds in 1994 to finance improvements to its transmission system. At the time D transfers operating control of its transmission system to the RTO, D chooses to apply the private activity bond regulations of §§ 1.141 through 1.141-15 to the 1994 bonds. The operation of D's facilities by the RTO results in private business use under § 1.141-3 and paragraph (g)(1)(i) of this section. Under the special exception in paragraph (g)(4)(ii) of this section, however, the transfer of control is not treated as a deliberate action. Accordingly, the transfer of control does not cause the 1994 bonds to meet the private activity bond tests.

Reg. § 1.141-7(i)

Tax Exempt. Requirements: State/Local Bonds   **25,323**

See p. 20,601 for regulations not amended to reflect law changes

→ *Caution: Reg. § 1.141-7, below, is generally applicable to bonds sold on or after November 22, 2002.*←

Example 8. Current refunding. The facts are the same as in *Example 7* of this paragraph (i), and in addition D issues bonds in 2004 to currently refund the 1994 bonds. The weighted average maturity of the 2004 bonds is not greater than the remaining weighted average maturity of the 1994 bonds. D chooses to apply the private activity bond regulations of § § 1.141 through 1.141-15 to the refunding bonds. In general, reasonable expectations must be separately tested on the date that refunding bonds are issued under

§ 1.141-2(d). Under the special exception in paragraph (g)(4)(iii) of this section, however, the transfer of the financed facilities to the RTO need not be taken into account in applying the reasonable expectations test to the refunding bonds.

[Reg. § 1.141-7.]

☐ [*T.D.* 9016, 9-19-2002 (*corrected* 11-26-2002).]

→ *Caution: Temporary Reg. § 1.141-7T, below, was removed by T.D. 9016, effective November 22, 2002.*←

[Reg. § 1.141-7T]

§ 1.141-7T. Special rules for output facilities (temporary).—(a) *Overview.* This section provides special rules to determine whether arrangements for the purchase of output from an output facility cause an issue of bonds to meet the private business tests. For this purpose, unless otherwise stated, water facilities are treated as output facilities. Sections 1.141-3 and 1.141-4 generally apply to determine whether other types of arrangements for use of an output facility cause an issue to meet the private business tests.

(b) *Definitions.* For purposes of this section and § 1.141-8T, the following definitions and rules apply:

(1) *Available output.* The available output of a facility financed by an issue is determined by multiplying the number of units produced or to be produced by the facility in one year by the number of years in the measurement period of that facility for that issue.

(i) *Generating facilities.* The number of units produced or to be produced by a generating facility in one year is determined by reference to its nameplate capacity or the equivalent (or where there is no nameplate capacity or the equivalent, its maximum capacity), which is not reduced for reserves, maintenance or other unutilized capacity.

(ii) *Transmission and other output facilities*—(A) *In general.* For transmission, cogeneration, and other output facilities, available output must be measured in a reasonable manner to reflect capacity.

(B) *Electric transmission facilities.* Measurement of the available output of all or a portion of electric transmission facilities may be determined in a manner consistent with the reporting rules and requirements for transmission networks promulgated by the Federal Energy

Regulatory Commission (FERC). For example, for a transmission network, the use of aggregate load and load share ratios in a manner consistent with the requirements of the FERC may be reasonable. In addition, depending on the facts and circumstances, measurement of the available output of transmission facilities using thermal capacity or transfer capacity may be reasonable.

(iii) *Special rule for facilities with significant unutilized capacity.* If an issuer reasonably expects on the issue date that persons that are treated as private business users will purchase more than 20 percent of the actual output of the facility financed with the issue, the Commissioner may determine the number of units produced or to be produced by the facility in one year on a reasonable basis other than by reference to nameplate capacity, such as the average expected annual output of the facility. For example, the Commissioner may determine the available output of a financed peaking electric generating unit by reference to the reasonably expected annual output of that unit if the issuer reasonably expects, on the issue date of bonds that finance the unit, that an investor-owned utility will purchase more than 20 percent of the actual output of the facility during the measurement period under a take or pay contract, even if the amount of output purchased is less than 10 percent of the available output determined by reference to nameplate capacity. The reasonably expected annual output of the generating facility must be consistent with the capacity reported for prudent reliability purposes.

(iv) *Special rule for facilities with a limited source of supply.* If a limited source of supply constrains the output of an output facility, the number of units produced or to be produced by the facility must be determined by reasonably taking into account those constraints. For this purpose, a limited source of supply shall include a

25,324   **Tax Exempt. Requirements: State/Local Bonds**

See p. 20,601 for regulations not amended to reflect law changes

→ *Caution: Temporary Reg. § 1.141-7T, below, was removed by T.D. 9016, effective November 22, 2002.*←

physical limitation (for example, flow of water), but not an economic limitation (for example, cost of coal or gas). For example, the available output of a hydroelectric unit must be determined by reference to the reasonably expected annual flow of water through the unit.

(2) *Measurement period.* The measurement period of an output facility financed by an issue is determined under § 1.141-3(g).

(3) *Sale at wholesale.* For purposes of this section, a sale at wholesale means a sale of output to any person for resale.

(4) *Take contract and take or pay contract.* A *take contract* is an output contract under which a purchaser agrees to pay for the output under the contract if the output facility is capable of providing the output. A *take or pay contract* is an output contract under which a purchaser agrees to pay for the output under the contract, whether or not the output facility is capable of providing the output.

(5) *Transmission facilities*—(i) *In general.* Transmission facilities are facilities for the transmission or distribution of output.

(ii) *Special rule for ancillary services.* For purposes of paragraph (f)(5), transmission facilities include facilities necessary to provide ancillary services required to be offered as part of open access transmission tariffs under rules promulgated by the FERC under sections 205 and 206 of the Federal Power Act (16 U.S.C. 824d and 824e). Thus, if a facility also serves another function (for example, a facility that provides for operating reserves for transmission and also provides generation) an allocable portion of the facility is treated as a transmission facility for purposes of paragraph (f)(5) of this section.

(6) *Nonqualified amount.* The nonqualified amount with respect to an issue is determined under section 141(b)(8).

(c) *Output contracts*—(1) *General rule.* The purchase by a nongovernmental person of available output of an output facility (output contract) financed with the proceeds of an issue is taken into account under the private business tests if the purchase has the effect of transferring substantial benefits of owning the facility and substantial burdens of paying the debt service on bonds used (directly or indirectly) to finance the facility (the benefits and burdens test). See paragraph (c)(5) of this section for the treatment of an output contract that is properly characterized as a lease for Federal income tax purposes. See paragraphs (d) and (e) of this section for rules

regarding measuring the use of, and payments of debt service for, an output facility for determining whether the private business tests are met. See also § 1.141-8T for rules for when an issue that finances an output facility (other than a water facility) meets the private business tests because the nonqualified amount of the issue exceeds $15 million.

(2) *Benefits and burdens test*—(i) *Benefits of ownership.* An output contract transfers substantial benefits of owning a facility if the contract gives the purchaser (directly or indirectly) rights to capacity of the facility on a basis that is preferential to the rights of the general public.

(ii) *Burdens of paying debt service.* An output contract transfers substantial burdens of paying debt service on an issue to the extent that the issuer reasonably expects that it is substantially certain that payments will be made under the terms of the contract (disregarding default, insolvency, or other similar circumstances). For example, an output contract is treated as transferring burdens of paying debt service on an issue if payments must be made upon contract termination.

(iii) *Payments pursuant to pledged contract.* Payments made or to be made under the terms of an output contract that is pledged as security for an issue are taken into account under the private business tests even if the issuer reasonably expects that it is not substantially certain that payments will be made under the contract (disregarding default, insolvency, or other similar circumstances). For this purpose, an output contract is pledged as security only if the bond documents provide that the pledged contract cannot be substantially amended without the consent of bondholders or a trustee for the bondholders. This paragraph (c)(2)(iii) applies to pledges made on or after February 23, 1998, with respect to bonds that are subject to this section.

(3) *Take contract or take or pay contract.* The benefits and burdens test is met if a nongovernmental person agrees pursuant to a take contract or a take or pay contract to purchase available output of a facility.

(4) *Requirements contracts*—(i) *In general.* A requirements contract under which a nongovernmental person agrees to purchase all or art of its output requirements is taken into account under the private business tests only to the extent that, based on all the facts and circumstances, the contract meets the benefits and burdens test. See § 1.141-15T(f)(2) for special effective dates for

Reg. § 1.141-7T(b)(2)

→ *Caution: Temporary Reg. § 1.141-7T, below, was removed by T.D. 9016, effective November 22, 2002.*←

the application of this paragraph (c)(4) to issues financing facilities subject to requirements contracts.

(ii) *Significant factors.* Significant factors that tend to establish that the benefits and burdens test is met under the rule set forth in paragraph (c)(4)(i) of this section include, but are not limited to—

(A) The purchaser's customer base has significant indicators of stability, such as large size, diverse composition, and a substantial residential component;

(B) The contract covers historical requirements of the purchaser, rather than only projected requirements that are in addition to historical requirements; and

(C) The purchaser agrees not to construct or acquire other power resources to meet the requirements covered by the contract.

(iii) *Special rule for retail requirements contracts.* In general, a requirements contract that is not a sale at wholesale (a *retail requirements contract*) does not meet the benefits and burdens test because the obligation to make payments on the contract is contingent on the output requirements of a single user. Such a requirements contract in general meets the benefits and burdens test, however, to the extent that it contains contractual terms that obligate the purchaser to make payments that are not contingent on the output requirements of the purchaser or that obligate the purchaser to have output requirements. For example, a requirements contract with an industrial purchaser meets the benefits and burdens test if the purchaser enters into additional contractual obligations with the issuer or another governmental unit not to cease operations. A retail requirements contract does not meet the benefits and burdens test by reason of a provision that requires the purchaser to pay reasonable and customary damages (including liquidated damages) in the event of a default, or a provision that permits the purchaser to pay a specified amount to terminate the contract while the purchaser has requirements, in each case if the amount of the payment is reasonably related to the purchaser's obligation to buy requirements that is discharged by the payment.

(5) *Output contract properly characterized as a lease.* Notwithstanding any other provision of this section, an output contract that is properly characterized as a lease for Federal income tax purposes shall be tested under the rules contained in § § 1.141-3 and 1.141-4 to determine whether it

is taken into account under the private business tests.

(d) *Measurement of private business use.* If an output contract results in private business use under this section, the amount of private business use generally is the amount of output purchased under the contract.

(e) *Measurement of private security or payment.* The measurement of payments made or to be made by nongovernmental persons under output contracts as a percent of the debt service of an issue is determined under the rules provided in § 1.141-4.

(f) *Exceptions for certain contracts*—(1) *Small purchases of output.* An output contract is not taken into account under the private business tests if the average annual payments under the contract that are substantially certain to be made under paragraph (c)(2)(ii) of this section do not exceed 0.5 percent of the average annual debt service on all outstanding tax-exempt bonds issued to finance the facility, determined as of the effective date of the contract.

(2) *Swapping and pooling arrangements.* An agreement that provides for swapping or pooling of output by one or more governmental persons and one or more nongovernmental persons does not result in private business use of the output facility owned by the governmental person to the extent that—

(i) The swapped output is reasonably expected to be approximately equal in value (determined over periods of one year or less); and

(ii) The purpose of the agreement is to enable each of the parties to satisfy different peak load demands, to accommodate temporary outages, to diversify supply, or to enhance reliability in accordance with prudent reliability standards.

(3) *Short-term output contracts.* An output contract with a nongovernmental person is not taken into account under the private business tests if—

(i) The term of the contract, including all renewal options, is not longer than 1 year;

(ii) The contract either is a negotiated, arm's-length arrangement that provides for compensation at fair market value, or is based on generally applicable and uniformly applied rates; and

(iii) The output facility is not financed for a principal purpose of providing that facility for use by that nongovernmental person.

Reg. § 1.141-7T(f)(3)

→ *Caution: Temporary Reg. § 1.141-7T, below, was removed by T.D. 9016, effective November 22, 2002.*←

(4) *Special 3-year exception for sales of output attributable to excess generating capacity resulting from participation in open access.* The purchase of output of an electric generating facility by a nongovernmental person is not treated as private business use if all of the following requirements are met:

(i) The term of the contract is not longer than 3 years, including all renewal options.

(ii) The issuer does not make expenditures to increase the generating capacity of its system during the term of the contract that are, or will be, financed with proceeds of tax-exempt bonds (other than expenditures for property that does not increase the generating capacity of the system by more than 3 percent).

(iii) The governmental owner offers non-discriminatory, open access transmission tariffs for use of its transmission system pursuant to rules promulgated by the FERC under sections 205 and 206 of the Federal Power Act (16 U.S.C. 824d and 824e) (or comparable provisions of state law).

(iv) All of the output sold under the contract is attributable to excess capacity resulting from the offer of the non-discriminatory, open access transmission-tariffs referred to in paragraph (f)(5)(iii) of this section.

(v) All payments received by the governmental owner under the contract (other than the portion of such payments described in § 1.141-4(c)(2)(C)) are applied as promptly as is reasonably practical to redeem tax-exempt bonds that financed the output facility in a manner consistent with § 1.141-12.

(5) *Special exceptions for transmission facilities—(i) Mandated wheeling.* Entering into a contract for the use of transmission facilities financed by an issue is not treated as a deliberate action under § 1.141-2(d) if—

(A) The contract is entered into in response to (or in anticipation of) an order by the United States under sections 211 and 212 of the Federal Power Act (16 U.S.C. 824j and 824k) (or a state regulatory authority under comparable provisions of state law); and

(B) The terms of the contract are bona fide and arm's length, and the consideration paid is consistent with the provisions of section 212(a) of the Federal Power Act.

(ii) *Actions taken to implement non-discriminatory, open access.* An action is not treated as a deliberate action under § 1.141-2(d) if it is taken to implement the offering of non-discrimi-

natory, open access tariffs for the use of transmission facilities financed by an issue in a manner consistent with rules promulgated by the FERC under sections 205 and 206 of the Federal Power Act (16 U.S.C. 824d and 824e) (or comparable provisions of state law). This paragraph (f)(5)(ii) does not apply, however, to the sale, exchange, or other disposition of transmission facilities to a nongovernmental person.

(iii) *Application of reasonable expectations test to certain current refunding bonds.* An action taken or to be taken with respect to transmission facilities refinanced by an issue is not taken into account under the reasonable expectations test of § 1.141-2(d) if—

(A) The action is described in paragraph (f)(5)(i) or (ii) of this section;

(B) The bonds of the issue are current refunding bonds that, directly or indirectly, refund bonds originally issued before February 23, 1998; and

(C) The weighted average maturity of the refunding bonds is not greater than the remaining weighted average maturity of those prior bonds.

(6) *Certain conduit parties disregarded.* A nongovernmental person acting solely as a conduit for the exchange of output among governmentally owned and operated utilities is disregarded in determining whether the private business tests are met with respect to financed facilities owned by a governmental person. Use of property by a power marketer in the trade or business of purchasing and reselling power, however, is taken into account under the private business tests.

(g) *Allocations of output facilities and systems—(1) Facts and circumstances analysis.* Whether output sold under an output contract is allocated to a particular facility (for example, a generating unit), to the entire system of the seller of that output (net of any uses of that system output allocated to a particular facility), or to a portion of a facility is based on all the facts and circumstances. Significant factors to be considered in determining the allocation of an output contract to financed property are the following:

(i) The extent to which it is physically possible to deliver output to or from a particular facility or system.

(ii) The terms of a contract relating to the delivery of output (such as delivery limitations and options or obligations to deliver power from additional sources).

→ *Caution: Temporary Reg. § 1.141-7T, below, was removed by T.D. 9016, effective November 22, 2002.*←

(iii) Whether a contract is entered into as part of a common plan of financing for a facility.

(iv) The method of pricing output under the contract, such as the use of market rates rather than rates designed to pay debt service of tax-exempt bonds used to finance a particular facility.

(2) *Illustrations.* The following illustrate the factors set forth in paragraph (g)(1) of this section:

(i) *Physical possibility.* Output from a generating unit that is fed directly into a low voltage distribution system of the owner of that unit and that cannot physically leave that distribution system generally must be allocated to those receiving electricity through that distribution system. Output may be allocated without regard to physical limitations, however, if exchange or similar agreements provide output to a purchaser where, but for the exchange agreements, it would not be possible for the seller to provide output to that purchaser.

(ii) *Contract terms relating to performance.* A contract to provide a specified amount of electricity from a system, but only when at least that amount of electricity is being generated by a particular unit, is allocated to that unit. For example, a contract to buy 20 MW of system power with a right to take up to 40 percent of the actual output of a specific 50 MW facility whenever total system output is insufficient to meet all of the seller's obligations generally is allocated to the specific facility rather than to the system.

(iii) *Common plan of financing.* A contract entered into as part of a common plan of financing for a facility generally is allocated to the facility if debt service for the issue of bonds is reasonably expected to be paid, directly or indirectly, from payments substantially certain to be made under the contract (disregarding default, insolvency, or other similar circumstances).

(iv) *Pricing method.* Pricing based on the capital and generating costs of a particular turbine tends to indicate that output under the contract is properly allocated to that turbine.

(3) *Transmission contracts.* Whether use under an output contract for transmission is allocated to a particular facility or to a transmission network is based on all the facts and circumstances, in a manner similar to paragraphs (g)(1) and (2) of this section. In general, the method used to determine payments under a contract is a more significant contract term for this purpose than nominal contract path. In general, if reason-able and consistently applied, the determination of use of transmission facilities under an output contract may be based on a method used by third parties, such as reliability councils.

(4) *Allocation of payments.* Payments for output provided by an output facility financed with two or more sources of funding are generally allocated under the rules in § 1.141-4(c).

(h) *Examples.* The following examples illustrate the application of this section:

Example 1. Joint ownership. Z, an investor-owned electric utility, and City H agree to construct an electric generating facility of a size sufficient to take advantage of the economies of scale. H will issue $50 million of its 24-year bonds, and Z will use $100 million of its funds for construction of a facility they will jointly own as tenants in common. Each of the participants will share in the ownership, output, and operating expenses of the facility in proportion to its contribution to the cost of the facility, that is, one-third by H and two-thirds by Z. H's bonds will be secured by H's ownership interest in the facility and by revenues to be derived from its share of the annual output of the facility. H will need only 50 percent of its share of the annual output of the facility during the first 20 years of operations. It agrees to sell 10 percent of its share of the annual output to Z for a period of 20 years pursuant to a contract under which Z agrees to take that power if available. The facility will begin operation, and Z will begin to receive power, 4 years after the H bonds are issued. The measurement period for the property financed by the issue is 20 years. H also will sell the remaining 40 percent of its share of the annual output to numerous other private utilities under contracts of one year or less that satisfy the exception under paragraph (f)(3) of this section. No other contracts will be executed obligating any person to purchase any specified amount of the power for any specified period of time. No person (other than Z) will make payments substantially certain to be made (disregarding default, insolvency, or other similar circumstances) under paragraph (c)(2) of this section that will result in a transfer of substantial burdens of paying debt service on bonds used directly or indirectly to provide H's share of the facilities. The bonds are not private activity bonds, because H's one-third interest in the facility is not treated as used by the other owners of the facility. Although 10 percent of H's share of the annual output of the facility will be used in the trade or business of Z, a nongovernmental person, under this section, that portion constitutes not more than 10 percent

Reg. § 1.141-7T(h)

25,328   **Tax Exempt. Requirements: State/Local Bonds**

See p. 20,601 for regulations not amended to reflect law changes

→ *Caution: Temporary Reg. § 1.141-7T, below, was removed by T.D. 9016, effective November 22, 2002.*←

of the available output of H's ownership interest in the facility.

Example 2. Requirements contract treated as take contract. (i) City J issues 20-year bonds to acquire an electric generating facility having a reasonably expected economic life substantially greater than 20 years and a nameplate capacity of 100 MW. The available output of the facility under paragraph (b)(1) of this section is approximately 17,520,000 MWh (100 MW × 24 hours × 365 days × 20 years). On the issue date, J enters into a contract with T, an investor-owned utility, to provide T with all of its power requirements for a period of 10 years, commencing on the issue date. J reasonably expects that T will actually purchase an average of 30 MW over the 10-year period. Based on all of the facts and circumstances, including the size, diversity, and composition of T's customer base, J reasonably expects that it is substantially certain (disregarding default, insolvency, or other similar circumstances) that T will actually purchase only an average of 26 MW over the 10-year period. The contract is a requirements contract that must be taken into account under the private business tests pursuant to paragraph (c)(4) of this section because it provides T with substantial benefits of ownership (rights to capacity) and obligates T with substantial burdens of making payments that the issuer reasonably expects are substantially certain.

(ii) Under paragraph (d) of this section, the amount of reasonably expected private business use under this contract is approximately 15 percent (30 MW × 24 hours × 365 days × 10 years, or 2,628,000 MWh) of the available output. Accordingly, the issue meets the private business use test. J reasonably expects that the amount to be paid for an average of 26 MW of power (less the operation and maintenance costs directly attributable to generating that 26 MW of power), will be more than 10 percent of debt service on the issue on a present-value basis. The payment for 26 MW of power is an amount that J reasonably expects is substantially certain to be made under paragraph (c)(2) of this section. Accordingly, the issue meets the private security or payment test because J reasonably expects that it is substantially certain that payment of more than 10 percent of the debt service will be indirectly derived from payments by T. The bonds are private activity bonds under paragraph (c) of this section. Further, if 15 percent of the sale proceeds of the issue is greater than $15 million and the issue meets the private security or payment test with respect to the $15 million output limitation, the bonds are also pri-

vate activity bonds under section 141(b)(4). See § 1.141-8T.

Example 3. Allocation of existing contracts to new facilities. Power Authority K, a political subdivision created by the legislature in State X to own and operate certain power generating facilities, sells all of the power from its existing facilities to four private utility systems under contracts executed in 1999, under which the four systems are required to take or pay for specified portions of the total power output until the year 2029. Existing facilities supply all of the present needs of the four utility systems, but their future power requirements are expected to increase substantially beyond the capacity of K's current generating system. K issues 20-year bonds in 2004 to construct a large generating facility. As part of the financing plan for the bonds, a fifth private utility system contracts with K to take or pay for 15 percent of the available output of the new facility. The balance of the output of the new facility will be available for sale as required, but initially it is not anticipated that there will be any need for that power. The revenues from the contract with the fifth private utility system will be sufficient to pay less than 10 percent of the debt service on the bonds (determined on a present value basis). The balance, which will exceed 10 percent of the debt service on the bonds, will be paid from revenues derived from the contracts with the four systems initially from sale of power produced by the old facilities. The output contracts with all the private utilities are allocated to K's entire generating system. See paragraphs (g)(1) and (2) of this section. Thus, the bonds meet the private business use test because more than 10 percent of the proceeds will be used in the trade or business of a nongovernmental person. In addition, the bonds meet the private security or payment test because payment of more than 10 percent of the debt service, pursuant to underlying arrangements, will be derived from payments in respect of property used for a private business use.

Example 4. Allocation to displaced resource. Municipal utility MU, a political subdivision, purchases all of the electricity required to meet the needs of its customers (1,000 MW) from B, an investor-owned utility that operates its own electric generating facilities, under a 50-year take or pay contract. MU does not anticipate that it will require additional electric resources, and any new resources would produce electricity at a higher cost to MU than its cost under its contract with B. Nevertheless, B encourages MU to construct a

Reg. § 1.141-7T(h)

Tax Exempt. Requirements: State/Local Bonds   25,329

See p. 20,601 for regulations not amended to reflect law changes

→ *Caution: Temporary Reg. § 1.141-7T, below, was removed by T.D. 9016, effective November 22, 2002.*←

new generating plant sufficient to meet MU's requirements. MU issues obligations to construct facilities that will produce 1,000 MW of electricity. MU, B, and I, another investor-owned utility, enter into an agreement under which MU assigns to I its rights under MU's take or pay contract with B. Under this arrangement, I will pay MU, and MU will continue to pay B, for the 1,000 MW. I's payments to MU will at least equal the amounts required to pay debt service on MU's bonds. In addition, under paragraph (g)(1)(iii) of this section, the contract among MU, B, and I is entered into as part of a common plan of financing of the MU facilities. Under all the facts and circumstances, MU's assignment to I of its rights under the original take or pay contract is allocable to MU's new facilities under paragraph (g) of this section. Because I is a nongovernmental person, MU's bonds are private activity bonds.

Example 5. Transmission facilities transferred to regional transmission organization. (i) In 2001, the public utilities commission of State C adopts a plan for restructuring its electric power industry. The plan fosters competition by providing both wholesale and retail customers with non-discriminatory access to transmission facilities within the State. The plan provides that investor-owned utilities will transfer operating control over all of their transmission assets to a regional transmission organization (RTO), which is a nongovernmental person that will operate those combined assets as a single, state-wide system. Municipally-owned utilities are eligible for, but are not required to participate in, the open access system implemented by the RTO. The functions of the RTO include control of transmission access and pricing, scheduling transmission, control area operations, and settlements and billing. The RTO's compensation under its operating agreement with transmission owners is based on a share of net profits from operating the facilities. The restructuring plan is approved by the FERC pursuant to sections 205 and 206 of the Federal Power Act.

(ii) In 1994, City D had issued bonds to finance improvements to its transmission system. In 2001, D transfers operating control of its transmission system to the RTO pursuant to the restructuring plan. At the same time, D chooses to apply the private activity bond regulations of §§ 1.141-1 through 1.141-15 to the 1994 bonds. The operation of the financed facilities by the RTO results in private business use under § 1.141-3. Under the special exception in paragraph (f)(5) of this section, however, the transfer of control is not treated as a deliberate action. Accordingly, the transfer of control does not cause the 1994 bonds to meet the private activity bond tests

Example 6. Current refunding. The facts are the same as in Example 5 of this paragraph (h), and in addition D issues bonds in 2003 to currently refund the 1994 bonds. The weighted average maturity of the 2003 bonds is not greater than the remaining weighted average maturity of the 1994 bonds. D chooses to apply the private activity bond regulations of §§ 1.141-1 through 1.141-15 to the refunding bonds. In general, reasonable expectations must be separately tested on the date that refunding bonds are issued under § 1.141-2(d). Under the special exception in paragraph (f)(5) of this section, however, the transfer of the financed facilities to the RTO need not be taken into account in applying the reasonable expectations test to the refunding bonds.

[Temporary Reg. § 1.141-7T.]

⫧ [*T.D. 8757, 1-21-98. Amended by T.D. 8941, 1-17-2001. Removed by T.D. 9016, 9-19-2002.*]

→ *Caution: Reg. § 1.141-8, below, is generally applicable to bonds sold on or after November 22, 2002.*←

[Reg. § 1.141-8]

§ 1.141-8. **$15 million limitation for output facilities.**—(a) *In general*—(1) *General rule.* Section 141(b)(4) provides a special private activity bond limitation (the $15 million output limitation) for issues 5 percent or more of the proceeds of which are to be used to finance output facilities (other than a facility for the furnishing of water). Under this rule, an issue consists of private activity bonds under the private business tests of section 141(b)(1) and (2) if the nonqualified amount with respect to output facilities financed by the proceeds of the issue exceeds $15 million. The $15 million output limitation applies in addition to the private business tests of section 141(b)(1) and (2). Under section 141(b)(4) and paragraph (a)(2) of this section, the $15 million output limitation is reduced in certain cases. Specifically, an issue meets the test in section 141(b)(4) if both of the following tests are met:

(i) More than $15 million of the proceeds of the issue to be used with respect to an output facility are to be used for a private business use. Investment proceeds are disregarded for this pur-

25,330   Tax Exempt. Requirements: State/Local Bonds

See p. 20,601 for regulations not amended to reflect law changes

→ *Caution: Reg. § 1.141-8, below, is generally applicable to bonds sold on or after November 22, 2002.*←

pose if they are not allocated disproportionately to the private business use portion of the issue.

(ii) The payment of the principal of, or the interest on, more than $15 million of the sale proceeds of the portion of the issue used with respect to an output facility is (under the terms of the issue or any underlying arrangement) directly or indirectly—

(A) Secured by any interest in an output facility used or to be used for a private business use (or payments in respect of such an output facility); or

(B) To be derived from payments (whether or not to the issuer) in respect of an output facility used or to be used for a private business use.

(2) *Reduction in $15 million output limitation for outstanding issues*—(i) *General rule.* In determining whether an issue 5 percent or more of the proceeds of which are to be used with respect to an output facility consists of private activity bonds under the $15 million output limitation, the $15 million limitation on private business use and private security or payments is applied by taking into account the aggregate nonqualified amounts of any outstanding bonds of other issues 5 percent or more of the proceeds of which are or will be used with respect to that output facility or any other output facility that is part of the same project.

(ii) *Bonds taken into account.* For purposes of this paragraph (a)(2), applying the $15 million output limitation to an issue (the later issue), a tax-exempt bond of another issue (the earlier issue) is taken into account if—

(A) That bond is outstanding on the issue date of the later issue;

(B) That bond will not be redeemed within 90 days of the issue date of the later issue in connection with the refunding of that bond by the later issue; and

(C) 5 percent or more of the sale proceeds of the earlier issue financed an output facility that is part of the same project as the output facility that is financed by 5 percent or more of the sale proceeds of the later issue.

(3) *Benefits and burdens test applicable*—(i) *In general.* In applying the $15 million output limitation, the benefits and burdens test of § 1.141-7 applies, except that "$15 million" is applied in place of "10 percent", or "5 percent" as appropriate.

(ii) *Earlier issues for the project.* If bonds of an earlier issue are outstanding and must be taken into account under paragraph (a)(2) of this section, the nonqualified amount for that earlier issue is multiplied by a fraction, the numerator of which is the adjusted issue price of the earlier issue as of the issue date of the later issue, and the denominator of which is the issue price of the earlier issue. Pre-issuance accrued interest as defined in § 1.148-1(b) is disregarded for this purpose.

(b) *Definition of project*—(1) *General rule.* For purposes of paragraph (a)(2) of this section, *project* has the meaning provided in this paragraph. Facilities that are functionally related and subordinate to a project are treated as part of that same project. Facilities having different purposes or serving different customer bases are not ordinarily part of the same project. For example, the following are generally not part of the same project—

(i) Generation, transmission and distribution facilities;

(ii) Separate facilities designed to serve wholesale customers and retail customers; and

(iii) A peaking unit and a baseload unit (regardless of the location of the units).

(2) *Separate ownership.* Except as otherwise provided in this paragraph (b)(2), facilities that are not owned by the same person are not part of the same project. If different governmental persons act in concert to finance a project, however (for example as participants in a joint powers authority), their interests are aggregated with respect to that project to determine whether the $15 million output limitation is met. In the case of undivided ownership interests in a single output facility, property that is not owned by different persons is treated as separate projects only if the separate interests are financed—

(i) With bonds of different issuers; and

(ii) Without a principal purpose of avoiding the limitation in this section.

(3) *Generating property*—(i) *Property on same site.* In the case of generation and related facilities, *project* means property located at the same site.

(ii) *Special rule for generating units.* Separate generating units are not part of the same project if one unit is reasonably expected, on the issue date of each issue that finances the units, to be placed in service more than 3 years before the other. Common facilities or property that will be functionally related to more than one generating

Reg. § 1.141-8(a)(2)

Tax Exempt. Requirements: State/Local Bonds   25,331

See p. 20,6C1 for regulations not amended to reflect law changes

→ *Caution: Reg. § 1.141-8, below, is generally applicable to bonds sold on or after November 22, 2002.*←

unit must be allocated on a reasonable basis. If a generating unit already is constructed or is under construction (the first unit) and bonds are to be issued to finance an additional generating unit (the second unit), all costs for any common facilities paid or incurred before the earlier of the issue date of bonds to finance the second unit or the commencement of construction of the second unit are allocated to the first unit. At the time that bonds are issued to finance the second unit (or, if earlier, upon commencement of construction of that unit), any remaining costs of the common facilities may be allocated between the first and second units so that in the aggregate the allocation is reasonable.

(4) *Transmission and distribution.* In the case of transmission or distribution facilities, *project* means functionally related or contiguous property. Separate transmission or distribution facilities are not part of the same project if one facility is reasonably expected, on the issue date of each issue that finances the facilities, to be placed in service more than 2 years before the other.

(5) *Subsequent improvements*—(i) *In general.* An improvement to generation, transmission or distribution facilities that is not part of the original design of those facilities (the original project) is not part of the same project as the original project if the construction, reconstruction, or acquisition of that improvement commences more than 3 years after the original project was placed in service and the bonds issued to finance that improvement are issued more than 3 years after the original project was placed in service.

(ii) *Special rule for transmission and distribution facilities.* An improvement to transmission or distribution facilities that is not part of the original design of that property is not part of the same project as the original project if the issuer did not reasonably expect the need to make that improvement when it commenced construction of the original project and the construction, reconstruction, or acquisition of that improvement is mandated by the federal government or a state regulatory authority to accommodate requests for wheeling.

(6) *Replacement property.* For purposes of this section, property that replaces existing property of an output facility is treated as part of the same project as the replaced property unless—

(i) The need to replace the property was not reasonably expected on the issue date or the need to replace the property occurred more than 3 years before the issuer reasonably expected (determined on the issue date of the bonds financing the property) that it would need to replace the property; and

(ii) The bonds that finance (and refinance) the output facility have a weighted average maturity that is not greater than 120 percent of the reasonably expected economic life of the facility.

(c) *Example.* The application of the provisions of this section is illustrated by the following example:

Example. (i) Power Authority K, a political subdivision, intends to issue a single issue of tax-exempt bonds at par with a stated principal amount and sale proceeds of $500 million to finance the acquisition of an electric generating facility. No portion of the facility will be used for a private business use, except that L, an investor-owned utility, will purchase 10 percent of the output of the facility under a take contract and will pay 10 percent of the debt service on the bonds. The nonqualified amount with respect to the bonds is $50 million.

(ii) The maximum amount of tax-exempt bonds that may be issued for the acquisition of an interest in the facility in paragraph (i) of this *Example* is $465 million (that is, $450 million for the 90 percent of the facility that is governmentally owned and used plus a nonqualified amount of $15 million).

[Reg. § 1.141-8.]

☐ [T.D. 9016, 9-19-2002.]

→ *Caution: Temporary Reg. § 1.141-8T, below, was removed by T.D. 9016, effective November 22, 2002.*←

[Reg. § 1.141-8T]

§ 1.141-8T. $15 million limitation for output facilities (temporary).—(a) *In general*—(1) *General rule.* Section 141(b)(4) provides a special private activity bond limitation (the $15 million output limitation) for issues 5 percent or more of the proceeds of which are to be used to finance output facilities (other than a facility for the furnishing of water). Under this rule, an issue consists of private activity bonds under the private business tests of section 141(b)(1) and (2) if the nonqualified amount with respect to output facilities financed by the proceeds of the issue exceeds $15 million. The $15 million output limitation applies in addition to the private business tests of section 141(b)(1) and (2). Under section

→ *Caution: Temporary Reg. § 1.141-8T, below, was removed by T.D. 9016, effective November 22, 2002.*←

141(b)(4) and paragraph (a)(2) of this section, the $15 million output limitation is reduced in certain cases. Specifically, an issue meets the test in section 141(b)(4) if both of the following tests are met:

(i) More than $15 million of the proceeds of the issue to be used with respect to an output facility are to be used for a private business use. Investment proceeds are disregarded for this purpose if they are not allocated disproportionately to the private business use portion of the issue.

(ii) The payment of the principal of, or the interest on, more than $15 million of the sales proceeds of the portion of the issue used with respect to an output facility is (under the terms of the issue or any underlying arrangement) directly or indirectly—

(A) Secured by any interest in an output facility used or to be used for a private business use (or payments in respect of such an output facility); or

(B) To be derived from payments (whether or not to the issuer) in respect of an output facility used or to be used for a private business use.

(2) *Reduction in $15 million output limitation for outstanding issues*—(i) *General rule.* In determining whether an issue 5 percent or more of the proceeds of which are to be used with respect to an output facility consists of private activity bonds under the $15 million output limitation, the $15 million limitation on private business use and private security or payments is applied by taking into account the aggregate nonqualified amounts of any outstanding bonds of other issues 5 percent or more of the proceeds of which are or will be used with respect to that output facility or any other output facility that is part of the same project.

(ii) *Bonds taken into account.* For purposes of this paragraph (a)(2), in applying the $15 million output limitation to an issue (the later issue), a tax-exempt bond of another issue (the earlier issue) is taken into account if—

(A) That bond is outstanding on the issue date of the later issue;

(B) That bond will not be redeemed within 90 days of the issue date of the later issue in connection with the refunding of that bond by the later issue; and

(C) 5 percent or more of the sale proceeds of the earlier issue financed an output facility that is part of the same project as the output

facility that is financed by 5 percent or more of the sale proceeds of the later issue.

(3) *Benefits and burdens test applicable*—(i) *In general.* In applying the $15 million output limitation, the benefits and burdens test of § 1.141-7T applies, except that "$15 million" is substituted for "10 percent", or "5 percent" as appropriate.

(ii) *Earlier issues for the project.* If bonds of an earlier issue are outstanding and must be taken into account under paragraph (a)(2) of this section, the nonqualified amount for that earlier issue is multiplied by a fraction, the numerator of which is the adjusted issue price of the earlier issue as of the issue date of the later issue, and the denominator of which is the issue price of the earlier issue. Pre-issuance accrued interest as defined in § 1.148-1(b) is disregarded for this purpose.

(b) *Definition of project*—(1) *General rule.* For purposes of paragraph (a)(2) of this section, *project* has the meaning provided in this paragraph. Facilities that are functionally related and subordinate to a project are treated as part of that same project. Facilities having different purposes or serving different customer bases are not ordinarily part of the same project. For example, the following are generally not part of the same project—

(i) Generation and transmission facilities;

(ii) Separate facilities designed to serve wholesale customers and retail customers; and

(iii) A peaking unit and a baseload unit.

(2) *Separate ownership.* Except as otherwise provided in this paragraph (b)(2), facilities that are not owned by the same person are not part of the same project. If different governmental persons act in concert to finance a project, however (for example as participants in a joint powers authority), their interests are aggregated with respect to that project to determine whether the $15 million output limitation is met. In the case of undivided ownership interests in a single output facility, property that is not owned by different persons is treated as separate projects only if the separate interests are financed—

(i) With bonds of different issuers; and

(ii) Without a principal purpose of avoiding the limitation in this section.

(3) *Generating property*—(i) *Property on same site.* In the case of generation and related facilities, *project* means property located at the same site.

Reg. § 1.141-8T(a)(2)

→ *Caution: Temporary Reg. § 1.141-8T, below, was removed by T.D. 9016, effective November 22, 2002.←*

(ii) *Special rule for generating units.* Separate generating units are not part of the same project if one unit is reasonably expected, on the issue date of each issue that finances the units, to be placed in service more than 3 years before the other. Common facilities or property that will be functionally related to more than one generating unit must be allocated on a reasonable basis. If a generating unit already is constructed or is under construction (the first unit) and bonds are to be issued to finance an additional generating unit (the second unit), all costs for any common facilities paid or incurred before the earlier of the issue date of bonds to finance the second unit or the commencement of construction of the second unit are allocated to the first unit. At the time that bonds are issued to finance the second unit (or, if earlier, upon commencement of construction of that unit), any remaining costs of the common facilities may be allocated between the first and second units so that in the aggregate the allocation is reasonable.

(4) *Transmission.* In the case of transmission facilities, *project* means functionally related or contiguous property. Separate transmission facilities are not part of the same project if one facility is reasonably expected, on the issue date of each issue that finances the facilities, to be placed in service more than 2 years before the other.

(5) *Subsequent improvements*—(i) *In general.* An improvement to generating or transmission facilities that is not part of the original design of those facilities (the original project) is not part of the same project as the original project if the construction, reconstruction, or acquisition of that improvement commences more than 3 years after the original project was placed in service and the bonds issued to finance that improvement are issued more than 3 years after the original project was placed in service.

(ii) *Special rule for transmission facilities.* An improvement to transmission facilities that is not part of the original design of that property is not part of the same project as the original project if the issuer did not reasonably expect the need to make that improvement when it commenced construction of the original project and the construction, reconstruction, or acquisition of that improvement is mandated by the federal government or a state regulatory authority to accommodate requests for wheeling.

(6) *Replacement property.* For purposes of this section, property that replaces existing property of an output facility is treated as part of the same project as the replaced property unless—

(i) The need to replace the property was not reasonably expected on the issue date or the need to replace the property occurred more than 3 years before the issuer reasonably expected (determined on the issue date of the bonds financing the property) that it would need to replace the property; and

(ii) The bonds that finance (and refinance) the output facility have a weighted average maturity that is not greater than 120 percent of the reasonably expected economic life of the facility.

(c) *Example.* The application of the provisions of this section is illustrated by the following example:

Example. (i) Power Authority K, a political subdivision, intends to issue a single issue of tax-exempt bonds at par with a stated principal amount and sale proceeds of $500 million to finance the acquisition of an electric generating facility. No portion of the facility will be used for a private business use, except that L, an investor-owned utility, will purchase 10 percent of the output of the facility under a take contract and will pay 10 percent of the debt service on the bonds. The nonqualified amount with respect to the bonds is $50 million.

(ii) The maximum amount of tax-exempt bonds that may be issued for the acquisition of an interest in the facility in paragraph (i) of this *Example* is $465 million (that is, $450 million for the 90 percent of the facility that is governmentally owned and used plus a nonqualified amount of $15 million).

[Temporary Reg. § 1.141-8T.]

☐ [*T.D.* 8757, 1-21-98. *Amended by T.D.* 8941, 1-17-2001. *Removed by T.D.* 9016, 9-19-2002.]

[Reg. § 1.141-9]

§ 1.141-9. **Unrelated or disproportionate use test**—(a) *General rules*—(1) *Description of test.* Under section 141(b)(3) (the unrelated or disproportionate use test), an issue meets the private business tests if the amount of private business use and private security or payments attributable to unrelated or disproportionate private business use exceeds 5 percent of the proceeds of the issue. For this purpose, the private business use test is applied by taking into account only use that is not related to any government use of proceeds of the issue (unrelated use) and use that is related but disproportionate to any government use of those proceeds (disproportionate use).

(2) *Application of unrelated or disproportionate use test*—(i) *Order of application.* The unre-

25,334   Tax Exempt. Requirements: State/Local Bonds

See p. 20,601 for regulations not amended to reflect law changes

lated or disproportionate use test is applied by first determining whether a private business use is related to a government use. Next, private business use that relates to a government use is examined to determine whether it is disproportionate to that government use.

(ii) *Aggregation of unrelated and disproportionate use.* All the unrelated use and disproportionate use financed with the proceeds of an issue are aggregated to determine compliance with the unrelated or disproportionate use test. The amount of permissible unrelated and disproportionate private business use is not reduced by the amount of private business use financed with the proceeds of an issue that is neither unrelated use nor disproportionate use.

(iii) *Deliberate actions.* A deliberate action that occurs after the issue date does not result in unrelated or disproportionate use if the issue meets the conditions of § 1.141-12(a).

(b) *Unrelated use*—(1) *In general.* Whether a private business use is related to a government use financed with the proceeds of an issue is determined on a case-by-case basis, emphasizing the operational relationship between the government use and the private business use. In general, a facility that is used for a related private business use must be located within, or adjacent to, the governmentally used facility.

(2) *Use for the same purpose as government use.* Use of a facility by a nongovernmental person for the same purpose as use by a governmental person is not treated as unrelated use if the government use is not insignificant. Similarly, a use of a facility in the same manner both for private business use that is related use and private business use that is unrelated use does not result in unrelated use if the related use is not insignificant. For example, a privately owned pharmacy in a governmentally owned hospital does not ordinarily result in unrelated use solely because the pharmacy also serves individuals not using the hospital. In addition, use of parking spaces in a garage by a nongovernmental person is not treated as unrelated use if more than an insignificant portion of the parking spaces are used for a government use (or a private business use that is related to a government use), even though the use by the nongovernmental person is not directly related to that other use.

(c) *Disproportionate use*—(1) *Definition of disproportionate use.* A private business use is disproportionate to a related government use only to the extent that the amount of proceeds used for that private business use exceeds the amount of proceeds used for the related government use. For example, a private use of $100 of proceeds that is

related to a government use of $70 of proceeds results in $30 of disproportionate use.

(2) *Aggregation of related uses.* If two or more private business uses of the proceeds of an issue relate to a single government use of those proceeds, those private business uses are aggregated to apply the disproportionate use test.

(3) *Allocation rule.* If a private business use relates to more than a single use of the proceeds of the issue (for example, two or more government uses of the proceeds of the issue or a government use and a private use), the amount of any disproportionate use may be determined by—

(i) Reasonably allocating the proceeds used for the private business use among the related uses;

(ii) Aggregating government uses that are directly related to each other; or

(iii) Allocating the private business use to the government use to which it is primarily related.

(d) *Maximum use taken into account.* The determination of the amount of unrelated use or disproportionate use of a facility is based on the maximum amount of reasonably expected government use of a facility during the measurement period. Thus, no unrelated use or disproportionate use arises solely because a facility initially has excess capacity that is to be used by a nongovernmental person if the facility will be completely used by the issuer during the term of the issue for more than an insignificant period.

(e) *Examples.* The following examples illustrate the application of this section:

Example 1. School and remote cafeteria. County X issues bonds with proceeds of $20 million and uses $18.1 million of the proceeds for construction of a new school building and $1.9 million of the proceeds for construction of a privately operated cafeteria in its administrative office building, which is located at a remote site. The bonds are secured, in part, by the cafeteria. The $1.9 million of proceeds is unrelated to the government use (that is, school construction) financed with the bonds and exceeds 5 percent of $20 million. Thus, the issue meets the private business tests.

Example 2. Public safety building and courthouse. City Y issues bonds with proceeds of $50 million for construction of a new public safety building ($32 million) and for improvements to an existing courthouse ($15 million). Y uses $3 million of the bond proceeds for renovations to an existing privately operated cafeteria located in the courthouse. The bonds are secured, in part, by the cafeteria. Y's use of the $3 million for the

Tax Exempt. Requirements: State/Local Bonds   **25,335**

See p. 20,601 for regulations not amended to reflect law changes

privately operated cafeteria does not meet the unrelated or disproportionate use test because these expenditures are neither unrelated use nor disproportionate use.

Example 3. Unrelated garage. City Y issues bonds with proceeds of $50 million for construction of a new public safety building ($30.5 million) and for improvements to an existing courthouse ($15 million). Y uses $3 million of the bond proceeds for renovations to an existing privately operated cafeteria located in the courthouse. The bonds are secured, in part, by the cafeteria. Y also uses $1.5 million of the proceeds to construct a privately operated parking garage adjacent to a private office building. The private business use of the parking garage is unrelated to any government use of proceeds of the issue. Since the proceeds used for unrelated uses and disproportionate uses do not exceed 5 percent of the proceeds, the unrelated or disproportionate use test is not met.

Example 4. Disproportionate use of garage. County Z issues bonds with proceeds of $20 million for construction of a hospital with no private business use ($17 million); renovation of an office building with no private business use ($1 million); and construction of a garage that is entirely used for a private business use ($2 million). The use of the garage is related to the use of the office building but not to the use of the hospital. The private business use of the garage results in $1 million of disproportionate use because the proceeds used for the garage ($2 million) exceed the proceeds used for the related government use ($1 million). The bonds are not private activity bonds, however, because the disproportionate use does not exceed 5 percent of the proceeds of the issue.

Example 5. Bonds for multiple projects. (i) County W issues bonds with proceeds of $80 million for the following purposes: (1) $72 million to construct a County-owned and operated waste incinerator; (2) $1 million for a County-owned and operated facility for the temporary storage of hazardous waste prior to final disposal; (3) $1 million to construct a privately owned recycling facility located at a remote site; and (4) $6 million to build a garage adjacent to the County-owned incinerator that will be leased to Company T to store and repair trucks that it owns and uses to haul County W refuse. Company T uses 75 percent of its trucks to haul materials to the incinerator and the remaining 25 percent of its trucks to haul materials to the temporary storage facility.

(ii) The $1 million of proceeds used for the recycling facility is used for an unrelated use. The garage is related use. In addition, 75 percent of the use of the $6 million of proceeds used for the garage is allocable to the government use of proceeds at the incinerator. The remaining 25 percent of the proceeds used for the garage ($1.5 million) relates to the government use of proceeds at the temporary storage facility. Thus, this portion of the proceeds used for the garage exceeds the proceeds used for the temporary storage facility by $0.5 million and this excess is disproportionate use (but not unrelated use). Thus, the aggregate amount of unrelated use and disproportionate use financed with the proceeds of the issue is $1.5 million. Alternatively, under paragraph (c)(3)(iii) of this section, the entire garage may be treated as related to the government use of the incinerator and, under that allocation, the garage is not disproportionate use. In either event, section 141(b)(3) limits the aggregate unrelated use and disproportionate use to $4 million. Therefore, the bonds are not private activity bonds under this section.

[Reg § 1.141-9.]

☐ [*T.D.* 8712, 1-10-97.]

[Reg. § 1.141-10]

§ 1.141-10. Coordination with volume cap.— [Reserved.]

☐ [*T.D.* 8712, 1-10-97.]

[Reg. § 1.141-11]

§ 1.141-11. Acquisition of nongovernmental output property.—[Reserved.]

☐ [*T.D.* 8712, 1-10-97.]

[Reg. § 1.141-12]

§ 1.141-12. Remedial actions.—(a) *Conditions to making remedial action.* An action that causes an issue to meet the private business tests or the private loan financing test is not treated as a deliberate action if the issuer takes a remedial action described in paragraph (d), (e), or (f) of this section with respect to the nonqualified bonds and if all of the requirements in paragraphs (a)(1) through (5) of this section are met.

(1) *Reasonable expectations test met.* The issuer reasonably expected on the issue date that the issue would meet neither the private business tests nor the private loan financing test for the entire term of the bonds. For this purpose, if the issuer reasonably expected on the issue date to take a deliberate action prior to the final maturity date of the issue that would cause either the private business tests or the private loan financing test to be met, the term of the bonds for this purpose may be determined by taking into account a redemption provision if the provisions of § 1.141-2(d)(2)(ii)(A) through (C) are met.

25,336   Tax Exempt. Requirements: State/Local Bonds

See p. 20,601 for regulations not amended to reflect law changes

(2) *Maturity not unreasonably long.* The term of the issue must not be longer than is reasonably necessary for the governmental purposes of the issue (within the meaning of § 1.148-1(c)(4)). Thus, this requirement is met if the weighted average maturity of the bonds of the issue is not greater than 120 percent of the average reasonably expected economic life of the property financed with the proceeds of the issue as of the issue date.

(3) *Fair market value consideration.* Except as provided in paragraph (f) of this section, the terms of any arrangement that results in satisfaction of either the private business tests or the private loan financing test are bona fide and arm's-length, and the new user pays fair market value for the use of the financed property. Thus, for example, fair market value may be determined in a manner that takes into account restrictions on the use of the financed property that serve a bona fide governmental purpose.

(4) *Disposition proceeds treated as gross proceeds for arbitrage purposes.* The issuer must treat any disposition proceeds as gross proceeds for purposes of section 148. For purposes of eligibility for temporary periods under section 148(c) and exemptions from the requirement of section 148(f) the issuer may treat the date of receipt of the disposition proceeds as the issue date of the bonds and disregard the receipt of disposition proceeds for exemptions based on expenditure of proceeds under § 1.148-7 that were met before the receipt of the disposition proceeds.

(5) *Proceeds expended on a governmental purpose.* Except for a remedial action under paragraph (d) of this section, the proceeds of the issue that are affected by the deliberate action must have been expended on a governmental purpose before the date of the deliberate action.

(b) *Effect of a remedial action*—(1) *In general.* The effect of a remedial action is to cure use of proceeds that causes the private business use test or the private loan financing test to be met. A remedial action does not affect application of the private security or payment test.

(2) *Effect on bonds that have been advance refunded.* If proceeds of an issue were used to advance refund another bond, a remedial action taken with respect to the refunding bond proportionately reduces the amount of proceeds of the advance refunded bond that is taken into account under the private business use test or the private loan financing test.

(c) *Disposition proceeds*—(1) *Definition.* Disposition proceeds are any amounts (including property, such as an agreement to provide services) derived from the sale, exchange, or other disposition (disposition) of property (other than investments) financed with the proceeds of an issue.

(2) *Allocating disposition proceeds to an issue.* In general, if the requirements of paragraph (a) of this section are met, after the date of the disposition, the proceeds of the issue allocable to the transferred property are treated as financing the disposition proceeds rather than the transferred property. If a disposition is made pursuant to an installment sale, the proceeds of the issue continue to be allocated to the transferred property. If an issue does not meet the requirements for remedial action in paragraph (a) of this section or the issuer does not take an appropriate remedial action, the proceeds of the issue are allocable to either the transferred property or the disposition proceeds, whichever allocation produces the greater amount of private business use and private security or payments.

(3) *Allocating disposition proceeds to different sources of funding.* If property has been financed by different sources of funding, for purposes of this section, the disposition proceeds from that property are first allocated to the outstanding bonds that financed that property in proportion to the principal amounts of those outstanding bonds. In no event may disposition proceeds be allocated to bonds that are no longer outstanding or to a source of funding not derived from a borrowing (such as revenues of the issuer) if the disposition proceeds are not greater than the total principal amounts of the outstanding bonds that are allocable to that property. For purposes of this paragraph (c)(3), principal amount has the same meaning as in § 1.148-9(b)(2) and outstanding bonds do not include advance refunded bonds.

(d) *Redemption or defeasance of nonqualified bonds*—(1) *In general.* The requirements of this paragraph (d) are met if all of the nonqualified bonds of the issue are redeemed. Proceeds of tax-exempt bonds must not be used for this purpose, unless the tax-exempt bonds are qualified bonds, taking into account the purchaser's use of the facility. If the bonds are not redeemed within 90 days of the date of the deliberate action, a defeasance escrow must be established for those bonds within 90 days of the deliberate action.

(2) *Special rule for dispositions for cash.* If the consideration for the disposition of financed property is exclusively cash, the requirements of this paragraph (d) are met if the disposition proceeds are used to redeem a pro rata portion of the nonqualified bonds at the earliest call date after the deliberate action. If the bonds are not redeemed within 90 days of the date of the deliberate action, the disposition proceeds must be used

Reg. § 1.141-12(a)(2)

Tax Exempt. Requirements: State/Local Bonds   25,337

See p. 20,601 for regulations not amended to reflect law changes

to establish a defeasance escrow for those bonds within 90 days of the deliberate action.

(3) *Notice of defeasance.* The issuer must provide written notice to the Commissioner of the establishment of the defeasance escrow within 90 days of the date the defeasance escrow is established.

(4) *Special limitation.* The establishment of a defeasance escrow does not satisfy the requirements of this paragraph (d) if the period between the issue date and the first call date of the bonds is more than 10 1/2 years.

(5) *Defeasance escrow defined.* A defeasance escrow is an irrevocable escrow established to redeem bonds on their earliest call date in an amount that, together with investment earnings, is sufficient to pay all the principal of, and interest and call premium on, bonds from the date the escrow is established to the earliest call date. The escrow may not be invested in higher yielding investments or in any investment under which the obligor is a user of the proceeds of the bonds.

(e) *Alternative use of disposition proceeds*—(1) *In general.* The requirements of this paragraph (e) are met if—

(i) The deliberate action is a disposition for which the consideration is exclusively cash;

(ii) The issuer reasonably expects to expend the disposition proceeds within two years of the date of the deliberate action;

(iii) The disposition proceeds are treated as proceeds for purposes of section 141 and are used in a manner that does not cause the issue to meet either the private business tests or the private loan financing test, and the issuer does not take any action subsequent to the date of the deliberate action to cause either of these tests to be met; and

(iv) If the issuer does not use all of the disposition proceeds for an alternative use described in paragraph (e)(1)(iii) of this section, the issuer uses those remaining disposition proceeds for a remedial action that meets paragraph (d) of this section.

(2) *Special rule for use by 501(c)(3) organizations.* If the disposition proceeds are to be used by a 501(c)(3) organization, the nonqualified bonds must in addition be treated as reissued for purposes of sections 141, 145, 147, 149, and 150 and, under this treatment, satisfy all of the applicable requirements for qualified 501(c)(3) bonds. Thus, beginning on the date of the deliberate action, nonqualified bonds that satisfy these requirements must be treated as qualified 501(c)(3) bonds for all purposes, including sections 145(b) and 150(b).

(f) *Alternative use of facility.* The requirements of this paragraph (f) are met if—

(1) The facility with respect to which the deliberate action occurs is used in an alternative manner (for example, used for a qualifying purpose by a nongovernmental person or used by a 501(c)(3) organization rather than a governmental person);

(2) The nonqualified bonds are treated as reissued, as of the date of the deliberate action, for purposes of sections 55 through 59 and 141, 142, 144, 145, 146, 147, 149 and 150, and under this treatment, the nonqualified bonds satisfy all the applicable requirements for qualified bonds throughout the remaining term of the nonqualified bonds;

(3) The deliberate action does not involve a disposition to a purchaser that finances the acquisition with proceeds of another issue of tax-exempt bonds; and

(4) Any disposition proceeds other than those arising from an agreement to provide services (including disposition proceeds from an installment sale) resulting from the deliberate action are used to pay the debt service on the bonds on the next available payment date or, within 90 days of receipt, are deposited into an escrow that is restricted to the yield on the bonds to pay the debt service on the bonds on the next available payment date.

(g) *Rules for deemed reissuance.* For purposes of determining whether bonds that are treated as reissued under paragraphs (e) and (f) of this section are qualified bonds—

(1) The provisions of the Code and regulations thereunder in effect as of the date of the deliberate action apply; and

(2) For purposes of paragraph (f) of this section, section 147(d) (relating to the acquisition of existing property) does not apply.

(h) *Authority of Commissioner to provide for additional remedial actions.* The Commissioner may, by publication in the Federal Register or the Internal Revenue Bulletin, provide additional remedial actions, including making a remedial payment to the United States, under which a subsequent action will not be treated as a deliberate action for purposes of § 1.141-2.

(i) *Effect of remedial action on continuing compliance.* Solely for purposes of determining whether deliberate actions that are taken after a remedial action cause an issue to meet the private business tests or the private loan financing test—

(1) If a remedial action is taken under paragraph (d), (e), or (f) of this section, the private business use or private loans resulting from the

Reg. § 1.141-12(i)(1)

deliberate action are not taken into account for purposes of determining whether the bonds are private activity bonds; and

(2) After a remedial action is taken, the amount of disposition proceeds is treated as equal to the proceeds of the issue that had been allocable to the transferred property immediately prior to the disposition. See paragraph (k) of this section, *Example 5.*

(j) *Nonqualified bonds*—(1) *Amount of nonqualified bonds.* The percentage of outstanding bonds that are nonqualified bonds equals the highest percentage of private business use in any 1-year period commencing with the deliberate action.

(2) *Allocation of nonqualified bonds.* Allocations to nonqualified bonds must be made on a pro rata basis, except that, for purposes of paragraph (d) of this section (relating to redemption or defeasance), an issuer may treat bonds with longer maturities (determined on a bond-by-bond basis) as the nonqualified bonds.

(k) *Examples.* The following examples illustrate the application of this section:

Example 1. Disposition proceeds less than outstanding bonds used to retire bonds. On June 1, 1997, City C issues 30-year bonds with an issue price of $10 million to finance the construction of a hospital building. The bonds have a weighted average maturity that does not exceed 120 percent of the reasonably expected economic life of the building. On the issue date, C reasonably expects that it will be the only user of the building for the entire term of the bonds. Six years after the issue date, C sells the building to Corporation P for $5 million. The sale price is the fair market value of the building, as verified by an independent appraiser. C uses all of the $5 million disposition proceeds to immediately retire a pro rata portion of the bonds. The sale does not cause the bonds to be private activity bonds because C has taken a remedial action described in paragraph (d) of this section so that P is not treated as a private business user of bond proceeds.

Example 2. Lease to nongovernmental person. The facts are the same as in *Example 1,* except that instead of selling the building, C, 6 years after the issue date, leases the building to P for 7 years and uses other funds to redeem all of the $10 million outstanding bonds within 90 days of the deliberate act. The bonds are not treated as private activity bonds because C has taken the remedial action described in paragraph (d) of this section.

Example 3. Sale for less than fair market value. The facts are the same as in *Example 1,* except that the fair market value of the building at the

time of the sale to P is $6 million. Because the transfer was for less than fair market value, the bonds are ineligible for the remedial actions under this section. The bonds are private activity bonds because P is treated as a user of all of the proceeds and P makes a payment ($6 million) for this use that is greater than 10 percent of the debt service on the bonds, on a present value basis.

Example 4. Fair market value determined taking into account governmental restrictions. The facts are the same as in *Example 1,* except that the building was used by C only for hospital purposes and C determines to sell the building subject to a restriction that it be used only for hospital purposes. After conducting a public bidding procedure as required by state law, the best price that C is able to obtain for the building subject to this restriction is $4.5 million from P. C uses all of the $4.5 million disposition proceeds to immediately retire a pro rata portion of the bonds. The sale does not cause the bonds to be private activity bonds because C has taken a remedial action described in paragraph (d) of this section so that P is not treated as a private business user of bond proceeds.

Example 5. Alternative use of disposition proceeds. The facts are the same as in *Example 1,* except that C reasonably expects on the date of the deliberate action to use the $5 million disposition proceeds for another governmental purpose (construction of governmentally owned roads) within two years of receipt, rather than using the $5 million to redeem outstanding bonds. C treats these disposition proceeds as gross proceeds for purposes of section 148. The bonds are not private activity bonds because C has taken a remedial action described in paragraph (e) of this section. After the date of the deliberate action, the proceeds of all of the outstanding bonds are treated as used for the construction of the roads, even though only $5 million of disposition proceeds was actually used for the roads.

Example 6. Alternative use of financed property. The facts are the same as in *Example 1,* except that C determines to lease the hospital building to Q, an organization described in section 501(c)(3), for a term of 10 years rather than to sell the building to P. In order to induce Q to provide hospital services, C agrees to lease payments that are less than fair market value. Before entering into the lease, an applicable elected representative of C approves the lease after a noticed public hearing. As of the date of the deliberate action, the issue meets all the requirements for qualified 501(c)(3) bonds, treating the bonds as reissued on that date. For example, the issue meets the two percent restriction on use of proceeds of finance issuance costs of section 147(g) because the issue pays no costs of issuance from disposition proceeds in connection with the deemed reissuance. C and Q treat the bonds as qualified 501(c)(3) bonds for all purposes commencing with the date of the deliberate action. The bonds are treated as qualified 501(c)(3) bonds commencing with the date of the deliberate action.

Example 7. Deliberate action before proceeds are expended on a governmental purpose. County J issues bonds with proceeds of $10 million that can be used only to finance a correctional facility. On the issue date of the bonds, J reasonably expects that it will be the sole user of the bonds for the useful life of the facility. The bonds have a weighted average maturity that does not exceed 120 percent of the reasonably expected economic life of the facility. After the issue date of the bonds, but before the facility is placed in service, J enters into a contract with the federal government pursuant to which the federal government will make a fair market value, lump sum payment equal to 25 percent of the cost of the facility. In exchange for this payment, J provides the federal government with priority rights to use of 25 percent of the facility. J uses the payment received from the federal government to defease the non-qualified bonds. The agreement does not cause the bonds to be private activity bonds because J has taken a remedial action described in paragraph (d) of this section. See paragraph (a)(5) of this section.

Example 8. Compliance after remedial action. In 1997, City G issues bonds with proceeds of $10 million to finance a courthouse. The bonds have a weighted average maturity that does not exceed 120 percent of the reasonably expected economic life of the courthouse. G uses $1 million of the proceeds for a private business use and more than 10 percent of the debt service on the issue is secured by private security or payments. G later sells one-half of the courthouse property to a non-governmental person for cash. G immediately redeems 60 percent of the outstanding bonds. This percentage of outstanding bonds is based on the highest private business use of the courthouse in any 1-year period commencing with the deliberate action. For purposes of subsequently applying section 141 to the issue, G may continue to use all of the proceeds of the outstanding bonds in the same manner (that is, for both the courthouse and the existing private business use) without causing the issue to meet the private business use test. The issue, however, continues to meet the private security or payment test. The result would be the same if D, instead of redeeming the bonds, established a defeasance escrow for those bonds, pro-

vided that the requirement of paragraph (d)(4) of this section was met.

[Reg. § 1.141-12.]

☐ [*T.D.* 8712, 1-10-97.]

[Reg. § 1.141-13]

§ 1.141-13. Refunding issues.—[Reserved.]

☐ [*T.D.* 8712, 1-10-97.]

[Reg. § 1.141-14]

§ 1.141-14. Anti-abuse rules.—(a) *Authority of Commissioner to reflect substance of transactions.* If an issuer enters into a transaction or series of transactions with respect to one or more issues with a principal purpose of transferring to nongovernmental persons (other than as members of the general public) significant benefits of tax-exempt financing in a manner that is inconsistent with the purposes of section 141, the Commissioner may take any action to reflect the substance of the transaction or series of transactions, including—

(1) Treating separate issues as a single issue for purposes of the private activity bond tests;

(2) Reallocating proceeds to expenditures, property, use, or bonds;

(3) Reallocating payments to use or proceeds;

(4) Measuring private business use on a basis that reasonably reflects the economic benefit in a manner different than as provided in § 1.141-3(g); and

(5) Measuring private payments or security on a basis that reasonably reflects the economic substance in a manner different than as provided in § 1.141-4.

(b) *Examples.* The following examples illustrate the application of this section:

Example 1. Reallocating proceeds to indirect use. City C issues bonds with proceeds of $20 million for the stated purpose of financing improvements to roads that it owns. As a part of the same plan of financing, however, C also agrees to make a loan of $7 million to Corporation M from its general revenues that it otherwise would have used for the road improvements. The interest rate of the loan corresponds to the interest rate on a portion of the issue. A principal purpose of the financing arrangement is to transfer to M significant benefits of the tax-exempt financing. Although C actually allocates all of the proceeds of the bonds to the road improvements, the Commissioner may reallocate a portion of the proceeds of the bonds to the loan to M because a principal purpose of the financing arrangement is to transfer to M significant benefits of tax-exempt financing in a manner that is inconsistent with the

Reg. § 1.141-14(b)

25,340   **Tax Exempt. Requirements: State/Local Bonds**

See p. 20,601 for regulations not amended to reflect law changes

purposes of section 141. The bonds are private activity bonds because the issue meets the private loan financing test. The bonds also meet the private business tests. See also §§ 1.141-3(a)(2), 1.141-4(a)(1), and 1.141-5(a), under which indirect use of proceeds and payments are taken into account.

Example 2. Taking into account use of amounts derived from proceeds that would be otherwise disregarded. County B issues bonds with proceeds of $10 million to finance the purchase of land. On the issue date, B reasonably expects that it will be the sole user of the land. Subsequently, the federal government acquires the land for $3 million in a condemnation action. B uses this amount to make a loan to Corporation M. In addition, the interest rate on the loan reflects the tax-exempt interest rate on the bonds and thus is substantially less than a current market rate. A principal purpose of the arrangement is to transfer to M significant benefits of the tax-exempt financing. Although the condemnation action is not a deliberate action, the Commissioner may treat the condemnation proceeds as proceeds of the issue because a principal purpose of the arrangement is to transfer to M significant benefits of tax-exempt financing in a manner inconsistent with the purposes of section 141. The bonds are private activity bonds.

Example 3. Measuring private business use on an alternative basis. City F issues bonds with a 30-year term to finance the acquisition of an industrial building having a remaining reasonably expected useful economic life of more than 30 years. On the issue date, F leases the building to Corporation G for 3 years. F reasonably expects that it will be the sole user of the building for the remaining term of the bonds. Because of the local market conditions, it is reasonably expected that the fair rental value of the industrial building will be significantly greater during the early years of the term of the bonds than in the later years. The annual rental payments are significantly less than fair market value, reflecting the interest rate on the bonds. The present value of these rental payments (net of operation and maintenance expenses) as of the issue date, however, is approximately 25 percent of the present value of debt service on the issue. Under § 1.141-3, the issue does not meet the private business tests, because only 10 percent of the proceeds are used in a trade or business by a nongovernmental person. A principal purpose of the issue is to transfer to G significant benefits of tax-exempt financing in a manner inconsistent with the purposes of section 141. The method of measuring private business use over the reasonably expected useful economic life of financed property is for the administrative convenience of issuers of state and local bonds. In cases where this method is used in a manner inconsistent with the purposes of section 141, the Commissioner may measure private business use on another basis that reasonably reflects economic benefit, such as in this case on an annual basis. If the Commissioner measures private business use on an annual basis, the bonds are private activity bonds because the private payment test is met and more than 10 percent of the proceeds are used in a trade or business by a nongovernmental person.

Example 4. Treating separate issues as a single issue. City D enters into a development agreement with Corporation T to induce T to locate its headquarters within D's city limits. Pursuant to the development agreement, in 1997 D will issue $20 million of its general obligation bonds (the 1997 bonds) to purchase land that it will grant to T. The development agreement also provides that, in 1998, D will issue $20 million of its tax increment bonds (the 1998 bonds), secured solely by the increase in property taxes in a special taxing district. Substantially all of the property within the special taxing district is owned by T or D. T will separately enter into an agreement to guarantee the payment of tax increment to D in an amount sufficient to retire the 1998 bonds. The proceeds of the 1998 bonds will be used to finance improvements owned and operated by D that will not give rise to private business use. Treated separately, the 1997 issue meets the private business use test, but not the private security or payment test; the 1998 issue meets the private security or payment test, but not the private business use test. A principal purpose of the financing plan including the two issues is to transfer significant benefits of tax-exempt financing to T for its headquarters. Thus, the 1997 issue and the 1998 issue may be treated by the Commissioner as a single issue for purposes of applying the private activity bond tests. Accordingly, the bonds of both the 1997 issue and the 1998 issue may be treated as private activity bonds.

Example 5. Reallocating proceeds. City E acquires an electric generating facility with a useful economic life of more than 40 years and enters into a 30-year take or pay contract to sell 30 percent of the available output to investor-owned utility M. E plans to use the remaining 70 percent of available output for its own governmental purposes. To finance the entire cost of the facility, E issues $30 million of its series A taxable bonds at taxable interest rates and $70 million series B bonds, which purport to be tax-exempt bonds, at tax-exempt interest rates. E allocates all of M's private business use to the proceeds of the series A bonds and all of its own government use to the proceeds of the series B bonds. The series A bonds

Tax Exempt. Requirements: State/Local Bonds 25,341

See p. 20,601 for regulations not amended to reflect law changes

have a weighted average maturity of 15 years, while the series B bonds have a weighted average maturity of 26 years. M's payments under the take or pay contract are expressly determined by reference to 30 percent of M's total costs (that is, the sum of the debt service required to be paid on both the series A and the series B bonds and all other operating costs). The allocation of all of M's private business use to the series A bonds does not reflect economic substance because the series of transactions transfers to M significant benefits of the tax-exempt interest rates paid on the series B bonds. A principal purpose of the financing arrangement is to transfer to M significant benefits of the tax-exempt financing. Accordingly, the Commissioner may allocate M's private business use on a pro rata basis to both the series B bonds as well as the series A bonds, in which case the series B bonds are private activity bonds.

Example 6. Allocations respected. The facts are the same as in *Example 5*, except that the debt service component of M's payments under the take or pay contract is based exclusively on the amounts necessary to pay the debt service on the taxable series A bonds. E's allocation of all of M's private business use to the series A bonds is respected because the series of transactions does not actually transfer benefits of tax-exempt interest rates to M. Accordingly, the series B bonds are not private activity bonds. The result would be the same if M's payments under the take or pay contract were based exclusively on fair market value pricing, rather than the tax-exempt interest rates on E's bonds. The result also would be the same if the series A bonds and the series B bonds had substantially equivalent weighted average maturities and E and M had entered into a customary contract providing for payments based on a ratable share of total debt service. E would not be treated by the Commissioner in any of these cases as entering into the contract with a principal purpose of transferring the benefits of tax-exempt financing to M in a manner inconsistent with the purposes of section 141.

[Reg. § 1.141-14.]

☐ [*T.D.* 8712, 1-10-97.]

[Reg. § 1.141-15]

§ 1.141-15. Effective dates.—(a) *Scope.* The effective dates of this section apply for purposes of §§ 1.141-1 through 1.141-6(a), 1.141-7 through 1.141-14, 1.145-1 through 1.145-2, 1.150-1(a)(3) and the definition of bond documents contained in § 1.150-1(b).

(b) *Effective dates—*(1) *In general.* Except as otherwise provided in this section, §§ 1.141-1 through 1.141-6(a), 1.141-9 through 1.141-14,

1.145-1 through 1.145-2, 1.150-1(a)(3) and the definition of bond documents contained in § 1.150-1(b) apply to bonds issued on or after May 16, 1997, that are subject to section 1301 of the Tax Reform Act of 1986 (100 Stat. 2602).

(2) *Certain short-term arrangements.* The provisions of § 1.141-3 that refer to arrangements for 200 days, 100 days, or 50 days apply to any bond sold on or after November 20, 2001 and may be applied to any bond outstanding on November 20, 2001 to which § 1.141-3 applies.

(c) *Refunding bonds.* Sections 1.141-1 through 1.141-6(a), 1.141-9 through 1.141-14, 1.145-1 through 1.145-2, 1.150-1(a)(3) and the definition of bond documents contained in § 1.150-1(b) do not apply to any bonds issued on or after May 16, 1997, to refund a bond to which those sections do not apply unless—

(1) The refunding bonds are subject to section 1301 of the Tax Reform Act of 1986 (100 Stat. 2602); and

(2)(i) The weighted average maturity of the refunding bonds is longer than—

(A) The weighted average maturity of the refunded bonds; or

(B) In the case of a short-term obligation that the issuer reasonably expects to refund with a long-term financing (such as a bond anticipation note), 120 percent of the weighted average reasonably expected economic life of the facilities financed; or

(ii) A principal purpose for the issuance of the refunding bonds is to make one or more new conduit loans.

(d) *Permissive application of regulations.* Except as provided in paragraph (e) of this section, §§ 1.141-1 through 1.141-6(a), 1.141-9 through 1.141-14, 1.145-1 through 1.145-2, 1.150-1(a)(3) and the definition of bond documents contained in § 1.150-1(b) may be applied in whole, but not in part, to actions taken before February 23, 1998, with respect to—

(1) Bonds that are outstanding on May 16, 1997, and subject to section 141; or

(2) Refunding bonds issued on or after May 16, 1997 that are subject to section 141.

(e) *Permissive application of certain sections.* The following sections may each be applied to any bonds—

(1) Section 1.141-3(b)(4);

(2) Section 1.141-3(b)(6); and

(3) Section 1.141-12.

(f) *Effective dates for certain regulations relating to output facilities—*(1) *General rule.* Except as otherwise provided in this section, §§ 1.141-7

25,342   **Tax Exempt. Requirements: State/Local Bonds**

See p. 20,601 for regulations not amended to reflect law changes

and 1.141-8 apply to bonds sold on or after November 22, 2002, that are subject to section 1301 of the Tax Reform Act of 1986 (100 Stat. 2602).

(2) *Transition rule for requirements contracts.* For bonds otherwise subject to §§ 1.141-7 and 1.141-8, § 1.141-7(c)(3) applies to output contracts entered into on or after September 19, 2002. An output contract is treated as entered into on or after that date if it is amended on or after that date, but only if the amendment results in a change in the parties to the contract or increases the amount of requirements covered by the contract by reason of an extension of the contract term or a change in the method for determining such requirements. For purposes of this paragraph (f)(2)—

(i) The extension of the term of a contract causes the contract to be treated as entered into on the first day of the additional term;

(ii) The exercise by a party of a legally enforceable right that was provided under a contract before September 19, 2002, on terms that were fixed and determinable before such date, is not treated as an amendment of the contract. For example, the exercise by a purchaser after September 19, 2002 of a renewal option that was provided under a contract before that date, on terms identical to the original contract, is not treated as an amendment of the contract; and

(iii) An amendment that increases the amount of requirements covered by the contract by reason of a change in the method for determining such requirements is treated as a separate contract that is entered into as of the effective date of the amendment, but only with respect to the increased output to be provided under the contract.

(g) *Refunding bonds for output facilities.* Except as otherwise provided in paragraph (h) or (i) of this section, §§ 1.141-7 and 1.141-8 do not

apply to any bonds sold on or after November 22, 2002, to refund a bond to which §§ 1.141-7 and 1.141-8 do not apply unless—

(1) The refunding bonds are subject to section 1301 of the Tax Reform Act of 1986 (100 Stat. 2602); and

(2)(i) The weighted average maturity of the refunding bonds is longer than—

(A) The weighted average maturity of the refunded bonds; or

(B) In the case of a short-term obligation that the issuer reasonably expects to refund with a long-term financing (such as a bond anticipation note), 120 percent of the weighted average reasonably expected economic life of the facilities financed; or

(ii) A principal purpose for the issuance of the refunding bonds is to make one or more new conduit loans.

(h) *Permissive retroactive application.* Except as provided in paragraphs (d), (e) or (i) of this section, §§ 1.141-1 through 1.141-6(a), 1.141-7 through 1.141-14, 1.145-1 through 1.145-2, 1.150-1(a)(3) and the definition of bond documents contained in § 1.150-1(b) may be applied by issuers in whole, but not in part, to—

(1) Outstanding bonds that are sold before November 22, 2002, and subject to section 141; or

(2) Refunding bonds that are sold on or after November 22, 2002, and subject to section 141.

(i) *Permissive application of certain regulations relating to output facilities.* Issuers may apply §§ 1.141-7(f)(3) and 1.141-7(g) to any bonds. [Reg. § 1.141-15.]

☐ [*T.D. 8712, 1-10-97. Amended by T.D. 8757, 1-21-98; T.D. 8941, 1-17-2001; T.D. 8967, 11-19-2001 and T.D. 9016, 9-19-2002.*]

→ *Caution: Temporary Reg. § 1.141-15T, below, was removed by T.D. 9016, effective November 22, 2002.*←

[Reg. § 1.141-15T]

§ 1.141-15T. Effective dates (temporary).— (a) through (e) [Reserved]. For further guidance see § 1.141-15.

(f) *Effective dates for certain regulations relating to output facilities*—(1) *General rule.* Except as otherwise provided in this section, §§ 1.141-7T and 1.141-8T apply to bonds sold on or after January 19, 2001, that are subject to section 1301 of the Tax Reform Act of 1986 (100 Stat. 2602).

(2) *Transition rule for requirements contracts.* For bonds otherwise subject to §§ 1.141-7T and 1.141-8T, § 1.141-7T(c)(4) applies to output

contracts entered into on or after February 23, 1998. An output contract is treated as entered into on or after that date if its term is extended, the parties to the contract change, or other material terms are amended on or after that date. For purposes of this paragraph (f)(2)—

(i) The extension of the term of a contract causes the contract to be treated as entered into on the first day of the additional term;

(ii) The exercise by a party of a legally enforceable right that was provided under a contract before February 23, 1998, on terms that were fixed and determinable before such date, is not treated as an amendment of the contract. For

Tax Exempt. Requirements: State/Local Bonds 25,343

See p. 20,601 for regulations not amended to reflect law changes

→ *Caution: Temporary Reg. § 1.141-15T, below, was removed by T.D. 9016, effective November 22, 2002.*←

example, the exercise by a purchaser after February 23, 1998 of a renewal option that was provided under a contract before that date, on terms identical to the original contract, is not treated as an amendment of the contract; and

(iii) An amendment that reduces the term of a contract, or the amount of requirements covered by a contract, is not, in and of itself, material.

(3) *Elective application of 1998 temporary regulations.* For an issue sold on or after January 19, 2001, and before February 15, 2001, an issuer may apply the provisions of §§ 1.141-7T and 1.141-8T in effect prior to January 19, 2001 (26 CFR part 1, revised April 1, 2000) in whole, but not in part, in lieu of applying §§ 1.141-7T and 1.141-8T.

(g) *Refunding bonds in general.* Except as otherwise provided in paragraph (h) or (i) of this section, §§ 1.141-7T and 1.141-8T do not apply to any bonds sold on or after January 19, 2001, to refund a bond to which §§ 1.141-7T and 1.141-8T do not apply unless—

(1) The refunding bonds are subject to section 1301 of the Tax Reform Act of 1986 (100 Stat. 2602); and

(2)(i) The weighted average maturity of the refunding bonds is longer than—

(A) The weighted average maturity of the refunded bonds; or

(B) In the case of a short-term obligation that the issuer reasonably expects to refund with a long-term financing (such as a bond anticipation note), 120 percent of the weighted average reasonably expected economic life of the facilities financed; or

(ii) A principal purpose for the issuance of the refunding bonds is to make one or more new conduit loans.

(h) *Permissive retroactive application.* Except as provided in § 1.141-15(d) or (e) or paragraph (i) of this section, §§ 1.141-1 through 1.141-6, 1.141-7T through 1.141-8T, 1.141-9 through 1.141-14, 1.145-1 through 1.145-2, 1.150-1(a)(3) and the definition of bond documents contained in § 1.150-1(b) may be applied in whole, but not in part to—

(1) Outstanding bonds that are sold before January 19, 2001, and subject to section 141; or

(2) Refunding bonds sold on or after January 19, 2001, that are subject to section 141.

(i) *Permissive application of certain regulations pertaining to output contracts.* Section

1,141-7T(f)(4) and (5) may be applied to any bonds. [Temporary Reg. § 1.141-15T.]

□ [T.D. 8757, 1-21-98. *Amended by T.D.* 8941, 1-17-2001. *Removed by T.D.* 9016, 9-19-2002.]

[Reg. § 1.141-16]

§ 1.141-16. **Effective dates for qualified private activity bond provisions.**—(a) *Scope.* The effective dates of this section apply for purposes of §§ 1.142-0 through 1.142-2, 1.144-0 through 1.144-2, 1.147-0 through 1.147-2, and 1.150-4.

(b) *Effective dates.* Except as otherwise provided in this section, the regulations designated in paragraph (a) of this section apply to bonds issued on or after May 16, 1997, (the effective date).

(c) *Permissive application.* The regulations designated in paragraph (a) of this section may be applied in whole, but not in part, to bonds outstanding on the effective date. [Reg. § 1.141-16.]

□ [T.D. 8712, 1-10-97.]

[Reg. § 1.142-0]

§ 1.142-0. **Table of contents.**—This section lists the captioned paragraphs contained in §§ 1.142-1 through 1.142-3.

[Reg. § 1.142-0.]

□ [T.D. 8712, 1-10-97.]

[Reg. § 1.142-1]

§ 1.142-1. **Exempt facility bonds.**—(a) *Overview.* Interest on a private activity bond is not excludable from gross income under section 103(a) unless the bond is a qualified bond. Under section 141(e)(1)(A), an exempt facility bond issued under section 142 may be a qualified bond. Under section 142(a), an exempt facility bond is any bond issued as a part of an issue using 95 percent or more of the proceeds for certain exempt facilities.

(b) *Scope.* Sections 1.142-0 through 1.142-3 apply for purposes of the rules for exempt facility bonds under section 142, except that, with respect to net proceeds that have been spent, § 1.142-2 does not apply to bonds issued under section 142(d) (relating to bonds issued to provide qualified residential rental projects) and section 142(f)(2) and (4) (relating to bonds issued to provide local furnishing of electric energy or gas).

(c) *Effective dates.* For effective dates of §§ 1.142-0 through 1.142-2, see § 1.141-16. [Reg. § 1.142-1.]

☐ [Reg. § 1.142-1, issued under Code Sec. 142 as it existed prior to repeal by P.L. 95-30, was removed from the CFR, and Reg. § 1.142-1, above, was adopted by *T.D.* 8712, 1-10-97.]

[Reg. § 1.142-2]

§ 1.142-2. **Remedial actions.**—(a) *General rule.* If less than 95 percent of the net proceeds of an exempt facility bond are actually used to provide an exempt facility, and for no other purpose, the issue will be treated as meeting the use of proceeds requirement of section 142(a) if the issue meets the condition of paragraph (b) of this section and the issuer takes the remedial action described in paragraph (c) of this section.

(b) *Reasonable expectations requirement.* The issuer must have reasonably expected on the issue date that 95 percent of the net proceeds of the issue would be used to provide an exempt facility and for no other purpose for the entire term of the bonds (disregarding any redemption provisions). To meet this condition the amount of the issue must have been based on reasonable estimates about the cost of the facility.

(c) *Redemption or defeasance*—(1) *In general.* The requirements of this paragraph (c) are met if all of the nonqualified bonds of the issue are redeemed on the earliest call date after the date on which the failure to properly use the proceeds occurs under paragraph (d) of this section. Proceeds of tax-exempt bonds (other than those described in paragraph (d)(1) of this section) must not be used for this purpose. If the bonds are not

redeemed within 90 days of the date on which the failure to properly use proceeds occurs, a defeasance escrow must be established for those bonds within 90 days of that date.

(2) *Notice of defeasance.* The issuer must provide written notice to the Commissioner of the establishment of the defeasance escrow within 90 days of the date the escrow is established.

(3) *Special limitation.* The establishment of a defeasance escrow does not satisfy the requirements of this paragraph (c) if the period between the issue date and the first call date is more than 10½ years.

(4) *Special rule for dispositions of personal property.* For dispositions of personal property exclusively for cash, the requirements of this paragraph (c) are met if the issuer expends the disposition proceeds within 6 months of the date of the disposition to acquire replacement property for the same qualifying purpose of the issue under section 142.

(5) *Definitions.* For purposes of paragraph (c)(4) of this section, *disposition proceeds* means disposition proceeds as defined in § 1.141-12(c).

(d) *When a failure to properly use proceeds occurs*—(1) *Proceeds not spent.* For net proceeds that are not spent, a failure to properly use proceeds occurs on the earlier of the date on which the issuer reasonably determines that the financed facility will not be completed or the date on which the financed facility is placed in service.

(2) *Proceeds spent.* For net proceeds that are spent, a failure to properly use proceeds occurs on the date on which an action is taken that causes the bonds not to be used for the qualifying purpose for which the bonds were issued.

(e) *Nonqualified bonds.* For purposes of this section, the nonqualified bonds are a portion of the outstanding bonds in an amount that, if the remaining bonds were issued on the date on which the failure to properly use the proceeds occurs, at least 95 percent of the net proceeds of the remaining bonds would be used to provide an exempt facility. If no proceeds have been spent to provide an exempt facility, all of the outstanding bonds are nonqualified bonds. The nonqualified bonds must be determined on a pro rata allocation basis, except that an issuer may treat bonds with longer maturities (determined on a bond-by-bond basis) as the nonqualified bonds. [Reg. § 1.142-2.]

☐ [Reg. § 1.142-2, issued under Code Sec. 142 as it existed prior to repeal by P.L. 95-30, was removed from the CFR, and Reg. § 1.142-2, above, was adopted by *T.D.* 8712, 1-10-97.]

Tax Exempt. Requirements: State/Local Bonds **25,345**

See p. 20,601 for regulations not amended to reflect law changes

[Reg. § 1.142-3]

§ 1.142-3. Refunding issues.—[Reserved.]

☐ [*T.D.* 8712, 1-10-97.]

[Reg. § 1.142-4]

§ 1.142-4. Use of proceeds to provide a facility.—(a) *In general.* [Reserved].

(b) *Reimbursement allocations.* If an expenditure for a facility is paid before the issue date of the bonds to provide that facility, the facility is described in section 142(a) only if the expenditure meets the requirements of § 1.150-2 (relating to reimbursement allocations). For purposes of this paragraph (b), if the proceeds of an issue are used to pay principal of or interest on an obligation other than a State or local bond (for example, temporary construction financing of the conduit borrower), that issue is not a refunding issue, and, thus, § 1.150-2(g) does not apply.

(c) *Limitation on use of facilities by substantial users*—(1) *In general.* If the original use of a facility begins before the issue date of the bonds to provide the facility, the facility is not described in section 142(a) if any person that was a substantial user of the facility at any time during the 5-year period before the issue date or any related person to that user receives (directly or indirectly) 5 percent or more of the proceeds of the issue for the user's interest in the facility and is a substantial user of the facility at any time during the 5-year period after the issue date, unless—

(i) An official intent for the facility is adopted under § 1.150-2 within 60 days after the date on which acquisition, construction, or reconstruction of that facility commenced; and

(ii) For an acquisition, no person that is a substantial user or related person after the acquisition date was also a substantial user more than 60 days before the date on which the official intent was adopted.

(2) *Definitions.* For purposes of paragraph (c)(1) of this section, *substantial user* has the meaning used in section 147(a)(1), *related person* has the meaning used in section 144(a)(3), and a user that is a governmental unit within the meaning of § 1.103-1 is disregarded.

(d) *Effective date*—(1) *In general.* This section applies to bonds sold on or after July 8, 1997. See § 1.103-8(a)(5) for rules applicable to bonds sold before that date.

(2) *Elective retroactive application.* An issuer may apply this section to any bond sold before July 8, 1997. [Reg. § 1.142-4.]

☐ [*T.D.* 8718, 5-8-97.]

[Reg. § 1.142(a)(5)-1]

§ 1.142(a)(5)-1. Exempt facility bonds: Sewage facilities.—(a) *In general.* Under section 103(a), a private activity bond is a tax-exempt bond only if it is a qualified bond. A qualified bond includes an exempt facility bond, defined as any bond issued as part of an issue 95 percent or more of the net proceeds of which are used to provide a facility specified in section 142. One type of facility specified in section 142(a) is a sewage facility. This section defines the term sewage facility for purposes of section 142(a).

(b) *Definitions*—(1) *Sewage facility defined.* A sewage facility is property—

(i) Except as provided in paragraphs (b)(2) and (d) of this section, used for the secondary treatment of wastewater; however, for property treating wastewater reasonably expected to have an average daily raw wasteload concentration of biochemical oxygen demand (BOD) that exceeds 350 milligrams per liter as oxygen (measured at the time the influent enters the facility) (the *BOD limit*), this paragraph (b)(1)(i) applies only to the extent the treatment is for wastewater having an average daily raw wasteload concentration of BOD that does not exceed the BOD limit;

(ii) Used for the preliminary and/or primary treatment of wastewater but only to the extent used in connection with secondary treatment (without regard to the BOD limit described in paragraph (b)(1)(i) of this section);

(iii) Used for the advanced or tertiary treatment of wastewater but only to the extent used in connection with and after secondary treatment;

(iv) Used for the collection, storage, use, processing, or final disposal of—

(A) Wastewater, which property is necessary for such preliminary, primary, secondary, advanced, or tertiary treatment; or

(B) Sewage sludge removed during such preliminary, primary, secondary, advanced, or tertiary treatment (without regard to the BOD limit described in paragraph (b)(1)(i) of this section;

(v) Used for the treatment, collection, storage, use, processing, or final disposal of septage (without regard to the BOD limit described in paragraph (b)(1)(i) of this section); and

(vi) Functionally related and subordinate to property described in this paragraph (b)(1), such as sewage disinfection property.

(2) *Special rules and exceptions*—(i) *Exception to BOD limit.* A facility treating wastewater with an average daily raw wasteload concentration of BOD exceeding the BOD limit will not fail

Reg. § 1.142(a)(5)-1(b)(2)

to qualify as a sewage facility described in paragraph (b)(1) of this section to the extent that the failure to satisfy the BOD limit results from the implementation of a federal, state, or local water conservation program (for example, a program designed to promote water use efficiency that results in BOD concentrations beyond the BOD limit).

(ii) *Anti-abuse rule for BOD limit.* A facility does not satisfy the BOD limit if there is any intentional manipulation of the BOD level to circumvent the BOD limit (for example, increasing the volume of water in the wastewater before the influent enters the facility with the intention of reducing the BOD level).

(iii) *Authority of Commissioner.* In appropriate cases upon application to the Commissioner, the Commissioner may determine that facilities employing technologically advanced or innovative treatment processes qualify as sewage facilities if it is demonstrated that these facilities perform functions that are consistent with the definition of sewage facilities described in paragraph (b)(1) of this section.

(3) *Other applicable definitions*—(i) *Advanced or tertiary treatment* means the treatment of wastewater after secondary treatment. Advanced or tertiary treatment ranges from biological treatment extensions to physical-chemical separation techniques such as denitrification, ammonia stripping, carbon adsorption, and chemical precipitation.

(ii) *Nonconventional pollutants* are any pollutants that are not listed in 40 CFR 401.15, 401.16, or app. A to part 423.

(iii) *Preliminary treatment* means treatment that removes large extraneous matter from incoming wastewater and renders the incoming wastewater more amenable to subsequent treatment and handling.

(iv) *Pretreatment* means a process that preconditions wastewater to neutralize or remove toxic, priority, or nonconventional pollutants that could adversely affect sewers or inhibit a preliminary, primary, secondary, advanced, or tertiary treatment operation.

(v) *Primary treatment* means treatment that removes material that floats or will settle, usually by screens or settling tanks.

(vi) *Priority pollutants* are those pollutants listed in app. A to 40 CFR part 423.

(vii) *Secondary treatment* means the stage in sewage treatment in which a bacterial process (or an equivalent process) consumes the organic parts of wastes, usually by trickling filters or an activated sludge process.

(viii) *Sewage sludge* is defined in 40 CFR 122.2 and includes septage.

(ix) *Toxic pollutants* are those pollutants listed in 40 CFR 401.15.

(c) *Other property not included in the definition of a sewage facility.* Property other than property described in paragraph (b)(1) of this section is not a sewage facility. Thus, for example, property is not a sewage facility, or functionally related and subordinate property, if the property is used for pretreatment of wastewater (whether or not this treatment is necessary to perform preliminary, primary, secondary, advanced, or tertiary treatment), or the related collection, storage, use, processing, or final disposal of the wastewater. In addition, property used to treat, process, or use wastewater subsequent to the time the wastewater can be discharged into navigable waters, as defined in 33 U.S.C. 1362, is not a sewage facility.

(d) *Allocation of costs.* In the case of property that has both a use described in paragraph (b)(1) of this section (a sewage treatment function) and a use other than sewage treatment, only the portion of the cost of the property allocable to the sewage treatment function is taken into account as an expenditure to provide sewage facilities. The portion of the cost of property allocable to the sewage treatment function is determined by allocating the cost of that property between the property's sewage treatment function and any other uses by any method which, based on all the facts and circumstances, reasonably reflects a separation of costs for each use of the property.

(e) *Effective date*—(1) *In general.* This section applies to issues of bonds issued after February 21, 1995.

(2) *Refundings.* In the case of a refunding bond issued to refund a bond to which this section does not apply, the issuer need not apply this section to that refunding bond. This paragraph (e)(2) applies only if the weighted average maturity of the refunding bonds, as described in section 147(b), is not greater than the remaining weighted average maturity of the refunded bonds. [Reg. § 1.142(a)(5)-1.]

☐ [*T.D.* 8576, 12-22-94.]

[Reg. § 1.142(f)(4)-1]

§ 1.142(f)(4)-1. **Manner of making election to terminate tax-exempt bond financing.**—(a) *Overview.* Section 142(f)(4) permits a person engaged in the local furnishing of electric energy or gas (a local furnisher) that uses facilities financed with exempt facility bonds under section 142(a)(8) and that expands its service area in a manner inconsistent with the requirements of sec-

Reg. § 1.142(f)(4)-1(a)

tions 142(a)(8) and (f) to make an election to ensure that those bonds will continue to be treated as exempt facility bonds. The election must meet the requirements of paragraphs (b) and (c) of this section.

(b) *Time for making election*—(1) *In general.* An election under section 142(f)(4)(B) must be filed with the Internal Revenue Service on or before 90 days after the date of the service area expansion that causes bonds to cease to meet the requirements of sections 142(a)(8) and (f).

(2) *Date of service area expansion.* For the purposes of this section, the date of the service area expansion is the first date on which the local furnisher is authorized to collect revenue for the provision of service in the expanded area.

(c) *Manner of making election.* An election under section 142(f)(4)(B) must be captioned "ELECTION TO TERMINATE TAX-EXEMPT BOND FINANCING", must be signed under penalties of perjury by a person who has authority to sign on behalf of the local furnisher, and must contain the following information—

(1) The name of the local furnisher;

(2) The tax identification number of the local furnisher;

(3) The complete address of the local furnisher;

(4) The date of the service area expansion;

(5) Identification of each bond issue subject to the election, including the complete name of each issue, the tax identification number of each issuer, the report number of the information return filed under section 149(e) for each issue, the issue date of each issue, the CUSIP number (if any) of the bond with the latest maturity of each issue, the issue price of each issue, the adjusted issue price of each issue as of the date of the election, the earliest date on which the bonds of each issue may be redeemed, and the principal amount of bonds of each issue to be redeemed on the earliest redemption date;

(6) A statement that the local furnisher making the election agrees to the conditions stated in section 142(f)(4)(B); and

(7) A statement that each issuer of the bonds subject to the election has received written notice of the election.

(d) *Effect on section 150(b).* Except as provided in paragraph (e) of this section, if a local furnisher files an election within the period specified in paragraph (b) of this section, section 150(b) does not apply to bonds identified in the election during and after that period.

(e) *Effect of failure to meet agreements.* If a local furnisher fails to meet any of the conditions

stated in an election pursuant to paragraph (c)(6) of this section, the election is invalid.

(f) *Corresponding provisions of the Internal Revenue Code of 1954.* Section 103(b)(4)(E) of the Internal Revenue Code of 1954 set forth corresponding requirements for the exclusion from gross income of the interest on bonds issued for facilities for the local furnishing of electric energy or gas. For the purposes of this section any reference to sections 142(a)(8) and (f) of the Internal Revenue Code of 1986 includes a reference to the corresponding portion of section 103(b)(4)(E) of the Internal Revenue Code of 1954.

(g) *Effective dates.* This section applies to elections made on or after January 19, 2001. [Reg. § 1.142(f)(4)-1.]

☐ [*T.D.* 8941, 1-17-2001.]

[Reg. § 1.144-0]

§ 1.144-0. **Table of contents.**—This section lists the captioned paragraphs contained in §§ 1.144-1 and 1.144-2.

§ 1.144-1 Qualified small issue bonds, qualified student loan bonds, and qualified redevelopment bonds.

(a) Overview.

(b) Scope.

(c) Effective dates.

§ 1.144-2 Remedial actions.

[Reg. § 1.144-0.]

☐ [*T.D.* 8712, 1-10-97.]

[Reg. § 1.144-1]

§ 1.144-1. **Qualified small issue bonds, qualified student loan bonds, and qualified redevelopment bonds.**—(a) *Overview.* Interest on a private activity bond is not excludable from gross income under section 103(a) unless the bond is a qualified bond. Under section 141(e)(1)(D), a qualified small issue bond issued under section 144(a) may be a qualified bond. Under section 144(a), any qualified small issue bond is any bond issued as a part of an issue 95 percent or more of the proceeds of which are to be used to provide certain manufacturing facilities or certain depreciable farm property and which meets other requirements. Under section 141(e)(1)(F) a qualified redevelopment bond issued under section 144(c) is a qualified bond. Under section 144(c), a qualified redevelopment bond is any bond issued as a part of an issue 95 percent or more of the net proceeds of which are to be used for one or more redevelopment purposes and which meets certain other requirements.

(b) *Scope.* Sections 1.144-0 through 1.144-2 apply for purposes of the rules for small issue bonds

25,348   Tax Exempt. Requirements: State/Local Bonds

See p. 20,601 for regulations not amended to reflect law changes

under section 144(a) and qualified redevelopment bonds under section 144(c), except that § 1.144-2 does not apply to the requirements for qualified small issue bonds under section 144(a)(4) (relating to the limitation on capital expenditures) or under section 144(a)(10) (relating to the aggregate limit of tax-exempt bonds per taxpayer).

(c) *Effective dates.* For effective dates of §§ 1.144-0 through 1.144-2, see § 1.141-16. [Reg. § 1.144-1.]

☐ [Reg. § 1.144-1, issued under Code Sec. 144 as it exsisted prior to repeal by P.L. 95-30, was removed from the CFR, and Reg. § 1.144-1, above, was adopted by *T.D.* 8712, 1-10-97.]

[Reg. § 1.144-2]

§ **1.144-2. Remedial actions.**—The remedial action rules of § 1.142-2 apply to qualified small issue bonds issued under section 144(a) and to qualified redevelopment bonds issued under section 144(c), for this purpose treating those bonds as exempt facility bonds and the qualifying purposes for those bonds as exempt facilities. [Reg. § 1.144-2.]

☐ [Reg. § 1.144-2, issued under Code Sec. 144 as it exsisted prior to repeal by P.L. 95-30, was removed from the CFR, and Reg. § 1.144-2, above, was adopted by *T.D.* 8712, 1-10-97.]

[Reg. § 1.145-0]

§ **1.145-0. Table of contents.**—This section lists the captioned paragraphs contained in §§ 1.145-1 and 1.145-2.

§ 1.145-1 Qualified 501(c)(3) bonds.

(a) Overview.

(b) Scope.

(c) Effective dates.

§ 1.145-2 Application of private activity bond regulations.

(a) In general.

(b) Modification of private business tests.

(c) Exceptions.

  (1) Certain provisions relating to governmental programs.

  (2) Costs of issuance.

[Reg. § 1.145-0.]

☐ [*T.D.* 8712, 1-10-97.]

[Reg. § 1.145-1]

§ **1.145-1. Qualified 501(c)(3) bonds.**—(a) *Overview.* Interest on a private activity bond is not excludable from gross income under section 103(a) unless the bond is a qualified bond. Under section 141(e)(1)(G), a qualified 501(c)(3) bond issued under section 145 is a qualified bond.

Under section 145, a qualified 501(c)(3) bond is any bond issued as a part of an issue that satisfies the requirements of sections 145(a) through (d).

(b) *Scope.* Sections 1.145-0 through 1.145-2 apply for purposes of section 145(a).

(c) *Effective dates.* For effective dates of §§ 1.145-0 through 1.145-2, see § 1.141-15. [Reg. § 1.145-1.]

☐ [*T.D.* 8712, 1-10-97.]

[Reg. § 1.145-2]

§ **1.145-2. Application of private activity bond regulations.**—(a) *In general.* Except as provided in this section, §§ 1.141-0 through 1.141-15 apply to section 145(a). For example, under this section, § 1.141-1, and § 1.141-2, an issue ceases to be an issue of qualified 501(c)(3) bonds if the issuer or a conduit borrower 501(c)(3) organization takes a deliberate action, subsequent to the issue date, that causes the issue to fail to comply with the requirements of sections 141(e) and 145 (such as an action that results in revocation of exempt status of the 501(c)(3) organization).

(b) *Modification of private business tests.* In applying §§ 1.141-0 through 1.141-15 to section 145(a)—

(1) References to governmental persons include 501(c)(3) organizations with respect to their activities that do not constitute unrelated trades or businesses under section 513(a);

(2) References to "10 percent" and "proceeds" in the context of the private business use test and the private security or payment test mean "5 percent" and "net proceeds"; and

(3) References to the private business use test in §§ 1.141-2 and 1.141-12 include the ownership test of section 145(a)(1).

(c) *Exceptions*—(1) *Certain provisions relating to governmental programs.* The following provisions do not apply to section 145: § 1.141-2(d)(4) (relating to the special rule for dispositions of personal property in the ordinary course of an established governmental program) and § 1.141-2(d)(5) (relating to the special rule for general obligation bond programs that finance a large number of separate purposes).

(2) *Costs of issuance.* Section 1.141-3(g)(6) does not apply to section 145(a)(2) to the extent that it provides that costs of issuance are allocated ratably among the other purposes for which the proceeds are used. For purposes of section 145(a)(2), costs of issuance are treated as private business use. [Reg. § 1.145-2.]

☐ [*T.D.* 8712, 1-10-97.]

Tax Exempt. Requirements: State/Local Bonds   25,349

See p. 20,601 for regulations not amended to reflect law changes

[Reg. § 1.147-0]

§ 1.147-0. Table of contents.—This section lists the captioned paragraphs contained in §§ 1.147-1 and 1.147-2.

§ 1.147-1 Other requirements applicable to certain private activity bonds.

(a) Overview.

(b) Scope.

(c) Effective dates.

§ 1.147-2 Remedial actions.

[Reg. § 1.147-0.]

☐ [*T.D.* 8712, 1-10-97.]

[Reg. § 1.147-1]

§ 1.147-1. Other requirements applicable to certain private activity bonds.—(a) *Overview.* Interest on a private activity bond is not excludable from gross income under section 103(a) unless the bond is a qualified bond. Under section 147, certain requirements must be met for a private activity bond to qualify as a qualified bond.

(b) *Scope.* Sections 1.147-0 through 1.147-2 apply for purposes of the rules in section 147 for qualified private activity bonds that permit use of proceeds to acquire land for environmental purposes (section 147(c)(3)), permit use of proceeds for certain rehabilitations (section 147(d)(2) and (3)), prohibit use of proceeds to finance skyboxes, airplanes, gambling establishments and similar facilities (section 147(e)), and require public approval (section 147(f)), but not for the rules limiting use of proceeds to acquire land or existing property under sections 147(c)(1) and (2), and (d)(1).

(c) *Effective dates.* For effective dates of §§ 1.147-0 through 1.147-2, see § 1.141-16. [Reg. § 1.147-1.]

☐ [*T.D.* 8712, 1-10-97.]

[Reg. § 1.147-2]

§ 1.147-2. Remedial actions.—The remedial action rules of § 1.142-2 apply to the rules in section 147 for qualified private activity bonds that permit use of proceeds to acquire land for environmental purposes (section 147(c)(3)), permit use of proceeds for certain rehabilitations (section 147(d)(2) and (3)), prohibit use of proceeds to finance skyboxes, airplanes, gambling establishments and similar facilities (section 147(e)), and require public approval (section 147(f)), for this purpose treating those private activity bonds subject to the rules under section 147 as exempt facility bonds and the qualifying purposes for those bonds as exempt facilities. [Reg. § 1.147-2.]

☐ [*T.D.* 8712, 1-10-97.]

[Reg. § 1.147(b)-1]

§ 1.147(b)-1. Bond maturity limitation-treatment of working capital.—Section 147(b) does not apply to proceeds of a private activity bond issue used to finance working capital expenditures. [Reg. § 1.147(b)-1.]

☐ [*T.D.* 8476, 6-14-93.]

[Reg. § 1.148-0]

§ 1.148-0. Scope and table of contents.—(a) *Overview.* Under section 103(a), interest on certain obligations issued by States and local governments is excludable from the gross income of the owners. Section 148 was enacted to minimize the arbitrage benefits from investing gross proceeds of tax-exempt bonds in higher yielding investments and to remove the arbitrage incentives to issue more bonds, to issue bonds earlier, or to leave bonds outstanding longer than is otherwise reasonably necessary to accomplish the governmental purposes for which the bonds were issued. To accomplish these purposes, section 148 restricts the direct and indirect investment of bond proceeds in higher yielding investments and requires that certain earnings on higher yielding investments be rebated to the United States. Violation of these provisions causes the bonds in the issue to become *arbitrage bonds*, the interest on which is not excludable from the gross income of the owners under section 103(a). The regulations in §§ 1.148-1 through 1.148-11 apply in a manner consistent with these purposes.

(b) *Scope.* Sections 1.148-1 through 1.148-11 apply generally for purposes of the arbitrage restrictions on State and local bonds under section 148.

(c) *Table of contents.* This paragraph (c) lists the table of contents for §§ 1.148-1, 1.148-2, 1.148-3, 1.148-4, 1.148-5, 1.148-6, 1.148-7, 1.148-8, 1.148-9, 1.148-10 and 1.148-11.

§ 1.148-1. Definitions and elections.

(a) In general.

(b) Certain definitions.

(c) Definition of replacement proceeds.

(1) In general.

(2) Sinking fund.

(3) Pledged fund.

(4) Other replacement proceeds.

(d) Elections.

(e) Investment-type property.

§ 1.148-2. General arbitrage yield restriction rules.

(a) In general.

(b) Reasonable expectations.

Reg. § 1.148-0(c)

(1) In general.

(2) Certification of expectations.

(c) Intentional acts.

(d) Materially higher yielding investments.

(1) In general.

(2) Definitions of materially higher yield.

(3) Mortgage loans.

(e) Temporary periods.

(1) In general.

(2) General 3-year temporary period for capital projects and qualified mortgage loans.

(3) Temporary period for restricted working capital expenditures.

(4) Temporary period for pooled financings.

(5) Temporary period for replacement proceeds.

(6) Temporary period for investment proceeds.

(7) Other amounts.

(f) Reserve or replacement funds.

(1) General 10 percent limitation on funding with sale proceeds.

(2) Exception from yield restriction for reasonably required reserve or replacement funds.

(3) Certain parity reserve funds.

(g) Minor portion.

(h) Certain waivers permitted.

§ 1.148-3. General arbitrage rebate rules.

(a) In general.

(b) Definition of rebate amount.

(c) Computation of future value of a payment or receipt.

(d) Payments and receipts.

(1) Definition of payments.

(2) Definition of receipts.

(3) Special rules for commingled funds.

(e) Computation dates.

(1) In general.

(2) Final computation date.

(f) Amount of required rebate installment payment.

(1) Amount of interim rebate payments.

(2) Amount of final rebate payment.

(3) Future value of rebate payments.

(g) Time and manner of payment.

(h) Penalty in lieu of loss of tax exemption.

(1) In general.

(2) Interest on underpayments.

(3) Waivers of the penalty.

(4) Application to alternative penalty under § 1.148-7.

(i) Recovery of overpayment of rebate.

(1) In general.

(2) Limitations on recovery.

(j) Examples.

(k) Bona fide debt service fund exception.

§ 1.148-4. Yield on an issue of bonds.

(a) In general.

(b) Computing yield on a fixed yield issue.

(1) In general.

(2) Yield on certain fixed yield bonds subject to mandatory or contingent early redemption.

(3) Yield on certain fixed yield bonds subject to optional early redemption.

(4) Yield recomputed upon transfer of certain rights associated with the bond.

(5) Special aggregation rule treating certain bonds as a single fixed yield bond.

(6) Examples.

(c) Computing yield on a variable yield issue.

(1) In general.

(2) Payments on bonds included in yield for a computation period.

(3) Example.

(d) Conversion from variable yield issue to fixed yield issue.

(e) Value of bonds.

(1) Plain par bonds.

(2) Other bonds.

(f) Qualified guarantees.

(1) In general.

(2) Interest savings.

(3) Guarantee in substance.

(4) Reasonable charge.

(5) Guarantee of purpose investments.

(6) Allocation of qualified guarantee payments.

(7) Refund or reduction of guarantee payments.

(g) Yield on certain mortgage revenue and student loan bonds.

(h) Qualified hedging transactions.

(1) In general.

(2) Qualified hedge defined.

(3) Accounting for qualified hedges.

(4) Certain variable yield bonds treated as fixed yield bonds.

(5) Contracts entered into before issue date of hedged bond.

Reg. § 1.148-0(c)

(6) Authority of the Commissioner.

§ 1.148-5. Yield and valuation of investments.

(a) In general.

(b) Yield on an investment.

(1) In general.

(2) Yield on a separate class of investments.

(3) Investments to be held beyond issue's maturity or beyond temporary period.

(4) Consistent redemption assumptions on purpose investments.

(5) Student loan special allowance payments included in yield.

(c) Yield reduction payments to the United States.

(1) In general.

(2) Manner of payment.

(3) Applicability of special yield reduction rule.

(d) Value of investments.

(1) In general.

(2) Mandatory valuation of yield restricted investments at present value.

(3) Mandatory valuation of certain investments at fair market value.

(4) Special transition rule for transferred proceeds.

(5) Definition of present value of an investment.

(6) Definition of fair market value.

(e) Administrative costs of investments.

(1) In general.

(2) Qualified administrative costs on nonpurpose investments.

(3) Qualified administrative costs on purpose investments.

§ 1.148-6. General allocation and accounting rules.

(a) In general.

(1) Reasonable accounting methods required.

(2) Bona fide deviations from accounting method.

(b) Allocation of gross proceeds to an issue.

(1) One-issue rule and general ordering rules.

(2) Universal cap on value of nonpurpose investments allocated to an issue.

(c) Fair market value limit on allocations to nonpurpose investments.

(d) Allocation of gross proceeds to expenditures.

(1) Expenditures in general.

(2) Treatment of gross proceeds invested in purpose investments.

(3) Expenditures for working capital purposes.

(4) Expenditures for grants.

(5) Expenditures for reimbursement purposes.

(6) Expenditures of certain commingled investment proceeds of governmental issues.

(7) Payments to related parties.

(e) Special rules for commingled funds.

(1) In general.

(2) Investments held by a commingled fund.

(3) Certain expenditures involving a commingled fund.

(4) Fiscal periods.

(5) Unrealized gains and losses on investments of a commingled fund.

(6) Allocations of commingled funds serving as common reserve funds or sinking funds.

§ 1.148-7. Spending exceptions to the rebate requirement.

(a) Scope of section.

(1) In general.

(2) Relationship of spending exceptions.

(3) Spending exceptions not mandatory.

(b) Rules applicable for all spending exceptions.

(1) Special transferred proceeds rules.

(2) Application of multipurpose issue rules.

(3) Expenditures for governmental purposes of the issue.

(4) De minimis rule.

(5) Special definition of reasonably required reserve or replacement fund.

(6) Pooled financing issue.

(c) 6-month exception.

(1) General rule.

(2) Additional period for certain bonds.

(3) Amounts not included in gross proceeds.

(4) Series of refundings.

(d) 18-month exception.

(1) General rule.

(2) Extension for reasonable retainage.

(3) Gross proceeds.

(4) Application to multipurpose issues.

(e) 2-year exception.

(1) General rule.

(2) Extension for reasonable retainage.

(3) Definitions.

(f) Construction issue.

(1) Definition.

(2) Use of actual facts.

Reg. § 1.148-0(c)

(3) Ownership requirement.

(g) Construction expenditures.

(1) Definition.

(2) Certain acquisitions under turnkey contracts treated as construction expenditures.

(3) Constructed personal property.

(4) Specially developed computer software.

(5) Examples.

(h) Reasonable retainage definition.

(i) Available construction proceeds.

(1) Definition in general.

(2) Earnings on a reasonably required reserve or replacement fund.

(3) Reasonable expectations test for future earnings.

(4) Issuance costs.

(5) One and one-half percent penalty in lieu of arbitrage rebate.

(6) Payments on purpose investments and repayments of grants.

(7) Examples.

(j) Election to treat portion of issue used for construction as separate issue.

(1) In general.

(2) Example.

(k) One and one-half percent penalty in lieu of arbitrage rebate.

(1) In general.

(2) Application to reasonable retainage.

(3) Coordination with rebate requirement.

(l) Termination of 1-1/2 percent penalty.

(1) Termination after initial temporary period.

(2) Termination before end of initial temporary period.

(3) Application to reasonable retainage.

(4) Example.

(m) Payment of penalties.

§ 1.148-8. Small issuer exception to rebate requirement.

(a) Scope.

(b) General taxing powers.

(c) Size limitation.

(1) In general.

(2) Aggregation rules.

(3) Certain refunding bonds not taken into account.

(d) Pooled financings.

(1) Treatment of pool issuer.

(2) Treatment of conduit borrowers.

(e) Refunding issues.

(1) In general.

(2) Multipurpose issues.

§ 1.148-9. Arbitrage rules for refunding issues.

(a) Scope of application.

(b) Transferred proceeds allocation rule.

(1) In general.

(2) Special definition of principal amount.

(3) Relation of transferred proceeds rule to universal cap rule.

(4) Limitation on multi-generational transfers.

(c) Special allocation rules for refunding issues.

(1) Allocations of investments.

(2) Allocations of mixed escrows to expenditures for principal, interest, and redemption prices on a prior issue.

(d) Temporary periods in refundings.

(1) In general.

(2) Types of temporary periods in refundings.

(e) Reasonably required reserve or replacement funds in refundings.

(f) Minor portions in refundings.

(g) Certain waivers permitted.

(h) Multipurpose issue allocations.

(1) Application of multipurpose issue allocation rules.

(2) Rules on allocations of multipurpose issues.

(3) Separate purposes of a multipurpose issue.

(4) Allocations of bonds of a multipurpose issue.

(5) Limitation on multi-generation allocations.

(i) Operating rules for separation of prior issues into refunded and unrefunded portions.

(1) In general.

(2) Allocations of proceeds and investments in a partial refunding.

(3) References to prior issue.

§ 1.148-10. Anti-abuse rules and authority of Commissioner.

(a) Abusive arbitrage device.

(1) In general.

(2) Abusive arbitrage device defined.

(3) Exploitation of tax-exempt interest rates.

(4) Overburdening the tax-exempt market.

(b) Consequences of overburdening the tax-exempt bond market.

Reg. § 1.148-0(c)

(1) In general.

(2) Application.

(c) Anti-abuse rules on excess gross proceeds of advance refunding issues.

(1) In general.

(2) Definition of excess gross proceeds.

(3) Special treatment of transferred proceeds.

(4) Special rule for crossover refundings.

(5) Special rule for gross refundings.

(d) Examples.

(e) Authority of the Commissioner to clearly reflect the economic substance of a transaction.

(f) Authority of the Commissioner to require an earlier date for payment of rebate.

(g) Authority of the Commissioner to waive regulatory limitations.

§ 1.148-11. Effective dates.

(a) In general.

(b) Elective retroactive application in whole.

(1) In general.

(2) No elective retroactive application for 18-month spending exception.

(a) No elective retroactive application for hedges of fixed rate issues.

(c) Elective retroactive application of certain provisions.

(1) Retroactive application of overpayment recovery provisions.

(2) Certain allocations of multipurpose issues.

(3) Special limitation.

(d) Transition rule excepting certain state guarantee funds from the definition of replacement proceeds.

(1) Certain perpetual trust funds.

(2) Permanent University Fund.

(e) Transition rule regarding special allowance payments.

(f) Transition rule regarding applicability of yield reduction rule.

(g) Provisions applicable to certain bonds sold before effective date.

[Reg. § 1.148-0.]

□ [T.D. 8418, 5-12-92. Amended by T.D. 8476, 6-14-93; T.D. 8538, 5-5-94 and T.D. 8718, 5-8-97.]

→ *Caution: Reg. § 1.148-1, below, is applicable to certain bonds sold on or after July 8, 1997.*←

[Reg. § 1.148-1]

§ 1.148-1. Definitions and elections.—(a) *In general.* The definitions in this section and the definitions under section 150 apply for purposes of section 148 and §§ 1.148-1 through 1.148-11.

(b) *Certain definitions.* The following definitions apply:

Accounting method means both the overall method used to account for gross proceeds of an issue (e.g., the cash method or a modified accrual method) and the method used to account for or allocate any particular item within that overall accounting method (e.g., accounting for investments, expenditures, allocations to and from different sources, and particular items of the foregoing).

Annuity contract means annuity contract as defined in section 72.

Available amount means available amount as defined in § 1.148-6(d)(3)(iii).

Bona fide debt service fund means a fund, which may include proceeds of an issue, that—

(1) Is used primarily to achieve a proper matching of revenues with principal and interest payments within each bond year; and

(2) Is depleted at least once each bond year, except for a reasonable carryover amount not to exceed the greater of:

(i) the earnings on the fund for the immediately preceding bond year; or

(ii) one-twelfth of the principal and interest payments on the issue for the immediately preceding bond year.

Bond year means, in reference to an issue, each 1-year period that ends on the day selected by the issuer. The first and last bond years may be short periods. If no day is selected by the issuer before the earlier of the final maturity date of the issue or the date that is 5 years after the issue date, bond years end on each anniversary of the issue date and on the final maturity date.

Capital project or capital projects means all capital expenditures, plus related working capital expenditures to which the de minimis rule under § 1.148-6(d)(3)(ii)(A) applies, that carry out the governmental purposes of an issue. For example, a capital project may include capital expenditures for one or more buildings, plus related start-up operating costs.

Commingled fund means any fund or account containing both gross proceeds of an issue and amounts in excess of $25,000 that are not gross proceeds of that issue if the amounts in the fund

→ *Caution: Reg. § 1.148-1, below, is applicable to certain bonds sold on or after July 8, 1997.*←

or account are invested and accounted for collectively, without regard to the source of funds deposited in the fund or account. An open-end regulated investment company under section 851, however, is not a commingled fund.

Computation date means each date on which the rebate amount for an issue is computed under § 1.148-3(e).

Computation period means the period between computation dates. The first computation period begins on the issue date and ends on the first computation date. Each succeeding computation period begins on the date immediately following the computation date and ends on the next computation date.

Consistently applied means applied uniformly within a fiscal period and between fiscal periods to account for gross proceeds of an issue and any amounts that are in a commingled fund.

De minimis amount means—

(1) In reference to original issue discount (as defined in section 1273(a)(1)) or premium on an obligation—

(i) An amount that does not exceed 2 percent multiplied by the stated redemption price at maturity; plus

(ii) Any original issue premium that is attributable exclusively to reasonable underwriters' compensation; and

(2) In reference to market discount (as defined in section 1278(a)(2)(A)) or premium on an obligation, an amount that does not exceed 2 percent multiplied by the stated redemption price at maturity.

Economic accrual method (also known as the *constant interest method* or *actuarial method*) means the method of computing yield that is based on the compounding of interest at the end of each compounding period.

Fair market value means fair market value as defined in § 1.148-5(d)(6).

Fixed rate investment means any investment whose yield is fixed and determinable on the issue date.

Fixed yield bond means any bond whose yield is fixed and determinable on the issue date using the assumptions and rules provided in § 1.148-4(b).

Fixed yield issue means any issue if each bond that is part of the issue is a fixed yield bond.

Gross proceeds means any proceeds and replacement proceeds of an issue.

Guaranteed investment contract includes any nonpurpose investment that has specifically negotiated withdrawal or reinvestment provisions and a specifically negotiated interest rate, and also includes any agreement to supply investments on two or more future dates (e.g., a forward supply contract).

Higher yielding investments means higher yielding investments as defined in section 148(b)(1).

Investment means any investment property as defined in sections 148(b)(2) and 148(b)(3), and any other tax-exempt bond.

Investment proceeds means any amounts actually or constructively received from investing proceeds of an issue.

Investment-type property is defined in paragraph (e) of this section.

Issue price means, except as otherwise provided, issue price as defined in sections 1273 and 1274. Generally, the issue price of bonds that are publicly offered is the first price at which a substantial amount of the bonds is sold to the public. Ten percent is a substantial amount. The public does not include bond houses, brokers, or similar persons or organizations acting in the capacity of underwriters or wholesalers. The issue price does not change if part of the issue is later sold at a different price. The issue price of bonds that are not substantially identical is determined separately. The issue price of bonds for which a bona fide public offering is made is determined as of the sale date based on reasonable expectations regarding the initial public offering price. If a bond is issued for property, the applicable Federal tax-exempt rate is used in lieu of the Federal rate in determining the issue price under section 1274. The issue price of bonds may not exceed their fair market value as of the sale date.

Issuer generally means the entity that actually issues the issue, and, unless the context or a provision clearly requires otherwise, each conduit borrower of the issue. For example, rules imposed on issuers to account for gross proceeds of an issue apply to a conduit borrower to account for any gross proceeds received under a purpose investment. Provisions regarding elections, filings, liability for the rebate amount, and certifications of reasonable expectations apply only to the actual issuer.

Multipurpose issue means an issue the proceeds of which are used for two or more separate purposes determined in accordance with § 1.148-9(h).

Reg. § 1.148-1(b)

Tax Exempt. Requirements: State/Local Bonds   **25,355**

See p. 20,601 for regulations not amended to reflect law changes

→ *Caution: Reg. § 1.148-1, below, is applicable to certain bonds sold on or after July 8, 1997.*←

Net sale proceeds means sale proceeds, less the portion of those sale proceeds invested in a reasonably required reserve or replacement fund under section 148(d) and as part of a minor portion under section 148(e).

Nonpurpose investment means any investment property, as defined in section 148(b), that is not a purpose investment.

Payment means a payment as defined in § 1.148-3(d) for purposes of computing the rebate amount, and a payment as defined in § 1.148-5(b) for purposes of computing the yield on an investment.

Plain par bond means a qualified tender bond or a bond—

(1) Issued with not more than a de minimis amount of original issue discount or premium;

(2) Issued for a price that does not include accrued interest other than pre-issuance accrued interest;

(3) That bears interest from the issue date at a single, stated, fixed rate or that is a variable rate debt instrument under section 1275, in each case with interest unconditionally payable at least annually; and

(4) That has a lowest stated redemption price that is not less than its outstanding stated principal amount.

Plain par investment means an investment that is an obligation—

(1) Issued with not more than a de minimis amount of original issue discount or premium, or, if acquired on a date other than the issue date, acquired with not more than a de minimis amount of market discount or premium;

(2) Issued for a price that does not include accrued interest other than pre-issuance accrued interest;

(3) That bears interest from the issue date at a single, stated, fixed rate or that is a variable rate debt instrument under section 1275, in each case with interest unconditionally payable at least annually; and

(4) That has a lowest stated redemption price that is not less than its outstanding stated principal amount.

Pre-issuance accrued interest means amounts representing interest that accrued on an obligation for a period not greater than one year before its issue date but only if those amounts are paid within one year after the issue date.

Proceeds means any sale proceeds, investment proceeds, and transferred proceeds of an issue.

Proceeds do not include, however, amounts actually or constructively received with respect to a purpose investment that are properly allocable to the immaterially higher yield under § 1.148-2(d) or section 143(g) or to qualified administrative costs recoverable under § 1.148-5(e).

Program investment means a purpose investment that is part of a governmental program in which—

(1) The program involves the origination or acquisition of purpose investments;

(2) At least 95 percent (90 percent for qualified student loans under section 144(b)(1)(A)) of the cost of the purpose investments acquired under the program represents one or more loans to a substantial number of persons representing the general public, States or political subdivisions, 501(c)(3) organizations, persons who provide housing and related facilities, or any combination of the foregoing;

(3) At least 95 percent of the receipts from purpose investments are used to pay principal, interest, or redemption prices on issues that financed the program, to pay or reimburse administrative costs of those issues or of the program, to pay or reimburse anticipated future losses directly related to the program, to finance additional purpose investments for the same general purposes of the program, or to redeem and retire governmental obligations at the next earliest possible date of redemption;

(4) The program documents prohibit any obligor on a purpose investment financed by the program or any related party to that obligor from purchasing bonds of an issue that finance the program in an amount related to the amount of the purpose investment acquired from that obligor; and

(5) The issuer has not waived the right to treat the investment as a program investment.

Purpose investment means an investment that is acquired to carry out the governmental purpose of an issue.

Qualified administrative costs means qualified administrative costs as defined in § 1.148-5(e).

Qualified guarantee means a qualified guarantee as defined in § 1.148-4(f).

Qualified hedge means a qualified hedge as defined in § 1.148-4(h)(2).

Reasonable expectations or reasonableness. An issuer's expectations or actions are reasonable only if a prudent person in the same circumstances as the issuer would have those same ex-

Reg. § 1.148-1(b)

→ *Caution: Reg. § 1.148-1, below, is applicable to certain bonds sold on or after July 8, 1997.*←

pectations or take those same actions, based on all the objective facts and circumstances. Factors relevant to a determination of reasonableness include the issuer's history of conduct concerning stated expectations made in connection with the issuance of obligations, the level of inquiry by the issuer into factual matters, and the existence of covenants, enforceable by bondholders, that require implementation of specific expectations. For a conduit financing issue, factors relevant to a determination of reasonableness include the reasonable expectations of the conduit borrower, but only if, under the circumstances, it is reasonable and prudent for the issuer to rely on those expectations.

Rebate amount means 100 percent of the amount owed to the United States under section 148(f)(2), as further described in § 1.148-3.

Receipt means a receipt as defined in § 1.148-3(d) for purposes of computing the rebate amount, and a receipt as defined in § 1.148-5(b) for purposes of computing yield on an investment.

Refunding escrow means one or more funds established as part of a single transaction or a series of related transactions, containing proceeds of a refunding issue and any other amounts to provide for payment of principal or interest on one or more prior issues. For this purpose, funds are generally not so established solely because of—

(1) The deposit of proceeds of an issue and replacement proceeds of the prior issue in an escrow more than 6 months apart, or

(2) The deposit of proceeds of completely separate issues in an escrow.

Replacement proceeds is defined in paragraph (c) of this section.

Restricted working capital expenditures means working capital expenditures that are subject to the proceeds-spent-last rule in § 1.148-6(d)(3)(i) and are ineligible for any exception to that rule.

Sale proceeds means any amounts actually or constructively received from the sale of the issue, including amounts used to pay underwriters' discount or compensation and accrued interest other than pre-issuance accrued interest. Sale proceeds also include, but are not limited to, amounts derived from the sale of a right that is associated with a bond, and that is described in § 1.148(b)(4). See also § 1.148-4(h)(5) treating amounts received upon the termination of certain hedges as sale proceeds.

Stated redemption price means the redemption price of an obligation under the terms of that obligation, including any call premium.

Transferred proceeds means transferred proceeds as defined in § 1.148-9 (or the applicable corresponding provision of prior law).

Unconditionally payable means payable under terms in which—

(1) Late payment or nonpayment results in a significant penalty to the borrower or reasonable remedies to the lender, and

(2) It is reasonably certain on the issue date that the payment will actually be made.

Value means value determined under § 1.148-4(e) for a bond, and value determined under § 1.148-5(d) for an investment.

Variable yield bond means any bond that is not a fixed yield bond.

Variable yield issue means any issue that is not a fixed yield issue.

Yield means yield computed under § 1.148-4 for an issue, and yield computed under § 1.148-5 for an investment.

Yield restricted means required to be invested at a yield that is not materially higher than the yield on the issue under section 148(a) and § 1.148-2.

(c) *Definition of replacement proceeds*—(1) *In general.* Amounts are replacement proceeds of an issue if the amounts have a sufficiently direct nexus to the issue or to the governmental purpose of the issue to conclude that the amounts would have been used for that governmental purpose if the proceeds of the issue were not used or to be used for that governmental purpose. For this purpose, governmental purposes include the expected use of amounts for the payment of debt service on a particular date. The mere availability or preliminary earmarking of amounts for a governmental purpose, however, does not in itself establish a sufficient nexus to cause those amounts to be replacement proceeds. Replacement proceeds include, but are not limited to, sinking funds, pledged funds, and other replacement proceeds described in paragraph (c)(4) of this section, to the extent that those funds or amounts are held by or derived from a substantial beneficiary of the issue. A substantial beneficiary of an issue includes the issuer and any related party to the issuer, and, if the issuer is not a state, the state in which the issuer is located. A person is not a substantial beneficiary of an issue solely because it is a guarantor under a qualified guarantee.

Reg. § 1.148-1(c)(1)

→ *Caution: Reg. § 1.148-1, below, is applicable to certain bonds sold on or after July 8, 1997.*←

(2) *Sinking fund.* Sinking fund includes a debt service fund, redemption fund, reserve fund, replacement fund, or any similar fund, to the extent reasonably expected to be used directly or indirectly to pay principal or interest on the issue.

(3) *Pledged fund*—(i) *In general.* A *pledged fund* is any amount that is directly or indirectly pledged to pay principal or interest on the issue. A pledge need not be cast in any particular form but, in substance, must provide reasonable assurance that the amount will be available to pay principal or interest on the issue, even if the issuer encounters financial difficulties. A pledge to a guarantor of an issue is an indirect pledge to secure payment of principal or interest on the issue. A pledge of more than 50 percent of the outstanding stock of a corporation that is a conduit borrower of the issue is not treated as a pledge for this purpose, unless the corporation is formed or availed of to avoid the creation of replacement proceeds.

(ii) *Negative pledges.* An amount is treated as pledged to pay principal or interest on an issue if it is held under an agreement to maintain the amount at a particular level for the direct or indirect benefit of the bondholders or a guarantor of the bonds. An amount is not treated as pledged under this paragraph (c)(3)(ii), however, if—

(A) The issuer or a substantial beneficiary may grant rights in the amount that are superior to the rights of the bondholders or the guarantor; or

(B) The amount does not exceed reasonable needs for which it is maintained, the required level is tested no more frequently than every 6 months, and the amount may be spent without any substantial restriction other than a requirement to replenish the amount by the next testing date.

(4) *Other replacement proceeds*—(i) *Bonds outstanding longer than necessary*—(A) *In general.* Replacement proceeds arise to the extent that the issuer reasonably expects as of the issue date that—

(*1*) The term of an issue will be longer than is reasonably necessary for the governmental purposes of the issue, and

(*2*) There will be available amounts during the period that the issue remains outstanding longer than necessary. Whether an issue is outstanding longer than necessary is determined under § 1.148-10. Replacement proceeds are cre-

ated under this paragraph (c)(4)(i)(A) at the beginning of each fiscal year during which an issue remains outstanding longer than necessary in an amount equal to available amounts of the issuer as of that date.

(B) *Safe harbor against creation of replacement proceeds.* As a safe harbor, replacement proceeds do not arise under paragraph (c)(4)(i)(A) of this section—

(*1*) For the portion of an issue that is to be used to finance restricted working capital expenditures, if that portion is not outstanding longer than 2 years;

(*2*) For the portion of an issue (including a refunding issue) that is to be used to finance or refinance capital projects, if that portion has a weighted average maturity that does not exceed 120 percent of the average reasonably expected economic life of the financed capital projects, determined in the same manner as under section 147(b); or

(*3*) For the portion of an issue that is a refunding issue, if that portion has a weighted average maturity that does not exceed the remaining weighted average maturity of the prior issue, and the issue of which the prior issue is a part satisfies paragraph (c)(4)(i)(B)(*1*) or (*2*) of this section.

(ii) *Bonds financing a working capital reserve*—(A) *In general.* Except as otherwise provided in paragraph (c)(4)(ii)(B) of this section, replacement proceeds arise to the extent a working capital reserve is, directly or indirectly, financed with the proceeds of the issue (regardless of the expenditure of proceeds of the issue). Thus, for example, if an issuer that does not maintain a working capital reserve borrows to fund a working capital reserve, the issuer will have replacement proceeds. To determine the amount of a working capital reserve maintained, an issuer may use the average amount maintained as a working capital reserve during annual periods of at least 1 year, the last of which ends within 1 year before the issue date. For example, the amount of a working capital reserve may be computed using the average of the beginning or ending monthly balances of the amount maintained as a reserve (net of unexpended gross proceeds) during the 1 year period preceding the issue date.

(B) *Exception to creation of replacement proceeds.* Replacement proceeds do not arise under paragraph (c)(4)(ii)(A) of this section with respect to an issue—

Reg. § 1.148-1(c)(4)

25,358 **Tax Exempt. Requirements: State/Local Bonds**

See p. 20,601 for regulations not amended to reflect law changes

→ *Caution: Reg. § 1.148-1, below, is applicable to certain bonds sold on or after July 8, 1997.*←

(*1*) All of the net proceeds of which are spent within 6 months of the issue date under section 148(f)(4)(B)(iii)(I); or

(*2*) That is not subject to the rebate requirement under the exception provided by section 148(f)(4)(D).

(d) *Elections.* Except as otherwise provided, any required elections must be made in writing, and, once made, may not be revoked without the permission of the Commissioner.

(e) *Investment-type property*—(1) *In general.* Investment-type property includes any property, other than property described in section 148(b)(2)(A), (B), (C), or (E), that is held principally as a passive vehicle for the production of income. For this purpose, production of income includes any benefit based on the time value of money, including the benefit from making a prepayment.

(2) *Non-customary prepayments.* Except as otherwise provided in this paragraph (e), a prepayment for property or services gives rise to investment-type property if a principal purpose for prepaying is to receive an investment return from the time the prepayment is made until the time payment otherwise would be made. A prepayment does not give rise to investment-type property if—

(i) The prepayment is made for a substantial business purpose other than investment return and the issuer has no commercially reasonable alternative to the prepayment; or

(ii) Prepayments on substantially the same terms are made by a substantial percentage of persons who are similarly situated to the issuer but who are not beneficiaries of tax-exempt financing.

(3) *Certain hedges.* Investment-type property also includes the investment element of a contract that is a hedge (within the meaning of § 1.148-4(h)(2)(i)(A)) and that contains a significant investment element because a payment by the issuer relates to a conditional or unconditional obligation by the hedge provider to make a payment on a later date. See § 1.148-4(h)(2)(ii) relating to hedges with a significant investment element. [Reg. § 1.148-1.]

☐ [*T.D.* 8418, 5-12-92. *Amended by T.D.* 8476, 6-14-93; *T.D.* 8538, 5-5-94 *and T.D.* 8718, 5-8-97.]

→ *Caution: Reg. § 1.148-1A, below, is applicable to certain bonds sold prior to July 8, 1997.*←

[Reg. § 1.148-1A]

§ 1.148-1A. **Definitions and elections.**—(a) [Reserved]. For guidance see § 1.148-1.

(b) *Certain definitions.*

Investment-type property. See § 1.148-1(b). Investment-type property also includes a contract that would be a hedge (within the meaning of § 1.148-4(h)) except that it contains a significant investment element.

(c) through (c)(4)(i) [Reserved]. For guidance see § 1.148-1.

(c)(4)(ii) *Bonds financing a working capital reserve*—(A) *In general.* Except as otherwise provided in § 1.148-1(c)(4)(ii)(B), replacement proceeds arise to the extent a working capital reserve is, directly or indirectly, financed with the proceeds of the issue (regardless of the expenditure of proceeds of the issue). Thus, for example, if an issuer that does not maintain a working capital reserve borrows to fund such a reserve, the issuer will have replacement proceeds. To determine the amount of a working capital reserve maintained, an issuer may use the average amount maintained as a working capital reserve during annual periods of at least one year, the last of which ends within a year before the issue date. For example, the amount of a working capital reserve may be computed using the average of the beginning or ending monthly balances of the amount maintained as a reserve (net of unexpended gross proceeds) during the one year period preceding the issue date. [Reg. § 1.148-1A.]

☐ [*T.D.* 8538, 5-5-94. *Redesignated and amended by T.D.* 8718, 5-8-97.]

→ *Caution: Reg. § 1.148-2, below, is applicable to certain bonds sold on or after July 8, 1997.*←

[Reg. § 1.148-2]

§ 1.148-2. **General arbitrage yield restriction rules.**—(a) *In general.* Under section 148(a), the direct or indirect investment of the gross proceeds of an issue in higher yielding investments causes the bonds of the issue to be arbitrage bonds. The investment of proceeds in higher yielding investments, however, during a temporary period described in paragraph (e) of this section, as part of a reasonably required reserve or replacement fund

Tax Exempt. Requirements: State/Local Bonds　　**25,359**

See p. 20,601 for regulations not amended to reflect law changes

→ *Caution: Reg. § 1.148-2, below, is applicable to certain bonds sold on or after July 8, 1997.*←

described in paragraph (f) of this section, or as part of a minor portion described in paragraph (g) of this section does not cause the bonds of the issue to be arbitrage bonds. Bonds are not arbitrage bonds under this section as a result of an inadvertent, insubstantial error.

(b) *Reasonable expectations*—(1) *In general.* Except as provided in paragraph (c) of this section, the determination of whether an issue consists of arbitrage bonds under section 148(a) is based on the issuer's reasonable expectations as of the issue date regarding the amount and use of the gross proceeds of the issue.

(2) *Certification of expectations*—(i) *In general.* An officer of the issuer responsible for issuing the bonds must, in good faith, certify the issuer's expectations as of the issue date. The certification must state the facts and estimates that form the basis for the issuer's expectations. The certification is evidence of the issuer's expectations, but does not establish any conclusions of law or any presumptions regarding either the issuer's actual expectations or their reasonableness.

(ii) *Exceptions to certification requirement.* An issuer is not required to make a certification for an issue under paragraph (b)(2)(i) of this section if—

(A) The issuer reasonably expects as of the issue date that there will be no unspent gross proceeds after the issue date, other than gross proceeds in a bona fide debt service fund (e.g., equipment lease financings in which the issuer purchases equipment in exchange for an installment payment note); or

(B) The issue price of the issue does not exceed $1,000,000.

(c) *Intentional acts.* The taking of any deliberate, intentional action by the issuer or person acting on its behalf after the issue date in order to earn arbitrage causes the bonds of the issue to be arbitrage bonds if that action, had it been expected on the issue date, would have caused the bonds to be arbitrage bonds. An intent to violate the requirements of section 148 is not necessary for an action to be intentional.

(d) *Materially higher yielding investments*—(1) *In general.* The yield on investments is materially higher than the yield on the issue to which the investments are allocated if the yield on the investments over the term of the issue exceeds the yield on the issue by an amount in excess of the applicable definition of *materially higher* set forth in paragraph (d)(2) of this section. If yield restricted investments in the same class are subject

to different definitions of *materially higher*, the applicable definition of *materially higher* that produces the lowest permitted yield applies to all the investments in the class. The yield on the issue is determined under § 1.148-4. The yield on investments is determined under § 1.148-5.

(2) *Definitions of materially higher yield*—(i) *General rule for purpose and nonpurpose investments.* For investments that are not otherwise described in this paragraph (d)(2), materially higher means one-eighth of 1 percentage point.

(ii) *Refunding escrows and replacement proceeds.* For investments in a refunding escrow or for investments allocable to replacement proceeds, materially higher means one-thousandth of 1 percentage point.

(iii) *Program investments.* For program investments that are not described in paragraph (d)(2)(iv) of this section, materially higher means 1 and one-half percentage points.

(iv) *Student loans.* For qualified student loans that are program investments, materially higher means 2 percentage points.

(v) *Tax-exempt investments.* For investments that are tax-exempt bonds and are not investment property under section 148(b)(3), no yield limitation applies.

(3) *Mortgage loans.* Qualified mortgage loans that satisfy the requirements of section 143(g) are treated as meeting the requirements of this paragraph (d).

(e) *Temporary periods*—(1) *In general.* During the temporary periods set forth in this paragraph (e), the proceeds and replacement proceeds of an issue may be invested in higher yielding investments without causing bonds in the issue to be arbitrage bonds. This paragraph (e) does not apply to refunding issues (see § 1.148-9).

(2) *General 3-year temporary period for capital projects and qualified mortgage loans*—(i) *In general.* The net sale proceeds and investment proceeds of an issue reasonably expected to be allocated to expenditures for capital projects qualify for a temporary period of 3 years beginning on the issue date (the *3-year temporary period*). The 3-year temporary period also applies to the proceeds of qualified mortgage bonds and qualified veterans' mortgage bonds by substituting *qualified mortgage loans* in each place that *capital projects* appears in this paragraph (e)(2). The 3-year temporary period applies only if the issuer reasonably expects to satisfy the expenditure test, the time test, and the due diligence test. These rules apply separately to each conduit loan fi-

25,360   **Tax Exempt. Requirements: State/Local Bonds**

See p. 20,601 for regulations not amended to reflect law changes

→ *Caution: Reg. § 1.148-2, below, is applicable to certain bonds sold on or after July 8, 1997.←*

nanced by an issue (other than qualified mortgage loans), with the expenditure and time tests measured from the issue date of the issue.

    (A) *Expenditure test.* The expenditure test is met if at least 85 percent of the net sale proceeds of the issue are allocated to expenditures on the capital projects by the end of the 3-year temporary period.

    (B) *Time test.* The time test is met if the issuer incurs within 6 months of the issue date a substantial binding obligation to a third party to expend at least 5 percent of the net sale proceeds of the issue on the capital projects. An obligation is not binding if it is subject to contingencies within the issuer's or a related party's control.

    (C) *Due diligence test.* The due diligence test is met if completion of the capital projects and the allocation of the net sale proceeds of the issue to expenditures proceed with due diligence.

    (ii) *5-year temporary period.* In the case of proceeds expected to be allocated to a capital project involving a substantial amount of construction expenditures (as defined in § 1.148-7), a 5-year temporary period applies in lieu of the 3-year temporary period if the issuer satisfies the requirements of paragraph (e)(2)(i) of this section applied by substituting "5 years" in each place that "3 years" appears, and both the issuer and a licensed architect or engineer certify that the longer period is necessary to complete the capital project.

    (3) *Temporary period for restricted working capital expenditures—(i) General rule.* The proceeds of an issue that are reasonably expected to be allocated to restricted working capital expenditures within 13 months after the issue date qualify for a temporary period of 13 months beginning on the issue date. Paragraph (e)(2) of this section contains additional temporary period rules for certain working capital expenditures that are treated as part of a capital project.

    (ii) *Longer temporary period for certain tax anticipation issues.* If an issuer reasonably expects to use tax revenues arising from tax levies for a single fiscal year to redeem or retire an issue, and the issue matures by the earlier of 2 years after the issue date or 60 days after the last date for payment of those taxes without interest or penalty, the temporary period under paragraph (e)(3)(i) of this section is extended until the maturity date of the issue.

    (4) *Temporary period for pooled financings—* (i) *In general.* Proceeds of a pooled financing issue

reasonably expected to be used to finance purpose investments qualify for a temporary period of 6 months while held by the issuer before being loaned to a conduit borrower. Any otherwise available temporary period for proceeds held by a conduit borrower, however, is reduced by the period of time during which those proceeds were held by the issuer before being loaned. For example, if the proceeds of a pooled financing issue loaned to a conduit borrower would qualify for a 3-year temporary period, and the proceeds are held by the issuer for 5 months before being loaned to the conduit borrower, the proceeds qualify for only an additional 31-month temporary period after being loaned to the conduit borrower. Except as provided in paragraph (e)(4)(iv) of this section, this paragraph (e)(4) does not apply to any qualified mortgage bond or qualified veterans' mortgage bond under section 143.

    (ii) *Loan repayments—(A) Amount held by the issuer.* The temporary period under this paragraph (e)(4) for proceeds from the sale or repayment of any loan that are reasonably expected to be used to make or finance new loans is 3 months.

    (B) *Amounts re-loaned to conduit borrowers.* Any temporary period for proceeds held by a conduit borrower under a new loan from amounts described in paragraph (e)(4)(ii)(A) of this section is determined by treating the date the new loan is made as the issue date and by reducing the temporary period by the period the amounts were held by the issuer following the last repayment.

    (iii) *Construction issues.* If all or a portion of a pooled financing issue qualifies as a construction issue under § 1.148-7(b)(6), paragraph (e)(4)(i) of this section is applied by substituting "2 years" for "6 months."

    (iv) *Amounts re-loaned for qualified mortgage loans.* The temporary period under this paragraph (e)(4) for proceeds from the sale, prepayment, or repayment of any qualified mortgage loan that are reasonably expected to be used to make or finance new qualified mortgage loans is 3 years.

    (5) *Temporary period for replacement proceeds—(i) In general.* Except as otherwise provided, replacement proceeds qualify for a temporary period of 30 days beginning on the date that the amounts are first treated as replacement proceeds.

    (ii) *Temporary period for bona fide debt service funds.* Amounts in a bona fide debt service

Reg. § 1.148-2(e)(3)

→ *Caution: Reg. § 1.148-2, below, is applicable to certain bonds sold on or after July 8, 1997.*←

fund for an issue qualify for a temporary period of 13 months. If only a portion of a fund qualifies as a bona fide debt service fund, only that portion qualifies for this temporary period.

(6) *Temporary period for investment proceeds.* Except as otherwise provided in this paragraph (e), investment proceeds qualify for a temporary period of 1 year beginning on the date of receipt.

(7) *Other amounts.* Gross proceeds not otherwise eligible for a temporary period described in this paragraph (e) qualify for a temporary period of 30 days beginning on the date of receipt.

(f) *Reserve or replacement funds*—(1) *General 10 percent limitation on funding with sale proceeds.* An issue consists of arbitrage bonds if sale proceeds of the issue in excess of 10 percent of the stated principal amount of the issue are used to finance any reserve or replacement fund, without regard to whether those sale proceeds are invested in higher yielding investments. If an issue has more than a de minimis amount of original issue discount or premium, the issue price (net of pre-issuance accrued interest) is used to measure the 10-percent limitation in lieu of stated principal amount. This rule does not limit the use of amounts other than sale proceeds of an issue to fund a reserve or replacement fund.

(2) *Exception from yield restriction for reasonably required reserve or replacement funds*—(i) *In general.* The investment of amounts that are part of a reasonably required reserve or replacement fund in higher yielding investments will not cause an issue to consist of arbitrage bonds. A reasonably required reserve or replacement fund may consist of all or a portion of one or more funds, however labelled, derived from one or more sources. Amounts in a reserve or replacement fund in excess of the amount that is reasonably required are not part of a reasonably required reserve or replacement fund.

(ii) *Size limitation.* The amount of gross proceeds of an issue that qualifies as a reasonably required reserve or replacement fund may not exceed an amount equal to the least of 10 percent of the stated principal amount of the issue, the maximum annual principal and interest requirements on the issue, or 125 percent of the average annual principal and interest requirements on the issue. If an issue has more than a de minimis amount of original issue discount or premium, the issue price of the issue (net of pre-issuance accrued interest) is used to measure the 10 percent limitation in lieu of its stated principal amount. For a reserve or replacement fund that secures

more than one issue (e.g. a parity reserve fund), the size limitation may be measured on an aggregate basis.

(iii) *Valuation of investments.* Investments in a reasonably required reserve or replacement fund may be valued in any reasonable, consistently applied manner that is permitted under § 1.148-5.

(iv) *150 percent debt service limitation on investment in nonpurpose investments for certain private activity bonds.* Section 148(d)(3) contains additional limits on the amount of gross proceeds of an issue of private activity bonds, other than qualified 501(c)(3) bonds, that may be invested in higher yielding nonpurpose investments without causing the bonds to be arbitrage bonds. For purposes of these rules, *initial temporary period* means the temporary periods under paragraphs (e)(2), (e)(3), and (e)(4) of this section and under § 1.148-9(d)(2)(i), (ii), and (iii).

(3) *Certain parity reserve funds.* The limitation contained in paragraph (f)(1) of this section does not apply to an issue if the master legal document authorizing the issuance of the bonds (e.g., a master indenture) was adopted before August 16, 1986, and that document—

(i) Requires a reserve or replacement fund in excess of 10 percent of the sale proceeds, but not more than maximum annual principal and interest requirements;

(ii) Is not amended after August 31, 1986 (other than to permit the issuance of additional bonds as contemplated in the master legal document); and

(iii) Provides that bonds having a parity of security may not be issued by or on behalf of the issuer for the purposes provided under the document without satisfying the reserve fund requirements of the indenture.

(g) *Minor portion.* Under section 148(e), a bond of an issue is not an arbitrage bond solely because of the investment in higher yielding investments of gross proceeds of the issue in an amount not exceeding the lesser of—

(1) 5 percent of the sale proceeds of the issue; or

(2) $100,000.

(h) *Certain waivers permitted.* On or before the issue date, an issuer may elect to waive the right to invest in higher yielding investments during any temporary period under paragraph (e) of this section or as part of a reasonably required reserve or replacement fund under paragraph (f) of this

25,362   **Tax Exempt. Requirements: State/Local Bonds**

See p. 20,601 for regulations not amended to reflect law changes

→ *Caution: Reg. § 1.148-2, below, is applicable to certain bonds sold on or after July 8, 1997.*←

section. At any time, an issuer may waive the right to invest in higher yielding investments as part of a minor portion under paragraph (g) of this section. [Reg. § 1.148-2.]

☐ [*T.D.* 8418, 5-12-92. *Amended by T.D.* 8476, 6-14-93; *T.D.* 8538, 5-5-94 *and T.D.* 8718, 5-8-97.]

→ *Caution: Reg. § 1.148-2A, below, is applicable to certain bonds sold prior to July 8, 1997.*←

[Reg. § 1.148-2A]

§ 1.148-2A. General arbitrage yield restriction rules.—(a) through (b)(2)(i) [Reserved]. For guidance see § 1.148-2.

(b)(2)(ii) *Exceptions to certification requirement.* An issuer is not required to make a certification for an issue under § 1.148-2(b)(2)(i) if—

(A) The issuer reasonably expects as of the issue date that there will be no unspent gross

proceeds after the issue date, other than gross proceeds in a bona fide debt service fund (e.g., *equipment lease* financings in which the issuer purchases equipment in exchange for an installment payment note); or

(B) The issue price of the issue does not exceed $1,000,000. [Reg. § 1.148-2A.]

☐ [*T.D.* 8538, 5-5-94. *Redesignated and amended by T.D.* 8718, 5-8-97.]

→ *Caution: Reg. § 1.148-3, below, is applicable to certain bonds sold on or after July 8, 1997.*←

[Reg. § 1.148-3]

§ 1.148-3. General arbitrage rebate rules.— (a) *In general.* Section 148(f) requires that certain earnings on nonpurpose investments allocable to the gross proceeds of an issue be paid to the United States to prevent the bonds in the issue from being arbitrage bonds. The arbitrage that must be rebated is based on the difference between the amount actually earned on nonpurpose investments and the amount that would have been earned if those investments had a yield equal to the yield on the issue.

(b) *Definition of rebate amount.* As of any date, the rebate amount for an issue is the excess of the future value, as of that date, of all receipts on nonpurpose investments over the future value, as of that date, of all payments on nonpurpose investments.

(c) *Computation of future value of a payment or receipt.* The future value of a payment or receipt at the end of any period is determined using the economic accrual method and equals the value of that payment or receipt when it is paid or received (or treated as paid or received), plus interest assumed to be earned and compounded over the period at a rate equal to the yield on the issue, using the same compounding interval and financial conventions used to compute that yield.

(d) *Payments and receipts*—(1) *Definition of payments.* For purposes of this section, payments are—

(i) Amounts actually or constructively paid to acquire a nonpurpose investment (or treated as paid to a commingled fund);

(ii) For a nonpurpose investment that is first allocated to an issue on a date after it is actually acquired (e.g., an investment that becomes allocable to transferred proceeds or to replacement proceeds) or that becomes subject to the rebate requirement on a date after it is actually acquired (e.g., an investment allocated to a reasonably required reserve or replacement fund for a construction issue at the end of the 2-year spending period), the value of that investment on that date;

(iii) For a nonpurpose investment that was allocated to an issue at the end of the preceding computation period, the value of that investment at the beginning of the computation period;

(iv) On the last day of each bond year during which there are amounts allocated to gross proceeds of an issue that are subject to the rebate requirement, and on the final maturity date, a computation credit of $1,000; and

(v) Yield reduction payments on nonpurpose investments made pursuant to § 1.148-5(c).

(2) *Definition of receipts.* For purposes of this section, receipts are—

(i) Amounts actually or constructively received from a nonpurpose investment (including amounts treated as received from a commingled fund), such as earnings and return of principal;

(ii) For a nonpurpose investment that ceases to be allocated to an issue before its disposition or redemption date (e.g., an investment that becomes allocable to transferred proceeds of another issue or that ceases to be allocable to the

Reg. § 1.148-2A(a)

Tax Exempt. Requirements: State/Local Bonds   25,363

See p. 20,601 for regulations not amended to reflect law changes

→ *Caution: Reg. § 1.148-3, below, is applicable to certain bonds sold on or after July 8, 1997.*←

issue pursuant to the universal cap under § 1.148-6) or that ceases to be subject to the rebate requirement on a date earlier than its disposition or redemption date (e.g. an investment allocated to a fund initially subject to the rebate requirement but that subsequently qualifies as a bona fide debt service fund), the value of that nonpurpose investment on that date; and

(iii) For a nonpurpose investment that is held at the end of a computation period, the value of that investment at the end of that period.

(3) *Special rules for commingled funds.* Section 1.148-6(e) provides special rules to limit certain of the required determinations of payments and receipts for investments of a commingled fund.

(e) *Computation dates*—(1) *In general.* For a fixed yield issue, an issuer may treat any date as a computation date. For a variable yield issue, an issuer:

(i) May treat the last day of any bond year ending on or before the latest date on which the first rebate amount is required to be paid under paragraph (f) of this section (the *first required payment date*) as a computation date but may not change that treatment after the first payment date; and

(ii) After the first required payment date, must consistently treat either the end of each bond year or the end of each fifth bond year as computation dates and may not change these computation dates after the first required payment date.

(2) *Final computation date.* The date that an issue is discharged is the final computation date. For an issue retired within 3 years of the issue date, however, the final computation date need not occur before the end of 8 months after the issue date or during the period in which the issuer reasonably expects that any of the spending exceptions under § 1.148-7 will apply to the issue.

(f) *Amount of required rebate installment payment*—(1) *Amount of interim rebate payments.* The first rebate installment payment must be made for a computation date that is not later than 5 years after the issue date. Subsequent rebate installment payments must be made for a computation date that is not later than 5 years after the previous computation date for which an installment payment was made. A rebate installment payment must be in an amount that, when added to the future value, as of the computation date, of previous rebate payments made for the

issue, equals at least 90 percent of the rebate amount as of that date.

(2) *Amount of final rebate payment.* For the final computation date, a final rebate payment must be paid in an amount that, when added to the future value of previous rebate payments made for the issue, equals 100 percent of the rebate amount as of that date.

(3) *Future value of rebate payments.* The future value of a rebate payment is determined under paragraph (c) of this section. This value is computed by taking into account recoveries of overpayments.

(g) *Time and manner of payment.* Each rebate payment must be paid no later than 60 days after the computation date to which the payment relates. Any rebate payment paid within this 60-day period may be treated as paid on the computation date to which it relates. A rebate payment is paid when it is filed with the Internal Revenue Service at the place or places designated by the Commissioner. A payment must be accompanied by the form provided by the Commissioner for this purpose.

(h) *Penalty in lieu of loss of tax exemption*—(1) *In general.* The failure to pay the correct rebate amount when required will cause the bonds of the issue to be arbitrage bonds, unless the Commissioner determines that the failure was not caused by willful neglect and the issuer promptly pays a penalty to the United States. If no bond of the issue is a private activity bond (other than a qualified 501(c)(3) bond), the penalty equals 50 percent of the rebate amount not paid when required to be paid, plus interest on that amount. Otherwise, the penalty equals 100 percent of the rebate amount not paid when required to be paid, plus interest on that amount.

(2) *Interest on underpayments.* Interest accrues at the underpayment rate under section 6621, beginning on the date the correct rebate amount is due and ending on the date 10 days before it is paid.

(3) *Waivers of the penalty.* The penalty is automatically waived if the rebate amount that the issuer failed to pay plus interest is paid within 180 days after discovery of the failure, unless, the Commissioner determines that the failure was due to willful neglect, or the issue is under examination by the Commissioner at any time during the period beginning on the date the failure first occurred and ending on the date 90 days after the receipt of the rebate amount. Generally, extensions of this 180-day period and waivers of the

25,364   Tax Exempt. Requirements: State/Local Bonds

See p. 20,601 for regulations not amended to reflect law changes

→ *Caution: Reg. § 1.148-3, below, is applicable to certain bonds sold on or after July 8, 1997.*←

penalty in other cases will be granted by the Commissioner only in unusual circumstances. See also § 1.148-3T(h)(3). For purposes of this paragraph (h)(3), willful neglect does not include a failure that is attributable solely to the permissible retroactive selection of a short first bond year if the rebate amount that the issuer failed to pay is paid within 60 days of the selection of that bond year.

(4) *Application to alternative penalty under § 1.148-7.* Paragraphs (h)(1), (2), and (3) of this section apply to failures to pay penalty payments under § 1.148-7 (*alternative penalty amounts*) by substituting *alternative penalty amounts* for *rebate amount* and *the last day of each spending period* for *computation date.*

(i) *Recovery of overpayment of rebate*—(1) *In general.* An issuer may recover an overpayment for an issue of tax-exempt bonds by establishing to the satisfaction of the Commissioner that the overpayment occurred. An overpayment is the excess of the amount paid to the United States for an issue under section 148 over the sum of the rebate amount for the issue as of the most recent computation date and all amounts that are other-

wise required to be paid under section 148 as of the date the recovery is requested.

(2) *Limitations on recovery.* (i) An overpayment may be recovered only to the extent that a recovery on the date that it is first requested would not result in an additional rebate amount if that date were treated as a computation date.

(ii) Except for overpayments of penalty in lieu of rebate under section 148(f)(4)(C)(vii) and § 1.148-7(k), an overpayment of less than $5,000 may not be recovered before the final computation date.

(j) *Examples.* The provisions of this section may be illustrated by the following examples.

Example 1. Calculation and payment of rebate for a fixed yield issue. (i) *Facts.* On January 1, 1994, City *A* issues a fixed yield issue and invests all the sale proceeds of the issue ($49 million). There are no other gross proceeds. The issue has a yield of 7.0000 percent per year compounded semiannually (computed on a 30 day month/360 day year basis). City *A* receives amounts from the investment and immediately expends them for the governmental purpose of the issue as follows:

Date	Amount
2/1/94	$3,000,000
5/1/94	5,000,000
1/1/95	5,000,000
9/1/95	20,000,000
3/1/96	22,000,000

(ii) *First computation date.* (A) City *A* chooses January 1, 1999, as its first computation date. This date is the latest date that may be used to compute the first required rebate installment payment. The rebate amount as of this date is computed by determining the future value of the receipts and the payments for the investment.

The compounding interval is each 6-month (or shorter) period and the 30 day month/360 day year basis is used because these conventions were used to compute yield on the issue. The future value of these amounts, plus the computation credit, as of January 1, 1999, is:

Date	Receipts (Payments)	FV (7.0000 percent)
1/1/94	($49,000,000)	($69,119,339)
2/1/94	3,000,000	4,207,602
5/1/94	5,000,000	6,893,079
1/1/95	5,000,000	6,584,045
1/1/95	(1,000)	(1,317)
9/1/95	20,000,000	25,155,464
1/1/96	(1,000)	(1,229)
3/1/96	22,000,000	26,735,275
1/1/97	(1,000)	(1,148)
Rebate amount (1/01/99)		$ 452,432

(B) City *A* pays 90 percent of the rebate amount ($407,189) to the United States within 60 days of January 1, 1999.

(iii) *Second computation date.* (A) On the next required computation date, January 1, 2004, the future value of the payments and receipts is:

Reg. § 1.148-3(h)(4)

Tax Exempt. Requirements: State/Local Bonds   25,365

See p. 20,601 for regulations not amended to reflect law changes

→ *Caution: Reg. § 1.148-3, below, is applicable to certain bonds sold on or after July 8, 1997.*←

Date	Receipts (Payments)	FV (7.0000 percent)
1/1/99..	$ 452,432	$ 638,200
Rebate amount (1/01/04)		$ 638,200

(B) As of this computation date, the future value of the payment treated as made on January 1, 1999, is $574,380, which equals at least 90 percent of the rebate amount as of this computation date ($638,200 × 0.9), and thus no additional rebate payment is due as of this date.

(iv) *Final computation date.* (A) On January 1, 2009, City A redeems all the bonds, and thus this date is the final computation date. The future value of the receipts and payments as of this date is:

Date	Receipts (Payments)	FV (7.0000 percent)
1/1/04..	$638,200	$900,244
1/1/09..	(1,000)	(1,000)
Rebate amount (1/01/09)		$899,244

(B) As of this computation date, the future value of the payment made on January 1, 1999, is $810,220 and thus an additional rebate payment of $89,024 is due. This payment reflects the future value of the 10 percent unpaid portion, and thus would not be owed had the issuer paid the full rebate amount as of any prior computation date.

Example 2. Calculation and payment of rebate for a variable yield issue. (i) *Facts.* On July 1,

Date	Amount
8/1/1994	$5,000,000
7/1/1995	8,000,000
12/1/1995	17,000,000
7/1/1999	650,000

(ii) *First computation date.* (A) City B treats the last day of the fifth bond year (July 1, 1999) as a computation date. The yield on the variable yield issue during the first computation period (the period beginning on the issue date and ending on the first computation date) is 6.0000 percent per year compounded semiannually. The value of the nonpurpose investments allocated to the issue as of July 1, 1999, is $3 million. The rebate

1994, City B issues a variable yield issue and invests all of the sale proceeds of the issue ($30 million). There are no other gross proceeds. As of July 1, 1999, there are nonpurpose investments allocated to the issue. Prior to July 1, 1999, City B receives amounts from nonpurpose investments and immediately expends them for the governmental purpose of the issue as follows:

amount as of July 1, 1999, is computed by determining the future value of the receipts and the payments for the nonpurpose investments. The compounding interval is each 6-month (or shorter) period and the 30 day month/360 day year basis is used because these conventions were used to compute yield on the issue. The future value of these amounts and of the computation date credits as of July 1, 1999, is:

Date	Receipts (Payments)	FV (6.0000 percent)
7/1/1994	($30,000,000)	($40,317,491)
8/1/1994	5,000,000	6,686,560
7/1/1995	(1,000)	(1,267)
7/1/1995	8,000,000	10,134,161
12/1/1995	17,000,000	21,011,112
7/1/1996	(1,000)	(1,194)
7/1/1997	(1,000)	(1,126)
7/1/1998	(1,000)	(1,061)
7/1/1999	3,000,000	3,000,000
7/1/1999	650,000	650,000
7/1/1999	(1,000)	(1,000)
Rebate amount (7/01/1999)		$1,158,694

Reg. § 1.148-3(j)

25,366   **Tax Exempt. Requirements: State/Local Bonds**

See p. 20,601 for regulations not amended to reflect law changes

→ *Caution: Reg. § 1.148-3, below, is applicable to certain bonds sold on or after July 8, 1997.*←

(B) City *B* pays 90 percent of the rebate amount ($1,042,824.60) to the United States within 60 days of July 1, 1999.

(iii) *Next computation date.* (A) On July 1, 2004, City *B* redeems all of the bonds. Thus, the next computation date is July 1, 2004. On July 30, 1999, City *B* chose to compute rebate for periods following the first computation period by treating the end of each fifth bond year as a computation date. The yield during the second computation period is 5.0000 percent per year compounded

semiannually. The computation of the rebate amount as of this date reflects the value of the nonpurpose investments allocated to the issue at the end of the prior computation period. On July 1, 2004, City *B* sells those nonpurpose investments for $3,925,000 and expends that amount for the governmental purpose of the issue.

(B) As of July 1, 2004, the future value of the rebate amount computed as of July 1, 1999, and of all other payments and receipts is:

Date	Receipts (Payments)	FV (5.0000 percent)
7/1/1999	$1,158,694	$1,483,226
7/1/1999	(3,000,000)	(3,840,254)
7/1/2000	(1,000)	(1,218)
7/1/2001	(1,000)	(1,160)
7/1/2002	(1,000)	(1,104)
7/1/2003	(1,000)	(1,051)
7/1/2004	(2,000)	(2,000)
7/1/2004	3,925,000	3,925,000
		$1,561,439

(C) As of this computation date, the future value of the payment made on July 1, 1999, is $1,334,904 and thus an additional rebate payment of $226,535 is due.

(D) If the yield during the second computation period were, instead, 7.0000 percent, the rebate amount computed as of July 1, 1999, would be $1,320,891. The future value of the payment made on July 1, 1999, would be $1,471.007, and, therefore, City B would have overpaid the rebate amount by $150,116.

(k) *Bona fide debt service fund exception.* Under section 148(f)(4)(A), the rebate requirement does not apply to amounts in certain bona fide debt service funds. An issue with an average annual debt service that is not in excess of $2,500,000 may be treated as satisfying the $100,000 limitation in section 148(f)(4)(A)(ii). [Reg. § 1.148-3.]

☐ [*T.D. 8418, 5-12-92. Amended by T.D. 8476, 6-14-93; T.D. 8538, 5-5-94 and T.D. 8718, 5-8-97.*]

→ *Caution: Reg. § 1.148-3A, below, is applicable to certain bonds sold prior to July 8, 1997.*←

[Reg. § 1.148-3A]

§ 1.148-3A. General arbitrage rebate rules.— (a) through (h)(2) [Reserved]. For guidance see § 1.148-3.

(h)(3) *Waivers of the penalty.* For purposes of § 1.148-3(h)(3), willful neglect does not include a failure that is attributable solely to the permis-

sible retroactive selection of a short first bond year if the rebate amount that the issuer failed to pay is paid within 60 days of the selection of that bond year. [Reg. § 1.148-3A.]

☐ [*T.D. 8538, 5-5-94. Redesignated and amended by T.D. 8718, 5-8-97.*]

→ *Caution: Reg. § 1.148-4, below, is applicable to certain bonds sold on or after July 8, 1997.*←

[Reg. § 1.148-4]

§ 1.148-4. Yield on an issue of bonds.—(a) *In general.* The yield on an issue of bonds is used to apply investment yield restrictions under section 148(a) and to compute rebate liability under section 148(f). Yield is computed under the economic accrual method using any consistently applied compounding interval of not more than one year.

A short first compounding interval and a short last compounding interval may be used. Yield is expressed as an annual percentage rate that is calculated to at least four decimal places (e.g., 5.2525 percent). Other reasonable, standard financial conventions, such as the 30 days per month/360 days per year convention, may be used in computing yield but must be consistently applied. The yield on an issue that would be a

Tax Exempt. Requirements: State/Local Bonds 25,367

See p. 20,601 for regulations not amended to reflect law changes

→ *Caution: Reg. § 1.148-4, below, is applicable to certain bonds sold on or after July 8, 1997.*←

purpose investment (absent section 148(b)(3)(A)) is equal to the yield on the conduit financing issue that financed that purpose investment. The Commissioner may permit issuers of qualified mortgage bonds or qualified student loan bonds to use a single yield for two or more issues.

(b) *Computing yield on a fixed yield issue*—(1) *In general*—(i) *Yield on an issue.* The yield on a fixed yield issue is the discount rate that, when used in computing the present value as of the issue date of all unconditionally payable payments of principal, interest, and fees for qualified guarantees on the issue and amounts reasonably expected to be paid as fees for qualified guarantees on the issue, produces an amount equal to the present value, using the same discount rate, of the aggregate issue price of bonds of the issue as of the issue date. Further, payments include certain amounts properly allocable to a qualified hedge. Yield on a fixed yield issue is computed as of the issue date and is not affected by subsequent unexpected events, except to the extent provided in paragraphs (b)(4) and (h)(3) of this section.

(ii) *Yield on a bond.* Yield on a fixed yield bond is computed in the same manner as yield on a fixed yield issue.

(2) *Yield on certain fixed yield bonds subject to mandatory or contingent early redemption*—(i) *In general.* The yield on a fixed yield issue that includes a bond subject to mandatory early redemption or expected contingent redemption is computed by treating that bond as redeemed on its reasonably expected early redemption date for an amount equal to its value on that date. Reasonable expectations are determined on the issue date. A bond is subject to mandatory early redemption if it is unconditionally payable in full before its final maturity date. A bond is subject to a contingent redemption if it must be, or is reasonably expected to be, redeemed prior to final maturity upon the occurrence of a contingency. A contingent redemption is taken into account only if the contingency is reasonably expected to occur, in which case the date of occurrence of the contingency must be reasonably estimated. For example, if bonds are reasonably expected to be redeemed early using excess revenues from general or special property taxes or benefit assessments or similar amounts, the reasonably expected redemption schedule is used to determine yield. For purposes of this paragraph (b)(2)(i), excess proceeds calls for issues for which the requirements of § 1.148-2(e)(2) or (3) are satisfied, calamity calls, and refundings do not cause a bond to be subject to early redemption. The

value of a bond is determined under paragraph (e) of this section.

(ii) *Substantially identical bonds subject to mandatory early redemption.* If substantially identical bonds of an issue are subject to specified mandatory redemptions prior to final maturity (e.g., a mandatory sinking fund redemption requirement), yield on that issue is computed by treating those bonds as redeemed in accordance with the redemption schedule for an amount equal to their value. Generally, bonds are substantially identical if the stated interest rate, maturity, and payment dates are the same. In computing the yield on an issue containing bonds described in this paragraph (b)(2)(ii), each of those bonds must be treated as redeemed at its present value, unless the stated redemption price at maturity of the bond does not exceed the issue price of the bond by more than one-fourth of one percent multiplied by the product of the stated redemption price at maturity and the number of years to the weighted average maturity date of the substantially identical bonds, in which case each of those bonds must be treated as redeemed at its outstanding stated principal amount, plus accrued, unpaid interest. Weighted average maturity is determined by taking into account the mandatory redemption schedule.

(3) *Yield on certain fixed yield bonds subject to optional early redemption*—(i) *In general.* If a fixed yield bond is subject to optional early redemption and is described in paragraph (b)(3)(ii) of this section, the yield on the issue containing the bond is computed by treating the bond as redeemed at its stated redemption price on the optional redemption date that would produce the lowest yield on the issue.

(ii) *Fixed yield bonds subject to special yield calculation rule.* A fixed yield bond is described in this paragraph (b)(3)(ii) only if it—

(A) Is subject to optional redemption within five years of the issue date, but only if the yield on the issue computed by assuming all bonds in the issue subject to redemption within 5 years of the issue date are redeemed at maturity is more than one-eighth of one percentage point higher than the yield on that issue computed by assuming all bonds subject to optional redemption within 5 years of the issue date are redeemed at the earliest date for their redemption;

(B) Is issued at an issue price that exceeds the stated redemption price at maturity by more than one-fourth of one percent multiplied by the product of the stated redemption price at

Reg. § 1.148-4(b)(3)

25,368   Tax Exempt. Requirements: State/Local Bonds

See p. 20,601 for regulations not amended to reflect law changes

→ *Caution: Reg. § 1.148-4, below, is applicable to certain bonds sold on or after July 8, 1997.*←

maturity and the number of complete years to the first optional redemption date for the bond; or

(C) Bears interest at increasing interest rates (i.e., a *stepped coupon bond*).

(4) *Yield recomputed upon transfer of certain rights associated with the bond.* For purposes of § 1.148-3, as of the date of any transfer, waiver, modification, or similar transaction (collectively, a *transfer*) of any right that is part of the terms of a bond or is otherwise associated with a bond (e.g., a redemption right), in a transaction that is separate and apart from the original sale of the bond, the issue is treated as if it were retired and a new issue issued on the date of the transfer (*reissued*). The redemption price of the retired issue and the issue price of the new issue equal the aggregate values of all the bonds of the issue on the date of the transfer. In computing yield on the new issue, any amounts received by the issuer as consideration for the transfer are taken into account.

(5) *Special aggregation rule treating certain bonds as a single fixed yield bond.* Two variable yield bonds of an issue are treated in the aggregate as a single fixed yield bond if—

(i) Aggregate treatment would result in the single bond being a fixed yield bond; and

(ii) The terms of the bonds do not contain any features that could distort the aggregate fixed

yield from what the yield would be if a single fixed yield bond were issued. For example, if an issue contains a bond bearing interest at a floating rate and a related bond bearing interest at a rate equal to a fixed rate minus that floating rate, those two bonds are treated as a single fixed yield bond only if neither bond may be redeemed unless the other bond is also redeemed at the same time.

(6) *Examples.* The provisions of this paragraph (b) may be illustrated by the following examples.

Example 1. No early call. (i) *Facts.* On January 1, 1994, City *A* issues an issue consisting of four identical fixed yield bonds. The stated final maturity date of each bond is January 1, 2004, and no bond is subject to redemption before this date. Interest is payable on January 1 of each year at a rate of 6.0000 percent per year on the outstanding principal amount. The total stated principal amount of the bonds is $20 million. The issue price of the bonds $20,060,000.

(ii) *Computation.* The yield on the issue is computed by treating the bonds as retired at the stated maturity under the general rule of § 1.148-4(b)(1). The bonds are treated as redeemed for their stated redemption prices. The yield on the issue is 5.8731 percent per year compounded semiannually, computed as follows:

Date	Payments	PV (5.8731 percent)
1/1/1995	$ 1,200,000	$ 1,132,510
1/1/1996	1,200,000	1,068,816
1/1/1997	1,200,000	1,008,704
1/1/1998	1,200,000	951,973
1/1/1999	1,200,000	898,433
1/1/2000	1,200,000	847,903
1/1/2001	1,200,000	800,216
1/1/2002	1,200,000	755,210
1/1/2003	1,200,000	712,736
1/1/2004	21,200,000	11,883,498
		$20,060,000

Example 2. Mandatory calls. (i) *Facts.* The facts are the same as in *Example 1.* In this case, however, the bonds are subject to mandatory sinking fund redemption on January 1 of each year, beginning January 1, 2001. On each sinking fund redemption date, one of the bonds is chosen by lottery and is required to be redeemed at par plus accrued interest.

(ii) *Computation.* Because the bonds are subject to specified redemptions, yield on the issue is computed by treating the bonds as redeemed in accordance with the redemption schedule under § 1.148-4(b)(2)(ii). Because the bonds are not sold at a discount, the bonds are treated as retired at their stated redemption prices. The yield on the issue is 5.8678 percent per year compounded semiannually, computed as follows:

Reg. § 1.148-4(b)(4)

→ *Caution: Reg. § 1.148-4, below, is applicable to certain bonds sold on or after July 8, 1997.*←

Date	Payments	PV (5.8678 percent)
1/1/1995	$1,200,000	$ 1,132,569
1/1/1996	1,200,000	1,068,926
1/1/1997	1,200,000	1,008,860
1/1/1998	1,200,000	952,169
1/1/1999	1,200,000	898,664
1/1/2000	1,200,000	848,166
1/1/2001	6,200,000	4,135,942
1/1/2002	5,900,000	3,714,650
1/1/2003	5,600,000	3,327,647
1/1/2004	5,300,000	2,972,407
		$20,060,000

Example 3. Optional early call. (i) *Facts.* On January 1, 1994, City C issues an issue consisting of three bonds. Each bond has a stated principal amount of $10 million dollars and is issued for par. Bond X bears interest at 5 percent per year and matures on January 1, 1999. Bond Y bears interest at 6 percent per year and matures on January 1, 2002. Bond Z bears interest at 7 per-

cent per year and matures on January 1, 2004. Bonds Y and Z are callable by the issuer at par plus accrued interest after December 31, 1998.

(ii) *Computation.* (A) The yield on the issue computed as if each bond is outstanding to its maturity is 6.0834 percent per year compounded semiannually, computed as follows:

Date	Payments	PV (6.0834 percent)
1/1/1995	$ 1,800,000	$ 1,695,299
1/1/1996	1,800,000	1,596,589
1/1/1997	1,800,000	1,503,814
1/1/1998	1,800,000	1,416,342
1/1/1999	11,800,000	8,744,830
1/1/2000	1,300,000	907,374
1/1/2001	1,300,000	854,595
1/1/2002	11,300,000	6,996,316
1/1/2003	700,000	408,190
1/1/2004	10,700,000	5,876,551
		$30,000,000

(B) The yield on the issue computed as if all bonds are called at the earliest date for redemp-

tion is 5.9126 percent per year compounded semiannually, computed as follows:

Date	Payments	PV (5.9126 percent)
1/1/1995	$ 1,800,000	$ 1,698,113
1/1/1996	1,800,000	1,601,994
1/1/1997	1,800,000	1,511,315
1/1/1998	1,800,000	1,425,769
1/1/1999	31,800,000	23,762,809
		$30,000,000

(C) Because the yield on the issue computed by assuming all bonds in the issue subject to redemption within 5 years of the issue date are redeemed at maturity is more than one-eighth of one percentage point higher than the yield on the issue computed by assuming all bonds subject to optional redemption within 5 years of the issue date are redeemed at the earliest date for their redemption, each bond is treated as redeemed on the date that would produce the lowest yield for the issue. The lowest yield on the issue would result from a redemption of all the bonds on

January 1, 1999. Thus, the yield on the issue is 5.9126 percent per year compounded semiannually.

(c) *Computing yield on a variable yield issue—* (1) *In general.* The yield on a variable yield issue is computed separately for each computation period. The yield for each computation period is the discount rate that, when used in computing the present value as of the first day of the computation period of all the payments of principal and interest and fees for qualified guarantees that are

Reg. § 1.148-4(c)(1)

25,370 **Tax Exempt. Requirements: State/Local Bonds**

See p. 20,601 for regulations not amended to reflect law changes

→ *Caution: Reg. § 1.148-4, below, is applicable to certain bonds sold on or after July 8, 1997.*←

attributable to the computation period, produces an amount equal to the present value, using the same discount rate, of the aggregate issue price (or deemed issue price, as determined in paragraph (c)(2)(iv) of this section) of the bonds of the issue as of the first day of the computation period. The yield on a variable yield bond is computed in the same manner as the yield on a variable yield issue. Except as provided in paragraph (c)(2) of this section, yield on any fixed yield bond in a variable yield issue is computed in the same manner as the yield on a fixed yield issue as provided in paragraph (b) of this section.

(2) *Payments on bonds included in yield for a computation period*—(i) *Payments in general.* The payments on a bond that are attributable to a computation period include any amounts actually paid during the period for principal on the bond. Payments also include any amounts paid during the current period both for interest accruing on the bond during the current period and for interest accruing during the prior period that was included in the deemed issue price of the bond as accrued unpaid interest at the start of the current period under this paragraph (c)(2). Further, payments include any amounts properly allocable to fees for a qualified guarantee of the bond for the period and to any amounts properly allocable to a qualified hedge for the period.

(ii) *Payments at actual redemption.* If a bond is actually redeemed during a computation period, an amount equal to the greater of its value on the redemption date or the actual redemption price is a payment on the actual redemption date.

(iii) *Payments for bonds outstanding at end of computation period.* If a bond is outstanding at the end of a computation period, a payment equal to the bond's value is taken into account on the last day of that period.

(iv) *Issue price for bonds outstanding at beginning of next computation period.* A bond outstanding at the end of a computation period is treated as if it were immediately reissued on the next day for a deemed issue price equal to the value from the day before as determined under paragraph (c)(2)(iii) of this section.

(3) *Example.* The provisions of this paragraph (c) may be illustrated by the following example.

Example. On January 1, 1994, City *A* issues an issue of identical plain par bonds in an aggregate principal amount of $1,000,000. The bonds pay interest at a variable rate on each June 1 throughout the term of the issue. The entire principal amount of the bonds plus accrued, unpaid interest is payable on the final maturity date of January 1, 2000. No bond year is selected. On June 1, 1994, 1995, 1996, 1997, and 1998, interest in the amounts of $30,000, $55,000, $57,000, $56,000, and $45,000 is paid on the bonds. From June 1, 1998, to January 1, 1999, $30,000 of interest accrues on the bonds. From January 1, 1999, to June 1, 1999, another $35,000 of interest accrues. On June 1, 1999, the issuer actually pays $65,000 of interest. On January 1, 2000, $1,000,000 of principal and $38,000 of accrued interest are paid. The payments for the computation period starting on the issue date and ending on January 1, 1999, include all annual interest payments paid from the issue date to June 1, 1998. Because the issue is outstanding on January 1, 1999, it is treated as redeemed on that date for [an] amount equal to its value ($1,000,000 plus accrued, unpaid interest of $30,000 under paragraph (e)(1) of this section). Thus, $1,030,000 is treated as paid on January 1, 1999. The issue is then treated as reissued on January 1, 1999, for $1,030,000. The payments for the next computation period starting on January 1, 1999, and ending on January 1, 2000, include the interest actually paid on the bonds during that period ($65,000 on June 1, 1999, plus $38,000 paid on January 1, 2000). Because the issue was actually redeemed on January 1, 2000, an amount equal to its stated redemption price is also treated as paid on January 1, 2000.

(d) *Conversion from variable yield issue to fixed yield issue.* For purposes of determining yield under this section, as of the first day on which a variable yield issue would qualify as a fixed yield issue if it were newly issued on that date (a *conversion date*), that issue is treated as if it were reissued as a fixed yield issue on the conversion date. The redemption price of the variable yield issue and the issue price of the fixed yield issue equal the aggregate values of all the bonds on the conversion date. Thus, for example, for plain par bonds (e.g., tender bonds), the deemed issue price would be the outstanding principal amount, plus accrued unpaid interest. If the conversion date occurs on a date other than a computation date, the issuer may continue to treat the issue as a variable yield issue until the next computation date, at which time it must be treated as converted to a fixed yield issue.

(e) *Value of bonds*—(1) *Plain par bonds.* Except as otherwise provided, the value of a plain par bond is its outstanding stated principal amount, plus accrued unpaid interest. The value

Reg. § 1.148-4(c)(2)

Tax Exempt. Requirements: State/Local Bonds 25,371

See p. 20,601 for regulations not amended to reflect law changes

→ *Caution: Reg. § 1.148-4, below, is applicable to certain bonds sold on or after July 8, 1997.*←

of a plain par bond that is actually redeemed or treated as redeemed is its stated redemption price on the redemption date, plus accrued, unpaid interest.

(2) *Other bonds.* The value of a bond other than a plain par bond on a date is its present value on that date. The present value of a bond is computed under the economic accrual method taking into account all the unconditionally payable payments of principal, interest, and fees for a qualified guarantee to be paid on or after that date and using the yield on the bond as the discount rate, except that for purposes of § 1.148-6(b)(2) (relating to the universal cap), these values may be determined by consistently using the yield on the issue of which the bonds are a part. To determine yield on fixed yield bonds, see paragraph (b)(1) of this section. The rules contained in paragraphs (b)(2) and (b)(3) of this section apply for this purpose. In the case of bonds described in paragraph (b)(2)(ii) of this section, the present value of those bonds on any date is computed using the yield to the final maturity date of those bonds as the discount rate. In determining the present value of a variable yield bond under this paragraph (e)(2), the initial interest rate on the bond established by the interest index or other interest rate setting mechanism is used to determine the interest payments on that bond.

(f) *Qualified guarantees*—(1) *In general.* Fees properly allocable to payments for a qualified guarantee for an issue (as determined under paragraph (f)(6) of this section) are treated as additional interest on that issue under section 148. A guarantee is a qualified guarantee if it satisfies each of the requirements of paragraphs (f)(2) through (f)(4) of this section.

(2) *Interest savings.* As of the date the guarantee is obtained, the issuer must reasonably expect that the present value of the fees for the guarantee will be less than the present value of the expected interest savings on the issue as a result of the guarantee. For this purpose, present value is computed using the yield on the issue, determined with regard to guarantee payments, as the discount rate.

(3) *Guarantee in substance.* The arrangement must create a guarantee in substance. The arrangement must impose a secondary liability that unconditionally shifts substantially all of the credit risk for all or part of the payments, such as payments for principal and interest, redemption prices, or tender prices, on the guaranteed bonds. Reasonable procedural or administrative require-

ments of the guarantee do not cause the guarantee to be conditional. In the case of a guarantee against failure to remarket a qualified tender bond, commercially reasonable limitations based on credit risk, such as limitations on payment in the event of default by the primary obligor or the bankruptcy of a long-term credit guarantor, do not cause the guarantee to be conditional. The guarantee may be in any form. The guarantor may not be a co-obligor. Thus, the guarantor must not expect to make any payments other than under a direct-pay letter of credit or similar arrangement for which the guarantor will be reimbursed immediately. The guarantor and any related parties together must not use more than 10 percent of the proceeds of the portion of the issue allocable to the guaranteed bonds.

(4) *Reasonable charge*—(i) *In general.* Fees for a guarantee must not exceed a reasonable, arm's-length charge for the transfer of credit risk. In complying with this requirement, the issuer may not rely on the representations of the guarantor.

(ii) *Fees for services other than transfer of credit risk must be separately stated.* A fee for a guarantee must not include any payment for any direct or indirect services other than the transfer of credit risk, unless the compensation for those other services is separately stated, reasonable, and excluded from the guarantee fee. Fees for the transfer of credit risk include fees for the guarantor's overhead and other costs relating to the transfer of credit risk. For example, a fee includes payment for services other than transfer of credit risk if—

(A) It includes payment for the cost of underwriting or remarketing bonds or for the cost of insurance for casualty to bond-financed property;

(B) It is refundable upon redemption of the guaranteed bond before the final maturity date and the amount of the refund would exceed the portion of the fee that had not been earned; or

(C) The requirements of § 1.148-2(e)(2) (relating to temporary periods for capital projects) are not satisfied, and the guarantor is not reasonably assured that the bonds will be repaid if the project to be financed is not completed.

(5) *Guarantee of purpose investments.* Except for guarantees of qualified mortgage loans and qualified student loans, a guarantee of payments on a purpose investment is a qualified guarantee of the issue if all payments on the

Reg. § 1.148-4(f)(5)

25,372   Tax Exempt. Requirements: State/Local Bonds

See p. 20,601 for regulations not amended to reflect law changes

→ *Caution: Reg. § 1.148-4, below, is applicable to certain bonds sold on or after July 8, 1997.*←

purpose investment reasonably coincide with payments on the related bonds and the payments on the purpose investment are unconditionally payable no more than 6 months before the corresponding interest payment and 12 months before the corresponding principal payments on the bonds. This paragraph (f)(5) only applies if, in addition to satisfying the other requirements of this paragraph (f), the guarantee is, in substance, a guarantee of the bonds allocable to that purpose investment and to no other bonds except for bonds that are equally and ratably secured by purpose investments of the same conduit borrower.

(6) *Allocation of qualified guarantee payments*—(i) *In general.* Payments for a qualified guarantee must be allocated to bonds and to computation periods in a manner that properly reflects the proportionate credit risk for which the guarantor is compensated. Proportionate credit risk for bonds that are not substantially identical may be determined using any reasonable, consistently applied method. For example, this risk may be based on the ratio of the total principal and interest paid and to be paid on a guaranteed bond to the total principal and interest paid and to be paid on all bonds of the guaranteed issue. An allocation method generally is not reasonable, for example, if a substantial portion of the fee is allocated to the construction portion of the issue and a correspondingly insubstantial portion is allocated to the later years covered by the guarantee. Reasonable letter of credit *set up* fees may be allocated ratably during the initial term of the letter of credit. Upon an early redemption of a variable yield bond, fees otherwise allocable to the period after the redemption are allocated to remaining outstanding bonds of the issue or, if none remain outstanding, to the period before the redemption.

(ii) *Safe harbor for allocation of qualified guarantee fees for variable yield issues.* An allocation of non-level payments for a qualified guarantee for variable yield bonds is treated as meeting the requirements of paragraph (f)(6)(i) of this section if, for each bond year for which the guarantee is in effect, an equal amount (or for any short bond year, a proportionate amount of the equal amount) is treated as paid as of the beginning of that bond year. The present value of the annual amounts must equal the fee for the guarantee allocated to that bond, with present value computed as of the first day the guarantee is in effect by using as the discount rate the yield on the variable yield bonds covered by the guarantee,

determined without regard to any fee allocated under this paragraph (f)(6)(ii).

(7) *Refund or reduction of guarantee payments.* If as a result of an investment of proceeds of a refunding issue in a refunding escrow, there will be a reduction in, or refund of, payments for a guarantee (*savings*), the savings must be treated as a reduction in the payments on the refunding issue.

(g) *Yield on certain mortgage revenue and student loan bonds.* For purposes of section 148 and this section, section 143(g)(2)(C)(ii) applies to the computation of yield on an issue of qualified mortgage bonds or qualified veterans' mortgage bonds. For purposes of applying section 148 and section 143(g) with respect to purpose investments allocable to a variable yield issue of qualified mortgage bonds, qualified veterans' mortgage bonds, or qualified student loan bonds that is reasonably expected as of the issue date to convert to a fixed yield issue, the yield may be computed over the term of the issue, and, if the yield is so computed, paragraph (d) of this section does not apply to the issue. As of any date, the yield over the term of the issue is based on—

(1) With respect to any bond of the issue that has not converted to a fixed and determinable yield on or before that date, the actual amounts paid or received to that date and the amounts that are reasonably expected (as of that date) to be paid or received with respect to that bond over the remaining term of the issue (taking into account prepayment assumptions under section 143(g)(2)(B)(iv), if applicable); and

(2) With respect to any bond of the issue that has converted to a fixed and determinable yield on or before that date, the actual amounts paid or received before that bond converted, if any, and the amount that was reasonably expected (on the date that bond converted) to be paid or received with respect to that bond over the remaining term of the issue (taking into account prepayment assumptions under section 143(g)(2)(B)(iv), if applicable).

(h) *Qualified hedging transactions*—(1) *In general.* Payments made or received by an issuer under a qualified hedge (as defined in paragraph (h)(2) of this section) relating to bonds of an issue are taken into account (as provided in paragraph (h)(3) of this section) to determine the yield on the issue. Except as provided in paragraphs (h)(4) and (h)(5)(ii)(E) of this section, the bonds to which a qualified hedge relates are treated as variable yield bonds from the issue date of the

Tax Exempt. Requirements: State/Local Bonds   25,373

See p. 20,601 for regulations not amended to reflect law changes

→ *Caution: Reg. § 1.148-4, below, is applicable to certain bonds sold on or after July 8, 1997.*←

bonds. This paragraph (h) applies solely for purposes of sections 143(g), 148, and 149(d).

(2) *Qualified hedge defined.* Except as provided in paragraph (h)(5) of this section, the term *qualified hedge* means a contract that satisfies each of the following requirements:

(i) *Hedge*—(A) *In general.* The contract is entered into primarily to modify the issuer's risk of interest rate changes with respect to a bond (a hedge). For example, the contract may be an interest rate swap, an interest rate cap, a futures contract, a forward contract, or an option.

(B) *Special rule for fixed rate issues.* If the contract modifies the issuer's risk of interest rate changes with respect to a bond that is part of an issue that, absent the contract, would be a fixed rate issue, the contract must be entered into—

(1) No later than 15 days after the issue date (or the deemed issue date under paragraph (d) of this section) of the issue; or

(2) No later than the expiration of a qualified hedge with respect to bonds of that issue that satisfies paragraph (h)(2)(i)(B)(1) of this section; or

(3) No later than the expiration of a qualified hedge with respect to bonds of that issue that satisfies either paragraph (h)(2)(i)(B)(2) of this section or this paragraph (h)(2)(i)(B)(3).

(C) *Contracts with certain acquisition payments.* If a hedge provider makes a single payment to the issuer (e.g., a payment for an off-market swap) in connection with the acquisition of a contract, the issuer may treat a portion of that contract as a hedge provided—

(1) The hedge provider's payment to the issuer and the issuer's payments under the contract in excess of those that it would make if the contract bore rates equal to the on-market rates for the contract (determined as of the date the parties enter into the contract) are separately identified in a certification of the hedge provider; and

(2) The payments described in paragraph (h)(2)(i)(C)(1) of this section are not treated as payments on the hedge.

(ii) *No significant investment element*—(A) *In general.* The contract does not contain a significant investment element. Except as provided in paragraph (h)(2)(ii)(B) of this section, a contract contains a significant investment element if a significant portion of any payment by one party relates to a conditional or unconditional obligation by the other party to make a payment on a different date. Examples of contracts that contain a significant investment element are a debt instrument held by the issuer; an interest rate swap requiring any payments other than periodic payments, within the meaning of § 1.446-3 (periodic payments) (e.g., a payment for an off-market swap or prepayment of part or all of one leg of a swap); and an interest rate cap requiring the issuer's premium for the cap to be paid in a single, up-front payment.

(B) *Special level payment rule for interest rate caps.* An interest rate cap does not contain a significant investment element if—

(1) All payments to the issuer by the hedge provider are periodic payments;

(2) The issuer makes payments for the cap at the same time as periodic payments by the hedge provider must be made if the specified index (within the meaning of § 1.446-3) of the cap is above the strike price of the cap; and

(3) Each payment by the issuer bears the same ratio to the notional principal amount (within the meaning of § 1.446-3) that is used to compute the hedge provider's payment, if any, on that date.

(iii) *Parties.* The contract is entered into between the issuer or the political subdivision on behalf of which the issuer issues the bonds (collectively referred to in this paragraph (h) as the *issuer*) and a provider that is not a related party (the *hedge provider*).

(iv) *Hedged bonds.* The contract covers, in whole or in part, all of one or more groups of substantially identical bonds in the issue (i.e., all of the bonds having the same interest rate, maturity, and terms). Thus, for example, a qualified hedge may include a hedge of all or a pro rata portion of each interest payment on the variable rate bonds in an issue for the first 5 years following their issuance. For purposes of this paragraph (h), unless the context clearly requires otherwise, *hedged bonds* means the specific bonds or portions thereof covered by a hedge.

(v) *Interest based contract.* The contract is primarily interest based. A contract is not primarily interest based unless—

(A) The hedged bond, without regard to the contract, is either a fixed rate bond, a variable rate debt instrument within the meaning of § 1.1275-5 provided the rate is not based on an objective rate other than a qualified inverse floating rate or a qualified inflation rate, a tax-exempt obligation described in § 1.1275-4(d)(2), or an in-

Reg. § 1.148-4(h)(2)

25,374   Tax Exempt. Requirements: State/Local Bonds

See p. 20,601 for regulations not amended to reflect law changes

→ *Caution: Reg. § 1.148-4, below, is applicable to certain bonds sold on or after July 8, 1997.←*

flation-indexed debt instrument within the meaning of § 1.1275-7; and

(B) As a result of treating all payments on (and receipts from) the contract as additional payments on (and receipts from) the hedged bond, the resulting bond would be substantially similar to either a fixed rate bond, a variable rate debt instrument within the meaning of § 1.1275-5 provided the rate is not based on an objective rate other than a qualified inverse floating rate or a qualified inflation rate, a tax-exempt obligation described in § 1.1275-4(d)(2), or an inflation-indexed debt instrument within the meaning of § 1.1275-7. For this purpose, differences that would not prevent the resulting bond from being substantially similar to another type of bond include a difference between the index used to compute payments on the hedged bond and the index used to compute payments on the hedge where one index is substantially the same, but not identical to, the other; the difference resulting from the payment of a fixed premium for a cap (e.g., payments for a cap that are made in other than level installments); and the difference resulting from the allocation of a termination payment where the termination was not expected as of the date the contract was entered into.

(vi) *Payments closely correspond.* The payments received by the issuer from the hedge provider under the contract correspond closely in time to either the specific payments being hedged on the hedged bonds or specific payments required to be made pursuant to the bond documents, regardless of the hedge, to a sinking fund, debt service fund, or similar fund maintained for the issue of which the hedged bond is a part.

(vii) *Source of payments.* Payments to the hedge provider are reasonably expected to be made from the same source of funds that, absent the hedge, would be reasonably expected to be used to pay principal and interest on the hedged bonds.

(viii) *Identification.* The contract must be identified by the actual issuer on its books and records maintained for the hedged bonds not later than 3 days after the date on which the issuer and the hedge provider enter into the contract. The identification must specify the hedge provider, the terms of the contract, and the hedged bonds. The identification must contain sufficient detail to establish that the requirements of this paragraph (h)(2) and, if applicable, paragraph (h)(4) of this section are satisfied. In addition, the existence of the hedge must be noted on the first form relating to the issue of which the hedged bonds are

a part that is filed with the Internal Revenue Service on or after the date on which the contract is identified pursuant to this paragraph (h)(2)(viii).

(3) *Accounting for qualified hedges*—(i) *In general.* Except as otherwise provided in paragraph (h)(4) of this section, payments made or received by the issuer under a qualified hedge are treated as payments made or received, as appropriate, on the hedged bonds that are taken into account in determining the yield on those bonds. These payments are reasonably allocated to the hedged bonds in the period to which the payments relate, as determined under paragraph (h)(3)(iii) of this section. Payments made or received by the issuer include payments deemed made or received when a contract is terminated or deemed terminated under this paragraph (h)(3). Payments reasonably allocable to the modification of risk of interest rate changes and to the hedge provider's overhead under this paragraph (h) are included as payments made or received under a qualified hedge.

(ii) *Exclusions from hedge.* If any payment for services or other items under the contract is not expressly treated by paragraph (h)(3)(i) of this section as a payment under the qualified hedge, the payment is not a payment with respect to a qualified hedge.

(iii) *Timing and allocation of payments.* Except as provided in paragraphs (h)(3)(iv) and (h)(5) of this section, payments made or received by the issuer under a qualified hedge are taken into account in the same period in which those amounts would be treated as income or deductions under § 1.446-4 (without regard to § 1.446-4(a)(2)(iv)) and are adjusted as necessary to reflect the end of a computation period and the start of a new computation period.

(iv) *Termination payments*—(A) *Termination defined.* A termination of a qualified hedge includes any sale or other disposition of the hedge by the issuer or the acquisition by the issuer of an offsetting hedge. A deemed termination occurs when the hedged bonds are redeemed or when a hedge ceases to be a qualified hedge of the hedged bonds. In the case of an assignment by a hedge provider of its remaining rights and obligations under the hedge to a third party or a modification of the hedging contract, the assignment or modification is treated as a termination with respect to the issuer only if it results in a deemed exchange of the hedge and a realization event under section 1001 to the issuer.

Reg. § 1.148-4(h)(3)

→ *Caution: Reg. § 1.148-4, below, is applicable to certain bonds sold on or after July 8, 1997.*←

(B) *General rule.* A payment made or received by an issuer to terminate a qualified hedge, including loss or gain realized or deemed realized, is treated as a payment made or received on the hedged bonds, as appropriate. The payment is reasonably allocated to the remaining periods originally covered by the terminated hedge in a manner that reflects the economic substance of the hedge.

(C) *Special rule for terminations when bonds are redeemed.* Except as otherwise provided in this paragraph (h)(3)(iv)(C) and in paragraph (h)(3)(iv)(D) of this section, when a qualified hedge is deemed terminated because the hedged bonds are redeemed, the fair market value of the qualified hedge on the redemption date is treated as a termination payment made or received on that date. When hedged bonds are redeemed, any payment received by the issuer on termination of a hedge, including a termination payment or a deemed termination payment, reduces, but not below zero, the interest payments made by the issuer on the hedged bonds in the computation period ending on the termination date. The remainder of the payment, if any, is reasonably allocated over the bond years in the immediately preceding computation period or periods to the extent necessary to eliminate the excess.

(D) *Special rules for refundings.* To the extent that the hedged bonds are redeemed using the proceeds of a refunding issue, the termination payment is accounted for under paragraph (h)(3)(iv)(B) of this section by treating it as a payment on the refunding issue, rather than the hedged bonds. In addition, to the extent that the refunding issue is redeemed during the period to which the termination payment has been allocated to that issue, paragraph (h)(3)(iv)(C) of this section applies to the termination payment by treating it as a payment on the redeemed refunding issue.

(E) *Safe harbor for allocation of certain termination payments.* A payment to terminate a qualified hedge does not result in that hedge failing to satisfy the applicable provisions of paragraph (h)(3)(iv)(B) of this section if the payment is allocated in accordance with this paragraph (h)(3)(iv)(E). For an issue that is a variable yield issue after termination of a qualified hedge, an amount must be allocated to each date on which the hedge provider's payment, if any, would have been made had the hedge not been terminated. The amounts allocated to each date must bear the same ratio to the notional principal amount (within the meaning of § 1.446-3) that would have

been used to compute the hedge provider's payment, if any, on that date, and the sum of the present values of those amounts must equal the present value of the termination payment. Present value is computed as of the day the qualified hedge is terminated, using the yield on the hedged bonds, determined without regard to the termination payment. The yield used for this purpose is computed for the period beginning on the first date the qualified hedge is in effect and ending on the date the qualified hedge is terminated. On the other hand, for an issue that is a fixed yield issue after termination of a qualified hedge, the termination payment is taken into account as a single payment on the date it is paid.

(4) *Certain variable yield bonds treated as fixed yield bonds*—(i) *In general.* Except as otherwise provided in this paragraph (h)(4), if the issuer of variable yield bonds enters into a qualified hedge, the hedged bonds are treated as fixed yield bonds paying a fixed interest rate if:

(A) *Maturity.* The term of the hedge is equal to the entire period during which the hedged bonds bear interest at variable interest rates, and the issuer does not reasonably expect that the hedge will be terminated before the end of that period.

(B) *Payments closely correspond.* Payments to be received under the hedge correspond closely in time to the hedged portion of payments on the hedged bonds. Hedge payments received within 15 days of the related payments on the hedged bonds generally so correspond.

(C) *Aggregate payments fixed.* Taking into account all payments made and received under the hedge and all payments on the hedged bonds (i.e., after netting all payments), the issuer's aggregate payments are fixed and determinable as of a date not later than 15 days after the issue date of the hedged bonds. Payments on bonds are treated as fixed for purposes of this paragraph (h)(4)(i)(C) if payments on the bonds are based, in whole or in part, on one interest rate, payments on the hedge are based, in whole or in part, on a second interest rate that is substantially the same as, but not identical to, the first interest rate and payments on the bonds would be fixed if the two rates were identical. Rates are treated as substantially the same if they are reasonably expected to be substantially the same throughout the term of the hedge. For example, an objective 30-day tax-exempt variable rate index or other objective index may be substantially the same as an issuer's individual 30-day interest rate.

Reg. § 1.148-4(h)(4)

25,376   **Tax Exempt. Requirements: State/Local Bonds**

See p. 20,601 for regulations not amended to reflect law changes

→ *Caution: Reg. § 1.148-4, below, is applicable to certain bonds sold on or after July 8, 1997.*←

(ii) *Accounting.* Except as otherwise provided in this paragraph (h)(4)(ii), in determining yield on the hedged bonds, all the issuer's payments on the hedged bonds and all payments made and received on a hedge described in paragraph (h)(4)(i) of this section are taken into account. If payments on the bonds and payments on the hedge are based, in whole or in part, on variable interest rates that are substantially the same within the meaning of paragraph (h)(4)(i)(C) of this section (but not identical), yield on the issue is determined by treating the variable interest rates as identical. For example, if variable rate bonds bearing interest at a weekly rate equal to the rate necessary to remarket the bonds at par are hedged with an interest rate swap under which the issuer receives payments based on a short-term floating rate index that is substantially the same as, but not identical to, the weekly rate on the bonds, the interest payments on the bonds are treated as equal to the payments received by the issuer under the swap for purposes of computing the yield on the bonds.

(iii) *Effect of termination*—(A) *In general.* Except as otherwise provided in this paragraph (h)(4)(iii) and paragraph (h)(5) of this section, the issue of which the hedged bonds are a part is treated as if it were reissued as of the termination date of the qualified hedge covered by paragraph (h)(4)(i) of this section in determining yield on the hedged bonds for purposes of § 1.148-3. The redemption price of the retired issue and the issue price of the new issue equal the aggregate values of all the bonds of the issue on the termination date. In computing the yield on the new issue for this purpose, any termination payment is accounted for under paragraph (h)(3)(iv) of this section, applied by treating the termination payment as made or received on the new issue under this paragraph (h)(4)(iii).

(B) *Effect of early termination.* Except as otherwise provided in this paragraph (h)(4)(iii), the general rules of paragraph (h)(4)(i) of this section do not apply in determining the yield on the hedged bonds for purposes of § 1.148-3 if the hedge is terminated or deemed terminated within 5 years after the issue date of the issue of which the hedged bonds are a part. Thus, the hedged bonds are treated as variable yield bonds for purposes of § 1.148-3 from the issue date.

(C) *Certain terminations disregarded.* This paragraph (h)(4)(iii) does not apply to a termination if, based on the facts and circumstances (e.g., taking into account both the termination and any qualified hedge that immediately replaces the terminated hedge), there is no change in the yield.

(5) *Contracts entered into before issue date of hedged bond*—(i) *In general.* A contract does not fail to be a hedge under paragraph (h)(2)(i) of this section solely because it is entered into before the issue date of the hedged bond. However, that contract must be one to which either paragraph (h)(5)(ii) or (h)(5)(iii) of this section applies.

(ii) *Contracts expected to be closed substantially contemporaneously with the issue date of hedged bond*—(A) *Application.* This paragraph (h)(5)(ii) applies to a contract if, on the date the contract is identified, the issuer reasonably expects to terminate or otherwise close (terminate) the contract substantially contemporaneously with the issue date of the hedged bond.

(B) *Contract terminated.* If a contract to which this paragraph (h)(5)(ii) applies is terminated substantially contemporaneously with the issue date of the hedged bond, the amount paid or received, or deemed to be paid or received, by the issuer in connection with the issuance of the hedged bond to terminate the contract is treated as an adjustment to the issue price of the hedged bond and as an adjustment to the sale proceeds of the hedged bond for purposes of section 148. Amounts paid or received, or deemed to be paid or received, before the issue date of the hedged bond are treated as paid or received on the issue date in an amount equal to the future value of the payment or receipt on that date. For this purpose, future value is computed using yield on the hedged bond without taking into account amounts paid or received (or deemed paid or received) on the contract.

(C) *Contract not terminated.* If a contract to which this paragraph (h)(5)(ii) applies is not terminated substantially contemporaneously with the issue date of the hedged bond, the contract is deemed terminated for its fair market value as of the issue date of the hedged bond. Once a contract has been deemed terminated pursuant to this paragraph (h)(5)(ii)(C), payments on and receipts from the contract are no longer taken into account under this paragraph (h) for purposes of determining yield on the hedged bond.

(D) *Relation to other requirements of a qualified hedge.* Payments made in connection with the issuance of a bond to terminate a contract to which this paragraph (h)(5)(ii) applies do not prevent the contract from satisfying the requirements of paragraph (h)(2)(vi) of this section.

Reg. § 1.148-4(h)(5)

Tax Exempt. Requirements: State/Local Bonds   25,377

See p. 20,601 for regulations not amended to reflect law changes

→ *Caution: Reg. § 1.148-4, below, is applicable to certain bonds sold on or after July 8, 1997.*←

(E) *Fixed yield treatment.* A bond that is hedged with a contract to which this paragraph (h)(5)(ii) applies does not fail to be a fixed yield bond if, taking into account payments on the contract and the payments to be made on the bond, the bond satisfies the definition of fixed yield bond. See also paragraph (h)(4) of this section.

(iii) *Contracts expected not to be closed substantially contemporaneously with the issue date of hedged bond*—(A) *Application.* This paragraph (h)(5)(iii) applies to a contract if, on the date the contract is identified, the issuer does not reasonably expect to terminate the contract substantially contemporaneously with the issue date of the hedge bond.

(B) *Contract terminated.* If a contract to which this paragraph (h)(5)(iii) applies is terminated in connection with the issuance of the hedged bond, the amount paid or received, or deemed to be paid or received, by the issuer to terminate the contract is treated as an adjustment to the issue price of the hedged bond and as an adjustment to the sale proceeds of the hedged bond for purposes of section 148.

(C) *Contract not terminated.* If a contract to which this paragraph (h)(5)(iii) applies is not terminated substantially contemporaneously with the issue date of the hedged bond, no payments with respect to the hedge made by the issuer before the issue date of the hedged bond are taken into account under this section.

(iv) *Identification.* The identification required under paragraph (h)(2)(viii) of this section must specify the reasonably expected governmental purpose, issue price, maturity, and issue date of the hedged bond, the manner in which interest is reasonably expected to be computed, and whether paragraph (h)(5)(ii) or (h)(5)(iii) of this section applies to the contract. If an issuer identifies a contract under this paragraph (h)(5)(iv) that would be a qualified hedge with respect to the anticipated bond, but does not issue the anticipated bond on the identified issue date, the contract is taken into account as a qualified hedge of any bond of the issuer that is issued for the identified governmental purpose within a reasonable interval around the identified issue date of the anticipated bond.

(6) *Authority of the Commissioner.* The Commissioner, by publication of a revenue ruling or revenue procedure (see § 601.601(d)(2) of this chapter), may specify contracts that, although they do not meet the requirements of paragraph (h)(2) of this section, are qualified hedges or, although they do not meet the requirements of paragraph (h)(4) of this section, cause the hedged bonds to be treated as fixed yield bonds. [Reg. § 1.148-4.]

☐ [*T.D.* 8418, 5-12-92. *Amended by T.D.* 8476, 6-14-93; *T.D.* 8538, 5-5-94; *T.D.* 8718, 5-8-97 *and T.D.* 8838, 9-3-99.]

→ *Caution: Reg. § 1.148-4A, below, is applicable to certain bonds sold prior to July 8, 1997.*←

[Reg. § 1.148-4A]

§ 1.148-4A. **Yield on an issue of bonds.**—(a) through (b)(4) [Reserved]. For guidance see § 1.148-4.

(b)(5) *Special aggregation rule treating certain bonds as a single fixed yield bond.* Two variable yield bonds of an issue are treated in the aggregate as a single fixed yield bond if—

(i) Aggregate treatment would result in the single bond being a fixed yield bond; and

(ii) The terms of the bonds do not contain any features that could distort the aggregate fixed yield from what the yield would be if a single fixed yield bond were issued. For example, if an issue contains a bond bearing interest at a floating rate and a related bond bearing interest at a rate equal to a fixed rate minus that floating rate, those two bonds are treated as a single fixed yield

bond only if neither bond may be redeemed unless the other bond is also redeemed at the same time.

(c) through (f) [Reserved]. For guidance see § 1.148-4.

(g) *Yield on certain mortgage revenue and student loan bonds.* For purposes of section 148 and § 1.148-4, section 143(g)(2)(C)(ii) applies to the computation of yield on an issue of qualified mortgage bonds or qualified veterans' mortgage bonds. For purposes of applying sections 148 and 143(g) to a variable yield issue of qualified mortgage bonds, qualified veterans' mortgage bonds, or qualified student loan bonds, the yield on that issue is computed over the term of the issue, and § 1.148-4(d) does not apply to the issue. As of any date before the final maturity date, the yield over the term of the issue is based on the actual amounts paid or received to that date and the amounts that are reasonably expected (as of that

25,378   **Tax Exempt. Requirements: State/Local Bonds**

See p. 20,601 for regulations not amended to reflect law changes

→ *Caution: Reg. § 1.148-4A, below, is applicable to certain bonds sold prior to July 8, 1997.*←

date) to be paid or received over the remaining term of the issue.

(h) *Qualified hedging transactions*—(1) *In general.* Payments made or received by an issuer under a qualified hedge (as defined in § 1.148-4(h)(2)) relating to bonds of an issue are taken into account (as provided in paragraph (h)(3) of this section) to determine the yield on the issue. Except as provided in paragraphs (h)(4) and (h)(5)(ii)(C) of this section, the bonds to which a qualified hedge relates are treated as variable yield bonds. These hedging rules apply solely for purposes of sections 143(g), 148, and 149(d).

(2)(i) through (vi) [Reserved]. For guidance see § 1.148-4(h)(2).

(2)(vii) *Timing and duration.* For a contract to be a qualified hedge under § 1.148-4(h)(2), payments must not begin to accrue under the contract on a date earlier than the issue date of the hedged bonds and must not accrue longer than the hedged interest payments on the hedged bonds.

(viii) [Reserved]. For guidance see § 1.148-4(h).

(ix) *Identification.* For a contract to be a qualified hedge under § 1.148-4(h)(2), the contract must be identified by the actual issuer on its books and records maintained for the hedged bonds not later than three days after the date on which the parties enter into the contract. The identification must specify the hedge provider, the terms of the contract, and the hedged bonds. The identification must contain sufficient detail to establish that the requirements of § 1.148-4(h)(2), and if applicable, paragraph (h)(4) of this section are satisfied. The existence of the hedge must be noted on all forms filed with the Internal Revenue Service for the issue on or after the date on which the hedge is entered into.

(3) *Accounting for qualified hedges*—(i) *In general.* Except as otherwise provided in paragraph (h)(4) of this section, payments made or received by the issuer under a qualified hedge are treated as payments made or received, as appropriate, on the hedged bonds that are taken into account in determining the yield on those bonds. These payments are reasonably allocated to the hedged bonds in the period to which the payments relate, as determined under paragraph (h)(3)(iii) of this section. Payments made or received by the issuer include payments deemed made or received when a contract is terminated or deemed terminated under this paragraph (h)(3). Payments rea-

sonably allocable to the reduction of risk of interest rate changes and to the hedge provider's overhead under this paragraph (h) are included as payments made or received under a qualified hedge.

(ii) *Exclusions from hedge.* Payments for services or other items under the contract that are not expressly treated as payments under the qualified hedge under paragraph (h)(3)(i) of this section are not payments with respect to a qualified hedge.

(iii) *Timing and allocation of payments.* The period to which a payment made by the issuer relates is determined under general Federal income tax principles, including, without limitation, § 1.446-3, and adjusted as necessary to reflect the end of a computation period and the start of a new computation period. Except as provided in paragraphs (h)(3)(iv) and (h)(5)(ii) of this section, a payment received by the issuer is taken into account in the period that the interest payment that the payment hedges is required to be made.

(iv) *Termination payments*—(A) *Termination defined.* A termination of a qualified hedge includes any sale or other disposition of the hedge by the issuer, or the acquisition by the issuer of an offsetting hedge. A deemed termination occurs when the hedged bonds are redeemed and when a hedge ceases to be a qualified hedge of the hedged bonds. In the case of an assignment by a hedge provider of its remaining rights and obligations on the hedge to a third party or a modification of the hedging contract, the assignment or modification is treated as a termination with respect to the issuer only if it results in a deemed exchange of the hedge and a realization event under section 1001.

(B) *General rule.* A payment made or received by an issuer to terminate a qualified hedge, including loss or gain realized or deemed realized, is treated as a payment made or received on the hedged bonds, as appropriate. The payment is reasonably allocated to the remaining periods originally covered by the terminated hedge in a manner that reflects the economic substance of the hedge.

(C) *Special rule for terminations when bonds are redeemed.* Except as otherwise provided in this paragraph (h)(3)(iv)(C) and in paragraph (h)(3)(iv)(D) of this section, when a qualified hedge is deemed terminated because the hedged bonds are redeemed, the fair market value of the contract on the redemption date is treated as a

Reg. § 1.148-4A(h)(1)

Tax Exempt. Requirements: State/Local Bonds   25,379

See p. 20,601 for regulations not amended to reflect law changes

→ *Caution: Reg. § 1.148-4A, below, is applicable to certain bonds sold prior to July 8, 1997.*←

termination payment made or received on that date. When hedged bonds are redeemed, any payment received by the issuer on termination of a hedge, including a termination payment or a deemed termination payment, reduces, but not below zero, the interest payments made by the issuer on the hedged bonds in the computation period ending on the termination date. The remainder of the payment, if any, is reasonably allocated over the bond years in the immediately preceding computation period or periods to the extent necessary to eliminate the excess.

(D) *Special rules for refundings.* To the extent that the hedged bonds are redeemed using the proceeds of a refunding issue, the termination payment is accounted for under paragraph (h)(3)(iv)(B) of this section by treating it as a payment on the refunding issue, rather than the hedged bonds. In addition, to the extent that the refunding issue, rather than the hedged bonds, has been redeemed, paragraph (h)(3)(iv)(C) of this section applies to the termination payment by treating it as a payment on the redeemed refunding issue.

(E) *Safe harbor for certain non-level payments.* A non-level payment to terminate a hedge does not result in that hedge failing to satisfy the applicable provisions of paragraph (h)(3)(iv)(B) of this section if the payment is allocated to each bond year for which the hedge would have been in effect in accordance with this paragraph (h)(3)(iv)(E). For a variable yield issue, an equal amount (or for any short bond year, a proportionate amount of the equal amount) must be allocated to each bond year such that the sum of the present values of the annual amounts equals the present value of the non-level payment. Present value is computed as of the day the hedge is terminated, using the yield on the hedged bonds, determined without regard to the non-level payment. The yield used for this purpose is computed for the period beginning on the first date the hedge is in effect and ending on the date the hedge is terminated. On the other hand, for a fixed yield issue, the non-level payment is taken into account as a single payment on the date it is paid.

(4) *Certain variable yield bonds treated as fixed yield bonds*—(i) *In general.* Except as otherwise provided in this paragraph (h)(4), if the issuer of variable yield bonds enters into a qualified hedge, the hedged bonds are treated as fixed yield bonds paying a fixed interest rate if:

(A) *Start date.* The date on which payments begin to accrue on the hedge is not later than 15 days after the issue date of the hedged bonds.

(B) *Maturity.* The term of the hedge is equal to the entire period during which the hedged bonds bear interest at variable interest rates.

(C) *Payments closely correspond.* Payments to be received under the hedge correspond closely in time to the hedged portion of the payments on the hedged bonds. Hedge payments received within 15 days of the related payments on the hedged bonds generally so correspond.

(D) *Aggregate payments fixed.* Taking into account all payments made and received under the hedge and all payments on the hedged bonds (i.e., after netting all payments), the issuer's aggregate payments are fixed and determinable as of a date not later than 15 days after the issue date of the hedged bonds. Payments on bonds are treated as fixed for purposes of this paragraph (h)(4)(i)(D) if payments on the bonds are based, in whole or in part, on one interest rate, payments on the hedge are based, in whole or in part, on a second interest rate that is substantially the same as, but not identical to, the first interest rate and payments on the bonds would be fixed if the two rates were identical. Rates are treated as substantially the same if they are reasonably expected to be substantially the same throughout the term of the hedge. For example, an objective 30-day tax-exempt variable rate index or other objective index (*e.g.,* J.J. Kenny Index, PSA Municipal swap index, a percentage of LIBOR) may be substantially the same as an issuer's individual 30-day interest rate.

(ii) *Accounting.* Except as otherwise provided in this paragraph (h)(4)(ii), in determining yield on the hedged bonds, all the issuer's actual interest payments on the hedged bonds and all payments made and received on a hedge described in paragraph (h)(4)(i) of this section are taken into account. If payments on the bonds and payments on the hedge are based, in whole or in part, on variable interest rates that are substantially the same within the meaning of paragraph (h)(4)(i)(D) of this section (but not identical), yield on the issue is determined by treating the variable interest rates as identical. For example, if variable rate bonds bearing interest at a weekly rate equal to the rate necessary to remarket the bonds at par are hedged with an interest rate swap under which the issuer receives payments based on a short-term floating rate index that is substantially the same as, but not identical to, the weekly rate on the bonds, the interest payments

Reg. § 1.148-4A(h)(4)

25,380   **Tax Exempt. Requirements: State/Local Bonds**

See p. 20,601 for regulations not amended to reflect law changes

→ *Caution: Reg. § 1.148-4A, below, is applicable to certain bonds sold prior to July 8, 1997.*←

on the bonds are treated as equal to the payments received by the issuer under the swap for purposes of computing the yield on the bonds.

(iii) *Effect of termination*—(A) *In general.* Except as otherwise provided in this paragraph (h)(4)(iii) and paragraph (h)(5) of this section, the issue of which the hedged bonds are a part is treated as if it were reissued as of the termination date of the qualified hedge covered by paragraph (h)(4)(i) of this section in determining yield on the hedged bonds for purposes of § 1.148-3. The redemption price of the retired issue and the issue price of the new issue equal the aggregate values of all the bonds of the issue on the termination date. In computing the yield on the new issue for this purpose, any termination payment is accounted for under paragraph (h)(3)(iv) of this section, applied by treating the termination payment as made or received on the new issue under this paragraph (h)(4)(iii).

(B) *Effect of early termination.* Except as otherwise provided in this paragraph (h)(4)(iii), the general rules of paragraph (h)(4)(i) of this section do not apply in determining the yield on the hedged bonds for purposes of § 1.148-3 if the hedge is terminated or deemed terminated within 5 years after the issue date of the issue of which the hedged bonds are a part. Thus, the hedged bonds are treated as variable yield bonds for purposes of § 1.148-3 from the issue date.

(C) *Certain terminations disregarded.* This paragraph (h)(4)(iii) does not apply to a termination if, based on the facts and circumstances (*e.g.*, taking into account both the termination and any qualified hedge that immediately replaces the terminated hedge), there is no change in the yield. In addition, this paragraph (h)(4)(iii) does not apply to a termination caused by the bankruptcy or insolvency of the hedge provider if the Commissioner determines that the termination occurred without any action by the issuer (other than to protect its rights under the hedge).

(5) *Special rules for certain hedges*—(i) *Certain acquisition payments.* A payment to the issuer by the hedge provider (*e.g.*, an up-front payment for an off-market swap) in connection with the acquisition of a hedge that, but for that payment, would be a qualified hedge, does not cause the hedge to fail to be a qualified hedge provided the payment to the issuer and the issuer's payments under the hedge in excess of those that it would make if the hedge bore rates equal to the on-market rates for the hedge are separately identified in a certification of the hedge provider and not taken into account in determin-

ing the yield on the issue of which the hedged bonds are a part. The on-market rates are determined as of the date the parties enter into the contract.

(ii) *Anticipatory hedges*—(A) *In general.* A contract does not fail to be a hedge under § 1.148-4(h)(2)(i)(A) solely because it is entered into with respect to an anticipated issuance of tax-exempt bonds. The identification required under § 1.148-4T(h)(2)(ix) must specify the reasonably expected governmental purpose, principal amount, and issue date of the hedged bonds, and the manner in which interest is reasonably expected to be computed.

(B) *Special rules.* Payments made in connection with the issuance of a bond to terminate or otherwise close (*terminate*) an anticipatory hedge of that bond do not prevent the hedge from satisfying the requirements of § 1.148-4(h)(2)(vi) and paragraph (h)(2)(vii) of this section. Amounts received or deemed to be received by the issuer in connection with the issuance of the hedged bonds to terminate an anticipatory hedge are treated as proceeds of the hedged bonds.

(C) *Fixed yield treatment.* A bond that is hedged with an anticipatory hedge is a fixed yield bond if, taking into account payments on the hedge that are made or fixed on or before the issue date of the bond and the payments to be made on the bond, the bond satisfies the definition of fixed yield bond. See also paragraph (h)(4) of this section.

(6) *Authority of the Commissioner*—(i) *In general.* A contract is not a qualified hedge if the Commissioner determines, based on all the facts and circumstances, that treating the contract as a qualified hedge would provide a material potential for arbitrage, or a principal purpose for entering into the contract is that arbitrage potential. For example, a contract that requires a substantial nonperiodic payment may constitute, in whole or part, an embedded loan, investment-type property, or other investment.

(ii) *Other qualified hedges.* The Commissioner, by publication of a revenue ruling or revenue procedure, may specify contracts that do not otherwise meet the requirements of § 1.148-4(h)(2) as qualified hedges and contracts that do not otherwise meet the requirements of paragraph (h)(4) of this section as causing the hedged bonds to be treated as fixed yield bonds.

(iii) *Recomputation of yield.* If an issuer enters into a hedge that is not properly identified,

Tax Exempt. Requirements: State/Local Bonds **25,381**

See p. 20,601 for regulations not amended to reflect law changes

→ *Caution: Reg. § 1.148-4A, below, is applicable to certain bonds sold prior to July 8, 1997.*←

fails to properly associate an anticipatory hedge with the hedged bonds, or otherwise fails to meet the requirements of this section, the Commissioner may recompute the yield on the issue taking the hedge into account if the failure to take the hedge into account distorts that yield or other-wise fails to clearly reflect the economic substance of the transaction. [Reg. § 1.148-4A.]

☐ [*T.D. 8538, 5-5-94. Redesignated and amended by T.D. 8718, 5-8-97.*]

→ *Caution: Reg. § 1.148-5, below, is applicable to certain bonds sold on or after July 8, 1997.*←

[Reg. § 1.148-5]

§ 1.148-5. Yield and valuation of investments.—(a) *In general.* This section provides rules for computing the yield and value of investments allocated to an issue for various purposes under section 148.

(b) *Yield on an investment*—(1) *In general.* Except as otherwise provided, the yield on an investment allocated to an issue is computed under the economic accrual method, using the same compounding interval and financial conventions used to compute the yield on the issue. The yield on an investment allocated to an issue is the discount rate that, when used in computing the present value as of the date the investment is first allocated to the issue of all unconditionally payable receipts from the investment, produces an amount equal to the present value of all unconditionally payable payments for the investment. For this purpose, *payments* means amounts to be actually or constructively paid to acquire the investment, and *receipts* means amounts to be actually or constructively received from the investment, such as earnings and return of principal. The yield on a variable rate investment is determined in a manner comparable to the determination of the yield on a variable rate issue. For an issue of qualified mortgage bonds, qualified veterans' mortgage bonds, or qualified student loan bonds on which interest is paid semiannually, all regular monthly loan payments to be received during a semiannual debt service period may be treated as received at the end of that period. In addition, for any conduit financing issue, payments made by the conduit borrower are not treated as paid until the conduit borrower ceases to receive the benefit of earnings on those amounts.

(2) *Yield on a separate class of investments*—(i) *In general.* For purposes of the yield restriction rules of section 148(a) and § 1.148-2, yield is computed separately for each class of investments. For this purpose, in determining the yield on a separate class of investments, the yield on each individual investment within the class is blended with the yield on other individual invest-ments within the class, whether or not held concurrently, by treating those investments as a single investment. The yields on investments that are not within the same class are not blended.

(ii) *Separate classes of investments.* Each of the following is a separate class of investments—

(A) Each category of yield restricted purpose investment and program investment that is subject to a different definition of *materially higher* under § 1.148-2(d)(2);

(B) Yield-restricted nonpurpose investments; and

(C) All other nonpurpose investments;

(iii) *Permissive application of single investment rules to certain yield restricted investments for all purposes of section 148.* For all purposes of section 148, if an issuer reasonably expects as of the issue date to establish and maintain a sinking fund solely to reduce the yield on the investments in a refunding escrow, then the issuer may treat all of the yield restricted nonpurpose investments in the refunding escrow and that sinking fund as a single investment having a single yield, determined under this paragraph (b)(2). Thus, an issuer may not treat the nonpurpose investments in a reasonably required reserve fund and a refunding escrow as a single investment having a single yield under this paragraph (b)(2)(iii).

(iv) *Mandatory application of single investment rules for refunding escrows for all purposes of section 148.* For all purposes of section 148, in computing the yield on yield restricted investments allocable to proceeds (i.e., sale proceeds, investment proceeds, and transferred proceeds) of a refunding issue that are held in one or more refunding escrows, the individual investments are treated as a single investment having a single yield, whether or not held concurrently. For example, this single investment includes both the individual investments allocable to sale and investment proceeds of a refunding issue that are held in one refunding escrow for a prior issue and the investments allocable to transferred proceeds

Reg. § 1.148-5(b)(2)

25,382   Tax Exempt. Requirements: State/Local Bonds

See p. 20,601 for regulations not amended to reflect law changes

→ *Caution: Reg. § 1.148-5, below, is applicable to certain bonds sold on or after July 8, 1997.*←

of that refunding issue that are held in another refunding escrow.

(3) *Investments to be held beyond issue's maturity or beyond temporary period.* In computing the yield on investments allocable to an issue that are to be held beyond the reasonably expected redemption date of the issue, those investments are treated as sold for an amount equal to their value on that date. In computing the yield on investments that are held beyond an applicable temporary period under § 1.148-2, for purposes of § 1.148-2 those investments may be treated as purchased for an amount equal to their fair market value as of the end of the temporary period.

(4) *Consistent redemption assumptions on purpose investments.* The yield on purpose investments allocable to an issue is computed using the same redemption assumptions used to compute the yield on the issue. Yield on purpose investments allocable to an issue of qualified mortgage bonds and qualified veterans' mortgage bonds must be determined in a manner that is consistent with, and using the assumptions required by, section 143(g)(2)(B).

(5) *Student loan special allowance payments included in yield.* Except as provided in § 1.148-11(e), the yield on qualified student loans is computed by including as receipts any special allowance payments made by the Secretary of Education pursuant to section 438 of the Higher Education Act of 1965.

(c) *Yield reduction payments to the United States*—(1) *In general.* In determining the yield on an investment to which this paragraph (c) applies, any amount paid to the United States in accordance with this paragraph (c), including a rebate amount, is treated as a payment for that investment that reduces the yield on that investment.

(2) *Manner of payment*—(i) *In general.* Except as otherwise provided in paragraph (c)(2)(ii) of this section, an amount is paid under this paragraph (c) if it is paid to the United States at the same time and in the same manner as rebate amounts are required to be paid or at such other time or in such manner as the Commissioner may prescribe. For example, yield reduction payments must be made on or before the date of required rebate installment payments as described in §§ 1.148-3(f), (g), and (h). The provisions of § 1.148-3(i) apply to payments made under this paragraph (c).

(ii) *Special rule for purpose investments.* For purpose investments allocable to an issue—

(A) No amounts are required to be paid to satisfy this paragraph (c) until the earlier of the end of the tenth bond year after the issue date of the issue or 60 days after the date on which the issue is no longer outstanding; and

(B) For payments made prior to the date on which the issue is retired, the issuer need not pay more than 75 percent of the amount otherwise required to be paid as of the date to which the payment relates.

(3) *Applicability of special yield reduction rule*—(i) *Covered investments.* This paragraph (c) applies to—

(A) Nonpurpose investments allocable to proceeds of an issue that qualified for one of the temporary periods available for capital projects, restricted working capital expenditures, pooled financings, or investment proceeds under § 1.148-2(e)(2), (e)(3), (e)(4), or (e)(6), respectively;

(B) Investments allocable to a variable yield issue during any computation period in which at least 5 percent of the value of the issue is represented by variable yield bonds, unless the issue is an issue of hedge bonds (as defined in section 149(g)(3)(A));

(C) Nonpurpose investments allocable to transferred proceeds of—

(*1*) A current refunding issue to the extent necessary to reduce the yield on those investments to satisfy yield restrictions under section 148(a); or

(*2*) An advance refunding issue to the extent that investment of the refunding escrows allocable to the proceeds, other than transferred proceeds, of the refunding issue in zero-yielding nonpurpose investments is insufficient to satisfy yield restrictions under section 148(a);

(D) Purpose investments allocable to qualified student loans under a program described in section 144(b)(1)(A);

(E) Nonpurpose investments allocable to gross proceeds of an issue in a reasonably required reserve or replacement fund in a fund that, except for its failure to satisfy the size limitation in § 1.148-2(f)(2)(ii), would qualify as a reasonably required reserve or replacement fund, but only to the extent that—

(*1*) The value of the nonpurpose investments in the fund is not greater than 15

Reg. § 1.148-5(b)(3)

Tax Exempt. Requirements: State/Local Bonds   25,383

See p. 20,601 for regulations not amended to reflect law changes

→ *Caution: Reg. § 1.148-5, below, is applicable to certain bonds sold on or after July 8, 1997.←*

percent of the stated principal amount of the issue, as computed under § 1.148-2(f)(2)(ii), or

(2) The amounts in the fund (other than investment earnings) are not reasonably expected to be used to pay debt service on the issue other than in connection with reductions in the amount required to be in that fund (e.g., a reserve fund for a revolving fund loan program);

(F) Nonpurpose investments allocated to replacement proceeds of a refunded issue as a result of the application of the universal cap to amounts in a refunding escrow (see § 1.148-11(c)(1)(ii)); and

(G) Investments described in § 1.148-11(f).

(ii) *Exception to yield reduction payments rule for advance refunding issues.* Paragraph (c)(1) of this section does not apply to investments allocable to gross proceeds of an advance refunding issue, other than—

(A) Transferred proceeds to which paragraph (c)(3)(i)(C) of this section applies;

(B) Replacement proceeds to which paragraph (c)(3)(i)(F) of this section applies; and

(C) Transferred proceeds to which paragraph (c)(3)(i)(E) of this section applies, but only to the extent necessary to satisfy yield restriction under section 148(a) on those proceeds treating all investments allocable to those proceeds as a separate class.

(d) *Value of investments*—(1) *In general.* Except as otherwise provided, the value of an investment (including a payment or receipt on the investment) on a date must be determined using one of the following valuation methods consistently for all purposes of section 148 to that investment on that date:

(i) *Plain par investment—outstanding principal amount.* A plain par investment may be valued at its outstanding stated principal amount, plus any accrued unpaid interest on that date.

(ii) *Fixed rate investment—present value.* A fixed rate investment may be valued at its present value on that date.

(iii) *Any investment—fair market value.* An investment may be valued at its fair market value on that date.

(2) *Mandatory valuation of yield restricted investments at present value.* Any yield restricted investment must be valued at present value. For example, a purpose investment or an investment allocable to gross proceeds in a refunding escrow

after the expiration of the initial temporary period must be valued at present value. See, however, paragraph (b)(3) of this section.

(3) *Mandatory valuation of certain investments at fair market value*—(i) *In general.* Except as provided in paragraphs (d)(2), (d)(3)(ii), and (d)(4) of this section, an investment must be valued at fair market value on the date that it is first allocated to an issue or first ceases to be allocated to an issue as a consequence of a deemed acquisition or deemed disposition. For example, if an issuer deposits existing investments into a sinking fund for an issue, those investments must be valued at fair market value as of the date first deposited into the fund.

(ii) *Exception to fair market value requirement for transferred proceeds allocations, universal cap allocations, and commingled funds.* Paragraph (d)(3)(i) of this section does not apply if the investment is allocated from one issue to another issue as a result of the transferred proceeds allocation rule under § 1.148-9(b) or the universal cap rule under § 1.148-6(b)(2), provided that both issues consist exclusively of tax-exempt bonds. In addition, paragraph (d)(3)(i) of this section does not apply to investments in a commingled fund (other than a bona fide debt service fund) unless it is an investment being initially deposited in or withdrawn from a commingled fund described in § 1.148-6(e)(5)(iii).

(4) *Special transition rule for transferred proceeds.* The value of a nonpurpose investment that is allocated to transferred proceeds of a refunding issue on a transfer date may not exceed the value of that investment on the transfer date used for purposes of applying the arbitrage restrictions to the refunded issue.

(5) *Definition of present value of an investment.* Except as otherwise provided, present value of an investment is computed under the economic accrual method, using the same compounding interval and financial conventions used to compute the yield on the issue. The present value of an investment on a date is equal to the present value of all unconditionally payable receipts to be received from and payments to be paid for the investment after that date, using the yield on the investment as the discount rate.

(6) *Definition of fair market value*—(i) *In general.* The fair market value of an investment is the price at which a willing buyer would purchase the investment from a willing seller in a bona fide, arm's-length transaction. Fair market value generally is determined on the date on which a contract to purchase or sell the nonpurpose

Reg. § 1.148-5(d)(6)

25,384   **Tax Exempt. Requirements: State/Local Bonds**

See p. 20,601 for regulations not amended to reflect law changes

→ *Caution: Reg. § 1.148-5, below, is applicable to certain bonds sold on or after July 8, 1997.*←

investment becomes binding (i.e., the trade date rather than the settlement date). Except as otherwise provided in this paragraph (d)(6), an investment that is not of a type traded on an established securities market, within the meaning of section 1273, is rebuttably presumed to be acquired or disposed of for a price that is not equal to its fair market value. The fair market value of a United States Treasury obligation that is purchased directly from the United States Treasury is its purchase price.

(ii) *Safe harbor for establishing fair market value for certificates of deposit.* This paragraph (d)(6)(ii) applies to a certificate of deposit that has a fixed interest rate, a fixed payment schedule, and a substantial penalty for early withdrawal. The purchase price of such a certificate of deposit is treated as its fair market value on the purchase date if the yield on the certificate of deposit is not less than—

(A) The yield on reasonably comparable direct obligations of the United States; and

(B) The highest yield that is published or posted by the provider to be currently available from the provider on reasonably comparable certificates of deposit offered to the public.

(iii) *Safe harbor for establishing fair market value for guaranteed investment contracts and investments purchased for a yield restricted defeasance escrow.* The purchase price of a guaranteed investment contract and the purchase price of an investment purchased for a yield restricted defeasance escrow will be treated as the fair market value of the investment on the purchase date if all of the following requirements are satisfied:

(A) The issuer makes a bona fide solicitation for the purchase of the investment. A bona fide solicitation is a solicitation that satisfies all of the following requirements:

(*1*) The bid specifications are in writing and are timely forwarded to potential providers.

(*2*) The bid specifications include all material terms of the bid. A term is material if it may directly or indirectly affect the yield or the cost of the investment.

(*3*) The bid specifications include a statement notifying potential providers that submission of a bid is a representation that the potential provider did not consult with any other potential provider about its bid, that the bid was determined without regard to any other formal or informal agreement that the potential provider

has with the issuer or any other person (whether or not in connection with the bond issue), and that the bid is not being submitted solely as a courtesy to the issuer or any other person for purposes of satisfying the requirements of paragraph (d)(6)(iii)(B)(*1*) or (*2*) of this section.

(*4*) The terms of the bid specifications are commercially reasonable. A term is commercially reasonable if there is a legitimate business purpose for the term other than to increase the purchase price or reduce the yield of the investment. For example, for solicitations of investments for a yield restricted defeasance escrow, the hold firm period must be no longer than the issuer reasonably requires.

(*5*) For purchases of guaranteed investment contracts only, the terms of the solicitation take into account the issuer's reasonably expected deposit and drawdown schedule for the amounts to be invested.

(*6*) All potential providers have an equal opportunity to bid. For example, no potential provider is given the opportunity to review other bids (i.e., a last look) before providing a bid.

(*7*) At least three reasonably competitive providers are solicited for bids. A reasonably competitive provider is a provider that has an established industry reputation as a competitive provider of the type of investments being purchased.

(B) The bids received by the issuer meet all of the following requirements:

(*1*) The issuer receives at least three bids from providers that the issuer solicited under a bona fide solicitation meeting the requirements of paragraph (d)(6)(iii)(A) of this section and that do not have a material financial interest in the issue. A lead underwriter in a negotiated underwriting transaction is deemed to have a material financial interest in the issue until 15 days after the issue date of the issue. In addition, any entity acting as a financial advisor with respect to the purchase of the investment at the time the bid specifications are forwarded to potential providers has a material financial interest in the issue. A provider that is a related party to a provider that has a material financial interest in the issue is deemed to have a material financial interest in the issue.

(*2*) At least one of the three bids described in paragraph (d)(6)(iii)(B)(*1*) of this section is from a reasonably competitive provider, within the meaning of paragraph (d)(6)(iii)(A)(*7*) of this section.

Reg. § 1.148-5(d)(6)

→ *Caution: Reg. § 1.148-5, below, is applicable to certain bonds sold on or after July 8, 1997.*←

(*3*) If the issuer uses an agent to conduct the bidding process, the agent did not bid to provide the investment.

(C) The winning bid meets the following requirements:

(*1*) *Guaranteed investment contracts.* If the investment is a guaranteed investment contract, the winning bid is the highest yielding bona fide bid (determined net of any broker's fees).

(*2*) *Other investments.* If the investment is not a guaranteed investment contract, the following requirements are met:

(*i*) The winning bid is the lowest cost bona fide bid (including any broker's fees). The lowest cost bid is either the lowest cost bid for the portfolio or, if the issuer compares the bids on an investment-by-investment basis, the aggregate cost of a portfolio comprised of the lowest cost bid for each investment. Any payment received by the issuer from a provider at the time a guaranteed investment contract is purchased (e.g., an escrow float contract) for a yield restricted defeasance escrow under a bidding procedure meeting the requirements of this paragraph (d)(6)(iii) is taken into account in determining the lowest cost bid.

(*ii*) The lowest cost bona fide bid (including any broker's fees) is not greater than the cost of the most efficient portfolio comprised exclusively of State and Local Government Series Securities from the United States Department of the Treasury, Bureau of Public Debt. The cost of the most efficient portfolio of State and Local Government Series Securities is to be determined at the time that bids are required to be submitted pursuant to the terms of the bid specifications.

(*iii*) If State and Local Government Series Securities from the United States Department of the Treasury, Bureau of Public Debt are not available for purchase on the day that bids are required to be submitted pursuant to terms of the bid specifications because sales of those securities have been suspended, the cost comparison of paragraph (d)(6)(iii) (C)(*2*)(*ii*) of this section is not required.

(D) The provider of the investments or the obligor on the guaranteed investment contract certifies the administrative costs that it pays (or expects to pay, if any) to third parties in connection with supplying the investment.

(E) The issuer retains the following records with the bond documents until three years after the last outstanding bond is redeemed:

(*1*) For purchases of guaranteed investment contracts, a copy of the contract, and for purchases of investments other than guaranteed investment contracts, the purchase agreement or confirmation.

(*2*) The receipt or other record of the amount actually paid by the issuer for the investments, including a record of any administrative costs paid by the issuer and the certification under paragraph (d)(6)(iii)(D) of this section.

(*3*) For each bid that is submitted, the name of the person and entity submitting the bid, the time and date of the bid, and the bid results.

(*4*) The bid solicitation form and, if the terms of the purchase agreement or the guaranteed investment contract deviated from the bid solicitation form or a submitted bid is modified, a brief statement explaining the deviation and stating the purpose for the deviation. For example, if the issuer purchases a portfolio of investments for a yield restricted defeasance escrow and, in order to satisfy the yield restriction requirements of section 148, an investment in the winning bid is replaced with an investment with a lower yield, the issuer must retain a record of the substitution and how the price of the substitute investment was determined. If the issuer replaces an investment in the winning bid portfolio with another investment, the purchase price of the new investment is not covered by the safe harbor unless the investment is bid under a bidding procedure meeting the requirements of this paragraph (d)(6)(iii).

(*5*) For purchases of investments other than guaranteed investment contracts, the cost of the most efficient portfolio of State and Local Government Series Securities, determined at the time that the bids were required to be submitted pursuant to the terms of the bid specifications.

(e) *Administrative costs of investments*—(1) *In general.* Except as otherwise provided in this paragraph (e), an allocation of gross proceeds of an issue to a payment or a receipt on an investment is not adjusted to take into account any costs or expenses paid, directly or indirectly, to purchase, carry, sell, or retire the investment (*administrative costs*). Thus, these administrative costs generally do not increase the payments for, or reduce the receipts from investments.

(2) *Qualified administrative costs on nonpurpose investments*—(i) *In general.* In determining payments and receipts on nonpurpose investments, qualified administrative costs are taken

→ *Caution: Reg. § 1.148-5, below, is applicable to certain bonds sold on or after July 8, 1997.*←

into account. Thus, qualified administrative costs increase the payments for, or decrease the receipts from, the investments. Qualified administrative costs are reasonable, direct administrative costs, other than carrying costs, such as separately stated brokerage or selling commissions, but not legal and accounting fees, recordkeeping, custody, and similar costs. General overhead costs and similar indirect costs of the issuer such as employee salaries and office expenses and costs associated with computing the rebate amount under section 148(f) are not qualified administrative costs. In general, administrative costs are not reasonable unless they are comparable to administrative costs that would be charged for the same investment or a reasonably comparable investment if acquired with a source of funds other than gross proceeds of tax-exempt bonds.

(ii) *Special rule for administrative costs of nonpurpose investments in certain regulated investment companies and commingled funds.* Qualified administrative costs include all reasonable administrative costs, without regard to the limitation on indirect costs under paragraph (e)(2)(i) of this section, incurred by:

(A) *Regulated investment companies.* A publicly offered regulated investment company (as defined in section 67(c)(2)(B)); and

(B) *External commingled funds.* A widely held commingled fund in which no investor in the fund owns more than 10 percent of the beneficial interest in the fund. For purposes of this paragraph (e)(2)(ii)(B), a fund is treated as widely held only if, during the immediately preceding fixed, semiannual period chosen by the fund (e.g., semiannual periods ending June 30 and December 31), the fund had a daily average of more than 15 investors that were not related parties, and the daily average amount each investor had invested in the fund was not less than the lesser of $500,000 and 1 percent of the daily average of the total amount invested in the fund. For purposes of this paragraph (e)(2)(ii)(B), an investor will be treated as owning not more than 10 percent of the beneficial interest in the fund if, on the date of each deposit by the investor into the fund, the total amount the investor and any related parties have on deposit in the fund is not more than 10 percent of the total amount that all investors have on deposit in the fund. For purposes of the preceding sentence, the total amount that all investors have on deposit in the fund is equal to the sum of all deposits made by the investor and any related parties on the date of those deposits and the closing balance in the fund

on the day before those deposits. If any investor in the fund owns more than 10 percent of the beneficial interest in the fund, the fund does not qualify under this paragraph (e)(2)(ii)(B) until that investor makes sufficient withdrawals from the fund to reduce its beneficial interest in the fund to 10 percent or less.

(iii) *Special rule for guaranteed investment contracts.* For a guaranteed investment contract, a broker's commission or similar fee paid on behalf of either an issuer or the provider is treated as an administrative cost and, except in the case of an issue that satisfies section 148(f)(4)(D)(i), is a qualified administrative cost to the extent that the present value of the commission, as of the date the contract is allocated to the issue, does not exceed the lesser of a reasonable amount within the meaning of paragraph (e)(2)(i) of this section or the present value of annual payments equal to .05 percent of the weighted average amount reasonably expected to be invested each year of the term of the contract. For this purpose, present value is computed using the taxable discount rate used by the parties to compute the commission or, if not readily ascertainable, the yield to the issuer on the investment contract or other reasonable taxable discount rate.

(iv) *Special rule for investments purchased for a yield restricted defeasance escrow.* For investments purchased for a yield restricted defeasance escrow, a fee paid to a bidding agent is a qualified administrative cost only if the following requirements are satisfied:

(A) The fee is comparable to a fee that would be charged for a reasonably comparable investment if acquired with a source of funds other than gross proceeds of tax-exempt bonds, and it is reasonable. The fee is deemed to be comparable to a fee that would be charged for a comparable investment acquired with a source of funds other than gross proceeds of tax-exempt bonds, and to be reasonable if the fee does not exceed the lesser of $10,000 or .1% of the initial principal amount of investments deposited in the yield restricted defeasance escrow.

(B) For transactions in which a guaranteed investment contract and other investments are purchased for a yield restricted defeasance escrow in a single investment (e.g., an issuer bids United States Treasury obligations and an escrow float contract collectively), a broker's fee described in paragraph (e)(2)(iv)(A) of this section will apply to the initial principal amount of the investment deposited in the yield restricted defeasance escrow, and a broker's fee described in para-

Reg. § 1.148-5(e)(2)

Tax Exempt. Requirements: State/Local Bonds 25,387

See p. 20,601 for regulations not amended to reflect law changes

→ *Caution: Reg. § 1.148-5, below, is applicable to certain bonds sold on or after July 8, 1997.*←

graph (e)(2)(iii) of this section will apply only to the guaranteed investment contract portion of the investment.

(3) *Qualified administrative costs on purpose investments*—(i) *In general.* In determining payments and receipts on purpose investments, qualified administrative costs described in this paragraph (e)(3) paid by the conduit borrower are taken into account. Thus, these costs increase the payments for, or decrease the receipts from, the purpose investments. This rule applies even if those payments merely reimburse the issuer. Although the actual payments by the conduit borrower may be made at any time, for this purpose, a pro rata portion of each payment made by a conduit borrower is treated as a reimbursement of reasonable administrative costs, if the present value of those payments does not exceed the present value of the reasonable administrative costs paid by the issuer, using the yield on the issue as the discount rate.

(ii) *Definition of qualified administrative costs on purpose investments*—(A) *In general.* Except as otherwise provided in this paragraph (e)(3)(i), qualified administrative costs of a purpose investment means—

(1) Costs or expenses paid, directly or indirectly, to purchase, carry, sell, or retire the investment; and

(2) Costs of issuing, carrying, or repaying the issue, and any underwriters' discount.

(B) *Limitation on program investments.* For a program investment, qualified administrative costs include only those costs described in paragraph (e)(3)(ii)(A)(2) of this section. [Reg. § 1.148-5.]

☐ [T.D. 8418, 5-12-92. Amended by T.D. 8476, 6-14-93 T.D. 8538, 5-5-94; T.D. 8718, 5-8-97 and T.D. 8801, 12-29-98.]

→ *Caution: Reg. § 1.148-5A, below, is applicable to certain bonds sold prior to July 8, 1997.*←

[Reg. § 1.148-5A]

§ 1.148-5A. Yield and valuation of investments.—(a) through (b)(2)(ii) [Reserved]. For guidance see § 1.148-5.

(b)(2)(iii) *Permissive application of single investment rules to certain yield restricted investments for all purposes of section 148.* For all purposes of section 148, an issuer may treat all of the yield restricted nonpurpose investments in a refunding escrow and a sinking fund that is reasonably expected as of the issue date to be maintained to reduce the yield on the investments in the refunding escrow as a single investment having a single yield, determined under § 1.148(b)(2).

(b)(2)(iv) through (c)(1) [Reserved]. For guidance see § 1.148-5.

(c)(2) *Manner of payment*—(i) *In general.* Except as otherwise provided in § 1.148-5(c)(2)(ii), an amount is paid under § 1.148-5(c) if it is paid to the United States at the same time and in the same manner as rebate amounts are required to be paid or at such other time or in such manner as the Commissioner may prescribe. For example, yield reduction payments must be made on or before the date of required rebate installment payments as described in § 1.148-3(f). The date a payment is required to be paid is determined without regard to § 1.148-3(h). An amount that is paid untimely is not taken into account under this paragraph (c) unless the Commissioner determines that the failure to pay timely is not due to willful neglect. The provisions of § 1.148-3(i) apply to payments made under § 1.148-5(c).

(c)(2)(ii) through (c)(3)(i) [Reserved]. For guidance see § 1.148-5.

(c)(3)(ii) *Exception to yield reduction payments rule for advance refunding issues.* Section 1.148-5(c)(1) does not apply to investments allocable to gross proceeds of an advance refunding issue, other than—

(A) Transferred proceeds to which § 1.148-5(c)(3)(i)(C) applies;

(B) Replacement proceeds to which § 1.148-5(c)(3)(i)(F) applies; and

(C) Transferred proceeds to which § 1.148-5(c)(3)(i)(E) applies, but only to the extent necessary to satisfy yield restriction under section 148(a) on those proceeds treating all investments allocable to those proceeds as a separate class.

(d)(1) through (d)(3)(i) [Reserved]. For guidance see § 1.148-5.

(d)(3)(ii) *Exception to fair market value requirement for transferred proceeds allocations, universal cap allocations, and commingled funds.* Section 1.148-5(d)(3)(i) does not apply if the investment is allocated from one issue to another issue as a result of the transferred proceeds allocation rule under § 1.148-9(b) or the universal cap rule under § 1.148-6(b)(2), provided that both is-

25,388   Tax Exempt. Requirements: State/Local Bonds

See p. 20,601 for regulations not amended to reflect law changes

→ *Caution: Reg. § 1.148-5A, below, is applicable to certain bonds sold prior to July 8, 1997.*←

sues consist exclusively of tax-exempt bonds. In addition, § 1.148-5(d)(3)(i) does not apply to investments in a commingled fund (other than a bona fide debt service fund) unless it is an investment being initially deposited in or withdrawn from a commingled fund described in § 1.148-6(e)(5)(iii).

(e)(1) through (e)(2)(ii)(A) [Reserved]. For guidance see § 1.148-5.

(e)(2)(ii)(B) *External commingled funds.* For any semiannual period, a commingled fund satisfies the 10 percent requirement of § 1.148-5(e)(2)(ii)(B) if—

(*1*) Based on average amounts on deposit, this requirement was satisfied for the prior semiannual period; and

(*2*) The fund does not accept deposits that would cause it to fail to meet this requirement.

(iii) *Special rule for guaranteed investment contracts.* For a guaranteed investment contract, a broker's commission or similar fee paid on behalf of either an issuer or the provider is treated as an administrative cost and, except in the case of an issue that satisfies section 148(f)(4)(D)(i), is not a qualified administrative cost to the extent that the present value of the commission, as of the date the contract is allocated to the issue, exceeds the present value of annual payments equal to .05 percent of the weighted average amount reasonably expected to be invested each year of the term of the contract. For this purpose, present value is computed using the taxable discount rate used by the parties to compute the commission or, if not readily ascertainable, a reasonable taxable discount rate. [Temporary Reg. § 1.148-5A.]

□ [*T.D. 8538, 5-5-94. Redesignated and amended by T.D. 8718, 5-8-97.*]

→ *Caution: Reg. § 1.148-6, below, is applicable to certain bonds sold on or after July 8, 1997.*←

[Reg. § 1.148-6]

§ 1.148-6. General allocation and accounting rules.—(a) *In general*—(1) *Reasonable accounting methods required.* An issuer may use any reasonable, consistently applied accounting method to account for gross proceeds, investments, and expenditures of an issue.

(2) *Bona fide deviations from accounting method.* An accounting method does not fail to be reasonable and consistently applied solely because a different accounting method is used for a bona fide governmental purpose to consistently account for a particular item. Bona fide governmental purposes may include special state law restrictions imposed on specific funds or actions to avoid grant forfeitures.

(3) *Absence of allocation and accounting methods.* If an issuer fails to maintain books and records sufficient to establish the accounting method for an issue and the allocation of the proceeds of that issue, the rules of this section are applied using the specific tracing method. This paragraph (a)(3) applies to bonds issued on or after May 16, 1997.

(b) *Allocation of gross proceeds to an issue*—(1) *One-issue rule and general ordering rules.* Except as otherwise provided, amounts are allocable to only one issue at a time as gross proceeds, and if amounts simultaneously are proceeds of one issue and replacement proceeds of another issue, those amounts are allocable to the issue of which they

are proceeds. Amounts cease to be allocated to an issue as proceeds only when those amounts are allocated to an expenditure for a governmental purpose, are allocated to transferred proceeds of another issue, or cease to be allocated to that issue at retirement of the issue or under the universal cap of paragraph (b)(2) of this section. Amounts cease to be allocated to an issue as replacement proceeds only when those amounts are allocated to an expenditure for a governmental purpose, are no longer used in a manner that causes those amounts to be replacement proceeds of that issue, or cease to be allocated to that issue because of the retirement of the issue or the application of the universal cap under paragraph (b)(2) of this section. Amounts that cease to be allocated to an issue as gross proceeds are eligible for allocation to another issue. Under § 1.148-10(a), however, the rules in this paragraph (b)(1) do not apply in certain cases involving abusive arbitrage devices.

(2) *Universal cap on value of nonpurpose investments allocated to an issue*—(i) *Application.* The rules in this paragraph (b)(2) provide an overall limitation on the amount of gross proceeds allocable to an issue. Although the universal cap generally may be applied at any time in the manner described in this paragraph (b)(2), it need not be applied on any otherwise required date of application if its application on that date would not result in a reduction or reallocation of gross proceeds of an issue. For this purpose, if an issuer reasonably expects as of the issue date that the

Reg. § 1.148-6(a)(1)

Tax Exempt. Requirements: State/Local Bonds   25,389

See p. 20,601 for regulations not amended to reflect law changes

→ *Caution: Reg. § 1.148-6, below, is applicable to certain bonds sold on or after July 8, 1997.←*

universal cap will not reduce the amount of gross proceeds allocable to the issue during the term of the issue, the universal cap need not be applied on any date on which an issue actually has all of the following characteristics—

(A) No replacement proceeds are allocable to the issue, other than replacement proceeds in a bona fide debt service fund or a reasonably required reserve or replacement fund;

(B) The net sale proceeds of the issue—

(*1*) Qualified for one of the temporary periods available for capital projects, restricted working capital expenditures, or pooled financings under § 1.148-2(e)(2), (e)(3), or (e)(4), and those net sales proceeds were in fact allocated to expenditures prior to the expiration of the longest applicable temporary period; or

(*2*) were deposited in a refunding escrow and expended as originally expected;

(C) The issue does not refund a prior issue that, on any transfer date, has unspent proceeds allocable to it;

(D) None of the bonds are retired prior to the date on which those bonds are treated as retired in computing the yield on the issue; and

(E) No proceeds of the issue are invested in qualified student loans or qualified mortgage loans.

(ii) *General rule.* Except as otherwise provided below, amounts that would otherwise be gross proceeds allocable to an issue are allocated (and remain allocated) to the issue only to the extent that the value of the nonpurpose investments allocable to those gross proceeds does not exceed the value of all outstanding bonds of the issue. For this purpose, gross proceeds allocable to cash, tax-exempt bonds that would be nonpurpose investments (absent section 148(b)(3)(A)), qualified student loans, and qualified mortgage loans are treated as nonpurpose investments. The values of bonds and investments are determined under § 1.148-4(e) and § 1.148-5(d), respectively. The value of all outstanding bonds of the issue is referred to as the *universal cap.* Thus, for example, the universal cap for an issue of plain par bonds is equal to the outstanding stated principal amount of those bonds plus accrued interest.

(iii) *Determination and application of the universal cap.* Except as otherwise provided, beginning with the first bond year that commences after the second anniversary of the issue date, the amount of the universal cap and the value of the nonpurpose investments must be determined as of the first day of each bond year. For refunding and

refunded issues, the cap and values must be determined as of each date that, but for this paragraph (b)(2), proceeds of the refunded issue would become transferred proceeds of the refunding issue, and need not otherwise be determined in the bond year in which that date occurs. All values are determined as of the close of business on each determination date, after giving effect to all payments on bonds and payments for and receipts on investments on that date.

(iv) *General ordering rule for allocations of amounts in excess of the universal cap*—(A) *In general* If the value of all nonpurpose investments allocated to the gross proceeds of an issue exceeds the universal cap for that issue on a date as of which the cap is determined under paragraph (b)(2)(iii) of this section, nonpurpose investments allocable to gross proceeds necessary to eliminate that excess cease to be allocated to the issue, in the following order of priority—

(*1*) First, nonpurpose investments allocable to replacement proceeds;

(*2*) Second, nonpurpose investments allocable to transferred proceeds; and

(*3*) Third, nonpurpose investments allocable to sale proceeds and investment proceeds.

(B) *Re-allocation of certain amounts.* Except as provided in § 1.148-9(b)(3), amounts that cease to be allocated to an issue as a result of the application of the universal cap may only be allocated to another issue as replacement proceeds.

(C) *Allocations of portions of investments.* Portions of investments to which this paragraph (b)(2)(iv) applies are allocated under either the ratable method or the representative method in the same manner as allocations of portions of investments to transferred proceeds under § 1.148-9(c).

(v) *Nonpurpose investments in a bona fide debt service fund not counted.* For purposes of this paragraph (b)(2), nonpurpose investments allocated to gross proceeds in a bona fide debt service fund for an issue are not taken into account in determining the value of the nonpurpose investments, and those nonpurpose investments remain allocated to the issue.

(c) *Fair market value limit on allocations to nonpurpose investments.* Upon a purchase or sale of a nonpurpose investment, gross proceeds of an issue are not allocated to a payment for that nonpurpose investment in an amount greater than, or to a receipt from that nonpurpose invest-

→ *Caution: Reg. § 1.148-6, below, is applicable to certain bonds sold on or after July 8, 1997.*←

ment in an amount less than, the fair market value of the nonpurpose investment as of the purchase or sale date. For purposes of this paragraph (c) only, the fair market value of a nonpurpose investment is adjusted to take into account qualified administrative costs allocable to the investment.

(d) *Allocation of gross proceeds to expenditures*—(1) *Expenditures in general*—(i) *General rule.* Reasonable accounting methods for allocating funds from different sources to expenditures for the same governmental purpose include any of the following methods if consistently applied: a specific tracing method; a gross proceeds spent first method; a first-in, first-out method; or a ratable allocation method.

(ii) *General limitation.* An allocation of gross proceeds of an issue to an expenditure must involve a current outlay of cash for a governmental purpose of the issue. A *current outlay of cash* means an outlay reasonably expected to occur not later than 5 banking days after the date as of which the allocation of gross proceeds to the expenditure is made.

(iii) *Timing.* An issuer must account for the allocation of proceeds to expenditures not later than 18 months after the later of the date the expenditure is paid or the date the project, if any, that is financed by the issue is placed in service. This allocation must be made in any event by the date 60 days after the fifth anniversary of the issue date or the date 60 days after the retirement of the issue, if earlier. This paragraph (d)(1)(iii) applies to bonds issued on or after May 16, 1997.

(2) *Treatment of gross proceeds invested in purpose investments*—(i) *In general.* Gross proceeds of an issue invested in a purpose investment are allocated to an expenditure on the date on which the conduit borrower under the purpose investment allocates the gross proceeds to an expenditure in accordance with this paragraph (d).

(ii) *Exception for qualified mortgage loans and qualified student loans.* If gross proceeds of an issue are allocated to a purpose investment that is a qualified mortgage loan or a qualified student loan, those gross proceeds are allocated to an expenditure for the governmental purpose of the issue on the date on which the issuer allocates gross proceeds to that purpose investment.

(iii) *Continuing allocation of gross proceeds to purpose investments.* Regardless of whether gross proceeds of a conduit financing issue invested in a purpose investment have been

allocated to an expenditure under paragraph (d)(2)(i) or (ii) of this section, with respect to the actual issuer those gross proceeds continue to be allocated to the purpose investment until the sale, discharge, or other disposition of the purpose investment.

(3) *Expenditures for working capital purposes*—(i) *In general.* Except as otherwise provided in this paragraph (d)(3) or paragraph (d)(4) of this section, proceeds of an issue may only be allocated to working capital expenditures as of any date to the extent that those working capital expenditures exceed available amounts (as defined in paragraph (d)(3)(iii) of this section) as of that date (i.e., a "proceeds-spent-last" method). For this purpose, proceeds include replacement proceeds described in § 1.148-1(c)(4).

(ii) *Exceptions*—(A) *General de minimis exception.* Paragraph (d)(3)(i) of this section does not apply to expenditures to pay—

(*1*) Any issuance costs of the issue or any qualified administrative costs within the meaning of § § 1.148-5(e)(2)(i) or (ii), or § 1.148-5(e)(3)(ii)(A);

(*2*) Fees for qualified guarantees of the issue or payments for a qualified hedge for the issue;

(*3*) Interest on the issue for a period commencing on the issue date and ending on the date that is the later of three years from the issue date or one year after the date on which the project is placed in service;

(*4*) Amounts paid to the United States under § § 1.148-3, 1.148-5(c), or 1.148-7 for the issue;

(*5*) Costs, other than those described in paragraphs (d)(3)(ii)(A)(*1*) through (*4*) of this section, that do not exceed 5 percent of the sale proceeds of an issue and that are directly related to capital expenditures financed by the issue (e.g., initial operating expenses for a new capital project);

(*6*) Principal or interest on an issue paid from unexpected excess sale or investment proceeds; and

(*7*) Principal or interest on an issue paid from investment earnings on a reserve or replacement fund that are deposited in a bona fide debt service fund.

(B) *Exception for extraordinary items.* Paragraph (d)(3)(i) of this section does not apply to expenditures for extraordinary, nonrecurring items that are not customarily payable from cur-

Reg. § 1.148-6(d)(1)

Tax Exempt. Requirements: State/Local Bonds **25,391**

See p. 20,601 for regulations not amended to reflect law changes

→ *Caution: Reg. § 1.148-6, below, is applicable to certain bonds sold on or after July 8, 1997.* ←

rent revenues, such as casualty losses or extraordinary legal judgments in amounts in excess of reasonable insurance coverage. If, however, an issuer or a related party maintains a reserve for such items (e.g., a self-insurance fund) or has set aside other available amounts for such expenses, gross proceeds within that reserve must be allocated to expenditures only after all other available amounts in that reserve are expended.

(C) *Exception for payment of principal and interest on prior issues.* Paragraph (d)(3)(i) of this section does not apply to expenditures for payment of principal, interest, or redemption prices on a prior issue and, for a crossover refunding issue, interest on that issue.

(D) *No exceptions if replacement proceeds created.* The exceptions provided in this paragraph (d)(3)(ii) do not apply if the allocation merely substitutes gross proceeds for other amounts that would have been used to make those expenditures in a manner that gives rise to replacement proceeds. For example, if a purported reimbursement allocation of proceeds of a reimbursement bond does not result in an expenditure under § 1.150-2, those proceeds may not be allocated to pay interest on an issue that, absent this allocation, would have been paid from the issuer's current revenues.

(iii) *Definition of available amount*—(A) *In general.* For purposes of this paragraph (d)(3), *available amount* means any amount that is available to an issuer for working capital expenditure purposes of the type financed by an issue. Except as otherwise provided, *available amount* excludes proceeds of the issue but includes cash, investments, and other amounts held in accounts or otherwise by the issuer or a related party if those amounts may be used by the issuer for working capital expenditures of the type being financed by an issue without legislative or judicial action and without a legislative, judicial, or contractual requirement that those amounts be reimbursed.

(B) *Reasonable working capital reserve treated as unavailable.* A reasonable working capital reserve is treated as unavailable. Any working capital reserve is reasonable if it does not exceed 5 percent of the actual working capital expenditures of the issuer in the fiscal year before the year in which the determination of available amounts is made. For this purpose only, in determining the working capital expenditures of an issuer for a prior fiscal year, any expenditures (whether capital or working capital expenditures) that are paid out of current revenues may be treated as working capital expenditures

(C) *Qualified endowment funds treated as unavailable.* For a 501(c)(3) organization, a qualified endowment fund is treated as unavailable. A fund is a qualified endowment fund if—

(1) The fund is derived from gifts or bequests, or the income thereon, that were neither made nor reasonably expected to be used to pay working capital expenditures;

(2) Pursuant to reasonable, established practices of the organization, the governing body of the 501(c)(3) organization designates and consistently operates the fund as a permanent endowment fund or quasi-endowment fund restricted as to use; and

(3) There is an independent verification that the fund is reasonably necessary as part of the organization's permanent capital.

(D) *Application to statutory safe harbor for tax and revenue anticipation bonds.* For purposes of section 148(f)(4)(B)(iii)(II), *available amount* has the same meaning as in paragraph (d)(3)(ii) of this section, except that the otherwise-permitted reasonable working capital reserve is treated as part of the available amount.

(4) *Expenditures for grants*—(i) *In general.* Gross proceeds of an issue that are used to make a grant are allocated to an expenditure on the date on which the grant is made.

(ii) *Characterization of repayments of grants.* If any amount of a grant financed by gross proceeds of an issue is repaid to the grantor, the repaid amount is treated as unspent proceeds of the issue as of the repayment date unless expended within 60 days of repayment.

(iii) *Definition of grant. Grant* means a transfer for a governmental purpose of money or property to a transferee that is not a related party to or an agent of the transferor. The transfer must not impose any obligation or condition to directly or indirectly repay any amount to the transferor. Obligations or conditions intended solely to assure expenditure of the transferred moneys in accordance with the governmental purpose of the transfer do not prevent a transfer from being a grant.

(5) *Expenditures for reimbursement purposes.* In allocating gross proceeds of issues of reimbursement bonds (as defined in § 1.150-2) to certain expenditures, § 1.150-2 applies. In allocating gross proceeds to an expenditure to reimburse a previously paid working capital expenditure, paragraph (d)(3) of this section applies. Thus, if the expenditure is described in paragraph (d)(3)(ii) of this section or there are no available

Reg. § 1.148-6(d)(5)

25,392 Tax Exempt. Requirements: State/Local Bonds

See p. 20,601 for regulations not amended to reflect law changes

→ *Caution: Reg. § 1.148-6, below, is applicable to certain bonds sold on or after July 8, 1997.*←

amounts on the date a working capital expenditure is made and there are no other available amounts on the date of the reimbursement of that expenditure, gross proceeds are allocated to the working capital expenditure as of the date of the reimbursement.

(6) *Expenditures of certain commingled investment proceeds of governmental issues.* This paragraph (d)(6) applies to any issue of governmental bonds, any issue of private activity bonds issued to finance a facility that is required by section 142 to be owned by a governmental unit, and any portion of an issue that is not treated as consisting of private activity bonds under section 141(b)(9). Investment proceeds of the issue (other than investment proceeds held in a refunding escrow) are treated as allocated to expenditures for a governmental purpose when the amounts are deposited in a commingled fund with substantial tax or other revenues from governmental operations of the issuer and the amounts are reasonably expected to be spent for governmental purposes within 6 months from the date of the commingling. In establishing these reasonable expectations, an issuer may use any reasonable accounting assumption and is not bound by the *proceeds-spent-last* assumption generally required for working capital expenditures under paragraph (d)(3) of this section.

(7) *Payments to related parties.* Any payment of gross proceeds of the issue to a related party of the payor is not an expenditure of those gross proceeds.

(e) *Special rules for commingled funds—*(1) *In general.* An accounting method for gross proceeds of an issue in a commingled fund, other than a bona fide debt service fund, is reasonable only if it satisfies the requirements of paragraphs (e)(2) through (6) of this section in addition to the other requirements of this section.

(2) *Investments held by a commingled fund—*(i) *Required ratable allocations.* Not less frequently than as of the close of each fiscal period, all payments and receipts (including deemed payments and receipts) on investments held by a commingled fund must be allocated (but not necessarily distributed) among the different investors in the fund. This allocation must be based on a consistently applied, reasonable ratable allocation method.

(ii) *Safe harbors for ratable allocation methods.* Reasonable ratable allocation methods include, without limitation, methods that allocate these items in proportion to either—

(A) The average daily balances of the amounts in the commingled fund from different investors during a fiscal period (as described in paragraph (e)(4) of this section); or

(B) The average of the beginning and ending balances of the amounts in the commingled fund from different investors for a fiscal period that does not exceed one month.

(iii) *Definition of investor.* For purposes of this paragraph (e), the term *investor* means each different source of funds invested in a commingled fund. For example, if a city invests gross proceeds of an issue and tax revenues in a commingled fund, it is treated as two different investors.

(3) *Certain expenditures involving a commingled fund.* If a ratable allocation method is used under paragraph (d) of this section to allocate expenditures from the commingled fund, the same ratable allocation method must be used to allocate payments and receipts on investments in the commingled fund under paragraph (e)(2) of this section.

(4) *Fiscal periods.* The fiscal year of a commingled fund is the calendar year unless the fund adopts another fiscal year. A commingled fund may use any consistent fiscal period that does not exceed three months (e.g., a daily, weekly, monthly, or quarterly fiscal period).

(5) *Unrealized gains and losses on investments of a commingled fund—*(i) *Mark-to-market requirement for internal commingled funds with longer-term investment portfolios.* Except as otherwise provided in this paragraph (e), in the case of a commingled fund in which the issuer and any related party own more than 25 percent of the beneficial interests in the fund (an *internal commingled fund*), the fund must treat all its investments as if sold at fair market value either on the last day of the fiscal year or the last day of each fiscal period. The net gains or losses from these deemed sales of investments must be allocated to all investors of the commingled fund during the period since the last allocation.

(ii) *Exception for internal commingled funds with shorter-term investment portfolios.* If the remaining weighted average maturity of all investments held by a commingled fund during a particular fiscal year does not exceed 18 months, and the investments held by the commingled fund during that fiscal year consist exclusively of obligations, the mark-to-market requirement of paragraph (e)(5)(i) of this section does not apply.

(iii) *Exception for commingled reserve funds and sinking funds.* The mark-to-market re-

→ *Caution: Reg. § 1.148-6, below, is applicable to certain bonds sold on or after July 8, 1997.*←

quirement of paragraph (e)(5)(i) of this section does not apply to a commingled fund that operates exclusively as a reserve fund, sinking fund, or replacement fund for two or more issues of the same issuer.

(6) *Allocations of commingled funds serving as common reserve funds or sinking funds*—(i) *Permitted ratable allocation methods.* If a commingled fund serves as a common reserve fund, replacement fund, or sinking fund for two or more issues (a *commingled reserve*), after making reasonable adjustments to account for proceeds allocated under paragraph (b)(1) or (b)(2) of this section, investments held by that commingled fund must be allocated ratably among the issues served by the commingled fund in accordance with one of the following methods—

(A) The relative values of the bonds of those issues under § 1.148-4(e);

(B) The relative amounts of the remaining maximum annual debt service requirements on the outstanding principal amounts of those issues; or

(C) The relative original stated principal amounts of the outstanding issues.

(ii) *Frequency of allocations.* An issuer must make any allocations required by this paragraph (e)(6) as of a date at least every 3 years and as of each date that an issue first becomes secured by the commingled reserve. If relative original principal amounts are used to allocate, allocations must also be made on the retirement of any issue secured by the commingled reserve. [Reg. § 1.148-6.]

☐ [*T.D.* 8418, 5-12-92. *Amended by T.D.* 8476, 6-14-93; *T.D.* 8538, 5-5-94; *T.D.* 8712, 1-10-97 and *T.D.* 8718, 5-8-97.]

→ *Caution: Reg. § 1.148-6A, below, is applicable to certain bonds sold prior to July 8, 1997.*←

[Reg. § 1.148-6A]
§ 1.148-6A. General allocation and accounting rules.—(a) through (d)(3)(iii)(B) [Reserved]. For guidance see § 1.148-6.

(d)(3)(iii)(C) *Qualified endowment funds treated as unavailable.* For a 501(c)(3) organization, a qualified endowment fund is treated as unavailable. A fund is a qualified endowment fund if—

(1) The fund is derived from gifts or bequests, or the income thereon, that were neither made nor reasonably expected to be used to pay working capital expenditures.

(2) Pursuant to reasonable, established practices of the organization, the governing body of the 501(c)(3) organization designates and consistently operates the fund as a permanent endowment fund or quasi-endowment fund restricted as to use; and

(3) There is an independent verification (e.g., from an independent certified public accountant) that the fund is reasonably necessary as part of the organization's permanent capital. [Reg. § 1.148-6A.]

☐ [*T.D.* 8538, 5-5-94. *Redesignated and amended by T.D.* 8718, 5-8-97.]

[Reg. § 1.148-7]
§ 1.148-7. Spending exceptions to the rebate requirement.—(a) *Scope of section*—(1) *In general.* This section provides guidance on the spending exceptions to the arbitrage rebate requirement

of section 148(f)(2). These exceptions are the 6-month exception in section 148(f)(4)(B) (the *6-month exception*), the 18-month exception under paragraph (d) of this section (the *18-month exception*), and the 2-year construction exception under section 148(f)(4)(C) (the *2-year exception*) (collectively, the *spending exceptions*).

(2) *Relationship of spending exceptions.* Each of the spending exceptions is an independent exception to arbitrage rebate. For example, a construction issue may qualify for the 6-month exception or the 18-month exception even though the issuer makes one or more elections under the 2-year exception with respect to the issue.

(3) *Spending exceptions not mandatory.* Use of the spending exceptions is not mandatory. An issuer may apply the arbitrage rebate requirement to an issue that otherwise satisfies a spending exception. If an issuer elects to pay penalty in lieu of rebate under the 2-year exception, however, the issuer must apply those penalty provisions.

(b) *Rules applicable for all spending exceptions.* The provisions of this paragraph (b) apply for purposes of applying each of the spending exceptions.

(1) *Special transferred proceeds rules*—(i) *Application to prior issues.* For purposes of applying the spending exceptions to a prior issue only, proceeds of the prior issue that become transferred proceeds of the refunding issue continue to be treated as unspent proceeds of the prior issue.

Reg. § 1.148-7(b)(1)

25,394   **Tax Exempt. Requirements: State/Local Bonds**

See p. 20,601 for regulations not amended to reflect law changes

If the prior issue satisfies one of the spending exceptions, the proceeds of the prior issue that are excepted from rebate under that spending exception are not subject to rebate either as proceeds of the prior issue or as transferred proceeds of the refunding issue.

(ii) *Application to refunding issues*—(A) *In general.* The only spending exception applicable to refunding issues is the 6-month exception. For purposes of applying the 6-month exception to a refunding issue only, proceeds of the prior issue that become transferred proceeds of the refunding issue generally are not treated as proceeds of the refunding issue and need not be spent for the refunding issue to satisfy that spending exception. Even if the refunding issue qualifies for that spending exception, those transferred proceeds are subject to rebate as proceeds of the refunding issue unless an exception to rebate applied to those proceeds as proceeds of the prior issue.

(B) *Exception.* For purposes of applying the 6-month exception to refunding issues, those transferred proceeds of the refunding issue excluded from the gross proceeds of the prior issue under the special definition of gross proceeds in paragraph (c)(3) of this section, and those that transferred from a prior taxable issue, are generally treated as gross proceeds of the refunding issue. Thus, for the refunding issue to qualify for the 6-month exception, those proceeds must be spent within 6 months of the issue date of the refunding issue, unless those amounts continue to be used in a manner that does not cause those amounts to be gross proceeds under paragraph (c)(3) of this section.

(2) *Application of multipurpose issue rules.* Except as otherwise provided, if any portion of an issue is treated as a separate issue allocable to refunding purposes under § 1.148-9(h) (relating to multipurpose issues), for purposes of this section, that portion is treated as a separate issue.

(3) *Expenditures for governmental purposes of the issue.* For purposes of this section, expenditures for the governmental purpose of an issue include payments for interest, but not principal, on the issue, and for principal or interest on another issue of obligations. The preceding sentence does not apply for purposes of the 18-month and 2-year exceptions if those payments cause the issue to be a refunding issue.

(4) *De minimis rule.* Any failure to satisfy the final spending requirement of the 18-month exception or the 2-year exception is disregarded if the issuer exercises due diligence to complete the project financed and the amount of the failure does not exceed the lesser of 3 percent of the issue price of the issue or $250,000.

(5) *Special definition of reasonably required reserve or replacement fund.* For purposes of this section only, a reasonably required reserve or replacement fund also includes any fund to the extent described in § 1.148-5(c)(3)(i)(E) or (G).

(6) *Pooled financing issue*—(i) *In general.* Except as otherwise provided in this paragraph (b)(6), the spending exceptions apply to a pooled financing issue as a whole, rather than to each loan separately.

(ii) *Election to apply spending exceptions separately to each loan*—(A) *In general.* At the election (made on or before the issue date) of the issuer of a pooled financing issue, the spending exceptions are applied separately to each conduit loan, and the applicable spending requirements for a loan begin on the earlier of the date the loan is made, or the first day following the 1-year period beginning on the issue date of the pooled financing issue. If this election is made, the rebate requirement applies to, and none of the spending exceptions are available for, gross proceeds of the pooled financing bonds before the date on which the spending requirements for those proceeds begin.

(B) *Application of spending exceptions.* If the issuer makes the election under this paragraph (b)(6)(ii), the rebate requirement is satisfied for proceeds used to finance a particular conduit loan to the extent that the loan satisfies a spending exception or the small issuer exception under § 1.148-8, regardless of whether any other conduit loans allocable to the issue satisfy such an exception. A pooled financing issue is an issue of arbitrage bonds, however, unless the entire issue satisfies the requirements of section 148. An issuer may pay rebate for some conduit loans and 1½ percent penalty for other conduit loans from the same pooled financing issue. The 1½ percent penalty is computed separately for each conduit loan.

(C) *Elections under 2-year exception.* If the issuer makes the election under this paragraph (b)(6)(ii), the issuer may make all elections under the 2-year exception separately for each loan. Elections regarding a loan that otherwise must be made by the issuer on or before the issue date instead may be made on or before the date the loan is made (but not later than 1 year after the issue date).

(D) *Example.* The operation of this paragraph (b)(6) is illustrated by the following example:

Example. Pooled financing issue. On January 1, 1994, Authority *J* issues bonds. As of the issue date, *J* reasonably expects to use the proceeds of the issue to make loans to City *K*,

Reg. § 1.148-7(b)(2)

County *L*, and City *M*. *J* does not reasonably expect to use more than 75 percent of the available construction proceeds of the issue for construction expenditures. On or before the issue date, *J* elects to apply the spending exceptions separately for each loan, with spending requirements beginning on the earlier of the date the loan is made or the first day following the 1-year period beginning on the issue date. On February 1, 1994, *J* loans a portion of the proceeds to *K*, and *K* reasonably expects that 45 percent of those amounts will be used for construction expenditures. On the date this loan is made, *J* elects under paragraph (j) of this section to treat 60 percent of the amount loaned to *K* as a separate construction issue, and also elects the 1½ percent penalty under paragraph (k) of this section for the separate construction issue. On March 1, 1994, *J* loans a portion of the proceeds to *L*, and *L* reasonably expects that more than 75 percent of those amounts will be used for construction expenditures. On March 1, 1995, *J* loans the remainder of the proceeds to *M*, and none of those amounts will be used for construction expenditures. *J* must satisfy the rebate requirement for all gross proceeds before those amounts are loaned. For the loan to *K*, the spending periods begin on February 1, 1994, and the 1½ percent penalty must be paid for any failure to meet a spending requirement for the portion of the loan to *K* that is treated as a separate construction issue. Rebate must be paid on the remaining portion of the loan to *K*, unless that portion qualifies for the 6-month exception. For the loan to *L*, the spending periods begin on March 1, 1994, and the rebate requirement must be satisfied unless the 6-month, 18-month, or the 2-year exception is satisfied with respect to those amounts. For the loan to *M*, the spending periods begin on January 2, 1995, and the rebate requirement must be satisfied for those amounts unless the 6-month or 18-month exception is satisfied.

(c) *6-month exception*—(1) *General rule.* An issue is treated as meeting the rebate requirement if—

(i) The gross proceeds (as modified by paragraph (c)(3) of this section) of the issue are allocated to expenditures for the governmental purposes of the issue within the 6-month period beginning on the issue date (the *6-month spending period*); and

(ii) The rebate requirement is met for amounts not required to be spent within the 6-month spending period (excluding earnings on a bona fide debt service fund).

(2) *Additional period for certain bonds.* The 6-month spending period is extended for an additional 6 months in certain circumstances specified under section 148(f)(4)(B)(ii).

(3) *Amounts not included in gross proceeds.* For purposes of paragraph (c)(1)(i) of this section only, gross proceeds has the meaning used in § 1.148-1, except it does not include amounts—

(i) In a bona fide debt service fund;

(ii) In a reasonably required reserve or replacement fund (see § 1.148-7(b)(5));

(iii) That, as of the issue date, are not reasonably expected to be gross proceeds but that become gross proceeds after the end of the 6-month spending period;

(iv) Representing sale or investment proceeds derived from payments under any purpose investment of the issue; and

(v) Representing repayments of grants (as defined in § 1.148-6(d)(4)) financed by the issue.

(4) *Series of refundings.* If a principal purpose of a series of refunding issues is to exploit the difference between taxable and tax-exempt interest rates by investing proceeds during the temporary periods provided in § 1.148-9(d), the 6-month spending period for all issues in the series begins on the issue date of the first issue in the series.

(d) *18-month exception*—(1) *General rule.* An issue is treated as meeting the rebate requirement if all of the following requirements are satisfied—

(i) *18-month expenditure schedule met.* The gross proceeds (as defined in paragraph (d)(3) of this section) are allocated to expenditures for a governmental purpose of the issue in accordance with the following schedule (the *18-month expenditure schedule*) measured from the issue date—

(A) At least 15 percent within 6 months (the *first spending period*);

(B) At least 60 percent within 12 months (the *second spending period*); and

(C) 100 percent within 18 months (the *third spending period*).

(ii) *Rebate requirement met for amounts not required to be spent.* The rebate requirement is met for all amounts not required to be spent in accordance with the 18-month expenditure schedule (other than earnings on a bona fide debt service fund).

(iii) *Issue qualifies for initial temporary period.* All of the gross proceeds (as defined in paragraph (d)(3)(i) of this section) of the issue qualify for the initial temporary period under § 1.148-2(e)(2).

(2) *Extension for reasonable retainage.* An issue does not fail to satisfy the spending requirement for the third spending period as a result of a reasonable retainage if the reasonable retainage is

allocated to expenditures within 30 months of the issue date. Reasonable retainage has the meaning under paragraph (h) of this section, as modified to refer to net sale proceeds on the date 18 months after the issue date.

(3) *Gross proceeds*—(i) *Definition of gross proceeds.* For purposes of paragraph (d)(1) of this section only, *gross proceeds* means gross proceeds as defined in paragraph (c)(3) of this section, as modified to refer to "18 months" in paragraph (c)(3)(iii) of this section in lieu of "6 months."

(ii) *Estimated earnings.* For purposes of determining compliance with the first two spending periods under paragraph (d)(1)(i) of this section, the amount of investment proceeds included in gross proceeds of the issue is determined based on the issuer's reasonable expectations on the issue date.

(4) *Application to multipurpose issues.* This paragraph (d) does not apply to an issue any portion of which is treated as meeting the rebate requirement under paragraph (e) of this section (relating to the 2-year exception).

(e) *2-year exception*—(1) *General rule.* A construction issue is treated as meeting the rebate requirement for available construction proceeds if those proceeds are allocated to expenditures for governmental purposes of the issue in accordance with the following schedule (the *2-year expenditure schedule*), measured from the issue date—

(i) At least 10 percent within 6 months (the *first spending period*);

(ii) At least 45 percent within 1 year (the *second spending period*);

(iii) At least 75 percent within 18 months (the *third spending period*); and

(iv) 100 percent within 2 years (the *fourth spending period*).

(2) *Extension for reasonable retainage.* An issue does not fail to satisfy the spending requirement for the fourth spending period as a result of unspent amounts for reasonable retainage (as defined in paragraph (h) of this section) if those amounts are allocated to expenditures within 3 years of the issue date.

(3) *Definitions.* For purposes of the 2-year exception, the following definitions apply:

(i) *Real property* means land and improvements to land, such as buildings or other inherently permanent structures, including interests in real property. For example, real property includes wiring in a building, plumbing systems, central heating or air-conditioning systems, pipes or ducts, elevators, escalators installed in a building, paved parking areas, roads, wharves and docks, bridges, and sewage lines.

(ii) *Tangible personal property* means any tangible property other than real property, including interests in tangible personal property. For example, tangible personal property includes machinery that is not a structural component of a building, subway cars, fire trucks, automobiles, office equipment, testing equipment, and furnishings.

(iii) *Substantially completed.* Construction may be treated as substantially completed when the issuer abandons construction or when at least 90 percent of the total costs of the construction reasonably expected, as of that date, to be financed with the available construction proceeds have been allocated to expenditures.

(f) *Construction issue*—(1) *Definition.* Construction issue means any issue that is not a refunding issue if—

(i) The issuer reasonably expects, as of the issue date, that at least 75 percent of the available construction proceeds of the issue will be allocated to construction expenditures (as defined in paragraph (g) of this section) for property owned by a governmental unit or a 501(c)(3) organization; and

(ii) Any private activity bonds that are part of the issue are qualified 501(c)(3) bonds or private activity bonds issued to finance property to be owned by a governmental unit or a 501(c)(3) organization.

(2) *Use of actual facts.* For the provisions of paragraphs (e) through (m) of this section that apply based on the issuer's reasonable expectations, an issuer may elect on or before the issue date to apply all of those provisions based on actual facts, except that this election does not apply for purposes of determining whether an issue is a construction issue under paragraph (f)(1) of this section if the 1 and ½ percent penalty election is made under paragraph (k) of this section.

(3) *Ownership requirement*—(i) *In general.* A governmental unit or 501(c)(3) organization is treated as the owner of property if it would be treated as the owner for Federal income tax purposes. For obligations issued on behalf of a State or local governmental unit, the entity that actually issues the bonds is treated as a governmental unit.

(ii) *Safe harbor for leases and management contracts.* Property leased by a governmental unit or a 501(c)(3) organization is treated as owned by the governmental unit or 501(c)(3) organization if the lessee complies with the requirements of section 142(b)(1)(B). For a bond described in section 142(a)(6), the requirements of section

Reg. § 1.148-7(d)(3)

Tax Exempt. Requirements: State/Local Bonds   **25,397**

See p. 20,60˙ for regulations not amended to reflect law changes

142(b)(1)(B) apply as modified by section 146(h)(2).

(g) *Construction expenditures*—(1) *Definition.* Except as otherwise provided, *construction expenditures* means capital expenditures (as defined in § 1.150-1) that are allocable to the cost of real property or constructed personal property (as defined in paragraph (g)(3) of this section). Except as provided in paragraph (g)(2) of this section, construction expenditures do not include expenditures for acquisitions of interests in land or other existing real property.

(2) *Certain acquisitions under turnkey contracts treated as construction expenditures.* Expenditures are not for the acquisition of an interest in existing real property other than land if the contract between the seller and the issuer requires the seller to build or install the property (e.g., a *turnkey contract*), but only to the extent that the property has not been built or installed at the time the parties enter into the contract.

(3) *Constructed personal property.* Constructed personal property means tangible personal property (or, if acquired pursuant to a single acquisition contract, properties) or specially developed computer software if—

(i) A substantial portion of the property or properties is completed more than 6 months after the earlier of the date construction or rehabilitation commenced and the date the issuer entered into an acquisition contract;

(ii) Based on the reasonable expectations of the issuer, if any, or representations of the person constructing the property, with the exercise of due diligence, completion of construction or rehabilitation (and delivery to the issuer) could not have occurred within that 6-month period; and

(iii) If the issuer itself builds or rehabilitates the property, not more than 75 percent of the capitalizable cost is attributable to property acquired by the issuer (e.g., components, raw materials, and other supplies).

(4) *Specially developed computer software.* Specially developed computer software means any programs or routines used to cause a computer to perform a desired task or set of tasks, and the documentation required to describe and maintain those programs, provided that the software is specially developed and is functionally related and subordinate to real property or other constructed personal property.

(5) *Examples.* The operation of this paragraph (g) is illustrated by the following examples:

Example 1. Purchase of construction materials. City *A* issues bonds to finance a new office building. *A* uses proceeds of the bonds to purchase materials to be used in constructing the building, such as bricks, pipes, wires, lighting, carpeting, heating equipment, and similar materials. Expenditures by *A* for the construction materials are construction expenditures because those expenditures will be capitalizable to the cost of the building upon completion, even though they are not initially capitalizable to the cost of existing real property. This result would be the same if *A* hires a third-party to perform the construction, unless the office building is partially constructed at the time that *A* contracts to purchase the building.

Example 2. Turnkey contract. City *B* issues bonds to finance a new office building. *B* enters into a turnkey contract with developer *D* under which *D* agrees to provide *B* with a completed building on a specified completion date on land currently owned by *D*. Under the agreement, *D* holds title to the land and building and assumes any risk of loss until the completion date, at which time title to the land and the building will be transferred to *B*. No construction has been performed by the date that *B* and *D* enter into the agreement. All payments by *B* to *D* for construction of the building are construction expenditures because all the payments are properly capitalized to the cost of the building, but payments by *B* to *D* allocable to the acquisition of the land are not construction expenditures.

Example 3. Right-of-way. *P*, a public agency, issues bonds to finance the acquisition of a right-of-way and the construction of sewage lines through numerous parcels of land. The right-of-way is acquired primarily through *P*'s exercise of its powers of eminent domain. As of the issue date, *P* reasonably expects that it will take approximately 2 years to acquire the entire right-of-way because of the time normally required for condemnation proceedings. No expenditures for the acquisition of the right-of-way are construction expenditures because they are costs incurred to acquire an interest in existing real property.

Example 4. Subway cars. City *C* issues bonds to finance new subway cars. *C* reasonably expects that it will take more than 6 months for the subway cars to be constructed to *C*'s specifications. The subway cars are constructed personal property. Alternatively, if the builder of the subway cars informs *C* that it will only take 3 months to build the subway cars to *C*'s specifications, no payments for the subway cars are construction expenditures.

Example 5. Fractional interest in property. *U*, a public agency, issues bonds to finance an undivided fractional interest in a newly constructed power-generating facility. *U* contributes its ratable share of the cost of building the new

Reg. § 1.148-7(g)(5)

25,398   Tax Exempt. Requirements: State/Local Bonds

See p. 20,601 for regulations not amended to reflect law changes

facility to the project manager for the facility. U's contributions are construction expenditures in the same proportion that the total expenditures for the facility qualify as construction expenditures.

Example 6. Park land. City D issues bonds to finance the purchase of unimproved land and the cost of subsequent improvements to the land, such as grading and landscaping, necessary to transform it into a park. The costs of the improvements are properly capitalizable to the cost of the land, and therefore, are construction expenditures, but expenditures for the acquisition of the land are not.

(h) *Reasonable retainage definition. Reasonable retainage* means an amount, not to exceed 5 percent of available construction proceeds as of the end of the fourth spending period, that is retained for reasonable business purposes relating to the property financed with the proceeds of the issue. For example, a reasonable retainage may include a retention to ensure or promote compliance with a construction contract in circumstances in which the retained amount is not yet payable, or in which the issuer reasonably determines that a dispute exists regarding completion or payment.

(i) *Available construction proceeds—*(1) *Definition in general. Available construction proceeds* has the meaning used in section 148(f)(4)(C)(vi). For purposes of this definition, earnings include earnings on any tax-exempt bond. Pre-issuance accrued interest and earnings thereon may be disregarded. Amounts that are not gross proceeds as a result of the application of the universal cap under § 1.148-6(b)(2) are not available construction proceeds.

(2) *Earnings on a reasonably required reserve or replacement fund.* Earnings on any reasonably required reserve or replacement fund are available construction proceeds only to the extent that those earnings accrue before the earlier of the date construction is substantially completed or the date that is 2 years after the issue date. An issuer may elect on or before the issue date to exclude from available construction proceeds the earnings on such a fund. If the election is made, the rebate requirement applies to the excluded amounts from the issue date.

(3) *Reasonable expectations test for future earnings.* For purposes of determining compliance with the spending requirements as of the end of each of the first three spending periods, available construction proceeds include the amount of future earnings that the issuer reasonably expected as of the issue date.

(4) *Issuance costs.* Available construction proceeds do not include gross proceeds used to pay issuance costs financed by an issue, but do include

earnings on such proceeds. Thus, an expenditure of gross proceeds of an issue for issuance costs does not count toward meeting the spending requirements. The expenditure of earnings on gross proceeds used to pay issuance costs does count toward meeting those requirements. If the spending requirements are met and the proceeds used to pay issuance costs are expended by the end of the fourth spending period, those proceeds and the earnings thereon are treated as having satisfied the rebate requirement.

(5) *One and one-half percent penalty in lieu of arbitrage rebate.* For purposes of the spending requirements of paragraph (e) of this section, available construction proceeds as of the end of any spending period are reduced by the amount of penalty in lieu of arbitrage rebate (under paragraph (k) of this section) that the issuer has paid from available construction proceeds before the last day of the spending period.

(6) *Payments on purpose investments and repayments of grants.* Available construction proceeds do not include—

(i) Sale or investment proceeds derived from payments under any purpose investment of the issue; or

(ii) Repayments of grants (as defined in § 1.148-6(d)(4)) financed by the issue.

(7) *Examples.* The operation of this paragraph (i) is illustrated by the following examples:

Example 1. Treatment of investment earnings. City F issues bonds having an issue price of $10,000,000. F deposits all of the proceeds of the issue into a construction fund to be used for expenditures other than costs of issuance. F estimates on the issue date that, based on reasonably expected expenditures and rates of investment, earnings on the construction fund will be $800,000. As of the issue date and the end of each of the first three spending periods, the amount of available construction proceeds is $10,800,000. To qualify as a construction issue, F must reasonably expect on the issue date that at least $8,100,000 (75 percent of $10,800,000) will be used for construction expenditures. In order to meet the 10 percent spending requirement at the end of the first spending period, F must spend at least $1,080,000. As of the end of the fourth spending period, F has received $1,100,000 in earnings. In order to meet the spending requirement at the end of the fourth spending period, however, F must spend all of the $11,100,000 of actual available construction proceeds (except for reasonable retainage not exceeding $555,000).

Example 2. Treatment of investment earnings without a reserve fund. City G issues bonds having an issue price of $11,200,000. G does not

Tax Exempt. Requirements: State/Local Bonds 25,399

See p. 20,601 for regulations not amended to reflect law changes

elect to exclude earnings on the reserve fund from available construction proceeds. G uses $200,000 of proceeds to pay issuance costs and deposits $1,000,000 of proceeds into a reasonably required reserve fund. G deposits the remaining $10,000,000 of proceeds into a construction fund to be used for construction expenditures. On the issue date, G reasonably expects that, based on the reasonably expected date of substantial completion and rates of investment total earnings on the construction fund will be $800,000, and total earnings on the reserve fund to the date of substantial completion will be $150,000. G reasonably expects that substantial completion will occur during the fourth spending period. As of the issue date, the amount of available construction proceeds is $10,950,000 ($10,000,000 originally deposited into the construction fund plus $800,000 expected earnings on the construction fund and $150,000 expected earnings on the reserve fund). To qualify as a construction issue, G must reasonably expect on the issue date that at least $8,212,500 will be used for construction expenditures.

Example 3. Election to exclude earnings on a reserve fund. The facts are the same as *Example 2*, except that G elects on the issue date to exclude earnings on the reserve fund from available construction proceeds. The amount of available construction proceeds as of the issue date is $10,800,000.

(j) *Election to treat portion of issue used for construction as separate issue*—(1) *In general.* For purposes of paragraph (e) of this section, if any proceeds of an issue are to be used for construction expenditures, the issuer may elect on or before the issue date to treat the portion of the issue that is not a refunding issue as two, and only two, separate issues, if—

(i) One of the separate issues is a construction issue as defined in paragraph (f) of this section;

(ii) The issuer reasonably expects, as of the issue date, that this construction issue will finance all of the construction expenditures to be financed by the issue; and

(iii) The issuer makes an election to apportion the issue under this paragraph (j)(1) in which it identifies the amount of the issue price of the issue allocable to the construction issue

(2) *Example.* The operation of this paragraph (j) is illustrated by the following example.

Example. City D issues bonds having an issue price of $19,000,000. On the issue date, D reasonably expects to use $10,800,000 of bond proceeds (including investment earnings) for construction expenditures for the project being fi-

nanced D deposits $10,000,000 in a construction fund to be used for construction expenditures and $9,000,000 in an acquisition fund to be used for acquisition of equipment not qualifying as construction expenditures. D estimates on the issue date, based on reasonably expected expenditures and rates of investment, that total earnings on the construction fund will be $800,000 and total earnings on the acquisition fund will be $200,000. Because the total construction expenditures to be financed by the issue are expected to be $10,800,000, the maximum available construction proceeds for a construction issue is $14,400,000 ($10,800,000 divided by 0.75). To determine the maximum amount of the issue price allocable to a construction issue, the estimated investment earnings allocable to the construction issue are subtracted The entire $800,000 of earnings on the construction fund are allocable to the construction issue. Only a portion of the $200,000 of earnings on the acquisition fund, however, are allocable to the construction issue. The total amount of the available construction proceeds that is expected to be used for acquisition is $3,600,000 ($14,400,000 − $10,800,000). The portion of earnings on the acquisition fund that is allocable to the construction issue is $78,261 ($200,000 × $3,600,000/$9,200,000). Accordingly, D may elect on or before the issue date to treat up to $13,521,739 of the issue price as a construction issue ($14,400,000 − $800,000 − $78,261). D's election must specify the amount of the issue price treated as a construction issue. The balance of the issue price is treated as a separate nonconstruction issue that is subject to the rebate requirement unless it meets another exception to arbitrage rebate. Because the financing of a construction issue is a separate governmental purpose under § 1.148-9(h), the election causes the issue to be a multipurpose issue under that section.

(k) *One and one-half percent penalty in lieu of arbitrage rebate*—(1) *In general.* Under section 148(f)(4)(C)(vii), an issuer of a construction issue may elect on or before the issue date to pay a penalty (the *1 1/2 percent penalty*) to the United States in lieu of the obligation to pay the rebate amount on available construction proceeds upon failure to satisfy the spending requirements of paragraph (e) of this section. The 1 1/2 percent penalty is calculated separately for each spending period, including each semiannual period after the end of the fourth spending period, and is equal to 1.5 percent times the underexpended proceeds as of the end of the spending period. For each spending period, underexpended proceeds equal the amount of available construction proceeds required to be spent by the end of the spending

25,400   **Tax Exempt. Requirements: State/Local Bonds**

See p. 20,601 for regulations not amended to reflect law changes

period, less the amount actually allocated to expenditures for the governmental purposes of the issue by that date. The 1 1/2 percent penalty must be paid to the United States no later than 90 days after the end of the spending period to which it relates. The 1 1/2 percent penalty continues to apply at the end of each spending period and each semiannual period thereafter until the earliest of the following—

(i) The termination of the penalty under paragraph (l) of this section;

(ii) The expenditure of all of the available construction proceeds; or

(iii) The last stated final maturity date of bonds that are part of the issue and any bonds that refund those bonds.

(2) *Application to reasonable retainage.* If an issue meets the exception for reasonable retainage except that all retainage is not spent within 3 years of the issue date, the issuer must pay the 1 1/2 percent penalty to the United States for any reasonable retainage that was not so spent as of the close of the 3-year period and each later spending period.

(3) *Coordination with rebate requirement.* The rebate requirement is treated as met with respect to available construction proceeds for a period if the 1 1/2 percent penalty is paid in accordance with this section.

(l) *Termination of 1 1/2 percent penalty—*(1) *Termination after initial temporary period.* The issuer may terminate the 1 1/2 percent penalty after the initial temporary period (a *section 148(f)(4)(C)(viii) penalty termination*) if—

(i) Not later than 90 days after the earlier of the end of the initial temporary period or the date construction is substantially completed, the issuer elects to terminate the 1 1/2 percent penalty; provided that solely for this purpose, the initial temporary period may be extended by the issuer to a date ending 5 years after the issue date;

(ii) Within 90 days after the end of the initial temporary period, the issuer pays a penalty equal to 3 percent of the unexpended available construction proceeds determined as of the end of the initial temporary period, multiplied by the number of years (including fractions of years computed to 2 decimal places) in the initial temporary period;

(iii) For the period beginning as of the close of the initial temporary period, the unexpended available construction proceeds are not invested in higher yielding investments; and

(iv) On the earliest date on which the bonds may be called or otherwise redeemed, with or without a call premium, the unexpended available construction proceeds as of that date (not including any amount earned after the date on which notice of the redemption was required to be given) must be used to redeem the bonds. Amounts used to pay any call premium are treated as used to redeem bonds. This redemption requirement may be met by purchases of bonds by the issuer on the open market at prices not exceeding fair market value. A portion of the annual principal payment due on serial bonds of a construction issue may be paid from the unexpended amount, but only in an amount no greater than the amount that bears the same ratio to the annual principal due that the total unexpended amount bears to the issue price of the construction issue.

(2) *Termination before end of initial temporary period.* If the construction to be financed by the construction issue is substantially completed before the end of the initial temporary period, the issuer may elect to terminate the 1 1/2 percent penalty before the end of the initial temporary period (a *section 148(f)(4)(C)(ix) penalty termination*) if—

(i) Before the close of the initial temporary period and not later than 90 days after the date the construction is substantially completed, the issuer elects to terminate the 1 1/2 percent penalty;

(ii) The election identifies the amount of available construction proceeds that will not be spent for the governmental purposes of the issue; and

(iii) The issuer has met all of the conditions for a section 148(f)(4)(C)(viii) penalty termination, applied as if the initial temporary period ended as of the date the required election for a section 148(f)(4)(C)(ix) penalty termination is made. That penalty termination election satisfies the required election for a section 148(f)(4)(C)(viii) termination.

(3) *Application to reasonable retainage.* Solely for purposes of determining whether the conditions for terminating the 1 1/2 percent penalty are met, reasonable retainage may be treated as spent for a governmental purpose of the construction issue. Reasonable retainage that is so treated continues to be subject to the 1 1/2 percent penalty.

(4) *Example.* The operation of this paragraph (l) is illustrated by the following example.

Example. City *I* issues a construction issue having a 20-year maturity and qualifying for a 3-year initial temporary period. The bonds are first subject to optional redemption 10 years after the issue date at a premium of 3 percent. *I* elects,

Reg. § 1.148-7(k)(2)

on or before the issue date, to pay the 1 1/2 percent penalty in lieu of arbitrage rebate. At the end of the 3-year temporary period, the project is not substantially completed, and $1,500,000 of available construction proceeds of the issue are unspent. At that time, *I* reasonably expects to need $500,000 to complete the project. *I* may terminate the 1 1/2 percent penalty in lieu of arbitrage rebate with respect to the excess $1,500,000 by electing to terminate within 90 days of the end of the initial temporary period; paying a penalty to the United States of $135,000 (3 percent of $1,500,000 multiplied by 3 years); restricting the yield on the investment of unspent available construction proceeds for 7 years until the first call date, although any portion of these proceeds may still be spent on the project prior to that call date; and using the available construction proceeds that, as of the first call date, have not been allocated to expenditures for the governmental purposes of the issue to redeem bonds on that call date. If *I* fails to make the termination election, *I* is required to pay the 1 1/2 percent penalty on unspent available construction proceeds every 6 months until the latest maturity date of bonds of the issue (or any bonds of another issue that refund such bonds).

(m) *Payment of penalties.* Each penalty payment under this section must be paid in the manner provided in § 1.148-3(g). See § 1.148-3(h) for rules on failures to pay penalties under this section. [Reg. § 1.148-7.]

☐ [*T.D.* 8418, 5-12-92. *Amended by T.D.* 8476, 6-14-93.]

[Reg. § 1.148-8]

§ **1.148-8. Small issuer exception to rebate requirement.**—(a) *Scope.* Under section 148(f)(4)(D), bonds issued to finance governmental activities of certain small issuers are treated as meeting the arbitrage rebate requirement of section 148(f)(2) (the "small issuer exception"). This section provides guidance on the small issuer exception.

(b) *General taxing powers.* The small issuer exception generally applies only to bonds issued by governmental units with general taxing powers. A governmental unit has general taxing powers if it has the power to impose taxes (or to cause another entity to impose taxes) of general applicability which, when collected, may be used for the general purposes of the issuer. The taxing power may be limited to a specific type of tax, provided that the applicability of the tax is not limited to a small number of persons. The governmental unit's exercise of its taxing power may be subject to procedural limitations, such as voter approval requirements, but may not be contingent on approval by another governmental unit. See, also, section 148(f)(4)(D)(iv).

(c) *Size limitation*—(1) *In general.* An issue (other than a refunding issue) qualifies for the small issuer exception only if the issuer reasonably expects, as of the issue date, that the aggregate face amount of all tax-exempt bonds (other than private activity bonds) issued by it during that calendar year will not exceed $5,000,000; or the aggregate face amount of all tax-exempt bonds of the issuer (other than private activity bonds) actually issued during that calendar year does not exceed $5,000,000. For this purpose, if an issue has more than a de minimis amount of original issue discount or premium, *aggregate face amount* means the aggregate issue price of that issue (determined without regard to pre-issuance accrued interest).

(2) *Aggregation rules.* The following aggregation rules apply for purposes of applying the $5,000,000 size limitation under paragraph (c)(1) of this section.

(i) *On-behalf-of issuers.* An issuer and all entities (other than political subdivisions) that issue bonds on behalf of that issuer are treated as one issuer.

(ii) *Subordinate entities*—(A) *In general.* Except as otherwise provided in paragraph (d) of this section and section 148(f)(4)(D)(iv), all bonds issued by a subordinate entity are also treated as issued by each entity to which it is subordinate. An issuer is subordinate to another governmental entity if it is directly or indirectly controlled by the other entity within the meaning of § 1.150-1(e).

(B) *Exception for allocations of size limitation.* If an entity properly makes an allocation of a portion of its $5,000,000 size limitation to a subordinate entity (including an [entity] on behalf of issuer) under section 148(f)(4)(D)(iv), the portion of bonds issued by the subordinate entity under the allocation is treated as issued only by the allocating entity and not by any other entity to which the issuing entity is subordinate. These allocations are irrevocable and must bear a reasonable relationship to the benefits received by the allocating unit from issues issued by the subordinate entity. The benefits to be considered include the manner in which—

(*1*) Proceeds are to be distributed;

(*2*) The debt service is to be paid;

(*3*) The facility financed is to be owned;

(*4*) The use or output of the facility is to be shared; and

25,402   Tax Exempt. Requirements: State/Local Bonds

See p. 20,601 for regulations not amended to reflect law changes

(5) Costs of operation and maintenance are to be shared.

(iii) *Avoidance of size limitation.* An entity formed or availed of to avoid the purposes of the $5,000,000 size limitation and all entities that would benefit from the avoidance are treated as one issuer. Situations in which an entity is formed or availed of to avoid the purposes of the $5,000,000 size limitation include those in which the issuer—

(A) Issues bonds which, but for the $5,000,000 size limitation, would have been issued by another entity; and

(B) Does not receive a substantial benefit from the project financed by the bonds.

(3) *Certain refunding bonds not taken into account.* In applying the $5,000,000 size limitation, there is not taken into account the portion of an issue that is a current refunding issue to the extent that the stated principal amount of the refunding bond does not exceed the portion of the outstanding stated principal amount of the refunded bond paid with proceeds of the refunding bond. For this purpose, *principal amount* means, in reference to a plain par bond, its stated principal amount plus accrued unpaid interest, and in reference to any other bond, its present value.

(d) *Pooled financings*—(1) *Treatment of pool issuer.* To the extent that an issuer of a pooled financing is not an ultimate borrower in the financing and the conduit borrowers are governmental units with general taxing powers and not subordinate to the issuer, the pooled financing is not counted towards the $5,000,000 size limitation of the issuer for purposes of applying the small issuer exception to its other issues. The issuer of the pooled financing issue is, however, subject to the rebate requirement for any unloaned gross proceeds.

(2) *Treatment of conduit borrowers.* A loan to a conduit borrower in a pooled financing qualifies for the small issuer exception, regardless of the size of either the pooled financing or of any loan to other conduit borrowers, only if—

(i) The bonds of the pooled financing are not private activity bonds;

(ii) None of the loans to conduit borrowers are private activity bonds; and

(iii) The loan to the conduit borrower meets all the requirements of the small issuer exception.

(e) *Refunding issues*—(1) *In general.* Sections 148(f)(4)(D)(v) and (vi) provide restrictions on application of the small issuer exception to refunding issues.

(2) *Multipurpose issues.* The multipurpose issue allocation rules of § 1.148-9(h) apply for purposes of determining whether refunding bonds meet the requirements of section 148(f)(4)(D)(v). [Reg. § 1.148-8.]

☐ [*T.D. 8418, 5-12-92. Amended by T.D. 8476, 6-14-93.*]

→ *Caution: Reg. § 1.148-9, below, is applicable to certain bonds sold on or after July 8, 1997.*←

[Reg. § 1.148-9]

§ 1.148-9. Arbitrage rules for refunding issues.—(a) *Scope of application.* This section contains special arbitrage rules for refunding issues. These rules apply for all purposes of section 148 and govern allocations of proceeds, bonds, and investments to determine transferred proceeds, temporary periods, reasonably required reserve or replacement funds, minor portions, and separate issue treatment of certain multipurpose issues.

(b) *Transferred proceeds allocation rule*—(1) *In general.* When proceeds of the refunding issue discharge any of the outstanding principal amount of the prior issue, proceeds of the prior issue become transferred proceeds of the refunding issue and cease to be proceeds of the prior issue. The amount of proceeds of the prior issue that becomes transferred proceeds of the refunding issue is an amount equal to the proceeds of the prior issue on the date of that discharge multiplied by a fraction—

(i) The numerator of which is the principal amount of the prior issue discharged with proceeds of the refunding issue on the date of that discharge; and

(ii) The denominator of which is the total outstanding principal amount of the prior issue on the date immediately before the date of that discharge.

(2) *Special definition of principal amount.* For purposes of this section, *principal amount* means, in reference to a plain par bond, its stated principal amount, and in reference to any other bond, its present value.

(3) *Relation of transferred proceeds rule to universal cap rule*—(i) *In general.* Paragraphs (b)(1) and (c) of this section apply to allocate transferred proceeds and corresponding investments to a refunding issue on any date required by those paragraphs before the application of the universal cap rule of § 1.148-6(b)(2) to reallocate any of those amounts. To the extent nonpurpose

Reg. § 1.148-9(a)

Tax Exempt. Requirements: S-ate/Local Bonds   25,403

See p. 20,601 for regulations not amended to reflect law changes

→ *Caution: Reg. § 1.148-9, be!ow, is applicable to certain bonds sold on or after July 8, 1997.*←

investments allocable to proceeds of a refunding issue exceed the universal cap for the issue on the date that amounts become transferred proceeds of the refunding issue, those transferred proceeds and corresponding investments are reallocated back to the issue from which they transferred on that same date to the extent of the unused universal cap on that prior issue.

(ii) *Example.* The following example illustrates the application of this paragraph of (b)(3):

Example. On January 1, 1995, $100,000 of nonpurpose investments allocable to proceeds of issue *A* become transferred proceeds of issue *B* under § 1.148-9, but the unused port on of issue *B*'s universal cap is $75,000 as of that date. On January 1, 1995, issue *A* has unused universal cap in excess of $25,000. Thus, $25,000 of nonpurpose investments representing the transferred proceeds are immediately reallocated back to issue *A* on January 1, 1995, and are proceeds of issue *A*. On the next transfer date under § 1.148-9, the $25,000 receives no priority in determining transferred proceeds as of that date but is treated the same as all other proceeds of issue *A* subject to transfer.

(4) *Limitation on multi-generat'onal transfers.* This paragraph (b)(4) contains limitations on the manner in which proceeds of a first generation issue that is refunded by a refunding issue (a *second generation issue*) become transferred proceeds of a refunding issue (a *third generation issue*) that refunds the second generation issue. Proceeds of the first generation issue that become transferred proceeds of the third generation issue are treated as having a yield equal to the yield on the refunding escrow allocated to the second generation issue (i.e., as determined under § 1.148-5(b)(2)(iv)). The determination of the transferred proceeds of the third generation issue does not affect compliance with the requirements of section 148, including the determination of the amount of arbitrage rebate with respect to or the yield on the refunding escrow, of the second generation issue.

(c) *Special allocation rules for refunding issues*—(1) *Allocations of investments*—(i) *In general.* Except as otherwise provided in this paragraph (c), investments purchased with sale proceeds or investment proceeds of a refunding issue must be allocated to those proceeds, and investments not purchased with these proceeds may not be allocated to those proceeds (i.e., a *specific tracing method*).

(ii) *Allocations to transferred proceeds.* When proceeds of a prior issue become transferred

proceeds of a refunding issue, investments (and the related payments and receipts) of proceeds of the prior issue that are held in a refunding escrow for ano her issue are allocated to the transferred proceeds under the ratable allocation method described in paragraph (c)(1)(iii) of this section. Investments of proceeds of the prior issue that are not held in a refunding escrow for another issue are allocated to the transferred proceeds by application of the allocation methods described in paragraph (c)(1)(iii) or (iv) of this section, consistently applied to all investments on a transfer date.

(iii) *Ratable allocation method.* Under the ratable allocation method, a ratable portion of each nonpurpose and purpose investment of proceeds of the prior issue is allocated to transferred proceeds of the refunding issue.

(iv) *Representative allocation method*—(A) *In general.* Under the representative allocation method, representative portions of the portfolio of nonpurpose investments and the portfolio of purpose investments of proceeds of the prior issue are allocated to transferred proceeds of the refunding issue. Unlike the ratable allocation method, this representative allocation method permits an allocation of particular whole investments. Whether a portion is representative is based on all the facts and circumstances, including, without limitation, whether the current yields, maturities, and current unrealized gains or losses on the particular allocated investments are reasonably comparable to those of the unallocated investments in the aggregate. In addition, if a portion of nonpurpose investments is otherwise representative, it is within the issuer's discretion to allocate the portion from whichever source of funds it deems appropriate, such as a reserve fund or a construction fund for a prior issue.

(B) *Mark-to-market safe harbor for representative allocation method.* In addition to other representative allocations, a specific allocation of a particular nonpurpose investment to transferred proceeds (e.g., of lower yielding investments) is treated as satisfying the representative allocation method if that investment is valued at fair market value on the transfer date in determining the payments and receipts on that date, but only if the portion of the nonpurpose investments that transfers is based on the relative fair market value of all nonpurpose investments.

(2) *Allocations of mixed escrows to expenditures for principal, interest, and redemption prices on a prior issue*—(i) *In general.* Except for amounts required or permitted to be accounted for under paragraph (c)(2)(ii) of this section, pro-

Reg. § 1.148-9(c)(2)

→ *Caution: Reg. § 1.148-9, below, is applicable to certain bonds sold on or after July 8, 1997.*←

ceeds of a refunding issue and other amounts that are not proceeds of a refunding issue that are deposited in a refunding escrow (a *mixed escrow*) must be accounted for under this paragraph (c)(2)(i). Those proceeds and other amounts must be allocated to expenditures for principal, interest, or stated redemption prices on the prior issue so that the expenditures of those proceeds do not occur faster than ratably with expenditures of the other amounts in the mixed escrow. During the period that the prior issue has unspent proceeds, however, these allocations must be ratable (with reasonable adjustments for rounding) both between sources for expenditures (i.e., proceeds and other amounts) and between uses (i.e., principal, interest, and stated redemption prices on the prior issue).

(ii) *Exceptions*—(A) *Mandatory allocation of certain non-proceeds to earliest expenditures.* If amounts other than proceeds of the refunding issue are deposited in a mixed escrow, but before the issue date of the refunding issue those amounts had been held in a bona fide debt service fund or a fund to carry out the governmental purpose of the prior issue (e.g., a construction fund), those amounts must be allocated to the earliest maturing investments in the mixed escrow.

(B) *Permissive allocation of non-proceeds to earliest expenditures.* Excluding amounts covered by paragraph (c)(2)(ii)(A) of this section and subject to any required earlier expenditure of those amounts, any amounts in a mixed escrow that are not proceeds of a refunding issue may be allocated to the earliest maturing investments in the mixed escrow, provided that those investments mature and the proceeds thereof are expended before the date of any expenditure from the mixed escrow to pay any principal of the prior issue.

(d) *Temporary periods in refundings*—(1) *In general.* Proceeds of a refunding issue may be invested in higher yielding investments under section 148(c) only during the temporary periods described in paragraph (d)(2) of this section.

(2) *Types of temporary periods in refundings.* The available temporary periods for proceeds of a refunding issue are as follows:

(i) *General temporary period for refunding issues.* Except as otherwise provided in this paragraph (d)(2), the temporary period for proceeds (other than transferred proceeds) of a refunding issue is the period ending 30 days after the issue date of the refunding issue.

(ii) *Temporary periods for current refunding issues*—(A) *In general.* Except as otherwise provided in paragraph (d)(2)(ii)(B) of this section, the temporary period for proceeds (other than transferred proceeds) of a current refunding issue is 90 days.

(B) *Temporary period for short-term current refunding issues.* The temporary period for proceeds (other than transferred proceeds) of a current refunding issue that has an original term to maturity of 270 days or less may not exceed 30 days. The aggregate temporary periods for proceeds (other than transferred proceeds) of all current refunding issues described in the preceding sentence that are part of the same series of refundings is 90 days. An issue is part of a series of refundings if it finances or refinances the same expenditures for a particular governmental purpose as another issue.

(iii) *Temporary periods for transferred proceeds*—(A) *In general.* Except as otherwise provided in paragraph (d)(2)(iii)(B) of this section, each available temporary period for transferred proceeds of a refunding issue begins on the date those amounts become transferred proceeds of the refunding issue and ends on the date that, without regard to the discharge of the prior issue, the available temporary period for those proceeds would have ended had those remained proceeds of the prior issue.

(B) *Termination of initial temporary period for prior issue in an advance refunding.* The initial temporary period under § 1.148-2(e)(2) and (3) for the proceeds of a prior issue that is refunded by an advance refunding issue (including transferred proceeds) terminates on the issue date of the advance refunding issue.

(iv) *Certain short-term gross proceeds.* Except for proceeds of a refunding issue held in a refunding escrow, proceeds otherwise reasonably expected to be used to pay principal or interest on the prior issue, replacement proceeds not held in a bona fide debt service fund, and transferred proceeds, the temporary period for gross proceeds of a refunding issue is the 13-month period beginning on the date of receipt.

(e) *Reasonably required reserve or replacement funds in refundings.* In addition to the requirements of § 1.148-2(f), beginning on the issue date of a refunding issue, a reserve or replacement fund for a refunding issue or a prior issue is a reasonably required reserve or replacement fund under section 148(d) that may be invested in higher yielding investments only if the aggregate

Reg. § 1.148-9(d)(1)

Tax Exempt. Requirements: State/Local Bonds   **25,405**

See p. 20,601 for regulations not amended to reflect law changes

→ *Caution: Reg. § 1.148-9, below, is applicable to certain bonds sold on or after July 8, 1997.*←

amount invested in higher yielding investments under this paragraph (e) for both the refunding issue and the prior issue does not exceed the size limitations under § 1.148-2(f)(2) and (f)(3), measured by reference to the refunding issue only (regardless of whether proceeds of the prior issue have become transferred proceeds of the refunding issue).

(f) *Minor portions in refundings.* Beginning on the issue date of the refunding issue, gross proceeds not in excess of a minor portion of the refunding issue qualify for investment in higher yielding investments under section 148(e), and gross proceeds not in excess of a minor portion of the prior issue qualify for investment in higher yielding investments under either section 148(e) or section 149(d)(3)(A)(v), whichever is applicable. *Minor portion* is defined in § 1.148-2(g).

(g) *Certain waivers permitted.* On or before the issue date, an issuer may waive the right to invest in higher yielding investments during any temporary period or as part of a reasonably required reserve or replacement fund. At any time, an issuer may waive the right to invest in higher yielding investments as part of a minor portion.

(h) *Multipurpose issue allocations*—(1) *Application of multipurpose issue allocation rules.* The portion of the bonds of a multipurpose issue reasonably allocated to any separate purpose under this paragraph (h) is treated as a separate issue for all purposes of section 148 except the following—

(i) *Arbitrage yield.* Except to the extent that the proceeds of an issue are allocable to two or more conduit loans that are tax-exempt bonds, determining the yield on a multipurpose issue and the yield on investments for purposes of the arbitrage yield restrictions of section 148 and the arbitrage rebate requirement of section 148(f);

(ii) *Rebate amount.* Except as provided in paragraph (h)(1)(i) of this section, determining the rebate amount for a multipurpose issue, including subsidiary matters with respect to that determination, such as the computation date credit under § 1.148-3(d)(1), the due date for payments, and the $100,000 bona fide debt service fund exception under section 148(f)(4)(A)(ii);

(iii) *Minor portion.* Determining the *minor portion* of an issue under section 148(e);

(iv) *Reasonably required reserve or replacement fund.* Determining the portion of an issue eligible for investment in higher yielding investments as part of a reasonably required re-

serve or replacement fund under section 148(d); and

(v) *Effective date.* Applying the provisions of § 1.148-11(b) (relating to elective retroactive application of §§ 1.148-1 through 1.148-10 to certain issues).

(2) *Rules on allocations of multipurpose issues*—(i) *In general.* This paragraph (h) applies to allocations of multipurpose issues, including allocations involving the refunding purposes of the issue. Except as otherwise provided in this paragraph (h), proceeds, investments, and bonds of a multipurpose issue may be allocated among the various separate purposes of the issue using any reasonable, consistently applied allocation method. An allocation is not reasonable if it achieves more favorable results under section 148 or 149(d) than could be achieved with actual separate issues. An allocation under this paragraph (h) may be made at any time, but once made may not be changed.

(ii) *Allocations involving certain common costs.* A ratable allocation of common costs (as described in paragraph (h)(3)(ii) of this section) among the separate purposes of the multipurpose issue is generally reasonable. If another allocation method more accurately reflects the extent to which any separate purpose of a multipurpose issue enjoys the economic benefit or bears the economic burden of certain common costs, that allocation method may be used.

(3) *Separate purposes of a multipurpose issue*—(i) *In general.* Separate purposes of a multipurpose issue include refunding a separate prior issue, financing a separate purpose investment, financing a construction issue (as defined in § 1.148-7(f)), and any clearly discrete governmental purpose reasonably expected to be financed by that issue. In general, all integrated or functionally related capital projects that qualify for the same initial temporary period under § 1.148-2(e)(2) are treated as having a single governmental purpose. The separate purposes of a refunding issue include the separate purposes of the prior issue, if any. Separate purposes may be treated as a single purpose if the proceeds used to finance those purposes are eligible for the same initial temporary period under section 148(c). For example, the use of proceeds of a multipurpose issue to finance separate qualified mortgage loans may be treated as a single purpose.

(ii) *Financing common costs.* Common costs of a multipurpose issue are not separate purposes. Common costs include issuance costs, accrued interest, capitalized interest on the issue,

Reg. § 1.148-9(h)(3)

25,406   Tax Exempt. Requirements: State/Local Bonds

See p. 20,601 for regulations not amended to reflect law changes

→ *Caution: Reg. § 1.148-9, below, is applicable to certain bonds sold on or after July 8, 1997.*←

a reserve or replacement fund, qualified guarantee fees, and similar costs properly allocable to the separate purposes of the issue.

(iii) *Example.* The following example illustrates the application of this paragraph (h)(3).

Example. On January 1, 1994, Housing Authority of State *A* issues a $10 million issue (the *1994 issue*) at an interest rate of 10 percent to finance qualified mortgage loans for owner-occupied residences under section 143. During 1994, *A* originates $5 million in qualified mortgage loans at an interest rate of 10 percent. In 1995, the market interest rates for housing loans falls to 8 percent and *A* is unable to originate further loans from the 1994 issue. On January 1, 1996, *A* issues a $5 million issue (the *1996 issue*) at an interest rate of 8 percent to refund partially the 1994 issue. Under paragraph (h) of this section, *A* treats the portion of the 1994 issue used to originate $5 million in loans as a separate issue comprised of that group of purpose investments. *A* allocates those purpose investments representing those loans to that separate unrefunded portion of the issue. In addition, *A* treats the unoriginated portion of the 1994 issue as a separate issue and allocates the nonpurpose investments representing the unoriginated proceeds of the 1994 issue to the refunded portion of the issue. Thus, when proceeds of the 1996 issue are used to pay principal on the refunded portion of the 1994 issue that is treated as a separate issue under paragraph (h) of this section, only the portion of the 1994 issue representing unoriginated loan funds invested in nonpurpose investments transfer to become transferred proceeds of the 1996 issue.

(4) *Allocations of bonds of a multipurpose issue*—(i) *Reasonable allocation of bonds to portions of issue.* After reasonable adjustment of the issue price of a multipurpose issue to account for common costs, the portion of the bonds of a multipurpose issue allocated to a separate purpose must have an issue price that bears the same ratio to the aggregate issue price of the multipurpose issue as the portion of the sale proceeds of the multipurpose issue used for that separate purpose bears to the aggregate sale proceeds of the multipurpose issue. For a refunding issue used to refund two or more prior issues, the portion of the sales proceeds allocated to the refunding of a separate prior issue is based on the present value of the refunded debt service on that prior issue, using the yield on investments in the refunding escrow allocable to the entire refunding issue as the discount rate.

(ii) *Safe harbor for pro rata allocation method for bonds.* The use of the relative amount of sales proceeds used for each separate purpose to ratably allocate each bond or a ratable number of substantially identical whole bonds is a reasonable method for allocating bonds of a multipurpose issue.

(iii) *Safe harbor for allocations of bonds used to finance separate purpose investments.* An allocation of a portion of the bonds of a multipurpose issue to a particular purpose investment is generally reasonable if that purpose investment has principal and interest payments that reasonably coincide in time and amount to principal and interest payments on the bonds allocated to that purpose investment.

(iv) *Rounding of bond allocations to next whole bond denomination permitted.* An allocation that rounds each resulting fractional bond up or down to the next integral multiple of a permitted denomination of bonds of that issue not in excess of $100,000 does not prevent the allocation from satisfying this paragraph (h)(4).

(v) *Restrictions on allocations of bonds to refunding purposes.* For each portion of a multipurpose issue that is used to refund a separate prior issue, a method of allocating bonds of that issue is reasonable under this paragraph (h) only if, in addition to the requirements of paragraphs (h)(1) and (h)(2) of this section, the portion of the bonds allocated to the refunding of that prior issue—

(A) Results from a pro rata allocation under paragraph (h)(4)(ii) of this section;

(B) Reflects aggregate principal and interest payable in each bond year that is less than, equal to, or proportionate to, the aggregate principal and interest payable on the prior issue in each bond year;

(C) Results from an allocation of all the bonds of the entire multipurpose issue in proportion to the remaining weighted average economic life of the capital projects financed or refinanced by the issue, determined in the same manner as under section 147(b); or

(D) Results from another reasonable allocation method, but only to the extent that the application of the allocation methods provided in this paragraph (h)(4)(v) is not permitted under state law restrictions applicable to the bonds, reasonable terms of bonds issued before, or subject to a master indenture that became effective prior to, July 1, 1993, or other similar restrictions or circumstances. This paragraph (h)(4)(v)(D) shall be

Reg. § 1.148-9(h)(4)

→ *Caution: Reg. § 1.148-9, below, is applicable to certain bonds sold on or after July 8, 1997.*←

strictly construed and is available only if it does not result in a greater burden on the market for tax-exempt bonds than would occur using one of the other allocation methods provided in this paragraph (h)(4)(v). (See also § 1.148-11(c)(2).)

(vi) *Exception for refundings of interim notes.* Paragraph (h)(4)(v) of this section need not be applied to refunding bonds issued to provide permanent financing for one or more projects if the prior issue had a term of less than 3 years and was sold in anticipation of permanent financing, but only if the aggregate term of all prior issues sold in anticipation of permanent financing was less than 3 years.

(5) *Limitation on multi-generation allocations.* This paragraph (h) does not apply to allocations of a multipurpose refunded issue unless that refunded issue is refunded directly by an issue to which this paragraph (h) applies. For example, if a 1994 issue refunds a 1984 multipurpose issue, which in turn refunded a 1980 multipurpose issue, this paragraph (h) applies to allocations of the 1984 issue for purposes of allocating the refunding purposes of the 1994 issue, but does not permit allocations of the 1980 issue.

(i) *Operating rules for separation of prior issue into refunded and unrefunded portions—*(1) *In general.* For purposes of paragraph (h)(3)(i) of this section, the separate purposes of a prior issue include the refunded and unrefunded portions of the prior issue. Thus, the refunded and unrefunded portions are treated as separate issues under paragraph (h)(1) of this section. Those separate issues must satisfy the requirements of paragraphs (h) and (i) of this section. The refunded portion of the bonds of a prior issue is based on a fraction the numerator of which is the principal amount of the prior issue to be paid with proceeds of the refunding issue and the denominator of which is the outstanding principal amount of the bonds of the prior issue, each determined as of the issue date of the refunding issue. (See also paragraph (b)(2) of this section.)

(2) *Allocations of proceeds and investments in a partial refunding.* As of the issue date of a partial refunding issue under this paragraph (i), unspent proceeds of the prior issue are allocated ratably between the refunded and unrefunded portions of the prior issue and the investments allocable to those unspent proceeds are allocated in the manner required for the allocation of investments to transferred proceeds under paragraph (c)(1)(ii) of this section.

(3) *References to prior issue.* If the refunded and unrefunded portions of a prior issue are treated as separate issues under this paragraph (i), then, except to the extent that the context clearly requires otherwise (e.g., references to the aggregate prior issue in the mixed escrow rule in paragraph (c)(2) of this section), all references in this section to a prior issue refer only to the refunded portion of that prior issue. [Reg. § 1.148-9.]

☐ [*T.D.* 8418, 5-12-92. *Amended by T.D.* 8476, 6-14-93; *T.D.* 8538, 5-5-94 *and T.D.* 8718, 5-8-97.]

→ *Caution: Reg. § 1.148-9A, below, is applicable to certain bonds sold prior to July 8, 1997.*←

[Reg. § 1.148-9A]

§ 1.148-9A. Arbitrage rules for refunding issues.—(a) through (c)(2)(ii)(A) [Reserved]. For guidance see § 1.148-9.

(c)(2)(ii)(B) *Permissive allocation of non-proceeds to earliest expenditures.* Excluding amounts covered by § 1.148-9(c)(2)(ii)(A) and subject to any required earlier expenditure of those amounts, any amounts in a mixed escrow that are not proceeds of a refunding issue may be allocated to the earliest maturing investments in the mixed escrow, provided that those investments mature and the proceeds thereof are expended before the date of any expenditure from the mixed escrow to pay any principal of the prior issue.

(d) through (h)(4)(v) [Reserved]. For guidance see § 1.148-9.

(h)(4)(vi) *Exception for refundings of interim notes.* Section 1.148-9(h)(4)(v) need not be applied to refunding bonds issued to provide permanent financing for one or more projects if the prior issue had a term of less than 3 years and was sold in anticipation of permanent financing, but only if the aggregate term of all prior issues sold in anticipation of permanent financing was less than 3 years. [Reg. § 1.148-9A.]

☐ [*T.D.* 8538, 5-5-94. *Redesignated and amended by T.D.* 8718, 5-8-97.]

→ *Caution: Reg. § 1.148-10, below, is applicable to certain bonds sold on or after July 8, 1997.*←

Reg. § 1.148-9A(a)

25,408   Tax Exempt. Requirements: State/Local Bonds

See p. 20,601 for regulations not amended to reflect law changes

→ *Caution: Reg. § 1.148-10, below, is applicable to certain bonds sold on or after July 8, 1997.*←

[Reg. § 1.148-10]

§ 1.148-10. Anti-abuse rules and authority of Commissioner.—(a) *Abusive arbitrage device*— (1) *In general.* Bonds of an issue are arbitrage bonds under section 148 if an abusive arbitrage device under paragraph (a)(2) of this section is used in connection with the issue. This paragraph (a) is to be applied and interpreted broadly to carry out the purposes of section 148, as further described in § 1.148-0. Except as otherwise provided in paragraph (c) of this section, any action that is expressly permitted by section 148 or §§ 1.148-1 through 1.148-11 is not an abusive arbitrage device (e.g., investment in higher yielding investments during a permitted temporary period under section 148(c)).

(2) *Abusive arbitrage device defined.* Any action is an abusive arbitrage device if the action has the effect of—

(i) Enabling the issuer to exploit the difference between tax-exempt and taxable interest rates to obtain a material financial advantage; and

(ii) Overburdening the tax-exempt bond market.

(3) *Exploitation of tax-exempt interest rates.* An action may exploit tax-exempt interest rates under paragraph (a)(2) of this section as a result of an investment of any portion of the gross proceeds of an issue over any period of time, notwithstanding that, in the aggregate, the gross proceeds of the issue are not invested in higher yielding investments over the term of the issue.

(4) *Overburdening the tax-exempt market.* An action overburdens the tax-exempt bond market under paragraph (a)(2)(ii) of this section if it results in issuing more bonds, issuing bonds earlier, or allowing bonds to remain outstanding longer than is otherwise reasonably necessary to accomplish the governmental purposes of the bonds, based on all the facts and circumstances. Whether an action is reasonably necessary to accomplish the governmental purposes of the bonds depends on whether the primary purpose of the transaction is a bona fide governmental purpose (e.g., an issue of refunding bonds to achieve a debt service restructuring that would be issued independent of any arbitrage benefit). An important factor bearing on this determination is whether the action would reasonably be taken to accomplish the governmental purpose of the issue if the interest on the issue were not excludable from gross income under section 103(a) (assuming that the hypothetical taxable interest rate would be the same as the actual tax-exempt interest rate). Factors evidencing an overissuance include the issuance of an issue the proceeds of which are reasonably expected to exceed by more than a minor portion the amount necessary to accomplish the governmental purposes of the issue, or an issue the proceeds of which are, in fact, substantially in excess of the amount of sale proceeds allocated to expenditures for the governmental purposes of the issue. One factor evidencing an early issuance is the issuance of bonds that do not qualify for a temporary period under § 1.148-2(e)(2), (e)(3), or (e)(4). One factor evidencing that bonds may remain outstanding longer than necessary is a term that exceeds the safe harbors against the creation of replacement proceeds under § 1.148-1(c)(4)(i)(B). These factors may be outweighed by other factors, however, such as bona fide cost underruns or long-term financial distress.

(b) *Consequences of overburdening the tax-exempt bond market*—(1) *In general.* An issue that overburdens the tax-exempt bond market (within the meaning of paragraph (a)(4) of this section) is subject to the following special limitations—

(i) *Special yield restriction.* Investments are subject to the definition of *materially higher* yield under § 1.148-2(d) that is equal to one-thousandth of 1 percent. In addition, each investment is treated as a separate class of investments under § 1.148-5(b)(2)(ii), the yield on which may not be blended with that of other investments.

(ii) *Certain regulatory provisions inapplicable.* The provisions of § 1.148-5(c) (relating to yield reduction payments) and § 1.148-5(e)(2) and (3) (relating to recovery of qualified administrative costs) do not apply.

(iii) *Restrictive expenditure rule.* Proceeds are not allocated to expenditures unless the proceeds-spent-last rule under § 1.148-6(d)(3)(i) is satisfied, applied by treating those proceeds as proceeds to be used for restricted working capital expenditures. For this purpose, available amount includes a reasonable working capital reserve as defined in § 1.148-6(d)(3)(iii)(B).

(2) *Application.* The provisions of this paragraph (b) only apply to the portion of an issue that, as a result of actions taken (or actions not taken) after the issue date, overburdens the market for tax-exempt bonds, except that for an issue that is reasonably expected as of the issue date to overburden the market, those provisions apply to all of the gross proceeds of the issue.

Tax Exempt. Requirements: State/Local Bonds   25,409

See p. 20,601 for regulations not amended to reflect law changes

→ *Caution: Reg. § 1.148-10, below, is applicable to certain bonds sold on or after July 8, 1997.* ←

(c) *Anti-abuse rules on excess gross proceeds of advance refunding issues*—(1) *In general.* Except as otherwise provided in this paragraph (c), an abusive arbitrage device is used and bonds of an advance refunding issue are arbitrage bonds if the issue has excess gross proceeds.

(2) *Definition of excess gross proceeds.* Excess gross proceeds means all gross proceeds of an advance refunding issue that exceed an amount equal to 1 percent of sale proceeds of the issue, other than gross proceeds allocable to—

(i) Payment of principal, interest, or call premium on the prior issue;

(ii) Payment of pre-issuance accrued interest on the refunding issue, and interest on the refunding issue that accrues for a period up to the completion date of any capital project for which the prior issue was issued, plus one year;

(iii) A reasonably required reserve or replacement fund for the refunding issue or investment proceeds of such a fund;

(iv) Payment of costs of issuance of the refunding issue;

(v) Payment of administrative costs allocable to repaying the prior issue, carrying and repaying the refunding issue, or investments of the refunding issue;

(vi) Transferred proceeds that will be used or maintained for the governmental purpose of the prior issue;

(vii) Interest on purpose investments;

(viii) Replacement proceeds in a sinking fund for the refunding issue;

(ix) Qualified guarantee fees for the refunding issue or the prior issue; and

(x) Fees for a qualified hedge for the refunding issue.

(3) *Special treatment of transferred proceeds.* For purposes of this paragraph (c), all unspent proceeds of the prior issue as of the issue date of the refunding issue are treated as transferred proceeds of the advance refunding issue.

(4) *Special rule for crossover refundings.* An advance refunding issue is not an issue of arbitrage bonds under this paragraph (c) if all excess gross proceeds of the refunding issue are used to pay interest that accrues on the refunding issue before the prior issue is discharged, and no gross proceeds of any refunding issue are used to pay interest on the prior issue or to replace funds used directly or indirectly to pay such interest (other than transferred proceeds used to pay interest on the prior issue that accrues for a period up to the completion date of the project for which the prior issue was issued, plus one year, or proceeds used to pay principal that is attributable to accrued original issue discount).

(5) *Special rule for gross refundings.* This paragraph (c)(5) applies if an advance refunding issue (the *series B issue*) is used together with one or more other advance refunding issues (the *series A issues*) in a gross refunding of a prior issue, but only if the use of a gross refunding method is required under bond documents that were effective prior to November 6, 1992. These advance refunding issues are not arbitrage bonds under this paragraph (c) if—

(i) All excess gross proceeds of the series B issue and each series A issue are investment proceeds used to pay principal and interest on the series B issue;

(ii) At least 99 percent of all principal and interest on the series B issue is paid with proceeds of the series B and series A issues or with the earnings on other amounts in the refunding escrow for the prior issue;

(iii) The series B issue is discharged not later than the prior issue; and

(iv) As of any date, the amount of gross proceeds of the series B issue allocated to expenditures does not exceed the aggregate amount of expenditures before that date for principal and interest on the series B issue, and administrative costs of carrying and repaying the series B issue, or of investments of the series B issue.

(d) *Examples.* The provisions of this section are illustrated by the following examples:

Example 1. Mortgage sale. In 1982, City issued its revenue issue (the *1982 issue*) and lent the proceeds to Developer to finance a low-income housing project under former section 103(b)(4)(A) of the 1954 Code. In 1994, Developer encounters financial difficulties and negotiates with City to refund the 1982 issue. City issues $10 million in principal amount of its 8 percent bonds (the *1994 issue*). City lends the proceeds of the 1994 issue to Developer. To evidence Developer's obligation to repay that loan, Developer, as obligor, issues a note to City (the *City note*). Bank agrees to provide Developer with a direct-pay letter of credit pursuant to which Bank will make all payments to the trustee for the 1994 issue necessary to meet Developer's obligations under the City note. Developer pays Bank a fee for the issuance of the letter of credit and issues a note to Bank (the *Bank note*). The Bank note is secured by a mortgage on the housing project and is guaranteed by

Reg. § 1.148-10(d)

25,410   Tax Exempt. Requirements: State/Local Bonds

See p. 20,601 for regulations not amended to reflect law changes

→ *Caution: Reg. § 1.148-10, below, is applicable to certain bonds sold on or after July 8, 1997.*←

FHA. The Bank note and the 1994 issue have different prepayment terms. The City does not reasonably expect to treat prepayments of the Bank note as gross proceeds of the 1994 issue. At the same time or pursuant to a series of related transactions, Bank sells the Bank note to Investor for $9.5 million. Bank invests these monies together with its other funds. In substance, the transaction is a loan by City to Bank, under which Bank enters into a series of transactions that, in effect, result in Bank retaining $9.5 million in amounts treated as proceeds of the 1994 issue. Those amounts are invested in materially higher yielding investments that provide funds sufficient to equal or exceed the Bank's liability under the letter of credit. Alternatively, the letter of credit is investment property in a sinking fund for the 1994 issue provided by Developer, a substantial beneficiary of the financing. Because, in substance, Developer acquires the $10 million principal amount letter of credit for a fair market value purchase price of $9.5 million, the letter of credit is a materially higher yielding investment. Neither result would change if Developer's obligation under the Bank note is contingent on Bank performing its obligation under the letter of credit. Each characterization causes the bonds to be arbitrage bonds.

Example 2. Bonds outstanding longer than necessary for yield-blending device. (i) *Longer bond maturity to create sinking fund.* In 1994, Authority issues an advance refunding issue (the *refunding issue*) to refund a 1982 prior issue (the *prior issue*). Under current market conditions, Authority will have to invest the refunding escrow at a yield significantly below the yield on the refunding issue. Authority issues its refunding issue with a longer weighted average maturity than otherwise necessary primarily for the purpose of creating a sinking fund for the refunding issue that will be invested in a guaranteed investment contract. The weighted average maturity of the refunding issue is less than 120 percent of the remaining average economic life of the facilities financed with the proceeds of the prior issue. The guaranteed investment contract has a yield that is higher than the yield on the refunding issue. The yield on the refunding escrow blended with the yield on the guaranteed investment contract does not exceed the yield on the issue. The refunding issue uses an abusive arbitrage device and the bonds of the issue are arbitrage bonds under section 148(a).

(ii) *Refunding of noncallable bonds.* The facts are the same as in paragraph (i) of this *Example 2*

except that instead of structuring the refunding issue to enable it to take advantage of sinking fund investments, Authority will also refund other long-term, non-callable bonds in the same refunding issue. There are no savings attributable to the refunding of the non-callable bonds (e.g., a *low-to-high* refunding). The Authority invests the portion of the proceeds of the refunding issue allocable to the refunding of the non-callable bonds in the refunding escrow at a yield that is higher than the yield on the refunding issue, based on the relatively long escrow period for this portion of the refunding. The Authority invests the other portion of the proceeds of the refunding issue in the refunding escrow at a yield lower than the yield on the refunding issue. The blended yield on all the investments in the refunding escrow for the prior issues does not exceed the yield on the refunding issue. The portion of the refunding issue used to refund the noncallable bonds, however, was not otherwise necessary and was issued primarily to exploit the difference between taxable and tax-exempt rates for that long portion of the refunding escrow to minimize the effect of lower yielding investments in the other portion of the escrow. The refunding issue uses an abusive arbitrage device and the bonds of the issue are arbitrage bonds.

(iii) *Governmental purpose.* In paragraphs (i) and (ii) of this *Example 2,* the existence of a governmental purpose for the described financing structures would not change the conclusions unless Authority clearly established that the primary purpose for the use of the particular structure was a bona fide governmental purpose. The fact that each financing structure had the effect of eliminating significant amounts of negative arbitrage is strong evidence of a primary purpose that is not a bona fide governmental purpose. Moreover, in paragraph (i) of this *Example 2,* the structure of the refunding issue coupled with the acquisition of the guaranteed investment contract to lock in the investment yield associated with the structure is strong evidence of a primary purpose that is not a bona fide governmental purpose.

Example 3. Window refunding. (i) Authority issues its 1994 refunding issue to refund a portion of the principal and interest on its outstanding 1985 issue. The 1994 refunding issue is structured using zero-coupon bonds that pay no interest or principal for the 5-year period following the issue date. The proceeds of the 1994 refunding issue are deposited in a refunding escrow to be used to pay only the interest requirements of the refunded

Reg. § 1.148-10(d)

Tax Exempt. Requirements: State/Local Bonds   25,411

See p. 20,601 for regulations not amended to reflect law changes

→ *Caution: Reg. § 1.148-10, below, is applicable to certain bonds sold on or after July 8, 1997.*←

portion of the 1985 issue. Authority enters into a guaranteed investment contract with a financial institution, *G*, under which *G* agrees to provide a guaranteed yield on revenues invested by Authority during the 5-year period following the issue date. The guaranteed investment contract has a yield that is no higher than the yield on the refunding issue. The revenues to be invested under this guaranteed investment contract consist of the amounts that Authority otherwise would have used to pay principal and interest on the 1994 refunding issue. The guaranteed investment contract is structured to generate receipts at times and in amounts sufficient to pay the principal and redemption requirements of the refunded portion of the 1985 issue. A principal purpose of these transactions is to avoid transferred proceeds. Authority will continue to invest the unspent proceeds of the 1985 issue that are on deposit in a refunding escrow for its 1982 issue at a yield equal to the yield on the 1985 issue and will not otherwise treat those unspent proceeds as transferred proceeds of the 1994 refunding issue. The 1994 refunding issue is an issue of arbitrage bonds since those bonds involve a transaction or series of transactions that overburdens the market by leaving bonds outstanding longer than is necessary to obtain a material financial advantage based on arbitrage. Specifically, Authority has structured the 1994 refunding issue to make available for the refunding of the 1985 issue replacement proceeds rather than proceeds so that the unspent proceeds of the 1985 issue will not become transferred proceeds of the 1994 refunding issue.

(ii) The result would be the same in each of the following circumstances:

(A) The facts are the same as in paragraph (i) of this *Example 3* except that Authority does not enter into the guaranteed investment contract but instead, as of the issue date of the 1994 refunding issue, reasonably expects that the released revenues will be available for investment until used to pay principal and interest on the 1985 issue.

(B) The facts are the same as in paragraph (i) of this *Example 3* except that there are no unspent proceeds of the 1985 issue and Authority invests the released revenues at a yield materially higher than the yield on the 1994 issue.

(C) The facts are the same as in paragraph (i) of this *Example 3* except that Authority uses the proceeds of the 1994 issue for capital projects instead of to refund a portion of the 1985 issue.

Example 4. Sale of conduit loan. On January 1, 1994, Authority issues a conduit financing issue

(the *1994 conduit financing issue*) and uses the proceeds to purchase from City, an unrelated party, a tax-exempt bond of City (the *City note*). The proceeds of the 1994 conduit financing issue are to be used to advance refund a prior conduit financing issue that was issued in 1988 and used to make a loan to City. The 1994 conduit financing issue and the City note each have a yield of 8 percent on January 1, 1994. On June 30, 1996, interest rates have decreased and Authority sells the City note to D, a person unrelated to either City or Authority. Based on the sale price of the City note and treating June 30, 1996 as the issue date of the City note, the City note has a 6 percent yield. Authority deposits the proceeds of the sale of the City note into an escrow to redeem the bonds of the 1994 conduit financing issue on January 1, 2001. The escrow is invested in nonpurpose investments having a yield of 8 percent. For purposes of section 149(d), City and Authority are related parties and, therefore, the issue date of the City note is treated as being June 30, 1996. Thus, the City note is an advance refunding of Authority's 1994 conduit financing issue. Interest on the City note is not exempt from Federal income tax from the date it is sold to D under section 149(d), because, by investing the escrow investments at a yield of 8 percent instead of a yield not materially higher than 6 percent, the sale of the City note employs a device to obtain a material financial advantage, based on arbitrage, apart from the savings attributable to lower interest rates. In addition, the City note is not a tax-exempt bond because the note is the second advance refunding of the original bond under section 149(d)(3). The City note also employs an abusive arbitrage device and is an arbitrage bond under section 148.

Example 5. Re-refunding. (i) On January 1, 1984, City issues a tax-exempt issue (the *1984 issue*) to finance the cost of constructing a prison. The 1984 issue has a 7 percent yield and a 30-year maturity. The 1984 issue is callable at any time on or after January 1, 1994. On January 1, 1990, City issues a refunding issue (the *1990 issue*) to advance refund the 1984 issue. The 1990 issue has an 8 percent yield and a 30-year maturity. The 1990 issue is callable at any time on or after January 1, 2000. The proceeds of the 1990 issue are invested at an 8 percent yield in a refunding escrow for the 1984 issue (the *original 1984 escrow*) in a manner sufficient to pay debt service on the 1984 issue until maturity (i.e., an escrow to maturity). On January 1, 1994, City issues a refunding issue (the *1994 issue*). The 1994 issue

25,412   Tax Exempt. Requirements: State/Local Bonds

See p. 20,601 for regulations not amended to reflect law changes

→ *Caution: Reg. § 1.148-10, below, is applicable to certain bonds sold on or after July 8, 1997.←*

has a 6 percent yield and a 30-year maturity. City does not invest the proceeds of the 1994 issue in a refunding escrow for the 1990 issue in a manner sufficient to pay a portion of the debt service until, and redeem a portion of that issue on, January 1, 2000. Instead, City invests those proceeds at a 6 percent yield in a new refunding escrow for a portion of the 1984 issue (the *new 1984 escrow*) in a manner sufficient to pay debt service on a portion of the 1984 issue until maturity. City also liquidates the investments allocable to the proceeds of the 1990 issue held in the original 1984 escrow and reinvests those proceeds in an escrow to pay a portion of the debt service on the 1990 issue itself until, and redeem a portion of that issue on, January 1, 2000 (the *1990 escrow*). The 1994 bonds are arbitrage bonds and employ an abusive device under section 149(d)(4). Although, in form, the proceeds of the 1994 issue are used to pay principal on the 1984 issue, this accounting for the use of the proceeds of the 1994 issue is an unreasonable, inconsistent accounting method under § 1.148-6(a). Moreover, since the proceeds of the 1990 issue were set aside in an escrow to be used to retire the 1984 issue, the use of proceeds of the 1994 issue for that same purpose involves a replacement of funds invested in higher yielding investments under section 148(a)(2). Thus, using a reasonable, consistent accounting method and giving effect to the substance of the transaction, the proceeds of the 1994 issue are treated as used to refund the 1990 issue and are allocable to the 1990 escrow. The proceeds of the 1990 issue are treated as used to refund the 1984 issue and are allocable to the investments in the new 1984 escrow. The proceeds of the 1990 issue allocable to the nonpurpose investments in the new 1984 escrow become transferred proceeds of the 1994 issue as principal is paid on the 1990 issue from amounts on deposit in the 1990 escrow. As a result, the yield on nonpurpose investments allocable to the 1994 issue is materially higher than the yield on the 1994 issue, causing the bonds of the 1994 issue to be arbitrage bonds. In addition, the transaction employs a device under section 149(d)(4) to obtain a material financial advantage based on arbitrage, other than savings attributable to lower interest rates.

(ii) The following changes in the facts do not affect the conclusion that the 1994 issue consists of arbitrage bonds—

(1) The 1990 issue is a taxable issue;

(2) The original 1984 escrow is used to pay the 1994 issue (rather than the 1990 issue); or

(3) The 1994 issue is used to retire the 1984 issue within 90 days of January 1, 1994.

(e) *Authority of the Commissioner to clearly reflect the economic substance of a transaction.* If an issuer enters into a transaction for a principal purpose of obtaining a material financial advantage based on the difference between tax-exempt and taxable interest rates in a manner that is inconsistent with the purposes of section 148, the Commissioner may exercise the Commissioner's discretion to depart from the rules of § 1.148-1 through § 1.148-11 as necessary to clearly reflect the economic substance of the transaction. For this purpose, the Commissioner may recompute yield on an issue or on investments, reallocate payments and receipts on investments, recompute the rebate amount on an issue, treat a hedge as either a qualified hedge or not a qualified hedge, or otherwise adjust any item whatsoever bearing upon the investments and expenditures of gross proceeds of an issue. For example, if the amount paid for a hedge is specifically based on the amount of arbitrage earned or expected to be earned on the hedged bonds, a principal purpose of entering into the contract is to obtain a material financial advantage based on the difference between tax-exempt and taxable interest rates in a manner that is inconsistent with the purposes of section 148.

(f) *Authority of the Commissioner to require an earlier date for payment of rebate.* If the Commissioner determines that an issue is likely to fail to meet the requirements of § 1.148-3 and that a failure to serve a notice of demand for payment on the issuer will jeopardize the assessment or collection of tax on interest paid or to be paid on the issue, the date that the Commissioner serves notice on the issuer is treated as a required computation date for payment of rebate for that issue.

(g) *Authority of the Commissioner to waive regulatory limitations.* Notwithstanding any specific provision in § § 1.148-1 through 1.148-11, the Commissioner may prescribe extensions of temporary periods, larger reasonably required reserve or replacement funds, or consequences of failures or remedial action under section 148 in lieu of or in addition to other consequences of those failures, or take other action, if the Commissioner finds that good faith or other similar circumstances so warrant, consistent with the purposes of section 148. [Reg. § 1.148-10.]

☐ [*T.D. 8284, 1-22-90. Amended by T.D. 8418, 5-12-92, T.D. 8476, 6-14-93; T.D. 8538, 5-5-94 and T.D. 8718, 5-8-97.*]

Reg. § 1.148-10(e)

→ *Caution: Reg. § 1.148-10A, below, is applicable to certain bonds sold prior to July 8, 1997.*←

[Reg. § 1.148-10A]

§ 1.148-10A. Anti-abuse rules and authority of Commissioner.—(a) through (b)(1) [Reserved]. For guidance see § 1.148-10.

(b)(2) *Application.* The provisions of § 1.148-10(b) only apply to the portion of an issue that, as a result of actions taken (or actions not taken) after the issue date, overburdens the market for tax-exempt bonds, except that for an issue that is reasonably expected as of the issue date to overburden the market, those provisions apply to all of the gross proceeds of the issue.

(c) through (c)(2)(viii) [Reserved]. For guidance see § 1.148-10.

(c)(2)(ix) For purposes of § 1.148-10(c)(2), excess gross proceeds do not include gross proceeds allocable to fees for a qualified hedge for the refunding issue. [Reg. § 1.148-10A.]

☐ [*T.D.* 8538, 5-5-94. *Redesignated and amended by T.D. 8718, 5-8-97.*]

[Reg. § 1.148-11]

§ 1.148-11. Effective dates.—(a) *In general.* Except as otherwise provided in this section, §§ 1.148-1 through 1.148-11 apply to bonds sold on or after July 8, 1997.

(b) *Elective retroactive application in whole*—(1) *In general.* Except as otherwise provided in this section, and subject to the applicable effective dates for the corresponding statutory provisions, an issuer may apply the provisions of §§ 1.148-1 through 1.148-11 in whole, but not in part, to any issue that is outstanding on July 8, 1997, and is subject to section 148(f) or to sections 103(c)(6) or 103A(i) of the Internal Revenue Code of 1954, in lieu of otherwise applicable regulations under those sections.

(2) *No elective retroactive application for 18-month spending exception.* The provisions of § 1.148-7(d) (relating to the 18-month spending exception) may not be applied to any issue issued on or before June 30, 1993.

(3) *No elective retroactive application for hedges of fixed rate issues.* The provisions of § 1.148-4(h)(2)(i)(B) (relating to hedges of fixed rate issues) may not be applied to any bond sold on or before July 8, 1997.

(4) *No elective retroactive application for safe harbor for establishing fair market value for guaranteed investment contracts and investments purchased for a yield restricted defeasance escrow.* The provisions of §§ 1.148-5(d)(6)(iii) (relating to the safe harbor for establishing fair market value of guaranteed investment contracts

and yield restricted defeasance escrow investments) and 1.148-5(e)(2)(iv) (relating to a special rule for yield restricted defeasance escrow investments) may not be applied to any bond sold before December 30, 1998.

(c) *Elective retroactive application of certain provisions and special rules*—(1) *Retroactive application of overpayment recovery provisions.* An issuer may apply the provisions of § 1.148-3(i) to any issue that is subject to section 148(f) or to sections 103(c)(6) or 103A(i) of the Internal Revenue Code of 1954.

(i) *Certain commingled funds.* If paragraph (a) of this section applies to an issue, and that issue has a commingled fund to which the provisions of § 1.148-6(e)(6) (relating to commingled reserves) apply, that provision may be applied to all issues secured by that commingled reserve.

(ii) *Certain applications of the universal cap.* The provisions of § 1.148-5(c)(3)(i)(F) (and related provisions) may be applied to satisfy the requirements of section 148 (or applicable prior law) if the application of the universal cap results in amounts in a refunding escrow becoming replacement proceeds of an issue issued on or before June 30, 1993.

(2) *Certain allocations of multipurpose issues.* An allocation of bonds to a refunding purpose under § 1.148-9(h) may be adjusted as necessary to reflect allocations made between May 18, 1992, and August 15, 1993, if the allocations satisfied the corresponding prior provision of § 1.148-11(j)(4) under applicable prior regulations.

(3) *Special limitation.* The provisions of § 1.148-9 apply to issues issued before August 15, 1993, only if the issuer in good faith estimates the present value savings, if any, associated with the effect of the application of that section on refunding escrows, using any reasonable accounting method, and applies those savings, if any, to redeem outstanding tax-exempt bonds of the applicable issue at the earliest possible date on which those bonds may be redeemed or otherwise retired. These savings are not reduced to take into account any administrative costs associated with applying these provisions retroactively.

(d) *Transition rule excepting certain state guarantee funds from the definition of replacement proceeds*—(1) *Certain perpetual trust funds.* A guarantee by a fund created and controlled by a State and established pursuant to its constitution does not cause the amounts in the fund to be

Reg. § 1.148-11(d)

25,414   Tax Exempt. Requirements: State/Local Bonds

See p. 20,601 for regulations not amended to reflect law changes

pledged funds treated as replacement proceeds if—

(i) Substantially all of the corpus of the fund consists of nonfinancial assets, revenues derived from these assets, gifts, and bequests;

(ii) The corpus of the guarantee fund may be invaded only to support specifically designated essential governmental functions (*designated functions*) carried on by political subdivisions with general taxing powers;

(iii) Substantially all of the available income of the fund is required to be applied annually to support designated functions;

(iv) The issue guaranteed consists of general obligations that are not private activity bonds substantially all of the proceeds of which are to be used for designated functions;

(v) The fund satisfied each of the requirements of paragraphs (d)(1)(i) through (d)(1)(iii) of this section on August 16, 1986; and

(vi) The guarantee is not attributable to a deposit to the fund made after May 14, 1989, unless—

(A) The deposit is attributable to the sale or other disposition of fund assets; or

(B) Prior to the deposit, the outstanding amount of the bonds guaranteed by the fund did not exceed 250 percent of the lower of the cost or fair market value of the fund.

(2) *Permanent University Fund.* Replacement proceeds do not include amounts allocable to investments of the fund described in section 648 of Public Law 98-369.

(e) *Transition rule regarding special allowance payments.* Section 1.148-5(b)(5) applies to any bond issued after January 5, 1990, except a bond issued exclusively to refund a bond issued before January 6, 1990, if the amount of the refunding bond does not exceed 101 percent of the amount of the refunded bond, and the maturity date of the refunding bond is not later than the date that is 17 years after the date on which the refunded bond was issued (or, in the case of a series of refundings, the date on which the original bond was issued), but only if § 1.148-2(d)(2)(iv) is applied by substituting *1 and one-half percentage points* for *2 percentage points.*

(f) *Transition rule regarding applicability of yield reduction rule.* Section 1.148-5(c) applies to nonpurpose investments allocable to replacement proceeds of an issue that are held in a reserve or replacement fund to the extent that—

(1) Amounts must be paid into the fund under a constitutional provision, statute, or ordinance adopted before May 3, 1978;

(2) Under that provision, amounts paid into the fund (and investment earnings thereon) can be used only to pay debt service on the issues; and

(3) The size of the payments made into the fund is independent of the size of the outstanding issues or the debt service thereon.

(g) *Provisions applicable to certain bonds sold before effective date.* Except for bonds to which paragraph (b)(1) of this section applies—

(1) Section 1.148-11A provides rules applicable to bonds sold after June 6, 1994, and before July 8, 1997; and

(2) Sections 1.148-1 through 1.148-11 as in effect on July 1, 1993 (see 26 CFR part 1 as revised April 1, 1994), and § 1.148-11A(i) (relating to elective retroactive application of certain provisions) provide rules applicable to certain issues issued before June 7, 1994.

(h) *Safe harbor for establishing fair market value for guaranteed investment contracts and investments purchased for a yield restricted defeasance escrow.* The provisions of § 1.148-5(d)(6)(iii) are applicable to bonds sold on or after March 1, 1999. Issuers may apply these provisions to bonds sold on or after December 30, 1998, and before March 1, 1999.

(i) *Special rule for investments purchased for a yield restricted defeasance escrow.* The provisions of § 1.148-5(e)(2)(iv) are applicable to bonds sold on or after March 1, 1999. Issuers may apply these provisions to bonds sold on or after December 30, 1998, and before March 1, 1999. [Reg. § 1.148-11.]

□ [*T.D.* 8418, 5-12-92 (*corrected* 9-29-92). Amended by T.D. 8476, 6-14-93 (*corrected* 8-18-93 and 7-8-99); T.D. 8538, 5-5-94 and T.D. 8718, 5-8-97.]

[Reg. § 1.148-11A]

§ 1.148-11A. **Effective dates.**—(a) through (c)(3) [Reserved]. For guidance see § 1.148-11.

(c)(4) *Retroactive application of overpayment recovery provisions.* An issuer may apply the provisions of § 1.148-3(i) to any issue that is subject to section 148(f) or to sections 103(c)(6) or 103A(i) of the Internal Revenue Code of 1954.

(d) through (h) [Reserved]. For guidance see § 1.148-11.

(i) *Transition rules for certain amendments*— (1) *In general.* Section 1.103-8(a)(5), § § 1.148-1, 1.148-2, 1.148-3, 1.148-4, 1.148-5, 1.148-6, 1.148-7, 1.148-8, 1.148-9, 1.148-10, 1.148-11, 1.149(d)-1, and 1.150-1 as in effect on June 7, 1994 (see 26 CFR part 1 as revised April 1, 1997), and § § 1.148-1A through 1.148-11A, 1.149(d)-1A, and 1.150-1A apply, in whole, but not in part—

Reg. § 1.148-11A(a)

Tax Exempt. Requirements: State/Local Bonds   **25,415**

See p. 20,601 for regulations not amended to reflect law changes

(i) To bonds sold after June 6, 1994, and before July 8, 1997;

(ii) To bonds issued before July 1, 1993, that are outstanding on June 7, 1994, if the first time the issuer applies §§1.148-1 through 1.148-11 as in effect on June 7, 1994 (see 26 CFR part 1 as revised April 1, 1997), to the bonds under §1.148-11(b) or (c) is after June 6, 1994, and before July 8, 1997;

(iii) At the option of the issuer, to bonds to which §§1.148-1 through 1.148-11, as in effect on July 1, 1993 (see 26 CFR part 1 as revised April 1, 1994), apply, if the bonds are outstanding on June 7, 1994, and the issuer applies §1.103-8(a)(5), §§1.148-1, 1.148-2, 1.148-3, 1.148-4, 1.148-5, 1.148-6, 1.148-7, 1.148-8, 1.148-9, 1.148-10, 1.148-11, 1.149(d)-1, and 1.150-1 as in effect on June 7, 1994 (see 26 CFR part 1 as revised April 1, 1997), and §§1.148-1A through 1.148-11A, 1.149(d)-1A, and 1.150-1A to the bonds before July 8, 1997.

(2) *Special rule.* For purposes of paragraph (i)(1) of this section, any reference to a particular paragraph of §§1.148-1T, 1.148-2T, 1.148-3T, 1.148-4T, 1.148-5T, 1.148-6T, 1.148-9T, 1.148-10T, 1.148-11T, 1.149(d)-1T, or 1.150-1T shall be applied as a reference to the corresponding paragraph of §§1.148-1A, 1.148-2A, 1.148-3A, 1.148-4A, 1.148-5A, 1.148-6A, 1.148-9A, 1.148-10A, 1.148-11A, 1.149(d)-1A, or 1.150-1A, respectively.

(3) *Identification of certain hedges.* For any hedge entered into after June 18, 1993, and on or before June 6, 1994, that would be a qualified hedge within the meaning of §1.148-4(h)(2), as in effect on June 7, 1994 (see 26 CFR part 1 as revised April 1, 1997), except that the hedge does not meet the requirements of §1.148-4A(h)(2)(ix) because the issuer failed to identify the hedge not later than 3 days after which the issuer and the provider entered into the contract, the requirements of §1.148-4A(h)(2)(ix) are treated as met if the contract is identified by the actual issuer on its books and records maintained for the hedged bonds not later than July 8, 1997. [Reg. §1.148-11A.]

☐ [*T.D. 8538, 5-5-94. Redesignated and amended by T.D. 8718, 5-8-97.*]

[Reg. § 1.149(b)-1]

§1.149(b)-1. **Federally guaranteed bonds.**— (a) *General rule.* Under section 149(b) and this section, nothing in section 103(a) or in any other provision of law shall be construed to provide an exemption from Federal income tax for interest on any bond issued as part of an issue that is federally guaranteed.

(b) *Exceptions.* Pursuant to section 149(b)(3)(B), section 149(b)(1) and paragraph (a) of this section do not apply to—

(1) Investments in obligations issued pursuant to §21B(d)(3) of the Federal Home Loan Bank Act, as amended by §511 of the Financial Institutions Reform, Recovery, and Enforcement Act of 1989, or any successor provision; or

(2) Any investments that are held in a refunding escrow (as defined in §1.148-1).

(c) *Effective date.* This section applies to investments made after June 30, 1993. [Reg. §1.149(b)-1.]

☐ [*T.D. 8476, 6-14-93.*]

→ *Caution: Reg. § 1.149(d)-1, below, is applicable to certain bonds sold on or after July 8, 1997.*←

[Reg. § 1.149(d)-1]

§1.149(d)-1. **Limitations on advance refundings.**—(a) *General rule.* Under section 149(d) and this section, nothing in section 103(a) or in any other provision of law shall be construed to provide an exemption from Federal income tax for interest on any bond issued as part of an issue described in paragraphs (2), (3) or (4) of section 149(d).

(b) *Advance refunding issues that employ abusive devices*—(1) *In general.* An advance refunding issue employs an abusive device and is described in section 149(d)(4) if the issue violates any of the anti-abuse rules under §1.148-10.

(2) *Failure to pay required rebate.* An advance refunding issue is described in section 149(d)(4) if the issue fails to meet the requirements of §1.148-3. This paragraph (b)(2) applies to any advance refunding issue issued after August 31, 1986.

(3) *Mixed escrows invested in tax-exempt bonds.* An advance refunding issue is described in section 149(d)(4) if—

(i) Any of the proceeds of the issue are invested in a refunding escrow in which a portion of the proceeds are invested in tax-exempt bonds and a portion of the proceeds are invested in nonpurpose investments;

(ii) The yield on the tax-exempt bonds in the refunding escrow exceeds the yield on the issue;

(iii) The yield on all the investments (including investment property and tax-exempt

Reg. § 1.149(d)-1(b)(3)

25,416   Tax Exempt. Requirements: State/Local Bonds

See p. 20,601 for regulations not amended to reflect law changes

→ *Caution: Reg. § 1.149(d)-1, below, is applicable to certain bonds sold on or after July 8, 1997.*←

bonds) in the refunding escrow exceeds the yield on the issue; and

(iv) The weighted average maturity of the tax-exempt bonds in the refunding escrow is more than 25 percent greater or less than the weighted average maturity of the nonpurpose investments in the refunding escrow, and the weighted average maturity of nonpurpose investments in the refunding escrow is greater than 60 days.

(4) *Tax-exempt conduit loans.* For purposes of applying section 149(d) to a conduit financing issue that finances any conduit loan that is a tax-exempt bond, the actual issuer of a conduit financing issue and the conduit borrower of that conduit financing issue are treated as related parties. Thus, the issue date of the conduit loan does not occur prior to the date on which the actual issuer of the conduit financing issue sells, exchanges, or otherwise disposes of that conduit loan, and the use of the proceeds of the disposition to pay debt service on the conduit financing issue causes the conduit loan to be a refunding issue. See § 1.148-10(d), *Example 4.*

(c) *Unrefunded debt service remains eligible for future advance refunding.* For purposes of section 149(d)(3)(A)(i), any principal or interest on a prior issue that has not been paid or provided for by any advance refunding issue is treated as not having been advance refunded.

(d) *Application of arbitrage regulations*—(1) *Application of multipurpose issue rules.* For purposes of sections 149(d)(2) and (3)(A)(i), (ii), and (iii), the provisions of the multipurpose issue rule in § 1.148-9(h) apply, except that the limitation in § 1.148-9(h)(5) is disregarded.

(2) *General mixed escrow rules.* For purposes of section 149(d), the provisions of § 1.148-9(c) (relating to mixed escrows) apply, except that those provisions do not apply for purposes of section 149(d)(2) and (d)(3)(A)(i) and (ii) to amounts that were not gross proceeds of the prior issue before the issue date of the refunding issue.

(3) *Temporary periods and minor portions.* Section 1.148-9(d) and (f) contains rules applicable to temporary periods and minor portions for advance refunding issues.

(4) *Definitions.* Section 1.148-1 applies for purposes of section 149(d).

(e) *Taxable refundings*—(1) *In general.* Except as provided in paragraph (e)(2) of this section, for purposes of section 149(d)(3)(A)(i), an advance refunding issue the interest on which is not excludable from gross income under section 103(a) (i.e., a taxable advance refunding issue) is not

taken into account. In addition, for this purpose, an advance refunding of a taxable issue is not taken into account unless the taxable issue is a conduit loan of a tax-exempt conduit financing issue.

(2) *Use to avoid section 149(d)(3)(A)(i).* A taxable issue is taken into account under section 149(d)(3)(A)(i) if it is issued to avoid the limitations of that section. For example, in the case of a refunding of a tax-exempt issue with a taxable advance refunding issue that is, in turn, currently refunded with a tax-exempt issue, the taxable advance refunding issue is taken into account under section 149(d)(3)(A)(i) if the two tax-exempt issues are outstanding concurrently for more than 90 days.

(f) *Redemption at first call date*—(1) *General rule.* Under sections 149(d)(3)(A)(ii) and (iii) (the *first call requirement*), bonds refunded by an advance refunding must be redeemed on their first call date if the savings test under section 149(d)(3)(B)(i) (the *savings test*) is satisfied. The savings test is satisfied if the issuer may realize present value debt service savings (determined without regard to administrative expenses) in connection with the issue of which the refunding bond is a part.

(2) *First call date. First call date* means the earliest date on which a bond may be redeemed (or, if issued before 1986, on the earliest date on which that bond may be redeemed at a redemption price not in excess of 103 percent of par). If, however, the savings test is not met with respect to the date described in the preceding sentence (i.e., there are no present value savings if the refunded bonds are retired on that date), the first call date is the first date thereafter on which the bonds can be redeemed and on which the savings test is met.

(3) *Application of savings test to multipurpose issues.* Except as otherwise provided in this paragraph (f)(3), the multipurpose issue rules in § 1.148-9(h) apply for purposes of the savings test. If any separate issue in a multipurpose issue increases the aggregate present value debt service savings on the entire multipurpose issue or reduces the present value debt service losses on that entire multipurpose issue, that separate issue satisfies the savings test.

(g) *Effective date*—(1) *In general.* Except as provided in paragraph (g)(2) of this section, this section applies to bonds issued after June 30, 1993, to which §§ 1.148-1 through 1.148-11 apply, including conduit loans that are treated as

Reg. § 1.149(d)-1(b)(4)

Tax Exempt. Requirements: State/Local Bonds **25,417**

See p. 20,601 for regulations not amended to reflect law changes

→ *Caution: Reg. § 1.149(d)-1, below, is applicable to certain bonds sold on or after July 8, 1997.*←

issued after June 30, 1993, under paragraph (b)(4) of this section. In addition, this section applies to any issue to which the election described in § 1.148-11(b)(1) is made.

(2) *Special effective date for paragraph (b)(3).* Paragraph (b)(3) of this section applies to any advance refunding issue issued after May 28, 1991.

(3) *Special effective date for paragraph (f)(3).* Paragraph (f)(3) of this section applies to

bonds sold on or after July 8, 1997, and to any issue to which the election described in § 1.148-11(b)(1) is made. See § 1.148-11A(i) for rules relating to certain bonds sold before July 8, 1997. [Reg. § 1.149(d)-1.]

☐ [*T.D. 8418, 5-12-92. Amended by T.D. 8476, 6-14-93. T.D. 8538, 5-5-94 and T.D. 8718, 5-8-97.*]

→ *Caution: Reg. § 1.149(d)-1A, below, is applicable to certain bonds sold prior to July 8, 1997.*←

[Reg. § 1.149(d)-1A]

§ 1.149(d)-1A. Limitations on advance refundings.—(a) through (f)(2) [Reserved]. For guidance see § 1.149(d)-1.

(f)(3) *Application of savings test to multipurpose issues.* Except as otherwise provided in this paragraph (f)(3), the multipurpose issue rules in § 1.148-9(h) apply for purposes of the savings test. If any separate issue in a multipurpose issue increases the aggregate present value debt service savings on the entire multipurpose issue or reduces the present value debt service losses on that entire multipurpose issue, that separate issue satisfies the savings test. [Reg. § 1.149(d)-1A.]

☐ [*T.D. 8538, 5-5-94. Redesignated and amended by T.D. 8718, 5-8-97.*]

[Reg. § 1.149(e)-1]

§ 1.149(e)-1. Information reporting requirements for tax-exempt bonds.—(a) *General rule.* Interest on a bond is included in gross income unless certain information with respect to the issue of which the bond is a part is reported to the Internal Revenue Service in accordance with the requirements of this section. This section applies to any bond if the issue of which the bond is a part is issued after December 31, 1986 (including any bond issued to refund a bond issued on or before December 31, 1986).

(b) *Requirements for private activity bonds—* (1) *In general.* If the issue of which the bond is a part is an issue of private activity bonds, the issuer must comply with the following requirements—

(i) Not later than the 15th day of the second calendar month after the close of the calendar quarter in which the issue is issued, the issuer must file with the Internal Revenue Service a completed information reporting form prescribed for this purpose;

ii) If any bond that is part of the issue is taken into account under section 146 (relating to volume cap on private activity bonds), the state certification requirement of paragraph (b)(2) of this section must be satisfied; and

iii) If any bond that is part of the issue is a qualified mortgage bond or qualified veterans' mortgage bond (within the meaning of section 143(a) or (b) or section 103A(c)(1) or (3) as in effect on the day before enactment of the Tax Reform Act of 1986), the issuer must submit the annual report containing information on the borrowers of the original proceeds of the issue as required under § 1.103A-2(k)(2)(ii) and (k)(3) through (k)(6).

(2) *State certification with respect to volume cap.*—( ) *In general.* If an issue is subject to the volume cap under section 146, a state official designated by state law (if there is no such official, then the governor or the governor's delegate) must certify that the issue meets the requirements of section 146, and a copy of this certification must be attached to the information reporting form filed with respect to the issue. In the case of any constitutional home rule city (as defined in section 146(d)(3)(C)), the preceding sentence is applied by substituting "city" for "state" and "chief executive officer" for "governor."

ii) *Certification.* The certifying official need not perform an independent investigation in order to certify that the issue meets the requirements of section 146. For example, if the certifying official receives an affidavit that was executed by an officer of the issuer who is responsible for issuing the bonds and that sets forth, in brief and summary terms, the facts necessary to determine that the issue meets the requirements of section 146 and if the certifying official has compared the information in that affidavit to other readily available information with respect to that issuer

25,418   Tax Exempt. Requirements: State/Local Bonds

See p. 20,601 for regulations not amended to reflect law changes

(e.g., previous affidavits and certifications for other private activity bonds issued by that issuer), the certifying official may rely on the affidavit.

(c) *Requirements for governmental bonds*—(1) *Issue price of $100,000 or more.* If the issue of which the bond is a part has an issue price of $100,000 or more and is not an issue of private activity bonds, then, not later than the 15th day of the second calendar month after the close of the calendar quarter in which the issue is issued, the issuer must file with the Internal Revenue Service a completed information reporting form prescribed for this purpose.

(2) *Issue price of less than $100,000*—(i) *In general.* If the issue of which the bond is a part has an issue price of less than $100,000 and is not an issue of private activity bonds, the issuer must file with the Internal Revenue Service one of the following information reporting forms within the prescribed period—

(A) *Separate return.* Not later than the 15th day of the second calendar month after the close of the calendar quarter in which the issue is issued, a completed information reporting form prescribed for this purpose with respect to that issue; or

(B) *Consolidated return.* Not later than February 15 of the calendar year following the calendar year in which the issue is issued, a completed information form prescribed for this purpose with respect to all issues to which this paragraph (c)(2) applies that were issued by the issuer during the calendar year and for which information was not reported on a separate information return pursuant to paragraph (c)(2)(i)(A) of this section.

(ii) *Bond issues issued before January 1, 1992.* Paragraph (c)(2)(i)(A) of this section does not apply if the issue of which the bond is a part is issued before January 1, 1992.

(iii) *Extended filing date for first and second calendar quarters of 1992.* If the issue of which the bond is a part is issued during the first or second calendar quarter of 1992, the prescribed period for filing an information reporting form with respect to that issue pursuant to paragraph (c)(2)(i)(A) of this section is extended until November 16, 1992.

(d) *Filing of forms and special rules*—(1) *Completed form.* For purposes of this section—

(i) *Good faith effort.* An information reporting form is treated as completed if the issuer (or a person acting on behalf of the issuer) has made a good faith effort to complete the form (taking into account the instructions to the form).

(ii) *Information.* In general, information reporting forms filed pursuant to this section must be completed on the basis of available information and reasonable expectations as of the date the issue is issued. Forms that are filed on a consolidated basis pursuant to paragraph (c)(2)(i)(B) of this section, however, may be completed on the basis of information readily available to the issuer at the close of the calendar year to which the form relates, supplemented by estimates made in good faith.

(iii) *Certain information not required.* An issuer need not report to the Internal Revenue Service any information specified in the first sentence of section 149(e)(2) that is not required to be reported to the Internal Revenue Service pursuant to the information reporting forms prescribed under that section and the instructions to those forms.

(2) *Manner of filing*—(i) *Place for filing.* The information reporting form must be filed with the Internal Revenue Service at the address specified on the form or in the instructions to the form.

(ii) *Extension of time.* The Commissioner may grant an extension of time to file any form or attachment required under this section if the Commissioner determines that the failure to file in a timely manner was not due to willful neglect. The Commissioner may make this determination with respect to an issue or to a class of issues.

(e) *Definitions.* For purposes of this section only—(1) *Private activity bond.* The term "private activity bond" has the meaning given that term in section 141(a) of the Internal Revenue Code, except that the term does not include any bond described in section 1312(c) of the Tax Reform Act of 1986 to which section 1312 or 1313 of the Tax Reform Act of 1986 applies.

(2) *Issue*—(i) *In general.* Except as otherwise provided in this paragraph (e)(2), bonds are treated as part of the same issue only if the bonds are issued—

(A) By the same issuer;

(B) On the same date; and

(C) Pursuant to a single transaction or to a series of related instructions.

(ii) *Draw-down loans, commercial paper, etc.*

(A) Bonds issued during the same calendar year may be treated as part of the same issue if the bonds are issued—

(1) Pursuant to a loan agreement under which amounts are to be advanced periodically ("draw-down loan"); or

(2) With a term not exceeding 270 days.

Reg. § 1.149(e)-1(c)(1)

(B) In addition, the bonds must be equally and ratably secured under a single indenture or loan agreement and issued pursuant to a common financing arrangement (*e.g.*, pursuant to the same official statement that is periodically updated to reflect changing factual circumstances). In the case of bonds issued pursuant to a draw-down loan that meets the requirements of the preceding sentence, bonds issued during different calendar years may be treated as part of the same issue if all the amounts to be advanced pursuant to the draw-down loan are reasonably expected to be advanced within three years of the date of issue of the first bond.

(iii) *Leases and installment sales.* Bonds other than private activity bonds may be treated as part of the same issue if—

(A) The bonds are issued pursuant to a single agreement that is in the form of a lease or installment sales agreement; and

(B) All of the property covered by that agreement is reasonably expected to be delivered within three years of the date of issue of the first bond.

(iv) *Qualified 501(c)(3) bonds.* If an issuer elects under section 141(b)(9) to treat a portion of an issue as a qualified 501(c)(3) bond, that portion is treated as a separate issue.

(3) *Date of issue*—(i) *Bond.* The date of issue of a bond is determined under § 1.150-1.

(ii) *Issue.* The date of issue of an issue of bonds is the date of issue of the first bond that is part of the issue. See paragraphs (e)(2)(ii) and (iii) of this section for rules relating to draw-down loans, commercial paper, *etc.*, and leases and installment sales.

(iii) *Bonds to which prior law applied.* Notwithstanding the provisions of this paragraph (e)(3), an issue for which an information report was required to be filed under section 103(l) or section 103A(j)(3) is treated as issued prior to January 1, 1987.

(4) *Issue price.* The term "issue price" has the same meaning given the term under § 1.148-1(b). [Reg. § 1.149(e)-1.]

☐ [*T.D.* 8425, 8-11-92.]

[Reg. § 1.149(g)-1]

§ 1.149(g)-1. Hedge bonds.—(a) *Certain definitions.* Except as otherwise provided, the definitions set forth in § 1.148-1 apply for purposes of section 149(g) and this section. In addition, the following terms have the following meanings:

Reasonable expectations means reasonable expectations (as defined in § 1.148-1), as modified to take into account the provisions of section 149(f)(2)(B).

Spendable proceeds means net sale proceeds (as defined in § 1.148-1).

(b) *Applicability of arbitrage allocation and accounting rules.* Section 1.148-6 applies for purposes of section 149(g), except that an expenditure that results in the creation of replacement proceeds (other than amounts in a bona fide debt service fund or a reasonably required reserve or replacement fund) is not an expenditure for purposes of section 149(g).

(c) *Refundings*—(1) *Investment in tax-exempt bonds.* A bond issued to refund a bond that is a tax-exempt bond by virtue of the rule in section 149(g)(3)(B) is not a tax-exempt bond unless the gross proceeds of that refunding bond (other than proceeds in a refunding escrow for the refunded bond) satisfy the requirements of section 149(g)(3)(B).

(2) *Anti-abuse rule.* A refunding bond is treated as a hedge bond unless there is a significant governmental purpose for the issuance of that bond (e.g., an advance refunding bond issued to realize debt service savings or to relieve the issuer of significantly burdensome document provisions, but not to otherwise hedge against future increases in interest rates).

(d) *Effective date.* This section applies to bonds issued after June 30, 1993 to which § § 1.148-1 through 1.148-11 apply. In addition, this section applies to any issue to which the election described in § 1.148-11(b)(1) is made. [Reg. § 1.149(g)-1.]

☐ [*T.D.* 8476, 6-14-93.]

→ *Caution: Reg. § 1.150-1, below, is applicable to certain bonds sold on or after July 8, 1997.*←

[Reg. § 1.150-1]

§ 1.150-1. Definitions—(a) *Scope and effective date*—(1) *In general.* Except as otherwise provided, the definitions in this section apply for all purposes of sections 103 and 141 through 150.

(2) *Effective date*—(i) *In general.* Except as otherwise provided in this paragraph (a)(2), this section applies to issues issued after June 30, 1993

to which § § 1.148-1 through 1.148-11 apply. In addition, this section (other than paragraph (c)(3) of this section) applies to any issue to which the election described in § 1.148-11(b)(1) is made.

(i) *Special effective date for paragraphs (c)(1), (c)(4)(iii), and (c)(6).* Paragraphs (c)(1), (c)(4)(iii), and (c)(6) of this section apply to bonds sold on or after July 8, 1997, and to any issue to

25,420   Tax Exempt. Requirements: State/Local Bonds

See p. 20,601 for regulations not amended to reflect law changes

→ *Caution: Reg. § 1.150-1, below, is applicable to certain bonds sold on or after July 8, 1997.←*

which the election described in § 1.148-11(b)(1) is made. See § 1.148-11A(i) for rules relating to certain bonds sold before July 8, 1997.

(3) *Exception to general effective date.* See § 1.141-15 for the effective date of the definition of bond documents contained in paragraph (b) of this section.

(b) *Certain general definitions.* The following definitions apply:

Bond means any obligation of a State or political subdivision thereof under section 103(c)(1).

Bond documents means the bond indenture or resolution, transcript of proceedings, and any related documents.

Capital expenditure means any cost of a type that is properly chargeable to capital account (or would be so chargeable with a proper election or with the application of the definition of placed in service under § 1.150-2(c)) under general Federal income tax principles. For example, costs incurred to acquire, construct, or improve land, buildings, and equipment generally are capital expenditures. Whether an expenditure is a capital expenditure is determined at the time the expenditure is paid with respect to the property. Future changes in law do not affect whether an expenditure is a capital expenditure.

Conduit borrower means the obligor on a purpose investment (as defined in § 1.148-1). For example, if an issuer invests proceeds in a purpose investment in the form of a loan, lease, installment sale obligation, or similar obligation to another entity and the obligor uses the proceeds to carry out the governmental purpose of the issue, the obligor is a conduit borrower.

Conduit financing issue means an issue the proceeds of which are used or are reasonably expected to be used to finance at least one purpose investment representing at least one conduit loan to one conduit borrower.

Conduit loan means a purpose investment (as defined in § 1.148-1).

Governmental bond means any bond of an issue of tax-exempt bonds in which none of the bonds are private activity bonds.

Issuance costs means costs to the extent incurred in connection with, and allocable to, the issuance of an issue within the meaning of section 147(g). For example, issuance costs include the following costs but only to the extent incurred in connection with, and allocable to, the borrowing: underwriters' spread; counsel fees; financial advisory fees; rating agency fees; trustee fees; paying agent fees; bond registrar, certification, and authentication fees; accounting fees; printing costs for bonds and offering documents; public approval process costs; engineering and feasibility study costs; guarantee fees, other than for qualified guarantees (as defined in § 1.148-4(f)); and similar costs.

Issue date means, in reference to an issue, the first date on which the issuer receives the purchase price in exchange for delivery of the evidence of indebtedness representing any bond included in the issue. Issue date means, in reference to a bond, the date on which the issuer receives the purchase price in exchange for that bond. In no event is the issue date earlier than the first day on which interest begins to accrue on the bond or bonds for Federal income tax purposes.

Obligation means any valid evidence of indebtedness under general Federal income tax principles.

Pooled financing issue means an issue the proceeds of which are to be used to finance purpose investments representing conduit loans to two or more conduit borrowers, unless those conduit loans are to be used to finance a single capital project.

Private activity bond means a private activity bond (as defined in section 141).

Qualified mortgage loan means a mortgage loan with respect to an owner-occupied residence acquired with the proceeds of an obligation described in section 143(a)(1) or 143(b) (or applicable prior law).

Qualified student loan means a student loan acquired with the proceeds of an obligation described in section 144(b)(1).

Related party means, in reference to a governmental unit or a 501(c)(3) organization, any member of the same controlled group, and, in reference to any person that is not a governmental unit or 501(c)(3) organization, a related person (as defined in section 144(a)(3)).

Taxable bond means any obligation the interest on which is not excludable from gross income under section 103.

Tax-exempt bond means any bond the interest on which is excludable from gross income under section 103(a). For purposes of section 148, tax-exempt bond includes:

(1) An interest in a regulated investment company to the extent that at least 95 percent of the income to the holder of the interest is interest that

Reg. § 1.150-1(a)(3)

→ *Caution: Reg. § 1.150-1, below, is applicable to certain bonds sold on or after July 8, 1997.*←

is excludable from gross income under section 103; and

(2) A certificate of indebtedness issued by the United States Treasury pursuant to the Demand Deposit State and Local Government Series program described in 31 CFR part 344.

Working capital expenditure means any cost that is not a capital expenditure. Generally, current operating expenses are working capital expenditures.

(c) *Definition of issue*—(1) *In general.* Except as otherwise provided in this paragraph (c), the term *issue* means two or more bonds that meet all of the following requirements:

(i) *Sold at substantially the same time.* The bonds are sold at substantially the same time. Bonds are treated as sold at substantially the same time if they are sold less than 15 days apart.

(ii) *Sold pursuant to the same plan of financing.* The bonds are sold pursuant to the same plan of financing. Factors material to the plan of financing include the purposes for the bonds and the structure of the financing. For example, generally—

(A) Bonds to finance a single facility or related facilities are part of the same plan of financing;

(B) Short-term bonds to finance working capital expenditures and long-term bonds to finance capital projects are not part of the same plan of financing; and

(C) Certificates of participation in a lease and general obligation bonds secured by tax revenues are not part of the same plan of financing.

(iii) *Payable from same source of funds.* The bonds are reasonably expected to be paid from substantially the same source of funds, determined without regard to guarantees from parties unrelated to the obligor.

(2) *Exception for taxable bonds.* Taxable bonds and tax-exempt bonds are not part of the same issue under this paragraph (c). The issuance of tax-exempt bonds in a transaction (or series of related transactions) that includes taxable bonds, however, may constitute an abusive arbitrage device under § 1.148-10(a) or a device to avoid other limitations in sections 103 and 141 through 150 (for example, structures involving *windows* or unreasonable allocations of bonds).

(3) *Exception for certain bonds financing separate purposes*—(i) *In general.* Bonds may be treated as part of separate issues if the requirements of this paragraph (c)(3) are satisfied. Each of these separate issues must finance a separate purpose (e.g., refunding a separate prior issue, financing a separate purpose investment, financing integrated or functionally related capital projects, and financing any clearly discrete governmental purpose). Each of these separate issues independently must be a tax-exempt bond (e.g., a governmental bond or a qualified mortgage bond). The aggregate proceeds, investments, and bonds in such a transaction must be allocated between each of the separate issues using a reasonable, consistently applied allocation method. If any separate issue consists of refunding bonds, the allocation rules in § 1.148-9(h) must be satisfied. An allocation is not reasonable if it achieves more favorable results under sections 103 and 141 to 150 than could be achieved with actual separate issues. All allocations under this paragraph (c)(3) must be made in writing on or before the issue date.

(ii) *Exceptions.* This paragraph (c)(3) does not apply for purposes of sections 141(b)(5), 141(c)(2), 141(d)(1), 144(a), 148, 149(d), and 149(g).

(4) *Special rules for certain financings*—(i) *Draw-down loans.* Bonds issued pursuant to a draw-down loan are treated as part of a single issue. The issue date of that issue is the first date on which the aggregate draws under the loan exceed the lesser of $50,000 or 5 percent of the issue price.

(ii) *Commercial paper*—(A) *In general.* Short-term bonds having a maturity of 270 days or less (*commercial paper*) issued pursuant to the same commercial paper program may be treated as part of a single issue, the issue date of which is the first date the aggregate amount of commercial paper issued under the program exceeds the lesser of $50,000 or 5 percent of the aggregate issue price of the commercial paper in the program. A commercial paper program is a program to issue commercial paper to finance or refinance the same governmental purpose pursuant to a single master legal document. Commercial paper is not part of the same commercial paper program unless issued during an 18-month period, beginning on the deemed issue date. In addition, commercial paper issued after the end of this 18-month period may be treated as part of the program to the extent issued to refund commercial paper that is part of the program, but only to the extent that—

(1) There is no increase in the principal amount outstanding; and

Reg. § 1.150-1(c)(4)

→ *Caution: Reg. § 1.150-1, below, is applicable to certain bonds sold on or after July 8, 1997.*←

(2) The program does not have a term in excess of—

(i) 30 years; or

(ii) The period reasonably necessary for the governmental purposes of the program.

(B) *Safe harbor.* The requirement of paragraph (c)(4)(ii)(A)(2) of this section is treated as satisfied if the weighted average maturity of the issue does not exceed 120 percent of the weighted average expected economic life of the property financed by the issue.

(iii) *Certain general obligation bonds.* Except as otherwise provided in paragraph (c)(2) of this section, bonds that are secured by a pledge of the issuer's full faith and credit (or a substantially similar pledge) and sold and issued on the same dates pursuant to a single offering document may be treated as part of the same issue if the issuer so elects on or before the issue date.

(5) *Anti-abuse rule.* In order to prevent the avoidance of sections 103 and 141 through 150 and the general purposes thereof, the Commissioner may treat bonds as part of the same issue or as part of separate issues to clearly reflect the economic substance of a transaction.

(6) *Sale date.* The sale date of a bond is the first day on which there is a binding contract in writing for the sale or exchange of the bond.

(d) *Definition of refunding issue and related definitions*—(1) *General definition of refunding issue. Refunding issue* means an issue of obligations the proceeds of which are used to pay principal, interest, or redemption price on another issue (a *prior issue,* as more particularly defined in paragraph (d)(5) of this section), including the issuance costs, accrued interest, capitalized interest on the refunding issue, a reserve or replacement fund, or similar costs, if any, properly allocable to that refunding issue.

(2) *Exceptions and special rules.* For purposes of paragraph (d)(1) of this section, the following exceptions and special rules apply—

(i) *Payment of certain interest.* An issue is not a refunding issue if the only principal and interest that is paid with proceeds of the issue (determined without regard to the multipurpose issue rules of § 1.148-9(h)) is interest on another issue that—

(A) Accrues on the other issue during a one-year period including the issue date of the issue that finances the interest;

(B) Is a capital expenditure; or

(C) Is a working capital expenditure to which the de minimis rule of § 1.148-6(d)(3)(ii)(A) applies.

(ii) *Certain issues with different obligors*— (A) *In general.* An issue is not a refunding issue to the extent that the obligor (as defined in paragraph (d)(2)(ii)(B) of this section) of one issue is neither the obligor of the other issue nor a related party with respect to the obligor of the other issue.

(B) *Definition of obligor.* The *obligor* of an issue means the actual issuer of the issue, except that the obligor of the portion of an issue properly allocable to an investment in a purpose investment means the conduit borrower under that purpose investment. The obligor of an issue used to finance qualified mortgage loans, qualified student loans, or similar program investments (as defined in § 1.148-1) does not include the ultimate recipient of the loan (e.g., the homeowner, the student).

(iii) *Certain special rules for purpose investments.* For purposes of this paragraph (d), the following special rules apply:

(A) *Refunding of a conduit financing issue by a conduit loan refunding issue.* Except as provided in paragraph (d)(2)(iii)(B) of this section, the use of the proceeds of an issue that is used to refund an obligation that is a purpose investment (a *conduit refunding issue*) by the actual issuer of the conduit financing issue determines whether the conduit refunding issue is a refunding of the conduit financing issue (in addition to a refunding of the obligation that is the purpose investment).

(B) *Recycling of certain payments under purpose investments.* A conduit refunding issue is not a refunding of a conduit financing issue to the extent that the actual issuer of the conduit financing issue reasonably expects as of the date of receipt of the proceeds of the conduit refunding issue to use those amounts within 6 months (or, if greater, during the applicable temporary period for those amounts under section 148(c) or under applicable prior law) to acquire a new purpose investment. Any new purpose investment is treated as made from the proceeds of the conduit financing issue.

(C) *Application to tax-exempt loans.* For purposes of this paragraph (d), obligations that would be purpose investments (absent section 148(b)(3)(A)) are treated as purpose investments.

(iv) *Substance of transaction controls.* In the absence of other applicable controlling rules

Reg. § 1.150-1(c)(5)

Tax Exempt. Requirements: State/Local Bonds 25,423

See p. 20,601 for regulations not amended to reflect law changes

→ *Caution: Reg. § 1.150-1, below, is applicable to certain bonds sold on or after July 8, 1997.*←

under this paragraph (d), the determination of whether an issue is a refunding issue is based on the substance of the transaction in light of all the facts and circumstances.

(v) *Certain integrated transactions in connection with asset acquisition not treated as refunding issues.* If, within six months before or after a person assumes (including taking subject to) obligations of an unrelated party in connection with an asset acquisition (other than a transaction to which section 381(a) applies if the person assuming the obligation is the acquiring corporation within the meaning of section 381(a)), the assumed issue is refinanced, the refinancing issue is not treated as a refunding issue.

(3) *Current refunding issue.* Current refunding issue means:

(i) Except as provided in paragraph (d)(3)(ii) of this section, a refunding issue that is issued not more than 90 days before the last expenditure of any proceeds of the refunding issue for the payment of principal or interest on the prior issue; and

(ii) In the case of a refunding issue issued before 1986—

(A) A refunding issue that is issued not more than 180 days before the last expenditure of any proceeds of the refunding issue for the payment of principal or interest on the prior issue; or

(B) A refunding issue if the prior issue had a term of less than 3 years and was sold in anticipation of permanent financing, but only if the aggregate term of all prior issues sold in anticipation of permanent financing was less than 3 years.

(4) *Advance refunding issue.* Advance refunding issue means a refunding issue that is not a current refunding issue.

(5) *Prior issue.* Prior issue means an issue of obligations all or a portion of the principal, interest, or call premium on which is paid or provided for with proceeds of a refunding issue. A prior issue may be issued before, at the same time as, or

after a refunding issue. If the refunded and unrefunded portions of a prior issue are treated as separate issues under § 1.148-9(i), for the purposes for which that section applies, except to the extent that the context clearly requires otherwise, references to a prior issue refer only to the refunded portion of that prior issue.

(e) *Controlled group* means a group of entities controlled directly or indirectly by the same entity or group of entities within the meaning of this paragraph (e).

(1) *Direct control.* The determination of direct control is made on the basis of all the relevant facts and circumstances. One entity or group of entities (the *controlling entity*) generally controls another entity or group of entities (the *controlled entity*) for purposes of this paragraph if the controlling entity possesses either of the following rights or powers and the rights or powers are discretionary and non-ministerial—

(i) The right or power both to approve and to remove without cause a controlling portion of the governing body of the controlled entity; or

(ii) The right or power to require the use of funds or assets of the controlled entity for any purpose of the controlling entity.

(2) *Indirect control.* If a controlling entity controls a controlled entity under the test in paragraph (e)(1) of this section, then the controlling entity also controls all entities controlled, directly or indirectly, by the controlled entity or entities.

(3) *Exception for general purpose governmental entities.* An entity is not a controlled entity under this paragraph (e) if the entity possesses substantial taxing, eminent domain, and police powers. For example, a city possessing substantial amounts of each of these sovereign powers is not a controlled entity of the state. [Reg. § 1.150-1.]

□ [*T.D. 8394, 1-27-92. Amended by T.D. 8418, 5-12-92; T.D. 8476, 6-14-93; T.D. 8538, 5-5-94; T.D. 8712, 1-10-97 and T.D. 8718, 5-8-97.*]

→ *Caution: Reg. § 1.150-1A, below, is applicable to certain bonds sold prior to July 8, 1997.*←

[Reg. § 1.150-1A]

§ 1.150-1A. **Definitions.**—(a) through (b) [Reserved]. For guidance see § 1.150-1.

(c) *Definition of issue*—(1) *In general.* Except as otherwise provided, the provisions of this paragraph (c) apply for all purposes of sections 103 and 141 through 150. Except as otherwise pro-

vided in this paragraph (c), two or more bonds are treated as part of the same issue if all of the following factors are present:

(i) *Sold at substantially the same time.* The bonds are sold at substantially the same time. Bonds are treated as sold at substantially the same time if they are sold less than 15 days apart.

25,424   Tax Exempt. Requirements: State/Local Bonds

See p. 20,601 for regulations not amended to reflect law changes

→ *Caution: Reg. § 1.150-1A, below, is applicable to certain bonds sold prior to July 8, 1997.*←

For this purpose only, a variable yield bond is treated as sold on its issue date.

(ii) *Sold pursuant to the same plan of financing.* The bonds are sold pursuant to the same plan of financing. Factors material to the plan of financing include the purposes for the bonds and the structure of the financing. For example, generally—

(A) Bonds to finance a single facility or related facilities are part of the same plan of financing;

(B) Short-term bonds to finance working capital expenditures and long-term bonds to finance capital projects are not part of the same plan of financing; and

(C) Certificates of participation in a lease and general obligation bonds secured by tax revenues are not part of the same plan of financing.

(iii) *Payable from same source of funds.* The bonds are reasonably expected to be paid from substantially the same source of funds, determined without regard to guarantees from parties unrelated to the obligor.

(2) through (4)(ii) [Reserved]. For guidance see § 1.150-1(c)(3) through (c)(4)(ii).

(c)(4)(iii) *Certain general obligation bonds.* Bonds are part of the same issue if secured by a pledge of the issuer's full faith and credit (or a substantially similar pledge) and sold and issued on the same dates pursuant to a single offering document.

(5) [Reserved]. For guidance see § 1.150-1(c)(5).

(6) *Sale date.* The sale date of a bond is the first day on which there is a binding contract in writing for the sale or exchange of the bond. [Reg. § 1.150-1A.]

□ [*T.D. 8538, 5-5-94. Redesignated and amended by T.D. 8718, 5-8-97.*]

[Reg. § 1.150-2]

§ 1.150-2. Proceeds of bonds used for reimbursement.—(a) *Table of contents.* This table of contents contains a listing of the headings contained in § 1.150-2.

(a) Table of contents.

(b) Scope.

(c) Definitions.

(d) General operating rules for reimbursement expenditures.

(1) Official intent.

(2) Reimbursement period.

(3) Nature of expenditure.

(e) Official intent rules.

(1) Form of official intent.

(2) Project description in official intent.

(3) Reasonableness of official intent.

(f) Exceptions to general operating rules.

(1) De minimis exception.

(2) Preliminary expenditures exception.

(g) Special rules on refundings.

(1) In general—once financed, not reimbursed.

(2) Certain proceeds of prior issue used for reimbursement treated as unspent.

(h) Anti-abuse rules.

(1) General rule.

(2) One-year step transaction rule.

(i) Authority of the Commissioner to prescribe rules.

(j) Effective date.

(1) In general.

(2) Transitional rules.

(b) *Scope.* This section applies to reimbursement bonds (as defined in paragraph (c) of this section) for all purposes of sections 103 and 141 to 150.

(c) *Definitions.* The following definitions apply:

Issuer means—

(1) For any private activity bond (excluding a qualified 501(c)(3) bond, qualified student loan bond, qualified mortgage bond, or qualified veterans' mortgage bond), the entity that actually issues the reimbursement bond; and

(2) For any bond not described in paragraph (1) of this definition, either the entity that actually issues the reimbursement bond or, to the extent that the reimbursement bond proceeds are to be loaned to a conduit borrower, that conduit borrower.

Official intent means an issuer's declaration of intent to reimburse an original expenditure with proceeds of an obligation.

Original expenditure means an expenditure for a governmental purpose that is originally paid from a source other than a reimbursement bond.

Placed in service means, with respect to a facility, the date on which, based on all the facts and circumstances—

Reg. § 1.150-2(a)

(1) The facility has reached a degree of completion which would permit its operation at substantially its design level; and

(2) The facility is, in fact, in operation at such level.

Reimbursement allocation means an allocation in writing that evidences an issuer's use of proceeds of a reimbursement bond to reimburse an original expenditure. An allocation made within 30 days after the issue date of a reimbursement bond may be treated as made on the issue date.

Reimbursement bond means the portion of an issue allocated to reimburse an original expenditure that was paid before the issue date.

(d) *General operating rules for reimbursement expenditures.* Except as otherwise provided, a reimbursement allocation is treated as an expenditure of proceeds of a reimbursement bond for the governmental purpose of the original expenditure on the date of the reimbursement allocation only if:

(1) *Official intent.* Not later than 60 days after payment of the original expenditure, the issuer adopts an official intent for the original expenditure that satisfies paragraph (e) of this section.

(2) *Reimbursement period*—(i) *In general.* The reimbursement allocation is made not later than 18 months after the later of—

(A) The date the original expenditure is paid; or

(B) The date the project is placed in service or abandoned, but in no event more than 3 years after the original expenditure is paid.

(ii) *Special rule for small issuers.* In applying paragraph (d)(2)(i) of this section to an issue that satisfies section 148(f)(4)(D)(i)(I) through (IV), the "18 month" limitation is changed to "3 years" and the "3-year" maximum reimbursement period is disregarded.

(iii) *Special rule for long-term construction projects.* In applying paragraph (d)(2)(i) to a construction project for which both the issuer and a licensed architect or engineer certify that at least 5 years is necessary to complete construction of the project, the maximum reimbursement period is changed from "3 years" to "5 years."

(3) *Nature of expenditure.* The original expenditure is a capital expenditure, a cost of issuance for a bond, an expenditure described in § 1.148-6(d)(3)(ii)(B) (relating to certain extraordinary working capital items), a grant (as defined in § 1.148-6(d)(4)), a qualified student loan, a qualified mortgage loan, or a qualified veterans' mortgage loan.

(e) *Official intent rules.* An official intent satisfies this paragraph (e) if:

(1) *Form of official intent.* The official intent is made in any reasonable form, including issuer resolution, action by an appropriate representative of the issuer (e.g., a person authorized or designated to declare official intent on behalf of the issuer), or specific legislative authorization for the issuance of obligations for a particular project.

(2) *Project description in official intent*—(i) *In general.* The official intent generally describes the project for which the original expenditure is paid and states the maximum principal amount of obligations expected to be issued for the project. A project includes any property, project, or program (e.g., *highway capital improvement program, hospital equipment acquisition, or school building renovation*).

(ii) *Fund accounting.* A project description is sufficient if it identifies, by name and functional purpose, the fund or account from which the original expenditure is paid (e.g., *parks and recreation fund—recreational facility capital improvement program*).

(iii) *Reasonable deviations in project description.* Deviations between a project described in an official intent and the actual project financed with reimbursement bonds do not invalidate the official intent to the extent that the actual project is reasonably related in function to the described project. For example, *hospital equipment* is a reasonable deviation from *hospital building improvements.* In contrast, a *city office building rehabilitation* is not a reasonable deviation from *highway improvements.*

(3) *Reasonableness of official intent.* On the date of the declaration, the issuer must have a reasonable expectation (as defined in § 1.148-1(b)) that it will reimburse the original expenditure with proceeds of an obligation. Official intents declared as a matter of course or in amounts substantially in excess of the amounts expected to be necessary for the project (e.g., *blanket declarations*) are not reasonable. Similarly, a pattern of failure to reimburse actual original expenditures covered by official intents (other than in extraordinary circumstances) is evidence of unreasonableness. An official intent declared pursuant to a specific legislative authorization is rebuttably presumed to satisfy this paragraph (e)(3).

(f) *Exceptions to general operating rules*—(1) *De minimis exception.* Paragraphs (d)(1) and (d)(2) of this section do not apply to costs of issuance of any bond or to an amount not in excess of the lesser of $100,000 or 5 percent of the proceeds of the issue.

Reg. § 1.150-2(f)(1)

25,426   **Tax Exempt. Requirements: State/Local Bonds**

See p. 20,601 for regulations not amended to reflect law changes

(2) *Preliminary expenditures exception.* Paragraphs (d)(1) and (d)(2) of this section do not apply to any preliminary expenditures, up to an amount not in excess of 20 percent of the aggregate issue price of the issue or issues that finance or are reasonably expected by the issuer to finance the project for which the preliminary expenditures were incurred. Preliminary expenditures include architectural, engineering, surveying, soil testing, reimbursement bond issuance, and similar costs that are incurred prior to commencement of acquisition, construction, or rehabilitation of a project, other than land acquisition, site preparation, and similar costs incident to commencement of construction.

(g) *Special rules on refundings*—(1) *In general—once financed, not reimbursed.* Except as provided in paragraph (g)(2) of this section, paragraph (d) of this section does not apply to an allocation to pay principal or interest on an obligation or to reimburse an original expenditure paid by another obligation. Instead, such an allocation is analyzed under rules on refunding issues. See § 1.148-9.

(2) *Certain proceeds of prior issue used for reimbursement treated as unspent.* In the case of a refunding issue (or series of refunding issues), proceeds of a prior issue purportedly used to reimburse original expenditures are treated as unspent proceeds of the prior issue unless the purported reimbursement was a valid expenditure under applicable law on reimbursement expenditures on the issue date of the prior issue.

(h) *Anti-abuse rules*—(1) *General rule.* A reimbursement allocation is not an expenditure of proceeds of an issue under this section if the allocation employs an abusive arbitrage device under § 1.148-10 to avoid the arbitrage restrictions or to avoid the restrictions under sections 142 through 147.

(2) *One-year step transaction rule*—(i) *Creation of replacement proceeds.* A purported reimbursement allocation is invalid and thus is not an expenditure of proceeds of an issue if, within 1 year after the allocation, funds corresponding to the proceeds of a reimbursement bond for which a reimbursement allocation was made are used in a manner that results in the creation of replacement proceeds (as defined in § 1.148-1) of that issue or another issue. The preceding sentence does not apply to amounts deposited in a bona fide debt service fund (as defined in § 1.148-1).

(ii) *Example.* The provisions of paragraph (h)(2)(i) are illustrated by the following example.

Example. On January 1, 1994, County A issues an issue of 7 percent tax-exempt bonds (the

1994 issue) and makes a purported reimbursement allocation to reimburse an original expenditure for specified capital improvements. *A* immediately deposits funds corresponding to the proceeds subject to the reimbursement allocation in an escrow fund to provide for payment of principal and interest on its outstanding 1991 issue of 9 percent tax-exempt bonds (the *prior issue*). The use of amounts corresponding to the proceeds of the reimbursement bonds to create a sinking fund for another issue within 1 year after the purported reimbursement allocation invalidates the reimbursement allocation. The proceeds retain their character as unspent proceeds of the 7 percent issue upon deposit in the escrow fund. Accordingly, the proceeds are subject to the 7 percent yield restriction of the 1994 issue instead of the 9 percent yield restriction of the prior issue.

(i) *Authority of the Commissioner to prescribe rules.* The Commissioner may by revenue ruling or revenue procedure (see § 601.601(d)(2)(ii)(b) of this chapter) prescribe rules for the expenditure of proceeds of reimbursement bonds in circumstances that do not otherwise satisfy this section.

(j) *Effective date*—(1) *In general.* The provisions of this section apply to all allocations of proceeds of reimbursement bonds issued after June 30, 1993.

(2) *Transitional rules*—(i) *Official intent.* An official intent is treated as satisfying the official intent requirement of paragraph (d)(1) of this section if it—

(A) Satisfied the applicable provisions of § 1.103-8(a)(5) as in effect prior to July 1, 1993, (as contained in 26 CFR part 1 revised as of April 1, 1993) and was made prior to that date, or

(B) Satisfied the applicable provisions of § 1.103-18 as in effect between January 27, 1992, and June 30, 1993, (as contained in 26 CFR part 1 revised as of April 1, 1993) and was made during that period.

(ii) *Certain expenditures of private activity bonds.* For any expenditure that was originally paid prior to August 15, 1993, and that would have qualified for expenditure by reimbursement from the proceeds of a private activity bond under T.D. 7199, section 1.103-8(a)(5), 1972-2 C.B. 45 (See § 601.601(d)(2)(i)(b) of this chapter.), the requirements of that section may be applied in lieu of this section. [Reg. § 1.150-2.]

☐ [*T.D.* 8476, 6-14-93.]

[Reg. § 1.150-4]

§ 1.150-4. **Change in use of facilities financed with tax-exempt private activity bonds.**—(a) *Scope.* This section applies for purposes of the rules for change of use of facilities financed with private activity bonds under sections 150(b)(3) (relating to qualified 501(c)(3) bonds), 150(b)(4) (relating to certain exempt facility bonds and small issue bonds), 150(b)(5) (relating to facilities required to be owned by governmental units or 501(c)(3) organizations), and 150(c).

(b) *Effect of remedial actions*—(1) *In general.* Except as provided in this section, the change of use provisions of sections 150(b)(3) through (5), and 150(c) apply even if the issuer takes a remedial action described in §§ 1.142-2, 1.144-2, or 1.145-2.

(2) *Exceptions*—(i) *Redemption.* If nonqualified bonds are redeemed within 90 days of a deliberate action under § 1.145-2(a) or within 90 days of the date on which a failure to properly use proceeds occurs under § 1.142-2 or § 1.144-2, sections 150(b)(3) through (5) do not apply during the period between that date and the date on which the nonqualified bonds are redeemed.

(ii) *Alternative qualifying use of facility.* If a bond-financed facility is used for an alternative qualifying use under §§ 1.145-2 and 1.141-12(f), sections 150(b)(3) and (5) do not apply because of the alternative use.

(iii) *Alternative use of disposition proceeds.* If disposition proceeds are used for a qualifying purpose under §§ 1.145-2 and 1.141-12(e), 1.142-2(c)(4), or 1.144-2, sections 150(b)(3) through (5) do not apply because of the deliberate action that gave rise to the disposition proceeds after the date on which all of the disposition proceeds have been expended on the qualifying purpose. If all of the disposition proceeds are so expended within 90 days of the date of the deliberate action, however, sections 150(b)(3) through (5) do not apply because of the deliberate action.

(c) *Allocation rules*—(1) *In general.* If a change in use of a portion of the property financed with an issue of qualified private activity bonds causes section 150(b)(3), (b)(4), or (b)(5) to apply to an issue, the bonds of the issue allocable to that portion under section 150(c)(3) are the same as the nonqualified bonds determined for purposes of §§ 1.142-1, 1.144-1, and 1.145-1, except that bonds allocable to all common areas are also allocated to that portion.

(2) *Special rule when remedial action is taken.* If an issuer takes a remedial action with respect to an issue of private activity bonds under §§ 1.142-2, 1.144-2, or 1.145-2, the bonds of the issue allocable to a portion of property are the same as the nonqualified bonds determined for purposes of those sections.

(d) *Effective dates.* For effective dates of this section, see § 1.141-16. [Reg. § 1.150-4.]

□ [*T.D.* 8712, 1-10-97.]

[Reg. § 1.150-5]

§ 1.150-5. **Filing notices and elections.**—(a) *In general.* Notices and elections under the following sections must be filed with the Internal Revenue Service, 1111 Constitution Avenue, NW, Attention: T:GE:TEB:O, Washington, DC 20224 or such other place designated by publication of a notice in the Internal Revenue Bulletin—

(1) Section 1.141-12(d)(3);

(2) Section 1.142(f)(4)-1; and

(3) Section 1.142-2(c)(2).

(b) *Effective dates.* This section applies to notices and elections filed on or after January 19, 2001. [Reg. § 1.150-5.]

□ [*T.D.* 8941, 1-17-2001.]

Deductions for Personal Exemptions

[Reg. § 1.151-1]

§ 1.151-1. **Deductions for personal exemptions.**—(a) *In general.* (1) In computing taxable income, an individual is allowed a deduction for the exemptions specified in section 151. Such exemptions are: (i) The exemptions for an individual taxpayer and spouse (the so-called personal exemptions); (ii) the additional exemptions for a taxpayer attaining the age of 65 years and spouse attaining the age of 65 years (the so-called old-age exemptions); (iii) the additional exemptions for a blind taxpayer and a blind spouse; and (iv) the exemptions for dependents of the taxpayer.

(2) A nonresident alien individual who is a bona fide resident of Puerto Rico during the entire taxable year and subject to tax under section 1 or 1201(b) is allowed as deductions the exemptions specified in section 151, even though as to the United States such individual is a nonresident alien. See section 876 and the regulations thereunder, relating to alien residents of Puerto Rico.

(b) *Exemptions for individual taxpayer and spouse (so-called personal exemptions).* Section 151(b) allows an exemption for the taxpayer and an additional exemption for the spouse of the taxpayer if a joint return is not made by the taxpayer and his spouse, and if the spouse, for the calendar year in which the taxable year of the taxpayer begins, has no gross income and is not the dependent of another taxpayer. Thus, a husband is not entitled to an exemption for his wife on his separate return for the taxable year beginning in a calendar year during which she has any gross income (though insufficient to require her to file a return). Since, in the case of a joint return, there are two taxpayers (although under section

6013 there is only one income for the two taxpayers on such return, *i.e.,* their aggregate income), two exemptions are allowed on such return, one for each taxpayer spouse. If in any case a joint return is made by the taxpayer and his spouse, no other person is allowed an exemption for such spouse even though such other person would have been entitled to claim an exemption for such spouse as a dependent if such joint return had not been made.

(c) *Exemptions for taxpayer attaining age of 65 and spouse attaining the age of 65 (so-called old-age exemptions).* (1) Section 151(c) provides an additional exemption for the taxpayer if he has attained the age of 65 before the close of his taxable year. An additional exemption is also allowed to the taxpayer for his spouse if a joint return is not made by the taxpayer and his spouse and if the spouse has attained the age of 65 before the close of the taxable year of the taxpayer and, for the calendar year in which the taxable year of the taxpayer begins, the spouse has no gross income and is not the dependent of another taxpayer. If a husband and wife make a joint return, an old-age exemption will be allowed as to each taxpayer spouse who has attained the age of 65 before the close of the taxable year for which the joint return is made. The exemptions under section 151(c) are in addition to the exemptions for the taxpayer and spouse under section 151(b).

(2) In determining the age of an individual for the purposes of the exemption for old age, the last day of the taxable year of the taxpayer is the controlling date. Thus, in the event of a separate return by a husband, no additional exemption for old age may be claimed for his spouse unless such spouse has attained the age of 65 on or before the close of the taxable year of the husband. In no event shall the additional exemption for old age be allowed with respect to a spouse who dies before attaining the age of 65 even though such spouse would have attained the age of 65 before the close of the taxable year of the taxpayer. For the purposes of the old-age exemption, an individual attains the age of 65 on the first moment of the day preceding his sixty-fifth birthday. Accordingly, an individual whose sixty-fifth birthday falls on January 1 in a given year attains the age of 65 on the last day of the calendar year immediately preceding.

(d) *Exemptions for the blind.* (1) Section 151(d) provides an additional exemption for the taxpayer if he is blind at the close of his taxable year. An additional exemption is also allowed to the taxpayer for his spouse if the spouse is blind and, for the calendar year in which the taxable year of the taxpayer begins, has no gross income and is not

the dependent of another taxpayer. The determination of whether the spouse is blind shall be made as of the close of the taxable year of the taxpayer, unless the spouse dies during such taxable year, in which case such determination shall be made as of the time of such death.

(2) The exemptions for the blind are in addition to the exemptions for the taxpayer and spouse under section 151(b) and are also in addition to the exemptions under section 151(c) for taxpayers and spouses attaining the age of 65 years. Thus, a single individual who has attained the age of 65 before the close of his taxable year and who is blind at the close of his taxable year is entitled, in addition to the so-called personal exemption, to two further exemptions, one by reason of his age and the other by reason of his blindness. If a husband and wife make a joint return, an exemption for the blind will be allowed as to each taxpayer spouse who is blind at the close of the taxable year for which the joint return is made.

(3) A taxpayer claiming an exemption allowed by section 151(d) for a blind taxpayer and a blind spouse shall, if the individual for whom the exemption is claimed is not totally blind as of the last day of the taxable year of the taxpayer (or in the case of a spouse who dies during such taxable year as of the time of such death), attach to his return a certificate from a physician skilled in the diseases of the eye or a registered optometrist stating that as of the applicable status determination date in the opinion of such physician or optometrist (i) the central visual acuity of the individual for whom the exemption is claimed did not exceed 20/200 in the better eye with correcting lenses or (ii) such individual's visual acuity was accompanied by a limitation in the fields of vision such that the widest diameter of the visual field subtends an angle no greater than 20 degrees. If such individual is totally blind as of the status determination date there shall be attached to the return a statement by the person or persons making the return setting forth such fact.

(4) Notwithstanding subparagraph (3) of this paragraph, this subparagraph may be applied where the individual for whom an exemption under section 151(d) is claimed is not totally blind, and in the certified opinion of an examining physician skilled in the diseases of the eye there is no reasonable probability that the individual's visual acuity will ever improve beyond the minimum standards described in subparagraph (3) of this paragraph. In this event, if the examination occurs during a taxable year for which the exemption is claimed, and the examining physician certifies that, in his opinion, the condition is irreversible, and a copy of this certification is filed

Reg. § 1.151-1(c)(2)

with the return for that taxable year, then a statement described in subparagraph (3) of this paragraph need not be attached to such individual's return for subsequent taxable years so long as the condition remains irreversible. The taxpayer shall retain a copy of the certified opinion in his records, and a statement referring to such opinion shall be attached to future returns claiming the section 151(d) exemption. [Reg. § 1.151-1.]

☐ [T.D. 6231, 4-25-57. Amended by T.D. 7114, 5-17-71 and T.D. 7230, 12-21-72.]

[Reg. § 1.151-2]

§ 1.151-2. Additional exemptions for dependents.—(a) Section 151(e) allows to a taxpayer an exemption for each dependent (as defined in section 152) whose gross income (as defined in section 61) for the calendar year in which the taxable year of the taxpayer begins is less than the amount provided in section 151(e)(1)(A) applicable to the taxable year of the taxpayer, or who is a child of the taxpayer and who—

(1) Has not attained the age of 19 at the close of the calendar year in which the taxable year of the taxpayer begins, or

(2) Is a student, as defined in paragraph (b) of § 1.151-3.

No exemption shall be allowed under section 151(e) for any dependent who has made a joint return with his spouse under section 6013 for the taxable year beginning in the calendar year in which the taxable year of the taxpayer begins. The amount provided in section 151(e)(1)(A) is $750 in the case of a taxable year beginning after December 31, 1972; $700 in the case of a taxable year beginning after December 31, 1971, and before January 1, 1973; $650 in the case of a taxable year beginning after December 31, 1970, and before January 1, 1972; $625 in the case of a taxable year beginning after December 31, 1969, and before January 1, 1971; and $600 in the case of a taxable year beginning before January 1, 1970. For special rules in the case of a taxpayer whose taxable year is a fiscal year ending after December 31, 1969, and beginning before January 1, 1973, see section 21(d) and the regulations thereunder.

(b) The only exemption allowed for a dependent of the taxpayer is that provided by section 151(e). The exemptions provided by section 151(c) (old-age exemptions) and section 151(d) (exemptions for the blind) are allowed only for the taxpayer or his spouse. For example, where a taxpayer provides the entire support for his father who meets all the requirements of a dependent, he is entitled to only one exemption for his father (section 151(e)), even though his father is over the age of 65. [Reg. § 1.151-2.]

☐ [T.D. 6231, 4-25-57. Amended by T.D. 7114, 5-17-71.]

[Reg. § 1.151-3]

§ 1.151-3. Definitions.—(a) *Child.* For purposes of sections 151(e), 152, and the regulations thereunder, the term "child" means a son, stepson, daughter, stepdaughter, adopted son, adopted daughter, or for taxable years beginning after December 31, 1958, a child who is a member of an individual's household if the child was placed with the individual by an authorized placement agency for legal adoption pursuant to a formal application filed by the individual with the agency (see paragraph (c)(2) of § 1.152-2), or, for taxable years beginning after December 31, 1969, a foster child (if such foster child satisfies the requirements set forth in paragraph (b) of § 1.152-1 with respect to the taxpayer) of the taxpayer.

(b) *Student.* For purposes of section 151(e) and section 152(d), and the regulations thereunder, the term "student" means an individual who during each of 5 calendar months during the calendar year in which the taxable year of the taxpayer begins is a full-time student at an educational institution or is pursuing a full-time course of institutional on-farm training under the supervision of an accredited agent of an educational insitution or of a State or political subdivision of a State. An example of "institutional on-farm training" is that authorized by 38 U. S. C. 1652 (formerly section 252 of the Veterans' Readjustment Assistance Act of 1952) as described in section 252 of such act. A full-time student is one who is enrolled for some part of 5 calendar months for the number of hours or courses which is considered to be full-time attendance. The 5 calendar months need not be consecutive. School attendance exclusively at night does not constitute full-time attendance. However, full-time attendance at an educational institution may include some attendance at night in connection with full-time course of study.

(c) *Educational institution.* For purposes of sections 151(e) and 152, and the regulations thereunder, the term "educational institution" means a school maintaining a regular faculty and established curriculum, and having an organized body of students in attendance. It includes primary and secondary schools, colleges, universities, normal schools, technical schools, mechanical schools, and similar institutions, but does not include noneducational institutions, on-the-job training, correspondence schools, night schools, and so forth. [Reg. § 1.151-3.]

☐ [T.D. 6231, 4-25-57. Amended by T.D. 7051, 7-8-70.]

[Reg. § 1.151-4]

§ 1.151-4. Amount of deduction for each exemption under section 151.—The amount allowed as a deduction for each exemption under section 151 is (a) $750 in the case of a taxable year beginning after December 31, 1972; (b) $700 in the case of a taxable year beginning after December 31, 1971, and before January 1, 1973; (c) $650 in the case of a taxable year beginning after December 31, 1970, and before January 1, 1972; (d) $625 in the case of a taxable year beginning after December 31, 1969, and before January 1, 1971; and (e) $600 in the case of a taxable year beginning before January 1, 1970. For special rules in the case of a fiscal year ending after December 31, 1969, and beginning before January 1, 1973, see section 21(d) and the regulations thereunder. [Reg. § 1.151-4.]

☐ [*T.D. 7114,* 5-17-71.]

[Reg. § 1.152-1]

§ 1.152-1. General definition of a dependent.—(a)(1) For purposes of the income taxes imposed on individuals by chapter 1 of the Code, the term "dependent" means any individual described in paragraphs (1) through (10) of section 152(a) over half of whose support, for the calendar year in which the taxable year of the taxpayer begins, was received from the taxpayer.

(2)(i) For purposes of determining whether or not an individual received, for a given calendar year, over half of his support from the taxpayer, there shall be taken into account the amount of support received from the taxpayer as compared to the entire amount of support which the individual received from all sources, including support which the individual himself supplied. The term "support" includes food, shelter, clothing, medical and dental care, education, and the like. Generally, the amount of an item of support will be the amount of expense incurred by the one furnishing such item. If the item of support furnished an individual is in the form of property or lodging, it will be necessary to measure the amount of such item of support in terms of its fair market value.

(ii) In computing the amount which is contributed for the support of an individual, there must be included any amount which is contributed by such individual for his own support, including income which is ordinarily excludable from gross income, such as benefits received under the Social Security Act. For example, a father receives $800 social security benefits, $400 interest, and $1,000 from his son during 1955, all of which sums represent his sole support during that

year. The fact that the social security benefits of $800 are not includible in the father's gross income does not prevent such amount from entering into the computation of the total amount contributed for the father's support. Consequently, since the son's contribution of $1,000 was less than one-half of the father's support ($2,200) he may not claim his father as a dependent.

(iii)(*a*) For purposes of determining the amount of support furnished for a child (or children) by a taxpayer for a given calendar year, an arrearage payment made in a year subsequent to a calendar year for which there is an unpaid liability shall not be treated as paid either during that calendar year or in the year of payment, but no amount shall be treated as an arrearage payment to the extent that there is an unpaid liability (determined without regard to such payment) with respect to the support of a child for the taxable year of payment; and

(*b*) Similarly, payments made prior to any calendar year (whether or not made in the form of a lump sum payment in settlement of the parent's liability for support) shall not be treated as made during such calendar year, but payments made during any calendar year from amounts set aside in trust by a parent in a prior year, shall be treated as made during the calendar year in which paid.

(b) Section 152(a)(9) applies to any individual (other than an individual who at any time during the taxable year was the spouse, determined without regard to section 153, of the taxpayer) who lives with the taxpayer and is a member of the taxpayer's household during the entire taxable year of the taxpayer. An individual is not a member of the taxpayer's household if at any time during the taxable year of the taxpayer the relationship between such individual and the taxpayer is in violation of local law. It is not necessary under section 152(a)(9) that the dependent be related to the taxpayer. For example, foster children may qualify as dependents. It is necessary, however, that the taxpayer both maintain and occupy the household. The taxpayer and dependent will be considered as occupying the household for such entire taxable year notwithstanding temporary absences from the household due to special circumstances. A nonpermanent failure to occupy the common abode by reason of illness, education, business, vacation, military service, or a custody agreement under which the dependent is absent for less than six months in the taxable year of the taxpayer, shall be considered temporary absence due to special circumstances. The fact that the dependent dies during the year

Reg. § 1.151-4

shall not deprive the taxpayer of the deduction if the dependent lived in the household for the entire part of the year preceding his death. Likewise, the period during the taxable year preceding the birth of an individual shall not prevent such individual from qualifying as a dependent under section 152(a)(9). Moreover, a child who actually becomes a member of the taxpayer's household during the taxable year shall not be prevented from being considered a member of such household for the entire taxable year, if the child is required to remain in a hospital for a period following its birth, and if such child would otherwise have been a member of the taxpayer's household during such period.

(c) In the case of a child of the taxpayer who is under 19 or who is a student, the taxpayer may claim the dependency exemption for such child provided he has furnished more than one-half of the support of such child for the calendar year in which the taxable year of the taxpayer begins, even though the income of the child for such calendar year may be equal to or in excess of the amount determined pursuant to § 1.151-2 applicable to such calendar year. In such a case, there may be two exemptions claimed for the child: One on the parent's (or stepparent's) return, and one on the child's return. In determining whether the taxpayer does in fact furnish more than one-half of the support of an individual who is a child, as defined in paragraph (a) of § 1.151-3, of the taxpayer and who is a student, as defined in paragraph (b) of § 1.151-3, a special rule regarding scholarships applies. Amounts received as scholarships, as defined in paragraph (a) of § 1.117-3, for study at an educational institution shall not be considered in determining whether the taxpayer furnishes more than one-half the support of such individual. For example, A has a child who receives a $1,000 scholarship to the X college for 1 year. A contributes $500, which constitutes the balance of the child's support for that year. A may claim the child as a dependent, as the $1,000 scholarship is not counted in determining the support of the child. For purposes of this paragraph, amounts received for tuition payments and allowances by a veteran under the provisions of the Servicemen's Readjustment Act of 1944 (58 Stat. 284) or the Veterans' Readjustment Assistance Act of 1952 (38 U.S.C. ch. 38) are not amounts received as scholarships. See also § 1.117-4. For definition of the terms "child," "student," and "educational institution," as used in this paragraph, see § 1.151-3. [Reg. § 1.152-1.]

☐ [*T.D.* 6231, 4-25-57. *Amended by T.D.* 6304, 8-22-58, *T.D.* 6441, 1-4-60, *T.D.* 6663, 7-10-63, *T.D.* 7099, 3-19-71 *and T.D.* 7114, 5-17-71.]

[Reg. § 1.152-2]

§ 1.152-2. Rules relating to general definition of dependent.—(a)(1) Except as provided in subparagraph (2) of this paragraph, to qualify as a dependent an individual must be a citizen or resident of the United States or be a resident of the Canal Zone, the Republic of Panama, Canada, or Mexico, or, for taxable years beginning after December 31, 1971, a national of the United States, at some time during the calendar year in which the taxable year of the taxpayer begins. A resident of the Republic of the Philippines who was born to or legally adopted by the taxpayer in the Philippine Islands before January 1, 1956, at a time when the taxpayer was a member of the Armed Forces of the United States, may also be claimed as a dependent if such resident otherwise qualifies as a dependent. For definition of "Armed Forces of the United States," see section 7701(a)(15).

(2)(i) For any taxable year beginning after December 31, 1957, a taxpayer who is a citizen, or, for any taxable year beginning after December 31, 1971, a national of the United States is permitted under section 152(b)(3)(B) to treat as a dependent his legally adopted child who lives with him, as a member of his household, for the entire taxable year and who, but for the citizenship, nationality, or residence requirements of section 152(b)(3) and subparagraph (1) of this paragraph, would qualify as a dependent of the taxpayer for such taxable year.

(ii) Under section 152(b)(3)(B) and this subparagraph, it is necessary that the taxpayer both maintain and occupy the household. The taxpayer and his legally adopted child will be considered as occupying the household for the entire taxable year of the taxpayer notwithstanding temporary absences from the household due to special circumstances. A nonpermanent failure to occupy the common abode by reason of illness, education, business, vacation, military service, or a custody agreement under which the legally adopted child is absent for less than six months in the taxable year of the taxpayer shall be considered temporary absence due to special circumstances. The fact that a legally adopted child dies during the year shall not deprive the taxpayer of the deduction if the child lived in the household for the entire part of the year preceding his death. The period during the taxable year preceding the birth of a child shall not prevent such child from qualifying as a dependent under this subparagraph. Moreover, a legally adopted child who actually becomes a member of the taxpayer's household during the taxable year shall not be prevented from being considered a member of

Reg. § 1.152-2(a)(2)

such household for the entire taxable year, if the child is required to remain in a hospital for a period following its birth and if such child would otherwise have been a member of the taxpayer's household during such period.

(iii) For purposes of section 152(b)(3)(B) and this subparagraph, any child whose legal adoption by the taxpayer (a citizen or national of the United States) becomes final at any time before the end of the taxable year of the taxpayer shall not be disqualified as a dependent of such taxpayer by reason of his citizenship, nationality, or residence, provided the child lived with the taxpayer and was a member of the taxpayer's household for the entire taxable year in which the legal adoption became final. For example, A, a citizen of the United States who makes his income tax returns on the basis of the calendar year, is employed in Brazil by an agency of the United States Government. In October 1958 he takes into his household C, a resident of Brazil who is not a citizen of the United States, for the purpose of initiating adoption proceedings. C lives with A and is a member of his household for the remainder of 1958 and for the entire calendar year 1959. On July 1, 1959, the adoption proceedings were completed and C became the legally adopted child of A. If C otherwise qualifies as a dependent, he may be claimed as a dependent by A for 1959.

(b) A payment to a wife which is includible in her gross income under section 71 or section 682 shall not be considered a payment by her husband for the support of any dependent.

(c)(1) For purposes of determining the existence of any of the relationships specified in section 152(a) or (b)(1), a legally adopted child of an individual shall be treated as a child of such individual by blood.

(2) For any taxable year beginning after December 31, 1958, a child who is a member of an individual's household also shall be treated as a child of such individual by blood if the child was placed with the individual by an authorized placement agency for legal adoption pursuant to a formal application filed by the individual with the agency. For purposes of this subparagraph an authorized placement agency is any agency which is authorized by a State, the District of Columbia, a possession of the United States, a foreign country, or a political subdivision of any of the foregoing to place children for adoption. A taxpayer who claims as a dependent a child placed with him for adoption shall attach to his income tax return a statement setting forth the name of the child for whom the dependency deduction is claimed, the name and address of the authorized placement

agency, and the date the formal application was filed with the agency.

(3) The application of this paragraph may be illustrated by the following example:

Example. On March 1, 1959, D, a resident of the United States, made formal application to an authorized child placement agency for the placement of E, a resident of the United States, with him for legal adoption. On June 1, 1959, E was placed with D for legal adoption. During the year 1959 E received over one-half of his support from D. D may claim E as a dependent for 1959. Since E was a resident of the United States, his qualification as a dependent is in no way based on the provisions of section 152(b)(3)(B). Therefore, it is immaterial that E was not a member of D's household during the entire taxable year.

(4) For purposes of determining the existence of any of the relationships specified in section 152(a) or (b)(1), a foster child of an individual (if such foster child satisfies the requirements set forth in paragraph (b) of § 1.152-1 with respect to such individual) shall, for taxable years beginning after December 31, 1969, be treated as a child of such individual by blood. For purposes of this subparagraph, a foster child is a child who is in the care of a person or persons (other than the parents or adopted parents of the child) who care for the child as their own child. Status as a foster child is not dependent upon or affected by the circumstances under which the child became a member of the household.

(d) In the case of a joint return it is not necessary that the prescribed relationship exist between the person claimed as a dependent and the spouse who furnishes the support; it is sufficient if the prescribed relationship exists with respect to either spouse. Thus, a husband and wife making a joint return may claim as a dependent a daughter of the wife's brother (wife's niece) even though the husband is the one who furnishes the chief support. The relationship of affinity once existing will not terminate by divorce or the death of a spouse. For example, a widower may continue to claim his deceased wife's father (his father-in-law) as a dependent provided he meets the other requirements of section 151. [Reg. § 1.152-2.]

☐ [*T.D. 6231, 4-25-57. Amended by T.D. 6441, 1-4-60, T.D. 6663, 7-10-63, T.D. 7051, 7-8-70 and T.D. 7291, 12-3-73.*]

[Reg. § 1.152-3]

§ 1.152-3. Multiple support agreements.—(a) Section 152(c) provides that a taxpayer shall be treated as having contributed over half of the support of an individual for the calendar year (in

Reg. § 1.152-3(a)

cases where two or more taxpayers contributed to the support of such individual) if:

(1) No one person contributed over half of the individual's support,

(2) Each member of the group which collectively contributed more than half of the support of the individual would have been entitled to claim the individual as a dependent but for the fact that he did not contribute more than one-half of such support,

(3) The member of the group claiming the individual as a dependent contributed more than 10 percent of the individual's support, and

(4) Each other person in the group who contributed more than 10 percent of such support files a written declaration that he will not claim the individual as a dependent for any taxable year beginning in such calendar year.

(b) Application of the rule contained in paragraph (a) of this section may be illustrated by the following examples:

Example (1). Brothers A, B, C, and D contributed the entire support of their mother in 1956 in the following percentages: A, 30 percent; B, 20 percent; C, 29 percent; and D, 21 percent. Any one of the brothers, except for the fact that he did not contribute more than half of her support, would have been entitled to claim his mother as a dependent. Consequently, any one of the brothers could claim a deduction for the exemption of the mother provided a written declaration (as provided in paragraph (c) of this section) from each of the other brothers is attached to his income tax return. Even though A and D together contributed more than one-half the support of the mother, A, if he wished to claim his mother as a dependent, would be required to attach written declarations from B, C, and D to his income tax return, since each of those three contributed more than 10 percent of the support and, but for the support requirement, would have been entitled to claim his mother as a dependent.

Example (2). E, an individual who resides with his son, received $1,500 during the calendar year 1956, which constituted his entire support for that year. The source of the $1,500 was as follows:

Source	Amount received	Percentage of total
Social Security	$ 375	25
N, an unrelated neighbor	165	11
B, a brother	210	14
D, a daughter	150	10
S, a son	600	40
Total received by E	$1,500	100

B, D, and S are persons each of whom, but for the fact that he did not contribute more than half of the $1,500, could claim E as a dependent for a

taxable year beginning in 1956. The three together contributed $960, or 64 percent of the $1,500, and, thus, each is a member of the group to be considered for the purpose of section 152(c). B and S are the only members of such group who can meet all the requirements of section 152(c) and either one could claim E as a dependent for his taxable year beginning in 1956 provided he attached to his income tax return a written declaration (as provided in paragraph (c) of this section) signed by the other, and furnished the other information required by the return with respect to all the contributions to E. Inasmuch as D did not contribute more than 10 percent of E's support, she is not entitled to claim E as a dependent for a taxable year beginning in 1956 nor is she required to file a written declaration with respect to her contributions to E. N contributed over 10 percent of the support of E in 1956 but, since he is an unrelated neighbor, he does not qualify as a member of the group for the purpose of the multiple support agreement under section 152(c).

(c) [Reserved] [Reg. § 1.152-3.]

☐ [T.D. 6231, 4-25-57. Amended by T.D. 6663, 7-10-63 and T.D. 8989, 4-23-2002.]

[Reg. § 1.152-3T]

§ 1.152-3T. Multiple support agreements (temporary).—(a) through (b) [Reserved] For further guidance, see § 1.152-3(a) and (b).

(c)(1) The member of a group of contributors who claims an individual as a dependent for a taxable year beginning before January 1, 2002, under the multiple support agreement provisions of section 152(c) must attach to the member's income tax return for the year of the deduction a written declaration from each of the other persons who contributed more than 10 percent of the support of such individual and who, but for the failure to contribute more than half of the support of the individual, would have been entitled to claim the individual as a dependent.

(2) The taxpayer claiming an individual as a dependent for a taxable year beginning after December 31, 2001, under the multiple support agreement provisions of section 152(c) must provide with the income tax return for the year of the deduction—

( ) A statement identifying each of the other persons who contributed more than 10 percent of the support of the individual and who, but for the failure to contribute more than half of the support of the individual, would have been entitled to claim the individual as a dependent; and

(i) A statement indicating that the taxpayer obtained a written declaration from each of the persons described in section 152(c)(2) waiving the right to claim the individual as a dependent.

(3) The taxpayer claiming the individual as a dependent for a taxable year beginning after December 31, 2001, must retain the waiver declarations and should be prepared to furnish the waiver declarations and any other information necessary to substantiate the claim of the taxpayer. Other information that will substantiate the dependency claim of the taxpayer may include a statement showing the names of all contributors (whether or not members of the group described in section 152(c)(2)) and the amount contributed by each to the support of the claimed dependent. [Temporary Reg. § 1.152-3T.]

☐ [*T.D.* 8989, 4-23-2002.]

[Reg. § 1.152-4]

§ 1.152-4. Support test in case of child of divorced or separated parents.—(a) *Applicability.* For taxable years beginning after December 31, 1966, the provisions of section 152(e) and this section relate to a determination of which of separated parents (that is, parents who are divorced or legally separated under a decree of divorce or separate maintenance, or separated under a written separation agreement) is to be treated for purposes of section 152(a) and § 1.152-1 of this chapter as having provided more than half of the support of a child, as defined in section 151(e)(3) and § 1.151-3(a) of this chapter. For section 152(e) and this section to apply either parent or both parents combined must provide more than one-half of the child's total support, within the meaning of § 1.152-1(a)(2)(i) of this chapter during the calendar year in which the taxable year of the parent who is claiming the child as a dependent begins; and such child must be in the custody of one or both of his parents for more than one-half of the calendar year. Thus, section 152(e) and this section do not apply if a person other than the parents provides one-half or more for the support of such child during the calendar year or has custody of the child for one-half or more of the calendar year. In addition, section 152(e) and this section do not apply in any case where over half of the support of the child is treated as having been received from a taxpayer pursuant to a multiple support agreement under the provisions of section 152(c) and § 1.152-3 of this chapter. Nor does section 152(e) and this section apply to a period for which a joint return signed by both parents if filed.

(b) *Custody.* "Custody", for purposes of this section, will be determined by the terms of the most recent decree of divorce or separate maintenance, or subsequent custody decree, or, if none, a written separation agreement. In the event of so-called "split" custody, or if neither a decree or agreement establishes who has custody, or if the validity or continuing effect of such decree or agreement is uncertain by reason of proceedings pending on the last day of the calendar year, "custody" will be deemed to be with the parent who, as between both parents, has the physical custody of the child for the greater portion of the calendar year.

(c) *General rule.* For purposes of section 152(a) and § 1.152-1 of this chapter, a child shall be treated as receiving over half of his support during the calendar year from the parent (hereinafter referred to as the "custodial parent") having custody within the meaning of paragraph (b) of this section for a greater portion of the calendar year unless the exceptions of paragraph (d) of this section apply. If the parents of such a child are divorced or separated for only a portion of a calendar year after having had joint custody of the child for the prior portion of the year, the parent who has custody for the greater portion of the remainder of the year after divorce or separation shall be treated as having custody for a greater portion of the calendar year. Except as provided in section 152(e)(2)(A) and paragraph (d)(2) of this section (relating to decree or agreement) parents who are unable to enter into a multiple support agreement under section 152(c) cannot enter into an agreement as to which parent is entitled to claim a child as a dependent. Therefore, in general, the custodial parent shall be allowed as a deduction the exemption for the dependent child, if the requirements of section 151(e) are met.

(d) *Exceptions*—(1) *In general.* Notwithstanding paragraph (c) of this section, a child shall be treated as receiving over half of his support during the calendar year from the parent who is not the custodial parent (hereinafter referred to as the "noncustodial parent") if the conditions of subparagraph (2) or (3) of this paragraph are met.

(2) *Decree or agreement.* A noncustodial parent who provides at least $600 for the support of a child during the calendar year shall be treated as having provided more than half the support of the child if the decree of divorce or of separate maintenance, or a written agreement between the parents applicable to the taxable year of the noncustodial parent beginning in such calendar year, provides that the noncustodial parent shall be entitled to any deduction allowable under section 151 as an exemption for the dependent child. In order for this subparagraph to apply, the noncustodial parent must provide at least $600 for the support of each child he claims as a dependent. For taxable years beginning after December

Reg. § 1.152-4(a)

31, 1970, in the case of a written agreement or portion of a written agreement between the parents which allocates the deduction to the noncustodial parent, the noncustodial parent must attach to his return (or amended return) a copy of such agreement or such portion of such agreement which is applicable to the calendar year in which the taxable year of the noncustodial parent begins.

(3) *Actual support.* A noncustodial parent who provides $1,200 or more support for the child (or, for taxable years beginning before October 5, 1976, if there is more than one child for which he claims an exemption, $1,200 or more for the combined support for all of such children) shall be treated as having provided more than half the support for the child (or children) notwithstanding any provision to the contrary contained in a decree of divorce or separation or in a written agreement, unless the custodial parent clearly establishes that the custodial parent provided, in fact, more for the support of the child during the calendar year than the noncustodial parent. Under section 152(e)(2)(B) and this subparagraph, if the noncustodial parent established that the noncustodial parent has provided $1,200 or more for support of the child, then the custodial parent has the burden of establishing by a clear preponderance of the evidence that the custodial parent has provided more for the support of the child than has been established by the noncustodial parent in order to be treated as having provided over half of the support of the child. See paragraph (e) of this section with regard to notification and submission of itemized statements.

(4) *Amount of support.* For purposes of this paragraph, amounts expended for the support of a child shall be treated as received from the noncustodial parent to the extent that the noncustodial parent provided amounts for the support of the child, whether or not such amounts provided by the noncustodial parent are actually expended for child support. Therefore, for example, if only the parents have provided support for the child during a calendar year, only the excess of the total amount expended for the support of the child over the amount so provided by the noncustodial parent shall be treated as provided by the custodial parent for the support of the child.

(e) *Itemized statement—*(1) *Exchange.* (i) If a parent intends to claim for a taxable year a child as a dependent or a parent is uncertain whether he is entitled to claim a child and desires either to determine whether the second parent intends to or has claimed the same child as a dependent, or if the first parent desires to receive an itemized statement as provided in subparagraph (3) of this paragraph from the second parent, the first parent is entitled to receive such information from the second parent in writing upon request provided he both notifies the second parent of his intention (or possible intention) to so claim the child and sends the second parent a copy of such an itemized statement upon which the first parent's claim is based. A failure to make such a request shall not affect the right of the first parent to claim the child as a dependent. However, if the first parent makes such a request, and the second parent does not respond within a reasonable time, and it is determined that the first parent is not entitled to claim the child as a dependent, the inability of the first parent to obtain information will be taken into account in determining whether the addition to tax under section 6653, relating to failure to pay tax, is applicable.

(ii) Upon receipt of such a request accompanied by an itemized statement, if the second parent intends to claim (with respect to the calendar year in which such taxable year of the first parent begins) or has claimed the same child as a dependent, the second parent shall so inform the first parent, and if so requested shall send him a copy of the itemized statement upon which the second parent's claim is based. A notification under this subparagraph that the parent is claiming or is not claiming the child as a dependent shall not affect the rights of the parent making such notification and does not constitute a waiver.

(2) *Attachment to return.* For taxable years beginning after December 31, 1970, if a parent intends to claim a child as a dependent and, prior to the filing of his return or the time prescribed by law for filing the return (determined without regard to any extension thereof), whichever is later, such parent makes or receives a request under the procedures provided under paragraph (e)(1) of this section, then unless he is reasonably certain that the other parent will not claim the child as a dependent, such parent must attach to his return (or if the return is already filed, to a corrected or amended return) a copy of the itemized statement upon which such parent's claim is based, as provided in subparagraph (3) of this paragraph, together with a copy of the other parent's itemized statement, if available, at the time the return is filed. Failure to attach an itemized statement to the extent required by this subparagraph will be taken into account in determining whether the addition to tax under section 6653, relating to failure to pay tax, is applicable in the event it is determined that the parent is not entitled to claim the child as a dependent.

(3) *Contents*. The itemized statement referred to in subparagraphs (1) and (2) of this paragraph shall include—

(i) The name of the child (or children) being claimed as a dependent as well as the name of both parents and, if known, the address and social security number of both parents;

(ii) If known, the number of months the dependent child (or children) lived during the calendar year in the home of each parent or person other than the parents;

(iii) If known, income for the taxable year of each dependent child;

(iv) If known, the total amount of support furnished the child (or children) (including amounts furnished by persons other than the parents);

(v) A list of amounts expended during the calendar year for the child (or children) made by the parent making the statement and itemized to show the amounts expended for medical and dental care, food, shelter, clothing, education, recreation, and transportation;

(vi) Amounts actually paid by the parent making the statement during the calendar year for the support of the child (or children) pursuant to a decree of divorce or separate maintenance, or a written separation agreement; and

(vii) Other amounts paid or expended by the parent making the statement during the calendar year, for the support of the child (or children).

(4) *Requirement by Officer*. Notwithstanding subparagraphs (1), (2), or (3) of this paragraph, an internal revenue officer may require the submission of an itemized statement from either parent and may make it available to the other parent. Such itemized statement shall contain the information requested by the internal revenue officer and shall be filed within such reasonable time as may be designated by him. If the required statement is not furnished pursuant to the instructions of the internal revenue officer, the claim of support of the parent failing to comply with such requirement may be disallowed by the Internal Revenue Service.

(f) *Illustration of principles*. The application of the provisions of this section may be illustrated by the following examples:

Example (1). A, a child of B and C, who were divorced June 1, 1970, received $1,000 for support during the calendar year 1970, of which $400 was provided by B and $300 was provided by C. No multiple support agreement was entered into. Prior to the divorce B and C jointly had custody of A, and for the remainder of 1970, B had custody

of A for the months of October through December, while C had custody of A for the months of June through September. Since C had custody for 4 of the 7 months following the divorce, C is the custodial parent for 1970 and is treated as having provided over half of the support for A during 1970.

Example (2). Assume the same facts as in example (1) and that for the calendar year 1971, of $1,000 support expended for A during 1971, $400 was provided by B and $300 was provided by C. Furthermore, assume that in addition to having custody of A for the months of October through December 1971, B had custody for the first 5 months of 1971. Since B had custody of A for a total of 8 months in 1971, B is the custodial parent for 1971 and is treated as having provided over half of the support for A during 1971.

Example (3). D received all of his support, $1,000, during the calendar year 1970, from his parents E and F, who are separated under a written separation agreement. F had custody of D for the entire year of 1970, but under the agreement E was to provide $600 for the support of D during 1970, and E is entitled to any deduction allowable under section 151 for the years 1970 and 1971. E, in fact, provides only $550 for the support of D during 1970, but makes up the arrearage of $50 early in 1971. Nevertheless, F is treated as having provided over half of the support for D during 1970.

Example (4). Assume the same facts as in example (3) and that F had custody of D for the entire year 1971, and of $2,350 expended for the support of D during 1971, E provided $650 while F provided $1,700. Since under the written separation agreement E is entitled to any deduction allowable under section 151 for D for the year 1971 and E provided at least $600 for the support of D, E is treated as having provided over half of the support of D, for 1971.

Example (5). G and H are legally separated under a decree of separate maintenance. G has custody of I, the child of G and H, for the entire year, and G and H enter into a written agreement that G is entitled to any deduction allowable under section 151 for I for the calendar year 1970. However, during 1970, of the $2,000 provided for the support of I, H provided $1,300 while G provided only $700. H has provided more than $1,200 for the support of I, and G cannot establish that G provided more for the support of I, than did H. Therefore, notwithstanding the agreement, since H does not have custody of I, H is treated as having provided over half of the support for I for 1970.

Reg. § 1.152-4(e)(3)

Example (6). J and K, the children of L and M, who are divorced, received a total of $3,400 for the support of both during the calendar year 1970 from their parents. L, who has custody of J and K for the entire year 1970, provided $1,800 for the support of both, while M, the noncustodial parent, provided $1,600 for such support. Under the decree of divorce, M is entitled to any deduction allowable under section 151 for such children. Since M has provided at least $600 for the support of each child, M is treated as having provided over half the support for J and K for 1970. Furthermore, as J and K are determined under section 152(e) and § 1.152-4 to be dependents of M for purposes of section 151(e), they are also considered to be dependents of M with respect to other provisions of the Code that are dependent upon such a determination for their operation. (For example, section 213.)

Example (7). N, O, and P are the children of divorced parents Q and R, both calendar year taxpayers. During calendar year 1976, the children received over half their support from Q and R. Q, who has custody of the three children for the entire year 1976, provided $800 for the support of each of the three children. R, the noncustodial parent, provided $2,700 during 1976 for the combined support of the three children under the terms of the decree of divorce. So, for calendar year 1976, although R, the noncustodial parent, did not provide support in the amount of $1,200 per child under paragraph (d)(3) of this section, R, the noncustodial parent, is treated as having provided more than half the support of each child during 1976, since R provided more than $1,200 for the combined support of all the children and Q did not provide more for the support of either N, O, or P ($800 per child) during 1976 than R provided during 1976 ($900 per child).

Example (8). Assume the same facts that occurred in 1976 in example 7 also occurred in 1977. For 1977 R does not satisfy the $1,200 support test under paragraph (d)(3) of this section because he has not provided $1,200 support for each individual child, N, O, or P for calendar year 1977. Therefore, R, the noncustodial parent, is not treated as having provided more than half the support of the children for calendar year 1977.

Example (9). A, B, and C, the children of divorced parents M and N, both calendar year taxpayers, receive all of their support, $5,900, from their parents during the calendar year 1979. M has custody of A, B, and C and provides $2,700 for their collective support during 1979. Pursuant to the terms of the decree of divorce N provided $1,200 for the support of A, $1,000 for the support of B, and $1,000 for the support of C. Since N has

provided $1,200 or more for the support of A, and M has provided $900 ($2,700 ÷ 3) for the support of A during 1979, N is treated as having provided more than half the support for A during 1979. However, since N has not provided $1,200 or more for the support of either B or C, N, the noncustodial parent, is not treated as having provided more than half the support of B or C during 1979. [Reg. § 1.152-4.]

☐ [*T.D.* 7099, 3-19-71. *Amended by T.D.* 7145, 10-14-71 *and T.D.* 7639, 8-17-79.]

[Reg. § 1.152-4T]

§ 1.152-4T. **Dependency exemption in the case of child of divorced parent, etc. (Temporary).—(a)** *In general.—*

Q-1. Which parent may claim the dependency exemption in the case of a child of divorced or separated parents?

A-1. Provided the parents together would have been entitled to the dependency exemption had they been married and filing a joint return, the parent having custody of a child for the greater portion of the year (the custodial parent) will generally be entitled to the dependency exemption. This rule applies to parents not living together during the last 6 months of the calendar year, as well as those divorced or separated under a separation agreement.

Q-2. Are there any exceptions to the general rule in A-1?

A-2. Yes, there are three exceptions. The general rule does not apply (i) if a multiple support agreement is in effect (see section 152(c)), (ii) if a decree or agreement executed prior to January 1, 1985 provides that the custodial parent has agreed to release his or her claim to the dependency exemption to the noncustodial parent and the noncustodial parent provides at least $600 of support to the child (see section 152(e)(4)), or (iii) if the custodial parent relinquishes the exemption in the manner described in A-3.

Q-3 How may the exemption for a dependent child be claimed by a noncustodial parent?

A-3 A noncustodial parent may claim the exemption for a dependent child only if the noncustodial parent attaches to his/her income tax return for the year of the exemption a written declaration from the custodial parent stating that he/she will not claim the child as a dependent for the taxable year beginning in such calendar year. The written declaration may be made on a form to be provided by the Service for this purpose. Once the Service has released the form, any declaration made other than on the official form shall conform to the substance of such form.

Reg. § 1.152-4T(a)

Q-4. For what period may a custodial parent release to the noncustodial parent a claim to the exemption for a dependent child?

A-4. The exemption may be released for a single year, for a number of specified years (for example, alternate years), or for all future years, as specified in the declaration. If the exemption is released for more than one year, the original release must be attached to the return of the noncustodial spouse and a copy of such release must be attached to his/her return for each succeeding taxable year for which he/she claims the dependency exemption.

Q-5. May only the custodial parent claim a deduction under section 213(d) for medical expenses paid by the parent or an income exclusion under section 105(b) for medical expenses paid by an employer for a dependent child?

A-5. No. Under the new rules, if a child receives over half of his support during the calendar year from his parents who are divorced or legally sepa-

rated under a decree of divorce or separate maintenance, or who are separated under a written separation agreement, that child will be treated as a dependent of both parents for purposes of sections 105(b) and 213(d). Thus, a parent can deduct medical expenses paid by that parent for a child even though a dependency exemption for the child is claimed by the other parent. The special rule of sections 105(b) and 213(d) does not apply where over half of the support of a child is treated as having been received from a person under the provisions of section 152(c) (relating to multiple support agreements).

Q-6. When does section 152(e), as amended by the Tax Reform Act of 1984, become effective?

A-6. Section 152(e), as amended, is effective with respect to dependency exemptions for taxable years beginning after December 31, 1984. [Temporary Reg. § 1.152-4T.]

□ [T.D. 7973, 8-30-84.]

Itemized Deductions for Individuals and Corporations

[Reg. § 1.161-1]

§ 1.161-1. Allowance of deductions.—Section 161 provides for the allowance as deductions, in computing taxable income under section 63(a), of the items specified in part VI (section 161 and following), subchapter B of chapter 1 of the Code, subject to the exceptions provided in part IX (section 261 and following), of such subchapter B, relating to the items not deductible. Double deductions are not permitted. Amounts deducted under one provision of the Internal Revenue Code of 1954 cannot again be deducted under any other provision thereof. See also section 7852(c), relating to the taking into account, both in computing a tax under subtitle A of the Internal Revenue Code of 1954 and a tax under chapter 1 or 2 of the Internal Revenue Code of 1939, of the same item of deduction. [Reg. § 1.161-1.]

□ [T.D. 6291, 4-3-58.]

[Reg. § 1.162-1]

§ 1.162-1. Business expenses.—(a) In general. Business expenses deductible from gross income include the ordinary and necessary expenditures directly connected with or pertaining to the taxpayer's trade or business, except items which are used as the basis for a deduction or a credit under provisions of law other than section 162. The cost of goods purchased for resale, with proper adjustment for opening and closing inventories, is deducted from gross sales in computing gross income. See paragraph (a) of § 1.61-3. Among the items included in business expenses are management expenses, commissions (but see section 263

and the regulations thereunder), labor, supplies, incidental repairs, operating expenses of automobiles used in the trade or business, traveling expenses while away from home solely in the pursuit of a trade or business (see § 1.162-2), advertising and other selling expenses, together with insurance premiums against fire, storm, theft, accident, or other similar losses in the case of a business, and rental for the use of business property. No such item shall be included in business expenses, however, to the extent that it is used by the taxpayer in computing the cost of property included in its inventory or used in determining the gain or loss basis of its plant, equipment, or other property. See section 1054 and the regulations thereunder. A deduction for an expense paid or incurred after December 30, 1969, which would otherwise be allowable under section 162 shall not be denied on the grounds that allowance of such deduction would frustrate a sharply defined public policy. See section 162(c), (f), and (g) and the regulations thereunder. The full amount of the allowable deduction for ordinary and necessary expenses in carrying on a business is deductible, even though such expenses exceed the gross income derived during the taxable year from such business. In the case of any sports program to which section 114 (relating to sports programs conducted for the American National Red Cross) applies, expenses described in section 114(a)(2) shall be allowable as deductions under section 162(a) only to the extent that such expenses exceed the amount excluded from gross income under section 114(a).

Reg. § 1.161-1

(b) *Cross references.* (1) For charitable contributions by individuals and corporations not deductible under section 162, see § 1.162-15.

(2) For items not deductible, see sections 261-276, inclusive, and the regulations thereunder.

(3) For research and experimental expenditures, see section 174 and regulations thereunder.

(4) For soil and water conservation expenditures, see section 175 and regulations thereunder.

(5) For expenditures attributable to grant or loan by United States for encouragement of exploration for, or development or mining of, critical and strategic minerals or metals, see section 621 and regulations thereunder.

(6) For treatment of certain rental payments with respect to public utility property see section 167(1) and § 1.167(1)-3.

(7) For limitations on the deductibility of miscellaneous itemized deductions, see section 67 and § § 1.67-1T through 1.67-4T.

(8) For the timing of deductions with respect to notional principal contracts, see § 1.446-3. [Reg. § 1.162-1.]

□ [*T.D.* 6291, 4-3-58. *Amended by T.D.* 6690, 11-18-63; *T.D.* 6996, 1-17-69; *T.D.* 7315, 6-6-74; *T.D.* 7345, 2-19-75; *T.D.* 8189, 3-25-88 *and T.D.* 8491, 10-8-93.]

[Reg. § 1.162-2]

§ 1.162-2. Traveling expenses.—(a) Traveling expenses include travel fares, meals and lodging, and expenses incident to travel such as expenses for sample rooms, telephone and telegraph, public stenographers, etc. Only such traveling expenses as are reasonable and necessary in the conduct of the taxpayer's business and directly attributable to it may be deducted. If the trip is undertaken for other than business purposes, the travel fares and expenses incident to travel are personal expenses and the meals and lodging are living expenses. If the trip is solely on business, the reasonable and necessary traveling expenses, including travel fares, meals and lodging, and expenses incident to travel, are business expenses. For the allowance of traveling expenses as deductions in determining adjusted gross income, see section 62(2)(B) and the regulations thereunder.

(b)(1) If a taxpayer travels to a destination and while at such destination engages in both business and personal activities, traveling expenses to and from such destination are deductible only if the trip is related primarily to the taxpayer's trade or business. If the trip is primarily personal in nature, the traveling expenses to and from the destination are not deductible even though the taxpayer engages in business activities while at such destination. However, expenses while at the destination which are properly allocable to the taxpayer's trade or business are deductible even though the traveling expenses to and from the destination are not deductible.

(2) Whether a trip is related primarily to the taxpayer's trade or business or is primarily personal in nature depends on the facts and circumstances in each case. The amount of time during the period of the trip which is spent on personal activity compared to the amount of time spent on activities directly relating to the taxpayer's trade or business is an important factor in determining whether the trip is primarily personal. If, for example, a taxpayer spends one week while at a destination on activities which are directly related to his trade or business and subsequently spends an additional five weeks for vacation or other personal activities, the trip will be considered primarily personal in nature in the absence of a clear showing to the contrary.

(c) Where a taxpayer's wife accompanies him on a business trip, expenses attributable to her travel are not deductible unless it can be adequately shown that the wife's presence on the trip has a bona fide business purpose. The wife's performance of some incidental service does not cause her expenses to qualify as deductible business expenses. The same rules apply to any other members of the taxpayer's family who accompany him on such a trip.

(d) Expenses paid or incurred by a taxpayer in attending a convention or other meeting may constitute an ordinary and necessary business expense under section 162 depending upon the facts and circumstances of each case. No distinction will be made between self-employed persons and employees. The fact that an employee uses vacation or leave time or that his attendance at the convention is voluntary will not necessarily prohibit the allowance of the deduction. The allowance of deductions for such expenses will depend upon whether there is a sufficient relationship between the taxpayer's trade or business and his attendance at the convention or other meeting so that he is benefiting or advancing the interests of his trade or business by such attendance. If the convention is for political, social or other purposes unrelated to the taxpayer's trade or business, the expenses are not deductible.

(e) Commuters' fares are not considered as business expenses and are not deductible.

(f) For rules with respect to the reporting and substantiation of traveling and other business expenses of employees for taxable years beginning after December 31, 1957, see § 1.162-17. [Reg. § 1.162-2.]

□ [*T.D. 6291, 4-3-58. Amended by T.D. 6306, 8-27-58.*]

[Reg. § 1.162-3]

§ 1.162-3. Cost of materials.—Taxpayers carrying materials and supplies on hand should include in expenses the charges for materials and supplies only in the amount that they are actually consumed and used in operation during the taxable year for which the return is made, provided that the costs of such materials and supplies have not been deducted in determining the net income or loss or taxable income for any previous year. If a taxpayer carries incidental materials or supplies on hand for which no record of consumption is kept or of which physical inventories at the beginning and end of the year are not taken, it will be permissible for the taxpayer to include in his expenses and to deduct from gross income the total cost of such supplies and materials as were purchased during the taxable year for which the return is made, provided the taxable income is clearly reflected by this method. [Reg. § 1.162-3.]

□ [*T.D. 6291, 4-3-58.*]

[Reg. § 1.162-4]

§ 1.162-4. Repairs.—The cost of incidental repairs which neither materially add to the value of the property nor appreciably prolong its life, but keep it in an ordinarily efficient operating condition, may be deducted as an expense, provided the cost of acquisition or production or the gain or loss basis of the taxpayer's plant, equipment, or other property, as the case may be, is not increased by the amount of such expenditures. Repairs in the nature of replacements, to the extent that they arrest deterioration and appreciably prolong the life of the property, shall either be capitalized and depreciated in accordance with section 167 or charged against the depreciation reserve if such an account is kept. [Reg. § 1.162-4.]

□ [*T.D. 6291, 4-3-58.*]

[Reg. § 1.162-5]

§ 1.162-5. Expenses for education.—(a) *General rule.* Expenditures made by an individual for education (including research undertaken as part of his educational program) which are not expenditures of a type described in paragraph (b)(2) or (3) of this section are deductible as ordinary and necessary business expenses (even though the education may lead to a degree) if the education—

(1) Maintains or improves skills required by the individual in his employment or other trade or business, or

(2) Meets the express requirements of the individual's employer, or the requirements of applicable law or regulations, imposed as a condition to the retention by the individual of an established employment relationship, status, or rate of compensation.

(b) *Nondeductible educational expenditures*—(1) *In general.* Educational expenditures described in subparagraphs (2) and (3) of this paragraph are personal expenditures or constitute an inseparable aggregate of personal and capital expenditures and, therefore, are not deductible as ordinary and necessary business expenses even though the education may maintain or improve skills required by the individual in his employment or other trade or business or may meet the express requirements of the individual's employer or of applicable law or regulations.

(2) *Minimum educational requirements.* (i) The first category of nondeductible educational expenses within the scope of subparagraph (1) of this paragraph are expenditures made by an individual for education which is required of him in order to meet the minimum educational requirements for qualification in his employment or other trade or business. The minimum education necessary to qualify for a position or other trade or business must be determined from a consideration of such factors as the requirements of the employer, the applicable law and regulations, and the standards of the profession, trade, or business involved. The fact that an individual is already performing service in an employment status does not establish that he has met the minimum educational requirements for qualification in that employment. Once an individual has met the minimum educational requirements for qualification in his employment or other trade or business (as in effect when he enters the employment or trade or business), he shall be treated as continuing to meet those requirements even though they are changed.

(ii) The minimum educational requirements for qualification of a particular individual in a position in an educational institution is the minimum level of education (in terms of aggregate college hours or degree) which under the applicable laws or regulations, in effect at the time this individual is first employed in such position, is normally required of an individual initially being employed in such a position. If there are no normal requirements as to the minimum level of education required for a position in an educational institution, then an individual in such a position shall be considered to have met the minimum educational requirements for qualification in that position when he becomes a member of the faculty of the educational institution. The determination of whether an individual is a member of the faculty of an educational institution must be made on the basis of the particular practices of the institution. However, an individual will ordinarily be considered to be a member of the faculty of an institution if (a) he has tenure or his years of service are being counted toward obtaining tenure; (b) the institution is making contributions to a retirement plan (other than Social Security or a similar program) in respect of his employment; or (c) he has a vote in faculty affairs.

(iii) The application of this subparagraph may be illustrated by the following examples:

Example (1). General facts: State X requires a bachelor's degree for beginning secondary school teachers which must include 30 credit hours of professional educational courses. In addition, in order to retain his position, a secondary school teacher must complete a fifth year of preparation within 10 years after beginning his employment. If an employing school official certifies to the State Department of Education that applicants having a bachelor's degree and the required courses in professional education cannot be found, he may hire individuals as secondary school teachers if they have completed a minimum of 90 semester hours of college work. However, to be retained in his position, such an individual must obtain his bachelor's degree and complete the required professional educational courses within 3 years after his employment commences. Under these facts, a bachelor's degree, without regard to whether it includes 30 credit hours of professional educational courses, is considered to be the minimum educational requirement for qualification as a secondary school teacher in State X. This is the case notwithstanding the number of teachers who are actually hired without such a degree. The following are examples of the application of these facts in particular situations:

Situation 1. A, at the time he is employed as a secondary school teacher in State X, has a bachelor's degree including 30 credit hours of professional educational courses. After his employment, A completes a fifth college year of education and, as a result, is issued a standard certificate. The fifth college year of education undertaken by A is not education required to meet the minimum educational requirements for qualification as a secondary school teacher. Accordingly, the expenditures for such education are deductible unless the expenditures are for education which is part of a program of study being pursued by A which will lead to qualifying him in a new trade or business.

Situation 2. Because of a shortage of applicants meeting the stated requirements, B, who has a bachelor's degree, is employed as a secondary school teacher in State X even though he has only 20 credit hours of professional educational courses. After his employment, B takes an additional 10 credit hours of professional educational courses. Since these courses do not constitute education required to meet the minimum educational requirements for qualification as a secondary school teacher which is a bachelor's degree and will not lead to qualifying B in a new trade or business, the expenditures for such courses are deductible.

Situation 3. Because of a shortage of applicants meeting the requirements, C is employed as a secondary school teacher in State X although he has only 90 semester hours of college work towards his bachelor's degree. After his employment, C undertakes courses leading to a bachelor's degree. These courses (including any courses in professional education) constitute education required to meet the minimum educational requirements for qualification as a secondary school teacher. Accordingly, the expenditures for such education are not deductible.

Situation 4. Subsequent to the employment of A, B, and C, but before they have completed a fifth college year of education, State X changes its requirements affecting secondary school teachers to provide that beginning teachers must have completed 5 college years of preparation. In the cases of A, B, and C, a fifth college year of education is not considered to be education undertaken to meet the minimum educational requirements for qualification as a secondary school teacher. Accordingly, expenditures for a fifth year of college will be deductible unless the expenditures are for education which is part of a program being pursued by A, B, or C which will lead to qualifying him in a new trade or business.

Example (2). D, who holds a bachelor's degree, obtains temporary employment as an instructor at University Y and undertakes graduate courses as a candidate for a graduate degree. D may become a faculty member only if he obtains a graduate degree and may continue to hold a position as instructor only so long as he shows satisfactory progress towards obtaining this graduate degree. The graduate courses taken by D constitute education required to meet the minimum educational requirements for qualification in D's trade or business and, thus, the expenditures for such courses are not deductible.

Example (3). E, who has completed 2 years of a normal 3-year law school course leading to a bachelor of laws degree (LL.B.), is hired by a

Reg. § 1.162-5(b)(2)

law firm to do legal research and perform other functions on a full-time basis. As a condition to continued employment, E is required to obtain an LL.B. and pass the State bar examination. E completes his law school education by attending night law school, and he takes a bar review course in order to prepare for the State bar examination. The law courses and bar review course constitute education required to meet the minimum educational requirements for qualification in E's trade or business and, thus, the expenditures for such courses are not deductible.

(3) *Qualification for new trade or business.* (i) The second category of nondeductible educational expenses within the scope of subparagraph (1) of this paragraph are expenditures made by an individual for education which is part of a program of study being pursued by him which will lead to qualifying him in a new trade or business. In the case of an employee, a change of duties does not constitute a new trade or business if the new duties involve the same general type of work as is involved in the individual's present employment. For this purpose, all teaching and related duties shall be considered to involve the same general type of work. The following are examples of changes in duties which do not constitute new trades or businesses:

(*a*) Elementary to secondary school classroom teacher.

(*b*) Classroom teacher in one subject (such as mathematics) to classroom teacher in another subject (such as science).

(*c*) Classroom teacher to guidance counselor.

(*d*) Classroom teacher to principal.

(ii) The application of this subparagraph to individuals other than teachers may be illustrated by the following examples:

Example (1). A, a self-employed individual practicing a profession other than law, for example, engineering, accounting, etc., attends law school at night and after completing his law school studies receives a bachelor of laws degree. The expenditures made by A in attending law school are nondeductible because this course of study qualifies him for a new trade or business.

Example (2). Assume the same facts as in example (1) except that A has the status of an employee rather than a self-employed individual, and that his employer requires him to obtain a bachelor of laws degree. A intends to continue practicing his nonlegal profession as an employee of such employer. Nevertheless, the expenditures made by A in attending law school are not deduct-

ible since this course of study qualifies him for a new trade or business.

Example (3). B, a general practitioner of medicine, takes a 2-week course reviewing new developments in several specialized fields of medicine. B's expenses for the course are deductible because the course maintains or improves skills required by him in his trade or business and does not qualify him for a new trade or business.

Example (4). C, while engaged in the private practice of psychiatry, undertakes a program of study and training at an accredited psychoanalytic institute which will lead to qualifying him to practice psychoanalysis. C's expenditures for such study and training are deductible because the study and training maintains or improves skills required by him in his trade or business and does not qualify him for a new trade or business.

(c) *Deductible educational expenditures*—(1) *Maintaining or improving skills.* The deduction under the category of expenditures for education which maintains or improves skills required by the individual in his employment or other trade or business includes refresher courses or courses dealing with current developments as well as academic or vocational courses provided the expenditures for the courses are not within either category of nondeductible expenditures described in paragraph (b) (2) or (3) of this section.

(2) *Meeting requirements of employer.* An individual is considered to have undertaken education in order to meet the express requirements of his employer, or the requirements of applicable law or regulations, imposed as a condition to the retention by the taxpayer of his established employment relationship, status, or rate of compensation only if such requirements are imposed for a bona fide business purpose of the individual's employer. Only the minimum education necessary to the retention by the individual of his established employment relationship, status, or rate of compensation may be considered as undertaken to meet the express requirements of the taxpayer's employer. However, education in excess of such minimum education may qualify as education undertaken in order to maintain or improve the skills required by the taxpayer in his employment or other trade or business (see subparagraph (1) of this paragraph). In no event, however, is a deduction allowable for expenditures for education which, even though for education required by the employer or applicable law or regulations, are within one of the categories of nondeductible expenditures described in paragraph (b)(2) and (3) of this section.

(d) *Travel as a form of education.* Subject to the provisions of paragraph (b) and (e) of this section, expenditures for travel (including travel while on sabbatical leave) as a form of education are deductible only to the extent such expenditures are attributable to a period of travel that is directly related to the duties of the individual in his employment or other trade or business. For this purpose, a period of travel shall be considered directly related to the duties of the individual in his employment or other trade or business only if the major portion of the activities during such period is of a nature which directly maintains or improves skills required by the individual in such employment or other trade or business. The approval of a travel program by an employer or the fact that travel is accepted by an employer in the fulfillment of its requirements for retention of rate of compensation, status or employment, is not determinative that the required relationship exists between the travel involved and the duties of the individual in his particular position.

(e) *Travel away from home.* (1) If an individual travels away from home primarily to obtain education the expenses of which are deductible under this section, his expenditures for travel, meals, and lodging while away from home are deductible. However, if as an incident of such trip the individual engages in some personal activity such as sightseeing, social visiting, or entertaining, or other recreation, the portion of the expenses attributable to such personal activity constitutes nondeductible personal or living expenses and is not allowable as a deduction. If the individual's travel away from home is primarily personal, the individual's expenditures for travel, meals and lodging (other than meals and lodging during the time spent in participating in deductible educational pursuits) are not deductible. Whether a particular trip is primarily personal or primarily to obtain education the expenses of which are deductible under this section depends upon all the facts and circumstances of each case. An important factor to be taken into consideration in making the determination is the relative amount of time devoted to personal activity as compared with the time devoted to educational pursuits. The rules set forth in this paragraph are subject to the provisions of section 162(a)(2), relating to deductibility of certain traveling expenses, and section 274(c) and (d), relating to allocation of certain foreign travel expenses and substantiation required, respectively, and the regulations thereunder.

(2) *Examples.* The application of this subsection may be illustrated by the following examples:

Example (1). A, a self-employed tax practitioner, decides to take a 1-week course in new developments in taxation, which is offered in City

X, 500 miles away from his home. His primary purpose in going to X is to take the course, but he also takes a side trip to City Y (50 miles from X) for 1 day, takes a sightseeing trip while in X, and entertains some personal friends. A's transportation expenses to City X and return to his home are deductible but his transportation expenses to City Y are not deductible. A's expenses for meals and lodging while away from home will be allocated between his educational pursuits and his personal activities. Those expenses which are entirely personal, such as sightseeing and entertaining friends, are not deductible to any extent.

Example (2). The facts are the same as in example (1) except that A's primary purpose in going to City X is to take a vacation. This purpose is indicated by several factors, one of which is the fact that he spends only 1 week attending the tax course and devotes 5 weeks entirely to personal activities. None of A's transportation expenses are deductible and his expenses for meals and lodging while away from home are not deductible to the extent attributable to personal activities. His expenses for meals and lodging allocable to the week attending the tax course are, however, deductible.

Example (3). B, a high school mathematics teacher in New York City, in the summertime travels to a university in California in order to take a mathematics course the expense of which is deductible under this section. B pursues only one-fourth of a full course of study and the remainder of her time is devoted to personal activities the expense of which is not deductible. Absent a showing by B of a substantial nonpersonal reason for taking the course in the university in California, the trip is considered taken primarily for personal reasons and the cost of traveling from New York City to California and return would not be deductible. However, one-fourth of the cost of B's meals and lodging while attending the university in California may be considered properly allocable to deductible educational pursuits and, therefore, is deductible. [Reg. § 1.162-5.]

☐ [*T.D.* 6291, 4-3-58. *Amended by T.D.* 6918, 5-1-67.]

[Reg. § 1.162-6]

§ 1.162-6. **Professional expenses.**—A professional man may claim as deductions the cost of supplies used by him in the practice of his profession, expenses paid or accrued in the operation and repair of an automobile used in making professional calls, dues to professional societies and subscriptions to professional journals, the rent paid or accrued for office rooms, the cost of the fuel, light, water, telephone, etc., used in such offices, and the hire of office assistants. Amounts currently paid or accrued for books, furniture, and professional instruments and equipment, the useful life of which is short, may be deducted. [Reg. § 1.162-6.]

☐ [*T.D.* 6291, 4-3-58.]

[Reg. § 1.162-7]

§ 1.162-7. **Compensation for personal services.**—(a) There may be included among the ordinary and necessary expenses paid or incurred in carrying on any trade or business a reasonable allowance for salaries or other compensation for personal services actually rendered. The test of deductibility in the case of compensation payments is whether they are reasonable and are in fact payments purely for services.

(b) The test set forth in paragraph (a) of this section and its practical application may be further stated and illustrated as follows:

(1) Any amount paid in the form of compensation, but not in fact as the purchase price of services is not deductible. An ostensible salary paid by a corporation may be a distribution of a dividend on stock. This is likely to occur in the case of a corporation having few shareholders, practically all of whom draw salaries. If in such a case the salaries are in excess of those ordinarily paid for similar services and the excessive payments correspond or bear a close relationship to the stockholdings of the officers or employees, it would seem likely that the salaries are not paid wholly for services rendered, but that the excessive payments are a distribution of earnings upon the stock. An ostensible salary may be in part payment for property. This may occur, for example, where a partnership sells out to a corporation, the former partners agreeing to continue in the service of the corporation. In such a case it may be found that the salaries of the former partners are not merely for services, but in part constitute payment for the transfer of their business.

(2) The form or method of fixing compensation is not decisive as to deductibility. While any form of contingent compensation invites scrutiny as a possible distribution of earnings of the enterprise, it does not follow that payments on a contingent basis are to be treated fundamentally on any basis different from that applying to compensation at a flat rate. Generally speaking, if contingent compensation is paid pursuant to a free bargain between the employer and the individual made before the services are rendered, not influenced by any consideration on the part of the employer other than that of securing on fair and advantageous terms the services of the individual, it should be allowed as a deduction even though in the actual working out of the contract it may

prove to be greater than the amount which would ordinarily be paid.

(3) In any event the allowance for the compensation paid may not exceed what is reasonable under all the circumstances. It is, in general, just to assume that reasonable and true compensation is only such amount as would ordinarily be paid for like services by like enterprises under like circumstances. The circumstances to be taken into consideration are those existing at the date when the contract for services was made, not those existing at the date when the contract is questioned.

(4) For disallowance of deduction in the case of certain transfers of stock pursuant to employees stock options, see section 421 and the regulations thereunder. [Reg. § 1.162-7.]

☐ [*T.D.* 6291, 4-3-58.]

[Reg. § 1.162-8]

§ 1.162-8. **Treatment of excessive compensation.**—The income tax liability of the recipient in respect of an amount ostensibly paid to him as compensation, but not allowed to be deducted as such by the payor, will depend upon the circumstances of each case. Thus, in the case of excessive payments by corporations, if such payments correspond or bear a close relationship to stockholders, and are found to be a distribution of earnings or profits, the excessive payments will be treated as a dividend. If such payments constitute payment for property, they should be treated by the payor as a capital expenditure and by the recipient as part of the purchase price. In the absence of evidence to justify other treatment, excessive payments for salaries or other compensation for personal services will be included in gross income of the recipient. [Reg. § 1.162-8.]

☐ [*T.D.* 6291, 4-3-58.]

[Reg. § 1.162-9]

§ 1.162-9. **Bonuses to employees.**—Bonuses to employees will constitute allowable deductions from gross income when such payments are made in good faith and as additional compensation for the services actually rendered by the employees, provided such payments, when added to the stipulated salaries, do not exceed a reasonable compensation for the services rendered. It is immaterial whether such bonuses are paid in cash or in kind or partly in cash and partly in kind. Donations made to employees and others, which do not have in them the element of compensation or which are in excess of reasonable compensation for services, are not deductible from gross income. [Reg. § 1.162-9.]

☐ [*T.D.* 6291, 4-3-58.]

Reg. § 1.162-7(a)

[Reg. § 1.162-10]

§ 1.162-10. Certain employee benefits—(a) *In general.* Amounts paid or accrued by a taxpayer on account of injuries received by employees and lump-sum amounts paid or accrued as compensation for injuries are proper deductions as ordinary and necessary expenses. Such deductions are limited to the amount not compensated for by insurance or otherwise. Amounts paid or accrued within the taxable year for dismissal wages, unemployment benefits, guaranteed annual wages, vacations, or a sickness, accident, hospitalization, medical expense, recreational, welfare, or similar benefit plan, are deductible under section 162(a) if they are ordinary and necessary expenses of the trade or business. However, except as provided in paragraph (b) of this section, such amounts shall not be deductible under section 162(a) if, under any circumstances, they may be used to provide benefits under a stock bonus, pension, annuity, profit-sharing, or other deferred compensation plan of the type referred to in section 404(a). In such an event, the extent to which these amounts are deductible from gross income shall be governed by the provisions of section 404 and the regulations issued thereunder.

(b) *Certain negotiated plans.* (1) Subject to the limitations set forth in subparagraphs (2) and (3) of this paragraph, contributions paid by an employer under a plan under which such contributions are held in a welfare trust for the purpose of paying (either from principal or income or both) for the benefit of employees, their families, and dependents, at least medical or hospital care, and pensions on retirement or death of employees, are deductible when paid as business expenses under section 162(a).

(2) For the purpose of subparagraph (1) of this paragraph, the word "plan" means any plan established prior to January 1, 1954, as a result of an agreement between employee representatives and the Government of the United States, during a period of Government operation, under seizure powers, of a major part of the productive facilities of the industry in which the employer claiming the deduction is engaged. The phrase 'plan established prior to January 1, 1954, as a result of an agreement" is intended primarily to cover a trust established under the terms of such an agreement. It also includes a trust established under a plan of an employer, or group of employers, who, by reason of producing the same commodity, are in competition with the employers whose facilities were seized and who would therefore be expected to establish such a trust as a reasonable measure to maintain a sound position in the labor market producing the commodity. For example, if a trust

was established under such an agreement in the bituminous coal industry, a similar trust established in the anthracite coal industry within a reasonable time, but before January 1, 1954, would qualify under subparagraph (1) of this paragraph.

(3) If any trust described in subparagraph (2) of this paragraph becomes qualified for exemption from tax under the provisions of section 501(a) the deductibility of contributions by an employer to such trust on or after any date of such qualification shall no longer be governed by the provisions of section 162, even though the trust may later lose its exemption from tax under section 501(a).

(c) *Other plans providing deferred compensation.* For rules relating to the deduction of amounts paid to or under a stock bonus, pension, annuity, or profit-sharing plan or amounts paid or accrued under any other plan deferring the receipt of compensation, see section 404 and the regulations thereunder. [Reg. § 1.162-10.]

☐ [T.D. 6291, 4-3-58.]

[Reg. § 1.162-10T]

§ 1.162-10T. Questions and answers relating to the deduction of employee benefits under the Tax Reform Act of 1984; certain limits on amounts deductible (Temporary).—

Q-1: How does the amendment of section 404(b) by the Tax Reform Act of 1984 affect the deduction of employee benefits under section 162 of the Internal Revenue Code?

A-1: As amended by the Tax Reform Act of 1984, section 404(b) clarifies that section 404(a) and (d) (in the case of employees and nonemployees, respectively) shall govern the deduction of contributions paid or compensation paid or incurred under a plan, or method or arrangement, deferring the receipt of compensation or providing for deferred benefits. Section 404(a) and (d) requires that such a contribution or compensation be paid or incurred for purposes of section 162 or 212 and satisfy the requirements for deductibility under either of these sections. However, notwithstanding the above, section 404 does not apply to contributions paid or accrued with respect to a "welfare benefit fund" (as defined in section 419(e) after July 18, 1984, in taxable years of employers (and payors) ending after that date. Also, section 463 shall govern the deduction of vacation pay by a taxpayer that has elected the application of such section. Section 404(b), as amended, generally applies to contributions paid and compensation paid or incurred after July 18, 1984, in taxable years of employers (and payors) ending after that date. See Q&A-3 of

§ 1.404(b)-1T. For rules relating to the deduction of contributions attributable to the provision of deferred benefits, see section 404(a), (b) and (d) and § 1.404(a)-1T, § 1.404(b)-1T and § 1.404(d)-1T. For rules relating to the deduction of contributions paid or accrued with respect to a welfare benefit fund, see section 419, § 1.419-1T and § 1.419A-2T. For rules relating to the deduction of vacation pay for which an election is made under section 463, see § 301.9100-16T of this chapter and § 1.463-1T.

Q-2: How does the enactment of section 419 by the Tax Reform Act of 1984 affect the deduction of employee benefits under section 162?

A-2: As enacted by the Tax Reform Act of 1984, section 419 shall govern the deduction of contributions paid or accrued by an employer (or a person receiving services under section 419(g)) with respect to a "welfare benefit fund" (within the meaning of section 419(e)) after December 31, 1985, in taxable years of the employer (or person receiving the services) ending after that date. Section 419(a) requires that such a contribution be paid or accrued for purposes of section 162 or 212 and satisfy the requirements for deductibility under either of those sections. Generally, subject to a binding contract exception (as described in section 511(e)(5) of the Tax Reform Act of 1984), section 419 shall also govern the deduction of the contribution of a facility (or other contribution used to acquire or improve a facility) to a welfare benefit fund after June 22, 1984. See Q&A-11 of § 1.419-1T. In the case of a welfare benefit fund maintained pursuant to a collective bargaining agreement, section 419 applies to the extent provided under the special effective date rule described in Q&A-2 of § 1.419-1T and the special rules of § 1.419A-2T. For rules relating to the deduction of contributions paid or accrued with respect to a welfare benefit fund, see section 419 and § 1.419-1T. [Temporary Reg. § 1.162-10T.]

☐ [T.D. 8073, 1-29-86. Amended by T.D. 8435, 9-18-92.]

[Reg. § 1.162-11]

§ 1.162-11. Rentals.—(a) *Acquisition of a leasehold.* If a leasehold is acquired for business purposes for a specified sum, the purchaser may take as a deduction in his return an aliquot part of such sum each year, based on the number of years the lease has to run. Taxes paid by a tenant to or for a landlord for business property are additional rent and constitute a deductible item to the tenant and taxable income to the landlord, the amount of the tax being deductible by the latter. For disallowance of deduction for income taxes paid by a lessee corporation pursuant to a lease arrangement with the lessor corporation, see

section 110 and the regulations thereunder. See section 178 and the regulations thereunder for rules governing the effect to be given renewal options in amortizing the costs incurred after July 28, 1958, of acquiring a lease. See § 1.197-2 for rules governing the amortization of costs to acquire limited interests in section 197 intangibles.

(b) *Improvements by lessee on lessor's property.* (1) The cost to a lessee of erecting buildings or making permanent improvements on property of which he is the lessee is a capital investment, and is not deductible as a business expense. If the estimated useful life in the hands of the taxpayer of the building erected or of the improvements made, determined without regard to the terms of the lease, is longer than the remaining period of the lease, an annual deduction may be made from gross income of an amount equal to the total cost of such improvements divided by the number of years remaining in the term of the lease, and such deduction shall be in lieu of a deduction for depreciation. If, on the other hand, the useful life of such buildings or improvements in the hands of the taxpayer is equal to or shorter than the remaining period of the lease, this deduction shall be computed under the provisions of section 167 (relating to depreciation).

(2) If the lessee began improvements on leased property before July 28, 1958, or if the lessee was on such date and at all times thereafter under a binding legal obligation to make such improvements, the matter of spreading the cost of erecting buildings or making permanent improvements over the term of the original lease, together with the renewal period or periods depends upon the facts in the particular case, including the presence or absence of an obligation of renewal and the relationship between the parties. As a general rule, unless the lease has been renewed or the facts show with reasonable certainty that the lease will be renewed, the cost or other basis of the lease, or the cost of improvements shall be spread only over the number of years the lease has to run without taking into account any right of renewal. The provisions of this subparagraph may be illustrated by the following examples:

Example (1). A subsidiary corporation leases land from its parent at a fair rental for a 25-year period. The subsidiary erects on the land valuable factory buildings having an estimated useful life of 50 years. These facts show with reasonable certainty that the lease will be renewed, even though the lease contains no option of renewal. Therefore, the cost of the buildings shall be depreciated over the estimated useful life of the buildings in accordance with section 167 and the regulations thereunder.

Reg. § 1.162-11(a)

Example (2). A retail merchandising corporation leases land at a fair rental from an unrelated lessor for the longest period that the lessor is willing to lease the land (30 years). The lessee erects on the land a department store having an estimated useful life of 40 years. These facts do not show with reasonable certainty that the lease will be renewed. Therefore, the cost of the building shall be spread over the remaining term of the lease. An annual deduction may be made of an amount equal to the cost of the building divided by the number of years remaining in the term of the lease, and such deduction shall be in lieu of a deduction for depreciation.

(3) See section 178 and the regulations thereunder for rules governing the effect to be given renewal options where a lessee begins improvements on leased property after July 28, 1958, other than improvements which on such date and at all times thereafter, the lessee was under a binding legal obligation to make. [Reg. § 1.162-11.]

☐ [*T.D.* 6291, 4-3-58. *Amended by T.D.* 6520, 12-30-60 *and T.D.* 8865, 1-20-2000.]

[Reg. § 1.162-12]

§ **1.162-12. Expenses of farmers.**—(a) *Farms engaged in for profit.* A farmer who operates a farm for profit is entitled to deduct from gross income as necessary expenses all amounts actually expended in the carrying on of the business of farming. The cost of ordinary tools of short life or small cost, such as hand tools. including shovels, rakes, etc., may be deducted. The purchase of feed and other costs connected with raising livestock may be treated as expense deductions insofar as such costs represent actual outlay, but not including the value of farm produce grown upon the farm or the labor of the taxpayer. For rules regarding the capitalization of expenses of producing property in the trade or business of farming, see section 263A and the regulations thereunder. For taxable years beginning after July 12, 1972, where a farmer is engaged in producing crops and the process of gathering and disposal of such crops is not completed within the taxable year in which such crops were planted, expenses deducted may, with the consent of the Commissioner (see section 446 and the regulations thereunder), be determined upon the crop method, and such deductions must be taken in the taxable year in which the gross income from the crop has been realized. For taxable years beginning on or before July 12, 1972, where a farmer is engaged in producing crops which take more than a year from the time of planting to the process of gathering and disposal, expenses deducted may, with the consent of the Commissioner (see section 446 and the regula-

tions thereunder), be determined upon the crop method, and such deductions must be taken in the taxable year in which the gross income from the crop has been realized. If a farmer does not compute income upon the crop method, the cost of seeds and young plants which are purchased for further development and cultivation prior to sale in later years may be deducted as an expense for the year of purchase, provided the farmer follows a consistent practice of deducting such costs as an expense from year to year. The preceding sentence does not apply to the cost of seeds and young plants connected with the planting of timber (see section 611 and the regulations thereunder). For rules regarding the capitalization of expenses of producing property in the trade or business of farming, see section 263A of the Internal Revenue Code and § 1.263A-4. The cost of farm machinery, equipment, and farm buildings represents a capital investment and is not an allowable deduction as an item of expense. Amounts expended in the development of farms, orchards and ranches prior to the time when the productive state is reached may, at the election of the taxpayer, be regarded as investments of capital. For the treatment of soil and water conservation expenditures as expenses which are not chargeable to capital account, see section 175 and the regulations thereunder. For taxable years beginning after December 31, 1959, in the case of expenditures paid or incurred by farmers for fertilizer. lime, etc., see section 180 and the regulations thereunder. Amounts expended in purchasing work, breeding, dairy, or sporting animals are regarded as investments of capital, and shall be depreciated unless such animals are included in an inventory in accordance with § 1.61-4. The purchase price of an automobile, even when wholly used in carrying on farming operations, is not deductible, but is regarded as an investment of capital. The cost of gasoline, repairs, and upkeep of an automobile if used wholly in the business of farming is deductible as an expense; if used partly for business purposes and partly for the pleasure or convenience of the taxpayer or his family, such cost may be apportioned according to the extent of the use for purposes of business and pleasure or convenience, and only the proportion of such cost justly attributable to business purposes is deductible as a necessary expense.

(b) *Farms not engaged in for profit; taxable years beginning before January 1, 1970*—(1) *In general.* If a farm is operated for recreation or pleasure and not on a commercial basis, and if the expenses incurred in connection with the farm are in excess of the receipts therefrom, the entire receipts from the sale of farm products may be

Reg. § 1.162-12(b)(1)

ignored in rendering a return of income, and the expenses incurred, being regarded as personal expenses, will not constitute allowable deductions.

(2) *Effective date.* The provisions of this paragraph shall apply with respect to taxable years beginning before January 1, 1970.

(3) *Cross reference.* For provisions relating to activities not engaged in for profit, applicable to taxable years beginning after December 31, 1969, see section 183 and the regulations thereunder. [Reg. § 1.162-12.]

☐ [*T.D. 6291, 4-3-58. Amended by T.D. 6548, 2-21-61; T.D. 7198, 7-12-72; T.D. 8729, 8-21-97 and T.D. 8897, 8-18-2000.*]

[Reg. § 1.162-13]

§ 1.162-13. Depositors' guaranty fund.—Banking corporations which pursuant to the laws of the State in which they are doing business are required to set apart, keep, and maintain in their banks the amount levied and assessed against them by the State authorities as a "Depositors' guaranty fund," may deduct from their gross income the amount so set apart each year to this fund provided that such fund, when set aside and carried to the credit of the State banking board or duly authorized State officer, ceases to be an asset of the bank and may be withdrawn in whole or in part upon demand by such board or State officer to meet the needs of these officers in reimbursing depositors in insolvent banks, and provided further that no portion of the amount thus set aside and credited is returnable under the laws of the State to the assets of the banking corporation. If, however, such amount is simply set up on the books of the bank as a reserve to meet a contingent liability and remains an asset of the bank, it will not be deductible except as it is actually paid out as required by law and upon demand of the proper State officers. [Reg. § 1.162-13.]

☐ [*T.D. 6291, 4-3-58.*]

[Reg. § 1.162-14]

§ 1.162-14. Expenditures for advertising or promotion of good will.—A corporation which has, for the purpose of computing its excess profits tax credit under subchapter E, chapter 2, or subchapter D, chapter 1 of the Internal Revenue Code of 1939, elected under section 733 or section 451 (applicable to the excess profits tax imposed by subchapter E of chapter 2, and subchapter D of chapter 1, respectively) to charge to capital account for taxable years in its base period expenditures for advertising or the promotion of good will which may be regarded as capital investments, may not deduct similar expenditures for the taxable year. See section 263(b). Such a tax-

payer has the burden of proving that expenditures for advertising or the promotion of good will which it seeks to deduct in the taxable year may not be regarded as capital investments under the provisions of the regulations prescribed under section 733 or section 451 of the Internal Revenue Code of 1939. See 26 CFR, 1938 ed., § 35.733-2 (Regulations 112) and 26 CFR (1939) § 40.451-2 (Regulations 130). For the disallowance of deductions for the cost of advertising in programs of certain conventions of political parties, or in publications part of the proceeds of which directly or indirectly inures (or is intended to inure) to or for the use of a political party or political candidate, see § 1.276-1. [Reg. § 1.162-14.]

☐ [*T.D. 6291, 4-3-58. Amended by T.D. 6996, 1-17-69.*]

[Reg. § 1.162-15]

§ 1.162-15. Contributions, dues, etc.—(a) *Contributions to organizations described in section 170—*(1) *In general.* No deduction is allowable under section 162(a) for a contribution or gift by an individual or a corporation if any part thereof is deductible under section 170. For example, if a taxpayer makes a contribution of $5,000 and only $4,000 of this amount is deductible under section 170(a) (whether because of the percentage limitation under either section 170(b)(1) or (2), the requirement as to time of payment, or both) no deduction is allowable under section 162(a) for the remaining $1,000.

(2) *Scope of limitations.* The limitations provided in section 162(b) and this paragraph apply only to payments which are in fact contributions or gifts to organizations described in section 170. For example, payments by a transit company to a local hospital (which is a charitable organization within the meaning of section 170) in consideration of a binding obligation on the part of the hospital to provide hospital services and facilities for the company's employees are not contributions or gifts within the meaning of section 170 and may be deductible under section 162(a) if the requirements of section 162(a) are otherwise satisfied.

(b) *Other contributions.* Donations to organizations other than those described in section 170 which bear a direct relationship to the taxpayer's business and are made with a reasonable expectation of a financial return commensurate with the amount of the donation may constitute allowable deductions as business expenses, provided the donation is not made for a purpose for which a deduction is not allowable by reason of the provisions of paragraph (b)(1)(i) or (c) of § 1.162-20. For example, a transit company may donate a sum of money to an organization (of a class not referred to in section 170) intending to hold a convention in the city in which it operates, with a reasonable expectation that the holding of such convention will augment its income through a greater number of people using its transportation facilities.

(c) *Dues.* Dues and other payments to an organization, such as a labor union or a trade association, which otherwise meet the requirements of the regulations under section 162, are deductible in full. For limitations on the deductibility of dues and other payments, see paragraph (b) and (c) of § 1.162-20.

(d) *Cross reference.* For provisions dealing with expenditures for institutional or "good will" advertising, see § 1.162-20. [Reg. § 1.162-15.]

☐ [*T.D.* 6291, 4-3-58. *Amended by T.D.* 6435, 12-28-59 *and T.D.* 6819, 4-19-65.]

[Reg. § 1.162-16]

§ 1.162-16. **Cross reference.**—For special rules relating to expenses in connection with subdividing real property for sale, see section 1237 and the regulations thereunder. [Reg. § 1.162-16.]

☐ [*T.D.* 6291, 4-3-58.]

[Reg. § 1.162-17]

§ 1.162-17. **Reporting and substantiation of certain business expenses of employees.**—(a) *Introductory.* The purpose of the regulations in this section is to provide rules for the reporting of information on income tax returns by taxpayers who pay or incur ordinary and necessary business expenses in connection with the performance of services as an employee and to furnish guidance as to the type of records which will be useful in compiling such information and in its substantiation, if required. The rules prescribed in this section do not apply to expenses paid or incurred for incidentals, such as office supplies for the employer or local transportation in connection with an errand. Employees incurring such incidental expenses are not required to provide substantiation for such amounts. The term "ordinary and necessary business expenses" means only those expenses which are ordinary and necessary in the conduct of the taxpayer's business and are directly attributable to such business. The term does not include nondeductible personal, living or family expenses.

(b) *Expenses for which the employee is required to account to his employer*—(1) *Reimbursements equal to expenses.* The employee need not report on his tax return (either itemized or in total amount) expenses for travel, transportation, entertainment, and similar purposes paid or incurred by him solely for the benefit of his employer for which he is required to account and does account to his employer and which are charged directly or indirectly to the employer (for example, through credit cards) or for which the employee is paid through advances, reimbursements, or otherwise, provided the total amount of such advances, reimbursements, and charges is equal to such expenses. In such a case the taxpayer need only state in his return that the total of amounts charged directly or indirectly to his employer through credit cards or otherwise and received from the employer as advances or reimbursements did not exceed the ordinary and necessary business expenses paid or incurred by the employee.

(2) *Reimbursements in excess of expenses.* In case the total of amounts charged directly or indirectly to the employer and received from the employer as advances, reimbursements, or otherwise, exceeds the ordinary and necessary business expenses paid or incurred by the employee and the employee is required to and does account to his employer for such expenses, the taxpayer must include such excess in income and state on his return that he has done so.

(3) *Expenses in excess of reimbursements.* If the employee's ordinary and necessary business expenses exceed the total of the amounts charged directly or indirectly to the employer and received from the employer as advances, reimbursements, or otherwise, and the employee is required to and does account to his employer for such expenses, the taxpayer may make the statement in his return required by subparagraph (1) of this paragraph unless he wishes to claim a deduction for such excess. If, however, he wishes to secure a deduction for such excess, he must submit a statement showing the following information as part of his tax return:

(i) The total of any charges paid or borne by the employer and of any other amounts received from the employer for payment of expenses, whether by means of advances, reimbursements or otherwise; and

(ii) The nature of his occupation, the number of days away from home on business, and the total amount of ordinary and necessary business expenses paid or incurred by him (including those charged directly or indirectly to the employer through credit cards or otherwise) broken down into such broad categories as transportation, meals and lodging while away from home overnight, entertainment expenses, and other business expenses.

(4) To "account" to his employer as used in this section means to submit an expense account or other required written statement to the em-

ployer showing the business nature and the amount of all the employee's expenses (including those charged directly or indirectly to the employer through credit cards or otherwise) broken down into such broad categories as transportation, meals and lodging while away from home overnight, entertainment expenses, and other business expenses. For this purpose, the Commissioner in his discretion may approve reasonable business practices under which mileage, per diem in lieu of subsistence, and similar allowances providing for ordinary and necessary business expenses in accordance with a fixed scale may be regarded as equivalent to an accounting to the employer.

(c) *Expenses for which the employee is not required to account to his employer.* If the employee is not required to account to his employer for his ordinary and necessary business expenses, e.g., travel, transportation, entertainment, and similar items, or, though required, fails to account for such expenses, he must submit, as a part of his tax return, a statement showing the following information:

(1) The total of all amounts received as advances or reimbursements from his employer in connection with the ordinary and necessary business expenses of the employee, including amounts charged directly or indirectly to the employer through credit cards or otherwise; and

(2) The nature of his occupation, the number of days away from home on business, and the total amount of ordinary and necessary business expenses paid or incurred by him (including those charged directly or indirectly to the employer through credit cards or otherwise) broken down into such broad categories as transportation, meals and lodging while away from home overnight, entertainment expenses, and other business expenses.

(d) *Substantiation of items of expense.* (1) Although the Commissioner may require any taxpayer to substantiate such information concerning expense accounts as may appear to be pertinent in determining tax liability, taxpayers ordinarily will not be called upon to substantiate expense account information except those in the following categories:

(i) A taxpayer who is not required to account to his employer, or who does not account;

(ii) A taxpayer whose expenses exceed the total of amounts charged to his employer and amounts received through advances, reimbursements or otherwise and who claims a deduction on his return for such excess;

(iii) A taxpayer who is related to his employer within the meaning of section 267(b); and

(iv) Other taxpayers in cases where it is determined that the accounting procedures used by the employer for the reporting and substantiation of expenses by employees are not adequate.

(2) The Code contemplates that taxpayers keep such records as will be sufficient to enable the Commissioner to correctly determine income tax liability. Accordingly, it is to the advantage of taxpayers who may be called upon to substantiate expense account information to maintain as adequate and detailed records of travel, transportation, entertainment, and similar business expenses as practical since the burden of proof is upon the taxpayer to show that such expenses were not only paid or incurred but also that they constitute ordinary and necessary business expenses. One method for substantiating expenses incurred by an employee in connection with his employment is through the preparation of a daily diary or record of expenditures, maintained in sufficient detail to enable him to readily identify the amount and nature of any expenditure, and the preservation of supporting documents, especially in connection with large or exceptional expenditures. Nevertheless, it is recognized that by reason of the nature of certain expenses or the circumstances under which they are incurred, it is often difficult for an employee to maintain detailed records or to preserve supporting documents for all his expenses. Detailed records of small expenditures incurred in traveling or for transportation, as for example, tips, will not be required.

(3) Where records are incomplete or documentary proof is unavailable, it may be possible to establish the amount of the expenditures by approximations based upon reliable secondary sources of information and collateral evidence. For example, in connection with an item of traveling expense a taxpayer might establish that he was in a travel status a certain number of days but that it was impracticable for him to establish the details of all his various items of travel expense. In such a case rail fares or plane fares can usually be ascertained with exactness and automobile costs approximated on the basis of mileage covered. A reasonable approximation of meals and lodging might be based upon receipted hotel bills or upon average daily rates for such accommodations and meals prevailing in the particular community for comparable accommodations. Since detailed records of incidental items are not required, deductions for these items may be based upon a reasonable approximation. In cases where a taxpayer is called upon to substantiate expense account information, the burden is on the taxpayer to establish that the amounts claimed as a deduction are reasonably accurate and constitute ordinary and necessary business expenses paid or

Reg. § 1.162-17(c)(1)

incurred by him in connection with his trade or business. In connection with the determination of factual matters of this type, due consideration will be given to the reasonableness of the stated expenditures for the claimed purposes in relation to the taxpayer's circumstances (such as his income and the nature of his occupation), to the reliability and accuracy of records in connection with other items more readily lending themselves to detailed record-keeping, and to all of the facts and circumstances in the particular case.

(e) *Applicability.* (1) Except as provided in subparagraph (2) of this paragraph, the provisions of the regulations in this section are supplemental to existing regulations relating to information required to be submitted with income tax returns, and shall be applicable with respect to taxable years beginning after December 31, 1957, notwithstanding any existing regulation to the contrary.

(2) With respect to taxable years ending after December 31, 1962, but only in respect of periods after such date, the provisions of the regulations in this section are superseded by the regulations under section 274(d) to the extent inconsistent therewith. See § 1.274-5.

(3) For taxable years beginning on or after January 1, 1989, the provisions of this section are superseded by the regulations under section 62(c) to the extent this section is inconsistent with those regulations. See § 1.62-2. [Reg. § 1.162-17.]

☐ [*T.D.* 6306, 8-27-58. *Amended by T.D.* 6630, 12-27-62; *T.D.* 8276, 12-7-89 *and T.D.* 8324, 12-14-90.]

[Reg. § 1.162-18]

§ 1.162-18. Illegal bribes and kickbacks.—(a) *Illegal payments to government officials or employees*—(1) *In general.* No deduction shall be allowed under section 162(a) for any amount paid or incurred, directly or indirectly, to an official or employee of any government, or of any agency or other instrumentality of any government, if—

(i) In the case of a payment made to an official or employee of a government other than a foreign government described in subparagraph (3)(ii) or (iii) of this paragraph, the payment constitutes an illegal bribe or kickback, or

(ii) In the case of a payment made to an official or employee of a foreign government described in subparagraph (3)(ii) or (iii) of this paragraph, the making of the payment would be unlawful under the laws of the United States (if such laws were applicable to the payment and to the official or employee at the time the expenses were paid or incurred).

No deduction shall be allowed for an accrued expense if the eventual payment thereof would fall within the prohibition of this section. The place where the expenses are paid or incurred is immaterial. For purposes of subdivision (ii) of this subparagraph, lawfulness or unlawfulness of the payment under the laws of the foreign country is immaterial.

(2) *Indirect payment.* For purposes of this paragraph, an indirect payment to an individual shall include any payment which inures to his benefit or promotes his interests, regardless of the medium in which the payment is made and regardless of the identity of the immediate recipient or payer. Thus, for example, payment made to an agent, relative, or independent contractor of an official or employee, or even directly into the general treasury of a foreign country of which the beneficiary is an official or employee, may be treated as an indirect payment to the official or employee, if in fact such payment inures or will inure to his benefit or promotes or will promote his financial or other interests. A payment made by an agent or independent contractor of the taxpayer which benefits the taxpayer shall be treated as an indirect payment by the taxpayer to the official or employee.

(3) *Official or employee of a government.* Any individual officially connected with—

(i) The government of the United States, a State, a territory or possession of the United States, the District of Columbia, or the Commonwealth of Puerto Rico,

(ii) The government of a foreign country, or

(iii) A political subdivision of, or a corporation or other entity serving as an agency or instrumentality of, any of the above,

in whatever capacity, whether on a permanent or temporary basis, and whether or not serving for compensation, shall be included within the term "official or employee of a government", regardless of the place of residence or post of duty of such individual. An independent contractor would not ordinarily be considered to be an official or employee. For purposes of section 162(c) and this paragraph, the term "foreign country" shall include any foreign nation, whether or not such nation has been accorded diplomatic recognition by the United States. Individuals who purport to act on behalf of or as the government of a foreign nation or an agency or instrumentality thereof, shall be treated under this section as officials or employees of a foreign government, whether or not such individuals in fact control such foreign nation agency, or instrumentality, and whether or not such individuals are accorded diplomatic recognition. Accordingly, a group in rebellion against an established government ment shall be treated as officials or employees of a foreign government, as shall officials or employees of the government against which the group is in rebellion.

(4) *Laws of the United States.* The term "laws of the United States", to which reference is made in paragraph (a)(1)(ii) of this section, shall be deemed to include only Federal statutes, including State laws which are assimilated into Federal law by Federal statute, and legislative and interpretative regulations thereunder. The term shall also be limited to statutes which prohibit some act or acts, for the violation of which there is a civil or criminal penalty.

(5) *Burden of proof.* In any proceeding involving the issue of whether, for purposes of section 162(c)(1), a payment made to a government official or employee constitutes an illegal bribe or kickback (or would be unlawful under the laws of the United States) the burden of proof in respect of such issue shall be upon the Commissioner to the same extent as he bears the burden of proof in civil fraud cases under section 7454 (*i.e.,* he must prove the illegality of the payment by clear and convincing evidence).

(6) *Example.* The application of this paragraph may be illustrated by the following example:

Example. X Corp. is in the business of selling hospital equipment in State Y. During 1970, X Corp. employed A who at the time was employed full time by State Y as Superintendent of Hospitals. The purpose of A's employment by X Corp. was to procure for it an improper advantage over other concerns in the making of sales to hospitals in respect of which A, as Superintendent, had authority. X Corp. paid A $5,000 during 1970. The making of this payment was illegal under the laws of State Y. Under section 162(c)(1), X Corp. is precluded from deducting as a trade or business expense the $5,000 paid to A.

(b) *Other illegal payments*—(1) *In general.* No deduction shall be allowed under section 162(a) for any payment (other than a payment described in paragraph (a) of this section) made, directly or indirectly, to any person, if the payment constitutes an illegal bribe, illegal kickback, or other illegal payment under the laws of the United States (as defined in paragraph (a)(4) of this section), or under any State law (but only if such State law is generally enforced), which subjects the payor to a criminal penalty or the loss (including a suspension) of license or privilege to engage in a trade or business (whether or not such penalty or loss is actually imposed upon the tax-

payer). For purposes of this paragraph, a kickback includes a payment in consideration of the referral of a client, patient, or customer. This paragraph applies only to payments made after December 30, 1969.

(2) *State law.* For purposes of this paragraph, State law means a statute of a State or the District of Columbia.

(3) *Generally enforced.* For purposes of this paragraph, a State law shall be considered to be generally enforced unless it is never enforced or the only persons normally charged with violations thereof in the State (or the District of Columbia) enacting the law are infamous or those whose violations are extraordinarily flagrant. For example, a criminal statute of a State shall be considered to be generally enforced unless violations of the statute which are brought to the attention of appropriate enforcement authorities do not result in any enforcement action in the absence of unusual circumstances.

(4) *Burden of proof.* In any proceeding involving the issue of whether, for purposes of section 162(c)(2), a payment constitutes an illegal bribe, illegal kickback, or other illegal payment the burden of proof in respect of such issue shall be upon the Commissioner to the same extent as he bears the burden of proof in civil fraud cases under section 7454 (*i.e.,* he must prove the illegality of the payment by clear and convincing evidence).

(5) *Example.* The application of this paragraph may be illustrated by the following example:

Example. X Corp., a calendar-year taxpayer, is engaged in the ship repair business in State Y. During 1970, repairs on foreign ships accounted for a substantial part of its total business. It was X Corp.'s practice to kick back approximately 10 percent of the repair bill to the captain and chief engineer of all foreign-owned vessels, which kickbacks are illegal under a law of State Y (which is generally enforced) and potentially subject X Corp. to fines. During 1970, X Corp. paid $50,000 in such kickbacks. On X Corp.'s return for 1970, a deduction under section 162 was taken for the $50,000. The deduction of the $50,000 of illegal kickbacks during 1970 is disallowed under section 162(c)(2), whether or not X Corp. is prosecuted with respect to the kickbacks.

(c) *Kickbacks, rebates, and bribes under medicare and medicaid.* No deduction shall be allowed under section 162(a) for any kickback, rebate, or bribe (whether or not illegal) made on or after December 10, 1971, by any provider of services, supplier, physician, or other person who furnishes items or services for which payment is or may be

Reg. § 1.162-18(a)(4)

made under the Social Security Act, as amended, or in whole or in part out of Federal funds under a State plan approved under such Act, if such kickback, rebate, or bribe is made in connection with the furnishing of such items or services or the making or receipt of such payments. For purposes of this paragraph, a kickback includes a payment in consideration of the referral of a client, patient, or customer. [Reg. § 1.162-18.]

☐ [*T.D. 6448, 1-26-60. Amended by T.D. 7345, 2-19-75.*]

[Reg. § 1.162-19]

§ 1.162-19. Capital contributions to Federal National Mortgage Association.—(a) *In general.* The initial holder of stock of the Federal National Mortgage Association (FNMA) which is issued pursuant to section 303(c) of the Federal National Mortgage Association Charter Act (12 U.S.C., sec. 1718) in a taxable year beginning after December 31, 1959, shall treat the excess, if any, of the issuance price (the amount of capital contributions evidenced by a share of stock) over the fair market value of the stock as of the issue date of such stock as an ordinary and necessary business expense paid or incurred during the year in which occurs the date of issuance of the stock. To the extent that a sale to FNMA of mortgage paper gives rise to the issuance of a share of FNMA stock during a taxable year beginning after December 31, 1959, such sale is to be treated in a manner consistent with the purpose for, and the legislative intent underlying the enactment of, the provisions of section 8, Act of September 14, 1960 (Public Law 86-779, 74 Stat. 1003). Thus, for the purpose of determining an initial holder's gain or loss from the sale to FNMA of mortgage paper, with respect to which a share of FNMA stock is issued in a taxable year beginning after December 31, 1959 (irrespective of when the sale is made), the amount realized by the initial holder from the sale of the mortgage paper is the amount of the "FNMA purchase price". The "FNMA purchase price" is the gross amount of the consideration agreed upon between FNMA and the initial holder for the purchase of the mortgage paper, without regard to any deduction therefrom as, for example, a deduction representing a capital contribution or a purchase or marketing fee. The date of issuance of the stock is the date which appears on the stock certificates of the initial holder as the date of issue. The initial holder is the original purchaser who is issued stock of the Federal National Mortgage Association pursuant to section 303(c) of the Act, and who appears on the books of FNMA as the initial holder. In determining the period for which the

initial holder has held such stock, such period shall begin with the date of issuance.

(b) *Examples.* The provisions of paragraph (a) of this section may be illustrated by the following examples:

Example (1). A, a banking institution which reports its income on a calendar year basis, sold mortgage paper with an outstanding principal balance of $12,500 to FNMA on October 17, 1960. The FNMA purchase price was $11,500. A's basis for the mortgage paper was $10,500. In accordance with the terms of the contract, FNMA deducted $375 ($250 representing capital contribution and $125 representing purchase and marketing fee) from the amount of the purchase price. FNMA credited A's account with the amount of the capital contribution. A stock certificate evidencing two shares of FNMA common stock of $100 par value was mailed to A and FNMA deducted $200 from A's account, leaving a net balance of $50 in such account. The stock certificate, bearing an issue date of November 1, 1960, was received by A on November 7, 1960. The fair market value of a share of FNMA stock on October 17, 1960, was $65, on November 1, 1960, was $67, and on November 7, 1960, was $68. A may deduct $66, the difference between the issuance price ($200) and the fair market value ($134) of the two shares of stock on the date of issuance (November 1, 1960), as a business expense for the taxable year 1960. The basis of each share of stock issued as of November 1, 1960 will be $67. See section 1054 and § 1.1054-1. A's gain from the sale of the mortgage paper is $875 computed as follows:

Amount realized (FNMA purchase price)	$11,500
A's basis in mortgage paper	$10,500
Purchase and marketing fee	125 10,625
Gain on sale	875

Example (2). Assume the same facts as in Example (1), and, in addition, that A sold to FNMA on December 15, 1960, additional mortgage paper having an outstanding principal balance of $12,500. FNMA deducted from the FNMA purchase price $250 representing capital contribution and credited A's account with this amount. A then had a total credit of $300 to his account consisting of the $50 balance from the transaction described in Example (1) and $250 from the December 15th transaction. A stock certificate evidencing three shares of FNMA common stock of $100 par value was mailed to A and FNMA deducted $300 from A's account. The stock certificate, bearing an issue date of January 1, 1961, was received by A on January 9, 1961. The fair market value of a share of FNMA stock on January 1, 1961, was $69. A may deduct $93, the difference between the issuance price ($300) and the fair market value ($207) of the three shares of stock on the date of issuance (January 1, 1961), as a business expense for the taxable year 1961. The gain or loss on the sale of mortgage paper on December 15, 1960, is reportable for the taxable year 1960. [Reg. § 1.162-19.]

☐ [*T.D.* 6690, 11-18-63.]

[Reg. § 1.162-20]

§ 1.162-20. **Expenditures attributable to lobbying, political campaigns, attempts to influence legislation, etc., and certain advertising.**—(a) *In general*—(1) *Scope of section.* This section contains rules governing the deductibility or non-deductibility of expenditures for lobbying purposes, for the promotion or defeat of legislation, for political campaign purposes (including the support of or opposition to any candidate for public office) or for carrying on propaganda (including advertising) related to any of the foregoing purposes. For rules applicable to such expenditures in respect of taxable years beginning before January 1, 1963, and for taxable years beginning after December 31, 1962, see paragraphs (b) and (c), respectively, of this section. This section also deals with expenditures for institutional or "good will" advertising.

(2) *Institutional or "good will" advertising.* Expenditures for institutional or "good will" advertising which keeps the taxpayer's name before the public are generally deductible as ordinary and necessary business expenses provided the expenditures are related to the patronage the taxpayer might reasonably expect in the future. For example, a deduction will ordinarily be allowed for the cost of advertising which keeps the taxpayer's name before the public in connection with encouraging contributions to such organizations as the Red Cross, the purchase of United States Savings Bonds, or participation in similar causes. In like fashion, expenditures for advertising which presents views on economic, financial, social, or other subjects of a general nature, but which does not involve any of the activities specified in paragraph (b) or (c) of this section for which a deduction is not allowable, are deductible if they otherwise meet the requirements of the regulations under section 162.

(b) *Taxable years beginning before January 1, 1963*—(1) *In general.* (i) For taxable years beginning before January 1, 1963, expenditures for lobbying purposes, for the promotion or defeat of legislation, for political campaign purposes (including the support of or opposition to any candidate for public office), or for carrying on

propaganda (including advertising) related to any of the foregoing purposes are not deductible from gross income. For example, the cost of advertising to promote or defeat legislation or to influence the public with respect to the desirability or undesirability of proposed legislation is not deductible as a business expense, even though the legislation may directly affect the taxpayer's business.

(ii) If a substantial part of the activities of an organization, such as a labor union or a trade association, consists of one or more of the activities specified in the first sentence of this subparagraph, deduction will be allowed only for such portion of the dues or other payments to the organization as the taxpayer can clearly establish is attributable to activities other than those so specified. The determination of whether such specified activities constitute a substantial part of an organization's activities shall be based on all the facts and circumstances. In no event shall special assessments or similar payments (including an increase in dues) made to any organization for any of such specified purposes be deductible. For other provisions relating to the deductibility of dues and other payments to an organization, such as a labor union or a trade association, see paragraph (c) of § 1.162-15.

(2) *Expenditures for promotion or defeat of legislation.* For purposes of this paragraph, expenditures for the promotion or the defeat of legislation include, but shall not be limited to, expenditures for the purpose of attempting to—

(i) Influence members of a legislative body directly, or indirectly by urging or encouraging the public to contact such members for the purpose of proposing, supporting, or opposing legislation, or

(ii) Influence the public to approve or reject a measure in a referendum, initiative, vote on a constitutional amendment, or similar procedure.

(c) *Taxable years beginning after December 31, 1962*—(1) *In general.* For taxable years beginning after December 31, 1962, certain types of expenses incurred with respect to legislative matters are deductible under section 162(a) if they otherwise meet the requirements of the regulations under section 162. These deductible expenses are described in subparagraph (2) of this paragraph. All other expenditures for lobbying purposes, for the promotion or defeat of legislation (see paragraph (b)(2) of this section), for political campaign purposes (including the support of or opposition to any candidate for public office), or for carrying on propaganda (including advertising) relating to any of the foregoing purposes are not deductible from gross income for such taxable years. For the disallowance of deductions for bad

Reg. § 1.162-20(a)(1)

debts and worthless securities of a political party, see § 1.271-1. For the disallowance of deductions for certain indirect political contributions, such as the cost of certain advertising and the cost of admission to certain dinners, programs, and inaugural events, see § 1.276-1.

(2) *Appearances, etc., with respect to legislation*—(i) *General rule.* Pursuant to the provisions of section 162(e), expenses incurred with respect to legislative matters which may be deductible are those ordinary and necessary expenses (including, but not limited to, traveling expenses described in section 162(a)(2) and the cost of preparing testimony) paid or incurred by the taxpayer during a taxable year beginning after December 31, 1962, in carrying on any trade or business which are in direct connection with—

(a) appearances before, submission of statements to, or sending communications to, the committees, or individual members of Congress or of any legislative body of a State, a possession of the United States, or a political subdivision of any of the foregoing with respect to legislation or proposed legislation of direct interest to the taxpayer, or

(b) communication of information between the taxpayer and an organization of which he is a member with respect to legislation or proposed legislation of direct interest to the taxpayer and to such organization.

For provisions relating to dues paid or incurred with respect to an organization of which the taxpayer is a member, see subparagraph (3) of this paragraph.

(ii) *Legislation or proposed legislation of direct interest to the taxpayer*—(a) *Legislation or proposed legislation.* The term "legislation or proposed legislation" includes bills and resolutions introduced by a member of Congress or other legislative body referred to in subdivision (i)(a) of this subparagraph for consideration by such body as well as oral or written proposals for legislative action submitted to the legislative body or to a committee or member of such body.

(b) *Direct interest*—(1) *In general.* (i) Legislation or proposed legislation is of direct interest to a taxpayer if the legislation or proposed legislation is of such a nature that it will, or may reasonably be expected to, affect the trade or business of the taxpayer. It is immaterial whether the effect, or expected effect, on the trade or business will be beneficial or detrimental to the trade or business or whether it will be immediate. If legislation or proposed legislation has such a relationship to a trade or business that the expenses of any appearance or communication in connection with the legislation meets the ordinary

and necessary test of section 162(a), then such legislation ordinarily meets the direct interest test of section 162(e). However, if the nature of the legislation or proposed legislation is such that the likelihood of its having an effect on the trade or business of the taxpayer is remote or speculative, the legislation or proposed legislation is not of direct interest to the taxpayer. Legislation or proposed legislation which will not affect the trade or business of the taxpayer is not of direct interest to the taxpayer even though such legislation will affect the personal, living, or family activities or expenses of the taxpayer. Legislation or proposed legislation is not of direct interest to a taxpayer merely because it may affect business in general; however, if the legislation or proposed legislation will, or may reasonably be expected to, affect the taxpayer's trade or business it will be of direct interest to the taxpayer even though it also will affect the trade or business of other taxpayers or business in general. To meet the direct interest test, it is not necessary that all provisions of the legislation or proposed legislation have an effect, or expected effect, on the taxpayer's trade or business. The test will be met if one of the provisions of the legislation has the specified effect. Legislation or proposed legislation will be considered to be of direct interest to a membership organization if it is of direct interest to the organization, as such, or if it is of direct interest to one or more of its members.

(ii) Legislation which would increase or decrease the taxes applicable to the trade or business, increase or decrease the operating costs or earnings of the trade or business, or increase or decrease the administrative burdens connected with the trade or business meets the direct interest test. Legislation which would increase the social security benefits or liberalize the right to such benefits meets the direct interest test because such changes in the social security benefits may reasonably be expected to affect the retirement benefits which the employer will be asked to provide his employees or to increase his taxes. Legislation which would impose a retailer's sales tax is of direct interest to a retailer because, although the tax may be passed on to his customers, collection of the tax will impose additional burdens on the retailer, and because the increased cost of his products to the consumer may reduce the demand for them. Legislation which would provide an income tax credit or exclusion for shareholders is of direct interest to a corporation, because those tax benefits may increase the sources of capital available to the corporation. Legislation which would favorably or adversely affect the business of a competitor so as to affect the taxpayer's competitive position is of direct interest to the taxpayer.

Reg. § 1.162-20(c)(2)

Legislation which would improve the school system of a community is of direct interest to a membership organization comprised of employers in the community because the improved school system is likely to make the community more attractive to prospective employees of such employers. On the other hand, proposed legislation relating to Presidential succession in the event of the death of the President has only a remote and speculative effect on any trade or business and therefore does not meet the direct interest test. Similarly, if a corporation is represented before a congressional committee to oppose an appropriation bill merely because of a desire to bring increased Government economy with the hope that such economy will eventually cause a reduction in the Federal income tax, the legislation does not meet the direct interest test because any effect it may have upon the corporation's trade or business is highly speculative.

(2) *Appearances, etc., by expert witnesses.* (*i*) An appearance or communication (of a type described in paragraph (c)(2)(i)(*a*) of this section) by an individual in connection with legislation or proposed legislation shall be considered to be with respect to legislation of direct interest to such individual if the legislation is in a field in which he specializes as an employee, if the appearance or communication is not on behalf of his employer, and if it is customary for individuals in his type of employment to publicly express their views in respect of matters in their field of competence. Expenses incurred by such an individual in connection with such an appearance or communication, including traveling expenses properly allocable thereto, represent ordinary and necessary business expenses and are, therefore, deductible under section 162. For example, if a university professor who teaches in the field of money and banking appears, on his own behalf, before a legislative committee to testify on proposed legislation regarding the banking system, his expenses incurred in connection with such appearance are deductible under section 162 since university professors customarily take an active part in the development of the law in their field of competence and publicly communicate the results of their work.

(*ii*) An appearance or communication (of a type described in paragraph (c)(2)(i)(*a*) of this section) by an employee or self-employed individual in connection with legislation or proposed legislation shall be considered to be with respect to legislation of direct interest to such person if the legislation is in the field in which he specializes in his business (or as an employee) and if the appearance or communication is made pursuant to an invitation extended to him individually for the purpose of receiving his expert testimony. Expenses incurred by an employee or self-employed individual in connection with such an appearance or communication, including traveling expenses properly allocable thereto, represent ordinary and necessary business expenses and are, therefore, deductible under section 162. For example, if a self-employed individual is personally invited by a congressional committee to testify on proposed legislation in the field in which he specializes in his business, his expenses incurred in connection with such appearance are deductible under section 162. If a self-employed individual makes an appearance, on his own behalf, before a legislative committee without having been extended an invitation his expenses will be deductible to the extent otherwise provided in this paragraph.

(3) *Nominations, etc.* A taxpayer does not have a direct interest in matters such as nominations, appointments, or the operation of the legislative body.

(iii) *Allowable expenses.* To be deductible under section 162(a), expenditures which meet the tests of deductibility under the provisions of this paragraph must also qualify as ordinary and necessary business expenses under section 162(a) and, in addition, be in direct connection with the carrying on of the activities specified in subdivision (i)(*a*) or (i)(*b*) of this subparagraph. For example, a taxpayer appearing before a committee of the Congress to present testimony concerning legislation or proposed legislation in which he has a direct interest may deduct the ordinary and necessary expenses directly connected with his appearance, such as traveling expenses described in section 162(a)(2), and the cost of preparing testimony.

(3) *Deductibility of dues and other payments to an organization.* If a substantial part of the activities of an organization, such as a labor union or a trade association, consists of one or more of the activities to which this paragraph relates (legislative matters, political campaigns, etc.,) exclusive of any activity constituting an appearance or communication with respect to legislation or proposed legislation of direct interest to the organization (see subparagraph (2)(ii)(*b*)(*1*)), a deduction will be allowed only for such portion of the dues or other payments to the organization as the taxpayer can clearly establish is attributable to activities to which this paragraph does not relate and to any activity constituting an appearance or communication with respect to legislation or proposed legislation of direct interest to the organization. The determination of whether a substantial part of an organization's activities consists of one

Reg. § 1.162-20(c)(3)

or more of the activities to which this paragraph relates (exclusive of appearance or communications with respect to legislation or proposed legislation of direct interest to the organization) shall be based on all the facts and circumstances. In no event shall a deduction be allowed for that portion of a special assessment or similar payment (including an increase in dues) made to any organization for any activity to which this paragraph relates if the activity does not constitute any appearance or communication with respect to legislation or proposed legislation of direct interest to the organization. If an organization pays or incurs expenses allocable to legislative activities which meet the tests of subdivisions (i) and (ii) of subparagraph (2) of this paragraph (appearances or communications with respect to legislation or proposed legislation of direct interest to the organization), on behalf of its members, the dues paid by a taxpayer are deductible to the extent used for such activities. Dues paid by a taxpayer will be considered to be used for such an activity, and thus deductible, although the legislation or proposed legislation involved is not of direct interest to the taxpayer, if, pursuant to the provisions of subparagraph (2)(ii)(*b*)(*1*) of this paragraph, the legislation or proposed legislation is of direct interest to the organization, as such, or is of direct interest to one or more members of the organization. For other provisions relating to the deductibility of dues and other payments to an organization, such as a labor union or a trade association, see paragraph (c) of § 1.162-15.

(4) *Limitations.* No deduction shall be allowed under section 162(a) for any amount paid or incurred (whether by way of contribution, gift, or otherwise) in connection with any attempt to influence the general public, or segments thereof, with respect to legislative matters, elections, or referendums. For example, no deduction shall be allowed for any expenses incurred in connection with "grassroot" campaigns or any other attempts to urge or encourage the public to contact members of a legislative body for the purpose of proposing, supporting, or opposing legislation.

(5) *Expenses paid or incurred after December 31, 1993, in connection with influencing legislation other than certain local legislation.* The provisions of paragraphs (c)(1) through (3) of this section are superseded for expenses paid or incurred after December 31, 1993, in connection with influencing legislation (other than certain local legislation) to the extent inconsistent with section 162(e)(1)(A) (as limited by section 162(e)(2)) and § § 1.162-20(d) and 1.162-29.

(d) *Dues allocable to expenditures after 1993.* No deduction is allowed under section 162(a) for the portion of dues or other similar amounts paid by the taxpayer to an organization exempt from tax (other than an organization described in section 501(c)(3)) which the organization notifies the taxpayer under section 6033(e)(1)(A)(ii) is allocable to expenditures to which section 162(e)(1) applies. The first sentence of this paragraph (d) applies to dues or other similar amounts whether or not paid on or before December 31, 1993. Section 1.162-20(c)(3) is superseded to the extent inconsistent with this paragraph (d). [Reg. § 1.162-20.]

☐ [*T.D.* 6819, 4-19-65. *Amended by T.D.* 6996, 1-17-69 *and T.D.* 8602, 7-20-95.]

[Reg. § 1.162-21]

§ 1.162-21. **Fines and penalties.**—(a) *In general.* No deduction shall be allowed under section 162(a) for any fine or similar penalty paid to—

(1) The government of the United States, a State, a territory or possession of the United States, the District of Columbia, or the Commonwealth of Puerto Rico;

(2) The government of a foreign country; or

(3) A political subdivision of, or

corporation or other entity serving as an agency or instrumentality of, any of the above.

(b) *Definition.* (1) For purposes of this section a fine or similar penalty includes an amount—

(i) Paid pursuant to conviction or a plea of guilty or *nolo contendere* for a crime (felony or misdemeanor) in a criminal proceeding;

(ii) Paid as a civil penalty imposed by Federal, State, or local law, including additions to tax and additional amounts and assessable penalties imposed by chapter 68 of the Internal Revenue Code of 1954;

(iii) Paid in settlement of the taxpayer's actual or potential liability for a fine or penalty (civil or criminal); or

(iv) Forfeited as collateral posted in connection with a proceeding which could result in imposition of such a fine or penalty.

(2) The amount of a fine or penalty does not include legal fees and related expenses paid or incurred in the defense of a prosecution or civil action arising from a violation of the law imposing the fine or civil penalty, nor court costs assessed against the taxpayer, or stenographic and printing charges. Compensatory damages (including damages under section 4A of the Clayton Act (15 U.S.C. 15a), as amended) paid to a government do not constitute a fine or penalty.

(c) *Examples.* The application of this section may be illustrated by the following examples:

Example (1). M Corp. was indicted under section 1 of the Sherman Anti-Trust Act (15 U.S.C. 1) for fixing and maintaining prices of certain electrical products. M Corp. was convicted and fined $50,000. The United States sued M Corp. under section 4A of the Clayton Act (15 U.S.C. 15a) for $100,000, the amount of the actual damages resulting from the price fixing of which M Corp. was convicted. Pursuant to a final judgment entered in the civil action, M Corp. paid the United States $100,000 in damages. Section 162(f) precludes M Corp. from deducting the fine of $50,000 as a trade or business expense. Section 162(f) does not preclude it from deducting the $100,000 paid to the United States as actual damages.

Example (2). N Corp. was found to have violated 33 U.S.C. 1321(b)(3) when a vessel it operated discharged oil in harmful quantities into the navigable waters of the United States. A civil penalty under 33 U.S.C. 1321(b)(6) of $5,000 was assessed against N Corp. with respect to the discharge. N Corp. paid $5,000 to the Coast Guard in payment of the civil penalty. Section 162(f) precludes N Corp. from deducting the $5,000 penalty.

Example (3). O Corp., a manufacturer of motor vehicles, was found to have violated 42 U.S.C. 1857f-2(a)(1) by selling a new motor vehicle which was not covered by the required certificate of conformity. Pursuant to 42 U.S.C. 1857f-4, O Corp. was required to pay, and did pay, a civil penalty of $10,000. In addition, pursuant to 42 U.S.C. 1857f-5a(c)(1), O Corp. was required to expend, and did expend, $500 in order to remedy the noncomformity of that motor vehicle. Section 162(f) precludes O Corp. from deducting the $10,000 penalty as a trade or business expense, but does not preclude it from deducting the $500 which it expended to remedy the nonconformity.

Example (4). P Corp. was the operator of a coal mine in which occurred a violation of a mandatory safety standard prescribed by the Federal Coal Mine Health and Safety Act of 1969 (30 U.S.C. 801 et seq.). Pursuant to 30 U.S.C. 819(a), a civil penalty of $10,000 was assessed against P Corp., and P Corp. paid the penalty. Section 162(f) precludes P Corp. from deducting the $10,000 penalty.

Example (5). Q Corp., a common carrier engaged in interstate commerce by railroad, hauled a railroad car which was not equipped with efficient hand brakes, in violation of 45 U.S.C. 11. Q Corp. was found to be liable for a penalty of $250 pursuant to 45 U.S.C. 13. Q Corp. paid that penalty. Section 162(f) precludes Q Corp. from deducting the $250 penalty.

Example (6). R Corp. owned and operated on the highways of State X a truck weighing in excess of the amount permitted under the law of State X. R Corp. was found to have violated the law and was assessed a fine of $85 which it paid to State X. Section 162(f) precludes R Corp. from deducting the amount so paid.

Example (7). S Corp. was found to have violated a law of State Y which prohibited the emission into the air of particulate matter in excess of a limit set forth in a regulation promulgated under that law. The Environmental Quality Hearing Board of State Y assessed a fine of $500 against S Corp. The fine was payable to State Y, and S Corp. paid it. Section 162(f) precludes S Corp. from deducting the $500 fine.

Example (8). T Corp. was found by a magistrate of City Z to be operating in such city an apartment building which did not conform to a provision of the city housing code requiring operable fire escapes on apartment buildings of that type. Upon the basis of the magistrate's finding, T Corp. was required to pay, and did pay, a fine of $200 to City Z. Section 162(f) precludes T Corp. from deducting the $200 fine. [Reg. § 1.162-21.]

□ [*T.D.* 7345, 2-19-75. Amended by *T.D.* 7366, 7-10-75.]

[Reg. § 1.162-22]

§ **1.162-22. Treble damage payments under the antitrust laws.**—(a) *In general.* In the case of a taxpayer who after December 31, 1969, either is convicted in a criminal action of a violation of the Federal antitrust laws or enters a plea of guilty or *nolo contendere* to an indictment or information charging such a violation, and whose conviction or plea does not occur in a new trial following an appeal of a conviction on or before such date, no deduction shall be allowed under section 162(a) for two-thirds of any amount paid or incurred after December 31, 1969, with respect to—

(1) Any judgment for damages entered against the taxpayer under section 4 of the Clayton Act (15 U.S.C. 15), as amended, on account of such violation or any related violation of the Federal antitrust laws, provided such related violation occurred prior to the date of the final judgment of such conviction, or

(2) Settlement of any action brought under such section 4 on account of such violation or related violation.

For purposes of this section, where a civil judgment has been entered or a settlement made with respect to a violation of the antitrust laws and a criminal proceeding is based upon the same viola-

Reg. § 1.162-22(a)(1)

tion, the criminal proceeding need not have been brought prior to the civil judgment or settlement. If, in his return for any taxable year, a taxpayer claims a deduction for an amount paid or incurred with respect to a judgment or settlement described in the first sentence of this paragraph and is subsequently convicted of a violation of the antitrust laws which makes a portion of such amount unallowable, then the taxpayer shall file an amended return for such taxable year on which the amount of the deduction is appropriately reduced. Attorney's fees, court costs, and other amounts paid or incurred in connection with a controversy under such section 4 which meet the requirements of section 162 are deductible under that section. For purposes of subparagraph (2) of this paragraph, the amount paid or incurred in settlement shall not include amounts attributable to the plaintiff's costs of suit and attorney's fees, to the extent that such costs or fees have actually been paid.

(b) *Conviction.* For purposes of paragraph (a) of this section, a taxpayer is convicted of a violation of the antitrust laws if a judgment of conviction (whether or not a final judgment) with respect to such violation has been entered against him, provided a subsequent final judgment of acquittal has not been entered or criminal prosecution with respect to such violation terminated without a final judgment of conviction. During the pendency of an appeal or other action directly contesting a judgment of conviction, the taxpayer should file a protective claim for credit or refund to avoid being barred by the period of limitations on credit or refund under section 6511.

(c) *Related violation.* For purposes of this section, a violation of the Federal antitrust laws is related to a subsequent violation if (1) with respect to the subsequent violation the United States obtains both a judgment in a criminal proceeding and an injunction against the taxpayer, and (2) the taxpayer's actions which constituted the prior violation would have contravened such injunction if such injunction were applicable at the time of the prior violation.

(d) *Settlement following a dismissal of an action or amendment of the complaint.* For purposes of paragraph (a)(2) of this section, an amount may be considered as paid in settlement of an action even though the action is dismissed or otherwise disposed of prior to such settlement or the complaint is amended to eliminate the claim with respect to the violation or related violation.

(e) *Antitrust laws.* The term "antitrust laws" as used in section 162(g) and this section shall include the Federal acts enumerated in paragraph

(1) of section 1 of the Clayton Act (15 U.S.C. 12), as amended.

(f) *Examples.* The application of this section may be illustrated by the following examples:

Example (1). In 1970, the United States instituted a criminal prosecution against X Co., Y Co., A, the president of X Co., and B, the president of Y Co., under section 1 of the Sherman Anti-Trust Act, 15 U.S.C. 1. In the indictment, the defendants were charged with conspiring to fix and maintain prices of electrical transformers from 1965 to 1970. All defendants entered pleas of *nolo contendere* to these charges. These pleas were accepted and judgments of conviction entered. In a companion civil suit, the United States obtained an injunction prohibiting the defendants from conspiring to fix and maintain prices in the electrical transformer market. Thereafter, Z Co. sued X Co. and Y Co. for $300,000 in treble damages under section 4 of the Clayton Act. Z Co's complaint alleged that the criminal conspiracy between X Co. and Y Co. forced Z Co. to pay excessive prices for electrical transformers. X Co. and Y Co. each paid Z Co. $85,000 in full settlement of Z Co.'s action. Of each $85,000 paid, $10,000 was attributable to court costs and attorney's fees actually paid by Z Co. Under section 162(g), X Co. and Y Co. are each precluded from deducting as a trade or business expense more than $35,000 of the $85,000 paid to Z Co. in settlement.

$$\left(\$10,000 + \frac{\$85,000 - \$10,000}{3} \right)$$

Example (2). Assume the same facts as in example (1) except that Z Co.'s claim for treble damages was based on a conspiracy to fix and maintain prices in the sale of electrical transformers during 1963. Although the criminal prosecution of the defendants did not involve 1963 (a year barred by the applicable criminal statute of limitations when the prosecution was instituted), Z Co.'s pleadings alleged that the civil statute of limitations had been tolled by the defendants' fraudulent concealment of their conspiracy. Since the United States has obtained both a judgment in a criminal proceeding and an injunction against the defendants in connection with their activities from 1965 to 1970, and the alleged actions of the defendants in 1963 would have contravened such injunction if it were applicable in 1963, the alleged violation in 1963 is related to the violation from 1965 to 1970. Accordingly, the tax consequences to X Co. and Y Co. of the payments of $85,000 in settlement of Z Co.'s claim against X Co. and Y Co. are the same as in example (1).

Reg. § 1.162-22(f)

Example (3). Assume the same facts as in example (1) except that Z Co.'s claim for treble damages was based on a conspiracy to fix and maintain prices with respect to electrical insulators for high-tension power poles. Since the civil action was not based on the same violation of the Federal antitrust laws as the criminal action, or on a related violation (a violation which would have contravened the injunction if it were applicable), X Co. and Y Co. are not precluded by section 162(g) from deducting as a trade or business expense the entire $85,000 paid by each in settlement of the civil action. [Reg. § 1.162-22.]

☐ [*T.D.* 7217, 11-9-72.]

[Reg. § 1.162-25]

§ 1.162-25. Deductions with respect to noncash fringe benefits.—(a) [Reserved]

(b) *Employee.* If an employer provides the use of a vehicle (as defined in § 1.61-21(e)(2)) to an employee as a noncash fringe benefit and includes the entire value of the benefit in the employee's gross income without taking into account any exclusion for a working condition fringe allowable under section 132 and the regulations thereunder, the employee may deduct that value multiplied by the percentage of the total use of the vehicle that is in connection with the employer's trade or business (business value). For taxable years beginning before January 1, 1990, the employee may deduct the business value from gross income in determining adjusted gross income. For taxable years beginning on or after January 1, 1990, the employee may deduct the business value only as a miscellaneous itemized deduction in determining taxable income, subject to the 2-percent floor provided in section 67. If the employer determines the value of the noncash fringe benefit under a special accounting rule that allows the employer to treat the value of benefits provided during the last two months of the calendar year or any shorter period as paid during the subsequent calendar year, then the employee must determine the deduction allowable under this paragraph (b) without regard to any use of the benefit during those last two months or any shorter period. The employee may not use a cents-per-mile valuation method to determine the deduction allowable under this paragraph (b). [Reg. § 1.162-25.]

☐ [*T.D.* 8451, 12-4-92.]

[Reg. § 1.162-25T]

§ 1.162-25T. Deductions with respect to noncash fringe benefits (temporary).—(a) *Employer.* If an employer includes the value of a noncash fringe benefit in an employee's gross income, the employer may not deduct this amount as compensation for services, but rather may de-

duct only the costs incurred by the employer in providing the benefit to the employee. The employer may be allowed a cost recovery deduction under section 168 or a deduction under section 179 for an expense not chargeable to capital account, or, if the noncash fringe benefit is property leased by the employer, a deduction for the ordinary and necessary business expense of leasing the property.

(b) [Reserved]

(c) *Examples.* The following examples illustrate the provisions of this section.

Example (1). On January 1, 1986, X Company owns and provides the use of an automobile with a fair market value of $20,000 to E, an employee, for the entire calendar year. Both X and E compute taxable income on the basis of the calendar year. Seventy percent of the use of the automobile by E is in connection with X's trade or business. If X uses the special rule provided in § 1.61-2T for valuing the availability of the automobile and takes into account the amount excludable as a working condition fringe, X would include $1,680 ($5,600, the Annual Lease Value, less 70 percent of $5,600) in E's gross income for 1986. X may not deduct the amount included in E's income as compensation for services. X may, however, determine a cost recovery deduction under section 168, subject to the limitations under section 280F, for taxable year 1986.

Example (2). The facts are the same as in example (1), except that X includes $5,600 in E's gross income, the value of the noncash fringe benefit without taking into account the amount excludable as a working condition fringe. X may not deduct that amount as compensation for services, but may determine a cost recovery deduction under section 168, subject to the limitations under section 280F. For purposes of determining adjusted gross income, E may deduct $3,920 ($5,600 multiplied by the percent of business use). [Temporary Reg. § 1.162-25T.]

☐ [*T.D.* 8004, 1-2-85. *Amended by T.D.* 8061, 11-1-85; *T.D.* 8063, 12-18-85; *T.D.* 8276, 12-7-89 *and T.D.* 8451, 12-4-92.]

[Reg. § 1.162-27]

§ 1.162-27. Certain employee remuneration in excess of $1,000,000.—(a) *Scope.* This section provides rules for the application of the $1 million deduction limit under section 162(m) of the Internal Revenue Code. Paragraph (b) of this section provides the general rule limiting deductions under section 162(m). Paragraph (c) of this section provides definitions of generally applicable terms. Paragraph (d) of this section provides an exception from the deduction limit for compensation payable on a commission basis. Paragraph (e) of this section provides an exception for qualified performance-based compensation. Paragraphs (f) and (g) of this section provide special rules for corporations that become publicly held corporations and payments that are subject to section 280G, respectively. Paragraph (h) of this section provides transition rules, including the rules for contracts that are grandfathered and not subject to section 162(m). Paragraph (j) of this section contains the effective date provisions. For rules concerning the deductibility of compensation for services that are not covered by section 162(m) and this section, see section 162(a)(1) and § 1.162-7. This section is not determinative as to whether compensation meets the requirements of section 162(a)(1).

(b) *Limitation on deduction.* Section 162(m) precludes a deduction under chapter 1 of the Internal Revenue Code by any publicly held corporation for compensation paid to any covered employee to the extent that the compensation for the taxable year exceeds $1,000,000.

(c) *Definitions*—(1) *Publicly held corporation*—(i) *General rule.* A *publicly held corporation* means any corporation issuing any class of common equity securities required to be registered under section 12 of the Exchange Act. A corporation is not considered publicly held if the registration of its equity securities is voluntary. For purposes of this section, whether a corporation is publicly held is determined based solely on whether, as of the last day of its taxable year, the corporation is subject to the reporting obligations of section 12 of the Exchange Act.

(ii) *Affiliated groups.* A publicly held corporation includes an affiliated group of corporations, as defined in section 1504 (determined without regard to section 1504(b)). For purposes of this section, however, an affiliated group of corporations does not include any subsidiary that is itself a publicly held corporation. Such a publicly held subsidiary, and its subsidiaries (if any), are separately subject to this section. If a covered employee is paid compensation in a taxable year by more than one member of an affiliated group, compensation paid by each member of the affiliated group is aggregated with compensation paid to the covered employee by all other members of the group. Any amount disallowed as a deduction by this section must be prorated among the payor corporations in proportion to the amount of compensation paid to the covered employee by each such corporation in the taxable year.

(2) *Covered employee*—(i) *General rule.* A *covered employee* means any individual who, on the last day of the taxable year, is—

(A) The chief executive officer of the corporation or is acting in such capacity; or

(B) Among the four highest compensated officers (other than the chief executive officer).

(ii) *Application of rules of the Securities and Exchange Commission.* Whether an individual is the chief executive officer described in paragraph (c)(2)(i)(A) of this section or an officer described in paragraph (c)(2)(i)(B) of this section is determined pursuant to the executive compensation disclosure rules under the Exchange Act.

(3) *Compensation*—(i) *In general.* For purposes of the deduction limitation described in paragraph (b) of this section, *compensation* means the aggregate amount allowable as a deduction under chapter 1 of the Internal Revenue Code for the taxable year (determined without regard to section 162(m)) for remuneration for services performed by a covered employee, whether or not the services were performed during the taxable year.

(ii) *Exceptions. Compensation* does not include—

(A) Remuneration covered in section 3121(a)(5)(A) through section 3121(a)(5)(D) (concerning remuneration that is not treated as *wages* for purposes of the Federal Insurance Contributions Act); and

(B) Remuneration consisting of any benefit provided to or on behalf of an employee if, at the time the benefit is provided, it is reasonable to believe that the employee will be able to exclude it from gross income. In addition, compensation does not include salary reduction contributions described in section 3121(v)(1).

(4) *Compensation Committee.* The *compensation committee* means the committee of directors (including any subcommittee of directors) of the publicly held corporation that has the authority to establish and administer performance goals described in paragraph (e)(2) of this section, and to certify that performance goals are attained, as described in paragraph (e)(5) of this section. A committee of directors is not treated as failing to have the authority to establish performance goals merely because the goals are ratified by the board of directors of the publicly held corporation or, if applicable, any other committee of the board of directors. See paragraph (e)(3) of this section for rules concerning the composition of the compensation committee.

(5) *Exchange Act.* The *Exchange Act* means the Securities Exchange Act of 1934.

(6) *Examples.* This paragraph (c) may be illustrated by the following examples:

Reg. § 1.162-27(c)(6)

Example 1. Corporation X is a publicly held corporation with a July 1 to June 30 fiscal year. For Corporation X's taxable year ending on June 30, 1995, Corporation X pays compensation of $2,000,000 to A, an employee. However, A's compensation is not required to be reported to shareholders under the executive compensation disclosure rules of the Exchange Act because A is neither the chief executive officer nor one of the four highest compensated officers employed on the last day of the taxable year. A's compensation is not subject to the deduction limitation of paragraph (b) of this section.

Example 2. C, a covered employee, performs services and receives compensation from Corporations X, Y, and Z, members of an affiliated group of corporations. Corporation X, the parent corporation, is a publicly held corporation. The total compensation paid to C from all affiliated group members is $3,000,000 for the taxable year, of which Corporation X pays $1,500,000; Corporation Y pays $900,000; and Corporation Z pays $600,000. Because the compensation paid by all affiliated group members is aggregated for purposes of section 162(m), $2,000,000 of the aggregate compensation paid is nondeductible. Corporations X, Y, and Z each are treated as paying a ratable portion of the nondeductible compensation. Thus, two thirds of each corporation's payment will be nondeductible. Corporation X has a nondeductible compensation expense of $1,000,000 ($1,500,000 x $2,000,000/$3,000,000). Corporation Y has a nondeductible compensation expense of $600,000 ($900,000 x $2,000,000/$3,000,000). Corporation Z has a nondeductible compensation expense of $400,000 ($600,000 x $2,000,000/$3,000,000).

Example 3. Corporation W, a calendar year taxpayer, has total assets equal to or exceeding $5 million and a class of equity security held of record by 500 or more persons on December 31, 1994. However, under the Exchange Act, Corporation W is not required to file a registration statement with respect to that security until April 30, 1995. Thus, Corporation W is not a publicly held corporation on December 31, 1994, but is a publicly held corporation on December 31, 1995.

Example 4. The facts are the same as in *Example 3*, except that on December 15, 1996, Corporation W files with the Securities and Exchange Commission to disclose that Corporation W is no longer required to be registered under section 12 of the Exchange Act and to terminate its registration of securities under that provision. Because Corporation W is no longer subject to Exchange Act reporting obligations as of December 31, 1996, Corporation W is not a publicly held corporation for taxable year 1996, even though the registration of Corporation W's securities does not terminate until 90 days after Corporation W files with the Securities and Exchange Commission.

(d) *Exception for compensation paid on a commission basis.* The deduction limit in paragraph (b) of this section shall not apply to any compensation paid on a commission basis. For this purpose, compensation is paid on a commission basis if the facts and circumstances show that it is paid solely on account of income generated directly by the individual performance of the individual to whom the compensation is paid. Compensation does not fail to be attributable directly to the individual merely because support services, such as secretarial or research services, are utilized in generating the income. However, if compensation is paid on account of broader performance standards, such as income produced by a business unit of the corporation, the compensation does not qualify for the exception provided under this paragraph (d).

(e) *Exception for qualified performance-based compensation—*

(1) *In general.* The deduction limit in paragraph (b) of this section does not apply to qualified performance-based compensation. Qualified performance-based compensation is compensation that meets all of the requirements of paragraphs (e)(2) through (e)(5) of this section.

(2) *Performance goal requirement—*(i) *Preestablished goal.* Qualified performance-based compensation must be paid solely on account of the attainment of one or more preestablished, objective performance goals. A performance goal is considered preestablished if it is established in writing by the compensation committee not later than 90 days after the commencement of the period of service to which the performance goal relates, provided that the outcome is substantially uncertain at the time the compensation committee actually establishes the goal. However, in no event will a performance goal be considered to be preestablished if it is established after 25 percent of the period of service (as scheduled in good faith at the time the goal is established) has elapsed. A performance goal is objective if a third party having knowledge of the relevant facts could determine whether the goal is met. Performance goals can be based on one or more business criteria that apply to the individual, a business unit, or the corporation as a whole. Such business criteria could include, for example, stock price, market share, sales, earnings per share, return on equity, or costs. A performance goal need not, however, be based upon an increase or positive result under a

Reg. § 1.162-27(d)

business criterion and could include, for example, maintaining the status quo or limiting economic losses (measured, in each case, by reference to a specific business criterion). A performance goal does not include the mere continued employment of the covered employee. Thus, a vesting provision based solely on continued employment would not constitute a performance goal. See paragraph (e)(2)(vi) of this section for rules on compensation that is based on an increase in the price of stock.

(ii) *Objective compensation formula.* A preestablished performance goal must state, in terms of an objective formula or standard, the method for computing the amount of compensation payable to the employee if the goal is attained. A formula or standard is objective if a third party having knowledge of the relevant performance results could calculate the amount to be paid to the employee. In addition, a formula or standard must specify the individual employees or class of employees to which it applies.

(iii) *Discretion.*

(A) The terms of an objective formula or standard must preclude discretion to increase the amount of compensation payable that would otherwise be due upon attainment of the goal. A performance goal is not discretionary for purposes of this paragraph (e)(2)(iii) merely because the compensation committee reduces or eliminates the compensation or other economic benefit that was due upon attainment of the goal. However, the exercise of negative discretion with respect to one employee is not permitted to result in an increase in the amount payable to another employee. Thus, for example, in the case of a bonus pool, if the amount payable to each employee is stated in terms of a percentage of the pool, the sum of these individual percentages of the pool is not permitted to exceed 100 percent. If the terms of an objective formula or standard fail to preclude discretion to increase the amount of compensation merely because the amount of compensation to be paid upon attainment of the performance goal is based, in whole or in part, on a percentage of salary or base pay and the dollar amount of the salary or base pay is not fixed at the time the performance goal is established, then the objective formula or standard will not be considered discretionary for purposes of this paragraph (e)(2)(iii) if the maximum dollar amount to be paid is fixed at that time.

(B) If compensation is payable upon or after the attainment of a performance goal, and a change is made to accelerate the payment of compensation to an earlier date after the attainment of the goal, the change will be treated as an increase in the amount of compensation, unless the amount of compensation paid is discounted to reasonably reflect the time value of money. If compensation is payable upon or after the attainment of a performance goal, and a change is made to defer the payment of compensation to a later date, any amount paid in excess of the amount that was originally owed to the employee will not be treated as an increase in the amount of compensation if the additional amount is based either on a reasonable rate of interest or on one or more predetermined actual investments (whether or not assets associated with the amount originally owed are actually invested therein) such that the amount payable by the employer at the later date will be based on the actual rate of return of a specific investment (including any decrease as well as any increase in the value of an investment). If compensation is payable in the form of property, a change in the timing of the transfer of that property after the attainment of the goal will not be treated as an increase in the amount of compensation for purposes of this paragraph (e)(2)(iii). Thus, for example, if the terms of a stock grant provide for stock to be transferred after the attainment of a performance goal and the transfer of the stock also is subject to a vesting schedule, a change in the vesting schedule that either accelerates or defers the transfer of stock will not be treated as an increase in the amount of compensation payable under the performance goal.

(C) Compensation attributable to a stock option, stock appreciation right, or other stock-based compensation does not fail to satisfy the requirements of this paragraph (e)(2) to the extent that a change in the grant or award is made to reflect a change in corporate capitalization, such as a stock split or dividend, or a corporate transaction, such as any merger of a corporation into another corporation, any consolidation of two or more corporations into another corporation, any separation of a corporation (including a spinoff or other distribution of stock or property by a corporation), any reorganization of a corporation (whether or not such reorganization comes within the definition of such term in section 368), or any partial or complete liquidation by a corporation.

(iv) *Grant-by-grant determination.* The determination of whether compensation satisfies the requirements of this paragraph (e)(2) generally shall be made on a grant-by-grant basis. Thus, for example, whether compensation attributable to a stock option grant satisfies the requirements of this paragraph (e)(2) generally is determined on the basis of the particular grant made and without regard to the terms of any other option grant, or other grant of compensation, to the same or another employee. As a further example, except as provided in paragraph (e)(2)(vi), whether a grant of restricted stock or other stock-based compensation satisfies the requirements of this paragraph (e)(2) is determined without regard to whether dividends, dividend equivalents, or other similar distributions with respect to stock, on such stock-based compensation are payable prior to the attainment of the performance goal. Dividends, dividend equivalents, or other similar distributions with respect to stock that are treated as separate grants under this paragraph (e)(2)(iv) are not performance-based compensation unless they separately satisfy the requirements of this paragraph (e)(2).

(v) *Compensation contingent upon attainment of performance goal.* Compensation does not satisfy the requirements of this paragraph (e)(2) if the facts and circumstances indicate that the employee would receive all or part of the compensation regardless of whether the performance goal is attained. Thus, if the payment of compensation under a grant or award is only nominally or partially contingent on attaining a performance goal, none of the compensation payable under the grant or award will be considered performance-based. For example, if an employee is entitled to a bonus under either of two arrangements, where payment under a nonperformance-based arrangement is contingent upon the failure to attain the performance goals under an otherwise performance-based arrangement, then neither arrangement provides for compensation that satisfies the requirements of this paragraph (e)(2). Compensation does not fail to be qualified performance-based compensation merely because the plan allows the compensation to be payable upon death, disability, or change of ownership or control, although compensation actually paid on account of those events prior to the attainment of the performance goal would not satisfy the requirements of this paragraph (e)(2). As an exception to the general rule set forth in the first sentence of paragraph (e)(2)(iv) of this section, the facts-and-circumstances determination referred to in the first sentence of this paragraph (e)(2)(v) is made taking into account all plans, arrangements, and agreements that provide for compensation to the employee.

(vi) *Application of requirements to stock options and stock appreciation rights*—(A) *In general.* Compensation attributable to a stock option or a stock appreciation right is deemed to satisfy the requirements of this paragraph (e)(2) if the grant or award is made by the compensation committee; the plan under which the option or right is granted states the maximum number of shares with respect to which options or rights may be granted during a specified period to any employee; and, under the terms of the option or right, the amount of compensation the employee could receive is based solely on an increase in the value of the stock after the date of the grant or award. Conversely, if the amount of compensation the employee will receive under the grant or award is not based solely on an increase in the value of the stock after the date of grant or award (e.g., in the case of restricted stock, or an option that is granted with an exercise price that is less than the fair market value of the stock as of the date of grant), none of the compensation attributable to the grant or award is qualified performance-based compensation because it does not satisfy the requirement of this paragraph (e)(2)(vi)(A). Whether a stock option grant is based solely on an increase in the value of the stock after the date of grant is determined without regard to any dividend equivalent that may be payable, provided that payment of the dividend equivalent is not made contingent on the exercise of the option. The rule that the compensation attributable to a stock option or stock appreciation right must be based solely on an increase in the value of the stock after the date of grant or award does not apply if the grant or award is made on account of, or if the vesting or exercisability of the grant or award is contingent on, the attainment of a performance goal that satisfies the requirements of this paragraph (e)(2).

(B) *Cancellation and repricing.* Compensation attributable to a stock option or stock appreciation right does not satisfy the requirements of this paragraph (e)(2) to the extent that the number of options granted exceeds the maximum number of shares for which options may be granted to the employee as specified in the plan. If an option is canceled, the canceled option continues to be counted against the maximum number of shares for which options may be granted to the employee under the plan. If, after grant, the exercise price of an option is reduced, the transaction is treated as a cancellation of the option and a grant of a new option. In such case, both the option that is deemed to be canceled and the option that is deemed to be granted reduce the maximum number of shares for which options may be granted to the employee under the plan. This paragraph (e)(2)(vi)(B) also applies in the case of a stock appreciation right where, after the award is made, the base amount on which stock appreciation is calculated is reduced to reflect a reduction in the fair market value of stock.

(vii) *Examples.* This paragraph (e)(2) may be illustrated by the following examples:

Reg. § 1.162-27(e)(2)

Example 1. No later than 90 days after the start of a fiscal year, but while the outcome is substantially uncertain, Corporation S establishes a bonus plan under which A, the chief executive officer, will receive a cash bonus of $500,000, if year-end corporate sales are increased by at least 5 percent. The compensation committee retains the right, if the performance goal is met, to reduce the bonus payment to A if, in its judgment, other subjective factors warrant a reduction. The bonus will meet the requirements of this paragraph (e)(2).

Example 2. The facts are the same as in *Example 1*, except that the bonus is based on a percentage of Corporation S's total sales for the fiscal year. Because Corporation S is virtually certain to have some sales for the fiscal year, the outcome of the performance goal is not substantially uncertain, and therefore the bonus does not meet the requirements of this paragraph (e)(2).

Example 3. The facts are the same as in *Example 1*, except that the bonus is based on a percentage of Corporation S's total profits for the fiscal year. Although some sales are virtually certain for virtually all public companies, it is substantially uncertain whether a company will have profits for a specified future period even if the company has a history of profitability. Therefore, the bonus will meet the requirements of this paragraph (e)(2).

Example 4. B is the general counsel of Corporation R, which is engaged in patent litigation with Corporation S. Representatives of Corporation S have informally indicated to Corporation R a willingness to settle the litigation for $50,000,000. Subsequently, the compensation committee of Corporation R agrees to pay B a bonus if B obtains a formal settlement for at least $50,000,000. The bonus to B does not meet the requirement of this paragraph (e)(2) because the performance goal was not established at a time when the outcome was substantially uncertain.

Example 5. Corporation S, a public utility, adopts a bonus plan for selected salaried employees that will pay a bonus at the end of a 3-year period of $750,000 each if, at the end of the 3 years, the price of S stock has increased by 10 percent. The plan also provides that the 10-percent goal will automatically adjust upward or downward by the percentage change in a published utilities index. Thus, for example, if the published utilities index shows a net increase of 5 percent over a 3-year period, then the salaried employees would receive a bonus only if Corporation S stock has increased by 15 percent. Conversely, if the published utilities index shows a net decrease of 5 percent over a 3-year period, then

the salaried employees would receive a bonus if Corporation S stock has increased by 5 percent. Because these automatic adjustments in the performance goal are preestablished, the bonus meets the requirement of this paragraph (e)(2), notwithstanding the potential changes in the performance goal.

Example 6. The facts are the same as in *Example 5*, except that the bonus plan provides that, at the end of the 3-year period, a bonus of $750,000 will be paid to each salaried employee if either the price of Corporation S stock has increased by 10 percent or the earnings per share on Corporation S stock have increased by 5 percent. If both the earnings-per-share goal and the stock-price goal are preestablished, the compensation committee's discretion to choose to pay a bonus under either of the two goals does not cause any bonus paid under the plan to fail to meet the requirement of this paragraph (e)(2) because each goal independently meets the requirements of this paragraph (e)(2). The choice to pay under either of the two goals is tantamount to the discretion to choose not to pay under one of the goals, as provided in paragraph (e)(2)(iii) of this section.

Example 7. Corporation U establishes a bonus plan under which a specified class of employees will participate in a bonus pool if certain preestablished performance goals are attained. The amount of the bonus pool is determined under an objective formula. Under the terms of the bonus plan, the compensation committee retains the discretion to determine the fraction of the bonus pool that each employee may receive. The bonus plan does not satisfy the requirements of this paragraph (e)(2). Although the aggregate amount of the bonus plan is determined under an objective formula, a third party could not determine the amount that any individual could receive under the plan.

Example 8. The facts are the same as in *Example 7*, except that the bonus plan provides that a specified share of the bonus pool is payable to each employee, and the total of these shares does not exceed 100% of the pool. The bonus plan satisfies the requirements of this paragraph (e)(2). In addition, the bonus plan will satisfy the requirements of this paragraph (e)(2) even if the compensation committee retains the discretion to reduce the compensation payable to any individual employee, provided that a reduction in the amount of one employee's bonus does not result in an increase in the amount of any other employee's bonus.

Example 9. Corporation V establishes a stock option plan for salaried employees. The terms of the stock option plan specify that no salaried employee shall receive options for more than 100,000 shares over any 3-year period. The compensation committee grants options for 50,000 shares to each of several salaried employees. The exercise price of each option is equal to or greater than the fair market value at the time of each grant. Compensation attributable to the exercise of the options satisfies the requirements of this paragraph (e)(2). If, however, the terms of the options provide that the exercise price is less than fair market value at the date of grant, no compensation attributable to the exercise of those options satisfies the requirements of this paragraph (e)(2) unless issuance or exercise of the options was contingent upon the attainment of a preestablished performance goal that satisfies this paragraph (e)(2).

Example 10. The facts are the same as in *Example 9*, except that, within the same 3-year grant period, the fair market value of Corporation V stock is significantly less than the exercise price of the options. The compensation committee reprices those options to that lower current fair market value of Corporation V stock. The repricing of the options for 50,000 shares held by each salaried employee is treated as the grant of new options for an additional 50,000 shares to each employee. Thus, each of the salaried employees is treated as having received grants for 100,000 shares. Consequently, if any additional options are granted to those employees during the 3-year period, compensation attributable to the exercise of those additional options would not satisfy the requirements of this paragraph (e)(2). The results would be the same if the compensation committee canceled the outstanding options and issued new options to the same employees that were exercisable at the fair market value of Corporation V stock on the date of reissue.

Example 11. Corporation W maintains a plan under which each participating employee may receive incentive stock options, nonqualified stock options, stock appreciation rights, or grants of restricted Corporation W stock. The plan specifies that each participating employee may receive options, stock appreciation rights, restricted stock, or any combination of each, for no more than 20,000 shares over the life of the plan. The plan provides that stock options may be granted with an exercise price of less than, equal to, or greater than fair market value on the date of grant. Options granted with an exercise price equal to, or greater than, fair market value on the date of grant do not fail to meet the requirements of this paragraph (e)(2) merely because the compensation committee has the discretion to determine the types of awards (i.e., options, rights, or restricted stock) to be granted to each employee

or the discretion to issue options or make other compensation awards under the plan that would not meet the requirements of this paragraph (e)(2). Whether an option granted under the plan satisfies the requirements of this paragraph (e)(2) is determined on the basis of the specific terms of the option and without regard to other options or awards under the plan.

Example 12. Corporation X maintains a plan under which stock appreciation rights may be awarded to key employees. The plan permits the compensation committee to make awards under which the amount of compensation payable to the employee is equal to the increase in the stock price plus a percentage "gross up" intended to offset the tax liability of the employee. In addition, the plan permits the compensation committee to make awards under which the amount of compensation payable to the employee is equal to the increase in the stock price, based on the highest price, which is defined as the highest price paid for Corporation X stock (or offered in a tender offer or other arms-length offer) during the 90 days preceding exercise. Compensation attributable to awards under the plan satisfies the requirements of paragraph (e)(2)(vi) of this section, provided that the terms of the plan specify the maximum number of shares for which awards may be made.

Example 13. Corporation W adopts a plan under which a bonus will be paid to the CEO only if there is a 10% increase in earnings per share during the performance period. The plan provides that earnings per share will be calculated without regard to any change in accounting standards that may be required by the Financial Accounting Standards Board after the goal is established. After the goal is established, such a change in accounting standards occurs. Corporation W's reported earnings, for purposes of determining earnings per share under the plan, are adjusted pursuant to this plan provision to factor out this change in standards. This adjustment will not be considered an exercise of impermissible discretion because it is made pursuant to the plan provision.

Example 14. Corporation X adopts a performance-based incentive pay plan with a four-year performance period. Bonuses under the plan are scheduled to be paid in the first year after the end of the performance period (year 5). However, in the second year of the performance period, the compensation committee determines that any bonuses payable in year 5 will instead, for bona fide business reasons, be paid in year 10. The compensation committee also determines that any compensation that would have been payable in year 5 will be adjusted to reflect the delay in payment.

Reg. § 1.162-27(e)(2)

The adjustment will be based on the greater of the future rate of return of a specified mutual fund that invests in blue chip stocks or of a specified venture capital investment over the five-year deferral period. Each of these investments, considered by itself, is a predetermined actual investment because it is based on the future rate of return of an actual investment. However, the adjustment in this case is not based on predetermined actual investments within the meaning of paragraph (e)(2)(iii)(B) of this section because the amount payable by Corporation X in year 10 will be based on the greater of the two investment returns and, thus, will not be based on the actual rate of return on either specific investment.

Example 15. The facts are the same as in *Example 14,* except that the increase will be based on Moody's Average Corporate Bond Yield over the five-year deferral period. Because this index reflects a reasonable rate of interest, the increase in the compensation payable that is based on the index's rate of return is not considered an impermissible increase in the amount of compensation payable under the formula.

Example 16. The facts are the same as in *Example 14,* except that the increase will be based on the rate of return for the Standard & Poor's 500 Index. This index does not measure interest rates and thus does not represent a reasonable rate of interest. In addition, this index does not represent an actual investment. Therefore, any additional compensation payable based on the rate of return of this index will result in an impermissible increase in the amount payable under the formula. If, in contrast, the increase were based on the rate of return of an existing mutual fund that is invested in a manner that seeks to approximate the Standard & Poor's 500 Index, the increase would be based on a predetermined actual investment within the meaning of paragraph (e)(2)(iii)(B) of this section and thus would not result in an impermissible increase in the amount payable under the formula.

(3) *Outside directors*—(i) *General rule.* The performance goal under which compensation is paid must be established by a compensation committee comprised solely of two or more outside directors. A director is an outside director if the director—

(A) Is not a current employee of the publicly held corporation;

(B) Is not a former employee of the publicly held corporation who receives compensation for prior services (other than benefits under a tax-qualified retirement plan) during the taxable year;

(C) Has not been an officer of the publicly held corporation; and

(D) Does not receive remuneration from the publicly held corporation, either directly or indirectly, in any capacity other than as a director. For this purpose, remuneration includes any payment in exchange for goods or services.

(ii) *Remuneration received.* For purposes of this paragraph (e)(3), remuneration is received, directly or indirectly, by a director in each of the following circumstances:

(A) If remuneration is paid, directly or indirectly, to the director personally or to an entity in which the director has a beneficial ownership interest of greater than 50 percent. For this purpose, remuneration is considered paid when actually paid (and throughout the remainder of that taxable year of the corporation) and, if earlier, throughout the period when a contract or agreement to pay remuneration is outstanding.

(B) If remuneration, other than de minimis remuneration, was paid by the publicly held corporation in its preceding taxable year to an entity in which the director has a beneficial ownership interest of at least 5 percent but not more than 50 percent. For this purpose, remuneration is considered paid when actually paid or, if earlier, when the publicly held corporation becomes liable to pay it.

(C) If remuneration, other than de minimis remuneration, was paid by the publicly held corporation in its preceding taxable year to an entity by which the director is employed or self-employed other than as a director. For this purpose, remuneration is considered paid when actually paid or, if earlier, when the publicly held corporation becomes liable to pay it.

(iii) *De minimis remuneration*—(A) *In general.* For purposes of paragraphs (e)(3)(ii)(B) and (C) of this section, remuneration that was paid by the publicly held corporation in its preceding taxable year to an entity is de minimis if payments to the entity did not exceed 5 percent of the gross revenue of the entity for its taxable year ending with or within that preceding taxable year of the publicly held corporation.

(B) *Remuneration for personal services and substantial owners.* Notwithstanding paragraph (e)(3)(iii)(A) of this section, remuneration in excess of $60,000 is not de minimis if the remuneration is paid to an entity described in paragraph (e)(3)(ii)(B) of this section, or is paid for personal services to an entity described in paragraph (e)(3)(ii)(C) of this section.

(iv) *Remuneration for personal services.* For purposes of paragraph (e)(3)(iii)(B) of this section, remuneration from a publicly held corporation is for personal services if—

(A) The remuneration is paid to an entity for personal or professional services, consisting of legal, accounting, investment banking, and management consulting services (and other similar services that may be specified by the Commissioner in revenue rulings, notices, or other guidance published in the Internal Revenue Bulletin), performed for the publicly held corporation, and the remuneration is not for services that are incidental to the purchase of goods or to the purchase of services that are not personal services; and

(B) The director performs significant services (whether or not as an employee) for the corporation, division, or similar organization (within the entity) that actually provides the services described in paragraph (e)(3)(iv)(A) of this section to the publicly held corporation, or more than 50 percent of the entity's gross revenues (for the entity's preceding taxable year) are derived from that corporation, subsidiary, or similar organization.

(v) *Entity defined.* For purposes of this paragraph (e)(3), entity means an organization that is a sole proprietorship, trust, estate, partnership, or corporation. The term also includes an affiliated group of corporations as defined in section 1504 (determined without regard to section 1504(b)) and a group of organizations that would be an affiliated group but for the fact that one or more of the organizations are not incorporated. However, the aggregation rules referred to in the preceding sentence do not apply for purposes of determining whether a director has a beneficial ownership interest of at least 5 percent or greater than 50 percent.

(vi) *Employees and former officers.* Whether a director is an employee or a former officer is determined on the basis of the facts at the time that the individual is serving as a director on the compensation committee. Thus, a director is not precluded from being an outside director solely because the director is a former officer of a corporation that previously was an affiliated corporation of the publicly held corporation. For example, a director of a parent corporation of an affiliated group is not precluded from being an outside director solely because that director is a former officer of an affiliated subsidiary that was spun off or liquidated. However, an outside director would no longer be an outside director if a corporation in which the director was previously an officer became an affiliated corporation of the publicly held corporation.

(vii) *Officer.* Solely for purposes of this paragraph (e)(3), *officer* means an administrative executive who is or was in regular and continued service. The term implies continuity of service and excludes those employed for a special and single transaction. An individual who merely has (or had) the title of officer but not the authority of an officer is not considered an officer. The determination of whether an individual is or was an officer is based on all the of facts and circumstances in the particular case, including without limitation the source of the individual's authority, the term for which the individual is elected or appointed, and the nature and extent of the individual's duties.

(viii) *Members of affiliated groups.* For purposes of this paragraph (e)(3), the outside directors of the publicly held member of an affiliated group are treated as the outside directors of all members of the affiliated group.

(ix) *Examples.* This paragraph (e)(3) may be illustrated by the following examples:

Example 1. Corporations X and Y are members of an affiliated group of corporations as defined in section 1504, until July 1, 1994, when Y is sold to another group. Prior to the sale, A served as an officer of Corporation Y. After July 1, 1994, A is not treated as a former officer of Corporation X by reason of having been an officer of Y.

Example 2. Corporation Z, a calendar-year taxpayer, uses the services of a law firm by which B is employed, but in which B has a less-than-5-percent ownership interest. The law firm reports income on a July 1 to June 30 basis. Corporation Z appoints B to serve on its compensation committee for calendar year 1998 after determining that, in calendar year 1997, it did not become liable to the law firm for remuneration exceeding the lesser of $60,000 or five percent of the law firm's gross revenue (calculated for the year ending June 30, 1997). On October 1, 1998, Corporation Z becomes liable to pay remuneration of $50,000 to the law firm on June 30, 1999. For the year ending June 30, 1998, the law firm's gross revenue was less than $1 million. Thus, in calendar year 1999, B is not an outside director. However, B may satisfy the requirements for an outside director in calendar year 2000, if, in calendar year 1999, Corporation Z does not become liable to the law firm for additional remuneration. This is because the remuneration actually paid on June 30, 1999 was considered paid on October 1, 1998 under paragraph (e)(3)(ii)(C) of this section.

Example 3. Corporation Z, a publicly held corporation, purchases goods from Corporation A. D, an executive and less-than-5-percent owner of

Reg. § 1.162-27(e)(3)

Corporation A, sits on the board of directors of Corporation Z and on its compensation committee. For 1997, Corporation Z obtains representations to the effect that D is not eligible for any commission for D's sales to Corporation Z and that, for purposes of determining D's compensation for 1997, Corporation A's sales to Corporation Z are not otherwise treated differently than sales to other customers of Corporation A (including its affiliates, if any) or are irrelevant. In addition, Corporation Z has no reason to believe that these representations are inaccurate or that it is otherwise paying remuneration indirectly to D personally. Thus, in 1997, no remuneration is considered paid by Corporation Z indirectly to D personally under paragraph (e)(3)(ii)(A) of this section.

Example 4. (i) Corporation W, a publicly held corporation, purchases goods from Corporation T. C, an executive and less-than5-percent owner of Corporation T, sits on the board of directors of Corporation W and on its compensation committee. Corporation T develops a new product and agrees on January 1, 1998 to pay C a bonus of $500,000 if Corporation W contracts to purchase the product. Even if Corporation W purchases the new product, sales to Corporation W will represent less than 5 percent of Corporation T's gross revenues. In 1999, Corporation W contracts to purchase the new product and, in 2000, C receives the $500,000 bonus from Corporation T. In 1998, 1999, and 2000, Corporation W does not obtain any representations relating to indirect remuneration to C personally (such as the representations described in *Example 3*).

(ii) Thus, in 1998, 1999, and 2000, remuneration is considered paid by Corporation W indirectly to C personally under paragraph (e)(3)(ii)(A) of this section. Accordingly, in 1998, 1999, and 2000, C is not an outside director of Corporation W. The result would have been the same if Corporation W had obtained appropriate representations but nevertheless had reason to believe that it was paying remuneration indirectly to C personally.

Example 5. Corporation R, a publicly held corporation, purchases utility service from Corporation Q, a public utility. The chief executive officer, and less-than-5-percent owner, of Corporation Q is a director of Corporation R. Corporation R pays Corporation Q more than $60,000 per year for the utility service, but less than 5 percent of Corporation Q's gross revenues. Because utility services are not personal services, the fees paid are not subject to the $60,000 *de minimis* rule for remuneration for personal services within the meaning of paragraph (e)(3)(iii)(B) of this section. Thus, the chief executive officer qualifies as an

outside director of Corporation R, unless disqualified on some other basis.

Example 6. Corporation A, a publicly held corporation, purchases management consulting services from Division S of Conglomerate P. The chief financial officer of Division S is a director of Corporation A. Corporation A pays more than $60,000 per year for the management consulting services, but less than 5 percent of Conglomerate P's gross revenues. Because management consulting services are personal services within the meaning of paragraph (e)(3)(iv)(A) of this section, and the chief financial officer performs significant services for Division S, the fees paid are subject to the $60,000 *de minimis* rule as remuneration for personal services. Thus, the chief financial officer does not qualify as an outside director of Corporation A.

Example 7. The facts are the same as in *Example 6*, except that the chief executive officer, and less-than-5-percent owner, of the parent company of Conglomerate P is a director of Corporation A and does not perform significant services for Division S. If the gross revenues of Division S do not constitute more than 50 percent of the gross revenues of Conglomerate P for P's preceding taxable year, the chief executive officer will qualify as an outside director of Corporation A, unless disqualified on some other basis.

(4) *Shareholder approval requirement*—(i) *General rule.* The material terms of the performance goal under which the compensation is to be paid must be disclosed to and subsequently approved by the shareholders of the publicly held corporation before the compensation is paid. The requirements of this paragraph (e)(4) are not satisfied if the compensation would be paid regardless of whether the material terms are approved by shareholders. The material terms include the employees eligible to receive compensation; a description of the business criteria on which the performance goal is based; and either the maximum amount of compensation that could be paid to any employee or the formula used to calculate the amount of compensation to be paid to the employee if the performance goal is attained (except that, in the case of a formula based, in whole or in part, on a percentage of salary or base pay, the maximum dollar amount of compensation that could be paid to the employee must be disclosed).

(ii) *Eligible employees.* Disclosure of the employees eligible to receive compensation need not be so specific as to identify the particular individuals by name. A general description of the class of eligible employees by title or class is sufficient, such as the chief executive officer and vice presidents, or all salaried employees, all executive officers, or all key employees.

(iii) *Description of business criteria*—(A) *In general.* Disclosure of the business criteria on which the performance goal is based need not include the specific targets that must be satisfied under the performance goal. For example, if a bonus plan provides that a bonus will be paid if earnings per share increase by 10 percent, the 10-percent figure is a target that need not be disclosed to shareholders. However, in that case, disclosure must be made that the bonus plan is based on an earnings-per-share business criterion. In the case of a plan under which employees may be granted stock options or stock appreciation rights, no specific description of the business criteria is required if the grants or awards are based on a stock price that is no less than current fair market value.

(B) *Disclosure of confidential information.* The requirements of this paragraph (e)(4) may be satisfied even though information that otherwise would be a material term of a performance goal is not disclosed to shareholders, provided that the compensation committee determines that the information is confidential commercial or business information, the disclosure of which would have an adverse effect on the publicly held corporation. Whether disclosure would adversely affect the corporation is determined on the basis of the facts and circumstances. If the compensation committee makes such a determination, the disclosure to shareholders must state the compensation committee's belief that the information is confidential commercial or business information, the disclosure of which would adversely affect the company. In addition, the ability not to disclose confidential information does not eliminate the requirement that disclosure be made of the maximum amount of compensation that is payable to an individual under a performance goal. Confidential information does not include the identity of an executive or the class of executives to which a performance goal applies or the amount of compensation that is payable if the goal is satisfied.

(iv) *Description of compensation.* Disclosure as to the compensation payable under a performance goal must be specific enough so that shareholders can determine the maximum amount of compensation that could be paid to any employee during a specified period. If the terms of the performance goal do not provide for a maximum dollar amount, the disclosure must include the formula under which the compensation would be calculated. Thus, for example, if compensation attributable to the exercise of stock options is

equal to the difference in the exercise price and the current value of the stock, disclosure would be required of the maximum number of shares for which grants may be made to any employee and the exercise price of those options (*e.g.,* fair market value on date of grant). In that case, shareholders could calculate the maximum amount of compensation that would be attributable to the exercise of options on the basis of their assumptions as to the future stock price.

(v) *Disclosure requirements of the Securities and Exchange Commission.* To the extent not otherwise specifically provided in this paragraph (e)(4), whether the material terms of a performance goal are adequately disclosed to shareholders is determined under the same standards as apply under the Exchange Act.

(vi) *Frequency of disclosure.* Once the material terms of a performance goal are disclosed to and approved by shareholders, no additional disclosure or approval is required unless the compensation committee changes the material terms of the performance goal. If, however, the compensation committee has authority to change the targets under a performance goal after shareholder approval of the goal, material terms of the performance goal must be disclosed to and reapproved by shareholders no later than the first shareholder meeting that occurs in the fifth year following the year in which shareholders previously approved the performance goal.

(vii) *Shareholder vote.* For purposes of this paragraph (e)(4), the material terms of a performance goal are approved by shareholders if, in a separate vote, a majority of the votes cast on the issue (including abstentions to the extent abstentions are counted as voting under applicable state law) are cast in favor of approval.

(viii) *Members of affiliated group.* For purposes of this paragraph (e)(4), the shareholders of the publicly held member of the affiliated group are treated as the shareholders of all members of the affiliated group.

(ix) *Examples.* This paragraph (e)(4) may be illustrated by the following examples:

Example 1. Corporation X adopts a plan that will pay a specified class of its executives an annual cash bonus based on the overall increase in corporate sales during the year. Under the terms of the plan, the cash bonus of each executive equals $100,000 multiplied by the number of percentage points by which sales increase in the current year when compared to the prior year. Corporation X discloses to its shareholders prior to the vote both the class of executives eligible to receive awards and the annual formula of $100,000 multiplied by the percentage increase in sales. This disclosure meets the requirements of this paragraph (e)(4). Because the compensation committee does not have the authority to establish a different target under the plan, Corporation X need not redisclose to its shareholders and obtain their reapproval of the material terms of the plan until those material terms are changed.

Example 2. The facts are the same as in *Example 1* except that Corporation X discloses only that bonuses will be paid on the basis of the annual increase in sales. This disclosure does not meet the requirements of this paragraph (e)(4) because it does not include the formula for calculating the compensation or a maximum amount of compensation to be paid if the performance goal is satisfied.

Example 3. Corporation Y adopts an incentive compensation plan in 1995 that will pay a specified class of its executives a bonus every 3 years based on the following 3 factors: increases in earnings per share, reduction in costs for specified divisions, and increases in sales by specified divisions. The bonus is payable in cash or in Corporation Y stock, at the option of the executive. Under the terms of the plan, prior to the beginning of each 3-year period, the compensation committee determines the specific targets under each of the three factors (i.e., the amount of the increase in earnings per share, the reduction in costs, and the amount of sales) that must be met in order for the executives to receive a bonus. Under the terms of the plan, the compensation committee retains the discretion to determine whether a bonus will be paid under any one of the goals. The terms of the plan also specify that no executive may receive a bonus in excess of $1,500,000 for any 3-year period. To satisfy the requirements of this paragraph (e)(4), Corporation Y obtains shareholder approval of the plan at its 1995 annual shareholder meeting. In the proxy statement issued to shareholders, Corporation Y need not disclose to shareholders the specific targets that are set by the compensation committee. However, Corporation Y must disclose that bonuses are paid on the basis of earnings per share, reductions in costs, and increases in sales of specified divisions. Corporation Y also must disclose the maximum amount of compensation that any executive may receive under the plan is $1,500,000 per 3-year period. Unless changes in the material terms of the plan are made earlier, Corporation Y need not disclose the material terms of the plan to the shareholders and obtain their reapproval until the first shareholders' meeting held in 2000.

Example 4. The same facts as in *Example 3,* except that prior to the beginning of the second 3-year period, the compensation committee determines that different targets will be set under the plan for that period with regard to all three of the performance criteria (i.e., earnings per share, reductions in costs, and increases in sales). In addition, the compensation committee raises the maximum dollar amount that can be paid under the plan for a 3-year period to $2,000,000. The increase in the maximum dollar amount of compensation under the plan is a changed material term. Thus, to satisfy the requirements of this paragraph (e)(4), Corporation Y must disclose to and obtain approval by the shareholders of the plan as amended.

Example 5. In 1998, Corporation Z establishes a plan under which a specified group of executives will receive a cash bonus not to exceed $750,000 each if a new product that has been in development is completed and ready for sale to customers by January 1, 2000. Although the completion of the new product is a material term of the performance goal under this paragraph (e)(4), the compensation committee determines that the disclosure to shareholders of the performance goal would adversely affect Corporation Z because its competitors would be made aware of the existence and timing of its new product. In this case, the requirements of this paragraph (e)(4) are satisfied if all other material terms, including the maximum amount of compensation, are disclosed and the disclosure affirmatively states that the terms of the performance goal are not being disclosed because the compensation committee has determined that those terms include confidential information, the disclosure of which would adversely affect Corporation Z.

(5) *Compensation committee certification.* The compensation committee must certify in writing prior to payment of the compensation that the performance goals and any other material terms were in fact satisfied. For this purpose, approved minutes of the compensation committee meeting in which the certification is made are treated as a written certification. Certification by the compensation committee is not required for compensation that is attributable solely to the increase in the value of the stock of the publicly held corporation.

(f) *Companies that become publicly held, spinoffs, and similar transactions*—(1) *In general.* In the case of a corporation that was not a publicly held corporation and then becomes a publicly held corporation, the deduction limit of paragraph (b) of this section does not apply to any remuneration paid pursuant to a compensation plan or agreement that existed during the period in which the corporation was not publicly held. However, in the case of such a corporation that becomes publicly held in connection with an initial public

Reg. § 1.162-27(f)(1)

offering, this relief applies only to the extent that the prospectus accompanying the initial public offering disclosed information concerning those plans or agreements that satisfied all applicable securities laws then in effect. In accordance with paragraph (c)(1)(ii) of this section, a corporation that is a member of an affiliated group that includes a publicly held corporation is considered publicly held and, therefore, cannot rely on this paragraph (f)(1).

(2) *Reliance period.* Paragraph (f)(1) of this section may be relied upon until the earliest of—

(i) The expiration of the plan or agreement;

(ii) The material modification of the plan or agreement, within the meaning of paragraph (h)(1)(iii) of this section;

(iii) The issuance of all employer stock and other compensation that has been allocated under the plan; or

(iv) The first meeting of shareholders at which directors are to be elected that occurs after the close of the third calendar year following the calendar year in which the initial public offering occurs or, in the case of a privately held corporation that becomes publicly held without an initial public offering, the first calendar year following the calendar year in which the corporation becomes publicly held.

(3) *Stock-based compensation.* Paragraph (f)(1) of this section will apply to any compensation received pursuant to the exercise of a stock option or stock appreciation right, or the substantial vesting of restricted property, granted under a plan or agreement described in paragraph (f)(1) of this section if the grant occurs on or before the earliest of the events specified in paragraph (f)(2) of this section.

(4) *Subsidiaries that become separate publicly held corporations*—(i) *In general.* If a subsidiary that is a member of the affiliated group described in paragraph (c)(1)(ii) of this section becomes a separate publicly held corporation (whether by spinoff or otherwise), any remuneration paid to covered employees of the new publicly held corporation will satisfy the exception for performance-based compensation described in paragraph (e) of this section if the conditions in either paragraph (f)(4)(ii) or (f)(4)(iii) of this section are satisfied.

(ii) *Prior establishment and approval.* Remuneration satisfies the requirements of this paragraph (f)(4)(ii) if the remuneration satisfies the requirements for performance-based compensation set forth in paragraphs (e)(2), (e)(3), and (e)(4) of this section (by application of paragraphs

(e)(3)(viii) and (e)(4)(viii) of this section) before the corporation becomes a separate publicly held corporation, and the certification required by paragraph (e)(5) of this section is made by the compensation committee of the new publicly held corporation (but if the performance goals are attained before the corporation becomes a separate publicly held corporation, the certification may be made by the compensation committee referred to in paragraph (e)(3)(viii) of this section before it becomes a separate publicly held corporation). Thus, this paragraph (f)(4)(ii) requires that the outside directors and shareholders (within the meaning of paragraphs (e)(3)(viii) and (e)(4)(viii) of this section) of the corporation before it becomes a separate publicly held corporation establish and approve, respectively, the performance-based compensation for the covered employees of the new publicly held corporation in accordance with paragraphs (e)(3) and (e)(4) of this section.

(iii) *Transition period.* Remuneration satisfies the requirements of this paragraph (f)(4)(iii) if the remuneration satisfies all of the requirements of paragraphs (e)(2), (e)(3), and (e)(5) of this section. The outside directors (within the meaning of paragraph (e)(3)(viii) of this section) of the corporation before it becomes a separate publicly held corporation, or the outside directors of the new publicly held corporation, may establish and administer the performance goals for the covered employees of the new publicly held corporation for purposes of satisfying the requirements of paragraphs (e)(2) and (e)(3) of this section. The certification required by paragraph (e)(5) of this section must be made by the compensation committee of the new publicly held corporation. However, a taxpayer may rely on this paragraph (f)(4)(iii) to satisfy the requirements of paragraph (e) of this section only for compensation paid, or stock options, stock appreciation rights, or restricted property granted, prior to the first regularly scheduled meeting of the shareholders of the new publicly held corporation that occurs more than 12 months after the date the corporation becomes a separate publicly held corporation. Compensation paid, or stock options, stock appreciation rights, or restricted property granted, on or after the date of that meeting of shareholders must satisfy all requirements of paragraph (e) of this section, including the shareholder approval requirement of paragraph (e)(4) of this section, in order to satisfy the requirements for performance-based compensation.

(5) *Example.* The following example illustrates the application of paragraph (f)(4)(ii) of this section:

Reg. § 1.162-27(f)(2)

Example. Corporation P, which is publicly held, decides to spin off Corporation S, a wholly owned subsidiary of Corporation P. After the spinoff, Corporation S will be a separate publicly held corporation. Before the spinoff, the compensation committee of Corporation P, pursuant to paragraph (e)(3)(viii) of this section, establishes a bonus plan for the executives of Corporation S that provides for bonuses payable after the spinoff and that satisfies the requirements of paragraph (e)(2) of this section. If, pursuant to paragraph (e)(4)(viii) of this section, the shareholders of Corporation P approve the plan prior to the spinoff, that approval will satisfy the requirements of paragraph (e)(4) of this section with respect to compensation paid pursuant to the bonus plan after the spinoff. However, the compensation committee of Corporation S will be required to certify that the goals are satisfied prior to the payment of the bonuses in order for the bonuses to be considered performance-based compensation.

(g) *Coordination with disallowed excess parachute payments.* The $1,000,000 limitation in paragraph (b) of this section is reduced (but not below zero) by the amount (if any) that would have been included in the compensation of the covered employee for the taxable year but for being disallowed by reason of section 280G. For example, assume that during a taxable year a corporation pays $1,500,000 to a covered employee and no portion satisfies the exception in paragraph (d) of this section for commissions or paragraph (e) of this section for qualified performance-based compensation. Of the $1,500,000, $600,000 is an excess parachute payment, as defined in section 280G(b)(1) and is disallowed by reason of that section. Because the excess parachute payment reduces the limitation of paragraph (b) of this section, the corporation can deduct $400,000, and $500,000 of the otherwise deductible amount is nondeductible by reason of section 162(m).

(h) *Transition rules*—(1) *Compensation payable under a written binding contract which was in effect on February 17, 1993*—(i) *General rule.* The deduction limit of paragraph (b) of this section does not apply to any compensation payable under a written binding contract that was in effect on February 17, 1993. The preceding sentence does not apply unless, under applicable state law, the corporation is obligated to pay the compensation if the employee performs services. However, the deduction limit of paragraph (b) of this section does apply to a contract that is renewed after February 17, 1993. A written binding contract that is terminable or cancelable by the corporation after February 17, 1993, without the employee's consent is treated as a new contract as

of the date that any such termination or cancellation, if made, would be effective. Thus, for example, if the terms of a contract provide that it will be automatically renewed as of a certain date unless either the corporation or the employee gives notice of termination of the contract at least 30 days before that date, the contract is treated as a new contract as of the date that termination would be effective if that notice were given. Similarly, for example, if the terms of a contract provide that the contract will be terminated or canceled as of a certain date unless either the corporation or the employee elects to renew within 30 days of that date, the contract is treated as renewed by the corporation as of that date. Alternatively, if the corporation will remain legally obligated by the terms of a contract beyond a certain date at the sole discretion of the employee, the contract will not be treated as a new contract as of that date if the employee exercises the discretion to keep the corporation bound to the contract. A contract is not treated as terminable or cancelable if it can be terminated or canceled only by terminating the employment relationship of the employee.

(ii) *Compensation payable under a plan or arrangement.* If a compensation plan or arrangement meets the requirements of paragraph (h)(1)(i) of this section, the compensation paid to an employee pursuant to the plan or arrangement will not be subject to the deduction limit of paragraph (b) of this section even though the employee was not eligible to participate in the plan as of February 17, 1993. However, the preceding sentence does not apply unless the employee was employed on February 17, 1993, by the corporation that maintained the plan or arrangement, or the employee had the right to participate in the plan or arrangement under a written binding contract as of that date.

(iii) *Material modifications.*

(A) Paragraph (h)(1)(i) of this section will not apply to any written binding contract that is materially modified. A material modification occurs when the contract is amended to increase the amount of compensation payable to the employee. If a binding written contract is materially modified, it is treated as a new contract entered into as of the date of the material modification. Thus, amounts received by an employee under the contract prior to a material modification are not affected, but amounts received subsequent to the material modification are not treated as paid under a binding, written contract described in paragraph (h)(1)(i) of this section.

(B) A modification of the contract that accelerates the payment of compensation will be

Reg. § 1.162-27(h)(1)

treated as a material modification unless the amount of compensation paid is discounted to reasonably reflect the time value of money. If the contract is modified to defer the payment of compensation, any compensation paid in excess of the amount that was originally payable to the employee under the contract will not be treated as a material modification if the additional amount is based on either a reasonable rate of interest or one or more predetermined actual investments (whether or not assets associated with the amount originally owed are actually invested therein) such that the amount payable by the employer at the later date will be based on the actual rate of return of the specific investment (including any decrease as well as any increase in the value of the investment).

(C) The adoption of a supplemental contract or agreement that provides for increased compensation, or the payment of additional compensation, is a material modification of a binding, written contract where the facts and circumstances show that the additional compensation is paid on the basis of substantially the same elements or conditions as the compensation that is otherwise paid under the written binding contract. However, a material modification of a written binding contract does not include a supplemental payment that is equal to or less than a reasonable cost-of-living increase over the payment made in the preceding year under that written binding contract. In addition, a supplemental payment of compensation that satisfies the requirements of qualified performance-based compensation in paragraph (e) of this section will not be treated as a material modification.

(iv) *Examples.* The following examples illustrate the exception of this paragraph (h)(1):

Example 1. Corporation X executed a 3-year compensation arrangement with C on February 15, 1993, that constitutes a written binding contract under applicable state law. The terms of the arrangement provide for automatic extension after the 3-year term for additional 1-year periods, unless the corporation exercises its option to terminate the arrangement within 30 days of the end of the 3-year term or, thereafter, within 30 days before each anniversary date. Termination of the compensation arrangement does not require the termination of C's employment relationship with Corporation X. Unless terminated, the arrangement is treated as renewed on February 15, 1996, and the deduction limit of paragraph (b) of this section applies to payments under the arrangement after that date.

Example 2. Corporation Y executed a 5-year employment agreement with B on January 1, 1992, providing for a salary of $900,000 per year. Assume that this agreement constitutes a written binding contract under applicable state law. In 1992 and 1993, B receives the salary of $900,000 per year. In 1994, Corporation Y increases B's salary with a payment of $20,000. The $20,000 supplemental payment does not constitute a material modification of the written binding contract because the $20,000 payment is less than or equal to a reasonable cost-of-living increase from 1993. However, the $20,000 supplemental payment is subject to the limitation in paragraph (b) of this section. On January 1, 1995, Corporation Y increases B's salary to $1,200,000. The $280,000 supplemental payment is a material modification of the written binding contract because the additional compensation is paid on the basis of substantially the same elements or conditions as the compensation that is otherwise paid under the written binding contract and it is greater than a reasonable, annual cost-of-living increase. Because the written binding contract is materially modified as of January 1, 1995, all compensation paid to B in 1995 and thereafter is subject to the deduction limitation of section 162(m).

Example 3. Assume the same facts as in *Example 2*, except that instead of an increase in salary, B receives a restricted stock grant subject to B's continued employment for the balance of the contract. The restricted stock grant is not a material modification of the binding written contract because any additional compensation paid to B under the grant is not paid on the basis of substantially the same elements and conditions as B's salary because it is based both on the stock price and B's continued service. However, compensation attributable to the restricted stock grant is subject to the deduction limitation of section 162(m).

(2) *Special transition rule for outside directors.* A director who is a disinterested director is treated as satisfying the requirements of an outside director under paragraph (e)(3) of this section until the first meeting of shareholders at which directors are to be elected that occurs on or after January 1, 1996. For purposes of this paragraph (h)(2) and paragraph (h)(3) of this section, a director is a disinterested director if the director is disinterested within the meaning of Rule 16b-3(c)(2)(i), 17 CFR 240.16b-3(c)(2)(i), under the Exchange Act (including the provisions of Rule 16b-3(d)(3), as in effect on April 30, 1991).

(3) *Special transition rule for previously-approved plans—*(i) *In general.* Any compensation paid under a plan or agreement approved by shareholders before December 20, 1993, is treated

Reg. § 1.162-27(h)(2)

as satisfying the requirements of paragraphs (e)(3) and (e)(4) of this section, provided that the directors administering the plan or agreement are disinterested directors and the plan was approved by shareholders in a manner consistent with Rule 16b-3(b), 17 CFR 240.16b-3(b), under the Exchange Act or Rule 16b-3(a), 17 CFR 240.16b-3(a) (as contained in 17 CFR part 240 revised April 1, 1990). In addition, for purposes of satisfying the requirements of paragraph (e)(2)(vi) of this section, a plan or agreement is treated as stating a maximum number of shares with respect to which an option or right may be granted to any employee if the plan or agreement that was approved by the shareholders provided for an aggregate limit, consistent with Rule 16b-3(b), 17 CFR 250.16b-3(b), on the shares of employer stock with respect to which awards may be made under the plan or agreement.

(ii) *Reliance period.* The transition rule provided in this paragraph (h)(3) shall continue and may be relied upon until the earliest of—

(A) The expiration or material modification of the plan or agreement;

(B) The issuance of all employer stock and other compensation that has been allocated under the plan; or

(C) The first meeting of shareholders at which directors are to be elected that occurs after December 31, 1996.

(iii) *Stock-based compensation.* This paragraph (h)(3) will apply to any compensation received pursuant to the exercise of a stock option or stock appreciation right, or the substantial vesting of restricted property, granted under a plan or agreement described in paragraph (h)(3)(i) of this section if the grant occurs on or before the earliest of the events specified in paragraph (h)(3)(ii) of this section.

(iv) *Example.* The following example illustrates the application of this paragraph (h)(3):

Example. Corporation Z adopted a stock option plan in 1991. Pursuant to Rule 16b-3 under the Exchange Act, the stock option plan has been administered by disinterested directors and was approved by Corporation Z shareholders. Under the terms of the plan, shareholder approval is not required again until 2001. In addition, the terms of the stock option plan include an aggregate limit on the number of shares available under the plan. Option grants under the Corporation Z plan are made with an exercise price equal to or greater than the fair market value of Corporation Z stock. Compensation attributable to the exercise of options that are granted under the plan before the earliest of the dates specified in paragraph (h)(3)(ii) of this section will be treated as

satisfying the requirements of paragraph (e) of this section for qualified performance-based compensation, regardless of when the options are exercised.

(i) *(Reserved)*

(j) *Effective date*—(1) *In general.* Section 162(m) and this section apply to compensation that is otherwise deductible by the corporation in a taxable year beginning on or after January 1, 1994.

(2) *Delayed effective date for certain provisions*—(i) *Date on which remuneration is considered paid.* Notwithstanding paragraph (j)(1) of this section, the rules in the second sentence of each of paragraphs (e)(3)(i)(A), (e)(3)(ii)(B), and (e)(3)(i)(C) of this section for determining the date or dates on which remuneration is considered paid to a director are effective for taxable years beginning on or after January 1, 1995. Prior to those taxable years, taxpayers must follow the rules in paragraphs (e)(3)(ii)(A), (e)(3)(ii)(B), and (e)(3)(i)(C) of this section or another reasonable, good faith interpretation of section 162(m) with respect to the date or dates on which remuneration is considered paid to a director.

(ii) *Separate treatment of publicly held subsidiaries.* Notwithstanding paragraph (j)(1) of this section, the rule in paragraph (c)(1)(ii) of this section that treats publicly held subsidiaries as separately subject to section 162(m) is effective as of the first regularly scheduled meeting of the shareholders of the publicly held subsidiary that occurs more than 12 months after December 2, 1994. The rule for stock-based compensation set forth in paragraph (f)(3) of this section will apply for this purpose, except that the grant must occur before the shareholder meeting specified in this paragraph (j)(2)(ii). Taxpayers may choose to rely on the rule referred to in the first sentence of this paragraph (j)(2)(ii) for the period prior to the effective date of the rule.

(iii) *Subsidiaries that become separate publicly held corporations.* Notwithstanding paragraph (j)(1) of this section, if a subsidiary of a publicly held corporation becomes a separate publicly held corporation as described in paragraph (f)(4)(i) of this section, then, for the duration of the reliance period described in paragraph (f)(2) of this section, the rules of paragraph (f)(1) of this section are treated as applying (and the rules of paragraph (f)(4) of this section do not apply) to remuneration paid to covered employees of that new publicly held corporation pursuant to a plan or agreement that existed prior to December 2, 1994, provided that the treatment of that remuneration as performance-based is in accordance with a reasonable, good faith interpretation of

Reg. § 1.162-27(j)(2)

section 162(m). However, if remuneration is paid to covered employees of that new publicly held corporation pursuant to a plan or agreement that existed prior to December 2, 1994, but that remuneration is not performance-based under a reasonable, good faith interpretation of section 162(m), the rules of paragraph (f)(1) of this section will be treated as applying only until the first regularly scheduled meeting of shareholders that occurs more than 12 months after December 2, 1994. The rules of paragraph (f)(4) of this section will apply as of that first regularly scheduled meeting. The rule for stock-based compensation set forth in paragraph (f)(3) of this section will apply for purposes of this paragraph (j)(2)(iii), except that the grant must occur before the shareholder meeting specified in the preceding sentence if the remuneration is not performance-based under a reasonable, good faith interpretation of section 162(m). Taxpayers may choose to rely on the rules of paragraph (f)(4) of this section for the period prior to the applicable effective date referred to in the first or second sentence of this paragraph (j)(2)(iii).

(iv) *Bonus Pools.* Notwithstanding paragraph (j)(1) of this section, the rules in paragraph (e)(2)(iii)(A) that limit the sum of individual percentages of a bonus pool to 100 percent will not apply to remuneration paid before January 1, 2001, based on performance in any performance period that began prior to December 20, 1995.

(v) *Compensation based on a percentage of salary or base pay.* Notwithstanding paragraph (j)(1) of this section, the requirement in paragraph (e)(4)(i) of this section that, in the case of certain formulas based on a percentage of salary or base pay, a corporation disclose to shareholders the maximum dollar amount of compensation that could be paid to the employee, will apply only to plans approved by shareholders after April 30, 1995. [Reg. § 1.162-27.]

☐ [*T.D.* 8650, 12-19-95.]

[Reg. § 1.162-28]

§ 1.162-28. Allocation of costs to lobbying activities.—(a) *Introduction*—(1) *In general.* Section 162(e)(1) denies a deduction for certain amounts paid or incurred in connection with activities described in section 162(e)(1)(A) and (D) (*lobbying activities*). To determine the nondeductible amount, a taxpayer must allocate costs to lobbying activities. This section describes costs that must be allocated to lobbying activities and prescribes rules permitting a taxpayer to use a reasonable method to allocate those costs. This section does not apply to taxpayers subject to section 162(e)(5)(A). In addition, this section does

not apply for purposes of sections 4911 and 4945 and the regulations thereunder.

(2) *Recordkeeping.* For recordkeeping requirements, see section 6001 and the regulations thereunder.

(b) *Reasonable method of allocating costs*—(1) *In general.* A taxpayer must use a reasonable method to allocate the costs described in paragraph (c) of this section to lobbying activities. A method is not reasonable unless it is applied consistently and is consistent with the special rules in paragraph (g) of this section. Except as provided in paragraph (b)(2) of this section, reasonable methods of allocating costs to lobbying activities include (but are not limited to)—

(i) The ratio method described in paragraph (d) of this section;

(ii) The gross-up method described in paragraph (e) of this section; and

(iii) A method that applies the principles of section 263A and the regulations thereunder (see paragraph (f) of this section).

(2) *Taxpayers not permitted to use certain methods.* A taxpayer (other than one subject to section 6033(e)) that does not pay or incur reasonable labor costs for persons engaged in lobbying activities may not use the gross-up method. For example, a partnership or sole proprietorship in which the lobbying activities are performed by the owners who do not receive a salary or guaranteed payment for services does not pay or incur reasonable labor costs for persons engaged in those activities and may not use the gross-up method.

(c) *Costs allocable to lobbying activities*—(1) *In general.* Costs properly allocable to lobbying activities include labor costs and general and administrative costs.

(2) *Labor costs.* For each taxable year, labor costs include costs attributable to full-time, part-time, and contract employees. Labor costs include all elements of compensation, such as basic compensation, overtime pay, vacation pay, holiday pay, sick leave pay, payroll taxes, pension costs, employee benefits, and payments to a supplemental unemployment benefit plan.

(3) *General and administrative costs.* For each taxable year, general and administrative costs include depreciation, rent, utilities, insurance, maintenance costs, security costs, and other administrative department costs (for example, payroll, personnel, and accounting).

(d) *Ratio method*—(1) *In general.* Under the ratio method described in this paragraph (d), a taxpayer allocates to lobbying activities the sum of its third-party costs (as defined in paragraph (d)(5) of this section) allocable to lobbying activities and the costs determined by using the following formula:

$$\frac{\text{Lobbying labor hours}}{\text{Total labor hours}} \times \text{Total costs of operations.}$$

(2) *Lobbying labor hours.* Lobbying labor hours are the hours that a taxpayer's personnel spend on lobbying activities during the taxable year. A taxpayer may use any reasonable method to determine the number of labor hours spent on lobbying activities and may use the de minimis rule of paragraph (g)(1) of this section. A taxpayer may treat as zero the lobbying labor hours of personnel engaged in secretarial, clerical, support, and other administrative activities (as opposed to activities involving significant judgment with respect to lobbying activities). Thus, for example, the hours spent on lobbying activities by para-professionals and analysts may not be treated as zero.

(3) *Total labor hours.* Total labor hours means the total number of hours that a taxpayer's personnel spend on a taxpayer's trade or business during the taxable year. A taxpayer may make reasonable assumptions concerning total hours spent by personnel on the taxpayer's trade or business. For example, it may be reasonable, based on all the facts and circumstances, to assume that all full-time personnel spend 1,800 hours per year on a taxpayer's trade or business. If, under paragraph (d)(2) of this section, a taxpayer treats as zero the lobbying labor hours of personnel engaged in secretarial, clerical, support, and other administrative activities, the taxpayer must also treat as zero the total labor hours of all personnel engaged in those activities.

(4) *Total costs of operations.* A taxpayer's total costs of operations means the total costs of

$$\frac{\text{Lobbying labor hours}}{\text{Total labor hours}} \times \text{Total costs of operations} +$$

$$\frac{[300 + 1,700 + 1,000]}{6,000} \times \$300,000] +$$

(e) *Gross-up method—(1) In general* Under the gross-up method described in this paragraph (e)(1), the taxpayer allocates to lobbying activities the sum of its third-party costs (as defined in paragraph (d)(5) of this section) allocable to lobbying activities and 175 percent of its basic lobbying labor costs (as defined in paragraph (e)(3) of this section) of all personnel.

(2) *Alternative gross-up method.* Under the alternative gross-up method described in this paragraph (e)(2), the taxpayer allocates to lobbying activities the sum of its third-party costs (as de-

the taxpayer's trade or business for a taxable year, excluding third-party costs (as defined in paragraph (d)(5) of this section).

(5) *Third-party costs.* Third-party costs are amounts paid or incurred in whole or in part for lobbying activities conducted by third parties (such as amounts paid to taxpayers subject to section 162(e)(5)(A) or dues or other similar amounts that are not deductible in whole or in part under section 162(e)(3)) and amounts paid or incurred for travel (including meals and lodging while away from home) and entertainment relating in whole or in part to lobbying activities.

(6) *Example.* The provisions of this paragraph (d) are illustrated by the following example.

Example. (i) In 1996, three full-time employees, A, B, and C, of Taxpayer W engage in both lobbying activities and nonlobbying activities. A spends 300 hours, B spends 1,700 hours, and C spends 1,000 hours on lobbying activities, for a total of 3,000 hours spent on lobbying activities for W. W reasonably assumes that each of its three employees spends 2,000 hours a year on W's business.

(ii) W's total costs of operations are $300,000. W has no third-party costs.

(iii) Under the ratio method, X allocates $150,000 to its lobbying activities for 1996, as follows:

$$\frac{\text{Allocable}}{\text{third-party costs}} = \frac{\text{Costs allocable}}{\text{to lobbying activities}}$$

$$[0] = \$150,000.$$

fined in paragraph (d)(5) of this section) allocable to lobbying activities and 225 percent of its basic lobbying labor costs (as defined in paragraph (e)(3)), excluding the costs of personnel who engage in secretarial, clerical, support, and other administrative activities (as opposed to activities involving significant judgment with respect to lobbying activities).

(3) *Basic lobbying labor costs.* For purposes of this paragraph (e), basic lobbying labor costs are the basic costs of lobbying labor hours (as defined in paragraph (d)(2) of this section) deter-

mined for the appropriate personnel. For purposes of this paragraph (e), basic costs of lobbying labor hours are wages or other similar costs of labor, including, for example, guaranteed payments for services. Basic costs do not include pension, profit-sharing, employee benefits, and supplemental unemployment benefit plan costs, or other similar costs.

(4) *Example.* The provisions of this paragraph (e) are illustrated by the following example.

Example. (i) In 1996, three employees, A, B, and C, of Taxpayer X engage in both lobbying activities and nonlobbying activities. A spends

$$175\% \quad \times \quad \begin{array}{c}\text{Basic lobbying labor}\\\text{costs of all personnel}\end{array} \quad + \quad \begin{array}{c}\text{Allocable third-}\\\text{party costs}\end{array} \quad = \quad \begin{array}{c}\text{Costs allocable}\\\text{to lobbying activities}\end{array}$$

$$[175\% \quad \times \quad \$82,000] \quad + \quad [0] \quad = \quad \$143,500.$$

(f) *Section 263A cost allocation methods*—(1) *In general.* A taxpayer may allocate its costs to lobbying activities under the principles set forth in section 263A and the regulations thereunder, except to the extent inconsistent with paragraph (g) of this section. For this purpose, lobbying activities are considered a service department or function. Therefore, a taxpayer may allocate costs to lobbying activities by applying the methods provided in § § 1.263A-1 through 1.263A-3. See § 1.263A-1(e)(4), which describes service costs generally; § 1.263A-1(f), which sets forth cost allocation methods available under section 263A; and § 1.263A-1(g)(4), which provides methods of allocating service costs.

(2) *Example.* The provisions of this paragraph (f) are illustrated by the following example.

Example. (i) Three full-time employees, A, B, and C, work in the Washington office of Taxpayer Y, a manufacturing concern. They each engage in lobbying activities and nonlobbying activities. In 1996, A spends 75 hours, B spends 1,750 hours, and C spends 2,000 hours on lobbying activities. A's hours are not spent on direct contact lobbying as defined in paragraph (g)(2) of this section. All three work 2,000 hours during 1996. The Washington office also employs one secretary, D, who works exclusively for A, B, and C.

(ii) In addition, three departments in the corporate headquarters in Chicago benefit the Washington office: public affairs, human resources, and insurance.

300 hours, B spends 1,700 hours, and C spends 1,000 hours on lobbying activities.

(ii) X has no third-party costs.

(iii) For purposes of the gross-up method, X determines that its basic labor costs are $20 per hour for A, $30 per hour for B, and $25 per hour for C. Thus, its basic lobbying labor costs are ($20 × 300) + ($30 × 1,700) + ($25 × 1,000), or ($6,000 + $51,000 + $25,000), for total basic lobbying labor costs for 1996 of $82,000.

(iv) Under the gross-up method, X allocates $143,500 to its lobbying activities for 1996, as follows:

(iii) Y is subject to section 263A and uses the step-allocation method to allocate its service costs. Prior to the amendments to section 162(e), the Washington office was treated as an overall management function for purposes of section 263A. As such, its costs were fully deductible and no further allocations were made under Y's step allocation. Following the amendments to section 162(e), Y adopts its 263A step-allocation methodology to allocate costs to lobbying activities. Y adds a lobbying department to its step-allocation program, which results in an allocation of costs to the lobbying department from both the Washington office and the Chicago office.

(iv) Y develops a labor ratio to allocate its Washington office costs between the newly defined lobbying department and the overall management department. To determine the hours allocable to lobbying activities, Y uses the de minimis rule of paragraph (g)(1) of this section. Under this rule, A's hours spent on lobbying activities are treated as zero because less than 5 percent of A's time is spent on lobbying (75/2,000 = 3.75%). In addition, because D works exclusively for personnel engaged in lobbying activities, D's hours are not used to develop the allocation ratio. Y assumes that D's allocation of time follows the average time of all the personnel engaged in lobbying activities. Thus, Y's labor ratio is determined as follows:

Departments

Employee	Lobbying Hours	Overall Management Hours	Total Hours
A	0	2,000	2,000
B	1,750	250	2,000
C	2,000	0	2,000
Totals	3,750	2,250	6,000

Reg. § 1.162-28(e)(4)

Lobbying Department Ratio $= \dfrac{3,750}{6,000} = 62.5\%$

Overall Management Department Ratio $= \dfrac{2,250}{6,000} = 37.5\%$

(v) In 1996, the Washington office has the following costs:

Account		Amount
Professional Salaries and Benefits	$	660,000
Clerical Salaries and Benefits		50,000
Rent Expense		100,000
Depreciation on Furniture and Equip.		40,000
Utilities		15,000
Outside Payroll Service		5,000
Miscellaneous		10,000
Third-Party Lobbying (Law Firm)		90,000
Total Washington Costs	$	970,000

(vi) In addition, $233,800 of costs from the public affairs department, $30,000 of costs from the insurance department, and $5,000 of costs from the human resources department are alloca-ble to the Washington office from departments in Chicago. Therefore, the Washington office costs are allocated to the Lobbying and Overall Management departments as follows:

Total Washington department costs from above	$	970,000
Plus Costs Allocated From Other Departments		268,800
Less third-party costs directly allocable to lobbying		(90,000)
Total Washington office costs	$	1,148,800

	Lobbying Department	Overall Mgmt. Department
Department Allocation Ratios	62.5%	37.5%
× Washington Office Costs	$ 1,148,800	$ 1,148,800
= Costs Allocated To Departments	$ 718,000	$ 430,800

(vii) Y's step-allocation for its Lobbying Department is determined as follows:

Y's Step-Allocation	Lobbying Department
Washington Costs Allocated To Lobbying Department	$ 718,000
Plus Third-Party Costs	90,000
Total Costs of Lobbying Activities	$ 808,000

(g) *Special rules.* The following rules apply to any reasonable method of allocating costs to lobbying activities.

(1) *De minimis rule for labor hours.* Subject to the exception provided in paragraph (g)(2) of this section, a taxpayer may treat time spent by an individual on lobbying activities as zero if less than five percent of the person's time is spent on lobbying activities. Reasonable methods must be used to determine if less than five percent of a person's time is spent on lobbying activities.

(2) *Direct contact lobbying labor hours.* Notwithstanding paragraph (g)(1) of this section, a taxpayer must treat all hours spent by a person on direct contact lobbying (as well as the hours that person spends in connection with direct contact lobbying, including time spent traveling that is allocable to the direct contact lobbying) as labor hours allocable to lobbying activities. An activity is direct contact lobbying if it is a meeting, telephone conversation, letter, or other similar means of communication with a legislator (other than a local legislator) or covered executive branch official (as defined in section 162(e)(6)) and otherwise qualifies as a lobbying activity. A person who engages in research, preparation, and other background activities related to direct contact lobbying but who does not make direct contact with a legislator or covered executive branch official is not engaged in direct contact lobbying.

(3) *Taxpayer defined.* For purposes of this section a taxpayer includes a tax-exempt organization subject to section 6033(e).

Reg. § 1.162-28(g)(3)

(h) *Effective date.* This section is effective for amounts paid or incurred on or after July 21, 1995. Taxpayers must adopt a reasonable interpretation of sections 162(e)(1)(A) and (D) for amounts paid or incurred before this date. [Reg. § 1.162-28.]

☐ [*T.D.* 8602, 7-20-95.]

[Reg. § 1.162-29]

§ 1.162-29. **Influencing legislation.**—(a) *Scope.* This section provides rules for determining whether an activity is influencing legislation for purposes of section 162(e)(1)(A). This section does not apply for purposes of sections 4911 and 4945 and the regulations thereunder.

(b) *Definitions.* For purposes of this section—

(1) *Influencing legislation.* Influencing legislation means—

(i) Any attempt to influence any legislation through a lobbying communication; and

(ii) All activities, such as research, preparation, planning, and coordination, including deciding whether to make a lobbying communication, engaged in for a purpose of making or supporting a lobbying communication, even if not yet made. See paragraph (c) of this section for rules for determining the purposes for engaging in an activity.

(2) *Attempt to influence legislation.* An attempt to influence any legislation through a lobbying communication is making the lobbying communication.

(3) *Lobbying communication.* A lobbying communication is any communication (other than any communication compelled by subpoena, or otherwise compelled by Federal or State law) with any member or employee of a legislative body or any other government official or employee who may participate in the formulation of the legislation that—

(i) Refers to specific legislation and reflects a view on that legislation; or

(ii) Clarifies, amplifies, modifies, or provides support for views reflected in a prior lobbying communication.

(4) *Legislation.* Legislation includes any action with respect to Acts, bills, resolutions, or other similar items by a legislative body. Legislation includes a proposed treaty required to be submitted by the President to the Senate for its advice and consent from the time the President's representative begins to negotiate its position with the prospective parties to the proposed treaty.

(5) *Specific legislation.* Specific legislation includes a specific legislative proposal that has not been introduced in a legislative body.

(6) *Legislative bodies.* Legislative bodies are Congress, state legislatures, and other similar governing bodies, excluding local councils (and similar governing bodies), and executive, judicial, or administrative bodies. For this purpose, administrative bodies include school boards, housing authorities, sewer and water districts, zoning boards, and other similar Federal, State, or local special purpose bodies, whether elective or appointive.

(7) *Examples.* The provisions of this paragraph (b) are illustrated by the following examples.

Example 1. Taxpayer P's employee, A, is assigned to approach members of Congress to gain their support for a pending bill. A drafts and P prints a position letter on the bill. P distributes the letter to members of Congress. Additionally, A personally contacts several members of Congress or their staffs to seek support for P's position on the bill. The letter and the personal contacts are lobbying communications. Therefore, P is influencing legislation.

Example 2. Taxpayer R is invited to provide testimony at a congressional oversight hearing concerning the implementation of The Financial Institutions Reform, Recovery, and Enforcement Act of 1989. Specifically, the hearing concerns a proposed regulation increasing the threshold value of commercial and residential real estate transactions for which an appraisal by a state licensed or certified appraiser is required. In its testimony, R states that it is in favor of the proposed regulation. Because R does not refer to any specific legislation or reflect a view on any such legislation, R has not made a lobbying communication. Therefore, R is not influencing legislation.

Example 3. State X enacts a statute that requires the licensing of all day-care providers. Agency B in State X is charged with writing rules to implement the statute. After the enactment of the statute, Taxpayer S sends a letter to Agency B providing detailed proposed rules that S recommends Agency B adopt to implement the statute on licensing of day-care providers. Because the letter to Agency B neither refers to nor reflects a view on any specific legislation, it is not a lobbying communication. Therefore, S is not influencing legislation.

Example 4. Taxpayer T proposes to a State Park Authority that it purchase a particular tract of land for a new park. Even if T's proposal would necessarily require the State Park Authority eventually to seek appropriations to acquire the land and develop the new park, T has not made a lobbying communication because there has been no reference to, nor any view reflected on, any specific legislation. Therefore, T's proposal is not influencing legislation.

Example 5. (i) Taxpayer U prepares a paper that asserts that lack of new capital is hurting State X's economy. The paper indicates that State X residents either should invest more in local businesses or increase their savings so that funds will be available to others interested in making investments. U forwards a summary of the unpublished paper to legislators in State X with a cover letter that states in part:

You must take action to improve the availability of new capital in the state.

(ii) Because neither the summary nor the cover letter refers to any specific legislative proposal and no other facts or circumstances indicate that they refer to an existing legislative proposal, forwarding the summary to legislators in State X is not a lobbying communication. Therefore, U is not influencing legislation.

(iii) Q, a member of the legislature of State X, calls U to request a copy of the unpublished paper from which the summary was prepared. U forwards the paper with a cover letter that simply refers to the enclosed materials. Because U's letter to Q and the unpublished paper do not refer to any specific legislation or reflect a view on any such legislation, the letter is not a lobbying communication. Therefore, U is not influencing legislation.

Example 6. (i) Taxpayer V prepares a paper that asserts that lack of new capital is hurting the national economy. The paper indicates that lowering the capital gains rate would increase the availability of capital and increase tax receipts from the capital gains tax. V forwards the paper to its representatives in Congress with a cover letter that says, in part:

I urge you to support a reduction in the capital gains tax rate.

(ii) V's communication is a lobbying communication because it refers to and reflects a view on a specific legislative proposal (i.e., lowering the capital gains rate). Therefore, V is influencing legislation.

Example 7. Taxpayer W, based in State A, notes in a letter to a legislator of State A that State X has passed a bill that accomplishes a stated purpose and then says that State A should pass such a bill. No such bill has been introduced into the State A legislature. The communication is a lobbying communication because it refers to and reflects a view on a specific legislative proposal. Therefore, W is influencing legislation.

Example 8. (i) Taxpayer Y represents citrus fruit growers. Y writes a letter to a United States senator discussing how pesticide O has benefited citrus fruit growers and disputing problems linked to its use. The letter discusses a bill pending in Congress and states in part:

This bill would prohibit the use of pesticide O. If citrus growers are unable to use this pesticide, their crop yields will be severely reduced, leading to higher prices for consumers and lower profits, even bankruptcy, for growers.

(ii) Y's views on the bill are reflected in this statement. Thus, the communication is a lobbying communication, and Y is influencing legislation.

Example 9. (i) B, the president of Taxpayer Z, an insurance company, meets with Q, who chairs the X state legislature's committee with jurisdiction over laws regulating insurance companies, to discuss the possibility of legislation to address current problems with surplus-line companies. B recommends that legislation be introduced that would create minimum capital and surplus requirements for surplus-line companies and create clearer guidelines concerning the risks that surplus-line companies can insure. B's discussion with Q is a lobbying communication because B refers to and reflects a view on a specific legislative proposal. Therefore, Z is influencing legislation.

(ii) Q is not convinced that the market for surplus-line companies is substantial enough to warrant such legislation and requests that B provide information on the amount and types of risks covered by surplus-line companies. After the meeting, B has employees of Z prepare estimates of the percentage of property and casualty insurance risks handled by surplus-line companies. B sends the estimates with a cover letter that simply refers to the enclosed materials. Although B's follow-up letter to Q does not refer to specific legislation or reflect a view on such legislation, B's letter supports the views reflected in the earlier communication. Therefore, the letter is a lobbying communication and Z is influencing legislation.

(c) *Purpose for engaging in an activity*—(1) *In general.* The purposes for engaging in an activity are determined based on all the facts and circumstances. Facts and circumstances include, but are not limited to—

(i) Whether the activity and the lobbying communication are proximate in time;

(ii) Whether the activity and the lobbying communication relate to similar subject matter;

(iii) Whether the activity is performed at the request of, under the direction of, or on behalf of a person making the lobbying communication;

Reg. § 1.162-29(c)(1)

(iv) Whether the results of the activity are also used for a nonlobbying purpose; and

(v) Whether, at the time the taxpayer engages in the activity, there is specific legislation to which the activity relates.

(2) *Multiple purposes.* If a taxpayer engages in an activity both for the purpose of making or supporting a lobbying communication and for some nonlobbying purpose, the taxpayer must treat the activity as engaged in partially for a lobbying purpose and partially for a nonlobbying purpose. This division of the activity must result in a reasonable allocation of costs to influencing legislation. See § 1.162-28 (allocation rules for certain expenditures to which section 162(e)(1) applies). A taxpayer's treatment of these multiple-purpose activities will, in general, not result in a reasonable allocation if it allocates to influencing legislation—

(i) Only the incremental amount of costs that would not have been incurred but for the lobbying purpose; or

(ii) An amount based solely on the number of purposes for engaging in that activity without regard to the relative importance of those purposes.

(3) *Activities treated as having no purpose to influence legislation.* A taxpayer that engages in any of the following activities is treated as having done so without a purpose of making or supporting a lobbying communication—

(i) Before evidencing a purpose to influence any specific legislation referred to in paragraph (c)(3)(i)(A) or (B) of this section (or similar legislation)—

(A) Determining the existence or procedural status of specific legislation, or the time, place, and subject of any hearing to be held by a legislative body with respect to specific legislation; or

(B) Preparing routine, brief summaries of the provisions of specific legislation;

(ii) Performing an activity for purposes of complying with the requirements of any law (for example, satisfying state or federal securities law filing requirements);

(iii) Reading any publications available to the general public or viewing or listening to other mass media communications; and

(iv) Merely attending a widely attended speech.

(4) *Examples.* The provisions of this paragraph (c) are illustrated by the following examples.

Example 1. (i) *Facts.* In 1997, Agency F issues proposed regulations relating to the business of Taxpayer W. There is no specific legislation during 1997 that is similar to the regulatory proposal. W undertakes a study of the impact of the proposed regulations on its business. W incorporates the results of that study in comments sent to Agency F in 1997. In 1998, legislation is introduced in Congress that is similar to the regulatory proposal. Also in 1998, W writes a letter to Senator P stating that it opposes the proposed legislation. W encloses with the letter a copy of the comments it sent to Agency F.

(ii) *Analysis.* W's letter to Senator P refers to and reflects a view on specific legislation and therefore is a lobbying communication. Although W's study of the impact of the proposed regulations is proximate in time and similar in subject matter to its lobbying communication, W performed the study and incorporated the results in comments sent to Agency F when no legislation with a similar subject matter was pending (a nonlobbying use). On these facts, W engaged in the study solely for a nonlobbying purpose.

Example 2. (i) *Facts.* The governor of State Q proposes a budget that includes a proposed sales tax on electricity. Using its records of electricity consumption, Taxpayer Y estimates the additional costs that the budget proposal would impose upon its business. In the same year, Y writes to members of the state legislature and explains that it opposes the proposed sales tax. In its letter, Y includes its estimate of the costs that the sales tax would impose on its business. Y does not demonstrate any other use of its estimates.

(ii) *Analysis.* The letter is a lobbying communication (because it refers to and reflects a view on specific legislation, the governor's proposed budget). Y's estimate of additional costs under the proposal supports the lobbying communication, is proximate in time and similar in subject matter to a specific legislative proposal then in existence, and is not used for a nonlobbying purpose. Based on these facts, Y estimated its additional costs under the budget proposal solely to support the lobbying communication.

Example 3. (i) *Facts.* A senator in the State Q legislature announces her intention to introduce legislation to require health insurers to cover a particular medical procedure in all policies sold in the state. Taxpayer Y has different policies for two groups of employees, one of which covers the procedure and one of which does not. After the bill is introduced, Y's legislative affairs staff asks Y's human resources staff to estimate the additional cost to cover the procedure for both groups of employees. Y's human resources staff prepares a

Reg. § 1.162-29(c)(2)

study estimating Y's increased costs and forwards it to the legislative affairs staff. Y's legislative staff then writes to members of the state legislature and explains that it opposes the proposed change in insurance coverage based on the study. Y's legislative affairs staff thereafter forwards the study, prepared for its use in opposing the statutory proposal, to its labor relations staff for use in negotiations with employees scheduled to begin later in the year.

(ii) *Analysis.* The letter to legislators is a lobbying communication (because it refers to and reflects a view on specific legislation). The activity of estimating Y's additional costs under the proposed legislation relate to the same subject as the lobbying communication, occurs close in time to the lobbying communication, is conducted at the request of a person making a lobbying communication, and relates to specific legislation then in existence. Although Y used the study in its labor negotiations, mere use for that purpose does not establish that Y estimated its additional costs under the proposed legislation in part for a nonlobbying purpose. Thus, based on all the facts and circumstances, Y estimated the additional costs it would incur under the proposal solely to make or support the lobbying communication.

Example 4. (i) *Facts.* After several years of developmental work under various contracts, in 1996, Taxpayer A contracts with the Department of Defense (DOD) to produce a prototype of a new generation military aircraft. A is aware that DOD will be able to fund the contract only if Congress appropriates an amount for that purpose in the upcoming appropriations process. In 1997, A conducts simulation tests of the aircraft and revises the specifications of the aircraft's expected performance capabilities, as required under the contract. A submits the results of the tests and the revised specifications to DOD. In 1998, Congress considers legislation to appropriate funds for the contract. In that connection, A summarizes the results of the simulation tests and of the aircraft's expected performance capabilities, and submits the summary to interested members of Congress with a cover letter that encourages them to support appropriations of funds for the contract.

(ii) *Analysis.* The letter is a lobbying communication (because it refers to specific legislation (i.e., appropriations) and requests passage). The described activities in 1996, 1997, and 1998 relate to the same subject as the lobbying communication. The summary was prepared specifically for, and close in time to, that communication. Based on these facts, the summary was prepared solely for a lobbying purpose. In contrast, A conducted the tests and revised the specifications to comply

with its production contract with DOD. A conducted the tests and revised the specifications solely for a nonlobbying purpose.

Example 5. (i) *Facts.* C, president of Taxpayer W, travels to the state capital to attend a two-day conference on new manufacturing processes. C plans to spend a third day in the capital meeting with state legislators to explain why W opposes a pending bill unrelated to the subject of the conference. At the meetings with the legislators, C makes lobbying communications by referring to and reflecting a view on the pending bill.

(ii) *Analysis.* C's traveling expenses (transportation and meals and lodging) are partially for the purpose of making or supporting the lobbying communications and partially for a nonlobbying purpose. As a result, under paragraph (c)(2) of this section, W must reasonably allocate C's traveling expenses between these two purposes. Allocating to influencing legislation only C's incremental transportation expenses (i.e., the taxi fare to meet with the state legislators) does not result in a reasonable allocation of traveling expenses.

Example 6. (i) *Facts.* On February 1, 1997, a bill is introduced in Congress that would affect Company E. Employees in E's legislative affairs department, as is customary, prepare a brief summary of the bill and periodically confirm the procedural status of the bill through conversations with employees and members of Congress. On March 31, 1997, the head of E's legislative affairs department meets with E's President to request that B, a chemist, temporarily help the legislative affairs department analyze the bill. The President agrees, and suggests that B also be assigned to draft a position letter in opposition to the bill. Employees of the legislative affairs department continue to confirm periodically the procedural status of the bill. On October 31, 1997, B's position letter in opposition to the bill is delivered to members of Congress.

(ii) *Analysis.* B's letter is a lobbying communication because it refers to and reflects a view on specific legislation. Under paragraph (c)(3)(i) of this section, the assignment of B to assist the legislative affairs department in analyzing the bill and in drafting a position letter in opposition to the bill evidences a purpose to influence legislation. Neither the activity of periodically confirming the procedural status of the bill nor the activity of preparing the routine, brief summary of the bill before March 31 constitutes influencing legislation. In contrast, periodically confirming the procedural status of the bill on or after March 31 relates to the same subject as, and is close in time to, the lobbying communication and is used for no nonlobbying purpose. Consequently, after March 31, E determined the procedural status of the bill for the purpose of supporting the lobbying communication by B.

(d) *Lobbying communication made by another.* If a taxpayer engages in activities for a purpose of supporting a lobbying communication to be made by another person (or by a group of persons), the taxpayer's activities are treated under paragraph (b) of this section as influencing legislation. For example, if a taxpayer or an employee of the taxpayer (as a volunteer or otherwise) engages in an activity to assist a trade association in preparing its lobbying communication, the taxpayer's activities are influencing legislation even if the lobbying communication is made by the trade association and not the taxpayer. If, however, the taxpayer's employee, acting outside the employee's scope of employment, volunteers to engage in those activities, then the taxpayer is not influencing legislation.

(e) *No lobbying communication.* Paragraph (e) of this section applies if a taxpayer engages in an activity for a purpose of making or supporting a lobbying communication, but no lobbying communication that the activity supports has yet been made.

(1) *Before the filing date.* Under this paragraph (e)(1), if on the filing date of the return for any taxable year the taxpayer no longer expects, under any reasonably foreseeable circumstances, that a lobbying communication will be made that is supported by the activity, then the taxpayer will be treated as if it did not engage in the activity for a purpose of making or supporting a lobbying communication. Thus, the taxpayer need not treat any amount allocated to that activity for that year under § 1.162-28 as an amount to which section 162(e)(1)(A) applies. The filing date for purposes of paragraph (e) of this section is the earlier of the time the taxpayer files its timely return for the year or the due date of the timely return.

(2) *After the filing date—(i) In general.* If, at any time after the filing date, the taxpayer no longer expects, under any reasonably foreseeable circumstances, that a lobbying communication will be made that is supported by the activity, then any amount previously allocated under § 1.162-28 to the activity and disallowed under section 162(e)(1)(A) is treated as an amount that is not subject to section 162(e)(1)(A) and that is paid or incurred only at the time the taxpayer no longer expects that a lobbying communication will be made.

(ii) *Special rule for certain tax-exempt organizations.* For a tax-exempt organization subject to section 6033(e), the amounts described in paragraph (e)(2)(i) of this section are treated as reducing (but not below zero) its expenditures to which section 162(e)(1) applies beginning with that year and continuing for subsequent years to the extent not treated in prior years as reducing those expenditures.

(f) *Anti-avoidance rule.* If a taxpayer, alone or with others, structures its activities with a principal purpose of achieving results that are unreasonable in light of the purposes of section 162(e)(1)(A) and section 6033(e), the Commissioner can recast the taxpayer's activities for federal tax purposes as appropriate to achieve tax results that are consistent with the intent of section 162(e)(1)(A), section 6033(e) (if applicable), and this section, and the pertinent facts and circumstances.

(g) *Taxpayer defined.* For purposes of this section, a taxpayer includes a tax-exempt organization subject to section 6033(e).

(h) *Effective date.* This section is effective for amounts paid or incurred on or after July 21, 1995. Taxpayers must adopt a reasonable interpretation of section 162(e)(1)(A) for amounts paid or incurred before this date. [Reg. § 1.162-29.]

☐ [*T.D. 8602, 7-20-95.*]

[Reg. § 1.163-1]

§ 1.163-1. **Interest deduction in general.—(a)** Except as otherwise provided in sections 264 to 267, inclusive, interest paid or accrued within the taxable year on indebtedness shall be allowed as a deduction in computing taxable income. For rules relating to interest on certain deferred payments, see section 483 and the regulations thereunder.

(b) Interest paid by the taxpayer on a mortgage upon real estate of which he is the legal or equitable owner, even though the taxpayer is not directly liable upon the bond or note secured by such mortgage, may be deducted as interest on his indebtedness. Pursuant to the provisions of section 163(c), any annual or periodic rental payment made by a taxpayer on or after January 1, 1962, under a redeemable ground rent, as defined in section 1055(c) and paragraph (b) of § 1.1055-1, is required to be treated as interest on an indebtedness secured by a mortgage and, accordingly, may be deducted by the taxpayer as interest on his indebtedness. Section 163(c) has no application in respect of any annual or periodic rental payment made prior to January 1, 1962, or pursuant to an arrangement which does not constitute a "redeemable ground rent" as defined in section 1055(c) and paragraph (b) of § 1.1055-1.

Accordingly, annual or periodic payments of Pennsylvania ground rents made before, on, or after January 1, 1962, are deductible as interest if the ground rent is redeemable. An annual or periodic rental payment under a Maryland redeemable ground rent made prior to January 1, 1962, is deductible in accordance with the rules and regulations applicable at the time such payment was made. Any annual or periodic rental payment under a Maryland redeemable ground rent made by the taxpayer on or after January 1, 1962, is, pursuant to the provisions of section 163(c), treated as interest on an indebtedness secured by a mortgage and, accordingly, is deductible by the taxpayer as interest on his indebtedness. In any case where the ground rent is irredeemable, any annual or periodic ground rent payment shall be treated as rent and shall be deductible only to the extent that the payment constitutes a proper business expense. Amounts paid in redemption of a ground rent shall not be treated as interest. For treatment of redeemable ground rents and real property held subject to liabilities under redeemable ground rents, see section 1055 and the regulations thereunder.

(c) Interest calculated for costkeeping or other purposes on account of capital or surplus invested in the business which does not represent a charge arising under an interest-bearing obligation, is not an allowable deduction from gross income. Interest paid by a corporation on scrip dividends is an allowable deduction. So-called interest on preferred stock, which is in reality a dividend thereon, cannot be deducted in computing taxable income. (See, however, section 583). In case of banks and loan or trust companies, interest paid within the year on deposits, such as interest paid on moneys received for investment and secured by interest-bearing certificates of indebtedness issued by such bank or loan or trust company, may be deducted from gross income.

(d) To the extent of assistance payments made in respect of an indebtedness of the taxpayer during the taxable year by the Department of Housing and Urban Development under section 235 of the National Housing Act (12 U.S.C. § 1715z), as amended, no deduction shall be allowed under section 163 and this section for interest paid or accrued with respect to such indebtedness. However, such payments shall not affect the amount of any deduction under any section of the Code other than section 163. The provisions of this paragraph shall apply to taxable years beginning after December 31, 1974. [Reg. § 1.163-1.]

☐ [*T.D.* 6223, 1-23-57. *Amended by T.D.* 6593, 2-28-62, *T.D.* 6821, 5-3-65, *T.D.* 6873, 1-24-66, *and T.D.* 7408, 3-4-76.]

[Reg. § 5f.163-1]

§ 5f.163-1. Denial of interest deduction on certain obligations issued after December 31, 1982, unless issued in registered form (temporary).—(a) *Denial of deduction generally.* Interest paid or accrued on a registration-required obligation (as defined in paragraph (b) of this section) shall not be allowed as a deduction under section 163 or any other provision of law unless such obligation is issued in registered form (as defined in § 5f.103-1(c)).

(b) *Registration-required obligation.* For purposes of this section, the term "registration-required obligation" means any obligation except any one of the following:

(1) An obligation issued by a natural person.

(2) An obligation not of a type offered to the public. The determination as to whether an obligation is not of a type offered to the public shall be based on whether similar obligations are in fact publicly offered or traded.

(3) An obligation that has a maturity at the date of issue of not more than 1 year.

(4) An obligation issued before January 1, 1983. An obligation first issued before January 1, 1983, shall not be considered to have been issued on or after such date merely as a result of the existence of a right on the part of the holder of such obligation to convert such obligation from registered form into bearer form, or as a result of the exercise of such a right.

(5) An obligation described in subparagraph (1) of paragraph (c) (relating to certain obligations issued to foreign persons).

(c) [Reserved.]

(d) *Effective date.* The provisions of this section shall apply to obligations issued after December 31, 1982, unless issued on an exercise of a warrant for the conversion of a convertible obligation if such warrant or obligation was offered or sold outside the United States without registration under the Securities Act of 1933 and was issued before August 10, 1982.

(e) *Obligations first issued after December 31, 1982, where the right exists for the holder to convert such obligation from registered form into bearer form.* [Reserved]

(f) *Examples.* The application of this section may be illustrated by the following examples:

Example (1). All of the shares of Corporation X are owned by two individuals, A and B. X desires

Reg. § 5f.163-1(f)

to sell all of its assets to Corporation Y, all of the shares of which are owned by individual C. Following the sale, Corporation X will be completely liquidated. As partial consideration for the Corporation X assets, Corporation Y delivers a promissory note to X, secured by a security interest and mortgage on the acquired assets. The note given by Y to X is not of a type offered to the public.

Example (2). Corporation 2 has a credit agreement with Bank M pursuant to which Corporation Z may borrow amounts not exceeding $10X upon delivery of Z's note to Bank M. The note Z delivers to M is not of a type offered to the public.

Example (3). Individuals D and E operate a retail business through partnership DE. D wishes to loan partnership DE $5X. DE's note evidencing the loan from D is not of a type offered to the public.

Example (4). Individual F owns one-third of the shares of Corporation W. F makes a cash advance to W. W's note evidencing F's cash advance is not of a type offered to the public.

Example (5). Closely-held Corporation R places its convertible debentures with 30 individuals who are United States persons. The offering is not required to be registered under the Securities Act of 1933. Similar debentures are publicly offered and traded. The obligations are not considered of a type not offered to the public.

Example (6). In 1980, Corporation V issued its bonds due in 1986 through an offering registered with the Securities and Exchange Commission. Although the bonds were initially issued in registered form, the terms of the bonds permit a holder, at his option, to convert a bond into bearer form at any time prior to maturity. Similarly, a person who holds a bond in bearer form may, at any time, have the bond converted into registered form.

    (i) Assume G bought one of Corporation V's bonds upon the original issuance in 1980. In 1983, G requests that V convert the bond into bearer form. Except for the change from registered to bearer form, the terms of the bond are unchanged. The bond held by G is not considered issued after December 31, 1982, under § 5f.163-1(b)(4).

    (ii) Assume H buys one of Corporation V's bonds in the secondary market in 1983. The bond H receives is in registered form, but H requests that V convert the obligation into bearer form. There is no other change in the terms of the instrument. The bond held by H is not considered issued after December 31, 1982, under § 5f.163-1(b)(4).

    (iii) Assume the same facts as in (ii) except that in 1984 I purchases H's V Corporation bond, which is in bearer form. I requests V to convert the bond into registered form. There is no other change in the terms of the instrument. In 1985, I requests V to convert the bond bank into bearer form. Again, there is no other change in the terms of the instrument. The bond purchased by I is not considered issued after December 31, 1982, under § 5f.163-1(b)(4).

Example (7). Corporation U wishes to make a public offering of its debentures to United States persons. U issues a master note to Bank N. The terms of the note require that any person who acquires an interest in the note must have such interest reflected in a book entry. Bank N offers for sale interests in the Corporation U note. Ownership interests in the note are reflected on the books of Bank N. Corporation U's debenture is considered issued in registered form.

Example (8). Issuer S wishes to make a public offering of its debt obligations to United States persons. The obligations will have a maturity in excess of one year. On November 1, 1982, the closing on the debt offering occurs. At the closing, the net cash proceeds of the offering are delivered to S, and S delivers a master note to the underwriter of the offering. On January 2, 1983, S delivers the debt obligations to the purchasers, in definitive form and the master note is cancelled. The obligations are not registration-required because they are considered issued before January 1, 1983.

Example (9). In July 1983, Corporation T sells an issue of debt obligations maturing in 1985 to the public in the United States. Three of the obligations of the issue are issued to J in bearer form. The balance of the obligations of the issue are issued in registered form. The terms of the registered and bearer obligations are identical. The obligations issued to J are of a type offered to the public and are registration-required obligations. Since the three obligations are issued in bearer form, T is subject to the tax imposed under section 4701 with respect to the three bearer obligations. In addition, interest paid or accrued on the three bearer obligations is not deductible by T. Moreover, since the issuance of the three bearer obligations is subject to tax under section 4701, J is not prohibited from deducting losses on the obligations under section 165(j) or from treating gain on the obligations as capital gain under section 1232(d). The balance of the obligations in the issue do not give rise to liability for the tax under section 4701, and the deductibility of interest on such obligations is not affected by section 163(f).

Reg. § 5f.163-1(f)

Example (10). Broker K acquires a bond issued in 1980 by the United States Treasury through the Bureau of Public Debt. Broker K sells interests in the bond to the public after December 31, 1982. A purchaser may acquire an interest in any interest payment falling due under the bond or an interest in the principal of the bond. The bond is held by Custodian L for the benefit of the persons acquiring these interests. On receipt of interest and principal payments under the bond, Custodian L transfers the amount received to the person whose ownership interest corresponds to the bond component giving rise to the payment. Under section 1232B, each bond component is treated as an obligation issued with original issue discount equal to the excess of the stated redemption price at maturity over the purchase price of the bond component. The interests sold by K are obligations of a type offered to the public. Further, the interests are, in accordance with section 1232B, considered issued after December 31, 1982. Accordingly, the interests are registration-required obligations under § 5f.163-1(b). [Temporary Reg. § 5f.163-1.]

□ [*T.D. 7852, 11-9-82. Amended by T.D. 7965, 8-17-84.*]

[Reg. § 1.163-2]

§ **1.163-2. Installment purchases where interest charge is not separately stated.—**(a) *In general.* (1) Whenever there is a contract with a seller for the purchase of personal property providing for payment of part or all of the purchase price in installments and there is a separately stated carrying charge (including a finance charge, service charge, and the like) but the actual interest charge cannot be ascertained, a portion of the payments made during the taxable year under the contract shall be treated as interest and is deductible under section 163 and this section. Section 163(b) contains a formula, described in paragraph (b) of this section, in accordance with which the amount of interest deductible in the taxable year must be computed. This formula is designed to operate automatically in the case of any installment purchase, without regard to whether payments under the contract are made when due or are in default. For applicable limitations when an obligation to pay is terminated, see paragraph (c) of this section.

(2) Whenever there is a contract with an educational institution for the purchase of educational services providing for payment of part or all of the purchase price in installments and there is a separately stated carrying charge (including a finance charge, service charge, and the like) but the actual interest charge cannot be ascertained,

a portion of the payments made during the taxable year under the contract shall be treated as interest and is deductible under section 163 and this section. See paragraphs (b) and (c) of this section for the applicable computation and limitations rules. For purposes of section 163(b) and this section, the term "educational services" means any service (including lodging), which is purchased from an educational institution (as defined in section 151(e)(4) and paragraph (c) of § 1.151-3) and which is provided for a student of such institution.

(3) Section 163(b) and this section do not apply to a contract for the loan of money, even if the loan is to be repaid in installments and even if the borrowed amount is used to purchase personal property or educational services. In cases to which the preceding sentence applies, the portion of the installment payment which constitutes interest (as distinguished from payments of principal and charges such as payments for credit life insurance) is deductible under section 163(a) and § 1.163-1.

(b) *Computation.* The portion of any such payments to be treated as interest shall be equal to 6 percent of the average unpaid balance under the contract during the taxable year. For purposes of this computation, the average unpaid balance under the contract is the sum of the unpaid balance outstanding on the first day of each month beginning during the taxable year, divided by 12.

(c) *Limitations.* The amount treated as interest under section 163(b) and this section for any taxable year shall not exceed the amount of the payments made under the contract during the taxable year nor the aggregate carrying charges properly attributable to each contract for such taxable year. In computing the amount to be treated as interest if the obligation to pay is terminated as, for example, in the case of a repossession of the property, the unpaid balance on the first day of the month during which the obligation is terminated shall be zero.

(d) *Illustrations.* The provisions of this section may be illustrated by the following examples:

Example (1). On January 20, 1955, A purchased a television set for $400, including a stated carrying charge of $25. The down payment was $50, and the balance was paid in 14 monthly installments of $25 each, on the 20th day of each month commencing with February. Assuming that A is a cash method, calendar year taxpayer and that no other installment purchases were made, the amount to be treated as interest in 1955 is $12.38, computed as follows:

Year 1955

First day of:	Unpaid balance outstanding
January	$ 0
February	350
March	325
April	300
May	275
June	250
July	225
August	200
September	175
October	150
November	125
December	100
	$2,475

Sum of unpaid balances $2,475 ÷ 12 = $206.25;
6 percent thereof = $12.38.

Example (2). On November 20, 1955, B purchased a furniture set for $1,250, including a stated carrying charge of $48. The down payment was $50 and the balance was payable in 12 monthly installments of $100 each, on the first day of each month commencing with December 1955. Assume that B is a cash method, calendar year taxpayer and that no other installment purchases were made. Assume further that B made the first payment when due, but made only one other payment on June 1, 1956. The amount to be treated as interest in 1955 is $4, and the amount to be treated as interest in 1956 is $33, computed as follows:

Year 1955

First day of:	Unpaid balance outstanding
December	$1,200

Sum of unpaid balances $1200 ÷ 12 = $100;
6 percent thereof = $6.
Carrying charges attributable to 1955 = $4.

Year 1956

First day of:	Unpaid balance outstanding
January	$1,100
February	1,000
March	900
April	800
May	700
June	600
July	500
August	400
September	300
October	200
November	100
	$6,600

Sum of unpaid balances $6,600 ÷ 12 = $550;
6 percent thereof = $33.

Carrying charges attributable to 1956 = $44.
($4 × 11).

Example (3). Assume the same facts as in example (2), except that the furniture was repossessed and B's obligation to pay terminated as of July 15, 1956. The amount to be treated as interest in 1955 is $4, computed as in example (2) above. The amount to be treated as interest in 1956 is $25.50, computed as follows:

Year 1956

First day of:	Unpaid balance outstanding
January	$1,100
February	1,000
March	900
April	800
May	700
June	600
July—November	0
	$5,100

Sum of unpaid balances $5,100 ÷ 12 = $425;
6 percent thereof = $25.50.
Carrying charges attributable to 1956 = $44
($4 × 11).

Example (4). (i) On September 15, 1968, C registered at X University for the 1968-69 academic year. C entered into an agreement with the X University for the purchase during such academic year of educational services (including lodging and tuition) for a total fee of $1,000, including a separately stated carrying charge of $50. Under the terms of the agreement, an initial payment of $200 was to be made by C on September 15, 1968, and the balance was to be paid in 8 monthly installments of $100 each, on the 15th day of each month commencing with October 1968. C made all of the required 1968 payments. Assuming that C is a cash method, calendar year taxpayer and that no other installment purchases of services or property were made, the amount to be treated as interest in 1968 is $10.50, computed as follows:

Year 1968

First day of:	Unpaid balance outstanding
January—September	$ 0
October	800
November	700
December	600
	$2,100

The sum of unpaid balances ($2,100) divided by 12 is $175; 6 percent thereof is $10.50. The carrying charges attributable to 1968 are $18.75 (i.e., the total carrying charges ($50), divided by the total number of payments (8), multiplied by the number of payments made in 1968 (3)). Since the

Reg. § 1.163-2(d)

amount to be treated as interest in 1968 ($10.50) does not exceed the carrying charges attributable to 1968 ($18.75), the limitation set forth in paragraph (c) of this section is not applicable.

(ii) The result in this example would be the same even if the X University assigned the agreement to a bank or other financial institution and C made his payments directly to the bank or other financial institution.

Example (5). On September 15, 1968, D registered at Y University for the 1968-69 academic year. The tuition for such year was $1,500. In order to pay his tuition, D borrowed $1,500 from the M Corporation, a lending institution, and remitted that sum to the Y University. The loan agreement between M Corporation and D provided that D was to repay the loan, plus a service charge, in 10 equal monthly installments, on the first day of each month commencing with October 1968. The service charge consisted of interest and the cost of credit life insurance on D's life. Since section 163(b) and this section do not apply to a contract for the loan of money, D is not entitled to compute his interest deduction with respect to his loan from M Corporation under such sections. D may deduct that portion of each installment payment which constitutes interest (as distinguished from payments of principal and the charge for credit life insurance) under section 163(a) and § 1.163-1, provided that the amount of such interest can be ascertained.

(e) *Effective date.* Except in the case of payments made under a contract for educational services, the rule provided in section 163(b) and this section applies to payments made during taxable years beginning after December 31, 1953, and ending after August 16, 1954, regardless of when the contract of sale was made. In the case of payments made under a contract for educational services, the rule provided in section 163(b) and this section applies to payments made during taxable years beginning after December 31, 1963, regardless of when the contract for educational services was made. [Reg. § 1.163-2.]

☐ *[T.D. 6223, 1-23-57. Amended by T.D. 6991, 1-16-69.]*

[Reg. § 1.163-3]

§ 1.163-3. Deduction for discount on bond issued on or before May 27, 1969.—(a) *Discount upon issuance.* (1) If bonds are issued by a corporation at a discount, the net amount of such discount is deductible and should be prorated or amortized over the life of the bonds. For purposes of this section, the amortizable bond discount equals the excess of the amount payable at maturity (or, in the case of a callable bond, at the earlier

call date) over the issue price of the bond (as defined in paragraph (b)(2) of § 1.1232-3).

(2) In the case of a bond issued by a corporation after December 31, 1954, as part of an investment unit consisting of an obligation and an option, the issue price of the bond is determined by allocating the amount received for the investment unit to the individual elements of the unit in the manner set forth in subdivision (ii)(*a*) of § 1.1232-3(b)(2). Discount with respect to bonds issued by a corporation as part of investment units consisting of obligations and options after December 31, 1954, and before December 24, 1968—

(i) Increased by any amount treated as bond premium which has been included in gross income with respect to such bonds prior to December 24, 1968, or

(ii) Decreased by any amount which has been deducted by the issuer as discount attributable to such bonds prior to December 24, 1968, and

(iii) Decreased by any amount which has been deducted by the issuer prior to December 24, 1968, upon the exercise or sale by investors of options issued in investment units with such bonds,

should be amortized, starting with the first taxable year ending on or after December 24, 1968, over the remaining life of such bonds.

(b) *Examples.* The rules in paragraph (a) of this section are illustrated by the following examples:

Example (1). M Corporation, on January 1, 1960, the beginning of its taxable year, issued for $95,000, 3 percent bonds, maturing 10 years from the date of issue, with a stated redemption price at maturity of $100,000. M Corporation should treat $5,000 ($100,000 − $95,000) as the total amount to be amortized over the life of the bonds.

Example (2). Assume the same facts as example (1), except that the bonds are convertible into common stock of M Corporation. Since the issue price of the bonds includes any amount attributable to the conversion privilege, the result is the same as in example (1).

Example (3). Assume the same facts as example (1), except that the bonds are issued as part of an investment unit consisting of an obligation and an option. Assume further that the issue price of the bonds as determined under the rules of allocation set forth in subdivision (ii)(*a*) of § 1.1232-3(b)(2) is $94,000. Accordingly, M Corporation should treat $6,000 ($100,000 − $94,000) as the total amount to be amortized over the life of the bonds.

Example (4). Assume in example (3), that prior to December 24, 1968, M Corporation had only treated $5,000 as the bond discount to be amortized and deducted only $4,000 of this amount. Starting with the first taxable year ending on or after December 24, 1968, M Corporation should amortize $2,000 ($6,000 discount, less $4,000 previously deducted) over the remaining life of the bonds.

Example (5). N Corporation, on January 1, 1956, for a consideration of $102,000, issued 20-year bonds in the face amount of $100,000, together with options to purchase stock of N Corporation. The issue price of the bonds as determined under the rules of allocation set forth in subdivision (ii)(*a*) of § 1.1232-3(b)(2) is $99,000. Until December 24, 1968, N Corporation has treated as bond premium, $2,000, representing the excess of the consideration received for the bond-option investment units over the maturity value of the bonds, and has accordingly prorated and included in income $1,200 of such amount. Starting with the first taxable year beginning on or after December 24, 1968, N Corporation may amortize as a deduction over the remaining life of the bonds the amount of $2,200 ($1,000 discount, plus $1,200 previously included in income).

Example (6). O Corporation, on January 1, 1956, for a consideration of $100,000, issued 20-year bonds with a $100,000 face value, together with options to purchase stock of O Corporation, which could be exercised at any time up to 5 years from the date of issue. The issue price of the bonds as determined under the rules of allocation set forth in subdivision (ii)(*a*) of § 1.1232-3(b)(2) is $98,000. O Corporation, upon the exercise of the options prior to December 24, 1968, had deducted from income their fair market value at the time of exercise, which is assumed for purposes of this example to have been $3,000. Even though the bonds are considered to have been issued at a discount under paragraph (a)(1) of this section, O Corporation would have no deduction over the remaining life of the bonds, inasmuch as O Corporation, in computing the amount of such deduction, is required under paragraph (a)(2)(iii) of this section to reduce the amount which would otherwise be treated as bond discount, $2,000 ($100,000 − $98,000), by the amount deducted from income upon the exercise of the options, in this case, $3,000.

(c) *Deduction upon repurchase.* (1) Except as provided in subparagraphs (2) and (3) of this paragraph, if bonds are issued by a corporation and are subsequently repurchased by the corporation at a price in excess of the issue price plus any amount of discount deducted prior to repurchase, or (in the case of bonds issued subsequent to Feb. 28, 1913) minus any amount of premium returned as income prior to repurchase, the excess of the purchase price over the issue price adjusted for amortized premium or discount is a deductible expense for the taxable year.

(2) In the case of a convertible bond (except a bond which the corporation, before September 5, 1968, has obligated itself to repurchase at a specified price), the deduction allowable under subparagraph (1) of this paragraph may not exceed an amount equal to one year's interest at the rate specified in the bond, except to the extent that the corporation can demonstrate to the satisfaction of the Commissioner or his delegate that an amount in excess of one year's interest does not include any amount attributable to the conversion feature.

(3) No deduction shall be allowed under subparagrah (1) of this paragraph to the extent a deduction is disallowed under subparagraph (2) of this paragraph or to the extent a deduction is disallowed by section 249 (relating to limitation on deduction of bond premium on repurchase of convertible obligation) and the regulations thereunder. See paragraph (f) of § 1.249-1 for effective date limitation on section 249.

(d) *Definition.* For purposes of this section, a debenture, note, certificate or other evidence of indebtedness, issued by a corporation and bearing interest shall be given the same treatment as a bond.

(e) *Effective date.* The provisions of this section shall not apply in respect of a bond issued after May 27, 1969, unless issued pursuant to a written commitment which was binding on that date and at all times thereafter. [Reg. § 1.163-3.]

☐ *[T.D. 6984, 12-23-68. Amended by T.D. 7154, 12-27-71 and T.D. 7259, 2-9-73.]*

[Reg. § 1.163-4]

§ 1.163-4. Deduction for original issue discount on certain obligations issued after May 27, 1969.—(a) *In general.* (1) If an obligation is issued by a corporation with original issue discount, the amount of such discount is deductible as interest and shall be prorated or amortized over the life of the obligation. For purposes of this section the term "obligation" shall have the same meaning as in § 1.1232-1 (without regard to whether the obligation is a capital asset in the hands of the holder) and the term "original issue discount" shall have the same meaning as in section 1232(b)(1) (without regard to the one-fourth-of-1-percent limitation in the second sentence thereof). Thus, in general, the amount of original issue discount equals the excess of the amount payable at maturity over the issue price of the bond (as defined in paragraph (b)(2) of § 1.1232-3), regardless of whether that amount is

Reg. § 1.163-4(a)

less than one-fourth of 1 percent of the redemption price at maturity multiplied by the number of complete years to maturity. For the rule as to whether there is original issue discount in the case of an obligation issued in an exchange for property other than money, and the amount thereof, see paragraph (b)(2)(iii) of § 1.1232-3. In any case in which original issue discount is carried over from one corporation to another corporation under section 381(c)(9) or from an obligation exchanged to an obligation received in any exchange under paragraph (b)(1)(iv) of § 1.1232-3, such discount shall be carried over for purposes of this section. The amount of original issue discount carried over in an exchange of obligations under the preceding sentence shall be prorated or amortized over the life of the obligation issued in such exchange. For computation of issue price and the amount of original issue discount in the case of serial obligations, see paragraph (b)(2)(iv) of § 1.1232-3.

(2) In the case of an obligation issued by a corporation as part of an investment unit (as defined in paragraph (b)(2)(ii)(a) of § 1.1232-3) consisting of an obligation and other property, the issue price of the obligation is determined by allocating the amount received for the investment unit to the individual elements of the unit in the manner set forth in paragraph (b)(2)(ii) of § 1.1232-3.

(3) *Recovery or retention of amounts previously deducted.* In any taxable year in which an amount of original issue discount which was deducted as interest under this section is retained or recovered by the taxpayer, such as, for example, by reason of a fine, penalty, forfeiture, or other withdrawal fee, such amount shall be includible in the gross income of such taxpayer for such taxable year.

(b) *Examples.* The rules in paragraph (a) of this section are illustrated by the following examples:

Example (1). N Corporation, which uses the calendar year as its taxable year, on January 1, 1970, issued for $99,000, 9 percent bonds maturing 10 years from the date of issue, with a stated redemption price at maturity of $100,000. The original issue discount on each bond (as determined under section 1232(b)(1) without regard to the one-fourth-of-1-percent limitation in the second sentence thereof) is $1,000, *i.e.,* redemption price, $100,000, minus issue price, $99,000. N shall treat $1,000 as the total amount to be amortized over the life of the bonds.

Example (2). Assume the same facts as example (1), except that the bonds are convertible into common stock of N Corporation. Since the issue price of the bonds includes any amount attributa-

ble to the conversion privilege, the result is the same as in example (1).

Example (3). Assume the same facts as example (1), except that the bonds are issued as part of an investment unit consisting of an obligation and an option. Assume further that the issue price of the bonds as determined under the rules of allocation set forth in paragraph (b)(2)(ii) of § 1.1232-3 is $94,000. The original issue discount on the bond (as determined under section 1232(b)(1) without regard to the one-fourth-of-1-percent limitation in the second sentence thereof) is $6,000, *i.e.,* redemption price, $100,000, minus issue price, $94,000. N shall treat $6,000 as the total amount to be amortized over the life of the bonds.

Example (4). On January 1, 1971, a commercial bank which uses the calendar year as its taxable year, issued a certificate of deposit for $10,000. The certificate of deposit is not redeemable until December 31, 1975, except in an emergency as defined in, and subject to the qualifications provided by, Regulations Q of the Board of Governors of the Federal Reserve. See 12 CFR § 217.4(d). The stated redemption price at maturity is $13,382.26. The certificate is an obligation to which section 1232(a)(3)(A) applies (see paragraph (d) of § 1.1232-1), and the original issue discount with respect to the certificate (as determined under section 1232(b)(1) without regard to the one-fourth-of-1-percent limitation in the second sentence thereof) is $3,382.26 (*i.e.,* redemption price, $13,382.26, minus issue price, $10,000). Y shall treat $3,382.26 as the total amount to be amortized over the life of the certificate.

(c) *Deduction upon repurchase.*—(1) Except as provided in subparagraph (2) of this paragraph, if bonds are issued by a corporation and are subsequently repurchased by the corporation at a price in excess of the issue price plus any amount of original issue discount deducted prior to repurchase, or minus any amount of premium returned as income prior to repurchase, the excess of the repurchase price over the issue price adjusted for amortized premium or deducted discount is deductible as interest for the taxable year.

(2) The provisions of subparagraph (1) of this paragraph shall not apply to the extent a deduction is disallowed by section 249 (relating to limitation on deduction of bond premium or repurchase of convertible obligation) and the regulations thereunder.

(d) *Effective date.* The provisions of this section shall apply in respect of obligations issued after May 27, 1969, other than—

Reg. § 1.163-4(d)

(1) Obligations issued pursuant to a written commitment which was binding on May 27, 1969, and at all times thereafter, and

(2) Deposits made before January 1, 1971, in the case of certificates of deposit, time deposits, bonus plans, and other deposit arrangements with banks, domestic building and loan associations, and similar financial institutions. [Reg. § 1.163-4.]

☐ [*T.D.* 7154, 12-27-71. *Amended by T.D.* 7213, 10-17-72 and *T.D.* 7259, 2-9-73.]

[Reg. § 1.163-5]

§ 1.163-5. Denial of interest deduction on certain obligations issued after December 31, 1982, unless issued in registered form.—(a) [Reserved]

(b) [Reserved]

(c) *Obligations issued to foreign persons after September 21, 1984.*—(1) *In general.* A determination of whether an obligation satisfies each of the requirements of this paragraph shall be made on an obligation-by-obligation basis. An obligation issued directly (or through affiliated entities) in bearer form by, or guaranteed by, a United States Government-owned agency or a United States Government-sponsored enterprise, such as the Federal National Mortgage Association, the Federal Home Loan Banks, the Federal Loan Mortgage Corporation, the Farm Credit Administration, and the Student Loan Marketing Association, may not satisfy this paragraph (c). An obligation issued after September 21, 1984 is described in this paragraph if—

(i) There are arrangements reasonably designed to ensure that such obligation will be sold (or resold in connection with its original issuance) only to a person who is not a United States person or who is a United States person that is a financial institution (as defined in § 1.165-12 (c)(1)(v)) purchasing for its own account or for the account of a customer and that agrees to comply with the requirements of section 165 (j)(3)(A), (B), or (C) and the regulations thereunder, and

(ii) In the case of an obligation which is not in registered form—

(A) Interest on such obligation is payable only outside the United States and its possessions, and

(B) Unless the obligation is described in subparagraph (2)(i)(C) of this paragraph or is a temporary global security, the following statement in English either appears on the face of the obligation and on any interest coupons which may be detached therefrom or, if the obligation is evidenced by a book entry, appears in the book or record in which the book entry is made: "Any United States person who holds this obligation will be subject to limitations under the United States income tax laws, including the limitations provided in sections 165(j) and 1287(a) of the Internal Revenue Code." For purposes of this paragraph, the term "temporary global security" means a security which is held for the benefit of the purchasers of the obligations of the issuer and interests in which are exchangeable for securities in definitive registered or bearer form prior to its stated maturity.

(2) *Rules for the application of this paragraph*—(i) *Arrangements reasonably designed to ensure sale to non-United States persons.* An obligation will be considered to satisfy paragraph (c)(1)(i) of this section if the conditions of paragraph (c)(2)(i)(A), (B), (C) or (D) of this section are met in connection with the original issuance of the obligation. An exchange of one obligation for another is considered an original issuance if and only if the exchange constitutes a disposition of property for purposes of section 1001 of the Code. However, an exchange of one obligation for another will not be considered a new issuance if the obligation received is identical in all respects to the obligation surrendered in exchange therefor, except that the obligor of the obligation received need not be the same obligor as the obligor of the obligation surrendered. Obligations that meet the conditions of paragraph (c)(2)(i)(A), (B), (C) or (D) of this section may be issued in a single public offering. The preceding sentence does not apply to certificates of deposit issued under the conditions of paragraph (c)(2)(i)(C) of this section by a United States person or by a controlled foreign corporation within the meaning of section 957(a) that is engaged in the active conduct of a banking business within the meaning of section 954(c)(3)(B) as in effect prior to the Tax Reform Act of 1986, and the regulations thereunder. A temporary global security need not satisfy the conditions of paragraph (c)(2)(i)(A), (B) or (C) of this section, but must satisfy the applicable requirements of paragraph (c)(2)(i)(D) of this section.

(A) In connection with the original issuance of an obligation, the obligation is offered for sale or resale only outside of the United States and its possessions, is delivered only outside the United States and its possessions and is not registered under the Securities Act of 1933 because it is intended for distribution to persons who are not United States persons. An obligation will not be considered to be required to be registered under the Securities Act of 1933 if the issuer, in reliance on the written opinion of counsel received prior to the issuance thereof, determines in good faith that

Reg. § 1.163-5(a)

the obligation need not be registered under the Securities Act of 1933 for the reason that it is intended for distribution to persons who are not United States persons. Solely fcr purposes of this subdivision (i)(A), the term "United States person" has the same meaning as it has for purposes of determining whether an obligation is intended for distribution to persons under the Securities Act of 1933. Except as provided in paragraph (c)(3) of this section, this paragraph (c)(2)(i)(A) applies only to obligations iss.ied on or before September 7, 1990.

(B) The obligation is registered under the Securi:ies Act of 1933, is exempt from registration by reason of section 3 or section 4 of such Act, or does not qualify as a security under the Securities Act of 1933; all of the conditions set forth in paragraph (c)(2)(i)(B)(*1*), (*2*), (*3*), (*4*), and (*5*) of this section are met with respect to such obligations; and, except as provided in paragraph (c)(3) of this section, the obligation is issued on or before September 7, 1990.

(*1*) In connection with the original issuance of an obligation in bearer form, the obligation is offered for sale or resale only outside the United States and its possess.ons.

(*2*) The issuer does not, and each underwriter and each member of the selling group, if any, covenants that it will not, in connection wizh the original issuance of the obligation, offer to sell or resell the obligation in bearer form to any person inside the United States or to a United States person unless such United States person is a financial institution as defined in § 1.165-12(c)(v) purchasing for i:s own account or for the account of a customer, which financial institution, as a condition of the purchase, agrees to provide on delivery of the obligation (or on issuance, if the obligation is not in definitive form) the certificate requir2d under paragraph (c)(2)(i)(B)(*4*).

(*3*) In connection with its sale or resale during the original issuance of the obligation in bearer form, each underw-ite- and each member of the selling group, if any, or the issuer, if there is no underwriter or selling group, sends a confirmation to the purchaser of the bearer obligation stating that the purchaser represents that it is not a United States persor or, if it is a United States person, it is a financial institution as defined in § 1.165-12(c)(v) purchasing for its own account or for the account of a customer and that the financial institution will comply with the requirements of section 165(j)(3)(A), (B), or (C) and the regulations thereunder. The confirmation must also state that, if the purchaser is a dealer,

it will send similar confirmations to whomever purchases from it.

(*4*) In connection with the original issuance of the obligation in bearer form it is delivered in definitive form (or issued, if the obligation is not in definitive form) to the person entitlec to physical delivery thereof only outside the United States and its possessions and only upon presentation of a certificate signed by such person to the issuer, underwriter, or member of the sell.ng group, which certificate states that the obligation is not being acquired by or on behalf of a United States person, or for offer to resell or for resale to a United States person or any person inside the United States, or, if a beneficial interest in the obligation is being acquired by a United States person, that such person is a financial institution as defined in § 1.165-12(c)(1)(v) or is acquiring through a financial institution and that the obligation is held by a financial institution that has agreed to comply with the requirements of section 165(j)(3)(A), (B), or (C) and the regulations thereunder and that is not purchasing for offer tc resell or for resale inside the United States. When a certificate is provided by a clearing organization, it must be based on statements provided to it by its member organizations. A clearing organization is an entity which is in the business of holding obligations for member organizations and transferring obligations among such members by credit or debit to the account of a member without the necessity of physical delivery of the obligation. For purposes of paragraph (c)(2)(i) B), the term "delivery" does not include the delivery of an obligation to an underwriter or member of the selling group, if any.

(*5*) The issuer, underwriter, or member of the selling group does not have actual knowledge that the certificate described in paragraph (c)(2)(i)(B)(*4*) of this section is false. The issuer, underwriter, or member of the selling group shall be deemed to have actual knowledge that the certificate described in paragraph (c)(2)(i) B)(*4*) of this section is false if the issuer, underwriter, or member of the selling group has a United States address for the beneficial owner (other than a financial institution as defined in § 1.165-12(c)(v) that represents that it will comply with the requirements of section 165(j)(3)(A), (B), or (C) and the regulations thereunder) and does not have documentary evidence as described in § 1.6C49-5(c)(1) that the beneficial owner is not a Unitec States person.

(C) The obligation is issued only outside the United States and its possessions by an issuer that does not significantly engage in interstate commerce with respect to the issuance of such obligation either directly or through its agent, an underwriter, or a member of the selling group. In the case of an issuer that is a United States person, such issuer may only satisfy the test set forth in this paragraph (c)(2)(i)(C) if—

(*1*) It is engaged through a branch in the active conduct of a banking business, within the meaning of section 954(c)(3)(B) as in effect before the Tax Reform Act of 1986, and the regulations thereunder, outside the United States;

(*2*) The obligation is issued outside of the United States by the branch in connection with that trade or business;

(*3*) The obligation that is so issued is sold directly to the public and is not issued as a part of a larger issuance made by means of a public offering; and

(*4*) The issuer either maintains documentary evidence as described in subdivision (iii) of A-5 of 35a.9999-4T that the purchaser is not a United States person (provided that the issuer has no actual knowledge that the documentary evidence is false) or on delivery of the obligation the issuer receives a statement signed by the person entitled to physical delivery thereof and stating either that the obligation is not being acquired by or on behalf of a United States person or that, if a beneficial interest in the obligation is being acquired by a United States person, such person is a financial institution as defined in § 1.165-12(c)(v) or is acquiring through a financial institution and the obligation is held by a financial institution that has agreed to comply with the requirements of 165 (j)(3)(A), (B), or (C) and the regulations thereunder and that it is not purchasing for offer to resell or for resale inside the United States (provided that the issuer has no actual knowledge that the statement is false).

In addition, an issuer that is a controlled foreign corporation within the meaning of section 957(a) that is engaged in the active conduct of a banking business outside the United States within the meaning of section 954(c)(3)(B) as in effect before the Tax Reform Act of 1986, and the regulations thereunder, can only satisfy the provisions of this paragraph (c)(2)(i)(C), if it meets the requirements of this paragraph (c)(2)(i)(C)(*2*), (*3*) and (*4*).

(D) The obligation is issued after September 7, 1990, and all of the conditions set forth in this paragraph (c)(2)(i)(D) are met with respect to such obligation.

(*1*) *Offers and sales*—(*i*) *Issuer.* The issuer does not offer or sell the obligation during the restricted period to a person who is within the United States or its possessions or to a United States person.

(*ii*) *Distributors.* (*A*) The distributor of the obligation does not offer or sell the obligation during the restricted period to a person who is within the United States or its possessions or to a United States person.

(*B*) The distributor of the obligation will be deemed to satisfy the requirements of paragraph (c)(2)(i)(D)(1)(*ii*)(*A*) of this section if the distributor of the obligation covenants that it will not offer or sell the obligation during the restricted period to a person who is within the United States or its possessions or to a United States person; and the distributor of the obligation has in effect, in connection with the offer and sale of the obligation during the restricted period, procedures reasonably designed to ensure that its employees or agents who are directly engaged in selling the obligation are aware that the obligation cannot be offered or sold during the restricted period to a person who is within the United States or its possessions or is a United States person.

(*iii*) *Certain rules.* For purposes of paragraph (c)(2)(i)(D)(*1*)(*i*) and (*ii*) of this section:

(*A*) An offer or sale will be considered to be made to a person who is within the United States or its possessions if the offeror or seller of the obligation has an address within the United States or its possessions for the offeree or buyer of the obligation with respect to the offer or sale.

(*B*) An offer or sale of an obligation will not be treated as made to a person within the United States or its possessions or to a United States person if the person to whom the offer or sale is made is: An exempt distributor, as defined in paragraph (c)(2)(i)(D)(*5*) of this section; An international organization as defined in section 7701(a)(18) and the regulations thereunder, or a foreign central bank as defined in section 895 and the regulations thereunder, or the foreign branch of a United States financial institution as described in paragraph (c)(2)(i)(D)(*6*)(*i*) of this section.

Paragraph (c)(2)(i)(D)(*1*)(*iii*)(*B*) regarding an exempt distributor will only apply to an offer to the United States office of an exempt distributor, and paragraph (c)(2)(i)(D)(*1*)(*iii*)(*B*) regarding an international organization or foreign central bank will only apply to an offer to an international organization or foreign central bank, if such offer is made directly and specifically to the United States office, organization or bank.

(*C*) A sale of an obligation will not be treated as made to a person within the United States or its possessions or to a United States person if the person to whom the sale is

Reg. § 1.163-5(c)(2)

made is a person described in paragraph (c)(2)(i)(D)(6)(ii) of this section.

(2) *Delivery.* In connection with the sale of the obligation during the restricted period, neither the issuer nor any distributor delivers the obligation in definitive form within the United States or its possessions.

(3) *Certification*—(i) *In general.* On the earlier of the date of the first actual payment of interest by the issuer on the obligation or the date of delivery by the issuer of the obligation in definitive form, a certificate is provided to the issuer of the obligation stating that on such date:

(A) The obligation is owned by a person that is not a United States person;

(B) The obligation is owned by a United States person described in paragraph (c)(2)(i)(D)(6) of this section; or

(C) The obligation is owned by a financial institution for purposes of resale during the restricted period, and such financial institution certifies in addition that it has not acquired the obligation for purposes of resale directly or indirectly to a United States person or to a person within the United States or its possessions.

A certificate described in paragraph (c)(2)(i)(D)(3)(i)(A) or (B) of this section may not be given with respect to an obligation that is owned by a financial institution for purposes of resale during the restricted period. For purposes of paragraph (c)(2)(i)(D)(2) and (3) of this section, a temporary global security (as defined in § 1.163-5(c)(1)(ii)(B)) is not considered to be an obligation in definitive form. If the issuer does not make the obligation available for delivery in definitive form within a reasonable period of time after the end of the restricted period, then the obligation shall be treated as not satisfying the requirements of this paragraph (c)(2)(i)(D)(3). The certificate must be signed (or sent, as provided in paragraph (c)(2)(i)(D)(3)(ii) of this section) either by the owner of the obligation or by a financial institution or clearing organization through which the owner holds the obligation, directly or indirectly. For purposes of this paragraph (c)(2)(i)(D)(3), the term "financial institution" means a financial institution described in § 1.165-12(c)(1)(v). When a certificate is provided by a clearing organization, the certificate must be based on statements provided to it by its member organizations. The requirement of this paragraph (c)(1)(D)(3) shall be deemed not to be satisfied with respect to an obligation if the issuer knows or has reason to know that the certificate with respect to such obligation is false. The certificate must be retained by the issuer (and statements by member organizations must be retained by the clearing organization, in the case of certificates based on such statements) for a period of four calendar years following the year in which the certificate is received.

(ii) *Electronic certification.* The certificate required by paragraph (c)(2)(i)(D)(3)(i) of this section (including a statement provided to a clearing organization by a member organization) may be provided electronically, but only if the person receiving such electronic certificate maintains adequate records, for the retention period described in paragraph (c)(2)(i)(D)(3)(i) of this section, establishing that such certificate was received in respect of the subject obligation, and only if there is a written agreement entered into prior to the time of certification (including the written membership rules of a clearing organization) to which the sender and recipient are subject, providing that the electronic certificate shall have the effect of a signed certificate described in paragraph (c)(2)(i)(D)(3)(i) of this section.

(iii) *Exception for certain obligations.* This paragraph (c)(2)(i)(D)(3) shall not apply, and no certificate shall be required, in the case of an obligation that is sold during the restricted period and that satisfies all of the following requirements:

(A) The interest and principal with respect to the obligation are denominated only in the currency of a single foreign country.

(B) The interest and principal with respect to the obligation are payable only within that foreign country (according to rules similar to those set forth in § 1.163-5(c)(2)(v)).

(C) The obligation is offered and sold in accordance with practices and documentation customary in that foreign country.

(D) The distributor covenants to use reasonable efforts to sell the obligation within that foreign country.

(E) The obligation is not listed, or the subject of an application for listing, on an exchange located outside that foreign country.

(F) The Commissioner has designated that foreign country as a foreign country in which certification under paragraph (c)(2)(i)(D)(3)(i) of this section is not permissible.

(G) The issuance of the obligation is subject to guidelines or restrictions imposed by governmental, banking or securities authorities in that foreign country.

(H) More than 80 percent by value of the obligations included in the offering of which the obligation is a part are offered and sold to non-distributors by distributors maintaining an office located in that foreign country. Foreign currency denominated obligations that are convertible into U.S. dollar denominated obligations or that by their terms are linked to the U.S. dollar in a way which effectively converts the obligations to U.S. dollar denominated obligations do not satisfy the requirements of this paragraph (c)(2)(i)(D)(3)(iii). A foreign currency denominated obligation will not be treated as linked, by its terms, to the U.S. dollar solely because the obligation is the subject of a swap transaction.

(4) *Distributor.* For purposes of this paragraph (c)(2)(i)(D), the term "distributor" means:

(i) a person that offers or sells the obligation during the restricted period pursuant to a written contract with the issuer;

(ii) any person that offers or sells the obligation during the restricted period pursuant to a written contract with a person described in paragraph (c)(2)(i)(D)(4)(i); and

(iii) any affiliate that acquires the obligation from another member of its affiliated group for the purpose of offering or selling the obligation during the restricted period, but only if the transferor member of the group is the issuer or a person described in paragraph (c)(2)(i)(D)(4)(i) or (ii) of this section. The terms "affiliate" and "affiliated group" have the same meanings as in section 1504(a) of the Code, but without regard to the exceptions contained in section 1504(b) and substituting "50 percent" for "80 percent" each time it appears.

For purposes of this paragraph (c)(2)(i)(D)(4), a written contract does not include a confirmation or other notice of the transaction.

(5) *Exempt distributor.* For purposes of this paragraph (c)(2)(i)(D), the term "exempt distributor" means a distributor that covenants in its contract with the issuer or with a distributor described in paragraph (c)(2)(i)(D)(4)(i) that it is buying the obligation for the purpose of resale in connection with the original issuance of the obligation, and that if it retains the obligation for its own account, it will only do so in accordance with the requirements of paragraph (c)(2)(i)(D)(6) of this section. In the latter case, the covenant will constitute the certificate required under paragraph (c)(2)(i)(D)(6). The provisions of paragraph (c)(2)(i)(D)(7) governing the restricted period for unsold allotments or subscriptions shall apply to any obligation retained for investment by an exempt distributor.

(6) *Certain United States persons.* A person is described in this paragraph (c)(2)(i)(D)(6) if the requirements of this paragraph are satisfied and the person is:

(i) The foreign branch of a United States financial institution purchasing for its own account or for resale, or

(ii) A United States person who acquired the obligation through the foreign branch of a United States financial institution and who, for purposes of the certification required in paragraph (c)(2)(i)(D)(3) of this section, holds the obligation through such financial institution on the date of certification.

For purposes of paragraph (c)(2)(i)(D)(6)(ii) of this section, a United States person will be considered to acquire and hold an obligation through the foreign branch of a United States financial institution if the United States person has an account with the United States office of a financial institution, and the transaction is executed by a foreign office of that financial institution, or by the foreign office of another financial institution acting on behalf of that financial institution. This paragraph (c)(2)(i)(D)(6) will apply, however, only if the United States financial institution (or the United States office of a foreign financial institution) holding the obligation provides a certificate to the issuer or distributor selling the obligation within a reasonable time stating that it agrees to comply with the requirements of section 165(j)(3)(A), (B), or (C) and the regulations thereunder. For purposes of this paragraph (c)(2)(i)(D)(6), the term "financial institution" means a financial institution as defined in § 1.165-12(c)(1)(v). As an alternative to the certification required above, a financial institution may provide a blanket certificate to the issuer or distributor selling the obligation stating that the financial institution will comply with the requirements of section 165(j)(3)(A), (B) or (C) and the regulations thereunder. A blanket certificate must be received by the issuer or the distributor in the year of the issuance of the obligation or in either of the preceding two calendar years, and must be retained by the issuer or distributor for at least four years after the end of the last calendar year to which it relates.

(7) *Restricted period.* For purposes of this paragraph (c)(2)(i)(D), the restricted period with respect to an obligation begins on the earlier of the closing date (or the date on which the issuer receives the loan proceeds, if there is no closing with respect to the obligation), or the first date on which the obligation is offered to persons other than a distributor. The restricted period with respect to an obligation ends on the expiration of the forty day period beginning on the closing date (or the date on which the issuer receives the loan proceeds, if there is no closing with respect to the obligation). Notwithstanding the preceding sen-

Reg. § 1.163-5(c)(2)

tence, any offer or sale of the obligation by the issuer or a distributor shall be deemed to be during the restricted period if the issuer or distributor holds the obligation as part of an unsold allotment or subscription.

(8) *Clearing organization.* For purposes of this paragraph (c)(2)(i)(D), a "clearing organization" is an entity which is in the business of holding obligations for member organizations and transferring obligations among such members by credit or debit to the account of a member without the necessity of physical delivery of the obligation.

(ii) *Special rules.* An obligation shall not be considered to be described in paragraph (c)(2)(i)(C) of this section if it is—

(A) Guaranteed by a United States shareholder of the issuer;

(B) Convertible into a debt or equity interest in a United States shareholder of the issuer; or

(C) Substantially identical to an obligation issued by a United States shareholder of the issuer.

For purposes of this paragraph (c)(2)(ii), the term "United States shareholder" is defined as it is defined in section 951(b) and the regulations thereunder. For purposes of this paragraph (c)(2)(ii)(C), obligations are substantially identical if the face amount, interest rate, term of the issue, due dates for payments, and maturity date of each is substantially identical to the other.

(iii) *Interstate commerce.* For purposes of this paragraph, the term "interstate commerce" means trade or commerce in obligations or any transportation or communication relating thereto between any foreign country and the United States or its possessions.

(A) An issuer will not be considered to engage significantly in interstate commerce with respect to the issuance of an obligation if the only activities with respect to which the issuer uses the means or instrumentalities of interstate commerce are activities of a preparatory or auxiliary character that do not involve communication between a prospective purchaser and an issuer, its agent, an underwriter, or member of the selling group if either is inside the United States or its possessions. Activities of a preparatory or auxiliary character include, but are not limited to, the following activities:

(1) Establishment or participation in establishment of policies concerning the issuance of obligations and the allocation of funding by a United States shareholder with respect to obligations issued by a foreign corporation or by a

United States office with respect to obligations issued by a foreign branch;

(2) Negotiation between the issuer and underwriters as to the terms and pricing of an issue;

(3) Transfer of funds to an office of an issuer in the United States or its possessions by a foreign branch or to a United States shareholder by a foreign corporation;

(4) Consultation by an issuer with accountants and lawyers or other financial advisors in the United States or its possessions regarding the issuance of an obligation;

(5) Document drafting and printing; and

(6) Provision of payment or delivery instructions to members of the selling group by an issuer's office or agent that is located in the United States or its possessions.

(B) Activities that will not be considered to be of a preparatory or auxiliary character include, but are not limited to, any of the following activities:

(1) Negotiation or communication between a prospective purchaser and an issuer, its agent, an underwriter, or a member of the selling group concerning the sale of an obligation if either is inside the United States or its possessions;

(2) Involvement of an issuer's office, its agent, an underwriter, or a member of the selling group in the United States or its possessions in the offer or sale of a particular obligation, either directly with the prospective purchaser, or through the issuer in a foreign country;

(3) Delivery of an obligation in the United States or its possessions; or

(4) Advertising or otherwise promoting an obligation in the United States or its possessions.

(C) The following examples illustrate the application of this subdivision (iii) of § 1.163-5(c)(2).

Example (1). Foreign corporation A, a corporation organized in and doing business in foreign country Z, and not a controlled foreign corporation within the meaning of section 957(a) that is engaged in the conduct of a banking business within the meaning of section 954(c)(3)(B) as in effect before the Tax Reform Act of 1986, issues its debentures outside the United States. The debentures are not guaranteed by a United States shareholder of A, nor are they convertible into a debt or equity interest of a United States shareholder of A, nor are they substantially identical to an obligation issued by a United States shareholder of A. A consults its accountants and lawyers in the United States for certain securities and tax advice regarding the debt offering. The underwriting and selling group in respect of A's offering is composed entirely of foreign securities firms, some of which are foreign subsidiaries of United States securities firms. A U.S. affiliate of the foreign underwriter communicates payment and delivery instruction to the selling group. All offering circulars for the offering are mailed and delivered outside the United States and its possessions. All debentures are delivered and paid for outside the United States and its possessions. No office located in the United States or in a United States possession is involved in the sale of debentures. Interest on the debentures is payable only outside the United States and its possessions. A is not significantly engaged in interstate commerce with respect to the offering.

Example (2). B, a United States bank, does business in foreign country X through a branch located in X. The branch is a staffed and operating unit engaged in the active conduct of a banking business consisting of one or more of the activities set forth in § 1.954-2(d)(2)(ii). As part of its ongoing business, the branch in X issues negotiable certificates of deposit with a maturity in excess of one year to customers upon request. The certificates of deposit are not guaranteed by a United States shareholder of B, nor are they convertible into a debt or equity interest of a United States shareholder of B, nor are they substantially identical to an obligation issued by a United States shareholder of B. Policies regarding the issuance of negotiable certificates of deposit and funding allocations for foreign branches are set in the United States at B's main office. Branch personnel decide whether to issue a negotiable certificate of deposit based on the guidelines established by the United States offices of B, but without communicating with the United States offices of B with respect to the issuance of a particular obligation. Negotiable certificates of deposits are delivered and paid for outside the United States and its possessions. Interest on the negotiable certificates of deposit is payable only outside the United States and its possessions. B maintains documentary evidence described in § 1.163-5(c)(2)(i)(C)(4). After the issuance of negotiable certificates of deposit by the foreign branch of B, the foreign branch sends the funds to a United States branch of B for use in domestic operations. B is not significantly engaged in interstate commerce with respect to the issuance of such obligation.

Example (3). The facts in Example (2) apply except that the foreign branch of B consulted, by telephone, the main office in the United States to request approval of the issuance of the certificate of deposit at a particular rate of interest. The main office granted permission to issue the negotiable certificate of deposit to the customer by a telex sent from the main office of B to the branch in X. B is significantly engaged in interstate commerce with respect to the issuance of the obligation as a result of the involvement of B's United States office in the issuance of the obligation.

Example (4). The facts in Example (2) apply with the additional fact that a customer contacted the foreign branch of B through a telex originating in the United States or its possessions. Subsequent to the telex, the foreign branch issued the negotiable certificate of deposit and recorded it on the books. B is significantly engaged in interstate commerce with respect to the issuance of the obligation as a result of its communication by telex with a customer in the United States.

(iv) *Possessions.* For purposes of this section, the term "possessions" includes Puerto Rico, the U.S. Virgin Islands, Guam, American Samoa, Wake Island, and Northern Mariana Islands.

(v) *Interest payable outside of the United States.* Interest will be considered payable only outside the United States and its possessions if payment of such interest can be made only upon presentation of a coupon, or upon making of any other demand for payment, outside of the United States and its possessions to the issuer or a paying agent. The fact that payment is made by a draft drawn on a United States bank account or by a wire or other electronic transfer from a United States account does not affect this result. Interest payments will be considered to be made within the United States if the payments are made by a transfer of funds into an account maintained by the payee in the United States or mailed to an address in the United States, if—

(A) The interest is paid on an obligation issued by either a United States person, a controlled foreign corporation as defined in section 957(a), or a foreign corporation if 50 percent or more of the gross income of the foreign corporation from all sources of the 3-year period ending with the close of its taxable year preceding the original issuance of the obligation (or for such part of the period that the foreign corporation has been in existence) was effectively connected with the conduct of a trade or business within the United States; and

(B) The interest is paid to a person other than—

(1) A person who may satisfy the requirements of section 165(j)(3)(A), (B), or (C) and the regulations thereunder; and

Reg. § 1.163-5(c)(2)

(*2*) A financial institution as a step in the clearance of funds and such interest is promptly credited to an account maintained outside the United States for such financial institution or for persons for which the financial institution has collected such interest.

Interest is considered to be paid within the United States and its possessions if a coupon is presented, or a demand for payment is otherwise made, to the issuer or a paying agent (whether a United States or foreign person) in the United States and its possessions even if the funds paid are credited to an account maintained by the payee outside the United States and its possessions. Interest will be considered payable only outside the United States and its possessions notwithstanding that such interest may become payable at the office of the issuer or its United States paying agent under the following conditions: the issuer has appointed paying agents located outside the United States and its possessions with the reasonable expectation that such paying agents will be able to pay the interest in United States dollars, and the full amount of such payment at the offices of all such paying agents is illegal or effectively precluded because of the imposition of exchange controls or other similar restrictions on the full payment or receipt of interest in United States dollars. A lawsuit brought in the United States or its possessions for payment of the obligation or interest thereon as a result of a default shall not be considered to be a demand for payment. For purposes of this subdivision (v), interest includes original issue discount as defined in section 1273(a). Therefore, an amount equal to the original issue discount as defined in section 1273(a) is payable only outside the United States and its possessions. The amount of market discount as defined in section 1278(a) does not affect the amount of interest to be considered payable only outside the United States and its possessions.

(vi) *Rules relating to obligations issued after December 31, 1982 and on or before September 21, 1984.* Whether an obligation originally issued after December 31, 1982 and on or before September 21, 1984, or an obligation originally issued after September 21, 1984 pursuant to the exercise of a warrant or the conversion of a convertible obligation, which warrant or obligation (including conversion privilege) was issued after December 31, 1982 and on or before September 21, 1984, is described in section 163(f)(2)(B) shall be determined under the rules provided in § 5f.163-1(c) as in effect prior to its removal. Notwithstanding the preceding sentence, an issuer will be considered to satisfy the requirements of section 163(f)(2)(B) with respect to an obligation issued after December 31, 1982 and on or

before September 21, 1984 or after September 21, 1984 pursuant to the exercise of a warrant or the conversion of a convertible obligation, which warrant or obligation (including conversion privilege) was issued after December 31, 1982 and on or before September 21, 1984, if the issuer substantially complied with the proposed regulations provided in § 1.163-5(c), which were published in the Federal Register on September 2, 1983 (48 FR 39953) and superseded by temporary regulations published in the Federal Register on August 22, 1984 (49 FR 33228).

(3) *Effective date—*(i) *In general.* These regulations apply generally to obligations issued after January 20, 1987. A taxpayer may choose to apply the rules of § 1.163-5(c) with respect to an obligation issued after December 31, 1982 and on or before January 20, 1987. If this choice is made, the rules of § 1.163-5(c) will apply in lieu of § 1.163-5T(c) except that the legend requirement under § 1.163-5(c)(1)(ii)(B) does not apply with respect to a bearer obligation evidenced exclusively by a book entry and that the certification requirement under § 1.163-5T(c)(2)(i)(B)(*4*) applies in lieu of the certification under § 1.163-5(c)(2)(i)(B)(*4*).

(ii) *Special rules.* If an obligation is originally issued after September 7, 1990 pursuant to the exercise of a warrant or the conversion of a convertible obligation, which warrant or obligation (including conversion privilege) was issued on or before May 10, 1990, then the issuer may choose to apply either the rules of § 1.163-5(c)(2)(i)(A) or § 1.163-5(c)(2)(i)(B), or the rules of § 1.163-5(c)(2)(i)(D). The issuer of an obligation may choose to apply either the rules of § 1.163-5(c)(2)(i)(A) or (B), or the rules of § 1.163-5(c)(2)(i)(D), to an obligation that is originally issued after May 10, 1990, and on or before September 7, 1990. However, any issuer choosing to apply the rules of § 1.163-5(c)(2)(i)(A) must apply the definition of United States person used for such purposes on December 31, 1989, and must obtain any certificates that would have been required under applicable law on December 31, 1989. [Reg. § 1.163-5.]

☐ [*T.D.* 8110, 12-16-86. *Amended by T.D.* 8203, 5-19-88; *T.D.* 8300, 5-9-90 *and T.D.* 8734, 10-6-97 (T.D. 8804 delayed the effective date of T.D. 8734 from January 1, 1999, to January 1, 2000; T.D. 8856 further delayed the effective date of T.D. 8734 until January 1, 2001).]

[Reg. § 1.163-5T]

§ 1.163-5T. **Denial of interest deduction on certain obligations issued after December 31, 1982, unless issued in registered form (Temporary).—**

(a) [Reserved]

(b) [Reserved]

(c) [Reserved]

(d) *Pass-through certificates.* (1) A pass-through or participation certificate evidencing an interest in a pool of mortgage loans which under Subpart E of Subchapter J of the Code is treated as a trust of which the grantor is the owner (or similar evidence of interest in a similar pooled fund or pooled trust treated as a grantor trust) ("pass-through certificate") is considered to be a "registration-required obligation" under section 163(f)(2)(A) and § 1.163-5(c) if the pass-through certificate is described in section 163(f)(2)(A) and § 1.163-5(c) without regard to whether any obligation held by the fund or trust to which the pass-through certificate relates is described in section 163(f)(2)(A) and § 1.163-5(c). A pass-through certificate is considered to be described in section 163(f)(2)(B) and § 1.163-5(c) if the pass-through certificate is described in section 163(f)(2)(B) and § 1.163-5(c) without regard to whether any obligation held by the fund or trust to which the pass-through certificate relates is described in section 163(f)(2)(B) and § 1.163-5(c).

(2) An obligation held by a fund or trust in which ownership interests are represented by pass-through certificates is considered to be in registered form under section 149(a) and the regulations thereunder or to be described in section 163(f)(2)(A) or (B), if the obligation held by the fund or trust is in registered form under section 149(a) and the regulations thereunder or is described in section 163(f)(2)(A) or (B), respectively, without regard to whether the pass-through certificates are so considered.

(3) For purposes of section 4701, a pass-through certificate is considered to be issued solely by the recipient of the proceeds from the issuance of the pass-through certificate (hereinafter the "sponsor"). The sponsor is therefore liable for any excise tax under section 4701 that may be imposed with reference to the principal amount of the pass-through certificate.

(4) In order to implement the purpose of section 163, § 1.163-5(c) and this section, the Commissioner may characterize a certificate or other evidence of interest in a fund or trust which under Subpart E of Subchapter J of the Code is treated as a trust of which the grantor is the owner and any obligation held by such fund or trust in accordance with the substance of the arrangement they represent and may impose the penalties provided under section 163(f)(1) and 4701 in the appropriate amounts and on the appropriate persons. This provision may be applied, for example, where a corporation issues obligations purportedly in registered form, contributes them to a grantor trust as its only assets, and arranges for the sale to investors of bearer certificates of interest in the trust which do not meet the requirements of section 163(f)(2)(B). If this provision is applied, the obligations held by the fund or trust will not be considered to be issued in registered form or to meet the requirements of section 163(f)(2)(B). The corporation will not be allowed a deduction for the payment of interest on the obligations held by the trust, and the excise tax under section 4701, calculated with reference to the principal amount of the obligations held by the trust will be imposed on the corporation may be collected from the corporation and its agents. This paragraph (d)(4) will not be applied so as to alter the tax consequences of transactions as to which rulings have been issued by the Internal Revenue Service prior to September 19, 1985.

(5) The rules set forth in this paragraph (d) apply solely for purposes of sections 4701, 163(f)(2)(A), 163(f)(2)(B), § 1.163-5(c), and any other section that refers to this section for the definition of the term "registration-required obligation" (such as the regulations under sections 871(h) and 881(c)). The treatment of obligations described in this paragraph (d) for purposes of section 163(f)(2)(A) and (B) does not affect the determination of whether bearer obligations that are issued or guaranteed by the United States Government, a United States Government-owned agency, a United States Government sponsored enterprise (within the meaning of § 1.163-5(c)(1)) or that are backed (as described in the Treasury Department News Release R-2835 of September 10, 1984 and Treasury Department News Release R-2847 of September 14, 1984) by obligations issued by the United States Government, a United States Government-owned agency, or a United States Government sponsored enterprise comply with the requirements of section 163(f)(2)(B) and the regulations thereunder.

(6) The provisions of this paragraph (d)(1) through (5) may be illustrated by the following example:

Commercial Bank K forms a pool of 1000 residential mortgage loans, each made to a different individual homeowner, by assigning them to Commercial Bank L, an unrelated entity serving as trustee of the pool. Commercial Bank L immediately sells in a public offering certificates of interest in the trust of a maturity of 10 years in registered form. Commercial Bank L transfers the cash proceeds of the offering to Commercial Bank K. The certificates of interest in the trust are of a type offered to the public and are not described in section 163(f)(2)(B). Pursuant to paragraph (d)(1), the certificates of interest in the pool are registration-required obligations without regard to the fact that the obligations held by the trust are not registration-required obligations.

(e) *Regular interests in REMICs.* (1) A regular interest in a REMIC, as defined in sections 860D and 860G and the regulations thereunder, is considered to be a "registration-required obligation" under section 163(f)(2)(A) and § 1.163-5(c) if the regular interest is described in section 163(f)(2)(A) and § 1.163-5(c), without regard to whether any obligation held by the REMIC to which the regular interest relates is described in section 163(f)(2)(A) and § 1.163-5(c). A regular interest in a REMIC is considered to be described in section 163(f)(2)(B) and § 1.163-5(c), if the regular interest is described in section 163(f)(2)(B) and § 1.163(c), without regard to whether any obligation held by the REMIC to which the regular interest relates is described in section 163(f)(2)(B) and § 1.163-5(c).

(2) An obligation held by a REMIC is considered to be described in section 163(f)(2)(A) or (B) if such obligation is described in section 163(f)(2)(A) or (B), respectively, without regard to whether the regular interests in the REMIC are so considered.

(3) For purposes of section 4701, a regular interest is considered to be issued solely by the recipient of the proceeds from the issuance of the regular interest (hereinafter the "sponsor"). The sponsor is therefore liable for any excise tax under section 4701 that may be imposed with reference to the principal amount of the regular interest.

(4) In order to implement the purpose of section 163, § 1.163-5(c), and this section, the Commissioner may characterize a regular interest in a REMIC and any obligation held by such REMIC in accordance with the substance of the arrangement they represent and may impose the penalties provided under sections 163(f)(1) and 4701 in the appropriate amounts and on the appropriate persons. This provision may be applied, for example, where a corporation issues an obligation that is purportedly in registered form and that will qualify as a "qualified mortgage" within the meaning of section 860G(a)(3) in the hands of a REMIC, contributes the obligation to a REMIC as its only asset, and arranges for the sale to investors of regular interests in the REMIC in bearer form that do not meet the requirements of section 163(f)(2)(B). If this provision is applied, the obligation held by the REMIC will not be considered to be issued in registered form or to meet the requirements of section 163(f)(2)(B). The corporation will not be allowed a deduction for the payment of interest on the obligation held

by the REMIC, and the excise tax under section 4701, calculated with reference to the principal amount of the obligation held by the REMIC, will be imposed on the corporation and may be collected from the corporation and its agents. [Temporary Reg. § 1.163-5T.]

☐ [*T.D. 8202*, 5-18-88. *Amended by T.D. 8300*, 5-9-90.]

[Reg. § 1.163-6T]

§ 1.163-6T. Reduction of deduction where section 25 credit taken (Temporary).—(a) *In general.* The amount of the deduction under section 163 for interest paid or accrued during any taxable year on a certified indebtedness amount with respect to a mortgage credit certificate which has been issued under section 25 shall be reduced by the amount of the credit allowable with respect to such interest under section 25 (determined without regard to section 26).

(b) *Cross reference.* See §§ 1.25-1T through 1.25-8T with respect to rules relating to mortgage credit certificates. [Temporary Reg. § 1.163-6T.]

☐ *T.D. 8023*, 5-3-85.]

[Reg. § 1.163-7]

§ 1.163-7. Deduction for OID on certain debt instruments.—(a) *General rule.* Except as otherwise provided in paragraph (b) of this section, an issuer (including a transferee) determines the amount of OID that is deductible each year under section 163(e)(1) by using the constant yield method described in § 1.1272-1(b). This determination, however, is made without regard to section 1272(a)(7) (relating to acquisition premium) and § 1.1273-1(d) (relating to de minimis OID). An issuer is permitted a deduction under section 163(e)(1) only to the extent the issuer is primarily liable on the debt instrument. For certain limitations on the deductibility of OID, see sections 163(e) and 1275(b)(2). To determine the amount of interest (OID) that is deductible each year on a debt instrument that provides for contingent payments, see § 1.1275-4.

(b) *Special rules for de minimis OID*—(1) *Stated interest.* If a debt instrument has a de minimis amount of OID (within the meaning of § 1.1273-1(d)), the issuer treats all stated interest on the debt instrument as qualified stated interest. See §§ 1.446-2(b) and 1.461-1 for the treatment of qualified stated interest.

(2) *Deduction of de minimis OID on other than a constant yield basis.* In lieu of deducting de minimis OID under the general rule of paragraph (a) of this section, an issuer of a debt instrument with a de minimis amount of OID (other than a de minimis amount treated as quali-

fied stated interest under paragraph (b)(1) of this section) may choose to deduct the OID at maturity, on a straight-line basis over the term of the debt instrument, or in proportion to stated interest payments. The issuer makes this choice by reporting the de minimis OID in a manner consistent with the method chosen on the issuer's timely filed Federal income tax return for the taxable year in which the debt instrument is issued.

(c) *Deduction upon repurchase.* Except to the extent disallowed by any other section of the Internal Revenue Code (e.g., section 249) or this paragraph (c), if a debt instrument is repurchased by the issuer for a price in excess of its adjusted issue price (as defined in § 1.1275-1(b)), the excess (repurchase premium) is deductible as interest for the taxable year in which the repurchase occurs. If the issuer repurchases a debt instrument in a debt-for-debt exchange, the repurchase price is the issue price of the newly issued debt instrument (reduced by any unstated interest within the meaning of section 483). However, if the issue price of the newly issued debt instrument is determined under either section 1273(b)(4) or section 1274, any repurchase premium is not deductible in the year of the repurchase, but is amortized over the term of the newly issued debt instrument in the same manner as if it were OID.

(d) *Choice of accrual periods to determine whether a debt instrument is an applicable high yield discount obligation (AHYDO).* Section 163(e)(5) affects an issuer's OID deductions for certain high yield debt instruments that have significant OID. For purposes of section 163(i)(2), which defines significant OID, the issuer's choice of accrual periods to determine OID accruals is used to determine whether a debt instrument has significant OID. See § 1.1275-2(e) for rules relating to the issuer's obligation to disclose certain information to holders.

(e) *Qualified reopening—*(1) *In general.* In a qualified reopening of an issue of debt instruments, if a holder pays more or less than the adjusted issue price of the original debt instruments to acquire an additional debt instrument, the issuer treats this difference as an adjustment to the issuer's interest expense for the original and additional debt instruments. As provided by paragraphs (e)(2) through (5) of this section, the adjustment is taken into account over the term of the instrument using constant yield principles.

(2) *Positive adjustment.* If the difference is positive (that is, the holder pays more than the adjusted issue price of the original debt instrument), then, with respect to the issuer but not the holder, the difference increases the aggregate ad-

justed issue prices of all of the debt instruments in the issue, both original and additional.

(3) *Negative adjustment.* If the difference is negative (that is, the holder pays less than the adjusted issue price of the original debt instrument), then, with respect to the issuer but not the holder, the difference reduces the aggregate adjusted issue prices of all of the debt instruments in the issue, both original and additional.

(4) *Determination of issuer's interest accruals.* As of the reopening date, the issuer must redetermine the yield of the debt instruments in the issue for purposes of applying the constant yield method described in § 1.1272-1(b) to determine the issuer's accruals of interest expense over the remaining term of the debt instruments in the issue. This redetermined yield is based on the aggregate adjusted issue prices of the debt instruments in the issue (as determined under this paragraph (e)) and the remaining payment schedule of the debt instruments in the issue. If the aggregate adjusted issue prices of the debt instruments in the issue (as determined under this paragraph (e)) are less than the aggregate stated redemption price at maturity of the instruments (determined as of the reopening date) by a de minimis amount (within the meaning of § 1.1273-1(d)), the issuer may use the rules in paragraph (b) of this section to determine the issuer's accruals of interest expense.

(5) *Effect of adjustments on issuer's adjusted issue price.* The adjustments made under this paragraph (e) are taken into account for purposes of determining the issuer's adjusted issue price under § 1.1275-1(b).

(6) *Definitions.* The terms *additional debt instrument, original debt instrument, qualified reopening,* and *reopening date* have the same meanings as in § 1.1275-2(k).

(f) *Effective dates.* This section (other than paragraph (e) of this section) applies to debt instruments issued on or after April 4, 1994. Taxpayers, however, may rely on this section (other than paragraph (e) of this section) for debt instruments issued after December 21, 1992, and before April 4, 1994. Paragraph (e) of this section applies to qualified reopenings where the reopening date is on or after March 13, 2001. [Reg. § 1.163-7.]

☐ [*T.D. 8517, 1-27-94. Amended by T.D. 8674, 6-11-96 and T.D. 8934, 1-11-2001.*]

[Reg. § 1.163-8T]

§1.163-8T. **Allocation of interest expense among expenditures (temporary).**—(a) *In general—*(1) *Application.* This section prescribes rules for allocating interest expense for purposes of applying sections 469 (the "passive loss limitation") and 163(d) and (h) (the "nonbusiness interest limitations").

(2) *Cross-references.* This paragraph provides an overview of the manner in which interest expense is allocated for the purposes of applying the passive loss limitation and nonbusiness interest limitations and the manner in which interest expense allocated under this section is treated. See paragraph (b) of this section for definitions of certain terms, paragraph (c) for the rules for allocating debt and interest expense among expenditures, paragraphs (d) and (e) for the treatment of debt repayments and refinancings, paragraph (j) for the rules for reallocating debt upon the occurrence of certain events, paragraph (m) for the coordination of the rules in this section with other limitations on the deductibility of interest expense, and paragraph (n) of this section for effective date and transitional rules.

(3) *Manner of allocation.* In general, interest expense on a debt is allocated in the same manner as the debt to which such interest expense relates is allocated. Debt is allocated by tracing disbursements of the debt proceeds to specific expenditures. This section prescribes rules for tracing debt proceeds to specific expenditures.

(4) *Treatment of interest expense*—(i) *General rule.* Except as otherwise provided in paragraph (m) of this section (relating to limitations on interest expense other than the passive loss and nonbusiness interest limitations), interest expense allocated under the rules of this section is treated in the following manner:

(A) Interest expense allocated to a trade or business expenditure (as defined in paragraph (b)(7) of this section) is taken into account under section 163(h)(2)(A);

(B) Interest expense allocated to a passive activity expenditure (as defined in paragraph (b)(4) of this section) or a former passive activity expenditure (as defined in paragraph (b)(2) of this section) is taken into account for purposes of section 469 in determining the income or loss from the activity to which such expenditure relates;

(C) Interest expense allocated to an investment expenditure (as defined in paragraph (b)(3) of this section) is treated for purposes of section 163(d) as investment interest;

(D) Interest expense allocated to a personal expenditure (as defined in paragraph (b)(5) of this section) is treated for purposes of section 163(h) as personal interest; and

(E) Interest expense allocated to a portfolio expenditure (as defined in paragraph (b)(6) of this section) is treated for purposes of section

469(e)(2)(B)(ii) as interest expense described in section 469(e)(1)(A)(i)(III).

(ii) *Examples.* The following examples illustrate the application of this paragraph (a)(4):

Example (1). Taxpayer A, an individual, incurs interest expense allocated under the rules of this section to the following expenditures:

$6,000	Passive activity expenditure
$4,000	Personal expenditure

The $6,000 interest expense allocated to the passive activity expenditure is taken into account for purposes of section 469 in computing A's income or loss from the activity to which such interest relates. Pursuant to section 163(h), A may not deduct the $4,000 interest expense allocated to the personal expenditure (except to the extent such interest is qualified residence interest, within the meaning of section 163(h)(3)).

Example (2). (i) Corporation M, a closely held C corporation (within the meaning of section 469(j)(1)) has $10,000 of interest expense for a taxable year. Under the rules of this section, M's interest expense is allocated to the following expenditures:

$2,000	Passive activity expenditure
$3,000	Portfolio expenditure
$5,000	Other expenditures

(ii) Under section 163(d)(3)(D) and this paragraph (a)(4), the $2,000 interest expense allocated to the passive activity expenditure is taken into account in computing M's passive activity loss for the taxable year, but, pursuant to section 469(e)(1) and this paragraph (a)(4), the interest expense allocated to the portfolio expenditure and the other expenditures is not taken into account for such purposes.

(iii) Since M is a closely held C corporation, its passive activity loss is allowable under section 469(e)(2)(A) as a deduction from net active income. Under section 469(e)(2)(B) and this paragraph (a)(4), the $5,000 interest expense allocated to other expenditures is taken into account in computing M's net active income, but the interest expense allocated to the passive activity expenditure and the portfolio expenditure is not taken into account for such purposes.

(iv) Since M is a corporation, the $3,000 interest expense allocated to the portfolio expenditure is allowable without regard to section 163(d). If M were an individual, however, the interest expense allocated to the portfolio expenditure would be treated as investment interest for purposes of applying the limitation of section 163(d).

(b) *Definitions.* For purposes of this section—

(1) "Former passive activity" means an activity described in section 469(f)(3), but only if an unused deduction or credit (within the meaning of section 469(f)(1)(A) or (B)) is allocable to the activity under section 469(b) for the taxable year.

(2) "Former passive activity expenditure" means an expenditure that is taken into account under section 469 in computing the income or loss from a former passive activity of the taxpayer or an expenditure (including an expenditure properly chargeable to capital account) that would be so taken into account if such expenditure were otherwise deductible.

(3) "Investment expenditure" means an expenditure (other than a passive activity expenditure) properly chargeable to capital account with respect to property held for investment (within the meaning of section 163(d)(5)(A)) or an expenditure in connection with the holding of such property.

(4) "Passive activity expenditure" means an expenditure that is taken into account under section 469 in computing income or loss from a passive activity of the taxpayer or an expenditure (including an expenditure properly chargeable to capital account) that would be so taken into account if such expenditure were otherwise deductible. For purposes of this section, the term passive activity expenditure does not include any expenditure with respect to any low-income housing project in any taxable year in which any benefit is allowed with respect to such project under section 502 of the Tax Reform Act of 1986.

(5) "Personal expenditure" means an expenditure that is not a trade or business expenditure, a passive activity expenditure, or an investment expenditure.

(6) "Portfolio expenditure" means an investment expenditure properly chargeable to capital account with respect to property producing income of a type described in section 469(e)(1)(A) or an investment expenditure for an expense clearly and directly allocable to such income.

(7) "Trade or business expenditure" means an expenditure (other than a passive activity expenditure or an investment expenditure) in connection with the conduct of any trade or business other than the trade or business of performing service as an employee.

(c) *Allocation of debt and interest expense—*(1) *Allocation in accordance with use of proceeds.* Debt is allocated to expenditures in accordance with the use of the debt proceeds and, except as provided in paragraph (m) of this section, interest expense accruing on a debt during any period is allocated to expenditures in the same manner as the debt is allocated from time to time during

such period. Except as provided in paragraph (m) of this section, debt proceeds and related interest expense are allocated solely by reference to the use of such proceeds, and the allocation is not affected by the use of an interest in any property to secure the repayment of such debt or interest. The following example illustrates the principles of this paragraph (c)(1):

Example. Taxpayer A, an individual, pledges corporate stock held for investment as security for a loan and uses the debt proceeds to purchase an automobile for personal use. Interest expense accruing on the debt is allocated to the personal expenditure to purchase the automobile even though the debt is secured by investment property.

(2) *Allocation period—*(i) *Allocation of debt.* Debt is allocated to an expenditure for the period beginning on the date the proceeds of the debt are used or treated as used under the rules of this section to make the expenditure and ending on the earlier of—

(A) The date the debt is repaid; or

(B) The date the debt is reallocated in accordance with the rules in paragraphs (c)(4) and (j) of this section.

(ii) *Allocation of interest expense—*(A) *In general.* Except as otherwise provided in paragraph (m) of this section, interest expense accruing on a debt for any period is allocated in the same manner as the debt is allocated from time to time, regardless of when the interest is paid.

(B) *Effect of compounding.* Accrued interest is treated as a debt until it is paid and any interest accruing on unpaid interest is allocated in the same manner as the unpaid interest is allocated. For the taxable year in which a debt is reallocated under the rules in paragraphs (c)(4) and (j) of this section, however, compound interest accruing on such debt (other than compound interest accruing on interest that accrued before the beginning of the year) may be allocated between the original expenditure and the new expenditure on a straight-line basis (i.e., by allocating an equal amount of such interest expense to each day during the taxable year). In addition, a taxpayer may treat a year as consisting of 12 30-day months for purposes of allocating interest on a straight-line basis.

(C) *Accrual of interest expense.* For purposes of this paragraph (c)(2)(ii), the amount of interest expense that accrues during any period is determined by taking into account relevant provisions of the loan agreement and any applicable law such as sections 163(e), 483, and 1271 through 1275.

Reg. § 1.163-8T(b)(1)

(iii) *Examples.* The following examples illustrate the principles of this paragraph (c)(2):

Example (1). (i) On January 1, taxpayer B, a calendar year taxpayer, borrows $1,000 at an interest rate of 11 percent, compounded semiannually. B immediately uses the debt proceeds to purchase an investment security. On July 1, B sells the investment security for $1,000 and uses the sales proceeds to make a passive activity expenditure. On December 31, B pays accrued interest on the $1,000 debt for the entire year.

(ii) Under this paragraph (c)(2) and paragraph (j) of this section, the $1,000 debt is allocated to the investment expenditure for the period from January 1 through June 30, and to the passive activity expenditure from July 1 through December 31. Interest expense accruing on the $1,000 debt is allocated in accordance with the allocation of the debt from time to time during the year even though the debt was allocated to the passive activity expenditure on the date the interest was paid. Thus, the $55 interest expense for the period from January 1 through June 30 is allocated to the investment expenditure. In addition, during the period from July 1 through December 31, the interest expense allocated to the investment expenditure is a debt, the proceeds of which are treated as used to make an investment expenditure. Accordingly, an additional $3 of interest expense for the period from July 1 through December 31 ($55 × .055) is allocated to the investment expenditure. The remaining $55 of

interest expense for the period from July 1 through December 31 ($1,000 × .055) is allocated to the passive activity expenditure.

(iii) Alternatively, under the rule in paragraph (c)(2)(ii)(B) of this section, B may allocate the interest expense on a straight-line basis and may also treat the year as consisting of 12 30-day months for this purpose. In that case, $56.50 of interest expense (180/360 × $113) would be allocated to the investment expenditure and the remaining $56.50 of interest expense would be allocated to the passive activity expenditure.

Example (2). On January 1, 1988, taxpayer C borrows $10,000 at an interest rate of 11 percent, compounded annually. All interest and principal on the debt is payable in a lump sum on December 31, 1992. C immediately uses the debt proceeds to make a passive activity expenditure. C materially participates in the activity in 1990, 1991, and 1992. Therefore, under paragraphs (c)(2)(i) and (j) of this section, the debt is allocated to a passive activity expenditure from January 1, 1988, through December 31, 1989, and to a former passive activity expenditure from January 1, 1990, through December 31, 1992. In accordance with the loan agreement (and consistent with § 1.1272-1(d)(1) of the proposed regulations), interest expense accruing during any period is determined on the basis of annual compounding. Accordingly, the interest expense on the debt is allocated as follows:

Year	Amount		Expenditure
1988	$10,000 × .11	$1,100	Passive activity
1989	11,100 × .11	1,221	Passive activity
1990	12,321 × .11 = 1,355		
	1,355 × 2,321/12,321	255	Passive activity
	1,355 × 10,000/12,321	1,100	Former passive activity
		1,355	
1991	13,676 × .11 = 1,504		
	1,504 × 2,576/13,676	283	Passive activity
	1,504 × 11,100/13,676	1,221	Former passive activity
		1,504	
1992	15,180 × .11 = 1,670		
	1,670 × 2,859/15,180	315	Passive activity
	1,670 × 12,321/15,180	1,355	Former passive activity
		1,670	

(3) *Allocation of debt; proceeds not disbursed to borrower*—(i) *Third-party financing.* If a lender disburses debt proceeds to a person other than the borrower in consideration for the sale or use of property, for services, or for any other purpose, the debt is treated for purposes of this section as if the borrower used an amount of the

debt proceeds equal to such disbursement to make an expenditure for such property, services, or other purpose.

(ii) *Debt assumptions not involving cash disbursements.* If a taxpayer incurs or assumes a debt in consideration for the sale or use of property, for services, or for any other purpose, or

Reg. § 1.163-8T(c)(3)

takes property subject to a debt, and no debt proceeds are disbursed to the taxpayer, the debt is treated for purposes of this section as if the taxpayer used an amount of the debt proceeds equal to the balance of the debt outstanding at such time to make an expenditure for such property, services, or other purpose.

(4) *Allocation of debt; proceeds deposited in borrower's account*—(i) *Treatment of deposit.* For purposes of this section, a deposit of debt proceeds in an account is treated as an investment expenditure, and amounts held in an account (whether or not interest bearing) are treated as property held for investment. Debt allocated to an account under this paragraph (c)(4)(i) must be reallocated as required by paragraph (j) of this section whenever debt proceeds held in the account are used for another expenditure. This paragraph (c)(4) provides rules for determining when debt proceeds are expended from the account. The following example illustrates the principles of this paragraph (c)(4)(i):

Example. Taxpayer C, a calendar year taxpayer, borrows $100,000 on January 1 and immediately uses the proceeds to open a noninterest-bearing checking account. No other amounts are deposited in the account during the year, and no portion of the principal amount of the debt is repaid during the year. On April 1, C uses $20,000 of the debt proceeds held in the account for a passive activity expenditure. On September 1, C uses an additional $40,000 of the debt proceeds held in the account for a personal expenditure. Under this paragraph (c)(4)(i), from January 1 through March 31 the entire $100,000 debt is allocated to an investment expenditure for the account. From April 1 through August 31, $20,000 of the debt is allocated to the passive activity expenditure, and $80,000 of the debt is allocated to the investment expenditure for the account. From September 1 through December 31, $40,000 of the debt is allocated to the personal expenditure, $20,000 is allocated to the passive activity expenditure, and $40,000 is allocated to an investment expenditure for the account.

(ii) *Expenditures from account; general ordering rule.* Except as provided in paragraph (c)(4)(iii)(B) or (C) of this section, debt proceeds deposited in an account are treated as expended before—

(A) Any unborrowed amounts held in the account at the time such debt proceeds are deposited; and

(B) Any amounts (borrowed or unborrowed) that are deposited in the account after such debt proceeds are deposited.

The following example illustrates the application of this paragraph (c)(4)(ii):

Example. On January 10, taxpayer E opens a checking account, depositing $500 of proceeds of Debt A and $1,000 of unborrowed funds. The following chart summarizes the transactions which occur during the year with respect to the account:

Date	Transaction
January 10	$ 500 proceeds of Debt A and $1,000 unborrowed funds deposited
January 11	$ 500 proceeds of Debt B deposited
February 17	$ 800 personal expenditure
February 26	$ 700 passive activity expenditure
June 21	$1,000 proceeds of Debt C deposited
November 24	$ 800 investment expenditure
December 20	$ 600 personal expenditure

The $800 personal expenditure is treated as made from the $500 proceeds of Debt A and $300 of the proceeds of Debt B. The $700 passive activity expenditure is treated as made from the remaining $200 proceeds of Debt B and $500 of unborrowed funds. The $800 investment expenditure is treated as made entirely from the proceeds of Debt C. The $600 personal expenditure is treated as made from the remaining $200 proceeds of Debt C and $400 of unborrowed funds. Under paragraph (c)(4)(i) of this section, debt is allocated to an investment expenditure for periods during which debt proceeds are held in the account.

(iii) *Expenditures from account; supplemental ordering rules*—(A) *Checking or similar accounts.* Except as otherwise provided in this paragraph (c)(4)(iii), an expenditure from a checking or similar account is treated as made at the time the check is written on the account, provided the check is delivered or mailed to the payee within a reasonable period after the writing of the check. For this purpose, the taxpayer may treat checks written on the same day as written in any order. In the absence of evidence to the contrary, a check is presumed to be written on the date appearing on the check and to be delivered or mailed to the payee within a reasonable period thereafter. Evidence to the contrary may include the fact that a check does not clear within a reasonable period after the date appearing on the check.

(B) *Expenditures within 15 days after deposit of borrowed funds.* The taxpayer may treat any expenditure made from an account

Reg. § 1.163-8T(c)(4)

within 15 days after debt proceeds are deposited in such account as made from such proceeds to the extent thereof even if under paragraph (c)(4)(ii) of this section the debt proceeds would be treated as used to make one or more other expenditures. Any such expenditures and the debt proceeds from which such expenditures are treated as made are disregarded in applying paragraph (c)(4)(ii) of this section. The following examples illustrate the application of this paragraph (c)(4)(iii)(B):

Example (1). Taxpayer D incurs a $1,000 debt on June 5 and immediately deposits the proceeds in an account ("Account A"). On June 17, D transfers $2,000 from Account A to another account ("Account B"). On June 30, D writes a $1,500 check on Account B for a passive activity expenditure. In addition, numerous deposits of borrowed and unborrowed amounts and expenditures occur with respect to both accounts throughout the month of June. Notwithstanding these other transactions, D may treat $1,000 of the deposit to Account B on June 17 as an expenditure from the debt proceeds deposited in Account A on June 5. In addition, D may similarly treat $1,000 of the passive activity expenditure on June 30 as made from debt proceeds treated as deposited in Account B on June 17.

Example (2). The facts are the same as in the example in paragraph (c)(4)(ii) of this section, except that the proceeds of Debt B are deposited on February 11 rather than on January 11. Since the $700 passive activity expenditure occurs within 15 days after the proceeds of Debt B are deposited in the account, E may treat such expenditure as being made from the proceeds of Debt B to the extent thereof. If E treats the passive activity expenditure in this manner, the expenditures from the account are treated as follows: The $800 personal expenditure is treated as made from the $500 proceeds of Debt A and $300 of unborrowed funds. The $700 passive activity expenditure is treated as made from the $500 proceeds of Debt B and $200 of unborrowed funds. The remaining expenditures are treated as in the example in paragraph (c)(4)(ii) of this section.

(C) *Interest on segregated account.* In the case of an account consisting solely of the proceeds of a debt and interest earned on such account, the taxpayer may treat any expenditure from such account as made first from amounts constituting interest (rather than debt proceeds) to the extent of the balance of such interest in the account at the time of the expenditure, determined by applying the rules in this paragraph (c)(4). To the extent any expenditure is treated as made from interest under this paragraph

(c)(4)(iii)(C), the expenditure is disregarded in applying paragraph (c)(4)(ii) of this section.

(iv) *Optional method for determining date of reallocation.* Solely for the purpose of determining the date on which debt allocated to an account under paragraph (c)(4)(i) of this section is reallocated, the taxpayer may treat all expenditures made during any calendar month from debt proceeds in the account as occurring on the later of the first day of such month or the date on which such debt proceeds are deposited in the account. This paragraph (c)(4)(iv) applies only if all expenditures from an account during the same calendar month are similarly treated. The following example illustrates the application of this paragraph (c)(4)(iv):

Example. On January 10, taxpayer G opens a checking account, depositing $500 of proceeds of Debt A and $1,000 of unborrowed funds. The following chart summarizes the transactions which occur during the year with respect to the account (note that these facts are the same as the facts of the example in paragraph (c)(4)(ii) of this section):

Date	Transaction
January 10	$500 proceeds of Debt A and $1,000 unborrowed funds deposited
January 11	$500 proceeds of Debt B deposited
February 17	$800 personal expenditure
February 26	$700 passive activity expenditure
June 21	$1,000 proceeds of Debt C deposited
November 24	$800 investment expenditure
December 20	$600 personal expenditure

Assume that G chooses to apply the optional rule of this paragraph (c)(4)(iv) to all expenditures. For purposes of determining the date on which debt is allocated to the $800 personal expenditure made on February 17, the $500 treated as made from the proceeds of Debt A and the $300 treated as made from the proceeds of Debt B are treated as expenditures occurring on February 1. Accordingly, Debt A is allocated to an investment expenditure for the account from January 10 through January 31 and to the personal expenditure from February 1 through December 31, and $300 of Debt B is allocated to an investment expenditure for the account from January 11 through January 31 and to the personal expenditure from February 1 through December 31. The remaining $200 of Debt B is allocated to an investment expenditure for the account from January 11 through January 31 and to the passive activity expenditure from February 1 through December 31. The $800 of Debt C used to make the investment expenditure

Reg. § 1.163-8T(c)(4)

on November 24 is allocated to an investment expenditure for the account from June 21 through October 31 and to an investment expenditure from November 1 through December 31. The remaining $200 of Debt C is allocated to an investment expenditure for the account from June 21 through November 30 and to a personal expenditure from December 1 through December 31.

(v) *Simultaneous deposits—(A) In general.* If the proceeds of two or more debts are deposited in an account simultaneously, such proceeds are treated for purposes of this paragraph (c)(4) as deposited in the order in which the debts were incurred.

(B) *Order in which debts incurred.* If two or more debts are incurred simultaneously or are treated under applicable law as incurred simultaneously, the debts are treated for purposes of this paragraph (c)(4)(v) as incurred in any order the taxpayer selects.

(C) *Borrowings on which interest accrues at different rates.* If interest does not accrue at the same fixed or variable rate on the entire amount of a borrowing, each portion of the borrowing on which interest accrues at a different fixed or variable rate is treated as a separate debt for purposes of this paragraph (c)(4)(v).

(vi) *Multiple accounts.* The rules in this paragraph (c)(4) apply separately to each account of a taxpayer.

(5) *Allocation of debt; proceeds received in cash—(i) Expenditure within 15 days of receiving debt proceeds.* If a taxpayer receives the proceeds of a debt in cash, the taxpayer may treat any cash expenditure made within 15 days after receiving the cash as made from such debt proceeds to the extent thereof and may treat such expenditure as made on the date the taxpayer received the cash. The following example illustrates the rule in this paragraph (c)(5)(i):

Example. Taxpayer F incurs a $1,000 debt on August 4 and receives the debt proceeds in cash. F deposits $1,500 cash in an account on August 15 and on August 27 writes a check on the account for a passive activity expenditure. In addition, F engages in numerous other cash transactions throughout the month of August, and numerous deposits of borrowed and unborrowed amounts and expenditures occur with respect to the account during the same period. Notwithstanding these other transactions, F may treat $1,000 of the deposit on August 15 as an expenditure made from the debt proceeds on August 4. In addition, under the rule in paragraph (c)(4)(v)(B) of this section, F may treat the passive activity expenditure on August 27 as made from the

$1,000 debt proceeds treated as deposited in the account.

(ii) *Other expenditures.* Except as provided in paragraphs (c)(5)(i) and (iii) of this section, any debt proceeds a taxpayer (other than a corporation) receives in cash are treated as used to make personal expenditures. For purposes of this paragraph (c)(5), debt proceeds are received in cash if, for example, a withdrawal of cash from an account is treated under the rules of this section as an expenditure of debt proceeds.

(iii) *Special rules for certain taxpayers.* [Reserved.]

(6) *Special rules—(i) Qualified residence debt.* [Reserved.]

(ii) *Debt used to pay interest.* To the extent proceeds of a debt are used to pay interest, such debt is allocated in the same manner as the debt on which such interest accrued is allocated from time to time. The following example illustrates the application of this paragraph (c)(6)(ii):

Example. On January 1, taxpayer H incurs a debt of $1,000, bearing interest at an annual rate of 10 percent, compounded annually, payable at the end of each year ("Debt A"). H immediately opens a checking account, in which H deposits the proceeds of Debt A. No other amounts are deposited in the account during the year. On April 1, H writes a check for a personal expenditure in the amount of $1,000. On December 31, H borrows $100 ("Debt B") and immediately uses the proceeds of Debt B to pay the accrued interest of $100 on Debt A. From January 1 through March 31, Debt A is allocated, under the rule in paragraph (c)(4)(i) of this section, to the investment expenditure for the account. From April 1 through December 31, Debt A is allocated to the personal expenditure. Under the rule in paragraph (c)(2)(ii) of this section, $25 of the interest on Debt A for the year is allocated to the investment expenditure, and $75 of the interest on Debt A for the year is allocated to the personal expenditure. Accordingly, for the purpose of allocating the interest on Debt B for all periods until Debt B is repaid, $25 of Debt B is allocated to the investment expenditure, and $75 of Debt B is allocated to the personal expenditure.

(iii) *Debt used to pay borrowing costs— (A) Borrowing costs with respect to different debt.* To the extent the proceeds of a debt (the "ancillary debt") are used to pay borrowing costs (other than interest) with respect to another debt (the "primary debt"), the ancillary debt is allocated in the same manner as the primary debt is allocated from time to time. To the extent the primary debt is repaid, the ancillary debt will continue to be allocated in the same manner as the primary debt

Reg. § 1.163-8T(c)(5)

was allocated immediately before its repayment. The following example illustrates the rule in this paragraph (c)(6)(iii)(A):

Example. Taxpayer I incurs debts of $60,000 ("Debt A") and $10,000 ("Debt B"). I immediately uses $30,000 of the proceeds of Debt A to make a trade or business expenditure, $20,000 to make a passive activity expenditure, and $10,000 to make an investment expenditure. I immediately uses $3,000 of the proceeds of Debt B to pay borrowing costs (other than interest) with respect to Debt A (such as loan origination, loan commitment, abstract, and recording fees) and deposits the remaining $7,000 in an account. Under the rule in this paragraph (c)(6)(iii)(A), the $3,000 of Debt B used to pay expenses of incurring Debt A is allocated $1,500 to the trade or business expenditure ($3,000 × $30,000/$60,000), $1,000 to the passive activity expenditure ($3,000 × $20,000/$60,000), and $500 ($3,000 × $10,000/$60,000) to the investment expenditure. The manner in which the $3,000 of Debt B used to pay expenses of incurring Debt A is allocated may change if the allocation of Debt A changes, but such allocation will be unaffected by any repayment of Debt A. The remaining $7,000 of Debt B is allocated to an investment expenditure for the account until such time, if any, as this amount is used for a different expenditure.

(B) *Borrowing costs with respect to same debt.* To the extent the proceeds of a debt are used to pay borrowing costs (other than interest) with respect to such debt, such debt is allocated in the same manner as the remaining debt is allocated from time to time. The remaining debt for this purpose is the portion of the debt that is not used to pay borrowing costs (other than interest) with respect to such debt. Any repayment of the debt is treated as a repayment of the debt allocated under this paragraph (c)(6)(iii)(B) and the remaining debt in the same proportion as such amounts bear to each other. The following example illustrates the application of this paragraph (c)(6)(iii)(B):

Example. (i) Taxpayer J borrows $85,000. The lender disburses $80,000 of this amount to J, retaining $5,000 for borrowing costs (other than interest) with respect to the loan. J immediately uses $40,000 of the debt proceeds to make a personal expenditure, $20,000 to make a passive activity expenditure, and $20,000 to make an investment expenditure. Under the rule in this paragraph (c)(6)(iii)(B), the $5,000 used to pay borrowing costs is allocated $2,500 ($5,000 × $40,000/$80,000) to the personal expenditure, $1,250 ($5,000 × $20,000/$80,000) to the passive

activity expenditure, and $1,250 ($5,000 × $20,000/$80,000) to the investment expenditure. The manner in which this $5,000 is allocated may change if the allocation of the remaining $80,000 of debt is changed.

(ii) Assume that J repays $50,000 of the debt. The repayment is treated as a repayment of $2,941 ($50,000 × $5,000/$85,000) of the debt used to pay borrowing costs and a repayment of $47,059 ($50,000 × $80,000/$85,000) of the remaining debt. Under paragraph (d) of this section, J is treated as repaying the $42,500 of debt allocated to the personal expenditure ($2,500 of debt used to pay borrowing costs and $40,000 of remaining debt). In addition, assuming that under paragraph (d)(2) J chooses to treat the allocation to the passive activity expenditure as having occurred before the allocation to the investment expenditure, J is treated as repaying $7,500 of debt allocated to the passive activity expenditure ($441 of debt used to pay borrowing costs and $7,059 of remaining debt).

(iv) *Allocation of debt before actual receipt of debt proceeds.* If interest properly accrues on a debt during any period before the debt proceeds are actually received or used to make an expenditure, the debt is allocated to an investment expenditure for such period.

(7) *Antiabuse rules.* [Reserved.]

(d) *Debt repayments—*(1) *General ordering rule.* If, at the time any portion of a debt is repaid, such debt is allocated to more than one expenditure, the debt is treated for purposes of this section as repaid in the following order:

(i) Amounts allocated to personal expenditures;

(ii) Amounts allocated to investment expenditures and passive activity expenditures (other than passive activity expenditures described in paragraph (d)(1)(iii) of this section).

(iii) Amounts allocated to passive activity expenditures in connection with a rental real estate activity with respect to which the taxpayer actively participates (within the meaning of section 469(i));

(iv) Amounts allocated to former passive activity expenditures; and

(v) Amounts allocated to trade or business expenditures and to expenditures described in the last sentence of paragraph (b)(4) of this section.

(2) *Supplemental ordering rules for expenditures in same class.* Amounts allocated to two or more expenditures that are described in the same subdivision of paragraph (d)(1) of this section (e.g., amounts allocated to different personal expenditures) are treated as repaid in the order in

Reg. § 1.163-8T(d)(2)

which the amounts were allocated (or reallocated) to such expenditures. For purposes of this paragraph (d)(2), the taxpayer may treat allocations and reallocations that occur on the same day as occurring in any order (without regard to the order in which expenditures are treated as made under paragraph (c)(4)(iii)(A) of this section).

(3) *Continuous borrowings.* In the case of borrowings pursuant to a line of credit or similar account or arrangement that allows a taxpayer to borrow funds periodically under a single loan agreement—

(i) All borrowings on which interest accrues at the same fixed or variable rate are treated as a single debt; and

(ii) Borrowings or portions of borrowings on which interest accrues at different fixed or variable rates are treated as different debts, and such debts are treated as repaid for purposes of this paragraph (d) in the order in which such borrowings are treated as repaid under the loan agreement.

(4) *Examples.* The following examples illustrate the application of this paragraph (d):

Example (1). Taxpayer B borrows $100,000 ("Debt A") on July 12, immediately deposits the proceeds in an account, and uses the debt proceeds to make the following expenditures on the following dates:

August 31	$40,000 passive activity expenditure #1
October 5	$20,000 passive activity expenditure #2
December 24	$40,000 personal expenditure

On January 19 of the following year, B repays $90,000 of Debt A (leaving $10,000 of Debt A outstanding). The $40,000 of Debt A allocated to the personal expenditure, the $40,000 allocated to passive activity expenditure # 1, and $10,000 of the $20,000 allocated to passive activity expenditure # 2 are treated as repaid.

Example (2). (i) Taxpayer A obtains a line of credit. Interest on any borrowing on the line of credit accrues at the lender's "prime lending rate" on the date of the borrowing plus two percentage points. The loan documents provide that borrowings on the line of credit are treated as repaid in the order the borrowings were made. A borrows $30,000 ("Borrowing # 1") on the line of credit and immediately uses $20,000 of the debt proceeds to make a personal expenditure ("personal expenditure # 1") and $10,000 to make a trade or business expenditure ("trade or business expenditure # 1"). A subsequently borrows another $20,000 ("Borrowing # 2") on the line of credit and immediately uses $15,000 of the debt

proceeds to make a personal expenditure ("personal expenditure # 2") and $5,000 to make a trade or business expenditure ("trade or business expenditure # 2"). A then repays $40,000 of the borrowings.

(ii) If the prime lending rate plus two percentage points was the same on both the date of Borrowing # 1 and the date of Borrowing # 2, the borrowings are treated for purposes of this paragraph (d) as a single debt, and A is treated as having repaid $35,000 of debt allocated to personal expenditure # 1 and personal expenditure # 2, and $5,000 of debt allocated to trade or business expenditure # 1.

(iii) If the prime lending rate plus two percentage points was different on the date of Borrowing # 1 and Borrowing # 2, the borrowings are treated as two debts, and, in accordance with the loan agreement, the $40,000 repaid amount is treated as a repayment of Borrowing # 1 and $10,000 of Borrowing # 2. Accordingly, A is treated as having repaid $20,000 of debt allocated to personal expenditure # 1, $10,000 of debt allocated to trade or business expenditure # 1, and $10,000 of debt allocated to personal expenditure # 2.

(e) *Debt refinancings*—(1) *In general.* To the extent proceeds of any debt (the "replacement debt") are used to repay any portion of a debt, the replacement debt is allocated to the expenditures to which the repaid debt was allocated. The amount of replacement debt allocated to any such expenditure is equal to the amount of debt allocated to such expenditure that was repaid with proceeds of the replacement debt. To the extent proceeds of the replacement debt are used for expenditures other than repayment of a debt, the replacement debt is allocated to expenditures in accordance with the rules of this section.

(2) *Example.* The following example illustrates the application of this paragraph (e):

Example. Taxpayer C borrows $100,000 ("Debt A") on July 12, immediately deposits the debt proceeds in an account, and uses the proceeds to make the following expenditures on the following dates (note that the facts of this example are the same as the facts of example (1) in paragraph (d)(4) of this section):

August 31	$40,000 passive activity expenditure #1
October 5	$20,000 passive activity expenditure #2
December 24	$40,000 personal expenditure #1

On January 19 of the following year, C borrows $120,000 ("Debt B") and uses $90,000 of the proceeds to repay $90,000 of Debt A (leaving $10,000 of Debt A outstanding). In addition, C

Reg. § 1.163-8T(d)(3)

uses $30,000 of the proceeds of Debt B to make a personal expenditure ("personal expenditure # 2"). Debt B is allocated $40,000 to personal expenditure # 1, $40,000 to passive activity expenditure # 1, $10,000 to passive activity expenditure # 2, and $30,000 to personal expenditure # 2. Under paragraph (d)(1) of this section, Debt B will be treated as repaid in the following order: (1) amounts allocated to personal expenditure # 1, (2) amounts allocated to personal expenditure # 2, (3) amounts allocated to passive activity expenditure # 1, and (4) amounts allocated to passive activity expenditure # 2.

(f) *Debt allocated to distributions by pass-through entities.* [Reserved.]

(g) *Repayment of passthrough entity debt.* [Reserved.]

(h) *Debt allocated to expenditures for interests in passthrough entities.* [Reserved.]

(i) *Allocation of debt to loans between pass-through entities and interest holders.* [Reserved.]

(j) *Reallocation of debt*—(1) *Debt allocated to capital expenditures*—(i) *Time of reallocation.* Except as provided in paragraph (j)(2) of this section, debt allocated to an expenditure properly chargeable to capital account with respect to an asset (the "first expenditure") is reallocated to another expenditure on the earlier of—

(A) The date on which proceeds from a disposition of such asset are used for another expenditure; or

(B) The date on which the character of the first expenditure changes (e.g., from a passive activity expenditure to an expenditure that is not a passive activity expenditure) by reason of a change in the use of the asset with respect to which the first expenditure was capitalized.

(ii) *Limitation on amount reallocated.* The amount of debt reallocated under paragraph (j)(1)(i)(A) of this section may not exceed the proceeds from the disposition of the asset. The amount of debt reallocated under paragraph (j)(1)(i)(B) of this section may not exceed the fair market value of the asset on the date of the change in use. In applying this paragraph (j)(1)(ii) with respect to a debt in any case in which two or more debts are allocable to expenditures properly chargeable to capital account with respect to the same asset, only a ratable portion (determined with respect to any such debt by dividing the amount of such debt by the aggregate amount of all such debts) of the fair market value or proceeds from the disposition of such asset shall be taken into account.

(iii) *Treatment of loans made by the tax-payer.* Except as provided in paragraph (j)(1)(iv)

of this section, an expenditure to make a loan is treated as an expenditure properly chargeable to capital account with respect to an asset, and for purposes of paragraph (j)(1)(i)(A) of this section any repayment of the loan is treated as a disposition of the asset. Paragraph (j)(3) of this section applies to any repayment of a loan in installments.

(iv) *Treatment of accounts.* Debt allocated to an account under paragraph (c)(4)(i) of this section is treated as allocated to an expenditure properly chargeable to capital account with respect to an asset, and any expenditure from the account is treated as a disposition of the asset. See paragraph (c)(4) of this section for rules under which debt proceeds allocated to an account are treated as used for another expenditure.

(2) *Disposition proceeds in excess of debt.* If the proceeds from the disposition of an asset exceed the amount of debt reallocated by reason of such disposition, or two or more debts are reallocated by reason of the disposition of an asset, the proceeds of the disposition are treated as an account to which the rules in paragraph (c)(4) of this section apply.

(3) *Special rule for deferred payment sales.* If any portion of the proceeds of a disposition of an asset are received subsequent to the disposition—

(i) The portion of the proceeds to be received subsequent to the disposition is treated for periods prior to the receipt as used to make an investment expenditure; and

(ii) Debt reallocated by reason of the disposition is allocated to such investment expenditure to the extent such debt exceeds the proceeds of the disposition previously received (other than proceeds used to repay such debt).

(4) *Examples.* The following examples illustrate the application of this paragraph (j):

Example (1). On January 1, 1988, taxpayer D sells an asset for $25,000. Immediately before the sale, the amount of debt allocated to expenditures properly chargeable to capital account with respect to the asset was $15,000. The proceeds of the disposition are treated as an account consisting of $15,000 of debt proceeds and $10,000 of unborrowed funds to which paragraph (c)(4) of this section applies. Thus, if D immediately makes a $10,000 personal expenditure from the proceeds and within 15 days deposits the remaining proceeds in an account, D may, pursuant to paragraph (c)(4)(iii)(B) of this section, treat the entire $15,000 deposited in the account as proceeds of a debt.

Example (2). The facts are the same as in example (1) except that, instead of receiving all

Reg. § 1.163-8T(j)(4)

$25,000 of the sale proceeds on January 1, 1988, D receives $5,000 on that date, $10,000 on January 1, 1989, and $10,000 on January 1, 1990. D does not use any portion of the sale proceeds to repay the debt. Between January 1, 1988, and December 31, 1988, D is treated under paragraph (j)(3) of this section as making an investment expenditure of $20,000 to which $10,000 of debt is allocated. In addition, the remaining $5,000 of debt is reallocated on January 1, 1988, in accordance with D's use of the sales proceeds received on that date. Between January 1, 1989, and December 31, 1989, D is treated as making an investment expenditure of $10,000 to which no debt is allocated. In addition, as of January 1, 1989, $10,000 of debt is reallocated in accordance with D's use of the sales proceeds received on that date.

Example (3). The facts are the same as in example (2), except that D immediately uses the $5,000 sale proceeds received on January 1, 1988, to repay $5,000 of the $15,000 debt. Between January 1, 1988, and December 31, 1988, D is treated as making an investment expenditure of $20,000 to which the remaining balance ($10,000) of the debt is reallocated. The results in 1989 are as described in example (2).

(k) *Modification of rules in the case of interest expense allocated to foreign source income.* [Reserved.]

(l) *Reserved.*

(m) *Coordination with other provisions*—(1) *Effect of other limitations*—(i) *In general.* All debt is allocated among expenditures pursuant to the rules in this section, without regard to any limitations on the deductibility of interest expense on such debt. The applicability of the passive loss and nonbusiness interest limitations to interest on such debt, however, may be affected by other limitations on the deductibility of interest expense.

(ii) *Disallowance provisions.* Interest expense that is not allowable as a deduction by reason of a disallowance provision (within the meaning of paragraph (m)(7)(ii) of this section) is not taken into account for any taxable year for purposes of applying the passive loss and nonbusiness interest limitations.

(iii) *Deferral provisions.* Interest expense that is not allowable as a deduction for the taxable year in which paid or accrued by reason of a deferral provision (within the meaning of paragraph (m)(7)(iii) of this section) is allocated in the same manner as the debt giving rise to the interest expense is allocated for such taxable year. Such interest expense is taken into account for purposes of applying the passive loss and nonbusi-

ness interest limitations for the taxable year in which such interest expense is allowable under such deferral provision.

(iv) *Capitalization provisions.* Interest expense that is capitalized pursuant to a capitalization provision (within the meaning of paragraph (m)(7)(i) of this section) is not taken into account as interest for any taxable year for purposes of applying the passive loss and nonbusiness interest limitations.

(2) *Effect on other limitations*—(i) *General rule.* Except as provided in paragraph (m)(2)(ii) of this section, any limitation on the deductibility of an item (other than the passive loss and nonbusiness interest limitations) applies without regard to the manner in which debt is allocated under this section. Thus, for example, interest expense treated under section 265(a)(2) as interest on indebtedness incurred or continued to purchase or carry obligations the interest on which is wholly exempt from Federal income tax is not deductible regardless of the expenditure to which the underlying debt is allocated under this section.

(ii) *Exception.* Capitalization provisions (within the meaning of paragraph (m)(7)(i) of this section) do not apply to interest expense allocated to any personal expenditure under the rules of this section.

(3) *Qualified residence interest.* Qualified residence interest (within the meaning of section 163(h)(3)) is allowable as a deduction without regard to the manner in which such interest expense is allocated under the rules of this section. In addition, qualified residence interest is not taken into account in determining the income or loss from any activity for purposes of section 469 or in determining the amount of investment interest for purposes of section 163(d). The following example illustrates the rule in this paragraph (m)(3):

Example. Taxpayer E, an individual, incurs a $20,000 debt secured by a residence and immediately uses the proceeds to purchase an automobile exclusively for E's personal use. Under the rules in this section, the debt and interest expense on the debt are allocated to a personal expenditure. If, however, the interest on the debt is qualified residence interest within the meaning of section 163(h)(3), the interest is not treated as personal interest for purposes of section 163(h).

(4) *Interest described in section 163(h)(2)(E).* Interest described in section 163(h)(2)(E) is allowable as a deduction without regard to the rules of this section.

(5) *Interest on deemed distributee debt.* [Reserved.]

Reg. § 1.163-8T(k)

(6) *Examples.* The following examples illustrate the relationship between the passive loss and nonbusiness interest limitations and other limitations on the deductibility of interest expense:

Example (1). Debt is allocated pursuant to the rules in this section to an investment expenditure for the purchase of taxable investment securities. Pursuant to section 265(a)(2), the debt is treated as indebtedness incurred or continued to purchase or carry obligations the interest on which is wholly exempt from Federal income tax, and, accordingly, interest on the debt is disallowed. If section 265(a)(2) subsequently ceases to apply (because, for example, the taxpayer ceases to hold any tax-exempt obligations), and the debt at such time continues to be allocated to an investment expenditure, interest on the debt that accrues after such time is subject to section 163(d).

Example (2). An accrual method taxpayer incurs a debt payable to a cash method lender who is related to the taxpayer within the meaning of section 267(b). During the period in which interest on the debt is not deductible by reason of section 267(a)(2), the debt is allocated to a passive activity expenditure. Thus, interest that accrues on the debt for such period is also allocated to the passive activity expenditure. When such interest expense becomes deductible under section 267(a)(2), it will be allocated to the passive activity expenditure, regardless of how the debt is allocated at such time.

Example (3). A taxpayer incurs debt that is allocated under the rules of this section to an investment expenditure. Under section 263A(f), however, interest expense on such debt is capitalized during the production period (within the meaning of section 263A(f)(4)(B)) of property used in a passive activity of the taxpayer. The capitalized interest expense is not allocated to the investment expenditure, and depreciation deductions attributable to the capitalized interest expense are subject to the passive loss limitation as long as the property is used in a passive activity. However, interest expense on the debt for periods after the production period is allocated to the investment expenditure as long as the debt remains allocated to the investment expenditure.

(7) *Other limitations on interest expense*—(i) *Capitalization provisions.* A capitalization provision is any provision that requires or allows interest expense to be capitalized. Capitalization provisions include sections 263(g), 263A(f), and 266.

(ii) *Disallowance provisions.* A disallowance provision is any provision (other than the passive loss and nonbusiness interest limitations)

that disallows a deduction for interest expense for all taxable years and is not a capitalization provision. Disallowance provisions include sections 163(f)(2), 264(a)(2), 264(a)(4), 265(a)(2), 265(b)(2), 279(a), 291(e)(1)(B)(ii), 805(b)(1), and 834(c)(5).

(iii) *Deferral provisions.* A deferral provision is any provision (other than the passive loss and nonbusiness interest limitations) that disallows a deduction for interest expense for any taxable year and is not a capitalization or disallowance provision. Deferral provisions include sections 267(a)(2), 465, 1277, and 1282.

(n) *Effective date*—(1) *In general.* This section applies to interest expense paid or accrued in taxable years beginning after December 31, 1986.

(2) *Transitional rule for certain expenditures.* For purposes of determining whether debt is allocated to expenditures made on or before August 3, 1987, paragraphs (c)(4)(iii)(B) and (c)(5)(i) of this section are applied by substituting "90 days" for "15 days."

(3) *Transitional rule for certain debt*—(i) *General rule.* Except as provided in paragraph (n)(3)(ii) of this section, any debt outstanding on December 31, 1986, that is properly attributable to a business or rental activity is treated for purposes of this section as debt allocated to expenditures properly chargeable to capital account with respect to the assets held for use or for sale to customers in such business or rental activity. Debt is properly attributable to a business or rental activity for purposes of this section (regardless of whether such debt otherwise would be allocable under this section to expenditures in connection with such activity) if the taxpayer has properly and consistently deducted interest expense (including interest subject to limitation under section 163(d) as in effect prior to the Tax Reform Act of 1986) on such debt on Schedule C, E, or F of Form 1040 in computing income or loss from such business or rental activity for taxable years beginning before January 1, 1987. For purposes of this paragraph (n)(3), amended returns filed after July 2, 1987, are disregarded in determining whether a taxpayer has consistently deducted interest expense on Schedule C, E, or F of Form 1040 in computing income or loss from a business or rental activity.

(ii) *Exceptions*—(A) *Debt financed distributions by pass-through entities.* [Reserved.]

(B) *Election out.* This paragraph (n)(3) does not apply with respect to debt of a taxpayer who elects under paragraph (n)(3)(viii) of this section to allocate debt outstanding on December 31 1986, in accordance with the provisions of this section other than this paragraph (n)(3) (i.e., in accordance with the use of the debt proceeds).

(iii) *Business or rental activity.* For purposes of this paragraph (n)(3), a business or rental activity is any trade or business or rental activity of the taxpayer. For this purpose—

(A) A trade or business includes a business or profession the income and deductions of which (or, in the case of a partner or S corporation shareholder, the taxpayer's share thereof) are properly reported on Schedule C, E, or F of Form 1040; and

(B) A rental activity includes an activity of renting property the income and deductions of which (or, in the case of a partner or S corporation shareholder, the taxpayer's share thereof) are properly reported on Schedule E of Form 1040.

(iv) Example. The following example illustrates the circumstances in which debt is properly attributable to a business or rental activity:

Example. Taxpayer H incurred a debt in 1979 and properly deducted the interest expense on the debt on Schedule C of Form 1040 for each year from 1979 through 1986. Under this paragraph (n)(3), the debt is properly attributable to the business the results of which are reported on Schedule C.

(v) *Allocation requirement*—(A) *In general.* Debt outstanding on December 31, 1986, that is properly attributable (within the meaning of paragraph (n)(3)(i) of this section) to a business or rental activity must be allocated in a reasonable and consistent manner among the assets held for use or for sale to customers in such activity on the last day of the taxable year that includes December 31, 1986. The taxpayer shall specify the manner in which such debt is allocated by filing a statement in accordance with paragraph (n)(3)(vii) of this section. If the taxpayer does not file such a statement or fails to allocate such debt in a reasonable and consistent manner, the Commissioner shall allocate the debt.

(B) *Reasonable and consistent manner—examples of improper allocation.* For purposes of this paragraph (n)(3)(v), debt is not treated as allocated in a reasonable and consistent manner if—

(1) The amount of debt allocated to goodwill exceeds the basis of the goodwill; or

(2) The amount of debt allocated to an asset exceeds the fair market value of the asset, and the amount of debt allocated to any other asset is less than the fair market value (lesser of basis or fair market value in the case of goodwill) of such other asset.

(vi) *Coordination with other provisions.* The effect of any events occurring after the last day of the taxable year that includes December 31, 1986, shall be determined under the rules of this section, applied by treating the debt allocated to an asset under paragraph (n)(3)(v) of this section as if proceeds of such debt were used to make an expenditure properly chargeable to capital account with respect to such asset on the last day of the taxable year that includes December 31, 1986. Thus, debt that is allocated to an asset in accordance with this paragraph (n)(3) must be reallocated in accordance with paragraph (j) of this section upon the occurrence with respect to such asset of any event described in such paragraph (j). Similarly, such debt is treated as repaid in the order prescribed in paragraph (d) of this section. In addition, a replacement debt (within the meaning of paragraph (e) of this section) is allocated to an expenditure properly chargeable to capital account with respect to an asset to the extent the proceeds of such debt are used to repay the portion of a debt allocated to such asset under this paragraph (n)(3).

(vii) *Form for allocation of debt.* A taxpayer shall allocate debt for purposes of this paragraph (n)(3) by attaching to the taxpayer's return for the first taxable year beginning after December 31, 1986, a statement that is prominently identified as a TRANSITIONAL ALLOCATION STATEMENT UNDER § 1.163-8T(n)(3) and includes the following information:

(A) A description of the business or rental activity to which the debt is properly attributable;

(B) The amount of debt allocated;

(C) The assets among which the debt is allocated;

(D) The manner in which the debt is allocated;

(E) The amount of debt allocated to each asset; and

(F) Such other information as the Commissioner may require.

(viii) *Form for election out.* A taxpayer shall elect to allocate debt outstanding on December 31, 1986, in accordance with the provisions of this section other than this paragraph (n)(3) by attaching to the taxpayer's return (or amended return) for the first taxable year beginning after December 31, 1986, a statement to that effect, prominently identified as an ELECTION OUT UNDER § 1.163-8T(n)(3).

(ix) *Special rule for partnerships and S corporations.* For purposes of paragraph (n)(3)(ii)(B), (v), (vii) and (viii) of this section

Reg. § 1.163-8T(n)(3)

(relating to the allocation of debt and election out), a partnership or S corporation shall be treated as the taxpayer with respect to the debt of the partnership or S corporation.

(x) *Irrevocability.* An allocation or election filed in accordance with paragraph (n)(3)(vii) or (viii) of this section may not be revoked or modified except with the consent of the Commissioner. [Temporary Reg. § 1.163-8T.]

☐ [*T.D.* 8145, 7-1-87.]

[Reg. § 1.163-9T]

§ 1.163-9T. Personal interest (temporary).—
(a) *In general.* No deduction under any provision of Chapter 1 of the Internal Revenue Code shall be allowed for personal interest paid or accrued during the taxable year by a taxpayer other than a corporation.

(b) *Personal interest*—(1) *Definition.* For purposes of this section, personal interest is any interest expense other than—

(i) Interest paid or accrued on indebtedness properly allocable (within the meaning of § 1.163-8T) to the conduct of a trade or business (other than the trade or business of performing services as an employee),

(ii) Any investment interest (within the meaning of section 163(d)(3)),

(iii) Any interest that is taken into account under section 469 in computing income or loss from a passive activity of the taxpayer,

(iv) Any qualified residence interest (within the meaning of section 163(h)(3) and § 1.163-10T), and

(v) Any interest payable under section 6601 with respect to the unpaid portion of the tax imposed by section 2001 for the period during which an extension of time for payment of such tax is in effect under section 6163, 6166, or 6166A (as in effect before its repeal by the Economic Recovery Tax Act of 1981).

(2) *Interest relating to taxes*—(i) *In general.* Except as provided in paragraph (b)(2)(iii) of this section, personal interest includes interest—

(A) Paid on underpayments of individual Federal, State or local income taxes and on indebtedness used to pay such taxes (within the meaning of § 1.168-8T), regardless of the source of the income generating the tax liability;

(B) Paid under section 453C(e)(4)(B) (interest on deferred tax resulting from certain installment sales) and section 1291(c) (interest on deferred tax attributable to passive foreign investment companies); or

(C) Paid by a trust, S corporation, or other pass-through entity on underpayments of State or local income taxes and on indebtedness used to pay such taxes.

(ii) *Example.* A, an individual, owns stock of an S corporation. On its return for 1987, the corporation underreports its taxable income. Consequently, A underreports A's share of that income on A's tax return. In 1989, A pays the resulting deficiency plus interest to the Internal Revenue Service. The interest paid by A in 1989 on the tax deficiency is personal interest, notwithstanding the fact that the additional tax liability may have arisen out of income from a trade or business. The result would be the same if A's business had been operated as a sole proprietorship.

(iii) *Certain other taxes.* Personal interest does not include interest—

(A) Paid with respect to sales, excise and similar taxes that are incurred in connection with a trade or business or an investment activity;

(B) Paid by an S corporation with respect to an underpayment of income tax from a year in which the S corporation was a C corporation or with respect to an underpayment of the taxes imposed by sections 1374 or 1375, or similar provision of State law; or

(C) Paid by a transferee under section 6901 (tax liability resulting from transferred assets), or a similar provision of State law, with respect to a C corporation's underpayment of income tax.

(3) *Cross references.* See § 1.163-8T for rules for determining the allocation of interest expense to various activities. See § 1.163-10T for rules concerning qualified residence interest.

(c) *Effective date*—(1) *In general.* The provisions of this section are effective for taxable years beginning after December 31, 1986. In the case of any taxable year beginning in calendar years 1987 through 1990, the amount of personal interest that is nondeductible under this section is limited to the applicable percentage of such amount.

(2) *Applicable percentage.* The applicable percentages for taxable years beginning in 1987 through 1990 are as follows:

    1987: 35 percent

    1988: 60 percent

    1989: 80 percent

    1990: 90 percent [Temporary Reg. § 1.163-9T.]

☐ [*T.D.* 8168, 12-21-87.]

[Reg. § 1.163-10T]

§ 1.163-10T. Qualified residence interest (temporary).—(a) *Table of contents.* This paragraph (a) lists the major paragraphs that appear in this section 1.163-10T.

(a) Table of contents.

(b) Treatment of qualified residence interest.

(c) Determination of qualified residence interest when secured debt does not exceed the adjusted purchase price.

(1) In general.

(2) Examples.

(d) Determination of qualified residence interest when secured debt exceeds adjusted purchase price—Simplified method.

(1) In general.

(2) Treatment of interest paid or accrued on secured debt that is not qualified residence interest.

(3) Example.

(e) Determination of qualified residence interest when secured debt exceeds adjusted purchase price—Exact method.

(1) In general.

(2) Determination of applicable debt limit.

(3) Example.

(4) Treatment of interest paid or accrued with respect to secured debt that is not qualified residence interest.

(i) In general.

(ii) Example.

(iii) Special rule if debt is allocated to more than one expenditure.

(iv) Example.

(f) Special rules.

(1) Special rules for personal property.

(i) In general.

(ii) Example.

(2) Special rule for real property.

(i) In general.

(ii) Example.

(g) Selection of method.

(h) Average balance.

(1) Average balance defined.

(2) Average balance reported by lender.

(3) Average balance computed on a daily basis.

(i) In general.

(ii) Example.

(4) Average balance computed using the interest rate.

(i) In general.

(ii) Points and prepaid interest.

(iii) Examples.

(5) Average balance computed using average of beginning and ending balance.

(i) In general.

(ii) Example.

(6) Highest principal balance.

(7) Other methods provided by the Commissioner.

(8) Anti-abuse rule.

(i) [Reserved.]

(j) Determination of interest paid or accrued during the taxable year.

(1) In general.

(2) Special rules for cash-basis taxpayers.

(i) Points deductible in year paid under section 461(g)(2).

(ii) Points and other prepaid interest described in section 461(g)(1).

(3) Examples.

(k) Determination of adjusted purchase price and fair market value.

(1) Adjusted purchase price.

(i) In general.

(ii) Adjusted purchase price of a qualified residence acquired incident to divorce.

(iii) Examples.

(2) Fair market value.

(i) In general.

(ii) Examples.

(3) Allocation of adjusted purchase price and fair market value.

(l) [Reserved].

(m) Grandfathered amount.

(1) Substitution for adjusted purchase price.

(2) Determination of grandfathered amount.

(i) In general.

(ii) Special rule for lines of credit and certain other debt.

(iii) Fair market value limitation.

(iv) Examples.

(3) Refinancing of grandfathered debt.

(i) In general.

(ii) Determination of grandfathered amount.

(4) Limitation on term of grandfathered debt.

(i) In general.

(ii) Special rule for nonamortizing debt.

Reg. § 1.163-10T(a)

(iii) Example.

(n) Qualified indebtedness (secured debt used for medical and educational purposes).

(1) In general.

(i) Treatment of qualified indebtedness.

(ii) Determination of amount of qualified indebtedness.

(iii) Determination of amount of qualified indebtedness for mixed-use debt.

(iv) Example.

(v) Prevention of double counting in year of refinancing.

(vi) Special rule for principal payments in excess of qualified expenses.

(2) Debt used to pay for qualified medical or educational expenses.

(i) In general.

(ii) Special rule for refinancing.

(iii) Other special rules

(iv) Examples.

(3) Qualified medical expenses.

(4) Qualified educational expenses.

(o) Secured debt.

(1) In general.

(2) Special rule for debt in certain States.

(3) Time at which debt is treated as secured.

(4) Partially secured debt.

(i) In general.

(ii) Example.

(5) Election to treat debt as not secured by a qualified residence.

(i) In general.

(ii) Example.

(iii) Allocation of debt secured by two qualified residences.

(p) Definition of qualified residence.

(1) In general.

(2) Principal residence.

(3) Second residence.

(i) In general.

(ii) Definition of residence.

(iii) Use as a residence.

(iv) Election of second residence.

(4) Allocations between residence and other property.

(i) In general.

(ii) Special rule for rental of residence.

(iii) Examples.

(5) Residence under construction.

(i) In general.

(ii) Example.

(6) Special rule for the time-sharing arrangements.

(q) Special rules for tenant-stockholders in co-operative housing corporations.

(1) In general.

(2) Special rule where stock may not be used to secure debt.

(3) Treatment of interest expense of the co-operative described in section 216(a)(2).

(4) Special rule to prevent tax avoidance.

(5) Other definitions.

(r) Effective date.

(b) *Treatment of qualified residence interest.* Except as provided below, qualified residence interest is deductible under section 163(a). Qualified residence interest is not subject to limitation or otherwise taken into account under section 163(d) (limitation on investment interest), section 163(h)(1) (disallowance of deduction for personal interest), section 263A (capitalization and inclusion in inventory costs of certain expenses) or section 469 (limitations on losses from passive activities). Qualified residence interest is subject to the limitation imposed by section 263(g) (certain interest in the case of straddles), section 264(a)(2) and (4) (interest paid in connection with certain insurance), section 265(a)(2) (interest relating to tax-exempt income), section 266 (carrying charges), section 267(a)(2) (interest with respect to transactions between related taxpayers), section 465 (deductions limited to amount at risk), section 1277 (deferral of interest deduction allocable to accrued market discount), and section 1282 (deferral of interest deduction allocable to accrued discount).

(c) *Determination of qualified residence interest when secured debt does not exceed adjusted purchase price—(1) In general.* If the sum of the average balances for the taxable year of all secured debts on a qualified residence does not exceed the adjusted purchase price (determined as of the end of the taxable year) of the qualified residence, all of the interest paid or accrued during the taxable year with respect to the secured debts is qualified residence interest. If the sum of the average balances for the taxable year of all secured debts exceeds the adjusted purchase price of the qualified residences (determined as of the end of the taxable year), the taxpayer must use either the simplified method (see paragraph (d) of this section) or the exact method (see paragraph (e) of this section) to determine the amount of interest that is qualified residence interest.

(2) *Examples.*

Reg. § 1.163-10T(c)(2)

Example (1). T purchases a qualified residence in 1987 for $65,000. T pays $6,500 in cash and finances the remainder of the purchase with a mortgage of $58,500. In 1988, the average balance of the mortgage is $58,000. Because the average balance of the mortgage is less than the adjusted purchase price of the residence ($65,000), all of the interest paid or accrued during 1988 on the mortgage is qualified residence interest.

Example (2). The facts are the same as in example (1), except that T incurs a second mortgage on January 1, 1988, with an initial principal balance of $2,000. The average balance of the second mortgage in 1988 is $1,900. Because the sum of the average balance of the first and second mortgages ($59,900) is less than the adjusted purchase price of the residence ($65,000), all of the interest paid or accrued during 1988 on both the first and second mortgages is qualified residence interest.

Example (3). P borrows $50,000 on January 1, 1988 and secures the debt by a qualified residence. P pays the interest on the debt monthly, but makes no principal payments in 1988. There are no other debts secured by the residence during 1988. On December 31, 1988, the adjusted purchase price of the residence is $40,000. The average balance of the debt in 1988 is $50,000. Because the average balance of the debt exceeds the adjusted purchase price ($10,000), some of the interest on the debt is not qualified residence interest. The portion of the total interest that is qualified residence interest must be determined in accordance with the rules of paragraph (d) or paragraph (e) of this section.

(d) *Determination of qualified residence interest when secured debt exceeds adjusted purchase price—Simplified method—*(1) *In general.* Under the simplified method, the amount of qualified residence interest for the taxable year is equal to the total interest paid or accrued during the taxable year with respect to all secured debts multiplied by a fraction (not in excess of one), the numerator of which is the adjusted purchase price (determined as of the end of the taxable year) of the qualified residence and the denominator of which is the sum of the average balances of all secured debts.

(2) *Treatment of interest paid or accrued on secured debt that is not qualified residence interest.* Under the simplified method, the excess of the total interest paid or accrued during the taxable year with respect to all secured debts over the amount of qualified residence interest is personal interest.

(3) *Example.* R's principal residence has an adjusted purchase price on December 31, 1988, of $105,000. R has two debts secured by the residence, with the following average balances and interest payments:

Debt	Date Secured	Average Balance	Interest
Debt 1	June 1983	$ 80,000	$ 8,000
Debt 2	May 1987	$ 40,000	$ 4,800
Total		$120,000	$12,800

The amount of qualified residence interest is determined under the simplified method by multiplying the total interest ($12,800) by a fraction (expressed as a decimal amount) equal to the adjusted purchase price ($105,000) of the residence divided by the combined average balances ($120,000). For 1988, this fraction is equal to 0.875 ($105,000/$120,000). Therefore, $11,200 ($12,800 × 0.875) of the total interest is qualified residence interest. The remaining $1,600 in interest ($12,800 − $11,200) is personal interest, even if (under the rules of § 1.163-8T) such remaining interest would be allocated to some other category of interest.

(e) *Determination of qualified residence interest when secured debt exceeds adjusted purchase price—Exact method—*(1) *In general.* Under the exact method, the amount of qualified residence interest for the taxable year is determined on a debt-by-debt basis by computing the applicable debt limit for each secured debt and comparing each such applicable debt limit to the average balance of the corresponding debt. If, for the taxable year, the average balance of a secured debt does not exceed the applicable debt limit for that debt, all of the interest paid or accrued during the taxable year with respect to the debt is qualified residence interest. If the average balance of the secured debt exceeds the applicable debt limit for that debt, the amount of qualified residence interest with respect to the debt is determined by multiplying the interest paid or accrued with respect to the debt by a fraction, the numerator of which is the applicable debt limit for that debt and the denominator of which is the average balance of the debt.

(2) *Determination of applicable debt limit.* For each secured debt, the applicable debt limit for the taxable year is equal to

(i) The lesser of—

(A) The fair market value of the qualified residence as of the date the debt is first secured, and

(B) The adjusted purchase price of the qualified residence as of the end of the taxable year,

Reg. § 1.163-10T(d)(2)

(ii) Reduced by the average balance of each debt previously secured by the qualified residence.

For purposes of paragraph (e)(2)(ii) of this section, the average balance of a debt shall be treated as not exceeding the applicable debt limit of such debt. See paragraph (n)(1)(i) of this section for the rule that increases the adjusted purchase price in paragraph (e)(2)(i)(B) of this section by the amount of any qualified indebtedness (certain medical and educational debt). See

Debt	Date Secured
Debt 1	June 1983
Debt 2	May 1987
Total	

(ii) The amount of qualified residence interest for 1988 under the exact method is determined as follows. Because there are no debts previously secured by the residence, the applicable debt limit for Debt 1 is $100,000 (the lesser of the adjusted purchase price as of the end of the taxable year and the fair market value of the residence at the time the debt was secured). Because the average balance of Debt 1 ($80,000) does not exceed its applicable debt limit ($100,000), all of the interest paid on the debt during 1988 ($8,000) is qualified residence interest.

(iii) The applicable debt limit for Debt 2 is $25,000 ($105,000 (the lesser of $140,000 fair market value and $105,000 adjusted purchase price) reduced by $80,000 (the average balance of Debt 1)). Because the average balance of Debt 2 ($40,000) exceeds its applicable debt limit, the amount of qualified residence interest on Debt 2 is determined by multiplying the amount of interest paid on the debt during the year ($4,800) by a fraction equal to its applicable debt limit divided by its average balance ($25,000/$40,000 = 0.625). Accordingly, $3,000 ($4,800 × 0.625) of the interest paid in 1988 on Debt 2 is qualified residence interest. The character of the remaining $1,800 of interest paid on Debt 2 is determined under the rules of paragraph (e)(4) of this section.

(4) *Treatment of interest paid or accrued with respect to secured debt that is not qualified residence interest*—(i) *In general.* Under the exact method, the excess of the interest paid or accrued during the taxable year with respect to a secured debt over the amount of qualified residence interest with respect to the debt is allocated under the rules of § 1.163-8T.

(ii) *Example.* T borrows $20,000 and the entire proceeds of the debt are disbursed by the lender to T's broker to purchase securities held for investment. T secures the debt with T's principal

paragraph (f) of this section for special rules relating to the determination of the fair market value of the qualified residence.

(3) *Example.* (i) R's principal residence has an adjusted purchase price on December 31, 1988, of $105,000. R has two debts secured by the residence. The average balances and interest payments on each debt during 1988 and fair market value of the residence on the date each debt was secured are as follows:

Fair Market Value	Average Balance	Interest
$100,000	$ 80,000	$ 8,000
$140,000	$ 40,000	$ 4,800
$120,000	$12,800

residence. In 1990, T pays $2,000 of interest on the debt. Assume that under the rules of paragraph (e) of this section, $1,500 of the interest is qualified residence interest. The remaining $500 in interest expense would be allocated under the rules of § 1.163-8T. Section 1.163-8T generally allocates debt (and the associated interest expense) by tracing disbursements of the debt proceeds to specific expenditures. Accordingly, the $500 interest expense on the debt that is not qualified residence interest is investment interest subject to section 163(d).

(iii) *Special rule if debt is allocated to more than one expenditure.* If—

(A) The average balance of a secured debt exceeds the applicable debt limit for that debt, and

(B) Under the rules of § 1.163-8T, interest paid or accrued with respect to such debt is allocated to more than one expenditure,

the interest expense that is not qualified residence interest may be allocated among such expenditures, to the extent of such expenditures, in any manner selected by the taxpayer.

(iv) *Example.* (i) C borrows $60,000 secured by a qualified residence. C uses (within the meaning of § 1.163-8T) $20,000 of the proceeds in C's trade or business, $20,000 to purchase stock held for investment and $20,000 for personal purposes. In 1990, C pays $6,000 in interest on the debt and, under the rules of § 1.163-8T, $2,000 in interest is allocable to trade or business expenses, $2,000 to investment expenses and $2,000 to personal expenses. Assume that under paragraph (e) of this section, $2,500 of the interest is qualified residence interest and $3,500 of the interest is not qualified residence interest.

(ii) Under paragraph (e)(4)(iii) of this section, C may allocate up to $2,000 of the interest that is not qualified residence interest to any of

Reg. § 1.163-10T(e)(4)

the three categories of expenditures up to a total of $3,500 for all three categories. Therefore, for example, C may allocate $2,000 of such interest to C's trade or business and $1,500 of such interest to the purchase of stock.

(f) *Special rules*—(1) *Special rules for personal property*—(i) *In general.* If a qualified residence is personal property under State law (*e.g.*, a boat or motorized vehicle)—

(A) For purposes of paragraphs (c)(1) and (d)(1) of this section, if the fair market value of the residence as of the date that any secured debt (outstanding during the taxable year) is first secured by the residence is less than the adjusted purchase price as of the end of the taxable year, the lowest such fair market value shall be substituted for the adjusted purchase price.

(B) For purposes of paragraphs (e)(2)(i)(A) and (f)(1)(i)(A) of this section, the fair market value of the residence as of the date the debt is first secured by the residence shall not exceed the fair market value as of any date on which the taxpayer borrows any additional amount with respect to the debt.

(ii) *Example.* D owns a recreational vehicle that is a qualified residence under paragraph (p)(4) of this section. The adjusted purchase price and fair market value of the recreational vehicle is $20,000 in 1989. In 1989, D establishes a line of credit secured by the recreational vehicle. As of June 1, 1992, the fair market value of the vehicle has decreased to $10,000. On that day, D borrows an additional amount on the debt by using the line of credit. Although under paragraphs (e)(2)(i) and (f)(1)(i)(A) of this section, fair market value is determined at the time the debt is first secured, under paragraph (f)(1)(i)(B) of this section, the fair market value is the lesser of that amount or the fair market value on the most recent date that D borrows any additional amount with respect to the line of credit. Therefore, the fair market value with respect to the debt is $10,000.

(2) *Special rule for real property*—(i) *In general.* For purposes of paragraph (e)(2)(i)(A) of this section, the fair market value of a qualified residence that is real property under State law is presumed irrebuttably to be not less than the adjusted purchase price of the residence as of the last day of the taxable year.

(ii) *Example.* (*i*) C purchases a residence on August 11, 1987, for $50,000, incurring a first mortgage. The residence is real property under State law. During 1987, C makes $10,000 in home improvements. Accordingly, the adjusted purchase price of the residence as of December 31, 1988, is $60,000. C incurs a second mortgage on

May 19, 1988, as of which time the fair market value of the residence is $55,000.

(*ii*) For purposes of determining the applicable debt limit for each debt, the fair market value of the residence is generally determined as of the time the debt is first secured. Accordingly, the fair market value would be $50,000 and $55,000 with respect to the first and second mortgage, respectively. Under the special rule of paragraph (f)(2)(i) of this section, however, the fair market value with respect to both debts in 1988 is $60,000, the adjusted purchase price on December 31, 1988.

(g) *Selection of method.* For any taxable year, a taxpayer may use the simplified method (described in paragraph (d) of this section) or the exact method (described in paragraph (e) of this section) by completing the appropriate portion of Form 8598. A taxpayer with two qualified residences may use the simplified method for one residence and the exact method for the other residence.

(h) *Average balance*—(1) *Average balance defined.* For purposes of this section, the term "average balance" means the amount determined under this paragraph (h). A taxpayer is not required to use the same method to determine the average balance of all secured debts during a taxable year or of any particular secured debt from one year to the next.

(2) *Average balance reported by lender.* If a lender that is subject to section 6050H (returns relating to mortgage interest received in trade or business from individuals) reports the average balance of a secured debt on Form 1098, the taxpayer may use the average balance so reported.

(3) *Average balance computed on a daily basis*—(i) *In general.* The average balance may be determined by—

(A) Adding the outstanding balance of a debt on each day during the taxable year that the debt is secured by a qualified residence, and

(B) Dividing the sum by the number of days during the taxable year that the residence is a qualified residence.

(ii) *Example.* Taxpayer A incurs a debt of $10,000 on September 1, 1989, securing the debt with A's principal residence. The residence is A's principal residence during the entire taxable year. A pays current interest on the debt monthly, but makes no principal payments. The debt is, therefore, outstanding for 122 days with a balance each day of $10,000. The residence is a qualified residence for 365 days. The average balance of the debt for 1989 is $3,342 (122 × $10,000/365).

Reg. § 1.163-10T(f)(1)

(4) *Average balance computed using the interest rate*—(i) *In general.* If all accrued interest on a secured debt is paid at least monthly, the average balance of the secured debt may be determined by dividing the interest paid or accrued during the taxable year while the debt is secured by a qualified residence by the annual interest rate on the debt. If the interest rate on a debt varies during the taxable year, the lowest annual interest rate that applies to the debt during the taxable year must be used for purposes of this paragraph (h)(4). If the residence securing the debt is a qualified residence for less than the entire taxable year, the average balance of any secured debt may be determined by dividing the average balance determined under the preceding sentence by the percentage of the taxable year that the debt is secured by a qualified residence.

(ii) *Points and prepaid interest.* For purposes of paragraph (h)(4)(i) of this section, the amount of interest paid during the taxable year does not include any amount paid as points and includes prepaid interest only in the year accrued.

(iii) *Examples—Example (1).* B has a line of credit secured by a qualified residence for the entire taxable year. The interest rate on the debt is 10 percent throughout the taxable year. The principal balance on the debt changes throughout the year. B pays the accrued interest on the debt monthly. B pays $2,500 in interest on the debt during the taxable year. The average balance of the debt ($25,000) may be computed by dividing the total interest paid by the interest rate ($25,000 = $2,500/0.10).

Example (2). Assume the same facts as in example 1, except that the residence is a qualified residence, and the debt is outstanding, for only one-half of the taxable year and B pays only $1,250 in interest on the debt during the taxable year. The average balance of the debt may be computed by first dividing the total interest paid by the interest rate ($12,500 = $1,250/0.10). Second, because the residence is not a qualified residence for the entire taxable year, the average balance must be determined by dividing this amount ($12,500) by the portion of the year that the residence is qualified (0.50). The average balance is therefore $25,000 ($12,500/0.50).

(5) *Average balance computed using average of beginning and ending balances*—(i) *In general.* If—

(A) A debt requires level payments at fixed equal intervals (*e.g.*, monthly, quarterly) no less often than semi-annually during the taxable year,

(B) The taxpayer prepays no more than one month's principal on the debt during the taxable year, and

(C) No new amounts are borrowed on the debt during the taxable year,

the average balance of the debt may be determined by adding the principal balance as of the first day of the taxable year that the debt is secured by the qualified residence and the principal balance as of the last day of the taxable year that the debt is secured by the qualified residence and dividing the sum by 2. If the debt is secured by a qualified residence for less than the entire period during the taxable year that the residence is a qualified residence, the average balance may be determined by multiplying the average balance determined under the preceding sentence by a fraction, the numerator of which is the number of days during the taxable year that the debt is secured by the qualified residence and the denominator of which is the number of days during the taxable year that the residence is a qualified residence. For purposes of this paragraph (h)(5)(i), the determination of whether payments are level shall disregard the fact that the amount of the payments may be adjusted from time to time to take into account changes in the applicable interest rate.

(ii) *Example.* C borrows $10,000 in 1988, securing the debt with a second mortgage on a principal residence. The terms of the loan require C to make equal monthly payments of principal and interest so as to amortize the entire loan balance over 20 years. The balance of the debt is $9,652 on January 1, 1990, and is $9,450 on December 31, 1990. The average balance of the debt during 1990 may be computed as follows:

Balance on first day of the year $9,652
Balance on last day of the year $9,450
Average balance . $9,652 + $9,450 = $9,551
$$\frac{\$9,652 + \$9,450}{2} = \$9,551$$

(6) *Highest principal balance.* The average balance of a debt may be determined by taking the highest principal balance of the debt during the taxable year.

(7) *Other methods provided by the Commissioner.* The average balance may be determined using any other method provided by the Commissioner by form, publication, revenue ruling, or revenue procedure. Such methods may include methods similar to (but with restrictions different from) those provided in paragraph (h) of this section.

(8) *Anti-abuse rule.* If, as a result of the determination of the average balance of a debt using any of the methods specified in paragraphs

Reg. § 1.163-10T(h)(8)

(h)(4), (5), or (6) of this section, there is a significant overstatement of the amount of qualified residence interest and a principal purpose of the pattern of payments and borrowing on the debt is to cause the amount of such qualified residence interest to be overstated, the district director may redetermine the average balance using the method specified under paragraph (h)(3) of this section.

(i) [Reserved.]

(j) *Determination of interest paid or accrued during the taxable year*—(1) *In general.* For purposes of determining the amount of qualified residence interest with respect to a secured debt, the amount of interest paid or accrued during the taxable year includes only interest paid or accrued while the debt is secured by a qualified residence.

(2) *Special rules for cash-basis taxpayers*—(i) *Points deductible in year paid under section 461(g)(2).* If points described in section 461(g)(2) (certain points paid in respect of debt incurred in connection with the purchase or improvement of a principal residence) are paid with respect to a debt, the amount of such points is qualified residence interest.

(ii) *Points and other prepaid interest described in section 461(g)(1).* The amount of points or other prepaid interest charged to capital account under section 461(g)(1) (prepaid interest) that is qualified residence interest shall be determined under the rules of paragraphs (c) through (e) of this section in the same manner as any other interest paid with respect to the debt in the taxable year to which such payments are allocable under section 461(g)(1).

(3) *Examples.*

Example (1). T designates a vacation home as a qualified residence as of October 1, 1987. The home is encumbered by a mortgage during the entire taxable year. For purposes of determining the amount of qualified residence interest for 1987, T may take into account the interest paid or accrued on the secured debt from October 1, 1987, through December 31, 1987.

Example (2). R purchases a principal residence on June 17, 1987. As part of the purchase price, R obtains a conventional 30-year mortgage, secured by the residence. At closing, R pays 2½ points on the mortgage and interest on the mortgage for the period June 17, 1987 through June 30, 1987. The points are actually paid by R and are not merely withheld from the loan proceeds. R incurs no additional secured debt during 1987. Assuming that the points satisfy the requirements of section 461(g)(2), the entire amount of points

and the interest paid at closing are qualified residence interest.

Example (3). (i) On July 1, 1987, W borrows $120,000 to purchase a residence to use as a vacation home. W secures the debt with the residence. W pays 2 points, or $2,400. The debt has a term of 10 years and requires monthly payments of principal and interest. W is permitted to amortize the points at the rate of $20 per month over 120 months. W elects to treat the residence as a second residence. W has no other debt secured by the residence. The average balance of the debt in each taxable year is less than the adjusted purchase price of the residence. W sells the residence on June 30, 1990, and pays off the remaining balance of the debt.

(ii) W is entitled to treat the following amounts of the points as interest paid on a debt secured by a qualified residence—

1987	$120 =	$20 × 6 months;
1988	$240 =	$20 × 12 months;
1989	$120 =	$20 × 6 months.
TOTAL	$480	

All of the interest paid on the debt, including the allocable points, is qualified residence interest. Upon repaying the debt, the remaining $1,920 ($2,400 − $480) in unamortized points is treated as interest paid in 1990 and, because the average balance of the secured debt in 1990 is less than the adjusted purchase price, is also qualified residence interest.

(k) *Determination of adjusted purchase price and fair market value*—(1) *Adjusted purchase price*—(i) *In general.* For purposes of this section, the adjusted purchase price of a qualified residence is equal to the taxpayer's basis in the residence as initially determined under section 1012 or other applicable sections of the Internal Revenue Code, increased by the cost of any improvements to the residence that have been added to the taxpayer's basis in the residence under section 1016(a)(1). Any other adjustments to basis, including those required under section 1033(b) (involuntary conversions), and 1034(e) (rollover of gain on sale of principal residence) are disregarded in determining the taxpayer's adjusted purchase price. If, for example, a taxpayer's second residence is rented for a portion of the year and its basis is reduced by depreciation allowed in connection with the rental use of the property, the amount of the taxpayer's adjusted purchase price in the residence is not reduced. See paragraph (m) of this section for a rule that treats the sum of the grandfathered amounts of all secured debts as the adjusted purchase price of the residence.

Reg. § 1.163-10T(i)

(ii) *Adjusted purchase price of a qualified residence acquired incident to divorce.* [Reserved.]

(iii) *Examples—Example (1).* X purchases a residence for $120,000. X's basis, as determined under section 1012, is the cost of the property, or $120,000. Accordingly, the adjusted purchase price of the residence is initially $120,000.

Example (2). Y owns a principal residence that has a basis of $30,000. Y sells the residence for $100,000 and purchases a new principal residence for a $120,000. Under section 1034, Y does not recognize gain on the sale of the former residence. Under section 1034(e), Y's basis in the new residence is reduced by the amount of gain not recognized. Therefore, under section 1034(e), Y's basis in the new residence is $50,000 ($120,000 − $70,000). For purposes of section 163(h), however, the adjusted purchase price of the residence is not adjusted under section 1034(e). Therefore, the adjusted purchase price of the residence is initially $120,000.

Example (3). Z acquires a residence by gift. The donor's basis in the residence was $30,000. Z's basis in the residence, determined under section 1015, is $30,000. Accordingly, the adjusted purchase price of the residence is initially $30,000.

(2) *Fair market value*—(i) *In general.* For purposes of this section, the fair market value of a qualified residence on any date is the fair market value of the taxpayer's interest in the residence on such date. In addition, the fair market value determined under this paragraph (k)(2)(i) shall be determined by taking into account the cost of improvements to the residence reasonably expected to be made with the proceeds of the debt.

(ii) *Example.* In 1988, the adjusted purchase price of P's second residence is $65,000 and the fair market value of the residence is $70,000. At that time, P incurs an additional debt of $10,000, the proceeds of which P reasonably expects to use to add two bedrooms to the residence. Because the fair market value is determined by taking into account the cost of improvements to the residence that are reasonably expected to be made with the proceeds of the debt, the fair market value of the residence with respect to the debt incurred in 1988 is $80,000 ($70,000 + $10,000).

(3) *Allocation of adjusted purchase price and fair market value.* If a property includes both a qualified residence and other property, the adjusted purchase price and the fair market value of such property must be allocated between the qualified residence and the other property. See

paragraph (p)(4) of this section for rules governing such an allocation.

(l) [Reserved].

(m) *Grandfathered amount*—(1) *Substitution for adjusted purchase price.* If, for the taxable year, the sum of the grandfathered amounts, if any, of all secured debts exceeds the adjusted purchase price of the qualified residence, such sum may be treated as the adjusted purchase price of the residence under paragraphs (c), (d) and (e) of this section.

(2) *Determination of grandfathered amount*—(i) *In general.* For any taxable year, the grandfathered amount of any secured debt that was incurred on or before August 16, 1986, and was secured by the residence continuously from August 16, 1986, through the end of the taxable year, is the average balance of the debt for the taxable year. A secured debt that was not incurred and secured on or before August 16, 1986, has no grandfathered amount.

(ii) *Special rule for lines of credit and certain other debt.* If, with respect to a debt described in paragraph (m)(2)(i) of this section, a taxpayer has borrowed any additional amounts after August 15, 1986, the grandfathered amount of such debt is equal to the lesser of—

(A) The average balance of the debt for the taxable year, or

(B) The principal balance of the debt as of August 16, 1986, reduced (but not below zero) by all principal payments after August 16, 1986, and before the first day of the current taxable year.

For purposes of this paragraph (m)(2)(ii), a taxpayer shall not be considered to have borrowed any additional amount with respect to a debt merely because accrued interest is added to the principal balance of the debt, so long as such accrued interest is paid by the taxpayer no less often than quarterly.

(iii) *Fair market value limitation.* The grandfathered amount of any debt for any taxable year may not exceed the fair market value of the residence on August 16, 1986, reduced by the principal balance on that day of all previously secured debt.

(iv) *Examples—Example (1).* As of August 16, 1986, T has one debt secured by T's principal residence. The debt is a conventional self-amortizing mortgage and, on August 16, 1986, it has an outstanding principal balance of $75,000. In 1987, the average balance of the mortgage is $73,000. The adjusted purchase price of the residence as of the end of 1987 is $50,000. Because the mortgage was incurred and secured on or before August 16, 1986 and T has not borrowed any additional amounts with respect to the mortgage, the grandfathered amount is the average balance, $73,000. Because the grandfathered amount exceeds the adjusted purchase price ($50,000), T may treat the grandfathered amount as the adjusted purchase price in determining the amount of qualified residence interest.

Example (2). (i) The facts are the same as in example (1), except that in May 1986, T also obtains a home equity line of credit that, on August 16, 1986, has a principal balance of $40,000. In November 1986, T borrows an additional $10,000 on the home equity line, increasing the balance to $50,000. In December 1986, T repays $5,000 of principal on the home equity line. The average balance of the home equity line in 1987 is $45,000.

(ii) Because T has borrowed additional amounts on the line of credit after August 16, 1986, the grandfathered amount for that debt must be determined under the rules of paragraph (m)(2)(ii) of this section. Accordingly, the grandfathered amount for the line of credit is equal to the lesser of $45,000, the average balance of the debt in 1987, and $35,000, the principal balance on August 16, 1986, reduced by all principal payments between August 17, 1986, and December 31, 1986 ($40,000 − $5,000). The sum of the grandfathered amounts with respect to the residence is $108,000 ($73,000 + $35,000). Because the sum of the grandfathered amounts exceeds the adjusted purchase price ($50,000), T may treat the sum as the adjusted purchase price in determining the qualified residence interest for 1987.

(3) Refinancing of grandfathered debt—(i) *In general.* A debt incurred and secured on or before August 16, 1986, is refinanced if some or all of the outstanding balance of such a debt (the "original debt") is repaid out of the proceeds of a second debt secured by the same qualified residence (the "replacement debt"). In the case of a refinancing, the replacement debt is treated as a debt incurred and secured on or before August 16, 1986, and the grandfathered amount of such debt is the amount (but not less than zero) determined pursuant to paragraph (m)(3)(ii) of this section.

(ii) Determination of grandfathered amount—(A) *Exact refinancing.* If—

(1) The entire proceeds of a replacement debt are used to refinance one or more original debts, and

(2) The taxpayer has not borrowed any additional amounts after August 16, 1986, with respect to the original debt or debts,

the grandfathered amount of the replacement debt is the average balance of the replacement debt. For purposes of the preceding sentence, the fact that proceeds of a replacement debt are used to pay costs of obtaining the replacement debt (including points or other closing costs) shall be disregarded in determining whether the entire proceeds of the replacement debt have been used to refinance one or more original debts.

(B) Refinancing other than exact refinancings—*(1) Year of refinancing.* In the taxable year in which an original debt is refinanced, the grandfathered amount of the original and replacement debts is equal to the lesser of—

(i) The sum of the average balances of the original debt and the replacement debt, and

(ii) The principal balance of the original debt as of August 16, 1986, reduced by all principal payments on the original debt after August 16, 1986, and before the first day of the current taxable year.

(2) In subsequent years. In any taxable year after the taxable year in which an original debt is refinanced, the grandfathered amount of the replacement debt is equal to the least of—

(i) The average balance of the replacement debt for the taxable year,

(ii) The amount of the replacement debt used to repay the principal balance of the original debt, reduced by all principal payments on the replacement debt after the date of the refinancing and before the first day of the current taxable year, or

(iii) The principal balance of the original debt on August 16, 1986, reduced by all principal payments on the original debt after August 16, 1986, and before the date of the refinancing, and further reduced by all principal payments on the replacement debt after the date of the refinancing and before the first day of the current taxable year.

(C) Example—*(i) Facts.* On August 16, 1986, T has a single debt secured by a principal residence with a balance of $150,000. On July 1, 1988, T refinances the debt, which still has a principal balance of $150,000, with a new secured debt. The principal balance of the replacement debt throughout 1988 and 1989 is $150,000. The adjusted purchase price of the residence is $100,000 throughout 1987, 1988 and 1989. The average balance of the original debt was $150,000 in 1987 and $75,000 in 1988. The average balance of the replacement debt is $75,000 in 1988 and $150,000 in 1989.

(ii) Grandfathered amount in 1987. The original debt was incurred and secured on or

before August 16, 1986 and T has not borrowed any additional amounts with respect to the debt. Therefore, its grandfathered amount in 1987 is its average balance ($150,000). This amount is treated as the adjusted purchase price for 1987 and all of the interest paid on the debt is qualified residence interest.

(iii) *Grandfathered amount in 1988.* Because the replacement debt was used to refinance a debt incurred and secured on or before August 16, 1986, the replacement debt is treated as a grandfathered debt. Because all of the proceeds of the replacement debt were used in the refinancing and because no amounts have been borrowed after August 16, 1986, on the original debt, the grandfathered amount for the original debt is its average balance ($75,000) and the grandfathered amount for the replacement debt is its average balance ($75,000). Since the sum of the grandfathered amounts ($150,000) exceeds the adjusted purchase price of the residence, the sum of the grandfathered amounts may be substituted for the adjusted purchase price for 1988 and all of the interest paid on the debt is qualified residence interest.

(iv) *Grandfathered amount in 1989.* The grandfathered amount for the replacement debt is its average balance ($150,000). This amount is treated as the adjusted purchase price for 1989 and all of the interest paid on the mortgage is qualified residence interest.

(4) *Limitation on term of grandfathered debt*—(i) *In general.* An original debt or replacement debt shall not have any grandfathered amount in any taxable year that begins after the date, as determined on August 16, 1986, that the original debt was required to be repaid in full (the "maturity date"). If a replacement debt is used to refinance more than one original debt, the maturity date is determined by reference to the original debt that, as of August 16, 1986, had the latest maturity date.

(ii) *Special rule for nonamortizing debt.* If an original debt was actually incurred and secured on or before August 16, 1986, and if as of such date the terms of such debt did not require the amortization of its principal over its original term, the maturity date of the replacement debt is the earlier of the maturity date of the replacement debt or the date 30 years after the date the original debt is first refinanced.

(iii) *Example.* C incurs a debt on May 10, 1986, the final payment of which is due May 1, 2006. C incurs a second debt on August 11, 1990, with a term of 20 years and uses the proceeds of the second debt to refinance the first debt. Because, under paragraph (m)(4)(i) of this section, a replacement debt will not have any grandfathered amount in any taxable year that begins after the maturity date of the original debt (May 1, 2006), the second debt has no grandfathered amount in any taxable year after 2006.

(n) *Qualified indebtedness (secured debt used for medical and educational purposes)*—(1) *In general*—(i) *Treatment of qualified indebtedness.* The amount of any qualified indebtedness resulting from a secured debt may be added to the adjusted purchase price under paragraph (e)(2)(i)(B) of this section to determine the applicable debt limit for that secured debt and any other debt subsequently secured by the qualified residence.

(ii) *Determination of amount of qualified indebtedness.* If, as of the end of the taxable year (or the last day in the taxable year that the debt is secured), at least 90 percent of the proceeds of a secured debt are used (within the meaning of paragraph (n)(2) of this section) to pay for qualified medical and educational expenses (within the meaning of paragraphs (n)(3) and (n)(4) of this section), the amount of qualified indebtedness resulting from that debt for the taxable year is equal to the average balance of such debt for the taxable year.

(iii) *Determination of amount of qualified indebtedness for mixed-use debt.* If, as of the end of the taxable year (or the last day in the taxable year that the debt is secured), more than ten percent of the proceeds of a secured debt are used to pay for expenses other than qualified medical and educational expenses, the amount of qualified indebtedness resulting from that debt for the taxable year shall equal the lesser of—

(A) The average balance of the debt, or

(B) The amount of the proceeds of the debt used to pay for qualified medical and educational expenses through the end of the taxable year, reduced by any principal payments on the debt before the first day of the current taxable year.

(iv) *Example.* (i) C incurs a $10,000 debt on April 20, 1987, which is secured on that date by C's principal residence. C immediately uses (within the meaning of paragraph (n)(2) of this section) $4,000 of the proceeds of the debt to pay for a qualified medical expense. C makes no principal payments on the debt during 1987. During 1988 and 1989, C makes principal payments of $1,000 per year. The average balance of the debt during 1988 is $9,500 and the average balance during 1989 is $8,500.

(ii) Under paragraph (n)(1)(iii) of this section, C determines the amount of qualified indebtedness for 1988 as follows:

Reg. § 1.163-10T(n)(1)

Average balance......................	$9,500
Amount of debt used to pay for qualified medical expenses $4,000	
Less payments of principal before 1988................. $ 0	
Net qualified expenses...............	$4,000

The amount of qualified indebtedness for 1988 is, therefore, $4,000 (lesser of $9,500 average balance or $4,000 net qualified expenses). This amount may be added to the adjusted purchase price of C's principal residence under paragraph (e)(2)(i)(B) of this section for purposes of computing the applicable debt limit for this debt and any other debt subsequently secured by the principal residence.

(*iii*) C determines the amount of qualified indebtedness for 1989 as follows:

Average balance......................	$8,500
Amount of debt used to pay qualified medical expenses $4,000	
Less payments of principal before 1989................. $1,000	
Net qualified expenses...............	$3,000

The amount of qualified indebtedness for 1989 is, therefore, $3,000 (lesser of $8,500 average balance or $3,000 net qualified expense).

(v) *Prevention of double counting in year of refinancing*—(A) *In general.* A debt used to pay for qualified medical or educational expenses is refinanced if some or all of the outstanding balance of the debt (the "original debt") is repaid out of the proceeds of a second debt (the "replacement debt"). If, in the year of a refinancing, the combined qualified indebtedness of the original debt and the replacement debt exceeds the combined qualified expenses of such debts, the amount of qualified indebtedness for each such debt shall be determined by multiplying the amount of qualified indebtedness for each such debt by a fraction, the numerator of which is the combined qualified expenses and the denominator of which is the combined qualified indebtedness.

(B) *Definitions.* For purposes of paragraph (n)(1)(v)(A) of this section—

(*1*) The term "combined qualified indebtedness" means the sum of the qualified indebtedness (determined without regard to paragraph (n)(1)(v) of this section) for the original debt and the replacement debt.

(*2*) The term "combined qualified expenses" means the amount of the proceeds of the original debt used to pay for qualified medical and educational expenses through the end of the current taxable year, reduced by any principal payments on the debt before the first day of the current taxable year, and increased by the

amount, if any, of the proceeds of the replacement debt used to pay such expenses through the end of the current taxable year other than as part of the refinancing.

(C) *Example.*—(*i*) On August 11, 1987, C incurs a $8,000 debt secured by a principal residence. C uses (within the meaning of paragraph (n)(2)(i) of this section) $5,000 of the proceeds of the debt to pay for qualified educational expenses. C makes no principal payments on the debt. On July 1, 1988, C incurs a new debt in the amount of $8,000 secured by C's principal residence and uses all of the proceeds of the new debt to repay the original debt. Under paragraph (n)(2)(ii) of this section $5,000 of the new debt is treated as being used to pay for qualified educational expenses. C makes no principal payments (other than the refinancing) during 1987 or 1988 on either debt and pays all accrued interest monthly. The average balance of each debt in 1988 is $4,000.

(*ii*) Under paragraph (n)(1)(iii) of this section, the amount of qualified indebtedness for 1988 with respect to the original debt is $4,000 (the lesser of its average balance ($4,000) and the amount of the debt used to pay for qualified medical and educational expenses ($5,000)). Similarly, the amount of qualified indebtedness for 1988 with respect to the replacement debt is also $4,000. Both debts, however, are subject in 1988 to the limitation in paragraph (n)(1)(v)(A) of this section. The combined qualified indebtedness, determined without regard to the limitation, is $8,000 ($4,000 of qualified indebtedness from each debt). The combined qualified expenses are $5,000 ($5,000 from the original debt and $0 from the replacement debt). The amount of qualified indebtedness from each debt must, therefore, be reduced by a fraction, the numerator of which is $5,000 (the combined qualified expenses) and the denominator of which is $8,000 (the combined qualified indebtedness). After application of the limitation, the amount of qualified indebtedness for the original debt is $2,500 ($4,000 × ⅝). Similarly, the amount of qualified indebtedness for the replacement debt is $2,500. Note that the total qualified indebtedness for both the original and the replacement debt is $5,000 ($2,500 + $2,500). Therefore, C is entitled to the same amount of qualified indebtedness as C would have been entitled to if C had not refinanced the debt.

(vi) *Special rule for principal payments in excess of qualified expenses.* For purposes of paragraph (n)(1)(iii)(B), (n)(1)(v)(B)(*2*) and (n)(2)(ii) of this section, a principal payment is taken into account only to the extent that the payment, when added to all prior payments, does not exceed

Reg. § 1.163-10T(n)(1)

the amount used on or before the date of the payment to pay for qualified medical and educational expenses.

(2) *Debt used to pay for qualified medical or educational expenses*—(i) *In general.* For purposes of this section, the proceeds of a debt are used to pay for qualified medical or educational expenses to the extent that—

(A) The taxpayer pays qualified medical or educational expenses within 90 days before or after the date that amounts are actually borrowed with respect to the debt, the proceeds of the debt are not directly allocable to another expense under § 1.163-8T(c)(3) (allocation of debt; proceeds not disbursed to borrower) and the proceeds of any other debt are not allocable to the medical or educational expenses under § 1.163-8T(c)(3), or

(B) The proceeds of the debt are otherwise allocated to such expenditures under § 1.163-8T.

(ii) *Special rule for refinancings.* For purposes of this section, the proceeds of a debt are used to pay for qualified medical and educational expenses to the extent that the proceeds of the debt are allocated under § 1.163-8T to the repayment of another debt (the "original debt"), but only to the extent of the amount of the original debt used to pay for qualified medical and educational expenses, reduced by any principal payments on such debt up to the time of the refinancing.

(iii) *Other special rules.* The following special rules apply for purposes of this section.

(A) Proceeds of a debt are used to pay for qualified medical or educational expenses as of the later of the taxable year in which such proceeds are borrowed or the taxable year in which such expenses are paid.

(B) The amount of debt which may be treated as being used to pay for qualified medical or educational expenses may not exceed the amount of such expenses.

(C) Proceeds of a debt may not be treated as being used to pay for qualified medical or educational expenses to the extent that:

(1) The proceeds have been repaid as of the time the expense is paid;

(2) The proceeds are actually borrowed before August 17, 1986; or

(3) The medical or educational expenses are paid before August 17, 1986.

(iv) *Examples—Example (1).* A pays a $5,000 qualified educational expense from a checking account that A maintains at Bank 1 on November 9, 1987. On January 1, 1988, A incurs a $20,000 debt that is secured by A's residence

and places the proceeds of the debt in a savings account that A also maintains at Bank 1. A pays another $5,000 qualified educational expense on March 15 from a checking account that A maintains at Bank 2. Under paragraph (n)(2) of this section, the debt proceeds are used to pay for both educational expenses, regardless of other deposits to, or expenditures from, the accounts, because both expenditures are made within 90 days before or after the debt was incurred.

Example (2). B pays a $5,000 qualified educational expense from a checking account on November 1, 1987. On November 30, 1987, B incurs a debt secured by B's residence, and the lender disburses the debt proceeds directly to a person who sells B a new car. Although the educational expense is paid within 90 days of the date the debt is incurred, the proceeds of the debt are not used to pay for the educational expense because the proceeds are directly allocable to the purchase of the new car under § 1.163-8T(c)(3).

Example (3). On November 1, 1987, C borrows $5,000 from C's college. The proceeds of this debt are not disbursed to C, but rather are used to pay tuition fees for C's attendance at the college. On November 30, 1987, C incurs a second debt and secures the debt by C's residence. Although the $5,000 educational expense is paid within 90 days before the second debt is incurred, the proceeds of the second debt are not used to pay for the educational expense, because the proceeds of the first debt are directly allocable to the educational expense under § 1.163-8T(c)(3).

Example (4). On January 1, 1988, D incurs a $20,000 debt secured by a qualified residence. D places the proceeds of the debt in a separate account (*i.e.*, the proceeds of the debt are the only deposit in the account). D makes payments of $5,000 each for qualified educational expenses on September 1, 1988, September 1, 1989, September 1, 1990, and September 1, 1991. Because the debt proceeds are allocated to educational expenses as of the date the expenses are paid, under the rules of § 1.163-8T(c)(4), the following amounts of the debt proceeds are used to pay for qualified educational expenses as of the end of each year:

1988:	$ 5,000
1989:	$10,000
1990:	$15,000
1991:	$20,000

Example (5). During 1987 E incurs a $10,000 debt secured by a principle [sic] residence. E uses (within the meaning of paragraph (n)(2)(i) of this section) all of the proceeds of the debt to pay for qualified educational expenses. On August 20, 1988, at which time the balance of the debt is $9,500, E incurs a new debt in the amount of $9,500 secured by E's principal residence and uses all of the proceeds of the new debt to repay the original debt. Under paragraph (n)(2)(ii) of this section, all of the proceeds of the new debt are used to pay for qualified educational expenses.

(3) *Qualified medical expenses.* Qualified medical expenses are amounts that are paid for medical care (within the meaning of section 213(d)(1)(A) and (B)) for the taxpayer, the taxpayer's spouse, or a dependent of the taxpayer (within the meaning of section 152), and that are not compensated for by insurance or otherwise.

(4) *Qualified educational expenses.* Qualified educational expenses are amounts that are paid for tuition, fees, books, supplies and equipment required for enrollment, attendance or courses of instruction at an educational organization described in section 170(b)(1)(A)(ii) and for any reasonable living expenses while away from home while in attendance at such an institution, for the taxpayer, the taxpayer's spouse or a dependent of the taxpayer (within the meaning of section 152) and that are not reimbursed by scholarship or otherwise.

(o) *Secured debt*—(1) *In general.* For purposes of this section, the term "secured debt" means a debt that is on the security of any instrument (such as a mortgage, deed of trust, or land contract)—

(i) That makes the interest of the debtor in the qualified residence specific security for the payment of the debt,

(ii) Under which, in the event of default, the residence could be subjected to the satisfaction of the debt with the same priority as a mortgage or deed of trust in the jurisdiction in which the property is situated, and

(iii) That is recorded, where permitted, or is otherwise perfected in accordance with applicable State law.

A debt will not be considered to be secured by a qualified residence if it is secured solely by virtue of a lien upon the general assets of the taxpayer or by a security interest, such as a mechanic's lien or judgment lien, that attaches to the property without the consent of the debtor.

(2) *Special rule for debt in certain States.* Debt will not fail to be treated as secured solely because, under an applicable State or local homestead law or other debtor protection law in effect on August 16, 1986, the security interest is ineffective or the enforceability of the security interest is restricted.

(3) *Time at which debt is treated as secured.* For purposes of this section, a debt is treated as secured as of the date on which each of the re-

quirements of paragraph (o)(1) of this section are satisfied, regardless of when amounts are actually borrowed with respect to the debt. For purposes of this paragraph (o)(3), if the instrument is recorded within a commercially reasonable time after the security interest is granted, the instrument will be treated as recorded on the date that the security interest was granted.

(4) *Partially secured debt*—(i) *In general.* If the security interest is limited to a prescribed maximum amount or portion of the residence, and the average balance of the debt exceeds such amount or the value of such portion, such excess shall not be treated as secured debt for purposes of this section.

(ii) *Example.* T borrows $80,000 on January 1, 1991. T secures the debt with a principal residence. The security in the residence for the debt, however, is limited to $20,000. T pays $8,000 in interest on the debt in 1991 and the average balance of the debt in that year is $80,000. Because the average balance of the debt exceeds the maximum amount of the security interest, such excess is not treated as secured debt. Therefore, for purposes of applying the limitation on qualified residence interest, the average balance of the secured debt is $20,000 (the maximum amount of the security interest) and the interest paid or accrued on the secured debt is $2,000 (the total interest paid on the debt multiplied by the ratio of the average balance of the secured debt ($20,000) and the average balance of the total debt ($80,000)).

(5) *Election to treat debt as not secured by a qualified residence*—(i) *In general.* For purposes of this section, a taxpayer may elect to treat any debt that is secured by a qualified residence as not secured by the qualified residence. An election made under this paragraph shall be effective for the taxable year for which the election is made and for all subsequent taxable years unless revoked with the consent of the Commissioner.

(ii) *Example.* T owns a principal residence with a fair market value of $75,000 and an adjusted purchase price of $40,000. In 1988, debt A, the proceeds of which were used to purchase the residence, has an average balance of $15,000. The proceeds of debt B, which is secured by a second mortgage on the property, are allocable to T's trade or business under § 1.163-8T and has an average balance of $25,000. In 1988, T incurs debt C, which is also secured by T's principal residence and which has an average balance in 1988 of $5,000. In the absence of an election to treat debt B as unsecured, the applicable debt limit for debt C in 1988 under paragraph (e) of this section would be zero dollars ($40,000 —

$15,000 — $25,000) and none of the interest paid on debt C would be qualified residence interest. If, however, T makes or has previously made an election pursuant to paragraph (o)(5)(i) of this section to treat debt B as not secured by the residence, the applicable debt limit for debt C would be $25,000 ($40,000 — $15,000), and all of the interest paid on debt C during the taxable year would be qualified residence interest. Since the proceeds of debt B are allocable to T's trade or business under § 1.163-8T, interest on debt B may be deductible under other sections of the Internal Revenue Code.

(iii) *Allocation of debt secured by two qualified residences.* [Reserved.]

(p) *Definition of qualified residence*—(1) *In general.* The term "qualified residence" means the taxpayer's principal residence (as defined in paragraph (p)(2) of this section), or the taxpayer's second residence (as defined in paragraph (p)(3) of this section).

(2) *Principal residence* The term "principal residence" means the taxpayer's principal residence within the meaning of section 1034. For purposes of this section, a taxpayer cannot have more than one principal residence at any one time.

(3) *Second residence*—(i) *In general.* The term "second residence" means—

(A) A residence within the meaning of paragraph (p)(3)(ii) of this section,

(B) That the taxpayer uses as a residence within the meaning of paragraph (p)(3)(iii) of this section, and

(C) That the taxpayer elects to treat as a second residence pursuant to paragraph (p)(3)(iv) of this section.

A taxpayer cannot have more than one second residence at any time.

(ii) *Definition of residence.* Whether property is a residence shall be determined based on all the facts and circumstances, including the good faith of the taxpayer. A residence generally includes a house, condominium, mobile home, boat, or house trailer, that contains sleeping space and toilet and cooking facilities. A residence does not include personal property, such as furniture or a television, that, in accordance with the applicable local law, is not a fixture.

(iii) *Use as a residence.* If a residence is rented at any time during the taxable year, it is considered to be used as a residence only if the taxpayer uses it during the taxable year as a residence within the meaning of section 280A(d). If a residence is not rented at any time during the taxable year, it shall be considered to be used as a

residence. For purposes of the preceding sentence, a residence will be deemed to be rented during any period that the taxpayer holds the residence out for rental or resale or repairs or renovates the residence with the intention of holding it out for rental or resale.

(iv) *Election of second residence.* A taxpayer may elect a different residence (other than the taxpayer's principal residence) to be the taxpayer's second residence for each taxable year. A taxpayer may not elect different residences as second residences at different times of the same taxable year except as provided below—

(A) If the taxpayer acquires a new residence during the taxable year, the taxpayer may elect the new residence as the taxpayer's second residence as of the date acquired;

(B) If property that was the taxpayer's principal residence during the taxable year ceases to qualify as the taxpayer's principal residence, the taxpayer may elect that property as the taxpayer's second residence as of the date that the property ceases to be the taxpayer's principal residence; or

(C) If property that was the taxpayer's second residence is sold during the taxable year or becomes the taxpayer's principal residence, the taxpayer may elect a new second residence as of such day.

(4) *Allocations between residence and other property*—(i) *In general.* For purposes of this section, the adjusted purchase price and fair market value of property must be allocated between the portion of the property that is a qualified residence and the portion that is not a qualified residence. Neither the average balance of the secured debt nor the interest paid or accrued on secured debt is so allocated. Property that is not used for residential purposes does not qualify as a residence. For example, if a portion of the property is used as an office in the taxpayer's trade or business, that portion of the property does not qualify as a residence.

(ii) *Special rule for rental of residence.* If a taxpayer rents a portion of his or her principal or second residence to another person (a "tenant"), such portion may be treated as used by the taxpayer for residential purposes if, but only if—

(A) Such rented portion is used by the tenant primarily for residential purposes,

(B) The rented portion is not a self-contained residential unit containing separate sleeping space and toilet and cooking facilities, and

(C) The total number of tenants renting (directly or by sublease) the same or different portions of the residence at any time during the taxable year does not exceed two. For this purpose, if two persons (and the dependents, as defined by section 152, of either of them) share the same sleeping quarters, they shall be treated as a single tenant.

(iii) *Examples—Example (1)*. D, a dentist, uses a room in D's principal residence as an office which qualifies under section 280A(c)(1)(B) as a portion of the dwelling unit used exclusively on a regular basis as a place of business for meeting with patients in the normal course of D's trade or business. D's adjusted purchase price of the property is $65,000; $10,000 of which is allocable under paragraph (o)(4)(i) of this section to the room used as an office. For purposes of this section, D's residence does not include the room used as an office. The adjusted purchase price of the residence is, accordingly, $55,000. Similarly, the fair market value of D's residence must be allocated between the office and the remainder of the property.

Example (2). J rents out the basement of property that is otherwise used as J's principal residence. The basement is a self-contained residential unit, with sleeping space and toilet and cooking facilities. The adjusted purchase price of the property is $100,000; $15,000 of which is allocable under paragraph (o)(4)(i) of this section to the basement. For purposes of this section, J's residence does not include the basement and the adjusted purchase price of the residence is $85,000. Similarly, the fair market value of the residence must be allocated between the basement unit and the remainder of the property.

(5) *Residence under construction*—(i) *In general*. A taxpayer may treat a residence under construction as a qualified residence for a period of up to 24 months, but only if the residence becomes a qualified residence, without regard to this paragraph (p)(5)(i), as of the time that the residence is ready for occupancy.

(ii) *Example*. X owns a residential lot suitable for the construction of a vacation home. On April 20, 1987, X obtains a mortgage secured by the lot and any property to be constructed on the lot. On August 9, 1987, X begins construction of a residence on the lot. The residence is ready for occupancy on November 9, 1989. The residence is used as a residence within the meaning of paragraph (p)(3)(iii) of this section during 1989 and X elects to treat the residence as his second residence for the period November 9, 1989, through December 31, 1989. Since the residence under construction is a qualified residence as of the first day that the residence is ready for occupancy (November 9, 1987), X may treat the residence as

his second residence under paragraph (p)(5)(i) of this section for up to 24 months of the period during which the residence is under construction, commencing on or after the date that construction is begun (August 9, 1987). If X treats the residence under construction as X's second residence beginning on August 9, 1987, the residence under construction would cease to qualify as a qualified residence under paragraph (p)(5)(i) on August 8, 1989. The residence's status as a qualified residence for future periods would be determined without regard to paragraph (p)(5)(i) of this section.

(6) *Special rule for time-sharing arrangements*. Property that is otherwise a qualified residence will not fail to qualify as such solely because the taxpayer's interest in or right to use the property is restricted by an arrangement whereby two or more persons with interests in the property agree to exercise control over the property for different periods during the taxable year. For purposes of determining the use of a residence under paragraph (p)(3)(iii) of this section, a taxpayer will not be considered to have used or rented a residence during any period that the taxpayer does not have the right to use the property or to receive any benefits from the rental of the property.

(q) *Special rules for tenant-stockholders in cooperative housing corporations*—(1) *In general*. For purposes of this section, a residence includes stock in a cooperative housing corporation owned by a tenant-stockholder if the house or apartment which the tenant-stockholder is entitled to occupy by virtue of owning such stock is a residence within the meaning of paragraph (p)(3)(ii) of this section.

(2) *Special rule where stock may not be used to secure debt*. For purposes of this section, if stock described in paragraph (q)(1) of this section may not be used to secure debt because of restrictions under local or State law or because of restrictions in the cooperative agreement (other than restrictions the principal purpose of which is to permit the tenant-stockholder to treat unsecured debt as secured debt under this paragraph (q)(2)), debt may be treated as secured by such stock to the extent that the proceeds of the debt are allocated to the purchase of the stock under the rules of § 1.163-8T. For purposes of this paragraph (q)(2), proceeds of debt incurred prior to January 1, 1987, may be treated as allocated to the purchase of such stock to the extent that the tenant-stockholder has properly and consistently deducted interest expense on such debt as home mortgage interest attributable to such stock on Schedule A of Form 1040 in determining his taxa-

Reg. § 1.163-10T(p)(5)

ble income for taxable years beginning before January 1, 1987. For purposes of this paragraph (q)(2), amended returns filed after December 22, 1987 are disregarded.

(3) *Treatment of interest expense of the co-operative described in section 216(a)(2).* For purposes of section 163(h) and § 1.163-9T (disallowance of deduction for personal interest) and section 163(d) (limitation on investment interest), any amount allowable as a deduction to a tenant-stockholder under section 216(a)(2) shall be treated as interest paid or accrued by the tenant-stockholder. If a tenant-stockholder's stock in a cooperative housing corporation is a qualified residence of the tenant-shareholder, any amount allowable as a deduction to the tenant-stockholder under section 216(a)(2) is qualified residence interest.

(4) *Special rule to prevent tax avoidance.* If the amount treated as qualified residence interest under this section exceeds the amount which would be so treated if the tenant-stockholder were treated as directly owning his proportionate share of the assets and liabilities of the cooperative and one of the principal purposes of the cooperative arrangement is to permit the tenant-stockholder to increase the amount of qualified residence interest, the district director may determine that such excess is not qualified residence interest.

(5) *Other definitions.* For purpose of this section, the terms "tenant-stockholder," "cooperative housing corporation" and "proportionate share" shall have the meaning given by section 216 and the regulations thereunder.

(r) *Effective date.* The provisions of this section are effective for taxable years beginning after December 31, 1986. [Temporary Reg. § 1.163-10T.]

☐ [*T.D.* 8168, 12-21-87.]

[Reg. § 1.163-12]

§ 1.163-12. Deduction of original issue discount on instrument held by related foreign person.—(a) *General rules*—(1) *Deferral of deduction.* Except as provided in paragraph (b) of this section, section 163(e)(3) requires a taxpayer to use the cash method of accounting with respect to the deduction of original issue discount owed to a related foreign person. A deduction for an otherwise deductible portion of original issue discount with respect to a debt instrument will not be allowable as a deduction to the issuer until paid if, at the close of the issuer's taxable year in which such amount would otherwise be deductible, the person holding the debt instrument is a related foreign person. For purposes of this section, a related foreign person is any person that is not a

United States person within the meaning of section 7701(a)(30), and that is related (within the meaning of section 267(b)) to the issuer at the close of the taxable year in which the amount incurred by the taxpayer would otherwise be deductible. Section 267(f) defines "controlled group" for purposes of section 267(b) without regard to the limitations of section 1563(b). An amount is treated as paid for purposes of this section if the amount is considered paid for purposes of section 1441 or section 1442 (including an amount taken into account pursuant to section 871(a)(1)(C), section 881(a)(3), or section 884(f)). The rules of this paragraph (a) apply even if the original issue discount is not subject to United States tax, or is subject to a reduced rate of tax, pursuant to a provision of the Internal Revenue Code or a treaty obligation of the United States. For purposes of this section, original issue discount is an amount described in section 1273, whether from sources inside or outside the United States.

(2) *Change in method of accounting.* A taxpayer that uses a method of accounting other than that required by the rules of this section must change its method of accounting to conform its method to the rules of this section. The taxpayer's change in method must be made pursuant to the rules of section 446(e), the regulations thereunder, and any applicable administrative procedures prescribed by the Commissioner. Because the rules of this section prescribe a method of accounting, these rules apply in the determination of a taxpayer's earnings and profits pursuant to § 1.312-6(a).

(b) *Exceptions and special rules*—(1) *Effectively connected income.* The provisions of section 267(a)(2) and the regulations thereunder, and not the provisions of paragraph (a) of this section, apply to an amount of original issue discount that is income of the related foreign person that is effectively connected with the conduct of a United States trade or business of such related foreign person. An amount described in this paragraph (b)(1) thus is allowable as a deduction as of the day on which the amount is includible in the gross income of the related foreign person as effectively connected income under sections 872(a)(2) or 882(b) (or, if later, as of the day on which the deduction would be so allowable but for section 267(a)(2)). However, this paragraph (b)(1) does not apply if the related foreign person is exempt from United States income tax on the amount owed, or is subject to a reduced rate of tax, pursuant to a treaty obligation of the United States (such as under an article relating to the taxation of business profits).

(2) *Certain obligations issued by natural persons.* This section does not apply to any debt instrument described in section 163(e)(4) (relating to obligations issued by natural persons before March 2, 1984, and to loans between natural persons).

(3) *Amounts owed to a foreign personal holding company, controlled foreign corporation, or passive foreign investment company*—(i) *Foreign personal holding companies.* If an amount to which paragraph (a) of this section otherwise applies is owed to a related foreign person that is a foreign personal holding company within the meaning of section 552, then the amount is allowable as a deduction as of the day on which the amount is includible in the income of the foreign personal holding company. The day on which the amount is includible in income is determined with reference to the method of accounting under which the foreign personal holding company computes its taxable income and earnings and profits for purposes of sections 551 through 558. See section 551(c) and the regulations thereunder for the reporting requirements of the foreign personal holding company provisions (sections 551 through 558).

(ii) *Controlled foreign corporations.* If an amount to which paragraph (a) of this section otherwise applies is owed to a related foreign person that is a controlled foreign corporation within the meaning of section 957, then the amount is allowable as a deduction as of the day on which the amount is includible in the income of the controlled foreign corporation. The day on which the amount is includible in income is determined with reference to the method of accounting under which the controlled foreign corporation computes its taxable income and earnings and profits for purposes of sections 951 through 964. See section 6038 and the regulations thereunder for the reporting requirements of the controlled foreign corporation provisions (sections 951 through 964).

(iii) *Passive foreign investment companies.* If an amount to which paragraph (a) of this section otherwise applies is owed to a related foreign person that is a passive foreign investment company within the meaning of section 1296, then the amount is allowable as a deduction as of the day on which [the] amount is includible in the income of the passive foreign investment company. The day on which the amount is includible in income is determined with reference to the method of accounting under which the earnings and profits of the passive foreign investment company are computed for purposes of sections 1291 through 1297. See sections 1291 through 1297 and the regulations thereunder for the reporting requirements of the passive foreign investment company provisions. This exception shall apply, however, only if the person that owes the amount at issue has made and has in effect an election pursuant to section 1295 with respect to the passive foreign investment company to which the amount at issue is owed.

(c) *Application of section 267.* Except as limited in paragraph (b)(1) of this section, the provisions of section 267 and the regulations thereunder shall apply to any amount of original issue discount to which the provisions of this section do not apply.

(d) *Effective date.* The rules of this section are effective with respect to all original issue discount on debt instruments issued after June 9, 1984. [Reg. § 1.163-12.]

□ [*T.D.* 8465, 12-31-92.]

[Reg. § 1.163-13]

§ 1.163-13. **Treatment of bond issuance premium.**—(a) *General rule.* If a debt instrument is issued with bond issuance premium, this section limits the amount of the issuer's interest deduction otherwise allowable under section 163(a). In general, the issuer determines its interest deduction by offsetting the interest allocable to an accrual period with the bond issuance premium allocable to that period. Bond issuance premium is allocable to an accrual period based on a constant yield. The use of a constant yield to amortize bond issuance premium is intended to generally conform the treatment of debt instruments having bond issuance premium with those having original issue discount. Unless otherwise provided, the terms used in this section have the same meaning as those terms in section 163(e), sections 1271 through 1275, and the corresponding regulations. Moreover, unless otherwise provided, the provisions of this section apply in a manner consistent with those of section 163(e), sections 1271 through 1275, and the corresponding regulations. In addition, the anti-abuse rule in § 1.1275-2(g) applies for purposes of this section. For rules dealing with the treatment of bond premium by a holder, see §§ 1.171-1 through 1.171-5.

(b) *Exceptions.* This section does not apply to—

(1) A debt instrument described in section 1272(a)(6)(C) (regular interests in a REMIC, qualified mortgages held by a REMIC, and certain other debt instruments, or pools of debt instruments, with payments subject to acceleration); or

(2) A debt instrument to which § 1.1275-4 applies (relating to certain debt instruments that provide for contingent payments).

Reg. § 1.163-13(a)

(c) *Bond issuance premium.* Bond issuance premium is the excess, if any, of the issue price of a debt instrument over its stated redemption price at maturity. For purposes of this section, the issue price of a convertible bond (as defined in § 1.171-1(e)(1)(iii)(C)) does not include an amount equal to the value of the conversion option (as determined under § 1.171-1(e)(1)(iii)(A)).

(d) *Offsetting qualified stated interest with bond issuance premium—*(1) *In general.* An issuer amortizes bond issuance premium by offsetting the qualified stated interest allocable to an accrual period with the bond issuance premium allocable to the accrual period. This offset occurs when the issuer takes the qualified stated interest into account under its regular method of accounting.

(2) *Qualified stated interest allocable to an accrual period.* See § 1.446-2(b) to determine the accrual period to which qualified stated interest is allocable and to determine the accrual of qualified stated interest within an accrual period.

(3) *Bond issuance premium allocable to an accrual period.* The bond issuance premium allocable to an accrual period is determined under this paragraph (d)(3). Within an accrual period, the bond issuance premium allocable to the period accrues ratably.

(i) *Step one: Determine the debt instrument's yield to maturity.* The yield to maturity of a debt instrument is determined under the rules of § 1.1272-1(b)(1)(i).

(ii) *Step two: Determine the accrual periods.* The accrual periods are determined under the rules of § 1.1272-1(b)(1)(ii).

(iii) *Step three: Determine the bond issuance premium allocable to the accrual period.* The bond issuance premium allocable to an accrual period is the excess of the qualified stated interest allocable to the accrual period over the product of the adjusted issue price at the beginning of the accrual period and the yield. In performing this calculation, the yield must be stated appropriately taking into account the length of the particular accrual period. Principles similar to those in § 1.1272-1(b)(4) apply in determining the bond issuance premium allocable to an accrual period.

(4) *Bond issuance premium in excess of qualified stated interest—*(i) *Ordinary income.* If the bond issuance premium allocable to an accrual period exceeds the qualified stated interest allocable to the accrual period, the excess is treated as ordinary income by the issuer for the accrual period. However, the amount treated as ordinary income is limited to the amount by which the issuer's total interest deductions on the debt instrument in prior accrual periods exceed the total

amount treated by the issuer as ordinary income on the debt instrument in prior accrual periods.

(ii) *Carryforward.* If the bond issuance premium allocable to an accrual period exceeds the sum of the qualified stated interest allocable to the accrual period and the amount treated as ordinary income for the accrual period under paragraph (d)(4)(i) of this section, the excess is carried forward to the next accrual period and is treated as bond issuance premium allocable to that period. If a carryforward exists on the date the debt instrument is retired, the carryforward is treated as ordinary income on that date.

(e) *Special rules—*(1) *Variable rate debt instruments.* An issuer determines bond issuance premium on a variable rate debt instrument by reference to the stated redemption price at maturity of the equivalent fixed rate debt instrument constructed for the variable rate debt instrument. The issuer also allocates any bond issuance premium among the accrual periods by reference to the equivalent fixed rate debt instrument. The issuer constructs the equivalent fixed rate debt instrument, as of the issue date, by using the principles of § 1.1275-5(e).

(2) *Inflation-indexed debt instruments.* An issuer determines bond issuance premium on an inflation-indexed debt instrument by assuming that there will be no inflation or deflation over the term of the instrument. The issuer also allocates any bond issuance premium among the accrual periods by assuming that there will be no inflation or deflation over the term of the instrument. The bond issuance premium allocable to an accrual period offsets qualified stated interest allocable to the period. Notwithstanding paragraph (d)(4) of this section, if the bond issuance premium allocable to an accrual period exceeds the qualified stated interest allocable to the period, the excess is treated as a deflation adjustment under § 1.1275-7(f)(1)(ii). See § 1.1275-7 for other rules relating to inflation-indexed debt instruments.

(3) *Certain debt instruments subject to contingencies—*(i) *In general.* Except as provided in paragraph (e)(3)(ii) of this section, the rules of § 1.1272-1(c) apply to determine a debt instrument's payment schedule for purposes of this section. For example, an issuer uses the payment schedule determined under § 1.1272-1(c) to determine the amount, if any, of bond issuance premium on the debt instrument, the yield and maturity of the debt instrument, and the allocation of bond issuance premium to an accrual period.

(ii) *Mandatory sinking fund provision.* Notwithstanding paragraph (e)(3)(i) of this section, if a debt instrument is subject to a mandatory sinking fund provision described in § 1.1272-1(c)(3), the issuer must determine the payment schedule by assuming that a pro rata portion of the debt instrument will be called under the sinking fund provision.

(4) *Remote and incidental contingencies.* For purposes of determining the amount of bond issuance premium and allocating bond issuance premium among accrual periods, if a bond provides for a contingency that is remote or incidental (within the meaning of § 1.1275-2(h)), the issuer takes the contingency into account under the rules for remote and incidental contingencies in § 1.1275-2(h).

(f) *Example.* The following example illustrates the rules of this section:

Example—(i) *Facts.* On February 1, 1999, X issues for $110,000 a debt instrument maturing on February 1, 2006, with a stated principal amount of $100,000, payable at maturity. The debt instrument provides for unconditional payments of interest of $10,000, payable on February 1 of each year. X uses the calendar year as its taxable year, X uses the cash receipts and disbursements method of accounting, and X decides to use annual accrual periods ending on February 1 of each year. X's calculations assume a 30-day month and 360-day year.

(ii) *Amount of bond issuance premium.* The issue price of the debt instrument is $110,000. Because the interest payments on the debt instrument are qualified stated interest, the stated redemption price at maturity of the debt instrument is $100,000. Therefore, the amount of bond issuance premium is $10,000 ($110,000 − $100,000).

(iii) *Bond issuance premium allocable to the first accrual period.* Based on the payment schedule and the issue price of the debt instrument, the yield of the debt instrument is 8.07 percent, compounded annually. (Although, for purposes of simplicity, the yield as stated is rounded to two decimal places, the computations do not reflect this rounding convention.) The bond issuance premium allocable to the accrual period ending on February 1, 2000, is the excess of the qualified stated interest allocable to the period ($10,000) over the product of the adjusted issue price at the beginning of the period ($110,000) and the yield (8.07 percent, compounded annually). Therefore, the bond issuance premium allocable to the accrual period is $1,118.17 ($10,000 − $8,881.83).

(iv) *Premium used to offset interest.* Although X makes an interest payment of $10,000 on February 1, 2000, X only deducts interest of $8,881.83, the qualified stated interest allocable

to the period ($10,000) offset with the bond issuance premium allocable to the period ($1,118.17).

(g) *Effective date.* This section applies to debt instruments issued on or after March 2, 1998.

(h) *Accounting method changes*—(1) *Consent to change.* An issuer required to change its method of accounting for bond issuance premium to comply with this section must secure the consent of the Commissioner in accordance with the requirements of § 1.446-1(e). Paragraph (h)(2) of this section provides the Commissioner's automatic consent for certain changes.

(2) *Automatic consent.* The Commissioner grants consent for an issuer to change its method of accounting for bond issuance premium on debt instruments issued on or after March 2, 1998. Because this change is made on a cut-off basis, no items of income or deduction are omitted or duplicated and, therefore, no adjustment under section 481 is allowed. The consent granted by this paragraph (h)(2) applies provided—

(i) The change is made to comply with this section;

(ii) The change is made for the first taxable year for which the issuer must account for a debt instrument under this section; and

(iii) The issuer attaches to its federal income tax return for the taxable year containing the change a statement that it has changed its method of accounting under this section. [Reg. § 1.163-13.]

☐ [*T.D.* 8746, 12-30-97. *Amended by T.D.* 8838, 9-3-99.]

[Reg. § 1.163(d)-1]

§ 1.163(d)-1. **Time and manner for making election under the Omnibus Budget Reconciliation Act of 1993.**—(a) *Description.* Section 163(d)(4)(B)(iii), as added by section 13206(d) of the Omnibus Budget Reconciliation Act of 1993 (Public Law 103-66, 107 Stat. 467), allows an electing taxpayer to take all or a portion of certain net capital gains, attributable to dispositions of property held for investment, into account as investment income. As a consequence, the capital gains affected by this election are not eligible for the maximum capital gain rate of 28 percent. The election may be made for net capital gains recognized by noncorporate taxpayers during any taxable year beginning after December 31, 1992.

(b) *Time and manner for making the election.* The election under section 163(d)(4)(B)(iii) must be made on or before the due date (including extensions) of the income tax return for the taxable year in which the net capital gain is recognized. The election is to be made on Form 4952,

Investment Interest Expense Deduction, in accordance with the Form and its instructions.

(c) *Revocability of election.* The election described in this section is revocable with the consent of the Commissioner.

(d) *Effective date.* The rules set forth in this section are effective December 12, 1996. [Reg. § 1.163(d)-1.]

☐ [*T.D.* 8688, 12-11-96.]

[Reg. § 1.164-1]

§ 1.164-1. **Deduction for taxes.**—(a) *In general.* Only the following taxes shall be allowed as a deduction under this section for the taxable year within which paid or accrued, according to the method of accounting used in computing taxable income:

(1) State and local, and foreign, real property taxes.

(2) State and local personal property taxes.

(3) State and local, and foreign, income, war profits, and excess profits taxes.

(4) State and local general sales taxes.

(5) State and local taxes on the sale of gasoline, diesel fuel, and other motor fuels.

In addition, there shall be allowed as a deduction under this section State and local, and foreign, taxes not described in subparagraphs (1) through (5) of this paragraph which are paid or accrued within the taxable year in carrying on a trade or business or an activity described in section 212 (relating to expenses for production of income). For example, dealers or investors in securities and dealers or investors in real estate may deduct State stock transfer and real estate transfer taxes, respectively, under section 164, to the extent they are expenses incurred in carrying on a trade or business or an activity for the production of income. In general, taxes are deductible only by the person upon whom they are imposed. However, see § 1.164-5 in the case of certain taxes paid by the consumer. Also, in the case of a qualified State individual income tax (as defined in section 6362 and the regulations thereunder) which is determined by reference to a percentage of the Federal income tax (pursuant to section 6362(c)), an accrual method taxpayer shall use the cash receipts and disbursements method to compute the amount of his deduction therefor. Thus, the deduction under section 164 is in the amount actually paid with respect to the qualified tax, rather than the amount accrued with respect thereto, during the taxable year even though the taxpayer uses the accrual method of accounting for other purposes. In addition, see paragraph (f)(1) of § 301.6361-1 of this chapter (Regulations on Procedure and Administration) with respect to rules relating to allocation and reallocation of amounts collected on account of the Federal income tax and qualified taxes.

(b) *Taxable years beginning before January 1, 1964.* For taxable years beginning before January 1, 1964, except as otherwise provided in §§ 1.164-2 through 1.164-8, inclusive, taxes imposed by the United States, any State, territory, possession of the United States, or a political subdivision of any of the foregoing, or by any foreign country, are deductible from gross income for the taxable year in which paid or accrued, according to the method of accounting used in computing taxable income. For this purpose, postage is not a tax and automobile license or registration fees are ordinarily taxes.

(c) *Cross references.* For the definition of the term "real property taxes", see paragraph (b) of § 1.164-3. For the definition of the term "foreign taxes", see paragraph (d) of § 1.164-3. For the definition of the term "general sales taxes", see paragraph (f) of § 1.164-3. For the treatment of gasoline, diesel fuel, and other motor fuel taxes, see § 1.164-5. For apportionment of taxes on real property between seller and purchaser, see section 164(d) and § 1.164-6. For the general rule for taxable year of deduction, see section 461. For provisions disallowing any deduction for the tax paid at the source on interest from tax-free covenant bonds, see section 1451(f). [Reg. § 1.164-1.]

☐ [*T.D.* 6256, 10-7-57. *Amended by T.D.* 6406, 8-14-59, *T.D.* 6780, 12-21-64 *and T.D.* 7577, 12-19-73.]

[Reg. § 1.164-2]

§ 1.164-2. **Deduction denied in case of certain taxes.**—This section and § 1.275 describe certain taxes for which no deduction is allowed. In the case of taxable years beginning before January 1, 1964, the denial is provided for by section 164(b) (prior to being amended by section 207 of the Revenue Act of 1964 (78 Stat. 40)). In the case of taxable years beginning after December 31, 1963, the denial is governed by sections 164 and 275. No deduction is allowed for the following taxes:

(a) *Federal income taxes.* Federal income taxes, including the taxes imposed by section 3101, relating to the tax on employees under the Federal Insurance Contributions Act (chapter 21 of the Code), sections 3201 and 3211, relating to taxes on railroad employees and railroad employee representatives; section 3402, relating to the tax withheld at source on wages; and by corresponding provisions of prior internal revenue laws.

(b) *Federal war profits and excess profits taxes.* Federal war profits and excess profits taxes including those imposed by Title II of the Revenue Act of 1917 (39 Stat. 1000), Title III of the Revenue Act of 1918 (40 Stat. 1088), Title III of the Revenue Act of 1921 (42 Stat. 271), section 216 of the National Industrial Recovery Act (48 Stat. 208), section 702 of the Revenue Act of 1934 (48 Stat. 770), subchapter D, chapter 1 of the Internal Revenue Code of 1939, and subchapter E, chapter 2 of the Internal Revenue Code of 1939.

(c) *Estate and gift taxes.* Estate, inheritance, legacy, succession, and gift taxes.

(d) *Foreign income, war profits, and excess profits taxes.* Income, war profits, and excess profits taxes imposed by the authority of any foreign country or possession of the United States, if the taxpayer chooses to take to any extent the benefits of section 901, relating to the credit for taxes of foreign countries and possessions of the United States.

(e) *Real property taxes.* Taxes on real property, to the extent that section 164(d) and § 1.164-6 require such taxes to be treated as imposed on another taxpayer.

(f) *Federal duties and excise taxes.* Federal import or tariff duties, business, license, privilege, excise, and stamp taxes (not described in paragraphs (a), (b), (c) or (h) of this section, of § 1.164-4) paid or accrued within the taxable year. The fact that any such tax is not deductible as a tax under section 164 does not prevent (1) its deduction under section 162 or section 212, provided it represents an ordinary and necessary expense paid or incurred during the taxable year by a corporation or an individual in the conduct of any trade or business or, in the case of an individual for the production or collection of income, for the management, conservation, or maintenance of property held for the production of income, or in connection with the determination, collection, or refund of any tax, or (2) its being taken into account during the taxable year by a corporation or an individual as a part of the cost of acquiring or producing property in the trade or business or, in the case of an individual, as a part of the cost of property held for the production of income with respect to which it relates.

(g) *Taxes for local benefits.* Except as provided in § 1.164-4, taxes assessed against local benefits of a kind tending to increase the value of the property assessed.

(h) *Excise tax on real estate investment trusts.* The excise tax imposed on certain real estate investment trusts by section 4981. [Reg. § 1.164-2.]

□ [*T.D.* 6256, 10-7-57. *Amended by T.D.* 6780, 12-21-64 *and T.D.* 7767, 2-3-81.]

[Reg. § 1.164-3]

§ 1.164-3. Definitions and special rules.—For purposes of section 164 and § 1.164-1 to § 1.164-8, inclusive—

(a) *State or local taxes.* A State or local tax includes only a tax imposed by a State, a possession of the United States, or a political subdivision of any of the foregoing, or by the District of Columbia.

(b) *Real property taxes.* The term "real property taxes" means taxes imposed on interests in real property and levied for the general public welfare, but it does not include taxes assessed against local benefits. See § 1.164-4.

(c) *Personal property taxes.* The term "personal property tax" means an ad valorem tax which is imposed on an annual basis in respect of personal property. To qualify as a personal property tax, a tax must meet the following three tests:

(1) The tax must be ad valorem—that is, substantially in proportion to the value of the personal property. A tax which is based on criteria other than value does not qualify as ad valorem. For example, a motor vehicle tax based on weight, model year, and horsepower, or any of these characteristics is not an ad valorem tax. However, a tax which is partly based on value and partly based on other criteria may qualify in part. For example, in the case of a motor vehicle tax of 1 per cent of value plus 40 cents per hundredweight, the part of the tax equal to 1 percent of value qualifies as an ad valorem tax and the balance does not qualify.

(2) The tax must be imposed on an annual basis, even if collected more frequently or less frequently.

(3) The tax must be imposed in respect of personal property. A tax may be considered to be imposed in respect of personal property even if in form it is imposed on the exercise of a privilege. Thus, for taxable years beginning after December 31, 1963, State and local taxes on the registration or licensing of highway motor vehicles are not deductible as personal property taxes unless and to the extent that the tests prescribed in this subparagraph are met. For example, an annual ad valorem tax qualifies as a personal property tax although it is denominated a registration fee imposed for the privilege of registering motor vehicles or of using them on the highways.

(d) *Foreign taxes.* The term "foreign tax" includes only a tax imposed by the authority of a foreign country. A tax imposed by a political

Reg. § 1.164-3(a)

subdivision of a foreign country is considered to be imposed by the authority of that foreign country.

(e) *Sales tax.* (1) The term "sales tax" means a tax imposed upon persons engaged in selling tangible personal property, or upon the consumers of such property, including persons selling gasoline or other motor vehicle fuels at wholesale or retail, which is a stated sum per unit of property sold or which is measured by the gross sales price or the gross receipts from the sale. The term also includes a tax imposed upon persons engaged in furnishing services which is measured by the gross receipts for furnishing such services.

(2) In general, the term "consumer" means the ultimate user or purchaser; it does not include a purchaser such as a retailer, who acquires the property for resale.

(f) *General sales tax.* A "general sales tax" is a sales tax which is imposed at one rate in respect of the sale at retail of a broad range of classes of items. No foreign sales tax is deductible under section 164(a) and paragraph (a)(4) of § 1.164-1. To qualify as a general sales tax, a tax must meet the following two tests:

(1) The tax must be a tax in respect of sales at retail. This may include a tax imposed on persons engaged in selling property at retail or furnishing services at retail, for example, if the tax is measured by gross sales price or by gross receipts from sales or services. Rentals qualify as sales at retail if so treated under applicable State sales tax laws.

(2) The tax must be general—that is, it must be imposed at one rate in respect of the retail sales of a broad range of classes of items. A sales tax is considered to be general although imposed on sales of various classes of items at more than one rate provided that one rate applies to the retail sales of a broad range of classes of items. The term "items" includes both commodities and services.

(g) *Special rules relating to general sales taxes.* (1) A sales tax which is general is usually imposed at one rate in respect of the retail sales of all tangible personal property (with exception and additions). However, a sales tax which is selective—that is, a tax which applies at one rate with respect to retail sales of specified classes of items also qualifies as general if the specified classes represent a broad range of classes of items. A selective sales tax which does not apply at one rate to the retail sales of a broad range of classes of items is not general. For example, a tax which applies only to sales of alcoholic beverages, tobacco, admissions, luxury items, and a few other items is not general. Similarly, a tax imposed solely on services is not general. However a selec-

tive sales tax may be deemed to be part of the general sales tax and hence may be deductible, even if imposed by a separate Title, etc., of the State or local law, if imposed at the same rate as the general rate of tax (as defined in subparagraph (4) of this paragraph) which qualifies a tax in the taxing jurisdiction as a general sales tax. For example, if a State has a 5 percent general sales tax and a separate selective sales tax of 5 percent on transient accommodations, the tax on transient accommodations is deductible.

(2) A tax is imposed at one rate only if it is imposed at that rate on generally the same base for all items subject to tax. For example, a sales tax imposed at a 3 percent rate on 100 percent of the sales price of some classes of items and at a 3 percent rate on 50 percent of the sales price of other classes of items would not be imposed at one rate with respect to all such classes. However, a tax is considered to be imposed at one rate although it allows dollar exemptions, if the exemptions are designed to exclude all sales under a certain dollar amount. For example, a tax may be imposed at one rate although it applies to all sales of tangible personal property but applies only to sales amounting to more than 10 cents.

(3) The fact that a sales tax exempts food, clothing, medical supplies, and motor vehicles, or any of them, shall not be taken into account in determining whether the tax applies to a broad range of classes of items. The fact that a sales tax applies to food, clothing, medical supplies, and motor vehicles, or any of them, at a rate which is lower than the general rate of tax (as defined in subparagraph (4) of this paragraph) is not taken into account in determining whether the tax is imposed at one rate on the retail sales of a broad range of classes of items. For purposes of this section, the term "food" means food for human consumption off the premises where sold, and the term "medical supplies" includes drugs, medicines, and medical devices.

(4) Except in the case of a lower rate of tax applicable in respect of food, clothing, medical supplies, and motor vehicles, or any of them, no deduction is allowed for a general sales tax in respect of any item if the tax is imposed on such item at a rate other than the general rate of tax. The general rate of tax is the one rate which qualifies a tax in a taxing jurisdiction as a general sales tax because the tax is imposed at such one rate on a broad range of classes of items. There can be only one general rate of tax in any one taxing jurisdiction. However, a general sales tax imposed at a lower rate or rates on food, clothing, motor vehicles, and medical supplies, or any of them, may nonetheless be deductible with respect

Reg. § 1.164-3(g)(4)

to such items. For example, a sales tax which is imposed at 1 percent with respect to food, imposed at 3 percent with respect to a broad range of classes of tangible personal property, and imposed at 4 percent with respect to transient accommodations would qualify as a general sales tax. Taxes paid at the 1 percent and the 3 percent rates are deductible, but tax paid at the 4 percent rate is not deductible. The fact that a sales tax provides for the adjustment of the general rate of tax to reflect the sales tax rate in another taxing jurisdiction shall not be taken into account in determining whether the tax is imposed at one rate on the retail sales of a broad range of classes of items. Moreover, a general sales tax imposed at a lower rate with respect to an item in order to reflect the tax rate in another jurisdiction is also deductible at such lower rate. For example, State E imposes a general sales tax whose general rate is 3 percent. The State E sales tax law provides that in areas bordering on States with general sales taxes, selective sales taxes, or special excise taxes, the rate applied in the adjoining State will be used if such rate is under 3 percent. State F imposes a 2 percent sales tax. The 2 percent sales tax paid by residents of State E in areas bordering on State F is deductible.

(h) *Compensating use taxes.* A compensating use tax in respect of any item is treated as a general sales tax. The term "compensating use tax" means, in respect of any item, a tax which is imposed on the use, storage, or consumption of such item and which is complementary to a general sales tax which is deductible with respect to sales of similar items.

(i) *Special rules relating to compensating use taxes.* (1) In general, a use tax on an item is complementary to a general sales tax on similar items if the use tax is imposed on an item which was not subject to such general sales tax but which would have been subject to such general sales tax if the sale of the item had taken place within the jurisdiction imposing the use tax. For example, a tax imposed by State A on the use of a motor vehicle purchased in State B is complementary to the general sales tax of State A on similar items, if the latter tax applies to motor vehicles sold in State A.

(2) Since a compensating use tax is treated as a general sales tax, it is subject to the rule of subparagraph (C) of section 164(b)(2) and paragraph (g)(4) of this section that no deduction is allowed for a general sales tax imposed in respect of an item at a rate other than the general rate of tax (except in the case of lower rates on the sale of food, clothing, medical supplies, and motor vehicles). The fact that a compensating use tax in

respect of any item provides for an adjustment in the rate of the compensating use tax or the amount of such tax to be paid on account of a sales tax on such item imposed by another taxing jurisdiction is not taken into account in determining whether the compensating use tax is imposed in respect of the item at a rate other than the general rate of tax. For example, a compensating use tax imposed by State C on the use of an item purchased in State D is considered to be imposed at the general rate of tax even though the tax imposed by State C allows a credit for any sales tax paid on such item in State D, or the rate of such compensating use tax is adjusted to reflect the rate of sales tax imposed by State D. [Reg. § 1.164-3.]

☐ [*T.D.* 6256, 10-7-57. *Amended by T.D.* 6780, 12-21-64.]

[Reg. § 1.164-4]

§ 1.164-4. Taxes for local benefits.—(a) So-called taxes for local benefits referred to in paragraph (g) of § 1.164-2 more properly assessments, paid for local benefits such as street, sidewalks, and other like improvements, imposed because of and measured by some benefit inuring directly to the property against which the assessment is levied are not deductible as taxes. A tax is considered assessed against local benefits when the property subject to the tax is limited to property benefited. Special assessments are not deductible, even though an incidental benefit may inure to the public welfare. The real property taxes deductible are those levied for the general public welfare by the proper taxing authorities at a like rate against all property in the territory over which such authorities have jurisdiction. Assessments under the statutes of California relating to irrigation, and of Iowa relating to drainage, and under certain statutes of Tennessee relating to levees, are limited to property benefited, and if the assessments are so limited, the amounts paid thereunder are not deductible as taxes. For treatment of assessments for local benefits as adjustments to the basis of property, see section 1016(a)(1) and the regulations thereunder.

(b) (1) Insofar as assessments against local benefits are made for the purpose of maintenance or repair or for the purpose of meeting interest charges with respect to such benefits, they are deductible. In such cases, the burden is on the taxpayer to show the allocation of the amounts assessed to the different purposes. If the allocation cannot be made, none of the amount so paid is deductible.

(2) Taxes levied by a special taxing district which was in existence on December 31, 1963, for the purpose of retiring indebtedness existing on

such date, are deductible, to the extent levied for such purpose, if (i) the district covers the whole of at least one county, (ii) if at least 1,000 persons are subject to the taxes levied by the district, and (iii) if the district levies its assessments annually at a uniform rate on the same assessed value of real property, including improvements, as is used for purposes of the real property tax generally. [Reg. § 1.164-4.]

☐ [*T.D.* 6256, 10-7-57. *Amended by T.D.* 6780, 12-21-64.]

[Reg. § 1.164-5]

§ 1.164-5. Certain retail sales taxes and gasoline taxes.—For taxable years beginning before January 1, 1964, any amount representing a State or local sales tax paid by a consumer of services or tangible personal property is deductible by such consumer as a tax, provided it is separately stated and not paid in connection with his trade or business. For taxable years beginning after December 31, 1963, only the amount of any separately stated State and local general sales tax (as defined in paragraph (g) of § 1.164-3) and tax on the sale of gasoline, diesel fuel or other motor fuel paid by the consumer (other than in connection with his trade or business) is deductible by the consumer as tax. The fact that, under the law imposing it, the incidence of such State or local tax does not fall on the consumer is immaterial. The requirement that the amount of tax must be separately stated will be deemed complied with where it clearly appears that at the time of sale to the consumer, the tax was added to the sales price and collected or charged as a separate item. It is not necessary, for the purpose of this section, that the consumer be furnished with a sales slip, bill, invoice, or other statement on which the tax is separately stated. For example, where the law imposing the State or local tax for which the taxpayer seeks a deduction contains a prohibition against the seller absorbing the tax, or a provision requiring a posted notice stating that the tax will be added to the quoted price, or a requirement that the tax be separately shown in advertisements or separately stated on all bills and invoices, it is presumed that the amount of the State or local tax was separately stated at the time paid by the consumer; except that such presumption shall have no application to a tax on the sale of gasoline, diesel fuel or other motor fuel imposed upon a wholesaler unless such provisions of law apply with respect to both the sale at wholesale and the sale at retail. [Reg. § 1.164-5.]

☐ [*T.D.* 6256, 10-7-57. *Amended by T.D.* 6780, 12-21-64.]

[Reg. § 1.164-6]

§ 1.164-6. Apportionment of taxes on real property between seller and purchaser.—(a) *Scope.* Except as provided otherwise in section 164(f) and § 1.164-8, when real property is sold, section 164(d)(1) governs the deduction by the seller and the purchaser of current real property taxes. Section 164(d)(1) performs two functions: (1) It provides a method by which a portion of the taxes for the real property tax year in which the property is sold may be deducted by the seller and a portion by the purchaser; and (2) it limits the deduction of the seller and the purchaser to the portion of the taxes corresponding to the part of the real property tax year during which each was the owner of the property. These functions are accomplished by treating a portion of the taxes for the real property tax year in which the property is sold as imposed on the seller and a portion as imposed on the purchaser. To the extent that the taxes are treated as imposed on the seller and the purchaser, each shall be allowed a deduction, under section 164(a), in the taxable year such tax is paid or accrued, or treated as paid or accrued under section 164(d)(2)(A) or (D) and this section. No deduction is allowed for taxes on real property to the extent that they are imposed on another taxpayer, or are treated as imposed on another taxpayer under section 164(d). For the election to accrue real property taxes ratably see section 461(c) and the regulations thereunder.

(b) *Application of rule of apportionment.*— (1)(i) For purposes of the deduction provided by section 164(a), if real property is sold during any real property tax year, the portion of the real property tax properly allocable to that part of the real property tax year which ends on the day before the date of the sale shall be treated as a tax imposed on the seller, and the portion of such tax properly allocable to that part of such real property tax year which begins on the date of the sale shall be treated as a tax imposed on the purchaser. For definition of "real property tax year" see paragraph (c) of this section. This rule shall apply whether or not the seller and the purchaser apportion such tax. The rule of apportionment contained in section 164(d)(1) applies even though the same real property is sold more than once during the real property tax year. (See paragraph (d)(5) of this section for rule requiring inclusion in gross income of excess deductions.)

(ii) Where the real property tax becomes a personal liability or a lien before the beginning of the real property tax year to which it relates and the real property is sold subsequent to the time the tax becomes a personal liability or a lien but

Reg. § 1.164-6(b)(1)

prior to the beginning of the related real property tax year—

   (a) The seller may not deduct any amount for real property taxes for the related real property tax year, and

   (b) To the extent that he holds the property for such real property tax year, the purchaser may deduct the amount of such taxes for the taxable year they are paid (or amounts representing such taxes are paid to the seller, mortgagee, trustee or other person having an interest in the property as security) or accrued by him according to his method of accounting.

   (iii) Similarly, where the real property tax becomes a personal liability or a lien after the end of the real property tax year to which it relates and the real property is sold prior to the time the tax becomes a personal liability or a lien but after the end of the related real property tax year—

   (a) The purchaser may not deduct any amount for real property taxes for the related real property tax year, and

   (b) To the extent that he holds the property for such real property tax year, the seller may deduct the amount of such taxes for the taxable year they are paid (or amounts representing such taxes are paid to the purchaser, mortgagee, trustee, or other person having an interest in the property as security) or accrued by him according to his method of accounting.

   (iv) Where the real property is sold (or purchased) during the related real property tax year the real property taxes for such year are apportioned between the parties to such sale and may be deducted by such parties in accordance with the provisions of paragraph (d) of this section.

   (2) Section 164(d) does not apply to delinquent real property taxes for any real property tax year prior to the real property tax year in which the property is sold.

   (3) The provisions of this paragraph may be illustrated by the following examples:

   Example (1). The real property tax year in County R is April 1 to March 31. A, the owner on April 1, 1954, of real property located in County R sells the real property to B on June 30, 1954. B owns the real property from June 30, 1954, through March 31, 1955. The real property tax for the real property tax year April 1, 1954-March 31, 1955 is $365. For purposes of section 164(a), $90 (90/365 × $365, April 1, 1954-June 29, 1954) of the real property tax is treated as imposed on A, the seller, and $275 (275/365 × $365, June 30, 1954-March 31, 1955) of such real property tax is treated as imposed on B, the purchaser.

   Example (2). In County S the real property tax year is the calendar year. The real property tax becomes a lien on June 1 and is payable on July 1 of the current real property tax year, but there is no personal liability for such tax. On April 30, 1955, C, the owner of real property in County S on January 1, 1955, sells the real property to D. On July 1, 1955, D pays the 1955 real property tax. On August 31, 1955, D sells the same real property to E. C, D, and E use the cash receipts and disbursements method of accounting. Under the provisions of section 164(d)(1), 119/365 (January 1-April 29, 1955) of the real property tax payable on July 1, 1955, for the 1955 real property tax year is treated as imposed on C, and, under the provisions of section 164(d)(2)(A), such portion is treated as having been paid by him on the date of sale. Under the provisions of section 164(d)(1), 123/365 (April 30-August 30, 1955) of the real property tax paid July 1, 1955, for the 1955 real property tax year is treated as imposed on D and may be deducted by him. Under the provisions of section 164(d)(1), 123/365 (August 31-December 31, 1955) of the real property tax due and paid on July 1, 1955, for the 1955 real property tax year is treated as imposed on E and, under the provisions of section 164(d)(2)(A) such portion is treated as having been paid by him on the date of sale.

   Example (3). In State X the real property tax year is the calendar year. The real property tax becomes a lien on November 1 of the preceding calendar year. On November 15, 1955, F sells real property in State X to G. G owns the real property through December 31, 1956. Under section 164(d)(1), the real property tax (which became a lien on November 1, 1954) for the 1955 real property tax year is apportioned between F and G. No part of the real property tax for the 1956 real property tax year may be deducted by F. The entire real property tax for the 1956 real property tax year may be deducted by G when paid or accrued, depending upon the method of accounting used by him. See subparagraph (6) of paragraph (d) and section 461(c) and the regulations thereunder.

   (c) *Real property tax year.* As used in section 164(d), the term "real property tax year" refers to the period which, under the law imposing the tax, is regarded as the period to which the tax imposed relates. Where the State and one or more local governmental units each imposes a tax on real property, the real property tax year for each tax must be determined for purposes of applying the rule of apportionment of section 164(d)(1) to each tax. The time when the tax rate is determined, the time when the assessment is made, the time when the tax becomes a lien, or the time when the tax becomes due or delinquent does not necessarily determine the real property tax year. The real property tax year may or may not correspond to the fiscal year of the governmental unit imposing the tax. In each case the State or local law determines what constitutes the real property tax year. Although the seller and the purchaser may or may not make an allocation of real property taxes, the meaning of "real property tax year" in section 164(d) and the application of section 164(d) do not depend upon what real property taxes were allocated nor the method of allocation used by the parties.

(d) *Special rules* —(1) *Seller using cash receipts and disbursements method of accounting.* Under the provisions of section 164(c), if the seller by reason of his method of accounting may not deduct any amount for taxes unless paid, and—

(i) The purchaser (under the law imposing the real property tax) is liable for the real property tax for the real property tax year, or

(ii) The seller (under the law imposing the real property tax) is liable for the real property tax for the real property tax year and the tax is not payable until after the date of sale,

then the portion of the tax treated under section 164(d)(1) as imposed upon the seller (whether or not actually paid by him in the taxable year in which the sale occurs) shall be considered as having been paid by him in such taxable year. Such portion may be deducted by him for the taxable year in which the sale occurs, or, if at a later time, for the taxable year (which would be proper under the taxpayer's method of accounting) in which the tax is actually paid, or an amount representing such tax is paid to the purchaser, mortgagee, trustee, or other person having an interest in the property as security.

(2) *Purchasers using the cash receipts and disbursements method of accounting.* Under the provisions of section 164(d), if the purchaser by reason of his method of accounting may not deduct any amount for taxes unless paid and the seller (under the law imposing the real property tax) is liable for the real property tax for the real property tax year, the portion of the tax treated under section 164(d)(1) as imposed upon the purchaser (whether or not actually paid by him in the taxable year in which the sale occurs) shall be considered as having been paid by him in such taxable year. Such portion may be deducted by him for the taxable year in which the sale occurs, or if at a later time, for the taxable year (which would be proper under the taxpayer's method of accounting) in which the tax is actually paid, or an amount representing such tax is paid to the

seller, mortgagee, trustee, or other person having an interest in the property as security.

(3) *Persons considered liable for tax.* Where the tax is not a liability of any person, the person who holds the property at the time the tax becomes a lien on the property shall be considered liable for the tax. As to a particular sale, in determining:

(i) Whether the other party to the sale is liable for the tax or,

(ii) The person who holds the property at the time the tax becomes a lien on the property (where the tax is not a liability of any person),

prior or subsequent sales of the property during the real property tax year shall be disregarded.

(4) *Examples.* The provisions of subparagraphs (1), (2), and (3) of this paragraph may be illustrated as follows:

Example (1). In County X the real property tax year is the calendar year. The real property tax is a personal liability of the owner of the real property on June 30 of the current real property tax year, but is not payable until February 28 of the following real property tax year. A, the owner of real property in County X on January 1, 1955, uses the cash receipts and disbursements method of accounting. On May 30, 1955, A sells the real property to B, who also uses the cash receipts and disbursements method of accounting. B retains ownership of the real property for the balance of the 1955 calendar year. Under the provisions of section 164(d)(1), 149/365 (January 1-May 29, 1955) of the real property tax payable on February 28, 1956, for the 1955 real property tax year is treated as imposed on A, the seller, and under the provisions of section 164(d)(2)(A) such portion is treated as having been paid by him on the date of sale and may be deducted by him for his taxable year in which the sale occurs (whether or not such portion is actually paid by him in that year) or for his taxable year in which the tax is actually paid or an amount representing such tax is paid. Under the provisions of section 164(d)(1), 216/365 (May 30-December 31, 1955) of the real property tax payable on February 28, 1956, for the 1955 real property tax year is treated as imposed on B, the purchaser, and may be deducted by him for his taxable year in which the tax is actually paid, or an amount representing such tax is paid.

Example (2). In County Y, the real property tax year is the calendar year. The real property tax becomes a lien on January 1, 1955, and is payable on April 30, 1955. There is no personal liability for the real property tax imposed by County Y. On April 30, 1955, C, the owner of real property in County Y on January 1, 1955, pays the real property tax for the 1955 real property tax year. On May 1, 1955, C sells the real property to D. On September 1, 1955, D sells the real property to E. C, D, and E use the cash receipts and disbursements method of accounting. Under the provisions of section 164(d)(1), 120/365 (January 1-April 30, 1955) of the real property tax is treated as imposed upon C and may be deducted by him for his taxable year in which the tax is actually paid. Under section 164(d)(1), 123/365 (May 1-August 31, 1955) of the real property tax is treated as imposed upon D and, under the provisions of section 164(d)(2)(A), is treated as having been paid by him on May 1, 1955, and may be deducted by D for his taxable year in which the sale from C to him occurs (whether or not such portion is actually paid by him in that year), or for his taxable year in which an amount representing such tax is paid. Since, according to paragraph (d)(3) of this section, the prior sale by C to D is disregarded, under the provisions of section 164(d)(1), 122/365 (September 1-December 31, 1955) of the real property tax is treated as imposed on E and, under the provisions of section 164(d)(2)(A), is treated as having been paid by him on September 1, 1955, and may be deducted by E for his taxable year in which the sale from D to him occurs (whether or not such portion is actually paid by him in that year), or for his taxable year in which an amount representing such tax is paid.

Example (3). In County X the real property tax year is the calendar year and the real property taxes are assessed and become a lien on June 30 of the current real property tax year, but are not payable until September 1 of that year. There is no personal liability for the real property tax imposed by County X. A, the owner on January 1, 1955, of real property in County X, uses the cash receipts and disbursements method of accounting. On July 15, 1955, A sells the real property to B. Under the provisions of section 164(d)(1), 195/365 (January 1-July 14, 1955) of the real property tax payable on September 1, 1955, for the 1955 real property tax year is treated as imposed on A, and may be deducted by him for his taxable year in which the sale occurs (whether or not such portion is actually paid by him in that year) or for his taxable year in which the tax is actually paid or an amount representing such tax is paid. Under the provisions of section 164(d)(1), 170/365 (July 15-December 31, 1955) of the real property tax is treated as imposed on B and may be deducted by him for his taxable year in which the sale occurs (whether or not such portion is actually paid by him in that year), or for his taxable year in which the tax is actually paid or an amount representing such tax is paid.

(5) *Treatment of excess deduction.* If, for a taxable year prior to the taxable year of sale of real property, a taxpayer has deducted an amount for real property tax in excess of the portion of such real property tax treated as imposed on him under the provisions of section 164(d), the excess of the amount deducted over the portion treated as imposed on him shall be included in his gross income for the taxable year of the sale, subject to the provisions of section 111, relating to the recovery of bad debts, prior taxes, and delinquency amounts. The provisions of this subparagraph may be illustrated as follows:

Example (1). In Borough Y the real property tax is due and payable on November 30 for the succeeding calendar year, which is also the real property tax year. On November 30, 1954, taxpayer A, who reports his income on a calendar year under the cash receipts and disbursements method of accounting, pays the real property tax on real property owned by him in Borough Y for the 1955 real property tax year. On June 30, 1955, A sells the real property. Under the provisions of section 164(d), only 180/365 (January 1-June 29, 1955) of the real property tax for the 1955 real property tax year is treated as imposed on A, and the excess of the amount of real property tax for 1955 deducted by A, on his 1954 income tax return, over the 180/365 portion of such tax treated as imposed on him under section 164(d), must be included in gross income in A's 1955 income tax return, subject to the provisions of section 111.

Example (2). In County Z the real property tax year is the calendar year. The real property tax becomes a personal liability of the owner of real property on January 1 of the current real property tax year, and is payable on July 1 of the current real property tax year. On May 1, 1955, A, the owner of real property in County Z on January 1, 1955, sells the real property to B. On November 1, 1955, B sells the same real property to C. B uses the cash receipts and disbursements method of accounting and reports his income on the basis of a fiscal year ending July 31. B, on July 1, 1955, pays the entire real property tax for the real property tax year ending December 31, 1955. Under the provisions of section 164(d), only 184/365 (May 1-October 31, 1955) of the real property tax for the 1955 real property tax year is treated as imposed on B, and the excess of the amount of real property tax for 1955 deducted by B on his income tax return for the fiscal year ending July 31, 1955, over the 184/365 portion of such tax treated as imposed on him under section 164(d), must be included in gross income in B's income tax return for his fiscal year ending July 31, 1956, subject to the provisions of section 111.

Reg. § 1.164-6(d)(5)

(6) *Persons using an accrual method of accounting.* Where real property is sold and the seller or the purchaser computes his taxable income (for the taxable year during which the sale occurs) on an accrual method of accounting, then, if the seller or the purchaser has not made the election provided in section 461(c) (relating to the accrual of real property taxes), the portion of any real property tax which is treated as imposed on him and which may not be deducted by him for any taxable year by reason of his method of accounting shall be treated as having accrued on the date of sale. The provisions of this subparagraph may be illustrated as follows:

Example. In County X the real property tax becomes a lien on property and is assessed on November 30 for the current calendar year, which is also the real property tax year. There is no personal liability for the real property tax imposed by County X. A owns, on January 1, 1955, real property in County X. A uses an accrual method of accounting and has not made any election under section 461(c) to accrue ratably real property taxes. A sells real property on June 30, 1955. By reason of A's method of accounting, he could not deduct any part of the real property tax for 1955 on the real property since he sold the real property prior to November 30, 1955, the accrual date. Under section 164(d)(1), 180/365 (January 1-June 29, 1955) of the real property tax for the 1955 real property tax year is treated as imposed on A, and under section 164(d)(2)(D) that portion is treated as having accrued on June 30, 1955, and may be deducted by A for his taxable year in which such date falls. B, the purchaser from A, who uses an accrual method of accounting, has likewise not made an election under section 461(c) to accrue real property taxes ratably. Under section 164(d)(1), 185/365 of the real property taxes may be accrued by B on November 30, 1955, and deducted for his taxable year in which such date falls.

(7) *Cross references.* For determination of amount realized on a sale of real property, see section 1001(b) and the regulations thereunder. For determination of basis of real property acquired by purchase, see section 1012 and the regulations thereunder.

(8) *Effective dates.* Section 164(c) applies to taxable years ending after December 31, 1953, but only in the case of sales made after December 31, 1953. However, section 164(d) does not apply to any real property tax to the extent that such tax was allowable as a deduction under the Internal Revenue Code of 1939 to the seller for any taxable year which ended before January 1, 1954. [Reg. § 1.164-6.]

☐ [*T.D.* 6256, 10-7-57. *Amended by T.D.* 6293, 5-20-58 *and T.D.* 6406, 8-14-59.]

[Reg. § 1.164-7]

§ 1.164-7. Taxes of shareholder paid by corporation.—Banks and other corporations paying taxes assessed against their shareholders on account of their ownership of the shares of stock issued by such corporations without reimbursement from such shareholders may deduct the amount of taxes so paid. In such cases no deduction shall be allowed to the shareholders for such taxes. The amount so paid should not be included in the gross income of the shareholder. [Reg. § 1.164-7.]

☐ [*T.D.* 6256, 10-7-57.]

[Reg. § 1.165-1]

§ 1.165-1. Losses.—(a) *Allowance of deduction.* Section 165(a) provides that, in computing taxable income under section 63, any loss actually sustained during the taxable year and not made good by insurance or some other form of compensation shall be allowed as a deduction subject to any provision of the internal revenue laws which prohibits or limits the amount of the deduction. This deduction for losses sustained shall be taken in accordance with section 165 and the regulations thereunder. For the disallowance of deductions for worthless securities issued by a political party, see § 1.271-1.

(b) *Nature of loss allowable.* To be allowable as a deduction under section 165(a), a loss must be evidenced by closed and completed transactions, fixed by identifiable events, and, except as otherwise provided in section 165(h) and § 1.165-11, relating to disaster losses, actually sustained during the taxable year. Only a bona fide loss is allowable. Substance and not mere form shall govern in determining a deductible loss.

(c) *Amount deductible.* (1) The amount of loss allowable as a deduction under section 165(a) shall not exceed the amount prescribed by § 1.1011-1 as the adjusted basis for determining the loss from the sale or other disposition of the property involved. In the case of each such deduction claimed, therefore, the basis of the property must be properly adjusted as prescribed by § 1.1011-1 for such items as expenditures, receipts, or losses, properly chargeable to capital account, and for such items as depreciation, obsolescence, amortization, and depletion, in order to determine the amount of loss allowable as a deduction. To determine the allowable loss in the case of property acquired before March 1, 1913, see also paragraph (b) of § 1.1053-1.

Reg. § 1.165-1(c)

(2) The amount of loss recognized upon the sale or exchange of property shall be determined for purposes of section 165(a) in accordance with § 1.1002-1.

(3) A loss from the sale or exchange of a capital asset shall be allowed as a deduction under section 165(a) but only to the extent allowed in section 1211 (relating to limitation on capital losses) and section 1212 (relating to capital loss carrybacks and carryovers), and in the regulations under those sections.

(4) In determining the amount of loss actually sustained for purposes of section 165(a), proper adjustment shall be made for any salvage value and for any insurance or other compensation received.

(d) *Year of deduction.* (1) A loss shall be allowed as a deduction under section 165(a) only for the taxable year in which the loss is sustained. For this purpose, a loss shall be treated as sustained during the taxable year in which the loss occurs as evidenced by closed and completed transactions and as fixed by identifiable events occurring in such taxable year. For provisions relating to situations where a loss attributable to a disaster will be treated as sustained in the taxable year immediately preceding the taxable year in which the disaster actually occurred, see section 165(h) and § 1.165-11.

(2)(i) If a casualty or other event occurs which may result in a loss and, in the year of such casualty or event, there exists a claim for reimbursement with respect to which there is a reasonable prospect of recovery, no portion of the loss with respect to which reimbursement may be received is sustained, for purposes of section 165, until it can be ascertained with reasonable certainty whether or not such reimbursement will be received. Whether a reasonable prospect of recovery exists with respect to a claim for reimbursement of a loss is a question of fact to be determined upon an examination of all facts and circumstances. Whether or not such reimbursement will be received will be ascertained with reasonable certainty, for example, by a settlement of the claim, by an adjudication of the claim, or by an abandonment of the claim. When a taxpayer claims that the taxable year in which a loss is sustained is fixed by his abandonment of the claim for reimbursement, he must be able to produce objective evidence of his having abandoned the claim, such as the execution of a release.

(ii) If in the year of the casualty or other event a portion of the loss is not covered by a claim for reimbursement with respect to which there is a reasonable prospect of recovery, then such portion of the loss is sustained during the taxable year in which the casualty or other event occurs. For example, if property having an adjusted basis of $10,000 is completely destroyed by fire in 1961, and if the taxpayer's only claim for reimbursement consists of an insurance claim for $8,000 which is settled in 1962, the taxpayer sustains a loss of $2,000 in 1961. However, if the taxpayer's automobile is completely destroyed in 1961 as a result of the negligence of another person and there exists a reasonable prospect of recovery on a claim for the full value of the automobile against such person, the taxpayer does not sustain any loss until the taxable year in which the claim is adjudicated or otherwise settled. If the automobile had an adjusted basis of $5,000 and the taxpayer secures a judgment of $4,000 in 1962, $1,000 is deductible for the taxable year 1962. If in 1963 it becomes reasonably certain that only $3,500 can ever be collected on such judgment, $500 is deductible for the taxable year 1963.

(iii) If the taxpayer deducted a loss in accordance with the provisions of this paragraph and in a subsequent taxable year receives reimbursement for such loss, he does not recompute the tax for the taxable year in which the deduction was taken but includes the amount of such reimbursement in his gross income for the taxable year in which received, subject to the provisions of section 111, relating to recovery of amounts previously deducted.

(3) Any loss arising from theft shall be treated as sustained during the taxable year in which the taxpayer discovers the loss (see § 1.165-8, relating to theft losses). However, if in the year of discovery there exists a claim for reimbursement with respect to which there is a reasonable prospect of recovery, no portion of the loss with respect to which reimbursement may be received is sustained, for purposes of section 165, until the taxable year in which it can be ascertained with reasonable certainty whether or not such reimbursement will be received.

(4) The rules of this paragraph are applicable with respect to a casualty or other event which may result in a loss and which occurs after January 16, 1960. If the casualty or other event occurs on or before such date, a taxpayer may treat any loss resulting therefrom in accordance with the rules then applicable, or, if he so desires, in accordance with the provisions of this paragraph; but no provision of this paragraph shall be construed to permit a deduction of the same loss or any part thereof in more than one taxable year or to extend the period of limitations within which a claim for credit or refund may be filed under section 6511.

Reg. § 1.165-1(c)(2)

(e) *Limitation on losses of individuals.* In the case of an individual, the deduction for losses granted by section 165(a) shall, subject to the provisions of section 165(c) and paragraph (a) of this section, be limited to:

(1) Losses incurred in a trade or business;

(2) Losses incurred in any transaction entered into for profit, though not connected with a trade or business; and

(3) Losses of property not connected with a trade or business and not incurred in any transaction entered into for profit, if such losses arise from fire, storm, shipwreck, or other casualty, or from theft, and if the loss involved has not been allowed for estate tax purposes in the estate tax return. For additional provisions pertaining to the allowance of casualty and theft losses, see §§ 1.165-7 and 1.165-8, respectively. For special rules relating to an election by a taxpayer to deduct disaster losses in the taxable year immediately preceding the taxable year in which the disaster occurred, see section 165(h) and § 1.165-11. [Reg. § 1.165-1.]

☐ [*T.D.* 6445, 1-15-60. *Amended by T.D.* 6753, 5-18-64, *T.D.* 6996, 1-17-69, *T.D.* 7301, 1-3-74 and *T.D.* 7522, 12-15-77.]

[Reg. § 1.165-2]

§ 1.165-2. Obsolescence of nondepreciable property.—(a) *Allowance of deduction.* A loss incurred in a business or in a transaction entered into for profit and arising from the sudden termination of the usefulness in such business or transaction of any nondepreciable property, in a case where such business or transaction is discontinued or where such property is permanently discarded from use therein, shall be allowed as a deduction under section 165(a) for the taxable year in which the loss is actually sustained. For this purpose, the taxable year in which the loss is sustained is not necessarily the taxable year in which the overt act of abandonment, or the loss of title to the property, occurs.

(b) *Exceptions.* This section does not apply to losses sustained upon the sale or exchange of property, losses sustained upon the obsolescence or worthlessness of depreciable property, casualty losses, or losses reflected in inventories required to be taken under section 471. The limitations contained in sections 1211 and 1212 upon losses from the sale or exchange of capital assets do not apply to losses allowable under this section.

(c) *Cross references.* For the allowance under section 165(a) of losses arising from the permanent withdrawal of depreciable property from use in the trade or business or in the production of income, see § 1.167(a)-8. For provisions respecting the obsolescence of depreciable property, see § 1.167(a)-9. For the allowance of casualty losses, see § 1.165-7. [Reg. § 1.165-2.]

☐ [*T.D.* 6445, 1-15-60.]

[Reg. § 1.165-3]

§ 1.165-3. Demolition of buildings.—(a) *Intent to demolish formed at time of purchase.* (1) Except as provided in subparagraph (2) of this paragraph, the following rule shall apply when, in the course of a trade or business or in a transaction entered into for profit, real property is purchased with the intention of demolishing either immediately or subsequently the buildings situated thereon: No deduction shall be allowed under section 165(a) on account of the demolition of the old buildings even though any demolition originally planned is subsequently deferred or abandoned. The entire basis of the property so purchased shall, notwithstanding the provisions of § 1.167(a)-5, be allocated to the land only. Such basis shall be increased by the net cost of demolition or decreased by the net proceeds from demolition.

(2)(i) If the property is purchased with the intention of demolishing the buildings and the buildings are used in a trade or business or held for the production of income before their demolition, a portion of the basis of the property may be allocated to such buildings and depreciated over the period during which they are so used or held. The fact that the taxpayer intends to demolish the buildings shall be taken into account in making the apportionment of basis between the land and buildings under § 1.167(a)-5. In any event, the portion of the purchase price which may be allocated to the buildings shall not exceed the present value of the right to receive rentals from the buildings over the period of their intended use. The present value of such right shall be determined at the time that the buildings are first used in the trade or business or first held for the production of income. If the taxpayer does not rent the buildings, but uses them in his own trade or business or in the production of his income, the present value of such right shall be determined by reference to the rentals which could be realized during such period of intended use. The fact that the taxpayer intends to rent or use the buildings for a limited period before their demolition shall also be taken into account in computing the useful life in accordance with paragraph (b) of § 1.167(a)-1.

(ii) Any portion of the purchase price which is allocated to the buildings in accordance with this subparagraph shall not be included in the basis of the land computed under subparagraph (1) of this paragraph, and any portion of the basis of the buildings which has not been recovered through depreciation or otherwise at the time of the demolition of the buildings is allowable as a deduction under section 165.

(iii) The application of this subparagraph may be illustrated by the following example:

Example. In January 1958, A purchased land and a building for $60,000 with the intention of demolishing the building. In the following April, A concludes that he will be unable to commence the construction of a proposed new building for a period of more than 3 years. Accordingly, on June 1, 1958, he leased the building for a period of 3 years at an annual rental of $1,200. A intends to demolish the building upon expiration of the lease. A may allocate a portion of the $60,000 basis of the property to the building to be depreciated over the 3-year period. That portion is equal to the present value of the right to receive $3,600 (3 times $1,200). Assuming that the present value of that right determined as of June 1, 1958, is $2,850, A may allocate that amount to the building and, if A files his return on the basis of a taxable year ending May 31, 1959, A may take a depreciation deduction with respect to such building of $950 for such taxable year. The basis of the land to A as determined under subparagraph (1) of this paragraph is reduced by $2,850. If on June 1, 1960, A ceases to rent the building and demolishes it, the balance of the undepreciated portion allocated to the buildings, $950, may be deducted from gross income under section 165.

(3) The basis of any building acquired in replacement of the old buildings shall not include any part of the basis of the property originally purchased even though such part was, at the time of purchase, allocated to the buildings to be demolished for purposes of determining allowable depreciation for the period before demolition.

(b) *Intent to demolish formed subsequent to the time of acquisition.* (1) Except as provided in subparagraph (2) of this paragraph, the loss incurred in a trade or business or in a transaction entered into for profit and arising from a demolition of old buildings shall be allowed as a deduction under section 165(a) if the demolition occurs as a result of a plan formed subsequent to the acquisition of the buildings demolished. The amount of the loss shall be the adjusted basis of the buildings demolished increased by the net cost of demolition or decreased by the net proceeds from demolition. See paragraph (c) of § 1.165-1 relating to amount deductible under section 165. The basis of any building acquired in replacement of the old buildings shall not include any part of the basis of the property demolished.

(2) If a lessor or lessee of real property demolishes the buildings situated thereon pursuant to a lease or an agreement which resulted in a lease, under which either the lessor was required or the lessee was required or permitted to demolish such buildings, no deduction shall be allowed to the lessor under section 165(a) on account of the demolition of the old buildings. However, the adjusted basis of the demolished buildings, increased by the net cost of demolition or decreased by the net proceeds from demolition, shall be considered as a part of the cost of the lease to be amortized over the remaining term thereof.

(c) *Evidence of intention.* (1) Whether real property has been purchased with the intention of demolishing the buildings thereon or whether the demolition of the buildings occurs as a result of a plan formed subsequent to their acquisition is a question of fact, and the answer depends upon an examination of all the surrounding facts and circumstances. The answer to the question does not depend solely upon the statements of the taxpayer at the time he acquired the property or demolished the buildings, but such statements, if made, are relevant and will be considered. Certain other relevant facts and circumstances that exist in some cases and the inferences that might reasonably be drawn from them are described in subparagraphs (2) and (3) of this paragraph. The question as to the taxpayer's intention is not answered by any inference that is drawn from any one fact or circumstance but can be answered only by a consideration of all relevant facts and circumstances and the reasonable inferences to be drawn therefrom.

(2) An intention at the time of acquisition to demolish may be suggested by:

(i) A short delay between the date of acquisition and the date of demolition;

(ii) Evidence of prohibitive remodeling costs determined at the time of acquisition;

(iii) Existence of municipal regulations at the time of acquisition which would prohibit the continued use of the buildings for profit purposes;

(iv) Unsuitability of the buildings for the taxpayer's trade or business at the time of acquisition; or

(v) Inability at the time of acquisition to realize a reasonable income from the buildings.

(3) The fact that the demolition occurred pursuant to a plan formed subsequent to the acquisition of the property may be suggested by:

(i) Substantial improvement of the buildings immediately after their acquisition;

(ii) Prolonged use of the buildings for business purposes after their acquisition;

Reg. § 1.165-3(a)(3)

(iii) Suitability of the buildings for investment purposes at the time of acquisition;

(iv) Substantial change in economic or business conditions after the date of acquisition;

(v) Loss of useful value occurring after the date of acquisition;

(vi) Substantial damage to the buildings occurring after their acquisition

(vii) Discovery of latent structural defects in the buildings after their acquisition;

(viii) Decline in the taxpayer's business after the date of acquisition;

(ix) Condemnation of the property by municipal authorities after the date of acquisition; or

(x) Inability after acquisition to obtain building material necessary for the improvement of the property. [Reg. § 1.165-3.]

☐ [*T.D.* 6445, 1-15-60. *Amended by T.D.* 7447, 12-21-76.]

[Reg. § 1.165-4]

§ 1.165-4. Decline in value of stock.—(a) *Deduction disallowed.* No deduction shall be allowed under section 165(a) solely on account of a decline in the value of stock owned by the taxpayer when the decline is due to a fluctuation in the market price of the stock or to other similar cause. A mere shrinkage in the value of stock owned by the taxpayer, even though extensive, does not give rise to a deduction under section 165(a) if the stock has any recognizable value on the date claimed as the date of loss. No loss for a decline in the value of stock owned by the taxpayer shall be allowed as a deduction under section 165(a) except insofar as the loss is recognized under § 1.1002-1 upon the sale or exchange of the stock and except as otherwise provided in § 1.165-5 with respect to stock which becomes worthless during the taxable year.

(b) *Stock owned by banks.* (1) In the regulation of banks and certain other corporations, Federal and State authorities may require that stock owned by such organizations be charged off as worthless or written down to a nominal value. If, in any such case, this requirement is premised upon the worthlessness of the stock, the charging off or writing down will be considered prima facie evidence of worthlessness for purposes of section 165(a); but, if the charging off or writing down is due to a fluctuation in the market price of the stock or if no reasonable attempt to determine the worthlessness of the stock has been made, then no deduction shall be allowed under section 165(a) for the amount so charged off or written down.

(2) This paragraph shall not be construed, however, to permit a deduction under section 165(a) unless the stock owned by the bank or other corporation actually becomes worthless in the taxable year. Such a taxpayer owning stock which becomes worthless during the taxable year is not precluded from deducting the loss under section 165(a) merely because, in obedience to the specific orders or general policy of such supervisory authorities, the value of the stock is written down to a nominal amount instead of being charged off completely.

(c) *Application to inventories.* This section does not apply to a decline in the value of corporate stock reflected in inventories required to be taken by a dealer in securities under section 471. See § 1.471-5.

(d) *Definition.* As used in this section, the term "stock" means a share of stock in a corporation or a right to subscribe for, or to receive, a share of stock in a corporation. [Reg. § 1.165-4.]

☐ [*T.D.* 6445, 1-15-60.]

[Reg. § 1.165-5]

§ 1.165-5. Worthless securities.—(a) *Definition of security.* As used in section 165(g) and this section, the term "security" means:

(1) A share of stock in a corporation;

(2) A right to subscribe for, or to receive, a share of stock in a corporation; or

(3) A bond, debenture, note, or certificate, or other evidence of indebtedness to pay a fixed or determinable sum of money, which has been issued with interest coupons or in registered form by a domestic or foreign corporation or by any government or political subdivision thereof.

(b) *Ordinary loss.* If any security which is not a capital asset becomes wholly worthless during the taxable year, the loss resulting therefrom may be deducted under section 165(a) as an ordinary loss.

(c) *Capital loss.* If any security which is a capital asset becomes wholly worthless at any time during the taxable year, the loss resulting therefrom may be deducted under section 165(a) but only as though it were a loss from a sale or exchange, on the last day of the taxable year, of a capital asset. See section 165(g)(1). The amount so allowed as a deduction shall be subject to the limitations upon capital losses described in paragraph (c)(3) of § 1.165-1.

(d) *Loss on worthless securities of an affiliated corporation*—(1) *Deductible as an ordinary loss.* If a taxpayer which is a domestic corporation owns any security of a domestic or foreign corporation which is affiliated with the taxpayer within the meaning of subparagraph (2) of this paragraph and such security becomes wholly worthless during the taxable year, the loss resulting therefrom may be deducted under section 165(a) as an ordinary loss in accordance with paragraph (b) of this section. The fact that the security is in fact a capital asset of the taxpayer is immaterial for this purpose, since section 165(g)(3) provides that such security shall be treated as though it were not a capital asset for the purposes of section 165(g)(1). A debt which becomes wholly worthless during the taxable year shall be allowed as an ordinary loss in accordance with the provisions of this subparagraph, to the extent that such debt is a security within the meaning of paragraph (a)(3) of this section.

(2) *Affiliated corporation defined.* For purposes of this paragraph, a corporation shall be treated as affiliated with the taxpayer owning the security if—

(i)(*a*) In the case of a taxable year beginning on or after January 1, 1970, the taxpayer owns directly—

(*1*) Stock possessing at least 80 percent of the voting power of all classes of such corporation's stock, and

(*2*) At least 80 percent of each class of such corporation's nonvoting stock

excluding for purposes of this subdivision (i)(*a*) nonvoting stock which is limited and preferred as to dividends (see section 1504(a)), or

(*b*) In the case of a taxable year beginning before January 1, 1970, the taxpayer owns directly at least 95 percent of each class of the stock of such corporation;

(ii) None of the stock of such corporation was acquired by the taxpayer solely for the purpose of converting a capital loss sustained by reason of the worthlessness of any such stock into an ordinary loss under section 165(g)(3), and

(iii) More than 90 percent of the aggregate of the gross receipts of such corporation for all the taxable years during which it has been in existence has been from sources other than royalties, rents (except rents derived from rental of properties to employees of such corporation in the ordinary course of its operating business), dividends, interest (except interest received on the deferred purchase price of operating assets sold), annuities and gains from sales or exchanges of stocks and securities. For this purpose, the term "gross receipts" means total receipts determined without any deduction for cost of goods sold, and gross receipts from sales or exchanges of stocks and securities shall be taken into account only to the extent of gains from such sales or exchanges.

(e) *Bonds issued by an insolvent corporation.* A bond of an insolvent corporation secured only by a mortgage from which nothing is realized for the

bondholders on foreclosure shall be regarded as having become worthless not later than the year of the foreclosure sale, and no deduction in respect of the loss shall be allowed under section 165(a) in computing a bondholder's taxable income for a subsequent year. See also paragraph (d) of § 1.165-1.

(f) *Decline in market value.* A taxpayer possessing a security to which this section relates shall not be allowed any deduction under section 165(a) on account of mere market fluctuation in the value of such security. See also § 1.165-4.

(g) *Application to inventories.* This section does not apply to any loss upon the worthlessness of any security reflected in inventories required to be taken by a dealer in securities under section 471. See § 1.471-5.

(h) *Special rules for banks.* For special rules applicable under this section to worthless securities of a bank, including securities issued by an affiliated bank, see § 1.582-1.

(i) *Examples.* The provisions of this section may be illustrated by the following examples:

Example (1). (i) X Corporation, a domestic manufacturing corporation which makes its return on the basis of the calendar year, owns 100 percent of each class of the stock of Y Corporation; and, in addition, 19 percent of the common stock (the only class of stock) of Z Corporation, which it acquired in 1948. Y Corporation, a domestic manufacturing corporation which makes its return on the basis of the calendar year, owns 81 percent of the common stock of Z Corporation, which it acquired in 1946. It is established that the stock of Z Corporation, which has from its inception derived all its gross receipts from manufacturing operations, became worthless during 1971.

(ii) Since the stock of Z Corporation which is owned by X Corporation is a capital asset and since X Corporation does not directly own at least 80 percent of the stock of Z Corporation, any loss sustained by X Corporation upon the worthlessness of such stock shall be deducted under section 165(g)(1) and paragraph (c) of this section as a loss from a sale or exchange on December 31, 1971, of a capital asset. The loss so sustained by X Corporation shall be considered a long-term capital loss under the provisions of section 1222(4), since the stock was held by that corporation for more than 6 months.

(iii) Since Z Corporation is considered to be affiliated with Y Corporation under the provisions of paragraph (d)(2) of this section, any loss sustained by Y Corporation upon the worthlessness of the stock of Z Corporation shall be deducted in

Reg. § 1.165-5(d)(2)

1971 under section 165(g)(3) and paragraph (d)(1) of this section as an ordinary loss.

Example (2). (i) On January 1, 1971, X Corporation, a domestic manufacturing corporation which makes its return on the basis of the calendar year, owns 60 percent of each class of the stock of Y Corporation, a foreign corporation, which it acquired in 1950. Y Corporation has, from the date of its incorporation, derived all of its gross receipts from manufacturing operations. It is established that the stock of Y Corporation became worthless on June 30, 1971. On August 1, 1971, X Corporation acquires the balance of the stock of Y Corporation for the purpose of obtaining the benefit of section 165(g)(3) with respect to the loss it has sustained on the worthlessness of the stock of Y Corporation.

(ii) Since the stock of Y Corporation which is owned by X Corporation is a capital asset and since Y Corporation is not to be treated as affiliated with X Corporation under the provisions of paragraph (d)(2) of this section, notwithstanding the fact that, at the close of 1971, X Corporation owns 100 percent of each class of stock of Y Corporation, any loss sustained by X Corporation upon the worthlessness of such stock shall be deducted under the provisions of section 165(g)(1) and paragraph (c) of this section as a loss from a sale or exchange on December 31, 1971, of a capital asset.

Example (3). (i) X Corporation, a domestic manufacturing corporation which makes its return on the basis of the calendar year, owns 80 percent of each class of the stock of Y Corporation, which from its inception has derived all of its gross receipts from manufacturing operations. As one of its capital assets, X Corporation owns $100,000 in registered bonds issued by Y Corporation payable at maturity on December 31, 1974. It is established that these bonds became worthless during 1971.

(ii) Since Y Corporation is considered to be affiliated with X Corporation under the provisions of paragraph (d)(2) of this section, any loss sustained by X Corporation upon the worthlessness of these bonds may be deducted in 1971 under section 165(g)(3) and paragraph (d)(1) of this section as an ordinary loss. The loss may not be deducted under section 166 as a bad debt. See section 166(e). [Reg. § 1.165-5.]

☐ [*T.D.* 6445, 1-15-60. *Amended by T.D.* 7224, 12-5-72.]

[Reg. § 1.165-6]

§ 1.165-6. **Farming losses.**—(a) *Allowance of losses.*—(1) Except as otherwise provided in this section, any loss incurred in the operation of a farm as a trade or business shall be allowed as a deduction under section 165(a) or as a net operating loss deduction in accordance with the provisions of section 172. See § 1.172-1.

(2) If the taxpayer owns and operates a farm for profit in addition to being engaged in another trade or business, but sustains a loss from the operation of the farming business, then the amount of loss sustained in the operation of the farm may be deducted from gross income, if any, from all other sources.

(3) Loss incurred in the operation of a farm for recreation or pleasure shall not be allowed as a deduction from gross income. See § 1.162-12.

(b) *Loss from shrinkage.* If, in the course of the business of farming, farm products are held for a favorable market, no deduction shall be allowed under section 165(a) in respect of such products merely because of shrinkage in weight, decline in value, or deterioration in storage.

(c) *Loss of prospective crop.* The total loss by frost, storm, flood, or fire of a prospective crop being grown in the business of farming shall not be allowed as a deduction under section 165(a).

(d) *Loss of livestock*—(1) *Raised stock.* A taxpayer engaged in the business of raising and selling livestock, such as cattle, sheep, or horses, may not deduct as a loss under section 165(a) the value of animals that perish from among those which were raised on the farm.

(2) *Purchased stock.* The loss sustained upon the death by disease, exposure, or injury of any livestock purchased and used in the trade or business of farming shall be allowed as a deduction under section 165(a). See, also, paragraph (e) of this section.

(e) *Loss due to compliance with orders of governmental authority.* The loss sustained upon the destruction by order of the United States, a State, or any other governmental authority, of any livestock, or other property, purchased and used in the trade or business of farming shall be allowed as a deduction under section 165(a).

(f) *Amount deductible*—(1) *Expenses of operation.* The cost of any feed, pasture, or care which is allowed under section 162 as an expense of operating a farm for profit shall not be included as a part of the cost of livestock for purposes of determining the amount of loss deductible under section 165(a) and this section. For the deduction of farming expenses, see § 1.162-12.

(2) *Losses reflected in inventories.* If inventories are taken into account in determining the income from the trade or business of farming, no deduction shall be allowed under this section for losses sustained during the taxable year upon live-

stock or other products, whether purchased for resale or produced on the farm, to the extent such losses are reflected in the inventory on hand at the close of the taxable year. Nothing in this section shall be construed to disallow the deduction of any loss reflected in the inventories of the taxpayer. For provisions relating to inventories of farmers, see section 471 and the regulations thereunder.

(3) *Other limitations.* For other provisions relating to the amount deductible under this section, see paragraph (c) of § 1.165-1, relating to the amount deductible under section 165(a); § 1.165-7, relating to casualty losses; and § 1.1231-1, relating to gains and losses from the sale or exchange of certain property used in the trade or business.

(g) *Other provisions applicable to farmers.* For other provisions relating to farmers, see § 1.61-4, relating to gross income of farmers; paragraph (b) of § 1.167(a)-6, relating to depreciation in the case of farmers; and § 1.175-1, relating to soil and water conservation expenditures. [Reg. § 1.165-6.]

☐ [*T.D.* 6445, 1-15-60.]

[Reg. § 1.165-7]

§ 1.165-7. Casualty losses.—(a) *In general—* (1) *Allowance of deduction.* Except as otherwise provided in paragraphs (b)(4) and (c) of this section, any loss arising from fire, storm, shipwreck, or other casualty is allowable as a deduction under section 165(a) for the taxable year in which the loss is sustained. However, see § 1.165-6, relating to farming losses, and § 1.165-11, relating to an election by a taxpayer to deduct disaster losses in the taxable year immediately preceding the taxable year in which the disaster occurred. The manner of determining the amount of a casualty loss allowable as a deduction in computing taxable income under section 63 is the same whether the loss has been incurred in a trade or business or in any transaction entered into for profit, or whether it has been a loss of property not connected with a trade or business and not incurred in any transaction entered into for profit. The amount of a casualty loss shall be determined in accordance with paragraph (b) of this section. For other rules relating to the treatment of deductible casualty losses, see § 1.1231-1, relating to the involuntary conversion of property.

(2) *Method of valuation—*(i) In determining the amount of loss deductible under this section, the fair market value of the property immediately before and immediately after the casualty shall generally be ascertained by competent appraisal. This appraisal must recognize the effects of any general market decline affecting undamaged as

well as damaged property which may occur simultaneously with the casualty, in order that any deduction under this section shall be limited to the actual loss resulting from damage to the property.

(ii) The cost of repairs to the property damaged is acceptable as evidence of the loss of value if the taxpayer shows that (*a*) the repairs are necessary to restore the property to its condition immediately before the casualty, (*b*) the amount spent for such repairs is not excessive, (*c*) the repairs do not care for more than the damage suffered, and (*d*) the value of the property after the repairs does not as a result of the repairs exceed the value of the property immediately before the casualty.

(3) *Damage to automobiles.* An automobile owned by the taxpayer, whether used for business purposes or maintained for recreation or pleasure, may be the subject of a casualty loss, including those losses specifically referred to in subparagraph (1) of this paragraph. In addition, a casualty loss occurs when an automobile owned by the taxpayer is damaged and when:

(i) The damage results from the faulty driving of the taxpayer or other person operating the automobile but is not due to the willful act or willful negligence of the taxpayer or of one acting in his behalf, or

(ii) The damage results from the faulty driving of the operator of the vehicle with which the automobile of the taxpayer collides.

(4) *Application to inventories.* This section does not apply to a casualty loss reflected in the inventories of the taxpayer. For provisions relating to inventories, see section 471 and the regulations thereunder.

(5) *Property converted from personal use.* In the case of property which originally was not used in the trade or business or for income-producing purposes and which is thereafter converted to either of such uses, the fair market value of the property on the date of conversion, if less than the adjusted basis of the property at such time, shall be used, after making proper adjustments in respect of basis, as the basis for determining the amount of loss under paragraph (b)(1) of this section. See paragraph (b) of § 1.165-9, and § 1.167(g)-1.

(6) *Theft losses.* A loss which arises from theft is not considered a casualty loss for purposes of this section. See § 1.165-8, relating to theft losses.

(b) *Amount deductible—*(1) *General rule.* In the case of any casualty loss whether or not incurred in a trade or business or in any transaction

Reg. § 1.165-7(a)(1)

entered into for profit, the amount of loss to be taken into account for purposes of section 165(a) shall be the lesser of either—

(i) The amount which is equal to the fair market value of the property immediately before the casualty reduced by the fair market value of the property immediately after the casualty; or

(ii) The amount of the adjusted basis prescribed in § 1.1011-1 for determining the loss from the sale or other disposition of the property involved. However, if the property used in a trade or business or held for the production of income is totally destroyed by casualty, and if the fair market value of such property immediately before the casualty is less than the adjusted basis of such property, the amount of the adjusted basis of such property shall be treated as the amount of the loss for purposes of section 165(a).

(2) *Aggregation of property for computing loss*—(i) A loss incurred in a trade or business or in any transaction entered into for profit shall be determined under subparagraph (1) of this paragraph by reference to the single identifiable property damaged or destroyed. Thus, for example, in determining the fair market value of the property before and after the casualty in a case where damage by casualty has occurred to a building and ornamental or fruit trees used in a trade or business, the decrease in value shall be measured

by taking the building and trees into account separately, and not together as an integral part of the realty, and separate losses shall be determined for such building and trees.

(ii) In determining a casualty loss involving real property and improvements thereon not used in a trade or business or in any transaction entered into for profit, the improvements (such as buildings and ornamental trees and shrubbery) to the property damaged or destroyed shall be considered an integral part of the property, for purposes of subparagraph (1) of this paragraph, and no separate basis need by apportioned to such improvements.

(3) *Examples.* The application of this paragraph may be illustrated by the following examples:

Example (1). In 1956 B purchases for $3,600 an automobile which he uses for nonbusiness purposes. In 1959 the automobile is damaged in an accidental collision with another automobile. The fair market value of B's automobile is $2,000 immediately before the collision and $1,500 immediately after the collision. B receives insurance proceeds of $300 to cover the loss. The amount of the deduction allowable under section 165(a) for the taxable year 1959 is $200, computed as follows:

Value of automobile immediately before casualty	$2,000
Less: Value of automobile immediately after casualty	1,500
Value of property actually destroyed	500
Loss to be taken into account for purposes of section 165(a): Lesser amount of property actually destroyed ($500) or adjusted basis of property ($3,600) ..	$ 500
Less: Insurance received	300
Deduction allowable	200

Example (2). In 1958 A purchases land containing an office building for the lump sum of $90,000. The purchase price is allocated between the land ($18,000) and the building ($72,000) for purposes of determining basis. After the purchase A planted trees and ornamental shrubs on the grounds surrounding the building. In 1961 the land, building, trees, and shrubs are damaged by hurricane. At the time of the casualty the adjusted basis of the land is $18,000 and the adjusted basis of the building is $66,000. At that time the trees and shrubs have an adjusted basis of $1,200. The fair market value of the land and building immediately before the casualty is

$18,000 and $70,000, respectively, and immediately after the casualty is $18,000 and $52,000, respectively. The fair market value of the trees and shrubs immediately before the casualty is $2,000 and immediately after the casualty is $400. In 1961 insurance of $5,000 is received to cover the loss to the building. A has no other gains or losses in 1961 subject to section 1231 and § 1.1231-1. The amount of the deduction allowable under section 165(a) with respect to the building for the taxable year 1961 is $13,000, computed as follows:

Value of property immediately before casualty	$70,000
Less: Value of property immediately after casualty	52,000
Value of property actually destroyed	18,000

Reg. § 1.165-7(b)(3)

Loss to be taken into account for purposes of section 165(a):

    Lesser amount of property actually destroyed ($18,000) or adjusted basis
        of property ($66,000) $18,000

    Less: Insurance received 5,000

Deduction allowable 13,000

The amount of the deduction allowable under section 165(a) with respect to the trees and shrubs for the taxable year 1961 is $1,200, computed as follows:

    Value of property immediately before casualty $2,000

    Less: Value of property immediately after casualty 400

    Value of property actually destroyed 1,600

Loss to be taken into account for purposes of section 165(a): Lesser amount of property actually destroyed ($1,600) or adjusted basis of property ($1,200) . $1,200

Example (3). Assume the same facts as in example (2) except that A purchases land containing a house instead of an office building. The house is used as his private residence. Since the property is used for personal purposes, no allocation of the purchase price is necessary for the land and house. Likewise, no individual determination of the fair market values of the land, house, trees, and shrubs is necessary. The amount of the deduction allowable under section 165(a) with respect to the land, house, trees, and shrubs for the taxable year 1961 is $14,600, computed as follows:

    Value of property immediately before casualty $90,000

    Less: Value of property immediately after casualty 70,400

    Value of property actually destroyed $19,600

Loss to be taken into account for purposes of section 165(a): Lesser amount of property actually destroyed ($19,600) or adjusted basis of property ($91,200) $19,600

    Less: Insurance received 5,000

Deduction allowable 14,600

(4) *Limitation on certain losses sustained by individuals after December 31, 1963*—(i) Pursuant to section 165(c)(3), the deduction allowable under section 165(a) in respect of a loss sustained—

    (a) After December 31, 1963, in a taxable year ending after such date,

    (b) In respect of property not used in a trade or business or for income producing purposes, and

    (c) From a single casualty

shall be limited to that portion of the loss which is in excess of $100. The nondeductibility of the first $100 of loss applies to a loss sustained after December 31, 1963, without regard to when the casualty occurred. Thus, if property not used in a trade or business or for income producing purposes is damaged or destroyed by a casualty which occurred prior to January 1, 1964, and loss resulting therefrom is sustained after December 31, 1963, the $100 limitation applies.

(ii) The $100 limitation applies separately in respect of each casualty and applies to the entire loss sustained from each casualty. Thus, if as a result of a particular casualty occurring in 1964, a taxpayer sustains in 1964 a loss of $40 and in 1965 a loss of $250, no deduction is allowable for the loss sustained in 1964 and the loss sustained in 1965 must be reduced by $60 ($100 − $40). The determination of whether damage to, or destruction of, property resulted from a single casualty or from two or more separate casualties will be made upon the basis of the particular facts of each case. However, events which are closely related in origin generally give rise to a single casualty. For example, if a storm damages a taxpayer's residence and his automobile parked in his driveway, any loss sustained results from a single casualty. Similarly, if a hurricane causes high waves, all wind and flood damage to a taxpayer's property caused by the hurricane and the waves results from a single casualty.

(iii) Except as otherwise provided in this subdivision, the $100 limitation applies separately to each individual taxpayer who sustains a loss even though the property damaged or destroyed is owned by two or more individuals. Thus, if a house occupied by two sisters and jointly owned by them is damaged or destroyed, the $100 limitation applies separately to each sister in respect of any loss sustained by her. However, for purposes of applying the $100 limitation, a husband and wife who file a joint return for the first taxable year in which the loss is allowable as a deduction are treated as one individual taxpayer. Accordingly, if property jointly owned by a husband and wife, or property separately owned by the husband or by the wife, is damaged or destroyed by a single casualty in 1964, and a loss is sustained in that year by either or both the husband or wife, only one $100 limitation applies if a joint return is filed for 1964. If, however, the husband and wife file separate returns for 1964, the $100 limitation applies separately in respect of any loss sustained by the husband and in respect of any loss sustained by the wife. Where losses from a single casualty are sustained in two or more separate tax years, the husband and wife shall, for purposes of applying the $100 limitation to such losses, be treated as one individual for all such years if they file a joint return for the first year in which a loss is sustained from the casualty; they shall be treated as separate individuals for all such years if they file separate returns for the first such year. If a joint return is filed in the first loss year but separate returns are filed in a subsequent year, any unused portion of the $100 limitation shall be allocated equally between the husband and wife in the latter year.

(iv) If a loss is sustained in respect of property used partially for business and partially for nonbusiness purposes, the $100 limitation applies only to that portion of the loss properly attributable to the nonbusiness use. For example, if a taxpayer sustains a $1,000 loss in respect of an automobile which he uses 60 percent for business and 40 percent for nonbusiness, the loss is allocated 60 percent to business use and 40 percent to nonbusiness use. The $100 limitation applies to the portion of the loss allocable to the nonbusiness loss.

(c) *Loss sustained by an estate.* A casualty loss of property not connected with a trade or business and not incurred in any transaction entered into for profit which is sustained during the settlement of an estate shall be allowed as a deduction under sections 165(a) and 641(b) in computing the taxable income of the estate if the loss has not been allowed under section 2054 in computing the taxable estate of the decedent and if the statement has been filed in accordance with § 1.642(g)-1. See section 165(c)(3).

(d) *Loss treated as though attributable to a trade or business.* For the rule treating a casualty loss not connected with a trade or business as though it were a deduction attributable to a trade or business for purposes of computing a net operating loss, see paragraph (a)(3)(iii) of § 1.172-3.

(e) *Effective date.* The rules of this section are applicable to any taxable year beginning after January 16, 1960. If, for any taxable year beginning on or before such date, a taxpayer computed the amount of any casualty loss in accordance with the rules then applicable, such taxpayer is not required to change the amount of the casualty loss allowable for any such prior taxable year. On the other hand, the taxpayer may, if he so desires, amend his income tax return for such year to compute the amount of a casualty loss in accordance with the provisions of this section, but no provision in this section shall be construed as extending the period of limitations within which a claim for credit or refund may be filed under section 6511. [Reg. § 1.165-7.]

☐ [*T.D.* 6445, 1-15-60. *Amended by T.D.* 6712, 3-23-64, *T.D.* 6735, 5-18-64, *T.D.* 6786, 12-28-64 *and T.D.* 7522, 12-15-77.]

[Reg. § 1.165-8]

§ 1.165-8. Theft losses.—(a) *Allowance of deduction.* (1) Except as otherwise provided in paragraphs (b) and (c) of this section, any loss arising from theft is allowable as a deduction under section 165(a) for the taxable year in which the loss is sustained. See section 165(c)(3).

(2) A loss arising from theft shall be treated under section 165(a) as sustained during the taxable year in which the taxpayer discovers the loss. See section 165(e). Thus, a theft loss is not deductible under section 165(a) for the taxable year in which the theft actually occurs unless that is also the year in which the taxpayer discovers the loss. However, if in the year of discovery there exists a claim for reimbursement with respect to which there is a reasonable prospect of recovery, see paragraph (d) of § 1.165-1.

(3) The same theft loss shall not be taken into account both in computing a tax under chapter 1, relating to the income tax, or chapter 2, relating to additional income taxes, of the Internal Revenue Code of 1939 and in computing the income tax under the Internal Revenue Code of 1954. See section 7852(c), relating to items not to be twice deducted from income.

(b) *Loss sustained by an estate.* A theft loss of property not connected with a trade or business and not incurred in any transaction entered into for profit which is discovered during the settlement of an estate, even though the theft actually occurred during a taxable year of the decedent, shall be allowed as a deduction under sections 165(a) and 641(b) in computing the taxable income of the estate if the loss has not been allowed under section 2054 in computing the taxable estate of the decedent and if the statement has been filed in accordance with § 1.642(g)-1. See section 165(c)(3). For purposes of determining the year of deduction, see paragraph (a)(2) of this section.

(c) *Amount deductible.* The amount deductible under this section in respect of a theft loss shall be determined consistently with the manner prescribed in § 1.165-7 for determining the amount of casualty loss allowable as a deduction under section 165(a). In applying the provisions of paragraph (b) of § 1.165-7 for this purpose, the fair market value of the property immediately after the theft shall be considered to be zero. In the case of a loss sustained after December 31, 1963, in a taxable year ending after such date, in respect of property not used in a trade or business or for income producing purposes, the amount deductible shall be limited to that portion of the loss which is in excess of $100. For rules applicable in applying the $100 limitation, see subparagraph (b)(4) of § 1.165-7. For other rules relating to the treatment of deductible theft losses, see § 1.1231-1, relating to the involuntary conversion of property.

(d) *Definition.* For purposes of this section the term "theft" shall be deemed to include, but shall not necessarily be limited to, larceny, embezzlement, and robbery.

(e) *Application to inventories.* This section does not apply to a theft loss reflected in the inventories of the taxpayer. For provisions relating to inventories, see section 471 and the regulations thereunder.

(f) *Example.* The application of this section may be illustrated by the following example:

Example. In 1955 B, who makes her return on the basis of the calendar year, purchases for personal use a diamond brooch costing $4,000. On November 30, 1961, at which time it has a fair market value of $3,500, the brooch is stolen; but B does not discover the loss until January 1962. The brooch was fully insured against theft. A controversy develops with the insurance company over its liability in respect of the loss. However, in 1962, B has a reasonable prospect of recovery of the fair market value of the brooch from the insurance company. The controversy is settled in March 1963, at which time B receives $2,000 in insurance proceeds to cover the loss from theft. No deduction for the loss is allowable for 1961 or 1962; but the amount of the deduction allowable under section 165(a) for the taxable year 1963 is $1,500, computed as follows:

Value of property immediately before theft	$3,500
Less: Value of property immediately after the theft	0
Balance	$3,500

Loss to be taken into account for purposes of section 165(a):

($3,500 but not to exceed adjusted basis of $4,000 at time of theft)	$3,500
Less: Insurance received in 1963	2,000
Deduction allowable for 1963	$1,500

[Reg. § 1.165-8.]

☐ [*T.D.* 6445, 1-15-60. *Amended by T.D.* 6786, 12-28-64.]

[Reg. § 1.165-9]

§ 1.165-9. Sale of residential property.—(a) *Losses not allowed.* A loss sustained on the sale of residential property purchased or constructed by the taxpayer for use as his personal residence and so used by him up to the time of the sale is not deductible under section 165(a).

(b) *Property converted from personal use.* (1) If property purchased or constructed by the taxpayer for use as his personal residence is, prior to its sale, rented or otherwise appropriated to income-producing purposes and is used for such purposes up to the time of its sale, a loss sustained on the sale of the property shall be allowed as a deduction under section 165(a).

(2) The loss allowed under this paragraph upon the sale of the property shall be the excess of the adjusted basis prescribed in § 1.1011-1 for determining loss over the amount realized from the sale. For this purpose, the adjusted basis for determining loss shall be the lesser of either of the following amounts, adjusted as prescribed in § 1.1011-1 for the period subsequent to the conversion of the property to income-producing purposes:

(i) The fair market value of the property at the time of conversion, or

(ii) The adjusted basis for loss, at the time of conversion, determined under § 1.1011-1 but without reference to the fair market value.

(3) For rules relating to casualty losses of property converted from personal use, see paragraph (a)(5) of § 1.165-7. To determine the basis for depreciation in the case of such property, see § 1.167(g)-1. For limitations on the loss from the sale of a capital asset, see paragraph (c)(3) of § 1.165-1.

(c) *Examples.* The application of paragraph (b) of this section may be illustrated by the following examples:

Example (1). Residential property is purchased by the taxpayer in 1943 for use as his personal residence at a cost of $25,000, of which $15,000 is allocable to the building. The taxpayer uses the property as his personal residence until January

1, 1952, at which time its fair market value is $22,000, of which $12,000 is allocable to the building. The taxpayer rents the property from January 1, 1952, until January 1, 1955, at which time it is sold for $16,000. On January 1, 1952, the building has an estimated useful life of 20 years. It is assumed that the building has no estimated salvage value and that there are no adjustments in respect of basis other than depreciation, which is computed on the straight-line method. The loss to be taken into account for purposes of section 165(a) for the taxable year 1955 is $4,200, computed as follows:

Basis of property at time of conversion for purposes of this section (that is, the lesser of $25,000 cost or $22,000 fair market value)	$22,000
Less: Depreciation allowable from January 1, 1952, to January 1, 1955 (3 years at 5 percent based on $12,000, the value of the building at time of conversion, as prescribed by § 1.167(g)-1)	$ 1,800
Adjusted basis prescribed in § 1.1011-1 for determining loss on sale of the property	$20,200
Less: Amount realized on sale ..	16,000
Loss to be taken into account for purposes of section 165(a) ...	$ 4,200

In this example the value of the building at the time of conversion is used as the basis for computing depreciation. See example (2) of this paragraph wherein the adjusted basis of the building is required to be used for such purpose.

Example (2). Residential property is purchased by the taxpayer in 1940 for use as his personal residence at a cost of $23,000, of which $10,000 is allocable to the building. The taxpayer uses the property as his personal residence until January 1, 1953, at which time its fair market value is $20,000, of which $12,000 is allocable to the building. The taxpayer rents the property from January 1, 1953, until January 1, 1957, at which time it is sold for $17,000. On January 1, 1953, the building has an estimated useful life of 20 years. It is assumed that the building has no estimated salvage value and that there are no adjustments in respect of basis other than depreciation, which is computed on the straight-line method. The loss to be taken into account for purposes of section 165(a) for the taxable year 1957 is $1,000, computed as follows:

Basis of property at time of conversion for purposes of this section (that is, the lesser of $23,000 cost or $20,000 fair market value)	$20,000
Less: Depreciation allowable from January 1, 1953, to January 1, 1957 (4 years at 5% based on $10,000, the cost of the building, as prescribed by § 1.167(g)-1)	2,000
Adjusted basis prescribed in § 1.1011-1 for determining loss on sale of the property	$18,000
Less: Amount realized on sale ..	17,000
Loss to be taken into account for purposes of section 165(a) ...	$ 1,000

[Reg. § 1.165-9.]

☐ [*T.D.* 6445, 1-15-60. *Amended by T.D. 6712,* 3-23-64.]

[Reg. § 1.165-10]

§ 1.165-10. **Wagering losses.**—Losses sustained during the taxable year on wagering transactions shall be allowed as a deduction but only to the extent of the gains during the taxable year from such transactions. In the case of a husband and wife making a joint return for the taxable year, the combined losses of the spouses from wagering transactions shall be allowed to the extent of the combined gains of the spouses from wagering transactions. [Reg. § 1.165-10.]

☐ [*T.D.* 6445, 1-15-60.]

[Reg. § 1.165-11]

§ 1.165-11. **Election in respect of losses attributable to a disaster.**—(a) *In general.* Section 165(h) provides that a taxpayer who has sustained a disaster loss which is allowable as a deduction under section 165(a) may, under certain circumstances, elect to deduct such loss for the taxable year immediately preceding the taxable year in which the disaster actually occurred.

(b) *Loss subject to election.* The election provided by section 165(h) and paragraph (a) of this section applies only to a loss:

(1) Arising from a disaster resulting in a determination referred to in subparagraph (2) of this paragraph and occurring—

(i) After December 31, 1971, or

(ii) After December 31, 1961, and before January 1, 1972, and during the period following the close of a particular taxable year of the taxpayer and on or before the due date for filing the income tax return for that taxable year (determined without regard to any extension of time granted the taxpayer for filing such return);

(2) Occurring in an area subsequently determined by the President of the United States to warrant assistance by the Federal Government under the Disaster Relief Act of 1974; and

Reg. § 1.165-11(b)(2)

(3) Constituting a loss otherwise allowable as a deduction for the year in which the loss occurred under section 165(a) and the provisions of § § 1.165-1 through 1.165-10 which are applicable to such losses.

(c) *Amount of loss to which election applies.* The amount of the loss to which section 165(h) and this section apply shall be the amount of the loss sustained during the period specified in paragraph (b)(1) of this section computed in accordance with the provisions of section 165 and those provisions of § § 1.165-1 through 1.165-10 which are applicable to such losses. However, for purposes of making such computation, the period specified in paragraph (b)(1) of this section shall be deemed to be a taxable year.

(d) *Scope and effect of election.* An election made pursuant to section 165(h) and this section in respect of a loss arising from a particular disaster shall apply to the entire loss sustained by the taxpayer from such disaster during the period specified in paragraph (b)(1) of this section in the area specified in paragraph (b)(2) of this section. If such an election is made, the disaster to which the election relates will be deemed to have occurred in the taxable year immediately preceding the taxable year in which the disaster actually occurred, and the loss to which the election applies will be deemed to have been sustained in such preceding taxable year.

(e) *Time and manner of making election.* An election to claim a deduction with respect to a disaster loss described in paragraph (b) of this section for the taxable year immediately preceding the taxable year in which the disaster actually occurred must be made by filing a return, an amended return, or a claim for refund clearly showing that the election provided by section 165(h) has been made. In general, the return or claim should specify the date or dates of the disaster which gave rise to the loss, and the city, town, county, and State in which the property which was damaged or destroyed was located at the time of the disaster. An election in respect of a loss arising from a particular disaster occurring after December 31, 1971, must be made on or before the later of (1) the due date for filing the income tax return (determined without regard to any extension of time granted the taxpayer for filing such return) for the taxable year in which the disaster actually occurred, or (2) the due date for filing the income tax return (determined with regard to any extension of time granted the taxpayer for filing such return) for the taxable year immediately preceding the taxable year in which the disaster actually occurred. Such election shall be irrevocable after the later of (1) 90 days after

the date on which the election was made, or (2) 90 days after the date of publication of final regulations conforming this section to section 2(a) of the Act of August 29, 1972 (Public Law 92-418, 86 Stat. 656). No revocation of such election shall be effective unless the amount of any credit or refund which resulted from such election is paid to the Internal Revenue Service within the revocation period described in the preceding sentence. However, in the case of a revocation made before receipt by the taxpayer of a refund claimed pursuant to such election, the revocation shall be effective if the refund is repaid within 30 calendar days after such receipt. An election in respect of a loss arising from a particular disaster occurring after December 31, 1961, and before January 1, 1972, must be made on or before the later of (1) the 15th day of the third month following the month in which falls the date prescribed for the filing of the income tax return (determined without regard to any extension of time granted the taxpayer for filing such return) for the taxable year immediately preceding the taxable year in which the disaster actually occurred, or, (2) the due date for filing the income tax return (determined with regard to any extension of time granted the taxpayer for filing such return) for the taxable year immediately preceding the taxable year in which the disaster actually occurred. Such election shall be irrevocable after the date by which it must be made. [Reg. § 1.165-11.]

☐ [*T.D. 6735, 5-18-64. Amended by T.D. 7224, 12-5-72 and T.D. 7522, 12-15-77.*

[Reg. § 1.165-12]

§ 1.165-12. Denial of deduction for losses on registration-required obligations not in registered form.—(a) *In general.* Except as provided in paragraph (c) of this section, nothing in section 165(a) and the regulations thereunder, or in any other provision of law, shall be construed to provide a deduction for any loss sustained on any registration-required obligation held after December 31, 1982, unless the obligation is in registered form or the issuance of the obligation was subject to tax under section 4701. The term "registration-required obligation" has the meaning given to that term in section 163(f)(2), except that clause (iv) of subparagraph (A) thereof shall not apply. Therefore, although an obligation that is not in registered form is described in § 1.163-5(c)(1), the holder of such an obligation shall not be allowed a deduction of any loss sustained on such obligation unless paragraph (c) of this section applies. The term "holder" means the person that would be denied a loss deduction under section 165(j)(1) or denied capital gain treatment under section 1287(a). For purposes of this section, the term

Reg. § 1.165-12(a)

United States means the United States and its possessions within the meaning of § 1.163-5(c)(2)(iv).

(b) *Registered form*—(1) *Obligations issued after September 21, 1984.* With respect to any obligation originally issued after September 21, 1984, the term "registered form" has the meaning given that term in section 103(j)(3) and the regulations thereunder. Therefore, an obligation that would otherwise be in registered form is not considered to be in registered form if it can be transferred at that time or at any time until its maturity by any means not described in § 5f.103-1(c). An obligation that, as of a particular time, is not considered to be in registered form because it can be transferred by any means not described in § 5f.103-1(c) is considered to be in registered form at all times during the period beginning with a later time and ending with the maturity of the obligation in which the obligation can be transferred only by a means described in § 5f.103-1(c).

(2) *Obligations issued after December 31, 1982 and on or before September 21, 1984.* With respect to any obligation originally issued after December 31, 1982 and on or before September 21, 1984 or an obligation originally issued after September 21, 1984 pursuant to the exercise of a warrant or the conversion of a convertible obligation, which warrant or obligation (including conversion privilege) was issued after December 31, 1982 and on or before September 21 1984, that obligation will be considered in registered form if it satisfied § 5f.163-1 or the proposed regulations provided in § 1.163-5(c) and published in the Federal Register on September 2, 1933 (48 FR 39953).

(c) *Registration-required obligations not in registered form which are not subject to section 165(j)(1).* Notwithstanding the fact that an obligation is a registration-required obligation that is not in registered form, the holder will not be subject to section 165(j)(1) if the holder meets the conditions of any one of the following subparagraphs (1), (2), (3), or (4) of this paragraph (c).

(1) *Persons permitted to hold in connection with the conduct of a trade or business.*—(i) The holder is an underwriter, broker, dealer, bank, or other financial institution (defined in paragraph (c)(1)(iv)) that holds such obligation in connection with its trade or business conducted outside the United States; or the holder is a broker-dealer (registered under Federal or State law or exempted from registration by the provisions of such law because it is a bank) that holds such obligation for sale to customers in the ordinary course of its trade or business.

(ii) The holder must offer to sell, sell and deliver the obligation in bearer form only outside of the United States except that a holder that is a registered broker-dealer as described in paragraph (c)(1)(ii) of this section may offer to sell and sell the obligation in bearer form inside the United States to a financial institution as defined in paragraph (c)(1)(iv) of this section for its own account or for the account of another financial institution or of an exempt organization as defined in section 501(c)(3).

(iii) The holder may deliver an obligation in bearer form that is offered or sold inside the United States only if the holder delivers it to a financial institution that is purchasing for its own account, or for the account of another financial institution or of an exempt organization, and the financial institution or organization that purchases the obligation for its own account or for whose account the obligation is purchased represents that it will comply with the requirements of section 165(j)(3)(A), (B), or (C). Absent actual knowledge that the representation is false, the holder may rely on a written statement provided by the financial institution or exempt organization, including a statement that is delivered in electronic form. The holder may deliver a registration-required obligation in bearer form that is offered and sold outside the United States to a person other than a financial institution only if the holder has evidence in its records that such person is not a U.S. citizen or resident and does not have actual knowledge that such evidence is false. Such evidence may include a written statement by that person, including a statement that is delivered electronically. For purposes of this paragraph (c), the term *deliver* includes a transfer of an obligation evidenced by a book entry including a book entry notation by a clearing organization evidencing transfer of the obligation from one member of the organization to another member. For purposes of this paragraph (c), the term *deliver* does not include a transfer of an obligation to the issuer or its agent for cancellation or extinguishment. The record-retention provisions in § 1.1441-1(e)(4)(iii) shall apply to any statement that a holder receives pursuant to this paragraph (c)(1)(iii).

(iv) For purposes of paragraph (c) of this section, the term "financial institution" means a person which itself is, or more than 50 percent of the total combined voting power of all classes of whose stock entitled to vote is owned by a person which is—

(A) Engaged in the conduct of a banking, financing, or similar business within the meaning of section 954(c)(3)(B) as in effect before the Tax Reform Act of 1986, and the regulations thereunder;

    (B) Engaged in business as a broker or dealer in securities;

    (C) An insurance company;

    (D) A person that provides pensions or other similar benefits to retired employees;

    (E) Primarily engaged in the business of rendering investment advice;

    (F) A regulated investment company or other mutual fund; or

    (G) A finance corporation a substantial part of the business of which consists of making loans (including the acquisition of obligations under a lease which is entered into primarily as a financing transaction), acquiring accounts receivable, notes or installment obligations arising out of the sale of tangible personal property or the performing of services, or servicing debt obligations.

    (2) *Persons permitted to hold obligations for their own investment account.* The holder is a financial institution holding the obligation for its own investment account that satisfies the conditions set forth in subdivisions (i), (ii), (iii), and (iv) of this paragraph (c)(2).

    (i) The holder reports on its Federal income tax return for the taxable year any interest payments received (including original issue discount includable in gross income for such taxable year) with respect to such obligation and gain or loss on the sale or other disposition of such obligation;

    (ii) The holder indicates on its Federal income tax return that income, gain or loss described in paragraph (c)(2)(i) is attributable to registration-required obligations held in bearer form for its own account;

    (iii) The holder of a bearer obligation that resells the obligation inside the United States resells the obligation only to another financial institution for its own account or for the account of another financial institution or exempt organization; and

    (iv) The holder delivers such obligation in bearer form to any other person in accordance with paragraph (c)(1)(ii) and (iii) of this section.

    (3) *Persons permitted to hold through financial institutions.* The holder is any person that purchases and holds a registration-required obligation in bearer form through a financial institution with which the holder maintains a customer, custodial or nominee relationship and such institution agrees to satisfy, and does in fact satisfy, the conditions set forth in subdivisions (i), (ii), (iii), (iv) and (v) of this paragraph (c)(3).

    (i) The financial institution makes a return of information to the Internal Revenue Service with respect to any interest payments received. The financial institution must report original issue discount includable in the holder's gross income for the taxable year on any obligation so held, but only if the obligation appears in an Internal Revenue Service publication of obligations issued at an original issue discount and only in an amount determined in accordance with information contained in that publication. An information return for any interest payment shall be made on a Form 1099 for the calendar year. It shall indicate the aggregate amount of the payment received, the name, address and taxpayer identification number of the holder, and such other information as is required by the form. No return of information is required under this subdivision if the financial institution reports payments under section 6041 or 6049.

    (ii) The financial institution makes a return of information on Form 1099B with respect to any disposition by the holder of such obligation. The return shall show the name, address, and taxpayer identification number of the holder of the obligation, Committee on Uniform Security Information Procedures (CUSIP), gross proceeds, sale date, and such other information as may be required by the form. No return of information is required under this subdivision if such financial institution reports with respect to the disposition under section 6045.

    (iii) In the case of a bearer obligation offered for resale or resold in the United States, the financial institution may resell the obligation only to another financial institution for its own account or for the account of an exempt organization.

    (iv) The financial institution covenants with the holder that the financial institution will deliver the obligation in bearer form in accordance with the requirements set forth in paragraph (c)(1)(ii) and (iii).

    (v) The financial institution delivers the obligation in bearer form in accordance with paragraph (c)(1)(ii) and (iv) as if the financial institution delivering the obligation were the holder referred to in such paragraph.

    (4) *Conversion of obligations into registered form.* The holder is not a person described in paragraph (c)(1), (2), or (3) of this section, and within thirty days of the date when the seller or other transferor is reasonably able to make the bearer obligation available to the holder, the holder surrenders the obligation to a transfer agent or the issuer for conversion of the obligation into registered form. If such obligation is not

registered within such 30 day period, the holder shall be subject to sections 165(j) and 1287(a).

(d) *Effective date.* These regulations apply generally to obligations issued after January 20, 1987. However, a taxpayer may choose to apply the rules of § 1.165-12 with respect to an obligation issued after December 31, 1982 and on or before January 20, 1987, which obligation is held after January 20, 1987. [Reg. § 1.165-12.]

☐ [*T.D. 8110, 12-16-86. Amended by T.D. 8734, 10-6-97 (T.D. 8804 delayed the effective date of T.D. 8734 from January 1, 1999, to January 1, 2000; T.D. 8856 further delayed the effective date of T.D. 8734 until January 1, 2001).]*

[Reg. § 1.165-13T]

§ 1.165-13T. Questions and answers relating to the treatment of losses on certain straddle transactions entered into before the effective date of the Economic Recovery Tax Act of 1981, under section 108 of the Tax Reform Act of 1984 (temporary).—The following questions and answers concern the treatment of losses on certain straddle transactions entered into before the effective date of the Economic Recovery Tax Act of 1981, under the Tax Reform Act of 1984 (98 Stat. 494).

Q-1. What is the scope of section 108 of the Tax Reform Act of 1984 (Act)?

A-1. Section 108 of the Act provides that in the case of any disposition of one or more positions, which were entered into before 1982 and form part of a straddle, and to which the provisions of Title V of the Economic Recovery Tax Act of 1981 (ERTA) do not apply, any loss from such disposition shall be allowed for the taxable year of the disposition if such position is part of a transaction entered into for profit. For purposes of section 108 of the Act, the term "straddle" has the meaning given to such term by section 1092(c) of the Internal Revenue Code of 1954 as in effect on the day after the date of enactment of ERTA; including a straddle all the positions of which are regulated futures contracts (as defined in Q&A-6 of this section). Straddles in certain listed stock options were not covered by ERTA and are not affected by this provision.

Q-2. What transactions are considered entered into for profit?

A-2. A transaction is considered entered into for profit if the transaction is entered into for profit within the meaning of section 165(c)(2) of the Code. In this respect, section 108 of the Act restates existing law applicable to straddle transactions. All the circumstances surrounding the transaction, including the magnitude and timing for entry into, and disposition of, the positions

comprising the transaction are relevant in making the determination whether a transaction is considered entered into for profit. Moreover, in order for section 108 of the Act to apply, the transaction must have sufficient substance to be recognized for Federal income tax purposes. Thus, for example, since a "sham" transaction would not be recognized for tax purposes, section 108 of the Act would not apply to such a transaction.

Q-3. If a loss is disallowed in a taxable year (year 1) because the transaction was not entered into for profit, is the entire gain from the straddle occurring in a later taxable year taxed?

A-3. No. Under section 108(c) of the Act the taxpayer is allowed to offset the gain in the subsequent taxable year by the amount of loss (including expenses) disallowed in year 1.

Q-4. In what manner does the for-profit test of Q&A-2 apply to losses from straddle transactions sustained by commodities dealers and persons regularly engaged in investing in regulated futures contracts?

A-4. In general, for a loss to be allowable with respect to positions that form part of a straddle, the for-profit test of Q&A-2 must be satisfied. However, certain positions (see Q&A-6) held by a commodities dealer or person regularly engaged in investing in regulated futures contracts are rebuttably presumed to be part of a transaction entered into for profit. Thus, the for profit test is applied to commodities dealers and persons regularly engaged in investing in regulated futures contracts in light of the factors relating to the applicability and rebuttal of the profit presumption, including, for example, the nature and extent of the taxpayer's trading activities.

Q-5. Under what circumstances is the presumption considered rebutted?

A-5. All the facts and circumstances of each case are to be considered in determining if the presumption is rebutted. The following factors are significant in making this determination: (1) the level of transaction costs; (2) the extent to which the transaction results from trading patterns different from the taxpayer's regular patterns; and (3) the extent of straddle transactions having tax results disproportionate to economic consequences. Factors other than the ones described above may be taken into account in making the determination. Moreover, a determination is not to be made solely on the basis of the number of factors indicating that the presumption is rebutted.

Q-6. Does a commodities dealer or person regularly engaged in investing in regulated futures contracts qualify for the profit presumption for all transactions?

A-6. No. The presumption is only applicable to regulated futures contract transactions in property that is the subject of the person's regular trading activity. For example, a commodities dealer who regularly trades only in agricultural futures will not qualify for the presumption for a silver futures straddle transaction. For purposes of this section, the term "regulated futures contracts" has the meaning given to such term by section 1256(b) of the Code as in effect before the enactment of the Tax Reform Act of 1984.

Q-7. Who qualifies as a commodities dealer or as a person regularly engaged in investing in regulated futures contracts for purposes of the profit presumption?

A-7. For purposes of this section, the term "commodities dealer" has the meaning given to such term by section 1402(i)(2)(B) of the Code. Section 1402(i)(2)(B) defines a commodities dealer as a person who is actively engaged in trading section 1256 contracts (which includes regulated futures contracts as defined in Q&A-6) and is registered with a domestic board of trade which is designated as a contract market by the Commodity Futures Trading Commission. To determine if a person is regularly engaged in investing in regulated futures contracts all the facts and circumstances should be considered including, but not limited to, the following factors: (1) regularity of trading at all times throughout the year; (2) the level of transaction costs; (3) substantial volume and economic consequences of trading at all times throughout the year; (4) percentage of time dedicated to commodity trading activites as compared to other activities; and (5) the person's knowledge of the regulated futures contract market.

Q-8. If a commodities dealer or a person regularly engaged in investing in regulated futures contracts participates in a syndicate, as defined in section 1256(e)(3)(B) of the Code, does the rebuttable presumption of "entered into for profit" apply to the transactions entered into through the syndicate?

A-8. No. A participant in a syndicate does not qualify for the rebuttable presumption of "entered into for profit" with respect to transactions entered into by or for the syndicate. A syndicate is defined in section 1256(e)(3)(B) of the Code as any partnership or other entity (other than a corporation which in not an S corporation) if more than 35 percent of the losses of such entity during the taxable year are allocable to limited partners or limited entrepreneurs (within the meaning of section 464(e)(2)).

Q-9. Will the Service continue to make the closed and completed transaction argument set forth in Rev. Rul. 77-185, 1977-1 C.B. 48, with respect to transactions covered by section 108 of the Act?

A-9. No. The closed and completed transaction argument will not be made regarding transactions subject to section 108 of the Act. In general, losses in such transactions will be allowed for the taxable year of disposition if the transaction is not viewed as a sham and satisfies the "entered into for profit" test described in Q&A-2. Nevertheless, for certain positions covered by section 108 of the Act, various Code sections may apply without regard to whether such position constitutes a straddle to disallow or limit the loss otherwise allowable in the year of the disposition. For example, dispositions of certain positions held by a partnership which resulted in a loss to a partner may be limited or disallowed under section 465 or 704(d). [Temporary Reg. § 1.165-13T.]

□ [T.D. 7968, 8-21-84.]

[Reg. § 1.166-1]

§ 1.166-1. Bad debts.—(a) *Allowance of deduction.* Section 166 provides that, in computing taxable income under section 63, a deduction shall be allowed in respect of bad debts owed to the taxpayer. For this purpose, bad debts shall, subject to the provisions of section 166 and the regulations thereunder, be taken into account either as—

(1) A deduction in respect of debts which become worthless in whole or in part; or as

(2) A deduction for a reasonable addition to a reserve for bad debts.

(b) *Manner of selecting method.* (1) A taxpayer filing a return of income for the first taxable year for which he is entitled to a bad debt deduction may select either of the two methods prescribed by paragraph (a) of this section for treating bad debts, but such selection is subject to the approval of the district director upon examination of the return. If the method so selected is approved, it shall be used in returns for all subsequent taxable years unless the Commissioner grants permission to use the other method. A statement of facts substantiating any deduction claimed under section 166 on account of bad debts shall accompany each return of income.

(2) Taxpayers who have properly selected one of the two methods for treating bad debts under provisions of prior law corresponding to section 166 shall continue to use that method for all subsequent taxable years unless the Commissioner grants permission to use the other method.

(3)(i) For taxable years beginning after December 31, 1959, application for permission to change the method of treating bad debts shall be made in accordance with section 446(e) and paragraph (e)(3) of § 1.446-1.

Reg. § 1.166-1(a)(1)

(ii) For taxable years beginning before January 1, 1960, application for permission to change the method of treating bad debts shall be made at least 30 days before the close of the taxable year for which the change is effective.

(4) Notwithstanding paragraph (b) (1), (2), and (3) of this section, a dealer in property currently employing the accrual method of accounting and currently maintaining a reserve for bad debts under section 166(c) (which may have included guaranteed debt obligations described in section 166(f)(1)(A)) may establish a reserve for section 165(f)(1)(A) guaranteed debt obligations for a taxable year ending after October 21, 1965 under section 166(f) and § 1.166-10 by filing on or before April 17, 1986, an amended return indicating that such a reserve has been established. The establishment of such a reserve will not be considered a change in method of accounting for purposes of section 446(e). However, an election by a taxpayer to establish a reserve for bad debts under section 166(c) shall be treated as a change in method of accounting. See also § 1.166-4, relating to reserve for bad debts, and § 1.166-10, relating to reserve for guaranteed debt obligations.

(c) *Bona fide debt required.* Only a bona fide debt qualifies for purposes of section 166. A bona fide debt is a debt which arises from a debtor-creditor relationship based upon a valid and enforceable obligation to pay a fixed or determinable sum of money. A debt arising out of the receivables of an accrual method taxpayer is deemed to be an enforceable obligation for purposes of the preceding sentence to the extent that the income such debt represents has been included in the return of income for the year for which the deduction as a bad debt is claimed or for a prior taxable year. For example, a debt arising out of gambling receivables that are unenforceable under state or local law, which an accrual method taxpayer includes in income under section 61, is an enforceable obligation for purposes of this paragraph. A gift or contribution to capital shall not be considered a debt for purposes of section 166. The fact that a bad debt is not due at the time of deduction shall not of itself prevent its allowance under section 166. For the disallowance of deductions for bad debts owed by a political party, see § 1.271-1.

(d) *Amount deductible* —(1) *General rule.* Except in the case of a deduction for a reasonable addition to a reserve for bad debts, the basis for determining the amount of deduction under section 166 in respect of a bad debt shall be the same as the adjusted basis prescribed by § 1.1011-1 for determining the loss from the sale or other disposition of property. To determine the allowable deduction in the case of obligations acquired before

March 1, 1913, see also paragraph (b) of § 1.1053-1.

(2) *Specific cases.* Subject to any provision of section 166 and the regulations thereunder which provides to the contrary, the following amounts are deductible as bad debts:

(i) *Notes or accounts receivable.*

(*a*) If, in computing taxable income, a taxpayer values his notes or accounts receivable at their fair market value when received, the amount deductible as a bad debt under section 166 in respect of such receivables shall be limited to such fair market value even though it is less than their face value.

(*b*) A purchaser of accounts receivable which become worthless during the taxable year shall be entitled under section 166 to a deduction which is based upon the price he paid for such receivables but not upon their face value.

(ii) *Bankruptcy claim.* Only the difference between the amount received in distribution of the assets of a bankrupt and the amount of the claim may be deducted under section 166 as a bad debt.

(iii) *Claim against decedent's estate.* The excess of the amount of the claim over the amount received by a creditor of a decedent in distribution of the assets of the decedent's estate may be considered a worthless debt under section 166.

(e) *Prior inclusion in income required.* Worthless debts arising from unpaid wages, salaries, fees, rents, and similar items of taxable income shall not be allowed as a deduction under section 166 unless the income such items represent has been included in the return of income for the year for which the deduction as a bad debt is claimed or for a prior taxable year.

(f) *Recovery of bad debts.* Any amount attributable to the recovery during the taxable year of a bad debt, or of a part of a bad debt, which was allowed as a deduction from gross income in a prior taxable year shall be included in gross income for the taxable year of recovery, except to the extent that the recovery is excluded from gross income under the provisions of § 1.111-1, relating to the recovery of certain items previously deducted or credited. This paragraph shall not apply, however, to a bad debt which was previously charged against a reserve by a taxpayer on the reserve method of treating bad debts.

(g) *Worthless securities.* (1) Section 166 and the regulations thereunder do not apply to a debt which is evidenced by a bond, debenture, note, or certificate, or other evidence of indebtedness, issued by a corporation, or by a government or political subdivision thereof, with interest coupons or in registered form. See section 166(e). For provisions allowing the deduction of a loss resulting from the worthlessness of such a debt, see § 1.165-5.

(2) The provisions of subparagraph (1) of this paragraph do not apply to any loss sustained by a bank and resulting from the worthlessness of a security described in section 165(g)(2)(C). See paragraph (a) of § 1.582-1. [Reg. § 1.166-1.]

☐ [*T.D.* 6403, 7-30-59. *Amended by T.D.* 6996, 1-17-69, *T.D.* 7902, 7-20-83 *and T.D.* 8071, 1-17-86.]

[Reg. § 1.166-2]

§ 1.166-2. **Evidence of worthlessness.**—(a) *General rule.* In determining whether a debt is worthless in whole or in part the district director will consider all pertinent evidence, including the value of the collateral, if any, securing the debt and the financial condition of the debtor.

(b) *Legal action not required.* Where the surrounding circumstances indicate that a debt is worthless and uncollectible and that legal action to enforce payment would in all probability not result in the satisfaction of execution on a judgment, a showing of these facts will be sufficient evidence of the worthlessness of the debt for purposes of the deduction under section 166.

(c) *Bankruptcy* —(1) *General rule.* Bankruptcy is generally an indication of the worthlessness of at least a part of an unsecured and unpreferred debt.

(2) *Year of deduction.* In bankruptcy cases a debt may become worthless before settlement in some instances; and in others, only when a settlement in bankruptcy has been reached. In either case, the mere fact that bankruptcy proceedings instituted against the debtor are terminated in a later year, thereby confirming the conclusion that the debt is worthless, shall not authorize the shifting of the deduction under section 166 to such later year.

(d) *Banks and other regulated corporations* — (1) *Worthlessness presumed in year of charge-off.* If a bank or other corporation which is subject to supervision by Federal authorities, or by State authorities maintaining substantially equivalent standards, charges off a debt in whole or in part, either—

(i) In obedience to the specific orders of such authorities, or

(ii) In accordance with established policies of such authorities, and, upon their first audit of the bank or other corporation subsequent to the charge-off, such authorities confirm in writing that the charge-off would have been subject to such specific orders if the audit had been made on the date of the charge-off,

then the debt shall, to the extent charged off during the taxable year, be conclusively presumed to have become worthless, or worthless only in part, as the case may be, during such taxable year. But no such debt shall be so conclusively presumed to be worthless, or worthless only in part, as the case may be, if the amount so charged off is not claimed as a deduction by the taxpayer at the time of filing the return for the taxable year in which the charge-off takes place.

(2) *Evidence of worthlessness in later taxable year.* If such a bank or other corporation does not claim a deduction for such a totally or partially worthless debt in its return for the taxable year in which the charge-off takes place, but claims the deduction for a later taxable year, then the charge-off in the prior taxable year shall be deemed to have been involuntary and the deduction under section 166 shall be allowed for the taxable year for which claimed, provided that the taxpayer produces sufficient evidence to show that—

(i) The debt became wholly worthless in the later taxable year, or became recoverable only in part subsequent to the taxable year of the involuntary charge-off, as the case may be; and,

(ii) To the extent that the deduction claimed in the later taxable year for a debt partially worthless was not involuntarily charged off in prior taxable years, it was charged off in the later taxable year.

(3) *Conformity election*—(i) *Eligibility for election.* In lieu of applying paragraphs (d)(1) and (2) of this section, a bank (as defined in paragraph (d)(4)(i) of this section) that is subject to supervision by Federal authorities, or by state authorities maintaining substantially equivalent standards, may elect under this paragraph (d)(3) to use a method of accounting that establishes a conclusive presumption of worthlessness for debts, provided that the bank meets the express determination requirement of paragraph (d)(3)(iii)(D) of this section for the taxable year of the election.

(ii) *Conclusive presumption*—(A) *In general.* If a bank satisfies the express determination requirement of paragraph (d)(3)(iii)(D) of this section and elects to use the method of accounting under this paragraph (d)(3)—

(*1*) Debts charged off, in whole or in part, for regulatory purposes during a taxable year are conclusively presumed to have become worthless, or worthless only in part, as the case may be, during that year, but only if the charge-off results from a specific order of the bank's

Reg. § 1.166-2(a)

supervisory authority or corresponds to the bank's classification of the debt, in whole or in part, as a loss asset, as described in paragraph (d)(3)(ii)(C) of this section; and

(2) A bad debt deduction for a debt that is subject to regulatory loss classification standards is allowed for a taxable year only to the extent that the debt is conclusively presumed to have become worthless under paragraph (d)(3)(ii)(A)(1) of this section during that year.

(B) *Charge-off should have been made in earlier year.* The conclusive presumption that a debt is worthless in the year that it is charged off for regulatory purposes applies even if the bank's supervisory authority determines in a subsequent year that the charge-off should have been made in an earlier year. A pattern of charge-offs in the wrong year, however, may result in revocation of the bank's election by the Commissioner pursuant to paragraph (d)(3)(iv)(D) of this section.

(C) *Loss asset defined.* A debt is classified as a loss asset by a bank if the bank assigns the debt to a class that corresponds to a loss asset classification under the standards set forth in the "Uniform Agreement on the Classification of Assets and Securities Held by Banks" (See Attachment to Comptroller of the Currency Banking Circular No. 127, Rev. 4-26-91, Comptroller of the Currency, Communications Department, Washington, DC 20219) or similar guidance issued by the Office of the Comptroller of the Currency, the Federal Deposit Insurance Corporation, the Board of Governors of the Federal Reserve, or the Farm Credit Administration; or for institutions under the supervision of the Office of Thrift Supervision, 12 CFR 563.160(b)(3).

(iii) *Election*—(A) *In general.* An election under this paragraph (d)(3) is to be made on a bank-by-bank basis and constitutes either the adoption of or a change in method of accounting, depending on the particular bank's facts. A change in method of accounting that results from the making of an election under this paragraph (d)(3) has the effects described in paragraph (d)(3)(iii)(B) of this section.

(B) *Effect of change in method of accounting.* A change in method of accounting resulting from an election under this paragraph (d)(3) does not require or permit an adjustment under section 481(a). Under this cut-off approach—

(1) There is no change in the § 1.1011-1 adjusted basis of the bank's existing debts (as determined under the bank's former method of accounting for bad debts) as a result of the change in method of accounting;

(2) With respect to debts that are subject to regulatory loss classification standards and are held by the bank at the beginning of the year of change (to the extent they have not been charged off for regulatory purposes), and with respect to debts subject to regulatory loss classification standards that are originated or acquired subsequent to the beginning of the year of change, bad debt deductions in the year of change and thereafter are determined under the method of accounting for bad debts prescribed by this paragraph (d)(3);

(3) With respect to debts that are not subject to regulatory loss classification standards or that have been totally charged off prior to the year of change, bad debt deductions are determined under the general rules of section 166; and

(4) If there was any partial charge-off of a debt in a pre-change year, any portion of which was not claimed as a deduction, the deduction reflecting that partial charge-off must be taken in the first year in which there is any further charge-off of the debt for regulatory purposes.

(C) *Procedures*—(1) *In general.* A new bank adopts the method of accounting under this paragraph (d)(3) for any taxable year ending on or after December 31, 1991 (and for all subsequent taxable years) when it adopts its overall method of accounting for bad debts, by attaching a statement to this effect to its income tax return for that year. Any other bank makes an election for any taxable year ending on or after December 31, 1991 (and for all subsequent taxable years) by filing a completed Form 3115 (Application for Change in Accounting Method) in accordance with the rules of paragraph (d)(3)(iii)(C)(2) or (3) of this section. The statement or Form 3115 must include the name, address, and taxpayer identification number of the electing bank and contain a declaration that the express determination requirement of paragraph (d)(3)(iii)(D) of this section is satisfied for the taxable year of the election. When a Form 3115 is used, the declaration must be made in the space provided on the form for "Other changes in method of accounting." The words "ELECTION UNDER § 1.166-2(d)(3)" must be typed or legibly printed at the top of the statement or page 1 of the Form 3115.

(2) *First election.* The first time a bank makes this election, the statement or Form 3115 must be attached to the bank's timely filed return (taking into account extensions of time to file) for the first taxable year covered by the election. The consent of the Commissioner to make a change in method of accounting under this

Reg. § 1.166-2(d)(3)

paragraph (d)(3) is granted, pursuant to section 446(e), to any bank that makes the election in accordance with this paragraph (d)(3)(iii)(C), provided the bank has not made a prior election under this paragraph (d)(3).

(3) *Subsequent elections.* The advance consent of the Commissioner is required to make any election under this paragraph (d)(3) after a previous election has been revoked pursuant to paragraph (d)(3)(iv) of this section. This consent must be requested under the procedures, terms, and conditions prescribed under the authority of section 446(e) and § 1.446-1(e) for requesting a change in method of accounting.

(D) *Express determination requirement.* In connection with its most recent examination involving the bank's loan review process, the bank's supervisory authority must have made an express determination (in accordance with any applicable administrative procedure prescribed hereunder) that the bank maintains and applies loan loss classification standards that are consistent with the regulatory standards of that supervisory authority. For purposes of this paragraph (d)(3)(iii)(D), the supervisory authority of a bank is the *appropriate Federal banking agency* for the bank, as that term is defined in 12 U.S.C. 1813(q), or, in the case of an institution in the Farm Credit System, the Farm Credit Administration.

(E) *Transition period election.* For taxable years ending before completion of the first examination of the bank by its supervisory authority (as defined in paragraph (d)(3)(iii)(D) of this section) that is after October 1, 1992, and that involves the bank's loan review process, the statement or Form 3115 filed by the bank must include a declaration that the bank maintains and applies loan loss classification standards that are consistent with the regulatory standards of that supervisory authority. A bank that makes this declaration is deemed to satisfy the express determination requirement of paragraph (d)(3)(iii)(D) of this section for those years, even though an express determination has not yet been made.

(iv) *Revocation of Election*—(A) *In general.* Revocation of an election under this paragraph (d)(3) constitutes a change in method of accounting that has the effects described in paragraph (d)(3)(iv)(B) of this section. If an election under this paragraph (d)(3) has been revoked, a bank may make a subsequent election only under the provisions of paragraph (d)(3)(iii)(C)(3) of this section.

(B) *Effect of change in method of accounting.* A change in method of accounting resulting from revocation of an election under this

paragraph (d)(3) does not require or permit an adjustment under section 481(a). Under this cutoff approach—

(1) There is no change in the § 1.1011-1 adjusted basis of the bank's existing debts (as determined under this paragraph (d)(3) method or any other former method of accounting used by the bank with respect to its bad debts) as a result of the change in method of accounting; and

(2) Bad debt deductions in the year of change and thereafter with respect to all debts held by the bank, whether in existence at the beginning of the year of change or subsequently originated or acquired, are determined under the new method of accounting.

(C) *Automatic revocation*—(1) *In general.* A bank's election under this paragraph (d)(3) is revoked automatically if, in connection with any examination involving the bank's loan review process by the bank's supervisory authority as defined in paragraph (d)(3)(iii)(D) of this section, the bank does not obtain the express determination required by that paragraph.

(2) *Year of revocation.* If a bank makes the conformity election under the transition rules of paragraph (d)(3)(iii)(E) of this section and does not obtain the express determination in connection with the first examination involving the bank's loan review process that is after October 1, 1992, the election is revoked as of the beginning of the taxable year of the election or, if later, the earliest taxable year for which tax may be assessed. In other cases in which a bank does not obtain an express determination in connection with an examination of its loan review process, the election is revoked as of the beginning of the taxable year that includes the date as of which the supervisory authority conducts the examination even if the examination is completed in the following taxable year.

(3) *Consent granted.* Under the Commissioner's authority in section 446(e) and § 1.446-1(e), the bank is directed to and is granted consent to change from this paragraph (d)(3) method as of the year of revocation (year of change) prescribed by paragraph (d)(3)(iv)(C)(2) of this section.

(4) *Requirements.* A bank changing its method of accounting under the automatic revocation rules of this paragraph (d)(3)(iv)(C) must attach a completed Form 3115 to its income tax return for the year of revocation prescribed by paragraph (d)(3)(iv)(C)(2) of this section. The words "REVOCATION OF § 1.166-2(d)(3) ELECTION" must be typed or legibly printed at the top of page 1 of the Form 3115. If the year of

Reg. § 1.166-2(d)(3)

revocation is a year for which the bank has already filed its income tax return, the bank must file an amended return for that year reflecting its change in method of accounting and must attach the completed Form 3115 to that amended return. The bank also must file amended returns reflecting the new method of accounting for all subsequent taxable years for which returns have been filed and tax may be assessed.

(D) *Revocation by Commissioner.* An election under this paragraph (d)(3) may be revoked by the Commissioner as of the beginning of any taxable year for which a bank fails to follow the method of accounting prescribed by this paragraph. In addition, the Commissioner may revoke an election as of the beginning of any taxable year for which the Commissioner determines that a bank has taken charge-offs and deductions that, under all facts and circumstances existing at the time, were substantially in excess of those warranted by the exercise of reasonable business judgment in applying the regulatory standards of the bank's supervisory authority as defined in paragraph (d)(3)(iii)(D) of this section.

(E) *Voluntary revocation.* A bank may apply for revocation of its election made under this paragraph (d)(3) by timely filing a completed Form 3115 for the appropriate year and obtaining the consent of the Commissioner in accordance with section 446(e) and §1.446-1(e) (including any applicable administrative procedures prescribed thereunder). The words "REVOCATION OF §1.166-2(d)(3) ELECTION" must be typed or legibly printed at the top of page 1 of the Form 3115. If any bank has had its election automatically revoked pursuant to paragraph (d)(3)(iv)(C) of this section and has not changed its method of accounting in accordance with the requirements of that paragraph, the Commissioner will require that any voluntary change in method of accounting under this paragraph (d)(3)(iv)(E) be implemented retroactively pursuant to the same amended return terms and conditions as are prescribed by paragraph (d)(3)(iv)(C) of this section.

(4) *Definitions.* For purposes of this paragraph (d)—

(i) *Bank.* The term "bank" has the meaning assigned to it by section 581. The term "bank" also includes any corporation that would be a bank within the meaning of section 581 except for the fact that it is a foreign corporation, but this paragraph (d) applies only with respect to loans the interest on which is effectively connected with the conduct of a banking business within the United States. In addition, the term "bank" includes a Farm Credit System institution

that is subject to supervision by the Farm Credit Administration.

(ii) *Charge-off.* For banks regulated by the Office of Thrift Supervision, the term "charge-off" includes the establishment of specific allowances for loan losses in the amount of 100 percent of the portion of the debt classified as loss. [Reg. § 1.166-2.]

□ [*T.D.* 6403, 7-30-59. *Amended by T.D.* 7254, 1-24-73; *T.D.* 8396, 2-21-92; *T.D.* 8441, 10-1-92 and *T.D.* 8492, 10-15-93.]

[Reg. § 1.166-3]

§ 1.166-3. **Partial or total worthlessness.**— (a) *Partial worthlessness*—(1) *Applicable to specific debts only.* A deduction under section 166 (a)(2) on account of partially worthless debts shall be allowed with respect to specific debts only.

(2) *Charge-off required.* (i) If, from all the surrounding and attending circumstances, the district director is satisfied that a debt is partially worthless, the amount which has become worthless shall be allowed as a deduction under section 166(a)(2) but only to the extent charged off during the taxable year.

(ii) If a taxpayer claims a deduction for a part of a debt for the taxable year within which that part of the debt is charged off and the deduction is disallowed for that taxable year, then, in a case where the debt becomes partially worthless after the close of that taxable year, a deduction under section 166(a)(2) shall be allowed for a subsequent taxable year but not in excess of the amount charged off in the prior taxable year plus any amount charged off in the subsequent taxable year. In such instance, the charge-off in the prior taxable year shall, if consistently maintained as such, be sufficient to that extent to meet the charge-off requirement of section 166(a)(2) with respect to the subsequent taxable year.

(iii) Before a taxpayer may deduct a debt in part, he must be able to demonstrate to the satisfaction of the district director the amount thereof which is worthless and the part thereof which has been charged off.

(3) *Significantly modified debt*—(i) *Deemed charge-off.* If a significant modification of a debt instrument (within the meaning of §1.1001-3) during a taxable year results in the recognition of gain by a taxpayer under §1.1001-1(a), and if the requirements of paragraph (a)(3)(ii) of this section are met, there is a deemed charge-off of the debt during that taxable year in the amount specified in paragraph (a)(3)(iii) of this section.

(ii) *Requirements for deemed charge-off.* A debt is deemed to have been charged off only if—

Reg. § 1.166-3(a)(3)

(A) The taxpayer (or, in the case of a debt that constitutes transferred basis property within the meaning of section 7701(a)(43), a transferor taxpayer) has claimed a deduction for partial worthlessness of the debt in any prior taxable year; and

(B) Each prior charge-off and deduction for partial worthlessness satisfied the requirements of paragraphs (a)(1) and (2) of this section.

(iii) *Amount of deemed charge-off.* The amount of the deemed charge-off, if any, is the amount by which the tax basis of the debt exceeds the greater of the fair market value of the debt or the amount of the debt recorded on the taxpayer's books and records reduced as appropriate for a specific allowance for loan losses. The amount of the deemed charge-off, however, may not exceed the amount of recognized gain described in paragraph (a)(3)(i) of this section.

(iv) *Effective date.* This paragraph (a)(3) applies to significant modifications of debt instruments occurring on or after September 23, 1996.

(b) *Total worthlessness.* If a debt becomes wholly worthless during the taxable year, the amount thereof which has not been allowed as a deduction from gross income for any prior taxable year shall be allowed as a deduction for the current taxable year. [Reg. § 1.166-3.]

☐ [*T.D. 6403, 7-30-59. Amended by T.D. 8763, 1-28-98.*]

[Reg. § 1.166-4]

§ 1.166-4. **Reserve for bad debts.**—(a) *Allowance of deduction.* A taxpayer who has established the reserve method of treating bad debts and has maintained proper reserve accounts for bad debts or who, in accordance with paragraph (b) of § 1.166-1, adopts the reserve method of treating bad debts may deduct from gross income a reasonable addition to a reserve for bad debts in lieu of deducting specific bad debt items. This paragraph applies both to bad debts owed to the taxpayer and to bad debts arising out of section 166(f)(1)(A) guaranteed debt obligations. If a reserve is maintained for bad debts arising out of section 166(f)(1)(A) guaranteed debt obligations, then a separate reserve must also be maintained for all other debt obligations of the taxpayer in the same trade or business, if any. A taxpayer may not maintain a reserve for bad debts arising out of section 166(f)(1)(A) guaranteed debt obligations if with respect to direct debt obligations in the same trade or business the taxpayer takes deductions when the debts become worthless in whole or in part rather than maintaining a reserve for such obligations. See § 1.166-10 for rules

concerning section 166(f)(1)(A) guaranteed debt obligations.

(b) *Reasonableness of addition to reserve*—(1) *Relevant factors.* What constitutes a reasonable addition to a reserve for bad debts shall be determined in the light of the facts existing at the close of the taxable year of the proposed addition. The reasonableness of the addition will vary as between classes of business and with conditions of business prosperity. It will depend primarily upon the total amount of debts outstanding as of the close of the taxable year, including those arising currently as well as those arising in prior taxable years, and the total amount of the existing reserve.

(2) *Correction of errors in prior estimates.* In the event that subsequent realizations upon outstanding debts prove to be more or less than estimated at the time of the creation of the existing reserve, the amount of the excess or inadequacy in the existing reserve shall be reflected in the determination of the reasonable addition necessary in the current taxable year.

(c) *Statement required.* A taxpayer using the reserve method shall file with his return a statement showing—

(1) The volume of his charge sales or other business transactions for the taxable year and the percentage of the reserve to such amount;

(2) The total amount of notes and accounts receivable at the beginning and close of the taxable year;

(3) The amount of the debts which have become wholly or partially worthless and have been charged against the reserve account; and

(4) The computation of the addition to the reserve for bad debts.

(d) *Special rules applicable to financial institutions*—(1) *Banks.* For special rules for the addition to the bad debt reserves of certain banks, see §§ 1.585-1 through 1.585-3.

(2) For special rules for the addition to the bad debt reserves of small business investment companies and business development corporations, see §§ 1.586-1 and 1.586-2.

(3) For special rules for the addition to the bad debts reserves of certain mutual savings banks, domestic building and loan associations, and cooperative banks, see §§ 1.593-1 through 1.593-11. [Reg. § 1.166-4.]

☐ [*T.D. 6403, 7-30-59. Amended by T.D. 6728, 5-4-64; T.D. 7444, 12-6-76 and T.D. 8071, 1-17-86.*]

Reg. § 1.166-4(a)

[Reg. § 1.166-5]

§ 1.166-5. Nonbusiness debts.—(a) *Allowance of deduction as capital loss.* (1) The loss resulting from any nonbusiness debt's becoming partially or wholly worthless within the taxable year shall not be allowed as a deduction under either section 166(a) or section 166(c) in determining the taxable income of a taxpayer other than a corporation. See section 166(d)(1)(A).

(2) If, in the case of a taxpayer other than a corporation, a non-business debt becomes wholly worthless within the taxable year, the loss resulting therefrom shall be treated as a loss from the sale or exchange, during the taxable year, of a capital asset held for not more than 1 year (6 months for taxable years beginning before 1977; 9 months for taxable years beginning in 1977). Such a loss is subject to the limitations provided in section 1211, relating to the limitation on capital losses, and section 1212, relating to the capital loss carryover, and in the regulations under those sections. A loss on a nonbusiness debt shall be treated as sustained only if and when the debt has become totally worthless, and no deduction shall be allowed for a nonbusiness debt which is recoverable in part during the taxable year.

(b) *Nonbusiness debt defined.* For purposes of section 166 and this section. a nonbusiness debt is any debt other than —

(1) A debt which is created, or acquired, in the course of a trade or business of the taxpayer, determined without regard to the relationship of the debt to a trade or business of the taxpayer at the time when the debt becomes worthless; or

(2) A debt the loss from the worthlessness of which is incurred in the taxpayer's trade or business.

The question whether a debt is a nonbusiness debt is a question of fact in each particular case. The determination of whether the loss on a debt's becoming worthless has been incurred in a trade or business of the taxpayer shall, for this pu:pose, be made in substantially the same manner for determining whether a loss has been incurred in a trade or business for purposes of section 165(c)(1). For purposes of subparagraph (2) of this paragraph, the character of the debt is to be determined by the relation which the loss resulting from the debt's becoming worthless bears to the trade or business of the taxpayer. If that relation is a proximate one in the conduct of the trade or business in which the taxpayer is engaged at the time the debt becomes worthless, the debt comes within the exception provided by that subparagraph. The use to which the borrowed funds are put by the debtor is of no consequence in making a determination under this paragraph. For pur-

poses of section 166 and this section, a nonbusiness debt does not include a debt described in section 165(g)(2)(C). See § 1.165-5, relating to losses on worthless securities.

(c) *Guaranty of obligations.* For provisions treating a loss sustained by a guarantor of obligations as a loss resulting from the worthlessness of a debt, see § § 1.166-8 and 1.166-9.

(d) *Examples.* The application of this section may be illustrated by the following examples involving a case where A, an individual who is engaged in the grocery business and who makes his return on the basis of the calendar year, extends credit to B in 1955 on an open account:

Example (1). In 1956 A sells the business but retains the claim against B. The claim becomes worthless in A's hands in 1957. A's loss is not controlled by the nonbusiness debt provisions, since the original consideration has been advanced by A in his trade or business.

Example (2). In 1956 A sells the business to C but sells the claim against B to the taxpayer, D. The claim becomes worthless in D's hands in 1957. During 1956 and 1957, D is not engaged in any trade or business. D's loss is controlled by the nonbusiness debt provisions even though the original consideratior. has been advanced by A in his trade or business, since the debt has not been created or acquired in connection with a trade or business of D and since in 1957 D is not engaged in a trade or business incident to the conduct of which a loss from the worthlessness of such claims is a proximate result.

Example (3). In 1956 A dies, leaving the business, including the accounts receivable, to his son, C, the taxpayer. The claim against B becomes worthless in C's hands in 1957. C's loss is not controlled by the nonbusiness debt provisions. While C does not advance any consideration for the claim, or create or acquire it in connection with his trade or business, the loss is sustained as a proximate incident to the conduct of the trade or business in which he is engaged at the time the debt becomes worthless.

Example (4). In 1956 A dies, leaving the business to his son, C, but leaving the claim against B to his son, D, the taxpayer. The claim against B becomes worthless in D's hands in 1957. During 1956 and 1957, D is not engaged in any trade or business. D's loss is controlled by the nonbusiness debt provisions even though the original consideration has been advanced by A in his trade or business, since the debt has not been created or acquired in connection with a trade or business of D and since in 1957 D is not engaged in a trade or business incident to the conduct of which a loss from the worthlessness of such claims is a proximate result.

Example (5). In 1956 A dies, and, while his executor, C, is carrying on the business, the claim against B becomes worthless in 1957. The loss sustained by A's estate is not controlled by the nonbusiness debt provisions. While C does not advance any consideration for the claim on behalf of the estate, or create or acquire it in connection with a trade or business in which the estate is engaged, the loss is sustained as a proximate incident to the conduct of the trade or business in which the estate is engaged at the time the debt becomes worthless.

Example (6). In 1956, A, in liquidating the business, attempts to collect the claim against B but finds that it has become worthless. A's loss is not controlled by the nonbusiness debt provisions, since the original consideration has been advanced by A in his trade or business and since a loss incurred in liquidating a trade or business is a proximate incident to the conduct thereof. [Reg. § 1.166-5.]

☐ [*T.D. 6403, 7-23-59. Amended by T.D. 7657, 11-28-79 and T.D. 7728, 10-31-80.*]

[Reg. § 1.166-6]

§ 1.166-6. Sale of mortgaged or pledged property.—(a) *Deficiency deductible as bad debts*—(1) *Principal amount.* If mortgaged or pledged property is lawfully sold (whether to the creditor or another purchaser) for less than the amount of the debt, and the portion of the indebtedness remaining unsatisfied after the sale is wholly or partially uncollectible, the mortgagee or pledgee may deduct such amount under section 166(a) (to the extent that it constitutes capital or represents an item the income from which has been returned by him) as a bad debt for the taxable year in which it becomes wholly worthless or is charged off as partially worthless. See § 1.166-3.

(2) *Accrued interest.* Accrued interest may be included as part of the deduction allowable under this paragraph, but only if it has previously been returned as income.

(b) *Realization of gain or loss*—(1) *Determination of amount.* If, in the case of a sale described in paragraph (a) of this section, the creditor buys in the mortgaged or pledged property, loss or gain is also realized, measured by the difference between the amount of those obligations of the debtor which are applied to the purchase or bid price of the property (to the extent that such obligations constitute capital or represent an item the income from which has been returned by the

creditor) and the fair market value of the property.

(2) *Fair market value defined.* The fair market value of the property for this purpose shall, in the absence of clear and convincing proof to the contrary, be presumed to be the amount for which it is bid in by the taxpayer.

(c) *Basis of property purchased.* If the creditor subsequently sells the property so acquired, the basis for determining gain or loss upon the subsequent sale is the fair market value of the property at the date of its acquisition by the creditor.

(d) *Special rules applicable to certain banking organizations.* For special rules relating to the treatment of mortgaged or pledged property by certain mutual savings banks, domestic building and loan associations, and cooperative banks, see section 595 and the regulations thereunder.

(e) *Special rules applicable to certain reacquisitions of real property.* Notwithstanding this section, special rules apply for taxable years beginning after September 2, 1964 (and for certain taxable years beginning after December 31, 1957), to the gain or loss on certain reacquisitions of real property, to indebtedness remaining unsatisfied as a result of such reacquisitions, and to the basis of the reacquired real property. See §§ 1.1038 through 1.1038-3. [Reg. § 1.166-6.]

☐ [*T.D. 6403, 7-30-59. Amended by T.D. 6814, 4-6-65 and T.D. 6916, 4-12-67.*]

[Reg. § 1.166-7]

§ 1.166-7. Worthless bonds issued by an individual.—(a) *Allowance of deduction.* A bond or other similar obligation issued by an individual, if it becomes worthless in whole or in part, is subject to the bad debt provisions of section 166. The loss from the worthlessness of any such bond or obligation is deductible in accordance with section 166(a), unless such bond or obligation is a nonbusiness debt as defined in section 166(d)(2). If the bond or obligation is a nonbusiness debt, it is subject to section 166(d) and § 1.166-5.

(b) *Decline in market value.* A taxpayer possessing debts evidenced by bonds or other similar obligations issued by an individual shall not be allowed any deduction under section 166 on account of mere market fluctuation in the value of such obligations.

(c) *Worthless bonds issued by corporation.* For provisions allowing the deduction under section 165(a) of the loss sustained upon the worthlessness of any bond or similar obligation issued by a corporation or a government, see § 1.165-5.

(d) *Application to inventories.* This section does not apply to any loss upon the worthlessness of any bond or similar obligation reflected in inventories required to be taken by a dealer in securities under section 471. See § 1.471-5. [Reg. § 1.166-7.]

☐ [T.D. 6403, 7-30-59.]

[Reg. § 1.166-8]

§ 1.166-8. Losses of guarantors, endorsers, and indemnitors.—(a) *Noncorporate obligations*—(1)*Deductible as bad debt.* A payment during the taxable year by a taxpayer other than a corporation in discharge of part or all of his obligation as a guarantor, endorser, or indemnitor of an obligation issued by a person other than a corporation shall, for purposes of section 166 and the regulations thereunder, be treated as a debt's becoming worthless within the taxable year, if—

(i) The proceeds of the obligation so issued have been used in the trade or business of the borrower, and

(ii) The borrower's obligation to the person to whom the taxpayer's payment is made is worthless at the time of payment except for the existence of the guaranty, endorsement, or indemnity, whether or not such obligation has in fact become worthless within the taxable year in which payment is made.

(2) *Nonbusiness debt rule not applicable.* If a payment is treated as a loss in accordance with the provisions of subparagraph (1) of this paragraph, section 166(d), relating to the special rule for losses sustained on the worthlessness of a nonbusiness debt, shall not apply. Accordingly, in each instance the loss shall be deducted under section 166(a)(1) as a wholly worthless debt even though there has been a discharge of only a part of the taxpayer's obligation. Thus, if the taxpayer makes a payment during the taxable year in discharge of only part of his obligation as a guarantor, endorser, or indemnitor, he may treat such payment under section 166(a)(1) as a debt's becoming wholly worthless within the taxable year, provided that he can establish that such part of the borrower's obligation to the person to whom the taxpayer's payment is made is worthless at the time of payment and the conditions of subparagraph (1) of this paragraph have otherwise been satisfied.

(3) *Other applicable provisions.* Other provisions of the internal revenue laws relating to bad debts, such as section 111, relating to the recovery of bad debts, shall be deemed to apply to any payment which, under the provisions of this paragraph, is treated as a bad debt. If the requirements of section 166(f) are not met, any loss sustained by a guarantor, endorser, or indemnitor upon the worthlessness of the debtor's obligation

shall be treated under the provisions of law applicable thereto. See, for example, paragraph (b) of this section.

(b) *Corporate obligations.* The loss sustained during the taxable year by a taxpayer other than a corporation in discharge of all of his obligation as a guarantor of an obligation issued by a corporation shall be treated, in accordance with section 166(d) and the regulations thereunder, as a loss sustained on the worthlessness of a nonbusiness debt if the debt created in the guarantor's favor as a result of the payment does not come within the exceptions prescribed by section 166(d)(2)(A) or (B). See paragraph (a)(2) of § 1.166-5.

(c) *Examples.* The application of this section may be illustrated by the following examples:

Example (1). During 1955, A, an individual who makes his return on the basis of the calendar year, guarantees payment of an obligation of B, an individual, to the X Bank, the proceeds of the obligation being used in B's business. B defaults on his obligation in 1956. A makes payment to the X Bank during 1957 in discharge of his entire obligation as a guarantor, the obligation of B to the X Bank being wholly worthless. For his taxable year 1957, A is entitled to a deduction under section 166(a)(1) as a result of his payment during that year.

Example (2). During 1955, A, an individual who makes his return on the basis of the calendar year, guarantees payment of an obligation of B, an individual, to the X Bank, the proceeds of the obligation being used in B's business. In 1956, B pays a part of his obligation to the X Bank but defaults on the remaining part. In 1957, A makes payment to the X Bank, in discharge of part of his obligation as a guarantor, of the remaining unpaid part of B's obligation to the bank, such part of B's obligation then being worthless. For his taxable year 1957, A is entitled to a deduction under section 166(a)(1) as a result of his payment of the remaining unpaid part of B's obligation.

Example (3). During 1955, A, an individual who makes his return on the basis of the calendar year, guarantees payment of an obligation of B, an individual, to the X Bank, the proceeds of the obligation being used for B's personal use. B defaults on his obligation in 1956. A makes payment to the X Bank during 1957 in discharge of his entire obligation as a guarantor, the obligation of B to X Bank being wholly worthless. A may not apply the benefit of section 166(f) to his loss, since the proceeds of B's obligation have not been used in B's trade or business.

Example (4). During 1955, A, an individual who makes his return on the basis of the calendar year, guarantees payment of an obligation of Y

Corporation to the X Bank, the proceeds of the obligation being used in Y Corporation's business. Y Corporation defaults on its obligation in 1956. A makes payment to the X Bank during 1957 in discharge of his entire obligation as a guarantor, the obligation of Y Corporation to the X Bank being wholly worthless. At no time during 1955 or 1957 is A engaged in a trade or business. For his taxable year 1957, A is entitled to deduct a capital loss in accordance with the provisions of section 166(d) and paragraph (a)(2) of § 1.166-5. He may not apply the benefit of section 166(f) to his loss, since his payment is in discharge of an obligation issued by a corporation.

(d) *Effective date.* This section applies only to losses, regardless of the taxable year in which incurred, on agreements made before January 1, 1976. [Reg. § 1.166-8.]

□ [*T.D.* 6403, 7-30-59. *Amended by T.D.* 7657, 11-28-79.]

[Reg. § 1.166-9]

§ 1.166-9. Losses of guarantors, endorsers, and indemnitors incurred, on agreements made after December 31, 1975, in taxable years beginning after such date.—(a) *Payment treated as worthless business debt.* This paragraph applies to taxpayers who, after December 31, 1975, enter into an agreement in the course of their trade or business to act as (or in a manner essentially equivalent to) a guarantor, endorser, or indemnitor of (or other secondary obligor upon) a debt obligation. Subject to the provisions of paragraphs (c), (d), and (e) of this section, a payment of principal or interest made during a taxable year beginning after December 31, 1975, by the taxpayer in discharge of part or all of the taxpayer's obligation as a guarantor, endorser, or indemnitor is treated as a business debt becoming worthless in the taxable year in which the payment is made or in the taxable year described in paragraph (e)(2) of this section. Neither section 163 (relating to interest) nor section 165 (relating to losses) shall apply with respect to such a payment.

(b) *Payment treated as worthless nonbusiness debt.* This paragraph applies to taxpayers (other than corporations) who, after December 31, 1975, enter into a transaction for profit, but not in the course of their trade or business, to act as (or in a manner essentially equivalent to) a guarantor, endorser, or indemnitor of (or other secondary obligor upon) a debt obligation. Subject to the provisions of paragraphs (c), (d), and (e) of this section, a payment of principal or interest made during a taxable year beginning after December 31, 1975, by the taxpayer in discharge of part or all of the taxpayer's obligation as a guarantor,

endorser, or indemnitor is treated as a worthless nonbusiness debt in the taxable year in which the payment is made or in the taxable year described in paragraph (e)(2) of this section. Neither section 163 nor section 165 shall apply with respect to such a payment.

(c) *Obligations issued by corporations.* No treatment as a worthless debt is allowed with respect to a payment made by the taxpayer in discharge of part or all of the taxpayer's obligation as a guarantor, endorser, or indemnitor of an obligation issued by a corporation if, on the basis of the facts and circumstances at the time the obligation was entered into, the payment constitutes a contribution to capital by a shareholder. The rule of this paragraph (c) applies to payments whenever made (see paragraph (f) of this section).

(d) *Certain payments treated as worthless debts.* A payment in discharge of part or all of taxpayer's agreement to act as guarantor, endorser, or indemnitor of an obligation is to be treated as a worthless debt only if—

(1) The agreement was entered into in the course of the taxpayer's trade or business or a transaction for profit;

(2) There was an enforceable legal duty upon the taxpayer to make the payment (except that legal action need not have been brought against the taxpayer); and

(3) The agreement was entered into before the obligation became worthless (or partially worthless in the case of an agreement entered into in the course of the taxpayer's trade or business). See §§ 1.166-2 and 1.166-3 for rules on worthless and partially worthless debts. For purposes of this paragraph (d)(3), an agreement is considered as entered into before the obligation became worthless (or partially worthless) if there was a reasonable expectation on the part of the taxpayer at the time the agreement was entered into that the taxpayer would not be called upon to pay the debt (subject to such agreement) without full reimbursement from the issuer of the obligation.

(e) *Special rules —(1) Reasonable consideration required.* Treatment as a worthless debt of a payment made by a taxpayer in discharge of part or all of the taxpayer's agreement to act as a guarantor, endorser, or indemnitor of an obligation is allowed only if the taxpayer demonstrates that reasonable consideration was received for entering into the agreement. For purposes of this paragraph (e)(1), reasonable consideration is not limited to direct consideration in the form of cash or property. Thus, where a taxpayer can demonstrate that the agreement was given without direct consideration in the form of cash or property

Reg. § 1.166-9(a)

but in accordance with normal business practice or for a good faith business purpose, worthless debt treatment is allowed with respect to a payment in discharge of part or all of the agreement if the conditions of this section are met. However, consideration received from a taxpayer's spouse or any individual listed in section 152(a) must be direct consideration in the form of cash or property.

(2) *Right of subrogation.* With respect to a payment made by a taxpayer in discharge of part or all of the taxpayer's agreement to act as a guarantor, endorser, or indemnitor where the agreement provides for a right of subrogation or other similar right against the issuer, treatment as a worthless debt is not allowed until the taxable year in which the right of subrogation or other similar right becomes totally worthless (or partially worthless in the case of an agreement which arose in the course of the taxpayer's trade or business).

(3) *Other applicable provisions.* Unless inconsistent with this section, other Internal Revenue laws concerning worthless debts, such as section 111 relating to the recovery of bad debts, apply to any payment which, under the provisions of this section, is treated as giving rise to a worthless debt.

(4) *Taxpayer defined.* For purposes of this section, except as otherwise provided, the term "taxpayer" means any taxpayer and includes individuals, corporations, partnerships, trusts and estates.

(f) *Effective date.* This section applies to losses incurred on agreements made after December 31, 1975, in taxable years beginning after such date. However, paragraph (c) of this section also applies to payments, regardless of the taxable year in which made, under agreements made before January 1, 1976. [Reg. § 1.166-9.]

☐ [*T.D. 7657, 11-28-79. Amended by T.D. 7747, 12-29-80 and T.D. 7920, 11-2-83.*]

[Reg. § 1.166-10]

§ 1.166-10. Reserve for guaranteed debt obligations.—(a) *Definitions.* The following provisions apply for purposes of this section and section 166(f):

(1) *Dealer in property.* A dealer in property is a person who regularly sells property in the ordinary course of the person's trade or business.

(2) *Guaranteed debt obligation.* A guaranteed debt obligation is a legal duty of one person as a guarantor, endorser or indemnitor of a second person to pay a third person. It does not include duties based solely on moral or good public relations considerations that are not legally binding.

A guaranteed debt obligation typically arises where a seller receives in payment for property or services the debt obligation of a purchaser and sells that obligation to a third party with recourse. However, a guaranteed debt obligation also may arise out of a sale in respect of which there is no direct debtor-creditor relationship between the debtor purchaser and the seller. For example, it arises where a purchaser borrows money from a third party to make payment to the seller and the seller guarantees the payment of the purchaser's debt. Generally, debt obligations which are sold without recourse do not result in any obligation of the seller as a guarantor, endorser, or indemnitor. However, there are certain without-recourse transactions which may give rise to a seller's liability as a guarantor or indemnitor. For example, such a liability may arise where a holder of a debt obligation holds money or other property of a seller which the holder may apply, without seeking permission of the seller, against any uncollectible debt obligations transferred to the holder by the seller without recourse, or where the seller is under a legal obligation to reacquire the real or tangible personal property from the holder of the debt obligation who repossessed property in satisfaction of the debt obligations.

(3) *Real or tangible personal property.* Real or tangible personal property generally does not include other forms of property, such as securities. However, if the sale of other property is related to the sale of actual real or tangible personal property, the other property will be considered to be real or tangible personal property. In order for the sale of other property to be related, it must be—

(i) Incidental to the sale of the actual real or tangible personal property; and

(ii) Made under an agreement, entered into at the same time as the sale of actual real or tangible personal property, between the dealer in that property and the customer with respect to that property.

The other property may be charged for as a part of, or in addition to, the sales price of the actual real or tangible personal property. If the value of the other property is not greater than 20 percent of the total sales price, including the value of all related services other than financing services, the sale of the other property is related to the sale of actual real or tangible personal property.

(4) *Related services.* In the case of a sale of both property and services a determination must be made as to whether the services are related to the property. Related services include only those services which are—

(i) Incidental to the sale of the real or tangible personal property; and

Reg. § 1.166-10(a)(4)

(ii) To be performed under an agreement, entered into at the same time as the sale of the property, between the dealer in property and the customer with respect to the property.

Delivery, financing, installation, maintenance, repair, or instructional services generally qualify as related services. The services may be charged for as a part of, or in addition to, the sales price of the property. Where the value of all services other than financing services is not greater than 20 percent of the total of the sales price of the property, including the value of all the services other than financing services, all of the services are considered to be incidental to the sale of the property. Where the value of the services is greater than 20 percent, the determination as to whether a service is a related service in a particular case is to be made on the basis of all relevant facts and circumstances.

(5) *Examples.* The following examples apply to paragraph (a)(4) of this section:

Example (1). A, a dealer in television sets, sells a television set to B, his customer. If at the time of the sale A, for a separate charge which is added to the sales price of the set and which is not greater than 20 percent of the total sales price, provides a 3-year service contract on only that television set, the service contract is a related service agreement. However, if A does not sell the service contract to B contemporaneously with the sale of the television set, as would be the case if the service agreement were entered into after the sale of the set were completed, or if the service contract includes services for a television set in addition to the one then sold by A to B, the service contract is not an agreement for a related service.

Example (2). C, an automobile dealer, at the time of the sale by C of an automobile to D, agrees to make available to D driving instructions furnished by the M driving school, the cost of which is included in the sale price of the automobile and is not greater than 20 percent of the total sales price. C also agrees to pay M for the driving instructions furnished to D. Since C's agreement with D to make available driving instructions is incidental to the sale of the automobile, is made contemporaneously with the sale, and is charged for as part of the sales price of the automobile, it is an agreement for a related service. In contrast, however, because M's agreement with C is not an agreement between the dealer in property and the customer, M's agreement with C to provide driving instructions to C's customers is not an agreement for a related service.

(b) *Incorporation by reference of section 166(c) rules.* A reserve for section 166(f)(1)(A) guaran-

teed debt obligations must be established and maintained under the rules applicable to the reserve for bad debts under section 166(c) (with the exception of the statement requirement under § 1.166-4(c)). For example, the rules in § 1.166-4(b), relating to what constitutes a reasonable addition to a reserve for bad debts and to correction of errors in prior estimates, apply to a reserve for section 166(f)(1)(A) guaranteed debt obligations as well.

(c) *Special requirements.* Any reserve for section 166(f)(1)(A) guaranteed debt obligations must be established and maintained separately from any reserve for other debt obligations. In addition, a taxpayer who charges off direct debts when they become worthless in whole or in part rather than maintaining a reserve for such obligations may not maintain a reserve for section 166(f)(1)(A) guaranteed debt obligations in the same trade or business.

(d) *Requirement of statement.* A taxpayer who uses the reserve method of treating section 166(f)(1)(A) guaranteed debt obligations must attach to his return for each taxable year, returns for which are filed after April 17, 1986, and for each trade or business for which the reserve is maintained a statement showing—

(1) The total amount of these obligations at the beginning of the taxable year;

(2) The total amount of these obligations incurred during the taxable year;

(3) The amount of the initial balance of the suspense account, if any, established with respect to these obligations;

(4) The balance of the suspense account, if any, at the beginning of the taxable year;

(5) The adjustment, if any, to that account;

(6) The adjusted balance, if any, at the close of the taxable year;

(7) The reconciliation of the beginning and closing balances of the reserve for these obligations and the computation of the addition to the reserve; and

(8) The taxable year for which the reserve for these obligations was established.

(e) *Computation of opening balance —*(1) *In general.* The opening balance of a reserve for section 166(f)(1)(A) guaranteed debt obligations established for the first taxable year for which a taxpayer maintains such a reserve shall be determined as if the taxpayer had maintained such a reserve for the taxable years preceding that taxable year. The amount of the opening balance may be determined under the following formula:

Reg. § 1.166-10(a)(5)

$$OB = CG \times \frac{SNL}{SG}$$

where—

OB = the opening balance at the beginning of the first taxable year

CG = the amount of these obligations at the close of the last preceding taxable year

SG = the sum of the amounts of these obligations at the close of the five preceding taxable years

SNL = the sum of the amounts of net losses arising from these obligations for the five preceding taxable years

Year	Obligations outstanding at close of year	Gross losses from these obligations	Recoveries from these obligations	Net losses from these obligations
1972	$ 0	$ 0	$ 0	$ 0
1973	780,000	9,700	1,000	8,700
1974	795,000	8,900	1,050	7,850
1975	850,000	8,850	850	8,000
1976	820,000	9,300	1,400	7,900
Totals	$3,245,000	$36,750	$4,300	$32,450

The opening balance for 1977 of A's reserve for these obligations is $8,200, determined as follows:

$$\$8,200 = \$820,000 \times \frac{\$\ 32,450}{\$3,245,000}$$

(3) *More appropriate balance.* A taxpayer may select a balance other than the one produced under paragraph (e)(1) of this section if it is more appropriate, based upon the taxpayer's actual experience, and in the event the taxpayer's return is examined, if the balance is approved by the district director.

(4) *No losses in the five preceding taxable years.* If a taxpayer is in the taxpayer's first taxable year of a particular trade or business, or if the taxpayer has no losses arising from section 166(f)(1)(A) guaranteed debt obligations in a particular trade or business for any other reason in the five preceding taxable years, then the taxpayer's opening balance is zero for that particular trade or business.

(5) *Where reserve method was used before October 22, 1965.* If for a taxable year ending before October 22, 1965, the taxpayer maintained a reserve for bad debts under section 166(c) which included guaranteed debt obligations described in section 166(f)(1)(A), and if the taxpayer is allowed a deduction referred to in paragraph (g)(2) of this section on account of those obligations, the amount of the opening balance of the reserve for

section 166(f)(1)(A) guaranteed debt obligations for the taxpayer's first taxable year ending after October 21, 1965, shall be an amount equal to that portion of the section 166(c) reserve at the close of the last taxable year which is attributable to those debt obligations. The amount of the balance of the section 166(c) reserve for the taxable year shall be reduced by the amount of the opening balance of the reserve for those guaranteed debt obligations.

(f) *Suspense account*—(1) *Zero opening balance cases.* No suspense account shall be maintained if the opening balance of the reserve for section 166(f)(1)(A) guaranteed debt obligations under section 166(f)(3) is zero.

(2) *Example.* The following example applies to section 166(f)(4)(B), relating to adjustments to the suspense account:

Example. In 1977, A, an individual who operates an appliance store and uses the calendar year as the taxable year, adopts the reserve method of treating section 166(f)(1)(A) guaranteed debt obligations. The initial balance of A's suspense account is $8,200. At the close of 1977, 1978, 1979, and 1980, the balance of A's reserve for these obligations is $8,400, $8,250, $8,150, and $8,175 respectively, after making the addition to the reserve for each year. The adjustments under section 166(f)(4)(B) to the suspense account at the close of each of the years involved are as follows:

(2) *Example.* The following example applies to paragraph (e)(1) of this section.

Example. For 1977, A, a dealer in automobiles who uses the calendar year as the taxable year, adopts in accordance with this section the reserve method of treating section 166(f)(1)(A) guaranteed debt obligations. A's first year in business as an automobile dealer is 1973. For 1972, 1973, 1974, 1975, and 1976, A's records disclose the following information with respect to these obligations:

	1977	1978	1979	1980
(1) Taxable year	1977	1978	1979	1980
(2) Closing reserve account balance	$8,400	$8,250	$8,150	$8,175
(3) Opening suspense account balance	$8,200	$8,200	$8,200	$8,150
(4) Line (2) less line (3)	$ 200	$ 50	$ (50)	$ 25
(5) Adjustment to suspense account balance	0	0	$ (50)	$ 25
(6) Closing suspense account balance (line 3 plus line 5)	$8,200	$8,200	$8,150	$8,175

(g) *Effective date* —(1) *In general.* This section is generally effective for taxable years ending after October 21, 1965.

(2) *Transitional rule.* Section 2(b) of the Act of November 2, 1966 (Pub. L. 89-722, 80 Stat. 1151) allows additions to section 166(c) bad debt reserves in earlier taxable years on account of section 166(f)(1)(A) guaranteed debt obligations to be deducted for those earlier taxable years. Paragraphs (c), (d), (e), and (f) of this section do not apply in determining whether a deduction is allowed under section 2(b) of the Act. See Rev. Rul. 68-313 (1968-1 C.B. 75) for rules relating to that deduction. [Reg. § 1.166-10.]

☐ [T.D. 8071, 1-17-86.]

[Reg. § 1.167(a)-1]

§ 1.167(a)-1. **Depreciation in general.**—(a) *Reasonable allowance.* Section 167(a) provides that a reasonable allowance for the exhaustion, wear and tear, and obsolescence of property used in the trade or business or of property held by the taxpayer for the production of income shall be allowed as a depreciation deduction. The allowance is that amount which should be set aside for the taxable year in accordance with a reasonably consistent plan (not necessarily at a uniform rate), so that the aggregate of the amounts set aside, plus the salvage value, will, at the end of the estimated useful life of the depreciable property, equal the cost or other basis of the property as provided in section 167(g) and § 1.167(g)-1. An asset shall not be depreciated below a reasonable salvage value under any method of computing depreciation. However, see section 167(f) and § 1.167(f)-1 for rules which permit a reduction in the amount of salvage value to be taken into account for certain personal property acquired after October 16, 1962. See also paragraph (c) of this section for definition of salvage. The allowance shall not reflect amounts representing a mere reduction in market value. See section 179 and § 1.179-1 for a further description of the term "reasonable allowance."

(b) *Useful life.* For the purpose of section 167 the estimated useful life of an asset is not necessarily the useful life inherent in the asset but is the period over which the asset may reasonably be expected to be useful to the taxpayer in his trade or business or in the production of his income. This period shall be determined by reference to his experience with similar property taking into account present conditions and probable future developments. Some of the factors to be considered in determining this period are (1) wear and tear and decay or decline from natural causes, (2) the normal progress of the art, economic changes, inventions, and current developments within the industry and the taxpayer's trade or business, (3) the climatic and other local conditions peculiar to the taxpayer's trade or business, and (4) the taxpayer's policy as to repairs, renewals, and replacements. Salvage value is not a factor for the purpose of determining useful life. If the taxpayer's experience is inadequate, the general experience in the industry may be used until such time as the taxpayer's own experience forms an adequate basis for making the determination. The estimated remaining useful life may be subject to modification by reason of conditions known to exist at the end of the taxable year and shall be redetermined when necessary regardless of the method of computing depreciation. However, estimated remaining useful life shall be redetermined only when the change in the useful life is significant and there is a clear and convincing basis for the redetermination. For rules covering agreements with respect to useful life, see section 167(d) and § 1.167(d)-1. If a taxpayer claims an investment credit with respect to an asset for a taxable year preceding the taxable year in which the asset is considered as placed in service under § 1.167(a)-10(b) or § 1.167(a)-11(e), the useful life of the asset under this paragraph shall be the same useful life assigned to the asset under § 1.46-3(e).

(c) *Salvage.* (1) Salvage value is the amount (determined at the time of acquisition) which is estimated will be realizable upon sale or other disposition of an asset when it is no longer useful in the taxpayer's trade or business or in the production of his income and is to be retired from service by the taxpayer. Salvage value shall not be changed at any time after the determination made at the time of acquisition merely because of changes in price levels. However, if there is a redetermination of useful life under the rules of paragraph (b) of this section, salvage value may

Reg. § 1.167(a)-1(a)

be redetermined based upon facts known at the time of such redetermination of useful life. Salvage, when reduced by the cost of removal, is referred to as net salvage. The time at which an asset is retired from service may vary according to the policy of the taxpayer. If the taxpayer's policy is to dispose of assets which are still in good operating condition, the salvage value may represent a relatively large proportion of the original basis of the asset. However, if the taxpayer customarily uses an asset until its inherent useful life has been substantially exhausted, salvage value may represent no more than junk value. Salvage value must be taken into account in determining the depreciation deduction either by a reduction of the amount subject to depreciation or by a reduction in the rate of depreciation, but in no event shall an asset (or an account) be depreciated below a reasonable salvage value. See, however, paragraph (a) of § 1.167(b)-2 for the treatment of salvage under the declining balance method, and § 1.179-1 for the treatment of salvage in computing the additional first-year depreciation allowance. The taxpayer may use either salvage or net salvage in determining depreciation allowances but such practice must be consistently followed and the treatment of the costs of removal must be consistent with the practice adopted. For specific treatment of salvage value, see §§ 1.167(b)-1, 1.167(b)-2, and 1.167(b)-3. When an asset is retired or disposed of, appropriate adjustments shall be made in the asset and depreciation reserve accounts. For example, the amount of the salvage adjusted for the costs of removal may be credited to the depreciation reserve.

(2) For taxable years beginning after December 31, 1961, and ending after October 16, 1962, see section 167(f) and § 1.167(f)-1 for rules applicable to the reduction of salvage value taken into account for certain personal property acquired after October 16, 1962. [Reg. § 1.167(a)-1.]

☐ [*T.D.* 6182, 6-11-56. *Amended by T.D.* 6507, 12-1-60, *T.D.* 6712, 3-23-64 *and T.D.* 7203, 8-24-72.]

[Reg. § 1.167(a)-2]

§ 1.167(a)-2. **Tangible property.**—The depreciation allowance in the case of tangible property applies only to that part of the property which is subject to wear and tear, to decay or decline from natural causes, to exhaustion, and to obsolescence. The allowance does not apply to inventories or stock in trade, or to land apart from the improvements of physical development added to it. The allowance does not apply to natural resources which are subject to the allowance for depletion provided in section 611. No deduction for depreciation shall be allowed on automobiles or other

vehicles used solely for pleasure, on a building used by the taxpayer solely as his residence, or on furniture or furnishings therein, personal effects, or clothing; but properties and costumes used exclusively in a business, such as a theatrical business, may be depreciated. [Reg. § 1.167(a)-2.]

☐ [*T.D.* 6182, 6-11-56.]

[Reg. § 1.167(a)-3]

§ 1.167(a)-3. **Intangibles.**—If an intangible asset is known from experience or other factors to be of use in the business or in the production of income for only a limited period, the length of which can be estimated with reasonable accuracy, such an intangible asset may be the subject of a depreciation allowance. Examples are patents and copyrights. An intangible asset, the useful life of which is not limited, is not subject to the allowance for depreciation. No allowance will be permitted merely because, in the unsupported opinion of the taxpayer, the intangible asset has a limited useful life. No deduction for depreciation is allowable with respect to good will. For rules with respect to organizational expenditures, see section 248 and the regulations thereunder. For rules with respect to trademark and trade name expenditures, see section 177 and the regulations thereunder. See sections 197 and 167(f) and, to the extent applicable, §§ 1.197-2 and 1.167(a)-14 for amortization of goodwill and certain other intangibles acquired after August 10, 1993, or after July 25, 1991, if a valid retroactive election under § 1.197-1T has been made. [Reg. § 1.167(a)-3.]

☐ [*T.D.* 6182, 6-11-56. *Amended by T.D.* 6452, 2-3-60 *and T.D.* 8865, 1-20-2000.]

[Reg. § 1.167(a)-4]

§ 1.167(a)-4 **Leased property.**—Capital expenditures made by a lessee for the erection of buildings or the construction of other permanent improvements on leased property are recoverable through allowances for depreciation or amortization. If the useful life of such improvements in the hands of the taxpayer is equal to or shorter than the remaining period of the lease, the allowances shall take the form of depreciation under section 167. See §§ 1.167(b)-0, 1.167(b)-1, 1.167(b)-2, 1.167(b)-3, and 1.167(b)-4 for methods of computing such depreciation allowances. If, on the other hand, the estimated useful life of such property in the hands of the taxpayer, determined without regard to the terms of the lease, would be longer than the remaining period of such lease, the allowances shall take the form of annual deductions from gross income in an amount equal to the unrecovered cost of such capital expenditures divided by the number of years remaining of the term of the lease. Such deductions shall be in lieu of allowances for depreciation. See section 162 and the regulations thereunder. See section 178 and the regulations thereunder for rules governing the effect to be given renewal options in determining whether the useful life of the improvement exceeds the remaining term of the lease where a lessee begins improvements on leased property after July 28, 1958, other than improvements which on such date and at all times thereafter, the lessee was under a binding legal obligation to make. Capital expenditures made by a lessor for the erection of buildings or other improvements shall, if subject to depreciation allowances, be recovered by him over the estimated life of the improvements without regard to the period of the lease. [Reg. § 1.167(a)-4.]

☐ [*T.D.* 6182, 6-11-56. *Amended by T.D.* 6520, 12-23-60.]

[Reg. § 1.167(a)-5]

§ 1.167(a)-5. **Apportionment of basis.**—In the case of the acquisition on or after March 1, 1913, of a combination of depreciable and nondepreciable property for a lump sum, as for example, buildings and land, the basis for depreciation cannot exceed an amount which bears the same proportion to the lump sum as the value of the depreciable property at the time of acquisition bears to the value of the entire property at that time. In the case of property which is subject to both the allowance for depreciation and amortization, depreciation is allowable only with respect to the portion of the depreciable property which is not subject to the allowance for amortization and may be taken concurrently with the allowance for amortization. After the close of the amortization period or after amortization deductions have been discontinued with respect to any such property, the unrecovered cost or other basis of the depreciable portion of such property will be subject to depreciation. For adjustments to basis, see section 1016 and other applicable provisions of law. For the adjustment to the basis of a structure in the case of a donation of a qualified conservation contribution under section 170(h), see § 1.170A-14(h)(3)(iii). [Reg. § 1.167(a)-5.]

☐ [*T.D.* 6182, 6-11-56. *Amended by T.D.* 8069, 1-13-86.]

[Reg. § 1.167(a)-5T]

§ 1.167(a)-5T. **Application of section 1060 to section 167 (temporary).**—In the case of an acquisition of a combination of depreciable and nondepreciable property for a lump sum in an applicable asset acquisition to which section 1060 applies, the basis for depreciation of the depreciable property cannot exceed the amount of consid-

eration allocated to that property under section 1060 and § 1.1060-1T. [Temporary Reg. § 1.167(a)-5T.]

☐ [*T.D.* 8215, 7-15-88.]

[Reg. § 1.167(a)-6]

§ 1.167(a)-6. **Depreciation in special cases.**—(a) *Depreciation of patents or copyrights.* The cost or other basis of a patent or copyright shall be depreciated over its remaining useful life. Its cost to the patentee includes the various Government fees, cost of drawings, models, attorneys' fees, and similar expenditures. For rules applicable to research and experimental expenditures, see sections 174 and 1016 and the regulations thereunder. If a patent or copyright becomes valueless in any year before its expiration the unrecovered cost or other basis may be deducted in that year. See § 1.167(a)-14(c)(4) for depreciation of a separately acquired interest in a patent or copyright described in section 167(f)(2) acquired after January 25, 2000. See § 1.197-2 for amortization of interests in patents and copyrights that constitute amortizable section 197 intangibles.

(b) *Depreciation in case of farmers.* A reasonable allowance for depreciation may be claimed on farm buildings (except a dwelling occupied by the owner), farm machinery, and other physical property but not including land. Livestock acquired for work, breeding, or dairy purposes may be depreciated unless included in an inventory used to determine profits in accordance with section 61 and the regulations thereunder. Such depreciation should be determined with reference to the cost or other basis, salvage value, and the estimated useful life of the livestock. See also section 162 and the regulations thereunder relating to trade or business expenses, section 165 and the regulations thereunder relating to losses of farmers, and section 175 and the regulations thereunder relating to soil or water conservation expenditures. [Reg. § 1.167(a)-6.]

☐ [*T.D.* 6182, 6-11-56. *Amended by T.D.* 8865, 1-20-2000.]

[Reg. § 1.167(a)-7]

§ 1.167(a)-7. **Accounting for depreciable property.**—(a) Depreciable property may be accounted for by treating each individual item as an account, or by combining two or more assets in a single account. Assets may be grouped in an account in a variety of ways. For example, assets similar in kind with approximately the same useful lives may be grouped together. Such an account is commonly known as a group account. Another appropriate grouping might consist of assets segregated according to use without regard to useful life, for example, machinery and equip-

Reg. § 1.167(a)-5

ment, furniture and fixtures, or transportation equipment. Such an account is commonly known as a classified account. A broader grouping, where assets are included in the same account regardless of their character or useful lives, is commonly referred to as a composite account. For example, all the assets used in a business may be included in a single account. Group, classified, or composite accounts may be further broken down on the basis of location, dates of acquisition, cost, character, use, etc.

(b) When group, classified, or composite accounts are used with average useful lives and a normal retirement occurs, the full cost or other basis of the asset retired, unadjusted for depreciation or salvage, shall be removed from the asset account and shall be charged to the depreciation reserve. Amounts representing salvage ordinarily are credited to the depreciation reserve. Where an asset is disposed of for reasons other than normal retirement, the full cost or other basis of the asset shall be removed from the asset account, and the depreciation reserve shall be charged with the depreciation applicable to the retired asset. For rules with respect to losses on normal retirements, see § 1.167(a)-8.

(c) A taxpayer may establish as many accounts for depreciable property as he desires. Depreciation allowances shall be computed separately for each account. Such depreciation preferably should be recorded in a depreciation reserve account; however, in appropriate cases it may be recorded directly in the asset account. Where depreciation reserves are maintained, a separate reserve account shall be maintained for each asset account. The regular books of account or permanent auxiliary records shall show for each account the basis of the property, including adjustments necessary to conform to the requirements of section 1016 and other provisions of law relating to adjustments to basis, and the depreciation allowances for tax purposes. In the event that reserves for book purposes do not correspond with reserves maintained for tax purposes, permanent auxiliary records shall be maintained with the regular books of account reconciling the differences in depreciation for tax and book purposes because of different methods of depreciation, bases, rates, salvage, or other factors. Depreciation schedules filed with the income tax return shall show the accumulated reserves computed in accordance with the allowances for income tax purposes.

(d) In classified or composite accounts, the average useful life and rate shall be redetermined whenever additions, retirements, or replacements substantially alter the relative proportion of types of assets in the accounts. See example (2) in paragraph (b) of § 1.167(b)-1 for a method of determining the depreciation rate for a classified or composite account. [Reg. § 1.167(a)-7.]

☐ [T.D. 6182, 6-11-56.]

[Reg. § 1.167(a)-8]

§ 1.167(a)-8. Retirements.—(a) *Gains and losses on retirements.* For the purposes of this section the term "retirement" means the permanent withdrawal of depreciable property from use in the trade or business or in the production of income. The withdrawal may be made in one of several ways. For example, the withdrawal may be made by selling or exchanging the asset, or by actual abandonment. In addition, the asset may be withdrawn from such productive use without disposition as, for example, by being placed in a supplies or scrap account. The tax consequences of a retirement depend upon the form of the transaction, the reason therefor, the timing of the retirement, the estimated useful life used in computing depreciation, and whether the asset is accounted for in a separate or multiple asset account. Upon the retirement of assets, the rules in this section apply in determining whether gain or loss will be recognized, the amount of such gain or loss, and the basis for determining gain or loss:

(1) Where an asset is retired by sale at arm's length, recognition of gain or loss will be subject to the provisions of sections 1002, 1231, and other applicable provisions of law.

(2) Where an asset is retired by exchange, the recognition of gain or loss will be subject to the provisions of sections 1002, 1031, 1231, and other applicable provisions of law.

(3) Where an asset is permanently retired from use in the trade or business or in the production of income but is not disposed of by the taxpayer or physically abandoned (as, for example, when the asset is transferred to a supplies or scrap account), gain will not be recognized. In such a case loss will be recognized measured by the excess of the adjusted basis of the asset at the time of retirement over the estimated salvage value or over the fair market value at the time of such retirement if greater, but only if—

(i) The retirement is an abnormal retirement or

(ii) The retirement is a normal retirement from a single asset account (but see paragraph (d) of this section for special rule for item accounts), or

(iii) The retirement is a normal retirement from a multiple asset account in which the depreciation rate was based on the maximum expected life of the longest lived asset contained in the account.

(4) Where an asset is retired by actual physical abandonment (as, for example, in the case of a building condemned as unfit for further occupancy or other use), loss will be recognized measured by the amount of the adjusted basis of the asset abandoned at the time of such abandonment. In order to qualify for the recognition of loss from physical abandonment, the intent of the taxpayer must be irrevocably to discard the asset so that it will neither be used again by him nor retrieved by him for sale, exchange, or other disposition.

Experience with assets which have attained an exceptional or unusual age shall, with respect to similar assets, be disregarded in determining the maximum expected useful life of the longest lived asset in a multiple asset account. For example, if a manufacturer establishes a proper multiple asset account for 50 assets which are expected to have an average life of 30 years but which will remain useful to him for varying periods between 20 and 40 years, the maximum expected useful life will be 40 years, even though an occasional asset of this kind may last 60 years.

(b) *Definition of normal and abnormal retirements.* For the purpose of this section the determination of whether a retirement is normal or abnormal shall be made in the light of all the facts and circumstances. In general, a retirement shall be considered a normal retirement unless the taxpayer can show that the withdrawal of the asset was due to a cause not contemplated in setting the applicable depreciation rate. For example, a retirement is considered normal if made within the range of years taken into consideration in fixing the depreciation rate and if the asset has reached a condition at which, in the normal course of events, the taxpayer customarily retires similar assets from use in his business. On the other hand, a retirement may be abnormal if the asset is withdrawn at an earlier time or under other circumstances, as, for example, when the asset has been damaged by casualty or has lost its usefulness suddenly as the result of extraordinary obsolescence.

(c) *Basis of assets retired.* The basis of an asset at the time of retirement for computing gain or loss shall be its adjusted basis for determining gain or loss upon a sale or other disposition as determined in accordance with the provisions of section 1011 and the following rules:

(1) In the case of a normal retirement of an asset from a multiple asset account where the depreciation rate is based on average expected useful life, the term "adjusted basis" means the salvage value estimated in determining the depreciation deduction in accordance with the provisions in paragraph (c) of § 1.167(a)-1.

(2) In the case of a normal retirement of an asset from a multiple asset account in which the depreciation rate was based on the maximum expected life of the longest lived asset in the account, the adjustment for depreciation allowed or allowable shall be made at the rate which would have been proper if the asset had been depreciated in a single asset account (under the method of depreciation used for the multiple asset account) using a rate based upon the maximum expected useful life of that asset, and

(3) In the case of an abnormal retirement from a multiple asset account the adjustment for depreciation allowed or allowable shall be made at the rate which would have been proper had the asset been depreciated in a single asset account (under the method of depreciation used for the multiple asset account) and using a rate based upon either the average expected useful life or the maximum expected useful life of the asset, depending upon the method of determining the rate of depreciation used in connection with the multiple asset account.

(d) *Special rule for item accounts.* (1) As indicated in paragraphs (a)(3)(ii) and (iii) of this section, a loss is recognized upon the normal retirement of an asset from a single asset account but a loss on the normal retirement of an asset in a multiple asset account is not allowable where the depreciation rate is based upon the average useful life of the assets in the account. Where a taxpayer with more than one depreciable asset chooses to set up a separate account for each such asset and the depreciation rate is based on the average useful life of such assets (so that he uses the same life for each account), the question arises whether his depreciation deductions in substance are the equivalent of those which would result from the use of multiple asset accounts and, therefore, he should be subject to the rules governing losses on retirements of assets from multiple asset accounts. Where a taxpayer has only a few depreciable assets which he chooses to account for in single asset accounts, particularly where such assets cover a relatively narrow range of lives, it cannot be said in the usual case that the allowance of losses on retirements from such accounts clearly will distort income. This results from the fact that where a taxpayer has only a few depreciable assets it is usually not possible clearly to determine that the depreciation rate is based upon the average useful life of such assets. Accordingly, it cannot be said that the taxpayer is in effect clearly operating with a multiple asset account using an average life rate so that losses should not be allowed on normal retirements. Therefore, losses normally will be allowed upon retirement of assets from single asset accounts where the taxpayer has only a few depreciable assets. On the other hand, when a taxpayer who has only a few depreciable assets chooses to account for them in single asset accounts, using for each account a depreciation rate based on the average useful life of such assets, and the assets cover a wide range of lives, the likelihood that income will be distorted is greater than where the group of assets covers a relatively narrow range of lives. In those cases where the allowance of losses would distort income, the rules with respect to the allowance of losses on normal retirement shall be applied to such assets in the same manner as though the assets had been accounted for in multiple asset accounts using a rate based upon average expected useful life.

(2) Where a taxpayer has a large number of depreciable assets and depreciation is based on the average useful life of such assets, then, whether such assets are similar or dissimilar and regardless of whether they are accounted for in individual asset accounts or multiple asset accounts the allowance of losses on the normal retirement of such assets would distort income. Such distortion would result from the fact that the use of average useful life (and, accordingly, average rate) assumes that while some assets normally will be retired before the expiration of the average life, others normally will be retired after expiration of the average life. Accordingly, if instead of accounting for a large number of similar or dissimilar depreciable assets in multiple asset accounts, the taxpayer chooses to account separately for such assets, using a rate based upon the average life of such assets, the rules with respect to the allowances of losses on normal retirements will be applied to such assets in the same manner as though the assets were accounted for in multiple asset accounts using a rate based upon average expected useful life.

(3) Where a taxpayer who does not have a large number of depreciable assets (and who therefore is not subject to subparagraph (2) of this paragraph) chooses to set up a separate account for each such asset, and has sought to compute an average life for such assets on which to base his depreciation deductions (so that he uses the same life for each account), the allowance of losses on normal retirements from such accounts may in some situations substantially distort income. Such distortion would result from the fact that the use of average useful life (and, accordingly, average rate) assumes that while some assets normally will be retired before expiration of the average life, others normally will be retired after expiration of

the average life. Accordingly, where a taxpayer chooses to account separately for such assets instead of accounting for them in multiple asset accounts, and the result is to substantially distort his income, the rules with respect to the allowance of losses on normal retirements shall be applied to such assets in the same manner as though the assets had been accounted for in multiple asset accounts using a rate based upon average expected useful life.

(4) Whenever a taxpayer is treated under this paragraph as though his assets were accounted for in a multiple asset account using an average life rate, and, therefore, he is denied a loss on retirements, the unrecovered cost less salvage of each asset which was accounted for separately may be amortized in accordance with the regulation stated in paragraph (e)(1)(ii) of this section.

(e) *Accounting treatment of asset retirements.* (1) In the case of a normal retirement where under the foregoing rules no loss is recognized and where the asset is retired without disposition or abandonment, (i) if the asset was contained in a multiple asset account, the full cost of such asset, reduced by estimated salvage, shall be charged to the depreciation reserve, or (ii) if the asset was accounted for separately, the unrecovered cost or other basis, less salvage, of the asset may be amortized through annual deductions from gross income in amounts equal to the unrecovered cost or other basis of such asset, divided by the average expected useful life (not the remaining useful life applicable to the asset at the time of retirement. For example, if an asset is retired after six years of use and at the time of retirement depreciation was being claimed on the basis of an average expected useful life of ten years, the unrecovered cost or other basis less salvage would be amortized through equal annual deductions over a period of ten years from the time of retirement.

(2) Where multiple asset accounts are used and acquisitions and retirements are numerous, if a taxpayer, in order to avoid unnecessarily detailed accounting for individual retirements, consistently follows the practice of charging the reserve with the full cost or other basis of assets retired and of crediting it with all receipts from salvage, the practice may be continued so long as, in the opinion of the Commissioner, it clearly reflects income. Conversely, where the taxpayer customarily follows a practice of reporting all receipts from salvage as ordinary taxable income such practice may be continued so long as, in the opinion of the Commissioner, it clearly reflects income.

(f) *Cross reference.* For special rules in connection with the retirement of the last asset of a

Reg. § 1.167(a)-8(f)

given year's acquisitions under the declining balance method, see example (2) in paragraph (b) of § 1.167(b)-2. [Reg. § 1.167(a)-8.]

☐ [*T.D. 6182, 6-11-56.*]

[Reg. § 1.167(a)-9]

§ 1.167(a)-9. Obsolescence.—The depreciation allowance includes an allowance for normal obsolescence which should be taken into account to the extent that the expected useful life of property will be shortened by reason thereof. Obsolescence may render an asset economically useless to the taxpayer regardless of its physical condition. Obsolescence is attributable to many causes, including technological improvements and reasonably foreseeable economic changes. Among these causes are normal progress of the arts and sciences, supersession or inadequacy brought about by developments in the industry, products, methods, markets, sources of supply, and other like changes, and legislative or regulatory action. In any case in which the taxpayer shows that the estimated useful life previously used should be shortened by reason of obsolescence greater than had been assumed in computing such estimated useful life, a change to a new and shorter estimated useful life computed in accordance with such showing will be permitted. No such change will be permitted merely because in the unsupported opinion of the taxpayer the property may become obsolete. For rules governing the allowance of a loss when the usefulness of depreciable property is suddenly terminated, see § 1.167(a)-8. If the estimated useful life and the depreciation rates have been the subject of a previous agreement, see section 167(d) and § 1.167(d)-1. [Reg. § 1.167(a)-9.]

☐ [*T.D. 6182, 6-11-56. Amended by T.D. 6445, 1-15-60.*]

[Reg. § 1.167(a)-10]

§ 1.167(a)-10. When depreciation deduction is allowable.—(a) A taxpayer should deduct the proper depreciation allowance each year and may not increase his depreciation allowances in later years by reason of his failure to deduct any depreciation allowance or of his action in deducting an allowance plainly inadequate under the known facts in prior years. The inadequacy of the depreciation allowance for property in prior years shall be determined on the basis of the allowable method of depreciation used by the taxpayer for such property or under the straight line method if no allowance has ever been claimed for such property. The preceding sentence shall not be construed as precluding application of any method provided in section 167 (b) if taxpayer's failure to claim any allowance for depreciation was due

solely to erroneously treating as a deductible expense an item properly chargeable to capital account. For rules relating to adjustments to basis, see section 1016 and the regulations thereunder.

(b) The period for depreciation of an asset shall begin when the asset is placed in service and shall end when the asset is retired from service. A proportionate part of one year's depreciation is allowable for that part of the first and last year during which the asset was in service. However, in the case of a multiple asset account, the amount of depreciation may be determined by using what is commonly described as an "averaging convention" that is, by using an assumed timing of additions and retirements. For example, it might be assumed that all additions and retirements to the asset account occur uniformly throughout the taxable year, in which case depreciation is computed on the average of the beginning and ending balances of the asset account for the taxable year. See example (3) under paragraph (b) of § 1.167(b)-1. Among still other averaging conventions which may be used is the one under which it is assumed that all additions and retirements during the first half of a given year were made on the first day of that year and that all additions and retirements during the second half of the year were made on the first day of the following year. Thus, a full year's depreciation would be taken on additions in the first half of the year and no depreciation would be taken on additions in the second half. Moreover, under this convention, no depreciation would be taken on retirements in the first half of the year and a full year's depreciation would be taken on the retirements in the second half. An averaging convention, if used, must be consistently followed as to the account or accounts for which it is adopted, and must be applied to both additions and retirements. In any year in which an averaging convention substantially distorts the depreciation allowance for the taxable year, it may not be used. [Reg. § 1.167(a)-10.]

☐ [*T.D. 6182, 6-11-56.*]

[Reg. § 1.167(a)-11]

§ 1.167(a)-11. Depreciation based on class lives and asset depreciation ranges for property placed in service after December 31, 1970.—(a) *In general*—(1) *Summary.* This section provides an asset depreciation range and class life system for determining the reasonable allowance for depreciation of designated classes of assets placed in service after December 31, 1970. The system is designed to minimize disputes between taxpayers and the Internal Revenue Service as to the useful life of property, and as to salvage value, repairs, and other matters. The system is optional with the taxpayer. The taxpayer has an annual election. Generally, an election for a taxable year must apply to all additions of eligible property during the taxable year of election, but does not apply to additions of eligible property in any other taxable year. The taxpayer's election, made with the return for the taxable year, may not be revoked or modified for any property included in the election. Generally, the taxpayer must establish vintage accounts for all eligible property included in the election, must determine the allowance for depreciation of such property in the taxable year of election, and in subsequent taxable years, on the basis of the asset depreciation period selected, and must apply the first-year convention specified in the election to determine the allowance for depreciation of such property. This section also contains special provisions for the treatment of salvage value, retirements, and the costs of the repair, maintenance, rehabilitation or improvement of property. In general, a taxpayer may not apply any provision of this section unless he makes an election and thereby consents to, and agrees to apply, all the provisions of this section. A taxpayer who elects to apply this section does, however, have certain options as to the application of specified provisions of this section. A taxpayer may elect to apply this section for a taxable year only if for such taxable year he complies with the requirements of paragraph (f)(4) of this section.

(2) *Definitions.* For the meaning of certain terms used in this section, see paragraphs (b)(2) ("eligible property"), (b)(3) ("vintage account" and "vintage"), (b)(4) ("asset depreciation range", "asset guideline class", "asset guideline period", and "asset depreciation period"), (b)(5)(iii)(c) ("used property"), (b)(6)(i) ("public utility property"), (c)(1)(iv) ("original use"), (c)(1)(v) ("unadjusted basis" and "adjusted basis"), (c)(2)(ii) ("modified half-year convention"), (c)(2)(iii) ("half-year convention"), (d)(1)(i) ("gross salvage value"), (d)(1)(ii) ("salvage value"), (d)(2)(iii) ("repair allowance", "repair allowance percentage", and "repair allowance property"), (d)(2)(vi) ("excluded addition"), (d)(2)(vii) ("property improvement"), (d)(3)(ii) ("ordinary retirement" and "extraordinary retirement"), (d)(3)(vi) ("special basis vintage account"), and (e)(1) ("first placed in service") of this section.

(b) *Reasonable allowance using asset depreciation ranges*—(1) *In general.* The allowance for depreciation of eligible property (as defined in subparagraph (2) of this paragraph) to which the taxpayer elects to apply this section shall be determined as provided in paragraph (c) of this section and shall constitute the reasonable allow-

ance for depreciation of such property under section 167(a).

(2) *Definition of eligible property.* For purposes of this section, the term "eligible property" means tangible property which is subject to the allowance for depreciation provided by section 167(a) but only if—

(i) An asset guideline class and asset guideline period are in effect for such property for the taxable year of election (see subparagraph (4) of this paragraph);

(ii) The property is first placed in service (as described in paragraph (e)(1) of this section) by the taxpayer after December 31, 1970 (but see subparagraph (7) of this paragraph for special rule where there is a mere change in the form of conducting a trade or business); and

(iii) The property is either—

(a) Section 1245 property as defined in section 1245(a)(3). or

(b) Section 1250 property as defined in section 1250(c).

See, however, subparagraph (6) of this paragraph for special rule for certain public utility property as defined in section 167(1)(3)(A). Property which meets the requirements of this subparagraph is eligible property even if depreciation with respect to such property, determined in accordance with this section, is allocated to or otherwise required to be reflected in the cost of a capitalized item. The term "eligible property" includes any property which meets the requirements of this subparagraph, whether such property is new property, "used property" (as described in subparagraph (5)(iii)(c) of this paragraph), a "property improvement" (as described in paragraph (d)(2)(vii) of this section), or an "excluded addition" (as described in paragraph (d)(2)(vi) of this section). For the treatment of expenditures for the repair, maintenance, rehabilitation or improvement of certain property, see paragraph (d)(2) of this section.

(3) *Requirement of vintage accounts*—(i) *In general.* For purposes of this section, a "vintage account" is a closed-end depreciation account containing eligible property to which the taxpayer elects to apply this section, first placed in service by the taxpayer during the taxable year of election. The "vintage" of an account refers to the taxable year during which the eligible property in the account is first placed in service by the taxpayer. Such an account will consist of an asset, or a group of assets, within a single asset guideline class established pursuant to subparagraph (4) of this paragraph and may contain only eligible property. Each item of eligible property to which

Reg. § 1.167(a)-11(b)(3)

the taxpayer elects to apply this section, first placed in service by the taxpayer during the taxable year of election (determined without regard to a convention described in paragraph (c)(2) of this section) shall be placed in a vintage account of the taxable year of election. For rule regarding "special basis vintage accounts" for certain property improvements, see paragraph (d)(2)(viii) and (3)(vi) of this section. Any number of vintage accounts of a taxable year may be established. More than one account of the same vintage may be established for different assets of the same asset guideline class. See paragraph (d)(3)(xi) of this section for special rule for treatment of certain multiple asset and item accounts.

(ii) *Special rule.* Section 1245 property may not be placed in a vintage account with section 1250 property. Property the original use of which does not commence with the taxpayer may not be placed in a vintage account with property the original use of which commences with the taxpayer. Property described in section 167(f)(2) may not be placed in a vintage account with property not described in section 167(f)(2). Property described in section 179(d)(1) for which the taxpayer elects the allowance for the first taxable year in accordance with section 179(c) may not be placed in a vintage account with property not described in section 179(d)(1) or for which the taxpayer does not elect such allowance for the first taxable year. For special rule for property acquired in a transaction to which section 381(a) applies, see paragraph (e)(3)(i) of this section. For additional rules with respect to accounting for eligible property, see paragraph (e) of this section.

(4) *Asset depreciation ranges and periods—*(i) *Selection of asset depreciation period.* The taxpayer's books and records must specify for each vintage account of the taxable year of election—

(a) In the case of vintage account for property in an asset guideline class for which no asset depreciation range is in effect for the taxable year, the asset depreciation period (which shall be equal to the asset guideline period for the assets in such account), or

(b) In the case of a vintage account for property in an asset guideline class for which an asset depreciation range is in effect for the taxable year, the asset depreciation period selected by the taxpayer from the asset depreciation range for the assets in such account.

Unless otherwise expressly provided in the establishment thereof, for purposes of this section, the term "asset guideline class" means a category of assets (including "subsidiary assets") for which a separate asset guideline period is in effect for the taxable year as provided in subdivision (ii) of this

subparagraph. The "asset depreciation range" is a period of years which extends from 80 percent of the asset guideline period to 120 percent of such period, determined in each case by rounding any fractional part of a year to the nearer of the nearest whole or half year. Except as provided in paragraph (e)(3)(iv) of this section, in the case of an asset guideline class for which an asset depreciation range is in effect, any period within the asset depreciation range which is a whole number of years or a whole number of years plus a half year, may be selected. The term "asset depreciation period" means the period selected from the asset depreciation range, or if no asset depreciation range is in effect for the class, the asset guideline period. The "asset guideline period" is established in accordance with subdivision (ii) of this subparagraph and is the class life under section 167(m). See Revenue Procedure 72-10 [superseded by Rev. Proc. 77-10, which was superseded by Rev. Proc. 83-35, which was obsoleted by Rev. Proc. 87-56; see ¶ 310A.01, 310B.01 and 310D.01] for special rules for section 1250 property and property predominately used outside the United States. In general, an asset guideline period, but no asset depreciation range, is in effect for such property.

(ii) *Establishment of asset guideline classes and periods.* The asset guideline classes and the asset guideline periods, and the asset depreciation ranges determined from such periods, in effect for taxable years ending before the effective date of the first supplemental asset guideline classes, asset guideline periods, and asset depreciation ranges, established pursuant to this section are set forth in Revenue Procedure 72-10 [superseded by Rev. Proc. 77-10, which was superseded by Rev. Proc. 83-35, which was obsoleted by Rev. Proc. 87-56; see ¶ 310A.01, 310B.01 and 310D.01]. Asset guideline classes and periods, and asset depreciation ranges, will from time to time be established, supplemented, and revised with express reference to this section, and will be published in the Internal Revenue Bulletin. The asset guideline classes, the asset guideline periods, and the asset depreciation ranges determined from such periods in effect as of the last day of a taxable year of election shall apply to all vintage accounts of such taxable year, except that neither the asset guideline period nor the lower limit of the asset depreciation range for any such account shall be longer than the asset guideline period or the lower limit of the asset depreciation range, as the case may be, for such account in effect as of the first day of the taxable year (or as of such later time in such year as an asset guideline class first established during such year becomes effective). Generally, the reasonable allowance for de-

Reg. § 1.167(a)-11(b)(4)

preciation of property for any taxable year in a vintage account shall not be changed to reflect any supplement or revision of the asset guideline classes or periods, and asset depreciation ranges, for the taxable year in which the account is established, which occurs after the end of such taxable year. However, if expressly provided in such a supplement or revision, the taxpayer may, at his option in the manner specified therein, apply the revised or supplemented asset guideline classes or periods and asset depreciation ranges to such property for such taxable year and succeeding taxable years.

(iii) *Applicable guideline classes and periods in special situations.* (a) An electric or gas utility which would in accordance with Revenue Procedure 64-21 be entitled to use a composite guideline class basis for applying Revenue Procedure 62-21 may, solely with respect to property for which an asset depreciation range is in effect for the taxable year, elect to apply this section on the basis of a composite asset guideline class and asset guideline period determined by applying the provisions of Revenue Procedure 64-21 to such property. The asset depreciation range for such a composite asset guideline class shall be determined by reference to the composite asset guideline period at the beginning of the first taxable year to which the taxpayer elects to apply this section and shall not be changed until such time as major variations in the asset mix or the asset guideline classes or periods justify some other composite asset guideline period. Except as provided in paragraph (d)(2)(iii) of this section with respect to buildings and other structures, for the purposes of this section, all property in the composite asset guideline class shall be treated as included in a single asset guideline class. If the taxpayer elects to apply this subdivision, the election shall be made on the tax return filed for the first taxable year for which the taxpayer elects to apply this section. An election to apply this subdivision for any taxable year shall apply to all succeeding taxable years to which the taxpayer elects to apply this section, except to the extent the election to apply this subdivision is with the consent of the Commissioner terminated with respect to a succeeding taxable year and all taxable years thereafter.

(b) For purposes of this section, property shall be included in the asset guideline class for the activity in which the property is primarily used. See paragraph (e)(3)(iii) of this section for rule for leased property. Property shall be classified according to primary use even though the activity in which such property is primarily used is insubstantial in relation to all the taxpayer's activities. No change in the classification of prop-

erty shall be made because of a change in primary use after the end of the taxable year in which property is first placed in service, including a change in use which results in section 1250 property becoming section 1245 property.

(c) An incorrect classification or characterization by the taxpayer of property for the purposes of this section (such as under (b) of this subdivision or under subparagraph (2) or (3)(ii) of this paragraph) shall not cause or permit a revocation of the election to apply this section for the taxable year in which such property was first placed in service. The classification or characterization of such property shall be corrected. All adjustments necessary to the correction shall be made, including adjustments of unadjusted basis, adjusted basis, salvage value, the reserve for depreciation of all vintage accounts affected, and the amount of depreciation allowable for all taxable years for which the period for assessment of tax prescribed in section 6501 has not expired. If because of incorrect classification or characterization property included in an election to apply this section was not placed in a vintage account and no asset depreciation period was selected for the property or the property was placed in a vintage account but an asset depreciation period was selected from an incorrect asset depreciation range, the taxpayer shall place the property in a vintage account and select an asset depreciation period for the account from the correct asset depreciation range.

(d) Generally, except as provided in subparagraph (5)(v)(a) of this paragraph, a taxpayer may not compute depreciation for eligible property first placed in service during the taxable year under a method of depreciation not described in section 167(b)(1), (2), or (3). (If the taxpayer computes depreciation with respect to such property under section 167(k), or amortizes such property, the property must be excluded from the election to apply this section.) (See subparagraph (5)(v)(b) of this paragraph.) However, if the taxpayer establishes to the satisfaction of the Commissioner that a method of depreciation not described in section 167(b)(1), (2), (3), or (k) was adopted for property in the asset guideline class on the basis of a good faith mistake as to the proper asset guideline class for the property, then, unless the requirements of subparagraph (5)(v)(a) of this paragraph are met, the taxpayer must terminate (as of the beginning of the taxable year) such method of depreciation with respect to all eligible property in the asset guideline class which was first placed in service during the taxable year. In such event, the taxpayer's election to apply this section shall include eligible property in the asset guideline class without regard to

Reg. § 1.167(a)-11(b)(4)

subparagraph (5)(v)(a) of this paragraph. The provisions of (c) of this subdivision shall apply to the correction in the classification of the property.

(e) If the provisions of section 167(j) apply to require a change in the method of depreciation with respect to an item of section 1250 property in a multiple asset vintage account, the asset shall be removed from the account and placed in a separate item vintage account. The unadjusted basis of the asset shall be removed from the unadjusted basis of the vintage account as of the first day of the taxable year in which the change in method of depreciation is required and the depreciation reserve established for the account shall be reduced by the depreciation allowable for the property computed in the manner prescribed in paragraph (c)(1)(v)(b) of this section for determination of the adjusted basis of property. See paragaraph (d)(3)(vii)(e) of this section for treatment of salvage value when property is removed from a vintage account.

(iv) *Examples.* The principles of this subparagraph may be illustrated by the following examples:

Example (1). Corporation X purchases a bulldozer for use in its construction business. The bulldozer is first placed in service in 1972. Since the bulldozer is tangible property for which an asset guideline class and period have been established, the bulldozer is eligible property. The bulldozer is in asset guideline class 15.1 of Revenue Procedure 72-10, and the asset depreciation range is 4-6 years.

Example (2). In 1972, corporation Y first places in service a factory building. Since the factory building is tangible property for which an asset guideline class and period have been established, it is eligible property. The factory building is in asset guideline class 65.11 of Revenue Procedure 72-10. Since no asset depreciation range is in

effect for the asset guideline class, the asset depreciation period is the asset guideline period of 45 years. (See subparagraph (5)(vi) of this paragraph for election to exclude certain section 1250 property during transition period.)

Example (3). In January of 1971, corporation Y, a calendar year taxpayer, pays or incurs $2,000 for the rehabilitation and improvement of machine A which was first placed in service in 1969. On January 1, 1971, corporation Y first placed in service machines B and C, each with an unadjusted basis of $10,000. Machines B and C are eligible property. Machine A would be eligible property but for the fact it was first placed in service prior to January 1, 1971 (that is, machine A is eligible property determined without regard to subparagraph (2)(ii) of this paragraph). Corporation Y elects to apply this section for the taxable year, and adopts the modified half-year convention described in paragraph (c)(2)(ii) of this section, but does not elect to apply the asset guideline class repair allowance described in paragraph (d)(2)(iii) of this section. Machines A, B, and C are in asset guideline class 24.4 under Revenue Procedure 72-10 for which the asset depreciation range is 8 to 12 years. The $2,000 expended on machine A substantially increases its capacity and is a capital expenditure under sections 162 and 263. The $2,000 is a property improvement (as defined in paragraph (d)(2)(vii)(b) of this section) which is eligible property. However, corporation Y by mistake treats the property improvement of $2,000 as a deductible repair. Also by mistake, corporation Y includes machine B in asset guideline class 24.3 under Revenue Procedure 72-10 for which the asset depreciation range is 5 to 7 years. Corporation Y establishes vintage accounts for 1971, and computes depreciation for 1971 and 1972 as follows:

	Dec. 31, 1972, reserve for depreciation	Dec. 31, 1972, adjusted basis
Vintage account for machine B, with an asset depreciation period of 5 years and an unadjusted basis of $10,000 for which corporation Y adopts the straight line method	$4,000	$6,000
Vintage account for machine C, with an asset depreciation period of 8 years and an unadjusted basis of $10,000 for which corporation Y adopts the straight line method	2,500	7,500

After audit in 1973 of corporation Y's taxable years 1971 and 1972, it is determined that the $2,000 paid in 1971 for the rehabilitation and improvement of machine A is a capital expenditure and that machine B is in asset guideline class 24.4. The incorrect classification is corrected. Corporation Y places machine B and the property improvement in a vintage account of 1971 and on its tax return filed for 1973 selects an asset depre-

ciation period of 8 years for that account. Giving effect to the correction in classification of the property in accordance with subdivision (iii)(c) of this subparagraph, at the end of 1972 the unadjusted basis, reserve for depreciation, and adjusted basis of the vintage account for machine B and the property improvement with respect to machine A are $12,000, $3,000 and $9,000, respectively. Corporation Y's deduction of the

Reg. § 1.167(a)-11(b)(4)

$2,000 property improvement in 1971 as a repair expense under section 162 was disallowed. For 1971 and 1972 depreciation deductions are disallowed in the amount of $500 each year (that is, $750 excess annual depreciation on machine B minus $250 annual depreciation on the property improvement).

Example (4). (*a*) In 1971, Corporation X, a calendar year taxpayer, first places in service machines A through M, all of which are eligible property. All the machines except machine A are in asset guideline class 24.3 under Revenue Procedure 72-10. Machine A is in asset guideline class 24.4 under Revenue Procedure 72-10. Machine B has an unadjusted basis equal to 80 percent of the total unadjusted basis of machines B through M. By good faith mistake as to proper classification, corporation X includes both machine A and machine B in asset guideline class 24.4. Corporation X consistently uses the machine hour method of depreciation on all property in asset guideline class 24.4, and for 1971 computes depreciation for machines A and B under that method. Corporation X elects to apply this section for 1971 on the assumption that the election includes machines C through M which are in asset guideline class 24.3. In 1973, upon audit of corporation X's taxable years 1971 and 1972, it is determined that machine B is included in asset guideline class 24.3 and that since for 1971 corporation X computed depreciation on machine B under the machine hour method, in accordance with subparagraph (5)(v)(*a*) of this paragraph, all property in asset guideline class 24.3 (machines B through M) is excluded from corporation X's election to apply this section for 1971. Although corporation X has consistently used the machine hour method for asset guideline class 24.4, corporation X has not in the past used the machine hour method for machines of the type and function of machines C through M which are in asset guideline class 24.3. Both machine A and machine B are used in connection with the manufacture of wood products. There is reasonable basis for corporation X having assumed that machine B is in asset guideline 24.4 along with machine A to which it is similar. Corporation X establishes to the satisfaction of the Commissioner that it used the machine hour method for machine B on the basis of a good faith mistake as to the proper classification of the machine. Corporation X may, at its option (see subparagraph (5)(v) of this paragraph), terminate the machine hour method of depreciation for machine B as of the beginning of 1971, and in that event corporation X's election to apply this section for 1971 will apply to machines B through M without regard to subparagraph (5)(v)(*a*) of this paragraph. The adjustments provided in subdivi-

sion (iii)(*c*) of this subparagraph will be made as a result of the correction in classification of property. If corporation X does not terminate the machine hour method with respect to machine B, machines B through M must be excluded from the election to apply this section (see subparagraph (5)(v) of this paragraph.)

(*b*) The facts are the same as in (*a*) of this example except that machine B has an unadjusted basis equal to only 65 percent of the total unadjusted basis of machines B through M. In this case, corporation X must either terminate the machine hour method of depreciation with respect to asset B (since the provisions of subparagraph (5)(v) of this paragraph do not permit the exclusion of the property from the election to apply this section) or otherwise comply with the provisions of subparagraph (5)(v) of this paragraph.

(See paragraph (c)(1)(iv) for limitation on methods which may be adopted for property included in the election to apply this section.)

(5) *Requirements of election*—(i) *In general.* Except as otherwise provided in paragraph (d)(2) of this section dealing with expenditures for the repair, maintenance, rehabilitation or improvement of certain property, no provision of this section shall apply to any property other than eligible property to which the taxpayer elects in accordance with this section, to apply this section. For the time and manner of election, and certain conditions to an election, see paragraph (f) of this section. Except as otherwise provided in subparagraph (4)(iii) of this paragraph, subdivision (v) of this subparagraph, and in subparagraph (6)(iii) of this paragraph, a taxpayer's election to apply this section may not be revoked or modified after the last day prescribed for filing the election. Thus, for example, after such day, a taxpayer may not cease to apply this section to property included in the election, establish different vintage accounts for the taxable year of election, select a different period from the asset depreciation range for any such account, or adopt a different first-year convention for any such account.

(ii) *Property required to be included in election.* Except as otherwise provided in subdivision (iii) of this subparagraph dealing with certain "used property", in subdivision (iv) of this subparagraph dealing with "section 38 property", in subdivision (v) of this subparagraph dealing with property subject to special depreciation or amortization, in subdivision (vi) of this subparagraph dealing with certain section 1250 property, in subdivision (vii) of this subparagraph dealing with certain subsidiary assets, and in paragraph (e)(3)(i) and (iv) of this section dealing with transactions to which section 381(a) applies, if the

Reg. § 1.167(a)-11(b)(5)

taxpayer elects to apply this section to any eligible property first placed in service by the taxpayer during the taxable year of election, the election shall apply to all such eligible property, whether placed in service in a trade or business or held for production of income.

(iii) *Special 10 percent used property rule.* (a) If (1) the unadjusted basis of eligible used section 1245 property (as defined in (c) of this subdivision) first placed in service by the taxpayer during the taxable year of election, for which no specific used property asset guideline class (as defined in (c) of this subdivision) is in effect for the taxable year, exceeds (2) 10 percent of the unadjusted basis of all eligible section 1245 property first placed in service during the taxable year of election, the taxpayer may exclude all (but not less than all) the property described in (a)(1) of this subdivision from the election to apply this section.

(b) If (1) the unadjusted basis of eligible used section 1250 property first placed in service by the taxpayer during the taxable year of election, for which no specific used property asset guideline class is in effect for the taxable year, exceeds (2) 10 percent of the unadjusted basis of all eligible section 1250 property first placed in service during the taxable year of election, the taxpayer may exclude all (but not less than all) the property described in (b)(1) of this subdivision from the election to apply this section.

(c) For the purposes of this section, the term "used property" means property the original use of which does not commence with the taxpayer. Solely for the purpose of determining whether the 10 percent rule of this subdivision is satisfied, (1) eligible used property first placed in service during the taxable year and excluded from the election to apply this section pursuant to subdivision (v)(a) of this subparagraph and (2) eligible property acquired during the taxable year in a transaction to which section 381(a) applies, shall all be treated as used property regardless of whether such property would be treated as new property under section 167(c) and the regulations thereunder. The term "specific used property asset guideline class" means a class established in accordance with subparagraph (4) of this paragraph solely for used property primarily used in connection with the activity to which the class relates.

(iv) *Property subject to investment tax credit.* The taxpayer may exclude from an election to apply this section all, or less than all, units of eligible property first placed in service during the taxable year which is—

(a) "Section 38 property" as defined in section 48(a) which meets the requirements of section 49 and which is not property described in section 50, or

(b) Property to which section 47(a)(5)(B) applies which would be section 38 property but for section 49 which is placed in service to replace section 38 property (other than property described in section 50) disposed of prior to August 15, 1971.

(v) *Property subject to special method of depreciation or amortization.* (a) In the case of eligible property first placed in service in a taxable year of election (and not otherwise properly excluded from an election to apply this section) the taxpayer may not compute depreciation for any of such property in the asset guideline class under a method not described in section 167(b)(1), (2), (3) or (k) unless he (1) computes depreciation under a method or methods not so described for eligible property first placed in service in the taxable year in the asset guideline class with an unadjusted basis at least equal to 75 percent of the unadjusted basis of all eligible property first placed in service in the taxable year in the asset guideline class and (2) agrees to continue to depreciate such property under such method or methods until the consent of the Commissioner is obtained to a change in method. The consent of the Commissioner must be obtained by filing Form 3115 with the Commissioner of Internal Revenue, Washington, D.C. 20224, within the first 180 days of the taxable year for which the change is desired. If for the taxable year of election the taxpayer computes depreciation under any method not described in section 167(b)(1), (2), (3) or (k) for any eligible property (other than property otherwise properly excluded from an election to apply this section) first placed in service during the taxable year, an election to apply this section for the taxable year shall not include such property or any other eligible property in the same asset guideline class as such property. With respect to a taxable year beginning before January 1, 1973, if the taxpayer has adopted a method of depreciation which is not permitted under this subdivision, the taxpayer may under this section adopt a method of depreciation permitted under this subdivision or otherwise comply with the provisions of this subdivision.

(b) An election to apply this section shall not include eligible property for which, for the taxable year of election, the taxpayer computes depreciation under section 167(k), or computes amortization under section 169, 184, 185, 187, 188 or paragraph (b) or § 1.162-11. If the taxpayer has elected to apply this section to eligi-

Reg. § 1.167(a)-11(b)(5)

ble property described in section 167(k), 169, 184, 185, or 187 and the taxpayer thereafter computes depreciation or amortization for such property for any taxable year in accordance with section 167(k), 169, 184,185, or 187, then the election to apply this section to such property shall terminate as of the beginning of the taxable year for which depreciation or amortization is computed under such section. Application of this section to the property for any period prior to the termination date will not be affected by the termination. The unadjusted basis of the property shall be removed as of the termination date from the unadjusted basis of the vintage account. The depreciation reserve established for the account shall be reduced by the depreciation allowable for the property, computed in the manner prescribed in paragraph (c)(1)(v)(b) of this section for determination of the adjusted basis of the property. See paragraph (d)(3)(vii)(e) of this section for treatment of salvage value when property is removed from a vintage account.

(vi) *Certain section 1250 property.* (a) The taxpayer may exclude from an election to apply this section all, or less than all, items of eligible section 1250 property first placed in service during the taxable year of election provided that—

(1) The item is first placed in service before the earlier of the effective date of the first supplemental asset guideline class including such property established in accordance with subparagraph (4)(ii) of this paragraph, or January 1, 1974, and

(2) The taxpayer establishes that a useful life shorter than the asset guideline period in effect on January 1, 1971, for such item of property is justified for such taxable year.

A useful life shorter than the asset guideline period in effect on January 1, 1971, will be considered justified only if such life is justified in accordance with the provisions of Revenue Procedure 62-21 (including all modifications, amendments or supplements thereto as of January 1, 1971), determined without application of the minimal adjustment rule in section 4, Part II, of Revenue Procedure 65-13. If an item of section 1250 property is excluded from an election to apply this section pursuant to this subdivision, any elevator or escalator which is a part of such item shall also be excluded from the election.

(b) If the taxpayer excludes an item of section 1250 property from an election to apply this section in accordance with this subdivision, the useful life justified under Revenue Procedure 62-21 in accordance with this subdivision for the taxable year of exclusion will be treated as justified for such item of section 1250 property for the

taxable year of the exclusion and all subsequent taxable years.

(vii) *Subsidiary assets.* The taxpayer may exclude from an election to apply this section all (but not less than all) subsidiary assets first placed in service during the taxable year of election in an asset guideline class, provided that—

(a) the unadjusted basis of eligible subsidiary assets first placed in service during the taxable year in the class is as much as 3 percent of the unadjusted basis of all eligible property first placed in service during the taxable year in the class and

(b) such subsidiary assets are first placed in service by the taxpayer before the earlier of (1) the effective date of the first supplemental asset guideline class including such subsidiary assets established in accordance with subparagraph (4)(ii) of this paragraph, or (2) January 1, 1974. For purposes of this subdivision the term "subsidiary assets" includes jigs, dies, molds, returnable containers, glassware, silverware, textile mill cam assemblies, and other equipment included in Group One, Class 5, of Revenue Procedure 62-21 which is usually and properly accounted for separately from other property and under a method of depreciation not expressed in terms of years.

(6) *Special rule for certain public utility property*—(i) *Requirement of normalization in certain cases.* Under section 167(l), in the case of public utility property (as defined in section 167(l)(3)(A)), if the taxpayer—

(a) Is entitled to use a method of depreciation other than a "subsection (1) method" of depreciation (as defined in section 167(l)(3)(F)) only if it uses the "normalization method of accounting" (as defined in section 167(l)(3)(G)) with respect to such property, or

(b) Is entitled for the taxable year to use only a "subsection (1) method" of depreciation,

such property shall be eligible property (as defined in subparagraph (2) of this paragraph) only if the taxpayer normalizes the tax deferral resulting from the election to apply this section.

(ii) *Normalization.* The taxpayer will be considered to normalize the tax deferral resulting from the election to apply this section only if it computes its tax expense for purposes of establishing its cost of service for rate-making purposes and for reflecting operating results in its regulated books of account using a period for depreciation no less than the lesser of—

(a) 100% of the asset guideline period in effect in accordance with subparagraph (4)(ii) of

Reg. § 1.167(a)-11(b)(6)

this paragraph for the first taxable year to which this section applies, or

(b) The period for computing its depreciation expense for rate-making purposes and for reflecting operating results in its regulated books of account,

and makes adjustments to a reserve to reflect the deferral of taxes resulting from the use of a period for depreciation under section 167 in accordance with an election to apply this section different from the lesser of the periods described in (a) and (b) of this subdivision. In the case of public utility property described in section 167(l)(3)(A)(iii) for which no guideline life was prescribed in Revenue Procedure 62-21 (or for which reference was made in Revenue Procedure 62-21 to lives or rates established by governmental regulatory agencies), for the purpose of (a) of this subdivision, the asset guideline period shall be deemed to be the period for computing the taxpayer's depreciation expense for rate-making purposes and for reflecting operating results in its regulated books of account instead of the asset guideline period in effect in accordance with subparagraph (4)(ii) of this paragraph for the first taxable year to which this section applies. A determination whether the taxpayer is considered to normalize under this subdivision the tax deferral resulting from the election to apply this section shall be made in a manner consistent with the principles for determining whether a taxpayer is using the "normalization" method of accounting (within the meaning of section 167(l)(3)(G)). See § 1.167(l)-1(h).

(iii) *Failure to normalize.* If a taxpayer, which has elected to apply this section to any eligible public utility property and is required under subdivision (i) of this subparagraph to normalize the tax deferral resulting from the election to apply this section to such property, fails to normalize such tax deferral, the election to apply this section to such property shall terminate as of the beginning of the taxable year for which the taxpayer fails to normalize such tax deferral. Application of this section to such property for any period prior to the termination date will not be affected by the termination. The unadjusted basis of the property shall be removed as of the termination date from the unadjusted basis of the vintage account. The depreciation reserve established for the account shall be reduced by the depreciation allowable for the property, computed in the manner prescribed in paragraph (c)(1)(v)(b) of this section for determination of the adjusted basis of the property. See paragraph (d)(3)(vii)(e) of this section for treatment of salvage value when property is removed from a vintage account.

(iv) *Examples.* The principles of this subparagraph may be illustrated by the following examples:

Example (1). Corporation A is a gas pipeline company, subject to the jurisdiction of the Federal Power Commission, which is entitled under section 167(l) to use a method of depreciation other than a "subsection (l) method" of depreciation (as defined in section 167(l)(3)(F)) only if it uses the "normalization method of accounting" (as defined in section 167 (l)(3)(G)). Corporation A elects to apply this section for 1972 with respect to all eligible property. In 1972, corporation A places in service eligible property with an unadjusted basis of $2 million. One hundred percent of the asset guideline period for such property is 22 years and the asset depreciation range is from 17.5 years to 26.5 years. The taxpayer uses the double declining balance method of depreciation, selects an asset depreciation period of 17.5 years and applies the half-year convention (described in paragraph (c)(2)(iii) of this section). The depreciation allowable under this section with respect to such property in 1972 is $114,285. The taxpayer will be considered to normalize the tax deferral resulting from the election to apply this section and to use the "normalization method of accounting" (within the meaning of section 167(l)(3)(G)) if it computes its tax expense for purposes of determining its cost of service for rate making purposes and for reflecting operating results in its regulated books of account using a "subsection (l) method" of depreciation, such as the straight line method, determined by using a depreciation period of 22 years (that is, 100 percent of the asset guideline period). A depreciation allowance computed in this manner is $45,454. The difference in the amount determined under this section ($114,285) and the amount used in computing its tax expense for purposes of estimating its cost of service for rate making purposes and for reflecting operating results in its regulated books of account ($45,454) is $68,831. Assuming a tax rate of 48 percent, the deferral of taxes resulting from an election to apply this section and using a different method of depreciation for tax purposes from that used for establishing its cost of service for rate making purposes and for reflecting operating results in its regulated books of account is 48 percent of $68,831, or $33,039, which amount should be added to a reserve to reflect the deferral of taxes resulting from the election to apply this section and from the use of a different method of depreciation in computing the allowance for depreciation under section 167 from that used in computing its depreciation expense for purposes of establishing its cost of service for rate making purposes and for reflect-

Reg. § 1.167(a)-11(b)(6)

ing operating results in its regulated books of account.

Example (2). Corporation B, a telephone company subject to the jurisdiction of the Federal Communications Commission used a "flow-through method of accounting" (as defined in section 167(l)(3)(H)) for its "July 1969 accounting period" (as defined in section 167(l)(3)(I)) with respect to all of its pre-1970 public utility property and did not make an election under section 167(l)(4)(A). Thus, corporation B is entitled under section 167(l) to use a method of depreciation other than a "subsection (l) method" with respect to certain property without using the "normalization method of accounting." In 1972, corporation B makes an election to apply this section with respect to all eligible property. Corporation B is not required to normalize the tax deferral resulting from the election to apply this section in the case of property for which it is not required to use the "normalization method of accounting" under section 167(l).

Example (3). Assume the same facts as in example (2) except that corporation B made a timely election under section 167(l)(4)(A) that section 167(l)(2)(C) not apply with respect to property which increases the productive or operational capacity of the taxpayer. Corporation B must normalize the tax deferral resulting from the election to apply this section with respect to such property.

(7) *Mere change in form of conducting a trade or business.* Property which was first placed in service by the transferor before January 1, 1971, shall not be eligible property if such property is first placed in service by the transferee after December 31, 1970, by reason of a mere change in the form of conducting a trade or business in which such property is used. A mere change in the form of conducting a trade or business in which such property is used will be considered to have occurred if—

(i) The transferor (or in a case where the transferor is a partnership, estate, trust, or corporation, the partners, beneficiaries, or shareholders) of such property retains a substantial interest in such trade or business, or

(ii) The basis of such property in the hands of the transferee is determined in whole or in part by reference to the basis of such property in the hands of the transferor.

For purposes of this subparagraph, a transferor (or in a case where the transferor is a partnership, estate, trust, or corporation, the partners, beneficiaries, or shareholders) shall be considered as having retained a substantial interest in the trade or business only if, after the change in form, his

(or their) interest in such trade or business is substantial in relation to the total interest of all persons in such trade or business. This subparagraph shall apply to property first placed in service prior to January 1, 1971, held for the production of income (within the meaning of section 167(a)(2)) as well as to property used in a trade or business. The principles of this subdivision may be illustrated by the following examples:

Example (1). Corporation X and corporation Y are includible corporations in an affiliated group as defined in section 1504(a). In 1971 corporation X sells property to corporation Y for cash. The property would meet the requirements of subparagraph (2) of this paragraph for eligible property except that it was first placed in service by corporation X in 1970. After the transfer, the property is first placed in service by corporation Y in 1971. The property is not eligible property because of the mere change in the form of conducting a trade or business.

Example (2). In 1971, in a transaction to which section 351 applies, taxpayer B transfers to corporation W property which would meet the requirements of subparagraph (2) of this paragraph for eligible property except that the property was first placed in service by B in 1969. Corporation W first places the property in service in 1971. The property is not eligible property because of the mere change in the form of conducting a trade or business.

(c) *Manner of determining allowance*—(1) *In general*—(i) *Computation of allowance.* (a) The allowance for depreciation of property in a vintage account shall be determined in the manner specified in this paragraph by using the method of depreciation adopted by the taxpayer for the account and a rate based upon the asset depreciation period for the account. (For limitations on methods of depreciation permitted with respect to property, see section 167(c) and (j) and subdivision (iv) of this subparagraph.) In applying the method of depreciation adopted by the taxpayer, the annual allowance for depreciation of a vintage account shall be determined without adjustment for the salvage value of the property in such account except that no account may be depreciated below the reasonable salvage value of the account. (For rules regarding estimation and treatment of salvage value, see paragraph (d)(1) and (3) (vii) and (viii) of this section.) Regardless of the method of depreciation adopted by the taxpayer, the depreciation allowable for a taxable year with respect to a vintage account may not exceed the amount by which (as of the beginning of the taxable year) the unadjusted basis of the account exceeds (*1*) the reserve for depreciation

Reg. § 1.167(a)-11(c)(1)

established for the account plus (2) the salvage value of the account. The unadjusted basis of a vintage account is defined in subdivision (v) of this subparagraph. The adjustments to the depreciation reserve are described in subdivision (ii) of this subparagraph.

(b) The annual allowance for depreciation of a vintage account using the straight line method of depreciation shall be determined by dividing the unadjusted basis of the vintage account (without reduction for salvage value) by the number of the years in the asset depreciation period selected for the account. See subdivision (iii)(b) of this subparagraph for the manner of computing the depreciation allowance following a change from the declining balance method or the sum of the years-digits method to the straight line method.

(c) In the case of the sum of the years-digits method, the annual allowance for depreciation of a vintage account shall be computed by multiplying the unadjusted basis of the vintage account (without reduction for salvage value) by a fraction, the numerator of which changes each year to a number which corresponds to the years remaining in the asset depreciation period for the account (including the year for which the allowance is being computed) and the denominator of which is the sum of all the year's digits corresponding to the asset depreciation period for the account. See subdivision (iii)(c) of this subparagraph for the manner of computing the depreciation allowance following a change from the declining balance method to the sum of the years-digits method.

(d) The annual allowance for depreciation of a vintage account using a declining balance method is determined by applying a uniform rate to the excess of the unadjusted basis of the vintage account over the depreciation reserve established for that account. The rate under the declining balance method may not exceed twice the straight line rate based upon the asset depreciation period for the vintage account.

(e) The allowance for depreciation under this paragraph shall constitute the amount of depreciation allowable under section 167. See section 179 for additional first-year allowance for certain property.

(ii) *Establishment of depreciation reserve.* The taxpayer must establish a depreciation reserve for each vintage account. The amount of the reserve for a guideline class must be stated on each income tax return on which depreciation with respect to such class is determined under this section. The depreciation reserve for a vintage account consists of the accumulated depreciation

allowable under this section with respect to the vintage account, increased by the adjustments for ordinary retirements prescribed by paragraph (d)(3)(iii) of this section, by the adjustments for reduction of the salvage value of a vintage account prescribed by paragraph (d)(3)(vii)(d) of this section, and by the adjustments for transfers to supplies or scrap prescribed by paragraph (d)(3)(viii)(b) of this section, and decreased by the adjustments for extraordinary retirements and certain special retirements as prescribed by paragraph (d)(3)(iv) and (v) of this section, by the adjustments for the amount of the reserve in excess of the unadjusted basis of a vintage account prescribed by paragraph (d)(3)(ix)(a) of this section, and by the adjustments for property removed from a vintage account prescribed by paragraph (b)(4)(iii)(e), (5)(v)(b) and (6)(iii) of this section. The adjustments to the depreciation reserve for ordinary retirements during the taxable year shall be made as of the beginning of the taxable year. The adjustments to the depreciation reserve for extraordinary retirements shall be made as of the date the retirement is treated as having occurred in accordance with the first-year convention (described in subparagraph (2) of this paragraph) adopted by the taxpayer for the vintage account. The adjustment to the depreciation reserve for reduction of salvage value and for transfers to supplies or scrap shall, in the case of an ordinary retirement, be made as of the beginning of the taxable year, and in the case of an extraordinary retirement the adjustment for reduction of salvage value shall be made as of the date the retirement is treated as having occurred in accordance with the first-year convention (described in subparagraph (2) of this paragraph) adopted by the taxpayer for the vintage account. The adjustment to the depreciation reserve for property removed from a vintage account in accordance with paragraph (b)(4)(iii)(e), (5)(v)(b) and (6)(iii) of this section shall be made as of the beginning of the taxable year. The depreciation reserve of a vintage account may not be decreased below zero.

(iii) *Consent to change in method of depreciation.* (a) During the asset depreciation period for a vintage account, the taxpayer is permitted to change under this section from a declining balance method of depreciation to the sum of the years-digits method of depreciation and from a declining balance method of depreciation or the sum of the years-digits method of depreciation to the straight line method of depreciation with respect to such account. Except as provided in section 167(j)(2) and (l) and paragraph (e)(3)(i) of this section, no other changes in the method of depreciation adopted for a vintage account will be

Reg. § 1.167(a)-11(c)(1)

permitted. The provisions of § 1.167(e)-1 shall not apply to any change in depreciation method permitted under this section. The change in method applies to all property in the vintage account and must be adhered to for the entire taxable year of the change.

(b) When a change is made to the straight line method of depreciation, the annual allowance for depreciation of the vintage account shall be determined by dividing the adjusted basis of the vintage account (without reduction for salvage value) by the number of years remaining (at the time as of which the change is made) in the asset depreciation period selected for the account. However, the depreciation allowable for any taxable year following a change to the straight line method may not exceed an amount determined by dividing the unadjusted basis of the vintage account (without reduction for salvage value) by the number of years in the asset depreciation period selected for the account.

(c) When a change is made from the declining balance method of depreciation to the sum of the years-digits method of depreciation, the annual allowance for depreciation of a vintage account shall be determined by multiplying the adjusted basis of the account (without reduction for salvage value) at the time as of which the change is made by a fraction, the numerator of which changes each year to a number which corresponds to the number of years remaining in the asset depreciation period selected for the account (including the year for which the allowance is being computed), and the denominator of which is the sum of all the year's digits corresponding to the number of years remaining in the asset depreciation period at the time as of which the change is made.

(d) The number of years remaining in the asset depreciation period selected for an account is equal to the asset depreciation period less the number of years of depreciation previously allowed. For this purpose, regardless of the first year convention adopted by the taxpayer, it will be assumed that depreciation was allowed for one-half of a year in the first year.

(e) The taxpayer shall furnish a statement setting forth the vintage accounts for which the change is made with the income tax return filed for the taxable year of the change.

(f) The principles of this subdivision may be illustrated by the following examples:

Example (1). A calendar year taxpayer, places new section 1245 property in service in a trade or business as follows:

Asset	Placed in service	Unadjusted basis	Estimated salvage
X	March 15, 1971	$400	$20
Y	June 13, 1971	$500	50
Z	July 30, 1971	$100	0

The property is eligible property and is properly included in a single vintage account. The asset depreciation range for such property is 5 to 7 years and the taxpayer selects an asset depreciation period of 51/2 years and adopts the 200-percent declining balance method of depreciation.

The taxpayer adopts the half-year convention described in subparagraph (2)(iii) of this paragraph. After 3 years, A changes from the 200-percent declining balance method to the straight line method of depreciation. Depreciation allowances would be as follows:

Year	Unadjusted basis	Rate	Depreciation	Reserve	Adjusted basis
1971	$1,000.00	.18182	$181.82	$181.82	$818.18
1972	1,000.00	.36363	297.52	479.34	520.66
1973	1,000.00	.36363	189.33	668.67	331.33
1974	1,000.00	.33333[1]	110.44	779.11	220.89
1975	1,000.00	.33333	110.44	889.56	110.44
1976	1,000.00	.33333	40.44[2]	930.00	70.00

[1] Rate applied to adjusted basis of the account (without reduction by salvage) at the time as of which the change is made to the straight line method.

[2] The allowable depreciation is limited by estimated salvage.

Example (2). The facts are the same as in example (1) except that A elects to use the modified half-year convention described in subparagraph (2)(ii) of this paragraph. The depreciation allowances would be as follows:

Reg. § 1.167(a)-11(c)(1)

Year	Unadjusted basis	Rate	Depreciation	Reserve	Adjusted basis
1971	$1,000.00	.36363[1]	$327.27	$327.27	$672.73
1972	1,000.00	.36363	244.63	571.90	428.10
1973	1,000.00	.36363	155.67	727.57	272.43
1974	1,000.00	.33333	90.8 1	818.38	181.62
1975	1,000.00	.33333	90.81	909.19	90.81
1976	1,000.00	.33333	20.81[2]	930.00	70.00

[1] Rate applied to $900.00, the amount of assets placed in service during the first half of the taxable year.

[2] The allowable depreciation is limited by estimated salvage.

Example (3). The facts are the same as in example (1) except that A adopted the sum of the years-digits method of depreciation and does not change to the straight-line method of depreciation. The depreciation allowances would be as follows:

Year	Unadjusted basis	Rate	Depreciation	Reserve	Adjusted basis
1971	$1,000.00	2.75/18 [1]	$152.78	$152.78	$847.22
1972	1,000.00	5/18	277.78	430.56	569.44
1973	1,000.00	4/18	222.22	652.78	347.22
1974	1,000.00	3/18	166.67	819.45	180.55
1975	1,000.00	2/18	110.55 [2]	930.00	70.00
1976	1,000.00	1/18	0.00	930.00	70.00
1977	1,000.00	0.25/18	0.00	930.00	70.00

[1] Rate is equal to one-half of 5.5/18. The denominator is equal to $5.5 + 4.5 + 3.5 + 2.5 + 1.5 + .5$.

[2] The allowable depreciation is limited by estimated salvage.

Example (4). The facts are the same as in example (3) except that A elects to use the modified half-year convention described in subparagraph (2)(ii) of this paragraph. The depreciation allowances would be as follows:

Year	Unadjusted basis	Rate	Depreciation	Reserve	Adjusted basis
1971	$1,000.00	5.5/18 [1]	$275.00	$275.00	$725.00
1972	1,000.00	5/18	277.78	552.78	447.22
1973	1,000.00	4/18	222.22	775.00	225.00
1974	1,000.00	3/18	155.00 [2]	930.00	70.00
1975	1,000.00	2/18	0.00	930.00	70.00
1976	1,000.00	1/18	0.00	930.00	70.00
1977	1,000.00	0.25/18	0.00	930.00	70.00

[1] Rate applied to $900.00, the amount of assets placed in service during the first half of the taxable year.

[2] The allowable depreciation is limited by estimated salvage.

Example (5). The facts are the same as in example (2) except that after 2 years A changes from the 200-percent declining balance method to the sum of the years-digits method of depreciation. The depreciation allowances would be as follows:

Year	Unadjusted basis	Rate	Depreciation	Reserve	Adjusted basis
1971	$1,000.00	.36363	$327.27	$327.27	$672.73
1972	1,000.00	.36363	244.63	571.90	428.10
1973	1,000.00	4/10	171.24	743.14	256.86
1974	1,000.00	3/10	128.43	871.57	128.43
1975	1,000.00	2/10	58.43 [1]	930.00	70.00
1976	1,000.00	1/10	0.00	930.00	70.00

[1] The allowable depreciation is limited by estimated salvage.

(iv) Limitation on methods. (a) The same method of depreciation must be adopted for all property in a single vintage account. Generally, the method of depreciation which may be adopted is subject to the limitations contained in section 167(c), (j) and (l).

Reg. § 1.167(a)-11(c)(1)

(b) Except as otherwise provided in section 167(j) with respect to certain eligible section 1250 property—

(1) In the case of a vintage account for which the taxpayer has selected an asset depreciation period of 3 years or more and which only contains property the original use of which commences with the taxpayer, any method of depreciation described in section 167(b)(1), (2), or (3) may be adopted, but if the vintage account contains property the original use of which does not commence with the taxpayer, or if the asset depreciation period for the account is less than 3 years, a method of depreciation described in section 167(b)(2) or (3) may not be adopted for the account, and

(2) The declining balance method using a rate not in excess of 150 percent of the straight line rate based upon the asset depreciation period for the vintage account may be adopted for the account even if the original use of the property does not commence with the taxpayer provided the asset depreciation period for the account is at least 3 years.

(c) The term "original use" means the first use to which the property is put, whether or not such use corresponds to the use of such property by the taxpayer. (See § 1.167(c)-1).

(v) *Unadjusted and adjusted basis.* (a) For purposes of this section, the unadjusted basis of an asset (including an "excluded addition" and a "property improvement" as described, respectively, in paragraph (d)(2)(vi) and (vii) of this section) is its cost or other basis without any adjustment for depreciation or amortization (other than depreciation under section 179) but with other adjustments required under section 1016 or other applicable provisions of law. The unadjusted basis of a vintage account is the total of the unadjusted bases of all the assets in the account. The unadjusted basis of a "special basis vintage account" as described in paragraph (d)(3)(vi) of this section is the amount of the property improvement determined in paragraph (d)(2)(vii)(a) of this section

(b) The adjusted basis of a vintage account is the amount by which the unadjusted basis of the account exceeds the reserve for depreciation for the account. The adjusted basis of an asset in a vintage account is the amount by which the unadjusted basis of the asset exceeds the amount of depreciation allowable for the asset under this section computed by using the method of depreciation and the rate applicable to the account. For purposes of this subdivision, the depreciation allowable for an asset shall include, to the extent identifiable, the amount of proceeds previously added to the depreciation reserve in

accordance with paragraph (d)(3)(iii) of this section upon the retirement of any portion of such asset. (See paragraph (d)(3)(vi) of this section for election under certain circumstances to allocate adjusted basis of an amount of property improvement determined under paragraph (d)(2)(vii) (a) of this section.)

(2) *Conventions applied to additions and retirements*—(i) *In general.* The allowance for depreciation of a vintage account (whether an item account or a multiple asset account) shall be determined by applying one of the conventions described in subdivisions (ii) and (iii) of this subparagraph. (For the manner of applying a convention in the case of taxable years beginning before and ending after December 31, 1970, see subparagraph (3) of this paragraph.) The same convention must be adopted for all vintage accounts of a taxable year, but the same convention need not be adopted for the vintage accounts of another taxable year. An election to apply this section must specify the convention adopted. (See paragraph (f) of this section for information required in making the election.) The convention adopted by the taxpayer is a method of accounting for purposes of section 446, but the consent of the Commissioner will be deemed granted to make an annual adoption of either of the conventions described in subdivisions (ii) and (iii) of this subparagraph.

(ii) *Modified half-year convention.* The depreciation allowance for a vintage account for which the taxpayer adopts the "modified half-year convention" shall be determined by treating: (a) all property in such account which is placed in service during the first half of the taxable year as placed in service on the first day of the taxable year; and (b) all property in such account which is placed in service during the second half of the taxable year as placed in service on the first day of the succeeding taxable year. The depreciation allowance for a vintage account for a taxable year in which there is an extraordinary retirement (as defined in paragraph (d)(3)(ii) of this section) of property first placed in service during the first half of the taxable year is determined by treating all such retirements from such account during the first half of the taxable year as occurring on the first day of the taxable year and all such retirements from such account during the second half of the taxable year as occurring on the first day of the second half of the taxable year. The depreciation allowance for a vintage account for a taxable year in which there is an extraordinary retirement (as defined in paragraph (d)(3)(ii) of this section) of property first placed in service during the second half of the taxable year is determined by treating all such retirements from such account

Reg. § 1.167(a)-11(c)(2)

during the first half of the taxable year as occurring on the first day of the second half of the taxable year and all such retirements in the second half of the taxable year as occurring on the first day of the succeeding taxable year.

(iii) *Half-year convention.* The depreciation allowance for a vintage account for which the taxpayer adopts the "half-year convention" shall be determined by treating all property in the account as placed in service on the first day of the second half of the taxable year and by treating all extraordinary retirements (as defined in paragraph (d)(3)(ii) of this section) from the account as occurring on the first day of the second half of the taxable year.

(iv) *Rules of application.* (*a*) The first-year convention adopted for a vintage account must be consistently applied to all additions to and all extraordinary retirements from such account. See paragraph (d)(3)(ii) and (iii) of this section for definition and treatment of ordinary retirements.

(*b*) If the actual number of months in a taxable year is other than 12 full calendar months, depreciation is allowed only for such actual number months and the term "taxable year", for purposes of this subparagraph, shall mean only such number of months. In such event, the first half of such taxable year shall be deemed to expire at the close of the last day of a calendar month which is the closest such last day to the middle of such taxable year and the second half of such taxable year shall be deemed to begin the day after the expiration of the first half of such taxable year. If a taxable year consists of a period which includes only one calendar month, the first half of the taxable year shall be deemed to expire on the first day which is nearest to the midpoint of the month, and the second half of the taxable year shall begin the day after the expiration of the first half of the month.

(*c*) For purposes of this subparagraph, for property placed in service after November 14, 1979, other than depreciable property described in paragraph (c)(2)(iv)(*e*) of this section, the taxable year of the person placing such property in service does not include any month before the month in which the person begins engaging in a trade or business or holding depreciable property for the production of income.

(*d*) For purposes of paragraph (c)(2)(iv)(*c*) of this section—

(*1*) For property placed in service after February 21, 1981, an employee is not considered engaged in a trade or business by virtue of employment.

(*2*) If a person engages in a small amount of trade or business activity after February 21, 1981, for the purpose of obtaining a disproportionately large depreciation deduction for

assets for the taxable year in which they are placed in service, and placing those assets in service represents a substantial increase in the person's level of business activity, then for purposes of depreciating those assets the person will not be treated as beginning a trade or business until the increased amount of business activity begins. For property held for the production of income, the principle of the preceding sentence applies.

(*3*) A person may elect to apply the rules of § 1.167(a)-11(c)(2)(iv)(*d*) as set forth in T.D. 7763 ("(*d*) rules in T.D. 7763"). This election shall be made by reflecting it under paragraph (f)(4) of this section in the books and records. If necessary, amended returns shall be filed.

(*4*) If an averaging convention was adopted in reliance on or in anticipation of the (*d*) rules in T.D. 7763, that convention may be changed without regard to paragraph (f)(3) of this section. Similarly, if an election is made under paragraph (c)(2)(iv)(*d*) (*3*) of this section to apply the (*d*) rules in T.D. 7763, the averaging convention adopted for the taxable years for which the election is made may be changed. The change shall be made by filing a timely amended return for the taxable year for which the convention was adopted. Notwithstanding the three preceding sentences, if an averaging convention was adopted in reliance on or in anticipation of the (*d*) rules in T.D. 7763, and if an election is made to apply those rules, the averaging convention adopted cannot be changed except as provided in paragraph (f) of this section.

(*e*) The rules in paragraph (c)(2)(iv)(*c*) of this section do not apply to depreciable property placed in service after November 14, 1979, and the rules in paragraph (c)(2)(iv)(*d*) of this section do not apply to depreciable property placed in service after February 21, 1981, with respect to which substantial expenditures were paid or incurred prior to November 15, 1979. For purposes of the preceding sentence, expenditures will not be considered substantial unless they exceed the lesser of 30 percent of the final cost of the property or $10 million. Expenditures that are not includible in the basis of the depreciable property will be considered expenditures with respect to property if they are directly related to a specific project involving such property. For purposes of determining whether expenditures were paid or incurred prior to November 15, 1979, expenditures made by a person (transferor) other than the person placing the property in service (transferee) will be taken into account only if the basis of the property in the hands of the transferee is determined in whole or in part by reference to the basis in the hands of the transferor. The principle of the preceding sentence also applies if there are multiple transfers.

Reg. § 1.167(a)-11(c)(2)

(v) *Mass assets.* In the case of mass assets, if extraordinary retirements of such assets in a guideline class during the first half of the taxable year are allocated to a particular vintage year for which the taxpayer applied the modified half-year convention, then that portion of the mass assets so allocated which bears the same ratio to the total number of mass assets so allocated as the mass assets in the same vintage and asset guideline class placed in service during the first half of that vintage year bear to the total mass assets in the same vintage and asset guideline class shall be treated as retired on the first day of the taxable year. The remaining mass assets which are subject to extraordinary retirement during the first half of the taxable year and which are allocated to that vintage year and asset guideline class shall be treated as retired on the first day of the second half of the taxable year. If extraordinary retirements of mass assets in a guideline class occur in the second half of the taxable year and are allocated to a particular vintage year for which the taxpayer applied the modified half-year convention, then that portion of the mass assets so allocated which bears the same ratio to the total number of mass assets so allocated as the mass assets in the same vintage and asset guideline class first placed in service during the first half of that vintage year bear to the total mass assets in the same vintage and asset guideline class shall be treated as retired on the first day of the second half of the taxable year. The remaining mass assets which are subject to extraordinary retirements during the second half of the taxable year and which are allocated to that same vintage and asset guideline class shall be treated as retired on the first day of the succeeding taxable year. If the taxpayer has applied the half-year convention for the vintage year to which the extraordinary retirements are allocated, the mass assets shall be treated as retired on the first day of the second half of the taxable year.

(3) *Taxable years beginning before and ending after December 31, 1970.* In the case of a taxable year which begins before January 1, 1971, and ends after December 31, 1970, property first placed in service after December 31, 1970, but treated as first placed in service before January 1, 1971, by application of a convention described in subparagraph (2) of this paragraph shall be treated as provided in this subparagraph. The depreciation allowed (or allowable) for the taxable year shall consist of the depreciation allowed (or allowable) for the period before January 1, 1971, determined without regard to this section plus the amount allowable for the period after December 31, 1970, determined under this section. However, neither the modified half-year convention described in subparagraph (2)(ii) of this paragraph, nor the half-year convention described in subparagraph (2)(iii) of this paragraph may for any such taxable year be applied with respect to property placed in service after December 31, 1970, to allow depreciation for any period prior to January 1, 1971, unless such convention is consistent with the convention applied by the taxpayer with respect to property placed in service in such taxable year prior to January 1, 1971.

(4) *Examples.* The principles of this paragraph may be illustrated by the following examples:

Example (1). Taxpayer A, a calendar year taxpayer, places new property in service in a trade or business as follows:

Asset	Placed in Service	Unadjusted Basis
W	April 1, 1971	$ 5,000
X	June 30, 1971	8,000
Y	July 15, 1971	12,000

Taxpayer A adopts the modified half-year convention described in subparagraph (2)(ii) of this paragraph. Assets W, X. and Y are placed in a multiple asset account for which the asset depreciation range is 8 to 12 years. A selects 8 years, the minimum asset depreciation period with respect to such assets, and adopts the declining balance method of depreciation using a rate twice the straight line rate (computed without reduction for salvage). The annual rate under this method using a period of 8 years is 25 percent. The depreciation allowance for assets W and X for 1971 is $3,250, a full year's depreciation under the modified half-year convention (that is, basis of $13,000 (unreduced by salvage) multiplied by 25 percent).

The depreciation allowance for asset Y for 1971 is zero under the modified half-year convention.

Example (2). The facts are the same as in example (1), except that the taxpayer adopts the half-year convention described in subparagraph (2)(iii) of this paragraph. The depreciation allowance with respect to asset Y is $1,500 (that is the basis of $12,000 multiplied by 25 percent, then multiplied by 1/2). Assets W and X are also entitled to a depreciation allowance for only a half year. Thus, the depreciation allowance for assets W and X for 1971 is $1,625 (that is, 1/2 of the $3,250 allowance computed in example (1)).

Reg. § 1.167(a)-11(c)(4)

Example (3). Asset Z is placed in service by a calendar year taxpayer on December 1, 1971. The taxpayer places asset Z in an item account and adopts the sum of the years-digits method and the half-year convention described in subparagraph (2)(iii) of this paragraph. The asset depreciation range for such asset is 4 to 6 years and the taxpayer selects an asset depreciation period of 5 years. The depreciation allowance for asset Z in 1971 is $10,000 (that is, basis of $60,000 (unreduced by salvage) multiplied by 5/15, the appropriate fraction using the sum of the years-digits method then multiplied by 1/2, since only

one half year's depreciation is allowable under the convention).

Example (4). A is a calendar year taxpayer. All taxpayer A's assets are placed in service in the first half of 1971. If the taxpayer selects the modified half-year convention described in subparagraph (2)(ii) of this paragraph, a full year's depreciation is allowable for all assets.

Example (5). (i) The taxpayer during his taxable year which begins April 1, 1970, and ends March 31, 1971, places new property in service in a trade or business as follows:

Asset	Placed in Service	Unadjusted Basis
A	April 30, 1970	$10,000
B	December 15, 1970	10,000
C	January 1, 1971	10,000

The taxpayer adopted a convention under § 1.167(a)-10(b) with respect to assets placed in service prior to January 1, 1971, which treats assets placed in service during the first half of the year as placed in service on the first day of such year and assets placed in service in the second half of the year as placed in service on the first day of the following year. If the taxpayer selects the half-year convention described in subparagraph (2)(iii) of this paragraph, one year's depreciation is allowable on asset A determined without regard to this section. No depreciation is allowable for asset B. No depreciation is allowable for asset C for the period prior to January 1, 1971.

Asset	
A	August 1, 1970
B	January 15, 1971
C	June 30, 1971

The taxpayer adopted a convention under § 1.167(a)-10(b) with respect to assets placed in service prior to January 1, 1971, which treats all assets as placed in service at the mid-point of the taxable year. If the taxpayer selects the half-year convention described in subparagraph (2)(iii) of this paragraph, one-half year's depreciation is allowable for asset A determined without regard to this section. One-half year's depreciation is allowable for assets B and C determined under this section.

Example (7). X, a calendar year corporation, is incorporated on July 1, 1978, and begins engaging in a trade or business in September 1979. X purchases asset A and places it in service on November 20, 1979. Substantial expenditures were not paid or incurred by X with respect to asset A prior to November 15, 1979. For purposes of applying the conventions under this section to determine depreciation for asset A, the 1979 taxable year is treated as consisting of 4 months. The

One-fourth year's depreciation is allowable on asset C determined under this section.

(ii) The facts are the same as in (i) of this example except that the taxpayer adopts the modified half-year convention described in subparagraph (2)(ii) of this paragraph for 1971. No depreciation is allowable for assets B and C which were placed in service in the second half of the taxable year.

Example (6). The taxpayer during his taxable year which begins August 1, 1970, and ends July 31, 1971, places new property in service in a trade or business as follows:

first half of the taxable year ends on October 31, 1979, and the second half begins on November 1, 1979. X adopts the half-year convention. Asset A is treated as placed in service on November 1, 1979.

Example (8). On January 20, 1982, A, B, and C enter an agreement to form partnership P for the purpose of purchasing and leasing a ship to a third party, Z. P uses the calendar year as its taxable year. On December 15, 1982, P acquires the ship and leases it to Z. For purposes of applying the conventions, P begins its leasing business in December 1982, and its taxable year begins on December 1, 1982. Assuming that P elects to apply this section and adopts the modified half-year convention, P depreciates the ship placed in service in 1982 for the 1-month period beginning December 1, 1982, and ending December 31, 1982.

Example (9). A and B form partnership P on December 15, 1981, to conduct a business of leas-

Reg. § 1.167(a)-11(c)(4)

ing small aircraft. P uses the calendar year as its taxable year. On January 15, 1982, P acquires and places in service a $25,000 aircraft. P begins engaging in business with only one aircraft for the purpose of obtaining a disproportionately large depreciation deduction for aircraft that P plans to acquire at the end of the year. On December 10, 1982, P acquires and places in service 4 aircraft, the total purchase price of which is $250,000. For purposes of applying the conventions to the aircraft acquired in December, P begins its leasing business in December 1982, and P's taxable year begins December 1, 1982, and ends December 31, 1982. Assuming that P elects to apply this section and adopts the modified half-year convention, P depreciates the aircraft placed in service in December 1982, for the 1-month period beginning December 1, 1982, and ending December 31, 1982. P depreciates the aircraft placed in service in January 1982, for the 12-month period beginning January 1, 1982, and ending December 31, 1982.

(d) *Special rules for salvage, repairs and retirements*—(1) *Salvage value*—(i) *Definition of gross salvage value.* "Gross salvage" value is the amount which is estimated will be realized upon a sale or other disposition of the property in the vintage account when it is no longer useful in the taxpayer's trade or business or in the production of his income and is to be retired from service, without reduction for the cost of removal, dismantling, demolition or similar operations. If a taxpayer customarily sells or otherwise disposes of property at a time when such property is still in good operating condition, the gross salvage value of such property is the amount expected to be realized upon such sale or disposition, and under certain circumstances, as where such property is customarily sold at a time when it is still relatively new, the gross salvage value may constitute a relatively large proportion of the unadjusted basis of such property.

(ii) *Definition of salvage value.* "Salvage value" means gross salvage value less the amount, if any, by which the gross salvage value is reduced by application of section 167(f). Generally, as provided in section 167(f), a taxpayer may reduce the amount of gross salvage value of a vintage account by an amount which does not exceed 10 percent of the unadjusted basis of the personal property (as defined in section 167(f)(2)) in the account. See paragraph (b)(3)(ii) of this section for requirement of separate vintage accounts for personal property described in section 167(f)(2).

(iii) *Estimation of salvage value.* The salvage value of each vintage account of the taxable year shall be estimated by the taxpayer at the time the election to apply this section is made, upon the basis of all the facts and circumstances existing at the close of the taxable year in which the account is established. The taxpayer shall specify the amount, if any, by which gross salvage value taken into account is reduced by application of section 167(f). The salvage value estimated by the taxpayer will not be redetermined merely as a result of fluctuations in price levels or as a result of other facts and circumstances occurring after the close of the taxable year of election. Salvage value for a vintage account need not be established or increased as a result of a property improvement as described in subparagraph (2)(vii) of this paragraph. The taxpayer shall maintain records reasonably sufficient to determine facts and circumstances taken into account in estimating salvage value.

(iv) *Salvage as limitation on depreciation.* In no case may a vintage account be depreciated below a reasonable salvage value after taking into account any reduction in gross salvage value permitted by section 167(f).

(v) *Limitation on adjustment of reasonable salvage value.* The salvage value established by the taxpayer for a vintage account will not be redetermined if it is reasonable. Since the determination of salvage value is a matter of estimation, minimal adjustments will not be made. The salvage value established by the taxpayer will be deemed to be reasonable unless there is sufficient basis in the facts and circumstances existing at the close of the taxable year in which the account is established for a determination of an amount of salvage value for the account which exceeds the salvage value established by the taxpayer for the account by an amount greater than 10 percent of the unadjusted basis of the account at the close of the taxable year in which the account is established. If the salvage value established by the taxpayer for the account is not within the 10 percent range, or if the taxpayer follows the practice of understating his estimates of gross salvage value to take advantage of this subdivision, and if there is a determination of an amount of salvage value for the account which exceeds the salvage value established by the taxpayer for the account, an adjustment will be made by increasing the salvage value established by the taxpayer for the account by an amount equal to the difference between the salvage value as determined and the salvage value established by the taxpayer for the account. For the purposes of this subdivision, a determination of salvage value shall include all determinations at all levels of audit and appellate proceedings, and as well as all final determinations within the meaning of section 1313(a)(1). This subdivision shall apply to each such determination. (See example (3) of subdivision (vi) of this subparagraph.)

(vi) *Examples.* The principles of this subparagraph may be illustrated by the following examples in which it is assumed that the taxpayer has not followed a practice of understating his estimates of gross salvage value:

Example (1). Taxpayer B elects to apply this section to assets Y and Z, which are placed in a multiple asset vintage account of 1971 for which the taxpayer selects an asset depreciation period of 8 years. The unadjusted basis of asset Y is $50,000 and the unadjusted basis of asset Z is $30,000. B estimates a gross salvage value of $55,000. The property qualifies under section 167(f)(2) and B reduces the amount of salvage taken into account by $8,000 (that is, 10 percent of $80,000 under section 167(f)). Thus, B establishes a salvage value of $47,000 for the account. Assume that there is not sufficient basis for determining a salvage value for the account greater than $52,000 (that is, $60,000 minus the $8,000 reduction under section 167(f)). Since the salvage value of $47,000 established by B for the account is within the 10 percent range, it is reasonable. Salvage value for the account will not be redetermined.

Example (2). The facts are the same as in example (1) except that B estimates a gross salvage value of $50,000 and establishes a salvage value of $42,000 for the account (that is, $50,000 minus the $8,000 reduction under section 167(f)). There is sufficient basis for determining an amount of salvage value greater than $50,000 (that is, $58,000 minus the $8,000 reduction under section 167(f)). The salvage value of $42,000 established by B for the account can be redetermined without regard to the limitation in subdivision (v) of this subparagraph, since it is not within the 10 percent range. Upon audit of B's tax return for a taxable year for which the redetermination would affect the amount of depreciation allowable for the account, salvage value is determined to be $52,000 after taking into account the reduction under section 167(f). Salvage value for the account will be adjusted to $52,000.

Example (3). The facts are the same as in example (1) except that upon audit of B's tax return for a taxable year the examining officer determines the salvage value to be $58,000 (that is, $66,000 minus the $8,000 reduction under section 167(f)), and proposes to adjust salvage value for the vintage account to $58,000 which will result in disallowing an amount of depreciation for the taxable year. B does not agree with the finding of the examining officer. After receipt of a "30-day letter", B waives a district conference and initiates proceedings before the Appellate Division. In consideration of the case by the Appellate Division it is concluded that there is not sufficient basis for determining an amount of salvage value for the account in excess of $55,000 (that is, $63,000 minus the $8,000 reduction under section 167(f)). Since the salvage of $47,000 established by B for the account is within the 10 percent range, it is reasonable. Salvage value for the account will not be redetermined.

Example (4). Taxpayer C elects to apply this section to factory building X which is placed in an item vintage account of 1971. The unadjusted basis of factory building X is $90,000. C estimates a gross salvage value for the account of $10,000. The property does not qualify under section 167(f)(2). C establishes a salvage value of $10,000 for the account. Assume that there is not sufficient basis for determining a salvage value for the account greater than $18,000. Since the salvage value of $10,000 established by B for the account is within the 10 percent range, it is reasonable. Salvage value for the account will not be redetermined.

(2) *Treatment of repairs—(i) In general. (a)* Sections 162, 212, and 263 provide general rules for the treatment of certain expenditures for the repair, maintenance, rehabilitation or improvement of property. In general, under those sections, expenditures which substantially prolong the life of an asset, or are made to increase its value or adapt it to a different use are capital expenditures. If an expenditure is treated as a capital expenditure under section 162, 212, or 263, it is subject to the allowance for depreciation. On the other hand, in general, expenditures which do not substantially prolong the life of an asset or materially increase its value or adapt it for a substantially different use may be deducted as an expense in the taxable year in which paid or incurred. Expenditures, or a series of expenditures, may have characteristics both of deductible expenses and capital expenditures. Other expenditures may have the characteristics of capital expenditures, as in the case of an "excluded addition" (as defined in subdivision (vi) of this subparagraph). This subparagraph provides a simplified procedure for determining whether expenditures with respect to certain property are to be treated as deductible expenses or capital expenditures.

(*b*) [Reserved]

(ii) *Election of repair allowance.* In the case of an asset guideline class which consists of "repair allowance property" as defined in subdivision (iii) of this subparagraph, subject to the provisions of subdivision (v) of this subparagraph, the taxpayer may elect to apply the asset guideline class repair allowance described in subdivision (iii) of this subparagraph for any taxable year ending after December 31, 1970, for which the taxpayer elects to apply this section.

(iii) *Repair allowance for an asset guideline class.* For a taxable year for which the taxpayer elects to apply this section, the "repair allowance" for an asset guideline class which consists of "repair allowance property" is an amount equal to—

(a) The average of (1) the unadjusted basis of all "repair allowance property" in the asset guideline class at the beginning of the taxable year, less in the case of such property in a vintage account the unadjusted basis of all such property retired in an ordinary retirement (as described in subparagraph (3)(ii) of this paragraph) in prior taxable years, and (2) the unadjusted basis of all "repair allowance property" in the asset guideline class at the end of the taxable year, less in the case of such property in a vintage account the unadjusted basis of all such property retired in an ordinary retirement (including ordinary retirements during the taxable year), multiplied by—

(b) The repair allowance percentage in effect for the asset guideline class for the taxable year.

In applying the asset guideline class repair allowance to buildings which are section 1250 property, for the purpose of this subparagraph each building shall be treated as in a separate guideline class. If two or more buildings are in the same asset guideline class determined without regard to the preceding sentence, and are operated as an integrated unit (as evidenced by their actual operation, management, financing, and accounting), they shall be treated as a single building for this purpose. The "repair allowance percentages" in effect for taxable years ending before the effective date of the first supplemental repair allowance percentages established pursuant to this section are set forth in Revenue Procedure 72-10 [superseded by Rev. Proc. 77-10; see ¶ 1732D.08]. Repair allowance percentages will from time to time be established, supplemented and revised with express reference to this section. These repair allowance percentages will be published in the Internal Revenue Bulletin. The repair allowance percentages in effect on the last day of the taxable year of election shall apply for the taxable year, except that the repair allowance percentage for a particular taxable year shall not be less than the repair allowance percentage in effect on the first day of such taxable year (or as of such later time in such year as a repair allowance percentage first established during such year becomes effective).

Generally, the repair allowance percentages for a taxable year shall not be changed to reflect any supplement or revision of the repair allowance percentages after the end of such taxable year. However, if expressly provided in such a supplement or revision of the repair allowance percentages, the taxpayer may, at his option in the manner specified therein, apply the revised or supplemented repair allowance percentages for such taxable year and succeeding taxable years. For the purposes of this section, "repair allowance property" means eligible property determined without regard to paragraph (b)(2)(ii) of this section (that is, without regard to whether such property was first placed in service by the taxpayer before or after December 31, 1970) in an asset guideline class for which a repair allowance percentage is in effect for the taxable year. The determination whether property is repair allowance property shall be made without regard to whether such property is excluded, under paragraph (b)(5) of this section, from an election to apply this section. Property in an asset guideline class for which the taxpayer elects to apply the asset guideline class repair allowance described in this subdivision, which results from expenditures in the taxable year of election for the repair, maintenance, rehabilitation, or improvement of property in an asset guideline class shall not be "repair allowance property" for such taxable year but shall be for each succeeding taxable year provided such property is a property improvement as described in subdivision (vii)(a) of this subparagraph and is in an asset guideline class for which a repair allowance percentage is in effect for such succeeding taxable year.

(iv) *Application of asset guideline class repair allowance.* In accordance with the principles of sections 162, 212, and 263, if the taxpayer pays or incurs any expenditures during the taxable year for the repair, maintenance, rehabilitation or improvement of eligible property (determined without regard to paragraph (b)(2)(ii) of this section), the taxpayer must either—

(a) If such property is repair allowance property and if the taxpayer elects to apply the repair allowance for the asset guideline class, treat an amount of all such expenditures in such taxable year with respect to all such property in the asset guideline class which does not exceed in total the repair allowance for that asset guideline class as deductible repairs, and treat the excess of all such expenditures with respect to all such property in the asset guideline class in the manner described for a property improvement in subdivision (viii) of this subparagraph, or

Reg. § 1.167(a)-11(d)(2)

(b) If such property is not repair allowance property or if the taxpayer does not elect to apply the repair allowance for the asset guideline class, treat each of such expenditures in such taxable year with respect to all such property in the asset guideline class as either a capital expenditure or as a deductible repair in accordance with the principles of sections 162, 212, and 263 (without regard to (a) of this subdivision), and treat the expenditures which are required to be capitalized under sections 162, 212, and 263 (without regard to (a) of this subdivision) in the manner described for a property improvement in subdivision (viii) of this subparagraph.

For the purposes of (a) of this subdivision expenditures for the repair, maintenance, rehabilitation or improvement of property do not include expenditures for an excluded addition or for which a deduction is allowed under section 167(k). (See subdivision (viii) of this subparagraph for treatment of an excluded addition.) The taxpayer shall elect each taxable year whether to apply the repair allowance and treat expenditures under (a) of this subdivision, or to treat expenditures under (b) of this subdivision. The treatment of expenditures under this subdivision for a taxable year for all asset guideline classes shall be specified in the books and records of the taxpayer for the taxable year. The taxpayer may treat expenditures under (a) of this subdivision with respect to property in one asset guideline class and treat expenditures under (b) of this subdivision with respect to property in some other asset guideline class. In addition, the taxpayer may treat expenditures with respect to property in an asset guideline class under (a) of this subdivision in one taxable year, and treat expenditures with respect to property in that asset guideline class under (b) of this subdivision in another taxable year.

(v) *Special rules for repair allowance.* (a) The asset guideline class repair allowance described in subdivision (iii) of this subparagraph shall apply only to expenditures for the repair, maintenance, rehabilitation or improvement of repair allowance property (as described in subdivision (iii) of this subparagraph). The taxpayer may apply the asset guideline class repair allowance for the taxable year only if he maintains books and records reasonably sufficient to determine:

(1) The amount of expenditures paid or incurred during the taxable year for the repair, maintenance, rehabilitation or improvement of repair allowance property in the asset guideline class, and

(2) The expenditures (and the amount thereof) with respect to such property which are for excluded additions (such as whether the expenditure is for an additional identifiable unit of property, or substantially increases the productivity or capacity of an existing identifiable unit of property or adapts it for a substantially different use).

In general, such books and records shall be sufficient to identify the amount and nature of expenditures with respect to specific items of repair allowance property or groups of similar properties in the same asset guideline class. However, in the case of such expenditures with respect to property, part of which is in one asset guideline class and part in another, or part of which is repair allowance property and part of which is not, and in comparable circumstances involving property in the same asset guideline class, to the extent books and records are not maintained identifying such expenditures with specific items of property or groups of similar properties and it is not practicable to do so, the total amount of such expenditures which is not specifically identified may be allocated by any reasonable method consistently applied. In any case, the cost or repair, maintenance, rehabilitation or improvement of property performed by production personnel may be allocated by any reasonable method consistently applied and, if performed incidental to production and not substantial in amount, no allocation to repair, maintenance, rehabilitation or improvement need be made. The types of expenditures for which specific identification would ordinarily be made include: substantial expenditures such as for major parts or major structural materials for which a work order is or would customarily be written; expenditures for work performed by an outside contractor; or expenditures under a specific down time program. Types of expenditures for which specific identification would ordinarily be impractical include: general maintenance costs of machinery, equipment, and plant in the case of a taxpayer having assets in more than one class (or different types of assets in the same class) which are located together and generally maintained by the same work crew; small supplies which are used with respect to various classes or types of property; labor costs of personnel who work on property in different classes, or different types of property in the same class, if the work is performed on a routine, as needed, basis and the only identification of the property repaired is by the personnel. Factors which will be taken into account in determining the reasonableness of the taxpayer's allocation of expenditures include prior experience of the taxpayer; relative bases of the assets in the guideline class; types of assets involved; and relationship to specifically identified expenditures.

Reg. § 1.167(a)-11(d)(2)

(b) If for the taxable year the taxpayer elects to deduct under section 263(e) expenditures with respect to repair allowance property consisting of railroad rolling stock (other than a locomotive) in a particular asset guideline class, the taxpayer may not, for such taxable year, use the asset guideline class repair allowance described in subdivision (iii) of this subparagraph for any property in such asset guideline class.

(c)(1) If the taxpayer repairs, rehabilitates or improves property for sale or resale to customers, the asset guideline class repair allowance described in subdivision (iii) of this subparagraph shall not apply to expenditures for the repair, maintenance, rehabilitation or improvement of such property, or

(2) if a taxpayer follows the practice of acquiring for his own use property (in need of repair, rehabilitation or improvement to be suitable for the use intended by the taxpayer) and of making expenditures to repair, rehabilitate or improve such property in order to take advantage of this subparagraph, the asset guideline class repair allowance described in subdivision (iii) of this subparagraph shall not apply to such expenditures. In either event, such property shall not be "repair allowance property" as described in subdivision (iii) of this subparagraph.

(vi) *Definition of excluded addition.* The term "excluded addition" means—

(a) An expenditure which substantially increases the productivity of an existing identifiable unit of property over its productivity when first acquired by the taxpayer;

(b) An expenditure which substantially increases the capacity of an existing identifiable unit of property over its capacity when first acquired by the taxpayer;

(c) An expenditure which modifies an existing identifiable unit of property for a substantially different use;

(d) An expenditure for an identifiable unit of property if (1) such expenditure is for an additional identifiable unit of property or (2) such expenditure (other than an expenditure described in (e) of this subdivision) is for replacement of an identifiable unit of property which was retired;

(e) An expenditure for replacement of a part in or a component or portion of an existing identifiable unit of property (whether or not such part, component or portion is also an identifiable unit of property) if such part, component or portion is for replacement of a part, component or portion which was retired in a retirement upon which gain or loss is recognized (or would be

recognized but for a special nonrecognition provision of the Code or § 1.1502-13).

(f) In the case of a building or other structure (in addition to (b), (c), (d) and (e) of this subdivision which also apply to such property), an expenditure for additional cubic or linear space; and

(g) In the case of those units of property of pipelines, electric utilities, telephone companies, and telegraph companies consisting of lines, cables and poles (in addition to (a) through (e) of this subdivision which also apply to such property), an expenditure for replacement of a material portion of the unit of property.

Except as provided in (d) and (e) of this subdivision, notwithstanding any other provision of this subdivision, the term "excluded addition" does not include any expenditure in connection with the repair, maintenance, rehabilitation or improvement of an identifiable unit of property which does not exceed $100. For this purpose all related expenditures with respect to the unit of property shall be treated as a single expenditure. For the purposes of (a) and (b) of this subdivision, an increase in productivity or capacity is substantial only if the increase is more than 25 percent. An expenditure which merely extends the productive life of an identifiable unit of property is not an increase in productivity within the meaning of (a) of this subdivision. Under (g) of this subdivision a replacement is material only if the portion replaced exceeds 5 percent of the unit of property with respect to which the replacement is made. For the purposes of this subdivision, a unit of property generally consists of each operating unit (that is, each separate machine or piece of equipment) which performs a discrete function and which the taxpayer customarily acquires for original installation and retires as a unit. The taxpayer's accounting classification of units of property will generally be accepted for purposes of this subdivision provided the classifications are reasonably consistent with the preceding sentence and are consistently applied. In the case of a building the unit of property generally consists of the building as well as its structural components; except that each building service system (such as an elevator, an escalator, the electrical system, or the heating and cooling system) is an identifiable unit for the purpose of (a), (b), (c), and (d) of this subdivision. However, both in the case of machinery and equipment and in the case of a building, for the purpose of applying (d)(1) of this subdivision a unit of property may consist of a part in or a component or portion of a larger unit of property. In the case of property described in (g) of this subdivision (such as a pipeline), a

Reg. § 1.167(a)-11(d)(2)

unit of property generally consists of each segment which performs a discreet function either as to capacity, service, transmission or distribution between identifiable points. Thus, for example, under this subdivision in the case of a vintage account of five automobiles each automobile is an identifiable unit of property which is not merely a part in or a component or portion of larger unit of property within the meaning of (e) of this subdivision). Accordingly, the replacement of one of the automobiles (which is retired) with another automobile is an excluded addition under (d)(2) of this subdivision. Also the purchase of a sixth automobile is an expenditure for an additional identifiable unit of property and is an excluded addition under (d)(1) of this subdivision. An automobile air conditioner is also an identifiable unit of property for the purposes of (d)(1) of this subdivision, but not for the purposes of (d)(2) of this subdivision. Accordingly, the addition of an air conditioner to an automobile is an excluded addition under (d)(1) of this subdivision, but the replacement of an existing air conditioner in an automobile is not an excluded addition under (d)(2) of this subdivision (since it is merely the replacement of a part in an existing identifiable unit of property). The replacement of the air conditioner may, however, be an excluded addition under (e) of this subdivision, if the air conditioner replaced was retired in a retirement upon which gain or loss was recognized. The principles of this subdivision may be further illustrated by the following examples in which it is assumed (unless otherwise stated) that (e) of this subdivision does not apply.

Example (1). For the taxable year, B pays or incurs only the following expenditures: (1) $5,000 for general maintenance of repair allowance property (as described in subdivision (iii) of this subparagraph) such as inspection, oiling, machine adjustments, cleaning, and painting; (2) $175 for replacement of the bearings and gears in an existing lathe; (3) $125 for replacement of an electric starter (of the same capacity) and certain electrical wiring in an automatic drill press; (4) $300 for modification of a metal fabricating machine (including replacement of certain parts) which substantially increases its capacity; (5) $175 for repair of the same metal fabricating machine which does not substantially increase its capacity; (6) $800 for the replacement of an existing lathe with a new lathe; and (7) $65 for the repair of a drill press. Expenditures (1) through (3) are expenditures for the repair, maintenance, rehabilitation or improvement of property to which B can elect to apply the asset guideline class repair allowance described in subdivision (iii) of this subparagraph. Expenditure (4) is an excluded addition under (b) of this

subdivision. Expenditure (5) is not an excluded addition. Expenditure (6) is an excluded addition under (d)(2) of this subdivision. Without regard to (a), (b) and (c) of this subdivision, expenditure (7) is not an excluded addition, since the expenditure does not exceed $100.

Example (2). Corporation M operates a steel plant which produces rails, blooms, billets, special bar sections, reinforcing bars, and large diameter line pipe. During the taxable year, corporation M: (1) relines an open-hearth furnace; (2) places in service 20 new ingot molds; (3) replaces one reversing roll in the blooming mill; (4) overhauls the rail and billet mill with no increase in capacity; (5) replaces a roll stand in the 20-inch bar mill; and (6) overhauls the 11-inch bar mill and reducing stands increasing billet speed from 1800 feet per minute to 2300 feet per minute. Assume that each expenditure exceeds $100. Expenditure (1) is not an excluded addition. Expenditure (2) is an excluded addition under (d)(1) of this subdivision. Expenditure (3) is not an excluded addition since the expenditure for the reversing roll merely replaces a part in an existing identifiable unit of property. Expenditure (4) is not an excluded addition. Expenditure (5) is an excluded addition under (d)(2) of this subdivision since the roll stand is not merely a part of an existing identifiable unit of property. Expenditure (6) is an excluded addition under (a) of this subdivision since it increases the billet speed by more than 25 percent.

Example (3). For the taxable year, corporation X pays or incurs the following expenditures: (1) $1,000 for two new temporary partition walls in the company's offices; (2) $1,400 for repainting the exterior of a terminal building; (3) $300 for repair of the roof of a warehouse; (4) $150 for replacement of two window frames and panes in the warehouse; and (5) $100 for plumbing repair. Expenditure (1) is an excluded addition under (d)(1) of this subdivision. None of the other expenditures are excluded additions.

Example (4). For the taxable year, corporation Y pays or incurs the following expenditures: (1) $10,000 for expansion of a loading dock from 600 square feet to 750 square feet; (2) $600 for replacement of two roof girders in a factory building; and (3) $9,500 for replacement of columns and girders supporting the floor of a second story loft storage area within the factory building in order to permit storage of supplies with a gross weight 50 percent greater than the previous capacity of the loft. Expenditure (1) is an excluded addition under (f) of this subdivision. Expenditure (2) is not an excluded addition. Expenditure

Reg. § 1.167(a)-11(d)(2)

(3) is an excluded addition under (b) of this subdivision.

Example (5). Corporation A has an office building with an unadjusted basis of $10,000,000. The building has 10 elevators, five of which are manually operated and five of which are automatic. During 1971, corporation A:

(1) replaces the five manually operated elevators with highspeed automatic elevators at a cost of $400,000;

(2) replaces the cable in one of the existing automatic elevators at a cost of $1,700.

The replacements of the elevators are excluded additions under (d)(2) of this subdivision. The replacement of the cable is not an excluded addition.

Example (6). Taxpayer W, a cement manufacturer, engages in the following modification and maintenance activities during the taxable year: (1) replaces eccentric-bearing, spindle, and wearing surface in a gyratory crusher; (2) places in service a new apron feeder and hammer mill; (3) replaces four buckets on a chain bucket elevator; (4) relines refractory surface in the burning zone of a rotary kiln; (5) installs additional new dust collectors; and (6) replaces two 16-inch x 90-foot belts on his conveyor system. Assume that there is no increase in productivity or capacity and that each expenditure exceeds $100. Expenditure (1) is not an excluded addition. Expenditure (2) [is] an excluded addition under (d)(1) of this subdivision. Expenditures (3) and (4) are not excluded additions. Expenditure (5) is an excluded addition under (d)(1) of this subdivision. Expenditure (6) is not an excluded addition.

Example (7). Corporation X, a gas pipeline company, has, in addition to others, the following units of property: (1) a gathering pipeline for a field consisting of 25 gas wells; (2) the main transmission line between compressor stations (that is, in the case of a 500 mile main transmission line with a compressor station every 100 miles, each one hundred miles section between compressor stations is a separate unit of property); (3) a lateral transmission line from the main transmission line to a city border station; (4) a medium pressure distribution line to the northern portion of the city; and (5) a low pressure distribution line serving a group of approximately 200 residential customers off the medium pressure distribution line. In 1971, corporation X pays or incurs the following expenditures in connection with the repair, maintenance rehabilitation or improvement of repair allowance property; (1) replaces a meter on a gas well; (2) in connection with the repair and rehabilitation of a unit of property consisting of a two-mile gathering pipe-

line, replaces a 3,000-foot section of the gathering line; (3) in connection with the repair of leaks in a unit of property consisting of a 100-mile gas transmission line (that is, the 100 miles between compressor stations), replaces a 2,000-foot section of pipeline at one point; and (4) at another point replaces a 7-mile section of the same 100-mile gas transmission line. Assume that none of these expenditures substantially increases capacity and that each expenditure exceeds $100. Expenditure (1) is an excluded addition under (d) of this subdivision. Expenditure (2) is an excluded addition under (g) of this subdivision since the portion replaced is more than 5 percent of the unit of property. Expenditure (3) is not an excluded addition Expenditure (4) is an excluded addition under (g) of this subdivision.

Example (8). Taxpayer Y, an electric utility company, has in addition to others, the following units of property: (1) a high voltage transmission circuit from the switching station (at the generating station) to the transmission station; (2) a series of 100 poles (fully dressed) supporting the circuit in (1); (3) a high voltage circuit from the transmission station to the distribution substation; (4) a high voltage distribution circuit (either radial or looped) from the distribution substation; (5) a transformer on a distribution pole; (6) a circuit breaker on a distribution pole; and (7) all 220 (and lower) volt circuit (including customer service connections) off the distribution circuit in (4). In 1971, taxpayer Y pays or incurs the following expenditures for the repair, maintenance, rehabilitation or improvement of repair allowance property: (1) replaces 25 adjacent poles in a unit of property consisting of the 300 poles supporting a radial distribution circuit from a distribution substation; (2) replaces a transformer on one of the poles in (1); (3) replaces a cross-arm on one of the poles in (1); (4) replaces a 200-foot section of a 2-mile radial distribution circuit serving 100 residential customers; and (5) replaces a 2,000-foot section on a 10-mile high voltage circuit from a transmission station to a distribution substation which was destroyed by a casualty which taxpayer Y treated as an extraordinary retirement under paragraph (d)(3)(ii) of this section. Expenditure (1) is an excluded addition under (g) of this subdivision. Expenditure (2) is an excluded addition under (d)(2) of this subdivision. Expenditures (3) and (4) are not excluded additions. Expenditure (5) is an excluded addition under (e) of this subdivision.

Example (9). Corporation Z, a telephone company, has in addition to others, the following units of property: (1) a buried feeder cable 3 miles in length off a local switching station; (2) a buried sub-feeder cable one mile in length off the feeder

Reg. § 1.167(a)-11(d)(2)

cable in (1); (3) all the distribution cable (and customer service drops) off the sub-feeder cable in (2); (4) the 300 poles (fully dressed) supporting the distribution cable in (3); (5) a 10-mile local trunk cable which interconnects two local tandem switching stations; (6) a toll connecting trunk cable from a local tandem switching station to a long distance tandem switching station; (7) a toll trunk cable 50 miles in length from the access point at one city to the access point at another city. In 1971, corporation Z pays or incurs the following expenditures in connection with the repair, maintenance, rehabilitation or improvement of repair allowance property: (1) replaces 100 feet of distribution cable in a unit of property consisting of 8 miles of local distribution cable (plus customer service drops); (2) replaces an amplifier in the distribution system; and (3) replaces 10 miles of a unit of property consisting of a toll trunk cable 50 miles in length.

Expenditure (1) is not an excluded addition. Expenditure (2) is an excluded addition under (d)(2) of this subdivision. Expenditure (3) is an excluded addition under (g) of this subdivision.

(vii) *Definition of property improvement.* The term "property improvement" means—

(a) If the taxpayer treats expenditures for the asset guideline class under subdivision (iv)(a) of this subparagraph, the amount of all expenditures paid or incurred during the taxable year for the repair, maintenance, rehabilitation or improvement of repair allowance property in the asset guideline class, which exceeds the asset guideline class repair allowance for the taxable year; and

(b) If the taxpayer treats expenditures for the asset guideline class under subdivision (iv)(b) of this subparagraph, the amount of each expenditure paid or incurred during the taxable year for the repair, maintenance, rehabilitation or improvements of property which is treated under sections 162, 212 and 263 as a capital expenditure.

The term "property improvement" does not include any expenditure for an excluded addition.

(viii) *Treatment of property improvements and excluded additions.* If for the taxable year there is a property improvement as described in subdivision (vii) of this subparagraph or an excluded addition as described in subdivision (vi) of this subparagraph, the following rules shall apply—

(a) The total amount of any property improvement for the asset guideline class determined under subdivision (vii)(a) of this subparagraph shall be capitalized in a single "special basis vintage account" of the taxable year in accordance with the taxpayer's election to apply this section for the taxable year (applied without regard to paragraph (b)(5)(v)(a) of this section). See subparagraph (3)(vi) of this paragraph for definition and treatment of a "special basis vintage account".

(b) Each property improvement determined under subdivision (vii)(b) of this subparagraph, if it is eligible property, shall be capitalized in a vintage account of the taxable year in accordance with the taxpayer's election to apply this section for the taxable year (applied without regard to paragraph (b)(5)(v)(a) of this section).

(c) Each excluded addition, if it is eligible property, shall be capitalized in a vintage account of the taxable year in accordance with the taxpayer's election to apply this section for the taxable year.

For rule as to date on which a property improvement or an excluded addition is first placed in service, see paragraph (e)(1)(iii) and (iv) of this section.

(ix) *Examples.* The principles of this subparagraph may be illustrated by the following examples:

Example (1). For the taxable year 1972, B elects to apply this section. B has repair allowance property (as described in subdivision (iii) of this subparagraph) in asset guideline class 20.2 under Revenue Procedure 72-10 with an average unadjusted basis determined as provided in subdivision (iii)(a) of this subparagraph of $100,000 and repair allowance property in asset guideline class 24.4 with an average unadjusted basis of $300,000. The repair allowance percentage for asset guideline class 20.2 is 4.5 percent and for asset guideline class 24.4 is 6.5 percent. The two asset guideline class repair allowances for 1972 are $4,500 and $19,500, respectively, determined as follows:

Asset Guideline Class 20.2

$100,000 average unadjusted basis multiplied by 4.5 percent . . . . $ 4,500

Asset Guideline Class 24.4

$300,000 average unadjusted basis multiplied by 6.5 percent $19,500

Example (2). The facts are the same as in example (1). During the taxable year 1972, B pays or incurs the following expenditures for the repair, maintenance, rehabilitation or improvement of repair allowance property in asset guideline class 20.2.

Reg. § 1.167(a)-11(d)(2)

General maintenance (including primarily labor costs)	$3,000
Replacement of parts in several machines (including labor costs of $1,650)	$4,000
	$7,000

In addition, in connection with the rehabilitation and improvement of two other machines B pays or incurs $6,000 (including labor costs of $2,000) which is treated as an excluded addition because the capacity of the machines was substantially increased. For 1972, B elects to apply this section and to apply the asset guideline class repair allowance to asset guideline class 20.2. Since the asset guideline class repair allowance is $4,500, B can deduct $4,500 in accordance with subdivision (iv)(a) of this subparagraph. B must capitalize $2,500 in a special basis vintage account in accordance with subdivisions (vii)(a) and (viii)(a) of this subparagraph. Since the excluded addition is a capital item and is eligible property, B must also capitalize $6,000 in a vintage account in accordance with subdivision (viii)(c) of this subparagraph. B selects from the asset depreciation range an asset depreciation period of 17 years for the special basis vintage account. B includes the excluded addition in a vintage account of 1972 for which he also selects an asset depreciation period of 17 years.

(3) *Treatment of retirements*—(i) *In general.* The rules of this subparagraph specify the treatment of all retirements from vintage accounts. The rules of § 1.167(a)-8 shall not apply to any retirement from a vintage account. An asset in a vintage account is retired when such asset is permanently withdrawn from use in a trade or business or in the production of income by the taxpayer. A retirement may occur as a result of a sale or exchange, by other act of the taxpayer amounting to a permanent disposition of an asset, or by physical abandonment of an asset. A retirement may also occur by transfer of an asset to supplies or scrap.

(ii) *Definitions of ordinary and extraordinary retirements.* The term 'ordinary retirement" means any retirement of section 1245 property from a vintage account which is not treated as an "extraordinary retirement" under this subparagraph. The retirement of an asset from a vintage account in a taxable year is an "extraordinary retirement" if—

(a) The asset is section 1250 property;

(b) The asset is section 1245 property which is retired as the direct result of fire, storm, shipwreck, or other casualty and the taxpayer, at his option consistently applied (taking into account type, frequency and the size of such casualties) treats such retirements as extraordinary; or

(c)(1) The asset is section 1245 property which is retired (other than by transfer to

supplies or scrap) in a taxable year as the direct result of a cessation, termination, curtailment, or disposition of a business, manufacturing, or other income producing process, operation, facility or unit, and (2) the unadjusted basis (determined without regard to subdivision (vi) of this subparagraph) of all such assets so retired in such taxable year from such account as a direct result of the event described in (c)(1) of this subdivision exceeds 20 percent of the unadjusted basis of such account immediately prior to such event.

(d) The asset is section 1245 property which is retired after December 30, 1980, by a charitable contribution for which a deduction is allowable under section 170.

For the purposes of (c) of this subdivision, all accounts (other than a special basis vintage account as described in subdivision (vi) of this subparagraph) containing section 1245 property of the same vintage in the same asset guideline class, and from which a retirement as a direct result of such event occurs within the taxable year, shall be treated as a single vintage account. See subdivision (xi) of this subparagraph for special rule for item accounts. The principles of this subdivision may be illustrated by the following examples:

Example (1). Taxpayer A is a processor and distributor of dairy products. Part of taxpayer A's operation is a bottle washing facility consisting of machines X, Y, and Z, each of which is in an item vintage account of 1971. Each item vintage account has an unadjusted basis of $1,000 Taxpayer A also has a 1971 multiple asset vintage account consisting of machines E, S, and C. Machines E and S, used in processing butter, each as an unadjusted basis of $10,000. Machine C used in capping bottles has an unadjusted basis of $1,000. In 1975, taxpayer A changes to the use of paper milk cartons and disposes of all bottle washing machines (X, Y, and Z) as well as machine C which was used in capping bottles. The sales of machines C, X, Y, and Z are the direct result of the termination of a manufacturing process. However, since the total unadjusted basis of the eligible section 1245 property retired as a direct result of such event is only $4,000 (which is less than 20 percent of the total unadjusted basis of machines E, S, C, X, Y, and Z, $24,000) the sales are ordinary retirements. All the assets are in the same asset guideline class and are of the same vintage. Accordingly, machines E, S, C, X, Y, and Z are for this purpose treated as being in a single vintage account.

Reg. § 1.167(a)-11(d)(3)

Example (2). The facts are the same as in example (1) except that in 1976, taxpayer A sells six of his 12 milk delivery trucks as a direct result of eliminating home deliveries to customers in the suburbs. Deliveries within the city require only six trucks. Each of the trucks has an unadjusted basis of $3,000. Six of the taxpayer's delivery trucks are in a multiple asset vintage account of 1974 and six are in a multiple asset vintage account of 1972. Neither account contains any other property. Four trucks are retired from the 1972 vintage account and two trucks are retired from the 1974 vintage account. The sales result from the curtailment of taxpayer A's home delivery operation. The unadjusted basis of the four trucks retired from the 1972 vintage exceeds 20 percent of the total unadjusted basis of the affected account. The same is true for the two trucks retired from the 1974 vintage account. The sales of the trucks are extraordinary retirements.

(iii) *Treatment of ordinary retirements.* No loss shall be recognized upon an ordinary retirement. Gain shall be recognized only to the extent specified in this subparagraph. All proceeds from ordinary retirements shall be added to the depreciation reserve of the vintage account from which the retirement occurs. See subdivision (vi) of this subparagraph for optional allocation of basis in the case of a special basis vintage account. See subdivision (ix) of this subparagraph for recognition of gain when the depreciation reserve exceeds the unadjusted basis of the vintage account. The amount of salvage value for a vintage account shall be reduced (but not below zero) as of the beginning of the taxable year by the excess of (*a*) the depreciation reserve for the account, after adjustment for depreciation allowable for such taxable year and all other adjustments prescribed by this section (other than the adjustment prescribed by subdivision (ix) of this subparagraph), over (*b*) the unadjusted basis of the account less the amount of salvage value for the account before such reduction. Thus, in the case of a vintage account with an unadjusted basis of $1,000 and a salvage value of $100, to the extent that proceeds from ordinary retirements increase the depreciation reserve above $900, the salvage value is reduced. If the proceeds increase the depreciation reserve for the account to $1,000, the salvage value is reduced to zero. The unadjusted basis of the asset retired in an ordinary retirement is not removed from the account and the depreciation reserve for the account is not reduced by the depreciation allowable for the retired asset. The previously unrecovered basis of the retired asset will be recovered through the allowance for depreciation with respect to the vintage account. See subdivision (v)(*a*) of this subparagraph for treat-

ment of retirements on which gain or loss is not recognized in whole or in part. See subdivision (v)(*b*) of this subparagraph for treatment of retirements by disposition to a member of an affiliated group as defined in section 1504(a). See subdivision (v)(*c*) of this subparagraph for treatment of transfers between members of an affiliated group of corporations or other related parties as extraordinary retirements.

(iv) *Treatment of extraordinary retirements.* (*a*) Unless the transaction is governed by a special nonrecognition section of the Code such as 1031 or 337 or is one to which subdivision (v)(*b*) of this subparagraph applies, gain or loss shall be recognized upon an extraordinary retirement in the taxable year in which such retirement occurs subject to section 1231, section 165, and all other applicable provisions of law such as sections 1245 and 1250. If the asset which is retired in an extraordinary retirement is the only or last asset in the account, the account shall terminate and no longer be an account to which this section applies. In all other cases, the unadjusted basis of the retired asset shall be removed from the unadjusted basis of the vintage account, and the depreciation reserve established for the account shall be reduced by the depreciation allowable for the retired asset computed in the manner prescribed in paragraph (c)(1)(v)(*b*) of this section for determination of the adjusted basis of the asset. See subdivision (ix) of this subparagraph for recognition of gain in the case of an account containing section 1245 property when the depreciation reserve exceeds the unadjusted basis of the vintage account. See subdivision (iii) of this subparagraph for reduction of salvage value for such an account when the depreciation reserve exceeds the unadjusted basis of the account minus salvage value. See subdivision (v)(*b*) of this subparagraph for treatment of retirements by disposition to a member of an affiliated group as defined in section 1504(a).

(*b*) The principles of this subdivision may be illustrated by the following examples:

Example (1). Corporation X has a multiple asset vintage account of 1971 consisting of assets K, R, A and P all of which are section 1245 property. The unadjusted basis of the account is $40,000. The unadjusted basis of asset A is $10,000. When the reserve for depreciation for the account is $20,000, asset A is sold in an extraordinary retirement for $8,000 in cash. The $10,000 unadjusted basis of asset A is removed from the account and the $5,000 depreciation allowable for asset A is removed from the reserve for depreciation. Gain in the amount of $3,000 (to which

Reg. § 1.167(a)-11(d)(3)

section 1245 applies) is recognized upon the sale of asset A.

Example (2). Corporation X has an item vintage account of 1972 consisting of residential apartment unit A. Unit A is section 1250 property. It is residential rental property and meets the requirements of section 167(j)(2). Corporation X adopts the declining balance method of depreciation using a rate twice the straight line rate. The asset depreciation period is 40 years. Unit A has an unadjusted basis of $200,000. On June 30, 1974, when the reserve for depreciation for the account is $19,500, unit A is sold for $220,000. Since unit A is section 1250 property, the sale is an extraordinary retirement in accordance with subdivision (ii)(a) of this subparagraph (without regard to subdivision (ii)(b) or (c) of this subparagraph). The adjusted basis of unit A is $180,500. Gain in the amount of $39,500 is recognized. The "additional depreciation" (as defined in section 1250(b)) for unit A is $9,500. Accordingly, $9,500 is in accordance with section 1250 treated as gain from the sale or exchange of an asset which is neither a capital asset nor property described in section 1231. The $30,000 balance of the gain from the sale of unit A may be gain to which section 1231 applies.

(v) *Special rule for certain retirements.* (a) In the case of an ordinary retirement on which gain or loss is in whole or in part not recognized because of a special nonrecognition section of the Code, such as 1031 or 337, no part of the proceeds from such retirement shall be added to the depreciation reserve of the vintage account in accordance with subdivision (iii) of this subparagraph. Instead, such retirement shall for all purposes of this section be treated as an extraordinary retirement.

(b) The provisions of § 1.1502-13 shall apply to a retirement. In the case of an ordinary retirement to which the provisions of § 1.1502-13 apply, no part of the proceeds from such retirement shall be added to the depreciation reserve of the vintage account in accordance with subdivision (iii) of this subparagraph. Instead, such retirement shall for all purposes of this section be treated as an extraordinary retirement.

(c) In a case in which property is transferred, in a transaction which would without regard to this subdivision be treated as an ordinary retirement, during the taxable year in which first placed in service to a person who bears a relationship described in section 179(d)(2)(A) or (B), such transfer shall for all purposes of this section be treated as an extraordinary retirement.

(d)(1) If, in the case of mass assets, it is impracticable for the taxpayer to maintain records from which he can establish the vintage of such assets as retirements occur, and if he adopts other reasonable recordkeeping practices, then the vintage of mass asset retirements may be determined by use of an appropriate mortality dispersion table. Such a mortality dispersion table may be based upon an acceptable sampling of the taxpayer's actual experience or other acceptable statistical or engineering techniques. Alternatively, the taxpayer may use a standard mortality dispersion table prescribed by the Commissioner for this purpose. If the taxpayer uses such standard mortality dispersion table for any taxable year of election, it must be used for all subsequent taxable years of election unless the taxpayer obtains the consent of the Commissioner to change to another dispersion table or to actual identification of retirements. For information requirements regarding mass assets, see paragraph (f)(5) of this section.

(2) For purposes of this section, the term "mass assets" has the same meaning as when used in paragraph (e)(4) of § 1.47-1.

(e) The principles of this subdivision may be illustrated by the following examples:

Example (1). Corporation X has a vintage account of 1971 consisting of machines A, B and C, each with an unadjusted basis of $1,000. The unadjusted basis of the account is $3,000 and at the end of 1977 the reserve for depreciation is $2,100. On January 1, 1978, machine A is transferred to corporation Y solely for stock in the amount of $1,400 in a transaction to which section 351 applies. Since the adjusted basis of machine A is $300, a gain of $1,100 is realized, but no gain is recognized under section 351. Even though machine A was transferred in an ordinary retirement in accordance with (a) of this subdivision, the rules for an extraordinary retirement are applied. The proceeds are not added to the reserve for depreciation for the account. Machine A is removed from the account, the unadjusted basis of the account is reduced by $1,000, and the reserve for depreciation for the account is reduced by $700.

Example (2). The facts are the same as in example (1) except that the consideration received for machine A is stock of corporation Y in the amount of $1,200 and cash in the amount of $200. The result is the same as in example (1) except that gain is recognized in the amount of $200 all of which is gain to which section 1245 applies.

Example (3). The facts are the same as in example (1) except that machine A is sold for $1,400 cash in an ordinary retirement and corporation X and corporation Y are includible corporations in an affiliated group as defined in section 1504(a) which files a consolidated return for 1978. Accordingly, (b) of this subdivision applies. The retirement is treated as an extraordinary retirement. Machine A is removed from the account, the unadjusted basis of the account is reduced by $1,000, and the reserve for depreciation for the account is reduced by $700. The gain of $1,100 is deferred gain to which § 1.1502-13 applies.

(vi) *Treatment of special basis vintage accounts.* A "special basis vintage account" is a vintage account for an amount of property improvement determined under subparagraph (2)(vii)(a) of this paragraph. In general, reference in this section to a "vintage account" shall include a special basis vintage account. The unadjusted basis of a special basis vintage account shall be recovered through the allowance for depreciation in accordance with this section over the asset depreciation period for the account. Except as provided in this subdivision, the unadjusted basis, adjusted basis and reserve for depreciation of such account shall not be allocated to any specific asset in the asset guideline class, and the provisions of this subparagraph shall not apply to such account. However, in the event of a sale, exchange or other disposition of "repair allowance property" (as described in subparagraph (2)(iii) of this paragraph) in an extraordinary retirement as described in subdivision (ii) of this subparagraph (or if the asset is not in a vintage account, in an

1972 special basis vintage account, for which the taxpayer selected an asset depreciation period of 10 years, adopted the straight line method, and used the half-year convention . . . .

By application of this subdivision, the adjusted basis of machines A, B, and C is increased to $10,100 each (that is, $10,000/$90,000×$900=$100). The unadjusted basis, reserve for depreciation and adjusted basis of the special basis vintage account are reduced, respectively, by 1/3 (that is, $300/$900 = 1/3) in order to reflect the allocation of basis from the special basis vintage account.

(vii) *Reduction in the salvage value of a vintage account.* (a) A taxpayer may apply this section without reducing the salvage value for a vintage account in accordance with this subdivision or in accordance with subdivision (viii) of this subparagraph (relating to transfers to supplies or scrap). See subdivision (iii) of this subparagraph for reduction of salvage value in certain circumstances in the amount of proceeds from ordinary retirements.

(b) However, the taxpayer may, at his option, follow the consistent practice of reducing,

abnormal retirement as described in § 1.167(a)-8, the taxpayer may, if consistently applied to all such retirements in the taxable year and adequately identified in the taxpayer's books and records, elect to allocate the adjusted basis (as of the end of the taxable year) of all special basis vintage accounts for the asset guideline class to each such retired asset in the proportion that the adjusted basis of the retired asset (as of the beginning of the taxable year) bears to the adjusted basis of all repair allowance property in the asset guideline class at the beginning of the taxable year. The election to allocate basis in accordance with this subdivision shall be made on the tax return filed for the taxable year. The principles of this subdivision may be illustrated by the following example:

Example. In addition to other property, the taxpayer has machines A, B, and C all in the same asset guideline class and each with an adjusted basis on January 1, 1977, of $10,000. The adjusted basis on January 1, 1977, of all repair allowance property (as described in subparagraph (2)(iii) of this paragraph) in the asset guideline class is $90,000. The machines are sold in an extraordinary retirement in 1977. The taxpayer is entitled to and does elect to allocate basis in accordance with this subdivision. There is also a 1972 special basis vintage account for the asset guideline class, as follows:

Unadjusted Basis	Reserve for Depreciation	Dec. 31, 1977, Adjusted Basis
$2,000	$1,100	$900

as retirements occur, the salvage value for a vintage account by the amount of salvage value attributable to the retired asset, or the taxpayer may consistently follow the practice of so reducing the salvage value for a vintage account as extraordinary retirements occur while not reducing the salvage value for the account as ordinary retirements occur. If the taxpayer does not reduce the salvage value for a vintage account as ordinary retirements occur, the taxpayer may be entitled to a deduction in the taxable year in which the last asset is retired from the account in accordance with subdivision (ix) (b) of this subparagraph.

(c) For purposes of this subdivision, the portion of the salvage value for a vintage account attributable to a retired asset may be determined by multiplying the salvage value for the account by a fraction, the numerator of which is the unadjusted basis of the retired asset and the denominator of which is the unadjusted basis of the

Reg. § 1.167(a)-11(d)(3)

account, or any other method consistently applied which reasonably reflects that portion of the salvage value for the account originally attributable to the retired asset.

(d) In the case of ordinary retirements the taxpayer may—

(1) In the case of retirements (other than by transfer to supplies or scrap) follow the consistent practice of reducing the salvage value for the account by the amount of salvage value attributable to the retired asset and not adding the same amount to the depreciation reserve for the account, and

(2) In the case of retirements by transfer to supplies or scrap, follow the consistent practice of reducing the salvage value for the account by the amount of salvage value attributable to the retired asset and not adding the same amount to the depreciation reserve for the account (in which case the basis in the supplies or scrap account of the retired asset will be zero) or follow the consistent practice of reducing the salvage value for the account by the amount of salvage value attributable to the retired asset and adding the same amount to the depreciation reserve for the account (up to an amount which does not increase the depreciation reserve to an amount in excess of the unadjusted basis of the account) in which case the basis in the supplies or scrap account of the retired asset will be the amount added to the depreciation reserve for the account.

Thus, for example, in the case of an ordinary retirement by transfer of an asset to supplies or scrap, the basis of the asset in the supplies or scrap account would either be zero or the amount added to the depreciation reserve of the vintage account from which the retirement occurred. When the depreciation reserve for the account equals the unadjusted basis of the account no further adjustment to salvage value for the account will be made. See subdivision (viii) of this subparagraph for special optional rule for reduction of salvage value in the case of an ordinary retirement by transfer of an asset to supplies or scrap.

(e) In the event of a removal of property from a vintage account in accordance with paragraph (b)(4)(iii)(e), (5)(v)(b) or (6)(iii) of this section the salvage value for the account may be reduced by the amount of salvage value attributable to the asset removed determined as provided in (c) of this subdivision.

(viii) *Special optional adjustments for transfers to supplies or scrap.* If the taxpayer does not follow the consistent practice of reducing, as ordinary retirements occur, the salvage value for a vintage account in accordance with subdivision (vii) of this subparagraph, the taxpayer may (in lieu of the method described in subdivision (vii)(c) and (d) of this subparagraph) follow the consistent practice of reducing salvage value as ordinary retirements occur by transfer of assets to supplies or scrap and of determining the basis (in the supplies or scrap account) as assets retired in an ordinary retirement by transfer to supplies or scrap, in the following manner—

(a) The taxpayer may determine the value of the asset (not to exceed its unadjusted basis) by any reasonable method consistently applied (such as average cost, conditioned cost, or fair market value) if such method is adequately identified in the taxpayer's books and records.

(b) The value attributable to the asset determined in accordance with (a) of this subdivision shall be subtracted from the salvage value for the account (to the extent thereof) and the greater of (1) the amount subtracted from the salvage value for the vintage account and (2) the value of the asset determined in accordance with (a) of this subdivision, shall be added to the reserve for depreciation of the vintage account.

(c) The amount added to the reserve for depreciation of the vintage account in accordance with (b) of this subdivision shall be treated as the basis of the retired asset in the supplies or scrap account. If the taxpayer makes the adjustments in accordance with this subdivision, the reserve for depreciation of the vintage account may exceed the unadjusted basis of the account, and in that event gain will be recognized in accordance with subdivision (ix) of this subparagraph.

(ix) *Recognition of gain or loss in certain situations.* (a) In the case of a vintage account for section 1245 property, if at the end of any taxable year after adjustment for depreciation allowable for such taxable year and all other adjustments prescribed by this section, the depreciation reserve established for such account exceeds the unadjusted basis of the account, the entire amount of such excess shall be recognized as gain in such taxable year. Such gain—

(1) Shall constitute gain to which section 1245 applies to the extent that it does not exceed the total amount of depreciation allowances in the depreciation reserve at the end of such taxable year, reduced by gain recognized pursuant to this subdivision with respect to the account previously treated as gain to which section 1245 applies, and

(2) May constitute gain to which section 1231 applies to the extent that it exceeds such total amount as so reduced.

Reg. § 1.167(a)-11(d)(3)

In such event, the depreciation reserve shall be reduced by the amount of gain recognized, so that after such reduction the amount of the depreciation reserve is equal to the unadjusted basis of the account.

(b) In the case of an account for section 1245 property, if at the time the last asset in the vintage account is retired the unadjusted basis of the account exceeds the depreciation reserve for the account (after all adjustments prescribed by this section), the entire amount of such excess shall be recognized in such taxable year as a loss under section 165 or as a deduction for depreciation under section 167. If the retirement of such asset occurs by sale or exchange on which gain or loss is recognized, the amount of such excess may constitute a loss subject to section 1231. Upon retirement of the last asset in a vintage account, the account shall terminate and no longer be an account to which this section applies. See subdivision (xi) of this subparagraph for treatment of certain multiple asset and item accounts.

(c) The principles of this subdivision may be illustrated by the following example:

Example. The taxpayer has a vintage account for section 1245 property with an unadjusted basis of $1,000 and a depreciation reserve of $700 (of which $600 represents depreciation allowances and $100 represents the proceeds of ordinary retirements from the account). If $500 is realized during the taxable year from ordinary retirements of assets from the account, the reserve is increased to $1,200, gain is recognized to the extent of $200 (the amount by which the depreciation reserve before further adjustment exceeds $1,000) and the depreciation reserve is then decreased to $1,000. The $200 of gain constitutes gain to which section 1245 applies. If the amount realized from ordinary retirements during the year had been $1,100 instead of $500, the gain of $800 would have consisted of $600 of gain to which section 1245 applies and $200 of gain to which section 1231 may apply.

(x) *Dismantling cost.* The cost of dismantling, demolishing, or removing an asset in the process of a retirement from the vintage account shall be treated as an expense deductible in the year paid or incurred, and such cost shall not be subtracted from the depreciation reserve for the account.

(xi) *Special rule for treatment of multiple asset and item accounts.* For the purposes of subdivision (ix)(b) of this subparagraph, all accounts (other than a special basis vintage account as described in subdivision (vi) of this subparagraph) of the same vintage in the same asset guideline class for which the taxpayer has selected the same

asset depreciation period and adopted the same method of depreciation, and which contain only section 1245 property permitted by paragraph (b)(3)(ii) of this section to be included in the same vintage account, shall be treated as a single multiple asset vintage account.

(4) *Examples.* The principles of this paragraph may be illustrated by the following examples:

Example (1). (a) Taxpayer A has a multiple asset vintage account for section 1245 property with an unadjusted basis of $1,000. All the assets were first placed in service by A on January 15, 1971. This account contains all of A's assets in a single asset guideline class. A elects to apply this section for 1971 and adopts the modified half-year convention. A estimates a salvage value for the account of $100 and this estimate is determined to be reasonable. (See subparagraph (1)(v) of this paragraph for limitation on adjustment of reasonable salvage value.) A adopts the straight line method of depreciation with respect to the account and selects a 10-year asset depreciation period. A does not follow a practice of reducing the salvage value for the account in the amount of salvage value attributable to each retired asset in accordance with subparagraph (3)(vii) of this paragraph. The depreciation allowance for each of the first 4 years is $100, that is 1/10 multiplied by the unadjusted basis of $1,000, without reduction for salvage.

(b) In the fifth year of the asset depreciation period, three assets are sold in an ordinary retirement for $300. Under paragraph (c)(1)(ii) of this section and subparagraph (3)(iii) of this paragraph, the proceeds of the retirement are added to the depreciation reserve as of the beginning of the fifth year. Accordingly, the reserve as of the beginning of the fifth year is $700, that is, $400 of depreciation as of the beginning of the year plus $300 proceeds from ordinary retirements. The depreciation allowance for the fifth year is $100, that is 1/10 multiplied by the unadjusted basis of $1,000, without reduction for salvage. Accordingly, the depreciation reserve at the end of the fifth year is $800.

(c) In the sixth year, asset X is sold in an extraordinary retirement for $30 and gain or loss is recognized. Under the first-year convention used by the taxpayer, the unadjusted basis of X, $300, is removed from the unadjusted basis of the vintage account as of the beginning of the sixth year and the depreciation reserve as of the beginning of such year is reduced to $650 by removing the depreciation applicable to asset X, $150 (see subparagraph (3)(iv) of this paragraph). Since the depreciation reserve ($650) exceeds the unad-

Reg. § 1.167(a)-11(d)(4)

justed basis of the account ($700) minus salvage value ($100) by $50, under subparagraph (3)(iii) of this paragraph, salvage value is reduced by $50. No depreciation is allowable for the sixth year.

(d) In the seventh year, an asset is sold in an ordinary retirement for $110. This would increase the reserve as of the beginning of the seventh year to $760 and under subparagraph (3)(iii) of this paragraph the salvage value is reduced to zero. Under subparagraph (3)(ix)(a) of this paragraph the depreciation reserve is then decreased to $700 (the unadjusted basis of the account) and $60 is reported as gain, without regard to the adjusted basis of the asset. No depreciation is allowable for the seventh year since the depreciation reserve ($700) equals the unadjusted basis of the account ($700).

(e)(1) In the eighth year, A elects to apply this section and to treat expenditures during the year for repair, maintenance, rehabilitation or improvement under subparagraph (2)(iii) and (iv)(a) of this paragraph (the "guideline class repair allowance"). This results in the treatment of $300 as a property improvement for the asset guideline class. (See subparagraph (2)(vii) of this paragraph for definition of a property improvement.) The property improvement is capitalized in a special basis vintage account of the eighth taxable year (see subparagraph (2)(viii)(a) of this paragraph). A selects an asset depreciation period of 10 years and adopts the straight line method for the special basis vintage account. A adopts the modified half-year convention for the eighth year.

(2) In the eighth year, A sells asset Y in an ordinary retirement for $175. Under paragraph (c)(1)(ii) of this section and subparagraph (3)(iii) of this paragraph, $175 is added to the depreciation reserve for the account as of the beginning of the taxable year. Since the depreciation reserve for the account ($875) exceeds the unadjusted basis of the account ($700) by $175, that amount of gain is recognized under subparagraph (3)(ix) of this paragraph. Upon recognition of gain in the amount of $175, the depreciation reserve for the account is reduced to $700.

(3) No depreciation is allowable in the eighth year for the vintage account since the depreciation reserve ($700) equals the unadjusted basis of the account ($700). The depreciation allowable in the eighth year for the special basis vintage account is $15, that is, unadjusted basis of $300, multiplied by 1/10, the asset depreciation period selected for the special basis vintage account, but limited to $15 under the modified half-year convention. (See paragraph (e)(1)(iv) of this section for treatment of $150 of the property

improvement as first placed in service in the first half of the taxable year and $150 of the property improvement as first placed in service in the last half of the taxable year.)

Example (2). Taxpayer B has a 1971 multiple asset vintage account for section 1245 property with an unadjusted basis of $100,000. B selects from the asset depreciation range an asset depreciation period of 10 years and adopts the straight line method of depreciation and the modified half-year convention. B establishes a salvage value for the account of $10,000. All the assets in the account are first placed in service on January 15, 1971. B follows the practice of reducing salvage value for the account as ordinary retirements occur in accordance with subparagraph (3)(vii) of this paragraph, but does not follow the optional practice of determining the basis of assets transferred to supplies or scrap in accordance with subparagraph (3)(viii) of this paragraph. No retirements occur during the first five years. The depreciation reserve at the beginning of the sixth year is $50,000. In the sixth year an asset with an unadjusted basis of $20,000 is transferred to supplies in an ordinary retirement. By application of subparagraph (3)(vii)(c) and (d)(2) of this paragraph 3 determines the reduction in salvage value for the account attributable to such asset to be $2,000 (that is, $20,000/$100,000 × $10,000 = $2,000).

B reduces the salvage value for the account by $2,000 and adds $2,000 to the depreciation reserve for the account. The basis of the retired asset in the supplies account is $2,000. The depreciation allowable for the account for the sixth year is $10,000. The depreciation reserve for the account at the beginning of the seventh year is $62,000. At the mid-point of the seventh year all the remaining assets in the account are sold in an ordinary retirement for $20,000, which is added to the depreciation reserve as of the beginning of the seventh year, thus increasing the reserve to $82,000. The $5,000 depreciation allowable for the account for the seventh year (one-half of a full-year's depreciation of $10,000) increases the depreciation reserve to $87,000. Under subparagraph (3)(ix)(b) of this paragraph, a loss of $13,000 subject to section 1231 is realized in the seventh year (that is, the excess of the unadjusted basis of $100,000 over the depreciation reserve of $87,000). No depreciation is allowable for the account after the mid-point of the seventh year since all the assets are retired and the account has terminated.

(e) Accounting for eligible property—(1) Definition of first placed in service—(i) In general. The term "first placed in service" refers to the

Reg. § 1.167(a)-11(e)(1)

time the property is first placed in service by the taxpayer, not to the first time the property is placed in service. Property is first placed in service when first placed in a condition or state of readiness and availability for a specifically assigned function, whether in a trade or business, in the production of income, in a tax-exempt activity, or in a personal activity. In general, the provisions of paragraph (d)(1)(ii) and (d)(2) of § 1.46-3 shall apply for the purpose of determining the date on which property is placed in service, but see subdivision (ii) of this subparagraph for special rule for certain replacement parts. In the case of a building which is intended to house machinery and equipment and which is constructed, reconstructed, or erected by or for the taxpayer and for the taxpayer's use, the building will ordinarily be placed in service on the date such construction, reconstruction, or erection is substantially complete and the building is in a condition or state of readiness and availability. Thus, for example, in the case of a factory building, such readiness and availability shall be determined without regard to whether the machinery or equipment which the building houses, or is intended to house, has been placed in service. However, in an appropriate case, as for example where the building is essentially an item of machinery or equipment, or the use of the building is so closely related to the use of the machinery or equipment that it clearly can be expected to be replaced or retired when the property it initially houses is replaced or retired, the determination of readiness or availability of the building shall be made by taking into account the readiness and availability of such machinery or equipment. The date on which depreciation begins under a convention used by the taxpayer or under a particular method of depreciation, such as the unit of production method or the retirement method, shall not determine the date on which the property is first placed in service. See paragraph (c)(2) of this section for application of a first-year convention to determine the allowance for depreciation of property in a vintage account.

(ii) *Certain replacement parts.* Property (such as replacement parts) the cost or other basis of which is deducted as a repair expense in accordance with the asset guideline repair allowance described in paragraph (d)(2)(iii) of this section shall not be treated as placed in service.

(iii) *Property improvements and excluded additions.* (a) Except as provided in (b) of this subdivision, a property improvement determined under paragraph (d)(2)(vii)(b) of this section, and an excluded addition (other than an excluded addition referred to in the succeeding sentence) is first placed in service when its cost is paid or

incurred. The general rule in subdivision (i) of this subparagraph applies to an excluded addition described in paragraph (d)(2)(vi)(d), (e), (f) or (g) of this section.

(b) If a property improvement or an excluded addition to which the first sentence of (a) of this subdivision applies is paid or incurred in part in one taxable year and in part in the succeeding taxable year (or in part in the first half of a taxable year and in part in the last half of the taxable year) the taxpayer may at his option consistently treat such property improvements and excluded additions under the general rule in subdivision (i) of this subparagraph.

(iv) *Certain property improvements.* In the case of an amount of property improvement determined under paragraph (d)(2)(vii)(a) of this section, one-half of such amount is first placed in service in the first half of the taxable year in which the cost is paid or incurred and one-half is first placed in service in the last half of such taxable year.

(v) *Special rules for clearing accounts.* In the case of public utilities which consistently account for certain property through "clearing accounts", the date on which such property is first placed in service shall be determined in accordance with rules to be prescribed by the Commissioner.

(2) *Special rules for transferred property.* If eligible property is first placed in service by the taxpayer during a taxable year of election, and the property is disposed of before the end of the taxable year, the election for such taxable year shall include such property unless such property is excluded in accordance with paragraph (b)(5)(iii), (iv), (v), (vi) or (vii) of this section.

(3) *Special rules in the case of certain transfers—*(i) *Transaction to which section 381(a) applies.* (a) In general the acquiring corporation in a transaction to which section 381(a) applies is for the purposes of this section treated as if it were the distributor or transferor corporation.

(b) If the distributor or transferor corporation (including any distributor or transferor corporation of any distributor or transferor corporation) has made an election to apply this section to eligible property transferred in a transaction to which section 381(a) applies, the acquiring corporation must segregate such eligible property (to which the distributor or transferor corporation elected to apply this section) into vintage accounts as nearly coextensive as possible with the vintage accounts created by the distributor or transferor corporation identified by reference to the year the property was first placed in service by the distributor or transferor corporation. The

Reg. § 1.167(a)-11(e)(2)

asset depreciation period for the vintage account in the hands of the distributor or transferor corporation must be used by the acquiring corporation. The method of depreciation adopted by the distributor or transferor corporation, shall be used by the acquiring corporation unless such corporation obtains the consent of the Commissioner to use another method of depreciation in accordance with paragraph (e) of § 1.445-1 or changes the method of depreciation under paragraph (c)(1)(iii) of this section.

(c) The acquiring corporation may apply this section to the property so acquired only if the distributor or transferor corporation elected to apply this section to such property.

(d) See paragraph (b)(7) of this section for special rule for certain property where there is a mere change in the form of conducting a trade or business.

(ii) *Partnerships, trusts, estates, donees, and corporations.* Except as provided in subdivision (i) of this subparagraph with respect to transactions to which section 381(a) applies, and subdivision (iv) of this subparagraph with respect to certain transfers between members of an affiliated group of corporations or other related parties, if eligible property is placed in service by an individual, trust, estate, partnership, or corporation, the election to apply this section shall be made by the individual, trust, estate, partnership, or corporation placing such property in service. For example, if a partnership places in service property contributed to the partnership by a partner, the partnership may elect to apply this section to such property. If the partnership does not make the election, this section will not apply to such property. See paragraph (b)(7) of this section for special rule for certain property where there is mere change in the form of conducting a trade or business.

(iii) *Leased property.* The asset depreciation range and the asset depreciation period for eligible property subject to a lease shall be determined without regard to the period for which such property is leased, including any extensions or renewals of such period. See paragraph (b)(5)(v) of this section for exclusion of property amortized under paragraph (b) of § 1.162-11 from an election to apply this section. In the case of a lessor of property, unless there is an asset guideline class in effect for lessors of such property, the asset guideline class for such property shall be determined as if the property were owned by the lessee. However, in the case of an asset guideline class based upon the type of property (such as trucks or railroad cars) as distinguished from the activity in which used, the property shall be classified with-

out regard to the activity of the lessee. Notwithstanding the preceding sentence, if a lease with respect to property, which would be includible in an asset guideline class based upon the type of property under the preceding sentence (such as trucks or railroad cars), is entered into after March 12, 1971, and before April 23, 1973, or a written contract to execute such a lease is entered into during such period and such contract is binding on April 23, 1973, and at all times thereafter, and if the rent or rate of return is based on a classification of such property as if it were owned by the lessee, then such property shall be classified as if it were owned by the lessee. However, the preceding sentence shall not apply if pursuant to the terms or conditions of the lease or binding contract the rent or rate of return may be adjusted to take account of a change in the period for depreciation with respect to the property resulting from inclusion of the property in an asset guideline class based upon the type of property rather than in an asset guideline class based upon the activity of the lessee. Similarly, where the terms of such a lease or contract provide that the obligation of the taxpayer to enter into the lease is subject to a condition that the property be included in an asset guideline class based upon the activity of the lessee, the contract or lease will not be considered as binding upon the taxpayer, for purposes of this subdivision. See paragraph (b)(4)(iii)(b) of this section for general rule for classification of property according to primary use.

(iv) *Treatment of certain transfers between members of affiliated groups or other related persons.* If section 38 property in an asset guideline class (determined without regard to whether the taxpayer elects to apply this section) is transferred by the taxpayer to a person who bears a relationship described in section 179(d)(2)(A) or (B), such property is in the same asset guideline class in the hands of transferee, and the transfer is neither described in section 381(a) nor treated as a disposition or cessation within the meaning of section 47, then the asset guideline period for such property selected by the taxpayer under this section shall not be shorter than the period used for computing the qualified investment with respect to the property under section 46(c). In a case in which the asset depreciation range for the asset guideline class which includes such property does not include the period for depreciation used by the transferor in computing the qualified investment with respect to such property, the transferee will not be permitted to include such property in an election under this section. However, in such a case, the transferor of the property may recompute the qualified investment for the year the property was placed in service using a period for depreciation which falls within the asset depreciation range.

(f) *Election with respect to eligible property—* (1) *Time and manner of election—*(i) *In general.* An election to apply this section to eligible property shall be made with the income tax return filed for the taxable year in which the property is first placed in service (see paragraph (e)(1) of this section) by the taxpayer. In the case of an affiliated group of corporations (as defined in section 1504(a)) which makes a consolidated return with respect to income tax in accordance with section 1502 and the regulations thereunder, each corporation which joins in the making of such return may elect to apply this section for a taxable year. An election to compute the allowance for depreciation under this section is a method of accounting but the consent of the Commissioner will be deemed granted to make an annual election. For election by a partnership see section 703(b) and paragraph (e)(3)(ii) of this section. If the taxpayer does not file a timely return (taking into account extensions of the time for filing) for the taxable year in which the property is first placed in service, the election shall be filed at the time the taxpayer files his first return for that year. The election may be made with an amended return filed within the time prescribed by law (including extensions) for filing the original return for the taxable year of election. If an election is not made within the time and in the manner prescribed in this paragraph, no election may be made for such taxable year (by the filing of an amended return or in any other manner) with respect to any eligible property placed in service in the taxable year.

(ii) *Other elections under this section.* All other elections under this section may be made only within the time and in the manner prescribed by subdivision (i) of this subparagraph with respect to an election to apply this section.

(iii) *Effective date.* See paragraph (f)(6) of this section for the effective date of this paragraph.

(2) *Information required.* A taxpayer who elects to apply this section must specify in the election:

(i) That the taxpayer makes such election and consents to, and agrees to apply, all the provisions of this section;

(ii) The asset guideline class for each vintage account of the taxable year;

(iii) The first-year convention adopted by the taxpayer for the taxable year of election;

(iv) Whether the special 10 percent used property rule described in paragraph (b)(5)(iii) of this section has been applied to exclude used property from the election;

(v) Whether the taxpayer elects to apply the asset guideline class repair allowance described in paragraph (d)(2)(iii) of this section;

(vi) Whether the taxpayer elects for the taxable year to allocate the adjusted basis of a special basis vintage account in accordance with paragraph (d)(3)(vi) of this section;

(vii) Whether any eligible property for which the taxpayer was not required or permitted to make an election was excluded because of the special rules of paragraph (b)(5)(v) or (6), or paragraph (e)(3)(i) or (iv) of this section;

(viii) Whether any "section 38 property" was excluded under paragraph (b)(5)(iv) of this section from the election to apply this section;

(ix) If the taxpayer is an electric or gas utility, whether the taxpayer elects to apply this section on the basis of a composite asset guideline class in accordance with paragraph (b)(4)(iii)(*a*) of this section; and

(x) Such other information as may reasonably be required.

The information required under this subparagraph may be provided in accordance with rules prescribed by the Commissioner for reasonable grouping of assets or accounts. Form 4832 is provided for making an election and for submission of the information required. An election may be made and the information submitted only in accordance with Form 4832. An election to apply this section will not be rendered invalid under this subparagraph so long as there is substantial compliance, in good faith, with the requirements of this subparagraph.

(3) *Irrevocable election.* An election to apply this section to eligible property for any taxable year may not be revoked or changed after the time for filing the election prescribed under subparagraph (1) of this paragraph has expired. No other election under this section may be revoked or changed after such time unless expressly provided for under this section. (See paragraph (b)(5)(v)(*b*) of this section for special rule.)

(4) *Special conditions to election to apply this section —*(i) *Maintenance of books and records.* The taxpayer may not elect to apply this section for a taxable year unless the taxpayer maintains the books and records required under this section. In addition to any other information required under this section, the taxpayer's books and records must specify—

Reg. § 1.167(a)-11(f)(1)

(*a*) The asset depreciation period selected by the taxpayer for each vintage account;

(*b*) If the taxpayer applies the modified half-year convention, the total cost or other basis of all eligible property first placed in service in the first half of the taxable year and the total cost or other basis of all eligible property first placed in service in the last half of the taxable year;

(*c*) The unadjusted basis and salvage value for each vintage account, and the amount, if any, by which gross salvage value was decreased under section 167(f);

(*d*) Each asset guideline class for which the taxpayer elects to apply the asset guideline class repair allowance described in paragraph (d)(2)(iii) of this section;

(*e*) The amount of property improvement, determined under paragraph (d)(2)(vii)(*a*) of this section, for each asset guideline class for which the taxpayer elects to apply the asset guideline class repair allowance;

(*f*) A reasonable description of property excluded from an election to apply this section and the basis for the exclusion;

(*g*) The total unadjusted basis of all assets retired during the taxable year from each asset guideline class, and the proceeds realized during the taxable year from such retirements; and

(*h*) The vintage (that is, the taxable year in which established) of the assets retired during the year from each asset guideline class.

For purposes of paragraph (f)(4)(i)(*g*) and (*h*) of this section, all accounts of the same vintage and asset guideline class may be treated as a single account. The taxpayer must specify the information required under paragraph (f)(4)(i)(*g*) and (*h*) without regard to the retirement of an asset by transfer to a supplies account for reuse.

(ii) *Response to survey.* Taxpayers who elect to apply this section must respond to infrequent data surveys conducted by the Treasury Department. These periodic surveys, which will be conducted on the basis of scientifically sound sampling methods, are designed to obtain data (including industry asset acquisitions and retirements) used to keep the asset guideline classes and periods up to date.

(iii) *Effect of noncompliance.* An election to apply this section will not be rendered invalid under this subparagraph so long as there is substantial compliance, in good faith, with the requirements of this subparagraph.

(5) *Mass assets.* In the case of mass assets, if the taxpayer assigns retirements to vintage accounts in the manner provided in paragraph

(d)(3)(v)(*c*) of this section, the following information must be supplied with Form 4832:

(i) Whether the taxpayer used the standard mortality dispersion curve or a curve based upon his own experience, and

(ii) Such other reasonable information as may be required by the Commissioner.

(6) *Effective date.* The rules in this paragraph apply to elections for taxable years ending on or after December 31, 1978. In the case of an election for a taxable year ending before December 31, 1978, the rules in paragraph (f) of this section, in effect before the amendments made by T.D. 7593, approved January 11, 1979, shall apply. See 26 C.F.R. § 1.167(a)-11(f) (1977) for paragraph (f) of this section as it appeared before the amendments made by T.D. 7593.

(*g*) *Relationship to other provisions*—(1) *Useful life*—(i) *In general.* Except as provided in subdivision (ii) of this subparagraph, an election to apply this section to eligible property constitutes an agreement under section 167(d) and this section to treat the asset depreciation period for each vintage account as the useful life of the property in such account for all purposes of the Code, including sections 46, 47, 48, 57, 163(d), 167(c), 167(f)(2), 179, 312(m), 514(a), and 4940(c). For example, since section 167(c) requires a useful life of at least 3 years and the asset depreciation period selected is treated as the useful life for purposes of section 167(c), the taxpayer may adopt a method of depreciation described in section 167(b)(2) or (3) for an account only if the asset depreciation period selected for the account is at least 3 years.

(ii) *Special rules.* (*a*) For the purposes of paragraph (d) of this section, the anticipated period of use (estimated at the close of the taxable year in which the asset is first placed in service) on the basis of which salvage value is estimated, shall be determined without regard to the asset depreciation period for the property.

(*b*) For the purposes of sections 162 and 263 and the regulations thereunder, whether an expenditure prolongs the life of an asset shall be determined on the basis of the anticipated period of use of the asset (estimated at the close of the taxable year in which the asset is first placed in service) without regard to the asset depreciation period for such asset.

(*c*) The determination whether a transaction with respect to qualified property constitutes a sale or a lease of such property shall be made without regard to the asset depreciation period for the property.

(*d*) The principles of this subdivision may be illustrated by the following example:

Example: Corporation X has assets in the asset guideline class 32.3 which are used in the manufacture of stone and clay products. The asset depreciation range for assets in asset guideline class 32.3 is from 12 to 18 years. Assume that corporation X selects 14 years as the asset depreciation period for all assets in asset guideline class 32.3. Under paragraph (d)(1)(i) of this section, corporation X must estimate salvage value on the basis of the anticipated period of use of the property (determined as of the close of the taxable year in which the property is first placed in service). The anticipated period of use must also be used for purposes of sections 162 and 263 in determining whether an expenditure materially prolongs the useful life of an asset. The anticipated period of use of an asset is determined without regard to the asset depreciation period of 14 years. Corporation X has, among other assets in the asset guideline class, machines A, B, and C. Corporation X estimates the anticipated period of use of machines A, B, and C as 8 years, 14 years, and 22 years, respectively. These estimates are reasonable and will be used for estimating salvage value and for purposes of sections 162 and 263.

(2) *Section 167 (d) agreements.* If the taxpayer has, prior to January 1, 1971, entered into a section 167(d) agreement which applies to any eligible property, the taxpayer will be permitted to withdraw the eligible property from the agreement provided that an election is made to apply this section to such property. The statement of intent to withdraw eligible property from such an agreement must be made in an election filed for the taxable year in which the property is first placed in service. The withdrawal, in accordance with this subparagraph, of any eligible property from a section 167(d) agreement shall not affect any other property covered by such an agreement.

(3) *Relationship to the straight line method* —(i) *In general.* For purposes of determining the amount of depreciation which would be allowable under the straight line method of depreciation, such amount shall be computed with respect to any property in a vintage account using the straight line method in the manner described in paragraph (c)(1)(i) of this section and a rate based upon the period for the vintage account selected from the asset depreciation range. Thus, for example, section 57(a)(3) requires a taxpayer to compute an amount using the straight line method of depreciation if the taxpayer uses an accelerated method of depreciation. For purposes of section 57(a)(3), the amount for property in a vintage account shall be computed using the asset

depreciation period for the vintage account selected from the asset depreciation range. In the case of property to which the taxpayer does not elect to apply this section, such amount computed by using the straight line method shall be determined under § 1.167(b)-1 without regard to this section.

(ii) *Examples.* The principles of this subparagraph may be illustrated by the following example:

Example. (*a*) Corporation X places a new asset in service to which it elects to apply this section. The cost of the asset is $200,000 and the estimated salvage value is zero. The taxpayer selects 9 years from the applicable asset depreciation range of 8 to 12 years. Corporation X adopts the double declining balance method of depreciation and thus the rate of depreciation is 22.2 percent (twice the applicable straight line rate). The depreciation allowance in the first year would be $44,400, that is, 22.2 percent of $200,000.

(*b*) Assume that the provisions of section 57(a)(3) apply to the property. The amount of the tax preference would be $22,200, that is, the excess of the depreciation allowed under this section ($44,400) over the depreciation which would have been allowable if the taxpayer had used the period selected from the asset depreciation range and the straight line rate ($22,200). [Reg. § 1.167(a)-11.]

☐ [*T.D. 7128, 6-22-71. Amended by T.D. 7272, 4-20-73; T.D. 7315, 6-6-74; T.D. 7593, 1-25-79; T.D. 7763, 1-19-81; T.D. 7828, 8-31-82; T.D. 7831, 9-8-82 and T.D. 8597, 7-12-95.*]

[Reg. § 1.167(a)-12]

§ 1.167(a)-12. **Depreciation based on class lives for property first placed in service before January 1, 1971.**—(a) *In general*—(1) *Summary.* This section provides an elective class life system for determining the reasonable allowance for depreciation of certain classes of assets for taxable years ending after December 31, 1970. The system applies only to assets placed in service before January 1, 1971. Depreciation for such assets during periods prior to January 1, 1971, may have been determined in accordance with Revenue Procedure 62-21. Accordingly, rules are provided which permit taxpayers to apply the system in taxable years ending after December 31, 1970, to such assets without the necessity of changing or regrouping their depreciation accounts other than as previously required by Revenue Procedure 62-21. The system is designed to minimize disputes between taxpayers and the Internal Revenue Service as to the useful life of assets, salvage value, and repairs. See § 1.167(a)-11 for a similar system for property placed in service after December 31, 1970. See paragraph (d)(2) of § 1.167(a)-11 for treatment of expenditures for the repair, maintenance, rehabilitation or improvement of certain property. The system provided by this section is optional with the taxpayer. An election under this section applies only to qualified property in an asset guideline class for which an election is made and only for the taxable year of election. The taxpayer's election is made with the income tax return for the taxable year. This section also revokes the reserve ratio test for taxable years ending after December 31, 1970, and provides transitional rules for taxpayers who after January 11, 1971, adopt Revenue Procedure 62-21 for a taxable year ending prior to January 1, 1971.

(2) *Revocation of reserve ratio test and other matters.* Except as otherwise expressly provided in this section and in paragraph (b)(5)(vi) of § 1.167(a)-11, the provisions of Revenue Procedure 62-21 shall not apply to any property for any taxable year ending after December 31, 1970, whether or not the taxpayer elects to apply this section to any property. See paragraph (f) of this section for rules for the adoption of Revenue Procedure 62-21 for taxable years ending prior to January 1, 1971.

(3) *Definition of qualified property.* The term "qualified property" means tangible property which is subject to the allowance for depreciation provided by section 167(a), but only if—

(i) An asset guideline class and asset guideline period are in effect for such property for the taxable year, and

(ii) The property is first placed in service by the taxpayer before January 1, 1971.

(iii) The property is placed in service before January 1, 1971, but first placed in service by the taxpayer after December 31, 1970, and is not includible in an election under § 1.167(a)-11 by reason of § 1.167(a)-11(b)(7) (property acquired as a result of a mere change in form) or § 1.167(a)-11(e)(3)(i) (certain property acquired in a transaction to which section 381(a) applies), or

(iv) The property is acquired and first placed in service by the taxpayer after December 31, 1970, pursuant to a binding written contract entered into prior to January 1, 1971, and is excluded in accordance with paragraph (b)(5)(iv) of § 1.167(a)-11 from an election to apply § 1.167(a)-11. The provisions of paragraph (e)(1) of § 1.167(a)-11 apply in determining whether property is first placed in service before January 1, 1971. See subparagraph (4)(ii) of this para-

graph for special rules for the exclusion of property from the definition of qualified property.

(4) *Requirements of election*—(i) *In general.* An election to apply this section to qualified property must be made within the time and in the manner specified in paragraph (e) of this section. The election must specify that the taxpayer consents to and agrees to apply all the provisions of this section. The election may be made separately for each asset guideline class. Thus, a taxpayer may for the taxable year elect to apply this section to one, more than one, or all asset guideline classes in which he has qualified property. An election to apply this section for a taxable year must include all qualified property in the asset guideline class for which the election is made.

(ii) *Special rules for exclusion of property from application of this section.* (a) If for the taxable year of election, the taxpayer computes depreciation under section 167(k) or computes amortization under section 169, 185, 186, 187, 188, or paragraph (b) of § 1.162-11 with respect to property, such property is not qualified property for such taxable year. If for the taxable year of election, the taxpayer computes depreciation under any method of depreciation (other than a method described in the preceding sentence) not permitted by subparagraph (5) (v) of this paragraph for any property in an asset guideline class (other than subsidiary assets excluded from an election under (b) of this subdivision), no property in such asset guideline class is qualified property for such taxable year.

(b) The taxpayer may exclude from an election to apply this section all (but not less than all) subsidiary assets. Subsidiary assets so excluded are not qualified property for such taxable year. For purposes of this subdivision the term "subsidiary assets" includes jigs, dies, molds, returnable containers, glassware, silverware, textile mill cam assemblies, and other equipment includable in Group One, Class 5, of Revenue Procedure 62-21 which is usually and properly accounted for separately from other property and under a method of depreciation not expressed in terms of years.

(iii) *Special rule for certain public utility property*—(a) In the case of public utility property described in section 167(1)(3)(A)(iii) for which no guideline life was prescribed in Revenue Procedure 62-21 (or for which reference was made in Revenue Procedure 62-21 to lives or rates established by governmental regulatory agencies) of a taxpayer which—

(1) Is entitled to use a method of depreciation other than a "subsection (l) method" of depreciation (as defined in section 167(l)(3)(F))

Reg. § 1.167(a)-12(a)(4)

only if it uses the "normalization method of accounting" (as defined in section 167(l)(3)(G)) with respect to such property, or

(2) Is entitled for the taxable year to use only a "subsection (l) method" of depreciation,

such property shall be qualified property (as defined in subparagraph (3) of this paragraph) only if the taxpayer normalizes the tax deferral resulting from the election to apply this section.

(b) The taxpayer will be considered to normalize the tax deferral resulting from the election to apply this section only if it computes its tax expense for purposes of establishing its cost of service for ratemaking purposes and for reflecting operating results in its regulated books of account using a period for depreciation no less than the period used for computing its depreciation expense for ratemaking purposes and for reflecting operating results in its regulated books of account for the taxable year, and the taxpayer makes adjustments to a reserve to reflect the deferral of taxes resulting from the use of a period for depreciation under section 167 in accordance with an election to apply this section different from the period used for computing its depreciation expense for ratemaking purposes and for reflecting operating results in its regulated books of account for the taxable year. A determination whether the taxpayer is considered to normalize under this subdivision the tax deferral resulting from the election to apply this section shall be made in a manner consistent with the principles for determining whether a taxpayer is using the "normalization method of accounting" (within the meaning of section 167(l)(3)(G)). See § 1.167(l)-1(h).

(c) If a taxpayer, which has elected to apply this section to any qualified public utility property and is required under (a) of this subdivision to normalize the tax deferral resulting from the election to apply this section to such property, fails to normalize such tax deferral, the election to apply this section to such property shall terminate as of the beginning of the taxable year for which the taxpayer fails to normalize such tax deferral. Application of this section to such property for any period prior to the termination date will not be affected by this termination.

(5) *Determination of reasonable allowance for depreciation*—(i) *In general.* The allowance for depreciation of qualified property to which the taxpayer elects to apply this section shall be determined in accordance with this section. The annual allowance for depreciation is determined by using the method of depreciation adopted by the taxpayer and rate based on a life permitted by

this section. In the case of the straight-line method of depreciation, the rate of depreciation shall be based upon the class life (or individual life if the taxpayer assigns individual depreciable lives in accordance with subdivision (iii) of this subparagraph) used by the taxpayer with respect to the assets in the asset guideline class. Such rate will be applied to the unadjusted basis of the asset guideline class (individual assets or depreciation accounts if the taxpayer assigns individual depreciable lives). In the case of the sum of the years-digits method of depreciation, the rate of depreciation will be determined based upon the remaining life of the class (or individual remaining lives if the taxpayer assigns such lives in accordance with subdivision (iii) of this subparagraph) and is applied to the adjusted basis of the class (or individual accounts or asset) as of the beginning of the taxable year of election. The remaining life of a depreciation account is determined by dividing the unrecovered cost or other basis of the account, as computed by straight-line depreciation, by the gross cost or unadjusted basis of the account, and multiplying the result by the class life used with respect to the account. In the case of the declining balance method of depreciation, the rate of depreciation for the asset guideline class shall be based upon the class life (or individual life if the taxpayer assigns such lives in accordance with subdivision (iii) of this subparagraph). Such rate is applied to the adjusted basis of the class (or individual accounts or assets) as of the beginning of the taxable year of election.

(ii) *Reasonable allowance by reference to class lives.* The amount of depreciation for all qualified property in an asset guideline class to which the taxpayer elects to apply this section will constitute the reasonable allowance provided by section 167(a) and the depreciation for the asset guideline class will not be adjusted if—

(a) The taxpayer's qualified property is accounted for in one or more depreciation accounts which conform to the asset guideline class, and the depreciation for each such account is determined by using a rate based upon a life not less than the class life, or

(b) The taxpayer's qualified property is accounted for in one or more depreciation accounts (whether or not conforming to the asset guideline class) for which depreciation is determined at a rate based upon the taxpayer's estimate of the lives of the assets (instead of the class life) and the total amount of depreciation so determined for the asset guideline class for the taxable year of election is not more than would be permitted under (a) of this subdivision for such

Reg. § 1.167(a)-12(a)(5)

year using the method of depreciation adopted by the taxpayer for the property.

See subdivision (vii) of this subparagraph for determination of reasonable allowance if depreciation exceeds the amount permitted by this subdivision. See paragraph (b) of this section for rules regarding the determination of "class life". For rules for regrouping depreciation accounts to conform to the asset guideline class, see subdivision (iv) of this subparagraph.

(iii) *Consistency when individual lives are used.* If the taxpayer assigns individual depreciable lives to assets in accordance with subdivision (ii)(*b*) of this subparagraph, even though the total amount of depreciation for the asset guideline class will not be adjusted, the lives assigned to the various assets in the asset guideline class must be reasonably in proportion to their relative expected periods of use in the taxpayer's business. Thus, although the taxpayer who uses individual asset lives normally has latitude in thereby allocating the depreciation for the asset guideline class among the assets, if the lives are grossly disproportionate (as where a short life is assigned to one asset and a long life to another even though the expected periods of use are the same), the taxpayer's allocation of depreciation to particular assets or depreciation accounts may be adjusted. For example, the taxpayer's allocation may be adjusted for purposes of determining adjusted basis under section 1016(a) or in allocating depreciation to the 50-percent limitation on percentage depletion provided by section 613(a). See paragraph (d) of this section for rules regarding the use of individual asset lives for purposes of classifying retirements as normal or abnormal.

(iv) *Regrouping depreciation accounts.* Without the consent of the Commissioner, the taxpayer may for any taxable year for which he elects to apply this section to an asset guideline class, regroup his accounts for that and all succeeding taxable years to conform to the asset guideline class. Other changes in accounting, including a change from item accounts to multiple-asset accounting, may be made with the consent of the Commissioner. No depreciation accounts for which the straight line or sum of the years-digits method of depreciation is adopted may be combined under this section which would not be permitted to be combined under part III of Revenue Procedure 65-13, as in effect on January 1, 1971. Accordingly, whether or not the taxpayer adopted the guideline system of Revenue Procedure 62-21 for a taxable year to which Part III of Revenue Procedure 65-13 is applicable, the depreciation allowance for any taxable year of election under this section may not exceed that amount which

would have been allowed for such year if the taxpayer had used item accounts or year of acquisition accounts. Thus, for example, if a calendar year taxpayer acquired a $90 asset on the first day of each year from 1966 through 1970, placed such assets in a single multiple asset account, adopted the sum of the years-digits method of depreciation and used a 5-year depreciable life for such assets, and in 1971 uses the 5-year class life determined under paragraph (b) of this section, the depreciation allowance for such assets in 1971 under this section may not exceed $60, that is, the amount which would be allowed if the taxpayer had used year of acquisition accounts for the assets for the years 1966 through 1970. For purposes of this subparagraph, a taxpayer's depreciation accounts conform to the asset guideline class if each depreciation account includes only assets of the same asset guideline class.

(v) *Method of depreciation.* The same method of depreciation must be applied to all property in a single depreciation account. The method of depreciation is subject to the limitations of section 167(c), (j) and (l). Except as otherwise provided in this subdivision, the taxpayer must apply a method of depreciation described in section 167(b)(1), (2), or (3) for qualified property to which the taxpayer elects to apply this section. A method of depreciation permitted under section 167(b)(4) may be used under this section if the method was used by the taxpayer with respect to the property for his last taxable year ending before January 1, 1971, the method is expressed in terms of years, the taxpayer establishes to the satisfaction of the Commissioner that the method is both a reasonable and consistent method, and if the taxpayer applies paragraph (b)(2) of this section (relating to class lives in special situations) to determine a class life, that the method of determining such class life is consistent with the principles of Revenue Procedure 62-21 as applied to such a method. If the taxpayer has applied a method of depreciation with respect to the property which is not described in section 167(b)(1), (2), (3), or (4) (as permitted under the preceding sentence), he must change under this section to a method of depreciation described in section 167(b)(1), (2), or (3) for the first taxable year for which an election is made under this section. Other changes in depreciation method may be made with the consent of the Commissioner (see section 446 and the regulations thereunder). (See also section 167(e).)

(vi) *Salvage value.* In applying the method of depreciation adopted by the taxpayer, the annual allowance for depreciation is determined without adjustment for the salvage value of the property, except that no depreciation account

Reg. § 1.167(a)-12(a)(5)

may be depreciated below a reasonable salvage value for the account. See paragraph (c) of this section for definition and treatment of salvage value.

(vii) *Reasonable allowance when depreciation exceeds amount based on class life.* In the event that the total amount of depreciation claimed by the taxpayer on his income tax return, in a claim for refund, or otherwise, for an asset guideline class with respect to which an election is made under this section for the taxable year, exceeds the maximum amount permitted under subdivision (ii)() of this subparagraph—

(a) If the excess is established to the satisfaction of the Commissioner to be the result of a good faith mistake by the taxpayer in determining the maximum amount permitted under subdivision (ii)(a) of this subparagraph, the taxpayer's election to apply this section will be treated as valid and only such excess will be disallowed, and

(b) In all other cases, the taxpayers' election to apply this section to the asset guideline class for the taxable year is invalid and the reasonable allowance for depreciation will be determined without regard to this section. (See § 1.167(a)-1(b) for rules regarding the estimated useful life of property.)

(b) *Determination of class lives—*(1) *Class lives in general.* The class life determined under this paragraph (without regard to any range or variance permitted with respect to class lives under § 1.167(a)-11) will be applied for purposes of determining whether the allowance for depreciation for qualified property included in an election under this section is subject to adjustment. The taxpayer is not required to use the class life determined under this paragraph for purposes of determining the allowance for depreciation. Except as provided in subparagraph (2) of this paragraph, the class life of qualified property to which the taxpayer elects to apply this section is the shorter of—

(i) The asset guideline period for the asset guideline class as set forth in Revenue Procedure 72-10 as in effect on March 1, 1972 (applied without regard to any special provision therein with respect to property predominantly used outside the United States), or

(ii) The asset guideline period for the asset guideline class as set forth in any supplement or revision of Revenue Procedure 72-10, but only if and to the extent by express reference in such supplement or revision made applicable for the purpose of changing the asset guideline period or classification of qualified property to which this section applies. See paragraph (e)(3)(iii) of this

section for requirement that the election for the taxable year specify the class life for each asset guideline class. Generally, the applicable asset guideline class and asset guideline period for qualified property to which the taxpayer has elected to apply this section will not be changed for the taxable year of election to reflect any supplement or revision thereof after the taxable year. However, if expressly provided in such a supplement or revision, the taxpayer may, at his option in the manner specified therein, apply the revised or supplemented asset guideline classes or periods to such property for such taxable year and succeeding taxable years. The principles of this subparagraph may be illustrated by the following example:

Example. (i) Corporation X, a calendar year taxpayer, has assets in asset guideline class 20.4 of Revenue Procedure 72-10 which were placed in service by corporation X in 1967, 1968, and 1970. Corporation X also has assets in asset guideline class 22.1 of Revenue Procedure 72-10 which were placed in service at various times prior to 1971. Corporation X has no other qualified property. Corporation X elects to apply this section for 1971 to both classes. Assume that the class lives are determined under this subparagraph and not under subparagraph (2) of this paragraph.

(ii) The class lives for asset guideline classes 20.4 and 22.1 are their respective asset guideline periods of 12 years and 9 years in Revenue Procedure 72-10.

(iii) Accordingly, in the election for the taxable year, in accordance with paragraph (e)(3)(iii) of this section, corporation X specifies a class life of 12 years for asset guideline class 20.4 and a class life of 9 years for asset guideline class 22.1.

(2) *Class lives in special situations.* Notwithstanding subparagraph (1) of this paragraph, for the purposes of this section the class life for the asset guideline class determined under this subparagraph shall be used if such class life is shorter than the class life determined under subparagraph (1) of this paragraph. If property described in paragraph (a)(2)(iii) of this section in an asset guideline class is acquired by the taxpayer in a transaction to which section 381(a) applies, for purposes of this subparagraph such property shall be segregated from other property in the class and treated as in a separate asset guideline class, and the class life for that asset guideline class under this subparagraph shall be the shortest class life the transferor was entitled to use under this section for such property on the date of such transfer. In all other cases, the class life for the asset

Reg. § 1.167(a)-12(b)(1)

guideline class for purposes of this subparagraph shall be the shortest class life (within the meaning of section 4, Part II, of Revenue Procedure 62-21) which can be justified by application of section 3.02(a), 3.03(a) or 3.05, Part II. of Revenue Procedure 62-21 (other than the portion of such section 3.05 dealing with justification of a class life by reference to facts and circumstances) for the taxpayer's last taxable year ending prior to January 1, 1971. A class life justified by application of section 3.03(a), Part II, of Revenue Procedure 62-21 shall not be shorter than can be justified under the Adjustment Table for Class Lives in Part III of such Revenue Procedure. For purposes of this subparagraph and paragraph (f)(1)(iii) of this section, the reserve ratio test is met only if the taxpayer's reserve ratio does not exceed the upper limit of the appropriate reserve ratio range or in the alternative during the transitional period there provided does not exceed the appropriate "transitional upper limit" in section 3, Part II, of Revenue Procedure 65-13. References to Revenue Procedure 62-21 include all modifications, amendments, and supplements thereto as of January 1, 1971. The guideline form of the reserve ratio test, as described in Revenue Procedure 65-13, may be applied for purposes of this subparagraph in a manner consistent with the rules contained in section 7, Part II, of Revenue Procedure 65-13 and sections 3.02, 3.03, and 3.05, Part II, of Revenue Procedure 62-21. The principles of this subparagraph may be illustrated by the following examples:

Example (1). Corporation X, a calendar year taxpayer, has all its assets in asset guideline class 20.4 of Revenue Procedure 72-10 which were placed in service by corporation X prior to 1971. Corporation X elects to apply this section for 1971. For taxable years 1967 through 1969, corporation X had used a class life (within the meaning of section 4, Part II, of Revenue Procedure 62-21) for asset guideline class 20.4 of 12 years. The asset guideline period in Revenue Procedure 72-10 in effect for 1971 is also 12 years. Assume that for 1969 corporation X's reserve ratio was below that appropriate reserve ratio lower limit. However, corporation X could not justify a class life shorter than the asset guideline period of 12 years for 1970 since corporation X had not used the 12-year class life for a period at least equal to one-half of 12 years. (See section 3.03(a), Part II, of Revenue Procedure 62-21.) Accordingly, the class life for asset guideline class 20.4 in 1971 is the asset guideline period of 12 years in accordance with subparagraph (1) or this paragraph.

Example (2). The facts are the same as in example (1) except that corporation X had used a class life of 10 years for guideline class 20.4 since

1967. Corporation X had not used the class life of 10 years for a period at least equal to one-half of 10 years. However, in 1968 corporation X's 10-year class life was accepted on audit by the Internal Revenue Service and corporation X met the reserve ratio test in 1970 for guideline class 20.4 using a test life of 10 years. (See section 3.05, Part II, of Revenue Procedure 62-21.) Accordingly, the class life of 10 years is justified for 1970 and the class life for 1971 is 10 years in accordance with this subparagraph. If the taxpayer's class life had not been audited and accepted for 1968, and in the absence of other circumstances, the taxpayer could not justify a class life shorter than the asset guideline period of 12 years since it had not used the 10-year class life for a period at least equal to one-half of 10 years. (See section 3.02, Part II, of Revenue Procedure 62-21.)

Example (3). Corporation Y, a calendar year taxpayer, has all its assets in asset guideline class 13.3 of Revenue Procedure 72-10 which were placed in service from 1960 through 1970. Corporation Y elects to apply this section for 1971. The asset guideline period in Revenue Procedure 72-10 in effect for 1971 is 16 years. Since 1963 corporation Y had used a class life of 16 years for asset guideline 13.3. At the end of 1969 corporation Y's reserve ratio for guideline class 13.3 was 36 percent. With a growth rate of 8 percent and a test life of 16 years the appropriate reserve ratio lower limit was 37 percent. Corporation Y's reserve ratio of 36 percent was below the lower limit of the appropriate reserve ratio range. Corporation Y had used the 16-year class life for at least eight years. A class life of 13.5 years for 1970 was justified by application of section 3.03(a), Part II, of Revenue Procedure 62-21 and the Adjustment Table for Class Lives in Part III, of Revenue Procedure 62-21. The class life for 1971 is 13.5 years in accordance with this subparagraph.

(3) *Classification of property*—(i) *In general.* Property to which this section applies shall be included in the asset guideline class for the activity in which the property is primarily used in the taxable year of election. See paragraph (d)(5) of this section for rule regarding the classification of leased property.

(ii) *Insubstantial activity.* The provisions of Revenue Procedure 62-21 with respect to classification of assets used in an activity which is insubstantial may be applied under this section.

(iii) *Special rule for certain public utilities.* An electric or gas utility which in accordance with Revenue Procedure 64-21 used a composite guideline class basis for applying Revenue Procedure 64-21 for its last taxable year prior to January 1, 1971, may apply Revenue Procedure 72-10 and

Reg. § 1.167(a)-12(b)(3)

this section on the basis of such composite asset guideline class determined as provided in Revenue Procedure 64-21. For the purposes of this section all property in the composite guideline class shall be treated as included in a single asset guideline class.

(c) *Salvage value—(1) In general—(i) Definition of gross salvage value.* "Gross salvage" value is the amount (determined at or as of the time of acquisition but without regard to the application of Revenue Procedure 62-21) which is estimated will be realized upon a sale or other disposition of qualified property when it is no longer useful in the taxpayer's trade or business or in the production of his income and is to be retired from service, without reduction for the cost of removal, dismantling, demolition, or similar operations. "Net salvage" is gross salvage reduced by the cost of removal, dismantling, demolition, or similar operations. If a taxpayer customarily sells or otherwise disposes of property at a time when such property is still in good operating condition, the gross salvage value of such property is the amount expected to be realized upon such sale or disposition, and under certain circumstances, as where such property is customarily sold at a time when it is still relatively new, the gross salvage value may constitute a relatively large proportion of the unadjusted basis of such property.

(ii) *Definition of salvage value.* "Salvage value" for purposes of this section means gross or net salvage value less the amount, if any, by which reduced by application of section 167(f). Generally, as provided in section 167(f), a taxpayer may reduce the gross or net salvage value for an account by an amount which does not exceed 10 percent of the unadjusted basis of the personal property (as defined in section 167(f)(2)) in the account.

(2) *Estimation of salvage value—(i) In general.* For the first taxable year for which he elects to apply this section, the taxpayer must (in accordance with paragraph (e)(3)(iv)(c) of this section) establish salvage value for all qualified property to which the election applies. The taxpayer may (in accordance with subparagraph (1) of this paragraph) determine either gross or net salvage, but an election under this section does not constitute permission to change the manner of estimating salvage. Permission to change the manner of estimating salvage must be obtained by filing Form 3115 with the Commissioner of Internal Revenue, Washington, D.C. 20224, within the time otherwise permitted for the taxable year or before September 6, 1973. Salvage value in succeeding taxable years of election will be determined by adjustments of such initial salvage value for the

account, as retirements occur. This salvage value established by the taxpayer for the first taxable year of election will not be redetermined merely as a result of fluctuations in price levels or as a result of other circumstances occurring after the close of such taxable year. See paragraph (e)(3)(iv) of this section for requirements that the taxpayer specify in his election the aggregate amount of salvage value for an asset guideline class and that the taxpayer maintain records reasonably sufficient to identify the salvage value established for each depreciation account in the class.

(ii) *Salvage as limitation on depreciation.* In no case may an account be depreciated under this section below a reasonable salvage value, after taking into account any reduction in gross or net salvage value permitted by section 167(f). For example, if the salvage value of an account for 1971 is $75, the unadjusted basis of the account is $500, and the depreciation reserve is $425, no depreciation is allowable for 1971.

(iii) *Special rule for first taxable year.* If for a taxable year ending prior to January 1, 1971, the taxpayer had adopted Revenue Procedure 62-21 prior to January 12, 1971 (see paragraph (f)(2) of this section), no adjustment in the amount of depreciation allowable for any taxable year ending prior to January 1, 1971, shall be made solely by reason of establishing salvage value under this paragraph for any taxable year ending after December 31, 1970. The principles of this subdivision may be illustrated by the following example:

Example: Taxpayer A had adopted Revenue Procedure 62-21 prior to January 12, 1971, for taxable years prior to 1971. Taxpayer A had not taken into account any salvage value for account No. 1 which is one of four depreciation accounts A has in the class. The reserve ratio test has been met for all years prior to 1971 and in accordance with Revenue Procedure 62-21 no adjustments in depreciable lives or salvage values were made. At the end of A's taxable year 1970, the unadjusted basis of account No. 1 was $10,000 and the reserve for depreciation was $9,800. Pursuant to this paragraph, A establishes a salvage value of $400 for account No. 1 (determined at or as of the time of acquisition). This salvage value is determined to be correct. No depreciation is allowable for account No. 1 in 1971. No depreciation is disallowed for any taxable year prior to 1971, solely by reason of establishing salvage value under this paragraph.

(3) *Limitation on adjustment of reasonable salvage value.* The salvage value established by the taxpayer for a depreciation account will not

Reg. § 1.167(a)-12(c)(1)

be redetermined if it is reasonable. Since the determination of salvage value is a matter of estimation, minimal adjustments will not be made. The salvage value established by the taxpayer will be deemed to be reasonable unless there is sufficient basis for a determination of an amount of salvage value for the account which exceeds the salvage value established by the taxpayer for the account by an amount greater than 10 percent of the unadjusted basis of the account at the close of such taxable year. If the salvage value established by the taxpayer for the account is not within the 10 percent range or if the taxpayer follows the practice of understating his estimates of salvage to take advantage of this subdivision, and if there is a determination of an amount of salvage value for the account for the taxable year which exceeds the salvage value established by the taxpayer for the account for such taxable year, an adjustment will be made by increasing the salvage value established by the taxpayer for the account by an amount equal to the difference between the salvage value as determined and the salvage value established by the taxpayer for the account. For the purposes of this subdivision, a determination of salvage value shall include all determinations at all levels of audit and appellate proceedings, as well as all final determinations within the meaning of section 1313(a)(1). This subparagraph shall apply to each such determination.

(4) *Examples.* The principles of this paragraph may be illustrated by the following examples in which it is assumed that the taxpayer has established salvage value in accordance with this paragraph and has not followed a practice of understating his estimates of salvage value:

Example (1). Taxpayer B elects to apply this section for 1971. Assets Y and Z are the only assets in a multiple asset account of 1967, the year in which the assets were acquired. The unadjusted basis of asset Y is $50,000 and the unadjusted basis of asset Z is $30,000. B estimated a gross salvage value of $55,000 at the time of acquisition. The property qualified under section 167(f)(2) and B reduced the amount of salvage taken into account by $8,000 (that is, 10 percent of $80,000, under section 167(f)). Thus, in accordance with this paragraph and paragraph (e)(3)(iv)(c) of this section, B establishes a salvage value of $47,000 for the account for 1971. Assume that there is not sufficient basis for determining a salvage value for the account greater than $52,000 (that is $60,000 minus the $8,000 reduction under section 167(f)). Since the salvage value of $47,000 established by B for the account is within the 10 percent range, it is reasonable. Salvage for the account will not be redetermined.

Example (2). The facts are the same as in example (1) except that B estimated a gross salvage value of $50,000 and establishes a salvage value of $42,000 for the account (that is $50,000 minus the $8,000 reduction under section 167(f)). There is sufficient basis for determining an amount of salvage value greater than $50,000 (that is, $58,000 minus the $8,000 reduction under section 167(f)). The salvage value of $42,000 established by B for the account can be redetermined without regard to the limitation in subparagraph (3) of this paragraph, since it is not within the 10 percent range. Upon audit of B's tax return for 1971 (a year in which the redetermination would affect the amount of depreciation allowable for the account), salvage value is determined to be $52,000 after taking into account the reduction under section 167(f). Salvage value for the account will be adjusted to $52,000.

Example (3). The facts are the same as in example (1) except that upon audit of B's tax return for 1971 the examining officer determines the salvage value to be $58,000 (that is $66,000 minus the $8,000 reduction under section 167(f)), and proposes to adjust salvage value for the account to $58,000 which will result in disallowing an amount of depreciation for the taxable year. B does not agree with the finding of the examining officer. After receipt of a "30-day letter," B waives a district conference and initiates proceedings before the Appellate Division. In consideration of the case by the Appellate Division it is concluded that there is not sufficient basis for determining an amount of salvage value for the account in excess of $55,000 (that is, $63,000 minus the $8,000 reduction under section 167(f)). Since the salvage value of $47,000 established by B for the account is within the 10 percent range, it is reasonable. Salvage value for the account will not be redetermined.

Example (4). For 1971, taxpayer C elects to apply this section to factory building X which is in an item account of 1965, the year in which the building was acquired. The unadjusted basis of factory building X is $90,000. C estimated a gross salvage value for the account of $10,000. The property did not qualify under section 167(f)(2). Thus, C establishes a salvage value of $10,000 for the account for 1971. Assume that there is not sufficient basis for determining a salvage value for the account greater than $14,000. Since the salvage value of $10,000 established by C for the account is within the 10 percent range, it is reasonable. Salvage value for the account will not be redetermined.

(d) *Accounting for qualified property*—(1) *In general.* Qualified property for which the tax-

Reg. § 1.167(a)-12(d)(1)

payer elects to apply this section may be accounted for in any number of item or multiple asset accounts.

(2) *Retirements of qualified property*—(i) *In general.* The provisions of this subparagraph and § 1.167(a)-8 apply to retirements of qualified property to which the taxpayer elects to apply this section for the taxable year. See subdivision (iii) of this subparagraph for special rule for normal retirements.

(ii) *Adjusted basis of assets retired.* In the case of a taxpayer who depreciates qualified property in a multiple asset account conforming to the asset guideline class at a rate based on the class life in accordance with paragraph (a)(5)(ii)(*a*) of this section, § 1.167(a)-8(c) (relating to basis of assets retired) shall be applied by assuming that the class life is the average expected useful life of the assets in the account. See § 1.167(a)-8, generally, for the basis of assets retired.

(iii) *Definition of normal retirements.* Notwithstanding § 1.167 (a)-8(b), the determination whether a retirement of qualified property is normal or abnormal shall be made in light of all facts and circumstances, primarily with reference to the expected period of use of the asset in the taxpayer's business without regard to paragraph (a)(5)(ii) of this section. A retirement is not abnormal unless the taxpayer can show that the withdrawal of the asset was not due to a cause which would customarily be contemplated (in light of the taxpayer's practice and experience) in setting a depreciation rate for the assets without regard to paragraph (a)(5)(ii) of this section. Thus, for example, a retirement is normal if made within the range of years which would customarily be taken into account in setting such depreciation rate and if the asset has reached a condition at which, in the normal course of events, the taxpayer customarily retires similar assets from use in his business. A retirement may be abnormal if the asset is withdrawn at an earlier time or under other circumstances, as, for example, when the asset has been damaged by casualty or has lost its usefulness suddenly as the result of extraordinary obsolescence.

(3) *Special rules*—(i) *In general.* The provisions of this subparagraph shall apply to qualified property in a taxable year for which an election to apply this section is made.

(ii) *Repairs.* For the purpose of sections 162 and 263 and the regulations thereunder, whether an expenditure prolongs the life of an asset shall be determined by reference to the expected period of use of the asset in the taxpayer's business without regard to paragraph (a)(5)(ii) of this section.

(iii) *Sale and lease.* For the purpose of comparison with the term of a lease of such property, the remaining life of qualified property shall be determined by reference to the expected period of use of the asset in the taxpayer's business without regard to paragraph (a)(5)(ii) of this section.

(4) *Expected period of use.* For the purposes of subparagraphs (2) and (3) of this paragraph, the determination of the expected period of use of an asset shall be made in light of all the facts and circumstances. The expected period of use of a particular asset will not necessarily coincide with the class life used for depreciation (or with the individual asset life for depreciation under the alternative method in paragraph (a)(5)(ii)(*b*) of this section for applying the class life). Thus, for example, if the question is whether an asset has been leased for a period less than, equal to or greater than its remaining life, the determination shall be based on the remaining expected period of use of the individual asset without regard to the fact that the asset is depreciated at a rate based on the class life in accordance with paragraph (a)(5)(ii)(*a*) of this section.

(5) *Leased property.* In the case of a lessor of qualified property, unless there is an asset guideline class in effect for such lessors, the asset guideline class for such property shall be determined by reference to the activity in which such property is primarily used by the lessee. See paragraph (b)(3) of this section for general rule for classification of qualified property according to primary use. However, in the case of an asset guideline class based upon the type of property (such as trucks or railroad cars), as distinguished from the activity in which used, the property shall be classified without regard to the activity of the lessee.

(e) *Election under this section*—(1) *Consent to change in method of accounting.* An election to apply this section for a taxable year ending after December 31, 1970, is a method of accounting but the consent of the Commissioner will be deemed granted to make an annual election.

(2) *Election for taxable years ending after December 31, 1976.* For taxable years ending after December 31, 1976, the election to apply this section for a taxable year shall be made by attaching to the income tax return a statement that an election under this section is being made. If the taxpayer does not file a timely return (taking into account extensions of time for filing) for the taxable year, the election shall be made at the time the taxpayer files his first return for the taxable year. The election may be made with an amended return only if such amended return is filed no later than the time prescribed by law (including

Reg. § 1.167(a)-12(d)(2)

extensions thereof) for filing the return for the taxable year. A taxpayer who makes an election under this subparagraph must maintain books and records reflecting the information described in paragraph (e)(3)(ii) and (iii) of this section.

(3) *Election for taxable years ending on or before December 31, 1976.* (i) For taxable years ending on or before December 31, 1976, the election to apply this section for a taxable year may be made by filing Form 5006 with the income tax return for the taxable year. If the taxpayer does not file a timely return (taking into account extensions of time for filing) for the taxable year, the election shall be filed at the time the taxpayer files his first return for the taxable year. The election may be made with an amended return only if such amended return is filed no later than the later of (a) the time prescribed by law (including extensions thereof) for filing the return for the taxable year, or (b) November 5, 1973.

(ii) The election to apply this section for a taxable year ending on or before December 31, 1976, will be deemed to be made if the tax return (filed within the periods referred to in paragraph (e)(3)(i) of this section) contains information sufficient to establish the following

(a) Each asset guideline class for which the election is intended to apply;

(b) The class life for each such asset guideline class and whether the class life is determined under paragraph (b)(1) or (2) of this section;

(c) For each asset guideline class, as of the end of the taxable year of election, (1) the total unadjusted basis of all qualified property, (2) the aggregate of the reserves for depreciation of all accounts in the asset guideline class, and (3) the aggregate of the salvage value established for all accounts in the asset guideline class; and

(d) Whether the taxpayer is an electric or gas utility using a composite asset guideline class basis in accordance with paragraph (b)(3)(iii) of this section.

If an election is deemed to be made under this subdivision (ii), the taxpayer will be deemed to have consented to apply all provisions of this section.

(iii) A taxpayer to whom the election applies shall maintain books and records for each asset guideline class reasonably sufficient to identify the unadjusted basis, reserve for depreciation and salvage value established for each depreciation account in such assset guideline class.

(f) *Depreciation for taxable years ending before January 1, 1971* —(1) *Adoption of Revenue Procedure 62-21* —(i) *In general.* Except as provided

in subdivision (ii) of this subparagraph, a taxpayer may elect to be examined under the provisions of Revenue Procedure 62-21 for a taxable year ending before January 1, 1971, only in accordance with the rules of this paragraph. The election must specify:

(a) That the taxpayer makes such election and consents to, and agrees to apply, all the provisions of this paragraph;

(b) Each guideline class and taxable year for which the taxpayer elects to be examined under Revenue Procedure 62-21;

(c) The class life claimed for each such guideline class;

(d) The class life and the total amount of the depreciation for the guideline class claimed on the last income tax return for such taxable year filed prior to January 12, 1971 (or in case no income tax return was filed prior to January 12, 1971, on the first income tax return filed for such taxable year);

(e) The class life claimed and the total amount of depreciation for the guideline class under the election to apply Revenue Procedure 62-21, in accordance with this paragraph, for the taxable year; and

(f) If the class life or total amount of depreciation for the guideline class is different in (d) and (e) of this subdivision, a reasonable description of the computation of the class life in (e) of this subdivision, the amount of difference in tax liability resulting therefrom, and the amount of any refund or reduction in any deficiency in tax.

The election shall be made in an amended tax return or claim for refund (or by a supplement to the tax return or claim) for the taxable year, and if the class life or total amount of depreciation for the guideline class is different in accordance with (f) of this subdivision, such difference shall be reflected in the amended tax return or claim for refund. Forms may be provided for making the election and submission of the information. In the case of an election made after issuance of such Forms and more than 30 days after publication of notice thereof in the Internal Revenue Bulletin, the election may be made and the information submitted only in accordance with such forms. An election will not otherwise be invalid under this paragraph so long as there is substantial compliance, in good faith, with the requirements of this paragraph.

(ii) *Special rule.* The provisions of this subparagraph shall not apply to a guideline class in any taxable year for which the taxpayer has prior to January 12, 1971, adopted Revenue Procedure

Reg. § 1.167(a)-12(f)(1)

62-21 for such class. See subparagraph (2) of this paragraph for determination of adoption of Revenue Procedure 62-21 prior to January 12, 1971.

(iii) *Justification of class life claimed and limitations on refunds.* If the taxpayer elects for a taxable year to be examined under the provisions of Revenue Procedure 62-21 in accordance with subdivision (i) of this subparagraph, any of the provisions of Revenue Procedure 62-21 may be applied to justify a class life claimed on the income tax return filed for such year or to offset an increase in tax liability for such year. Unless it meets the reserve ratio test, no class life will be accepted on audit which (after all other adjustments in tax liability for such year) results in a reduction (or further reduction) in the amount of tax liability shown on the income tax return (specified in subdivision (i)(*d*) of this subparagraph) for such taxable year, or results in an amount of loss carryback or carryover to any taxable year, but if it is justified under Revenue Procedure 62-21 and meets the reserve ratio test, a class life will be accepted on audit without regard to the foregoing limitations and, for example, may produce a refund or credit against tax. For example, if a class life of 9 years is otherwise justified under Revenue Procedure 62-21 for 1969, but the taxpayer does not meet the reserve ratio test for 1969 using a test life of 9 years, a class life of 9 years (or any class life justified under Revenue Procedure 62-21) will be accepted on audit under Revenue Procedure 62-21 pursuant to an election in accordance with this paragraph provided it does not result in the reduction or further reduction in tax liability or in an amount of loss carryback or carryover as described in the preceding sentence. On the other hand, for example, if a class life of 10 years is justified under Revenue Procedure 62-21 for 1969 and the taxpayer meets the reserve ratio test for 1969 using a test life of 10 years, a class life of 10 years will be accepted on audit under Revenue Procedure 62-21 pursuant to an election in accordance with this paragraph even though it results in a reduction or further reduction in tax liability or in an amount of loss carryback or carryover as described above and produces a refund of tax. For purposes of this section, the term "audit" includes examination of claims for refund or credit against tax.

(iv) *Definitions.* For purposes of this paragraph, the determination whether the reserve ratio test is met shall be made in accordance with that portion of paragraph (b)(2) of this section which is by express reference therein made applicable to this paragraph. In addition, the guideline form of the reserve ratio test, as described in Revenue Procedure 65-13, may be applied.

For purposes of this paragraph, references to Revenue Procedure 62-21 include all modifications, amendments, and supplements thereto as of January 11, 1971. The terms "class life" and "guideline class" have the same meaning as in Revenue Procedure 62-21.

(2) *Determination whether Revenue Procedure 62-21 adopted prior to January 12, 1971*—(i) *In general.* For the purposes of this paragraph, a taxpayer will be treated as having adopted prior to January 12, 1971, Revenue Procedure 62-21 for a guideline class for a taxable year ending before January 1, 1971, only if—

(*a*) For the guideline class and taxable year, the taxpayer adopted Revenue Procedure 62-21 by expressly so indicating on the income tax return filed for such taxable year prior to January 12, 1971;

(*b*) For the guideline class and taxable year, the taxpayer adopted Revenue Procedure 62-21 prior to January 12, 1971, by expressly so indicating in a proceeding before the Internal Revenue Service (such as upon examination of the income tax return for such taxable year) and there is reasonable evidence to that effect; or

(*c*) There is other reasonable evidence that prior to January 12, 1971, the taxpayer adopted Revenue Procedure 62-21 for the guideline class and taxable year.

If not treated under (*b*) or (*c*) of this subdivision as having done so for the last taxable year ending before January 1, 1971, and if the taxpayer files his first income tax return for such taxable year after January 11, 1971, the taxpayer will be treated as having adopted Revenue Procedure 62-21 prior to January 12, 1971, for a guideline class for such taxable year if he expressly so indicated on that return, or is treated under this subparagraph as having adopted Revenue Procedure 62-21 prior to January 12, 1971, for that guideline class for the immediately preceeding taxable year.

(ii) *Examples.* The principles of this subparagraph may be illustrated by the following examples:

Example (1). Taxpayer A, an individual who uses the calendar year as his taxable year, has property in Group Three, Class 16(a), of Revenue Procedure 62-21. On A's income tax return for 1968, filed prior to January 12, 1971, he adopted Revenue Procedure 62-21 for the guideline class by so indicating under "Summary of Depreciation" in the appropriate schedule of Form 1040 for 1968. Under subdivision (i)(*a*) of this subparagraph, A is treated as having adopted Revenue Procedure 62-21 for the guideline class for 1968 prior to January 12, 1971.

Reg. § 1.167(a)-12(f)(2)

Example (2). Taxpayer B, an individual who uses the calendar year as his taxable year, has property in Group Two, Class 5, of Revenue Procedure 62-21. B filed timely income tax returns for 1966 through 1968 but did not adopt Revenue Procedure 62-21 on any of such returns. In 1969 upon audit of B's taxable years 1966 through 1968, B exercised his option to be examined under the provisions of Revenue Procedure 62-21. The Revenue Agent's report shows that B was examined under Revenue Procedure 62-21 for taxable years 1966 through 1968. B will be treated under subdivision (i)(*b*) of this subparagraph as having adopted Revenue Procedure 62-21 for such years prior to January 12, 1971.

Example (3). The facts are the same as in example (2) except that B did not upon examination by the Revenue Agent in 1969 exercise his option to be examined under Revenue Procedure 62-21. B has six accounts in the guideline class, Nos. 1 through 6. The Revenue Agent proposed to lengthen the depreciable lives on accounts Nos. 2 and 3 from 8 years to 12 years. In proceedings before the Appellate Division in 1970, B exercised his option to be examined under the provisions of Revenue Procedure 62-21. This is shown by correspondence between B and the Appellate Conferee as well as by other documents in the case before the Appellate Division. The case was settled on that basis before the Appellate Division without adjustment of the depreciable lives for B's accounts Nos. 2 and 3. B will be treated under subdivision (ii)(*b*) of this subparagraph as having adopted Revenue Procedure 62-21 for taxable years 1966 through 1968 prior to January 12, 1971.

Example (4). Corporation X uses the calendar year as its taxable year and has assets in Group Two, Class 5, of Revenue Procedure 62-21. Beginning in 1964, corporation X used the guideline life of 10 years as the depreciable life for all assets in the guideline class. In 1967, corporation X's taxable years 1964 through 1966 were examined and corporation X exercised its option to be examined under the provisions of Revenue Procedure 62-21. Corporation X did not adopt Revenue Procedure 62-21 on any of its income tax returns, for the years 1964 through 1970. Corporation X has not been examined since 1967, but has continued to use the guideline life of 10 years for all property in the guideline class including additions since 1966. Corporation X will be treated under subdivision (ii)(*c*) and (*d*) of this subparagraph as having adopted Revenue Procedure 62-21 prior to January 12, 1971 for taxable years 1964 through 1970.

Example (5). Corporation Y uses the calendar year as its taxable year and has assets in Group Two, Class 5, of Revenue Procedure 62-21. Since 1964, corporation Y has used various depreciable lives, based on the facts and circumstances, for different accounts in the guideline class. Corporation Y was examined in 1968 for taxable years 1965 through 1967. Corporation Y was also examined in 1970 for taxable years 1968 and 1969. Corporation Y did not exercise its option to be examined under the provisions of Revenue Procedure 62-21. Corporation Y has not adopted Revenue Procedure 62-21 on any income tax return. For taxable years 1964 through 1970, corporation Y's class life (within the meaning of section 4, Part I, of Revenue Procedure 62-21) was between 12 and 14 years. In August of 1971, corporation Y filed amended income tax returns for 1968 and 1969, and an income tax return for 1970, using a depreciable life of 10 years (equal to the guideline life) for all assets in the guideline class. Corporation Y will not be treated as having adopted Revenue Procedure 62-21 prior to January 12, 1971.

Example (6). Corporation Z uses the calendar year as its taxable year and has assets in Group Two, Class 5, of Revenue Procedure 62-21. Corporation Z adopted Revenue Procedure 62-21 for this guideline class by expressly so indicating on its tax return for 1966, which was filed before January 12, 1971. Corporation Z computed its allowable depreciation for 1966 as if it adopted Rev. Proc. 62-21 for this guideline class for its taxable years 1962 through 1965, although it had earlier filed its tax returns for those years without regard to Rev. Proc. 62-21. The depreciation thus claimed in 1966 was less than what would have been allowed if corporation Z first adopted Rev. Proc. 62-21 in 1966. This was the result of certain accounts becoming fully depreciated through use of Rev. Proc. 62-21 in computing depreciation for 1962 through 1965. In addition, in deferred tax accounting procedures employed before January 12, 1971, for financial reporting purposes, corporation Z calculated its tax deferrals on the basis that it had adopted Rev. Proc. 62-21 for the years 1962 through 1965. Corporation Z will be treated under subdivision (i)(*c*) of this subparagraph as having adopted Rev. Proc. 62-21 for taxable years 1962 through 1965 prior to January 12, 1971. [Reg. § 1.167(a)-12.]

☐ [*T.D.* 7278, 6-6-73. *Amended by T.D.* 7315, 6-6-74 *and T.D.* 7517, 11-11-77.]

[Reg. § 1.167(a)-13T]

§ 1.167(a)-13T. Certain elections for intangible property (temporary).—For rules applying the elections under section 13261(g)(2) and (3) of

Reg. § 1.167(a)-13T

the Omnibus Budget Reconciliation Act of 1993 to intangible property described in section 167(f), see § 1.197-1T. [Temporary Reg. § 1.167(a)-13T.]

□ *T.D.* 8528, 3-10-94.]

[Reg. § 1.167(a)-14]

§ 1.167(a)-14. **Treatment of certain intangible property excluded from section 197.**—(a) *Overview.* This section provides rules for the amortization of certain intangibles that are excluded from section 197 (relating to the amortization of goodwill and certain other intangibles). These excluded intangibles are specifically described in § 1.197-2(c)(4), (6), (7), (11), and (13) and include certain computer software and certain other separately acquired rights, such as rights to receive tangible property or services, patents and copyrights, certain mortgage servicing rights, and rights of fixed duration or amount. Intangibles for which an amortization amount is determined under section 167(f) and intangibles otherwise excluded from section 197 are amortizable only if they qualify as property subject to the allowance for depreciation under section 167(a).

(b) *Computer software*—(1) *In general.* The amount of the deduction for computer software described in section 167(f)(1) and § 1.197-2(c)(4) is determined by amortizing the cost or other basis of the computer software using the straight line method described in § 1.167(b)-1 (except that its salvage value is treated as zero) and an amortization period of 36 months beginning on the first day of the month that the computer software is placed in service. If costs for developing computer software that the taxpayer properly elects to defer under section 174(b) result in the development of property subject to the allowance for depreciation under section 167, the rules of this paragraph (b) will apply to the unrecovered costs. In addition, this paragraph (b) applies to the cost of separately acquired computer software where these costs are separately stated and the costs are required to be capitalized under section 263(a).

(2) *Exceptions.* Paragraph (b)(1) of this section does not apply to the cost of computer software properly and consistently taken into account under § 1.162-11. The cost of acquiring an interest in computer software that is included, without being separately stated, in the cost of the hardware or other tangible property is treated as part of the cost of the hardware or other tangible property that is capitalized and depreciated under other applicable sections of the Internal Revenue Code.

(3) *Additional rules.* Rules similar to those in § 1.197-2(f)(1)(iii), (f)(1)(iv), and (f)(2) (relating to the computation of amortization deductions and the treatment of contingent amounts) apply for purposes of this paragraph (b).

(c) *Certain interests or rights not acquired as part of a purchase of a trade or business*—(1) *Certain rights to receive tangible property or services.* The amount of the deduction for a right (other than a right acquired as part of a purchase of a trade or business) to receive tangible property or services under a contract or from a governmental unit (as specified in section 167(f)(2) and § 1.197-2(c)(6)) is determined as follows:

(i) *Amortization of fixed amounts.* The basis of a right to receive a fixed amount of tangible property or services is amortized for each taxable year by multiplying the basis of the right by a fraction, the numerator of which is the amount of tangible property or services received during the taxable year and the denominator of which is the total amount of tangible property or services received or to be received under the terms of the contract or governmental grant. For example, if a taxpayer acquires a favorable contract right to receive a fixed amount of raw materials during an unspecified period, the taxpayer must amortize the cost of acquiring the contract right by multiplying the total cost by a fraction, the numerator of which is the amount of raw materials received under the contract during the taxable year and the denominator of which is the total amount of raw materials received or to be received under the contract.

(ii) *Amortization of unspecified amount over fixed period.* The cost or other basis of a right to receive an unspecified amount of tangible property or services over a fixed period is amortized ratably over the period of the right. (See paragraph (c)(3) of this section regarding renewals).

(iii) *Amortization in other cases.* [Reserved]

(2) *Rights of fixed duration or amount.* The amount of the deduction for a right (other than a right acquired as part of a purchase of a trade or business) of fixed duration or amount received under a contract or granted by a governmental unit (specified in section 167(f)(2) and § 1.197-2(c)(13)) and not covered by paragraph (c)(1) of this section is determined as follows:

(i) *Rights to a fixed amount.* The basis of a right to a fixed amount is amortized for each taxable year by multiplying the basis by a fraction, the numerator of which is the amount received during the taxable year and the denominator of which is the total amount received or to be received under the terms of the contract or governmental grant.

(ii) *Rights to an unspecified amount over fixed duration of less than 15 years.* The basis of a

Reg. § 1.167(a)-14(a)

right to an unspecified amount over a fixed duration of less than 15 years is amortized ratably over the period of the right.

(3) *Application of renewals*—(i) For purposes of paragraphs (c)(1) and (2) of this section, the duration of a right under a contract (or granted by a governmental unit) includes any renewal period if, based on all of the facts and circumstances in existence at any time during the taxable year in which the right is acquired, the facts clearly indicate a reasonable expectancy of renewal.

(ii) The mere fact that a taxpayer will have the opportunity to renew a contract right or other right on the same terms as are available to others, in a competitive auction or similar process that is designed to reflect fair market value and in which the taxpayer is not contractually advantaged, will generally not be taken into account in determining the duration of such right provided that the bidding produces a fair market value price comparable to the price that would be obtained if the rights were purchased immediately after renewal from a person (other than the person granting the renewal) in an arm's-length transaction.

(iii) The cost of a renewal not included in the terms of the contract or governmental grant is treated as the acquisition of a separate intangible asset.

(4) *Patents and copyrights.* If the purchase price of a interest (other than an interest acquired as part of a purchase of a trade or business) in a patent or copyright described in section 167(f)(2) and § 1.197-2(c)(7) is payable on at least an annual basis as either a fixed amount per use or a fixed percentage of the revenue derived from the use of the patent or copyright, the depreciation deduction for a taxable year is equal to the amount of the purchase price paid or incurred during the year. Otherwise, the basis of such patent or copyright (or an interest therein) is depreciated either ratably over its remaining useful life or under section 167(g) (income forecast method). If a patent or copyright becomes valueless in any year before its legal expiration, the adjusted basis may be deducted in that year.

(5) *Additional rules.* The period of amortization under paragraphs (c)(1) through (4) of this section begins when the intangible is placed in service, and rules similar to those in § 1.197-2(f)(2) apply for purposes of this paragraph (c).

(d) *Mortgage servicing rights*—(1) *In general.* The amount of the deduction for mortgage servicing rights described in section 167(f)(3) and § 1.197-2(c)(11) is determined by using the straight line method described in § 1.167(b)-1 (except that the salvage value is treated as zero) and an amortization period of 108 months beginning on the first day of the month that the rights are placed in service. Mortgage servicing rights are not depreciable to the extent the rights are stripped coupons under section 1286.

(2) *Treatment of rights acquired as a pool*—(i) *In general.* Except as provided in paragraph (d)(2)(i) of this section, all mortgage servicing rights acquired in the same transaction or in a series of related transactions are treated as a single asset (the pool) for purposes of determining the depreciation deduction under this paragraph (d) and any gain or loss from the sale, exchange, or other disposition of the rights. Thus, if some (but not all) of the rights in a pool become worthless as a result of prepayments, no loss is recognized by reason of the prepayment and the adjusted basis of the pool is not affected by the unrecognized loss. Similarly, any amount realized from the sale or exchange of some (but not all) of the mortgage servicing rights is included in income and the adjusted basis of the pool is not affected by the realization.

(ii) *Multiple accounts.* If the taxpayer establishes multiple accounts within a pool at the time of its acquisition, gain or loss is recognized on the sale or exchange of all mortgage servicing rights within any such account.

(3) *Additional rules.* Rules similar to those in § 1.197-2(f)(1)(iii), (f)(1)(iv), and (f)(2) (relating to the computation of amortization deductions and the treatment of contingent amounts) apply for purposes of this paragraph (d).

(e) *Effective date*—(1) *In general.* This section applies to property acquired after January 25, 2000, except that § 1.167(a)-14(c)(2) (depreciation of the cost of certain separately acquired rights) and so much of § 1.167(a)-14(c)(3) as relates to § 1.167(a)-14(c)(2) apply to property acquired after August 10, 1993 (or July 25, 1991, if a valid retroactive election has been made under § 1.197-1T).

(2) *Change in method of accounting.* See § 1.197-2(l)(4) for rules relating to changes in method of accounting for property to which § 1.167(a)-14 applies. [Reg. § 1.167(a)-14.]

☐ [*T.D.* 8865, 1-20-2000.]

[Reg. § 1.167(b)-0]

§ 1.167(b)-0. **Methods of computing depreciation.**—(a) *In general.* Any reasonable and consistently applied method of computing depreciation may be used or continued in use under section 167. Regardless of the method used in computing depreciation, deductions for depreciation shall not exceed such amounts as may be necessary to recover the unrecovered cost or other basis less salvage during the remaining useful life of the property. The reasonableness of any claim for depreciation shall be determined upon the basis of conditions known to exist at the end of the period for which the return is made. It is the responsibility of the taxpayer to establish the reasonableness of the deduction for depreciation claimed. Generally, depreciation deductions so claimed will be changed only where there is a clear and convincing basis for a change.

(b) *Certain methods.* Methods previously found adequate to produce a reasonable allowance under the Internal Revenue Code of 1939 or prior revenue laws will, if used consistently by the taxpayer, continue to be acceptable under section 167(a). Examples of such methods which continue to be acceptable are the straight line method, the declining balance method with the rate limited to 150 percent of the applicable straight line rate, and under appropriate circumstances, the unit of production method. The methods described in section 167(b) and §§ 1.167(b)-1, 1.167(b)-2, 1.167(b)-3, and 1.167(b)-4 shall be deemed to produce a reasonable allowance for depreciation except as limited under section 167(c) and § 1.167(c)-1. See also § 1.167(e)-1 for rules relating to change in method of computing depreciation.

(c) *Application of methods.* In the case of item accounts, any method which results in a reasonable allowance for depreciation may be selected for each item of property, but such method must thereafter be applied consistently to that particular item. In the case of group, classified, or composite accounts, any method may be selected for each account. Such method must be applied to

that particular account consistently thereafter but need not necessarily be applied to acquisitions of similar property in the same or subsequent years, provided such acquisitions are set up in separate accounts. See, however, § 1.167(e)-1 and section 446 and the regulations thereunder, for rules relating to changes in the method of computing depreciation, and § 1.167(c)-1 for restriction on the use of certain methods. See also § 1.167(a)-7 for definition of account. [Reg. § 1.167(b)-0.]

☐ [*T.D.* 6182, 6-11-56.]

[Reg. § 1.167(b)-1]

§ 1.167(b)-1. **Straight line method.**—(a) *Application of method.* Under the straight line method the cost or other basis of the property less its estimated salvage value is deductible in equal annual amounts over the period of the estimated useful life of the property. The allowance for depreciation for the taxable year is determined by dividing the adjusted basis of the property at the beginning of the taxable year, less salvage value, by the remaining useful life of the property at such time. For convenience, the allowance so determined may be reduced to a percentage or fraction. The straight line method may be used in determining a reasonable allowance for depreciation for any property which is subject to depreciation under section 167 and it shall be used in all cases where the taxpayer has not adopted a different acceptable method with respect to such property.

(b) *Illustrations.* The straight line method is illustrated by the following examples:

Example (1). Under the straight line method items may be depreciated separately:

Year	Item	Cost or other basis less salvage	Useful life Years	Depreciation allowable 1954	1955	1954
1954	Asset A	$ 1,600	4	$200 [1]	$400	$400
	Asset B	12,000	40	150 [1]	300	300

[1] In this example it is assumed that the assets were placed in service on July 1, 1954.

Example (2). In group, classified, or composite accounting, a number of assets with the same or different useful lives may be combined into one account, and a single rate of depreciation, i.e., the group, classified, or composite rate used for the entire account. In the case of group accounts, i.e., accounts containing assets which are similar in kind and which have approximately the same estimated useful lives, the group rate is determined from the average of the useful lives of the assets. In the case of classified or composite ac-

counts, the classified or composite rate is generally computed by determining the amount of one year's depreciation for each item or each group of similar items, and by dividing the total depreciation thus obtained by the total cost or other basis of the assets. The average rate so obtained is to be used as long as subsequent additions, retirements, or replacements do not substantially alter the relative proportions of different types of assets in the account. An example of the computation of a classified or composite rate follows:

Reg. § 1.167(b)-1(a)

Cost or other basis	Estimated useful life	Annual depreciation
	Years	
$10,000	5	$2,000
10,000	15	667
20,000		2,667

Average rate is 13.33 percent ($2,667 ÷ $20,000) unadjusted for salvage. Assuming the estimated salvage value is 10 percent of the cost or other basis, the rate adjusted for salvage will be 13.33 percent minus 10 percent of 13.33 percent (13.33% — 1.33%), or 12 percent.

Example (3). The use of the straight line method for group, classified, or composite accounts is illustrated by the following example: A taxpayer filing his returns on a calendar year basis maintains an asset account for which a group rate of 20 percent has been determined, before adjustment for salvage. Estimated salvage is determined to be 6⅔ percent, resulting in an adjusted rate of 18.67 percent During the years illustrated, the initial investment, additions, re-

tirements, and salvage recoveries, which were determined not to change the composition of the group sufficiently to require a change in rate, were assumed to have been made as follows:

1954—Initial investment of $12,000

1957—Retirement $2,000, salvage realized $200

1958—Retirement $2,000, salvage realized $200

1959—Retirements $4,000, salvage realized $400

1959—Additions $10,000

1960—Retirement $2,000, no salvage realized

1961—Retirement $2,000, no salvage realized

Depreciable Asset Account and Depreciation Computation on Average Balances

Year	Asset balance Jan. 1	Current additions	Current retirements	Asset balance Dec. 31	Average balance	Rate (percent)	Allowable depreciation
1954	—	$12,000	—	$12,000	$ 6,000	18.67	$1,120
1955	$12,000	—	—	12,000	12,000	18.67	2,240
1956	12,000	—	—	12,000	12,000	18.67	2,240
1957	12,000	—	$2,000	10,000	11,000	18.67	2,054
1958	10,000	—	2,000	8,000	9,000	18.67	1,680
1959	8,000	10,000	4,000	14,000	11,000	18.67	2,054
1960	14,000	—	2,000	12,000	13,000	18.67	2,427
1961	12,000	—	2,000	10,000	11,000	18.67	2,054

Corresponding Depreciation Reserve Account

Year	Depreciation reserve Jan. 1	Depreciation allowable	Current retirements	Salvage realized	Depreciation reserve Dec. 31
1954	—	$1,120	—	—	$1,120
1955	$1,120	2,240	—	—	3,360
1956	3,360	2,240	—	—	5,600
1957	5,600	2,054	$2,000	$200	5,854
1958	5,854	1,680	2,000	200	5,734
1959	5,734	2,054	4,000	400	4,188
1960	4,188	2,427	2,000	—	4,615
1961	4,615	2,054	2,000	—	4,669

[Reg. § 1.167(b)-1.]

☐ [*T.D.* 6182, 6-11-56.]

[Reg. § 1.167(b)-2]

§ 1.167(b)-2. Declining balance method.—(a) *Application of method.* Under the declining balance method a uniform rate is applied each year to the unrecovered cost or other basis of the property. The unrecovered cost or other basis is the basis provided by section 167(g), adjusted for depreciation previously allowed or allowable, and for all other adjustments provided by section 1016 and other applicable provisions of law. The declining balance rate may be determined without re-

sort to formula. Such rate determined under section 167(b)(2) shall not exceed twice the appropriate straight line rate computed without adjustment for salvage. While salvage is not taken into account in determining the annual allowances under this method, in no event shall an asset (or an account) be depreciated below a reasonable salvage value. However, see section 167(f) and § 1.167(f)-1 for rules which permit a reduction in the amount of salvage value to be taken into account for certain personal property acquired after October 16, 1962. Also, see section 167(c) and § 1.167(c)-1 for restrictions on the use of the declining balance method.

Reg. § 1.167(b)-2(a)

(b) *Illustrations.* The declining balance method is illustrated by the following examples:

Example (1). A new asset having an estimated useful life of 20 years was purchased on January 1, 1954, for $1,000. The normal straight line rate (without adjustment for salvage) is 5 percent, and the declining balance rate at twice the normal straight line rate is 10 percent. The annual depreciation allowances for 1954, 1955, and 1956 are as follows:

Year	Basis	Declining balance rate (percent)	Depreciation allowance
1954	$1,000	10	$100
1955	900	10	90
1956	810	10	81

Example (2). A taxpayer filing his returns on a calendar year basis maintains a group account to which a 5 year life and a 40 percent declining balance rate are applicable. Original investment, additions, retirements, and salvage recoveries are the same as those set forth in example (3) of paragraph (b) of § 1.167(b)-1. Although salvage value is not taken into consideration in computing a declining balance rate, it must be recognized and accounted for when assets are retired.

Depreciable Asset Account and Depreciation Computation Using Average Asset and Reserve Balances

Year	Asset balance Jan. 1	Current additions	Current retirements	Asset balance Dec. 31	Average balance	Average reserve before depreciation	Net depreciable balance	Rate (percent)	Allowable depreciation
1954	—	$12,000	—	$12,000	$ 6,000	—	$6,000	40	$2,400
1955	$12,000	—	—	12,000	12,000	$2,400	9,600	40	3,840
1956	12,000	—	—	12,000	12,000	6,240	5,760	40	2,304
1957	12,000	—	$2,000	10,000	11,000	7,644	3,356	40	1,342
1958	10,000	—	2,000	8,000	9,000	7,186	1,814	40	726
1959	8,000	10,000	4,000	14,000	11,000	5,212	5,788	40	2,315
1960	14,000	—	2,000	12,000	13,000	4,727	8,273	40	3,309
1961	12,000	—	2,000	10,000	11,000	6,036	4,964	40	1,986

Depreciation Reserve

Year	Reserve Jan. 1	Current retirements	Salvage realized	Reserve Dec. 31, before depreciation	Average reserve before depreciation	Allowable depreciation	Reserve Dec. 31, after depreciation
1954	—	—	—	—	—	$2,400	$2,400
1955	$2,400	—	—	$2,400	$2,400	3,840	6,240
1956	6,240	—	—	6,240	6,240	2,304	8,544
1957	8,544	$2,000	$200	6,744	7,644	1,342	8,086
1958	8,086	2,000	200	6,286	7,186	726	7,012
1959	7,012	4,000	400	3,412	5,212	2,315	5,727
1960	5,727	2,000	—	3,727	4,727	3,309	7,036
1961	7,036	2,000	—	5,036	6,036	1,986	7,022

Where separate depreciation accounts are maintained by year of acquisition and there is an unrecovered balance at the time of the last retirement, such unrecovered balance may be deducted as part of the depreciation allowance for the year of such retirement. Thus, if the taxpayer had kept separate depreciation accounts by year of acquisition and all the retirements shown in the example above were from 1954 acquisitions, depreciation would be computed on the 1954 and 1959 acquisitions as follows:

Reg. § 1.167(b)-2(b)

1954 ACQUISITIONS

Year	Asset balance Jan. 1	Acquisitions	Current retirements	Asset balance Dec. 31	Average balance	Average reserve before depreciation	Net depreciable balance	Rate (percent)	Allowable depreciation
1954	—	$12,000	—	$12,000	$ 6,000	—	$6,000	40	$2,400
1955	$12,000	—	—	12,000	12,000	$2,400	9,600	40	3,840
1956	12,000	—	—	12,000	12,000	6,240	5,760	40	2,304
1957	12,000	—	$2,000	10,000	11,000	7,644	3,356	40	1,342
1958	10,000	—	2,000	8,000	9,000	7,186	1,814	40	726
1959	8,000	—	4,000	4,000	6,000	5,212	788	40	315
1960	4,000	—	2,000	2,000	3,000	2,727	273	40	109
1961	2,000	—	2,000	—	1,000	836	164	40	164[1]

[1] Balance allowable as depreciation in the year of retirement of the last survivor of the 1954 acquisitions.

Reg. § 1.167(b)-2(b)

Depreciation Reserve for 1954 Acquisitions

Year	Reserve Jan. 1	Current retirements	Salvage realized	Reserve Dec. 31, before depreciation	Average reserve before depreciation	Allowable depreciation	Reserve Dec. 31, after depreciation
1954	—	—	—	—	—	$2,400	$2,400
1955	$2,400	—	—	$2,400	$2,400	3,840	6,240
1956	6,240	—	—	6,240	6,240	2,304	8,544
1957	8,544	$2,000	$200	6,744	7,644	1,342	8,086
1958	8,086	2,000	200	6,286	7,186	726	7,012
1959	7,012	4,000	400	3,412	5,212	315	3,727
1960	3,727	2,000	—	1,727	2,727	109	1,836
1961	1,836	2,000	—	(164)	836	164	—

Reg. § 1.167(b)-2(b)

1959 ACQUISITIONS

Year	Asset balance Jan. 1	Acquisitions	Asset balance Dec. 31	Average balance	Reserve Dec. 31, before depreciation	Net depreciable balance	Rate (percent)	Allowable depreciation	Reserve Dec. 31, after depreciation
1959		$10,000	$10,000	$ 5,000	None	$5,000	40	$2,000	$2,000
1960	$10,000	—	10,000	10,000	$2,000	8,000	40	3,200	5,200
1961	10,000	—	10,000	10,000	5,200	4,800	40	1,920	7,120

In the above example, the allowable depreciation on the 1954 acquisitions totals $11,200. This amount when increased by salvage realized in the amount of $800, equals the entire cost or other basis of the 1954 acquisitions ($12,000).

(c) *Change in estimated useful life.* In the declining balance method when a change is justified in the useful life estimated for an account, subsequent computations shall be made as though the revised useful life had been originally estimated. For example, assume that an account has an estimated useful life of ten years and that a declining balance rate of 20 percent is applicable. If, at the end of the sixth year, it is determined that the remaining useful life of the account is six years, computations shall be made as though the estimated useful life was originally determined as twelve years. Accordingly, the applicable depreciation rate will be 162/3 percent. This rate is thereafter applied to the unrecovered cost or other basis. [Reg. § 1.167(b)-2.]

☐ *[T.D. 6182, 6-11-56. Amended by T.D. 6712, 3-23-64.]*

[Reg. § 1.167(b)-3]

§ 1.167(b)-3. Sum of the years-digits method.—(a) *Applied to a single asset.*—(1) *Gen-*

eral rule. Under the sum of the years-digits method annual allowances for depreciation are computed by applying changing fractions to the cost or other basis of the property reduced by estimated salvage. The numerator of the fraction changes each year to a number which corresponds to the remaining useful life of the asset (including the year for which the allowance is being computed), and the denominator which remains constant is the sum of all the years digits corresponding to the estimated useful life of the asset. See section 167(c) and § 1.167(c)-1 for restrictions on the use of the sum of the years-digits method.

(i) *Illustrations.* Computation of depreciation allowances on a single asset under the sum of the years-digits method is illustrated by the following examples:

Example (1). A new asset having an estimated useful life of five years was acquired on January 1, 1954, for $1,750. The estimated salvage is $250. For a taxpayer filing his returns on a calendar year basis, the annual depreciation allowances are as follows:

Year	Cost or other basis less salvage	Fraction [1]	Allowable depreciation	Depreciation reserve
1954	$1,500	5/15	$500	$ 500
1955	1,500	4/15	400	900
1956	1,500	3/15	300	1,200
1957	1,500	2/15	200	1,400
1958	1,500	1/15	100	1,500

Uncovered value (salvage)	250

[1] The denominator of the fraction is the sum of the digits representing the years of useful life, i.e., 5, 4, 3, 2, and 1, or 15.

Example (2). Assume in connection with an asset acquired in 1954 that 3/4 of a year's depreciation is allowable in that year. The follow-

ing illustrates a reasonable method of allocating depreciation:

	Depreciation for 12 months		Allowable depreciation				
			1954		1955		1956
1st year	$500	(3/4)	$375	(1/4)	$125		
2nd year	400			(3/4)	300	(1/4)	$100
3rd year	300					(3/4)	225
			375		425		325

(ii) *Change in useful life.* Where in the case of a single asset, a change is justified in the useful life, subsequent computations shall be made as though the remaining useful life at the beginning of the taxable year of change were the useful life of a new asset acquired at such time and with a basis equal to the unrecovered cost or other basis of the asset at that time. For example, assume that a new asset with an estimated useful life of ten years is purchased in 1954. At the time of

making out his return for 1959, the taxpayer finds that the asset has a remaining useful life of seven years from January 1, 1959. Depreciation for 1959 should then be computed as though 1959 were the first year of the life on an asset estimated to have a useful life of seven years, and the allowance for 1959 would be 7/28 of the unrecovered cost or other basis of the asset after adjustment for salvage.

Reg. § 1.167(b)-3(a)(1)

(2) *Remaining life*—(i) *Application.* Under the sum of the years-digits method, annual allowances for depreciation may also be computed by applying changing fractions to the unrecovered cost or other basis of the asset reduced by estimated salvage. The numerator of the fraction changes each year to a number which corresponds to the remaining useful life of the asset (including the year for which the allowance is being computed), and the denominator changes each year to a number which represents the sum of the digits corresponding to the years of estimated remaining useful life of the asset. For decimal equivalents of such fractions, see Table I of subdivision (ii) of

this subparagraph. For example, a new asset with an estimated useful life of 10 years is purchased January 1, 1954, for $6,000. Assuming a salvage value of $500, the depreciation allowance for 1954 is $1,000 ($5,500 × 0.1818, the applicable rate from Table I). For 1955, the unrecovered balance is $4,500, and the remaining life is 9 years. The depreciation allowance for 1955 would then be $900 ($4,500 × .2000, the applicable rate from Table I).

(ii) *Table I.* This table shows decimal equivalents of sum of the years digits fractions corresponding to remaining lives from 1 to 100 years.

TABLE I—DECIMAL EQUIVALENTS FOR USE OF SUM OF THE YEARS-DIGITS METHOD, BASED ON REMAINING LIFE

Remaining life (years)	Decimal equivalent	Remaining life (years)	Decimal equivalent	Remaining life (years)	Decimal equivalent
100.0	.0198	95.5	.0207	91.0	.0217
99.9	.0198	95.4	.0207	90.9	.0218
99.8	.0198	95.3	.0208	90.8	.0218
99.7	.0199	95.2	.0208	90.7	.0218
99.6	.0199	95.1	.0208	90.6	.0218
99.5	.0199	95.0	.0208	90.5	.0219
99.4	.0199	94.9	.0209	90.4	.0219
99.3	.0199	94.8	.0209	90.3	.0219
99.2	.0200	94.7	.0209	90.2	.0219
99.1	.0200	94.6	.0209	90.1	.0220
99.0	.0200	94.5	.0209	90.0	.0220
98.9	.0200	94.4	.0210	89.9	.0220
98.8	.0200	94.3	.0210	89.8	.0220
98.7	.0201	94.2	.0210	89.7	.0221
98.6	.0201	94.1	.0210	89.6	.0221
98.5	.0201	94.0	.0211	89.5	.0221
98.4	.0201	93.9	.0211	89.4	.0221
98.3	.0201	93.8	.0211	89.3	.0221
98.2	.0202	93.7	.0211	89.2	.0222
98.1	.0202	93.6	.0211	89.1	.0222
98.0	.0202	93.5	.0212	89.0	.0222
97.9	.0202	93.4	.0212	88.9	.0222
97.8	.0202	93.3	.0212	88.8	.0223
97.7	.0203	93.2	.0212	88.7	.0223
97.6	.0203	93.1	.0213	88.6	.0223
97.5	.0203	93.0	.0213	88.5	.0223
97.4	.0203	92.9	.0213	88.4	.0224
97.3	.0203	92.8	.0213	88.3	.0224
97.2	.0204	92.7	.0213	88.2	.0224
97.1	.0204	92.6	.0214	88.1	.0224
97.0	.0204	92.5	.0214	88.0	.0225
96.9	.0204	92.4	.0214	87.9	.0225
96.8	.0204	92.3	.0214	87.8	.0225
96.7	.0205	92.2	.0215	87.7	.0225
96.6	.0205	92.1	.0215	87.6	.0226
96.5	.0205	92.0	.0215	87.5	.0226
96.4	.0205	91.9	.0215	87.4	.0226
96.3	.0206	91.8	.0216	87.3	.0226
96.2	.0206	91.7	.0216	87.2	.0227
96.1	.0206	91.6	.0216	87.1	.0227
96.0	.0206	91.5	.0216	87.0	.0227
95.9	.0206	91.4	.0216	86.9	.0228
95.8	.0207	91.3	.0217	86.8	.0228
95.7	.0207	91.2	.0217	86.7	.0228
95.6	.0207	91.1	.0217	86.6	.0228

Reg. § 1.167(b)-3(a)(2)

Remaining life (years)	Decimal equivalent	Remaining life (years)	Decimal equivalent	Remaining life (years)	Decimal equivalent
86.5	.0229	79.9	.0247	73.3	.0269
86.4	.0229	79.8	.0248	73.2	.0270
86.3	.0229	79.7	.0248	73.1	.0270
86.2	.0229	79.6	.0248	73.0	.0270
86.1	.0230	79.5	.0248	72.9	.0271
86.0	.0230	79.4	.0249	72.8	.0271
85.9	.0230	79.3	.0249	72.7	.0271
85.8	.0230	79.2	.0249	72.6	.0272
85.7	.0231	79.1	.0250	72.5	.0272
85.6	.0231	79.0	.0250	72.4	.0272
85.5	.0231	78.9	.0250	72.3	.0273
85.4	.0231	78.8	.0251	72.2	.0273
85.3	.0232	78.7	.0251	72.1	.0274
85.2	.0232	78.6	.0251	72.0	.0274
85.1	.0232	78.5	.0252	71.9	.0274
85.0	.0233	78.4	.0252	71.8	.0275
84.9	.0233	78.3	.0252	71.7	.0275
84.8	.0233	78.2	.0253	71.6	.0275
84.7	.0233	78.1	.0253	71.5	.0276
84.6	.0234	78.0	.0253	71.4	.0276
84.5	.0234	77.9	.0253	71.3	.0277
84.4	.0234	77.8	.0254	71.2	.0277
84.3	.0234	77.7	.0254	71.1	.0277
84.2	.0235	77.6	.0254	71.0	.0278
84.1	.0235	77.5	.0255	70.9	.0278
84.0	.0235	77.4	.0255	70.8	.0279
83.9	.0236	77.3	.0255	70.7	.0279
83.8	.0236	77.2	.0256	70.6	.0279
83.7	.0236	77.1	.0256	70.5	.0280
83.6	.0236	77.0	.0256	70.4	.0280
83.5	.0237	76.9	.0257	70.3	.0280
83.4	.0237	76.8	.0257	70.2	.0281
83.3	.0237	76.7	.0257	70.1	.0281
83.2	.0238	76.6	.0258	70.0	.0282
83.1	.0238	76.5	.0258	69.9	.0282
83.0	.0238	76.4	.0258	69.8	.0282
82.9	.0238	76.3	.0259	69.7	.0283
82.8	.0239	76.2	.0259	69.6	.0283
82.7	.0239	76.1	.0259	69.5	.0284
82.6	.0239	76.0	.0260	69.4	.0284
82.5	.0240	75.9	.0260	69.3	.0284
82.4	.0240	75.8	.0260	69.2	.0285
82.3	.0240	75.7	.0261	69.1	.0285
82.2	.0240	75.6	.0261	69.0	.0286
82.1	.0241	75.5	.0261	68.9	.0286
82.0	.0241	75.4	.0262	68.8	.0287
81.9	.0241	75.3	.0262	68.7	.0287
81.8	.0242	75.2	.0262	68.6	.0287
81.7	.0242	75.1	.0263	68.5	.0288
81.6	.0242	75.0	.0263	68.4	.0288
81.5	.0242	74.9	.0264	68.3	.0289
81.4	.0243	74.8	.0264	68.2	.0289
81.3	.0243	74.7	.0264	68.1	.0289
81.2	.0243	74.6	.0265	68.0	.0290
81.1	.0244	74.5	.0265	67.9	.0290
81.0	.0244	74.4	.0265	67.8	.0291
80.9	.0244	74.3	.0266	67.7	.0291
80.8	.0244	74.2	.0266	67.6	.0292
80.7	.0245	74.1	.0266	67.5	.0292
80.6	.0245	74.0	.0267	67.4	.0292
80.5	.0245	73.9	.0267	67.3	.0293
80.4	.0246	73.8	.0267	67.2	.0293
80.3	.0246	73.7	.0268	67.1	.0294
80.2	.0246	73.6	.0268	67.0	.0294
80.1	.0247	73.5	.0268	66.9	.0295
80.0	.0247	73.4	.0269	66.8	.0295

Reg. § 1.167(b)-3(a)(2)

Remaining life (years)	Decimal equivalent	Remaining life (years)	Decimal equivalent	Remaining life (years)	Decimal equivalent
66.7	.0295	60.1	.0327	53.3	.0368
66.6	.0296	60.0	.0328	53.2	.0369
66.5	.0296	59.9	.0328	53.1	.0370
66.4	.0297	59.8	.0329	53.0	.0370
66.3	.0297	59.7	.0329	52.9	.0371
66.2	.0298	59.6	.0330	52.8	.0372
66.1	.0298	59.5	.0331	52.7	.0372
66.0	.0299	59.4	.0331	52.6	.0373
65.9	.0299	59.3	.0332	52.5	.0374
65.8	.0299	59.2	.0332	52.4	.0374
65.7	.0300	59.1	.0333	52.3	.0375
65.6	.0300	58.8	.0334	52.2	.0376
65.5	.0301	58.7	.0335	52.1	.0377
65.4	.0301	58.6	.0336	52.0	.0377
65.3	.0302	58.5	.0336	51.9	.0378
65.2	.0302	58.4	.0337	51.8	.0379
65.1	.0303	58.3	.0337	51.7	.0379
65.0	.0303	58.2	.0338	51.6	.0380
64.9	.0303	58.1	.0338	51.5	.0381
64.8	.0304	58.0	.0339	51.4	.0382
64.7	.0304	57.9	.0340	51.3	.0382
64.6	.0305	57.8	.0340	51.2	.0383
64.5	.0305	57.7	.0341	51.1	.0384
64.4	.0306	57.6	.0341	51.0	.0385
64.3	.0306	57.5	.0342	50.9	.0385
64.2	.0307	57.4	.0342	50.8	.0386
64.1	.0307	57.3	.0343	50.7	.0387
64.0	.0308	57.2	.0344	50.6	.0388
63.9	.0308	57.1	.0344	50.5	.0388
63.8	.0309	57.0	.0345	50.4	.0389
63.7	.0309	56.9	.0345	50.3	.0390
63.6	.0310	56.8	.0346	50.2	.0391
63.5	.0310	56.7	.0347	50.1	.0391
63.4	.0311	56.6	.0347	50.0	.0392
63.3	.0311	56.5	.0348	49.9	.0393
63.2	.0312	56.4	.0348	49.8	.0394
63.1	.0312	56.3	.0349	49.7	.0394
63.0	.0313	56.2	.0350	49.6	.0395
62.9	.0313	56.1	.0350	49.5	.0396
62.8	.0313	56.0	.0351	49.4	.0397
62.7	.0314	55.9	.0351	49.3	.0398
62.6	.0314	55.8	.0352	49.2	.0398
62.5	.0315	55.7	.0353	49.1	.0399
62.4	.0315	55.6	.0353	49.0	.0400
62.3	.0316	55.5	.0354	48.9	.0401
62.2	.0316	55.4	.0355	48.8	.0402
62.1	.0317	55.3	.0355	48.7	.0402
62.0	.0317	55.2	.0356	48.6	.0403
61.9	.0318	55.1	.0356	48.5	.0404
61.8	.0318	55.0	.0357	48.4	.0405
61.7	.0319	54.9	.0358	48.3	.0406
61.6	.0319	54.8	.0358	48.2	.0406
61.5	.0320	54.7	.0359	48.1	.0407
61.4	.0320	54.6	.0360	48.0	.0408
61.3	.0321	54.5	.0360	47.9	.0409
61.2	.0322	54.4	.0361	47.8	.0410
61.1	.0322	54.3	.0362	47.7	.0411
61.0	.0323	54.2	.0362	47.6	.0411
60.9	.0323	54.1	.0363	47.5	.0412
60.8	.0324	54.0	.0364	47.4	.0413
60.7	.0324	53.9	.0364	47.3	.0414
60.6	.0325	53.8	.0365	47.2	.0415
60.5	.0325	53.7	.0366	47.1	.0416
60.4	.0326	53.6	.0366	47.0	.0417
60.3	.0326	53.5	.0367	46.9	.0418
60.2	.0327	53.4	.0368	46.8	.0418

Reg. § 1.167(b)-3(a)(2)

Itemized Deductions for Individuals and Corps.

See p. 20,601 for regulations not amended to reflect law changes

Remaining life (years)	Decimal equivalent	Remaining life (years)	Decimal equivalent	Remaining life (years)	Decimal equivalent
46.7	.0419	40.1	.0487	33.5	.0580
46.6	.0420	40.0	.0488	33.4	.0581
46.5	.0421	39.9	.0489	33.3	.0583
46.4	.0422	39.8	.0490	33.2	.0585
46.3	.0423	39.7	.0491	33.1	.0586
46.2	.0424	39.6	.0493	33.0	.0588
46.1	.0425	39.5	.0494	32.9	.0590
46.0	.0426	39.4	.0495	32.8	.0592
45.9	.0426	39.3	.0496	32.7	.0593
45.8	.0427	39.2	.0497	32.6	.0595
45.7	.0428	39.1	.0499	32.5	.0597
45.6	.0429	39.0	.0500	32.4	.0599
45.5	.0430	38.9	.0501	32.3	.0600
45.4	.0431	38.8	.0502	32.2	.0602
45.3	.0432	38.7	.0504	32.1	.0604
45.2	.0433	38.6	.0505	32.0	.0606
45.1	.0434	38.5	.0506	31.9	.0608
45.0	.0435	38.4	.0508	31.8	.0610
44.9	.0436	38.3	.0509	31.7	.0611
44.8	.0437	38.2	.0510	31.6	.0613
44.7	.0438	38.1	.0511	31.5	.0615
44.6	.0439	38.0	.0513	31.4	.0617
44.5	.0440	37.9	.0514	31.3	.0619
44.4	.0440	37.8	.0515	31.2	.0621
44.3	.0441	37.7	.0517	31.1	.0623
44.2	.0442	37.6	.0518	31.0	.0625
44.1	.0443	37.5	.0519	30.9	.0627
44.0	.0444	37.4	.0521	30.8	.0629
43.9	.0445	37.3	.0522	30.7	.0631
43.8	.0446	37.2	.0524	30.6	.0633
43.7	.0447	37.1	.0525	30.5	.0635
43.6	.0448	37.0	.0526	30.4	.0637
43.5	.0449	36.9	.0528	30.3	.0639
43.4	.0450	36.8	.0529	30.2	.0641
43.3	.0451	36.7	.0530	30.1	.0643
43.2	.0452	36.6	.0532	30.0	.0645
43.1	.0453	36.5	.0533	29.9	.0647
43.0	.0455	36.4	.0535	29.8	.0649
42.9	.0456	36.3	.0536	29.7	.0651
42.8	.0457	36.2	.0538	29.6	.0653
42.7	.0458	36.1	.0539	29.5	.0656
42.6	.0459	36.0	.0541	29.4	.0658
42.5	.0460	35.9	.0542	29.3	.0660
42.4	.0461	35.8	.0543	29.2	.0662
42.3	.0462	35.7	.0545	29.1	.0664
42.2	.0463	35.6	.0546	29.0	.0667
42.1	.0464	35.5	.0548	28.9	.0669
42.0	.0465	35.4	.0549	28.8	.0671
41.9	.0466	35.3	.0551	28.7	.0673
41.8	.0467	35.2	.0552	28.6	.0675
41.7	.0468	35.1	.0554	28.5	.0678
41.6	.0469	35.0	.0556	28.4	.0680
41.5	.0471	34.9	.0557	28.3	.0682
41.4	.0472	34.8	.0559	28.2	.0685
41.3	.0473	34.7	.0560	28.1	.0687
41.2	.0474	34.6	.0562	28.0	.0690
41.1	.0475	34.5	.0563	27.9	.0692
41.0	.0476	34.4	.0565	27.8	.0694
40.9	.0477	34.3	.0566	27.7	.0697
40.8	.0478	34.2	.0568	27.6	.0699
40.7	.0480	34.1	.0570	27.5	.0702
40.6	.0481	34.0	.0571	27.4	.0704
40.5	.0482	33.9	.0573	27.3	.0707
40.4	.0483	33.8	.0575	27.2	.0709
40.3	.0484	33.7	.0576	27.1	.0712
40.2	.0485	33.6	.0578	27.0	.0714

Reg. § 1.167(b)-3(a)(2)

Remaining life (years)	Decimal equivalent	Remaining life (years)	Decimal equivalent	Remaining life (years)	Decimal equivalent
26.9	.0717	20.3	.0939	13.7	.1359
26.8	.0719	20.2	.0943	13.6	.1368
26.7	.0722	20.1	.0948	13.5	.1378
26.6	.0724	20.0	.0952	13.4	.1387
26.5	.0727	19.9	.0957	13.3	.1397
26.4	.0730	19.8	.0961	13.2	.1407
26.3	.0732	19.7	.0966	13.1	.1418
26.2	.0735	19.6	.0970	13.0	.1429
26.1	.0738	19.5	.0975	12.9	.1438
26.0	.0741	19.4	.0980	12.8	.1448
25.9	.0743	19.3	.0985	12.7	.1458
25.8	.0746	19.2	.0990	12.6	.1469
25.7	.0749	19.1	.0995	12.5	.1479
25.6	.0752	19.0	.1000	12.4	.1490
25.5	.0754	18.9	.1005	12.3	.1502
25.4	.0757	18.8	.1010	12.2	.1514
25.3	.0760	18.7	.1015	12.1	.1526
25.2	.0763	18.6	.1020	12.0	.1538
25.1	.0756	18.5	.1025	11.9	.1549
25.0	.0759	18.4	.1030	11.8	.1561
24.9	.0772	18.3	.1036	11.7	.1573
24.8	.0775	18.2	.1041	11.6	.1585
24.7	.0778	18.1	.1047	11.5	.1597
24.6	.0781	18.0	.1053	11.4	.1610
24.5	.0784	17.9	.1058	11.3	.1624
24.4	.0787	17.8	.1063	11.2	.1637
24.3	.0790	17.7	.1069	11.1	.1652
24.2	.0793	17.6	.1074	11.0	.1667
24.1	.0797	17.5	.1080	10.9	.1680
24.0	.0800	17.4	.1086	10.8	.1693
23.9	.0803	17.3	.1092	10.7	.1707
23.8	.0806	17.2	.1098	10.6	.1721
23.7	.0809	17.1	.1105	10.5	.1736
23.6	.0813	17.0	.1111	10.4	.1751
23.5	.0816	16.9	.1117	10.3	.1767
23.4	.0819	16.8	.1123	10.2	.1783
23.3	.0823	16.7	.1129	10.1	.1800
23.2	.0826	16.6	.1135	10.0	.1818
23.1	.0830	16.5	.1142	9.9	.1833
23.0	.0833	16.4	.1148	9.8	.1849
22.9	.0837	16.3	.1155	9.7	.1865
22.8	.0840	16.2	.1162	9.6	.1882
22.7	.0844	16.1	.1169	9.5	.1900
22.6	.0847	16.0	.1176	9.4	.1918
22.5	.0851	15.9	.1183	9.3	.1938
22.4	.0854	15.8	.1190	9.2	.1957
22.3	.0858	15.7	.1197	9.1	.1978
22.2	.0862	15.6	.1204	9.0	.2000
22.1	.0866	15.5	.1211	8.9	.2018
22.0	.0870	15.4	.1218	8.8	.2037
21.9	.0873	15.3	.1226	8.7	.2057
21.8	.0877	15.2	.1234	8.6	.2077
21.7	.0881	15.1	.1242	8.5	.2099
21.6	.0885	15.0	.1250	8.4	.2121
21.5	.0888	14.9	.1257	8.3	.2145
21.4	.0892	14.8	.1265	8.2	.2169
21.3	.0896	14.7	.1273	8.1	.2195
21.2	.0901	14.6	.1281	8.0	.2222
21.1	.0905	14.5	.1289	7.9	.2244
21.0	.0909	14.4	.1297	7.8	.2267
20.9	.0913	14.3	.1306	7.7	.2292
20.8	.0917	14.2	.1315	7.6	.2317
20.7	.0921	14.1	.1324	7.5	.2344
20.6	.0925	14.0	.1333	7.4	.2372
20.5	.0930	13.9	.1342	7.3	.2401
20.4	.0934	13.8	.1350	7.2	.2432

Remaining life (years)	Decimal equivalent	Remaining life (years)	Decimal equivalent	Remaining life (years)	Decimal equivalent
7.1	.2465	5.0	.3333	2.9	.5088
7.0	.2500	4.9	.3379	2.8	.5185
6.9	.2527	4.8	.3429	2.7	.5294
6.8	.2556	4.7	.3481	2.6	.5417
6.7	.2587	4.6	.3538	2.5	.5556
6.6	.2619	4.5	.3600	2.4	.5714
6.5	.2653	4.4	.3667	2.3	.5897
6.4	.2689	4.3	.3739	2.2	.6111
6.3	.2727	4.2	.3818	2.1	.6364
6.2	.2768	4.1	.3905	2.0	.6667
6.1	.2811	4.0	.4000	1.9	.6786
6.0	.2857	3.9	.4063	1.8	.6923
5.9	.2892	3.8	.4130	1.7	.7083
5.8	.2929	3.7	.4205	1.6	.7273
5.7	.2969	3.6	.4286	1.5	.7500
5.6	.3011	3.5	.4375	1.4	.7778
5.5	.3056	3.4	.4474	1.3	.8125
5.4	.3103	3.3	.4583	1.2	.8571
5.3	.3155	3.2	.4706	1.1	.9167
5.2	.3210	3.1	.4844	1.0	1.0000
5.1	.3269	3.0	.5000		

Note: For determination of decimal equivalents of remaining lives falling between those shown in the above table, the taxpayer may use the next longest life shown in the table, interpolate from the table, or use the following formula from which the table was derived.

$$D = \frac{2R}{(W + 2F)(W + 1)}$$

where

D = Decimal equivalent
R = Remaining life
W = Whole number of years in remaining life
F = Fractional part of year in remaining life

If the taxpayer desires to carry his calculations of decimal equivalents to a greater number of decimal places than is provided in the table, he may use the formula. The procedure adopted must be consistently followed thereafter.

(b) *Applied to group, classified, or composite accounts.*—(1) *General rule.* The sum of the years-digits method may be applied to group, classified, or composite accounts in accordance with the plan described in subparagraph (2) of this paragraph or in accordance with other plans as explained in subparagraph (3) of this paragraph.

(2) *Remaining life plan.* The remaining life plan as applied to a single asset is described in paragraph (a)(2) of this section. This plan may also be applied to group, classified, or composite accounts. Under this plan the allowance for depreciation is computed by applying changing fractions to the unrecovered cost or other basis of the account reduced by estimated salvage. The numerator of the fraction changes each year to a number which corresponds to the remaining useful life of the account (including the year for which the allowance is being computed), and the denominator changes each year to a number which represents the sum of the years digits corresponding to the years of estimated remaining useful life of the account. Decimal equivalents of such fractions can be obtained by use of Table I under paragraph (a)(2)(ii) of this section. The proper application of this method requires that the estimated remaining useful life of the account be determined each year. This determination, of course, may be made each year by analysis, i.e., by determining the remaining lives for each of the components in the account, and averaging them. The estimated remaining life of any account, however, may also be determined arithmetically. For example, it may be computed by dividing the unrecovered cost or other basis of the account, as computed by straight line depreciation, by the gross cost or other basis of the account, and multiplying the result by the average life of the assets in the account. Salvage value is not a factor for the purpose of determining remaining life. Thus, if a group account with an average life of ten years had at January 1, 1958, a gross asset balance of $12,600 and a depreciation reserve computed on the straight line method of $9,450, the remaining life of the account at January 1, 1958, would be computed as follows:

Reg. § 1.167(b)-3(b)(1)

$$\frac{\$12,600 - \$9,450}{\$12,600} \text{ times 10 years equals 2.50 years.}$$

Example. The use of the sum of the years-digits method with group, classified, or composite accounts under the remaining life plan is illustrated by the following example: A calendar year taxpayer maintains a group account to which a five-year life is applicable. Original investment, additions, retirements, and salvage recoveries are the same as those set forth in example (3) of paragraph (b) of § 1.167(b)-1.

DEPRECIATION COMPUTATIONS ON A GROUP ACCOUNT UNDER REMAINING LIFE PLAN

	1	2	3	4	5	6	7	8	9	10	Sum of the years digits depreciation			
											11	12	13	14
Year	Asset balance Jan. 1	Current additions	Current retirements	Average asset balance	Straight line amount — Col. (4) ÷ life	Straight line reserve — Col. (5) − Col. (3) accumulated Jan. 1	Remaining life — [Col. (1) − Col. (6) ÷ Col. (1)] × average service life	Asset balance reduced by salvage — Col. (1) × (100% − 6.67%)	Current additions reduced by salvage — Col. (2) × (100% − 6.67%)	Salvage realized	Accumulated reserve Jan. 1 — Prior reserve + Col. (14) + Col. (10) − Col. (3)	Unrecovered Jan. 1 — Col. (8) − Col. (11)	Rate based on Col. (7) from Table I	Allowable depreciation — Col. (12) × Col. (13) + ½ Col. (9) × F[2]
1954	.....	$12,000	.....	$ 6,000	$1,200[1]	.....	5.00	.....	$11,200	.....	.....	.....	.3333	$1,866
1955	$12,000	.....	.....	12,000	2,400	$1,200	4.50	$11,200	.....	.....	$1,866	$9,334	.3600	3,360
1956	12,000	.....	.....	12,000	2,400	3,600	3.50	11,200	.....	.....	5,226	5,974	.4375	2,614
1957	12,000	.....	$2,000	11,000	2,200	6,000	2.50	11,200	.....	$200	7,840	3,360	.5556	1,867
1958	10,000	.....	2,000	9,000	1,800	6,200	1.90	9,333	.....	200	7,907	1,426	.6786	968
1959	8,000	10,000	4,000	11,000	2,200	6,000	1.25	7,466	9,333	400	7,075	391	.8125	1,874
1960	14,000	.....	2,000	13,000	2,600	4,200	3.50	13,066	.....	.....	5,349	7,717	.4375	3,376
1961	12,000	.....	2,000	11,000	2,200	4,800	3.00	11,200	.....	.....	6,725	4,475	.5000	2,238
1962						5,000					6,963			

1 ½ year's amount.
2 F = Rate based on average service life (.3333 in this example).

Reg. § 1.167(b)-3(b)(2)

(3) Other plans for application of the sum of the years-digits method. Taxpayers who wish to use the sum of the years-digits method in computing depreciation for group, classified, or composite accounts in accordance with a sum of the years digits plan other than the remaining life plan described herein may do so only with the consent of the Commissioner. Request for permission to use plans other than that described shall be addressed to the Commissioner of Internal Revenue, Washington 25, D.C. [Reg. § 1 167(b)-3.]

☐ [*T.D.* 6182, 6-11-56.]

[Reg. § 1.167(b)-4]

§ 1.167(b)-4. **Other methods.**—(a) Under section 167(b)(4) a taxpayer may use any consistent method of computing depreciation, such as the sinking fund method, provided depreciation allowances computed in accordance with such method do not result in accumulated allowances at the end of any taxable year greater than the total of the accumulated allowances which could have resulted from the use of the declining balance method described in section 167(b)(2). This limitation applies only during the first two-thirds of the useful life of the property. For example, an asset costing $1,000 having a useful life of six years may be depreciated under the declining balance method in accordance with § 1.167(b)-2, at a rate of 33⅓ percent. During the first four years or ⅔ of its useful life, maximum depreciation allowances under the declining balance method would be as follows:

	Current depreciation	Accumulated depreciation	Balance
Cost of asset	. $1,000		
First year	$333	$ 333	$667
Second year	222	555	445
Third year	148	703	297
Fourth year	99	802	198

An annual allowance computed by any other method under section 167(b)(4) could not exceed $333 for the first year, and at the end of the second year the total allowances for the two years could not exceed $555. Likewise, the total allowances for the three years could not exceed $703 and for the four years could not exceed $802. This limitation would not apply in the fifth and sixth years. See section 167(c) and § 1.167(c)-1 for restrictions on the use of certain methods.

(b) It shall be the responsibility of the taxpayer to establish to the satisfaction of the Commissioner that a method of depreciation under section 167(b)(4) is both a reasonable and consistent method and that it does not produce depreciation allowances in excess of the amount permitted under the limitations provided in such section. [Reg. § 1.167(b)-4.]

☐ [*T.D.* 6182, 6-11-56.]

[Reg. § 1.167(c)-1]

§ 1.167(c)-1. **Limitations on methods of computing depreciation under section 167(b)(2), (3), and (4).**—(a) *In general.* (1) Section 167(c) provides limitations on the use of the declining balance method described in section 167(b)(2), the sum of the years-digits method described in section 167(b)(3), and certain other methods authorized by section 167(b)(4). These methods are applicable only to tangible property having a useful life of three years or more. If construction, reconstruction, or erection by the taxpayer began before January 1, 1954, and was completed after December 31, 1953, these methods apply only to that portion of the basis of the property which is properly attributable to such construction, reconstruction, or erection after December 31, 1953. Property is considered as constructed, reconstructed, or erected by the taxpayer if the work is done for him in accordance with his specifications. The portion of the basis of such property attributable to construction, reconstruction, or erection after December 31, 1953, consists of all costs of the property allocable to the period after December 31, 1953, including the cost or other basis of materials entering into such work. It is not necessary that such materials be acquired after December 31, 1953, or that they be new in use. If construction or erection by the taxpayer began after December 31, 1953, the entire cost or other basis of such construction or erection qualifies for these methods of depreciation. In the case of reconstruction of property, these methods do not apply to any part of the adjusted basis of such property on December 31, 1953. For purposes of this section, construction, reconstruction, or erection by the taxpayer begins when physical work is started on such construction, reconstruction, or erection.

(2) If the property was not constructed, reconstructed, or erected by the taxpayer, these methods apply only if it was acquired after December 31, 1953, and if the original use of the property commences with the taxpayer and commences after December 31, 1953. For the purpose of the preceding sentence, property shall be deemed to be acquired when reduced to physical possession, or control. The term "original use" means the first use to which the property is put, whether or not such use corresponds to the use of such property by the taxpayer. For example, a reconditioned or rebuilt machine acquired after December 31, 1953, will not be treated as being put to original use by the taxpayer even though it is put to a different use, nor will a horse acquired for breeding purposes be treated as being put to

original use by the taxpayer if prior to the purchase the horse was used for racing purposes. See §§ 1.167(b)-2, 1.167(b)-3, and 1.167(b)-4 for application of the various methods.

(3) Assets having an estimated average useful life of less than three years shall not be included in a group, classified, or composite account to which the methods described in §§ 1.167(b)-2, 1.167(b)-3, and 1.167(b)-4 are applicable. However, an incidental retirement of an asset from such an account prior to the expiration of a useful life of three years will not prevent the application of these methods to such an account.

(4) See section 381(c)(6) and the regulations thereunder for rules covering the use of depreciation methods by acquiring corporations in the case of certain corporate acquisitions.

(5) See §§ 1.1502-12(g) and 1.1502-13 for provisions dealing with depreciation of property received by a member of an affiliated group from another member of the group during a consolidated return period.

(6) Except in the cases described in subparagraphs (4) and (5) of this paragraph, the methods of depreciation described in §§ 1.167(b)-2, 1.167(b)-3, and 1.167(b)-4 are not applicable to property in the hands of a distributee, vendee, transferee, donee, or grantee unless the original use of the property begins with such person and the conditions required by section 167(c) and this section are otherwise met. For example, these methods of depreciation may not be used by a corporation with respect to property which it acquires from an individual or partnership in exchange for its stock. Similarly, if an individual or partnership receives property in a distribution upon dissolution of a corporation, these methods of depreciation may not be used with respect to property so acquired by such individual or partnership. As a further example, these methods of depreciation may not be used by a partnership with respect to contributed property, nor by a partner with respect to partnership property distributed to him. Moreover, where a partnership is entitled to use these depreciation methods, and the optional adjustment to basis of partnership property provided by section 743 is applicable, (i) in the case of an increase in the adjusted basis of the partnership property under such section, the transferee partner with respect to whom such adjustment is applicable shall not be entitled to use such methods with respect to such increase, and (ii) in the case of a decrease in the adjusted basis of the partnership property under such section, the transferee partner with respect to whom such adjustment is applicable shall include in his income an amount equal to the portion of the depreciation deducted by the partnership which is attributable to such decrease.

(b) *Illustrations.* (1) The application of these methods to property constructed, reconstructed, or erected by the taxpayer after December 31, 1953, may be illustrated by the following examples:

Example (1). If a building with a total cost of $100,000 is completed after December 31, 1953, and the portion attributable to construction after December 31, 1953, is determined by engineering estimates or by cost accounting records to be $30,000, the methods referred to in paragraph (a)(1) of this section, are applicable only to the $30,000 portion of the total.

Example (2). In 1954, a taxpayer has an old machine with an unrecovered cost of $1,000. If he contracts to have it reconditioned, or reconditions it himself, at a cost of an additional $5,000, only the $5,000 may be depreciated under the methods referred to in paragraph (a)(1) of this section, whether or not the materials used for reconditioning are new in use.

Example (3). A taxpayer who acquired a building in 1940 makes major maintenance or repair expenditures in 1954 of a type which must be capitalized. For these expenditures the taxpayer may use a method of depreciation different from that used on the building (for example, the methods referred to in paragraph (a)(1) of this section) only if he accounts for such expenditures separately from the account which contained the original building. In such case, the unadjusted basis on any parts replaced shall be removed from the asset account and shall be charged to the appropriate depreciation reserve account. In the alternative he may capitalize such expenditures by charging them to the depreciation reserve account for the building.

(2) The application of these methods to property which was not constructed, reconstructed, or erected by the taxpayer but which was acquired after December 31, 1953, may be illustrated by the following examples:

Example (1). A taxpayer contracted in 1953 to purchase a new machine which he acquired in 1954 and put into first use in that year. He may use the methods referred to in paragraph (a)(1) of this section, in recovering the cost of the new machine.

Example (2). A taxpayer instead of reconditioning his old machine buys a "factory reconditioned" machine in 1954 to replace it. He cannot apply the methods referred to in paragraph (a)(1) of this section, to any part of the cost of the reconditioned machine since he is not the first user of the machine.

Reg. § 1.167(c)-1(a)(3)

Example (3). In 1954, a taxpayer buys a house for $20,000 which had been used as a personal residence and thus had not been subject to depreciation allowances. He makes a capital addition of $5,000 and rents the property to another. The taxpayer may use the methods referred to in paragraph (a)(1) of this section, only with respect to the $5,000 cost of the addition.

(c) *Election to use methods.* Subject to the limitations set forth in paragraph (a) of this section, the methods of computing the allowance for depreciation specified in section 167(b)(2), (3), and (4) may be adopted without permission and no formal election is required. In order for a taxpayer to elect to use these methods for any property described in paragraph (a) of this section, he need only compute depreciation thereon under any of these methods for any taxable year ending after December 31, 1953, in which the property may first be depreciated by him. The election with respect to any property shall not be binding with respect to acquisitions of similar property in the same year or subsequent year which are set up in separate accounts. If a taxpayer has filed his return for a taxable year ending after December 31, 1953, for which the return is required to be filed on or before September 15, 1956, an election to compute the depreciation allowance under any of the methods specified in section 167(b) or a change in such an election may be made in an amended return or claim for refund filed on or before September 15, 1956. [Reg. § 1.167(c)-1.]

☐ [*T.D.* 6182, 6-11-56. *Amended by T.D.* 7244, 12-29-72; *T.D.* 8560, 8-12-94 *and T.D.* 8597, 7-12-95.]

[Reg. § 1.167(d)-1]

§ 1.167(d)-1. **Agreement as to useful life and rates of depreciation.**—After August 16, 1954, a taxpayer may, for taxable years ending after December 31, 1953, enter into an agreement with respect to the estimated useful life, method and rate of depreciation, and treatment of salvage of any property which is subject to the allowance for depreciation. An application for such agreement may be made to the district director for the internal revenue district in which the taxpayer's return is required to be filed. Such application shall be filed in quadruplicate and shall contain in such detail as may be practical the following information:

(a) The character and location of the property.

(b) The original cost or other basis and date of acquisition.

(c) Proper adjustments to the basis including depreciation accumulated to the first taxable year to be covered by the agreement.

(d) Estimated useful life and estimated salvage value.

(e) Method and rate of depreciation.

(f) Any other facts and circumstances pertinent to making a reasonable estimate of the useful life of the property and its salvage value.

The agreement must be in writing and must be signed by the taxpayer and by the district director. The agreement must be signed in quadruplicate, and two of the signed copies will be returned to the taxpayer. The agreement shall set forth its effective date, the estimated remaining useful life, the estimated salvage value, and rate and method of depreciation of the property and the facts and circumstances taken into consideration in adoption of the agreement, and shall relate only to depreciation allowances for such property on and after the effective date of the agreement. Such an agreement shall be binding on both parties until such time as facts and circumstances which were not taken into account in making the agreement are shown to exist. The party wishing to modify or change the agreement shall have the responsibility of establishing the existence of such facts and circumstances. Any change in the useful life or rate specified in such agreement shall be effective only prospectively, that is, it shall be effective beginning with the taxable year in which notice of the intention to change, including facts and circumstances warranting the adjustment of useful life and rate, is sent by the party proposing the change to the other party and is sent by registered mail, if such notice is mailed before September 3, 1958, or is sent by certified mail or registered mail, if such notice is mailed after September 2, 1958. A copy of the agreement (and any modification thereof) shall be filed with the taxpayer's return for the first taxable year which is affected by the agreement (or any modification thereof). A signed copy should be retained with the permanent records of the taxpayer. For rules relating to changes in method of depreciation, see § 1.167(e)-1 and section 446 and the regulations thereunder. [Reg. § 1.167(d)-1.]

☐ [*T.D.* 6182, 6-11-56. *Amended by T.D.* 6426, 11-30-59.]

[Reg. § 1.167(e)-1]

§ 1.167(e)-1. **Change in method.**—(a) *In general.* Any change in the method of computing the depreciation allowances with respect to a particular account (other than a change in method permitted or required by reason of the operation of section 167(j)(2) and § 1.167(j)-3(c)) is a change in method of accounting, and such a change will be permitted only with the consent of the Commissioner, except that certain changes to the straight line method of depreciation will be permitted without consent as provided in section 167(e)(1), (2), and (3). Except as provided in paragraphs (c) and (d) of this section, a change in method of computing depreciation will be permitted only with respect to all the assets contained in a particular account as defined in § 1.167(a)-7. Any change in the percentage of the current straight line rate under the declining balance method, as for example, from 200 percent of the straight line rate to any other percent of the straight line rate, or any change in the interest factor used in connection with a compound interest or sinking fund method, will constitute a change in method of depreciation. Any request for a change in method of depreciation shall be made in accordance with section 446 and the regulations thereunder and shall state the character and location of the property, method of depreciation being used and the method proposed, the date of acquisition, the cost or other basis and adjustments thereto, amount recovered through depreciation and other allowances, the estimated salvage value, the estimated remaining life of the property, and such other information as may be required. For rules covering the use of depreciation methods by acquiring corporations in the case of certain corporate acquisitions, see section 381(c)(6) and the regulations thereunder.

(b) *Declining balance to straight line.* In the case of an account to which the method described in section 167(b)(2) is applicable, a taxpayer may change without the consent of the Commissioner from the declining balance method of depreciation to the straight line method at any time during the useful life of the property under the following conditions. Such a change may not be made if a provision prohibiting such a change is contained in an agreement under section 167(d). When the change is made, the unrecovered cost or other basis (less a reasonable estimate for salvage) shall be recovered through annual allowances over the estimated remaining useful life determined in accordance with the circumstances existing at the time. With respect to any account, this change will be permitted only if applied to all the assets in the account as defined in section 1.167(a)-7. If the method of depreciation described in section 167(b)(2) (the declining balance method of depreciation using a rate not exceeding 200 percent of the straight line rate) is an acceptable method of depreciation with respect to a particular account, the taxpayer may elect under this paragraph to change to the straight line method of depreciation, even if with respect to that particular ac-

count, the declining balance method is permitted under a provision other than section 167(b)(2). Thus, for example, in the case of section 1250 property to which section 167(j)(1) is applicable, section 167(b) does not apply, but the declining balance method of depreciation using 150 percent of the straight line rate is an acceptable method of depreciation under section 167(j)(1)(B). Accordingly, the taxpayer may elect under this paragraph to change to the straight line method of depreciation with respect to such property. Similarly, if the taxpayer acquired used property before July 25, 1969, and adopted the 150 percent declining balance method of depreciation permitted with respect to such property under § 1.167(b)-0(b), the taxpayer may elect under this paragraph to change to the straight line method of depreciation with respect to such property. The taxpayer shall furnish a statement with respect to the property which is the subject of the change showing the date of acquisition, cost or other basis, amounts recovered through depreciation and other allowances, the estimated salvage value, the character of the property, the remaining useful life of the property, and such other information as may be required. The statement shall be attached to the taxpayer's return for the taxable year in which the change is made. A change to the straight line method must be adhered to for the entire taxable year of the change and for all subsequent taxable years unless, with the consent of the Commissioner, a change to another method is permitted.

(c) *Change with respect to section 1245 property.* (1) In respect of his first taxable year beginning after December 31, 1962, a taxpayer may elect, without the consent of the Commissioner, to change the method of depreciation of section 1245 property (as defined in section 1245(a)(3)) from any declining balance method or sum of the years-digits method to the straight line method. With respect to any account (as defined in § 1.167(a)-7), this change may be made notwithstanding any provision to the contrary in an agreement under section 167(d), but such change shall constitute (as of the first day of such taxable year) a termination of such agreement as to all property in such account. With respect to any account, this change will be permitted only if applied to all the section 1245 property in the account. The election shall be made by a statement on, or attached to, the return for such taxable year filed on or before the last day prescribed by law, including any extensions thereof, for filing such return.

(2) When an election under this paragraph is made in respect of section 1245 property in an account, the unrecovered cost or other basis (less a

Reg. § 1.167(e)-1(b)

reasonable estimate for salvage) of al the section 1245 property in the account shall be recovered through annual allowances over the estimated remaining useful life determined in accordance with the circumstances existing at that time. If there is other property in such account, the other property shall be placed in a separate account and depreciated by using the same method as was used before the change permitted by this paragraph, but the estimated useful life of such property shall be redetermined in accordance with § 1.167(b)-2 or 1.167(b)-3, whichever is applicable. The taxpayer shall maintain records which permit specific identification of the section 1245 property in the account with respect to which the election is made, and any other property in such account. The records shall also show for all the property in the account the date of acquisition, cost or other basis, amounts recovered through depreciation and other allowances, the estimated salvage value, the character of the property, and the remaining useful life of the property. A charge to the straight line method under this paragraph must be adhered to for the entire taxable year of the change and for all subsequent taxable years unless, with the consent of the Commissioner, a change to another method is permitted.

(d) *Change with respect to section 1250 property.* (1) In respect of his first taxable year beginning after July 24, 1969, a taxpayer may elect, without the consent of the Commissioner, to change the method of depreciation of section 1250 property (as defined in section 1250(c)) from any declining balance method or sum of the years-digits method to the straight line method. With respect to any account (as defined in § 1.167(a)-7) this change may be made notwithstanding any provision to the contrary in an agreement under section 167(d), but such change will constitute (as of the first day of such taxable year) a termination of such agreement as to all property in such account. With respect to any account, this change will be permitted only if applied to all the section 1250 property in the account. The election shall be made by a statement on, or attached to, the return for such taxable year filed on or before the last day prescribed by law, including extensions thereof, for filing such return.

(2) When an election under this paragraph is made in respect of section 1250 property in an account, the unrecovered cost or other basis (less a reasonable estimate for salvage) of all the section 1250 property in the account shall be recovered through annual allowances over the estimated remaining useful life determined in accordance with the circumstances existing at that time. If there is other property in such account, the other property shall be placed in a separate account and depreci-

ated by using the same method as was used before the change permitted by this paragraph, but the estimated useful life of such property shall be redetermined in accordance with § 1.167(b)-2 or § 1.167(b)-3, whichever is applicable. The taxpayer shall maintain records which permit specific identification of the section 1250 property in the account with respect to which the election is made and any other property in such account. The records shall also show for all the property in the account the date of the acquisition, cost or other basis, amounts recovered through depreciation and other allowances, the estimated salvage value, the character of the property, and the estimated remaining useful life of the property. A change to the straight line method under this paragraph must be adhered to for the entire taxable year of the change and for all subsequent taxable years unless, with the consent of the Commissioner, a change to another method is permitted. [Reg. § 1.167(e)-1.]

☐ [*T.D.* 6182, 6-11-56. *Amended by T.D.* 6832, 7-6-65 *and T.D.* 7166, 3-10-72.]

[Reg. § 1.167(f)-1]

§ 1.167(f)-1. **Reduction of salvage value taken into account for certain personal property.**—(a) *In general.* For taxable years beginning after December 31, 1961, and ending after October 16, 1962, a taxpayer may reduce the amount taken into account as salvage value in computing the allowance for depreciation under section 167(a) with respect to "personal property" as defined in section 167(f)(2) and paragraph (b) of this section. The reduction may be made in an amount which does not exceed 10 percent of the basis of the property for determining depreciation, as of the time as of which salvage value is required to be determined (or when salvage value is redetermined), taking into account all adjustments under section 1016 other than (1) the adjustment under section 1016(a)(2) for depreciation allowed or allowable to the taxpayer, and (2) the adjustment under section 1016(a)(19) for a credit earned by the taxpayer under section 38, to the extent such adjustment is reflected in the basis for depreciation. See paragraph (c) of § 1.167(a)-1 for the definition of salvage value, the time for making the determination, the redetermination of salvage value, and the general rules with respect to the treatment of salvage value. See also section 167(g) and § 1.167(g)-1 for basis for depreciation. A reduction of the amount taken into account as salvage value with respect to any property shall not be binding with respect to other property. In no event shall an asset (or an account) be depreciated below a reasonable salvage value after taking into account the reduction in salvage value permitted by section 167(f) and this section.

(b) *Definitions and special rules.* The following definitions and special rules apply for purposes of section 167(f) and this section.

(1) *Personal property.* The term "personal property" shall include only depreciable—

(i) Tangible personal property (as defined in section 48 and the regulations thereunder) and

(ii) Intangible personal property

which has an estimated useful life (determined at the time of acquisition) of 3 years or more and which is acquired after October 16, 1962. Such term shall not include livestock. The term "livestock" includes horses, cattle, hogs, sheep, goats, and mink and other fur-bearing animals, irrespective of the use to which they are put or the purpose for which they are held. The original use of the property need not commence with the taxpayer so long as he acquired it after October 16, 1962; thus, the property may be new or used. For purposes of determining the estimated useful life, the provisions of paragraph (b) of § 1.167(a)-1 shall be applied. For rules determining when property is acquired, see subparagraph (2) of this paragraph. For purposes of determining the types of intangible personal property which are subject to the allowance for depreciation, see § 1.167(a)-3.

(2) *Acquired.* In determining whether property is acquired after October 16, 1962, property shall be deemed to be acquired when reduced to physical possession, or control. Property which has not been used in the taxpayer's trade or business or held for the production of income and which is thereafter converted by the taxpayer to such use shall be deemed to be acquired on the date of such conversion. In addition, property shall be deemed to be acquired if constructed, reconstructed, or erected by the taxpayer. If construction, reconstruction, or erection by the taxpayer began before October 17, 1962, and was completed after October 16, 1962, section 167(f) and this section apply only to that portion of the basis of the property which is properly attributable to such construction, reconstruction, or erection after October 16, 1962. Property is considered as constructed, reconstructed, or erected by the taxpayer if the work is done for him in accordance with his specifications. The portion of the basis of such property attributable to construction, reconstruction, or erection after October 16, 1962, consists of all costs of the property allocable to the period after October 16, 1962, including the cost or other basis of materials entering into such work. It is not necessary that such materials be acquired after October 16, 1962, or that they be new in use. If construction

or erection by the taxpayer began after October 16, 1962, the entire cost or other basis of such construction or erection qualifies for the reduction provided for by section 167(f) and this section. In the case of reconstruction of property, section 167(f) and this section do not apply to any part of the adjusted basis of such property on October 16, 1962. For purposes of this section, construction, reconstruction, or erection by the taxpayer begins when physical work is started on such construction, reconstruction, or erection.

(c) *Illustrations.* The provisions of paragraphs (a) and (b) of this section may be illustrated by the following examples:

Example (1). Taxpayer A purchases a new asset for use in his business on January 1, 1963, for $10,000. The asset qualifies for the investment credit under section 38 and for the additional first-year depreciation allowance under section 179. A is entitled to an investment credit of $700 (7% × $10,000) and elects to take an additional first-year depreciation allowance of $2,000 (20% × $10,000). The basis for depreciation (determined in accordance with the provisions of section 167(g) and § 1.167(g)-1) is computed as follows:

Purchase price		$10,000
Less: Adjustment required for taxable years beginning before Jan. 1, 1964, under section 1016(a) (19) for the investment credit ...	$ 700	
Adjustment required under section 1016(a)(2) for the additional first-year depreciation allowance	2,000	2,700
Basis for depreciation for the taxable year 1963		$ 7,300

However, the basis of the property for determining depreciation as of the time as of which salvage value is required to be determined is $10,000, the purchase price of the property. A files his income tax returns on a calendar year basis and uses the straight line method of depreciation. A estimates that he will use the asset in his business for 10 years after which it will have a salvage value of $500, which is less than $1,000 (10% × $10,000, the basis of the property for determining depreciation as of the time as of which salvage value is required to be determined). For the taxable year 1963 A may deduct $730 as the depreciation allowance. As of January 1, 1964, the basis of the asset is increased by $700 in accordance with paragraph (d) of § 1.48-7. In computing his total depreciation allowance on the asset, A may reduce the amount taken into account as salvage value to zero and may claim depreciation deductions (including the additional first-year depreciation allowance) totaling $10,000. See paragraph (d) of § 1.48-7 for the computation of depreciation for taxable years beginning after December 31, 1963, where there is an increase in basis of property subject to the investment credit.

Example (2). Assume the same facts as in example (1) except that A in a subsequent taxable year redetermines the estimate of the useful life of the asset and at the same time also redetermines the estimate of salvage value. Assume also that at such time the only reductions reflected in the basis are for depreciation allowed or allowable. Accordingly, the reduction under section 167(f) and this section will be computed with regard to the purchase price and not the unrecovered basis for depreciation at the time of the redetermination.

Example (3). Assume the same facts as in example (1) except that A estimates that the asset will have a salvage value of $1,200 at the end of its useful life. In computing his depreciation for the asset, A may reduce the amount to be taken into account as salvage value to $200 ($1,200 − $1,000). Accordingly, A may claim depreciation deductions (including the additional first-year depreciation allowance) totaling $9,800, i.e., the purchase price of the property ($10,000) less the amount taken into account as salvage value ($200).

Example (4). Assume the same facts as in example (1) except that the taxpayer had taken into account salvage value of only $200 but that the estimated salvage value had actually been $700. The amount of salvage value taken into account by the taxpayer is permissible since the reduction of salvage value by $500 ($700 − $200) would be within the limit provided for in section 167(f), i.e., $1,000 (10% × $10,000).

Example (5). On January 1, 1963, taxpayer B, a taxicab operator, traded his old taxicab plus cash for a new one, which had an estimated useful life of three years, in a transaction qualifying as a nontaxable exchange. The old taxicab had an adjusted basis of $2,500. B was allowed $3,000 for his old taxicab and paid $1,000 in cash. The basis of the new taxicab for determining depreciation (as determined under section 167(g) and § 1.167(g)-1) is the adjusted basis of the old taxicab at the time of trade-in ($2,500) plus the additional cash paid out ($1,000), or $3,500. In computing his depreciation allowance on the new taxicab, B may reduce the amount taken into account as salvage value by $350 (10% of $3,500).

Example (6). Taxpayer C purchases a new asset for use in his business on January 1, 1963, for $10,000. At the time of purchase, the asset has an estimated useful life of 10 years and an estimated salvage value of $1,500. C elects to compute his depreciation allowance for the asset by the declining balance method of depreciation, using a rate of 20% which is twice the normal straight line rate of 10% (without adjustment for salvage value). C files his income tax returns on a calendar year basis. In computing his depreciation allowance for the year 1966, C changes his method of determining the depreciation allowance for the asset from the declining balance method to the straight line method (in which salvage value is accounted for in determining the annual depreciation allowances) in accordance with the provisions of section 167(e) and paragraph (b) of § 1.167(e)-1. He also wishes to reduce the amount of salvage value taken into account in accordance with the provisions of section 167(f) and this section. At the close of the year 1966, the only reductions reflected in the basis of the asset are for depreciation allowances. Thus, C may reduce the amount of salvage value taken into account by $1,000 (10% × $10,000, the basis of the asset when it was acquired), and, therefore, will account for salvage value of only $500 in computing his depreciation allowance for the asset in 1966 and subsequent years.

Example (7). Taxpayer D purchases a station wagon for his personal use on January 1, 1962, for $4,500. On January 1, 1963, D converts the use of the station wagon to his business, and at that time it has an estimated useful life of 4 years, an estimated salvage value of $500, and a basis of $3,000 (as determined under section 167(g) and § 1.167(g)-1). Thus, for purposes of section 167(f) and this section, D is deemed to have acquired the station wagon on January 1, 1963. D elects the straight line method of depreciation in computing the depreciation allowance for the station wagon and also wishes to reduce the amount of salvage value taken into account in accordance with the provisions of section 167(f) and this section. Accordingly, D may reduce the amount of salvage value taken into account by $300 (10% of $3,000). D files his income tax returns on a calendar year basis. His depreciation allowance for the year 1963 would be computed as follows:

Basis for depreciation		$3,000
Less: Salvage value	$ 500	
Reduction permitted by		
section 167(f)	300	200
Amount to be depreciated over the		
useful life		2,800

D's depreciation allowance on the station wagon for the year 1963 would be $700 ($2,800 divided by 4, the remaining useful life). [Reg. § 1.167(f)-1.]

□ [*T.D.* 6712, 3-23-64. *Amended by T.D.* 6838, 7-19-65.]

Reg. § 1.167(f)-1(c)

[Reg. § 1.167(g)-1]

§ 1.167(g)-1. Basis for depreciation.—The basis upon which the allowance for depreciation is to be computed with respect to any property shall be the adjusted basis provided in section 1011 for the purpose of determining gain on the sale or other disposition of such property. In the case of property which has not been used in the trade or business or held for the production of income and which is thereafter converted to such use, the fair market value on the date of such conversion, if less than the adjusted basis of the property at that time, is the basis for computing depreciation. [Reg. § 1.167(g)-1.]

□ [*T.D. 6182, 6-11-56. Amended by T.D. 6712, 3-23-64.*]

[Reg. § 1.167(h)-1]

§ 1.167(h)-1. Life tenants and beneficiaries of trusts and estates.—(a) *Life tenants.* In the case of property held by one person for life with remainder to another person, the deduction for depreciation shall be computed as if the life tenant were the absolute owner of the property so that he will be entitled to the deduction during his life, and thereafter the deduction, if any, shall be allowed to the remainderman.

(b) *Trusts.* If property is held in trust, the allowable deduction is to be apportioned between the income beneficiaries and the trustee on the basis of the trust income allocable to each, unless the governing instrument (or local law) requires or permits the trustee to maintain a reserve for depreciation in any amount. In the latter case, the deduction is first allocated to the trustee to the extent that income is set aside for a depreciation reserve, and any part of the deduction in excess of the income set aside for the reserve shall be apportioned between the income beneficiaries and the trustee on the basis of the trust income (in excess of the income set aside for the reserve) allocable to each. For example:

(1) If under the trust instrument or local law the income of a trust computed without regard to depreciation is to be distributed to a named beneficiary, the beneficiary is entitled to the deduction to the exclusion of the trustee.

(2) If under the trust instrument or local law the income of a trust is to be distributed to a named beneficiary, but the trustee is directed to maintain a reserve for depreciation in any amount, the deduction is allowed to the trustee (except to the extent that income set aside for the reserve is less than the allowable deduction). The same result would follow if the trustee sets aside income for a depreciation reserve pursuant to

discretionary authority to do so in the governing instrument.

No effect shall be given to any allocation of the depreciation deduction which gives any beneficiary or the trustee a share of such deduction greater than his pro rata share of the trust income, irrespective of any provisions in the trust instrument, except as otherwise provided in this paragraph when the trust instrument or local law requires or permits the trustee to maintain a reserve for depreciation.

(c) *Estates.* In the case of an estate, the allowable deduction shall be apportioned between the estate and the heirs, legatees, and devisees on the basis of income of the estate which is allocable to each. [Reg. § 1.167(h)-1.]

□ [*T.D. 6182, 6-11-56. Amended by T.D. 6712, 3-23-64.*]

[Reg. § 1.167(i)-1]

§ 1.167(i)-1. Depreciation of improvements in the case of mines, etc.—Property used in the trade or business or held for the production of income which is subject to the allowance for depreciation provided in section 611 shall be treated for all purposes of the Code as if it were property subject to the allowance for depreciation under section 167. The preceding sentence shall not limit the allowance for depreciation otherwise allowable under section 611. [Reg. § 1.167(i)-1.]

□ [*T.D. 6182, 6-11-56. Amended by T.D. 6712, 3-23-64.*]

[Reg. § 1.167(l)-1]

§ 1.167(l)-1. Limitations on reasonable allowance in case of property of certain public utilities.—(a) *In general*—(1) *Scope.* Section 167(l) in general provides limitations on the use of certain methods of computing a reasonable allowance for depreciation under section 167(a) with respect to "public utility property" (see paragraph (b) of this section) for all taxable years for which a Federal income tax return was not filed before August 1, 1969. The limitations are set forth in paragraph (c) of this section for "pre-1970 public utility property" and in paragraph (d) of this section for "post-1969 public utility property." Under section 167(l), a taxpayer may always use a straight line method (or other "subsection (l) method" as defined in paragraph (f) of this section). In general, the use of a method of depreciation other than a subsection (l) method is not prohibited by section 167(l) for any taxpayer if the taxpayer uses a "normalization method of regulated accounting" (described in paragraph (h) of this section). In certain cases, the use of a method of depreciation other than a subsection (l) method is not prohibited by section 167(l) if the taxpayer used a "flow-through method of regulated accounting" (described in paragraph (i) of this section) for its "July 1969 regulated accounting period" (described in paragraph (g) of this section) whether or not the taxpayer uses either a normalization or a flow-through method of regulated accounting after its July 1969 regulated accounting period. However, in no event may a method of depreciation other than a subsection (l) method be used in the case of pre-1970 public utility property unless such method of depreciation is the "applicable 1968 method" (within the meaning of paragraph (e) of this section). The normalization requirements of section 167(l) with respect to public utility property defined in section 167(l)(3)(A) pertain only to the deferral of Federal income tax liability resulting from the use of an accelerated method of depreciation for computing the allowance for depreciation under section 167 and the use of straight line depreciation for computing tax expense and depreciation expense for purposes of establishing cost of services and for reflecting operating results in regulated books of account. Regulations under section 167(l) do not pertain to other book-tax timing differences with respect to State income taxes, F.I.C.A. taxes, construction costs, or any other taxes and items. The rules provided in paragraph (h)(6) of this section are to insure that the same time period is used to determine the deferred tax reserve amount resulting from the use of an accelerated method of depreciation for cost of service purposes and the reserve amount that may be excluded from the rate base or included in no-cost capital in determining such cost of services. The formula provided in paragraph (h)(6)(ii) of this section is to be used in conjunction with the method of accounting for the reserve for deferred taxes (otherwise proper under paragraph (h)(2) of this section) in accordance with the accounting requirements prescribed or approved, if applicable, by the regulatory body having jurisdiction over the taxpayer's regulated books of account. The formula provides a method to determine the period of time during which the taxpayer will be treated as having received amounts credited or charged to the reserve account so that the disallowance of earnings with respect to such amounts through rate base exclusion or treatment as no-cost capital will take into account the factor of time for which such amounts are held by the taxpayer. The formula serves to limit the amount of such disallowance.

(2) *Methods of depreciation.* For purposes of section 167(l), in the case of declining balance method each different uniform rate applied to the unrecovered cost or other basis of the property is a different method of depreciation. For purposes of section 167(l), a change in a uniform rate of depreciation due to a change in the useful life of the property or a change in the taxpayer's unrecovered cost or other basis for the property is not a change in the method of depreciation. The use of "guideline lives" or "class lives" for Federal income tax purposes and different lives on the taxpayer's regulated books of account is generally not treated for purposes of section 167(l) as a different method of depreciation. Further, the use of an unrecovered cost or other basis or salvage value for Federal income tax purposes different from the basis or salvage value used on the taxpayer's regulated books of account is not treated as a different method of depreciation.

(3) *Application of certain other provisions to public utility property.* For rules with respect to application of the investment credit to public utility property, see section 46(e). For rules with respect to the application of the class life asset depreciation range system, including the treatment of the use of "class lives" for Federal income tax purposes and different lives on the taxpayer's regulated books of account, see § 1.167(a)-11 and § 1.167(a)-12.

(4) *Effect on agreements under section 167(d).* If the taxpayer has entered into an agreement under section 167(d) as to any public utility property and such agreement requires the use of a method of depreciation prohibited by section 167(l), such agreement shall terminate as to such property. The termination, in accordance with this subparagraph, shall not affect any other property (whether or not public utility property) covered by the agreement.

(5) *Effect of change in method of depreciation.* If, because the method of depreciation used by the taxpayer with respect to public utility property is prohibited by section 167(l), the taxpayer changes to a method of depreciation not prohibited by section 167(l), then when the change is made the unrecovered cost or other basis shall be recovered through annual allowances over the estimated remaining useful life determined in accordance with the circumstances existing at that time.

(b) *Public utility property.*—(1) *In general.* Under section 167(l)(3)(A), property is "public utility property" during any period in which it is used predominantly in a "section 167(l) public utility activity." The term "section 167(l) public utility activity" means the trade or business of the furnishing or sale of—

(i) Electrical energy, water, or sewage disposal services,

(ii) Gas or steam through a local distribution system,

(iii) Telephone services,

(iv) Other communication services (whether or not telephone services) if furnished or sold by the Communications Satellite Corporation for purposes authorized by the Communications Satellite Act of 1962 (47 U.S.C. 701), or

(v) Transportation of gas or steam by pipeline,

if the rates for such furnishing or sale, as the case may be, are regulated, i.e., have been established or approved by a regulatory body described in section 167(l)(3)(A). The term "regulatory body described in section 167(l)(3)(A)" means a State (including the District of Columbia) or political subdivision thereof, any agency or instrumentality of the United States, or a public service or public utility commission or other body of any State or political subdivision thereof similar to such a commission. The term "established or approved" includes the filing of a schedule of rates with a regulatory body which has the power to approve such rates, even though such body has taken no action on the filed schedule or generally leaves undisturbed rates filed by the taxpayer involved.

(2) *Classification of property.* If property is not used solely in a section 167(l) public utility activity, such property shall be public utility property if its predominant use is in a section 167(l) public utility activity. The predominant use of property for any period shall be determined by reference to the proper accounts to which expenditures for such property are chargeable under the system of regulated accounts required to be used for the period for which the determination is made and in accordance with the principles of § 1.46-3(g)(4) (relating to credit for investment in certain depreciable property). Thus, for example, for purposes of determining whether property is used predominantly in the trade or business of the furnishing or sale of transportation of gas by pipeline, or furnishing or sale of gas through a local distribution system, or both, the rules prescribed in § 1.46-3(g)(4) apply, except that accounts 365 through 371, inclusive (Transmission Plant), shall be added to the accounts enumerated in subdivision (i) of such paragraph (g)(4).

(c) *Pre-1970 public utility property*—(1) *Definition.* (i) Under section 167(l)(3)(B), the term "pre-1970 public utility property" means property which was public utility property at any time before January 1, 1970. If a taxpayer acquires pre-1970 public utility property, such property shall be pre-1970 public utility property in the hands of the taxpayer even though such prop-

erty may have been acquired by the taxpayer in an arm's-length cash sale at fair market value or in a tax-free exchange. Thus, for example, if corporation X which is a member of the same controlled group of corporations (within the meaning of section 1563(a)) as corporation Y sells pre-1970 public utility property to Y, such property is pre-1970 public utility property in the hands of Y. The result would be the same if X and Y were not members of the same controlled group of corporations.

(ii) If the basis of public utility property acquired by the taxpayer in a transaction is determined in whole or in part by reference to the basis of any of the taxpayer's pre-1970 public utility property by reason of the application of any provision of the code, and if immediately after the transaction the adjusted basis of the property acquired is less than 200 percent of the adjusted basis of such pre-1970 public utility property immediately before the transaction, the property acquired is pre-1970 public utility property.

(2) *Methods of depreciation not prohibited.* Under section 167(l)(1), in the case of pre-1970 public utility property, the term "reasonable allowance" as used in section 167(a) means, for a taxable year for which a Federal income tax return was not filed before August 1, 1969, and in which such property is public utility property, an allowance (allowable without regard to section 167(l)) computed under—

(i) A subsection (l) method, or

(ii) The applicable 1968 method (other than a subsection (l) method) used by the taxpayer for such property, but only if—

(a) The taxpayer uses in respect of such taxable year a normalization method of regulated accounting for such property.

(b) The taxpayer used a flow-through method of regulated accounting for such property for its July 1969 regulated accounting period, or

(c) The taxpayer's first regulated accounting period with respect to such property is after the taxpayer's July 1969 regulated accounting period and the taxpayer used a flow-through method of regulated accounting for its July 1969 regulated accounting period for public utility property of the same kind (or if there is no property of the same kind, property of the most similar kind) most recently placed in service. See paragraph (e)(5) of this section for determination of same (or similar) kind.

(3) *Flow-through method of regulated accounting in certain cases.* See paragraph (e)(6) of this section for treatment of certain taxpayers with pending applications for change in method of

accounting as being deemed to have used a flow-through method of regulated accounting for the July 1969 regulated accounting period.

(4) *Examples.* The provisions of this paragraph may be illustrated by the following examples:

Example (1). Corporation X, a calendar-year taxpayer subject to the jurisdiction of a regulatory body described in section 167(l)(3)(A), used the straight line method of depreciation (a subsection (l) method) for all of its public utility property for which depreciation was allowable on its Federal income tax return for 1967 (the latest taxable year for which X, prior to August 1, 1969, filed a return). Assume that under paragraph (e) of this section, X's applicable 1968 method is a subsection (l) method with respect to all of its public utility property. Thus, with respect to its pre-1970 public utility property, X may only use a straight line method (or any other subsection (l) method) of depreciation for all taxable years after 1967.

Example (2). Corporation Y, a calendar-year taxpayer subject to the jurisdiction of the Federal Power Commission, is engaged exclusively in the transportation of gas by pipeline. On its Federal income tax return for 1967 (the latest taxable year for which Y, prior to August 1, 1969, filed a return), Y used the declining balance method of depreciation using a rate of 150 percent of the straight line rate for all of its nonsection 1250 public utility property with respect to which depreciation was allowable. Assume that with respect to all of such property, Y's applicable 1968 method under paragraph (e) of this section is such 150 percent declining balance method. Assume that Y used a normalization method of regulated accounting for all relevant regulated accounting periods. If Y continues to use a normalization method of regulated accounting, Y may compute its reasonable allowance for purposes of section 167(a) using such 150 percent declining balance method for its non-section 1250 pre-1970 public utility property for all taxable years beginning with 1968, provided the use of such method is allowable without regard to section 167(l). Y may also use a subsection (l) method for any of such pre-1970 public utility property for all taxable years beginning after 1967. However, because each different uniform rate applied to the basis of the property is a different method of depreciation, Y may not use a declining balance method of depreciation using a rate of twice the straight line rate for any of such pre-1970 public utility property for any taxable year beginning after 1967.

Example (3). Assume the same facts as in example (2) except that with respect to all of its

nonsection 1250 pre-1970 public utility property accounted for in its July 1969 regulated accounting period Y used a flow-through method of regulated accounting for such period. Assume further that such property is the property on the basis of which the applicable 1968 method is established for pre-1970 public utility property of the same kind, but having a first regulated accounting period after the taxpayer's July 1969 regulated accounting period. Beginning with 1968, with respect to such property Y may compute its reasonable allowance for purposes of section 167(a) using the declining balance method of depreciation and a rate of 150 percent of the straight line rate, whether it uses a normalization or flow-through method of regulated accounting after its July 1969 regulated accounting period, provided the use of such method is allowable without regard to section 167(l).

(d) *Post-1969 public utility property—*(1) *In general.* Under section 167(l)(3)(C), the term "post-1969 public utility property" means any public utility property which is not pre-1970 public utility property.

(2) *Methods of depreciation not prohibited.* Under section 167(l)(2), in the case of post-1969 public utility property, the term "reasonable allowance" as used in section 167(a) means, for a taxable year, an allowance (allowable without regard to section 167(l)) computed under—

(i) A subsection (l) method,

(ii) A method of depreciation otherwise allowable under section 167 if, with respect to the property, the taxpayer uses in respect of such taxable year a normalization method of regulated accounting, or

(iii) The taxpayer's applicable 1968 method (other than a subsection (l) method) with respect to the property in question, if the taxpayer used a flow-through method of regulated accounting for its July 1969 regulated accounting period for the property of the same (or similar) kind most recently placed in service, provided that the property in question is not property to which an election under section 167(l)(4)(A) applies. See § 1.167(l)-2 for rules with respect to an election under section 167(l)(4)(A). See paragraph (e)(5) of this section for definition of same (or similar) kind.

(3) *Examples.* The provisions of this paragraph may be illustrated by the following examples:

Example (1). Corporation X is engaged exclusively in the trade or business of the transportation of gas by pipeline and is subject to the jurisdiction of the Federal Power Commission. With respect to all its public utility property, X's applicable 1968 method (as determined under paragraph (e) of this section) is the straight line method of depreciation. X may determine its reasonable allowance for depreciation under section 167(a) with respect to its post-1969 public utility property under a straight line method (or other subsection (l) method) or, if X uses a normalization method of regulated accounting, any other method of depreciation, provided that the use of such other method is allowable under section 167 without regard to section 167(l).

Example (2). Assume the same facts as in example (1) except that with respect to all of X's post-1969 public utility property the applicable 1968 method (as determined under paragraph (e) of this section) is the declining balance method using a rate of 150 percent of the straight line rate. Assume further that all of X's pre-1970 public utility property was accounted for in its July 1969 regulated accounting period, and that X used a flow-through method of regulated accounting for such period. X may determine its reasonable allowance for depreciation under section 167 with respect to its post-1969 public utility property by using the straight-line method of depreciation (or any other subsection (l) method), by using any method otherwise allowable under section 167 (such as a declining balance method) if X uses a normalization method of regulated accounting, or, by using the declining balance method using a rate of 150 percent of the straight line rate, whether or not X uses a normalization or a flow-through method of regulated accounting.

(e) *Applicable 1968 method* —(1) *In general.* Under section 167(l)(3)(D), except as provided in subparagraphs (3) and (4) of this paragraph, the term "applicable 1968 method" means with respect to any public utility property—

(i) The method of depreciation properly used by the taxpayer in its Federal income tax return with respect to such property for the latest taxable year for which a return was filed before August 1, 1969,

(ii) If subdivision (i) of this subparagraph does not apply, the method of depreciation properly used by the taxpayer in its Federal income tax return for the latest taxable year for which a return was filed before August 1, 1969, with respect to public utility property of the same kind (or if there is no property of the same kind, property of the most similar kind) most recently placed in service before the end of such latest taxable year, or

(iii) If neither subdivision (i) nor (ii) of this subparagraph applies, a subsection (l) method.

If, on or after August 1, 1969, the taxpayer files an amended return for the taxable year referred to in subdivisions (i) and (ii) of this subparagraph, such amended return shall not be taken into consideration in determining the applicable 1968 method. The term "applicable 1968 method" also means with respect to any public utility property, for the year of change and subsequent years, a method of depreciation otherwise allowable under section 167 to which the taxpayer changes from an applicable 1968 method, if such new method results in a lesser allowance for depreciation for such property under section 167 in the year of change and the taxpayer secures the Commissioner's consent to the change in accordance with the procedures of section 446(e) and § 1.446-1.

(2) *Placed in service.* For purposes of this section, property is placed in service on the date on which the period for depreciation begins under section 167. See, for example, § 1.167(a)-10(b) and proposed § 1.167(a)-11(c)(2). If under an averaging convention, property which is placed in service (as defined in § 1.46-3(d)(ii)) by the taxpayer on different dates is treated as placed in service on the same date, then for purposes of section 167(l) the property shall be treated as having been placed in service on the date the period for depreciation with respect to such property would begin under section 167 absent such averaging convention. Thus, for example, if, except for the fact that the averaging convention used assumes that all additions and retirements made during the first half of the year were made on the first day of the year, the period of depreciation for two items of public utility property would begin on January 10 and March 15, respectively, then for purposes of determining the property of the same (or similar) kind most recently placed in service, such items of property shall be treated as placed in service on January 10 and March 15, respectively.

(3) *Certain section 1250 property.* If a taxpayer is required under section 167(j) to use a method of depreciation other than its applicable 1968 method with respect to any section 1250 property, the term "applicable 1968 method" means the method of depreciation allowable under section 167(j) which is the most nearly comparable method to the applicable 1968 method determined under subparagraph (1) of this paragraph. For example, if the applicable 1968 method on new section 1250 property is the declining balance method using 200 percent of the straight line rate, the most nearly comparable method allowable for new section 1250 property under section 167(j) would be the declining balance method using 150 percent of the straight line rate. If the applicable 1968 method determined under subparagraph (1) of this paragraph is the sum of the years-digits method, the term "most nearly comparable

method" refers to any method of depreciation allowable under section 167(j).

(4) *Applicable 1968 method in certain cases.* (i) (*a*) Under section 167(l)(3)(E), if the taxpayer evidenced within the time and manner specified in (*b*) of this subdivision (i) the intent to use a method of depreciation under section 167 (other than its applicable 1968 method as determined under subparagraph (1) or (3) of this paragraph or a subsection (l) method) with respect to any public utility property, such method of depreciation shall be deemed to be the taxpayer's applicable 1968 method with respect to such public utility property and public utility property of the same (or most similar) kind subsequently placed in service.

(*b*) Under this subdivision (i), the intent to use a method of depreciation under section 167 is evidenced—

(*1*) By a timely application for permission for a change in method of accounting filed by the taxpayer before August 1, 1969, or

(*2*) By the use of such method of depreciation in the computation by the taxpayer of its tax expense for purposes of reflecting operating results in its regulated books of account for its July 1969 regulated accounting period, as established in the manner prescribed in subparagraph (g)(1)(i), (ii), or (iii) of this section.

(ii)(*a*) If public utility property is acquired in a transaction in which its basis in the hands of the transferee is determined in whole or in part by reference to its basis in the hands of the transferor by reason of the application of any provision of the Code, or in a transfer (including any purchase for cash or in exchange) from a related person, then in the hands of the transferee the applicable 1968 method with respect to such property shall be determined by reference to the treatment in respect of such property in the hands of the transferor.

(*b*) For purposes of this subdivision (ii), the term "related person" means a person who is related to another person if either immediately before or after the transfer—

(*1*) The relationship between such persons would result in a disallowance of losses under section 267 (relating to disallowance of losses, etc., between related taxpayers) or section 707(b) (relating to losses disallowed, etc., between partners and controlled partnerships) and the regulations thereunder, or

(*2*) Such persons are members of the same controlled group of corporations, as defined in section 1563(a) (relating to definition of controlled group of corporations), except that "more

than 50 percent" shall be substituted for "at least 80 percent" each place it appears in section 1563(a) and the regulations thereunder.

(5) *Same or similar.* The classification of property as being of the same (or similar) kind shall be made by reference to the function of the public utility to which the primary use of the property relates. Property which performs the identical function in the identical manner shall be treated as property of the same kind. The determination that property is of a similar kind shall be made by reference to the proper account to which expenditures for the property are chargeable under the system of regulated accounts required to be used by the taxpayer for the period in which the property in question was acquired. Property, the expenditure for which is chargeable to the same account, is property of the most similar kind. Property, the expenditure for which is chargeable to an account for property which serves the same general function, is property of a similar kind. Thus, for example, if corporation X, a natural gas company, subject to the jurisdiction of the Federal Power Commission, had property properly chargeable to account 366 (relating to transmission plant structures and improvements) acquired an additional structure properly chargeable to account 366, under the uniform system of accounts prescribed for natural gas companies (class A and class B) by the Federal Power Commission, effective September 1, 1968, the addition would constitute property of the same kind if it performed the identical function in the identical manner. If, however, the addition did not perform the identical function in the identical manner, it would be property of the most similar kind.

(6) *Regulated method of accounting in certain cases.* Under section 167(l)(4)(B), if with respect to any pre-1970 public utility property the taxpayer filed a timely application for change in method of accounting referred to in subparagraph (4)(i)(*b*)(*1*) of this paragraph and with respect to property of the same (or similar) kind most recently placed in service the taxpayer used a flow-through method of regulated accounting for its July 1969 regulated accounting period, then for purposes of section 167(l)(1)(B) and paragraph (c) of this section the taxpayer shall be deemed to have used a flow-through method of regulated accounting with respect to such pre-1970 public utility property.

(7) *Examples.* The provisions of this paragraph may be illustrated by the following examples:

Example (1). Corporation X is a calendar-year taxpayer. On its Federal income tax return for 1967 (the latest taxable year for which X, prior to August 1, 1969, filed a return) X used a straight line method of depreciation with respect to certain public utility property placed in service before 1965 and used the declining balance method of depreciation using 200 percent of the straight line rate (double declining balance) with respect to the same kind of public utility property placed in service after 1964. In 1968 and 1970, X placed in service additional public utility property of the same kind. The applicable 1968 method with respect to the above described public utility property is shown in the following chart:

Property held in 1970	Placed in service	Method on 1967 return	Applicable 1968 method
	Before 1965		
Group 1	....	Straight line	Straight line
Group 2	After 1964 . and before 1968.	Double declining balance.	Double declining balance.
Group 3	After 1967 and before 1969.	....	Do.
Group 4	After 1968	....	Do.

Example (2). Corporation Y is a calendar-year taxpayer engaged exclusively in the trade or business of the furnishing of electrical energy. In 1954, Y placed in service hydroelectric generators and for all purposes Y has taken straight line depreciation with respect to such generators. In 1960, Y placed in service fossil fuel generators and for all purposes since 1960 has used the declining balance method of depreciation using a rate of 150 percent of the straight line rate (computed without reduction for salvage) with respect to such generators. After 1960 and before 1970 Y did not place in service any generators. In 1970, Y placed in service additional hydroelectric generators. The applicable 1968 method with respect to the hydroelectric generators placed in service in 1970 would be the straight line method because it was the method used by Y on its return for the latest taxable year for which Y filed a return before August 1, 1969, with respect to property of the same kind (i.e., hydroelectric generators) most recently placed in service.

Example (3). Assume the same facts as in example (2), except that the generators placed in service in 1970 were nuclear generators. The applicable 1968 method with respect to such generators is the declining balance method using a rate of 150 percent of the straight line rate because, with respect to property of the most similar kind (fossil fuel generators) most recently placed in service, Y used such declining balance method on its return for the latest taxable year for which it filed a return before August 1, 1969.

(f) *Subsection (l) method.* Under section 167(l)(3)(F), the term "subsection (l) method" means a reasonable and consistently applied rata-

ble method of computing depreciation which is allowable under section 167(a), such as, for example, the straight-line method or a unit of production method or machine-hour method. The term "subsection (l) method" does not include any declining balance method (regardless of the uniform rate applied), sum of the years-digits method, or method of depreciation which is allowable solely by reason of section 167(b)(4) or (j)(1)(C).

(g) *July 1969 regulated accounting period* —(1) *In general.* Under section 167(l)(3)(I), the term "July 1969 regulated accounting period" means the taxpayer's latest accounting period ending before August 1, 1969, for which the taxpayer regularly computed, before January 1, 1970, its tax expense for purposes of reflecting operating results in its regulated books of account. The computation by the taxpayer of such tax expense may be established by reference to the following:

(i) The most recent periodic report of a period ending before August 1, 1969, required by a regulatory body described in section 167(l)(3)(A) having jurisdiction over the taxpayer's regulated books of account which was filed with such body before January 1, 1970 (whether or not such body has jurisdiction over rates).

(ii) If subdivision (i) of the subparagraph does not apply, the taxpayer's most recent report to its shareholders for a period ending before August 1, 1969, but only if such report was distributed to the shareholders before January 1, 1970, and if the taxpayer's stocks or securities are traded in an established securities market during such period. For purposes of this subdivision, the term "established securities market" has the meaning assigned to such term in § 1.453-3(d)(4).

(iii) If subdivisions (i) and (ii) of this subparagraph do not apply, entries made to the satisfaction of the district director before January 1, 1970, in its regulated books of account for its most recent accounting period ending before August 1, 1969.

(2) *July 1969 method of regulated accounting in certain acquisitions.* If public utility property is acquired in a transaction in which its basis in the hands of the transferee is determined in whole or in part by reference to its basis in the hands of the transferor by reason of the application of any provision of the Code, or in a transfer (including any purchase for cash or in exchange) from a related person, then in the hands of the transferee the method of regulated accounting for such property's July 1969 regulated accounting period shall be determined by reference to the treatment in respect of such property in the hands of the transferor. See paragraph (e)(4)(ii) of this section for definition of "related person."

Reg. § 1.167(l)-1(f)

(3) *Determination date.* For purposes of section 167(l), any reference to a method of depreciation under section 167(a), or a method of regulated accounting, taken into account by the taxpayer in computing its tax expense for its July 1969 regulated accounting period shall be a reference to such tax expense as shown on the periodic report or report to shareholders to which subparagraph (l)(i) or (ii) of this paragraph applies or the entries made on the taxpayer's regulated books of account to which subparagraph (l)(iii) of this paragraph applies. Thus, for example, assume that regulatory body A having jurisdiction over public utility property with respect to X's regulated books of account requires X to reflect its tax expense in such books using the same method of depreciation which regulatory body B uses for determining X's cost of service for ratemaking purposes. If in 1971, in the course of approving a rate change for X, B retroactively determines X's cost of service for ratemaking purposes for X's July 1969 regulated accounting period using a method of depreciation different from the method reflected in X's regulated books of account as of January 1, 1970, the method of depreciation used by X for its July 1969 regulated accounting period would be determined without reference to the method retroactively used by B in 1971.

(h) *Normalization method of accounting*—(1) *In general.* (i) Under section 167(l), a taxpayer uses a normalization method of regulated accounting with respect to public utility property—

(a) If the same method of depreciation (whether or not a subsection (l) method) is used to compute both its tax expense and its depreciation expense for purposes of establishing cost of service for ratemaking purposes and for reflecting operating results in its regulated books of account, and

(b) If to compute its allowance for depreciation under section 167 it uses a method of depreciation other than the method it used for purposes described in (a) of this subdivision, the taxpayer makes adjustments consistent with subparagraph (2) of this paragraph to a reserve to reflect the total amount of the deferral of Federal income tax liability resulting from the use with respect to all of its public utility property of such different methods of depreciation.

(ii) In the case of a taxpayer described in section 167(l) (1)(B) or (2)(C), the reference in subdivision (i) of this subparagraph shall be a reference only to such taxpayer's "qualified public utility property." See § 1.167(l)-2(b) for definition of "qualified public utility property."

(iii) Except as provided in this subparagraph, the amount of Federal income tax liability deferred as a result of the use of different method

of depreciation under subdivision (i) of this subparagraph is the excess (computed without regard to credits) of the amount the tax liability would have been had a subsection (l) method been used over the amount of the actual tax liability. Such amount shall be taken into account for the taxable year in which such different methods of depreciation are used. If, however, in respect of any taxable year the use of a method of depreciation other than a subsection (l) method for purposes of determining the taxpayer's reasonable allowance under section 167(a) results in a net operating loss carryover (as determined under section 172) to a year succeeding such taxable year which would not have arisen (or an increase in such carryover which would not have arisen) had the taxpayer determined his reasonable allowance under section 167(a) using a subsection (l) method, then the amount and time of the deferral of tax liability shall be taken into account in such appropriate time and manner as is satisfactory to the district director.

(2) *Adjustments to reserve.* (i) The taxpayer must credit the amount of deferred Federal income tax determined under subparagraph (l)(i) of this paragraph for any taxable year to a reserve for deferred taxes, a depreciation reserve, or other reserve account. The taxpayer need not establish a separate reserve account for such amount but the amount of deferred tax determined under subparagraph (l)(i) of this paragraph must be accounted for in such a manner so as to be readily identifiable. With respect to any account, the aggregate amount allocable to deferred tax under section 167(l) shall not be reduced except to reflect the amount for any taxable year by which Federal income taxes are greater by reason of the prior use of different methods of depreciation under subparagraph (l)(i) of this paragraph. An additional exception is that the aggregate amount allocable to deferred tax under section 167(l) may be properly adjusted to reflect asset retirements or the expiration of the period for depreciation used in determining the allowance for depreciation under section 167(a).

(ii) The provisions of this subparagraph may be illustrated by the following examples:

Example (1). Corporation X is exclusively engaged in the transportation of gas by pipeline subject to the jurisdiction of the Federal Power Commission. With respect to its post-1969 public utility property, X is entitled under section 167(l)(2)(B) to use a method of depreciation other than a subsection (l) method if it uses a normalization method of regulated accounting. With respect to such property, X has not made any election under § 1.167(a)-11 (relating to depreciation based on class lives and asset depreciation ranges). In 1972, X places in service public utility property with an unadjusted basis of $2 million, and an estimated useful life of 20 years. X uses the declining-balance method of depreciation with a rate twice the straight line rate. If X uses a normalization method of regulated accounting, the amount of depreciation allowable under section 167(a) with respect to such property for 1972 computed under the double declining balance method would be $200,000. X computes its tax expense and depreciation expense for purposes of determining its cost of service for ratemaking purposes and for reflecting operating results in its regulated books of account using the straight line method of depreciation (a subsection (l) method). A depreciation allowance computed in this manner is $100,000. The excess of the depreciation allowance determined under the double declining balance method ($200,000) over the depreciation expense computed using the straight line method ($100,000) is $100,000. Thus, assuming a tax rate of 48 percent, X used a normalization method of regulated accounting for 1972 with respect to property placed in service that year if for 1972 it added to a reserve $48,000 as taxes deferred as a result of the use by X of a method of depreciation for Federal income tax purposes different from that used for establishing its cost of service for ratemaking purposes and for reflecting operating results in its regulated books of account.

Example (2). Assume the same facts as in example (l), except that X elects to apply § 1.167(a)-11 with respect to all eligible property placed in service in 1972. Assume further that all property X placed in service in 1972 is eligible property. One hundred percent of the asset guideline period for such property is 22 years and the asset depreciation range is from 17.5 years to 26.5 years. X uses the double declining balance method of depreciation, selects an asset depreciation period of 17.5 years, and applies the half-year convention (described in § 1.167(a)-11(c)(2)(iii)). In 1972, the depreciation allowable under section 167(a) with respect to property placed in service in 1972 is $114,285 (determined without regard to the normalization requirements in § 1.167(a)-11(b)(6) and in section 167(l)). X computes its tax expense for purposes of determining its cost of service for ratemaking purposes and for reflecting operating results in its regulated books of account using the straight-line method of depreciation (a subsection (l) method), an estimated useful life of 22 years (that is, 100 percent of the asset guideline period), and the half-year convention. A depreciation allowance computed in this manner is $45,454. Assuming a tax rate of 48 percent, the amount that X must add to a reserve

for 1972 with respect to property placed in service that year in order to qualify as using a normalization method of regulated accounting under section 167(l)(3)(G) is $27,429 and the amount in order to satisfy the normalization requirements of proposed § 1.167(a)-11(b)(6) is $5,610. X determined such amounts as follows:

(1) Depreciation allowance on tax return (determined without regard to section 167(1) and § 1.167(a)-11(b)(6)) $114,285
(2) Line (1), recomputed using a straight line method 57,142

(3) Difference in depreciation allowance attributable to different methods (line (1) minus line (2)) . . . . $ 57,143
(4) Amount to add to reserve under this paragraph (48 percent of line (3)) . . . . $ 27,429

(5) Amount in line (2) . . . . $ 57,142
(6) Line (5), recomputed by using an estimated useful life of 22 years and the half-year convention 45,454

(7) Difference in depreciation allowance attributable to difference in depreciation periods . . . . $ 11,688
(8) Amount to add to reserve under § 1.167(a)-11(b)(6)(ii) (48 percent of line (7)) 5,610

If, for its depreciation expense for purposes of determining its cost of service for ratemaking purposes and for reflecting operating results in its regulated books of account, X had used a period in excess of the asset guideline period of 22 years, the total amount in lines (4) and (8) in this example would not be changed.

Example (3). Corporation Y, a calendar-year taxpayer which is engaged in furnishing electrical energy, made the election provided by section 167(l)(4)(a) with respect to its "qualified public utility property" (as defined in § 1.167(l)-2(b)). In 1971, Y placed in service qualified public utility property which had an adjusted basis of $2 million, estimated useful life of 20 years, and no salvage value. With respect to property of the same kind most recently placed in service, Y used a flow-through method of regulated accounting for its July 1969 regulated accounting period and the applicable 1968 method is the declining balance method of depreciation using 200 percent of the straight line rate. The amount of depreciation allowable under the double declining balance method with respect to the qualified public utility property would be $200,000. Y computes its tax expense and depreciation expense for purposes of determining its cost of service for ratemaking purposes and for reflecting operating results in its regulated books of account using the straight line method of depreciation. A depreciation allowance with respect to the qualified public utility property determined in this manner is $100,000. The excess of the depreciation allowance determined under the double declining balance method ($200,000) over the depreciation expense computed using the straight line method ($100,000) is $100,000. Thus, assuming a tax rate of 48 percent, Y used a normalization method of regulated accounting for 1971 if for 1971 it added to a reserve $48,000 as tax deferred as a result of the use by Y of a method of depreciation for Federal income tax purposes with respect to its qualified public utility property which method was different from that used for establishing its cost of service for ratemaking purposes and for reflecting operating results in its regulated books of account for such property.

Example (4). Corporation Z, exclusively engaged in a public utility activity did not use a flow-through method of regulated accounting for its July 1969 regulated accounting period. In 1971, a regulatory body having jurisdiction over all of Z's property issued an order applicable to all years beginning with 1968 which provided, in effect, that Z use an accelerated method of depreciation for purposes of section 167 and for determining its tax expenses for purposes of reflecting operating results in its regulated books of account. The order further provided that Z normalize 50 percent of the tax deferral resulting from the use of the accelerated method of depreciation and that Z flow-through 50 percent of the tax deferral resulting therefrom. Under section 167(l), the method of accounting provided in the order would not be a normalization method of regulated accounting because Z would not be permitted to normalize 100 percent of the tax deferral resulting from the use of an accelerated method of depreciation. Thus, with respect to its public utility property for purposes of section 167, Z may only use a subsection (l) method of depreciation.

Example (5). Assume the same facts as in example (4) except that the order of the regulatory body provided, in effect, that Z normalize 100 percent of the tax deferral with respect to 50 percent of its public utility property and flow-through the tax savings with respect to the other 50 percent of its property. Because the effect of such an order would allow Z to flow-through a portion of the tax savings resulting from the use of an accelerated method of depreciation, Z would not be using a normalization method of regulated accounting with respect to any of its properties. Thus, with respect to its public utility property for purposes of section 167, Z may only use a subsection (l) method of depreciation.

(3) *Establishing compliance with normalization requirements in respect of operating books of account.* The taxpayer may establish compliance with the requirement in subparagraph (1)(i) of this paragraph in respect of reflecting operating results, and adjustments to a reserve, in its operating books of account by reference to the following:

(i) The most recent periodic report for a period beginning before the end of the taxable year, required by a regulatory body described in section 167(l)(3)(A) having jurisdiction over the taxpayer's regulated operating books of account which was filed with such body before the due date (determined with regard to extensions) of the taxpayer's Federal income tax return for such taxable year (whether or not such body has jurisdiction over rates).

(ii) If subdivision (i) of this subparagraph does not apply, the taxpayer's most recent report to its shareholders for the taxable year but only if (a) such report was distributed to the shareholders before the due date (determined with regard to extensions) of the taxpayer's Federal income tax return for the taxable year and (b) the taxpayer's stocks or securities are traded in an established securities market during such taxable year. For purposes of this subdivision, the term "established securities market" has the meaning assigned to such term in § 1.453-3(d)(4).

(iii) If neither subdivision (i) nor (ii) of this subparagraph applies, entries made to the satisfaction of the district director before the due date (determined with regard to extensions) of the taxpayer's Federal income tax return for the taxable year in its regulated books of account for its most recent period beginning before the end of such taxable year.

(4) *Establishing compliance with normalization requirements in computing cost of service for ratemaking purposes.* (i) In the case of a taxpayer which used a flow-through method of regulated accounting for its July 1969 regulated accounting period or thereafter, with respect to all or a portion if its pre-1970 public utility property, if a regulatory body having jurisdiction to establish the rates of such taxpayer as to such property (or a court which has jurisdiction over such body) issues an order of general application (or an order of specific application to the taxpayer) which states that such regulatory body (or court) will permit a class of taxpayers of which such taxpayer is a member (or such taxpayer) to use the normalization method of regulated accounting to establish cost of service for ratemaking purposes with respect to all or a portion of its public utility property, the taxpayer will be presumed to be

Reg. § 1.167(l)-1(h)(4)

using the same method of depreciation to compute both its tax expense and its depreciation expense for purposes of establishing its cost of service for ratemaking purposes with respect to the public utility property to which such order applies. In the event that such order is in any way conditional, the preceding sentence shall not apply until all of the conditions contained in such order which are applicable to the taxpayer have been fulfilled. The taxpayer shall establish to the satisfaction of the Commissioner or his delegate that such conditions have been fulfilled.

(ii) In the case of a taxpayer which did not use the flow-through method of regulated accounting for its July 1969 regulated accounting period or thereafter (including a taxpayer which used a subsection (l) method of depreciation to compute its allowance for depreciation under section 167(a) and to compute its tax expense for purposes of reflecting operating results in its regulated books of account), with respect to any of its public utility property, it will be presumed that such taxpayer is using the same method of depreciation to compute both its tax expense and its depreciation expense for purposes of establishing its cost of service for ratemaking purposes with respect to its post-1969 public utility property. The presumption described in the preceding sentence shall not apply in any case where there is (a) an expression of intent (regardless of the manner in which such expression of intent is indicated) by the regulatory body (or bodies), having jurisdiction to establish the rates of such taxpayer, which indicates that the policy of such regulatory body is in any way inconsistent with the use of the normalization method of regulated accounting by such taxpayer or by a class of taxpayers of which such taxpayer is a member, or (b) a decision by a court having jurisdiction over such regulatory body which decision is any way inconsistent with the use of the normalization method of regulated accounting by such taxpayer or a class of taxpayers of which such taxpayer is a member. The presumption shall be applicable on January 1, 1970, and shall, unless rebutted, be effective until an inconsistent expression of intent is indicated by such regulatory body or by such court. An example of such an inconsistent expression of intent is the case of a regulatory body which has, after the July 1969 regulated accounting period and before January 1, 1970, directed public utilities subject to its ratemaking jurisdiction to use a flow-through method of regulated accounting, or has issued an order of general application which states that such agency will direct a class of public utilities of which the taxpayer is a member to use a flow-through method of regulated accounting. The presumption described in

this subdivision may be rebutted by evidence that the flow-through method of regulated accounting is being used by the taxpayer with respect to such property.

(iii) The provisions of this subparagraph may be illustrated by the following examples:

Example (1). Corporation X is a calendar-year taxpayer and its "applicable 1968 method" is a straight line method of depreciation. Effective January 1, 1970, X began collecting rates which were based on a sum of the years-digits method of depreciation and a normalization method of regulated accounting which rates had been approved by a regulatory body having jurisdiction over X. On October 1, 1971, a court of proper jurisdiction annulled the rate order prospectively, which annulment was not appealed, on the basis that the regulatory body had abused its discretion by determining the rates on the basis of a normalization method of regulated accounting. As there was no inconsistent expression of intent during 1970 or prior to the due date of X's return for 1970, X's use of the sum of the years-digits method of depreciation for purposes of section 167 on such return was proper. For 1971, the presumption is in effect through September 30. During 1971, X may use the sum of the years-digits method of depreciation for purposes of section 167 from January 1 through September 30, 1971. After September 30, 1971, and for taxable years after 1971, X must use a straight line method of depreciation until the inconsistent court decision is on longer in effect.

Example (2). Assume the same facts as in example (1), except that pursuant to the order of annulment, X was required to refund the portion of the rates attributable to the use of the normalization method of regulated accounting. As there was no inconsistent expression of intent during 1970 or prior to the due date of X's return for 1970, X has the benefit of the presumption with respect to its use of the sum of the years-digits method of depreciation for purposes of section 167, but because of the retroactive nature of the rate order X must file an amended return for 1970 using a straight line method of depreciation. As the inconsistent decision by the court was handed down prior to the due date of X's Federal income tax return for 1971, for 1971 and thereafter the presumption of subdivision (ii) of this subparagraph does not apply. X must file its Federal income tax returns for such years using a straight line method of depreciation.

Example (3). Assume the same facts as in example (2), except that the annulment order was stayed pending appeal of the decision to a court of proper appellate jurisdiction. X has the benefit of

Reg. § 1.167(l)-1(h)(4)

the presumption as described in example (2) for the year 1970, but for 1971 and thereafter the presumption of subdivision (ii) of this subparagraph does not apply. Further, X must file an amended return for 1970 using a straight line method of depreciation and for 1971 and thereafter X must file its returns using a straight line method of depreciation unless X and the district director have consented in writing to extend the time for assessment of tax for 1970 and thereafter with respect to the issue of normalization method of regulated accounting for as long as may be necessary to allow for resolution of the appeal with respect to the annulment of the rate order.

(5) *Change in method of regulated accounting.* The taxpayer shall notify the district director of a change in its method of regulated accounting, an order by a regulatory body or court that such method be changed, or an interim or final rate determination by a regulatory body which determination is inconsistent with the method of regulated accounting used by the taxpayer immediately prior to the effective date of such rate determination. Such notification shall be made within 90 days of the date that the change in method, the order, or the determination is effective. In the case of a change in the method of regulated accounting, the taxpayer shall recompute its tax liability for any affected taxable year and such recomputation shall be made in the form of an amended return where necessary unless the taxpayer and the district director have consented in writing to extend the time for assessment of tax with respect to the issue of normalization method of regulated accounting.

(6) *Exclusion of normalization reserve from rate base.* (i) Notwithstanding the provisions of subparagraph (1) of this paragraph, a taxpayer does not use a normalization method of regulated accounting if, for ratemaking purposes, the amount of the reserve for deferred taxes under section 167(l) which is excluded from the base to which the taxpayer's rate of return is applied, or which is treated as no-cost capital in those rate cases in which the rate of return is based upon the cost of capital, exceeds the amount of such reserve for deferred taxes for the period used in determining the taxpayer's tax expense in computing cost of service in such ratemaking.

(ii) For the purpose of determining the maximum amount of the reserve to be excluded from the rate base (or to be included as no-cost capital) under subdivision (i) of this subparagraph, if solely an historical period is used to determine depreciation for Federal income tax expense for ratemaking purposes, then the amount of the reserve account for the period is the

amount of the reserve (determined under subparagraph (2) of this paragraph) at the end of the historical period. If solely a future period is used for such determination, the amount of the reserve account for the period is the amount of the reserve at the beginning of the period and a pro rata portion of the amount of any projected increase to be credited or decrease to be charged to the account during such period. If such determination is made by reference both to an historical portion and to a future portion of a period, the amount of the reserve account for the period is the amount of the reserve at the end of the historical portion of the period and a pro rata portion of the amount of any projected increase to be credited or decrease to be charged to the account during the future portion of the period. The pro rata portion of any increase to be credited or decrease to be charged during a future period (or the future portion of a part-historical and part-future period) shall be determined by multiplying any such increase or decrease by a fraction, the numerator of which is the number of days remaining in the period at the time such increase or decrease is to be accrued, and the denominator of which is the total number of days in the period (or future portion).

(iii) The provisions of subdivision (i) of this subparagraph shall not apply in the case of a final determination of a rate case entered on or before May 31, 1973. For this purpose, a determination is final if all rights to request a review, a rehearing, or a redetermination by the regulatory body which makes such determination have been exhausted or have lapsed. The provisions of subdivision (ii) of this subparagraph shall not apply in the case of a rate case filed prior to June 7, 1974, for which a rate order is entered by a regulatory body having jurisdiction to establish the rates of the taxpayer prior to September 5, 1974, whether or not such order is final, appealable, or subject to further review or reconsideration.

(iv) The provisions of this subparagraph may be illustrated by the following examples:

Example (1). Corporation X is exclusively engaged in the transportation of gas by pipeline subject to the jurisdiction of the Z Power Commission. With respect to its post-1969 public utility property, X is entitled under section 167(l)(2)(B) to use a method of depreciation other than a subsection (l) method if it uses a normalization method of regulated accounting. With respect to X the Z Power Commission for purposes of establishing cost of service uses a recent consecutive 12-month period ending not more than 4 months prior to the date of filing a rate case adjusted for certain known changes occurring within a 9-month period subsequent to the base period. X's

Reg. § 1.167(l)-1(h)(6)

rate case is filed on January 1, 1975. The year 1974 is the recorded test period for X's rate case and is the period used in determining X's tax expense in computing cost of service. The rates are contemplated to be in effect for the years 1975, 1976, and 1977. The adjustments for known changes relate only to wages and salaries. X's rate base at the end of 1974 is $145,000,000. The amount of the reserve for deferred taxes under section 167(l) at the end of 1974 is $1,300,000, and the reserve is projected to be $4,400,000 at the end of 1975, $6,500,000 at the end of 1976, and $9,800,000 at the end of 1977. X does not use a normalization method of regulated accounting if the Z Power Commission excludes more than $1,300,000 from the rate base to which X's rate of return is applied. Similarly, X does not use a normalization method of regulated accounting if, instead of the above, the Z Power Commission, in determining X's rate of return which is applied to the rate base, assigns to no-cost capital an amount that represents the reserve account for deferred tax that is greater than $1,300,000.

Example (2). Assume the same facts as in example (1) except that the adjustments for known changes in cost of service made by the Z Power Commission include an additional depreciation expense that reflects the installation of new equipment put into service on January 1, 1975. Assume further that the reserve for deferred taxes under section 167(l) at the end of 1974 is $1,300,000 and that the monthly net increases for the first 9 months of 1975 are projected to be

January	1-31	$	310,000
February	1-28		300,000
March	1-31		300,000
April	1-30		280,000
May	1-31		270,000
June	1-30		260,000
July	1-31		260,000
August	1-31		250,000
Sept.	1-30		240,000
			$2,470,000

For its regulated books of account X accrues such increases as of the last day of the month but as a matter of convenience credits increases or charges decreases to the reserve account on the 15th day of the month following the whole month for which such increase or decrease is accrued. The maximum amount that may be excluded from the rate base is $2,470,879 (the amount in the reserve at the end of the historical portion of the period ($1,300,000) and a pro rata portion of the amount of any projected increase for the future portion of the period to be credited to the reserve ($1,170,879)). Such pro rata portion is computed (without regard to the date such increase will actually be posted to the account) as follows:

$310,000	×	243/273	=	$ 275,934
300,000	×	215/273	=	236,264
300,000	×	184/273	=	202,198
280,000	×	154/273	=	157,949
270,000	×	123/273	=	121,648
260,000	×	93/273	=	88,571
260,000	×	62/273	=	59,048
250,000	×	31/273	=	28,388
240,000	×	1/273	=	879
				$1,170,879

Example (3). Assume the same facts as in example (1) except that for purposes of establishing cost of service the Z Power Commission uses a future test year (1975). The rates are contemplated to be in effect for 1975, 1976, and 1977. Assume further that plant additions, depreciation expense, and taxes are projected to the end of 1975 and that the reserve for deferred taxes under section 167(l) is $1,300,000 for 1974 and is projected to be $4,400,000 at the end of 1975. Assume also that the Z Power Commission applies the rate of return to X's 1974 rate base of $145,000,000. X and the Z Power Commission through negotiation arrive at the level of approved rates. X uses a normalization method of regulated accounting only if the settlement agreement, the rate order, or record of the proceedings of the Z Power Commission indicates that the Z Power Commission did not exclude an amount representing the reserve for deferred taxes from X's rate base ($145,000,000) greater than $1,300,000 plus a pro rata portion of the projected increases and decreases that are to be credited or charged to the reserve account for 1975. Assume that for 1975 quarterly net increases are projected to be

1st quarter	$	910,000
2nd quarter		810,000
3rd quarter		750,000
4th quarter		630,000
Total		$3,100,000

For its regulated books of account X will accrue such increases as of the last day of the quarter but as a matter of convenience will credit increases or charge decreases to the reserve account on the 15th day of the month following the last month of the quarter for which suce reserve account on the 15th day of the month following the last month of the quarter for which such increase or decrease will be accrued. The maximum amount that may be excluded from the rate base is $2,591,480 (the amount of the reserve at the beginning of the period ($1,300,000) plus a pro rata portion ($1,291,480) of the $3,100,000 projected increase to be credited to the reserve during the period). Such portion is computed (without regard to the date such increase will actually be posted to the account) as follows:

Reg. § 1.167(l)-1(h)(6)

$910,000	× 276/365	=	$ 688,110
810,000	× 185/365	=	410,548
750,000	× 93/365	=	191,096
630,000	× 1/365	=	1,726
			$1,291,480

(i) *Flow-through method of regulated accounting.* Under section 167(l)(3)(H), a taxpayer uses a flow-through method of regulated accounting with respect to public utility property if it uses the same method of depreciation (other than a subsection (l) method) to compute its allowance for depreciation under section 167 and to compute its tax expense for purposes of reflecting operating results in its regulated books of account unless such method is the same method used by the taxpayer to determine its depreciation expense for purposes of reflecting operating results in its regulated books of account. Except as provided in the preceding sentence, the method of depreciation used by a taxpayer with respect to public utility property for purposes of determining cost of service for ratemaking purposes or rate base for ratemaking purposes shall not be considered in determining whether the taxpayer used a flow-through method of regulated accounting. A taxpayer may establish use of a flow-through method of regulated accounting in the same manner that compliance with normalization requirements in respect of operating books of account may be established under paragraph (h)(4) of this section. [Reg. § 1.167(l)-1.]

☐ [*T.D.* 7315, 6-6-74.]

[Reg. § 1.167(l)-2]

§ 1.167(l)-2. **Public utility property; election as to post-1969 property representing growth in capacity.**—(a) *In general.* Section 167(l)(2) prescribes the methods of depreciation which may be used by a taxpayer with respect to its post-1969 public utility property. Under section 167(l)(2)(A) and (B) the taxpayer may use a subsection (l) method of depreciation (as defined in section 167(l)(3)(F)) or any other method of depreciation which is otherwise allowable under section 167 if, in conjunction with the use of such other method, such taxpayer uses the normalization method of accounting (as defined in section 167(l)(3)(G)). Paragraph (2)(C) of section 167(l) permits a taxpayer which used the flow-through method of accounting for its July 1969 accounting period (as these terms are defined in section 167(l)(3)(H) and (I), respectively) to use its applicable 1968 method of depreciation with respect to certain property. Section 167(l)(3)(D) describes the term "applicable 1968 method." Accordingly, a regulatory agency is not precluded by section 167(l) from requiring such a taxpayer subject to its jurisdiction to continue to use the flow-through method of accounting unless the taxpayer makes

the election pursuant to section 167(l)(4)(A) and this section. Whether or not the election is made, if such regulatory agency permits the taxpayer to change from the flow-through method of accounting, subsection (l)(2)(A) or (B) would apply and such taxpayer could, subject to the provisions of section 167(e) and the regulations thereunder (relating to change in method), use a subsection (l) method of depreciation or, if the taxpayer uses the normalization method of accounting, any other method of depreciation otherwise allowable under section 167.

(1) *Election.* Under subparagraph (A) of section 167(l)(4), if the taxpayer so elects, the provisions of paragraph (2)(C) of section 167(l) shall not apply to its qualified public utility property (as such term is described in paragraph (b) of this section). In such case the taxpayer making the election shall use a method of depreciation prescribed by section 167(l)(2)(A) or (B) with respect to such property.

(2) *Property to which election shall apply.* (i) Except as provided in subdivision (ii) of this subparagraph the election provided by section 167(l)(4)(A) shall apply to all of the qualified public utility property of the taxpayer.

(ii) In the event that the taxpayer wishes the election provided by section 167(l)(4)(A) to apply to only a portion of its qualified public utility property, it must clearly identify the property to be subject to the election in the statement of election described in paragraph (e) of this section. Where all property which performs a certain function is included within the election, the election shall apply to all future acquisitions of qualified public utility property which performs the same function. Where only certain property within a functional group of property is included within the election, the election shall apply only to property which is of the same kind as the included property.

(iii) The provisions of subdivision (ii) of this subparagraph may be illustrated by the following examples:

Example (1). Corporation A, an electric utility company, wishes to have the election provided by section 167(l)(4)(A) apply only with respect to its production plant. A statement that the election shall apply only with respect to production plant will be sufficient to include within the election all of the taxpayer's qualified production plant of any kind. All public utility property of the taxpayer other than production plant will not be subject to the election.

Example (2). Corporation B, an electric utility company, wishes to have the election provided by section 167(l)(4)(A) apply only with respect to nuclear production plant. A statement which clearly indicates that only nuclear production plant will be included in the election will be sufficient to exclude from the election all public utility property other than nuclear production plant.

(b) *Qualified public utility property—*(1) *Definition.* For purposes of this section the term "qualified public utility property" means post-1969 public utility property to which section 167(l)(2)(C) applies, or would apply if the election described in section 167(l)(4)(A) had not been made, to the extent that such property constitutes property which increases the productive or operational capacity of the taxpayer with respect to the goods or services described in section 167(l)(3)(A) and does not represent the replacement of existing capacity. In the event that particular assets which are post-1969 public utility property both replace existing public utility property and increase the productive or operational capacity of the taxpayer, only that portion of each such asset which is properly allocable, pursuant to the provisions of subparagraph (3)(v) of this paragraph or paragraph (c)(2) of this section (as the case may be), to increasing the productive or operational capacity of the taxpayer shall be qualified public utility property.

(2) *Limitation on use of formula method.* A taxpayer which makes the election with respect to all of its post-1969 public utility property may determine the amount of its qualified public utility property by using the formula method described in paragraph (c) of this section or, where the taxpayer so chooses, it may use any other method based on engineering data which is satisfactory to the Commissioner. A taxpayer which chooses to include only a portion of its post-1969 public utility property in the election described in paragraph (a)(1) of this section shall, in a manner satisfactory to the Commissioner and consistent with the provisions of subparagraph (3) of this paragraph, use a method based on engineering data. If the taxpayer uses the formula method described in paragraph (c) of this section, it must continue to use such method with respect to additions made in subsequent taxable years. The tax-

payer may change from an engineering method to the formula method described in paragraph (c) of this section by filing a statement described in paragraph (h) of this section if it could have used such formula method for the prior taxable year.

(3) *Measuring capacity under an engineering method in the case of a general election.* (i) The provisions of this subparagraph apply in the case of an election made with respect to all of the post-1969 public utility property of the taxpayer.

(ii) A taxpayer which uses a method based on engineering data to determine the portion of its additions for a taxable year which constitutes qualified public utility property shall make such determination with reference to its "adjusted capacity" as of the first day of the taxable year during which such additions are placed in service. For purposes of this subparagraph, the term "adjusted capacity" means the taxpayer's capacity as of January 1, 1970, adjusted upward in the manner described in subdivision (iii) of this subparagraph for each taxpayer year ending after December 31, 1969, and before the first day of the taxable year during which the additions described in the preceding sentence are placed in service.

(iii) The adjustment described in this subdivision for each taxable year shall be equal to the number of units of capacity by which additions for the taxable year of public utility property with respect to which the election had been made exceed the number of units of capacity of retirements for such taxable year of public utility property with respect to which the flow-through method of accounting was being used at the time of their retirement. If for any taxable year the computation in the preceding sentence results in a negative amount, such negative amount shall be taken into account as a reduction in the amount of the adjustment (computed without regard to this sentence) in succeeding taxable years.

(iv) The provisions of this subparagraph may be illustrated by the following table which assumes that the taxpayer's adjusted capacity as of January 1, 1970, was 5,000 units:

1 Year	2 Additions	3 Flow-through Retirements	4 Net Additions	5 Adjusted Capacity [1]	6 Actual Capacity	7 Units of Qualified Additions [2]
1970	1000	700	300	5000	5300	300
1971	300	500	(200)	5300	5100	...
1972	500	200	300	5300	5400	100
1973	400	800	(400)	5400	5000	...
1974	600	400	200	5400	5200	...
1975	800	300	500	5400	5700	300

[1] Capacity as of January 1, 1970 plus amounts in column 7 for years prior to the year for which determination is being made.

[2] Column 6 minus column 5.

Reg. § 1.167(l)-2(b)(1)

(v) The qualified portion of the basis for depreciation (as defined in section 167(g)) of each asset or group of assets (if group or composite

$$\frac{\text{Qualified portion of basis}}{\text{Total basis of asset}} =$$

(c) *Formula method of determining amount of property subject to election*—(1) *In general.* The following formula method may be used to determine the amount of qualified public utility property:

Step 1. Find the total cost (within the meaning of section 1012) to the taxpayer of additions during the taxable year of all post-1969 public utility property with respect to which section 167(l)(2)(C) would apply if the election had not been made.

Step 2. Aggregate the cost (within the meaning of section 1012) to the taxpayer of all retirements during the taxable year of public utility property with respect to which the flow-through method of accounting was being used at the time of their retirement.

Step 3. Subtract the figure reached in step 2 from the figure reached in step 1.

$$\frac{\text{Amount of qualified additions computed in step 3}}{\text{Amount of total additions computed in step 1}} =$$

(d) *Examples:* The provisions of this section may be illustrated by the following examples:

Example (1). Corporation A, a telephone company subject to the jurisdiction of the Federal Communications Commission, elected, pursuant to the provisions of section 167(l)(4)(A) and this section, with respect to all of its qualified post-1969 public utility property, to have the provisions of paragraph (2)(C) of section 167(l) not apply. In 1971 the Corporation added new underground cable with a cost (within the meaning of section 1012) to it of $4.0 million to its underground cable account. In the same year it retired public utility property with a cost (within the meaning of section 1012) to Corporation A of $1.5 million. The flow-through method of accounting was being used with respect to all of the retired property at the time of retirement. Using

accounting is used by the taxpayer) subject to the election shall be determined using the following ratio:

$$\frac{\text{Units of qualified additions computed in column 7 on chart}}{\text{Units of capacity of additions computed in column 2 on chart}}$$

In the event that the figure reached in step 2 exceeds the figure reached in step 1 such excess shall be carried forward to the next taxable year and shall be aggregated with the cost (within the meaning of section 1012) to the taxpayer of all retirements referred to in step 2 for such next taxable year.

(2) *Allocation of bases.* The amount of qualified public utility property as determined in accordance with the formula method described in subparagraph (1) of this paragraph shall be allocated to the basis for depreciation (as defined in section 167(g)) of each asset or group of assets (if group or composite accounting is used by the taxpayer) subject to the election using the following ratio:

$$\frac{\text{Qualified portion of basis}}{\text{Total basis of asset}} =$$

the formula method described in paragraph (c) of this section, the amount of qualified underground cable would be determined as follows:

Step 1.	Aggregate cost of flow-through additions	$4.0 million
Step 2.	Cost of all flow-through retirements	1.5 million
Step 3.	Figure reached in step 1 less figure reached in step 2	$2.5 million

The amount of qualified public utility property to which section 167(l)(2)(C) will not apply is $2.5 million. Pursuant to the provisions of paragraph (c)(2) of this section, the amount of qualified public utility property would be allocated to the basis for depreciation (as defined in section 167(g)) of an asset with a total basis for depreciation of $2 million as follows:

$$\frac{\$2.5 \text{ million (figure in step 3)}}{\$4 \text{ million (figure in step 1)}} = \frac{\text{Qualified portion of basis of asset}}{\$2 \text{ million}}$$

Qualified portion of basis of asset = $1.25 million

Example (2). In 1972 Corporation A (the corporation described in example (1)) added underground cable with a cost (within the meaning of section 1012) to it of $1.0 million. In the same

Reg. § 1.167(l)-2(d)

year the cost (within the meaning of section 1012) to the corporation of retirements of public utility property with respect to which the flow-through method of accounting was being used was $3.0 million. There were no other additions or retirements. The amount of qualified public utility property would be determined as follows:

Step 1.	Aggregate cost of flow-through additions	$1.0 million
Step 2.	Cost of all flow-through retirements	3.0 million
Step 3.	Figure reached in step 1 less figure reached in step 2 . . .	($2.0 million)

Since retirements of flow-through public utility property for the year 1972 exceeded additions made during such year, the excess retirements, $2.0 million, must be carried forward to be aggregated with retirements for 1973.

Example (3). Corporation *B*, a gas pipeline company subject to the jurisdiction of the Federal Power Commission, made the election provided by section 167(l)(4)(A) and this section with respect to all of its post-1969 public utility property. Corporation *B* chose to use an engineering data method of determining which property was subject to the election provided by this section. In 1970, the corporation replaced a portion of its pipeline with respect to which the flow-through method of accounting was being used at the time of its retirement which had a peak capacity on January 1, 1970 of 100,000 thousand cubic feet (MCF) per day at a pressure of 14.73 pounds per square inch absolute (PSIA) with pipe with a capacity of 125.000 MCF per day at 14.73 PSIA. Assuming that there were no other additions or retirements, using an engineering data method one-fifth of the new pipeline would be property subject to the election of this section effective for its taxable year beginning on January 1, 1971.

Example (4). In 1970 Corporation *C* (with the same characteristics as the corporation described in example (3)) extended its pipeline five miles further than it extended on January 1, 1970. Assuming that there were no other additions or retirements, the entire extension would be property subject to the election provided by this section effective for its taxable year beginning on January 1, 1971.

Example (5). As a result of a change of service areas between two corporations, in 1970 Corporation *D* (with the same characteristics as the corporation described in example (3)) retired a pipeline running north and south and replaced it with a pipeline of equal length and capacity running east and west. No part of the pipeline running east and west is property subject to the election.

(e) *Manner of making election.* The election described in paragraph (a) of this section shall be made by filing, in duplicate, with the Commissioner of Internal Revenue, Washington, D.C. 20224, Attention, T:I:E, a statement of such election.

(f) *Content of statement.* The statement described in paragraph (e) of this section shall indicate that an election is being made under section 167(l) of the Internal Revenue Code of 1954, and it shall contain the following information:

(1) The name, address, and taxpayer identification number of the taxpayer,

(2) Whether the taxpayer will use the formula method of determining the amount of its qualified public utility property described in paragraph (c) of this section, or an engineering method, and

(3) Where the taxpayer wishes to include only a portion of its pubic utility property in the election pursuant to the provisions of paragraph (a)(2) of this section, a description sufficient to clearly identify the property to be included.

(g) *Time for making election.* The election permitted by this section shall be made by filing the statement described in paragraph (e) of this section not later than Monday, June 29, 1970.

(h) *Change of method of determining amount of qualified property.* Where a taxpayer which has elected pursuant to the provisions of section 167(l)(4)(A) wishes to change, pursuant to the provisions of paragraph (b)(2) of this section, from an engineering data method of determining which of its property is qualified public utility property to the formula method described in paragraph (c) of this section, it may do so by filing a statement to that effect at the time that it files its income tax return, with the district director or director of the regional service center, with whom the taxpayer's income tax return is required to be filed.

(i) *Revocability of election.* An election made under section 167(l) shall be irrevocable.

(j) *Effective date.* The election prescribed by section 167(l)(4)(A) and this section shall be effective for taxable years beginning after December 31, 1970. [Reg. § 1.167(l)-2.]

☐ [*T.D. 7045, 6-5-70. Amended by T.D. 7315,* 6-6-74.]

[Reg. § 1.167(l)-3]

§ 1.167(l)-3. **Multiple regulation, asset acquisitions, reorganizations, etc.**—(a) *Property not entirely subject to jurisdiction of one regulatory body*—(1) *In general.* If a taxpayer which uses a method of depreciation other than a subsection (l) method of depreciation is required by regulatory body having jurisdiction over less than all of its property to use, or not to use a method of regulated accounting (i.e., normalization or flow-through), such taxpayer shall be considered as using, or not using, such method of regulated accounting only with respect to property subject to the jurisdiction of such regulatory body. In the case of property which is contained in a multiple asset account, the provisions of § 1.167(a)-7(c) and § 1.167(a)-11(c)(1)(iv) to prohibit depreciating a single account by two or more different methods.

(2) *Jurisdiction of regulatory body.* For purposes of this paragraph, a regulatory body is considered to have jurisdiction over property of a taxpayer if expenses with respect to the property area included in cost of service as determined by the regulatory body for ratemaking purposes or for reflecting operating results in its regulated books of account. For example, if regulatory body A, having jurisdiction over 60 percent of an item of X corporation's public utility property, required X to use the flow-through method of regulated accounting in circumstances which would bar X from using a method of depreciation under section 167(a) other than a subsection (l) method, and if regulatory body B, having jurisdiction over the remaining 40 percent of such item of property does not so require X to use the flow-through method of regulated accounting (or if the remaining 40 percent is not subject to the jurisdiction of any regulatory body), then with respect to 60 percent of the adjusted basis of the property X is prohibited from using a method of depreciation for purposes of section 167(a) other than a subsection (l) method. If in such example, A, having jurisdiction over 60 percent of X's public utility property, had jurisdiction over 100 percent of a particular generator, then with respect to the generator X would be prohibited from using a method of depreciation other than a subsection (l) method.

(3) *Public utility property subject to more than one regulatory body.* If a regulatory body having jurisdiction over public utility property with respect to the taxpayer's regulated books of account requires the taxpayer to reflect its tax expense in such books in the manner used by the regulatory body having jurisdiction over the public utility property for purposes of determining the taxpayer's cost of service for ratemaking purposes, the rules of subparagraphs (1) and (2) of this paragraph shall apply.

(b) *Leasing transactions—*(1) *Leased property.* Public utility property as defined in paragraph (b) of § 1.167(l)-1 includes property which is leased by a taxpayer where the leasing of such property is part of the lessor's section 167(l) public utility activity. Thus, such leased property qualifies as public utility property even though the predominant use of such property by the lessee is in other than a section 167(l) public utility activity. Further, leased property qualifies as public utility property under section 167(l) even though the leasing is not part of the lessor's public utility activity if the predominant use of such property by the lessee or any sublessee is in a section 167(l) public utility activity. However, the limitations of section 167(l) apply to a taxpayer only if such taxpayer is subject to the jurisdiction of a regulatory body described in section 167(l)(3)(A). For example, if a financial institution purchases property which it then leases to a lessee which uses such property predominantly in a section 167(l) public utility activity, the property qualifies as public utility property. However, because the financial institution's rates for leasing the property are not subject to the jurisdiction of a regulatory body described in section 167(l)(3)(A), the provisions of section 167(l) do not apply to the depreciation deductions taken with respect to the property by the financial institution. For possible application of section 167(l) to the lessee, see subparagraph (2) of this paragraph.

(2) *Certain rental payments.* Under section 167(l)(5), if a taxpayer leases property which is public utility property and the regulatory body having jurisdiction over such property for purposes of determining the taxpayer's operating results in its regulated books of account or for ratemaking purposes allows only an amount of such lessee's expenses with respect to the lease which is less than the amount which the taxpayer deducts for purposes of its Federal income tax liability, then a portion of the difference between such amounts shall not be allowed as a deduction by the taxpayer for purposes of its Federal income tax liability in such manner and time as the Commissioner or his delegate may determine consistent with the principles of § 1.167(l)-1 and this section applicable as to when a method of depreciation other than a subsection (l) method may be used for purposes of section 167(a).

(c) *Certain partnership arrangements.* Under section 167(l)(5), if property held by a partnership is not public utility property in the hands of the partnership but would be public utility property if an election was made under section 761 to be excluded from partnership treatment, then section 167(l) shall be applied by treating the partners as directly owning the property in proportion to their partnership interests.

(d) *Cross reference.* See § 1.167(l)-1(c)(1) for treatment of certain property as "pre-1970 public utility property" and § 1.167(l)-1(e)(4)(ii) for applicable 1968 method in the case of property acquired in certain transactions. [Reg. § 1.167(l)-3.]

□ [*T.D. 7315, 6-6-74.*]

[Reg. § 1.167(l)-4]

§ 1.167(l)-4. Public utility property; election to use asset depreciation range system.—(a) *Application of section 167(l) to certain property subject to asset depreciation range system.* If the taxpayer elects to compute depreciation under the asset depreciation range system described in § 1.167(a)-11 with respect to certain public utility property placed in service after December 31, 1970, see § 1.167(a)-11(b)(6). [Reg. § 1.167(l)-4.]

□ [*T.D. 7128, 6-22-71. Amended by T.D. 7315, 6-6-74.*]

[Reg. § 1.167(m)-1]

§ 1.167(m)-1. Class lives.—(a) For rules regarding the election to use the class life system

If the recovery year is:			
1	100		
2			
3			
4			

(ii) The provisions of paragraph (a)(1)(i) of this section do not apply to any taxpayer who did not use the RRB method of depreciation under section 167 as of December 31, 1980. In such case, RRB replacement property placed in service by the taxpayer after December 31, 1980, shall be treated as other 5-year recovery property under section 168.

(2) *RRB replacement property placed in service after December 31, 1984.* RRB replacement property placed in service after December 31, 1984, is treated as other 5-year recovery property under section 168.

(3) *RRB replacement property defined.* RRB replacement property, for purposes of section 168, means replacement track material (including rail, ties, other track material, and ballast) installed by a railroad (including a railroad switching or terminal company) if—

(i) The replacement is made pursuant to a scheduled program for replacement,

(ii) The replacement is made pursuant to observations by maintenance-of-way personnel of specific track material needing replacement,

(iii) The replacement is made pursuant to the detection by a rail-test car of specific track material needing replacement, or

authorized by section 167(m), see the provisions of § 1.167(a)-11. [Reg. § 1.167(m)-1.]

□ [*T.D. 7272, 4-20-73.*]

[Reg. § 1.168-5]

§ 1.168-5. Special rules.—(a) *Retirement-replacement-betterment (RRB) property*—(1) *RRB replacement property placed in service before January 1, 1985.* (i) Except as provided in paragraph (a)(1)(ii) of this section, the recovery deduction for the taxable year for retirement-replacement-betterment (RRB) replacement property (as defined in paragraph (a)(3) of this section) placed in service before January 1, 1985, shall be (in lieu of the amount determined under section 168(b)) an amount determined by applying to the unadjusted basis (as defined in section 168(d)(1) and regulations thereunder) of such property the applicable percentage determined in accordance with the following table:

	And the year the property is placed in service is:			
	1981	1982	1983	1984
	The applicable percentage is:			
1	100	50	33	25
2		50	45	38
3			22	25
4				12

(iv) The replacement is made as a result of a casualty.

Replacements made as a result of a casualty shall be RRB replacement property only to the extent that, in the case of each casualty, the replacement cost with respect to the replacement track material exceeds $50,000.

(4) *Recovery of adjusted basis of RRB property as of December 31, 1980.* The taxpayer shall recover the adjusted basis of RRB property (as defined in section 168(g)(6)) as of December 31, 1980, over a period of not less than 5 years and not more than 50 years, using a rate of recovery consistent with any method described in section 167(b), including the method described in section 167(b)(2), switching to the method described in section 167(b)(3) at a time to maximize the deduction. For purposes of determining the recovery allowance under this subparagraph, salvage value shall be disregarded and, in the case of a taxpayer that depreciated RRB property placed in service before January 1, 1981, using the RRB method consistently for all periods after February 28, 1913, the adjusted basis of RRB property is the adjusted basis for purposes of determining the deduction for retirements under the RRB method, with no adjustment for depreciation sustained prior to March 1, 1913.

Reg. § 1.167(l)-4(a)

(5) *RRB property (which is not RRB replacement property) placed in service after December 31, 1980.* Property placed in service by the taxpayer after December 31, 1980, which is not RRB replacement property and which, under the taxpayer's method of depreciation as of December 31, 1980, would have been depreciated by the taxpayer under the RRB method, is treated as other property under section 168.

(b)-(f) [Reserved]

[Reg. § 1.168-5.]

☐ [*T.D.* 8116, 12-23-86.]

[Reg. § 1.168(d)-0]

§ 1.168(d)-0. **Table of contents for the applicable convention rules.**—This section lists the major paragraphs in § 1.168(d)-1.

§ *1.168(d)-1. Applicable conventions—Half-year and mid-quarter conventions.*

(a) In general.

(b) Additional rules for determining whether the mid-quarter convention applies and for applying the applicable convention.

(1) Property described in section 168(f).

(2) Listed property.

(3) Property placed in service and disposed of in the same taxable year.

(4) Aggregate basis of property.

(5) Special rules for affiliated groups.

(6) Special rule for partnerships and S corporations.

(7) Certain nonrecognition transactions.

(c) Disposition of property subject to the half-year or mid-quarter convention.

(1) In general.

(2) Example.

(d) Effective date. [Reg. § 1.158(d)-0.]

☐ [*T.D.* 8444, 10-28-92.]

[Reg. § 1.168(d)-1]

§ 1.168(d)-1. **Applicable conventions—Half-year and mid-quarter conventions.**—(a) *In general.* Under section 168(d), the half-year convention applies to depreciable property (other than certain real property described in section 168(d)(2)) placed in service during a taxable year, unless the mid-quarter convention applies to the property. Under section 168(d)(3)(A), the mid-quarter convention applies to depreciable property (other than certain real property described in section 168(d)(2)) placed in service during a taxable year if the aggregate basis of property placed in service during the last three months of the taxable year exceeds 40 percent of the aggregate

basis of property placed in service during the taxable year ("the 40-percent test"). Thus, if the depreciable property is placed in service during a taxable year that consists of three months or less, the mid-quarter convention applies to the property. Under section 168(d)(3)(B)(i), the depreciable basis of nonresidential real property, residential rental property, and any railroad grading or tunnel bore is disregarded in applying the 40-percent test. For rules regarding property that is placed in service and disposed of in the same taxable year, see paragraph (b)(3) of this section. For the definition of "aggregate basis of property," see paragraph (b)(4) of this section.

(b) *Additional rules for determining whether the mid-quarter convention applies and for applying the applicable convention*—(1) *Property described in section 168(f).* In determining whether the 40-percent test is satisfied for a taxable year, the depreciable basis of property described in section 168(f) (property to which section 168 does not apply) is not taken into account.

(2) *Listed property.* The depreciable basis of listed property (as defined in section 280F(d)(4) and the regulations thereunder) placed in service during a taxable year is taken into account (unless otherwise excluded) in applying the 40-percent test.

(3) *Property placed in service and disposed of in the same taxable year*—(i) Under section 168(d)(3)(B)(ii), the depreciable basis of property placed in service and disposed of in the same taxable year is not taken into account in determining whether the 40-percent test is satisfied. However, the depreciable basis of property placed in service, disposed of, subsequently reacquired, and again placed in service in the same taxable year must be taken into account in applying the 40-percent test, but the basis of the property is only taken into account on the later of the dates that the property is placed in service during the taxable year.

(ii) The applicable convention, as determined under this section, applies to all depreciable property (except nonresidential real property, residential rental property, and any railroad grading or tunnel bore) placed in service during the taxable year, excluding property placed in service and disposed of in the same taxable year. No depreciation deduction is allowed for property placed in service and disposed of during the same taxable year.

(iii) The provisions of this paragraph (b)(3) are illustrated by the following examples.

Example 1. During 1990, A, a calendar-year taxpayer, purchases a light general purpose truck costing $8,000, an office desk costing $500,

Reg. § 1.168(d)-1(b)(3)

a safe costing $1,000, and a computer costing $3,000. The truck is placed in service in January, the desk and safe in August, and the computer in November. These are the only items placed in service during 1990. In September, A sells the truck and the desk. Thus, the truck and the desk were placed in service and disposed of in the same taxable year. Therefore, the depreciable basis of the truck and the desk are not taken into account in determining whether the mid-quarter convention applies to depreciable property placed in service during 1990. Because the computer was placed in service during the last three months of the taxable year and its basis ($3,000) exceeds 40 percent of the aggregate basis of depreciable property placed in service during the taxable year (safe and computer with an aggregate basis of $4,000), the mid-quarter convention applies to the safe and the computer. No depreciation is allowed with respect to the truck and desk because they were placed in service and disposed of in the same taxable year.

Example 2. The facts are the same as in *Example 1,* except that, in December, A reacquires the truck for $7,000. Thus, the truck is considered placed in service in December and its basis is included in determining whether the mid-quarter convention applies. The mid-quarter convention is applicable, because the computer ($3,000) and the truck ($7,000) are placed in service during the last three months of the taxable year and their aggregate basis ($10,000) exceeds 40 percent of the aggregate basis of property placed in service during the taxable year (safe, computer, and truck with an aggregate basis of $11,000).

(4) *Aggregate basis of property.* For purposes of the 40-percent test, the term "aggregate basis of property" means the sum of the depreciable bases of all items of depreciable property that are taken into account in applying the 40-percent test. "Depreciable basis" means the basis of depreciable property for purposes of determining gain under sections 1011 through 1024. The depreciable basis for the taxable year the property is placed in service reflects the reduction in basis for—

(i) Any portion of the basis the taxpayer properly elects to treat as an expense under section 179;

(ii) Any adjustment to basis under section 48(q); and

(iii) The percentage of the taxpayer's use of property for the taxable year other than in the taxpayer's trade or business (or for the production of income), but is determined before any reduc-

tion for depreciation under section 167(a) for that taxable year.

(5) *Special rules for affiliated groups*—(i) In the case of a consolidated group (as defined in § 1.1502-1(h)), all members of the group that are included on the consolidated return are treated as one taxpayer for purposes of applying the 40-percent test. Thus, the depreciable bases of all property placed in service by members of a consolidated group during a consolidated return year are taken into account (unless otherwise excluded) in applying the 40-percent test to determine whether the mid-quarter convention applies to property placed in service by the members during the consolidated return year. The 40-percent test is applied separately to the depreciable bases of property placed in service by any member of an affiliated group that is not included in a consolidated return for the taxable year in which the property is placed in service.

(ii) In the case of a corporation formed by a member or members of a consolidated group and that is itself a member of the consolidated group ("newly-formed subsidiary"), the depreciable bases of property placed in service by the newly-formed subsidiary in the consolidated return year in which it is formed is included with the depreciable bases of property placed in service during the consolidated return year by the other members of the consolidated group in applying the 40-percent test. If depreciable property is placed in service by a newly-formed subsidiary during the consolidated return year in which it was formed, the newly-formed subsidiary is considered as being in existence for the entire consolidated return year for purposes of applying the applicable convention to determine when the recovery period begins.

(iii) The provisions of paragraph (b)(5)(ii) of this section are illustrated by the following example.

Example. Assume a member of a consolidated group that files its return on a calendar-year basis forms a subsidiary on August 1. The subsidiary places depreciable property in service on August 5. If the mid-quarter convention applies to property placed in service by the members of the consolidated group (including the newly-formed subsidiary), the property placed in service by the subsidiary on August 5 is deemed placed in service on the mid-point of the third quarter of the consolidated return year (*i.e.,* August 15). If the mid-quarter convention does not apply, the property is deemed placed in service on the mid-point of the consolidated return year (*i.e.,* July 1).

(iv) In the case of a corporation that joins or leaves a consolidated group, the depreciable

Reg. § 1.168(d)-1(b)(4)

bases of property placed in service by the corporation joining or leaving the group during the portion of the consolidated return year that the corporation is a member of the consolidated group is included with the depreciable bases of property placed in service during the consolidated return year by the other members in applying the 40-percent test. The depreciable bases of property placed in service by the joining or leaving member in the taxable year before it joins or after it leaves the consolidated group is not taken into account by the consolidated group in applying the 40-percent test for the consolidated return year. If a corporation leaves a consolidated group and joins another consolidated group, each consolidated group takes into account, in applying the 40-percent test, the depreciable bases of property placed in service by the corporation while a member of the group.

(v) The provisions of paragraph (b)(5)(iv) of this section are illustrated by the following example.

Example. Assume Corporations A and B file a consolidated return on a calendar-year basis. Corporation C, also a calendar-year taxpayer, enters the consolidated group on July 1 and is included on the consolidated return for that taxable year. The depreciable bases of property placed in service by C during the period of July 1 to December 31 is included with the depreciable bases of property placed in service by A and B during the entire consolidated return year in applying the 40-percent test. The depreciable bases of property placed in service by C from January 1 to June 30 is not taken into account by the consolidated group in applying the 40-percent test. If C was a member of another consolidated group during the period from January 1 to June 30, that consolidated group would include the depreciable bases of property placed in service by C during that period.

(vi) A corporation that joins or leaves a consolidated group during a consolidated year is considered as being a member of the consolidated group for the entire consolidated return year for purposes of applying the applicable convention to determine when the recovery period begins for depreciable property placed in service by the corporation during the portion of the consolidated return year that the corporation is a member of the group.

(vii) If depreciable property is placed in service by a corporation in the taxable year ending immediately before it joins a consolidated group or beginning immediately after it leaves a consolidated group, the applicable convention is applied to the property under either the full taxable year rules or the short taxable year rules, as applicable.

(viii) The provisions of paragraphs (d)(5)(vi) and (vii) of this section are illustrated by the following example.

Example. Assume that on July 1, C, a calendar-year corporation, joins a consolidated group that files a return on a calendar-year basis. The short taxable year rules apply to C for the period of January 1 to June 30. However, in applying the applicable convention to determine when the recovery period begins for depreciable property placed in service for the period of July 1 to December 31, C is considered as being a member of the consolidated group for the entire consolidated return year. Thus, if the half-year convention applies to depreciable property placed in service by the consolidated group (taking into account the depreciable bases of property placed in service by C after June 30), the property is deemed placed in service on the mid-point of the consolidated return year (*i.e.,* July 1, if the group did not have a short taxable year).

(ix) In the case of a transfer of depreciable property between members of a consolidated group, the following special rules apply for purposes of applying the 40-percent test. Property that is placed in service by one member of a consolidated group and transferred to another member of the same group is considered as placed in service on the date that it is placed in service by the transferor member, and the date it is placed in service by the transferee member is disregarded. In the case of multiple transfers of property between members of a consolidated group, the property is considered as placed in service on the date that the first member places the property in service, and the dates it is placed in service by other members are disregarded. The depreciable basis of the transferred property that is taken into account in applying the 40-percent test is the depreciable basis of the property in the hands of the transferor member (as determined under paragraph (b)(4) of this section), or, in the case of multiple transfers of property between members, the depreciable basis in the hands of the first member that placed the property in service.

(x) The provisions of paragraph (b)(5)(ix) of this section are illustrated by the following example.

Example. Assume the ABC consolidated group files its return on a calendar-year basis. A, a member of the consolidated group, purchases depreciable property costing $50,000 and places the property in service on January 5, 1991. On December 1, 1991, the property is transferred for $75,000 to B, another member of the consolidated group. In applying the 40-percent test to the members of the consolidated group for 1991, the property is considered as placed in service on January 5, the date that A placed the property in service, and the depreciable basis of the property that is taken into account is $50,000.

(6) *Special rule for partnerships and S corporations.* In the case of property placed in service by a partnership or an S corporation, the 40-percent test is generally applied at the partnership or corporate level. However, if a partnership or an S corporation is formed or availed of for the principal purpose of either avoiding the application of the mid-quarter convention or having the mid-quarter convention apply where it otherwise would not, the 40-percent test is applied at the partner, shareholder, or other appropriate level.

(7) *Certain nonrecognition transactions*—(i) Except as provided in paragraph (b)(6) of this section, if depreciable property is transferred in a transaction described in section 168(i)(7)(B)(i) (other than in a transaction between members of a consolidated group) in the same taxable year that the property is placed in service by the transferor, the 40-percent test is applied by treating the transferred property as placed in service by the transferee on the date of transfer. Thus, if the aggregate basis of property (including the transferred property) placed in service by the transferee during the last three months of its taxable year exceeds 40 percent of the aggregate basis of property (including the transferred property) placed in service by the transferee during the taxable year, the mid-quarter convention applies to the transferee's depreciable property, including the transferred property. The depreciable basis of the transferred property is not taken into account by the transferor in applying the 40-percent test for the taxable year that the transferor placed the property in service.

(ii) In applying the applicable convention to determine when the recovery period for the transferred property begins, the date on which the transferor placed the property in service must be used. Thus, for example, if the mid-quarter convention applies, the recovery period for the transferred property begins on the mid-point of the quarter of the taxable year that the transferor placed the property in service. If the transferor placed the transferred property in service in a short taxable year, then for purposes of applying the applicable convention and allocating the depreciation deduction between the transferor and the transferee, the transferor is treated as having a full 12-month taxable year commencing on the first day of the short taxable year. The depreciation deduction for the transferor's taxable year in

which the property was placed in service is allocated between the transferor and the transferee based on the number of months in the transferor's taxable year that each party held the property in service. For purposes of allocating the depreciation deduction, the transferor takes into account the month in which the property was placed in service but does not take into account the month in which the property was transferred. The transferee is allocated the remaining portion of the depreciation deduction for the transferor's taxable year in which the property was transferred. For the remainder of the transferee's current taxable year (if the transferee has a different taxable year than the transferor) and for subsequent taxable years, the depreciation deduction for the transferee is calculated by allocating to the transferee's taxable year the depreciation attributable to each recovery year, or portion thereof, that falls within the transferee's taxable year.

(iii) If the applicable convention for the transferred property has not been determined by the time the transferor files its income tax return for the year of transfer because the transferee's taxable year has not ended, the transferor may use either the mid-quarter or the half-year convention in determining the depreciation deduction for the property. However, the transferor must specify on the depreciation form filed for the taxable year that the applicable convention has not been determined for the property. If the transferee determines that a different convention applies to the transferred property, the transferor should redetermine the depreciation deduction on the property, and, within the period of limitation, should file an amended income tax return for the taxable year and pay any additional tax due plus interest.

(iv) The provisions of this paragraph (b)(7) are illustrated by the following example.

Example. (i) During 1991, C, a calendar-year taxpayer, purchases satellite equipment costing $100,000, and computer equipment costing $15,000. The satellite equipment is placed in service in January, and the computer equipment in February. On October 1, C transfers the computer equipment to Z Partnership in a transaction described in section 721. During 1991, Z, a calendar-year partnership, purchases 30 office desks for a total of $15,000. The desks are placed in service in June. These are the only items of depreciable property placed in service by C and Z during 1991.

(ii) In applying the 40-percent test, because C transferred the computer equipment in a transaction described in section 168(i)(7)(B)(i) in the same taxable year that C placed it in service,

Reg. § 1.168(d)-1(b)(6)

the computer equipment is treated as placed in service by the transferee, Z, on the date of transfer, October 1. The 40-percent test is satisfied with respect to Z, because the computer equipment is placed in service during the last three months of Z's taxable year and its basis ($15,000) exceeds 40 percent of the aggregate basis of property placed in service by Z during the taxable year (desks and computer equipment with an aggregate basis of $30,000).

(iii) In applying the mid-quarter convention to determine when the computer equipment is deemed to be placed in service, the date on which C placed the property in service is used. Accordingly, because C placed the computer equipment in service during the first quarter of its taxable year, the computer equipment is deemed placed in service on February 15, 1991, the mid-point of the first quarter of C's taxable year. The depreciation deduction allowable for C's 1991 taxable year, $5,250 ($15,000 × 40 percent × 10.5/12), is allocated between C and Z based on the number of months in C's taxable year that C and Z held the property in service. Thus, because the property was in service for 11 months during C's 1991 taxable year and C held it for 8 of those 11 months, C is allocated $3,818 (8/11 × $5,250). Z is allocated $1,432, the remaining 3/11 of the $5,250 depreciation deduction for C's 1991 taxable year. For 1992, Z's depreciation deduction for the computer equipment is $3,900, the sum of the remaining 1.5 months of depreciation deduction for the first recovery year and 10.5 months of depreciation deduction for the second recovery year (($15,000 × 40 percent × 1.5/12) + ($9,000 × 40 percent × 10.5/12)).

(c) *Disposition of property subject to the half-year or mid-quarter convention*—(1) *In general.* If depreciable property is subject to the half-year (or mid-quarter) convention in the taxable year in which it is placed in service, it also is subject to the half-year (or mid-quarter) convention in the taxable year in which it is disposed of.

(2) *Example.* The provisions of paragraph (c)(1) of this section are illustrated by the following example.

Example. In October 1991, B, a calendar-year taxpayer, purchases and places in service a light general purpose truck costing $10,000. B does not elect to expense any part of the cost of the truck, and this is the only item of depreciable property placed in service by B during 1991. The 40-percent test is satisfied and the mid-quarter convention applies, because the truck is placed in service during the last three months of the taxable year and no other assets are placed in service in

that year. In April 1993 (prior to the end of the truck's recovery period), B sells the truck. The mid-quarter convention applies in determining the depreciation deduction for the truck in 1993, the year of disposition.

(d) *Effective date.* This section applies to depreciable property placed in service in taxable years ending after January 30, 1991. For depreciable property placed in service after December 31, 1986, in taxable years ending on or before January 30, 1991, a taxpayer may use a method other than the method provided in this section in applying the 40-percent test and the applicable convention, provided the method is reasonable and is consistently applied to the taxpayer's property. [Reg. § 1.168(d)-1.]

☐ [*T.D.* 8444, 1C-28-92.]

[Reg. § 5c.168(f)(8)-1]

§ 5c.168(f)(8)-1 **Special rules for leases (Temporary).**—(a) *In general.* Section 168(f)(8) of the Internal Revenue Code of 1954 provides special rules for characterizing certain agreements as leases and characterizing the parties to the agreement as lessors and lessees for Federal tax law purposes. These rules apply only with respect to qualified leased property. If all the requirements of section 168(f)(8) and §§ 5c.168(f)(8)-2 through 5c.168(f)(8)-11 are met, then the agreement shall be treated as a lease, and the party characterized as the lessor shall be treated as the owner of the property. In such case, the lessor shall be deemed to have entered into the lease in the course of carrying on a trade or business and shall be allowed accelerated cost recovery system (ACRS) deductions under section 168 and the investment tax credit under section 38 with respect to the leased property.

(b) *Exception for qualified research expenditures.* For purposes of section 44F(b)(2)(A)(iii), the determination of whether any amount is paid or incurred to another person for the right to use personal property in the conduct of qualified research shall be made without regard to the characterization of the transaction as a lease under section 168(f)(8). Thus, if a lessee would be considered the owner of the property without regard to section 168(f)(8), any amounts paid by the lessee under the lease shall not be considered amounts paid or incurred for the right to use the property.

(c) *Other factors disregarded.* If an agreement meets the requirements of section 168(f)(8) and §§ 5c.168(f)(8)-2 through 5c.168(f)(8)-11, the following factors will not be taken into account in determining whether the transaction is a lease:

(1) Whether the lessor or lessee must take the tax benefits into account in order to determine that a profit is made from the transaction;

(2) The fact that the lessee is the nominal owner of the property for State or local law purposes (e.g., has legal title to the property) and retains the burdens, benefits, and incidents of ownership (such as payment of taxes and maintenance charges with respect to the property);

(3) Whether or not a person other than the lessee may be able to use the property after the lease term;

(4) The fact that the property may (or must) be bought or sold at the end of the lease term at a fixed or determinable price that is more or less than its fair market value at that time;

(5) The fact that the lessee or related party has provided financing or has guaranteed financing for the transaction (other than for the lessor's minimum 10 percent investment); and

(6) The fact that the obligation of any person is subject to any contingency or offset agreement. See, for example, the rent and debt service offset in Example (2) of paragraph (e).

An agreement that meets the requirements of section 168(f)(8) and §§ 5c.168(f)(8)-2 through §§ 5c.168(f)(8)-11 may be treated by the parties as a lease for Federal tax law purposes only. Similarly, a sale by the lessee of the leased property to the lessor in a transaction where the property is leased back under an agreement that meets the requirements of section 168(f)(8) may be treated by the parties as a sale for Federal tax law purposes only. The agreements need not comply with State law requirements concerning transfer of title, recording, etc.

(d) *Ownership in one of the parties.* Notwithstanding any other section, if neither the lessor nor the lessee would be the owner of the property without regard to section 168(f)(8), or, if any party with an economic interest in the property (other than the lessor or lessee or any subsequent transferee of their interests) claims ACRS deductions or any investment tax credit with respect to the leased property, an election under section 168(f)(8) with respect to such property shall be void as of the date of the execution of the lease agreement.

(e) *Examples.* The application of section 168(f)(8) and §§ 5c.168(f)(8)-2 through 5c.168(f)(8)-11 may be illustrated by the following examples:

Example (1). X Corp. wishes to acquire a $1 million piece of equipment which is "qualified leased property" as defined in section 168(f)(8)(D). The equipment has a 10-year eco-

nomic life and falls within the 5-year ACRS class. Y Corp. is a person meeting the qualifications set forth in section 168(f)(8)(B)(i) and § 5c.168(f)(8)-3 and wishes to be the owner of the property for Federal tax law purposes. Y therefore purchases the equipment from the manufacturer for $1 million, paying $200,000 in cash and borrowing $800,000 from a bank (payable over 9 years and requiring nine equal annual payments of principal and interest of $168,000). Y then leases the equipment to X under an agreement providing for nine annual rental payments of $168,000, and the parties elect in accordance with the provisions of § 5c.168(f)(8)-2 to have the provisions of section 168(f)(8) apply. The timing and amount of the rental payments required to be made by X (the "lessee-user") under the lease will be exactly equal to the timing and amount of the principal and interest payments that Y (the "lessor") will be required to make to the bank under its purchase money note. Under these circumstances, Y is treated as the owner and lessor of the property for Federal tax law purposes; it therefore is entitled to the investment tax credit and the ACRS deductions with respect to the property. Y's basis in the property is $1 million. Y must report the rent as income and will be entitled to deduct the interest on the purchase money note. The aggregate payments required to be made by X under the lease are treated as rent in accordance with § 5c.168(f)(8)-7 and are deductible as such.

Example (2). The facts are the same as in example (1) except that X purchases the equipment for $1 million and wishes to transfer ownership of the property for Federal tax law purposes to Y under a sale and leaseback arrangement. Accordingly, X sells the property to Y for $200,000 in cash (which represents the agreed upon compensation for the tax benefits to be enjoyed by Y as lessor) plus a 9-year, $800,000 note calling for nine $168,000 annual payments of principal and interest. Y then leases the property back to X under an agreement providing for nine annual rental payments of $168,000. The parties elect in accordance with the provisions of § 5c.168(f)(8)-2 to have the provisions of section 168(f)(8) apply. The timing and amount of the rental payments required to be made by X (as the lessee-user) under the lease will be exactly equal to the timing and amount of the principal and interest payments that Y will be required to make to X under Y's purchase money note, so that the only cash transferred between X and Y is the $200,000 down payment. Y's obligation to make debt service payments on the note is contingent on X's obligation to make rental payments under the lease. Under these circumstances, Y is treated

Reg. § 5c.168(f)(8)-1(c)(1)

as the owner and lessor of the property for Federal tax law purposes; it therefore is entitled to the investment tax credit and ACRS deductions with respect to the property. Y's basis in the property is $1 million. Y must report the rent as income and will be entitled to deduct the interest on the purchase money note. No gain or loss will be recognized by X on the sale of the property since the sale price equals X's basis in the property. X must report as income the interest paid by Y on the note and will be entitled to a deduction for the rental payments it makes under the lease in accordance with § 5c.168(f)(8)-7.

Example (3). Assume that in both examples (1) and (2) X has an option to purchase the equipment at the end of the lease term for $1.00. The fact that the property may (or must) be bought or sold at the end of the lease term at a fixed or determinable price that is more or less than its fair market value is not taken into account in determining the status of the transactions as leases under section 168(f)(8). [Temporary Reg. § 5c.168(f)(8)-1.]

☐ *[T.D. 7791, 10-20-81. Amended by T.D. 7795, 11-10-81.]*

[Reg. § 5f.168(f)(8)-1]

§ 5f.168(f)(8)-1. Questions and answers concerning transitional rules and related matters regarding certain safe harbor leases (Temporary).—The following questions and answers concern the transitional rules and related matters regarding certain safe harbor leases under section 208(d) of the Tax Equity and Fiscal Responsibility Act of 1982 (Public Law 97-248) ("TEFRA"):

Q-1: If a lessee, prior to the period beginning after December 31, 1980, and ending before July 2, 1982 (the "window period"), enters into a binding contract to acquire property and the property is delivered to the lessee during the window period, is the property eligible for the transitional rule provided in section 208(d)(3) of TEFRA which applies the safe harbor leasing rules of section 168(f)(8) of the Internal Revenue Code of 1954 as in effect before the enactment of TEFRA?

A-1: Yes, assuming all other requirements of the TEFRA transitional rules are met. Section 208(d)(3)(A)(i) and (ii) of TEFRA provide alternative tests under which an item of property may constitute "transitional safe harbor lease property" for purposes of the transitional rules under the modifications to the safe harbor lease provisions of section 168(f)(8). The tests are:

(i) The lessee entered into a binding contract to acquire the property;

(ii) The lessee entered into a binding contract to construct the property;

(iii) The property was acquired by the lessee; or

(iv) Construction of the property was commenced by or for the lessee.

These tests are stated in the alternative, and, accordingly, property may be eligible for pre-TEFRA safe harbor leasing if any one of the tests is satisfied. Thus, if a lessee acquired property during the window period, the property may be eligible for pre-TEFRA safe harbor leasing even though a binding contract to acquire the property was executed before the window period. Similarly, if construction of property commences during the window period, the property may be eligible for pre-TEFRA safe harbor leasing even though a binding contract to construct the property was executed before the window period.

Q-2: How do the transitional rules apply to components of an integrated manufacturing, production, or extraction process, none of which would be considered "placed in service" until all of the components are placed in service?

A-2: (i) The transitional rules regarding acquisition, binding contracts, and commencement of construction are applied to each separate item of property which is part of a manufacturing, production, or extraction process. What constitutes a separate item will be determined on a case-by-case basis, taking into account all relevant factors. In general, a discrete component capable of performing a function which is separate from or in addition to the function of other components to which it may be related is a separate item of property; but an item that is integrated into a component which performs a function separate from other components to which it is related is not itself a separate item of property. For example, a bolt or a nut that is used to construct a machine does not constitute a separate item of property. On the other hand, the transitional rules will not be applied to an entire facility as a whole, as was the case under the investment tax credit transition rule of section 50 in *Hawaiian Independent Refinery, Inc. v. United States,* 49 AFTR2d 675 (Ct. Cl. Tr. Judge 1982), where the taxpayer was held to have constructed a property which consisted of an entire refinery complex. Thus, for example, for purposes of these transitional rules, an oil or gas well, storage tanks, and pipeline located on a lease would not be considered a single item of property. Although each item is related to the production of oil or gas, each is discrete and each is capable of performing a separate function from the other. In addition, in the case of an integrated manufacturing, production, or extraction process, commencement of construction of one item of property within the process would not be considered construction of any other item of property that is part of the process.

(ii) If property qualifies as transitional safe harbor lease property, all direct and indirect costs allocable to the property (except for those described in § 5c.168(f)(8)-6(a)(2)(ii)) and required to be capitalized for Federal income tax purposes will also qualify as transitional safe harbor lease property to the extent such costs are incurred on or before the date on which the property is leased under section 168(f)(8).

(iii) The adjusted basis to the lessor of property leased on or prior to December 1, 1982, under a transitional safe harbor lease shall be deemed to include all direct and indirect costs (including installation costs) described in subdivision (ii) allocable to such property that were incurred before it was leased despite the fact that such costs were not included in the lessor's adjusted basis of such property under the terms of the lease agreement, provided that the parties to such agreement reasonably believed that they had leased the whole of such property. Such costs will be treated as having been included in the lessor's adjusted basis of such safe harbor lease property on the date the lease agreement was executed without regard to any provisions in the lease agreement that limits the dollar amount of the permissible adjustment of the lessor's adjusted basis to such property. To qualify for inclusion of such direct and indirect costs within the basis of such property, the parties to such agreement must file an amended Form 6793, the Safe Harbor Lease Information Return, no later than April 21, 1983, which reflects the parties' intent to include installation and other such costs within the basis of such property. For purposes of this subdivision, a transitional safe harbor lease is a lease either which was executed after July 1, 1982, and on or prior to December 1, 1982, or which includes some transitional safe harbor lease property, as defined in TEFRA section 208(d)(3), that was placed in service after July 1, 1982, and on or prior to December 1, 1982.

Q-3: What test will be applied in determining whether an item of property is constructed or acquired?

A-3: Except as expressly provided in section 208(d)(3)(D) or (E) of TEFRA, the determination of whether and when any such events occurred with respect to an item of property will generally be made in accordance with the principles and precedents prior to TEFRA under the investment tax credit and depreciation allowance transitional provisions. See § § 1.48-2(b)(6) and 1.167(c)-1(a)(2), which provide definitions of the term "acquired", and § § 1.48-2(b)(1) and 1.167(c)-1(a)(1), which provide definitions of the term "constructed". Also see Rev. Rul. 80-312, 1980-2 C.B. 21, which discusses the factors to be considered in determining when a taxpayer has control over a project being constructed.

In general, for purposes of TEFRA section 208(d)(3), construction of an item of property is considered to have commenced when physical work of a significant nature has begun with respect to the property. Thus, construction does not begin when parts or components which enter into construction are acquired. If property is assembled from purchased parts or components, the commencement of construction occurs when actual assembly of the property begins. If a taxpayer manufactures a major part or component of an item of property for itself, construction will be considered to have begun when the manufacturing of that part or component commences. However, construction of an item of property will not be considered as begun if physical work by the taxpayer relates to minor parts or components. Clearing and grading of land will be considered in determining when construction begins on an item of property only if they are directly associated with the construction of the property.

Q-4: Under section 168(f)(8)(J), the at-risk rules are liberalized for closely held lessors that engage in safe harbor leasing. These rules apply "in the case of property placed in service after the date of enactment of this subparagraph," namely, after September 3, 1982.

Do the liberalized at-risk rules apply in the case where otherwise qualified property is placed in service by a lessee in August of 1982 but is leased by a corporate lessor subject to the at-risk rules after September 3, 1982?

A-4: The liberalized at-risk rule in section 168(f)(8)(J) is applicable in this case because, in determining whether property is placed in service before or after the date of enactment of section 168(f)(8)(J), the relevant date is the date the property is placed in service by the lessor. Additionally, a closely held corporate lessor, which is not a personal service corporation, may lease transitional safe harbor lease property placed in service after September 3, 1982, under the liberalized at-risk rule.

Q-5: Is it necessary for property placed in service by a lessee in December of 1982 to be leased before January 1, 1983, in order to qualify under the general transitional rule of section 208(d)(3)(A) of TEFRA, which requires that the property be placed in service before January 1, 1983?

A-5: The legislative intent of this transitional rule was to provide a 3-month period after prop-

Reg. § 5f.168(f)(8)-1

erty is placed in service by a lessee in which a safe harbor lease could be entered into. *Cf.* section 209(c) of TEFRA (3-month window applies to true leases entered into after 1983). The legislative intent further was to permit property to qualify as transitional safe harbor lease property if it was placed in service by the end of 1982 by a lessee. Accordingly, transitional safe harbor lease property placed in service in 1982 by a lessee may be leased in a safe harbor lease transaction within 3 months after it is placed in service by the lessee without losing its status as transitional safe harbor lease property.

However, for all other purposes of the Code other than section 168(f)(8)(D)(i), section 168(f)(8)(D)(viii)(II) will apply and the property will be treated as originally placed in service not earlier than the date that the property is used under the lease. Thus, for example, if transitional safe harbor lease property is placed in service in December of 1982 and leased under section 168(f)(8) in January of 1983, the property will not lose its status as transitional safe harbor lease property, but the basis adjustment rules of section 48(g) will apply with respect to the property.

Q-6: Will a contract to acquire property be considered "binding" for purposes of section 208(d)(3)(A)(i) of TEFRA if the contract contains no liquidated damages clause?

A-6: Generally, an irrevocable contract which contains no provision for liquidated damages in the event of breach or cancellation would be considered binding. Moreover, in determining the amount of the lessee's potential liability, the fair market value of the property will not be taken into account. For example, if a lessee entered into an irrevocable contract to purchase an asset for $100 and the contract contained no provision for liquidated damages, the contract would be considered binding notwithstanding the fact that the property at all times after July 1, 1982, had a value of $99 and under local law the seller could only recover the difference in the event the lessee failed to perform. On the other hand, if the contract by its terms provided for liquidated damages of less than 5 percent of the purchase price which is in lieu of any damages allowable by law, in the event of breach or cancellation, the contract would not be considered binding.

Q-7: How does the 50-percent limitation on lessors in section 168(i)(1) and the 45-percent limitation on lessees in section 168(f)(8)(D)(ii) apply to corporations which are part of an affiliated group filing consolidated returns?

A-7: Both the 50-percent limitation on lessors and the 45-percent limitation on lessees will be applied on a consolidated basis for corporations filing consolidated returns.

Q-8: Section 168(f)(8)(J) liberalized the at-risk rules for safe harbor leasing and provides that in cases where the safe harbor lessee would be considered the owner of the property without regard to the safe harbor lease, the lessor is considered to be at risk with respect to the property in an amount equal to the amount the lessee is considered at risk with respect to such property as determined under section 465.

Will a corporate lessor that would ordinarily be subject to the at-risk rules under section 465 be exempt from such rules under section 168(f)(8)(J) in a situation where acquisition of the leased property is financed with nonrecourse debt by a lessee that is not subject to the at-risk rules?

A-8: Yes. The liberalized at-risk rules of section 168(f)(8)(J) will apply in cases where the lessee's ACRS deductions and investment tax credit with respect to the property would not have been limited under the at-risk rules had the parties not elected treatment under section 168(f)(8).

Q-9: Section 168(f)(8)(J)(ii) excepts certain service corporations from the liberalized at-risk rules of section 168(f)(8)(J)(i). Does the exception in subdivision (ii) also extend to subsidiaries of such service corporations that file consolidated returns?

A-9: Yes. The liberalized at-risk rules of section 168(f)(8)(J)(i) will not apply to any subsidiary filing a consolidated return with a service organization described in section 168(f)(8)(J)(ii).

Q-10: Will property lose its status as transitional safe harbor lease property under section 208(d)(3) of TEFRA solely by reason of the fact that the person who is a party to a binding contract to acquire the property assigns his rights in the contract to another person?

A-10: When a person who is a party to a binding contract transfers his rights in the contract (or the property covered by the contract) to another person and the transferor (or a corporation which is a member of the same affiliated group as the transferor) will use the property under a lease for a period not less than 50 percent of the appropriate recovery period for the leased property under section 168(c), then to the extent of the transferred rights, this other person will succeed to the position of the transferor with respect to the binding contract and the property. Accordingly, under these circumstances, property will not lose its status as transitional safe harbor lease property.

In addition, property will not be disqualified as transitional safe harbor lease property solely by reason of a transfer by a person of his rights in a contract (or the property covered by the contract) in a transaction in which the basis of the property in the hands of the transferee is determined by reference to its basis in the hands of the transferor (e.g., transfers governed by sections 332, 351, 361, 721, and 731). Thus, for example, if a corporation entered into a binding contract for the construction or acquisition of property prior to July 1, 1982, and after such date assigned the contract to a corporation within the same affiliated group which files consolidated returns, the assignee will be entitled to treat the property acquired pursuant to the contract as transitional safe harbor lease property, assuming the property would have so qualified in the hands of the transferor. Similarly, if a joint venture or partnership between two corporations entered into a binding contract or commenced construction of property before July 2, 1982, but dissolved and distributed its assets to the partners or joint venturers after July 2, 1982, the joint venturers or partners may treat the asset as transitional safe harbor lease property, assuming the property would have so qualified had the joint venture or partnership remained in existence.

Q-11: During 1982, Corporation Y placed in service section 38 property with a total cost of $100X. On August 15, 1982, Corporation Y placed in service the last component of an entire facility within the meaning of § 5c.168(f)(8)-6(b)(2). The facility had a total cost basis of $40X, of which $30X was transitional safe harbor lease property within the meaning of section 208(d)(3) of TEFRA and $10X was not transitional safe harbor lease property. On November 1, 1982, Corporation Y sold and leased back under a section 168(f)(8) lease the $30X of transitional safe harbor lease property in the facility.

Will the entire facility rule in § 5c.168(f)(8)-6(b)(2) apply in this situation where the taxpayer has not leased all of the section 38 property in the facility?

A-11: No. The placed in service date, for purposes of the rule requiring that property be leased within 3 months after such property was placed in service by the lessee, would be determined under the entire facility rule in § 5c.168(f)(8)-6(b)(2) only if Corporation Y had leased all the qualified leased property in the facility. Since Corporation Y leased only the $30X of transitional section 38 property of the facility and did not lease the $10X of nontransitional property, Corporation Y may not rely on the entire facility rule of § 5c.168(f)(8)-6(b)(2) for purposes of determining the placed in service date for the property under the section 168(f)(8) lease.

Q-12: Assume the same facts as in Q-11, except that Corporation Y had also placed in service by August 15, 1982, $30X of miscellaneous machinery and equipment all of which was transitional safe harbor lease property within the meaning of section 208(d)(3) of TEFRA. On November 1, 1982, in addition to the $30X of transitional property in the facility, Corporation Y also sold and leased back under a separate section 168(f)(8) lease the $30X of miscellaneous machinery and equipment. Will the entire facility rule in § 5c.168(f)(8)-6(b)(2) apply in this situation to the $30X of transitional property in the facility?

A-12: Yes. Since Corporation Y leased $30X of transitional machinery and equipment and the $30X of the facility which consisted of transitional property, Corporation Y can lease none of the nontransitional property in the facility because, by reason of the 45-percent cap on lessees contained in section 168(f)(8)(D)(ii) and (iii) and (I), it is not qualified leased property for purposes of section 168(f)(8). Thus, on the facts, Corporation Y has leased all the qualified leased property in the facility.

Q-13: Corporation X constructed a manufacturing complex consisting of three integrated operational components, each with a different ADR present class life midpoint, which together constitute an "entire facility" within the meaning of § 5c.168(f)(8)-6(b)(2). The last components of the facility were placed in service on August 15, 1982. On October 1, 1982, Corporation X sold to Corporation Z and leased back under section 168(f)(8) all the qualified leased property of the facility.

For purposes of the rule requiring that property be leased within 3 months after such property was placed in service by the lessee, will the leased components of the entire facility be considered placed in service by the lessee on August 15, 1982, the date the last components were placed in service, if the components are leased at one time pursuant to documents consisting of three section 168(f)(8) leases with different terms to reflect the different ADR midpoint lives of the qualified leased property in the facility?

A-13: Yes. If the entire facility rule in § 5c.168(f)(8)-6(b)(2) applies, the facility components which were placed in service prior to August 15, 1982, will be treated as placed in service by the lessee on August 15, 1982, for purposes of the 3-month rule. This rule will apply if all the qualified leased property of the facility is leased at one time. The documentation may be in the form of multiple, simultaneously executed agreements or may be in the form of an agreement comprised of one or more parts or schedules. Each of the multiple agreements, or each of the parts or schedules

Reg. § 5f.168(f)(8)-1

of an agreement, may have different lease terms for property with different ADR midpoint lives, so long as each such agreement or part of schedule individually would be treated as a lease under section 168(f)(8), taking into account the entire facility rule, with lease terms commencing on the same date. A single transaction effected by multiple agreements or by an agreement with one or more parts or schedules will meet the maximum lease term requirement of § 5c.168(f)(8)-5(b) so long as each agreement or each part or schedule of an agreement meets the maximum lease term requirement.

Q-14: Under § 5c.168(f)(8)-6(b)(2), the special rule for facilities applies only if the entire facility is leased under a section 168(f)(8) lease.

Will a transaction not qualify under section 168(f)(8) if the parties, acting in good faith, omit an insubstantial portion of the qualified lease property from the lease?

A-14: No. The facility rule of § 5c.168(f)(8)-6(b)(2) will apply if the parties, acting in good faith, substantially comply with its terms.

Q-15: When will construction of an aircraft be considered to have been begun after June 25, 1981, and before February 20, 1982, for purposes of TEFRA section 208(d)(3)(D)?

A-15: Construction of an aircraft will be considered to have been begun after June 25, 1981, and before February 20, 1982, if during such period any of the following events occurred:

(i) Construction or reconstruction of a subassembly designated for the aircraft was commenced;

(ii) Construction of a lot increment of subassemblies (one or more of which was designated for the aircraft) was commenced; or

(iii) The stub wing join occurred.

Q-16: Does the definition of assets used in the manufacture or production of steel for purposes of TEFRA section 208(d)(2)(F) include all assets used in this function (such as electrical and steam generators and distribution equipment, coke oven by-product equipment) although not necessarily includible in the former ADR guideline class for primary steel mill products?

A-16: Yes, all assets that are used, in their primary function, as an integral part of the steel manufacturing or production process are included. Cf. § 1.48-1(d)(4). However, the steel manufacturing or production process does not include processing beyond the production of primary ferrous metals (as defined by the ADR Class for Manufacture of Primary Ferrous Metals).

Q-17: Where a qualified mass commuting vehicle meets the requirements for both the TEFRA section 208(d)(2) transitional rule and the TEFRA section 208(d)(5) special rule for mass commuting vehicles, which provision will control?

A-17: The general transitional rule of TEFRA section 208(d)(2) will apply. Thus, pursuant to TEFRA section 208(d)(2)(B), the provisions of section 168(f)(8)(J) but not the provisions of section 168(i)(1), will apply only to such property. If the general transitional rule does not apply to a specific mass commuting vehicle, the provision of section 168(i)(1) applies to the lessor who leases such vehicle.

Q-18: Does the definition of a qualified mass commuting vehicle include component parts of a qualified mass commuting vehicle—such as an undercarriage of a subway car or the costs of rehabilitation or reconstruction of a mass commuting vehicle (or component part thereof)?

A-18: Yes.

[Temporary Reg. § 5f.168(f)(8)-1.]

☐ [T.D. 7850, 11-5-82. Amended by T.D. 7879, 3-21-83.]

[Reg. § 1.168(f)(8)-1T]

§ 1.168(f)(8)-1T. Safe-harbor lease information returns concerning qualified mass commuting vehicles (Temporary).—In general. Form 6793, Safe Harbor Lease Information Return, is obsolete for safe harbor lease agreements executed after June 30, 1985. The parties to a safe harbor lease agreement under section 168(f)(8) executed after June 30, 1985 must file with their timely filed (including extensions) Federal income tax returns for the taxable year during which the lease term begins a statement containing the following information:

(a) The name, address, and taxpayer identification number of the lessor and the lessee;

(b) A description of the property with respect to which safe-harbor lease treatment is claimed;

(c) The date on which the lessee places the property in service, the date on which the lease begins, and the term of the lease;

(d) The recovery property class of the leased property under section 168(c)(2) (for example, 5-year);

(e) The terms of the payments between the parties to the lease transaction;

(f) The unadjusted basis of the property as defined in section 168(d)(1) and its adjusted basis as determined under § 5c.168(f)(8)-6(b)(3); and

(g) If the lessor is a partnership or grantor trust, the name, address, and taxpayer identification number of the partners or beneficiaries and the service center at which the income tax return of each partner or beneficiary is filed.

The lessor's failure to file the above-described statement shall void such agreement as a safe-harbor lease under section 168(f)(8) as of the date of the execution of the lease agreement. For rules regarding extensions of time for filing elections, see § 1.9100-1. [Temporary Reg. § 1.168(f)(8)-1T.]

☐ [*T.D.* 8033, 6-28-85.]

[Reg. § 5c.168(f)(8)-2]

§ 5c.168(f)(8)-2. **Election to characterize transaction as a section 168(f)(8) lease (Temporary).**—(a) *Election*—(1) *In general.* The election to characterize a transaction as a lease qualifying under section 168(f)(8) shall be made within the time and manner as set forth in this section without regard to section 168(f)(4).

(2) *Lease agreement.* For an agreement to be treated as a lease under section 168(f)(8) and this section, the lease agreement must be executed not later than 3 months after the property was first placed in service, as defined in § 5c.168(f)(8)-6(b)(2)(i) (or prior to November 14, 1981, if the property was first placed in service by the lessee after December 31, 1980, and before August 14, 1981). The agreement must be in writing and must state that all of the parties to the agreement agree to characterize it as a lease for purposes of Federal tax law and elect to have the provisions of section 168(f)(8) apply to the transaction. The agreement must also name the party who will be treated as the lessor and the party who will be treated as the lessee.

(3) *Information return concerning the election.* (i) Except as provided in subdivision (ii), for each lease agreement, the lessor and lessee must jointly file Form 6793, Safe Harbor Lease Information Return, concerning their election under section 168(f)(8). The information return must be signed by both the lessor and the lessee and filed not later than the 30th day after the agreement is executed with the Commission of Internal Revenue, 1111 Constitution Avenue, N.W., Washington, D.C. 20224 (Attn: Form 6793). Unless the failure to file timely is shown to be due to reasonable cause, the failure to file the information return timely shall void the section 168(f)(8) election as of the date of the execution of the lease agreement. The information return shall include the following items:

(A) The name, address, and taxpayer identifying number of the lessor and the lessee (and the common parent company if a consolidated return is filed);

(B) The service center with which the income tax returns of the lessor and lessee are filed;

(C) A description of each property with respect to which the election is made;

(D) The date on which the lessee places the property in service (determined as defined in § 5c.168(f)(8)-6(b)(2)(i)), the date on which the lease begins, and the term of the lease;

(E) The recovery property class of the leased property under section 168(c)(2) (for example, 5 years) and the ADR midpoint life of the leased property;

(F) The terms of the payments between the parties to the lease transaction;

(G) Whether the ACRS deductions and the investment tax credit are allowable to the same taxpayer;

(H) The aggregate amount paid to outside parties to arrange or carry out the transaction, such as, for example, legal and investment banking fees;

(I) For the lessor only: the unadjusted basis of the property as defined in section 168(d)(1);

(J) For the lessor only: if the lessor is a partnership or a grantor trust, the name, address, and taxpayer identifying number of the partners or the beneficiaries, and the Service Center with which the income tax return of each partner or beneficiary is filed; and

(K) Such other information as may be required by the return or its instructions. The aggregate amount paid to outside parties which is described in subdivision (H) need not be disclosed unless it is reasonable to estimate that either the lessor or the lessee will lease property under section 168(f)(8) for the calendar year which has an aggregate adjusted basis to such person of more than $1,000,000. If either the lessor or the lessee reasonably expects to lease property with an aggregate basis of more than $1,000,000, then both parties must disclose their transaction costs.

(ii) In the case of an agreement executed before January 1, 1982, only the lessor is required to file the information return described in subdivision (i) of this paragraph (a)(3) and the return must be postmarked not later than January 31, 1982. Unless the failure to file timely is shown to be due to reasonable cause, or unless the lessee files the information return postmarked by January 31, 1982, the lessor's failure to file the information return timely shall be a disqualifying event as of February 1, 1982, which shall cause an agreement to cease to be treated as a lease under section 168(f)(8). For the Federal income tax consequences of a disqualifying event, see § 5c.168(f)(8)-8.

(iii) A copy of the information return described in subdivisions (i) and (ii) shall be filed by each party with its timely filed Federal income tax return for its taxable year during which the lease term begins. However, for taxable years ending in 1981 with respect to lease agreements executed during calendar year 1981, such statement shall be filed by the later of (A) the due date (taking extensions into account) of the party's 1981 Federal income tax return, or (B) where the filing of an amended return is required, with the amended return within 3 months following the execution of the lease agreement. For the requirement to file an amended return within 3 months and the consequences of the failure to so file, see § 5c.168(f)(8)-6(b)(2)(ii). A taxpayer that is required to file the information return with its Federal income tax return before an information return form is available shall file, in lieu of the required information return, a statement which contains the information set forth in subdivisions (A) through J of paragraph (a)(3)(i). The failure by the lessor to file the information return (or, if applicable, the statement referred to in the preceding sentence) with its timely filed Federal income tax return shall be a disqualifying event which shall cause an aggrement to cease to be treated as a lease under section 168(f)(8). For the Federal income tax consequences of a disqualifying event, see § 5c.168(f)(8)-8.

(4) *Election is irrevocable.* An agreement made pursuant to paragraph (a)(2) of this section shall be irrevocable as of the later of the date such agreement was executed or November 23, 1981.

(5) *Disposition by lessee.* Except in the case of transactions described in subparagraph (6), of this paragraph, if the lessee (or any transferee of the lessee's interest) sells or assigns its interest in the lease or in the property, the agreement will cease to be characterized as a lease under Section 168(f)(8) as of the time of the sale or assignment unless the transferee furnishes to the lessor within 60 days following the transfer the transferee's written consent to take the property subject to the lease, and the transferee and lessor file a statement with their timely filed Federal income tax returns for the taxable year in which the transfer occurs containing the following information:

(i) The name, address, and taxpayer identifying number of the lessor and the transferee;

(ii) The district director's office with which the income tax returns of the lessor and transferee are filed;

(iii) A description of the property; and

(iv) Confirmation of the transferee's consent.

See § 5c.168(f)(8)-8 for the Federal income tax consequences where an agreement ceases to be characterized as a lease under section 168(f)(8).

(6) *Disposition of lessee's interest in bankruptcy, etc., or similar proceeding.* In the case of an agreement executed after May 31, 1982, where the lessee's interest in the lease or in the property is sold or assigned in a bankruptcy, liquidation, receivership, a court-supervised foreclosure, or in any similar proceeding for the relief or protection of insolvent debtors in Federal or State court, the agreement will continue to be characterized as a lease under section 168(f)(8) and the purchaser or assignee shall take the property subject to the lease if—

(i) Prior to the consummation of the sale or assignment, the lessor gives written notice of its Federal income tax ownership to the judicial or administrative body having jurisdiction over the proceeding and to the debtor in possession of the interest or, if at such time a trustee, receiver or similar person has been appointed by the court, to the person appointed. The notice must contain a request that the court and the debtor or the person appointed provide a copy of the notice to the purchaser or assignee prior to the consummation of the sale or assignment. Within 60 days following the sale or assignment, the lessor must provide notice of its Federal income tax ownership and copies of the lease agreement, and, in the case of a sale and leaseback transaction, the lessor's purchase money obligation, to the purchaser or assignee;

(ii) The lessor files a statement with its timely filed Federal income tax return for the taxable year in which the sale or assignment occurs containing the following information:

(A) The name, address, and taxpayer identifying number of the lessor and the purchaser or assignee;

(B) The district director's office with which the Federal income tax returns of the lessor and purchaser or assignee are filed;

(C) A description of the property; and

(iii) Prior to the consummation of the sale or assignment, all secured lenders of the lessee with interests in the property, which interests arose not later than the time the lessee first used the property under the lease (and which were perfected in accordance with applicable local law), specifically either exclude or release in writing the Federal income tax ownership of the property from their interests.

Reg. § 5c.168(f)(8)-2(a)(6)

The purchaser or assignee of the interest with respect to which this paragraph applies shall file a statement with its timely filed Federal income tax return for the taxable year in which the sale or assignment occurs containing the information described in subdivision (ii). If the interest is subsequently transferred (other than in a bankruptcy, liquidation, receivership, court-supervised foreclosure, or similar proceeding) during the term of the lease, the agreement will continue to be characterized as a lease under section 168(f)(8) and the transferee will take the property subject to the lease if either (A) the lessor gives the transferee, prior to the transfer, a copy of the lease, written notice of its Federal income tax ownership, and, in the case of a sale and leaseback transaction, a copy of the lessor's purchase money obligation, and the lessor files a statement with its timely filed Federal income tax return as described in subdivision (ii), or (B) within 60 days following the transfer, the transferee agrees in writing to take the property subject to the lease and the lessor and transferee file a statement with their timely filed Federal income tax returns within the time and in the manner described in paragraph (a)(5). However, an agreement will not continue to be characterized as a lease under this subparagraph if, under another applicable provision, it would cease to be characterized as a lease. See § 5c.168(f)(8)-8 for the Federal income tax consequences where an agreement ceases to be characterized as a lease under section 168(f)(8).

(7) *Consequences of taking the property subject to the lease agreement.* For purposes of § 5c.168(f)(8)-1 through § 5c.168(f)(8)-11, in a situation where a transferee of a lessee's interest acquires the property subject to the lease, the transferee shall be deemed to have acquired a leasehold interest in the property equal to the remaining lease term, any unpaid obligation of the lessor arising in connection with the sale of the property by the original lessee in a sale and leaseback transaction, and any option of the lessee to purchase the property. Any consideration paid by the transferee for the property shall be allocated to the lessor's obligation to the extent of the unpaid balance of the obligation. Any excess over the unpaid balance shall be allocated between the leasehold interest and the purchase option in proportion to their relative fair market values. As the new lessee, the transferee shall not be entitled to claim any ACRS deduction with respect to the property while the lease remains in effect and shall not be entitled to any investment tax credit with respect to the property. The transferee shall report interest income on the lessor's obligation, and shall be entitled to deduct the rent paid under the lease, in accordance with § 5c.168(f)(8)-7. In

addition, the transferee shall be entitled to amortize the portion of its cost allocable to the leasehold interest. Conversely, as long as the lease remains in effect, the lessor will continue to be recognized as the owner of the property for Federal income tax purposes, shall be required to report rents due under the lease, and shall be entitled to deduct interest on its obligation.

(8) *Election to treat certain leases under subparagraph (6) rules.* The lessor under a section 168(f)(8) lease executed on or before May 31, 1982, may elect to have the provisions of paragraph (a)(6) of this section apply in the case of a sale or assignment of the lessee's interest in the lease or in the property in a bankruptcy, receivership, liquidation, court-supervised foreclosure, or similar proceeding. The election of the lessor with respect to any leased property may be made at any time prior to the consummation of any sale or assignment of such property in a bankruptcy, etc., or similar proceeding, by complying with the provisions of subparagraph (6) of this paragraph.

(b) *Examples.* The application of the provisions of this section may be illustrated by the following examples:

Example (1). X Corp. maintains its books and records for Federal tax law purposes on a calendar year basis. On February 1, 1981, X acquires certain equipment for use in its business, and the equipment is deemed to be placed in service on that date within the meaning of § 5c.168(f)(8)-6(b)(2)(i). On November 1, 1981, X sells the equipment to Y and leases it back under a lease in which the parties elect to have the provisions of section 168(f)(8) apply. The election is considered timely for purposes of making Y the owner of the property under section 168(f)(8) since the lease agreement was executed before November 14, 1981.

Example (2). The facts are the same as in example (1) except that X Corp.'s taxable year ends on February 28, 1981. X claimed the investment tax credit and depreciation deductions with respect to the property in its return filed April 1, 1981. The lease will qualify for safe harbor treatment under section 168(f)(8) provided X, within 3 months after the lease agreement was executed, files an amended return pursuant to § 5c.168(f)(8)-6(b)(2)(ii) for its taxable year ending February 28, 1981, in which X foregoes its right to claim any investment tax credit or ACRS deductions with respect to the property subject to the lease.

Example (3). X Corp. (as lessee) sells certain new equipment to Y Corp. (as lessor) and leases it back under a section 168(f)(8) lease. During the term of the lease X sells its interest in the prop-

Reg. § 5c.168(f)(8)-2(a)(7)

erty to T Corp. (other than in a bankruptcy or similar proceeding), and T does not give Y a written consent to take the property subject to the lease. The agreement ceases to be treated as a lease under section 168(f)(8) as of the date of the sale.

Example (4). The facts are the same as in example (3) except that the sale of the property takes place while X is under the jurisdiction of a court in a bankruptcy proceeding. All lenders of X having perfected interests in the property that arose by the time the property was first used under the lease have specifically either excluded or released the ownership of the property for Federal income tax purposes from their interests. Within the required time periods, Y gives appropriate notification to the court, the bankruptcy trustee, and T that the property is subject to the lease and files the required statement with its Federal income tax return for the taxable year in which the sale occurs. The agreement continues to be treated as a lease under section 168(f)(8). T will take the property subject to the lease. T must allocate the purchase price among the lessor's note, the leasehold interest, and the option (if any) to purchase the property.

Example (5). The facts are the same as in example (4), except that one lender of X having a perfected and timely interest in the property does not specifically exclude or release the Federal income tax ownership of the property from its interest. The agreement will cease to be treated as a lease under section 168(f)(8) as of the date of the transfer to T. The result would be the same if Y failed to furnish any of the notices required by subdivision (i) of paragraph (a) and (6) or failed to file a statement as required by subdivision (ii) of paragraph (a)(6).

Example (6). The facts are the same as in example (4). In addition, during the term of the lease T transfers the property to U Corp. and Y fails to furnish U with written notice that the property is subject to the lease prior to the sale and U refuses to agree to consent to the lease agreement. The agreement will cease to be treated as a lease under section 168(f)(8) as of the date of the transfer to U. The result would be the same if Y furnished U with timely written notice of its tax ownership but failed to file the required statement with its income tax return for its taxable year in which the sale occurred. [Temporary Reg. § 5c.168(f)(8)-2.]

□ [*T.D. 7791, 10-20-81. Amended by T.D. 7795, 11-10-81 and T.D. 7800, 12-28-81.*]

[Reg. § 5c.168(f)(8)-3]

§ 5c.168(f)(8)-3. Requirements for lessor (Temporary).—(a) *Qualified lessor.* In order for an agreement to be treated as a lease under section 168(f)(8), the party characterized in the agreement as the lessor must be a qualified lessor. The term "qualified lessor" means—

(1) A corporation which is neither an electing small business corporation under section 1371(b) nor a personal holding company under section 542(a), or

(2) A partnership all of whose partners are corporations described in subparagraph (1), or

(3) A grantor trust whose grantor and beneficiaries are all corporations described in paragraph (a)(1) or partnerships described in paragraph (a)(2).

(b) *Effect of disqualification of lessor.* If at any time during the term of the agreement the lessor ceases to be a qualified lessor, the agreement will lose its characterization as a lease under section 168(f)(8) as of the date of the event causing such disqualification. If any partner of a partnership described in paragraph (a)(2) ceases to be a corporation described in paragraph (a)(1), the partnership entity shall cease to be a qualified lessor. Similarly, if any beneficiary of a trust described in paragraph (a)(3) ceases to be a corporation described in paragraph (a)(1), the trust shall cease to be a qualified lessor. See § 5c.168(f)(8)-8 for the Federal income tax consequences of such a disqualification.

(c) *One tax owner per property.* Only one person may be a qualified lessor under section 168(f)(8) with respect to leased property. Thus, property that is subject to a lease under section 168(f)(8) may not be subleased under a lease for which a section 168(f)(8) election is made. In addition, if a lessor sells or assigns in a taxable transaction its interest in a section 168(f)(8) lease or in the underlying property, the lease shall cease to qualify under section 168(f)(8) and no other lease may be executed under section 168(f)(8) with respect to the property. The preceding sentence applies to a sale or assignment of its interest by a partner of a lessor that is a partnership described in paragraph (a)(2) of this section or by a beneficiary of a lessor that is a trust described in paragraph (a)(3) of this section. See § 5c.168(f)(8)-8 for the Federal income tax consequences where a lease ceases to qualify under section 168(f)(8). However, lease brokers, agents, etc., may, for example, prepare executory contracts with the lessee whereby the broker's assignee may execute a lease as lessor, and, if the requirements of section 168(f)(8) and

Reg. § 5c.168(f)(8)-3(c)

§ § 5c.168(f)(8)-1 through 5c.168(f)(8)-11 are met, the lease will qualify under section 168(f)(8).

(d) *Examples*. The application of paragraph (c) may be illustrated by the following examples:

Example (1). X Corp. (as lessee) sells certain new equipment to Y Corp. (as lessor) and leases it back under a section 168(f)(8) lease. Within 3 months after the property was placed in service, Y assigns its interest in the lease to Z. Upon the transfer to Z, the lease will no longer qualify for treatment under section 168(f)(8). The property may not thereafter be the subject of a section 168(f)(8) lease.

Example (2). X Corp., which wishes to acquire certain equipment for use in its business and to transfer ownership of the property for Federal income tax law purposes, purchases the equipment and enters into an executory contract with LB, a lease broker, under which X agrees to execute a section 168(f)(8) lease as lessee with a third party lessor. At a later date (but within the prescribed 3-month period), LB arranges for X and T Corp. (which wishes to secure Federal income tax law ownership) to execute a lease agreement in accordance with § 5c.168(f)(8)-2. The lease will qualify for treatment under section 168(f)(8). [Temporary Reg. § 5c.168(f)(8)-3.]

□ [*T.D. 7791*, 10-20-81. *Amended by T.D. 7795*, 11-10-81.]

[Reg. § 5c.168(f)(8)-4]

§ 5c.168(f)(8)-4. **Minimum investment of lessor (Temporary).**—(a) *Minimum investment.* Under section 168(f)(8)(B)(ii), an agreement will not be characterized as a lease for purposes of section 168(f)(8) unless the qualified lessor has a minimum at risk investment which, at the time the property is placed in service under the lease and at all times during the term of the lease, is not less than 10 percent of the adjusted basis of the leased property. As the adjusted basis of the leased property is reduced by capital cost recovery deductions, the minimum investment required will also be reduced to 10 percent of the revised adjusted basis, until the adjusted basis has been completely recovered, at which time no minimum investment will be required. Financing provided by the lessee or a party related to the lessee, such as a recourse note given by the lessor to the lessee, will not be taken into account in determining the lessor's minimum investment.

(b) *At risk amount*. The minimum investment which the lessor has at risk with respect to the leased property for purposes of paragraph (a) of this section includes only consideration paid and recourse indebtedness incurred by the lessor to purchase the property. The lessor must have suffi-

cient net worth (without regard to the value of any leases which qualify under section 168(f)(8)) to satisfy any personal liability incurred. Any tax benefits which the lessor derives from the leased property shall not be taken into account to reduce the amount the lessor has at risk. An agreement between the lessor and the lessee requiring either or both parties to purchase or sell the qualified leased property at some price (whether or not fixed in the agreement) at the end of the lease term shall not affect the amount the lessor has at risk with respect to the property. However, an option held by the lessor to sell the property that is exercisable before the end of the period prescribed under section 168(c)(2) for the recovery property class of the leased property (taking into account any election by the lessor or lessee under section 168(b)(3)) shall reduce the amount the lessor is considered to have at risk by the amount of the option price at the time the option becomes exercisable. [Temporary Reg. § 5c.168(f)(8)-4.]

□ [*T.D. 7791*, 10-20-81.]

[Reg. § 5c.168(f)(8)-5]

§ 5c.168(f)(8)-5. **Term of lease (Temporary).**—(a) *Term of lease—Basic rules.* To qualify as a lease under section 168(f)(8) and § 5c.168(f)(8)-1(a), the lease agreement must provide for a term that does not exceed the maximum term described in paragraph (b) of this section; such term must also at least equal the minimum term described in paragraph (c).

(b) *Maximum term.* For purposes of section 168(f)(8)(B)(iii) and this section, the term of the lease may not exceed the greater of—

(1) 90 percent of the useful life of the property under section 167, or

(2) 150 percent of the asset depreciation range (ADR) present class life ("midpoint") of such property, applicable as of January 1, 1981 (without regard to section 167(m)(4)), published in Rev. Proc. 77-10, 1977-1 C.B. 548, and revisions thereto.

Solely for purposes of this paragraph (b), "useful life" means the period when the leased asset can reasonably be expected to be economically useful in anyone's trade or business; such term does not mean the period during which the lessor expects to lease the property. Any option to extend the term of the lease, whether or not at fair market value rent, must be included in the term of the lease for purposes of this paragraph. If several different pieces of property are the subject of a single lease, the maximum allowable term for such lease will be measured with respect to the property with the shortest life. In no case, however, will the lease term qualify under this section if

Reg. § 5c.168(f)(8)-4(a)

such term with respect to any piece of property is less than the minimum term described in paragraph (c).

(c) *Minimum term.* For purposes of this section, the term of the lease must at least equal the period prescribed under section 168(c)(2) for the recovery property class of the leased property. For example, if a piece of leased equipment is in the 5-year recovery property class, the lease agreement must have a minimum term of 5 years. In general, the determination of whether property is 3-year recovery property, 5-year recovery property, etc., in the hands of the lessor will be based on the characterization of the property in the hands of the owner as determined without regard to the section 168(f)(8) lease. Thus, for example, property which is public utility property or RRB replacement property absent the section 168(f)(8) lease will be characterized as such in the hands of the lessor for purposes of section 168(f)(8). However, with respect to RRB replacement property, the transitional rule of section 168(f)(3) shall be inapplicable to the lessor. In addition, any election under section 168(b)(3) by the lessor with respect to the class of recovery property to which the qualified leased property is assigned shall apply to the leased property in determining the term of the lease. A lease term that does not exceed the term required to satisfy the minimum lease term of this paragraph will be deemed to comply with the maximum lease term described in paragraph (b) if such minimum lease term exceeds such maximum lease term.

(d) *Examples.* The application of this section may be illustrated by the following examples:

Example (1). X Corp. (as lessee) and Y Corp. (as lessor) enter into a lease which they elect to be treated under section 168(f)(8) with respect to a chemical manufacturing facility that will also generate steam for use in the production of electricity. The assets comprising the chemical plant are described in ADR guideline class 28.0 (midpoint life of 9.5 years), and the assets comprising the steam plant are described in ADR class 00.4 (midpoint life of 22 years). To satisfy the maximum lease term requirement of section 168(f)(8)(B)(iii)(II) and § 5c.168(f)(8)-5(b), the lease term may not exceed 14.25 years (150 percent of the 9.5 year midpoint life of the chemical plant).

Example (2). The facts are the same as in example (1) except that the chemical plant and the steam plant are the subject of separate leases. For purposes of section 168(f)(8)(B)(iii)(II) and § 5c.168(f)(8)-5(b), the maximum term of the lease with respect to the chemical plant is 14.25 years (150 percent of 9.5 years) and the maximum

term of the lease with respect to the steam plant is 33 years (150 percent of 22 years). [Temporary Reg. § 5c.168(f)(8)-5.]

☐ [*T.D. 7791*, 10-20-81.]

[Reg. § 5c.168(f)(8)-6]

§ 5c.168(f)(8)-6. **Qualified leased property (Temporary).**—(a) *Basic rules*—(1) *In general.* An agreement shall be treated as a section 168(f)(8) lease only if the property which is leased is qualified leased property. Qualified leased property is recovery property as defined in section 168(c) and is either—

(i) Except as provided in subparagraph (2), new section 38 property of the lessor which is leased no later than 3 months after the date the property was placed in service (or prior to November 14, 1981, if the property was placed in service after December 31, 1980, and before August 14, 1981) and which, if acquired by the lessee, would have been new section 38 property of the lessee, or

(ii) Property which is a qualified mass commuting vehicle (as defined in section 103(b)(9)) and which is financed in whole or in part by proceeds from an issue of obligations the interest on which is excludable from income under section 103(a).

(2) *Sale and leaseback arrangement.* (i) Where the leased property is purchased, directly or indirectly, by the lessor from the lessee (or a party related to the lessee), the property will not be qualified leased property unless the property was (or would have been) new section 38 property of the lessee and was purchased and leased no later than 3 months after the date the property was placed in service by the lessee (or prior to November 14, 1981, if the property was placed in service by the lessee after December 31, 1980 and before August 14, 1981) and with respect to which the lessor's adjusted basis does not exceed the adjusted basis of the lessee (or a party related to the lessee) at the time of the lease. If the lessor's adjusted basis in the property exceeds the seller's adjusted basis with respect to the property at the beginning of the lease, the property will not be qualified leased property.

(ii) For purposes of this paragraph (a)(2) and paragraph (b)(3)(ii) of this section, transactional costs with respect to a sale and leaseback arrangement that are not currently deductible shall be allocated to the lease agreement (and not included in the lessor's adjusted basis with respect to the property) and amortized over the term of the lease. These costs include legal and investment banking fees and printing costs.

(iii) [*Examples*.] The application of this paragraph (a)(2) may be illustrated by the following examples:

Example (1). X, an airline, contracts to have an airplane constructed for a fixed price of $10 million. Prior to completion of construction of the airplane, the value of the airplane increases to $11 million. X buys the airplane at the contract price of $10 million and, before it is placed in service, sells the airplane at its fair market value of $11 million to Y and then leases it back. The lease will not qualify for safe harbor protection under section 168(f)(8) because the lessor's adjusted basis in the airplane exceeds the lessee's adjusted basis. This result obtains even though the airplane qualifies as new section 38 property of X airline.

Example (2). Assume the same facts as in example (1) except that, prior to completion of the construction of the airplane, X assigns its contract to Y for $1 million, and Y thereafter buys the airplane at the contract price of $10 million. The acquisition by Y is treated as an indirect purchase from the lessee. Because Y's adjusted basis in the airplane would exceed the lessee's adjusted basis, the lease will not qualify under section 168(f)(8).

(b) *Special rules*—(1) *New section 38 property.* (i) New section 38 property is section 38 property described in subsection (b) of section 48 and the regulations thereunder other than a qualified rehabilitated building (within the meaning of section 48(g)(1)). Qualified leased property must be new section 38 property at the beginning of the lease and must continue to be section 38 property in the hands of the lessor and the lessee throughout the lease term. The fact that the lessee used the property within the 3-month period prior to the lease will not disqualify the property as new section 38 property of the lessee.

(ii) [*Examples*.] The application of this paragraph (b)(1) may be illustrated by the following examples:

Example (1). N is a hospital exempt from Federal income tax and wishes to purchase certain equipment for use in furtherance of its exempt functions (*i.e.*, other than for use in an unrelated trade or business). O, a qualified lessor as defined in § 5c.168(f)(8)-3(a), acquires the property and leases it to N. Since the equipment would not be new section 38 property of N if N had acquired it by virtue of section 48(a)(4) (relating to exception from definition of section 38 property for certain property used by certain tax-exempt organizations), the equipment is not qualified leased property and the lease does not qualify under section 168(f)(8). Whether O is considered the owner of the property for Federal tax law purposes will be

determined without regard to the provisions of section 168(f)(8).

Example (2). P Corp. is constructing progress expenditure property as defined in section 46(d)(2) for R Corp. Progress expenditure property is property which it is reasonable to believe will be section 38 property in the hands of the taxpayer when it is placed in service. Before the date that the property is placed in service (as defined in § 5c.168(f)(8)-6(b)(2)(i)), the property is not new section 38 property. Accordingly, progress expenditure property cannot be qualified leased property.

Example (3). R Corp., a foreign railroad, acquires new rolling stock and enters into a sale and leaseback transaction with B Corp., a domestic corporation. R uses the rolling stock within and without the United States, but predominantly outside the United States within the meaning of section 48(a)(2)(A). Section 48(a)(2)(B)(ii) is inapplicable to R because R is neither a domestic railroad corporation nor a United States person; therefore, the rolling stock cannot be section 38 property to R. The property is not qualified leased property.

(2) *Placed in service.* (i) Property shall be considered as placed in service at the time the property is placed in a condition or state of readiness and availability for a specifically assigned function. If an entire facility is leased under one lease, property which is part of the facility will not be considered placed in service under this rule until the entire facility is placed in service. If the lessee claims any investment tax credit or ACRS deductions with respect to any component which is part of an entire facility that is subsequently leased, the lessee must file an amended return within the time prescribed in paragraph (b)(2)(ii) of this section in which it foregoes its claim to the investment tax credit and ACRS deductions. If such amended return may not be filed because the time for filing a claim for refund with respect to any component under section 6511 has expired, each component of the facility will be considered as placed in service at the time the individual component is placed in a condition or state of readiness and availability for a specifically assigned function and not when the entire facility is placed in service.

(ii) For purposes other than determining whether property is qualified leased property, property subject to a lease under section 168(f)(8) will be deemed to have been placed in service not earlier than the date such property is used under the lease. If the lessee claims any investment tax credit or ACRS deductions with respect to property placed in service under a lease, the lessee

Reg. § 5c.168(f)(8)-6(b)(1)

must file an amended return within 3 months following the execution of the lease agreement in which the lessee foregoes its claim to the investment tax credit and ACRS deductions with respect to the leased property or the election under section 168(f)(8) will be void.

(iii) The application of this paragraph (b)(2) may be illustrated by the following examples:

Example (1). X Corp. acquires equipment on December 31, 1982, and places the equipment in service. X's taxable year ends December 31. On March 20, 1983, X sells the equipment to Y Corp. and leases it back in a transaction that qualifies under section 168(f)(8). The property is considered to be new section 38 property to X under paragraph (b)(1). X is not allowed any investment tax credit or ACRS deductions with respect to the property in 1982 because the property is not considered to have been placed in service for purposes other than determining whether it is qualified leased property until it is used under the lease under subdivision (ii) of this subparagraph (2). If X has claimed credits or deductions on its 1982 return, it must file an amended return for 1982 within 3 months following the execution of the lease agreement or the election will be void.

Example (2). In March 1985, K Corp. completes reconditioning of a machine, which it constructed and placed in service in 1982 and which has an adjusted basis in 1985 of $10,000. The cost of reconditioning amounts to an additional $20,000. K would be entitled to a basis of $20,000 in computing its qualified investment in new section 38 property for 1985. In May 1985, K enters into a sale and leaseback transaction with L Corp. with respect to the reconditioned parts of the machine that are new section 38 property to K. K and L elect to have section 168(f)(8) apply. Assuming that the adjusted basis of the leased property is the same to L as it is to K, the property qualifies as qualified leased property under section 168(f)(8)(D)(ii) and L is considered the tax owner of the property. Since, for purposes other than determining whether property is qualified leased property, the property is deemed originally placed in service not earlier than the date the property is used under the lease, the property is new section 38 property to L and L may claim the investment tax credit (and ACRS deductions) with respect to the leased property.

(3) *Qualified mass commuting vehicle.* (i) A qualified mass commuting vehicle as defined in section 103(b)(9) will constitute qualified leased property for purposes of section 168(f)(8)(D)(iii) and this section provided all of the following requirements are met:

(A) At least part (as, for example, 5 percent) of the financing for the purchase of such vehicle must be derived from proceeds of obligations the interest on which is excludable from income under section 103(a)(1) (whether or not such obligations are described in section 103(b)(4)(I));

(B) The vehicle must be recovery property (i.e., it must have been first placed in service by the lessee after December 31, 1980); and

(C) The vehicle must not have been previously leased under a section 168(f)(8) lease by the lessee.

A qualified mass commuting vehicle that is qualified leased property may be leased under section 168(f)(8) at any time after December 31, 1980. The requirement of paragraph (b)(3)(i)(A) of this section may be satisfied where the vehicles leased under a section 168(f)(8) lease are refinanced with proceeds of an obligation the interest on which is excludable from income under section 103(a)(1).

(ii) Where the leased property is purchased, directly or indirectly, by the lessor from the lessee (or a party related to the lessee), the property will not qualify under this subsection unless the lessor's adjusted basis in the property does not exceed the adjusted basis of the lessee (or related party) at the time of the execution of the lease. The adjusted basis of property to a lessee (or related party) shall be determined under part II of subchapter O of chapter 1 of the Code for purposes of determining gain, except that the adjustment described in section 1016(a)(3) and § 1.1016-4 need not be made for property acquired during calendar year 1981 and leased no later than March 1, 1982.

(iii) In a transaction characterized as a lease under section 168(f)(8), the lessor's adjusted basis may not include that portion, if any, of the cost of the vehicle to the lessee (or related party) that is financed, directly or indirectly, with an Urban Mass Transportation Administration (UMTA) grant (excluding a grant under the interstate transfer provision of the Federal-Aid Highway Act (FAHA)), a FAHA grant, or any other Federal grant. Where a vehicle is included as part of an UMTA-funded project, 80 percent of the vehicle's cost will be deemed to be financed with an UMTA grant and 20 percent will be deemed to be financed from non-Federal sources without regard to whether the UMTA funds or the non-Federal funds are traceable to any particular vehicle included within the project. For purposes of this subparagraph and paragraph (b)(3)(ii) of this section, amounts originating from non-Federal sources which are paid or incurred with respect to leased property by a State or political subdivision

Reg. § 5c.168(f)(8)-6(b)(3)

of the State (or political subdivision created by the joint authorization of two or more States) shall be taken into account in computing the lessee's adjusted basis in the leased property as if the lessee had paid or incurred such amounts.

(iv) If a vehicle is purchased pending approval of an UMTA grant, the lessor's unadjusted basis in the vehicle may equal the lessee's unadjusted basis unreduced by any subsequently approved UMTA grant; however, if an UMTA grant is later approved and the vehicle is included as part of an UMTA-funded project, except as provided hereinafter in this subparagraph, the lease shall terminate with respect to an undivided 80 percent interest in the vehicle. For the Federal income tax consequences of the termination of a lease, see § 5c.168(f)(8)-8. If such a subsequently approved UMTA grant is used to purchase additional qualified mass commuting vehicles, the portion of each vehicle deemed to be allocable to non-UMTA financing (i.e., 20 percent) may be leased under section 168(f)(8). If a vehicle is purchased pending approval of an UMTA grant and leased under section 168(f)(8), the lease will not be deemed to have terminated with respect to 80 percent of the vehicle when the UMTA grant is later approved if the total interest leased before the grant is approved did not exceed 20 percent of the lessee's adjusted basis in the vehicle (unadjusted basis prior to March 1, 1982) unreduced by any subsequently approved UMTA grant. For purposes of this subparagraph and paragraph (b)(3)(iii) of this section, the allocation principles applicable to UMTA grants shall apply in the case of FAHA grants except that 85 percent and 15 percent shall be substituted for 80 percent and 20 percent, respectively. Similar allocation rules shall also apply to other Federal grants used to finance the acquisition of qualified mass commuting vehicles.

(v) (A) Notwithstanding the provisions of § 5c.168(f)(8)-2(a)(3)(iii), the lessee in a transaction to which this paragraph (b)(3) applies is not required to file an information return or a statement concerning its election under section 168(f)(8).

(B) Notwithstanding the provisions of § 5c.168(f)(8)-2(a)(5), if the transfer of a qualified mass commuting vehicle is not otherwise a disqualifying event, the transferee is not required to file the statement mentioned therein.

(C) The fact that a qualified mass commuting vehicle is not section 38 property because it is used by an exempt entity will not disqualify the lease under § 5c.168(f)(8)-8(b)(4); however, a disqualifying event will occur, and the agreement will cease to be characterized as a lease under

section 168(f)(8), with respect to a vehicle which (1) ceases to be a qualified mass commuting vehicle or (2) would cease to be section 38 property if used by a taxable entity as, for example, a vehicle used predominantly outside the United States. For the Federal income tax consequences of a disqualifying event, see § 5c.168(f)(8)-8.

(vi) The lessor of a qualified vehicle will not be allowed an investment tax credit with respect to it under section 38.

(vii) The application of this paragraph (b)(3) may be illustrated by the following examples:

Example (1). On July 1, 1981, a unit of city X, X Transit Authority (XTA), purchases 100 buses after receiving an UMTA grant for 80 percent of their purchase price. Fifteen percent of the purchase price is financed with a combination of State and local governmental grants and 5 percent is financed with proceeds from an issue of tax-exempt obligations described in section 103(b)(4)(I). Because UMTA financed an 80 percent interest in the 100 buses, XTA may lease under section 168(f)(8) only a 20 percent interest in each bus. If XTA were to lease 100 percent of 20 buses, only 20 percent of such buses would be deemed to be leased under a safe harbor lease.

Example (2). The facts are the same as in example (1) except that UMTA has not yet approved XTA's application in 1981. Pending the UMTA approval, XTA purchases and places in service 20 buses in July 1981. The 20 buses are financed with tax-exempt obligations described in section 103(b)(4)(I). On December 15, 1981, XTA sells a 100 percent interest in these 20 buses to Corporation M and leases them back under a lease in which the parties elect to have the provisions of section 168(f)(8) apply. M is a calendar-year taxpayer and claims an ACRS deduction with respect to the buses on its return for taxable year 1981. On July 1, 1982, UMTA approves XTA's grant application, thus enabling XTA to purchase an additional 80 buses. Because 80 percent of the original 20 buses are deemed to have been financed by UMTA beginning on July 1, 1982, the safe harbor lease terminates with respect to an undivided 80 percent interest in the 20 buses. If XTA would be considered the owner of the buses without regard to section 168(f)(8), the termination will result in a deemed sale of an undivided 80 percent interest in the 20 buses by M to XTA. The amoung realized by M on the sale will include a proportionate part of the outstanding amount of M's debt plus the sum of any other consideration received by M. M will realize gain or loss, depending upon its basis, with applicable section 1245 recapture. However, XTA may lease the 20 per-

Reg. § 5c.168(f)(8)-6(b)(3)

cent interest in the 80 new buses it purchased in 1982 which is deemed to have been financed with non-Federal funds.

Example (3). The facts are the same as in example (2) except that the grant approved by UMTA is used to purchase and renovate a bus garage facility. Eighty percent of the original 20 buses are deemed to have been financed by UMTA beginning on July 1, 1982. The lease would still terminate with respect to an undivided 80 percent interest in the vehicles. XTA cannot lease the garage facility under 168(f)(8) because it does not constitute a qualified mass commuting vehicle.

Example (4). The facts are the same as in example (2) except that on December 15, 1981, XTA sells and leases back only a 20 percent interest in the 20 buses acquired in July 1981. When the UMTA grant is later approved, the lease will not terminate with respect to any portion of the 20 buses. In addition, XTA may lease the 20 percent interest in the 80 new buses purchased in 1982 and deemed to have been financed with non-Federal funds.

Example (5). On August 1, 1982, UMTA approves a grant for a major 5-year capital expenditure program to improve city Y's rapid rail transit system. None of the funds relating to this UMTA-funded project, provided either by UMTA or by city Y, will be used to purchase qualified mass commuting vehicles. Instead, a number of rapid rail cars and buses will be purchased entirely with funds provided with a combination of grants by the State and city governments and of proceeds from an issue of tax-exempt obligations described in section 103(a). Because none of the rapid rail cars and buses are included as part of the UMTA-funded project, no part of them is deemed to be financed by UMTA. If at least 5 percent of the cost of the qualified mass commuting vehicles is provided by tax-exempt obligations under section 103(a), the vehicles will be qualified leased property in their entirety.

Example (6). City Z has a mass transit agency (ZTA) which purchases on July 1, 1982, 10 buses for which it pays $1,000,000 95 percent of which is derived from grants from city Z and 5 percent from tax-exempt obligations described in section 103(a). The buses have a useful life within the meaning of § 1.167(a)-1(b) of 10 years and their salvage value is zero. On July 1, 1983, ZTA sells these buses to corporation P and leases them back in a transaction which the parties elect to have treated as a lease under section 168(f)(8). At the time of the sale and leaseback, ZTA's adjusted basis in the 10 buses under section 1016(a)(3) and § 1.1016-4 is $900,000 ($1,000,000 cost less

$100,000 of depreciation sustained, computed on a straight-line basis). Before the transaction will qualify under section 168(f)(8) and § 5c.168(f)(8)-6(b)(3)(ii), P's adjusted basis in the vehicles may not exceed ZTA's basis, or $900,000. Assuming that the transaction qualifies under section 168(f)(8) and that corporation P is a calendar year taxpayer, P may claim ACRS deductions for 1982 of $135,000 (15 percent of $900,000).

Example (7). The facts are the same as in example (6) except that the sale and leaseback transaction is closed on December 31, 1982. P's adjusted basis in the vehicles may not exceed ZTA's basis, or $950,000 ($1,000,000 cost less $50,000 of depreciation sustained, computed on a straight-line basis).

Example (8). The facts are the same as in example (6) except that ZTA purchases the buses on June 1, 1981, and enters into the sale and leaseback transaction with corporation P on December 31, 1981. Under § 5c.168(f)(8)-6(b)(3)(ii), no adjustment is made to ZTA's basis in the buses for depreciation sustained. Therefore, P's basis in the buses may equal ZTA's cost of $1,000,000.

Example (9). On July 1, 1981, a unit of city W, W Transit Authority (WTA), purchases 100 buses with local grants derived entirely from a city W sales tax. The buses do not constitute qualified leased property under § 5c.168(f)(8)-6(b)(3) because no part of the financing for their purchase was derived from the proceeds of tax-exempt obligations.

Example (10). The facts are the same as in example (9) except that on November 1, 1981, WTA borrows 5 percent of the cost of the buses and pledges them as security. The interest on WTA's obligation is excludable from income under section 103(a)(1). On December 31, 1981, WTA sells to T Corp. all 100 buses and leases them back. Under § 5c.168(f)(8)-6(b)(3)(i), each bus is deemed to be financed with the proceeds of tax-exempt obligations. Therefore, if the vehicles otherwise meet the definition of qualified leased property, all the vehicles will be qualified leased property under this section.

(4) *Foreign lessees.* In addition to the other provisions of this section, property which is leased under a section 168(f)(8) lease to a foreign person shall not be qualified leased property unless the gross income attributable to the property from all sources (determined without regard to section 872(a) or 882 (b)) is effectively connected with a trade or business within the United States, and the taxable income, if any, attributable to the property is subject to tax under section 871(b)(1) or 822(a)(1). For this purpose, if income attributable to the property is not included in gross income

of a foreign lessee, and is exempt from taxation, under sections 872 or 883, or if the income is otherwise exempt from taxation under any income tax convention to which the United States is a party, then the property shall not be qualified leased property.

(5) *Other rules.* (i) Qualified leased property may include undivided interests in property or property regardless of whether or not it is considered separate property under State or local law. If property subject to a section 168(f)(8) lease is later determined not to be qualified leased property, disqualification of the lease under section 168(f)(8) will apply only as to that property.

(ii) The application of this subparagraph (5) may be illustrated by the following examples:

Example (1). On July 1, 1981, X Corp. contracts to have a manufacturing facility constructed for use in its business. Construction of the facility is completed on July 1, 1982, and the facility is deemed to be placed in service as of that date under § 5c.168(f)(8)-6(b)(2)(i). The facility is comprised of a mixture of new section 38 property and buildings that do not qualify as section 38 property. On August 1, 1982, X sells the new section 38 property in the facility to Y and leases it back under an agreement in which the parties elect to be treated as a lease described in section 168(f)(8). Assuming that the other requirements of this paragraph are met, the new section 38 property contained in the facility will be qualified leased property. If it is later determined that property subject to the section 168(f)(8) lease is not new section 38 property (and thus not qualified leased property), the safe harbor protection will be lost only as to that property.

Example (2). X Corp. acquires a certain piece of equipment (which is new section 38 property) for use in its business. Within 3 months, X sells a 70 percent undivided interest in the property to lessor A and a 10 percent undivided interest in the property to lessor B and leases both portions back under separate section 168(f)(8) leases. The investment tax credit and ACRS deductions associated with the property will be divided among X, lessor A, and lessor B, on a basis of 20 percent, 70 percent, and 10 percent, respectively. [Temporary Reg. § 5c.168(f)(8)-6.]

☐ [*T.D. 7791*, 10-20-81. *Amended by T.D.* 7795, 11-10-81 *and T.D. 7800*, 12-28-81.]

[Reg. § 5c.168(f)(8)-7]

§ 5c.168(f)(8)-7. **Reporting of income, deductions and investment tax credit; at risk rules (Temporary).**—(a) *In general.* The fact that the lessor's payments of interest and principal and the lessee's rental payments under the lease are not equal in amount will not prevent the lease from qualifying under section 168(f)(8). However, see paragraph (b) for special requirements in sale and leaseback transactions. In determining the parties' income, deductions, and investment tax credit under the lease, the rules in paragraphs (c) through (g) of this section shall apply regardless of the overall method of accounting otherwise used by the parties.

* * * * *

(b) *Requirements for sale and leaseback transaction.* If the property leased is financed by the lessee (or a related party of the lessee) in a sale and leaseback transaction, the lease will not qualify under section 168(f)(8) unless—

(1) The term of the lessor's purchase money obligation is coterminous with the term of the lease, and

(2) The lesser's obligation bears a reasonable rate of interest. For this purpose, a rate of interest shall be presumed to be reasonable if, on the date the agreement is executed, it is within 3 percentage points of (i) the rate in effect under section 6621, the prime rate in effect at any local commercial bank, or the most recent applicable rate determined by the Secretary under § 1.385-6(e)(2)(i), or (ii) an arm's-length rate as defined in § 1.482-2, or (iii) any rate between any two of the rates described by subdivisions (i) and (ii) of this paragraph (b)(2).

(c) *Interest deductions and income*—(1) *Deductibility from income.* In determining the amount of interest that a lessor may deduct in a taxable year with respect to its purchase money obligation given to the lessee or to a third party creditor, the lessor may not claim a deduction that would be—

(i) Greater than a deduction that would be allowed to an accrual basis taxpayer under a level-payment mortgage, amortized over a period equal to the term of the lessor's obligation, or

(ii) Less than a deduction that would be allowed to an accrual basis taxpayer under a straight line amortization of the principal over the term of the lessor's obligation.

In cases in which the property is not financed by the lessee or a party related to the lessee, the computation of the interest deduction may take into account fluctuations in the interest rate which are dependent on adjustments in the prime rate or events outside the control of the lessor and the third party creditor.

(2) *Includibility in income.* The lessee shall include interest on the lessor's purchase money obligation in income at the same time and in the

same amount as the lessor's interest deductions, as determined under paragraph (c)(1).

(d) *Rental income and deductions*—(1) *Deductibility from income.* The amount of the lessee's rent deduction under a section 168(f)(8) lease with respect to any taxable year shall be a pro rata portion of the aggregate amount required to be paid by the lessee to the lessor under the terms of the lease agreement.

If the lessee is required to purchase the leased property at the end of the lease term, or if the lessor has an option to sell the property to the lessee, rent shall not include the lesser of—

(A) The amount of the lessee's purchase obligation, whether fixed by the terms of the lease agreement or conditioned on the exercise of the lessor's option to sell the property to the lessee, or

(B) The fair market value of the property at the end of the lease term determined at the beginning of the lease term

For this purpose, fair market value shall be determined without taking into account any increase or decrease for inflation or deflation during the lease term. Rent deductions may be adjusted pursuant to the terms of the lease agreement to account for fluctuations which are dependent on events outside the control of the lessor and lessee, such as a change in the interest rate charged by a third party creditor of the lessor on the debt incurred to finance the purchase of the leased property.

(2) *Includibility in income.* The lessor shall include rent in income as follows:

(A) In the case of prepayments of rent, the earlier of when such rent is paid by the lessee or accrued under the lease, and

(B) In the case of other rent, at the same time and in the same amount as the lessee's rent deductions, as determined under paragraph (d)(1).

(e) *ACRS deductions.* The deductions that the lessor is allowed under section 168(a) with respect to property subject to a section 168(f)(8) lease shall be determined without regard to the limitation in section 168(f)(10)(B)(iii). The recovery class of qualified leased property in the hands of the lessor shall be determined by the character of the property in the hands of the owner of the property without regard to section 168(f)(8). Any elections under section 168(b)(3) by the lessor with respect to the class of recovery property to which the qualified leased property is assigned shall apply to the leased property. However, with respect to RRB replacement property, the transitional rule of section 168(f)(3) shall be inapplicable to the lessor.

(f) *At risk requirements.* The amount of the investment credit and ACRS deductions that a lessor shall be allowed with respect to the leased property shall be limited to the extent the at risk rules under the investment tax credit provisions and section 465 apply to the lessee or to the lessor. In determining the amount the lessee would be at risk, the at risk rules will be applied as if the lessee had not elected to have section 168(f)(8) apply. Thus, for example, if, without regard to section 168(f)(8), an individual lessee would be treated as the owner of the leased property for Federal tax law purposes, the lessor under a section 168(f)(8) lease would be allowed ACRS deductions or investment tax credits with respect to the property only to the extent that the lessee may have claimed them had the parties not elected treatment under section 168(f)(8). In addition, the ACRS deductions and investment tax credits that a lessor is allowed with respect to the property are further limited to the extent that the at risk rules apply to the lessor as owner of the property under the section 168(f)(8) lease. If the lessor and the lessee are subject to the at risk rules, the lessor is allowed only the lesser of ACRS deductions and investment tax credits allowable to the lessor and the lessee.

(g) *Limitation on section 48(d) amount.* If in a sale and leaseback transaction the lessor elects pursuant to section 48(d) to treat the lessee (which is the user of the property) as having acquired the property for purposes of claiming the investment tax credit, the lessee shall be treated as acquiring the property for an amount equal to the basis of the property to the lessor (and not for an amount equal to its fair market value). The investment tax credit allowable to the lessee is further limited to the extent the at risk rules apply to either the lessor or to the lessee. See paragraph (f) of this section.

(h) *Examples.* The application of the provisions of this section may be illustrated by the following examples.

Example (1). Y, a qualified lessor, acquires a piece of equipment which is qualified leased property for $1 million and leases it to X under a lease which the parties properly elect to have characterized as a lease described in section 168(f)(8). The equipment has a 10-year economic life and falls within the 5-year ACRS class. Under the terms of the lease, X, the lessee-user, is obligated to pay Y nine annual payments of $10,000 and, at the end of the lease term, Y has the option to sell the property to X for $2,160,000. Under § 5c.168(f)(8)-7(d), the aggregate payments required to be made by X under the lease are $2,250,000 ($90,000 rent plus $2,160,000 option

Reg. § 5c.168(f)(8)-7(h)

price) and are treated as rent to Y (less a reasonable estimate for the residual value of the property) and taxable as such. Assuming a reasonable estimate of the residual value is zero, the full $2,250,000 will be treated as rent, and under § 5c.168(f)(8)-7(d), such amount is deductible by X and includible in Y's income ratably over the term of the lease, i.e., at a rate of $250,000 per year ($2,250,000 divided by 9).

Example (2). The facts are the same as in example (1) except that under the terms of the lease X is obligated to make rental payments of $100,000 for each of the first 5 years of the lease and $300,000 for each of the 4 remaining years under the lease. Further, X has an option to purchase the equipment for $1.00 at the end of the lease term. Pursuant to § 5c.168(f)(8)-7(d), X's aggregate rental payments are deductible by X and are includible in Y's income ratably over the term of the lease. Thus, the annual rental payments are deemed to be $188,000 per year ($1,700,000 divided by 9). [Temporary Reg. § 5c.168(f)(8)-7.]

☐ [T.D. 7791, 10-20-81. Amended by T.D. 7795, 11-10-81.]

[Reg. § 5c.168(f)(8)-8]

§ 5c.168(f)(8)-8. **Loss of section 168(f)(8) protection; recapture (Temporary).**—(a) *In general.* Upon the occurrence of an event that causes an agreement to cease to be characterized as a lease under section 168(f)(8), the characterization of the lessor and lessee shall be determined without regard to section 168(f)(8).

(b) *Events which cause an agreement to cease to be characterized as a lease.* A disqualifying event shall cause an agreement to cease to be treated as a lease under section 168(f)(8) as of the date of the disqualifying event. A disqualifying event shall include the following:

(1) The lessor sells or assigns its interest in the lease or in the qualified leased property in a taxable transaction.

(2) The failure by the lessor to file a copy of the information return (or applicable statement) with its income tax return as required in § 5c.168(f)(8)-2(a)(3)(iii).

(3) The lessee (or any transferee of the lessee's interest) sells or assigns its interest in the lease or in the qualified leased property in a transaction not described in § 5c.168(f)(8)-2(a)(6) and the transferee fails to execute, within the prescribed time, the consent described in § 5c.168(f)(8)-2(a)(5), or either the lessor or the transferee fail to file statements with their income tax returns as required by that paragraph.

(4) The property ceases to be section 38 property as defined in § 1.48-1 in the hands of the lessor or lessee, for example, due to its conversion to personal use or to use predominantly outside the United States, or to use by a lessee exempt from Federal income taxation.

(5) The lessor ceases to be a qualified lessor by becoming an electing small business corporation or a personal holding company (within the meaning of section 542(a)).

(6) The minimum investment of the lessor becomes less than 10 percent of the adjusted basis of the qualified leased property as described in section 168(f)(8)(B)(ii) and § 5c.168(f)(8)-4.

(7) The lease terminates.

(8) The property becomes subject to more than one lease for which an election is made under section 168(f)(8).

(9) Retirements and casualties. [Reserved]

(10) The property is transferred in a bankruptcy or similar proceeding and the lessor fails either to furnish the appropriate notification or to file a statement with its income tax return as required by § 5c.168(f)(8)-2(a)(6).

(11) The property is transferred in a bankruptcy or similar proceeding and not all lenders with perfected and timely interests in the property specifically exclude or release the Federal income tax ownership of the property as required under § 5c.168(f)(8)-2(a)(6)(iii).

(12) The property is transferred subsequent to a bankruptcy or similar proceeding and the lessor fails to furnish notice to the transferee prior to the transfer or fails to file a statement with its income tax return, and either the lessor fails to secure the transferee's consent or the lessor or the transferee fail to file statements with their returns.

(13) The property is leased under the provisions of section 168(f)(8)(D)(iii) and § 5c.168(f)(8)-6(b)(3) and ceases to be a qualified mass commuting vehicle.

(14) The failure by the lessor to file the required information return described in § 5c.168(f)(8)-2(a)(3)(ii) by January 31, 1982, unless the lessee files such return by January 31, 1982.

(c) *Recapture.* The required amount of recapture of the investment tax credit and of accelerated cost recovery deductions after a disqualifying event shall be determined under sections 47 and 1245, respectively.

(d) *Consequences of loss of safe harbor protection.* The tax consequences of a disqualifying event depend upon the characterization of the parties without regard to section 168(f)(8). If the lessee would be the owner of the property without regard to section 168(f)(8), the disqualifying event will be deemed to be a sale of the qualified leased property by the lessor to the lessee. The amount realized by the lessor on the sale will include the outstanding amount (if any) of the lessor's debt on the property plus the sum of any other consideration received by the lessor. A disposition that results from a disqualifying event shall not be treated as an installment sale under section 453.

(e) *Examples*. The application of the provisions of this section may be illustrated by the following examples:

Example (1). M Corp. and N Corp. enter into a sale and leaseback transaction in which the lease-back agreement is characterized as a lease under section 168(f)(8) and M is treated as the lessor. In the second year of the lease, M becomes an electing small business corporation under subchapter S. The agreement ceases to be treated as a lease under section 168(f)(8) as of the date of the subchapter S election. Without respect to section 168(f)(8), N would be considered the owner of the property. The disqualification of M will be treated as a sale of the qualified leased property from M to N for the amount of the purchase money debt on the property then outstanding. M will realize gain or loss, depending upon its basis, with applicable investment tax credit and section 1245 recapture. N will acquire the property with a basis equal to the amount of the outstanding obligation. The property will not be used section 38 property to N under § 1.48-3(a)(2).

Example (2). Q Corp. (as lessor) and P Corp. (as lessee) enter into a lease that is characterized as a lease under section 168(f)(8). The lease has a 6-year term. P has no option to renew the lease or to purchase the property. At the end of 6 years, if P would be considered the owner of the property without regard to section 168(f)(8), upon the termination of the lease the property will be deemed to be sold by Q to P for the amount of the purchase money debt outstanding with respect to the property. [Temporary Reg. § 5c.168(f)(8)-8.]

☐ [*T.D. 7791, 10-20-81. Amended by T.D. 7795, 11-10-81 and T.D. 7800, 12-28-81.*]

[Reg. § 5c.168(f)(8)-9]

§ 5c.168(f)(8)-9. **Pass-through leases—transfer of only the investment tax credit to a party other than the ultimate user of the property.** [Reserved]

[Reg. § 5c.168(f)(8)-10]

§ 5c.168(f)(8)-10. **Leases between related parties.** [Reserved]

[Reg. § 5c.168(f)(8)-11]

§ 5c.168(f)(8)-11. **Consolidated returns.** [Reserved]

[Reg. § 1.168(h)-1]

§ 1.168(h)-1. **Like-kind exchanges involving tax-exempt use property.**—(a) *Scope*—(1) This section applies with respect to a direct or indirect transfer of property among related persons, including transfers made through a qualified intermediary (as defined in § 1.1031(k)-1(g)(4)) or other unrelated person, (a transfer) if—

(i) Section 1031 applies to any party to the transfer or to any related transaction; and

(ii) A principal purpose of the transfer or any related transaction is to avoid or limit the application of the alternative depreciation system (within the meaning of section 168(g)).

(2) For purposes of this section, a person is related to another person if they bear a relationship specified in section 267(b) or section 707(b)(1).

(b) *Allowable depreciation deduction for property subject to this section*—(1) *In general.* Property (tainted property) transferred directly or indirectly to a taxpayer by a related person (related party) as part of, or in connection with, a transaction in which the related party receives tax-exempt use property (related tax-exempt use property) will, if the tainted property is subject to an allowance for depreciation, be treated in the same manner as the related tax-exempt use property for purposes of determining the allowable depreciation deduction under section 167(a). Under this paragraph (b), the tainted property is depreciated by the taxpayer over the remaining recovery period of, and using the same depreciation method and convention as that of, the related tax-exempt use property.

(2) *Limitations*—(i) *Taxpayer's basis in related tax-exempt use property.* The rules of this paragraph (b) apply only with respect to so much of the taxpayer's basis in the tainted property as does not exceed the taxpayer's adjusted basis in the related tax-exempt use property prior to the transfer. Any excess of the taxpayer's basis in the tainted property over its adjusted basis in the related tax-exempt use property prior to the transfer is treated as property to which this section does not apply. This paragraph (b)(2)(i) does not apply if the related tax-exempt use property is not acquired from the taxpayer (e.g., if the taxpayer acquires the tainted property for cash

Reg. § 1.168(h)-1(b)(2)

but section 1031 nevertheless applies to the related party because the transfer involves a qualified intermediary).

(ii) *Application of section 168(i)(7).* This section does not apply to so much of the taxpayer's basis in the tainted property as is subject to section 168(i)(7).

(c) *Related tax-exempt use property.* (1) For purposes of paragraph (b) of this section, related tax-exempt use property includes—

(i) Property that is tax-exempt use property (as defined in section 168(h)) at the time of the transfer; and

(ii) Property that does not become tax-exempt use property until after the transfer if, at the time of the transfer, it was intended that the property become tax-exempt use property.

(2) For purposes of determining the remaining recovery period of the related tax-exempt use property in the circumstances described in paragraph (c)(1)(ii) of this section, the related tax-exempt use property will be treated as having, prior to the transfer, a lease term equal to the term of any lease that causes such property to become tax-exempt use property.

(d) *Examples.* The following examples illustrate the application of this section. The examples do not address common law doctrines or other authorities that may apply to recharacterize or alter the effects of the transactions described therein. Unless otherwise indicated, parties to the transactions are not related to one another.

Example 1. (i) X owns all of the stock of two subsidiaries, B and Z. X, B and Z do not file a consolidated federal income tax return. On May 5, 1995, B purchases an aircraft (*FA*) for $1 million and leases it to a foreign airline whose income is not subject to United States taxation and which is a tax-exempt entity as defined in section 168(h)(2). On the same date, Z owns an aircraft (*DA*) with a fair market value of $1 million, which has been, and continues to be, leased to an airline that is a United States taxpayer. Z's adjusted basis in DA is $0. The next day, at a time when each aircraft is still worth $1 million, B transfers FA to Z (subject to the lease to the foreign airline) in exchange for DA (subject to the lease to the airline that is a United States taxpayer). Z realizes gain of $1 million on the exchange, but that gain is not recognized pursuant to section 1031(a) because the exchange is of like-kind properties. Assume that a principal purpose of the transfer of DA to B or of FA to Z is to avoid the application of the alternative depreciation system. Following the exchange, Z has a $0 basis in FA pursuant to section 1031(d). B has a $1 million basis in DA.

(ii) B has acquired property from Z, a related person; Z's gain is not recognized pursuant to section 1031(a); Z has received tax-exempt use property as part of the transaction; and a principal purpose of the transfer of DA to B or of FA to Z is to avoid the application of the alternative depreciation system. Accordingly, the transaction is within the scope of this section. Pursuant to paragraph (b) of this section, B must recover its $1 million basis in DA over the remaining recovery period of, and using the same depreciation method and convention as that of, FA, the related tax-exempt use property.

(iii) If FA did not become tax-exempt use property until after the exchange, it would still be related tax-exempt use property and paragraph (b) of this section would apply if, at the time of the exchange, it was intended that FA become tax-exempt use property.

Example 2. (i) X owns all of the stock of two subsidiaries, B and Z. X, B and Z do not file a consolidated federal income tax return. B and Z each own identical aircraft. B's aircraft (*FA*) is leased to a tax-exempt entity as defined in section 168(h)(2) and has a fair market value of $1 million and an adjusted basis of $500,000. Z's aircraft (DA) is leased to a United States taxpayer and has a fair market value of $1 million and an adjusted basis of $10,000. On May 1, 1995, B and Z exchange aircraft, subject to their respective leases. B realizes gain of $500,000 and Z realizes gain of $990,000, but neither person recognizes gain because of the operation of section 1031(a). Moreover, assume that a principal purpose of the transfer of DA to B or of FA to Z is to avoid the application of the alternative depreciation system.

(ii) As in *Example 1*, B has acquired property from Z, a related person; Z's gain is not recognized pursuant to section 1031(a); Z has received tax-exempt use property as part of the transaction; and a principal purpose of the transfer of DA to B or of FA to Z is to avoid the application of the alternative depreciation system. Thus, the transaction is within the scope of this section even though B has held tax-exempt use property for a period of time and, during that time, has used the alternative depreciation system with respect to such property. Pursuant to paragraph (b) of this section, B, which has a substituted basis determined pursuant to section 1031(d) of $500,000 in DA, must depreciate the aircraft over the remaining recovery period of FA, using the same depreciation method and convention. Z holds tax-exempt use property with a basis of $10,000, which must be depreciated under the alternative depreciation system.

Reg. § 1.168(h)-1(c)(2)

(iii) Assume the same facts as in paragraph (i) of this *Example 2*, except that B and Z are members of an affiliated group that files a consolidated federal income tax return. Of B's $500,000 basis in DA, $10,000 is subject to section 168(i)(7) and therefore not subject to this section. The remaining $490,000 of basis is subject to this section. But see § 1.1502-80(f) making section 1031 inapplicable to intercompany transactions occurring in consolidated return years beginning on or after July 12, 1995.

(e) *Effective date.* This section applies to transfers made on or after April 20, 1995. [Reg. § 1.168(h)-1.]

□ [*T.D.* 8667, 4-26-96.]

[Reg. § 1.168(i)-0]

§ 1.168(i)-0. **Table of contents for the general asset account rules.**—This section lists the major paragraphs contained in § 1.168(i)-1.

§ 1.168(i)-1. General asset accounts.

(a) Scope.

(b) Definitions.

(1) Unadjusted depreciable basis.

(2) Unadjusted depreciable basis of the general asset account.

(3) Adjusted depreciable basis of the general asset account.

(4) Expensed cost.

(c) Establishment of general asset accounts.

(1) Assets eligible for general asset accounts.

(i) General rules.

(ii) Special rules for assets generating foreign source income.

(2) Grouping assets in general asset accounts.

(i) General rules.

(ii) Special rules.

(d) Determination of depreciation allowance.

(1) In general.

(2) Special rule for passenger automobiles.

(e) Disposition of an asset from a general asset account.

(1) Scope.

(2) General rules for a disposition.

(i) No immediate recovery of basis.

(ii) Treatment of amount realized.

(iii) Effect of disposition on a general asset account.

(iv) Coordination with nonrecognition provisions.

(v) Examples.

(3) Special rules.

(i) In general.

(ii) Disposition of all assets remaining in a general asset account.

(iii) Disposition of an asset in a qualifying disposition.

(iv) Transactions subject to section 168(i)(7).

(v) Anti-abuse rule.

(f) Assets generating foreign source income.

(1) In general.

(2) Source of ordinary income, gain, or loss.

(i) Source determined by allocation and apportionment of depreciation allowed.

(ii) Formula for determining foreign source income, gain, or loss.

(3) Section 904(d) separate categories.

(g) Assets subject to recapture.

(h) Changes in use.

(1) Conversion to personal use.

(2) Other changes in use.

(i) Identification of disposed or converted asset.

(j) Effect of adjustments on prior dispositions.

(k) Election.

(1) Irrevocable election.

(2) Time for making election.

(3) Manner of making election.

(l) Effective date.

[Reg. § 1.168(i)-0.]

□ [*T.D.* 8566, 10-7-94.]

[Reg. § 1.168(i)-1]

§ 1.168(i)-1. **General asset accounts.**—(a) *Scope.* This section provides rules for general asset accounts under section 168(i)(4). The provisions of this section apply only to assets for which an election has been made under paragraph (k) of this section.

(b) *Definitions.* For purposes of this section, the following definitions apply:

(1) *Unadjusted depreciable basis* is the basis of an asset for purposes of section 1011 without regard to any adjustments described in sections 1016(a)(2) and (3).

(2) *Unadjusted depreciable basis of the general asset account* is the sum of the unadjusted depreciable bases of all assets included in the general asset account.

(3) *Adjusted depreciable basis of the general asset account* is the unadjusted depreciable basis of the general asset account less the adjustments to basis described in sections 1016(a)(2) and (3).

Reg. § 1.168(i)-1(b)(3)

(4) *Expensed cost* is the amount of any allowable credit or deduction treated as a deduction allowable for depreciation or amortization for purposes of section 1245 (for example, a credit allowable under section 30 or a deduction allowable under section 179, 179A, or 190).

(c) *Establishment of general asset accounts*— (1) *Assets eligible for general asset accounts*—(i) *General rules.* Assets that are subject to either the general depreciation system of section 168(a) or the alternative depreciation system of section 168(g) may be accounted for in one or more general asset accounts. An asset may be included in a general asset account only to the extent of the asset's unadjusted depreciable basis (for example, if, in 1995, a taxpayer places in service an asset that costs $20,000 and elects under section 179 to expense $17,500 of that asset's cost, the unadjusted depreciable basis of the asset is $2,500 and, therefore, only $2,500 of the asset's cost may be included in a general asset account). However, an asset is not to be included in a general asset account if the asset is used both in a trade or business (or for the production of income) and in a personal activity at any time during the taxable year in which the asset is first placed in service by the taxpayer.

(ii) *Special rules for assets generating foreign source income*—(A) Assets that generate foreign source income, both United States and foreign source income, or combined gross income of a FSC (as defined in section 922), DISC (as defined in section 992(a)), or possessions corporation (as defined in section 936) and its related supplier, may be included in a general asset account if the requirements of paragraph (c)(2)(i) of this section are satisfied. If, however, the inclusion of these assets in a general asset account results in a substantial distortion of income, the Commissioner may disregard the general asset account election and make any reallocations of income or expense necessary to clearly reflect income.

(B) A general asset account shall be treated as a single asset for purposes of applying the rules in § 1.861-9T(g)(3) (relating to allocation and apportionment of interest expense under the asset method). A general asset account that generates income in more than one grouping of income (statutory and residual) is a multiple category asset (as defined in § 1.861-9T(g)(3)(ii)), and the income yield from the general asset account must be determined by applying the rules for multiple category assets as if the general asset account were a single asset.

(2) *Grouping assets in general asset accounts*—(i) *General rules.* If a taxpayer makes the

election under paragraph (k) of this section, assets that are subject to the election are grouped into one or more general asset accounts. Assets that are eligible to be grouped into a single general asset account may be divided into more than one general asset account. Each general asset account must include only assets that—

(A) Have the same asset class (for further guidance, see Rev. Proc. 87-56, 1987-2 C.B. 674, and § 601.601(d)(2)(ii)(*b*) of this chapter);

(B) Have the same applicable depreciation method;

(C) Have the same applicable recovery period;

(D) Have the same applicable convention; and

(E) Are placed in service by the taxpayer in the same taxable year.

(ii) *Special rules.* In addition to the general rules in paragraph (c)(2)(i) of this section, the following rules apply when establishing general asset accounts—

(A) Assets without an asset class, but with the same characteristics described in paragraphs (c)(2)(i)(B), (C), (D), and (E) of this section, may be grouped into a general asset account;

(B) Assets subject to the mid-quarter convention may only be grouped into a general asset account with assets that are placed in service in the same quarter of the taxable year;

(C) Assets subject to the mid-month convention may only be grouped into a general asset account with assets that are placed in service in the same month of the taxable year; and

(D) Passenger automobiles for which the depreciation allowance is limited under section 280F(a) must be grouped into a separate general asset account.

(d) *Determination of depreciation allowance*—(1) *In general.* Depreciation allowances are determined for each general asset account by using the applicable depreciation method, recovery period, and convention for the assets in the account. The depreciation allowances are recorded in a depreciation reserve account for each general asset account. The allowance for depreciation under this section constitutes the amount of depreciation allowable under section 167(a).

(2) *Special rule for passenger automobiles.* For purposes of applying section 280F(a), the depreciation allowance for a general asset account established for passenger automobiles is limited for each taxable year to the amount prescribed in section 280F(a) multiplied by the excess of the number of automobiles originally included in the

Reg. § 1.168(i)-1(b)(4)

account over the number of automobiles disposed of during the taxable year or in any prior taxable year in a transaction described in paragraph (e)(3)(iii) (disposition of an asset in a qualifying disposition), (e)(3)(iv) (transactions subject to section 168(i)(7)), (e)(3)(v) (anti-abuse rule), (g) (assets subject to recapture), or (h)(1) (conversion to personal use) of this section.

(e) *Disposition of an asset from a general asset account*—(1) *Scope.* This paragraph (e) provides rules applicable to dispositions of assets included in a general asset account. For purposes of this paragraph (e), an asset in a general asset account is disposed of when ownership of the asset is transferred or when the asset is permanently withdrawn from use either in the taxpayer's trade or business or in the production of income. A disposition includes the sale, exchange, retirement, physical abandonment, or destruction of an asset. A disposition also occurs when an asset is transferred to a supplies, scrap, or similar account. A disposition does not include, however, the retirement of a structural component of real property.

(2) *General rules for a disposition*—(i) *No immediate recovery of basis.* Immediately before a disposition of any asset in a general asset account, the asset is treated as having an adjusted basis of zero for purposes of section 1011. Therefore, no loss is realized upon the disposition of an asset from the general asset account. Similarly, where an asset is disposed of by transfer to a supplies, scrap, or similar account, the basis of the asset in the supplies, scrap, or similar account will be zero.

(ii) *Treatment of amount realized.* Any amount realized on a disposition is recognized as ordinary income (notwithstanding any other provision of subtitle A of the Internal Revenue Code (Code)) to the extent the sum of the unadjusted depreciable basis of the general asset account and any expensed cost (as defined in paragraph (b)(4) of this section) for assets in the account exceeds any amounts previously recognized as ordinary income upon the disposition of other assets in the account. The recognition and character of any excess amount realized are determined under other applicable provisions of the Code (other than sections 1245 and 1250 or provisions of the Code that treat gain on a disposition as subject to section 1245 or 1250).

(iii) *Effect of disposition on a general asset account.* The unadjusted depreciable basis and the depreciation reserve of the general asset account are not affected as a result of a disposition of an asset from the general asset account.

(iv) *Coordination with nonrecognition provisions.* For purposes of determining the basis of an asset acquired in a transaction described in paragraph (e)(3)(iii)(B)(4) of this section (relating to certain nonrecognition provisions), the amount of ordinary income recognized under this paragraph (e)(2) is treated as the amount of gain recognized on the disposition.

(v) *Examples.* The following examples illustrate the application of this paragraph (e)(2).

Example 1. (i) R, a calendar-year corporation, maintains one general asset account for ten machines. The machines cost a total of $10,000 and were placed in service in June 1995. Of the ten machines, one machine costs $8,200 and nine machines cost a total of $1,800. Assume this general asset account has a depreciation method of 200 percent declining balance, a recovery period of 5 years, and a half-year convention. R does not make a section 179 election for any of the machines. As of January 1, 1996, the depreciation reserve of the account is $2,000 [(($10,000 − $0) × 40%) / 2].

(ii) On February 8, 1996, R sells the machine that cost $8,200 to an unrelated party for $9,000. Under paragraph (e)(2)(i) of this section, this machine has an adjusted basis of zero.

(iii) On its 1996 tax return, R recognizes the amount realized of $9,000 as ordinary income because such amount does not exceed the unadjusted depreciable basis of the general asset account ($10,000), plus any expensed cost for assets in the account ($0), less amounts previously recognized as ordinary income ($0). Moreover, the unadjusted depreciable basis and depreciation reserve of the account are not affected by the disposition of the machine. Thus, the depreciation allowance for the account in 1996 is $3,200 (($10,000 − $2,000) × 40%).

Example 2. (i) The facts are the same as in *Example 1.* In addition, on June 4, 1997, R sells seven machines to an unrelated party for a total of $1,100. In accordance with paragraph (e)(2)(i) of this section, these machines have an adjusted basis of zero.

(ii) On its 1997 tax return, R recognizes $1,000 as ordinary income (the unadjusted depreciable basis of $10,000, plus the expensed cost of $0, less the amount of $9,000 previously recognized as ordinary income). The recognition and character of the excess amount realized of $100 ($1,100 − $1,000) are determined under applicable provisions of the Code other than section 1245 (such as section 1231). Moreover, the unadjusted depreciable basis and depreciation reserve of the account are not affected by the disposition of the machines. Thus, the depreciation allowance for

Reg. § 1.168(i)-1(e)(2)

the account in 1997 is $1,920 (($10,000 − $5,200) × 40%).

(3) *Special rules*—(i) *In general.* This paragraph (e)(3) provides the rules for terminating general asset account treatment upon certain dispositions. While the rules under paragraphs (e)(3)(ii) and (iii) of this section are optional rules, the rules under paragraphs (e)(3)(iv) and (v) of this section are mandatory rules. A taxpayer applies paragraph (e)(3)(ii) or (iii) of this section by reporting the gain, loss, or other deduction on the taxpayer's timely filed (including extensions) income tax return for the taxable year in which the disposition occurs. For purposes of applying paragraph (e)(3)(iii) through (v) of this section, see paragraph (i) of this section for identifying the unadjusted depreciable basis of a disposed asset.

(ii) *Disposition of all assets remaining in a general asset account*—(A) *Optional termination of a general asset account.* Upon the disposition of all of the assets, or the last asset, in a general asset account, a taxpayer may apply this paragraph (e)(3)(ii) to recover the adjusted depreciable basis of the general asset account (rather than having paragraph (e)(2) of this section apply). Under this paragraph (e)(3)(ii), the general asset account terminates and the amount of gain or loss for the general asset account is determined under section 1001(a) by taking into account the adjusted depreciable basis of the general asset account at the time of the disposition. The recognition and character of the gain or loss are determined under other applicable provisions of the Code, except that the amount of gain subject to section 1245 (or section 1250) is limited to the excess of the depreciation allowed or allowable for the general asset account, including any expensed cost (or the excess of the additional depreciation allowed or allowable for the general asset account), over any amounts previously recognized as ordinary income under paragraph (e)(2) of this section.

(B) *Example.* The following example illustrates the application of this paragraph (e)(3)(ii).

Example. (i) *T*, a calendar-year corporation, maintains a general asset account for 1,000 calculators. The calculators cost a total of $60,000 and were placed in service in 1995. Assume this general asset account has a depreciation method of 200 percent declining balance, a recovery period of 5 years, and a half-year convention. *T* does not make a section 179 election for any of the calculators. In 1996, *T* sells 200 of the calculators to an unrelated party for a total of $10,000 and recognizes the $10,000 as ordinary income in accordance with paragraph (e)(2) of this section.

(ii) On March 26, 1997, *T* sells the remaining calculators in the general asset account to an unrelated party for $35,000. *T* chooses to apply paragraph (e)(3)(ii) of this section. As a result, the account terminates and gain or loss is determined for the account.

(iii) On the date of disposition, the adjusted depreciable basis of the account is $23,040 (unadjusted depreciable basis of $60,000 less the depreciation allowed or allowable of $36,960). Thus, in 1997, *T* recognizes gain of $11,960 (amount realized of $35,000 less the adjusted depreciable basis of $23,040). The gain of $11,960 is subject to section 1245 to the extent of the depreciation allowed or allowable for the account (plus the expensed cost for assets in the account) less the amounts previously recognized as ordinary income ($36,960 + $0 − $10,000 = $26,960). As a result, the entire gain of $11,960 is subject to section 1245.

(iii) *Disposition of an asset in a qualifying disposition*—(A) *Optional determination of the amount of gain, loss, or other deduction.* In the case of a qualifying disposition of an asset (described in paragraph (e)(3)(iii)(B) of this section), a taxpayer may apply this paragraph (e)(3)(iii) (rather than having paragraph (e)(2) of this section apply). Under this paragraph (e)(3)(iii), general asset account treatment for the asset terminates as of the first day of the taxable year in which the qualifying disposition occurs, and the amount of gain, loss, or other deduction for the asset is determined by taking into account the asset's adjusted basis. The adjusted basis of the asset at the time of the disposition equals the unadjusted depreciable basis of the asset less the depreciation allowed or allowable for the asset, computed by using the depreciation method, recovery period, and convention applicable to the general asset account in which the asset was included. The recognition and character of the gain, loss, or other deduction are determined under other applicable provisions of the Code, except that the amount of gain subject to section 1245 (or section 1250) is limited to the lesser of—

(*1*) The depreciation allowed or allowable for the asset, including any expensed cost (or the additional depreciation allowed or allowable for the asset); or

(*2*) The excess of—

(*i*) The original unadjusted depreciable basis of the general asset account plus, in the case of section 1245 property originally included in the general asset account, any expensed cost; over

(*ii*) The cumulative amounts of gain previously recognized as ordinary income under either paragraph (e)(2) of this section or section 1245 (or section 1250).

(B) *Qualifying dispositions.* A qualifying disposition is a disposition that does not involve all the assets, or the last asset, remaining in a general asset account and that is—

(1) A direct result of a fire, storm, shipwreck, or other casualty, or from theft;

(2) A charitable contribution for which a deduction is allowable under section 170;

(3) A direct result of a cessation, termination, or disposition of a business, manufacturing or other income producing process, operation, facility, plant, or other unit (other than by transfer to a supplies, scrap, or similar account); or

(4) A transaction, other than a transaction described in paragraph (e)(3)(iv) of this section (pertaining to transactions subject to section 168(i)(7)), to which a nonrecognition section of the Code applies (determined without regard to this section), such as section 1031 or 1033.

(C) *Effect of a qualifying disposition on a general asset account.* If the taxpayer applies this paragraph (e)(3)(iii) to a qualifying disposition of an asset, then—

(1) The asset is removed from the general asset account as of the first day of the taxable year in which the qualifying disposition occurs;

(2) The unadjusted depreciable basis of the general asset account is reduced by the unadjusted depreciable basis of the asset as of the first day of the taxable year in which the disposition occurs;

(3) The depreciation reserve of the general asset account is reduced by the depreciation allowed or allowable for the asset as of the end of the taxable year immediately preceding the year of disposition, computed by using the depreciation method, recovery period, and convention applicable to the general asset account in which the asset was included; and

(4) For purposes of determining the amount of gain realized on subsequent dispositions that is subject to ordinary income treatment under paragraph (e)(2)(i) of this section, the amount of any expensed cost with respect to the asset is disregarded.

(D) *Example.* The provisions of this paragraph (e)(3)(iii) are illustrated by the following example.

Example. (i) Z, a calendar-year corporation, maintains one general asset account for 12 machines. Each machine costs $15,000 and was placed in service in 1995. Of the 12 machines,

nine machines that cost a total of $135,000 are used in Z's Kentucky plant, and three machines that cost a total of $45,000 are used in Z's Ohio plant. Assume this general asset account has a depreciation method of 200 percent declining balance, a recovery period of 5 years, and a half-year convention. Z does not make a section 179 election for any of the machines. As of January 1, 1997, the depreciation reserve for the account is $93,600.

(ii) On May 27, 1997, Z sells its entire manufacturing plant in Ohio to an unrelated party. The sales proceeds allocated to each of the three machines at the Ohio plant is $5,000. Because this transaction is a qualifying disposition under paragraph (e)(3)(iii)(B)(3) of this section, Z chooses to apply paragraph (e)(3)(iii) of this section.

(iii) For Z's 1997 return, the depreciation allowance for the account is computed as follows. As of December 31, 1996, the depreciation allowed or allowable for the three machines at the Ohio plant is $23,400. Thus, as of January 1, 1997, the unadjusted depreciable basis of the account is reduced from $180,000 to $135,000 ($180,000 less the unadjusted depreciable basis of $45,000 for the three machines), and the depreciation reserve of the account is decreased from $93,600 to $70,200 ($93,600 less the depreciation allowed or allowable of $23,400 for the three machines as of December 31, 1996). Consequently, the depreciation allowance for the account in 1997 is $25,920 (($135,000 − $70,200) × 40%).

(iv) For Z's 1997 return, gain or loss for each of the three machines at the Ohio plant is determined as follows. The depreciation allowed or allowable in 1997 for each machine is $1,440 [(($15,000 − $7,800) × 40%) / 2]. Thus, the adjusted basis of each machine under section 1011 is $5,760 (the adjusted depreciable basis of $7,200 removed from the account less the depreciation allowed or allowable of $1,440 in 1997). As a result, the loss recognized in 1997 for each machine is $760 ($5,000 − $5,760), which is subject to section 1231.

(iv) *Transactions subject to section 168(i)(7).* If an asset in a general asset account is transferred in a transaction described in section 168(i)(7)(B) (pertaining to treatment of transferees in certain nonrecognition transactions), the transferor must remove the transferred asset from the general asset account as of the first day of the taxable year in which the transaction occurs. In addition, the adjustments to the general asset account described in paragraph (e)(3)(iii)(C)(2) through (4) of this section must be made. The transferee is bound by the transferor's election

Reg. § 1.168(i)-1(e)(3)

under paragraph (k) of this section with respect to so much of the asset's basis in the hands of the transferee as does not exceed the asset's adjusted basis in the hands of the transferor. If all of the assets, or the last asset, in a general asset account are transferred, the transferee's basis in the assets or asset transferred is equal to the adjusted depreciable basis of the general asset account as of the beginning of the transferor's taxable year in which the transaction occurs, decreased by the amount of depreciation allocable to the transferor for the year of the transfer.

(v) *Anti-abuse rule*—(A) *In general.* If an asset in a general asset account is disposed of by a taxpayer in a transaction described in paragraph (e)(3)(v)(B) of this section, general asset account treatment for the asset terminates as of the first day of the taxable year in which the disposition occurs. Consequently, the taxpayer must determine the amount of gain, loss, or other deduction attributable to the disposition in the manner described in paragraph (e)(3)(iii)(A) of this section (notwithstanding that paragraph (e)(3)(iii)(A) of this section is an optional rule) and must make the adjustments to the general asset account described in paragraph (e)(3)(iii)(C)(*1*) through (*4*) of this section.

(B) *Abusive transactions.* A transaction is described in this paragraph (e)(3)(v)(B) if the transaction is not described in paragraph (e)(3)(iv) of this section and the transaction is entered into, or made, with a principal purpose of achieving a tax benefit or result that would not be available absent an election under this section. Examples of these types of transactions include—

(*1*) A transaction entered into with a principal purpose of shifting income or deductions among taxpayers in a manner that would not be possible absent an election under this section in order to take advantage of differing effective tax rates among the taxpayers; or

(*2*) An election made under this section with a principal purpose of disposing of an asset from a general asset account in order to utilize an expiring net operating loss or credit. The fact that a taxpayer with a net operating loss carryover or a credit carryover transfers an asset to a related person or transfers an asset pursuant to an arrangement where the asset continues to be used (or is available for use) by the taxpayer pursuant to a lease (or otherwise) indicates, absent strong evidence to the contrary, that the

transaction is described in this paragraph (e)(3)(v)(B).

(f) *Assets generating foreign source income*— (1) *In general.* This paragraph (f) provides the rules for determining the source of any income, gain, or loss recognized, and the appropriate section 904(d) separate limitation category or categories for any foreign source income, gain, or loss recognized, on a disposition (within the meaning of paragraph (e)(1) of this section) of an asset in a general asset account that consists of assets generating both United States and foreign source income. These rules apply only to a disposition to which paragraph (e)(2) (general disposition rules), (e)(3)(ii) (disposition of all assets remaining in a general asset account), (e)(3)(iii) (disposition of an asset in a qualifying disposition), or (e)(3)(v) (anti-abuse rule) of this section applies.

(2) *Source of ordinary income, gain, or loss*— (i) *Source determined by allocation and apportionment of depreciation allowed.* The amount of any ordinary income, gain, or loss that is recognized on the disposition of an asset in a general asset account must be apportioned between United States and foreign sources based on the allocation and apportionment of the—

(A) Depreciation allowed for the general asset account as of the end of the taxable year in which the disposition occurs if paragraph (e)(2) of this section applies to the disposition;

(B) Depreciation allowed for the general asset account as of the time of the disposition if the taxpayer applies paragraph (e)(3)(ii) of this section to the disposition of all of the assets, or the last asset, in the general asset account; or

(C) Depreciation allowed for the disposed asset for only the taxable year in which the disposition occurs if the taxpayer applies paragraph (e)(3)(iii) to the disposition of the asset in a qualifying disposition or if the asset is disposed in a transaction described in paragraph (e)(3)(v) (anti-abuse rule) of this section.

(ii) *Formula for determining foreign source income, gain, or loss.* The amount of ordinary income, gain, or loss recognized on the disposition that shall be treated as foreign source income, gain, or loss must be determined under the formula in this paragraph (f)(2)(ii). For purposes of this formula, the allowed depreciation deductions are determined for the applicable time period provided in paragraph (f)(2)(i) of this section. The formula is:

$$\begin{array}{l}\text{Foreign Source} \\ \text{Income, Gain, or} \\ \text{Loss from the} \\ \text{Disposition of} \\ \text{an Asset}\end{array} = \begin{array}{l}\text{Total Ordinary} \\ \text{Income, Gain, or} \\ \text{Loss from} \\ \text{Disposition of an} \\ \text{Asset}\end{array} \times \frac{\begin{array}{l}\text{Allowed Depreciation} \\ \text{Deductions Allocated and} \\ \text{Apportioned to} \\ \text{Foreign Source Income}\end{array}}{\begin{array}{l}\text{Total Allowed Depreciation} \\ \text{Deductions for the General} \\ \text{Asset Account or for the} \\ \text{Disposed Asset (as} \\ \text{applicable)}\end{array}}$$

(3) *Section 904(d) separate categories.* If the assets in the general asset account generate foreign source income in more than one separate category under section 904(d)(1) or another section of the Code (for example, income treated as foreign source income under section 904(g)(10)), or under a United States income tax treaty that requires the foreign tax credit limitation to be determined separately for specified types of income, the amount of "foreign source income, gain, or loss from the disposition of an asset" (as determined under the formula in paragraph (f)(2)(ii) of this section) must be allocated and apportioned to the applicable separate category or categories under the formula in this paragraph (f)(3). For purposes of this formula, the allowed depreciation deductions are determined for the applicable time period provided in paragraph (f)(2)(i) of this section. The formula is:

$$\begin{array}{l}\text{Foreign Source} \\ \text{Income, Gain, or} \\ \text{Loss In a Separate} \\ \text{Category}\end{array} = \begin{array}{l}\text{Foreign Source} \\ \text{Income, Gain, or} \\ \text{Loss from the} \\ \text{Disposition of an} \\ \text{Asset}\end{array} \times \frac{\begin{array}{l}\text{Allowed Depreciation} \\ \text{Deductions Allocated and} \\ \text{Apportioned to a} \\ \text{Separate Category}\end{array}}{\begin{array}{l}\text{Total Allowed Depreciation} \\ \text{Deductions Allocated and} \\ \text{Apportioned to Foreign} \\ \text{Source Income}\end{array}}$$

(g) *Assets subject to recapture.* If the basis of an asset in a general asset account is increased as a result of the recapture of any allowable credit or deduction (for example, the basis adjustment for the recapture amount under section 30(d)(2), 50(c)(2), 179(d)(10), or 179A(e)(4)), general asset account treatment for the asset terminates as of the first day of the taxable year in which the recapture event occurs. Consequently, the taxpayer must remove the asset from the general asset account as of that day and must make the adjustments to the general asset account described in paragraph (e)(3)(iii)(C)(2) through (4) of this section.

(h) *Changes in use*—(1) *Conversion to personal use.* An asset in a general asset account becomes ineligible for general asset account treatment if a taxpayer uses the asset in a personal activity during a taxable year. Upon a conversion to personal use, the taxpayer must remove the asset from the general asset account as of the first day of the taxable year in which the change in use occurs and must make the adjustments to the general asset account described in paragraph (e)(3)(iii)(C)(2) through (4) of this section.

(2) *Other changes in use.* [Reserved].

(i) *Identification of disposed or converted asset.* A taxpayer may use any reasonable method that is consistently applied to the taxpayer's general asset accounts for purposes of determining the unadjusted depreciable basis of a disposed or converted asset in a transaction described in paragraph (e)(3)(iii) (disposition of an asset in a qualifying disposition), (e)(3)(iv) (transactions subject to section 168(i)(7)), (e)(3)(v) (anti-abuse rule), (g) (assets subject to recapture), or (h)(1) (conversion to personal use) of this section.

(j) *Effect of adjustments on prior dispositions.* The adjustments to a general asset account under paragraph (e)(3)(iii), (e)(3)(iv), (e)(3)(v), (g), or (h)(1) of this section have no effect on the recognition and character of prior dispositions subject to paragraph (e)(2) of this section.

(k) *Election*—(1) *Irrevocable election.* If a taxpayer makes an election under this paragraph (k), the taxpayer consents to, and agrees to apply, all of the provisions of this section to the assets included in a general asset account. Except as provided in paragraph (c)(1)(ii)(A), (e)(3), (g), or (h)(1) of this section, an election made under this section is irrevocable and will be binding on the taxpayer for computing taxable income for the taxable year for which the election is made and for all subsequent taxable years. An election under this paragraph (k) is made separately by each person owning an asset to which this section applies (for example, by each member of a consolidated group, at the partnership level (and not by the partner separately), or at the S corporation level (and not by the shareholder separately)).

Reg. § 1.168(i)-1(k)(1)

(2) *Time for making election.* The election to apply this section shall be made on the taxpayer's timely filed (including extensions) income tax return for the taxable year in which the assets included in the general asset account are placed in service by the taxpayer.

(3) *Manner of making election.* In the year of election, a taxpayer makes the election under this section by typing or legibly printing at the top of the Form 4562, "GENERAL ASSET ACCOUNT ELECTION MADE UNDER SECTION 168(i)(4)," or in the manner provided for on Form 4562 and its instructions. The taxpayer shall maintain records (for example, "General Asset Account #1—all 1995 additions in asset class 00.11 for Salt Lake City, Utah facility") that identify the assets included in each general asset account, that establish the unadjusted depreciable basis and depreciation reserve of the general asset account, and that reflect the amount realized during the taxable year upon dispositions from each general asset account. (But see section 179(c) and § 1.179-5 for the recordkeeping requirements for section 179 property.) The taxpayer's record-keeping practices should be consistently applied to the general asset accounts. If Form 4562 is revised or renumbered, any reference in this section to that form shall be treated as a reference to the revised or renumbered form.

(l) *Effective date.* This section applies to depreciable assets placed in service in taxable years ending on or after October 11, 1994. For depreciable assets placed in service after December 31, 1986, in taxable years ending before October 11, 1994, the Internal Revenue Service will allow any reasonable method that is consistently applied to the taxpayer's general asset accounts. [Reg. § 1.168(i)-1.]

☐ [*T.D.* 8566, 10-7-94.]

[Reg. § 1.168(i)-2]

§ 1.168(i)-2. Lease term.—(a) *In general.* For purposes of section 168, a lease term is determined under all the facts and circumstances. Paragraph (b) of this section and § 1.168(j)-1T, Q&A 17, describe certain circumstances that will result in a period of time not included in the stated duration of an original lease (additional period) nevertheless being included in the lease term. These rules do not prevent the inclusion of an additional period in the lease term in other circumstances.

(b) *Lessee retains financial obligation*—(1) *In general.* An additional period of time during which a lessee may not continue to be the lessee will nevertheless be included in the lease term if the lessee (or a related person)—

(i) Has agreed that one or both of them will or could be obligated to make a payment of rent or a payment in the nature of rent with respect to such period; or

(ii) Has assumed or retained any risk of loss with respect to the property for such period (including, for example, by holding a note secured by the property).

(2) *Payments in the nature of rent.* For purposes of paragraph (b)(1)(i) of this section, a payment in the nature of rent includes a payment intended to substitute for rent or to fund or supplement the rental payments of another. For example, a payment in the nature of rent includes a payment of any kind (whether denominated as supplemental rent, as liquidated damages, or otherwise) that is required to be made in the event that—

(i) The leased property is not leased for the additional period;

(ii) The leased property is leased for the additional period under terms that do not satisfy specified terms and conditions;

(iii) There is a failure to make a payment of rent with respect to such additional period; or

(iv) Circumstances similar to those described in paragraph (b)(2)(i), (ii), or (iii) of this section occur.

(3) *De minimis rule.* For the purposes of this paragraph (b), obligations to make de minimis payments will be disregarded.

(c) *Multiple leases or subleases.* If property is subject to more than one lease (including any sublease) entered into as part of a single transaction (or a series of related transactions), the lease term includes all periods described in one or more of such leases. For example, if one taxable corporation leases property to another taxable corporation for a 20-year term and, as part of the same transaction, the lessee subleases the property to a tax-exempt entity for a 10-year term, then the lease term of the property for purposes of section 168 is 20 years. During the period of tax-exempt use, the property must be depreciated under the alternative depreciation system using the straight line method over the greater of its class life or 25 years (125 percent of the 20-year lease term).

(d) *Related person.* For purposes of paragraph (b) of this section, a person is related to the lessee if such person is described in section 168(h)(4).

(e) *Changes in status.* Section 168(i)(5) (changes in status) applies if an additional period is included in a lease term under this section and the leased property ceases to be tax-exempt use property for such additional period.

Reg. § 1.168(i)-2(a)

(f) *Example.* The following example illustrates the principles of this section. The example does not address common law doctrines or other authorities that may apply to cause an additional period to be included in the lease term or to recharacterize a lease as a conditional sale or otherwise for federal income tax purposes. Unless otherwise indicated, parties to the transactions are not related to one another.

Example. Financial obligation with respect to an additional period—(i) *Facts.* X, a taxable corporation, and Y, a foreign airline whose income is not subject to United States taxation, enter into a lease agreement under which X agrees to lease an aircraft to Y for a period of 10 years. The lease agreement provides that, at the end of the lease period, Y is obligated to find a subsequent lessee (replacement lessee) to enter into a subsequent lease (replacement lease) of the aircraft from X for an additional 10-year period. The provisions of the lease agreement require that any replacement lessee be unrelated to Y and that it not be a tax-exempt entity as defined in section 168(h)(2). The provisions of the lease agreement also set forth the basic terms and conditions of the replacement lease, including its duration and the required rental payments. In the event Y fails to secure a replacement lease, the lease agreement requires Y to make a payment to X in an amount determined under the lease agreement.

(ii) *Application of this section.* The lease agreement between X and Y obligates Y to make a payment in the event the aircraft is not leased for the period commencing after the initial 10-year lease period and ending on the date the replacement lease is scheduled to end. Accordingly, pursuant to paragraph (b) of this section, the term of the lease between X and Y includes such additional period, and the lease term is 20 years for purposes of section 168.

(iii) *Facts modified.* Assume the same facts as in paragraph (i) of this *Example,* except that Y is required to guarantee the payment of rentals under the 10-year replacement lease and to make a payment to X equal to the present value of any excess of the replacement lease rental payments specified in the lease agreement between X and Y,

over the rental payments actually agreed to be paid by the replacement lessee. Pursuant to paragraph (b) of this section, the term of the lease between X and Y includes the additional period, and the lease term is 20 years for purposes of section 168.

(iv) *Changes in status.* If, upon the conclusion of the stated duration of the lease between X and Y, the aircraft either is returned to X or leased to a replacement lessee that is not a tax-exempt entity as defined in section 168(h)(2), the subsequent method of depreciation will be determined pursuant to section 168(i)(5).

(g) *Effective date*—(1) *In general.* Except as provided in paragraph (g)(2) of this section, this section applies to leases entered into on or after April 20, 1995.

(2) *Special rules.* Paragraphs (b)(1)(ii) and (c) of this section apply to leases entered into after April 26, 1996. [Reg. § 1.168(i)-2.]

☐ T.D. 8667, 4-26-96.]

[Reg. § 1.168(j)-1T]

§ 1.168(j)-1T. Questions and answers concerning tax-exempt entity leasing rules (Temporary).—The following questions and answers concern tax-exempt entity leasing under section 168(j) of the Internal Revenue Code of 1954, as enacted by section 31 of the Tax Reform Act of 1984 ("TRA") (Pub. L. 98-369): *Consequences of tax-exempt use status:*

Q-1. If recovery property is subject to the tax-exempt entity leasing provisions of section 168(j), how must the taxpayer compute the property's recovery deductions?

A-1. The taxpayer must compute the property's recovery deductions in accordance with section 168(j)(1) and (2); that is, the taxpayer must use the straight line method and the specified recovery period. For property other than 18-year real property, the applicable recovery percentages for the specified recovery period are to be determined with reference to the tables contained in Prop. Treas. Reg. § 1.168-2(g)(3)(iv)(A). For 18-year real property for which a 40-year recovery period is required, the applicable recovery percentages are to be determined under the following table:

40-Year Straight Line Method (Assuming Mid-Month Convention)

If the recovery year is:	And the month in the first recovery year the property is placed in service is:											
	1	2	3	4	5	6	7	8	9	10	11	12
	The applicable recovery percentage is:											
1	2.4	2.2	2.0	1.8	1.6	1.4	1.1	0.9	0.7	0.5	0.3	0.1
2	2.5	2.5	2.5	2.5	2.5	2.5	2.5	2.5	2.5	2.5	2.5	2.5
3	2.5	2.5	2.5	2.5	2.5	2.5	2.5	2.5	2.5	2.5	2.5	2.5
4	2.5	2.5	2.5	2.5	2.5	2.5	2.5	2.5	2.5	2.5	2.5	2.5
5	2.5	2.5	2.5	2.5	2.5	2.5	2.5	2.5	2.5	2.5	2.5	2.5
6	2.5	2.5	2.5	2.5	2.5	2.5	2.5	2.5	2.5	2.5	2.5	2.5
7	2.5	2.5	2.5	2.5	2.5	2.5	2.5	2.5	2.5	2.5	2.5	2.5
8	2.5	2.5	2.5	2.5	2.5	2.5	2.5	2.5	2.5	2.5	2.5	2.5
9	2.5	2.5	2.5	2.5	2.5	2.5	2.5	2.5	2.5	2.5	2.5	2.5
10	2.5	2.5	2.5	2.5	2.5	2.5	2.5	2.5	2.5	2.5	2.5	2.5
11	2.5	2.5	2.5	2.5	2.5	2.5	2.5	2.5	2.5	2.5	2.5	2.5
12	2.5	2.5	2.5	2.5	2.5	2.5	2.5	2.5	2.5	2.5	2.5	2.5
13	2.5	2.5	2.5	2.5	2.5	2.5	2.5	2.5	2.5	2.5	2.5	2.5
14	2.5	2.5	2.5	2.5	2.5	2.5	2.5	2.5	2.5	2.5	2.5	2.5
15	2.5	2.5	2.5	2.5	2.5	2.5	2.5	2.5	2.5	2.5	2.5	2.5
16	2.5	2.5	2.5	2.5	2.5	2.5	2.5	2.5	2.5	2.5	2.5	2.5
17	2.5	2.5	2.5	2.5	2.5	2.5	2.5	2.5	2.5	2.5	2.5	2.5
18	2.5	2.5	2.5	2.5	2.5	2.5	2.5	2.5	2.5	2.5	2.5	2.5
19	2.5	2.5	2.5	2.5	2.5	2.5	2.5	2.5	2.5	2.5	2.5	2.5
20	2.5	2.5	2.5	2.5	2.5	2.5	2.5	2.5	2.5	2.5	2.5	2.5
21	2.5	2.5	2.5	2.5	2.5	2.5	2.5	2.5	2.5	2.5	2.5	2.5
22	2.5	2.5	2.5	2.5	2.5	2.5	2.5	2.5	2.5	2.5	2.5	2.5
23	2.5	2.5	2.5	2.5	2.5	2.5	2.5	2.5	2.5	2.5	2.5	2.5
24	2.5	2.5	2.5	2.5	2.5	2.5	2.5	2.5	2.5	2.5	2.5	2.5
25	2.5	2.5	2.5	2.5	2.5	2.5	2.5	2.5	2.5	2.5	2.5	2.5
26	2.5	2.5	2.5	2.5	2.5	2.5	2.5	2.5	2.5	2.5	2.5	2.5
27	2.5	2.5	2.5	2.5	2.5	2.5	2.5	2.5	2.5	2.5	2.5	2.5
28	2.5	2.5	2.5	2.5	2.5	2.5	2.5	2.5	2.5	2.5	2.5	2.5
29	2.5	2.5	2.5	2.5	2.5	2.5	2.5	2.5	2.5	2.5	2.5	2.5
30	2.5	2.5	2.5	2.5	2.5	2.5	2.5	2.5	2.5	2.5	2.5	2.5
31	2.5	2.5	2.5	2.5	2.5	2.5	2.5	2.5	2.5	2.5	2.5	2.5
32	2.5	2.5	2.5	2.5	2.5	2.5	2.5	2.5	2.5	2.5	2.5	2.5
33	2.5	2.5	2.5	2.5	2.5	2.5	2.5	2.5	2.5	2.5	2.5	2.5
34	2.5	2.5	2.5	2.5	2.5	2.5	2.5	2.5	2.5	2.5	2.5	2.5
35	2.5	2.5	2.5	2.5	2.5	2.5	2.5	2.5	2.5	2.5	2.5	2.5
36	2.5	2.5	2.5	2.5	2.5	2.5	2.5	2.5	2.5	2.5	2.5	2.5
37	2.5	2.5	2.5	2.5	2.5	2.5	2.5	2.5	2.5	2.5	2.5	2.5
38	2.5	2.5	2.5	2.5	2.5	2.5	2.5	2.5	2.5	2.5	2.5	2.5
39	2.5	2.5	2.5	2.5	2.5	2.5	2.5	2.5	2.5	2.5	2.5	2.5
40	2.5	2.5	2.5	2.5	2.5	2.5	2.5	2.5	2.5	2.5	2.5	2.5
41	0.1	0.3	0.5	0.7	0.9	1.1	1.4	1.6	1.8	2.0	2.2	2.4

Q-2. If recovery property that was placed in service after December 31, 1980 by a taxable entity subsequently becomes tax-exempt use property, how are such property's cost recovery deductions under section 168 affected?

A-2. A change to tax-exempt use property, as defined in section 168(j)(3), will cause the cost recovery deductions under the accelerated cost recovery system (ACRS) to be recomputed. The allowable recovery deduction for the taxable year in which the change occurs (and for subsequent taxable years) must be determined as if the property had originally been tax-exempt use property. Proper adjustment must be made under the principles of Prop. Treas. Reg. § 1.168-2(j)(3)(i)(B) to account for the difference between the deductions allowable with respect to the property prior to the year of change and those which would have been allowable had the taxpayer used the recovery period and method for tax-exempt use property under section 168(j)(1) and (2). However, no adjustment is made pursuant to the provisions of this A-2 if section 168(j)(2)(C) applies, that is, if the taxpayer had selected a longer recovery period in the year the property was placed in service than the recovery period prescribed for such property under section 168(j)(1).

Example (1). On July 1, 1983, X, a calendar year taxpayer, places in service 5-year recovery property with an unadjusted basis of $100. For 1983, X's allowable deduction is $15 (i.e., .15 × $100). In 1984, the property becomes tax-exempt use property. Under section 168(j), assume the prescribed recovery period is 12 years. For 1984

Reg. § 1.168(j)-1T

(and subsequent taxable years), X's allowable deduction is determined as if the property had been tax-exempt use property since 1983, that is, the year it was placed in service. Thus, taxable year 1984 is the property's second recovery year of its 12-year recovery period. Additionally, X must account for the excess allowable recovery deduction of $11 (*i.e.*, the difference between the recovery allowance for 1983 ($15) and the allowance for that year had the property been tax-exempt use property ($4)) in accordance with the principles of Prop. Treas. Reg. § 1.168-2(j)(3)(i)(B). Thus, the recovery allowances in 1984 and 1985 are $7.97, determined as follows:

Unadjusted basis multiplied by the applicable recovery percentage for second recovery year ($100 × .09)	$9.00
Excess allowable recovery deduction multiplied by the applicable recovery percentage for second recovery year divided by the sum of the remaining unused applicable percentages for tax-exempt use property existing as of the taxable year of change (1984) (($11 × .09)/.96)	− 1.03
Difference—allowable deduction for 1984	$7.97
Unadjusted basis multiplied by the applicable recovery percentage for third recovery year ($100 × .09)	$9.00
Excess allowable recovery deduction multiplied by the applicable recovery percentage for third recovery year divided by the sum of the remaining unused applicable percentages for tax-exempt use property existing as of the taxable year of change (1984) (($11 × .09)/.96)	− 1.03
Difference—allowable deduction for 1985	$7.97

Additionally, X must make a similar adjustment for the taxable years 1986 through 1995, that is, his fourth through thirteenth recovery years.

Example (2). Assume the same facts as in Example (1) except that in 1983, X elected under section 168(b)(3) with respect to the 5-year property to use the optional recovery percentages over a 25-year recovery period. Based on these facts, the provisions of this A-2 do not apply.

Definition of tax-exempt use property

—Mixed leases of real and personal property:

Q-3. How is a mixed lease of real property and personal property (*e.g.*, a building with furniture) to be treated for purposes of applying the rules of section 168(j)(3) defining which property constitutes tax-exempt use property?

A-3. The general rule is that 18-year real property and property other than 18-year real property are tested separately to determine whether each constitutes tax-exempt use property. However, if a lease of section 1245 class property is incidental to a lease of 18-year real property, and the 18-year real property is not tax-exempt use property, then the section 1245 class property also does not constitute tax-exempt use property. A lease of section 1245 class property will be considered incidental if the adjusted basis of all section 1245 class property leased in the same transaction is 1 percent or less of the adjusted basis of all 18-year real property leased in such transaction.

—Buildings which are partially tax-exempt use property:

Q-4. If part of a building is leased to a tax-exempt entity in a disqualified lease and part of the building is leased other than to a tax-exempt entity in a disqualified lease, to what extent do the tax-exempt entity leasing rules apply to such building?

A-4. The taxpayer must determine the amount of the building's unadjusted basis that is properly allocable to the portion of the building that is tax-exempt use property; the section 168(j) rules apply to the allocated amount. Solely for purposes of determining what percentage of the building's basis is subject to the tax-exempt entity leasing rules, no part of the basis is allocated to common areas.

Example. A constructs a 3-story building in 1984 at a cost of $900,000. Each floor consists of 30,000 square feet. The only common area (10,000 square feet) in the building is on the first floor. A leases the first floor (other than the common areas) to a firm that is not a tax-exempt entity. A leases the top two floors to a tax-exempt entity in a 25-year lease. The top two floors constitute tax-exempt use property. Assume that square footage is the appropriate method for allocating basis in this case. Thus, A must allocate $675,000 of the $900,000 basis to the tax-exempt use portion, determined as follows:

$$\frac{\text{square footage of building which is tax-exempt use property (excluding common areas)}}{\text{total square footage in the building (excluding common areas)}} = \frac{60{,}000 \text{ sq. feet}}{80{,}000 \text{ sq. feet}} = 3/4$$

$$3/4 \times \$900{,}000 = \$675{,}000$$

Reg. § 1.168(j)-1T

A must compute his recovery deductions on this portion of the basis ($675,000) in accordance with the rules of section 168(j)(1) and (2).

—Requirement of a lease:

Q-5. Can the use of property by a party other than a tax-exempt entity result in the property being treated as tax-exempt use property within the meaning of section 168(j)(3)?

A-5. Yes, if based on all the facts and circumstances it is more appropriate to characterize the transaction as a lease to a tax-exempt entity. A transaction can be characterized as a lease to a tax-exempt entity under section 168(j)(6)(A), which provides that "the term 'lease' includes any grant of a right to use property"; or under the service contract rules of section 7701(e). See Q & A #18 for rules regarding service contracts.

Example. A trust is executed on January 1, 1984, to create a pooled income fund (P) that meets the requirements of section 642(c)(5). A university (U) that is tax-exempt under section 501(c)(3) is the remainderman of the pooled income fund. P's purpose is to construct and operate an athletic center on land adjacent to U's campus. Construction of the athletic center, which has a 50-year useful life, was completed and the center was placed in service on February 1, 1985. The athletic center is managed for a fee by M, an unrelated taxable organization which operates athletic facilities open to the public. Office space at the facility is occupied rent-free by both the U athletic department and M. Scheduling of activities at the center is handled jointly by members of U's athletic department and M. General operating expenses of the athletic center are paid by P. Although the athletic center is open to the public for a membership fee, the majority of members are U's students who pay membership fees as part of their tuition. These fees are remitted by U to P. This arrangement is in substance a grant to U of a right to use the facility, and therefore a lease to U under section 168(j)(6)(A). U, as remainderman, will have obtained title to the entire building when the last pooled income fund donor dies. This arrangement is a disqualified lease because either (1) U has the equivalent of a fixed price purchase option under section 168(j)(3)(B)(ii)(II) (if U receives title as remainderman before the end of the useful life of the building), or (2) the lease has a term in excess of 20 years under section 168(j)(3)(B)(ii)(III) (if U does not receive title as remainderman until 20 years have elapsed), or both. Therefore, the allowable recovery deductions (without regard to salvage value) must be computed in accordance with section 168(j)(1) and (2). In addition, because this arrangement is treated as a lease under section 168(j), the facility is used by U for purposes of section 48(a)(4), and thus no investment tax credit is permitted with respect to any portion of the facility. This arrangement also may be treated as a lease to U for all purposes of chapter 1 of the Internal Revenue Code under section 7701(e).

—"More than 35 percent of the property" test:

Q-6. How is the percentage of 18-year real property leased to a tax-exempt entity in a disqualified lease to be determined for purposes of the "more than 35 percent of the property" test of section 168(j)(3)(B)(iii)?

A-6. The phrase "more than 35 percent of the property" means more than 35 percent of the net rentable floor space of the property. The net rentable floor space in a building does not include the common areas of the building, regardless of the terms of the lease. For purposes of the "more than 35 percent of the property" rule, two or more buildings will be treated as separate properties unless they are part of the same project, in which case they will be treated as one property. Two or more buildings will be treated as part of the same project if the buildings are constructed, under a common plan, within a reasonable time of each other on the same site and will be used in an integrated manner.

Q-7. Are disqualified leases to different tax-exempt entities (regardless of whether they are related) aggregated in determining whether 18-year real property is tax-exempt use property?

A-7. Yes.

Example. A tax-exempt entity participates in industrial development bond financing for the acquisition of a new building by a taxable entity. The tax-exempt entity leases 60 percent of the net rentable floor space in the building for 5 years. Sixty percent of the building is tax-exempt use property. If the same tax-exempt entity leased only 19 percent of the net rentable floor space in the building for 5 years, no portion of the building would be tax-exempt use property because not more than 35 percent of the property is leased to a tax-exempt entity pursuant to a disqualified lease. If such tax-exempt entity leased only 19 percent of the net rentable floor space in the building for 5 years and another tax-exempt entity leased 20 percent of the net rentable floor space in the building for a term in excess of 20 years (or a related entity leased 20 percent of the building for 5 years), 39 percent of the building would be tax-exempt use property. See A-4 regarding the determination of the amount of the building unadjusted basis that is properly allocable to the portion of the building that is tax-exempt use property.

—"*Predominantly used*" test:

Q-8. What does the term "predominantly used" mean for purposes of the section 168(j)(3)(D) exception to the tax-exempt use property rules?

A-8. "Predominantly used" means that for more than 50 percent of the time used, as determined for each taxable year, the real or personal property is used in an unrelated trade or business the income of which is subject to tax under section 511 (determined without regard to the debt-financed income rules of section 514). If only a portion of property is predominantly used in an unrelated trade or business, the remainder may nevertheless be tax-exempt use property.

Q-9. How is the "predominantly used" test of section 168(j)(3)(D) to be applied to a building?

A-9. The "predominantly used" test is to be applied to a building in the following manner:

(i) Identify the discrete portions (excluding common areas) of the building which are leased to a tax-exempt entity in a disqualified lease under section 168(j)(3)(B)(ii). A discrete portion of a building is an area physically separated from other areas. An area is physically separated from other areas if separated by permanent walls or by partitions serving as room dividers if such partitions remain in place throughout the taxable year. A discrete portion can be the entire building, floors, wings, offices, rooms, or a combination thereof. For example, a building whose entire internal space consists of a single large room used as a gymnasium has only one discrete portion. On the other hand, if the building has 3 stories with 10 offices on each floor, each of the 30 offices is a discrete portion.

(ii) Determine whether each discrete portion is predominantly used in an unrelated trade or business subject to tax under section 511. See A-8 for the rules regarding how to make this determination.

(iii) Once the discrete portions of the building that constitute tax-exempt use property have been identified, an appropriate allocation of basis must be made to such discrete portions. See A-4 for rules regarding how to make such allocation.

(iv) The application of these rules is illustrated by the following example:

Example. A building, constructed in 1985, is leased in its entirety to a tax-exempt entity (E) pursuant to a 25-year lease. The building has 25,000 square feet of net rentable floor space and consists of an auditorium (15,000 square feet), a retail shop (10,000 square feet), plus common area of 5,000 square feet. E uses the auditorium 80 percent of the time in its exempt activity and 20 percent of the time in an unrelated trade or business subject to tax under section 511. The retail shop is used 90 percent of the time in an unrelated trade or business subject to tax under section 511 and 10 percent of the time in an exempt activity. Thus, the auditorium is tax-exempt use property; the retail shop is not. An appropriate allocation of basis to the auditorium must be made. See A-4.

Definition of tax-exempt entity:

Q-10. What elections must be made in order to avoid the "5-year lookback" rule of section 168(j)(4)(E)(i)?

A-10. Only organizations which were exempt from tax under section 501(a) as organizations described in section 501(c)(12) (and which are no longer tax-exempt) may avoid the 5-year lookback rule of section 168(j)(4)(E)(i). In order to avoid the 5-year lookback rule with respect to any property, two elections are required. First, the organization must elect not to be exempt from tax under section 501(a) during the tax-exempt use period (as defined in section 168(j)(4)(E)(ii)(II)) with respect to the property. Second, the organization must elect to be taxed on the exempt arbitrage profits as provided in section 31(g)(16) of the Tax Reform Act of 1984. See Temp. Treas. Reg. § 301.9100-6T(a) for the time and manner of making these elections. These elections, once made, are irrevocable.

Q-11. Does the term "tax-exempt entity" include tax-exempt plans of deferred compensation and similar arrangements?

A-11. Yes. For purposes of section 168(j), the term "tax-exempt entity" includes trusts or other entities that are tax-qualified under section 401(a), individual retirement accounts, simplified employee pensions, and other tax-exempt arrangements described in subchapter D of chapter 1 of the Internal Revenue Code.

Special rules for high technology equipment:

Q-12. What effect do the tax-exempt entity leasing provisions have on "qualified technological equipment"?

A-12. "Qualified technological equipment" which is leased to a tax-exempt entity for a term of 5 years or less shall not constitute tax-exempt use property. If "qualified technological equipment" which is leased to a tax-exempt entity for a term of more than 5 years constitutes tax-exempt use property (as defined in section 168(j)(3)) and is not used predominantly outside the United States, the rules of section 168(j)(1) and (2) apply except that the recovery period to be used for such equipment shall be 5 years regardless of the length of the lease term. For purposes of section 168(j)(5), "qualified technological equipment" means (1) any computer or peripheral equipment,

Reg. § 1.168(j)-1T

(2) any high technology telephone station equipment installed on the customer's premises, and (3) any high technology medical equipment. For definitions of these terms, see A-13 through A-16.

Q-13. What is a "computer" as that term is used in section 168(j)(5)(C)(i)(I)?

A-13. Computers are electronically activated devices that are programmable by the user and that are capable of accepting information, applying prescribed processes to it, and supplying the results of those processes with or without human intervention. Computers consist of a central processing unit containing extensive storage, logic, arithmetic, and control capabilities. A computer does not include any equipment which is an integral part of property that is not a user-programmable device, any video games or other devices used by the user primarily for amusement or entertainment purposes, or any typewriters, calculators, adding or accounting machines, copiers, duplicating equipment, or similar equipment. A computer does not include any equipment that is not tangible personal property.

Q-14. What is "peripheral equipment" as that term is used in section 168(j)(5)(C)(i)(I)?

A-14. Peripheral equipment means tangible personal property such as auxiliary machines, whether on-line or off-line, that are designed to be placed under the control of the central processing unit of the computer. Some examples of peripheral equipment are: card readers, card punches, magnetic tape feeds, high speed printers, optical character readers, tape cassettes, mass storage units, paper tape equipment, keypunches, data entry devices, teleprinters, terminals, tape drives, disc drives, disc files, disc packs, visual image projector tubes, card sorters, plotters, and collators. Peripheral equipment does not include equipment not included in Asset Depreciation Range (ADR) 00.12 listed in section 3 of Rev. Proc. 83-35, 1983-1 C.B. 745, 746. Peripheral equipment also does not include any equipment that is an integral part of property that is not a user-programmable device, any video games or other devices used by the user primarily for amusement or entertainment purposes, or any typewriters, calculators, adding or accounting machines, copiers, duplicating equipment, or similar equipment.

Q-15. What does "high technology telephone station equipment" mean as that term is used in section 168(j)(5)(C)(i)(II)?

A-15. High technology telephone station equipment includes only tangible personal property described in asset depreciation range (ADR) class 48.13 listed in section 3 of Rev. Proc. 83-35, 1983-1 C.B. 745, 758 that has a high technology content and which, because of such high technol-

ogy content, can reasonably be expected to become obsolete before the expiration of its physical useful life. For example, telephone booths and telephones which include only a standard dialing feature are not high technology equipment. However, telephones with features such as an abbreviated dialing short program, an automatic callback, or conference call feature may qualify as high technology equipment. High technology telephone station equipment may include terminal equipment including such extra features but not terminal equipment used in conjunction with features offered through central office capacity. There are no current plans to utilize the regulatory authority provided in section 168(j)(5)(C)(iv).

Q-16. What is "high technology medical equipment" as that term is used in section 168(j)(5)(C)(i)(III)?

A-16. High technology medical equipment is any electronic, electromechanical, or computer-based high technology equipment which is tangible personal property used in the screening, monitoring, observation, diagnosis, or treatment of human patients in a laboratory, medical, or hospital environment. High technology medical equipment includes only equipment that has a high technology content and which, because of such high technology content, can reasonably be expected to become obsolete before the expiration of its physical useful life. High technology medical equipment may include computer axial tomography (C.A.T.) scanners, nuclear magnetic resonance equipment, clinical chemistry analyzers, drug monitors, diagnostic ultrasound scanners, nuclear cameras, radiographic and fluoroscopic systems, Holter monitors, and bedside monitors. Incidental use of any such equipment for other purposes, such as research, will not prevent it from qualifying as high technology medical equipment. There are no current plans to utilize the regulatory authority provided in section 168(j)(5)(C)(iv).

Lease term:

Q-17. What is included in determining the length of a lease term?

A-17. (i) The lease term starts when the property is first made available to the lessee under the lease. The lease term includes not only the stated duration, but also any additional period of time which is within the "realistic contemplation of the parties at the time the property is first put into service." *Hokanson v. Commissioner,* 730 F.2d 1245, 1248 (9th Cir. 1984). A subsequent period of time is included in the term of the original lease if the circumstances indicate that the parties, upon entering into the original lease, had infor-

Reg. § 1.168(j)-1T

mally agreed that there would be an extension of the original lease.

(ii) With respect to personal property, the lease term includes all periods for which the tax-exempt lessee or a related party (as defined under section 168(j)(7)) has a legally enforceable option to renew the lease, or the lessor has a legally enforceable option to compel its renewal by the tax-exempt entity or a related party. This is true regardless of the renewal terms of the lease agreement or whether the lease is in fact renewed.

(iii) With respect to real property, the lease term includes all periods for which the tax-exempt lessee or a related party (as defined under section 168(j)(7)) has a legally enforceable option to renew the lease, or the lessor has a legally enforceable option to compel its renewal by the tax-exempt entity or a related party, unless the option to renew is at fair market value, determined at the time of renewal. The *Hokanson* facts and circumstances test (see (i) above) may cause the term of a fair market value renewal option to be treated as part of the original lease term.

(iv) Successive leases that are part of the same transaction or a series of related transactions concerning the same or substantially similar property shall be treated as one lease. This rule applies if at substantially the same time or as part of one arrangement the parties enter into multiple leases covering the same or substantially similar property, each having a different term. If so, then the original lease term will be treated as running through the term of the lease that has the last expiration date of the multiple leases. The multiple lease rule will not apply merely because the parties enter into a new lease at fair market rental value at the end of the original lease term.

(v) The application of the above rules is illustrated by the following examples:

Example (1). On December 30, 1984, X, a taxable corporation, and Y, a tax-exempt entity, enter into a requirements contract for a period of 3 years. The requirements contract sets the terms and conditions under which X and Y will do business on those occasions when X actually leases items of personal property to Y. The requirements contract imposes no obligation on either party to actually enter into a lease agreement. Pursuant to this requirements contract, on January 1, 1985, X and Y enter into three separate leases. Under the leases, Y obtained the use of three identical items of personal property, each for a term of six months beginning on January 1, 1985. On March 1, 1985, Y entered into a fourth lease for the use of a fourth item of personal property substantially similar to the other three items for a term of 20 months beginning on that date. The mere fact

that all 4 leases were entered into pursuant to the same requirements contract and involved the same or substantially similar property does not require aggregation of the terms of such leases under section 168( )(6)(B).

Example (2). Assume the same facts as in Example (1) except that, instead of the 4 leases entered into in Example (1), on January 1, 1985, pursuant to the requirements contract, X and Y enter into a lease for an item of personal property for one year. On January 10, 1986, after the end of the one-year lease term, X and Y enter into a second lease with respect to the same or substantially similar equipment. Assuming that the requirements contract itself is not a lease and assuming that the parties did not have any informal or implicit understanding (other than the general expectation of doing some business in the future) to enter into the second lease when the first lease was entered into, these two leases are not aggregated. The mere fact that the parties entered into two leases under the requirements contract does not result in the application of the section 168(j)(6)(B) rules for successive leases.

Example (3). The facts are the same as in Example (2) except that the parties did have an understanding, informal or otherwise, at the time of the first lease that they would enter into a second lease of the same personal property. The terms of the leases are aggregated.

Example (4). The facts are the same as in Example (2) except that, instead of the leases entered into in Example (2), on January 1, 1985, X and Y enter into two separate leases, each for a term of one year. One lease is for the period beginning on January 1, 1985 and ending on December 31, 1985. The other lease is for the period beginning on January 1, 1986 and ending on December 31, 1986. Both leases involve the same or substantially similar personal property. Under the successive lease rule, the terms of both leases are aggregated for purposes of determining the term of either lease under section 168(j)(6)(B). This result occurs because the two leases were entered into as part of the same transaction, and they relate to the same or substantially similar personal property.

Service contract issues:

Q-18. How is the treatment of service contracts affected by the service contract rules set forth in section 7701(e)?

A-18. If a contract which purports to be a service contract is treated as a lease under section 7701(e), such contract is to be treated as a lease for all purposes of Chapter 1 of the Internal Revenue Code (including, for example, section 158(j) and section 48(a)(4) and (5)).

Reg. § 1.168(j)-1T

Q-19. Does a contract to provide heating, maintenance, etc. services in low-income housing come within the low-income housing exception in section 7701(e)(5) to the service contract rules set forth in section 7701(e)?

A-19. No. Although certain low-income housing operated by or for an organization described in paragraphs (3) or (4) of section 501(c) is not subject to the service contract rules in section 7701(e), a contract, for instance, to provide heating services to low-income housing units, such as by installing and operating a furnace, does not constitute "low-income housing" within the meaning of section 7701(e)(5). Thus, the rules of section 7701(e) apply to such contracts in determining whether they are properly treated as leases.

Partnership issues:

Q-20. Do the provisions applicable to property leased to partnerships, set forth in section 168(j)(8), and the provisions applicable to property owned by partnerships, set forth in section 168(j)(9), apply to pass-through entities other than partnerships?

A-20. Yes. Rules similar to those provided in paragraphs (8), (9)(A), (9)(B), and (9)(C) of section 168(j) and those provided in Q & A's 21-26 apply to pass-through entities other than partnerships.

Q-21. What rules apply to property owned by a partnership in which one or more partners is a tax-exempt entity?

A-21. If property is owned by a partnership having both taxable and tax-exempt entities as partners, and any allocation to a tax-exempt entity partner is not a "qualified allocation" under section 168(j)(9)(B), then such entity's proportionate share of the property is to be treated as tax-exempt use property for all purposes. However, the property will not be tax-exempt use property if it is predominantly used by the partnership in an activity which, with respect to the tax-exempt entity, is an unrelated trade or business. An activity is an unrelated trade or business with respect to a tax-exempt entity if such entity's distributive share of the partnership's gross income from the activity is includible in computing its unrelated business taxable income under section 512(c) (determined without regard to the debt-financed income rules of section 514). A tax-exempt entity partner's proportionate share of property of a partnership equals such partner's share of that item of the partnership's income or gain (excluding income or gain allocated under section 704(c)) in which the tax-exempt entity has the highest share. If the tax-exempt entity partner's share of any item of income or gain (excluding income or gain allocated under section 704(c)) may vary

during the period it is a partner, the previous sentence shall be applied with reference to the highest share of any such item that it may receive at any time during such period. The application of these rules is illustrated by the following example:

Example. A partnership (P) operates a factory, which consists of a building and various items of machinery. P has one tax-exempt entity (E) as a partner, and E's proportionate share is 10 percent (*i.e.,* 10 percent is the largest share of any item of income or gain that E may receive during the time E is a partner). Unless P's allocations to E are qualified under section 168(j)(9)(B), 10 percent of each item of partnership property (including the building) is tax-exempt use property, notwithstanding the 35 percent threshold test of section 168(j)(3)(B)(iii) that is otherwise applicable to 18-year real property. However, the property will not be tax-exempt use property if it is predominantly used by the partnership in an activity which, with respect to E, is an unrelated trade or business (determined without regard to the debt-financed income rules of section 514).

Q-22. What constitutes a "qualified allocation" under section 168(j)(9)(B)?

A-22. (i) A "qualified allocation" means any allocation to a tax-exempt entity which is consistent with such entity's being allocated the same share (*i.e.,* the identical percentage) of each and every item of partnership income, gain, loss, deduction, credit, and basis during the entire period such entity is a partner. Except as provided in A-23, an allocation is not qualified if it does not have substantial economic effect under section 704(b). However, for purposes of the two preceding sentences, items allocated under section 704(c) (relating to contributed property) are not taken into account. An allocation is not a "qualified allocation" under section 168(j)(9)(B) if the partnership agreement provides for, or the partners have otherwise formally or informally agreed to, any change (regardless of whether such change is contingent upon the happening of one or more events) in the tax-exempt entity's distributive share of income, gain, loss, deduction, credit, or basis at any time during the entire period the tax-exempt entity is a partner.

(ii) A change in a tax-exempt entity's distributive share of income, gain, loss, deduction, credit, or basis which occurs as a result of a sale or redemption of a partnership interest (or portion thereof) or a contribution of cash or property to the partnership shall be disregarded in determining whether the partnership allocations are qualified, provided that such transaction is based on fair market value at the time of the transaction

Reg. § 1.168(j)-1T

and that the allocations are qualified after the change. For this purpose, the consideration determined by the parties dealing at arm's length and with adverse interests normally will be deemed to satisfy the fair market value requirement. In addition, a change in a tax-exempt entity's distributive share which occurs as a result of a partner's default (other than a prearranged default) under the terms of the partnership agreement will be disregarded, provided that the allocations are qualified after the change, and that the change does not have the effect of avoiding the restrictions of section 168(j)(9). Any of the above-described transactions between existing partners (and parties related to them) will be closely scrutinized.

Example (1). A, a taxable entity, and B, a tax-exempt entity, form a partnership in 1985. A contributes $800,000 to the partnership; B contributes $200,000. The partnership agreement allocates 95 percent of each item of income, gain, loss, deduction, credit, and basis to A; B's share of each of these items is 5 percent. Liquidation proceeds are, throughout the term of the partnership, to be distributed in accordance with the partner's capital account balances, and any partner with a deficit in his capital account following the distribution of liquidation proceeds is required to restore the amount of such deficit to the partnership. Assuming that these allocations have substantial economic effect within the meaning of section 704(b)(2), they are qualified because B's distributive share of each item of income, gain, loss, deduction, credit, and basis will remain the same during the entire period that B is a partner. The fact that the liquidation proceeds may be distributed in a ratio other than 95 percent/5 percent does not cause the allocations not to be qualified.

Example (2). A, B, and E are members of a partnership formed on July 1, 1984. On that date the partnership places in service a building and section 1245 class property. A and B are taxable entities; E is a tax-exempt entity. The partnership agreement provides that during the first 5 years of the partnership, A and B are each allocated 40 percent of each item of income, gain, loss, deduction, credit, and basis; E is allocated 20 percent. Thereafter, A, B, and E are each allocated 33 1/3 percent of each item of income, gain, loss, deduction, credit, and basis. Assume that these allocations meet the substantial economic effect test of section 704(b)(2) and E's distributive share of the partnership's income is not unrelated trade or business income subject to tax under section 511. The allocations to E are not qualified allocations under section 168(j)(9)(B) because E's distributive share of partnership items does not remain

the same during the entire period that E is a partner in the partnership. Thus, 33 1/3 percent of the building and 33 1/3 percent of the section 1245 class property are tax-exempt use property from the time each is placed in service by the partnership and are thus subject to the cost recovery rules of section 168(j)(1) and (2). In addition, no investment tax credit is allowed for 33 1/3 percent of the section 1245 class property because of section 48(a)(4).

Q-23. In determining whether allocations constitute qualified allocations, what rules are applied to test allocations that are not governed by the substantial economic effect rules?

A-23. A-22 provides the general rules to be used in determining whether an allocation is a qualified allocation, including the rule that the allocation must have substantial economic effect. However, certain allocations are not governed by the substantial economic effect rules (*e.g.,* an allocation of basis of an oil and gas property is generally governed by section 613A(c)(7)(D), rather than section 704(b)), and other allocations cannot satisfy the substantial economic effect rules (*e.g.,* allocations of credits, allocations of deduction and loss attributable to nonrecourse debt, and allocations of percentage depletion in excess of basis). Since allocations in either of these categories cannot be tested under the substantial economic effect test, these allocations, in order to be qualified, must comply with the relevant Code or regulation section that governs the particular allocation (*e.g.,* in the case of an allocation of basis of an oil and gas property, section 613A(c)(7)(D)).

Q-24. Will the Internal Revenue Service issue letter rulings on the issue of whether an allocation is a "qualified allocation" for purposes of section 168(j)(9)?

A-24. The Internal Revenue Service will accept requests for rulings on the question of whether an allocation is a "qualified allocation" for purposes of section 168(j)(9). Such requests should be submitted in accordance with the appropriate revenue procedure. One requirement of a qualified allocation is that such allocation must have substantial economic effect under section 704(b)(2). Currently, the Service will not rule on the question of whether an allocation has substantial economic effect under section 704(b)(2). Therefore, unless and until this policy is changed, a ruling request regarding a qualified allocation must contain a representation that the subject allocation has substantial economic effect (or complies with A-23, if applicable).

Q-25. Do priority cash distributions which constitute guaranteed payments under section 707(c) disqualify an otherwise qualified allocation?

Reg. § 1.168(j)-1T

A-25. Priority cash distributions to partners which constitute guaranteed payments will not disqualify an otherwise qualified allocation if the priority cash distributions are reasonable in amount (*e.g.,* equal to the Federal short-term rate described in section 1274(d)) and are made in equal priorities to all partners in proportion to their capital in the partnership. Other guaranteed payments will be closely scrutinized and, in appropriate cases, will disqualify an otherwise qualified allocation.

Example. A and B form Partnership AB to operate a manufacturing business. A is a tax-exempt entity; B is a taxable person. A contributes $500,000 to the partnership; B contributes $100,000. The partnership agreement provides that A and B are each entitled to cash distributions each year, in equal priority, in an amount equal to 8 percent of their capital contribution. Assume that these payments are reasonable in amount and constitute guaranteed payments under section 707(c). Without taking into consideration the guaranteed payments, all allocations constitute qualified allocations under section 168(j)(9)(B) and A-22. These guaranteed payments will not disqualify such allocations.

Q-26. Can property be treated as tax-exempt use property under both the general rule of section 168(j)(3) and the partnership provisions of section 168(j)(9)?

A-26. Yes. For example, a tax-exempt entity may be a partner in a partnership that owns a building 60 percent of which is tax-exempt use property because it is leased to an unrelated tax-exempt entity under a 25-year lease. The status of the remaining 40 percent depends on whether or not allocations under the parntership agreement are qualified under section 168(j)(9). If the allocations are not qualified under section 168(j)(9), the tax-exempt entity's proportionate share (as determined under section 168(j)(9)(C)) of the remaining 40 percent will be tax-exempt use property. For example, if the tax-exempt entity's proportionate share is 30 percent, then 12 percent of the remaining 40 percent (*i.e.*, .30 times .40) is tax-exempt use property and a total of 72 percent of the property (60 percent + 12 percent) is tax-exempt use property.

Effective date questions:

Q-27. Does an amendment to a lease (or sublease) to a tax-exempt entity of property which, pursuant to the effective date provisions of section 31(g) of TRA, is not subject to section 168(j) cause such property to be subject to the provisions of section 168(j)?

A-27. An amendment to such a lease (or sublease) does not cause such property to be subject to the provisions of section 168(j) unless the amendment increases the term of the lease (or sublease). However, if the amendment increases the amount of property subject to the lease, the additional property must be tested independently under the effective date provisions of section 31(g) of TRA. See A-31 for special rules regarding improvements to property.

Example. On May 1, 1983, X, a taxable entity, and E, a tax-exempt entity, enter into a lease whereby X will lease to E the top 4 floors of a ten-story building for a lease term of 25 years. In 1985, the lease is amended to provide that E will lease an additional floor for the balance of the lease term. At that time the annual rent due under the lease is increased. Pursuant to the provisions of section 31(g)(2)(A) of TRA, section 168(j) does not apply to the lease to E of the top 4 floors of the building. Assuming that no other provision of section 31(g) of TRA provides otherwise, the floor added to the lease in 1985 is subject to the provisions of section 168(j).

Q-28. If property which is not subject to section 168(j) by virtue of the effective date provisions of section 31(g) of TRA is sold, subject to the lease to the tax-exempt entity, what are the consequences?

A-28. Property to which section 168(j) does not apply by virtue of the effective date provisions set forth in section 31(g)(2), (3), and (4) of TRA will not become subject to section 168(j) merely by reason of a transfer of the property subject to the lease by the lessor (or a transfer of the contract to acquire, construct, reconstruct, or rehabilitate the property), so long as the lessee (or party obligated to lease) does not change. For purposes of the preceding sentence, the term "transfer" includes the sale-leaseback by a taxable lessor of its interest in the property, subject to the underlying lease to the tax-exempt entity. However, if property is transferred to a partnership or other pass-through entity after the effective date of section 168(j)(9) (see section 31(g) of TRA), such property is subject to the provisions of section 168(j)(9).

Q-29. Can property which was leased to a tax-exempt entity after May 23, 1983 and acquired by a partnership before October 22, 1983 be tax-exempt use property?

A-29. Yes. Because the property was leased to a tax-exempt entity after May 23, 1983 it may be tax-exempt use property under section 168(j)(3) and section 31(g)(1) of TRA. However, if the partnership included a tax-exempt entity as a partner, section 168(j)(9) would be inapplicable under section 31(g)(3)(B) of TRA because the partnership acquired the property before October 22, 1983.

Reg. § 1.168(j)-1T

Q-30. What is a binding contract for purposes of the transitional rules in section 31(g) of TRA?

A-30. (i) A contract is binding only if it is enforceable under State law against the taxpayer or a predecessor and does not limit damages to a specified amount, as for example, by a liquidated damages provision. A contract that limits damages to an amount equal to at least 5 percent of the total contract price will not be treated as limiting damages for this purpose. In determining whether a contract limits damages, the fact that there may be little or no damages because the contract price does not significantly differ from fair market value will not be taken into account. For example, if a taxpayer entered into an irrevocable contract to purchase an asset for $100 and the contract contained no provision for liquidated damages, the contract is considered binding notwithstanding the fact that the property had a fair market value of $99 and under local law the seller would only recover the difference in the event the purchaser failed to perform. If the contract provided for a refund of the purchase price in lieu of any damages allowable by law in the event of breach or cancellation, the contract is not considered binding.

(ii) A contract is binding even if subject to a condition, so long as the condition is not within the control of either party or a predecessor in interest. A contract will not be treated as ceasing to be binding merely because the parties make insubstantial changes in its terms or because any term is to be determined by a standard beyond the control of either party. A contract which imposes significant obligations on the taxpayer (or a predecessor) will be treated as binding notwithstanding the fact that insubstantial terms remain to be negotiated by the parties to the contract.

(iii) A binding contract to acquire a component part of a larger piece of property will not be treated as a binding contract to acquire the larger piece of property. For example, if a tax-exempt entity entered into a binding contract on May 1, 1983 to acquire a new aircraft engine, there would be a binding contract to acquire only the engine, not the entire aircraft.

Q-31. If an improvement is made to a property that is "grandfathered" (i.e., property that is not subject to section 168(j) because of the effective date provisions of section 31(g) of TRA), to what extent will such improvement be grandfathered?

A-31. Section 31(g)(20)(B) provides that a "substantial improvement" to property is treated as a separate property for purposes of the effective date provisions of section 31(g) of TRA. As a result, a "substantial improvement" will not be grandfathered unless such 'substantial improve-

ment" is grandfathered under a provision other than section 31(g)(20)(B). A property that is grandfathered will not become subject to section 168(j) merely because an improvement is made to such property, regardless of whether the improvement is a "substantial improvement". If an improvement other than a "substantial improvement" is made to property (other than land) that is grandfathered, that improvement also will be grandfathered. The determination of whether new construction constitutes an improvement to property or the creation of a new separate property will be based on all facts and circumstances. Furthermore, any improvement to land will be treated as a separate property.

Example. On January 3, 1983, T, a taxable entity, entered into a lease of a parking lot to E, a tax-exempt entity On January 1, 1985, T begins construction of a building for use by E on the site of the parking lot. The building is completed and placed in service in November 1985. The building is treated as a separate property, and is thus subject to the provisions of section 168(j), unless the building is grandfathered under a provision other than section 31(g)(20)(B) of TRA.

Q-32. What is "significant official governmental action" for purposes of the section 31(g)(4) transitional rule of TRA?

A-32. (i) "Significant official governmental action" involves three separate requirements. First, the action must be an official action. Second, the action must be specific action with respect to a particular project. Third, the action must be taken by a governmental entity having authority to commit the tax-exempt entity to the project, to provide funds for it, or to approve the project under State or local law.

(ii) The first requirement of official action means that the governing body must adopt a resolution or ordinance, or take similar official action, on or before November 1, 1983. The action qualifies only if it conforms with Federal, State, and local law (as applicable) and is a proper exercise of the powers of the governing body. Moreover, the action must not have been withdrawn. There must be satisfactory written evidence of the action that was in existence on or before November 1, 1983. Satisfactory written evidence includes a formal resolution or ordinance, minutes of meetings, and binding contracts with third parties pursuant to which third parties are to render services in furtherance of the project.

(iii) The second requirement of specific action is directed at the substance of the action taken. The action must be a specific action with respect to a particular project in which the governing body indicates an intent to have the project (or the design work for it) proceed. This requires that a specific project have been formulated and that the significant official action be a step toward consummation of the project. If the action does not relate to a specific project or merely directs that a proposal or recommendation be formulated, it will not qualify. The following set of actions with respect to a particular project constitute specific action: the hiring of bond counsel or bond underwriters necessary to assist in the issuance and sale of bonds to finance a particular project or the adoption of an inducement resolution relating to bonds to be issued for such a project; applying for an Urban Development Action Grant on behalf of the project described in the application, receiving such a grant concerning the project, or the recommendation of a city planning authority to proceed with a project; the enactment of a State law authorizing the sale, lease, or construction of the property; the appropriation of funds for the property or authorization of a feasibility study or a development services contract with respect to it; the approval of financing arrangements by a regulatory agency; the enactment of a State law designed to provide funding for a project; the certification of a building as a historic structure by a State agency and the Department of the Interior; or the endorsement of the application for a certification of need with respect to a medical facility by a regulatory agency other than the agency empowered to issue such a certificate.

(iv) The third requirement for significant official governmental action is that the action must be taken by a Federal, State, or local governing body having authority to commit the tax-exempt entity to the project, to provide funds for it, or to approve the project under applicable law. If the chief executive or another representative of a governing body has such authority, action by such representative would satisfy the requirement of this (iv). A governing body may have the authority to commit the tax-exempt entity to a project notwithstanding the fact that the project cannot be consummated without other governmental action being taken. For example, a city council will be treated as having authority to commit a city to do a sale-leaseback of its city hall notwithstanding the fact that State law needs to be amended to permit such a transaction. Similarly, if a local project cannot be completed without Federal approval, either legislative or administrative, the obtaining of such approval satisfies the requirements of this (iv).

(v) Routine governmental action at a local level will not qualify as significant official governmental action. Routine governmental action in-

cludes the granting of building permits or zoning changes and the issuance of environmental impact statements.

(vi) In order to qualify under the transitional rule of TRA section 31(g)(4), a sale and leaseback pursuant to a building contract entered into before January 1, 1985 must be part of the project as to which there was significant official governmental action. Except as provided in the following sentence, where there has been significant official governmental action on or before November 1, 1983 with respect to the construction, reconstruction or rehabilitation of a property, the sale and leaseback of such property pursuant to a binding contract entered into before January 1, 1985 will be treated as part of the project which was the subject of the significant official governmental action. However, if the construction, reconstruction or rehabilitation was substantially completed prior to January 1, 1983, the sale and leaseback of such property will be treated as a separate project, unless the sale and leaseback was contemplated at the time of the significant official governmental action. Nevertheless, where the sale and leaseback is treated as a separate project, section 31(g)(4) may apply if there was significant official governmental action on or before November 1, 1983, with respect to such sale and leaseback. The application of this provision is illustrated by the following example:

Example. In the summer of 1927, the Board of Aldermen of City C passed a resolution authorizing the design and construction of a new city hall and appropriated the funds necessary for such project. Construction was completed in 1928. At the time of the significant official governmental action, City C had no plan to enter into a sale-leaseback arrangement with respect to the facility. On December 15, 1984, City C entered into a binding sale-leaseback arrangement concerning the city hall. This transaction will not qualify for exclusion from section 168(j) under section 31(g)(4) of TRA since construction of the facility in question was substantially completed before January 1, 1983. If, however, there had been significant official governmental action on or before November 1, 1983 with respect to the sale-leaseback project, then the transitional rule of section 31(g)(4) of TRA would apply. [Temporary Reg. § 1.168(j)-1T.]

☐ [*T.D.* 8033, 6-28-85. *Amended by T.D.* 8435, 9-18-92.]

[Reg. § 1.169-1]

§ 1.169-1. Amortization of pollution control facilities.—(a) *Allowance of deduction*—(1) *In general.* Under section 169(a), every person, at his election, shall be entitled to a deduction with respect to the amortization of the amortizable basis (as defined in § 1.169-3) of any certified pollution control facility (as defined in § 1.169-2), based on a period of 60 months. Under section 169(b) and paragraph (a) of § 1.169-4, the taxpayer may further elect to begin such 60-month period either with the month following the month in which the facility is completed or acquired or with the first month of the taxable year succeeding the taxable year in which such facility is completed or acquired. Under section 169(c), a taxpayer who has elected under section 169(b) to take the amortization deduction provided by section 169(a) may, at any time after making such election and prior to the expiration of the 60-month amortization period, elect to discontinue the amortization deduction for the remainder of the 60-month period in the manner prescribed in paragraph (b)(1) of § 1.169-4. In addition, if on or before May 18, 1971, an election under section 169(a) has been made, consent is hereby given to revoke such election without the consent of the Commissioner in the manner prescribed in paragraph (b)(2) of § 1.169-4.

(2) *Amount of deduction.* With respect to each month of such 60-month period which falls within the taxable year, the amortization deduction shall be an amount equal to the amortizable basis of the certified pollution control facility at the end of such month divided by the number of months (including the month for which the deduction is computed) remaining in such 60-month period. The amortizable basis at the end of any month shall be computed without regard to the amortization deduction for such month. The total amortization deduction with respect to a certified pollution control facility for a taxable year is the sum of the amortization deductions allowable for each month of the 60-month period which falls within such taxable year. If a certified pollution control facility is sold or exchanged or otherwise disposed of during one month, the amortization deduction (if any) allowable to the original holder in respect of such month shall be that portion of the amount to which such person would be entitled for a full month which the number of days in such month during which the facility was held by such person bears to the total number of days in such month.

(3) *Effect on other deductions.* (i) The amortization deduction provided by section 169 with respect to any month shall be in lieu of the depreciation deduction which would otherwise be allowable under section 167 or a deduction in lieu of depreciation which would otherwise be allowable under paragraph (b) of § 1.162-11 for such month.

(ii) If the adjusted basis of such facility as computed under section 1011 for purposes other than the amortization deduction provided by section 169 is in excess of the amortizable basis, as computed under § 1.169-3, such excess shall be recovered through depreciation deductions under the rules of section 167. See section 169(g).

(iii) See section 179 and paragraph (e)(1)(ii) of § 1.179-1 and paragraph (b)(2) of § 1.169-3 for additional first-year depreciation in respect of a certified pollution control facility.

(4) [Deleted.]

(5) *Special rules.* (i) In the case of a certified pollution control facility held by one person for life with the remainder to another person, the amortization deduction under section 169(a) shall be computed as if the life tenant were the absolute owner of the property and shall be allowable to the life tenant during his life.

(ii) If the assets of a corporation which has elected to take the amortization deduction under section 169(a) are acquired by another corporation in a transaction to which section 381 (relating to carryovers in certain corporate acquisitions) applies, the acquiring corporation is to be treated as if it were the distributor or transferor corporation for purposes of this section.

(iii) For the right of estates and trusts to amortize pollution control facilities see section 642 f) and § 1.642(f)-1. For the allowance of the amortization deduction in the case of pollution control facilities of partnerships, see section 703 and § 1.703-1.

(6) *Depreciation subsequent to discontinuance or in the case of revocation of amortization.* A taxpayer which elects in the manner prescribed under paragraph (b)(1) of § 1.169-4 to discontinue amortization deductions or under paragraph (b)(2) of § 1.169-4 to revoke an election under section 169(a) with respect to a certified pollution control facility is entitled, if such facility is of a character subject to the allowance for depreciation provided in section 167, to a deduction for depreciation (to the extent allowable) with respect to such facility. In the case of an election to discontinue an amortization deduction, the deduction for depreciation shall begin with the first month as to which such amortization deduction is not applicable and shall be computed on the adjusted basis of the property as of the beginning of such month (see section 1011 and the regulations thereunder). Such depreciation deduction shall be based upon the remaining portion of the period authorized under section 167 for the facility, as determined, as of the first day of the first month as of which the amortization deduction is not applicable. If the taxpayer so elects to discontinue

Reg. § 1.169-1(a)(6)

the amortization deduction under section 169(a), such taxpayer shall not be entitled to any further amortization deduction under this section and section 169(a) with respect to such pollution control facility. In the case of a revocation of an election under section 169(a), the deduction for depreciation shall begin as of the time such depreciation deduction would have been taken but for the election under section 169(a). See paragraph (b)(2) of § 1.169-4 for rules as to filing amended returns for years for which amortization deductions have been taken.

(7) *Definitions.* Except as otherwise provided in § 1.169-2, all terms used in section 169 and the regulations thereunder shall have the meaning provided by this section and §§ 1.169-2 through 1.169-4.

(b) *Examples.* This section may be illustrated by the following examples:

Example (1). On September 30, 1970, the X Corporation, which uses the calendar year as its taxable year, completes the installation of a facility all of which qualifies as a certified pollution control facility within the meaning of paragraph (a) of § 1.169-2. The cost of the facility is $120,000 and the period referred to in paragraph (a)(6) of § 1.169-2 is 10 years. In accordance with the rules set forth in paragraph (a) of § 1.169-4, on its income tax return filed for 1970, X elects to take amortization deductions under section 169(a) with respect to the facility and to begin the 60-month amortization period with October 1970, the month following the month in which it was completed. The amortizable basis at the end of October 1970 (determined without regard to the amortization deduction under section 169(a) for that month) is $120,000. The allowable amortization deduction with respect to such facility for the taxable year 1970 is $6,000, computed as follows:

Monthly amortization deductions:

October: $120,000 divided by 60	$2,000
November: $118,000 (that is, $120,000 minus $2,000) divided by 59	2,000
December: $116,000 (that is, $118,000 minus $2,000) divided by 58	2,000
Total amortization deduction for 1970	$6,000

Example (2). Assume the same facts as in example (1). Assume further that on May 20, 1972, X properly files notice of its election to discontinue the amortization deductions with the month of June 1972. The adjusted basis of the facility as of June 1, 1972, is $80,000, computed as follows:

Yearly amortization deductions:

1970 (as computed in example (1)) . . . . $	6,000
1971 (computed in accordance with example (1))	24,000
1972 (for the first five months of 1972 computed in accordance with example (1))	10,000
Total amortization deduction for 20 months	40,000

Adjusted basis at beginning of amortization period	120,000
Less: Amortization deductions	40,000
Adjusted basis as of June 1, 1972 . . . . . . $	80,000

Beginning as of June 1, 1972, the deduction for depreciation under section 167 is allowable with respect to the property on its adjusted basis of $80,000. [Reg. § 1.169-1.]

☐ [*T.D.* 7116, 5-17-71. *Amended by T.D.* 7203, 8-24-72.]

[Reg. § 1.169-2]

§ 1.169-2. Definitions.—(a) *Certified pollution control facility* —(1) *In general.* Under section 169(d), the term "certified pollution control facility" means a facility which—

(i) The Federal certifying authority certifies, in accordance with the rules prescribed in paragraph (c) of this section, is a "treatment facility" described in subparagraph (2) of this paragraph, and

(ii) Is "a new identifiable facility" (as defined in paragraph (b) of this section).

For profitmaking abatement works limitation, see paragraph (d) of this section.

(2) *Treatment facility.* For purposes of subparagraph (1)(i) of this paragraph, a "treatment facility" is a facility which (i) is used to abate or control water or atmospheric pollution or contamination by removing, altering, disposing, or storing of pollutants, contaminants, wastes, or heat and (ii) is used in connection with a plant or other property in operation before January 1, 1969. Determinations under subdivision (i) of this subparagraph shall be made solely by the Federal certifying authority. See subparagraph (3) of this paragraph. For meaning of the phrases "plant or other property" and "in operation before January 1, 1969," see subparagraphs (4) and (5), respectively, of this paragraph.

(3) *Facilities performing multiple functions or used in connection with several plants, etc.* (i) If a facility is designed to perform or does perform a function in addition to abating or controlling water or atmospheric pollution or contamination by removing, altering, disposing or storing pollutants, contaminants, wastes, or heat, such facility shall be a treatment facility only with respect to that part of the cost thereof which is certified by

year in which such facility is completed or acquired and a depreciation deduction is allowable under section 167 (including an additional first-year depreciation allowance under section 179) with respect to the facility for the taxable year in which it is completed or acquired, the amount determined under subparagraph (1) of this paragraph shall be reduced by an amount equal to (i) the amount of such allowable depreciation multiplied by (ii) a fraction the numerator of which is the amount determined under subparagraph (1) of this paragraph, and the denominator of which is its total cost. The additional first-year allowance for depreciation under section 179 will be allowable only for the year in which the facility is completed or acquired and only if the taxpayer elects to begin the amortization deduction under section 169 with the taxable year succeeding the taxable year in which such facility is completed or acquired. See paragraph (e)(1)(i) of § 1.179-1.

(c) *Modification for profitmaking abatement works, etc.* If it appears that by reason of estimated profits to be derived through the recovery of wastes or otherwise (as determined by applying the rules prescribed in paragraph (d) of § 1.169-2) a portion or all of the total costs of the certified pollution control facility will be recovered over the period referred to in paragraph (a)(6) of § 1.169-2, its amortizable basis (computed without regard to this paragraph and paragraph (d) of this section) shall be reduced by an amount equal to (1) its amortizable basis (so computed) multiplied by (2) a fraction the numerator of which is such estimated profits and the denominator of which is its adjusted basis for purposes of determining gain. See section 169(e).

(d) *Cases in which the period referred to in paragraph (a)(6) of § 1.169-2 exceeds 15 years.* If as to a certified pollution control facility the period referred to in paragraph (a)(6) of § 1.169-2 exceeds 15 years (determined as of the first day of the first month for which a deduction is allowable under the election made under section 169(b) and paragraph (a) of § 1.169-4), the amortizable basis of such facility shall be an amount equal to (1) its amortizable basis (computed without regard to this paragraph) multiplied by (2) a fraction the numerator of which is 15 years and the denominator of which is the number of years of such period. See section 169(f)(2)(A).

(e) *Examples.* This section may be illustrated by the following examples:

Example (1). The X Corporation, which uses the calendar year as its taxable year, began the installation of a facility on November 1, 1968, and completed the installation on June 30, 1970, at a cost of $400,000. All of the facility qualifies

as a certified pollution control facility within the meaning of paragraph (a) of § 1.169-2. $40,000 of such cost is attributable to construction prior to January 1, 1969. The X Corporation elects to take amortization deductions under section 169(a) with respect to the facility and to begin the 60-month amortization period with January 1, 1971. The corporation takes a depreciation deduction under sections 167 and 179 of $10,000 (the amount allowable, of which $2,000 is for additional first year depreciation under section 179) for the last 6 months of 1970. It is estimated that over the period referred to in paragraph (a)(6) of § 1.169-2) (20 years) as to such facility, $80,000 in profits will be realized from the sale of wastes recovered in its operation. The amortizable basis of the facility for purposes of computing the amortization deduction as of January 1, 1971, is $210,600, computed as follows:

(1) Portion of $400,000 cost attributable to post-1968 construction, reconstruction, or erection	$360,000
(2) Reduction for portion of depreciation deduction taken for the taxable year in which the facility was completed:	
(a) $10,000 depreciation deduction taken for last 6 months of 1970 including $2,000 for additional first year depreciation under section 179 . $10,000	
(b) Multiplied by the amount in line (1) and divided by the total cost of the facility ($360,000/$400,000) 0.9	$ 9,000
(3) Subtotal	$351,000
(4) Modification for profitmaking abatement works: Multiply line (3) by estimated profits through waste recovery ($80,000) and divide by the adjusted basis for determining gain of the facility ($400,000)	
(5) Reduction	70,200
(6) Subtotal	$280,800
(7) Modification for period referred to in paragraph (a)(6) of § 1.169-2 exceeding 15 years: Multiply by 15 years and divide by such period (determined in accordance with paragraph (d) of this section) (20 years).......................	$ 0.75
(8) Amortizable basis	$210,600

Reg. § 1.169-3(e)

Example (2). Assume the same facts as in example (1), except that the facility is used in connection with a number of separate plants some of which were in operation before January 1, 1969, that the Federal certifying authority certifies that 80 percent of the capacity of the facility is allocable to the plants which were in operation before such date, and that all of the waste recovery is allocable to the portion of the facility used in connection with the plants in operation before January 1, 1969. The amortizable basis of such facility, for purposes of computing the amortization deduction as of January 1, 1971, is $157,950 computed as follows:

(1) Adjusted basis for purposes of determining gain: Multiply percent certified as allocable to plants in operation before January 1, 1969 (80 percent) by cost of entire facility ($400,000) $320,000

(2) Portion of adjusted basis for determining gain attributable to post-1968 construction, reconstruction, or erection: Multiply line (1) by portion of total cost of facility attributable to post-1968 construction, reconstruction, or erection ($360,000) and divide by the total cost of the facility ($400,000) $288,000

(3) Reduction for portion of depreciation deduction taken for the taxable year in which the facility was completed:
  (a) $10,000 depreciation deduction taken for last 6 months of 1970 including $2,000 for additional first year depreciation under section 170 . $10,000
  (b) Multiplied by the amount in line (2) and divided by the total cost of the facility ($288,000/$400,000)   0.72   7,200

(4) Subtotal $280,800
(5) Modification for profit making abatement works; Multiply line (4) by estimated profits through waste recovery ($80,000) and divide by the amount in line (1) ($320,000)
(6) Reduction . . . . $ 70,200
(7) Subtotal $210,600

(8) Modification for period referred to in paragraph (a)(6) of § 1.169-2 exceeding 15 years: Multiply by 15 years and divide by such period (determined in accordance with paragraph (d) of this section) (20 years) 0.75

(9) Amortizable basis $157,950

(f) *Additions or improvements.* (1) If after the completion or acquisition of a certified pollution control facility further expenditures are made for additional construction, reconstruction, or improvements, the cost of such additions or improvements made prior to the beginning of the amortization period shall increase the amortizable basis of such facility, but the cost of additions or improvements made after the amortization period has begun shall not increase the amortizable basis. See section 169(f)(2)(B).

(2) If expenditures for such additional construction, reconstruction, or improvements result in a facility which is new and is separately certified as a certified pollution control facility as defined in section 169(d)(1) and paragraph (a) of § 1.169-2, and, if proper election is made, such expenditures shall be taken into account in computing under paragraph (a) of this section the amortizable basis of such new and separately certified pollution control facility. [Reg. § 1.169-3.]

☐ [*T.D.* 7116, 5-17-71.]

[Reg. § 1.169-4]

§ 1.169-4. **Time and manner of making elections.**—(a) *Election of amortization* —(1) *In general.* Under section 169(b), an election by the taxpayer to take an amortization deduction with respect to a certified pollution control facility and to begin the 60-month amortization period (either with the month following the month in which the facility is completed or acquired, or with the first month of the taxable year succeeding the taxable year in which such facility is completed or acquired) shall be made by a statement to that effect attached to its return for the taxable year in which falls the first month of the 60-month amortization period so elected. Such statement shall include the following information (if not otherwise included in the documents referred to in subdivision (ix) of this subparagraph):

(i) A description clearly identifying each certified pollution control facility for which an amortization deduction is claimed;

(ii) The date on which such facility was completed or acquired (see paragraph (b)(2)(iii) of § 1.169-2);

(iii) The period referred to in paragraph (a)(6) of § 1.169-2 for the facility as of the date the property is placed in service;

(iv) The date as of which the amortization period is to begin;

(v) The date the plant or other property to which the facility is connected began operating (see paragraph (a)(5) of § 1.169-2);

(vi) The total costs and expenditures paid or incurred in the acquisition, construction, and installation of such facility;

(vii) A description of any wastes which the facility will recover during the course of its operation, and a reasonable estimate of the profits which will be realized by the sale of such wastes whether pollutants or otherwise, over the period referred to in paragraph (a)(6) of § 1.169-2 as to the facility. Such estimate shall include a schedule setting forth a detailed computation illustrating how the estimate was computed including every element prescribed in the definition of estimated profits in paragraph (d)(2) of § 1.169-2;

(viii) A computation showing the amortizable basis (as defined in § 1.169-3) of the facility as of the first month for which the amortization deduction provided for by section 169(a) is elected; and

(ix) (a) A statement that the facility has been certified by the Federal certifying authority, together with a copy of such certification, and a copy of the application for certification which was filed with and approved by the Federal certifying authority or (b), if the facility has not been certified by the Federal certifying authority, a statement that application has been made to the proper State certifying authority (see paragraph (c)(2) of § 1.169-2) together with a copy of such application and (except in the case of an election to which subparagraph (4) of this paragraph applies) a copy of the application filed or to be filed with the Federal certifying authority.

If subdivision (ix)(b) of this subparagraph applies, within 90 days after receipt by the taxpayer, the certification from the Federal certifying authority shall be filed by the taxpayer with the district director, or with the director of the internal revenue service center, with whom the return referred to in this subparagraph was filed.

(2) *Special rule.* If the return for the taxable year in which falls the first month of the 60-month amortization period to be elected is filed before November 16, 1971, without making the election for such year, then on or before December 31, 1971 (or if there is no State certifying authority in existence on November 16 1971, on or before the 90th day after such authority is estab-

lished), the election may be made by a statement attached to an amended income tax return for the taxable year in which falls the first month of the 60-month amortization period so elected. Amended income tax returns or claims for credit or refund must also be filed at this time for other taxable years which are within the amortization period and which are subsequent to the taxable year for which the election is made. Nothing in this paragraph should be construed as extending the time specified in section 6511 within which a claim for credit or refund may be filed.

(3) *Other requirements and considerations.* No method of making the election provided for in section 169(a) other than that prescribed in this section shall be permitted on or after May 18, 1971. A taxpayer which does not elect in the manner prescribed in this section to take amortization deductions with respect to a certified pollution control facility shall not be entitled to such deductions. In the case of a taxpayer which elects prior to May 18, 1971, the statement required by subparagraph (1) of this paragraph shall be attached to its income tax return for either its taxable year in which December 31, 1971 occurs or its taxable year preceding such year.

(4) *Elections filed before February 29, 1972.* If a statement of election required by subparagraph (1) of this paragraph is attached to a return (including an amended return referred to in subparagraph (2) of this paragraph) filed before February 29, 1972, such statement of election need not include a copy of the Federal application to be filed with the Federal certifying authority but a copy of such application must be filed no later than February 29, 1972, by the taxpayer with the district director, or with the director of the internal revenue service center, with whom the return or amended return referred to in this subparagraph was filed.

(b) *Election to discontinue or revoke amortization* —(1) *Election to discontinue.* An election to discontinue the amortization deduction provided by section 169(c) and paragraph (a)(1) of § 1.169-1 shall be made by a statement in writing filed with the district director, or with the director of the internal revenue service center, with whom the return of the taxpayer is required to be filed for its taxable year in which falls the first month for which the election terminates. Such statement shall specify the month as of the beginning of which the taxpayer elects to discontinue such deductions. Unless the election to discontinue amortization is one to which subparagraph (2) of this paragraph applies, such statement shall be filed before the beginning of the month specified therein. In addition, such statement shall contain a description clearly identifying the certified pollution control facility with respect to which the taxpayer elects to discontinue the amortization deduction, and, if a certification has previously been issued, a copy of the certification by the Federal certifying authority. If at the time of such election a certification has not been issued (or if one has been issued but has not been filed as provided in paragraph (a)(1) of this section), the taxpayer shall file, with respect to any taxable year or years for which a deduction under section 169 has been taken, a copy of such certification within 90 days after receipt thereof. For purposes of this paragraph, notification to the Secretary or his delegate from the Federal certifying authority that the facility no longer meets the requirements under which certification was originally granted by the State or Federal certifying authority shall have the same effect as a notice from the taxpayer electing to terminate amortization as of the month following the month such facility ceased functioning in accordance with such requirements.

(2) *Revocation of elections made prior to May 18, 1971.* If on or before May 18, 1971, an election under section 169(a) has been made, such election may be revoked (see paragraph (a)(1) of § 1.169-1) by filing on or before August 16, 1971, a statement of revocation of an election under section 169(a) in accordance with the requirements in subparagraph (1) of this paragraph for filing a notice to discontinue an election. If such election to revoke is for a period which falls within one or more taxable years for which an income tax return has been filed, amended income tax returns shall be filed for any such taxable years in which deductions were taken under section 169 on or before August 16, 1971. [Reg. § 1.169-4.]

☐ [*T.D.* 7116, 5-17-71. *Amended by T.D.* 7135, 7-30-71 *and T.D.* 7153, 12-27-71.]

[Reg. § 20.1]

§ 20.1. **Applicability.**—The regulations of this part apply to certifications by the Administrator of water or air pollution control facilities for purposes of section 169 of the Internal Revenue Code of 1954, as amended, 26 U.S.C. 169. Applicable regulations of the Department of the Treasury are set forth at 26 CFR 1.169 et seq. [Reg. § 20.1.]

☐ [*Adopted by the EPA on May* 26, 1971.]

[Reg. § 20.2]

§ 20.2. **Definitions.**—As used in this part, the following terms shall have the meaning indicated below:

(a) "Act" means, when used in connection with water pollution control facilities, the Federal Water Pollution Control Act, as amended (33 U.S.C. 1151 et seq.) or, when used in connection with air pollution control facilities, the Clean Air Act, as amended (42 U.S.C. 1857 et seq.).

(b) "State certifying authority" means:

(1) For water pollution control facilities, the State health authority, except that, in the case of any State in which there is a single State agency, other than the State health authority, charged with responsibility for enforcing State laws relating to the abatement of water pollution, it means such other State agency; or

(2) For air pollution control facilities, the air pollution control agency designated pursuant to section 302(b)(1) of the Act; or

(3) For both air and water pollution control facilities, any interstate agency authorized to act in place of the certifying agency of a State.

(c) "Applicant" means any person who files an application with the Administrator for certification that a facility is in compliance with the applicable regulations of Federal agencies and in furtherance of the general policies of the United States for cooperation with the States in the prevention and abatement of water or air pollution under the Act.

(d) "Administrator" means the Administrator, Environmental Protection Agency.

(e) "Regional Administrator" means the Regional designee appointed by the Administrator to certify facilities under this part.

(f) "Facility" means property comprising any new identifiable treatment facility which removes, alters, disposes of or stores pollutants, contaminants, wastes, or heat.

(g) "State" means the States, the District of Columbia, the Commonwealth of Puerto Rico, the Canal Zone, Guam, American Samoa, the Virgin Islands, and the Trust Territory of the Pacific Islands. [Reg. § 20.2.]

☐ [*Adopted by the EPA on May* 26, 1971.]

[Reg. § 20.3]

§ 20.3. **General provisions.**—(a) An applicant shall file an application in accordance with this part for each separate facility for which certification is sought: *Provided,* That one application shall suffice in the case of substantially identical facilities which the applicant has installed or plans to install in connection with substantially identical properties: *Provided further,* That an application may incorporate by reference material contained in an application previously submitted by the applicant under this part and pertaining to substantially identical facilities.

Reg. § 20.1

(b) The applicant shall, at the time of application to the State certifying authority, submit an application in the form prescribed by the Administrator to the Regional Administrator for the region in which the facility is located.

(c) Applications will be considered complete and will be processed when the Regional Administrator receives the completed State certification.

(d) Applications may be filed prior or subsequent to the commencement of construction, acquisition, installation, or operation of the facility.

(e) An amendment to an application shall be submitted in the same manner as the original application and shall be considered a part of the original application.

(f) If the facility is certified by the Regional Administrator, notice of certification will be issued to the Secretary of the Treasury or his delegate, and a copy of the notice shall be forwarded to the applicant and to the State certifying authority. If the facility is denied certification, the Regional Administrator will advise the applicant and State certifying authority in writing of the reasons therefor.

(g) No certification will be made by the Regional Administrator for any facility prior to the time it is placed in operation and the application, or amended application, in connection with such facility so states.

(h) An applicant may appeal any decision of the Regional Administrator which:

(1) Denies certification;

(2) Disapproves the applicant's suggested method of allocating costs pursuant to § 602.8(e) [20.8(e)]; or

(3) Revokes a certification pursuant to § 602.10 [20.10].

Any such appeal may be taken by filing with the Administrator within 30 days from the date of the decision of the Regional Administrator a written statement of objections to the decision appealed from. Within 60 days, the Administrator shall affirm, modify, or revoke the decision of the Regional Administrator, stating in writing his reasons therefor. [Reg. § 20.3.]

□ [Adopted by the EPA on May 26, 1971.]

[Reg. § 20.4]

§ 20.4. **Notice of intent to certify.**—(a) On the basis of applications submitted prior to the construction, reconstruction, erection, acquisition, or operation of a facility, the Regional Administrator may notify applicants that such facility will be certified if:

(1) The Regional Administrator determines that such facility, if constructed, reconstructed,

erected, acquired, installed, and operated in accordance with such application, will be in compliance with requirements identified in § 602.8 [20.8]; and if

(2) The application is accompanied by a statement from the State certifying authority that such facility, if constructed, reconstructed, acquired, erected, installed, and operated in accordance with such application, will be in conformity with the State program or requirements for abatement or control of water or air pollution.

(b) Notice of actions taken under this section will be given to the appropriate State certifying authority. [Reg. § 20.4.]

□ [Adopted by the EPA on May 26, 1971.]

[Reg. § 20.5]

§ 20.5. **Applications.**—Applications for certification under this part shall be submitted in such manner as the Administrator may prescribe, shall be signed by the applicant or agent thereof, and shall include the following information:

(a) Name, address, and Internal Revenue Service identifying number of the applicant;

(b) Type and narrative description of the new identifiable facility for which certification is (or will be) sought, including a copy of schematic or engineering drawings, and a description of the function and operation of such facility;

(c) Address (or proposed address) of facility location;

(d) A general description of the operation in connection with which such facility is (or will be) used and a description of the specific process or processes resulting in discharges or emissions which are (or will be) controlled by the facility;

(e) If the facility is (or will be) used in connection with more than one plant or other property, one or more of which were not in operation prior to January 1, 1969, a description of the operations of the facility in respect to each plant or other property, including a reasonable allocation of the costs of the facility among the plants being serviced, and a description of the reasoning and accounting method or methods used to arrive at such allocation;

(f) Description of the effect of such facility in terms of type and quantity of pollutants, contaminants, wastes or heat, removed, altered, stored, or disposed of by such facility;

(g) If the facility performs a function other than removal, alteration, storage, or disposal of pollutants, contaminants, wastes or heat, a description of all functions performed by the facility, including a reasonable identification of the costs of the facility allocable to removal, alteration, storage, or disposal of pollutants, contaminants, wastes or heat, and a description of the reasoning and the accounting method or methods used to arrive at such allocation;

(h) Date when such construction, reconstruction, or erection will be completed or when such facility was (or will be) acquired;

(i) Date when such facility is placed (or is intended to be placed) in operation;

(j) Identification of the applicable State and local water or air pollution control requirements and standards, if any;

(k) Expected useful life of facility;

(l) Cost of construction, acquisition, installation, operation, and maintenance of the facility;

(m) Estimated profits reasonably expected to be derived through the recovery of wastes or otherwise in the operation of the facility over the period referred to in paragraph (a)(6) of 26 CFR 1.169-2;

(n) Such other information as the Administrator deems necessary for certification. [Reg. § 20.5.]

☐ [Adopted by the EPA on May 26, 1971.]

[Reg. § 20.6]

§ 20.6. State certification.—The State certification shall be by the State certifying authority having jurisdiction with respect to the facility in accordance with 26 U.S.C. 169(d)(1)(A) and (d)(2). The certification shall state that the facility described in the application has been constructed, reconstructed, erected, or acquired in conformity with the State program or requirements for abatement or control of water or air pollution. It shall be executed by an agent or officer authorized to act on behalf of the State certifying authority. [Reg. § 20.6.]

☐ [Adopted by the EPA on May 26, 1971.]

[Reg. § 20.7]

§ 20.7. General policies.—(a) The general policies of the United States for cooperation with the States in the prevention and abatement of water pollution are: To enhance the quality and value of our water resources; to eliminate or reduce the pollution of the nation's waters and tributaries thereof; to improve the sanitary condition of surface and underground waters; and to conserve such waters for public water supplies, propagation of fish and aquatic life and wildlife, recreational purposes, and agricultural, industrial, and other legitimate uses.

(b) The general policy of the United States for cooperation with the States in the prevention and abatement of air pollution is to cooperate with

and to assist the States and local governments in protecting and enhancing the quality of the Nation's air resources by the prevention and abatement of conditions which cause or contribute to air pollution which endangers the public health or welfare. [Reg. § 20.7.]

☐ [Adopted by the EPA on May 26, 1971.]

[Reg. § 20.8]

§ 20.8. Requirements for certification.—(a) Subject to § 602.9 [20.9], the Regional Administrator will certify a facility if he makes the following determinations:

(1) It has been certified by the State certifying authority.

(2) It removes, alters, disposes of, or stores pollutants, contaminants, wastes or heat, which, but for the facility, would be released into the environment.

(3) The applicant is in compliance with all regulations of Federal agencies applicable to use of the facility, including conditions specified in any permit issued to the applicant under section 13 of the Rivers and Harbors Act of 1899, as amended.

(4) The facility furthers the general policies of the United States and the States in the prevention and abatement of pollution.

(5) The applicant has complied with all the other requirements of this part and has submitted all requested information.

(b) In determining whether use of a facility furthers the general policies of the United States and the States in the prevention and abatement of water pollution, the Regional Administrator shall consider whether such facility is consistent with the following, insofar as they are applicable to the waters which will be affected by the facility:

(1) All applicable water quality standards, including water quality criteria and plans of implementation and enforcement established pursuant to section 10 (c) of the Act or State laws or regulations;

(2) Recommendations issued pursuant to section 10(e) and (f) of the Act;

(3) Water pollution control programs established pursuant to section 3 or 7 of the Act.

(c) In determining whether use of a facility furthers the general policies of the United States and the States in the prevention and abatement of air pollution, the Regional Administrator shall consider whether such facility is consistent with and meets the following requirements, insofar as they are applicable to the air which will be affected by the facility;

(1) Plans for the implementation, maintenance, and enforcement of ambient air quality standards adopted or promulgated pursuant to section 110 of the Act;

(2) Recommendations issued pursuant to sections 103(e) and 115 of the Act which are applicable to facilities of the same type and located in the area to which the recommendations are directed;

(3) Local government requirements for control of air pollution, including emission standards;

(4) Standards promulgated by the Administrator pursuant to the Act.

(d) A facility which removes elements or compounds from fuels which would be released as pollutants when such fuels are burned may not be certified whether or not such facility is used in connection with the applicant's plant or property where such fuels are burned.

(e) Where a facility is used in connection with more than one plant or other property, one or more of which were not in operation prior to January 1, 1969, or where a facility will perform a function other than the removal, alteration, storage or disposal of pollutants, contaminants, wastes, or heat, the Regional Administrator will so indicate on the notice of certification and will approve or disapprove the applicant's suggested method of allocation of costs. If the Regional Administrator disapproves the applicant's suggested method, he shall identify the proportion of costs allocable to each such plant, or to the removal, alteration, storage or disposal of pollutants, contaminants, wastes, or heat. [Reg. § 20.8.]

☐ [*Adopted by the EPA on May 26, 1971.*]

[Reg. § 20.9]

§ 20.9. **Cost recovery.**—Where it appears that, by reason of estimated profits to be derived through the recovery of wastes, through separate charges for use of the facility in question, or otherwise in the operation of such facility, all or a portion of its costs may be recovered over the period referred to in paragraph (a)(6) of 26 CFR 1.169-2, the Regional Administrator shall so signify in the notice of certification. Determinations as to the meaning of the term "estimated profits" and as to the percentage of the cost of a certified facility which will be recovered over such period shall be made by the Secretary of the Treasury, or his delegate: *Provided,* That in no event shall estimated profits be deemed to arise from the use or reuse by the applicant of recovered waste. [Reg. § 20.9.]

☐ [*Adopted by the EPA on May 26, 1971.*]

[Reg. § 20.10]

§ 20.10. **Revocation.**—Certification hereunder may be revoked by the Regional Administrator on 30 days' written notice to the applicant, served by certified mail, whenever the Regional Administrator shall determine that the facility in question is no longer being operated consistent with the § 602.8(b) and (c) [20.8(b) and (c)] criteria in effect at the time the facility was placed in service. Within such 30-day period, the applicant may submit to the Regional Administrator such evidence, data or other written materials as the applicant may deem appropriate to show why the certification hereunder should not be revoked. Notification of a revocation under this section shall be given to the Secretary of the Treasury or his delegate. See 26 CFR 1.169-4(b)(1). [Reg. § 20.10.]

☐ [*Adopted by the EPA on May 26, 1971.*]

[Reg. § 1.170-0]

§ 1.170-0. **Effective dates.**—Except as otherwise provided in this section, the provisions of section 170 and § § 1.170-1 through 1.170-3 are applicable to contributions paid in taxable years beginning before January 1, 1970, and all references therein to sections of the Code are to sections of the Internal Revenue Code of 1954 prior to the amendments made by section 201(a) of the Tax Reform Act of 1969 (83 Stat. 549). Except as otherwise provided therein, § § 1.170A through 1.170A-11 are applicable to contributions paid in taxable years beginning after December 31, 1969. In a case where a provision in § § 1.170A through 1.170A-11 is applicable to a contribution paid in a taxable year beginning before January 1, 1970, such provision shall apply to the contribution and § § 1.170-1 through 1.170-3 shall not apply to the contribution. [Reg. § 1.170-0.]

☐ [*T.D. 7207, 10-3-72.*]

[Reg. § 1.170-1]

§ 1.170-1. **Charitable, etc., contributions and gifts; allowance of deduction (before amendment by Tax Reform Act of 1969).**—[The text of Reg. § 1.170-1, pertaining to taxable years beginning before January 1, 1970, is no longer reproduced by CCH.]

[Reg. § 1.170-2]

§ 1.170-2. **Charitable deductions by individuals; limitations (before amendment by Tax Reform Act of 1969).**—[The text of Reg. § 1.170-2, pertaining to taxable years beginning before January 1, 1970, is no longer reproduced by CCH.]

[Reg. § 1.170A-1]

§ 1.170A-1. Charitable, etc., contributions and gifts; allowance of deduction.—(a) *Allowance of deduction.* Any charitable contribution, as defined in section 170(c), actually paid during the taxable year is allowable as a deduction in computing taxable income irrespective of the method of accounting employed or of the date on which the contribution is pledged. However, charitable contributions by corporations may under certain circumstances be deductible even though not paid during the taxable year, as provided in section 170(a)(2) and § 1.170A-11. For rules relating to record keeping and return requirements in support of deductions for charitable contributions (whether by an itemizing or nonitemizing taxpayer) see § 1.170A-13. The deduction is subject to the limitations of section 170(b) and § 1.170A-8 or § 1.170A-11. Subject to the provisions of section 170(d) and §§ 1.170A-10 and 1.170A-11, certain excess charitable contributions made by individuals and corporations shall be treated as paid in certain succeeding taxable years. For provisions relating to direct charitable deductions under section 63 by nonitemizers, see section 63(b)(1)(C) and (i) and section 170(i). For rules relating to the determination of, and the deduction for, amounts paid to maintain certain students as members of the taxpayer's household and treated under section 170(g) as paid for the use of an organization described in section 170(c)(2), (3), or (4), see § 1.170A-2. For the reduction of any charitable contributions for interest on certain indebtedness, see section 170(f)(5) and § 1.170A-3. For a special rule relating to the computation of the amount of the deduction with respect to a charitable contribution of certain ordinary income or capital gain property, see section 170(e) and § 1.170A-4 and § 1.170A-4A. For rules for postponing the time for deduction of a charitable contribution of a future interest in tangible personal property, see section 170(a)(3) and § 1.170A-5. For rules with respect to transfers in trust and of partial interests in property, see section 170(e), section 170(f)(2) and (3), § 1.170A-4, § 1.170A-6, and § 1.170A-7. For definition of the term "section 170(b)(1)(A) organization," see § 1.170A-9. For valuation of a remainder interest in real property, see section 170(f)(4) and the regulations thereunder. The deduction for charitable contributions is subject to verification by the district director.

(b) *Time of making contribution.* Ordinarily, a contribution is made at the time delivery is effected. The unconditional delivery or mailing of a check which subsequently clears in due course will constitute an effective contribution on the date of delivery or mailing. If a taxpayer unconditionally delivers or mails a properly endorsed stock certifi-

cate to a charitable donee or the donee's agent, the gift is completed on the date of delivery or, if such certificate is received in the ordinary course of the mails, on the date of mailing. If the donor delivers the stock certificate to his bank or broker as the donor's agent, or to the issuing corporation or its agent, for transfer into the name of the donee, the gift is completed on the date the stock is transferred on the books of the corporation. For rules relating to the date of payment of a contribution consisting of a future interest in tangible personal property, see section 170(a)(3) and § 1.170A-5.

(c) *Value of a contribution in property*—(1) If a charitable contribution is made in property other than money, the amount of the contribution is the fair market value of the property at the time of the contribution reduced as provided in section 170(e)(1) and paragraph (a) of § 1.170A-4, or section 170(e)(3) and paragraph (c) of § 1.170A-4A.

(2) The fair market value is the price at which the property would change hands between a willing buyer and a willing seller, neither being under any compulsion to buy or sell and both having reasonable knowledge of relevant facts. If the contribution is made in property of a type which the taxpayer sells in the course of his business, the fair market value is the price which the taxpayer would have received if he had sold the contributed property in the usual market in which he customarily sells, at the time and place of the contribution and, in the case of a contribution of goods in quantity, in the quantity contributed. The usual market of a manufacturer or other producer consists of the wholesalers or other distributors to or through whom he customarily sells, but if he sells only at retail the usual market consists of his retail customers.

(3) If the donor makes a charitable contribution of property, such as stock in trade, at a time when he could not reasonably have been expected to realize its usual selling price, the value of the gift is not the usual selling price but is the amount for which the quantity of property contributed would have been sold by the donor at the time of the contribution.

(4) Any costs and expenses pertaining to the contributed property which were incurred in taxable years preceding the year of contribution and are properly reflected in the opening inventory for the year of contribution must be removed from inventory and are not a part of the cost of goods sold for purposes of determining gross income for the year of contribution. Any costs and expenses pertaining to the contributed property which are incurred in the year of contribution and would, under the method of accounting used, be properly

Reg. § 1.170A-1(a)

reflected in the cost of goods sold for such year are to be treated as part of the cost of goods sold for such year. If costs and expenses incurred in producing or acquiring the contributed property are, under the method of accounting used, properly deducted under section 162 or other section of the Code, such costs and expenses will be allowed as deductions for the taxable year in which they are paid or incurred, whether or not such year is the year of the contribution. Any such costs and expenses which are treated as part of the cost of goods sold for the year of contribution, and any such costs and expenses which are properly deducted under section 162 or other section of the Code, are not to be treated under any section of the Code as resulting in any basis for the contributed property. Thus, for example, the contributed property has no basis for purposes of determining under section 170(e)(1)(A) and paragraph (a) of § 1.170A-4 the amount of gain which would have been recognized if such property had been sold by the donor at its fair market value at the time of its contribution. The amount of any charitable contribution for the taxable year is not to be reduced by the amount of any costs or expenses pertaining to the contributed property which was properly deducted under section 162 or other section of the Code for any taxable year preceding the year of the contribution. This subparagraph applies only to property which was held by the taxpayer for sale in the course of a trade or business. The application of this subparagraph may be illustrated by the following examples:

Example (1). In 1970, A, an individual using the calendar year as the taxable year and the accrual method of accounting, contributed to a church property from inventory having a fair market value of $600. The closing inventory at the end of 1969 properly included $400 of costs attributable to the acquisition of such property, and in 1969 A properly deducted under section 162 $50 of administrative and other expenses attributable to such property. Under section 170(e)(1)(A) and paragraph (a) of § 1.170A-4, the amount of the charitable contribution allowed for 1970 is $400 ($600 − [$600 − $400]). Pursuant to this subparagraph, the cost of goods sold to be used in determining gross income for 1970 may not include the $400 which was included in opening inventory for that year.

Example (2). The facts are the same as in example (1) except that the contributed property was acquired in 1970 at a cost of $400. The $400 cost of the property is included in determining the cost of goods sold for 1970, and $50 is allowed as a deduction for that year under section 162. A is not allowed any deduction under section 170 for the contributed property, since under section 170(e)(1)(A) and paragraph (a) of § 1.170A-4 the amount of the charitable contribution is reduced to zero ($600 − [$600 − $0]).

Example (3). In 1970, B, an individual using the calendar year as the taxable year and the accrual method of accounting, contributed to a church property from inventory having a fair market value of $600. Under § 1.471-3(c), the closing inventory at the end of 1969 properly included $450 costs attributable to the production of such property, including $50 of administrative and other indirect expenses which, under his method of accounting, was properly added to inventory rather than deducted as a business expense. Under section 170(e)(1)(A) and paragraph (a) of § 1.170A-4, the amount of the charitable contribution allowed for 1970 is $450 ($600 − [$600 − $450]). Pursuant to this subparagraph, the cost of goods sold to be used in determining gross income for 1970 may not include the $450 which was included in opening inventory for that year.

Example (4). The facts are the same as in example (3) except that the contributed property was produced in 1970 at a cost of $450, including $50 of administrative and other indirect expenses. The $450 cost of the property is included in determining the cost of goods sold for 1970. B is not allowed any deduction under section 170 for the contributed property, since under section 170(e)(1)(A) and paragraph (a) of § 1.170A-4 the amount of the charitable contribution is reduced to zero ($600 − [$600 − $0]).

Example (5). In 1970, C, a farmer using the cash method of accounting and the calendar year as the taxable year, contributed to a church a quantity of grain which he had raised having a fair market value of $600. In 1969, C paid expenses of $450 in raising the property which he properly deducted for such year under section 162. Under section 170(e)(1)(A) and paragraph (a) of § 1.170A-4, the amount of the charitable contribution in 1970 is reduced to zero ($600 − [$600 − $0]). Accordingly, C is not allowed any deduction under section 170 for the contributed property.

Example (6). The facts are the same as in example (5) except that the $450 expenses incurred in raising the contributed property were paid in 1970. The result is the same as in example (5), except the amount of $450 is deductible under section 162 for 1970.

(5) Transfers of property to an organization described in section 170(c) which bear a direct relationship to the taxpayer's trade or business and which are made with a reasonable expectation of financial return commensurate with the

Reg. § 1.170A-1(c)(5)

amount of the transfer may constitute allowable deductions as trade or business expenses rather than as charitable contributions. See section 162 and the regulations thereunder.

(d) *Purchase of an annuity*—(1) In the case of an annuity or portion thereof purchased from an organization described in section 170(c), there shall be allowed as a deduction the excess of the amount paid over the value at the time of purchase of the annuity or portion purchased.

(2) The value of the annuity or portion is the value of the annuity determined in accordance with paragraph (e)(1)(iii)(*b*)(*2*) of § 1.101-2.

(3) For determining gain on any such transaction constituting a bargain sale, see section 1011(b) and § 1.1011-2.

(e) *Transfers subject to a condition or power.* If as of the date of a gift a transfer for charitable purposes is dependent upon the performance of some act or the happening of a precedent event in order that it might become effective, no deduction is allowable unless the possibility that the charitable transfer will not become effective is so remote as to be negligible. If an interest in property passes to, or is vested in, charity on the date of the gift and the interest would be defeated by the subsequent performance of some act or the happening of some event, the possibility of occurrence of which appears on the date of the gift to be so remote as to be negligible, the deduction is allowable. For example, A transfers land to a city government for as long as the land is used by the city for a public park. If on the date of the gift the city does plan to use the land for a park and the possibility that the city will not use the land for a public park is so remote as to be negligible, A is entitled to a deduction under section 170 for his charitable contribution.

(f) *Special rules applicable to certain contributions*—(1) See section 14 of the Wild and Scenic Rivers Act (Public Law 90-542, 82 Stat. 918) for provisions relating to the claim and allowance of the value of certain easements as a charitable contribution under section 170.

(2) For treatment of gifts accepted by the Secretary of State or the Secretary of Commerce, for the purpose of organizing and holding an international conference to negotiate a Patent Corporation Treaty, as gifts to or for the use of the United States, see section 3 of Joint Resolution of December 24, 1969 (Public Law 91-160, 83 Stat. 443).

(3) For treatment of gifts accepted by the Secretary of the Department of Housing and Urban Development, for the purpose of aiding or facilitating the work of the Department, as gifts to or for the use of the United States, see section 7(k) of the Department of Housing and Urban Development Act (42 U.S.C. 3535), as added by section 905 of Public Law 91-609 (84 Stat. 1809).

(g) *Contributions of services.* No deduction is allowable under section 170 for a contribution of services. However, unreimbursed expenditures made incident to the rendition of services to an organization contributions to which are deductible may constitute a deductible contribution. For example, the cost of a uniform without general utility which is required to be worn in performing donated services is deductible. Similarly, out-of-pocket transportation expenses necessarily incurred in performing donated services are deductible. Reasonable expenditures for meals and lodging necessarily incurred while away from home in the course of performing donated services also are deductible. For the purposes of this paragraph, the phrase "while away from home" has the same meaning as that phrase is used for purposes of section 162 and the regulations thereunder.

(h) *Payment in exchange for consideration*—(1) *Burden on taxpayer to show that all or part of payment is a charitable contribution or gift.* No part of a payment that a taxpayer makes to or for the use of an organization described in section 170(c) that is in consideration for (as defined in § 1.170A-13(f)(6)) goods or services (as defined in § 1.170A-13(f)(5)) is a contribution or gift within the meaning of section 170(c) unless the taxpayer—

(i) Intends to make a payment in an amount that exceeds the fair market value of the goods or services; and

(ii) Makes a payment in an amount that exceeds the fair market value of the goods or services.

(2) *Limitation on amount deductible*—(i) *In general.* The charitable contribution deduction under section 170(a) for a payment a taxpayer makes partly in consideration for goods or services may not exceed the excess of—

(A) The amount of any cash paid and the fair market value of any property (other than cash) transferred by the taxpayer to an organization described in section 170(c); over

(B) The fair market value of the goods or services the organization provides in return.

(ii) *Special rules.* For special limits on the deduction for charitable contributions of ordinary income and capital gain property, see section 170(e) and § § 1.170A-4 and 1.170A-4A.

(3) *Certain goods or services disregarded.* For purposes of section 170(a) and paragraphs (h)(1) and (h)(2) of this section, goods or services de-

scribed in § 1.170A-13(f)(8)(i) or § 1.170A-13(f)(9)(i) are disregarded.

(4) *Donee estimates of the value of goods or services may be treated as fair market value*—(i) *In general.* For purposes of section 170(a), a taxpayer may rely on either a contemporaneous written acknowledgment provided under section 170(f)(8) and § 1.170A-13(f) or a written disclosure statement provided under section 6115 for the fair market value of any goods or services provided to the taxpayer by the donee organization.

(ii) *Exception.* A taxpayer may not treat an estimate of the value of goods or services as their fair market value if the taxpayer knows, or has reason to know, that such treatment is unreasonable. For example, if a taxpayer knows, or has reason to know, that there is an error in an estimate provided by an organization described in section 170(c) pertaining to goods or services that have a readily ascertainable value, it is unreasonable for the taxpayer to treat the estimate as the fair market value of the goods or services. Similarly, if a taxpayer is a dealer in the type of goods or services provided in consideration for the taxpayer's payment and knows, or has reason to know, that the estimate is in error, it is unreasonable for the taxpayer to treat the estimate as the fair market value of the goods or services.

(5) *Examples.* The following examples illustrate the rules of this paragraph (h).

Example 1. Certain goods or services disregarded. Taxpayer makes a $50 payment to Charity *B*, an organization described in section 170(c), in exchange for a family membership. The family membership entitles Taxpayer and members of Taxpayer's family to certain benefits. These benefits include free admission to weekly poetry readings, discounts on merchandise sold by *B* in its gift shop or by mail order, and invitations to special events for members only, such as lectures or informal receptions. When *B* first offers its membership package for the year, *B* reasonably projects that each special event for members will have a cost to *B*, excluding any allocable overhead, of $5 or less per person attending the event. Because the family membership benefits are disregarded pursuant to § 1.170A-13(f)(8)(i), Taxpayer may treat the $50 payment as a contribution or gift within the meaning of section 170(c), regardless of Taxpayer's intent and whether or not the payment exceeds the fair market value of the goods or services. Furthermore, any charitable contribution deduction available to Taxpayer may be calculated without regard to the membership benefits.

Example 2. Treatment of good faith estimate at auction as the fair market value. Taxpayer attends an auction held by Charity *C*, an organization described in section 170(c). Prior to the auction, *C* publishes a catalog that meets the requirements for a written disclosure statement under section 6115(a) (including *C*'s good faith estimate of the value of items that will be available for bidding). A representative of *C* gives a copy of the catalog to each individual (including Taxpayer) who attends the auction. Taxpayer notes that in the catalog *C*'s estimate of the value of a vase is $100. Taxpayer has no reason to doubt the accuracy of this estimate. Taxpayer successfully bids and pays $500 for the vase. Because Taxpayer knew, prior to making her payment, that the estimate in the catalog was less than the amount of her payment, Taxpayer satisfies the requirement of paragraph (h)(1)(i) of this section. Because Taxpayer makes a payment in an amount that exceeds that estimate, Taxpayer satisfies the requirements of paragraph (h)(1)(ii) of this section. Taxpayer may treat *C*'s estimate of the value of the vase as its fair market value in determining the amount of her charitable contribution deduction.

Example 3. Good faith estimate not in error. Taxpayer makes a $200 payment to Charity *D*, an organization described in section 170(c). In return for Taxpayer's payment, *D* gives Taxpayer a book that Taxpayer could buy at retail prices typically ranging from $18 to $25. *D* provides Taxpayer with a good faith estimate, in a written disclosure statement under section 6115(a), of $20 for the value of the book. Because the estimate is within the range of typical retail prices for the book, the estimate contained in the written disclosure statement is not in error. Although Taxpayer knows that the book is sold for as much as $25, Taxpayer may treat the estimate of $20 as the fair market value of the book in determining the amount of his charitable contribution deduction.

(i) [Reserved]

(j) *Exceptions and other rules*—(1) The provisions of section 170 do not apply to contributions by an estate; nor do they apply to a trust unless the trust is a private foundation which, pursuant to section 642(c)(6) and § 1.642(c)-4, is allowed a deduction under section 170 subject to the provisions applicable to individuals.

(2) No deduction shall be allowed under section 170 for a charitable contribution to or for the use of an organization or trust described in section 508(d) or 4943(c)(4), subject to the conditions specified in such sections and the regulations thereunder.

Reg. § 1.170A-1(j)(2)

(3) For disallowance of deductions for contributions to or for the use of communist controlled organizations, see section 11(a) of the Internal Security Act of 1950, as amended (50 U.S.C. 790).

(4) For denial of deductions for charitable contributions as trade or business expenses and rules with respect to treatment of payments to organizations other than those described in section 170(c), see section 162 and the regulations thereunder.

(5) No deduction shall be allowed under section 170 for amounts paid to an organization:

(i) Which is disqualified for tax exemption under section 501(c)(3) by reason of attempting to influence legislation, or

(ii) Which participates in, or intervenes in (including the publishing or distributing of statements), any political campaign on behalf of or in opposition to any candidate for public office.

For purposes of determining whether an organization is attempting to influence legislation or is engaging in political activities, see sections 501(c)(3), 501(h), 4911 and the regulations thereunder.

(6) No deduction shall be allowed under section 170 for expenditures for lobbying purposes, the promotion or defeat of legislation, etc. See also the regulations under sections 162 and 4945.

(7) No deduction for charitable contributions is allowed in computing the taxable income of a common trust fund or of a partnership. See sections 584(d)(3) and 703(a)(2)(D). However, a partner's distributive share of charitable contributions actually paid by a partnership during its taxable year may be allowed as a deduction in the partner's separate return for his taxable year with or within which the taxable year of the partnership ends, to the extent that the aggregate of his share of the partnership contributions and his own contributions does not exceed the limitations in section 170(b).

(8) For charitable contributions paid by a nonresident alien individual or a foreign corporation, see § 1.170A-4(b)(5) and sections 873, 876, 877, and 882(c), and the regulations thereunder.

(9) For charitable contributions paid by a citizen of the United States or a domestic corporation entitled to the benefits of section 931 (relating to income from sources within possessions of the United States), see section 931(d) and the regulations thereunder.

(10) For carryover of excess charitable contributions in certain corporate acquisitions, see section 381(c)(19) and the regulations thereunder.

(11) No deduction shall be allowed under section 170 for out-of-pocket expenditures on behalf of an eligible organization (within the meaning of § 1.501(h)-2(b)(1)) if the expenditure is made in connection with influencing legislation (within the meaning of section 501(c)(3) or § 56.4911-2), or in connection with the payment of the organization's tax liability under section 4911. For the treatment of similar expenditures on behalf of other organizations see paragraph (h)(6) of this section.

(k) *Effective date.* In general this section applies to contributions made in taxable years beginning after December 31, 1969. Paragraph (j)(11) of this section, however, applies only to out-of-pocket expenditures made in taxable years beginning after December 31, 1976. In addition, paragraph (h) of this section applies only to payments made on or after December 16, 1996. However, taxpayers may rely on the rules of paragraph (h) of this section for payments made on or after January 1, 1994. [Reg. § 1.170A-1.]

☐ [*T.D.* 7207, 10-3-72. *Amended by T.D.* 7340, 1-6-75; *T.D.* 7807, 1-29-82; *T.D.* 8002, 12-26-84; *T.D.* 8308, 8-30-90 *and T.D.* 8690, 12-13-96.]

[Reg. § 1.170A-2]

§ 1.170A-2. Amounts paid to maintain certain students as members of the taxpayer's household.—(a) *In general*—(1) The term "charitable contributions" includes amounts paid by the taxpayer during the taxable year to maintain certain students as members of his household which, under the provisions of section 170(h) and this section, are treated as amounts paid for the use of an organization described in section 170(c)(2), (3), or (4), and such amounts, to the extent they do not exceed the limitations under section 170(h)(2) and paragraph (b) of this section, are contributions deductible under section 170. In order for such amounts to be so treated, the student must be an individual who is neither a dependent (as defined in section 152) of the taxpayer nor related to the taxpayer in a manner described in any of the paragraphs (1) through (8) of section 152(a), and such individual must be a member of the taxpayer's household pursuant to a written agreement between the taxpayer and an organization described in section 170(c)(2), (3), or (4) to implement a program of the organization to provide educational opportunities for pupils or students placed in private homes by such organization. Furthermore, such amounts must be paid to maintain such individual during the period in the taxable year he is a member of the taxpayer's household and is a full-time pupil or student in the twelfth or any lower grade at an educational institution, as defined in section 151(e)(4) and § 1.151-3, located in the United States. Amounts paid outside of such period, but within the taxable year, for expenses necessary for the maintenance of the student during the period will qualify for the charitable contributions deduction if the other limitation requirements of the section are met.

(2) For purposes of subparagraph (1) of this paragraph, amounts treated as charitable contributions include only those amounts actually paid by the taxpayer during the taxable year which are directly attributable to the maintenance of the student while he is a member of the taxpayer's household and is attending an educational institution on a full-time basis. This would include amounts paid to ensure the well-being of the individual and to carry out the purpose for which the individual was placed in the taxpayer's home. For example, a deduction under section 170 would be allowed for amounts paid for books, tuition, food, clothing, transportation, medical and dental care, and recreation for the individual. Amounts treated as charitable contributions under this section do not include amounts which the taxpayer would have expended had the student not been in the household. They would not include, for example, amounts paid in connection with the taxpayer's home for taxes, insurance, interest on a mortgage, repairs, etc. Moreover, such amounts do not include any depreciation sustained by the taxpayer in maintaining such student or students in his household, nor do they include the value of any services rendered on behalf of such student or students by the taxpayer or any member of the taxpayer's household.

(3) For purposes of section 170(h) and this section, an individual will be considered to be a full-time pupil or student at an educational institution only if he is enrolled for a course of study prescribed for a full-time student at such institution and is attending classes on a full-time basis. Nevertheless, such individual may be absent from school due to special circumstances and still be considered to be in full-time attendance. Periods during the regular school term when the school is closed for holidays, such as Christmas and Easter, and for periods between semesters are treated as periods during which the pupil or student is in full-time attendance at the school. Also, absences during the regular school term due to illness of such individual shall not prevent him from being considered as a full-time pupil or student. Similarly, absences from the taxpayer's household due to special circumstances will not disqualify the student as a member of the household. Summer vacations between regular school terms are not considered periods of school attendance.

(4) When claiming a deduction for amounts described in section 170(h) and this section, the taxpayer must submit with his return a copy of his agreement with the organization sponsoring the individual placed in the taxpayer's household, together with a summary of the various items for which amounts were paid to maintain such individual and a statement as to the date the individual became a member of the household and the period of his full-time attendance at school and the name and location of such school. Substantiation of amounts claimed must be supported by adequate records of the amounts actually paid. Due to the nature of certain items, such as food, a record of amounts spent for all members of the household, with an equal portion thereof allocated to each member, will be acceptable.

(b) *Limitations.* Section 170(h) and this section shall apply to amounts paid during the taxable year only to the extent that the amounts paid in maintaining each pupil or student do not exceed $50 multiplied by the number of full calendar months in the taxable year that the pupil or student is maintained in accordance with the provisions of this section. For purposes of such limitation if 15 or more days of a calendar month fall within the period to which the maintenance of such pupil or student relates, such month is considered as a full calendar month. To the extent that such amounts qualify as charitable contributions under section 170(c), the aggregate of such amounts plus other contributions made during the taxable year for the use of an organization described in section 170(c) is deductible under section 170 subject to the limitation provided in section 170(b)(1)(B) and paragraph (c) of § 1 170A-8.

(c) *Compensation or reimbursement.* Amounts paid during the taxable year to maintain a pupil or student as a member of the taxpayer's household as provided in paragraph (a) of this section, shall not be taken into account under section 170(h) and this section, if the taxpayer receives any money or other property as compensation or reimbursement for any portion of such amounts. The taxpayer will not be denied the benefits of section 170(h) if he prepays an extraordinary or non-recurring expense, such as a hospital bill or vacation trip, at the request of the individual's parents or the sponsoring organization and is reimbursed for such prepayment. The value of services performed by the pupil or student in attending to ordinary chores of the household will generally not be considered to constitute compensation or reimbursement. However, if the pupil or student is taken into the taxpayer's household to replace a former employee of the taxpayer or gratuitously to perform substantial services for the taxpayer, the facts and circumstances may warrant a conclusion that the taxpayer received reimbursement for maintaining the pupil or student.

(d) *No other amount allowed as deduction.* Except to the extent that amounts described in section 170(h) and this section are treated as charitable contributions under section 170(c) and, therefore, deductible under section 170(a), no deduction is allowed for any amount paid to maintain an individual, as a member of the taxpayer's household, in accordance with the provisions of section 170(h) and this section.

(e) *Illustrations.* The application of this section may be illustrated by the following examples:

Example (1). The X organization is an organization described in section 170(c)(2) and is engaged in a program under which a number of European children are placed in the homes of U.S. residents in order to further the children's high school education. In accordance with paragraph (a) of this section, the taxpayer, A, who reports his income on the calendar year basis, agreed with X to take two of the children, and they were placed in the taxpayer's home on January 2, 1970, where they remained until January 21, 1971, during which time they were fully maintained by the taxpayer. The children enrolled at the local high school for the full course of study prescribed for 10th grade students and attended the school on a full-time basis for the spring semester starting January 18, 1970, and ending June 3, 1970, and for the fall semester starting September 1, 1970, and ending January 13, 1971. The total cost of food paid by A in 1970 for himself, his wife, and the two children amounted to $1,920, or $40 per month for each member of the household. Since the children were actually full-time students for only 8½ months during 1970, the amount paid for food for each child during that period amounted to $340. Other amounts paid during the 8½ month period for each child for laundry, lights, water, recreation, and school supplies amounted to $160. Thus, the amounts treated under section 170(h) and this section as paid for the use of X would, with respect to each child, total $500 ($340 + $160), or a total for both children of $1,000, subject to the limitations of paragraph (b) of this section. Since, for purposes of such limitations, the children were full-time students for only 8 full calendar months during 1970 (less than 15 days in January 1970), the taxpayer may treat only $800 as a charitable contribution made in 1970, that is, $50 multiplied by the 8 full calendar months, or $400 paid for the maintenance of each child. Neither the excess payments nor amounts paid to maintain the children during the period before school opened and for the period in summer between regular school

terms is taken into account by reason of section 170(h). Also, because the children were full-time students for less than 15 days in January 1971 (although maintained in the taxpayer's household for 21 days), amounts paid to maintain the children during 1971 would not qualify as a charitable contribution.

Example (2). A religious organization described in section 170(c)(2) has a program for providing educational opportunities for children it places in private homes. In order to implement the program, the taxpayer, H, who resides with his wife, son, and daughter of high school age in a town in the United States, signs an agreement with the organization to maintain a girl sponsored by the organization as a member of his household while the child attends the local high school for the regular 1970-71 school year. The child is a full-time student at the school during the school year starting September 6, 1970, and ending June 6, 1971, and is a member of the taxpayer's household during that period. Although the taxpayer pays $200 during the school period falling in 1970, and $240 during the school period falling in 1971, to maintain the child, he cannot claim either amount as a charitable contribution because the child's parents, from time to time during the school year, send butter, eggs, meat, and vegetables to H to help defray the expenses of maintaining the child. This is considered property received as reimbursement under paragraph (c) of this section. Had her parents not contributed the food, the fact that the child, in addition to the normal chores she shared with the taxpayer's daughter, such as cleaning their own rooms and helping with the shopping and cooking, was responsible for the family laundry and for the heavy cleaning of the entire house while the taxpayer's daughter had no comparable responsibilities would also preclude a claim for a charitable contributions deduction. These substantial gratuitous services are considered property received as reimbursement under paragraph (c) of this section.

Example (3). A taxpayer resides with his wife in a city in the eastern United States. He agrees, in writing, with a fraternal society described in section 170(c)(4) to accept a child selected by the society for maintenance by him as a member of his household during 1971 in order that the child may attend the local grammar school as a part of the society's program to provide elementary education for certain children selected by it. The taxpayer maintains the child, who has as his principal place of abode the home of the taxpayer, and is a member of the taxpayer's household, during the entire year 1971. The child is a full-time student at the local grammar school for 9 full calendar months during the year. Under the

Reg. § 1.170A-2(d)

agreement, the society pays the taxpayer $30 per month to help maintain the child. Since the $30 per month is considered as compensation or reimbursement to the taxpayer for some portion of the maintenance paid on behalf of the child, no amounts paid with respect to such maintenance can be treated as amounts paid in accordance with section 170(h). In the absence of the $30 per month payments, if the child qualifies as a dependent of the taxpayer under section 152(a)(9), that fact would also prevent the maintenance payments from being treated as charitable contributions paid for the use of the fraternal society.

(f) *Effective date.* This section applies only to contributions paid in taxable years beginning after December 31, 1969. [Reg. § 1.170A-2.]

☐ [*T.D.* 7207, 10-3-72.]

[Reg. § 1.170A-3]

§ 1.170A-3. **Reduction of charitable contribution for interest on certain indebtedness.**— (a) *In general.* Section 170(f)(5) requires that the amount of a charitable contribution be reduced for certain interest to the extent necessary to avoid the deduction of the same amount both as an interest deduction under section 163 and as a deduction for charitable contributions under section 170. The reduction is to be determined in accordance with paragraphs (b) and (c) of this section.

(b) *Interest attributable to postcontribution period.* In determining the amount to be taken into account as a charitable contribution for purposes of section 170, the amount determined without regard to section 170(f)(5) or this section shall be reduced by the amount of interest which has been paid, or is to be paid, by the taxpayer, which is attributable to any liability connected with the contribution, and which is attributable to any period of time after the making of the contribution. The deduction otherwise allowable for charitable contributions under section 170 is required to be reduced pursuant to section 170(f)(5) and this section only if, in connection with a charitable contribution, a liability is assumed by the recipient of the contribution or by any other person or if the charitable contribution is of property which is subject to a liability. Thus, if a charitable contribution is made in property and the transfer is conditioned upon the assumption of a liability by the donee or by some other person, the contribution must be reduced by the amount of any interest which has been paid, or will be paid, by the taxpayer, which is attributable to the liability, and which is attributable to any period after the making of the contribution. The adjustment referred to in this paragraph must also be made where the contributed property is subject to a liability and the value of the property reflects the payment by the donor of interest with respect to a period of time after the making of the contribution.

(c) *Interest attributable to precontribution period.* If, in connection with the charitable contribution of a bond, a liability is assumed by the recipient or by any other person, or if the bond is subject to a liability, then, in determining the amount to be taken into account as a charitable contribution under section 170, the amount determined without regard to section 170(f)(5) and this section shall, without regard to whether any reduction may be required by paragraph (b) of this section, also be reduced for interest which has been paid, or is to be paid, by the taxpayer on indebtedness incurred or continued to purchase or carry such bond, and which is attributable to any period before the making of the contribution. However, the reduction referred to in this paragraph shall be made only to the extent that such reduction does not exceed the interest (including bond discount and other interest equivalent) receivable on the bond, and attributable to any period before the making of the contribution which is not, by reason of the taxpayer's method of accounting, includible in the taxpayer's gross income for any taxable year. For purposes of section 170(f)(5) and this section the term "bond" means any bond, debenture, note, or certificate or other evidence of indebtedness.

(d) *Illustrations.* The application of this section may be illustrated by the following examples:

Example (1). On January 1, 1970, A, a cash basis taxpayer using the calendar year as the taxable year, contributed to a charitable organization real estate having a fair market value and adjusted basis of $10,000. In connection with the contribution the charitable organization assumed an indebtedness of $8,000 which A had incurred. On December 31, 1969, A prepaid one year's interest on that indebtedness for 1970, amounting to $960, and took an interest deduction of $960 for such amount. The amount of the gift, determined without regard to this section, is $2,960 ($10,000 less $8,000, the outstanding indebtedness, plus $960, the amount of prepaid interest). In determining the amount of the deduction for the charitable contribution, the value of the gift ($2,960) must be reduced by $960 to eliminate from the computation of such deduction that portion thereof for which A has been allowed an interest deduction.

Example (2). (a) On January 1, 1970, B, an individual using the cash receipts and disbursements method of accounting, purchased for $9,950 a 5½ percent $10,000, 20-year M Corporation bond, the interest on which was payable semi-annually on June 30 and December 31. The M Corporation had issued the bond on January 1, 1960, at a discount of $720 from the principal amount. On December 1, 1970, B donated the bond to a charitable organization, and, in connection with the contribution, the charitable organization assumed an indebtedness of $7,000 which B had incurred to purchase and carry the bond.

(b) During the calendar year 1970 B paid accrued interest of $330 on the indebtedness for the period from January 1, 1970, to December 1, 1970, and has taken an interest deduction of $330 for such amount. No portion of the bond discount of $36 a year ($720 divided by 20 years) has been included in B's income, and of the $550 of annual interest receivable on the bond, he included in income only the June 30, 1970, payment of $275.

(c) The market value of the bond on December 1, 1970, was $9,902. Such value includes $229 of interest receivable which had accrued from July 1 to December 1, 1970.

(d) The amount of the charitable contribution determined without regard to this section is $2,902 ($9,902, the value of the property on the date of gift, less $7,000, the amount of the liability assumed by the charitable organization). In determining the amount of the allowable deduction for charitable contributions, the value of the gift ($2,902) must be reduced to eliminate from the deduction that portion thereof for which B has been allowed an interest deduction. Although the amount of such interest deduction was $330, the reduction required by this section is limited to $262, since the reduction is not in excess of the amount of interest income on the bond ($229 of accrued interest plus $33, the amount of bond discount attributable to the 11-month period B held the bond).

(e) *Effective date.* This section applies only to contributions paid in taxable years beginning after December 31, 1969. [Reg. § 1.170A-3.]

☐ [*T.D. 7207*, 10-3-72.]

[Reg. § 1.170A-4]

§ 1.170A-4. **Reduction in amount of charitable contributions of certain appreciated property.**—(a) *Amount of reduction.* Section 170(e)(1) requires that the amount of the charitable contribution which would be taken into account under section 170(a) without regard to section 170(e) shall be reduced before applying the percentage limitations under section 170(b)—

(1) In the case of a contribution by an individual or by a corporation of ordinary income property, as defined in paragraph (b)(1) of this section, by the amount of gain (hereinafter in this section referred to as ordinary income) which would have been recognized as gain which is not long-term capital gain if the property had been sold by the donor at its fair market value at the time of its contribution to the charitable organization,

(2) In the case of a contribution by an individual of section 170(e) capital gain property, as defined in paragraph (b)(2) of this section, by 50 percent of the amount of gain (hereinafter in this section referred to as long-term capital gain) which would have been recognized as long-term capital gain if the property had been sold by the donor at its fair market value at the time of its contribution to the charitable organization, and

(3) In the case of a contribution by a corporation of section 170(e) capital gain property, as defined in paragraph (b)(2) of this section by 62½ percent of the amount of gain (hereinafter in this section referred to as long-term capital gain) which would have been recognized as long-term capital gain if the property had been sold by the donor at its fair market value at the time of its contribution to the charitable organization,

Section 170(e)(1) and this paragraph do not apply to reduce the amount of the charitable contribution where, by reason of the transfer of the contributed property, ordinary income or capital gain is recognized by the donor in the same taxable year in which the contribution is made. Thus, where income or gain is recognized under section 453(d) upon the transfer of an installment obligation to a charitable organization, or under section 454(b) upon the transfer of an obligation issued at a discount to such an organization, or upon the assignment of income to such an organization, section 170(e)(1) and this paragraph do not apply if recognition of the income or gain occurs in the same taxable year in which the contribution is made. Section 170(e)(1) and this paragraph apply to a charitable contribution of an interest in ordinary income property or section 170(e) capital gain property which is described in paragraph (b) of § 1.170A-6 or paragraph (b) of § 1.170A-7. For purposes of applying section 170(e)(1) and this paragraph it is immaterial whether the charitable contribution is made "to" the charitable organization or whether it is made "for the use of" the charitable organization. See § 1.170A-8(a)(2).

(b) *Definitions and other rules.* For purposes of this section—

(1) *Ordinary income property.* The term "ordinary income property" means property any portion of the gain on which would not have been long-term capital gain if the property had been sold by the donor at its fair market value at the time of its contribution to the charitable organiza-

tion. Such term includes, for example, property held by the donor primarily for sale to customers in the ordinary course of his trade or business, a work of art created by the donor, a manuscript prepared by the donor, letters and memorandums prepared by or for the donor, a capital asset held by the donor for not more than 1 year (6 months for taxable years beginning before 1977; 9 months for taxable years beginning in 1977), and stock described in section 306(a), 341(a), or 1248(a) to the extent that, after applying such section, gain on its disposition would not have been long-term capital gain. The term does not include an income interest in respect of which a deduction is allowed under section 170(f)(2)(B) and paragraph (c) of § 1.170A-6.

(2) *Section 170(e) capital gain property.* The term "section 170(e) capital gain property" means property any portion of the gain on which would have been treated as long-term capital gain if the property had been sold by the donor at its fair market value at the time of its contribution to the charitable organization and which—

(i) Is contributed to or for the use of a private foundation, as defined in section 509(a) and the regulations thereunder, other than a private foundation described in section 170(b)(1)(E),

(ii) Constitutes tangible personal property contributed to or for the use of a charitable organization, other than a private foundation to which subdivision (i) of this subparagraph applies, which is put to an unrelated use by the charitable organization within the meaning of subparagraph (3) of this paragraph, or

(iii) Constitutes property not described in subdivision (i) or (ii) of this subparagraph which is 30-percent capital gain property to which an election under paragraph (d)(2) of § 1.170A-8 applies.

For purposes of this subparagraph a fixture which is intended to be severed from real property shall be treated as tangible personal property.

(3) *Unrelated use*—(i) *In general.* The term "unrelated use" means a use which is unrelated to the purpose or function constituting the basis of the charitable organization's exemption under section 501 or, in the case of a contribution of property to a governmental unit, the use of such property by such unit for other than exclusively public purposes. For example, if a painting contributed to an educational institution is used by that organization for educational purposes by being placed in its library for display and study by art students, the use is not an unrelated use; but if the painting is sold and the proceeds used by the organization for educational purposes, the use of the property is an unrelated use. If furnishings

contributed to a charitable organization are used by it in its offices and buildings in the course of carrying out its functions, the use of the property is not an unrelated use. If a set or collection of items of tangible personal property is contributed to a charitable organization or governmental unit, the use of the set or collection is not an unrelated use if the donee sells or otherwise disposes of only an insubstantial portion of the set or collection. The use by a trust of tangible personal property contributed to it for the benefit of a charitable organization is an unrelated use if the use by the trust is one which would have been unrelated if made by the charitable organization.

(ii) *Proof of use.* For purposes of applying subparagraph (2)(ii) of this paragraph, a taxpayer who makes a charitable contribution of tangible personal property to or for the use of a charitable organization or governmental unit may treat such property as not being put to an unrelated use by the donee if—

(a) He establishes that the property is not in fact put to an unrelated use by the donee, or

(b) At the time of the contribution or at the time the contribution is treated as made, it is reasonable to anticipate that the property will not be put to an unrelated use by the donee. In the case of a contribution of tangible personal property to or for the use of a museum, if the object donated is of a general type normally retained by such museum or other museums for museum purposes, it will be reasonable for the donor to anticipate, unless he has actual knowledge to the contrary, that the object will not be put to an unrelated use by the donee, whether or not the object is later sold or exchanged by the donee.

(4) *Property used in trade or business.* For purposes of applying subparagraphs (1) and (2) of this paragraph, property which is used in the trade or business, as defined in section 1231(b), shall be treated as a capital asset, except that any gain in respect of such property which would have been recognized if the property had been sold by the donor at its fair market value at the time of its contribution to the charitable organization shall be treated as ordinary income to the extent that such gain would have constituted ordinary income by reason of the application of section 617(d)(1), 1245(a), 1250(a), 1251(c), 1252(a), or 1254(a).

(5) *Nonresident alien individuals and foreign corporations.* The reduction in the case of a nonresident alien individual or a foreign corporation shall be determined by taking into account the gain which would have been recognized and subject to tax under chapter 1 of the Code if the

property had been sold or disposed of within the United States by the donor at its fair market value at the time of its contribution to the charitable organization. However, the amount of such gain which would have been subject to tax under section 871(a) or 881 (relating to gain not effectively connected with the conduct of a trade or business within the United States) if there had been a sale or other disposition within the United States shall be treated as long-term capital gain. Thus, a charitable contribution by a nonresident alien individual or a foreign corporation of property the sale or other disposition of which within the United States would have resulted in gain subject to tax under section 871(a) or 881 will be reduced only as provided in section 170(e)(1)(B) and paragraph (a)(2) or (3) of this section, but only if the property contributed is described in subdivision (i), (ii), or (iii) of subparagraph (2) of this paragraph. A charitable contribution by a nonresident alien individual or a foreign corporation of property the sale or other disposition of which within the United States would have resulted in gain subject to tax under section 871(a) or 881 will in no case be reduced under section 170(e)(1)(A) and paragraph (a)(1) of this section.

(c) *Allocation of basis and gain*—(1) *In general.* Except as provided in subparagraph (2) of this paragraph—

(i) If a taxpayer makes a charitable contribution of less than his entire interest in appreciated property, whether or not the transfer is made in trust, as, for example, in the case of a transfer of appreciated property to a pooled income fund described in section 642(c)(5) and § 1.642(c)-5, and is allowed a deduction under section 170 for a portion of the fair market value of such property, then for purposes of applying the reduction rules of section 170(e)(1) and this section to the contributed portion of the property the taxpayer's adjusted basis in such property at the time of the contribution shall be allocated under section 170(e)(2) between the contributed portion of the property and the noncontributed portion.

(ii) The adjusted basis of the contributed portion of the property shall be that portion of the adjusted basis of the entire property which bears the same ratio to the total adjusted basis as the fair market value of the contributed portion of the property bears to the fair market value of the entire property.

(iii) The ordinary income and the long-term capital gain which shall be taken into account in applying section 170(e)(1) and paragraph (a) of this section to the contributed portion of the property shall be the amount of gain which would have been recognized as ordinary income

and long-term capital gain if such contributed portion had been sold by the donor at its fair market value at the time of its contribution to the charitable organization.

(2) *Bargain sale.* (i) Section 1011(b) and § 1.1011-2 apply to bargain sales of property to charitable organizations. For purposes of applying the reduction rules of section 170(e)(1) and this section to the contributed portion of the property in the case of a bargain sale, there shall be allocated under section 1011(b) to the contributed portion of the property that portion of the adjusted basis of the entire property that bears the same ratio to the total adjusted basis as the fair market value of the contributed portion of the property bears to the fair market value of the entire property. For purposes of applying section 170(e)(1) and paragraph (a) of this section to the contributed portion of the property in such a case, there shall be allocated to the contributed portion the amount of gain that is not recognized on the bargain sale but that would have been recognized if such contributed portion had been sold by the donor at its fair market value at the time of its contribution to the charitable organization.

(ii) The term "bargain sale", as used in this subparagraph, means a transfer of property which is in part a sale or exchange of the property and in part a charitable contribution, as defined in section 170(c), of the property.

(3) *Ratio of ordinary income and capital gain.* For purposes of applying subparagraphs (1)(iii) and (2)(i) of this paragraph, the amount of ordinary income (or long-term capital gain) which would have been recognized if the contributed portion of the property had been sold by the donor at its fair market value at the time of its contribution shall be that amount which bears the same ratio to the ordinary income (or long-term capital gain) which would have been recognized if the entire property had been sold by the donor at its fair market value at the time of its contribution as (i) the fair market value of the contributed portion at such time bears to (ii) the fair market value of the entire property at such time. In the case of a bargain sale, the fair market value of the contributed portion for purposes of subdivision (i) is the amount determined by subtracting from the fair market value of the entire property the amount realized on the sale.

(4) *Donee's basis of property acquired.* The adjusted basis of the contributed portion of the property as determined under subparagraph (1) or (2) of this paragraph, shall be used by the donee in applying to the contributed portion such provisions as section 514(a)(1), relating to adjusted basis of debt-financed property; section

Reg. § 1.170A-4(c)(1)

1015(a), relating to basis of property acquired by gift; section 4940(c)(4), relating to capital gains and losses in determination of net investment income; and section 4942(f)(2)(B), relating to net short-term capital gain in determination of tax on failure to distribute income. The fair market value of the contributed portion of the property at the time of the contribution shall not be used by the donee as the basis of such contributed portion.

Property	Fair Market Value	Adjusted Basis	Recognized Gain if Sold
Ordinary income property	$ 50,000	$35,000	$15,000
Property which, if sold, would produce long-term capital gain:			
(1) Stock held more than 6 months contributed to—			
(i) A church	25,000	21,000	4,000
(ii) A private foundation not described in section 170(b)( )(E) .	15,000	10,000	5,000
(2) Tangible personal property held more than 6 months put to			
unrelated use by church)	12,000	6,000	6,000
Total	$102,000	$72,000	$30,000

(b) After making the reductions required by paragraph (a) of this section, the amount of charitable contributions allowed (before application of section 170(b) limitations) is as follows:

Property	Fair Market Value	Reduction	Contribution Allowed
Ordinary income property	$ 50,000	$15,000	$35,000
Property which, if sold, would produce long-term capital gain:			
(1) Stock contributed to—			
(i) The church	25,000	.	25,000
(ii) The private foundation	15,000	2,500	12,500
(2) Tangible personal property........................	12,000	3,000	9,000
Total	$102,000	$20,500	$81,500

(c) If C were a corporation, rather than an individual, the amount of charitable contributions allowed (before application of section 170(b) limitation) would be as follows:

Property	Fair Market Value	Reduction	Contribution Allowed
Ordinary income property	$ 50,000	$15,000	$35,000
Property which, if sold, would produce long-term capital gain:			
(1) Stock contributed to—			
(i) The church	25,000	.	25,000
(ii)The private foundation	15,000	3,125	11,875
(2) Tangible personal property.......................	12,000	3,750	8,250
Total	$102,000	$21,875	$80,125

(d) Illustrations. The application of this section may be illustrated by the following examples:

Example (1). (a) On July 1, 1970, C, an individual, makes the following charitable contributions, all of which are made to a church except in the case of the stock (as indicated):

Example (2). On March 1, 1970, D, an individual, contributes to a church intangible property to which section 1245 applies which has a fair market value of $60,000 and an adjusted basis of $10,000. At the time of the contribution D has used the property in his business for more than 6 months. If the property had been sold by D at its fair market value at the time of its contribution, it is assumed that under section 1245 $20,000 of the gain of $50,000 would have been treated as ordinary income and $30,000 would have been

long-term capital gain. Under paragraph (a)(1) of this section, D's contribution of $60,000 is reduced by $20,000.

Example (3). The facts are the same as in example (2) except that the property is contributed to a private foundation not described in section 170(b)(1)(E). Under paragraph (a)(1) and (2) of this section, D's contribution is reduced by $35,000 (100% of the ordinary income of $20,000 and 50% of the long-term capital gain of $30,000).

Reg. § 1.170A-4(d)

Example (4). (a) In 1971, E, an individual calendar-year taxpayer, contributes to a church stock held for more than 6 months which has a fair market value of $90,000 and an adjusted basis of $10,000. In 1972, E also contributes to a church stock held for more than 6 months which has a fair market value of $20,000 and an adjusted basis of $10,000. E's contribution base for 1971 is $200,000; and for 1972, is $150,000. E makes no other charitable contributions for these 2 taxable years.

(b) For 1971 the amount of the contribution which may be taken into account under section 170(a) is limited by section 170(b)(1)(D)(i) to $60,000 ($200,000 × 30%), and A is allowed a deduction for $60,000. Under section 170(b)(1)(D)(ii), E has a $30,000 carryover to 1972 of 30-percent capital gain property, as defined in paragraph (d)(3) of § 1.170A-8. For 1972 the amount of the charitable contributions deduction is $45,000 (total contributions of $50,000 [$30,000 + $20,000] but not to exceed 30% of $150,000).

(c) Assuming, however, that in 1972 E elects under section 170(b)(1)(D)(iii) and paragraph (d)(2) of § 1.170A-8 to have section 170(e)(1)(B) apply to his contributions and carryovers of 30-percent capital gain property, he must apply section 170(d)(1) as if section 170(e)(1)(B) had applied to the contribution for 1971. If section 170(e)(1)(B) had applied in 1971 to his contributions of 30-percent capital gain property, E's contribution would have been reduced from $90,000 to $50,000, the reduction of $40,000 being 50 percent of the gain of $80,000 ($90,000 − $10,000) which would have been recognized as long-term capital gain if the property had been sold by E at its fair market value at the time of its contribution to the church. Accordingly, by taking the election into account, E has no carryover of 30-percent capital gain property to 1972 since the charitable contributions deduction of $60,000 allowed for 1971 in respect of that property exceeds the reduced contribution of $50,000 for 1971 which may be taken into account by reason of the election. The charitable contributions deduction of $60,000 allowed for 1971 is not reduced by reason of the election.

(d) Since by reason of the election E is allowed under paragraph (a)(2) of this section a charitable contributions deduction for 1972 of $15,000 ($20,000 − [($20,000 − $10,000) × 50%]) and since the $30,000 carryover from 1971 is eliminated, it would not be to E's advantage to make the election under section 170(b)(1)(D)(iii) in 1972.

Example (5). In 1970, F, an individual calendar-year taxpayer, sells to a church for $4,000 ordinary income property with a fair market value of $10,000 and an adjusted basis of $4,000. F's contribution base for 1970 is $20,000, and F makes no other charitable contributions in 1970. Thus, F makes a charitable contribution to the church of $6,000 ($10,000 − $4,000 amount realized), which is 60% of the value of the property. The amount realized on the bargain sale is 40% ($4,000/$10,000) of the value of the property. In applying section 1011(b) to the bargain sale, adjusted basis in the amount of $1,600 ($4,000 adjusted basis × 40%) is allocated under § 1.1011-2(b) to the noncontributed portion of the property, and F recognizes $2,400 ($4,000 amount realized less $1,600 adjusted basis) of ordinary income. Under paragraphs (a)(1) and (c)(2)(i) of this section, F's contribution of $6,000 is reduced by $3,600 ($6,000 − [$4,000 adjusted basis × 60%]) (*i.e.,* the amount of ordinary income that would have been recognized on the contributed portion had the property been sold). The reduced contribution of $2,400 consists of the portion ($4,000 × 60%) of the adjusted basis not allocated to the noncontributed portion of the property. That is, the reduced contribution consists of the portion of the adjusted basis allocated to the contributed portion. Under sections 1012 and 1015(a) the basis of the property to the church is $6,400 ($4,000 + $2,400).

Example (6). In 1970, G, an individual calendar-year taxpayer, sells to a church for $6,000 ordinary income property with a fair market value of $10,000 and an adjusted basis of $4,000. G's contribution base for 1970 is $20,000, and G makes no other charitable contributions in 1970. Thus, G makes a charitable contribution to the church of $4,000 ($10,000 − $6,000 amount realized), which is 40% of the value of the property. The amount realized on the bargain sale is 60% ($6,000/$10,000) of the value of the property. In applying section 1011(b) to the bargain sale, adjusted basis in the amount of $2,400 ($4,000 adjusted basis × 60%) is allocated under § 1.1011-2(b) to the noncontributed portion of the property, and G recognizes $3,600 ($6,000 amount realized less $2,400 adjusted basis) of ordinary income. Under paragraphs (a)(1) and (c)(2)(i) of this section, G's contribution of $4,000 is reduced by $2,400 ($4,000 − [$4,000 adjusted basis × 40%]) (*i.e.,* the amount of ordinary income that would have been recognized on the contributed portion had the property been sold). The reduced contribution of $1,600 consists of the portion ($4,000 × 40%) of the adjusted basis not allocated to the noncontributed portion of the property. That is, the reduced contribution con-

Reg. § 1.170A-4(d)

sists of the portion of the adjusted basis allocated to the contributed portion. Under sections 1012 and 1015(a) the basis of the property to the church is $7,600 ($6,000 + $1,600).

Example (7). In 1970, H, an individual calendar-year taxpayer, sells to a church for $2,000 stock held for not more than 6 months which has an adjusted basis of $4,000 and a fair market value of $10,000. H's contribution base for 1970 is $20,000, and H makes no other charitable contributions in 1970. Thus, H makes a charitable contribution to the church of $8,000 ($10,000 — $2,000 amount realized), which is 80% of the value of the property. The amount realized on the bargain sale is 20% ($2,000/$10,000) of the value of the property. In applying section 1011(b) to the bargain sale, adjusted basis in the amount of $800 ($4,000 adjusted basis × 20%) is allocated under § 1.1011-2(b) to the noncontributed portion of the property, and H recognizes $1,200 ($2,000 amount realized less $800 adjusted basis) of ordinary income. Under paragraphs (a)(1) and (c)(2)(i) of this section, H's contribution of $8,000 is reduced by $4,800 ($8,000 — [$4,000 adjusted basis × 80%]) (*i.e.*, the amount of ordinary income that would have been recognized on the contributed portion had the property been sold). The reduced contribution of $3,200 consists of the portion ($4,000 × 80%) of the adjusted basis not allocated to the noncontributed portion of the property. That is, the reduced contribution consists of the portion of the adjusted basis allocated to the contributed portion. Under sections 1012 and 1015(a) the basis of the property to the church is $5,200 ($2,000 + $3,200).

Example (8). In 1970, F, an individual calendar-year taxpayer, sells for $4,000 to a private foundation not described in section 170(b)(1)(E) property to which section 1245 applies which has a fair market value of $10,000 and an adjusted basis of $4,000. F's contribution base for 1970 is $20,000, and F makes no other charitable contributions in 1970. At the time of the bargain sale, F has used the property in his business for more than 6 months. Thus, F makes a charitable contribution of $6,000 ($10,000 — $4,000 amount realized), which is 60% of the value of the property. The amount realized on the bargain sale is 40% ($4,000/$10,000) of the value of the property. If the property had been sold by F at its fair market value at the time of its contribution, it is assumed that under section 1245 $4,000 of the gain of $6,000 ($10,000 — $4,000 adjusted basis) would have been treated as ordinary income and $2,000 would have been long-term capital gain. In applying section 1011(b) to the bargain sale, adjusted basis in the amount of $1,600 ($4,000 adjusted basis × 40%) is allocated under § 1.1011-2(b) to

the noncontributed portion of the property, and F's recognized gain of $2,400 ($4,000 amount realized less $1,600 adjusted basis) consists of $1,600 ($4,000 × 40%) of ordinary income and $800 ($2,000 × 40%) of long-term capital gain. Under paragraphs (a) and (c)(2)(i) of this section, F's contribution of $6,000 is reduced by $3,000 (the sum of $2,400 ($4,000 × 60%) of ordinary income and $600 ([$2,000 × 60%] × 50%) of long-term capital gain) (*i.e.*, the amount of gain that would have been recognized on the contributed portion had the property been sold). The reduced contribution of $3,000 consists of $2,400 ($4,000 × 60%) of adjusted basis and $600 ([$2,000 × 60%] × 50%) of long-term capital gain not used as a reduction under paragraph (a)(2) of this section. Under sections 1012 and 1015(a) the basis of the property to the private foundation is $6,400 ($4,000 + $2,400).

Example (9). On January 1, 1970, A, an individual, transfers to a charitable remainder annuity trust described in section 664(d)(1) stock which he has held for more than 6 months and which has a fair market value of $250,000 and an adjusted basis of $50,000, an irrevocable remainder interest in the property being contributed to a private foundation not described in section 170(b)(1)(E). The trust provides that an annuity of $12,500 a year is payable to A at the end of each year for 20 years. By reference to § 20.2031-7A(c) of this chapter (Estate Tax Regulations) the figure in column (2) opposite 20 years is 11.4699. Therefore, under § 1.664-2 the fair market value of the gift of the remainder interest to charity is $106,626.25 ($250,000 — [$12,500 × 11.4699]). Under paragraph (c)(1)(ii) of this section, the adjusted basis allocated to the contributed portion of the property is $21,325.25 ($50,000 × $106,626.25/$250,000). Under paragraphs (a)(2) and (c)(1) of this section, A's contribution is reduced by $42,650.50 (50% × [$106,626.25 — $21,325.25]) to $63,975.75 ($106,626.25 — $42,650.50). If, however, the irrevocable remainder interest in the property had been contributed to a section 170(b)(1)(A) organization, A's contribution of $106,626.25 would not be reduced under paragraph (a) of this section.

Example (10). (a) On July 1, 1970, B, a calendar-year individual taxpayer, sells to a church for $75,000 intangible property to which section 1245 applies which has a fair market value of $250,000 and an adjusted basis of $75,000. Thus, B makes a charitable contribution to the church of $175,000 ($250,000 — $75,000 amount realized), which is 70% ($175,000/$250,000) of the value of the property, the amount realized on the bargain sale is 30% ($75,000/$250,000) of the value of the property. At the time of the bargain sale, B has used the property in his business for more than 6 months. B's contribution base for 1970 is $500,000, and B makes no other charitable contributions in 1970. If the property had been sold by B at its fair market value at the time of its contribution, it is assumed that under section 1245 $105,000 of the gain of $175,000 ($250,000 − $75,000 adjusted basis) would have been treated as ordinary income and $70,000 would have been long-term capital gain. In applying section 1011(b) to the bargain sale, adjusted basis in the amount of $22,500 ($75,000 adjusted basis × 30%) is allocated under § 1.1011-2(b) to the noncontributed portion of the property, and B's recognized gain of $52,500 ($75,000 amount realized less $22,500 adjusted basis) consists of $31,500 ($105,000 × 30%) of ordinary income and $21,000 ($70,000 × 30%) of long-term capital gain.

(b) Under paragraphs (a)(1) and (c)(2)(i) of this section B's contribution of $175,000 is reduced by $73,500 ($105,000 × 70%) (*i.e.,* the amount of ordinary income that would have been recognized on the contributed portion had the property been sold). The reduced contribution of $101,500 consists of $52,500 [$75,000 × 70%] of adjusted basis allocated to the contributed portion of the property and $49,000 [$70,000 × 70%] of long-term capital gain allocated to the contributed portion. Under sections 1012 and 1015(a) the basis of the property to the church is $127,500 ($75,000 + $52,500).

(e) *Effective date.* This section applies only to contributions paid after December 31, 1969, except that, in the case of a charitable contribution of a letter, memorandum, or property similar to a letter or memorandum, it applies to contributions paid after July 25, 1969. [Reg. § 1.170A-4.]

☐ [*T.D. 7207*, 10-3-72. *Amended by T.D. 7728*, 10-31-80, *T.D. 7807*, 1-29-82, *T.D. 8176*, 2-24-88 *and T.D. 8540*, 6-9-94.]

[Reg. § 1.170A-4A]

§ 1.170A-4A. **Special rule for the deduction of certain charitable contributions of inventory and other property.**—(a) *Introduction.* Section 170(e)(3) provides a special rule for the deduction of certain qualified contributions of inventory and certain other property. To be treated as a "qualified contribution," a contribution must meet the restrictions and requirements of section 170(e)(3)(A) and paragraph (b) of this section. Paragraph (b)(1) of this section describes the corporations whose contributions may be subject to this section, the exempt organizations to which these contributions may be made, and the kinds of property which may be contributed. Under paragraph (b)(2) of this section, the use of the prop-

erty must be related to the purpose or function constituting the ground for the exemption of the organization to which the contribution is made. Also, the property must be used for the care of the ill, needy, or infants. Under paragraph (b)(3) of this section, the recipient organization may not, except as there provided, require or receive in exchange money, property, or services for the transfer or use of property contributed under section 170(e)(3). Under paragraph (b)(4) of this section, the recipient organization must provide the contributing taxpayer with a written statement representing that the organization intends to comply with the restrictions set forth in paragraph (b)(2) and (3) of this section on the use and transfer of the property. Under paragraph (b)(5) of this section, the contributed property must conform to any applicable provisions of the Federal Food, Drug, and Cosmetic Act (as amended), and the regulations thereunder, at the date of contribution and for the immediately preceding 180 days. Paragraph (c) of this section provides the rules for determining the amount of reduction of the charitable contribution under section 170(e)(3). In general, the amount of the reduction is equal to one-half of the amount of gain (other than gain described in paragraph (d) of this section) which would not have been long-term capital gain if the property had been sold by the donor-taxpayer at fair market value at the date of contribution. If, after this reduction, the amount of the deduction would be more than twice the basis of the contributed property, the amount of the deduction is accordingly further reduced under paragraph (c)(1) of this section. The basis of contributed property which is inventory is determined under paragraph (c)(2) of this section, and the donor's cost of goods sold for the year of contribution must be adjusted under paragraph (c)(3) of this section. Under paragraph (d) of this section, a deduction is not allowed for any amount which, if the property had been sold by the donor-taxpayer, would have been gain to which the recapture provisions of section 617, 1245, 1250, 1251, or 1252 would have applied. For purposes of section 170(e)(3), the rules of § 1.170A-4 apply where not inconsistent with the rules of this section.

(b) *Qualified contributions*—(1) *In general.* A contribution of property qualifies under section 170(e)(3) of this section only if it is a charitable contribution—

(i) By a corporation, other than a corporation which is an electing small business corporation within the meaning of section 1371(b);

(ii) To an organization described in section 501(c)(3) and exempt under section 501(a), other than a private foundation, as defined in section 509(a), which is not an operating foundation, as defined in section 4942(j)(e);

(iii) Of property described in section 1221(1) or (2);

(iv) Which contribution meets the restrictions and requirements of paragraph (b)(2) through (5) of this section.

(2) *Restrictions on use of contributed property.* In order for the contribution to qualify under this section, the contributed property is subject to the following restrictions in use. If the transferred property is used or transferred by the donee organization (or by any subsequent transferee that furnished to the donee organization the written statement described in paragraph (b)(4)(ii) of this section) in a manner inconsistent with the requirements of subdivision (i) or (ii) of this paragraph (b)(2) or the requirements of paragraph (b)(3) of this section, the donor's deduction is reduced to the amount allowable under section 170 of the regulations thereunder, determined without regard to section 170(e)(3) of this section. If, however, the donor establishes that, at the time of the contribution, the donor reasonably anticipated that the property would be used in a manner consistent with those requirements, then the donor's deduction is not reduced.

(i) *Requirement of use for exempt purpose.* The use of the property must be related to the purpose or function constituting the ground for exemption under section 501(c)(3) of the organization to which the contribution is made. The property may not be used in connection with any activity which gives rise to unrelated trade or business income, as defined in sections 512 and 513 and the regulations thereunder.

(ii) *Requirement of use for care of the ill, needy, or infants* —(A) *In general.* The property must be used for the care of the ill, needy, or infants, as defined in this subdivision (ii). The property itself must ultimately either be transferred to (or for the use of) the ill, needy, or infants for their care or be retained for their care. No other person may use the contributed property except as incidental to primary use in the care of the ill, needy, or infants. The organization may satisfy the requirement of this subdivision by transferring the property to a relative, custodian, parent or guardian of the ill or needy individual or infant, or to any other individual if it makes a reasonable effort to ascertain that the property will ultimately be used primarily for the care of the ill or needy individual, or infant, and not for the primary benefit of any other person. The recipient organization may transfer the property to another exempt organization within the juris-

diction of the United States which meets the description contained in paragraph (b)(1)(ii) of this section, or to an organization not within the jurisdiction of the United States that, but for the fact that it is not within the jurisdiction of the United States, would be described in paragraph (b)(1)(ii) of this section. If an organization transfers the property to another organization, the transferring organization must obtain a written statement from the transferee organization as set forth in paragraph (b)(4) of this section. If the property is ultimately transferred to, or used for the benefit of, ill or needy persons, or infants, not within the jurisdiction of the United States, the organization which so transfers the property outside the jurisdiction of the United States must necessarily be a corporation. See section 170(c)(2) and §1.170A-11(a). For purposes of this subdivision, if the donee-organization charges for its transfer of contributed property (other than a fee allowed by paragraph (b)(3)(ii) of this section) the requirement of this subdivision is not met. See paragraph (b)(3) of this section.

(B) *Definition of the ill.* An ill person is a person who requires medical care within the meaning of §1.213-1(e). Examples of ill persons include a person suffering from physical injury, a person with a significant impairment of a bodily organ, a person with an existing handicap, whether from birth or later injury, a person suffering from malnutrition, a person with a disease, sickness, or infection which significantly impairs physical health, a person partially or totally incapable of self-care (including incapacity due to old age). A person suffering from mental illness is included if the person is hospitalized or institutionalized for the mental disorder, or, although the person is nonhospitalized or noninstitutionalized, if the person's mental illness constitutes a significant health impairment.

(C) *Definition of care of the ill.* Care of the ill means alleviation or cure of an existing illness and includes care of the physical, mental, or emotional needs of the ill.

(D) *Definition of the needy.* A needy person is a person who lacks the necessities of life, involving physical, mental, or emotional well-being, as a result of poverty or temporary distress. Examples of needy persons include a person who is financially impoverished as a result of low income and lack of financial resources, a person who temporarily lacks food or shelter (and the means to provide for it), a person who is the victim of a natural disaster (such as fire or flood), a person who is the victim of a civil disaster (such as a civil disturbance), a person who is temporarily not self-sufficient as a result of a sudden and severe per-

Reg. § 1.170A-4A(b)(2)

sonal or family crisis (such as a person who is the victim of a crime of violence or who has been physically abused), a person who is a refugee or immigrant and who is experiencing language, cultural, or financial difficulties, a minor child who is not self-sufficient and who is not cared for by a parent or guardian, and a person who is not self-sufficient as a result of previous institutionalization (such as a former prisoner or a former patient in a mental institution).

(E) *Definition of care of the needy.* Care of the needy means alleviation or satisfaction of an existing need. Since a person may be needy in some respects and not needy in other respects, care of the needy must relate to the particular need which causes the person to be needy. For example, a person whose temporary need arises from a natural disaster may need temporary shelter and food but not recreational facilities.

(F) *Definition of infant.* An infant is a minor child (as determined under the laws of the jurisdiction in which the child resides).

(G) *Definition of care of an infant.* Care of an infant means performance of parental functions and provision for the physical, mental, and emotional needs of the infant.

(3) *Restrictions on transfer of contributed property* —(i) *In general.* Except as otherwise provided in subdivision (ii) of this paragraph (b)(3), a contribution will not qualify under this section, if the donee-organization or any transferee of the donee-organization requires or receives any money, property, or services for the transfer or use of property contributed under section 170(e)(3). For example, if an organization provides temporary shelter for a fee, and also provides free meals to ill or needy individuals, or infants using food contributed under this section the contribution of food is subject to this section (if the other requirements of this section are met). However, the fee charged by the organization for the shelter may not be increased merely because meals are served to the ill or needy individuals or infants.

(ii) *Exception.* A contribution may qualify under this section if the donee-organization charges a fee to another organization in connection with its transfer of the donated property, if—

(A) The fee is small or nominal in relation to the value of the transferred property and is not determined by this value; and

(B) The fee is designed to reimburse the donee-organization for its administrative, warehousing, or other similar costs.

For example, if a charitable organization (such as a food bank) accepts surplus food to distribute to other charities which give the food to needy persons, a small fee may be charged to cover administrative, warehousing, and other similar costs. This fee may be charged on the basis of the total number of pounds of food distributed to the transferee charity but not on the basis of the value of the food distributed. The provisions of this subdivision (ii) do not apply to a transfer of donated property directly from an organization to ill or needy individuals, or infants.

(4) *Requirement of a written statement* —(i) *Furnished to taxpayer.* In the case of any contribution made on or after [Date which is 30 days after the issuance of these regulations by Treasury decision], the donee-organization must furnish to the taxpayer a written statement which—

(A) Describes the contributed property, stating the date of its receipt;

(B) Represents that the property will be used in compliance with section 170(e)(3) and paragraphs (b)(2) and (3) of this section;

(C) Represents that the donee-organization meets the requirements of paragraph (b)(1)(ii) of this section; and

(D) Represents that adequate books and records will be maintained, and made available to the Internal Revenue Service upon request.

The written statement must be furnished within a reasonable period after the contribution, but not later than the date (including extensions) by which the donor is required to file a United States corporate income tax return for the year in which the contribution was made. The books and records described in (D) of this subdivision (i) need not trace the receipt and disposition of specific items of donated property if they disclose compliance with the requirements by reference to aggregate quantities of donated property. The books and records are adequate if they reflect total amounts received and distributed (or used), and outline the procedure used for determining that the ultimate recipient of the property is an ill or needy individual, or infant. However, the books and records need not reflect the names of the ultimate individual recipients or the property distributed to (or used by) each one.

(ii) *Furnished to transferring organization.* If an organization that received a contribution under this section transfers the contributed property to another organization on or after [Date which is 30 days after the issuance of these regulations by Treasury decision], the transferee organization must furnish to the transferring organization a written statement which contains the information required in paragraph (b)(4)(i)(A), (B) and (D) of this section. The statement must also represent that the transferee or-

Reg. § 1.170A-4A(b)(3)

ganization meets the requirements of paragraph (b)(1)(ii) of this section (or, in the case of a transferee organization which is a foreign organization not within the jurisdiction of the United States, that, but for such fact, the organization would meet the requirements of paragraph (b)(1)(ii) of this section). The written statement must be furnished within a reasonable period after the transfer.

(5) *Requirement of compliance with the Federal Food, Drug, and Cosmetic Act* —(i) *In general.* With respect to property contributed under this section which is subject to the Federal Food, Drug, and Cosmetic Act (as amended), and regulations thereunder, the contributed property must comply with the applicable provisions of that Act and regulations thereunder at the date of the contribution and for the immediately preceding 180 days. In the case of specific items of contributed property not in existence for the entire period of 180 days immediately preceding the date of contribution, the requirement of this paragraph (b)(5) is considered met if the contributed property complied with that Act and the regulations thereunder during the period of its existence and at the date of contribution and if, for the 180 day period prior to contribution other property (if any) held by the taxpayer at any time during that period, which property was fungible with the contributed property, complied with that Act and the regulations thereunder during the period held by the taxpayer.

(ii) *Example.* The rule of this paragraph (b)(5) may be illustrated by the following example.

Example. Corporation X, a grocery store, contributes 12 crates of navel oranges. The oranges were picked and placed in the grocery store's stock two weeks prior to the date of contribution. The contribution satisfies the requirements of this paragraph (b)(5) if X complied with the Act and regulations thereunder for 180 days prior to the date of contribution with respect to all navel oranges in stock during that period.

(c) *Amount of reduction* —(1) *In general.* Section 170(e)(3)(B) requires that the amount of the charitable contribution subject to this section which would be taken into account under section 170(a), without regard to section 170(e), must be reduced before applying the percentage limitations under section 170(b) The amount of the first reduction is equal to one-half of the amount of gain which would not have been long-term capital gain if the property had been sold by the donor-taxpayer at its fair market value on the date of its contribution, excluding, however, any amount described in paragraph (d) of this section.

If the amount of the charitable contribution which remains after this reduction exceeds twice the basis of the contributed property, then the amount of the charitable contribution is reduced a second time to an amount which is equal to twice the amount of the basis of the property.

(2) *Basis of contributed property which is inventory.* For the purposes of this section, notwithstanding the rules of § 1.170A-1(c)(4), the basis of contributed property which is inventory must be determined under the donor's method of accounting for inventory for purposes of United States income tax. The donor must use as the basis of the contributed item the inventoriable carrying cost assigned to any similar item not included in closing inventory. For example, under the LIFO dollar value method of accounting for inventory, where there has been an invasion of a prior year's layer, the donor may choose to treat the item contributed as having a basis of the unit's cost with reference to the layer(s) of prior year(s) cost or with reference to the current year cost.

(3) *Adjustment to cost of goods sold.* Notwithstanding the rules of § 1.170A-1(c)(4), the donor of the property which is inventory contributed under this section must make a corresponding adjustment to cost of goods sold by decreasing the cost of goods sold by the lesser of the fair market value of the contributed item or the amount of basis determined under paragraph (c)(2) of this section.

(4) *Examples* The rules of this paragraph (c) may be illustrated by the following examples:

Example (1). During 1978 corporation X, a calendar year taxpayer, makes a qualified contribution of women's coats which were section 1221(1) property. The fair market value of the property at the date of contribution is $1,000, and the basis of the property is $200. The amount of the charitable contribution which would be taken into account under section 170(a) is the fair market value ($1,000). The amount of gain which would not have been long-term capital gain if the property had been sold is $800 ($1,000 − $200). The amount of the contribution is reduced by one-half the amount which would not have been capital gain if the property had been sold ($800/2 = $400).

After this reduction, the amount of the contribution which may be taken into account is $600 ($1 000 − $400). A second reduction is made in the amount of the charitable contribution because this amount (as first reduced to $600) is more than $400 which is an amount equal to twice the basis of the property. The amount of the further reduction is $200 [$600 − (2 × $200)], and the

Reg. § 1.170A-4A(c)(4)

amount of the contribution as finally reduced is $400 [$1,000 − ($400 + $200)]. X would also have to decrease its cost of goods sold for the year of contribution by $200.

Example (2). Assume the same facts as set forth in example (1) except that the basis of the property is $600. The amount of the first reduction is $200 (($1,000 − $600)/2).

As reduced, the amount of the contribution which may be taken into account is $800 ($1,000 − $200). There is no second reduction because $800 is less than $1,200 which is twice the basis of the property. However, X would have to decrease its cost of goods sold for the year of contribution by $600.

(d) *Recapture excluded.* A deduction is not allowed under section 170(e)(3) or this section for any amount which, if the property had been sold by the donor-taxpayer on the date of its contribution for an amount equal to its fair market value, would have been treated as ordinary income under section 617, 1245, 1250, 1251, or 1252. Thus, before making either reduction required by section 170(e)(3)(B) and paragraph (c) of this section, the fair market value of the contributed property must be reduced by the amount of gain that would have been recognized (if the property had been sold) as ordinary income under section 617, 1245, 1250, 1251, or 1252.

(e) *Effective date.* This section applies to qualified contributions made after October 4, 1976. [Reg. § 1.170A-4A.]

☐ [T.D. 7807, 1-29-82. *Amended by T.D. 7962,* 6-28-84.]

[Reg. § 1.170A-5]

§ 1.170A-5. **Future interests in tangible personal property.**—(a) *In general.* (1) A contribution consisting of a transfer of a future interest in tangible personal property shall be treated as made only when all intervening interests in, and rights to the actual possession or enjoyment of, the property—

(i) Have expired, or

(ii) Are held by persons other than the taxpayer or those standing in a relationship to the taxpayer described in section 267(b) and the regulations thereunder, relating to losses, expenses, and interest with respect to transactions between related taxpayers.

(2) Section 170(a)(3) and this section have no application in respect of a transfer of an undivided present interest in property. For example, a contribution of an undivided one-quarter interest in a painting with respect to which the donee is entitled to possession during three months of each

year shall be treated as made upon the receipt by the donee of a formally executed and acknowledged deed of gift. However, the period of initial possession by the donee may not be deferred in time for more than one year.

(3) Section 170(a)(3) and this section have no application in respect of a transfer of a future interest in intangible personal property or in real property. However, a fixture which is intended to be severed from real property shall be treated as tangible personal property. For example, a contribution of a future interest in a chandelier which is attached to a building is considered a contribution which consists of a future interest in tangible personal property if the transferor intends that it be detached from the building at or prior to the time when the charitable organization's right to possession or enjoyment of the chandelier is to commence.

(4) For purposes of section 170(a)(3) and this section, the term "future interest" has generally the same meaning as it has when used in section 2503 and § 25.2503-3 of this chapter (Gift Tax Regulations); it includes reversions, remainders, and other interests or estates, whether vested or contingent, and whether or not supported by a particular interest or estate, which are limited to commence in use, possession, or enjoyment at some future date or time. The term "future interest" includes situations in which a donor purports to give tangible personal property to a charitable organization, but has an understanding, arrangement, agreement, etc., whether written or oral, with the charitable organization which has the effect of reserving to, or retaining in, such donor a right to the use, possession, or enjoyment of the property.

(5) In the case of a charitable contribution of a future interest to which section 170(a)(3) and this section apply, the other provisions of section 170 and the regulations thereunder are inapplicable to the contribution until such time as the contribution is treated as made under section 170(a)(3).

(b) *Illustrations.* The application of this section may be illustrated by the following examples:

Example (1). On December 31, 1970, A, an individual who reports his income on the calendar year basis, conveys by deed of gift to a museum title to a painting, but reserves to himself the right to use, possession, and enjoyment of the painting during his lifetime. It is assumed that there was no intention to avoid the application of section 170(f)(3)(A) by the conveyance. At the time of the gift the value of the painting is $90,000. Since the contribution consists of a future interest in tangible personal property in

Reg. § 1.170A-5(a)(2)

which the donor has retained an intervening interest, no contribution is considered to have been made in 1970.

Example (2). Assume the same facts as in example (1) except that on December 31, 1971, A relinquishes all of his right to the use, possession, and enjoyment of the painting and delivers the painting to the museum. Assuming that the value of the painting has increased to $95,000, A is treated as having made a charitable contribution of $95,000 in 1971 for which a deduction is allowable without regard to section 170(f)(3)(A).

Example (3). Assume the same facts as in example (1) except A dies without relinquishing his right to the use, possession, and enjoyment of the painting. Since A did not relinquish his right to the use, possession, and enjoyment of the property during his life, A is treated as not having made a charitable contribution of the painting for income tax purposes.

Example (4). Assume the same facts as in example (1) except A, on December 31, 1971, transfers his interest in the painting to his son, B, who reports his income on the calendar year basis. Since the relationship between A and B is one described in section 267(b), no contribution of the remainder interest in the painting is considered to have been made in 1971.

Example (5). Assume the same facts as in example (4). Also assume that on December 31, 1972, B conveys to the museum the interest measured by A's life. B has made a charitable contribution of the present interest in the painting conveyed to the museum. In addition, since all intervening interests in, and rights to the actual possession or enjoyment of the property, have expired, a charitable contribution of the remainder interest is treated as having been made by A in 1972 for which a deduction is allowable without regard to section 170(f)(3)(A). Such remainder interest is valued according to § 20.2031-7A(c) of this chapter (Estate Tax Regulations), determined by subtracting the value of B's interest measured by A's life expectancy in 1972, and B receives a deduction in 1972 for the life interest measured by A's life expectancy and valued according to Table A (1) in such section.

Example (6). On December 31, 1970, C, an individual who reports his income on the calendar year basis, transfers a valuable painting to a pooled income fund described in section 642(c)(5), which is maintained by a university. C retains for himself for life an income interest in the painting, the remainder interest in the painting being contributed to the university. Since the contribution consists of a future interest in tangible personal property in which the donor has retained an inter-

vening interest, no charitable contribution is considered to have been made in 1970.

Example (7). On January 15, 1972, D, an individual who reports his income on the calendar year basis, transfers a capital asset held for more than 6 months consisting of a valuable painting to a pooled income fund described in section 642(c) 5), which is maintained by a university, and creates an income interest in such painting for E for life. E is an individual not standing in a relationship to D described in section 267(b). The remainder interest in the property is contributed by D to the university. The trustee of the pooled income fund puts the painting to an unrelated use within the meaning of paragraph (b)(3) of § 1.170A-4. Accordingly, D is allowed a deduction under section 170 in 1972 for the present value of the remainder interest in the painting, after reducing such amount under section 170(e)(1)(B)(i) and paragraph (a)(2) of § 1.170A-4. This reduction in the amount of the contribution is required since under paragraph (b)(3) of that section the use by the pooled income fund of the painting is a use which would have been an unrelated use if it had been made by the university.

(c) *Effective date.* This section applies only to contributions paid in taxable years beginning after December 31, 1969. [Reg. § 1.170A-5.]

☐ [*T.D. 7207, 10-3-72. Amended by T.D. 8540, 6-9-94.*]

[Reg. § 1.170A-6]

§ 1.170A-6. **Charitable contributions in trust.**—(a) *In general*—(1) No deduction is allowed under section 170 for the fair market value of a charitable contribution of any interest in property which is less than the donor's entire interest in the property and which is transferred in trust unless the transfer meets the requirements of paragraph (b) or (c) of this section. If the donor's entire interest in the property is transferred in trust and is contributed to a charitable organization described in section 170(c), a deduction is allowed under section 170. Thus, if on July 1, 1972, property is transferred in trust with the requirement that the income of the trust be paid for a term of 20 years to a church and thereafter the remainder be paid to an educational organization described in section 170(b)(1)(A), a deduction is allowed for the value of such property. See section 170(f)(2) and (3)(B), and paragraph (b)(1) of § 1.170A-7.

(2) A deduction is allowed without regard to this section for a contribution of a partial interest in property if such interest is the taxpayer's entire interest in the property, such as an income interest or a remainder interest. If, however, the

property in which such partial interest exists was divided in order to create such interest and thus avoid section 170(f)(2), the deduction will not be allowed. Thus, for example, assume that a taxpayer desires to contribute to a charitable organization the reversionary interest in certain stocks and bonds which he owns. If the taxpayer transfers such property in trust with the requirement that the income of the trust be paid to his son for life and that the reversionary interest be paid to himself and immediately after creating the trust contributes the reversionary interest to a charitable organization, no deduction will be allowed under section 170 for the contribution of the taxpayer's entire interest consisting of the reversionary interest in the trust.

(b) *Charitable contribution of a remainder interest in trust*—(1) *In general.* No deduction is allowed under section 170 for the fair market value of a charitable contribution of a remainder interest in property which is less than the donor's entire interest in the property and which the donor transfers in trust unless the trust is—

(i) A pooled income fund described in section 642(c)(5) and § 1.642(c)-5,

(ii) A charitable remainder annuity trust described in section 664(d)(1) and § 1.664-2, or

(iii) A charitable remainder unitrust described in section 664(d)(2) and § 1.664-3.

(2) *Value of a remainder interest.* The fair market value of a remainder interest in a pooled income fund shall be computed under § 1.642(c)-6. The fair market value of a remainder interest in a charitable remainder annuity trust shall be computed under § 1.664-2. The fair market value of a remainder interest in a charitable remainder unitrust shall be computed under § 1.664-4. However, in some cases a reduction in the amount of a charitable contribution of the remainder interest may be required. See section 170(e) and § 1.170A-4.

(c) *Charitable contribution of an income interest in trust*—(1) *In general.* No deduction is allowed under section 170 for the fair market value of a charitable contribution of an income interest in property which is less than the donor's entire interest in the property and which the donor transfers in trust unless the income interest is either a guaranteed annuity interest or a unitrust interest, as defined in paragraph (c) (2) of this section, and the grantor is treated as the owner of such interest for purposes of applying section 671, relating to grantors and others treated as substantial owners. See section 4947(a)(2) for the application to such income interests in trust of the provisions relating to private foundations and sec-

tion 508(e) for rules relating to provisions required in the governing instruments.

(2) *Definitions.* For purposes of this paragraph—

(i) *Guaranteed annuity interest*—(A) An income interest is a "guaranteed annuity interest" only if it is an irrevocable right pursuant to the governing instrument of the trust to receive a guaranteed annuity. A guaranteed annuity is an arrangement under which a determinable amount is paid periodically, but not less often than annually, for a specified term of years or for the life or lives of certain individuals, each of whom must be living at the date of transfer and can be ascertained at such date. Only one or more of the following individuals may be used as measuring lives: the donor, the donor's spouse, and an individual who, with respect to all remainder beneficiaries (other than charitable organizations described in section 170, 2055, or 2522), is either a lineal ancestor or the spouse of a lineal ancestor of those beneficiaries. A trust will satisfy the requirement that all noncharitable remainder beneficiaries are lineal descendants of the individual who is the measuring life, or that individual's spouse, if there is less than a 15% probability that individuals who are not lineal descendants will receive any trust corpus. This probability must be computed, based on the current applicable Life Table contained in § 20.2031-7, at the time property is transferred to the trust taking into account the interests of all primary and contingent remainder beneficiaries who are living at that time. An interest payable for a specified term of years can qualify as a guaranteed annuity interest even if the governing instrument contains a savings clause intended to ensure compliance with a rule against perpetuities. The savings clause must utilize a period for vesting of 21 years after the deaths of measuring lives who are selected to maximize, rather than limit, the term of the trust. The rule in this paragraph that a charitable interest may be payable for the life or lives of only certain specified individuals does not apply in the case of a charitable guaranteed annuity interest payable under a charitable remainder trust described in section 664. An amount is determinable if the exact amount which must be paid under the conditions specified in the governing instrument of the trust can be ascertained as of the date of transfer. For example, the amount to be paid may be a stated sum for a term of years, or for the life of the donor, at the expiration of which it may be changed by a specified amount, but it may not be redetermined by reference to a fluctuating index such as the cost of living index. In further illustration, the amount to be paid may be expressed in

Reg. § 1.170A-6(b)(1)

terms of a fraction or percentage of the cost of living index on the date of transfer.

(B) An income interest is a guaranteed annuity interest only if it is a guaranteed annuity interest in every respect. For example, if the income interest is the right to receive from a trust each year a payment equal to the lesser of a sum certain or a fixed percentage of the net fair market value of the trust assets, determined annually, such interest is not a guaranteed annuity interest.

(C) Where a charitable interest is in the form of a guaranteed annuity interest, the governing instrument of the trust may provide that income of the trust which is in excess of the amount required to pay the guaranteed annuity interest shall be paid to or for the use of a charitable organization. Nevertheless, the amount of the deduction under section 170(f)(2)(B) shall be limited to the fair market value of the guaranteed annuity interest as determined under paragraph (c)(3) of this section. For a rule relating to treatment by the grantor of any contribution made by the trust in excess of the amount required to pay the guaranteed annuity interest, see paragraph (d)(2)(ii) of this section.

(D) If the present value on the date of transfer of all the income interests for a charitable purpose exceeds 60 percent of the aggregate fair market value of all amounts in the trust (after the payment of liabilities), the income interest will not be considered a guaranteed annuity interest unless the governing instrument of the trust prohibits both the acquisition and the retention of assets which would give rise to a tax under section 4944 if the trustee had acquired such assets. The requirement in this subdivision (D) for a prohibition in the governing instrument against the retention of assets which would give rise to a tax under section 4944 if the trustee had acquired the assets shall not apply to a transfer in trust made on or before May 21, 1972.

(E) An income interest consisting of an annuity transferred in trust after May 21, 1972, will not be considered a guaranteed annuity interest if any amount other than an amount in payment of a guaranteed annuity interest may be paid by the trust for a private purpose before the expiration of all the income interests for a charitable purpose, unless such amount for a private purpose is paid from a group of assets which, pursuant to the governing instrument of the trust, are devoted exclusively to private purposes and to which section 4947(a)(2) is inapplicable by reason of section 4947(a)(2)(B). The exception in the immediately preceding sentence with respect to any guaranteed annuity for a private purpose shall apply only if the obligation to pay the annu-

ity for a charitable purpose begins as of the date of creation of the trust and the obligation to pay the guaranteed annuity for a private purpose does not precede in point of time the obligation to pay the annuity for a charitable purpose and only if the governing instrument of the trust does not provide for any preference or priority in respect of any payment of the guaranteed annuity for a private purpose as opposed to any payment of any annuity for a charitable purpose. For purposes of this subdivision (E), an amount is not paid for a private purpose if it is paid for an adequate and full consideration in money or money's worth. See § 53.4947-1(c) of this chapter (Foundation Excise Tax Regulations) for rules relating to the inapplicability of section 4947(a)(2) to segregated amounts in a split-interest trust.

Example. In 1975, E transfers $75,000 in trust with the requirement that an annuity of $5,000 a year, payable annually at the end of each year, be paid to B, an individual, for a period of 5 years and thereafter an annuity of $5,000 a year, payable annually at the end of each year, be paid to M Charity for a period of 5 years. The remainder is to be paid to C, an individual. No deduction is allowed under subparagraph (1) of this paragraph with respect to the charitable annuity because it is not a "guaranteed annuity interest" with the meaning of this subdivision.

(F) For rules relating to certain governing instrument requirements and to the imposition of certain excise taxes where the guaranteed annuity interest is in trust and for rules governing payment of private income interests by a split-interest trust, see section 4947(a)(2) and (b)(3)(A), and the regulations thereunder.

(ii) *Unitrust interest*—(A) An income interest is a "unitrust interest" only if it is an irrevocable right pursuant to the governing instrument of the trust to receive payment, not less often than annually, of a fixed percentage of the net fair market value of the trust assets, determined annually. In computing the net fair market value of the trust assets, all assets and liabilities shall be taken into account without regard to whether particular items are taken into account in determining the income of the trust. The net fair market value of the trust assets may be determined on any one date during the year or by taking the average of valuations made on more than one date during the year, provided that the same valuation date or dates and valuation methods are used each year. Where the governing instrument of the trust does not specify the valuation date or dates, the trustee shall select such date or dates and shall indicate his selection on the first return on Form 1041 which the trust is required to file. Payments under a unitrust interest may be paid for a specified term of years or for the life or lives of certain individuals, each of whom must be living at the date of transfer and can be ascertained at such date. Only one or more of the following individuals may be used as measuring lives: the donor, the donor's spouse, and an individual who, with respect to all remainder beneficiaries (other than charitable organizations described in section 170, 2055, or 2522), is either a lineal ancestor or the spouse of a lineal ancestor of those beneficiaries. A trust will satisfy the requirement that all noncharitable remainder beneficiaries are lineal descendants of the individual who is the measuring life, or that individual's spouse, if there is less than a 15% probability that individuals who are not lineal descendants will receive any trust corpus. This probability must be computed, based on the current applicable Life Table contained in § 20.2031-7, at the time property is transferred to the trust taking into account the interests of all primary and contingent remainder beneficiaries who are living at that time. An interest payable for a specified term of years can qualify as a unitrust interest even if the governing instrument contains a savings clause intended to ensure compliance with a rule against perpetuities. The savings clause must utilize a period for vesting of 21 years after the deaths of measuring lives who are selected to maximize, rather than limit, the term of the trust. The rule in this paragraph that a charitable interest may be payable for the life or lives of only certain specified individuals does not apply in the case of a charitable unitrust interest payable under a charitable remainder trust described in section 664.

(B) An income interest is a unitrust interest only if it is a unitrust interest in every respect. For example, if the income interest is the right to receive from a trust each year a payment equal to the lesser of a sum certain or a fixed percentage of the net fair market value of the trust assets, determined annually, such interest is not a unitrust interest.

(C) Where a charitable interest is in the form of a unitrust interest, the governing instrument of the trust may provide that income of the trust which is in excess of the amount required to pay the unitrust interest shall be paid to or for the use of a charitable organization. Nevertheless, the amount of the deduction under section 170(f)(2)(B) shall be limited to the fair market value of the unitrust interest as determined under paragraph (c)(3) of this section. For a rule relating to treatment by the grantor of any contribution made by the trust in excess of the amount

required to pay the unitrust interest, see paragraph (d)(2)(ii) of this section.

(D) An income interest in the form of a unitrust interest will not be considered a unitrust interest if any amount other than an amount in payment of a unitrust interest may be paid by the trust for a private purpose before the expiration of all the income interests for a charitable purpose, unless such amount for a private purpose is paid from a group of assets which, pursuant to the governing instrument of the trust, are devoted exclusively to private purposes and to which section 4947(a)(2) is inapplicable by reason of section 4947(a)(2)(B). The exception in the immediately preceding sentence with respect to any unitrust interest for a private purpose shall apply only if the obligation to pay the unitrust interest for a charitable purpose begins as of the date of creation of the trust and the obligation to pay the unitrust interest for a private purpose does not precede in point of time the obligation to pay the unitrust interest for a charitable purpose and only if the governing instrument of the trust does not provide for any preference or priority in respect of any payment of the unitrust interest for a private purpose as opposed to any payments of any unitrust interest for a charitable purpose. For purposes of this subdivision (D), an amount is not paid for a private purpose if it is paid for an adequate and full consideration in money or money's worth. See § 53.4947-1(c) of this chapter (Foundation Excise Tax Regulations) for rules relating to the inapplicability of section 4947(a)(2) to segregated amounts in a split-interest trust.

(E) For rules relating to certain governing instrument requirements and to the imposition of certain excise taxes where the unitrust interest is in trust and for rules governing payment of private income interests by a split-interest trust, see section 4947(a)(2) and (b)(3)(A), and the regulations thereunder.

(3) *Valuation of income interest*—(i) The deduction allowed by section 170(f)(2)(B) for a charitable contribution of a guaranteed annuity interest is limited to the fair market value of such interest on the date of contribution, as computed under § 20.2031-7 or, for certain prior periods, § 20.2031-7A of this chapter (Estate Tax Regulations).

(ii) The deduction allowed under section 170(f)(2)(B) for a charitable contribution of a unitrust interest is limited to the fair market value of the unitrust interest on the date of contribution. The fair market value of the unitrust interest shall be determined by subtracting the present value of all interests in the transferred property other than the unitrust interest from the fair market value of the transferred property.

(iii) If by reason of all the conditions and circumstances surrounding a transfer of an income interest in property in trust it appears that the charity may not receive the beneficial enjoyment of the interest, a deduction will be allowed under paragraph (c) (1) of this section only for the minimum amount it is evident the charity will receive. The application of this subdivision may be illustrated by the following examples:

Example (1). In 1972, B transfers $20,000 in trust with the requirement that M Church be paid a guaranteed annuity interest (as defined in subparagraph (2)(i) of this paragraph) of $4,000, payable annually at the end of each year for 9 years, and that the residue revert to himself. Since the fair market value of an annuity of $4,000 a year for a period of 9 years, as determined under § 20.2031-7A(c) of this chapter, is $27,206.80 ($4,000 × 6.8017), it appears that M will not receive the beneficial enjoyment of the income interest. Accordingly, even though B is treated as the owner of the trust under section 673, he is allowed a deduction under subparagraph (1) of this paragraph for only $20,000, which is the minimum amount it is evident M will receive.

Example (2). In 1975, C transfers $40,000 in trust with the requirement that D, an individual, and X Charity be paid simultaneously guaranteed annuity interests (as defined in subparagraph (2)(i) of this paragraph) of $5,000 a year each, payable annually at the end of each year, for a period of 5 years and that the remainder be paid to C's children. The fair market value of two annuities of $5,000 each a year for a period of 5 years is $42,124 ([$5,000 × 4.2124] × 2), as determined under § 20.2031-7A(c) of this chapter. The trust instrument provides that in the event the trust fund is insufficient to pay both annuities in a given year, the trust fund will be evenly divided between the charitable and private annuitants. The deduction under subparagraph (1) of this paragraph with respect to the charitable annuity will be limited to $20,000, which is the minimum amount it is evident X will receive.

Example (3). In 1975, D transfers $65,000 in trust with the requirement that a guaranteed annuity interest (as defined in subparagraph (2)(i) of this paragraph) of $5,000 a year, payable annually at the end of each year, be paid to Y Charity for a period of 10 years and that a guaranteed annuity interest (as defined in subparagraph (2)(i) of this paragraph) of $5,000 a year, payable annually at the end of each year, be paid to W, his wife, aged 62, for 10 years or until her

prior death. The annuities are to be paid simultaneously, and the remainder is to be paid to D's children. The fair market value of the private annuity is $33,877 ($5,000 × 6.7754), as determined pursuant to § 20.2031-7A(c) of this chapter and by the use of factors involving one life and a term of years as published in Publication 723A (12-70). The fair market value of the charitable annuity is $36,800.50 ($5,000 × 7.3601), as determined under § 20.2031-7A(c) of this chapter. It is not evident from the governing instrument of the trust or from local law that the trustee would be required to apportion the trust fund between the wife and charity in the event the fund were insufficient to pay both annuities in a given year. Accordingly, the deduction under subparagraph (1) of this paragraph with respect to the charitable annuity will be limited to $31,123 ($65,000 less $33,877 [the value of the private annuity]), which is the minimum amount it is evident Y will receive.

(iv) See paragraph (b)(1) of § 1.170A-4 for rule that the term "ordinary income property" for purposes of section 170(e) does not include an income interest in respect of which a deduction is allowed under section 170(f)(2)(B) and this paragraph.

(4) *Recapture upon termination of treatment as owner.* If for any reason the donor of an income interest in property ceases at any time before the termination of such interest to be treated as the owner of such interest for purposes of applying section 671, as for example, where he dies before the termination of such interest, he shall for purposes of this chapter be considered as having received, on the date he ceases to be so treated, an amount of income equal to (i) the amount of any deduction he was allowed under section 170 for the contribution of such interest reduced by (ii) the discounted value of all amounts which were required to be, and actually were, paid with respect to such interest under the terms of trust to the charitable organization before the time at which he ceases to be treated as the owner of the interest. The discounted value of the amounts described in subdivision (ii) of this subparagraph shall be computed by treating each such amount as a contribution of a remainder interest after a term of years and valuing such amount as of the date of contribution of the income interest by the donor, such value to be determined under § 20.2031-7 of this chapter consistently with the manner in which the fair market value of the income interest was determined pursuant to subparagraph (3)(i) of this paragraph. The application of this subparagraph will not be construed to disallow a deduction to the trust for amounts paid by the trust to the charitable organization after

Reg. § 1.170A-6(c)(4)

the time at which the donor ceased to be treated as the owner of the trust.

(5) *Illustrations.* The application of this paragraph may be illustrated by the following examples:

Example (1). On January 1, 1971, A contributes to a church in trust a 9-year irrevocable income interest in property. Both A and the trust report income on a calendar year basis. The fair market value of the property placed in trust is $10,000. The trust instrument provides that the church will receive an annuity of $500, payable annually at the end of each year for 9 years. The income interest is a guaranteed annuity interest as defined in subparagraph (2)(i) of this paragraph; upon termination of such interest the residue of the trust is to revert to A. By reference to § 20.2031-7A(c) of this chapter, it is found that the figure in column (2) opposite 9 years is 6.8017. The present value of the annuity is therefore $3,400.85 ($500 × 6.8017). The present value of the income interest and A's charitable contribution for 1971 is $3,400.85.

Example (2). (a) On January 1, B contributes to a church in trust a 9-year irrevocable income interest in property. Both B and the trust report income on a calendar year basis. The fair market value of the property placed in trust is $10,000. The trust instrument provides that the trust will pay to the church at the end of each year for 9 years 5 percent of the fair market value of all property in the trust at the beginning of the year. The income interest is a unitrust interest as defined in subparagraph (2)(ii) of this paragraph; upon termination of such interest the residue of the trust is to revert to B.

(b) The section 7520 rate at the time of the transfer was 6.0 percent. By reference to Table F(6.0) in § 1.664-4(e)(6), the adjusted payout rate is 4.717% (5% × 0.943396). The present value of the reversion is $6,473.75, computed by reference to Table D in § 1.664-4(e)(6), as follows:

Factor at 4.6 percent for 9 years	0.654539
Factor at 4.8 percent for 9 years	.642292
Difference	.012247

Interpolation adjustment:

$$\frac{4.717\% - 4.6\%}{0.2\%} = \frac{x}{0.012247}$$

$$x = 0.007164$$

Factor at 4.6 percent for 9 years	0.654539
Less: Interpolation adjustment	.007164
Interpolated factor	.647375

Present value of reversion
($10,000 × 0.647375) $6,473.75

(c) The present value of the income interest and B's charitable contribution is $3,526.25 ($10,000 − $6,473.75).

Example (3). (a) On January 1, 1971, C contributes to a church in trust a 9-year irrevocable income interest in property. Both C and the trust report income on a calendar year basis. The fair market value of the property placed in trust is $10,000. The trust instrument provides that the church will receive an annuity of $500, payable annually at the end of each year for 9 years. The income interest is a guaranteed annuity interest as defined in subparagraph (2)(i) of this paragraph; upon termination of such interest the residue of the trust is to revert to C. C's charitable contribution for 1971 is $3,400.85, determined as provided in example (1). The trust earns income of $600 in 1971, $400 in 1972, and $500 in 1973, all of which is taxable to C under section 671. The church is paid $500 at the end of 1971, 1972, and 1973, respectively. On December 31, 1973, C dies and ceases to be treated as the owner of the income interest under section 673.

(b) Pursuant to subparagraph (4) of this paragraph, the discounted value as of January 1, 1971, of the amounts paid to the church by the trust is $1,336.51, determined by reference to column (4) of Table B in § 20.2031-7A(c) of this chapter, as follows:

Annuity Payment date	Amount paid	Years from 1/1/71 to payment date	Discount factor	Discounted value as of 1/1/71
12/31/71	$500	1	.943396	$471.70
12/31/72	500	2	.889996	445.00
12/31/73	500	3	.839619	419.81
Total discounted value				$1,336.51

(c) Pursuant to subparagraph (4) of this paragraph, there must be included in C's gross income for 1973 the amount of $2,064.34 ($3,400.85 less $1,336.51).

(d) For deduction by the trust for amounts paid to the church after December 31, 1973, see section 642(c)(1) and the regulations thereunder.

(d) *Denial of deduction for certain contributions by a trust*—(1) If by reason of section 170(f)(2)(B) and paragraph (c) of this section a charitable contributions deduction is allowed under section 170 for the fair market value of an income interest transferred in trust, neither the grantor of the income interest, the trust, nor any other person shall be allowed a deduction under

Reg. § 1.170A-6(c)(5)

section 170 or any other section for the amount of any charitable contribution made by the trust with respect to, or in fulfillment of, such income interest.

(2) Section 170(f)(2)(C) and subparagraph (1) of this paragraph shall not be construed, however, to—

(i) Disallow a deduction to the trust, pursuant to section 642(c)(1) and the regulations thereunder, for amounts paid by the trust after the grantor ceases to be treated as the owner of the income interest for purposes of applying section 671 and which are not taken into account in determining the amount of recapture under paragraph (c)(4) of this section, or

(ii) Disallow a deduction to the grantor under section 671 and § 1.571-2(c) for a charitable contribution made by the trust in excess of the contribution required to be made by the trust under the terms of the trust instrument with respect to, or in fulfillment of, the income interest.

(3) Although a deduction for the fair market value of an income interest in property which is less than the donor's entire interest in the property and which the donor transfers in trust is disallowed under section 170 because such interest is not a guaranteed annuity interest, or a unitrust interest, as defined in paragraph (c)(2) of this section, the donor may be entitled to a deduction under section 671 and § 1.671-2(c) for any charitable contributions made by the trust if he is treated as the owner of such interest for purposes of applying section 671.

(e) *Effective date.* This section applies only to transfers in trust made after July 31, 1969. In addition, the rule in paragraphs (c)(2)(i)(A) and (ii)(A) of this section that guaranteed annuity interests and unitrust interests, respectively, may be payable for a specified term of years or for the life or lives of only certain individuals applies to transfers made on or after April 4, 2000. If a transfer is made to a trust on or after April 4, 2000 that uses an individual other than one permitted in paragraphs (c)(2)(i)(A) and (ii)(A) of this section, the trust may be reformed to satisfy this rule. As an alternative to reformation, rescission may be available for a transfer made on or before March 6, 2001. See § 25.2522(c)-3(e) of this chapter for the requirements concerning reformation or possible rescission of these interests. [Reg. § 1.170A-6.]

☐ [*T.D. 7207, 10-3-72. Amended by T.D. 7340, 1-6-75; T.D. 7955, 5-10-84; T.D. 8540, 6-9-94; T.D. 8819, 4-29-99 (corrected 6-21-99) and T.D. 8923, 1-4-2001.*]

[Reg. § 1.170A-7]

§ 1.170A-7. Contributions not in trust of partial interests in property.—(a) *In general.*—(1) In the case of a charitable contribution, not made by a transfer in trust, of any interest in property which consists of less than the donor's entire interest in such property, no deduction is allowed under section 170 for the value of such interest unless the interest is an interest described in paragraph (b) of this section. See section 170(f)(3)(A). For purposes of this section, a contribution of the right to use property which the donor owns, for example, a rent-free lease, shall be treated as a contribution of less than the taxpayer's entire interest in property.

(2)(i) A deduction is allowed without regard to this section for a contribution of a partial interest in property if such interest is the taxpayer's entire interest in the property, such as an income interest or a remainder interest. Thus, if securities are given to A for life, with the remainder over to B, and B makes a charitable contribution of his remainder interest to an organization described in section 170(c), a deduction is allowed under section 170 for the present value of B's remainder interest in the securities. If, however, the property in which such partial interest exists was divided in order to create such interest and thus avoid section 170(f)(3)(A), the deduction will not be allowed. Thus, for example, assume that a taxpayer desires to contribute to a charitable organization an income interest in property held by him which is not of a type described in paragraph (b)(2) of this section. If the taxpayer transfers the remainder interest in such property to his son and immediately thereafter contributes the income interest to a charitable organization, no deduction shall be allowed under section 170 for the contribution of the taxpayer's entire interest consisting of the retained income interest. In further illustration, assume that a taxpayer desires to contribute to a charitable organization the reversionary interest in certain stocks and bonds held by him, which is not of a type described in paragraph (b)(2) of this section. If the taxpayer grants a life estate in such property to his son and immediately thereafter contributes the reversionary interest to a charitable organization, no deduction will be allowed under section 170 for the contribution of the taxpayer's entire interest consisting of the reversionary interest.

(ii) A deduction is allowed without regard to this section for a contribution of a partial interest in property if such contribution constitutes part of a charitable contribution not in trust in which all interests of the taxpayer in the property are given to a charitable organization described in section 170(c). Thus, if on March 1, 1971, an income interest in property is given not in trust to a church and the remainder interest in the property is given not in trust to an educational organization described in section 170(b)(1)(A), a deduction is allowed for the value of such property.

(3) A deduction shall not be disallowed under section 170(f)(3)(A) and this section merely because the interest which passes to, or is vested in, the charity may be defeated by the performance of some act or the happening of some event, if on the date of the gift it appears that the possibility that such act or event will occur is so remote as to be negligible. See paragraph (e) of § 1.170A-1.

(b) *Contributions of certain partial interests in property for which a deduction is allowed.* A deduction is allowed under section 170 for a contribution not in trust of a partial interest which is less than the donor's entire interest in property and which qualifies under one of the following subparagraphs:

(1) *Undivided portion of donor's entire interest.* (i) A deduction is allowed under section 170 for the value of a charitable contribution not in trust of an undivided portion of a donor's entire interest in property. An undivided portion of a donor's entire interest in property must consist of a fraction or percentage or each and every substantial interest or right owned by the donor in such property and must extend over the entire term of the donor's interest in such property and in other property into which such property is converted. For example, assuming that in 1967 B has been given a life estate in an office building for the life of A and that B has no other interest in the office building, B will be allowed a deduction under section 170 for his contribution in 1972 to charity of a one-half interest in such life estate in a transfer which is not made in trust. Such contribution by B will be considered a contribution of an undivided portion of the donor's entire interest in property. In further illustration, assuming that in 1968 C has been given the remainder interest in a trust created under the will of his father and C has no other interest in the trust, C will be allowed a deduction under section 170 for his contribution in 1972 to charity of a 20-percent interest in such remainder interest in a transfer which is not made in trust. Such contribution by C will be considered a contribution of an undivided portion of the donor's entire interest in property. If a taxpayer owns 100 acres of land and makes a contribution of 50 acres to a charitable organization, the charitable contribution is allowed as a deduction under section 170. A deduction is allowed under section 170 for a contribution of

property to a charitable organization whereby such organization is given the right, as a tenant in common with the donor, to possession, dominion, and control of the property for a portion of each year appropriate to its interest in such property. However, for purposes of this subparagraph a charitable contribution in perpetuity of an interest in property not in trust where the donor transfers some specific rights and retains other substantial rights will not be considered a contribution of an undivided portion of the donor's entire interest in property to which section 170(f)(3)(A) does not apply. Thus, for example, a deduction is not allowable for the value of an immediate and perpetual gift not in trust of an interest in original historic motion picture films to a charitable organization where the donor retains the exclusive right to make reproductions of such films and to exploit such reproductions commercially.

(ii) With respect to contributions made on or before December 17, 1980, for purposes of this subparagraph a charitable contribution of an open space easement in gross in perpetuity shall be considered a contribution of an undivided portion of the donor's entire interest in property to which section 170(f)(3)(A) does not apply. For this purpose an easement in gross is a mere personal interest in, or right to use, the land of another; it is not supported by a dominant estate but is attached to, and vested in, the person to whom it is granted. Thus, for example, a deduction is allowed under section 170 for the value of a restrictive easement gratuitously conveyed to the United States in perpetuity whereby the donor agrees to certain restrictions on the use of his property, such as, restrictions on the type and height of buildings that may be erected, the removal of trees, the erection of utility lines, the dumping of trash, and the use of signs. For the deductibility of a qualified conservation contribution, see § 1.170A-14.

(2) *Partial interests in property which would be deductible in trust.* A deduction is allowed under section 170 for the value of a charitable contribution not in trust of a partial interest in property which is less than the donor's entire interest in the property and which would be deductible under section 170(f)(2) and § 1.170A-6 if such interest had been transferred in trust.

(3) *Contribution of a remainder interest in a personal residence.* A deduction is allowed under section 170 for the value of a charitable contribution not in trust of an irrevocable remainder interest in a personal residence which is not the donor's entire interest in such property. Thus, for example, if a taxpayer contributes not in trust to an

Reg. § 1.170A-7(a)(3)

organization described in section 170(c) a remainder interest in a personal residence and retains an estate in such property for life or for a term of years, a deduction is allowed under section 170 for the value of such remainder interest not transferred in trust. For purposes of section 170(f)(3)(B)(i) and this subparagraph, the term "personal residence" means any property used by the taxpayer as his personal residence even though it is not used as his principal residence. For example, the taxpayer's vacation home may be a personal residence for purposes of this subparagraph. The term "personal residence" also includes stock owned by a taxpayer as a tenant-stockholder in a cooperative housing corporation (as those terms are defined in section 216(b)(1) and (2)) if the dwelling which the taxpayer is entitled to occupy as such stockholder is used by him as his personal residence.

(4) *Contribution of a remainder interest in a farm.* A deduction is allowed under section 170 for the value of a charitable contribution not in trust of an irrevocable remainder interest in a farm which is not the donor's entire interest in such property. Thus, for example, if a taxpayer contributes not in trust to an organization described in section 170(c) a remainder interest in a farm and retains an estate in such farm for life or for a term of years, a deduction is allowed under section 170 for the value of such remainder interest not transferred in trust. For purposes of section 170(f)(3)(B)(i) and this subparagraph, the term "farm" means any land used by the taxpayer or his tenant for the production of crops, fruits, or other agricultural products or for the sustenance of livestock. The term "livestock" includes cattle, hogs, horses, mules, donkeys, sheep, goats, captive fur-bearing animals, chickens, turkeys, pigeons, and other poultry. A farm includes the improvements thereon.

(5) *Qualified conservation contribution.* A deduction is allowed under section 170 for the value of a qualified conservation contribution. For the definition of a qualified conservation contribution, see § 1.170A-14.

(c) *Valuation of a partial interest in property.* Except as provided in § 1.170A-14, the amount of the deduction under section 170 in the case of a charitable contribution of a partial interest in property to which paragraph (b) of this section applies is the fair market value of the partial interest at the time of the contribution. See § 1.170A-1(c). the fair market value of such partial interest must be determined in accordance with § 20.2031-7 of this chapter (Estate Tax Regulations), except that, in the case of a charitable contribution of a remainder interest in real property which is not transferred in trust, the fair market value of such interest must be determined in accordance with section 170(f)(4) and § 1.170A-12. In the case of a charitable contribution of a remainder interest in the form of a remainder interest in a pooled income fund, a charitable remainder annuity trust, or a charitable remainder unitrust, the fair market value of the remainder interest must be determined as provided in paragraph (b)(2) of § 1.170A-6. However, in some cases a reduction in the amount of a charitable contribution of the remainder interest may be required. See section 170(e) and paragraph (a) of § 1.170A-4.

(d) *Illustrations.* The application of this section may be illustrated by the following examples:

Example (1). A, an individual owning a 10-story office building, donates the rent-free use of the top floor of the building for the year 1971 to a charitable organization. Since A's contribution consists of a partial interest to which section 170(f)(3)(A) applies, he is not entitled to a charitable contributions deduction for the contribution of such partial interest.

Example (2). In 1971, B contributes to a charitable organization an undivided one-half interest in 100 acres of land, whereby as tenants in common they share in the economic benefits from the property. The present value of the contributed property is $50,000. Since B's contribution consists of an undivided portion of his entire interest in the property to which section 170(f)(3)(B) applies, he is allowed a deduction in 1971 for his charitable contribution of $50,000.

Example (3). In 1971, D loans $10,000 in cash to a charitable organization and does not require the organization to pay any interest for the use of the money. Since D's contribution consists of a partial interest to which section 170(f)(3)(A) applies he is not entitled to a charitable contributions deduction for the contribution of such partial interest.

(e) *Effective date.* This section applies only to contributions made after July 31, 1969. The deduction allowable under § 1.170A-7(b)(1)(ii) shall be available only for contributions made on or before December 17, 1980. Except as otherwise provided in § 1.170A-14(g)(4)(ii), the deduction allowable under § 1.170A-7(b)(5) shall be available for contributions made on or after December 18, 1980. [Reg. § 1.170A-7.]

☐ [*T.D.* 7207, 10-3-72. *Amended by T.D.* 7955, 5-10-84 *T.D.* 8069, 1-14-86 *and T.D.* 8540, 6-9-94.]

Reg. § 1.170A-7(e)

[Reg. § 1.170A-8]

§ 1.170A-8. Limitations on charitable deductions by individuals.—(a) *Percentage limitations* —(1) *In general.* An individual's charitable contributions deduction is subject to 20, 30, and 50-percent limitations unless the individual qualifies for the unlimited charitable contributions deduction under section 170(b)(1)(C). For a discussion of these limitations and examples of their application, see paragraphs (b) through (f) of this section. If a husband and wife make a joint return, the deduction for contributions is the aggregate of the contributions made by the spouses, and the limitations in section 170(b) and this section are based on the aggregate contribution base of the spouses. A charitable contribution by an individual to an organization described in section 170(c) is deductible even though all, or some portion, of the funds of the organization may be used in foreign countries for charitable or educational purposes.

(2) *"To" or "for the use of" defined.* For purposes of section 170, a contribution of an income interest in property, whether or not such contributed interest is transferred in trust, for which a deduction is allowed under section 170(f)(2)(B) or (3)(A) shall be considered as made "for the use of" rather than "to" the charitable organization. A contribution of a remainder interest in property, whether or not such contributed interest is transferred in trust, for which a deduction is allowed under section 170(f)(2)(A) or (3)(A), shall be considered as made "to" the charitable organization except that, if such interest is transferred in trust and, pursuant to the terms of the trust instrument, the interest contributed is, upon termination of the predecessor estate, to be held in trust for the benefit of such organization, the contribution shall be considered as made "for the use of" such organization. Thus, for example, assume that A transfers property to a charitable remainder annuity trust described in section 664(d)(1) which is required to pay to B for life an annuity equal to 5 percent of the initial fair market value of the property transferred in trust. The trust instrument provides that after B's death the remainder interest in the trust is to be transferred to M Church or, in the event M Church is not an organization described in section 170(c) when the amount is to be irrevocably transferred to such church, to an organization which is described in section 170(c) at that time. The contribution by A of the remainder interest shall be considered as made "to" M Church. However, if in the trust instrument A had directed that after B's death the remainder interest is to be held in trust for the benefit of M Church, the contribution shall be considered as made "for the use of" M Church. This subparagraph does not apply to the contribution of a partial interest in property, or of an undivided portion of such partial interest, if such partial interest is the donor's entire interest in the property and such entire interest was not created to avoid section 170(f)(2) or (3)(A). See paragraph (a)(2) of § 1.170A-6 and paragraphs (a)(2)(i) and (b)(1) of § 1.170A-7.

(b) *50-percent limitation.* An individual may deduct charitable contributions made during a taxable year to any one or more section 170(b)(1)(A) organizations, as defined in § 1.170A-9, to the extent that such contributions in the aggregate do not exceed 50-percent of his contribution base, as defined in section 170(b)(1)(F) and paragraph (e) of this section, for the taxable year. However, see paragraph (d) of this section for a limitation on the amount of charitable contributions of 30-percent capital gain property. To qualify for the 50-percent limitation the contributions must be made "to", and not merely "for the use of", one of the specified organizations. A contribution to an organization referred to in section 170(c)(2), other than a section 170(b)(1)(A) organization, will not qualify for the 50-percent limitation even though such organization makes the contribution available to an organization which is a section 170(b)(1)(A) organization. For provisions relating to the carryover of contributions in excess of 50-percent of an individual's contribution base see section 170(d)(1) and paragraph (b) of § 1.170A-10.

(c) *20-percent limitation.* (1) An individual may deduct charitable contributions made during a taxable year—

(i) To any one or more charitable organizations described in section 170(c) other than section 170(b)(1)(A) organizations, as defined in § 1.170A-9, and,

(ii) For the use of any charitable organization described in section 170(c),

to the extent that such contributions in the aggregate do not exceed the lesser of the limitations under subparagraph (2) of this paragraph.

(2) For purposes of subparagraph (1) of this paragraph the limitations are—

(i) 20 percent of the individual's contribution base, as defined in paragraph (e) of this section, for the taxable year, or

(ii) The excess of 50 percent of the individual's contribution base, as so defined, for the taxable year over the total amount of the charitable contributions allowed under section 170(b)(1)(A) and paragraph (b) of this section, determined by first reducing the amount of such contributions under section 170(e)(1) and paragraph (a) of

§ 1.170A-4 but without applying the 30-percent limitation under section 17C(b)(1)(D)(i) and paragraph (d)(1) of this section.

However, see paragraph (d) of this section for a limitation on the amount of charitable contributions of 30-percent capital gain property. If an election under section 170(b)(1)(D)(iii) and paragraph (d)(2) of this section applies to any contributions of 30-percent capital gain property made during the taxable year or carried over to the taxable year, the amount allowed for the taxable year under paragraph (b) of this section with respect to such contributions for purposes of applying subdivision (ii) of this subparagraph shall be the reduced amount of such contributions determined by applying paragraph (d)(2) of this section.

(d) *30-percent limitation* —(1) *In general.* An individual may deduct charitable contributions of 30-percent capital gain property, as defined in subparagraph (3) of this paragraph, made during a taxable year to or for the use of any charitable organization described in section 170(c) to the extent that such contributions in the aggregate do not exceed 30-percent of his contribution base, as defined in paragraph (e) of this section, subject, however, to the 50 and 20-percent limitations prescribed by paragraphs (b) and (c) of this section. For purposes of applying the 50-percent and 20-percent limitations described in paragraphs (b) and (c) of this section, charitable contributions of 30-percent capital gain property paid during the taxable year, and limited as provided by this subparagraph, shall be taken into account after all other charitable contributions paid during the taxable year. For provisions relating to the carryover of certain contributions of 30-percent capital gain property in excess of 30-percent of an individual's contribution base, see section 170(b)(1)(D)(ii) and paragraph (c) of § 1.170A-10.

(2) *Election by an individual to have section 170(e)(1)(B) apply to contributions* —(i) *In general.* (a) An individual may elect under section 170(b)(1)(D)(iii) for any taxable year to have the reduction rule of section 17C(e)(1)(B) and paragraph (a) of § 1.170A-4 apply to all his charitable contributions of 30-percent capital gain property made during such taxable year or carried over to such taxable year from a taxable year beginning after December 31, 1969. If such election is made such contributions shall be treated as contributions of section 170(e) capital gain property in accordance with paragraph (b)(2)(iii) of § 1.170A-4. The election may be made with respect to contributions of 30-percent capital gain property carried over to the taxable year even though the individual has not made any contribu-

tion of 30-percent capital gain property in such year. If such an election is made, section 170(b)(1)(D)(i) and (ii) and subparagraph (1) of this paragraph shall not apply to such contributions made during such year. However, such contributions must be reduced as required under section 170(e)(1)(B) and paragraph (a) of § 1.17CA-4.

(b) If there are carryovers to such taxable year of charitable contributions of 30-percent capital gain property made in preceding taxable years beginning after December 31, 1969, the amount of such contributions in each such preceding year shall be reduced as if section 170(e)(1)(B) had applied to them in the preceding year and shall be carried over to the taxable year and succeeding taxable years under section 170(d)(1) and paragraph (b) of § 1.170A-10 as contributions of property other than 30-percent capital gain property. For purposes of applying the immediately preceding sentence, the percentage limitations under section 170(b) for the preceding taxable year and for any taxable years intervening between such year and the year of the election shall not be redetermined and the amount of any deduction allowed for such years under section 170 in respect of the charitable contributions of 30-percent capital gain property in the preceding taxable year shall not be redetermined. However, the amount of the deduction so allowed under section 170 in the preceding taxable year must be subtracted from the reduced amount of the charitable contributions made in such year in order to determine the excess amount which is carried over from such year under section 170(d)(1). If the amount of the deduction so allowed in the preceding taxable year equals or exceeds the reduced amount of the charitable contributions, there shall be no carryover from such year to the year of the election.

(c) An election under this subparagraph may be made for each taxable year in which charitable contributions of 30-percent capital gain property are made or to which they are carried over under section 170(b)(1)(D)(ii). If there are also carryovers under section 170(d)(1) to the year of the election by reason of an election made under this subparagraph for a previous taxable year, such carryovers under section 170(d)(1) shall not be redetermined by reason of the subsequent election.

(ii) *Husband and wife making joint return.* If a husband and wife make a joint return of income for a contribution year and one of the spouses elects under this subparagraph in a later year when he files a separate return, or if a spouse dies after a contribution year for which a joint

Reg. § 1.170A-8(d)(2)

return is made, any excess contribution of 30-percent capital gain property which is carried over to the election year from the contribution year shall be allocated between the husband and wife as provided in paragraph (d)(4)(i) and (iii) of § 1.170A-10. If a husband and wife file separate returns in a contribution year, any election under this subparagraph in a later year when a joint return is filed shall be applicable to any excess contributions of 30-percent capital gain property of either taxpayer carried over from the contribution year to the election year. The immediately preceding sentence shall also apply where two single individuals are subsequently married and file a joint return. A remarried individual who filed a joint return with his former spouse for a contribution year and thereafter files a joint return with his present spouse shall treat the carryover to the election year as provided in paragraph (d)(4)(ii) of § 1.170A-10.

(iii) *Manner of making election.* The election under subdivision (i) of this subparagraph shall be made by attaching to the income tax return for the election year a statement indicating that the election under section 170(b)(1)(D)(iii) and this subparagraph is being made. If there is a carryover to the taxable year of any charitable contributions of 30-percent capital gain property from a previous taxable year or years, the statement shall show a recomputation, in accordance with this subparagraph and § 1.170A-4, of such carryover, setting forth sufficient information with respect to the previous taxable year or any intervening year to show the basis of the recomputation. The statement shall indicate the district director, or the director of the internal revenue service center, with whom the return for the previous taxable year or years was filed, the name or names in which such return or returns were filed, and whether each such return was a joint or separate return.

(3) *30-percent capital gain property defined.* If there is a charitable contribution of a capital asset which, if it were sold by the donor at its fair market value at the time of its contribution, would result in the recognition of gain all, or any portion, of which would be long-term capital gain and if the amount of such contribution is not required to be reduced under section 170(e)(1)(B) and § 1.170A-4(a)(2), such capital asset shall be treated as "30-percent capital gain property" for purposes of section 170 and the regulations thereunder. For such purposes any property which is property used in the trade or business, as defined in section 1231(b), shall be treated as a capital asset. However, see paragraph (b)(4) of § 1.170A-4. For the treatment of such property as

section 170(e) capital gain property, see paragraph (b)(2)(iii) of § 1.170A-4.

(e) *Contribution base defined.* For purposes of section 170 the term "contribution base" means adjusted gross income under section 62, computed without regard to any net operating loss carryback to the taxable year under section 172. See section 170(b)(1)(F).

(f) *Illustrations.* The application of this section may be illustrated by the following examples:

Example (1). B, an individual, reports his income on the calendar-year basis and for 1970 has a contribution base of $100,000. During 1970 he makes charitable contributions of $70,000 in cash, of which $40,000 is given to section 170(b)(1)(A) organizations and $30,000 is given to other organizations described in section 170(c). Accordingly, B is allowed a charitable contributions deduction of $50,000 (50% of $100,000), which consists of the $40,000 contributed to section 170(b)(1)(A) organizations and $10,000 of the $30,000 contributed to the other organizations. Under paragraph (c) of this section, only $10,000 of the $30,000 contributed to the other organizations is allowed as a deduction since such contribution of $30,000 is allowed to the extent of the lesser of $20,000 (20% of $100,000) or $10,000 ([50% of $100,000] − $40,000 (contributions allowed under section 170(b)(1)(A) and paragraph (b) of this section)). Under section 170(b)(1)(D)(ii) and (d)(1) and § 1.170A-10, B is not allowed a carryover to 1971 or to any other taxable year for any of the $20,000 ($30,000 − $10,000) not deductible under section 170(b)(1)(B) and paragraph (c) of this section.

Example (2). C, an individual, reports his income on the calendar-year basis and for 1970 has a contribution base of $100,000. During 1970 he makes charitable contributions of $40,000 in 30-percent capital gain property to section 170(b)(1)(A) organizations and of $30,000 in cash to other organizations described in section 170(c). The 20-percent limitation in section 170(b)(1)(B) and paragraph (c) of this section is applied before the 30-percent limitation in section 170(b)(1)(D)(i) and paragraph (d) of this section; accordingly section 170(b)(1)(B)(ii) limits the deduction for the $30,000 cash contribution to $10,000 ([50% of $100,000] − $40,000). The amount of the contribution of 30-percent capital gain property is limited by section 170(b)(1)(D)(i) and paragraph (d) of this section to $30,000 (30% of $100,000). Accordingly, C's charitable contributions deduction for 1970 is limited to $40,000 ($10,000 + $30,000). Under section 170(b)(1)(D)(ii) and paragraph (c) of § 1.170A-10, C is allowed a carryover to 1971 of $10,000 ($40,000 − $30,000) in respect of his contribu-

Reg. § 1.170A-8(d)(3)

tions of 30-percent capital gain property. C is not allowed a carryover to 1971 or to any other taxable year for any of the $20,000 cash ($30,000 − $10,000) not deductible under section 170(b)(1)(B) and paragraph (c) of this section.

Example (3). (a) D, an individual, reports his income on the calendar-year basis and for 1970 has a contribution base of $100,000. During 1970 he makes charitable contributions of $70,000 in cash, of which $40,000 is given to section 170(b)(1)(A) organizations and $30,000 is given to other organizations described in section 170(c). During 1971 D makes charitable contributions to a section 170(b)(1)(A) organization of $12,000, consisting of cash of $1,000 and $11,000 in 30-percent capital gain property. His contribution base for 1971 is $10,000.

(b) For 1970, D is allowed a charitable contributions deduction of $50,000 (50% of $100,000), which consists of the $40,000 contributed to section 170(b)(1)(A) organizations and $10,000 of the $30,000 contributed to the other organizations. Under paragraph (c) of this section, only $10,000 of the $30,000 contributed to the other organizations is allowed as a deduction since such contribution of $30,000 is allowed to the extent of the lesser of $20,000 (20% of $100,000) or $10,000 ([50% of $100,000] − $40,000 (contributions allowed under section 170(b)(1)(A) and paragraph (d) of this section)). D is not allowed a carryover to 1971 or to any other taxable year for any of the $20,000 ($30,000 − $10,000) not deductible under section 170(b)(1)(B) and paragraph (c) of this section.

(c) For 1971, D is allowed a charitable contributions deduction of $4,000, consisting of $1,000 cash and $3,000 of the 30-percent capital gain property (30% of $10,000). Under section 170(b)(1)(D)(ii) and paragraph (c) of § 1.170A-10, D is allowed a carryover to 1972 of $8,000 ($11,000 − $3,000) in respect of his contribution of 30-percent capital gain property in 1971.

Example (4). (a) E, an individual, reports his income on the calendar-year basis and for 1970 has a contribution base of $100,000. During 1970 he makes charitable contributions of $70,000 in cash, of which $40,000 is given to section 170(b)(1)(A) organizations and $30,000 is given to other organizations described in section 170(c). During 1971 E makes charitable contributions to a section 170(b)(1)(A) organization of $14,000 consisting of cash of $3,000 and $11,000 in 30-percent capital gain property. His contribution base for 1971 is $10,000.

(b) For 1970, E is allowed a charitable contributions deduction of $50,000 (50% of $100,000), which consists of the $40,000 contributed to sec-

tion 170(b)(1)(A) organizations and $10,000 of the $30,000 contributed to the other organizations. Under paragraph (c) of this section, only $10,000 of the $30,000 contributed to the other organizations is allowed as a deduction since such contribution of $30,000 is allowed to the extent of the lesser of $20,000 (20% of $100,000) or $10,000 ([50% of $100,000] − $40,000 (contributions allowed under section 170(b)(1)(A) and paragraph (b) of this section)). E is not allowed a carryover to 1971 or to any other taxable year for any of the $20,000 ($30,000 − $10,000) not deductible under section 170(b)(1)(B) and paragraph (c) of this section.

(c) For 1971, E is allowed a charitable contribution deduction of $5,000 (50% of $10,000), consisting of $3,000 cash and $2,000 of the $3,000 (30% of $10,000) 30-percent capital gain property which is taken into account. This result is reached because, as provided in section 170(b)(1)(D)(i) and paragraph (d)(1) of this section, cash contributions are taken into account before charitable contributions of 30-percent capital gain property. Under section 170(b)(1)(D)(ii) and (d)(1) and paragraphs (b) and (c) of § 1.170A-10, E is allowed a carryover of $9,000 ([$11,000 − $3,000] plus [$6,000 − $5,000]) to 1972 in respect of his contribution of 30-percent capital gain property in 1971.

Example (5). In 1970, C, a calendar-year individual taxpayer, contributes to section 170(b)(1)(A) organizations the amount of $8,000, consisting of $3,000 in cash and $5,000 in 30-percent capital gain property. In 1970, C also makes charitable contributions of $8,500 in 30-percent capital gain property to other organizations described in section 170(c). C's contribution base for 1970 is $20,000. The 20-percent limitation in section 170(b)(1)(B) and paragraph (c) of this section is applied before the 30-percent limitation in section 170(b)(1)(D)(i) and paragraph (d) of this section; accordingly, section 170(b)(1)(B)(ii) limits the deduction for the $8,500 of contributions to the other organizations described in section 170(c) to $2,000 ([50% of $20,000] − [$3,000 + $5,000]). However, the total amount of contributions of 30-percent capital gain property which is allowed as a deduction for 1970 is limited by section 170(b)(1)(D)(i) and paragraph (d) of this section to $6,000 (30% of $20,000), consisting of the $5,000 contribution to the section 170(c)(1)(A) organizations and $1,000 of the contributions to the other organizations described in section 170(c). Accordingly, C is allowed a charitable contributions deduction for 1970 of $9,000, which consists of $3,000 cash and $6,000 of the $13,500 of 30-percent capital gain property. C is not allowed to carry over to 1971 or any other

Reg. § 1.170A-8(f)

year the remaining $7,500 because his contributions of 30-percent capital gain property for 1970 to section 170(b)(1)(A) organizations amount only to $5,000 and do not exceed $6,000 (30% of $20,000). Thus, the requirement of section 170(b)(1)(D)(ii) is not satisfied.

Example (6). During 1971, D, a calendar-year individual taxpayer, makes a charitable contribution to a church of $8,000, consisting of $5,000 in cash and $3,000 in 30-percent capital gain property. For such year, D's contribution base is $10,000. Accordingly, D is allowed a charitable contributions deduction for 1971 of $5,000 (50% of $10,000) of cash. Under section 170(d)(1) and paragraph (b) of § 1.170A-10, D is allowed a carryover to 1972 of his $3,000 contribution of 30-percent capital gain property, even though such amount does not exceed 30 percent of his contribution base for 1971.

Example (7). In 1970, E, a calendar-year individual taxpayer, makes a charitable contribution to a section 170(b)(1)(A) organization in the amount of $10,000, consisting of $8,000 in 30-percent capital gain property and of $2,000 (after reduction under section 170(e)) in other property. E's contribution base of 1970 is $20,000. Accordingly, E is allowed a charitable contributions deduction for 1970 of $8,000, consisting of the $2,000 of property the amount of which was reduced under section 170(e) and $6,000 (30% of $20,000) of the 30-percent capital gain property. Under section 170(b)(1)(D)(ii) and paragraph (c) of § 1.170A-10, E is allowed to carry over to 1971 $2,000 ($8,000 − $6,000) of his contribution of 30-percent capital gain property.

Example (8). (a) In 1972, F, a calendar-year individual taxpayer, makes a charitable contribution to a church of $4,000, consisting of $1,000 in cash and $3,000 in 30-percent capital gain property. In addition, F makes a charitable contribution in 1972 of $2,000 in cash to an organization described in section 170(c)(4). F also has a carryover from 1971 under section 170(d)(1) of $5,000 (none of which consists of contributions of 30-percent capital gain property) and a carryover from 1971 under section 170(b)(1)(D)(ii) of $6,000 of contributions of 30-percent capital gain property. F's contribution base for 1972 is $11,000. Accordingly, F is allowed a charitable contributions deduction for 1972 of $5,500 (50% of $11,000), which consists of $1,000 cash contributed in 1972 to the church, $3,000 of 30-percent capital gain property contributed in 1972 to the church, and $1,500 (carryover of $5,000 but not to exceed [$5,500 − ($1,000 + $3,000)]) of the carryover from 1971 under section 170(d)(1).

(b) No deduction is allowed for 1972 for the contribution in that year of $2,000 cash to the section 170(c)(4) organization since section 170(b)(1)(B)(ii) and paragraph (c) of this section limit the deduction for such contribution to $0 ([50% of $11,000] − [$1,000 + $1,500 + $3,000]). Moreover, F is not allowed a carryover to 1973 or to any other year for any of such $2,000 cash contributed to the section 170(c)(4) organization.

(c) Under section 170(d)(1) and paragraph (b) of § 1.170A-10, F is allowed a carryover to 1973 from 1971 of $3,500 ($5,000 − $1,500) of contributions of other than 30-percent capital gain property. Under section 170(b)(1)(D)(ii) and paragraph (c) of § 1.170A-10, F is allowed a carryover to 1973 from 1971 of $6,000 ($6,000 − $0 of such carryover treated as paid in 1972) of contributions of 30-percent capital gain property. The portion of such $6,000 carryover from 1971 which is treated as paid in 1972 is $0 ([50% of $11,000] − [$4,000 contributions to the church in 1972 plus $1,500 of section 170(d)(1) carryover treated as paid in 1972]).

Example (9). (a) In 1970, A, a calendar-year individual taxpayer, makes a charitable contribution to a church of 30-percent capital gain property having a fair market value of $60,000 and an adjusted basis of $10,000. A's contribution base for 1970 is $50,000, and he makes no other charitable contributions in that year. A does not elect for 1970 under paragraph (d)(2) of this section to have section 170(e)(1)(B) apply to such contribution. Accordingly, under section 170(b)(1)(D)(i) and paragraph (d) of this section, A is allowed a charitable contributions deduction for 1970 of $15,000 (30% of $50,000). Under section 170(b)(1)(D)(ii) and paragraph (c) of § 1.170A-10, A is allowed a carryover to 1971 of $45,000 ($60,000 − $15,000) for his contribution of 30-percent capital gain property.

(b) In 1971, A makes a charitable contribution to a church of 30-percent capital gain property having a fair market value of $11,000 and an adjusted basis of $10,000. A's contribution base for 1971 is $60,000, and he makes no other charitable contributions in that year. A elects for 1971 under paragraph (d)(2) of this section to have section 170(e)(1)(B) and § 1.170A-4 apply to his contribution of $11,000 in that year and to his carryover of $45,000 from 1970. Accordingly, he is required to recompute his carryover from 1970 as if section 170(e)(1)(B) had applied to his contribution of 30-percent capital gain property in that year.

(c) If section 170(e)(1)(B) had applied in 1970 to his contribution of 30-percent capital gain

Reg. § 1.170A-8(f)

property, A's contribution would have been reduced from $60,000 to $35,000, the reduction of $25,000 being 50 percent of the gain of $50,000 ($60,000 – $10,000) which would have been recognized as long-term capital gain if the property had been sold by A at its fair market value at the time of the contribution in 1970. Accordingly, by taking the election under paragraph (d)(2) of this section into account, A has a recomputed carryover to 1971 of $20,000 ($35,000 – $15,000) of his contribution of 30-percent capital gain property in 1970. However, A's charitable contributions deduction of $15,000 allowed for 1970 is not recomputed by reason of the election.

(d) Pursuant to the election for 1971, the contribution of 30-percent capital gain property for 1971 is reduced from $11,000 to $10,500, the reduction of $500 being 50 percent of the gain of $1,000 ($11,000 – $10,000) which would have been recognized as long-term capital gain if the property had been sold by A at its fair market value at the time of its contribution in 1971.

(e) Accordingly, A is allowed a charitable contributions deduction for 1971 of $30,000 (total contributions of $30,500 [$20,000+$10,500] but not to exceed 50% of $60,000).

(f) Under section 170(d)(1) and paragraph (b) of § 1.170A-10, A is allowed a carryover of $500 ($30,500 – $30,000) to 1972 and the 3 succeeding taxable years. The $500 carryover, which by reason of the election is no longer treated as a contribution of 30-percent capital gain property, is treated as carried over under paragraph (b) of § 1.170A-10 from 1970 since in 1971 current year contributions are deducted before contributions which are carried over from preceding taxable years.

Example (10). The facts are the same as in example (9) except that A also makes a charitable contribution in 1971 of $2,000 cash to a private foundation not described in section 170(b)(1)(E) and that A's contribution base for that year is $62,000, instead of $60,000. Accordingly, A is allowed a charitable contributions deduction for 1971 of $31,000, determined in the following manner. Under section 170(b)(1)(A) and paragraph (b) of this section, A is allowed a charitable contributions deduction for 1971 of $30,500, consisting of $10,500 of property contributed to the church in 1971 and of $20,000 (carryover of $20,000 but not to exceed [($62,000×50%) – $10,500]) of contributions of property carried over to 1971 under section 170(d)(1) and paragraph (b) of § 1.170A-10. Under section 170(b)(1)(B) and paragraph (c) of this section, A is allowed a charitable contributions deduction for 1971 of $500 ([50% of $62,000] – [$10,500+$20,000]) of cash

contributed to the private foundation in that year. A is not allowed a carryover to 1972 or to any other taxable year for any of the $1,500 ($2,000 – $500) cash not deductible in 1971 under section 170(b)(1)(B) and paragraph (c) of this section.

Example (11). The facts are the same as in example (9) except that A's contribution base for 1970 is $120,000. Thus, before making the election under paragraph (d)(2) of this section for 1971, A is allowed a charitable contributions deduction for 1970 of $36,000 (30% of $120,000) and is allowed a carryover to 1971 of $24,000 ($60,000 – $36,000). By making the election for 1971, A is required to recompute the carryover from 1970, which is reduced from $24,000 to zero, since the charitable contributions deduction of $36,000 allowed for 1970 exceeds the reduced $35,000 contribution for 1970 which may be taken into account by reason of the election for 1971. Accordingly, A is allowed a deduction for 1971 of $10,500 and is allowed no carryover to 1972, since the reduced contribution for 1971 ($10,500) does not exceed the limitation of $30,000 (50% of $60,000) for 1971 which applies under section 170(d)(1) and paragraph (b) of § 1.170A-10. A's charitable contributions deduction of $36,000 allowed for 1970 is not recomputed by reason of the election. Thus, it is not to A's advantage to make the election under paragraph (d)(2) of this section.

Example (12). (a) B, an individual, reports his income on the calendar year basis and for 1970 has a contribution base of $100,000. During 1970 he makes charitable contributions of $70,000, consisting of $50,000 in 30-percent capital gain property contributed to a church and $20,000 in cash contributed to a private foundation not described in section 170(b)(1)(E). For 1971, B's contribution base is $40,000, and in that year he makes a charitable contribution of $5,000 in cash to such private foundation. During the years involved B makes no other charitable contributions.

(b) The amount of the contribution of 30-percent capital gain property which may be taken into account for 1970 is limited by section 170(b)(1)(D)(i) and paragraph (d) of this section to $30,000 (30% of $100,000). Accordingly, under section 170(b)(1)(A) and paragraph (b) of this section B is allowed a deduction for 1970 of $30,000 of 30-percent capital gain property (contribution of $30,000 but not to exceed $50,000 [50% of $100,000]). No deduction is allowed for 1970 for the contribution in that year of $20,000 of cash to the private foundation since section 170(b)(1)(B)(ii) and paragraph (c) of this section limit the deduction for such contribution to $0

([50% of $100,000]—$50,000, the amount of the contribution of 30-percent capital gain property).

(c) Under section 170(b)(1)(D)(ii) and paragraph (c) of § 1.170A-10, B is allowed a carryover to 1971 of $20,000 ($50,000 − [30% of $100,000]) of his contribution in 1970 of 30-percent capital gain property. B is not allowed a carryover to 1971 or to any other taxable year for any of the $20,000 cash contribution in 1970 which is not deductible under section 170(b)(1)(B) and paragraph (c) of this section.

(d) The amount of the contribution of 30-percent capital gain property which may be taken into account for 1971 is limited by section 170(b)(1)(D)(i) and paragraph (d) of this section to $12,000 (30% of $40,000). Accordingly, under section 170(b)(1)(A) and paragraph (b) of this section B is allowed a deduction for 1971 of $12,000 of 30-percent capital gain property (contribution of $12,000 but not to exceed $20,000 [50% of $40,000]). No deduction is allowed for 1971 for the contribution in that year of $5,000 of cash to the private foundation, since section 170(b)(1)(B)(ii) and paragraph (c) of this section limit the deduction for such contribution to $0 ([50% of $40,000] − $20,000 carryover of 30-percent capital gain property from 1970).

(e) Under section 170(b)(1)(D)(ii) and paragraph (c) of § 1.170A-10, B is allowed a carryover to 1972 of $8,000 ($20,000 − [30% of $40,000]) of his contribution in 1970 of 30-percent capital gain property. B is not allowed a carryover to 1972 or to any other taxable year for any of the $5,000 cash contribution for 1971 which is not deductible under section 170(b)(1)(B) and paragraph (c) of this section.

Example (13). D, an individual, reports his income on the calendar-year basis and for 1970 has a contribution base of $100,000. On March 1, 1970, he contributes to a church intangible property to which section 1245 applies which has a fair market value of $60,000 and an adjusted basis of $10,000. At the time of the contribution D has used the property in his business for more than 6 months. If the property had been sold by D at its fair market value at the time of its contribution, it is assumed that under section 1245 $20,000 of the gain of $50,000 would have been treated as ordinary income and $30,000 would have been long-term capital gain. Since the property contributed is ordinary income property within the meaning of paragraph (b)(1) of § 1.170A-4, D's contribution of $60,000 is reduced under paragraph (a)(1) of such section to $40,000 ($60,000 − $20,000 ordinary income). However, since the property contributed is also 30-percent capital gain property within the meaning of para-

graph (d)(3) of this section, D's deduction for 1970 is limited by section 170(b)(1)(D)(i) and paragraph (d) of this section to $30,000(30% of $100,000). Under section 170(b)(1)(D)(ii) and paragraph (c) of § 1.170A-10, D is allowed to carry over to 1971 $10,000 ($40,000 − $30,000) of his contribution of 30-percent capital gain property.

Example (14). C, an individual, reports his income on the calendar-year basis and for 1970 has a contribution base of $50,000. During 1970 he makes charitable contributions to a church of $57,000, consisting of $2,000 cash and of 30-percent capital gain property with a fair market value of $55,000 and an adjusted basis of $15,000. In addition, C contributes $3,000 cash in 1970 to a private foundation not described in section 170(b)(1)(E). For 1970, C elects under paragraph (d)(2) of this section to have section 170(e)(1)(B) and § 1.170A-4(a) apply to his contribution of property to the church. Accordingly, for 1970 C's contribution of property to the church is reduced from $55,000 to $35,000, the reduction of $20,000 being 50 percent of the gain of $40,000 ($55,000 − $15,000) which would have been recognized as long-term capital gain if the property had been sold by C at its fair market value at the time of its contribution to the church. Under section 170(b)(1)(A) and paragraph (b) of this section, C is allowed a charitable contributions deduction for 1970 of $25,000 ([$2,000 + $35,000] but not to exceed [$50,000 × 50%]). Under section 170(d)(1) and paragraph (b) of § 1.170A-10, C is allowed a carryover from 1970 to 1971 of $12,000 ($37,000 − $25,000). No deduction is allowed for 1970 for the contribution in that year of $3,000 cash to the private foundation since section 170(b)(1)(B) and paragraph (c) of this section limit the deduction for such contribution to the smaller of $10,000 ($50,000 × 20%) or $0 ([$50,000 × 50%] − $25,000). C is not allowed a carryover from 1970 for any of the $3,000 cash contribution in that year which is not deductible under section 170(b)(1)(B) and paragraph (c) of this section.

Example (15). (a) D, an individual, reports his income on the calendar-year basis and for 1970 has a contribution base of $100,000. During 1970 he makes a charitable contribution to a church of 30-percent capital gain property with a fair market value of $40,000 and an adjusted basis of $21,000. In addition, he contributes $23,000 cash in 1970 to a private foundation not described in section 170(b)(1)(E). For 1970, D elects under paragraph (d)(2) of this section to have section 170(e)(1)(B) and § 1.170A-4(a) apply to his contribution of property to the church. Accordingly, for 1970 D's contribution of property to the church is reduced from $40,000 to $30,500, the

Reg. § 1.170A-8(f)

reduction of $9,500 being 50 percent of the gain of $19,000 ($40,000 — $21,000) which would have been recognized as long-term capital gain if the property had been sold by D at its fair market value at the time of its contribution to the church. Under section 170(b)(1)(A) and paragraph (b) of this section, D is allowed a charitable contributions deduction for 1970 of $30,500 for the property contributed to the church. In addition, under section 170(b)(1)(B) and paragraph (c) of this section, D is allowed a deduction of $19,500 for the cash contributed to the private foundation, since such contribution of $23,000 is allowed to the extent of the lesser of $20,000 (20% of $100,000) or $19,500 ([$100,000 × 50%] — $30,500). D is not allowed a carryover to 1971 or to any other taxable year for any of the $3,500 (23,000 — $19,500) of cash not deductible under section 170(b)(1)(B) and paragraph (c) of this section.

(b) If D had not made the election under paragraph (d)(2) of this section for 1970, his deduction for 1970 under section 170(a) for the $40,000 contribution of property to the church would have been limited by section 170(b)(1)(D)(i) and paragraph (d) of this section to $30,000 (30% of $100,000), and under section 170(b)(1)(D)(ii) and paragraph (c) of § 1.17CA-10 he would have been allowed a carryover to 1971 of $10,000 ($40,000 — $30,000) for his contribution of such property. In addition, he would have been allowed under section 170(b)(1)(B)(ii) and paragraph (c) of this section for 1970 a charitable contributions deduction of $10,000 ([$100,000 × 50%] — $40,000) for the cash contributed to the private foundation. In such case, D would not have been allowed a carryover to 1971 or to any other taxable year for any of the $13,000 ($23,000 — $10,000) of cash not deductible under section 170(b)(1)(B) and paragraph (c) of this section.

(g) *Effective date.* This section applies only to contributions paid in taxable years beginning after December 31, 1969. [Reg. § 1.170A-8.]

☐ [*T.D. 7207*, 10-3-72.]

[Reg. § 1.170A-9]

§ 1.170A-9. **Definition of section 170(b)(1)(A) organization.**—The term "section 170(b)(1)(A) organization" as used in the regulations under section 170 means any organization described in paragraph (a) through (i) of this section, effective with respect to taxable years beginning after December 31, 1969, except as otherwise provided. Section 1.170-2(b) shall continue to be applicable with respect to taxable years beginning prior to January 1, 1970. The term "one or more organizations described in section 170(b)(1)(A) (other than in clauses (vii) and

(viii))" as used in sections 507 and 509 of the Code and the regulations thereunder means one or more organizations described in paragraphs (a) through (e) of this section, except as modified by the regulations under part II of subchapter F of chapter I or under chapter 42.

(a) *Church or a convention or association of churches.* An organization is described in section 170(b)(1)(A)(i) if it is a church or a convention or association of churches.

(b) *Educational organization and organizations for the benefit of certain State and municipal colleges and universities* —(1) *Educational organization.* An educational organization is described in section 170(b)(1)(A)(ii) if its primary function is the presentation of formal instruction and it normally maintains a regular faculty and curriculum and normally has a regularly enrolled body of pupils or students in attendance at the place where its educational activities are regularly carried on. The term includes institutions such as primary, secondary, preparatory, or high schools, and colleges and universities. It includes Federal, State, and other public-supported schools which otherwise come within the definition. It does not include organizations engaged in both educational and noneducational activities unless the latter are merely incidental to the educational activities. A recognized university which incidentally operates a museum or sponsors concerts is an educational organization within the meaning of section 170(b)(1)(A)(ii). However, the operation of a school by a museum does not necessarily qualify the museum as an educational organization within the meaning of this subparagraph.

(2) *Organizations for the benefit of certain State and municipal colleges and universities.* (i) An organization is described in section 170(b)(1)(A)(iv) if it meets the support requirements of subdivision (ii) of this subparagraph and is organized and operated exclusively to receive, hold, invest, and administer property and to make expenditures to or for the benefit of a college or university which is an organization described in subdivision (iii) of this subparagraph. The phrase "expenditures to or for the benefit of a college or university" includes expenditures made for any one or more of the normal functions of colleges and universities such as the acquisition and maintenance of real property comprising part of the campus area; the erection of, or participation in the erection of, college or university buildings; the acquisition and maintenance of equipment and furnishings used for, or in conjunction with, normal functions of colleges and universities; or expenditures for scholarships, libraries and student loans.

(ii) To qualify under section 170(b)(1)(A)(iv), the organization receiving the contribution must normally receive a substantial part of its support from the United States or any State or political subdivision thereof or from direct or indirect contributions from the general public, or from a combination of two or more of such sources. For such purposes, the term "support" does not include income received in the exercise or performance by the organization of its charitable, educational, or other purpose or function constituting the basis for its exemption under section 501(a). An example of an indirect contribution from the public is the receipt by the organization of its share of the proceeds of an annual collection campaign of a community chest, community fund, or united fund. In determining the amount of support received by such organization with respect to a contribution of property which is subject to reduction under section 170(e), the fair market value of the property shall be taken into account.

(iii) The college or university (including a land grant college or university) to be benefited must be an educational organization referred to in section 170(b)(1)(A)(ii) and subparagraph (1) of this paragraph which is an agency or instrumentality of a State or political subdivision thereof, or which is owned or operated by a State or political subdivision thereof or by an agency or instrumentality of one more States or political subdivisions.

(c) *Hospitals and medical research organizations* —(1) *Hospitals.* An organization (other than one described in subparagraph (2) of this paragraph) is described in section 170(b)(1)(A)(iii) if:

(i) It is a hospital, and

(ii) Its principal purpose or function is the providing of medical or hospital care or medical education or medical research.

The term "hospital" includes (A) Federal hospitals and (B) State, county, and municipal hospitals which are instrumentalities of governmental units referred to in section 170(c)(1) and otherwise come within the definition. A rehabilitation institution, outpatient clinic, or community mental health or drug treatment center may qualify as a "hospital" within the meaning of subdivision (i) of this subparagraph if its principal purpose or function is the providing of hospital or medical care. For purposes of this subdivision, the term "medical care" shall include the treatment of any physical or mental disability or condition, whether on an inpatient or outpatient basis, provided the cost of such treatment is deductible under section 213 by the person treated. An organization, all the accommodations of which qualify as being part of a "skilled nursing facility"

within the meaning of 42 U.S.C. 1395x(j), may qualify as a "hospital" within the meaning of subdivision (i) of this subparagraph if its principal purpose or function is the providing of hospital or medical care. For taxable years ending after June 28, 1968, the term "hospital" also includes cooperative hospital service organizations which meet the requirements of section 501(e) and § 1.501(e)-1. The term "hospital" does not, however, include convalescent homes or homes for children or the aged, nor does the term include institutions whose principal purpose or function is to train handicapped individuals to pursue some vocation. An organization whose principal purpose or function is the providing of medical education or medical research will not be considered a "hospital" within the meaning of subdivision (i) of this subparagraph, unless it is also actively engaged in providing medical or hospital care to patients on its premises or in its facilities, on an inpatient or outpatient basis, as an integral part of its medical education or medical research functions. See, however, subparagraph (2) of this paragraph with respect to certain medical research organizations.

(2) *Certain medical research organizations* —(i) *Introduction.* A medical research organization is described in section 170(b)(1)(A)(iii) if the principal purpose or functions of such organization are medical research and if it is directly engaged in the continuous active conduct of medical research in conjunction with a hospital. In addition, for purposes of the 50 percent limitation of section 170(b)(1)(A) with respect to a contribution, during the calendar year in which the contribution is made such organization must be committed to spend such contribution for such research before January 1 of the fifth calendar year which begins after the date such contribution is made. An organization need not receive contributions deductible under section 170 to qualify as a medical research organization and such organization need not be committed to spend amounts to which the limitation of section 170(b)(1)(A) does not apply within the 5-year period referred to in this subdivision. However, the requirement of continuous active conduct of medical research indicates that the type of organization contemplated in this subparagraph is one which is primarily engaged directly in the continuous active conduct of medical research, as compared to an inactive medical research organization or an organization primarily engaged in funding the programs of other medical research organizations. As in the case of a hospital, since an organization is ordinarily not described in section 170(b)(1)(A)(iii) as a hospital unless it functions primarily as a hospital, similarly a medical re-

Reg. § 1.170A-9(c)(1)

search organization is not so described unless it is primarily engaged directly in the continuous active conduct of medical research in conjunction with a hospital. Accordingly, the rules of this subparagraph shall only apply with respect to such medical research organizations.

(ii) *General rule.* An organization (other than a hospital described in subparagraph (1) of this paragraph) is described in section 170(b)(1)(A)(iii) only if within the meaning of this subparagraph:

(a) The principal purpose or functions of such organization are to engage primarily in the conduct of medical research, and

(b) It is primarily engaged directly in the continuous active conduct of medical research in conjunction with a hospital which is (1) described in section 501(c)(3), (2) a federal hospital, or (3) an instrumentality of a governmental unit referred to in section 170(c)(1).

However, in order for a contribution to such organization to qualify for purposes of the 50 percent limitation of section 170(b)(1)(A), during the calendar year in which such contribution is made or treated as made, such organization must be committed (within the meaning of subdivision (viii) of this subparagraph) to spend such contribution for such active conduct of medical research before January 1 of the fifth calendar year beginning after the date such contribution is made. For the meaning of the term "medical research" see subdivision (iii) of this subparagraph. For the meaning of the term "principal purpose or functions" see subdivision (iv) of this subparagraph. For the meaning of the term "primarily engaged directly in the continuous active conduct of medical research" see subdivision (v) of this subparagraph. For the meaning of the term "medical research in conjunction with a hospital" see subdivision (vii) of this subparagraph.

(iii) *Definition of medical research.* Medical research means the conduct of investigations, experiments, and studies to discover, develop, or verify knowledge relating to the causes, diagnosis, treatment, prevention, or control of physical or mental diseases and impairments of man. To qualify as a medical research organization, the organization must have or must have continuously available for its regular use the appropriate equipment and professional personnel necessary to carry out its principal function. Medical research encompasses the associated disciplines spanning the biological, social and behavioral sciences. Such disciplines include chemistry (biochemistry, physical chemistry, bio-organic chemistry, etc.), behavioral sciences (psychiatry, physiological psychology, neurophysiology, neurol-

ogy, neurobiology, and social psychology, etc.), biomedical engineering (applied biophysics, medical physics, and medical electronics, *e.g.,* developing pacemakers and other medically related electrical equipment), virology, immunology, biophysics, cell biology, molecular biology, pharmacology, toxicology, genetics, pathology, physiology, microbiology, parasitology, endocrinology, bacteriology, and epidemiology.

(iv) *Principal purpose or functions.* An organization must be organized for the principal purpose of engaging primarily in the conduct of medical research in order to be an organization meeting the requirements of this subparagraph. An organization will normally be considered to be so organized if it is expressly organized for the purpose of conducting medical research and is actually engaged primarily in the conduct of medical research. Other facts and circumstances, however, may indicate that an organization does not meet the principal purpose requirement of this subdivision even where its governing instrument so expressly provides. An organization that otherwise meets all of the requirements of this subparagraph (including this subdivision) to qualify as a medical research organization will not fail to so qualify solely because its governing instrument does not specifically state that its principal purpose is to conduct medical research.

(v) *Primarily engaged directly in the continuous active conduct of medical research.* (a) In order for an organization to be primarily engaged directly in the continuous active conduct of medical research, the organization must either devote a substantial part of its assets to, or expend a significant percentage of its endowment for, such purposes, or both. Whether an organization devotes a substantial part of its assets to, or makes significant expenditures for, such continuous active conduct depends upon the facts and circumstances existing in each specific case. An organization will be treated as devoting a substantial part of its assets to, or expending a significant percentage of its endowment for, such purposes if it meets the appropriate test contained in paragraph (c)(2)(v)(b) of this section. If an organization fails to satisfy both of such tests, in evaluating the facts and circumstances, the factor given most weight is the margin by which the organization failed to meet such tests. Some of the other facts and circumstances to be considered in making such a determination are:

(1) If the organization fails to satisfy the tests because it failed to properly value its assets or endowment, then upon determination of the improper valuation it devotes additional assets to, or makes additional expenditures for, such

purposes, so that it satisfies such tests on an aggregate basis for the prior year in addition to such tests for the current year.

(2) The organization acquires new assets or has a significant increase in the value of its securities after it had developed a budget in a prior year based on the assets then owned and the then current values.

(3) The organization fails to make expenditures in any given year because of the interrelated aspects of its budget and long-term planning requirements, for example, where an organization prematurely terminates an unsuccessful program and because of long-term planning requirements it will not be able to establish a fully operational replacement program immediately.

(4) The organization has as its objective to spend less than a significant percentage in a particular year but make up the difference in the subsequent few years, or to budget a greater percentage in an earlier year and a lower percentage in a later year.

(b) For purposes of this section, an organization which devotes more than one-half of its assets to the continuous active conduct of medical research will be considered to be devoting a substantial part of its assets to such conduct within the meaning of paragraph (c)(2)(v)(a) of this section. An organization which expends funds equaling 3.5 percent or more of the the fair market value of its endowment for the continuous active conduct of medical research will be considered to have expended a significant percentage of its endowment for such purposes within the meaning of paragraph (c)(2)(v)(a) of this section.

(c) Engaging directly in the continuous active conduct of medical research does not include the disbursing of funds to other organizations for the conduct of research by them or the extending of grants or scholarships to others. Therefore, if an organization's primary purpose is to disburse funds to other organizations for the conduct of research by them or to extend grants or scholarships to others, it is not primarily engaged directly in the continuous active conduct of medical research.

(vi) *Special rules.* The following rules shall apply in determining whether a substantial part of an organization's assets are devoted to, or its endowment is expended for, the continuous active conduct of medical research activities:

(a) An organization may satisfy the tests of paragraph (c)(2)(v)(b) of this section by meeting such tests either for a computation period consisting of the immediately preceding taxable year, or for the computation period consisting of the immediately preceding four taxable years. In

addition, for taxable years beginning in 1970, 1971, 1972, 1973, and 1974, if an organization meets such tests for the computation period consisting of the first four taxable years beginning after December 31, 1969, an organization will be treated as meeting such tests, not only for the taxable year beginning in 1974, but also for the preceding four taxable years. Thus, for example, if a calendar year organization failed to satisfy such tests for a computation period consisting of 1969, 1970, 1971, or 1972, but on the basis of a computation period consisting of the years 1970 through 1973, it expended funds equalling 3.5 percent or more of the fair market value of its endowment for the continuous active conduct of medical research, such organization will be considered to have expended a significant percentage of its endowment for such purposes for the taxable years 1970 through 1974. In applying such tests for a four-year computation period, although the organization's expenditures for the entire four-year period shall be aggregated, the fair market value of its endowment for each year shall be summed, even though, in the case of an asset held throughout the four-year period, the fair market value of such an asset will be counted four times. Similarly, the fair market value of an organization's assets for each year of a four-year computation period shall be summed.

(b) Any property substantially all the use of which is "substantially related" (within the meaning of section 514(b)(1)(A)) to the exercise or performance of the organization's medical research activities will not be treated as part of its endowment.

(c) The valuation of assets must be made with commonly accepted methods of valuation. A method of valuation made in accordance with the principles stated in the regulations under section 2031 constitutes an acceptable method of valuation. Assets may be valued as of any day in the organization's taxable year to which such valuation applies, provided the organization follows a consistent practice of valuing such asset as of such date in all taxable years. For purposes of paragraph (c)(2)(v) of this section, an asset held by the organization for part of a taxable year shall be taken into account by multiplying the fair market value of such asset by a fraction, the numerator of which is the number of days in such taxable year that the foundation held such asset and the denominator of which is the number of days in such taxable year.

(vii) *Medical research in conjunction with a hospital.* The organization need not be formally affiliated with a hospital to be considered primarily engaged directly in the continuous active con-

Reg. § 1.170A-9(c)(2)

duct of medical research in conjunction with a hospital, but in any event there must be a joint effort on the part of the research organization and the hospital pursuant to an understanding that the two organizations will maintain continuing close cooperation in the active conduct of medical research. For example, the necessary joint effort will normally be found to exist if the activities of the medical research organization are carried on in space located within or adjacent to a hospital, the organization is permitted to utilize the facilities (including equipment, case studies, etc.) of the hospital on a continuing basis directly in the active conduct of medical research, and there is substantial evidence of the close cooperation of the members of the staff of the research organization and members of the staff of the particular hospital or hospitals. The active participation in medical research by members of the staff of the particular hospital or hospitals will be considered to be evidence of such close cooperation. Because medical research may involve substantial investigation, experimentation and study not immediately connected with hospital or medical care, the requisite joint effort will also normally be found to exist if there is an established relationship between the research organization and the hospital which provides that the cooperation of appropriate personnel and the use of facilities of the particular hospital or hospitals will be required whenever it would aid such research.

(viii) *Commitment to spend contributions.* The organization's commitment that the contribution will be spent within the prescribed time only for the prescribed purposes must be legally enforceable. A promise in writing to the donor in consideration of his making a contribution that such contribution will be so spent within the prescribed time will constitute a commitment. The expenditure of contributions received for plant, facilities, or equipment, used solely for medical research purposes (within the meaning of subdivision (ii) of this subparagraph), shall ordinarily be considered to be an expenditure for medical research. If a contribution is made in other than money, it shall be considered spent for medical research if the funds from the proceeds of a disposition thereof are spent by the organization within the five-year period for medical research; or, if such property is of such a kind that it is used on a continuing basis directly in connection with such research, it shall be considered spent for medical research in the year in which it is first so used. A medical research organization will be presumed to have made the commitment required under this subdivision with respect to any contribution if its governing instrument or by-laws require that every contribution be spent for medical research

before January 1 of the fifth year which begins after the date such contribution is made.

(ix) *Organizational period for new organizations.* A newly created organization, for its "organizational" period, shall be considered to be primarily engaged directly in the continuous active conduct of medical research in conjunction with a hospital within the meaning of subdivisions (v) and (vii) of this subparagraph if during such period the organization establishes to the satisfaction of the Commissioner that it reasonably can be expected to be so engaged by the end of such period. The information to be submitted shall include detailed plans showing the proposed initial medical research program, architectural drawings for the erection of buildings and facilities to be used for medical research in accordance with such plans, plans to assemble a professional staff and detailed projections showing the timetable for the expected accomplishment of the foregoing. The "organizational" period shall be that period which is appropriate to implement the proposed plans, giving effect to the proposed amounts involved and the magnitude and complexity of the projected medical research program, but in no event in excess of three years following organization.

(x) *Examples.* The application of this subparagraph may be illustrated by the following examples:

Example (1). N, an organization referred to in section 170(c)(2), was created to promote human knowledge within the field of medical research and medical education. All of N's assets were contributed to it by A and consist of a diversified portfolio of stocks and bonds. N's endowment earns 3.5 percent annually, which N expends in the conduct of various medical research programs in conjunction with Y hospital. N is located adjacent to Y hospital makes substantial use of Y's facilities and there is close cooperation between the staffs of N and Y. N is directly engaged in the continuous active conduct of medical research in conjunction with a hospital, meets the principal purpose test described in subdivision (iv) of this subparagraph, and is therefore an organization described in section 170(b)(1)(A)(iii).

Example (2). O, an organization referred to in section 170(c)(2), was created to promote human knowledge within the field of medical research and medical education. All of O's assets consist of a diversified portfolio of stocks and bonds. O's endowment earns 3.5 percent annually, which O expends in the conduct of various medical research programs in conjunction with certain hospitals. However, in 1974, O receives a substantial bequest of additional stocks and bonds. O's

Reg. § 1.170A-9(c)(2)

budget for 1974 does not take into account the bequest and as a result O expends only 3.1 percent of its endowment in 1974. However, O establishes that it will expend at least 3.5 percent of its endowment for the active conduct of medical research for taxable years 1975 through 1978. O is therefore directly engaged in the continuous active conduct of medical research in conjunction with a hospital for taxable year 1975. Since O also meets the principal purpose test described in subdivision (iv) of this subparagraph, it is therefore an organization described in section 170(b)(1)(A)(iii) for taxable year 1975.

Example (3). M, an organization referred to in section 170(c)(2), was created to promote human knowledge within the field of medical research and medical education. M's activities consist of the conduct of medical research programs in conjunction with various hospitals. Under such programs, researchers employed by M engage in research at laboratories set aside for M within the various hospitals. Substantially all of M's assets consists of 100 percent of the stock of X corporation, which has a fair market value of approximately 100 million dollars. X pays M approximately 3.3 million dollars in dividends annually, which M expends in the conduct of its medical research programs. Since M expends only 3.3 percent of its endowment, which does not constitute a significant percentage, in the active conduct of medical research, M is not an organization described in section 170(b)(1)(A)(iii) because M is not engaged in the continuous active conduct of medical research.

(xi) *Special rule for organizations with existing ruling.* This subdivision shall apply to an organization that prior to January 1, 1970, had received a ruling or determination letter which has not been expressly revoked holding the organization to be a medical research organization described in section 170(b)(1)(A)(iii) and with respect to which the facts and circumstances on which the ruling was based have not substantially changed. An organization to which this subdivision applies shall be treated as an organization described in section 170(b)(1)(A)(iii) for a period not ending prior to 90 days after February 13, 1976 (or, where appropriate, for taxable years beginning before such 90th day). In addition, with respect to a grantor or contributor under sections 170, 507, 545(b)(2), 556(b)(2), 642(c), 4942, 4945, 2055, 2106(a)(2), and 2522, the status of an organization to which this subdivision applies will not be affected until notice of change of status under section 170(b)(1)(A)(iii) is made to the public (such as by publication in the Internal Revenue Bulletin). The preceding sentence shall not apply if the grantor or contributor had previously acquired knowledge that the Internal Revenue Service had given notice to such organization that it would be deleted from classification as a section 170(b)(1)(A)(iii) organization.

(d) *Governmental unit.* A governmental unit is described in section 170(b)(1)(A)(v) if it is referred to in section 170(c)(1).

(e) *Definition of section 170(b)(1)(A)(vi) organization.*

(1) *In general.* An organization is described in section 170(b)(1)(A)(vi) if it is:

(i) A corporation, trust, or community chest, fund, or foundation, referred to in section 170(c)(2) (other than an organization specifically described in paragraphs (a) through (d) of this section), and

(ii) A "publicly supported" organization. For purposes of this paragraph, an organization is "publicly supported" if it normally receives a substantial part of its support from a governmental unit referred to in section 170(c)(1) or from direct or indirect contributions from the general public. An organization will be treated as being "publicly supported" if it meets the requirements of either subparagraph (2) or subparagraph (3) of this paragraph. Types of organizations which, subject to the provisions of this paragraph, generally qualify under section 170(b)(1)(A)(vi) as "publicly supported" are publicly or governmentally supported museums of history, art, or science, libraries, community centers to promote the arts, organizations providing facilities for the support of an opera, symphony orchestra, ballet, or repertory drama or for some other direct service to the general public, and organizations such as the American Red Cross or the United Givers Fund.

(2) *Determination whether an organization is "publicly supported"; 33⅓ percent-of-support test.* An organization will be treated as a "publicly supported" organization if the total amount of support which the organization "normally" (as defined in subparagraph (4) of this paragraph) receives from governmental units referred to in section 170(c)(1), from contributions made directly or indirectly by the general public, or from a combination of these sources, equals at least 33⅓ percent of the total support "normally" received by the organization. See subparagraphs (6), (7), and (8) of this paragraph for the definition of "support." The application of this test is illustrated by Example (1) of subparagraph (9) of this paragraph.

(3) *Determination whether an organization is "publicly supported"; facts and circumstances test for organizations failing to meet 33⅓ percent-of-support test.* Even if an organization fails

Reg. § 1.170A-9(d)

to meet the 33⅓ percent-of-support test described in subparagraph (2) of this paragraph, it will be treated as a "publicly supported" organization if it normally receives a substantial part of its support from government units, from direct or indirect contributions from the general public, or from a combination of these sources, and meets the other requirements of this subparagraph. In order to satisfy this subparagraph, an organization must meet the requirements of subdivisions (i) and (ii) of this subparagraph in order to establish, under all the facts and circumstances, that it normally receives a substantial part of its support from governmental units or from direct or indirect contributions from the general public, and it must be in the nature of a "publicly supported" organization, taking into account the factors described in subdivisions (iii) through (vii) of this subparagraph. The requirements and factors referred to in the preceding sentence with respect to a "publicly supported" organization (other than one described in subparagraph (2) or (10) of this paragraph) are:

(i) *Ten percent-of-support limitation.* The percentage of support "normally" (as defined in subparagraph (4) of this paragraph) received by an organization from governmental units, from contributions made directly or indirectly by the general public, or from a combination of these sources, must be "substantial."

For purposes of this subparagraph, an organization will not be treated as "normally" receiving a "substantial" amount of governmental or public support unless the total amount of governmental and public support "normally" received equals at least 10 percent of the total support "normally" received by such organization. See subparagraphs (6), (7), and (8) of this paragraph for the definition of "support."

(ii) *Attraction of public support.* An organization must be so organized and operated as to attract new and additional public or governmental support on a continuous basis. An organization will be considered to meet this requirement if it maintains a continuous and bona fide program for solicitation of funds from the general public, community, or membership group involved, or if it carries on activities designed to attract support from governmental units or other organizations described in section 170(b)(1)(A)(i) through (vi). In determining whether an organization maintains a continuous and bona fide program for solicitation of funds from the general public or community, consideration will be given to whether the scope of its fund-raising activities is reasonable in light of its charitable activities. Consideration will also be given to the fact that

an organization may, in its early years of existence, limit the scope of its solicitation to persons deemed most likely to provide seed money in an amount sufficient to enable it to commence its charitable activities and expand its solicitation program.

In addition to the requirements set forth in subdivisions (i) and (ii) of this subparagraph which must be satisfied, all pertinent facts and circumstances, including the following factors, will be taken into consideration in determining whether an organization is "publicly supported" within the meaning of subparagraph (1) of this paragraph. However, an organization is not generally required to satisfy all of the factors in subdivisions (iii) through (vii) of this subparagraph. The factors relevant to each case and the weight accorded to any one of them may differ depending upon the nature and purpose of the organization and the length of time it has been in existence.

(iii) *Percentage of financial support.* The percentage of support received from public or governmental sources will be taken into consideration in determining whether an organization is "publicly supported." The higher the percentage of support above the 10 percent requirement of subdivision (i) of this subparagraph from public or governmental sources the lesser will be the burden of establishing the publicly supported nature of the organization through other factors described in this subparagraph, while the lower the percentage, the greater will be the burden. If the percentage of the organization's support from public or governmental sources is low because it receives a high percentage of its total support from investment income on its endowment funds, such fact will be treated as evidence of compliance with this subdivision if such endowment funds were originally contributed by a governmental unit or by the general public. However, if such endowment funds were originally contributed by a few individuals or members of their families, such fact will increase the burden on the organization of establishing compliance with the other factors described in this subparagraph.

(iv) *Sources of support.* The fact that an organization meets the requirement of subdivision (i) of this subparagraph through support from governmental units or directly or indirectly from a representative number of persons, rather than receiving almost all of its support from the members of a single family, will be taken into consideration in determining whether an organization is "publicly supported." In determining what is a "representative number of persons," consideration will be given to the type of organization involved, the length of time it has been in existence, and whether it limits its activities to a particular community or region or to a special field which can be expected to appeal to a limited number of persons.

(v) *Representative governing body.* The fact that an organization has a governing body which represents the broad interests of the public, other than the personal or private interests of a limited number of donors (or persons standing in a relationship to such donors which is described in section 4946(a)(1)(C) through (G)), will be taken into account in determining whether an organization is "publicly supported." An organization will be treated as meeting this requirement if it has a governing body (whether designated in the organization's governing instrument or bylaws as a Board of Directors, Board of Trustees, etc.) which is comprised of public officials acting in their capacities as such; of individuals selected by public officials acting in their capacities as such; of persons having special knowledge or expertise in the particular field or discipline in which the organization is operating; of community leaders, such as elected or appointed officials, clergymen, educators, civic leaders, or other such persons representing a broad cross-section of the views and interests of the community; or, in the case of a membership organization, of individuals elected pursuant to the organization's governing instrument or by-laws by a broadly based membership.

(vi) *Availability of public facilities or services; public participation in programs or policies.* (a) The fact that an organization is of the type which generally provides facilities or services directly for the benefit of the general public on a continuing basis (such as a museum or library which holds open its building to the public, a symphony orchestra which gives public performances, a conservation organization which provides educational services to the public through the distribution of educational materials, or an old age home which provides domiciliary or nursing services for members of the general public) will be considered evidence that such organization is "publicly supported."

(b) The fact that an organization is an educational or research institution which regularly publishes scholarly studies that are widely used by colleges and universities or by members of the general public will also be considered evidence that such organization is "publicly supported."

(c) Similarly, the following factors will also be considered evidence that an organization is "publicly supported":

(1) The participation in, or sponsorship of, the programs of the organization by members of the public having special knowledge or

expertise, public officials, or civic or community leaders;

(2) The maintenance of a definitive program by an organization to accomplish its charitable work in the community, such as slum clearance or defeloping employment opportunities; and

(3) The receipt of a significant part of its funds from a public charity or governmental agency to which it is in some way held accountable as a condition of the grant, contract, or contribution.

(vii) *Additional factors pertinent to membership organizations.* The following are additional factors to be considered in determining whether a membership organization is "publicly supported":

(a) Whether the solicitation for dues-paying members is designed to enroll a substantial number of persons in the community or area, or in a particular profession or field of special interest (taking into account the size of the area and the nature of the organization's activities);

(b) Whether membership dues for individual (rather than institutional) members have been fixed at rates designed to make membership available to a broad cross-section of the interested public, rather than to restrict membership to a limited number of persons; and

(c) Whether the activities of the organization will be likely to appeal to persons having some broad common interest or purpose, such as educational activities in the case of alumni associations, musical activities, symphony societies, or civic affairs in the case of parent-teacher associations. See Examples (2) through (5) contained in subparagraph (9) of this paragraph for illustration of this subparagraph.

(4) *Definition of "normally"; general rule.* (i) *Normally; 1/3 support test.* For purposes of subparagraph (2) of this paragraph, an organization will be considered as "normally" meeting the 33⅓ percent-of-support test for its current taxable year and the taxable year immediately succeeding its current year, if, for the four taxable years immediately preceding the current taxable year, the organization meets the 33⅓ percent-of-support test described in subparagraph (2) of this paragraph on an aggregate basis.

(ii) *Normally; facts and circumstances test.* For purposes of subparagraph (3) of this paragraph, an organization will be considered as "normally" meeting the requirements of subparagraph (3) of this paragraph for its current taxable year and the taxable year immediately succeeding its current year, if, for the four taxable years

Reg. § 1.170A-9(e)(4)

immediately preceding the current taxable year, the organization meets the requirements of subparagraph (3)(i) and (ii) of this paragraph on an aggregate basis and satisfies a sufficient combination of the factors set forth in subparagraph (3)(iii) through (vii) of this paragraph. In the case of subparagraph (3)(iii) and (iv) of this paragraph, facts pertinent to years preceding four taxable years immediately preceding the current taxable year may also be taken into consideration. The combination of factors set forth in subparagraph (3)(iii) through (vii) of this paragraph which an organization "normally" must meet does not have to be the same for each four-year period so long as there exists a sufficient combination of factors to show compliance with subparagraph (3) of this paragraph.

(iii) *Special rule.* The fact that an organization has "normally" met the requirements of subparagraph (2) of this paragraph for a current taxable year, but is unable "normally" to meet such requirements for a succeeding taxable year, will not in itself prevent such organization from meeting the requirements of subparagraph (3) of this paragraph for such succeeding taxable year.

(iv) *Illustration.* The application of subdivisions (i), (ii), and (iii) of this subparagraph may be illustrated by the following example:

Example. X, an organization described in section 170(c)(2), meets the 33⅓ percent-of-support test described in subparagraph (2) of this paragraph in taxable year 1975 on the basis of support received during taxable years 1971, 1972, 1973, and 1974. It therefore "normally" meets the requirements of subparagraph (2) of this paragraph for 1975 and 1976 (the taxable year immediately succeeding 1975, the current taxable year). For the taxable year 1976, X is unable to meet the 33⅓ percent-of-support test described in subparagraph (2) of this paragraph on the basis of support received during taxable years 1972, 1973, 1974, and 1975. If X can meet the requirements of subparagraph (3) of this paragraph on the basis of taxable years 1972, 1973, 1974, and 1975, X will meet the requirements of subparagraph (3) of this paragraph for 1977 (the taxable year immediately succeeding 1976, the current taxable year) under subdivision (ii) of this subparagraph. However, if on the basis of both the taxable years 1972 through 1975 and 1973 through 1976, X fails to meet the requirements of both subparagraphs (2) and (3) of this paragraph, X will not be described in section 170(b)(1)(A)(vi) for 1977. However, X will not be disqualified as a section 170(b)(1)(A)(vi) organization for taxable year 1976, because it "normally" met the requirements of subparagraph (2) of this paragraph on the basis

of the taxable years 1971 through 1974, unless the provisions of subdivision (v) of this subparagraph become applicable.

(v) *Exception for material changes in sources of support—(a) In general.* If for the current taxable year there are substantial and material changes in an organization's sources of support other than changes arising from unusual grants excluded under subparagraph (6)(ii) of this paragraph, then in applying subparagraph (2) or (3) of this paragraph, neither the 4-year computation period applicable to such year as an immediately succeeding taxable year or as a current taxable year shall apply, and in lieu of such computation periods there shall be applied a computation period consisting of the taxable year of substantial and material changes and the four taxable years immediately preceding such year. Thus, for example, if there are substantial and material changes in an organization's sources of support for taxable year 1976, then even though such organization meets the requirements of subparagraph (2) or (3) of this paragraph based on a computation period of taxable years 1971—1974 or 1972—1975, such an organization will not meet the requirements of section 170(b)(1)(A)(vi) unless it meets the requirements of subparagraph (2) or (3) of this paragraph for a computation period consisting of the taxable years 1972—1976. See Example (3) in § 1.509(a)-3(c)(6) for an illustration of a similar rule. An example of a substantial and material change is the receipt of an unusually large contribution or bequest which does not qualify as an unusual grant under subparagraph (6)(ii) of this paragraph. See subparagraph (6)(iv)(*b*) of this paragraph as to the procedure for obtaining a ruling whether an unusually large grant may be excluded as an unusual grant.

(*b*) *Status of grantors and contributors.* If as a result of (*a*) of this subdivision, an organization is not able to meet the requirements of either the 33⅓ percent-of-support test described in subparagraph (2) of this paragraph, or the facts and circumstances test described in subparagraph (3) of this paragraph for its current taxable year, its status (with respect to a grantor or contributor under sections 170, 507, 545(b)(2), 556(b)(2), 642(c), 4942, 4945, 2055, 2106(a)(2), and 2522) will not be affected until notice of change of status under section 170(b)(1)(A)(vi) is made to the public (such as by publication in the Internal Revenue Bulletin). The preceding sentence shall not apply, however, if the grantor or contributor was responsible for, or was aware of, the substantial and material change referred to in (*a*) of this subdivision, or acquired knowledge that the Internal Revenue Service had given notice to such

Reg. § 1.170A-9(e)(4)

organization that it would be deleted from classification as a section 170(b)(1)(A)(vi) organization.

(c) *Reliance by grantors and contributors.* A grantor or contributor (other than one of the organization's founders, creators, or foundation managers (within the meaning of section 4946(b))) will not be considered to be responsible for, or aware of, the substantial and material change referred to in *(a)* of this subdivision, if such grantor or contributor has made such grant or contribution in reliance upon a written statement by the grantee organization that such grant or contribution will not result in the loss of such organization's classification as a publicly supported organization as described in section 170(b)(1)(A)(vi). Such statement must be signed by a responsible officer of the grantee organization and must set forth sufficient information, including a summary of the pertinent financial data for the four preceding years, to assure a reasonably prudent man that his grant or contribution will not result in the loss of the grantee organization's classification as a publicly supported organization as described in section 170(b)(1)(A)(vi). If a reasonable doubt exists as to the effect of such grant or contribution, or if the grantor or contributor is one of the organizations' founders, creators, or foundation managers, the procedure set forth in subparagraph (6)(vi)(*b*) of this paragraph may be followed by the grantee organization for the protection of the grantor or contributor.

(vi) *Special rule for new organizations.* If an organization has been in existence for at least one taxable year consisting of at least 8 months, but for fewer than 5 taxable years, the number of years for which the organization has been in existence immediately preceding each current taxable year being tested will be substituted for the 4-year period described in subdivision (i) or (ii) of this subparagraph to determine whether the organization "normally" meets the requirements of subparagraph (2) or (3) of this paragraph. However, if subdivision (v) *(a)* of this subparagraph applies, then the period consisting of the number of years for which the organization has been in existence (up to and including the current year) will be substituted for the 4-year period described in subdivision (i) or (ii) of this subparagraph. An organization which has been in existence for at least one taxable year, consisting of 8 or more months, may be issued a ruling or determination letter if it "normally" meets the requirements of subparagraph (2) or (3) of this paragraph for the number of years described in this subdivision. Such an organization may apply for a ruling or determination letter under the provisions of this subparagraph, rather than under the provisions of

subparagraph (5) of this paragraph. The issuance of a ruling or determination letter will be discretionary with the Commissioner. See subparagraph (5)(v) of this paragraph as to the initial determination of the status of a newly created organization. This subdivision shall not apply to those organizations receiving an extended advance ruling under subparagraph (5)(iv) of this paragraph.

(vii) *Special rule for organizations with existing ruling.* This subdivision shall apply to an organization that prior to January 1, 1970, had received a ruling or determination letter which has not been expressly revoked holding the organization to be a publicly supported organization described in section 170(b)(1)(A)(vi) and with respect to which the facts and circumstances on which the ruling was based have not substantially changed. An organization to which this subdivision applies shall be treated as an organization described in section 170(b)(1)(A)(vi) for a period not ending prior to 90 days after December 29, 1972. In addition, with respect to a grantor or contributor under sections 170, 507, 545(b)(2), 556(b)(2), 642(c), 4942, 4945, 2055, 2106(a)(2), and 2522, the status of an organization to which this subdivision applies will not be affected until notice of change of status under section 170(b)(1)(A)(vi) is made to the public (such as by publication in the Internal Revenue Bulletin). The preceding sentence shall not apply if the grantor or contributor had previously acquired knowledge that the Internal Revenue Service had given notice to such organization that it would be deleted from classification as a section 170(b)(1)(A)(vi) organization.

(viii) *Termination of status.* For the transitional rules applicable to an organization that is unable to meet the requirements of this paragraph for its first taxable year beginning after December 31, 1969 (as extended by § 1.507-2(j)) and wishes to terminate its private foundation status, see § 1.507-2(c)(2) and (3).

(ix) *Status of ruling.* The provisions of this subparagraph do not require an organization to file a new application with the Internal Revenue Service every two years in order to maintain or reaffirm its status as a "publicly supported" organization described in section 170(b)(1)(A)(vi).

(5) *Advance rulings to newly created organizations* —(i) *In general.* A ruling or determination letter that an organization is described in section 170(b)(1)(A)(vi) will not be issued to a newly created organization prior to the close of its first taxable year consisting of at least 8 months. However, such organization may request a ruling or determination letter that it will be treated as a section 170(b)(1)(A)(vi) organization for its first 2

taxable years (or its first 3 taxable years, if its first taxable year consists of less than 8 months). For purposes of this section, such 2- or 3-year period, whichever is applicable, shall be referred to as the advance ruling period. Such an advance ruling or determination letter may be issued if the organization can reasonably be expected to meet the requirements of subparagraph (2) or (3) of this paragraph during the advance ruling period. The issuance of a ruling or determination letter will be discretionary with the Commissioner.

(ii) *Basic consideration.* In determining whether an organization can reasonably be expected (within the meaning of subdivision (i) of this subparagraph) to meet the requirements of subparagraph (2) or (3) of this paragraph for its advance ruling period or extended advance ruling period as provided in subdivision (iv) of this subparagraph, if applicable, the basic consideration is whether its organizational structure, proposed programs or activities, and intended method of operation are such as to attract the type of broadly based support from the general public, public charities, and governmental units which is necessary to meet such tests. The information to be considered for this purpose shall consist of all pertinent facts and circumstances relating to the requirements set forth in subparagraph (3) of this paragraph.

(iii) *Status of newly created organizations—(a) Advance ruling.* This subdivision shall apply to a newly created organization which has received an advance ruling or determination letter under subdivision (i) of this subparagraph, or an extended advance ruling or determination letter under subdivision (iv) of this subparagraph, that it will be treated as a section 170(b)(1)(A)(vi) organization for its advance or extended advance ruling period. So long as such an organization's ruling or determination letter has not been terminated by the Commissioner before the expiration of the advance or extended advance ruling period, then whether or not such organization has satisfied the requirements of subparagraph (2) or (3) of this paragraph during such advance or extended advance ruling period, such an organization will be treated as an organization described in section 170(b)(1)(A)(vi) in accordance with (b) and (c) of this subdivision, both for purposes of the organization and any grantor or contributor to such organization.

(b) *Reliance period.* Except as provided in (a) and (c) of this subdivision, an organization described in (a) of this subdivision will be treated as an organization described in section 170(b)(1)(A)(vi) for all purposes other than sections 507(d) and 4940 for the period beginning

with its inception and ending 90 days after its advance or extended advance ruling period. Such period will be extended until a final determination is made of such an organization's status only if the organization submits, within the 90-day period, information needed to determine whether it meets the requirements of subparagraph (2) or (3) of this paragraph for its advance or extended advance ruling period (even if such organization fails to meet the requirements of such subparagraph (2) or (3)). However, since this subparagraph does not apply to the tax imposed by section 4940, if it is subsequently determined that the organization was a private foundation from its inception, then the tax imposed by section 4940 shall be due without regard to the advance or extended advance ruling or determination letter. Consequently, if any amount of tax under section 4940 in such a case is not paid on or before the last date prescribed for payment, the organization is liable for interest in accordance with section 6601. However, since any failure to pay such tax during the period referred to in this subparagraph is due to reasonable cause, the penalty under section 6651 with respect to the tax imposed by section 4940 shall not apply.

(c) *Grantors or contributors.* If a ruling or determination letter is terminated by the Commissioner prior to the expiration of the period described in (b) of this subdivision, for purposes of sections 170, 507, 545(b)(2), 556(b)(2), 642(c), 4942, 4945, 2055, 2106(a)(2), and 2522, the status of grants or contributions with respect to grantors or contributors to such organizations will not be affected until notice of change of status of such organization is made to the public (such as by publication of the Internal Revenue Bulletin). The preceding sentence shall not apply, however, if the grantor or contributor was responsible for, or aware of, the act or failure to act that resulted in the organization's loss of classification under section 170(b)(1)(A)(vi) or acquired knowledge that the Internal Revenue Service had given notice to such organization that it would be deleted from such classification. Prior to the making of any grant or contribution which allegedly will not result in the grantee's loss of classification under section 170(b)(1)(A)(vi), a potential grantee organization may request a ruling whether such grant or contribution may be made without such loss of classification. A request for such ruling may be filed by the grantee organization with the district director. The issuance of such ruling will be at the sole discretion of the Commissioner. The organization must submit all information necessary to make a determination on the factors referred to in subparagraph (6)(iii) of this paragraph. If a favorable ruling is issued, such

Reg. § 1.170A-9(e)(5)

ruling may be relied upon by the grantor or contributor of the particular contribution in question for purposes of sections 170, 507, 545(b)(2), 556(b)(2), 642(c), 4942, 4945, 2055, 2106(a)(2), and 2522 and by the grantee organization for purposes of subparagraph (6)(ii) of this paragraph.

(iv) *Extension of advance ruling period.* (a) The advance ruling period described in subdivision (i) of this subparagraph shall be extended for a period of three taxable years after the close of the unextended advance ruling period if the organization so requests, but only if such organization's request accompanies its request for an advance ruling and is filed with a consent under section 6501(c)(4) to the effect that the period of limitation upon assessment under section 4940 for any taxable year within the extended advance ruling period shall not expire prior to one year after the date of the expiration of the time prescribed by law for the assessment of a deficiency for the last taxable year within the extended advance ruling period. An organization's extended advance ruling period is 5 taxable years if its first taxable year consists of at least 8 months, or is 6 years if its first taxable year is less than 8 months.

(b) Notwithstanding (a) of this subdivision, an organization which has received or applied for an advance ruling prior to January 29, 1973, may file its request for the 3-year extension within 90 days from such date, but only if it files the consents required in this section.

(c) See subdivision (v) of this subparagraph for the effect upon the initial determination of status of an organization which receives a ruling for an extended advance ruling period.

(v) *Initial determination of status.* (a) The initial determination of status of a newly created organization is the first determination (other than by issuance of an advance ruling or determination letter under subdivision (i) of this subparagraph or an extended advance ruling or determination letter under subdivision (iv) of this subparagraph) that the organization will be considered as "normally" meeting the requirements of subparagraph (2) or (3) of this paragraph for a period beginning with its first taxable year.

(b) In the case of a new organization whose first taxable year is at least eight months, except as provided for in subdivision (v)(d) of this subparagraph, the initial determination of status shall be based on a computation period of either the first taxable year or the first and second taxable years.

(c) In the case of a new organization whose first taxable year is less than eight taxable months, except as provided for in subdivision

(v)(d) of this subparagraph, the initial determination of status shall be based on a computation period of either the first and second taxable years or the first, second and third taxable years.

(d) In the case of an organization which has received a ruling or determination letter for an extended advance ruling period under subdivision (iv) of this subparagraph, the initial determination of status shall be based on a computation period of all of the taxable years in the extended advance ruling period. However, where the ruling or determination letter for an extended advance ruling period under subdivision (iv) of this subparagraph is terminated by the Commissioner prior to the expiration of the relevant period described in subdivision (iii)(b) of this subparagraph, the initial determination of status shall be based on a computation period of the period provided in (b) or (c) of this subdivision or, if greater, the number of years to which the advance ruling applies.

(e) An initial determination that an organization will be considered as "normally" meeting the requirements of subparagraph (2) or (3) of this paragraph shall be effective for each taxable year in the computation period plus (except as provided by subparagraph (4)(v)(a) of this paragraph, relating to material changes in sources of support) the two taxable years immediately succeeding the computation period. Therefore, in the case of an organization referred to in (b) of this subdivision to which subparagraph (4)(v)(a) of this paragraph does not apply, with respect to its first, second and third taxable years, such an organization shall be described in section 170(b)(1)(A)(vi) if it meets the requirements of subparagraph (2) or (3) of this paragraph for either its first taxable year or for its first and second taxable years on an aggregate basis. In addition, if it meets the requirements of subparagraph (2) or (3) of this paragraph for its first and second taxable years, it shall be described in section 170(b)(1)(A)(vi) for its fourth taxable year. Once an organization is considered as "normally" meeting the requirements of subparagraph (2) or (3) of this paragraph for a period specified under this subdivision, subparagraph (4)(i), (ii), (v) or (vi) of this paragraph shall apply.

(f) The provisions of this subdivision may be illustrated by the following examples:

Example (1). X, a calendar year organization described in section 501(c)(3), is created in February 1972. The support received from the public in 1972 by X will satisfy the one-third support test described in subparagraph (4)(i) of this paragraph over its first taxable year, 1972. X may therefore get an initial determination that it

Reg. § 1.170A-9(e)(5)

meets the requirements of subparagraph (2) of this paragraph for its first taxable year beginning in February 1972 and ending on December 31, 1972. This determination will be effective for taxable years 1972, 1973 and 1974.

Example (2). Assume the same facts as in example (1) except that X also receives a substantial contribution from one individual in 1972 which is not excluded from the denominator of the one-third support fraction described in subparagraph (4)(i) of this paragraph by reason of the unusual grant provision of subparagraph (6)(ii) of this paragraph. Because of this substantial contribution, X fails to satisfy the one-third support test over its first taxable year, 1972. X also fails to satisfy the "facts and circumstances" test described in subparagraph (4)(ii) of this paragraph for its first taxable year, 1972. However, the support received from the public over X's first and second taxable years in the aggregate will satisfy the one-third support test. X may therefore get an initial determination that it meets the requirements of subparagraph (2) of this paragraph for its first and second taxable years in the aggregate beginning in Febuary 1972 and ending on December 31, 1973. This determination will be effective for taxable years 1972, 1973, 1974 and 1975.

Example (3). Y, a calendar year organization described in section 501(c)(3), is created in July 1972. Y requests and receives an extended advance ruling period of five full taxable years plus its initial short taxable year of six months under subparagraph (5)(iv) of this paragraph. The extended advance ruling period begins in July 1972 and ends on December 31, 1977. The support received from the public over Y's first through sixth taxable years in the aggregate will satisfy the one-third support test described in subparagraph (4)(i) of this paragraph. Therefore, Y in 1978 may get an initial determination that it meets the requirements of subparagraph (2) of this paragraph in the aggregate over all the taxable years in its extended advance ruling period beginning in July 1972 and ending on December 31, 1977. This determination will be effective for taxable years 1972 through 1979.

Example (4). Assume the same facts as in example (3) except that the ruling for the extended advance ruling period is terminated prospectively at the end of 1975, so that Y may not rely upon such ruling for 1976 or any succeeding year. The support received from the public over Y's first through fourth taxable years (1972 through 1975) will not satisfy either the one-third support test described in subparagraph (4)(i) of this paragraph, or the "facts and circumstances" test described in subparagraph (4)(ii) of this para-

graph. Because the ruling was terminated, the computation period for Y's initial determination of status is the period 1972 through 1975. Since Y has not met the requirements of either subparagraph (2) or (3) of this paragraph for such computation period, Y is not described in section 170(b)(1)(A)(vi) for purposes of its initial determination of status. If Y is not described in section 170(b)(1)(A)(i) through (v) or section 509(a)(2), (3), or (4), then Y is a private foundation. As of 1976, Y shall be treated as a private foundation for all purposes (except as provided in subdivision (iii)(c) of this subparagraph with respect to grantors and contributors), and as of July 1972 for purposes of the tax imposed by section 4940 and for purposes of section 507(d) (relating to aggregate tax benefit).

(vi) *Failure to obtain advance ruling. (a)* Unless a newly created organization has obtained an advance ruling or determination letter under subdivision (i) of this subparagraph, or an extended advance ruling or determination letter under subdivision (iv) of this subparagraph, that it will be treated as a section 170(b)(1)(A)(vi) organization for its advance or extended advance ruling period, it cannot rely upon the possibility it will meet the requirements of subparagraph (2) or (3) of this paragraph for a taxable year which begins before the close of either applicable computation period provided for in subdivision (v)(b) or (c) of this subparagraph. Therefore, such an organization, in order to avoid the risk of subsequently being determined to be a private foundation because of failure to qualify under section 170(b)(1)(A)(vi) and therefore under section 509(a)(1), may comply with the rules applicable to private foundations and may pay, for example, the tax imposed by section 4940. In that event, if the organization subsequently meets the requirements of subparagraph (2) or (3) of this paragraph for either applicable computation period, it shall be treated as a section 170(b)(1)(A)(vi) organization from its inception and, therefore, any tax imposed under chapter 42 shall be refunded and section 509(b) shall not apply.

(b) if a newly created organization fails to obtain an advance ruling or determination letter under subdivision (i) of this subparagraph, or an extended advance ruling or determination letter under subdivision (iv) of this subparagraph, and fails to meet the requirements of subparagraph (2) or (3) of this paragraph for the first applicable computation period provided for in subdivision (v)(b) or (c) of this subparagraph, see section 6651 for penalty for failure to file return and pay tax.

Reg. § 1.170A-9(e)(5)

(6) *Definition of support; meaning of general public* —(i) *In general.* In determining whether the 33⅓ percent-of-support test described in subparagraph (2) of this paragraph or the 10 percent-of-support limitation described in subparagraph (3)(i) of this paragraph is "normally" met, contributions by an individual, trust, or corporation shall be taken into account as "support" from direct or indirect contributions from the general public only to the extent that the total amount of the contributions by any such individual, trust, or corporation during the period described in subparagraph (4)(i), (ii), (v) or (vi) or (5)(v) of this paragraph does not exceed 2 percent of the organization's total support for such period, except as provided in subdivision (ii) of this subparagraph. Therefore, any contribution by one individual will be included in full in the denominator of the fraction determining the 33⅓ percent-of-support or the 10 percent-of-support limitation, but will only be includible in the numerator of such fraction to the extent that such amount does not exceed 2 percent of the denominator. In applying the 2 percent limitation, all contributions made by a donor and by any person or persons standing in a relationship to the donor which is described in section 4946(a)(1)(C) through (G) and the regulations thereunder shall be treated as made by one person. The 2 percent limitation shall not apply to support received from governmental units referred to in section 170(c)(1) or to contributions from organizations described in section 170(b)(1)(A)(vi), except as provided in subdivision (v) of this subparagraph. For purposes of subparagraphs (2), (3)(i) and (7)(ii)(*b*) of this paragraph, the term "indirect contributions from the general public" includes contributions received by the organization from organizations (such as section 170(b)(1)(A)(vi) organizations) which normally receive a substantial part of their support from direct contributions from the general public, except as provided in subdivision (v) of this subparagraph. See the examples in subparagraph (9) of this paragraph for the application of this subdivision. For purposes of this paragraph (e), the term *contributions* includes qualified sponsorship payments (as defined in § 1.513-4) in the form of money or property (but not services).

(ii) *Exclusion of unusual grants.* For purposes of applying the 2 percent limitation described in subdivision (i) of this subparagraph to determine whether the 33⅓ percent-of-support test in subparagraph (2) of this paragraph or the 10 percent-of-support limitation in subparagraph (3)(i) of this paragraph is satisfied, one or more contributions may be excluded from both the numerator and the denominator of the applicable percent-of-support fraction if such contributions

meet the requirements of subdivision (iii) of this subparagraph. The exclusion provided by this subdivision is generally intended to apply to substantial contributions or bequests from disinterested parties which contributions or bequests:

(*a*) Are attracted by reason of the publicly supported nature of the organization;

(*b*) Are unusual or unexpected with respect to the amount thereof; and

(*c*) Would, by reason of their size, adversely affect the status of the organization as normally being publicly supported for the applicable period described in subparagraph (4) or (5) of this paragraph. In the case of a grant (as defined in § 1.509(a)-3(g)) which meets the requirements of this subdivision, if the terms of the granting instrument (whether executed before or after 1969) require that the funds be paid to the recipient organization over a period of years, the amount received by the organization each year pursuant to the terms of such grant may be excluded for such year. However, no item of gross investment income may be excluded under this subparagraph. The provisions of this subparagraph shall apply to exclude unusual grants made during any of the applicable periods described in subparagraph (4), (5), or (6) of this paragraph. See subdivision (iv) of this subparagraph as to reliance by a grantee organization upon an unusual grant ruling under this subparagraph.

(iii) *Determining factors.* In determining whether a particular contribution may be excluded under subdivision (ii) of this subparagraph all pertinent facts and circumstances will be taken into consideration. No single factor will necessarily be determinative. For some of the factors similar to the factors to be considered, see § 1.509(a)-3(c)(4).

(iv) *Grantors and contributors.* (a) As to the status of grants and contributions which result in substantial and material changes in the organization (as described in subparagraph (4)(v)(*a*) of this paragraph) and which fail to meet the requirements for exclusion under subdivision (ii) of this subparagraph, see the rules prescribed in subparagraph (4)(v)(*b*) and (c) of this paragraph.

(*b*) Prior to the making of any grant or contribution which will allegedly meet the requirements for exclusion under subdivision (ii) of this subparagraph, a potential grantee organization may request a ruling whether such grant or contribution may be so excluded. Requests for such ruling may be filed by the grantee organization with the district director. The issuance of such ruling will be at the sole discretion of the Commissioner. The organization must submit all

Reg. § 1.170A-9(e)(6)

information necessary to make a determination on the factors referred to in subdivision (iii) of this subparagraph. If a favorable ruling is issued, such ruling may be relied upon by the grantor or contributor of the particular contribution in question for purposes of sections 170, 507, 545(b)(2), 556(b)(2), 642(c), 4942, 4945, 2055, 2106(a)(2), and 2522 and by the grantee organization for purposes of subdivision (ii) of this subparagraph.

(v) *Grants from public charities.* Pursuant to subdivision (i) of this subparagraph, contributions received from a governmental unit or from a section 170(b)(1)(A)(vi) organization are not subject to the 2 percent limitation described in that subdivision unless such contributions represent amounts which have been expressly or impliedly earmarked by a donor to such governmental unit or section 170(b)(1)(A)(vi) organization as being for, or for the benefit of, the particular organization claiming section 170(b)(1)(A)(vi) status. See § 1.509(a)-3(j)(3) for examples illustrating the rules of this subdivision.

(7) *Definition of support; special rules and meaning of terms* —(i) *Definition of support.* For purposes of this paragraph, the term "support" shall be as defined in section 509(d) (without regard to section 509(d)(2)). The term "support" does not include:

(a) Any amounts received from the exercise or performance by an organization of its charitable, educational, or other purpose or function constituting the basis for its exemption under section 501(a). In general, such amounts include amounts received from any activity the conduct of which is substantially related to the furtherance of such purpose or function (other than through the production of income), or

(b) Contributions of services for which a deduction is not allowable.

For purposes of the 33⅓ percent-of-support test in subparagraph (2) of this paragraph and the 10 percent-of-support limitation in subparagraph (3)(i) of this paragraph, all amounts received which are described in (a) or (b) of this division are to be excluded from both the numerator and the denominator of the fractions determining compliance with such tests, except as provided in subdivision (ii) of this subparagraph.

(ii) *Organizations dependent primarily on gross receipts from related activities.* Notwithstanding the provisions of subdivision (i) of this subparagraph, an organization will not be treated as satisfying the 33⅓ percent-of-support test in subparagraph (3)(i) of this paragraph or the 10 percent-of-support limitation in subparagraph (3)(i) of this paragraph if it receives:

(a) Almost all of its support (as defined in section 509(d)) from gross receipts from related activities; and

(b) An insignificant amount of its support from governmental units (without regard to amounts referred to in subdivision (i)(a) of this subparagraph) and contributions made directly or indirectly by the general public.

For example, X, an organization described in section 501(c)(3), is controlled by A, its president. X received $500,000 during the four taxable years immediately preceding its current taxable year under a contract with the Department of Transportation, pursuant to which X has engaged in research to improve a particular vehicle used primarily by the Federal Government. During this same period, the only other support received by X consisted of $5,000 in small contributions primarily from X's employees and business associates. The $500,000 amount constitutes support under section 509(d)(2) and 502(d)(2)(a) of this subdivision. Under these circumstances, X meets the conditions of (a) and (b) of this subdivision and will not be treated as meeting the requirements of either subparagraph (2) or subparagraph (3) of this paragraph. As to the rules applicable to organizations which fail to qualify under section 170(b)(1)(A)(vi) because of the provisions of this subdivison, see section 509(a)(2) and the regulations thereunder. For the distinction between gross receipts (as referred to in section 509(d)(2)) and gross investment income (as referred to in section 509(d)(4)), see § 1.509(a)-3(m).

(iii) *Membership fees.* For purposes of this subparagraph, the term "support" shall include "membership fees" within the meaning of § 1.509(a)-3(h) (that is, if the basic purpose for making a payment is to provide support for the organization rather than to purchase admissions, merchandise, services, or the use of facilities).

(8) *Support from a governmental unit.* (i) For purposes of subparagraphs (2) and (3)(i) of this paragraph, the term "support from a governmental unit" includes any amounts received from a governmental unit, including donations or contributions and amounts received in connection with a contract entered into with a Governmental unit for the performance of services or in connection with a government research grant. However, such amounts will not constitute "support from a governmental unit" for such purposes if they constitute amounts received from the exercise or performance of the organization's exempt functions as provided in subparagraph (7)(i)(a) of this paragraph.

Reg. § 1.170A-9(e)(8)

(ii) For purposes of subdivision (i) of this subparagraph, any amount paid by a governmental unit to an organization is not to be treated as received from the exercise or performance of its charitable, educational, or other purpose or function constituting the basis for its exemption under section 501(a) (within the meaning of subparagraph (7)(i)(*a*) of this paragraph) if the purpose of the payment is primarily to enable the organization to provide a service to, or maintain a facility for, the direct benefit of the public (regardless of whether part of the expense of providing such service or facility is paid for by the public), rather than to serve the direct and immediate needs of the payor. For example:

(*a*) Amounts paid for the maintenance of library facilities which are open to the public,

(*b*) Amounts paid under Government programs to nursing homes or homes for the aged in order to provide health care or domiciliary services to residents of such facilities, and

(*c*) Amounts paid to child placement or child guidance organizations under Government programs for services rendered to children in the community,

are considered payments the purpose of which is primarily to enable the recipient organization to provide a service or maintain a facility for the direct benefit of the public, rather than to serve the direct and immediate needs of the payor. Furthermore, any amount received from a governmental unit under circumstances such that the amount would be treated as a "grant" within the meaning of § 1.509(1)-3(g) will generally constitute "support from a governmental unit" described in this subdivision, rather than an amount described in subparagraph (7)(i)(*a*) of this paragraph.

(9) *Examples.* The application of subparagraphs (1) through (8) of this paragraph may be illustrated by the following examples:

Example (1). (a) M is an organization referred to in section 170(c)(2). For the years 1970 through 1973 (the applicable period with respect to the taxable year 1974 under subparagraph (4) of this paragraph), M received support (as defined in subparagraphs (6) through (8) of this paragraph) of $600,000 from the following sources:

Investment Income	$300,000
City Y (a governmental unit referred to in section 170(c)(1))	$ 40,000
United Fund (an organization referred to in section 170(b)(1)(A)(vi))	$ 40,000
Contributions	$220,000
Total Support	$600,000

(*b*) With respect to the taxable year 1974, M "normally" received in excess of 33⅓ percent of its support from a governmental unit referred to in section 170(c)(1) and from direct and indirect contributions from the general public (as defined in subparagraph (6) of this paragraph) computed as follows:

33⅓ percent of total support	$200,000
Support from a governmental unit referred to in section 170(c)(1)....	$ 40,000
Indirect contributions from the general public (United Fund)	$ 40,000
Contributions by various donors (no one having made contributions which total in excess of $12,000—2 percent of total support)	$ 50,000
Six contributions (each in excess of $12,000—2 percent total support) 6 × $12,000	$ 72,000
	$202,000

(*c*) Since the amount of X's support from governmental units referred to in section 170(c)(1) and from direct and indirect contributions from the general public with respect to the taxable year 1974 "normally" exceeds 33⅓ percent of M's total support for the applicable period (1970-1973), X meets the 33⅓ percent-of-support test under subparagraph (2) of this paragraph and is therefore treated as satisfying the requirments for classification as a "publicly supported" organization under subparagraph (2) of this paragraph for the taxable years 1974 and 1975 (there being no substantial and material changes in the organization's character, purposes, methods of operation, or sources of support in these years).

Example (2). N is an organization referred to in section 170(c)(2). It was created to maintain public gardens containing botanical specimens and displaying statuary and other art objects. The facilities, works of art, and a large endowment were all contributed by a single contributor. The members of the governing body of the organization are unrelated to its creator. The gardens are open to the public without charge and attract a substantial number of visitors each year. For the four taxable years immediately preceding the current taxable year, 95 percent of the organization's total support was received from investment income from its original endowment. N also maintains a membership society which is supported by members of the general public who wish to contribute to the upkeep of the gardens by paying a small annual membership fee. Over the four-year period in question, these fees from the general public constituted the remaining 5 percent of the organization's total support for such period. Under these circumstances, N does not meet the 33⅓ percent-of-support test under subparagraph

Reg. § 1.170A-9(e)(9)

(2) of this paragraph for its current taxable year. Furthermore, since only 5 percent of its total support is, with respect to the current taxable year, normally received from the general public, N does not satisfy the 10 percent-of-support limitation described in subparagraph (3)(i) of this paragraph and cannot therefore be classified as "publicly supported" under subparagraph (3) of this paragraph. For its current taxable year, N therefore, is not an organization described in section 170(b)(1)(A)(vi). Since N has failed to satisfy the 10 percent-of-support limitation under subparagraph (3)(i) of this paragraph, none of the other requirements or factors set forth in subparagraph (3)(iii) through (vii) of this paragraph can be considered in determining whether N qualifies as a "publicly supported" organization.

Example (3). (a) O, an art museum, is an organization referred to in section 170(c)(2). In 1930, O was founded in Y City by the members of a single family to collect, preserve, interpret, and display to the public important works of art. O is governed by a Board of Trustees which originally consisted almost entirely of members of the founding family. However, since 1945, members of the founding family or persons standing in a relationship to the members of such family described in section 4946(a)(1)(C) through (G) have annually constituted less than one-fifth of the Board of Trustees. The remaining board members are citizens of Y City from a variety of professions and occupations who represent the interests and views of the people of Y City in the activities carried on by the organization rather than the personal or private interests of the founding family. O solicits contributions from the general public and for each of its four most recent taxable years has received total contributions (in small sums of less than $100, none of which exceeds 2 percent of O's total support for such period) in excess of $10,000. These contributions from the general public (as defined in subparagraph (6) of this paragraph) represent 25 percent of the organization's total support for such four-year period. For this same period, investment income from several large endowment funds has constituted 75 percent of its total support. O expends substantially all of its annual income for its exempt purposes and thus depends upon the funds it annually solicits from the public as well as its investment income in order to carry out its activities on a normal and continuing basis and to acquire new works of art. O has, for the entire period of its existence, been open to the public and more than 300,000 people (from Y City and elsewhere) have visited the museum in each of its four most recent taxable years.

(b) Under these circumstances, O does not meet the 33⅓ percent-of-support test under subparagraph (2) of this paragraph for its current taxable year since it has received only 25 percent of its total support for the applicable four-year period from the general public. However, under the facts set forth above, O has met the 10 percent-of-support limitation under subparagraph (3)(i), as well as the requirements of subparagraph (3)(ii), of this paragraph. Under all of the facts set forth in this example, O is considered as meeting the requirements of subparagraph (3) of this paragraph on the basis of satisfying subparagraph (3)(i) and (ii) of this paragraph and the factors set forth in subparagraph (3)(iii), (iv), (v) and (vi) of this paragraph, and is therefore classified as a "publicly supported organization" under subparagraph (1) of this paragraph for its current taxable year and the immediately succeeding taxable year (there being no substantial and material changes in the organization's character, purposes, methods of operation, or sources of support in these years).

Example (4). (a) In 1960, the P Philharmonic Orchestra was organized in Z City through the combined efforts of a local music society and a local women's club to present to the public a wide variety of musical programs intended to foster music appreciation in the community. P is an organization referred to in section 170(c)(2). The orchestra is composed of professional musicians who are paid by the association. Twelve performances open to the public are scheduled each year. A small admission charge is made for each of these performances. In addition, several performances are staged annually without charge. During its four most recent taxable years, P has received separate contributions of $200,000 each from A and B (not members of a single family) and support of $120,000 from the Z Community Chest, a public federated fund-raising organization operating in Z City. P depends on these funds in order to carry out its activities and will continue to depend on contributions of this type to be made in the future. P has also begun a fund-raising campaign in an attempt to expand its activities for the coming years. P is governed by a Board of Directors comprised of five individuals. A faculty member of a local college, the president of a local music society, the head of a local banking institution, a prominent doctor, and a member of the governing body of the local Chamber of Commerce currently serve on the Board and represent the interests and views of the community in the activities carried on by P.

(b) With respect to P's current taxable year, P's sources of support are computed on the basis of the four immediately preceding years, as follows:

Reg. § 1.170A-9(e)(9)

Contributions	$520,000
Receipts from performances . .	100,000
Total support	$620,000

Less:

Receipts from performances (excluded under subparagraph (7)(i)(a) of this paragraph)	$100,000
Total support for purposes of subparagraphs (2) and (3)(i) of this paragraph	$520,000

(c) For purposes of subparagraphs (2) and (3)(i) of this paragraph, P's support is computed as follows:

Z Community Chest (indirect support from the general public) . .	$120,000
Two contributions (each in excess of $10,400—2 percent of total support) 2 × $10,400	20,800
Total	$140,800

(d) P's support from the general public, directly and indirectly, does not meet the 33⅓ percent-of-support test under subparagraph (2) of this paragraph ($140,800/$520,000 = 27 percent of total support). However, since P receives 27 percent of its total support from the general public, it meets the 10 percent-of-support limitation under subparagraph (3)(i) of this paragraph. P also meets the requirements of subparagraph (3)(ii) of this paragraph. As a result of satisfying these requirements and the factors set forth in subparagraph (3)(iii), (iv), (v) and (vi) of this paragraph, P is considered as meeting the requirements of subparagraph (3) of this paragraph and is therefore considered to be a "publicly supported" organization under subparagraph (1) of this paragraph.

(e) If, instead of the above facts, P were a newly created organization, P could obtain a ruling pursuant to subparagraph (5) of this paragraph by reason of its purposes, organizational structure and proposed method of operation. Even if P had initially been founded by the contributions of a few individuals, such fact would not, in and of itself, disqualify P from receiving a ruling under subparagraph (5) of this paragraph.

Example (5). (a) Q is an organization referred to in section 170(c)(2). It is a philanthropic organization founded in 1965 by A for the purpose of making annual contributions to worthy charities. A created Q as a charitable trust by the transfer of $500,000 worth of appreciated securities to Q.

Pursuant to the trust agreement, A and two other members of his family are the sole trustees and are vested with the right to appoint successor trustees. In each of its four most recent taxable years, Q received $15,000 in investment income from its original endowment. Each year Q makes a solicitation for funds by operating a charity ball at A's residence. Guests are invited and requested to make contributions of $100 per couple. During the four-year period involved, $15,000 was received from the proceeds of these events. A and his family have also made contributions to Q of $25,000 over the course of the organization's four most recent taxable years. Q makes disbursements each year of substantially all of its net income to the public charities chosen by the trustees.

(b) With respect to Q's current taxable year, Q's sources of support are computed on the basis of the four immediately preceding years as follows:

Investment income	$ 60,000
Contributions	$ 40,000
Total Support	$100,000

(c) For purposes of subparagraphs (2) and (3)(i) of this paragraph, Q's support is computed as follows:

Contributions from the general public	$ 15,000
One contribution (in excess of $2,000—2 percent of total support) 1 × $2,000	$ 2,000
Total	$ 17,000

(d) Q's support from the general public does not meet the 33⅓ percent-of-support test under subparagraph (2) of this paragraph ($17,000/$100,000 = 17 percent of total support). Thus, Q's classification as a "publicly supported" organization depends on whether it meets the requirements of subparagraph (3) of this paragraph. Even though it satisfies the 10 percent-of-support limitation under subparagraph (3)(i) of this paragraph, its method of solicitation makes it questionable whether Q satisfies the requirements of subparagraph (3)(ii) of this paragraph. Because of its method of operating, Q also has a greater burden of establishing its publicly supported nature under subparagraph (3)(iii) of this paragraph. Based upon the foregoing and upon Q's failure to receive favorable consideration under the factors set forth in subparagraph (3)(iv), (v) and (vi) of this paragraph, Q does not satisfy the requirements of subparagraph (3) of this paragraph as a "publicly supported" organization.

(e) If, instead of the above facts, Q were a newly created organization, Q would not be able to receive a ruling pursuant to subparagraph (5) of this paragraph. Its purposes, organizational structure, and method of operation would be insufficient to establish that Q could reasonably be expected to meet the requirements of subpara-

Reg. § 1.170A-9(e)(9)

graph (2) or (3) of this paragraph for its first two or its first five taxable years.

(10) *Community trust; introduction.* Community trusts have often been established to attract large contributions of a capital or endowment nature for the benefit of a particular community or area, and often such contributions have come initially from a small number of donors. While the community trust generally has a governing body comprised of representatives of the particular community or area, its contributions are often received and maintained in the form of separate trusts or funds, which are subject to varying degrees of control by the governing body. To qualify as a "publicly supported" organization, a community trust must meet the 33⅓ percent-of-support test of paragraph (e)(2) of this section, or, if it cannot meet that test, be organized and operated so as to attract new and additional public or governmental support on a continuous basis sufficient to meet the facts and circumstances test of paragraph (e)(3) of this section. Such facts and circumstances test includes a requirement of attraction of public support in paragraph (e)(3)(ii) of this section which, as applied to community trusts, will generally be satisfied if they seek gifts and bequests from a wide range of potential donors in the community or area served, through banks or trust companies, through attorneys or other professional persons, or in other appropriate ways which call attention to the community trust as a potential recipient of gifts and bequests made for the benefit of the community or area served. A community trust is not required to engage in periodic, community-wide, fund-raising campaigns directed toward attracting a large number of small contributions in a manner similar to campaigns conducted by a community chest or united fund. Paragraph (e)(12) and (13) of this section provide[s] a transitional ruling period for certain community trusts in existence before November 11, 1976 that had irregular public support, so that they can meet the requirements of paragraph (e)(2) or (3) of this section based on the 4-year computation period described in paragraph (e)(4) of this section. Paragraph (e)(11) of this section provides rules for determining the extent to which separate trusts or funds may be treated as component parts of a community trust, fund or foundation (herein collectively referred to as a "community trust", and sometimes referred to as an "organization") for purposes of meeting the requirements of this paragraph for classification as a "publicly supported" organization. Paragraph (e)(14) of this section contains rules for trusts or funds which are prevented from qualifying as component parts of a community trust by paragraph (e)(11) of this section.

(11) *Community trusts; requirements for treatment as a single entity*—(*i*) *General rule.* For purposes of sections 170, 501, 507, 508, 509, and chapter 42, any organization that meets the requirements contained in paragraph (e)(11)(iii) through (vi) of this section will be treated as a single entity, rather than as an aggregation of separate funds, and except as otherwise provided, all funds associated with such organization (whether a trust, not-for-profit corporation, unincorporated association, or a combination thereof) which meet the requirements of paragraph (e)(11)(ii) of this section will be treated as component parts of such organization.

(ii) *Component part of a community trust.* In order to be treated as a component part of a community trust referred to in paragraph (e)(11) of this section (rather than as a separate trust or not-for-profit corporation or association) a trust or fund:

(A) Must be created by a gift, bequest, legacy, devise, or other transfer to a community trust which is treated as a single entity under paragraph (e)(11) of this section; and

(B) May not be directly subjected by the transferor to any material restriction or condition (within the meaning of § 1.507-2(a)(8)) with respect to the transferred assets.

For the purposes of paragraph (e)(11)(ii)(B) of this section, if the transferor is not a private foundation, the provisions of § 1.507-2(a)(8) shall be applied to the trust or fund as if the transferor were a private foundation established and funded by the person establishing the trust or fund and such foundation transferred all its assets to the trust or fund. Any transfer made to a fund or trust which is treated as a component part of a community trust under paragraph (e)(11)(ii) of this section will be treated as a transfer made "to" a "publicly supported" community trust for purposes of section 170(b)(1)(A) and 507(b)(1)(A) if such community trust meets the requirements of section 170 (b)(1)(A)(vi) as a "publicly supported" organization at the time of the transfer, except as provided in § 1.170A-9(e)(4)(v)(*b*) or § 1.508-1(b)(4) and (6) relating, generally, to reliance by grantors and contributors. See, also, paragraph (e)(14)(ii) and (iii) of this section for special provisions relating to split-interest trusts and certain private foundations described in section 170 (b)(1)(E)(iii).

(iii) *Name.* The organization must be commonly known as a community trust, fund, foundation or other similar name conveying the concept of a capital or endowment fund to support chari-

Reg. § 1.170A-9(e)(11)

table activities (within the meaning of section 170(c)(1) or (2)(B)) in the community or area it serves.

(iv) *Common instrument.* All funds of the organization must be subject to a common governing instrument or a master trust or agency agreement (herein referred to as the "governing instrument"), which may be embodied in a single document or several documents containing common language. Language in an instrument of transfer to the community trust making a fund subject to the community trust's governing instrument or master trust or agency agreement will satisfy the requirements of paragraph (e)(11)(iv) of this section. In addition, if a community trust adopts a new governing instrument (or creates a corporation) to put into effect new provisions (applying to future transfers to the community trust), the adoption of such new governing instrument (or creation of a corporation with a governing instrument) which contains common language with the existing governing instrument shall not preclude the community trust from meeting the requirements of such paragraph (e)(11)(iv).

(v) *Common governing body.* (A) *In general.* The organization must have a common governing body or distribution committee (herein referred to as the "governing body") which either directs or, in the case of a fund designated for specified beneficiaries, monitors the distribution of all of the funds exclusively for charitable purposes (within the meaning of section 170(c)(1) or (2)(B)).

For purposes of this (v) a fund is designated for specified beneficiaries only if no person is left with the discretion to direct the distribution of the fund.

(B) *Powers of modification and removal.* Except as provided in paragraph (e)(11)(v)(C) of this section, the governing body must have the power in the governing instrument, the instrument of transfer, the resolutions or by-laws of the governing body, a written agreement, or otherwise—

(1) To modify any restriction or condition on the distribution of funds for any specified charitable purposes or to specified organizations if in the sole judgment of the governing body (without the necessity of the approval of any participating trustee, custodian, or agent), such restriction or condition becomes, in effect, unnecessary, incapable of fulfillment, or inconsistent with the charitable needs of the community or area served;

(2) To replace any participating trustee, custodian, or agent for breach of fiduciary duty under State law; and

(3) To replace any participating trustee, custodian, or agent for failure to produce a reasonable (as determined by the governing body) return of net income (within the meaning of paragraph (e)(11)(v)(F) of this section) over a reasonable period of time (as determined by the governing body).

The fact that the exercise of any such power in paragraph (e)(11)(v)(B)(1), (2) or (3) of this section is reviewable by an appropriate State authority will not preclude the community trust from meeting the requirements of paragraph (e)(11)(v)(B) of this section.

(C) *Transitional rule.* (1) Notwithstanding paragraph (e)(11)(v)(B) of this section, if a community trust meets the requirements of paragraph (e)(11)(v)(C)(2) of this section, then in the case of any instrument of transfer which is executed before July 19, 1977 and is not revoked or amended thereafter (with respect to any dispositive provision affecting the transfer to the community trust), and in the case of any instrument of transfer which is irrevocable on January 19, 1982, the governing body must have the power to cause proceedings to be instituted (by request to the appropriate State authority)—

(i) To modify any restriction or condition on the distribution of funds for any specified charitable purposes or to specified organizations if in the judgment of the governing body such restriction or condition becomes, in effect, unnecessary, incapable of fulfillment, or inconsistent with the charitable needs of the community or area served; and

(ii) To remove any participating trustee, custodian, or agent for breach of fiduciary duty under State law.

The necessity of the governing body to obtain the approval of a participating trustee to exercise such a power shall be treated as not preventing the governing body from having such power, unless (and until) such approval has been (or is) requested by the governing body and has been (or is) denied.

(2) Paragraph (e)(11)(v)(C)(1) of this section shall not apply unless the community trust meets the requirements of paragraph (e)(11)(v)(B) of this section, with respect to funds other than those under instruments of transfer described in the first sentence of such paragraph (e)(11)(v)(C)(1), by January 19, 1978, or such later date as the Commissioner may provide for such community trust, and unless the community trust does not, once it so complies, thereafter

Reg. § 1.170A-9(e)(11)

solicit for funds that will not qualify under the requirements of such paragraph (e)(11)(v)(B).

(D) *Inconsistent State law.* (*1*) For purposes of paragraph (e)(11)(v)(B)(*1*) (*2*), or (*3*) or (C)(*1*)(*i*) or (*ii*) or (E) of this section, if a power described in such a provision is inconsistent with State law even if such power were expressly granted to the governing body by the governing transfer, then the community trust will be treated as meeting the requirements instrument and were accepted without limitation under an instrument of such a provision if it meets such requirements to the fullest extent possible consistent with State law (if such power is or had been so expressly granted).

(*2*) For example, if, under the conditions of paragraph (e)(11)(v)(D)(*1*) of this section, the power to modify is inconsistent with State law, but the power to institute proceedings to modify, if so expressly granted, would be consistent with State law, the community trust will be treated as meeting such requirements to the fullest extent possible if the governing body has the power (in the governing instrument or otherwise) to institute proceedings to modify a condition or restriction. On the other hand, if in such a case the community trust has only the power to cause proceedings to be instituted to modify a condition or restriction, it will not be treated as meeting such requirements to the fullest extent possible.

(*3*) In addition, if for example, under the conditions of paragraph (e)(11)(v)(D)(*1*) of this section, the power to modify and the power to institute proceedings to modify a condition or restriction is inconsistent with State law, but the power to cause such proceedings to be instituted would be consistent with State law, if it were expressly granted in the governing instrument and if the approval of the State Attorney General were obtained, then the community trust will be treated as meeting such requirements to the fullest extent possible if it has the power (in the governing instrument or otherwise) to cause such proceedings to be instituted, even if such proceedings can be instituted only with the approval of the State Attorney General.

(E) *Exercise of powers.* The governing body shall (by resolution or otherwise) commit itself to exercise the powers described in paragraph (e)(11)(v)(B), (C) and (D) of this section in the best interests of the community trust. The governing body will be considered not to be so committed where it has grounds to exercise such a power and fails to exercise it by taking appropriate action. Such appropriate action may include, for example, consulting with the appropriate

State authority prior to taking action to replace a participating trustee.

(F) *Reasonable return.* In addition to the requirements of paragraph (e)(11)(v)(B), (C), (D) or (E) of this section, the governing body shall (by resolution or otherwise) commit itself to obtain information and take other appropriate steps with the view to seeing that each participating trustee, custodian, or agent, with respect to each restricted (within the meaning of paragraph (e)(_3)(x) of this section) trust or fund that is, and with respect to the aggregate of the unrestricted trusts or funds that are, a component part of the community trust, administers such trust or fund in accordance with the terms of its governing instrument and accepted standards of fiduciary conduct to produce a reasonable return of net income (or appreciation where not inconsistent with the community trust's need for current income), with due regard to safety of principal, in furtherance of the exempt purposes of the community trust (except for assets held for the active conduct of the community trust's exempt activities). In the case of a low return of net income (and, where appropriate, appreciation), the Internal Revenue Service will examine carefully whether the governing body has, in fact, committed itself to take the appropriate steps.

(vi) *Common reports.* The organization must prepare periodic financial reports treating all of the funds which are held by the community trust, either directly or in component parts, as funds of the organization.

(vii) *Transitional rule.* If the governing instrument of a community trust (or an instrument of transfer) is inconsistent with the requirements of paragraph (e)(11)(iv) or (v) of this section but with respect to gifts or bequests acquired before January 1, 1982, the community trust changes its governing instrument (or instrument of transfer) by the later of November 11, 1977, or one year after the gift or bequest is acquired, in order to conform such instruments to such provisions, then such an instrument shall be treated as consistent with paragraph (e)(11)(iv) or (v) of this section for taxable years beginning after December 31, 1969. In addition, if prior to the later of such dates, the organization has instituted court proceedings in order to conform such an instrument, then it may apply (prior to the later of such dates) for an extension of the period to conform such instrument to such provisions. Such application shall be made to the Commissioner of Internal Revenue, Attention: E:EO, Washington, D.C. 20224. The Commissioner, at the Commissioner's discretion, may grant such an extension, if in the Commissioner's opinion such a

Reg. § 1.170A-9(e)(11)

change will conform the instrument to such provisions and will be made within a reasonable time.

(12) *Community trusts qualifying for 5-year transitional ruling period* —(i) *In general.* Paragraph (e)(12) and (13) of this section contain[s] transitional rules for certain community trusts in existence before November 11, 1976 which are unable to meet the requirements of paragraph (e)(2) or (3) of this section based upon a 4-year computation period under paragraph (e)(4) of this section. A community trust that satisfies the requirements of paragraph (e)(12)(ii) of this section will be eligible for a transitional ruling or determination letter that it will be treated as a section 170(b)(1)(A)(vi) organization for a 5-year transitional ruling period (referred to in this section as a "transitional ruling or determination letter"). These transitional rules apply to—

(A) A community trust which has been in existence less than 9 taxable years before November 11, 1976; and

(B) Other community trusts that for each taxable year beginning after December 31, 1969, and before January 1, 1978, qualify as "publicly supported" under paragraph (e)(2) or (3) of this section based upon a computation period of either—

(*1*) 10 taxable years, or

(*2*) The number of taxable years (but not more than 20 nor less then 10) preceding such taxable year that the organization was in existence.

For special rules in applying the requirements of paragraph (e)(2) or (3) of this section based upon such computation periods, see paragraph (e)(12)(v) of this section. For purposes of paragraph (e)(12) of this section the initial taxable year of the 5-year transitional ruling period (hereinafter referred to as the "transitional ruling period") shall be the organization's taxable year beginning in 1977, and (unless terminated earlier) the last year of the transitional ruling period is the organization's taxable year which begins in 1981.

(ii) *Transitional 5-year ruling.* (A) If a community trust meets the requirements of paragraph (e)(11), (12) and (13) of this section and can reasonably be expected to meet the requirements of paragraph (e)(2) or (3) of this section—

(*1*) For each of its taxable years (if such a year begins after its tenth taxable year) beginning in 1978, 1979, 1980, and 1981 based upon a 10-year computation period, and

(*2*) For its taxable year beginning in 1982 based upon a 4-year computation period under paragraph (e)(4) of this section,

it may, at the discretion of the Commissioner, receive a transitional ruling or determination letter for a 5-year transitional ruling period.

(B)(*1*) However, if for the taxable year beginning in 1977, a community trust can meet the requirements of paragraph (e)(12)(i)(B) of this section only by using the computation period of its existence described in paragraph (e)(12)(i)(B)(*2*) of this section, then the community trust may meet the requirements of paragraph (e)(12)(ii)(A)(*1*) of this section if it is reasonably expected to meet the requirements of paragraph (e)(2) or (3) of this section for each of its taxable years beginning in 1978, 1979, 1980 and 1981 based upon a computation period consisting of the number of taxable years (but not more than 20 nor less than 10) preceding such taxable year that the organization was in existence.

(*2*) In the case of a community trust that will not have been in existence more than ten taxable years as of its taxable year beginning in 1981, a transitional ruling or determination letter for the transitional ruling period will not be granted unless the community trust can reasonably be expected to meet the requirements of paragraph (e)(2) or (3) of this section for its taxable year beginning in 1982 based upon a 4-year computation period under paragraph (e)(4) of this section and also a computation period consisting of the taxable year the organization has been in existence (other than the organization's taxable year beginning in 1982).

(C) A community trust that is eligible for a transitional ruling or determination letter must apply with the district director for such ruling or determination letter within one year after November 11, 1976. A transitional ruling or determination letter will be granted only if the requesting organization files with its request for such ruling or determination letter a consent letter under section 6501(c)(4) to the effect that the period of limitation upon assessment under section 4940 for all taxable years beginning before January 1, 1982 during the transitional ruling period shall not expire prior to 1 year after the date of the expiration of the time prescribed by law for the assessment of a deficiency for its taxable year beginning in 1981. The provisions of paragraph (e)(5)(iii) of this section (relating to reliance upon ruling) shall apply with respect to a community trust which receives a transitional ruling or determination letter and with respect to its grantors and contributors, except that the transitional ruling period described in paragraph (e)(12)(ii) of this section shall be substituted for the advance ruling period described in paragraph (e)(5)(i) or (iv) of this section.

(D) A community trust does not have to meet the requirements of paragraph (e)(13) of this section for taxable years beginning prior to the date of its application for a transitional ruling or determination letter or for any taxable year beginning after the expiration or termination of its transitional ruling or determination letter. In applying paragraph (e)(13) of this section to organizations applying for a transitional ruling or determination letter, paragraph (e)(13)(x) and (xii) of this section (relating to unrestricted gifts and excess holdings, respectively) shall be applied without regard to assets acquired prior to November 11, 1976. In addition, if within 1 year from acquiring any asset, the community trust removes any restriction inconsistent with paragraph (e)(13) of this section, such asset shall be treated as if it were not subject to such restriction as of the time it was acquired. Since under paragraph (e)(12)(ii)(D) of this section, a community trust does not have to meet the requirements of paragraph (e)(13) of this section for taxable years beginning prior to the date of its application for the transitional ruling or determination letter, then if the community trust makes such application in its taxable year beginning in 1977 and it terminates such ruling or determination letter in such year as well, such a community trust does not have to meet such requirements for any taxable year.

(E) After the transitional ruling or determination letter of an organization has expired or been terminated under paragraph (e)(12)(iii) of this section, the organization must qualify as a "publicly supported" organization pursuant to the rules set forth in paragraph (e)(1) through (11) of this section. Thus, since the transitional ruling period of a community trust expires with its taxable year beginning in 1981, for its taxable year beginning in 1982 and thereafter, the community trust must meet the requirements of paragraph (e)(2) or (3) of this section based upon the 4-year computation period under paragraph (e)(4) of this section.

(iii) *Termination of transitional ruling.* (A) The transitional ruling or determination letter issued under this paragraph is subject to termination under paragraph (e)(12)(iii)(B) or (D) of this section without a request from the organization. In addition, such a ruling or determination letter is subject to termination under paragraph (e)(12)(iii)(E) of this section at the request of the organization. A transitional ruling or determination letter is subject to termination for any taxable year beginning after December 31, 1976, and

before January 1, 1982, under paragraph (e)(12)(iii)(B), (D) or (E) of this section.

(B) The transitional ruling or determination letter issued under this paragraph shall be terminated for any taxable year (if such a year begins after its tenth taxable year) beginning in 1978 1979, 1980 or 1981 for which the community trust receiving such a ruling or determination letter fails to meet the requirements of paragraph (e)(2) or (3) of this section for a 10-year computation period, except as provided in paragraph (e)(12)(iii)(C) of this section.

(C) In applying paragraph (e)(12)(iii)(B) of this section to a community trust described in paragraph (e)(12)(ii)(B)(*1*) of this section, a computation period consisting of the number of taxable years (but not more than 20 nor less than 10) preceding such taxable year that the organization was in existence shall be substituted for the 10-year computation period until the first taxable year beginning in 1978, 1979, 1980 or 1981 that the community trust can meet the requirements of paragraph (e)(2) or (3) of this section based upon a 10-year computation period.

(D) The Commissioner may, at the discretion of the Commissioner, terminate the transitional ruling or determination letter of any community trust for any taxable year beginning prior to January 1, 1982, for which the organization fails to meet the requirements of paragraph (e)(11), (12) or (13) of this section, as provided in paragraph (e)(12)(ii) of this section.

(E) A community trust may request an immediate termination of the community trust's transitional ruling or determination letter in order that, for the current taxable year, it may be determined if such community trust meets the requirements of paragraph (e)(2) or (3) of this section based upon a 4-year computation period under paragraph (e)(4) of this section. Such a request shall be granted and the transitional ruling or determination letter terminated only if the community trust meets such requirements, and in the case of an organization that has been in existence less than 11 taxable years at the time of such request, the organization also meets the requirements of paragraph (e)(2) or (3) of this section for the computation period consisting of the taxable years that the organization has been in existence.

(iv) *Initial determination of status.* (A) The initial determination of status of a community trust is the first determination (other than by issuance of an advance ruling or determination letter under paragraph (e)(5) or a transitional ruling or determination letter under paragraph (e)(12)(ii) of this section) that the community trust will be considered as "normally" meeting the requirements of paragraph (e)(2) or (3) of this section for a period beginning with its first taxable year.

(B) (*1*) In the case of a community trust described in paragraph (e)(12)(i)(B) of this section, the initial determination of status shall be made for the community trust's taxable year beginning in 1977 if such community trust has met the requirements of paragraph (e)(2) or (3) of this section for its taxable year beginning in 1977, based upon a 10-year computation period.

(*2*) In the case of any other community trust described in paragraph (e)(12)(i)(B) of this section (but not described in paragraph (e)(12)(v)(B)(*1*) of this section), the initial determination of status shall be made for its first taxable year beginning after December 31, 1976, and before January 1, 1982, for which it meets the requirements of paragraph (e)(2) or (3) of this section based upon a 10-year computation period (if the community trust has received a transitional ruling or determination letter that has not been terminated before such taxable year).

(C) In the case of a community trust described in paragraph (e)(12)(i)(A) of this section (relating to an organization in existence less than 9 taxable years) that reaches its 11th taxable year before its taxable year beginning in 1982, its initial determination of status shall be for its 11th taxable year based upon a 10-year computation period (if it has received a transitional ruling or determination letter that has not been terminated before such taxable year).

(D) If a community trust has not received an initial determination of status prior to the expiration or termination of its transitional ruling period, the initial determination of status shall be made—

(*1*) In the case of an expiration, for the taxable year beginning in 1982, or

(*2*) In the case of a termination, for the last taxable year of the terminated transitional period, based upon a 4-year computation period under paragraph (e)(4) of this section. In the case of an organization that has been in existence less than 11 taxable years at such time, the initial determination of status shall also be based upon a computation period consisting of the taxable years it has been in existence.

For example, if the initial determination of status (for an organization that has been in existence for at least 11 taxable years) is made for its taxable year beginning in 1982, then, except as provided in paragraph (e)(4)(v) of this section (relating to exception for material changes of support), such determination shall be based upon a

4-year computation period ending with the taxable year beginning in 1980 or 1981 (treating the taxable year beginning in 1982, as the subsequent year or current year, respectively).

On the other hand, if, for example, the transitional ruling or determination letter is terminated in the taxable year beginning in 1980, then, except as provided in such paragraph (e)(4)(v), the initial determination of status shall be made for the taxable year beginning in 1980 based upon the 4-year computation period ending with the taxable year beginning in 1978 or 1979.

(v) *Special rules* —(A) *Consequences of organization failing to meet requirements at end of transitional period.* If upon the expiration (or termination) of the transitional period an organization with a transitional ruling or determination letter fails to meet the requirements of paragraph (e)(2) or (3) of this section based upon the 4-year computation period of paragraph (e)(4) of this section, it shall not be treated as an organization described in section 170(b)(1)(A)(vi) for its taxable year beginning in 1982 (or for the last taxable year of its terminated transitional period, as the case may be). If, by reason of failing to qualify as an organization described in section 170(b)(1)(A)(vi), such organization becomes a private foundation, then the organization will be a private foundation for its taxable year beginning in 1982 (or the last taxable year of its terminated transitional period, as the case may be) and all subsequent taxable years, unless and until it terminates its status under section 507. In addition, such an organization is a private foundation for all taxable years beginning prior to its taxable year beginning in 1982 (or for the last taxable year of the terminated transitional period, as the case may be), except—

(*1*) That if the organization had received an initial determination of status that it met the requirements of paragraph (e)(2) or (3) of this section, then the organization will be treated as "publicly supported" for the taxable years to which the initial determination of status is effective, as well as for all taxable years beginning after the last of such years and before January 1, 1982, for which the organization consecutively meets the requirements of paragraph (e)(2) or (3) of this section based upon a 10-year computation period,

(*2*) That in the case of an organization that has reached its tenth taxable year of existence before January 1, 1970, if the organization has not received an initial determination of status prior to its taxable year beginning in 1982, then the organization will be treated as "publicly supported" for each taxable year beginning before

Reg. § 1.170A-9(e)(12)

January 1, 1977, that the organization, beginning with the taxable year beginning in 1970, consecutively met the requirements of paragraph (e)(2) or (3) of this section based upon a 10-year computation period, or

(3) That in the case of an organization whose 11th taxable year of its existence began after December 31, 1970 and before January 1, 1977, if the organization has not received an initial determination of status prior to its taxable year beginning in 1982, but the organization for its 11th taxable year of existence met the requirements of paragraph (e)(2) or (3) of this section based upon a 10-year computation period, then the organization will be treated as "publicly supported" for the first 12 taxable years of its existence. In addition, such an organization will be so treated for its 13th taxable year and each subsequent taxable year (if such year begins before January 1, 1977) that the organization, beginning with its 12th taxable year, consecutively met the requirements of paragraph (e)(2) or (3) of this section based upon a 10-year computation period.

(4) To the extent provided in paragraph (e)(4)(vii) of this section (relating to special rule for organization with existing rulings), § 1.508-1(b) (relating to notice that an organization is not a private foundation) or § 1.509(a)-7 (relating to reliance by grantors and contributors to section 509(a)(1), (2), and (3) organizations).

(B) *Computation period.* In applying the requirements of paragraph (e)(2) or (3) of this section to a 10-year or other computation period under paragraph (e)(12) or (13) of this section, such 10-year or other computation period shall be substituted for the 4-year computation period of paragraph (e)(4) of this section. Thus, for example, an organization will (except as provided in paragraph (e)(4)(v) of this section relating to exemption for material changes in sources of support) meet the "publicly supported" test of this paragraph for the taxable year beginning in 1977 based upon a 10-year computation period, if it met the requirements of paragraph (e)(2) or (3) of this section for a computation period consisting of either the taxable years beginning in the years 1966 through 1975 or the years 1967 through 1976, since under paragraph (e)(4) of this section, meeting the requirements for a computation period is effective for the current taxable year and the immediately succeeding taxable year. However, in substituting a 10-year or other computation period for the 4-year computation period of paragraph (e)(4) of this section, the rules of such paragraph (e)(4) and (6) apply, including the 2-percent limitation under paragraph (e)(6)(i) of this section and the exclusion for unusual grants

under paragraph (e)(6)(ii) of this section. In applying such provisions, the fact that the computation period is other than a 4-year computation period shall be taken into account, so that, for example, the 2-percent limitation shall be applied, in the case of a 10-year computation period, with reference to 2 percent of the organization's total support for the 10-year computation period rather than a 4-year computation period.

In addition, in substituting a 10-year or other computation period for purposes of paragraph (e)(3) of this section, all of the facts and circumstances referred to in such paragraph (e)(3) shall be considered with respect to such period, viewing such period as a whole. See, also, paragraph (e)(10) of this section with respect to the organization being organized and operated to attract public support.

(C) *First taxable year of less than 8 months.* In the case of an organization whose first taxable year consisted of less than 8 months, in order to coordinate the rules of paragraph (e)(12) of this section with the rules paragraph (e)(5) of this section, in applying the rules of paragraph (e)(12) of this section, such an organization shall be treated as organized at the beginning of its succeeding taxable year, so that such succeeding taxable year shall be treated as its first taxable year of existence. However, the support received for the period preceding such succeeding taxable year shall be taken into account with the support received in such succeeding taxable year.

(13) *Community trusts; requirements for 5-year transitional ruling period* —(i) *In general.* In order for a community trust to be eligible for a transitional ruling or determination letter for the transitional ruling period under paragraph (e)(12) of this section, it must establish that it is organized, and will be operated, in such manner that it can reasonably be expected to meet the requirements of paragraph (e)(13) of this section, and can reasonably be expected to meet the requirements of paragraph (e)(2) or (3) of this section, for each taxable year during and immediately following the transitional ruling period, as provided in paragraph (e)(12)(ii) of this section. In determining whether an organization can reasonably be expected to meet the requirements of paragraph (e)(2) or (3) of this section for each such taxable year, the basic consideration is whether its organizational structure, proposed programs or activities, and intended method of operation are such as to attract the type of broadly based support from the general public, public charities, and governmental units which is necessary to meet such tests. The information to be considered for this purpose shall consist of all pertinent facts and

circumstances relating to the requirements set forth in paragraph (e)(3) of this section. For purposes of meeting the requirements of paragraph (e)(13) of this section, a community trust may, prior to its application for a transitional ruling or determination letter under paragraph (e)(12)(ii)(C) of this section, adopt a resolution stating that, as a matter of policy, it will attempt to meet the conditions set forth in paragraph (e)(13) of this section during the transitional ruling period. A community trust will not be treated as failing to satisfy the requirements of paragraph (e)(13) of this section merely because the governing body, or any of its trustees, agents, or custodians, fails to meet one or more of the requirements contained in paragraph (e)(13)(ii) through (xiii) of this section by reason of isolated and nonrepetitive acts. However, any continuing pattern on the part of the governing body, or its trustees, agents or custodians, indicating a continued and repetitive failure to comply with a policy of meeting such requirements will result in termination of the transitional ruling or determination letter under paragraph (e)(12)(iii)(D) of this section.

(ii) *Area.* The community trust is organized and operated exclusively to carry out charitable purposes (within the meaning of section 170(c)(1) or (2)(B)) primarily within a broad geographical area which it serves, such as municipality, county, metropolitan area, State or region.

(iii) *General composition of governing body.* The governing body must represent the broad interests of the public rather than the personal or private interests of a limited number of donors. An organization will be treated as meeting this requirement if it has a governing body comprised of public officials acting in their capacities as such; individuals selected by public officials acting in their capacities as such; persons having special knowledge or expertise in a particular field or discipline in which the community trust operates; community leaders, such as elected or appointed officials, clergymen, educators, civic leaders; or other such persons representing a broad cross-section of the views and interests of the area served.

(iv) *Rules for governing body.* With respect to terms of office beginning after the date of the application of the community trust for a transitional ruling or determination letter—

(A) Its governing body is comprised of members who may serve a period of not more than ten consecutive years;

(B) Upon completion of a period of service (beginning before or after such date) no person may serve within a period consisting of the lesser of 5 years or the number of consecutive years the member has immediately completed serving;

(C) Persons who would be described in section 4946(a)(1)(A) or (C) through (G) if the community trust were a private foundation do not constitute more than one-third of its governing body; and

(D) Representatives of banks or trust companies which serve as trustees, investment managers, custodians, or agents, plus persons described in paragraph (e)(13)(iv)(C) of this section, do not constitute a majority of the governing body.

No term of office beginning on or before the date of such application may continue for more than 10 years from such date.

(v) *Fiduciary responsibility.* Fiduciary responsibility with respect to the funds of the community trust is imposed, either by the master trust or agency agreement or by State law, on either its governing body or its trustee banks or trust companies or both.

(vi) *Ultimate control of assets.* Neither its governing body, nor any of its trustees, investment managers, custodians or agents may be subjected by any donor to the community trust to any material condition or restriction within the meaning of § 1.507(a)(8) which would prevent it from exercising ultimate control over its assets.

(vii) *Administration.* Administration and investment of all gifts and bequests are accomplished through:

(A) A governing body which directly holds, administers or invests such gifts and bequests exclusively for charitable purposes;

(B) Banks or trust companies (acting or appointed as trustees), investment managers, custodians or agents of the community trust or one or more components thereof; or

(C) A combination of such persons.

(viii) *Annual distributions.* It makes annual distributions for purposes described in section 170(c)(1) or (2)(B), including administrative expenses and amounts paid to acquire an asset used (or held for use) directly in carrying out one or more of such purposes, in an amount not less than its adjusted net income (as defined in section 4942(f)). For purposes of paragraph (e)(13)(viii) of this section, the term "distributions" shall include amounts set aside for a specific project, but only if prior to making the set-aside the organization has, pursuant to a request for a ruling, established to the satisfaction of the Commissioner that:

Reg. § 1.170A-9(e)(13)

(A) The amount will be paid for the specific project within 5 years; and

(B) The project is one which can be better accomplished by such set-aside than by immediate distribution of funds.

All annual distributions required to be made pursuant to paragraph (e)(13)(viii) of this section, except for set-asides, must be made no later than the close of the organization's first taxable year after the taxable year for which the adjusted net income is computed. Thus, in the case of a calendar year community trust which has received a transitional ruling or determination letter upon an application made in 1977, it must make distributions under paragraph (e)(13)(vii) of this section for 1978, 1979, 1980 and 1981 based upon its adjusted net income for 1977, 1978, 1979 and 1980, respectively, unless its transitional ruling or determination letter is terminated. If such a community trust's transitional ruling or determination letter is terminated in 1979, it must make distributions under paragraph (e)(13)(viii) of this section only for 1978 based upon its adjusted net income for 1977.

On the other hand, if such ruling or letter is terminated in 1977 or 1978, no distribution under paragraph (e)(13)(viii) of this section need be made.

(ix) *Net income.* The community trust's funds must, on an aggregate basis, be invested to produce an annual adjusted net income (as defined in section 4942(f)) of not less than two-thirds of what would be its minimum investment return (within the meaning of section 4942(e)) if such organization were a private foundation.

(x) *Unrestricted gifts.* At least one-half of the total income which the community trust derives from the investment of gifts and bequests received must be unrestricted (within the meaning of this (x)) with respect to its availability for distribution by the governing body. For purposes of this (x), any income which has been designated by the donor of the gift or bequest to which such income is attributable as being available only for the use or benefit of a broad charitable purpose, such as the encouragement of higher education or the promotion of better health care in the community, will be treated as unrestricted. However, any income which has been designated for the use or benefit of a named charitable organization or agency or for the use or benefit of a particular class of charitable organizations or agencies, the members of which are readily ascertainable and are less than five in number, will be treated as restricted.

(xi) *Self-dealing.* The community trust may not engage in any act with any person (other than a foundation manager acting only in such capacity) which would constitute self-dealing within the meaning of section 4941 if such community trust were a private foundation.

(xii) *Excess holdings.* The community trust must dispose of any holdings which would constitute excess business holdings (within the meaning of section 4943—applied on a component-by-component basis as if each component were a private foundation, except that components will be combined for purposes of this paragraph if such components would have been described in section 4946(a)(1)(H)(ii)).

(xiii) *Expenditure responsibility.* The community trust must exercise expenditure responsibility (within the meaning of section 4945(h)) through either its governing body, trustees, investment managers, custodians, or agents with respect to any grant which would otherwise constitute a taxable expenditure under section 4945(d)(4) if the community trust were a private foundation, except that it need not make the reports required of private foundations by section 4945(h)(3).

(14) *Community trusts; treatment of trusts and not-for-profit corporations and associations not included as components.* (i) For purposes of sections 170, 501, 507, 508, 509 and chapter 42, any trust or not-for-profit corporation or association which is alleged to be a component part of a community trust, but which fails to meet the requirements of paragraph (e)(11)(ii) of this section, shall not be treated as a component part of a community trust and, if a trust, shall be treated as a separate trust and be subject to the provisions of section 501 or section 4947(a)(1) or (2), as the case may be. If such organization is a not-for-profit corporation or association, it will be treated as a separate entity, and, if it is described in section 501(c)(3), it will be treated as a private foundation unless it is described in section 509(a)(1), (2), (3), or (4). Any transfer made in connection with the creation of such separate trust or not-for-profit organization, or to such entity, will not be treated as being made "to" the community trust or one of its components for purposes of sections 170(b)(1)(A) and 507(b)(1)(A) even though a deduction with respect to such transfer is allowable under § 1.170-1(e), § 20.2055-2(b), or § 25.2522(a)-2(b), unless such treatment is permitted under § 1.170A-9(e)(4)(v)(*b*) or § 1.508-1(b)(4). In the case of a fund which is ultimately treated as not being a component part of a community trust pursuant to paragraph (e) (14) of this section, if the Form 990 filed annually by the community trust included financial information with respect

Reg. § 1.170A-9(e)(14)

to such fund and treated such fund in the same manner as other component parts thereof, such returns filed by the community trust prior to the taxable year in which the Commissioner notifies such fund that it will not be treated as a component part will be treated as its separate return for purpose of subchapter A of chapter 61 of Subtitle F, and the first such return filed by the community trust will be treated as the notification required of the separate entity for purposes of section 508(a).

(ii) If a transfer is made in trust to a community trust to make income or other payments for a period of a life or lives in being or a term of years to any individual or for any noncharitable purpose, followed by payments to or for the use of the community trust (such as in the case of a charitable remainder annuity trust or a charitable remainder unitrust described in section 664 or a pooled income fund described in section 642(c)(5)), such trust will be treated as a component part of the community trust upon the termination of all intervening noncharitable interests and rights to the actual possession or enjoyment of the property if such trust satisfies the requirements of paragraph (e)(11) of this section at such time. Until such time, the trust will be treated as a separate trust. If a transfer is made in trust to a community trust to make income or other payments to or for the use of the community trust, followed by payments to any individual or for any noncharitable purpose, such trust will be treated as a separate trust rather than as a component part of the community trust. See section 4947(a)(2) and the regulations thereunder for the treatment of such split-interest trusts. The provisions of this (ii) only provide rules for determining when a charitable remainder trust or pooled income fund may be treated as a component part of a community trust and are not intended to preclude a community trust from maintaining a charitable remainder trust or pooled income fund. Thus, for purposes of grantors and contributors, a pooled income fund of a "publicly supported" community trust shall be treated no differently than a pooled income fund of any other "publicly supported" organization.

(iii) An organization described in section 170(b)(1)(E)(iii) will not ordinarily satisfy the requirements of paragraph (e)(11)(ii) of this section because of the unqualified right of the donor to designate the recipients of the income and principal of the trust. Such organization will therefore ordinarily be treated as other than a component part of a community trust under paragraph (e)(14)(i) of this section. However, see section 170(b)(1)(E)(iii) and the regulations

thereunder with respect to the treatment of contributions of such organizations.

(f) *Private operating foundation.* An organization is described in section 170(b)(1)(A)(vii) and (E)(i) if it is a private "operating foundation" as defined in section 4942(j)(3) and the regulations thereunder.

(g) *Private nonoperating foundation distributing amount equal to all contributions received —* (1) *In general.* (i) An organization is described in section 170(b)(1)(A)(vii) and (E)(ii) if it is a private foundation which, not later than the 15th day of the third month after the close of its taxable year in which any contributions are received, distributes an amount equal in value to 100 percent of all contributions received in such year. Such distributions must be qualifying distributions (as defined in section 4942(g) without regard to paragraph (3) thereof) which are treated, after the application of section 4942(g)(3), as distributions out of corpus in accordance with section 4942(h). Qualifying distributions, as defined in section 4942(g) without regard to paragraph (3) thereof, cannot be made to (i) an organization controlled directly or indirectly by the foundation or by one or more disqualified persons (as defined in section 4946) with respect to the foundation or (ii) a private foundation which is not an operating foundation (as defined in section 4942(j)(3)). The phrase "after the application of section 4942(g)(3)" means that every contribution described in section 4942(g)(3) received by a private foundation described in this subparagraph in a particular taxable year must be distributed (within the meaning of section 4942(g)(3)(A)) by such foundation not later than the 15th day of the third month after the close of such taxable year in order for any other distribution by such foundation to be counted toward the 100-percent requirement described in this subparagraph.

(ii) In order for an organization to meet the distribution requirements of subdivision (i) of this subparagraph, it must, not later than the 15th day of the third month after the close of its taxable year in which any contributions are received, distribute (within the meaning of subdivision (i) of this subparagraph) an amount equal in value to 100 percent of all contributions received in such year and have no remaining undistributed income for such year.

(iii) The provisions of this subparagraph may be illustrated by the following examples:

Example (1). X is a private foundation on a calendar year basis. As of January 1, 1971, X had no undistributed income for 1970. X's distributable amount for 1971 was $600,000. In July

Reg. § 1.170A-9(f)

1971, A, an individual, contributed $500,000 (fair market value determined at the time of the contribution) of appreciated property to X (which, if sold, would give rise to long-term capital gain). X did not receive any other contribution in either 1970 or 1971. During 1971, X made qualifying distributions of $700,000 which were treated as made out of the undistributed income for 1971 and $100,000 out of corpus. X will meet the requirements of section 170(b)(1)(E)(ii) for 1971 if it makes additional qualifying distributions of $400,000 out of corpus by March 15, 1972.

Example (2). Assume the facts as stated in Example (1), except that as of January 1, 1971, X had $100,000 of undistributed income for 1970. Under these circumstances, the $700,000 distributed by X in 1971 would be treated as made out of the undistributed income for 1970 and 1971. X would therefore have to make additional qualifying distributions of $500,000 out of corpus between January 1, 1972, and March 15, 1972, in order to meet the requirements of section 170(b)(1)(E)(ii) for 1971.

(2) *Special rules.* In applying subparagraph (1) of this paragraph—

(i) For purposes of section 170(b)(1)(A)(vii), an organization described in section 170(b)(1)(E)(ii) must distribute all contributions received in any year, whether of cash or property. However, solely for purposes of section 170(e)(1)(B)(ii), an organization described in section 170(b)(1)(E)(ii) is required to distribute all contributions of property only received in any year. Contributions for purposes of this paragraph do not include bequests, legacies, devises, or transfers within the meaning of section 2055 or 2106(a)(2) with respect to which a deduction was not allowed under section 170.

(ii) Any distributions made by a private foundation pursuant to subparagraph (1) of this paragraph with respect to a particular taxable year shall be treated as made first out of contributions of property and then out of contributions of cash received by such foundation in such year.

(iii) A private foundation is not required to trace specific contributions of property, or amounts into which such contributions are converted, to specific distributions.

(iv) For purposes of satisfying the requirements of section 170(b)(1)(D)(ii), except as provided to the contrary in this subdivision (iv), the fair market value of contributed property, determined on the date of contribution, is required to be used for purposes of determining whether an amount equal in value to 100 percent of the contributions received has been distributed. However, reasonable selling expenses, if any, incurred

by the foundation in the sale of the contributed property may be deducted from the fair market value of the contributed property on the date of contribution, and distribution of the balance of the fair market value will satisfy the 100 percent distribution requirement. If a private foundation receives a contribution of property and, within 30 days thereafter, either sells the property or makes an in kind distribution of the property to a public charity, then at the choice of the private foundation the gross amount received on the sale (less reasonable selling expenses incurred) or the fair market value of the contributed property at the date of its distribution to the public charity, and not the fair market value of the contributed property on the date of contribution (less reasonable selling expenses, if any), is considered to be the amount of the fair market value of the contributed property for purposes of the requirements of section 170(b)(1)(D)(ii).

(v) A private foundation may satisfy the requirements of subparagraph (1) of this paragraph for a particular taxable year by electing (pursuant to section 4942(h)(2) and the regulations thereunder) to treat a portion or all of one or more distributions, made not later than the 15th day of the third month after the close of such year, as made out of corpus.

(3) *Transitional rules* —(i) *Taxable years beginning before January 1, 1970, and ending after December 31, 1969.* In order for an organization to meet the distribution requirements of subparagraph (1)(i) of this paragraph for a taxable year which begins before January 1, 1970 and ends after December 31, 1969, it must, not later than the 15th day of the third month after the close of such taxable year, distribute (within the meaning of subparagraph (1)(i) of this paragraph) an amount equal in value to 100 percent of all contributions (other than contributions described in section 4942(g)(3)) which were received between January 1, 1970 and the last day of such taxable year. Because the organization is not subject to the provisions of section 4942 for such year, the organization need not satisfy subparagraph (1)(ii) of this paragraph or the phrase "after the application of section 4942(g)(3)" for such year.

(ii) *Extension of period.* For purposes of section 170(b)(1)(A)(vii) and (e)(1)(B)(ii), in the case of a taxable year ending in either 1970, 1971 or 1972, the period referred to in section 170(b)(1)(E)(ii) for making distributions shall not expire before April 2, 1973.

(4) *Adequate records required.* A taxpayer claiming a deduction under section 170 for a charitable contribution to a foundation described in subparagraph (1) of this paragraph must obtain

Reg. § 1.170A-9(g)(4)

adequate records or other sufficient evidence from such foundation showing that the foundation made the required qualifying distributions within the time prescribed. Such records or other evidence must be attached to the taxpayer's return for the taxable year for which the charitable contribution deduction is claimed. If necessary, an amended income tax return or claim for refund may be filed in accordance with § 301.6402-2 and § 301.6402-3 of this chapter (Procedure and Administration Regulations).

(h) *Private foundation maintaining a common fund*—(1) *Designation by substantial contributors.* An organization is described in section 170(b)(1)(A)(vii) and (E)(iii) if it is a private foundation all of the contributions to which are pooled in a common fund and which would be described in section 509(a)(3) but for the right of any donor who is a substantial contributor or his spouse to designate annually the recipients, from among private charities, of the income attributable to the donor's contribution to the fund and to direct (by deed or by will) the payment, to public charities, of the corpus in the common fund attributable to the donor's contribution. For purposes of this paragraph the private foundation is to be treated as meeting the requirements of section 509(a)(3)(A) and (B) even though donors to the foundation, or their spouses, retain the right to, and in fact do, designate public charities to receive income or corpus from the fund.

(2) *Distribution requirements.* To qualify under subparagraph (1) of this paragraph, the private foundation described therein must be required by its governing instrument to distribute, and it must in fact distribute (including administrative expenses)—

(i) All of the adjusted net income (as defined in section 4942(f)) of the common fund to one or more public charities not later than the 15th day of the third month after the close of the taxable year in which such income is realized by the fund, and

(ii) All the corpus attributable to any donor's contribution to the fund to one or more public charities not later than one year after the donor's death or after the death of the donor's surviving spouse if such surviving spouse has the right to designate the recipients of such corpus.

(3) *Failure to designate.* A private foundation will not fail to qualify under this paragraph merely because a substantial contributor or his spouse fails to exercise his right to designate the recipients of income or corpus of the fund, provided that the income and corpus attributable to his contribution are distributed as required by subparagraph (2) of this paragraph.

(4) *Definitions.* For purposes of this paragraph—

(i) The term "substantial contributor" is as defined in section 507(d)(2) and the regulations thereunder.

(ii) The term "public charity" means an organization described in section 170(b)(1)(A)(i) through (vi). If an organization is described in section 170(b)(1)(A)(i) through (vi), and is also described in section 170(b)(1)(A)(viii), it shall be treated as a public charity for purposes of this paragraph.

(iii) The term "income attributable to" means the income earned by the fund which is properly allocable to the contributed amount by any reasonable and consistently applied method. See, for example, § 1.642(c)-5(c).

(iv) The term "corpus attributable to" means the portion of the corpus of the fund attributable to the contributed amount. Such portion may be determined by any reasonable and consistently applied method.

(v) The term "donor" means any individual who makes a contribution (whether of cash or property) to the private foundation, whether or not such individual is a substantial contributor.

(i) *Section 509(a)(2) or (3) organization.* An organization is described in section 170(b)(1)(A)(viii) if it is described in section 509(a)(2) or (3) and the regulations thereunder. [Reg. § 1.170A-9].

□ [*T.D. 7242, 12-29-72. Amended by T.D. 7406, 2-13-76; T.D. 7440, 11-11-76; T.D. 7465, 1-19-77; T.D. 7679, 2-28-80; T.D. 8100, 9-3-86 and T.D. 8991, 4-24-2002.*]

[Reg. § 1.170A-10]

§ 1.170A-10. Charitable contributions carryovers of individuals.—(a) *In general.* (1) Section 170(d)(1), relating to carryover of charitable contributions in excess of 50 percent of contribution base, and section 170(b)(1)(D)(ii), relating to carryover of charitable contributions in excess of 30 percent of contribution base, provide for excess charitable contributions carryovers by individuals of charitable contributions to section 170(b)(1)(A) organizations described in § 1.170A-9. These carryovers shall be determined as provided in paragraphs (b) and (c) of this section. No excess charitable contributions carryover shall be allowed with respect to contributions "for the use of", rather than "to", section 170(b)(1)(A) organizations or with respect to contributions "to" or "for the use of" organizations which are not section 170(b)(1)(A) organizations. See § 1.170A-8(a)(2) for definitions of "to" or "for the use of" a charitable organization.

Reg. § 1.170A-10(a)

(2) The carryover provisions apply with respect to contributions made during a taxable year in excess of the applicable percentage limitation even though the taxpayer elects under section 144 to take the standard deduction in that year instead of itemizing the deduction allowable in computing taxable income for that year.

(3) For provisions requiring a reduction of the excess charitable contribution computed under paragraph (b)(1) or (c)(1) of this section when there is a net operating loss carryover to the taxable year, see paragraph (d)(1) of this section.

(4) The provisions of section 170(b)(1)(D)(ii) and (d)(1) and this section do not apply to contributions by an estate; nor do they apply to a trust unless the trust is a private foundation which, pursuant to § 1.642(c)-4, is allowed a deduction under section 170 subject to the provisions applicable to individuals.

(b) *50-percent charitable contributions carryover of individuals* —(1) *Computation of excess of charitable contributions made in a contribution year.* Under section 170(d)(1), subject to certain conditions and limitations, the excess of—

(i) The amount of the charitable contributions made by an individual in a taxable year (hereinafter in this paragraph referred to as the "contribution year") to section 170(b)(1)(A) organizations described in § 1.170A-9, over

(ii) 50 percent of his contribution base, as defined in section 170(b)(1)(F), for such contribution year,

shall be treated as a charitable contribution paid by him to a section 170(b)(1)(A) organization in each of the 5 taxable years immediately succeeding the contribution year in order of time. However, such excess to the extent it consists of contributions of 30-percent capital gain property, as defined in § 1.170-A-8(d)(3), shall be subject to the rules of section 170(b)(1)(D)(ii) and paragraph (c) of this section in the years to which it is carried over. A charitable contribution made in a taxable year beginning before January 1, 1970, to a section 170(b)(1)(A) organization and carried over to a taxable year beginning after December 31, 1969, under section 170(b)(5) (before its amendment by the Tax Reform Act of 1969) shall be treated in such taxable year beginning after December 31, 1969, as a charitable contribution of cash subject to the limitations of this paragraph, whether or not such carryover consists of contributions of 30-percent capital gain property or of ordinary income property described in § 1.170A-4(b)(1). For purposes of applying this paragraph and paragraph (c) of this section, such a carryover from a taxable year beginning before January 1, 1970, which is so treated as paid to a

section 170(b)(1)(A) organization in a taxable year beginning after December 31, 1969, shall be treated as paid to such an organization under section 170(d)(1) of this section. The provisions of this subparagraph may be illustrated by the following examples:

Example (1). Assume that H and W (husband and wife) have a contribution base for 1970 of $50,000 and for 1971 of $40,000 and file a joint return for each year. Assume further that in 1970 they make a charitable contribution in cash of $26,500 to a church and $1,000 to X (not a section 170(b)(1)(A) organization) and in 1971 they make a charitable contribution in cash of $19,000 to a church and $600 to X. They may claim a charitable contributions deduction of $25,000 in 1970, and the excess of $26,500 (contribution to the church) over $25,000 (50 percent of contribution base), or $1,500, constitutes a charitable contributions carryover which shall be treated as a charitable contribution paid by them to a section 170(b)(1)(A) organization in each of the 5 succeeding taxable years in order of time. No carryover is allowed with respect to the $1,000 contribution made to X in 1970. Since 50 percent of their contribution base for 1971 ($20,000) exceeds the charitable contributions of $19,000 made by them in 1971 to section 170(b)(1)(A) organizations (computed without regard to section 170(b)(1)(D)(ii) and (d)(1) and this section), the portion of the 1970 carryover equal to such excess of $1,000 ($20,000 minus $19,000) is treated, pursuant to the provisions of subparagraph (2) of this paragraph, as paid to a section 170(b)(1)(A) organization in 1971; the remaining $500 constitutes an unused charitable contributions carryover. No deduction for 1971, and no carryover, are allowed with respect to the $600 contribution made to X in 1971.

Example (2). Assume the same facts as in example (1) except that H and W have a contribution base for 1971 of $42,000. Since 50 percent of their contribution base for 1971 ($21,000) exceeds by $2,000 the charitable contribution of $19,000 made by them in 1971 to the section 170(b)(1)(A) organization (computed without regard to section 170(b)(1)(D)(ii) and (d)(1) and this section), the full amount of the 1970 carryover of $1,500 is treated, pursuant to the provisions of subparagraph (2) of this paragraph, as paid to a section 170(b)(1)(A) organization in 1971. They may also claim a charitable contribution of $500 ($21,000 − $20,500 [$19,000 + $1,500]) with respect to the gift to X in 1971. No carryover is allowed with respect to the $100 ($600 − $500) of the contribution to X which is not deductible in 1971.

Reg. § 1.170A-10(b)(1)

(2) *Determination of amount treated as paid in taxable years succeeding contribution year.* In applying the provisions of subparagraph (1) of this paragraph, the amount of the excess computed in accordance with the provisions of such subparagraph and paragraph (d)(1) of this section which is to be treated as paid in any one of the 5 taxable years immediately succeeding the contribution year to a section 170(b)(1)(A) organization shall not exceed the lesser of the amounts computed under subdivision (i) to (iii), inclusive, of this subparagraph:

(i) The amount by which 50 percent of the taxpayer's contribution base for such succeeding taxable year exceeds the sum of—

(a) The charitable contributions actually made (computed without regard to the provisions of section 170(b)(1)(D)(ii) and (d)(1) and this section) by the taxpayer in such succeeding taxable year to section 170(b)(1)(A) organizations, and

(b) The charitable contributions, other than contributions of 30 percent capital gain property, made to section 170(b)(1)(A) organizations in taxable years preceding the contribution year which, pursuant to the provisions of section 170(d)(1) and this section, are treated as having been paid to a section 170(b)(1)(A) organization in such succeeding year.

(ii) In the case of the first taxable year succeeding the contribution year, the amount of the excess charitable contribution in the contribution year, computed under subparagraph (1) of this paragraph and paragraph (d)(1) of this section.

(iii) In the case of the second, third, fourth, and fifth taxable years succeeding the contribution year, the portion of the excess charitable contribution in the contribution year, computed under subparagraph (1) of this paragraph and paragraph (d)(1) of this section, which has not been treated as paid to a section 170(b)(1)(A)

organization in a year intervening between the contribution year and such succeeding taxable year.

For purposes of applying subdivision (i)(a) of this subparagraph, the amount of charitable contributions of 30-percent capital gain property actually made in a taxable year succeeding the contribution year shall be determined by first applying the 30-percent limitation of section 170(b)(1)(D)(i) and paragraph (d) of § 1.170A-8. If a taxpayer, in any one of the 4 taxable years succeeding a contribution year, elects under section 144 to take the standard deduction instead of itemizing the deductions allowable in computing taxable income, there shall be treated as paid (but not allowable as a deduction) in such standard deduction year the lesser of the amounts determined under subdivisions (i) to (iii), inclusive, of this subparagraph. The provisions of this subparagraph may be illustrated by the following examples:

Example (1). Assume that B has a contribution base for 1970 of $20,000 and for 1971 of $30,000. Assume further that in 1970 B contributed $12,000 in cash to a church and in 1971 he contributed $13,500 in cash to the church. B may claim a charitable contributions deduction of $10,000 in 1970, and the excess of $12,000 (contribution to the church) over $10,000 (50 percent of B's contribution base), or $2,000, constitutes a charitable contributions carryover which shall be treated as a charitable contribution paid by B to a section 170(b)(1)(A) organization in the 5 taxable years succeeding 1970 in order of time. B may claim a charitable contributions deduction of $15,000 in 1971. Such $15,000 consists of the $13,500 contribution to the church in 1971 and $1,500 carried over from 1970 and treated as a charitable contribution paid to a section 170(b)(1)(A) organization in 1971. The $1,500 contribution treated as paid in 1971 is computed as follows:

1970 excess contributions		$ 2,000
50 percent of B's contribution base for 1971		15,000
Less:		
Contributions actually made in 1971 to section 170(b)(1)(A) organizations . . .	$13,500	
Contributions made to section 170(b)(1)(A) organizations in taxable years prior to 1970 treated as having been paid in 1971	0	$13,500
Balance		1,500
Amount of 1970 excess treated as paid in 1971—the lesser of $2,000 (1970 excess contributions) or $1,500 (excess of 50 percent of contribution base for 1971 ($15,000) over the sum of the section 170(b)(1)(A) contributions actually made in 1971 ($13,500) and the section 170(b)(1)(A) contributions made in years prior to 1970 treated as having been paid in 1971 ($0))		1,500

Reg. § 1.170A-10(b)(2)

If the excess contributions made by B in 1971 had been $1,000 instead of $2,000, then, for purposes of this example, the amount of the 1970 excess treated as paid in 1971 would be $1,000 rather than $1,500.

Example (2). Assume the same facts as in example (1), and, in addition, that B has a contribution base for 1972 of $10,000 and for 1973 of $20,000. Assume further with respect to 1972 that B elects under section 144 to take the standard deduction in computing taxable income and that his actual contributions to section 170(b)(1)(A) organizations in that year are $300 in cash. Assume further that with respect to 1973 that B itemizes his deductions, which include a $5,000 cash contribution to a church. B's deductions for 1972 are not increased by reason of the $500 available as a charitable contribution carryover from 1970 (excess contributions made in 1970 ($2,000) less the amount of such excess treated as paid in 1971 ($1,500)), since B elected to take the standard deduction in 1972. However, for purposes of determining the amount of the excess charitable contributions made in 1970 which is available as a carryover to 1973, B is required to treat such $500 as a charitable contribution paid in 1972—the lesser of $500 or $4,700 (50 percent of contribution base ($5,000) over contributions actually made in 1972 to section 170(b)(1)(A) organizations ($300)). Therefore, even though the $5,000 contribution made by B in 1973 to a church does not amount to 50 percent of B's contribution base for 1973 (50 percent of $20,000), B may claim a charitable contributions deduction of only the $5,000 actually paid in 1973 since the entire excess charitable contribution made in 1970 ($2,000) has been treated as paid in 1971 ($1,500) and 1972 ($500).

Example (3). Assume the following factual situation for C who itemizes his deductions in computing taxable income for each of the years set forth in the example:

	1970	1971	1972	1973	1974
Contribution base	$10,000	$7,000	$15,000	$10,000	$9,000
Contributions of cash to section 170(b)(1)(A) organizations (no other contributions)	$ 6,000	$4,400	$ 8,000	$ 3,000	$1,500
Allowable charitable contributions deductions computed without regard to carryover of contribution	5,000	3,500	7,500	3,000	1,500
Excess contributions for taxable year to be treated as paid in 5 succeeding taxable years	1,000	900	500	0	0

Since C's contributions in 1973 and 1974 to section 170(b)(1)(A) organizations are less than 50 percent of his contribution base for such years, the excess contributions for 1970, 1971, and 1972 are treated as having been paid to section 170(b)(1)(A) organizations in 1973 and 1974 as follows:

1970	$1,000	0	$1,000
1971	900	0	900
1972	500	0	500
Total			2,400
50 percent of B's contribution base for 1973			5,000
Less: Charitable contributions made in 1973 to section 170(b)(1)(A) organizations			3,000
			2,000

Amount of excess contributions treated as paid in 1973—lesser of $2,400 (available carryovers to 1973) or $2,000 (excess of 50 percent of contribution base ($5,000) over contributions actually made in 1973 to section 170(b)(1)(A) organizations ($3,000)) ... $2,000

1970	$1,000	$1,000	0
1971	900	900	0
1972	500	100	$ 400
1973	0	0	0
Total			400
50 percent of B's contribution base for 1974			$4,500
Less: Charitable contributions made in 1974 to section 170(b)(1)(A) organizations			1,500
			3,000

Reg. § 1.170A-10(b)(2)

Amount of excess contributions treated as paid in 1974— the lesser of $400 (available carryovers to 1974) or $3,000 (excess of 50 percent of contribution base ($4,500) over contributions actually made in 1974 to section 170(b)(1)(A) organizations ($1,500)) .... $ 400

(c) *30-percent charitable contributions carryover of individuals.* —(1) *Computation of excess of charitable contributions made in a contribution year.* Under section 170(b)(1)(D)(ii), subject to certain conditions and limitations, the excess of—

(i) The amount of the charitable contributions of 30-percent capital gain property, as defined in § 1.170A-8(d)(3), made by an individual in a taxable year (hereinafter in this paragraph referred to as the "contribution year") to section 170(b)(1)(A) organizations described in § 1.170A-9, over

(ii) 30 percent of his contribution base for such contribution year, shall, subject to section 170(b)(1)(A) and paragraph (b) of § 1.170A-8, be treated as a charitable contribution of 30-percent capital gain property paid by him to a section 170(b)(1)(A) organization in each of the 5 taxable years immediately succeeding the contribution year in order of time. In addition, any charitable contribution of 30-percent capital gain property which is carried over to such years under section 170(d)(1) and paragraph (b) of this section shall also be treated as though it were a carryover of 30-percent capital gain property under section 170(b)(1)(D)(ii) and this paragraph. The provisions of this subparagraph may be illustrated by the following examples:

Example (1). Assume that H and W (husband and wife) have a contribution base for 1970 of $50,000 and for 1971 of $40,000 and file a joint return for each year. Assume further that in 1970 they contribute $20,000 cash and $13,000 of 30-percent capital gain property to a church, and that in 1971 they contribute $5,000 cash and $10,000 of 30-percent capital gain property to a church. They may claim a charitable contributions deduction of $25,000 in 1970 and the excess of $33,000 (contributed to the church) over $25,000 (50 percent of contribution base), or $8,000, constitutes a charitable contributions carryover which shall be treated as a charitable contribution of 30-percent capital gain property paid by them to a section 170(b)(1)(A) organization in each of the 5 succeeding taxable years in order of time. Since 30 percent of their contribution base for 1971 ($12,000) exceeds the charitable contributions of 30-percent capital gain property ($10,000) made by them in 1971 to section 170(b)(1)(A) organizations (computed without regard to section 170(b)(1)(D)(ii) and (d)(1) and this section), the portion of the 1970 carryover equal to such excess of $2,000 ($12,000 —

$10,000) is treated, pursuant to the provisions of subparagraph (2) of this paragraph, as paid to a section 170(b)(1)(A) organization in 1971; the remaining $6,000 constitutes an unused charitable contributions carryover in respect of 30-percent capital gain property from 1970.

Example (2). Assume the same facts as in example (1) except the $33,000 of charitable contributions in 1970 are all 30-percent capital gain property. Since their charitable contributions in 1970 exceed 30 percent of their contribution base ($15,000) by $18,000 ($33,000 — $15,000), they may claim a charitable contributions deduction of $15,000 in 1970, and the excess of $33,000 over $15,000, or $18,000, constitutes a charitable contributions carryover which shall be treated as a charitable contribution of 30-percent capital gain property paid by them to a section 170(b)(1)(A) organization in each of the 5 succeeding taxable years in order of time. Since they are allowed to treat only $2,000 of their 1970 contribution as paid in 1971, they have a remaining unused charitable contributions carryover of $16,000 in respect to 30-percent capital gain property from 1970.

(2) *Determination of amount treated as paid in taxable years succeeding contribution year.* In applying the provisions of subparagraph (1) of this paragraph, the amount of the excess computed in accordance with the provisions of such subparagraph and paragraph (d)(1) of this section which is to be treated as paid in any one of the 5 taxable years immediately succeeding the contribution year to a section 170(b)(1)(A) organization shall not exceed the least of the amounts computed under subdivisions (i) to (iv), inclusive, of this subparagraph:

(i) The amount by which 30 percent of the taxpayer's contribution base for such succeeding taxable year exceeds the sum of—

(*a*) The charitable contributions of 30-percent capital gain property actually made (computed without regard to the provisions of section 170(b)(1)(D)(ii) and (d)(1) and this section) by the taxpayer in such succeeding taxable year to section 170(b)(1)(A) organizations, and

(*b*) The charitable contributions of 30-percent capital gain property made to section 170(b)(1)(A) organizations in taxable years preceding the contribution year, which, pursuant to the provisions of section 170(b)(1)(D)(ii) and (d)(1) and this section, are treated as having been

Reg. § 1.170A-10(c)(1)

paid to a section 170(b)(1)(A) organization in such succeeding year.

(ii) The amount by which 50 percent of the taxpayer's contribution base for such succeeding taxable year exceeds the sum of—

(a) The charitable contributions actually made (computed without regard to the provisions of section 170(b)(1)(D)(ii) and (d)(1) and this section) by the taxpayer in such succeeding taxable year to section 170(b)(1)(A) organizations,

(b) The charitable contributions of 30-percent capital gain property made to section 170(b)(1)(A) organizations in taxable years preceding the contribution year which, pursuant to the provisions of section 170(b)(1)(D)(ii) and (d)(1) and this section, are treated as having been paid to a section 170(b)(1)(A) organization in such succeeding year, and

(c) The charitable contributions, other than contributions of 30-percent capital gain property, made to section 170(b)(1)(A) organizations which, pursuant to the provisions of section 170(d)(1) and paragraph (b) of this section, are treated as having been paid to a section 170(b)(1)(A) organization in such succeeding year.

(iii) In the case of the first taxable year succeeding the contribution year, the amount of the excess charitable contribution of 30-percent capital gain property in the contribution year, computed under subparagraph (1) of this paragraph and paragraph (d)(1) of this section.

(iv) In the case of the second, third, fourth, and fifth succeeding taxable years succeeding the contribution year, the portion of the excess charitable contribution of 30-percent capital gain property in the contribution year (computed under subparagraph (1) of this paragraph and paragraph (d)(1) of this section) which has not been treated as paid to a section 170(b)(1)(A) organization in a year intervening between the contribution year and such succeeding taxable year.

For purposes of applying subdivisions (i) and (ii) of this subparagraph, the amount of charitable contributions of 30-percent capital gain property actually made in a taxable year succeeding the contribution year shall be determined by first applying the 30-percent limitation of section 170(b)(1)(D)(i) and paragraph (d) of § 1.170A-8. If a taxpayer, in any one of the four taxable years succeeding a contribution year, elects under section 144 to take the standard deduction instead of itemizing the deductions allowable in computing taxable income, there shall be treated as paid (but not allowable as a deduction) in the standard deduction year the least of the amounts determined under subdivisions (1) to (iv), inclusive, of this subparagraph. The provisions of this subparagraph may be illustrated by the following example:

Example. Assume the following factual situation for C who itemizes his deductions in computing taxable income for each of the years set forth in the example:

	1970	1971	1972	1973	1974
Contribution base	$10,000	$15,000	$20,000	$15,000	$33,000
Contributions of cash to section 170(b)(1)(A) organizations	2,000	8,500	0	14,000	700
Contributions of 30-percent capital gain property to section 170(b)(1)(A) organizations	5,000	0	7,800	0	6,400
Allowable charitable contributions deductions (computed without regard to carryover of contributions) subject to limitations of:					
50 percent	2,000	7,500	0	7,500	700
30 percent	3,000	0	6,000	0	6,400
Total	5,000	7,500	6,000	7,500	7,100
Excess of contributions for taxable year to be treated as paid in 5 succeeding taxable years:					
Carryover of contributions of property other than 30-percent capital gain property		0	$ 1,000	0	$ 6,500	0
Carryover of contributions of 30-percent capital gain property	$ 2,000	0	$ 1,800	0	0

C's excess contributions for 1970, 1971, 1972, and 1973 which are treated as having been paid to section 170(b)(1)(A) organizations in 1972, 1973 and 1974 are indicated below. The portion of the excess charitable contribution for 1972 of 30-percent capital gain property which is not treated as paid in 1974 ($1,800 — $900) is available as a carryover to 1975.

Reg. § 1.170A-10(c)(2)

1971

Contribution year	Total excess 50%	30%	Less: Amount treated as paid in years prior to 1971	Available charitable contributions carryovers 50%	30%
1970	0	$2,000	0	0	$2,000

50 percent of C's contribution base for 1971	$ 7,500	
30 percent of C's contribution base for 1971		4,500
Less: Charitable contributions actually made in 1971 to section 170(b)(1)(A) organizations ($8,500, but not to exceed 50% of contribution base)	7,500	0
Excess	0	4,500

The amount of excess contributions for 1970 of 30-percent capital gain property which is treated as paid in 1971 is the least of—

    (i) Available carryover from 1970 to 1971 of contributions of 30-percent capital gain property   2,000

    (ii) Excess of 50 percent of contribution base for 1971 ($7,500) over sum of contributions actually made in 1971 to section 170(b)(1)(A) organizations ($7,500)..   0

    (iii) Excess of 30 percent of contribution base for 1971 ($4,500) over contributions of 30-percent capital gain property actually made in 1971 to section 170(b)(1)(A) organizations ($0) .... $ 4,500

    Amount treated as paid   0

1972

Contribution year	Total excess 50%	30%	Less: Amount treated as paid in years prior to 1972	Available charitable contributions carryovers 50%	30%
1970	0	$2,000	0	0	$2,000
1971	$1,000	0	0	$ 1,000	0
				1,000	2,000

50 percent of C's contribution base for 1972..	10,000	
30 percent of C's contribution base for 1972		6,000
Less: Charitable contributions actually made in 1972 to section 170(b)(1)(A) organizations ($7,800, but not to exceed 30% of contribution base)	0	6,000
Excess	10,000	0

(1) The amount of excess contributions for 1971 of property other than 30-percent capital gain property which is treated as paid in 1972 is the lesser of—

    (i) Available carryover from 1971 to 1972 of contributions of property other than 30-percent capital gain property .... $ 1,000

    (ii) Excess of 50 percent of contribution base for 1972 ($10,000) over contributions actually made in 1972 to section 170(b)(1)(A) organizations ($6,000)   4,000

    Amount treated as paid $1,000

(2) The amount of excess contributions for 1970 of 30-percent capital gain property which is treated as paid in 1972 is the least of—

    (i) Available carryover from 1970 to 1972 of contributions of 30-percent capital gain property .... $ 2,000

    (ii) Excess of 50 percent of contribution base for 1972 ($10,000) over sum of contributions actually made in 1972 to section 170(b)(1)(A) organizations ($6,000) and excess contributions for 1971 treated under item (1) above as paid in 1972 ($1,000)   3,000

    (iii) Excess of 30 percent of contribution base for 1972 ($6,000) over contributions of 30-percent capital gain property actually made in 1972 to section 170(b)(1)(A) organizations ($6,000)   0

    Amount treated as paid......................................   0

Reg. § 1.170A-10(c)(2)

1973

Contribution year	Total excess		Less: Amount treated as paid in years prior to 1973	Available charitable contributions carryovers	
	50%	30%		50%	30%
1970	0	$2,000	0	0	$2,000
1971	$1,000	0	$1,000	0	0
1972	0	1,800	0	0	1,800
				0	3,800

50 percent of C's contribution base for 1973	$7,500	
30 percent of C's contribution base for 1973		4,500
Less: Charitable contributions actually made in 1973 to section 170(b)(1)(A) organizations ($14,000, but not to exceed 50% of contribution base)	7,500	0
Excess	0	4,500

(1) The amount of excess contributions for 1970 of 30-percent capital gain property which is treated as paid in 1973 is the least of ....
   (i) Available carryover from 1970 to 1973 of contributions of 30-percent capital gain property $2,000
   (ii) Excess of 50 percent of contribution base for 1973 ($7,500) over contributions actually made in 1973 to section 170(b)(1)(A) organizations ($7,500) 0
   (iii) Excess of 30 percent of contribution base for 1973 ($4,500) over contributions of 30-percent capital gain property actually made in 1973 to section 170(b)(1)(A) organizations ($0) 4,500

   Amount treated as paid 0

(2) The amount of excess contributions for 1972 of 30-percent capital gain property which is treated as paid in 1973 is the least of—
   (i) Available carryover from 1972 to 1973 of contributions of 30-percent capital gain property $1,800
   (ii) Excess of 50 percent of contribution base for 1973 ($7,500) over contributions actually made in 1973 to section 170(b)(1)(A) organizations ($7,500) 0
   (iii) Excess of 30 percent of contribution base for 1973 ($4,500) over sum of contributions of 30-percent capital gain property actually made in 1973 to section 170(b)(1)(A) organizations ($0) and excess contributions for 1970 treated under item (1) above as paid in 1973 ($0) $4,500

   Amount treated as paid 0

1974

Contribution year	Total excess		Less: Amount treated as paid in years prior to 1974	Available charitable contributions carryovers	
	50%	30%		50%	30%
1970	0	$2,000	0	0	$2,000
1971	$1,000	0	$1,000	0	0
1972	0	1,800	0	0	1,800
1973	6,500	0	0	$ 6,500	0
				$ 6,500	$3,800

50 percent of C's contribution base of 1974	$16,500	
30 percent of C's contribution base for 1974		$9,900
Less: Charitable contributions actually made in 1974 to section 170(b)(1)(A) organizations	700	6,400
Excess	15,800	3,500

(1) The amount of excess contributions for 1973 of property other than 30-percent capital gain property which is treated as paid in 1974 is the lesser of ....
   (i) Available carryover from 1973 to 1974 of contributions of property other than 30-percent capital gain property 6,500
   (ii) Excess of 50 percent of contribution base for 1974 ($16,500) over contributions actually made in 1974 to section 170(b)(1)(A) organizations ($7,100) 9,400

   Amount treated as paid 6,500

Reg. § 1.170A-10(c)(2)

(2) The amount of excess contributions for 1970 of 30-percent capital gain property which is treated as paid in 1974 is the least of—

    (i) Available carryover from 1970 to 1974 of contributions of 30-percent capital gain property .... $ 2,000

    (ii) Excess of 50 percent of contribution base for 1974 ($16,500) over sum of contributions actually made in 1974 to section 170(b)(1)(A) organizations ($7,100) and excess contributions for 1973 of property other than 30-percent capital gain property treated under item (1) above as paid in 1974 ($6,500) 2,900

    (iii) Excess of 30 percent of contribution base for 1974 ($9,900) over contributions of 30-percent capital gain property actually made in 1974 to section 170(b)(1)(A) organizations ($6,400) 3,500

        Amount treated as paid 2,000

(3) The amount of excess contributions for 1972 of 30-percent capital gain property which is treated as paid in 1974 is the least of—

    (i) Available carryover from 1972 to 1974 of contributions of 30-percent capital gain property 1,800

    (ii) Excess of 50 percent of contribution base for 1974 ($16,500) over sum of contributions actually made in 1974 to section 170(b)(1)(A) organizations ($7,100) and excess contributions for 1973 and 1970 treated under items (1) and (2) above as paid in 1974 ($8,500)................................... $ 900

    (iii) Excess of 30 percent of contribution base for 1974 ($9,900) over sum of contributions of 30-percent capital gain property actually made in 1974 to section 170(b)(1)(A) organizations ($6,400) and excess contributions for 1970 of 30-percent capital gain property treated under item (2) above as paid in 1974 ($2,000) 1,500

        Amount treated as paid .... $ 900

(d) *Adjustments*—(1) *Effect of net operating loss carryovers on carryover of excess contributions.* An individual having a net operating loss carryover from a prior taxable year which is available as a deduction in a contribution year must apply the special rule of section 170(d)(1)(B) and this subparagraph in computing the excess described in paragraph (b)(1) or (c)(1) of this section for such contribution year. In determining the amount of excess charitable contributions that shall be treated as paid in each of the 5 taxable years succeeding the contribution year, the excess charitable contributions described in paragraph (b)(1) or (c)(1) of this section must be reduced by the amount by which such excess reduces taxable income (for purposes of determining the portion of a net operating loss which shall be carried to taxable years succeeding the contribution year under the second sentence of section 172(b)(2)) and increases the net operating loss which is carried to a succeeding taxable year. In reducing taxable income under the second sentence of section 172(b)(2), an individual who has made charitable contributions in the contribution year to both section 170(b)(1)(A) organizations, as defined in § 1.170A-9, and to organizations which are not section 170(b)(1)(A) organizations must first deduct contributions made to the section 170(b)(1)(A) organizations from his adjusted gross income computed without regard to his net operating loss deduction before any of the contributions made to organizations which are not section 170(b)(1)(A) organizations may be deducted from such adjusted gross income. Thus, if the excess of the contributions made in the contribution year to section 170(b)(1)(A) organizations over the amount deductible in such contribution year is utilized to reduce taxable income (under the provisions of section 172(b)(2)) for such year, thereby serving to increase the amount of the net operating loss carryover to a succeeding year or years, no part of the excess charitable contributions made in such contribution year shall be treated as paid in any of the 5 immediately succeeding taxable years. If only a portion of the excess charitable contributions is so used, the excess charitable contributions shall be reduced only to that extent. The provisions of this subparagraph may be illustrated by the following examples:

Example (1). B, an individual, reports his income on the calendar year basis and for the year 1970 has adjusted gross income (computed without regard to any net operating loss deduction) of $50,000. During 1970 he made charitable contributions of cash in the amount of $30,000 all of which were to section 170(b)(1)(A) organizations. B has a net operating loss carryover from 1969 of $50,000. In the absence of the net operating loss deduction B would have been allowed a deduction for charitable contributions of $25,000. After the application of the net operating loss deduction, B is allowed no deduction for charitable contributions, and there is (before applying the special rule of section 170(d)(1)(B) and this subparagraph) a tentative excess charitable contribution of $30,000. For purposes of determining the net operating loss which remains to be carried over to 1971, B computes his taxable income for 1970 under section 172(b)(2) by deducting the $25,000 charitable contribution. After the $50,000 net op-

Reg. § 1.170A-10(d)(1)

erating loss carryover is applied against the $25,000 of taxable income for 1970 (computed in accordance with section 172(b)(2), assuming no deductions other than the charitable contributions deduction are applicable in making such computation) there remains a $25,000 net operating loss carryover to 1971. Since the application of the net operating loss carryover of $50,000 from 1969 reduces the 1970 adjusted gross income (for purposes of determining 1970 tax liability) to zero, no part of the $25,000 of charitable contributions in that year is deductible under section 170(b)(1). However, in determining the amount of the excess charitable contributions which shall be treated as paid in taxable years 1971, 1972, 1973, 1974, and 1975, the $30,000 must be reduced to $5,000 by the portion of the excess charitable contributions ($25,000) which was used to reduce taxable income for 1970 (as computed for purposes of the second sentence of section 172(b)(2)) and which thereby served to increase the net operating loss carryover to 1971 from zero to $25,000.

Example (2). Assume the same facts as in example (1), except that B's total charitable contributions of $30,000 in cash made during 1970 consisted of $25,000 to section 170(b)(1)(A) organizations and $5,000 to organizations other than section 170(b)(1)(A) organizations. Under these facts there is a tentative excess charitable contribution of $25,000, rather than $30,000 as in example (1). For purposes of determining the net operating loss which remains to be carried over to 1971, B computes his taxable income for 1970 under section 172(b)(2) by deducting the $25,000 of charitable contributions made to section 170(b)(1)(A) organizations. Since the excess charitable contribution of $25,000 determined in accordance with paragraph (b)(1) of this section was used to reduce taxable income for 1970 (as computed for purposes of the second sentence of section 172(b)(2)) and thereby served to increase the net operating loss carryover to 1971 from zero to $25,000, no part of such excess charitable contributions made in the contribution year shall be treated as paid in any of the five immediately succeeding taxable years. No carryover is allowed with respect to the $5,000 of charitable contributions made in 1970 to organizations other than section 170(b)(1)(A) organizations.

Example (3). Assume the same facts as in example (1), except that B's total contributions of $30,000 made during 1970 were of 30-percent capital gain property. Under these facts there is a tentative excess charitable contribution of $30,000. For purposes of determining the net op-

erating loss which remains to be carried over to 1971, B computes his taxable income for 1970 under section 172(b)(2)(B) by deducting the $15,000 (30 percent of $50,000) contribution of 30-percent capital gain property which would have been deductible in 1970 absent the net operating loss deduction. Since $15,000 of the excess charitable contribution of $30,000 determined in accordance with paragraph (c)(1) of this section was used to reduce taxable income for 1970 (as computed for purposes of the second sentence of section 172(b)(2)) and thereby served to increase the net operating loss carryover to 1971 from zero to $15,000, only $15,000 ($30,000 − $15,000) of such excess shall be treated as paid in taxable years 1971, 1972, 1973, 1974, and 1975.

(2) *Effect of net operating loss carryback to contribution year.* The amount of the excess contribution for a contribution year computed as provided in paragraph (b)(1) or (c)(1) of this section and subparagraph (1) of this paragraph shall not be increased because a net operating loss carryback is available as a deduction in the contribution year. Thus, for example, assuming that in 1970 there is an excess contribution of $50,000 (determined as provided in paragraph (b)(1) of this section) which is to be carried to the 5 succeeding taxable years and that in 1973 the taxpayer has a net operating loss which may be carried back to 1970, the excess contribution of $50,000 for 1970 is not increased by reason of the fact that the adjusted gross income for 1970 (on which such excess contribution was based) is subsequently decreased by the carryback of the net operating loss from 1973. In addition, in determining under the provisions of section 172(b)(2) the amount of the net operating loss for any year subsequent to the contribution year which is a carryback or carryover to taxable years succeeding the contribution year, the amount of contributions made to section 170(b)(1)(A) organizations shall be limited to the amount of such contributions which did not exceed 50 percent or, in the case of 30-percent capital gain property, 30 percent of the donor's contribution base, computed without regard to any of the modifications referred to in section 172(d), for the contribution year. Thus, for example, assume that the taxpayer has a net operating loss in 1973 which is carried back to 1970 and in turn to 1971 and that he has made charitable contributions in 1970 to section 170(b)(1)(A) organizations. In determining the maximum amount of such charitable contributions which may be deducted in 1970 for purposes of determining the taxable income for

Reg. § 1.170A-10(d)(2)

1970 which is deducted under section 172(b)(2) from the 1973 loss in order to ascertain the amount of such loss which is carried back to 1971, the 50-percent limitation of section 170(b)(1)(A) is based upon the adjusted gross income for 1970 computed without taking into account the net operating loss carryback from 1973 and without making any of the modifications specified in section 172(d).

(3) *Effect of net operating loss carryback to taxable years succeeding the contribution year.* The amount of the charitable contribution from a preceding taxable year which is treated as paid, as provided in paragraph (b)(2) or (c)(2) of this section, in a current taxable year (hereinafter referred to in this subparagraph as the "deduction year") shall not be reduced because a net operating loss carryback is available as a deduction in the deduction year. In addition, in determining under the provisions of section 172(b)(2) the amount of the net operating loss for any taxable year subsequent to the deduction year which is a carryback or carryover to taxable years succeeding the deduction year, the amount of contributions made to section 170(b)(1)(A) organizations in the deduction year shall be limited to the amount of such contributions, which were actually made in such year and those which were treated as paid in such year, which did not exceed 50 percent or, in the case of 30-percent capital gain property, 30 percent of the donor's contribution based, computed without regard to any of the modifications referred to in section 172(d), for the deduction year.

(4) *Husband and wife filing joint returns —* (i) *Change from joint return to separate returns.* If a husband and wife—

(*a*) Make a joint return for a contribution year and compute an excess charitable contribution for such year in accordance with the provisions of paragraph (b)(1) or (c)(1) of this section and subparagraph (1) of this paragraph, and

(*b*) Make separate returns for one or more of the 5 taxable years immediately succeeding such contribution year,

any excess charitable contribution for the contribution year which is unused at the beginning of the first such taxable year for which separate returns are filed shall be allocated between the husband and wife. For purposes of the allocation, a computation shall be made of the amount of any

excess charitable contribution which each spouse would have computed in accordance with paragraph (b)(1) or (c)(1) of this section and subparagraph (1) of this paragraph if separate returns (rather than a joint return) had been filed for the contribution year. The portion of the total unused excess charitable contribution for the contribution year allocated to each spouse shall be an amount which bears the same ratio to such unused excess charitable contribution as such spouse's excess contribution, based on the separate return computation, bears to the total excess contributions of both spouses, based on the separate return computation. To the extent that a portion of the amount allocated to either spouse in accordance with the foregoing provisions of this subdivision is not treated in accordance with the provisions of paragraph (b)(2) or (c)(2) of this section as a charitable contribution paid to a section 170(b)(1)(A) organization in the taxable year in which a separate return or separate returns are filed, each spouse shall for purposes of paragraph (b)(2) or (c)(2) of this section treat his respective unused portion as the available charitable contributions carryover to the next succeeding taxable year in which the joint excess charitable contribution may be treated as paid in accordance with paragraph (b)(1) or (c)(1) of this section. If such husband and wife make a joint return in one of the five taxable years immediately succeeding the contribution year with respect to which a joint excess charitable contribution is computed and following such first taxable year for which such husband and wife filed a separate return, the amounts allocated to each spouse in accordance with this subdivision for such first year reduced by the portion of such amounts treated as paid to a section 170(b)(1)(A) organization in such first year and in any taxable year intervening between such first year and the succeeding taxable year in which the joint return is filed shall be aggregated for purposes of determining the amount of the available charitable contributions carryover to such succeeding taxable year. The provisions of this subdivision may be illustrated by the following example:

Example. (a) H and W file joint returns for 1970, 1971, and 1972, and in 1973 they file separate returns. In each such year H and W itemize their deductions in computing taxable income. Assume the following factual situation with respect to H and W for 1970:

1970

	H	W	Joint return
Contribution base	$50,000	$40,000	$90,000
Contributions of cash to section 170(b)(1)(A) organizations (no other contributions)	37,000	28,000	65,000
Allowable charitable contributions deductions	$25,000	$20,000	$45,000
Excess contributions for taxable year to be treated as paid in 5 succeeding taxable years	$12,000	$8,000	$20,000

(b) The joint excess charitable contribution of $20,000 is to be treated as having been paid to a section 170(b)(1)(A) organization in the five succeeding taxable years. Assume that in 1971 the portion of such excess treated as paid by H and W is $3,000, and that in 1972 the portion of such excess treated as paid is $7,000. Thus, the unused portion of the excess charitable contribution made in the contribution year is $10,000 ($20,000 less $3,000 [amount treated as paid in 1971] and $7,000 [amount treated as paid in 1972]). Since H and W file separate returns in 1973, $6,000 of such $10,000 is allocable to H, and $4,000 is allocable to W. Such allocation is computed as follows:

$$\frac{\$12,000 \text{ (excess charitable contributions made by H (based on separate return computation) in 1970)}}{\$20,000 \text{ (total excess charitable contributions made by H and W (based on separate return computation) in 1970)}} \times \$10,000 = \$6,000$$

$$\frac{\$8,000 \text{ (excess charitable contributions made by W (based on separate return computation) in 1970)}}{\$20,000 \text{ (Total excess charitable contributions made by H and W (based on separate return computation) in 1970)}} \times \$10,000 = \$4,000$$

(c) In 1973 H has a contribution base of $70,000, and he contributes $14,000 in cash to a section 170(b)(1)(A) organization. In 1973 W has a contribution base of $50,000, and she contributes $10,000 in cash to a section 170(b)(1)(A) organization. Accordingly, H may claim a charitable contributions deduction of $20,000 in 1973, and W may claim a charitable contributions deduction of $14,000 in 1973. H's $20,000 deduction consists of the $14,000 contribution made to the section 170(b)(1)(A) organization in 1973 and the $6,000 carried over from 1970 and treated as a charitable contribution paid by him to a section 170(b)(1)(A) organization in 1973. W's $14,000 deduction consists of the $10,000 contribution made to a section 170(b)(1)(A) organization in 1973 and the $4,000 carried over from 1970 and treated as a charitable contribution paid by her to a section 170(b)(1)(A) organization in 1973.

(d) The $6,000 contribution treated as paid in 1973 by H, and the $4,000 contribution treated as paid in 1973, by W, are computed as follows:

	H	W
Available charitable contribution carryover (see computations in (b))	$ 6,000	$ 4,000
50-percent of contribution base	35,000	25,000
Contributions of cash made in 1973 to section 170(b)(1)(A) organizations (no other contributions)	14,000	10,000
	21,000	15,000

Amount of excess contributions treated as paid in 1973:

The lesser of $6,000 (available carryover of H to 1973) or $21,000 (excess of 50 percent of contribution base ($35,000) over contributions actually made in 1973 to section 170(b)(1)(A) organizations ($14,000))		$ 6,000
The lesser of $4,000 (available carryover of W to 1973) or $15,000 (excess of 50 percent of contribution base ($25,000) over contributions actually made in 1973 to section 170(b)(1)(A) organizations ($10,000))		$ 4,000

(e) It is assumed that H and W made no contributions of 30-percent capital gain property during these years. If they had made such contributions, there would have been similar adjustments based on 30 percent of the contribution base.

(ii) *Change from separate returns to joint return.* If in the case of a husband and wife—

(a) Either or both of the spouses make a separate return for a contribution year and compute an excess charitable contribution for such year in accordance with the provisions of paragraph (b)(1) or (c)(1) of this section and subparagraph (1) of this paragraph, and

(b) Such husband and wife make a joint return for one or more of the taxable years succeeding such contribution year,

the excess charitable contribution of the husband and wife for the contribution year which is unused at the beginning of the first taxable year for which a joint return is filed shall be aggregated for purposes of determining the portion of such unused charitable contribution which shall be treated in accordance with paragraph (b)(2) or (c)(2) of this section as a charitable contribution paid to a section 170(b)(1)(A) organization. The provisions of this subdivision also apply in the case of two single individuals who are subsequently married and file a joint return. A remarried taxpayer who filed a joint return with a former spouse in a contribution year with respect to which an excess charitable contribution was computed and who in any one of the five taxable years succeeding such contribution year files a joint return with his or her present spouse shall treat the unused portion of such excess charitable contribution allocated to him or her in accordance with subdivision (i) of this subparagraph in the same manner as the unused portion of an excess charitable contribution computed in a contribution year in which he filed a separate return, for purposes of determining the amount which in accordance with paragraph (b)(2) or (c)(2) of this section shall be treated as paid to an organization specified in section 170(b)(1)(A) in such succeeding year.

(iii) *Unused excess charitable contribution of deceased spouse.* In case of the death of one spouse, any unused portion of an excess charitable contribution which is allocable in accordance with subdivision (i) of this subparagraph to such spouse shall not be treated as paid in the taxable year in which such death occurs or in any subsequent taxable year except on a separate return made for the deceased spouse by a fiduciary for the taxable year which ends with the date of death or on a joint return for the taxable year in which such death occurs. The application of this subdivision may be illustrated by the following example:

Example. Assume the same facts as in the example in subdivision (i) of this subparagraph except that H dies in 1972 and W files a separate

return for 1973. W made a joint return for herself and H for 1972. In that example, the unused excess charitable contribution as of January 1, 1973, was $10,000, $6,000 of which was allocable to H and $4,000 to W. No portion of the $6,000 allocable to H may be treated as paid by W or any other person in 1973 or any subsequent year.

(e) *Information required in support of a deduction of an amount carried over and treated as paid.* If, in a taxable year, a deduction is claimed in respect of an excess charitable contribution which, in accordance with the provisions of paragraph (b)(2) or (c)(2) of this section, is treated (in whole or in part) as paid in such taxable year, the taxpayer shall attach to his return a statement showing:

(1) The contribution year (or years) in which the excess charitable contributions were made,

(2) The excess charitable contributions made in each contribution year, and the amount of such excess charitable contributions consisting of 30-percent capital gain property,

(3) The portion of such excess, or of each such excess, treated as paid in accordance with paragraph (b)(2) or (c)(2) of this section in any taxable year intervening between the contribution year and the taxable year for which the return is made, and the portion of such excess which consists of 30-percent capital gain property.

(4) Whether or not an election under section 170(b)(1)(D)(iii) has been made which affects any of such excess contributions of 30-percent capital gain property, and

(5) Such other information as the return or the instructions relating thereto may require.

(f) *Effective date.* This section applies only to contributions paid in taxable years beginning after December 31, 1969. For purposes of applying section 170(d)(1) with respect to contributions paid in a taxable year beginning before January 1, 1970, subsection (b)(1)(D), subsection (e), and paragraphs (1), (2), (3), and (4) of subsection (f) of section 170 shall not apply. See section 201(g)(1)(D) of the Tax Reform Act of 1969 (83 Stat. 564). [Reg. § 1.170A-10.]

☐ [*T.D. 7207, 10-3-72. Amended by T.D. 7340, 1-6-75.*]

[Reg. § 1.170-3]

§ 1.170-3. Contributions or gifts by corporations (before amendment by Tax Reform Act of 1969).—[The text of Reg. § 1.170-3, pertaining to taxable years beginning before January 1, 1970, is no longer reproduced by CCH.]

[Reg. § 1.170A-11]

§ 1.170A-11. Limitation on, and carryover of, contributions by corporations.—(a) *In gen-*

eral. The deduction by a corporation in any taxable year for charitable contributions, as defined in section 170(c), is limited to 5 percent of its taxable income for the year, computed without regard to—

(1) The deduction under section 170 for charitable contributions,

(2) The special deductions for corporations allowed under part VIII (except section 248), subchapter B, chapter 1 of the Code,

(3) Any net operating loss carryback to the taxable year under section 172, and

(4) Any capital loss carryback to the taxable year under section 1212(a)(1).

A charitable contribution by a corporation to a trust, chest, fund, or foundation described in section 170(c)(2) is deductible under section 170 only if the contribution is to be used in the United States or its possessions exclusively for religious, charitable, scientific, literary, or educational purposes or for the prevention of cruelty to children or animals. For the purposes of section 170, amounts excluded from the gross income of a corporation under section 114, relating to sports programs conducted for the American National Red Cross, are not to be considered contributions or gifts.

(b) *Election by corporations on an accrual method.* (1) A corporation reporting its taxable income on an accrual method may elect to have a charitable contribution treated as paid during the taxable year, if payment is actually made on or before the 15th day of the third month following the close of such year and if, during such year, its board of directors authorizes the charitable contribution. If by reason of such an election a charitable contribution (other than a contribution of a letter, memorandum, or property similar to a letter or memorandum) paid in a taxable year beginning after December 31, 1969, is treated as paid during a taxable year beginning before January 1, 1970, the provisions of § 1.170A-4 shall not be applied to reduce the amount of such contribution. However, see section 170(e) before its amendment by the Tax Reform Act of 1969.

(2) The election must be made at the time the return for the taxable year is filed, by reporting the contribution on the return. There shall be attached to the return when filed a written declaration that the resolution authorizing the contribution was adopted by the board of directors during the taxable year, and the declaration shall be vertified by a statement signed by an officer authorized to sign the return that it is made under the penalties of perjury. There shall also be attached to the return when filed a copy of the resolution of the board of directors authorizing the contribution.

(c) *Charitable contributions carryover of corporations* —(1) *In general.* Subject to the reduction provided in subparagraph (2) of this paragraph, any charitable contributions made by a corporation in a taxable year (hereinafter in this paragraph referred to as the "contribution year") in excess of the amount deductible in such contribution year under the 5-percent limitation of section 170(b)(2) are deductible in each of the five succeeding taxable years in order of time, but only to the extent of the lesser of the following amounts:

(i) The excess of the maximum amount deductible for such succeeding taxable year under the 5-percent limitation of section 170(b)(2) over the sum of the charitable contributions made in that year plus the aggregate of the excess contributions which were made in taxable years before the contribution year and which are deductible under this paragraph in such succeeding taxable year; or

(ii) In the case of the first taxable year succeeding the contribution year, the amount of the excess charitable contributions, and in the case of the second, third, fourth, and fifth taxable years succeeding the contribution year, the portion of the excess charitable contributions not deductible under this subparagraph for any taxable year intervening between the contribution year and such succeeding taxable year.

This paragraph applies to excess charitable contributions by a corporation, whether or not such contributions are made to, or for the use of, the donee organization and whether or not such organization is a section 170(b)(1)(A) organization, as defined in § 1.170A-9. For purposes of applying this paragraph, a charitable contribution made in a taxable year beginning before January 1, 1970, which is carried over to a taxable year beginning after December 31, 1969, under section 170(b)(2) (before its amendment by the Tax Reform Act of 1969) and is deductible in such taxable year beginning after December 31, 1969, shall be treated as deductible under section 170(d)(1) and this paragraph. The application of this subparagraph may be illustrated by the following example:

Example. A corporation which reports its income on the calendar year basis makes a charitable contribution of $20,000 in 1970. Its taxable income (determined without regard to any deduction for charitable contributions) for 1970 is $100,000. Accordingly, the charitable contributions deduction for that year is limited to $5,000 (5 percent of $100,000). The excess charitable contribution not deductible in 1970 ($15,000) is a carryover to 1971. The corporation has taxable income (determined without regard to any deduction for charitable contributions) of $150,000 in

1971 and makes a charitable contribution of $5,000 in that year. For 1971 the corporation may deduct as a charitable contribution the amount of $7,500 (5 percent of $150,000). This amount consists of the $5,000 contribution made in 1971 and of the $2,500 carried over from 1970. The remaining $12,500 carried over from 1970 and not allowable as a deduction for 1971 because of the 5-percent limitation may be carried over to 1972. The corporation has taxable income (determined without regard to any deduction for charitable contributions) of $200,000 in 1972 and makes a charitable contribution of $5,000 in that year. For 1972 the corporation may deduct the amount of $10,000 (5 percent of $200,000). This amount consists of the $5,000 contributed in 1972, and $5,000 of the $12,500 carried over from 1970 to 1972. The remaining $7,500 of the carryover from 1970 is available for purposes of computing the charitable contributions carryover from 1970 to 1973, 1974, and 1975.

(2) *Effect of net operating loss carryovers on carryover of excess contributions.* A corporation having a net operating loss carryover from any taxable year must apply the special rule of section 170(d)(2)(B) and this subparagraph before computing under subparagraph (1) of this paragraph the excess charitable contributions carryover from any taxable year. In determining the amount of excess charitable contributions that may be deducted in accordance with subparagraph (1) of this paragraph in taxable years succeeding the contribution year, the excess of the charitable contributions made by a corporation in the contributions year over the amount deductible in such year must be reduced by the amount by which such excess reduces taxable income for purposes of determining the net operating loss carryover under the second sentence of section 172(b)(2) and increases a net operating loss carryover to a succeeding taxable year. Thus, if the excess of the contributions made in a taxable year over the amount deductible in the taxable year is utilized to reduce taxable income (under the provisions of section 172(b)(2)) for such year, thereby serving to increase the amount of the net operating loss carryover to a succeeding taxable year or years, no charitable contributions carryover will be allowed. If only a portion of the excess charitable contributions is so used, the charitable contributions carryover will be reduced only to that extent. The application of this subparagraph may be illustrated by the following example:

Example. A corporation, which reports its income on the calendar year basis, makes a charitable contribution of $10,000 during 1971. Its taxable income for 1971 is $80,000 (computed without regard to any net operating loss deduc-

tion and computed in accordance with section 170(b)(2) without regard to any deduction for charitable contributions). The corporation has a net operating loss carryover from 1970 of $80,000. In the absence of the net operating loss deduction the corporation would have been allowed a deduction for charitable contributions of $4,000 (5 percent of $80,000). After the application of the net operating loss deduction the corporation is allowed no deduction for charitable contributions, and there is a tentative charitable contribution carryover from 1971 of $10,000. For purposes of determining the net operating loss carryover to 1972 the corporation computes its taxable income for 1971 under section 172 (b)(2) by deducting the $4,000 charitable contribution. Thus, after the $80,000 net operating loss carryover is applied against the $76,000 of taxable income for 1971 (computed in accordance with section 172(b)(2)), there remains a $4,000 net operating loss carryover to 1972. Since the application of the net operating loss carryover of $80,000 from 1970 reduces the taxable income for 1971 to zero, no part of the $10,000 of charitable contributions in that year is deductible under section 170(b)(2). However, in determining the amount of the allowable charitable contributions carryover from 1971 to 1972, 1973, 1974, 1975, and 1976, the $10,000 must be reduced by the portion thereof ($4,000) which was used to reduce taxable income for 1971 (as computed for purposes of the second sentence of section 172(b)(2)) and which thereby served to increase the net operating loss carryover from 1970 to 1972 from zero to $4,000.

(3) *Effect of net operating loss carryback to contribution year.* The amount of the excess contribution for a contribution year computed as provided in subparagraph (1) of this paragraph shall not be increased because a net operating loss carryback is available as a deduction in the contribution year. In addition, in determining under the provisions of section 172(b)(2) the amount of the net operating loss for any year subsequent to the contribution year which is a carryback or carryover to taxable years succeeding the contribution year, the amount of any charitable contributions shall be limited to the amount of such contributions which did not exceed 5 percent of the donor's taxable income, computed as provided in paragraph (a) of this section and without regard to any of the modifications referred to in section 172(d), for the contribution year. For illustrations see paragraph (d)(2) of § 1.170A-10.

(4) *Effect of net operating loss carryback to taxable year succeeding the contribution year.* The amount of the charitable contribution from a preceding taxable year which is deductible (as provided in this paragraph) in a current taxable

Reg. § 1.170A-11(c)(2)

year (hereinafter referred to in this subparagraph as the "deduction year") shall not be reduced because a net operating loss carryback is available as a deduction in the deduction year. In addition, in determining under the provisions of section 172(b)(2) the amount of the net operating loss for any taxable year subsequent to the deduction year which is a carryback or a carryover to taxable years succeeding the deduction year, the amount of contributions made in the deduction year shall be limited to the amount of such contributions, which were actually made in such year and those which were deductible in such year under section 170(d)(2), which did not exceed 5 percent of the donor's taxable income, computed as provided in paragraph (a) of this section and without regard to any of the modifications referred to in section 172(d), for the deduction year.

(5) *Year contribution is made.* For purposes of this paragraph, contributions made by a corporation in a contribution year include contributions which, in accordance with the provisions of section 170(a)(2) and paragraph (b) of this section, are considered as paid during such contribution year.

(d) *Effective date.* This section applies only to contributions paid in taxable years beginning after December 31, 1969. For purposes of applying section 170(d)(2) with respect to contributions paid, or treated under section 170(a)(2) as paid, in a taxable year beginning before January 1, 1970, subsection (e), and paragraphs (1), (2), (3), and (4) of subsection (f) of section 170 shall not apply. See section 201(g)(1)(D) of the Tax Reform Act of 1969 (83 Stat. 564). [Reg. § 1.170A-11.]

□ [*T.D. 7207, 10-3-72. Amended by T.D. 7807, 1-29-82.*]

[Reg. § 1.170A-12]

§ 1.170A-12. Valuation of a remainder interest in real property for contributions made after July 31, 1969.—(a) *In general*—(1) Section 170(f)(4) provides that, in determining the value of a remainder interest in real property for purposes of section 170, depreciation and depletion of such property shall be taken into account. Depreciation shall be computed by the straight line method and depletion shall be computed by the cost depletion method. Section 170(f)(4) and this section apply only in the case of a contribution, not made in trust, of a remainder interest in real property made after July 31, 1969, for which a deduction is otherwise allowable under section 170.

(2) In the case of the contribution of a remainder interest in real property consisting of a combination of both depreciable and nondeprecia-

ble property, or of both depletable and nondepletable property, and allocation of the fair market value of the property at the time of the contribution shall be made between the depreciable and nondepreciable property, or the depletable and nondepletable property, and depreciation or depletion shall be taken into account only with respect to the depreciable or depletable property. The expected value at the end of its "estimated useful life" (as defined in paragraph (d) of this section) of that part of the remainder interest consisting of depreciable property shall be considered to be nondepreciable property for purposes of the required allocation. In the case of the contribution of a remainder interest in stock in a cooperative housing corporation (as defined in section 216(b)(1)), an allocation of the fair market value of the stock at the time of the contribution shall be made to reflect the respective values of the depreciable and nondepreciable property underlying such stock, and depreciation on the depreciable part shall be taken into account for purposes of valuing the remainder interest in such stock.

(3) If the remainder interest that has been contributed follows only one life, the value of the remainder interest shall be computed under the rules contained in paragraph (b) of this section. If the remainder interest that has been contributed follows a term for years, the value of the remainder interest shall be computed under the rules contained in paragraph (c) of this section. If the remainder interest that has been contributed is dependent upon the continuation or the termination of more than one life or upon a term certain concurrent with one or more lives, the provisions of paragraph (e) of this section shall apply. In every case where it is provided in this section that the rules contained in § 25.2512-5 (or, for certain prior periods, § 25.2512-5A) of this chapter (Gift Tax Regulations) apply, such rules shall apply notwithstanding the general effective date for such rules contained in paragraph (a) of such sections. Except as provided in § 1.7520-3(b) of this chapter, for transfers of remainder interests after April 30, 1989, the present value of the remainder interest is determined under § 25.2512-5 of this chapter by use of the interest rate component on the date the interest is transferred unless an election is made under section 7520 and § 1.7520-2 of this chapter to compute the present value of the interest transferred by use of the interest rate component for either of the 2 months preceding the month in which the interest is transferred. In some cases, a reduction in the amount of a charitable contribution of a remainder interest, after the computation of its value under section 170(f)(4) and this section,

Reg. § 1.170A-12(a)(3)

may be required. See section 170(e) and § 1.170A-4.

(b) *Valuation of a remainder interest following only one life*—(1) *General rule.* The value of a remainder interest in real property following only one life is determined under the rules provided in § 20.2031-7 (or for certain prior periods, § 20.2031-7A) of this chapter (Estate Tax Regulations), using the interest rate and life contingencies prescribed for the date of the gift. See, however, § 1.7520-3(b) (relating to exceptions to the use of prescribed tables under certain circumstances). However, if any part of the real property is subject to exhaustion, wear and tear, or obsolescence, the special factor determined under paragraph (b)(2) of this section shall be used in valuing the remainder interest in that part. Further, if any part of the property is subject to depletion of its natural resources, such depletion is taken into account in determining the value of the remainder interest.

(2) *Computation of depreciation factor.* If the valuation of the remainder interest in depreciable property is dependent upon the continuation of one life, a special factor must be used. The factor determined under this paragraph (b)(2) is carried to the fifth decimal place. The special factor is to be computed on the basis of the interest rate and life contingencies prescribed in § 20.2031-7 of this chapter (or for periods before May 1, 1999, § 20.2031-7A) and on the assump-

tion that the property depreciates on a straight-line basis over its estimated useful life. For transfers for which the valuation date is after April 30, 1999, special factors for determining the present value of a remainder interest following one life and an example describing the computation is contained in Internal Revenue Service Publication 1459, "Actuarial Values, Book Gimel," (7-1999). A copy of this publication is available for purchase from the Superintendent of Documents, United States Government Printing Office, Washington, DC 20402. For transfers for which the valuation date is after April 30, 1989, and before May 1, 1999, special factors for determining the present value of a remainder interest following one life and an example describing the computation is contained in Internal Revenue Service Publication 1459, "Actuarial Values, Gamma Volume," (8-89). This publication is no longer available for purchase from the Superintendent of Documents. However, it may be obtained by requesting a copy from: CC:DOM:CORP:R (IRS Publication 1459), room 5226, Internal Revenue Service, POB 7604, Ben Franklin Station, Washington, DC 20044. See, however, § 1.7520-3(b) (relating to exceptions to the use of prescribed tables under certain circumstances). Otherwise, in the case of the valuation of a remainder interest following one life, the special factor may be obtained through use of the following formula:

$$\left(1 + \frac{i}{2}\right) \sum_{t=0}^{n-1} v^{(t+1)} \left[\left(1 - \frac{l_{x+t+1}}{l_x}\right) - \left(1 - \frac{l_{x+t}}{l_x}\right)\right]\left(1 - \frac{1}{2n} - \frac{t}{n}\right)$$

Where:

n = the estimated number of years of useful life,

i = the applicable interest rate under section 7520 of the Internal Revenue Code,

v = 1 divided by the sum of 1 plus the applicable interest rate under section 7520 of the Internal Revenue Code,

x = the age of the life tenant, and

l_x = number of persons living at age x as set forth in Table 90CM of § 20.2031-7 (or, for periods before May 1, 1999, the tables set forth under § 20.2031-7A) of this chapter.

(3) *Example.* The following example illustrates the provisions of this paragraph (b):

Example. A, who is 62, donates to Y University a remainder interest in a personal residence, consisting of a house and land, subject to a reserved life estate in A. At the time of the gift, the land has a value of $30,000 and the house has a value of $100,000 with an estimated useful life of 45 years, at the end of which the value of the house is expected to be $20,000. The portion of the property considered to be depreciable is $80,000 (the value of the house ($100,000) less its expected value at the end of 45 years ($20,000)). The portion of the property considered to be non-

depreciable is $50,000 (the value of the land at the time of the gift ($30,000) plus the expected value of the house at the end of 45 years ($20,000)). At the time of the gift, the interest rate prescribed under section 7520 is 8.4 percent. Based on an interest rate of 8.4 percent, the remainder factor for $1.00 prescribed in § 20.2031-7(d) of this chapter for a person age 62 is 0.27925. The value of the nondepreciable remainder interest is $13,962.50 (0.27925 times $50,000). The value of the depreciable remainder interest is $16,148.80 (0.20186, computed under the formula described in paragraph (b)(2) of this

Reg. § 1.170A-12(b)(1)

section, times $80,000). Therefore, the value of the remainder interest is $30,111.30.

(c) *Valuation of a remainder interest following a term for years.* The value of a remainder interest in real property following a term for years shall be determined under the rules provided in § 25.2512-5 (or, for certain prior periods, § 25.2512-5A) of this chapter (Gift Tax Regulations) using Table B provided in § 20 2031-7(d)(6) of this chapter. However, if any part of the real property is subject to exhaustion, wear and tear, or obsolescence, in valuing the remainder interest in that part the value of such part is adjusted by subtracting from the value of such part the amount determined by multiplying such value by a fraction, the numerator of which is the number of years in the term or, if less, the estimated useful life of the property, and the denominator of which is the estimated useful life of the property. The resultant figure is the value of the property to be used in § 25.2512-5 (or, for certain prior periods, § 25.2512-5A) of this chapter (Gift Tax Regulations). Further, if any part of the property is subject to depletion of its natural resources, such depletion shall be taken into account in determining the value of the remainder interest. The provisions of this paragraph as it relates to depreciation are illustrated by the following example:

Example. In 1972, B donates to Z University a remainder interest in his personal residence, consisting of a house and land, subject to a 20 year term interest provided for his sister. At such time the house has a value of $60,000, and an expected useful life of 45 years, at the end of which time it is expected to have a value of 10,000, and the land has a value of $8,000. The value of the portion of the property considered to be depreciable is $50,000 (the value of the house ($60,000) less its expected value at the end of 45 years ($10,000)), and this is multiplied by the fraction 20/45. The product, $22,222.22, is subtracted from $68,000, the value of the entire property, and the balance, $45,777.78, is multiplied by the factor .311805 (see § 25.2512-5A(c)). The result, $14,273.74, is the value of the remainder interest in the property.

(d) *Definition of estimated useful life.* For the purposes of this section, the determination of the estimated useful life of depreciable property shall take account of the expected use of such property during the period of the life estate or term for years. The term "estimated useful life" means the estimated period (beginning with the date of the contribution) over which such property may reasonably be expected to be useful for such expected use. This period shall be determined by reference

to the experience based on any prior use of the property for such purposes if such prior experience is adequate. If such prior experience is inadequate or if the property has not been previously used for such purposes, the estimated useful life shall be determined by reference to the general experience of persons normally holding similar property for such expected use, taking into account present conditions and probable future developments. The estimated useful life of such depreciable property is not limited to the period of the life estate or term for years preceding the remainder interest. In determining the expected use and the estimated useful life of the property, consideration is to be given to the provisions of the governing instrument creating the life estate or term for years or applicable local law, if any, relating to use, preservation, and maintenance of the property during the life estate or term for years In arriving at the estimated useful life of the property, estimates, if available, of engineers or other persons skilled in estimating the useful life of similar property may be taken into account. At the option of the taxpayer, the estimated useful life of property contributed after December 31, 1970, for purposes of this section, shall be an asset depreciation period selected by the taxpayer that is within the permissible asset depreciation range for the relevant asset guideline class established pursuant to § 1.167(a)-11(b)(4)(ii). For purposes of the preceding sentence, such period, range, and class shall be those which are in effect at the time that the contribution of the remainder interest was made. At the option of the taxpayer, in the case of property contributed before January 1, 1971, the estimated useful life, for purposes of this section, shall be the guideline life provided in Revenue Procedure 62-21 for the relevant asset guideline class.

(e) *Valuation of a remainder interest following more than one life or a term certain concurrent with one or more lives.*—(1)(i) If the valuation of the remainder interest in the real property is dependent upon the continuation or the termination of more than one life or upon a term certain concurrent with one or more lives, a special factor must be used.

(ii) The special factor is to be computed on the basis of—

(A) Interest at the rate prescribed under § 25.2512-5 (or for certain prior periods, § 25.2512-5A) of this chapter, compounded annually;

(B) Life contingencies determined from the values that are set forth in the mortality table in § 20.2031-7 (or, for certain prior periods, § 20.2031-7A) of this chapter; and

(C) If depreciation is involved, the assumption that the property depreciates on a straight-line basis over its estimated useful life.

(iii) If any part of the property is subject to depletion of its natural resources, such deple-

tion must be taken into account in determining the value of the remainder interest.

(2) In the case of the valuation of a remainder interest following two lives, the special factor may be obtained through use of the following formula:

$$\left(1 + \frac{i}{2}\right) \sum_{t=0}^{n-1} v^{(t+1)} \left[\left(1 - \frac{l_{x+t+1}}{l_x}\right)\left(1 - \frac{l_{y+t+1}}{l_y}\right) - \left(1 - \frac{l_{x+t}}{l_x}\right)\left(1 - \frac{l_{y+t}}{l_y}\right)\right]\left(1 - \frac{1}{2n} - \frac{t}{n}\right)$$

Where:

n = the estimated number of years of useful life,

i = the applicable interest rate under section 7520 of the Internal Revenue Code,

v = 1 divided by the sum of 1 plus the applicable interest rate under section 7520 of the Internal Revenue Code,

x and y = the ages of the life tenants, and

lx and ly = the number of persons living at ages x and y as set forth in Table 90CM in § 20.2031-7 (or, for prior periods, in § 20.2031-7A) of this chapter.

(3) Notwithstanding that the taxpayer may be able to compute the special factor in certain cases under paragraph (2), if a special factor is required in the case of an actual contribution, the Commissioner will furnish the factor to the donor upon request. The request must be accompanied by a statement of the sex and date of birth of each person the duration of whose life may affect the value of the remainder interest, copies of the relevant instruments, and, if depreciation is involved, a statement of the estimated useful life of the depreciable property. However, since remainder interests in that part of any property which is depletable cannot be valued on a purely actuarial basis, special factors will not be furnished with respect to such part. Requests should be forwarded to the Commissioner of Internal Revenue, Attention: OP:E:EP:A:1, Washington, D.C. 20224. [Reg. § 1.170A-12.]

☐ [*T.D. 7370, 7-14-75. Amended by T.D. 7955, 5-10-84; T.D. 8540, 6-9-94; T.D. 8819, 4-29-99 and T.D. 8886, 6-9-2000.*]

[Reg. § 1.170A-13]

§ 1.170A-13. Recordkeeping and return requirements for deductions for charitable contributions.—(a) *Charitable contributions of money made in taxable years beginning after December 31, 1982*—(1) *In general.* If a taxpayer makes a charitable contribution of money in a taxable year beginning after December 31, 1982, the taxpayer shall maintain for each contribution one of the following:

(i) A cancelled check.

(ii) A receipt from the donee charitable organization showing the name of the donee, the

date of the contribution, and the amount of the contribution. A letter or other communication from the donee charitable organization acknowledging receipt of a contribution and showing the date and amount of the contribution constitutes a receipt for purposes of this paragraph (a).

(iii) In the absence of a canceled check or receipt from the donee charitable organization, other reliable written records showing the name of the donee, the date of the contribution, and the amount of the contribution.

(2) *Special rules*—(i) *Reliability of records.* The reliability of the written records described in paragraph (a)(1)(iii) of this section is to be determined on the basis of all of the facts and circumstances of a particular case. In all events, however, the burden shall be on the taxpayer to establish reliability. Factors indicating that the written records are reliable include, but are not limited to:

(A) The contemporaneous nature of the writing evidencing the contribution.

(B) The regularity of the taxpayer's recordkeeping procedures. For example, a contemporaneous diary entry stating the amount and date of the donation and the name of the donee charitable organization made by a taxpayer who regularly makes such diary entries would generally be considered reliable.

(C) In the case of a contribution of a small amount, the existence of any written or other evidence from the donee charitable organization evidencing receipt of a donation that would not otherwise constitute a receipt under paragraph (a)(1)(ii) of this section (including an emblem, button, or other token traditionally associated with a charitable organization and regularly given by the organization to persons making cash donations).

(ii) *Information stated in income tax return.* The information required by paragraph (a)(1)(iii) of this section shall be stated in the taxpayer's income tax return if required by the return form or its instructions.

(3) *Taxpayer option to apply paragraph (d)(1) to pre-1985 contributions.* See paragraph (d)(1) of this section with regard to contributions of money made on or before December 31, 1984.

(b) *Charitable contributions of property other than money made in taxable years beginning after December 31, 1982*—(1) *In general.* Except in the case of certain charitable contributions of property made after December 31, 1984, to which paragraph (c) of this section applies, any taxpayer who makes a charitable contribution of property other than money in a taxable year beginning after December 31, 1982, shall maintain for each contribution a receipt from the donee showing the following information:

(i) The name of the donee.

(ii) The date and location of the contribution.

(iii) A description of the property in detail reasonably sufficient under the circumstances. Although the fair market value of the property is one of the circumstances to be taken into account in determining the amount of detail to be included on the receipt, such value need not be stated on the receipt.

A letter or other written communication from the donee acknowledging receipt of the contribution, showing the date of the contribution, and containing the required description of the property contributed constitutes a receipt for purposes of this paragraph. A receipt is not required if the contribution is made in circumstances where it is impractical to obtain a receipt (*e.g.*, by depositing property at a charity's unattended drop site). In such cases, however, the taxpayer shall maintain reliable written records with respect to each item of donated property that include the information required by paragraph (b)(2)(ii) of this section.

(2) *Special rules*—(i) *Reliability of records.* The rules described in paragraph (a)(2)(i) of this section also apply to this paragraph (b) for determining the reliability of the written records described in paragraph (b)(1) of this section.

(ii) *Content of records.* The written records described in paragraph (b)(1) of this section shall include the following information and such information shall be stated in the taxpayer's income

tax return if required by the return form or its instructions:

(A) The name and address of the donee organization to which the contribution was made.

(B) The date and location of the contribution.

(C) A description of the property in detail reasonable under the circumstances (including the value of the property), and, in the case of securities, the name of the issuer, the type of security, and whether or not such security is regularly traded on a stock exchange or in an over-the-counter market.

(D) The fair market value of the property at the time the contribution was made, the method utilized in determining the fair market value, and, if the valuation was determined by appraisal, a copy of the signed report of the appraiser.

(E) In the case of property to which section 170(e) applies, the cost or other basis, adjusted as provided by section 1016, the reduction by reason of section 170(e)(1) in the amount of the charitable contribution otherwise taken into account, and the manner in which such reduction was determined. A taxpayer who elects under paragraph (d)(2) of § 1.170A-8 to apply section 170(e)(1) to contributions and carryovers of 30 percent capital gain property shall maintain a written record indicating the years for which the election was made and showing the contributions in the current year and carryovers from preceding years to which it applies. For the definition of the term "30-percent capital gain property," see paragraph (d)(3) of § 1.170A-8.

(F) If less than the entire interest in the property is contributed during the taxable year, the total amount claimed as a deduction for the taxable year due to the contribution of the property, and the amount claimed as a deduction in any prior year or years for contributions of other interests in such property, the name and address of each organization to which any such contribution was made, the place where any such property which is tangible property is located or kept, and the name of any person, other than the organization to which the property giving rise to the deduction was contributed, having actual possession of the property.

(G) The terms of any agreement or understanding entered into by or on behalf of the taxpayer which relates to the use, sale, or other disposition of the property contributed, including for example, the terms of any agreement or understanding which—

Reg. § 1.170A-13(b)(2)

(1) Restricts temporarily or permanently the donee's right to use or dispose of the donated property,

(2) Reserves to, or confers upon, anyone (other than the donee organization or an organization participating with the donee organization in cooperative fund-raising) any right to the income from donated property or to the possession of the property, including the right to vote donated securities, to acquire the property by purchase or otherwise, or to designate the person having such income, possession, or right to acquire, or

(3) Earmarks donated property for a particular use.

(3) *Deductions in excess of $500 claimed for a charitable contribution of property other than money*—(i) *In general*. In addition to the information required under paragraph (b)(2)(ii) of this section, if a taxpayer makes a charitable contribution of property other than money in a taxable year beginning after December 31, 1982, and claims a deduction in excess of $500 in respect of the contribution of such item, the taxpayer shall maintain written records that include the following information with respect to such item of donated property, and shall state such information in his or her income tax return if required by the return form or its instructions:

(A) The manner of acquisition, as, for example by purchase, gift, bequest, inheritance, or exchange, and the approximate date of acquisition of the property by the taxpayer or, if the property was created, produced, or manufactured by or for the taxpayer, the approximate date the property was substantially completed.

(B) The cost or other basis, adjusted as provided by section 1016, of property, other than publicly traded securities, held by the taxpayer for a period of less than 12 months (6 months for property contributed in taxable years beginning after December 31, 1982, and on or before June 6, 1988) immediately preceding the date on which the contribution was made and, when the information is available, of property, other than publicly traded securities, held for a period of 12 months or more (6 months or more for property contributed in taxable years beginning after December 31, 1982, and on or before June 6, 1988) preceding the date on which the contribution was made.

(ii) *Information on acquisition date or cost basis not available.* If the return form or its instructions require the taxpayer to provide information on either the acquisition date or the cost basis as described in paragraph (b)(3)(i)(A) and (B), respectively, of this section, and the taxpayer has reasonable cause for not being able to provide such information, the taxpayer shall attach an explanatory statement to the return. If a taxpayer has reasonable cause for not being able to provide such information, the taxpayer shall not be disallowed a charitable contribution deduction under section 170 for failure to comply with paragraph (b)(3)(i)(A) and (B) of the section.

(4) *Taxpayer option to apply paragraph (d)(1) and (2) to pre-1985 contributions.* See paragraph (d)(1) and (2) of this section with regard to contributions of property made on or before December 31, 1984.

(c) *Deductions in excess of $5,000 for certain charitable contributions of property made after December 31, 1984*—(1) *General Rule*—(i) *In general.* This paragraph applies to any charitable contribution made after December 31, 1984, by an individual, closely held corporation, personal service corporation, partnership, or S corporation of an item of property (other than money and publicly traded securities to which § 1.170A-13(c)(7)(xi)(B) does not apply) if the amount claimed or reported as a deduction under section 170 with respect to such item exceeds $5,000. This paragraph also applies to charitable contributions by C corporations (as defined in section 1361(a)(2) of the Code) to the extent described in paragraph (c)(2)(ii) of this section. No deduction under section 170 shall be allowed with respect to a charitable contribution to which this paragraph applies unless the substantiation requirements described in paragraph (c)(2) of this section are met. For purposes of this paragraph (c), the amount claimed or reported as a deduction for an item of property is the aggregate amount claimed or reported as a deduction for a charitable contribution under section 170 for such items of property and all similar items of property (as defined in paragraph (c)(7)(iii) of this section) by the same donor for the same taxable year (whether or not donated to the same donee).

(ii) *Special rule for property to which section 170(e)(3) or (4) applies.* For purposes of this paragraph (c), in computing the amount claimed or reported as a deduction for donated property to which section 170(e)(3) or (4) applies (pertaining to certain contributions of inventory and scientific equipment) there shall be taken into account only the amount claimed or reported as a deduction in excess of the amount which would have been taken into account for tax purposes by the donor as costs of goods sold if the donor had sold the contributed property to the donee. For example, assume that a donor makes a contribution from inventory of clothing for the care of the needy to which section 170(e)(3) applies. The cost of the property to the donor was $5,000, and, pursuant to section 170(e)(3)(B), the donor claims a charitable contribution deduction of $8,000 with respect to the property. Therefore, $3,000 ($8,000 − $5,000) is the amount taken into account for purposes of determining whether the $5,000 threshold of this paragraph (c)(1) is met.

(2) *Substantiation requirements*—(i) *In general.* Except as provided in paragraph (c)(2)(ii) of this section, a donor who claims or reports a deduction with respect to a charitable contribution to which this paragraph (c) applies must comply with the following three requirements:

(A) Obtain a qualified appraisal (as defined in paragraph (c)(3) of this section) for such property contributed. If the contributed property is a partial interest, the appraisal shall be of the partial interest.

(B) Attach a fully completed appraisal summary (as defined in paragraph (c)(4) of this section) to the tax return (or, in the case of a donor that is a partnership or S corporation, the information return) on which the deduction for the contribution is first claimed (or reported) by the donor.

(C) Maintain records containing the information required by paragraph (b)(2)(ii) of this section.

(ii) *Special rules for certain nonpublicly traded stock, certain publicly traded securities, and contributions by certain C corporations.* (A) In cases described in paragraph (c)(2)(ii)(B) of this section, a qualified appraisal is not required, and only a partially completed appraisal summary form (as described in paragraph (c)(4)(iv)(A) of this section) is required to be attached to the tax or information return specified in paragraph (c)(2)(i)(B) of this section. However, in all cases donors must maintain records containing the information required by paragraph (b)(2)(ii) of this section.

(B) This paragraph (c)(2)(ii) applies in each of the following cases:

(1) The contribution of nonpublicly traded stock, if the amount claimed or reported as a deduction for the charitable contribution of such stock is greater than $5,000 but does not exceed $10,000;

(2) The contribution of a security to which paragraph (c)(7)(xi)(B) of this section applies; and

(3) The contribution of an item of property or of similar items of property described in paragraph (c)(1) of this section made after June 6, 1988, by a C corporation (as defined in

section 1361(a)(2) of the Code), other than a closely held corporation or a personal service corporation.

(3) *Qualified appraisal*—(i) *In general.* For purposes of this paragraph (c), the term "qualified appraisal" means an appraisal document that—

(A) Relates to an appraisal that is made not earlier than 60 days prior to the date of contribution of the appraised property nor later than the date specified in paragraph (c)(3)(iv)(B) of this section;

(B) Is prepared, signed, and dated by a qualified appraiser (within the meaning of paragraph (c)(5) of this section);

(C) Includes the information required by paragraph (c)(3)(ii) of this section; and

(D) Does not involve an appraisal fee prohibited by paragraph (c)(5) of this section.

(ii) *Information included in qualified appraisal.* A qualified appraisal shall include the following information:

(A) A description of the property in sufficient detail for a person who is not generally familiar with the type of property to ascertain that the property that was appraised is the property that was (or will be) contributed;

(B) In the case of tangible property, the physical condition of the property;

(C) The date (or expected date) of contribution to the donee;

(D) The terms of any agreement or understanding entered into (or expected to be entered into) by or on behalf of the donor or donee that relates to the use, sale, or other disposition of the property contributed, including, for example, the terms of any agreement or understanding that—

(1) Restricts temporarily or permanently a donee's right to use or dispose of the donated property,

(2) Reserves to, or confers upon, anyone (other than a donee organization or an organization participating with a donee organization in cooperative fund-raising) any right to the income from the contributed property or to the possession of the property, including the right to vote donated securities, to acquire the property by purchase or otherwise, or to designate the person having such income, possession, or right to acquire, or

(3) Earmarks donated property for a particular use;

(E) The name, address, and (if a taxpayer identification number is otherwise required

Reg. § 1.170A-13(c)(3)

by section 6109 and the regulations thereunder) the identifying number of the qualified appraiser; and, if the qualified appraiser is acting in his or her capacity as a partner in a partnership, an employee of any person (whether an individual, corporation, or partnerships), or an independent contractor engaged by a person other than the donor, the name, address, and taxpayer identification number (if a number is otherwise required by section 6109 and the regulations thereunder) of the partnership or the person who employs or engages the qualified appraiser;

(F) The qualifications of the qualified appraiser who signs the appraisal, including the appraiser's background, experience, education, and membership, if any, in professional appraisal associations;

(G) A statement that the appraisal was prepared for income tax purposes;

(H) The date (or dates) on which the property was appraised;

(I) The appraised fair market value (within the meaning of § 1.170A-1(c)(2)) of the property on the date (or expected date) of contribution;

(J) The method of valuation used to determine the fair market value, such as the income approach, the market-data approach, and the replacement-cost-less-depreciation approach; and

(K) The specific basis for the valuation, such as specific comparable sales transactions or statistical sampling, including a justification for using sampling and an explanation of the sampling procedure employed.

(iii) *Effect of signature of the qualified appraiser.* Any appraiser who falsely or fraudulently overstates the value of the contributed property referred to in a qualified appraisal or appraisal summary (as defined in paragraph (c)(3) and (4), respectively, of this section) that the appraiser has signed may be subject to a civil penalty under section 6701 for aiding and abetting an understatement of tax liability and, moreover, may have appraisals disregarded pursuant to 31 U.S.C. § 330(c).

(iv) *Special rules*—(A) *Number of qualified appraisals.* For purposes of paragraph (c)(2)(i)(A) of this section, a separate qualified appraisal is required for each item of property that is not included in a group of similar items of property. See paragraph (c)(7)(iii) of this section for the definition of similar items of property. Only one qualified appraisal is required for a group of similar items of property contributed in

the same taxable year of the donor, although a donor may obtain separate qualified appraisals for each item of property. A qualified appraisal prepared with respect to a group of similar items of property shall provide all the information required by paragraph (c)(3)(ii) of this section for each item of similar property, except that the appraiser may select any items whose aggregate value is appraised at $100 or less and provide a group description of such items.

(B) *Time of receipt of qualified appraisal.* The qualified appraisal must be received by the donor before the due date (including extensions) of the return on which a deduction is first claimed (or reported in the case of a donor that is a partnership or S corporation) under section 170 with respect to the donated property, or, in the case of a deduction first claimed (or reported) on an amended return, the date on which the return is filed.

(C) *Retention of qualified appraisal.* The donor must retain the qualified appraisal in the donor's records for so long as it may be relevant in the administration of any internal revenue law.

(D) *Appraisal disregarded pursuant to 31 U.S.C. § 330(c).* If an appraisal is disregarded pursuant to 31 U.S.C. § 330(c) it shall have no probative effect as to the value of the appraised property. Such appraisal will, however, otherwise constitute a "qualified appraisal" for purposes of this paragraph (c) if the appraisal summary includes the declaration described in paragraph (c)(4)(ii)(L)(*2*) and the taxpayer had no knowledge that such declaration was false as of the time described in paragraph (c)(4)(i)(B) of this section.

(4) *Appraisal summary*—(i) *In general.* For purposes of this paragraph (c), except as provided in paragraph (c)(4)(iv)(A) of this section, the term "appraisal summary" means a summary of a qualified appraisal that—

(A) Is made on the form prescribed by the Internal Revenue Service;

(B) Is signed and dated (as described in paragraph (c)(4)(iii) of this section) by the donee (or presented to the donee for signature in cases described in paragraph (c)(4)(iv)(C)(*2*) of this section);

(C) Is signed and dated by the qualified appraiser (within the meaning of paragraph (c)(5) of this section) who prepared the qualified appraisal (within the meaning of paragraph (c)(3) of this section); and

(D) Includes the information required by paragraph (c)(4)(ii) of this section.

Reg. § 1.170A-13(c)(4)

(ii) *Information included in an appraisal summary.* An appraisal summary shall include the following information:

(A) The name and taxpayer identification number of the donor (social security number if the donor is an individual or employer identification number if the donor is a partnership or corporation);

(B) A description of the property in sufficient detail for a person who is not generally familiar with the type of property to ascertain that the property that was appraised is the property that was contributed;

(C) In the case of tangible property, a brief summary of the overall physical condition of the property at the time of the contribution;

(D) The manner of acquisition (*e.g.*, purchase, exchange, gift, or bequest) and the date of acquisition of the property by the donor, or, if the property was created, produced, or manufactured by or for the donor, a statement to that effect and the approximate date the property was substantially completed;

(E) The cost or other basis of the property adjusted as provided by section 1016;

(F) The name, address, and taxpayer identification number of the donee;

(G) The date the donee received the property;

(H) For charitable contributions made after June 6, 1988, a statement explaining whether or not the charitable contribution was made by means of a bargain sale and the amount of any consideration received from the donee for the contribution;

(I) The name, address, and (if a taxpayer identification number is otherwise required by section 6109 and the regulations thereunder) the identifying number of the qualified appraiser who signs the appraisal summary and of other persons as required by paragraph (c)(3)(ii)(E) of this section;

(J) The appraised fair market value of the property on the date of contribution;

(K) The declaration by the appraiser described in paragraph (c)(5)(i) of this section;

(L) A declaration by the appraiser stating that—

(*1*) The fee charged for the appraisal is not of a type prohibited by paragraph (c)(6) of this section; and

(*2*) Appraisals prepared by the appraiser are not being disregarded pursuant to 31 U.S.C. § 330(c) on the date the appraisal summary is signed by the appraiser; and

(M) Such other information as may be specified by the form.

(iii) *Signature of the original donee.* The person who signs the appraisal summary for the donee shall be an official authorized to sign the tax or information returns of the donee, or a person specifically authorized to sign appraisal summaries by an official authorized to sign the tax or information returns of such donee. In the case of a donee that is a governmental unit, the person who signs the appraisal summary for such donee shall be the official authorized by such donee to sign appraisal summaries. The signature of the donee on the appraisal summary does not represent concurrence in the appraised value of the contributed property. Rather, it represents acknowledgment of receipt of the property described in the appraisal summary on the date specified in the appraisal summary and that the donee understands the information reporting requirements imposed by section 6050L and § 1.6050L-1. In general, § 1.6050L-1 requires the donee to file an information return with the Internal Revenue Service in the event the donee sells, exchanges, consumes, or otherwise disposes of the property (or any portion thereof) described in the appraisal summary within 2 years after the date of the donor's contribution of such property.

(iv) *Special rules—(A) Content of appraisal summary required in certain cases.* With respect to contributions of nonpublicly traded stock described in paragraph (c)(2)(ii)(B)(*1*) of this section, contributions of securities described in paragraph (c)(7)(xi)(B) of this section, and contributions by C corporations described in paragraph (c)(2)(ii)(B)(*3*) of this section, the term "appraisal summary" means a document that—

(*1*) Complies with the requirements of paragraph (c)(4)(i)(A) and (B) of this section,

(*2*) Includes the information required by paragraph (c)(4)(ii)(A) through (H) of this section,

(*3*) Includes the amount claimed or reported as a charitable contribution deduction, and

(*4*) In the case of securities described in paragraph (c)(7)(xi)(B) of this section, also includes the pertinent average trading price (as described in paragraph (c)(7)(xi)(B)(*2*)(*iii*) of this section).

(B) *Number of appraisal summaries.* A separate appraisal summary for each item of property described in paragraph (c)(1) of this section must be attached to the donor's return. If, during the donor's taxable year, the donor contributes similar items of property described in paragraph (c)(1) of this section to more than one

Reg. § 1.170A-13(c)(4)

donee, the donor shall attach to the donor's return a separate appraisal summary for each donee. See paragraph (c)(7)(iii) of this section for the definition of similar items of property. If, however, during the donor's taxable year, a donor contributes similar items of property described in paragraph (c)(1) of this section to the same donee, the donor may attach to the donor's return a single appraisal summary with respect to all similar items of property contributed to the same donee. Such an appraisal summary shall provide all the information required by paragraph (c)(4)(ii) of this section for each item of property, except that the appraiser may select any items whose aggregate value is appraised at $100 or less and provide a group description for such items.

(C) *Manner of acquisition, cost basis and donee's signature.* (1) If a taxpayer has reasonable cause for being unable to provide the information required by paragraph (c)(4)(ii)(D) and (E) of this section (relating to the manner of acquisition and basis of the contributed property), an appropriate explanation should be attached to the appraisal summary. The taxpayer's deduction will not be disallowed simply because of the inability (for reasonable cause) to provide these items of information.

(2) In rare and unusual circumstances in which it is impossible for the taxpayer to obtain the signature of the donee on the appraisal summary as required by paragraph (c)(4)(i)(B) of this section, the taxpayer's deduction will not be disallowed for that reason provided that the taxpayer attaches a statement to the appraisal summary explaining, in detail, why it was not possible to obtain the donee's signature. For example, if the donee ceases to exist as an entity subsequent to the date of the contribution and prior to the date when the appraisal summary must be signed, and the donor acted reasonably in not obtaining the donee's signature at the time of the contribution, relief under this paragraph (c)(4)(iv)(C)(2) would generally be appropriate.

(D) *Information excluded from certain appraisal summaries.* The information required by paragraph (c)(4)(i)(C), paragraph (c)(4)(ii)(D), (E), (H) through (M), and paragraph (c)(4)(iv)(A)(3), and the average trading price referred to in paragraph (c)(4)(iv)(A)(4) of this section do not have to be included on the appraisal summary at the time it is signed by the donee or a copy is provided to the donee pursuant to paragraph (c)(4)(iv)(E) of this section.

(E) *Statement to be furnished by donors to donees.* Every donor who presents an appraisal summary to a donee for signature after June 6, 1988, in order to comply with paragraph (c)(4)(i)(B) of this section shall furnish a copy of the appraisal summary to such donee.

(F) *Appraisal summary required to be provided to partners and S corporation shareholders.* If the donor is a partnership or S corporation, the donor shall provide a copy of the appraisal summary to every partner or shareholder, respectively, who receives an allocation of a charitable contribution deduction under section 170 with respect to the property described in the appraisal summary.

(G) *Partners and S corporation shareholders.* A partner of a partnership or shareholder of an S corporation who receives an allocation of a deduction under section 170 for a charitable contribution of property to which this paragraph (c) applies must attach a copy of the partnership's or S corporation's appraisal summary to the tax return on which the deduction for the contribution is first claimed. If such appraisal summary is not attached, the partner's or shareholder's deduction shall not be allowed except as provided for in paragraph (c)(4)(iv)(H) of this section.

(H) *Failure to attach appraisal summary.* In the event that a donor fails to attach to the donor's return an appraisal summary as required by paragraph (c)(2)(i)(B) of this section, the Internal Revenue Service may request that the donor submit the appraisal summary within 90 days of the request. If such a request is made and the donor complies with the request within the 90-day period, the deduction under section 170 shall not be disallowed for failure to attach the appraisal summary, provided that the donor's failure to attach the appraisal summary was a good faith omission and the requirements of paragraph (c)(3) and (4) of this section are met (including the completion of the qualified appraisal prior to the date specified in paragraph (c)(3)(iv)(B) of this section).

(5) *Qualified appraiser*—(i) *In general.* The term "qualified appraiser" means an individual (other than a person described in paragraph (c)(5)(iv) of this section) who includes on the appraisal summary (described in paragraph (c)(4) of this section), a declaration that—

(A) The individual either holds himself or herself out to the public as an appraiser or performs appraisals on a regular basis;

(B) Because of the appraiser's qualifications as described in the appraisal (pursuant to paragraph (c)(3)(ii)(F) of this section), the appraiser is qualified to make appraisals of the type of property being valued;

(C) The appraiser is not one of the persons described in paragraph (c)(5)(iv) of this section; and

Reg. § 1.170A-13(c)(5)

(D) The appraiser understands that an intentionally false or fraudulent overstatement of the value of the property described in the qualified appraisal or appraisal summary may subject the appraiser to a civil penalty under section 6701 for aiding and abetting an understatement of tax liability, and, moreover, the appraiser may have appraisals disregarded pursuant to 31 U.S.C. § 330(c) (see paragraph (c)(3)(iii) of this section).

(ii) *Exception.* An individual is not a qualified appraiser with respect to a particular donation, even if the declaration specified in paragraph (c)(5)(i) of this section is provided in the appraisal summary, if the donor had knowledge of facts that would cause a reasonable person to expect the appraiser falsely to overstate the value of the donated property (e.g., the donor and the appraiser make an agreement concerning the amount at which the property will be valued and the donor knows that such amount exceeds the fair market value of the property).

(iii) *Numbers of appraisers.* More than one appraiser may appraise the donated property. If more than one appraiser appraises the property, the donor does not have to use each appraiser's appraisal for purposes of substantiating the charitable contribution deduction pursuant to this paragraph (c). If the donor uses the appraisal of more than one appraiser, or if two or more appraisers contribute to a single appraisal, each appraiser shall comply with the requirements of this paragraph (c), including signing the qualified appraisal and appraisal summary as required by paragraphs (c)(3)(i)(B) and (c)(4)(i)(C) of this section, respectively.

(iv) *Qualified appraiser exclusions.* The following persons cannot be qualified appraisers with respect to particular property:

(A) The donor or the taxpayer who claims or reports a deduction under section 170 for the contribution of the property that is being appraised.

(B) A party to the transaction in which the donor acquired the property being appraised (i.e., the person who sold, exchanged, or gave the property to the donor, or any person who acted as an agent for the transferor or for the donor with respect to such sale, exchange, or gift), unless the property is donated within 2 months of the date of acquisition and its appraised value does not exceed its acquisition price.

(C) The donee of the property.

(D) Any person employed by any of the foregoing persons (e.g., if the donor acquired a painting from an art dealer, neither the art dealer nor persons employed by the dealer can be qualified appraisers with respect to that painting).

(E) Any person related to any of the foregoing persons under section 267(b), or with respect to appraisals made after June 6, 1988, married to a person who is in a relationship described in section 267(b) with any of the foregoing persons.

(F) An appraiser who is regularly used by any person described in paragraph (c)(5)(iv)(A), (B), or (C) of this section and who does not perform a majority of his or her appraisals made during his or her taxable year for other persons.

(6) *Appraisal fees—*(i) *In general.* Except as otherwise provided in paragraph (c)(6)(ii) of this section, no part of the fee arrangement for a qualified appraisal can be based, in effect, on a percentage (or set of percentages) of the appraised value of the property. If a fee arrangement for an appraisal is based in whole or in part on the amount of the appraised value of the property, if any, that is allowed as a deduction under section 170, after Internal Revenue Service examination or otherwise, it shall be treated as a fee based on a percentage of the appraised value of the property. For example, an appraiser's fee that is subject to reduction by the same percentage as the appraised value may be reduced by the Internal Revenue Service would be treated as a fee that violates this paragraph (c)(6).

(ii) *Exception.* Paragraph (c)(6)(i) of this section does not apply to a fee paid to a generally recognized association that regulates appraisers provided all of the following requirements are met:

(A) The association is not organized for profit and no part of the net earnings of the association inures to the benefit of any private shareholder or individual (these terms have the same meaning as in section 501(c)),

(B) The appraiser does not receive any compensation from the association or any other persons for making the appraisal, and

(C) The fee arrangement is not based in whole or in part on the amount of the appraised value of the donated property, if any, that is allowed as a deduction under section 170 after Internal Revenue Service examination or otherwise.

(7) *Meaning of terms.* For purposes of this paragraph (c)—

(i) *Closely held corporation.* The term "closely held corporation" means any corporation (other than an S corporation) with respect to which the stock ownership requirement of paragraph (2) of section 542(a) of the Code is met.

Reg. § 1.170A-13(c)(7)

(ii) *Personal service corporation.* The term "personal service corporation" means any corporation (other than an S corporation) which is a service organization (within the meaning of section 414(m)(3) of the Code).

(iii) *Similar items of property.* The phrase "similar items of property" means property of the same generic category or type, such as stamp collections (including philatelic supplies and books on stamp collecting), coin collections (including numismatic supplies and books on coin collecting), lithographs, paintings, photographs, books, nonpublicly traded stock, nonpublicly traded securities other than nonpublicly traded stock, land, buildings, clothing, jewelry, furniture, electronic equipment, household appliances, toys, everyday kitchenware, china, crystal, or silver. For example, if a donor claims on her return for the year deductions of $2,000 for books given by her to College A, $2,500 for books given by her to College B, and $900 for books given by her to College C, the $5,000 threshold of paragraph (c)(1) of this section is exceeded. Therefore, the donor must obtain a qualified appraisal for the books and attach to her return three appraisal summaries for the books donated to A, B, and C. For rules regarding the number of qualified appraisals and appraisal summaries required when similar items of property are contributed, see paragraphs (c)(3)(iv)(A) and (c)(4)(iv)(B), respectively, of this section.

(iv) *Donor.* The term "donor" means a person or entity (other than an organization described in section 170(c) to which the donated property was previously contributed) that makes a charitable contribution of property.

(v) *Donee.* The term "donee" means—

(A) Except as provided in paragraph (c)(7)(v)(B) and (C) of this section, an organization described in section 170(c) to which property is contributed,

(B) Except as provided in paragraph (c)(7)(v)(C) of this section, in the case of a charitable contribution of property placed in trust for the benefit of an organization described in section 170(c), the trust, or

(C) In the case of a charitable contribution of property placed in trust for the benefit of an organization described in section 170(c) made on or before June 6, 1988, the beneficiary that is an organization described in section 170(c), or if the trust has assumed the duties of a donee by signing the appraisal summary pursuant to paragraph (c)(4)(i)(B) of this section, the trust.

In general, the term refers only to the original donee. However, with respect to paragraph (c)(3)(ii)(D), the last sentence of paragraph (c)(4)(iii), and paragraph (c)(5)(iv)(C) of this section, the term "donee" means the original donee and all successor donees in cases where the original donee transfers the contributed property to a successor donee after June 6, 1988.

(vi) *Original donee.* The term "original donee" means the donee to or for which property is initially donated by a donor.

(vii) *Successor donee.* The term "successor donee" means any donee of property other than its original donee (*i.e.*, a transferee of property for less than fair market value from an original donee or another successor donee).

(viii) *Fair market value.* For the meaning of the term "fair market value," see section 1.170A-1(c)(2).

(ix) *Nonpublicly traded securities.* The term "nonpublicly traded securities" means securities (within the meaning of section 165(g)(2) of the Code) which are not publicly traded securities as defined in paragraph (c)(7)(xi) of this section.

(x) *Nonpublicly traded stock.* The term "nonpublicly traded stock" means any stock of a corporation (evidence by a stock certificate) which is not a publicly traded security. The term stock does not include a debenture or any other evidence of indebtedness.

(xi) *Publicly traded securities*—(A) *In general.* Except as provided in paragraph (c)(7)(xi)(C) of this section, the term "publicly traded securities" means securities (within the meaning of section 165(g)(2) of the Code) for which (as of the date of the contribution) market quotations are readily available on an established securities market. For purposes of this section, market quotations are readily available on an established securities market with respect to a security if:

(*1*) The security is listed on the New York Stock Exchange, the American Stock Exchange, or any copy or regional exchange in which quotations are published on a daily basis, including foreign securities listed on a recognized foreign, national, or regional exchange in which quotations are published daily basis;

(*2*) The security is regularly traded in the national or regional over-the-counter market, for which published quotations are available; or

(*3*) The security is a share of an open-end investment company (commonly known as a mutual fund) registered under the Investment Company Act of 1940, as amended (15 U.S.C. 80a-1 to 80b-2), for which quotations are published on a daily basis in a newspaper of general circulation throughout the United States.

Reg. § 1.170A-13(c)(7)

(If the market value of an issue of a security is reflected only on an interdealer quotation system, the issue shall not be considered to be publicly traded unless the special rule described in paragraph (c)(7)(xi)(B) of this section is satisfied.)

(B) *Special rule—(1) In General.* An issue of a security that does not satisfy the requirements of paragraph (c)(7)(xi)(A)(*1*), (*2*), or (*3*) of this section shall nonetheless be considered to have market quotations readily available on an established securities market for purposes of paragraph (c)(7)(xi)(A) of this section if all of the following five requirements are met:

(*i*) The issue is regularly traded during the computational period (as defined in paragraph (c)(7)(xi)(B)(*2*)(*iv*) of this section) in a market that is reflected by the existence of an interdealer quotation system for the issue,

(*ii*) The issuer or an agent of the issuer computes the average trading price (as defined in paragraph (c)(7)(xi)(B)(*2*)(*iii*) of this section) for the issue for the computational period,

(*iii*) The average trading price and total volume of the issue during the computational period are published in a newspaper of general circulation throughout the United States not later than the last day of the month following the end of the calendar quarter in which the computational period ends,

(*iv*) The issuer or its agent keeps books and records that list for each transaction during the computational period involving each issue covered by this procedure the date of the settlement of the transaction, the name and address of the broker or dealer making the market in which the transaction occurred, and the trading price and volume, and

(*v*) The issuer or its agent permits the Internal Revenue Service to review the books and records described in paragraph (c)(7)(xi)(B)(*1*)(*iv*) of this section with respect to transactions during the computational period upon giving reasonable notice to the issuer or agent.

(*2*) *Definitions.* For purposes of this paragraph (c)(7)(xi)(B)—

(*i*) *Issue of a security.* The term "issue of a security" means a class of debt securities with the same obligor and identical terms except as to their relative denominations (amounts) or a class of stock having identical rights.

(*ii*) *Interdealer quotation system.* The term "interdealer quotation system" means any system of general circulation to brokers and dealers that regularly disseminates quotations of obligations by two or more identified brokers or dealers who are not related to either the issuer of the security or to the issuer's agent, who compute the average trading price of the security. A quotation sheet prepared and distributed by a broker or dealer in the regular course of its business and containing only quotations of such broker or dealer s not an interdealer quotation system.

(*iii*) *Average trading price.* The term 'average trading price" means the mean price of all transactions (weighted by volume), other than original issue or redemption transactions, conducted through a United States office of a broker or dealer who maintains a market in the issue of the security during the computational period For this purpose, bid and asked quotations are not taken into account.

(*iv*) *Computational period.* For calendar quarters beginning on or after June 6, 1988, the term "computational period" means weekly during October through December (beginning with the first Monday in October and ending with the first Sunday following the last Monday in December) and monthly during January through September (beginning January 1). For calendar quarters beginning before June 6, 1988, the term "computational period" means weekly during October through December and monthly during January through September.

(C) *Exception.* Securities described in paragraph (c)(7)(xi)(A) or (B) of this section shall not be considered publicly traded securities if—

(*1*) The securities are subject to any restrictions that materially affect the value of the securities to the donor or prevent the securities from being freely traded, or

(*2*) If the amount claimed or reported as a deduction with respect to the contribution of the securities is different than the amount listed in the market quotations that are readily available on an established securities market pursuant to paragraph (c)(7)(xi)(A) or (B) of this section.

(D) *Market quotations and fair market value.* The fair market value of a publicly traded security, as defined in this paragraph (c)(7)(xi), is not necessarily equal to its market quotation, its average trading price (as defined in paragraph (c)(7)(xi)(B)(*2*)(*iii*) of this section), or its face value, if any. See section 1.170A-1(c)(2) for the definition of "fair market value."

(d) *Charitable contributions; information required in support of deductions for taxable years beginning before January 1, 1983—(1) In general.* This paragraph (d)(1) shall apply to deductions for charitable contributions made in taxable years beginning before January 1, 1983. At the option of the taxpayer the requirements of this paragraph (d)(1) shall also apply to all charitable contributions made on or before December 31, 1984 (in lieu of the requirements of paragraphs (a) and (b) of this section). In connection with claims for deductions for charitable contributions, taxpayers shall state in their income tax returns the name of each organization to which a contribution was made and the amount and date of the actual payment of each contribution. If a contribution is made in property other than money, the taxpayer shall state the kind of property contributed, for example, used clothing, paintings, or securities, the method utilized in determining the fair market value of the property at the time the contribution was made, and whether or not the amount of the contribution was reduced under section 170(e). If a taxpayer makes more than one cash contribution to an organization during the taxable year, then in lieu of listing each cash contribution and the date of payment the taxpayer may state the total cash payments made to such organization during the taxable year. A taxpayer who elects under paragraph (d)(2) of § 1.170A-8 to apply section 170(e)(1) to his contributions and carryovers of 30-percent capital gain property must file a statement with his return indicating that he has made the election and showing the contributions in the current year and carryovers from preceding years to which it applies. For the definition of the term "30-percent capital gain property", see paragraph (d)(3) of § 1.170A-8.

(2) *Contribution by individual of property other than money.* This paragraph (d)(2) shall apply to deductions for charitable contributions made in taxable years beginning before January 1, 1983. At the option of the taxpayer, the requirements of this paragraph (d)(2) shall also apply to contributions of property made on or before December 31, 1984 (in lieu of the requirements of paragraph (b) of this section).

(i) The name and address of the organization to which the contribution was made.

(ii) The date of the actual contribution.

(iii) A description of the property in sufficient detail to identify the particular property contributed, including in the case of tangible property the physical condition of the property at the time of contribution, and, in the case of securities, the name of the issuer, the type of security, and whether or not such security is regularly traded on a stock exchange or in an over-the-counter market.

(iv) The manner of acquisition, as, for example, by purchase, gift, bequest, inheritance, or exchange, and the approximate date of acquisition of the property by the taxpayer or, if the property was created, produced, or manufactured by or for the taxpayer, the approximate date the property was substantially completed.

(v) The fair market value of the property at the time the contribution was made, the method utilized in determining the fair market value, and, if the valuation was determined by appraisal, a copy of the signed report of the appraiser.

(vi) The cost or other basis, adjusted as provided by section 1016, of property, other than securities, held by the taxpayer for a period of less than five years immediately preceding the date on which the contribution was made and, when the information is available, of property, other than securities, held for a period of five years or more preceding the date on which the contribution was made.

(vii) In the case of property to which section 170(e) applies, the cost or other basis, adjusted as provided by section 1016, the reduction by reason of section 170(e)(1) in the amount of the charitable contribution otherwise taken into account, and the manner in which such reduction was determined.

(viii) The terms of any agreement or understanding entered into by or on behalf of the taxpayer which relates to the use, sale, or disposition of the property contributed, as, for example, the terms of any agreement or understanding which—

(A) Restricts temporarily or permanently the donee's right to dispose of the donated property.

(B) Reserves to, or confers upon, anyone other than the donee organization or other than an organization participating with such organization in cooperative fund raising, any right to the income from such property, to the possession of the property, including the right to vote securities, to acquire such property by purchase or otherwise, or to designate the person to have such income, possession, or right to acquire, or

(C) Earmarks contributed property for a particular charitable use, such as the use of donated furniture in the reading room of the donee organization's library.

(ix) The total amount claimed as a deduction for the taxable year due to the contribution of the property and, if less than the entire interest in the property is contributed during the taxable year, the amount claimed as a deduction in any prior year or years for contributions of other interests in such property, the name and address of each organization to which any such contribution was made, the place where any such property which is tangible property is located or kept, and

Reg. § 1.170A-13(d)(2)

the name of any person, other than the organization to which the property giving rise to the deduction was contributed, having actual possession of the property.

(e) [Reserved]

(f) *Substantiation of charitable contributions of $250 or more*—(1) *In general.* No deduction is allowed under section 170(a) for all or part of any contribution of $250 or more unless the taxpayer substantiates the contribution with a contemporaneous written acknowledgment from the donee organization. A taxpayer who makes more than one contribution of $250 or more to a donee organization in a taxable year may substantiate the contributions with one or more contemporaneous written acknowledgments. Section 170(f)(8) does not apply to a payment of $250 or more if the amount contributed (as determined under § 1.170A-1(h)) is less than $250. Separate contributions of less than $250 are not subject to the requirements of section 170(f)(8), regardless of whether the sum of the contributions made by a taxpayer to a donee organization during a taxable year equals $250 or more.

(2) *Written acknowledgment.* Except as otherwise provided in paragraphs (f)(8) through (f)(11) and (f)(13) of this section, a written acknowledgment from a donee organization must provide the following information—

(i) The amount of any cash the taxpayer paid and a description (but not necessarily the value) of any property other than cash the taxpayer transferred to the donee organization;

(ii) A statement of whether or not the donee organization provides any goods or services in consideration, in whole or in part, for any of the cash or other property transferred to the donee organization;

(iii) If the donee organization provides any goods or services other than intangible religious benefits (as described in section 170(f)(8)), a description and good faith estimate of the value of those goods or services; and

(iv) If the donee organization provides any intangible religious benefits, a statement to that effect.

(3) *Contemporaneous.* A written acknowledgment is contemporaneous if it is obtained by the taxpayer on or before the earlier of—

(i) The date the taxpayer files the original return for the taxable year in which the contribution was made; or

(ii) The due date (including extensions) for filing the taxpayer's original return for that year.

(4) *Donee organization.* For purposes of this paragraph (f), a donee organization is an organization described in section 170(c).

(5) *Goods or services.* Goods or services means cash, property, services, benefits, and privileges.

(6) *In consideration for.* A donee organization provides goods or services in consideration for a taxpayer's payment if, at the time the taxpayer makes the payment to the donee organization, the taxpayer receives or expects to receive goods or services in exchange for that payment. Goods or services a donee organization provides in consideration for a payment by a taxpayer include goods or services provided in a year other than the year in which the taxpayer makes the payment to the donee organization.

(7) *Good faith estimate.* For purposes of this section, good faith estimate means a donee organization's estimate of the fair market value of any goods or services, without regard to the manner in which the organization in fact made that estimate. See § 1.170A-1(h)(4) for rules regarding when a taxpayer may treat a donee organization's estimate of the value of goods or services as the fair market value.

(3) *Certain goods or services disregarded*—(i) *In general.* For purposes of section 170(f)(8), the following goods or services are disregarded—

(A) Goods or services that have insubstantial value under the guidelines provided in Revenue Procedures 90-12, 1990-1 C.B. 471, 92-49 1992-1 C.B. 987, and any successor documents. (See § 601.601(d)(2)(ii) of the Statement of Procedural Rules, 26 CFR part 601.); and

(B) Annual membership benefits offered to a taxpayer in exchange for a payment of $75 or less per year that consist of—

(1) Any rights or privileges, other than those described in section 170(l), that the taxpayer can exercise frequently during the membership period. Examples of such rights and privileges may include, but are not limited to, free or discounted admission to the organization's facilities or events, free or discounted parking, preferred access to goods or services, and discounts on the purchase of goods or services; and

(2) Admission to events during the membership period that are open only to members of a donee organization and for which the donee organization reasonably projects that the cost per person (excluding any allocable overhead) attending each such event is within the limits established for "low cost articles" under section 513(h)(2). The projected cost to the donee organization is determined at the time the organization

first offers its membership package for the year (using section 3.07 of Revenue Procedure 90-12, or any successor documents, to determine the cost of any items or services that are donated).

(ii) *Examples.* The following examples illustrate the rules of this paragraph (f)(8).

Example 1. Membership benefits disregarded. Performing Arts Center *E* is an organization described in section 170(c). In return for a payment of $75, *E* offers a package of basic membership benefits that includes the right to purchase tickets to performances one week before they go on sale to the general public, free parking in *E*'s garage during evening and weekend performances, and a 10% discount on merchandise sold in *E*'s gift shop. In return for a payment of $150, *E* offers a package of preferred membership benefits that includes all of the benefits in the $75 package as well as a poster that is sold in *E*'s gift shop for $20. The basic membership and the preferred membership are each valid for twelve months, and there are approximately 50 performances of various productions at *E* during a twelve-month period. *E*'s gift shop is open for several hours each week and at performance times. *F*, a patron of the arts, is solicited by *E* to make a contribution. *E* offers *F* the preferred membership benefits in return for a payment of $150 or more. *F* makes a payment of $300 to *E*. *F* can satisfy the substantiation requirement of section 170(f)(8) by obtaining a contemporaneous written acknowledgment from *E* that includes a description of the poster and a good faith estimate of its fair market value ($20) and disregards the remaining membership benefits.

Example 2. Contemporaneous written acknowledgment need not mention rights or privileges that can be disregarded. The facts are the same as in Example 1, except that *F* made a payment of $300 and received only a basic membership. *F* can satisfy the section 170(f)(8) substantiation requirement with a contemporaneous written acknowledgment stating that no goods or services were provided.

Example 3. Rights or privileges that cannot be exercised frequently. Community Theater Group *G* is an organization described in section 170(c). Every summer, *G* performs four different plays. Each play is performed two times. In return for a membership fee of $60, *G* offers its members free admission to any of its performances. Non-members may purchase tickets on a performance by performance basis for $15 a ticket. *H*, an individual who is a sponsor of the theater, is solicited by *G* to make a contribution. *G* tells *H* that the membership benefit will be provided in return for any payment of $60 or

more. *H* chooses to make a payment of $350 to *G* and receives in return the membership benefit. *G*'s membership benefit of free admission is not described in paragraph (f)(8)(i)(B) of this section because it is not a privilege that can be exercised frequently (due to the limited number of performances offered by *G*). Therefore, to meet the requirements of section 170(f)(8), a contemporaneous written acknowledgment of *H*'s $350 payment must include a description of the free admission benefit and a good faith estimate of its value.

Example 4. Multiple memberships. In December of each year, *K*, an individual, gives each of her six grandchildren a junior membership in Dinosaur Museum, an organization described in section 170(c). Each junior membership costs $50, and *K* makes a single payment of $300 for all six memberships. A junior member is entitled to free admission to the museum and to weekly films, slide shows, and lectures about dinosaurs. In addition, each junior member receives a bi-monthly, non-commercial quality newsletter with information about dinosaurs and upcoming events. *K*'s contemporaneous written acknowledgment from Dinosaur Museum may state that no goods or services were provided in exchange for *K*'s payment.

(9) *Goods or services provided to employees or partners of donors*—(i) *Certain goods or services disregarded.* For purposes of section 170(f)(8), goods or services provided by a donee organization to employees of a donor, or to partners of a partnership that is a donor, in return for a payment to the organization may be disregarded to the extent that the goods or services provided to each employee or partner are the same as those described in paragraph (f)(8)(i) of this section.

(ii) *No good faith estimate required for other goods or services.* If a taxpayer makes a contribution of $250 or more to a donee organization and, in return, the donee organization offers the taxpayer's employees or partners goods or services other than those described in paragraph (f)(9)(i) of this section, the contemporaneous written acknowledgment of the taxpayer's contribution is not required to include a good faith estimate of the value of such goods or services but must include a description of those goods or services.

(iii) *Example.* The following example illustrates the rules of this paragraph (f)(9).

Example. Museum *J* is an organization described in section 170(c). For a payment of $40, *J* offers a package of basic membership benefits that includes free admission and a 10% discount

Reg. § 1.170A-13(f)(9)

on merchandise sold in J's gift shop. J's other membership categories are for supporters who contribute $100 or more. Corporation K makes a payment of $50,000 to J and, in return, J offers K's employees free admission for one year, a tee-shirt with J's logo that costs J $4.50, and a gift shop discount of 25% for one year. The free admission for K's employees is the same as the benefit made available to holders of the $40 membership and is otherwise described in paragraph (f)(8)(i)(B) of this section. The tee-shirt given to each of K's employees is described in paragraph (f)(8)(i)(A) of this section. Therefore, the contemporaneous written acknowledgment of K's payment is not required to include a description or good faith estimate of the value of the free admission or the tee-shirts. However, because the gift shop discount offered to K's employees is different than that offered to those who purchase the $40 membership, the discount is not described in paragraph (f)(8)(i) of this section. Therefore, the contemporaneous written acknowledgment of K's payment is required to include a description of the 25% discount offered to K's employees.

(10) *Substantiation of out-of-pocket expenses.* A taxpayer who incurs unreimbursed expenditures incident to the rendition of services, within the meaning of § 1.170A-1(g), is treated as having obtained a contemporaneous written acknowledgment of those expenditures if the taxpayer—

(i) Has adequate records under paragraph (a) of this section to substantiate the amount of the expenditures; and

(ii) Obtains by the date prescribed in paragraph (f)(3) of this section a statement prepared by the donee organization containing—

(A) A description of the services provided by the taxpayer;

(B) A statement of whether or not the donee organization provides any goods or services in consideration, in whole or in part, for the unreimbursed expenditures; and

(C) The information required by paragraphs (f)(2)(iii) and (iv) of this section.

(11) *Contributions made by payroll deduction*—(i) *Form of substantiation.* A contribution made by means of withholding from a taxpayer's wages and payment by the taxpayer's employer to a donee organization may be substantiated, for purposes of section 170(f)(8), by both—

(A) A pay stub, Form W-2, or other document furnished by the employer that sets forth the amount withheld by the employer for the purpose of payment to a donee organization; and

(B) A pledge card or other document prepared by or at the direction of the donee organization that includes a statement to the effect that the organization does not provide goods or services in whole or partial consideration for any contributions made to the organization by payroll deduction.

(ii) *Application of $250 threshold.* For the purpose of applying the $250 threshold provided in section 170(f)(8)(A) to contributions made by the means described in paragraph (f)(11)(i) of this section, the amount withheld from each payment of wages to a taxpayer is treated as a separate contribution.

(12) *Distributing organizations as donees.* An organization described in section 170(c), or an organization described in 5 CFR 950.105 (a Principal Combined Fund Organization for purposes of the Combined Federal Campaign) and acting in that capacity, that receives a payment made as a contribution is treated as a donee organization solely for purposes of section 170(f)(8), even if the organization (pursuant to the donor's instructions or otherwise) distributes the amount received to one or more organizations described in section 170(c). This paragraph (f)(12) does not apply, however, to a case in which the distributee organization provides goods or services as part of a transaction structured with a view to avoid taking the goods or services into account in determining the amount of the deduction to which the donor is entitled under section 170.

(13) *Transfers to certain trusts.* Section 170(f)(8) does not apply to a transfer of property to a trust described in section 170(f)(2)(B), a charitable remainder annuity trust (as defined in section 664(d)(1)), or a charitable remainder unitrust (as defined in section 664(d)(2) or (d)(3) or § 1.664-(3)(a)(1)(i)(b)). Section 170(f)(8) does apply, however, to a transfer to a pooled income fund (as defined in section 642(c)(5)); for such a transfer, the contemporaneous written acknowledgment must state that the contribution was transferred to the donee organization's pooled income fund and indicate whether any goods or services (in addition to an income interest in the fund) were provided in exchange for the transfer. The contemporaneous written acknowledgment is not required to include a good faith estimate of the income interest.

(14) *Substantiation of payments to a college or university for the right to purchase tickets to athletic events.* For purposes of paragraph (f)(2)(iii) of this section, the right to purchase tickets for seating at an athletic event in exchange for a payment described in section 170(l) is treated as having a value equal to twenty

Reg. § 1.170A-13(f)(14)

percent of such payment. For example, when a taxpayer makes a payment of $312.50 for the right to purchase tickets for seating at an athletic event, the right to purchase tickets is treated as having a value of $62.50. The remaining $250 is treated as a charitable contribution, which the taxpayer must substantiate in accordance with the requirements of this section.

(15) *Substantiation of charitable contributions made by a partnership or an S corporation.* If a partnership or an S corporation makes a charitable contribution of $250 or more, the partnership or S corporation will be treated as the taxpayer for purposes of section 170(f)(8). Therefore, the partnership or S corporation must substantiate the contribution with a contemporaneous written acknowledgment from the donee organization before reporting the contribution on its income tax return for the year in which the contribution was made and must maintain the contemporaneous written acknowledgment in its records. A partner of a partnership or a shareholder of an S corporation is not required to obtain any additional substantiation for his or her share of the partnership's or S corporation's charitable contribution.

(16) *Purchase of an annuity.* If a taxpayer purchases an annuity from a charitable organization and claims a charitable contribution deduction of $250 or more for the excess of the amount paid over the value of the annuity, the contemporaneous written acknowledgment must state whether any goods or services in addition to the annuity were provided to the taxpayer. The contemporaneous written acknowledgment is not required to include a good faith estimate of the value of the annuity. See § 1.170A-1(d)(2) for guidance in determining the value of the annuity.

(17) *Substantiation of matched payments—*(i) *In general.* For purposes of section 170, if a taxpayer's payment to a donee organization is matched, in whole or in part, by another payor, and the taxpayer receives goods or services in consideration for its payment and some or all of the matching payment, those goods or services will be treated as provided in consideration for the taxpayer's payment and not in consideration for the matching payment.

(ii) *Example.* The following example illustrates the rules of this paragraph (f)(17).

Example. Taxpayer makes a $400 payment to Charity L, a donee organization. Pursuant to a matching payment plan, Taxpayer's employer matches Taxpayer's $400 payment with an additional payment of $400. In consideration for the combined payments of $800, L gives Taxpayer an item that it estimates has a fair market value of $100. L does not give the employer any goods or services in consideration for its contribution. The contemporaneous written acknowledgment provided to the employer must include a statement that no goods or services were provided in consideration for the employer's $400 payment. The contemporaneous written acknowledgment provided to Taxpayer must include a statement of the amount of Taxpayer's payment, a description of the item received by Taxpayer, and a statement that L's good faith estimate of the value of the item received by Taxpayer is $100.

(18) *Effective date.* This paragraph (f) applies to contributions made on or after December 16, 1996. However, taxpayers may rely on the rules of this paragraph (f) for contributions made on or after January 1, 1994. [Reg. § 1.170A-13.]

□ [*T.D. 8002, 12-26-84. Amended by T.D. 8003, 12-26-84; T.D. 8199, 5-4-88; T.D. 8623, 10-11-95 and T.D. 8690, 12-13-96.*]

[Reg. § 1.170A-14]

§ 1.170A-14. **Qualified conservation contributions.**—(a) *Qualified conservation contributions.* A deduction under section 170 is generally not allowed for a charitable contribution of any interest in property that consists of less than the donor's entire interest in the property other than certain transfers in trust (see § 1.170A-6 relating to charitable contributions in trust and § 1.170A-7 relating to contributions not in trust of partial interests in property). However, a deduction may be allowed under section 170(f)(3)(B)(iii) for the value of a qualified conservation contribution if the requirements of this section are met. A qualified conservation contribution is the contribution of a qualified real property interest to a qualified organization exclusively for conservation purposes. To be eligible for a deduction under this section, the conservation purpose must be protected in perpetuity.

(b) *Qualified real property interest—*(1) *Entire interest of donor other than qualified mineral interest.* (i) The entire interest of the donor other than a qualified mineral interest is a qualified real property interest. A qualified mineral interest is the donor's interest in subsurface oil, gas, or other minerals and the right of access to such minerals.

(ii) A real property interest shall not be treated as an entire interest other than a qualified mineral interest by reason of section 170(h)(2)(A) and this paragraph (b)(1) if the property in which the donor's interest exists was divided prior to the contribution in order to enable the donor to retain control of more than a qualified mineral interest or to reduce the real property interest donated.

Reg. § 1.170A-14(a)

See Treasury regulations § 1.170A-7(a)(2)(i). An entire interest in real property may consist of an undivided interest in the property. But see section 170(h)(5)(A) and the regulations thereunder (relating to the requirement that the conservation purpose which is the subject of the donation must be protected in perpetuity).

Minor interests, such as rights-of-way, that will not interfere with the conservation purposes of the donation, may be transferred prior to the conservation contribution without affecting the treatment of a property interest as a qualified real property interest under this paragraph (b)(1).

(2) *Perpetual conservation restriction.* A perpetual conservation restriction is a qualified real property interest. A "perpetual conservation restriction" is a restriction granted in perpetuity on the use which may be made of real property—including, an easement or other interest in real property that under state law has attributes similar to an easement (e.g., a restrictive covenant or equitable servitude). For purposes of this section, the terms "easement", "conservation restriction", and "perpetual conservation restriction" have the same meaning. The definition of "perpetual conservation restriction" under this paragraph (b)(3) is not intended to preclude the deductibility of a donation of affirmative rights to use a land or water area under § 1.170A-13(d)(2). Any rights reserved by the donor in the donation of a perpetual conservation restriction must conform to the requirements of this section. See *e.g.*, paragraphs (d)(4)(ii), (d)(5)(i), (e)(3), and (g)(4) of this section.

(c) *Qualified organization*—(1) *Eligible donee.* To be considered an eligible donee under this section, an organization must be a qualified organization, have a commitment to protect the conservation purposes of the donation, and have the resources to enforce the restrictions. A conservation group organized or operated primarily or substantially for one of the conservation purposes specified in section 170(b)(4)(A) will be considered to have the commitment required by the preceding sentence. A qualified organization need not set aside funds to enforce the restrictions that are the subject of the contribution. For purposes of this section, the term "qualified organization" means:

(i) A governmental unit described in section 170(b)(1)(A)(v);

(ii) An organization described in section 170(b)(1)(A)(vi);

(iii) A charitable organization described in section 501(c)(3) that meets the public support test of section 509(a)(2);

(iv) A charitable organization described in section 501(c)(3) that meets the requirements of section 509(a)(3) and is controlled by an organization described in paragraphs (c)(1)(i), (ii), or (iii) of this section.

(2) *Transfers by donee.* A deduction shall be allowed for a contribution under this section only if in the instrument of conveyance the donor prohibits the donee from subsequently transferring the easement (or, in the case of a remainder interest or the reservation of a qualified mineral interest, the property), whether or not for consideration, unless the donee organization, as a condition of the subsequent transfer, requires that the conservation purposes which the contribution was originally intended to advance continue to be carried out. Moreover, subsequent transfers must be restricted to organizations qualifying, at the time of the subsequent transfer, as an eligible donee under paragraph (c)(1) of this section. When a later unexpected change in the conditions surrounding the property that is the subject of a donation under paragraphs (b)(1), (2), or (3) of this section makes impossible or impractical the continued use of the property for conservation purposes, the requirements of this paragraph will be met if the property is sold or exchanged and any proceeds are used by the donee organization in a manner consistent with the conservation purposes of the original contribution. In the case of a donation under paragraph (b)(3) of this section to which the preceding sentence applies, see also paragraph (g)(5)(ii) of this section.

(c) *Conservation purposes*—(1) *In general.* For purposes of section 170(h) and this section, the term "conservation purposes" means—

(i) The preservation of land areas for outdoor recreation by, or the education of, the general public, within the meaning of paragraph (d)(2) of this section,

(ii) The protection of a relatively natural habitat of fish, wildlife, or plants, or similar ecosystem, within the meaning of paragraph (d)(3) of this section,

(iii) The preservation of certain open space (including farmland and forest land) within the meaning of paragraph (d)(4) of this section, or

(iv) The preservation of an historically important land area or a certified historic structure, within the meaning of paragraph (d)(5) of this section.

(2) *Recreation or education*—(i) *In general.* The donation of a qualified real property interest to preserve land areas for the outdoor recreation of the general public or for the education of the general public will meet the conservation purposes test of this section. Thus, conservation pur-

Reg. § 1.170A-14(d)(2)

poses would include, for example, the preservation of a water area for the use of the public for boating or fishing, or a nature or hiking trail for the use of the public.

(ii) *Access.* The preservation of land areas for recreation or education will not meet the test of this section unless the recreation or education is for the substantial and regular use of the general public.

(3) *Protection of environmental system*—(i) *In general.* The donation of a qualified real property interest to protect a significant relatively natural habitat in which a fish, wildlife, or plant community, or similar ecosystem, normally lives will meet the conservation purposes test of this section. The fact that the habitat or environment has been altered to some extent by human activity will not result in a deduction being denied under this section if the fish, wildlife, or plants continue to exist there in a relatively natural state. For example, the preservation of a lake formed by a man-made dam or a salt pond formed by a man-made dike would meet the conservation purposes test if the lake or pond were a natural feeding area for a wildlife community that included rare, endangered, or threatened native species.

(ii) *Significant habitat or ecosystem.* Significant habitats and ecosystems include, but are not limited to, habitats for rare, endangered, or threatened species of animals, fish, or plants; natural areas that represent high quality examples of a terrestrial community or aquatic community, such as islands that are undeveloped or not intensely developed where the coastal ecosystem is relatively intact; and natural areas which are included in, or which contribute to, the ecological viability of a local, state, or national park, nature preserve, wildlife refuge, wilderness area, or other similar conservation area.

(iii) Limitations on public access to property that is the subject of a donation under this paragraph (d)(3) shall not render the donation nondeductible. For example, a restriction on all public access to the habitat of a threatened native animal species protected by a donation under this paragraph (d)(3) would not cause the donation to be nondeductible.

(4) *Preservation of open space*—(i) *In general.* The donation of a qualified real property interest to preserve open space (including farmland and forest land) will meet the conservation purposes test of this section if such a preservation is—

(A) Pursuant to a clearly delineated federal, state, or local governmental conservation

policy and will yield a significant public benefit, or

(B) For the scenic enjoyment of the general public and will yield a significant public benefit.

An open space easement donated on or after December 18, 1980, must meet the requirements of section 170(h) in order to be deductible.

(ii) *Scenic enjoyment*—(A) *Factors.* A contribution made for the preservation of open space may be for the scenic enjoyment of the general public. Preservation of land may be for the scenic enjoyment of the general public if development of the property would impair the scenic character of the local rural or urban landscape or would interfere with a scenic panorama that can be enjoyed from a park, nature preserve, road, waterbody, trail, or historic structure or land area, and such area or transportation way is open to, or utilized by, the public. "Scenic enjoyment" will be evaluated by considering all pertinent facts and circumstances germane to the contribution. Regional variations in topography, geology, biology, and cultural and economic conditions require flexibility in the application of this test, but do not lessen the burden on the taxpayer to demonstrate the scenic characteristics of a donation under this paragraph. The application of a particular objective factor to help define a view as "scenic" in one setting may in fact be entirely inappropriate in another setting. Among the factors to be considered are:

(*1*) The compatibility of the land use with other land in the vicinity;

(*2*) The degree of contrast and variety provided by the visual scene;

(*3*) The openness of the land (which would be a more significant factor in an urban or densely populated setting or in a heavily wooded area);

(*4*) Relief from urban closeness;

(*5*) The harmonious variety of shapes and textures;

(*6*) The degree to which the land use maintains the scale and character of the urban landscape to preserve open space, visual enjoyment, and sunlight for the surrounding area;

(*7*) The consistency of the proposed scenic view with a methodical state scenic identification program, such as a state landscape inventory; and

(*8*) The consistency of the proposed scenic view with a regional or local landscape inventory made pursuant to a sufficiently rigorous review process, especially if the donation is endorsed by an appropriate state or local governmental agency.

(B) *Access.* To satisfy the requirement of scenic enjoyment by the general public, visual (rather than physical) access to or across the property by the general public is sufficient. Under the terms of an open space easement on scenic property, the entire property need not be visible to the public for a donation to qualify under this section, although the public benefit from the donation may be insufficient to qualify for a deduction if only a small portion of the property is visible to the public.

(iii) *Governmental conservation policy—* (A) *In general.* The requirement that the preservation of open space be pursuant to a clearly delineated Federal, state, or local governmental policy is intended to protect the types of property identified by representatives of the general public as worthy of preservation or conservation. A general declaration of conservation goals by a single official or legislative body is not sufficient. However, a governmental conservation policy need not be a certification program that identifies particular lots or small parcels of individually owned property. This requirement will be met by donations that further a specific, identified conservation project, such as the preservation of land within a state or local landmark district that is locally recognized as being significant to that district; the preservation of a wild or scenic river; the preservation of farmland pursuant to a state program for flood prevention and control; or the protection of the scenic, ecological, or historic character of land that is contiguous to, or an integral part of, the surroundings of existing recreation or conservation sites. For example, the donation of a perpetual conservation restriction to a qualified organization pursuant to a formal resolution or certification by a local governmental agency established under state law specifically identifying the subject property as worthy of protection for conservation purposes will meet the requirement of this paragraph. A program need not be funded to satisfy this requirement, but the program must involve a significant commitment by the government with respect to the conservation project. For example, a governmental program according preferential tax assessment or preferential zoning for certain property deemed worthy of protection for conservation purposes would constitute a significant commitment by the government.

(B) *Effect of acceptance by governmental agency.* Acceptance of an easement by an agency of the Federal Government or by an agency of a state or local government (or by a commission, authority, or similar body duly constituted by the state or local government and acting on behalf of the state or local government) tends to establish the requisite clearly delineated governmental policy, although such acceptance, without more, is not sufficient. The more rigorous the review process by the governmental agency, the more the acceptance of the easement tends to establish the requisite clearly delineated governmental policy. For example, in a state where the legislature has established an Environmental Trust to accept gifts to the state which meet certain conservation purposes and to submit the gifts to a review that requires the approval of the state's highest officials, acceptance of a gift by the Trust tends to establish the requisite clearly delineated governmental policy. However, if the Trust merely accepts such gifts without a review process, the requisite clearly delineated governmental policy is not established.

(C) *Access.* A limitation on public access to property subject to a donation under this paragraph (d)(4)(iii) shall not render the deduction nondeductible unless the conservation purpose of the donation would be undermined or frustrated without public access. For example, a donation pursuant to a governmental policy to protect the scenic character of land near a river requires visual access to the same extent as would a donation under paragraph (d)(4)(ii) of this section.

(iv) *Significant public benefit—*(A) *Factors.* All contributions made for the preservation of open space must yield a significant public benefit. Public benefit will be evaluated by considering all pertinent facts and circumstances germane to the contribution. Factors germane to the evaluation of public benefit from one contribution may be irrelevant in determining public benefit from another contribution. No single factor will necessarily be determinative. Among the factors to be considered are:

(*1*) The uniqueness of the property to the area;

(*2*) The intensity of land development in the vicinity of the property (both existing development and foreseeable trends of development);

(*3*) The consistency of the proposed open space use with public programs (whether Federal, state or local) for conservation in the region, including programs for outdoor recreation, irrigation or water supply protection, water quality maintenance or enhancement, flood prevention and control, erosion control, shoreline protection, and protection of land areas included in, or related to, a government approved master plan or land management area;

Reg. § 1.170A-14(d)(4)

(4) The consistency of the proposed open space use with existing private conservation programs in the area, as evidenced by other land, protected by easement or fee ownership by organizations referred to in § 1.170A-14(c)(1), in close proximity to the property;

(5) The likelihood that development of the property would lead to or contribute to degradation of the scenic, natural, or historic character of the area;

(6) The opportunity for the general public to use the property or to appreciate its scenic values;

(7) The importance of the property in preserving a local or regional landscape or resource that attracts tourism or commerce to the area;

(8) The likelihood that the donee will acquire equally desirable and valuable substitute property or property rights;

(9) The cost to the donee of enforcing the terms of the conservation restriction;

(10) The population density in the area of the property; and

(11) The consistency of the proposed open space use with a legislatively mandated program identifying particular parcels of land for future protection.

(B) *Illustrations.* The preservation of an ordinary tract of land would not in and of itself yield a significant public benefit, but the preservation of ordinary land areas in conjunction with other factors that demonstrate significant public benefit or the preservation of a unique land area for public enjoyment would yield a significant public benefit. For example, the preservation of a vacant downtown lot would not by itself yield a significant public benefit, but the preservation of the downtown lot as a public garden would, absent countervailing factors, yield a significant public benefit. The following are other examples of contributions which would, absent countervailing factors, yield a significant public benefit: the preservation of farmland pursuant to a state program for flood prevention and control; the preservation of a unique natural land formation for the enjoyment of the general public; the preservation of woodland along a public highway pursuant to a government program to preserve the appearance of the area so as to maintain the scenic view from the highway; and the preservation of a stretch of undeveloped property located between a public highway and the ocean in order to maintain the scenic ocean view from the highway.

(v) *Limitation.* A deduction will not be allowed for the preservation of open space under section 170(h)(4)(A)(iii), if the terms of the easement permit a degree of intrusion or future development that would interfere with the essential scenic quality of the land or with the governmental conservation policy that is being furthered by the donation. See § 1.170A-14(e)(2) for rules relating to inconsistent use.

(vi) *Relationship of requirements—(A) Clearly delineated governmental policy and significant public benefit.* Although the requirements of "clearly delineated governmental policy" and "significant public benefit" must be met independently, for purposes of this section the two requirements may also be related. The more specific the governmental policy with respect to the particular site to be protected, the more likely the governmental decision, by itself, will tend to establish the significant public benefit associated with the donation. For example, while a statute in State X permitting preferential assessment for farmland is, by definition, governmental policy, it is distinguishable from a state statute, accompanied by appropriations, naming the X River as a valuable resource and articulating the legislative policy that the X River and the relatively natural quality of its surroundings be protected. On these facts, an open space easement on farmland in State X would have to demonstrate additional factors to establish "significant public benefit." The specificity of the legislative mandate to protect the X River, however, would by itself tend to establish the significant public benefit associated with an open space easement on land fronting the X River.

(B) *Scenic enjoyment and significant public benefit.* With respect to the relationship between the requirements of "scenic enjoyment" and "significant public benefit," since the degrees of scenic enjoyment offered by a variety of open space easements are subjective and not as easily delineated as are increasingly specific levels of governmental policy, the significant public benefit of preserving a scenic view must be independently established in all cases.

(C) *Donations may satisfy more than one test.* In some cases, open space easements may be both for scenic enjoyment and pursuant to a clearly delineated governmental policy. For example, the preservation of a particular scenic view identified as part of a scenic landscape inventory by a rigorous governmental review process will meet the tests of both paragraphs (d)(4)(i)(A) and (d)(4)(i)(B) of this section.

(5) *Historic preservation—(i) In general.* The donation of a qualified real property interest to

Reg. § 1.170A-14(d)(5)

preserve an historically important land area or a certified historic structure will meet the conservation purposes test of this section. When restrictions to preserve a building or land area within a registered historic district permit future development on the site, a deduction will be allowed under this section only if the terms of the restrictions require that such development conform with appropriate local, state, or Federal standards for construction or rehabilitation within the district. See also, § 1.170A-14(h)(3)(ii).

(ii) *Historically important land area.* The term "historically important land area" includes:

(A) An independently significant land area including any related historic resources (for example, an archaeological site or a Civil War battlefield with related monuments, bridges, cannons, or houses) that meets the National Register Criteria for Evaluation in 36 CFR 60.4 (Pub. L. 89-665, 80 Stat. 915);

(B) Any land area within a registered historic district including any buildings on the land area that can reasonably be considered as contributing to the significance of the district; and

(C) Any land area (including related historic resources) adjacent to a property listed individually in the National Register of Historic Places (but not within a registered historic district) in a case where the physical or environmental features of the land area contribute to the historic or cultural integrity of the property.

(iii) *Certified historic structure—(A) Definition.* The term "certified historic structure," for purposes of this section, means any building, structure or land area which is—

(A) Listed in the National Register, or

(B) Located in a registered historic district (as defined in section 48(g)(3)(B)) and is certified by the Secretary of the Interior (pursuant to 36 CFR 67.4) to the Secretary of the Treasury as being of historic significance to the district.

A "structure" for purposes of this section means any structure, whether or not it is depreciable. Accordingly, easements on private residences may qualify under this section. In addition, a structure would be considered to be a certified historic structure if it were certified either at the time the transfer was made or at the due date (including extensions) for filing the donor's return for the taxable year in which the contribution was made.

(iv) *Access—(A)* In order for a conservation contribution described in section 170(h)(4)(A)(iv) and this paragraph (d)(5) to be deductible, some visual public access to the

donated property is required. In the case of an historically important land area, the entire property need not be visible to the public for a donation to qualify under this section. However, the public benefit from the donation may be insufficient to qualify for a deduction if only a small portion of the property is so visible. Where the historic land area or certified historic structure which is the subject of the donation is not visible from a public way (e.g., the structure is hidden from view by a wall or shrubbery, the structure is too far from the public way, or interior characteristics and features of the structure are the subject of the easement), the terms of the easement must be such that the general public is given the opportunity on a regular basis to view the characteristics and features of the property which are preserved by the easement to the extent consistent with the nature and condition of the property.

(B) Factors to be considered in determining the type and amount of public access required under paragraph (d)(5)(iv)(A) of this section include the historical significance of the donated property, the nature of the features that are the subject of the easement, the remoteness or accessibility of the site of the donated property, the possibility of physical hazards to the public visiting the property (for example, an unoccupied structure in a dilapidated condition), the extent to which public access would be an unreasonable intrusion on any privacy interests of individuals living on the property, the degree to which public access would impair the preservation interests which are the subject of the donation, and the availability of opportunities for the public to view the property by means other than visits to the site.

(C) The amount of access afforded the public by the donation of an easement shall be determined with reference to the amount of access permitted by the terms of the easement which are established by the donor, rather than the amount of access actually provided by the donee organization. However, if the donor is aware of any facts indicating that the amount of access that the donee organization will provide is significantly less than the amount of access permitted under the terms of the easement, then the amount of access afforded the public shall be determined with reference to this lesser amount.

(v) *Examples.* The provisions of paragraph (d)(5)(iv) of this section may be illustrated by the following examples:

Example (1). A and his family live in a house in a certified historic district in the State of X. The entire house, including its interior, has architectural features representing classic Victorian period architecture. A donates an exterior and interior easement on the property to a qualified organization but continues to live in the house with his family. A's house is surrounded by a high stone wall which obscures the public's view of it from the street. Pursuant to the terms of the easement, the house may be opened to the public from 10:00 a.m. to 4:00 p.m. on one Sunday in May and one Sunday in November each year for house and garden tours. These tours are to be under the supervision of the donee and open to members of the general public upon payment of a small fee. In addition, under the terms of the easement, the donee organization is given the right to photograph the interior and exterior of the house and distribute such photographs to magazines, newsletters, or other publicly available publications. The terms of the easement also permit persons affiliated with educational organizations, professional architectural associations, and historical societies to make an appointment through the donee organization to study the property. The donor is not aware of any facts indicating that the public access to be provided by the donee organization will be significantly less than that permitted by the terms of the easement. The 2 opportunities for public visits per year, when combined with the ability of the general public to view the architectural characteristics and features that are the subject of the easement through photographs, the opportunity for scholarly study of the property, and the fact that the house is used as an occupied residence, will enable the donation to satisfy the requirement of public access.

Example (2). B owns an unoccupied farmhouse built in the 1840's and located on a property that is adjacent to a Civil War battlefield. During the Civil War the farmhouse was used as quarters for Union troops. The battlefield is visited year round by the general public. The condition of the farmhouse is such that the safety of visitors will not be jeopardized and opening it to the public will not result in significant deterioration. The farmhouse is not visible from the battlefield or any public way. It is accessible only by way of a private road owned by B. B donates a conservation easement on the farmhouse to a qualified organization. The terms of the easement provide that the donee organization may open the property (via B's road) to the general public on four weekends each year from 8:30 a.m. to 4:00 p.m. The donation does not meet the public access requirement because the farmhouse is safe, unoccupied, and easily accessible to the general public who have come to the site to visit Civil War historic land areas (and related resources), but

will only be open to the public on four weekends each year. However, the donation would meet the public access requirement if the terms of the easement permitted the donee organization to open the property to the public every other weekend during the year and the donor is not aware of any facts indicating that the donee organization will provide significantly less access than that permitted.

(e) *Exclusively for conservation purposes*—(1) *In general.* To meet the requirements of this section, a donation must be exclusively for conservation purposes. See paragraphs (c)(1) and (g)(1) through (g)(6)(ii) of this section. A deduction will not be denied under this section when incidental benefit inures to the donor merely as a result of conservation restrictions limiting the uses to which the donor's property may be put.

(2) *Inconsistent use.* Except as provided in paragraph (e)(4) of this section, a deduction will not be allowed if the contribution would accomplish one of the enumerated conservation purposes but would permit destruction of other significant conservation interests. For example, the preservation of farmland pursuant to a state program for flood prevention and control would not qualify under paragraph (d)(4) of this section if under the terms of the contribution a significant naturally occurring ecosystem could be injured or destroyed by the use of pesticides in the operation of the farm. However, this requirement is not intended to prohibit uses of the property, such as selective timber harvesting or selective farming if, under the circumstances, those uses do not impair significant conservation interests.

(3) *Inconsistent use permitted.* A use that is destructive of conservation interests will be permitted only if such use is necessary for the protection of the conservation interests that are the subject of the contribution. For example, a deduction for the donation of an easement to preserve an archaeological site that is listed on the National Register of Historic Places will not be disallowed if site excavation consistent with sound archaeological practices may impair a scenic view of which the land is a part. A donor may continue a pre-existing use of the property that does not conflict with the conservation purposes of the gift.

(f) *Examples.* The provisions of this section relating to conservation purposes may be illustrated by the following examples.

Example (1). State S contains many large tract forests that are desirable recreation and scenic areas for the general public. The forests' scenic values attract millions of people to the State. However, due to the increasing intensity of land development in State S, the continued existence of forestland parcels greater than 45 acres is threatened. J grants a perpetual easement on a 100-acre parcel of forestland that is part of one of the State's scenic areas to a qualifying organization. The easement imposes restrictions on the use of the parcel for the purpose of maintaining its scenic values. The restrictions include a requirement that the parcel be maintained forever as open space devoted exclusively to conservation purposes and wildlife protection, and that there be no commercial, industrial, residential, or other development use of such parcel. The law of State S recognizes a limited public right to enter private land, particularly for recreational pursuits, unless such land is posted or the landowner objects. The easement specifically restricts the landowner from posting the parcel, or from objecting, thereby maintaining public access to the parcel according to the custom of the State. J's parcel provides the opportunity for the public to enjoy the use of the property and appreciate its scenic values. Accordingly, J's donation qualifies for a deduction under this section.

Example (2). A qualified conservation organization owns Greenacre in fee as a nature preserve. Greenacre contains a high quality example of a tall grass prairie ecosystem. Farmacre, an operating farm, adjoins Greenacre and is a compatible buffer to the nature preserve. Conversion of Farmacre to a more intense use, such as a housing development, would adversely affect the continued use of Greenacre as a nature preserve because of human traffic generated by the development. The owner of Farmacre donates an easement preventing any future development on Farmacre to the qualified conservation organization for conservation purposes. Normal agricultural uses will be allowed on Farmacre. Accordingly, the donation qualifies for a deduction under this section.

Example (3). H owns Greenacre, a 900-acre parcel of woodland, rolling pasture, and orchards on the crest of a mountain. All of Greenacre is clearly visible from a nearby national park. Because of the strict enforcement of an applicable zoning plan, the highest and best use of Greenacre is as a subdivision of 40-acre tracts. H wishes to donate a scenic easement on Greenacre to a qualifying conservation organization, but H would like to reserve the right to subdivide Greenacre into 90-acre parcels with no more than one single-family home allowable on each parcel. Random building on the property, even as little as one home for each 90 acres, would destroy the scenic character of the view. Accordingly, no deduction would be allowable under this section.

Example (4). Assume the same facts as in example (3), except that not all of Greenacre is visible from the park and the deed of easement allows for limited cluster development of no more than five nine-acre clusters (with four houses on each cluster) located in areas generally not visible from the national park and subject to site and building plan approval by the donee organization in order to preserve the scenic view from the park. The donor and the donee have already identified sites where limited cluster development would not be visible from the park or would not impair the view. Owners of homes in the clusters will not have any rights with respect to the surrounding Greenacre property that are not also available to the general public. Accordingly, the donation qualifies for a deduction under this section.

Example (5). In order to protect State S's declining open space that is suited for agricultural use from increasing development pressure that has led to a marked decline in such open space, the Legislature of State S passed a statute authorizing the purchase of "agricultural land development rights" on open acreage. Agricultural land development rights allow the State to place agricultural preservation restrictions on land designated as worthy of protection in order to preserve open space and farm resources. Agricultural preservation restrictions prohibit or limit construction or placement of buildings except those used for agricultural purposes or dwellings used for family living by the farmer and his family and employees; removal of mineral substances in any manner that adversely affects the land's agricultural potential; or other uses detrimental to retention of the land for agricultural use. Money has been appropriated for this program and some landowners have in fact sold their "agricultural land development rights" to State S. K owns and operates a small dairy farm in State S located in an area designated by the Legislature as worthy of protection. K desires to preserve his farm for agricultural purposes in perpetuity. Rather than selling the development rights to State S, K grants to a qualified organization an agricultural preservation restriction on his property in the form of a conservation easement. K reserves to himself, his heirs and assigns the right to manage the farm consistent with sound agricultural and management practices. The preservation of K's land is pursuant to a clearly delineated governmental policy of preserving open space available for agricultural use, and will yield a significant public benefit by preserving open space against increasing development pressures. Accordingly, a deduction is allowed under this section.

(g) *Enforceable in perpetuity*—(1) *In general.* In the case of any donation under this section, any interest in the property retained by the donor (and the donor's successors in interest) must be subject to legally enforceable restrictions (for example, by recordation in the land records of the jurisdiction in which the property is located) that will prevent uses of the retained interest inconsistent with the conservation purposes of the donation. In the case of a contribution of a remainder interest, the contribution will not qualify if the tenants, whether they are tenants for life or a term of years, can use the property in a manner that diminishes the conservation values which are intended to be protected by the contributions.

(2) *Protection of a conservation purpose in case of donation of property subject to a mortgage.* In the case of conservation contributions made after February 13, 1986, no deduction will be permitted under this section for an interest in property which is subject to a mortgage unless the mortgagee subordinates its rights in the property to the right of the qualified organization to enforce the conservation purposes of the gift in perpetuity. For conservation contributions made prior to February 14, 1986, the requirement of section 170(h)(5)(A) is satisfied in the case of mortgaged property (with respect to which the mortgagee has not subordinated its rights) only if the donor can demonstrate that the conservation purpose is protected in perpetuity without subordination of the mortgagee's rights.

(3) *Remote future event.* A deduction shall not be disallowed under section 170(f)(3)(B)(iii) and this section merely because the interest which passes to, or is vested in, the donee organization may be defeated by the performance of some act or the happening of some event, if on the date of the gift it appears that the possibility that such act or event will occur is so remote as to be negligible. See paragraph (e) of § 1.170A-1. For example, a state's statutory requirement that use restrictions must be rerecorded every 30 years to remain enforceable shall not, by itself, render an easement nonperpetual.

(4) *Retention of qualified mineral interest—* (i) *In general.* Except as otherwise provided in paragraph (g)(4)(ii) of this section, the requirements of this section are not met and no deduction shall be allowed in the case of a contribution of any interest when there is a retention by any person of a qualified mineral interest (as defined in paragraph (b)(1)(i) of this section) if at any time there may be extractions or removal of minerals by any surface mining method. Moreover, in the case of a qualified mineral interest gift, the requirement that the conservation purposes be protected in perpetuity is not satisfied if any method of mining that is inconsistent with the particular conservation purposes of a contribution is permitted at any time. See also

§ 1.170A-14(e)(2). However, a deduction under this section will not be denied in the case of certain methods of mining that may have limited, localized impact on the real property but that are not irremediably destructive of significant conservation interests. For example, a deduction will not be denied in a case where production facilities are concealed or compatible with existing topography and landscape and when surface alteration is to be restored to its original state.

(ii) *Exception for qualified conservation contributions after July 1984.* (A) A contribution made after July 18, 1984, of a qualified real property interest described in section 170(h)(2)(A) shall not be disqualified under the first sentence of paragraph (g)(4)(i) of this section if the following requirements are satisfied.

(*1*) The ownership of the surface estate and mineral interest were separated before June 13, 1976, and remain so separated up to and including the time of the contribution.

(*2*) The present owner of the mineral interest is not a person whose relationship to the owner of the surface estate is described at the time of the contribution in section 267(b) or section 707(b), and

(*3*) The probability of extraction or removal of minerals by any surface mining method is so remote as to be negligible.

Whether the probability of extraction or removal of minerals by surface mining is so remote as to be negligible is a question of fact and is to be made on a case by case basis. Relevant factors to be considered in determining if the probability of extraction or removal of minerals by surface mining is so remote as to be negligible include: geological, geophysical or economic data showing the absence of mineral reserves on the property, or the lack of commercial feasibility at the time of the contribution of surface mining the mineral interest.

(B) If the ownership of the surface estate and mineral interest first became separated after June 12, 1976, no deduction is permitted for a contribution under this section unless surface mining on the property is completely prohibited.

(iii) *Examples.* The provisions of paragraph (g)(4)(i) and (ii) of this section may be illustrated by the following examples.

Example (1). K owns 5,000 acres of bottomland hardwood property along a major watershed system in the southern part of the United States. Agencies within the Department of the Interior have determined that southern bottomland hardwoods are a rapidly diminishing resource and a critical ecosystem in the south

Reg. § 1.170A-14(g)(2)

because of the intense pressure to cut the trees and convert the land to agricultural use. These agencies have further determined (and have indicated in correspondence with K) that bottomland hardwoods provide a superb habitat for numerous species and play an important role in controlling floods and in purifying rivers. K donates to a qualified organization his entire interest in this property other than his interest in the gas and oil deposits that have been identified under K's property. K covenants and can ensure that, although drilling for gas and oil on the property may have some temporary localized impact on the real property, the drilling will not interfere with the overall conservation purpose of the gift, which is to protect the unique bottomland hardwood ecosystem. Accordingly, the donation qualifies for a deduction under this section.

Example (2). Assume the same facts as in example (1), except that in 1979, K sells the mineral interest to A, an unrelated person, in an arm's-length transaction, subject to a recorded prohibition on the removal of any minerals by any surface mining method and a recorded prohibition against any mining technique that will harm the bottomland hardwood ecosystem. After the sale to A, K donates a qualified real property interest to a qualified organization to protect the bottomland hardwood ecosystem. Since at the time of the transfer, surface mining and any mining technique that will harm the bottomland hardwood ecosystem are completely prohibited, the donation qualifies for a deduction under this section.

(5) *Protection of conservation purpose where taxpayer reserves certain rights.* (i) *Documentation.* In the case of a donation made after February 13, 1986, of any qualified real property interest when the donor reserves rights the exercise of which may impair the conservation interests associated with the property, for a deduction to be allowable under this section the donor must make available to the donee, prior to the time the donation is made, documentation sufficient to establish the condition of the property at the time of the gift. Such documentation is designed to protect the conservation interests associated with the property, which although protected in perpetuity by the easement, could be adversely affected by the exercise of the reserved rights. Such documentation may include:

(A) The appropriate survey maps from the United States Geological Survey, showing the property line and other contiguous or nearby protected areas;

(B) A map of the area drawn to scale showing all existing man-made improvements or incursions (such as roads, buildings, fences, or gravel pits), vegetation and identification of flora and fauna (including, for example, rare species locations, animal breeding and roosting areas, and migration routes), land use history (including present uses and recent past disturbances), and distinct natural features (such as large trees and aquatic areas);

(C) An aerial photograph of the property at an appropriate scale taken as close as possible to the date the donation is made; and

(D) On-site photographs taken at appropriate locations on the property.

If the terms of the donation contain restrictions with regard to a particular natural resource to be protected, such as water quality or air quality, the condition of the resource at or near the time of the gift must be established. The documentation, including the maps and photographs, must be accompanied by a statement signed by the donor and a representative of the donee clearly referencing the documentation and in substance saying "This natural resources inventory is an accurate representation of [the protected property] at the time of the transfer."

(ii) *Donee's right to inspection and legal remedies.* In the case of any donation referred to in paragraph (g)(5)(i) of this section, the donor must agree to notify the donee, in writing, before exercising any reserved right, *e.g.,* the right to extract certain minerals which may have an adverse impact on the conservation interests associated with the qualified real property interest. The terms of the donation must provide a right of the donee to enter the property at reasonable times for the purpose of inspecting the property to determine if there is compliance with the terms of the donation. Additionally, the terms of the donation must provide a right of the donee to enforce the conservation restrictions by appropriate legal proceedings including, but not limited to, the right to require the restoration of the property to its condition at the time of the donation.

(6) *Extinguishment.* (i) *In general.* If a subsequent unexpected change in the conditions surrounding the property that is the subject of a donation under this paragraph can make impossible or impractical the continued use of the property for conservation purposes, the conservation purpose can nonetheless be treated as protected in perpetuity if the restrictions are extinguished by judicial proceeding and all of the donee's proceeds (determined under paragraph (g)(6)(ii) of this section) from a subsequent sale or exchange of the property are used by the donee organization in a manner consistent with the conservation purposes of the original contribution.

Reg. § 1.170A-14(g)(6)

(ii) *Proceeds.* In the case of a donation made after February 13, 1986, for a deduction to be allowed under this section, at the time of the gift the donor must agree that the donation of the perpetual conservation restriction gives rise to a property right, immediately vested in the donee organization, with a fair market value that is at least equal to the proportionate value that the perpetual conservation restriction at the time of the gift bears to the value of the property as a whole at that time. See § 1.170A-14(h)(3)(iii) relating to the allocation of basis. For purposes of this paragraph (g)(6)(ii), that proportionate value of the donee's property rights shall remain constant. Accordingly, when a change in conditions gives rise to the extinguishment of a perpetual conservation restriction under paragraph (g)(6)(i) of this section, the donee organization, on a subsequent sale, exchange,or involuntary conversion of the subject property, must be entitled to a portion of the proceeds at least equal to that proportionate value of the perpetual conservation restriction, unless state law provides that the donor is entitled to the full proceeds from the conversion without regard to the terms of the prior perpetual conservation restriction.

(h) *Valuation*—(1) *Entire interest of donor other than qualified mineral interest.* The value of the contribution under section 170 in the case of a contribution of a taxpayer's entire interest in property other than a qualified mineral interest is the fair market value of the surface rights in the property contributed. The value of the contribution shall be computed without regard to the mineral rights. See paragraph (h)(4), *example (1),* of this section.

(2) *Remainder interest in real property.* In the case of a contribution of any remainder interest in real property, section 170(f)(4) provides that in determining the value of such interest for purposes of section 170, depreciation and depletion of such property shall be taken into account. See § 170A-12. In the case of the contribution of a remainder interest for conservation purposes, the current fair market value of the property (against which the limitations of § 1.170A-12 are applied) must take into account any pre-existing or contemporaneously recorded rights limiting, for conservation purposes, the uses to which the subject property may be put.

(3) *Perpetual conservation restriction*—(i) *In general.* The value of the contribution under section 170 in the case of a charitable contribution of a perpetual conservation restriction is the fair market value of the perpetual conservation restriction at the time of the contribution. See § 1.170A-7(c). If there is a substantial record of sales of easements comparable to the donated easement (such as purchases pursuant to a governmental program), the fair market value of the donated easement is based on the sales prices of such comparable easements. If no substantial record of market-place sales is available to use as a meaningful or valid comparison, as a general rule (but not necessarily in all cases) the fair market value of a perpetual conservation restriction is equal to the difference between the fair market value of the property it encumbers before the granting of the restriction and the fair market value of the encumbered property after the granting of the restriction. The amount of the deduction in the case of a charitable contribution of a perpetual conservation restriction covering a portion of the contiguous property owned by a donor and the donor's family as defined in section 267(c)(4) is the difference between the fair market value of the entire contiguous parcel of property before and after the granting of the restriction. If the granting of a perpetual conservation restriction after January 14, 1986, has the effect of increasing the value of any other property owned by the donor or a related person, the amount of the deduction for the conservation contribution shall be reduced by the amount of the increase in the value of the other property, whether or not such property is contiguous. If, as a result of the donation of a perpetual conservation restriction, the donor or a related person receives, or can reasonably expect to receive, financial or economic benefits that are greater than those that will inure to the general public from the transfer, no deduction is allowable under this section. However, if the donor or a related person receives, or can reasonably expect to receive, a financial or economic benefit that is substantial, but it is clearly shown that the benefit is less than the amount of the transfer, then a deduction under this section is allowable for the excess of the amount transferred over the amount of the financial or economic benefit received or reasonably expected to be received by the donor or the related person. For purposes of this paragraph (h)(3)(i), related person shall have the same meaning as in either section 267(b) or section 707(b). (See *example (10)* of paragraph (h)(4) of this section.)

(ii) *Fair market value of property before and after restriction.* If before and after valuation is used, the fair market value of the property before contribution of the conservation restriction must take into account not only the current use of the property but also an objective assessment of how immediate or remote the likelihood is that the property, absent the restriction, would in fact be developed, as well as any effect from zoning, con-

Reg. § 1.170A-14(h)(1)

servation, or historic preservation laws that already restrict the property's potential highest and best use. Further, there may be instances where the grant of a conservation restriction may have no material effect on the value of the property or may in fact serve to enhance, rather than reduce, the value of property. In such instances, no deduction would be allowable. In the case of a conservation restriction that allows for any development, however limited, on the property to be protected, the fair market value of the property after contribution of the restriction must take into account the effect of the development. In the case of a conservation easement such as an easement on a certified historic structure, the fair market value of the property after contribution of the restriction must take into account the amount of access permitted by the terms of the easement. Additionally, if before and after valuation is used, an appraisal of the property after contribution of the restriction must take into account the effect of restrictions that will result in a reduction of the potential fair market value represented by highest and best use but will, nevertheless, permit uses of the property that will increase its fair market value above that represented by the property's current use. The value of a perpetual conservation restriction shall not be reduced by reason of the existence of restrictions on transfer designed solely to ensure that the conservation restriction will be dedicated to conservation purposes. See § 1.170A-14(c)(3).

(iii) *Allocation of basis.* In the case of the donation of a qualified real property interest for conservation purposes, the basis of the property retained by the donor must be adjusted by the elimination of that part of the total basis of the property that is properly allocable to the qualified real property interest granted. The amount of the basis that is allocable to the qualified real property interest shall bear the same ratio to the total basis of the property as the fair market value of the qualified real property interest bears to the fair market value of the property before the granting of the qualified real property interest. When a taxpayer donates to a qualifying conservation organization an easement on a structure with respect to which deductions are taken for depreciation, the reduction required by this paragraph (h)(3)(ii) in the basis of the property retained by the taxpayer must be allocated between the structure and the underlying land.

(4) *Examples.* The provisions of this section may be illustrated by the following examples. In examples illustrating the value or deductibility of donations, the applicable restrictions and limitations of § 1.170A-4, with respect to reduction in amount of charitable contributions of certain ap-

preciated property, and § 1.170A-8, with respect to limitations on charitable deductions by individuals, must also be taken into account.

Example (1). A owns Goldacre, a property adjacent to a state park. A wants to donate Goldacre to the state to be used as part of the park, but A wants to reserve a qualified mineral interest in the property, to exploit currently and to devise at death. The fair market value of the surface rights in Goldacre is $200,000 and the fair market value of the mineral rights is $100,000. In order to ensure that the quality of the park will not be degraded, restrictions must be imposed on the right to extract the minerals that reduce the fair market value of the mineral rights to $80,000. Under this section, the value of the contribution is $200,000 (the value of the surface rights).

Example (2). In 1984, B, who is 62, donates a remainder interest in Greenacre to a qualifying organization for conservation purposes. Greenacre is a tract of 200 acres of undeveloped woodland that is valued at $200,000 at its highest and best use. Under § 1.170A-12(b), the value of a remainder interest in real property following one life is determined under § 25.2512-5 of this chapter (Gift Tax Regulations). (See § 25.2512-5A of this chapter with respect to the valuation of annuities, interests for life or term of years, and remainder or reversionary interests transferred before May 1, 1999). Accordingly, the value of the remainder interest, and thus the amount eligible for an income tax deduction under section 170(f), is $55,996 ($200,000 × .27998).

Example (3). Assume the same facts as in *example (2)*, except that Greenacre is B's 200-acre estate with a home built during the colonial period. Some of the acreage around the home is cleared; the balance of Greenacre, except for access roads, is wooded and undeveloped. See section 170(f)(3)(B)(i). However, B would like Greenacre to be maintained in its current state after his death, so he donates a remainder interest in Greenacre to a qualifying organization for conservation purposes pursuant to sections 170(f)(3)(B)(iii) and (h)(2)(B). At the time of the gift the land has a value of $200,000 and the house has a value of $100,000. The value of the remainder interest, and thus the amount eligible for an income tax deduction under section 170(f), is computed pursuant to § 1.170A-12. See § 1.170A-12(b)(3).

Example (4). Assume the same facts as in *example (2)*, except that at age 62 instead of donating a remainder interest B donates an easement in Greenacre to a qualifying organization for conservation purposes. The fair market value of Greenacre after the donation is reduced to

$110,000. Accordingly, the value of the easement, and thus the amount eligible for a deduction under section 170(f), is $90,000 ($200,000 less $110,000).

Example (5). Assume the same facts as in *example (4),* and assume that three years later, at age 65, B decides to donate a remainder interest in Greenacre to a qualifying organization for conservation purposes. Increasing real estate values in the area have raised the fair market value of Greenacre (subject to the easement) to $130,000. Accordingly, the value of the remainder interest, and thus the amount eligible for a deduction under section 170(f), is $41,639 ($130,000 × .32030).

Example (6). Assume the same facts as in *example (2),* except that at the time of the donation of a remainder interest in Greenacre, B also donates an easement to a different qualifying organization for conservation purposes. Based on all the facts and circumstances, the value of the easement is determined to be $100,000. Therefore, the value of the property after the easement is $100,000 and the value of the remainder interest, and thus the amount eligible for deduction under section 170(f), is $27,998 ($100,000 × .27998).

Example (7). C owns Greenacre, a 200-acre estate containing a house built during the colonial period. At its highest and best use, for home development, the fair market value of Greenacre is $300,000. C donates an easement (to maintain the house and Greenacre in their current state) to a qualifying organization for conservation purposes. The fair market value of Greenacre after the donation is reduced to $125,000. Accordingly, the value of the easement and the amount eligible for a deduction under section 170(f) is $175,000 ($300,000 less $125,000).

Example (8). Assume the same facts as in *example (7),* and assume that three years later, C decides to donate a remainder interest in Greenacre to a qualifying organization for conservation purposes. Increasing real estate values in the area have raised the fair market value of Greenacre to $180,000. Assume that because of the perpetual easement prohibiting any development of the land, the value of the house is $120,000 and the value of the land is $60,000. The value of the remainder interest, and thus the amount eligible for an income tax deduction under section 170(f), is computed pursuant to § 1.170A-12. See § 1.170A-12(b)(3).

Example (9). D owns property with a basis of $20,000 and a fair market value of $80,000. D donates to a qualifying organization an easement for conservation purposes that is determined under this section to have a fair market value of

$60,000. The amount of basis allocable to the easement is $15,000 ($60,000/$80,000 = $15,000/$20,000). Accordingly, the basis of the property is reduced to $5,000 ($20,000 minus $15,000).

Example (10). E owns 10 one-acre lots that are currently woods and parkland. The fair market value of each of E's lots is $15,000 and the basis of each lot is $3,000. E grants to the county a perpetual easement for conservation purposes to use and maintain eight of the acres as a public park and to restrict any future development on those eight acres. As a result of the restrictions, the value of the eight acres is reduced to $1,000 an acre. However, by perpetually restricting development on this portion of the land, E has ensured that the two remaining acres will always be bordered by parkland, thus increasing their fair market value to $22,500 each. If the eight acres represented all of E's land, the fair market value of the easement would be $112,000, an amount equal to the fair market value of the land before the granting of the easement (8 × $15,000 = $120,000) minus the fair market value of the encumbered land after the granting of the easement (8 × $1,000 = $8,000). However, because the easement only covered a portion of the taxpayer's contiguous land, the amount of the deduction under section 170 is reduced to $97,000 ($150,000 − $53,000), that is, the difference between the fair market value of the entire tract of land before ($150,000) and after ((8 × $1,000) + (2 × $22,500)) the granting of the easement.

Example (11). Assume the same facts as in *example (10).* Since the easement covers a portion of E's land, only the basis of that portion is adjusted. Therefore, the amount of basis allocable to the easement is $22,400 ((8 × $3,000) × ($112,000/$120,000)). Accordingly, the basis of the eight acres encumbered by the easement is reduced to $1,600 ($24,000 − $22,400), or $200 for each acre. The basis of the two remaining acres is not affected by the donation.

Example (12). F owns and uses as professional offices a two-story building that lies within a registered historic district. F's building is an outstanding example of period architecture with a fair market value of $125,000. Restricted to its current use, which is the highest and best use of the property without making changes to the facade, the building and lot would have a fair market value of $100,000, of which $80,000 would be allocable to the building and $20,000 would be allocable to the lot. F's basis in the property is $50,000, of which $40,000 is allocable to the building and $10,000 is allocable to the lot. F's neighborhood is a mix of residential and commer-

Reg. § 1.170A-14(h)(4)

cial uses, and it is possible that F (or another owner) could enlarge the building for more extensive commercial use, which is its highest and best use. However, this would require changes to the facade. F would like to donate to a qualifying preservation organization an easement restricting any changes to the facade and promising to maintain the facade in perpetuity. The donation would qualify for a deduction under this section. The fair market value of the easement is $25,000 (the fair market value of the property before the easement, $125,000, minus the fair market value of the property after the easement, $100,000). Pursuant to § 1.170A-14(h)(3)(iii), the basis allocable to the easement is $10,000 and the basis of the underlying property (building and lot) is reduced to $40,000.

(i) *Substantiation requirement.* If a taxpayer makes a qualified conservation contribution and claims a deduction, the taxpayer must maintain written records of the fair market value of the underlying property before and after the donation and the conservation purpose furthered by the donation and such information shall be stated in the taxpayer's income tax return if required by the return or its instructions. See also § 1.170A-13(c) (relating to substantiation requirements for deductions in excess of $5,000 for charitable contributions made after 1984), and section 6659 (relating to additions to tax in the case of valuation overstatements).

(i)[j] *Effective date.* Except as otherwise provided in § 1.170A-14(g)(4)(ii), this section applies only to contributions made on or after December 18, 1980. [Reg. § 1.170A-14.]

☐ [T.D. 8069, 1-13-86. Amended by T.D. 8199, 5-4-88; T.D. 8540, 6-9-94 and T.D. 8819, 4-29-99.]

[Reg. § 1.171-1]

§ 1.171-1. Bond premium.—(a) *Overview—* (1) *In general.* This section and §§ 1.171-2 through 1.171-5 provide rules for the determination and amortization of bond premium by a holder. In general, a holder amortizes bond premium by offsetting the interest allocable to an accrual period with the premium allocable to that period. Bond premium is allocable to an accrual period based on a constant yield. The use of a constant yield to amortize bond premium is intended to generally conform the treatment of bond premium to the treatment of original issue discount under sections 1271 through 1275. Unless otherwise provided, the terms used in this section and §§ 1.171-2 through 1.171-5 have the same meaning as those terms in sections 1271 through 1275 and the corresponding regulations. Moreover, unless otherwise provided, the provisions of this section and §§ 1.171-2 through

1.171-5 apply in a manner consistent with those of sections 1271 through 1275 and the corresponding regulations. In addition, the anti-abuse rule in § 1.1275-2(g) applies for purposes of this section and §§ 1.171-2 through 1.171-5.

(2) *Cross-references.* For rules dealing with the adjustments to a holder's basis to reflect the amortization of bond premium, see § 1.1016-5(b). For rules dealing with the treatment of bond issuance premium by an issuer, see § 1.163-13.

(b) *Scope*—(1) *In general.* Except as provided in paragraph (b)(2) of this section and § 1.171-5, this section and §§ 1.171-2 through 1.171-4 apply to any bond that, upon its acquisition by the holder, is held with bond premium. For purposes of this section and §§ 1.171-2 through 1.171-5, the term *bond* has the same meaning as the term *debt instrument* in § 1.1275-1(d).

(2) *Exceptions.* This section and §§ 1.171-2 through 1.171-5 do not apply to—

(i) A bond described in section 1272(a)(6)(C) (regular interests in a REMIC, qualified mortgages held by a REMIC, and certain other debt instruments, or pools of debt instruments, with payments subject to acceleration);

(ii) A bond to which § 1.1275-4 applies (relating to certain debt instruments that provide for contingent payments);

(iii) A bond held by a holder that has made a § 1.1272-3 election with respect to the bond;

(iv) A bond that is stock in trade of the holder, a bond of a kind that would properly be included in the inventory of the holder if on hand at the close of the taxable year, or a bond held primarily for sale to customers in the ordinary course of the holder's trade or business; or

(v) A bond issued before September 28, 1985, unless the bond bears interest and was issued by a corporation or by a government or political subdivision thereof.

(c) *General rule*—(1) *Tax-exempt obligations.* A holder must amortize bond premium on a bond that is a tax-exempt obligation. See § 1.171-2(c) Example 4.

(2) *Taxable bonds.* A holder may elect to amortize bond premium on a taxable bond. Except as provided in paragraph (c)(3) of this section, a taxable bond is any bond other than a tax-exempt obligation. See § 1.171-4 for rules relating to the election to amortize bond premium on a taxable bond.

(3) *Bonds the interest on which is partially excludable.* For purposes of this section and §§ 1.171-2 through 1.171-5, a bond the interest on which is partially excludable from gross income is

treated as two instruments, a tax-exempt obligation and a taxable bond. The holder's basis in the bond and each payment on the bond are allocated between the two instruments based on a reasonable method.

(d) *Determination of bond premium*—(1) *In general.* A holder acquires a bond at a premium if the holder's basis in the bond immediately after its acquisition by the holder exceeds the sum of all amounts payable on the bond after the acquisition date (other than payments of qualified stated interest). This excess is bond premium, which is amortizable under § 1.171-2.

(2) *Additional rules for amounts payable on certain bonds.* Additional rules apply to determine the amounts payable on a variable rate debt instrument, an inflation-indexed debt instrument, a bond that provides for certain alternative payment schedules, and a bond that provides for remote or incidental contingencies. See § 1.171-3.

(e) *Basis.* A holder determines its basis in a bond under this paragraph (e). This determination of basis applies only for purposes of this section and §§ 1.171-2 through 1.171-5. Because of the application of this paragraph (e), the holder's basis in the bond for purposes of these sections may differ from the holder's basis for determining gain or loss on the sale or exchange of the bond.

(1) *Determination of basis*—(i) *In general.* In general, the holder's basis in the bond is the holder's basis for determining loss on the sale or exchange of the bond.

(ii) *Bonds acquired in certain exchanges.* If the holder acquired the bond in exchange for other property (other than in a reorganization defined in section 368) and the holder's basis in the bond is determined in whole or in part by reference to the holder's basis in the other property, the holder's basis in the bond may not exceed its fair market value immediately after the exchange. See paragraph (f) *Example 1* of this section. If the bond is acquired in a reorganization, see section 171(b)(4)(B).

(iii) *Convertible bonds*—(A) *General rule.* If the bond is a convertible bond, the holder's basis in the bond is reduced by an amount equal to the value of the conversion option. The value of the conversion option may be determined under any reasonable method. For example, the holder may determine the value of the conversion option by comparing the market price of the convertible bond to the market prices of similar bonds that do not have conversion options. See paragraph (f) *Example 2* of this section.

(B) *Convertible bonds acquired in certain exchanges.* If the bond is a convertible bond

acquired in a transaction described in paragraph (e)(1)(ii) of this section, the holder's basis in the bond may not exceed its fair market value immediately after the exchange reduced by the value of the conversion option.

(C) *Definition of convertible bond.* A convertible bond is a bond that provides the holder with an option to convert the bond into stock of the issuer, stock or debt of a related party (within the meaning of section 267(b) or 707(b)(1)), or into cash or other property in an amount equal to the approximate value of such stock or debt.

(2) *Basis in bonds held by certain transferees.* Notwithstanding paragraph (e)(1) of this section, if the bond is transferred basis property (as defined in section 7701(a)(43)) and the transferor had acquired the bond at a premium, the holder's basis in the bond is—

(i) The holder's basis for determining loss on the sale or exchange of the bond; reduced by

(ii) Any amounts that the transferor could not have amortized under this paragraph (e) or under § 1.171-4(c), except to the extent that the holder's basis already reflects a reduction attributable to such nonamortizable amounts.

(f) *Examples.* The following examples illustrate the rules of this section:

Example 1. Bond received in liquidation of a partnership interest—(i) *Facts.* PR is a partner in partnership PRS. PRS does not have any unrealized receivables or inventory items as defined in section 751. On January 1, 1998, PRS distributes to PR a taxable bond, issued by an unrelated corporation, in liquidation of PR's partnership interest. At that time, the fair market value of PR's partnership interest is $40,000 and the basis is $100,000. The fair market value of the bond is $40,000.

(ii) *Determination of basis.* Under section 732(b), PR's basis in the bond is equal to PR's basis in the partnership interest. Therefore, PR's basis for determining loss on the sale or exchange of the bond is $100,000. However, because the distribution is treated as an exchange for purposes of section 171(b)(4), PR's basis in the bond is $40,000 for purposes of this section and §§ 1.171-2 through 1.171-5. See paragraph (e)(1)(ii) of this section.

Example 2. Convertible bond—(i) *Facts.* On January 1, 1998, A purchases for $1,100 B corporation's bond maturing on January 1, 2001, with a stated principal amount of $1,000, payable at maturity. The bond provides for unconditional payments of interest of $30 on January 1 and July 1 of each year. In addition, the bond is convertible into 15 shares of B corporation stock at the option of the holder. On January 1, 1998, B corporation's nonconvertible, publicly-traded, three-year debt with a similar credit rating trades at a price that reflects a yield of 6.75 percent, compounded semiannually.

(ii) *Determination of basis.* A's basis for determining loss on the sale or exchange of the bond is $1,100. As of January 1, 1998, discounting the remaining payments on the bond at the yield at which B's similar nonconvertible bonds trade (6.75 percent, compounded semiannually) results in a present value of $980. Thus, the value of the conversion option is $120. Under paragraph (e)(1)(iii)(A) of this section, A's basis is $980 ($1,100 − $120) for purposes of this section and §§ 1.171-2 through 1.171-5. The sum of all amounts payable on the bond other than qualified stated interest is $1,000. Because A's basis (as determined under paragraph (e)(1)(iii)(A) of this section) does not exceed $1,000, A does not acquire the bond at a premium.

[Reg. § 1.171-1.]

☐ [*T.D.* 6278, 12-10-57. *Amended by T.D.* 8746, 12-30-97.]

[Reg. § 1.171-2]

§ 1.171-2. Amortization of bond premium.— (a) *Offsetting qualified stated interest with premium*—(1) *In general.* A holder amortizes bond premium by offsetting the qualified stated interest allocable to an accrual period with the bond premium allocable to the accrual period. This offset occurs when the holder takes the qualified stated interest into account under the holder's regular method of accounting.

(2) *Qualified stated interest allocable to an accrual period.* See § 1.446-2(b) to determine the accrual period to which qualified stated interest is allocable and to determine the accrual of qualified stated interest within an accrual period.

(3) *Bond premium allocable to an accrual period.* The bond premium allocable to an accrual period is determined under this paragraph (a)(3). Within an accrual period, the bond premium allocable to the period accrues ratably.

(i) *Step one: Determine the holder's yield.* The holder's yield is the discount rate that, when used in computing the present value of all remaining payments to be made on the bond (including payments of qualified stated interest), produces an amount equal to the holder's basis in the bond as determined under § 1.171-1(e) For this purpose, the remaining payments include only payments to be made after the date the holder acquires the bond. The yield is calculated as of the date the holder acquires the bond, must be con-

stant over the term of the bond, and must be calculated to at least two decimal places when expressed as a percentage.

(ii) *Step two: Determine the accrual periods.* A holder determines the accrual periods for the bond under the rules of § 1.1272-1(b)(1)(ii).

(iii) *Step three: Determine the bond premium allocable to the accrual period.* The bond premium allocable to an accrual period is the excess of the qualified stated interest allocable to the accrual period over the product of the holder's adjusted acquisition price (as defined in paragraph (b) of this section) at the beginning of the accrual period and the holder's yield. In performing this calculation, the yield must be stated appropriately taking into account the length of the particular accrual period. Principles similar to those in § 1.1272-1(b)(4) apply in determining the bond premium allocable to an accrual period.

(4) *Bond premium in excess of qualified stated interest*—(i) *Taxable bonds*—(A) *Bond premium deduction.* In the case of a taxable bond, if the bond premium allocable to an accrual period exceeds the qualified stated interest allocable to the accrual period the excess is treated by the holder as a bond premium deduction under section 171(a)(1) for the accrual period. However, the amount treated as a bond premium deduction is limited to the amount by which the holder's total interest inclusions on the bond in prior accrual periods exceed the total amount treated by the holder as a bond premium deduction on the bond in prior accrual periods. A deduction determined under this paragraph (a)(4)(i)(A) is not subject to section 67 (the 2-percent floor on miscellaneous itemized deductions). See *Example 1* of § 1.171-3(e).

(B) *Carryforward.* If the bond premium allocable to an accrual period exceeds the sum of the qualified stated interest allocable to the accrual period and the amount treated as a deduction for the accrual period under paragraph (a)(4)(i)(A) of this section, the excess is carried forward to the next accrual period and is treated as bond premium allocable to that period.

(ii) *Tax-exempt obligations.* In the case of a tax-exempt obligation, if the bond premium allocable to an accrual period exceeds the qualified stated interest allocable to the accrual period, the excess is a nondeductible loss. If a regulated investment company (RIC) within the meaning of section 851 has excess bond premium for an accrual period that would be a nondeductible loss under the prior sentence, the RIC must use this excess bond premium to reduce its tax-exempt interest income on other tax-exempt obligations held during the accrual period.

(5) *Additional rules for certain bonds.* Additional rules apply to determine the amortization of bond premium on a variable rate debt instrument, an inflation-indexed debt instrument, a bond that provides for certain alternative payment schedules, and a bond that provides for remote or incidental contingencies. See § 1.171-3.

(b) *Adjusted acquisition price.* The adjusted acquisition price of a bond at the beginning of the first accrual period is the holder's basis as determined under § 1.171-1(e). Thereafter, the adjusted acquisition price is the holder's basis in the bond decreased by—

(1) The amount of bond premium previously allocable under paragraph (a)(3) of this section; and

(2) The amount of any payment previously made on the bond other than a payment of qualified stated interest.

(c) *Examples.* The following examples illustrate the rules of this section. Each example assumes the holder uses the calendar year as its taxable year and has elected to amortize bond premium, effective for all relevant taxable years. In addition, each example assumes a 30-day month and 360-day year. Although, for purposes of simplicity, the yield as stated is rounded to two decimal places, the computations do not reflect this rounding convention. The examples are as follows:

Example 1. Taxable bond—(i) *Facts.* On February 1, 1999, A purchases for $110,000 a taxable bond maturing on February 1, 2006, with a stated principal amount of $100,000, payable at maturity. The bond provides for unconditional payments of interest of $10,000, payable on February 1 of each year. A uses the cash receipts and disbursements method of accounting, and A decides to use annual accrual periods ending on February 1 of each year.

(ii) *Amount of bond premium.* The interest payments on the bond are qualified stated interest. Therefore, the sum of all amounts payable on the bond (other than the interest payments) is $100,000. Under § 1.171-1, the amount of bond premium is $10,000 ($110,000 − $100,000).

(iii) *Bond premium allocable to the first accrual period.* Based on the remaining payment schedule of the bond and A's basis in the bond, A's yield is 8.07 percent, compounded annually. The bond premium allocable to the accrual period ending on February 1, 2000, is the excess of the qualified stated interest allocable to the period ($10,000) over the product of the adjusted acquisition price at the beginning of the period ($110,000) and A's yield (8.07 percent, compounded annually). Therefore, the bond premium allocable to the accrual period is $1,118.17 ($10,000 − $8,881.83).

(iv) *Premium used to offset interest.* Although A receives an interest payment of $10,000 on February 1, 2000, A only includes in income $8,881.83, the qualified stated interest allocable to the period ($10,000) offset with bond premium allocable to the period ($1,118.17). Under § 1.1016-5(b), A's basis in the bond is reduced by $1,118.17 on February 1, 2000.

Example 2. Alternative accrual periods—(i) *Facts.* The facts are the same as in *Example 1* of this paragraph (c) except that A decides to use semiannual accrual periods ending on February 1 and August 1 of each year.

(ii) *Bond premium allocable to the first accrual period.* Based on the remaining payment schedule of the bond and A's basis in the bond, A's yield is 7.92 percent, compounded semiannually. The bond premium allocable to the accrual period ending on August 1, 1999, is the excess of the qualified stated interest allocable to the period ($5,000) over the product of the adjusted acquisition price at the beginning of the period ($110,000) and A's yield, stated appropriately taking into account the length of the accrual period (7.92 percent/2). Therefore, the bond premium allocable to the accrual period is $645.29 ($5,000 − $4,354.71). Although the accrual period ends on August 1, 1999, the qualified stated interest of $5,000 is not taken into income until February 1, 2000, the date it is received. Likewise, the bond premium of $645.29 is not taken into account until February 1, 2000. The adjusted acquisition price of the bond on August 1, 1999, is $109,354.71 (the adjusted acquisition price at the beginning of the period ($110,000) less the bond premium allocable to the period ($645.29)).

(iii) *Bond premium allocable to the second accrual period.* Because the interval between payments of qualified stated interest contains more than one accrual period, the adjusted acquisition price at the beginning of the second accrual period must be adjusted for the accrued but unpaid qualified stated interest. See paragraph (a)(3)(iii) of this section and § 1.1272-1(b)(4)(i)(B). Therefore, the adjusted acquisition price on August 1, 1999, is $114,354.71 ($109,354.71 + $5,000). The bond premium allocable to the accrual period ending on February 1, 2000, is the excess of the qualified stated interest allocable to the period ($5,000) over the product of the adjusted acquisition price at the beginning of the period ($114,354.71) and A's yield, stated appropriately taking into account the length of the accrual period (7.92 percent/2). Therefore, the bond premium allocable to the accrual period is $472.88 ($5,000 − $4,527.12).

Reg. § 1.171-2(a)(5)

(iv) *Premium used to offset interest.* Although A receives an interest payment of $10,000 on February 1, 2000, A only includes in income $8,881.83, the qualified stated interest of $10,000 ($5,000 allocable to the accrual period ending on August 1, 1999, and $5,000 allocable to the accrual period ending on February 1, 2000) offset with bond premium of $1,118.17 ($645.29 allocable to the accrual period ending on August 1, 1999, and $472.88 allocable to the accrual period ending on February 1, 2000) As indicated in *Example 1* of this paragraph (c), this same amount would be taken into income at the same time had A used annual accrual periods.

Example 3. Holder uses accrual method of accounting—(i) *Facts.* The facts are the same as in *Example 1* of this paragraph (c) except that A uses an accrual method of accounting. Thus, for the accrual period ending on February 1, 2000, the qualified stated interest allocable to the period is $10,000, and the bond premium allocable to the period is $1,118.17. Because the accrual period extends beyond the end of A's taxable year, A must allocate these amounts between the two taxable years.

(ii) *Amounts allocable to the first taxable year.* The qualified stated interest allocable to the first taxable year is $9,166.67 ($10,000 × 11/12). The bond premium allocable to the first taxable year is $1,024.99 ($1,118.17 × 11/12).

(iii) *Premium used to offset interest.* For 1999, A includes in income $8,141.68, the qualified stated interest allocable to the period ($9,166.67) offset with bond premium allocable to the period ($1,024.99). Under § 1.1016-5(b), A's basis in the bond is reduced by $1,024.99 in 1999.

(iv) *Amounts allocable to the next taxable year.* The remaining amounts of qualified stated interest and bond premium allocable to the accrual period ending on February 1, 2000, are taken into account for the taxable year ending on December 31, 2000.

Example 4. Tax-exempt obligation—(i) *Facts.* On January 15, 1999, C purchases for $120,000 a tax-exempt obligation maturing on January 15, 2006, with a stated principal amount of $100,000, payable at maturity. The obligation provides for unconditional payments of interest of $9,000, payable on January 15 of each year. C uses the cash receipts and disbursements method of accounting, and C decides to use annual accrual periods ending on January 15 of each year.

(ii) *Amount of bond premium.* The interest payments on the obligation are qualified stated interest. Therefore, the sum of all amounts payable on the obligation (other than the interest payments)

is $100,000. Under § 1.171-1, the amount of bond premium is $20,000 ($120,000 − $100,000).

(iii) *Bond premium allocable to the first accrual period.* Based on the remaining payment schedule of the obligation and C's basis in the obligation, C's yield is 5.48 percent, compounded annually. The bond premium allocable to the accrual period ending on January 15, 2000, is the excess of the qualified stated interest allocable to the period ($9,000) over the product of the adjusted acquisition price at the beginning of the period ($120,000) and C's yield (5.48 percent, compounded annually). Therefore, the bond premium allocable to the accrual period is $2,420.55 ($9,000 − $6,579.45).

(iv) *Premium used to offset interest.* Although C receives an interest payment of $9,000 on January 15, 2000, C only receives tax-exempt interest income of $6,579.45, the qualified stated interest allocable to the period ($9,000) offset with bond premium allocable to the period ($2,420.55). Under § 1.1016-5(b), C's basis in the obligation is reduced by $2,420.55 on January 15, 2000.

[Reg. § 1.171-2.]

☐ [*T.D.* 6278, 12-10-57. *Amended by T.D.* 6647, 4-10-63; *T.D.* 6984, 12-23-68 *and T.D.* 8746, 12-30-97.]

[Reg. § 1.171-3]

§ 1.171-3. Special rules for certain bonds.— (a) *Variable rate debt instruments.* A holder determines bond premium on a variable rate debt instrument by reference to the stated redemption price at maturity of the equivalent fixed rate debt instrument constructed for the variable rate debt instrument. The holder also allocates any bond premium among the accrual periods by reference to the equivalent fixed rate debt instrument. The holder constructs the equivalent fixed rate debt instrument, as of the date the holder acquires the variable rate debt instrument, by using the principles of § 1.1275-5(e). See paragraph (e) *Example 1* of this section.

(b) *Inflation-indexed debt instruments.* A holder determines bond premium on an inflation-indexed debt instrument by assuming that there will be no inflation or deflation over the remaining term of the instrument. The holder also allocates any bond premium among the accrual periods by assuming that there will be no inflation or deflation over the remaining term of the instrument. The bond premium allocable to an accrual period offsets qualified stated interest allocable to the period. Notwithstanding § 1.171-2(a)(4), if the bond premium allocable to an accrual period exceeds the qualified stated interest allocable to the period, the excess is treated as a deflation adjustment under § 1.1275-7(f)(1)(i). See § 1.1275-7 for other rules relating to inflation-indexed debt instruments.

(c) *Yield and remaining payment schedule of certain bonds subject to contingencies—*(1) *Applicability.* This paragraph (c) provides rules that apply in determining the yield and remaining payment schedule of certain bonds that provide for an alternative payment schedule (or schedules) applicable upon the occurrence of a contingency (or contingencies). This paragraph (c) applies, however, only if the timing and amounts of the payments that comprise each payment schedule are known as of the date the holder acquires the bond (the acquisition date) and the bond is subject to paragraph (c)(2), (3), or (4) of this section. A bond does not provide for an alternative payment schedule merely because there is a possibility of impairment of a payment (or payments) by insolvency, default, or similar circumstances. See § 1.1275-4 for the treatment of a bond that provides for a contingency that is not described in this paragraph (c).

(2) *Remaining payment schedule that is significantly more likely than not to occur.* If, based on all the facts and circumstances as of the acquisition date, a single remaining payment schedule for a bond is significantly more likely than not to occur, this remaining payment schedule is used to determine and amortize bond premium under §§ 1.171-1 and 1.171-2.

(3) *Mandatory sinking fund provision.* Notwithstanding paragraph (c)(2) of this section, if a bond is subject to a mandatory sinking fund provision described in § 1.1272-1(c)(3), the provision is ignored for purposes of determining and amortizing bond premium under §§ 1.171-1 and 1.171-2.

(4) *Treatment of certain options—*(i) *Applicability.* Notwithstanding paragraphs (c)(2) and (3) of this section, the rules of this paragraph (c)(4) determine the remaining payment schedule of a bond that provides the holder or issuer with an unconditional option or options, exercisable on one or more dates during the remaining term of the bond, to alter the bond's remaining payment schedule.

(ii) *Operating rules.* A holder determines the remaining payment schedule of a bond by assuming that each option will (or will not) be exercised under the following rules:

(A) *Issuer options.* In general, the issuer is deemed to exercise or not exercise an option or combination of options in the manner that minimizes the holder's yield on the obligation. However, the issuer of a taxable bond is deemed to exercise or not exercise a call option or combina-

tion of call options in the manner that maximizes the holder's yield on the bond.

(B) *Holder options.* A holder is deemed to exercise or not exercise an option or combination of options in the manner that maximizes the holder's yield on the bond.

(C) *Multiple options.* If both the issuer and the holder have options, the rules of paragraphs (c)(4)(ii)(A) and (B) of this section are applied to the options in the order that they may be exercised. Thus, the deemed exercise of one option may eliminate other options that are later in time.

(5) *Subsequent adjustments—*(i) *In general.* Except as provided in paragraph (c)(5)(ii) of this section, if a contingency described in this paragraph (c) (including the exercise of an option described in paragraph (c)(4) of this section) actually occurs or does not occur, contrary to the assumption made pursuant to paragraph (c) of this section (a change in circumstances), then solely for purposes of section 171, the bond is treated as retired and reacquired by the holder on the date of the change in circumstances for an amount equal to the adjusted acquisition price of the bond as of that date. If, however, the change in circumstances results in a substantially contemporaneous pro-rata prepayment as defined in § 1.1275-2(f)(2), the pro-rata prepayment is treated as a payment in retirement of a portion of the bond. See paragraph (e) *Example 2* of this section.

(ii) *Bond premium deduction on the issuer's call of a taxable bond.* If a change in circumstances results from an issuer's call of a taxable bond or a partial call that is a pro-rata prepayment, the holder may deduct as bond premium an amount equal to the excess, if any, of the holder's adjusted acquisition price of the bond over the greater of—

(A) The amount received on redemption; and

(B) The amounts that would have been payable under the bond (other than payments of qualified stated interest) if no change in circumstances had occurred.

(d) *Remote and incidental contingencies.* For purposes of determining and amortizing bond premium, if a bond provides for a contingency that is remote or incidental (within the meaning of § 1.1275-2(h)), the holder takes the contingency into account under the rules for remote and incidental contingencies in § 1.1275-2(h).

(e) *Examples.* The following examples illustrate the rules of this section. Each example assumes the holder uses the calendar year as its taxable

Reg. § 1.171-3(c)(1)

year and has elected to amortize bond premium, effective for all relevant taxable years. In addition, each example assumes a 30-day month and 360-day year. Although, for purposes of simplicity, the yield as stated is rounded to two decimal places, the computations do not reflect this rounding convention. The examples are as follows:

Example 1. Variable rate debt instrument—(i) *Facts.* On March 1, 1999, E purchases for $110,000 a taxable bond maturing on March 1, 2007, with a stated principal amount of $100,000, payable at maturity. The bond provides for unconditional payments of interest on March 1 of each year based on the percentage appreciation of a nationally-known commodity index. On March 1, 1999, it is reasonably expected that the bond will yield 12 percent, compounded annually. E uses the cash receipts and disbursements method of accounting, and E decides to use annual accrual periods ending on March 1 of each year. Assume that the bond is a variable rate debt instrument under § 1.1275-5.

(ii) *Amount of bond premium.* Because the bond is a variable rate debt instrument, E determines and amortizes its bond premium by reference to the equivalent fixed rate debt instrument constructed for the bond as of March 1, 1999. Because the bond provides for interest at a single objective rate that is reasonably expected to yield 12 percent, compounded annually, the equivalent fixed rate debt instrument for the bond is an eight-year bond with a principal amount of $100,000, payable at maturity. It provides for annual payments of interest of $12,000. E's basis in the equivalent fixed rate debt instrument is $110,000. The sum of all amounts payable on the equivalent fixed rate debt instrument (other than payments of qualified stated interest) is $100,000. Under § 1.171-1, the amount of bond premium is $10,000 ($110,000 − $100,000).

(iii) *Bond premium allocable to each accrual period.* E allocates bond premium to the remaining accrual periods by reference to the payment schedule on the equivalent fixed rate debt instrument. Based on the payment schedule of the equivalent fixed rate debt instrument and E's basis in the bond, E's yield is 10.12 percent, compounded annually. The bond premium allocable to the accrual period ending on March 1, 2000, is the excess of the qualified stated interest allocable to the period for the equivalent fixed rate debt instrument ($12,000) over the product of the adjusted acquisition price at the beginning of the period ($110,000) and E's yield (10.12 percent, compounded annually). Therefore, the bond premium allocable to the accrual period is $870.71 ($12,000 − $11,129.29). The bond premium allocable to all the accrual periods is listed in the following schedule:

Accrual period ending	Adjusted acquisition price at beginning of accrual period	Premium allocable to accrual period
3/1/00	$110,000.00	$ 870.71
3/1/01	109,129.29	958.81
3/1/02	108,170.48	1,055.82
3/1/03	107,114.66	1,162.64
3/1/04	105,952.02	1,280.27
3/1/05	104,671.75	1,409.80
3/1/06	103,261.95	1,552.44
3/1/07	101,709.51	1,709.51
		$10,000.00

(iv) *Qualified stated interest for each accrual period.* Assume the bond actually pays the following amounts of qualified stated interest:

Accrual period ending	Qualified stated interest
3/1/00	$ 2,000.00
3/1/01	0.00
3/1/02	0.00
3/1/03	10,000.00
3/1/04	8,000.00
3/1/05	12,000.00
3/1/06	15,000.00
3/1/07	8,500.00

(v) *Premium used to offset interest.* E's interest income for each accrual period is determined by offsetting the qualified stated interest allocable to the period with the bond premium allocable to the period. For the accrual period ending on March 1, 2000 E includes in income $1,129.29, the qualified stated interest allocable to the period ($2,000) offset with the bond premium allocable to the period ($870.71). For the accrual period ending on March 1, 2001, the bond premium allocable to the accrual period ($958.81) exceeds the qualified stated interest allocable to the period ($0) and, therefore, E does not have interest income for this accrual period. However, under § 1.171-2(a)(4)(i)(A), E may deduct as bond premium $958.81, the excess of the bond premium allocable to the accrual period ($958.81) over the qualified stated interest allocable to the accrual period ($0). For the accrual period ending on March 1, 2002, the bond premium allocable to the accrual period ($1,055.82) exceeds the qualified stated interest allocable to the accrual period ($0) and, therefore, E does not have interest income for the accrual period. Under § 1.171-2(a)(4)(i)(A), E's deduction for bond premium for the accrual period is limited to $170.48, the excess of E's total interest inclusions on the bond in prior accrual periods ($1,129.29) over the total amount treated by E as a bond premium

Accrual period ending	Qualified stated interest	Premium allocable to accrual period
3/1/00	$ 2,000.00	$ 870.71
3/1/01	0.00	958.81
3/1/02	0.00	1,055.82
3/1/03	10,000.00	1,162.64
3/1/04	8,000.00	1,280.27
3/1/05	12,000.00	1,409.80
3/1/06	15,000.00	1,552.44
3/1/07	8,500.00	1,709.51
		$10,000.00

Example 2. Partial call that results in a pro-rata prepayment—(i) *Facts.* On April 1, 1999, M purchases for $110,000 N's taxable bond maturing on April 1, 2006, with a stated principal amount of $100,000, payable at maturity. The bond provides for unconditional payments of interest of $10,000, payable on April 1 of each year. N has the option to call all or part of the bond on April 1, 2001, at a 5 percent premium over the principal amount. M uses the cash receipts and disbursements method of accounting.

(ii) *Determination of yield and the remaining payment schedule.* M's yield determined without regard to the call option is 8.07 percent, compounded annually. M's yield determined by assuming N exercises its call option is 6.89 percent, compounded annually. Under paragraph (c)(4)(ii)(A) of this section, it is assumed N will not exercise the call option because exercising the option would minimize M's yield. Thus, for purposes of determining and amortizing bond premium, the bond is assumed to be a seven-year bond with a single principal payment at maturity of $100,000.

(iii) *Amount of bond premium.* The interest payments on the bond are qualified stated interest. Therefore, the sum of all amounts payable on the bond (other than the interest payments) is $100,000. Under § 1.171-1, the amount of bond premium is $10,000 ($110,000 − $100,000).

(iv) *Bond premium allocable to the first two accrual periods.* For the accrual period ending on April 1, 2000, M includes in income $8,881.83, the qualified stated interest allocable to the period ($10,000) offset with bond premium allocable to the period ($1,118.17). The adjusted acquisition price on April 1, 2000, is $108,881.83 ($110,000

deduction in prior accrual periods ($958.81). Under § 1.171-2(a)(4)(i)(B), E must carry forward the remaining $885.34 of bond premium allocable to the period ending March 1, 2002, and treat it as bond premium allocable to the period ending March 1, 2003. The amount E includes in income for each accrual period is shown in the following schedule:

Interest income	Premium deduction	Premium carryforward
$ 1,129.29	$958.81	
0.00		
0.00		$885.34
7,951.93	170.48	
6,719.73		
10,590.20		
13,447.56		
6,790.49		

− $1,118.17). For the accrual period ending on April 1, 2001, M includes in income $8,791.54, the qualified stated interest allocable to the period ($10,000) offset with bond premium allocable to the period ($1,208.46). The adjusted acquisition price on April 1, 2001, is $107,673.37 ($108,881.83 − $1,208.46).

(v) *Partial call.* Assume N calls one-half of M's bond for $52,500 on April 1, 2001. Because it was assumed the call would not be exercised, the call is a change in circumstances. However, the partial call is also a pro-rata prepayment within the meaning of § 1.1275-2(f)(2). As a result, the call is treated as a retirement of one-half of the bond. Under paragraph (c)(5)(ii) of this section, M may deduct $1,336.68, the excess of its adjusted acquisition price in the retired portion of the bond ($107,673.37/2, or $53,836.68) over the amount received on redemption ($52,500). M's adjusted basis in the portion of the bond that remains outstanding is $53,836.68 ($107,673.37 − $53,836.68).

[Reg. § 1.171-3.]

☐ [*T.D. 6278, 12-10-57. Amended by T.D. 8746, 12-30-97 and T.D. 8838, 9-3-99.*]

[Reg. § 1.171-4]

§ 1.171-4. **Election to amortize bond premium on taxable bonds.**—(a) *Time and manner of making the election*—(1) *In general.* A holder makes the election to amortize bond premium by offsetting interest income with bond premium in the holder's timely filed federal income tax return for the first taxable year to which the holder desires the election to apply. The holder should attach to the return a statement that the holder is making the election under this section.

(2) *Coordination with OID election.* If a holder makes an election under § 1.1272-3 for a bond with bond premium, the holder is deemed to have made the election under this section.

(b) *Scope of election.* The election under this section applies to all taxable bonds held during or after the taxable year for which the election is made.

(c) *Election to amortize made in a subsequent taxable year*—(1) *In general.* If a holder elects to amortize bond premium and holds a taxable bond acquired before the taxable year for which the election is made, the holder may not amortize amounts that would have been amortized in prior taxable years had an election been in effect for those prior years.

(2) *Example.* The following example illustrates the rule of this paragraph (c):

Example—(i) *Facts.* On May 1, 1999, C purchases for $130,000 a taxable bond maturing on May 1, 2006, with a stated principal amount of $100,000, payable at maturity. The bond provides for unconditional payments of interest of $15,000, payable on May 1 of each year. C uses the cash receipts and disbursements method of accounting and the calendar year as its taxable year. C has not previously elected to amortize bond premium, but does so for 2002.

(ii) *Amount to amortize.* C's basis for determining loss on the sale or exchange of the bond is $130,000. Thus, under § 1.171-1, the amount of bond premium is $30,000. Under § 1.171-2, if a bond premium election were in effect for the prior taxable years, C would have amortized $3,257.44 of bond premium on May 1, 2000, and $3,551.68 of bond premium on May 1, 2001, based on annual accrual periods ending on May 1. Thus, for 2002 and future years to which the election applies, C may amortize only $23,190.88 ($30,000 − $3,257.44 − $3,551.68).

(d) *Revocation of election.* The election under this section may not be revoked unless approved by the Commissioner. Because a revocation of the election is a change in accounting method, a taxpayer must follow the rules under § 1.446-1(e)(3)(i) to request the Commissioner's consent to revoke the election. A revocation of the election applies to all taxable bonds held during or after the taxable year for which the revocation is effective. The holder may not amortize any remaining bond premium on bonds held at the beginning of the taxable year for which the revocation is effective. Therefore, no adjustment under section 481 is allowed upon the revocation of the election because no items of income or deduction are omitted or duplicated. [Reg. § 1.171-4.]

☐ [T.D. 6278, 12-10-57. Amended by T.D. 8746, 2-30-97.]

[Reg. § 1.171-5]

§ 1.171-5. Effective date and transition rules.—(a) *Effective date*—(1) *In general.* Sections 1.171-1 through 1.171-4 apply to bonds acquired on or after March 2, 1998. However, if a holder makes the election under § 1.171-4 for the taxable year containing March 2, 1998, or any subsequent taxable year, §§ 1.171-1 through 1.171-4 apply to bonds held on or after the first day of the taxable year in which the election is made.

(2) *Transition rule for use of constant yield.* Notwithstanding paragraph (a)(1) of this section, § 1.171-2(a)(3) (providing that the bond premium allocable to an accrual period is determined with reference to a constant yield) does not apply to a bond issued before September 28, 1985.

(b) *Coordination with existing election.* A holder is deemed to have made the election under § 1.171-4 for the taxable year containing March 2, 1998, if the holder elected to amortize bond premium under section 171 and that election is effective on March 2, 1998. If the holder is deemed to have made the election under § 1.171-4 for the taxable year containing March 2, 1998, §§ 1.171-1 through 1.171-4 apply to bonds acquired on or after the first day of that taxable year. See § 1.171-4(d) for rules relating to a revocation of an election under section 171.

(c) *Accounting method changes*—(1) *Consent to change.* A holder required to change its method of accounting for bond premium to comply with §§ 1.171-1 through 1.171-3 must secure the consent of the Commissioner in accordance with the requirements of § 1.446-1(e). Paragraph (c)(2) of this section provides the Commissioner's automatic consent for certain changes. A holder making the election under § 1.171-4 does not need the Commissioner's consent to make the election.

(2) *Automatic consent.* The Commissioner grants consent for a holder to change its method of accounting for bond premium with respect to taxable bonds to which §§ 1.171-1 through 1.171-3 apply. Because this change is made on a cut-off basis, no items of income or deduction are omitted or duplicated and, therefore, no adjustment under section 481 is allowed. The consent granted by this paragraph (c)(2) applies provided—

(i) The holder elected to amortize bond premium under section 171 for a taxable year prior to the taxable year containing March 2, 1998, and that election has not been revoked;

(ii) The change is made for the first taxable year for which the holder must account for a bond under §§ 1.171-1 through 1.171-3; and

(iii) The holder attaches to its return for the taxable year containing the change a statement that it has changed its method of accounting under this section. [Reg. § 1.171-5.]

☐ [*T.D. 8746, 12-30-97.*]

[Reg. § 1.172-1]

§ 1.172-1. Net operating loss deduction.—(a) *Allowance of deduction.* Section 172(a) allows as a deduction in computing taxable income for any taxable year subject to the Code the aggregate of the net operating loss carryovers and net operating loss carrybacks to such taxable year. This deduction is referred to as the net operating loss deduction. The net operating loss is the basis for the computation of the net operating loss carryovers and net operating loss carrybacks and ultimately for the net operating loss deduction itself. The net operating loss deduction shall not be disallowed for any taxable year merely because the taxpayer has no income from a trade or business for the taxable year.

(b) *Steps in computation of net operating loss deduction.* The three steps to be taken in the ascertainment of the net operating loss deduction for any taxable year subject to the Code are as follows:

(1) Compute the net operating loss for any preceding or succeeding taxable year from which a net operating loss may be carried over or carried back to such taxable year.

(2) Compute the net operating loss carryovers to such taxable year from such preceding taxable years and the net operating loss carrybacks to such taxable year from such succeeding taxable years.

(3) Add such net operating loss carryovers and carrybacks in order to determine the net operating loss deduction for such taxable year.

(c) *Statement with tax return.* Every taxpayer claiming a net operating loss deduction for any taxable year shall file with his return for such year a concise statement setting forth the amount of the net operating loss deduction claimed and all material and pertinent facts relative thereto, including a detailed schedule showing the computation of the net operating loss deduction.

(d) *Ascertainment of deduction dependent upon net operating loss carryback.* If the taxpayer is entitled in computing his net operating loss deduction to a carryback which he is not able to ascertain at the time his return is due, he shall compute the net operating loss deduction on his return without regard to such net operating loss carryback. When the taxpayer ascertains the net operating loss carryback, he may within the applicable period of limitations file a claim for credit or refund of the overpayment, if any, resulting from the failure to compute the net operating loss deduction for the taxable year with the inclusion of such carryback; or he may file an application under the provisions of section 6411 for a tentative carryback adjustment.

(e) *Law applicable to computations.* (1) In determining the amount of any net operating loss carryback or carryover to any taxable year, the necessary computations involving any other taxable year shall be made under the law applicable to such other taxable year.

(2) The net operating loss for any taxable year shall be determined under the law applicable to that year without regard to the year to which it is to be carried and in which, in effect, it is to be deducted as part of the net operating loss deduction.

(3) The amount of the net operating loss deduction which shall be allowed for any taxable year shall be determined under the law applicable to that year.

(f) *Electing small business corporations.* In determining the amount of the net operating loss deduction of any corporation, there shall be disregarded the net operating loss of such corporation for any taxable year for which such corporation was an electing small business corporation under subchapter S (section 1371 and following), chapter 1 of the Code. In applying section 172(b)(1) and (2) to a net operating loss sustained in a taxable year in which the corporation was not an electing small business corporation, a taxable year in which the corporation was an electing small business corporation is counted as a taxable year to which such net operating loss is carried back or over. However, the taxable income for such year as determined under section 172(b)(2) is treated as if it were zero for purposes of computing the balance of the loss available to the corporation as a carryback or carryover to other taxable years in which the corporation is not an electing small business corporation. See section 1374 and the regulations thereunder for allowance of a deduction to shareholders for a net operating loss sustained by an electing small business corporation.

(g) *Husband and wife.* The net operating loss deduction of a husband and wife shall be determined in accordance with this section, but subject also to the provisions of § 1.172-7. [Reg. § 1.172-1.]

☐ [*T.D. 6192, 7-23-56. Amended by T.D. 6486, 8-12-60 and T.D. 8107, 12-1-86.*]

[Reg. § 1.172-2]

§ 1.172-2. Net operating loss in case of a corporation.—(a) *Modification of deductions.* A net operating loss is sustained by a corporation in any taxable year if and to the extent that, for such year, there is an excess of deductions allowed by chapter 1 of the Code over gross income computed thereunder. In determining the excess of deductions over gross income for such purpose—

(1) *Items not deductible.* No deduction shall be allowed under—

(i) Section 172 for the net operating loss deduction, and

(ii) Section 922 in respect of Western Hemisphere trade corporations.

(2) *Dividends received.* The 85-percent limitation provided by section 246(b) shall not apply to the deductions otherwise allowed under—

(i) Section 243(a) in respect of dividends received from domestic corporations,

(ii) Section 244 in respect of dividends received on preferred stock of public utilities, and

(iii) Section 245 in respect of dividends received from foreign corporations; and

(3) *Dividends paid.* The deduction granted by section 247 in respect of dividends paid on the preferred stock of public utilities shall be computed without regard to subsection (a)(1)(B) of section 247.

(b) *Example.* The following example illustrates the application of paragraph (a):

Example. For the calendar year 1981, the X corporation has gross income of $400,000 and total deductions allowed by chapter 1 of the Code of $375,000, exclusive of any net operating loss deduction and exclusive of any deduction for dividends received or paid. Corporation X in 1981 received $100,000 of dividends entitled to the benefits of section 243(a). These dividends are included in Corporation X's $400,000 gross income. Corporation X has no other deductions to which section 172(d) applies.

On the basis of these facts, Corporation X has a net operating loss for the year 1981 of $60,000, computed as follows:

Deductions for 1981	$375,000
Plus: Deduction for dividends received, computed without regard to the limitation provided in section 246(b) (85% of $100,000).................	85,000
Total	460,000
Less: Gross income for 1981 (including $100,000 dividends)	400,000
Net operating loss for 1981	$60,000

(c) *Qualified real estate investment trusts.* For taxable years ending after October 4, 1976, the net operating loss of a qualified real estate investment trust (as defined in § 1.172-10(b)) is computed by taking into account the adjustments described in section 857(b)(2) (other than the deduction for dividends paid, as defined in section 561), as well as the modifications required by paragraph (a)(1) of this section. Thus, for example, the special deductions for dividends received, etc., provided in part VIII of subchapter B (other than section 248), as well as the net operating loss deduction under section 172, are not allowed in computing the net operating loss of a qualified real estate investment trust. [Reg. § 1.172-2.]

☐ [T.D. 6192, 7-23-56. *Amended by T.D. 6486, 8-12-60, T.D. 7767, 2-3-81 and T.D. 8107, 12-1-85.*]

[Reg. § 1.172-3]

§ 1.172-3. Net operating loss in case of a taxpayer other than a corporation.—(a) *Modification of deductions.* A net operating loss is sustained by a taxpayer other than a corporation in any taxable year if and to the extent that, for such year, there is an excess of deductions allowed by chapter 1 of the Internal Revenue Code over gross income computed thereunder. In determining the excess of deductions over gross income for such purpose—

(1) *Items not deductible.* No deduction shall be allowed under—

(i) Section 151 for the personal exemptions or under any other section which grants a deduction in lieu of the deductions allowed by section 151,

(ii) Section 172 for the net operating loss deduction, and

(iii) Section 1202 in respect of net long-term capital gain.

(2) *Capital losses.* (i) The amount deductible on account of business capital losses shall not exceed the sum of the amount includible on account of business capital gains and that portion of nonbusiness capital gains which is computed in accordance with paragraph (c) of this section.

(ii) The amount deductible on account of nonbusiness capital losses shall not exceed the amount includible on account of nonbusiness capital gains.

(3) *Nonbusiness deductions*—(i) *Ordinary deductions.* Ordinary nonbusiness deductions shall be taken into account without regard to the amount of business deductions and shall be allowed in full to the extent, but not in excess, of that amount which is the sum of the ordinary

nonbusiness gross income and the excess of nonbusiness capital gains over nonbusiness capital losses. See paragraph (c) of this section. For purposes of section 172, nonbusiness deductions and income are those deductions and that income which are not attributable to, or derived from, a taxpayer's trade or business. Wages and salary constitute income attributable to the taxpayer's trade or business for such purposes.

(ii) *Sale of business property.* Any gain or loss on the sale or other disposition of property which is used in the taxpayer's trade or business and which is of a character that is subject to the allowance for depreciation provided in section 167, or of real property used in the taxpayer's trade or business, shall be considered, for purposes of section 172(d)(4), as attributable to, or derived from, the taxpayer's trade or business. Such gains and losses are to be taken into account fully in computing a net operating loss without regard to the limitation on nonbusiness deductions. Thus, a farmer who sells at a loss land used in the business of farming may, in computing a net operating loss, include in full the deduction otherwise allowable with respect to such loss, without regard to the amount of his nonbusiness income and without regard to whether he is engaged in the trade or business of selling farms. Similarly, an individual who sells at a loss machinery which is used in his trade or business and which is of a character that is subject to the allowance for depreciation may, in computing the net operating loss, include in full the deduction otherwise allowable with respect to such loss.

(iii) *Casualty losses.* Any deduction allowable under section 165(c)(3) for losses of property not connected with a trade or business shall not be considered, for purposes of section 172(d)(4), to be a nonbusiness deduction but shall be treated as a deduction attributable to the taxpayer's trade or business.

(iv) *Self-employed retirement plans.* Any deduction allowed under section 404, relating to contributions of an employer to an employees' trust or annuity plan, or under section 405(c), relating to contributions to a bond purchase plan, to the extent attributable to contributions made on behalf of an individual while he is an employee within the meaning of section 401(c)(1), shall not be treated, for purposes of section 172(d)(4), as attributable to, or derived from, the taxpayer's trade or business, but shall be treated as a nonbusiness deduction.

(v) *Limitation.* The provisions of this subparagraph shall not be construed to permit the deduction of items disallowed by subparagraph (1) of this paragraph.

(b) *Treatment of capital loss carryovers.* Because of the distinction between business and nonbusiness capital gains and losses, a taxpayer who has a capital loss carryover from a preceding taxable year, includible by virtue of section 1212 among the capital losses for the taxable year in issue, is required to determine how much of such capital loss carryover is a business capital loss and how much is a nonbusiness capital loss. In order to make this determination, the taxpayer shall first ascertain what proportion of the net capital loss for such preceding taxable year was attributable to an excess of business capital losses over business capital gains for such year, and what proportion was attributable to an excess of nonbusiness capital losses over nonbusiness capital gains. The same proportion of the capital loss carryover from such preceding taxable year shall be treated as a business capital loss and a nonbusiness capital loss, respectively. In order to determine the composition (business—nonbusiness) of a net capital loss for a taxable year, for purposes of this paragraph, if such net capital loss is computed under paragraph (b) of § 1.1212-1 and takes into account a capital loss carryover from a preceding taxable year, the composition (business—nonbusiness) of the net capital loss for such preceding taxable year must also be determined. For purposes of this paragraph, the term "capital loss carryover" means the sum of the short-term and long-term capital loss carryovers from such year This paragraph may be illustrated by the following examples:

Example (1). (i) A, an individual, has $5,000 ordinary taxable income (computed without regard to the deductions for personal exemptions) for the calendar year 1954 and also has the following capital gains and losses for such year: Business capital gains of $2,000; business capital losses of $3,200; nonbusiness capital gains of $1,000; and nonbusiness capital losses of $1,200.

(ii) A's net capital loss for the taxable year 1954 is $400, computed as follows:

Capital losses $4,400
Capital gains 3,000

Excess of capital losses over capital gains ... $1,400
Less: $1,000 of such ordinary taxable income 1,000

Net capital loss for 1954............. $ 400

(iii) A's capital losses for 1954 exceeded his capital gains for such year by $1,400. Since A's business capital losses for 1954 exceeded his business capital gains for such year by $1,200, 6/7ths ($1,200/$1,400) of A's net capital loss for 1954 is attributable to an excess of his business capital losses over his business capital gains for such year. Similarly, 1/7th of the net capital loss is attributable to the excess of nonbusiness capital losses

Reg. § 1.172-3(b)

over nonbusiness capital gains. Since the capital loss carryover for 1954 to 1955 is $400, 6/7ths of $400, or $342.86, shall be treated as a business capital loss in 1955; and 1/7th of $400, or $57.14, as a nonbusiness capital loss.

Example (2). (i) A, an individual who is computing a net operating loss for the calendar year 1966, has a capital loss carryover from 1965 of $8,000. In order to apply the provisions of this paragraph, A must determine what portion of the $8,000 carryover is attributable to the excess of business capital losses over business capital gains and what portion thereof is attributable to the excess of nonbusiness capital losses over nonbusiness capital gains. For 1965, A had $10,000 ordinary taxable income (computed without regard to the deductions for personal exemptions), and a short-term capital loss carryover of $6,000 from 1964. In order to determine the composition (business—nonbusiness) of the $8,000 carryover from 1965, A first determines that of the $6,000 carryover from 1964, $5,000 is a business capital loss and $1,000 is a nonbusiness capital loss. This must be done since, under paragraph (b) of § 1.1212-1, the net capital loss for 1965 is computed by taking into account the capital loss carryover from 1964. A's capital gains and losses for 1965 are as follows:

	1965	Carried over from 1964
Business capital gains	$2,000	
Business capital losses	3,000	$5,000
Nonbusiness capital gains	4,000	
Nonbusiness capital losses	6,000	1,000

(ii) A's net capital loss for the taxable year 1965 is $8,000, computed as follows:

Capital losses (including carryovers)	$15,000
Capital gains	6,000
Excess of capital losses over capital gains	$ 9,000
Less: $1,000 of such ordinary taxable income	1,000
Net capital loss for 1965	$ 8,000

(iii) A's capital losses, including carryovers, for 1965 exceeded his capital gains for such year by $9,000. Since A's business capital losses for 1965 exceeded his business capital gains for such year by $6,000, 2/3rds ($6,000/$9,000) of A's net capital loss for 1965 is attributable to an excess of his business capital losses over his business capital gains for such year. Similarly, 1/3rd of the net capital loss is attributable to the excess of nonbusiness capital losses over nonbusiness capital gains. Since the total capital loss carryover from 1965 to 1966 is $8,000, 2/3rds of $8,000, or $5,333.33, shall be treated as a business capital

loss in 1966; and 1/3rd of $8,000, or $2,666.67, as a nonbusiness capital loss.

(c) *Determination of portion of nonbusiness capital gains available for the deduction of business capital losses.* In the computation of a net operating loss a taxpayer other than a corporation must use his nonbusiness capital gains for the deduction of his nonbusiness capital losses. Any amount not necessary for this purpose shall then be used for the deduction of any excess of ordinary nonbusiness deductions over ordinary nonbusiness gross income. The remainder, computed by applying the excess ordinary nonbusiness deductions against the excess nonbusiness capital gains, shall be treated as nonbusiness capital gains and used for the purpose of determining the deductibility of business capital losses under paragraph (a)(2)(i) of this section. This principle may be illustrated by the following example:

Example. (1) A, an individual, has a total nonbusiness gross income of $20,500, computed as follows:

Ordinary gross income	$ 7,500
Capital gains	13,000
Total gross income	20,500

(2) A also has total nonbusiness deductions of $16,000, computed as follows:

Ordinary deductions	$ 9,000
Capital loss	7,000
Total deductions	16,000

(3) The portion of nonbusiness capital gains to be used for the purpose of determining the deductibility of business capital losses is $4,500, computed as follows:

Nonbusiness capital gains		$13,000
Less: Nonbusiness capital loss		7,000
Excess to be taken into account for purposes of paragraph (a)(3)(i) of this section		6,000
Ordinary nonbusiness deductions	$9,000	
Less: Ordinary nonbusiness gross income	7,500	1,500
Portion of nonbusiness capital gains to be used for purposes of paragraph (a)(2)(i) of this section		4,500

(d) *Joint net operating loss of husband and wife.* In the case of a husband and wife, the joint net operating loss for any taxable year for which a joint return is filed is to be computed on the basis of the combined income and deductions of both spouses, and the modifications prescribed in paragraph (a) of this section are to be computed as if the combined income and deductions of both spouses were the income and deductions of one individual.

Reg. § 1.172-3(d)

(e) *Illustration of computation of net operating loss of a taxpayer other than a corporation*—(1) *Facts.* For the calendar year 1954, A, an individual, has gross income of $483,000 and allowable deductions of $540,000. The latter amount does not include the net operating loss deduction or any deduction on account of the sale or exchange of capital assets. Included in gross income are business capital gains of $50,000 and ordinary nonbusiness income of $10,000. Included among the deductions are ordinary nonbusiness deductions of $12,000 and a deduction of $600 for his personal exemption. A has a business capital loss of $60,000 in 1954. A has no other items of income or deductions to which section 172(d) applies.

(2) *Computation.* On the basis of these facts, A has a net operating loss for 1954 of $104,400, computed as follows:

Deductions for 1954 (as specified in first sentence of subparagraph (1)) ..		$540,000
Plus: Amount of business capital loss ($60,000) to extent such amount does not exceed business capital gains ($50,000)		50,000
Total		590,000
Less: Excess of ordinary nonbusiness deductions over ordinary nonbusiness gross income ($12,000 minus $10,000)	$2,000	
Deduction for personal exemption.................	600	2,600
Deductions for 1954 adjusted as required by section 172(d)		587,400
Gross income for 1954		483,000
Net operating loss for 1954		104,400

[Reg. § 1.172-3.]

☐ [*T.D.* 6192, 7-23-56. *Amended by T.D.* 6828, 6-16-65, *T.D.* 6862, 11-17-65 *and T.D.* 8107, 12-1-86.]

[Reg. § 1.172-4]

§ 1.172-4. Net operating loss carrybacks and net operating loss carryovers.—(a) *General provisions*—(1) *Years to which loss may be carried*—(i) *In general.* In order to compute the net operating loss deduction the taxpayer must first determine the part of any net operating losses for any preceding or succeeding taxable years which are carrybacks or carryovers to the taxable year in issue.

(ii) *General rule for carrybacks and carryovers.* Except as provided in section 172(b)(1)(C), (D), (E), (F), (G), (H), (I), and (J), paragraphs (a)(1)(iii), (iv), (v), and (vi) of this section, and § 1.172-10(a), a net operating loss shall be carried back to the 3 preceding taxable years and carried over to the 15 succeeding taxable years (5 suc-

ceeding taxable years for a loss sustained in a taxable year ending before January 1, 1976).

(iii) *Loss of a regulated transportation corporation.* Except as provided in subdivision (iv) of this subparagraph and § 1.172-10(a), a net operating loss sustained by a taxpayer which is a regulated transportation corporation (as defined in section 172(g)(1)) in a taxable year ending before January 1, 1976, shall, subject to the provisions of section 172(g) and § 1.172-8, be carried back to the taxable years specified in paragraph (a)(1)(ii) of this section and shall be carried over to the 7 succeeding taxable years.

(iv) *Loss attributable to foreign expropriation.* If the provisions of section 172(b)(3)(A) and § 1.172-8 are satisfied, the portion of a net operating loss attributable to a foreign expropriation loss (as defined in section 172(h)) shall not be a net operating loss carryback to any taxable year preceding the taxable year of such loss and shall be a net operating loss carryover to each of the 10 taxable years following the taxable year of such loss.

(v) *Loss of a financial institution.* A net operating loss sustained in a taxable year beginning after December 31, 1975, by a taxpayer to which section 585, 586, or 593 applies shall be carried back (except as provided in § 1.172-10(a)) to the 10 preceding taxable years and shall be carried over to the 5 succeeding taxable years.

(vi) *Loss of a Bank for Cooperatives.* A net operating loss sustained by a taxpayer which is a Bank for Cooperatives (organized and chartered pursuant to section 2 of the Farm Credit Act of 1933 (12 U.S.C. 1134)) shall be carried back (except as provided in § 1.172-10(a)) to the 10 preceding taxable years and shall be carried over to the 5 succeeding taxable years.

(2) *Periods of less than 12 months.* A fractional part of a year which is a taxable year under sections 441(b) and 7701(a)(23) is a preceding or a succeeding taxable year for the purpose of determining under section 172 the first, second, etc., preceding or succeeding taxable year.

(3) *Amount of loss to be carried.* The amount which is carried back or carried over to any taxable year is the net operating loss to the extent it was not absorbed in the computation of the taxable (or net) income for other taxable years, preceding such taxable year, to which it may be carried back or carried over. For the purpose of determining the taxable (or net) income for any such preceding taxable year, the various net operating loss carryovers and carrybacks to such taxable year are considered to be applied in reduction of the taxable (or net) income in the order of the taxable years from which such losses are carried over or

carried back, beginning with the loss for the earliest taxable year.

(4) *Husband and wife.* The net operating loss carryovers and carrybacks of a husband and wife shall be determined in accordance with this section, but subject also to the provisions of § 1.172-7.

(5) *Corporate acquisitions.* For the computation of the net operating loss carryovers in the case of certain acquisitions of the assets of a corporation by another corporation. see section 381 and the regulations thereunder.

(6) *Special limitations.* For special limitations on the net operating loss carryovers in certain cases of change in both the ownership and the trade or business of a corporation and in certain cases of corporate reorganization lacking specified continuity of ownership, see section 382 and the regulations thereunder.

(7) *Electing small business corporations.* For special rule applicable to corporations which were electing small business corporations under subchapter S (section 1361 and following), chapter 1 of the Code, during one or more of the taxable years described in section 172(b)(1), see paragraph (f) of § 1.172-1.

(b) *Portion of net operating loss which is a carryback or a carryover to the taxable year in issue.* (1) A net operating loss shall first be carried to the earliest of the several taxable years for which such loss is allowable as a carryback or a carryover, and shall then be carried to the next earliest of such several taxable years, etc. Except as provided in § 1.172-9, the entire net operating loss shall be carried back to such earliest year.

(2) The portion of the loss which shall be carried to any of such several taxable years subsequent to the earliest taxable year is the excess of such net operating loss over the sum of the taxable incomes (computed as provided in § 1.172-3) for all of such several taxable years preceding such subsequent taxable year.

(3) If a portion of the net operating loss for a taxable year is attributable to a foreign expropriation loss (as defined in section 172(h)) and if an election under paragraph (c) of § 1.172-9 is made with respect to such portion of the net operating loss, then see § 1.172-9 for the separate treatment of such portion of the net operating loss.

(c) *Illustration.* The principles of this section are illustrated in § 1.172-6. [Reg. § 1.172-4.]

☐ [*T.D.* 6192, 7-23-56. *Amended by T.D.* 6486, 8-12-60, *T.D.* 6862, 11-17-65, *T.D.* 7444, 12-6-76, *T.D.* 7767, 2-3-81, *T.D.* 8096, 8-27-86 *and T.D.* 8107, 12-1-86.]

[Reg. § 1.172-5]

§ 1.172-5. **Taxable income which is subtracted from net operating loss to determine carryback or carryover.**—(a) *Taxable year subject to Internal Revenue Code of 1954.* The taxable income for any taxable year subject to the Internal Revenue Code of 1954 which is subtracted from the net operating loss for any other taxable year to determine the portion of such net operating loss which is a carryback or a carryover to a particular taxable year is computed with the modifications prescribed in this paragraph. These modifications shall be made independently of, and without reference to, the modifications required by §§ 1.172-2(a) and 1.172-3(a) for purposes of computing the net operating loss itself.

(1) *Modifications applicable to unincorporated taxpayers only.* In the case of a taxpayer other than a corporation, in computing taxable income and adjusted gross income—

(i) No deduction shall be allowed under section 151 for the personal exemptions (or under any other section which grants a deduction in lieu of the deductions allowed by section 151) and under section 1202 in respect of net long-term capital gain.

(ii) The amount deductible on account of losses from sales or exchanges of capital assets shall not exceed the amount includible on account of gains from sales or exchanges of capital assets.

(2) *Modifications applicable to all taxpayers.* In the case either of a corporation or of a taxpayer other than a corporation—

(i) *Net operating loss deduction.* The net operating loss deduction for such taxable year shall be computed by taking into account only such net operating losses otherwise allowable as carrybacks or carryovers to such taxable year as were sustained in taxable years preceding the taxable year in which the taxpayer sustained the net operating loss from which the taxable income is to be deducted. Thus, for such purposes, the net operating loss for the loss year or any taxable year thereafter shall not be taken into account.

Example. The taxpayer's income tax returns are made on the basis of the calendar year. In computing the net operating loss deduction for 1954, the taxpayer has a carryover from 1952 of $9,000, a carryover from 1953 of $6,000, a carryback from 1955 of $18,000, and a carryback from 1956 of $10,000, or an aggregate of $43,000 in carryovers and carrybacks. Thus, the net operating loss deduction for 1954, for purposes of determining the tax liability for 1954, is $43,000. However, in computing the taxable income for 1954 which is subtracted from the net operating loss for 1955 for the purpose of determining the portion of such loss which may be carried over to subsequent taxable years, the net operating loss deduction for 1954 is $15,000, that is, the aggregate of the $9,000 carryover from 1952 and the $6,000 carryover from 1953. In computing the net operating loss deduction for such purpose, the $18,000 carryback from 1955 and the $10,000 carryback from 1956 are disregarded. In computing the taxable income for 1954, however, which is subtracted from the net operating loss for 1956 for the purpose of determining the portion of such loss which may be carried over to subsequent taxable years, the net operating loss deduction for 1954 is $33,000, that is, the aggregate of the $9,000 carryover from 1952, the $6,000 carryover from 1953, and the $18,000 carryback from 1955. In computing the net operating loss deduction for such purpose, the $10,000 carryback from 1956 is disregarded.

(ii) *Recomputation of percentage limitations.* Unless otherwise specifically provided in this subchapter, any deduction which is limited in amount to a percentage of the taxpayer's taxable income or adjusted gross income shall be recomputed upon the basis of the taxable income or adjusted gross income, as the case may be, determined with the modifications prescribed in this paragraph. Thus, in the case of an individual the deduction for medical expenses would be recomputed after making all the modifications prescribed in this paragraph, whereas the deduction for charitable contributions would be determined without regard to any net operating loss carryback but with regard to any other modifications so prescribed. See, however, the regulations under paragraph (g) of § 1.170-2 (relating to charitable contributions carryover of individuals) and paragraph (c) of § 1.170-3 (relating to charitable contributions carryover of corporations) for special rules regarding charitable contributions in excess of the percentage limitations which may be treated as paid in succeeding taxable years.

Example (1). For the calendar year 1954 the taxpayer, an individual, files a return showing taxable income of $4,800, computed as follows:

Salary		$5,000
Net long-term capital gain		4,000
Total gross income		9,000
Less: Deduction allowed by section 1202 in respect of net long-term capital gain ...		$2,000
Adjusted gross income		7,000
Less:		
Deduction for personal exemption ....$ 600		

Deduction for medical expense ($410 actually paid but allowable only to extent in excess of 3 percent of adjusted gross income)	200	
Deduction for charitable contributions ($2,000 actually paid but allowable only to extent not in excess of 20 percent of adjusted gross income)	1,400	2,200
Taxable income		4,800

In 1955 the taxpayer undertakes the operation of a trade or business and sustains therein a net operating loss of $3,000. Under section 172(b)(2), it is determined that the entire $3,000 is a carryback to 1954. In 1956 he sustains a net operating loss of $10,000 in the operation of the business. In determining the amount of the carryover of the 1956 loss to 1957, the taxable income for 1954 as computed under this paragraph is $3,970, determined as follows:

Salary		$5,000
Net long-term capital gain		4,000
Total gross income		9,000
Less: Deduction for carryback of 1955 net operating loss		3,000
Less:		
Deduction for medical expense ($410 actually paid but allowable only to extent in excess of 3 percent of adjusted gross income as modified under this paragraph) .....$	230	
Deduction for charitable contributions ($2,000 actually paid but allowable only to extent not in excess of 20 percent of adjusted gross income determined with all the modifications prescribed in this paragraph other than the net operating loss carryback) ...$1,800		$2,030
Taxable income		3,970

Example (2). For the calendar year 1959 the taxpayer, an individual, files a return showing taxable income of $5,700, computed as follows:

Salary		$5,000
Net long-term capital gain		4,000
Total gross income		9,000
Less: Deduction allowed by section 1202 in respect of net long-term capital gain ...		2,000
Adjusted gross income		7,000
Less:		
Deduction for personal exemption ....$ 600		
Standard deduction allowed by section 141	700	1,300
Taxable income		5,700

Reg. § 1.172-5(a)(2)

In 1960 the taxpayer undertakes the operation of a trade or business and sustains therein a net operating loss of $4,700. In 1961 he sustains a net operating loss of $10,000 in the operation of the business. Under section 172(b)(2), it is determined that the entire amount of each loss, $4,700 and $10,000, is a carryback to 1959. In determining the amount of the carryover of the 1961 less to 1962, the taxable income for 1959 as computed under this paragraph is $3,870, determined as follows:

Salary	$5,000
Net long-term capital gain	4,000
Total gross income	9,000
Less: Deduction for carryback of 1960 net operating loss	4,700
Adjusted gross income	4,300
Less: Standard deduction	430
Taxable income	3,870

(iii) *Minimum limitation.* The taxable income, as modified under this paragraph, shall in no case be considered less than zero.

(3) *Electing small business corporations.* For special rule applicable to corporations which were electing small business corporations under subchapter S (section 1361 and following), chapter 1 of the Code, during one or more of the taxable years described in section 172(b)(1), see paragraph (f) of § 1.172-1.

(4) *Qualified real estate investment trust.* Where a net operating loss is carried over to a qualified taxable year (as defined in § 1.172-10(b)) ending after October 4, 1976, the real estate investment trust taxable income (as defined in section 857(b)(2)) shall be used as the "taxable income" for that taxable year to determine, under section 172(b)(2), the balance of the net operating loss available as a carryover to a subsequent taxable year. The real estate investment trust taxable income, however, is computed by applying the rules applicable to corporations in paragraph (a)(2) of this section. Thus, in computing real estate investment trust taxable income for purposes of section 172(b)(2), the net operating loss deduction for the taxable year shall be computed in accordance with paragraph (a)(2)(i) of this section. The principles of this subparagraph may be illustrated by the following examples:

Example (1). Corporation X, a calendar year taxpayer, is formed on January 1, 1977. X incurs a net operating loss of $100,000 for its taxable year 1977, which, under section 172(b)(2), is a carryover to 1978. For 1978 X is a qualified real estate investment trust (as defined in § 1.172-10(b)) and has real estate investment

trust taxable income (determined without regard to the deduction for dividends paid or the net operating loss deduction) of $150,000, all of which consists of ordinary income. X pays dividends in 1978 totaling $120,000 that qualify for the deduction for dividends paid under section 857(b)(2)(B). The portion of the 1977 net operating less available as a carryover to 1979 and subsequent years is $70,000 (*i.e.*, the excess of the amount of the net operating loss ($100,000) over the amount of the real estate investment trust taxable income for 1978 ($30,000), determined by taking into account the deduction for dividends paid allowable under section 857(b)(2)(B) and without taking into account the net operating loss for 1977).

Example (2). (i) Assume the same facts as in example (1), except that the $150,000 of real estate investment trust taxable income (determined without the net operating loss deduction or the dividends paid deduction) consists of $80,000 of ordinary income and $70,000 of net capital gain. The amount of capital gain dividends which may be paid for 1978 is limited to $50,000, that is, the amount of the real estate investment trust taxable income for 1978, determined by taking into account the net operating loss deduction for the taxable year, but not the deduction for dividends paid ($150,000 minus $100,000). See § 1.857-6(e)(1)(ii).

(ii) X designated $50,000 of the $120,000 of dividends paid as capital gains dividends (as defined in section 857(b)(3)(C) and § 1.857-6(e)). Thus, $70,000 is an ordinary dividend. Since both ordinary dividends and capital gains dividends are taken into account in computing the deduction for dividends paid under section 857(b)(2)(B), the result will be the same as in example (1); that is, the portion of the 1977 net operating loss available as a carryover to 1979 and subsequent years is $70,000.

(b) Reserved.

[Reg. § 1.172-5]

[*[T.D. 6192, 7-23-56. Amended by T.D. 6486, 8-12-60, T.D. 6862, 11-17-65, T.D. 6900, 11-16-66, T.D. 7767, 2-3-81 and T.D. 8107, 12-1-86.]*

[Reg. § 1.172-6]

§ 1.172-6. Illustration of net operating loss carrybacks and carryovers.—The application of § 1.172-4 may be illustrated by the following example:

(a) *Facts.* The books of the taxpayer, whose return is made on the basis of the calendar year, reveal the following facts:

Reg. § 1.172-6(a)

Taxable year	Taxable income	Net operating loss
1954	$15,000	....
1955	30,000	....
1956	......	($ 75,000)
1957	20,000	....
1958	......	(150,000)
1959	30,000	....
1960	35,000	....
1961	75,000	....
1962	17,000	....
1963	53,000	....

The taxable income thus shown is computed without any net operating loss deduction. The assumption is also made that none of the other modifications prescribed in § 1.172-5 apply. There are no net operating losses for 1950, 1951, 1952, 1953, 1964, or 1966.

(b) *Loss sustained in 1956.* The portions of the $75,000 net operating loss for 1956 which shall be used as carrybacks to 1954 and 1955 and as carryovers to 1957, 1958, 1959, 1960, and 1961 are computed as follows:

(1) *Carryback to 1954.* The carryback to this year is $75,000, that is, the amount of the net operating loss.

(2) *Carryback to 1955.* The carryback to this year is $60,000, computed as follows:

Net operating loss $75,000
Less:
    Taxable income for 1954 (computed
    without the deduction of the car-
    ryback from 1956) 15,000

Carryback 60,000

(3) *Carryover to 1957.* The carryover to this year is $30,000, computed as follows:

Net operating loss $75,000
Less:
    Taxable income for 1954
    (computed without the
    deduction of the car-
    ryback from 1956) $15,000
    Taxable income for 1955
    (computed without the
    deduction of the car-
    ryback from 1956 or
    the carryback from
    1958) 30,000   45,000

Carryover 30,000

(4) *Carryover to 1958.* The carryover to this year is $10,000, computed as follows:

Net operating loss $75,000
Less:
    Taxable income for 1954
    (computed without the
    deduction of the car-
    ryback from 1956) $15,000

Taxable income for 1955
(computed without the
deduction of the car-
ryback from 1956 or
the carryback from
1958) 30,000
Taxable income for 1957
(computed without the
deduction of the carry-
over from 1956 or the
carryback from 1958) . 20,000

         65,000

Carryover 10,000

(5) *Carryover to 1959.* The carryover to this year is $10,000, computed as follows:

Net operating loss $75,000
Less:
    Taxable income for 1954
    (computed without the
    deduction of the car-
    ryback from 1956) $15,000
    Taxable income for 1955
    (computed without the
    deduction of the car-
    ryback from 1956 or
    the carryback from
    1958) 30,000
    Taxable income for 1957
    (computed without the
    deduction of the carry-
    over from 1956 or the
    carryback from 1958) . 20,000
    Taxable income for 1958
    (a year in which a net
    operating loss was
    sustained) 0

         65,000

         10,000

(6) *Carryover to 1960.* The carryover to this year is $0, computed as follows:

Net operating loss .... $ 75,000
Less:
    Taxable income for
    1954 (computed
    without the deduc-
    tion of the carryback
    from 1956) $15,000
    Taxable income for
    1955 (computed
    without the deduc-
    tion of the carryback
    from 1956 or the car-
    ryback from 1958) .. $30,000
    Taxable income for
    1957 (computed
    without the deduc-
    tion of the carryover
    from 1956 or the car-
    ryback from 1958) .. 20,000

Reg. § 1.172-6(b)(1)

Taxable income for 1958 (a year in which a net operating loss was sustained) 0

Taxable income for 1959 (computed without the deduction of the carryover from 1956 or the carryover from 1958) .. 30,000

$ 95,000

Carryover 0

(7) *Carryover to 1961.* The carryover to this year is $0, computed as follows:

Net operating loss .... $ 75,000
Less:

Taxable income for 1954 (computed without the deduction of the carryback from 1956) $15,000

Taxable income for 1955 (computed without the deduction of the carryback from 1956 or the carryback from 1958) .. 30,000

Taxable income for 1957 (computed without the deduction of the carryover from 1956 or the carryback from 1958) .. 20,000

Taxable income for 1958 (a year in which a net operating loss was sustained) 0

Taxable income for 1959 (computed without the deduction of the carryover

Taxable income for 1960 (computed without the deduction of the carryover from 1956 or the carryover from 1958) .. 35,000

$130,000

Carryover 0

(c) *Loss sustained in 1958.* The portions of the $150,000 net operating loss for 1958 which shall be used as carrybacks to 1955, 1956, and 1957 and as carryovers to 1959, 1960, 1961, 1962, and 1963 are computed as follows:

(1) *Carryback to 1955.* The carryback to this year is $150,000, that is, the amount of the net operating loss.

(2) *Carryback to 1956.* The carryback to this year is $150,000, computed as follows:

Net operating loss $150,000
Less:

Taxable income for 1955 (the $30,000 taxable income for such year reduced by the carryback to such year of $60,000 from 1956, the carryback from 1958 to 1955 not being taken into account).... 0

Carryback............... 150,000

(3) *Carryback to 1957.* The carryback to this year is $150,000, computed as follows:

Net operating loss $150,000
Less

Taxable income for 1955 (the $30,000 taxable income for such year reduced by the carryback to such year of $60,000 from 1956, the carryback from 1958 to 1955 not being taken into account) ...... $ 0

Taxable income for 1956 (a year in which a net operating loss was sustained) 0

0

Carryback............... 150,000

(4) *Carryover to 1959.* The carryover to this year is $150,000, computed as follows:

Net operating loss $150,000
Less:

Taxable income for 1955 (the $30,000 taxable income for such year reduced by the carryback to such year of $60,000 from 1956, the carryback from 1958 to 1955 not being taken into account) .... $ 0

Taxable income for 1956 (a year in which a net operating loss was sustained)...... 0

Taxable income for 1957 (the $20,000 taxable income for such year reduced by the carryover to such year of $30,000 from 1956, the carryback from 1958 to 1957 not being taken into account)   0

    0

Carryover   150,000

(5) *Carryover to 1960.* The carryover to this year is $130,000, computed as follows:

Net operating loss $150,000
Less:

Taxable income for 1955 (the $30,000 taxable income for such year reduced by the carryback to such year of $60,000 from 1956, the carryback from 1958 to 1955 not being taken into account) . . . . $ 0

Taxable income for 1956 (a year in which a net operating loss was sustained)   0

Taxable income for 1957 (the $20,000 taxable income for such year reduced by the carryover to such year of $30,000 from 1956, the carryback from 1958 to 1957 not being taken into account)   0

Taxable income for 1959 (the $30,000 taxable income for such year reduced by the carryover to such year of $10,000 from 1956, the carryover from 1958 to 1959 not being taken into account) $20,000

$ 20,000

Carryover   130,000

(6) *Carryover to 1961.* The carryover to this year is $95,000, computed as follows:

Net operating loss $150,000
Less:

Taxable income for 1955 (the $30,000 taxable income for such year reduced by the carryback to such year of $60,000 from 1956, the carryback from 1958 to 1955 not being taken into account) . . . . $ 0

Taxable income for 1956 (a year in which a net operating loss was sustained)   0

Taxable income for 1957 (the $20,000 taxable income for such year reduced by the carryover to such year of $30,000 from 1956, the carryback from 1958 to 1957 not being taken into account)   0

Taxable income for 1959 (the $30,000 taxable income for such year reduced by the carryover to such year of $10,000 from 1956, the carryover from 1958 to 1959 not being taken into account)   20,000

Taxable income for 1960 (the $35,000 taxable income for such year reduced by the carryover to such year of $0 from 1956, the carryover from 1958 to 1960 not being taken into account)   35,000

55,000

Carryover   95,000

(7) *Carryover to 1962.* The carryover to this year is $20,000, computed as follows:

Net operating loss $150,000
Less:

Taxable income for 1955 (the $30,000 taxable income for such year reduced by the carryback to such year of $60,000 from 1956, the carryback from 1958 to 1955 not being taken into account) . . . . $ 0

Taxable income for 1956 (a year in which a net operating loss was sustained) . . . . $ 0

Taxable income for 1957 (the $20,000 taxable income for such year reduced by the carryover to such year of $30,000 from 1956, the carryback from 1958 to 1957 not being taken into account) 0

Taxable income for 1959 (the $30,000 taxable income for such year reduced by the carryover to such year of $10,000 from 1956, the carryover from 1958 to 1959 not being taken into account) 20,000

Taxable income for 1960 (the $35,000 taxable income for such year reduced by the carryover to such year of $0 from 1956, the carryover from 1958 to 1960 not being taken into account) 35,000

Taxable income for 1961 (the $75,000 taxable income for such year reduced by the carryover to such year of $0 from 1956, the carryover from 1958 to 1961 not being taken into account) 75,000

$130,000

Carryover 20,000

(8) *Carryover to 1963.* The carryover to this year is $3,000, computed as follows:

Net operating loss $150,000
Less:
Taxable income for 1955 (the $30,000 taxable income for such year reduced by the carryback to such year of $60,000 from 1956, the carryback from 1958 to 1955 not being taken into account) ... $ 0

Taxable income for 1956 (a year in which a net operating loss was sustained) 0

Taxable income for 1957 (the $20,000 taxable income for such year reduced by the carryover to such year of $30,000 from 1956, the carryback from 1958 to 1957 not being taken into account) ... 0

Taxable income for 1959 (the $30,000 taxable income for such year reduced by the carryover to such year of $10,000 from 1956, the carryover from 1958 to 1959 not being taken into account) ... 20,000

Taxable income for 1960 (the $35,000 taxable income for such year reduced by the carryover to such year of $0 from 1956, the carryover from 1958 to 1960 not being

Taxable income for 1961 (the $75,000 taxable income for such year reduced by the carryover to such year of $0 from 1956, the carryover from 1958 to 1961 not being taken into account) 75,000

Taxable income for 1962 (computed without the deduction of the carryover from 1958) . 17,000

147,000

Carryover 3,000

(d) *Determination of net operating loss deduction for each year.* The carryovers and carrybacks computed under paragraphs (b) and (c) of this section are used as a basis for the computation of the net operating loss deduction in the following manner:

Taxable year	Carryover From 1956	Carryover From 1958	Carryback From 1956	Carryback From 1958	Net operating loss deduction
1954	......	......	$75,000	......	$ 75,000
1955	......	......	60,000	$150,000	210,000
1957	$30,000	......	......	150,000	180,000
1959	10,000	$150,000	......	......	160,000
1960	......	130,000	......	......	130,000
1961	......	95,000	......	......	95,000
1962	......	20,000	......	......	20,000
1963	......	3,000	......	......	3,000

[Reg. § 1.172-6.]

□ [*T.D.* 6192, 7-23-56. Amended by T.D. 6486, 8-12-60.]

Reg. § 1.172-6(d)

[Reg. § 1.172-7]

§ 1.172-7. **Joint return by husband and wife.**—(a) *In general.* This section prescribes additional rules for computing the net operating loss carrybacks and carryovers of a husband and wife making a joint return for one or more of the taxable years involved in the computation of the net operating loss deduction.

(b) *From separate to joint return.* If a husband and wife, making a joint return for any taxable year, did not make a joint return for any of the taxable years involved in the computation of a net operating loss carryover or a net operating loss carryback to the taxable year for which the joint return is made, such separate net operating loss carryover or separate net operating loss carryback is a joint net operating loss carryover or joint net operating loss carryback to such taxable year.

(c) *Continuous use of joint return.* If a husband and wife making a joint return for a taxable year made a joint return for each of the taxable years involved in the computation of a net operating loss carryover or net operating loss carryback to such taxable year, the joint net operating loss carryover or joint net operating loss carryback to such taxable year is computed in the same manner as the net operating loss carryover or net operating loss carryback of an individual under § 1.172-4 but upon the basis of the joint net operating losses and the combined taxable income of both spouses.

(d) *From joint to separate return.* If a husband and wife making separate returns for a taxable year made a joint return for any, or all, of the taxable years involved in the computation of a net operating loss carryover or net operating loss carryback to such taxable year, the separate net operating loss carryover or separate net operating loss carryback of each spouse to the taxable year is computed in the manner set forth in § 1.172-4 but with the following modifications:

(1) *Net operating loss.* The net operating loss of each spouse for a taxable year for which a joint return was made shall be deemed to be that portion of the joint net operating loss (computed in accordance with paragraph (d) of § 1.172-3) which is attributable to the gross income and deductions of such spouse, gross income and deductions being taken into account to the same extent that they are taken into account in computing the joint net operating loss.

(2) *Taxable income to be subtracted*—(i) *Net operating loss of other spouse.* The taxable income of a particular spouse for any taxable year which is subtracted from the net operating loss of such spouse for another taxable year in order to determine the amount of such loss which may be carried back or carried over to still another taxable year is deemed to be, in a case in which such taxable income was reported in a joint return, the sum of the following:

(a) That portion of the combined taxable income of both spouses for such year for which the joint return was made which is attributable to the gross income and deductions of the particular spouse, gross income and deductions being taken into account to the same extent that they are taken into account in computing such combined taxable income, and

(b) That portion of such combined taxable income which is attributable to the other spouse; but, if such other spouse sustained a net operating loss in a taxable year beginning on the same date as the taxable year in which the particular spouse sustained the net operating loss from which the taxable income is subtracted, then such portion shall first be reduced by such net operating loss of such other spouse.

(ii) *Modifications.* For purposes of this subparagraph, the combined taxable income shall be computed as though the combined income and deductions of both spouses were those of one individual. The provisions of § 1.172-5 shall apply in computing the combined taxable income for such purposes except that the net operating loss deduction shall be determined without taking into account any separate net operating loss of either spouse, or any joint net operating loss of both spouses, which was sustained in a taxable year beginning on or after the date of the beginning of the taxable year in which the particular spouse sustained the net operating loss from which the taxable income is subtracted.

(e) *Recurrent use of joint return.* If a husband and wife making a joint return for any taxable year made a joint return for one or more, but not all, of the taxable years involved in the computation of a net operating loss carryover or net operating loss carryback to such taxable year, such net operating loss carryover or net operating loss carryback to the taxable year is computed in the manner set forth in paragraph (d) of this section. Such net operating loss carryover or net operating loss carryback is considered a joint net operating loss carryover or joint net operating loss carryback to such taxable year.

(f) *Joint carryovers and carrybacks.* The joint net operating loss carryovers and the joint net operating loss carrybacks to any taxable year for which a joint return is made are all the net operating loss carryovers and net operating loss carrybacks of both spouses to such taxable year. For example, a husband and wife file a joint return for the calendar year 1956, having a joint taxable

Reg. § 1.172-7(a)

income for such year. The wife filed a separate return for the calendar years 1954 and 1955, in which years she sustained net operating losses. The husband filed separate returns for his fiscal year ending June 30, 1955, and, having received permission to change his accounting period to a calendar year basis, for the 6-month period ending December 31, 1955. The husband sustained net operating losses in both such taxable years. Since the husband and wife did not file a joint return for any taxable year involved in the computation of the net operating loss carryovers to 1956 from 1954 and 1955, the joint net operating loss carryovers to 1956 are the separate net operating loss carryovers of the wife from the calendar years 1954 and 1955 and the separate net operating loss carryovers of the husband from the fiscal year ending June 30, 1955, and from the short taxable year ending December 31, 1955. If the husband and wife also file joint returns for the calendar years 1957, 1958, and 1959, having a joint taxable income in 1957 and 1958 and a joint net operating loss in 1959, the joint net operating loss carrybacks to 1956, 1957, and 1958 from 1959 are computed on the basis of the joint net operating loss for 1959, since separate returns were not made for any taxable year involved in the computation of such carrybacks.

(g) *Illustration of principles.* In the following examples, which illustrate the application of this section, it is assumed that there are no items of adjustment under section 172(b)(2)(A) and that the taxable income or loss in each case is the taxable income or loss determined without any net operating loss deduction. The taxpayers in each example, H, a husband, and W, his wife, report their income on the calendar-year basis.

Example (1). H and W filed joint returns for 1954 and 1955. They sustained a joint net operating loss of $1,000 for 1954 and a joint net operating loss of $2,000 for 1955. For 1954 the deductions of H exceeded his gross income by $700, and the deductions of W exceeded her gross income by $300, the total of such amounts being $1,000. Therefore, $700 of the $1,000 joint net operating loss for 1954 is considered the net operating loss of H for 1954, and $300 of such joint net operating loss is considered the net operating loss of W for 1954. For 1955 the gross income of H exceeded his deductions, so that his separate taxable income would be $1,500, and the deductions of W exceeded her gross income by $3,500. Therefore, all of the $2,000 joint net operating loss for 1955 is considered the separate net operating loss of W for 1955.

Example (2). (i) H and W filed joint returns for 1954 and 1956, and separate returns for 1955 and 1957. For the years 1954, 1955, 1956, and 1957 they had taxable incomes and net operating losses as follows, losses being indicated in parentheses:

	1954	1955	1956	1957
H	($5,000)	($2,500)	$6,500	($4,000)
W	(3,000)	2,000	3,000	(1,500)
Total	(8,000)	.....	9,500	.....

(ii) The net operating loss carryover of H from 1957 to 1958 is $4,000, that is, his $4,000 net operating loss for 1957 which is not reduced by any part of the taxable income for 1956, since none of such taxable income is attributable to H and the portion attributable to W is entirely offset by her separate net operating loss for her taxable year 1957, which taxable year begins on the same date as H's taxable year 1957. H's $4,000 net operating loss for 1957 likewise is not reduced by reference to 1955 since H sustained a loss in 1955. The $0 taxable income for 1956 which reduces H's net operating loss for 1957 is computed as follows:

(iii) The combined taxable income of $9,500 for 1956 is reduced to $1,000 by the net operating loss deduction for such year of $8,500. This net operating loss deduction is computed without taking into account any net operating loss of either H or W sustained in a taxable year beginning on or after January 1, 1957, the date of the beginning of the taxable year in which H sustained the net operating loss from which the taxable income is subtracted. This $8,500 is composed of H's carryovers of $5,000 from 1954 and $2,500 from 1955, and of W's carryover of $1,000 from 1954 (the excess of W's $3,000 loss for 1954 over her $2,000 income for 1955). None of the $1,000 combined taxable income for 1956 (computed with the net operating loss deduction described above) is attributable to H since it is caused by W's income (computed after deducting her separate carryover) offsetting H's loss (computed by deducting from his income his separate carryovers). No part of the $1,000 combined taxable income for 1956 which is attributable to W is used to reduce H's net operating loss for 1957 since such taxable income attributable to W must first be reduced by W's $1,500 net operating loss for 1957, her taxable year beginning on the same date as the taxable year of H in which he sustained the net operating loss from which the taxable income is subtracted.

(iv) The net operating loss carryover of W from 1957 to 1958 is $500, her $1,500 loss reduced by the sum of her $0 taxable income for 1955 (computed by taking into account her $3,000 carryover from 1954) and her $1,000 taxable income for 1956, that is, the portion of the combined taxable income for 1956 which is attributable to her.

Example (3). (i) Assume the same facts as in example (2) except that for 1957 the net operating loss of W is $200 instead of $1,500.

(ii) The net operating loss carryover of H from 1957 to 1958 is $3,200, that is, his $4,000 net operating loss for 1957 reduced by the sum of his $0 taxable income for 1955 (a year in which he sustained a loss) and his $800 taxable income for 1956. Such $800 is computed as follows:

(iii) The combined taxable income for 1956, computed with the net operating loss deduction in the manner described in example (2), remains $1,000, no part of which is attributable to H. To the $0 taxable income attributable to H for 1956 there is added $800, the excess of the $1,000 taxable income for such year attributable to W over her $200 net operating loss sustained in 1957, a taxable year beginning on the same date as the taxable year of H in which he sustained the $4,000 net operating loss from which the taxable income is subtracted.

(iv) W has no net operating loss carryover from 1957 to 1958 since her net operating loss of $200 for 1957 does not exceed the $1,000 taxable income for 1956 attributable to her.

Example (4). (i) Assume the same facts as in example (2), except that W changes her accounting period in 1957 to a fiscal year ending on January 31, and has neither income nor losses for the taxable year January 1, 1957, to January 31, 1957, or for the fiscal year February 1, 1957, to January 31, 1958, but has a net operating loss of $200 for the fiscal year February 1, 1958, to January 31, 1959.

(ii) The net operating loss carryover of H from 1957 to 1958 is $3,000, that is, his net operating loss of $4,000 for 1957 reduced by the sum of his $0 taxable income for 1955 (a year in which he sustained a loss) and his $1,000 taxable income for 1956. Such $1,000 is computed as follows:

(iii) The combined taxable income for 1956, computed with the net operating loss deduction in the manner described in example (2), remains $1,000, no part of which is attributable to H. To the $0 taxable income attributable to H for 1956 there is added the $1,000 taxable income attributable to W for such year. The taxable income attributable to W is not reduced by any amount since she does not have a net operating loss for her taxable year beginning on January 1, 1957, the date of the beginning of the taxable year of H in which he sustained the $4,000 net operating loss from which his taxable income is subtracted.

(iv) The net operating loss carryover of W from the fiscal year beginning February 1, 1958, to her next fiscal year is $200, that is, her net

operating loss of $200 for the fiscal year beginning February 1, 1958, reduced by the sum of her $0 taxable income for 1956, her $0 taxable income for the taxable year January 1, 1957, to January 31, 1957 (a year in which she had neither income nor loss), and her $0 taxable income for the fiscal year February 1, 1957, to January 31, 1958 (also a year in which she had neither income nor loss). The $0 taxable income for 1956 is computed as follows:

(v) The combined taxable income of $9,500 for 1956 is reduced to $0 amount by the net operating loss deduction for such year of $12,500. This net operating loss deduction is computed by taking into account the net operating loss of H for 1957 since it was sustained in a taxable year beginning before February 1, 1958, the date of the beginning of the taxable year of W in which she sustained the $200 net operating loss from which her taxable income is subtracted. This $12,500 is composed of H's carryovers of $5,000 from 1954 and $2,500 from 1955 and of his carryback of $4,000 from 1957, plus W's carryover of $1,000 from 1954 (the excess of W's $3,000 loss for 1954 over her $2,000 income for 1955). Since there is no combined taxable income for 1956, there is no taxable income attributable to W for such year. [Reg. § 1.172-7.]

☐ [*T.D.* 6192, 7-23-56. *Amended by T.D.* 6486, 8-12-60, and *T.D.* 8170, 12-1-86.]

[Reg. § 1.172-8]

§ 1.172-8. Net operating loss carryovers for regulated transportation corporations.—(a) *In general.* A net operating loss sustained in a taxable year ending before January 1, 1976, shall be a carryover to the 7 succeeding taxable years if the taxpayer is a regulated transportation corporation (as defined in paragraph (b) of this section) for the loss year and for the 6th and 7th succeeding taxable years. If, however, the taxpayer is a regulated transportation corporation for the loss year and for the 6th succeeding taxable year, but not for the 7th succeeding taxable year, then the loss shall be a carryover to the 6 succeeding taxable years. If the taxpayer is not a regulated transportation corporation for the 6th succeeding taxable year then this section shall not apply. A net operating loss sustained in a taxable year ending after December 31, 1975, shall be a carryover to the 15 succeeding taxable years.

(b) *Regulated transportation corporations.* A corporation is a "regulated transportation corporation" for a taxable year if it is included within one or more of the following categories:

(1) Eighty percent or more of the corporation's gross income (computed without regard to

dividends and capital gains and losses) for such taxable year is income from transportation sources described in paragraph (c) of this section.

(2) The corporation is a railroad corporation, subject to Part I of the Interstate Commerce Act, which is either a lessor railroad corporation described in section 7701(a)(33)(G) or a common parent railroad corporation described in section 7701(a)(33)(H).

(3) The corporation is a member of a regulated transportation system for the taxable year. For purposes of this section, a member of a regulated transportation system for a taxable year means a member of an affiliated group of corporations making a consolidated return for such year, if 80 percent or more of the sum of the gross incomes of the members of the affiliated group for such year (computed without regard to dividends, capital gains and losses, or eliminations for intercompany transactions) is derived from transportation sources described in paragraph (c) of this section. For purposes of this subparagraph, income derived by a corporation described in subparagraph (2) of this paragraph from leases described in section 7701(a)(33)(G) shall be considered as income from transportation sources described in paragraph (c) of this section.

(c) *Transportation sources.* For purposes of this section, income from "transportation sources" means income received directly in consideration for transportation services, and income from the furnishing or sale of essential facilities, products, and other services which are directly necessary and incidental to the furnishing of transportation services. For purposes of the preceding sentence, the term "transportation services" means—

(1) Transportation by railroad as a common carrier subject to the jurisdiction of the Interstate Commerce Commission;

(2)(i) Transportation, which is not included in subparagraph (1) of this paragraph—

(a) On an intrastate, suburban, municipal, or interurban electric railroad,

(b) On an intrastate, municipal, or suburban trackless trolley system,

(c) On a municipal or suburban bus system, or

(d) By motor vehicle not otherwise included in this subparagraph,

if the rates for the furnishing or sale of such transportation are established or approved by a regulatory body described in section 7701(a)(33)(A);

(ii) In the case of a corporation which establishes to the satisfaction of the district director that—

(a) Its revenue from regulated rates from transportation services described in subdivision (i) of this subparagraph and its revenue derived from unregulated rates are derived from its operation of a single interconnected and coordinated system or from the operation of more than one such system, and

(b) The unregulated rates have been and are substantially as favorable to users and consumers as are the regulated rates,

transportation, which is not included in subparagraph (1) of this paragraph, from which such revenue from unregulated rates is derived.

(3) Transportation by air as a common carrier subject to the jurisdiction of the Civil Aeronautics Board; and

(4) Transportation by water by common carrier subject to the jurisdiction of either the Interstate Commerce Commission under Part III of the Interstate Commerce Act (54 Stat. 929), or the Federal Maritime Board under the Intercoastal Shipping Act, 1933 (52 Stat. 965).

(d) *Corporate acquisitions.* This section shall apply to a carryover of a net operating loss sustained by a regulated transportation corporation (as defined in paragraph (b) of this section) to which an acquiring corporation succeeds under section 381(a) only if the acquiring corporation is a regulated transportation corporation (as defined in paragraph (b) of this section)—

(1) For the sixth succeeding taxable year in the case of a carryover to the sixth succeeding taxable year, and

(2) For the sixth and seventh succeeding taxable years in the case of a carryover to the seventh succeeding taxable year. [Reg. § 1.172-8.]

☐ [*T.D. 6862, 11-17-65. Amended by T.D. 8107, 12-1-86.*]

[Reg. § 1.172-9]

§ 1.172-9. **Election with respect to portion of net operating loss attributable to foreign expropriation loss.**—(a) *In general.* If a taxpayer has a net operating loss for a taxable year ending after December 31, 1958, and if the foreign expropriation loss for such year (as defined in paragraph (b)(1) of this section) equals or exceeds 50 percent of the net operating loss for such year, then the taxpayer may elect (at the time and in the manner provided in paragraph (c)(1) or (2) of this section, whichever is applicable) to have the provisions of this section apply. If the taxpayer so elects, the portion of the net operating loss for such taxable year attributable (under paragraph (b)(2) of this section) to such foreign expropriation loss shall not be a net operating loss carryback to any taxable year preceding the taxable year of such loss and shall be a net operating loss carry-over to each of the ten taxable years following the taxable year of such loss. In such case, the portion, if any, of the net operating loss not attributable to a foreign expropriation loss shall be carried back or carried over as provided in paragraph (a)(1)(ii) of § 1.172-4.

(b) *Determination of "foreign expropriation loss"*—(1) *Definition of "foreign expropriation loss".* The term "foreign expropriation loss" means, for any taxable year, the sum of the losses allowable as deductions under section 165 (other than losses from, or which under section 165(g) or 1231(a) are treated or considered as losses from, sales or exchanges of capital assets and other than losses described in section 165(i)(1)) sustained by reason of the expropriation, intervention, seizure, or similar taking of property by the government of any foreign country, any political subdivision thereof, or any agency or instrumentality of the foregoing. For purposes of the preceding sentence, a debt which becomes worthless in whole or in part, shall, to the extent of any deduction allowed under section 166(a), be treated as a loss allowable as a deduction under section 165.

(2) *Portion of the net operating loss attributable to a foreign expropriation loss.* (i) Except as provided in subdivision (ii) of this subparagraph, the portion of the net operating loss for any taxable year attributable to a foreign expropriation loss is the amount of the foreign expropriation loss for such taxable year (determined under subparagraph (1) of this paragraph).

(ii) The portion of the net operating loss for a taxable year attributable to a foreign expropriation loss shall not exceed the amount of the net operating loss, computed under section 172(c), for such year.

(3) *Examples.* The application of this paragraph may be illustrated by the following examples:

Example (1). M Corporation, a domestic calendar year corporation manufacturing cigars in the United States, owns, in country X, a tobacco plantation having an adjusted basis of $400,000 and farm equipment having an adjusted basis of $300,000. On January 15, 1961, country X expropriates the plantation and equipment without any allowance for compensation. For the taxable year 1961, M Corporation sustains a loss from the operation of its business (not including losses from the seizure of its plantation and equipment in country X) of $200,000, which loss would not have been sustained in the absence of the seizure. Accordingly, M has a net operating loss of $900,000 (the sum of $400,000, $300,000, and $200,000). For purposes of section 172(k)(1), M Corporation

has a foreign expropriation loss for 1961 of $700,000 (the sum of $400,000 and $300,000, the losses directly sustained by reason of the seizure of its property by country X). Since the foreign expropriation loss for 1961, $700,000, equals or exceeds 50 percent of the net operating loss for such year, or $450,000 (*i.e.*, 50 percent of $900,000) M Corporation may make the election under paragraph (c)(2) of this section with respect to $700,000, the portion of the net operating loss attributable to the foreign expropriation loss.

Example (2). Assume the same facts as in example (1) except that for 1961, M Corporation has operating profits of $300,000 (not including losses from the seizure of its plantation and equipment in country X) so that its net operating loss (as defined in section 172(c)) is only $400,000. Under the provisions of section 172(k)(2) and paragraph (b)(2) of this section, the portion of the net operating loss for 1961 attributable to a foreign expropriation loss is limited to $400,000, the amount of the net operating loss.

(c) *Time and manner of making election*—(1) *Taxable years ending after December 31, 1963.* In the case of a taxpayer who has a foreign expropriation loss for a taxable year ending after December 31, 1963, the election referred to in paragraph (a) of this section shall be made by attaching to the taxpayer's income tax return (filed within the time prescribed by law, including extensions of time) for the taxable year of such foreign expropriation loss a statement containing the information required by subparagraph (3) of this paragraph. Such election shall be irrevocable after the due date (including extensions of time) of such return.

(2) *Information required.* The statement referred to in subparagraph (1) of this paragraph shall contain the following information:

(i) The name, address, and taxpayer account number of the taxpayer;

(ii) A statement that the taxpayer elects under section 172(b)(3)(A)(ii) or (iii), whichever is applicable, to have section 172(b)(1)(D) of the Code apply;

(iii) The amount of the net operating loss for the taxable year; and

(iv) The amount of the foreign expropriation loss for the taxable year, including a schedule showing the computation of such foreign expropriation loss.

(d) *Amount of foreign expropriation loss which is a carryover to the taxable year in issue*—(1) *General.* If a portion of a net operating loss for the taxable year is attributable to a foreign expropriation loss and if an election under paragraph (a) of

Reg. § 1.172-9(b)(1)

this section has been made with respect to such portion of the net operating loss, then such portion shall be considered to be a separate net operating loss for such year, and, for the purpose of determining the amount of such separate loss which may be carried over to other taxable years, such portion shall be applied after the other portion (if any) of such net operating loss. Such separate loss shall be carried to the earliest of the several taxable years to which such separate loss is allowable as a carryover under the provisions of paragraph (a)(1)(iv) of § 1.172-4, and the amount of such separate loss which shall be carried over to any taxable year subsequent to such earliest year is an amount (not exceeding such separate loss) equal to the excess of—

(i) The sum of (a) such separate loss and (b) the other portion (if any) of the net operating loss (i.e., that portion not attributable to a foreign expropriation loss) to the extent such other portion is a carryover to such earliest taxable year, over

(ii) The sum of the aggregate of the taxable incomes (computed as provided in § 1.172-5) for all of such several taxable years preceding such subsequent taxable year

(2) *Cross reference.* The portion of a net operating loss which is not attributable to a foreign expropriation loss shall be carried back or carried over, in accordance with the rules provided in paragraph (b)(1) of § 1.172-4, as if such portion were the only net operating loss for such year.

(3) *Examples.* The application of this paragraph may be illustrated by the following examples:

Example (1). Corporation A, organized in 1960 and whose return is made on the basis of the calendar year, incurs for 1960 a net operating loss of $10,000, of which $7,500 is attributable to a foreign expropriation loss. With respect to such $7,500, A makes the election described in paragraph (a) of this section. In each of the years 1961, 1962, 1963, 1964, and 1965, A has taxable income in the amount of $600 (computed without any net operating loss deduction). The assumption is made that none of the other modifications prescribed in § 1.172-5 apply. The portion of the net operating loss attributable to the foreign expropriation loss which is a carryover to the year 1966 is $7,000, which is the sum of $7,500 (the portion of the net operating loss attributable to the foreign expropriation loss) and $2,500 (the other portion of the net operating loss available as a carryover to 1961), minus $3,000 (the aggregate of the taxable incomes for taxable years 1961 through 1965).

Example (2). Assume the same facts as in example (1) except that taxable income for each of the years 1961 through 1965 is $400 (computed without any net operating loss deduction). The carryover to the year 1966 is $7,500, that is, the sum of $7,500 (the portion of the net operating loss attributable to the foreign expropriation loss) and $2,500 (the other portion of the net operating loss available as a carryover to 1961), minus $2,000 (the aggregate of the taxable incomes for taxable years 1961 through 1965), but limited to $7,500 (the portion of the net operating loss attributable to the foreign expropriation loss).

(e) *Taxable income which is subtracted from net operating loss to determine carryback or carryover.* In computing taxable income for a taxable year (hereinafter called a "prior taxable year") for the purpose of determining the portion of a net operating loss for another taxable year which shall be carried to each of the several taxable years subsequent to the earliest taxable year to which such loss may be carried, the net operating loss deduction for any such prior taxable year shall be determined without regard to that portion, if any, of a net operating loss for a taxable year attributable to a foreign expropriation loss, if such portion may not, under the provisions of section 172(b)(1)(D) and paragraph (a)(1)(iv) of § 1.172-4, be carried back to such prior taxable year. Thus, if the taxpayer has a foreign expropriation loss for 1962 and elects the 10-year carryover with respect to the portion of his net operating loss for 1962 attributable to the foreign expropriation loss, then in computing taxable income for the year 1960 for the purpose of determining the portion of a net operating loss for 1963 which is carried to years subsequent to 1960, the net operating loss deduction for 1960 is determined without regard to the portion of the net operating loss for 1962 attributable to the foreign expropriation loss, since under the provisions of section 172(b)(1)(D) and paragraph (a)(1)(iv) of § 1.172-4 such portion of the net operating loss for 1962 may not be carried back to 1960. [Reg. § 1.172-9.]

□ [*T.D.* 6862, 11-17-65. *Amended by T.D.* 8107, 12-1-86.]

[Reg. § 1.172-10]

§ 1.172-10. **Net operating losses of real estate investment trusts.**—(a) *Taxable years to which a loss may be carried.*—(1) A net operating loss sustained by a qualified real estate investment trust (as defined in paragraph (b)(1) of this section) in a qualified taxable year (as defined in paragraph (b)(2) of this section) ending after October 4, 1976, shall not be carried back to a preceding taxable year.

(2) A net operating loss sustained by a qualified real estate investment trust in a qualified taxable year ending before October 5, 1976, shall be carried back to the 3 preceding taxable years. However, see § 1.857-2(a)(5), which does not allow the net operating loss deduction in computing real estate investment trust taxable income for taxable years ending before October 5, 1976.

(3) A net operating loss sustained by a qualified real estate investment trust in a qualified taxable year ending after December 31, 1972, shall be carried over to the 15 succeeding taxable years. However, see § 1.857-2(a)(5).

(4) A net operating loss sustained by a qualified real estate investment trust in a qualified taxable year ending before January 1, 1973, shall be carried over to the 8 succeeding taxable years. However, see § 1.857-2(a)(5).

(5) A net operating loss sustained in a taxable year for which the taxpayer is not a qualified real estate investment trust generally may be carried back to the 3 preceding taxable years; however, a net operating loss sustained in a taxable year ending after December 31, 1975, shall not be carried back to any qualified taxable year. However, see § 1.857-2(a)(5) with respect to a net operating loss sustained in a taxable year ending before January 1, 1976.

(6) A net operating loss sustained in a taxable year ending after December 31, 1975, for which the taxpayer is not a qualified real estate investment trust generally may be carried over to the 15 succeeding taxable years.

(7)(i) A net operating loss sustained in a taxable year ending before January 1, 1976, for which the taxpayer is not a qualified real estate investment trust generally may be a net operating loss carryover to each of the 5 succeeding taxable years. However, where the loss was a net operating loss carryback to one or more qualified taxable years, the net operating loss, in accordance with paragraph (a)(7)(ii) of this section, shall be—

(A) Carried over to the 15 succeeding taxable years if the loss could be a net operating loss carryover to a taxable year ending in 1981, or

(B) Carried over to the 5, 6, 7, or 8 succeeding taxable years if paragraph (a)(7)(i)(A) of this section does not apply.

(ii) For purposes of determining whether a net operating loss could be a carryover to a taxable year ending in 1981 under paragraph (a)(7)(i)(A) of this section or, where paragraph (a)(7)(i)(A) of this section does not apply, to determine the actual carryover period under paragraph (a)(7)(i)(B) of this section, the net operating loss shall have a carryover period of 5

years, and such period shall be increased (to a number not greater than 8) by the number of qualified taxable years to which such loss was a net operating loss carryback; however, where the taxpayer acted so as to cause itself to cease to be a qualified real estate investment trust and the principal purpose for such action was to secure the benefit of the allowance of a net operating loss carryover under section 172(b)(1)(B), the net operating loss carryover period shall be limited to 5 years. However, see § 1.857-2(a)(5).

(8) A qualified taxable year is a taxable year preceding or following the taxable year of the net operating loss, for purposes of section 172(b)(1), even though the loss may not be carried to, or allowed as a deduction in, such qualified taxable year. Thus, a qualified taxable year ending before October 5, 1976 (for which no net operating loss deduction is allowable) is nevertheless a preceding or following taxable year for purposes of section 172(b)(1). Moreover, a qualified taxable year ending after October 4, 1976 (to which a net operating loss cannot be carried back because of section 172(b)(1)(E)) is nevertheless a preceding taxable year for purposes of section 172(b)(1). For purposes of determining, under section 172(b)(2), the balance of the loss available as a carryback or carryover to other taxable years, however, the net operating loss is not reduced on account of such qualified taxable year being a preceding or following taxable year.

(b) *Definitions*—For purposes of this section and § § 1.172-2 and 1.172-5—

(1) The term "qualified real estate investment trust" means, with respect to any taxable year, a real estate investment trust within the meaning of part II of subchapter M which is taxable for such year under that part as a real estate investment trust, and

(2) The term "qualified taxable year" means a taxable year for which the taxpayer is a qualified real estate investment trust.

(c) *Examples.* The provisions of this section may be illustrated by the following examples:

Example (1)-(i) *Facts.* X was a qualified real estate investment trust for the taxable years ending on December 31, 1972, and December 31, 1973. X was not a qualified real estate investment trust for the taxable years ending on December 31, 1971, and December 31, 1974. X sustained a net operating loss for the taxable year ending on December 31, 1974.

(ii) *Applicable carryback and carryover periods.* The net operating loss must be carried back to the 3 preceding taxable years. Under § 1.857-2(a)(5) the net operating loss deduction shall not be allowed in computing real estate

Reg. § 1.172-10(a)(2)

investment trust taxable income for the years ending December 31, 1972, and December 31, 1973. Where a net operating loss is sustained in a taxable year ending before January 1, 1976, for which the taxpayer is not a qualified real estate investment trust and the loss is a net operating loss carryback to one or more qualified taxable years, the carryover period is determined under § 1.172-10(a)(7); the carryover period is determined by first applying the rule provided in paragraph (a)(7)(ii) of this section to obtain the carryover period for purposes of determining whether the net operating loss could have been a net operating loss carryover to a taxable year ending in 1981. Under these facts, paragraph (a)(7)(ii) of this section provides for a 7-year carryover period (5 years increased by the 2 qualified taxable years to which the loss was a net operating loss carryback); therefore, since the carryover period provided for by paragraph (a)(7)(ii) of this section would allow the net operating loss to be a net operating loss carryover to a taxable year ending in 1981, under paragraph (a)(7)(ii)(A) of this section the applicable carryover period is 15 years (provided that X did not act so as to cause itself to cease to qualify as a real estate investment trust for the principal purpose of securing the benefit of a net operating loss carryover under section 172(b)(1)(B)).

Example (2)-(i) *Facts.* The facts are the same as in *example* (1) except that the taxable year ending December 31, 1973, was not a qualified taxable year for X.

(ii) *Applicable carryback and carryover periods.* The net operating loss must be carried back to the 3 preceding taxable years. Section 1.857-2(a)(5) provides that the net operating loss deduction shall not be allowed in computing real estate investment trust taxable income for the year ending December 31, 1972. Under these facts the carryover period is determined under § 1.172-10(a)(7). Paragraph (a)(7)(ii) of this section provides for a 6 year carryover period (5 years increased by the 1 qualified taxable year to which the loss was a net operating loss carryback); therefore, since a 6 year carryover period would not allow the net operating loss to be a net operating loss carryover to a taxable year ending in 1981, under paragraph (a)(7)(ii)(A) of this section the applicable carryover period is 15 years (provided that X did not act so as to cause itself to cease to qualify as a real estate investment trust for the principal purpose of securing the benefit of a net operating loss carryover under section 172(b)(1)(B)).

(d) *Cross references.* See §§ 1.172-2(e) and 1.172-5(a)(5) for the computation of the net oper-

ating loss of a qualified real estate investment trust for a taxable year ending after October 4, 1976, and the amount of a net operating loss which is absorbed when carried over to a qualified taxable year ending after October 4, 1976. See § 1.857-2(a)(5), which provides that for a taxable year ending before October 5, 1976, the net operating loss deduction is not allowed in computing the real estate investment trust taxable income of a qualified real estate investment trust. [Reg. § 1.172-10.]

   ☐ *[T.D. 7767, 2-3-81. Amended by T.D. 8107, 12-1-86.]*

[Reg. § 1.172-13]

§ 1.172-13. **Product liability losses.**—(a) *Entitlement to 10-year carryback*—(1) *In general.* Unless an election is made pursuant to paragraph (c) of this section, in the case of a taxpayer which has a product liability loss (as defined in section 172(j) and paragraph (b)(1) of this section) for a taxable year beginning after September 30, 1979 (hereinafter "loss year"), the product liability loss shall be a net operating loss carryback to each of the 10 taxable years preceding the loss year.

(2) *Years to which loss may be carried.* A product liability loss shall first be carried to the earliest of the taxable years to which such loss is allowable as a carryback and shall then be carried to the next earliest of such taxable years, etc.

(3) *Example.* The application of this paragraph may be illustrated as follows:

Example. Taxpayer A incurs a net operating loss for taxable year 1980 of $80,000, of which $60,000 is a product liability loss. A's taxable income for each of the 10 years immediately preceding taxable year 1980 was $5,000. The product liability loss of $60,000 is first carried back to the 10th through the 4th preceding taxable years ($5,000 per year) thus offsetting $35,000 of the loss. The remaining $25,000 of product liability loss is added to the remaining portion of the total net operating loss for taxable year 1980 which was not a product liability loss ($20,000), and the total is then carried back to the 3rd through 1st years preceding taxable year 1980, which offsets $15,000 of this loss. The remaining loss ($30,000) is carried forward pursuant to section 172(b)(1) and the regulations thereunder without regard to whether all or any portion thereof originated as a product liability loss.

(b) *Definitions*—(1) *Product liability loss.* The term "product liability loss" means, for any taxable year, the lesser of—

(i) The net operating loss for the current taxable year (not including the portion of such net operating loss attributable to foreign expropriation losses, as defined in § 1.172-11), or

(ii) The total of the amounts allowable as deductions under sections 162 and 165 directly attributable to—

(A) Product liability (as defined in paragraph (b)(2) of this section), and

(B) Expenses (including settlement payments) incurred in connection with the investigation or settlement of or opposition to claims against the taxpayer on account of alleged product liability.

Indirect corporate expense, or overhead, is not to be allocated to product liability claims so as to become a product liability loss.

(2) *Product liability.* (i) The term "product liability" means the liability of a taxpayer for damages resulting from physical injury or emotional harm to individuals, or damage to or loss of the use of property, on account of any defect in any product which is manufactured, leased, or sold by the taxpayer. The preceding sentence applies only to the extent that the injury, harm, or damage occurs after the taxpayer has completed or terminated operations with respect to the product, including, but not limited to the manufacture, installation, delivery, or testing of the product, and has relinquished possession of such product.

(ii) The term "product liability" does not include liabilities arising under warranty theories relating to repair or replacement of the property that are essentially contract liabilities. For example, the costs incurred by a taxpayer in repairing or replacing defective products under the terms of a warranty, express or implied, are not product liability losses. On the other hand, the taxpayer's liability for damage done to other property or for harm done to persons that is attributable to a defective product may be product liability losses regardless of whether the claim sounds in tort or contract. Further, liability incurred as a result of services performed by a taxpayer is not product liability. For purposes of the preceding sentence, where both a product and services are integral parts of a transaction, product liability does not arise until all operations with respect to the product are completed and the taxpayer has relinquished possession of it. On the other hand, any liability that arises after completion of the initial delivery, installation, servicing, testing, etc., is considered "product liability" even if such liability arises during the subsequent servicing of the product pursuant to a service agreement or otherwise.

(iii) Liability for injury, harm, or damage due to a defective product as described in this subparagraph shall be "product liability" notwithstanding that the liability is not considered product liability under the law of the State in which such liability arose.

(iv) Amounts paid for insurance against product liability risks are not paid on account of product liability.

(v) Notwithstanding subparagraph (iv), an amount is paid on account of product liability (even if such amount is paid to an insurance company) if the amount satisfies the provisions of paragraph (b)(2)(i) through (iii) of this section and the amount—

(A) Is paid on account of specific claims against the taxpayer (or on account of expenses incurred in connection with the investigation or settlement of or opposition to such claims), subsequent to the events giving rise to the claims and pursuant to a contract entered into before those events,

(B) Is not refundable, and

(C) Is not applicable to other claims, other expenses or to subsequent coverage.

(3) *Examples.* Paragraph (b)(2) of this section is illustrated by the following examples:

Example (1). X, a manufacturer of heating equipment, sells a boiler to A, a homeowner. Subsequent to the sale and installation of the boiler, the boiler explodes due to a defect causing physical injury to A. A sues X for damages for the injuries sustained in the explosion and is awarded $250,000, which X pays. The payment was made on account of product liability.

Example (2). Assume the same facts as in example (1) and that A also sues under the contract with X to recover for the cost of the boiler and recovers $1,000, the boiler's replacement cost. The $1,000 payment is not a payment on account of product liability. Similarly, if X agrees to repair the destroyed boiler, any amount expended by X for such repair is not payment made on account of product liability.

Example (3). Y, a professional medical association, is sued by B, a patient, in an action based on the malpractice of one of its doctors. B recovers $25,000. Because the suit was based on the service of B, the payment is not made on account of product liability.

Example (4). R, a retailer of communications equipment, sells a telecommunication device to C. R also contracts with C to service the equipment for 3 years. While R is installing the equipment, the unit catches on fire due to faulty wiring within the unit and destroys C's office. Because R had not relinquished possession of this equipment when the fire started, any amount paid to C by R for the damage to C's property on account of the defective product is not payment on account of product liability.

Example (5). Assume the same facts as in example (4) except that the fire and resulting property damages occurred after R had installed the equipment and relinquished possession of it. Any amount paid for the property damages sustained on account of the defective product is payment on account of product liability.

Example (6). Assume the same facts as in example (4) except that the equipment catches on fire during the subsequent servicing of the unit. Because C is in possession of the unit during the servicing, any amount paid for the property damage sustained on account of the defective product would be payment on account of product liability.

Example (7). X, a manufacturer of computers, sells a computer to A. X also has its employees periodically service the computer for A from time to time after it is placed in service. After the initial delivery, installation, servicing, and testing of the computer is completed, the computer catches on fire while X's employee is servicing the equipment. This fire causes property damage to A's office and physical injury to A. Any amount paid for the property or physical damage sustained on account of the defective product is payment on account of product liability.

(c) *Election*—(1) *In general.* The 10-year carryback provision of this section applies, except as provided in this paragraph, to any taxpayer who, for a taxable year beginning after September 30, 1979, incurs a product liability loss. Any taxpayer entitled to a 10-year carryback under paragraph (a) of this section in any loss year may elect (at the time and in the manner provided in paragraph (c)(2) of this section) to have the carryback period with respect to the product liability loss determined without regard to the carryback rules provided by paragraph (a) of this section. If the taxpayer so elects, the product liability loss shall not be carried back to the 10th through the 4th taxable years preceding the loss year. In such case, the product liability loss shall be carried back or carried over as provided by section 172(b) (except subparagraph (1)(I) thereof) and the regulations thereunder.

(2) *Time and manner of making election.* An election by any taxpayer entitled to the 10-year carryback for the product liability loss to have the carryback with respect to such loss determined without regard to the 10-year carryback provision of paragraph (a) of this section must be made by attaching to the taxpayer's tax return (filed within the time prescribed by law, including extensions of time) for the taxable year in which

such product liability loss is sustained, a statement containing the information required by paragraph (c)(3) of this section. Such election, once made for any taxable year, shall be irrevocable after the due date (including extensions of time) of the taxpayer's tax return for that taxable year.

(3) *Information required.* In the case of a statement filed after April 25, 1983, the statement referred to in paragraph (c)(2) of this section shall contain the following information:

(i) The name, address, and taxpayer identifying number of the taxpayer; and

(ii) A statement that the taxpayer elects under section 172(j)(3) not to have section 172(b)(1)(I) apply.

(4) *Relationship with section 172(b)(3)(C) election.* If a taxpayer sustains during the taxable year both a net operating loss not attributable to product liability and a product liability loss (as defined in section 172(j)(1) and paragraph (b)(1) of this section), an election pursuant to section 172(b)(3)(C) (relating to election to relinquish the entire carryback period) does not preclude the product liability loss from being carried back 10 years under section 172(b)(1)(I) and paragraph (a)( ) of this section. [Reg. § 1.172-13.]

☐ [*T.D.* 8096, 8-26-86.]

[Reg. § 1.173-1]

§1.173-1. **Circulation expenditures.**—(a) *Allowance of deduction.* Section 173 provides for the deduction from gross income of all expenditures to establish, maintain, or increase the circulation of a newspaper, magazine, or other periodical, subject to the following limitations:

(1) No deduction shall be allowed for expenditures for the purchase of land or depreciable property or for the acquisition of circulation through the purchase of any part of the business of another publisher of a newspaper, magazine, or other periodical;

(2) The deduction shall be allowed only to the publisher making the circulation expenditures; and

(3) The deduction shall be allowed only for the taxable year in which such expenditures are paid or incurred.

Subject to the provisions of paragraph (c) of this section, the deduction permitted under section 173 and this paragraph shall be allowed without regard to the method of accounting used by the taxpayer and notwithstanding the provisions of section 263 and the regulations thereunder, relating to capital expenditures.

(b) *Deferred expenditures.* Notwithstanding the provisions of paragraph (a)(3) of this section, expenditures paid or incurred in a taxable year subject to the Internal Revenue Code of 1939 which are deferrable pursuant to I.T. 3369 (C.B. 1940-1, 46), as modified by Rev. Rul. 57-87 (C.B. 1957-1, 507), may be deducted in the taxable year subject to the Internal Revenue Code of 1954 to which so deferred.

(c) *Election to capitalize.* (1) A taxpayer entitled to the deduction for circulation expenditures provided in section 173 and paragraph (a) of this section may, in lieu of taking such deduction, elect to capitalize the portion of such circulation expenditures which is properly chargeable to capital account. As a general rule, expenditures normally made from year to year in an effort to maintain circulation are not properly chargeable to capital account; conversely, expenditures made in an effort to establish or to increase circulation are properly chargeable to capital account. For example, if a newspaper normally employs five persons to obtain renewals of subscriptions by telephone, the expenditures in connection therewith would not be properly chargeable to capital account. However, if such newspaper, in a special effort to increase its circulation, hires for a limited period 20 additional employees to obtain new subscriptions by means of telephone calls to the general public, the expenditures in connection therewith would be properly chargeable to capital account. If an election is made by a taxpayer to treat any portion of his circulation expenditures as chargeable to capital account, the election must apply to all such expenditures which are properly so chargeable. In such case, no deduction shall be allowed under section 173 for any such expenditures. In particular cases, the extent to which any deductions attributable to the amortization of capital expenditures are allowed may be determined under sections 162, 263, and 461.

(2) A taxpayer may make the election referred to in subparagraph (1) of this paragraph by attaching a statement to his return for the first taxable year to which the election is applicable. Once an election is made, the taxpayer must continue in subsequent taxable years to charge to capital account all circulation expenditures properly so chargeable, unless the Commissioner, on application made to him in writing by the taxpayer, permits a revocation of such election for any subsequent taxable year or years. Permission to revoke such election may be granted subject to such conditions as the Commissioner deems necessary.

(3) Elections filed under section 23(bb) of the Internal Revenue Code of 1939 shall be given the same effect as if they were filed under section 173. (See section 7807(b)(2).) [Reg. § 1.173-1.]

☐ [*T.D.* 6254, 9-27-57.]

[Reg. § 1.174-1]

§ 1.174-1. Research and experimental expenditures; in general.—Section 174 provides two methods for treating research or experimental expenditures paid or incurred by the taxpayer in connection with his trade or business. These expenditures may be treated as expenses not chargeable to capital account and deducted in the year in which they are paid or incurred (see § 1.174-3), or they may be deferred and amortized (see § 1.174-4). Research or experimental expenditures which are neither treated as expenses nor deferred and amortized under section 174 must be charged to capital account. The expenditures to which section 174 applies may relate either to a general research program or to a particular project. See § 1.174-2 for the definition of research and experimental expenditures. The term "paid or incurred", as used in section 174 and in §§ 1.174-1 to 1.174-4, inclusive, is to be construed according to the method of accounting used by the taxpayer in computing taxable income. See section 7701(a)(25). [Reg. § 1.174-1.]

☐ [*T.D.* 6255, 10-3-57.]

[Reg. § 1.174-2]

§ 1.174-2. Definition of research and experimental expenditures.—(a) *In general.*—(1) The term *research or experimental expenditures*, as used in section 174, means expenditures incurred in connection with the taxpayer's trade or business which represent research and development costs in the experimental or laboratory sense. The term generally includes all such costs incident to the development or improvement of a product. The term includes the costs of obtaining a patent, such as attorneys' fees expended in making and perfecting a patent application. Expenditures represent research and development costs in the experimental or laboratory sense if they are for activities intended to discover information that would eliminate uncertainty concerning the development or improvement of a product. Uncertainty exists if the information available to the taxpayer does not establish the capability or method for developing or improving the product or the appropriate design of the product. Whether expenditures qualify as research or experimental expenditures depends on the nature of the activity to which the expenditures relate, not the nature of the product or improvement being developed or the level of technological advancement the product or improvement represents.

(2) For purposes of this section, the term *product* includes any pilot model, process, formula, invention, technique, patent, or similar

Reg. § 1.174-1

property, and includes products to be used by the taxpayer in its trade or business as well as products to be held for sale, lease, or license.

(3) The term *research or experimental expenditures* does not include expenditures for—

(i) The ordinary testing or inspection of materials or products for quality control (quality control testing);

(ii) Efficiency surveys;

(iii) Management studies;

(iv) Consumer surveys;

(v) Advertising or promotions;

(vi) The acquisition of another's patent, model, production or process; or

(vii) Research in connection with literary, historical, or similar projects.

(4) For purposes of paragraph (a)(3)(i) of this section, testing or inspection to determine whether particular units of materials or products conform to specified parameters is quality control testing. However, quality control testing does not include testing to determine if the design of the product is appropriate.

(5) See section 263A and the regulations thereunder for cost capitalization rules which apply to expenditures paid or incurred for research in connection with literary, historical, or similar projects involving the production of property, including the production of films, sound recordings, video tapes, books, or similar properties.

(6) Section 174 applies to a research or experimental expenditure only to the extent that the amount of the expenditure is reasonable under the circumstances. In general, the amount of an expenditure for research or experimental activities is reasonable if the amount would ordinarily be paid for like activities by like enterprises under like circumstances. Amounts supposedly paid for research that are not reasonable under the circumstances may be characterized as disguised dividends, gifts, loans, or similar payments. The reasonableness requirement of this paragraph (a)(6) does not apply to the reasonableness of the type or nature of the activities themselves.

(7) This paragraph (a) applies to taxable years beginning after October 3, 1994.

(8) The provisions of this section apply not only to costs paid or incurred by the taxpayer for research or experimentation undertaken directly by him but also to expenditures paid or incurred for research or experimentation carried on in his behalf by another person or organization (such as a research institute, foundation, engineering company, or similar contractor). However, any expenditures for research or experimentation carried on in the taxpayer's behalf by another person are not expenditures to which section 174 relates, to the extent that they represent expenditures for the acquisition or improvement of land or depreciable property, used in connection with the research or experimentation, to which the taxpayer acquires rights of ownership.

(9) The application of subparagraph (2) of this paragraph may be illustrated by the following examples:

Example (1). A engages B to undertake research and experimental work in order to create a particular product. B will be paid annually a fixed sum plus an amount equivalent to his actual expenditures. In 1957, A pays to B in respect of the project the sum of $150,000 of which $25,000 represents an addition to B's laboratory and the balance represents charges for research and experimentation on the project. It is agreed between the parties that A will absorb the entire cost of this addition to B's laboratory which will be retained by B. A may treat the entire $150,000 as expenditures under section 174.

Example (2). X Corporation, a manufacturer of explosives, contracts with the Y research organization to attempt through research and experimentation the creation of a new process for making certain explosives. Because of the danger involved in such an undertaking, Y is compelled to acquire an isolated tract of land on which to conduct the research and experimentation. It is agreed that upon completion of the project Y will transfer this tract, including any improvements thereon, to X. Section 174 does not apply to the amount paid to Y representing the costs of the tract of land and improvements.

(b) *Certain expenditures with respect to land and other property.* (1) Expenditures by the taxpayer for the acquisition or improvement of land, or for the acquisition or improvement of property which is subject to an allowance for depreciation under section 167 or depletion under section 611, are not deductible under section 174, irrespective of the fact that the property or improvements may be used by the taxpayer in connection with research or experimentation. However, allowances for depreciation or depletion of property are considered as research or experimental expenditures, for purposes of section 174, to the extent that the property to which the allowances relate is used in connection with research or experimentation. If any part of the cost of acquisition or improvement of depreciable property is attributable to research or experimentation (whether made by the taxpayer or another), see subparagraphs (2), (3), and (4) of this paragraph.

Reg. § 1.174-2(b)

(2) Expenditures for research or experimentation which result, as an end product of the research or experimentation, in depreciable property to be used in the taxpayer's trade or business may, subject to the limitations of subparagraph (4) of this paragraph, be allowable as a current expense deduction under section 174(a). Such expenditures cannot be amortized under section 174(b) except to the extent provided in paragraph (a)(4) of § 1.174-4.

(3) If expenditures for research or experimentation are incurred in connection with the construction or manufacture of depreciable property by another, they are deductible under section 174(a) only if made upon the taxpayer's order and at his risk. No deduction will be allowed (i) if the taxpayer purchases another's product under a performance guarantee (whether express, implied, or imposed by local law) unless the guarantee is limited, to engineering specifications or otherwise, in such a way that economic utility is not taken into account; or (ii) for any part of the purchase price of a product in regular production. For example, if a taxpayer orders a specially-built automatic milling machine under a guarantee that the machine will be capable of producing a given number of units per hour, no portion of the expenditure is deductible since none of it is made at the taxpayer's risk. Similarly, no deductible expense is incurred if a taxpayer enters into a contract for the construction of a new type of chemical processing plant under a turn-key contract guaranteeing a given annual production and a given consumption of raw material and fuel per unit. On the other hand, if the contract contained no guarantee of quality of production and of quantity of units in relation to consumption of raw material and fuel, and if real doubt existed as to the capabilities of the process, expenses for research or experimentation under the contract are at the taxpayer's risk and are deductible under section 174(a). However, see subparagraph (4) of this paragraph.

(4) The deductions referred to in subparagraphs (2) and (3) of this paragraph for expenditures in connection with the acquisition or production of depreciable property to be used in the taxpayer's trade or business are limited to amounts expended for research or experimentation. For the purpose of the preceding sentence, amounts expended for research or experimentation do not include the costs of the component materials of the depreciable property, the costs of labor or other elements involved in its construction and installation, or costs attributable to the acquisition or improvement of the property. For example, a taxpayer undertakes to develop a new machine for use in his business. He expends $30,000 on the project of which $10,000 represents the actual costs of material, labor, etc., to construct the machine, and $20,000 represents research costs which are not attributable to the machine itself. Under section 174(a) the taxpayer would be permitted to deduct the $20,000 as expenses not chargeable to capital account, but the $10,000 must be charged to the asset account (the machine).

(c) *Exploration expenditures.* The provisions of section 174 are not applicable to any expenditures paid or incurred for the purpose of ascertaining the existence, location, extent, or quality of any deposit of ore, oil, gas or other mineral. See sections 617 and 263. [Reg. § 1.174-2.]

☐ [*T.D. 6255, 10-3-57. Amended by T.D. 8131, 3-24-87 and T.D. 8562, 9-30-94.*]

[Reg. § 1.174-3]

§ 1.174-3. **Treatment as expenses.**—(a) *In general.* Research or experimental expenditures paid or incurred by a taxpayer during the taxable year in connection with his trade or business are deductible as expenses, and are not chargeable to capital account, if the taxpayer adopts the method provided in section 174(a). See paragraph (b) of this section. If adopted, the method shall apply to all research and experimental expenditures paid or incurred in the taxable year of adoption and all subsequent taxable years, unless a different method is authorized by the Commissioner under section 174(a)(3) with respect to part or all of the expenditures. See paragraph (b)(3) of this section. Thus, if a change to the deferred expense method under section 174(b) is authorized by the Commissioner with respect to research or experimental expenditures attributable to a particular project or projects, the taxpayer, for the taxable year of the change and for subsequent taxable years, must apply the deferred expense method to all such expenditures paid or incurred during any of those taxable years in connection with the particular project or projects, even though all other research and experimental expenditures are required to be deducted as current expenses under this section. In no event will the taxpayer be permitted to adopt the method described in this section as to part of the expenditures relative to a particular project and adopt for the same taxable year a different method of treating the balance of the expenditures relating to the same project.

(b) *Adoption and change of method* —(1) *Adoption without consent.* The method described in this section may be adopted for any taxable year beginning after December 31, 1953, and ending after August 16, 1954. The consent of the Commissioner is not required if the taxpayer adopts the method for the first such taxable year in which he pays or incurs research or experimental expenditures. The taxpayer may do so by claiming in his income tax return for such year a deduction for his research or experimental expenditures. If the taxpayer fails to adopt the method for the first taxable year in which he incurs such expenditures, he cannot do so in subsequent taxable years unless he obtains the consent of the Commissioner under section 174(a)(2)(B) and subparagraph (2) of this paragraph. See, however, subparagraph (4) of this paragraph, relating to extensions of time.

(2) *Adoption with consent.* A taxpayer may, with the consent of the Commissioner, adopt at any time the method provided in section 174(a). The method adopted in this manner shall be applicable only to expenditures paid or incurred during the taxable year for which the request is made and in subsequent taxable years. A request to adopt this method shall be in writing and shall be addressed to the Commissioner of Internal Revenue, Attention: T:R, Washington 25, D.C. The request shall set forth the name and address of the taxpayer, the first taxable year for which the adoption of the method is requested, and a description of the project or projects with respect to which research or experimental expenditures are to be, or have already been, paid or incurred. The request shall be signed by the taxpayer (or his duly authorized representative) and shall be filed not later than the last day of the first taxable year for which the adoption of the method is requested. See, however, subparagraph (4) of this paragraph, relating to extensions of time.

(3) *Change of method.* An application for permission to change to a different method of treating research or experimental expenditures shall be in writing and shall be addressed to the Commissioner of Internal Revenue, Attention: T:R, Washington 25, D.C. The application shall include the name and address of the taxpayer, shall be signed by the taxpayer (or his duly authorized representative), and shall be filed not later than the last day of the first taxable year for which the change in method is to apply. See, however, subparagraph (4) of this paragraph, relating to extensions of time. The application shall—

(i) State the first year to which the requested change is to be applicable;

(ii) State whether the change is to apply to all research or experimental expenditures paid or incurred by the taxpayer, or only to expenditures attributable to a particular project or projects;

(iii) Include such information as will identify the project or projects to which the change is applicable;

(iv) Indicate the number of months (not less than 60) selected for amortization of the expenditures, if any, which are to be treated as deferred expenses under section 174(b);

(v) State that, upon approval of the application, the taxpayer will make an accounting segregation on his books and records of the research or experimental expenditures to which the change in method is to apply; and

(vi) State the reasons for the change.

If permission is granted to make the change, the taxpayer shall attach a copy of the letter granting permission to his income tax return for the first taxable year in which the different method is effective.

(4) *Special rules.* If the last day prescribed by law for filing a return for any taxable year (including extensions thereof) to which section 174(a) is applicable falls before January 2, 1958, consent is hereby given for the taxpayer to adopt the expense method or to change from the expense method to a different method. In the case of a change from the expense method to a different method, the taxpayer, on or before January 2, 1958, must submit to the district director for the internal revenue district in which the return was filed the information required by subparagraph (3) of this paragraph. For any taxable year for which the expense method or a different method is adopted pursuant to this subparagraph, an amended return reflecting such method shall be filed on or before January 2, 1958, if such return is necessary. [Reg. § 1.174-3.]

☐ [*T.D.* 6255, 10-3-57.]

[Reg. § 1.174-4]

§ 1.174-4. Treatment as deferred expenses.— (a) *In general.* (1) If a taxpayer has not adopted the method provided in section 174(a) of treating research or experimental expenditures paid or incurred by him in connection with his trade or business as currently deductible expenses, he may, for any taxable year beginning December 31, 1953, elect to treat such expenditures as deferred expenses under section 174(b), subject to the limitations of subparagraph (2) of this paragraph. If a taxpayer has adopted the method of treating such expenditures as expenses under section 174(a), he may not elect to defer and amortize any such expenditures unless permission to do so is granted under section 174(a)(3). See paragraph (b) of this section.

(2) The election to treat research or experimental expenditures as deferred expenses under

section 174(b) applies only to those expenditures which are chargeable to capital account but which are not chargeable to property of a character subject to an allowance for depreciation or depletion under section 167 or 611, respectively. Thus, the election under section 174(b) applies only if the property resulting from the research or experimental expenditures has no determinable useful life. If the property resulting from the expenditures has a determinable useful life, section 174(b) is not applicable, and the capitalized expenditures must be amortized or depreciated over the determinable useful life. Amounts treated as deferred expenses are properly chargeable to capital account for purposes of section 1016(a)(1), relating to adjustments to basis of property. See section 1016(a)(14). See section 174(c) and paragraph (b)(1) of § 1.174-2 for treatment of expenditures for the acquisition or improvement of land or of depreciable or depletable property to be used in connection with the research or experimentation.

(3) Expenditures which are treated as deferred expenses under section 174(b) are allowable as a deduction ratably over a period of not less than 60 consecutive months beginning with the month in which the taxpayer first realizes benefits from the expenditures. The length of the period shall be selected by the taxpayer at the time he makes the election to defer the expenditures. If a taxpayer has two or more separate projects, he may select a different amortization period for each project. In the absence of a showing to the contrary, the taxpayer will be deemed to have begun to realize benefits from the deferred expenditures in the month in which the taxpayer first puts the process, formula, invention, or similar property to which the expenditures relate to an income-producing use. See section 1016(a)(14) for adjustments to basis of property for amounts allowed as deductions under section 174(b) and this section. See section 165 and the regulations thereunder for rules relating to the treatment of losses resulting from abandonment.

(4) If expenditures which the taxpayer has elected to defer and deduct ratably over a period of time in accordance with section 174(b) result in the development of depreciable property, deductions for the unrecovered expenditures, beginning with the time the asset becomes depreciable in character, shall be determined under section 167 (relating to depreciation) and the regulations thereunder. For example, for the taxable year 1954, A, who reports his income on the basis of a calendar year, elects to defer and deduct ratably over a period of 60 months research and experimental expenditures made in connection with a particular project. In 1956, the total of the deferred expenditures amounts to $60,000. At that

time, A has developed a process which he seeks to patent. On July 1, 1956, A first realized benefits from the marketing of products resulting from this process. Therefore, the expenditures deferred are deductible ratably over the 60-month period beginning with July 1, 1956 (when A first realized benefits from the project). In his return for the year 1956, A deducted $6,000; in 1957, A deducted $12,000 ($1,000 per month). On July 1, 1958, a patent protecting his process is obtained by A. In his return for 1958, A is entitled to a deduction of $6,000, representing the amortizable portion of the deferred expenses attributable to the period prior to July 1, 1958. The balance of the unrecovered expenditures ($60,000 minus $24,000, or $36,000) is to be recovered as a depreciation deduction over the life of the patent commencing with July 1, 1958. Thus, one-half of the annual depreciation deduction based upon the useful life of the patent is also deductible for 1958 (from July 1 to December 31).

(5) The election shall be applicable to all research and experimental expenditures paid or incurred by the taxpayer or, if so limited by the taxpayer's election, to all such expenditures with respect to the particular project, subject to the limitations of subparagraph (2) of this paragraph. The election shall apply for the taxable year for which the election is made and for all subsequent taxable years, unless a change to a different treatment is authorized by the Commissioner under section 174(b)(2). See paragraph (b)(2) of this section. Likewise, the taxpayer shall adhere to the amortization period selected at the time of the election unless a different period of amortization with respect to a part or all of the expenditures is similarly authorized. However, no change in method will be permitted with respect to expenditures paid or incurred before the taxable year to which the change is to apply. In no event will the taxpayer be permitted to treat part of the expenditures with respect to a particular project as deferred expenses under section 174(b) and to adopt a different method of treating the balance of the expenditures relating to the same project for the same taxable year. The election under this section shall not apply to any expenditures paid or incurred before the taxable year for which the taxpayer makes the election.

(b) *Election and change of method* —(1) *Election.* The election under section 174(b) shall be made not later than the time (including extensions) prescribed by law for filing the return for the taxable year for which the method is to be adopted. The election shall be made by attaching a statement to the taxpayer's return for the first taxable year to which the election is applicable.

Reg. § 1.174-4(a)(3)

The statement shall be signed by the taxpayer (or his duly authorized representative), and shall—

(i) Set forth the name and address of the taxpayer;

(ii) Designate the first taxable year to which the election is to apply;

(iii) State whether the election is intended to apply to all expenditures within the permissible scope of the election, or only to a particular project or projects, and, if the latter, include such information as will identify the project or projects as to which the election is to apply;

(iv) Set forth the amount of all research or experimental expenditures paid or incurred during the taxable year for which the election is made;

(v) Indicate the number of months (not less than 60) selected for amortization of the deferred expenses for each project; and

(vi) State that the taxpayer will make an accounting segregation in his books and records of the expenditures to which the election relates.

(2) *Change to a different method or period.* Application for permission to change to a different method of treating research or experimental expenditures or to a different period of amortization for deferred expenses shall be in writing and shall be addressed to the Commissioner of Internal Revenue, Attention: T:R, Washington 25, D.C. The application shall include the name and address of the taxpayer, shall be signed by the taxpayer (or his duly authorized representative), and shall be filed not later than the end of the first taxable year in which the different method or different amortization period is to be used (unless subparagraph (3) of this paragraph, relating to extensions of time, is applicable). The application shall set forth the following information with regard to the research or experimental expenditures which are being treated under section 174(b) as deferred expenses:

(i) Total amount of research or experimental expenditures attributable to each project;

(ii) Amortization period applicable to each project; and

(iii) Unamortized expenditures attributable to each project at the beginning of the taxable year in which the application is filed.

In addition, the application shall set forth the length of the new period or periods proposed, or the new method of treatment proposed, the reasons for the proposed change, and such information as will identify the project or projects to which the expenditures affected by the change relate. If permission is granted to make the change, the taxpayer shall attach a copy of the letter granting the permission to his income tax return for the first taxable year in which the different method or period is to be effective.

(3) *Special rules.* If the last day prescribed by law for filing a return for any taxable year for which the deferred method provided in section 174(b) has been adopted falls before January 2, 1958, consent is hereby given for the taxpayer to change from such method and adopt a different method of treating research or experimental expenditures, provided that on or before January 2, 1958, he submits to the district director for the district in which the return was filed the information required by subparagraph (2) of this paragraph, relating to a change to a different method or period. For any taxable year for which the different method is adopted pursuant to this subparagraph, an amended return reflecting such method shall be filed on or before January 2, 1958.

(c) *Example.* The application of this section is illustrated by the following example:

Example. N Corporation is engaged in the business of manufacturing chemical products. On January 1, 1955, work is begun on a special research project. N Corporation elects, pursuant to section 174(b), to defer the expenditures relating to the special project and to amortize the expenditures over a period of 72 months beginning with the month in which benefits from the expenditures are first realized. On January 1, 1955, N Corporation also purchased for $57,600 a building having a remaining useful life of 12 years as of the date of purchase and no salvage value at the end of the period. Fifty per cent of the building's facilities are to be used in connection with the special research project. During 1955, N Corporation pays or incurs the following expenditures relating to the special research project:

Salaries	$15,000
Heat, light and power	700
Drawings	2,000
Models	6,500
Laboratory materials	8,000
Attorneys' fees	1,400
Depreciation on building attributable to project (50 percent of $4,800 allowable depreciation)	2,400
Total research and development expenditures	$36,000

The above expenditures result in a process which is marketable but not patentable and which has no determinable useful life. N Corporation first realizes benefits from the process in January 1956. N Corporation is entitled to deduct the amount of $6,000

Reg. § 1.174-4(c)

$$\left(\frac{\$36,000 \times 12 \text{ months}}{72 \text{ months}}\right)$$

as deferred expenses under section 174(b) in computing taxable income for 1956. [Reg. § 1.174-4.]

☐ [*T.D.* 6255, 10-3-57.]

[Reg. § 1.175-1]

§ 1.175-1. Soil and water conservation expenditures; in general.—Under section 175, a farmer may deduct his soil or water conservation expenditures which do not give rise to a deduction for depreciation and which are not otherwise deductible. The amount of the deduction is limited annually to 25 percent of the taxpayer's gross income from farming. Any excess may be carried over and deducted in succeeding taxable years. As a general rule, once a farmer has adopted this method of treating soil and water conservation expenditures, he must deduct all such expenditures (subject to the 25-percent limitation) for the current and subsequent taxable years. If a farmer does not adopt this method, such expenditures increase the basis of the property to which they relate. For rules relating to the allocation of expenditures that benefit both land used in farming and other land of the taxpayer, see § 1.175-7. [Reg. § 1.175-1.]

☐ [*T.D.* 6235, 5-31-57. *Amended by T.D.* 7740, 12-21-80.]

[Reg. § 1.175-2]

§ 1.175-2. Definition of soil and water conservation expenditures.—(a) *Expenditures treated as a deduction.* (1) The method described in section 175 applies to expenditures paid or incurred for the purpose of soil or water conservation in respect of land used in farming, or for the prevention or erosion of land used in farming, but only if such expenditures are made in the furtherance of the business of farming. More specifically, a farmer may deduct expenditures made for these purposes which are for (i) the treatment or moving of earth, (ii) the construction, control, and protection of diversion channels, drainage ditches, irrigation ditches, earthen dams, watercourses, outlets, and ponds, (iii) the eradication of brush, and (iv) the planting of windbreaks. Expenditures for the treatment or moving of earth include but are not limited to expenditures for leveling, conditioning, grading, terracing, contour furrowing, and restoration of soil fertility.

(2) The following are examples of soil and water conservation: (i) constructing terraces, or the like, to detain or control the flow of water, to check soil erosion on sloping land, to intercept run-off, and to divert excess water to protected outlets; (ii) constructing water detention or sediment retention dams to prevent or fill gullies, to retard or reduce run-off of water, or to collect stock water; and (iii) constructing earthen floodways, levees, or dikes, to prevent flood damage to farmland.

(b) *Expenditures not subject to section 175 treatment.* (1) The method described in section 175 applies only to expenditures for nondepreciable items. Accordingly, a taxpayer may not deduct expenditures for the purchase, construction, installation, or improvement of structures, appliances, or facilities subject to the allowance for depreciation. Thus, the method does not apply to depreciable nonearthen items such as those made of masonry or concrete (see section 167). For example, expenditures in respect of depreciable property include those for materials, supplies, wages, fuel, hauling, and dirt moving for making structures such as tanks, reservoirs, pipes, conduits, canals, dams, wells, or pumps composed of masonry, concrete, tile, metal, or wood. However, the method applies to expenditures for earthen items which are not subject to a depreciation allowance. For example, expenditures for earthen terraces and dams which are nondepreciable are deductible under section 175. For taxable years beginning after December 31, 1959, in the case of expenditures paid or incurred by farmers for fertilizer, lime, etc., for purposes other than soil or water conservation, see section 180 and the regulations thereunder.

(2) The method does not apply to expenses deductible apart from section 175. Adoption of the method is not necessary in order to deduct such expenses in full without limitation. Thus, the method does not apply to interest (deductible under section 163), nor to taxes (deductible under section 164). It does not apply to expenses for the repair of completed soil or water conservation structures, such as costs of annual removal of sediment from a drainage ditch. It does not apply to expenditures paid or incurred primarily to produce an agricultural crop even though they incidentally conserve soil. Thus, the cost of fertilizing (the effectiveness of which does not last beyond one year) used to produce hay is deductible without adoption of the method prescribed in section 175. For taxable years beginning after December 31, 1959, in the case of expenditures paid or incurred by farmers for fertilizer, lime, etc., for purposes other than soil or water conservation. See section 180 and the regulations thereunder. However, the method would apply to expenses incurred to produce vegetation primarily to conserve soil or water or to prevent erosion. Thus, for example, the method would apply to such expenditures as the cost of dirt moving, lime, fertilizer, seed and planting stock used in gulley stabiliza-

Reg. § 1.175-1

tion, or in stabilizing severely eroded areas, in order to obtain a soil binding stand of vegetation on raw or infertile land.

(c) *Assessments.* The method applies also to that part of assessments levied by a soil or water conservation or drainage district to reimburse it for its expenditures which, if actually paid or incurred during the taxable year by the taxpayer directly, would be deductible under section 175. Depending upon the farmer's method of accounting, the time when the farmer pays or incurs the assessment, and not the time when the expenditures are paid or incurred by the district, controls the time the deduction must be taken. The provisions of this paragraph may be illustrated by the following example:

Example. In 1955 a soil and water conservation district levies an assessment of $700 upon a farmer on the cash method of accounting. The assessment is to reimburse the district for its expenditures in 1954. The farmer's share of such expenditures is as follows: $400 for digging drainage ditches for soil conservation and $300 for assets subject to the allowance for depreciation. If the farmer pays the assessment in 1955 and has adopted the method of treating expenditures for soil or water conservation as current expenses under section 175, he may deduct in 1955 the $400 attributable to the digging of drainage ditches as a soil conservation expenditure subject to the 25-percent limitation. [Reg. § 1.175-2.]

□ [*T.D.* 6235, 5-31-57. *Amended by T.D.* 6548, 2-21-61.]

[Reg. § 1.175-3]

§ 1.175-3. Definition of "the business of farming".—The method described in section 175 is available only to a taxpayer engaged in "the business of farming". A taxpayer is engaged in the business of farming if he cultivates, operates, or manages a farm for gain or profit, either as owner or tenant. For the purpose of section 175, a taxpayer who receives a rental (either in cash or in kind) which is based upon farm production is engaged in the business of farming. However, a taxpayer who receives a fixed rental (without reference to production) is engaged in the business of farming only if he participates to a material extent in the operation or management of the farm. A taxpayer engaged in forestry or the growing of timber is not thereby engaged in the business of farming. A person cultivating or operating a farm for recreation on pleasure rather than a profit is not engaged in the business of farming. For the purpose of this section, the term "farm" is used in its ordinary, accepted sense and includes stock, dairy, poultry, fish, fruit, and truck farms, and also plantations, ranches, ranges, and orchards. A

fish farm is an area where fish are grown or raised, as opposed to merely caught or harvested; that is, an area where they are artificially fed, protected, cared for, etc. A taxpayer is engaged in "the business of farming" if he is a member of a partnership engaged in the business of farming. See paragraphs (a)(8)(i) and (c)(1)(iv) of § 1.702-1. [Reg. § 1 175-3.]

□ [*T.D.* 6235, 5-31-57. *Amended by T.D.* 6649, 4-17-63.]

[Reg. § 1.175-4]

§ 1.175-4. Definition of "land used in farming".—(a) *Requirements.* For purposes of section 175, the term "land used in farming" means land which is used in the business of farming and which meets both of the following requirements:

(1) The land must be used for the production of crops, fruits, or other agricultural products, including fish, or for the sustenance of livestock. The term "livestock" includes cattle, hogs, horses, mules, donkeys, sheep, goats, captive fur-bearing animals, chickens, turkeys, pigeons, and other poultry. Land used for the sustenance of livestock includes land used for grazing such livestock.

(2) The land must be or have been so used either by the taxpayer or his tenant at some time before, or at the same time as, the taxpayer makes the expenditure for soil or water conservation or for the prevention of the erosion of land. The taxpayer will be considered to have used the land in farming before making such expenditure if he or his tenant has employed the land in a farming use in the past. If the expenditures are made by the taxpayer in respect to land newly acquired from one who immediately prior to the acquisition was using it in farming, the taxpayer will be considered to be using the land in farming at the time that such expenditures are made, if the use which is made by the taxpayer of the land from the time of its acquisition by him is substantially a continuation of its use in farming, whether for the same farming use as that of the taxpayer's predecessor or for one of the other uses specified in paragraph (a)(1) of this section.

(b) *Example.* The provisions of paragraph (a) of this section may be illustrated by the following examples:

Example (1). A purchases an operating farm from B in the autumn after B has harvested his crops. Prior to spring plowing and planting when the land is idle because of the season, A makes certain soil and water conservation expenditures on this farm. At the time such expenditures are made the land is considered to be used by A in farming, and A may deduct such expenditures under section 175, subject to the other requisite conditions of such section.

Example (2). C acquires uncultivated land, not previously used in farming, which he intends to develop for farming. Prior to putting this land into production it is necessary for C to clear brush, construct earthern terraces and ponds, and make other soil and water conservation expenditures. The land is not used in farming at the same time that such expenditures are made. Therefore, C may not deduct such expenditures under section 175.

Example (3). D acquires several tracts of land from persons who had used such land immediately prior to D's acquisition for grazing cattle. D intends to use the land for growing grapes. In order to make the land suitable for this use, D constructs earthen terraces, builds drainage ditches and irrigation ditches, extensively treats the soil, and makes other soil and water conservation expenditures. The land is considered to be used in farming by D at the time he makes such expenditures, even though it is being prepared for a different type of farming activity than that engaged in by D's predecessors. Therefore, D may deduct such expenditures under section 175, subject to the other requisite conditions of such section.

(c) *Cross reference.* For rules relating to the allocation of expenditures that benefit both land used in farming and other land of the taxpayer, see § 1.175-7. [Reg. § 1.175-4.]

☐ [*T.D. 6235, 5-31-57. Amended by T.D. 6649, 4-17-63 and T.D. 7740, 11-21-80.*]

[Reg. § 1.175-5]

§ 1.175-5. Percentage limitation and carryover.—(a) *The limitation*—(1) *General rule.* The amount of soil and water conservation expenditures which the taxpayer may deduct under section 175 in any one taxable year is limited to 25 percent of his "gross income from farming".

(2) *Definition of "gross income from farming".* For the purpose of section 175, the term "gross income from farming" means the gross income of the taxpayer, derived in "the business of farming" as defined in § 1.175-3, from the production of crops, fruits, or other agricultural products, including fish, or from livestock (including livestock held for draft, breeding, or dairy purposes). It includes such income from land used in farming other than that upon which expenditures are made for soil or water conservation or for the prevention or erosion of land. It does not include gains from sales of assets such as farm machinery or gains from the disposition of land. A taxpayer shall compute his "gross income from

farming" in accordance with his accounting method used in determining gross income. (See the regulations under section 61 relating to accounting methods used by farmers in determining gross income.) The provisions of this subparagraph may be illustrated by the following example:

Example. A, who uses the cash receipts and disbursements method of accounting, includes in his "gross income from farming" for purposes of determining the 25-percent limitation the following items:

Proceeds from sale of his 1955 yield of corn	$10,000
Gain from disposition of old breeding cows replaced by younger cows	500
Total gross income from farming	10,500

A must exclude from "gross income from farming" the following items which are included in his gross income:

Gain from sale of tractor	$ 100
Gain from sale of 40 acres of taxpayer's farm	8,000
Interest on loan to neighboring farmer	100

(3) *Deduction qualifies for net operating loss deduction.* Any amount allowed as a deduction under section 175, either for the year in which the expenditure is paid or incurred or for the year to which it is carried, is taken into account in computing a net operating loss for such taxable year. If a deduction for soil or water conservation expenditures has been taken into account in computing a net operating loss carryback or carryover, it shall not be considered a soil or water conservation expenditure for the year to which the loss is carried, and therefore, is not subject to the 25-percent limitation for that year. The provisions of this subparagraph may be illustrated by the following example:

Example. Assume that in 1956 A has gross income from farming of $4,000, soil and water conservation expenditures of $1,600, and deductible farm expenses of $3,500. Of the soil and water conservation expenditures, $1,000 is deductible in 1956. The $600 in excess of 25 percent of A's gross income from farming is carried over into 1957. Assuming that A has no other income, his deductions of $4,500 ($1,000 pluc $3,500) exceed his gross income of $4,000 by $500. This $500 will constitute a net operating loss which he must carry back two years and carry forward five years, until it has offset $500 of taxable income. No part of this $500 net operating loss carryback or carryover will be taken into account in determining the amount of soil and water conservation expenditures in the years to which it is carried.

Reg. § 1.175-5(a)(1)

(b) *Carryover of expenditures in excess of deduction.* The deduction for soil and water conservation expenditures in any one taxable year is limited to 25 percent of the taxpayer's gross income from farming. The taxpayer may carry over the excess of such expenditures over 25 percent of his gross income from farming into his next taxable year, and, if not deductible in that year, into the next year, and so on without limit as to time. In determining the deductible amount of such expenditures for any taxable year, the actual expenditures of that year shall be added to any such expenditures carried over from prior years, before applying the 25-percent limitation. Any such expenditures in excess of the deductible amount may be carried over during the taxpayer's entire existence. For this purpose in a farm partnership, since the 25-percent limitation is applied to each partner, not the partnership, the carryover may be carried forward during the life of the partner. The provisions of this paragraph may be illustrated by the following example:

Example. Assume the expenditures and income shown in the following table:

Year	Paid or incurred during taxable year	Carried forward from prior year	Total	25 percent of gross income from farming	Excess to be carried forward
	Deductible soil and water conservation expenditures				
1954	$ 900	None	$ 900	$ 800	$ 100
1955	1,000	$ 100	1,100	900	200
1956	None	200	200	1,000	None

The deduction for 1954 is limited to $800. The remainder, $100 ($900 minus $800), not being deductible for 1954, is a carryover to 1955. For 1955, accordingly, the total of the expenditures to be taken into account is $1,100 (the $100 carryover and the $1,000 actually paid in that year). The deduction for 1955 is limited to $900, and the remainder of the $1,100 total, or $200, is a carryover to 1956. The deduction for 1956 consists solely of this carryover of $200. Since the total expenditures, actual and carried-over, for 1956 are less than 25 percent of gross income from farming, there is no carryover into 1957. [Reg. § 1.175-5.]

☐ [*T.D.* 6235, 5-31-57. *Amended by T.D.* 6649, 4-17-63.]

[Reg. § 1.175-6]

§ 1.175-6. Adoption or change of method.—
(a) *Adoption without consent.* A taxpayer may, without consent, adopt the method of treating expenditures for soil or water conservation as expenses for the first taxable year:

(1) Which begins after December 31, 1953, and ends after August 16, 1954, and

(2) For which soil or water conservation expenditures described in section 175(a) are paid or incurred.

Such adoption shall be made by claiming the deduction on his income tax return. For a taxable year ending prior to May 31, 1957, the adoption of the method described in section 175 shall be made by claiming the deduction on such return for that year, or by claiming the deduction on an amended return filed for that year on or before August 30, 1957.

(b) *Adoption with consent.* A taxpayer may adopt the method of treating soil and water conservation expenditures as provided by section 175 for any taxable year to which the section is applicable if consent is obtained from the district director for the internal revenue district in which the taxpayer's return is required to be filed.

(c) *Change of method.* A taxpayer who has adopted the method of treating expenditures for soil or water conservation, as provided by section 175, may change from this method and capitalize such expenditures made after the effective date of the change, if he obtains the consent of the district director for the internal revenue district in which his return is required to be filed.

(d) *Request for consent to adopt or change method.* Where the consent of the district director is required under paragraph (b) or (c) of this section, the request for his consent shall be in writing, signed by the taxpayer or his authorized representative, and shall be filed not later than the date prescribed by law for filing the income tax return for the first taxable year to which the adoption of, or change of, method is to apply, or not later than August 20, 1957, following their adoption, whichever is later. The request shall:

(1) Set forth the name and address of the taxpayer;

(2) Designate the first taxable year to which the method or change of method is to apply;

(3) State whether the method or change of method is intended to apply to all expenditures

Reg. § 1.175-6(d)(3)

within the permissible scope of section 175, or only to a particular project or farm and, if the latter, include such information as will identify the project or farm as to which the method or change of method is to apply;

(4) Set forth the amount of all soil and water conservation expenditures paid or incurred during the first taxable year for which the method or change of method is to apply; and

(5) State that the taxpayer will make an accounting segregation in his books and records of the expenditures to which the election relates.

(e) *Scope of method.* Except with the consent of the district director as provided in paragraph (b) or (c) of this section, the taxpayer's method of treating soil and water conservation expenditures described in section 175 shall apply to all such expenditures for the taxable year of adoption and all subsequent taxable years. Although a taxpayer may have elected to deduct soil and water conservation expenditures, he may request an authorization to capitalize his soil and water conservation expenditures attributable to a special project or single farm. Similarly, a taxpayer who has not elected to deduct such expenditures may request an authorization to deduct his soil and water conservation expenditures attributable to a special project or single farm. The authorization with respect to the special project or single farm will not affect the method adopted with respect to the taxpayer's regularly incurred soil and water conservation expenditures. No adoption of, or change of, the method under section 175 will be permitted as to expenditures actually paid or incurred before the taxable year to which the method or change of method is to apply. Thus, if a taxpayer adopts such method for 1956, he cannot deduct any part of such expenditures which he capitalized, or should have capitalized, in 1955. Likewise, if a taxpayer who has adopted such method has an unused carryover of such expenditures in excess of the 25-percent limitation, and is granted consent to capitalize soil and water conservation expenditures beginning in 1956, he cannot capitalize any part of the unused carryover. The excess expenditures carried over continue to be deductible to the extent of 25 percent of the taxpayer's gross income from farming. No adjustment to the basis of land shall be made under section 1016 for expenditures to which the method under section 175 applies. For example, A has an unused carryover of soil and water conservation expenditures amounting to $5,000 as of December 31, 1956. On January 1, 1957, A sells his farm and goes out of the business of farming. The unused carryover of $5,000 cannot be added to the basis of the farm for purposes of determining gain or loss on its sale. In 1959, A purchases another farm and resumes the business of farming. In such year, A may deduct the amount of the unused carryover to the extent of 25 percent of his gross income from farming and may carry over any excess to subsequent years. [Reg. § 1.175-6.]

☐ [*T.D.* 6235, 5-31-57.]

[Reg. § 1.175-7]

§ 1.175-7. Allocation of expenditures in certain circumstances.—(a) *General rule.* If at the time the taxpayer paid or incurred expenditures for the purpose of soil or water conservation, or for the prevention of erosion of land, it was reasonable to believe that such expenditures would directly and substantially benefit land of the taxpayer which does not qualify as "land used in farming", as defined in § 1.175-4, as well as land of the taxpayer which does so qualify, then, for purposes of section 175, only a part of the taxpayer's total expenditures is in respect of "land used in farming".

(b) *Method of allocation.* The part of expenditures allocable to "land used in farming" generally equals the amount which bears the same proportion to the total amount of such expenditures as the area of land of the taxpayer used in farming which it was reasonable to believe would be directly and substantially benefited as a result of the expenditures bears to the total area of land of the taxpayer which it was reasonable to believe would be so benefited. If it is established by clear and convincing evidence that, in the light of all the facts and circumstances, another method of allocation is more reasonable than the method provided in the preceding sentence, the taxpayer may allocate the expenditures under that other method. For purposes of this section, the term "land of the taxpayer" means land with respect to which the taxpayer has title, leasehold, or some other substantial interest.

(c) *Examples.* The provisions of this section may be illustrated by the following examples:

Example (1). A owns a 200-acre tract of land, 80 acres of which qualify as "land used in farming". A makes expenditures for the purpose of soil and water conservation which can reasonably be expected to directly and substantially benefit the entire 200-acre tract. In the absence of clear and convincing evidence that a different allocation is more reasonable, A may deduct 40 percent (80/200) of such expenditures under section 175. The same result would obtain if A had made the expenditures after newly acquiring the tract from a person who had used 80 of the 200 acres in farming immediately prior to A's acquisition.

Reg. § 1.175-7(a)

Example (2). Assume the same facts as in example (1), except that A's expenditures for the purpose of soil and water conservation can reasonably be expected to directly and substantially benefit only the 80 acres which qualify as land used in farming; any benefit to the other 120 acres would be minor and incidental. A may deduct all of such expenditures under section 175.

Example (3). Assume the same facts as in example (1), except that A's expenditures for the purpose of soil and water conservation can reasonably be expected to directly and substantially benefit only the 120 acres which do not qualify as land used in farming. A may not deduct any of such expenditures under section 175. The same result would obtain even if A had leased the 200-acre tract to B in the expectation that B would farm the entire tract. [Reg. § 1.175-7.]

☐ [*T.D. 7740,* 11-21-80.]

[Reg. § 1.177-1]

§ 1.177-1. Election to amortize trademark and trade name expenditures.—(a) *In general.*—(1) Section 177 provides that a taxpayer may elect to treat any trademark or trade name expenditure (defined in section 177(b) and paragraph (b) of this section) paid or incurred during a taxable year beginning after December 31, 1955, as a deferred expense. Any expenditure so treated shall be allowed as a deduction ratably over the number of continuous months (not less than 60) selected by the taxpayer, beginning with the first month of the taxable year in which the expenditure is paid or incurred. The term "paid or incurred", as used in section 177 and this section, is to be construed according to the method of accounting used by the taxpayer in computing taxable income. See section 77C1(a)(25). An election under section 177 is irrevocable insofar as it applies to a particular trademark or trade name expenditure, but separate elections may be made with respect to other trademark or trade name expenditures. See subparagraph (3) of this paragraph. See also paragraph (c) of this section for time and manner of making election.

(2) The number of continuous months selected by the taxpayer may be equal to or greater, but not less, than 60, but in any event the deduction must begin with the first month of the taxable year in which the expenditure is paid or incurred. The number of months selected by the taxpayer at the time he makes the election may not be subsequently changed but shall be adhered to in computing taxable income for the taxable year for which the election is made and all subsequent taxable years.

(3) Section 177 permits an election by the taxpayer for each separate trademark or trade name expenditure. Thus, a taxpayer who has several trademark or trade name expenditures in a taxable year may elect under section 177 with respect to some of such expenditures and not elect with respect to the other expenditures. Also, a taxpayer may choose different amortization periods for different trademark or trade name expenditures with respect to which he has made the election under section 177.

(4) All trademark and trade name expenditures are properly chargeable to capital account for purposes of section 1016(a)(1), relating to adjustments to basis of property, whether or not they are to be amortized under section 177. However, the trademark and trade name expenditures with respect to which the taxpayer has made an election under section 177 must be kept in a separate account in the taxpayer's books and records. See paragraph (c) of this section. See also section 1016(a)(16) and paragraph (m) of § 1.1016-5 for adjustments to basis of property for amounts allowed as deductions under section 177 and this section.

(b) *Trademark and trade name expenditures defined.* (1) The term "trademark and trade name expenditure", as used in section 177 and this section, means any expenditure which—

(i) Is directly connected with the acquisition, protection, expansion, registration (Federal, State, or foreign), or defense of a trademark or trade name;

(ii) Is chargeable to capital account; and

(iii) Is not part of the consideration or purchase price paid for a trademark, trade name, or a business (including goodwill) already in existence.

An expenditure which fails to meet one or more of these tests is not a trademark or trade name expenditure for purposes of section 177 and this section. Amounts paid in connection with the acquisition of an existing trademark or trade name may not be amortized under section 177 even though such amounts may be paid to protect or expand a previously owned trademark or trade name through purchase of a competitive trademark. Similarly, the provisions of section 177 and this section are not applicable to expenditures paid or incurred for an agreement to discontinue the use of a trademark or trade name (if the effect of the agreement is the purchase of a trademark or trade name) nor to expenditures paid or incurred in acquiring franchises or rights to the use of a trademark or trade name. Generally, section 177 will apply to expenditures such as legal fees and other costs in connection with the acquisition

Reg. § 1.177-1(b)

of a certificate of registration of a trademark from the United States or other government, artists' fees and similar expenses connected with the design of a distinctive mark for a product or service, litigation expenses connected with infringement proceedings, and costs in connection with the preparation and filing of an application for renewal of registration and continued use of a trademark.

(2) Expenditures for a trademark or trade name which has a determinable useful life and which would otherwise be depreciable under section 167 must be deferred and amortized under section 177 if an election under section 177 is made with respect to such expenditures.

(3) The following examples illustrate the application of section 177:

Example (1). X Corporation engages an artist to design a distinctive trademark for its product. At the same time it retains an attorney to prepare the papers necessary for registration of this trademark with the Federal Government. The fees of both the artist and the attorney may be amortized under section 177 over a period of not less than 60 continuous months.

Example (2). Y Corporation wishes to expand the market served by its product. It acquires a competing firm in a neighboring State. The contract of sale provides for a purchase price of $250,000 of which $225,000 shall constitute payment for physical assets and $25,000 for the trademark and goodwill. No part of the purchase price may be amortized under section 177.

Example (3). M Corporation brings suit against N Corporation for infringement of M's trademark. The costs of this litigation may be amortized under section 177.

(c) *Time and manner of making election.* (1) A taxpayer who elects to defer and amortize any trademark or trade name expenditure paid or incurred during a taxable year beginning after December 31, 1955, shall, within the time prescribed by law (including extensions thereof) for filing his income tax return for that year, attach to his income tax return a statement signifying his election under section 177 and setting forth the following:

(i) Name and address of the taxpayer, and the taxable year involved;

(ii) An identification of the character and amount of each expenditure to which the election applies and the number of continuous months (not less than 60) during which the expenditures are to be ratably deducted; and

(iii) A declaration by the taxpayer that he will make an accounting segregation on his books

and records of the trademark and trade name expenditures for which the election has been made, sufficient to permit an identification of the character and amount of each such expenditure and the amortization period selected for each expenditure.

(2) The provisions of subparagraph (1) of this paragraph shall apply to income tax returns and statements required to be filed after May 4, 1960. Elections properly made in accordance with the provisions of Treasury Decision 6209, approved October 26, 1956 (21 F.R. 8319, C.B. 1956-2, 1370), continue in effect. [Reg. § 1.177-1.]

☐ [*T.D.* 6452, 2-3-60.]

[Reg. § 1.178-1]

§ 1.178-1. Depreciation or amortization of improvements on leased property and cost of acquiring a lease.—(a) *In general.* Section 178 provides rules for determining the amount of the deduction allowable for any taxable year to a lessee for depreciation or amortization of improvements made on leased property and as amortization of the cost of acquiring a lease. For purposes of section 178 the term "depreciation" means the deduction allowable for exhaustion, wear and tear, or obsolescence under provisions of the Code such as section 167 or 611 and the regulations thereunder and the term "amortization" means the deduction allowable for amortization of buildings or other improvements made on leased property or for amortization of the cost of acquiring a lease under provisions of the Code such as section 162 or 212 and the regulations thereunder. The provisions of section 178 are applicable with respect to costs of acquiring a lease incurred, and improvements begun, after July 28, 1958, other than improvements which, on July 28, 1958, and at all times thereafter, the lessee was under a binding legal obligation to make.

(b) *Determination of amount of deduction.* (1) In determining the amount of the deduction allowable to a lessee (other than a lessee who is related to the lessor within the meaning of § 1.178-2) for any taxable year for depreciation or amortization of improvements made on leased property, or for amortization in respect of the cost of acquiring a lease, the term of the lease shall, except as provided in subparagraph (2) of this paragraph, be treated as including all periods for which the lease may be renewed, extended, or continued pursuant to an option or options exercisable by the lessee (whether or not specifically provided for in the lease) if—

(i) In the case of any building erected, or other improvements made, by the lessee on the leased property, the portion of the term of the lease (excluding all periods for which the lease may subsequently be renewed, extended, or continued pursuant to an option or options exercisable by the lessee) remaining upon the completion of such building or other improvements is less than 60 percent of the estimated useful life of such building or other improvements; or

(ii) In the case of any cost of acquiring the lease, less than 75 percent of such cost is attributable to the portion of the term of the lease (excluding all periods for which the lease may be renewed, extended, or continued pursuant to an option or options exercisable by the lessee) remaining on the date of its acquisition.

(2) The rules provided in subparagraph (1) of this paragraph shall not apply if the lessee establishes that, as of the close of the taxable year, it is more probable that the lease will not be renewed, extended, or continued than that the lease will be renewed, extended, or continued. In such case, the cost of improvements made on leased property or the cost of acquiring a lease shall be amortized over the remaining term of the lease without regard to any options exercisable by the lessee to renew, extend, or continue the lease. The probability test referred to in the first sentence of this subparagraph shall be applicable to each option period to which the lease may be renewed, extended, or continued. The establishment by a lessee as of the close of the taxable year that it is more probable that the lease will not be renewed, extended, or continued will ordinarily be effective as of the close of such taxable year and any subsequent taxable year, and the deduction for amortization will be based on the term of the lease without regard to any periods for which the lease may be renewed, extended, or continued pursuant to an option or options exercisable by the lessee. However, in appropriate cases, if the facts as of the close of any subsequent taxable year indicate that it is more probable that the lease will be renewed, extended, or continued, the deduction for amortization (or depreciation) shall, beginning with the first day of such subsequent taxable year, be determined by including in the remaining term of the lease all periods for which it is more probable that the lease will be renewed, extended, or continued.

(3) If at any time the remaining term of the lease determined in accordance with section 178 and this section is equal to or of longer duration than the then estimated useful life of the improvements made on the leased property by the lessee, the cost of such improvements shall be depreciated over the estimated useful life of such improvements under the provisions of section 167 and the regulations thereunder.

(4) For purposes of section 178(a)(1) and this section, the date on which the building erected or other improvements made are completed is the date on which the building or improvements are usable whether or not used.

(5) (i) For purposes of section 178(a)(2) and this section, the portion of the cost of acquiring a lease which is attributable to the term of the lease remaining on the date of its acquisition without regard to options exercisable by the lessee to renew, extend, or continue the lease shall be determined on the basis of the facts and circumstances of each case. In some cases, it may be appropriate to determine such portion of the cost of acquiring a lease by applying the principles used to measure the present value of an annuity. Where that method is used, such portion shall be determined by multiplying the cost of the lease by a fraction, the numerator comprised of a factor representing the present value of an annually recurring savings of $1 per year for the period of the remaining term of the lease (without regard to options to renew, extend, or continue the lease) at an appropriate rate of interest (determined on the basis of all the facts and circumstances in each case), and the denominator comprised of a factor representing the present value of $1 per year for the period of the remaining term of the lease including the options to renew, extend, or continue the lease at an appropriate rate of interest.

(ii) The provisions of this subparagraph may be illustrated by the following example:

Example. Lessee A acquires a lease with respect to unimproved property at a cost of $100,000 at which time there are 21 years remaining in the original term of the lease with two renewal options of 21 years each. The lease provides for a uniform annual rental for the remaining term of the lease and the renewal periods. It has been determined that this is an appropriate case for the application of the principles used to measure the present value of an annuity. Assume that in this case appropriate rate of interest is 5 percent. By applying the tables (Inwood) used to measure the present value of an annuity of $1 per year the factor representing the present value of $1 per annum for 21 years at 5% is ascertained to be 12.821, and the factor representing the present value of $1 per annum for 63 years at 5% is 19.075. The portion of the cost of the lease ($100,000) attributable to the remaining term of the original lease (21 years)

is 67.21% or $67,210 determined as follows: $\dfrac{12.821}{19.075}$ or 67.21%.

Reg. § 1.178-1(b)(5)

(6) The provisions of this paragraph may be illustrated by the following examples:

Example (1). Lessee A constructs a building on land leased from lessor B. The construction is commenced on August 1, 1958, and is completed and placed in service on December 31, 1958, at which time A has 15 years remaining on his lease with an option to renew for an additional 20 years. Lessee A computes his taxable income on a calendar year basis. Lessee A was not, on July 28, 1958, under a binding legal obligation to erect the building. The building has an estimated useful life of 30 years. A is not related to B. Since the portion of the term of the lease (without regard to any renewals) remaining upon completion of the building (15 years) is less than 60 percent of the estimated useful life of the building (60 percent of 30 years, or 18 years), the term of the lease shall be treated as including the remaining portion of the original lease period and the renewal period, or 35 years. Since the estimated useful life of the building (30 years) is less than 35 years, the cost of the building shall, in accord with paragraph (b)(3) of this section, be depreciated under the provisions of section 167, over its estimated useful life. If, however, lessee A establishes, as of the close of the taxable year 1958, it is more probable that the lease will not be renewed than that it will be renewed, then in such case the remaining term of the lease shall be treated as including only the 15-year period remaining in the original lease. Since this is less than the estimated useful life of the building, the remaining cost of the building would be amortized over such 15-year period under the provisions of section 162 and the regulations thereunder.

Example (2). Assume the same facts as in example (1), except that A has 21 years remaining on his lease with an option to renew for an additional 10 years. Section 178(a) and paragraph (b)(1) of this section do not apply since the term of the lease remaining on the date of completion of the building (21 years) is not less than 60 percent of the estimated useful life of the building (60 percent of 30 years, or 18 years).

Example (3). Assume the same facts as in example (1), except that A has no renewal option until July 1, 1961, when lessor B grants A an option to renew the lease for a 10-year period. Because there is no option to renew the lease, the term of the lease is, for the taxable years 1959 and 1960 and for the first six months of the taxable year 1961, determined without regard to section 178(a). However, as of July 1, 1961, the date the renewal option is granted, section 178(a) and paragraph (b)(1) of this section become applicable since the portion of the term of the lease remain-

ing upon completion of the building (15 years) was less than 60 percent of the estimated useful life of the building (60 percent of 30 years, or 18 years). As of July 1, 1961, the term of the lease shall be treated as including the remaining portion of the original lease period (12½ years) and the 10-year renewal period, of 22½ years, unless lessee A can establish that, as of the close of 1961, it is more probable that the lease will not be renewed than that it will be.

Example (4). On January 1, 1959, lessee A pays $10,000 to acquire a lease for 20 years with two options exercisable by him to renew for periods of 5 years each. Of the total $10,000 cost to acquire the lease, $7,000 was paid for the original 20-year lease period and the balance of $3,000 was paid for the renewal options. Since the $7,000 cost of acquiring the initial lease is less than 75 percent of the $10,000 cost of the lease ($7,500), the term of the lease shall be treated as including the original lease period and the 2 renewal periods, or 30 years. However, if lessee A establishes that, as of the close of the taxable year 1959, it is more probable that the lease will not be renewed than that it will be renewed, the term of the lease shall be treated as including only the original lease period, or 20 years.

Example (5). Assume the same facts as in example (4), except that the portion of the total cost ($10,000) paid for the 20-year original lease period is $8,000. Since the $8,000 cost of acquiring the original lease is not less than 75 percent of the $10,000 cost of the lease ($7,500), section 178(a) and paragraph (b)(1) of this section do not apply.

(c) *Application of section 178(a) where lessee gives notice to lessor of intention to exercise option.* (1) If the lessee has given notice to the lessor of his intention to renew, extend, or continue a lease, the lessee shall, for purposes of applying the provisions of section 178(a) and paragraph (b)(1) of this section, take into account such renewal or extension in determining the portion of the term of the lease remaining upon the completion of the improvements or on the date of the acquisition of the lease.

(2) The application of the provisions of this paragraph may be illustrated by the following examples:

Example (1). Lessee A constructs a building on land leased from lessor B. The construction was commenced on September 1, 1958, and was completed and placed in service on December 31, 1958. Lessee A was not, on July 28, 1958, under a binding legal obligation to erect the building. A and B are not related. At the time the building was completed (December 31, 1958), lessee A had

3 years remaining on his lease with 2 options to renew for periods of 20 years each. The estimated useful life of the building is 50 years. Prior to completion of the building, lessee A gives notice to lessor B of his intention to exercise the first 20-year option. Therefore, the portion of the term of the lease remaining on January 1, 1959, shall be the 3 years remaining in the original lease period plus the 20-year renewal period, or 23 years. Since the term of the lease remaining upon completion of the building (23 years) is less than 60 percent of the estimated useful life of the building (60 percent of 50 years, or 30 years), the provisions of section 178(a) and paragraph (b)(1) of this section are applicable. Accordingly, the term of the lease shall be treated as including the aggregate of the remaining term of the original lease (23 years) and the second 20-year renewal period or 43 years, unless lessee A establishes that it is more probable that the lease will not be renewed, extended, or continued under the second 20-year option than that it will be so renewed, extended, or continued under such option. If this is established by lessee A, then the term of the lease shall be treated as including only the remaining portion of the original lease period and the first 20-year renewal period, or 23 years.

Example (2). Assume the same facts as in example (1), except that the estimated useful life of the building is 30 years. Since the term of the lease remaining upon completion of the building (23 years) is not less than 60 percent of the estimated life of the building (60 percent of 30 years, or 18 years), the provisions of section 178(a) and paragraph (b)(1) of this section do not apply.

Example (3). If in examples (1) and (2), the lessee failed to give notice of his intention to exercise the renewal option, the renewal period would not be taken into account in computing the percentage requirements under section 178(a) and paragraph (b)(1) of this section. Thus, unless lessee A establishes the required probability, the provisions of section 178(a) and paragraph (b)(1) of this section would apply in both examples since the term of the lease remaining upon completion of the building (3 years) is less than 60 percent of the estimated useful life of the building in either example (60 percent of 50 years, or 30 years; 60 percent of 30 years, or 18 years).

(d) *Application of section 178 where lessee is related to lessor.*—(1) (i) If the lessee and lessor are related persons within the meaning of section 178(b)(2) and § 1.178-2 at any time during the taxable year, the lease shall be treated as including a period of not less duration than the remaining estimated useful life of improvements made by the lessee on leased property for purposes of determining the amount of deduction allowable to the lessee for such taxable year for depreciation or amortization in respect of any building erected or other improvements made on leased property. If the lessee and lessor cease to be related persons during any taxable year, then for the immediately following and subsequent taxable years during which they continue to be unrelated, the amount allowable to the lessee as a deduction shall be determined without reference to section 178(b) and in accordance with section 178(a) or section 178(c) whichever is applicable.

(ii) Although the related lessee and lessor rule of section 178(b) and § 1.178-2 does not apply in determining the period over which the cost of acquiring a lease may be amortized, the relationship between a lessee and lessor will be a significant factor in applying section 178(a) and (c) in cases in which the lease may be renewed, extended, or continued pursuant to an option or options exercisable by the lessee.

(2) The application of the provisions of this paragraph may be illustrated by the following examples:

Example (1). Lessee A constructs a building on land leased from lessor B. The construction was commenced on August 1, 1958, and was completed and put in service on December 31, 1958. Lessee A was not on July 28, 1958, under a binding legal obligation to erect the building. On the completion date of the building, lessee A had 20 years remaining in his original lease period with an option to renew for an additional 20 years The building has an estimated useful life of 50 years. During the taxable years 1959 and 1960, A and B are related persons within the meaning of section 178(b)(2) and § 1.178-2, but they are not related persons at any time during the taxable year 1961 or during any subsequent taxable year. Since A and B are related persons during the taxable years 1959 and 1960, the term of the lease shall, for each of those years, be treated as 50 years. Section 178(a) and paragraph (b)(1) of this section become applicable in the taxable year 1961 since A and B are not related persons at any time during that year and because the portion of the original lease period remaining at the time the building was completed (20 years) is less than 60 percent of the estimated useful life of the building (60 percent of 50 years, or 30 years). Thus, the term of the lease shall, beginning on January 1, 1961, be treated as including the remaining portion of the original lease period (18 years) and the renewal period (20 years), or 38 years, unless lessee A can establish that, as of the close of the taxable year 1961 or any subsequent taxable year, it is more probable that the lease will not be renewed than that it will be renewed.

Example (2). Assume the same facts as in example (1), except that the estimated useful life of the building is 30 years. During the taxable years 1959 and 1960, the term of the lease shall be treated as 30 years. For the taxable year 1961, however, neither section 178(a) nor section 178(b) apply since the percentage requirement of section 178(a) and paragraph (b) of this section are not satisfied and A and B are not related persons within the meaning of section 178(b)(2) and § 1.178-2. [Reg. § 1.178-1.]

☐ [*T.D.* 6520, 12-23-60.]

[Reg. § 1.178-2]

§ **1.178-2. Related lessee and lessor.**—(a) For purposes of section 178 and § 1.178-1, a lessor and lessee shall be considered to be related persons if—

(1) The lessor and lessee are members of an affiliated group, as defined in section 1504 and the regulations thereunder; or

(2) The relationship between the lessor and lessee is one described in section 267(b), except that the phrase "80 percent or more" shall be substituted for the phrase "more than 50 percent" wherever such phrase appears in section 267(b).

(b) In the application of section 267(b) for purposes of section 178, the rules provided in section 267(c) shall apply, except that the family of an individual shall include only his spouse, ancestors, and lineal descendants. Thus, if the lessee is the brother or sister of the lessor, the lessee and lessor will not be considered to be related persons for purposes of section 178 and § 1.178-1. If the lessor leases property to a corporation of which he owns 80 percent or more in value of the outstanding stock, the lessor and lessee shall be considered to be related persons. On the other hand, if the lessor leases property to a corporation of which he owns less than 80 percent in value of the outstanding stock and his brother owns the remaining stock, the lessor and lessee will not be considered to be related persons.

(c) If a relationship described in section 267(b) exists independently of family status, the brother-sister exception does not apply. For example, if the lessor leases property to the fiduciary of a trust of which he is the grantor, the lessor and lessee will be considered to be related persons for purposes of section 178. This result obtains whether or not the fiduciary is the brother or sister of the lessor since the disqualifying relationship exists because of the grantor-fiduciary status and not because of family status. [Reg. § 1.178-2.]

☐ [*T.D.* 6520, 12-23-60.]

[Reg. § 1.178-3]

§ **1.178-3. Reasonable certainty test.**—(a) In any case in which neither section 178(a) nor (b) applies, the determination as to the amount of the deduction allowable to a lessee for any taxable year for depreciation or amortization in respect of any building erected, or other improvements made, on leased property, or in respect of any cost of acquiring a lease, shall be made with reference to the original term of the lease (excluding any period for which the lease may subsequently be renewed, extended, or continued pursuant to an option exercisable by the lessee) unless the lease has been renewed, extended, or continued, or the facts show with reasonable certainty that the lease will be renewed, extended, or continued. In a case in which the facts show with reasonable certainty that the lease will be renewed, extended, or continued, the term of the lease shall, beginning with the taxable year in which such reasonable certainty is shown, be treated as including the period or periods for which it is reasonably certain that the lease will be renewed, extended, or continued. If the lessee has given notice to the lessor of his intention to renew, extend, or continue a lease, the lease shall be considered as renewed, extended, or continued for the periods specified in the notice. See paragraph (c) of § 1.178-1.

(b) The reasonable certainty test is applicable to each option to which the lease is subject. Thus, in a case of two successive options, the facts in a particular taxable year may show with reasonable certainty that the lease will be renewed pursuant to an exercise of only the first option; and, beginning with such year, the term of the lease will be treated as including the first option, but not the second. If in a subsequent taxable year the facts show with reasonable certainty that the second option will also be exercised, the term of the lease shall, beginning with such subsequent taxable year, be treated as including both options. Although the related lessee and lessor rule of section 178(b) and paragraph (d) of § 1.178-1 does not apply in determining the period over which the cost of acquiring a lease may be amortized, the relationship between the lessee and lessor will be a significant factor in determining whether the "reasonable certainty" rule of section 178(c) and this section applies.

(c) The application of the provisions of this section may be illustrated by the following examples:

Example (1). Corporation A leases land from lessor B for a period of 30 years beginning with January 1, 1958. Corporation A and lessor B are

Reg. § 1.178-2(a)(1)

not related persons. The lease provides that Corporation A will have two renewal options of 5 years each at the same annual rental as specified in the lease for the initial 30 years. Corporation A constructs a factory building on the leased land at a cost of $100,000. Corporation A was not, on July 28, 1958, under a binding legal obligation to erect the building. The construction was commenced on August 1, 1958, and was completed and placed in service on December 31, 1958. On January 1, 1959, Corporation A has 29 years remaining in the initial term of the lease. The estimated useful life of the building on January 1, 1959, is 40 years. The location of the leased property is particularly suitable for Corporation A's business and the annual rental of the property is lower than A would have to pay for other suitable property. No facts are present which establish that these conditions will not continue to exist beyond initial term of the lease. Since the period remaining in the initial term of the lease on January 1, 1959 (29 years) is not less than 60 percent of the estimated useful life of the building (60 percent of 40 years, or 24 years), the provisions of section 178(a) and paragraph (b)(1) of § 1.178-1 do not apply, and since Corporation A and lessor B are not related, section 178(b) and paragraph (d) of § 1.178-1 do not apply. However, since the facts show with reasonable certainty that Corporation A will renew the lease for the period of the two options (10 years), the cost of the building shall be amortized over the term of the lease, including the two renewal options, or 39 years.

Example (2). Assume the same facts as in example (1), except that a term of 30 years is the longest period that lessor B is willing to lease the unimproved property; that there was no agreement that Corporation A will have any renewal options; and that any other location would be as suitable for Corporation A's business as the leased property. Since the facts do not show with reasonable certainty that the initial term of the lease will be renewed, extended, or continued, Corporation A shall amortize the cost of the building over the remaining term of the lease, or 29 years. [Reg. § 1.178-3.]

□ [*T.D.* 6520, 12-23-60.]

[Reg. § 1.179-0]

§ **1.179-0. Table of contents.**—This section lists captioned paragraphs contained in §§ 1.179-1 through 1.179-6.

§ 1.179-1. Election to expense certain depreciable assets.

§ 1.179-2. Limitations on amount subject to section 179 election.

Reg. § 1.179-0

(ii) Example.

(7) Component members of a controlled group.

(i) In general.

(ii) Statement to be filed.

(iii) Revocation.

(c) Taxable income limitation.

(1) In general.

(2) Application to partnerships and partners.

(i) In general.

(ii) Taxable year.

(iii) Example.

(iv) Taxable income of a partnership.

(v) Partner's share of partnership taxable income.

(3) S corporations and S corporation shareholders.

(i) In general.

(ii) Taxable income of an S corporation.

(iii) Shareholder's share of S corporation taxable income.

(4) Taxable income of a corporation other than an S corporation.

(5) Ordering rule for certain circular problems.

(i) In general.

(ii) Example.

(6) Active conduct by the taxpayer of a trade or business.

(i) Trade or business.

(ii) Active conduct.

(iii) Example.

(iv) Employees.

(7) Joint returns.

(i) In general.

(ii) Joint returns filed after separate returns.

(8) Married individuals filing separately.

(d) Examples.

§ 1.179-3. Carryover of disallowed deduction.

(a) In general.

(b) Deduction of carryover of disallowed deduction.

(1) In general.

(2) Cross references.

(c) Unused section 179 expense allowance.

(d) Example.

(e) Recordkeeping requirement and ordering rule.

(f) Dispositions and other transfers of section 179 property.

(1) In general.

(2) Recapture under section 179(d)(10).

(g) Special rules for partnerships and S corporations.

(1) In general.

(2) Basis adjustment.

(3) Dispositions and other transfers of section 179 property by a partnership or an S corporation.

(4) Example.

(h) Special rules for partners and S corporation shareholders.

(1) In general.

(2) Dispositions and other transfers of a partner's interest in a partnership or a shareholder's interest in an S corporation.

(3) Examples.

§ 1.179-4. Definitions.

(a) Section 179 property.

(b) Section 38 property.

(c) Purchase.

(d) Cost.

(e) Placed in service.

(f) Controlled group of corporations and component member of controlled group.

§ 1.179-5. Time and manner of making election.

(a) Election.

(b) Revocation.

§ 1.179-6. Effective date.

[Reg. § 1.179-0.]

□ [T.D. 8455, 12-23-92.]

[Reg. § 1.179-1]

§ 1.179-1. Election to expense certain depreciable assets.—(a) In general. Section 179(a) allows a taxpayer to elect to expense the cost (as defined in § 1.179-4(d)), or a portion of the cost, of section 179 property (as defined in § 1.179-4(a)) for the taxable year in which the property is placed in service (as defined in § 1.179-4(e)). The election is not available for trusts, estates, and certain noncorporate lessors. See paragraph (i)(2) of this section for rules concerning noncorporate lessors. However, section 179(b) provides certain limitations on the amount that a taxpayer may elect to expense in any one taxable year. See §§ 1.179-2 and 1.179-3 for rules relating to the dollar and taxable income limitations and the carryover of disallowed deduction rules. For rules describing the time and manner of making an

Reg. § 1.179-1(a)

election under section 179, see § 1.179-5. For the effective date, see § 1.179-6.

(b) *Cost subject to expense.* The expense deduction under section 179 is allowed for the entire cost or a portion of the cost of one or more items of section 179 property. This expense deduction is subject to the limitations of section 179(b) and § 1.179-2. The taxpayer may select the properties that are subject to the election as well as the portion of each property's cost to expense.

(c) *Proration not required*—(1) *In general.* The expense deduction under section 179 is determined without any proration based on—

(i) The period of time the section 179 property has been in service during the taxable year; or

(ii) The length of the taxable year in which the property is placed in service.

(2) *Example.* The following example illustrates the provisions of paragraph (c)(1) of this section.

Example. On December 1, 1991, X, a calendar-year corporation, purchases and places in service section 179 property costing $20,000. For the taxable year ending December 31, 1991, X may elect to claim a section 179 expense deduction on the property (subject to the limitations imposed under section 179(b)) without proration of its cost for the number of days in 1991 during which the property was in service.

(d) *Partial business use*—(1) *In general.* If a taxpayer uses section 179 property for trade or business as well as other purposes, the portion of the cost of the property attributable to the trade or business use is eligible for expensing under section 179 provided that more than 50 percent of the property's use in the taxable year is for trade or business purposes. The limitations of section 179(b) and § 1.179-2 are applied to the portion of the cost attributable to the trade or business use.

(2) *Example.* The following example illustrates the provisions of paragraph (d)(1) of this section.

Example. A purchases section 179 property costing $10,000 in 1991 for which 80 percent of its use will be in A's trade or business. The cost of the property adjusted to reflect the business use of the property is $8,000 (80 percent × $10,000). Thus, A may elect to expense up to $8,000 of the cost of the property (subject to the limitations imposed under section 179(b) and § 1.179-2).

(3) *Additional rules that may apply.* If a section 179 election is made for "listed property" within the meaning of section 280F(d)(4) and there is personal use of the property, section 280F(d)(1), which provides rules that coordinate sec-

tion 179 with the section 280F limitation on the amount of depreciation, may apply. If section 179 property is no longer predominantly used in the taxpayer's trade or business, paragraphs (e)(1) through (4) of this section, relating to recapture of the section 179 deduction, may apply.

(e) *Change in use; recapture*—(1) *In general.* If a taxpayer's section 179 property is not used predominantly in a trade or business of the taxpayer at any time before the end of the property's recovery period, the taxpayer must recapture in the taxable year in which the section 179 property is not used predominantly in a trade or business any benefit derived from expensing such property. The benefit derived from expensing the property is equal to the excess of the amount expensed under this section over the total amount that would have been allowable for prior taxable years and the taxable year of recapture as a deduction under section 168 (had section 179 not been elected) for the portion of the cost of the property to which the expensing relates (regardless of whether such excess reduced the taxpayer's tax liability). For purposes of the preceding sentence, (i) the "amount expensed under this section" shall not include any amount that was not allowed as a deduction to a taxpayer because the taxpayer's aggregate amount of allowable section 179 expenses exceeded the section 179(b) dollar limitation, and (ii) in the case of an individual who does not elect to itemize deductions under section 63(g) in the taxable year of recapture, the amount allowable as a deduction under section 168 in the taxable year of recapture shall be determined by treating property used in the production of income other than rents or royalties as being property used for personal purposes. The amount to be recaptured shall be treated as ordinary income for the taxable year in which the property is no longer used predominantly in a trade or business of the taxpayer. For taxable years following the year of recapture, the taxpayer's deductions under section 168(a) shall be determined as if no section 179 election with respect to the property had been made. However, see section 280F(d)(1) relating to the coordination of section 179 with the limitation on the amount of depreciation for luxury automobiles and where certain property is used for personal purposes. If the recapture rules of both section 280F(b)(2) and this paragraph (e)(1) apply to an item of section 179 property, the amount of recapture for such property shall be determined only under the rules of section 280F(b)(2).

(2) *Predominant use.* Property will be treated as not used predominantly in a trade or business of the taxpayer if 50 percent or more of the use of such property during any taxable year

within the recapture period is for a use other than in a trade or business of the taxpayer. If during any taxable year of the recapture period the taxpayer disposes of the property (other than in a disposition to which section 1245(a) applies) or ceases to use the property in a trade or business in a manner that had the taxpayer claimed a credit under section 38 for such property such disposition or cessation in use would cause recapture under section 47, the property will be treated as not used in a trade or business of the taxpayer. However, for purposes of applying the recapture rules of section 47 pursuant to the preceding sentence, converting the use of the property from use in a trade or business to use in the production of income will be treated as a conversion to personal use.

(3) *Basis; application with section 1245.* The basis of property with respect to which there is recapture under paragraph (e)(1) of this section shall be increased immediately before the event resulting in such recapture by the amount recaptured. If section 1245(a) applies to a disposition of property, there is no recapture under paragraph (e)(1) of this section.

(4) *Carryover of disallowed deduction.* See § 1.179-3 for rules on applying the recapture provisions of this paragraph (e) when a taxpayer has a carryover of disallowed deduction.

(5) *Example.* The following example illustrates the provisions of paragraphs (e)(1) through (e)(4) of this section.

Example. A, a calendar-year taxpayer, purchases and places in service on January 1, 1991, section 179 property costing $15,000. The property is 5-year property for section 168 purposes and is the only item of depreciable property placed in service by A during 1991. A properly elects to expense $10,000 of the cost and elects under section 168(b)(5) to depreciate the remaining cost under the straight-line method. On January 1, 1992, A converts the property from use in A's business to use for the production of income, and A uses the property in the latter capacity for the entire year. A elects to itemize deductions for 1992. Because the property was not predominantly used in A's trade or business in 1992, A must recapture any benefit derived from expensing the property under section 179. Had A not elected to expense the $10,000 in 1991, A would have been entitled to deduct, under section 168, 10 percent of the $10,000 in 1991, and 20 percent of the $10,000 in 1992. Therefore, A must include $7,000 in ordinary income for the 1992 taxable year, the excess of $10,000 (the section 179 expense amount) over $3,000 (30 percent of $10,000).

(f) *Basis*—(1) *In general.* A taxpayer who elects to expense under section 179 must reduce the depreciable basis of the section 179 property by the amount of the section 179 expense deduction.

(2) *Special rules for partnerships and S. Corporations.*—Generally the basis of a partnership or S corporation's section 179 property must be reduced to reflect the amount of section 179 expense elected by the partnership or S corporation. This reduction must be made in the basis of partnership or S corporation property even if the limitations of section 179(b) and § 1.179-2 prevent a partner in a partnership or a shareholder in an S corporation from deducting all or a portion of the amount of the section 179 expense allocated by the partnership or S corporation. See § 1.179-3 for rules on applying the basis provisions of this paragraph (f) when a person has a carryover of disallowed deduction.

(3) *Special rules with respect to trusts and estates which are partners or S corporation shareholders.* Since the section 179 election is not available for trusts or estates, a partner or S corporation shareholder that is a trust or estate, may not deduct its allocable share of the section 179 expense elected by the partnership or S corporation. The partnership or S corporation's basis in section 179 property shall not be reduced to reflect any portion of the section 179 expense that is allocable to the trust or estate. Accordingly, the partnership or S corporation may claim a depreciation deduction under section 168 or a section 38 credit (if available) with respect to any depreciable basis resulting from the trust or estate's inability to claim its allocable portion of the section 179 expense.

(g) *Disallowance of the section 38 credit.* If a taxpayer elects to expense under section 179, no section 38 credit is allowable for the portion of the cost expensed. In addition, no section 38 credit shall be allowed under section 48(d) to a lessee of property for the portion of the cost of the property that the lessor expensed under section 179.

(h) *Partnerships and S corporations.*—(1) *In general.* In the case of property purchased and placed in service by a partnership or an S corporation, the determination of whether the property is section 179 property is made at the partnership or S corporation level. The election to expense the cost of section 179 property is made by the partnership or the S corporation. See sections 703(b), 1363(c), 6221, 6231(a)(3), 6241, and 6245.

(2) *Example.* The following example illustrates the provisions of paragraph (h)(1) of this section.

Example. A owns certain residential rental property as an investment. A and others form

Reg. § 1.179-1(e)(3)

ABC partnership whose function is to rent and manage such property. A and ABC partnership file their income tax returns on a calendar-year basis. In 1991, ABC partnership purchases and places in service office furniture costing $20,000 to be used in the active conduct of ABC's business. Although the office furniture is used with respect to an investment activity of A, the furniture is being used in the active conduct of ABC's trade or business. Therefore, because the determination of whether property is section 179 property is made at the partnership level, the office furniture is section 179 property and ABC may elect to expense a portion of its cost under section 179.

(i) *Leasing of section 179 property*—(1)*In general*. A lessor of section 179 property who is treated as the owner of the property for Federal tax purposes will be entitled to the section 179 expense deduction if the requirements of section 179 and the regulations thereunder are met. These requirements will not be met if the lessor merely holds the property for the production of income. For certain leases entered prior to January 1, 1984, the safe harbor provisions of section 168(f)(8) apply in determining whether an agreement is treated as a lease for Federal tax purposes.

(2) *Noncorporate lessor*. In determining the class of taxpayers (other than an estate or trust) for which section 179 is applicable, section 179(d)(5) provides that if a taxpayer is a noncorporate lessor (*i.e.*, a person who is not a corporation and is a lessor), the taxpayer shall not be entitled to claim a section 179 expense for section 179 property purchased and leased by the taxpayer unless the taxpayer has satisfied all of the requirements of section 179(d)(5)(A) or (B).

(j) *Application of sections 263 and 263A*. Under section 263(a)(1)(G), expenditures for which a deduction is allowed under section 179 and this section are excluded from capitalization under section 263(a). Under this paragraph (j), amounts allowed as a deduction under section 179 and this section are excluded from the application of the uniform capitalization rules of section 263A.

(k) *Cross references*. See section 453(i) and the regulations thereunder with respect to installment sales of section 179 property. See section 1033(g)(3) and the regulations thereunder relating to the condemnation of outdoor advertising displays. See section 1245(a) and the regulations thereunder with respect to recapture rules for section 179 property. [Reg. § 1.179-1.]

☐ [*T.D.* 8121, 1-5-87. *Amended by T.D.* 8455, 12-23-92.]

[Reg. § 1.179-2]

§ 1.179-2. Limitations on amount subject to section 179 election.—(a) *In general*. Sections 179(b)(1) and (2) limit the aggregate cost of section 179 property that a taxpayer may elect to expense under section 179 for any one taxable year (dollar limitation). See paragraph (b) of this section. Section 179(b)(3)(A) limits the aggregate cost of section 179 property that a taxpayer may deduct in any taxable year (taxable income limitation). See paragraph (c) of this section. Any cost that is elected to be expensed but that is not currently deductible because of the taxable income limitation may be carried forward to the next taxable year (carryover of disallowed deduction). See § 1.179-3 for rules relating to carryovers of disallowed deductions. See also sections 280F(a), (b), and (d)(1) relating to the coordination of section 179 with the limitations on the amount of depreciation for luxury automobiles and other listed property. The dollar and taxable income limitations apply to each taxpayer and not to each trade or business in which the taxpayer has an interest.

(b) *Dollar limitation*—(1) *In general*. The aggregate cost of section 179 property that a taxpayer may elect to expense under section 179 for any taxable year is $10,000, reduced (but not below zero) by the amount of any excess section 179 property (described in paragraph (b)(2) of this section) placed in service during the taxable year.

(2) *Excess section 179 property*. The amount of any excess section 179 property for a taxable year equals the excess (if any) of—

(i) The cost of section 179 property placed in service by the taxpayer in the taxable year; over

(ii) $200,000.

(3) *Application to partnerships*—(i) *In general*. The dollar limitation of this paragraph (b) applies to the partnership as well as to each partner. In applying the dollar limitation to a taxpayer that is a partner in one or more partnerships, the partner's share of section 179 expenses allocated to the partner from each partnership is aggregated with any nonpartnership section 179 expenses of the taxpayer for the taxable year. However, in determining the excess section 179 property placed in service by a partner in a taxable year, the cost of section 179 property placed in service by the partnership is not attributed to any partner.

(ii) *Example*. The following example illustrates the provisions of paragraph (b)(3)(i) of this section.

Reg. § 1.179-2(b)(3)

Example. During 1991, CD, a calendar-year partnership, purchases and places in service section 179 property costing $150,000 and elects under section 179(c) and § 1.179-5 to expense $10,000 of the cost of that property. CD properly allocates to C, a calendar-year taxpayer and a partner in CD, $5,000 of section 179 expenses (C's distributive share of CD's section 179 expenses for 1991). In applying the dollar limitation to C for 1991, C must include the $5,000 of section 179 expenses allocated from CD. However, in determining the amount of any excess section 179 property C placed in service during 1991, C does not include any of the cost of section 179 property placed in service by CD, including the $5,000 of cost represented by the $5,000 of section 179 expenses allocated to C by the partnership.

(iii) *Partner's share of section 179 expenses.* Section 704 and the regulations thereunder govern the determination of a partner's share of a partnership's section 179 expenses for any taxable year. However, no allocation among partners of the section 179 expenses may be modified after the due date of the partnership return (without regard to extensions of time) for the taxable year for which the election under section 179 is made.

(iv) *Taxable year.* If the taxable years of a partner and the partnership do not coincide, then for purposes of section 179, the amount of the partnership's section 179 expenses attributable to a partner for a taxable year is determined under section 706 and the regulations thereunder (generally the partner's distributive share of partnership section 179 expenses for the partnership year that ends with or within the partner's taxable year).

(v) *Example.* The following example illustrates the provisions of paragraph (b)(3)(iv) of this section.

Example. AB partnership has a taxable year ending January 31. A, a partner of AB, has a taxable year ending December 31. AB purchases and places in service section 179 property on March 10, 1991, and elects to expense a portion of the cost of that property under section 179. Under section 706 and § 1.706-1(a)(1), A will be unable to claim A's distributive share of any of AB's section 179 expenses attributable to the property placed in service on March 10, 1991, until A's taxable year ending December 31, 1992.

(4) *S Corporations.* Rules similar to those contained in paragraph (b)(3) of this section apply in the case of S corporations (as defined in section 1361(a)) and their shareholders. Each shareholder's share of the section 179 expenses of

an S corporation is determined under section 1366.

(5) *Joint returns*—(i) *In general.* A husband and wife who file a joint income tax return under section 6013(a) are treated as one taxpayer in determining the amount of the dollar limitation under paragraph (b)(1) of this section, regardless of which spouse purchased the property or placed it in service.

(ii) *Joint returns filed after separate returns.* In the case of a husband and wife who elect under section 6013(b) to file a joint income tax return for a taxable year after the time prescribed by law for filing the return for such taxable year has expired, the dollar limitation under paragraph (b)(1) of this section is the lesser of—

(A) The dollar limitation (as determined under paragraph (b)(5)(i) of this section); or

(B) The aggregate cost of section 179 property elected to be expensed by the husband and wife on their separate returns.

(iii) *Example.* The following example illustrates the provisions of paragraph (b)(5)(ii) of this section.

Example. During 1991, Mr. and Mrs. B, both calendar-year taxpayers, purchase and place in service section 179 property costing $100,000. On their separate returns for 1991, Mr. B elects to expense $3,000 of section 179 property as an expense and Mrs. B elects to expense $4,000. After the due date of the return they elect under section 6013(b) to file a joint income tax return for 1991. The dollar limitation for their joint income tax return is $7,000, the lesser of the dollar limitation ($10,000) or the aggregate cost elected to be expensed under section 179 on their separate returns ($3,000 elected by Mr. B plus $4,000 elected by Mrs. B, or $7,000).

(6) *Married individuals filing separately*—(i) *In general.* In the case of an individual who is married but files a separate income tax return for a taxable year, the dollar limitation of this paragraph (b) for such taxable year is the amount that would be determined under paragraph (b)(5)(i) of this section if the individual filed a joint income tax return under section 6013(a) multiplied by either the percentage elected by the individual under this paragraph (b)(6) or 50 percent. The election in the preceding sentence is made in accordance with the requirements of section 179(c) and § 1.179-5. However, the amount determined under paragraph (b)(5)(i) of this section must be multiplied by 50 percent if either the individual or the individual's spouse does not elect a percentage under this paragraph (b)(6) or the sum of the percentages elected by the individual and the individual's spouse does not equal 100

Reg. § 1.179-2(b)(4)

percent. For purposes of this paragraph (b)(5), marital status is determined under section 7703 and the regulations thereunder.

(ii) *Example.* The following example illustrates the provisions of paragraph (b)(6)(i) of this section.

Example. Mr. and Mrs. D, both calendar-year taxpayers, file separate income tax returns for 1991. During 1991, Mr. D places $195,000 of section 179 property in service and Mrs. D places $9,000 of section 179 property in service. Neither of them elects a percentage under paragraph (b)(6)(i) of this section. The 1991 dollar limitation for both Mr. D and Mrs. D is determined by multiplying by 50 percent the dollar limitation that would apply had they filed a joint income tax return. Had Mr. and Mrs. D filed a joint return for 1991, the dollar limitation would have been $6,000, $10,000 reduced by the excess section 179 property they placed in service during 1991 ($195,000 placed in service by Mr. D plus $9,000 placed in service by Mrs. D less $200,000, or $4,000). Thus, the 1991 dollar limitation for Mr. and Mrs. D is $3,000 each ($6,000 multiplied by 50 percent).

(7) *Component members of a controlled group*— (i) *In general.* Component members of a controlled group (as defined in § 1.179-4(f)) on a December 31 are treated as one taxpayer in applying the dollar limitation of sections 179(b)(1) and (2) and this paragraph (b). The expense deduction may be taken by any one component member or allocated (for the taxable year of each member that includes that December 31) among the several members in any manner. Any allocation of the expense deduction must be pursuant to an allocation by the common parent corporation if a consolidated return is filed for all component members of the group, or in accordance with an agreement entered into by the members of the group if separate returns are filed. If a consolidated return is filed by some component members of the group and separate returns are filed by other component members, the common parent of the group filing the consolidated return must enter into an agreement with those members that do not join in filing the consolidated return allocating the amount between the group filing the consolidated return and the other component members of the controlled group that do not join in filing the consolidated return. The amount of the expense allocated to any component member, however, may not exceed the cost of section 179 property actually purchased and placed in service by the member in the taxable year. If the component members have different taxable years, the term "taxable year" in sections 179(b)(1) and (2)

means the taxable year of the member whose taxable year begins on the earliest date.

(ii) *Statement to be filed.* If a consolidated return is filed, the common parent corporation must file a separate statement attached to the income tax return on which the election is made to claim an expense deduction under section 179. See § 1.179-5. If separate returns are filed by some or all component members of the group, each component member not included in a consolidated return must file a separate statement attached to the income tax return on which an election is made to claim a deduction under section 179. The statement must include the name, address, employee identification number, and the taxable year of each component member of the controlled group, a copy of the allocation agreement signed by persons duly authorized to act on behalf of the component members, and a description of the manner in which the deduction under section 179 has been divided among the component members.

(iii) *Revocation.* If a consolidated return is filed for all component members of the group, an allocation among such members of the expense deduction under section 179 may not be revoked after the due date of the return (including extensions of time) of the common parent corporation for the taxable year for which an election to take an expense deduction is made. If some or all of the component members of the controlled group file separate returns for taxable years including a particular December 31 for which an election to take the expense deduction is made, the allocation as to all members of the group may not be revoked after the due date of the return (including extensions of time) of the component member of the controlled group whose taxable year that includes such December 31 ends on the latest date.

c) *Taxable income limitation*—(1) *In general.* The aggregate cost of section 179 property elected to be expensed under section 179 that may be deducted for any taxable year may not exceed the aggregate amount of taxable income of the taxpayer for such taxable year that is derived from the active conduct by the taxpayer of any trade or business during the taxable year. For purposes of section 179(b)(3) and this paragraph (c), the aggregate amount of taxable income derived from the active conduct by an individual, a partnership, or an S corporation of any trade or business is computed by aggregating the net income (or less) from all of the trades or businesses actively conducted by the individual, partnership, or S corporation during the taxable year. Items of income that are derived from the active conduct of a trade or business include section 1231 gains (or losses) from the trade or business and interest

Reg. § 1.179-2(c)(1)

from working capital of the trade or business. Taxable income derived from the active conduct of a trade or business is computed without regard to the deduction allowable under section 179, any section 164(f) deduction, any net operating loss carryback or carryforward, and deductions suspended under any section of the Code. See paragraph (c)(6) of this section for rules on determining whether a taxpayer is engaged in the active conduct of a trade or business for this purpose.

(2) *Application to partnerships and partners*—(i) *In general.* The taxable income limitation of this paragraph (c) applies to the partnership as well as to each partner. Thus, the partnership may not allocate to its partners as a section 179 expense deduction for any taxable year more than the partnership's taxable income limitation for that taxable year, and a partner may not deduct as a section 179 expense deduction for any taxable year more than the partner's taxable income limitation for that taxable year.

(ii) *Taxable year.* If the taxable year of a partner and the partnership do not coincide, then for purposes of section 179, the amount of the partnership's taxable income attributable to a partner for a taxable year is determined under section 706 and the regulations thereunder (generally the partner's distributive share of partnership taxable income for the partnership year that ends with or within the partner's taxable year).

(iii) *Example.* The following example illustrates the provisions of paragraph (c)(2)(ii) of this section.

Example. AB partnership has a taxable year ending January 31. A, a partner of AB, has a taxable year ending December 31. For AB's taxable year ending January 31, 1992, AB has taxable income from the active conduct of its trade or business of $100,000, $90,000 of which was earned during 1991. Under section 706 and § 1.706-1(a)(1), A includes A's entire share of partnership taxable income in computing A's taxable income limitation for A's taxable year ending December 31, 1992.

(iv) *Taxable income of a partnership.* The taxable income (or loss) derived from the active conduct by a partnership of any trade or business is computed by aggregating the net income (or loss) from all of the trades or businesses actively conducted by the partnership during the taxable year. The net income (or loss) from a trade or business actively conducted by the partnership is determined by taking into account the aggregate amount of the partnership's items described in section 702(a) (other than credits, tax-exempt income, and guaranteed payments under section

707(c)) derived from that trade or business. For purposes of determining the aggregate amount of partnership items, deductions and losses are treated as negative income. Any limitation on the amount of a partnership item described in section 702(a) which may be taken into account for purposes of computing the taxable income of a partner shall be disregarded in computing the taxable income of the partnership.

(v) *Partner's share of partnership taxable income.* A taxpayer who is a partner in a partnership and is engaged in the active conduct of at least one of the partnership's trades or businesses includes as taxable income derived from the active conduct of a trade or business the amount of the taxpayer's allocable share of taxable income derived from the active conduct by the partnership of any trade or business (as determined under paragraph (c)(2)(iv) of this section).

(3) *S corporations and S corporation shareholders*—(i) *In general.* Rules similar to those contained in paragraphs (c)(2)(i) and (ii) of this section apply in the case of S corporations (as defined in section 1361(a)) and their shareholders. Each shareholder's share of the taxable income of an S corporation is determined under section 1366.

(ii) *Taxable income of an S corporation.* The taxable income (or loss) derived from the active conduct by an S corporation of any trade or business is computed by aggregating the net income (or loss) from all of the trades or businesses actively conducted by the S corporation during the taxable year. The net income (or loss) from a trade or business actively conducted by an S corporation is determined by taking into account the aggregate amount of the S corporation's items described in section 1366(a) (other than credits, tax-exempt income, and deductions for compensation paid to an S corporation's shareholder-employees) derived from that trade or business. For purposes of determining the aggregate amount of S corporation items, deductions and losses are treated as negative income. Any limitation on the amount of an S corporation item described in section 1366(a) which may be taken into account for purposes of computing the taxable income of a shareholder shall be disregarded in computing the taxable income of the S corporation.

(iii) *Shareholder's share of S corporation taxable income.* Rules similar to those contained in paragraph (c)(2)(v) and (c)(6)(ii) of this section apply to a taxpayer who is a shareholder in an S corporation and is engaged in the active conduct of the S corporation's trades or businesses.

(4) *Taxable income of a corporation other than an S corporation.* The aggregate amount of

Reg. § 1.179-2(c)(2)

taxable income derived from the active conduct by a corporation other than an S corporation of any trade or business is the amount of the corporation's taxable income before deducting its net operating loss deduction and special deductions (as reported on the corporation's income tax return), adjusted to reflect those items of income or deduction included in that amount that were not derived by the corporation from a trade or business actively conducted by the corporation during the taxable year.

(5) *Ordering rule for certain circular problems*—(i) *In general.* A taxpayer who elects to expense the cost of section 179 property (the deduction of which is subject to the taxable income limitation) also may have to apply another Internal Revenue Code section that has a limitation based on the taxpayer's taxable income. Except as provided in paragraph (c)(1) of this section, this section provides rules for applying the taxable income limitation under section 179 in such a case. First, taxable income is computed for the other section of the Internal Revenue Code. In computing the taxable income of the taxpayer for the other section of the Internal Revenue Code, the taxpayer's section 179 deduction is computed by assuming that the taxpayer's taxable income is determined without regard to the deduction under the other Internal Revenue Code section. Next, after reducing taxable income by the amount of the section 179 deduction so computed, a hypothetical amount of deduction is determined for the other section of the Internal Revenue Code. The taxable income limitation of the taxpayer under section 179(b)(3) and this paragraph (c) then is computed by including that hypothetical amount in determining taxable income.

(ii) *Example.* The following example illustrates the ordering rule described in paragraph (c)(5)(i) of this section.

Example. X, a calendar-year corporation, elects to expense $10,000 of the cost of section 179 property purchased and placed in service during 1991. Assume X's dollar limitation is $10,000. X also gives a charitable contribution of $5,000 during the taxable year. X's taxable income for purposes of both sections 179 and 170(b)(2), but without regard to any deduction allowable under either section 179 or section 170, is $11,000. In determining X's taxable income limitation under section 179(b)(3) and this paragraph (c), X must first compute its section 170 deduction. However, section 170(b)(2) limits X's charitable contribution to 10 percent of its taxable income determined by taking into account its section 179 deduction. Paragraph (c)(5)(i) of this section provides that in determining X's section 179 deduc-

tion for 1991, X first computes a hypothetical section 170 deduction by assuming that its section 179 deduction is not affected by the section 170 deduction. Thus, in computing X's hypothetical section 170 deduction, X's taxable income limitation under section 179 is $11,000 and its section 179 deduction is $10,000. X's hypothetical section 170 deduction is $100 (10 percent of $1,000 ($11,000 less $10,000 section 179 deduction)). X's taxable income limitation for section 179 purposes is then computed by deducting the hypothetical charitable contribution of $100 for 1991. Thus, X's section 179 taxable income limitation is $10,900 ($11,000 less hypothetical $100 section 170 deduction), and its section 179 deduction for 1991 is $10,000. X's section 179 deduction so calculated applies for all purposes of the Code, including the computation of its actual section 170 deduction.

(6) *Active conduct by the taxpayer of a trade or business*—(i) *Trade or business.* For purposes of this section and § 1.179-4(a), the term "trade or business" has the same meaning as in section 162 and the regulations thereunder. Thus, property held merely for the production of income or used in an activity not engaged in for profit (as described in section 183) does not qualify as section 179 property and taxable income derived from property held for the production of income or from an activity not engaged in for profit is not taken into account in determining the taxable income limitation.

(ii) *Active conduct.* For purposes of this section, the determination of whether a trade or business is actively conducted by the taxpayer is to be made from all the facts and circumstances and is to be applied in light of the purpose of the active conduct requirement of section 179(b)(3)(A). In the context of section 179, the purpose of the active conduct requirement is to prevent a passive investor in a trade or business from deducting section 179 expenses against taxable income derived from that trade or business. Consistent with this purpose, a taxpayer generally is considered to actively conduct a trade or business if the taxpayer meaningfully participates in the management or operations of the trade or business. Generally, a partner is considered to actively conduct a trade or business of the partnership if the partner meaningfully participates in the management or operations of the trade or business. A mere passive investor in a trade or business does not actively conduct the trade or business.

(iii) *Example.* The following example illustrates the provisions of paragraph (c)(6)(ii) of this section.

Reg. § 1.179-2(c)(6)

Example. A owns a salon as a sole proprietorship and employs B to operate it. A periodically meets with B to review developments relating to the business. A also approves the salon's annual budget that is prepared by B. B performs all the necessary operating functions, including hiring beauticians, acquiring the necessary beauty supplies, and writing the checks to pay all bills and the beauticians' salaries. In 1991, B purchased, as provided for in the salon's annual budget, equipment costing $9,500 for use in the active conduct of the salon. There were no other purchases of section 179 property during 1991. A's net income from the salon, before any section 179 deduction, totaled $8,000. A also is a partner in PRS, a calendar-year partnership, which owns a grocery store. C, a partner in PRS, runs the grocery store for the partnership, making all the management and operating decisions. PRS did not purchase any section 179 property during 1991. A's allocable share of partnership net income was $6,000. Based on the facts and circumstances, A meaningfully participates in the management of the salon. However, A does not meaningfully participate in the management or operations of the trade or business of PRS. Under section 179(b)(3)(A) and this paragraph (c), A's aggregate taxable income derived from the active conduct by A of any trade or business is $8,000, the net income from the salon.

(iv) *Employees.* For purposes of this section, employees are considered to be engaged in the active conduct of the trade or business of their employment. Thus, wages, salaries, tips, and other compensation (not reduced by unreimbursed employee business expenses) derived by a taxpayer as an employee are included in the aggregate amount of taxable income of the taxpayer under paragraph (c)(1) of this section.

(7) *Joint returns*—(i) *In general.* The taxable income limitation of this paragraph (c) is applied to a husband and wife who file a joint income tax return under section 6013(a) by aggregating the taxable income of each spouse (as determined under paragraph (c)(1) of this section).

(ii) *Joint returns filed after separate returns.* In the case of a husband and wife who elect under section 6013(b) to file a joint income tax return for a taxable year after the time prescribed by law for filing the return for such taxable year, the taxable income limitation of this paragraph (c) for the taxable year for which the joint return is filed is determined under paragraph (c)(7)(i) of this section.

(8) *Married individuals filing separately.* In the case of an individual who is married but files a separate tax return for a taxable year, the taxable income limitation for that individual is determined under paragraph (c)(1) of this section by treating the husband and wife as separate taxpayers.

(d) *Examples.* The following examples illustrate the provisions of paragraphs (b) and (c) of this section.

Example 1. (i) During 1991, PRS, a calendar-year partnership, purchases and places in service $50,000 of section 179 property. The taxable income of PRS derived from the active conduct of all its trades or businesses (as determined under paragraph (c)(1) of this section) is $8,000.

(ii) Under the dollar limitation of paragraph (b) of this section, PRS may elect to expense $10,000 of the cost of section 179 property purchased in 1991. Assume PRS elects under section 179(c) and § 1.179-5 to expense $10,000 of the cost of section 179 property purchased in 1991.

(iii) Under the taxable income limitation of paragraph (c) of this section, PRS may allocate to its partners as a deduction only $8,000 of the cost of section 179 property in 1991. Under section 179(b)(3)(B) and § 1.179-3(a), PRS may carry forward the remaining $2,000 it elected to expense, which would have been deductible under section 179(a) for 1991 absent the taxable income limitation.

Example 2. (i) The facts are the same as in *Example 1,* except that on December 31, 1991, PRS allocates to A, a calendar-year taxpayer and a partner in PRS, $7,000 of section 179 expenses and $2,000 of taxable income. A was engaged in the active conduct of a trade or business of PRS during 1991.

(ii) In addition to being a partner in PRS, A conducts a business as a sole proprietor. During 1991, A purchases and places in service $201,000 of section 179 property in connection with the sole proprietorship. A's 1991 taxable income derived from the active conduct of this business is $6,000.

(iii) Under the dollar limitation, A may elect to expense only $9,000 of the cost of section 179 property purchased in 1991, the $10,000 limit reduced by $1,000 (the amount by which the cost of section 179 property placed in service during 1991 ($201,000) exceeds $200,000). Under paragraph (b)(3)(i) of this section, the $7,000 of section 179 expenses allocated from PRS is subject to the $9,000 limit. Assume that A elects to expense $2,000 of the cost of section 179 property purchased by A's sole proprietorship in 1991. Thus, A has elected to expense under section 179 an amount equal to the dollar limitation for 1991 ($2,000 elected to be expensed by A's sole proprietorship plus $7,000, the amount of PRS's section 179 expenses allocated to A in 1991).

Reg. § 1.179-2(c)(7)

(iv) Under the taxable income limitation, A may only deduct $8,000 of the cost of section 179 property elected to be expensed in 1991, the aggregate taxable income derived from the active conduct of A's trades or businesses in 1991 ($2,000 from PRS and $6,000 from A's sole proprietorship). The entire $2,000 of taxable income allocated from PRS is included by A as taxable income derived from the active conduct by A of a trade or business because it was derived from the active conduct of a trade or business by PRS and A was engaged in the active conduct of a trade or business of PRS during 1991. Under section 179(b)(3)(B) and § 1.179-3(a), A may carry forward the remaining $1,000 A elected to expense, which would have been deductible under section 179(a) for 1991 absent the taxable income limitation. [Reg. § 1.179-2.]

□ [*T.D.* 8121, 1-5-87. *Amended by T.D.* 8455, 12-23-92.]

[Reg. § 1.179-3]

§ 1.179-3. Carryover of disallowed deduction.—(a) *In general.* Under section 179(b)(3)(B), a taxpayer may carry forward for an unlimited number of years the amount of any cost of section 179 property elected to be expensed in a taxable year but disallowed as a deduction in that taxable year because of the taxable income limitation of section 179(b)(3)(A) and § 1.179-2(c) ("carryover of disallowed deduction"). This carryover of disallowed deduction may be deducted under section 179(a) and § 1.179-1(a) in a future taxable year as provided in paragraph (b) of this section.

(b) *Deduction of carryover of disallowed deduction*—(1) *In general.* The amount allowable as a deduction under section 179(a) and § 1.179-1(a) for any taxable year is increased by the lesser of—

(i) The aggregate amount disallowed under section 179(b)(3)(A) and § 1.179-2(c) for all prior taxable years (to the extent not previously allowed as a deduction by reason of this section); or

(ii) The amount of any unused section 179 expense allowance for the taxable year (as described in paragraph (c) of this section).

(2) *Cross references.* See paragraph (f) of this section for rules that apply when a taxpayer disposes of or otherwise transfers section 179 property for which a carryover of disallowed deduction is outstanding. See paragraph (g) of this section for special rules that apply to partnerships and S corporations and paragraph (h) of this section for special rules that apply to partners and S corporation shareholders.

(c) *Unused section 179 expense allowance.* The amount of any unused section 179 expense allow-

ance for a taxable year equals the excess (if any) of—

(1) The maximum cost of section 179 property that the taxpayer may deduct under section 179 and § 1.179-1 for the taxable year after applying the limitations of section 179(b) and § 1.179-2; over

(2) The amount of section 179 property that the taxpayer actually elected to expense under section 179 and § 1.179-1(a) for the taxable year.

(d) *Example.* The following example illustrates the provisions of paragraphs (b) and (c) of this section.

Example. A, a calendar-year taxpayer, has a $3,000 carryover of disallowed deduction for an item of section 179 property purchased and placed in service in 1991. In 1992, A purchases and places in service an item of section 179 property costing $25,000. A's 1992 taxable income from the active conduct of all A's trades or businesses is $100,000. A elects, under section 179(c) and § 1.179-5, to expense $8,000 of the cost of the item of section 179 property purchased in 1992. Under paragraph (b) of this section, A may deduct $2,000 of A's carryover of disallowed deduction from 1991 (the lesser of A's total outstanding carryover of disallowed deductions ($3,000), or the amount of any unused section 179 expense allowance for 1992 ($10,000 limit less $8,000 elected to be expensed, or $2,000)). For 1993, A has a $1,000 carryover of disallowed deduction for the item of section 179 property purchased and placed in service in 1991.

(e) *Recordkeeping requirement and ordering rule.* The properties and the apportionment of cost that will be subject to a carryover of disallowed deduction are selected by the taxpayer in the year the properties are placed in service. This selection must be evidenced on the taxpayer's books and records and be applied consistently in subsequent years. If no selection is made, the total carryover of disallowed deduction is apportioned equally over the items of section 179 property elected to be expensed for the taxable year. For this purpose, the taxpayer treats any section 179 expense amount allocated from a partnership (or an S corporation) for a taxable year as one item of section 179 property. If the taxpayer is allowed to deduct a portion of the total carryover of disallowed deduction under paragraph (b) of this section, the taxpayer must deduct the cost of section 179 property carried forward from the earliest taxable year.

(f) *Dispositions and other transfers of section 179 property*—(1) *In general.* Upon a sale or other disposition of section 179 property, or a transfer of section 179 property in a transaction in which gain or loss is not recognized in whole or in part (including transfers at death), immediately before the transfer the adjusted basis of the section 179 property is increased by the amount of any outstanding carryover of disallowed deduction with respect to the property. This carryover of disallowed deduction is not available as a deduction to the transferor or the transferee of the section 179 property.

(2) *Recapture under section 179(d)(10).* Under § 1.179-1(e), if a taxpayer's section 179 property is subject to recapture under section 179(d)(10), the taxpayer must recapture the benefit derived from expensing the property. Upon recapture, any outstanding carryover of disallowed deduction with respect to the property is no longer available for expensing. In determining the amount subject to recapture under section 179(d)(10) and § 1.179-1(e), any outstanding carryover of disallowed deduction with respect to that property is not treated as an amount expensed under section 179.

(g) *Special rules for partnerships and S corporations*—(1) *In general.* Under section 179(d)(8) and § 1.179-2(c), the taxable income limitation applies at the partnership level as well as at the partner level. Therefore, a partnership may have a carryover of disallowed deduction with respect to the cost of its section 179 property. Similar rules apply to S corporations. This paragraph (g) provides special rules that apply when a partnership or an S corporation has a carryover of disallowed deduction.

(2) *Basis adjustment.* Under § 1.179-1(f)(2), the basis of a partnership's section 179 property must be reduced to reflect the amount of section 179 expense elected by the partnership. This reduction must be made for the taxable year for which the election is made even if the section 179 expense amount, or a portion thereof, must be carried forward by the partnership. Similar rules apply to S corporations.

(3) *Dispositions and other transfers of section 179 property by a partnership or an S corporation.* The provisions of paragraph (f) of this section apply in determining the treatment of any outstanding carryover of disallowed deduction with respect to section 179 property disposed of, or transferred in a nonrecognition transaction, by a partnership or an S corporation.

(4) *Example.* The following example illustrates the provisions of this paragraph (g).

Example. ABC, a calendar-year partnership, owns and operates a restaurant business. During 1992, ABC purchases and places in service two items of section 179 property—a cash register costing $4,000 and office furniture costing $6,000.

ABC elects to expense under section 179(c) the full cost of the cash register and the office furniture. For 1992, ABC has $6,000 of taxable income derived from the active conduct of its restaurant business. Therefore, ABC may deduct only $6,000 of section 179 expenses and must carry forward the remaining $4,000 of section 179 expenses at the partnership level. ABC must reduce the adjusted basis of the section 179 property by the full amount elected to be expensed. However, ABC may not allocate to its partners any portion of the carryover of disallowed deduction until ABC is able to deduct it under paragraph (b) of this section.

(h) *Special rules for partners and S corporation shareholders*—(1) *In general.* Under section 179(d)(8) and § 1.179-2(c), a partner may have a carryover of disallowed deduction with respect to the cost of section 179 property elected to be expensed by the partnership and allocated to the partner. A partner who is allocated section 179 expenses from a partnership must reduce the basis of his or her partnership interest by the full amount allocated regardless of whether the partner may deduct for the taxable year the allocated section 179 expenses or is required to carry forward all or a portion of the expenses. Similar rules apply to S corporation shareholders.

(2) *Dispositions and other transfers of a partner's interest in a partnership or a shareholder's interest in an S corporation.* A partner who disposes of a partnership interest, or transfers a partnership interest in a transaction in which gain or loss is not recognized in whole or in part (including transfers of a partnership interest at death), may have an outstanding carryover of disallowed deduction of section 179 expenses allocated from the partnership. In such a case, immediately before the transfer the partner's basis in the partnership interest is increased by the amount of the partner's outstanding carryover of disallowed deduction with respect to the partnership interest. This carryover of disallowed deduction is not available as a deduction to the transferor or transferee partner of the section 179 property. Similar rules apply to S corporation shareholders.

(3) *Examples.* The following examples illustrate the provisions of this paragraph (h).

Example 1. (i) G is a general partner in GD, a calendar-year partnership, and is engaged in the active conduct of GD's business. During 1991, GD purchases and places section 179 property in service and elects to expense a portion of the cost of the property under section 179. GD allocates $2,500 of section 179 expenses and $15,000 of taxable income (determined without regard to the

Reg. § 1.179-3(f)(2)

section 179 deduction) to G. The income was derived from the active conduct by GD of a trade or business.

(ii) In addition to being a partner in GD, G conducts a business as a sole proprietor. During 1991, G purchases and places in service office equipment costing $25,000 and a computer costing $10,000 in connection with the sole proprietorship. G elects under section 179(c) and § 1.179-5 to expense $7,500 of the cost of the office equipment. G has a taxable loss (determined without regard to the section 179 deduction) derived from the active conduct of this business of $12,500.

(iii) G has no other taxable income (or loss) derived from the active conduct of a trade or business during 1991. G's taxable income limitation for 1991 is $2,500 ($15,000 taxable income allocated from GD less $12,500 taxable loss from the sole proprietorship). Therefore, G may deduct during 1991 only $2,500 of the $10,000 of section 179 expenses. G notes on the appropriate books and records that G expenses the $2,500 of section 179 expenses allocated from GD and carries forward the $7,500 of section 179 expenses with respect to the office equipment purchased by G's sole proprietorship.

(iv) On January 1, 1992, G sells the office equipment G's sole proprietorship purchased and placed in service in 1991. Under paragraph (f) of this section, immediately before the sale G increases the adjusted basis of the office equipment by $7,500, the amount of the outstanding carryover of disallowed deduction with respect to the office equipment.

Example 2. (i) Assume the same facts as in *Example 1,* except that G notes on the appropriate books and records that G expenses $2,500 of section 179 expenses relating to G's sole proprietorship and carries forward the remaining $5,000 of section 179 expenses relating to G's sole proprietorship and $2,500 of section 179 expenses allocated from GD.

(ii) On January 1, 1992, G sells G's partnership interest to A. Under paragraph (h)(2) of this section, immediately before the sale G increases the adjusted basis of G's partnership interest by $2,500, the amount of the outstanding carryover of disallowed deduction with respect to the partnership interest. [Reg. § 1.179-3.]

☐ [*T.D.* 8455, 12-23-92.]

[Reg. § 1.179-4]

§ 1.179-4. Definitions.—The following definitions apply for purposes of section 179 and §§ 1.179-1 through 1.179-6:

(a) *Section 179 property.* The term "section 179 property" means any tangible property described

in section 179(d)(1) that is acquired by purchase for use in the active conduct of the taxpayer's trade or business (as described in § 1.179-2(c)(6)). For purposes of this paragraph (a), the term "trade or business" has the same meaning as in section 162 and the regulations thereunder.

(b) *Section 38 property.* The term "section 38 property" shall have the same meaning assigned to it in section 48(a) and the regulations thereunder.

(c) *Purchase.* (1)(i) Except as otherwise provided in paragraph (c)(2) of this section, the term "purchase" means any acquisition of the property, but only if all the requirements of paragraphs (c)(1)(ii), (iii), and (iv) of this section are satisfied.

(ii) Property is not acquired by purchase if it is acquired from a person whose relationship to the person acquiring it would result in the disallowance of losses under section 267 or 707(b). The property is considered not acquired by purchase only to the extent that losses would be disallowed under section 267 or 707(b). Thus, for example, if property is purchased by a husband and wife jointly from the husband's father, the property will be treated as not acquired by purchase only to the extent of the husband's interest in the property. However, in applying the rules of section 267(b) and (c) for this purpose, section 267(c)(4) shall be treated as providing that the family of an individual will include only his spouse, ancestors, and lineal descendants. For example, a purchase of property from a corporation by a taxpayer who owns, directly or indirectly, more than 50 percent in value of the outstanding stock of such corporation does not qualify as a purchase under section 179(d)(2); nor does the purchase of property by a husband from his wife. However, the purchase of section 179 property by a taxpayer from his brother or sister does qualify as a purchase for purposes of section 179(d)(2).

(iii) The property is not acquired by purchase if acquired from a component member of a controlled group of corporations (as defined in paragraph (g) of this section) by another component member of the same group.

(iv) The property is not acquired by purchase if the basis of the property in the hands of the person acquiring it is determined in whole or in part by reference to the adjusted basis of such property in the hands of the person from whom acquired, or is determined under section 1014(a), relating to property acquired from a decedent. For example, property acquired by gift or bequest does not qualify as property acquired by purchase for purposes of section 179(d)(2); nor does property received in a corporate distribution the basis of which is determined under section 301(d)(2)(B), property acquired by a corporation in a transaction to which section 351 applies, property acquired by a partnership through contribution (section 723), or property received in a partnership distribution which has a carryover basis under section 732(a)(1).

(2) Property deemed to have been acquired by a new target corporation as a result of a section 338 election (relating to certain stock purchases treated as asset acquisitions) will be considered acquired by purchase.

(d) *Cost.* The cost of section 179 property does not include so much of the basis of such property as is determined by reference to the basis of other property held at any time by the taxpayer. For example, X Corporation purchases a new drill press costing $10,000 in November 1984 which qualifies as section 179 property, and is granted a trade-in allowance of $2,000 on its old drill press. The old drill press had a basis of $1,200. Under the provisions of sections 1012 and 1031(d), the basis of the new drill press is $9,200 ($1,200 basis of old drill press plus cash expended of $8,000). However, only $8,000 of the basis of the new drill press qualifies as cost for purposes of the section 179 expense deduction; the remaining $1,200 is not part of the cost because it is determined by reference to the basis of the old drill press.

(e) *Placed in service.* The term "placed in service" means the time that property is first placed by the taxpayer in a condition or state of readiness and availability for a specifically assigned function, whether for use in a trade or business, for the production of income, in a tax-exempt activity, or in a personal activity. See § 1.46-3(d)(2) for examples regarding when property shall be considered in a condition or state of readiness and availability for a specifically assigned function.

(f) *Controlled group of corporations and component member of controlled group.* The terms "controlled group of corporations" and "component member" of a controlled group of corporations shall have the same meaning assigned to those terms in section 1563(a) and (b), except that the phrase "more than 50 percent" shall be substituted for the phrase "at least 80 percent" each place it appears in section 1563(a)(1). [Reg. § 1.179-4.]

☐ [*T.D. 8121, 1-5-87. Amended by T.D. 8455, 12-23-92.*]

[Reg. § 1.179-5]

§ 1.179-5. **Time and manner of making election.—(a)** *Election.* A separate election must be made for each taxable year in which a section 179 expense deduction is claimed with respect to sec-

tion 179 property. The election under section 179 and § 1.179-1 to claim a section 179 expense deduction for section 179 property shall be made on the taxpayer's first income tax return for the taxable year to which the election applies (whether or not the return is timely) or on an amended return filed within the time prescribed by law (including extensions) for filing the return for such taxable year. The election shall be made by showing as a separate item on the taxpayer's income tax return the following items:

(1) The total section 179 expense deduction claimed with respect to all section 179 property selected; and

(2) The portion of that deduction allocable to each specific item.

The person shall maintain records which permit specific identification of each piece of section 179 property and reflect how and from whom such property was acquired and when such property was placed in service. However, for this purpose a partner (or an S corporation shareholder) treats partnership (or S corporation) section 179 property for which section 179 expenses are allocated from a partnership (or an S corporation) as one item of section 179 property. The election to claim a section 179 expense deduction under this section, with respect to any property, is irrevocable and will be binding on the taxpayer with respect to such property for the taxable year for which the election is made and for all subsequent taxable years, unless the Commissioner consents to the revocation of the election. Similarly, the selection of section 179 property by the taxpayer to be subject to the expense deduction and apportionment scheme must be adhered to in computing the taxpayer's taxable income for the taxable year for which the election is made and for all subsequent taxable years, unless consent to change is given by the Commissioner.

(b) *Revocation.* Any election made under section 179, and any specification contained in such election, may not be revoked except with the consent of the Commissioner. Such consent will be granted only in extraordinary circumstances. Requests for consent must be filed with the Commissioner of Internal Revenue, Washington, D.C., 20224. The request must include the name, address, and taxpayer identification number of the taxpayer and must be signed by the taxpayer or his duly authorized representative. It must be accompanied by a statement showing the year and property involved, and must set forth in detail the reasons for the request. [Reg. § 1.179-5.]

☐ [*T.D. 8121, 1-5-87. Amended by T.D. 8455, 12-23-92.*]

[Reg. § 1.179-6]

§ 1.179-6. Effective date.—The provisions of §§ 1.179-1 through 1.179-5 are effective for property placed in service in taxable years ending after January 25, 1993. However, a taxpayer may apply the provisions of §§ 1.179-1 through 1.179-5 to property placed in service after December 31, 1986, in taxable years ending on or before January 25, 1993. Otherwise, for property placed in service after December 31, 1986, in taxable years ending on or before January 25, 1993, the final regulations under section 179 as in effect for the year the property was placed in service apply, except to the extent modified by the changes made to section 179 by the Tax Reform Act of 1986, the Technical and Miscellaneous Revenue Act of 1988, and the Revenue Reconciliation Act of 1990. For that property, a taxpayer may apply any reasonable method that clearly reflects income in applying the changes to section 179, provided the taxpayer consistently applies the method to the property. [Reg. § 1.179-6.]

☐ [*T.D. 8121, 1-5-87. Amended by T.D. 8455, 12-23-92.*]

[Reg. § 1.179A-1]

§ 1.179A-1. Recapture of deduction for qualified clean-fuel vehicle property and qualified clean-fuel vehicle refueling property.—(a) *In general.* If a recapture event occurs with respect to a taxpayer's qualified clean-fuel vehicle property or qualified clean-fuel vehicle refueling property, the taxpayer must include the recapture amount in taxable income for the taxable year in which the recapture event occurs.

(b) *Recapture event*—(1) *Qualified clean-fuel vehicle property*—(i) *In general.* A recapture event occurs if, within 3 full years from the date a vehicle of which qualified clean-fuel vehicle property is a part is placed in service, the property ceases to be qualified clean-fuel vehicle property. Property ceases to be qualified clean-fuel vehicle property if—

(A) The vehicle is modified by the taxpayer so that it may no longer be propelled by a clean-burning fuel;

(B) The vehicle is used by the taxpayer in a manner described in section 50(b);

(C) The vehicle otherwise ceases to qualify as property defined in section 179A(c); or

(D) The taxpayer receiving the deduction under section 179A sells or disposes of the vehicle and knows or has reason to know that the vehicle will be used in a manner described in paragraph (b)(1)(i)(A), (B), or (C) of this section.

(ii) *Exception for disposition.* Except as provided in paragraph (b)(1)(i)(D) of this section, a sale or other disposition (including a disposition by reason of an accident or other casualty) of qualified clean-fuel vehicle property is not a recapture event.

(2) *Qualified clean-fuel vehicle refueling property*—(i) *In general.* A recapture event occurs if, at any time before the end of its recovery period, the property ceases to be qualified clean-fuel vehicle refueling property. Property ceases to be qualified clean-fuel vehicle refueling property if—

(A) The property no longer qualifies as property described in section 179A(d);

(B) The property is no longer used predominantly in a trade or business (property will be treated as no longer used predominantly in a trade or business if 50 percent or more of the use of the property in a taxable year is for use other than in a trade or business);

(C) The property is used by the taxpayer in a manner described in section 50(b); or

(D) The taxpayer receiving the deduction under section 179A sells or disposes of the property and knows or has reason to know that the property will be used in a manner described in paragraph (b)(2)(i)(A), (B), or (C) of this section.

(ii) *Exception for disposition.* Except as provided in paragraph (b)(2)(i)(D) of this section, a sale or other disposition (including a disposition by reason of an accident or other casualty) of qualified clean-fuel vehicle refueling property is not a recapture event.

(c) *Recapture date*—(1) *Qualified clean-fuel vehicle property* The recapture date is the actual date of the recapture event unless an event described in paragraph (b)(1)(i)(B) of this section occurs, in which case the recapture date is the first day of the recapture year.

(2) *Qualified clean-fuel vehicle refueling property.* The recapture date is the actual date of the recapture event unless the recapture occurs as a result of an event described in paragraph (b)(2)(i)(B) or (C) of this section, in which case the recapture date is the first day of the recapture year.

(d) *Recapture amount*—(1) *Qualified clean-fuel vehicle property.* The recapture amount is equal to the benefit of the section 179A deduction allowable multiplied by the recapture percentage. The recapture percentage is—

Reg. § 1.179A-1(d)(1)

(i) 100, if the recapture date is within the first full year after the date the vehicle is placed in service;

(ii) 66⅔, if the recapture date is within the second full year after the date the vehicle is placed in service; or

(iii) 33⅓, if the recapture date is within the third full year after the date the vehicle is placed in service.

(2) *Qualified clean-fuel vehicle refueling property.* The recapture amount is equal to the benefit of the section 179A deduction allowable multiplied by the following fraction. The numerator of the fraction equals the total recovery period for the property minus the number of recovery years prior to, but not including, the recapture year. The denominator of the fraction equals the total recovery period.

(e) *Basis adjustment.* As of the first day of the taxable year in which the recapture event occurs, the basis of the vehicle of which qualified clean-fuel vehicle property is a part or the basis of qualified clean-fuel vehicle refueling property is increased by the recapture amount. For a vehicle or refueling property that is of a character that is subject to an allowance for depreciation, this increase in basis is recoverable over its remaining recovery period beginning as of the first day of the taxable year in which the recapture event occurs.

(f) *Application of section 1245 for sales and other dispositions.* For purposes of section 1245, the amount of the deduction allowable under section 179A(a) with respect to any property that is (or has been) of a character subject to an allowance for depreciation is treated as a deduction allowed for depreciation under section 167. Therefore, upon a sale or other disposition of depreciable qualified clean-fuel vehicle refueling property or a depreciable vehicle of which qualified clean-fuel vehicle property is a part, section 1245 will apply to any gain recognized to the extent the basis of the depreciable property or vehicle was reduced under section 179A(e)(6) net of any basis increase described in paragraph (e) of this section.

(g) *Examples.* The following examples illustrate the provisions of this section:

Example 1. A, a calendar-year taxpayer, purchases and places in service for personal use on January 1, 1995, a clean-fuel vehicle, a portion of which is qualified clean-fuel vehicle property, costing $25,000. The qualified clean-fuel vehicle property costs $11,000. On A's 1995 federal income tax return, A claims a section 179A deduction of $2,000. On January 2, 1996, A sells the vehicle to an unrelated third party who subsequently converts the vehicle into a gasoline-pro-

pelled vehicle on October 15, 1996. There is no recapture upon the sale of the vehicle by A provided A did not know or have reason to know that the purchaser intended to convert the vehicle to a gasoline-propelled vehicle.

Example 2. B, a calendar-year taxpayer, purchases and places in service for personal use on October 11, 1994, a clean-fuel vehicle costing $20,000, a portion of which is qualified clean-fuel vehicle property. The qualified clean-fuel vehicle property costs $10,000. On B's 1994 federal income tax return, B claims a deduction of $2,000, which reduces B's gross income by $2,000. The basis of the vehicle is reduced to $18,000 ($20,000 − $2,000). On January 31, 1996, B sells the vehicle to a tax-exempt entity. Because B knowingly sold the vehicle to a tax-exempt entity described in section 50(b) in the second full year from the date the vehicle was placed in service, B must recapture $1,333 ($2,000 × 66⅔ percent). This recapture amount increases B's gross income by $1,333 on B's 1996 federal income tax return and is added to the basis of the motor vehicle as of January 1, 1996, the beginning of the taxable year of recapture.

Example 3. X, a calendar-year taxpayer, purchases and places in service for its business use on January 1, 1994, qualified clean-fuel vehicle refueling property costing $400,000. Assume this property has a 5-year recovery period. On X's 1994 federal income tax return, X claims a deduction of $100,000, which reduces X's gross income by $100,000. The basis of the property is reduced to $300,000 ($400,000 − $100,000) prior to any adjustments for depreciation. In 1996, more than 50 percent of the use of the property is other than in X's trade or business. Because the property is no longer used predominantly in X's business, X must recapture three-fifths of the section 179A deduction or $60,000 ($100,000 × (5-2)/5 = $60,000) and include that amount in gross income on its 1996 federal income tax return. The recapture amount of $60,000 is added to the basis of the property as of January 1, 1996, the beginning of the taxable year of recapture, and to the extent the property remains depreciable, the adjusted basis is recoverable over the remaining recovery period.

Example 4. X, a calendar-year taxpayer, purchases and places in service for business use on January 1, 1994, qualified clean-fuel vehicle refueling property costing $350,000. Assume this property has a 5-year recovery period. On X's 1994 federal income tax return, X claims a deduction of $100,000, which reduces X's gross income by $100,000. The basis of the property is reduced to $250,000 ($350,000 − $100,000) prior to any

Reg. § 1.179A-1(d)(2)

adjustments for depreciation. In 1995, X converts the property to store and dispense gasoline. Because the property is no longer used as qualified clean-fuel vehicle refueling property in 1995, X must recapture four-fifths of the section 179A deduction or $80,000 ($100,000 × (5-1)/5 = $80,000) and include that amount in gross income on its 1995 federal income tax return. The recapture amount of $80,000 is added to the basis of the property as of January 1, 1995, the beginning of the taxable year of recapture, and to the extent the property remains depreciable, the adjusted basis is recoverable over the remaining recovery period.

Example 5. The facts are the same as in *Example 4.* In 1996, X sells the refueling property for $351,000, recognizing a gain from this sale. Under paragraph (f) of this section, section 1245 will apply to any gain recognized on the sale of depreciable property to the extent the basis of the property was reduced by the section 179A deduction net of any basis increase from recapture of the section 179A deduction. Accordingly, the gain from the sale of the property is subject to section 1245 to the extent of the depreciation allowance for the property plus the deduction allowed under section 179A ($100,000), less the previous recapture amount ($80,000). Any remaining amount of gain may be subject to other applicable provisions of the Internal Revenue Code.

(h) *Effective date.* This section is effective on October 14, 1994. If the recapture date is before the effective date of this section, a taxpayer may use any reasonable method to recapture the benefit of any deduction allowable under section 179A(a) consistent with section 179A and its legislative history. For this purpose, the recapture date is defined in paragraph (c) of this section. [Reg. § 1.179A-1.]

□ [T.D. 8606, 8-2-95.]

[Reg. § 1.180-1]

§ 1.180-1. Expenditures by farmers for fertilizer, etc.—(a) *In general.* A taxpayer engaged in the business of farming may elect, for any taxable year beginning after December 31, 1959, to treat as deductible expenses those expenditures otherwise chargeable to capital account which are paid or incurred by him during the taxable year for the purchase or acquisition of fertilizer, lime, ground limestone, marl, or other materials to enrich, neutralize, or condition land used in farming, and those expenditures otherwise chargeable to capital account paid or incurred for the application of such items and materials to such land. No election is required to be made for those expenditures which are not capital in nature. Section 180, § 1.180-2, and this section are not applicable to those expenses which are deductible under section

162 and the regulations thereunder or which are subject to the method described in section 175 and the regulations thereunder.

(b) *Land used in farming.* For purposes of section 180(a) and of paragraph (a) of this section, the term "land used in farming" means land used (before or simultaneously with the expenditures described in such section and such paragraph) by the taxpayer or his tenant for the production of crops, fruits, or other agricultural products or for the sustenance of livestock. See section 180(b). Expenditures for the initial preparation of land never previously used for farming purposes by the taxpayer or his tenant (although chargeable to capital account) are not subject to the election. The principles stated in §§ 1.175-3 and 1.175-4 are equally applicable under this section in determining whether the taxpayer is engaged in the business of farming and whether the land is used in farming. [Reg. § 1.180-1.]

□ T.D. 6548, 2-21-61.]

[Reg. § 1.180-2]

§ 1.180-2. Time and manner of making election and revocation.—(a) *Election.* The claiming of a deduction on the taxpayer's return for an amount to which section 180 applies for amounts (otherwise chargeable to capital account) expended for fertilizer, lime, etc., shall constitute an election under section 180 and paragraph (a) of § 1.180-1. Such election shall be effective only for the taxable year for which the deduction is claimed.

(b) *Revocation.* Once the election is made for any taxable year such election may not be revoked without the consent of the district director for the district in which the taxpayer's return is required to be filed. Such requests for consent shall be in writing and signed by the taxpayer or his authorized representative and shall set forth—

(1) The name and address of the taxpayer;

(2) The taxable year to which the revocation of the election is to apply;

(3) The amount of expenditures paid or incurred during the taxable year, or portions thereof (where applicable), previously taken as a deduction on the return in respect of which the revocation of the election is to be applicable; and

(4) The reasons for the request to revoke the election. [Reg. § 1.180-2.]

□ [T.D. 6548, 2-21-61.]

[Reg. § 1.182-1]

§ 1.182-1. Expenditures by farmers for clearing land; in general.—Under section 182, a taxpayer engaged in the business of farming may elect, in the manner provided in § 1.182-6, to deduct certain expenditures paid or incurred by him in any taxable year beginning after December 31, 1962, in the clearing of land. The expenditures to which the election applies are all expenditures paid or incurred during the taxable year in clearing land for the purpose of making the "land suitable for use in farming" (as defined in § 1.182-4) which are not otherwise deductible (exclusive of expenditures for or in connection with depreciable items referred to in paragraph (b)(1) of § 1.182-3), but only if such expenditures are made in furtherance of the taxpayer's business of farming. The term "expenditures" to which the election applies also includes a reasonable allowance for depreciation (not otherwise allowable) on equipment used in the clearing of land provided such equipment, if used in the carrying on of a trade or business, would be subject to the allowance for depreciation under section 167. (See paragraph (c) of § 1.182-3.) (See section 175 and the regulations thereunder for deductibility of certain expenditures for treatment or moving of earth by a farmer where the land already qualifies as land used in farming as defined in § 1.175.4.) The amount deductible for any taxable year is limited to the lesser of $5,000 or 25 percent of the taxable income derived from farming (as defined in paragraph (a)(2) of § 1.182-5) during the taxable year. Expenditures paid or incurred in a taxable year in excess of the amount deductible under section 182 for such taxable year shall be treated as capital expenditures and shall constitute an adjustment to the basis of the land under section 1016(a). [Reg. § 1.182-1.]

☐ [T.D. 6794, 1-25-65.]

[Reg. § 1.182-2]

§ 1.182-2. Definition of "the business of farming."—Under section 182, the election to deduct expenditures incurred in the clearing of land is applicable only to a taxpayer who is engaged in "the business of farming" during the taxable year. A taxpayer is engaged in the business of farming if he cultivates, operates, or manages a farm for gain or profit, either as owner or tenant. For purposes of section 182, a taxpayer who receives a rental (either in cash or in kind) which is based upon farm production is engaged in the business of farming. However, a taxpayer who receives a fixed rental (without reference to production) is engaged in the business of farming only if he participates to a material extent in the operation or management of the farm. A taxpayer engaged in forestry or the growing of timber is not thereby engaged in the business of farming. A person cultivating or operating a farm for recreation or pleasure rather than for profit is not engaged in the business of farming. For purposes of section 182 and this section, the term "farm" is used in its ordinary, accepted sense and includes

stock, dairy, poultry, fish, fruit, and truck farms, and also plantations, ranches, ranges, and orchards. A fish farm is an area where fish are grown or raised, as opposed to merely caught or harvested; that is, an area where they are artificially fed, protected, cared for, etc. A taxpayer is engaged in "the business of farming" if he is a member of a partnership engaged in the business of farming. See § 1.702-1. [Reg. § 1.182-2.]

☐ [T.D. 6794, 1-25-65.]

[Reg. § 1.182-3]

§ 1.182-3. Definition, exceptions, etc., relating to deductible expenditures.—(a) "Clearing of land." (1) For purposes of section 182, the term "clearing of land" includes (but is not limited to)—

(i) The removal of rocks, stones, trees, stumps, brush or other natural impediments to the use of the land in farming through blasting, cutting, burning, bulldozing, plowing, or in any other way;

(ii) The treatment or moving of earth, including the construction, repair or removal of nondepreciable earthen structures, such as dikes or levies, if the purpose of such treatment or moving of earth is to protect, level, contour, terrace, or condition the land so as to permit its use as farming land; and

(iii) The diversion of streams and watercourses, including the construction of nondepreciable drainage facilities, provided that the purpose is to remove or divert water from the land so as to make it available for use in farming.

(2) The following are examples of land clearing activities:

(i) The cutting of trees, the blasting of the resulting stumps, and the burning of the residual undergrowth;

(ii) The leveling of land so as to permit irrigation or planting;

(iii) The removal of salt or other minerals which might inhibit cultivation of the soil;

(iv) The draining and filling in of a swamp or marsh; and

(v) The diversion of a stream from one watercourse to another.

(b) Expenditures not allowed as a deduction under section 182. (1) Section 182 applies only to expenditures for nondepreciable items. Accordingly, a taxpayer may not deduct expenditures for the purchase, construction, installation, or improvement of structures, appliances, or facilities which are of a character which is subject to the allowance for depreciation under section 167 and the regulations thereunder. Expenditures in respect of such depreciable property include those

Reg. § 1.182-2

for materials, supplies, wages, fuel, freight, and the moving of earth, paid or incurred with respect to tanks, reservoirs, pipes, conduits, canals, dams, wells, or pumps constructed of masonry, concrete, tile, metal, wood, or other nonearthen material.

(2) Expenditures which are deductible without regard to section 182 are not deductible under section 182. Thus, such expenditures are deductible without being subject to the limitations imposed by section 182(b) and § 1.182-5. For example, section 182 does not apply to the ordinary and necessary expenses incurred in the business of farming which are deductible under section 162 even though they might otherwise be considered to be clearing of land expenditures. Section 182 also does not apply to interest (deductible under section 163) nor to taxes (deductible under section 164). Similarly, section 182 does not apply to any expenditures (whether or not currently deductible) paid or incurred for the purpose of soil or water conservation in respect of land used in farming, or for the prevention of erosion of land used in farming, within the meaning of section 175 and the regulations thereunder, nor to expenditures deductible under section 180 and the regulations thereunder relating to expenditures for fertilizer, etc.

(c) *Depreciation.* In addition to expenditures for the activities described in paragraph (a) of this section, there also shall be treated as an expenditure to which section 182 applies a reasonable allowance for depreciation not otherwise deductible on property of the taxpayer which is used in the clearing of land for the purpose of making such land suitable for use in farming, provided the property is property which, if used in a trade or business, would be subject to the allowance for depreciation under section 167. Depreciation allowable as a deduction under section 182 is limited to the portion of depreciation which is attributable to the use of the property in the clearing of land. The depreciation shall be computed in accordance with section 167 and the regulations thereunder. To the extent an amount representing a reasonable allowance for depreciation with respect to property used in clearing land is treated as an expenditure to which section 182 applies, such depreciation shall for purposes of chapter 1 of the Code, be treated as an amount allowed under section 167 for depreciation. Thus, if a deduction is allowed for depreciation under section 182 in respect of property used in clearing land, proper adjustment to the basis of the property so used shall be made under section 1016(a). [Reg. § 1.182-3.]

☐ [*T.D.* 6794, 1-25-65.]

[Reg. § 1.182-4]

§ 1.182-4. **Definition of "land suitable for use in farming"**, etc.—For purposes of section 182, the term "land suitable for use in farming" means land which, as a result of the land clearing activities described in paragraph (a) of § 1.182-3, could be used by the taxpayer or his tenant for the production of crops, fruits, or other agricultural products, including fish, or for the sustenance of livestock. The term "livestock" includes cattle, hogs, horses, mules, donkeys, sheep, goats, captive fur-bearing animals, chickens, turkeys, pigeons, and other poultry. Land used for the sustenance of livestock includes land used for grazing such livestock. Expenditures are considered to be for the purpose of making land suitable for use in farming by the taxpayer or his tenant only if made to prepare the land which is cleared for use by the taxpayer or his tenant in farming. Thus, if the taxpayer pays or incurs expenditures to clear land for the purpose of sale (whether or not for use in farming by the purchaser) or to be held by the taxpayer or his tenant other than for use in farming, section 182 does not apply to such expenditures. Whether the land is cleared for the purpose of making it suitable for use in farming by the taxpayer or his tenant, is a question of fact which must be resolved on the basis of all the relevant facts and circumstances. For purposes of section 182, it is not necessary that the land cleared actually be used in farming following the clearing activities. However, the fact that following the clearing operation, the land is used by the taxpayer or his tenant in the business of farming will, in most cases, constitute evidence that the purpose of the clearing was to make land suitable for use in farming by the taxpayer or his tenant. On the other hand, if the land cleared is sold or converted to nonfarming use soon after the taxpayer has completed his clearing activities, there will be a presumption that the expenditures were not made for the purpose of making the land suitable for use in farming by the taxpayer or his tenant. Other factors which will be considered in determining the taxpayer's purpose for clearing the land are, for example, the acreage, location, and character of the land cleared, the nature of the taxpayer's farming operation, and the use to which adjoining or nearby land is put. [Reg. § 1.182-4.]

☐ [*T.D.* 6794, 1-25-65.]

[Reg. § 1.182-5]

§ 1.182-5. **Limitation.**—(a) *Limitation*—(1) *General rule.* The amount of land clearing expenditures which the taxpayer may deduct under section 182 in any one taxable year is limited to the lesser of $5,000 or 25 percent of his "taxable income derived from farming". Expenditures in excess of the applicable limitation are to be charged to the capital account and constitute additions to the taxpayer's basis in the land.

(2) *Definition of "taxable income derived from farming".* For purposes of section 182, the term "taxable income derived from farming" means the gross income derived from the business of farming reduced by the deductions attributable to such gross income. Gross income derived from the business of farming is the gross income of the taxpayer derived from the production of crops, fruits, or other agricultural products, including fish, or from livestock (including livestock held for draft, breeding or dairy purposes). It does not include gains from sales of assets such as farm machinery or gains from the disposition of land. The deductions attributable to the business of farming are all the deductions allowed by chapter 1 of the Code (other than the deduction allowed by section 182) for expenditures or charges (including depreciation and amortization) paid or incurred in connection with the production or raising of crops, fruits, or other agricultural products, including fish, or livestock. However, the deduction under section 1202 (relating to the capital gains deduction) attributable to gain on the sale or other disposition of assets (other than draft, breeding, or dairy stock), and the net operating loss deduction (computed under section 172) shall not be taken into account in computing "taxable income derived from farming." Similarly, deductible losses on the sale, disposition, destruction, condemnation, or abandonment of assets (other than draft, breeding, or dairy stock) shall not be considered as deductions attributable to the business of farming. A taxpayer shall compute his gross income from farming in accordance with his accounting method used in determining gross income. (See the regulations under section 61 relating to accounting methods used by farmers in determining gross income.)

(b) *Examples.* The provisions of paragraph (a) of this section may be illustrated by the following examples:

Example 1. For the taxable year 1963, A, who uses the cash receipts and disbursements method of accounting, incurs expenditures to which section 182 applies in the amount of $2,000 and makes the election under section 182. A has the following items of income and deductions (without regard to section 182 expenditures).

Income:

Proceeds from sale of his 1963 yield of corn	$10,000
Proceeds from sale of milk	8,000
Gain from disposition of old breeding cows	500
Gain from sale of tractor	100
Gain from sale of farmland	5,000
Interest on loan to brother	100
	$23,700

Deductions:

Cost of labor	$ 4,000	
Cost of feed	3,000	
Depreciation on farm equipment and buildings	2,500	
Cost of maintenance, fuel, etc	2,000	
Interest paid, mortgage on farm buildings	1,000	
Interest paid, personal loan	500	
Loss on destruction of barn	2,000	
Loss on sale of truck	300	
Section 1202 deduction—gain on sale of cows ($500 × 1/2)	250	
Section 1202 deduction—net gain on disposition of section 1231 property, other than cows [$2,800 ($5,100 − $2,300) × 1/2]	1,400	$16,950
Net income before section 182 deduction		$ 6,750

For purposes of computing taxable income derived from farming under section 182, the following items of income and deductions are not taken into account:

Income:

Gain from the sale of tractor	$ 100	
Gain from the sale of farmland	5,000	
Interest on loan to brother	100	$5,200

Deductions:

Interest paid, personal loan	$ 500	
Loss on destruction of barn	2,000	
Loss on sale of truck	300	
Section 1202 deduction—Net gain from disposition of section 1231 assets other than cows	1,400	$4,200

Reg. § 1.182-5(a)(2)

A's "taxable income derived from farming" for purposes of section 182 is $5,750; income of $18,500 ($23,700 − $5,200), less deductions of $12,750 ($16,950 − $4,200). A may deduct $1,437.50 (25% of $5,750) under section 182. The excess expenditures in the amount of $562.50 are to be charged to capital account and serve to increase the taxpayer's basis of the land.

Example 2. Assume the same facts as in example (1) and in addition, assume that A is allowed a deduction for a net operating loss carryback from the taxable year 1966 in the amount of $3,000. The net operating loss deduction will not be taken into account in computing A's "taxable income derived from farming" for 1963. Accordingly, A will not be required to recompute such taxable income for purposes of applying the limitation on the deduction provided in section 182 and the deduction of $1,437.50 will not be reduced. [Reg. § 1.182-5.]

□ [*T.D.* 6794, 1-25-66.]

[Reg. § 1.182-6]

§ 1.182-6. Election to deduct land clearing expenditures.—(a) *Manner of making election.* The election to deduct expenditures for land clearing provided by section 182(a) shall be made by means of a statement attached to the taxpayer's income tax return for the taxable year for which such election is to apply. The statement shall include the name and address of the taxpayer, shall be signed by the taxpayer (or his duly authorized representative), and shall be filed not later than the time prescribed by law for filing the income tax return (including extensions thereof) for the taxable year for which the election is to apply. The statement shall also set forth the amount and description of the expenditures for land clearing claimed as a deduction under section 182, and shall include a computation of "taxable income derived from farming", if the amount of such income is not the same as the net income from farming shown on Schedule F of Form 1040, increased by the amount of the deduction claimed under section 182.

(b) *Scope of election.* An election under section 182(a) shall apply only to the taxable year for which made. However, once made, an election applies to all expenditures described in § 1.182-3 paid or incurred during the taxable year, and is binding for such taxable year unless the district director consents to a revocation of such election. Requests for consent to revoke an election under section 182 shall be made by means of a letter to the district director for the district in which the taxpayer is required to file his return, setting forth the taxpayer's name, address and identification number, the year for which it is desired to

revoke the election and the reasons therefor. However, consent will not be granted where the only reason therefor is a change in tax consequences. [Reg. § 1.182-6.]

□ [*T.D.* 6794, 1-25-65.]

[Reg. § 1.183-1]

§ 1.183-1. Activities not engaged in for profit—(a) *In general.* Section 183 provides rules relating to the allowance of deductions in the case of activities (whether active or passive in character) not engaged in for profit by individuals and electing small business corporations, creates a presumption that an activity is engaged in for profit if certain requirements are met, and permits the taxpayer to elect to postpone determination of whether such presumption applies until he has engaged in the activity for at least five taxable years. or, in certain cases, seven taxable years. Whether an activity is engaged in for profit is determined under section 162 and section 212(1) and (2) except insofar as section 183(d) creates a presumption that the activity is engaged in for profit. If deductions are not allowable under sections 162 and 212(1) and (2), the deduction allowance rules of section 183(b) and this section apply. Pursuant to section 641(b), the taxable income of an estate or trust is computed in the same manner as in the case of an individual, with certain exceptions not here relevant. Accordingly, where an estate or trust engages in an activity or activities which are not for profit, the rules of section 183 and this section apply in computing the allowable deductions of such trust or estate. No inference is to be drawn from the provisions of section 183 and the regulations thereunder that any activity of a corporation (other than an electing small business corporation) is or is not a business or engaged in for profit. For rules relating to the deductions that may be taken into account by taxable membership organizations which are operated primarily to furnish services, facilities, or goods to members, see section 277 and the regulations thereunder. For the definition of an activity not engaged in for profit, see § 1.183-2. For rules relating to the election contained in section 183(e), see § 1.183-3.

(b) *Deductions allowable*—(1) *Manner and extent.* If an activity is not engaged in for profit, deductions are allowable under section 183(b) in the following order and only to the following extent:

(i) Amounts allowable as deductions during the taxable year under chapter 1 of the Code without regard to whether the activity giving rise to such amounts was engaged in for profit are allowable to the full extent allowed by the relevant sections of the Code, determined after taking into account any limitations or exceptions with respect to the allowability of such amounts. For example, the allowability-of-interest expenses incurred with respect to activities not engaged in for profit is limited by the rules contained in section 163(d).

(ii) Amounts otherwise allowable as deductions during the taxable year under chapter 1 of the Code, but only if such allowance does not result in an adjustment to the basis of property, determined as if the activity giving rise to such amounts was engaged in for profit, are allowed only to the extent the gross income attributable to such activity exceeds the deductions allowed or allowable under subdivision (i) of this subparagraph.

(iii) Amounts otherwise allowable as deductions for the taxable year under chapter 1 of the Code which result in (or if otherwise allowed would have resulted in) an adjustment to the basis of property, determined as if the activity giving rise to such deductions was engaged in for profit, are allowed only to the extent the gross income attributable to such activity exceeds the deductions allowed or allowable under subdivisions (i) and (ii) of this subparagraph. Deductions falling within this subdivision include such items as depreciation, partial losses with respect to property, partially worthless debts, amortization, and amortizable bond premium.

(2) *Rule for deductions involving basis adjustments*—(i) *In general.* If deductions are allowed under subparagraph, (1)(iii) of this paragraph, and such deductions are allowed with respect to more than one asset, the deduction allowed with respect to each asset shall be determined separately in accordance with the computation set forth in subdivision (ii) of this paragraph.

(ii) *Basis adjustment fraction.* The deduction allowed under subparagraph (1)(iii) of this paragraph is computed by multiplying the amount which would have been allowed, had the activity been engaged in for profit, as a deduction with respect to each particular asset which involves a basis adjustment, by the basis adjustment fraction—

(a) The numerator of which is the total of deductions allowable under subparagraph (1)(iii) of this paragraph, and

(b) The denominator of which is the total of deductions which involve basis adjustments which would have been allowed with respect to the activity had the activity been engaged in for profit.

The amount resulting from this computation is the deduction allowed under subparagraph (1)(iii) of this paragraph with respect to the particular

asset. The basis of such asset is adjusted only to the extent of such deduction.

(3) *Examples.* The provisions of subparagraphs (1) and (2) of this paragraph may be illustrated by the following examples:

Example (1). A, an individual, maintains a herd of dairy cattle, which is an "activity not engaged in for profit" within the meaning of section 183(c). A sold milk for $1,000 during the year. During the year A paid $300 State taxes on gasoline used to transport the cows, milk, etc., and paid $1,200 for feed for the cows. For the year A also had a casualty loss attributable to this activity of $500. A determines the amount of his allowable deductions under section 183 as follows:

(i) First, A computes his deductions allowable under subparagraph (1)(i) of this paragraph as follows:

State gasoline taxes specifically allowed under section 164(a)(5) without regard to whether the activity is engaged in for profit	$ 300
Casualty loss specifically allowed under section 165(c)(3) without regard to whether the activity is engaged in for profit ($500 less $100 limitation)	400
Deductions allowable under subparagraph (1)(i) of this paragraph	$ 700

(ii) Second, A computes his deductions allowable under subparagraph (1)(ii) of this paragraph (deductions which would be allowed under chapter 1 of the Code if the activity were engaged in for profit and which do not involve basis adjustments) as follows:

Maximum amount of deductions allowable under subparagraph (1)(ii) of this paragraph: Income from milk sales	$1,000
Gross income from activity	$1,000
Less: deductions allowable under subparagraph (1)(i) of this paragraph	700
Maximum amount of deductions allowable under subparagraph (1)(ii) of this paragraph	$ 300
Feed for cows	$1,200
Deduction allowed under subparagraph (1)(ii) of this paragraph	$ 300

$900 of the feed expense is not allowed as a deduction under section 183 because the total feed expense ($1,200) exceeds the maximum amount of deductions allowable under subparagraph (1)(ii) of this paragraph ($300). In view of these circumstances, it is not necessary to determine deductions allowable under subparagraph (1)(iii) of this paragraph which would be allowable under chapter 1 of the Code if the activity were engaged in

Reg. § 1.183-1(b)(2)

for profit and which involve basis adjustment (the $100 of casualty loss not allowable under subparagraph (1)(i) of this paragraph because of the limitation in section 165(c)(3)) because none of such amount will be allowed as a deduction under section 183.

Example (2). Assume the same facts as in example (1), except that A also had income from sales of hay grown on the farm of $1,200 and that depreciation of $750 with respect to a barn, and $650 with respect to a tractor would have been allowed with respect to the activity had it been engaged in for profit. A determines the amount of his allowable deductions under section 183 as follows:

(i) First, A computes his deductions allowable under subparagraph (1)(i) of this paragraph as follows:

State gasoline taxes specifically allowed under section 164(a)(5) without regard to whether the activity is engaged in for profit	$ 300
Casualty loss specifically allowed under section 165(c)(3) without regard to whether the activity is engaged in for profit ($500 less $100 limitation)	400
Deductions allowable under subparagraph (1)(i) of this paragraph	$ 700

(ii) Second, A computes his deductions allowable under subparagraph (1)(ii) of this paragraph (deductions which would be allowable under chapter 1 of the Code if the activity were engaged in for profit and which do not involve basis adjustments) as follows:

Maximum amount of deductions allowable under subparagraph (1)(ii) of this paragraph:	
Income from milk sales	$1,000
Income from hay sales	1,200
Gross income from activity	$2,200
Less: deductions allowable under subparagraph (1)(i) of this paragraph	700
Maximum amount of deductions allowable under subparagraph (1)(ii) of this paragraph	$1,500
Feed for cows	$1,200

The entire $1,200 of expenses relating to feed for cows is allowable as a deduction under subparagraph (1)(ii) of this paragraph, since it does not exceed the maximum amount of deductions allowable under such subparagraph.

(iii) Last, A computes the deductions allowable under subparagraph (1)(iii) of this paragraph (deductions which would be allowable under chapter 1 of the Code if the activity were

engaged in for profit and which involve basis adjustments) as follows:

Maximum amount of deductions allowable under subparagraph (1)(ii) of this paragraph:		
Gross income from farming		$2,200
Less: Deductions allowed under subparagraph (1)(i) of this paragraph	$ 700	
Deductions allowed under subparagraph (1)(ii) of this paragraph	1,200	1,900
Maximum amount of deductions allowable under subparagraph (1)(ii) of this paragraph		$ 300

(iv) Since the total of A's deductions under chapter 1 of the Code (determined as if the activity was engaged in for profit) which involve basis adjustments ($750 with respect to barn, $650 with respect to tractor, and $100 with respect to limitation on casualty loss) exceeds the maximum amount of the deductions allowable under subparagraph (1)(iii) of this paragraph ($300), A computes his allowable deductions with respect to such assets as follows:

A first computes his basis adjustment fraction under subparagraph (2)(ii) of this paragraph as follows:

The numerator of the fraction is the maximum of deductions allowable under subparagraph (1)(iii) of this paragraph which involve basis adjustments	$ 300
The denominator of the fraction is the total of deductions that involve basis adjustments which would have been allowed with respect to the activity had the activity been engaged in for profit	$1,500

The basis adjustment fraction is then applied to the amount of each deduction which would have been allowable if the activity were engaged in for profit and which involves a basis adjustment as follows:

Depreciation allowed with respect to barn (300/1,500 × $750)	$ 150
Depreciation allowed with respect to tractor (300/1,500 × $650)	$ 130
Deduction allowed with respect to limitation on casualty loss (300/1,500 × $100)	$ 20

The basis of the barn and of the tractor are adjusted only by the amount of depreciation actually allowed under section 183 with respect to each (as determined by the above computation). The basis of the asset with regard to which the casualty loss was suffered is adjusted only to the extent of the amount of the casualty loss actually allowed as a deduction under subparagraph (1)(i) and (iii) of this paragraph.

Reg. § 1.183-1(b)(3)

(4) *Rule for capital gains and losses*—(i) *In general.* For purposes of section 183 and the regulations thereunder, the gross income from any activity not engaged in for profit includes the total of all capital gains attributable to such activity determined without regard to the section 1202 deduction. Amounts attributable to an activity not engaged in for profit which would be allowable as a deduction under section 1202, without regard to section 183, shall be allowable as a deduction under section 183(b)(1) in accordance with the rules stated in this subparagraph.

(ii) *Cases where deduction not allowed under section 183.* No deduction is allowable under section 183(b)(1) with respect to capital gains attributable to an activity not engaged in for profit if—

(a) Without regard to section 183 and the regulations thereunder, there is no excess of net long-term capital gain over net short-term capital loss for the year, or

(b) There is no excess of net long-term capital gain attributable to the activity over net short-term capital loss attributable to the activity.

(iii) *Allocation of deduction.* If there is—

(a) An excess of net long-term capital gain over net short-term capital loss attributable to an activity not engaged in for profit, and

(b) Such an excess attributable to all activities, determined without regard to section 183 and the regulations thereunder,

the deduction allowable under section 183(b)(1) attributable to capital gains with respect to each activity not engaged in for profit (with respect to which there is an excess of net long-term capital gain over net short-term capital loss for the year) shall be an amount equal to the deduction allowable under section 1202 for the taxable year (determined without regard to section 183) multiplied by a fraction the numerator of which is the excess of the net long-term capital gain attributable to the activity over the net short-term capital loss attributable to the activity and the denominator of which is an amount equal to the total excess of net long-term capital gain over net short-term capital loss for all activities with respect to which there is such excess. The amount of the total section 1202 deduction allowable for the year shall be reduced by the amount determined to be allocable to activities not engaged in for profit and accordingly allowed as a deduction under section 183(b)(1).

(iv) *Example.* The provisions of this subparagraph may be illustrated by the following example:

Example. A, an individual who uses the cash receipts and disbursement method of accounting and the calendar year as the taxable year, has three activities not engaged in for profit. For his taxable year ending on December 31, 1973, A has a $200 net long-term capital gain from activity No. 1, a $100 net short-term capital loss from activity No. 2, and a $300 net long-term capital gain from activity No. 3. In addition, A has a $500 net long-term capital gain from another activity which he engages in for profit. A computes his deductions for capital gains for calendar year 1973 as follows:

Section 1202 deduction without regard to section 183 is determined as follows:

Net long-term capital gain from activity No. 1	$ 200
Net long-term capital gain from activity No. 3	300
Net long-term capital gain from activity engaged in for profit	500
Total net long-term capital gain from all activities	$1,000
Less: Net short-term capital loss attributable to activity No. 2	$ 100
Aggregate net long-term capital gain over net short-term capital loss from all activities	$ 900
Section 1202 deduction determined without regard to section 183 (one-half of $900)	$ 450

Allocation of the total section 1202 deduction among A's various activities:

Portion allocable to activity No. 1 which is deductible under section 183(b)(1) (Excess net long-term capital gain attributable to activity No. 1 ($200) over total excess net long-term capital gain attributable to all of A's activities with respect to which there is such an excess ($1,000) times amount of section 1202 deduction ($450))	$ 90
Portion allocable to activity No. 3 which is deductible under section 183(b)(1) (Excess net long-term capital gain attributable to activity No. 3 ($300) over total excess net long-term capital gain attributable to all of A's activities with respect to which there is such an excess ($1,000) times amount of section 1202 deduction ($450))	135
Portion allocable to all activities engaged in for profit (total section 1202 deduction ($450) less section 1202 deduction allowable to activities No. 1 and 3 ($225)	225
Total section 1202 deduction deductible under sections 1202 and 183(b)(1)	$ 450

Reg. § 1.183-1(b)(4)

(c) *Presumption that activity is engaged in for profit* —(1) *In general.* If for—

(i) Any two of seven consecutive taxable years, in the case of an activity which consists in major part of the breeding, training, showing, or racing of horses, or

(ii) Any two of five consecutive taxable years, in the case of any other activity, the gross income derived from an activity exceeds the deductions attributable to such activity which would be allowed or allowable if the activity were engaged in for profit, such activity is presumed, unless the Commissioner establishes to the contrary, to be engaged in for profit. For purposes of this determination the deduction permitted by section 1202 shall not be taken into account. Such presumption applies with respect to the second profit year and all years subsequent to the second profit year within the five- or seven-year period beginning with the first profit year. This presumption arises only if the activity is substantially the same activity for each of the relevant taxable years, including the taxable year in question. If the taxpayer does not meet the requirements of section 183(d) and this paragraph, no inference that the activity is not engaged in for profit shall arise by reason of the provisions of section 183. For purposes of this paragraph, a net operating loss deduction is not taken into account as a deduction. For purposes of this subparagraph a short taxable year constitutes a taxable year.

(2) *Examples.* The provisions of subparagraph (1) of this paragraph may be illustrated by the following examples, in each of which it is assumed that the taxpayer has not elected, in accordance with section 183(e), to postpone determination of whether the presumption described in section 183(d) and this paragraph is applicable.

Example (1). For taxable years 1970-74, A, an individual who uses the cash receipts and disbursement method of accounting and the calendar year as the taxable year, is engaged in the activity of farming. In taxable years 1971, 1973, and 1974, A's deductible expenditures with respect to such activity exceed his gross income from the activity. In taxable years 1970 and 1972 A has income from the sale of farm produce of $30,000 for each year. In each of such years A had expenses for feed for his livestock of $10,000, depreciation of equipment of $10,000, and fertilizer cost of $5,000 which he elects to take as a deduction. A also has a net operating loss carryover to taxable year 1970 of $6,000. A is presumed, for taxable years 1972, 1973, and 1974, to have engaged in the activity of farming for profit, since for 2 years of a 5-consecutive-year period the gross income from the activity ($30,000 for each year)

exceeded the deductions (computed without regard to the net operating loss) which are allowable in the case of the activity ($25,000 for each year).

Example (2). For the taxable years 1970 and 1971, B, an individual who uses the cash receipts and disbursement method of accounting and the calendar year as the taxable year, engaged in raising pure-bred Charolais cattle for breeding purposes. The operation showed a loss during 1970. At the end of 1971, B sold a substantial portion of his herd and the cattle operation showed a profit for that year. For all subsequent relevant taxable years B continued to keep a few Charolais bulls at stud. In 1972, B started to raise Tennessee Walking Horses for breeding and show purposes, utilizing substantially the same pasture land, barns, and (with structural modifications) the same stalls. The Walking Horse operations showed a small profit in 1973 and losses in 1972 and 1974 through 1976.

(i) Assuming that under paragraph (d)(1) of this section the raising of cattle and raising of horses are determined to be separate activities, no presumption that the Walking Horse operation was carried on for profit arises under section 183(d) and this paragraph since this activity was not the same activity that generated the profit in 1971 and there are not, therefore, 2 profit years attributable to the horse activity.

(ii) Assuming the same facts as in (i) above, if there were no stud fees received in 1972 with respect to Charolais bulls, but for 1973 stud fees with respect to such bulls exceed deductions attributable to maintenance of the bulls in that year, the presumption will arise under section 183(d) and this paragraph with respect to the activity of raising and maintaining Charolais cattle for 1973 and for all subsequent years within the five-year period beginning with taxable year 1971, since the activity of raising and maintaining Charolais cattle is the same activity in 1971 and in 1973, although carried on by B on a much reduced basis and in a different manner. Since it has been assumed that the horse and cattle operations are separate activities, no presumption will arise with respect to the Walking Horse operation because there are not 2 profit years attributable to such horse operation during the period in question.

(iii) Assuming, alternatively, that the raising of cattle and raising of horses would be considered a single activity under paragraph (d)(1) of this section, B would receive the benefit of the presumption beginning in 1973 with respect to both the cattle and horses since there were profits in 1971 and 1973. The presumption would be effective through 1977 (and longer if there is an excess of income over deductions in this activity in 1974, 1975, 1976, or 1977 which would extend the presumption) if, under section 183(d) and subparagraph (3) of this paragraph, it was determined that the activity consists in major part of the breeding, training, showing, or racing of horses. Otherwise, the presumption would be effective only through 1975 (assuming no excess of income over deductions in this activity in 1974 or 1975 which would extend the presumption).

(3) *Activity which consists in major part of the breeding, training, showing, or racing of horses.* For purposes of this paragraph an activity consists in major part of the breeding, training, showing, or racing of horses for the taxable year if the average of the portion of expenditures attributable to breeding, training, showing, and racing of horses for the 3 taxable years preceding the taxable year (or, in the case of an activity which has not been conducted by the taxpayer for 3 years, for so long as it has been carried on by him) was at least 50 percent of the total expenditures attributable to the activity for such prior taxable years.

(4) *Transitional rule.* In applying the presumption described in section 183(d) and this paragraph, only taxable years beginning after December 31, 1969, shall be taken into account. Accordingly, in the case of an activity referred to in subparagraph (1)(i) or (ii) of this paragraph, section 183(d) does not apply prior to the second profitable taxable year beginning after December 31, 1969, since taxable years prior to such date are not taken into account.

(5) *Cross reference.* For rules relating to section 183(e) which permits a taxpayer to elect to postpone determination of whether any activity shall be presumed to be "an activity engaged in for profit" by operation of the presumption described in section 183(d) and this paragraph until after the close of the fourth taxable year (sixth taxable year, in the case of activity which consists in major part of breeding, training, showing, or racing of horses) following the taxable year in which the taxpayer first engages in the activity, see § 1.183-3.

(d) *Activity defined* —(1) *Ascertainment of activity.* In order to determine whether, and to what extent, section 183 and the regulations thereunder apply, the activity or activities of the taxpayer must be ascertained. For instance, where the taxpayer is engaged in several undertakings, each of these may be a separate activity, or several undertakings may constitute one activity. In ascertaining the activity or activities of the taxpayer, all the facts and circumstances of the case must be taken into account. Generally, the most signifi-

cant facts and circumstances in making this determination are the degree of organizational and economic interrelationship of various undertakings, the business purpose which is (or might be) served by carrying on the various undertakings separately or together in a trade or business or in an investment setting, and the similarity of various undertakings. Generally, the Commissioner will accept the characterization by the taxpayer of several undertakings either as a single activity or as separate activities. The taxpayer's characterization will not be accepted, however, when it appears that his characterization is artificial and cannot be reasonably supported under the facts and circumstances of the case. If the taxpayer engages in two or more separate activities, deductions and income from each separate activity are not aggregated either in determining whether a particular activity is engaged in for profit or in applying section 183. Where land is purchased or held primarily with the intent to profit from increase in its value, and the taxpayer also engages in farming on such land, the farming and the holding of the land will ordinarily be considered a single activity only if the farming activity reduces the net cost of carrying the land for its appreciation in value. Thus, the farming and holding of the land will be considered a single activity only if the income derived from farming exceeds the deductions attributable to the farming activity which are not directly attributable to the holding of the land (that is, deductions other than those directly attributable to the holding of the land such as interest on a mortgage secured by the land, annual property taxes attributable to the land and improvements, and depreciation of improvements to the land).

(2) *Rules for allocation of expenses.* If the taxpayer is engaged in more than one activity, an item of deduction or income may be allocated between two or more of these activities. Where property is used in several activities, and one or more of such activities is determined not to be engaged in for profit, deductions relating to such property must be allocated between the various activities on a reasonable and consistently applied basis.

(3) *Example.* The provisions of this paragraph may be illustrated by the following example:

Example. (i) A, an individual, owns a small house located near the beach in a resort community. Visitors come to the area for recreational purposes during only three months of the year. During the remaining 9 months of the year houses such as A's are not rented. Customarily, A arranges that the house will be leased for 2 months

Reg. § 1.183-1(c)(3)

of 3-month recreational season to vacationers and reserves the house for his own vacation during the remaining month of the recreational season. In 1971, A leases the house for 2 months for $1,000 per month and actually uses the house for his own vacation during the other month of the recreational season. For 1971, the expenses attributable to the house are $1,200 interest, $600 real estate taxes, $600 maintenance. $300 utilities, and $1,200 which would have been allowed as depreciation had the activity been engaged in for profit. Under these facts and circumstances, A is engaged in a single activity, holding the beach house primarily for personal purposes, which is an "activity not engaged in for profit" within the meaning of section 183(c). See paragraph (b)(9) of § 1.183-2.

(ii) Since the $1,200 of interest and the $600 of real estate taxes are specifically allowable as deductions under sections 163 and 164(a) without regard to whether the beach house activity is engaged in for profit, no allocation of these expenses between the uses of the beach house is necessary. However, since section 262 specifically disallows personal, living, and family expenses as deductions, the maintenance and utilities expenses and the depreciation from the activity must be allocated between the rental use and the personal use of the beach house. Under the particular facts and circumstances, 2/3 (2 months of rental use over 3 months of total use) of each of these expenses are allocated to the rental use, and 1/3 (1 month of personal use over 3 months of total use) of each of these expenses are allocated to the personal use as follows:

	Rental use 2/3— expenses allocable to section 183(b)(2)	Personal use 1/3— expenses allocable to section 262
Maintenance expense $600	$ 400	$200
Utilities expense $300	200	100
Depreciation $1,200	800	400
Total	$1,400	$700

The $700 of expenses and depreciation allocated to the personal use of the beach house are disallowed as a deduction under section 262. In addition, the allowability of each of the expenses and the depreciation allocated to section 183(b)(2) is determined under paragraph (b)(1)(ii) and (iii) of this section. Thus, the maximum amount allowable as a deduction under section 183(b)(2) is $200 ($2,000 gross income from activity, less $1,800 deductions under section 183(b)(1)). Since the amounts described in section 183(b)(2) ($1,400) exceed the maximum amount allowable ($200), and since the amounts described in paragraph (b)(1)(ii) of this section ($600) exceed such maximum amount allowable ($200), none of the depreciation (an amount described in paragraph (b)(1)(iii) of this section) is allowable as a deduction.

(e) *Gross income from activity not engaged in for profit defined.* For purposes of section 183 and the regulations thereunder, gross income derived from an activity not engaged in for profit includes the total of all gains from the sale, exchange, or other disposition of property, and all other gross receipts derived from such activity. Such gross income shall include, for instance, capital gains, and rents received for the use of property which is held in connection with the activity. The taxpayer may determine gross income from any activity by subtracting the cost of goods sold from the gross receipts so long as he consistently does so and follows generally accepted methods of accounting in determining such gross income.

(f) *Rule for electing small business corporations.* Section 183 and this section shall be applied at the corporate level in determining the allowable deductions of an electing small business corporation. [Reg. § 1.183-1.]

☐ [T.D. 7198, 7-12-72.]

[Reg. § 1.183-2]

§ 1.183-2. **Activity not engaged in for profit defined.**—(a) *In general.* For purposes of section 183 and the regulations thereunder, the term "activity not engaged in for profit" means any activity other than one with respect to which deductions are allowable for the taxable year under section 162 or under paragraph (1) or (2) of section 212. Deductions are allowable under section 162 for expenses of carrying on activities which constitute a trade or business of the taxpayer and under section 212 for expenses incurred in connection with activities engaged in for the production or collection of income or for the management, conservation, or maintenance of property held for the production of income. Except as provided in section 183 and § 1.183-1, no deductions are allowable for expenses incurred in connection with activities which are not engaged in for profit. Thus, for example, deductions are not allowable under section 162 or 212 for activities which are carried on primarily as a sport, hobby, or for recreation. The determination whether an activity is engaged in for profit is to be made by reference to objective standards, taking into account all of the facts and circumstances of each case. Although a reasonable expectation of profit is not required, the facts and circumstances must indicate that the taxpayer entered into the activity, or continued the activity, with the objective of making a profit. In determining whether such an objective exists, it may be sufficient that there is a small chance of making a large profit. Thus it may be found that an investor in a wildcat oil well who incurs very substantial expenditures is in the venture for profit even though the expectation of a profit might be considered unreasonable. In determining whether an activity is engaged in for profit, greater weight is given to objective facts than to the taxpayer's mere statement of his intent.

(b) *Relevant factors.* In determining whether an activity is engaged in for profit, all facts and circumstances with respect to the activity are to be taken into account. No one factor is determinative in making this determination. In addition, it is not intended that only the factors described in this paragraph are to be taken into account in making the determination, or that a determination is to be made on the basis that the number of factors (whether or not listed in this paragraph) indicating a lack of profit objective exceeds the number of factors indicating a profit objective, or vice versa. Among the factors which should normally be taken into account are the following:

(1) *Manner in which the taxpayer carries on the activity.* The fact that the taxpayer carries on the activity in a businesslike manner and maintains complete and accurate books and records may indicate that the activity is engaged in for profit. Similarly, where an activity is carried on in a manner substantially similar to other activities of the same nature which are profitable, a profit motive may be indicated. A change of operating methods, adoption of new techniques or abandonment of unprofitable methods in a manner consistent with an intent to improve profitability may also indicate a profit motive.

(2) *The expertise of the taxpayer or his advisors.* Preparation for the activity by extensive study of its accepted business, economic, and scientific practices, or consultation with those who are expert therein, may indicate that the taxpayer has a profit motive where the taxpayer carries on the activity in accordance with such practices. Where a taxpayer has such preparation or procures such expert advice, but does not carry on the activity in accordance with such practices, a lack of intent to derive profit may be indicated unless it appears that the taxpayer is attempting to develop new or superior techniques which may result in profits from the activity.

(3) *The time and effort expended by the taxpayer in carrying on the activity.* The fact that the taxpayer devotes much of his personal time and effort to carrying on an activity, particularly if the activity does not have substantial personal or recreational aspects, may indicate an intention to derive a profit. A taxpayer's withdrawal from another occupation to devote most of his energies to the activity may also be evidence that the activity is engaged in for profit. The fact that the taxpayer devotes a limited amount of time to an activity does not necessarily indicate a lack of profit motive where the taxpayer employs competent and qualified persons to carry on such activity.

(4) *Expectation that assets used in activity may appreciate in value.* The term "profit" encompasses appreciation in the value of assets, such as land, used in the activity. Thus, the taxpayer may intend to derive a profit from the operation of the activity, and may also intend that, even if no profit from current operations is derived, an overall profit will result when appreciation in the value of land used in the activity is realized since income from the activity together with the appreciation of land will exceed expenses of operation. See, however, paragraph (d) of § 1.183-1 for definition of an activity in this connection.

(5) *The success of the taxpayer in carrying on other similar or dissimilar activities.* The fact that the taxpayer has engaged in similar activities in the past and converted them from unprofitable to profitable enterprises may indicate that he is engaged in the present activity for profit, even though the activity is presently unprofitable.

(6) *The taxpayer's history of income or losses with respect to the activity.* A series of losses during the initial or start-up stage of an activity may not necessarily be an indication that the activity is not engaged in for profit. However, where losses continue to be sustained beyond the period which customarily is necessary to bring the

Reg. § 1.183-2(b)(1)

operation to profitable status such continued losses, if not explainable, as due to customary business risks or reverses, may be indicative that the activity is not being engaged in for profit. If losses are sustained because of unforeseen or fortuitous circumstances which are beyond the control of the taxpayer, such as drought, disease, fire, theft, weather damages, other involuntary conversions, or depressed market conditions, such losses would not be an indication that the activity is not engaged in for profit. A series of years in which net income was realized would of course be strong evidence that the activity is engaged in for profit.

(7) *The amount of occasional profits, if any, which are earned.* The amount of profits in relation to the amount of losses incurred, and in relation to the amount of the taxpayer's investment and the value of the assets used in the activity, may provide useful criteria in determining the taxpayer's intent. An occasional small profit from an activity generating large losses, or from an activity in which the taxpayer has made a large investment, would not generally be determinative that the activity is engaged in for profit. However, substantial profit, though only occasional, would generally be indicative that an activity is engaged in for profit, where the investment or losses are comparatively small. Moreover, an opportunity to earn a substantial ultimate profit in a highly speculative venture is ordinarily sufficient to indicate that the activity is engaged in for profit even though losses or only occasional small profits are actually generated.

(8) *The financial status of the taxpayer.* The fact that the taxpayer does not have substantial income or capital from sources other than the activity may indicate that an activity is engaged in for profit. Substantial income from sources other than the activity (particularly if the losses from the activity generate substantial tax benefits) may indicate that the activity is not engaged in for profit especially if there are personal or recreational elements involved.

(9) *Elements of personal pleasure or recreation.* The presence of personal motives in carrying on of an activity may indicate that the activity is not engaged in for profit, especially where there are recreational or personal elements involved. On the other hand, a profit motivation may be indicated where an activity lacks any appeal other than profit. It is not, however, necessary that an activity be engaged in with the exclusive intention of deriving a profit or with the intention of maximizing profits. For example, the availability of other investments which would yield a higher return, or which would be more likely to be profitable, is not evidence that an activity is not engaged in for profit. An activity will not be treated as not engaged in for profit merely because the taxpayer has purposes or motivations other than solely to make a profit. Also, the fact that the taxpayer derives personal pleasure from engaging in the activity is not sufficient to cause the activity to be classified as not engaged in for profit if the activity is in fact engaged in for profit as evidenced by other factors whether or not listed in this paragraph.

(c) *Examples.* The provisions of this section may be illustrated by the following examples:

Example (1). The taxpayer inherited a farm from her husband in an area which was becoming largely residential, and is now nearly all so. The farm had never made a profit before the taxpayer inherited it, and the farm has since had substantial losses in each year. The decedent from whom the taxpayer inherited the farm was a stockbroker, and he also left the taxpayer substantial stock holdings which yield large income from dividends. The taxpayer lives on an area of the farm which is set aside exclusively for living purposes. A farm manager is employed to operate the farm, but modern methods are not used in operating the farm. The taxpayer was born and raised on a farm, and expresses a strong preference for living on a farm. The taxpayer's activity of farming, based on all the facts and circumstances, could be found not to be engaged in for profit.

Example (2). The taxpayer is a wealthy individual who is greatly interested in philosophy. During the past thirty years he has written and published at his own expense several pamphlets, and he has engaged in extensive lecturing activity, advocating and disseminating his ideas. He has made a profit from these activities in only occasional years, and the profits in those years were small in relation to the amounts of the losses in all other years. The taxpayer has very sizable income from securities (dividends and capital gains) which constitutes the principal source of his livelihood. The activity of lecturing, publishing pamphlets, and disseminating his ideas is not an activity engaged in by the taxpayer for profit.

Example (3). The taxpayer, very successful in the business of retailing soft drinks, raises dogs and horses. He began raising a particular breed of dogs many years ago in the belief that the breed was in danger of declining, and he has raised and sold the dogs in each year since. The taxpayer recently began raising and racing thoroughbred horses. The losses from the taxpayer's dog and horse activities have increased in magnitude over the years, and he has not made a profit on these operations during any of the last 15 years. The taxpayer generally sells the dogs only to friends, does not advertise the dogs for sale, and shows the dogs only infrequently. The taxpayer races his horses only at the "prestige" tracks at which he combines his racing activities with social and recreational activities. The horse and dog operations are conducted at a large residential property on which the taxpayer also lives, which includes substantial living quarters and attractive recreational facilities for the taxpayer and his family. Since (i) the activity of raising dogs and horses and racing the horses is of a sporting and recreational nature, (ii) the taxpayer has substantial income from his business activities of retailing soft drinks, (iii) the horse and dog operations are not conducted in a businesslike manner, and (iv) such operations have a continuous record of losses, it could be determined that the horse and dog activities of the taxpayer are not engaged in for profit.

Example (4). The taxpayer inherited a farm of 65 acres from his parents when they died 6 years ago. The taxpayer moved to the farm from his house in a small nearby town, and he operates it in the same manner as his parents operated the farm before they died. The taxpayer is employed as a skilled machine operator in a nearby factory, for which he is paid approximately $8,500 per year. The farm has not been profitable for the past 15 years because of rising costs of operating farms in general, and because of the decline in the price of the produce of this farm in particular. The taxpayer consults the local agent of the State agricultural service from time-to-time, and the suggestions of the agent have generally been followed. The manner in which the farm is operated by the taxpayer is substantially similar to the manner in which farms of similar size, and which grow similar crops in the area are operated. Many of these other farms do not make profits. The taxpayer does much of the required labor around the farm himself, such as fixing fences, planting crops, etc. The activity of farming could be found, based on all the facts and circumstances, to be engaged in by the taxpayer for profit.

Example (5). A, an independent oil and gas operator, frequently engages in the activity of searching for oil on undeveloped and unexplored land which is not near proven fields. He does so in a manner substantially similar to that of others who engage in the same activity. The chances, based on the experience of A and others who engaged in this activity, are strong that A will not find a commercially profitable oil deposit when he drills on land not established geologically to be proven oil bearing land. However, on the rare occasions that these activities do result in discovering a well, the operator generally realizes a very large return from such activity. Thus, there is a

small chance that A will make a large profit from his oil exploration activity. Under these circumstances, A is engaged in the activity of oil drilling for profit.

Example (6). C, a chemist, is employed by a large chemical company and is engaged in a wide variety of basic research projects for his employer. Although he does no work for his employer with respect to the development of new plastics, he has always been interested in such development and has outfitted a workshop in his home at his own expense which he uses to experiment in the field. He has patented several developments at his own expense but as yet has realized no income from his inventions or from such patents. C conducts his research on a regular, systematic basis, incurs fees to secure consultation on his projects from time to time, and makes extensive efforts to "market" his developments. C has devoted substantial time and expense in an effort to develop a plastic sufficiently hard, durable, and malleable that it could be used in lieu of sheet steel in many major applications, such as automobile bodies. Although there may be only a small chance that C will invent new plastics, the return from any such development would be so large that it induces C to incur the costs of his experimental work. C is sufficiently qualified by his background that there is some reasonable basis for his experimental activities. C's experimental work does not involve substantial personal or recreational aspects and is conducted in an effort to find practical applications for his work. Under these circumstances, C may be found to be engaged in the experimental activities for profit. [Reg. § 1.183-2.]

☐ [*T.D.* 7198, 7-12-72.]

[Reg. § 1.183-3]

§ 1.183-3. **Election to postpone determination with respect to the presumption described in section 183(d).** [Reserved]

[Reg. § 12.9]

§ 12.9. **Election to postpone determination with respect to the presumption described in section 183(d).**—(a) *In general.* An individual, electing small business corporation, trust or estate may elect in accordance with the rules set forth in this section to postpone a determination whether the presumption described in section 183(d) applies with respect to any activity in which the taxpayer engages until after the close of the fourth taxable year (sixth taxable year, in the case of an activity described in § 1.183-1(c)(3)) following the taxable year in which the taxpayer first engages in such activity. The election must be made in accordance with the applicable requirements of paragraphs (b), (c) and (d) of this section. Except as otherwise provided in paragraphs (c) and (e) of this section, an election made pursuant to this section shall be binding for the first taxable year in which the taxpayer first engages in the activity and for all subsequent taxable years in the five (or seven) year period referred to in the first sentence of this paragraph. For purposes of this section, a taxpayer shall be treated as not having engaged in an activity during any taxable year beginning before January 1, 1970.

(b) *Period to which an election applies.* An individual, trust, estate, or small business corporation may make the election. The five year presumption period (seven year presumption period in the case of an activity described in § 1.183-1(c)(3)) to which the election shall apply shall be the five (or seven) consecutive taxable years of such taxpayer beginning with the taxable year in which such taxpayer first engages in the activity. For purposes of this section, a taxpayer who engages in an activity as a partner, engages in it in each of his taxable years with or within which ends a partnership year during which the activity was carried on by the partnership.

(c) *Time for making an election.* A taxpayer who is an individual, trust, estate or small business corporation may make the election provided in section 183(e) by filing the statement and consents required by paragraph (d) of this section within—

(1) 3 years after the due date of such taxpayer's return (determined without extensions) for the taxable year in which such taxpayer first engages in the activity, but not later than

(2) 60 days after such taxpayer receives a written notice (if any) from a district director that the district director proposes to disallow deductions attributable to an activity not engaged in for profit under section 183. The provisions of paragraph (c)(2) of this section shall in no event be construed to extend the period described in (c)(1) of this section for making such election. Notwithstanding the time periods prescribed in paragraph (c)(1) and (2) of this section, if no election has been made before a suit or proceeding described in section 7422(a) is maintained or a petition is filed in the Tax Court for a redetermination of a deficiency for any taxable year within the presumption period to which the election would apply, no election may be made except with the consent of the Commissioner which will not be given unless no appreciable delay in the suit or proceeding will be caused.

(d) *Manner of making election.* (1) The election shall be made by the individual, trust, estate, or electing small business corporation, as the case

may be, engaged in the activity, by filing a statement which sets forth the following information—

i) The name, address, and taxpayer identification number of such taxpayer, and, if applicable, of the partnership in which he engages in the activity,

(ii) A declaration stating that the taxpayer elects to postpone a determination as to whether the presumption described in section 183(d) applies until after the close of the taxpayer's fourth taxable year (sixth taxable year, in the case of an activity described in § 1.183-1(c)(3)) following the taxable year in which the taxpayer first engaged in such activity and identifying that first such taxable year, and,

(iii) A description of each activity (as defined in § 1.183-1(d)(1)) with respect to which the election is being made.

(2) For an election to be effective, there must be attached to the statement properly executed consents, in the form prescribed by the Commissioner, extending the period prescribed by section 6501 for the assessment of any tax to a date which is not earlier than 18 months after the due date of the return (determined without extensions) for the final year in the presumption period to which the election applies, as follows:

(i) Consents for each of the taxpayer's taxable years in the presumption period to which the election applies,

(ii) If the election is made by an electing small business corporation, a consent of each person who is a shareholder during any taxable year to which the election applies, for each of such shareholder's taxable years with or within which end each of the corporation's taxable years in the presumption period,

(iii) If a taxpayer referred to in paragraph (d)(2)(i) of this section or shareholder referred to in paragraph (d)(2)(ii) of this section is married at the time of the election, in the case of his present spouse, a consent for each of such spouse's taxable years which correspond to the taxable years (other than prior years of the shareholder during no part of which he was a shareholder) for which consents are required by paragraph (d)(2)(i) or (ii) of this section as the case may be. Such consents shall not be construed to shorten the period described in section 6501 for any taxable year within the presumption period to which the election applies.

(3) The statement, with the required consents attached, shall be filed—

(i) With the service center at which the taxpayer making the election is required to file his return, or

(ii) If the taxpayer is notified by a district director that, pursuant to section 183, he is proposing to disallow deductions with respect to an activity not engaged in for profit, with such district director.

(e) *Subsequent invalidations.* If, after a timely election has been made, but still within the presumption period, a suit or proceeding (as described in section 7422(a)) is maintained by the electing taxpayer, a shareholder referred to in paragraph (d)(2)(ii) of this section, or spouse referred to in paragraph (d)(2)(iii) of this section for any taxable year for which a consent is required by this section and the taxpayer, shareholder, or spouse has not been issued a notice of deficiency (as described in section 6212(a)) with respect to such taxable year, such election shall not be effective to postpone the determination whether the presumption applies, for such taxable year, but the consents extending the statute of limitations filed with the election shall not thereby be invalidated. The immediately preceding sentence shall not apply to a suit or proceeding maintained by the spouse of an electing taxpayer for a taxable year for which such spouse has filed a separate return, or a suit or proceeding maintained by a shareholder for a taxable year in which he was not such a shareholder. An election by an individual taxpayer or electing small business corporation, shall be subsequently invalidated for all years in the presumption period to which it had applied if—

(1) The electing taxpayer or shareholder taxpayer files a joint return for one of the first three (five, in the case of an activity described in § 1.183-1(c)(3)) taxable years in such presumption period, and

(2) The spouse with whom he files such joint return has not previously executed a consent described in paragraph (d)(2)(iii) of this section, and

(3) Within one year after the filing of such joint return (or, if later, 90 days after March 14, 1974), such spouse has not filed a consent described in paragraph (d)(2) of this section.

An election by an electing small business corporation shall be invalidated for all years in the presumption period to which it applies if a person who was not a shareholder on the date of election becomes a shareholder during the first three (or five) years of the presumption period to which the election applies and does not, within 90 days after the date on which he becomes a shareholder (or, if later, 90 days after March 14, 1974), file a consent required by paragraph (d)(2) of this section. Invalidation of the election by operation of this paragraph will in no case affect the validity of the consents filed with such election.

(f) *Extension of time for filing election in hardship cases.* The Commissioner may, upon application by a taxpayer, consent to an extension of time prescribed in this section for making an election if he finds that such an extension would be justified by hardship incurred by reason of the time at which this section is published. The burden will be on the taxpayer to establish that under the relevant facts the Commissioner should so consent. [Temporary Reg. § 12.9.]

☐ [*T.D.* 7308, 3-14-74.]

[Reg. § 1.183-4]

§ 1.183-4. Taxable years affected.—The provisions of section 183 and the regulations thereunder shall apply only with respect to taxable years beginning after December 31, 1969. For provisions applicable to prior taxable years, see section 270 and § 1.270-1. [Reg. § 1.183-4.]

☐ [*T.D.* 7198, 7-12-72.]

[Reg. § 1.186-1]

§ 1.186-1. Recoveries of damages for antitrust violations, etc.—(a) *Allowance of deduction.* Under section 186, when a compensatory amount which is included in gross income is received or accrued during a taxable year for a compensable injury, a deduction is allowed in an amount equal to the lesser of (1) such compensatory amount, or (2) the unrecovered losses sustained as a result of such compensable injury.

(b) *Compensable injury*—(1) *In general.* For purposes of this section, the term "compensable injury" means any of the injuries described in subparagraph (2), (3), or (4) of this paragraph.

(2) *Patent infringement.* An injury sustained as a result of an infringement of a patent issued by the United States (whether or not issued to the taxpayer or another person or persons) constitutes a compensable injury. The term "patent issued by the United States" means any patent issued or granted by the United States under the authority of the Commissioner of Patents pursuant to 35 U.S.C. 153.

(3) *Breach of contract or of fiduciary duty or relationship.* An injury sustained as a result of a breach of contract (including an injury sustained by a third party beneficiary) or a breach of fiduciary duty or relationship constitutes a compensable injury.

(4) *Injury suffered under certain antitrust law violations.* An injury sustained in business, or to property, by reason of any conduct forbidden in the antitrust laws for which a civil action may be brought under section 4 of the Act of October 15, 1914 (15 U.S.C. 15), commonly known as the Clayton Act, constitutes a compensable injury.

Reg. § 1.183-4

(c) *Compensatory amount* —(1) *In general.* For purposes of this section, the term "compensatory amount" means any amount received or accrued during the taxable year as damages as a result of an award in, or in settlement of, a civil action for recovery for a compensable injury, reduced by any amounts paid or incurred in the taxable year in securing such award or settlement. The term "compensatory amount" includes only amounts compensating for actual economic injury. Thus, additional amounts representing punitive, exemplary, or treble damages are not included within the term. Where, for example, a taxpayer recovers treble damages under section 4 of the Clayton Act, only one-third of the recovery representing economic injury constitutes a compensatory amount. In the absence of any indication to the contrary, amounts received in settlement of an action shall be deemed to be a recovery for an actual economic injury except to the extent such settlement amounts exceed actual damages claimed by the taxpayer in such action.

(2) *Interest on a compensatory amount.* Interest attributable to a compensatory amount shall not be included within the term "compensatory amount."

(3) *Settlement of a civil action for damages*—(i) *Necessity for an action.* The term "compensatory amount" does not include an amount received or accrued in settlement of a claim for a compensable injury if the amount is received or accrued prior to institution of an action. An action shall be considered as instituted upon completion of service of process, in accordance with the laws and rules of the court in which the action has been commenced or to which the action has been removed, upon all defendants who pay or incur an obligation to pay a compensatory amount.

(ii) *Specifications of the parties.* If an action for a compensable injury is settled, the specifications of the parties will generally determine compensatory amounts unless such specifications are not reasonably supported by the facts and circumstances of the case. For example, the parties may provide that the sum of $1,000 represents actual damages sustained as the result of antitrust violations and that the total amount of the settlement after the trebling of damages is $3,000. In such case, only the sum of $1,000 would be a compensatory amount. In the absence of specifications of the parties, the complaint filed by the taxpayer may be considered in determining what portion of the amount of the settlement is a compensatory amount.

(4) *Amounts paid or incurred in securing the award or settlement.* For purposes of this section, the term "amounts paid or incurred in the taxable

year in securing such award or settlement" shall include legal expenses such as attorney's fees, witness fees, accountant fees, and court costs. Expenses incurred in securing a recovery of both a compensatory amount and other amounts from the same action shall be allocated among such amounts in the ratio each of such amounts bears to the total recovery. For instance, where a taxpayer incurs attorney's fees and other expenses of $3,000 in recovering $10,000 as a compensatory amount, $5,000 as a return of capital, and $25,000 as punitive damages from the same action, the taxpayer shall allocate $750 of the expenses to the compensatory amount (10,000/40,000 × 3,000), $375 to the return of capital (5,000/40,000 × 3,000), and $1,875 to the punitive damages (25,000/40,000 × 3,000).

(d) *Unrecovered losses*—(1) *In general.* For purposes of this section, the term "unrecovered losses sustained as a result of such compensable injury" means the sum of the amounts of the net operating losses for each taxable year in whole or in part within the injury period, to the extent that such net operating losses are attributable to such compensable injury, reduced by (i) the sum of any amounts of such net operating losses which were allowed as a net operating loss carryback or carryover for any prior taxable year under the provisions of section 172, and (ii) the sum of any amounts allowed as deductions under section 186(a) and this section for all prior taxable years with respect to the same compensable injury. Accordingly, a deduction is permitted under section 186(a) and this section with respect to net operating losses whether or not the period for carryover under section 172 has expired.

(2) *Injury period.* For purposes of this section, the term "injury period" means (i) with respect to an infringement of a patent, the period during which the infringement of the patent continued, (ii) with respect to a breach of contract or breach of fiduciary duty or relationship, the period during which amounts would have been received or accrued but for such breach of contract or breach of fiduciary duty or relationship, or (iii) with respect to injuries sustained by reason of a violation of section 4 of the Clayton Act, the period during which such injuries were sustained. The injury period will be determined on the basis of the facts and circumstances of the taxpayer's situation. The injury period may include periods before and after the period covered by the civil action instituted.

(3) *Net operating losses attributable to compensable injuries.* A net operating loss for any taxable year shall be treated as attributable (whether actually attributable or not) to a com-

Reg. § 1.186-1(d)(3)

pensable injury to the extent the compensable injury is sustained during the taxable year. For purposes of determining the extent of the compensable injury sustained during a taxable year, a judgment for a compensable injury apportioning the amount of the recovery (not reduced by any amounts paid or incurred in securing such recovery) to specific taxable years within the injury period will be conclusive. If a judgment for a compensable injury does not apportion the amount of the recovery to specific taxable years within the injury period, the amount of the recovery will be prorated among the years within the injury period in the proportion that the net operating loss sustained in each of such years bears to the total net operating losses sustained for all such years. If an action is settled, the specifications of the parties will generally determine the apportionment of the amount of the recovery unless such specifications are not reasonably supported by the facts and circumstances of the case. In the absence of specifications of the parties, the amount of the recovery will be prorated among the years within the injury period in the proportion that the net operating loss sustained in each of such years bears to the total net operating losses sustained for all such years.

(4) *Application of losses attributable to a compensable injury.* If only a portion of a net operating loss for any taxable year is attributable to a compensable injury, such portion shall (in applying section 172 for purposes of this section) be considered to be a separate net operating loss for such year to be applied after the other portion of such net operating loss. If, for example, in the year of the compensable injury the net operating loss was $1,000 and the amount of the compensable injury was $600, the amount of $400 not attributable to the compensable injury would be used first to offset profits in the carryover or carryback periods as prescribed by section 172. After the amount not attributable to the compensable injury is used to offset profits in other years, then the amount attributable to the compensable injury will be applied against profits in the carryover or carryback periods.

(e) *Effect on net operating loss carryovers—(1) In general.* Under section 186(e) if for the taxable year in which a compensatory amount is received or accrued any portion of the net operating loss carryovers to such year are attributable to the compensable injury for which such amount is received or accrued, such portion of the net operating loss carryovers must be reduced by the excess, if any, of (i) the amount computed under section 186(e)(1) with respect to such compensatory amount, over (ii) the amount computed under

section 186(e)(2) with respect to such compensable injury.

(2) *Amount computed under section 186(e)(1).* The amount computed under section 186(e)(1) is equal to the deduction allowed under section 186(a) with respect to the compensatory amount received or accrued for the taxable year.

(3) *Amount computed under section 186(e)(2).* The amount computed under section 186(e)(2) is equal to that portion of the unrecovered losses sustained as a result of the compensable injury with respect to which, as of the beginning of the taxable year, the period for carryover under section 172 has expired without benefit to the taxpayer, but only to the extent that such portion of the unrecovered losses did not reduce an amount computed under section 186(e)(1) for any prior taxable year.

(4) *Increase in income under section 172(b)(2).* If there is a reduction for any taxable year under subparagraph (1) of this paragraph in the portion of the net operating loss carryovers to such year attributable to a compensable injury, then, solely for purposes of determining the amount of such portion which may be carried to subsequent taxable years, the income of such taxable year, as computed under section 172(b)(2), shall be increased by the amount of the reduction computed under subparagraph (1) of this paragraph, for such year.

(f) *Illustration.* The provisions of section 186 and this section may be illustrated by the following example:

Example. (i) As of the beginning of this taxable year 1969, taxpayer A has a net operating loss carryover from his taxable year 1966 of $550 of which $250 is attributable to a compensable injury. In addition, he has a net operating loss attributable to the compensable injury of $150 with respect to which the period for carryover under section 172 has expired without benefit to the taxpayer. In 1969, he receives a $100 compensatory amount with respect to that injury and he has $75 in other income. Thus, A has gross income of $175 and he is entitled to a $100 deduction (the compensatory amount received) under section 186(a) and this section since this amount is less than the unrecovered losses sustained as a result of the compensable injury ($250 + $150 = $400). No portion of the net operating loss carryover to the current taxable year attributable to the compensable injury is reduced under section 186(e) since the amount determined under section 186(e)(1) ($100) does not exceed the amount determined under section 186(e)(2) ($150). Therefore, A applies a net operating loss carryover of $550 against his remaining income of $75 and

Reg. § 1.186-1(d)(4)

retains a net operating loss carryover of $475 to following years of which amount $250 remains attributable to the compensable injury. In addition, he retains $50 of net operating losses attributable to the compensable injury with respect to which the period for carryover under section 172 has expired without benefit to the taxpayer.

(ii) In 1970, A receives a $200 compensatory amount with respect to the same compensable injury and has $75 of other income. Thus, A has gross income of $275 and he is entitled to a $200 deduction (the compensatory amount received) under section 186(a) and this section since this amount is less than the remaining unrecovered loss sustained as a result of the compensable injury ($250 + $50 = $300). The net operating loss carryover to the current taxable year of $250 attributable to the compensable injury is reduced under section 186(e) by $150, which is the excess of the amount determined under section 186(e)(1) ($200) over the amount determined under section 186(e)(2) ($50). Therefore, A applies net operating loss carryovers of $325 ($225 not attributable to the compensable injury, + $100 attributable to such injury) against his remaining income of $75. A retains net operating loss carryovers of $250 for following years, of which amount $100 is attributable to the compensable injury. A has used all of his net operating losses attributable to the compensable injury with respect to which the period for carryover under section 172 has expired without benefit to the taxpayer.

(iii) In 1971, A receives a $200 compensatory amount with respect to the same compensable injury and has $75 of other income. Thus, A has gross income of $275 and he is entitled to a $100 deduction (the amount of unrecovered losses) under section 186(a) and this section since this amount is less than the compensatory amount received ($200). The net operating loss carryover to the current taxable year of $100 attributable to the compensable injury is reduced under section 186(e) by $100, which is the excess of the amount determined under section 186(e)(1) ($100) over the amount determined under section 186(e)(2) ($0). Therefore, A applies net operating loss carryovers of $150 against his remaining income of $175 ($100 compensatory amount plus $75 other income) which leaves $25 taxable income. No net operating loss carryover remains for following years.

(g) *Effective date.* The provisions of this section are applicable as to compensatory amounts received or accrued in taxable years beginning after December 31, 1968, even though the compensable injury was sustained in taxable years beginning before such date. [Reg. § 1.186-1.]

□ [T.D. 7220, 11-20-72.]

[Reg. § 1.190-1]

§ 1.190-1. **Expenditures to remove architectural and transportation barriers to the handicapped and elderly.**—(a) *In general.* Under section 190 of the Internal Revenue Code of 1954, a taxpayer may elect, in the manner provided in § 1.190-3 of this chapter, to deduct certain amounts paid or incurred by him in any taxable year beginning after December 31, 1976, and before January 1, 1980, for qualified architectural and transportation barrier removal expenses (as defined in § 1.190-2(b) of this chapter). In the case of a partnership, the election shall be made by the partnership. The election applies to expenditures paid or incurred during the taxable year which (but for the election) are chargeable to capital account.

(b) *Limitation.* The maximum deduction for a taxpayer (including an affiliated group of corporations filing a consolidated return) for any taxable year is $25,000. The $25,000 limitation applies to a partnership and to each partner. Expenditures paid or incurred in a taxable year in excess of the amount deductible under section 190 for such taxable year are capital expenditures and are adjustments to basis under section 1016(a). A partner must combine his distributive share of the partnership's deductible expenditures (after application of the $25,000 limitation at the partnership level) with that partner's distributive share of deductible expenditures from any other partnership plus that partner's own section 190 expenditures, if any (if he makes the election with respect to his own expenditures), and apply the partner's $25,000 limitation to the combined total to determine the aggregate amount deductible by that partner. In so doing, the partner may allocate the partner's $25,000 limitation among the partner's own section 190 expenditures and the partner's distributive share of partnership deductible expenditures in any manner. If such allocation results in all or a portion of the partner's distributive share of a partnership's deductible expenditures not being an allowable deduction by the partner, the partnership may capitalize such unallowable portion by an appropriate adjustment to the basis of the relevant partnership property under section 1016. For purposes of adjustments to the basis of properties held by a partnership, however, it shall be presumed that each partner's distributive share of partnership deductible expenditures (after application of the $25,000 limitation at the partnership level) was allowable in full to the partner. This presumption can be rebutted only by clear and convincing evidence that all or any portion of a partner's distributive share of the partnership section 190 deduction was not allowable as a deduction to the partner because it exceeded that partner's $25,000 limitation as allocated by him. For example, suppose for 1978 A's distributive share of the ABC partnership's deductible section 190 expenditures (after application of the $25,000 limitation at the partnership level) is $15,000. A also made section 190 expenditures of $20,000 in 1978 which he elects to deduct. A allocates $10,000 of his $25,000 limitation to his distributive share of the ABC expenditures and $15,000 to his own expenditures. A may capitalize the excess $5,000 of his own expenditures. In addition, if ABC obtains from A evidence which meets the requisite burden of proof, it may capitalize the $5,000 of A's distributive share which is not allowable as a deduction to A. [Reg. § 1.190-1.]

☐ [*T.D.* 7634, 7-19-79.]

[Reg. § 1.190-2]

§ 1.190-2. Definitions.—For purposes of section 190 and the regulations thereunder—

(a) *Architectural and transportation barrier removal expenses.* The term "architectural and transportation barrier removal expenses" means expenditures for the purpose of making any facility, or public transportation vehicle, owned or leased by the taxpayer for use in connection with his trade or business more accessible to, or usable by, handicapped individuals or elderly individuals. For purposes of this section—

(1) The term "facility" means all or any portion of buildings, structures, equipment, roads, walks, parking lots, or similar real or personal property.

(2) The term "public transportation vehicle" means a vehicle, such as a bus, a railroad car, or other conveyance, which provides to the public general or special transportation service (including such service rendered to the customers of a taxpayer who is not in the trade or business of rendering transportation services).

(3) The term "handicapped individual" means any individual who has—

(i) A physical or mental disability (including, but not limited to, blindness or deafness) which for such individual constitutes or results in a functional limitation to employment, or

(ii) A physical or mental impairment (including, but not limited to, a sight or hearing impairment) which substantially limits one or more of such individual's major life activities, such as performing manual tasks, walking, speaking, breathing, learning, or working.

(4) The term "elderly individual" means an individual age 65 or over.

(b) *Qualified architectural and transportation barrier removal expense*—(1) *In general.* The term "qualified architectural and transportation barrier removal expense" means an architectural or transportation barrier removal expenses (as defined in paragraph (a) of this section) with respect to which the taxpayer establishes, to the satisfaction of the Commissioner or his delegate, that the resulting removal of any such barrier conforms a facility or public transportation vehicle to all the requirements set forth in one or more of paragraphs (b)(2) through (22) of this section or in one or more of the subdivisions of paragraph (b)(20) or (21). Such term includes only expenses specifically attributable to the removal of an existing architectural or transportation barrier. It does not include any part of any expense paid or incurred in connection with the construction or comprehensive renovation of a facility or public transportation vehicle or the normal replacement of depreciable property. Such term may include expenses of construction, as, for example, the construction of a ramp to remove the barrier posed for wheelchair users by steps. Major portions of the standards set forth in this paragraph were adapted from "American National Standard Specifications for Making Buildings and Facilities Accessible to, and Usable by, the Physically Handicapped" (1971), the copyright for which is held by the American National Standards Institute, 1430 Broadway, New York, New York 10018.

(2) *Grading.* The grading of ground, even contrary to existing topography, shall attain a level with a normal entrance to make a facility accessible to individuals with physical disabilities.

(3) *Walks.* (i) A public walk shall be at least 48 inches wide and shall have a gradient not greater than 5 percent. A walk of maximum or near maximum grade and of considerable length shall have level areas at regular intervals. A walk or driveway shall have a nonslip surface.

(ii) A walk shall be of a continuing common surface and shall not be interrupted by steps or abrupt changes in level.

(iii) Where a walk crosses a walk, a driveway, or a parking lot, they shall blend to a common level. However, the preceding sentence does not require the elimination of those curbs which are a safety feature for the handicapped, particularly the blind.

(iv) An inclined walk shall have a level platform at the top and at the bottom. If a door swings out onto the platform toward the walk, such platform shall be at least 5 feet deep and 5 feet wide. If a door does not swing onto the platform or toward the walk, such platform shall be at least 3 feet deep and 5 feet wide. A platform shall extend at least 1 foot beyond the strike jamb side of any doorway.

(4) *Parking lots.* (i) At least one parking space that is accessible and approximate to a facility shall be set aside and identified for use by the handicapped.

(ii) A parking space shall be open on one side to allow room for individuals in wheelchairs and individuals on braces or crutches to get in and out of an automobile onto a level surface which is suitable for wheeling and walking.

(iii) A parking space for the handicapped, when placed between two conventional diagonal or head-on parking spaces, shall be at least 12 feet wide.

(iv) A parking space shall be positioned so that individuals in wheelchairs and individuals on braces or crutches need not wheel or walk behind parked cars.

(5) *Ramps.* (i) A ramp shall not have a slope greater than 1 inch rise in 12 inches.

(ii) A ramp shall have at least one handrail that is 32 inches in height, measured from the surface of the ramp, that is smooth, and that extends 1 foot beyond the top and bottom of the ramp. However, the preceding sentence does not require a handrail extension which is itself a hazard.

(iii) A ramp shall have a nonslip surface.

(iv) A ramp shall have a level platform at the top and at the bottom. If a door swings out onto the platform or toward the ramp, such platform shall be at least 5 feet deep and 5 feet wide. If a door does not swing onto the platform or toward the ramp, such platform shall be at least 3 feet deep and 5 feet wide. A platform shall extend at least 1 foot beyond the strike jamb side of any doorway.

(v) A ramp shall have level platforms at not more than 30-foot intervals and at any turn.

(vi) A curb ramp shall be provided at an intersection. The curb ramp shall not be less than 4 feet wide; it shall not have a slope greater than 1 inch rise in 12 inches. The transition between the two surfaces shall be smooth. A curb ramp shall have a nonslip surface.

(6) *Entrances.* A building shall have at least one primary entrance which is usable by individuals in wheelchairs and which is on a level accessible to an elevator.

(7) *Doors and doorways.* (i) A door shall have a clear opening of no less than 32 inches and shall be operable by a single effort.

(ii) The floor on the inside and outside of a doorway shall be level for a distance of at least 5 feet from the door in the direction the door swings and shall extend at least 1 foot beyond the strike jamb side of the doorway.

(iii) There shall be no sharp inclines or abrupt changes in level at a doorway. The threshold shall be flush with the floor. The door closer shall be selected, placed, and set so as not to impair the use of the door by the handicapped.

(8) *Stairs.* (i) Stairsteps shall have round nosing of between 1 and $1\frac{1}{2}$ inch radius.

(ii) Stairs shall have a handrail 32 inches high as measured from the tread at the face of the riser.

(iii) Stairs shall have at least one handrail that extends at least 18 inches beyond the top step and beyond the bottom step. The preceding sentence does not require a handrail extension which is itself a hazard.

(iv) Steps shall have risers which do not exceed 7 inches.

(9) *Floors.* (i) Floors shall have a nonslip surface.

(ii) Floors on a given story of a building shall be of a common level or shall be connected by a ramp in accordance with subparagraph (5) of this paragraph.

(10) *Toilet rooms.* (i) A toilet room shall have sufficient space to allow traffic of individuals in wheelchairs.

(ii) A toilet room shall have at least one toilet stall that—

(A) Is at least 36 inches wide;

(B) Is at least 56 inches deep;

(C) Has a door, if any, that is at least 32 inches wide and swings out;

(D) Has handrails on each side, 33 inches high and parallel to the floor, $1\frac{1}{2}$ inches in outside diameter, $1\frac{1}{2}$ inches clearance between rail and wall, and fastened securely at ends and center; and

(E) Has a water closet with a seat 19 to 20 inches from the finished floor.

(iii) A toilet room shall have, in addition to or in lieu of a toilet stall described in (ii), at least one toilet stall that—

(A) Is at least 66 inches wide;

(B) Is at least 60 inches deep;

(C) Has a door, if any, that is at least 32 inches wide and swings out;

(D) Has a handrail on one side, 33 inches high and parallel to the floor, $1\frac{1}{2}$ inches in outside diameter, $1\frac{1}{2}$ inches clearance between

Reg. § 1.190-2(b)(10)

rail and wall, and fastened securely at ends and center; and

(E) Has a water closet with a seat 19 to 20 inches from the finished floor, centerline located 18 inches from the side wall on which the handrail is located.

(iv) A toilet room shall have lavatories with narrow aprons. Drain pipes and hot water pipes under a lavatory shall be covered or insulated.

(v) A mirror and a shelf above a lavatory shall be no higher than 40 inches above the floor, measured from the top of the shelf and the bottom of the mirror.

(vi) A toilet room for men shall have wall-mounted urinals with the opening of the basin 15 to 19 inches from the finished floor or shall have floor-mounted urinals that are level with the main floor of the toilet room.

(vii) Towel racks, towel dispensers, and other dispensers and disposal units shall be mounted no higher than 40 inches from the floor.

(11) *Water fountains.* (i) A water fountain and a cooler shall have upfront spouts and controls.

(ii) A water fountain and a cooler shall be hand-operated or hand-and-foot-operated.

(iii) A water fountain mounted on the side of a floor-mounted cooler shall not be more than 30 inches above the floor.

(iv) A wall-mounted, hand-operated water cooler shall be mounted with the basin 36 inches from the floor.

(v) A water fountain shall not be fully recessed and shall not be set into an alcove unless the alcove is at least 36 inches wide.

(12) *Public telephones.* (i) A public telephone shall be placed so that the dial and the headset can be reached by individuals in wheelchairs.

(ii) A public telephone shall be equipped for those with hearing disabilities and so identified with instructions for use.

(iii) Coin slots of public telephones shall be not more than 48 inches from the floor.

(13) *Elevators.* (i) An elevator shall be accessible to, and usable by, the handicapped or the elderly on the levels they use to enter the building and all levels and areas normally used.

(ii) Cab size shall allow for the turning of a wheelchair. It shall measure at least 54 by 68 inches.

(iii) Door clear opening width shall be at least 32 inches.

(iv) All essential controls shall be within 48 to 54 inches from cab floor. Such controls shall be usable by the blind and shall be tactilely identifiable.

(14) *Controls.* Switches and controls for light, heat, ventilation, windows, draperies, fire alarms, and all similar controls of frequent or essential use, shall be placed within the reach of individuals in wheelchairs. Such switches and controls shall be no higher than 48 inches from the floor.

(15) *Identification.* (i) Raised letters or numbers shall be used to identify a room or an office. Such identification shall be placed on the wall to the right or left of the door at a height of 54 inches to 66 inches, measured from the finished floor.

(ii) A door that might prove dangerous if a blind person were to exit or enter by it (such as a door leading to a loading platform, boiler room, stage, or fire escape) shall be tactilely identifiable.

(16) *Warning signals.* (i) An audible warning signal shall be accompanied by a simultaneous visual signal for the benefit of those with hearing disabilities.

(ii) A visual warning signal shall be accompanied by a simultaneous audible signal for the benefit of the blind.

(17) *Hazards.* Hanging signs, ceiling lights, and similar objects and fixtures shall be placed at a minimum height of 7 feet, measured from the floor.

(18) *International accessibility symbol.* The international accessibility symbol (see illustration) shall be displayed on routes to and at wheelchair-accessible entrances to facilities and public transportation vehicles.

(19) *Additional standards for rail facilities.* (i) A rail facility shall contain a fare control area

with at least one entrance with a clear opening at least 36 inches wide.

(ii) A boarding platform edge bordering a drop-off or other dangerous condition shall be marked with a warning device consisting of a strip of floor material differing in color and texture from the remaining floor surface. The gap between boarding platform and vehicle doorway shall be minimized.

(20) *Standards for buses.* (i) A bus shall have a level change mechanism (*e.g.,* lift or ramp) to enter the bus and sufficient clearance to permit a wheelchair user to reach a secure location.

(ii) A bus shall have a wheelchair securement device. However, the preceding sentence does not require a wheelchair securement device which is itself a barrier or hazard.

(iii) The vertical distance from a curb or from street level to the first front door step shall not exceed 8 inches; the riser height for each front doorstep after the first step up from the curb or street level shall also not exceed 8 inches; and the tread depth of steps at front and rear doors shall be no less than 12 inches.

(iv) A bus shall contain clearly legible signs that indicate that seats in the front of the bus are priority seats for handicapped or elderly persons, and that encourage other passengers to make such seats available to handicapped and elderly persons who wish to use them.

(v) Handrails and stanchions shall be provided in the entranceway to the bus in a configuration that allows handicapped and elderly persons to grasp such assists from outside the bus while starting to board and to continue to use such assists throughout the boarding and fare collection processes. The configuration of the passenger assist system shall include a rail across the front of the interior of the bus located to allow passengers to lean against it while paying fares. Overhead handrails shall be continuous except for a gap at the rear doorway.

(vi) Floors and steps shall have nonslip surfaces. Step edges shall have a band of bright contrasting color running the full width of the step.

(vii) A stepwell immediately adjacent to the driver shall have, when the door is open, at least 2 foot-candles of illumination measured on the step tread. Other stepwells shall have, at all times, at least 2 foot-candles of illumination measured on the step tread.

(viii) The doorways of the bus shall have outside lighting that provides at least 1 foot-candle of illumination on the street surface for a distance of 3 feet from all points on the bottom step tread edge. Such lighting shall be located below window level and shall be shielded to protect the eyes of entering and exiting passengers.

(ix) The fare box shall be located as far forward as practicable and shall not obstruct traffic in the vestibule.

(21) *Standards for rapid and light rail vehicles.* (i) Passenger doorways on the vehicle sides shall have clear openings at least 32 inches wide.

(ii) Audible or visual warning signals shall be provided to alert handicapped and elderly persons of closing doors.

(iii) Handrails and stanchions shall be sufficient to permit safe boarding, onboard circulation, seating and standing assistance, and unboarding by handicapped and elderly persons. On a level entry vehicle, handrails, stanchions, and seats shall be located so as to allow a wheelchair user to enter the vehicle and position the wheelchair in a location which does not obstruct the movement of other passengers. On a vehicle that requires the use of steps in the boarding process, handrails and stanchions shall be provided in the entranceway to the vehicle in a configuration that allows handicapped and elderly persons to grasp such assists from outside the vehicle while starting to board, and to continue using such assists throughout the boarding process.

(iv) Floors shall have nonslip surfaces. Step edges on a light rail vehicle shall have a band of bright contrasting color running the full width of the step.

(v) A stepwell immediately adjacent to the driver shall have, when the door is open, at least 2 foot-candles of illumination measured on the step tread. Other stepwells shall have, at all times, at least 2 foot-candles of illumination measured on the step tread.

(vi) Doorways on a light rail vehicle shall have outside lighting that provides at least 1 foot-candle of illumination on the street surface for a distance of 3 feet from all points on the bottom step tread edge. Such lighting shall be located below window level and shall be shielded to protect the eyes of entering and exiting passengers.

(22) *Other barrier removals.* The provisions of this subparagraph apply to any barrier which would not be removed by compliance with paragraphs (b)(2) through (21) of this section. The requirements of this subparagraph are:

(i) A substantial barrier to the access to or use of a facility or public transportation vehicle by handicapped or elderly individuals is removed;

(ii) The barrier which is removed had been a barrier for one or more major classes of such

Reg. § 1.190-2(b)(22)

individuals (such as the blind, deaf, or wheelchair users); and

(iii) The removal of that barrier is accomplished without creating any new barrier that significantly impairs access to or use of the facility or vehicle by such class or classes. [Reg. § 1.190-2.]

☐ [T.D. 7634, 7-19-79.]

[Reg. § 1.190-3]

§ 1.190-3. **Election to deduct architectural and transportation barrier removal expenses.**—(a) *Manner of making election.* The election to deduct expenditures for removal of architectural and transportation barriers provided by section 190(a) shall be made by claiming the deduction as a separate item identified as such on the taxpayer's income tax return for the taxable year for which such election is to apply (or, in the case of a partnership, to the return of partnership income for such year). For the election to be valid, the return must be filed not later than the time prescribed by law for filing the return (including extensions thereof) for the taxable year for which the election is to apply.

(b) *Scope of election.* An election under section 190(a) shall apply to all expenditures described in § 1.190-2 (or, in the case of a taxpayer whose architectural and transportation barrier removal expenses exceed $25,000 for the taxable year, to the $25,000 of such expenses with respect to which the deduction is claimed) paid or incurred during the taxable year for which made and shall be irrevocable after the date by which any such election must have been made.

(c) *Records to be kept.* In any case in which an election is made under section 190(a), the taxpayer shall have available, for the period prescribed by paragraph (e) of § 1.6001-1 of this chapter (Income Tax Regulations), records and documentation, including architectural plans and blueprints, contracts, and any building permits, of all the facts necessary to determine the amount of any deduction to which he is entitled by reason of the election, as well as the amount of any adjustment to basis made for expenditures in excess of the amount deductible under section 190. [Reg. § 1.190-3.]

☐ [T.D. 7634, 7-19-79.]

[Reg. § 1.193-1]

§ 1.193-1. **Deduction for tertiary injectant expenses.**—(a) *In general.* Subject to the limitations and restrictions of paragraphs (c) and (d) of this section, there shall be allowed as a deduction from gross income an amount equal to the quali-

fied tertiary injectant expenses of the taxpayer. This deduction is allowed for the later of—

(1) The taxable year in which the injectant is injected, or

(2) The taxable year in which the expenses are paid or incurred.

(b) *Definitions*—(1) *Qualified tertiary injectant expenses.* Except as otherwise provided in this section, the term "qualified tertiary injectant expense" means any cost paid or incurred for any tertiary injectant which is used as part of a tertiary recovery method.

(2) *Tertiary recovery method.* "Tertiary recovery method" means—

(i) Any method which is described in subparagraphs (1) through (9) of section 212.78(c) of the June 1979 energy regulations (as defined by section 4996(b)(8)(C)),

(ii) Any method for which the taxpayer has obtained the approval of the Associate Chief Counsel (Technical), under section 4993(d)(1)(B) for purposes of Chapter 45 of the Internal Revenue Code,

(iii) Any method which is approved in the regulations under section 4993(d)(1)(B), or

(iv) Any other method to provide tertiary enhanced recovery for which the taxpayer obtains the approval of the Associate Chief Counsel (Technical) for purposes of section 193.

(c) *Special rules for hydrocarbons*—(1) *In general.* If an injectant contains more than an insignificant amount of recoverable hydrocarbons, the amount deductible under section 193 and paragraph (a) of this section shall be limited to the cost of the injectant reduced by the lesser of—

(i) The fair market value of the hydrocarbon component in the form in which it is recovered, or

(ii) The cost to the taxpayer of the hydrocarbon component of the injectant. Price levels at the time of injection are to be used in determining the fair market value of the recoverable hydrocarbons.

(2) *Presumption of recoverability.* Except to the extent that the taxpayer can demonstrate otherwise, all hydrocarbons shall be presumed recoverable and shall be presumed to have the same value on recovery that they would have if separated from the other components of the injectant before injection. Estimates based on generally accepted engineering practices may provide evidence of limitations on the amount or value of recoverable hydrocarbons.

(3) *Significant amount.* For purposes of section 193 and this section, an injectant contains

Reg. § 1.190-3(a)

more than an insignificant amount of recoverable hydrocarbons if the fair market value of the recoverable hydrocarbon component of the injectant, in the form in which it is recovered, equals or exceeds 25 percent of the cost of the injectant.

(4) *Hydrocarbon defined.* For purposes of section 193 and this section, the term hydrocarbon means all forms of natural gas and crude oil (which includes oil recovered from sources such as oil shale and condensate).

(5) *Injectant defined.* For purposes of applying this paragraph (c), an injectant is the substance or mixture of substances injected at a particular time. Substances injected at different times are not treated as components of a single injectant even if the injections are part of a single tertiary recovery process.

(d) *Application with other deductions.* No deduction shall be allowed under section 193 and this section for any expenditure—

(1) With respect to which the taxpayer has made an election under section 263(c) or

(2) With respect to which a deduction is allowed or allowable under any other provision of chapter 1 of the Code.

(e) *Examples.* The application of this section may be illustrated by the following examples:

Example (1). B, a calendar year taxpayer who uses the cash receipts and disbursements method of accounting, uses an approved tertiary recovery method for the enhanced recovery of crude oil from one of B's oil properties. During 1980, B pays $100x for a tertiary injectant which contains 1,000y units of hydrocarbon; if separated from the other components of the injectant before injection, the hydrocarbons would have a fair market value of $80x. B uses this injectant during the recovery effort during 1981. B has not made any election under section 263(c) with respect to the expenditures for the injectant, and no section of chapter 1 of the Code other than section 193 allows a deduction for the expenditure. B is unable to demonstrate that the value of the injected hydrocarbons recovered during production will be less than $80x. B's deduction under section 193 is limited to the excess of the cost for the injectant over the fair market value of the hydrocarbon component expected to be recovered ($100x − $80x=$20x). B may claim the deduction only for 1981, the year of the injection.

Example (2). Assume the same facts as in example (1) except that through engineering studies B has shown that 700y units or 70 percent of the hydrocarbon injected is nonrecoverable. The recoverable hydrocarbons have a fair market value

of $24x (30 percent of $80x). The recoverable hydrocarbon portion of the injectant is 24 percent of the cost of the injectant ($24x divided by $100x). The injectant does not contain a significant amount of recoverable hydrocarbons. B may claim a deduction for $100x, the entire cost of the injectant.

Example (3). Assume the same facts as in example (1) except that through laboratory studies B has shown that because of chemical changes in the course of production the injected hydrocarbons that are recovered will have a fair market value of only $40x. B may claim a deduction for $60x, the excess of the cost of the injectant ($100x) over the fair market value of the recoverable hydrocarbons ($40x).

Example (4). B prepares an injectant from crude oil and certain nonhydrocarbon materials purchased by B. The total cost of the injectant to B is $100x, of which $24x is attributable to the crude oil. The fair market value of the crude oil used in the injectant is $27x. B is unable to demonstrate that the value of the crude oil from the injectant that will be recovered is less than $27x. The injectant contains more than an insignificant amount of recoverable hydrocarbons because the value of the recoverable crude oil ($27x) exceeds $25x (25 percent of $100x, the cost of the injectant). Because the cost to B of the hydrocarbon component of the injectant ($24x) is less than the fair market value of the hydrocarbon component in the form in which it is recovered ($27x), the cost rather than the value is taken into account in the adjustment required under paragraph (c)(1) of this section. B's deduction under section 193 is limited to the excess of the cost of the injectant over the cost of the hydrocarbon component ($100x − $24x = $76x). [Reg. § 1.193-1]

☐ [*T.D.* 7980, 10-2-84.]

[Reg. § 1.194-1]

§ 1.194-1. **Amortization of reforestation expenditures.**—(a) *In general.* Section 194 allows taxpayer to elect to amortize over an 84-mon period, up to $10,000 of reforestation exper tures (as defined in § 1.194-3(c)) incurred by taxpayer in a taxable year in connection qualified timber property (as define § 1.194-3(a)). The election is not availab trusts. Only those reforestation expend which result in additions to capital accoun December 31, 1979 are eligible for this amortization.

(b) *Determination of amortization pe* amortization period must begin on the f the first month of the last half of the ta during which the taxpayer incurs the reforestation expenditures. For example, the 84-month amortization period begins on July 1 of a taxable year for a calendar year taxpayer, regardless of whether the reforestation expenditures are incurred in January or December of that taxable year. Therefore, a taxpayer will be allowed to claim amortization deductions for only six months of each of the first and eighth taxable years of the period over which the reforestation expenditures will be amortized.

(c) *Recapture.* If a taxpayer disposes of qualified timber property within ten years of the year in which the amortizable basis was created and the taxpayer has claimed amortization deductions under section 194, part or all of any gain on the disposition may be recaptured as ordinary income. See section 1245. [Reg. § 1.194-1.]

☐ [*T.D.* 7927, 12-15-83.]

[Reg. § 1.194-2]

§ 1.194-2. **Amount of deduction allowable.**— (a) *General rule.* The allowable monthly deduction with respect to reforestation expenditures made in a taxable year is determined by dividing the amount of reforestation expenditures made in such taxable year (after applying the limitations of paragraph (b) of this section) by 84. In order to determine the total allowable amortization deduction for a given month, a taxpayer should add the monthly amortization deductions computed under the preceding sentence for qualifying expenditures made by the taxpayer in the taxable year and the preceding seven taxable years.

(b) *Dollar limitation*—(1) *Maximum amount subject to election.* A taxpayer may elect to amortize up to $10,000 of qualifying reforestation expenditures each year under section 194. However, the maximum amortizable amount is $5,000 in the case of a married individual (as defined in section 143) filing a separate return. No carryover or carryback of expenditures in excess of $10,000 is permitted. The maximum annual amortization deduction for expenditures incurred in any taxable year is $1,428.57 ($10,000/7). The maximum deduction in the first and eighth taxable years of the amortization period is one-half that amount, because of the half-year convention of § 1.194-1(b). Total deductions for any year under this section will reach $10,000 if a taxpayer incurs and elects to amortize $10,000 of expenditures each year

...mortizable basis among ...es. The limit of $10,000 ...expenditures applies ...ed during a taxable

year on all of the taxpayer's timber properties. A taxpayer who incurs more than $10,000 in qualifying expenditures in connection with more than one qualified timber property during a taxable year may select the properties for which section 194 amortization will be elected as well as the manner in which the $10,000 limitation on amortizable basis is allocated among such properties. For example, A incurred $10,000 of qualifying reforestation expenditures on each of four properties in 1981. A may elect under section 194 to amortize $2,500 of the amount spent on each property, $5,000 of the amount spent on any two properties, the entire $10,000 spent on any one property, or A may allocate the $10,000 maximum amortizable basis among some or all of the properties in any other manner.

(3) *Basis*—(i) *In general.* Except as provided in paragraph (b)(3)(ii) of this section, the basis of a taxpayer's interest in qualified timber property for which an election is made under section 194 shall be adjusted to reflect the amount of the section 194 amortization deduction allowable to the taxpayer.

(ii) *Special rule for trusts.* Although a trust may be a partner of a partnership, income beneficiary of an estate, or (for taxable years beginning after December 31, 1982) shareholder of an S corporation, it may not deduct its allocable share of a section 194 amortization deduction allowable to such partnership, estate, or S corporation. In addition, the basis of the interest held by the partnership, estate, or S corporation in the qualified timber property shall not be adjusted to reflect the portion of the section 194 amortization deduction that is allocable to the trust.

(4) *Allocation of amortizable basis among component members of a controlled group.* Component members of a controlled group (as defined in § 1.194-3(d)) on a December 31 shall be treated as one taxpayer in applying the $10,000 limitation of paragraph (b)(1) of this section. The amortizable basis may be allocated to any one such member or allocated (for the taxable year of each such member which includes such December 31) among the several members in any manner, provided that the amount of amortizable basis allocated to any member does not exceed the amount of amortizable basis actually acquired by the member in the taxable year. The allocation is to be made (1) by the common parent corporation if a consolidated return is filed for all component members of the group, or (2) in accordance with an agreement entered into by the members of the group if separate returns are filed. If a consolidated return is filed by some component members of the group and separate returns are filed by

other component members, then the common parent of the group filing the consolidated return shall enter into an agreement with those members who do not join in filing the consolidated return allocating the amount between the group filing the return and the other component members of the controlled group who do not join in filing the consolidated return. If a consolidated return is filed, the common parent corporation shall file a separate statement attached to the income tax return on which an election is made to amortize reforestation costs under section 194. See § 1.194-4. If separate returns are filed by some or all component members of the group, each component member to which is allocated any part of the deduction under section 194 shall file a separate statement attached to the income tax return in which an election is made to amortize reforestation expenditures. See § 1.194-4. Such statement shall include the name, address, employer identification number, and the taxable year of each component member of the controlled group, a copy of the allocation agreement signed by persons duly authorized to act on behalf of those members who file separate returns, and a description of the manner in which the deduction under section 194 has been divided among them.

(5) *Partnerships*—(i) *Election to be made by partnership.* A partnership makes the election to amortize qualified reforestation expenditures of the partnership. See section 703(b).

(ii) *Dollar limitations applicable to partnerships.* The dollar limitations of section 194 apply to the partnership as well as to each partner. Thus, a partnership may not elect to amortize more than $10,000 of reforestation expenditures under section 194 in any taxable year.

(iii) *Partner's share of amortizable basis.* Section 704 and the regulations thereunder shall govern the determination of a partner's share of a partnership's amortizable reforestation expenditures for any taxable year.

(iv) *Dollar limitation applicable to partners.* A partner shall in no event be entitled in any taxable year to claim a deduction for amortization based on more than $10,000 ($5,000 in the case of a married taxpayer who files a separate return) of amortizable basis acquired in such taxable year regardless of the source of the amortizable basis. In the case of a partner who is a member of two or more partnerships that elect under section 194, the partner's aggregate share of partnership amortizable basis may not exceed $10,000 or $5,000, whichever is applicable. In the case of a member of a partnership that elects under section 194 who also has separately acquired qualified

timber property, the aggregate of the member's partnership and nonpartnership amortizable basis may not exceed $10,000 or $5,000, whichever is applicable.

(6) *S corporations.* For taxable years beginning after December 31, 1982, rules similar to those contained in paragraph (b)(5)(ii) and (iv) of this section shall apply in the case of S corporations (as defined in section 1361(a)) and their shareholders.

(7) *Estates.* Estates may elect to amortize in each taxable year up to a maximum of $10,000 of qualifying reforestation expenditures under section 194. Any amortizable basis acquired by an estate shall be apportioned between the estate and the income beneficiary on the basis of the income of the estate allocable to each. The amount of amortizable basis apportioned from an estate to a beneficiary shall be taken into account in determining the $10,000 (or $5,000) amount of amortizable basis allowable to such beneficiary under this section.

(c) *Life tenant and remainderman.* If property is held by one person for life with remainder to another person, the life tenant is entitled to the full benefit of any amortization allowable under section 194 on qualifying expenditures he or she makes. Any remainder interest in the property is ignored for this purpose. [Reg. § 1.194-2.]

☐ [*T.D. 7927*, 12-15-83.]

[Reg. § 1.194-3]

§ 1.194-3. **Definitions.**—(a) *Qualified timber property.* The term "qualified timber property" means property located in the United States which will contain trees in significant commercial quantities. The property may be a woodlot or other site but must consist of at least one acre which is planted with tree seedlings in the manner normally used in forestation or reforestation. The property must be held by the taxpayer for the growing and cutting of timber which will either be sold for use in, or used by the taxpayer in, the commercial production of timber products. A taxpayer does not have to own the property in order to be eligible to elect to amortize costs attributable to it under section 194. Thus, a taxpayer may elect to amortize qualifying reforestation expenditures incurred by such taxpayer on leased qualified timber property. Qualified timber property does not include property on which the taxpayer has planted shelter belts (for which current deductions are allowed under section 175) or ornamental trees, such as Christmas trees.

(b) *Amortizable basis.* The term "amortizable basis" means that portion of the basis of qualified timber property which is attributable to reforestation expenditures.

(c) *Reforestation expenditures*—(1) *In general.* The term "reforestation expenditures" means direct costs incurred to plant or seed for forestation or reforestation purposes. Qualifying expenditures include amounts spent for site preparation, seed or seedlings, and labor and tool costs, including depreciation on equipment used in planting or seeding. Only those costs which must be capitalized and are included in the adjusted basis of the property qualify as reforestation expenditures. Costs which are currently deductible do not qualify.

(2) *Cost-sharing programs.* Any expenditures for which the taxpayer has been reimbursed under any governmental reforestation cost-sharing program do not qualify as reforestation expenditures unless the amounts reimbursed have been included in the gross income of the taxpayer.

(d) *Definitions of controlled group of corporations and component member of controlled group.* For purposes of section 194, the terms "controlled group of corporations" and "component member" of a controlled group of corporations shall have the same meaning assigned to those terms in section 1563(a) and (b), except that the phrase "more than 50 percent" shall be substituted for the phrase "at least 80 percent" each place it appears in section 1563(a)(1). [Reg. § 1.194-3.]

☐ [*T.D.* 7927, 12-15-83.]

[Reg. § 1.194-4]

§ 1.194-4. Time and manner of making election.—(a) *In general.* Except as provided in paragraph (b) of this section, an election to amortize reforestation expenditures under section 194 shall be made by entering the amortization deduction claimed at the appropriate place on the taxpayer's income tax return for the year in which the expenditures were incurred, and by attaching a statement to such return. The statement should state the amounts of the expenditures, describe the nature of the expenditures, and give the date on which each was incurred. The statement should also state the type of timber being grown and the purpose for which it is being grown. A separate statement must be included for each property for which reforestation expenditures are being amortized under section 194. The election may only be made on a timely return (taking into account extensions of the time for filing) for the taxable year in which the amortizable expenditures were made.

(b) *Special rule.* With respect to any return filed before March 15, 1984 on which a taxpayer was eligible to, but did not make an election under

section 194, the election to amortize reforestation expenditures under section 194 may be made by a statement on, or attached to, the income tax return (or an amended return) for the taxable year, indicating that an election is being made under section 194 and setting forth the information required under paragraph (a) of this section. An election made under the provisions of this paragraph (b) must be made not later than,

(1) The time prescribed by law (including extension thereof) for filing the income tax return for the year in which the reforestation expenditures were made, or

(2) March 15, 1984, whichever is later. Nothing in this paragraph shall be construed as extending the time specified in section 6511 within which a claim for credit or refund may be filed.

(c) *Revocation.* An application for consent to revoke an election under section 194 shall be in writing and shall be addressed to the Commissioner of Internal Revenue, Washington, D.C. 20224. The application shall set forth the name and address of the taxpayer, state the taxable years for which the election was in effect, and state the reason for revoking the election. The application shall be signed by the taxpayer or a duly authorized representative of the taxpayer and shall be filed at least 90 days prior to the time prescribed by law (without regard to extensions thereof) for filing the income tax return for the first taxable year for which the election is to terminate. Ordinarily, the request for consent to revoke the election will not be granted if it appears from all the facts and circumstances that the only reason for the desired change is to obtain a tax advantage. [Reg. § 1.194-4.]

☐ [*T.D.* 7927, 12-15-83.]

[Reg. § 1.195-1]

§ 1.195-1. Election to amortize start-up expenditures.—(a) *In general.* Under section 195(b), a taxpayer may elect to amortize start-up expenditures (as defined in section 195(c)(1)). A taxpayer who elects to amortize start-up expenditures must, at the time of the election, select an amortization period of not less than 60 months, beginning with the month in which the active trade or business begins. The election applies to all of the taxpayer's start-up expenditures with respect to the trade or business. The election to amortize startup expenditures is irrevocable, and the amortization period selected by the taxpayer in making the election may not subsequently be changed.

(b) *Time and manner of making election.* The election to amortize start-up expenditures under section 195 shall be made by attaching a statement containing the information described in paragraph (c) of this section to the taxpayer's return. The statement must be filed no later than the date prescribed by law for filing the return (including any extensions of time) for the taxable year in which the active trade or business begins. The statement may be filed with a return for any taxable year prior to the year in which the taxpayer's active trade or business begins, but no later than the date prescribed in the preceding sentence. Accordingly, an election under section 195 filed for any taxable year prior to the year in which the taxpayer's active trade or business begins (and pursuant to which the taxpayer commenced amortizing start-up expenditures in that prior year) will become effective in the month of the year in which the taxpayer's active trade or business begins.

(c) *Information required.* The statement shall set forth a description of the trade or business to which it relates with sufficient detail so that expenses relating to the trade or business can be identified properly for the taxable year in which the statement is filed and for all future taxable years to which it relates. The statement also shall include the number of months (not less than 60) over which the expenditures are to be amortized, and to the extent known at the time the statement is filed, a description of each start-up expenditure incurred (whether or not paid) and the month in which the active trade or business began (or was acquired). A revised statement may be filed to include any start-up expenditures not included in the taxpayer's original election statement, but the revised statement may not include any expenditures for which the taxpayer had previously taken a position on a return inconsistent with their treatment as start-up expenditures. The revised statement may be filed with a return filed after the return that contained the election.

(d) *Effective date.* This section applies to elections filed on or after December 17, 1998. [Reg. § 1.195-1.]

☐ [*T.D.* 8797, 12-16-98.]

[Reg. § 1.197-0]

§ 1.197-0. **Table of contents.**—This section lists the headings that appear in § 1.197-2.

§ *1.197-2 Amortization of goodwill and certain other intangibles.*

(a) Overview.

  (1) In general.

  (2) Section 167(f) property.

  (3) Amounts otherwise deductible.

(b) Section 197 intangibles; in general.

  (1) Goodwill.

  (2) Going concern value.

  (3) Workforce in place.

  (4) Information base.

  (5) Know-how, etc.

  (6) Customer-based intangibles.

  (7) Supplier-based intangibles.

  (8) Licenses, permits, and other rights granted by governmental units.

  (9) Covenants not to compete and other similar arrangements.

  (10) Franchises, trademarks, and trade names.

  (11) Contracts for the use of, and term interests in, other section 197 intangibles.

  (12) Other similar items.

(c) Section 197 intangibles; exceptions.

  (1) Interests in a corporation, partnership, trust, or estate.

  (2) Interests under certain financial contracts.

  (3) Interests in land.

  (4) Certain computer software.

    (i) Publicly available.

    (ii) Not acquired as part of trade or business.

    (iii) Other exceptions.

    (iv) Computer software defined.

  (5) Certain interests in films, sound recordings, video tapes, books, or other similar property.

  (6) Certain rights to receive tangible property or services.

  (7) Certain interests in patents or copyrights.

  (8) Interests under leases of tangible property.

    (i) Interest as a lessor.

    (ii) Interest as a lessee.

  (9) Interests under indebtedness.

    (i) In general.

    (ii) Exceptions.

  (10) Professional sports franchises.

  (11) Mortgage servicing rights.

  (12) Certain transaction costs.

  (13) Rights of fixed duration or amount.

(d) Amortizable section 197 intangibles.

  (1) Definition.

  (2) Exception for self-created intangibles.

    (i) In general.

    (ii) Created by the taxpayer.

      (A) Defined.

      (B) Contracts for the use of intangibles.

(C) Improvements and modifications.

(iii) Exceptions.

(3) Exception for property subject to anti-churning rules.

(e) Purchase of a trade or business.

(1) Goodwill or going concern value.

(2) Franchise, trademark, or trade name.

(i) In general.

(ii) Exceptions.

(3) Acquisitions to be included.

(4) Substantial portion.

(5) Deemed asset purchases under section 338.

(6) Mortgage servicing rights.

(7) Computer software acquired for internal use.

(f) Computation of amortization deduction.

(1) In general.

(2) Treatment of contingent amounts.

(i) Amounts added to basis during 15-year period.

(ii) Amounts becoming fixed after expiration of 15-year period.

(iii) Rules for including amounts in basis.

(3) Basis determinations for certain assets.

(i) Covenants not to compete.

(ii) Contracts for the use of section 197 intangibles; acquired as part of a trade or business.

(A) In general.

(B) Know-how and certain information base.

(iii) Contracts for the use of section 197 intangibles; not acquired as part of a trade or business.

(iv) Applicable rules.

(A) Franchises, trademarks, and trade names.

(B) Certain amounts treated as payable under a debt instrument.

(*1*) In general.

(*2*) Rights granted by governmental units.

(*3*) Treatment of other parties to transaction.

(*4*) Basis determinations in certain transactions.

(*i*) Certain renewal transactions.

(*ii*) Transactions subject to section 338 or 1060.

(*iii*)   Certain   reinsurance transactions.

(g) Special rules.

(1) Treatment of certain dispositions.

(i) Loss disallowance rules.

(A) In general.

(B) Abandonment or worthlessness.

(C) Certain nonrecognition transfers.

(ii) Separately acquired property.

(iii) Disposition of a covenant not to compete.

(iv) Taxpayers under common control.

(A) In general.

(B) Treatment of disallowed loss.

(2) Treatment of certain nonrecognition and exchange transactions.

(i) Relationship to anti-churning rules.

(ii) Treatment of nonrecognition and exchange transactions generally.

(A) Transfer disregarded.

(B) Application of general rule.

(C) Transactions covered.

(iii) Certain exchanged-basis property.

(iv) Transfers under section 708(b)(1).

(A) In general.

(B) Termination by sale or exchange of interest.

(C) Other terminations.

(3) Increase in the basis of partnership property under section 732(b), 734(b), 743(b), or 732(d).

(4) Section 704(c) allocations.

(i) Allocations where the intangible is amortizable by the contributor.

(ii) Allocations where the intangible is not amortizable by the contributor.

(5) Treatment of certain reinsurance transactions.

(i) In general.

(ii) Determination of adjusted basis.

(A) Acquisitions (other than under section 338) of specified insurance contracts.

(B) Insolvent ceding company

(C) Other acquisitions. [Reserved]

(6) Amounts paid or incurred for a franchise, trademark, or trade name.

(7) Amounts properly taken into account in determining the cost of property that is not a section 197 intangible.

Reg. § 1.197-0

(8) Treatment of amortizable section 197 intangibles as depreciable property.

(h) Anti-churning rules.

(1) Scope and purpose.

(i) Scope.

(ii) Purpose.

(2) Treatment of section 197(f)(9) intangibles.

(3) Amounts deductible under section 1253(d) or § 1.162-11.

(4) Transition period.

(5) Exceptions.

(6) Related person.

(i) In general.

(ii) Time for testing relationships.

(iii) Certain relationships disregarded.

(iv) De minimis rule.

(A) In general.

(B) Determination of beneficial ownership interest.

(7) Special rules for entities that owned or used property at any time during the transition period and that are no longer in existence.

(8) Special rules for section 338 deemed acquisitions.

(9) Gain-recognition exception.

(i) Applicability.

(ii) Effect of exception.

(iii) Time and manner of election.

(iv) Special rules for certain entities.

(v) Effect of nonconforming elections.

(vi) Notification requirements.

(vii) Revocation.

(viii) Election Statement.

(ix) Determination of highest marginal rate of tax and amount of other Federal income tax on gain.

(A) Marginal rate.

(1) Noncorporate taxpayers.

(2) Corporations and tax-exempt entities.

(B) Other Federal income tax on gain.

(x) Coordination with other provisions.

(A) In general.

(B) Section 1374.

(C) Procedural and administrative provisions.

(D) Installment method.

(xi) Special rules for persons not otherwise subject to Federal income tax.

(10) Transactions subject to both anti-churning and nonrecognition rules.

(11) Avoidance purpose.

(12) Additional partnership anti-churning rules.

(i) In general.

(ii) Section 732(b) adjustments. [Reserved]

(iii) Section 732(d) adjustments.

(iv) Section 734(b) adjustments. [Reserved]

(v) Section 743(b) adjustments.

(vi) Partner is or becomes a user of partnership intangible.

(A) General rule.

(B) Anti-churning partner.

(C) Effect of retroactive elections.

(vii) Section 704(c) elections.

(A) Allocations where the intangible is amortizable by the contributor.

(B) Allocations where the intangible is not amortizable by the contributor.

(viii) Operating rule for transfers upon death.

(i) Reserved

(j) General anti-abuse rule.

(k) Examples.

(l) Effective dates.

(1) In general.

(2) Application to pre-effective acquisitions.

(3) Application of regulation REG-209709-94 to pre-effective date acq[...]

(4) Change in method of accounting

(i) In general.

(ii) Application to pre-eff[...] transactions.

(iii) Automatic change proc[...] [Reg. § 1.197-0.]

☐ [T.D. 8865, 1-20-2000.]

[Reg. § 1.197-[...]

§ 1.197-1T. Certain elect[...] property (temporary).—(a[...] tion provides rules for ma[...] under section 13261 of th[...] onciliation Act of 1993 (C[...] of this section provides [...] tion 13261(g)(2) electio[...] to apply the intangible[...] property acquired af[...] before August 10, 1[...]

OBRA '93). Paragraph (d) of this section provides rules for making the section 13261(g)(3) election (binding contract election) to apply prior law to property acquired pursuant to a written binding contract in effect on August 10, 1993, and at all times thereafter before the date of acquisition. The provisions of this section apply only to property for which an election is made under paragraph (c) or (d) of this section.

(b) *Definitions and special rules*—(1) *Intangibles provisions of OBRA '93.* The intangibles provisions of OBRA '93 are sections 167(f) and 197 of the Internal Revenue Code (Code) and all other pertinent provisions of section 13261 of OBRA '93 (e.g., the amendment of section 1253 in the case of a franchise, trademark, or trade name).

(2) *Transition period property.* The transition period property of a taxpayer is any property that was acquired by the taxpayer after July 25, 1991, and on or before August 10, 1993.

(3) *Eligible section 197 intangibles.* The eligible section 197 intangibles of a taxpayer are any section 197 intangibles that—

(i) Are transition period property; and

(ii) Qualify as amortizable section 197 intangibles (within the meaning of section 197(c)) if ~~...~~ tion under section 13261(g)(2) of OBRA '93

~~...~~tion date. The election date is the ~~...~~ed after application of section ~~...~~ the taxpayer files the original ~~...~~ return to which the election statement ~~...~~ paragraph (e) of this section is

~~...~~ election year is the ~~...~~ that includes August

~~...~~yer is under ~~...~~ayer if, at ~~...~~r before (b)(4) ~~...~~ be ~~...~~ion

(ii) Property is not eligible for depreciation or amortization in the month of disposition.

(8) *Application to adjustment to basis of partnership property under section 734(b) or 743(b).* Any increase in the basis of partnership property under section 734(b) (relating to the optional adjustment to basis of undistributed partnership property) or section 743(b) (relating to the optional adjustment to the basis of partnership property) will be taken into account under this section by a partner as if the increased portion of the basis were attributable to the partner's acquisition of the underlying partnership property on the date the distribution or transfer occurs. For example, if a section 754 election is in effect and, as a result of its acquisition of a partnership interest, a taxpayer obtains an increased basis in an intangible held through the partnership, the increased portion of the basis in the intangible will be treated as an intangible asset newly acquired by that taxpayer on the date of the transaction.

(9) *Former member.* A former member of a consolidated group is a corporation that was a member of the consolidated group at any time after July 25, 1991, and on or before August 2, 1993, but that is not under common control with the common parent of the group for purposes of paragraph (c)(1)(ii) of this section.

(c) *Retroactive election*—(1) *Effect of election*—(i) *On taxpayer.* Except as provided in paragraph (c)(1)(v) of this section, if a taxpayer makes the retroactive election, the intangibles provisions of OBRA '93 will apply to all the taxpayer's transition period property. Thus, for example, section 197 will apply to all the taxpayer's eligible section 197 intangibles.

(ii) *On taxpayers under common control.* If a taxpayer makes the retroactive election, the election applies to each taxpayer that is under common control with the electing taxpayer. If the retroactive election applies to a taxpayer under common control, the intangibles provisions of OBRA '93 apply to that taxpayer's transition period property in the same manner as if that taxpayer had itself made the retroactive election. However, a retroactive election that applies to a non-electing taxpayer under common control is not treated as an election by that taxpayer for purposes of re-applying the rule of this paragraph (c)(1)(ii) to any other taxpayer.

(iii) *On former members of consolidated group.* A retroactive election by the common parent of a consolidated group applies to transition period property acquired by a former member while it was a member of the consolidated group and continues to apply to that property in each

Reg. § 1.197

subsequent consolidated or separate return year of the former member.

(iv) *On transferred assets*—(A) *In general.* If property is transferred in a transaction described in paragraph (c)(1)(iv)(C) of this section and the intangibles provisions of OBRA '93 applied to such property in the hands of the transferor, the property remains subject to the intangibles provisions of OBRA '93 with respect to so much of its adjusted basis in the hands of the transferee as does not exceed its adjusted basis in the hands of the transferor. The transferee is not required to apply the intangibles provisions of OBRA '93 to any other transition period property that it owns, however, unless such provisions are otherwise applicable under the rules of this paragraph (c)(1).

(B) *Transferee election.* If property is transferred in a transaction described in paragraph (c)(1)(iv)(C)(*1*) of this section and the transferee makes the retroactive election, the transferor is not required to apply the intangibles provisions of OBRA '93 to any of its transition period property (including the property transferred to the transferee in the transaction described in paragraph (c)(1)(iv)(C)(*1*) of this section), unless such provisions are otherwise applicable under the rules of this paragraph (c)(1).

(C) *Transactions covered.* This paragraph (c)(1)(iv) applies to—

(*1*) Any transaction described in section 332, 351, 361, 721, 731, 1031, or 1033; and

(*2*) Any transaction between corporations that are members of the same consolidated group immediately after the transaction.

(D) *Exchanged basis property.* In the case of a transaction involving exchanged basis property (e.g., a transaction subject to section 1031 or 1033)—

(*1*) Paragraph (c)(1)(iv)(A) of this section shall not apply; and

(*2*) If the intangibles provisions of OBRA '93 applied to the property by reference to which the exchanged basis is determined (the predecessor property), the exchanged basis property becomes subject to the intangibles provisions of OBRA '93 with respect to so much of its basis as does not exceed the predecessor property's basis.

(E) *Acquisition date.* For purposes of paragraph (b)(2) of this section (definition of transition period property), property (other than exchanged basis property) acquired in a transaction described in paragraph (c)(1)(iv)(C)(*1*) of this section generally is treated as acquired when the transferor acquired (or was treated as acquir-

ing) the property (or predecessor property). However, if the adjusted basis of the property in the hands of the transferee exceeds the adjusted basis of the property in the hands of the transferor, the property, with respect to that excess basis, is treated as acquired at the time of the transfer. The time at which exchanged basis property is considered acquired is determined by applying similar principles to the transferee's acquisition of predecessor property.

(v) *Special rule for property of former member of consolidated group*—(A) *Intangibles provisions inapplicable for certain periods.* If a former member of a consolidated group makes a retroactive election pursuant to paragraph (c)(1)(i) of this section or if an election applies to the former member under the common control rule of paragraph (c)(1)(ii) of this section, the intangibles provisions of OBRA '93 generally apply to all transition period property of the former member. The intangibles provisions of OBRA '93 do not apply, however, to the transition period property of a former member (including a former member that makes or is bound by a retroactive election) during the period beginning immediately after July 25, 1991, and ending immediately before the earlier of—

(*1*) The first day after July 25, 1991, that the former member was not a member of a consolidated group; or

(*2*) The first day after July 25, 1991, that the former member was a member of a consolidated group that is otherwise required to apply the intangibles provisions of OBRA '93 to its transition period property (e.g., because the common control election under paragraph (c)(1)(ii) of this section applies to the group).

(B) *Subsequent adjustments.* See paragraph (c)(5) of this section for adjustments when the intangibles provisions of OBRA '93 first apply to the transition period property of the former member after the property is acquired.

(2) *Making the election*—(i) *Partnerships, S corporations, estates, and trusts.* Except as provided in paragraph (c)(2)(ii) of this section, in the case of transition period property of a partnership, S corporation, estate, or trust, only the entity may make the retroactive election for purposes of paragraph (c)(1)(i) of this section.

(ii) *Partnerships for which a section 754 election is in effect.* In the case of increased basis that is treated as transition period property of a partner under paragraph (b)(8) of this section, only that partner may make the retroactive election for purposes of paragraph (c)(1)(i) of this section.

Reg. § 1.197-1T(c)(2)

(iii) *Consolidated groups.* An election by the common parent of a consolidated group applies to members and former members as described in paragraphs (c)(1)(ii) and (iii) of this section. Further, for purposes of paragraph (c)(1)(ii) of this section, an election by the common parent is not treated as an election by any subsidiary member. A retroactive election cannot be made by a corporation that is a subsidiary member of a consolidated group on August 10, 1993, but an election can be made on behalf of the subsidiary member under paragraph (c)(1)(ii) of this section (e.g., by the common parent of the group). See paragraph (c)(1)(iii) of this section for rules concerning the effect of the common parent's election on transition period property of a former member.

(3) *Time and manner of election*—(i) *Time.* In general, the retroactive election must be made by the due date (including extensions of time) of the electing taxpayer's Federal income tax return for the election year. If, however, the taxpayer's original Federal income tax return for the election year is filed before April 14, 1994, the election may be made by amending that return no later than September 12, 1994.

(ii) *Manner.* The retroactive election is made by attaching the election statement described in paragraph (e) of this section to the taxpayer's original or amended income tax return for the election year. In addition, the taxpayer must—

(A) Amend any previously filed return when required to do so under paragraph (c)(4) of this section; and

(B) Satisfy the notification requirements of paragraph (c)(6) of this section.

(iii) *Effect of nonconforming elections.* An attempted election that does not satisfy the requirements of this paragraph (c)(3) (including an attempted election made on a return for a taxable year prior to the election year) is not valid.

(4) *Amended return requirements*—(i) *Requirements.* A taxpayer subject to this paragraph (c)(4) must amend all previously filed income tax returns as necessary to conform the taxpayer's treatment of transition period property to the treatment required under the intangibles provisions of OBRA '93. See paragraph (c)(5) of this section for certain adjustments that may be required on the amended returns required under this paragraph (c)(4) in the case of certain consolidated group member dispositions and tax-free transactions.

(ii) *Applicability.* This paragraph (c)(4) applies to a taxpayer if—

(A) The taxpayer makes the retroactive election; or

(B) Another person's retroactive election applies to the taxpayer or to any property acquired by the taxpayer.

(5) *Adjustment required with respect to certain consolidated group member dispositions and tax-free transactions*—(i) *Application.* This paragraph (c)(5) applies to transition period property if the intangibles provisions of OBRA '93 first apply to the property while it is held by the taxpayer but do not apply to the property for some period (the "interim period") after the property is acquired (or considered acquired) by the taxpayer. For example, this paragraph (c)(5) may apply to transition period property held by a former member of a consolidated group if a retroactive election is made by or on behalf of the former member but is not made by the consolidated group. See paragraph (c)(1)(v) of this section.

(ii) *Required adjustment to income.* If this paragraph (c)(5) applies, an adjustment must be taken into account in computing taxable income of the taxpayer for the taxable year in which the intangibles provisions of OBRA '93 first apply to the property. The amount of the adjustment is equal to the difference for the transition period property between—

(A) The sum of the depreciation, amortization, or other cost recovery deductions that the taxpayer (and its predecessors) would have been permitted if the intangibles provisions of OBRA '93 applied to the property during the interim period; and

(B) The sum of the depreciation, amortization, or other cost recovery deductions that the taxpayer (and its predecessors) claimed during that interim period.

(iii) *Required adjustment to basis.* The taxpayer also must make a corresponding adjustment to the basis of its transition period property to reflect any adjustment to taxable income with respect to the property under this paragraph (c)(5).

(6) *Notification requirements*—(i) *Notification of commonly controlled taxpayers.* A taxpayer that makes the retroactive election must provide written notification of the retroactive election (on or before the election date) to each taxpayer that is under common control with the electing taxpayer.

(ii) *Notification of certain former members, former consolidated groups, and transferees.* This paragraph (c)(6)(ii) applies to a common parent of a consolidated group that makes or is

Reg. § 1.197-1T(c)(3)

notified of a retroactive election that applies to transition period property of a former member, a corporation that makes or is notified of a retroactive election that affects any consolidated group of which the corporation is a former member, or a taxpayer that makes or is notified of a retroactive election that applies to transition period property the taxpayer transfers in a transaction described in paragraph (c)(1)(iv)(C) of this section. Such common parent, former member, or transferor must provide written notification of the retroactive election to any affected former member, consolidated group, or transferee. The written notification must be provided on or before the election date in the case of an election by the common parent, former member, or transferor, and within 30 days of the election date in the case of an election by a person other than the common parent, former member, or transferor.

(7) *Revocation*. Once made, the retroactive election may be revoked only with the consent of the Commissioner.

(8) *Examples*. The following examples illustrate the application of this paragraph (c).

Example 1. (i) X is a partnership with 5 equal partners, A through E. X acquires in 1989, as its sole asset, intangible asset M. X has a section 754 election in effect for all relevant years. F, an unrelated individual, purchases A's entire interest in the X partnership in January 1993 for $700. At the time of F's purchase, X's inside basis for M is $2,000, and its fair market value is $3,500.

(ii) Under section 743(b), X makes an adjustment to increase F's basis in asset M by $300, the difference between the allocated purchase price and M's inside basis ($700 − $400 = $300). Under paragraphs (b)(8) and (c)(2)(ii) of this section, if F makes the retroactive election, the section 743(b) basis increase of $300 in M is an amortizable section 197 intangible even though asset M is not an amortizable section 197 intangible in the hands of X. F's increase in the basis of asset M is amortizable over 15 years beginning with the month of F's acquisition of the partnership interest. With respect to the remaining $400 of basis, F is treated as stepping into A's shoes and continues A's amortization (if any) in asset M. F's retroactive election applies to all other intangibles acquired by F or a taxpayer under common control with F.

Example 2. A, a calendar year taxpayer, is under common control with B, a June 30 fiscal year taxpayer. A files its original election year Federal income tax return on March 15, 1994, and does not make either the retroactive election or the binding contract election. B files its election year tax return on September 15, 1994, and makes the retroactive election. B is required by paragraph (c)(6)(i) of this section to notify A of its election. Even though A had already filed its election year return, A is bound by B's retroactive election under the common control rules. Additionally, if A had made a binding contract election, it would have been negated by B's retroactive election. Because of B's retroactive election, A must comply with the requirements of this paragraph (c), and file amended returns for the election year and any affected prior years as necessary to conform the treatment of transition period property to the treatment required under the intangibles provisions of OBRA '93.

Example 3. (i) P and Y, calendar year taxpayers, are the common parents of unrelated calendar year consolidated groups. On August 15, 1991, S, a subsidiary member of the P group, acquires a section 197 intangible with an unadjusted basis of $180. Under prior law, no amortization or depreciation was allowed with respect to the acquired intangible. On November 1, 1992, a member of the Y group acquires the S stock in a taxable transaction. On the P group's 1993 consolidated return, P makes the retroactive election. The P group also files amended returns for its affected prior years. Y does not make the retroactive election for the Y group.

(ii) Under paragraph (c)(1)(iii) of this section, a retroactive election by the common parent of a consolidated group applies to all transition period property acquired by a former member while it was a member of the group. The section 197 intangible acquired by S is transition period property that S, a former member of the P group, acquired while a member of the P group. Thus, P's election applies to the acquired asset. P must notify S of the election pursuant to paragraph (c)(6)(ii) of this section.

(iii) S amortizes the unadjusted basis of its eligible section 197 intangible ($180) over the 15-year amortization period using the applicable convention beginning as of the first day of the month of acquisition (August 1, 1991). Thus, the P group amends its 1991 consolidated tax return to take into account $5 of amortization ($180/15 years × $5/12 year = $5) for S.

(iv) For 1992, S is entitled to $12 of amortization ($180/15). Assume that under § 1.1502-76, $10 of S's amortization for 1992 is allocated to the P group's consolidated return and $2 is allocated to the Y group's return. The P group amends its 1992 consolidated tax return to reflect the $10 deduction for S. The Y group must amend its 1992 return to reflect the $2 deduction for S.

Reg. § 1.197-1T(c)(8)

Example 4. (i) The facts are the same as in *Example 3,* except that the retroactive election is made for the *Y* group, not for the *P* group.

(ii) The *Y* group amends its 1992 consolidated return to claim a section 197 deduction of $2 ($180/15 years × 2/12 year = $2) for *S.*

(iii) Under paragraph (c)(1)(ii) of this section, the retroactive election by *Y* applies to all transition period property acquired by *S.* However, under paragraph (c)(1)(v)(A) of this section, the intangibles provisions of OBRA '93 do not apply to *S*'s transition period property during the period when it held such property as a member of *P* group. Instead, these provisions become applicable to *S*'s transition period property beginning on November 1, 1992, when *S* becomes a member of *Y* group.

(iv) Because the *P* group did not make the retroactive election, there is an interim period during which the intangibles provisions of OBRA '93 do not apply to the asset acquired by *S.* Thus, under paragraph (c)(5) of this section, the *Y* group must take into account in computing taxable income in 1992 an adjustment equal to the difference between the section 197 deduction that would have been permitted if the intangibles provisions of OBRA '93 applied to the property for the interim period (i.e., the period for which *S* was included in the *P* group's 1991 and 1992 consolidated returns) and any amortization or depreciation deductions claimed by *S* for the transferred intangible for that period. The retroactive election does not affect the *P* group, and the *P* group is not required to amend its returns.

Example 5. The facts are the same as in *Example 3,* except that both *P* and *Y* make the retroactive election. *P* must notify *S* of its election pursuant to paragraph (c)(6)(ii) of this section. Further, both the *P* and *Y* groups must file amended returns for affected prior years. Because there is no period of time during which the intangibles provisions of OBRA '93 do not apply to the asset acquired by *S,* the *Y* group is permitted no adjustment under paragraph (c)(5) of this section for the asset.

(d) *Binding contract election*—(1) *General rule*—(i) *Effect of election.* If a taxpayer acquires property pursuant to a written binding contract in effect on August 10, 1993, and at all times thereafter before the acquisition (an eligible acquisition) and makes the binding contract election with respect to the contract, the law in effect prior to the enactment of OBRA '93 will apply to all property acquired pursuant to the contract. A separate binding contract election must be made with respect to each eligible acquisition to which

the law in effect prior to the enactment of OBRA '93 is to apply.

(ii) *Taxpayers subject to retroactive election.* A taxpayer may not make the binding contract election if the taxpayer or a person under common control with the taxpayer makes the retroactive election under paragraph (c) of this section.

(iii) *Revocation.* A binding contract election, once made, may be revoked only with the consent of the Commissioner.

(2) *Time and manner of election*—(i) *Time.* In general, the binding contract election must be made by the due date (including extensions of time) of the electing taxpayer's Federal income tax return for the election year. If, however, the taxpayer's original Federal income tax return for the election year is filed before April 14, 1994, the election may be made by amending that return no later than September 12, 1994.

(ii) *Manner.* The binding contract election is made by attaching the election statement described in paragraph (e) of this section to the taxpayer's original or amended income tax return for the election year.

(iii) *Effect of nonconforming election.* An attempted election that does not satisfy the requirements of this paragraph (d)(2) is not valid.

(e) *Election statement*—(1) *Filing requirements.* For an election under paragraph (c) or (d) of this section to be valid, the electing taxpayer must:

(i) File (with its Federal income tax return for the election year and with any affected amended returns required under paragraph (c)(4) of this section) a written election statement, as an attachment to Form 4562 (Depreciation and Amortization), that satisfies the requirements of paragraph (e)(2) of this section; and

(ii) Forward a copy of the election statement to the Statistics Branch (QAM:S:6111), IRS Ogden Service Center, ATTN: Chief, Statistics Branch, P.O. Box 9941, Ogden, UT 84409.

(2) *Content of the election statement.* The written election statement must include the information in paragraphs (e)(2)(i) through (vi) and (ix) of this section in the case of a retroactive election, and the information in paragraphs (e)(2)(i) and (vii) through (ix) of this section in the case of a binding contract election. The required information should be arranged and identified in accordance with the following order and numbering system—

(i) The name, address and taxpayer identification number (TIN) of the electing taxpayer (and the common parent if a consolidated return is filed).

(ii) A statement that the taxpayer is making the retroactive election.

(iii) Identification of the transition period property affected by the retroactive election, the name and TIN of the person from which the property was acquired, the manner and date of acquisition, the basis at which the property was acquired, and the amount of depreciation, amortization, or other cost recovery under section 167 or any other provision of the Code claimed with respect to the property.

(iv) Identification of each taxpayer under common control (as defined in paragraph (b)(6) of this section) with the electing taxpayer by name, TIN, and Internal Revenue Service Center where the taxpayer's income tax return is filed.

(v) If any persons are required to be notified of the retroactive election under paragraph (c)(6) of this section, identification of such persons and certification that written notification of the election has been provided to such persons.

(vi) A statement that the transition period property being amortized under section 197 is not subject to the anti-churning rules of section 197(f)(9).

(vii) A statement that the taxpayer is making the binding contract election.

(viii) Identification of the property affected by the binding contract election, the name and TIN of the person from which the property was acquired, the manner and date of acquisition, the basis at which the property was acquired, and whether any of the property is subject to depreciation under section 167 or to amortization or other cost recovery under any other provision of the Code.

(ix) The signature of the taxpayer or an individual authorized to sign the taxpayer's Federal income tax return.

(f) *Effective date.* These regulations are effective March 15, 1994. [Temporary Reg. § 1.197-1T.]

☐ [*T.D.* 8528, 3-10-94.]

[Reg. § 1.197-2]

§ 1.197-2. Amortization of goodwill and certain other intangibles.—(a) *Overview*—(1) *In general.* Section 197 allows an amortization deduction for the capitalized costs of an amortizable section 197 intangible and prohibits any other depreciation or amortization with respect to that property. Paragraphs (b), (c), and (e) of this section provide rules and definitions for determining whether property is a section 197 intangible, and

paragraphs (d) and (e) of this section provide rules and definitions for determining whether a section 197 intangible is an amortizable section 197 intangible. The amortization deduction under section 197 is determined by amortizing basis ratably over a 15-year period under the rules of paragraph (f) of this section. Section 197 also includes various special rules pertaining to the disposition of amortizable section 197 intangibles, nonrecognition transactions, anti-churning rules, and anti-abuse rules. Rules relating to these provisions are contained in paragraphs (g), (h), and (j) of this section. Examples demonstrating the application of these provisions are contained in paragraph (k) of this section. The effective date of the rules in this section is contained in paragraph (l) of this section.

(2) *Section 167(f) property.* Section 167(f) prescribes rules for computing the depreciation deduction for certain property to which section 197 does not apply. See § 1.167(a)-14 for rules under section 167(f) and paragraphs (c)(4), (6), (7), (11), and (13) of this section for a description of the property subject to section 167(f).

(3) *Amounts otherwise deductible.* Section 197 does not apply to amounts that are not chargeable to capital account under paragraph (c)(3) (relating to basis determinations for covenants not to compete and certain contracts for the use of section 197 intangibles) of this section and are otherwise currently deductible. For this purpose, an amount described in § 1.162-11 is not currently deductible if, without regard to § 1.162-11, such amount is properly chargeable to capital account.

(b) *Section 197 intangibles; in general.* Except as otherwise provided in paragraph (c) of this section, the term *section 197 intangible* means any property described in section 197(d)(1). The following rules and definitions provide guidance concerning property that is a section 197 intangible unless an exception applies:

(1) *Goodwill.* Section 197 intangibles include goodwill. Goodwill is the value of a trade or business attributable to the expectancy of continued customer patronage. This expectancy may be due to the name or reputation of a trade or business or any other factor.

(2) *Going concern value.* Section 197 intangibles include going concern value. Going concern value is the additional value that attaches to property by reason of its existence as an integral part of an ongoing business activity. Going concern value includes the value attributable to the ability of a trade or business (or a part of a trade or business) to continue functioning or generating income without interruption notwithstanding a

Reg. § 1.197-2(b)(2)

change in ownership, but does not include any of the intangibles described in any other provision of this paragraph (b). It also includes the value that is attributable to the immediate use or availability of an acquired trade or business, such as, for example, the use of the revenues or net earnings that otherwise would not be received during any period if the acquired trade or business were not available or operational.

(3) *Workforce in place.* Section 197 intangibles include workforce in place. Workforce in place (sometimes referred to as agency force or assembled workforce) includes the composition of a workforce (for example, the experience, education, or training of a workforce), the terms and conditions of employment whether contractual or otherwise, and any other value placed on employees or any of their attributes. Thus, the amount paid or incurred for workforce in place includes, for example, any portion of the purchase price of an acquired trade or business attributable to the existence of a highly-skilled workforce, an existing employment contract (or contracts), or a relationship with employees or consultants (including, but not limited to, any key employee contract or relationship). Workforce in place does not include any covenant not to compete or other similar arrangement described in paragraph (b)(9) of this section.

(4) *Information base.* Section 197 intangibles include any information base, including a customer-related information base. For this purpose, an information base includes business books and records, operating systems, and any other information base (regardless of the method of recording the information) and a customer-related information base is any information base that includes lists or other information with respect to current or prospective customers. Thus, the amount paid or incurred for information base includes, for example, any portion of the purchase price of an acquired trade or business attributable to the intangible value of technical manuals, training manuals or programs, data files, and accounting or inventory control systems. Other examples include the cost of acquiring customer lists, subscription lists, insurance expirations, patient or client files, or lists of newspaper, magazine, radio, or television advertisers.

(5) *Know-how, etc.* Section 197 intangibles include any patent, copyright, formula, process, design, pattern, know-how, format, package design, computer software (as defined in paragraph (c)(4)(iv) of this section), or interest in a film, sound recording, video tape, book, or other similar property. (See, however, the exceptions in paragraph (c) of this section.)

(6) *Customer-based intangibles.* Section 197 intangibles include any customer-based intangible. A customer-based intangible is any composition of market, market share, or other value resulting from the future provision of goods or services pursuant to contractual or other relationships in the ordinary course of business with customers. Thus, the amount paid or incurred for customer-based intangibles includes, for example, any portion of the purchase price of an acquired trade or business attributable to the existence of a customer base, a circulation base, an undeveloped market or market growth, insurance in force, the existence of a qualification to supply goods or services to a particular customer, a mortgage servicing contract (as defined in paragraph (c)(11) of this section), an investment management contract, or other relationship with customers involving the future provision of goods or services. (See, however, the exceptions in paragraph (c) of this section.) In addition, customer-based intangibles include the deposit base and any similar asset of a financial institution. Thus, the amount paid or incurred for customer-based intangibles also includes any portion of the purchase price of an acquired financial institution attributable to the value represented by existing checking accounts, savings accounts, escrow accounts, and other similar items of the financial institution. However, any portion of the purchase price of an acquired trade or business attributable to accounts receivable or other similar rights to income for goods or services provided to customers prior to the acquisition of a trade or business is not an amount paid or incurred for a customer-based intangible.

(7) *Supplier-based intangibles.* Section 197 intangibles include any supplier-based intangible. A supplier-based intangible is the value resulting from the future acquisition, pursuant to contractual or other relationships with suppliers in the ordinary course of business, of goods or services that will be sold or used by the taxpayer. Thus, the amount paid or incurred for supplier-based intangibles includes, for example, any portion of the purchase price of an acquired trade or business attributable to the existence of a favorable relationship with persons providing distribution services (such as favorable shelf or display space at a retail outlet), the existence of a favorable credit rating, or the existence of favorable supply contracts. The amount paid or incurred for supplier-based intangibles does not include any amount required to be paid for the goods or services themselves pursuant to the terms of the agreement or other relationship. In addition, see the exceptions in paragraph (c) of this section, including the exception in paragraph (c)(6) of this

Reg. § 1.197-2(b)(3)

section for certain rights to receive tangible property or services from another person.

(8) *Licenses, permits, and other rights granted by governmental units.* Section 197 intangibles include any license, permit, or other right granted by a governmental unit (including, for purposes of section 197, an agency or instrumentality thereof) even if the right is granted for an indefinite period or is reasonably expected to be renewed for an indefinite period. These rights include, for example, a liquor license, a taxi-cab medallion (or license), an airport landing or take-off right (sometimes referred to as a slot), a regulated airline route, or a television or radio broadcasting license. The issuance or renewal of a license, permit, or other right granted by a governmental unit is considered an acquisition of the license, permit, or other right. (See, however, the exceptions in paragraph (c) of this section, including the exceptions in paragraph (c)(3) of this section for an interest in land, paragraph (c)(6) of this section for certain rights to receive tangible property or services, paragraph (c)(8) of this section for an interest under a lease of tangible property, and paragraph (c)(13) of this section for certain rights granted by a governmental unit. See paragraph (b)(10) of this section for the treatment of franchises.)

(9) *Covenants not to compete and other similar arrangements.* Section 197 intangibles include any covenant not to compete, or agreement having substantially the same effect entered into in connection with the direct or indirect acquisition of an interest in a trade or business or a substantial portion thereof. For purposes of this paragraph (b)(9), an acquisition may be made in the form of an asset acquisition (including a qualified stock purchase that is treated as a purchase of assets under section 338), a stock acquisition or redemption, and the acquisition or redemption of a partnership interest. An agreement requiring the performance of services for the acquiring taxpayer or the provision of property or its use to the acquiring taxpayer does not have substantially the same effect as a covenant not to compete to the extent that the amount paid under the agreement represents reasonable compensation for the services actually rendered or for the property or use of the property actually provided.

(10) *Franchises, trademarks, and trade names*—(i) Section 197 intangibles include any franchise, trademark, or trade name. The term *franchise* has the meaning given in section 1253(b)(1) and includes any agreement that provides one of the parties to the agreement with the right to distribute, sell, or provide goods, services, or facilities, within a specified area. The term

trademark includes any word, name, symbol, or device, or any combination thereof, adopted and used to identify goods or services and distinguish them from those provided by others. The term *trade name* includes any name used to identify or designate a particular trade or business or the name or title used by a person or organization engaged in a trade or business. A license, permit, or other right granted by a governmental unit is a franchise if it otherwise meets the definition of a franchise. A trademark or trade name includes any trademark or trade name arising under statute or applicable common law, and any similar right granted by contract. The renewal of a franchise, trademark, or trade name is treated as an acquisition of the franchise, trademark, or trade name.

(ii) Notwithstanding the definitions provided in paragraph (b)(10)(i) of this section, any amount that is paid or incurred on account of a transfer, sale, or other disposition of a franchise, trademark, or trade name and that is subject to section 1253(d)(1) is not included in the basis of a section 197 intangible. (See paragraph (g)(6) of this section.)

(11) *Contracts for the use of, and term interests in, section 197 intangibles.* Section 197 intangibles include any right under a license, contract, or other arrangement providing for the use of property that would be a section 197 intangible under any provision of this paragraph (b) (including this paragraph (b)(11)) after giving effect to all of the exceptions provided in paragraph (c) of this section. Section 197 intangibles also include any term interest (whether outright or in trust) in such property.

(12) *Other similar items.* Section 197 intangibles include any other intangible property that is similar in all material respects to the property specifically described in section 197(d)(1)(C)(i) through (v) and paragraphs (b)(3) through (7) of this section. (See paragraph (g)(5) of this section for special rules regarding certain reinsurance transactions.)

(c) *Section 197 intangibles; exceptions.* The term *section 197 intangible* does not include property described in section 197(e). The following rules and definitions provide guidance concerning property to which the exceptions apply:

(1) *Interests in a corporation, partnership, trust, or estate.* Section 197 intangibles do not include an interest in a corporation, partnership, trust, or estate. Thus, for example, amortization under section 197 is not available for the cost of acquiring stock, partnership interests, or interests in a trust or estate, whether or not the interests are regularly traded on an established market.

Reg. § 1.197-2(c)(1)

(See paragraph (g)(3) of this section for special rules applicable to property of a partnership when a section 754 election is in effect for the partnership.)

(2) *Interests under certain financial contracts.* Section 197 intangibles do not include an interest under an existing futures contract, foreign currency contract, notional principal contract, interest rate swap, or other similar financial contract, whether or not the interest is regularly traded on an established market. However, this exception does not apply to an interest under a mortgage servicing contract, credit card servicing contract, or other contract to service another person's indebtedness, or an interest under an assumption reinsurance contract. (See paragraph (g)(5) of this section for the treatment of assumption reinsurance contracts. See paragraph (c)(11) of this section and § 1.167(a)-14(d) for the treatment of mortgage servicing rights.)

(3) *Interests in land.* Section 197 intangibles do not include any interest in land. For this purpose, an interest in land includes a fee interest, life estate, remainder, easement, mineral right, timber right, grazing right, riparian right, air right, zoning variance, and any other similar right, such as a farm allotment, quota for farm commodities, or crop acreage base. An interest in land does not include an airport landing or takeoff right, a regulated airline route, or a franchise to provide cable television service. The cost of acquiring a license, permit, or other land improvement right, such as a building construction or use permit, is taken into account in the same manner as the underlying improvement.

(4) *Certain computer software—*(i) *Publicly available.* Section 197 intangibles do not include any interest in computer software that is (or has been) readily available to the general public on similar terms, is subject to a nonexclusive license, and has not been substantially modified. Computer software will be treated as readily available to the general public if the software may be obtained on substantially the same terms by a significant number of persons that would reasonably be expected to use the software. This requirement can be met even though the software is not available through a system of retail distribution. Computer software will not be considered to have been substantially modified if the cost of all modifications to the version of the software that is readily available to the general public does not exceed the greater of 25 percent of the price at which the unmodified version of the software is readily available to the general public or $2,000. For the purpose of determining whether computer software has been substantially modified—

(A) Integrated programs acquired in a package from a single source are treated as a single computer program; and

(B) Any cost incurred to install the computer software on a system is not treated as a cost of the software. However, the costs for customization, such as tailoring to a user's specifications (other than embedded programming options) are costs of modifying the software.

(ii) *Not acquired as part of trade or business.* Section 197 intangibles do not include an interest in computer software that is not acquired as part of a purchase of a trade or business.

(iii) *Other exceptions.* For other exceptions applicable to computer software, see paragraph (a)(3) of this section (relating to otherwise deductible amounts) and paragraph (g)(7) of this section (relating to amounts properly taken into account in determining the cost of property that is not a section 197 intangible).

(iv) *Computer software defined.* For purposes of this section, computer software is any program or routine (that is, any sequence of machine-readable code) that is designed to cause a computer to perform a desired function or set of functions, and the documentation required to describe and maintain that program or routine. It includes all forms and media in which the software is contained, whether written, magnetic, or otherwise. Computer programs of all classes, for example, operating systems, executive systems, monitors, compilers and translators, assembly routines, and utility programs as well as application programs, are included. Computer software also includes any incidental and ancillary rights that are necessary to effect the acquisition of the title to, the ownership of, or the right to use the computer software, and that are used only in connection with that specific computer software. Such incidental and ancillary rights are not included in the definition of trademark or trade name under paragraph (b)(10)(i) of this section. For example, a trademark or trade name that is ancillary to the ownership or use of a specific computer software program in the taxpayer's trade or business and is not acquired for the purpose of marketing the computer software is included in the definition of computer software and is not included in the definition of trademark or trade name. Computer software does not include any data or information base described in paragraph (b)(4) of this section unless the data base or item is in the public domain and is incidental to a computer program. For this purpose, a copyrighted or proprietary data or information base is treated as in the public domain if its availability through the computer program does not contribute significantly to

Reg. § 1.197-2(c)(2)

the cost of the program. For example, if a word-processing program includes a dictionary feature used to spell-check a document or any portion thereof, the entire program (including the dictionary feature) is computer software regardless of the form in which the feature is maintained or stored.

(5) *Certain interests in films, sound recordings, video tapes, books, or other similar property.* Section 197 intangibles do not include any interest (including an interest as a licensee) in a film, sound recording, video tape, book, or other similar property (such as the right to broadcast or transmit a live event) if the interest is not acquired as part of a purchase of a trade or business. A film, sound recording, video tape, book, or other similar property includes any incidental and ancillary rights (such as a trademark or trade name) that are necessary to effect the acquisition of title to, the ownership of, or the right to use the property and are used only in connection with that property. Such incidental and ancillary rights are not included in the definition of trademark or trade name under paragraph (b)(10)(i) of this section. For purposes of this paragraph (c)(5), computer software (as defined in paragraph (c)(4)(iv) of this section) is not treated as other property similar to a film, sound recording, video tape, or book. (See section 167 for amortization of excluded intangible property or interests.)

(6) *Certain rights to receive tangible property or services.* Section 197 intangibles do not include any right to receive tangible property or services under a contract or from a governmental unit if the right is not acquired as part of a purchase of a trade or business. Any right that is described in the preceding sentence is not treated as a section 197 intangible even though the right is also described in section 197(d)(1)(D) and paragraph (b)(8) of this section (relating to certain governmental licenses, permits, and other rights) and even though the right fails to meet one or more of the requirements of paragraph (c)(13) of this section (relating to certain rights of fixed duration or amount). (See § 1.167(a)-14(c)(1) and (3) for applicable rules.)

(7) *Certain interests in patents or copyrights.* Section 197 intangibles do not include any interest (including an interest as a licensee) in a patent, patent application, or copyright that is not acquired as part of a purchase of a trade or business. A patent or copyright includes any incidental and ancillary rights (such as a trademark or trade name) that are necessary to effect the acquisition of title to, the ownership of, or the right to use the property and are used only in connection with that property. Such incidental and ancillary rights are not included in the defini-

tion of trademark or trade name under paragraph (b)(10)(i) of this section. (See § 1.167(a)-14(c)(4) for applicable rules.)

(8) *Interests under leases of tangible property*—(i) *Interest as a lessor.* Section 197 intangibles do not include any interest as a lessor under an existing lease or sublease of tangible real or personal property. In addition, the cost of acquiring an interest as a lessor in connection with the acquisition of tangible property is taken into account as part of the cost of the tangible property. For example, if a taxpayer acquires a shopping center that is leased to tenants operating retail stores, any portion of the purchase price attributable to favorable lease terms is taken into account as part of the basis of the shopping center and in determining the depreciation deduction allowed with respect to the shopping center. (See section 167(c)(2).)

(ii) *Interest as a lessee.* Section 197 intangibles do not include any interest as a lessee under an existing lease of tangible real or personal property. For this purpose, an airline lease of an airport passenger or cargo gate is a lease of tangible property. The cost of acquiring such an interest is taken into account under section 178 and § 1.162-11(a). If an interest as a lessee under a lease of tangible property is acquired in a transaction with any other intangible property, a portion of the total purchase price may be allocable to the interest as a lessee based on all of the relevant facts and circumstances.

(9) *Interests under indebtedness*—(i) *In general.* Section 197 intangibles do not include any interest (whether as a creditor or debtor) under an indebtedness in existence when the interest was acquired. Thus, for example, the value attributable to the assumption of an indebtedness with a below-market interest rate is not amortizable under section 197. In addition, the premium paid for acquiring a debt instrument with an above-market interest rate is not amortizable under section 197. See section 171 for rules concerning the treatment of amortizable bond premium.

(ii) *Exceptions.* For purposes of this paragraph (c)(9), an interest under an existing indebtedness does not include the deposit base (and other similar items) of a financial institution. An interest under an existing indebtedness includes mortgage servicing rights, however, to the extent the rights are stripped coupons under section 1286.

(10) *Professional sports franchises.* Section 197 intangibles do not include any franchise to engage in professional baseball, basketball, football, or any other professional sport, and any item (even though otherwise qualifying as a section 197

intangible) acquired in connection with such a franchise.

(11) *Mortgage servicing rights.* Section 197 intangibles do not include any right described in section 197(e)(7) (concerning rights to service indebtedness secured by residential real property that are not acquired as part of a purchase of a trade or business). (See § 1.167(a)-14(d) for applicable rules.)

(12) *Certain transaction costs.* Section 197 intangibles do not include any fees for professional services and any transaction costs incurred by parties to a transaction in which all or any portion of the gain or loss is not recognized under part III of subchapter C of the Internal Revenue Code.

(13) *Rights of fixed duration or amount*—(i) Section 197 intangibles do not include any right under a contract or any license, permit, or other right granted by a governmental unit if the right—

(A) Is acquired in the ordinary course of a trade or business (or an activity described in section 212) and not as part of a purchase of a trade or business;

(B) Is not described in section 197(d)(1)(A), (B), (E), or (F);

(C) Is not a customer-based intangible, a customer-related information base, or any other similar item; and

(D) Either—

(*1*) Has a fixed duration of less than 15 years; or

(*2*) Is fixed as to amount and the adjusted basis thereof is properly recoverable (without regard to this section) under a method similar to the unit-of-production method.

(ii) See § 1.167(a)-14(c)(2) and (3) for applicable rules.

(d) *Amortizable section 197 intangibles*—(1) *Definition.* Except as otherwise provided in this paragraph (d), the term *amortizable section 197 intangible* means any section 197 intangible acquired after August 10, 1993 (or after July 25, 1991, if a valid retroactive election under § 1.197-1T has been made), and held in connection with the conduct of a trade or business or an activity described in section 212.

(2) *Exception for self-created intangibles*—(i) *In general.* Except as provided in paragraph (d)(2)(iii) of this section, amortizable section 197 intangibles do not include any section 197 intangible created by the taxpayer (a self-created intangible).

(ii) *Created by the taxpayer*—(A) *Defined.* A section 197 intangible is created by the tax-

payer to the extent the taxpayer makes payments or otherwise incurs costs for its creation, production, development, or improvement, whether the actual work is performed by the taxpayer or by another person under a contract with the taxpayer entered into before the contracted creation, production, development, or improvement occurs. For example, a technological process developed specifically for a taxpayer under an arrangement with another person pursuant to which the taxpayer retains all rights to the process is created by the taxpayer.

(B) *Contracts for the use of intangibles.* A section 197 intangible is not a self-created intangible to the extent that it results from the entry into (or renewal of) a contract for the use of an existing section 197 intangible. Thus, for example, the exception for self-created intangibles does not apply to capitalized costs, such as legal and other professional fees, incurred by a licensee in connection with the entry into (or renewal of) a contract for the use of know-how or similar property.

(C) *Improvements and modifications.* If an existing section 197 intangible is improved or otherwise modified by the taxpayer or by another person under a contract with the taxpayer, the existing intangible and the capitalized costs (if any) of the improvements or other modifications are each treated as a separate section 197 intangible for purposes of this paragraph (d).

(iii) *Exceptions*—(A) The exception for self-created intangibles does not apply to any section 197 intangible described in section 197(d)(1)(D) (relating to licenses, permits or other rights granted by a governmental unit), 197(d)(1)(E) (relating to covenants not to compete), or 197(d)(1)(F) (relating to franchises, trademarks, and trade names). Thus, for example, capitalized costs incurred in the development, registration, or defense of a trademark or trade name do not qualify for the exception and are amortized over 15 years under section 197.

(B) The exception for self-created intangibles does not apply to any section 197 intangible created in connection with the purchase of a trade or business (as defined in paragraph (e) of this section).

(C) If a taxpayer disposes of a self-created intangible and subsequently reacquires the intangible in an acquisition described in paragraph (h)(5)(ii) of this section, the exception for self-created intangibles does not apply to the reacquired intangible.

(3) *Exception for property subject to anti-churning rules.* Amortizable section 197 intangibles do not include any property to which

the anti-churning rules of section 197(f)(9) and paragraph (h) of this section apply.

(e) *Purchase of a trade or business.* Several of the exceptions in section 197 apply only to property that is not acquired in (or created in connection with) a transaction or series of related transactions involving the acquisition of assets constituting a trade or business or a substantial portion thereof. Property acquired in (or created in connection with) such a transaction or series of related transactions is referred to in this section as property acquired as part of (or created in connection with) a purchase of a trade or business. For purposes of section 197 and this section, the applicability of the limitation is determined under the following rules:

(1) *Goodwill or going concern value.* An asset or group of assets constitutes a trade or business or a substantial portion thereof if their use would constitute a trade or business under section 1060 (that is, if goodwill or going concern value could under any circumstances attach to the assets). See § 1.1060-1(b)(2). For this purpose, all the facts and circumstances, including any employee relationships that continue (or covenants not to compete that are entered into) as part of the transfer of the assets, are taken into account in determining whether goodwill or going concern value could attach to the assets.

(2) *Franchise, trademark, or trade name*—(i) *In general.* The acquisition of a franchise, trademark, or trade name constitutes the acquisition of a trade or business or a substantial portion thereof.

(ii) *Exceptions.* For purposes of this paragraph (e)(2)—

(A) A trademark or trade name is disregarded if it is included in computer software under paragraph (c)(4) of this section or in an interest in a film, sound recording, video tape, book, or other similar property under paragraph (c)(5) of this section;

(B) A franchise, trademark, or trade name is disregarded if its value is nominal or the taxpayer irrevocably disposes of it immediately after its acquisition; and

(C) The acquisition of a right or interest in a trademark or trade name is disregarded if the grant of the right or interest is not, under the principles of section 1253, a transfer of all substantial rights to such property or of an undivided interest in all substantial rights to such property.

(3) *Acquisitions to be included.* The assets acquired in a transaction (or series of related transactions) include only assets (including a beneficial or other indirect interest in assets where the interest is of a type described in paragraph (c)(1) of this section) acquired by the taxpayer and persons related to the taxpayer from another person and persons related to that other person. For purposes of this paragraph (e)(3), persons are related only if their relationship is described in section 267(b) or 707(b) or they are engaged in trades or businesses under common control within the meaning of section 41(f)(1).

(4) *Substantial portion.* The determination of whether acquired assets constitute a substantial portion of a trade or business is to be based on all of the facts and circumstances, including the nature and the amount of the assets acquired as well as the nature and amount of the assets retained by the transferor. The value of the assets acquired relative to the value of the assets retained by the transferor is not determinative of whether the acquired assets constitute a substantial portion of a trade or business.

(5) *Deemed asset purchases under section 338.* A qualified stock purchase that is treated as a purchase of assets under section 338 is treated as a transaction involving the acquisition of assets constituting a trade or business only if the direct acquisition of the assets of the corporation would have been treated as the acquisition of assets constituting a trade or business or a substantial portion thereof.

(6) *Mortgage servicing rights.* Mortgage servicing rights acquired in a transaction or series of related transactions are disregarded in determining for purposes of paragraph (c)(11) of this section whether the assets acquired in the transaction or transactions constitute a trade or business or substantial portion thereof.

(7) *Computer software acquired for internal use.* Computer software acquired in a transaction or series of related transactions solely for internal use in an existing trade or business is disregarded in determining for purposes of paragraph (c)(4) of this section whether the assets acquired in the transaction or series of related transactions constitute a trade or business or substantial portion thereof.

(f) *Computation of amortization deduction*—(1) *In general.* Except as provided in paragraph (f)(2) of this section, the amortization deduction allowable under section 197(a) is computed as follows:

(i) The basis of an amortizable section 197 intangible is amortized ratably over the 15-year period beginning on the later of—

(A) The first day of the month in which the property is acquired; or

Reg. § 1.197-2(f)(1)

(B) In the case of property held in connection with the conduct of a trade or business or in an activity described in section 212, the first day of the month in which the conduct of the trade or business or the activity begins.

(ii) Except as otherwise provided in this section, basis is determined under section 1011 and salvage value is disregarded.

(iii) Property is not eligible for amortization in the month of disposition.

(iv) The amortization deduction for a short taxable year is based on the number of months in the short taxable year.

(2) *Treatment of contingent amounts*—(i) *Amounts added to basis during 15-year period.* Any amount that is properly included in the basis of an amortizable section 197 intangible after the first month of the 15-year period described in paragraph (f)(1)(i) of this section and before the expiration of that period is amortized ratably over the remainder of the 15-year period. For this purpose, the remainder of the 15-year period begins on the first day of the month in which the basis increase occurs.

(ii) *Amounts becoming fixed after expiration of 15-year period.* Any amount that is not properly included in the basis of an amortizable section 197 intangible until after the expiration of the 15-year period described in paragraph (f)(1)(i) of this section is amortized in full immediately upon the inclusion of the amount in the basis of the intangible.

(iii) *Rules for including amounts in basis.* See §§ 1.1275-4(c)(4) and 1.483-4(a) for rules governing the extent to which contingent amounts payable under a debt instrument given in consideration for the sale or exchange of an amortizable section 197 intangible are treated as payments of principal and the time at which the amount treated as principal is included in basis. See § 1.461-1(a)(1) and (2) for rules governing the time at which other contingent amounts are taken into account in determining the basis of an amortizable section 197 intangible.

(3) *Basis determinations for certain assets*—(i) *Covenants not to compete.* In the case of a covenant not to compete or other similar arrangement described in paragraph (b)(9) of this section (a covenant), the amount chargeable to capital account includes, except as provided in this paragraph (f)(3), all amounts that are required to be paid pursuant to the covenant, whether or not any such amount would be deductible under section 162 if the covenant were not a section 197 intangible.

(ii) *Contracts for the use of section 197 intangibles; acquired as part of a trade or business*—(A) *In general.* Except as provided in this paragraph (f)(3), any amount paid or incurred by the transferee on account of the transfer of a right or term interest described in paragraph (b)(11) of this section (relating to contracts for the use of, and term interests in, section 197 intangibles) by the owner of the property to which such right or interest relates and as part of a purchase of a trade or business is chargeable to capital account, whether or not such amount would be deductible under section 162 if the property were not a section 197 intangible.

(B) *Know-how and certain information base.* The amount chargeable to capital account with respect to a right or term interest described in paragraph (b)(11) of this section is determined without regard to the rule in paragraph (f)(3)(ii)(A) of this section if the right or interest relates to property (other than a customer-related information base) described in paragraph (b)(4) or (5) of this section and the acquiring taxpayer establishes that—

(*1*) The transfer of the right or interest is not, under the principles of section 1235, a transfer of all substantial rights to such property or of an undivided interest in all substantial rights to such property; and

(*2*) The right or interest was transferred for an arm's-length consideration.

(iii) *Contracts for the use of section 197 intangibles; not acquired as part of a trade or business.* The transfer of a right or term interest described in paragraph (b)(11) of this section by the owner of the property to which such right or interest relates but not as part of a purchase of a trade or business will be closely scrutinized under the principles of section 1235 for purposes of determining whether the transfer is a sale or exchange and, accordingly, whether amounts paid on account of the transfer are chargeable to capital account. If under the principles of section 1235 the transaction is not a sale or exchange, amounts paid on account of the transfer are not chargeable to capital account under this paragraph (f)(3).

(iv) *Applicable rules*—(A) *Franchises, trademarks, and trade names.* For purposes of this paragraph (f)(3), section 197 intangibles described in paragraph (b)(11) of this section do not include any property that is also described in paragraph (b)(10) of this section (relating to franchises, trademarks, and trade names).

(B) *Certain amounts treated as payable under a debt instrument*—(*1*) *In general.* For purposes of applying any provision of the Internal

Reg. § 1.197-2(f)(2)

Revenue Code to a person making payments of amounts that are otherwise chargeable to capital account under this paragraph (f)(3) and are payable after the acquisition of the section 197 intangible to which they relate, such amounts are treated as payable under a debt instrument given in consideration for the sale or exchange of the section 197 intangible.

(2) *Rights granted by governmental units.* For purposes of applying any provision of the Internal Revenue Code to any amounts that are otherwise chargeable to capital account with respect to a license, permit, or other right described in paragraph (b)(8) of this section (relating to rights granted by a governmental unit or agency or instrumentality thereof) and are payable after the acquisition of the section 197 intangible to which they relate, such amounts are treated, except as provided in paragraph (f)(4)(i) of this section (relating to renewal transactions), as payable under a debt instrument given in consideration for the sale or exchange of the section 197 intangible.

(3) *Treatment of other parties to transaction.* No person shall be treated as having sold, exchanged, or otherwise disposed of property in a transaction for purposes of any provision of the Internal Revenue Code solely by reason of the application of this paragraph (f)(3) to any other party to the transaction.

(4) *Basis determinations in certain transactions—(i) Certain renewal transactions.* The costs paid or incurred for the renewal of a franchise, trademark, or trade name or any license, permit, or other right granted by a governmental unit or an agency or instrumentality thereof are amortized over the 15-year period that begins with the month of renewal. Any costs paid or incurred for the issuance, or earlier renewal, continue to be taken into account over the remaining portion of the amortization period that began at the time of the issuance, or earlier renewal. Any amount paid or incurred for the protection, expansion, or defense of a trademark or trade name and chargeable to capital account is treated as an amount paid or incurred for a renewal.

(ii) *Transactions subject to section 338 or 1060.* In the case of a section 197 intangible deemed to have been acquired as the result of a qualified stock purchase within the meaning of section 338(d)(3), the basis shall be determined pursuant to section 338(b)(5) and the regulations thereunder. In the case of a section 197 intangible acquired in an applicable asset acquisition within the meaning of section 1060(c), the basis shall be determined pursuant to section 1060(a) and the regulations thereunder.

(iii) *Certain reinsurance transactions.* See paragraph (g)(5)(ii) of this section for special rules regarding the adjusted basis of an insurance contract acquired through an assumption reinsurance transaction.

(g) *Special rules—(1) Treatment of certain dispositions—(i) Loss disallowance rules—(A) In general.* No loss is recognized on the disposition of an amortizable section 197 intangible if the taxpayer has any retained intangibles. The retained intangibles with respect to the disposition of any amortizable section 197 intangible (the transferred intangible) are all amortizable section 197 intangibles, or rights to use or interests (including beneficial or other indirect interests) in amortizable section 197 intangibles (including the transferred intangible) that were acquired in the same transaction or series of related transactions as the transferred intangible and are retained after its disposition. Except as otherwise provided in paragraph (g)(1)(iv)(B) of this section, the adjusted basis of each of the retained intangibles is increased by the product of—

(1) The loss that is not recognized solely by reason of this rule; and

(2) A fraction, the numerator of which is the adjusted basis of the retained intangible on the date of the disposition and the denominator of which is the total adjusted bases of all the retained intangibles on that date.

(B) *Abandonment or worthlessness.* The abandonment of an amortizable section 197 intangible, or any other event rendering an amortizable section 197 intangible worthless, is treated as a disposition of the intangible for purposes of this paragraph (g)(1), and the abandoned or worthless intangible is disregarded (that is, it is not treated as a retained intangible) for purposes of applying this paragraph (g)(1) to the subsequent disposition of any other amortizable section 197 intangible.

(C) *Certain nonrecognition transfers.* The loss disallowance rule in paragraph (g)(1)(i)(A) of this section also applies when a taxpayer transfers an amortizable section 197 intangible from an acquired trade or business in a transaction in which the intangible is transferred basis property and, after the transfer, retains other amortizable section 197 intangibles from the trade or business. Thus, for example, the transfer of an amortizable section 197 intangible to a corporation in exchange for stock in the corporation in a transaction described in section 351, or to a partnership in exchange for an interest in the partnership in a transaction described in section

Reg. § 1.197-2(g)(1)

721, when other amortizable section 197 intangibles acquired in the same transaction are retained, followed by a sale of the stock or partnership interest received, will not avoid the application of the loss disallowance provision to the extent the adjusted basis of the transferred intangible at the time of the sale exceeds its fair market value at that time.

(ii) *Separately acquired property.* Paragraph (g)(1)(i) of this section does not apply to an amortizable section 197 intangible that is not acquired in a transaction or series of related transactions in which the taxpayer acquires other amortizable section 197 intangibles (a separately acquired intangible). Consequently, a loss may be recognized upon the disposition of a separately acquired amortizable section 197 intangible. However, the termination or worthlessness of only a portion of an amortizable section 197 intangible is not the disposition of a separately acquired intangible. For example, neither the loss of several customers from an acquired customer list nor the worthlessness of only some information from an acquired data base constitutes the disposition of a separately acquired intangible.

(iii) *Disposition of a covenant not to compete.* If a covenant not to compete or any other arrangement having substantially the same effect is entered into in connection with the direct or indirect acquisition of an interest in one or more trades or businesses, the disposition or worthlessness of the covenant or other arrangement will not be considered to occur until the disposition or worthlessness of all interests in those trades or businesses. For example, a covenant not to compete entered into in connection with the purchase of stock continues to be amortized ratably over the 15-year recovery period (even after the covenant expires or becomes worthless) unless all the trades or businesses in which an interest was acquired through the stock purchase (or all the purchaser's interests in those trades or businesses) also are disposed of or become worthless.

(iv) *Taxpayers under common control*—(A) *In general.* Except as provided in paragraph (g)(1)(iv)(B) of this section, all persons that would be treated as a single taxpayer under section 41(f)(1) are treated as a single taxpayer under this paragraph (g)(1). Thus, for example, a loss is not recognized on the disposition of an amortizable section 197 intangible by a member of a controlled group of corporations (as defined in section 41(f)(5)) if, after the disposition, another member retains other amortizable section 197 intangibles acquired in the same transaction as the amortizable section 197 intangible that has been disposed of.

(B) *Treatment of disallowed loss.* If retained intangibles are held by a person other than the person incurring the disallowed loss, only the adjusted basis of intangibles retained by the person incurring the disallowed loss is increased, and only the adjusted basis of those intangibles is included in the denominator of the fraction described in paragraph (g)(1)(i)(A) of this section. If none of the retained intangibles are held by the person incurring the disallowed loss, the loss is allowed ratably, as a deduction under section 197, over the remainder of the period during which the intangible giving rise to the loss would have been amortizable, except that any remaining disallowed loss is allowed in full on the first date on which all other retained intangibles have been disposed of or become worthless.

(2) *Treatment of certain nonrecognition and exchange transactions*—(i) *Relationship to antichurning rules.* This paragraph (g)(2) provides rules relating to the treatment of section 197 intangibles acquired in certain transactions. If these rules apply to a section 197(f)(9) intangible (within the meaning of paragraph (h)(1)(i) of this section), the intangible is, notwithstanding its treatment under this paragraph (g)(2), treated as an amortizable section 197 intangible only to the extent permitted under paragraph (h) of this section.

(ii) *Treatment of nonrecognition and exchange transactions generally*—(A) *Transfer disregarded.* If a section 197 intangible is transferred in a transaction described in paragraph (g)(2)(ii)(C) of this section, the transfer is disregarded in determining—

(1) Whether, with respect to so much of the intangible's basis in the hands of the transferee as does not exceed its basis in the hands of the transferor, the intangible is an amortizable section 197 intangible; and

(2) The amount of the deduction under section 197 with respect to such basis.

(B) *Application of general rule.* If the intangible described in paragraph (g)(2)(ii)(A) of this section was an amortizable section 197 intangible in the hands of the transferor, the transferee will continue to amortize its adjusted basis, to the extent it does not exceed the transferor's adjusted basis, ratably over the remainder of the transferor's 15-year amortization period. If the intangible was not an amortizable section 197 intangible in the hands of the transferor, the transferee's adjusted basis, to the extent it does not exceed the transferor's adjusted basis, cannot be amortized under section 197. In either event, the intangible is treated, with respect to so much of its adjusted basis in the hands of the transferee as exceeds its

Reg. § 1.197-2(g)(2)

adjusted basis in the hands of the transferor, in the same manner for purposes of section 197 as an intangible acquired from the transferor in a transaction that is not described in paragraph (g)(2)(ii)(C) of this section. The rules of this paragraph (g)(2)(ii) also apply to any subsequent transfers of the intangible in a transaction described in paragraph (g)(2)(ii)(C) of this section.

(C) *Transactions covered.* The transactions described in this paragraph (g)(2)(ii)(C) are—

(1) Any transaction described in section 332, 351, 361, 721, or 731; and

(2) Any transaction between corporations that are members of the same consolidated group immediately after the transaction.

(iii) *Certain exchanged-basis property.* This paragraph (g)(2)(iii) applies to property that is acquired in a transaction subject to section 1031 or 1033 and is permitted to be acquired without recognition of gain (replacement property). Replacement property is treated as if it were the property by reference to which its basis is determined (the predecessor property) in determining whether, with respect to so much of its basis as does not exceed the basis of the predecessor property, the replacement property is an amortizable section 197 intangible and the amortization period under section 197 with respect to such basis. Thus, if the predecessor property was an amortizable section 197 intangible, the taxpayer will amortize the adjusted basis of the replacement property, to the extent it does not exceed the adjusted basis of the predecessor property, ratably over the remainder of the 15-year amortization period for the predecessor property. If the predecessor property was not an amortizable section 197 intangible, the adjusted basis of the replacement property, to the extent it does not exceed the adjusted basis of the predecessor property, may not be amortized under section 197. In either event, the replacement property is treated, with respect to so much of its adjusted basis as exceeds the adjusted basis of the predecessor property, in the same manner for purposes of section 197 as property acquired from the transferor in a transaction that is not subject to section 1031 or 1033.

(iv) *Transfers under section 708(b)(1)*—(A) *In general.* Paragraph (g)(2)(ii) of this section applies to transfers of section 197 intangibles that occur or are deemed to occur by reason of the termination of a partnership under section 708(b)(1).

(B) *Termination by sale or exchange of interest.* In applying paragraph (g)(2)(ii) of this section to a partnership that is terminated pursu-

ant to section 708(b)(1)(B) (relating to deemed terminations from the sale or exchange of an interest), the terminated partnership is treated as the transferor and the new partnership is treated as the transferee with respect to any section 197 intangible held by the terminated partnership immediately preceding the termination. (See paragraph (g)(3) of this section for the treatment of increases in the bases of property of the terminated partnership under section 743(b).)

(C) *Other terminations.* In applying paragraph (g)(2)(ii) of this section to a partnership that is terminated pursuant to section 708(b)(1)(A) (relating to cessation of activities by a partnership), the terminated partnership is treated as the transferor and the distributee partner is treated as the transferee with respect to any section 197 intangible held by the terminated partnership immediately preceding the termination.

(3) *Increase in the basis of partnership property under section 732(b), 734(b), 743(b), or 732(d).* Any increase in the adjusted basis of a section 197 intangible under sections 732(b) or 732(d) (relating to a partner's basis in property distributed by a partnership), section 734(b) (relating to the optional adjustment to the basis of undistributed partnership property after a distribution of property to a partner), or section 743(b) (relating to the optional adjustment to the basis of partnership property after transfer of a partnership interest) is treated as a separate section 197 intangible. For purposes of determining the amortization period under section 197 with respect to the basis increase, the intangible is treated as having been acquired at the time of the transaction that causes the basis increase, except as provided in § 1.743-1(j)(4)(i)(B)(2). The provisions of paragraph (f)(2) of this section apply to the extent that the amount of the basis increase is determined by reference to contingent payments. For purposes of the effective date and anti-churning provisions (paragraphs (l)(1) and (h) of this section) for a basis increase under section 732(d), the intangible is treated as having been acquired by the transferee partner at the time of the transfer of the partnership interest described in section 732(d).

(4) *Section 704(c) allocations*—(i) *Allocations where the intangible is amortizable by the contributor.* To the extent that the intangible was an amortizable section 197 intangible in the hands of the contributing partner, a partnership may make allocations of amortization deductions with respect to the intangible to all of its partners under any of the permissible methods described in the regulations under section 704(c). See § 1.704-3.

Reg. § 1.197-2(g)(4)

(ii) *Allocations where the intangible is not amortizable by the contributor.* To the extent that the intangible was not an amortizable section 197 intangible in the hands of the contributing partner, the intangible is not amortizable under section 197 by the partnership. However, if a partner contributes a section 197 intangible to a partnership and the partnership adopts the remedial allocation method for making section 704(c) allocations of amortization deductions, the partnership generally may make remedial allocations of amortization deductions with respect to the contributed section 197 intangible in accordance with § 1.704-3(d). See paragraph (h)(12) of this section to determine the application of the anti-churning rules in the context of remedial allocations.

(5) *Treatment of certain reinsurance transactions*—(i) *In general.* Section 197 applies to any insurance contract acquired from another person through an assumption reinsurance transaction. For purposes of section 197, an assumption reinsurance transaction is—

(A) Any arrangement in which one insurance company (the reinsurer) becomes solely liable to policyholders on contracts transferred by another insurance company (the ceding company); and

(B) Any acquisition of an insurance contract that is treated as occurring by reason of an election under section 338.

(ii) *Determination of adjusted basis*—(A) *Acquisitions (other than under section 338) of specified insurance contracts.* The amount taken into account for purposes of section 197 as the adjusted basis of specified insurance contracts (as defined in section 848(e)(1)) acquired in an assumption reinsurance transaction that is not described in paragraph (g)(5)(i)(B) of this section is equal to the excess of—

(*1*) The amount paid or incurred (or treated as having been paid or incurred) by the reinsurer for the purchase of the contracts (as determined under § 1.817-4(d)(2)); over

(*2*) The amount of the specified policy acquisition expenses that are attributable to the reinsurer's net positive consideration for the reinsurance agreement (as determined under § 1.848-2(f)(3)).

(B) *Insolvent ceding company.* The reduction of the amount of specified policy acquisition expenses by the reinsurer with respect to an assumption reinsurance transaction with an insolvent ceding company where the ceding company and reinsurer have made a valid joint election under section 1.848-2(i)(4) is disregarded in deter-

mining the amount of specified policy acquisition expenses for purposes of this paragraph (g)(5)(ii).

(C) *Other acquisitions.* [Reserved]

(6) *Amounts paid or incurred for a franchise, trademark, or trade name.* If an amount to which section 1253(d) (relating to the transfer, sale, or other disposition of a franchise, trademark, or trade name) applies is described in section 1253(d)(1)(B) (relating to contingent serial payments deductible under section 162), the amount is not included in the adjusted basis of the intangible for purposes of section 197. Any other amount, whether fixed or contingent, to which section 1253(d) applies is chargeable to capital account under section 1253(d)(2) and is amortizable only under section 197.

(7) *Amounts properly taken into account in determining the cost of property that is not a section 197 intangible.* Section 197 does not apply to an amount that is properly taken into account in determining the cost of property that is not a section 197 intangible. The entire cost of acquiring the other property is included in its basis and recovered under other applicable Internal Revenue Code provisions. Thus, for example, section 197 does not apply to the cost of an interest in computer software to the extent such cost is included, without being separately stated, in the cost of the hardware or other tangible property and is consistently treated as part of the cost of the hardware or other tangible property.

(8) *Treatment of amortizable section 197 intangibles as depreciable property.* An amortizable section 197 intangible is treated as property of a character subject to the allowance for depreciation under section 167. Thus, for example, an amortizable section 197 intangible is not a capital asset for purposes of section 1221, but if used in a trade or business and held for more than one year, gain or loss on its disposition generally qualifies as section 1231 gain or loss. Also, an amortizable section 197 intangible is section 1245 property and section 1239 applies to any gain recognized upon its sale or exchange between related persons (as defined in section 1239(b)).

(h) *Anti-churning rules*—(1) *Scope and purpose*—(i) *Scope.* This paragraph (h) applies to section 197(f)(9) intangibles. For this purpose, section 197(f)(9) intangibles are goodwill and going concern value that was held or used at any time during the transition period and any other section 197 intangible that was held or used at any time during the transition period and was not depreciable or amortizable under prior law.

(ii) *Purpose.* To qualify as an amortizable section 197 intangible, a section 197 intangible must be acquired after the applicable date (July

25, 1991, if the acquiring taxpayer has made a valid retroactive election pursuant to § 1.197-1T; August 10, 1993, in all other cases). The purpose of the anti-churning rules of section 197(f)(9) and this paragraph (h) is to prevent the amortization of section 197(f)(9) intangibles unless they are transferred after the applicable effective date in a transaction giving rise to a significant change in ownership or use. (Special rules apply for purposes of determining whether transactions involving partnerships give rise to a significant change in ownership or use. See paragraph (h)(12) of this section.) The anti-churning rules are to be applied in a manner that carries out their purpose.

(2) *Treatment of section 197(f)(9) intangibles.* Except as otherwise provided in this paragraph (h), a section 197(f)(9) intangible acquired by a taxpayer after the applicable effective date does not qualify for amortization under section 197 if—

(i) The taxpayer or a related person held or used the intangible or an interest therein at any time during the transition period;

(ii) The taxpayer acquired the intangible from a person that held the intangible at any time during the transition period and, as part of the transaction, the user of the intangible does not change; or

(iii) The taxpayer grants the right to use the intangible to a person that held or used the intangible at any time during the transition period (or to a person related to that person), but only if the transaction in which the taxpayer grants the right and the transaction in which the taxpayer acquired the intangible are part of a series of related transactions.

(3) *Amounts deductible under section 1253(d) or § 1.162-11.* For purposes of this paragraph (h), deductions allowable under section 1253(d)(2) or pursuant to an election under section 1253(d)(3) (in either case as in effect prior to the enactment of section 197) and deductions allowable under § 1.162-11 are treated as deductions allowable for amortization under prior law.

(4) *Transition period.* For purposes of this paragraph (h), the transition period is July 25, 1991, if the acquiring taxpayer has made a valid retroactive election pursuant to § 1.197-1T and the period beginning on July 25, 1991, and ending on August 10, 1993, in all other cases.

(5) *Exceptions.* The anti-churning rules of this paragraph (h) do not apply to—

(i) The acquisition of a section 197(f)(9) intangible if the acquiring taxpayer's basis in the intangible is determined under section 1014(a); or

(ii) The acquisition of a section 197(f)(9) intangible that was an amortizable section 197 intangible in the hands of the seller (or transferor), but only if the acquisition transaction and the transaction in which the seller (or transferor) acquired the intangible or interest therein are not part of a series of related transactions.

(6) *Related person*—(i) *In general.* Except as otherwise provided in paragraph (h)(6)(ii) of this section, a person is related to another person for purposes of this paragraph (h) if—

(A) The person bears a relationship to that person that would be specified in section 267(b) (determined without regard to section 267(e)) and, by substitution, section 267(f)(1), if those sections were amended by substituting 20 percent for 50 percent; or

(B) The person bears a relationship to that person that would be specified in section 707(b)(1) if that section were amended by substituting 20 percent for 50 percent; or

(C) The persons are engaged in trades or businesses under common control (within the meaning of section 41(f)(1)(A) and (B)).

(ii) *Time for testing relationships.* Except as provided in paragraph (h)(6)(iii) of this section, a person is treated as related to another person for purposes of this paragraph (h) if the relationship exists—

(A) In the case of a single transaction, immediately before or immediately after the transaction in which the intangible is acquired; and

(B) In the case of a series of related transactions (or a series of transactions that together comprise a qualified stock purchase within the meaning of section 338(d)(3)), immediately before the earliest such transaction or immediately after the last such transaction.

(iii) *Certain relationships disregarded.* In applying the rules in paragraph (h)(7) of this section, if a person acquires an intangible in a series of related transactions in which the person acquires stock (meeting the requirements of section 1504(a)(2)) of a corporation in a fully taxable transaction followed by a liquidation of the acquired corporation under section 331, any relationship created as part of such series of transactions is disregarded in determining whether any person is related to such acquired corporation immediately after the last transaction.

(iv) *De minimis rule*—(A) *In general.* Two corporations are not treated as related persons for purposes of this paragraph (h) if—

(1) The corporations would (but for the application of this paragraph (h)(6)(iv)) be treated as related persons solely by reason of substituting "more than 20 percent" for "more than 50 percent" in section 267(f)(1)(A); and

(2) The beneficial ownership interest of each corporation in the stock of the other corporation represents less than 10 percent of the total combined voting power of all classes of stock entitled to vote and less than 10 percent of the total value of the shares of all classes of stock outstanding.

(B) *Determination of beneficial ownership interest.* For purposes of this paragraph (h)(6)(iv), the beneficial ownership interest of one corporation in the stock of another corporation is determined under the principles of section 318(a), except that—

(1) In applying section 318(a)(2)(C), the 50-percent limitation contained therein is not applied; and

(2) Section 318(a)(3)(C) is applied by substituting "20 percent" for "50 percent".

(7) *Special rules for entities that owned or used property at any time during the transition period and that are no longer in existence.* A corporation, partnership, or trust that owned or used a section 197 intangible at any time during the transition period and that is no longer in existence is deemed, for purposes of determining whether a taxpayer acquiring the intangible is related to such entity, to be in existence at the time of the acquisition.

(8) *Special rules for section 338 deemed acquisitions.* In the case of a qualified stock purchase that is treated as a deemed sale and purchase of assets pursuant to section 338, the corporation treated as purchasing assets as a result of an election thereunder (new target) is not considered the person that held or used the assets during any period in which the assets were held or used by the corporation treated as selling the assets (old target). Thus, for example, if a corporation (the purchasing corporation) makes a qualified stock purchase of the stock of another corporation after the transition period, new target will not be treated as the owner during the transition period of assets owned by old target during that period even if old target and new target are treated as the same corporation for certain other purposes of the Internal Revenue Code or old target and new target are the same corporation under the laws of the State or other jurisdiction of its organization. However, the anti-churning rules of this paragraph (h) may nevertheless apply to a deemed asset purchase resulting from a section 338 election if new target is related (within the meaning of paragraph (h)(6) of this section) to old target.

(9) *Gain-recognition exception*—(i) *Applicability.* A section 197(f)(9) intangible qualifies for the gain-recognition exception if—

(A) The taxpayer acquires the intangible from a person that would not be related to the taxpayer but for the substitution of 20 percent for 50 percent under paragraph (h)(6)(i)(A) of this section; and

(B) That person (whether or not otherwise subject to Federal income tax) elects to recognize gain on the disposition of the intangible and agrees, notwithstanding any other provision of law or treaty, to pay for the taxable year in which the disposition occurs an amount of tax on the gain that, when added to any other Federal income tax on such gain, equals the gain on the disposition multiplied by the highest marginal rate of tax for that taxable year.

(ii) *Effect of exception.* The anti-churning rules of this paragraph (h) apply to a section 197(f)(9) intangible that qualifies for the gain-recognition exception only to the extent the acquiring taxpayer's basis in the intangible exceeds the gain recognized by the transferor.

(iii) *Time and manner of election.* The election described in this paragraph (h)(9) must be made by the due date (including extensions of time) of the electing taxpayer's Federal income tax return for the taxable year in which the disposition occurs. The election is made by attaching an election statement satisfying the requirements of paragraph (h)(9)(viii) of this section to the electing taxpayer's original or amended income tax return for that taxable year (or by filing the statement as a return for the taxable year under paragraph (h)(9)(xi) of this section). In addition, the taxpayer must satisfy the notification requirements of paragraph (h)(9)(vi) of this section. The election is binding on the taxpayer and all parties whose Federal tax liability is affected by the election.

(iv) *Special rules for certain entities.* In the case of a partnership, S corporation, estate or trust, the election under this paragraph (h)(9) is made by the entity rather than by its owners or beneficiaries. If a partnership or S corporation makes an election under this paragraph (h)(9) with respect to the disposition of a section 197(f)(9) intangible, each of its partners or shareholders is required to pay a tax determined in the manner described in paragraph (h)(9)(i)(B) of this section on the amount of gain that is properly allocable to such partner or shareholder with respect to the disposition.

Reg. § 1.197-2(h)(7)

(v) *Effect of nonconforming elections.* An attempted election that does not substantially comply with each of the requirements of this paragraph (h)(9) is disregarded in determining whether a section 197(f)(9) intangible qualifies for the gain-recognition exception.

(vi) *Notification requirements.* A taxpayer making an election under this paragraph (h)(9) with respect to the disposition of a section 197(f)(9) intangible must provide written notification of the election on or before the due date of the return on which the election is made to the person acquiring the section 197 intangible. In addition, a partnership or S corporation making an election under this paragraph (h)(9) must attach to the Schedule K-1 furnished to each partner or shareholder a written statement containing all information necessary to determine the recipient's additional tax liability under this paragraph (h)(9).

(vii) *Revocation.* An election under this paragraph (h)(9) may be revoked only with the consent of the Commissioner.

(viii) *Election Statement.* An election statement satisfies the requirements of this paragraph (h)(9)(viii) if it is in writing and contains the information listed below. The required information should be arranged and identified in accordance with the following order and numbering system:

(A) The name and address of the electing taxpayer.

(B) Except in the case of a taxpayer that is not otherwise subject to Federal income tax, the taxpayer identification number (TIN) of the electing taxpayer.

(C) A statement that the taxpayer is making the election under section 197(f)(9)(B).

(D) Identification of the transaction and each person that is a party to the transaction or whose tax return is affected by the election (including, except in the case of persons not otherwise subject to Federal income tax, the TIN of each such person).

(E) The calculation of the gain realized, the applicable rate of tax, and the amount of the taxpayer's additional tax liability under this paragraph (h)(9).

(F) The signature of the taxpayer or an individual authorized to sign the taxpayer's Federal income tax return.

(ix) *Determination of highest marginal rate of tax and amount of other Federal income tax on gain*—(A) *Marginal rate.* The following rules apply for purposes of determining the highest marginal rate of tax applicable to an electing taxpayer:

(1) *Noncorporate taxpayers.* In the case of an individual, estate, or trust, the highest marginal rate of tax is the highest marginal rate of tax in effect under section 1, determined without regard to section 1(h).

(2) *Corporations and tax-exempt entities.* In the case of a corporation or an entity that is exempt from tax under section 501(a), the highest marginal rate of tax is the highest marginal rate of tax in effect under section 11, determined without regard to any rate that is added to the otherwise applicable rate in order to offset the effect of the graduated rate schedule.

(B) *Other Federal income tax on gain.* The amount of Federal income tax (other than the tax determined under this paragraph (h)(9)) imposed on any gain is the lesser of—

(1) The amount by which the taxpayer's Federal income tax liability (determined without regard to this paragraph (h)(9)) would be reduced if the amount of such gain were not taken into account; or

(2) The amount of the gain multiplied by the highest marginal rate of tax for the taxable year.

(x) *Coordination with other provisions*—(A) *In general.* The amount of gain subject to the tax determined under this paragraph (h)(9) is not reduced by any net operating loss deduction under section 172(a), any capital loss under section 1212, or any other similar loss or deduction. In addition, the amount of tax determined under this paragraph (h)(9) is not reduced by any credit of the taxpayer. In computing the amount of any net operating loss, capital loss, or other similar loss or deduction, or any credit that may be carried to any taxable year, any gain subject to the tax determined under this paragraph (h)(9) and any tax paid under this paragraph (h)(9) is not taken into account.

(B) *Section 1374.* No provision of paragraph (h)(9)(iv) of this section precludes the application of section 1374 (relating to a tax on certain built-in gains of S corporations) to any gain with respect to which an election under this paragraph (h)(9) is made. In addition, neither paragraph (h)(9)(iv) nor paragraph (h)(9)(x)(A) of this section precludes a taxpayer from applying the provisions of section 1366(f)(2) (relating to treatment of the tax imposed by section 1374 as a loss sustained by the S corporation) in determining the amount of tax payable under paragraph (h)(9) of this section.

Reg. § 1.197-2(h)(9)

(C) *Procedural and administrative provisions.* For purposes of subtitle F, the amount determined under this paragraph (h)(9) is treated as a tax imposed by section 1 or 11, as appropriate.

(D) *Installment method.* The gain subject to the tax determined under paragraph (h)(9)(i) of this section may not be reported under the method described in section 453(a). Any such gain that would, but for the application of this paragraph (h)(9)(x)(D), be taken into account under section 453(a) shall be taken into account in the same manner as if an election under section 453(d) (relating to the election not to apply section 453(a)) had been made.

(xi) *Special rules for persons not otherwise subject to Federal income tax.* If the person making the election under this paragraph (h)(9) with respect to a disposition is not otherwise subject to Federal income tax, the election statement satisfying the requirements of paragraph (h)(9)(viii) of this section must be filed with the Philadelphia Service Center. For purposes of this paragraph (h)(9) and subtitle F, the statement is treated as an income tax return for the calendar year in which the disposition occurs and as a return due on or before March 15 of the following year.

(10) *Transactions subject to both anti-churning and nonrecognition rules.* If a person acquires a section 197(f)(9) intangible in a transaction described in paragraph (g)(2) of this section from a person in whose hands the intangible was an amortizable section 197 intangible, and immediately after the transaction (or series of transactions described in paragraph (h)(6)(ii)(B) of this section) in which such intangible is acquired, the person acquiring the section 197(f)(9) intangible is related to any person described in paragraph (h)(2) of this section, the intangible is, notwithstanding its treatment under paragraph (g)(2) of this section, treated as an amortizable section 197 intangible only to the extent permitted under this paragraph (h). (See, for example, paragraph (h)(5)(ii) of this section.)

(11) *Avoidance purpose.* A section 197(f)(9) intangible acquired by a taxpayer after the applicable effective date does not qualify for amortization under section 197 if one of the principal purposes of the transaction in which it is acquired is to avoid the operation of the anti-churning rules of section 197(f)(9) and this paragraph (h). A transaction will be presumed to have a principal purpose of avoidance if it does not effect a significant change in the ownership or use of the intangible. Thus, for example, if section 197(f)(9) intangibles are acquired in a transaction (or series of related transactions) in which an option to

acquire stock is issued to a party to the transaction, but the option is not treated as having been exercised for purposes of paragraph (h)(6) of this section, this paragraph (h)(11) may apply to the transaction.

(12) *Additional partnership anti-churning rules*—(i) *In general.* In determining whether the anti-churning rules of this paragraph (h) apply to any increase in the basis of a section 197(f)(9) intangible under section 732(b), 732(d), 734(b), or 743(b), the determinations are made at the partner level and each partner is treated as having owned and used the partner's proportionate share of partnership property. In determining whether the anti-churning rules of this paragraph (h) apply to any transaction under another section of the Internal Revenue Code, the determinations are made at the partnership level, unless under § 1.701-2(e) the Commissioner determines that the partner level is more appropriate.

(ii) *Section 732(b) adjustments*—(A) *In general.* The anti-churning rules of this paragraph (h) apply to any increase in the adjusted basis of a section 197(f)(9) intangible under section 732(b) to the extent that the basis increase exceeds the total unrealized appreciation from the intangible allocable to—

(1) Partners other than the distributee partner or persons related to the distributee partner;

(2) The distributee partner and persons related to the distributee partner if the distributed intangible is a section 197(f)(9) intangible acquired by the partnership on or before August 10, 1993, to the extent that—

(i) The distributee partner and related persons acquired an interest or interests in the partnership after August 10, 1993;

(ii) Such interest or interests were held after August 10, 1993, by a person or persons other than either the distributee partner or persons who were related to the distributee partner; and

(iii) The acquisition of such interest or interests by such person or persons was not part of a transaction or series of related transactions in which the distributee partner (or persons related to the distributee partner) subsequently acquired such interest or interests; and

(3) The distributee partner and persons related to the distributee partner if the distributed intangible is a section 197(f)(9) intangible acquired by the partnership after August 10, 1993, that is not amortizable with respect to the partnership, to the extent that—

Reg. § 1.197-2(h)(10)

(*i*) The distributee partner and persons related to the distributee partner acquired an interest or interests in the partnership after the partnership acquired the distributed intangible;

(*ii*) Such interest or interests were held after the partnership acquired the distributed intangible, by a person or persons other than either the distributee partner or persons who were related to the distributee partner; and

(*iii*) The acquisition of such interest or interests by such person or persons was not part of a transaction or series of related transactions in which the distributee partner (or persons related to the distributee partner) subsequently acquired such interest or interests.

(B) *Effect of retroactive elections.* For purposes of paragraph (h)(12)(ii)(A) of this section, references to August 10, 1993, are treated as references to July 25, 1991, if the relevant party made a valid retroactive election under § 1.197-1T.

(C) *Intangible still subject to anti-churning rules.* Notwithstanding paragraph (h)(12)(ii) of this section, in applying the provisions of this paragraph (h) with respect to subsequent transfers, the distributed intangible remains subject to the provisions of this paragraph (h) in proportion to a fraction (determined at the time of the distribution), as follows—

(*1*) The numerator of which is equal to the sum of—

(*i*) The amount of the distributed intangible's basis that is nonamortizable under paragraph (g)(2)(ii)(B) of this section; and

(*ii*) The total unrealized appreciation inherent in the intangible reduced by the amount of the increase in the adjusted basis of the distributed intangible under section 732(b) to which the anti-churning rules do not apply; and

(*2*) The denominator of which is the fair market value of such intangible.

(D) *Partner's allocable share of unrealized appreciation from the intangible.* The amount of unrealized appreciation from an intangible that is allocable to a partner is the amount of taxable gain that would have been allocated to that partner if the partnership had sold the intangible immediately before the distribution for its fair market value in a fully taxable transaction.

(E) *Acquisition of partnership interest by contribution.* Solely for purposes of paragraphs (h)(12)(ii)(A)(*2*) and (*3*) of this section, a partner who acquires an interest in a partnership in exchange for a contribution of property to the partnership is deemed to acquire a pro rata portion of that interest in the partnership from each person

who is a partner in the partnership at the time of the contribution based on each partner's respective proportionate interest in the partnership.

(iii) *Section 732(d) adjustments.* The anti-churning rules of this paragraph (h) do not apply to an increase in the basis of a section 197(f)(9) intangible under section 732(d) if, had an election been in effect under section 754 at the time of the transfer of the partnership interest, the distributee partner would have been able to amortize the basis adjustment made pursuant to section 743(b).

(iv) *Section 734(b) adjustments*—(A) *In general.* The anti-churning rules of this paragraph (h) do not apply to a continuing partner's share of an increase in the basis of a section 197(f)(9) intangible held by a partnership under section 734(b) to the extent that the continuing partner is an eligible partner.

(B) *Eligible partner.* For purposes of this paragraph (h)(12)(iv), eligible partner means—

(*1*) A continuing partner that is not the distributee partner or a person related to the distributee partner;

(*2*) A continuing partner that is the distributee partner or a person related to the distributee partner, with respect to any section 197(f)(9) intangible acquired by the partnership on or before August 10, 1993, to the extent that—

(*i*) The distributee partner's interest in the partnership was acquired after August 10, 1993;

(*ii*) Such interest was held after August 10, 1993 by a person or persons who were not related to the distributee partner; and

(*iii*) The acquisition of such interest by such person or persons was not part of a transaction or series of related transactions in which the distributee partner or persons related to the distributee partner subsequently acquired such interest; or

(*3*) A continuing partner that is the distributee partner or a person related to the distributee partner, with respect to any section 197(f)(9) intangible acquired by the partnership after August 10, 1993, that is not amortizable with respect to the partnership, to the extent that—

(*i*) The distributee partner's interest in the partnership was acquired after the partnership acquired the relevant intangible;

(*ii*) Such interest was held after the partnership acquired the relevant intangible by a person or persons who were not related to the distributee partner; and (*iii*) The acquisition of such interest by such person or persons was not part of a transaction or series of related transactions in which the distributee partner or persons related to the distributee partner subsequently acquired such interest.

(C) *Effect of retroactive elections.* For purposes of paragraph (h)(12)(iv)(A) of this section, references to August 10, 1993, are treated as references to July 25, 1991, if the distributee partner made a valid retroactive election under § 1.197-1T.

(D) *Partner's share of basis increase—* (*1*) *In general.* Except as provided in paragraph (h)(12)(iv)(D)(*2*) of this section, for purposes of this paragraph (h)(12)(iv), a continuing partner's share of a basis increase under section 734(b) is equal to—

(*i*) The total basis increase allocable to the intangible; multiplied by

(*ii*) A fraction the numerator of which is the amount of the continuing partner's post-distribution capital account (determined immediately after the distribution in accordance with the capital accounting rules of § 1.704-1(b)(2)(iv)), and the denominator of which is the total amount of the post-distribution capital accounts (determined immediately after the distribution in accordance with the capital accounting rules of § 1.704-1(b)(2)(iv)) of all continuing partners.

(*2*) *Exception where partnership does not maintain capital accounts.* If a partnership does not maintain capital accounts in accordance with § 1.704-1(b)(2)(iv), then for purposes of this paragraph (h)(12)(iv), a continuing partner's share of a basis increase is equal to—

(*i*) The total basis increase allocable to the intangible; multiplied by

(*ii*) The partner's overall interest in the partnership as determined under § 1.704-1(b)(3) immediately after the distribution.

(E) *Interests acquired by contribution—*(*1*) *Application of paragraphs (h)(12)(iv)(B)(2) and (3) of this section.* Solely for purposes of paragraphs (h)(12)(iv)(B)(*2*) and (*3*) of this section, a partner who acquires an interest in a partnership in exchange for a contribution of property to the partnership is deemed to acquire a pro rata portion of that interest in the partnership from each person who is a partner in the partnership at the time of the contribution based on each such partner's proportionate interest in the partnership.

(*2*) *Special rule with respect to paragraph (h)(12)(iv)(B)(1) of this section.* Solely for purposes of paragraph (h)(12)(iv)(B)(*1*) of this section, if a distribution that gives rise to an increase in the basis under section 734(b) of a section 197(f)(9) intangible held by the partnership is undertaken as part of a series of related transactions that include a contribution of the intangible to the partnership by a continuing partner, the continuing partner is treated as related to the distributee partner in analyzing the basis adjustment with respect to the contributed section 197(f)(9) intangible.

(F) *Effect of section 734(b) adjustments on partners' capital accounts.* If one or more partners are subject to the anti-churning rules under this paragraph (h) with respect to a section 734(b) adjustment allocable to an intangible asset, taxpayers may use any reasonable method to determine amortization of the asset for book purposes, provided that the method used does not contravene the purposes of the anti-churning rules under section 197 and this paragraph (h). A method will be considered to contravene the purposes of the anti-churning rules if the effect of the book adjustments resulting from the method is such that any portion of the tax deduction for amortization attributable to the section 734 adjustment is allocated, directly or indirectly, to a partner who is subject to the anti-churning rules with respect to such adjustment.

(v) *Section 743(b) adjustments—*(A) *General rule.* The anti-churning rules of this paragraph (h) do not apply to an increase in the basis of a section 197 intangible under section 743(b) if the person acquiring the partnership interest is not related to the person transferring the partnership interest. In addition, the anti-churning rules of this paragraph (h) do not apply to an increase in the basis of a section 197 intangible under section 743(b) to the extent that—

(*1*) The partnership interest being transferred was acquired after August 10, 1993, provided—

(*i*) The section 197(f)(9) intangible was acquired by the partnership on or before August 10, 1993;

(*ii*) The partnership interest being transferred was held after August 10, 1993, by a person or persons (the post-1993 person or persons) other than the person transferring the partnership interest or persons who were related to the person transferring the partnership interest; and

(*iii*) The acquisition of such interest by the post-1993 person or persons was not part of a transaction or series of related transactions in which the person transferring the partnership in-

Reg. § 1.197-2(h)(12)

terest or persons related to the person transferring the partnership interest acquired such interest; or

(2) The partnership interest being transferred was acquired after the partnership acquired the section 197(f)(9) intangible, provided—

(i) The section 197(f)(9) intangible was acquired by the partnership after August 10, 1993, and is not amortizable with respect to the partnership;

(ii) The partnership interest being transferred was held after the partnership acquired the section 197(f)(9) intangible by a person or persons (the post-contribution person or persons) other than the person transferring the partnership interest or persons who were related to the person transferring the partnership interest; and

(iii) The acquisition of such interest by the post-contribution person or persons was not part of a transaction or series of related transactions in which the person transferring the partnership interest or persons related to the person transferring the partnership interest acquired such interest.

(B) *Acquisition of partnership interest by contribution.* Solely for purposes of paragraph (h)(12)(v)(A)(1) and (2) of this section, a partner who acquires an interest in a partnership in exchange for a contribution of property to the partnership is deemed to acquire a pro rata portion of that interest in the partnership from each person who is a partner in the partnership at the time of the contribution based on each such partner's proportionate interest in the partnership.

(C) *Effect of retroactive elections.* For purposes of paragraph (h)(12)(v)(A) of this section, references to August 10, 1993, are treated as references to July 25, 1991, if the transferee partner made a valid retroactive election under § 1.197-1T.

(vi) *Partner is or becomes a user of partnership intangible—*(A) *General rule.* If, as part of a series of related transactions that includes a transaction described in paragraph (h)(12)(ii), (iii), (iv), or (v) of this section, an anti-churning partner or related person (other than the partnership) becomes (or remains) a direct user of an intangible that is treated as transferred in the transaction (as a result of the partners being treated as having owned their proportionate share of partnership assets), the anti-churning rules of this paragraph (h) apply to the proportionate share of such intangible that is treated as transferred by such anti-churning partner, notwithstanding the application of paragraph (h)(12)(ii), (iii), (iv), or (v) of this section.

(B) *Anti-churning partner.* For purposes of this paragraph (h)(12)(vi), anti-churning partner means—

(1) With respect to all intangibles held by a partnership on or before August 10, 1993, any partner, but only to the extent that

(i) The partner's interest in the partnership was acquired on or before August 10, 1993, or

(ii) The interest was acquired from a person related to the partner on or after August 10, 1993, and such interest was not held by any person other than persons related to such partner at any time after August 10, 1993 (disregarding, for this purpose, a person's holding of an interest if the acquisition of such interest was part of a transaction or series of related transactions in which the partner or persons related to the partner subsequently acquired such interest),

(2) With respect to any section 197(f)(9) intangible acquired by a partnership after August 10, 1993, that is not amortizable with respect to the partnership, any partner, but only to the extent that

(i) The partner's interest in the partnership was acquired on or before the date the partnership acquired the section 197(f)(9) intangible, or

(ii) The interest was acquired from a person related to the partner on or after the date the partnership acquired the section 197(f)(9) intangible, and such interest was not held by any person other than persons related to such partner at any time after the date the partnership acquired the section 197(f)(9) intangible (disregarding, for this purpose, a person's holding of an interest if the acquisition of such interest was part of a transaction or series of related transactions in which the partner or persons related to the partner subsequently acquired such interest).

(C) *Effect of retroactive elections.* For purposes of paragraph (h)(12)(vi)(B) of this section, references to August 10, 1993, are treated as references to July 25, 1991, if the relevant party made a valid retroactive election under § 1.197-1T.

(vii) *Section 704(c) allocations—*(A) *Allocations where the intangible is amortizable by the contributor.* The anti-churning rules of this paragraph (h) do not apply to the curative or remedial allocations of amortization with respect to a section 197(f)(9) intangible if the intangible was an amortizable section 197 intangible in the hands of the contributing partner (unless paragraph (h)(10) of this section applies so as to cause the intangible to cease to be an amortizable section 197 intangible in the hands of the partnership).

(B) *Allocations where the intangible is not amortizable by the contributor.* If a section 197(f)(9) intangible was not an amortizable section 197 intangible in the hands of the contributing partner, a non-contributing partner generally may receive remedial allocations of amortization under section 704(c) that are deductible for Federal income tax purposes. However, such a partner may not receive remedial allocations of amortization under section 704(c) if that partner is related to the partner that contributed the intangible or if, as part of a series of related transactions that includes the contribution of the section 197(f)(9) intangible to the partnership, the contributing partner or related person (other than the partnership) becomes (or remains) a direct user of the contributed intangible. Taxpayers may use any reasonable method to determine amortization of the asset for book purposes, provided that the method used does not contravene the purposes of the anti-churning rules under section 197 and this paragraph (h). A method will be considered to contravene the purposes of the anti-churning rules if the effect of the book adjustments resulting from the method is such that any portion of the tax deduction for amortization attributable to section 704(c) is allocated, directly or indirectly, to a partner who is subject to the anti-churning rules with respect to such adjustment.

(viii) *Operating rule for transfers upon death.* For purposes of this paragraph (h)(12), if the basis of a partner's interest in a partnership is determined under section 1014(a), such partner is treated as acquiring such interest from a person who is not related to such partner, and such interest is treated as having previously been held by a person who is not related to such partner.

(i) [Reserved]

(j) *General anti-abuse rule.* The Commissioner will interpret and apply the rules in this section as necessary and appropriate to prevent avoidance of the purposes of section 197. If one of the principal purposes of a transaction is to achieve a tax result that is inconsistent with the purposes of section 197, the Commissioner will recast the transaction for Federal tax purposes as appropriate to achieve tax results that are consistent with the purposes of section 197, in light of the applicable statutory and regulatory provisions and the pertinent facts and circumstances.

(k) *Examples.* The following examples illustrate the application of this section:

Example 1. Advertising costs. (i) Q manufactures and sells consumer products through a series of wholesalers and distributors. In order to increase sales of its products by encouraging consumer loyalty to its products and to enhance the value of the goodwill, trademarks, and trade names of the business, Q advertises its products to the consuming public. It regularly incurs costs to develop radio, television, and print advertisements. These costs generally consist of employee costs and amounts paid to independent advertising agencies. Q also incurs costs to run these advertisements in the various media for which they were developed.

(ii) The advertising costs are not chargeable to capital account under paragraph (f)(3) of this section (relating to costs incurred for covenants not to compete, rights granted by governmental units, and contracts for the use of section 197 intangibles) and are currently deductible as ordinary and necessary expenses under section 162. Accordingly, under paragraph (a)(3) of this section, section 197 does not apply to these costs.

Example 2. Computer software. (i) X purchases all of the assets of an existing trade or business from Y. One of the assets acquired is all of Y's rights in certain computer software previously used by Y under the terms of a nonexclusive license from the software developer. The software was developed for use by manufacturers to maintain a comprehensive accounting system, including general and subsidiary ledgers, payroll, accounts receivable and payable, cash receipts and disbursements, fixed asset accounting, and inventory cost accounting and controls. The developer modified the software for use by Y at a cost of $1,000 and Y made additional modifications at a cost of $500. The developer does not maintain wholesale or retail outlets but markets the software directly to ultimate users. Y's license of the software is limited to an entity that is actively engaged in business as a manufacturer.

(ii) Notwithstanding these limitations, the software is considered to be readily available to the general public for purposes of paragraph (c)(4)(i) of this section. In addition, the software is not substantially modified because the cost of the modifications by the developer and Y to the version of the software that is readily available to the general public does not exceed $2,000. Accordingly, the software is not a section 197 intangible.

Example 3. Acquisition of software for internal use. (i) B, the owner and operator of a worldwide package-delivery service, purchases from S all rights to software developed by S. The software will be used by B for the sole purpose of improving its package-tracking operations. B does not purchase any other assets in the transaction or any related transaction.

(ii) Because B acquired the software solely for internal use, it is disregarded in determining for purposes of paragraph (c)(4)(ii) of this section whether the assets acquired in the transaction or series of related transactions constitute a trade or business or substantial portion thereof. Since no other assets were acquired, the software is not acquired as part of a purchase of a trade or business and under paragraph (c)(4)(ii) of this section is not a section 197 intangible.

Example 4. Governmental rights of fixed duration. (i) City M operates a municipal water system. In order to induce X to locate a new manufacturing business in the city, M grants X the right to purchase water for 16 years at a specified price.

(ii) The right granted by M is a right to receive tangible property or services described in section 197(e)(4)(B) and paragraph (c)(6) of this section and, thus, is not a section 197 intangible. This exclusion applies even though the right does not qualify for exclusion as a right of fixed duration or amount under section 197(e)(4)(D) and paragraph (c)(13) of this section because the duration exceeds 15 years and the right is not fixed as to amount. It is also immaterial that the right would not qualify for exclusion as a self-created intangible under section 197(c)(2) and paragraph (d)(2) of this section because it is granted by a governmental unit.

Example 5. Separate acquisition of franchise. (i) S is a franchiser of retail outlets for specialty coffees. G enters into a franchise agreement (within the meaning of section 1253(b)(1)) with S pursuant to which G is permitted to acquire and operate a store using the S trademark and trade name at the location specified in the agreement. G agrees to pay S $100,000 upon execution of the agreement and also agrees to pay, throughout the term of the franchise, additional amounts that are deductible under section 1253(d)(1). The agreement contains detailed specifications for the construction and operation of the business, but G is not required to purchase from S any of the materials necessary to construct the improvements at the location specified in the franchise agreement.

(ii) The franchise is a section 197 intangible within the meaning of paragraph (b)(10) of this section. The franchise does not qualify for the exclusion relating to self-created intangibles described in section 197(c)(2) and paragraph (d)(2) of this section because the franchise is described in section 197(d)(1)(F). In addition, because the acquisition of the franchise constitutes the acquisition of an interest in a trade or business or a substantial portion thereof, the franchise may not be excluded under section 197(e)(4). Thus, the

franchise is an amortizable section 197 intangible, the basis of which must be recovered over a 15-year period. However, the amounts that are deductible under section 1253(d)(1)are not subject to the provisions of section 197 by reason of section 197(f)(4)(C) and paragraph (b)(10)(ii) of this section.

Example 6. Acquisition and amortization of covenant not to compete. (i) As part of the acquisition of a trade or business from C, B and C enter into an agreement containing a covenant not to compete. Under this agreement, C agrees that it will not compete with the business acquired by B within a prescribed geographical territory for a period of three years after the date on which the business is sold to B. In exchange for this agreement, B agrees to pay C $90,000 per year for each year in the term of the agreement. The agreement further provides that, in the event of a breach by C of his obligations under the agreement, B may terminate the agreement, cease making any of the payments due thereafter, and pursue any other legal or equitable remedies available under applicable law. The amounts payable to C under the agreement are not contingent payments for purposes of § 1.1275-4. The present fair market value of B's rights under the agreement is $225,000. The aggregate consideration paid excluding any amount treated as interest or original issue discount under applicable provisions of the Internal Revenue Code, for all assets acquired in the transaction (including the covenant not to compete) exceeds the sum of the amount of Class I assets and the aggregate fair market value of all Class II, Class III, Class IV, Class V, and Class VI assets by $50,000. See § 1.338-6(b) for rules for determining the assets in each class.

(ii) Because the covenant is acquired in an applicable asset acquisition (within the meaning of section 1060(c)), paragraph (f)(4)(ii) of this section applies and the basis of B in the covenant is determined pursuant to section 1060(a) and the regulations thereunder. Under § § 1.1060-1(c)(2) and 1.338-6(c)(1), B's basis in the covenant cannot exceed its fair market value. Thus, B's basis in the covenant immediately after the acquisition is $225,000. This basis is amortized ratably over the 15-year period beginning on the first day of the month in which the agreement is entered into. All of the remaining consideration after allocation to the covenant and other Class VI assets, ($50,000) is allocated to Class VII assets (goodwill and going concern value). See § § 1.1060-1(c)(2) and 1.338-6(b).

Example 7. Stand-alone license of technology. (i) X is a manufacturer of consumer goods that does business throughout the world through sub-

Reg. § 1.197-2(k)

sidiary corporations organized under the laws of each country in which business is conducted. X licenses to Y, its subsidiary organized and conducting business in Country K, all of the patents, formulas, designs, and know-how necessary for Y to manufacture the same products that X manufactures in the United States. Assume that the license is not considered a sale or exchange under the principles of section 1235. The license is for a term of 18 years, and there are no facts to indicate that the license does not have a fixed duration. Y agrees to pay X a royalty equal to a specified, fixed percentage of the revenues obtained from selling products manufactured using the licensed technology. Assume that the royalty is reasonable and is not subject to adjustment under section 482. The license is not entered into in connection with any other transaction. Y incurs capitalized costs in connection with entering into the license.

(ii) The license is a contract for the use of a section 197 intangible within the meaning of paragraph (b)(11) of this section. It does not qualify for the exception in section 197(e)(4)(D) and paragraph (c)(13) of this section (relating to rights of fixed duration or amount) because it does not have a term of less than 15 years, and the other exceptions in section 197(e) and paragraph (c) of this section are also inapplicable. Accordingly, the license is a section 197 intangible.

(iii) The license is not acquired as part of a purchase of a trade or business. Thus, under paragraph (f)(3)(iii) of this section, the license will be closely scrutinized under the principles of section 1235 for purposes of determining whether the transfer is a sale or exchange and, accordingly, whether the payments under the license are chargeable to capital account. Because the license is not a sale or exchange under the principles of section 1235, the royalty payments are not chargeable to capital account for purposes section 197. The capitalized costs of entering into the license are not within the exception under paragraph (d)(2) of this section for self-created intangibles, and thus are amortized under section 197.

Example 8. License of technology and trademarks. (i) The facts are the same as in *Example 7*, except that the license also includes the use of the trademarks and trade names that X uses to manufacture and distribute its products in the United States. Assume that under the principles of section 1253 the transfer is not a sale or exchange of the trademarks and trade names or an undivided interest therein and that the royalty payments are described in section 1253(d)(1)(B).

(ii) As in *Example 7*, the license is a section 197 intangible. Although the license conveys an interest in X's trademarks and trade names to Y, the transfer of the interest is disregarded for purposes of paragraph (e)(2) of this section unless the transfer is considered a sale or exchange of the trademarks and trade names or an undivided interest therein. Accordingly, the licensing of the technology and the trademarks and trade names is not treated as part of a purchase of a trade or business under paragraph (e)(2) of this section.

(iii) Because the technology license is not part of the purchase of a trade or business, it is treated in the manner described in *Example 7*. The royalty payments for the use of the trademarks and trade names are deductible under section 1253(d)(1) and, under section 197(f)(4)(C) and paragraph (b)(10)(ii) of this section, are not chargeable to capital account for purposes of section 197. The capitalized costs of entering into the license are treated in the same manner as in example 7.

Example 9. Disguised sale. (i) The facts are the same as in *Example 7*, except that Y agrees to pay X, in addition to the contingent royalty, a fixed minimum royalty immediately upon entering into the agreement and there are sufficient facts present to characterize the transaction, for federal tax purposes, as a transfer of ownership of the intellectual property from X to Y.

(ii) The purported license of technology is, in fact, an acquisition of an intangible described in section 197(d)(1)(C)(iii) and paragraph (b)(5) of this section (relating to know-how, etc.). As in *Example 7*, the exceptions in section 197(e) and paragraph (c) of this section do not apply to the transfer. Accordingly, the transferred property is a section 197 intangible. Y's basis in the transferred intangible includes the capitalized costs of entering into the agreement and the fixed minimum royalty payment payable at the time of the transfer. In addition, except to the extent that a portion of any payment will be treated as interest or original issue discount under applicable provisions of the Internal Revenue Code, all of the contingent payments under the purported license are properly chargeable to capital account for purposes of section 197 and this section. The extent to which such payments are treated as payments of principal and the time at which any amount treated as a payment of principal is taken into account in determining basis are determined under the rules of § 1.1275-4(c)(4) or 1.483-4(a), whichever is applicable. Any contingent amount that is included in basis after the month in which the acquisition occurs is amortized under the rules of paragraph (f)(2)(i) or (ii) of this section.

Reg. § 1.197-2(k)

Example 10. License of technology and customer list as part of sale of a trade or business. (i) X is a computer manufacturer that produces, in separate operating divisions, personal computers, servers, and peripheral equipment. In a transaction that is the purchase of a trade or business for purposes of section 197, Y (who is unrelated to X) purchases from X all assets of the operating division producing personal computers, except for certain patents that are also used in the division manufacturing servers and customer lists that are also used in the division manufacturing peripheral equipment. As part of the transaction, X transfers to Y the right to use the retained patents and customer lists solely in connection with the manufacture and sale of personal computers. The transfer agreement requires annual royalty payments contingent on the use of the patents and also requires a payment for each use of the customer list. In addition, Y incurs capitalized costs in connection with entering into the licenses.

(ii) The rights to use the retained patents and customer lists are contracts for the use of section 197 intangibles within the meaning of paragraph (b)(11) of this section. The rights do not qualify for the exception in 197(e)(4)(D) and paragraph (c)(13) of this section (relating to rights of fixed duration or amount) because they are transferred as part of a purchase of a trade or business and the other exceptions in section 197(e) and paragraph (c) of this section are also inapplicable. Accordingly, the licenses are section 197 intangibles.

(iii) Because the right to use the retained patents is described in paragraph (b)(11) of this section and the right is transferred as part of a purchase of a trade or business, the treatment of the royalty payments is determined under paragraph (f)(3)(ii) of this section. In addition, however, the retained patents are described in paragraph (b)(5) of this section. Thus, the annual royalty payments are chargeable to capital account under the general rule of paragraph (f)(3)(ii)(A) of this section unless Y establishes that the license is not a sale or exchange under the principles of section 1235 and the royalty payments are an arm's length consideration for the rights transferred. If these facts are established, the exception in paragraph (f)(3)(ii)(B) of this section applies and the royalty payments are not chargeable to capital account for purposes of section 197. The capitalized costs of entering into the license are treated in the same manner as in Example 7.

(iv) The right to use the retained customer list is also described in paragraph (b)(11) of this section and is transferred as part of a purchase of a trade or business. Thus, the treatment of the payments for use of the customer list is also determined under paragraph (f)(3)(ii) of this section. The customer list, although described in paragraph (b)(6) of this section, is a customer-related information base. Thus, the exception in paragraph (f)(3)(ii)(B) of this section does not apply. Accordingly, payments for use of the list are chargeable to capital account under the general rule of paragraph (f)(3)(ii)(A) of this section and are amortized under section 197. In addition, the capitalized costs of entering into the contract for use of the customer list are treated in the same manner as in *Example 7*.

Example 11. Loss disallowance rules involving related persons. (i) Assume that X and Y are treated as a single taxpayer for purposes of paragraph (g)(1) of this section. In a single transaction, X and Y acquired from Z all of the assets used by Z in a trade or business. Z had operated this business at two locations, and X and Y each acquired the assets used by Z at one of the locations. Three years after the acquisition, X sold all of the assets it acquired, including amortizable section 197 intangibles, to an unrelated purchaser. The amortizable section 197 intangibles are sold at a loss of $120,000.

(ii) Because X and Y are treated as a single taxpayer for purposes of the loss disallowance rules of section 197(f)(1) and paragraph (g)(1) of this section, X's loss on the sale of the amortizable section 197 intangibles is not recognized. Under paragraph (g)(1)(iv)(B) of this section, X's disallowed loss is allowed ratably, as a deduction under section 197, over the remainder of the 15-year period during which the intangibles would have been amortized, and Y may not increase the basis of the amortizable section 197 intangibles that it acquired from Z by the amount of X's disallowed loss.

Example 12. Disposition of retained intangibles by related person. (i) The facts are the same as in *Example 11*, except that 10 years after the acquisition of the assets by X and Y and 7 years after the sale of the assets by X, Y sells all of the assets acquired from Z, including amortizable section 197 intangibles, to an unrelated purchaser.

(ii) Under paragraph (g)(1)(iv)(B) of this section, X may recognize, on the date of the sale by Y, any loss that has not been allowed as a deduction under section 197. Accordingly, X recognizes a loss of $50,000, the amount obtained by reducing the loss on the sale of the assets at the end of the third year ($120,000) by the amount allowed as a deduction under paragraph (g)(1)(iv)(B) of this section during the 7 years following the sale by X ($70,000).

Example 13. Acquisition of an interest in partnership with no section 754 election. (i) A, B, and

C each contribute $1,500 for equal shares in general partnership P. On January 1, 1998, P acquires as its sole asset an amortizable section 197 intangible for $4,500. P still holds the intangible on January 1, 2003, at which time the intangible has an adjusted basis to P of $3,000, and A, B, and C each have an adjusted basis of $1,000 in their partnership interests. D (who is not related to A) acquires A's interest in P for $1,600. No section 754 election is in effect for 2003.

(ii) Because there is no change in the basis of the intangible under section 743(b), D merely steps into the shoes of A with respect to the intangible. D's proportionate share of P's adjusted basis in the intangible is $1,000, which continues to be amortized over the 10 years remaining in the original 15-year amortization period for the intangible.

Example 14. Acquisition of an interest in partnership with a section 754 election. (i) The facts are the same as in *Example 13*, except that a section 754 election is in effect for 2003.

(ii) Pursuant to paragraph (g)(3) of this section, for purposes of section 197, D is treated as if P owns two assets. D's proportionate share of P's adjusted basis in one asset is $1,000, which continues to be amortized over the 10 years remaining in the original 15-year amortization period. For the other asset, D's proportionate share of P's adjusted basis is $600 (the amount of the basis increase under section 743 as a result of the section 754 election), which is amortized over a new 15-year period beginning January 2003. With respect to B and C, P's remaining $2,000 adjusted basis in the intangible continues to be amortized over the 10 years remaining in the original 15-year amortization period.

Example 15. Payment to a retiring partner by partnership with a section 754 election. (i) The facts are the same as in *Example 13*, except that a section 754 election is in effect for 2003 and, instead of D acquiring A's interest in P, A retires from P. A, B, and C are not related to each other within the meaning of paragraph (h)(6) of this section. P borrows $1,600, and A receives a payment under section 736 from P of such amount, all of which is in exchange for A's interest in the intangible asset owned by P. (Assume, for purposes of this example, that the borrowing by P and payment of such funds to A does not give rise to a disguised sale of A's partnership interest under section 707(a)(2)(B).) P makes a positive basis adjustment of $600 with respect to the section 197 intangible under section 734(b).

(ii) Pursuant to paragraph (g)(3) of this section, because of the section 734 adjustment, P is treated as having two amortizable section 197 intangibles, one with a basis of $3,000 and a

remaining amortization period of 10 years and the other with a basis of $600 and a new amortization period of 15 years.

Example 16. Termination of partnership under section 708(b)(1)(B). (i) A and B are partners with equal shares in the capital and profits of general partnership P. P's only asset is an amortizable section 197 intangible, which P had acquired on January 1, 1995. On January 1, 2000, the asset had a fair market value of $100 and a basis to P of $50. On that date, A sells his entire partnership interest in P to C, who is unrelated to A, for $50. At the time of the sale, the basis of each of A and B in their respective partnership interests is $25.

(ii) The sale causes a termination of P under section 708(b)(1)(B). Under section 708, the transaction is treated as if P transfers its sole asset to a new partnership in exchange for the assumption of its liabilities and the receipt of all of the interests in the new partnership. Immediately thereafter, P is treated as if it is liquidated, with B and C each receiving their proportionate share of the interests in the new partnership. The contribution by P of its asset to the new partnership is governed by section 721, and the liquidating distributions by P of the interests in the new partnership are governed by section 731. C does not realize a basis adjustment under section 743 with respect to the amortizable section 197 intangible unless P had a section 754 election in effect for its taxable year in which the transfer of the partnership interest to C occurred or the taxable year in which the deemed liquidation of P occurred.

(iii) Under section 197, if P had a section 754 election in effect, C is treated as if the new partnership had acquired two assets from P immediately preceding its termination. Even though the adjusted basis of the new partnership in the two assets is determined solely under section 723, because the transfer of assets is a transaction described in section 721, the application of sections 743(b) and 754 to P immediately before its termination causes P to be treated as if it held two assets for purposes of section 197. See paragraph (g)(3) of this section. B's and C's proportionate share of the new partnership's adjusted basis is $25 each in one asset, which continues to be amortized over the 10 years remaining in the original 15-year amortization period. For the other asset, C's proportionate share of the new partnership's adjusted basis is $25 (the amount of the basis increase resulting from the application of section 743 to the sale or exchange by A of the interest in P), which is amortized over a new 15-year period beginning in January 2000.

(iv) If P did not have a section 754 election in effect for its taxable year in which the sale of the partnership interest by A to C occurred or the taxable year in which the deemed liquidation of P occurred, the adjusted basis of the new partnership in the amortizable section 197 intangible is determined solely under section 723, because the transfer is a transaction described in section 721, and P does not have a basis increase in the intangible. Under section 197(f)(2) and paragraph (g)(2)(ii) of this section, the new partnership continues to amortize the intangible over the 10 years remaining in the original 15-year amortization period. No additional amortization is allowable with respect to this asset.

Example 17. Disguised sale to partnership. (i) E and F are individuals who are unrelated to each other within the meaning of paragraph (h)(6) of this section. E has been engaged in the active conduct of a trade or business as a sole proprietor since 1990. E and F form EF Partnership. E transfers all of the assets of the business, having a fair market value of $100, to EF, and F transfers $40 of cash to EF. E receives a 60 percent interest in EF and the $40 of cash contributed by F, and F receives a 40 percent interest in EF, under circumstances in which the transfer by E is partially treated as a sale of property to EF under § 1.707-3(b).

(ii) Under § 1.707-3(a)(1), the transaction is treated as if E had sold to EF a 40 percent interest in each asset for $40 and contributed the remaining 60 percent interest in each asset to EF in exchange solely for an interest in EF. Because E and EF are related persons within the meaning of paragraph (h)(6) of this section, no portion of any transferred section 197(f)(9) intangible that E held during the transition period (as defined in paragraph (h)(4) of this section) is an amortizable section 197 intangible pursuant to paragraph (h)(2) of this section. Section 197(f)(9)(E) and paragraph (g)(3) of this section do not apply to any portion of the section 197 intangible in the hands of EF because the basis of EF in these assets was not increased under any of sections 732, 734, or 743.

Example 18. Acquisition by related person in nonrecognition transaction. (i) A owns a nonamortizable intangible that A acquired in 1990. In 2000, A sells a one-half interest in the intangible to B for cash. Immediately after the sale, A and B, who are unrelated to each other, form partnership P as equal partners. A and B each contribute their one-half interest in the intangible to P.

(ii) P has a transferred basis in the intangible from A and B under section 723. The nonrecognition transfer rule under paragraph (g)(2)(ii) of this section applies to A's transfer of its one-half interest in the intangible to P, and consequently P steps into A's shoes with respect to A's nonamor-

tizable transferred basis. The anti-churning rules of paragraph (h) of this section apply to B's transfer of its one-half interest in the intangible to P, because A, who is related to P under paragraph (h)(6) of this section immediately after the series of transactions in which the intangible was acquired by P, held B's one-half interest in the intangible during the transition period. Pursuant to paragraph (h)(10) of this section, these rules apply to B's transfer of its one-half interest to P even though the nonrecognition transfer rule under paragraph (g)(2)(ii) of this section would have permitted P to step into B's shoes with respect to B's otherwise amortizable basis. Therefore, P's entire basis in the intangible is nonamortizable. However, if A (not B) elects to recognize gain under paragraph (h)(9) of this section on the transfer of each of the one-half interests in the intangible to B and P, then the intangible would be amortizable by P to the extent provided in section 197(f)(9)(B) and paragraph (h)(9) of this section.

Example 19. Acquisition of partnership interest following formation of partnership. (i) The facts are the same as in *Example 18* except that, in 2000, A formed P with an affiliate, S, and contributed the intangible to the partnership and except that in a subsequent year, in a transaction that is properly characterized as a sale of a partnership interest for Federal tax purposes, B purchases a 50 percent interest in P from A. P has a section 754 election in effect and holds no assets other than the intangible and cash.

(ii) For the reasons set forth in *Example 16*(iii), B is treated as if P owns two assets. B's proportionate share of P's adjusted basis in one asset is the same as A's proportionate share of P's adjusted basis in that asset, which is not amortizable under section 197. For the other asset, B's proportionate share of the remaining adjusted basis of P is amortized over a new 15-year period.

Example 20. Acquisition by related corporation in nonrecognition transaction. (i) The facts are the same as *Example 18*, except that A and B form corporation P as equal owners.

(ii) P has a transferred basis in the intangible from A and B under section 362. Pursuant to paragraph (h)(10) of this section, the application of the nonrecognition transfer rule under paragraph (g)(2)(ii) of this section and the anti-churning rules of paragraph (h) of this section to the facts of this *Example 18* is the same as in *Example 16*. Thus, P's entire basis in the intangible is nonamortizable.

Example 21. Acquisition from corporation related to purchaser through remote indirect interest. (i) X, Y, and Z are each corporations that have only one class of issued and outstanding stock. X owns 25 percent of the stock of Y and Y owns 25 percent of the outstanding stock of Z. No other shareholder of any of these corporations is related to any other shareholder or to any of the corporations. On June 30, 2000, X purchases from Z section 197(f)(9) intangibles that Z owned during the transition period (as defined in paragraph (h)(4) of this section).

(ii) Pursuant to paragraph (h)(6)(iv)(B) of this section, the beneficial ownership interest of X in Z is 6.25 percent, determined by treating X as if it owned a proportionate (25 percent) interest in the stock of Z that is actually owned by Y. Thus, even though X is related to Y and Y is related to Z, X and Z are not considered to be related for purposes of the anti-churning rules of section 197.

Example 22. Gain recognition election. (i) B owns 25 percent of the stock of S, a corporation that uses the calendar year as its taxable year. No other shareholder of B or S is related to each other. S is not a member of a controlled group of corporations within the meaning of section 1563(a). S has section 197(f)(9) intangibles that it owned during the transition period. S has a basis of $25,000 in the intangibles. In 2001, S sells these intangibles to B for $75,000. S recognizes a gain of $50,000 on the sale and has no other items of income, deduction, gain, or loss for the year, except that S also has a net operating loss of $20,000 from prior years that it would otherwise be entitled to use in 2001 pursuant to section 172(b). S makes a valid gain recognition election pursuant to section 197(f)(9)(B) and paragraph (h)(9) of this section. In 2001, the highest marginal tax rate applicable to S is 35 percent. But for the election, all of S's taxable income would be taxed at a rate of 15 percent.

(ii) If the gain recognition election had not been made, S would have taxable income of $30,000 for 2001 and a tax liability of $4,500. If the gain were not taken into account, S would have no tax liability for the taxable year. Thus, the amount of tax (other than the tax imposed under paragraph (h)(9) of this section) imposed on the gain is also $4,500. The gain on the disposition multiplied by the highest marginal tax rate is $17,500 ($50,000 × .35). Accordingly, S's tax liability for the year is $4,500 plus an additional tax under paragraph (h)(9) of this section of $13,000 ($17,500 − $4,500).

(iii) Pursuant to paragraph (h)(9)(x)(A) of this section, S determines the amount of its net operating loss deduction in subsequent years without regard to the gain recognized on the sale of the section 197 intangible to B. Accordingly, the entire $20,000 net operating loss deduction that would have been available in 2001 but for the

gain recognition election may be used in 2002, subject to the limitations of section 172.

(iv) B has a basis of $75,000 in the section 197(f)(9) intangibles acquired from S. As the result of the gain recognition election by S, B may amortize $50,000 of its basis under section 197. Under paragraph (h)(9)(ii) of this section, the remaining basis does not qualify for the gain-recognition exception and may not be amortized by B.

Example 23. Section 338 election. (i) Corporation P makes a qualified stock purchase of the stock of T corporation from two shareholders in July 2000, and a section 338 election is made by P. No shareholder of either T or P owns stock in both of these corporations, and no other shareholder is related to any other shareholder of either corporation.

(ii) Pursuant to paragraph (h)(8) of this section, in the case of a qualified stock purchase that is treated as a deemed sale and purchase of assets pursuant to section 338, the corporation treated as purchasing assets as a result of an election thereunder (new target) is not considered the person that held or used the assets during any period in which the assets were held or used by the corporation treated as selling the assets (old target). Because there are no relationships described in paragraph (h)(6) of this section among the parties to the transaction, any nonamortizable section 197(f)(9) intangible held by old target is an amortizable section 197 intangible in the hands of new target.

(iii) Assume the same facts as set forth in paragraph (i) of this *Example 23*, except that one of the selling shareholders is an individual who owns 25 percent of the total value of the stock of each of the T and P corporation.

(iv) Old target and new target (as these terms are defined in § 1.338-2(c)(17)) are members of a controlled group of corporations under section 267(b)(3), as modified by section 197(f)(9)(C)(i), and any nonamortizable section 197(f)(9) intangible held by old target is not an amortizable section 197 intangible in the hands of new target. However, a gain recognition election under paragraph (h)(9) of this section may be made with respect to this transaction.

Example 24. Relationship created as part of public offering. (i) On January 1, 2001, Corporation X engages in a series of related transactions to discontinue its involvement in one line of business. X forms a new corporation, Y, with a nominal amount of cash. Shortly thereafter, X transfers all the stock of its subsidiary conducting the unwanted business (Target) to Y in exchange for 100 shares of Y common stock and a Y promissory note. Target owns a nonamortizable section

Reg. § 1.197-2(k)

197(f)(9) intangible. Prior to January 1, 2001, X and an underwriter (U) had entered into a binding agreement pursuant to which U would purchase 85 shares of Y common stock from X and then sell those shares in a public offering. On January 6, 2001, the public offering closes. X and Y make a section 338(h)(10) election for Target.

(ii) Pursuant to paragraph (h)(8) of this section, in the case of a qualified stock purchase that is treated as a deemed sale and purchase of assets pursuant to section 338, the corporation treated as purchasing assets as a result of an election thereunder (new target) is not considered the person that held or used the assets during any period in which the assets were held or used by the corporation treated as selling the assets (old target). Further, for purposes of determining whether the nonamortizable section 197(f)(9) intangible is acquired by new target from a related person, because the transactions are a series of related transactions, the relationship between old target and new target must be tested immediately before the first transaction in the series (the formation of Y) and immediately after the last transaction in the series (the sale to U and the public offering). See paragraph (h)(6)(ii)(B) of this section. Because there was no relationship between old target and new target immediately before the formation of Y (because the section 338 election had not been made) and only a 15% relationship between old target and new target immediately after, old target is not related to new target for purposes of applying the anti-churning rules of paragraph (h) of this section. Accordingly, Target may amortize the section 197 intangible.

Example 25. Other transfers to controlled corporations. (i) In 2001, Corporation A transfers a section 197(f)(9) intangible that it held during the transition period to X, a newly formed corporation, in exchange for 15% of X's stock. As part of the same transaction, B transfers property to X in exchange for the remaining 85% of X stock.

(ii) Because the acquisition of the intangible by X is part of a qualifying section 351 exchange, under section 197(f)(2) and paragraph (g)(2)(ii) of this section, X is treated in the same manner as the transferor of the asset. Accordingly, X may not amortize the intangible. If, however, at the time of the exchange, B has a binding commitment to sell 25 percent of the X stock to C, an unrelated third party, the exchange, including A's transfer of the section 197(f)(9) intangible, would fail to qualify as a section 351 exchange. Because the formation of X, the transfers of property to X, and the sale of X stock by B are part of a series of related transactions, the relationship between A and X must be tested immediately before the first transaction in the series (the transfer of property

to X) and immediately after the last transaction in the series (the sale of X stock to C). See paragraph (h)(6)(ii)(B) of this section. Because there was no relationship between A and X immediately before and only a 15% relationship immediately after, A is not related to X for purposes of applying the anti-churning rules of paragraph (h) of this section. Accordingly, X may amortize the section 197 intangible.

Example 26. Relationship created as part of stock acquisition followed by liquidation. (i) In 2001, Partnership P purchases 100 percent of the stock of Corporation X. P and X were not related prior to the acquisition. Immediately after acquiring the X stock, and as part of a series of related transactions, P liquidates X under section 331. In the liquidating distribution, P receives a section 197(f)(9) intangible that was held by X during the transition period.

(ii) Because the relationship between P and X was created pursuant to a series of related transactions where P acquires stock (meeting the requirements of section 1504(a)(2)) in a fully taxable transaction followed by a liquidation under section 331, the relationship immediately after the last transaction in the series (the liquidation) is disregarded. See paragraph (h)(6)(iii) of this section. Accordingly, P is entitled to amortize the section 197(f)(9) intangible.

Example 27. Section 743(b) adjustment with no change in user. (i) On January 1, 2001, A forms a partnership (PRS) with B in which A owns a 40-percent, and B owns a 60-percent, interest in profits and capital. A contributes a nonamortizable section 197(f)(9) intangible with a value of $80 and an adjusted basis of $0 to PRS in exchange for its PRS interest and B contributes $120 cash. At the time of the contribution, PRS licenses the section 197(f)(9) intangible to A. On February 1, 2001, A sells its entire interest in PRS to C, an unrelated person, for $80. PRS has a section 754 election in effect.

(ii) The section 197(f)(9) intangible contributed to PRS by A is not amortizable in the hands of PRS. Pursuant to section (g)(2)(ii) of this section, PRS steps into the shoes of A with respect to A's nonamortizable transferred basis in the intangible.

(iii) When A sells the PRS interest to C, C will have a basis adjustment in the PRS assets under section 743(b) equal to $80. The entire basis adjustment will be allocated to the intangible because the only other asset held by PRS is cash. Ordinarily, under paragraph (h)(12)(v) of this section, the anti-churning rules will not apply to an increase in the basis of partnership property under section 743(b) if the person acquiring the partnership interest is not related to the person transferring the partnership interest. However, A is an anti-churning partner under paragraph (h)(12)(vi)(B)(2)(i) of this section. As a result of the license agreement, A remains a direct user of the section 197(f)(9) intangible after the transfer to C. Accordingly, paragraph (h)(12)(vi)(A) of this section will cause the anti-churning rules to apply to the entire basis adjustment under section 743(b).

Example 28. Distribution of section 197(f)(9) intangible to partner who acquired partnership interest prior to the effective date. (i) In 1990, A, B, and C each contribute $150 cash to form general partnership ABC for the purpose of engaging in a consulting business and a software manufacturing business. The partners agree to share partnership profits and losses equally. In 2000, the partnership distributes the consulting business to A in liquidation of A's entire interest in ABC. The only asset of the consulting business is a nonamortizable intangible, which has a fair market value of $180 and a basis of $0. At the time of the distribution, the adjusted basis of A's interest in ABC is $150. A is not related to B or C. ABC does not have a section 754 election in effect.

(ii) Under section 732(b), A's adjusted basis in the intangible distributed by ABC is $150, a $150 increase over the basis of the intangible in ABC's hands. In determining whether the anti-churning rules apply to any portion of the basis increase, A is treated as having owned and used A's proportionate share of partnership property. Thus, A is treated as holding an interest in the intangible during the transition period. Because the intangible was not amortizable prior to the enactment of section 197, the section 732(b) increase in the basis of the intangible may be subject to the anti-churning provisions. Paragraph (h)(12)(ii) of this section provides that the anti-churning provisions apply to the extent that the section 732(b) adjustment exceeds the total unrealized appreciation from the intangible allocable to partners other than A or persons related to A, as well as certain other partners whose purchase of their interests meet certain criteria. Because B and C are not related to A, and A's acquisition of its partnership interest does not satisfy the necessary criteria, the section 732(b) basis increase is subject to the anti-churning provisions to the extent that it exceeds B and C's proportionate share of the unrealized appreciation from the intangible. B and C's proportionate share of the unrealized appreciation from the intangible is $120 (2/3 of $180). This is the amount of gain that would be allocated to B and C if the partnership sold the intangible immediately before the distribution for its fair market value of $180. Therefore, $120 of the section 732(b) basis increase is not subject to the anti-churning rules.

The remaining $30 of the section 732(b) basis increase is subject to the anti-churning rules. Accordingly, A is treated as having two intangibles, an amortizable section 197 intangible with an adjusted basis of $120 and a new amortization period of 15 years and a nonamortizable intangible with an adjusted basis of $30.

(iii) In applying the anti-churning rules to future transfers of the distributed intangible, under paragraph (h)(12)(ii)(C) of this section, one-third of the intangible will continue to be subject to the anti-churning rules, determined as follows: The sum of the amount of the distributed intangible's basis that is nonamortizable under paragraph (g)(2)(ii)(B) of this section ($0) and the total unrealized appreciation inherent in the intangible reduced by the amount of the increase in the adjusted basis of the distributed intangible under section 732(b) to which the anti-churning rules do not apply ($180 − $120 = $60), over the fair market value of the distributed intangible ($180).

Example 29. Distribution of section 197(f)(9) intangible to partner who acquired partnership interest after the effective date. (i) The facts are the same as in *Example 28*, except that B and C form ABC in 1990. A does not acquire an interest in ABC until 1995. In 1995, A contributes $150 to ABC in exchange for a one-third interest in ABC. At the time of the distribution, the adjusted basis of A's interest in ABC is $150.

(ii) As in *Example 28*, the anti-churning rules do not apply to the increase in the basis of the intangible distributed to A under section 732(b) to the extent that it does not exceed the unrealized appreciation from the intangible allocable to B and C. Under paragraph (h)(12)(ii) of this section, the anti-churning provisions also do not apply to the section 732(b) basis increase to the extent of A's allocable share of the unrealized appreciation from the intangible because A acquired the ABC interest from an unrelated person after August 10, 1993, and the intangible was acquired by the partnership before A acquired the ABC interest. Under paragraph (h)(12)(ii)(E) of this section, A is deemed to acquire the ABC partnership interest from an unrelated person because A acquired the ABC partnership interest in exchange for a contribution to the partnership of property other than the distributed intangible and, at the time of the contribution, no partner in the partnership was related to A. Consequently, the increase in the basis of the intangible under section 732(b) is not subject to the anti-churning rules to the extent of the total unrealized appreciation from the intangible allocable to A, B, and C. The total unrealized appreciation from the intangible allocable to A, B, and C is $180 (the gain the partnership would have recognized if it had sold the intangible for its

Reg. § 1.197-2(k)

fair market value immediately before the distribution). Because this amount exceeds the section 732(b) basis increase of $150, the entire section 732(b) basis increase is amortizable.

(iii) In applying the anti-churning rules to future transfers of the distributed intangible, under paragraph (h)(12)(ii)(C) of this section, one-sixth of the intangible will continue to be subject to the anti-churning rules, determined as follows: The sum of the amount of the distributed intangible's basis that is nonamortizable under paragraph (g)(2)(ii)(B) of this section ($0) and the total unrealized appreciation inherent in the intangible reduced by the amount of the increase in the adjusted basis of the distributed intangible under section 732(b) to which the anti-churning rules do not apply ($180 − $150=$30), over the fair market value of the distributed intangible ($180).

Example 30. Distribution of section 197(f)(9) intangible contributed to the partnership by a partner. (i) The facts are the same as in *Example 29,* except that C purchased the intangible used in the consulting business in 1988 for $60 and contributed the intangible to ABC in 1990. At that time, the intangible had a fair market value of $150 and an adjusted tax basis of $60. When ABC distributes the intangible to A in 2000, the intangible has a fair market value of $180 and a basis of $60.

(ii) As in *Examples 28* and *29,* the adjusted basis of the intangible in A's hands is $150 under section 732(b). However, the increase in the adjusted basis of the intangible under section 732(b) is only $90 ($150 adjusted basis after the distribution compared to $60 basis before the distribution). Pursuant to paragraph (g)(2)(ii)(B) of this section, A steps into the shoes of ABC with respect to the $60 of A's adjusted basis in the intangible that corresponds to ABC's basis in the intangible and this portion of the basis is nonamortizable. B and C are not related to A, A acquired the ABC interest from an unrelated person after August 10, 1993, and the intangible was acquired by ABC before A acquired the ABC interest. Therefore, under paragraph (h)(12)(ii) of this section, the section 732(b) basis increase is amortizable to the extent of A, B, and C's allocable share of the unrealized appreciation from the intangible. The total unrealized appreciation from the intangible that is allocable to A, B, and C is $120. If ABC had sold the intangible immediately before the distribution to A for its fair market value of $180, it would have recognized gain of $120, which would have been allocated $10 to A, $10 to B, and $100 to C under section 704(c). Because A, B, and C's allocable share of the unrealized appreciation from the intangible exceeds the section 732(b) basis increase in the intangible, the entire $90 of

basis increase is amortizable by A. Accordingly, after the distribution, A will be treated as having two intangibles, an amortizable section 197 intangible with an adjusted basis of $90 and a new amortization period of 15 years and a nonamortizable intangible with an adjusted basis of $60.

(iii) In applying the anti-churning rules to future transfers of the distributed intangible, under paragraph (h)(12)(ii)(C) of this section, one-half of the intangible will continue to be subject to the anti-churning rules, determined as follows: The sum of the amount of the distributed intangible's basis that is nonamortizable under paragraph (g)(2)(ii)(B) of this section ($60) and the total unrealized appreciation inherent in the intangible reduced by the amount of the increase in the adjusted basis of the distributed intangible under section 732(b) to which the anti-churning rules do not apply ($120 − $90=$30), over the fair market value of the distributed intangible ($180).

Example 31. Partnership distribution causing section 734(b) basis adjustment to section 197(f)(9) intangible. (i) On January 1, 2001, A, B, and C form a partnership (ABC) in which each partner shares equally in capital and income, gain, loss, and deductions. On that date, A contributes a section 197(f)(9) intangible with a zero basis and a value of $150, and B and C each contribute $150 cash. A and B are related, but neither A nor B is related to C. ABC does not adopt the remedial allocation method for making section 704(c) allocations of amortization expenses with respect to the intangible. On December 1, 2004, when the value of the intangible has increased to $600, ABC distributes $300 to B in complete redemption of B's interest in the partnership. ABC has an election under section 754 in effect for the taxable year that includes December 1, 2004. (Assume that, at the time of the distribution, the basis of A's partnership interest remains zero, and the basis of each of B's and C's partnership interest remains $150.)

(ii) Immediately prior to the distribution, the assets of the partnership are revalued pursuant to § 1.704-1(b)(2)(iv)(*f),* so that the section 197(f)(9) intangible is reflected on the books of the partnership at a value of $600. B recognizes $150 of gain under section 731(a)(1) upon the distribution of $300 in redemption of B's partnership interest. As a result, the adjusted basis of the intangible held by ABC increases by $150 under section 734(b). A does not satisfy any of the tests set forth under paragraph (h)(12)(iv)(B) and thus is not an eligible partner. C is not related to B and thus is an eligible partner under paragraph (h)(12)(iv)(B)(*1)* of this section. The capital accounts of A and C are equal immediately after the distribution, so, pursuant to paragraph (h)(12)(iv)(D)(*1)* of this section, each partner's share of the basis increase is equal to $75. Because A is not an eligible partner, the anti-churning rules apply to A's share of the basis increase. The anti-churning rules do not apply to C's share of the basis increase.

(iii) For book purposes, ABC determines the amortization of the asset as follows: First, the intangible that is subject to adjustment under section 734(b) will be divided into three assets: the first, with a basis and value of $75 will be amortizable for both book and tax purposes; the second, with a basis and value of $75 will be amortizable for book, but not tax purposes; and a third asset with a basis of zero and a value of $450 will not be amortizable for book or tax purposes. Any subsequent revaluation of the intangible pursuant to § 1.704-1(b)(2)(iv)(f) will be made solely with respect to the third asset (which is not amortizable for book purposes). The book and tax attributes from the first asset (i.e., book and tax amortization) will be specially allocated to C. The book and tax attributes from the second asset (i.e., book amortization and non-amortizable tax basis) will be specially allocated to A. Upon disposition of the intangible, each partner's share of gain or loss will be determined first by allocating among the partners an amount realized equal to the book value of the intangible attributable to such partner, with any remaining amount realized being allocated in accordance with the partnership agreement. Each partner then will compare its share of the amount realized with its remaining basis in the intangible to arrive at the gain or loss to be allocated to such partner. This is a reasonable method for amortizing the intangible for book purposes, and the results in allocating the income, gain, loss, and deductions attributable to the intangible do not contravene the purposes of the anti-churning rules under section 197 or paragraph (h) of this section.

(l) *Effective dates*—(1) *In general.* This section applies to property acquired after January 25, 2000, except that paragraph (c)(13) of this section (exception from section 197 for separately acquired rights of fixed duration or amount) applies to property acquired after August 10, 1993 (or July 25, 1991, if a valid retroactive election has been made under § 1.197-IT), and paragraphs (h)(12)(ii), (iii), (iv), (v), (vi)(A), and (vii)(B) of this section (anti-churning rules applicable to partnerships) apply to partnership transactions occurring on or after November 20, 2000.

(2) *Application to pre-effective date acquisitions.* A taxpayer may choose, on a transaction-by-transaction basis, to apply the provisions of this section and § 1.167(a)-14 to property acquired (or partnership transactions occurring) after August 10, 1993 (or July 25, 1991, if a valid retroactive election has been made under § 1.197-IT) and—

(i) On or before January 25, 2000; or

(ii) With respect to paragraphs (h)(12)(ii), (iii), (iv), (v), (vi) (A), and (vii) (B) of this section, before November 20, 2000.

(3) *Application of regulation project REG-209709-94 to pre-effective date acquisitions.* A taxpayer may rely on the provisions of regulation project REG-209709-94 (1997-1 C.B. 731) for property acquired after August 10, 1993 (or July 25, 1991, if a valid retroactive election has been made under § 1.197-1T) and on or before January 25, 2000.

(4) *Change in method of accounting*—(i) *In general.* For the first taxable year ending after January 25, 2000, a taxpayer that has acquired property to which the exception in § 1.197-2(c)(13) applies is granted consent of the Commissioner to change its method of accounting for such property to comply with the provisions of this section and § 1.167(a)-14 unless the proper treatment of such property is an issue under consideration (within the meaning of Rev. Proc. 97-27 (1997-21 IRB 10)(see § 601.601(d)(2) of this chapter)) in an examination, before an Appeals office, or before a Federal court.

(ii) *Application to pre-effective date acquisitions.* For the first taxable year ending after January 25, 2000, a taxpayer is granted consent of the Commissioner to change its method of accounting for all property acquired in transactions described in paragraph (l)(2) of this section to comply with the provisions of this section and § 1.167(a)-14 unless the proper treatment of any such property is an issue under consideration (within the meaning of Rev. Proc. 97-27 (1997-21 IRB 10)(see § 601.601(d)(2) of this chapter)) in an examination, before an Appeals office, or before a Federal court.

(iii) *Automatic change procedures.* A taxpayer changing its method of accounting in accordance with this paragraph (l)(4) must follow the automatic change in accounting method provisions of Rev. Proc. 99-49 (1999-52 IRB 725) (see § 601.601(d)(2) of this chapter) except, for purposes of this paragraph (l)(4), the scope limitations in section 4.02 of Rev. Proc. 99-49 (1999-52 IRB 725) are not applicable. However, if the taxpayer is under examination, before an appeals office, or before a Federal court, the taxpayer must provide a copy of the application to the examining agent(s), appeals officer, or counsel for the government, as appropriate, at the same time that it files the copy of the application with the National Office. The application must contain the name(s) and telephone number(s) of the examining agent(s), appeals officer, or counsel for the government, as appropriate. [Reg. § 1.197-2.]

☐ [*T.D.* 8865, 1-20-2000 (*corrected* 3-27-2000 *and* 10-11-2000). *Amended by T.D.* 8907, 11-17-2000 *and T.D.* 8940, 2-12-2001.]